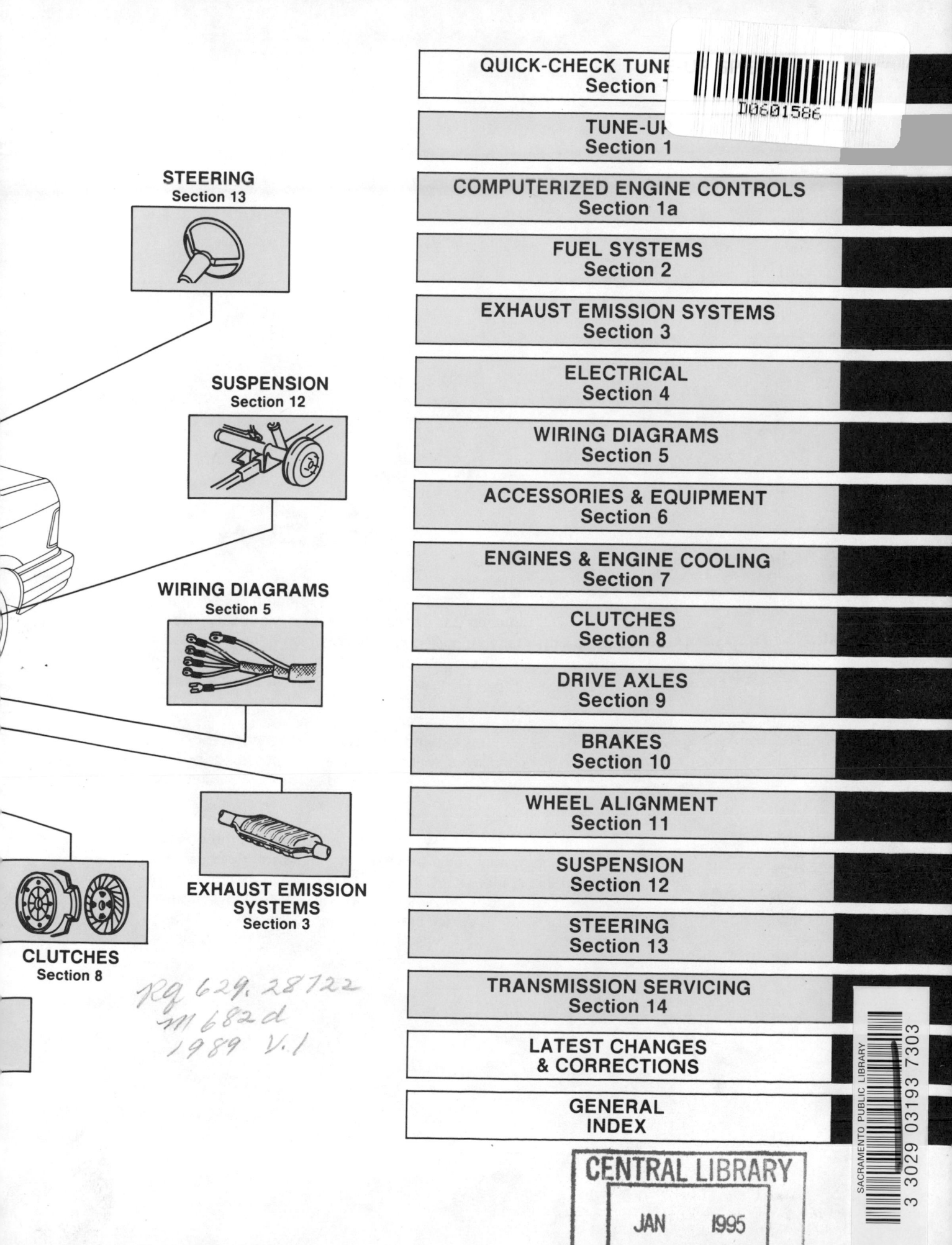

STEERING
Section 13

SUSPENSION
Section 12

WIRING DIAGRAMS
Section 5

EXHAUST EMISSION
SYSTEMS
Section 3

CLUTCHES
Section 8

Rg 629. 28722
m 682 d
1989 V. 1

QUICK-CHECK TUNE
Section

TUNE-UP
Section 1

COMPUTERIZED ENGINE CONTROLS
Section 1a

FUEL SYSTEMS
Section 2

EXHAUST EMISSION SYSTEMS
Section 3

ELECTRICAL
Section 4

WIRING DIAGRAMS
Section 5

ACCESSORIES & EQUIPMENT
Section 6

ENGINES & ENGINE COOLING
Section 7

CLUTCHES
Section 8

DRIVE AXLES
Section 9

BRAKES
Section 10

WHEEL ALIGNMENT
Section 11

SUSPENSION
Section 12

STEERING
Section 13

TRANSMISSION SERVICING
Section 14

LATEST CHANGES
& CORRECTIONS

GENERAL
INDEX

PREFACE

This is the 1989 edition of Mitchell's
Domestic Car Service and Repair Manual, Volume I.
This manual, like the many Mitchell publications which have preceded it,
represents our commitment to professionalism
in the automotive service market.

The automotive industry advances every year,
and we at Mitchell pledge to improve our product
to keep abreast of the industry.

We cordially acknowledge the goodwill
and mutual goals that exist in the automotive business,
and it is in this spirit that we thank the automotive manufacturers,
distributors, dealers and the entire automotive industry
for their fine cooperation and assistance
which have made this manual possible.

CHRYSLER MOTORS
EAGLE
FORD MOTOR CO.

1989 DOMESTIC CARS SERVICE & REPAIR

Published by
MITCHELL INTERNATIONAL, INC.
P.O. BOX 26260
SAN DIEGO, CALIFORNIA 92126
ISBN 0-8470-0880-0
© 1989 MITCHELL INTERNATIONAL, INC.

The Standard in Professional Estimating and Repair Information.

Mitchell International, Inc.

ACKNOWLEDGEMENT | Mitchell International, Inc. thanks the domestic manufacturers, distributors, and dealers for their generous cooperation and assistance which make this manual possible.

Chrysler Motors
Ford Motor Company
General Motors Corporation
Jeep/Eagle

EDITORIAL

Executive Editor
  Terry L. Blomquist

Product Manager
  David R. Koontz

Quality Assurance Manager
  Daryl F. Visser

Detroit Editors
  Lynn D. Meeker
  Andy Henry

Senior Editors
  David L. Skora
  Eddie Santangelo
  Roger Leftridge
  Chuck Vedra
  Ronald E. Garrett
  Ramiro Gutierrez
  John M. Fisher

Technical Editors
  Scott A. Olsen
  Bob Reel
  Don Brudos
  Brian Styve
  David W. Himes
  Christopher C. Chaney
  James A. Hawes
  Tom L. Hall
  Patrick G. San Nicolas
  Alex A. Solis
  Gary Dugan
  Paul B. Young
  Gregory P. Hanlon
  David C. Rust
  Serge G. Pirino

PRODUCT TECHNICAL SUPPORT
Senior Editor
  David R. Costantino
Technical Editors
  Eddie L. Dorszynski, Jr.
  James A. Wafford
  Robert Rooney

ELECTRICAL

Senior Editor
  Matthew Krimple
Electrical Editors
  Leonard McVicker
  Santiago Llano
  Harry Piper
  Michael Wertz
  Lloyd Adams
  Richard B. Speake
  Mark Zdeb
  Roy P. Gardetto

ART & COMPOSITION

Graphics Manager
  Gary Nicks
Graphics Supervisor
  Judie LaPierre

Published By

MITCHELL INTERNATIONAL, INC.
9889 Willow Creek Road
P.O. Box 26260
San Diego, California 92126-0260

For Subscription Information:
CALL TOLL FREE 800–854-7030.
Or WRITE: P.O. Box 26260, San Diego, CA 92126-0260

ISBN 0-8470-0880-0

© 1989 MITCHELL INTERNATIONAL, INC.

Introduction

You now have the most complete and up-to-date Service and Repair Manual available to the professional mechanic. Our staff of experts has spent thousands of hours gathering and processing service and repair information from sources throughout the automotive industry. More than 500 separate articles, providing step-by-step procedures and technical information for 1989 Domestic Cars, are contained in this year's two-volume edition.

To use this manual most efficiently, please read the following instruction, "How To Find the Information". This will enable you to quickly locate the car model and technical information you need, without wasting time thumbing through unnecessary pages.

HOW TO FIND THE INFORMATION

3 Quick Steps

(1) On the inside cover, you'll find the contents of this manual. Locate the section you want, and notice that it has a Black square next to it.

THUMB INDEX SPOT

TUNE-UP
Section 1

(2) Looking along the right edge of the book, you'll notice additional Black squares.

Match the Black square of the section listed on the cover with the Black square on the book's edge, then turn directly to that section.

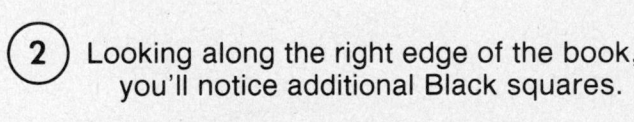

(3) Review the section contents page. After finding the article and page you want, turn to that page.

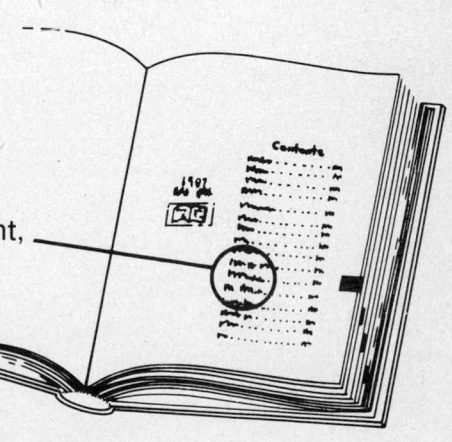

OR...

Determine which volume you need...Volume I for Chrysler Motors, Eagle and Ford Motor Co., Volume II for General Motors. Go directly to the expanded GENERAL INDEX at the rear of that manual.

Go to the section covering the vehicle make on which you are working. Use the alphabetical guide as you would any reference index.

Section G

GENERAL INFORMATION

CONTENTS

	Page
Maintenance Reminder Lights	G-2
VIN Code Explanation	G-5
Engine & Model Conversion	G-6
Mitchell's Abbreviations	G-7
Tool Applications	G-12

NOTE: **ALSO SEE GENERAL INDEX**

MAINTENANCE REMINDER LIGHTS
1980-89 Reset Procedures Domestic Cars & Trucks

AMERICAN MOTORS

1980-81 MODELS

Every 30,000 miles, an emission maintenance reminder light will illuminate on the instrument panel, indicating oxygen sensor requires servicing. If sensor is faulty, it must be replaced. After servicing sensor, reset light activating switch.

Locate switch in engine compartment, between upper and lower speedometer cables, next to firewall. Slide rubber boot up. With small screwdriver, turn reset screw clockwise 1/4 turn until detent resets in switch. *See Fig. 1.*

1982-84 MODELS
(EXCEPT ALLIANCE & ENCORE)

The emission maintenance light illuminates after 1000 HOURS of engine operation, indicating service of the oxygen sensor is required. After servicing sensor, emission maintenance E-cell timer must be replaced.

Locate timer in passenger compartment within the wire harness leading to the microprocessor. Remove E-cell timer from its enclosure and insert a replacement timer.

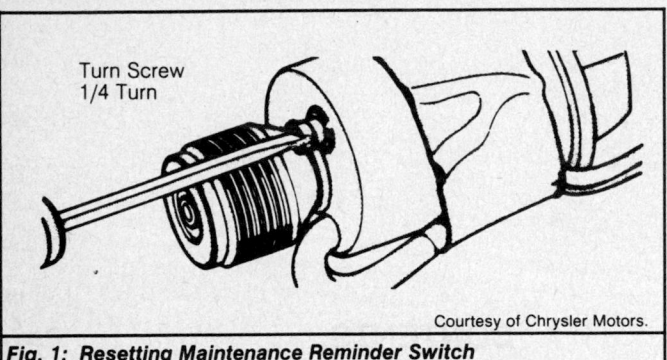

Turn Screw
1/4 Turn

Courtesy of Chrysler Motors.

Fig. 1: Resetting Maintenance Reminder Switch

1987 EAGLE WAGON

An emission light timer will start flashing the O_2 sensor service light at 82,500 miles. At this time, O_2 sensor and timer should both be replaced. Locate timer under the dash panel (to right of steering column). Remove mounting screws and disconnect wiring. To install, reverse procedure.

CHRYSLER MOTORS

1980 PASSENGER CARS, 1980-87 LIGHT DUTY TRUCKS & VANS

A mileage counter activates the emission reminder light between 12,000 and 30,000 mile intervals, depending on model. Two types are used. If equipped with mechanical type, see AMERICAN MOTORS 1980-81 MODELS reset procedure. *See Fig. 1.* The electronic type uses a 9-volt battery which supplies power to the electronic counter, preventing memory loss when the vehicle battery is disconnected.

Electronic Type – On 1987 Dakota models, mileage counter in the odometer will illuminate reminder light at 52,500, 82,500 and 105,000 miles. On all other models reminder light will illuminate between 12,000 and 30,000 mile intervals.

NOTE: Vehicle battery MUST be connected during resetting procedure to prevent power loss to memory.

To reset electronic type, locate Green, Red, White or Tan plastic case behind instrument panel in lower left cluster area. Slide case from bracket and open cover. Remove 9-volt battery and insert a small rod or screwdriver into hole in switch, closing contacts.

Replace battery with a new 9-volt alkaline type. Close case. Slide switch back into bracket. *See Fig. 2.*

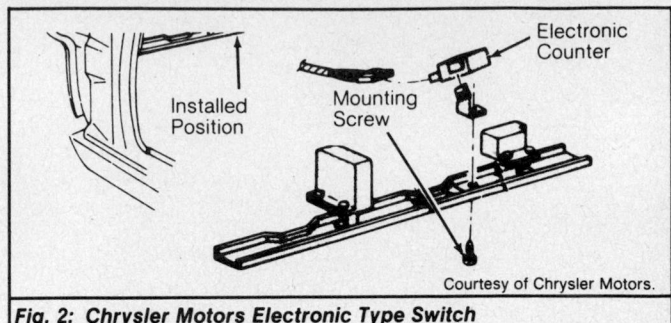

Installed Position

Electronic Counter

Mounting Screw

Courtesy of Chrysler Motors.

Fig. 2: Chrysler Motors Electronic Type Switch

1988 LIGHT DUTY TRUCKS & VANS

CAUTION: There is no test procedure for this system. Any attempt to test this system will damage system components.

The Emission Maintenance Reminder (EMR) module is designed to be a reminder to service the vehicle emissions control system. It is not an emissions warning system, only a reminder to perform emissions servicing. The components to be serviced include the EGR system, PCV valve, oxygen sensor, delay valves, and bi-level purge valve.

The EMR module will illuminate the "MAINT REQD" dash light after a predetermined time. Mileage will not cause the light to come on. The light will remain on until the EMR module is reset by inserting a small screwdriver into the hole in the module (RWD only) and depressing the reset switch (FWD and RWD).

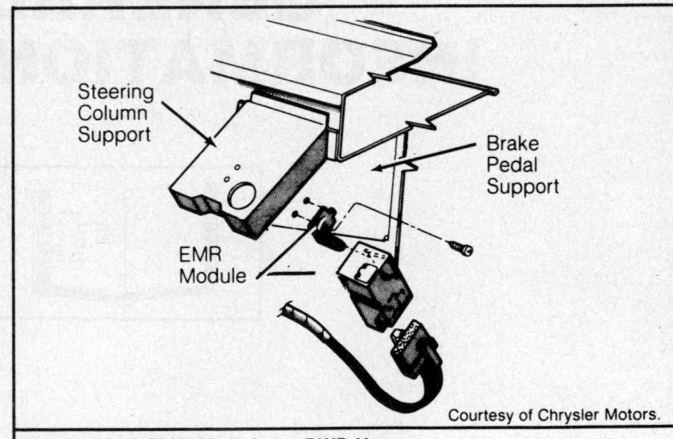

Steering Column Support

Brake Pedal Support

EMR Module

Courtesy of Chrysler Motors.

Fig. 3: 1988 EMR Module – RWD Van

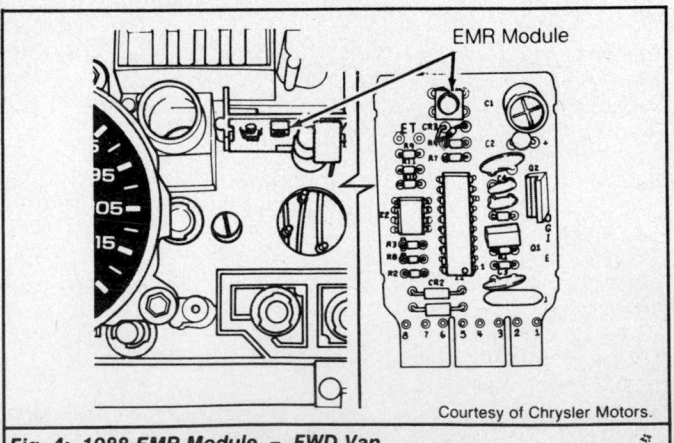

EMR Module

Courtesy of Chrysler Motors.

Fig. 4: 1988 EMR Module – FWD Van

MAINTENANCE REMINDER LIGHT
1980-89 Reset Procedures Domestic Cars & Trucks (Cont.)

G-3

The EMR module is located on the steering column behind instrument panel on RWD vans and in the instrument cluster on FWD vans. *See Fig. 3 and 4.* On trucks, it is located behind the far right side of dash panel next to the glove box. *See Fig. 5.* On Dakota models, module is located on bracket below headlight switch on rear of instrument panel. *See Fig. 6.*

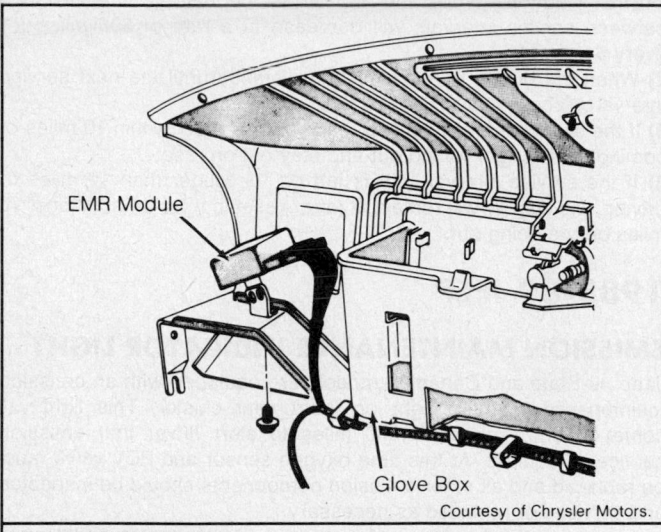

Fig. 5: 1988 EMR Module – Light Trucks (Exc. Dakota)

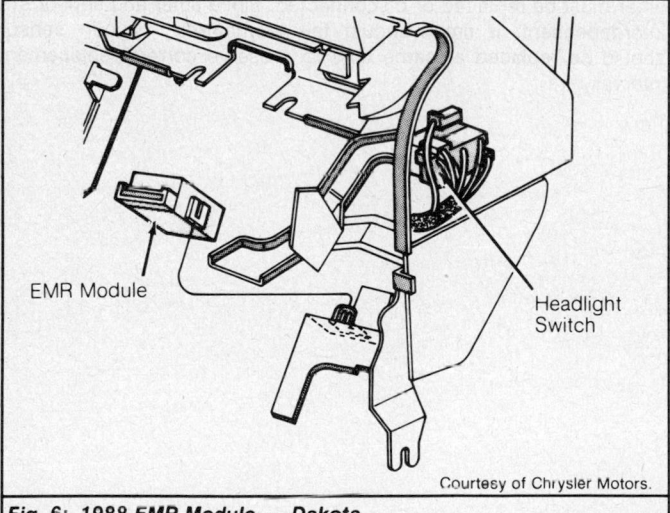

Fig. 6: 1988 EMR Module – Dakota

1989 LIGHT DUTY TRUCKS & VANS

The Emission Maintenance Reminder (EMR) light is designed to be a reminder to service the vehicle emissions control system. It is not an emissions warning system, only a reminder to perform emissions servicing.

1) Using the Chrysler DRB-II Tester (C-4805), select "EMISSIONS EMR TESTS". Select "EMR MEMORY CHECK". DRB-II display will read, "EMR MEMORY CHECK ARE YOU SURE ?". Press "Yes" key on DRB-II.

2) DRB-II display will read, "IS INSTRUMENT PANEL MILEAGE BETWEEN 9953 AND 10051 ?". If odometer mileage on vehicle is within specification, press "Yes" key on DRB-II. DRB-II will display "EMR MEMORY CHECK TEST COMPLETE". EMR light is reset. If odometer mileage on vehicle is not within specification shown on DRB-II, go to next step.

3) Press "No" key on DRB-II. DRB-II will read "DO YOU WANT TO CORRECT EMR MILEAGE ?". Press "Yes" key on DRB-II. DRB-II

will display "ENTER MILEAGE SHOWN ON INSTRUMENT PANEL USE ENTER KEY TO END".

4) Enter mileage shown on instrument panel. Do not enter tenths. Press "Enter" key on DRB-II. DRB-II will ask for verification of entry. If mileage entry was correct, DRB-II will display "EMR MEMORY CHECK TEST COMPLETE". Vehicle must be driven for at least 8 miles for mileage reset to take place.

EAGLE

PREMIER (1988-89)

Service Interval Reminder Light – Every 7500 miles, a Vehicle Maintenance Monitor (VMM) will illuminate a "SERVICE" interval reminder light. This indicates regular maintance is due. After required service is performed, press "RESET" button on dash below VMM display. Hold button until a "beep" is heard. VMM display will now be clear.

FORD MOTOR CO.

1980-89 PASSENGER CARS

NOTE: Ford Motor Co. 1980-89 passenger cars do not use an emission maintenance reminder. See SERVICE INTERVAL REMINDER LIGHT.

SERVICE INTERVAL REMINDER LIGHT

1985-89 Ford Passenger Cars – Every 5000 or 7500 miles, depending upon engine application, a "SERVICE" interval reminder light will illuminate (for approximately 30 seconds) on the dash, or begin flashing depending on model, indicating an oil change is due. To reset reminder light, turn ignition on. Simultaneously depress and hold "TRIP" ("ODO SEL" on Taurus and Sable), ("SYSTEM CHECK" on Continental) and "TRIP RESET" buttons. On Probe models, depress and hold service reset button located on speed alarm keyboard. On all models, three beeps will verify that reminder light has been reset.

1985-87 LIGHT DUTY TRUCKS, 1988 NON-EEC LIGHT DUTY TRUCKS & 1989 HEAVY DUTY TRUCKS

NOTE: 1980-84 trucks do not use an emission maintenance reminder light.

Ford Motor Co. 1985-87 light duty trucks (Aerostar vans, and Federal light and medium duty trucks), 1988 non-EEC equipped light duty trucks and 1989 heavy duty trucks use a maintenance reminder light to indicate emission system maintenance is required. Control unit (timer) for maintenance light is located under dash near steering column or behind glove box. Control unit may be hidden behind bracket on some truck models. Maintenance light is triggered after 2000 key starts (about 60,000 miles). After servicing emission system, reset light on models with resettable timer.

1) Turn ignition off. Remove tape over reset hole in timer. Lightly push a small Phillips screwdriver into hole in timer unit marked "RESET". With light pressure on screwdriver, turn ignition switch to "RUN" position.

2) Light should stay on while screwdriver is pressed down. Hold screwdriver down for approximately 5 seconds. Remove screwdriver. Light should go out within 2-5 seconds. If not, repeat steps **1)** and **2)**.

3) Cycle ignition from "OFF" to "RUN" position. Light should glow for 2 to 5 seconds. This verifies proper reset of maintenance reminder light.

G-4

MAINTENANCE REMINDER LIGHT
1980-89 Reset Procedures Domestic Cars & Trucks (Cont.)

NOTE: Some models use a non-resettable control unit. Replace it with a resettable type. Non-EEC vehicles for 1988 are the 2.0L Ranger, 6.1L and 7.0L gasoline trucks.

GENERAL MOTORS

Every 30,000 miles (15,000 for Cadillac), a reminder "flag" appears in speedometer face, indicating service of oxygen sensor is necessary. *See Fig. 7.*

1980 EXCEPT CADILLAC

Remove instrument panel trim plate. Remove instrument cluster lens. Using pointed tool, apply light downward pressure on notches of flag until it is reset. An alignment mark will appear in left center of odometer window when flag is fully reset.

1980 CADILLAC

Remove lower steering column cover. Sensor reset cable is located to the left of the speedometer cluster. Pull cable lightly (maximum 2 lbs. force). Reinstall lower steering column cover.

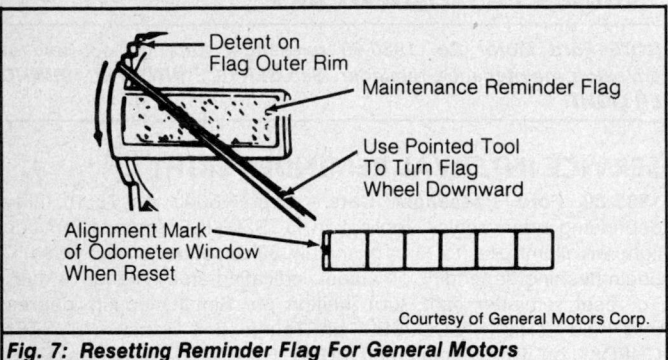

Courtesy of General Motors Corp.

Fig. 7: Resetting Reminder Flag For General Motors

1989 PONTIAC BONNEVILLE & 1987-89 6000 STE

Service Interval Reminder Light – A "SERVICE" light is used on models with a Driver's Information Center (DIC). After performing necessary services, reset service reminder light.

1) Display the desired item on the DIC. Press and hold down the "RESET" button. While the button is depressed, the distance between service intervals will decrease at a rate of 500 miles for every 5 seconds.

2) When the button is released, the distance until the next service interval will be displayed on the DIC.

3) If the service interval light for each item is reset within 10 miles of coming on, the light will go out and stay out on reset.

4) If the service interval light is left on for longer than 10 miles of driving, the display will remain lit (after resetting) for an additional 10 miles before going out.

1988-89 JEEP

EMISSION MAINTENANCE INDICATOR LIGHT

Jeep 49-State and Canadian models are equipped with an emission maintenance indicator light on instrument cluster. This light will come on one time at 82,500 miles to alert driver that emission service is required. At this time oxygen sensor and PCV valve must be replaced and all other emission components should be inspected and serviced or replaced as necessary.

Indicator timer is located under dash near accelerator pedal or to right of steering column. Timer cannot be reset. To turn off light, timer must be replaced or disconnected. Since timer and sensor are interdependent, if timer should fail prematurely, oxygen sensor should be replaced at same time to preserve correct replacement interval.

1989 VIN CODE EXPLANATION
All Manufacturers

1G1AZ37AGE5 100001
① ② ③ ④ ⑤ ⑥ ⑦ ⑧ ⑨ ⑩ ⑪ ⑫ ⑬ ⑭ ⑮ ⑯ ⑰

① FIRST CHARACTER – Indicates Nation of Origin.
② SECOND CHARACTER – Indicates Manufacturer.
③ THIRD CHARACTER – Indicates Make and Type.
④ FOURTH CHARACTER – Indicates Restraint System.
⑤ FIFTH CHARACTER – Indicates Carline/Series.
⑥⑦ SIXTH & SEVENTH CHARACTER – Indicates Body Types.
⑧ EIGHTH CHARACTER – Indicates Engine Type and Make.
⑨ NINTH CHARACTER – Indicates Check Digit.
⑩ TENTH CHARACTER – Indicates Model Year.
⑪ ELEVENTH CHARACTER – Indicates Assembly Plant.
⑫⑬⑭⑮⑯⑰ LAST SIX CHARACTERS – Indicates Plant Sequential Number.

CHRYSLER MOTORS VIN ENGINE CODES ⑧

Code Digit	Engine
A	2.2L 4-Cyl. MPFI Turbo II
D	2.2L 4-Cyl. TBI
J	2.5L 4-Cyl. MPFI Turbo I
K	2.5L 4-Cyl. TBI
3	3.0L V6 MPFI
P	5.2L V8 2-Bbl. Std.
4	5.2L V8 4-Bbl. Std.
S	5.2L V8 4-Bbl. Police

EAGLE PREMIER VIN ENGINE CODES ⑧

Code Digit	Engine
H	2.5L 4-Cyl. TBI
U	3.0L V6 MPFI

FORD MOTOR CO. VIN ENGINE CODES ⑧

Code Digit	Engine
9	1.9L 4-Cyl. CFI
J	1.9L 4-Cyl. MPFI H.O.
C	2.2L 4-Cyl. CFI
L	2.2L 4-Cyl. MPFI Turbo
A	2.3L 4-Cyl. MPFI OHC
X	2.3L 4-Cyl. MPFI HSC
S	2.3L 4-Cyl. MPFI HSO
D	2.5L 4-Cyl. CFI HSC
U	3.0L V6 MPFI
Y	3.0L V6 SEFI-MA SHO
3	3.8L V6 SEFI
4	3.8L V6 SEFI
R	3.8L V6 SEFI-MA SC
E	5.0L V8 SEFI-MA H.O.
F	5.0L V8 SEFI
G	5.8L V8 2-Bbl. VV Police

VIN DATE CODES ⑩

Code	Model Year
A	1980
B	1981
C	1982
D	1983
E	1984
F	1985
G	1986
H	1987
J	1988
K	1989

1989 ENGINE & MODEL CONVERSIONS
All Manufacturers

ENGINE SIZE CONVERSIONS

CHRYSLER MOTORS ENGINES

Liters	Cubic Inches
2.2 4-Cyl.	135
2.5 4-Cyl.	153
3.0 V6	181
5.2 V8	318

EAGLE ENGINES

Liters	Cubic Inches
2.5 4-Cyl.	150
3.0 V6	180

FORD MOTOR CO. ENGINES

Liters	Cubic Inches
1.9 4-Cyl.	116
2.2 4-Cyl.	135
2.3 4-Cyl.	140
2.5 4-Cyl.	153
3.0 V6	182
3.8 V6	232
5.0 V8	302
5.8 V8	351

MODEL USAGE

Because many models produced by the domestic manufacturers share the same frame, powertrain and chassis components, Mitchell does not always list all the models in a given article. The following charts show the models as they are called out by Mitchell, and the complete model list for those same models according to the manufacturer.

CHRYSLER MOTORS MODELS

Mitchell Application	Actual Models
Acclaim	Sedan
Aries	"LE" Sedan
Daytona	Base, "ES" & Shelby Hatchbacks
Dynasty	Sedan
Diplomat	Salon & "SE" Sedan
Fifth Avenue	Hardtop Sedan
Gran Fury	Salon Sedan
Horizon	Hatchback
Lancer	Base & "ES" Sedan
LeBaron	Sedan & Convertible
LaBaron GTS	Hatchback
New Yorker	Base & Landau Sedan
Omni	Hatchback
Reliant	"LE" Sedan
Shadow	Hatchback
Spirit	Sedan
Sundance	Hatchback

EAGLE MODELS

Mitchell Application	Actual Models
Premier	"ES", "ES" Limited & "LX" Sedans

FORD MOTOR CO. MODELS

Mitchell Application	Actual Models
Continental	Base & Signature Series Sedans
Cougar	"LS" & XR7 Coupes
Escort	"GT", "LX" & Pony Hatchbacks & Wagons
Grand Marquis	"GS" & "LS" Sedans, & Colony Park "GS" & "LS" Wagons
Lincoln Town Car	Base, Signature & Cartier Sedans
Crown Victoria	Base, "LX" & "S" Sedans & Wagons, Country Squire & Country Squire "LX" Wagons
Mark VII	Bill Blass Designer & "LSC" Sedans
Mustang	"LX" & "GT" Hatchbacks, Sedan & Convertibles
Probe	"GL", "LX" & "GT" Hatchbacks
Sable	"GS" & "LS" Sedans & Wagons
Taurus	"GL", "L" & "LX" Sedans, & Wagons SHO Sedan
Tempo	"GL", "GLS", "LX", & 4WD Sedans
Thunderbird	Base, "LX" & Super Coupes
Topaz	"GS", "LS", "LTS" & XR5 Sedans
Town Car	Base, Signature & Cartier Designer Series Sedans

NOTE: The following list of abbreviations, used most frequently in Mitchell's Service & Repair Manuals, is provided for your assistance. Although the majority of these abbreviations will be found in Mitchell's Wiring Diagrams, you may also find some of them used in articles dealing with Tune-Up, CEC, Emissions, Fuel Systems, Electrical, Air Conditioning, Body Repair and other such subjects.

CAUTION: As some abbreviations may have more than one application and some applications may have more than one abbreviation over the years, exercise caution that the definition provided here is logical for your vehicle's situation. For example, reason would help you determine whether "Alt." stands for Alternator, Altitude or for neither (an unlisted) definition.

A

A – Amperes
AAC – Auxiliary Air Control
AAP – Auxiliary Acceleration Pump
AAS – Aspirator Air System
AAS – Auto Adjust Suspension
AAV – Anti-Afterburn Valve
AB – Air Bleed
ABAV – Air Bleed Actuator Valve
ABDC – After Bottom Dead Center
ABS – Acrylonitrile Butadian Styrene Resin (Type of Plastic Used in Cars)
ABS – Altitude Barometric Switch
ABS – Anti-Lock Brake System
Abs. – Absolute
ABV – Air By-Pass Valve
AC – Alternating Current
AC – Altiutude Compensator
ACCWM – Air Cleaner Cold Weather Modulator
A/C – Air Conditioner
A/C – Air Conditioning
A/C Cltch. – A/C Clutch
Accel. – Accelerator
ACCS – A/C Clutch Cycling Switch
Accum. – Accumulator
Accy. – Accessory
Ack. – Acknowledge
ACD – Auxiliary Control Device
ACDV – Air Cleaner Diverter Valve
ACkV – Air Check Valve
A/CL – Air Cleaner
A/CL-BM – Air Cleaner Bimetal Sensor
A/CL-BMS – Air Cleaner Bimetal Sensor
A/CL-CWM – Air Cleaner Cold Weather Modulator
A/CL-DV – Air Cleaner Duct Valve Vacuum Motor
A/CL-TSOV – Air Cleaner Temperature Sensor Override Valve
A/CL-VCD – Air Cleaner Vacuum Control Delay
A/CL-VCV – Air Cleaner Vacuum Control Valve
A/CL-VM – Air Cleaner Vacuum Motor
ACT – Air Charge Temperature
Actu. – Actuator
Actv. – Active
ACV – Air Control Valve
Adj. – Adjust or Adjustable
ADL – Automatic Door Lock
ADS – Anti-Dieseling Solenoid
Adv. – Advance
AFC – Airflow Controlled Fuel Injection
AGE – Air Guard
AI – Air Injection
AICV – Air Injection Check Valve
AID – Air Injection Dual
A.I.R. or AIR – Air Injection Reactor
AIR-BPV – AIR By-Pass Valve
AIR-ChV – AIR Check Valve
AIR-DVLV – AIR Diverter Valve
AIR-IVV – AIR Idle Vacuum Valve

AIR. Sel. – AIR Selector
AIS – Air Injection System
AIS – Air Injection Single
AIV – Air Injection Valve
AIVV – Air Idle Vacuum Valve
ALCL – Assembly Line Communication Link
ALDL – Assembly Line Data (Diagnostic) Link
Alm. – Alarm
Alt. – Alternator
Alt. or Alti. – High Altitude Emissions
Amb. – Ambient
AMC – American Motors Corporation
AMgV – Air Management Valve
Amm. – Ammeter
Amp – Ampere
Amp. – Amplifier
Ant. – Antenna
ANTBV or ANTI-BFV – Anti-Backfire Valve
Anti-Dsl. – Anti-Diesel
APCV – Air Pump Control Valve
APDV – Air Pump Diverter Valve
APD-VLV – Air Pump Diverter Valve
APREVLV – Air Pump Relief Valve
AS – Airflow Sensor
AS – Air Suction
ASCPS – Air Switch Canister Purge Solenoid
ASCPT – Air Switch Canister Purge Timer
ASDV – Air Switching Diverter Valve
ASM – Assembly
ASRV – Air Switching Relief Valve
ASS – Air Switching Solenoid
Assy. – Assembly
ASV – Air Switching Valve
ASVS – Air Switching Vacuum Solenoid
A/T – Automatic Transaxle or Transmission
ATC – Automatic Temperature Control
ATDC – After Top Dead Center
ATF – Automatic Transmission Fluid
ATS – Air Temperature Sensor
Auto. – Automatic
Auto. Trans. – Automatic Transaxle or Transmission
Aux. – Auxiliary
Avg. – Average
AWD – Air Warning Device
AXOD – Automatic Overdrive Transaxle

B

Bap. Sens. – Barometric Absolute Pressure Sensor
Baro. – Barometric
Batt. – Battery
BBDC – Before Bottom Dead Center
Bbl. – Barrel
BCDD – Boost Controlled Deceleration Device
BCM – Body Control Module
BHP – Brake Horsepower
Bi. Met. – Bi-Metallic Air Temperature Control Sensor
Bk. – Back
Bk. Rest – Back Rest
Blst. – Ballast

Blwr. – Blower
BMAP or BMAPS – Barometric and Manifold Absolute Pressure Sensor
B/P – EGR Back Pressure Transducer
BPEGR – Back Pressure EGR
BPS – Exhaust Back Pressure Sensor
BPS – Barometric Pressure Sensor
BPT – Back Pressure Transducer
PBV – By-Pass Valve
Brkr. – Breaker
BS – Barometric Switch
BS – Bimetal Sensor
BTDC – Before Top Dead Center
Bulkhd. – Bulkhead
BTU – British Thermal Units
B/U or B-U – Back-Up
Buz. – Buzzer
BV – Bowl Vent Port
BVT – Backpressure Variable Transducer

C

C or C° – Celcius
C³I – Computer Controlled Coil Ignition
C4 – Computer Controlled Catalytic Converter
CAC or CACV – Combined Air Control Valve
Calib. – Calibration
Calif. – California
Can. – Canada
Can. – Canister
Canc. – Cancel
CanCV – Canister Control Valve
Can. Prg. – Canister Purge
Cap. – Capacitor or Capacity
Carb. – Carburetor
CARB – California Air Resources Board
CAT or Cat. – Catalytic Converter
CATV – Cold Temperature Activated Vacuum
CB – Circuit Breaker
CB – Choke Breaker
CBS – Coasting By-Pass System
CC – Cruise Control
cc – Cubic Centimeters
CCC – Computer Command Control
CCS – Controlled Combustion System
CEAB – Cold Engine Air Bleed
CC EGR – Coolant Controlled EGR
CCEV or CCEVS – Coolant Control Engine Vacuum Switch
CCEVV – Coolant Control Engine Vacuum Valve
CCIV – Coolant Control Idle Enrichment Valve
CCOT – Cycling Clutch Orifice Tube
CCP – Controlled Canister Purge
CCS – Controlled Combustion System

CCW – Counterclockwise
CD-REGVLV – Crankcase Depression
    Regulator Valve
CEAB – Cold Engine Air Bleed
CEC – Combined Emission
    Control (Valve)
CEC – Computerized Emission Control
CEC – Computerized Engine Control
Cent. – Center
CESS – Cold Engine Sensor Switch
CFI – Central Fuel Injection
CFI – Cross Fire Injection
Chk. – Check
Chk. Eng. – Check Engine
Chng. – Change
Chrg. – Charge or Charging
ChVLV – Check Valve
CI – Cubic Inches
CID – Cubic Inch Displacement
Cig. – Cigarette
Cig. Ltr. – Cigarette Lighter
Circ. – Circuit
Circ. Brkr. – Circuit Breaker
CIS – Continuous Injection System
CIS-E – CIS-Electronic
CkDL-VLV – Check Delay Valve
Ckt. – Circuit
Ck-VLV – Check Valve
CL – Closed Loop
CLCC – Closed Loop
    Carburetor Control
Clch. – Clutch
CLEC – Closed Loop
    Emission Control
Clk. – Clock
Clmn. – Column
Clmt. – Climate
Clrnc. – Clearance
Clstr. – Cluster
CMH – Cold Mixture Heater
Cmpnstr. – Compensator
Cmptr. – Computer
Cncld. – Concealed
Cntr. – Central or Center
Cnvnc. – Convenience
CO – Carbon Monoxide
CO – Choke Opener
CO_2 – Carbon Dioxide
COC – Conventional Oxidation
    Catalyst
Colng. – Cooling
Colnt. – Coolant
Comb. – Combination
Comp. – Compressor
Compens – Compensation
Compt. – Compartment
Cond. – Condenser
Conn. – Connector or Connection
Cont. – Continued or Control
Conv. – Convertible or
    Converter
Count. – Counter
CoV – Control Valve
CP – Canister Purge
CPCV – Canister Purge Control
    Valve
CPS – Canister Purge Solenoid
CPS – Central Power Supply
CP-TVS – Canister Purge TVS
CPU – Central Processing Unit
CPV – Canister Purge Valve
CPVVV – Choke Pulldown
    Vacuum Vent Valve
CRS – Choke Return System
Crnr. – Corner
Crnrng. – Cornering
CRT – Cathode Ray Tube
CRTC – Cathode Ray Tube
    Controller
CRV – Coasting Richer Valve
CSCS – Cold Start Control
    Solenoid
CSSA – Cold Start Spark
    Advance
CT – Cold Temperature

CTAV – Cold Temperature
    Actuated Vacuum or
    Ignition Advance
CTO – Coolant Temperature
    Override
Ctrl. – Control
Ctrlld. – Controlled
Ctrllr. – Controller
CTS or CTSW – Coolant Temperature
    Switch
CTSWH – Closed Throttle Switch
Ctsy. – Courtesy
CTTS – Coolant Temperature
    Thermo Switch
CTVS – Choke Thermal
    Vacuum Switch
Cu. In. – Cubic Inches
CV – Check Valve
CV – Constant Velocity
CVSCC – Coolant Vacuum Switch
    Cold Closed
CVSCO – Coolant Vacuum Switch
    Cold Open
CVS3P – Cold Vacuum Spark, 3-Port
CW – Clockwise
Cyl. – Cylinder

D

"D" – Drive
Damp. – Damper
DAS – Distributor Advance
    Solenoid
DBC – Dual Bed Catalytic
DC – Direct Current
DC – Digijet Control
DCLV or DC-VLV – Deceleration Valve
DCM/C-VLV – Deceleration Mixture
    Control Valve
DCP-TVS – Distributor &
    Canister Purge TVS
DCS – Deceleration Control System
DCTO – Dual Coolant
    Temperature Override
DD – Dual Distributors
DDD – Dual Diaphragm
    Distributor
DDV – Distributor Decel Valve
DEC – Digital Engine Control
Decel. – Deceleration
Def. – Defroster
Defog. – Defogger
Deg. – Degree
De-Ice. – De-Icer
Del. – Delay
Desig. – Designation
Detec. – Detector
Deton. – Detonation
Detrnt. – Deterrent
DFI – Digital Fuel Injection
Dft. – Defeat
DI – Deceleration Idle
Diag. – Diagnostic
DIDV – Dual Ignition Delay Valve
Diff. – Differential
Dig. – Digital
Dim. – Dimmer
Dir. – Direction or Directional
Disp. – Display
Dist. – Distribution
Distr. – Distributor
Dlx. – Deluxe
Dly. – Delay
DME – Digital Motor Electronics
DMS – Dual Manifold System
Dn. – Down
Dnshft. – Downshift
DP – Dashpot
DPD – Dual Point Distributor
Dr. – Door
Drop. – Dropping
DRS – Distributor Retard
    Solenoid
Drvr. – Driver

DS – Detonation Sensor
DS – Distributor Spark
Dsl. – Diesel
Dstnc. – Distance
DTM – Decel Throttle Modulator
DTVS – Distributor Thermal
    Vacuum Switch
DV – Decel Valve
DV – Delay Valve
DV – Diverter Valve
DVAS – Distributor Vacuum
    Advance Solenoid
DVCS – Distributor Vacuum
    Control Switch
DVCV – Differential Vacuum
    Control Valve
DVD – Differential Delay Valve
DVDSV – Differential Vacuum
    Delay Separator Valve
DVDV – Distributor Vacuum
    Delay Valve
DVRV – Distributor Vacuum
    Regulating Valve
DVTR-VLV – Diverter Valve
DVTW – Delay Valve Two-Way
DVVV – Distributor Vacuum
    Vent Valve

E

EAC – Electronic Air
    Control
EAC – Electric Assist Choke
EAVS – Electrically Actuated
    Vacuum Switch
EBCV – Electric Air
    Bleed Control Valve
EC – Electric Choke
ECA – Electronic Control
    Assembly
ECC – Electronic Chassis Control
ECC – Electronic Climate Control
ECC – Electronic Computer Control
ECC – Electronic Controlled
    Carburetor
ECCS – Electronic Concentrated
    Control System
ECI – Electronic Controlled
    Ignition
ECI – Electronic Controlled
    Injection
ECM – Electronic Control
    Module
Econ. – Economy
ECRV – Emission Control
    Regulator Valve
ECS – Electronic Control
    Suspension
ECS – Emission Control System
ECT – Electronic Control
    Transmission
ECT – Engine Coolant Temperature
ECU – Electronic Control Unit
EDF – Electro Drive Fan
EDM – Electronic Distributor
    Modulator
EEC – Electronic Engine Control
EEC – Evaporative Emission
    Control
EFC – Electronic Fuel Control
EFE – Early Fuel Evaporator
EFI – Electronic Fuel Injection
EGO – Exhaust Gas Oxygen
EGO Sens. Gnd. – EGO Sensor Ground
EGR – Exhaust Gas Recirculation
EGR-BldSOL – EGR Bleed Solenoid
EGRC or EGRCS – EGR Control
    Solenoid
EGR-CLR – EGR Cooler
EGR-CTS – EGR Charge
    Temperature Sensor
EGR-DV – EGR Delay Valve
EGR-EPV – EGR External
    Pressure Valve

EGR-EVR – EGR Electronic Vacuum Regulator
EGR-RSR – EGR Reservoir
EGRV – EGR Vent Solenoid
EGR-VSOL – EGR Vacuum Solenoid
EGR-VVA – EGR Venturi Vacuum Amplifier
EIS – Electronic Ignition System
ELB – Electronic Lean Burn
ELC – Electronic Level or Load Control
Elec. – Electric
Elect. – Electronic
Emis. or **Emiss.** – Emission
Eng. – Engine
EPA – Environmental Protection Agency
EPS – Electronic Power Steering
EPR – Exhaust Pressure Regulator
ESA – Electronic Spark Advance
ESC – Electronic Spark Control
ESS – Electronic Spark Selection
ESS – Engine Speed Sensor
ESSM – Engine Speed Switch Module
EST – Electronic Spark Timing
ETC – Electronic Throttle Control
ETS – Engine Temperature Switch
Evap. – Evaporative
EVCR – Emission Vacuum Control Regulator
EVRV – Electronic Vacuum Regulator Valve
EVS – Economy Vacuum Switch
Ex. or **Exc.** – Except or Excluding
Exch. – Exchange
Exh. – Exhaust
Ext. – Exterior
EZF – Performance Graph Ignition

F

F or **F°** – Fahrenheit
FAI – Fresh Air Intake
F/B – Feedback
F/B – Fuse Box or Block
FBC or **FC** – Feedback Carburetor
FCO – Fuel Cut-Off
FCS – Fuel Control System
FDC – Fuel Deceleration Control
FDLV – Forward Delay Valve
FDV – Fuel Decel Valve
FDV – Forward Delay Valve
Fed. – Federal
FES – Fuel Evaporation System
FFOT – Ford Fixed Orifice Tube
FIA – Fast Idle Actuator
FICD – Fast Idle Control Device
FISR – Fast Idle Solenoid Relay
FJEGR – Floor Jet EGR
Flshr. – Flasher
Fnt. – Front
Fnt. WD – Front Wheel Drive
FR – Fuel Return
Freq. – Frequency
F/Rly. Pnl. – Fuse/Relay Panel
Frwd. – Forward
FS – Forward Spark
FS – Fuel Separator
FSS – Fuel Shutoff System
Ft. Lbs. or **ft. lbs.** – Foot Pounds
FTVC – Fuel Tank Vapor Control
Func. – Function
Fus. – Fusible
Fus. Link – Fusible Link

FVEC – Fuel Vapor Emission Control
FVR – Fuel Vapor Return
4WD – Four-Wheel Drive
4WS – Four-Wheel Steering
FWD – Front Wheel Drive

G

g – Grams
Ga. – Gauge
Gals. – gallons
Gen. – Generator
Gnd. – Ground
Gov. – Governor

H

HAC – High Altitude Compensator
HADV – Heated Air Delay Valve
HAI – Heated Air Intake
Harn. – Harness
HAS – High Altitude System
HATSV – Heated Air Temperature Sensing Valve
Haz. – Hazard
HC – Hydrocarbons
H/D – Heavy Duty
HDC – Heavy Duty Cooling
HDSP-CT – Heavy Duty Spark Coolant Temperature Override
HDSP-CTO – Heavy Duty Spark Coolant Temperature Override
HDVA-CTO – Heavy Duty Vacuum Advance CTO
Headlt. – Headlight
HEDF – High Electro Drive Fan
HEI – High Energy Ignition
HEGO – Heated Exhaust Gas Oxygen Sensor
Hg – Mercury
Hgt. – Height
Hi. – High Beam
Hi. Alt. or **High Alt.** – High Altitude
HIC – Hot Idle Compensator
HICV – HIC Valve
Hi-Spd. – High Speed
Hndl. – Handle
HO – High Output
HP – Horsepower
HP – High Performance
Hrn. – Horn
Hsg. – Housing
HSLA – High Strength Low Alloy (Steel)
HT – High Temperature
Htr. – Heater
HTR – Heavy Truck
HW-AFC – Hot Wire AFC
Hyd. – Hydraulic
Hz – Hertz (Cycles Per Second)

I

IAC – Idle Air Control
IAS – Idle Air Stepper
IC – Idle Compensator
IC – Integrated Circuit
ICM – Ignition Control Module
ICVS – Idle Control Solenoid Vacuum Switch
I.D. – Inside Diameter
IDI – Integrated Direct Ignition
IES – Idle Enrichment System
Ign. – Ignition
Ign. Gnd. – Ignition Ground
Ign. Mod. Sens. – Ignition Module Sensor
II – Instrumented Injector
IIA – Integrated Ignition Assembly
ILC – Idle Load Control
Illum. – Illumination

IMCO – Improved Combustion System
IMPCO – Improved Combustion System
In. – Inches
In. – Input
Incand. – Incandescent
INCH Lbs. – Inch Pounds
Ind. – Indicator
Infl. – Inflate
Info. – Information
In. Hg – Inches of Mercury
Inhib. – Inhibitor
Inj. – Injector or Injection
Inst. – Instrument
Inst. Clstr. – Instrument Cluster
Int. – Interior
Interm. – Intermittent
Intgrtd. – Integrated
Intgrtn. – Integration
Intrpt. – Interrupt
Invrtr. – Inverter
IPC – Instrument Panel Cluster
IPS – Ignition Pressure Switch
IS – Idle Switch
ISC or **ISCS** – Idle Speed Control
ISC – Idle Speed Compensator
ISS – Idle Stop Solenoid
ITCS or **ITS** – Ignition Timing Control System
ITEC – ITEC Fuel System
ITVS – Ignition Timing Vacuum Switch
IVV – Idle Vacuum Valve

J

JAS – Jet Air System
J/B – Junction Box
Jmpr. – Jumper
Junc. – Junction

K

KAPWR – Keep Alive Power
kg – Kilograms
kg/cm² – Kilograms Per Square Centimeter
k/ohms – 1000 ohms
Key. – Keyless
KS – Knock Sensor

L

L – Liter
Lat. – Latched
Lbs. – Pounds
LCD – Liquid Crystal Display
LCV – Load Control Valve
L/D – Light Duty (Emissions)
LED – Light Emitting Diode
L. Fnt. – Left Front
LFT – Left
Lftgte. – Liftgate
LH – Left-hand
LH-AFC – Bosch LH-Jetronic
Lic. – License
Lk. – Lock
Lmtr. – Limiter
Lo. – Low
Lps. – Lamps
LR – Left Rear
Lt. – Light
Lt. Duty – Light Duty
Ltr. – Lighter
Ltr. – Limiter
Lug. – Luggage
Lvl. – Level
L4 – 4-Cylinder
L6 – 6-Cylinder

M

Ma – Milliamps
MAF – Mass Airflow
MAFS – Mass Airflow Sensor
MAFTS – Manifold Air/Fuel
    Temperature Sensor
Mag. – Magnetic
Maint. – Maintenance
MAJC – Main Air Jet Control
Man. – Manual
Man. – Manifold
Man. Stg. – Manual Steering
Man. Trans. – Manual Transaxle
    or Transmission
MAP – Manifold Absolute Pressure
MAT – Manifold Air Temperature
MCU – Microprocessor Control Unit
MCV – Mixture Control Valve
MEC – Motronic Engine Control
Mem. – Memory
Merc. – Mercury
Mesg. – Message
Mfd. – Microfarads
MFI – Mechanical Fuel Injection
MFI – Multi-Port Fuel
    Injection
MHC or MHCV – Manifold Heat Control
    Valve
Mic. – Microphone
MIG – Metal Inert Gas (Welding)
Mir. – Mirror
Mixt. – Mixture
mkg – Meter Kilogram
mm – Millimeters
Mod. – Module
Mon. – Monitor
MPC – Manifold Pressure
    Controlled Fuel Injection
MPH – Miles Per Hour
MPI – Multi-Point Injection
Mtr. – Motor
M/T – Manual Transaxle or
    Transmission
MTA – Managed Thermactor Air
MVS – Manifold Vacuum Switch

N

"N" – Neutral Position
NC – Normally Closed
NCA – No Color Available
Neut. – Neutral
NLV – Non-Linear Valve
NLVR – NLV Regulator
N.m – Newton Meter
NO – Normally Open
No. or # – Number
Norm. – Normal
NOx – Oxides of Nitrogen

O

O – Oxygen
O₂ – Oxygen
OBC – On-Board Computer
OC – Oxidation Catalyst
O.D. – Outside Diameter
O/D – Overdrive
OL – Open Loop
Oper. – Operated
Opt. – Options or Optional
OS – Oxygen Sensor
OSAC – Orifice Spark
    Advance Control
OTCS – Over-Temperature
    Control System
OTS – Oil Temperature Switch
OXS or OXY – Oxygen Sensor
Ozs. – Ounces

P

"P" – Park Position
PACV – Pulse Air Check Valve
PAF – Pulse Air Feeder
PAI or PAIR – Pulse Air Injection
PAS – Pulse Air Solenoid
    or System
Pass. – Passenger
P/C – Printed Circuit
PCOV – Purge Control Valve
PCV – Positive Crankcase
    Ventilation
PCV – Purge Control Valve
PCVS – Positive Crankcase
    Ventilation Solenoid
PEVR – Power Enrichment
    Vacuum Regulator
PFI – Port Fuel Injection
PFI – Programmed Fuel Injection
PGCV – Purge Control Valve
PGM-FI – Programmed
    Fuel Injection
PHCV – Power Heat Control Valve
PHDV – Power Heat
    Delay Valve
PIP – Profile Ignition Pick-Up
Pkg. – Package
PLBS – Partial Lean Burn
    System
P/N – Park/Neutral
Pneu. – Pneumatic
Pnl. – Panel
Pos. – Positive
Postn. – Position
Pot. – Potentiometer
PPM – Parts Per Million
PPS – Ported Pressure Switch
PR-CV – Pressure Control Valve
Pres. – Pressure
Prgmr. – Programmer
Pri. – Primary
PRNDL – Park, Reverse,
    Neutral, Drive, Low
PROM – Programmable Read
    Only Memory
Prtl. – Partial
PS – Push Switch
P/S – Power Steering
psi – Pounds Per Square Inch
P/S Pres. Sw. – Power Steering
    Pressure Switch
PSV – Pulse Air Shutoff Valve
PTO – Power Take Off
Pts. – Pints
PV – Pulse Air Valve
PV – Purge Control Valve
PVA – Ported Vacuum Advance
PVBrk – Primary Vacuum Break
PVCS – Ported Vacuum
    Control System
PVCS – Power Valve
    Control System
PVFFC – Pressure/Vacuum
    Fuel Filler Cap
PVS – Ported Vacuum Switch
PVTS – Purge TVS
Pwr. – Power

Q

Qts. – Quarts

R

R – Rear
Rad. – Radiator
Rcvr. – Receiver
Rdcr. – Reducer
RDLV – Reverse Delay Valve
RDLVD – RDLV Dual
RDLVS – RDLV Single

RDO – Retard Delay Orifice
RDV or R-DLV – Retard Delay Valve
Recirc. – Recirculator
Reduct. – Reduction
Ref. – Reference
Reg. – Regulator
Rel. – Release
Res. – Resistor
Resist – Resistance
Retrac. – Retract or Retractor
Rev. – Revolution
RH or RTH – Right-hand
Rheo. – Rheostat
Rly. – Relay
Rly. Up – Relay Up
Rplnsg. – Replenishing
RPM – Revolutions Per Minute
RS – Reverse Spark
Rsm. – Resume
Rt. – Right
Rtd. – Retard
Rt. Fnt. – Right Front
Rtrn. – Return
RV – Rollover Valve
RVSV – Rollover/Vapor
    Separator Valve
RWD – Rear Wheel Drive

S

SADV-TVS – Spark Advance TVS
SA-FV – Separator Assembly
    Fuel Vacuum
SAS – Secondary Air Supply
Satlt. – Satellite
SAVM – Spark Advance
    Vacuum Modulator
S/B – Seat Belt
SBC – Single Bed Catalytic
SC – Signal Conditioner
SC – Stratified Charge
SCC – Spark Control Computer
SCS – Speed Control Switch
SCS – Spark Control System
SCS – Speed Controlled Spark
SCTO – Spark Coolant
    Temperature Override
SDV – Spark Delay Valve
Sec. – Secondary
SEC ACT – Secondary Actuator
SEFI – Sequential Electronic
    Fuel Injection
SEGR – Sub EGR or
    Secondary EGR
Sel. – Selector or Selection
Sen. or Sens. – Sensor
Send. – Sender
Sfty. – Safety
Shld. – Shield
Sig. – Signal
SO – Sensor Override
Sol. – Solenoid
Sole-Vac. or SLV – Solenoid Vacuum
Sol. V. – Solenoid Valve
Spd. – Speed
Speedo. – Speedometer
SPFI – Sequential Port
    Fuel Injection
SPK – Spark
Spk. Ret. – Spark Retard
SP-TVS – Spark Thermal
    Vacuum Switch
SRDV or SRD-VLV – Spark Retard
    Delay Valve
SRS – Supplementary
    Restraint System
SS – Start Control System
SSC ACT – Stepped Speed
    Control Actuator
SSC SOL – Stepped Speed
    Control Solenoid
SSI – Solid State Ignition
St. – Start
Stab. – Stabilizer

Sta. Wag. – Station Wagon
STC or **STCS** – Spark Timing Control
Std. – Standard
Stop Lt. – Stop Light
Strkr. – Striker
Strng. – Steering
Strtr. – Starter
STVS – Spark Thermal
Vacuum Switch
STVS – Secondary Throttle
Valve System
SUCS – Shift-Up Control System
Supp. – Supply
Susp. – Suspension
S-V – Sol-Vac
SVB – Secondary Vacuum Break
SVBrk – Secondary Vacuum Break
SV-CBV – Solenoid Valve
Carb Bowl Vent
SVV – Solenoid Vent Valve
Sw. – Switch
Swover. – Switchover
SWV – Switching Valve
Sys. – System

T

TAB – Thermactor Air By-Pass
TAC – Thermostatic Air
Cleaner
Tach. – Tachometer
TAD – Thermactor Air Diverter
Taillt. – Taillight
TBI – Throttle Body Injection
TBVV – Thermal Bowl Vent Valve
TC – Throttle Closer
TCC – Transmission Converter Clutch
TCCS – Toyota Computer
Control System
TCDV – Thermal Check
& Delay Valve
TC-DVLV – Torque Converter
Delay Valve
TCE – Transmission Controlled EGR
TCS – Transmission
Controlled Spark
TCS – Transmission Converter
Switch
TC-TVS – Torque Converter TVS
TCV – Thermal Control Valve
TCVS – Torque Converter
Vacuum Switch
TDC – Top Dead Center
TDS – Time Delay Sensor
Temp. – Temperature
TEMS – Toyota Electronic
Modulated Suspension
Tens. – Tension
Tens. Rdcr. – Tension Reducer
Term. – Terminal
TES – Thermal Electric Switch
TFI – Thick Film Integrated
Therm. – Thermostat or Thermistor
THM – Turbo Hydra-Matic
Throt. – Throttle
TIC – Thermal Ignition
Control Valve
TIDC – Thermostatic Ignition
Distributor Control
TIG – Tungsten Inert
Gas (Welding)
TIV – Thermal Idle Valve
TK – Throttle Kicker
TLA – Throttle Lever Actuator
TO – Thermal Override
TOCS – Throttle Opener
Control System
TP – Throttle Positioner

TPBPV – Tank Pressure By-Pass
Valve
TP-CV – Tank Pressure
Control Valve
TPI – Tuned Port Injection
TPS or **Th. Sens.** – Throttle
Position Sensor
TPSW – Throttle Position
Switch
TPV – Throttle Poppet Valve
T-Q – Thermo-Quad
TR – Thermal Reactor
Trans. – Transaxle/Transmission
Transis. – Transistor
TRC – Throttle Return Control
TRC-SOL-CVLV – TRC Solenoid
Control Valve
TrC-TVS – Transmission Lock-Up
Converter TVS
TrC-VS – Transmission Lock-Up
Converter Vacuum Switch
TRest – Tee Restrictor
Tripmdr. – Tripminder
Trnsmtr. – Transmitter
TS – Trapped Spark
TSD – Throttle Solenoid
TSP – Throttle Solenoid Positioner
Turbo – Turbocharger
TV – Thermo Valve
T.V. – Throttle Valve
TV-RST – Hose Tee Vacuum
Restrictor
TVS – Thermal Vacuum Switch
TVV – Thermal Vent Valve
TVV – Temperature Vacuum
System Valve
TWC – Three Way Catalytic
Twilt. – Twilight
2WD – 2-Wheel Drive
Typ. – Typical

U

UIC – Universal Integrated
Circuit
Unlat. – Unlatched
UVS – Underhood Vent System

V

V – Volts
V6 – V6 Engine
V8 – V8 Engine
VA – Vacuum Amplifier
Vac. – Vacuum
VAC – Vacuum Advance Control
VACP – Vacuum Pump
VA-CTO – Vacuum Advance CTO
Vac.VV – Vacuum Vent Valve
Var. – Variable
VASC – Vacuum Advance
SparkControl
VATS – Vehicle Anti-Theft System
VB – Vacuum Break
VCC – Viscous Clutch
Converter
VCkV – Vacuum Check Valve
VCS – Vacuum Controlled Switch
VCV – Vacuum Control Valve
VDV or **VDVLV** – Vacuum Delay Valve
VDV – Vacuum Differential Valve
VDV – Vacuum Diverter Valve
Veh. – Vehicle
Vert. – Vertical
VHC – Vacuum Exhaust
Heat Control Valve

VIN – Vehicle Identification
Number
VIS – Vacuum Input Switch
VLDL or **VLDV** – Vacuum Delay Valve
Vlv. – Valve
VM – Vacuum Modulator
VMCV – Vacuum Modulator
Check Valve
VMV – Vacuum Modulator
Valve
VMVS – Vacuum Modulator
Valve Switch
Volt. – Voltage
VOTM – Vacuum Operated
Throttle Modulator
VP – Vacuum Pump
VPOC – Vacuum Pull-Off Choke
V. Pwr. – Vehicle Power
VPWR – Vehicle Power
VR – Vacuum Reservoir
VRCkV – Vacuum Reverse
Check Valve
VRDV – Vacuum Retard Delay Valve
VReser – Vacuum Reservoir
VRest – Vacuum Restrictor
VRS – Vacuum Regulator/Solenoid
VRS – Vacuum Retard Switch
VRV – Vacuum Reducer Valve
VRV – Vacuum Regulator Valve
VS – Vacuum Solenoid
VS – Vacuum Switch
VSA – Vacuum Switch Assembly
VSD – Vacuum Switch Dump
VSDV – Vacuum Source
(or Signal) Dump Valve
V-RSR – Vacuum Reservoir
V-RST – Vacuum Restrictor
VSS – Vehicle Speed Sensor
VSV – Vacuum Solenoid Valve
VTK – Vacuum Throttle Kicker
VTM – Vacuum Throttle Modulator
VTP – Vacuum Throttle Positioner
VVA – Venturi Vacuum Amplifier
VVCS – Vacuum Vent Control System
VVCV – Vacuum Vent Control Valve
VVV – Vacuum Vent Valve
VVVac. – Vent Valve Vacuum

W

W/ – With
Warn. – Warning
W/B – Wheelbase
Wdo. – Window
Wip. – Wiper
W/O – Without
WOT – Wide Open Throttle
WOTC – WOT Cutout
WOTS or **WOT-SW** – WOT Switch
WOTV – WOT Valve
W/Shield – Windshield
Wshr. – Washer
WST – Wastegate
WSTGT ACT – Wastegate Actuator
W/W – Wiper/Washer

X

Xcvr. – Transceiver
Xmit. – Transmitter

Y

YFA – Carburetor

1989 TOOL APPLICATIONS
All Manufacturers

DESCRIPTION

Tool applications used in this manual are noted in the text of all articles where applicable. These tools are usually specific tools that must be used to perform a specific function in Removal, Installation, Overhaul or Testing of a component.

For example; "Using Spline Adapter (J-28513) and Holding Wrench (J-28514), tighten pinion nut until end play is taken up." Although other tools could possibly be substituted, the tool references are those that are recommended by the vehicle manufacturer. These tools should be used whenever possible.

Normally, in cases where a non-specific tool is called for, no tool number will be given. For example; "Place bearing insert in rod and install guides on rod bolts. Compress piston rings using ring compressor." Since about any ring compressor that works and does not damage the components can be used, normally no specific tool number will be called out.

The following descriptions show an example of the reference in text, the maker of the tools recommended by the manufacturer and the tool maker's address. Further information on tools and local suppliers of the tools can be obtained from the tool maker. It is also possible, for example, that a Kent-Moore tool may be cross-referenced to another tool maker. In this case it is imperative that the tools be exactly the same in design, or the specific function of the tool may not be able to be performed.

CHRYSLER MOTORS

Chrysler Motors tool applications called out in this manual will appear as follows: "Assemble Pinion Locating Spacer (SP-6030) over body of main tool (SP-5385). Install Shaft Locating Sleeve (L-4507), Washer (C-4656) and Compression Nut (SP-533)."

The prefixes "C", "L" and "SP" mean that the tools are manufactured by Miller Special Tools. The number after the letter prefix is the basic tool part number. Any letters or numbers after the basic part number designate either a revised tool number or that the tool is part of a set.

CHRYSLER MOTORS
TOOL MANUFACTURER

Miller Special Tools
Division of Utica Tool Co., Inc.
32615 Park Lane
Garden City, Mich. 48135
Telephone (313) 522-6717

FORD MOTOR CO.

Ford Motor Co. tool applications called out in this manual will appear as follows: "Remove pinion bearing with Slide Hammer (T50T-100A with Attachment T58L-101-A). Remove bearing with Puller (T81P-3504-S, T58L-101-A and T81P-3504-T)."

Ford Motor Co. tools are manufactured by Owatonna Tools. The prefix used with Ford tool numbers means that the tools are essential tools. The number after the prefix is the basic tool part number. Any letters or numbers after the basic part number designate either a revised tool number or that the tool is part of a set.

FORD MOTOR CO.
TOOL MANUFACTURER

Owatonna Tool Co. Inc.
Owatonna, Minn. 55060
Telephone (507) 455-2626
Telex 29-0876

JEEP/EAGLE

Eagle Premier tool applications called out in this manual will appear as follows: "Use Bearing Remover (J-21473-1) and Extension (J-21054-1) to drive out bearing." The "J" in front of the first set of numbers means that it is a Kent-Moore tool. The second set of numbers is the basic tool part number. Part numbers with no additional characters after the basic part number means that the tool listed is a complete tool. The last number means that it is either part of a set (-2,-3 etc.), or a revised tool number (-02,-03, or -B,-C etc.).

JEEP/EAGLE
TOOL MANUFACTURER

Kent-Moore Tool Division
29784 Little Mack
Roseville, Mich., 48066-2298
Telephone (313) 774-9500
Telex 23-5377

Eagle Premier tool applications called out in this manual may also appear as follows: "Install Spring Retainer (Sus.594-02). Adjust rocker arms using Adjuster (Mot.567)." The two or three letter code at the front of the number stands for the mechanical application, such as Mot. = Motor and Sus. = Suspension. The three digit number after the letters is the tool part number abbreviation. Renault tool numbers are actually listed as 00 00 047 600. The 476 is used for the tool abbreviation as shown in this manual. Any numbers after the three digit part number mean that there is more than one part to the tool.

RENAULT TOOL MANUFACTURER

Facom Tools Inc.
2177-0 Flintstone Dr.
Tucker, (Atlanta) Ga. 30084

NOTE: Eagle Premier may also use Chrysler Motors tools.

Section T

QUICK-CHECK TUNE-UP SPECIFICATIONS

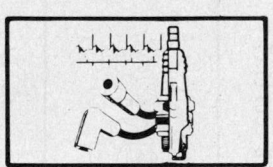

CONTENTS

AUTOMOBILE MANUFACTURERS   Page
Chrysler Motors T-2
Eagle T-2
Ford Motor Co. T-2

NOTE: ALSO SEE GENERAL INDEX

1989 TUNE-UP SPECIFICATIONS
Chrysler Motors, Eagle & Ford Motor Co.

TUNE-UP SPECIFICATIONS

ENGINE	IGNITION TIMING *		SPARK PLUGS		TPS ADJUSTMENT	No.
	Man. Trans.	Auto. Trans.	Type	Gap In. (mm)	Voltage	
CHRYSLER MOTORS						
4-Cyl.						
2.2L (135") TBI	12 @ 850	12 @ 850	RN12YC	.035 (.9)	.16	1
2.2L (135") Turbo II	12 @ 900	12 @ 900	RN12YC	.035 (.9)	.16	2
2.5L (152") TBI	12 @ 850	12 @ 850	RN12YC	.035 (.9)	.16	3
2.5L (152") Turbo I	12 @ 900	12 @ 900	RN12YC	.035 (.9)	.16	4
V6						
3.0L (181") MPFI	.....	12 @ 800	RN11YC4	[1]	[2]	5
V8						
5.2L (318") 2-Bbl.	.....	5-9 @ 680	RN12YC	.035 (.9)	.....	6
5.2L (318") 4-Bbl.	.....	14-18 @ 750	RN12YC	.035 (.9)	.....	7
EAGLE						
4-Cyl.						
2.5L (151") TBI	[2]	[2]	RN12LYC	.035 (.9)	.5	8
V6						
3.0L (182") MPFI	[2]	[2]	RS9YC	.035 (.9)	.4	9
FORD MOTOR CO.						
4-Cyl.						
1.9L (116") CFI						
Exc. Calibration Code						
8-07E-R10	10 @ 760-840	10 @ 760-840	AGSF-34C	[1]	.9-1.1	10
Calibration Code						
8-07E-R10	10 @ 900-1000	10 @ 900-1000	AGSF-24C	[1]	.9-1.1	11
2.2L (133") MPFI	6 @ 750	[3] 6 @ 750	AGSP-33C	[4]	[5]	12
2.3L OHC (140") MPFI	10 @ 770-830	[3] 10 @ 680-760	AWSF-44C	[1]	.9-1.1	13
2.3L HSC (140") MPFI	15 @ 810-890	[3] 15 @ 680-760	AWFS-42C	[1]	.9-1.1	14
2.3L HSC HO (140")						
Calibration Code						
8-25C-R00	15 @ 810-890	15 @ 680-760	AWFS-42C	[1]	.9-1.1	15
8-26D-R10	15 @ 810-890	[3] 15 @ 680-760	AWFS-42C	[1]	.9-1.1	16
2.5L (153") CFI	10 @ 675-725	10 @ 675-725	AWSF-32C	[1]	.9-1.1	17
V6						
3.0L (182") MPFI	.....	[3] 10 @ 740-780	AWSF-32P	.044 (1.1)	.9-1.1	18
3.0L SHO (182") MPFI	10 @ 760-830	.....	AGSP-32P	[1]	.9-1.1	19
3.8L (232") SEFI						
Calibration Code						
9-16C-R10	.....	[3] 10 @ 650-750	AWSF-44C	.054 (1.4)	.9-1.1	20
9-16D-R10	.....	[3] 10 @ 620-720	AWSF-44C	.054 (1.4)	.9-1.1	21
9-16F-R00	.....	[3] 10 @ 500-650	AWSF-44C	.054 (1.4)	.9-1.1	22
3.8L (232") [6] SEFI	[7] 10	[7] 10	AWSF-44P	[1]	.9-1.1	23
V8						
5.0L (302") SEFI						
Calibration Code						
8-22C-R00	10 @ 525-650	[3] 10 @ 525-650	AWSF-44C	.050 (1.3)	.9-1.1	24
Calibration Code						
8-22L-R00	10 @ 550-675	[3] 10 @ 550-675	AWSF-44C	.050 (1.3)	.9-1.1	25
Calibration Code						
8-22M-R00	10 @ 525-650	[3] 10 @ 525-650	AWSF-44C	.050 (1.3)	.9-1.1	26
Calibration Code						
9-22A-R00	10 @ 625-775	[3] 10 @ 575-725	AWSF-44C	.050 (1.3)	.9-1.1	27
5.8L (351") VV	.....	[3] 14 @ 600	ASF-42	.044 (1.1)	.....	28

TUNE-UP SPECIFICATIONS (Cont.)

No.	HOT IDLE •		FAST IDLE †			REMARKS
	Man. Trans.	Auto. Trans.	M/T RPM	Cam Step	A/T RPM	
1	850	850	.....	.....	.....	[1] – Refer to Emission Label.
2	900	900				[2] – Information not available from manufacturer.
3	850	850	.....	.....	.....	[3] – In Drive.
4	900	900	.....	.....	.....	[4] – Gap is .039-.043" (1.0-1.1 mm).
5	.....	[3] 800	.....	.....	.....	[5] – See TUNE-UP article.
6	.....	[3] 680	.....	2nd	1700	[6] – Supercharged engine.
7	.....	750	.....	2nd	1450	[7] – Refer to Emission Label for RPM specification.
8	750	750	.....	.....	.....	★ – All specifications given are Before Top Dead Center (BTDC); A/T in Neutral, unless otherwise specified.
9	.....	790				• – When idle solenoid is used, lower RPM is with solenoid disconnected, higher RPM is with solenoid connected.
10	760-840	[3] 760-840	.....	.....	.....	† – All specifications are with transmission in Neutral, unless otherwise noted.
11	900-1000	900-1000	.....	.....	.....	
12	700-750	[3] 700-750	.....	.....	.....	
13	810-890	[3] 810-890	.....	.....	.....	
14	820-880	[3] 820-880	.....	.....	.....	
15	810-890	[3] 810-890	.....	.....	.....	
16	810-890	[3] 810-890	.....	.....	.....	**SPARK PLUGS:**
17	675-725	[3] 675-725	.....	.....	.....	**AGSF** – Motorcraft.
18	.....	[3] 740-780	.....	.....	.....	**AGSP** – Motorcraft. **ASF** – Motorcraft.
19	760-830	.....	.....	.....	.....	**AWSF** – Motorcraft.
20	.....	[3] 650-750	.....	.....	.....	**RN** – Champion. **RS** – Champion.
21	.....	[3] 620-720	.....	.....	.....	
22	.....	[3] 500-650	.....	.....	.....	**FUEL INJECTION:**
23	[1]	[1]	.....	.....	.....	**CFI** – Central Fuel Injection. **MPFI** – Multi-Point Fuel Injection. **SFI** – Sequential Electronic Fuel Injection.
24	525-650	[3] 525-650	.....	.....	.....	**TBI** – Throttle Body Injection. **VV** – Variable Venturi Carburetor.
25	550-675	[3] 550-675	.....	.....	.....	**OHC** – Overhead Camshaft.
26	525-650	[3] 525-650	.....	.....	.....	**HSC** – High Swirl Combustion. **SHO** – Super High Output.
27	625-775	[3] 625-775	.....	.....	.....	
28	.....	[3] 600	.....	2nd	1750	

Section 1

TUNE-UP

CONTENTS

TROUBLE SHOOTING

Page

Engine Trouble Shooting 1-2

TUNE-UP

Chrysler Motors 4-Cylinder 1-5
Chrysler Motors V6 1-8
Chrysler Motors V8 1-10
Eagle 4-Cylinder 1-14
Eagle V6 1-16
Ford Motor Co. 4-Cylinder 1-18
Ford Motor Co. V6 1-24
Ford Motor Co. V8 1-28

NOTE: ALSO SEE GENERAL INDEX

1989 TUNE-UP
Engine Trouble Shooting

CONDITION	POSSIBLE CAUSE	CORRECTION
SPARK PLUG DIAGNOSIS		
Normal Spark Plug Condition	Light Tan or Gray deposits on insulator	
	Electrode not burned or fouled	
	Gap tolerance not changed	
Cold Fouling or Carbon Deposits	Overrich air/fuel mixture	Adjust air/fuel mixture, see TUNE-UP
	Clogged air filter	Clean and/or replace air filter
	Incorrect idle speed or dirty carburetor	Reset idle speed and/or clean carburetor
	Faulty ignition wires	Replace ignition wiring
	Prolonged operation at idle	Shut engine off during long idle
	Sticking valves or worn seals	Check valve train
Wet Fouling or Oil Deposits	Worn rings and pistons	Install new rings and pistons
	Excessive valve guide clearance	Worn or loose bearings
Gap Bridged	Deposits in combustion chamber	Clean combustion chamber of deposits
Blistered Electrode or Overheating	Engine overheating	Check cooling system
	Wrong type of fuel	Replace with correct fuel
	Loose spark plugs	Retighten spark plugs
	Over-advanced ignition timing	Reset ignition timing, see TUNE-UP
Pre-Ignition or Melted Electrodes	Incorrect type of fuel	Replace with correct fuel
	Incorrect ignition timing	Reset ignition timing, see TUNE-UP
	Engine overheating	Check cooling system
	Wrong type of spark plug, too hot	Replace with correct spark plug, see TUNE-UP
Chipped Insulators	Severe detonation	Check for over-advanced timing
	Improper gapping procedure	Re-gap spark plugs
Rust Colored Deposits	Additives in unleaded fuel	Try different fuel brand
Water In Combustion Chamber	Blown head gasket or cracked head	Repair or replace head and head gasket

ELECTRONIC IGNITION DIAGNOSIS

Before diagnosing an electronic ignition system, ensure that all wiring is connected properly between distributor, wiring connector and spark plugs. Ignition problem will show up either as: Engine Will Not Start or Engine Runs Rough.

CONDITION	POSSIBLE CAUSE	CORRECTION
Engine Will Not Start	Open in primary ignition circuit	Repair circuit
	No or low fuel pressure	Check fuel system, see FUEL
	No secondary ignition spark	Check ignition system, see TUNE-UP
Engine Runs Rough	Vacuum leaks	Check and repair all vacuum hoses
	Initial timing incorrect	Reset ignition timing, see TUNE-UP
	Defective spark plugs or wiring	Replace plugs or plug wiring

ELECTRONIC IGNITION DIAGNOSIS BY OSCILLOSCOPE PATTERN

CONDITION	POSSIBLE CAUSE	CORRECTION
Firing Voltage Lines are the Same, but Abnormally High	Fuel mixture too lean	Check fuel system, see TUNE-UP
	High resistance in coil wire	Replace coil wire
	Corrosion in coil tower terminal	Clean and/or replace coil
	Corrosion in distributor coil terminal	Clean and/or replace distributor cap
Firing Voltage Lines are the Same, but Abnormally Low	Spark plug gap too small	Set spark plug gap to specification
	Fuel mixture too rich	Check fuel system, see TUNE-UP
	Coil wire arcing to ground	Replace coil wire
	Cracked coil tower causing arcing	Replace coil
	Low coil output	Replace coil
	Low engine compression	Determine cause and repair
One or More, But Not All Firing Voltage Lines are Higher Than Others	Vacuum leak	Check and repair vacuum hoses
	EGR valve leaking	Clean and/or replace EGR valve
	High resistance in spark plug wire	Replace spark plug wires
	Defective spark plugs	Replace spark plugs
	Corroded spark plug terminals	Replace spark plugs

CONDITION	POSSIBLE CAUSE	CORRECTION
ELECTRONIC IGNITION DIAGNOSIS BY OSCILLOSCOPE PATTERN (Cont.)		
One or More, But Not All Firing Voltage Lines are Lower Than Others	Plug wire arcing to ground	Replace plug wires
	Cracked coil tower causing arching	Replace coil
	Low compression	Determine cause and repair
	Defective spark plugs	Replace spark plugs
Cylinders Not Firing	Cracked distributor cap terminals	Replace distributor cap
	Shorted spark plug wire	Determine cause of short and replace wiring
	Mechanical problem in engine	Determine cause and repair
	Defective spark plugs	Replace spark plugs
GENERAL DIAGNOSIS		
Hard Starting	Improper fuel pressure	Check fuel system, see TUNE-UP
	Vacuum leaks	Check and repair all vavuum leaks
	Defective coil	Replace coil
	Improper spark plug gap	Regap spark plugs
	Incorrect ignition timing	Reset ignition timing, see TUNE-UP
Detonation	Over-advanced ignition timing	Reset ignition timing, see TUNE-UP
	Defective spark plugs	Replace spark plugs
	EGR system malfunction	Check and repair EGR system
	PCV system malfunction	Repair PCV system
	Vacuum leaks	Check and repair vacuum system
	Restricted airflow	Remove restriction
Dieseling	Binding throttle linkage	Eliminate binding
	Binding choke linkage or fast idle cam	Eliminate binding
	Defective idle solenoid	Replace idle solenoid, see FUEL
	Improper base idle speed	Reset idle speed, see TUNE-UP
	Improper fuel	Ensure proper fuel is used
	Incorrect ignition timing	Reset ignition timing, see TUNE-UP
Faulty Acceleration	Incorrect ignition timing	Reset ignition timing, see TUNE-UP
	Improper throttle linkage adjustment	Adjust throttle linkage
	Defective spark plugs	Replace spark plugs
	Defective coil	Replace coil
Faulty Low Speed Operation	Vacuum leaks	Check and repair all vacuum leaks
	Faulty EGR operation	Check EGR operation
	Restricted idle air bleeds and passages	Disassemble and clean carburetor, see FUEL
	Defective spark plugs	Replace spark plugs
	Defective ignition wires	Replace ignition wires, see TUNE-UP
	Defective distributor cap	Replace distributor cap
Faulty High Speed Operation	Incorrect ignition timing	Reset ignition timing, see TUNE-UP
	Improper ignition advance	Check and repair advance.
	Incorrect spark plugs or plug gap	Check gap and/or replace spark plugs
	Low fuel pressure	Check fuel system, see FUEL
	Restricted air cleaner	Check filter and replace as necessary
	Defective distributor cap, rotor or coil	Replace cap, rotor or coil
	Worn distributor shaft	Replace distributor
Misfire at All Speeds	Defective spark plugs	Replace spark plugs
	Defective spark plug wires	Replace spark plug wires
	Defective distributor cap, rotor or coil	Replace cap, rotor or coil
	Vacuum leaks	Repair vacuum leaks
	Fuel lines restricted	Remove restriction
Hesitation	Vacuum leaks	Repair vacuum leaks
	Low fuel pressure	Check fuel system, see FUEL
	Faulty EGR operation	Check EGR operation
	Cracked or broken ignition wires	Replace ignition wires

1989 TUNE-UP
Engine Trouble Shooting (Cont.)

CONDITION	POSSIBLE CAUSE	CORRECTION
	GENERAL DIAGNOSIS (Cont.)	
Rough Idle, Missing or Stalling	Incorrect curb idle or fast idle speed	Reset idle speed, see TUNE-UP
	Incorrect basic timing	Reset ignition timing, see TUNE-UP
	Improper idle mixture adjustment	Reset idle mixture, see TUNE-UP
	Low fuel pressure	Check fuel system, see FUEL
	Incorrect spark plug gap	Reset spark plug gap, see TUNE-UP
	Moisture in ignition components	Dry components
	Loose or broken ignition wires	Replace ignition wires
	Damaged distributor cap or rotor	Replace distributor cap or rotor
	Faulty ignition coil	Replace ignition coil
	Improper EGR valve operation	Replace EGR valve
	Faulty PCV valve airflow	Replace PCV valve
	Choke binding or improper choke setting	Reset choke or eliminate binding
	Vacuum leak	Repair vacuum leak
	Exhaust manifold heat valve inoperative	Replace heat valve
	Improper distributor spark advance	Check distributor operation
	Leaking valves or valve components	Check and repair valvetrain
	Excessive play in distributor shaft	Replace distributor
	Loose or corroded wiring connections	Repair or replace as required
Engine Surges	Improper PCV valve airflow	Replace PCV valve
	Vacuum leaks	Repair vacuum leaks
	Low fuel pressure	Check fuel system, see FUEL
	EGR valve malfunction	Replace EGR valve
	Cracked or broken ignition wires	Replace ignition wires
	Vacuum advance malfunction	Check unit and replace as necessary
	Defective or fouled spark plugs	Replace spark plugs
Ping or Spark Knock	Incorrect ignition timing	Reset ignition timing, see TUNE-UP
	Distributor advance malfunction	Check operation and replace as necessary
	Improper fuel	Ensure proper fuel is used
	Vacuum leak	Eliminate vacuum leak
	EGR valve malfunction	Replace EGR valve
Poor Gasoline Mileage	Vacuum leaks	Repair vacuum leaks
	Defective ignition wires	Replace wires
	Incorrect choke setting	Readjust setting, see FUEL
	Defective vacuum advance	Replace vacuum advance
	Defective spark plugs	Replace spark plugs
	Incorrect float adjustment	Readjust float setting, see FUEL
	Defective power valve	Replace power valve, see FUEL
Engine Stalls	Incorrect idle speed	Readjust idle speed
	Leaking EGR valve	Repair or replace EGR valve
	Vacuum leaks	Eliminate vacuum leaks

Tune-Up

ENGINE IDENTIFICATION

VEHICLE IDENTIFICATION NUMBER CODE

Engine can be identified by the 8th character of Vehicle Identification Number (VIN). The VIN is stamped on a plate on top left corner of instrument panel, and is visible through windshield.

VIN ENGINE CODES

Application	Code
2.2L (135") TBI [1]	D
2.2L (135") MPFI Turbo II [2]	A
2.5L (152") TBI [1]	K
2.5L (135") MPFI Turbo I [2]	J

[1] – Throttle Body Injection.
[2] – Multi-Point Fuel Injection.

TUNE-UP NOTES

NOTE: When performing any tune-up procedures, the following notes and precautions should be used as guidelines.

Always refer to Engine Tune-Up Decal in engine compartment, before performing tune-up. If manual and decal differ, use decal specifications.

Avoid creating engine misfire in more than one cylinder for an extended period of time. Damage to converter may occur due to loading converter with unburned air/fuel mixture.

Do not use fuel system cleaning compounds that are not recommended by manufacturer. Damage to gaskets, diaphragm materials and catalytic converter could result.

ENGINE COMPRESSION

Before making a compression test or cranking engine with a remote starting switch, remove coil wire from distributor and attach to ground. Check compression pressure with engine warm, spark plugs removed, and throttle valve wide open.

COMPRESSION SPECIFICATIONS

Application	Compression Ratio
2.2L TBI	9.5:1
2.2L MPFI Turbo II	8.1:1
2.5L TBI	8.9:1
2.5L MPFI Turbo I	7.8:1
Compression Pressure	
2.2L & 2.5L	Minimum 100 psi (7 kg/cm²)
Maximum Cylinder Variation	
2.2L & 2.5L	25 psi (1.7 kg/cm²)

VALVE CLEARANCE

All engine use hydraulic lifters. No adjustment is possible.

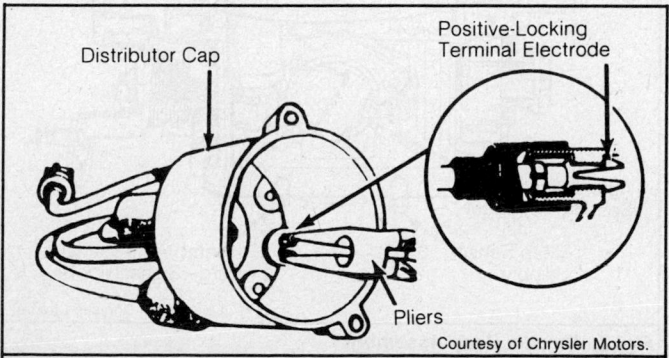

Fig. 1: Spark Plug Wire Removal From Distributor Cap

Distributor Cap

Positive-Locking Terminal Electrode

Pliers

Courtesy of Chrysler Motors.

VALVE CLEARANCE ADJUSTMENT

Application	Intake In. (mm)	Exhaust In. (mm)
2.2L & 2.5L	Zero Lash	Zero Lash

VALVE ARRANGEMENT

E-I-E-I-E-I-E-I (Front-to-rear).

IGNITION SYSTEM

SPARK PLUGS

SPARK PLUG TYPE

Application	Champion No.
2.2 & 2.5L	RN12YC

SPARK PLUG INSTALLATION

Application	Gap In. (mm)	Torque Ft. Lbs. (N.m)
2.2 & 2.5L	.035 (.9)	20 (27)

HIGH TENSION WIRE RESISTANCE

1) Carefully remove spark plug wire from spark plug. Remove distributor cap from distributor with spark plug wires attached. Connect ohmmeter leads between end of wire and its terminal inside distributor cap.
2) If resistance exceeds 7200 ohms per foot, remove wire from distributor cap and measure wire resistance. If resistance still exceeds 7200 ohms per foot, replace with wire identified as Electronic Suppression.

NOTE: Do not pull on secondary wires when servicing. To remove wires from distributor cap, release positive locking terminals from inside distributor cap. See Fig. 1.

IGNITION COIL WIRE

1) Remove distributor cap leaving all secondary wires connected. Connect ohmmeter leads between center contact inside distributor cap and either primary terminal of ignition coil.
2) If resistance exceeds 25,000 ohms, remove wire from ignition coil tower and recheck resistance. If resistance is over 15,000 ohms, replace ignition coil wire.

HIGH TENSION WIRE RESISTANCE

Applications	Maximum Ohms
Spark Plug Wires	7200 per ft.
Coil Wire	
Installed	25,000
Removed	15,000

IGNITION COIL RESISTANCE [1]

Application	Primary Ohms	Secondary Ohms
Diamond	1.34-1.55	15,000-19,000
Essex	1.34-1.55	9000-12,200
Prestolite	1.34-1.55	9400-11,700

[1] – Resistance measured at 70-80°F (21-27°C).

DISTRIBUTOR

All models use the Hall Effect distributor. The only adjustment that can be made is the ignition timing (changing distributor position). The system consists of a Hall Effect distributor, electronic control

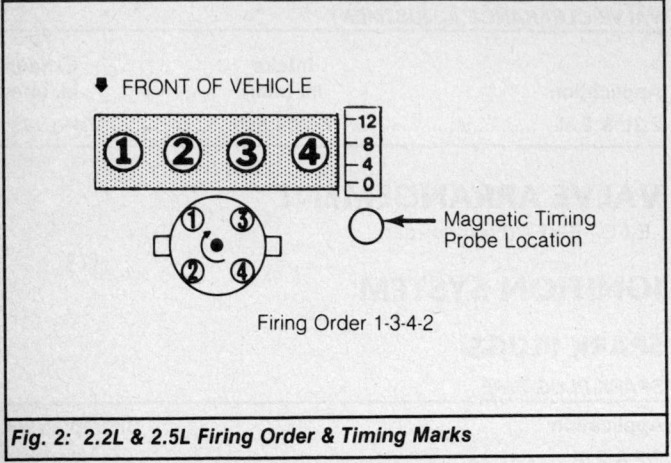

♦ FRONT OF VEHICLE

① ② ③ ④

Magnetic Timing Probe Location

Firing Order 1-3-4-2

Fig. 2: 2.2L & 2.5L Firing Order & Timing Marks

unit (module), and conventional coil. The distributor rotor is of special design and must be grounded through the distributor shaft for the system to operate.

IGNITION TIMING

CAUTION: *Timing light secondary connection should be made with inductive pick-up. Do not puncture cables, boots or nipples with test probes.*

1) Place gear selector in Neutral. Turn off all lights and accessories. If magnetic probe timing light is being used, refer to equipment manufacturer's instructions for service procedure. If conventional timing light is used, connect timing light to No. 1 cylinder.
2) Start engine and warm to normal temperature. Connect tachometer to engine and adjust idle RPM to specification. Disconnect engine coolant sensor lead wire.
3) Check timing through timing window in bellhousing. If timing is within 2 degrees of specification, do not adjust. If timing is incorrect, loosen distributor hold-down bolt and turn housing until specified timing is obtained.
4) Recheck timing after distributor hold-down bolt has been tightened. Reconnect coolant lead wire. Erase any fault codes. Recheck curb idle and adjust (if necessary). Remove diagnostic equipment and test drive vehicle.

NOTE: *The magnetic probe timing socket is located at 10 degrees ATDC. This socket is only for use with special electronic timing equipment. Do not use this socket when checking timing with conventional timing light.*

IGNITION TIMING SPECIFICATIONS
(DEGREES BTDC @ RPM ¹)

Application	Man. Trans.	Auto. Trans.
2.2L TBI	12 @ 850	12 @ 850
2.2L MPFI Turbo II	12 @ 900	12 @ 900
2.5L TBI	12 @ 850	12 @ 850
2.5L MPFI Turbo I	12 @ 900	12 @ 900

¹ – ±2 degrees.

ELECTRONIC SPARK ADVANCE CHECK

Check ignition timing and adjust (if necessary). Increase engine speed to 2000 RPM and check that ignition timing advances properly. See ELECTRONIC SPARK ADVANCE table.

ELECTRONIC SPARK ADVANCE

Application	Degrees BTDC
2.2L TBI	26-33
2.2L MPFI Turbo II	40
2.5L TBI	28-30
2.5L MPFI Turbo I	25

FUEL SYSTEM

FUEL INJECTION

Application	Model
Non-Turbo Models	Chrysler Throttle Body Injection
Turbo Models	Chrysler Multi-Point Injection

FUEL SYSTEM

For fuel system pressure relief procedures and fuel system diagnosis, see appropriate article in FUEL SYSTEMS section.

FUEL PUMP PERFORMANCE

Application	Specification
Pressure	
TBI (2.2L & 2.5L)	14.5 psi. (1.0 kg/cm²)
MPFI (2.2L & 2.5L)	55 psi (3.9 kg/cm²)

HOT (SLOW) IDLE RPM

Electronically fuel injected vehicles use an Automatic Idle Speed (AIS) motor to regulate idle RPM. The AIS is controlled by the Logic Module which uses information received from various sensors to determine among other things, idle speed. *See Fig. 3.* Idle speed is not adjustable. See appropriate article in COMPUTERIZED ENGINE CONTROLS section for diagnosis of incorrect idle speed.

CURB IDLE SPEED (RPM)

Application	Man. Trans.	Auto. Trans.
2.2L & 2.5L TBI	850	850
2.2L & 2.5L MPFI Turbo	900	900

THROTTLE POSITION SENSOR (TPS)

TPS is not adjustable and a break-off screw head is used upon installation. Using a DVOM, check that TPS reading at idle is approximately .16 volt. Move throttle to wide open, reading should be approximately 4.7 volts. If not within specifications, replace TPS.

IDLE MIXTURE ADJUSTMENT

No idle mixture adjustment is possible on fuel injected models.

COLD (FAST) IDLE RPM

Fast idle speed is nonadjustable on fuel injected engines.

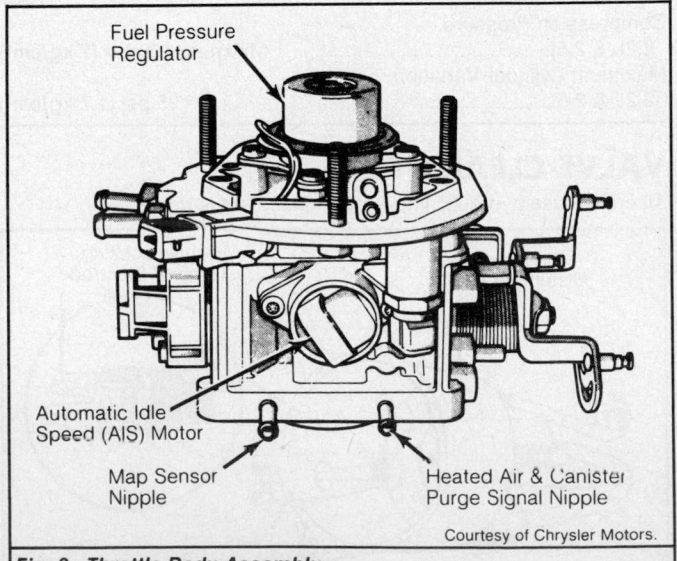

Fuel Pressure Regulator

Automatic Idle Speed (AIS) Motor

Map Sensor Nipple

Heated Air & Canister Purge Signal Nipple

Courtesy of Chrysler Motors.

Fig. 3: Throttle Body Assembly

BATTERY

BATTERY SPECIFICATIONS

Application	Cold Cranking Amps @ 0°F (-18°C)	Reserve Capacity (Minutes)
Standard	400	100
Standard	500	110
Optional	625	120

SERVICE INTERVALS

REPLACEMENT INTERVALS

Component	Interval (Miles)
Oil & Filter	
Turbo	3000
All Others	7500
Air Filter	15,000
PCV Filter	50,000
Fuel Filter	50,000
Spark Plugs	30,000

ADJUSTMENTS

BELT TENSION ADJUSTMENT [1]

Application	New Belt Lbs. (kg)	Used Belt Lbs. (kg)
2.2L & 2.5L		
A/C Compressor	105 (48)	80 (36)
Air Pump	[1]	[1]
Alternator	115 (52)	80 (36)
Power Steering	105 (48)	80 (36)

[1] - Information not available from manufacturer.

CAPACITIES

ENGINE OIL CAPACITIES

Application	Quantity Qts. (L)
Crankcase (Includes Filter)	
2.2L & 2.5L Non-Turbo	4.0 (3.8)
2.2L & 2.5L Turbo	5.0 (4.8)

TRANSAXLE CAPACITIES

Application	Quantity Qts. (L)
Auto. Trans. (Dextron II)	
A-413	
Except Fleet Models	8.9 (8.4)
Fleet Models	9.2 (8.7)
With Lock-Up	8.5 (8.0)

COOLING SYSTEM CAPACITY

Application	Quanity
2.2L	8.5 qts. (8.1L)
2.5L	8.0 qts. (7.6L)

1989 CHRYSLER MOTORS V6 TUNE-UP
Tune-Up

ENGINE IDENTIFICATION

Identification can be made by a number stamped on a pad on right side of block (below No. 6 spark plug). Engine can also be identified by 8th character of Vehicle Identifiction Number (VIN). VIN is located on a Gray metal plate attached to left corner of instrument panel, visible through windshield.

VIN ENGINE CODE

Engine	Code
3.0L (181") MPFI	3

TUNE-UP NOTES

NOTE: Always refer to Emission Control Label in engine compartment before attempting tune-up. If manual and label differ, always use emission label specifications. When performing tune-up procedures, the following notes and precautions must be followed:

When performing tune-up on vehicles equipped with catalytic converters, do not allow or create a condition of engine misfire in more than one cylinder for an extended period of time. Total test time must not exceed 10 minutes or damage to converter may occur due to loading converter with unburned air/fuel mixture.

When inspecting distributor rotor, a Black silicone varnish will be noticed covering .20-.30" (.50-.80 mm) of rotor electrode tip. This replaces earlier silicone grease used to suppress electro-magnetic radiation. Grease will darken with age, has an ash-like appearance and should not be removed. Ash formation (on both types of coverage) is normal and does not affect engine performance.

If it is determined that Spark Control Computer (SCC) is faulty, do not attempt to service. Computer is not serviceable and must be replaced as an assembly.

ENGINE COMPRESSION

Before performing compression test or cranking engine using remote starting switch, disconnect coil wire from distributor and secure to good ground. Check compression with engine warm, spark plugs removed and throttle wide open.

COMPRESSION SPECIFICATIONS

Application	Specification
Compression Ratio	8.9:1
Comp. Pressure	178 psi (12.5 kg/cm²) @ 250 RPM
Max. Variation Between Cylinders	25%

VALVE ARRANGEMENT

I-E-I-E-I-E (Right bank, front-to-rear).
E-I-E-I-E-I (Left bank, front-to-rear).

VALVE CLEARANCE

The 3.0L engine uses hydraulic lifters. Valve clearance is NOT adjustable.

IGNITION SYSTEM

DISTRIBUTOR

All 3.0L engines use Mitsubishi Electronic Ignition Systems (EIS). The only adjustments that can be made are initial ignition timing (changing distributor position) and spark plug gap. *See Fig. 1.*

IGNITION COIL

IGNITION COIL RESISTANCE (OHMS) [1]

Application	Primary	Secondary
Diamond	1.34-1.55	15,000-19,000
Essex	1.34-1.55	9000-12,200
Prestolite	1.34-1.55	9400-11,700

[1] – Resistance measured at 70-80°F (21-27°C).

SPARK PLUGS

SPARK PLUG TYPE

Application	Champion No.
3.0L	RN11YC4

SPARK PLUG SPECIFICATIONS

Application	Gap In. (mm)	Torque Ft. Lbs. (N.m)
3.0L	.039-.044 (1.0-1.1)	20 (28)

HIGH TENSION WIRE RESISTANCE

NOTE: Resistance spark plug wires are identified by the words "Electronic Suppression" printed on cable jacket. Use an ohmmeter to check condition of plug wires.

1) Carefully remove each spark plug wire from spark plugs. Detach coil wire from coil. Remove distributor cap without removing coil and spark plug wires.
2) Connect one ohmmeter lead to coil or spark plug end of wire. Connect other ohmmeter lead to electrode inside distributor cap. Repeat procedure for coil wire.
3) If resistance is not within specification, replace spark plug wire assembly and/or coil cable. Be sure to check ignition coil tower for carbon tracking, cracks and oil leaks.

HIGH TENSION WIRE RESISTANCE (OHMS)

Application	Minimum	Maximum
All Wires	3000 per ft.	7200 per ft.

IGNITION TIMING

NOTE: Do not puncture cables, boots or nipples with test probes. Use proper adapters. Probe can separate conductor and cause high resistance. In addition, breaking rubber insulator may permit secondary current to arc to ground.

1) If a magnetic probe timing light is used, refer to equipment manufacturer's instruction for proper hookup. Use a 10 degree offset when required.
2) Turn off all lights and accessories. Start engine and run until normal operating temperature is obtained. Unplug coolant sensor connector. The "CHECK ENGINE" light must turn on. Do not reconnect sensor or stop and restart engine at this time. Cooling fan should turn on and remain on until engine is turned off.
3) Aim power timing light at timing marks or read magnetic timing unit. If timing is not to specification, loosen distributor hold-down arm bolt and rotate distributor housing to obtain correct timing. Tighten distributor hold-down bolt when timing is correct.
4) Recheck timing. Turn engine off. Reconnect coolant sensor and erase fault codes. Start engine and let speed stabilize for one minute. "CHECK ENGINE" light should be off.

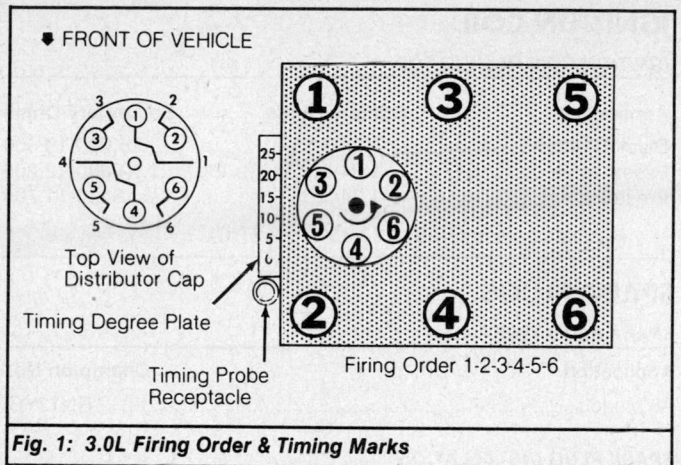

Fig. 1: 3.0L Firing Order & Timing Marks

FRONT OF VEHICLE

Top View of Distributor Cap

Timing Degree Plate

Timing Probe Receptacle

Firing Order 1-2-3-4-5-6

IGNITION TIMING SPECIFICATIONS (Degrees BTDC @ RPM)

Application	Man. Trans.	Auto. Trans.
3.0L MPFI	.....	[1] 12@800

[1] – Ignition timing at 2000 RPM should be 38 degrees.

FUEL SYSTEM

FUEL INJECTION

Application	Model
3.0L	Bosch/Holley MPFI

CURB IDLE SPEED

Fuel system adjustments on the 3.0L MPFI engine are not part of a normal tune-up.

IDLE MIXTURE

Idle mixture is not adjustable.

FUEL PUMP

CAUTION: Release fuel system pressure before disconnecting fuel lines. For fuel system diagnosis, see appropriate article in FUEL SYSTEMS section.

FUEL PUMP SPECIFICATIONS

Application	Pressure psi (kg/cm²)
3.0L	48 (3.4)

General Servicing

BATTERY

BATTERY SPECIFICATIONS

Application	Cold Cranking [1] Amps	Reserve Capacity Minutes
All Models	500	110

[1] – Tested at 0°F (-18°C).

ADJUSTMENTS

DRIVE BELT ADJUSTMENT

Application	[1] Deflection In. (mm)
All Models	
New Belts	1/4-1/2 (6.4-12.7)
Used Belts [2]	1/4-5/16 (6.4-7.9)

[1] – Deflection is 10 lbs. (4.5 kg) with push/pull spring scale.
[2] – Used belts are any belts operated more than 15 minutes.

SERVICE INTERVALS

REPLACEMENT INTERVALS

Component	Interval (Miles)
Air Filter	52,500
Engine Oil [1]	7500
Engine Oil Filter [2]	7500
EGR Valve	52,500
Emission System Components [3]	52,500
Fuel Filter	52,500
Oxygen Sensor	52,500
PCV Valve	52,500
Spark Plugs	37,500

[1] – Or every 12 months, whichever comes first.
[2] – If mileage is less than 7500 miles each 12 months, replace filter with each oil change.
[3] – Inspect or replace as necessary.

CAPACITIES

COOLING SYSTEM CAPACITY

Application	Quantity Qts. (L)
3.0L	9.5 (9.0)

ENGINE OIL CAPACITY

Application	Quantity Qts. (L)
Crankcase	[1] 4 (3.8)

[1] – With or without filter change.

TRANSAXLE CAPACITY

Application	Quantity Qts. (L)
A-604	9.1 (8.6)

1989 CHRYSLER MOTORS V8 TUNE-UP
Tune-Up

ENGINE IDENTIFICATION

VEHICLE IDENTIFICATION NUMBER CODE

Engine can be identified by the 8th digit of the Vehicle Identification Number (VIN). The VIN is located on plate, on upper left corner of instrument panel, visible through the windshield.

VIN ENGINE CODES

Application	Code
5.2L (318") 2-Bbl.	P
5.2L (318") 4-Bbl.	
Standard	4
Heavy Duty	S

TUNE-UP NOTES

NOTE: When performing any tune-up procedures, the following notes and precautions should be used as guidelines.

Refer to Engine Tune-Up Decal in engine compartment before performing tune-up. If manual and decal differ, always use decal specifications.

Avoid creating engine misfire in more than one cylinder for an extended period of time. Damage to the converter may occur due to loading converter with unburned air/fuel mixture.

Do not use fuel system cleaning compounds that are not recommended by manufacturer. Damage to gaskets, diaphragm materials and catalytic converter could result.

ENGINE COMPRESSION

Before performing compression test or cranking engine using remote starter switch, disconnect coil wire from distributor and secure to ground. Check compression pressure with engine at normal operating temperature, all spark plugs removed and throttle valve open.

COMPRESSION SPECIFICATIONS

Application	Compression Ratio
5.2L	
2-Bbl.	9.0:1
4-Bbl.	8.4:1
Compression Pressure	Minimum 100 psi (7 kg/cm²)
Maximum Cylinder Variation	25 psi (1.7 kg/cm²)

VALVE CLEARANCE

The 5.2L engine uses hydraulic lifters. Valve clearance is NOT adjustable.

VALVE CLEARANCE ADJUSTMENT

Application	Intake In. (mm)	Exhaust In. (mm)
All Models	Zero Lash	Zero Lash

VALVE ARRANGEMENT

E-I-I-E-E-I-I-E (Front-to-rear, both banks).

IGNITION SYSTEM

DISTRIBUTOR

All models are equipped with Chrysler Motors Electronic Spark Control ignition system. Vacuum transducer is with Spark Control Computer and mounted on the air cleaner housing. Disconnect and plug hose to the vacuum transducer when checking ignition timing. *See Fig. 1.*

IGNITION COIL

IGNITION COIL RESISTANCE [1]

Application	Primary Ohms	Secondary Ohms
Diamond	1.34-1.55	15,000-19,000
Essex	1.34-1.55	9000-12,200
Prestolite	1.34-1.55	9400-11,700

[1] – Resistance measured at 70-80°F (21-27°C).

SPARK PLUGS

SPARK PLUG TYPE

Application	Champion No.
All Models	RN12YC

SPARK PLUG INSTALLATION

Application	Gap In. (mm)	Torque Ft. Lbs. (N.m)
All Models	.035 (.9)	30 (41)

HIGH TENSION WIRE RESISTANCE

1) Carefully remove spark plug wire from spark plug. Remove distributor cap from distributor with spark plug wires attached. Connect ohmmeter leads between end of wire and its terminal inside distributor cap.
2) If spark plug wire resistance is more than 50,000 ohms, remove wire from distributor cap and connect ohmmeter lead to wire. If resistance is still more than 50,000 ohms, replace wire.
3) If coil wire resistance is more than 25,000 ohms, remove wire from distributor cap center terminal and recheck resistance. If resistance is more than 15,000 ohms, replace ignition coil wire.

HIGH TENSION WIRE RESISTANCE

Application	Maximum Ohms
Spark Plug Wires	50,000
Coil Wire	
Installed	25,000
Removed	15,000

DISTRIBUTOR

All models are equipped with Chrysler Motors Electronic Spark Control ignition system with either single or dual pick-up coils. On the 2 pick-up coil distributor, there is a start pick-up coil and a run pick-up coil. The only adjustments that can be made to this system are spark plug gap, pick-up coil air gap, and initial ignition timing (changing distributor position).

DUAL PICK-UP COIL ADJUSTMENT

NOTE: Start pick-up is identified by a two-pronged male connector. Run pick-up is identified by a male and female plug.

1) Align reluctor tooth with pick-up coil tooth. Loosen coil hold-down screw. Place non-metallic feeler gauge between the 2 teeth. Do not force gauge into air gap. Set air gap with adjustment gauge.
2) Adjust air gap until contact is made between the reluctor tooth, feeler gauge, and pick-up coil. Recheck air gap with check gauge. Fasten hold-down screw. Check that clearance is correct.

PICK-UP COIL ADJUSTMENT

Pick-Up Coil	Adjust Gauge In. (mm)	Check Gauge In. (mm)
Start	.006 (.15)	.008 (.20)
Run	.012 (.30)	.014 (.35)

IGNITION TIMING

CAUTION: Use inductive type timing light. Do not puncture cables, boots or nipples with test probes.

1) Connect timing light to No. 1 plug wire or magnetic timing unit to probe receptacle. Connect jumper wire between carburetor switch and ground. On 2-Bbl. models, disconnect vacuum hose to Spark Control Computer.

2) On all models, set parking brake. Place transmission in Neutral. Start engine and warm to normal operating temperature. If necessary, adjust curb idle speed. With engine running at or below curb idle RPM, check timing at timing plate.

3) Adjust timing by loosening distributor hold-down bolt and turning distributor housing. After timing has been set, recheck curb idle and adjust as necessary. Turn off engine.

NOTE: The magnetic timing probe receptacle is located 10 degrees ATDC. Do not use this to check timing with conventional timing light.

IGNITION TIMING SPECIFICATIONS
(Degrees BTDC @ RPM)

Application	Specification
5.2L	
2-Bbl.	5-9 @ 680
4-Bbl.	14-18 @ 750

ELECTRONIC SPARK ADVANCE TEST

1) Ensure engine is fully warmed and ignition timing is set to specification. Connect a variable advance timing light to engine. Insert a piece of paper between curb idle adjusting screw and carburetor switch to insulate adjusting screw from carburetor.

2) Disconnect and plug vacuum hose at vacuum transducer. Connect vacuum pump to transducer and apply 16 in. Hg vacuum. Increase engine speed to 2000 RPM. Wait one minute and check reading. See ELECTRONIC SPARK ADVANCE SPECIFICATIONS table. Advance specifications are in addition to basic timing. Replace computer if it fails to obtain specification.

3) On systems with an accumulator, specified timing must be reached with the carburetor switch ungrounded before checking spark advance specifications.

ELECTRONIC SPARK ADVANCE SPECIFICATIONS

RPM	Degrees Advance
2000	[1] 46

[1] – Total advance. Includes base timing.

FUEL SYSTEM

CARBURETOR

Application	Model
5.2L	
2-Bbl.	Holley 6280
4-Bbl.	Rochester Quadrajet

HOT (SLOW) IDLE RPM

NOTE: For curb idle speed, See Engine Tune-Up Decal.

Solenoid Idle Speed & Curb Idle Speed (2-Bbl. Carburetor) – 1) With ignition timing properly set, disconnect and plug vacuum hose at EGR valve. Disconnect and plug hose from carburetor at heated air temperature sensor. Remove air cleaner. Disconnect and plug canister purge hose at canister.

2) Remove PCV valve from valve cover and allow it to draw fresh air. Disconnect and plug vacuum advance at ESA (Electronic Spark Advance) computer. Connect tachometer to engine. Separate

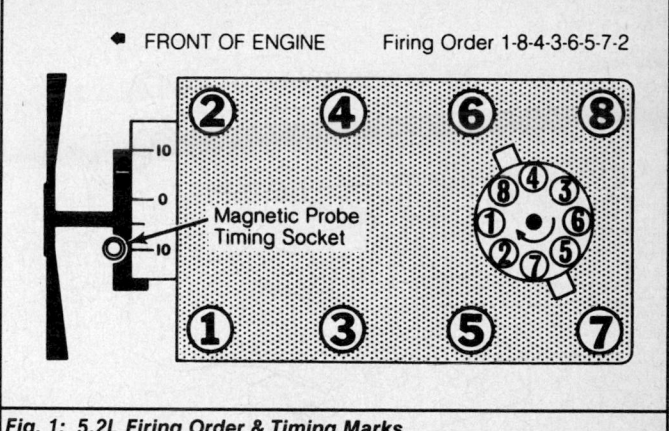

FRONT OF ENGINE   Firing Order 1-8-4-3-6-5-7-2

Magnetic Probe Timing Socket

Fig. 1: 5.2L Firing Order & Timing Marks

carburetor connector from engine harness. From carburetor connector, remove Green duty cycle wire and Blue idle solenoid wire.

CAUTION: Do not pull on O_2 sensor wire. Use caution working near sensor as exhaust manifold is very hot.

3) Reconnect carburetor connector to engine harness minus the Green and Blue wires. Ground carburetor switch with jumper wire. Connect jumper wire between battery positive post and Blue idle stop wire.

CAUTION: Use care in jumping to the proper solenoid wire. Applying battery voltage to the incorrect wire will damage the wiring harness.

4) Operate engine with transmission in Neutral and fast idle screw on 2nd step of fast idle cam for 5-10 minutes. Return engine to idle and quickly proceed with solenoid idle adjustment. Open throttle slightly allowing solenoid plunger to extend. Remove solenoid outer screw and spring. Insert 1/8" Allen wrench into solenoid and adjust to specification.

5) Install screw and spring, turning screw until it lightly bottoms out. Remove jumper wire. Set idle speed to specification by turning solenoid screw out. Remove tachometer and reconnect all hoses. Install PCV valve and air cleaner. Disconnect carburetor connector from engine harness and reconnect Green and Blue wires. Reinstall connector to engine harness.

Solenoid Idle Speed & Curb Idle Speed (4-Bbl. Carburetor) – 1) Verify ignition timing is properly set. Disconnect and plug vacuum hose at EGR valve and plug canister purge hose at canister. Disconnect and plug hose from carburetor at heated air temperature sensor. Remove air cleaner.

2) Remove PCV valve from valve cover and allow it to draw fresh air. Connect tachometer to engine. Start engine and warm to operating temperature. Disconnect carburetor electrical connector. Attach jumper wire between ground switch terminal of wiring harness connector (Violet wire) and ground.

3) Disconnect O_2 sensor from engine harness. Ground engine harness lead. Allow engine to run for 4 minutes, to allow the effect of grounding O_2 sensor lead to occur. Attach jumper wire between solenoid coil terminal on carburetor connector (Red wire) and battery positive post.

4) Open throttle slightly to allow solenoid plunger to extend. Remove outer screw and spring from solenoid. Insert 1/8" Allen wrench into solenoid and adjust solenoid idle speed to specification.

5) Install screw and spring and turn in outer screw until it lightly bottoms out. Remove jumper wire from carburetor connector and battery. Turn outer solenoid screw until correct idle RPM is obtained.

6) Remove remaining jumper wire and reconnect carburetor connector. Remove tachometer and reconnect all hoses. Reinstall PCV valve and air cleaner.

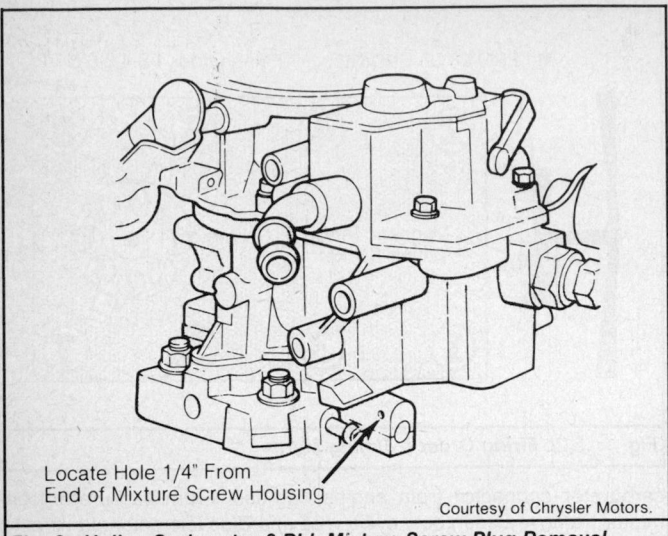

Locate Hole 1/4" From
End of Mixture Screw Housing

Courtesy of Chrysler Motors.

Fig. 2: Holley Carburetor 2-Bbl. Mixture Screw Plug Removal

SOLENOID IDLE SPECIFICATIONS

Application	RPM
5.2L	
2-Bbl.	775
4-Bbl.	900

IDLE MIXTURE ADJUSTMENT

Mixture Screw Plug Removal (2-Bbl. Carburetor) – **1)** Remove air cleaner. Remove vacuum hoses from front of carburetor base. Center punch a mark on mixture screw housing 1/4" (6.3 mm) from front end of housing for both mixture screws. Punch mark should be at 10 o'clock position on right housing and 2 o'clock position on left housing.
2) Using 3/16" drill bit, bore through outer surface of both mixture screw housings at a 90 degree angle toward plug. Use small drift punch to pry mixture screw plug from housing. Reinstall hoses and air cleaner. After mixture adjustment has been performed, reinstall plugs. See Fig. 2.

Mixture Screw Plug Removal(4-Bbl. Carburetor) – **1)** Remove carburetor. Invert carburetor and use hacksaw to make 2 parallel cuts in throttle body. Make cuts on each side on locator points beneath concealment plug. Cuts should reach the plug but not extend over 1/8" (3.2 mm) beyond locator points.
2) Place flat punch at point near the ends of the saw marks in the throttle body until casting breaks away, exposing steel plug. Repeat procedure for both concealment plugs. See Fig. 3.

PROPANE ENRICHMENT PROCEDURE

NOTE: See Engine Tune-Up Decal for propane enrichment RPM settings.

Quadrajet (4-Bbl. Carburetor) – **1)** Remove concealment plugs. Set parking brake. Shift transmission to "N". Turn all lights and accessories off. Connect a tachometer to engine. Operate engine with transmission in Neutral and fast idle screw on 2nd step of fast idle cam until engine reaches normal operating temperature. Return engine to idle. Ground carburetor switch (Black wire).
2) Disconnect and plug vacuum hose at EGR valve. Remove air cleaner assembly. Disconnect vacuum supply hose from choke diaphragm and install propane supply hose. Other connections at vacuum tee must remain in place.
3) Make sure propane bottle is upright and in a safe location. Remove PCV valve from valve cover and allow to draw fresh air. Disconnect engine harness lead from O_2 sensor and ground harness lead. Allow engine to run for 2 minutes to allow for effect of grounding O_2 sensor to occur.

CAUTION: Do not pull on O_2 sensor connecting wire. The bullet connector to be disconnected is approximately 4" from sensor. Use care in working around O_2 sensor as the exhaust manifold is extremely hot.

4) Open main propane valve. Slowly open metering valve until maximum engine RPM is obtained. When too much propane is added, engine speed will decrease. Adjust propane metering valve to obtain highest RPM.
5) With propane flowing, turn idle speed adjusting screw on solenoid for the correct propane enriched idle speed. If maximum RPM changes, readjust screw on solenoid to specification. Turn propane metering valve off. Allow idle speed to stabilize. Slowly adjust both mixture screws in equal amounts to obtain specified curb idle speed.

NOTE: Pause between mixture screw adjustments to allow idle to stabilize.

6) Open main propane valve. Adjust propane metering valve to obtain highest engine speed. If highest engine speed is not within 25 RPM of propane RPM, repeat steps **4)** and **5)** until proper propane RPM is obtained.
7) Close propane metering valve. Install PCV valve. Reconnect all vacuum hoses and wires to their original locations. Remove all test equipment. Install new concealment plugs to prevent unnecessary adjustment. Reconnect O_2 sensor.

Holley 6280 (2-Bbl. Carburetor) – **1)** Remove concealment plugs. Set parking brake. Shift transmission to "N". Turn all lights and accessories off. Connect a tachometer to engine. Operate engine in Neutral on 2nd step of fast idle cam until engine reaches normal operating temperature. Return engine to idle and turn ignition off.
2) Disconnect and plug vacuum hose at EGR valve and ESA computer. Disconnect and plug canister purge hose at vapor canister. Ground carburetor ground switch using a jumper wire. Separate carburetor electrical connector from wiring harness. Remove Green and Blue wires from carburetor electrical connector.
3) Reconnect carburetor electrical connector to engine harness with the 2 wires disconnected. Start and run engine for at least 4 minutes. Disconnect vacuum supply hose from choke diaphragm and tee propane supply hose in its place. Other connections at vacuum tee must remain in place. Make sure propane bottle is upright and in a safe location.
4) Remove PCV valve from valve cover and allow it to draw fresh air. Open main propane valve. Slowly open metering valve until maximum engine RPM is obtained. When too much propane is added, engine speed will decrease. Adjust propane metering valve to obtain highest RPM.
5) With propane flowing, turn idle speed adjusting screw on solenoid for the correct propane enriched idle speed. If maximum

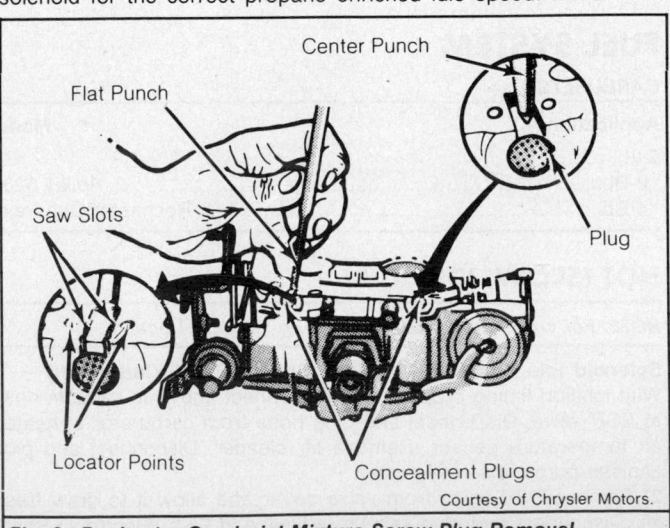

Center Punch

Flat Punch

Saw Slots

Plug

Locator Points

Concealment Plugs

Courtesy of Chrysler Motors.

Fig. 3: Rochester Quadrajet Mixture Screw Plug Removal

RPM changes, readjust screw on solenoid to specification. Turn main propane valve off. Allow idle speed to stabilize. Slowly adjust both mixture screws in equal amounts to obtain specified curb idle speed.

NOTE: Pause between mixture screw adjustments to allow idle to stabilize.

6) Open main propane valve. Adjust propane metering valve to obtain highest engine speed. If highest engine speed is not within 25 RPM of propane RPM, repeat steps 4) and 5) until proper propane RPM is obtained.

7) Close propane metering valve. Install PCV valve. Reconnect all vacuum hoses and wires to their original locations. Remove all test equipment. Install new concealment plugs to prevent unnecessary adjustment. Perform HOT (SLOW) IDLE RPM adjustment in this article.

COLD (FAST) IDLE RPM

NOTE: When all wires and vacuum hoses are reconnected, idle speed may change. DO NOT readjust.

Holley (2-Bbl. Carburetor) – 1) Ensure ignition timing is properly set. Disconnect and plug vacuum hose at EGR valve. Disconnect and plug vacuum hose from carburetor at heated air temperature sensor. Remove air cleaner.

2) Disconnect and plug 3/16" control hose at the canister. Remove PCV valve from valve cover and allow it to draw fresh air. Disconnect and plug vacuum hose at distributor. Connect tachometer to engine. Start engine and warm to operating temperature.

3) Separate carburetor connector from harness. Remove Green duty cycle wire and Blue idle solenoid wire. Reconnect carburetor to engine harness without Green and Blue wires. Ground carburetor switch with jumper wire.

4) Open throttle slightly. Place fast idle adjusting screw on second highest step of fast idle cam. With choke fully open, adjust fast idle speed using fast idle speed adjusting screw.

5) Return to idle speed. Reposition adjusting screw on second highest step of fast idle cam to verify fast idle speed. Readjust if necessary. Return to idle and stop engine.

6) Install air cleaner. Reconnect all wires and vacuum hoses to their original locations. Remove jumper wire and tachometer. Remove carburetor connector from engine harness to reconnect Green and Blue wires.

Quadrajet (4-Bbl. Carburetor) – 1) Ensure ignition timing is properly set. Disconnect and plug vacuum hose at EGR valve. Connect a jumper wire between carburetor switch and ground. Disconnect and plug 3/16" vacuum hose at canister.

2) Remove PCV valve from valve cover allow it to draw fresh air. Connect tachometer to engine. Start engine and warm to operating temperature. Disconnect engine harness lead from O$_2$ sensor. Attach engine harness lead to ground.

3) Allow engine to run 4 minutes to compensate for O$_2$ sensor removal. Open throttle slightly. Place fast idle adjusting screw on second highest step of fast idle cam. With choke fully open, turn fast idle adjusting screw until correct fast idle RPM is obtained.

4) Return to idle. Reposition fast idle adjusting screw on second highest step of fast idle cam to verify fast idle speed. Readjust if necessary. Return to idle. Turn engine off. Reconnect all vacuum hoses and wiring. Remove jumper wire from carburetor switch. Reconnect O$_2$ sensor.

FAST IDLE SPEED SPECIFICATIONS

Application	RPM
2-Bbl.	1700
4-Bbl.	1450

AUTOMATIC CHOKE

All carburetors are equipped with nonadjustable choke covers.

FUEL PUMP

FUEL PUMP PERFORMANCE

Application	Specification
Pressure (at Idle)	6.5 psi (.45 kg/cm²)
Volume (at Idle)	1 qt. (.94L) /minute

General Servicing

BATTERY

BATTERY SPECIFICATIONS

Application	Cold Cranking Amps @ 0°F (-18°C)	Reserve Capacity (Minutes)
Standard	400	100
Optional	500	110

SERVICE INTERVALS

REPLACEMENT INTERVALS

Component	Interval (Miles)
Oil & Filter	7500
Air Filter	30,000
PCV Filter	50,000
Fuel Filter	50,000
Spark Plugs	30,000

ADJUSTMENTS

BELT ADJUSTMENT
Tension in Lbs. (Kg)

	New Belt	Used Belt
All Models	120 (54)	70 (32)

CAPACITIES

COOLING SYSTEM CAPACITIES

Application	Quantity Qts. (L)
Standard	15.5 (14.7)
Heavy Duty	16.5 (15.6)

ENGINE OIL CAPACITY

Application	Quantity Qts. (L)
Crankcase (With Filter)	5.0 (4.7)

TRANSMISSION CAPACITIES

Application	Quanity Qts. (L)
Auto. Trans. (Dexron II)	
A-727 w/Lock-Up	[1] 8.4 (7.9)
A-904 w/Lock-Up	[1] 8.1 (7.7)

[1] – Add .5 pts. (.2L) for auxiliary oil coolers.

1989 EAGLE PREMIER 4 TUNE-UP
Tune-Up

ENGINE IDENTIFICATION

VEHICLE IDENTIFICATION NUMBER CODE

Engine can be identified by the 8th character of Vehicle Identification Number (VIN), which is stamped on a plate attached to top left corner of instrument panel, visible through windshield.

VIN ENGINE CODES

Application	Code
2.5L (151")	H

TUNE-UP NOTES

NOTE: When performing tune-up procedures described in this article, the following notes and precautions must be followed:

Always refer to Engine Tune-Up Decal in engine compartment before performing tune-up. If manual and decal differ, always use decal specifications.

Do not allow or create a condition of engine misfire in more than one cylinder for an extended period of time. Damage to converter may occur due to loading converter with unburned air/fuel mixture.

ENGINE COMPRESSION

COMPRESSION SPECIFICATIONS

Application	Specification
Compression Ratio	9.2:1

VALVE CLEARANCE

Engine uses hydraulic lifters. Adjustment is not possible.

VALVE CLEARANCE ADJUSTMENT

Application	Clearance
Hydraulic Lifters	Zero Lash

VALVE ARRANGEMENT

E-I-I-E-E-I-I-E (Front-to-rear).

IGNITION SYSTEM

DISTRIBUTOR

The distributor cap and rotor are the only servicable parts. Vehicle uses a toothed flywheel ring and pick-up sensor to trigger ignition coil. Ignition timing cannot be adjusted. See Fig. 1.

IGNITION COIL

NOTE: Information not available from manufacturer.

SPARK PLUGS

SPARK PLUG TYPE

Application	Champion No.
2.5L	RC12LYC

SPARK PLUG INSTALLATION

Application	Gap In. (mm)	Torque Ft. Lbs. (N.m)
2.5L	.035 (9)	28 (38)

HIGH TENSION WIRE RESISTANCE

Do not puncture spark plug wires with any type of probe. Use proper adapters. Remove spark plug wire and check resistance with ohmmeter.

HIGH TENSION WIRE RESISTANCE

Wire Length (In.)	Minimum Ohms	Maximum Ohms
1-15	3000	10,000
15-25	4000	15,000
25-35	6000	20,000
Over 35	8000	25,000

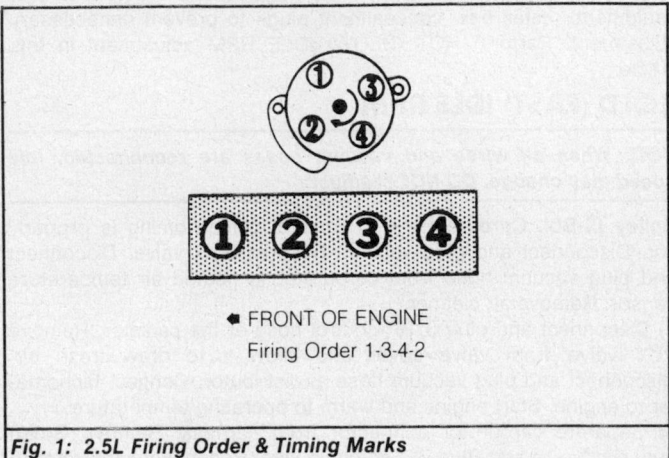

FRONT OF ENGINE
Firing Order 1-3-4-2

Fig. 1: 2.5L Firing Order & Timing Marks

IGNITION TIMING

The ignition timing is controlled by the engine ECU (Electronic Control Unit) and is not adjustable. This system is also equipped with Knock and Speed Sensors which supply the ECU with data that will alter ignition timing.

FUEL SYSTEM

CAUTION: Release fuel pressure before servicing any fuel components. For fuel system pressure relief procedures and fuel system diagnosis, see appropriate article in FUEL SYSTEMS section.

Fuel pressure is tested at the test port on the side of the fuel pressure regulator, next to the fuel return line. Remove test port plug from throttle body to test. See Fig. 2. Using Test Adapter (6173)

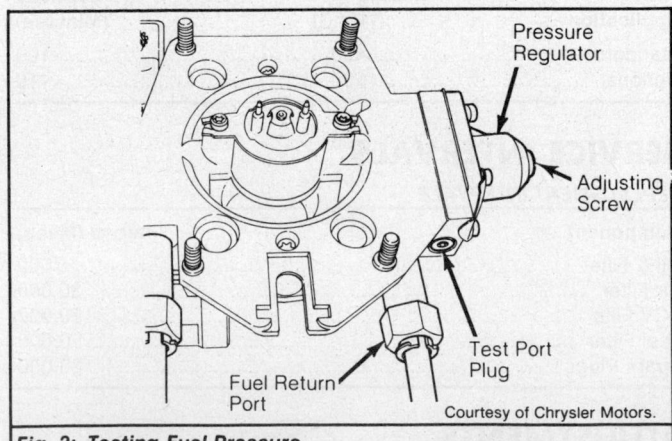

Courtesy of Chrysler Motors.

Fig. 2: Testing Fuel Pressure

Tune-Up (Cont.)

installed in throttle body, test fuel pressure. If fuel pressure is not to specification, turn pressure regulator adjusting screw in to increase pressure. Turn adjusting screw out to decrease pressure.

FUEL INJECTION

Application	Model
2.5L	Throttle Body Injection

FUEL PUMP PERFORMANCE

Application	Pressure
2.5L	14-15 psi (.99-1.07 kg/cm²)

HOT (SLOW) IDLE RPM

Idle Adjustments – 1) Disconnect ISC motor connector. Connect Idle Motor Tester (7088) to ISC motor. For proper connection, it will be necessary to modify Idle Motor Tester (7088). Cut a groove in terminal "A" the same size and shape as grooves in teminals "B" and "D".
2) Connect Idle Motor Tester (7088) to vehicle battery. Start engine and warm to normal operating temperature. Disconnect Idle Speed Control (ISC) motor wire connector. Adjust plunger screw until engine RPM is 3500. *See Fig. 3.*
3) Remove ISC tester and connect idle speed motor electrical connector. Idle speed should automatically return to normal within a few seconds.

CURB IDLE SPEED

Application	RPM
2.5L	750

IDLE MIXTURE ADJUSTMENT

No idle mixture adjustment is possible on fuel injected models.

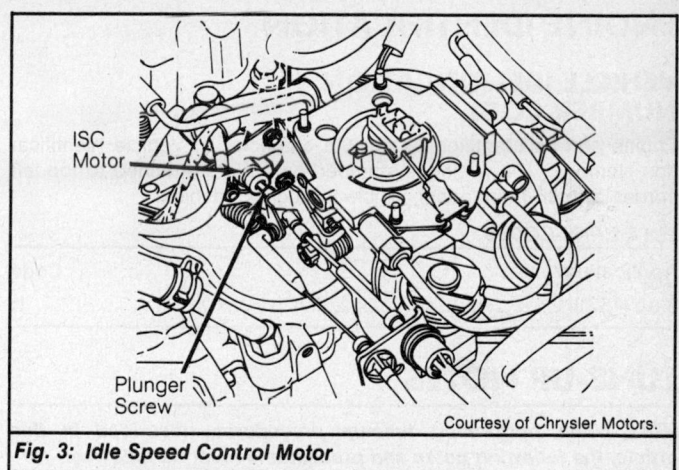
Courtesy of Chrysler Motors.

Fig. 3: Idle Speed Control Motor

COLD (FAST) IDLE RPM

Fast idle speed is not adjustable on fuel injected engines.

THROTTLE POSITION SENSOR (TPS)

1) The use of Diagnostic Tester (M.S. 1700) is preferred when adjusting the TPS.
2) If digital voltmeter is used, disconnect Idle Speed Control (ISC) motor electrical connector. Connect ISC Tester (AB.99) and Harness Adapter (Ele.CT.02). Retract ISC plunger until throttle lever contacts the idle stop screw and plunger does not contact the throttle lever.
3) Turn ignition on. Insert negative lead of voltmeter in terminal "D" and positive lead to terminal "A" of TPS. Voltmeter reading should be 5 volts. Insert voltmeter positive lead to terminal "B", reading should be 4.65 volts.
4) To adjust, loosen TPS retaining screws and pivot sensor to obtain correct reading.

General Servicing

BATTERY

BATTERY SPECIFICATIONS

Group Size	Cold Crank Amps @ 0°F (-18°C)	Reserve Capacity Minutes
34	525	125
58	390-475	75-82

SERVICE INTERVALS

REPLACEMENT INTERVALS

Component	Interval (Miles)
Air Filter	30,000
Engine Oil	7500
Fuel Filter	30,000
Oil Filter	7500
Oxygen Sensor	50,000
PCV Valve	50,000
Spark Plugs	30,000

ADJUSTMENTS

BELT ADJUSTMENT
Lbs. (kg) of Tension Using Gauge (8981-320-975)

Application [1]	Tension
New Belt	180-200 (81-90)
Used Belts	140-160 (63-72)

[1] – All models use serpentine belts.

CAPACITIES

COOLING SYSTEM CAPACITY

Application	Quantity Qts. (L)
All Models	8.6 (8.2)

ENGINE OIL CAPACITY

Application	Quantity Qts. (L)
Crankcase (With Filter)	5 (4.8)

TRANSMISSION CAPACITY

Application [1]	Quantity Qts. (L)
ZF 4HP 18	2.8 (2.6)

[1] – Use only MERCON transmission fluid.

1989 EAGLE V6 TUNE-UP
Tune-Up

ENGINE IDENTIFICATION

VEHICLE IDENTIFICATION NUMBER CODE

Engine can be identified by the 8th character of Vehicle Identification Number (VIN), which is stamped on a plate attached to top left corner of instrument panel, visible through windshield.

VIN ENGINE CODES

Application	Code
3.0L (182")	U

TUNE-UP NOTES

NOTE: When performing tune-up procedures described in this article, the following notes and precautions must be followed:

Always refer to Engine Tune-Up Decal in engine compartment before performing tune-up. If manual and decal differ, always use decal specifications.

Do not allow or create a condition of engine misfire in more than one cylinder for an extended period of time. Damage to converter may occur due to loading converter with unburned air/fuel mixture.

ENGINE COMPRESSION

COMPRESSION SPECIFICATIONS

Application	Specification
Compression Ratio	9.3:1

VALVE CLEARANCE

Engine uses hydraulic lifters. Adjustment is not possible.

VALVE CLEARANCE ADJUSTMENT

Application	Clearance
Hydraulic Lifters	Zero Lash

VALVE ARRANGEMENT

NOTE: "Right" and "Left" refer to right and left side of the engine NOT, the vehicle.

Right Bank – E-I-E-I-E-I (Front-to-rear).
Left Bank – I-E-I-E-I-E (Front-to-rear).

IGNITION SYSTEM

DISTRIBUTOR

The distributor cap and rotor are the only serviceable parts. Vehicle uses a toothed flywheel ring and pick-up sensor to trigger ignition coil. Ignition timing cannot be adjusted. *See Fig. 1.*

SPARK PLUGS

SPARK PLUG TYPE

Application	Champion No.
3.0L	RS9YC

SPARK PLUG INSTALLATION

Application	Gap In. (mm)	Torque Ft. Lbs. (N.m)
3.0L	.035 (9)	11 (15)

HIGH TENSION WIRE RESISTANCE

Do not puncture spark plug wires with any type of probe. Use proper adapters. Remove spark plug wire and check resistance with ohmmeter.

HIGH TENSION WIRE RESISTANCE

Wire Length (In.)	Minimum Ohms	Maximum Ohms
1-15	3000	10,000
15-25	4000	15,000
25-35	6000	20,000
Over 35	8000	25,000

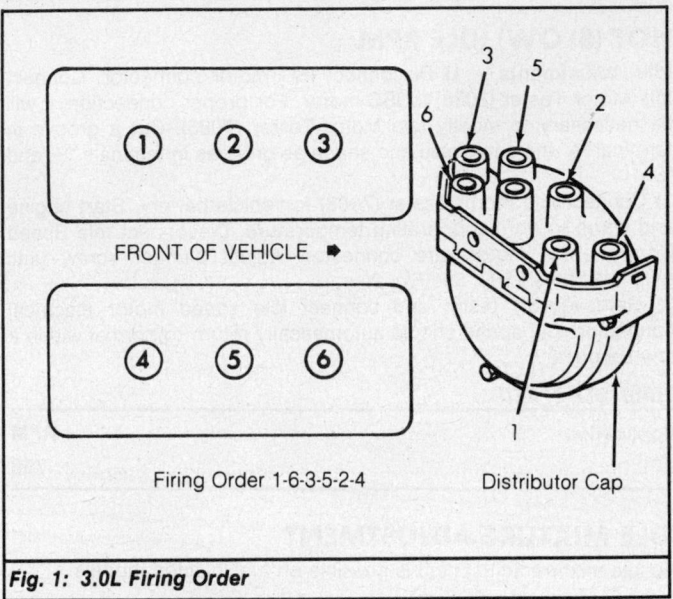

FRONT OF VEHICLE ➡

Firing Order 1-6-3-5-2-4

Distributor Cap

Fig. 1: 3.0L Firing Order

IGNITION COIL

NOTE: Information not available from manufacturer.

IGNITION TIMING

The ECU (Electronic Control Unit) operates the ignition power module. Ignition timing is modified by the ECU to meet engine operating condition. No adjustment is possible.

FUEL SYSTEM

CAUTION: Release fuel pressure before servicing any fuel components. For fuel system pressure relief procedures and fuel system diagnosis, see appropriate article in FUEL SYSTEMS section.

FUEL INJECTION

Application	Model
3.0L	Multi-Point Injection

FUEL PRESSURE

To check fuel pressure, relieve fuel pressure. Using Fuel Connector Remover (6182), disconnect fuel line quick connector at fuel rail. Install Fuel Line Adapter (6175). Connect fuel pressure gauge to adapter. Start and run engine and observe fuel pressure. See FUEL PUMP PERFORMANCE table.

FUEL PUMP PERFORMANCE

Application	Pressure
3.0L	28-30 psi (2.0-2.1 kg/cm²)

HOT (SLOW) IDLE RPM

1) Disconnect idle speed regulator wire connector. Attach Idle Speed Tester (7195) and Idle Speed Exerciser (7088) to idle speed regulator. Attach exerciser electrical leads to battery.

2) Start engine. Move tester switch in extend position and then the retract position. Engine speed should change if idle speed regulator is working.

3) If engine idle speed does not change, remove regulator and watch if valve inside the regulator port is working while cycling the ISC tester. If not, replace idle speed regulator.

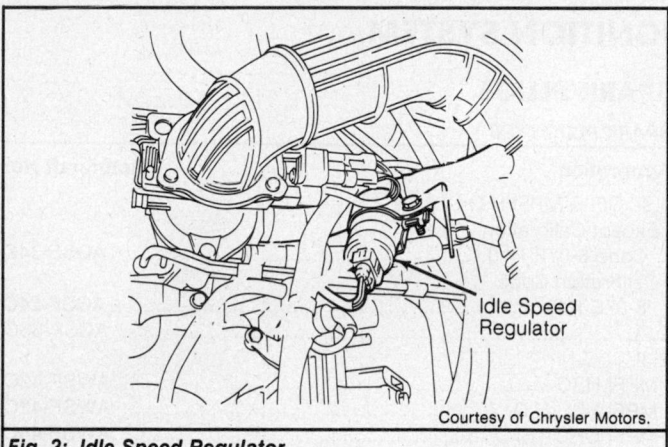

Idle Speed Regulator

Courtesy of Chrysler Motors.

Fig. 2: Idle Speed Regulator

CURB IDLE SPEED

Application	RPM
3.0L	790

IDLE MIXTURE ADJUSTMENT

No idle mixture adjustment is possible on fuel injected models.

COLD (FAST) IDLE RPM

Fast idle speed is not adjustable on fuel injected engines.

THROTTLE POSITION SENSOR (TPS)

1) Turn ignition on, engine off. Do not unplug the TPS wire harness connector. Insert DVOM leads through the back of the wire harness connector.

2) TPS connector is marked "A", "B" and "C". Insert negative lead of voltmeter in terminal "B" and positive lead to terminal "C", reading should be 5 volts.

3) Insert voltmeter positive lead to terminal "A", reading should be .4 volt. To adjust, loosen TPS retaining screws and pivot sensor to obtain correct reading.

General Servicing

BATTERY

BATTERY SPECIFICATIONS

Group Size	Cold Crank Amps @ 0°F (-18°C)	Reserve Capacity Minutes
34	525	125
58	390-475	75-82

SERVICE INTERVALS

REPLACEMENT INTERVALS

Component	Interval (Miles)
Air Filter	30,000
Engine Oil	7500
Fuel Filter	30,000
Oil Filter	7500
Oxygen Sensor	50,000
PCV Valve	50,000
Spark Plugs	30,000

ADJUSTMENTS

BELT ADJUSTMENT
Lbs. (kg)

Application [1]	Tension
New Belt	180-200 (81-90)
Used Belts	140-160 (63-72)

[1] – All models use serpentine belts.

CAPACITIES

COOLING SYSTEM CAPACITY

Application	Quantity Qts. (L)
All Models	8.7 (8.2)

ENGINE OIL CAPACITY

Application	Quantity Qts. (L)
Crankcase (With Filter)	6 (5.8)

TRANSMISSION CAPACITIES

Application	Quantity Qts. (L)
Dry Fill [1]	7.4 (7.0)
Fluid Change [1]	2.8 (2.6)

[1] – Use only MERCON transmission fluid.

1989 FORD MOTOR CO. 4 TUNE-UP
Tune-Up

ENGINE IDENTIFICATION

Engine can be identified by 8th character of Vehicle Identification Number (VIN). The VIN is stamped on a metal plate on top left corner of instrument panel cover, and is visible through windshield.

An Engine Calibration Label located on the engine timing belt cover or valve cover provides specific information required for tune-up parts application.

VIN ENGINE CODES

Application	Code
1.9L (116") CFI [1]	9
1.9L (116") MPFI [2] High Output	J
2.2L (133") MPFI	C
2.2L (133") MPFI Turbo	L
2.3L (140") MPFI [2] HSC [3]	X
2.3L (140") MPFI [2] HSC [3] High Output	S
2.3L (140") MPFI [2] OHC	A
2.5L (153") CFI [1] HSC [3]	D

[1] – Central Fuel Injection.
[2] – Multi-Port Fuel Injection.
[3] – High Swirl Combustion.

TUNE-UP NOTES

NOTE: When performing tune-up procedures described in this article, the following notes and precautions must be followed:

Due to late changes and corrections, always refer to Engine Tune-Up Decal and Engine Calibration Label in engine compartment before performing tune-up. If manual and decal differ, always use decal specifications.

Do not allow or create a condition of engine misfire in more than one cylinder for an extended period of time. Damage to catalytic converter may occur due to loading converter with unburned air/fuel mixture.

Use only fuel system cleaning materials recommended by manufacturer to avoid damage to fuel system and catalytic converter.

Before making a compression test or cranking engine using a remote starting switch, disconnect coil wire from distributor and secure to a good ground.

ENGINE COMPRESSION

Test compression with all spark plugs removed and engine warm. Crank engine through at least 5 compression strokes before recording pressure. Maximum compression variation between highest and lowest cylinder must not exceed 25%.

VALVE CLEARANCE

All engines use hydraulic lifters and are not adjustable.

VALVE CLEARANCE ADJUSTMENT

Application	Clearance
All Models (Hydraulic Lifters)	Zero Lash

VALVE ARRANGEMENT

NOTE: "Right" and "Left" refer to right and left side of the engine, NOT the vehicle.

1.9L CFI & MPFI

Exhaust - Left side.
Intake - Right side.

2.2L MPFI

Exhaust – Left side.
Intake – Right side.

2.3L MPFI

E-I-E-I-E-I-E-I (Front-to-rear).

2.5L CFI

I-E-I-E-E-I-E-I (Front-to-rear).

IGNITION SYSTEM

SPARK PLUGS

SPARK PLUG TYPE

Application	Motorcraft No.
1.9L CFI & MPFI H.O.	
Except Calibration	
Code 8-07E-R10	[1] AGSF-34C
Calibration Code	
8-07E-R10	[1] AGSF-24C
2.2L	AGSP-33C
2.3L	
MPFI HSC	AWSF-42C
MPFI HSC H.O.	AWSF-42C
MPFI OHC	AWSF-44C
2.5L CFI HSC	AWSF-32C

[1] – Spark plug has an extended tip with a full thread tapered seat.

SPARK PLUG INSTALLATION

Application	Gap In. (mm)	Torque Ft. Lbs. (N.m)
1.9L		
Escort	[1]	7-15 (9-20)
2.2L		
Probe	.039-.043 (1.0-1.1)	11-17 (15-23)
2.3L		
Mustang	[1]	[2] 7-15 (9-20)
Tempo & Topaz	[1]	7-15 (9-20)
2.5L		
Sable & Taurus	[1]	7-15 (9-20)

[1] – Refer to underhood decal for specification.
[2] – If spark plug threads are 18 mm, tighten to 15-20 ft. lbs. (20-27 N.m).

HIGH TENSION WIRE RESISTANCE

1) Loosen wires from spark plugs by twisting spark plug boot carefully to loosen seal on spark plug. Remove wires by pulling on plug boot. Remove distributor cap from distributor, leaving wires connected to cap.

NOTE: DO NOT disconnect wires from distributor cap unless replacement is necessary.

2) Using an ohmmeter, check resistance of each wire by connecting one ohmmeter lead to spark plug terminal and other lead to distributor cap insert. On Probe, replace wire if resistance is greater than 5000 ohms per foot. On all other models, if there is more than 7000 ohms resistance per foot, remove wire and test again. If resistance is still more than 7000 ohms per foot, replace wire.

NOTE: Whenever a high tension wire is disconnected, the interior of the spark plug terminal boot must be coated with silicone grease before reconnection.

DISTRIBUTOR

Probe uses an Electronic Control Assembly (ECA), and an electronic control distributor. The non-turbo model has a centrifugal and vacuum advance. All other models use Thick Film Integrated (TFI-IV) ignition systems. The TFI-IV system uses a small module attached to the distributor body.

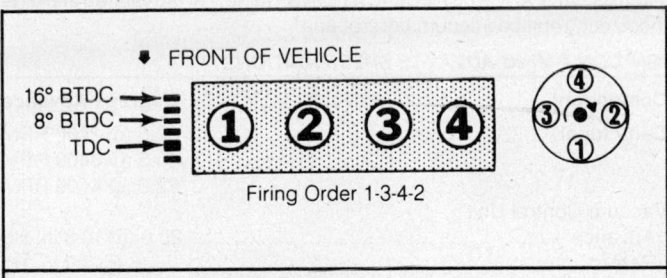

Fig. 1: 1.9L Firing Order & Timing Marks

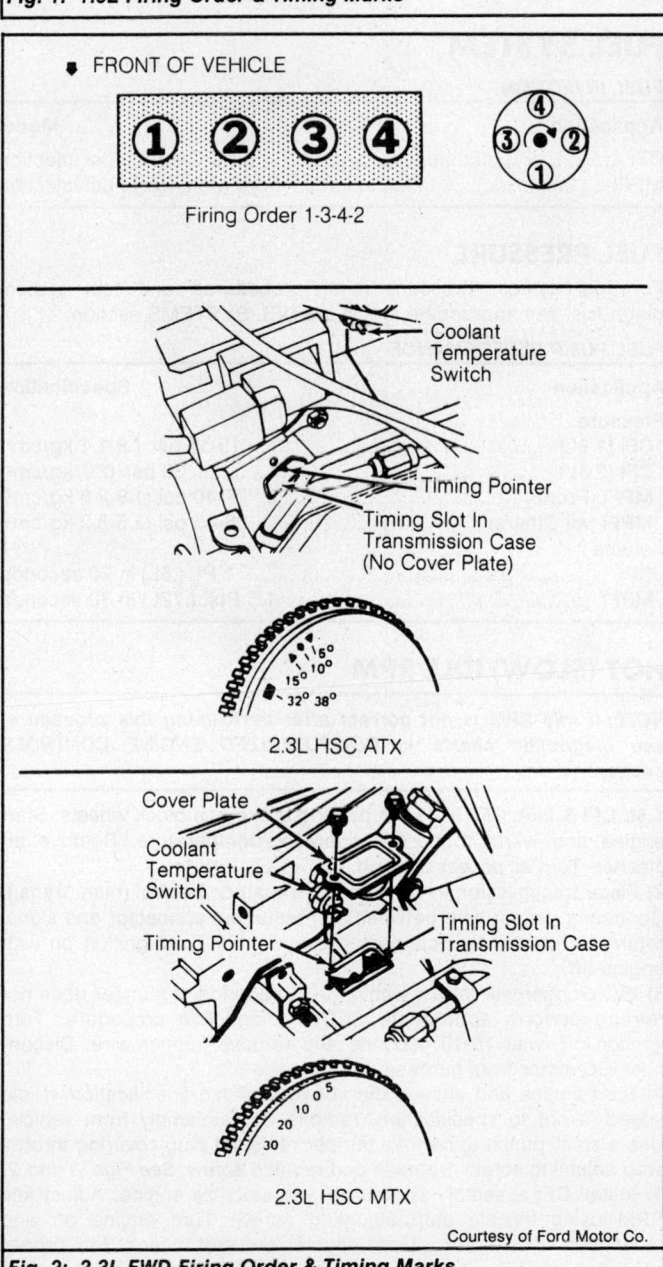

Courtesy of Ford Motor Co.

Fig. 2: 2.3L FWD Firing Order & Timing Marks

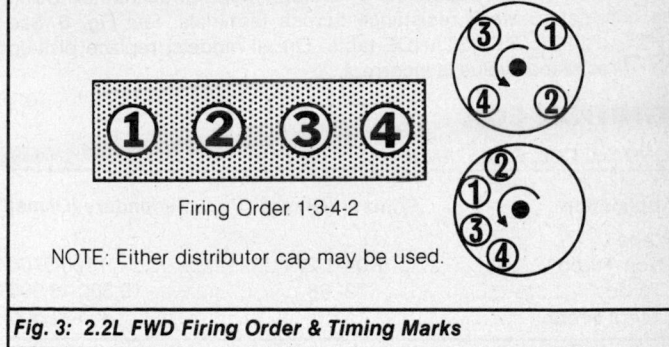

Fig. 3: 2.2L FWD Firing Order & Timing Marks

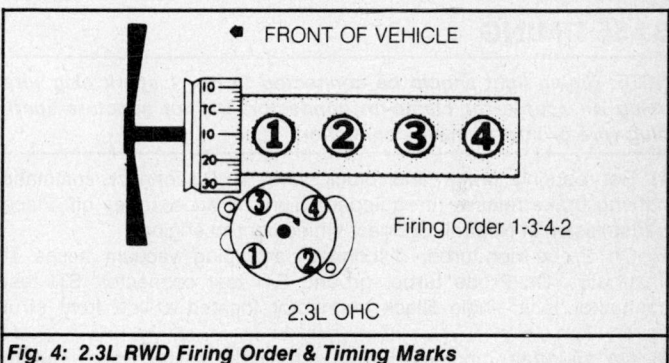

Fig. 4: 2.3L RWD Firing Order & Timing Marks

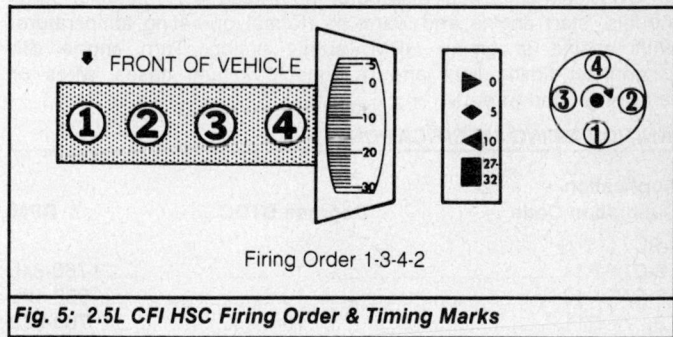

Fig. 5: 2.5L CFI HSC Firing Order & Timing Marks

DISTRIBUTOR PICK-UP COIL

1) On Probe non-turbo, remove distributor cap and rotor. Using an ohmmeter, check resistance across pick-up coil connectors. See PICK-UP COIL RESISTANCE table.

PICK-UP COIL RESISTANCE

Model	Ohms
Non-Turbo	900-1200
Turbo	
A-B	210-260
C-D	210-260
E-F	210-260

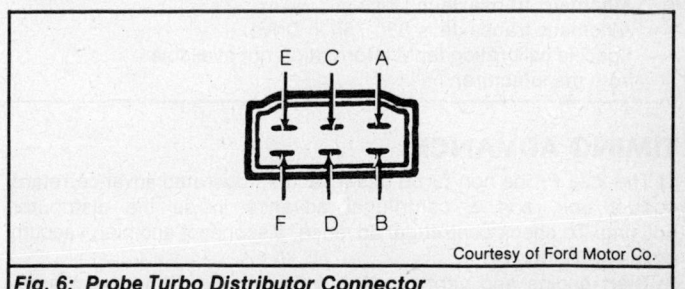

Courtesy of Ford Motor Co.

Fig. 6: Probe Turbo Distributor Connector

2) On Probe turbo, disconnect 6-wire connector at distributor. Using an ohmmeter, check resistance across terminals. *See Fig. 6.* See PICK-UP COIL RESISTANCE table. On all models, replace pick-up coil if resistance value is incorrect.

IGNITION COIL

IGNITION COIL RESISTANCE

Application	Primary (Ohms)	Secondary (Ohms)
Probe		
Non-Turbo	1.04-1.27	7100-9700
Turbo	.72-.88	10,300-13,900
Except Probe	.3-1.0	800-11,500

BASE TIMING

NOTE: Timing light should be connected to No. 1 spark plug wire using an adapter or clamp-on connector. Do not puncture spark plug wire or boot to make connection.

1) Set parking brake and block wheels. Disconnect automatic parking brake release (if equipped). Turn all accessories off. Place transmission in Neutral. Connect timing light to engine.
2) On Probe non-turbo, disconnect and plug vacuum hoses at distributor. On Probe turbo, ground STI test connector. STI test connector is a single Black connector located at left front strut tower.
3) On all other models, disconnect single in-line Spark Output (SPOUT) connector near distributor in harness to TFI module. On all models, start engine and warm to normal operating temperature. With engine at timing RPM, adjust timing. Turn engine off. Disconnect timing light and reconnect vacuum hoses, wires or remove ground wire.

IGNITION TIMING SPECIFICATIONS

Application Calibration Code	Degrees BTDC	RPM
1.9L		
8-07A-R11	10	[1] 760-840
8-07E-R10	10	900-100
8-07F-R11	10	760-840
8-08A-R11	10	[1] 760-840
2.2L [3]		
Exc. Turbo	6	750
Turbo	9	750
2.3L HSC HO		
8-25C-R00	15	[2] 810-890
8-26D-R10	15	[2] 810-890
2.3L HSC		
8-26E-R00	15	[2] 820-880
8-25F-R00	15	[2] 820-880
2.3L OHC [3]	10	770-830
2.5L		
9-20F-R00	10	675-725
9-20T-R00	10	675-725

[1] – Automatic transaxle in Drive.
[2] – Automatic transaxle is 680-760 in Drive.
[3] – Specific calibration label information not available from manufacturer.

TIMING ADVANCE

1) The 2.2L Probe non-turbo has a vacuum operated advance/retard control unit, and a centrifugal advance inside the distributor housing. To check centrifugal advance, disconnect and plug vacuum hoses at distributor.
2) Start engine and verify proper timing at idle. Slowly accelerate engine and observe timing advance at designated RPM. See IGNITION TIMING ADVANCE SPECIFICATIONS table. If advance is incorrect, repair or replace distributor as necessary.
3) To check vacuum advance/retard control unit, disconnect and plug vacuum hoses at distributor. Install timing light. Start engine and verify base timing. Using a vacuum pump, apply vacuum to advance/retard control unit and observe timing. See IGNITION TIMING ADVANCE SPECIFICATIONS table. If advance/retard is incorrect, replace vacuum control unit.

IGNITION TIMING ADVANCE SPECIFICATIONS

Component	Degrees Advance
Centrifugal	12.5 @ 2400 RPM
	15.5 @ 3400 RPM
	22.0 @ 4500 RPM
Vacuum Control Unit	
Advance	20.0 @ 10.8 in. Hg
Retard	6 @ 7.9 in. Hg

FUEL SYSTEM

FUEL INJECTION

Application	Model
CFI	Ford Central Fuel Injection
MPFI	Ford Multi-Port Fuel Injection

FUEL PRESSURE

For fuel system pressure relief procedures and fuel system diagnosis, see appropriate article in FUEL SYSTEMS section.

FUEL PUMP PERFORMANCE

Application	Specification
Pressure	
CFI (1.9L)	13-16 psi. (.9-1.1 kg/cm²)
CFI (2.5L)	39 psi. (2.7 kg/cm²)
MPFI (Probe)	27-40 psi (1.9-2.8 kg/cm²)
MPFI (All Others)	35-45 psi (2.5-3.2 kg/cm²)
Volume	
CFI	1 Pt. (.5L) in 20 seconds
MPFI	1.5 Pts. (.72L) in 30 seconds

HOT (SLOW) IDLE RPM

NOTE: If idle RPM is not correct after performing this procedure, see diagnostic charts in COMPUTERIZED ENGINE CONTROLS section.

1.9L CFI & 2.5L CFI – 1) Set parking brake and block wheels. Start engine and warm to normal operating temperature. Remove air cleaner. Turn all accessories off.
2) Place transmission in Drive (auto. trans.) or Neutral (man. trans.). Connect a jumper wire between self-test input connector and signal return pin on self-test connector. *See Fig. 7.* Turn ignition on with engine off.
3) ISC plunger will retract within 10-15 seconds. If plunger does not retract, perform appropriate EEC-IV diagnostic procedure. Turn ignition off, wait 10-15 seconds and remove jumper wire. Disconnect ISC motor from harness.
4) Start engine and ensure idle speed is within specification. If idle speed is not to specification, remove CFI assembly from vehicle. Use a small punch to remove tamper resistant plug covering throttle stop adjusting screw. Remove and replace screw. *See Figs. 8 and 9.*
5) Install CFI assembly on vehicle and stabilize engine. Adjust idle RPM using throttle stop adjusting screw. Turn engine off and reconnect ISC motor. Turn engine on and check for proper operation of ISC motor. Install a new tamper resistant plug over throttle stop adjusting screw.

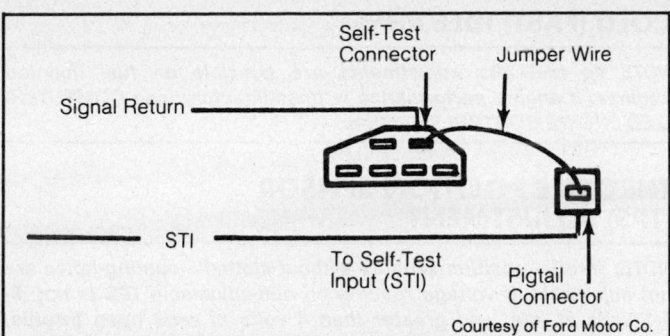

Fig. 7: Retracting ISC Plunger (1.9L CFI & 2.5L CFI)

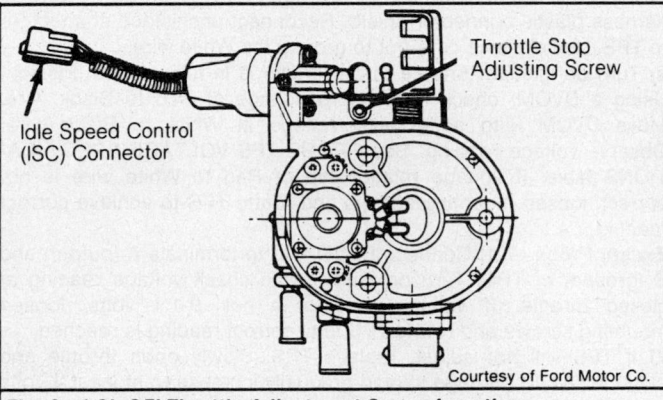

Fig. 8: 1.9L CFI Throttle Adjustment Screw Location

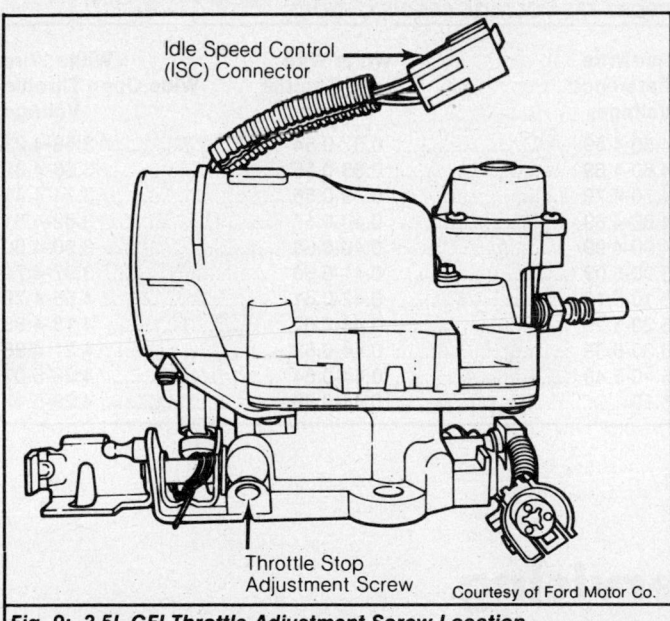

Fig. 9: 2.5L CFI Throttle Adjustment Screw Location

1.9L MPFI H.O. – 1) Turn all accessories off. Place transmission in Neutral. Apply parking brake and block wheels. Allow engine to idle and reach normal operating temperature. Turn ignition off.

2) Disconnect ISC connector. Start engine and run at 2000 RPM for one minute and return to idle. With transmission in Drive (auto. trans.) or Neutral (man. trans.), ensure idle speed is 900-1000 RPM. If idle speed is not to specification, ensure electric cooling fan is off.

3) Turn throttle plate adjusting screw until idle is within specification. *See Fig. 10.* Adjustment must be made within 2 minutes after returning to idle.

4) If idle speed adjustment was necessary, repeat steps **2)** and **3)**. When idle speed is set to specification, turn ignition off. Reconnect

ISC connector. Ensure throttle plate is not binding in bore or that linkage is preventing throttle plate from closing.

5) To check for proper adjustment, run engine at 2000 RPM for one minute and return to idle. Refer to underhood engine decal for engine idle RPM specification.

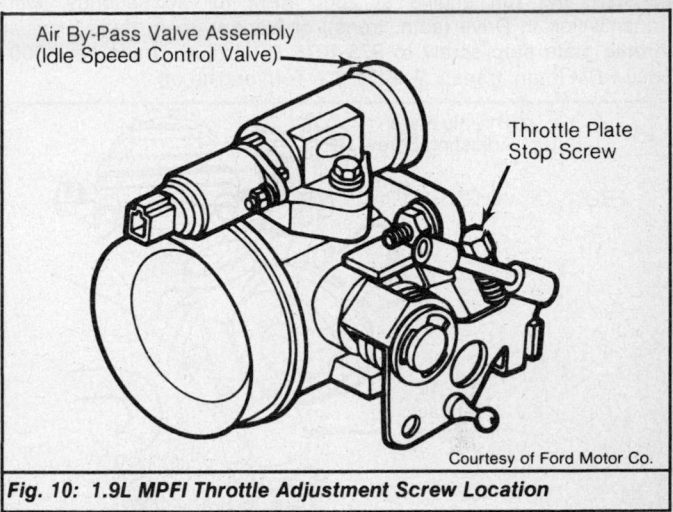

Fig. 10: 1.9L MPFI Throttle Adjustment Screw Location

2.2L – 1) Connect a tachometer to engine. Start and run engine until normal operating temperature is reached. Using a jumper wire, ground the STI connector. Place transaxle in Park or Neutral. Ensure cooling fan is not running.

2) Observe tachometer. If idle speed is not correct, remove adjusting screw blind cap and adjust idle speed to specification. See IDLE SPEED SPECIFICATIONS table. After adjustment is complete, replace blind cap and remove STI jumper wire.

2.3L OHC – 1) Turn all accessories off. Place transmission in Neutral. Apply parking brake and block wheels. Allow engine to idle and reach normal operating temperature. Turn ignition off.

2) Disconnect idle speed control air by-pass valve assembly connector. Start and run engine at 1500 RPM for 20 seconds and return to idle. With transmission in Drive (auto. trans.) or Neutral (man. trans.), ensure idle speed is 500-550 RPM.

3) If idle speed is not to specification, ensure electric cooling fan is off. Turn throttle plate adjusting screw until idle is within specification. *See Fig. 11.*

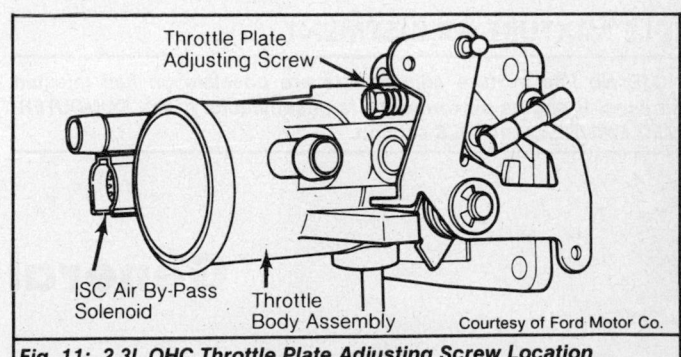

Fig. 11: 2.3L OHC Throttle Plate Adjusting Screw Location

4) If idle speed adjustment was necessary, repeat steps **2)** and **3)**. When idle speed is set to specification, turn ignition off. Reconnect idle speed control air by-pass valve assembly connector. Ensure throttle plate is not binding in bore or that linkage is preventing throttle plate from closing.

5) To check for proper adjustment, run engine at 1500 RPM for 20 seconds and return to idle. Refer to underhood engine decal for engine idle RPM specification.

2.3L HSC & 2.3L HSC H.O. – 1) Turn all accessories off. Place transmission in Neutral. Apply parking brake and block wheels. Allow engine to idle and reach normal operating temperature.

Ensure ignition timing is set to specifications. After checking ignition timing, leave in-line spout connector disconnected. Turn ignition off.
2) Remove PCV hose and install Orifice (T86P-9600-A) or an orifice with a .200" diameter opening. Disconnect idle speed control air by-pass valve assembly.
3) Start and run engine at 2500 RPM for 30 seconds. With transmission in Drive (auto. trans.) or Neutral (man. trans.), adjust throttle plate stop screw to 975-1075 RPM (auto. trans.) or 1500-1600 RPM (man. trans.). See Fig. 12. Turn engine off.

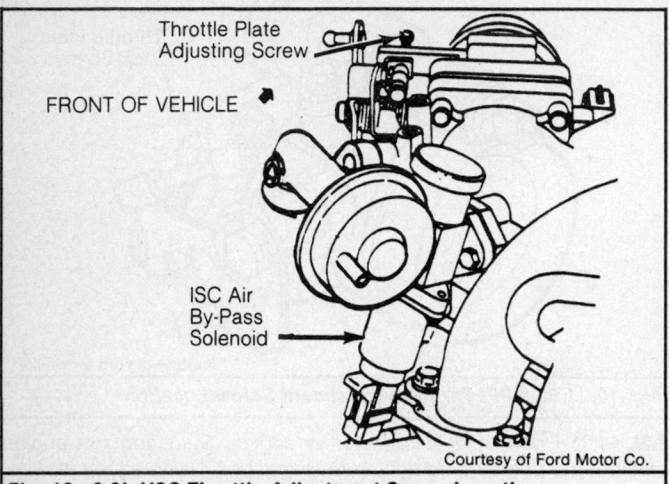

Throttle Plate Adjusting Screw

FRONT OF VEHICLE

ISC Air By-Pass Solenoid

Courtesy of Ford Motor Co.

Fig. 12: 2.3L HSC Throttle Adjustment Screw Location

4) Reconnect ignition timing in-line spout connector. Remove orifice from PCV hose and reconnect PCV hose. Reconnect idle speed control air by-pass valve assembly connector. Ensure throttle plate is not binding in bore or that linkage is preventing throttle plate from closing. To check for proper adjustment, start and run engine at 2500 RPM for 30 seconds. Refer to underhood engine decal for engine idle RPM specification.

IDLE SPEED SPECIFICATIONS

Model	RPM
Except 2.2L	1
2.2L	700-750

1 – Refer to underhood decal for specification.

IDLE MIXTURE ADJUSTMENT

NOTE: No idle mixture adjustments are possible on fuel injected engines. If engine performance is unsatisfactory, see COMPUTERIZED ENGINE CONTROLS section.

COLD (FAST) IDLE RPM

NOTE: No fast idle adjustments are possible on fuel injected engines. If engine performance is unsatisfactory, see COMPUTERIZED ENGINE CONTROLS section.

THROTTLE POSITION SENSOR (TPS) ADJUSTMENT

NOTE: Throttle position sensors without slotted mounting holes are not adjustable. If voltage reading on non-adjustable TPS is not .9-1.1 volts at idle, and greater than 4 volts at wide open throttle, replace throttle position sensor.

Probe – 1) Disconnect 3-wire connector at TPS. Remove TPS harness plastic connector shield. Reconnect unshielded connectors to TPS. Use extreme care not to ground the White wire.
2) Turn on ignition. Ensure throttle valve is in fully closed position. Using a DVOM, check and record voltage at Red to Black wire. Move DVOM lead and check voltage at White to Black wire. Observe voltage reading. See PROBE TPS VOLTAGE SPECIFICATIONS table. If voltage relationship of Red to White wire is not correct, loosen mounting screws and rotate TPS to achieve correct reading.
Except Probe – 1) Connect a DVOM to to terminals A (output) and B (ground) of TPS. Turn on ignition and check voltage reading at closed throttle. If voltage reading is not .9-1.1 volts, loosen mounting screws and rotate TPS until correct reading is reached.
2) If TPS will not adjust, replace TPS. Slowly open throttle and observe DVOM. Voltage should gradually increase to at least 4 volts at wide open throttle.

PROBE TPS VOLTAGE SPECIFICATIONS

Red Wire Reference Voltage	White Wire Closed Throttle Voltage	White Wire Wide Open Throttle Voltage
4.50-4.59	0.37-0.54	3.58-4.23
4.60-4.69	0.83-0.55	3.66-4.32
4.70-4.79	0.39-0.56	3.74-4.41
4.80-4.89	0.40-0.57	3.82-4.51
4.90-4.99	0.40-0.58	3.90-4.60
5.00-5.09	0.41-0.60	3.97-4.70
5.10-5.19	0.42-0.61	4.05-4.79
5.20-5.29	0.43-0.62	4.13-4.88
5.30-5.39	0.44-0.63	4.21-4.98
5.40-5.49	0.44-0.64	4.29-5.07
5.50	0.44-0.66	4.29-5.17

General Servicing

BATTERY
BATTERY SPECIFICATIONS

Rated Amps All Models	Cold Crank. Amps	Discharge Rate Amps
36	310	155
45	380	190
48	410	205
54	450	225
58	540	270
71	535	268
72	850	425

SERVICE INTERVALS

NOTE: On some vehicles, the Service Interval Light will come on after 5000-7000 miles. To reset, depress both Trip and Trip Reset buttons. Light will go out and 3 beeps will be heard.

1989 FORD MOTOR CO. 4 TUNE-UP
General Servicing (Cont.)

1-23

REPLACEMENT INTERVALS

Component	Interval (Miles)
Air Filter	30,000
Engine Oil	[1] 7500
Fuel Filter	30,000
Oil Filter	[1] 7500
PCV Filter	30,000
Spark Plugs	30,000

[1] – Replace at 5000 mile intervals on turbo model.

ADJUSTMENTS

BELT TENSION ADJUSTMENT [1]

Application	New Belt Lbs. (kg)	Used Belt Lbs. (kg)
All Models		
Standard "V" Belts		
1/4"	50-80 (23-36)	40-60 (18-27)
All Others	120-160 (54-73)	90-120 (41-54)
Ribbed "V" Belts		
4-Rib		
Air Pump Only	90-130 (41-59)	90-120 (41-54)
All Others	110-150 (50-68)	110-130 (50-59)
5-Rib	130-170 (59-77)	120-150 (54-68)
6-Rib		
Fixed	150-190 (68-85)	140-160 (64-75)
With Tensioner	85-140 (39-64)	80-140 (36-64)

[1] – Using standard belt tension gauge.

CAPACITIES

COOLING SYSTEM CAPACITIES

Application	Quantity Qts. (L)
1.9L	
Without A/C	7.9 (7.5)
With A/C	
Man. Trans.	6.8 (6.4)
Auto. Trans.	7.3 (6.9)
2.2L	7.9 (7.5)
2.3L HSC (Incl. H.O.)	7.3 (6.9)
2.3L OHC	8.3 (7.9)
2.5L CFI	8.3 (7.9)

ENGINE OIL CAPACITIES

Application	Quantity Qts. (L)
Crankcase (Includes Filter)	
1.9L	4.0 (3.8)
2.2L	5.0 (4.7)
2.3L	5.0 (4.7)
2.5L	4.5 (4.2)

TRANSMISSION CAPACITIES

Application	[1] Quantity Qts. (L)
Automatic Transaxle	
ATX	[2] 8.3 (7.9)
C3	[2] 8.0 (7.6)
4EC-AT (Probe)	[2] 7.2 (6.8)

[1] – Total capacity.
[2] – Use only MERCON transmission fluid.

ENGINE IDENTIFICATION

VEHICLE IDENTIFICATION NUMBER CODE

The engine can be identified by the 8th character of the Vehicle Identification Number (VIN). The VIN is located on the upper left corner of the dash panel. Metal plate is visible through left corner of windshield.

An Engine Calibration Label located on the engine valve cover provides specific information required for tune-up parts application.

VIN ENGINE CODES

Application	Code
3.0L (182") MPFI [1]	U
3.0L SHO (182") SEFI [2]	Y
3.8L (232") SEFI [2]	4
3.8L Supercharged (232") SEFI [2]	[3] R

[1] – Multi-Port Fuel Injection.
[2] – Sequential Electronic Fuel Injection.
[3] – Early production may be code C.

TUNE-UP NOTES

NOTE: When performing tune-up procedures described in this article, the following notes and precautions must be followed.

Always refer to Engine Tune-Up Decal in engine compartment, before tune-up procedures are attempted. In the event manual specifications and decal specifications are different, always use specifications on Engine Tune-Up Decal.

Before making a compression check or cranking engine with a remote starter switch, disconnect ignition wire at distributor or disconnect feed wire in DIS systems.

Do not remove ignition wires while engine is running. Ignition voltage is extremely high and can cause harmful electrical shock and electronic ignition system damage.

When performing tune-up on vehicles equipped with catalytic converters, do not allow or create a condition of engine misfire in more than one cylinder for an extended period of time. Damage to converter may occur due to loading converter with unburned air/fuel mixture.

ENGINE COMPRESSION

Test compression with all spark plugs removed and engine at normal operating temperature. Crank engine through at least 5 compression strokes before recording reading. Maximum variation between cylinders should not exceed 25%.

VALVE CLEARANCE

3.0L SHO – 1) Disconnect negative battery cable and partially drain cooling system. Mark and disconnect electrical connectors and vacuum hoses from intake manifold. Remove air intake duct. Disconnect coolant lines and cable from throttle body.
2) Note location and remove bolts and one stud retaining brackets to intake manifold. Bolts and studs MUST be installed to original location.
3) Mark brackets and remove lower bracket bolts with brackets. Remove 12 bolts retaining intake manifold to cylinder heads. Remove intake manifold and gaskets.
4) Mark and disconnect spark plug wires from spark plugs. Remove spark plugs. Remove valve covers. For left valve cover, remove oil fill cap and ignition coil pack cover. For right valve cover, disconnect fuel lines. On both sides, remove valve cover bolts and remove valve cover(s).
5) Rotate crankshaft, in direction of normal operation only, until camshaft lobe is as shown. *See Fig. 1.* Using a feeler gauge, check

clearance between camshaft and lifter shim. If not within specifications, replace shim. See VALVE CLEARANCE table in this article.
6) To replace shim, insert Lifter Compressor (T89P-6500-A) under camshaft, next to lobe and rotate down to depress lifter. Insert Lifter Holder (T86P-6500-B) and remove lifter compressor. Using a pick, lift and remove shim.
7) Determine size of removed shim by either the number on bottom side of shim or measuring with micrometer. Install appropriate shim with numbers facing downward. Repeat procedure for each valve.

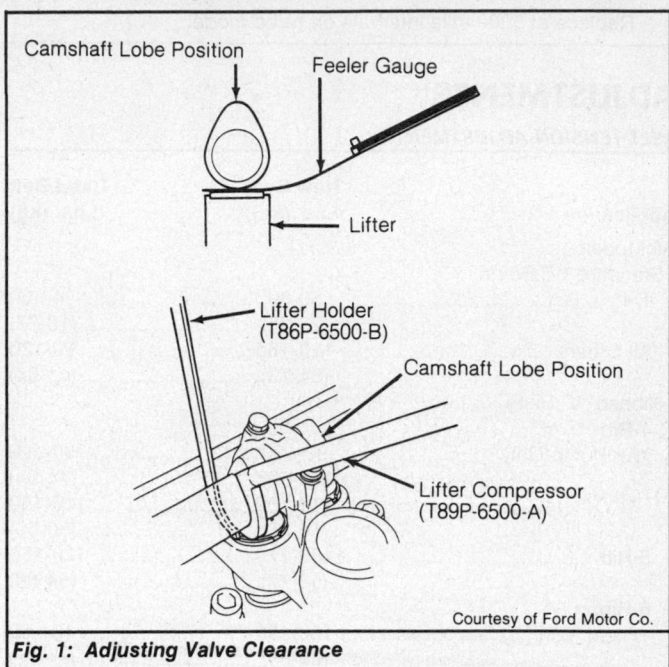

Fig. 1: Adjusting Valve Clearance

Courtesy of Ford Motor Co.

8) Lightly oil bolt/stud threads prior to installation. Using solvent, clean valve cover gasket and intake mating surfaces. Install new valve cover gasket and spark plug hold gaskets on valve cover. To complete installation, reverse removal procedure. Tighten all bolts and nuts to specification. See TIGHTENING SPECIFICATIONS table.

VALVE CLEARANCE

Application	Clearance (Hot)
Except 3.0L SHO	Non-Adjustable (Zero Lash)
3.0 SHO (24 Valve)	
Exhaust	.010-.014" (.25-.35 mm)
Intake	.006-.010" (.15-.25 mm)

TIGHTENING SPECIFICATIONS

Application	Ft. Lbs. (N.m)
Front Intake Section-to-Intake Manifold	11-17 (15-23)
Fuel Rail Assembly	11-17 (15-23)
Intake Manifold & Brackets	11-17 (15-23)
Spark Plugs	17-19 (23-26)

	INCH Lbs. (N.m)
Throttle Body-to-Intake	18-26 (2-3)
Valve Cover	96-132 (11-15)

VALVE ARRANGEMENT

NOTE: Right and left refers to right and left side of engine, NOT vehicle.

3.0L (EXC. SHO)

Left Bank – I-E-I-E-I-E (Front-to-rear).
Right Bank – E-I-E-I-E-I (Front-to-rear).

3.0L SHO

Exhaust – Outboard (both banks).
Intake – Inboard (both banks).

3.8L

Right Bank – I-E-I-E-I-E (Front-to-rear).
Left Bank – E-I-E-I-E-I (Front-to-rear).

IGNITION SYSTEM

NOTE: The 3.0L SHO and 3.8L supercharged models have a Distributorless Ignition System (DIS). Operation is the same except a crankshaft sensor, camshaft sensor and coil pack are used in place of the conventional electronic distributor and coil.

SPARK PLUGS

SPARK PLUG TYPE

Application	Motorcraft No.
3.0L	AWSF-32P
3.0L SHO	AGSP-32P
3.8L	AWSF-44C
3.8L Supercharged	AWSF-44P

SPARK PLUG INSTALLATION

Application	Gap In. (mm)	Torque Ft. Lbs. (N.m)
3.0L	.044 (1.1)	5-14 (7-20)
3.0L SHO	.042-.046 (1.0-1.2)	17-19 (23-26)
3.8L	.054 (1.4)	5-11 (7-15)
3.8L Supercharged	[1]	5-11 (7-15)

[1] – Information not available from manufacturer.

HIGH TENSION WIRE RESISTANCE

Except DIS System – Remove spark plug wires from plugs. Remove distributor cap with wires attached. Check resistance of each wire by connecting one ohmmeter lead to cap terminal and the other lead to spark plug end of wire. If resistance is more than 7000 ohms per foot, remove wire from cap and retest. If still more than 7000 ohms per foot, replace wire.

DIS System – Disconnect spark plug wire at plug. Remove ignition coil pack cover. Carefully squeeze the locking tabs and disconnect wire. Using an ohmmeter, check wire resistance. Replace any wire that exceeds 30,000 ohms resistance.

NOTE: Whenever a high tension wire is disconnected, the interior of the terminal boot must be coated with silicone grease before reconnection.

IGNITION COIL

IGNITION COIL RESISTANCE

Application	Primary Ohms	Secondary Ohms
All Models	.3-1.0	8700-11,500

DISTRIBUTOR

All models are equipped with TFI-IV ignition systems and no adjustments are required. The 3.0L SHO and 3.8L supercharged engines have a Distributorless Ignition System (DIS) which uses a crankshaft and camshaft sensor in place of a distributor.

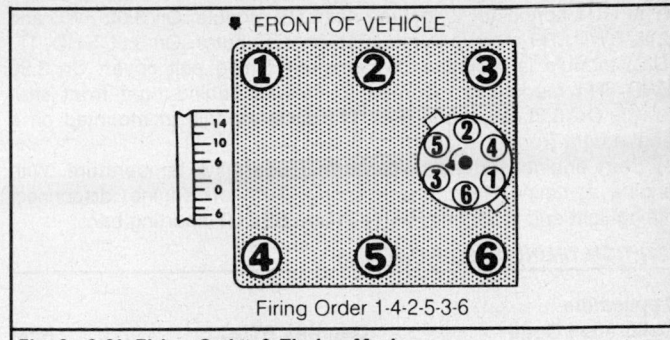

Firing Order 1-4-2-5-3-6

Fig. 2: 3.0L Firing Order & Timing Marks

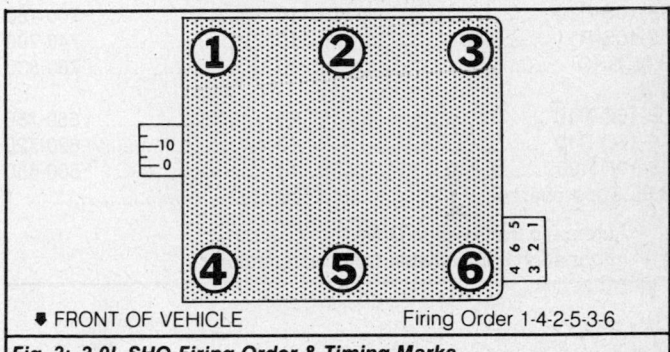

FRONT OF VEHICLE   Firing Order 1-4-2-5-3-6

Fig. 3: 3.0L SHO Firing Order & Timing Marks

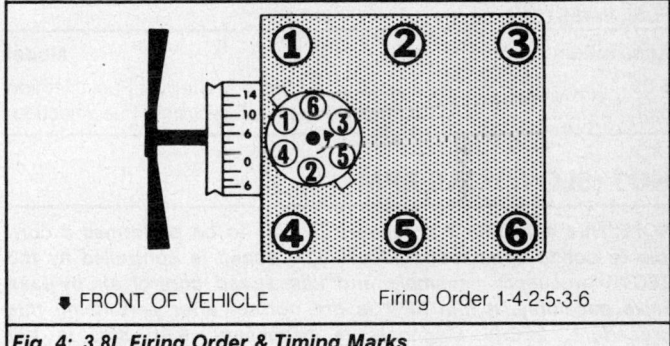

FRONT OF VEHICLE   Firing Order 1-4-2-5-3-6

Fig. 4: 3.8L Firing Order & Timing Marks

FRONT OF VEHICLE

Firing Order 1-4-2-5-3-6

Fig. 5: 3.8L Supercharged Firing Order & Timing Marks

IGNITION TIMING

1) – Connect timing light to No. 1 spark plug using inductive pickup, adapter or snap-on connector. Do not puncture spark plug wire or boot to make connection. Set parking brake and block wheels. Disconnect automatic parking brake release (if equipped). Turn all accessories off. Connect timing light to engine. Disconnect single in-line Spark Output (SPOUT) connector shorting bar. Wire color of SPOUT connector is Yellow/Light Green.

2) SPOUT connector is located near TFI module. On 3.0L FWD and 3.8L RWD, TFI module is mounted on distributor. On 3.0L SHO, TFI (DIS) module is mounted on camshaft timing belt cover. On 3.8L FWD, TFI module is mounted to firewall behind right front strut tower. On 3.8L supercharged, TFI (DIS) module in mounted on a pad at right front of engine.

3) Start engine and warm to normal operating temperature. With engine at timing RPM, check timing. Turn off engine, disconnect timing light and reconnect single in-line SPOUT shorting bar.

IGNITION TIMING SPECIFICATIONS

Application Calibration Code	Degrees BTDC	RPM
3.0L		
9-10S-R10	10	740-780
9-10S-R11	10	740-780
3.0L SHO	10	760-830
3.8L		
9-16C-R10	10	[1] 650-750
9-16D-R10	10	[1] 620-720
9-16F-R00	10	[1] 500-650
3.8L Supercharged	10	[2]

[1] – Automatic transaxle in Drive.
[2] – Information not available from manufacturer.

FUEL SYSTEM

FUEL INJECTION

Application	Model
3.0L	Ford Multi-Port Fuel Injection
3.8L	Ford Sequential Electronic Fuel Injection.

HOT (SLOW) IDLE RPM

NOTE: This adjustment procedure is only to be performed if curb idle is not to specification. Curb idle speed is controlled by the EEC-IV processor assembly and idle speed control air by-pass valve assembly. If idle RPM is not correct after performing this procedure, EEC-IV diagnosis is necessary. 3.0L SHO is not adjustable.

3.0L MPFI – 1) Turn all accessories off. Place transmission in Neutral. Apply parking brake and block wheels. Allow engine to idle and reach normal operating temperature. Ensure ignition timing is set to specifications. After checking ignition timing, leave in-line SPOUT connector disconnected. Turn ignition off.

2) Remove PCV hose and install Orifice (T86P-9600-A) or an orifice with a .200" diameter opening. Disconnect idle speed control air by-pass valve assembly.

3) Start engine. With transmission in Drive (auto. trans.) or Neutral (man. trans.), adjust throttle plate stop screw to specification. See IGNITION TIMING SPECIFICATIONS table. See engine tune-up decal. *See Fig. 6.* Turn engine off. Disconnect battery for a minimum of 3 minutes.

4) Reconnect battery and ignition timing in-line SPOUT connector. Remove orifice from PCV hose and reconnect PCV hose. Reconnect idle speed control air by-pass valve assembly connector. Ensure throttle plate is not binding in bore or that linkage is preventing throttle plate from closing. If vehicle is equipped with an Automatic Overdrive Transmission (AXOD), check T.V. pressure adjustment.

3.8L FWD & RWD SEFI (Includes Supercharged) – 1) Turn all accessories off. Place transmission in Neutral. Apply parking brake and block wheels. Allow engine to idle and reach normal operating temperature.

2) Stop engine. Back off throttle stop screw until clearance is obtained. Using a .010" (3 mm) feeler gauge inserted between screw

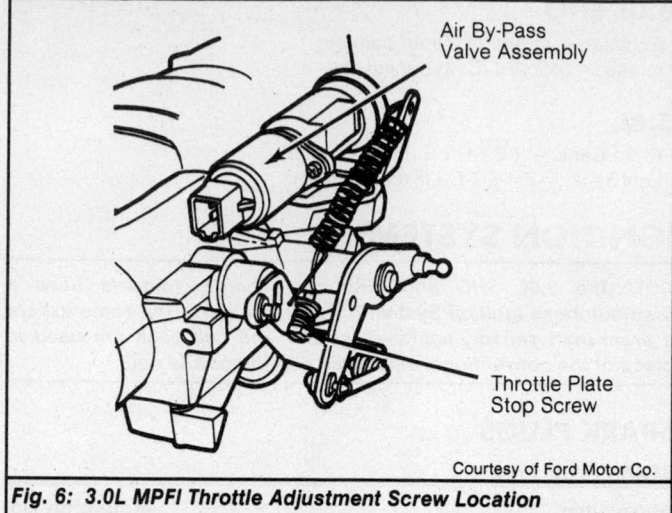

Fig. 6: 3.0L MPFI Throttle Adjustment Screw Location

Courtesy of Ford Motor Co.

and stop, turn throttle stop screw in until screw contacts feeler gauge. Turn screw in an additional 1 1/2 turns.

3) Start and run engine at 2500 RPM for 30 seconds. With transmission in Drive (auto. trans.) or Neutral (man. trans.), adjust throttle plate stop screw to specification. See IGNITION TIMING SPECIFICATIONS table. See engine tune-up decal. *See Fig. 7.*

4) Ensure throttle plate is not binding in bore or that linkage is preventing throttle plate from closing. To check for proper adjustment, start and run engine at 2500 RPM for 30 seconds. Allow engine to return to idle.

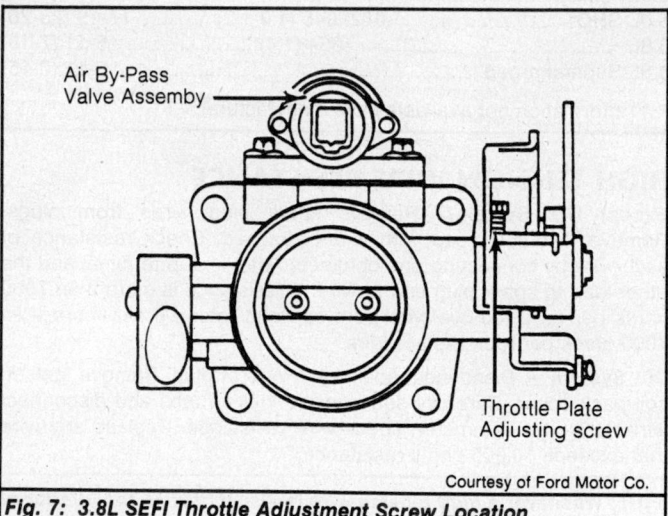

Fig. 7: 3.8L SEFI Throttle Adjustment Screw Location

Courtesy of Ford Motor Co.

IDLE MIXTURE ADJUSTMENT

No idle mixture adjustments are possible on 3.0L and 3.8L fuel injected engines.

COLD (FAST) IDLE RPM

No fast idle adjustments are possible on 3.0L and 3.8L fuel injected engines.

THROTTLE POSITION SENSOR (TPS)

NOTE: Two types of Throttle Position Sensors (TPS) are used on EEC-IV system. "Level C" is adjustable and "Level D/RD" is non-adjustable.

1) To adjust "Level C" sensors the use of EEC-IV Breakout Box (Rotunda T83L-50-EEC-IV) should be used.

2) Connect and set digital voltmeter to 20-volt scale. Connect positive lead of voltmeter to pin 47 and negative lead to pin 46.

3) Turn ignition on. Loosen TPS hold down screws. Rotate to adjust TPS until voltmeter reads 1.0 volt. Tighten hold down screws.

4) Move throttle wide open (WOT) and back to idle position. Voltmeter should read from 1.0 volt to at least 4.0 volts and back to 1.0 volt at idle position. Perform EEC-IV Quick Test if not to specification. See appropriate article in COMPUTERIZED ENGINE CONTROLS section

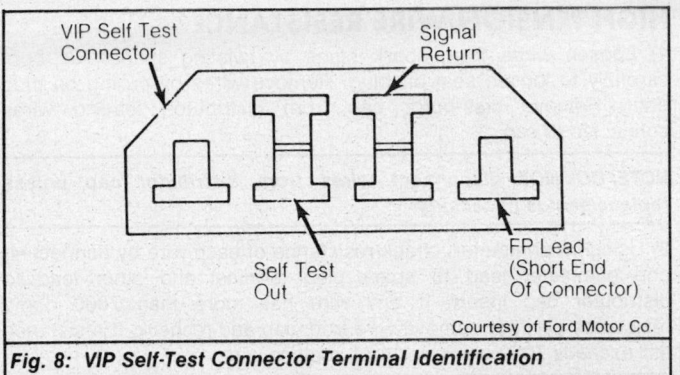

Fig. 8: VIP Self-Test Connector Terminal Identification

FUEL PUMP

Disconnect fuel return line at fuel rail. Connect fuel hose to fuel container. Connect fuel pressure gauge at diagnostic valve on fuel rail. Install jumper wire to FP lead of VIP Self-Test connector. See Fig. 8. Turn ignition on. Ground jumper wire to FP lead. Note fuel pump pressure. See FUEL PUMP SPECIFICATIONS table.

FUEL PUMP SPECIFICATIONS

Application	Specification [1] psi (kg/cm²)
3.0L MPFI	35-45 (2.5-3.2)
3.0L SHO	30-45 (2.1-3.2)
3.8L SEFI	35-45 (2.5-3.2)
3.8L Supercharged	35-40 (2.5-2.8)
Volume	
Except Supercharged	1 Pt. (.5L) in 30 seconds
Supercharged	1.5 Pt. (.72L) in 30 seconds

[1] – Key on, engine off. Engine running pressure may be 5 psi (.4 kg/cm²) less

General Servicing

SERVICE INTERVALS

REPLACEMENT INTERVALS

Component	Interval (Miles)
Air Filter	30,000
Engine Oil	7500
Fuel Filter	30,000
Oil Filter	7500
PCV Filter	30,000
Spark Plugs	30,000

CAPACITIES

COOLING SYSTEM CAPACITIES

Application	Quantity Qts. (L)
3.0L	11.0 (10.4)
3.0L SHO	1.6 (11.0)
3.8L	11.8 (11.2)
3.8L Supercharged	12.0 (11.3)

ENGINE OIL CAPACITIES

Application	Quantity Qts. (L)
Crankcase (Includes Filter)	
3.0L	4.5 (4.3)
3.8L	5.0 (4.7)

TRANSMISSION CAPACITIES

Application	Quantity Qts. (L)
Auto. Trans.	
AXOD	[1] 13.3 (12.6)
AOD	[1] 12.3 (11.7)

[1] – Use only MERCON transmission fluid.

ADJUSTMENTS

BELT TENSION ADJUSTMENT [1]

Application	New Belt Lbs. (kg)	[1] Used Belt Lbs. (kg)
3.0L Models		
Alternator Belt	100-140 (44-62)	80-100 (36-44)
P/S & A/C	150-190 (67-84)	140-160 (62-73)
3.8L Models		
Standard "V" Belts		
1/4"	50-90 (23-41)	40-60 (18-27)
All Others	120-160 (54-73)	90-120 (41-54)
Ribbed "V" Belts		
4-Rib		
Air Pump Only	90-130 (41-59)	90-120 (41-54)
5 Rib	120-170 (54-77)	110-130 (50-59)
6-Rib		
Fixed	150-190 (67-84)	140-160 (62-73)
With Tensioner	100-130 (44-59)	100-180 (44-82)

[1] – Any belt operated for 10 minutes.

BATTERY

BATTERY SPECIFICATIONS

Rated Amps	Cold Crank. Amps	Discharge Rate Amps
45	380	190
54	450	225
58	540	270
72	850	425

1989 FORD MOTOR CO. V8 TUNE-UP
Tune-Up

ENGINE IDENTIFICATION

VEHICLE IDENTIFICATION NUMBER CODE

Engine can be identified by the 8th character of the Vehicle Identification Number (VIN). The VIN is stamped on a plate on top left corner of instrument panel, visible through the windshield.

An Engine Calibration Label located on the engine valve cover provides specific information required for tune-up parts application.

VIN ENGINE CODES

Application	Code
5.0L (302") SEFI [1]	F
5.0L (302") H.O. SEFI [1]	E
5.8L (351") 2-Bbl. (Police Only)	G

[1] – Sequential Electronic Fuel Injection.

TUNE-UP NOTES

NOTE: When performing tune-up procedures described in this article, the following notes and precautions must be followed:

Always refer to Engine Tune-Up Decal in engine compartment, before attempting tune-up. In the event manual specifications and decal specifications differ, always use specifications on the Engine Tune-Up Decal.

On 5.8L engines, if the Dura Spark 2-piece distributor cap must be removed, first remove top portion, then rotor, and then bottom portion. If any spark plug wire is disconnected with this system, the connection must first be coated with silicone grease before reconnection.

When connecting a tachometer to Dura Spark ignition coil, install the alligator clip on tachometer into "DEC" (TACH TESTING) cavity of coil.

Do not allow or create a condition of engine misfire in more than one cylinder for more than 30 seconds. Damage to converter may result due to loading converter with unburned air/fuel mixture.

ENGINE COMPRESSION

Test compression with all spark plugs removed and engine at normal operating temperature. Crank engine through at least 5 compression strokes before recording reading. Maximum variation between cylinders should not exceed 25%.

VALVE CLEARANCE

All engines use hydraulic valve lifters and no adjustment is required.

VALVE CLEARANCE ADJUSTMENT

Application	Clearance
5.0L & 5.8L (Hydraulic)	Zero Lash

VALVE ARRANGEMENT

Right Bank – I-E-I-E-I-E-I-E (Front-to-rear).
Left Bank – E-I-E-I-E-I-E-I (Front-to-rear).

IGNITION SYSTEM

SPARK PLUGS

SPARK PLUG TYPE

Application	Motorcraft No.
5.0L & 5.0L H.O.	AWSF-44C
5.8L	ASF-42

SPARK PLUG INSTALLATION

Application	Gap In. (mm)	Torque Ft. Lbs. (N.m)
5.0L & 5.0L H.O.	.050 (1.3)	10-15 (14-20)
5.8L	.044 (1.1)	10-15 (14-20)

HIGH TENSION WIRE RESISTANCE

1) Loosen wires from spark plugs by twisting spark plug boot carefully to loosen seal on plug. Remove wires by pulling on plug boot. Remove distributor cap from distributor, leaving wires connected to cap.

NOTE: DO NOT disconnect wires from distributor cap unless replacement is necessary.

2) Using an ohmmeter, check resistance of each wire by connecting one ohmmeter lead to spark plug terminal and other lead to distributor cap insert. If any wire has more than 7000 ohms resistance per foot, remove wire from cap and recheck. If resistance still exceeds 7000 ohms per foot, replace wire.

NOTE: Whenever a high tension wire is disconnected, the interior of spark plug terminal boot must be coated with silicone grease before reconnection.

DISTRIBUTOR

On 5.0L models, the TFI-IV ignition system is used. On 5.8L Police models, the Dura Spark II with Universal Integrated Circuit (UIC) ignition system is used. Only basic ignition timing is adjustable on either system.

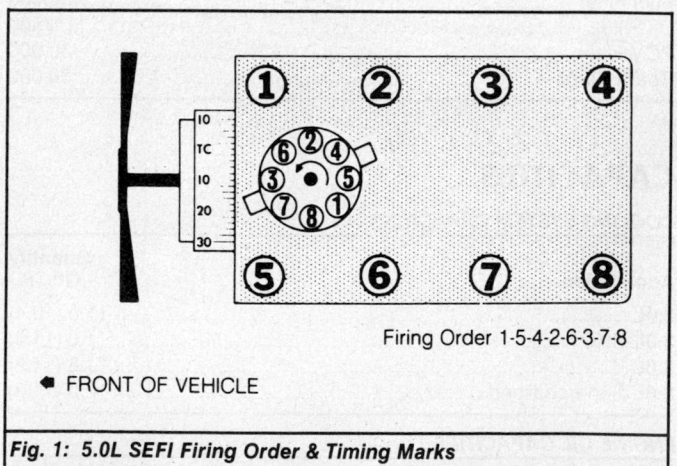

Firing Order 1-5-4-2-6-3-7-8

◄ FRONT OF VEHICLE

Fig. 1: 5.0L SEFI Firing Order & Timing Marks

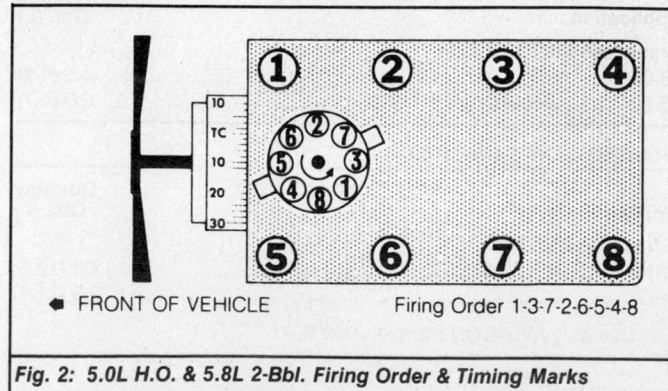

◄ FRONT OF VEHICLE   Firing Order 1-3-7-2-6-5-4-8

Fig. 2: 5.0L H.O. & 5.8L 2-Bbl. Firing Order & Timing Marks

IGNITION COIL

IGNITION COIL RESISTANCE

Application	Primary	Secondary
5.0L TFI-IV	.3-1.0	8000-11,500
5.8L Dura Spark II w/UIC	.8-1.6	7700-10,500

IGNITION TIMING

NOTE: Timing light should be connected to No. 1 spark plug using inductive adapter or clamp-on connector. Do not puncture spark plug wire or boot to make connection.

Carbureted Models – 1) With engine off, set parking brake and block wheels. Disconnect automatic parking brake release. Place transmission in Park (auto. trans.). Turn all accessories off. Disconnect and plug vacuum lines at distributor. Connect timing light and tachometer to engine.

2) Disconnect 2-wire connector from ignition module and install a jumper wire between the 2 pins (Yellow and Black wires).

3) Start engine and warm to normal operating temperature. With engine at timing RPM, adjust timing. Remove jumper wire. Reconnect all connectors and vacuum hoses. Remove all test equipment.

Fuel Injected Models – 1) With engine off, set parking brake and block wheels. Disconnect and plug automatic parking brake vacuum hose (if equipped). Turn all accessories off. Connect timing light to engine. Disconnect single in-line SPOUT connector shorting bar near near TFI module at distributor. Wire color of SPOUT connector is Yellow/Light Green.

2) Start engine and warm to normal operating temperature. Place transmission in Drive (auto. trans.) or Neutral (man. trans.). With engine at timing RPM, adjust timing. Turn off engine, disconnect timing light and reconnect single in-line SPOUT connector.

IGNITION TIMING SPECIFICATIONS

Application Calibration Code	Degrees BTDC	RPM
5.0L		
8-22C-R00	10	[1] 525-650
8-22L-R00	10	[1] 550-675
8-22M-R00	10	[1] 525-650
922A-R00	10	[2] 625-775
5.8L 2-Bbl.	14	600

[1] – Automatic transmission in Drive.
[2] – Manual transmission in Neutral. Automatic tranmission is 575-725 in Drive.

FUEL SYSTEM

CARBURETOR

Application	Model
5.8L 2-Bbl.	Motorcraft 7200VV

FUEL INJECTION

Application	Model
5.0L & 5.0L H.O.	Sequential Electronic Fuel Injection

HOT (SLOW) IDLE RPM

Carbureted Models (Curb Idle) – 1) Set parking brake and block wheels. Disconnect and plug automatic brake release vacuum hose (if equipped). Start engine and warm to normal operating temperature.

2) Place transmission in Neutral. Place A/C heater selector in "OFF" position. Disconnect and plug vacuum hose at throttle kicker. Adjust curb idle using curb idle speed adjusting screw on throttle lever. *See Fig. 3.*

3) Increase engine speed momentarily. Let engine return to idle and recheck curb idle speed. Refer to underhood engine decal for engine idle RPM specification. Apply slight pressure on top of nylon nut located on accelerator pump to take up linkage clearance.

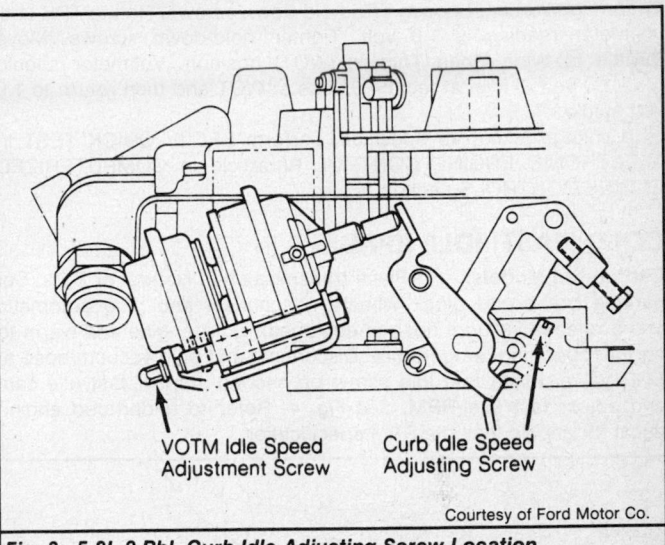

VOTM Idle Speed Adjustment Screw   Curb Idle Speed Adjusting Screw

Courtesy of Ford Motor Co.

Fig. 3: 5.8L 2-Bbl. Curb Idle Adjusting Screw Location

4) Turn nylon nut on accelerator pump rod clockwise until a .010 ± .005 in. (.25 ± .13 mm) clearance is obtained between top of accelerator pump and pump lever.

5) Turn accelerator pump rod one turn counterclockwise to set lever lash preload. Remove plug from throttle kicker vacuum hose and reconnect.

Carbureted Models (Throttle Kicker Adjustment) – 1) Set parking brake and block wheels. Start engine and warm to normal operating temperature. Place transmission in Neutral or Park. Place A/C-heater selector in "OFF" position.

2) Disconnect and plug vacuum hose at Vacuum Operated Throttle Modulator (VOTM) kicker. Connect a vacuum pump to VOTM and apply a minimum of 10 in. Hg to VOTM kicker.

3) Check/adjust VOTM kicker idle speed. Refer to underhood engine decal for RPM specification. If adjustment is required, turn saddle bracket adjustment screw. *See Fig. 3.* Remove vacuum pump. Remove vacuum hose plug and connect vacuum hose to throttle kicker.

Fuel Injected Models – 1) Turn all accessories off. Place transmission in Neutral. Apply parking brake and block wheels. Allow engine to idle and reach normal operating temperature. Stop engine. Disconnect idle speed control air by-pass valve assembly connector.

2) Start and run engine at 1800 RPM for 30 seconds. With transmission in Drive (auto. trans.) or Neutral (man. trans.), adjust throttle plate stop screw to 530-570 RPM (605-645 RPM on auto. trans. high output, 680-720 RPM on man. trans. high output). After throttle plate adjustment, back out throttle plate adjustment screw an additional 1/2 turn. Turn engine off.

3) Disconnect battery for a minimum of 3 minutes. Reconnect battery. Ensure throttle plate is not binding in bore or that linkage is preventing throttle plate from closing. To check for proper adjustment, start and run engine at 1800 RPM for 30 seconds. Refer to underhood engine decal for engine idle RPM specification.

IDLE MIXTURE ADJUSTMENT

NOTE: No idle mixture adjustment is possible 5.0L SEFI or 5.8L 2-Bbl. engines.

THROTTLE POSITION SENSOR (TPS)

NOTE: Two types of TPS are used on EEC-IV system. "Level C" type is adjustable and "Level D/RD" type is nonadjustable.

1) To adjust "Level C" type sensors, use EEC-IV Breakout Box (Rotunda T83L-50-EEC-IV). Connect digital voltmeter and set to 20-volt scale. Connect positive voltmeter lead to pin No. 47 and negative voltmeter lead to pin No. 46.

2) Turn ignition on. Loosen TPS hold-down screws. Rotate TPS until voltmeter reading is 1.0 volt. Tighten hold-down screws. Move throttle to Wide Open Throttle (WOT) position. Voltmeter should read 1.0 volt at idle, at least 4.0 volts at WOT and then return to 1.0 volt at idle.

3) If voltage is not as specified, perform EEC-IV QUICK TEST in ELECTRONIC ENGINE CONTROL IV article in COMPUTERIZED ENGINE CONTROLS section.

COLD (FAST) IDLE RPM

Carbureted Models – 1) Place transmission in Neutral or Park. Set parking brake and block wheels. Disconnect and plug automatic brake release vacuum hose (if equipped). Start engine and warm to normal operating temperature. Disconnect and plug vacuum hose at EGR valve. Place fast idle screw on second step of fast idle cam and adjust fast idle RPM. *See Fig. 4.* Refer to underhood engine decal for engine fast idle RPM specification.

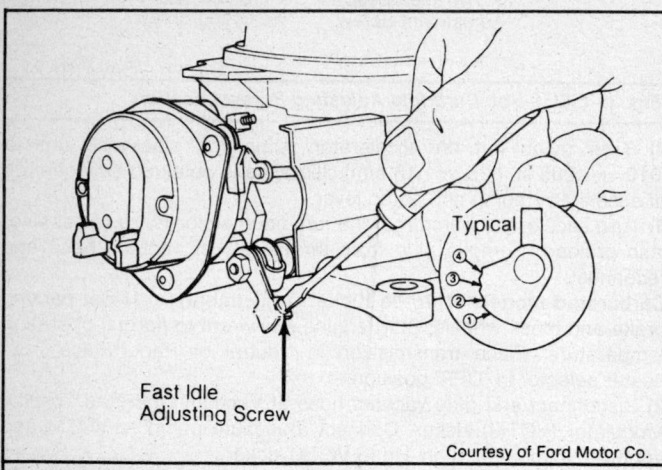

Fast Idle Adjusting Screw

Typical

Courtesy of Ford Motor Co.

Fig. 4: 5.8L 2-Bbl. Fast Idle Adjusting Screw Location

2) Increase engine speed momentarily. After engine has returned to idle, again place fast idle screw on second step of fast idle cam. Recheck fast idle RPM. Reconnect vacuum line to EGR valve and remove test equipment.

Fuel Injected Models – No fast idle adjustments are possible on fuel injected models.

AUTOMATIC CHOKE

Choke spring is set on index mark. For carburetor choke adjustment procedures, refer to appropriate article in FUEL SYSTEMS section.

NOTE: No on-car choke adjustment is possible on 5.8L engines.

FUEL PUMP

Carbureted Models – Check fuel pump volume and pressure with pump on engine, engine at idle RPM, and engine warmed to normal operating temperature. See FUEL PUMP SPECIFICATIONS table.

Fuel Injected Models – 1) Release fuel pressure prior to disconnecting any fuel lines. Remove fuel filler cap. Attach a fuel pressure gauge to pressure relief valve on fuel rail. Release fuel pressure through fuel gauge into a container.

2) Disconnect fuel return line at fuel rail. Connect fuel hose to fuel container. Connect fuel pressure gauge at pressure relief valve on fuel rail. Install jumper wire to FP lead of VIP test connector. *See Fig. 5.* Turn ignition on. Ground jumper wire to FP lead. Note fuel pump pressure. See FUEL PUMP SPECIFICATIONS table.

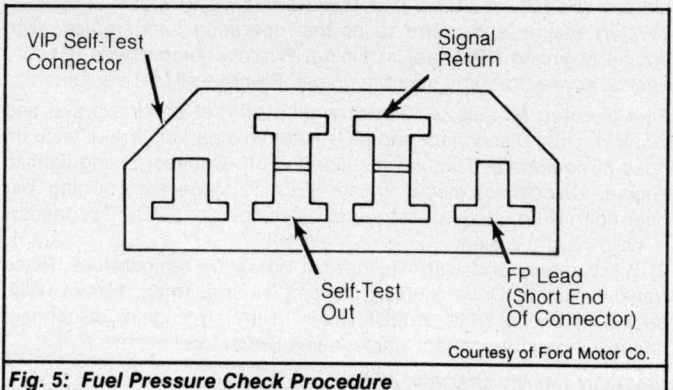

VIP Self-Test Connector

Signal Return

Self-Test Out

FP Lead (Short End Of Connector)

Courtesy of Ford Motor Co.

Fig. 5: Fuel Pressure Check Procedure

FUEL PUMP SPECIFICATIONS

Application	Specification
Carbureted Models	
Pressure	6-8 psi (.42-.56 kg/cm²)
Fuel Injected Models	[1] 35-45 psi (2.5-3.2 kg/cm²)
Volume	
Carbureted Models	1 Pt. (.5L) in 20 seconds
Fuel Injected Models	1.5 Pts. (.72L) in 30 seconds

[1] – Key on, engine off. Engine running pressure may be 5 psi (.4 kg/cm²) less.

General Servicing

BATTERY

BATTERY SPECIFICATIONS

Rated Amps	Cold Crank. Amps	Discharge Rate Amps
36	310	155
45	380	190
54	450	225
71	535	268
72	850	425

SERVICE INTERVALS

REPLACEMENT INTERVALS

Component	Interval (Miles)
Air Filter	30,000
Engine Oil	7500
Fuel Filter	30,000
Oil Filter	7500
PCV Filter	30,000
Spark Plugs	30,000

1989 FORD MOTOR CO. V8 TUNE-UP
General Servicing (Cont.)

1-31

ADJUSTMENTS

BELT TENSION ADJUSTMENT [1]

Application	New Belt Lbs. (kg)	[1] Used Belt Lbs. (kg)
All Models		
Standard "V" Belts		
1/4"	50-90 (23-41)	40-60 (18-27)
All Others	120-160 (54-73)	90-120 (41-54)
Ribbed "V" Belts		
4-Rib		
Air Pump Only	90-130 (41-59)	90-120 (41-54)
5-Rib	120-170 (54-77)	110-130 (50-59)
6-Rib		
Fixed	150-190 (68-84)	140-160 (64-73)
With Tensioner	100-130 (44-59)	100-180 (44-82)

[1] – Any belt operated for 10 minutes.

CAPACITIES

COOLING SYSTEM CAPACITIES

Application	Quantity Qts, (L)
5.0L & 5.8L	14.1 (13.3)

ENGINE OIL CAPACITY

Application	Quantity Qts. (L)
Crankcase (Includes Filter)	5.0 (4.7)

TRANSMISSION CAPACITY

Application	Quantity Qts. (L)
Auto. Trans.	
AOD & A4LD	[1] 12.3 (11.6)

[1] – Total capacity. Use only MERCON transmission fluid.

Section 1a

COMPUTERIZED ENGINE CONTROLS

CONTENTS

INTRODUCTION   Page
Computerized Engine Controls 1a-2

CHRYSLER MOTORS
FWD Models
2.2L Turbo II MPFI 1a-4
2.2L & 2.5L SPFI 1a-37
2.5L Turbo I MPFI 1a-83
3.0L MPFI 1a-126
RWD Models 1a-169
Body Control Computer 1a-189

EAGLE
Premier
2.5L TBI 1a-275
3.0L MPFI 1a-320

FORD MOTOR CO.
Probe EEC 1a-365
EEC-IV 1a-404
V8 MCU 1a-513

NOTE: **ALSO SEE GENERAL INDEX**

COMPUTERIZED ENGINE CONTROLS

One of the most important developments in the automotive service industry is the use of computerized engine controls. These systems constantly adjust fuel, ignition and emission controls. The result is better fuel economy, improved performance, and better driveability. Another result is an ever-increasing load of wiring, sensors, and "Black boxes" in the engine compartment. The aim of this section is to help untangle both the computer systems and the fear with which most service people approach them.

The traditional "tune-up" is performed to help improve engine operating efficiency. In vehicles with computerized systems, the computer is constantly tuning the engine. Some systems affect only air/fuel ratios, while others control air injection, EGR, transmission shifting and many other functions.

This introduction will cover the major components of computer systems, some basic servicing tips, and list some necessary tools.

CONTROL UNITS

The heart of any computer system is the control unit, or control module. These computers are usually sealed in a metal box and are linked to the system by a wiring harness with multi-pin connector. The computers are usually located in the passenger compartment for protection from moisture, vibration and temperature extremes.

The job of the computer is to coordinate vehicle operation and equipment. When engineers develop the systems, they simulate every conceivable driving condition and determine the best adjustments for economy, driveability and low emissions. These selected adjustments are in the computer's program and are used by the vehicle at certain times.

Systems are said to operate in either "Open Loop" or "Closed Loop". In an open loop condition, the instructions and decisions made by the designers are used to run the engine. The computer just follows their orders. In closed loop, the computer reads the values from a number of sensors and makes tuning decisions based on past experience and present conditions. This ability makes the system more responsive, and allows the computer to compensate for unusual or severe driving conditions.

SENSORS

The computer gets its information from a network of sensors. Most are simple sending units just like an oil pressure switch or fuel level gauge. Either the sensor is off/on or it gives the computer a variable resistance reading. Many systems use existing engine sensors, while some systems have specialized sensors that provide input on engine "knocking", atmospheric pressure or outside air temperature.

The control unit checks sensor inputs constantly and makes its decisions based on both pre-programmed input and the sensor readings. Common sensor inputs include:

- Air/Fuel Ratio (from exhaust gas oxygen sensor)
- Engine Speed (from distributor or crankshaft sensor)
- Engine Temperature (from oil or coolant sensors)
- Engine Load (from throttle position or vacuum level sensors)

Other sensors are used by some systems to provide additional information. These may include:

- Intake Air Temperature
- Intake Air Volume
- Barometric/Manifold Pressure
- Vehicle Speed
- Fuel Temperature and Pressure
- Detonation
- Transmission Gear

Two different systems may require the same kind of information, but get it from different sensors. For example, one of Ford's MCU systems uses an idle switch to tell the computer when the throttle is against the idle stop. Another MCU system uses a vacuum sensor to provide the same information. Despite the variety of sensors, computers make their decisions based on the same kind of inputs.

ENGINE CONTROLS

Computer commands are carried out by solenoids, motors and other control devices. Solenoids are used to control vacuum, air bleeds, the carburetor fuel flow, etc. Motors are used for the idle speed control and mixture adjustments.

Some computers control functions directly, while others use indirect means. For example, when a detonation sensor hears "knocking", the computer will retard timing. On some systems, it will tell a solenoid to cut off vacuum to the distributor vacuum advance solenoid. Timing is retarded. On other systems, the computer may be directly involved in controlling engine timing, and it just retards the firing slightly until "knocking" stops. The method used is different, but the effect is the same.

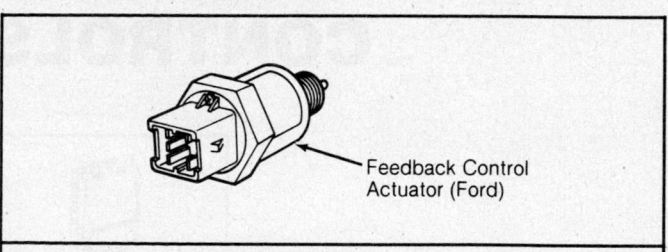

Feedback Control Actuator (Ford)

Fig. 2: Engine Control Solenoid & Motor

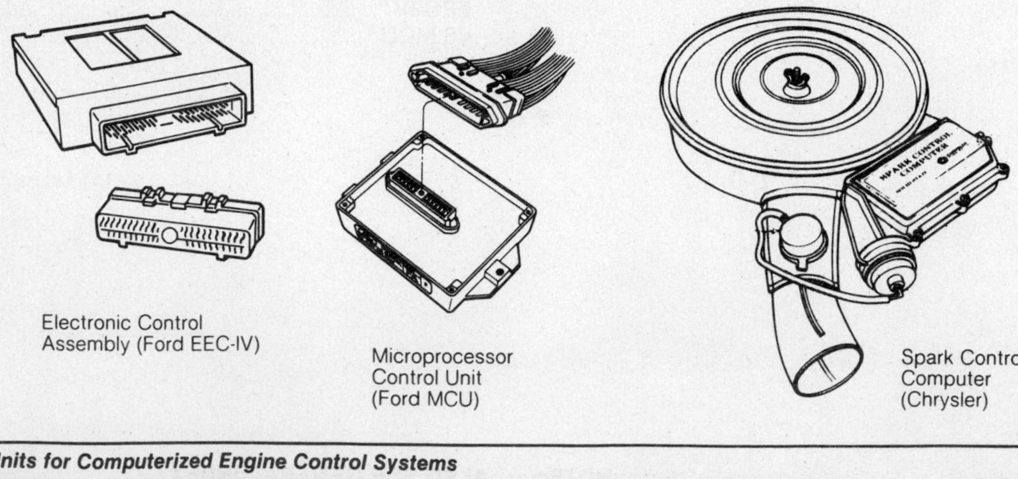

Electronic Control Assembly (Ford EEC-IV)

Microprocessor Control Unit (Ford MCU)

Spark Control Computer (Chrysler)

Fig. 1: Control Units for Computerized Engine Control Systems

SERVICING

The first step in servicing is to eliminate possible causes of trouble. Be sure that mechanical systems (compression, valves, plugs, transmission) are okay before suspecting the computer system. It has no control over these problems.

Most computer control systems have no serviceable parts. The technician's job is to locate the part that doesn't work and to replace it. Since these systems can be quite complicated, manufacturers have built in some self-diagnostic features. The computer looks for and indicates its own problems.

With these systems, the technician starts the computer diagnostic program and watches for service codes that indicate a problem. These code numbers can be indicated by flashes of a dash mounted light or pulses on a voltmeter. Small diagnostic testers are now available that will show a direct indication of the code.

Once the codes are known, trouble shooting procedures and charts are used to locate the specific component failure. Without the procedures and charts, troublesome components are harder to locate, but repairs can still be made. One danger is that traditional obvious causes of poor driveability may no longer be the cause now, and parts replacement to resolve a problem is very expensive. The diagnostic programs MUST be used to ensure profitable and accurate repairs.

TOOLS

Some systems require special testers (Ford EEC-IV), but most only require common shop equipment. The following items are necessary for most servicing:
- Analog Volt-Ohmmeter
- Digital Volt-Ohmmeter
- Vacuum Gauge
- Hand Vacuum Pump
- Timing Light
- Test Light
- Tachometer/Dwell Meter
- Jumper Wires

Several aftermarket tool manufacturers now make testers that will plug into these computer systems and allow faster reading of codes and system problems. If you service systems frequently, these may save time.

The most important tool in servicing is the alertness of the service technician. Most problems are caused by poor connections, damaged wiring or leaky vacuum lines. Only a very small percentage of computers ever fail. Most of the computers returned for rebuilding are in fine working condition, which means they were replaced unnecessarily. Be sure a complete visual check is made before deciding any part of the system is faulty.

COMPONENT TESTING

Since it is not possible to test a computer in the car, most servicing approaches are designed to eliminate all other causes of trouble. If everything else tests out okay, then the computer is the last possible cause. In order to do this, some components must be tested first.

Sensors can be checked to see if they open or close, or if their resistance values are correct at specified temperatures. Solenoids can be checked by applying voltage and observing their operation. Solenoids should also have a measureable resistance across the windings. They should not be shorted to ground or open.

If sensors and solenoids are okay, the system circuits should be checked. Disconnect wiring at both ends of a circuit and measure resistance. If more than about 5 ohms is measured, then the connections need to be cleaned or wires repaired. Next, connect the ohmmeter between one end of the wire and ground. There should be at least several hundred thousand ohms resistance. If not, the wire is shorted to ground and must be repaired. Wiring diagrams are available for all systems and should be used to check connections and resistance values.

If all sensors, control devices and wiring check out okay, then the computer may be the problem. If possible, substitute a known good computer. If performace is restored, install a new unit. Once again, since control units are very expensive and RARELY fail, be sure ALL other causes are eliminated before replacing.

SUMMARY

Computerized engine controls are used on all engines. The computer is just a decision-making device that acts according to a complicated set of instructions. Although computers have taken over many of the tuning chores once performed by service people, they are not perfect and have not replaced the competent service technician. A great opportunity is waiting for people who can accurately diagnose and repair computerized engine control systems.

1989 COMPUTERIZED ENGINE CONTROLS
Chrysler Motors 2.2L Turbo II MPFI

Daytona, Lancer, LeBaron

DESCRIPTION

The 2.2L Turbo II Multi-Point Fuel Injection (MPFI) computerized engine control system controls the fuel system, ignition system and emission control system.

The engine control system utilizes a Single Module Engine Controller (SMEC) to regulate air/fuel ratio, charging system, cooling fan, emission control components, idle speed, ignition timing and turbocharger wastegate control.

OPERATION

AIR CONDITIONING (A/C) CLUTCH RELAY

The A/C clutch relay is powered by the radiator fan relay, A/C switch and SMEC. The relay is energized to closed (on) position during engine operation with A/C switch closed and blower switch on. When the SMEC senses wide open throttle or low engine RPM through the throttle position sensor, SMEC will de-energize the A/C clutch relay, disengaging A/C clutch.

AUTO SHUTDOWN (ASD) RELAY

When distributor signal is not present with ignition switch in "RUN" position, the ASD relay turns power off to the electric fuel pump, fuel injectors, ignition coil and O_2 sensor heating element.

AUTOMATIC IDLE SPEED (AIS) MOTOR

The AIS motor adjusts idle speed to compensate for engine load and ambient temperature. The AIS motor varies the amount of air by-pass through the throttle body. The SMEC uses coolant temperature sensor, distance (speed) sensor, throttle position sensor, and various switch inputs to adjust the AIS to obtain optimum idle conditions.

BAROMETRIC READ SOLENOID

Barometric pressure information is used primarily for boost control. The solenoid is mounted in the vacuum line next to the Manifold Absolute Pressure (MAP) sensor. SMEC controls barometric read solenoid.

Atmospheric pressure is supplied to MAP sensor to periodically measure barometric pressure. This occurs once per throttle closure, but not more often than once every 3 minutes within a specified RPM range.

CANISTER PURGE SOLENOID

The canister purge solenoid is controlled by the SMEC. During engine warm-up and after hot restarts, the SMEC completes a ground, energizing the purge solenoid. When purge solenoid is energized, this prevents vacuum from reaching canister valve.

After engine reaches operating temperature and a timer has run out, the SMEC de-energizes the solenoid by turning off the ground, allowing fuel vapors to be drawn into the throttle body. The SMEC will also energize purge solenoid under certain idle conditions, this updates fuel delivery calibration.

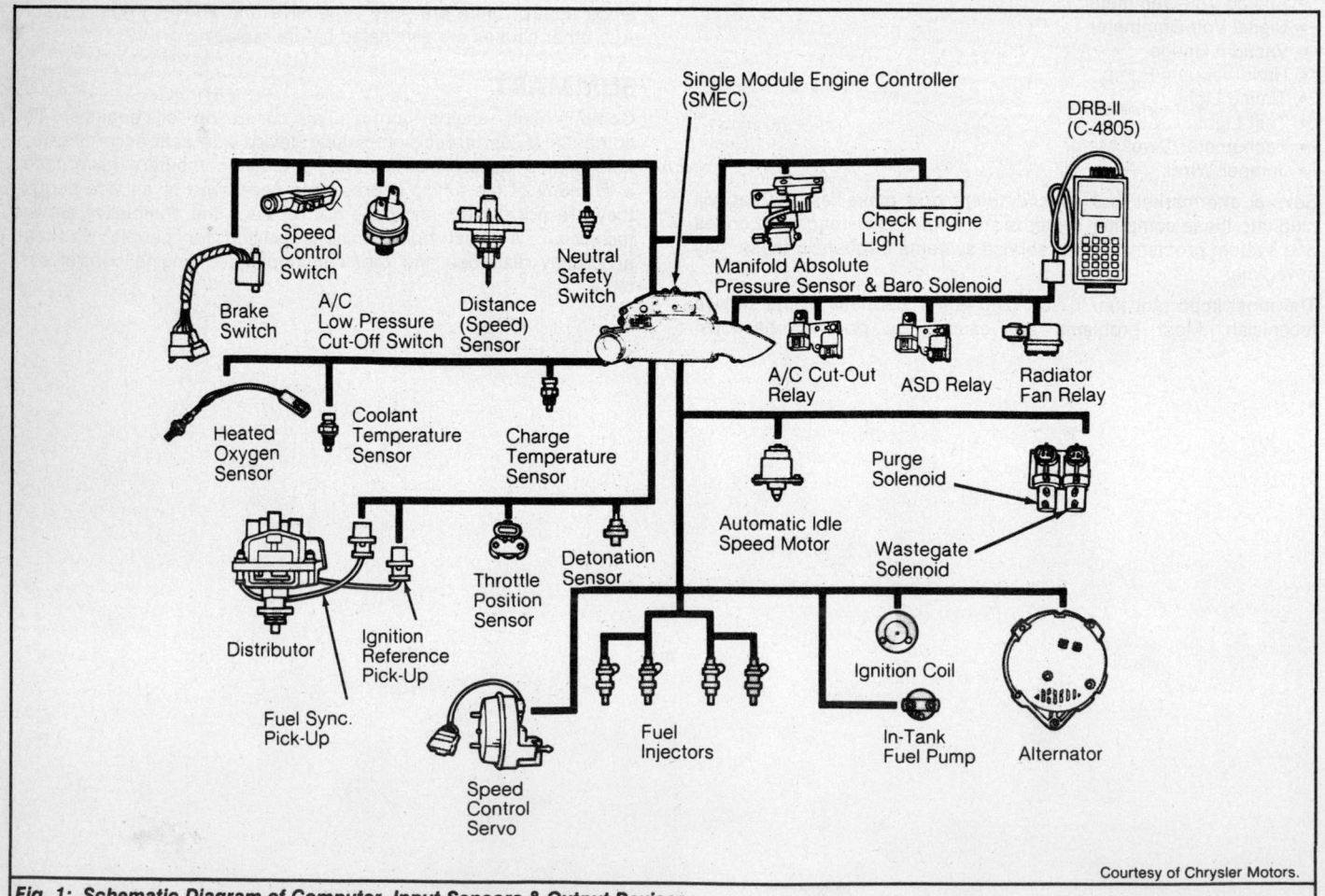

Courtesy of Chrysler Motors.

Fig. 1: Schematic Diagram of Computer, Input Sensors & Output Devices

1989 COMPUTERIZED ENGINE CONTROLS
Chrysler Motors 2.2L Turbo II MPFI (Cont.)

1a-5

CHARGE TEMPERATURE SENSOR

The charge temperature sensor is mounted in the intake manifold. This sensor measures temperature of incoming air/fuel mixture. The SMEC uses this information to adjust air/fuel mixture.

CHECK ENGINE LIGHT

The check engine light will illuminate for 3 seconds as a bulb test every time the ignition is turned on. If the SMEC receives an incorrect or no signal from coolant temperature sensor, manifold absolute pressure sensor, throttle position sensor, battery voltage input or emission related systems on California vehicles, the check engine light will be illuminated. This warns driver that SMEC has gone into a limp-in mode to keep system operational.

COOLANT TEMPERATURE SENSOR

The coolant temperature sensor is located in the thermostat housing. Input from this sensor allows SMEC to richen air/fuel mixtures until normal operating temperature is reached. The sensor is a variable resistor with a range of -40°F (-40°C) to 265°F (129°C). This sensor is also used to turn on radiator fan.

DETONATION SENSOR

The detonation sensor is mounted in the intake manifold in such a position so sensor can detect detonation in any cylinder. This sensor generates an input signal to SMEC when detonation occurs. This allows SMEC to adjust spark advance and boost schedules to eliminate detonation.

DISTANCE (SPEED) SENSOR

This sensor is located on transaxle extension housing. The sensor generates 8 pulses per axle shaft revolution. The SMEC will interpret distance (speed) sensor input along with throttle position sensor closed throttle input.

This will allow SMEC to differentiate between closed throttle decel and closed throttle idle (vehicle stopped) conditions. During decel, the SMEC controls Automatic Idle Speed (AIS) motor to maintain a desired manifold absolute pressure value. During idle (vehicle stopped), the SMEC controls AIS motor to maintain a desired idle speed.

LIMP-IN MODE

If SMEC senses incorrect data or no data from battery voltage, coolant temperature sensor, Manifold Absolute Pressure (MAP) sensor or Throttle Position Sensor (TPS), SMEC will put system in limp-in mode and illuminate check engine light.

MANIFOLD ABSOLUTE PRESSURE (MAP) SENSOR

The MAP sensor is connected to the intake manifold with a vacuum hose that runs through the barometric pressure solenoid. MAP sensor is electrically connected to SMEC. The SMEC uses MAP sensor to monitor manifold pressure and other sensors to calibrate the air/fuel mixture.

OXYGEN SENSOR

The O_2 sensor is used by SMEC to measure oxygen content in the turbo outlet. The sensor is electrically heated for faster switching during engine operation. If O_2 sensor measures a lean mixture, sensor will produce a low voltage. If O_2 sensor measures a rich mixture, sensor will produce a high voltage.

SINGLE MODULE ENGINE CONTROLLER (SMEC)

The SMEC is a digital computer containing a microprocessor. The SMEC receives input from the following sensors: coolant temperature sensor, detonation sensor, Manifold Absolute Pressure (MAP) sensor, oxygen sensor, Throttle Position Sensor (TPS), and Vehicle Speed Sensor (VSS).

The SMEC also receives input from the following switches: air conditioning clutch switch, brake switch, speed control switches, and neutral safety switch. During operation, the SMEC monitors many of its own input and output circuits. If a fault is detected, the computer will go into limp-in mode and store a trouble code to help in diagnosis of the system.

THROTTLE POSITION SENSOR (TPS)

The TPS is an electronic variable resistor. The SMEC uses TPS input and input from other sensors to adjust air/fuel ratio for varying driveability conditions.

WASTEGATE CONTROL SOLENOID

The wastegate control solenoid is controlled by SMEC. The SMEC adjusts maximum boost by varying the duty cycle (on time) of the control solenoid.

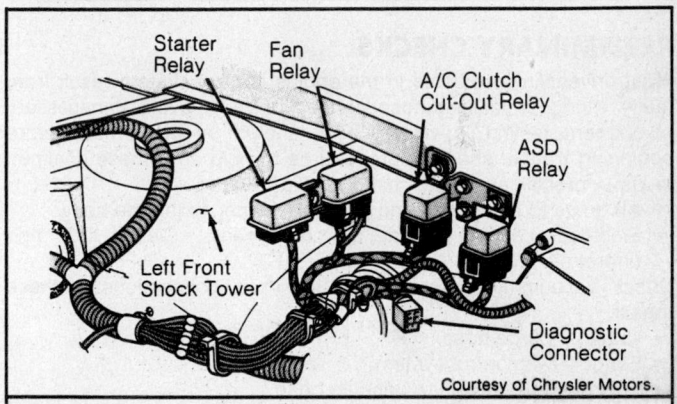

Fig. 2: Location Of Diagnostic Connector & Relays

Courtesy of Chrysler Motors.

REMOVAL & INSTALLATION

AIS MOTOR

Removal & Installation – Disconnect negative battery cable. Disconnect 4-pin connector on AIS. Remove 2 screws and AIS motor from throttle body. Ensure "O" ring is removed with AIS motor. To install, reverse removal procedure. Ensure that pintle is in retracted position, measuring not more than 1" (25 mm).

ASD RELAY

Removal & Installation – ASD relay is located on left fenderwell by the SMEC. Disconnect wiring harness from components. Remove attaching screws and component. To install, reverse removal procedure.

MAP SENSOR

Removal & Installation – Remove vacuum hose and screws from sensor. Remove electrical connector from sensor. Remove sensor from underhood, near right shock tower. To install, reverse removal procedure.

OXYGEN SENSOR

Removal & Installation – Oxygen sensor is located in exhaust manifold. Use Wrench (C-4907) to remove sensor. The threads in exhaust manifold must be cleaned with a tap prior to installation of sensor. If old sensor is being reinstalled, threads on sensor must be coated with anti-seize compound. Tighten sensor to 20 ft. lbs. (27 N.m).

SINGLE MODULE ENGINE CONTROLLER (SMEC)

Removal & Installation – Remove air cleaner duct from SMEC. Remove battery and 2 module mounting bolts. Remove 14-pin and 60-pin wiring connectors from module. Remove module. To install, reverse removal procedure.

1a-6

1989 COMPUTERIZED ENGINE CONTROLS
Chrysler Motors 2.2L Turbo II MPFI (Cont.)

THROTTLE POSITION SENSOR (TPS)

Removal & Installation – Disconnect negative battery cable. Disconnect 3-pin connector at throttle position sensor. Remove 2 screws mounting throttle position sensor to throttle body. Lift throttle position sensor from throttle shaft. To install, reverse removal procedure.

TESTING & DIAGNOSIS

NOTE: When diagnosing 1989 vehicles with DRB-II (C-4805), use 1988 cartridge for trouble shooting vehicle. If using a diagnostic readout box other than Chrysler's DRB-II, follow manufacturer's instructions on how to obtain codes. Some other readout boxes may display information that is not contained in this testing. This information may not be relative to diagnosising a problem. Only information in this article should be used during diagnosis.

PRELIMINARY CHECKS

Most driveability problems in the engine control system result from faulty wiring or leaking hose connections. To avoid unnecessary component testing, a visual check should be performed before beginning trouble shooting procedures to help spot these common faults. A preliminary visual check should include:

- Air ducts to air cleaner and from air cleaner to throttle body.
- Electrical connections at all components. Clean, tight and unbroken.

Check vacuum lines for secure, leak-free connections in these areas:

- Canister purge hose.
- Evaporative control system.
- Fuel pressure regulator vacuum hose.
- MAP sensor.
- PCV valve hose and correct PCV valve.
- Power brake, speed control, heater and A/C system vacuum hoses.
- Throttle body.
- Wastegate control diaphragm and vacuum hoses.

Ensure the following electrical connectors are securely attached:

- 14-pin and 60-pin connectors at Single Module Engine Controller (SMEC).
- A/C clutch relay connector.
- AIS motor connector.
- ASD relay connector.
- Barometric read, wastegate and purge solenoid connector.
- Black distributor reference connector.
- Charge temperature sensor connector.
- Check engine light.
- Coolant temperature sensor connector.
- Detonation sensor connector.
- Distance (speed) sensor connector.
- Distributor pick-up connector.
- Heated O$_2$ sensor connector.
- MAP sensor connector.
- Radiator fan relay connector.
- TPS connector.

SYSTEM DIAGNOSIS

The self-diagnostic capabilities of this system, if properly utilized, can greatly simplify testing. The SMEC has been programmed to monitor several different circuits of the fuel injection system. If a problem is sensed with a monitored circuit often enough to indicate an actual problem, a fault code is stored in the SMEC.

A check engine light will illuminate or light could be activated for display of trouble codes. This light acts as a warning device to inform the operator that a malfunction in the system has occurred and immediate service is required.

When certain malfunctions occur, the SMEC enters the limp-in mode. In this mode, the SMEC attempts to compensate for the failure of the particular component by substituting information from other sources. This will allow the vehicle to be operated until proper repairs can be made.

Once these codes are known, refer to the TROUBLE CODES in this article to determine the questionable circuit. Then use the wiring diagrams to locate testing points for each circuit. Test circuits and repair or replace as needed. If the problem is repaired or ceases to exist, the logic module cancels the trouble code after 50-100 ignition on/off cycles. If DRB-II is being used, refer to CLEARING CODES in this article to clear trouble codes.

The setting of a specific fault code is the result of a particular system failure, NOT the reason for that failure, such as failure of a specific component. The existence of a particular code denotes the probable area of the malfunction, not necessarily the failed component itself.

ENTERING ON-BOARD DIAGNOSIS

Diagnostic Test Mode – **1)** Attach the Chrysler DRB-II Tester (C-4805) to diagnostic connector. The connector is located in the engine compartment near the right side shock tower. If DRB-II is not available, codes may be read off of the check engine light.

2) Start engine (if possible). Move transmission shift lever through all positions, ending in Park. Turn A/C switch on, then off (if equipped).

3) Stop the engine and, without starting it again, turn key on, off, on, off and on. Record 2-digit trouble codes as displayed on tester or by counting flashes on check engine light.

4) The 2-digit codes displayed by the check engine light are indicated by a series of flashes. For example, code 23 is displayed as flash, flash, 4-second pause, flash, flash, flash. After a slightly longer pause, any other codes stored are displayed in numerical order. Once the light begins to display trouble codes, it cannot be stopped. If you lose count, it will be necessary to start over with step **2)**.

5) If DRB-II is being used, code 88 indicates start of test. If 88-12-55 is displayed, this indicates that there are no fault codes stored. If check engine light is being used, code 88 will NOT be displayed. If 12-55 is displayed, this indicates that no fault codes are present.

6) The setting of a specific trouble code is the result of a particular system failure, NOT the reason for that failure, such as failure of a specific component. Therefore, the existence of a particular code denotes the probable area of the malfunction, not necessarily the failed component itself.

Switch Test Mode – Put system in Diagnostic Test Mode. Wait for code 55 to appear on DRB-II. Press "Read/Hold" key on DRB-II until "READ" is displayed. Turn on desired switch input. The DRB-II display must change between "00" and "88" and the check engine light should flash when the following switches are activated and released:

- Brake switch.
- Gearshift selector.
- A/C switch (if equipped).

Circuit Actuation Test Mode (ATM) – **1)** Put system into Diagnostic Test Mode. Wait for code 55 to appear on DRB-II display. Press "Read/Hold" key on DRB-II until "READ" is displayed. Press "F3" key to determine which ATM test is desired. To enter ATM test, press "Enter" key.

2) The SMEC will continue to turn the selected circuit on and off at 2 second intervals for as long as 5 minutes. To enter another ATM test, press "F3" key on DRB-II. To stop ATM test, turn ignition off.

Sensor Test Mode – **1)** The Sensor Test Mode allows the output of 7 sensors and the state of 3 switches to be displayed on the tester while the engine is not running. This provides a means by which the entire circuit for each individual sensor and switch can be checked, including the wiring and SMEC circuitry.

2) Put system in Diagnostic Test Mode. Wait for code 55 to appear on DRB-II. Press "Read/Hold" key on DRB-II until "READ" is

1989 COMPUTERIZED ENGINE CONTROLS
Chrysler Motors 2.2L Turbo II MPFI (Cont.)

1a-7

displayed. Press "F3" key to determine which Sensor Test is desired. To enter, press "Enter" key.

3) Press "Read/Hold" key until "HOLD" is displayed. Since Sensor Test codes are the same as ATM Test codes, the ATM test circuit will turn on before "HOLD" appears on display.

4) The SMEC will now use the DRB-II to display the output of the selected sensor. To select another Sensor Test, press "Read/Hold" key until "READ" is displayed. Press "F3" key to select another Sensor Test.

Engine Running Test Mode – 1) Engine Running Test Mode can be performed with engine at idle, transmission in Neutral and parking brake on, or while driving the car. Connect DRB-II to engine harness connector. Set DRB-II to Engine Running Test Mode.

2) To select a test code, press "Read/Hold" key until "READ" is displayed. When the oxygen sensor is at operating temperature, the DRB-II will display "0" for a lean signal and "1" for a rich signal.

3) When the engine is running in Park or Neutral and O_2 switching is displayed, the AIS motor can be checked by pressing "Read/Hold" key until "HOLD" is displayed. Engine speed should increase to 1500 RPM.

4) With engine running, O_2 switching and "READ" displayed on DRB-II, select Engine Running Test codes by pressing "F3" key. To enter desired Engine Running Test code, press "Enter" key. Press "Read/Hold" key until "HOLD" is displayed.

5) The SMEC will now use DRB-II to display the output of a selected sensor or run engine in a specific mode for diagnosis. To select another Engine Running Test code, press "Read/Hold" key until "READ" is displayed and press "F3" key.

6) To return to O_2 sensor switching, press "Read/Hold" key until "READ" is displayed. Press and hold "ATM" key until "0" or "1" appears on display.

TROUBLE CODES

The MPFI injection system is equipped with a self-diagnostic capability which stores certain trouble codes in the SMEC when system malfunctions occur. Trouble codes are 2-digit numbers that will tell you if certain sequences or conditions have occured. Fault codes indicate the results of a failure but do not always identify the failed component.

Code 88 – First code displayed to indicate start of test. When using DRB-II, this code must appear first or trouble codes will be incorrect. If check engine light is being used to diagnose vehicle, code 88 will NOT be displayed.

Code 11 – Distributor reference pick-up. Monitored by SMEC during cranking. Displayed if no distributor signal is sent to SMEC after restoration of battery voltage.

Code 12 – Battery feed to SMEC. Monitored by SMEC all the time when ignition is on. Displayed if battery feed to SMEC has been disconnected within last 50-100 engine starts.

Code 13 – MAP sensor pneumatic system. Monitored by SMEC during engine operation between 600-1500 RPM with MAP signal within electrical range. Check engine light is illuminated. Displayed if no variance in vacuum signal is detected between ignition pulses.

Code 14 – MAP sensor electrical system. Monitored by SMEC when engine speed is 400-1500 RPM. Check engine light is illuminated. Displayed if MAP sensor signal is outside range of .02-4.7 volts.

Code 15 – Code indicates a problem with vehicle distance (speed) sensor circuit. Check engine light will illumnate on California models. Monitored by SMEC with engine speed more than 1800 RPM and MAP signal less than 10 in. Hg. Displayed if no speed sensor signal is detected over a 13 second period.

Code 16 – Battery voltage sensing (charging system). Monitored by SMEC all the time after one minute from engine start. Displayed if battery sensing voltage drops below 4 volts for more than 14 seconds.

Code 17 – Engine running too cool. Monitored by SMEC after 12 minutes from engine start. Displayed if engine coolant temperature does not reach 160°F (71°C) after 8 minutes of vehicle speeds greater than 28 MPH.

Code 21 – Oxygen sensor feedback circuit. Monitored by SMEC with engine temperature more than 170°F (76.6°C) and engine speed more than 1500 RPM. Check engine light will illuminate on California models. Displayed if no rich or lean condition is indicated for a 2 minute time period.

Code 22 – Coolant temperature sensor circuit. Monitored by SMEC all the time when ignition is on. Check engine light is illuminated. Displayed if sensor voltage is more than 4.96 volts on cold engine or less than .51 volt on warm engine.

Code 23 – Problem with charge temperature sensor circuit. Monitored by SMEC all the time when ignition is on. Displayed if sensor voltage is more than 4.96 volts or less than .51 volt.

Code 24 – TPS circuit. Monitored by SMEC all the time when ignition is on. Check engine light is illuminated. Displayed if sensor signal less than .16 volt or more than 4.7 volts.

Code 25 – AIS motor driver circuit. Monitored by SMEC when AIS system is required to control engine speed. Check engine light will illuminate on California models. Displayed if proper voltage is not present in AIS circuit. Open circuit will not set this code.

Code 26 – Fuel injector driver circuit. Monitored by SMEC when engine is running. Check engine light is illuminated. Displayed if current through injectors does not reach proper peak level.

Code 27 – Fuel control circuit. Monitored by SMEC when engine speed is less than 2000 RPM. Check engine light is illuminated. Displayed if fuel control interface does not switch properly.

Code 31 – Canister purge solenoid circuit. Monitored by SMEC when ignition is on. Check engine light is illuminated on California models. Displayed if solenoid does not turn on and off at correct time.

Code 33 – A/C WOT cut-out relay. Monitored by SMEC when ignition is on. Displayed if relay does not turn on and off at correct time.

Code 34 – Problem in speed control servo circuit. Monitored by SMEC when cruise control is engaged. Displayed if servo does not turn on and off at correct time.

Code 35 – Radiator fan relay circuit. Monitored by SMEC when ignition is on. Displayed if relay does not turn on and off at correct time.

Code 36 – Wastegate control solenoid circuit. Monitored by SMEC when ignition is on. Check engine light is illuminated. Displayed if solenoid does not turn on and off at correct time.

Code 37 – Baro read solenoid circuit. Monitored by SMEC when ignition is on. Check engine light is illuminated on California models. Displayed if solenoid does not turn on and off at correct time.

Code 41 – Alternator field control circuit (charging system). Monitored by SMEC when ignition is on. Displayed if field control interface does not switch properly.

Code 42 – Auto Shutdown (ASD) relay circuit. Monitored by SMEC when ignition is on. Displayed if relay does not turn on and off at correct time.

Code 43 – Spark control circuit. Monitored by SMEC only during engine cranking. Displayed if spark control interface does not switch properly.

Code 44 – Fused J2 circuit (loss of power to SMEC). Monitored by SMEC when ignition is on. Displayed if fused J2 is not present in logic board of SMEC.

Code 45 – Overboost monitor circuit. Monitored by SMEC when engine is running. Displayed when MAP signal exceeds a predetermined amount of boost.

Code 46 – Battery voltage sensing circuit (charging system). Monitored by SMEC when engine is running. Check engine light is illuminated. Displayed if sensed battery voltage is greater than one volt above desired control voltage for longer than 20 seconds.

Code 47 – Battery voltage sensing circuit (charging system). Monitored by SMEC with engine running for more than 6 minutes,

1a-8

1989 COMPUTERIZED ENGINE CONTROLS
Chrysler Motors 2.2L Turbo II MPFI (Cont.)

engine temperature greater than 160°F (71°C) and engine speed more than 1500 RPM. Displayed if sensed battery voltage is more than one volt below desired control voltage for more than 35 seconds.

Code 51 – Oxygen feedback system circuit. Monitored by SMEC during closed loop operation. Check engine light is illuminated on California models. Displayed if system stays lean for more than 2 minutes.

Code 52 – Oxygen feedback system circuit. Monitored by SMEC during closed loop operation. Check engine light is illuminated on California models. Displayed if system stays rich for more than 2 minutes.

Code 53 – Single Module Engine Controller (SMEC). Monitored by SMEC when system is in Diagnostic Test Mode. Displayed if logic board fails its self-test.

Code 54 – Distributor sync pick-up circuit. Monitored by SMEC when engine is running. Check engine light is displayed on California models. Displayed if there is not a distributor sync pick-up signal.

Code 55 – End of Diagnostic Test Mode. Always displayed as final code after all other fault codes have been displayed.

CLEARING CODES

Using DRB-II, put system into ATM test "10". Press "Read/Hold" key until "HOLD" is displayed. DRB-II display will flash alternating "0" (zeros). When flashing "0" (zeros) stop, display will show "00". All codes have now been cleared.

If DRB-II is not available, fault codes may be cleared by allowing 50-100 key on/off cycles to occur. This will allow SMEC to clear fault codes.

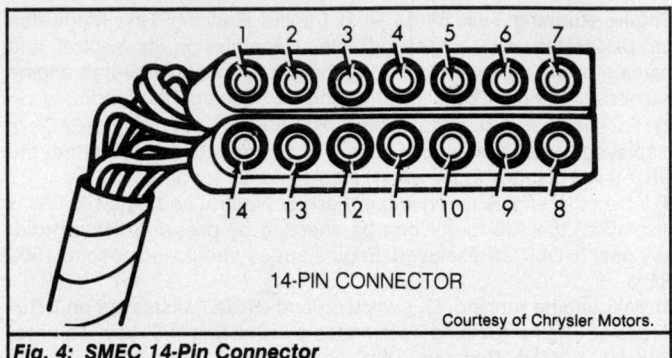

Courtesy of Chrysler Motors.

Fig. 4: SMEC 14-Pin Connector

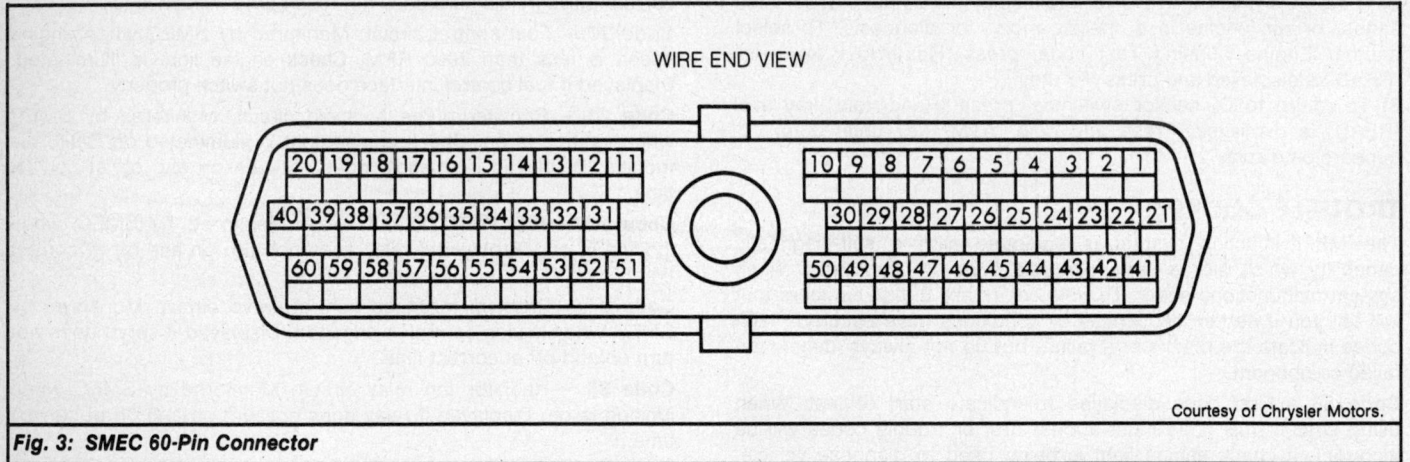

WIRE END VIEW

Courtesy of Chrysler Motors.

Fig. 3: SMEC 60-Pin Connector

1989 COMPUTERIZED ENGINE CONTROLS
Chrysler Motors 2.2L Turbo II MPFI (Cont.)

1a-9

NOTE: In the following diagnostic testing, illustrations are supplied courtesy of Chrysler Motors.

NO START TEST NO. 1

IGNITION SYSTEM CHECK

NOTE: Before replacing major components, be sure connector pins or cavities are not damaged, preventing proper voltage and resistance readings.

1) Disconnect any spark plug wire. Insert an insulated screwdriver or a spark tester into spark plug terminal. If using screwdriver, hold screwdriver shaft about 1/4" from a good ground. Have an assistant crank engine.

CAUTION: Fault/Trouble Codes may erase and SMEC damage may occur if spark plug wire is held more than 1/4" from ground while cranking.

2) If there is good spark between screwdriver and ground as long as engine is cranking, go to NO START TEST NO. 2. Treat 1-2 sparks as no spark. If there is no spark, go to step 3). If there is good spark, but engine is hard to start or starts and stalls, go to NO START TEST NO. 9.

3) Disconnect coil wire from distributor cap. Hold wire 1/4" away from ground. Crank engine. If there is good spark from coil wire, repair secondary ignition system. Check or replace distributor cap, rotor and spark plug wires. Treat 1-2 sparks as no spark.

4) If there is no spark from coil wire, connect voltmeter between Dark Green/Black wire at positive terminal of coil and ground. Crank engine for at least 7 seconds. If voltmeter reading is within one volt of battery voltage as long as engine is cranking, go to NO START TEST NO. 6. If voltmeter reads zero volts or cranking voltage for about one second, go to NO START TEST NO. 12.

NO START TEST NO. 2

FUEL SYSTEM CHECK

1) Relieve fuel system pressure. Install pressure gauge to fitting on fuel rail. Crank engine for at least 7 seconds. Fuel pressure should be at least 40 psi. If pressure is okay, go to step 2). If fuel pressure is less than 40 psi, go to NO START TEST NO. 5.

2) Connect Diagnostic Readout Box II (C-4805) to engine harness connector. Put system into Sensor Test Mode "05". If display reads .5-1.5 volts, go to step 3). If reading is greater than 1.5 volts, replace throttle position sensor. If system will not go into Sensor Test Mode (no code 88), replace SMEC.

3) With DRB-II connected to engine harness connector, connect a voltmeter to Dark Green/Black wire of injector harness 6-pin connector and ground. Put system in ATM Test Mode "02". If voltmeter reading is zero, repair open circuit in injector harness connector to wiring harness splice. If voltmeter reading is within one volt of battery voltage, go to NO START TEST NO. 3.

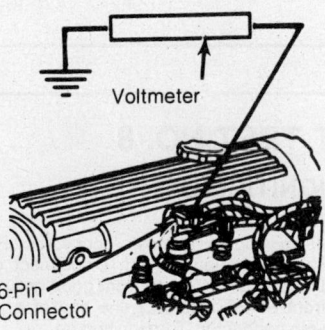

Voltmeter

6-Pin Connector

NO START TEST NO. 3

CHECKING FOR FUEL FOULED SPARK PLUGS

1) Remove spark plugs. Inspect spark plug tips for wet fuel. If spark plugs are wet with fuel, clean and reinstall plugs. Go to step 2). If spark plugs are not wet with fuel, go to NO START TEST NO. 4.

NOTE: It is normal for spark plugs to be Black after engine is started cold.

2) With DRB-II connected to vehicle, put system in Sensor Test Mode "08". Disconnect vacuum hose from MAP sensor. Connect an auxiliary vacuum pump to MAP sensor. Apply vacuum to MAP sensor while watching display on DRB-II.

3) If DRB-II is showing MAP voltage dropping to less than one volt as vacuum is applied, go to NO START TEST NO. 4. If DRB-II is not showing MAP voltage dropping as vacuum is applied, check for 5 volts at MAP sensor connector Violet wire. If 5 volts is present, replace MAP sensor.

NO START TEST NO. 4

CHECKING ENGINE TIMING

1) Connect timing light. Have an assistant crank engine while you observe timing marks. If timing is 0-16 degrees BTDC, remove distributor cap and crank engine to ensure rotor is turning and is indexed correctly. Check engine compression and valve timing.

2) If timing is not between 0-16 degrees BTDC, set timing to 10 degrees BTDC during cranking. If engine starts, reset timing to specification. If engine does not start, remove distributor cap and crank engine to ensure distributor rotor is turning and is indexed correctly. Check engine compression and valve timing.

NO START TEST NO. 5

FUEL PUMP CHECK

1) Connect DRB-II to engine harness connector. Put system in Diagnostic Test Mode. Press and hold ATM key on DRB-II. If fuel pump is running, check all fuel lines for kinks, restrictions and leaks. Check for a plugged fuel filter. If fuel lines and filter check okay, remove and inspect fuel pump. Check for fuel contamination.

2) If fuel pump was not running, leave DRB-II connected to engine harness connector and in Diagnostic Test Mode. Raise vehicle on a hoist. Disconnect in-tank fuel pump connector. Connect positive voltmeter lead to Dark Green/Black wire in fuel pump connector. Connect negative voltmeter lead to Gray wire in connector.

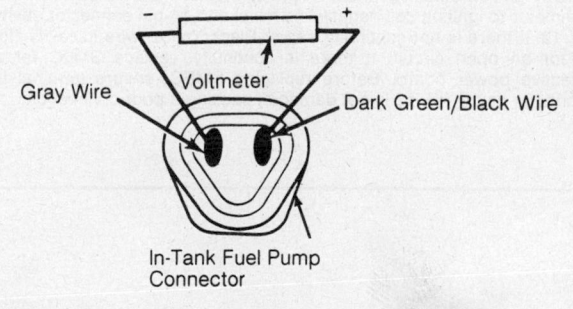

Gray Wire — Voltmeter — Dark Green/Black Wire

In-Tank Fuel Pump Connector

1a-10

1989 COMPUTERIZED ENGINE CONTROLS
Chrysler Motors 2.2L Turbo II MPFI (Cont.)

NO START TEST NO. 5 (Cont.)

3) If voltmeter is reading within one volt of battery voltage, replace fuel pump. If voltmeter reading is zero volts, move negative voltmeter lead to ground. Press ATM key on DRB-II. If voltage reading is within one volt of battery voltage, repair Gray wire for an open circuit. If voltage reading is still zero, repair Dark Green/Black wire for an open circuit.

NO START TEST NO. 6

IGNITION CONTROL SYSTEM FAULT CODE CHECK

Connect DRB-II to engine harness connector. Put system in Diagnostic Test Mode. Record all codes. If 88-12-55 is displayed (no fault codes), go to NO START TEST NO. 7. If 88-12-43-55 is displayed (spark control circuit), go to NO START TEST NO. 8.

NO START TEST NO. 7

IGNITION CONTROL CIRCUIT CHECK

1) Connect DRB-II to engine harness connector. Connect analog voltmeter to ignition coil negative terminal and ground. Put system in ATM Test "01". If voltmeter reading is pulsating between 10-14 volts, replace ignition coil.

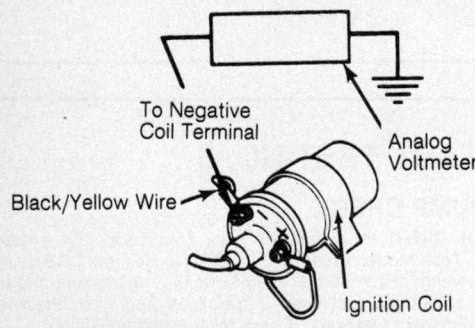

2) If voltmeter reading is not pulsating, but reads battery voltage, go to step **3)**. If voltmeter reading is pulsating between 5-10 volts, replace ignition coil. If voltmeter reading is pulsating between 0-2 volts, go to step **4)**.

3) Turn ignition off. Disconnect 14-pin connector from SMEC. Connect ohmmeter to ignition coil negative terminal and 14-pin connector cavity No. 12. If there is not continuity, repair Black/Yellow wire in cavity No. 12 for an open circuit. If there is continuity, replace SMEC for a defective power board. Before replacing SMEC, ensure terminal in connector cavity No. 12 is not damaged causing a poor connection.

NO START TEST NO. 7 (Cont.)

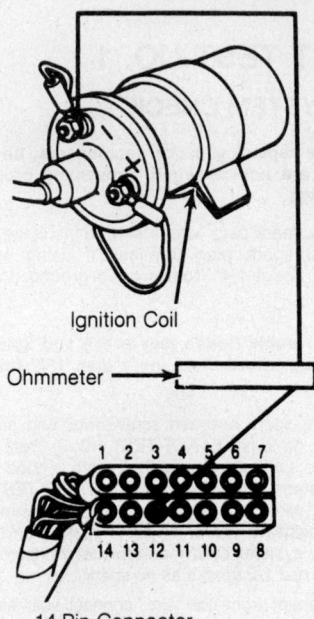

4) With DRB-II connected to engine harness connector, turn ignition off. Disconnect wire from negative side of ignition coil. Connect voltmeter to ignition coil negative terminal and ground. Put system in ATM Test "01". If voltmeter reading is between 0-2 volts, replace ignition coil.

5) If voltmeter reading is greater than 10 volts, turn ignition off. Disconnect 14-pin connector from SMEC. Connect ohmmeter to 14-pin connector cavity No. 12 and ground. If there is no continuity, replace SMEC for a defective power board. If there is continuity, repair Black/Yellow wire to cavity No. 12 for a short circuit to ground.

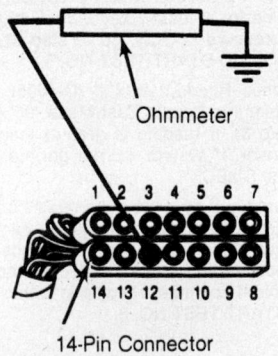

NO START TEST NO. 8

CODE 43 – IGNITION CONTROL CIRCUIT CHECK

1) Connect DRB-II to engine harness connector. Put system in Diagnostic Test Mode. Turn ignition off. Disconnect coil wire from distributor cap and hold wire 1/4" away from good ground. Disconnect 60-pin connector from SMEC. Connect one end of a jumper wire to cavity No. 34 of 60-pin connector. Turn ignition on.

1989 COMPUTERIZED ENGINE CONTROLS
Chrysler Motors 2.2L Turbo II MPFI (Cont.)

1a-11

NO START TEST NO. 8 (Cont.)

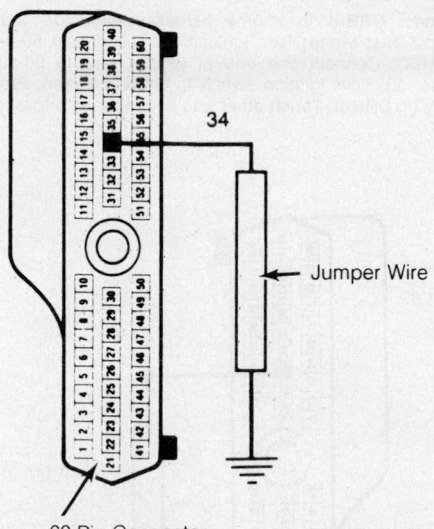

34

← Jumper Wire

60-Pin Connector

2) Press and hold ATM key on DRB-II. Touch other end of jumper wire to ground. Make and break this connection several times. If there is spark as you make and break this connection, replace SMEC for a defective logic board. Before replacing SMEC, ensure terminal in cavity No. 34 is not damaged causing a poor connection.

3) If there is no spark as you make and break the connection, turn ignition off. Remove jumper wire from 60-pin connector. Disconnect 14-pin connector from SMEC. Connect ohmmeter leads to 60-pin connector cavity No. 34 and 14-pin connector cavity No. 13.

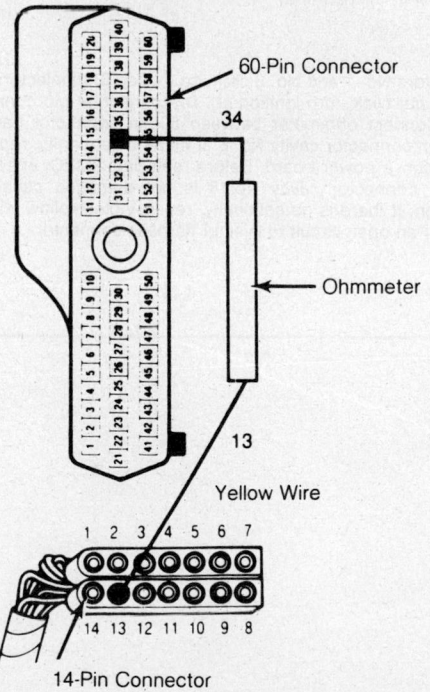

60-Pin Connector

34

← Ohmmeter

13

Yellow Wire

14-Pin Connector

4) If there is continuity, replace SMEC for a defective power board. Before replacing SMEC, ensure terminal in cavity No. 13 is not damaged causing a poor connection. If there is no continuity, repair Yellow wire to cavity No. 13 for an open circuit.

NO START TEST NO. 9

CHECKING FUEL SYSTEM FOR FAULT CODES

Connect DRB-II to engine harness connector. Put system in Diagnostic Test Mode. Record all codes. If there are no fault codes, go to DRIVEABILITY TEST NO. 1. If codes 88-12-26-55 (fuel injector driver circuit) are shown, go to NO START TEST NO. 10. If codes 88-12-27-55 (fuel injector control circuit) are shown, go to NO START TEST NO. 11.

NO START TEST NO. 10

CHECKING INJECTOR DRIVER CIRCUITS

1) Connect DRB-II to engine harness connector. Disconnect all injectors. Put system in ATM Test Mode "02". Connect negative voltmeter lead to ground and touch positive voltmeter lead to Dark Green/Black wire in each injector connector. If there is no voltage at one or more of the connectors, repair Dark Green/Black wire for an open circuit to injector connector.

Disconnect Injectors

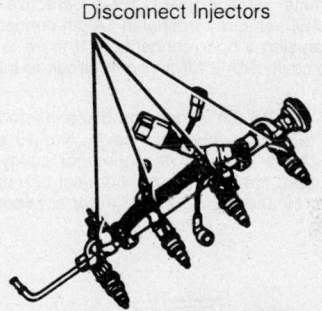

2) If there is battery voltage at each connector, connect No. 1 injector and listen for a click. Disconnect No. 1 injector. Connect No. 2 injector and listen for a click. Disconnect No. 2 injector. Connect No. 3 injector and listen for a click. Disconnect No. 3 injector. Connect No. 4 injector and listen for a click.

3) If any injector does not click, replace injector. Before replacing injector, check Tan and White wires to injectors for an open circuit. If No. 1 and No. 2 injectors do not click, go to next step. If injectors No. 3 and No. 4 do not click, go to step **6)**.

4) Turn ignition off. Disconnect 14-pin connector from SMEC. Connect ohmmeter to 14-pin connector cavity No. 9 and ground. If there is continuity, repair White wire to cavity No. 9 for a short to ground. If there is no continuity, connect ohmmeter to 14-pin connector cavity No. 9 and White wire of injector harness connectors No. 1 and No. 2.

1a-12

1989 COMPUTERIZED ENGINE CONTROLS
Chrysler Motors 2.2L Turbo II MPFI (Cont.)

NO START TEST NO. 10 (Cont.)

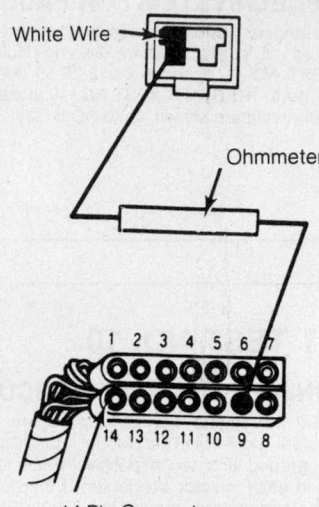

White Wire

Ohmmeter

1 2 3 4 5 6 7

14 13 12 11 10 9 8

14-Pin Connector

5) If there is continuity, replace SMEC for a defective power board. Before replacing SMEC, ensure terminal in 14-pin connector cavity No. 9 is not damaged causing a poor connection. If there is no continuity, repair White wire to cavity No. 9 for an open circuit to injector harness connector.

6) With ignition off and 14-pin connector disconnected from SMEC, connect ohmmeter to 14-pin connector cavity No. 10 and ground. If there is continuity, repair Tan wire to connector cavity No. 10 for a short to ground. If there is no continuity, connect ohmmeter to 14-pin connector cavity No. 10 and Tan wire of injector connectors No. 3 and No. 4.

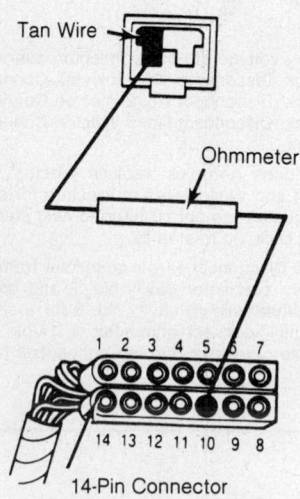

Tan Wire

Ohmmeter

1 2 3 4 5 6 7

14 13 12 11 10 9 8

14-Pin Connector

7) If there is continuity, replace SMEC for a defective power board. Before replacing SMEC, ensure terminal in 14-pin connector cavity No. 10 is not damaged causing a poor connection. If there is no continuity, repair Tan wire to cavity No. 10 for an open circuit to injector harness connector.

NO START TEST NO. 11

CHECKING INJECTOR CONTROL CIRCUITS

1) Connect DRB-II to engine harness connector. Put system in Diagnostic Test Mode. Turn ignition off. Disconnect 60-pin connector from SMEC. Connect one end of jumper wire to 60-pin connector cavity No. 33. Turn ignition switch to "RUN" position. Press and hold ATM key on DRB-II. Touch other end of jumper wire to positive battery terminal.

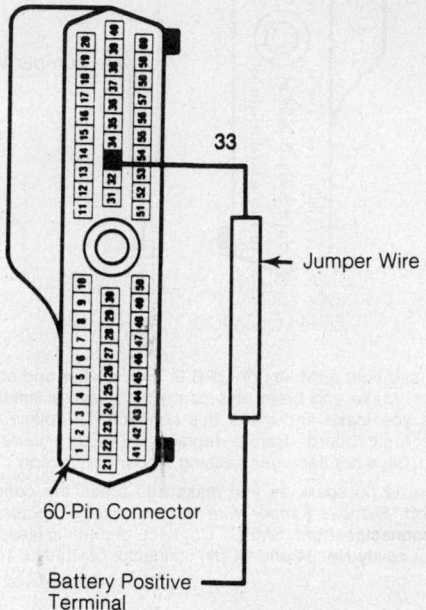

33

Jumper Wire

60-Pin Connector

Battery Positive Terminal

2) If injectors No. 1 and No. 2 click, go to step **3)**. If injectors No. 1 and No. 2 do not click, turn ignition off. Disconnect 14-pin connector from SMEC. Connect ohmmeter between 60-pin connector cavity No. 33 and 14-pin connector cavity No. 8. If there is continuity, replace SMEC for a defective power board. Before replacing SMEC, ensure terminal in 14-pin connector cavity No. 8 is not damaged causing a poor connection. If there is no continuity, repair Violet/Yellow wire to cavity No. 10 for an open circuit to injector harness connector.

1989 COMPUTERIZED ENGINE CONTROLS
Chrysler Motors 2.2L Turbo II MPFI (Cont.)

1a-13

NO START TEST NO. 11 (Cont.)

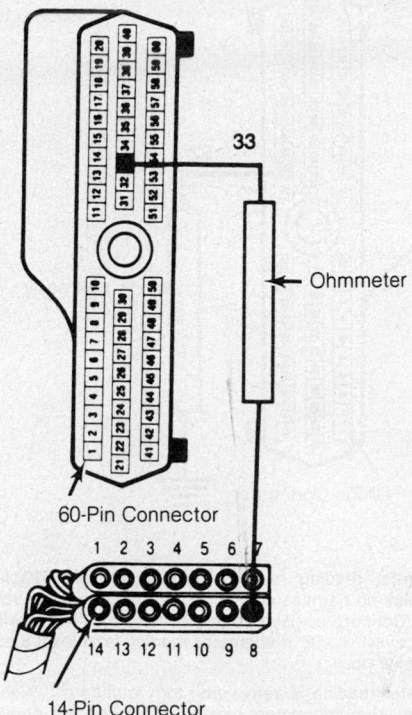

33

← Ohmmeter

60-Pin Connector

1 2 3 4 5 6 7

14 13 12 11 10 9 8

14-Pin Connector

3) With DRB-II connected and system in Diagnostic Test Mode and 60-pin connector disconnected from SMEC. Connect one end of jumper wire to 60-pin connector cavity No. 32. Press and hold ATM key on DRB-II. Touch other end of jumper wire to positive battery terminal. If injectors No. 3 and No. 4 click, replace SMEC for a defective logic board.

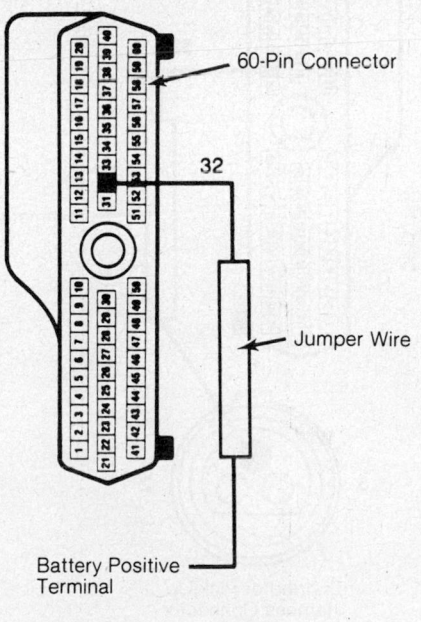

60-Pin Connector

32

← Jumper Wire

Battery Positive Terminal

NO START TEST NO. 11 (Cont.)

4) If injectors No. 3 and No. 4 do not click, turn ignition off. Disconnect 14-pin connector from SMEC. Connect ohmmeter to 60-pin connector cavity No. 32 and 14-pin connector cavity No. 5. If there is continuity, replace SMEC for a defective power board. Before replacing SMEC, ensure terminal in 14-pin connector cavity No. 5 is not damaged causing a poor connection. If there is no continuity, repair Gray/White wire between 14-pin and 60-pin connectors for an open circuit.

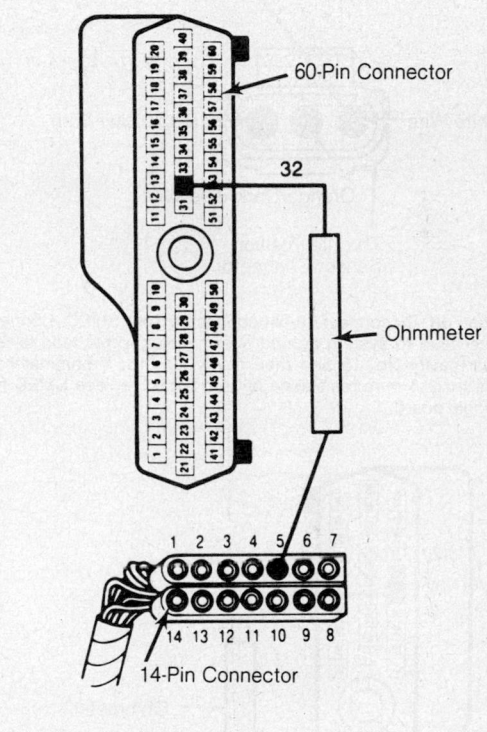

← 60-Pin Connector

32

← Ohmmeter

1 2 3 4 5 6 7

14 13 12 11 10 9 8

14-Pin Connector

NO START TEST NO. 12

CHECKING SYSTEM FOR FAULT CODES

1) Connect DRB-II to engine harness connector. Erase fault codes. Turn ignition switch to "RUN" position for 5 seconds. Crank engine for 7 seconds and return ignition switch to "RUN" position for 5 seconds. Turn ignition off. Put system in Diagnostic Test Mode. Record all codes. If 88-12-55 (no fault codes) is displayed, repair the Dark Green/Black wire of auto shutdown relay for an open circuit.

2) If no code 88 or 00 (system power circuits), go to NO START TEST NO. 13. If code 88-11-12-55 (distributor reference pick-up circuit) is displayed, go to NO START TEST NO. 14. If code 88-42-55 (auto shutdown relay pull-in coil circuit) is displayed, go to NO START TEST NO. 15. If code 88-44-55 is displayed, go to NO START TEST NO. 17.

3) If codes 88-12-14-22-24-55 or 88-12-14-22-23-24-55 are displayed, repair Black/Light Blue wire to 60-pin connector cavity No. 4 for an open circuit. If code 88-12-54-55 (distributor sync pick-up circuit) is displayed, go to NO START TEST NO. 16.

NO START TEST NO. 13

CHECKING SUPPLY & GROUND CIRCUITS

1) Turn ignition off. Disconnect Throttle Position Sensor (TPS) connector. Turn ignition on. Connect voltmeter to Violet/White wire at TPS connector and ground. If there is at least 4.5 volts, go to next step. If there is no voltage, go to step **4)**.

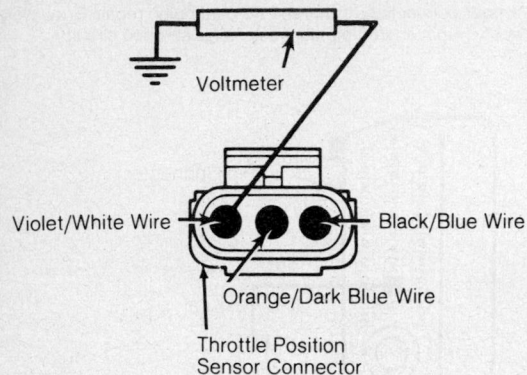

Voltmeter

Violet/White Wire — ● ● ● — Black/Blue Wire

Orange/Dark Blue Wire

Throttle Position
Sensor Connector

2) Turn ignition off. Disconnect 60-pin connector from SMEC. Connect one ohmmeter lead to system ground eyelet. Touch other lead to 60-pin connector cavity No. 15 and then cavity No. 16. If ohmmeter is showing less than .5 ohm resistance in both wires, replace SMEC for a defective logic board.

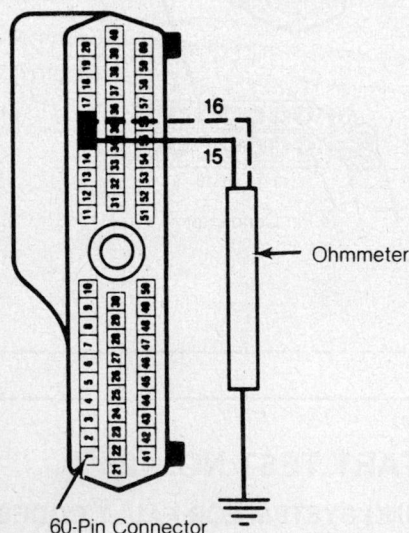

16
15

Ohmmeter

60-Pin Connector

3) If there is no continuity, repair Black wires for an open circuit to wiring harness splice. Replace SMEC. If ohmmeter is showing more than .5 ohm resistance, repair Black wire for high resistance to ground eyelet.

4) If voltmeter reading in step **1)** was zero volts, disconnect MAP sensor connector. Touch positive voltmeter lead to Violet/White wire at TPS sensor connector. If voltmeter reading is at least 4.5 volts, replace MAP sensor. If voltmeter reading is zero volts, turn ignition off.

5) Disconnect 60-pin connector from SMEC. Connect negative voltmeter lead to ground. Turn ignition on. Touch positive voltmeter lead to cavity No. 52 (Orange wire) of 60-pin connector. If voltmeter reading is at least 8 volts, replace SMEC for a defective logic board. Before replacing SMEC, check for a damaged terminal in 60-pin connector cavity No. 52 causing a poor connection.

NO START TEST NO. 13 (Cont.)

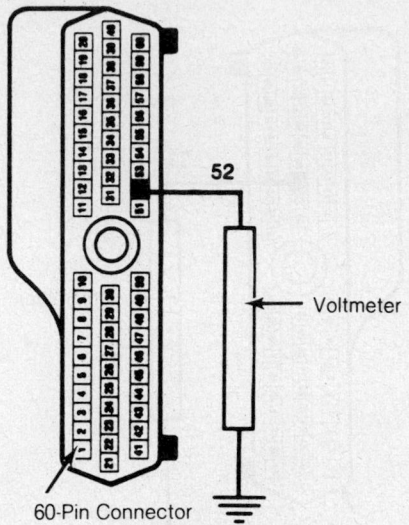

52

Voltmeter

60-Pin Connector

6) If voltmeter reading is zero volts, disconnect Black distributor reference pick-up harness connector. Connect negative voltmeter lead to ground. Connect positive voltmeter lead to Orange wire in 60-pin connector cavity No. 52. If voltmeter reading is at least 8 volts, replace distributor pick-up.

7) If voltmeter reading is zero volts, turn ignition off. With 60-pin and distributor pick-up connectors disconnected, connect ohmmeter to 60-pin connector cavity No. 52 and Orange wire terminal of distributor harness connector. If there is no continuity, repair Orange wire to 60-pin connector for an open circuit to wiring harness splice.

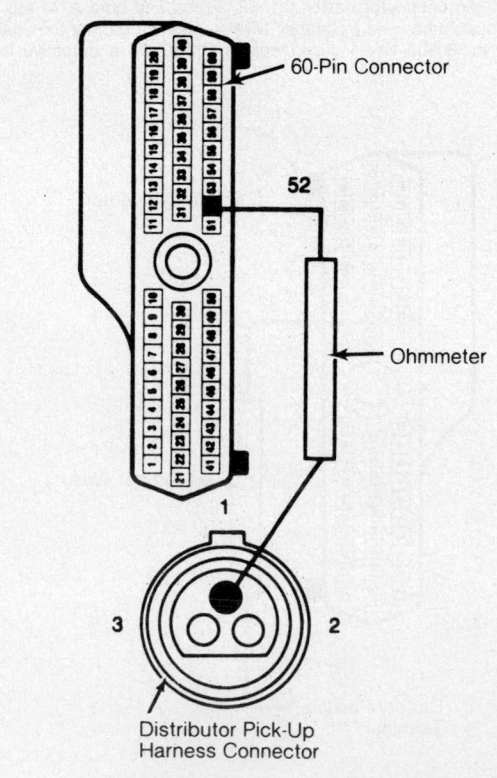

60-Pin Connector

52

Ohmmeter

1

3   2

Distributor Pick-Up
Harness Connector

1989 COMPUTERIZED ENGINE CONTROLS
Chrysler Motors 2.2L Turbo II MPFI (Cont.)

1a-15

NO START TEST NO. 13 (Cont.)

8) If there is continuity, disconnect 14-pin connector from SMEC. Connect negative voltmeter lead to ground. Turn ignition on. Touch positive voltmeter lead to Dark Blue wire in 14-pin connector cavity No. 4. If voltmeter reading is not within one volt of battery voltage, repair Dark Blue wire to 14-pin connector for an open circuit to wiring harness splice.

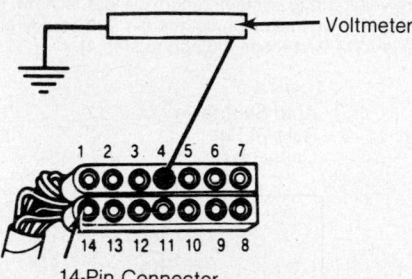

Voltmeter

14-Pin Connector

9) If voltmeter reading is within one volt of battery voltage, turn ignition off. Connect one ohmmeter lead to system ground eyelet. Connect other lead to 14-pin connector cavity No. 6 and then to cavity No. 7. If ohmmeter is showing continuity at both cavities with less than .5 ohm resistance, replace SMEC for defective power board. Before replacing SMEC, ensure terminals in connector cavities No. 6 and No. 7 are not damaged causing a poor connection.

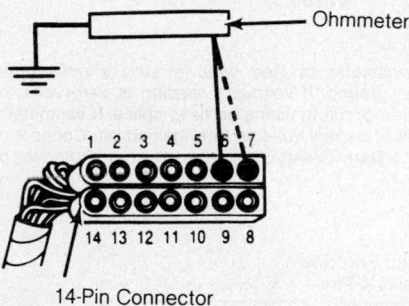

Ohmmeter

14-Pin Connector

10) If ohmmeter is not showing continuity at both cavities, repair Black wires in 14-pin connector cavities No. 6 and No. 7 for an open circuit to wiring harness splice. Replace SMEC. If ohmmeter is showing continuity with greater then .5 ohm resistance, repair ground circuit for high resistance to system ground eyelet.

NO START TEST NO. 14

CODE 11 – CHECKING DISTRIBUTOR PICK-UP HARNESS

1) Turn ignition off. Connect DRB-II to engine harness connector. Disconnect Black distributor reference pick-up coil connector. Turn ignition switch to "RUN" position. Connect a jumper wire between distributor reference pick-up coil connector cavities No. 2 and No. 3. Make and break this connection several times. Put system in Diagnostic Test Mode. Record all codes.

NO START TEST NO. 14 (Cont.)

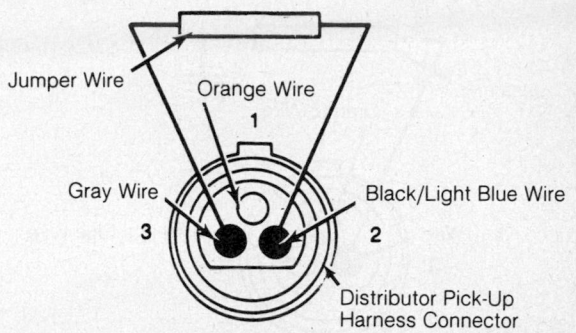

Jumper Wire
Orange Wire
Gray Wire
Black/Light Blue Wire
Distributor Pick-Up Harness Connector

2) If 88-11-12-54-55 is displayed, disregard code 54 and go to step **4)**. If 88-12-54-55 is displayed, disregard code 54. With distributor pick-up coil connector disconnected, connect voltmeter to distributor pick-up coil connector cavity No. 1 and ground.

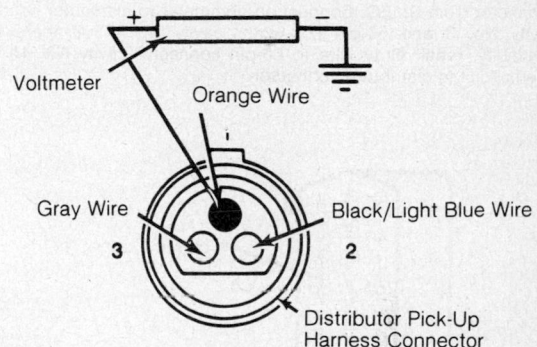

Voltmeter
Orange Wire
Gray Wire
Black/Light Blue Wire
Distributor Pick-Up Harness Connector

3) If voltmeter reading is at least 7 volts, replace distributor reference pick-up. Before replacing pick-up, ensure distributor harness connector terminals are not spread apart causing a poor connection. Also ensure distributor rotor turns while cranking engine. If yoltmeter reading is zero volts, repair Orange wire to connector cavity No. 1 for an open circuit to wiring harness splice.

4) With ignition on, connect positive voltmeter lead to distributor connector cavity No. 3. Connect negative voltmeter lead to distributor connector cavity No. 2. If voltmeter reading is at least 4 volts, replace SMEC.

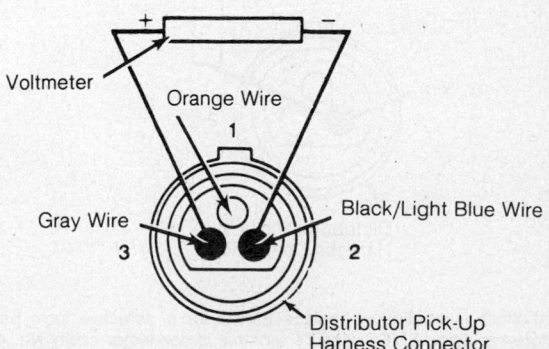

Voltmeter
Orange Wire
Gray Wire
Black/Light Blue Wire
Distributor Pick-Up Harness Connector

5) If voltmeter reading is zero volts, connect positive voltmeter lead to distributor connector cavity No. 3. Connect negative voltmeter lead to engine ground. If voltmeter reading is at least 4 volts, repair Black/Light Blue wire in distributor connector cavity No. 2 for an open circuit to wiring harness splice.

1a-16

1989 COMPUTERIZED ENGINE CONTROLS
Chrysler Motors 2.2L Turbo II MPFI (Cont.)

NO START TEST NO. 14 (Cont.)

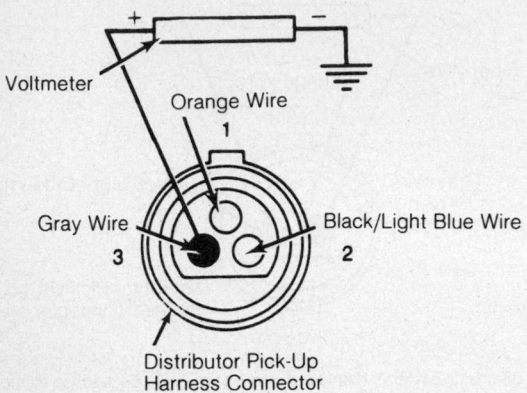

Voltmeter

Orange Wire
1

Gray Wire
3

Black/Light Blue Wire
2

Distributor Pick-Up
Harness Connector

6) If voltmeter reading is zero volts, turn ignition off. Disconnect 60-pin connector from SMEC. Connect an ohmmeter to distributor connector cavity No. 3 and 60-pin connector cavity No. 47. If there is no continuity, repair Gray wire to 60-pin connector cavity No. 47 or an open circuit to distributor connector.

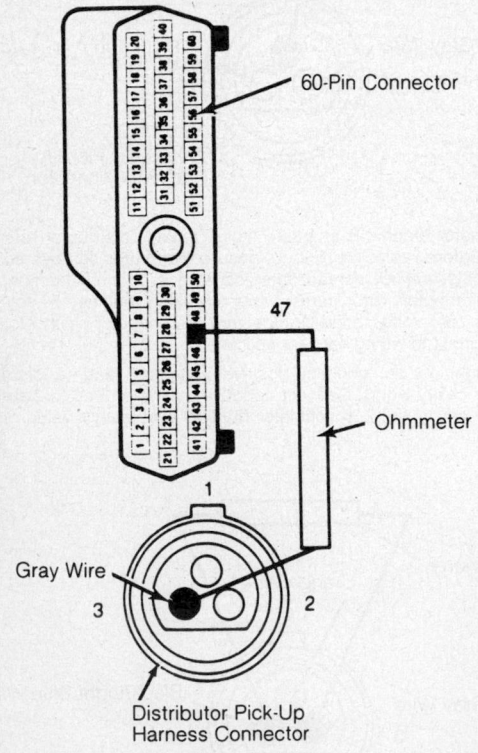

60-Pin Connector

47

Ohmmeter

Gray Wire

3   2

1

Distributor Pick-Up
Harness Connector

7) If there is continuity, replace SMEC for a defective logic board. Before replacing SMEC, ensure terminal in connector cavity No. 47 is not damaged causing a poor connection.

NO START TEST NO. 15

CODE 42 – CHECKING AUTO SHUTDOWN RELAY

1) Connect DRB-II to engine harness connector. Connect voltmeter to Dark Blue/Yellow wire in auto shutdown relay 4-pin connector and ground. Put system in ATM Test Mode "06". If voltmeter pulsates between 0-12 volts, go to next step. If voltmeter reading is within one volt of battery voltage and system cannot be put in ATM Test Mode "06", go to step **6)**. If voltmeter reading is 0-1 volt steady and system cannot be put in ATM Test Mode "06", go to step **4)**.

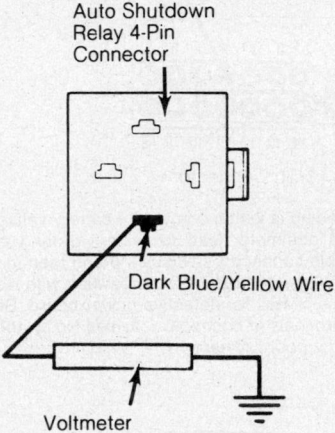

Auto Shutdown
Relay 4-Pin
Connector

Dark Blue/Yellow Wire

Voltmeter

2) Connect voltmeter to Red wire in auto shutdown relay 4-pin connector and ground. If voltmeter reading is zero volts, repair Red wire for an open circuit to wiring harness splice. If voltmeter reading is within one volt of battery voltage, turn ignition off. Connect one end of jumper wire to Dark Green/Black wire of auto shutdown relay 4-pin connector.

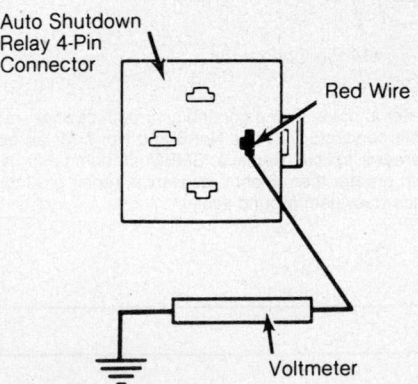

Auto Shutdown
Relay 4-Pin
Connector

Red Wire

Voltmeter

3) Touch other end of jumper wire to Red wire in auto shutdown relay 4-pin connector. If fuel pump turns on, replace auto shutdown relay. If fuel pump does not turn on, repair Dark Green/Black wire in auto shutdown relay connector for an open circuit to wiring harness splice.

1989 COMPUTERIZED ENGINE CONTROLS
Chrysler Motors 2.2L Turbo II MPFI (Cont.)

1a-17

NO START TEST NO. 15 (Cont.)

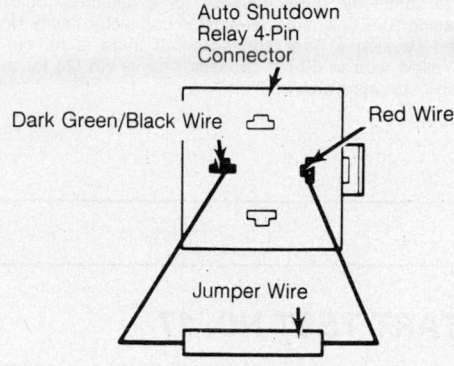

Auto Shutdown Relay 4-Pin Connector

Dark Green/Black Wire — Red Wire

Jumper Wire

4) Turn ignition off. Connect negative voltmeter lead to ground. Connect positive voltmeter lead to Dark Blue/White wire of auto shutdown relay 4-pin connector. Turn ignition on. If voltmeter reading is within one volt of battery voltage, replace auto shutdown relay.

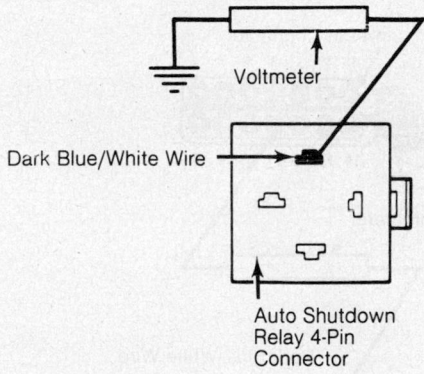

Voltmeter

Dark Blue/White Wire

Auto Shutdown Relay 4-Pin Connector

5) If voltmeter reading is zero volts, turn ignition off. Disconnect 14-pin connector from SMEC. Connect ohmmeter to 14-pin connector cavity No. 3 and Dark Blue/White wire of auto shutdown relay 4-pin connector. If there is no continuity, repair Dark Blue/White wire in 14-pin connector cavity No. 3 for an open circuit to auto shutdown relay. If there is continuity, replace SMEC for a defective power board. Before replacing SMEC, ensure terminal in connector cavity No. 3 is not damaged causing a poor connection.

NO START TEST NO. 15 (Cont.)

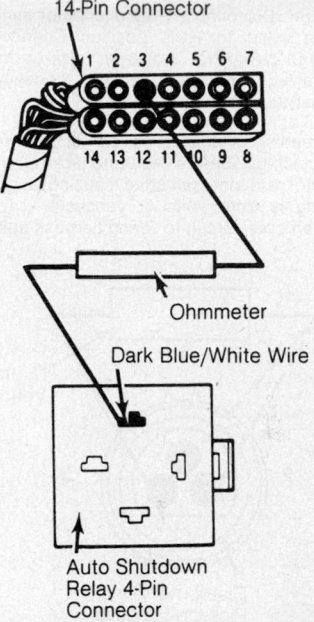

14-Pin Connector

Ohmmeter

Dark Blue/White Wire

Auto Shutdown Relay 4-Pin Connector

6) Turn ignition off. Disconnect 60-pin connector from SMEC. Connect voltmeter to Dark Blue/Yellow wire in 60-pin connector cavity No. 58 and ground. Turn ignition on. If voltmeter reading is zero volts, repair Dark Blue/Yellow wire for an open circuit to auto shutdown relay. If voltmeter reading is within one volt of battery voltage, replace SMEC. Before replacing SMEC, ensure terminal in connector cavity No. 58 is not damaged causing a poor connection.

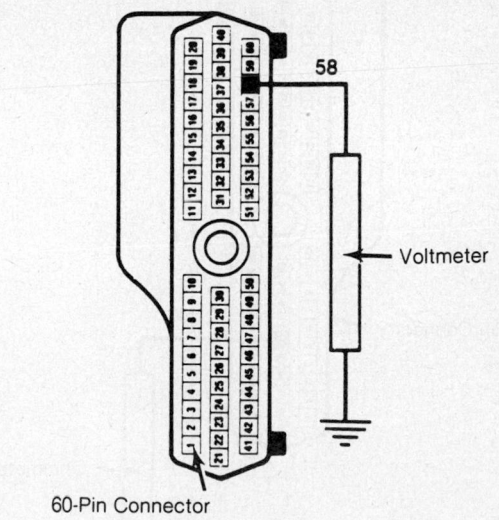

58

Voltmeter

60-Pin Connector

1989 COMPUTERIZED ENGINE CONTROLS
Chrysler Motors 2.2L Turbo II MPFI (Cont.)

NO START TEST NO. 16

CODE 54 – CHECKING DISTRIBUTOR SYNC PICK-UP

1) Turn ignition off. Disconnect Gray distributor sync pick-up connector. Turn ignition switch to "RUN" position. Connect negative lead of digital voltmeter to cavity No. 3 of sync. pick-up harness connector. Connect positive lead of digital voltmeter to cavity No. 1 and then cavity No. 2 of harness connector.

2) If voltmeter reading is at least 7 volts at both terminals. Replace distributor sync. pick-up. Before replacing pick-up, ensure terminals in harness connector are not damaged causing a poor connection. If voltmeter reading is zero volts at connector cavity No. 1, repair Orange wire for an open circuit to wiring harness splice.

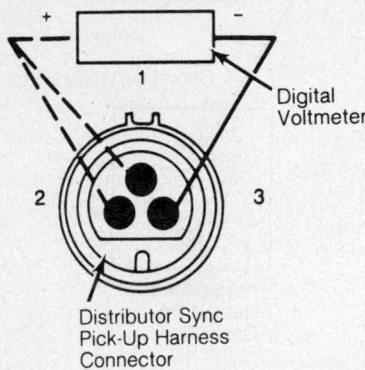

Digital Voltmeter

Distributor Sync Pick-Up Harness Connector

3) If voltmeter reading is zero volts at cavities No. 1 and No. 2, repair Black/Light Blue wire in cavity No. 3 for an open circuit to wiring harness splice. If voltmeter reading is zero volts at connector cavity No. 2, turn ignition off. Disconnect 60-pin connector from SMEC. Connect ohmmeter to Tan/Yellow wire in 60-pin connector cavity No. 26 and to Tan/Yellow wire in sync. pick-up connector cavity No. 3.

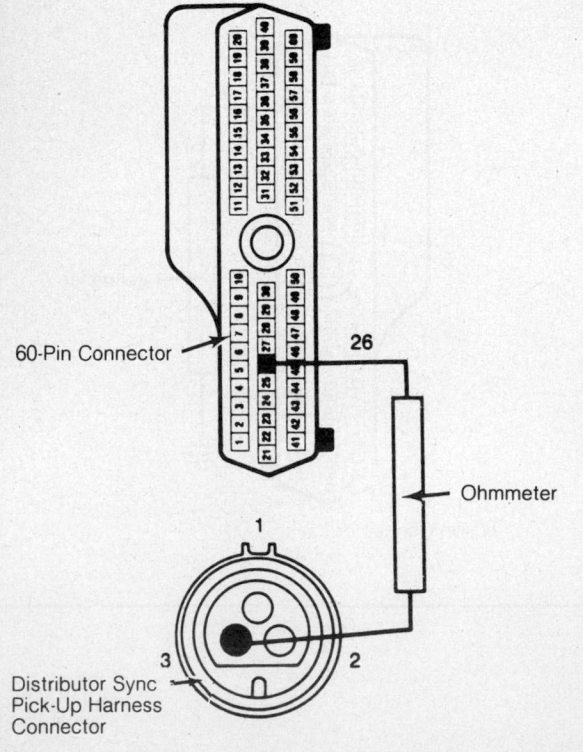

60-Pin Connector

26

Ohmmeter

Distributor Sync Pick-Up Harness Connector

NO START TEST NO. 16 (Cont.)

4) If there is continuity, replace SMEC for a defective logic board. Before replacing SMEC, ensure terminal in connector cavity No. 26 is not damaged causing a poor connection. If there is no continuity, repair Tan/Yellow wire to 60-pin connector cavity No. 26 for an open circuit to distributor sync pick-up.

NO START TEST NO. 17

CODE 44 – CHECKING FUSED J2 CIRCUIT

Turn ignition off. Disconnect 14-pin connector from SMEC. Connect ohmmeter to Dark Blue/White wire in auto shutdown relay 4-pin connector and 14-pin cavity No. 3. If there is no continuity, repair Dark Blue/White wire to 14-pin connector cavity No. 3 for an open circuit to wiring harness splice. If there is continuity, replace SMEC for a defective power board. Before replacing SMEC, ensure terminal in 14-pin connector cavity No. 3 is not damaged causing a poor connection.

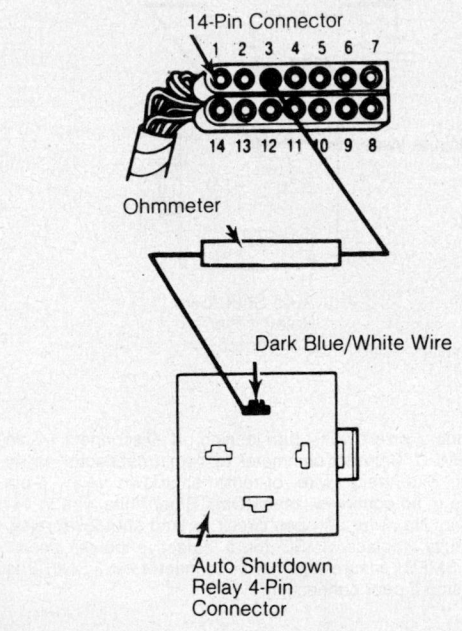

14-Pin Connector

Ohmmeter

Dark Blue/White Wire

Auto Shutdown Relay 4-Pin Connector

DRIVEABILITY TEST NO. 1

CHECKING SYSTEM FOR FAULT CODES

1) Connect DRB-II. Put system in Diagnostic Test Mode. Record all codes. If "88-12-55" (no fault codes) is displayed, go to DRIVEABILITY TEST NO. 2. For following fault codes, proceed to specified tests:
Code 15 – Speed sensor, go to DRIVEABILITY TEST NO. 3.
Code 17 – Coolant sensor, go to DRIVEABILITY TEST NO. 5.
Code 21 – Oxygen sensor, go to DRIVEABILITY TEST NO. 4.
Code 33 – A/C cut-out relay, go to DRIVEABILITY TEST NO. 10. This code will be displayed if vehicle is not equipped with A/C.
Code 51 – Oxygen feedback system locked lean, go to DRIVEABILITY TEST NO. 18.

1989 COMPUTERIZED ENGINE CONTROLS
Chrysler Motors 2.2L Turbo II MPFI (Cont.)

1a-19

DRIVEABILITY TEST NO. 1 (Cont.)

Code 52 – Oxygen feedback system locked rich, go to DRIVEABILITY TEST NO. 18.

2) Erase fault codes. Without depressing accelerator, start engine. Raise engine speed to 2000 RPM for 10 seconds and then return to idle. Cycle transmission gear selector. Turn A/C on and off (if equipped).

3) Turn ignition off. Put system into Diagnostic Test Mode. Record all codes. If the same code appears before and after the engine is started, the problem still exists. Proceed as follows:

Code 12 – No fault codes, go to step 4).
Code 13-14 – MAP sensor, go to DRIVEABILITY TEST NO. 2.
Code 15 – Speed sensor, go to DRIVEABILITY TEST NO. 3.
Code 16 – Battery voltage sense, SMEC memory circuit. Go to CHARGING SYSTEM TEST, NO. 3.
Code 17 – Engine running too cool, check engine cooling system.
Code 21 – Oxygen sensor, go to DRIVEABILITY TEST NO. 4.
Code 22 – Engine coolant sensor, go to DRIVEABILITY TEST NO. 5.
Code 17-22 – Engine coolant sensor, go to DRIVEABILITY TEST NO. 5.
Code 23 – Charge temperature sensor, go to DRIVEABILITY TEST NO. 6.
Code 24 – Throttle position sensor, go to DRIVEABILITY TEST NO. 7.
Code 25 – AIS motor, go to DRIVEABILITY TEST NO. 8.
Code 26 – Injector driver, go to NO START TEST NO. 9.
Code 27 – Injector interface, go to NO START TEST NO. 9.
Code 31 – Canister purge solenoid, go to DRIVEABILITY TEST NO. 9.
Code 33 – A/C cut-out relay, go to DRIVEABILITY TEST NO. 10. This code will display on vehicles without A/C.
Code 35 – Radiator fan relay, go to DRIVEABILITY TEST NO. 11.
Code 36 – Wastegate solenoid, go to DRIVEABILITY TEST NO. 12.
Code 37 – Baro read solenoid, go to DRIVEABILITY TEST NO. 13.
Code 42 – ASD relay, repair wire in SMEC 60-pin connector, cavity No. 10 for an open circuit.
Code 44 – Fused J2 circuit, go to DRIVEABILITY TEST NO. 14.
Code 45 – Overboost shutdown, go to DRIVEABILITY TEST NO. 15.
Code 51 – Oxygen feedback system locked lean, go to DRIVEABILITY TEST NO. 18.
Code 52 – Oxygen feedback system locked rich, go to DRIVEABILITY TEST NO. 18.
Code 53 – Replace SMEC.

NOTE: If code does not reappear, problem is not recorded, go to step 19).

4) With DRB-II connected, enter Actuator Test Mode (ATM). Perform the following tests:

Actuator Test "04" – The radiator fan should be cycling on/off every 2 seconds. If fan cycles, press and hold ATM key until code "07" (equipped with A/C) or code "05" (without A/C) appears. If fan is not on, check fan relay. If relay clicks, repair wiring to fan. If relay does not click, replace relay.

Actuator Test "05" – The A/C cut-out relay should click, every 2 seconds. Replace relay if it does not click. If relay clicks, hold ATM key until code "07" appears.

Actuator Test "07" – Listen for clicking from canister purge solenoid. Replace solenoid if it does not click. If relay clicks, hold ATM key until code "10" appears.

Actuator Test "10" – Baro read solenoid should be clicking. If solenoid is not clicking, replace baro read solenoid. If solenoid clicks, hold ATM key until code "11" appears.

Actuator Test "11" – – Wastegate solenoid should be clicking. If solenoid clicks, go to next step. If solenoid does not click, replace it.

5) With DRB-II connected, enter Switch Test Mode. Check switch inputs as follows:
- Depress brake pedal.
- Move gear selector from Park, to Reverse, Neutral and Drive.
- With A/C on, turn blower on and press A/C button.

DRIVEABILITY TEST NO. 1 (Cont.)

DRB-II display should change as each switch is activated. Disregard what is displayed, ensure only that a change in display occurs. If switch inputs are okay, go to step 10). If one or all of the switches do not pass, proceed to the following tests:
- Brake switch w/o speed control, go to next step.
- Brake switch with speed control, go to step 7).
- Park/Neutral switch, go to step 8).
- A/C button, go to step 9).

6) With ignition off, disconnect 60-pin connector from SMEC. Connect a voltmeter to White/Pink wire in connector cavity No. 29. Turn ignition switch to "RUN" position. Depress brake pedal. If voltmeter shows within one volt of battery voltage, replace SMEC for a defective logic board. If voltmeter reads zero volts, check brake switch, switch circuits and voltage supply.

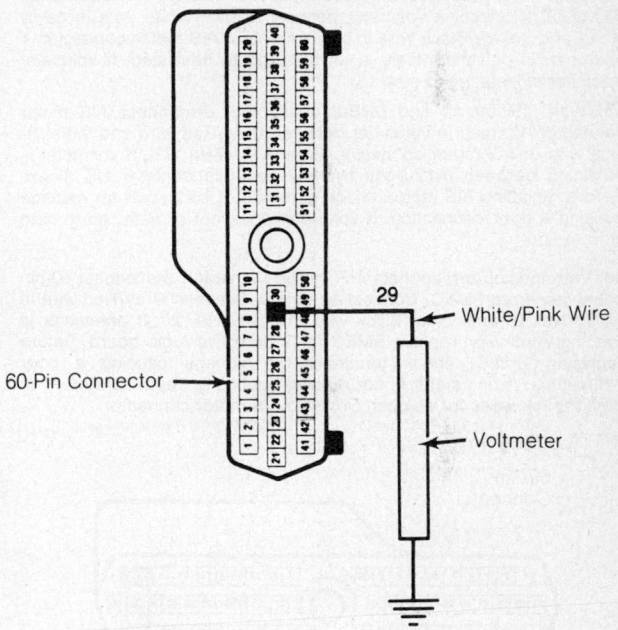

29 — White/Pink Wire

60-Pin Connector — Voltmeter

7) With ignition off, disconnect 60-pin connector from SMEC. Connect ohmmeter between White/Pink wire in connector cavity No. 29 and ground. Depress and release brake pedal. If ohmmeter shows an open when pedal is depressed and has continuity when pedal is released, replace SMEC for a defective logic board. If ohmmeter does not read as described above, check brake switch, switch circuits and stoplight bulbs.

8) With ignition off, disconnect 60-pin connector from SMEC. Connect ohmmeter between Brown/Yellow wire in connector cavity No. 30 and ground. Disconnect the battery quick disconnect. Turn ignition switch to "RUN" position. Shift gear selector to Park, Reverse, Neutral, and Drive positions and check ohmmeter readings in each position. If ohmmeter shows continuity or an open circuit in each position, check for defective Neutral Safety Switch (NSS) or short to ground in Brown/Yellow wire in connector cavity No. 30. If ohmmeter shows an open circuit in all positions, repair Brown/Yellow wire in connector cavity No. 30 or replace NSS. If the ohmmeter reads as follows, replace SMEC for a defective logic board:

Park • Continuity
Reverse • Open
Neutral • Continuity
Drive • Open

9) With ignition off, disconnect 60-pin connector from SMEC. Connect ohmmeter between Brown wire in connector cavity No. 45 and ground. Turn blower switch on, press A/C button and then press "OFF" button.

If ohmmeter shows continuity when A/C button is pressed, and open when blower motor switch is turned off, replace SMEC for a defective logic board. If ohmmeter reading is not as specified, repair Brown wire in connector cavity No. 45 for an open or short to wiring harness splice.

1a-20

1989 COMPUTERIZED ENGINE CONTROLS
Chrysler Motors 2.2L Turbo II MPFI (Cont.)

DRIVEABILITY TEST NO. 1 (Cont.)

NOTE: A/C system must have adequate freon charge to complete this test.

10) With ignition on, disconnect MAP sensor electrical connector. Connect a DVOM to Violet/White wire of MAP sensor harness connector and ground. If DVOM reading is at least 4 volts, go to next step. If DVOM reading is zero volts, repair Violet/White wire for an open circuit to harness splice.

11) Connect DRB-II, ensure "READ" is displayed. Reconnect MAP sensor connector. Connect a tachometer to engine. Start engine and disconnect coolant sensor. Press Read/Hold key and display "HOLD". Record engine RPM. Press key and display "READ". If engine speed increases to about 1500 RPM on "HOLD" and returns to idle on "READ", go to step **16)**. If engine speed does not increase and decrease as described, go to next step.

12) With DRB-II connected, disconnect AIS motor connector. Enter ATM "03". Connect a voltmeter between Brown/White wire in cavity No. 2 and Yellow/Black wire in cavity No. 3 of AIS motor connector. If voltmeter is pulsating every 4 seconds, go to next step. If voltmeter does not pulsate, go to step **15)**.

13) With ignition off and DRB-II connected, disconnect AIS motor connector. Connect a voltmeter between Gray/Red wire and Violet/Black wire of AIS motor connector. Enter ATM Test "03". If voltmeter is pulsating between 0-12 volts every 2 seconds, replace AIS motor. Before replacing AIS motor, check terminals of connector for damage causing a poor connection. If voltmeter does not pulsate, go to next step.

14) With ignition off, connect AIS motor connector. Disconnect 60-pin connector from SMEC. Connect ohmmeter between Gray/Red wire in cavity No. 19 and Violet/Black wire in cavity No. 20. If ohmmeter is reading continuity, replace SMEC for a defective logic board. Before replacing SMEC, check terminals for damage causing a poor connection. If ohmmeter is not reading continuity, repair Gray/Red or Violet/Black wires for an open circuit to AIS motor connector.

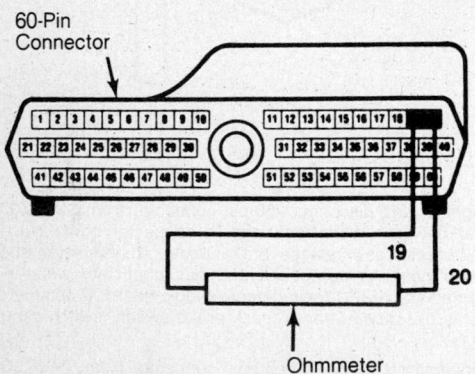

60-Pin Connector

Ohmmeter

15) With ignition off, disconnect 60-pin connector from SMEC. Ensure AIS motor is connected. Connect ohmmeter between Brown/White wire in connector cavity No. 17 and Yellow/Black wire in connector cavity No. 18. If ohmmeter shows continuity, replace SMEC for a defective logic board. If circuit is open, repair open in Brown/White or Yellow/Black wires.

DRIVEABILITY TEST NO. 1 (Cont.)

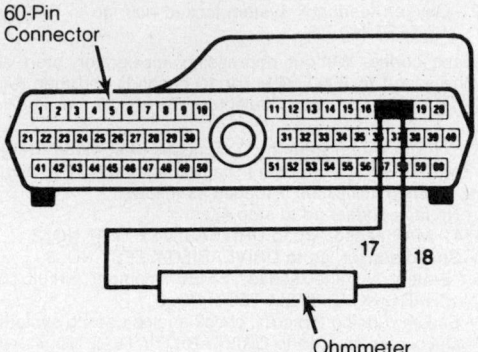

60-Pin Connector

Ohmmeter

16) With DRB-II connected, disconnect all 4 injector connectors. Enter ATM "02". Connect and disconnect each injector one at a time. When an injector is connected you should hear it click. If injectors click, go to next step. If any injector does not click, replace injector.

17) Disconnect DRB-II from vehicle. With ignition off, disconnect both SMEC connectors. Connect one lead of ohmmeter to ground. Connect other lead to the following circuits, and test resistance:

14-Pin Connector
Black/White wire in connector cavity No. 2.
Black wire in connector cavities No. 6 and 7.

60-Pin Connector
Black/White wire in connector cavity No. 5.
Light Blue/Red wire in connector cavities No. 15 and 16.

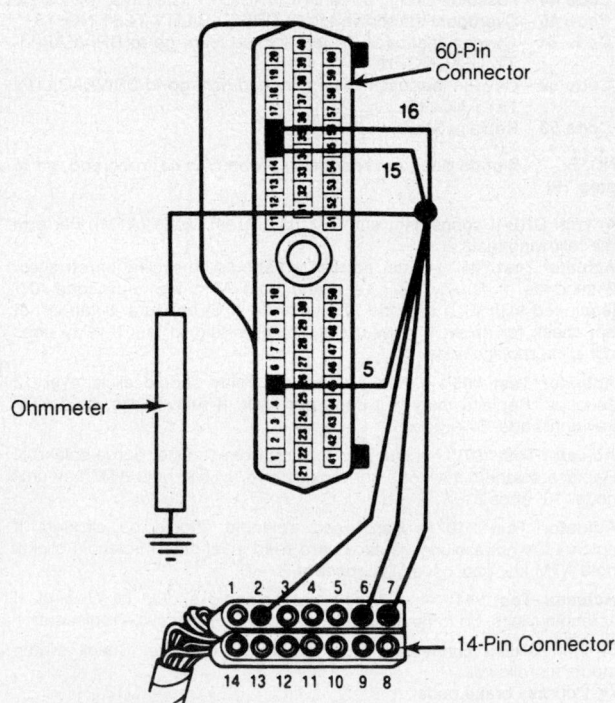

60-Pin Connector

Ohmmeter

14-Pin Connector

18) If ohmmeter shows less than .5 ohm resistance at all cavities, go to DRIVEABILITY TEST NO. 16 (cold engine driveability problems) or DRIVEABILITY TEST NO. 18 (warm engine driveability problems). If ohmmeter reading indicates an open in one or more of the connector cavities, check for an open ground circuit and replace SMEC. If ohmmeter indicates a resistance greater than .5 ohm, repair faulty ground connection.

1989 COMPUTERIZED ENGINE CONTROLS
Chrysler Motors 2.2L Turbo II MPFI (Cont.)

1a-21

DRIVEABILITY TEST NO. 1 (Cont.)

19) The majority of intermittent failures are caused by wiring and connections. One way to find them is to duplicate the problem. Since the SMEC can remember where they are, the ATM and Sensor Tests can be used in an attempt to locate them. Once in the correct test mode, wiggle all connectors and wires in the circuit. The DRB-II display will change, or ATM test will be interrupted when the bad connection or wire is located. When checking the MAP sensor circuit (Code 14), apply 10 inches of vacuum to MAP sensor before testing.

If the following codes do not reappear, go to the indicated test:

Sensor Tests
Code 14 – Sensor Test "08"
Code 22 – Sensor Test "04"
Code 23 – Sensor Test "03"
Code 24 – Sensor Test "05"
ATM Tests
Code 25 – ATM Test "03"
Code 26 – ATM Test "02"
Code 27 – ATM Test "02"
Code 31 – ATM Test "07"
Code 33 – ATM Test "05"
Code 35 – ATM Test "04"
Code 36 – ATM Test "11"
Code 37 – ATM Test "10"
Code 42 – ATM Test "06"
Code 43 – ATM Test "01"
Code 45 – ATM Test "11"

DRIVEABILITY TEST NO. 2

CODES 13 OR 14 – MAP SENSOR CIRCUIT

1) Turn ignition off. Tee vacuum gauge into vacuum line at MAP sensor. Start engine and observe vacuum gauge with engine at idle. Observe gauge while snapping throttle open and closed.

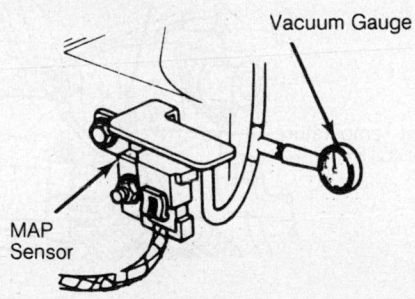

Vacuum Gauge

MAP Sensor

2) If gauge reads manifold vacuum at idle and drops to zero when throttle is snapped open, go to next step. If vacuum reads zero at idle, repair leak in vacuum line to throttle body. If vacuum slowly drops to zero when throttle is snapped open, repair restriction in vacuum supply line to MAP sensor.

3) Connect DRB-II and disconnect MAP sensor connector. Put system into Sensor Test Mode "08". If display reads zero volts, replace SMEC. Ensure Dark Green/Red wire of connector cavity No. 1, of 60-pin connector, is not shorted to ground. If reading is at least 4 volts, SMEC is okay, go to next step.

4) Connect DRB-II and put system in Sensor Test Mode "08". Disconnect MAP sensor. Connect jumper wire to Dark Green/Red wire and Black/Light Blue wire of the MAP sensor harness connector. If DRB-II displays "0" volts, go to step 6). If reading is not "0" volts, go to next step.

DRIVEABILITY TEST NO. 2 (Cont.)

5) Connect DRB-II and put system in Sensor Test Mode "08". Disconnect MAP sensor. Connect a jumper between battery negative terminal and Dark Green/Red wire at MAP sensor harness connector. If display is "0" volts, repair Black/Light Blue wire of the MAP sensor connector to the wiring harness splice. If display is "5" volts, repair Dark Green/Red wire of MAP sensor connector for an open circuit to SMEC.

6) Disconnect MAP sensor connector and turn ignition switch to "RUN" position. Connect a DVOM between Violet/White wire of MAP sensor harness and ground. If it reads zero volts, repair open in Violet/White wire. If reading is at least 4 volts, replace MAP sensor.

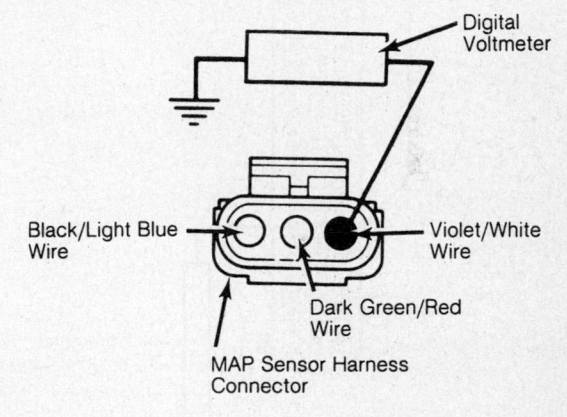

Digital Voltmeter

Black/Light Blue Wire

Violet/White Wire

Dark Green/Red Wire

MAP Sensor Harness Connector

DRIVEABILITY TEST NO. 3

CODE 15 – SPEED SENSOR CIRCUIT

1) Connect DRB-II. Start engine. Disconnect speed sensor connector. Put system into Engine Running Test "71". Connect jumper wire between the Black and White/Orange wire terminals of speed sensor. Make and break this connection. If display on DRB-II changes, replace speed sensor. If display does not change, go to next step.

2) Turn engine off with speed sensor disconnected. Disconnect 60-pin connector from SMEC. Connect an ohmmeter between White/Orange wire at cavity No. 48 of 60-pin connector and White/Orange wire at speed sensor connector. If ohmmeter reads continuity, go to next step. If ohmmeter is not reading continuity, repair White/Orange wire in cavity No. 48 of 60-pin connector for an open circuit to speed sensor connector.

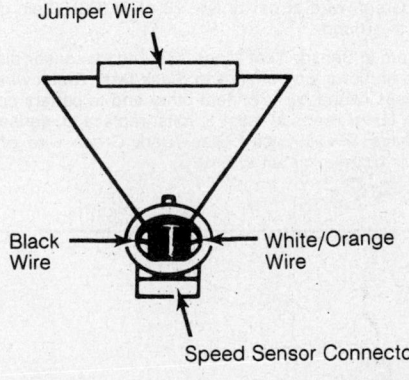

Jumper Wire

Black Wire

White/Orange Wire

Speed Sensor Connector

DRIVEABILITY TEST NO. 3 (Cont.)

3) With engine off, leave speed sensor and 60-pin SMEC connectors disconnected. Connect an ohmmeter between Black/Light Blue wire at cavity No. 4 of 60-pin connector and Black wire terminal of speed sensor harness connector. If ohmmeter reads continuity, replace SMEC. Before replacing SMEC, ensure cavity No. 48 is not damaged causing a poor connection. If ohmmeter is not reading continuity, repair Black/Light Blue or Black wire of speed sensor harness connector for an open circuit to wiring harness splice.

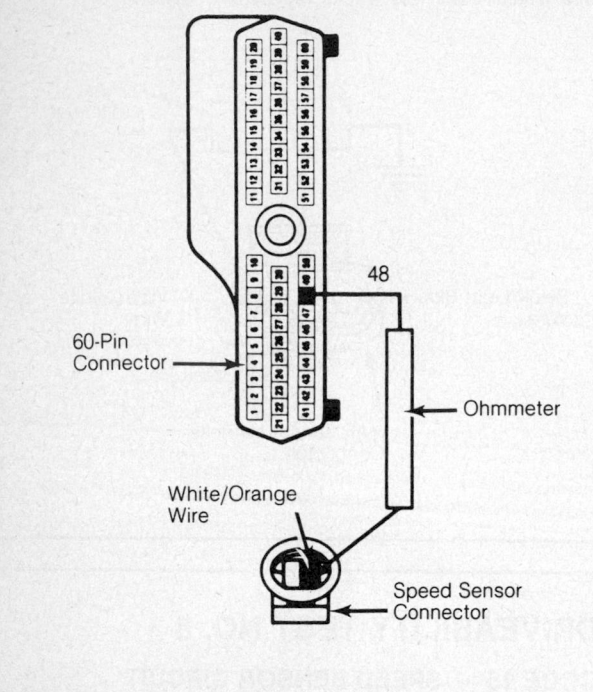

DRIVEABILITY TEST NO. 4

CODE 21 – OXYGEN SENSOR (O₂) CIRCUIT

1) Turn ignition off, connect DRB-II and disconnect O$_2$ sensor connector. Turn ignition on. Put system in Sensor Test Mode "02". Refer to ENTERING ON-BOARD DIAGNOSTICS in this article. If display on tester is at least .4 volt, go to next step. If display on tester reads zero volts, replace SMEC. Before replacing SMEC, ensure Black/Dark Green wire at cavity No. 23 of SMEC 60-pin connector is not shorted to ground.

2) With system in Sensor Test Mode "02" and O$_2$ sensor disconnected, connect one end of a jumper wire to Black/Dark Green wire of oxygen sensor harness connector. Connect other end to battery positive post. If display on tester reads at least 5 volts, replace O$_2$ sensor. If display on tester reads .4 volt, repair Black/Dark Green wire of O$_2$ sensor connector for an open circuit to SMEC.

DRIVEABILITY TEST NO. 4 (Cont.)

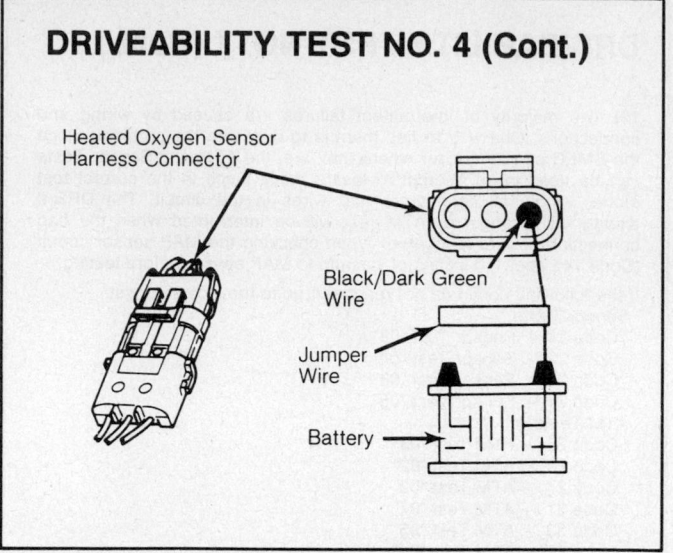

DRIVEABILITY TEST NO. 5

CODE 22 – COOLANT TEMPERATURE SENSOR CIRCUIT (CTS)

1) With DRB-II connected to diagnostic connector, turn ignition off. Disconnect CTS sensor connector. Put system in Sensor Test Mode "04". Refer to ENTERING ON-BOARD DIAGNOSTICS in this article. If display on tester reads "00°", go to next step. If display on tester reads "260°", replace SMEC for a defective logic board. Before replacing SMEC, ensure Tan/White wire at cavity No. 3 of 60-pin connector is not shorted to ground.

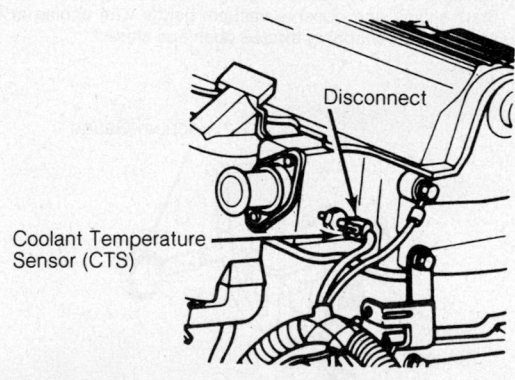

2) Connect a jumper wire between Tan/White and Black/Light Blue wire terminals of CTS. If display on tester reads "260°", replace CTS. If display on tester reads "00°", go to next step.

1989 COMPUTERIZED ENGINE CONTROLS
Chrysler Motors 2.2L Turbo II MPFI (Cont.)

1a-23

DRIVEABILITY TEST NO. 5 (Cont.)

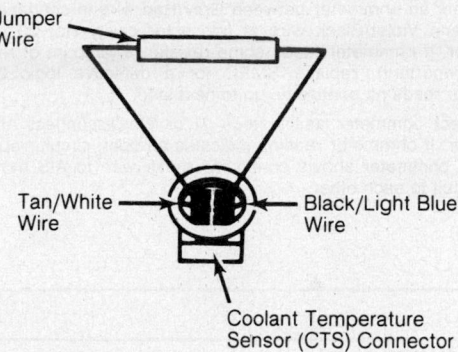

Jumper Wire

Tan/White Wire

Black/Light Blue Wire

Coolant Temperature Sensor (CTS) Connector

3) With DRB-II connected and system in Sensor Test Mode "04", disconnect CTS. Connect one end of a jumper wire to ground. Connect other end of wire to Tan/White wire terminal of CTS harness connector. If display on tester reads "260°", repair Black/Light Blue wire of CTS harness connector for an open circuit to wiring harness splice. If display on tester reads "00°", repair Tan/White wire of CTS harness connector for an open circuit to SMEC.

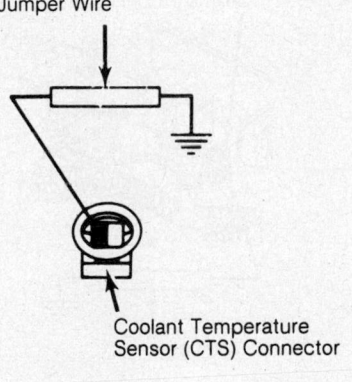

Jumper Wire

Coolant Temperature Sensor (CTS) Connector

DRIVEABILITY TEST NO. 6

CODE 23 – CHARGE TEMPERATURE SENSOR

1) With DRB-II connected to diagnostic connector, disconnect charge temperature sensor connector. Put system in Sensor Test "03". Refer to ENTERING ON-BOARD DIAGNOSTICS in this article. If display on tester reads 5 volts, go to next step. If display on tester reads zero volts, or zero volts and then increases, replace SMEC. Before replacing SMEC, ensure cavity No. 21 of 60-pin connector is not shorted to ground.

DRIVEABILITY TEST NO. 6 (Cont.)

2) With DRB-II connected and system in Sensor Test Mode "03", connect a jumper wire between Black/Red and Black/Light Blue wire terminals of charge temperature sensor harness connector. If display on tester reads zero volts, replace charge temperature sensor. If display on tester reads 5 volts, go to next step.

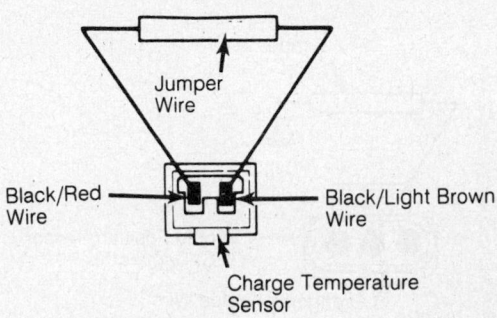

Jumper Wire

Black/Red Wire

Black/Light Brown Wire

Charge Temperature Sensor

3) Connect one end of a jumper wire to ground. Connect other end of wire to Black/Red wire terminal of charge temperature sensor connector. If display reads zero volts, repair Black/Light Blue wire of charge temperature sensor connector for an open circuit to wiring harness splice. If display on tester reads 5 volts, repair wire of charge temperature sensor connector for an open circuit to SMEC.

DRIVEABILITY TEST NO. 7

CODE 24 – THROTTLE POSITION SENSOR (TPS) CIRCUIT

1) With DRB-II connected to diagnostic connector and TPS sensor disconnected, put system in Sensor Test Mode "05". Refer to ENTERING ON-BOARD DIAGNOSTICS in this article. If display on tester reads between 4-5 volts, go to next step. If display on tester reads zero volts, replace SMEC for a defective logic board. Before replacing SMEC, ensure Orange/Dark Blue wire at connector cavity No. 22 of 60-pin connector is not shorted to ground.

2) Connect a jumper wire between Orange/Dark Blue and Black/Light Blue wire terminals of TPS connector. If display on tester reads zero volts, go to step 4). If display on tester reads 5 volts, go to next step.

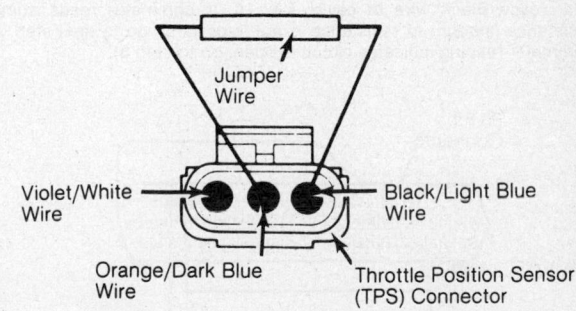

Jumper Wire

Violet/White Wire

Black/Light Blue Wire

Orange/Dark Blue Wire

Throttle Position Sensor (TPS) Connector

1a-24

1989 COMPUTERIZED ENGINE CONTROLS
Chrysler Motors 2.2L Turbo II MPFI (Cont.)

DRIVEABILITY TEST NO. 7 (Cont.)

3) Connect one end of a jumper wire to ground. Connect other end of wire to Orange/Dark Blue wire terminal of TPS harness connector. If display on tester reads zero volts, repair Black/Light Blue wire of TPS connector for an open circuit to wiring harness splice. If display on tester reads 5 volts, repair Orange/Dark Blue wire of TPS connector for an open circuit to SMEC.

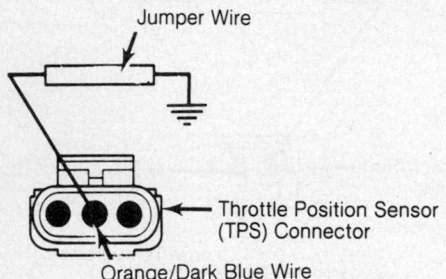

Jumper Wire

Throttle Position Sensor (TPS) Connector

Orange/Dark Blue Wire

4) With TPS disconnected, turn ignition switch to "RUN" position. Connect a digital voltmeter between Violet/White wire of TPS harness connector and ground. If voltmeter reads at least 4 volts, replace TPS. If voltmeter reads zero volts, repair Violet/White wire for an open circuit to wiring harness splice.

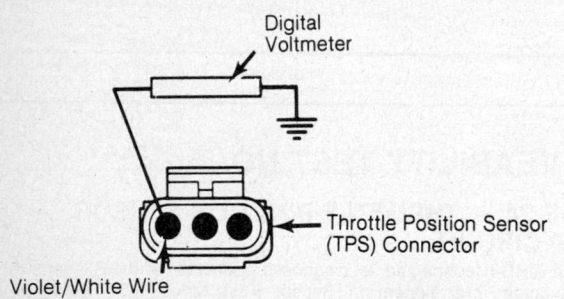

Digital Voltmeter

Throttle Position Sensor (TPS) Connector

Violet/White Wire

DRIVEABILITY TEST NO. 8

CODE 25 – AUTOMATIC IDLE SPEED CIRCUIT

1) Turn ignition off. Disconnect 60-pin connector from SMEC. Connect an ohmmeter between Brown/White wire in connector cavity No. 17 and Yellow/Black wire in cavity No. 18. If ohmmeter reads some resistance (amount of resistance is not important), go to next step. If ohmmeter reading indicates circuit is open, go to step 3).

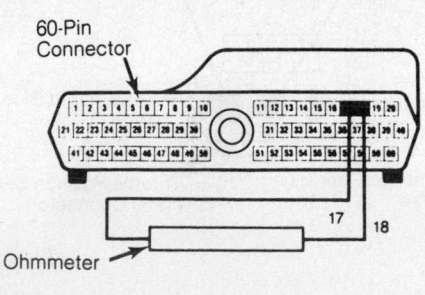

60-Pin Connector

17 18

Ohmmeter

DRIVEABILITY TEST NO. 8 (Cont.)

2) Connect an ohmmeter between Gray/Red wire in connector cavity No. 19 and Violet/Black wire in connector cavity No. 20 of 60-pin connector. If ohmmeter reads some resistance (amount of resistance is not important), replace SMEC for a defective logic board. If ohmmeter reads no continuity, go to next step.

3) Connect ohmmeter as in steps **1)** or **2)**. Disconnect AIS motor connector. If ohmmeter reading indicates an open circuit, replace AIS motor. If ohmmeter shows continuity, repair wire to AIS motor for a short circuit to each other.

DRIVEABILITY TEST NO. 9

CODE 31 – CANISTER PURGE SOLENOID

1) Connect a voltmeter between Pink/Black wire of canister purge solenoid connector and ground. Turn ignition switch to "RUN" position. If voltmeter reads battery voltage, go to next step. If voltmeter reads zero volts, go to step 3).

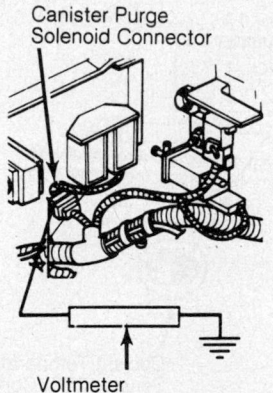

Canister Purge Solenoid Connector

Voltmeter

2) Turn ignition off. Disconnect 60-pin connector from SMEC. Connect a voltmeter between Pink/Black wire in connector cavity No. 54 and ground. Turn ignition switch to "RUN" position. If voltmeter reads battery voltage, replace SMEC. Before replacing SMEC, ensure connector cavity No. 54 is not damaged causing a poor connection. If voltmeter reads zero volts, repair Pink/Black wire in connector cavity No. 54 for an open circuit to canister purge solenoid.

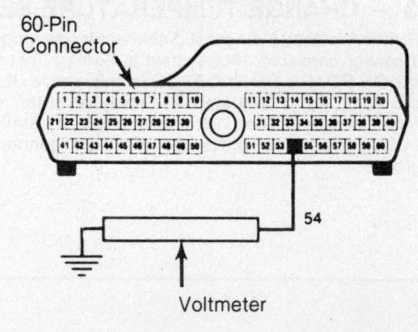

60-Pin Connector

54

Voltmeter

1989 COMPUTERIZED ENGINE CONTROLS
Chrysler Motors 2.2L Turbo II MPFI (Cont.)

1a-25

DRIVEABILITY TEST NO. 9 (Cont.)

3) Turn ignition switch to "RUN" position. Connect a voltmeter between Dark Blue wire of canister purge solenoid and ground. If voltmeter reads battery voltage, go to next step. If voltmeter reads zero volts, repair Dark Blue wire for an open circuit to wiring harness splice.

4) Turn ignition off. Connect a voltmeter between Pink/Black wire at canister purge solenoid connector and ground. Disconnect 60-pin connector from SMEC. Turn ignition switch to "RUN" position. If voltmeter reads battery voltage, replace SMEC. Before replacing SMEC, ensure Pink/Black wire is not shorted to ground. If voltmeter reads zero volts, replace canister purge solenoid.

DRIVEABILITY TEST NO. 10

CODE 33 – A/C CUT-OUT RELAY CIRCUIT

1) For the A/C cut-out relay to operate properly, the radiator fan relay must be operating properly. Disregard Fault Code 33 if it is not working properly. Connect a voltmeter to Dark Blue/Orange wire of A/C cut-out relay single connector and ground. Turn ignition on. Turn blower motor and A/C button on. Ensure radiator fan is running. If voltmeter reads battery voltage, go to next step. If voltmeter reads 0-1 volt, go to step **3)**.

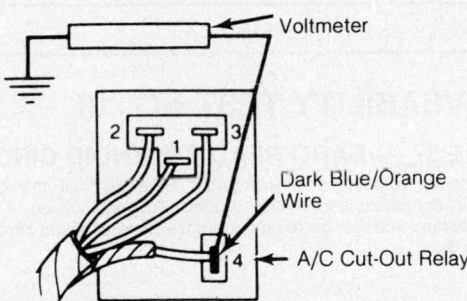

Voltmeter
Dark Blue/Orange Wire
A/C Cut-Out Relay

2) Turn ignition off. Disconnect 60-pin connector from SMEC. Connect a voltmeter between Dark Blue/Orange wire in cavity No. 56 and ground. Connect a jumper wire between cavity No. 57 of 60-pin connector and ground. Turn ignition on. The radiator fan will run. If voltmeter reads battery voltage, replace SMEC for a bad logic board. Before replacing SMEC, ensure cavity No. 56 of 60-pin connector is not damaged causing a poor connection. If voltmeter reads zero volts, repair Dark Blue/Orange wire of cavity No. 56 for an open circuit to A/C cut-out relay.

NOTE: A/C cut-out relay wire has a diode in it. Ensure diode has not failed causing an open circuit.

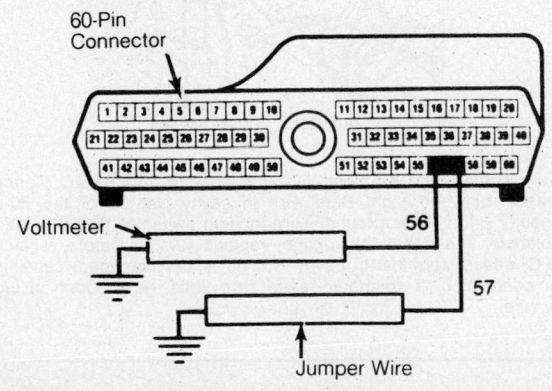

60-Pin Connector
Voltmeter
56
57
Jumper Wire

DRIVEABILITY TEST NO. 10 (Cont.)

3) Turn ignition off. With voltmeter connected to Dark Blue/Orange wire of A/C cut-out relay connector, disconnect 60-pin connector from SMEC. Connect a jumper wire between cavity No. 57 of 60-pin connector and ground. Turn ignition on. The radiator fan will run. If voltmeter reads battery voltage, replace SMEC. If voltmeter reads zero volts, go to next step.

4) With jumper wire connected as in previous step, connect a voltmeter between Light Green wire of A/C cut-out relay 3-pin connector and ground. If voltmeter reads battery voltage, replace A/C cut-out relay. If voltmeter reads zero volts, repair Light Green wire to radiator fan relay for an open circuit.

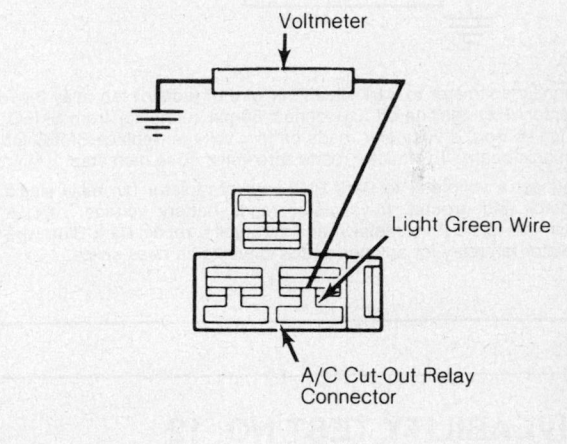

Voltmeter
Light Green Wire
A/C Cut-Out Relay Connector

DRIVEABILITY TEST NO. 11

CODE 35 – RADIATOR FAN RELAY CONTROL CIRCUIT

1) Connect a voltmeter to Dark Blue/Pink wire of radiator fan relay 3-pin connector and ground. Turn ignition on. If voltmeter reads battery voltage, go to next step. If voltmeter reads 0-1 volt, go to step **3)**.

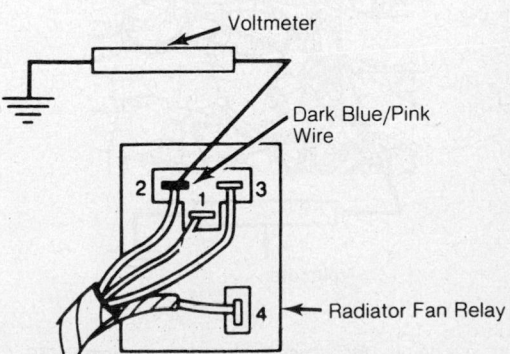

Voltmeter
Dark Blue/Pink Wire
Radiator Fan Relay

2) Turn ignition off. Disconnect 60-pin connector from SMEC. Connect a voltmeter between Dark Blue/Pink wire in cavity No. 57 and ground. Turn ignition on. If voltmeter reads battery voltage, replace SMEC for a defective logic board. Before replacing SMEC, ensure terminal in cavity No. 57 of 60-pin connector is not damaged causing a poor connection. If voltmeter reads zero volts, repair Dark Blue/Pink wire of cavity No. 57 for an open circuit to radiator fan relay.

1a-26

1989 COMPUTERIZED ENGINE CONTROLS
Chrysler Motors 2.2L Turbo II MPFI (Cont.)

DRIVEABILITY TEST NO. 11 (Cont.)

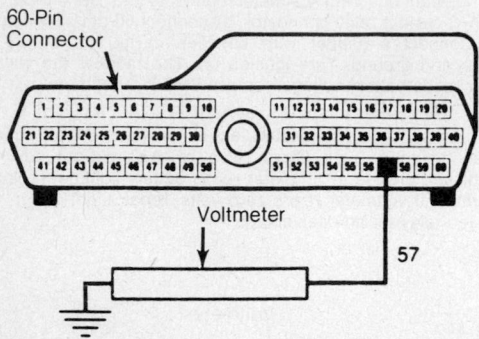

60-Pin Connector

Voltmeter

57

3) Connect voltmeter to Dark Blue/Pink wire of radiator fan relay 3-pin connector. Turn ignition off. Disconnect 60-pin connector from SMEC. Turn ignition on. If voltmeter reads battery voltage, replace SMEC for a bad logic board. If voltmeter reads zero volts, go to next step.

4) Connect a voltmeter to Dark Blue wire of radiator fan relay single connector and ground. If voltmeter reads battery voltage, replace radiator fan relay. If voltmeter reads zero volts, repair Dark Blue wire of radiator fan relay for an open circuit to wiring harness splice.

DRIVEABILITY TEST NO. 12

CODE 36 – WASTEGATE SOLENOID CIRCUIT

1) Connect a voltmeter to Light Green/Black wire of wastegate solenoid connector and ground. Turn ignition on. If voltmeter reads battery voltage, go to next step. If voltmeter reads zero, go to step 3).

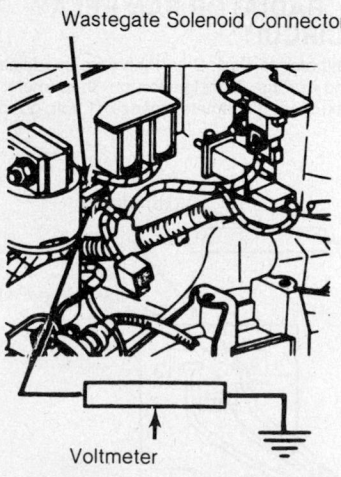

Wastegate Solenoid Connector

Voltmeter

2) Turn ignition off. Disconnect 60-pin connector from SMEC. Connect voltmeter to Light Green/Black wire in cavity No. 39 of the 60-pin connector and vehicle ground. Turn ignition switch to "RUN" position. If voltmeter reads battery voltage, replace SMEC. Before replacing the SMEC, check terminal in cavity No. 39 for damage. If voltmeter does not read battery voltage, repair open in Light Green/Black wire.

DRIVEABILITY TEST NO. 12 (Cont.)

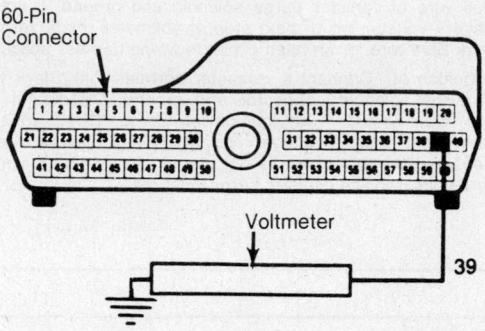

60-Pin Connector

Voltmeter

39

3) Turn ignition switch to "RUN" position. Connect voltmeter between the Dark Blue wire at the wastegate solenoid connector and vehicle ground. If voltmeter reads battery voltage, go to next step. If voltmeter reads zero volts, repair open in Dark Blue wire between wastegate connector and wiring harness splice.

4) Turn ignition off. Connect voltmeter between Light Blue/Black wire of the wastegate solenoid connector and vehicle ground. Disconnect 60-pin connector from SMEC. Turn ignition on. If voltmeter reads battery voltage, logic board is defective, replace SMEC. If voltmeter reads zero volts, replace wastegate solenoid.

DRIVEABILITY TEST NO. 13

CODE 37 – BARO READ SOLENOID CIRCUIT

1) Connect voltmeter between Light Blue wire of the baro read solenoid connector and vehicle ground. Turn ignition on. If voltmeter reads battery voltage, go to next step. If voltmeter reads zero volts, go to step 3).

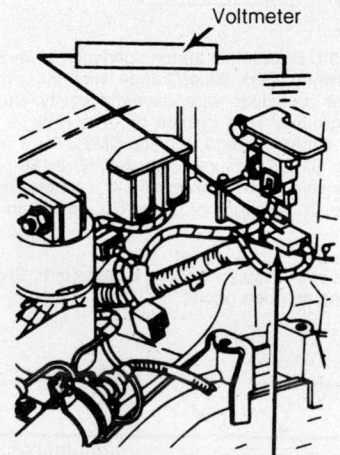

Voltmeter

Baro Read Solenoid Connector

2) Turn ignition off. Disconnect 60-pin connector from SMEC. Connect voltmeter between Light Blue wire in cavity No. 38 of the 60-pin connector and vehicle ground. Turn ignition switch to "RUN" position. If voltmeter reads battery voltage, replace SMEC. Before replacing SMEC, ensure terminal in cavity No. 38 is not damaged, causing a poor connection. If voltmeter reads zero volts, repair open in Light Blue wire.

1989 COMPUTERIZED ENGINE CONTROLS
Chrysler Motors 2.2L Turbo II MPFI (Cont.)

1a-27

DRIVEABILITY TEST NO. 13 (Cont.)

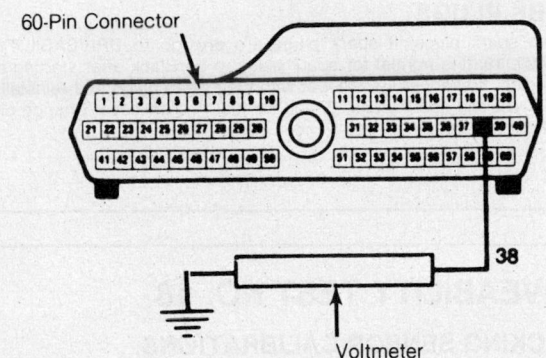

60-Pin Connector

38

Voltmeter

3) Connect voltmeter between Dark Blue wire of baro read solenoid connector and vehicle ground. If voltmeter reads battery voltage, go to next step. If voltmeter reads zero volts, repair open in Dark Blue wire.

4) Turn ignition off. Connect voltmeter between Light Blue wire at baro read connector and vehicle ground. Disconnect 60-pin connector from SMEC. Turn ignition switch to "RUN" position. If voltmeter reads battery voltage, logic board is defective, replace SMEC. Before replacing SMEC, ensure Light Blue wire is not shorted to ground. If voltmeter reads zero volts, replace the baro read solenoid.

DRIVEABILITY TEST NO. 14

CODE 44 – FUSED "J2" CIRCUIT TO SMEC

Turn ignition off. Disconnect 60-pin connector from SMEC. Connect a voltmeter to Dark Blue/White wire in cavity No. 12 of the 60-pin connector and ground. Turn ignition on. If voltmeter reads battery voltage, logic board is defective, replace SMEC. Before replacing SMEC, ensure terminal in cavity No. 12 of 60-pin connector is not damaged causing a poor connection. If voltmeter reads zero volts, repair Dark Blue/White wire of cavity No. 12 for an open circuit to wiring harness splice.

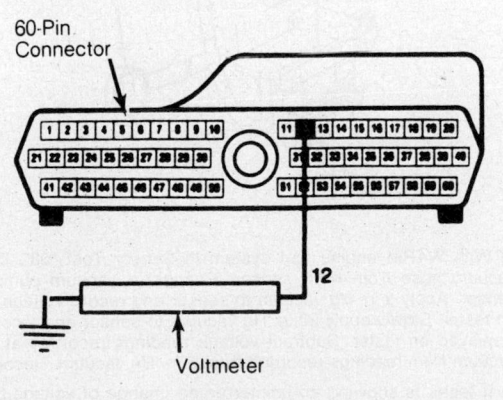

60-Pin Connector

12

Voltmeter

DRIVEABILITY TEST NO. 15

CODE 45 – OVERBOOST SHUTOFF

1) Disconnect vacuum line from wastegate diaphragm. Connect vacuum gauge to vacuum line that was removed. Disconnect vacuum line from the side of the wastegate solenoid and connect vacuum pump to it. Apply 15 in. Hg vacuum. Release vacuum. If vacuum gauge reads within one in. Hg of applied vacuum and drops to zero immediately when vacuum is released, system is okay, go to next step. If vacuum gauge does not read within one in. Hg of applied vacuum or drops slowly to zero, repair vacuum line for restriction or break.

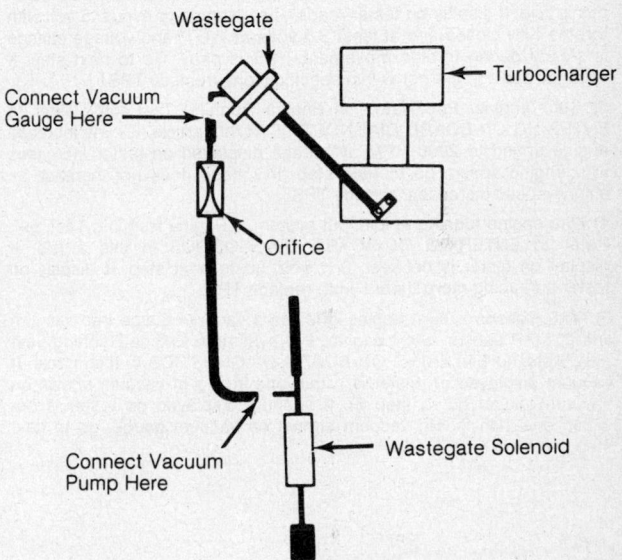

Wastegate

Turbocharger

Connect Vacuum Gauge Here

Orifice

Connect Vacuum Pump Here

Wastegate Solenoid

2) Disconnect vacuum line connector from top of wastegate solenoid and connect vacuum gauge to it. Start engine. If vacuum gauge reads manifold vacuum, check wastegate and MAP sensor calibration. If vacuum gauge reads zero, repair vacuum line to manifold for restriction or break.

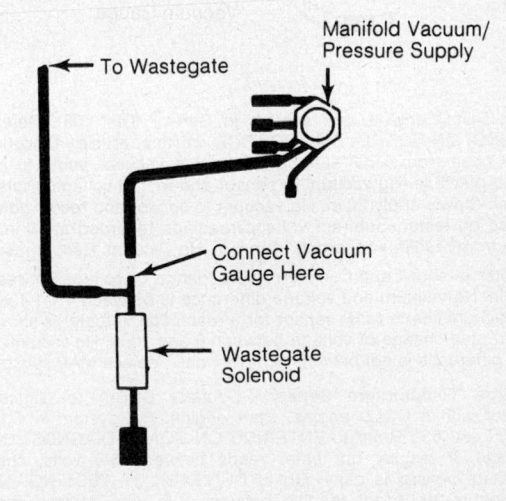

Manifold Vacuum/ Pressure Supply

To Wastegate

Connect Vacuum Gauge Here

Wastegate Solenoid

1a-28

1989 COMPUTERIZED ENGINE CONTROLS
Chrysler Motors 2.2L Turbo II MPFI (Cont.)

DRIVEABILITY TEST NO. 16

CHECKING SENSOR CALIBRATIONS (COLD ENGINE)

1) Coolant Temperature Sensor - Connect DRB-II Tester (C-4805) to diagnostic connector. With a COLD engine, put system in Engine Running Test "64". Refer to ENTERING ON-BOARD DIAGNOSTICS in this article. If display on tester is reading ambient temperature ±10°F (12.2°C), go to next step. If display on tester is reading more than 10°F (12.2°C) greater than or less than ambient temperature, replace coolant temperature sensor.

2) Throttle Position Sensor - With a COLD engine, put system in Sensor Test "05". Refer to ENTERING ON-BOARD DIAGNOSTICS in this article. If display on tester reads one volt plus or minus .5 volt with throttle fully closed and at least 3.5 volts at WOT, and voltage change is steady during throttle movement, TPS is okay. Go to next step. If voltage readings are not within specifications, replace TPS.

3) Start engine. Put system in Engine Running Test "65". Refer to ENTERING ON-BOARD DIAGNOSTICS in this article. Slowly increase engine speed to 2000 RPM. If voltage displayed on tester increases with engine speed, go to next step. If voltage does not increase as engine speed increases, replace TPS.

4) With engine running at idle, put system in Engine Running Test "69". Refer to ENTERING ON-BOARD DIAGNOSTICS in this article. If display on tester is between 0-.1 volt, go to next step. If display on tester is reading more than .1 volt, replace TPS.

5) MAP Sensor - Turn engine off. Tee a vacuum gauge into vacuum line at MAP sensor. Start engine. Put system in Engine Running Test "68". Refer to ENTERING ON-BOARD DIAGNOSTICS in this article. If vacuum displayed on tester is within one in. Hg of vacuum shown on vacuum gauge, go to step **8)**. If vacuum displayed on tester is not within one inch in. Hg vacuum shown on vacuum gauge, go to next step.

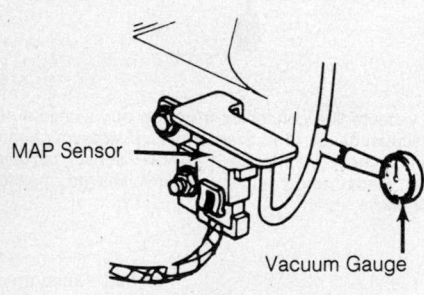

MAP Sensor

Vacuum Gauge

6) With COLD engine, put system in Sensor Test "08". Refer to ENTERING ON-BOARD DIAGNOSTICS in this article. Disconnect vacuum hose from MAP sensor. Connect a vacuum pump to MAP sensor. Apply 5 in. Hg vacuum to sensor and record voltage displayed on tester. Slowly apply 20 in. Hg vacuum to sensor and record voltage displayed on tester. Subtract voltage readings recorded at 20 in. Hg vacuum from readings recorded from 5 in. Hg vacuum. Record result.

7) If tester is showing an uninterrupted change of voltage between 5 and 20 in. Hg vacuum and voltage difference is between 1.1-1.4 volts, repair vacuum line to MAP sensor for a restriction. If tester is showing an interrupted change of voltage between 5 and 20 in. Hg vacuum and voltage difference is not between 1.1-1.4 volts, replace MAP sensor.

8) Charge Temperature Sensor - Connect DRB-II to diagnostic connector with a COLD engine. Start engine. Put system in Engine Running Test "63". Refer to ENTERING ON-BOARD DIAGNOSTICS in this article. If display on tester reads between 3-5 volts, charge temperature sensor is okay. Go to DRIVEABILITY TEST NO. 17. If display on tester is not reading between 3-5 volts, replace charge temperature sensor.

DRIVEABILITY TEST NO. 17

CHECKING FOR FUEL FOULED SPARK PLUGS

Remove spark plugs. If spark plugs are dry, go to DRIVEABILITY TEST NO. 19. It is normal for spark plugs to be Black after starting a cold engine. If spark plugs are wet with fuel, clean plugs and reinstall. DO NOT replace spark plugs. Check for fuel in crankcase. Change oil and filter if required.

DRIVEABILITY TEST NO. 18

CHECKING SENSOR CALIBRATIONS (WARM ENGINE)

1) Coolant Temperature Sensor - Connect DRB-II Tester (C-4805) to diagnostic connector. With a WARM engine, put system in Engine Running Test "64". Refer to ENTERING ON-BOARD DIAGNOSTICS in this article. If display on tester reads between 180-250°F (82-121°C), go to next step. If display on tester is not reading between 180-250°F (82-121°C), replace coolant temperature sensor.

2) Throttle Position Sensor - With a WARM engine, put system in Sensor Test "05". If display on tester reads one volt plus or minus .5 volt with throttle fully closed and at least 3.5 volts at WOT, and voltage changes steadily during throttle movement, TPS is okay. Go to next step. If voltage readings are not within specifications, replace TPS.

3) Start engine. Put system in Engine Running Test "65". Slowly increase engine speed to 2000 RPM. If voltage displayed on tester increases with engine speed, go to next step. If voltage does not increase as engine speed increases, replace TPS.

4) With engine running at idle, put system in Engine Running Test "69". If display on tester is between 0-.1 volt, go to next step. If display on tester is reading more than .1 volt, replace TPS.

5) MAP Sensor - Turn engine off. Tee a vacuum gauge into vacuum line at MAP sensor. Start engine. Put system in Engine Running Test "68". If vacuum displayed on tester is within one in. Hg vacuum shown on vacuum gauge, go to step **8)**. If vacuum displayed on tester is not within one in. Hg of vacuum shown on vacuum gauge, go to next step.

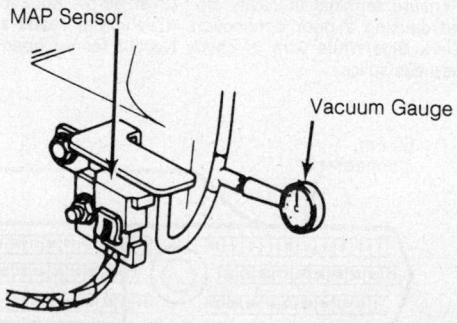

MAP Sensor

Vacuum Gauge

6) With WARM engine, put system in Sensor Test "08". Disconnect vacuum hose from MAP sensor. Connect a vacuum pump to MAP sensor. Apply 5 in. Hg vacuum to sensor and record voltage displayed on tester. Slowly apply 20 in. Hg vacuum to sensor and record voltage displayed on tester. Subtract voltage readings recorded at 20 in. Hg vacuum from readings recorded from 5 in. Hg vacuum. Record result.

7) If tester is showing an uninterrupted change of voltage between 5 and 20 in. Hg vacuum and voltage difference is between 1.1-1.4 volts, repair vacuum line to MAP sensor for a restriction. If tester is showing an interrupted change of voltage between 5 and 20 in. Hg vacuum and voltage difference is not between 1.1-1.4 volts, replace MAP sensor.

1989 COMPUTERIZED ENGINE CONTROLS
Chrysler Motors 2.2L Turbo II MPFI (Cont.)

1a-29

DRIVEABILITY TEST NO. 18 (Cont.)

8) Charge Temperature Sensor - With tester connected to diagnostic connector on a WARM engine. Start engine. Put system in Engine Running Test "63". If display on tester reads between 1-4 volts, go to DRIVEABILITY TEST NO. 19. If display on tester is not reading between 1-4 volts, replace charge temperature sensor.

DRIVEABILITY TEST NO. 19

SECONDARY IGNITION SYSTEM CHECK

Connect engine analyzer to engine. Start engine and allow engine speed to stabilize for 2 minutes. Following equipment manufacturer's instructions, test secondary ignition system. Ensure ignition coil output is checked during this test. If secondary ignition system is okay, perform DRIVEABILITY TEST NO. 20. If secondary ignition system does not test okay, repair as required.

DRIVEABILITY TEST NO. 20

BASIC IGNITION TIMING CHECK

1) Connect a tachometer and powered timing light to engine. Start and run engine until normal operating temperature is obtained. Disconnect engine coolant temperature sensor. The "CHECK ENGINE" light must come on. If basic timing is within 2 degrees of specification shown on emission label, go to next step. If basic timing is not within specification, adjust timing.

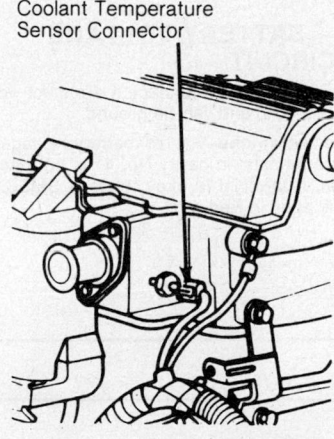

Coolant Temperature Sensor Connector

2) Remove air cleaner if necessary. Ensure engine is at normal operating temperature. Reconnect coolant temperature sensor. The "CHECK ENGINE" light will not go out until engine is restarted. Raise engine speed to 2000 RPM. If timing is between 20-42 degrees BTDC, go to DRIVEABILITY TEST NO. 21. If ignition timing is not within minimum specification, logic board is defective, replace SMEC.

DRIVEABILITY TEST NO. 21

CHECKING FUEL SUPPLY & RETURN SYSTEM

CAUTION: Fuel system is under approximately 55 psi (3.9 kg/cm²) pressure. Relieve pressure before servicing any fuel system component. Refer to REMOVAL & INSTALLATION section in this article for procedure on releasing fuel pressure.

1) With DRB-II connected to diagnostic connector, install Pressure Gauge (C-3292) with Adapter (C-4799) in fuel supply hose at fuel rail. Enter Diagnostic Test Mode. Refer to ENTERING ON-BOARD DIAGNOSTICS in this article. Press and hold "ATM" key on tester. If fuel pressure is 53-57 psi, go to DRIVEABILITY TEST NO. 22. If fuel pressure is less than 53 psi, record reading and go to next step. If fuel pressure is more than 57 psi, go to step **4)**.

2) Turn ignition off. Release fuel system pressure. Tee pressure gauge into fuel line before fuel filter. Turn ignition on. Press and hold "ATM" key on tester. If fuel pressure is 5 psi higher than in step **1)**, replace fuel filter. If fuel pressure is still less than 53 psi, go to next step.

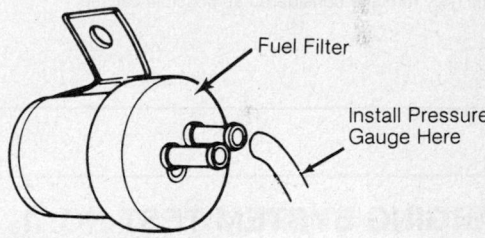

Fuel Filter

Install Pressure Gauge Here

3) Turn ignition off. Release fuel system pressure. Remove pressure gauge. Tee pressure gauge into line after fuel filter. Turn ignition switch to "RUN" position. Press and hold "ATM" key on tester. VERY GENTLY squeeze fuel return line at fuel rail and IMMEDIATELY release. Fuel pressure must not exceed 72 psi or damage to pressure regulator will result. If fuel pressure increases to more than operating pressure, replace pressure regulator. If fuel pressure does not increase, replace in-tank fuel pump. Before replacing in-tank fuel pump, look for contamination in fuel tank that may be plugging pump filter. Also ensure electrical connections are not corroded.

4) Turn ignition off. With pressure gauge connected, remove fuel return hose (small one) from fuel rail. Connect a 3 foot length of fuel hose to fuel rail and place other end of hose into a receptacle (2 gallon minimum). Turn ignition on. Press and hold "ATM" key on tester. If fuel pressure is 53-57 psi, check fuel return lines for kinks or restrictions, including return line check valve inside fuel tank. If fuel pressure is more than 57 psi, replace pressure regulator.

DRIVEABILITY TEST NO. 22

CHECKING THROTTLE BODY MINIMUM AIR FLOW

1) With DRB-II connected to vehicle, start engine and run to operating temperature. Put system into Engine Running Test "70". If vehicle has less than 1000 miles on odometer, engine speed should be 600-900 RPM. If vehicle has more than 1000 miles on odometer, engine speed should be 650-900 RPM. If engine RPM is within specification, go to DRIVEABILITY TEST NO. 23. If engine RPM is not within specification, replace throttle body.

1a-30

1989 COMPUTERIZED ENGINE CONTROLS
Chrysler Motors 2.2L Turbo II MPFI (Cont.)

DRIVEABILITY TEST NO. 23

NON-ENGINE CONTROL RELATED PROBLEMS

At this point in driveability testing procedures, all engine control systems have been determined to be operating properly. Therefore, engine control system devices are not the cause of the driveability problem. Check the following items as possible causes of driveability problem:

- Engine vacuum MUST be at least 13 in. Hg in Neutral.
- Valve timing must be set to specifications.
- Engine compression must be within specifications.
- Engine exhaust system must be free of restrictions.
- Engine PCV system must flow freely.
- Ensure engine drive sprockets (camshaft and crankshaft) are properly installed, meshed and timed.
- Torque converter stall speed must be within specifications.
- Power brake booster must not have any internal vacuum leaks.
- Fuel must not be contaminated (high alcohol and water content).
- Crossed fuel injector control wires (wrong wire connected to injector) may cause rough idle.

Any one or more of these conditions can cause a driveability related problem. They must be considered as possible causes.

CHARGING SYSTEM TEST NO. 1

CHECKING CHARGING SYSTEM FOR FAULT CODES

1) Connect DRB-II to diagnostic connector. Enter Diagnostic Test Mode. Record all codes. If Fault Code 47 is stored, check for a loose fan belt. Check battery and alternator output.

2) Turn ignition off. Erase fault codes. See ERASING CODES FROM SMEC MEMORY in this article. Start engine and let idle for 7 minutes. Raise engine speed to 1500 RPM for 30 seconds. Stop engine. Enter Diagnostic Test Mode. Refer to ENTERING ON-BOARD DIAGNOSTICS in this article. Record all codes.

3) If same code(s) were stored before and after memory was cleared, problem still exists. If Code 88-12-55 is stored, proceed to CHARGING SYSTEM TEST NO. 2. If Code 88-12-16-55 is stored, proceed to CHARGING SYSTEM TEST NO. 3. If Codes 88-12-41-46-55 or 88-12-46-55 are stored, proceed to CHARGING SYSTEM TEST NO. 4.

4) If Codes 88-12-41-55, 88-12-41-47-55 or 88-12-47-55 are stored, proceed to CHARGING SYSTEM TEST NO. 5. If there is no Code 88, ensure diagnostic readout box is operating properly and that there is not an open circuit between SMEC and DRB-II diagnostic connector.

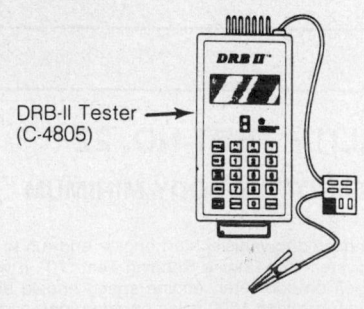

DRB-II Tester → (C-4805)

CHARGING SYSTEM TEST NO. 1 (Cont.)

5) Connect DRB-II as in previous steps. If Code 16 or 41 appeared before fault codes were erased in step 2), fault is intermittent. Enter ATM Test Mode "09" for Code 41 or ATM Test Mode "07" for Code 16. Connect voltmeter to the field control wire of alternator. Wiggle wires and connectors in charging circuit while observing voltage pulsations on voltmeter. When voltage pulsates while a circuit is being wiggled, this indicates an intermittent fault. Repair wire and/or connector. Retest circuits.

CHARGING SYSTEM TEST NO. 2

CHECKING BATTERY TEMPERATURE SENSOR CALIBRATION

1) Connect DRB-II to diagnostic connector. Put system in Engine Running Test Mode "61". Refer to ENTERING ON-BOARD DIAGNOSTICS in this article. If DRB-II display is between .2-3 volts, go to next step. If DRB-II display is not between .2-3 volts, logic board is defective, replace SMEC.

2) Put system in Engine Running Test Mode "67". If DRB-II display is between 13-15 volts, check condition of battery. Check for battery drain condition. If display on DRB-II is not between 13-15 volts, check alternator for low output.

CHARGING SYSTEM TEST NO. 3

CODE 16 – BATTERY VOLTAGE SENSING CIRCUIT

1) Disconnect 60-pin SMEC connector. Connect voltmeter between cavity No. 41 (Red Wire) and vehicle ground.

2) If display is within one volt of battery voltage, logic board is defective, ensure terminal in cavity No. 41 is not damaged, causing a poor connection. If terminal is okay, replace SMEC. If display reads zero volts, repair open in Red wire.

CHARGING SYSTEM TEST NO. 4

CODES 46 OR 41/46 – ALTERNATOR FIELD OUTPUT

1) Disconnect 14-pin connector from SMEC. Separate the 14-pin connector halves. Reconnect the half of connector containing cavities No. 1-7 to SMEC. Using an analog voltmeter, connect positive lead to cavity No. 14 (Dark Green wire). Connect negative lead to cavity No. 11 (Dark Green/Orange wire). Enter ATM Test Mode "09". Refer to ENTERING ON-BOARD DIAGNOSTICS in this article.

1989 COMPUTERIZED ENGINE CONTROLS
Chrysler Motors 2.2L Turbo II MPFI (Cont.)

1a-31

CHARGING SYSTEM TEST NO. 4 (Cont.)

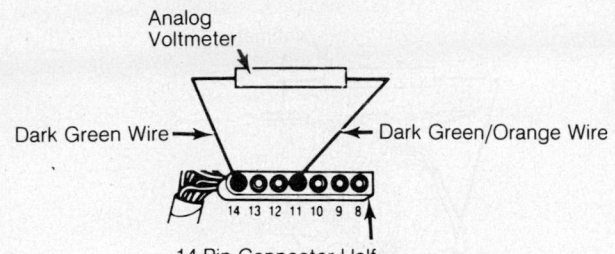

Analog Voltmeter

Dark Green Wire → ← Dark Green/Orange Wire

14 13 12 11 10 9 8

14-Pin Connector Half

2) If voltmeter reading pulsates between 0-12 volts, check terminals in cavities No. 11 and 14 for damage. If terminals are not damaged, power board is defective, replace SMEC. If voltmeter reads zero volts, go to next step.

3) Turn ignition switch to "RUN" position. Connect positive lead of analog voltmeter to cavity No. 14 (Dark Green wire). Connect negative lead to vehicle ground. If voltmeter reads battery voltage, go to next step. If voltmeter reads 0-1 volt, repair short in alternator field circuit.

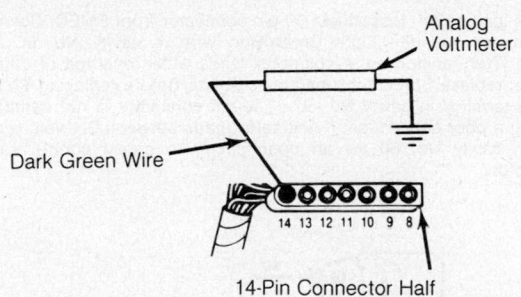

Analog Voltmeter

Dark Green Wire →

14 13 12 11 10 9 8

14-Pin Connector Half

4) Turn ignition off. Disconnect 60-pin connector from SMEC. Connect an ohmmeter between cavity No. 14 (Dark Green wire) of 60-pin connector and vehicle ground. If ohmmeter reads no continuity, check terminal in cavity No. 14 for damage. If terminal in cavity No. 14 is okay, logic board is defective, replace SMEC. If ohmmeter shows continuity, repair short from cavity No. 14 (Dark Green wire) to ground.

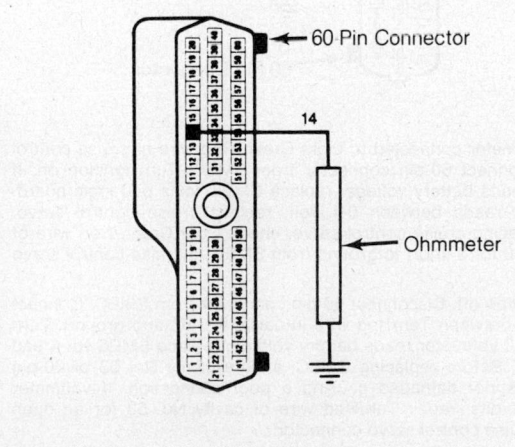

← 60-Pin Connector

14

← Ohmmeter

CHARGING SYSTEM TEST NO. 5

CODES 41 OR 41/47 – ALTERNATOR FIELD LOW CHARGING SYSTEM OUTPUT

1) Connect DRB-II to diagnostic connector. Connect negative lead of voltmeter to battery ground. Enter ATM Test Mode "09". Refer to ENTERING ON-BOARD DIAGNOSTICS in this article. Connect positive lead to each of the alternator field terminals.

2) If voltmeter reads zero volts at both terminals, repair open in Dark Blue wire. If voltmeter reads battery voltage at one terminal and pulsates between 0-12 volts at other terminal, check alternator drive belt for looseness. Check condition of battery and alternator. If voltmeter reads battery voltage at both terminals, go to next step.

3) Turn ignition off. Disconnect 14-pin connector from SMEC. Separate 14-pin connector halves. Connect voltmeter between cavity No. 14 (Dark Green wire) and vehicle ground. Turn ignition switch to "RUN" position. If voltmeter reads battery voltage, go to next step. If voltmeter reads zero volts, repair open in Dark Green wire.

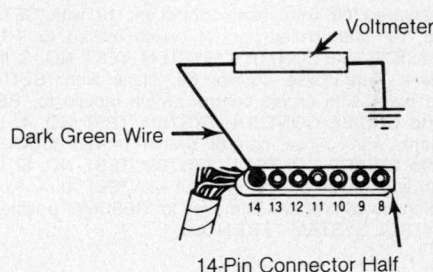

Voltmeter

Dark Green Wire →

14 13 12 11 10 9 8

14-Pin Connector Half

4) Turn ignition switch to "OFF" position. Reconnect the half of connector containing cavities No. 1-7 to SMEC. Connect voltmeter negative lead to cavity No. 11 (Dark Green/Orange wire) and voltmeter positive lead to cavity No. 14 (Dark Green) of 14-pin connector.

5) If voltmeter is pulsating between 0-12 volts, replace SMEC for a defective power board. Before replacing SMEC, check wires in cavities No. 11 and 14 of 14-pin connector for damaged terminals causing a poor connection. If voltmeter reads zero volts, go to next step.

6) With 14-pin connector disconnected from SMEC, turn ignition off. Disconnect 60-pin connector from SMEC. Connect an ohmmeter between Dark Green/Orange wire in cavity No. 11 of 14-pin connector and Dark Green/Orange wire in cavity No. 14 of 60-pin connector. If ohmmeter shows continuity, replace SMEC for a defective logic board.

7) Before replacing SMEC, check cavity No. 14 of 60-pin connector for damage. If terminal in cavity No. 14 of 60-pin connector is not damaged, logic board is defective, replace SMEC. If ohmmeter shows no continuity, repair open in Dark Green/Orange wire for an open between 14-pin connector and 60-pin connector.

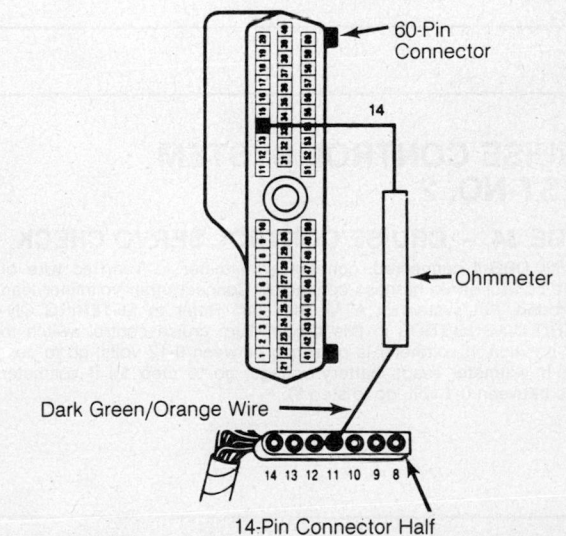

← 60-Pin Connector

14

← Ohmmeter

Dark Green/Orange Wire →

14 13 12 11 10 9 8

14-Pin Connector Half

1a-32

1989 COMPUTERIZED ENGINE CONTROLS
Chrysler Motors 2.2L Turbo II MPFI (Cont.)

CRUISE CONTROL SYSTEM TEST NO. 1

CHECKING CRUISE CONTROL SYSTEM FOR FAULT CODES

1) Connect DRB-II to diagnostic connector. Enter Diagnostic Test Mode. Refer to ENTERING ON-BOARD DIAGNOSTICS in this article. Record all codes. If codes 88-55 or 88-12-55 are displayed (no fault codes), go to next step. If codes 88-34-55 or 88-12-34-55 are displayed (cruise control servo), go to CRUISE CONTROL SYSTEM TEST NO. 2. If codes 88-15-55 or 88-12-15-55 are displayed (speed sensor), go to DRIVEABILITY TEST NO. 3.

2) Put system in Sensor Test "09". Refer to ENTERING ON-BOARD DIAGNOSTICS in this article. Ensure cruise control switch is in "OFF" position. While observing DRB-II, move cruise control switch to "ON" position. Press "SET" button. Move cruise control switch to "RESUME" position. Record displays on tester.

3) If tester displayed "00" with cruise control on, "10" with "SET" button pressed, and "01" with cruise control switch moved to "RESUME" position, go to CRUISE CONTROL SYSTEM TEST NO. 3. If tester displayed blank with cruise control on, blank with "SET" button pressed, and blank with cruise control switch moved to "RESUME" position, go to CRUISE CONTROL SYSTEM TEST NO. 4. If tester displayed blank with cruise control switch moved to "RESUME" position, go to CRUISE CONTROL SYSTEM TEST NO. 5. If tester displayed "00" with cruise control on, "00" with "SET" button pressed, and "00" with cruise control switch moved to "RESUME" position, go to CRUISE CONTROL SYSTEM TEST NO. 6.

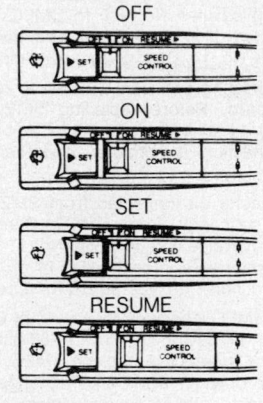

OFF

ON

SET

RESUME

CRUISE CONTROL SYSTEM TEST NO. 2

CODE 34 – CRUISE CONTROL SERVO CHECK

1) With DRB-II connected, connect a voltmeter to Tan/Red wire of cruise control servo harness connector. Connect other voltmeter lead to ground. Put system in ATM Test "08". Refer to ENTERING ON-BOARD DIAGNOSTICS in this article. Turn cruise control switch to "ON" position. If voltmeter is pulsating between 0-12 volts, go to next step. If voltmeter reads battery voltage, go to step **5)**. If voltmeter reads between 0-1 volt, go to step **6)**.

CRUISE CONTROL SYSTEM TEST NO. 2 (Cont.)

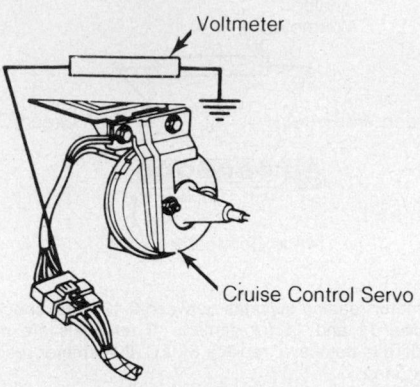

Voltmeter

Cruise Control Servo

2) Turn ignition off. Connect a voltmeter between Light Green/Red wire at cruise control servo harness connector and ground. Turn ignition on. Turn cruise control on. If voltmeter reads battery voltage, go to next step. If voltmeter reads between 0-1 volt, go to step **4)**.

3) Turn ignition off. Disconnect 60-pin connector from SMEC. Connect a voltmeter between Light Green/Red wire in cavity No. 60 and ground. Turn ignition on. If voltmeter reads within one volt of battery voltage, replace SMEC for a bad logic board. Before replacing SMEC, ensure terminal in cavity No. 60 of 60-pin connector is not damaged causing a poor connection. If voltmeter reads between 0-1 volt, repair wire in cavity No. 60 for an open circuit to cruise control servo connector.

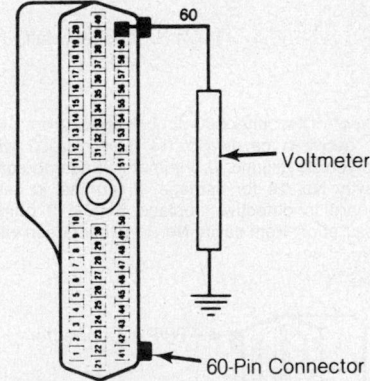

60

Voltmeter

60-Pin Connector

4) With voltmeter connected to Light Green/Red wire of cruise control servo, disconnect 60-pin connector from SMEC. Turn ignition on. If voltmeter reads battery voltage, replace SMEC for a bad logic board. If voltmeter reads between 0-1 volt, replace cruise control servo. Before replacing cruise control servo, check Light Green/Red wire of cavity No. 60 for a short to ground from SMEC to cruise control servo connector.

5) Turn ignition off. Disconnect 60-pin connector from SMEC. Connect a voltmeter between Tan/Red wire in cavity No. 53 and ground. Turn ignition on. If voltmeter reads battery voltage, replace SMEC for a bad logic board. Before replacing SMEC, ensure cavity No. 53 of 60-pin connector is not damaged causing a poor connection. If voltmeter reads zero volts, repair Tan/Red wire of cavity No. 53 for an open circuit to cruise control servo connector.

1989 COMPUTERIZED ENGINE CONTROLS
Chrysler Motors 2.2L Turbo II MPFI (Cont.)

1a-33

CRUISE CONTROL SYSTEM
TEST NO. 2 (Cont.)

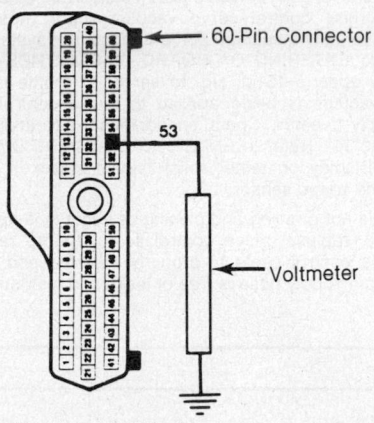

60-Pin Connector

53

Voltmeter

6) With voltmeter connected to Tan/Red wire of cruise control servo harness and ground, disconnect 60-pin connector from SMEC. Turn ignition on. If voltmeter reads battery voltage, replace SMEC for a bad logic board. If voltmeter reads between 0-1 volt, go to next step.

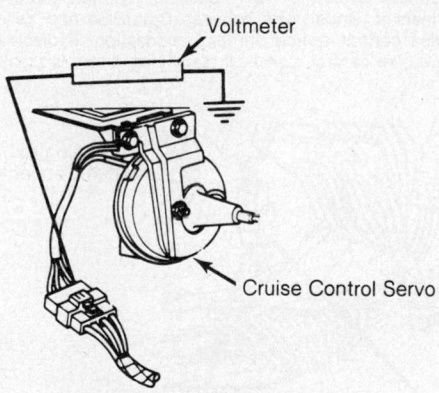

Voltmeter

Cruise Control Servo

7) With cruise control switch in "ON" position, turn ignition off. Connect a voltmeter between Dark Blue/Red wire of cruise control servo connector and ground. Turn ignition on. If voltmeter still reads between 0-1 volt, go to next step.

8) With cruise control and ignition on, connect a voltmeter between Dark Blue/Red wire of brake switch harness connector and ground. If voltmeter reads battery voltage, repair Dark Blue/Red wire for an open circuit to cruise control servo. If voltmeter still reads between 0-1 volt, go to next step.

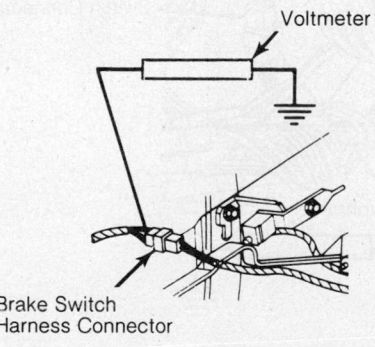

Voltmeter

Brake Switch
Harness Connector

CRUISE CONTROL SYSTEM
TEST NO. 2 (Cont.)

9) Connect a voltmeter between Yellow/Red wire of brake switch harness connector and ground. If voltmeter reads battery voltage, check brake switch adjustment. If brake switch adjustment is okay, replace brake switch. If voltmeter reads zero volts, repair Yellow/Red wire for an open circuit to wiring harness splice. Make sure fuse for Yellow/Red wire is not blown.

CRUISE CONTROL SYSTEM
TEST NO. 3

GROUND CIRCUIT CHECK

1) Turn ignition off. Disconnect cruise control servo connector. Connect an ohmmeter between Black wire of cruise control servo connector and ground. If ohmmeter is reading continuity, go to next step. If ohmmeter reads no continuity, repair Black wire for an open circuit to wiring harness splice.

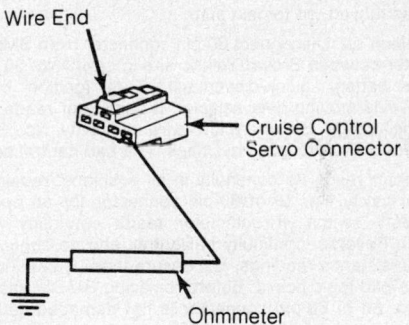

Wire End

Cruise Control
Servo Connector

Ohmmeter

2) With DRB-II connected to diagnostic connector, put system in Switch Test Mode. Refer to ENTERING ON-BOARD DIAGNOSTICS in this article. Press down on brake pedal. If display on tester changes as brake pedal was depressed (not important what display changes to, just ensure display changes), go to step **4)**. If display on tester did not change as brake pedal was depressed, go to next step.

3) Turn ignition off. Disconnect 60-pin connector. Connect an ohmmeter between White/Pink wire in cavity No. 29 and ground. Press down on brake pedal and then release. If ohmmeter reads no continuity when brake pedal is pressed down and continuity when brake pedal is released, replace SMEC for a bad logic board. Before replacing SMEC, ensure cavity No. 29 of 60-pin connector is not damaged causing a poor connection. If ohmmeter does not indicate as described, check White/Pink wire of cavity No. 29 for an open circuit through stoplight bulb circuit to ground.

1a-34

1989 COMPUTERIZED ENGINE CONTROLS
Chrysler Motors 2.2L Turbo II MPFI (Cont.)

CRUISE CONTROL SYSTEM
TEST NO. 3 (Cont.)

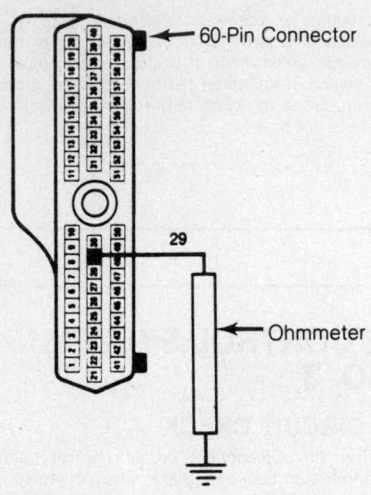

60-Pin Connector

29

Ohmmeter

4) While observing display on tester, put gear selector in Park, Reverse, Neutral, and Drive. If display on tester changes as gear selector is moved, go to step 7) (disregard what tester displays, just ensure display changes). If display on tester did not change when gear selector was moved, go to next step.

5) Turn ignition off. Disconnect 60-pin connector from SMEC. Connect an ohmmeter between Brown/Yellow wire in cavity No. 30 and ground. Disconnect battery quick-disconnect. Turn ignition on. Observe ohmmeter while moving gear selector. If ohmmeter reads continuity in all positions, check Brown/Yellow wire of cavity No. 30 of 60-pin connector for a short to ground. Check for a bad neutral safety switch.

6) If ohmmeter reads no continuity in all positions, repair Brown/Yellow wire of cavity No. 30 of 60-pin connector for an open circuit to neutral safety switch. If ohmmeter reads continuity in Park, no continuity in Reverse, continuity in Neutral, and no continuity in Drive (disregard resistance readings, just ensure there is continuity), replace SMEC for a bad logic board. Before replacing SMEC, ensure terminal in cavity No. 30 of 60-pin connector is not damaged causing a poor connection.

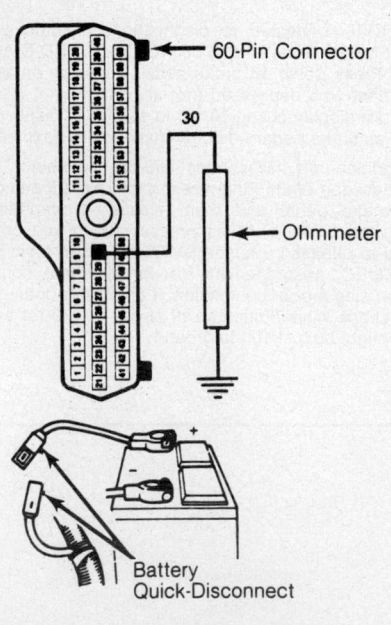

60-Pin Connector

30

Ohmmeter

Battery
Quick-Disconnect

CRUISE CONTROL SYSTEM
TEST NO. 3 (Cont.)

7) Connect cruise control servo connector. With DRB-II connected, disconnect cruise control servo vacuum supply hose from brake booster and connect a vacuum pump to hose. Put system in ATM Test "08". Refer to ENTERING ON-BOARD DIAGNOSTICS in this article. Continuously apply 5-15 in. Hg. to servo. If throttle is opening and closing as vacuum is being applied to cruise control servo, check vacuum supply to servo. Check speed sensor operation using Engine Running Test "71". Refer to ENTERING ON-BOARD DIAGNOSTICS in this article. Display on tester must remain stable. If display is not stable, replace speed sensor.

8) If throttle is not opening and closing as vacuum is applied to cruise control servo, replace cruise control servo. Before replacing servo, ensure cruise control cable is properly adjusted and not damaged. Ensure vacuum supply hose is free of leaks and restrictions.

CRUISE CONTROL SYSTEM
TEST NO. 4

POWER SUPPLY CHECK

1) With DRB-II connected to vehicle, put system in Sensor Test "09". Put speed control switch in "ON" position. Without disconnecting harness, connect a jumper wire between Dark/Blue and Yellow/Red wires of cruise control switch harness connection. If display reads "00", replace cruise control switch. If display on tester is blank, go to next step.

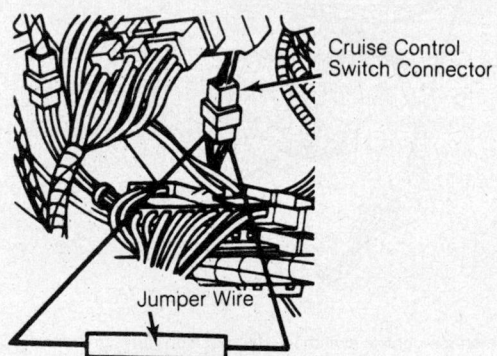

Cruise Control
Switch Connector

Jumper Wire

2) Turn ignition off. Without disconnecting connector, connect a voltmeter between Dark Blue/Red wire of cruise control switch harness connector and ground. Turn ignition on. If voltmeter reads within one volt of battery voltage, go to next step. If voltmeter reads zero volts, repair Dark Blue/Red wire for an open circuit to fuse box.

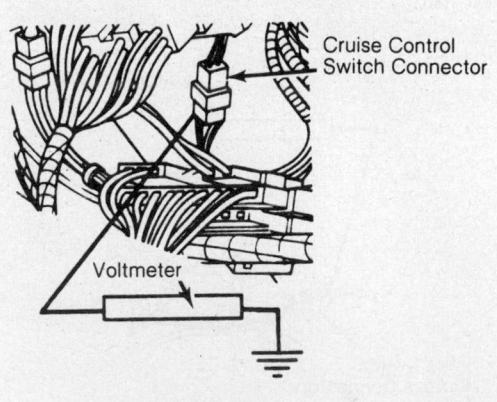

Cruise Control
Switch Connector

Voltmeter

1989 COMPUTERIZED ENGINE CONTROLS
Chrysler Motors 2.2L Turbo II MPFI (Cont.)

1a-35

CRUISE CONTROL SYSTEM
TEST NO. 4 (Cont.)

3) Turn ignition off. Disconnect 60-pin connector. Connect a voltmeter between Yellow/Red wire in cavity No. 8 and ground. Turn ignition on. If voltmeter reads battery voltage, replace SMEC for a bad logic board. Before replacing SMEC, ensure terminal in cavity No. 8 of 60-pin connector is not damaged causing a poor connection. If voltmeter reads zero volts, repair Yellow/Red wire in cavity No. 8 for an open circuit to cruise control switch.

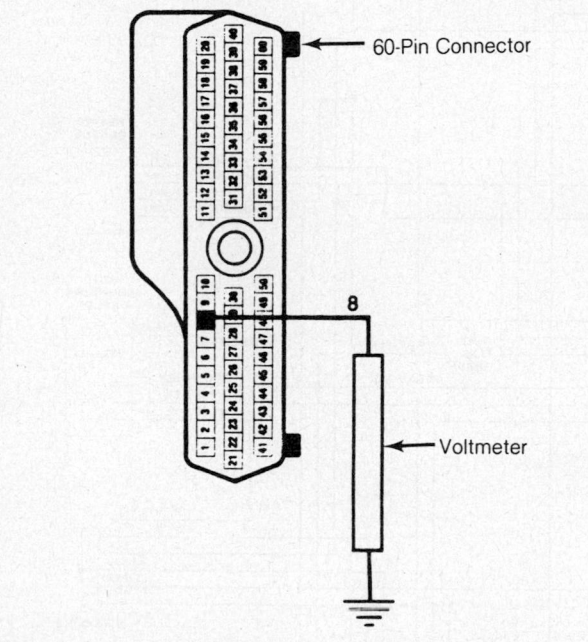

CRUISE CONTROL SYSTEM
TEST NO. 5

SET CIRCUIT CHECK

1) With DRB-II connected to diagnostic connector, put system in Sensor Test "09". Refer to ENTERING ON-BOARD DIAGNOSTICS in this article. Turn cruise control on. Without disconnecting connector, connect a jumper wire between Dark Blue/Red and Brown/Red wires of cruise control switch harness connector. If display on tester is "00", replace cruise control switch. If display on tester is "10", go to next step.

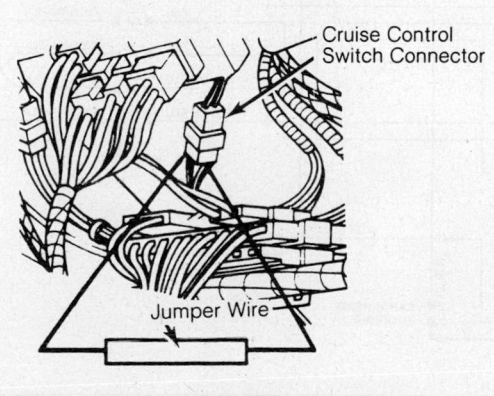

CRUISE CONTROL SYSTEM
TEST NO. 5 (Cont.)

2) Turn ignition off. Disconnect 60-pin connector from SMEC. Connect a voltmeter between Brown/Red wire in cavity No. 9 and ground. Turn ignition on. If voltmeter reads battery voltage, replace SMEC for a bad logic board. Before replacing SMEC, check cavity No. 9 of 60-pin connector for an open circuit to cruise control switch. If voltmeter reads zero volts, repair Brown/Red wire of cavity No. 9 for an open circuit to cruise control switch.

CRUISE CONTROL SYSTEM
TEST NO. 6

RESUME CIRCUIT CHECK

1) With DRB-II connected to diagnostic connector, put system in Sensor Test "09". Refer to ENTERING ON-BOARD DIAGNOSTICS in this article. Turn cruise control on. Without disconnecting connector connect a jumper wire between White and Dark Blue/Red wires of cruise control switch harness connector. If tester displays "01", replace cruise control switch. If tester displays "00", go to next step.

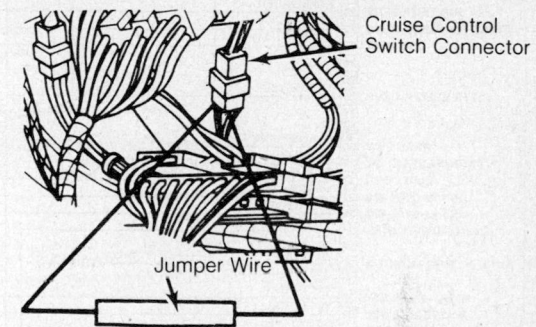

2) Turn ignition off. Disconnect 60-pin connector from SMEC. Connect a voltmeter between White/Light Green wire in cavity No. 7 of 60-pin connector and ground. Turn ignition on. Move cruise control switch to "RESUME" position. If voltmeter reads battery voltage, replace SMEC for a bad logic board. Before replacing SMEC, check terminal in cavity No. 7 of 60-pin connector for an open circuit to cruise control switch. If voltmeter reads zero volts, repair White/Light Green wire in cavity No. 7 for an open circuit to cruise control swtich.

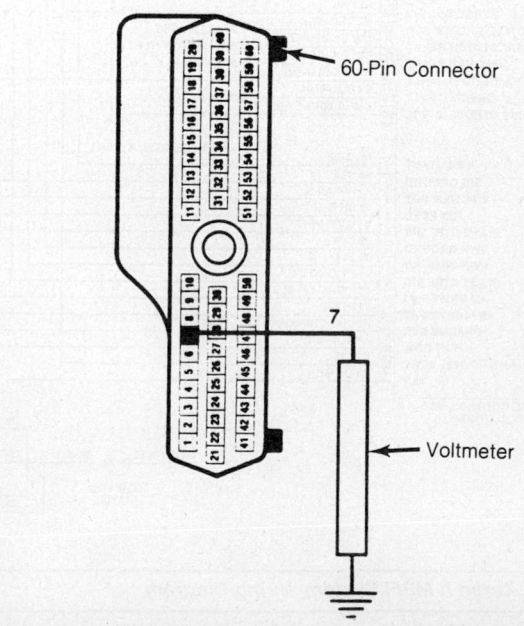

1989 Computerized ENGINE CONTROLS
Chrysler Motors 2.2L Turbo II MPFI (Cont.)

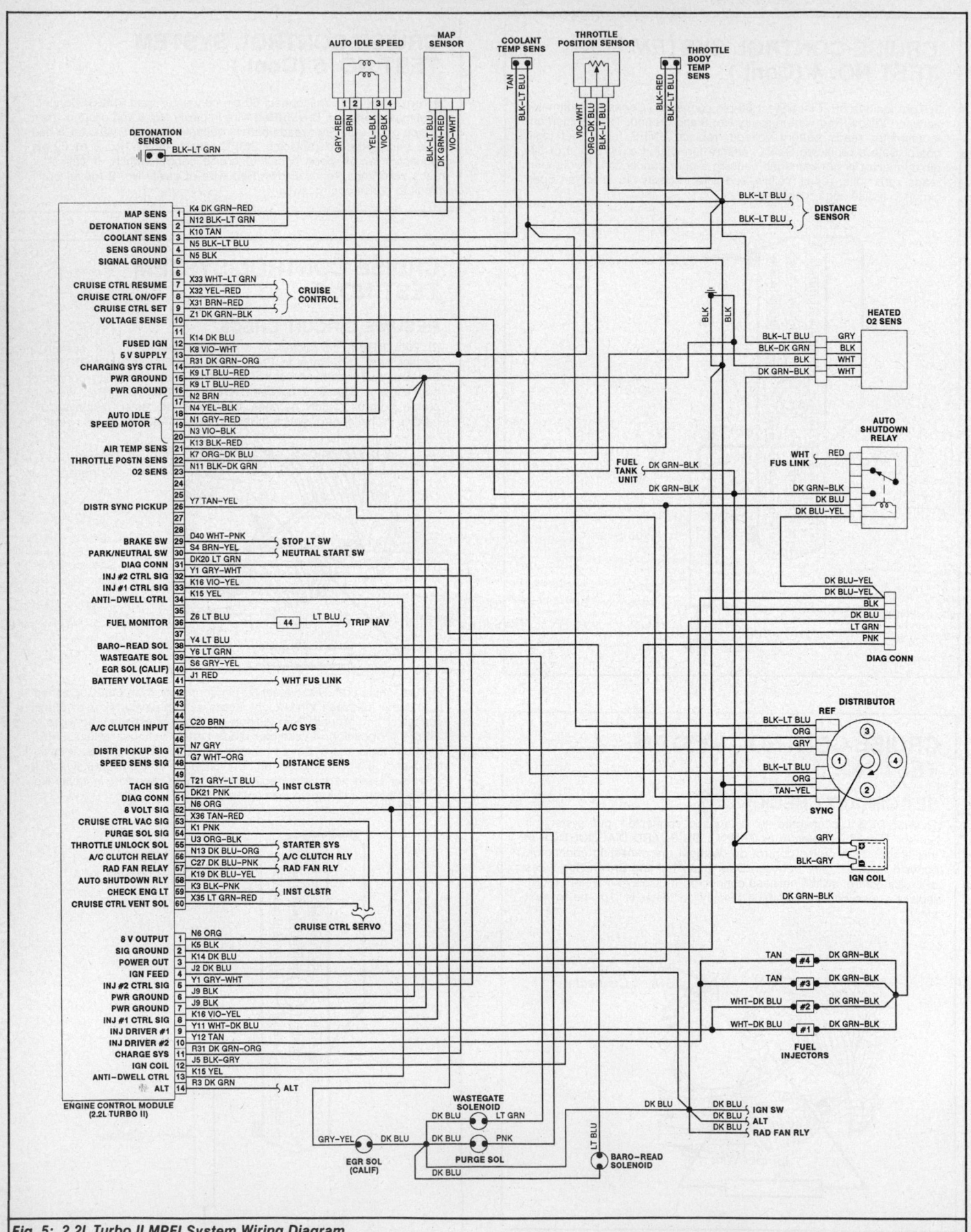

Fig. 5: 2.2L Turbo II MPFI System Wiring Diagram

Acclaim, Aries, Daytona, Dynasty, Horizon, Lancer, LeBaron, New Yorker, Omni, Reliant, Shadow, Spirit, Sundance

MODEL IDENTIFICATION

VEHICLE BODY IDENTIFICATION

Model Name	Body Type
Acclaim & Spirit	A Body
Aries & Reliant	K Body
Daytona	G Body
Dynasty & New Yorker	C Body
Horizon & Omni	L Body
Lancer & LeBaron GTS	H Body
LeBaron	J Body
Shadow & Sundance	P Body

DESCRIPTION

The Single Point Fuel Injection (SPFI) computerized engine control system controls the fuel system, ignition system and emission control system.

The engine control system utilizes a Single Module Engine Controller (SMEC) to regulate air/fuel ratio, charging system, cooling fan, emission control components, idle speed and ignition timing.

OPERATION

AIR CONDITIONING CLUTCH RELAY

The A/C clutch relay is powered by the radiator fan relay, A/C switch and SMEC. The relay is energized to closed position (on) during engine operation with A/C switch closed and blower switch on. When the SMEC senses wide open throttle or low engine RPM through the throttle position sensor, SMEC will de-energize the A/C clutch relay, disengaging A/C clutch.

AUTO SHUTDOWN (ASD) RELAY

When distributor signal is not present with ignition switch in "RUN" position, the ASD relay turns power off to the electric fuel pump, fuel injectors, ignition coil and O_2 sensor heating element.

AUTOMATIC IDLE SPEED (AIS) MOTOR

AIS motor adjusts idle speed to compensate for engine load and ambient temperature. The AIS motor varies the amount of air by-pass through throttle body. SMEC uses coolant temperature, distance (speed) sensor, throttle position sensor, and various switch inputs to adjust AIS to obtain optimum idle conditions.

CANISTER PURGE SOLENOID

The canister purge solenoid is controlled by the SMEC. During engine warm-up and after hot restarts, the SMEC completes a ground, energizing the purge solenoid. When purge solenoid is energized, this prevents vacuum from reaching canister valve.

After engine reaches operating temperature and a timer has run out, the SMEC de-energizes the solenoid by turning off the ground, allowing fuel vapors to be drawn into the throttle body. The SMEC will also energize purge solenoid under certain idle conditions, this updates fuel delivery calibration.

CHECK ENGINE LIGHT

The check engine light will illuminate for 3 seconds as a bulb test every time the ignition is turned on. If the SMEC receives an

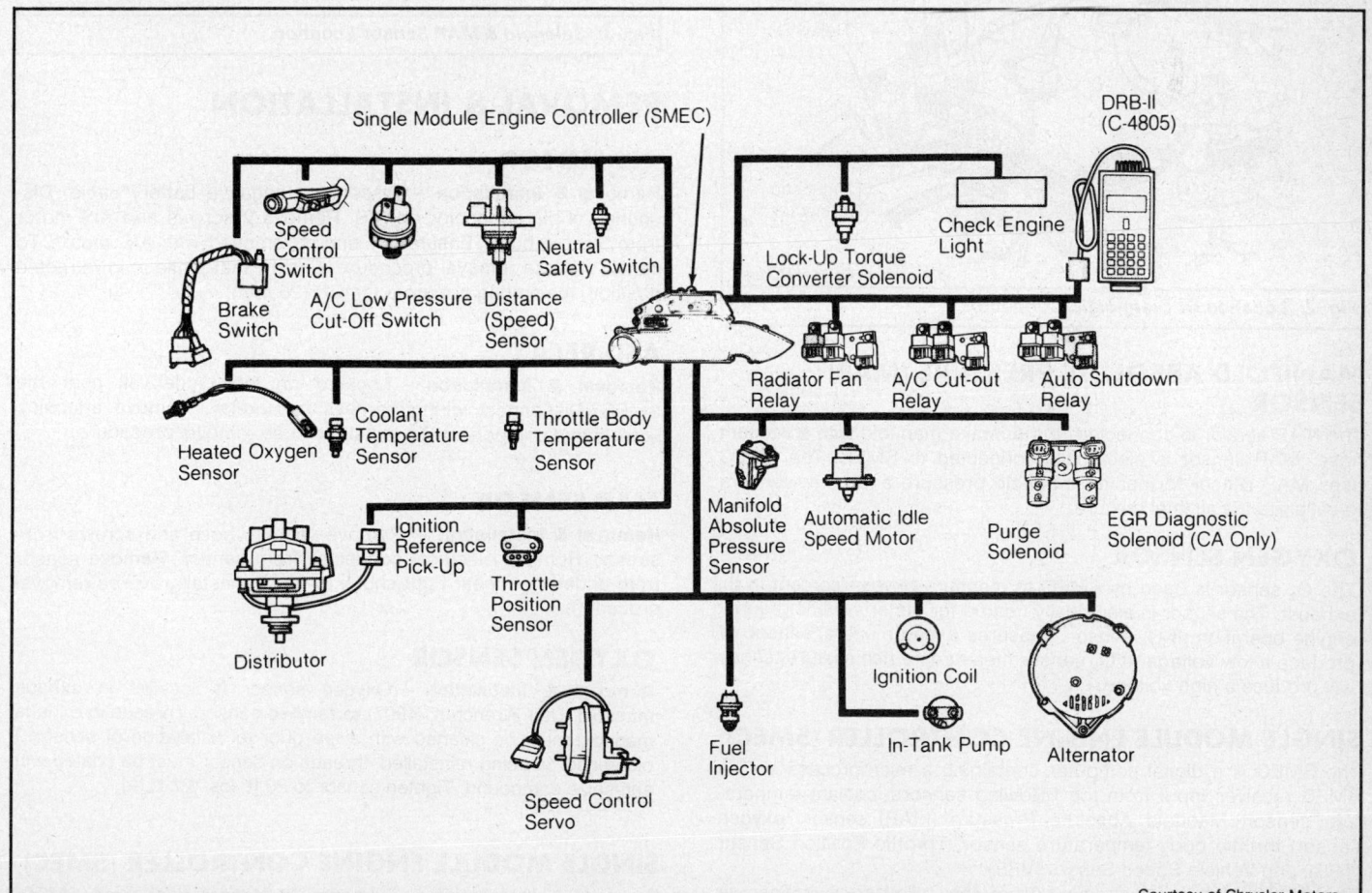

Fig. 1: Schematic Diagram of Computer, Input Sensors & Output Devices (SPFI)

1a-38

1989 COMPUTERIZED ENGINE CONTROLS
Chrysler Motors 2.2L & 2.5L SPFI (Cont.)

incorrect or no signal from certain sensors or emission related systems on California vehicles, the check engine light will be illuminated. This warns driver that SMEC has gone into a limp-in mode to keep system operational.

COOLANT TEMPERATURE SENSOR

The coolant temperature sensor is located in the thermostat housing. Input from this sensor allows SMEC to richen air/fuel mixtures until normal operating temperature is reached. The sensor is a variable resistor with a range of -40°F (-40°C) to 265°F (129°C). This sensor is also used to turn on radiator fan.

DISTANCE (SPEED) SENSOR

This sensor is located on transaxle extension housing. The sensor generates 8 pulses per axle shaft revolution. The SMEC will interpret distance (speed) sensor input along with throttle position sensor closed throttle input.

This will allow SMEC to differentiate between closed throttle decel and closed throttle idle (vehicle stopped) conditions. During decel, SMEC controls Automatic Idle Speed (AIS) motor to maintain a desired manifold absolute pressure value. During idle (vehicle stopped), the SMEC controls AIS motor to maintain a desired idle speed.

LIMP-IN MODE

If SMEC senses incorrect data or no data from certain sensors or emission related systems on California vehicles, SMEC will put system in limp-in mode and illuminate check engine light.

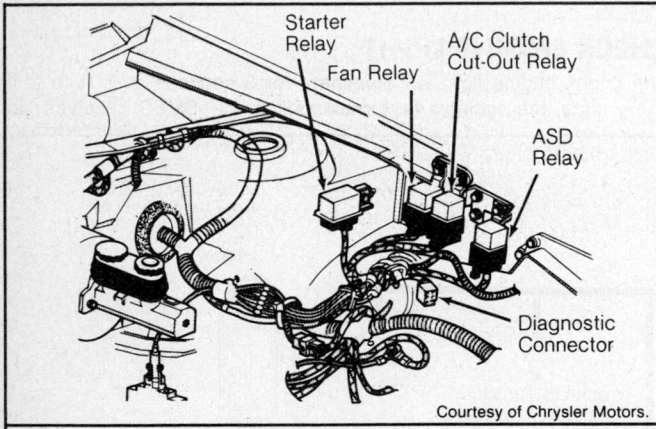

Fig. 2: Location Of Diagnostic Connector

MANIFOLD ABSOLUTE PRESSURE (MAP) SENSOR

The MAP sensor is connected to the intake manifold with a vacuum hose. MAP sensor is electrically connected to SMEC. The SMEC uses MAP sensor to monitor manifold pressure and other sensors to calibrate the air/fuel mixture.

OXYGEN SENSOR

The O_2 sensor is used by SMEC to measure oxygen content in the exhaust. The sensor is electrically heated for faster switching during engine operation. If O_2 sensor measures a lean mixture, sensor will produce a low voltage. If O_2 sensor measures a rich mixture, sensor will produce a high voltage.

SINGLE MODULE ENGINE CONTROLLER (SMEC)

The SMEC is a digital computer containing a microprocessor. The SMEC receives input from the following sensors: coolant temperature sensor, Manifold Absolute Pressure (MAP) sensor, oxygen sensor, throttle body temperature sensor, Throttle Position Sensor (TPS), and Vehicle Speed Sensor (VSS).

The SMEC also receives input from the following switches: air conditioning clutch switch, brake switch, speed control switches,

and neutral safety switch. During operation, the SMEC monitors many of its own input and output circuits. If a fault is detected, the computer will go into limp-in mode and store a trouble code to help in diagnosis of the system.

THROTTLE BODY TEMPERATURE SENSOR

The throttle body temperature sensor is mounted in throttle body. Throttle body temperature is the same as fuel temperature. This sensor allows SMEC to slightly richen air/fuel ratio during a hot restart condition.

THROTTLE POSITION SENSOR (TPS)

The TPS is an electronic variable resistor. The SMEC uses TPS input and input from other sensors to adjust air/fuel ratio for varying driveability conditions.

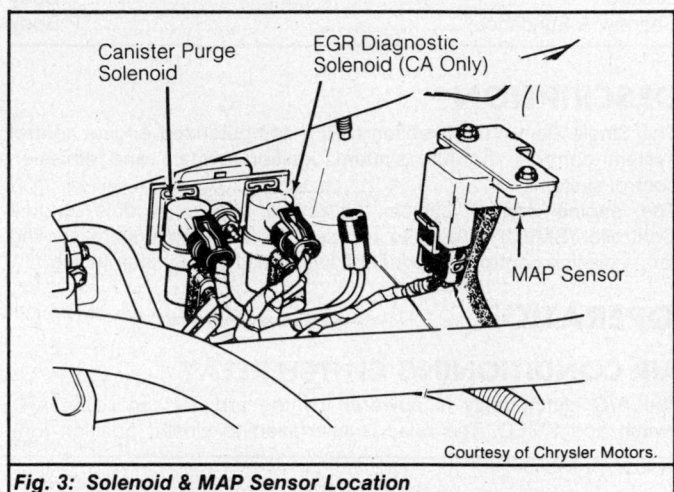

Fig. 3: Solenoid & MAP Sensor Location

REMOVAL & INSTALLATION

AIS MOTOR

Removal & Installation – Disconnect negative battery cable. Disconnect 4-pin connector on AIS. Remove 2 screws and AIS motor from throttle body. Ensure "O" ring is removed with AIS motor. To install, reverse removal procedure. Ensure that pintle is in retracted position, measuring not more than 1" (25 mm).

ASD RELAY

Removal & Installation – Located on left fenderwell near the SMEC. Disconnect wiring harness from relay. Remove attaching screws and component. To install, reverse removal procedure.

MAP SENSOR

Removal & Installation – Remove vacuum hose and screws from sensor. Remove electrical connector from sensor. Remove sensor from underhood, near right shock tower. To install, reverse removal procedure.

OXYGEN SENSOR

Removal & Installation – Oxygen sensor is located in exhaust manifold. Use Wrench (C-4907) to remove sensor. Threads in exhaust manifold must be cleaned with a tap prior to installation of sensor. If old sensor is being reinstalled, threads on sensor must be coated with anti-seize compound. Tighten sensor to 20 ft. lbs. (27 N.m).

SINGLE MODULE ENGINE CONTROLLER (SMEC)

Removal & Installation – Remove air cleaner duct from SMEC. Remove battery and 2 module mounting bolts. Remove 14-pin and

60-pin wiring connectors from module. Remove module. To install, reverse removal procedure.

THROTTLE BODY TEMPERATURE SENSOR

Removal & Installation – Remove air cleaner. Disconnect throttle cables from throttle body. Remove 2 screws from throttle cable bracket. Lay throttle cable bracket aside. Disconnect electrical connector from sensor. Unscrew sensor from throttle body.

THROTTLE POSITION SENSOR (TPS)

Removal & Installation – Disconnect negative battery cable and remove air cleaner. Disconnect 3-pin connector at throttle position sensor. Remove 2 screws mounting throttle position sensor to throttle body. Lift throttle position sensor from throttle shaft. To install, reverse removal procedure.

TESTING & DIAGNOSIS

PRELIMINARY CHECKS

Most driveability problems in the engine control system result from faulty wiring or leaking hose connections. To avoid unnecessary component testing, a visual check should be performed before beginning trouble shooting procedures to help spot these common faults. A preliminary visual check should include:
- Air ducts to air cleaner and from air cleaner to throttle body.
- Electrical connections at all components. Clean, tight and unbroken.

Check vacuum lines for secure, leak-free connections in these areas:
- Canister purge hose (this hose has a tee connector in it.)
- EGR vacuum line on EGR valve and EGR solenoid. Check hose between backpressure valve and exhaust supply tube on EGR.
- Evaporative control system.
- Fuel pressure regulator vacuum hose.
- MAP sensor.
- PCV valve hose and correct PCV valve.
- Power brake, speed control, heater and A/C system vacuum hoses.
- Throttle body.

Ensure the following electrical connectors are securely attached:
- 14-pin and 60-pin connectors at Single Module Engine Controller (SMEC).
- A/C clutch relay connector.
- AIS motor connector.
- ASD relay connector.
- Canister purge solenoid connector.
- Charge temperature sensor connector.
- Check engine light.
- Coolant temperature sensor connector.
- Distance (speed) sensor connector.
- Distributor connector.
- EGR diagnostic solenoid connector (California only).
- Fuel injector connector.
- Heated O_2 sensor connector.
- MAP sensor connector.
- Radiator fan relay connector.
- TPS connector.

SYSTEM DIAGNOSIS

The self-diagnostic capabilities of this system, if properly utilized, can greatly simplify testing. The SMEC has been programmed to monitor several different circuits of the engine control system. If a problem is sensed with a monitored circuit, a fault code is stored in the SMEC.

The check engine light will illuminate and SMEC will enter limp-in mode. In this mode, SMEC attempts to compensate for the failure of a particular component by substituting information from other sources. This will allow vehicle to be operated until proper repairs can be made.

Once these codes are known, refer to FAULT CODES listed in this article to determine the questionable circuit. Test circuits and repair or replace as necessary. If problem is repaired or ceases to exist, the logic module cancels fault codes after 50-100 ignition on/off cycles. If DRB-II is being used, refer to CLEARING CODES in this article.

The setting of a specific fault code is the result of a particular system failure, NOT the reason for that failure, such as failure of a specific component. The existence of a particular code denotes the probable area of the malfunction, not necessarily the failed component itself.

DIAGNOSTIC PROCEDURE

Refer to ENTERING ON-BOARD DIAGNOSTICS to retrieve fault codes. When using check engine light to retrieve fault codes, refer to description of DRB-II display under FAULT CODES for an explanation of fault code. Once description of fault code is obtained, refer to appropriate trouble shooting chart to diagnose problem. Use trouble shooting chart titles to find appropriate chart.

If no fault codes are present, but vehicle still displays one of the following conditions, go to appropriate test.
- No start condition. Go to NS-1.
- Cold driveability problem. Go to DR-1.
- Warm driveability problem. Go to DR-1.
- Check engine light is illuminated. Go to DR-1.
- Charging system problem. Go to CH-1.
- Speed control system problem. Go to SP-1.

NOTE: When using trouble shooting charts for diagnosis, DO NOT skip any steps in chart, as incorrect diagnosis will result.

Before proceeding with diagnosis, the following precautions must be followed:
- Vehicle must have a fully charged battery.
- When performing a cold driveability test, engine must not have been started for at least 7 hours.
- When performing a warm driveability test, engine must be at normal operating temperature.
- When probing SMEC connectors, probe connectors from pin side. DO NOT backprobe connectors.
- When performing electrical tests, be careful to not cause any short circuits. This will set more fault codes, making diagnosis of original problem more difficult.
- DO NOT use a test light in place of a voltmeter.
- When checking for spark, ensure coil wire is no more than 1/4" from ground. If wire is farther away from ground, damage to SMEC may result.
- DO NOT prolong testing of fuel injectors as engine may hydrostatically lock.
- Always repair lowest fault number (check engine light) or first fault displayed (DRB-II), first.
- Always perform indicated verification test after repairs are made.

ENTERING ON-BOARD DIAGNOSTICS

Using Check Engine Light – 1) Start engine (if possible). Move transmission shift lever through all positions, ending in Park. Turn A/C switch on, then off (if equipped).

2) Turn engine off. Without starting engine again, turn ignition on, off, on, off and on. Record 2-digit fault codes as displayed by flashing check engine light.

3) For example, Code 23 is displayed as flash, flash, 4 second pause, flash, flash, flash. After a slightly longer pause, any other codes stored are displayed in numerical order.

4) Once check engine light begins to flash fault codes, it cannot be stopped. If you loose count, it will be necessary to start over. Code 55 indicates end of fault code display. Refer to FAULT CODES in this article.

1a-40

1989 COMPUTERIZED ENGINE CONTROLS
Chrysler Motors 2.2L & 2.5L SPFI (Cont.)

Using DRB-II – 1) Attach DRB-II Tester (C-4805) to self-test connector. Connector is located in engine compartment near left shock tower.

2) Start engine (if possible). Move transmission shift lever through all positions, ending in Park. Turn A/C switch on, then off (if equipped).

3) Turn engine off. Without starting engine again, turn ignition on. Enter vehicle model year and engine size. Read fault data on DRB-II. Refer to FAULT CODES in this article.

DRB-II Switch Test Mode – The SMEC can only recognize high and low states on switch circuits. SMEC cannot tell the difference between an open or short circuit, or a defective switch.

The DRB-II display must change between "00" and "88" and flash check engine light when brake switch, gear shift selector and A/C switch (if equipped) are activated and released.

DRB-II Read Input States – This state on DRB-II allows technician to read input states of Z1 voltage sense, park/neutral switch, brake switch, A/C switch and speed control resume, on/off and set switches. DRB-II will display "INPUT LOW" or "INPUT HIGH" as SMEC senses component status changing.

DRB-II Read Output States – This state on DRB-II allows technician to read output states of speed control vacuum solenoid, purge solenoid, Part Throttle Unlock (PTU) solenoid, A/C clutch relay, radiator fan relay, ASD relay, check engine light, speed control vent solenoid and EGR solenoid. DRB-II will display "ENERGIZED" OR "DE-ENERGIZED" as SMEC senses component status changing.

DRB-II Actuate Solenoids & Relays – This state on DRB-II allows SMEC to actuate radiator fan relay, A/C clutch relay, ASD relay, purge solenoid, speed control servo solenoids, Part Throttle Unlock (PTU) solenoid and EGR solenoid. With tester in this state, SMEC can also actuate all solenoids and relays simultaneously. This test allows technician to visually and physically observe components under operation.

DRB-II Actuate Outputs – This state on DRB-II allows SMEC to actuate ignition coil, fuel injector, AIS motor open and close, alternator field, tachometer output (tach should read 1364 RPM) and fuel monitor signal. During this test, DRB-II will read "ACTUATING".

DRB-II Read Sensor Voltages – This state on DRB-II allows technician to read battery temperature sensor, oxygen sensor, coolant temperature sensor, TPS sensor, minimum throttle position in volts, battery voltage, MAP sensor and throttle body temperature sensor in volts.

DRB-II Read Sensor Values – This state on DRB-II allows technician to read throttle body temperature sensor in degrees fahrenheit or centigrade, coolant temperature in degrees fahrenheit or centigrade, manifold pressure in inches of vacuum or kilopascals, AIS motor in steps, added adaptive fuel in microseconds, adaptive fuel factor in percent, barometric pressure in inches of mercury or or kilopascals, engine speed in RPM, SMEC spark advance in

degrees, vehicle speed given in MPH and oxygen sensor state given as center, rich or lean.

DRB-II Set Engine RPM – This state on DRB-II allows technician to set engine RPM at a fixed speed from 900-2000 in 100 RPM increments. This allows for accuracy of AIS motor control to be checked.

DRB-II Minimum Airflow Speed – This state on DRB-II allows technician to completely close AIS motor to check minimum idle speed.

DRB-II Emissions EMR Tests – This state on DRB-II allows technician to reset emission reminder light and mileage. This is only used on trucks.

DRB-II Read Module Information – This state on DRB-II allows technician to read SMEC part number and application.

DRB-II PROBLEMS & ERROR MESSAGES

Blank Message Screen – 1) Connect DRB-II to a different vehicle. If message screen is still blank, DRB-II or cable adapter are faulty. Substitute to find faulty component. If message screen is not blank, DRB-II and cable adapter are functioning properly.

2) Inspect diagnostic connector for proper wire placement, damaged terminals or pushed out pins. Repair as necessary. If connector is okay, check Black/White ground wire of diagnostic connector for continuity to ground. Repair as necessary.

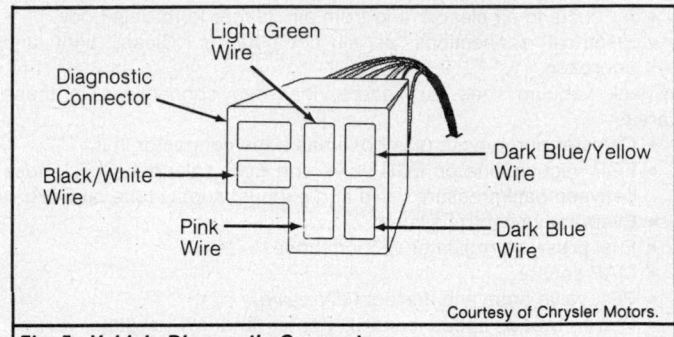

Courtesy of Chrysler Motors.

Fig. 5: Vehicle Diagnostic Connector

"NO RESPONSE" Message – 1) Disconnect SMEC 60-pin connector. Ensure ignition is turned on. Using an ohmmeter, check Pink wire of diagnostic connector for continuity to SMEC 60-pin connector cavity No. 51.

2) Check Light Green wire of diagnostic connector for continuity to SMEC 60-pin connector cavity No. 31. If continuity is not present, repair circuit as necessary. If continuity is present, replace SMEC. Attempt retest.

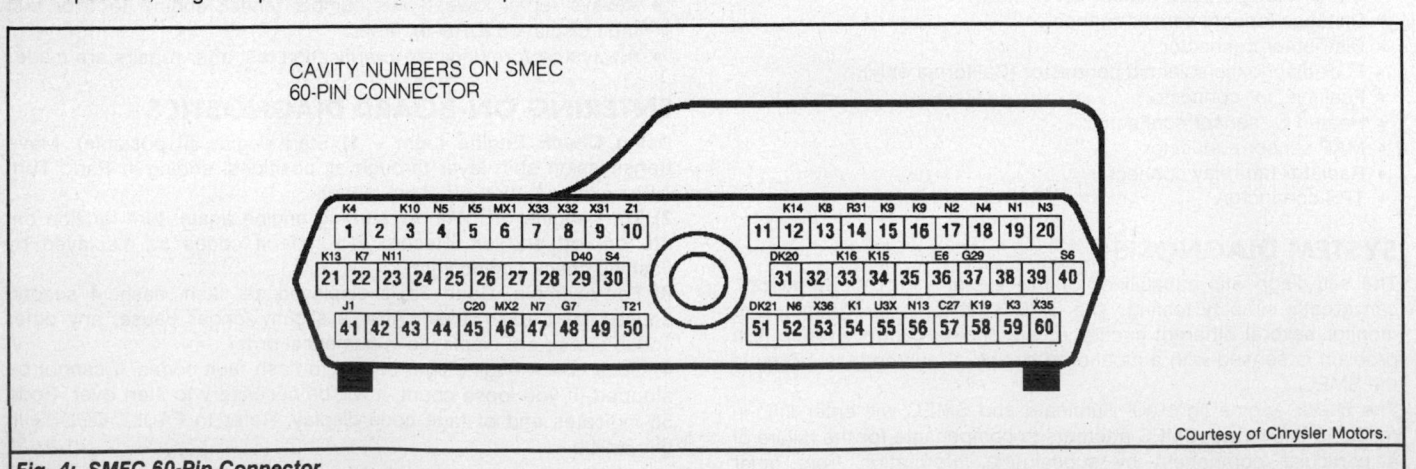

Courtesy of Chrysler Motors.

Fig. 4: SMEC 60-Pin Connector

1989 COMPUTERIZED ENGINE CONTROLS
Chrysler Motors 2.2L & 2.5L SPFI (Cont.)

1a-41

"RAM TEST FAILURE" Message – Replace DRB-II.

"CARTRIDGE ERROR" Message – Replace DRB-II cartridge.

"KEY PAD TEST FAILURE" Message – Power up DRB-II again with fingers off keypad. If error message returns, replace DRB-II.

"HIGH OR LOW BATTERY" Message – Correct condition of vehicle battery and reconnect DRB-II.

CLEARING CODES

Using DRB-II, select test "ERASE FAULT DATA". Press "YES" key on DRB-II. DRB-II will display "ARE YOU SURE? YES/NO". Press "YES" key on tester. Tester will display "ERASING FAULT DATA X". When DRB-II is finished erasing fault codes, it will display "FAULT DATA ERASED".

If DRB-II is not available, fault codes may be cleared by allowing 50-100 key on/off cycles to occur. This will allow SMEC to clear fault codes.

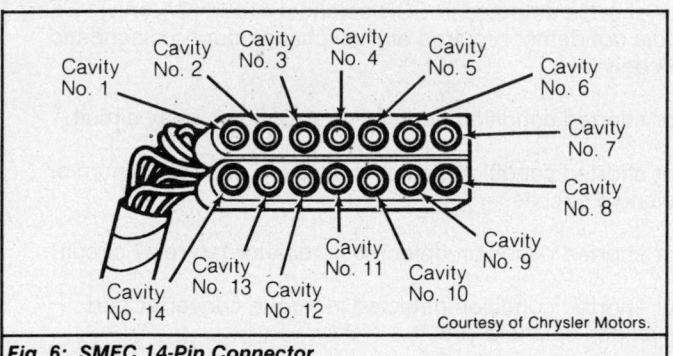

Courtesy of Chrysler Motors.

Fig. 6: SMEC 14-Pin Connector

EMISSION MAINTENANCE REMINDER (EMR) MILEAGE TRANSFER

1) When vehicle engine controller is replaced, vehicle mileage must be copied from odometer to a memory location within the replacement engine controller. Transfer of vehicle mileage will enable new engine controller to operate EMR light properly.

2) Using DRB-II, enter "EMISSIONS EMR TESTS". Press "Yes" key. Select test item "EMR MEMORY CHECK". Press "Yes" key. DRB-II display will read "EMR MEMORY CHECK ARE YOU SURE ? Yes,No". Press "Yes" key.

3) DRB-II will display "IS INSTRUMENT PANEL MILEAGE BETWEEN 9953 AND 10051 ?". If vehicle mileage is within specification, EMR memory check is complete. Press "Yes" key. If vehicle mileage is not within specification, go to next step.

4) Press "No" key. DRB-II will display "DO YOU WANT TO CORRECT EMR MILEAGE ?". Press "Yes" key. DRB-II will display "ENTER MILEAGE SHOWN ON INSTRUMENT PANEL USE ENTER KEY TO END".

5) Enter vehicle mileage. DO NOT enter tenths. When correct vehicle mileage is entered, press "Enter" key. DRB-II will ask for verification of mileage entry. If mileage entry was accurate, press "Enter" key. DRB-II will display "EMR MEMORY CHECK TEST COMPLETE". Vehicle must travel at least 8 miles for reset to occur.

NOTE: The following trouble shooting charts and illustrations are courtesy of Chrysler Motors.

FAULT CODES

CODE	DISPLAY ON DRB-II	FAULT CONDITION
11	IGN REFERENCE SIGNAL	No distributor reference signal picked up during cranking.
12	Number of key-ons since last fault or since faults were erased.	Direct battery input to SMEC was disconnected within last 50-100 ignition key-ons.
13	MAP PNEUMATIC SIGNAL or MAP PNEUMATIC CHANGE	No difference in MAP sensor signal is detected. No difference is detected between MAP reading and stored barometric pressure reading.
14	MAP VOLTAGE TOO LOW or MAP VOLTAGE TOO HIGH	MAP sensor input less than minimum acceptable voltage. MAP sensor input more than maximum acceptable voltage.
15	VEHICLE SPEED SIGNAL	No distance sensor signal detected with road load conditions.
16	BATTERY INPUT SENSE	Battery voltage sense input not detected with engine running.
17	LOW ENGINE TEMP	Coolant temperature stays below normal operating temperature during vehicle operation.
21	OXYGEN SENSOR SIGNAL	No rich or lean signal is detected from O_2 sensor input.
22	COOLANT VOLTAGE LOW or COOLANT VOLTAGE HIGH	Coolant temp. sensor input below minimum acceptable voltage. Coolant temp. sensor input above maximum acceptable voltage.
23	T/B TEMP VOLTAGE LOW	Throttle body temperature sensor input less than minimum acceptable voltage.
	or T/B TEMP VOLTAGE HI	Throttle body temperature sensor input more than maximum acceptable voltage.

1a-42

1989 COMPUTERIZED ENGINE CONTROLS
Chrysler Motors 2.2L & 2.5L SPFI (Cont.)

FAULT CODES (Cont.)

CODE	DISPLAY ON DRB-II	FAULT CONDITION
24	TPS VOLTAGE LOW or TPS VOLTAGE HIGH	TPS sensor output less than minimum acceptable voltage. TPS sensor output more than maximum acceptable voltage.
25	AIS MOTOR CIRCUITS	Shorted condition detected in one or more AIS control circuits.
26	INJ 1 PEAK CURRENT	High resistance detected in injector output circuit.
27	INJ 1 CONTROL CIRCUIT	Injector output driver stage does not respond correctly to SMEC control signal.
31	PURGE SOLENOID CKT	Open or shorted condition is detected in purge solenoid circuit.
32	EGR SOLENOID CIRCUIT or EGR SYSTEM FAILURE	Open or short is detected in EGR solenoid circuit (CA only). SMEC did not detect required air/fuel change during diagnostic test (CA only).
33	A/C CLUTCH RELAY CKT	Open or shorted condition detected in A/C clutch relay circuit.
34	S/C SERVO SOLENOIDS	Open or shorted condition detected in speed control vacuum or vent solenoid circuits.
35	RADIATOR FAN RELAY	Open or shorted condition detected in radiator fan relay circuit.
37	PTU SOLENOID CIRCUIT	Open or shorted condition detected in torque converter part throttle unlock solenoid circuit.
41	CHARGING SYSTEM CKT	Output driver stage does not respond correctly to voltage regulator control signal.
42	ASD RELAY CIRCUIT	Open or shorted condition detected in ASD relay circuit.
43	IGNITION CONTROL CIRCUIT	Output driver stage for ignition coil does not respond properly to dwell control signal.
44	FJ2 VOLTAGE SENSE	No FJ2 voltage present at logic board during SMEC operation.
46	BATTERY VOLTAGE HIGH	Battery voltage sense input more than target charging voltage during engine operation.
47	BATTERY VOLTAGE LOW	Battery voltage sense input less than target charging voltage during engine operation.
51	LEAN F/A CONDITION	Oxygen sensor input indicates lean air/fuel ratio during engine operation.
52	RICH F/A CONDITON or EXCESSIVE LEANING	Oxygen sensor input indicates rich air/fuel ratio during engine operation. Adaptive fuel value leaned excessively from a sustained rich condition.
53	INTERNAL SELF-TEST	SMEC detects internal failure.
55		Completion of fault code display by check engine light.
62	EMR MILEAGE ACCUM	Attempt is unsuccessful to update EMR mileage in SMEC EEPROM (trucks only).
63	EEPROM WRITE DENIED	Attempt is unsuccessful to write to an EEPROM location by SMEC.
N/A	FAULT CODE ERROR	DRB-II does not recognize fault identification.

1989 COMPUTERIZED ENGINE CONTROLS
Chrysler Motors 2.2L & 2.5L SPFI (Cont.)

1a-43

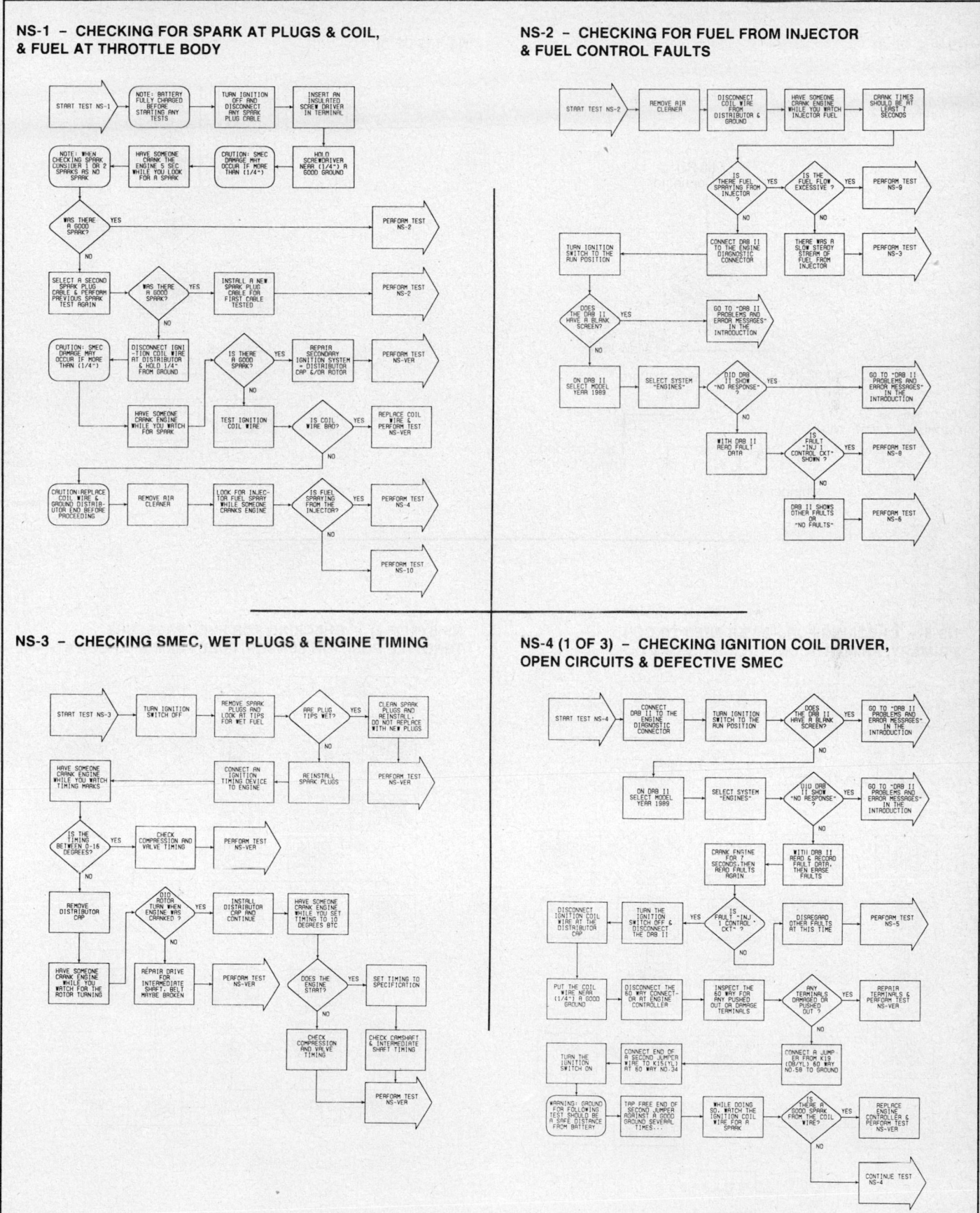

NS-1 – CHECKING FOR SPARK AT PLUGS & COIL, & FUEL AT THROTTLE BODY

NS-2 – CHECKING FOR FUEL FROM INJECTOR & FUEL CONTROL FAULTS

NS-3 – CHECKING SMEC, WET PLUGS & ENGINE TIMING

NS-4 (1 OF 3) – CHECKING IGNITION COIL DRIVER, OPEN CIRCUITS & DEFECTIVE SMEC

1a-44

1989 COMPUTERIZED ENGINE CONTROLS
Chrysler Motors 2.2L & 2.5L SPFI (Cont.)

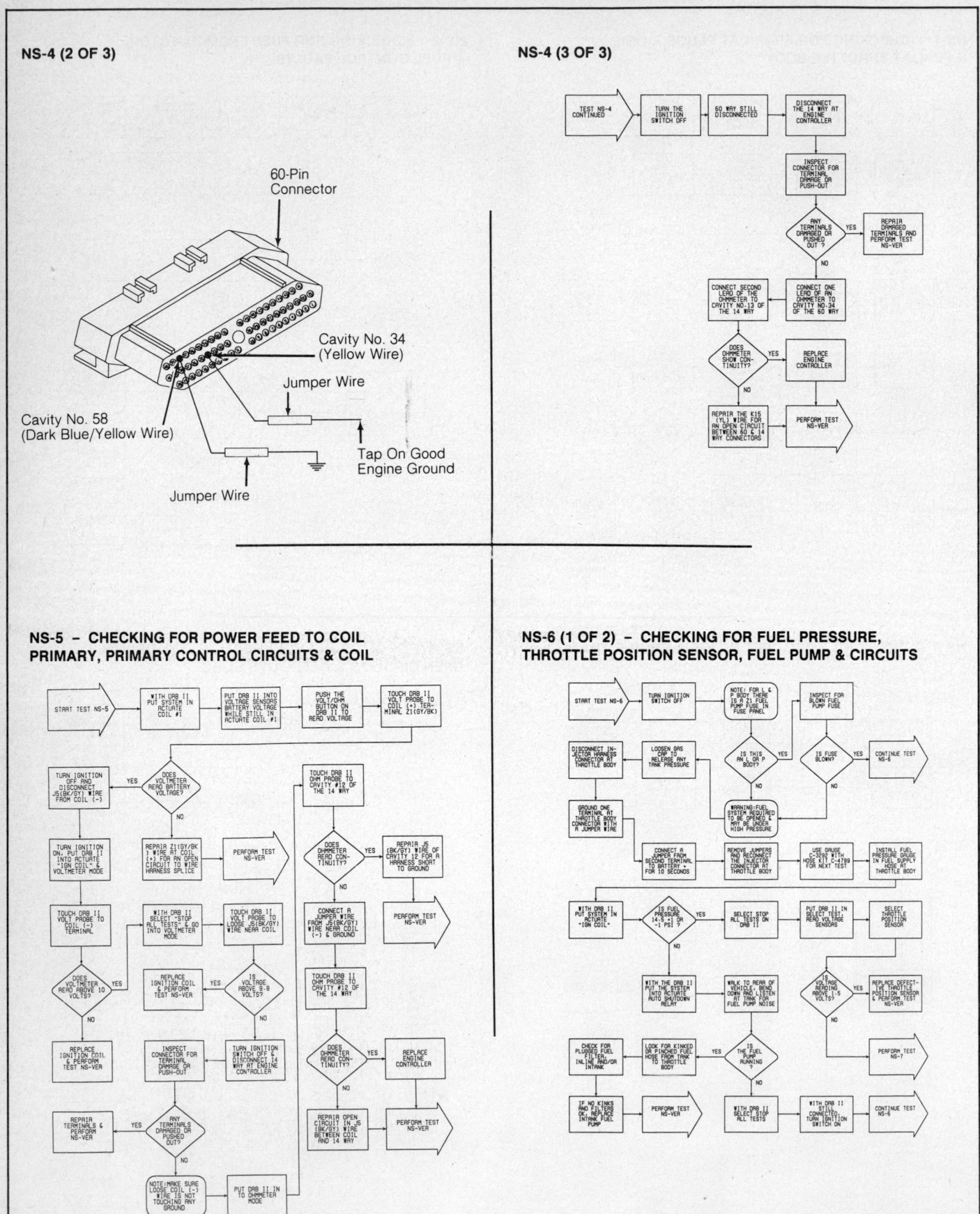

NS-4 (2 OF 3)

NS-4 (3 OF 3)

60-Pin Connector

Cavity No. 34 (Yellow Wire)

Jumper Wire

Cavity No. 58 (Dark Blue/Yellow Wire)

Tap On Good Engine Ground

Jumper Wire

NS-5 – CHECKING FOR POWER FEED TO COIL PRIMARY, PRIMARY CONTROL CIRCUITS & COIL

NS-6 (1 OF 2) – CHECKING FOR FUEL PRESSURE, THROTTLE POSITION SENSOR, FUEL PUMP & CIRCUITS

1989 COMPUTERIZED ENGINE CONTROLS
Chrysler Motors 2.2L & 2.5L SPFI (Cont.)

1a-45

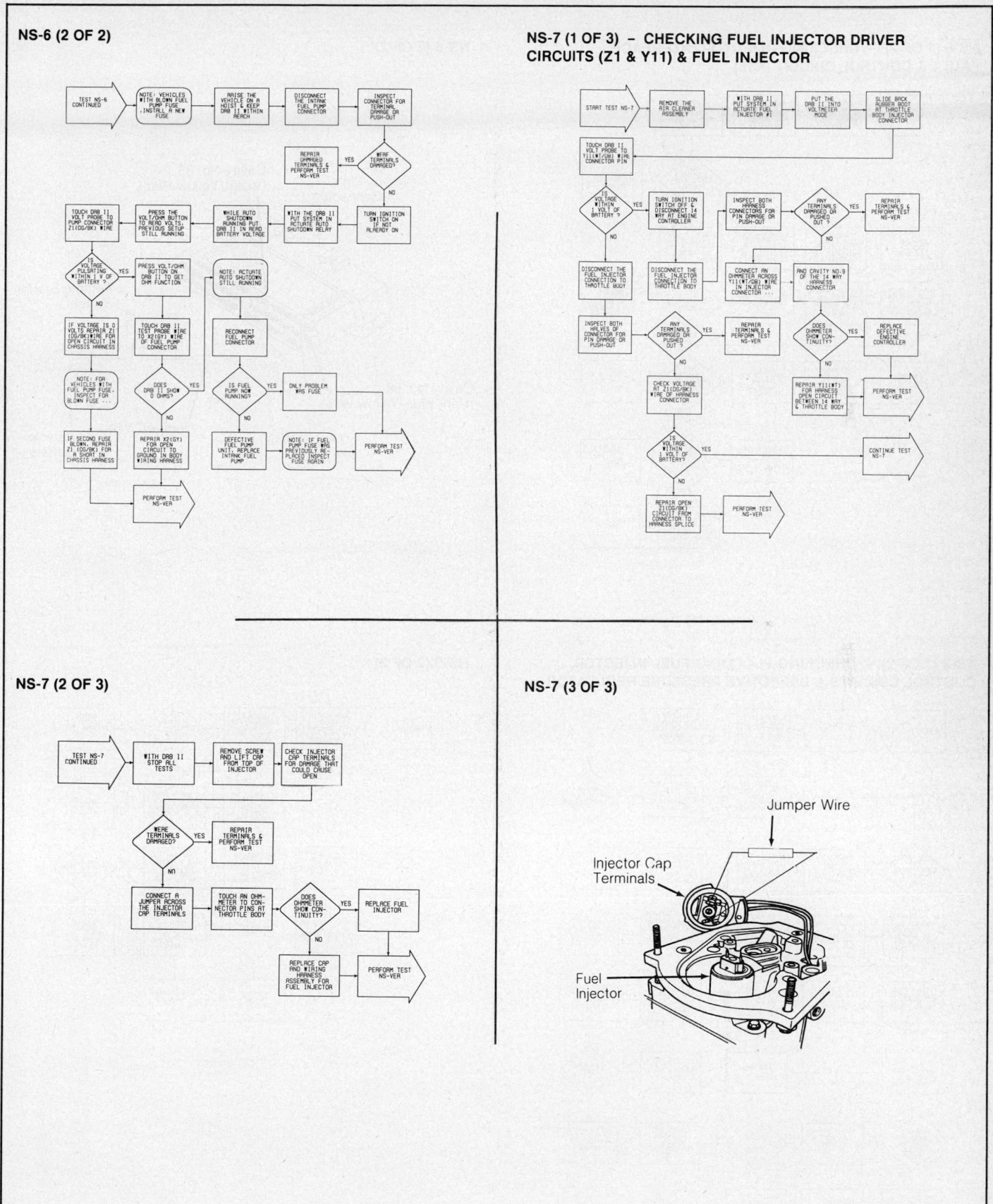

NS-6 (2 OF 2)

NS-7 (1 OF 3) – CHECKING FUEL INJECTOR DRIVER CIRCUITS (Z1 & Y11) & FUEL INJECTOR

NS-7 (2 OF 3)

NS-7 (3 OF 3)

Jumper Wire

Injector Cap Terminals

Fuel Injector

1a-46

1989 COMPUTERIZED ENGINE CONTROLS
Chrysler Motors 2.2L & 2.5L SPFI (Cont.)

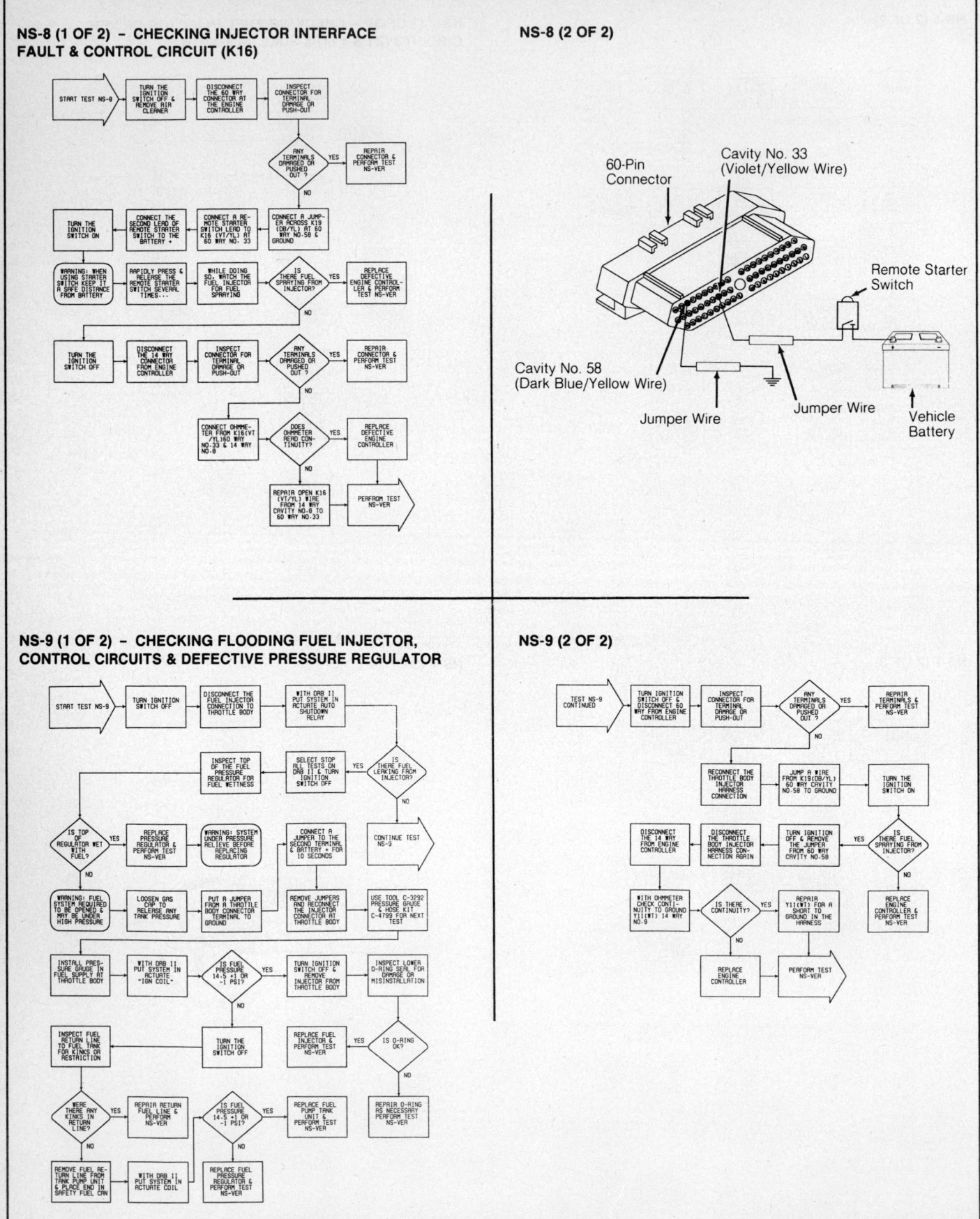

NS-8 (1 OF 2) – CHECKING INJECTOR INTERFACE FAULT & CONTROL CIRCUIT (K16)

NS-8 (2 OF 2)

NS-9 (1 OF 2) – CHECKING FLOODING FUEL INJECTOR, CONTROL CIRCUITS & DEFECTIVE PRESSURE REGULATOR

NS-9 (2 OF 2)

1989 COMPUTERIZED ENGINE CONTROLS
Chrysler Motors 2.2L & 2.5L SPFI (Cont.)

1a-47

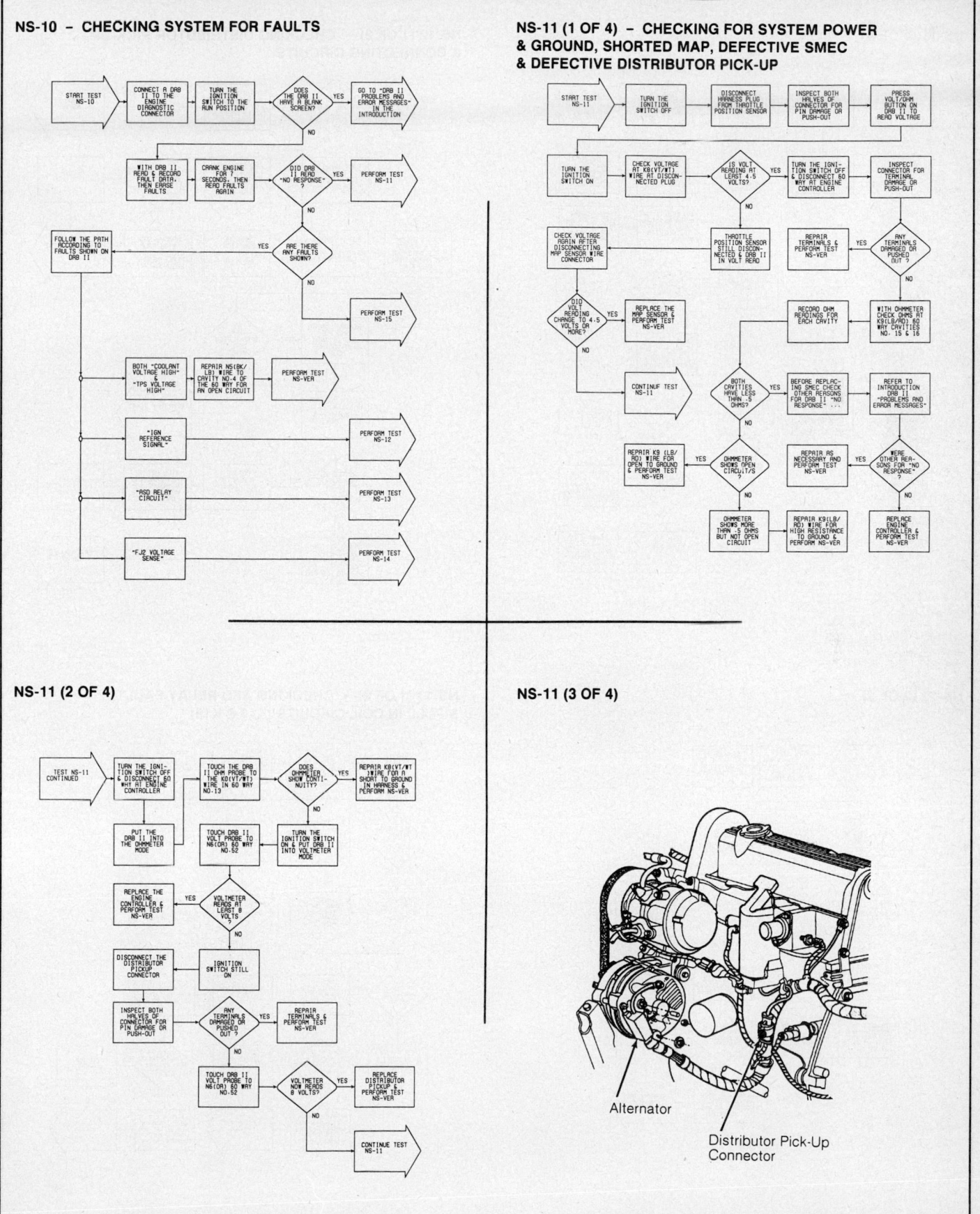

NS-10 – CHECKING SYSTEM FOR FAULTS

START TEST NS-10 → CONNECT A DRB II TO THE ENGINE DIAGNOSTIC CONNECTOR → TURN THE IGNITION SWITCH TO THE RUN POSITION → DOES THE DRB II HAVE A BLANK SCREEN? — YES → GO TO "DRB II PROBLEMS AND ERROR MESSAGES" IN THE INTRODUCTION

NO → WITH DRB II READ & RECORD FAULT DATA, THEN ERASE FAULTS → CRANK ENGINE FOR 2 SECONDS, THEN READ FAULTS AGAIN → DID DRB II READ "NO RESPONSE"? — YES → PERFORM TEST NS-11

NO → ARE THERE ANY FAULTS SHOWN? — YES → FOLLOW THE PATH ACCORDING TO FAULTS SHOWN ON DRB II

NO → PERFORM TEST NS-15

BOTH "COOLANT VOLTAGE HIGH" & "TPS VOLTAGE HIGH" → REPAIR NS(BK/LB) WIRE TO CAVITY NO.4 OF THE 60 WAY FOR AN OPEN CIRCUIT → PERFORM TEST NS-VER

"IGN REFERENCE SIGNAL" → PERFORM TEST NS-12

"ASD RELAY CIRCUIT" → PERFORM TEST NS-13

"FJ2 VOLTAGE SENSE" → PERFORM TEST NS-14

NS-11 (1 OF 4) – CHECKING FOR SYSTEM POWER & GROUND, SHORTED MAP, DEFECTIVE SMEC & DEFECTIVE DISTRIBUTOR PICK-UP

START TEST NS-11 → TURN THE IGNITION SWITCH OFF → DISCONNECT HARNESS PLUG FROM THROTTLE POSITION SENSOR → INSPECT BOTH HALVES OF CONNECTOR FOR PIN DAMAGE OR PUSH-OUT → PRESS VOLT/OHM BUTTON ON DRB II TO READ VOLTAGE

TURN THE IGNITION SWITCH ON → CHECK VOLTAGE AT K8(VT/WT) WIRE AT DISCONNECTED PLUG → IS VOLT READING AT LEAST 4.5 VOLTS? — YES → TURN THE IGNITION SWITCH OFF & DISCONNECT 60 WAY AT ENGINE CONTROLLER → INSPECT CONNECTOR FOR TERMINAL DAMAGE OR PUSH-OUT

NO → CHECK VOLTAGE AGAIN AFTER DISCONNECTING MAP SENSOR WIRE CONNECTOR ← THROTTLE POSITION SENSOR STILL DISCONNECTED & DRB II IN VOLT READ

REPAIR TERMINALS & PERFORM TEST NS-VER — YES → ANY TERMINALS DAMAGED OR PUSHED OUT?

DID VOLT READING CHANGE TO 4.5 VOLTS OR MORE? — YES → REPLACE THE MAP SENSOR & PERFORM TEST NS-VER

RECORD OHM READINGS FOR EACH CAVITY → WITH OHMMETER CHECK OHMS AT K9(LB/RD) 60 WAY CAVITIES NO. 15 & 16

NO → CONTINUE TEST NS-11 → BOTH CAVITIES HAVE LESS THAN .5 OHMS? — YES → BEFORE REPLACING SMEC CHECK OTHER REASONS FOR DRB II "NO RESPONSE" ... → REFER TO INTRODUCTION DRB II "PROBLEMS AND ERROR MESSAGES"

REPAIR K9 (LB/RD) WIRE FOR OPEN TO GROUND & PERFORM TEST NS-VER — YES → OHMMETER SHOWS OPEN CIRCUIT/S?

REPAIR AS NECESSARY AND PERFORM TEST NS-VER — YES → WERE OTHER REASONS FOR "NO RESPONSE"?

NO → OHMMETER SHOWS MORE THAN .5 OHMS BUT NOT OPEN CIRCUIT → REPAIR K9(LB/RD) WIRE FOR HIGH RESISTANCE TO GROUND & PERFORM NS-VER

NO → REPLACE ENGINE CONTROLLER & PERFORM TEST NS-VER

NS-11 (2 OF 4)

TEST NS-11 CONTINUED → TURN THE IGNITION SWITCH OFF & DISCONNECT 60 WAY AT ENGINE CONTROLLER → TOUCH THE DRB II OHM PROBE TO THE K0(VT/WT) WIRE IN 60 WAY NO.13 → DOES OHMMETER SHOW CONTINUITY? — YES → REPAIR K0(VT/WT) WIRE FOR A SHORT TO GROUND IN HARNESS & PERFORM NS-VER

PUT THE DRB II INTO THE OHMMETER MODE → TOUCH DRB II VOLT PROBE TO N6(OR) 60 WAY NO.52 → TURN THE IGNITION SWITCH ON & PUT DRB II INTO VOLTMETER MODE

REPLACE THE ENGINE CONTROLLER & PERFORM TEST NS-VER — YES → VOLTMETER READS AT LEAST 8 VOLTS?

NO → DISCONNECT THE DISTRIBUTOR PICKUP CONNECTOR ← IGNITION SWITCH STILL ON

INSPECT BOTH HALVES OF CONNECTOR FOR PIN DAMAGE OR PUSH-OUT → ANY TERMINALS DAMAGED OR PUSHED OUT? — YES → REPAIR TERMINALS & PERFORM TEST NS-VER

NO → TOUCH DRB II VOLT PROBE TO N6(OR) 60 WAY NO.52 → VOLTMETER NOW READS 8 VOLTS? — YES → REPLACE DISTRIBUTOR PICKUP & PERFORM NS-VER

NO → CONTINUE TEST NS-11

NS-11 (3 OF 4)

Alternator

Distributor Pick-Up Connector

1a-48

1989 COMPUTERIZED ENGINE CONTROLS
Chrysler Motors 2.2L & 2.5L SPFI (Cont.)

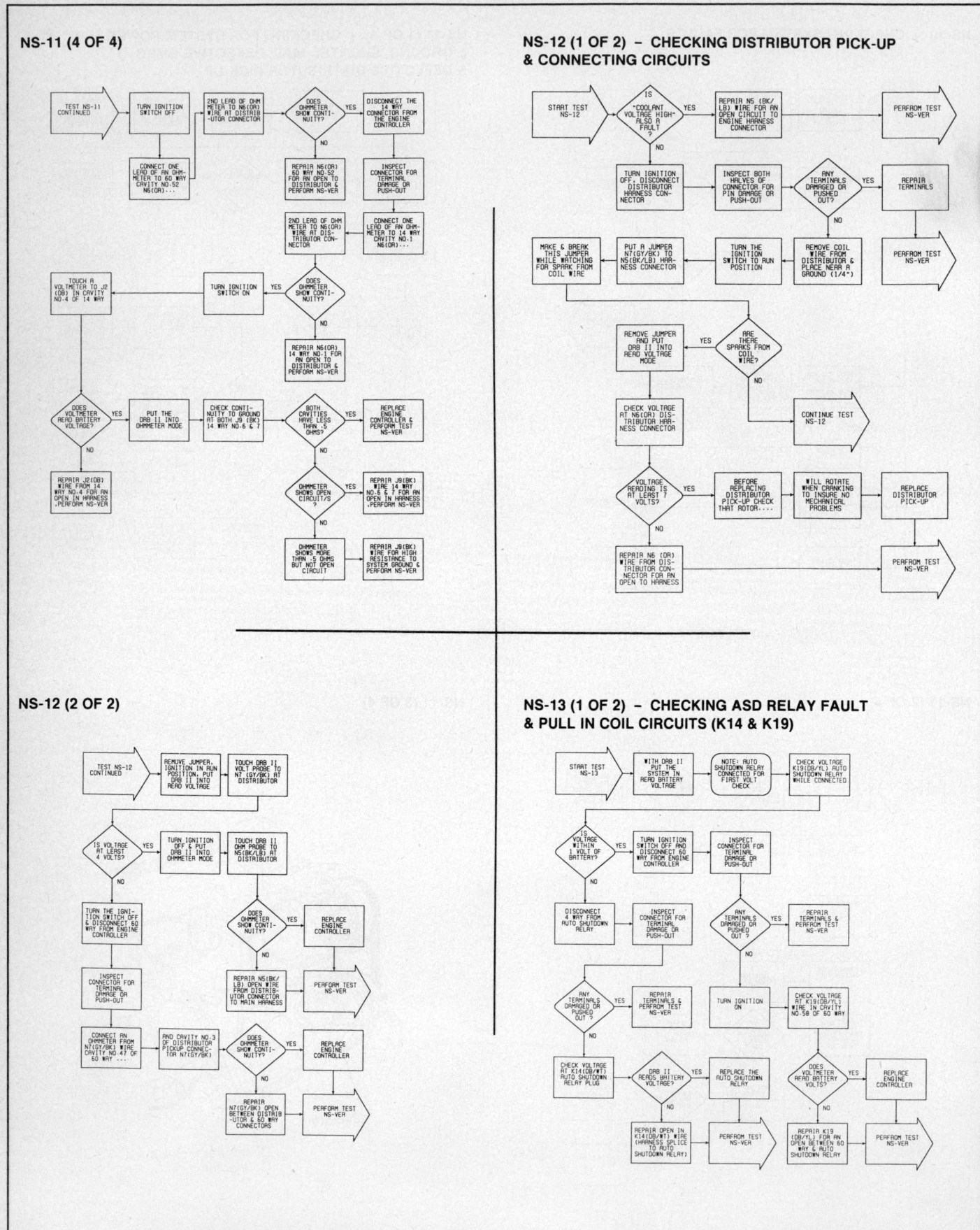

NS-11 (4 OF 4)

NS-12 (1 OF 2) – CHECKING DISTRIBUTOR PICK-UP & CONNECTING CIRCUITS

NS-12 (2 OF 2)

NS-13 (1 OF 2) – CHECKING ASD RELAY FAULT & PULL IN COIL CIRCUITS (K14 & K19)

1989 COMPUTERIZED ENGINE CONTROLS
Chrysler Motors 2.2L & 2.5L SPFI (Cont.)

1a-49

NS-13 (2 OF 2)

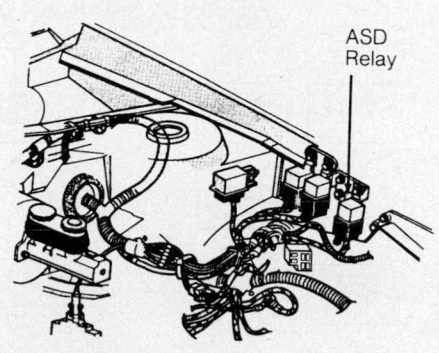

ASD Relay

NS-14 (1 OF 2) – CHECKING POWER CIRCUIT (K14) TO PULL IN COIL & ASD RELAY

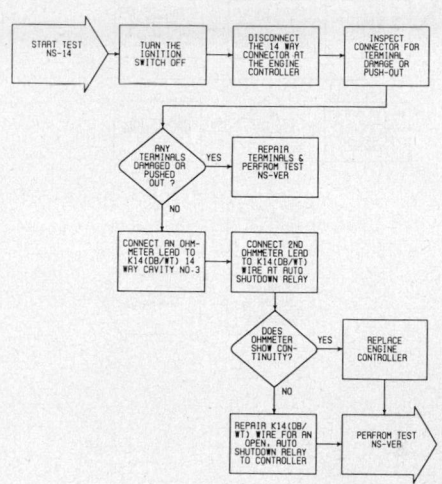

START TEST NS-14 → TURN THE IGNITION SWITCH OFF → DISCONNECT THE 14 WAY CONNECTOR AT THE ENGINE CONTROLLER → INSPECT CONNECTOR FOR TERMINAL DAMAGE OR PUSH-OUT

ANY TERMINALS DAMAGED OR PUSHED OUT? — YES → REPAIR TERMINALS & PERFORM TEST NS-VER

NO → CONNECT AN OHMMETER LEAD TO K14(DB/WT) 14 WAY CAVITY NO-3 → CONNECT 2ND OHMMETER LEAD TO K14(DB/WT) WIRE AT AUTO SHUTDOWN RELAY

DOES OHMMETER SHOW CONTINUITY? — YES → REPLACE ENGINE CONTROLLER

NO → REPAIR K14(DB/WT) WIRE FOR AN OPEN, AUTO SHUTDOWN RELAY TO CONTROLLER → PERFORM TEST NS-VER

NS-14 (2 OF 2)

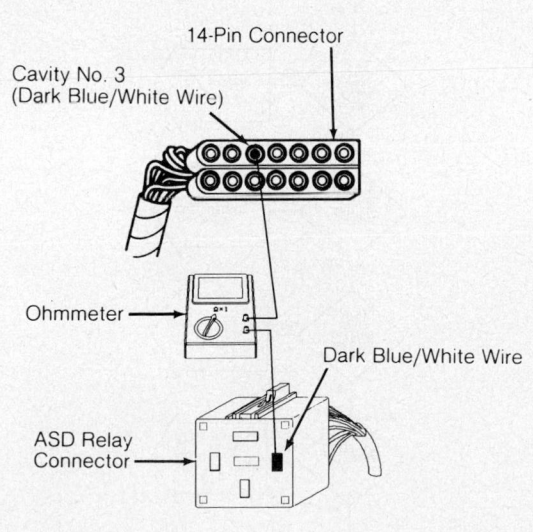

14-Pin Connector

Cavity No. 3 (Dark Blue/White Wire)

Ohmmeter

Dark Blue/White Wire

ASD Relay Connector

NS-15 (1 OF 2) – CHECKING POWER FEED CIRCUITS (J2 & Z1) TO ASD RELAY & DEFECTIVE ASD RELAY

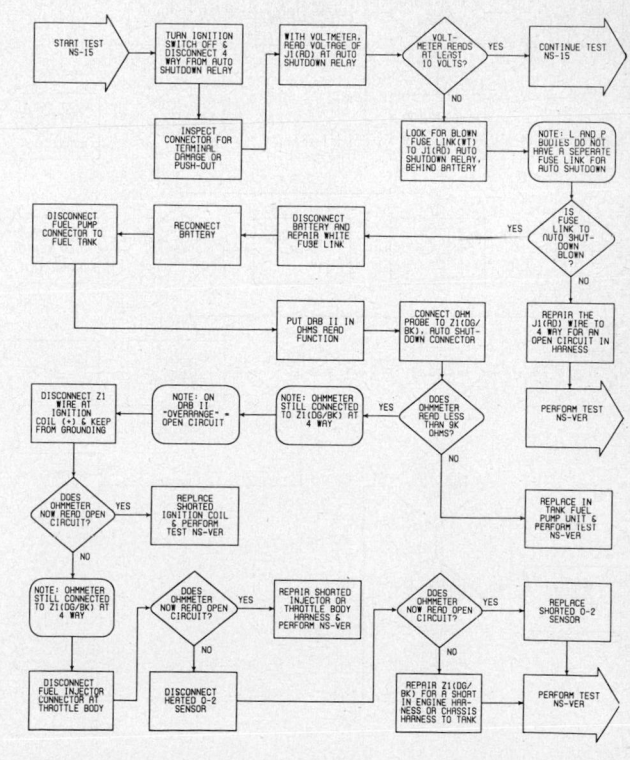

START TEST NS-15 → TURN IGNITION SWITCH OFF & DISCONNECT 4 WAY FROM AUTO SHUTDOWN RELAY → WITH VOLTMETER, READ VOLTAGE OF J1(RD) AT AUTO SHUTDOWN RELAY → VOLTMETER READS AT LEAST 10 VOLTS? — YES → CONTINUE TEST NS-15

INSPECT CONNECTOR FOR TERMINAL DAMAGE OR PUSH-OUT

NO → LOOK FOR BLOWN FUSE LINK(WT) TO J1(RD) AUTO SHUTDOWN RELAY, BEHIND BATTERY → NOTE: L AND P BODIES DO NOT HAVE A SEPERATE FUSE LINK FOR AUTO SHUTDOWN

DISCONNECT FUEL PUMP CONNECTOR TO FUEL TANK → RECONNECT BATTERY → DISCONNECT BATTERY AND REPAIR WHITE FUSE LINK — YES → IS FUSE LINK TO AUTO SHUTDOWN BLOWN?

NO → REPAIR THE J1(RD) WIRE TO 4 WAY FOR AN OPEN CIRCUIT IN HARNESS → PERFORM TEST NS-VER

PUT DRB II IN OHMS READ FUNCTION → CONNECT OHM PROBE TO Z1(DG/BK), AUTO SHUTDOWN CONNECTOR

DISCONNECT Z1 WIRE AT IGNITION COIL (+) KEEP FROM GROUNDING → NOTE: ON DRB II "OVERRANGE" = OPEN CIRCUIT → NOTE: OHMMETER STILL CONNECTED TO Z1(DG/BK) AT 4 WAY → DOES OHMMETER READ LESS THAN 9K OHMS? — YES

NO → REPLACE IN TANK FUEL PUMP UNIT & PERFORM TEST NS-VER

DOES OHMMETER NOW READ OPEN CIRCUIT? — YES → REPLACE SHORTED IGNITION COIL & PERFORM TEST NS-VER

NO → NOTE: OHMMETER STILL CONNECTED TO Z1(DG/BK) AT 4 WAY → DOES OHMMETER NOW READ OPEN CIRCUIT? — YES → REPAIR SHORTED INJECTOR OR THROTTLE BODY HARNESS & PERFORM NS-VER → DOES OHMMETER NOW READ OPEN CIRCUIT? — YES → REPLACE SHORTED O-2 SENSOR

NO → DISCONNECT FUEL INJECTOR CONNECTOR AT THROTTLE BODY → DISCONNECT HEATED O-2 SENSOR → REPAIR Z1(DG/BK) FOR A SHORT IN ENGINE HARNESS OR CHASSIS HARNESS TO TANK → PERFORM TEST NS-VER

1a-50

1989 COMPUTERIZED ENGINE CONTROLS
Chrysler Motors 2.2L & 2.5L SPFI (Cont.)

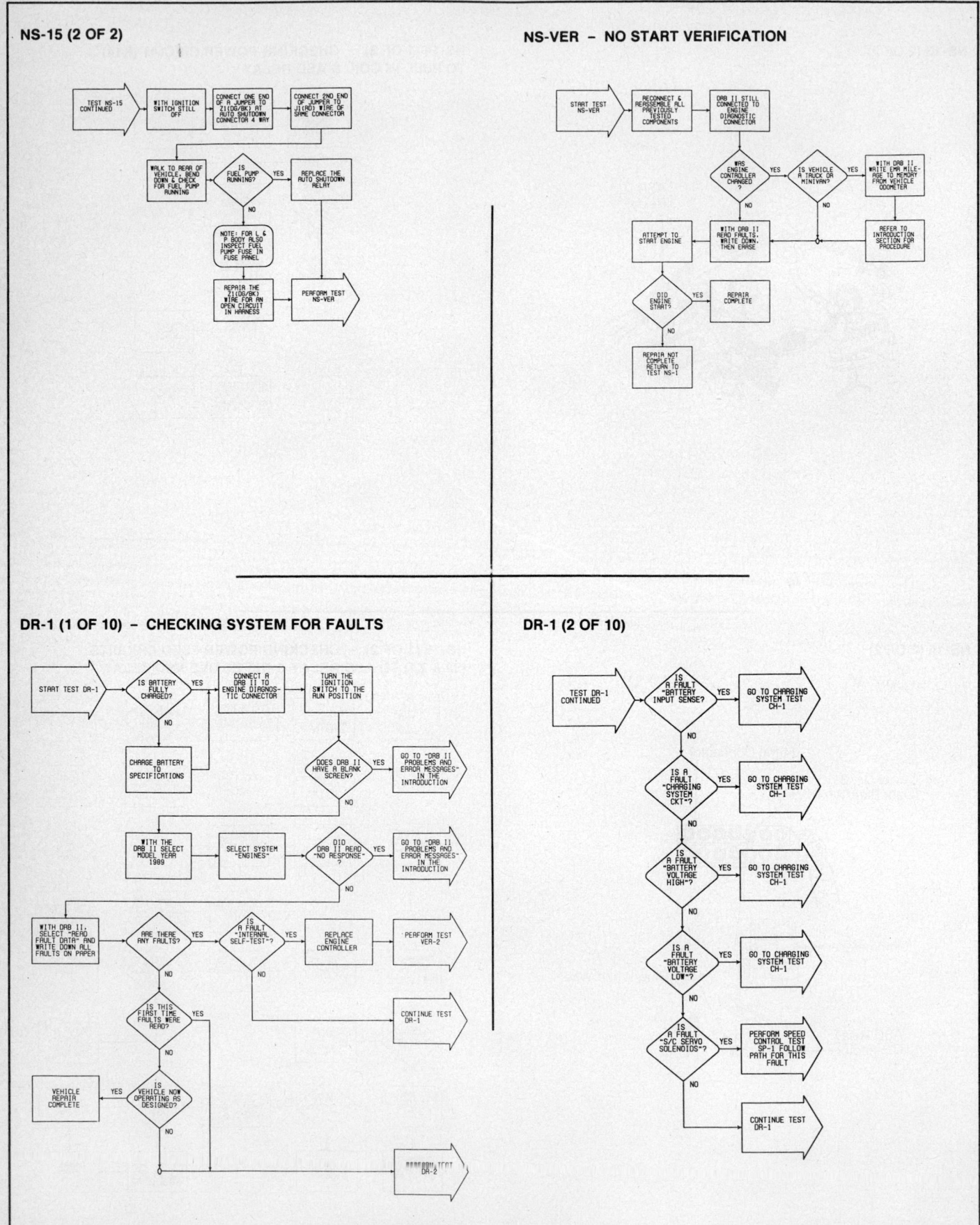

NS-15 (2 OF 2)

NS-VER – NO START VERIFICATION

DR-1 (1 OF 10) – CHECKING SYSTEM FOR FAULTS

DR-1 (2 OF 10)

1989 COMPUTERIZED ENGINE CONTROLS
Chrysler Motors 2.2L & 2.5L SPFI (Cont.)

1a-51

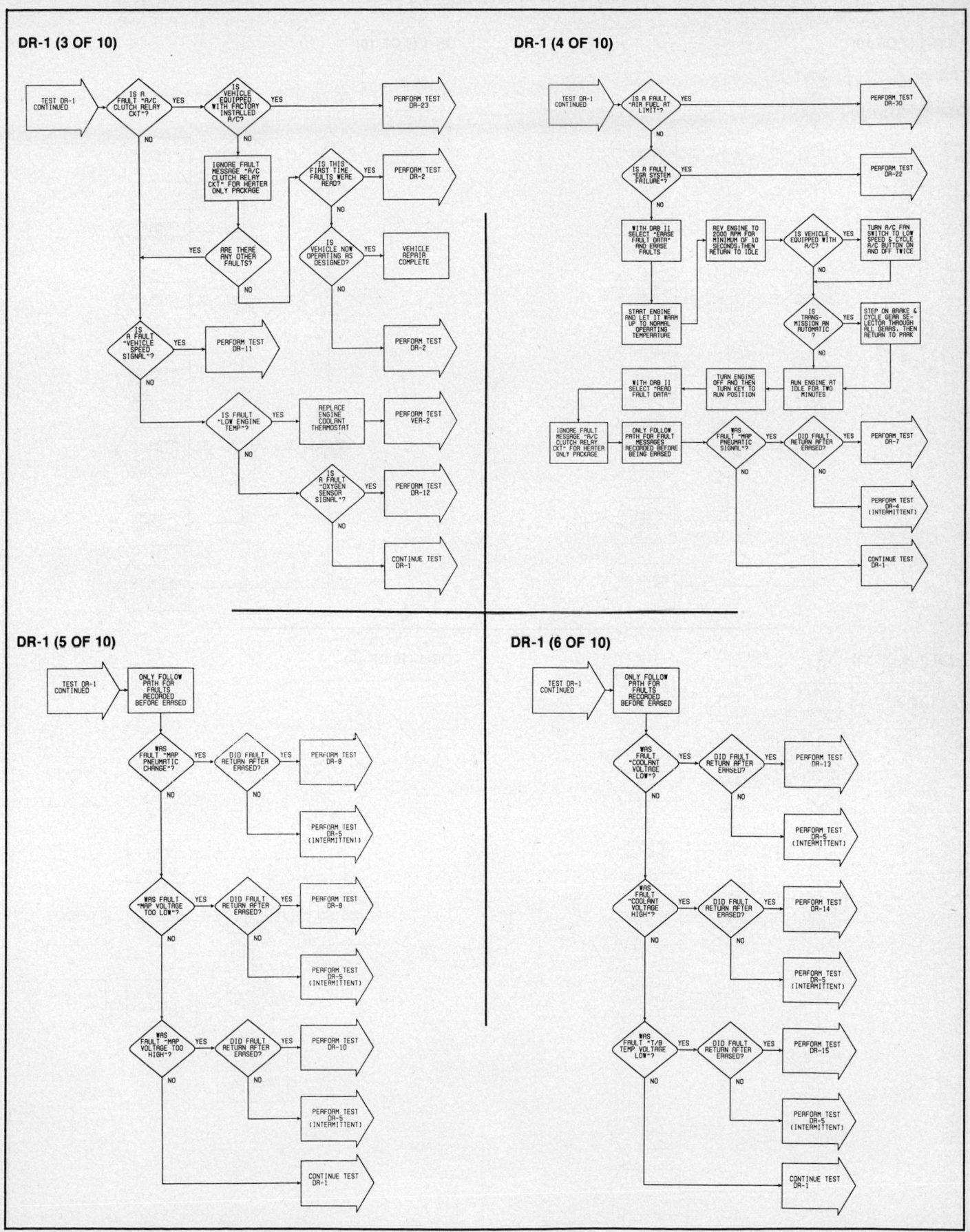

1a-52

1989 COMPUTERIZED ENGINE CONTROLS
Chrysler Motors 2.2L & 2.5L SPFI (Cont.)

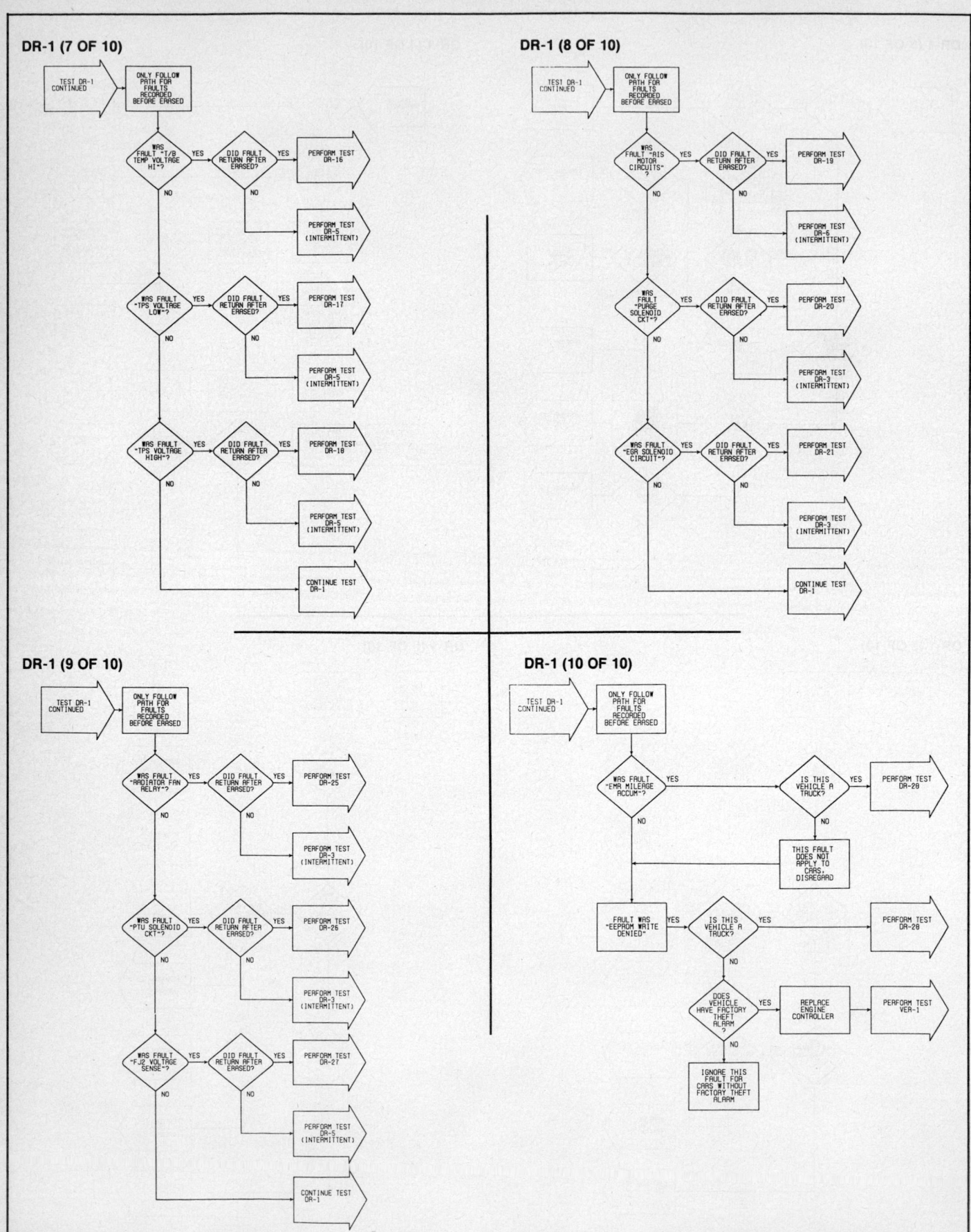

1989 COMPUTERIZED ENGINE CONTROLS
Chrysler Motors 2.2L & 2.5L SPFI (Cont.)

1a-53

DR-2 (1 OF 14) – CHECKING OUTPUT CIRCUITS OF SMEC

DR-2 (2 OF 14)

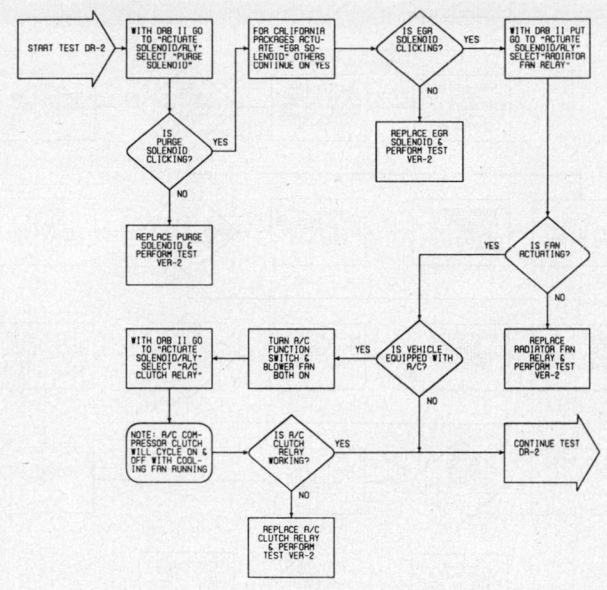

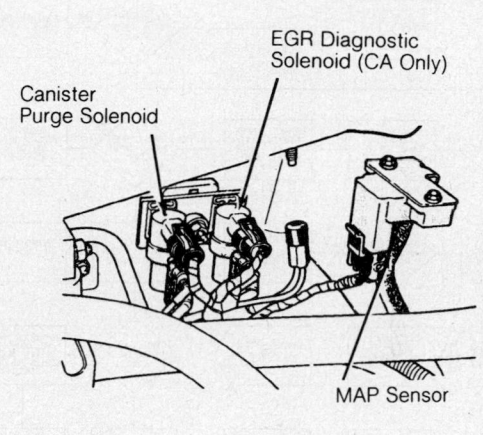

Canister Purge Solenoid

EGR Diagnostic Solenoid (CA Only)

MAP Sensor

DR-2 (3 OF 14)

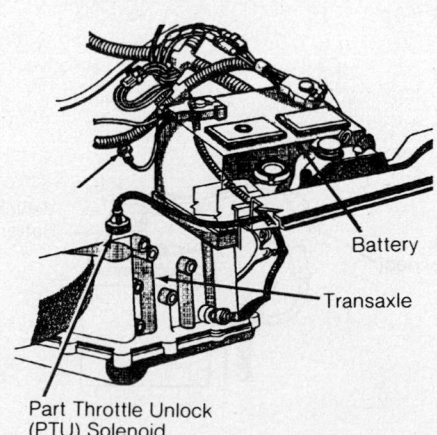

Battery

Transaxle

Part Throttle Unlock (PTU) Solenoid

NOTE: SOLENOID IS HARD TO HEAR.

DR-2 (4 OF 14) – CHECKING OUTPUT CIRCUITS OF SMEC & SHIFT INDICATOR LIGHT

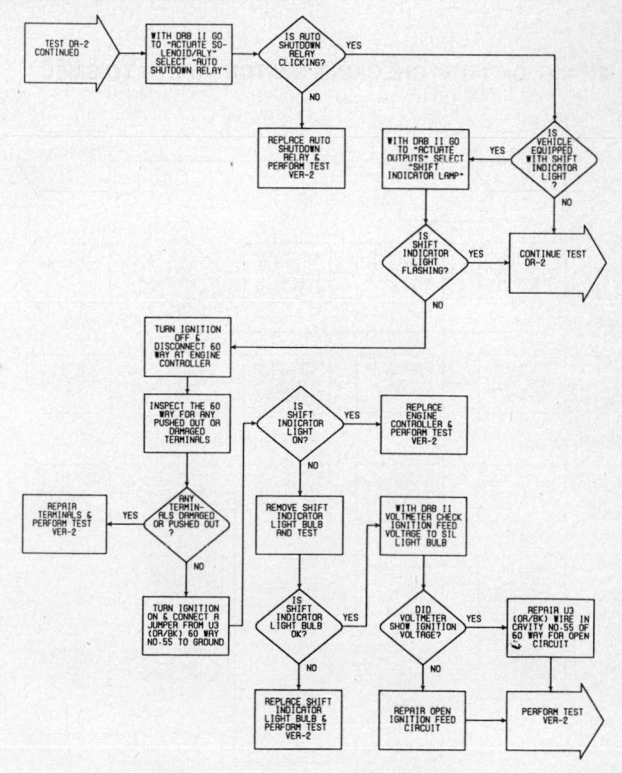

1a-54

1989 COMPUTERIZED ENGINE CONTROLS
Chrysler Motors 2.2L & 2.5L SPFI (Cont.)

DR-2 (5 OF 14) – CHECKING BRAKE SWITCH INPUT CIRCUIT TO SMEC

DR-2 (6 OF 14)

DR-2 (7 OF 14) – CHECKING SWITCH INPUTS TO SMEC

DR-2 (8 OF 14)

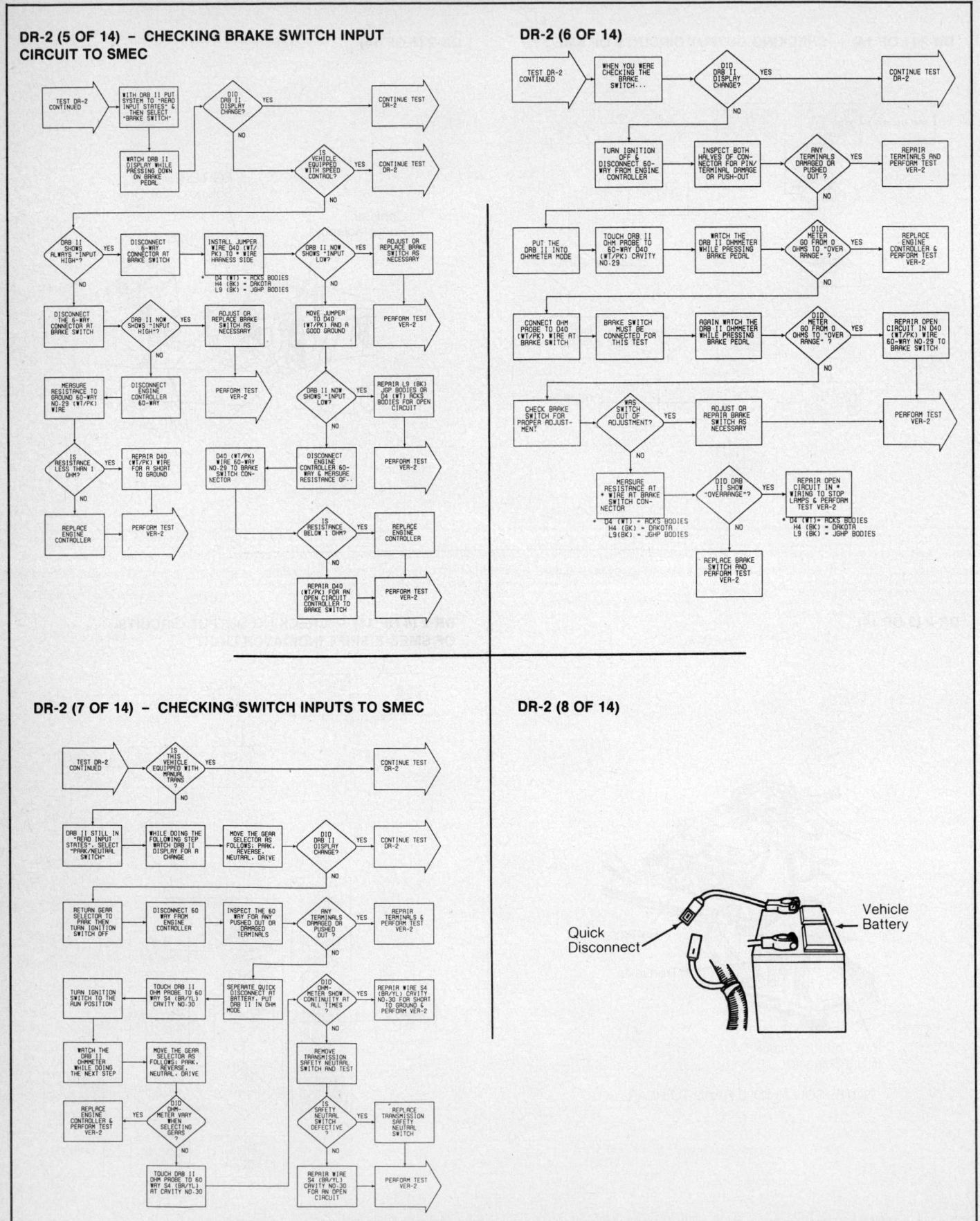

1989 COMPUTERIZED ENGINE CONTROLS
Chrysler Motors 2.2L & 2.5L SPFI (Cont.)

1a-55

DR-2 (9 OF 14) – CHECKING A/C PUSH BUTTON SWITCH INPUT

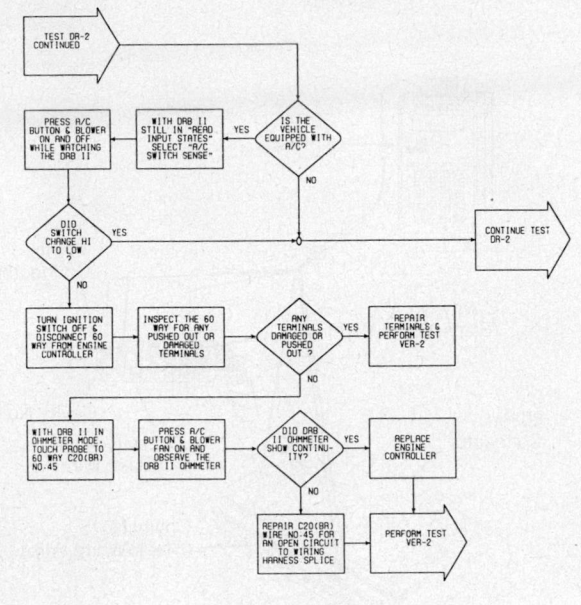

DR-2 (10 OF 14) – CHECKING EMISSION MAINTENANCE REMINDER LIGHT

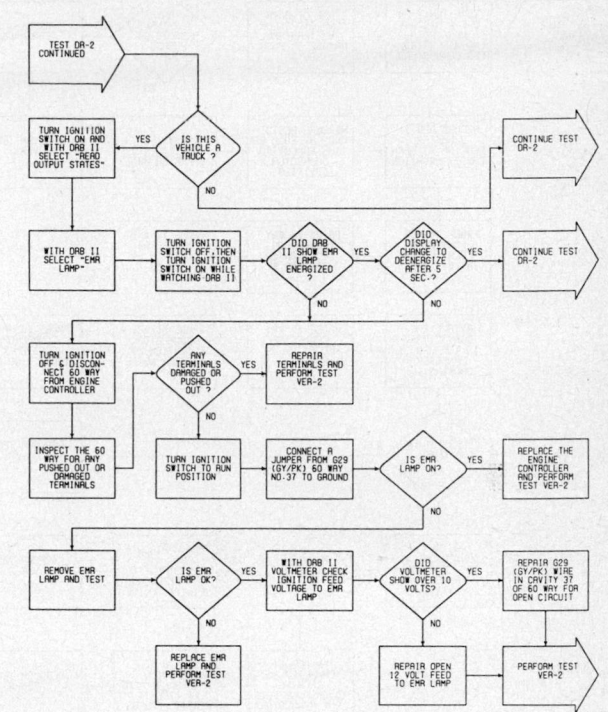

DR-2 (11 OF 14) – CHECKING AUTOMATIC IDLE SPEED MOTOR OPERATION

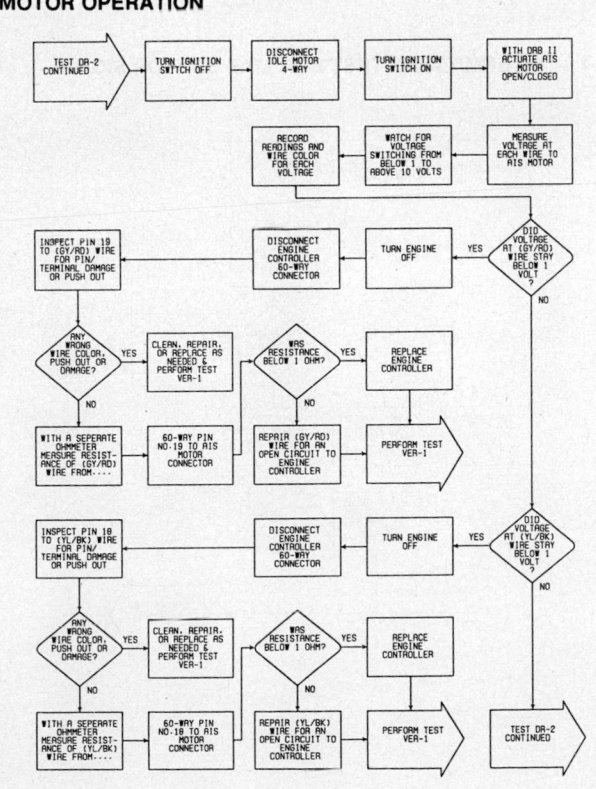

DR-2 (12 OF 14)

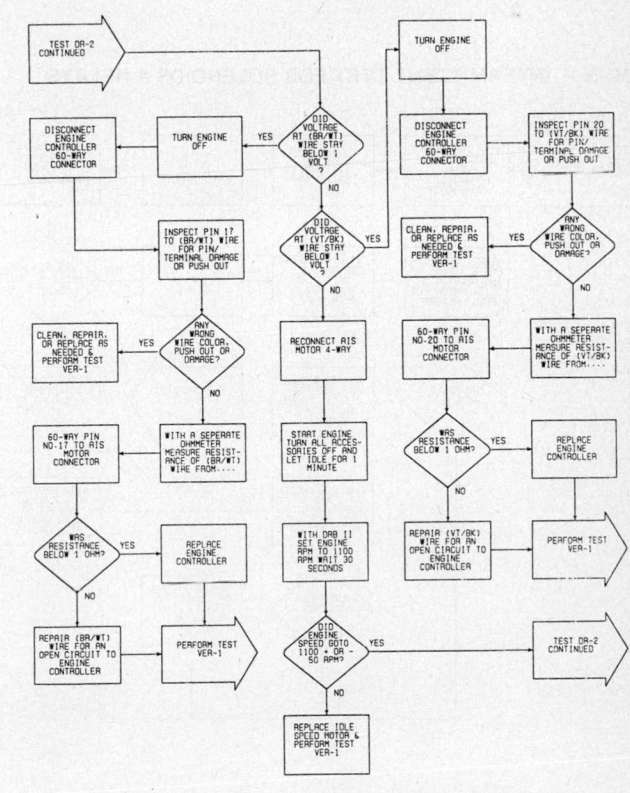

1a-56

1989 COMPUTERIZED ENGINE CONTROLS
Chrysler Motors 2.2L & 2.5L SPFI (Cont.)

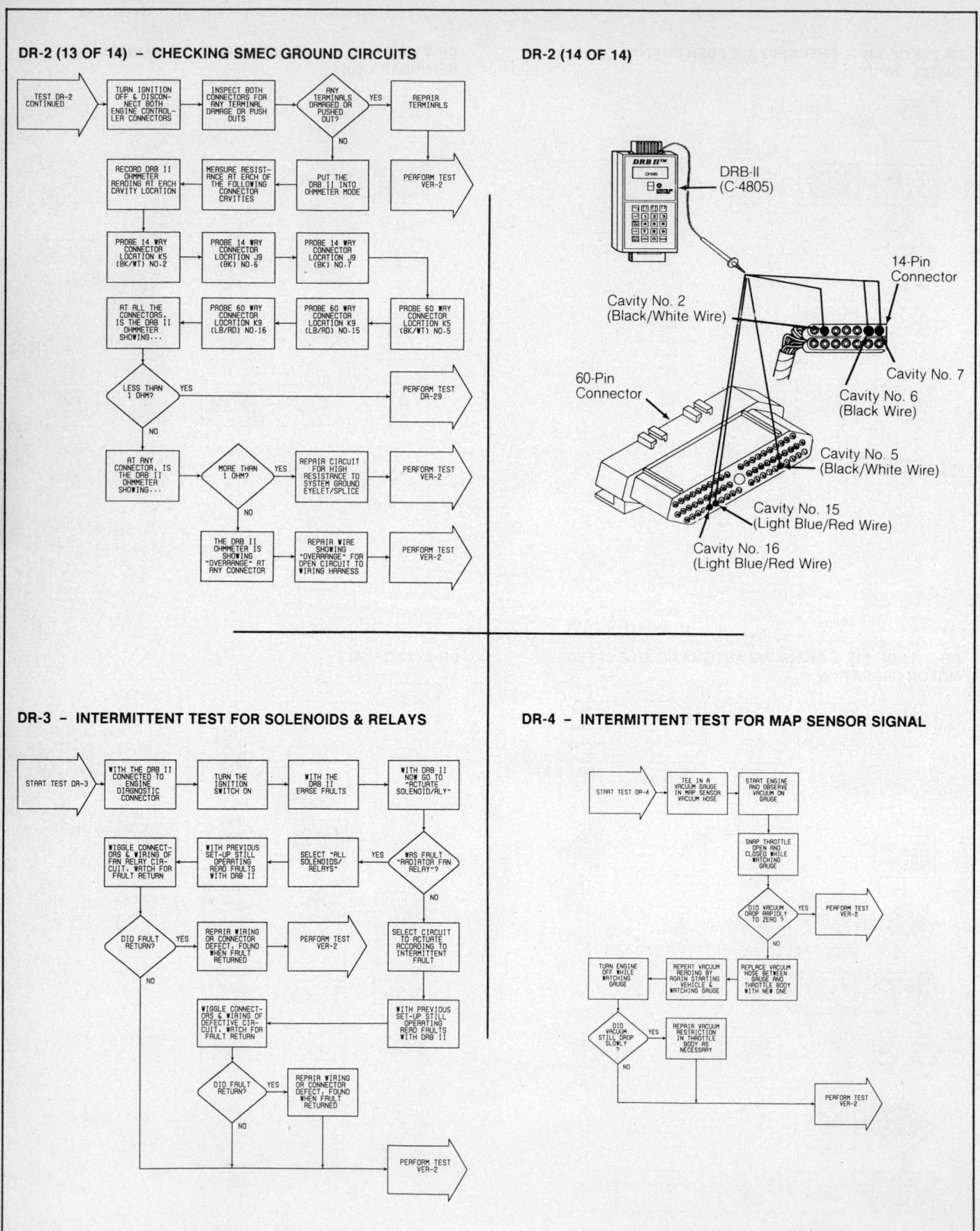

DR-2 (13 OF 14) – CHECKING SMEC GROUND CIRCUITS

TEST DR-2 CONTINUED → TURN IGNITION OFF & DISCONNECT BOTH ENGINE CONTROLLER CONNECTORS → INSPECT BOTH CONNECTORS FOR ANY TERMINAL DAMAGE OR PUSH OUTS → ANY TERMINALS DAMAGED OR PUSHED OUT? — YES → REPAIR TERMINALS

ANY TERMINALS DAMAGED OR PUSHED OUT? — NO

RECORD DRB II OHMMETER READING AT EACH CAVITY LOCATION ← MEASURE RESISTANCE AT EACH OF THE FOLLOWING CONNECTOR CAVITIES ← PUT THE DRB II INTO OHMMETER MODE → PERFORM TEST VER-2

PROBE 14 WAY CONNECTOR LOCATION K5 (BK/WT) NO.2 → PROBE 14 WAY CONNECTOR LOCATION J9 (BK) NO.6 → PROBE 14 WAY CONNECTOR LOCATION J9 (BK) NO.7

AT ALL THE CONNECTORS, IS THE DRB II OHMMETER SHOWING... ← PROBE 60 WAY CONNECTOR LOCATION K9 (LB/RD) NO.16 ← PROBE 60 WAY CONNECTOR LOCATION K9 (LB/RD) NO.15 ← PROBE 60 WAY CONNECTOR LOCATION K5 (BK/WT) NO.5

LESS THAN 1 OHM? — YES → PERFORM TEST DR-29

LESS THAN 1 OHM? — NO

AT ANY CONNECTOR, IS THE DRB II OHMMETER SHOWING... → MORE THAN 1 OHM? — YES → REPAIR CIRCUIT FOR HIGH RESISTANCE TO SYSTEM GROUND EYELET/SPLICE → PERFORM TEST VER-2

MORE THAN 1 OHM? — NO

THE DRB II OHMMETER IS SHOWING "OVERRANGE" AT ANY CONNECTOR → REPAIR WIRE SHOWING "OVERRANGE" FOR OPEN CIRCUIT TO WIRING HARNESS → PERFORM TEST VER-2

DR-2 (14 OF 14)

DRB-II (C-4805)

14-Pin Connector

Cavity No. 2 (Black/White Wire)

Cavity No. 7

Cavity No. 6 (Black Wire)

60-Pin Connector

Cavity No. 5 (Black/White Wire)

Cavity No. 15 (Light Blue/Red Wire)

Cavity No. 16 (Light Blue/Red Wire)

DR-3 – INTERMITTENT TEST FOR SOLENOIDS & RELAYS

START TEST DR-3 → WITH THE DRB II CONNECTED TO ENGINE DIAGNOSTIC CONNECTOR → TURN THE IGNITION SWITCH ON → WITH THE DRB II ERASE FAULTS → WITH DRB II NOW GO TO "ACTUATE SOLENOID/RLY"

WIGGLE CONNECTORS & WIRING OF FAN RELAY CIRCUIT. WATCH FOR FAULT RETURN ← WITH PREVIOUS SET-UP STILL OPERATING READ FAULTS WITH DRB II ← SELECT "ALL SOLENOIDS/RELAYS" — YES ← WAS FAULT "RADIATOR FAN RELAY"?

WAS FAULT "RADIATOR FAN RELAY"? — NO

DID FAULT RETURN? — YES → REPAIR WIRING OR CONNECTOR DEFECT, FOUND WHEN FAULT RETURNED → PERFORM TEST VER-2

SELECT CIRCUIT TO ACTUATE ACCORDING TO INTERMITTENT FAULT

DID FAULT RETURN? — NO

WIGGLE CONNECTORS & WIRING OF DEFECTIVE CIRCUIT. WATCH FOR FAULT RETURN ← WITH PREVIOUS SET-UP STILL OPERATING READ FAULTS WITH DRB II

DID FAULT RETURN? — YES → REPAIR WIRING OR CONNECTOR DEFECT, FOUND WHEN FAULT RETURNED

DID FAULT RETURN? — NO

PERFORM TEST VER-2

DR-4 – INTERMITTENT TEST FOR MAP SENSOR SIGNAL

START TEST DR-4 → TEE IN A VACUUM GAUGE IN MAP SENSOR VACUUM HOSE → START ENGINE AND OBSERVE VACUUM ON GAUGE

SNAP THROTTLE OPEN AND CLOSED WHILE WATCHING GAUGE

DID VACUUM DROP RAPIDLY TO ZERO? — YES → PERFORM TEST VER-2

DID VACUUM DROP RAPIDLY TO ZERO? — NO

TURN ENGINE OFF WHILE WATCHING GAUGE ← REPEAT VACUUM READING BY AGAIN STARTING VEHICLE & WATCHING GAUGE ← REPLACE VACUUM HOSE BETWEEN GAUGE AND THROTTLE BODY WITH NEW ONE

DID VACUUM STILL DROP SLOWLY? — YES → REPAIR VACUUM RESTRICTION IN THROTTLE BODY AS NECESSARY

DID VACUUM STILL DROP SLOWLY? — NO

PERFORM TEST VER-2

1989 COMPUTERIZED ENGINE CONTROLS
Chrysler Motors 2.2L & 2.5L SPFI (Cont.)

1a-57

DR-5 – INTERMITTENT TEST FOR SENSOR VOLTAGES

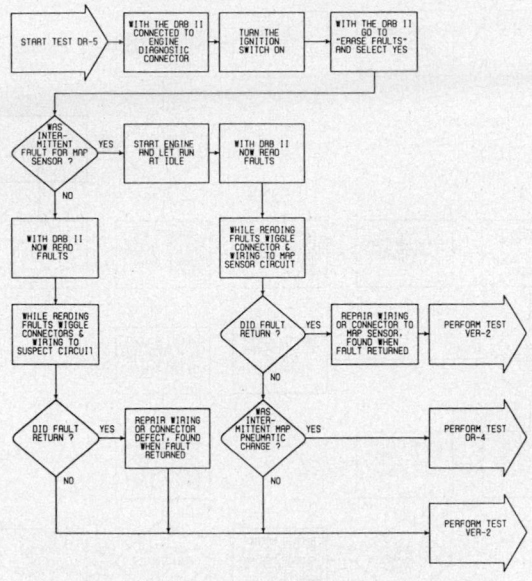

DR-6 – INTERMITTENT TEST FOR INJECTORS & AIS MOTOR

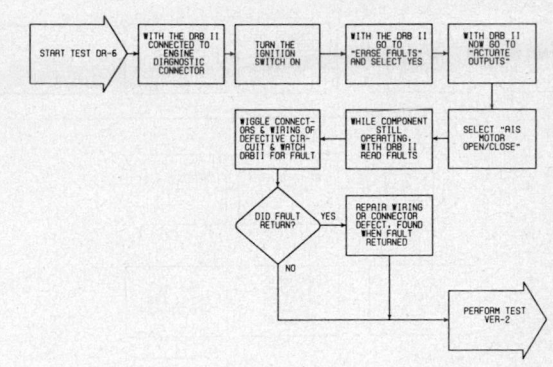

DR-7 – CHECKING FOR FAULT MESSAGE "MAP PNEUMATIC SIGNAL"

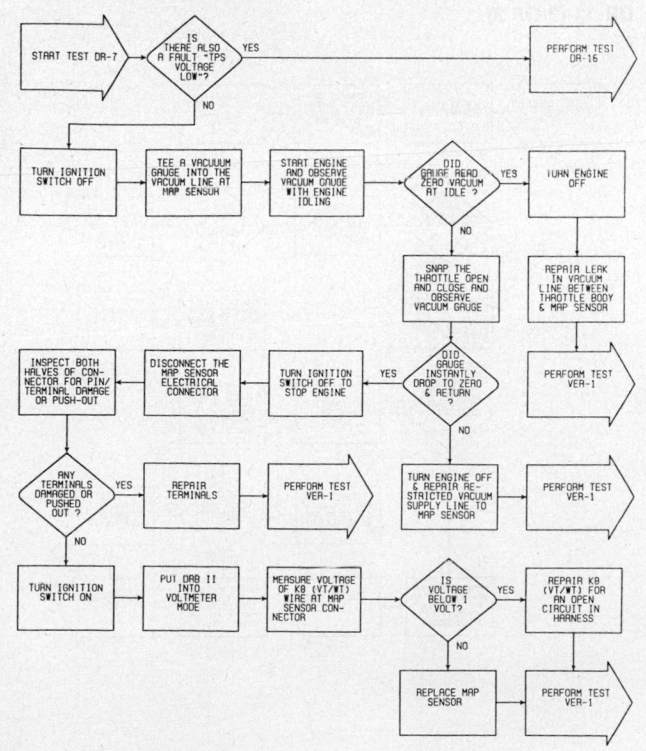

DR-8 – CHECKING FOR FAULT MESSAGE "MAP PNEUMATIC CHANGE"

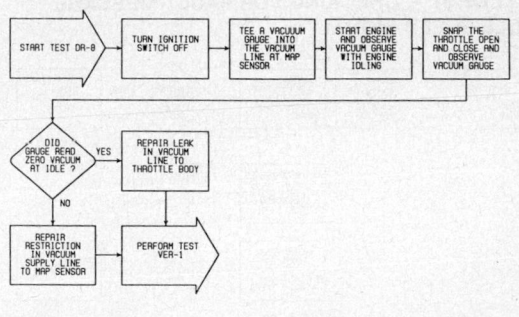

1989 COMPUTERIZED ENGINE CONTROLS
Chrysler Motors 2.2L & 2.5L SPFI (Cont.)

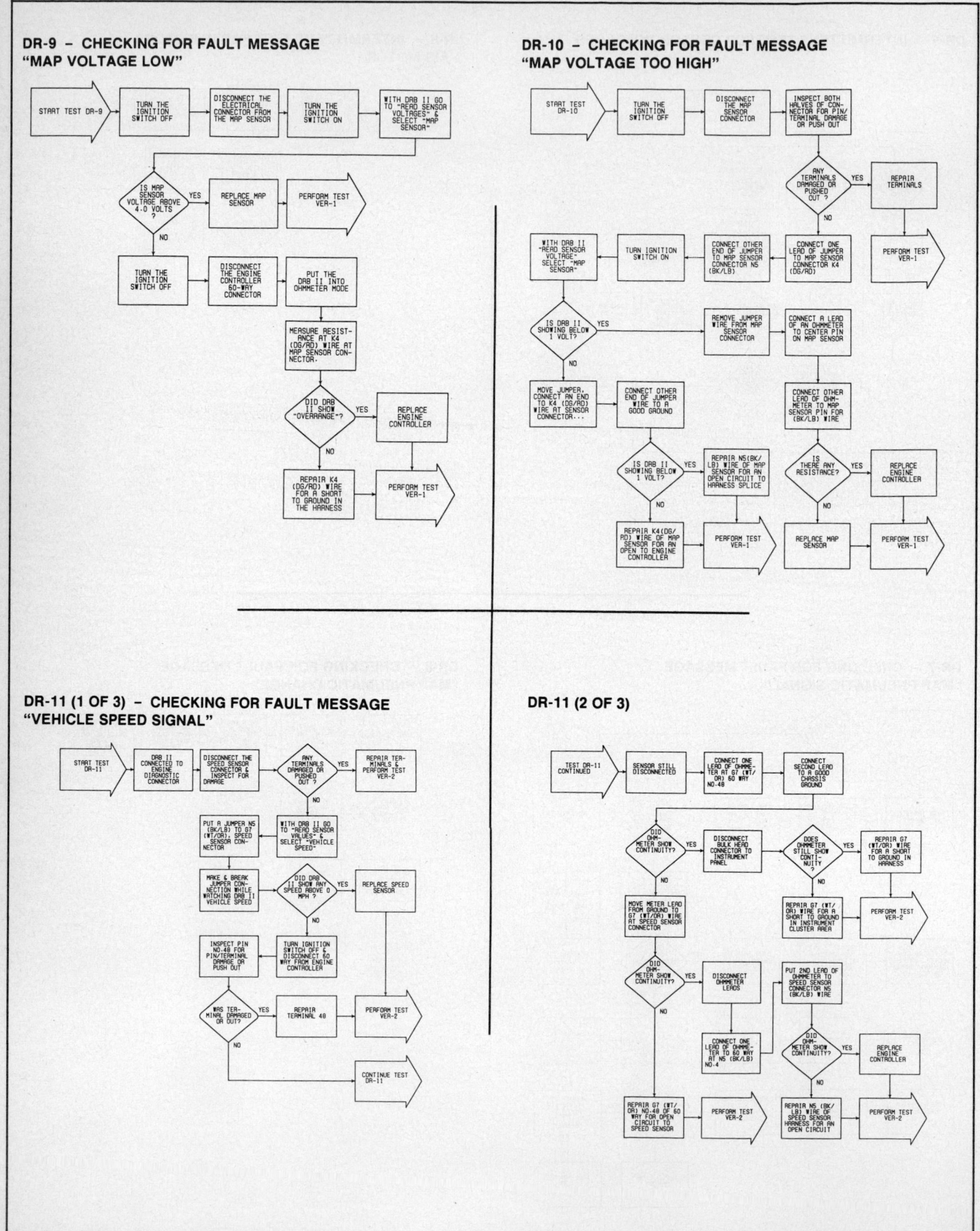

DR-9 – CHECKING FOR FAULT MESSAGE "MAP VOLTAGE LOW"

DR-10 – CHECKING FOR FAULT MESSAGE "MAP VOLTAGE TOO HIGH"

DR-11 (1 OF 3) – CHECKING FOR FAULT MESSAGE "VEHICLE SPEED SIGNAL"

DR-11 (2 OF 3)

1989 COMPUTERIZED ENGINE CONTROLS
Chrysler Motors 2.2L & 2.5L SPFI (Cont.)

1a-59

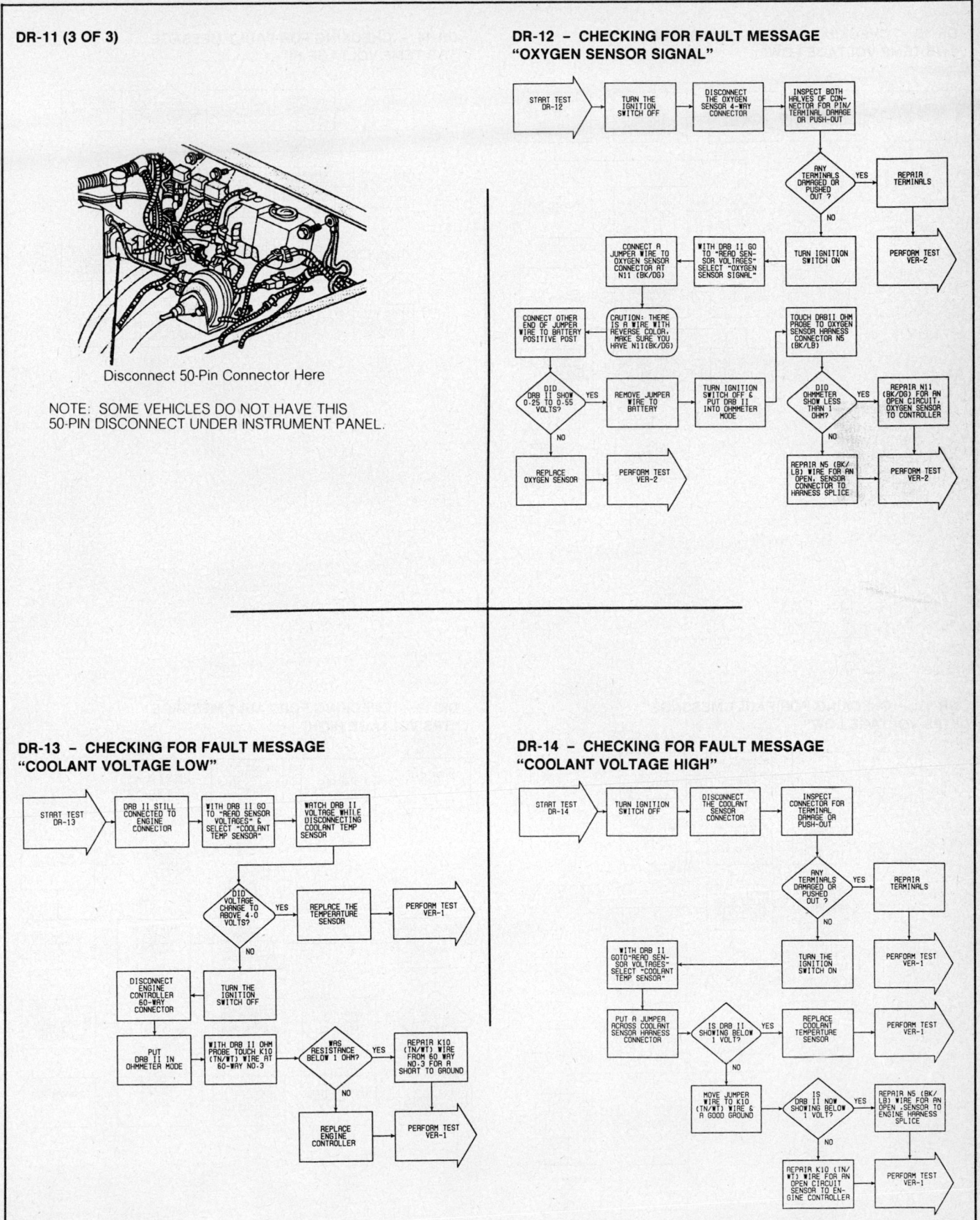

DR-11 (3 OF 3)

Disconnect 50-Pin Connector Here

NOTE: SOME VEHICLES DO NOT HAVE THIS
50-PIN DISCONNECT UNDER INSTRUMENT PANEL.

**DR-12 – CHECKING FOR FAULT MESSAGE
"OXYGEN SENSOR SIGNAL"**

**DR-13 – CHECKING FOR FAULT MESSAGE
"COOLANT VOLTAGE LOW"**

**DR-14 – CHECKING FOR FAULT MESSAGE
"COOLANT VOLTAGE HIGH"**

1989 COMPUTERIZED ENGINE CONTROLS
Chrysler Motors 2.2L & 2.5L SPFI (Cont.)

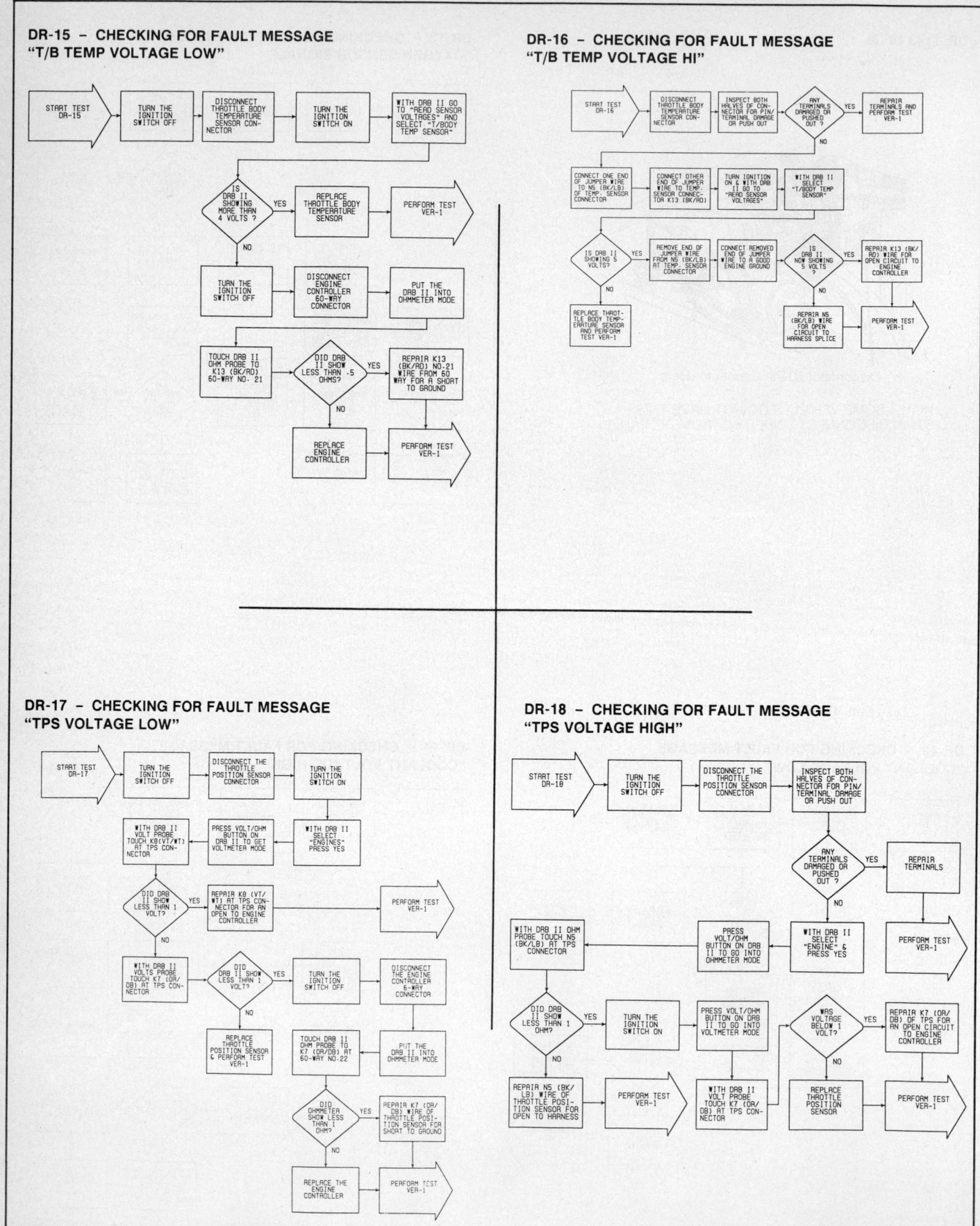

DR-15 – CHECKING FOR FAULT MESSAGE "T/B TEMP VOLTAGE LOW"

DR-16 – CHECKING FOR FAULT MESSAGE "T/B TEMP VOLTAGE HI"

DR-17 – CHECKING FOR FAULT MESSAGE "TPS VOLTAGE LOW"

DR-18 – CHECKING FOR FAULT MESSAGE "TPS VOLTAGE HIGH"

1989 COMPUTERIZED ENGINE CONTROLS
Chrysler Motors 2.2L & 2.5L SPFI (Cont.)

1a-61

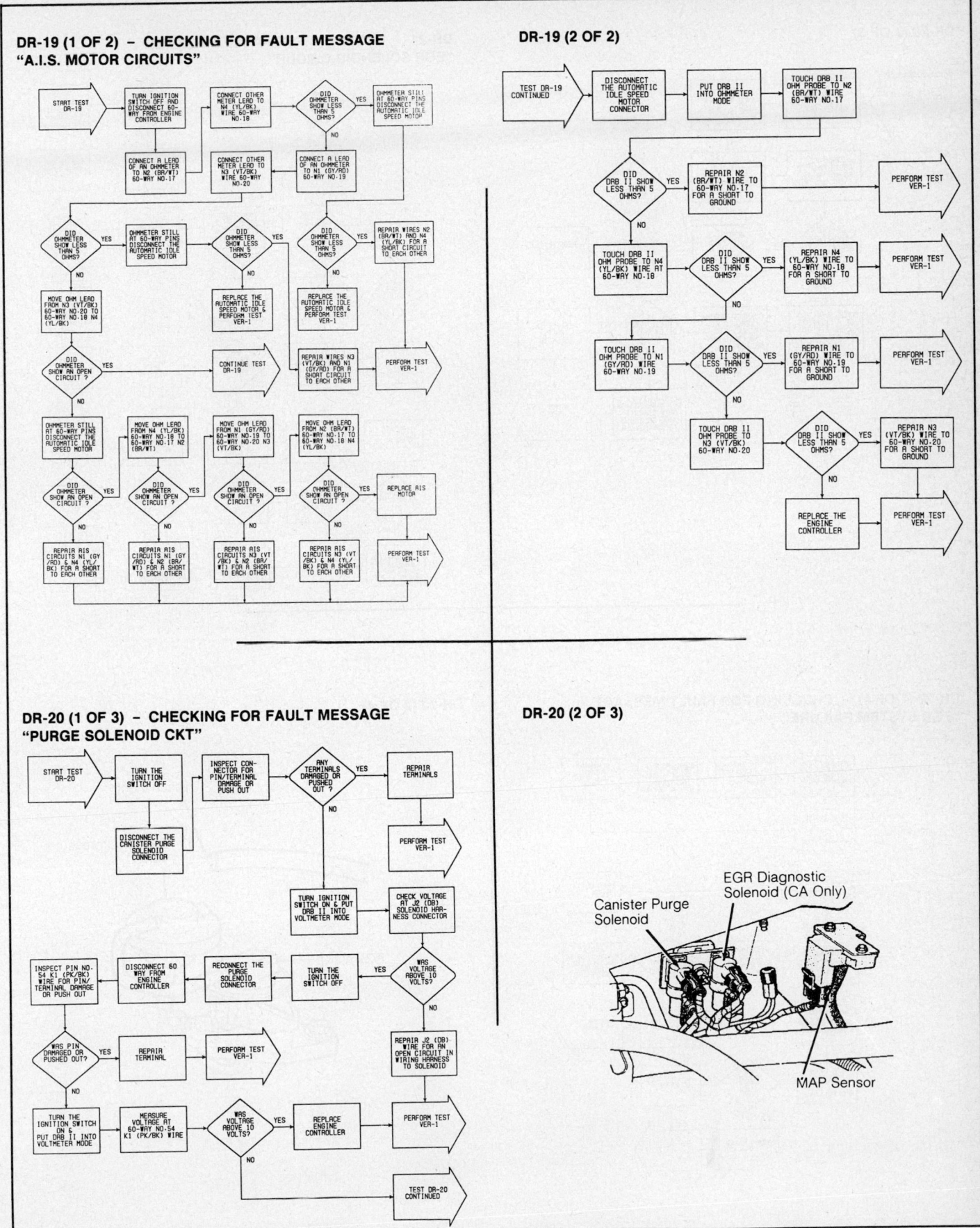

DR-19 (1 OF 2) – CHECKING FOR FAULT MESSAGE "A.I.S. MOTOR CIRCUITS"

DR-19 (2 OF 2)

DR-20 (1 OF 3) – CHECKING FOR FAULT MESSAGE "PURGE SOLENOID CKT"

DR-20 (2 OF 3)

Canister Purge Solenoid

EGR Diagnostic Solenoid (CA Only)

MAP Sensor

1989 COMPUTERIZED ENGINE CONTROLS
Chrysler Motors 2.2L & 2.5L SPFI (Cont.)

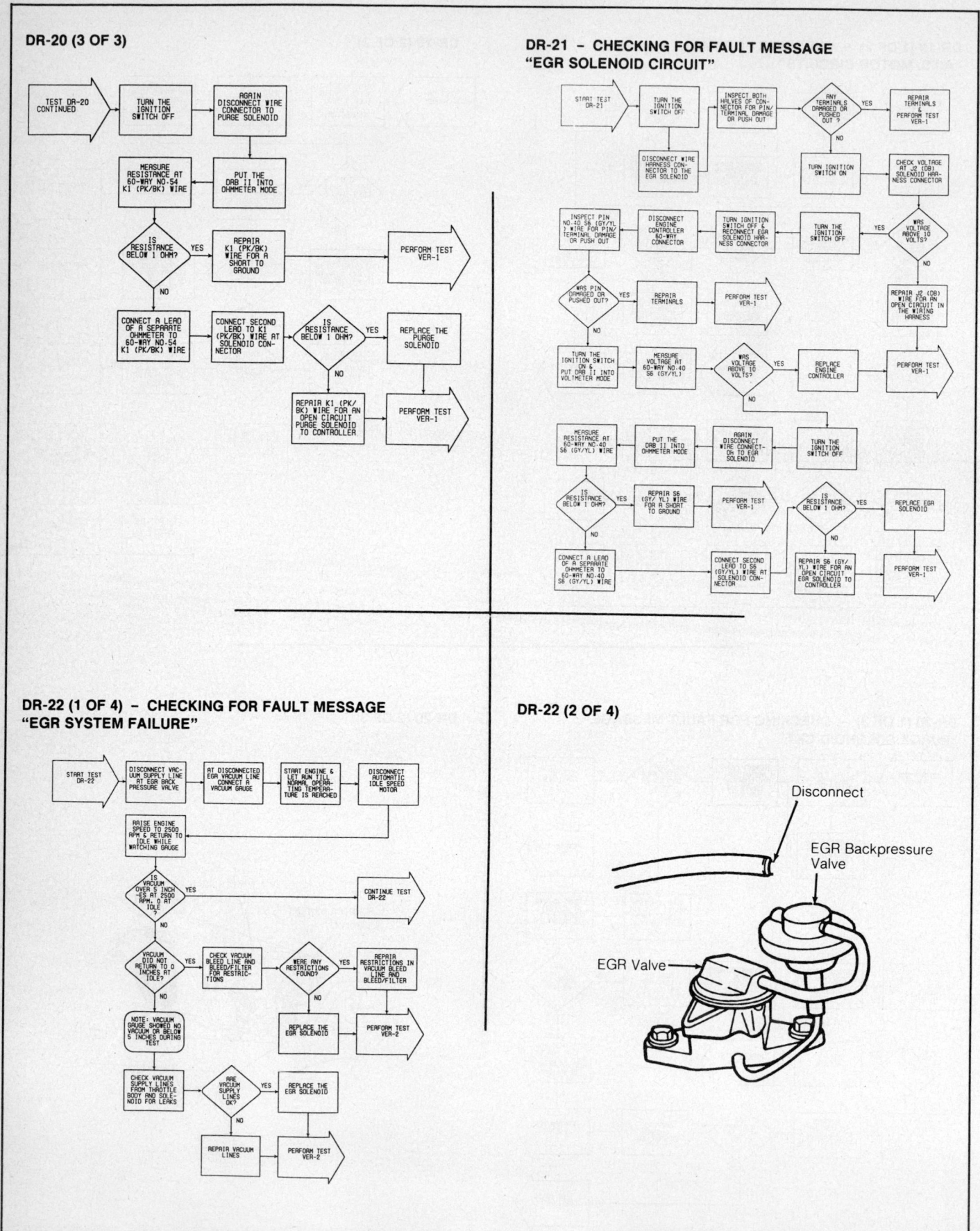

DR-20 (3 OF 3)

DR-21 – CHECKING FOR FAULT MESSAGE "EGR SOLENOID CIRCUIT"

DR-22 (1 OF 4) – CHECKING FOR FAULT MESSAGE "EGR SYSTEM FAILURE"

DR-22 (2 OF 4)

Disconnect

EGR Backpressure Valve

EGR Valve

1989 COMPUTERIZED ENGINE CONTROLS
Chrysler Motors 2.2L & 2.5L SPFI (Cont.)

1a-63

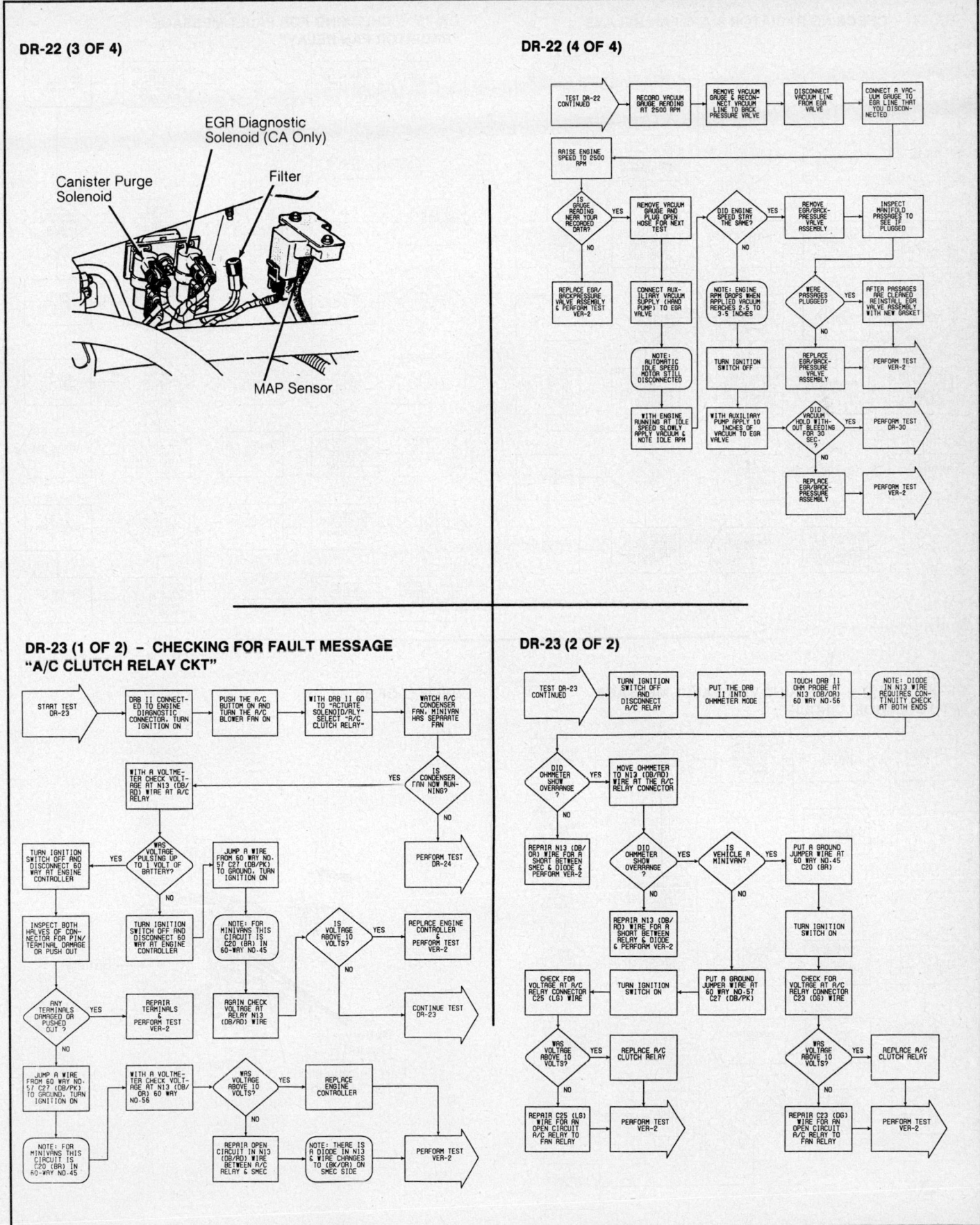

DR-22 (3 OF 4)

Canister Purge Solenoid

EGR Diagnostic Solenoid (CA Only)

Filter

MAP Sensor

DR-22 (4 OF 4)

DR-23 (1 OF 2) – CHECKING FOR FAULT MESSAGE "A/C CLUTCH RELAY CKT"

DR-23 (2 OF 2)

1989 COMPUTERIZED ENGINE CONTROLS
Chrysler Motors 2.2L & 2.5L SPFI (Cont.)

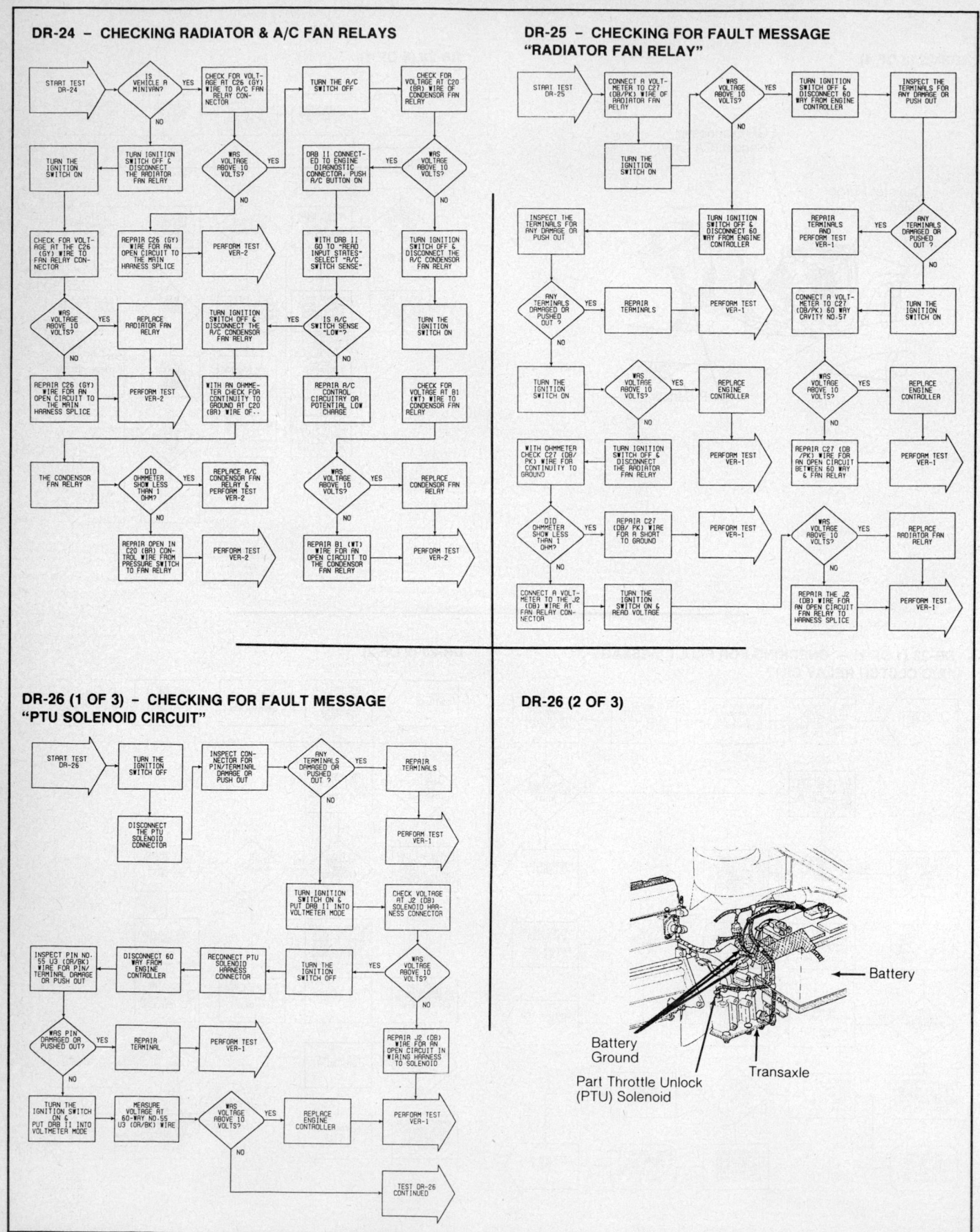

DR-24 – CHECKING RADIATOR & A/C FAN RELAYS

DR-25 – CHECKING FOR FAULT MESSAGE "RADIATOR FAN RELAY"

DR-26 (1 OF 3) – CHECKING FOR FAULT MESSAGE "PTU SOLENOID CIRCUIT"

DR-26 (2 OF 3)

Battery

Battery Ground

Transaxle

Part Throttle Unlock (PTU) Solenoid

1989 COMPUTERIZED ENGINE CONTROLS
Chrysler Motors 2.2L & 2.5L SPFI (Cont.)

1a-65

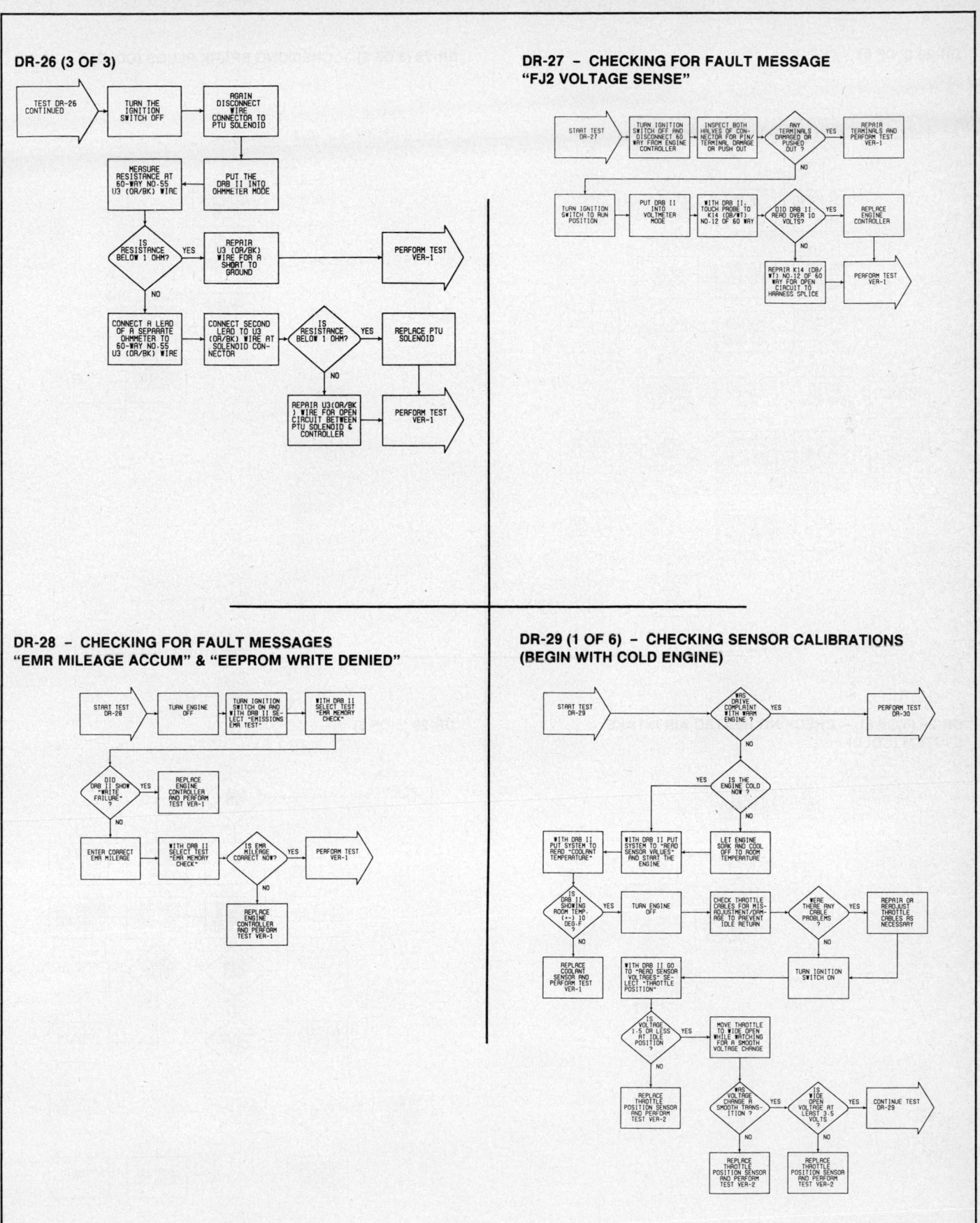

DR-26 (3 OF 3)

DR-27 – CHECKING FOR FAULT MESSAGE "FJ2 VOLTAGE SENSE"

DR-28 – CHECKING FOR FAULT MESSAGES "EMR MILEAGE ACCUM" & "EEPROM WRITE DENIED"

DR-29 (1 OF 6) – CHECKING SENSOR CALIBRATIONS (BEGIN WITH COLD ENGINE)

1a-66

1989 COMPUTERIZED ENGINE CONTROLS
Chrysler Motors 2.2L & 2.5L SPFI (Cont.)

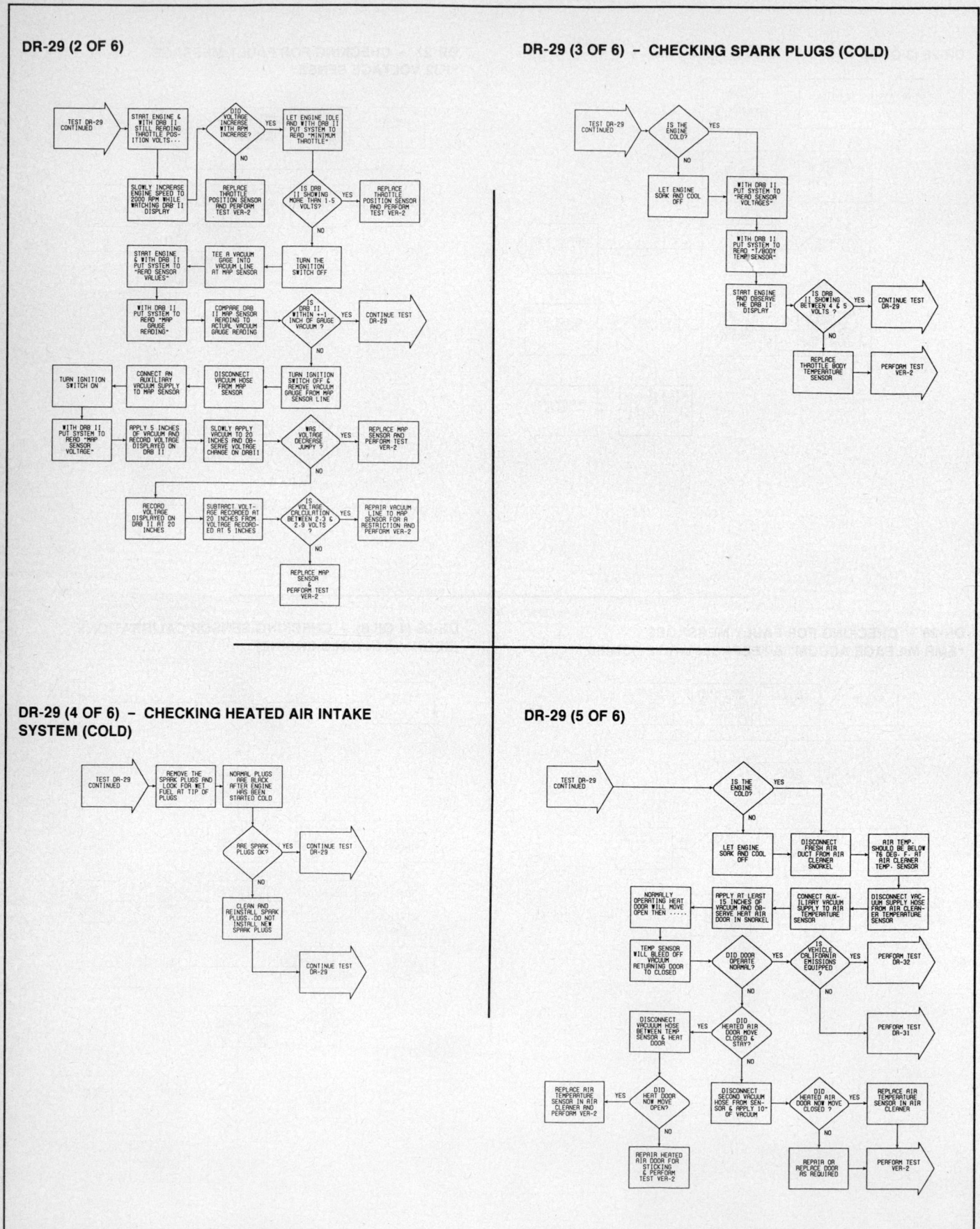

DR-29 (2 OF 6)

DR-29 (3 OF 6) – CHECKING SPARK PLUGS (COLD)

DR-29 (4 OF 6) – CHECKING HEATED AIR INTAKE SYSTEM (COLD)

DR-29 (5 OF 6)

1989 COMPUTERIZED ENGINE CONTROLS
Chrysler Motors 2.2L & 2.5L SPFI (Cont.)

1a-67

DR-29 (6 OF 6)

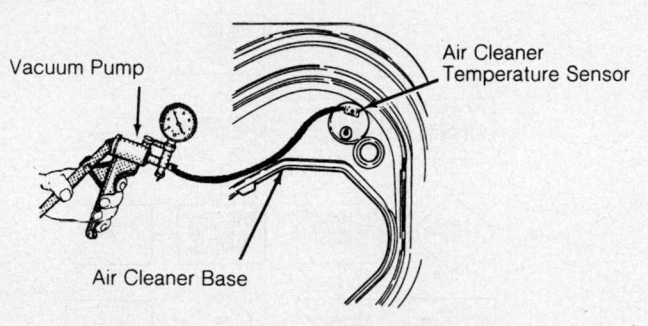

Vacuum Pump

Air Cleaner Temperature Sensor

Air Cleaner Base

DR-30 (1 OF 3) – CHECKING SENSOR CALIBRATIONS (BEGIN WARM ENGINE)

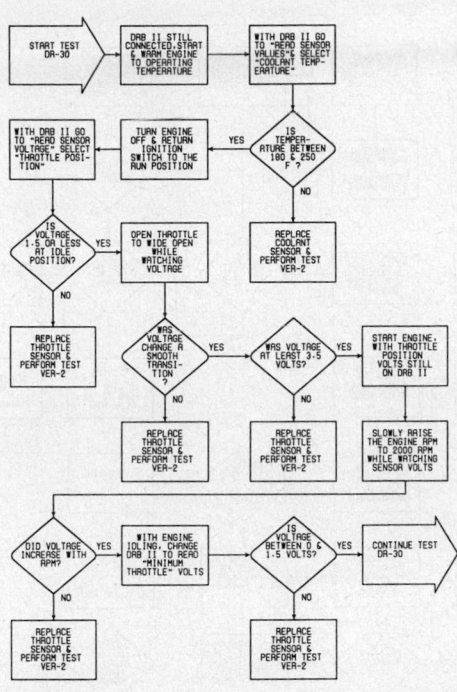

DR-30 (2 OF 3)

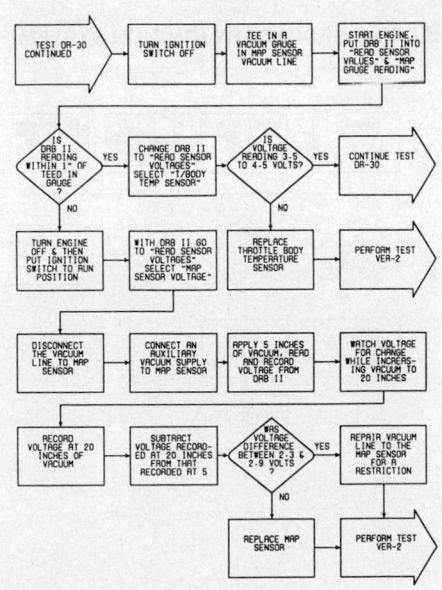

DR-30 (3 OF 3) – CHECKING HEATED AIR INTAKE SYSTEM (WARM)

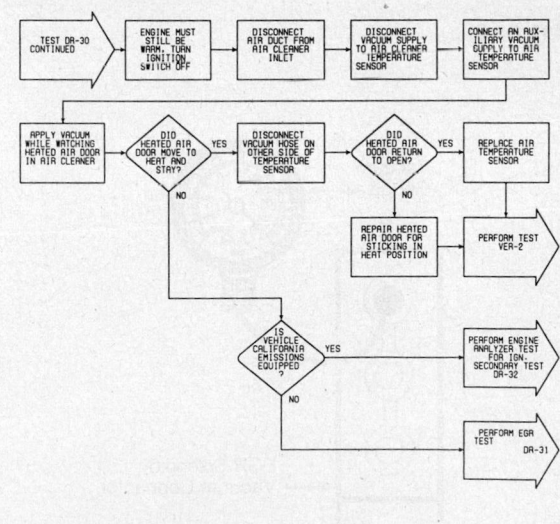

1a-68

1989 COMPUTERIZED ENGINE CONTROLS
Chrysler Motors 2.2L & 2.5L SPFI (Cont.)

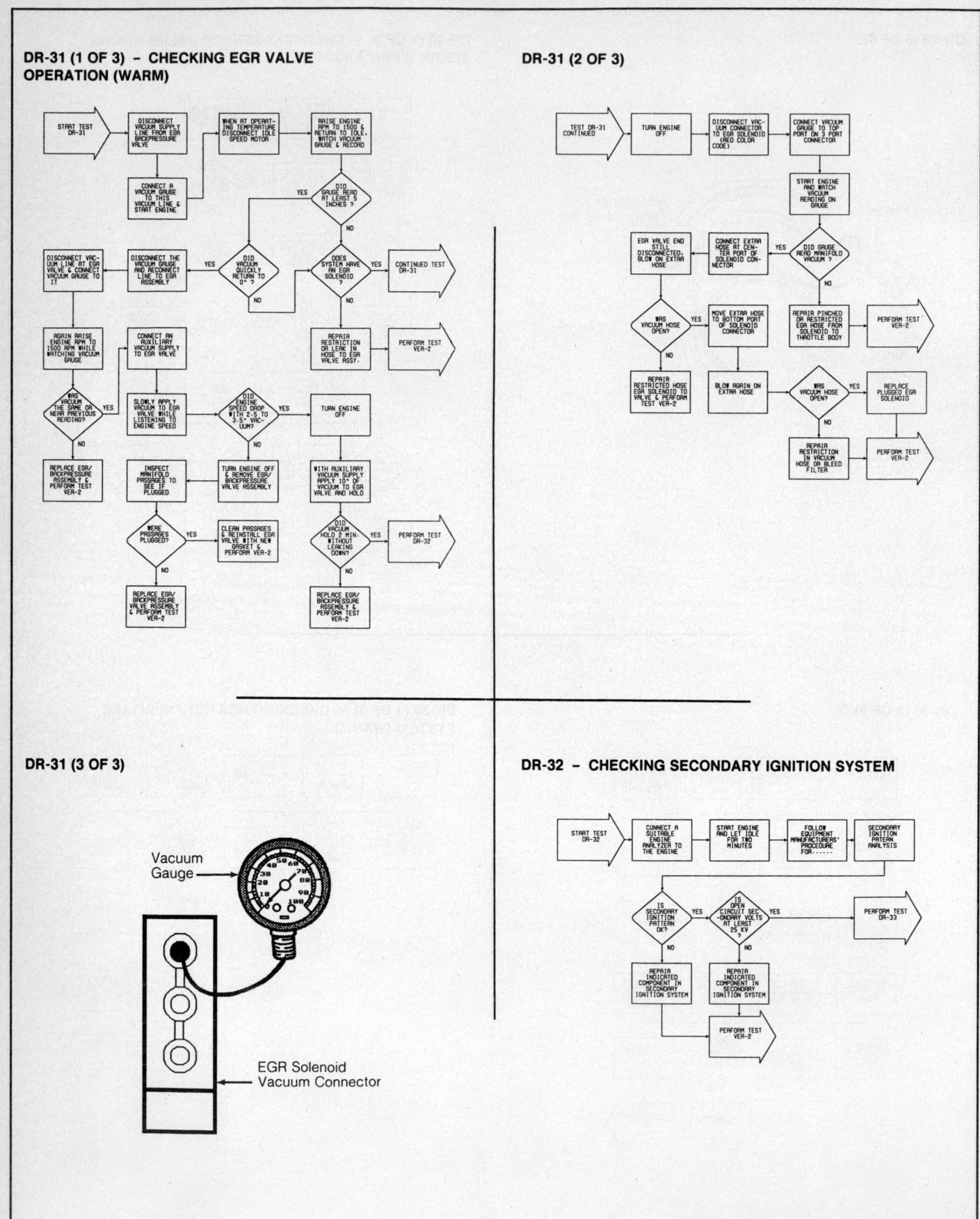

DR-31 (1 OF 3) – CHECKING EGR VALVE OPERATION (WARM)

DR-31 (2 OF 3)

DR-31 (3 OF 3)

Vacuum Gauge

EGR Solenoid Vacuum Connector

DR-32 – CHECKING SECONDARY IGNITION SYSTEM

1989 COMPUTERIZED ENGINE CONTROLS
Chrysler Motors 2.2L & 2.5L SPFI (Cont.)

1a-69

DR-33 (1 OF 5) – CHECKING BASIC TIMING & FUEL SYSTEM

DR-33 (2 OF 5)

DR-33 (3 OF 5)

DR-33 (4 OF 5)

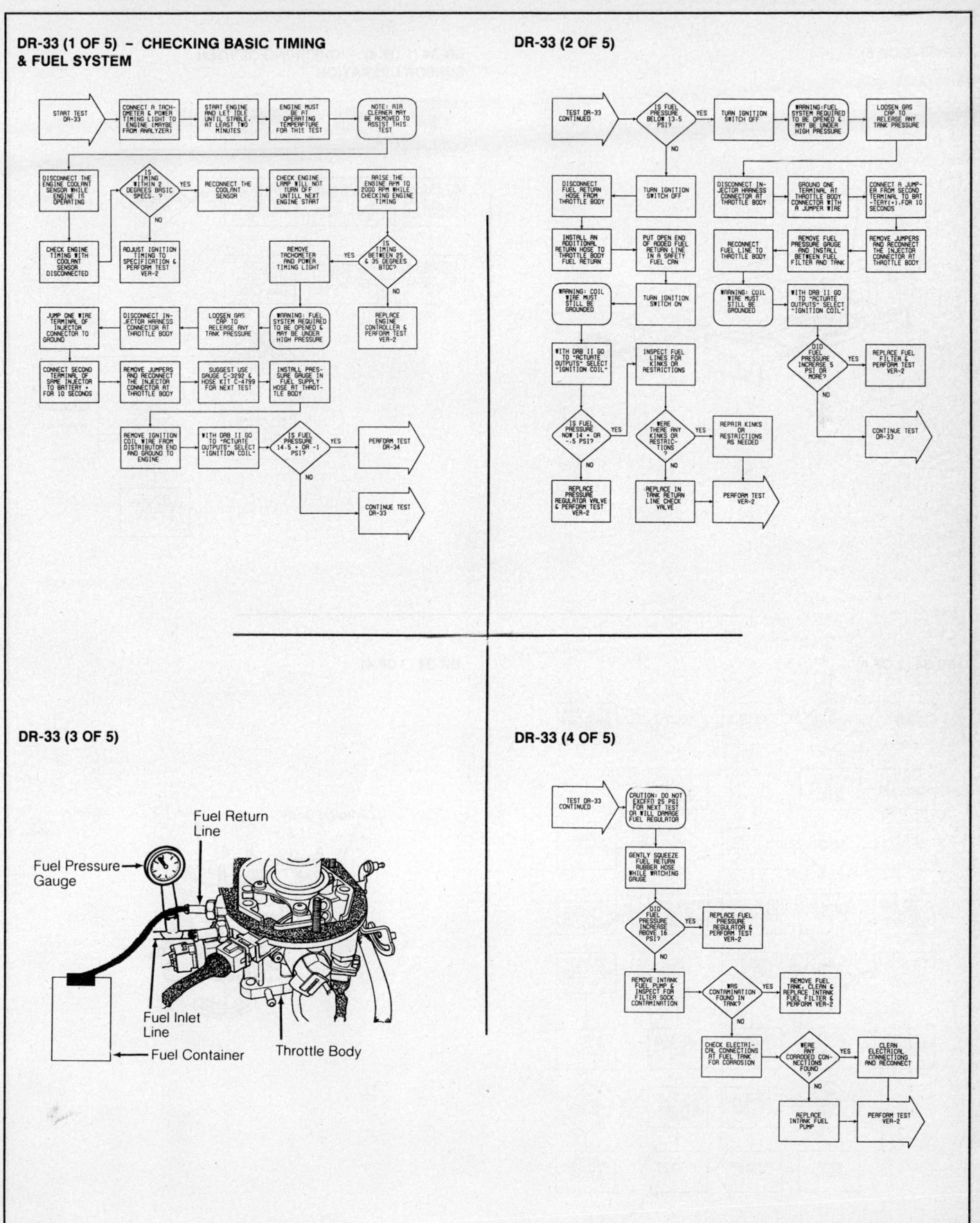

Fuel Return Line

Fuel Pressure Gauge

Fuel Inlet Line

Fuel Container

Throttle Body

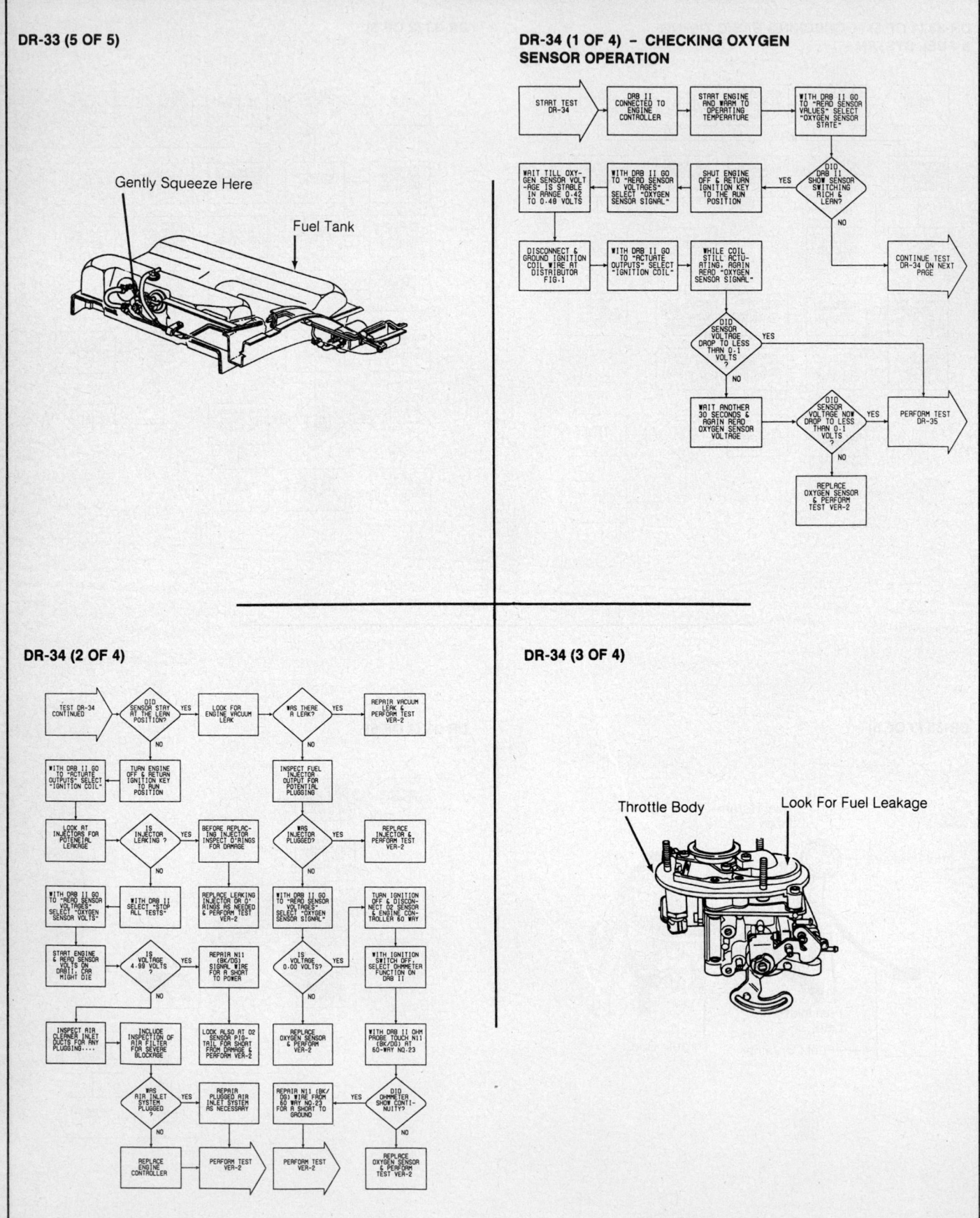

DR-33 (5 OF 5)

Gently Squeeze Here

Fuel Tank

DR-34 (1 OF 4) – CHECKING OXYGEN SENSOR OPERATION

DR-34 (2 OF 4)

DR-34 (3 OF 4)

Throttle Body

Look For Fuel Leakage

1989 COMPUTERIZED ENGINE CONTROLS
Chrysler Motors 2.2L & 2.5L SPFI (Cont.)

1a-71

DR-34 (4 OF 4)

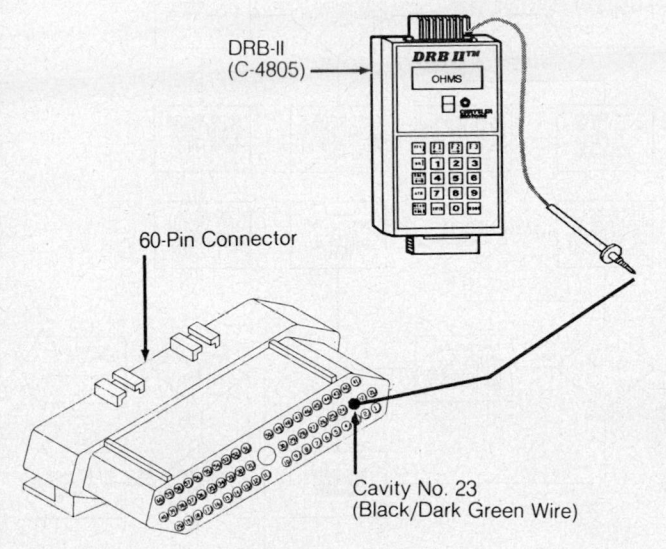

DRB-II
(C-4805)

60-Pin Connector

Cavity No. 23
(Black/Dark Green Wire)

DR-35 (1 OF 2) – CHECKING THROTTLE BODY MINIMUM AIRFLOW

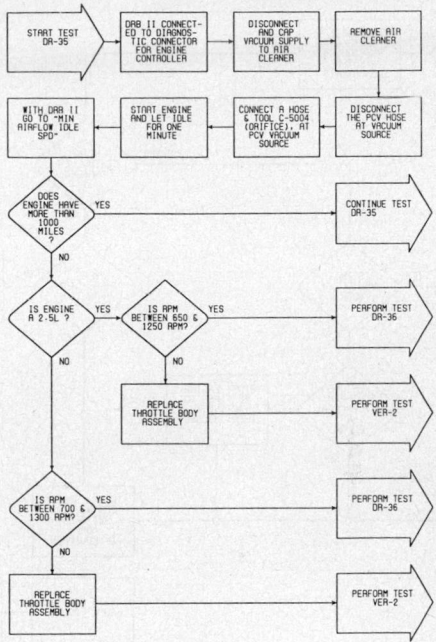

DR-35 (2 OF 2)

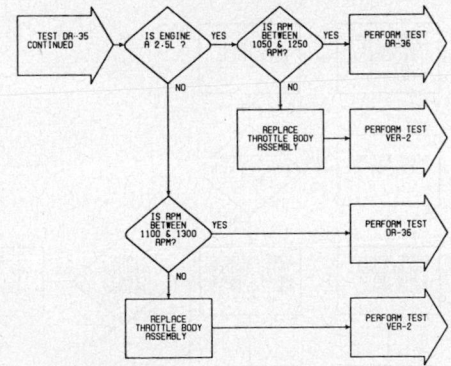

DR-36 – OTHER POSSIBLE CAUSES OF DRIVEABILITY RELATED PROBLEMS

AT THIS POINT IN THE DRIVEABILITY TEST PROCEDURE YOU HAVE DETERMINED THAT ALL OF THE ENGINE CONTROL SYSTEMS ARE OPERATING AS THEY WERE DESIGNED. THEREFORE, THEY ARE **NOT THE CAUSE OF THE DRIVEABILITY PROBLEM.**

THE FOLLOWING ADDITIONAL ITEMS SHOULD BE CHECKED AS POSSIBLE CAUSES:

1. **ENGINE VACUUM** - MUST BE AT LEAST 13 INCHES IN NEUTRAL.
2. **ENGINE VALVE TIMING** - TO SPECIFICATIONS.
3. **ENGINE COMPRESSION** - TO SPECIFICATIONS.
4. **ENGINE EXHAUST SYSTEM** - MUST BE FREE OF ANY RESTRICTIONS.
5. **ENGINE PCV SYSTEM** - MUST FLOW FREELY.
6. **ENGINE DRIVE SPROCKETS** - CAM, CRANK AND INTERMEDIATE SHAFTS.
7. **TORQUE CONVERTOR STALL SPEED** - TO SPECIFICATIONS.
8. **POWER BRAKE BOOSTER** - NO INTERNAL VACUUM LEAKS.
9. **FUEL CONTAMINATION** - HIGH ALCOHOL AND WATER CONTENT.
10. **TECHNICAL SERVICE BULLETINS** - ANY THAT MAY APPLY TO VEHICLE.

ANY ONE OR MORE OF THESE ITEMS CAN CREATE A DRIVEABILITY RELATED PROBLEM. THEY CAN NOT BE OVERLOOKED AS POSSIBLE CAUSES.

1989 COMPUTERIZED ENGINE CONTROLS
Chrysler Motors 2.2L & 2.5L SPFI (Cont.)

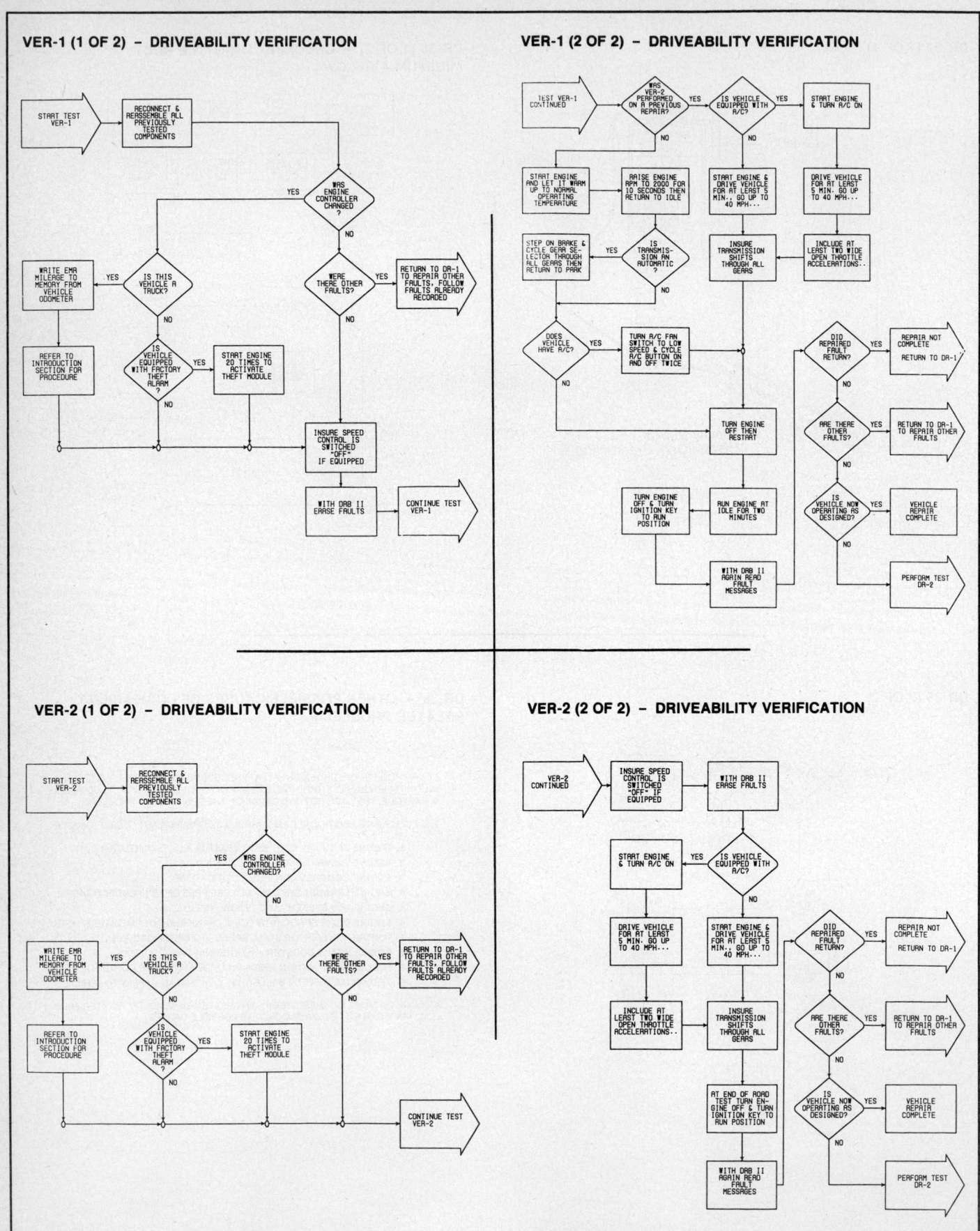

VER-1 (1 OF 2) – DRIVEABILITY VERIFICATION

VER-1 (2 OF 2) – DRIVEABILITY VERIFICATION

VER-2 (1 OF 2) – DRIVEABILITY VERIFICATION

VER-2 (2 OF 2) – DRIVEABILITY VERIFICATION

1989 COMPUTERIZED ENGINE CONTROLS
Chrysler Motors 2.2L & 2.5L SPFI (Cont.)

1a-73

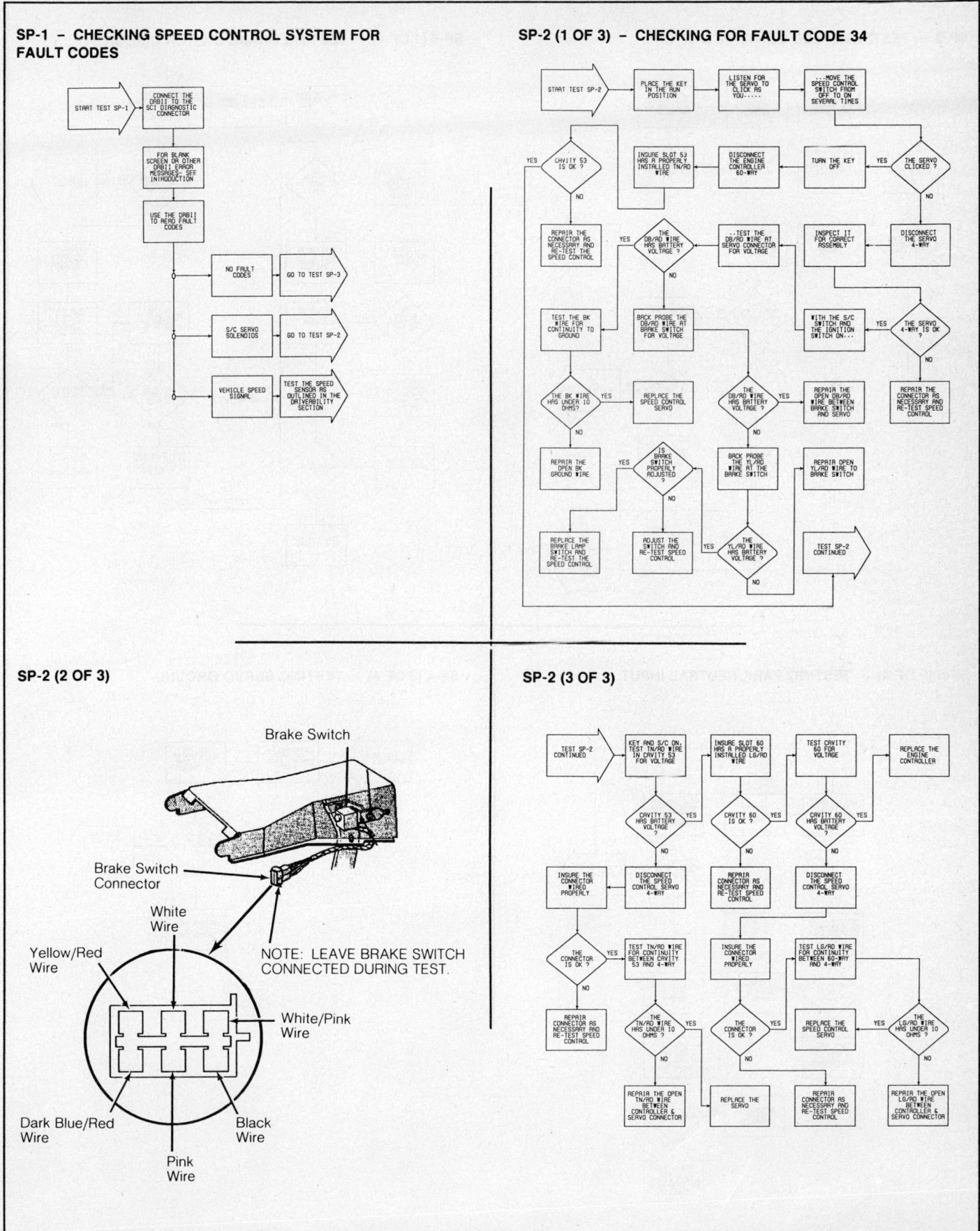

SP-1 – CHECKING SPEED CONTROL SYSTEM FOR FAULT CODES

SP-2 (1 OF 3) – CHECKING FOR FAULT CODE 34

SP-2 (2 OF 3)

Brake Switch

Brake Switch Connector

White Wire

Yellow/Red Wire

White/Pink Wire

NOTE: LEAVE BRAKE SWITCH CONNECTED DURING TEST.

Dark Blue/Red Wire

Pink Wire

Black Wire

SP-2 (3 OF 3)

1a-74

1989 COMPUTERIZED ENGINE CONTROLS
Chrysler Motors 2.2L & 2.5L SPFI (Cont.)

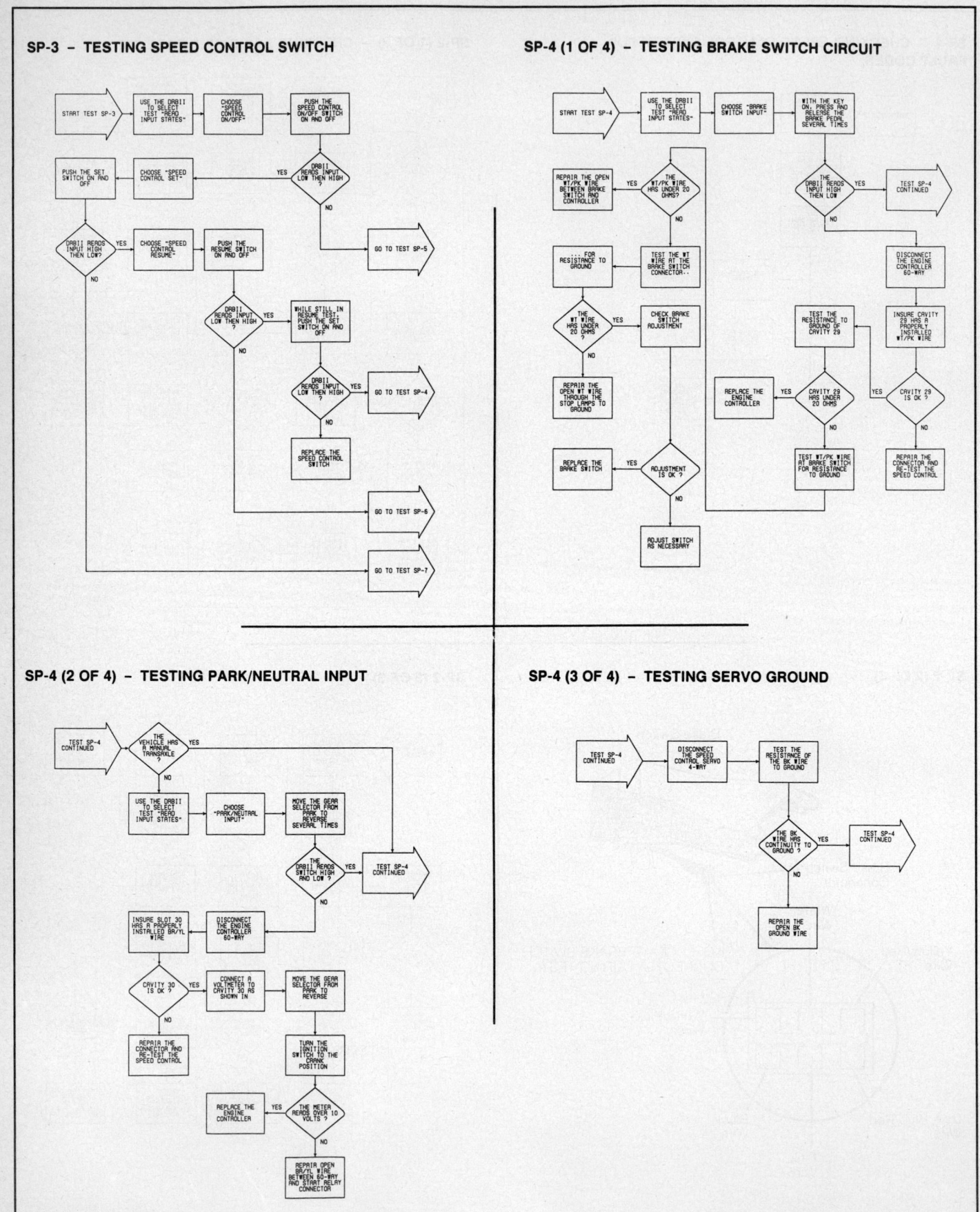

SP-3 – TESTING SPEED CONTROL SWITCH

SP-4 (1 OF 4) – TESTING BRAKE SWITCH CIRCUIT

SP-4 (2 OF 4) – TESTING PARK/NEUTRAL INPUT

SP-4 (3 OF 4) – TESTING SERVO GROUND

1989 COMPUTERIZED ENGINE CONTROLS
Chrysler Motors 2.2L & 2.5L SPFI (Cont.)

1a-75

SP-4 (4 OF 4) – SERVO ACTUATOR TEST

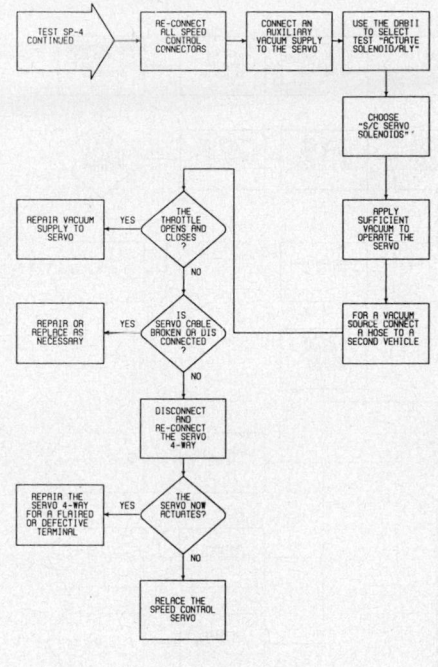

SP-5 (1 OF 2) – CHECKING ON/OFF SWITCH & STALK FEED

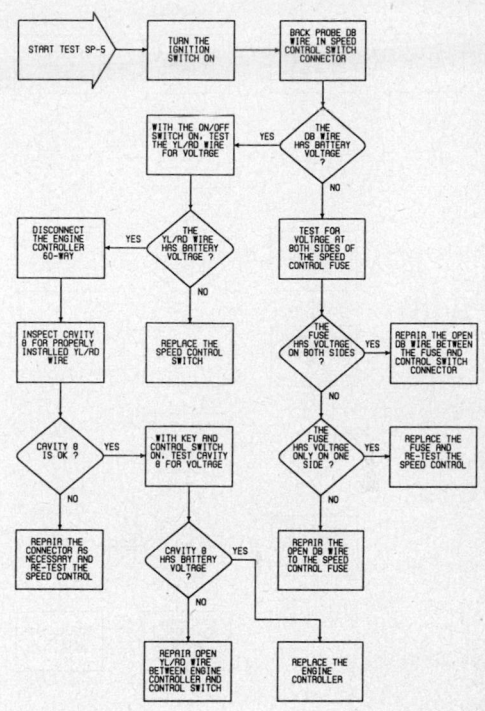

SP-5 (2 OF 2)

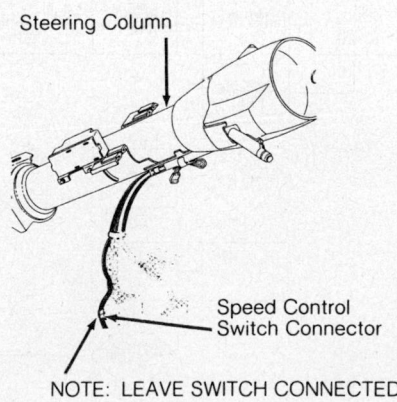

Steering Column

Speed Control Switch Connector

NOTE: LEAVE SWITCH CONNECTED.

SP-6 – TESTING "RESUME" SWITCH

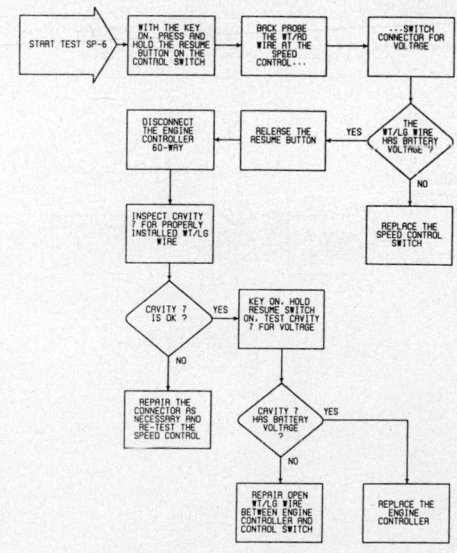

1a-76

1989 COMPUTERIZED ENGINE CONTROLS
Chrysler Motors 2.2L & 2.5L SPFI (Cont.)

SP-7 – TESTING "SET" SWITCH

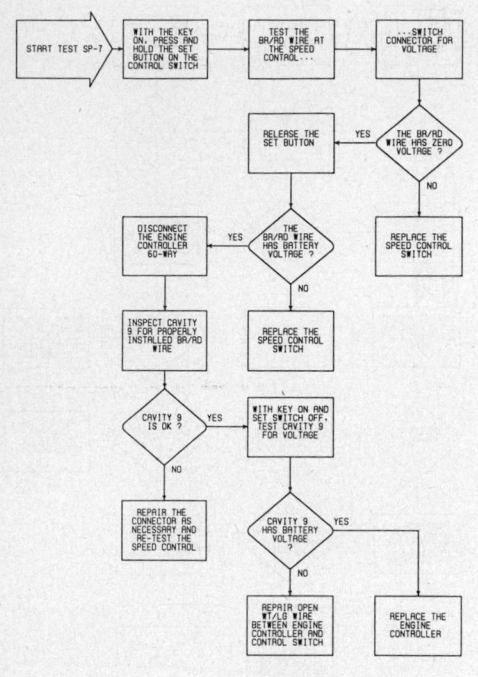

CH-1 – CHECKING CHARGING SYSTEM FOR FAULT CODES

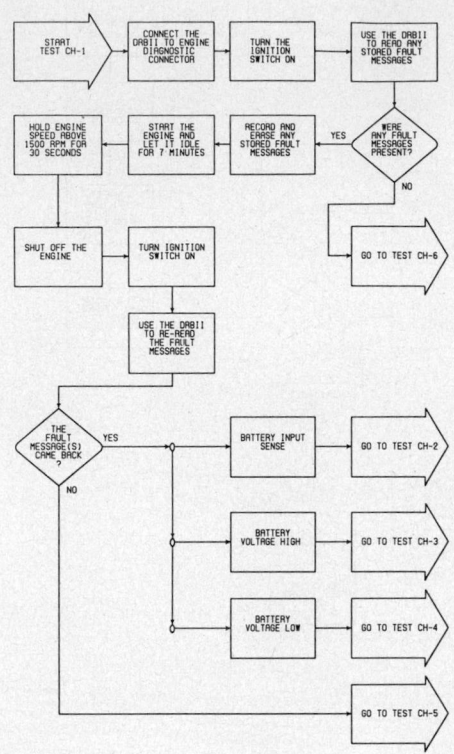

CH-2 – CHECKING FOR FAULT CODE 16
LOSS OF BATTERY VOLTAGE SENSE

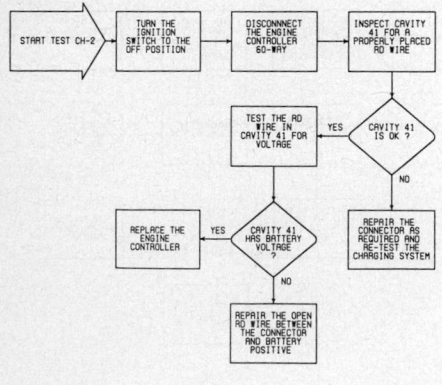

CH-3 (1 OF 2) – CHECKING FOR FAULT CODE 46
BATTERY VOLTAGE TOO HIGH

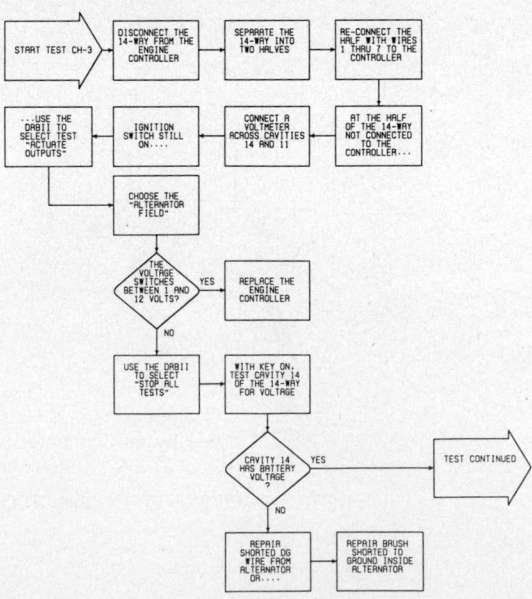

1989 COMPUTERIZED ENGINE CONTROLS
Chrysler Motors 2.2L & 2.5L SPFI (Cont.)

1a-77

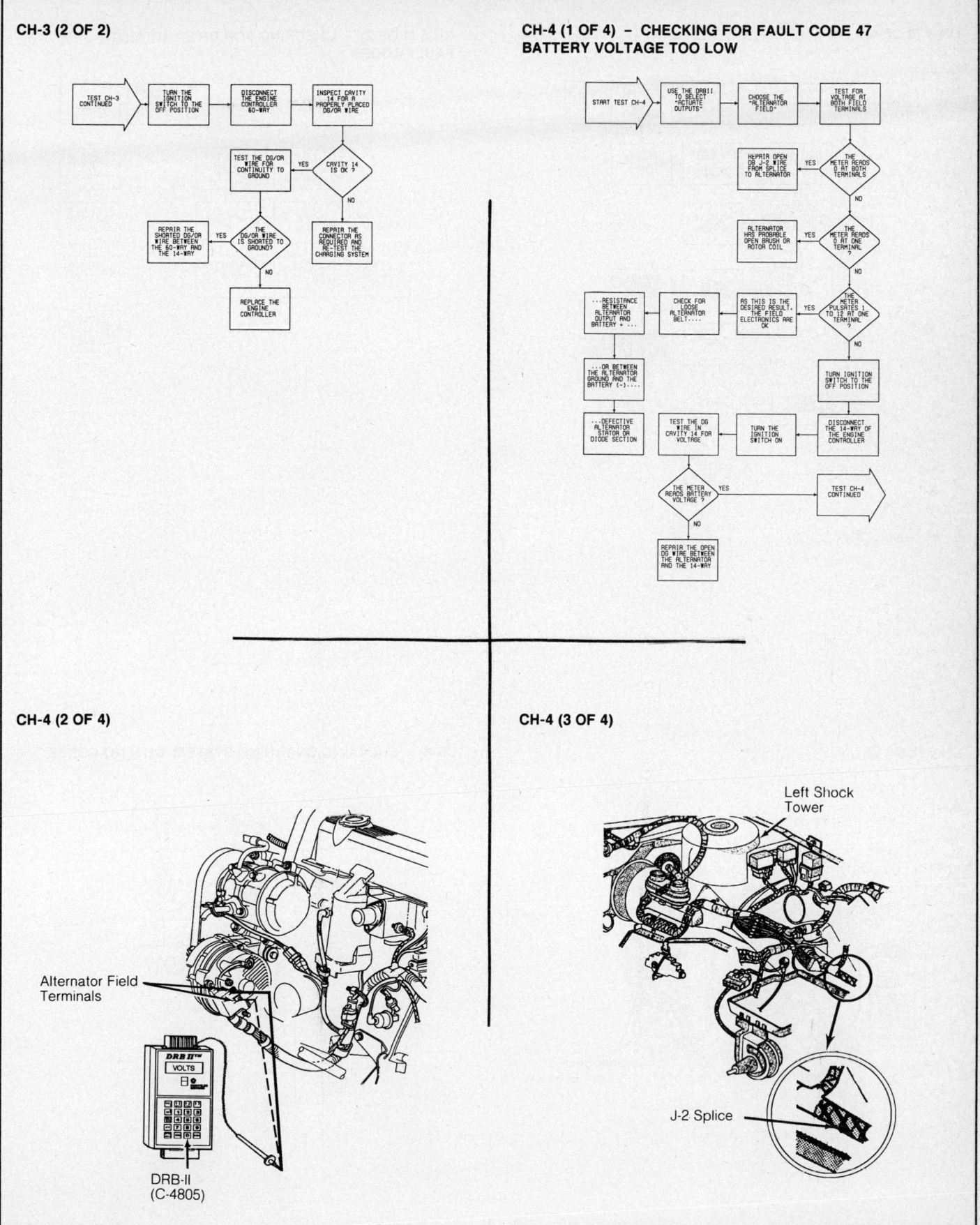

CH-3 (2 OF 2)

TEST CH-3 CONTINUED → TURN THE IGNITION SWITCH TO THE OFF POSITION → DISCONNECT THE ENGINE CONTROLLER 60-WAY → INSPECT CAVITY 14 FOR A PROPERLY PLACED DG/OR WIRE

TEST THE DG/OR WIRE FOR CONTINUITY TO GROUND ← CAVITY 14 IS OK ?

YES → CAVITY 14 IS OK ?

NO → REPAIR THE CONNECTOR AS REQUIRED AND RE-TEST THE CHARGING SYSTEM

REPAIR THE SHORTED DG/OR WIRE BETWEEN THE 60-WAY AND THE 14-WAY ← YES ← THE DG/OR WIRE IS SHORTED TO GROUND?

NO → REPLACE THE ENGINE CONTROLLER

CH-4 (1 OF 4) – CHECKING FOR FAULT CODE 47 BATTERY VOLTAGE TOO LOW

START TEST CH-4 → USE THE DRBII TO SELECT "ACTUATE OUTPUTS" → CHOOSE THE "ALTERNATOR FIELD" → TEST FOR VOLTAGE AT BOTH FIELD TERMINALS

REPAIR OPEN DB J-2 WIRE FROM SPLICE TO ALTERNATOR ← YES ← THE METER READS 0 AT BOTH TERMINALS

NO → ALTERNATOR HAS PROBABLE OPEN BRUSH OR ROTOR COIL ← YES ← THE METER READS 0 AT ONE TERMINAL ?

NO → THE METER PULSATES 1 TO 12 AT ONE TERMINAL ?

...RESISTANCE BETWEEN ALTERNATOR OUTPUT AND BATTERY + ... ← CHECK FOR LOOSE ALTERNATOR BELT..... ← AS THIS IS THE DESIRED RESULT, THE FIELD ELECTRONICS ARE OK ← YES

...OR BETWEEN THE ALTERNATOR GROUND AND THE BATTERY (-).....

...DEFECTIVE ALTERNATOR STATOR OR DIODE SECTION ← TEST THE DG WIRE IN CAVITY 14 FOR VOLTAGE ← TURN THE IGNITION SWITCH ON ← DISCONNECT THE 14-WAY OF THE ENGINE CONTROLLER

TURN IGNITION SWITCH TO THE OFF POSITION (from NO on meter pulsates)

THE METER READS BATTERY VOLTAGE ? → YES → TEST CH-4 CONTINUED

NO → REPAIR THE OPEN DG WIRE BETWEEN THE ALTERNATOR AND THE 14-WAY

CH-4 (2 OF 4)

Alternator Field Terminals

DRB-II (C-4805)

DRB II

VOLTS

CH-4 (3 OF 4)

Left Shock Tower

J-2 Splice

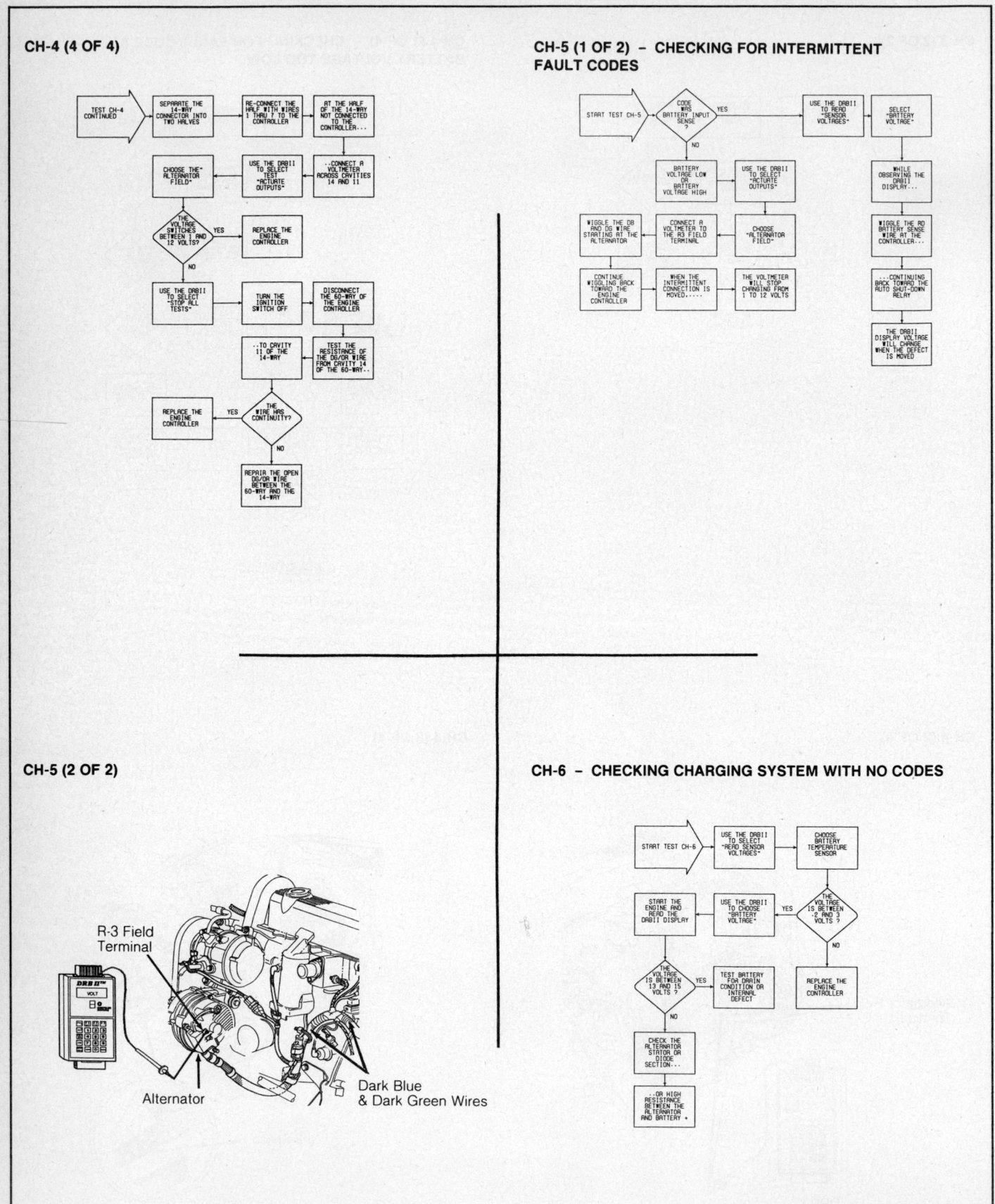

CH-4 (4 OF 4)

TEST CH-4 CONTINUED → SEPARATE THE 14-WAY CONNECTOR INTO TWO HALVES → RE-CONNECT THE HALF WITH WIRES 1 THRU 7 TO THE CONTROLLER → AT THE HALF OF THE 14-WAY NOT CONNECTED TO THE CONTROLLER...

CHOOSE THE "ALTERNATOR FIELD" → USE THE DRBII TO SELECT TEST "ACTUATE OUTPUTS" → ...CONNECT A VOLTMETER ACROSS CAVITIES 14 AND 11

THE VOLTAGE SWITCHES BETWEEN 1 AND 12 VOLTS? — YES → REPLACE THE ENGINE CONTROLLER

NO

USE THE DRBII TO SELECT "STOP ALL TESTS" → TURN THE IGNITION SWITCH OFF → DISCONNECT THE 60-WAY OF THE ENGINE CONTROLLER

..TO CAVITY 11 OF THE 14-WAY ← TEST THE RESISTANCE OF THE DG/OR WIRE FROM CAVITY 14 OF THE 60-WAY..

REPLACE THE ENGINE CONTROLLER ← YES — THE WIRE HAS CONTINUITY?

NO

REPAIR THE OPEN DG/OR WIRE BETWEEN THE 60-WAY AND THE 14-WAY

CH-5 (1 OF 2) – CHECKING FOR INTERMITTENT FAULT CODES

START TEST CH-5 → CODE WAS BATTERY INPUT SENSE ? — YES → USE THE DRBII TO READ "SENSOR VOLTAGES" → SELECT "BATTERY VOLTAGE"

NO

BATTERY VOLTAGE LOW OR BATTERY VOLTAGE HIGH → USE THE DRBII TO SELECT "ACTUATE OUTPUTS"

WHILE OBSERVING THE DRBII DISPLAY...

WIGGLE THE DB AND DG WIRE STARTING AT THE ALTERNATOR ← CONNECT A VOLTMETER TO THE R3 FIELD TERMINAL ← CHOOSE "ALTERNATOR FIELD"

WIGGLE THE RD BATTERY SENSE WIRE AT THE CONTROLLER...

CONTINUE WIGGLING BACK TOWARD THE ENGINE CONTROLLER → WHEN THE INTERMITTENT CONNECTION IS MOVED..... → THE VOLTMETER WILL STOP CHANGING FROM 1 TO 12 VOLTS

...CONTINUING BACK TOWARD THE AUTO SHUT-DOWN RELAY

THE DRBII DISPLAY VOLTAGE WILL CHANGE WHEN THE DEFECT IS MOVED

CH-5 (2 OF 2)

R-3 Field Terminal

Alternator

Dark Blue & Dark Green Wires

CH-6 – CHECKING CHARGING SYSTEM WITH NO CODES

START TEST CH-6 → USE THE DRBII TO SELECT "READ SENSOR VOLTAGES" → CHOOSE BATTERY TEMPERATURE SENSOR

START THE ENGINE AND READ THE DRBII DISPLAY ← USE THE DRBII TO CHOOSE "BATTERY VOLTAGE" ← YES — THE VOLTAGE IS BETWEEN -2 AND 3 VOLTS ?

NO

REPLACE THE ENGINE CONTROLLER

THE VOLTAGE IS BETWEEN 13 AND 15 VOLTS ? — YES → TEST BATTERY FOR DRAIN CONDITION OR INTERNAL DEFECT

NO

CHECK THE ALTERNATOR STATOR OR DIODE SECTION...

..OR HIGH RESISTANCE BETWEEN THE ALTERNATOR AND BATTERY +

1989 Computerized ENGINE CONTROLS
Chrysler Motors 2.2L & 2.5L SPFI (Cont.)

1a-79

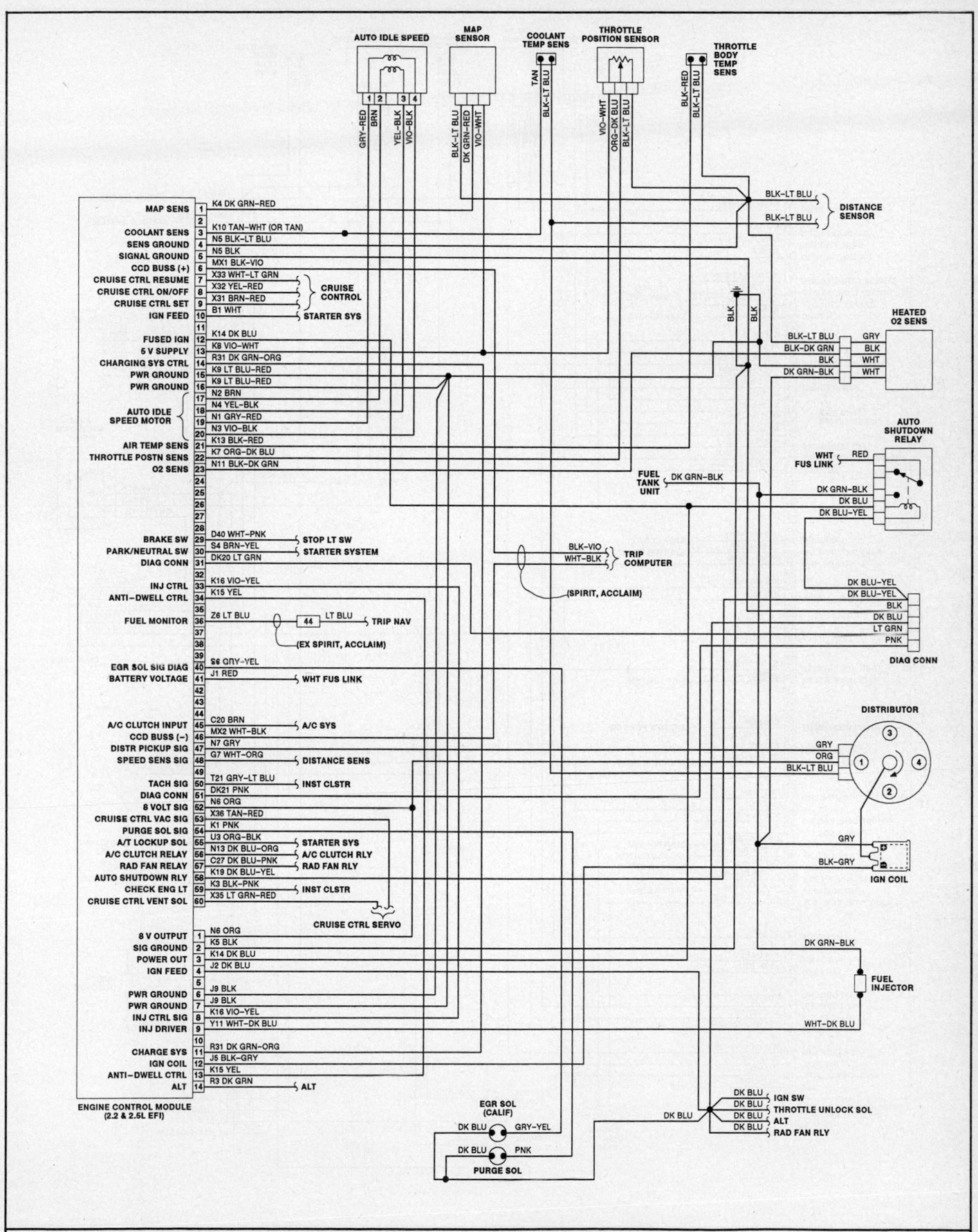

Fig. 7: Acclaim, Daytona, Lancer, LeBaron, Shadow, Spirit & Sundance 2.2L & 2.5L Wiring Diagram

1989 Computerized Engine Controls
Chrysler Motors 2.2L & 2.5L SPFI (Cont.)

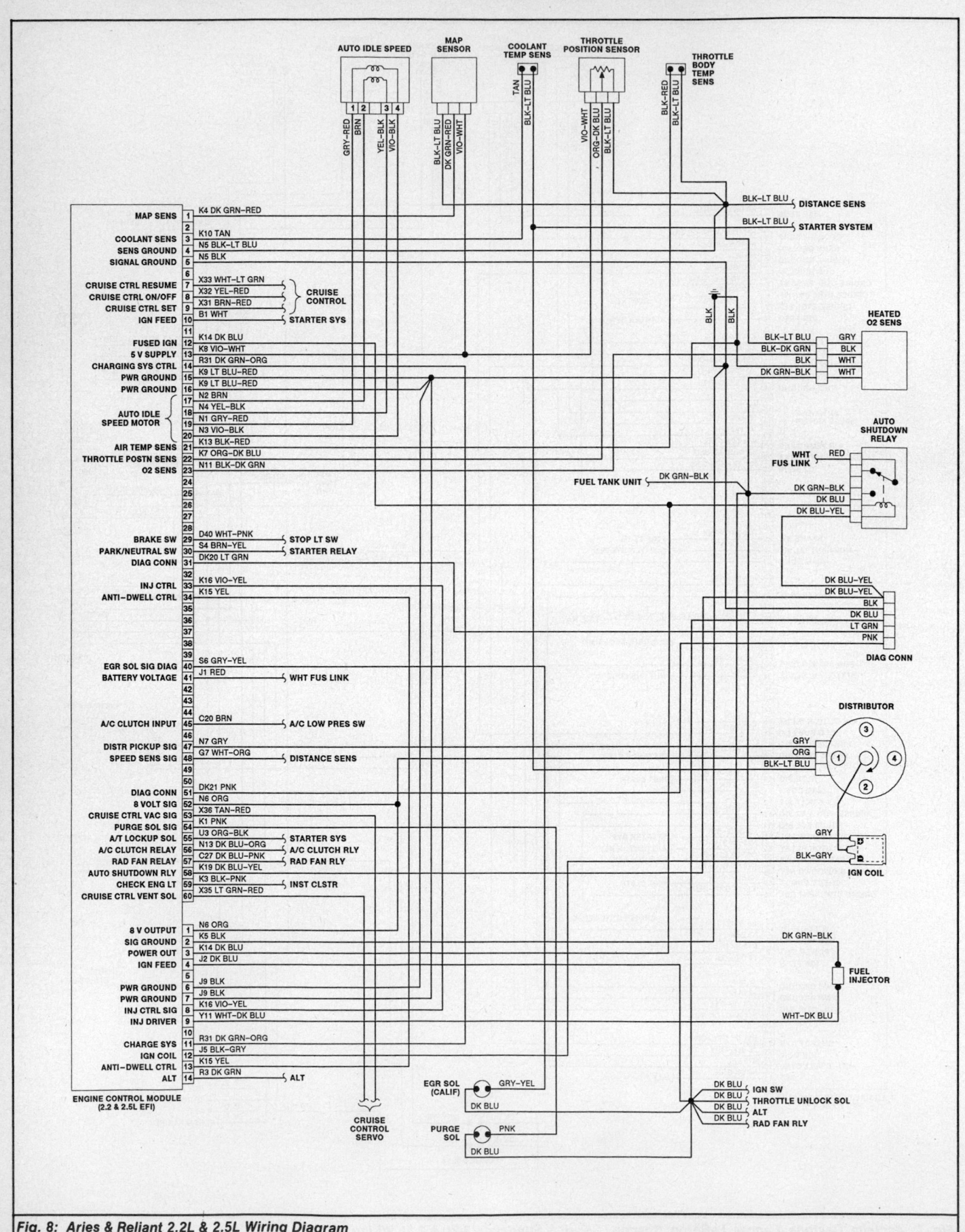

Fig. 8: Aries & Reliant 2.2L & 2.5L Wiring Diagram

1989 Computerized ENGINE CONTROLS
Chrysler Motors 2.2L & 2.5L SPFI (Cont.)

1a-81

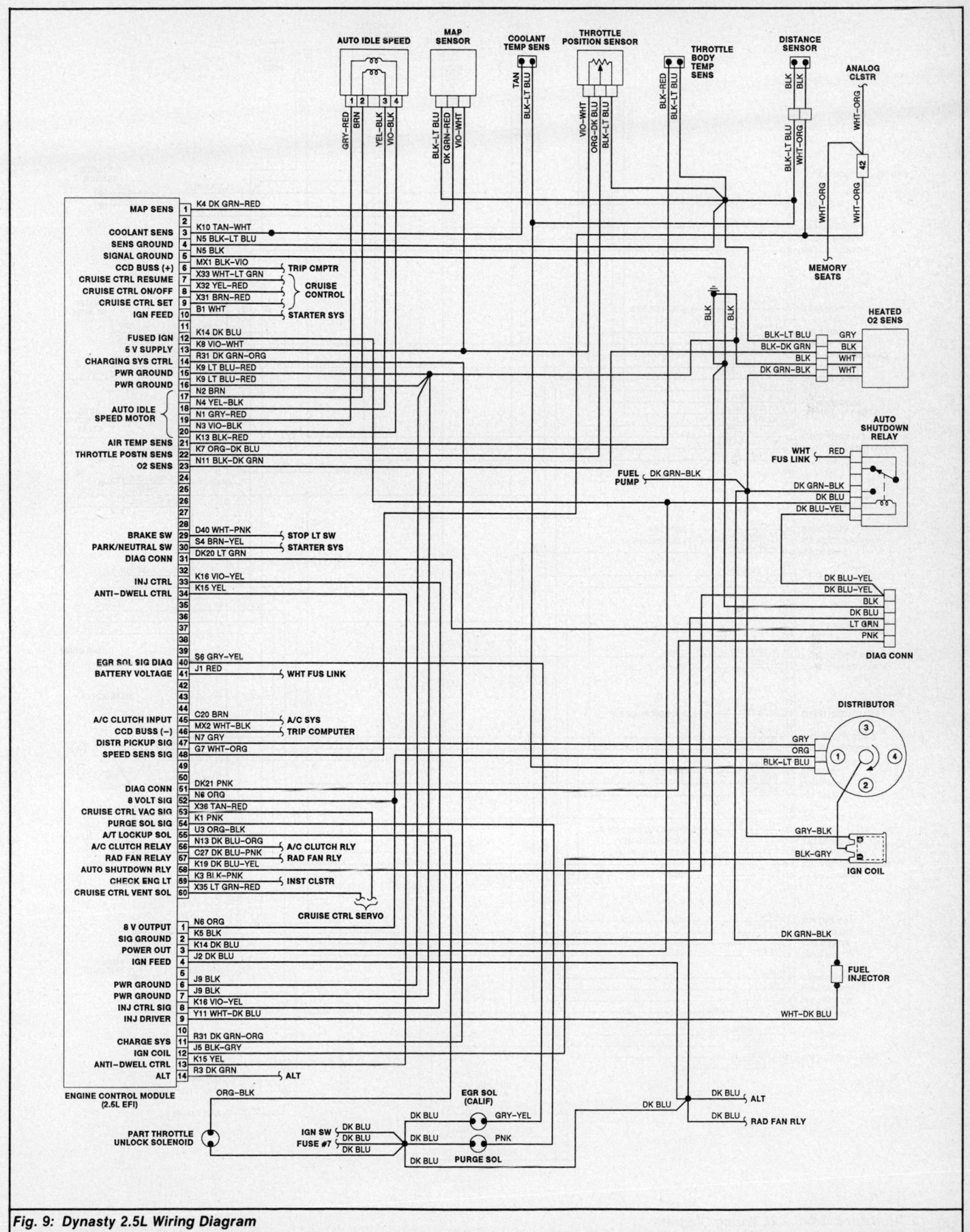

Fig. 9: Dynasty 2.5L Wiring Diagram

1989 Computerized ENGINE CONTROLS
Chrysler Motors 2.2L & 2.5L SPFI (Cont.)

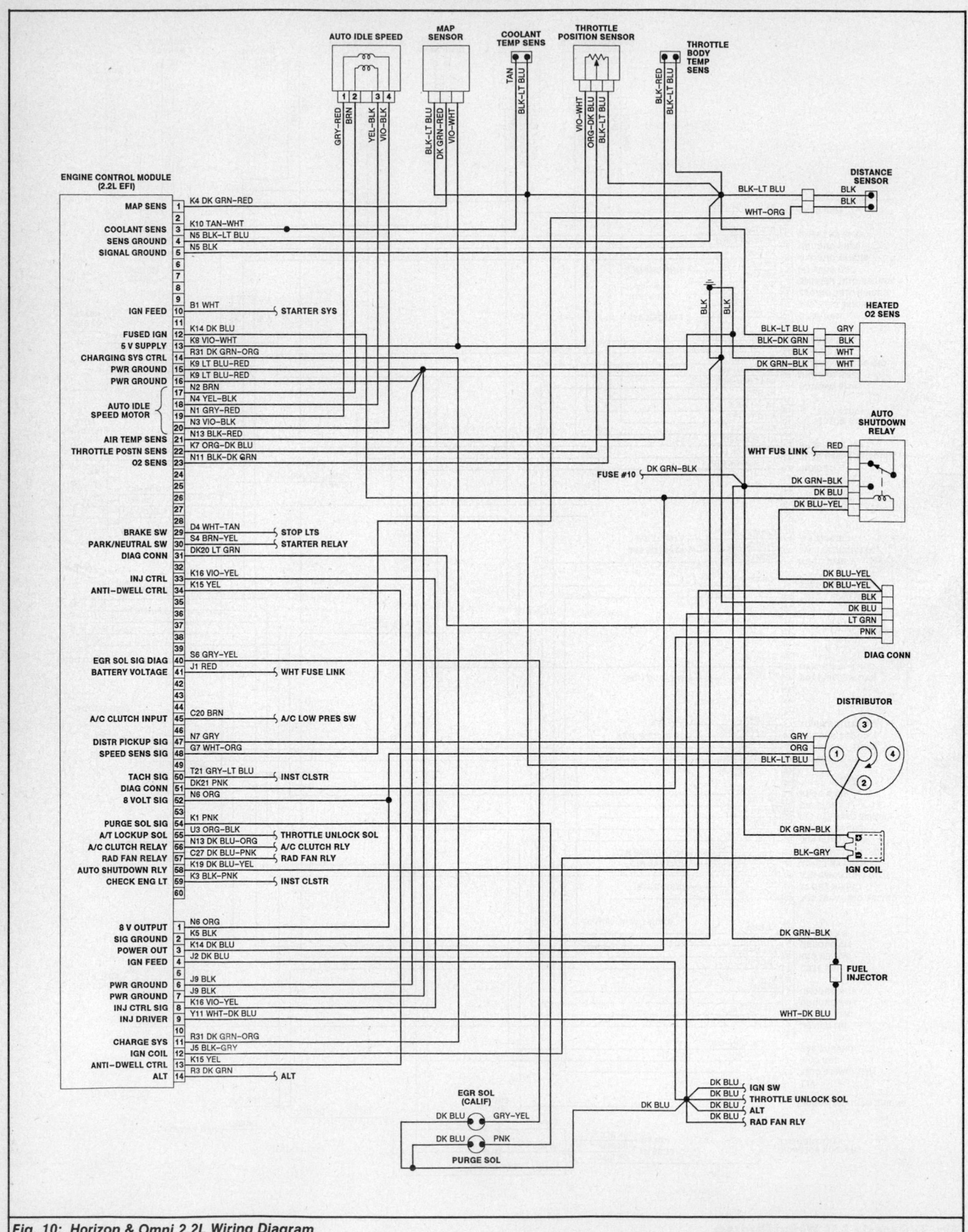

Fig. 10: *Horizon & Omni 2.2L Wiring Diagram*

Acclaim, Daytona, Lancer, LeBaron, Shadow, Spirit, Sundance

DESCRIPTION

The 2.5L Turbo I Multi-Point Fuel Injection (MPFI) computerized engine control system controls the fuel system, ignition system and emission control system.

The engine control system utilizes a Single Module Engine Controller (SMEC) to regulate air/fuel ratio, charging system, cooling fan, emission control components, idle speed, ignition timing and turbocharger wastegate control.

OPERATION

AIR CONDITIONING CLUTCH RELAY

The A/C clutch relay is powered by the radiator fan relay, A/C switch and SMEC. The relay is energized to closed (on) position during engine operation with A/C switch closed and blower switch on. When the SMEC senses wide open throttle or low engine RPM through the throttle position sensor, SMEC will de-energize the A/C clutch relay disengaging A/C clutch.

AUTO SHUTDOWN (ASD) RELAY

When distributor signal is not present with ignition switch in "RUN" position, the ASD relay turns power off to the electric fuel pump, fuel injectors, ignition coil and O_2 sensor heating element.

AUTOMATIC IDLE SPEED (AIS) MOTOR

The AIS motor adjusts idle speed to compensate for engine load and ambient temperature. The AIS motor varies the amount of air by-pass through the throttle body. The SMEC uses coolant temperature, distance (speed) sensor, throttle position, and various switch input operations to adjust the AIS to obtain optimum idle conditions.

BAROMETRIC READ SOLENOID

Barometric pressure information is used primarily for boost control. The solenoid is mounted in the vacuum line next to the Manifold Absolute Pressure (MAP) sensor. SMEC controls barometric read solenoid.

Atmospheric pressure is supplied to MAP sensor to periodically measure barometric pressure. This occurs once per throttle closure, but not more often than once every 3 minutes within a specified RPM range.

CANISTER PURGE SOLENOID

The canister purge solenoid is controlled by the SMEC. During engine warm-up and after hot restarts, the SMEC completes a ground, energizing the purge solenoid. When purge solenoid is energized, this prevents vacuum from reaching canister valve.

After engine reaches operating temperature and a timer has run out, the SMEC de-energizes the solenoid by turning off the ground allowing fuel vapors to be drawn into the throttle body. The SMEC will also energize purge solenoid under certain idle conditions, this updates fuel delivery calibration.

CHECK ENGINE LIGHT

The check engine light will illuminate for 3 seconds as a bulb test every time the ignition is turned on. If the SMEC receives an incorrect or no signal from coolant temperature sensor, manifold absolute pressure sensor, throttle position sensor, battery voltage input or emission related systems on California vehicles, the check engine light will be illuminated. This warns driver that SMEC has gone into a limp-in mode to keep system operational.

COOLANT TEMPERATURE SENSOR

The coolant temperature sensor is located in the thermostat housing. Input from this sensor allows SMEC to richen air/fuel mixtures until normal operating temperature is reached. The sensor

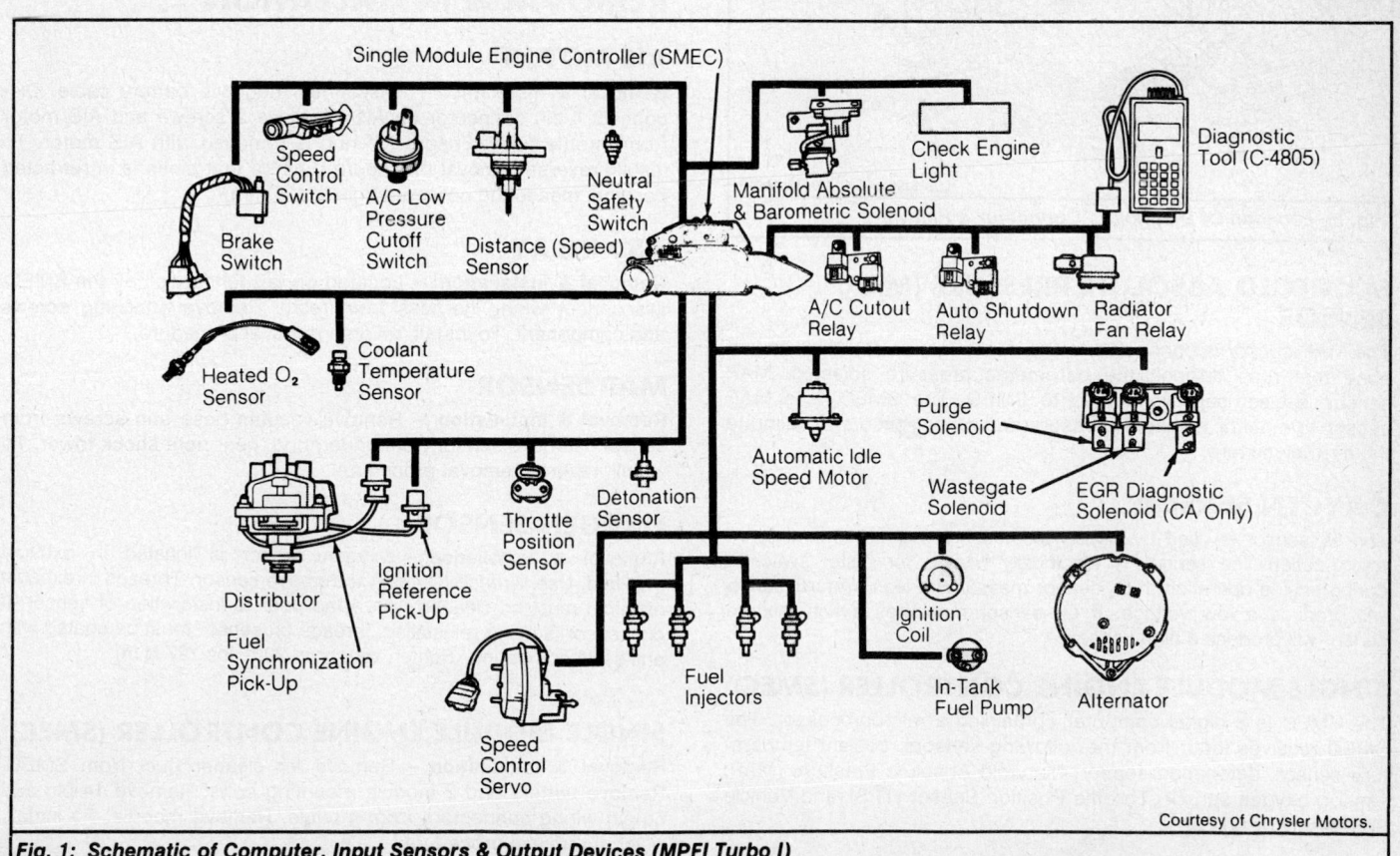

Courtesy of Chrysler Motors.

Fig. 1: Schematic of Computer, Input Sensors & Output Devices (MPFI Turbo I)

is a variable resistor with a range of -40°F (-40°C) to 265°F (129°C). This sensor is also used to turn on radiator fan.

DETONATION SENSOR

The detonation sensor is mounted in the intake manifold in such a position so sensor can detect detonation in any cylinder. This sensor generates an input signal to SMEC when detonation occurs. This allows SMEC to adjust spark advance and boost schedules to eliminate detonation.

DISTANCE (SPEED) SENSOR

This sensor is located on transaxle extension housing. The sensor generates 8 pulses per axle shaft revolution. The SMEC will interpret distance (speed) sensor input along with throttle position sensor closed throttle input.

This will allow SMEC to differentiate between closed throttle decel and closed throttle idle (vehicle stopped) conditions. During decel, the SMEC controls Automatic Idle Speed (AIS) motor to maintain a desired manifold absolute pressure value. During idle (vehicle stopped), the SMEC controls AIS motor to maintain a desired idle speed.

LIMP-IN MODE

If SMEC senses incorrect data or no data from battery voltage, coolant temperature sensor, Manifold Absolute Pressure (MAP) sensor or Throttle Position Sensor (TPS), SMEC will put system in limp-in mode and illuminate check engine light.

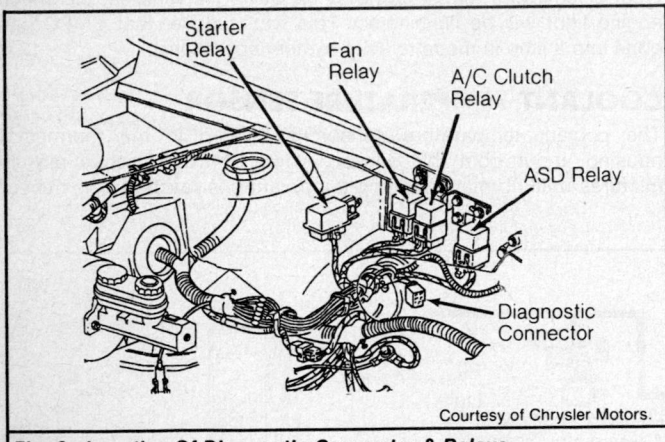

Fig. 2: Location Of Diagnostic Connector & Relays

MANIFOLD ABSOLUTE PRESSURE (MAP) SENSOR

The MAP sensor is connected to the intake manifold with a vacuum hose that runs through the barometric pressure solenoid. MAP sensor is electrically connected to SMEC. The SMEC uses MAP sensor to monitor manifold pressure and other sensors to calibrate the air/fuel mixture.

OXYGEN SENSOR

The O_2 sensor is used by SMEC to measure oxygen content in the turbo outlet. The sensor is electrically heated for faster switching during engine operation. If O_2 sensor measures a lean mixture, sensor will produce a low voltage. If O_2 sensor measures a rich mixture, sensor will produce a high voltage.

SINGLE MODULE ENGINE CONTROLLER (SMEC)

The SMEC is a digital computer containing a microprocessor. The SMEC receives input from the following sensors: coolant temperature sensor, detonation sensor, Manifold Absolute Pressure (MAP) sensor, oxygen sensor, Throttle Position Sensor (TPS), and Vehicle Speed sensor (VSS).

The SMEC also receives input from the following switches: air conditioning clutch switch, brake switch, speed control switches, and neutral safety switch. During operation, the SMEC monitors many of its own input and output circuits. If a fault is detected, the computer will go into limp-in mode and store a trouble code to help in diagnosis of the system.

THROTTLE POSITION SENSOR (TPS)

The TPS is an electronic variable resistor. The SMEC uses TPS input and input from other sensors to adjust air/fuel ratio for varying driveability conditions.

WASTEGATE CONTROL SOLENOID

The wastegate control solenoid is controlled by SMEC. The SMEC adjusts maximum boost by varying the duty cycle (on time) of the control solenoid.

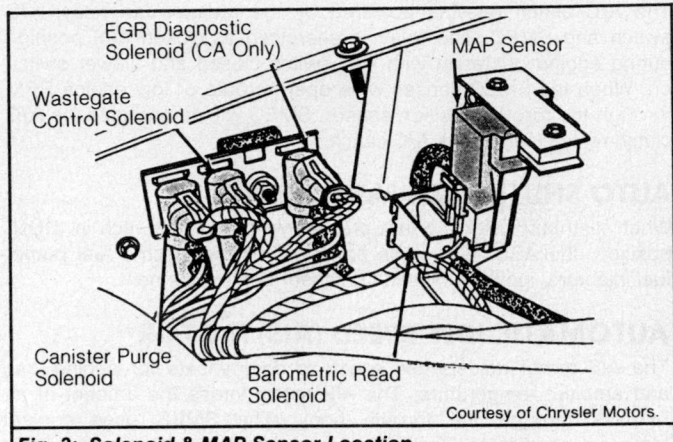

Fig. 3: Solenoid & MAP Sensor Location

REMOVAL & INSTALLATION

AIS MOTOR

Removal & Installation – Disconnect negative battery cable. Disconnect 4-pin connector on AIS. Remove 2 screws and AIS motor from throttle body. Ensure "O" ring is removed with AIS motor. To install, reverse removal procedure. Ensure that pintle is in retracted position, measuring not more than 1" (25 mm).

ASD RELAY

Removal & Installation – Located on left fenderwell by the SMEC. Disconnect wiring harness from relay. Remove attaching screws and component. To install, reverse removal procedure.

MAP SENSOR

Removal & Installation – Remove vacuum hose and screws from sensor. Remove sensor from underhood, near right shock tower. To install, reverse removal procedure.

OXYGEN SENSOR

Removal & Installation – Oxygen sensor is located in exhaust manifold. Use Wrench (C-4907) to remove sensor. Threads in exhaust manifold must be cleaned with a tap prior to installation of sensor. If old sensor is being reinstalled, threads on sensor must be coated with anti-seize compound. Tighten sensor to 20 ft. lbs. (27 N.m).

SINGLE MODULE ENGINE CONTROLLER (SMEC)

Removal & Installation – Remove air cleaner duct from SMEC. Remove battery and 2 module mounting bolts. Remove 14-pin and 60-pin wiring connectors from module. Remove module. To install, reverse removal procedure.

1989 COMPUTERIZED ENGINE CONTROLS
Chrysler Motors 2.5L Turbo I MPFI (Cont.)

1a-85

THROTTLE POSITION SENSOR (TPS)

Removal & Installation – Disconnect negative battery cable and remove air cleaner. Disconnect 3-pin connector at throttle position sensor. Remove 2 screws mounting throttle position sensor to throttle body. Lift throttle position sensor from throttle shaft. To install, reverse removal procedure.

TESTING & DIAGNOSIS

PRELIMINARY CHECKS

Most driveability problems in the engine control system result from faulty wiring or leaking hose connections. To avoid unnecessary component testing, a visual check should be performed before beginning trouble shooting procedures to help spot these common faults. A preliminary visual check should include:

- Air ducts to air cleaner and from air cleaner to throttle body.
- Electrical connections at all components. Clean, tight and unbroken.

Check vacuum lines for secure, leak-free connections in these areas:

- Canister purge hose (this hose has a check valve and tee connector in it.)
- EGR vacuum line on EGR valve and EGR solenoid. Check hose between backpressure valve and exhaust supply tube on EGR.
- Evaporative control system.
- Fuel pressure regulator vacuum hose.
- MAP sensor.
- PCV valve hose and correct PCV valve.
- Power brake, speed control, heater and A/C system vacuum hoses.
- Throttle body.
- Wastegate control diaphragm and vacuum hoses.

Ensure the following electrical connectors are securely attached:

- 14-pin and 60-pin connectors at Single Module Engine Controller (SMEC).
- A/C clutch relay connector.
- AIS motor connector.
- ASD relay connector.
- Barometric read, wastegate and purge solenoid connector.
- Black distributor reference connector.
- Canister purge solenoid connector.
- Charge temperature sensor connector.
- Check engine light.
- Coolant temperature sensor connector.
- Distance (speed) sensor connector.
- Distributor connector.
- EGR diagnostic solenoid connector (California only).
- Fuel synchronization pick-up connector (Gray connector).
- Heated O_2 sensor connector.
- Ignition reference pick-up connector.
- MAP sensor connector.
- Radiator fan relay connector.
- TPS connector.

SYSTEM DIAGNOSIS

The self-diagnostic capabilities of this system, if properly utilized, can greatly simplify testing. The SMEC has been programmed to monitor several different circuits of the engine control system. If a problem is sensed with a monitored circuit a fault code is stored in the SMEC.

The check engine light will illuminate and SMEC will enter "Limp-In Mode". In this mode, SMEC attempts to compensate for the failure of a particular component by substituting information from other sources. This will allow vehicle to be operated until proper repairs can be made.

Once these codes are known, refer to FAULT CODES listed in this article to determine the questionable circuit. Test circuits and repair or replace as necessary. If problem is repaired or ceases to exist, the logic module cancels fault codes after 50-100 ignition on/off cycles. If DRB-II is being used, refer to CLEARING CODES in this article.

The setting of a specific fault code is the result of a particular system failure, NOT the reason for that failure, such as failure of a specific component. The existence of a particular code denotes the probable area of the malfunction, not necessarily the failed component itself.

DIAGNOSTIC PROCEDURE

Refer to ENTERING ON-BOARD DIAGNOSTICS to retrieve fault codes. When using check engine light to retrieve fault codes, refer to description of DRB-II display under FAULT CODES for an explanation of fault code. Once description of fault code is obtained, refer to appropriate trouble shooting chart to diagnose problem. Use trouble shooting chart titles to find appropriate chart.

If no fault codes are present, but vehicle still displays one of the following conditions:

- No start condition. Go to NS-1.
- Cold driveability problem. Go to DR-1.
- Warm driveability problem. Go to DR-1.
- Check engine light is illuminated. Go to DR-1.
- Charging system problem. Go to CH-1.
- Speed control system problem. Go to SP-1.

NOTE: When using trouble shooting charts for diagnosis, DO NOT skip any steps in chart as incorrect diagnosis will result.

Before proceeding with diagnosis, the following precautions must be followed:

- Vehicle must have a fully charged battery.
- When performing a cold driveability test, engine must not have been started for at least 7 hours.
- When performing a warm driveability test, engine must be at normal operating temperature.
- When probing SMEC connectors, probe connectors from pin side DO NOT backprobe connectors.
- When performing electrical tests, be careful to not cause any short circuits. This will set more fault codes, making diagnosis of original problem more difficult.
- DO NOT use a test light in place of a voltmeter.
- When checking for spark, ensure coil wire is no more than 1/4" from ground. If wire is farther away from ground, damage to SMEC may result.
- DO NOT prolong testing of fuel injectors as engine may hydrostatically lock.
- Always repair lowest fault number (check engine light) or first fault displayed (DRB-II), first.
- Always perform indicated verification test after repairs are made.

ENTERING ON-BOARD DIAGNOSTICS

Check Engine Light Diagnostic Mode – 1) Start engine (if possible). Move transmission shift lever through all positions, ending in Park. Turn A/C switch on, then off (if equipped).

2) Turn engine off. Without starting engine again, turn ignition on, off, on, off and on. Record 2-digit fault codes as displayed by flashing check engine light.

3) For example, Code 23 is displayed as flash, flash, 4 second pause, flash, flash, flash. After a slightly longer pause, any other codes stored are displayed in numerical order.

4) Once check engine light begins to flash fault codes, it cannot be stopped. If you loose count, it will be necessary to start over. Code 55 indicates end of fault code display. Refer to FAULT CODES in this article.

DRB-II Diagnostic Mode – 1) Attach DRB-II Tester (C-4805) to self-test connector. Connector is located in engine compartment near left shock tower.

1a-86

1989 COMPUTERIZED ENGINE CONTROLS
Chrysler Motors 2.5L Turbo I MPFI (Cont.)

2) Start engine (if possible). Move transmission shift lever through all positions, ending in Park. Turn A/C switch on, then off (if equipped).

3) Turn engine off. Without starting engine again, turn ignition on. Enter vehicle model year and engine size. Read fault data on DRB-II. Refer to FAULT CODES in this article.

DRB-II Switch Test Mode – The SMEC can only recognize high and low states on switch circuits. SMEC cannot tell the difference between an open or short circuit or a defective switch.

The DRB-II display must change between "00" and "88" and flashing check engine light when brake switch, gear shift selector and A/C switch (if equipped) are activated and released.

DRB-II Read Input States – This state on DRB-II allows technician to read input states of Z1 voltage sense, park/neutral switch, brake switch, fuel synchronization pick-up, A/C switch, speed control resume, on/off and set switches. DRB-II will display "INPUT LOW" or "INPUT HIGH" as SMEC senses component status changing.

DRB-II Read Output States – This state on DRB-II allows technician to read output states of speed control vacuum solenoid, purge solenoid, A/C clutch relay, radiator fan relay, ASD relay, check engine light, speed control vent solenoid, barometric read solenoid, wastegate solenoid and EGR solenoid. DRB-II will display "ENERGIZED" OR "DE-ENERGIZED" as SMEC senses component status changing.

DRB-II Actuate Solenoids & Relays – This state on DRB-II allows SMEC to actuate radiator fan relay, A/C clutch relay, ASD relay, purge solenoid, speed control servo solenoids, EGR solenoid, wastegate solenoid and baro read solenoid. With tester in this state, SMEC can also actuate all solenoids and relays simultaneously. This test allows technician to visually and physically observe components under operation.

DRB-II Actuate Outputs – This state on DRB-II allows SMEC to actuate ignition coil, fuel injectors (#1), fuel injectors (#2), AIS motor open and close, alternator field, tachometer output (tach should read 1364 RPM) and fuel monitor signal. During this test DRB-II will read "ACTUATING".

DRB-II Read Sensor Voltages – This state on DRB-II allows technician to read battery temperature sensor, oxygen sensor, coolant temperature sensor, TPS sensor, minimum throttle position in volts, knock sensor, battery voltage and MAP sensor.

DRB-II Read Sensor Values – This state on DRB-II allows technician to read coolant temperature in degrees fahrenheit or centigrade, manifold pressure in inches of vacuum or kilopascals, AIS motor in steps, adaptive fuel factor in percent, barometric pressure in inches of mercury or or kilopascals, engine speed in RPM, SMEC spark advance in degrees, cylinder retard given in degrees (cylinders are given individually), boost pressure goal given in psi, vehicle speed given in MPH, oxygen sensor state given as center, rich or lean, baro read update performed or update denied.

DRB-II Set Engine RPM – This state on DRB-II allows technician to set engine RPM at a fixed speed from 900-2000 in 100 RPM increments. This allows for accuracy of AIS motor control to be checked.

DRB-II Minimum Airflow Speed – This state on DRB-II allows technician to completely close AIS motor to check minimum idle speed.

DRB-II Emissions EMR Tests – This state on DRB-II allows technician to reset emission reminder light and mileage. This is only used on trucks.

DRB-II Read Module Information – This state on DRB-II allows technician to read SMEC part number and application.

DRB-II PROBLEMS & ERROR MESSAGES

Blank Message Screen – **1)** Connect DRB-II to a different vehicle. If message screen is still blank, DRB-II or cable adapter are faulty. Substitute to find faulty component. If message screen is not blank, DRB-II and cable adapter are functioning properly.

2) Inspect diagnostic connector for proper wire placement, damaged terminals or pushed out pins. Repair as necessary. If connector is okay, using an ohmmeter, check Black/White ground wire of diagnostic connector for continuity to ground. Repair as necessary.

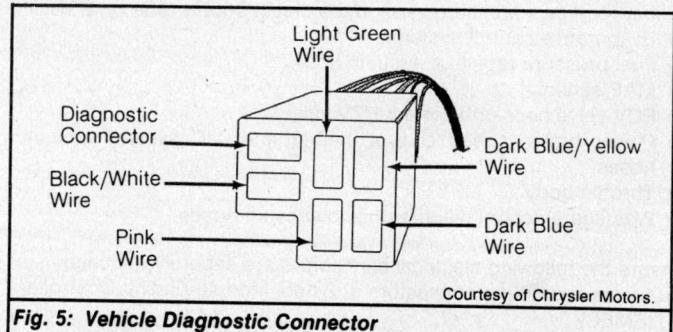

Fig. 5: Vehicle Diagnostic Connector

Courtesy of Chrysler Motors.

"NO RESPONSE" Message – **1)** Ensure ignition is turned on. Disconnect SMEC 60-pin connector. Using an ohmmeter, check Pink wire of diagnostic connector for continuity to SMEC 60-pin connector cavity No. 51.

2) Check Light Green wire of diagnostic connector for continuity to SMEC 60-pin connector cavity No. 31. If continuity is not present, repair circuit as necessary. If continuity is present, replace SMEC. Attempt retest.

"RAM TEST FAILURE" Message – Replace DRB-II.

"CARTRIDGE ERROR" Message – Replace DRB-II cartridge.

"KEY PAD TEST FAILURE" Message – Power up DRB-II again with fingers off keypad. If error message returns, replace DRB-II.

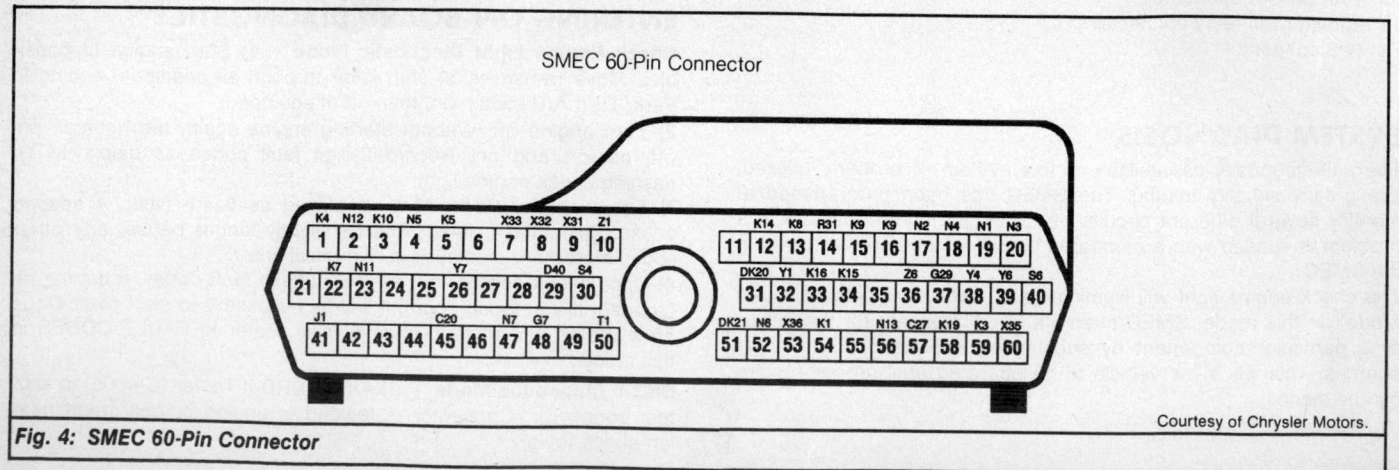

Fig. 4: SMEC 60-Pin Connector

Courtesy of Chrysler Motors.

1989 COMPUTERIZED ENGINE CONTROLS
Chrysler Motors 2.5L Turbo I MPFI (Cont.)

1a-87

"HIGH OR LOW BATTERY" Message – Correct condition of vehicle battery and reconnect DRB-II.

CLEARING CODES

Using DRB-II, select test "ERASE FAULT DATA". Press "YES" key on DRB-II. DRB-II will display "ARE YOU SURE? YES/NO". Press "YES" key on tester. Tester will display "ERASING FAULT DATA X". When DRB-II is finished erasing fault codes, it will display "FAULT DATA ERASED".

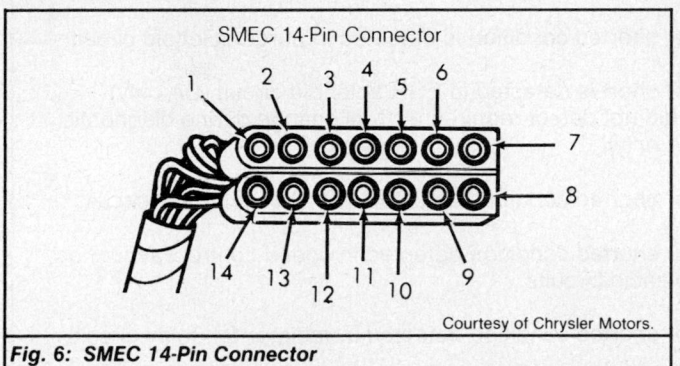

SMEC 14-Pin Connector

Courtesy of Chrysler Motors.

Fig. 6: SMEC 14-Pin Connector

NOTE: The following trouble shooting charts and illustrations are courtesy of Chrysler Motors.

If DRB-II is not available, fault codes may be cleared by allowing 50-100 key on/off cycles to occur. This will allow SMEC to clear fault codes.

EMISSION MAINTENANCE REMINDER (EMR) MILEAGE TRANSFER

1) When vehicle engine controller is replaced, vehicle mileage must be copied from odometer to a memory location within the replacement engine controller. Transfer of vehicle mileage will enable new engine controller to operate EMR light properly.

2) Using DRB-II, enter "EMISSIONS EMR TESTS". Press "Yes" key. Select test item "EMR MEMORY CHECK". Press "Yes" key. DRB-II display will read "EMR MEMORY CHECK ARE YOU SURE ? Yes,No". Press "Yes" key.

3) DRB-II will display "IS INSTRUMENT PANEL MILEAGE BETWEEN 9953 AND 10051 ?". If vehicle mileage is within specification, EMR memory check is complete. Press "Yes" key. If vehicle mileage is not within specification, go to next step.

4) Press "No" key. DRB-II will display "DO YOU WANT TO CORRECT EMR MILEAGE ?". Press "Yes" key. DRB-II will display "ENTER MILEAGE SHOWN ON INSTRUMENT PANEL USE ENTER KEY TO END".

5) Enter vehicle mileage. DO NOT enter tenths. When correct vehicle mileage is entered, press "Enter" key. DRB-II will ask for verification of mileage entry. If mileage entry was accurate, press "Enter" key. DRB-II will display "EMR MEMORY CHECK TEST COMPLETE". Vehicle must travel at least 8 miles for reset to occur.

FAULT CODES

CODE	DISPLAY ON DRB-II	FAULT CONDITION
11	IGN REFERENCE SIGNAL	No distributor reference signal picked up during cranking.
12	Number of key-ons since last fault or since faults were erased.	Direct battery input to SMEC was disconnected within last 50-100 ignition key-ons.
13	MAP PNEUMATIC SIGNAL OR MAP PNEUMATIC CHANGE	No difference in MAP sensor signal is detected. No difference is detected between MAP reading and stored barometric pressure reading.
14	MAP VOLTAGE TOO LOW OR MAP VOLTAGE TOO HIGH	MAP sensor input less than minimum acceptable voltage. MAP sensor input more than maximum acceptable voltage.
15	VEHICLE SPEED SIGNAL	No distance sensor signal detected with road load conditions.
16	BATTERY INPUT SENSE	Battery voltage sense input not detected with engine running.
17	LOW ENGINE TEMP	Coolant temperature stays below normal operating temperature during vehicle operation.
21	OXYGEN SENSOR SIGNAL	No rich or lean signal is detected from O_2 sensor input.
22	COOLANT VOLTAGE LOW OR COOLANT VOLTAGE HIGH	Coolant temp. sensor input below minimum acceptable voltage. Coolant temp. sensor input above maximum acceptable voltage.
24	TPS VOLTAGE LOW OR TPS VOLTAGE HIGH	TPS sensor output less than minimum acceptable voltage. TPS sensor output more than maximum acceptable voltage.
25	AIS MOTOR CIRCUITS	Shorted condition detected in one or more AIS control circuits.
26	INJ 1 PEAK CURRENT OR INJ 2 PEAK CURRENT	High resistance detected in INJ 1 injector bank circuit. High resistance detected in INJ 2 injector bank circuit.

1989 COMPUTERIZED ENGINE CONTROLS
Chrysler Motors 2.5L Turbo I MPFI (Cont.)

FAULT CODES (Cont.)

CODE	DISPLAY ON DRB-II	FAULT CONDITION
27	INJ 1 CONTROL CIRCUIT	INJ 1 injector bank output driver stage does not respond correctly to SMEC control signal.
	OR INJ 2 CONTROL CIRCUIT	INJ 2 injector bank output driver stage does not respond correctly to SMEC control signal.
31	PURGE SOLENOID CKT	Open or shorted condition is detected in purge solenoid circuit.
32	EGR SOLENOID CIRCUIT OR EGR SYSTEM FAILURE	Open or short is detected in EGR solenoid circuit (CA only). SMEC did not detect required air/fuel change during diagnostic test (CA only).
33	A/C CLUTCH RELAY CKT	Open or shorted condition detected in A/C clutch relay circuit.
34	S/C SERVO SOLENOIDS	Open or shorted condition detected in speed control vacuum or vent solenoid circuits.
35	RADIATOR FAN RELAY	Open or shorted condition detected in radiator fan relay circuit.
36	WASTEGATE SOLENOID	Open or shorted condition detected in turbocharger wastegate control solenoid circuit.
41	CHARGING SYSTEM CKT	Output driver stage does not respond correctly to voltage regulator control signal.
42	ASD RELAY CIRCUIT OR Z1 VOLTAGE SENSE	Open or shorted condition detected in ASD relay circuit. No battery voltage sensed when ASD relay is energized.
43	IGNITION CONTROL CIRCUIT	Output driver stage for ignition coil does not respond properly to dwell control signal.
44	FJ2 VOLTAGE SENSE	No FJ2 voltage present at logic board during SMEC operation.
45	BOOST LIMIT EXCEEDED	MAP reading above overboost limit detected during engine operation.
46	BATTERY VOLTAGE HIGH	Battery voltage sense input more than target charging voltage during engine operation.
47	BATTERY VOLTAGE LOW	Battery voltage sense input less than target charging voltage during engine operation.
51	LEAN F/A CONDITION	Oxygen sensor input indicates lean air/fuel ratio during engine operation.
52	RICH F/A CONDITON	Oxygen sensor input indicates rich air/fuel ratio during engine operation.
53	INTERNAL SELF-TEST	SMEC detects internal failure.
54	SYNC PICK-UP SIGNAL	Fuel synchronization signal not detected during engine rotation.
55		Completion of fault code display by check engine light.
61	BARO READ SOLENOID	Open or shorted condition detected in baro read solenoid circuit.
62	EMR MILEAGE ACCUM	Attempt is unsuccessful to update EMR mileage in SMEC EEPROM (trucks only).
63	EEPROM WRITE DENIED	Attempt is unsuccessful to write to an EEPROM location by SMEC.
N/A	FAULT CODE ERROR	DRB-II does not recognize fault identification.

1989 COMPUTERIZED ENGINE CONTROLS
Chrysler Motors 2.5L Turbo I MPFI (Cont.)

1a-89

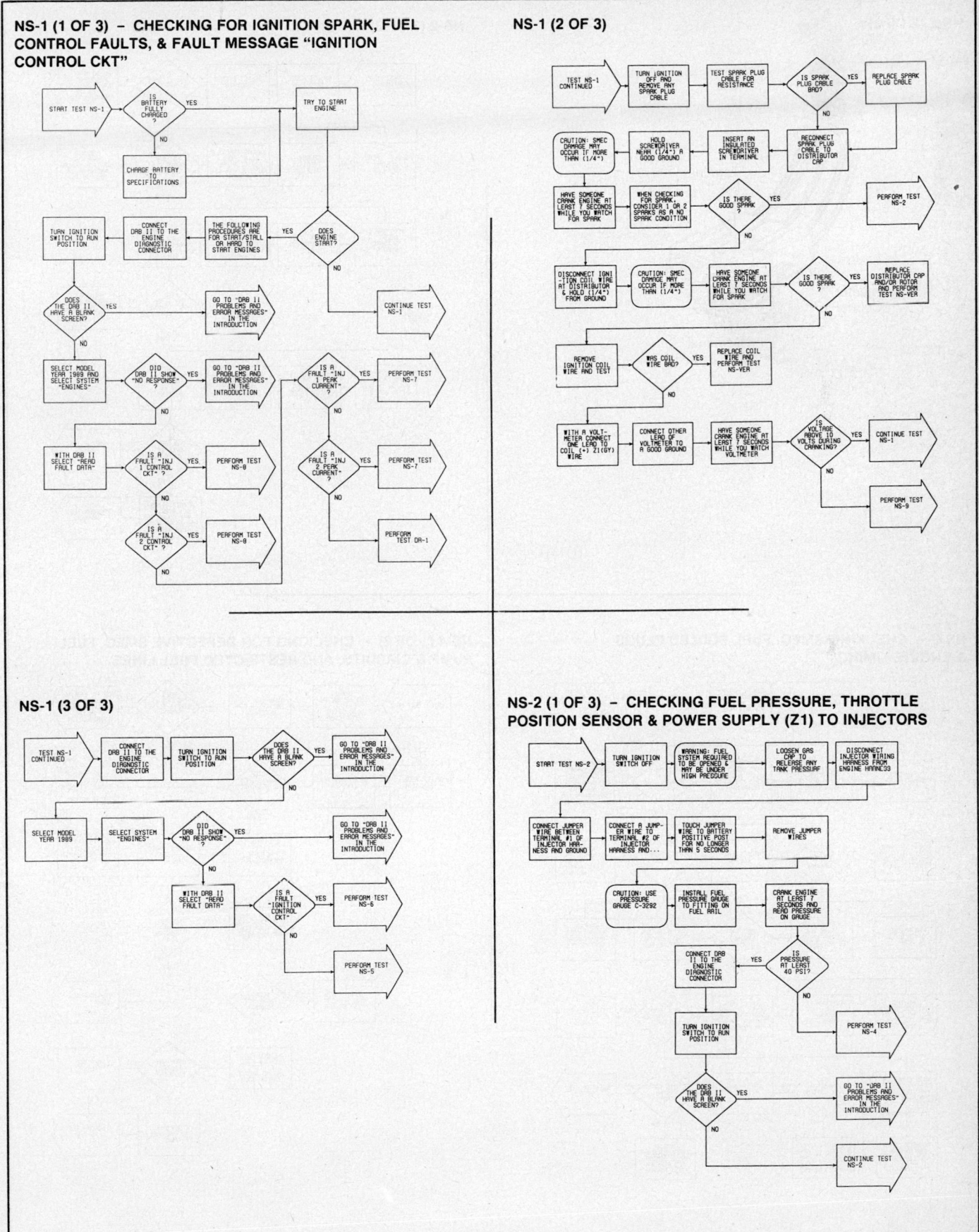

NS-1 (1 OF 3) – CHECKING FOR IGNITION SPARK, FUEL CONTROL FAULTS, & FAULT MESSAGE "IGNITION CONTROL CKT"

NS-1 (2 OF 3)

NS-1 (3 OF 3)

NS-2 (1 OF 3) – CHECKING FUEL PRESSURE, THROTTLE POSITION SENSOR & POWER SUPPLY (Z1) TO INJECTORS

1a-90

1989 COMPUTERIZED ENGINE CONTROLS
Chrysler Motors 2.5L Turbo I MPFI (Cont.)

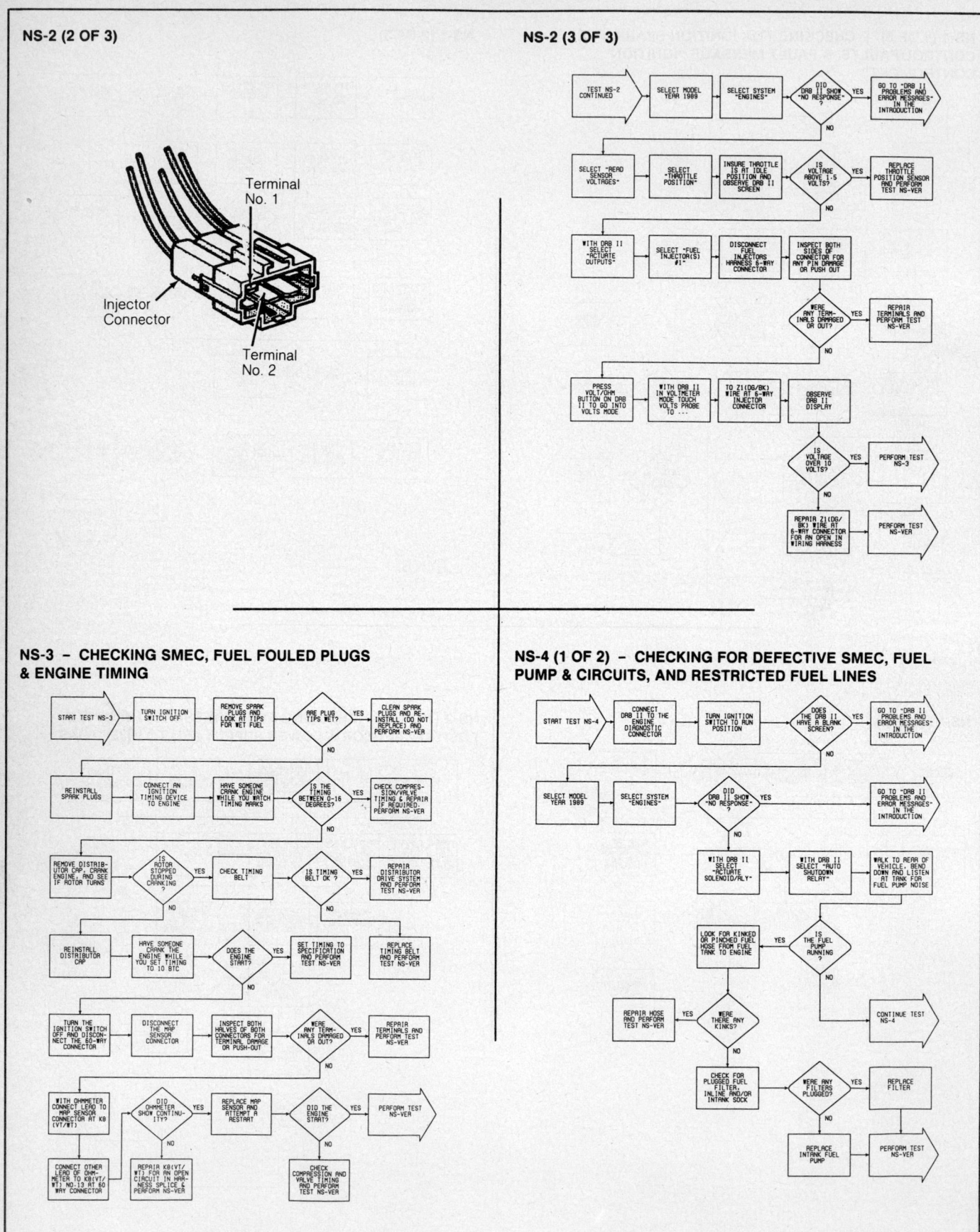

NS-2 (2 OF 3)

Terminal No. 1

Injector Connector

Terminal No. 2

NS-2 (3 OF 3)

NS-3 – CHECKING SMEC, FUEL FOULED PLUGS & ENGINE TIMING

NS-4 (1 OF 2) – CHECKING FOR DEFECTIVE SMEC, FUEL PUMP & CIRCUITS, AND RESTRICTED FUEL LINES

1989 COMPUTERIZED ENGINE CONTROLS
Chrysler Motors 2.5L Turbo I MPFI (Cont.)

1a-91

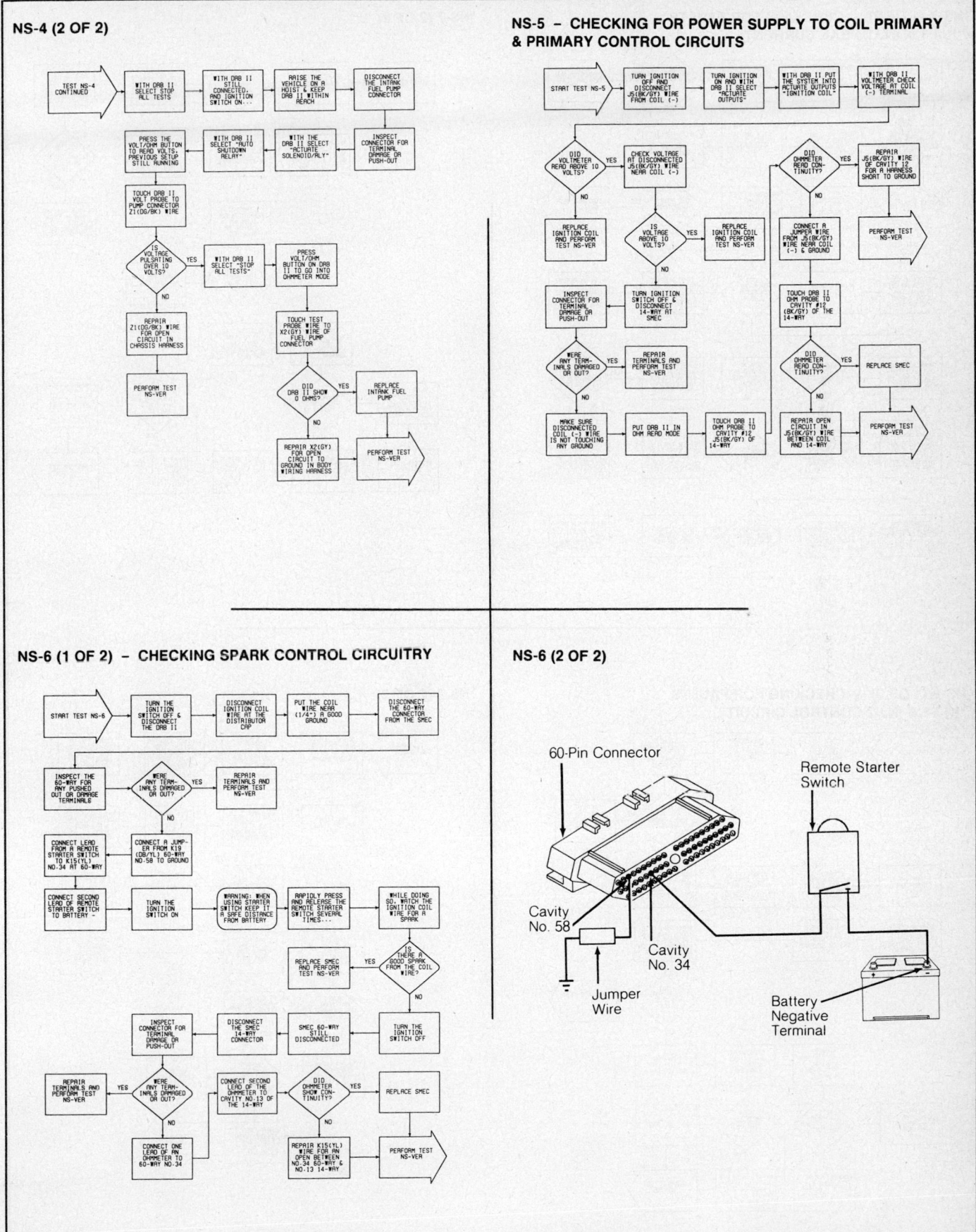

NS-4 (2 OF 2)

NS-5 – CHECKING FOR POWER SUPPLY TO COIL PRIMARY & PRIMARY CONTROL CIRCUITS

NS-6 (1 OF 2) – CHECKING SPARK CONTROL CIRCUITRY

NS-6 (2 OF 2)

NS-7 (1 OF 2) – CHECKING FOR FAULTS "INJ 1 & INJ 2 PEAK CURRENT"

NS-7 (2 OF 2)

NS-8 (1 OF 2) – CHECKING FOR FAULTS "INJ 1 & INJ 2 CONTROL CIRCUIT"

NS-8 (2 OF 2)

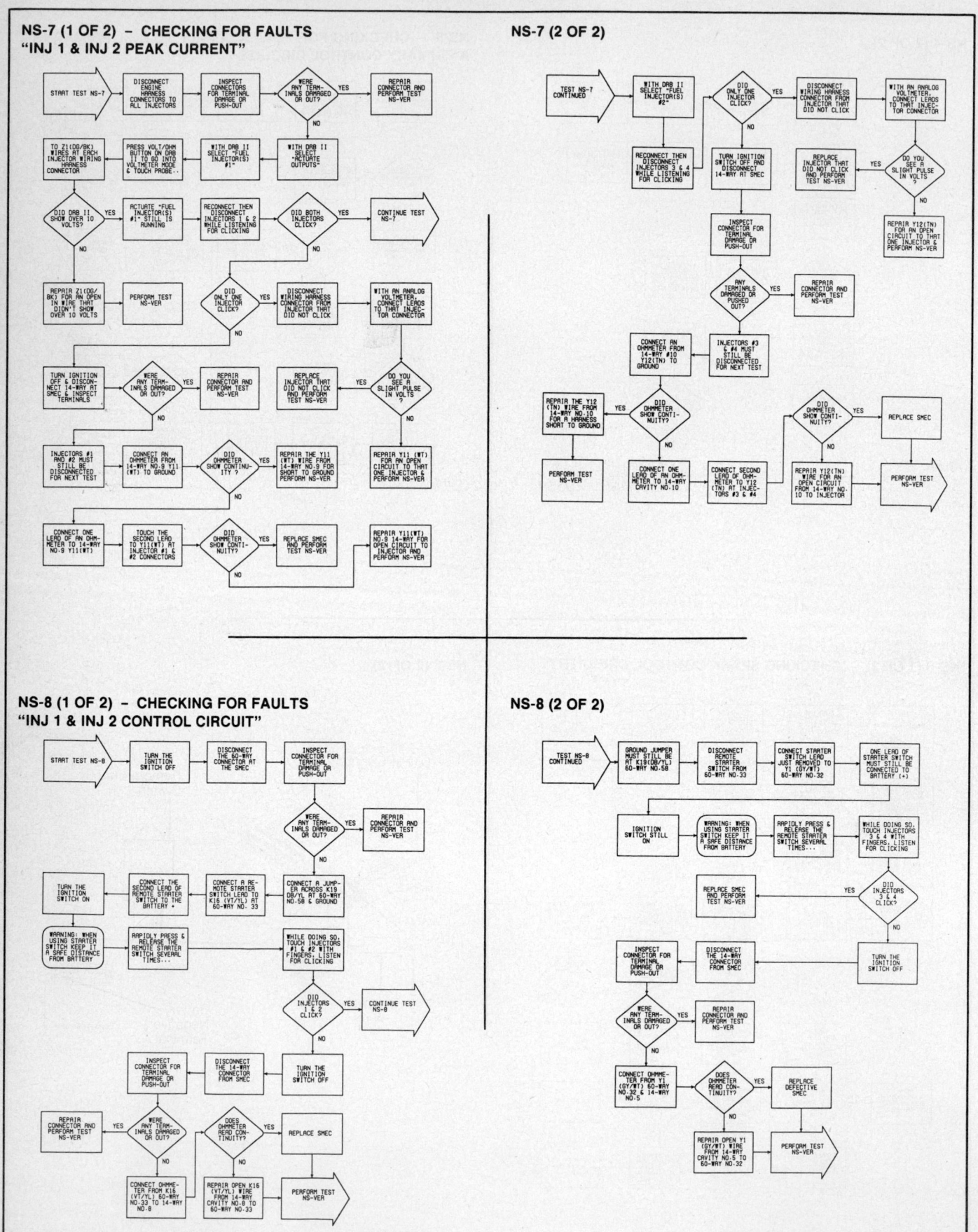

1989 COMPUTERIZED ENGINE CONTROLS
Chrysler Motors 2.5L Turbo I MPFI (Cont.)

1a-93

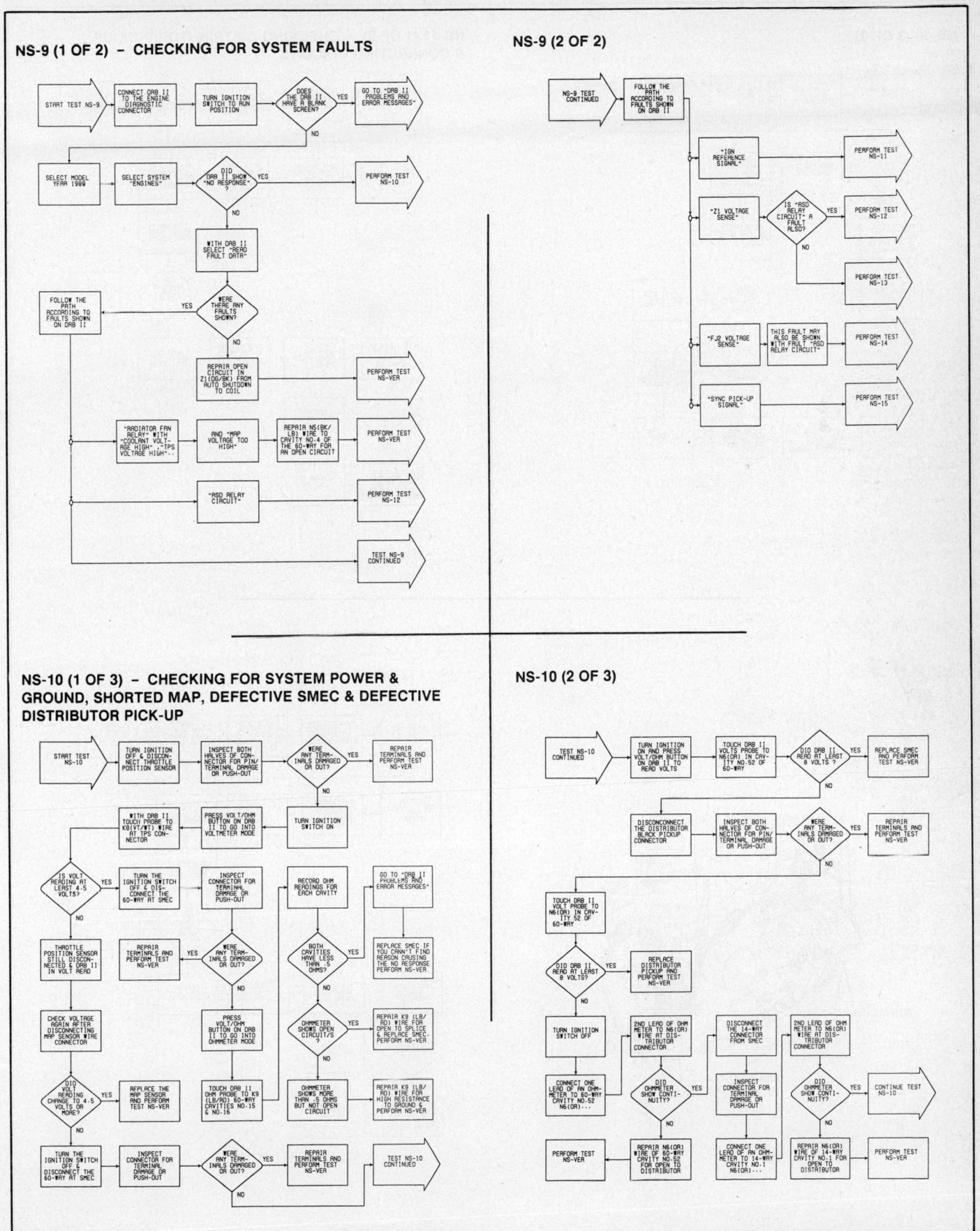

NS-9 (1 OF 2) – CHECKING FOR SYSTEM FAULTS

NS-9 (2 OF 2)

NS-10 (1 OF 3) – CHECKING FOR SYSTEM POWER & GROUND, SHORTED MAP, DEFECTIVE SMEC & DEFECTIVE DISTRIBUTOR PICK-UP

NS-10 (2 OF 3)

1a-94

1989 COMPUTERIZED ENGINE CONTROLS
Chrysler Motors 2.5L Turbo I MPFI (Cont.)

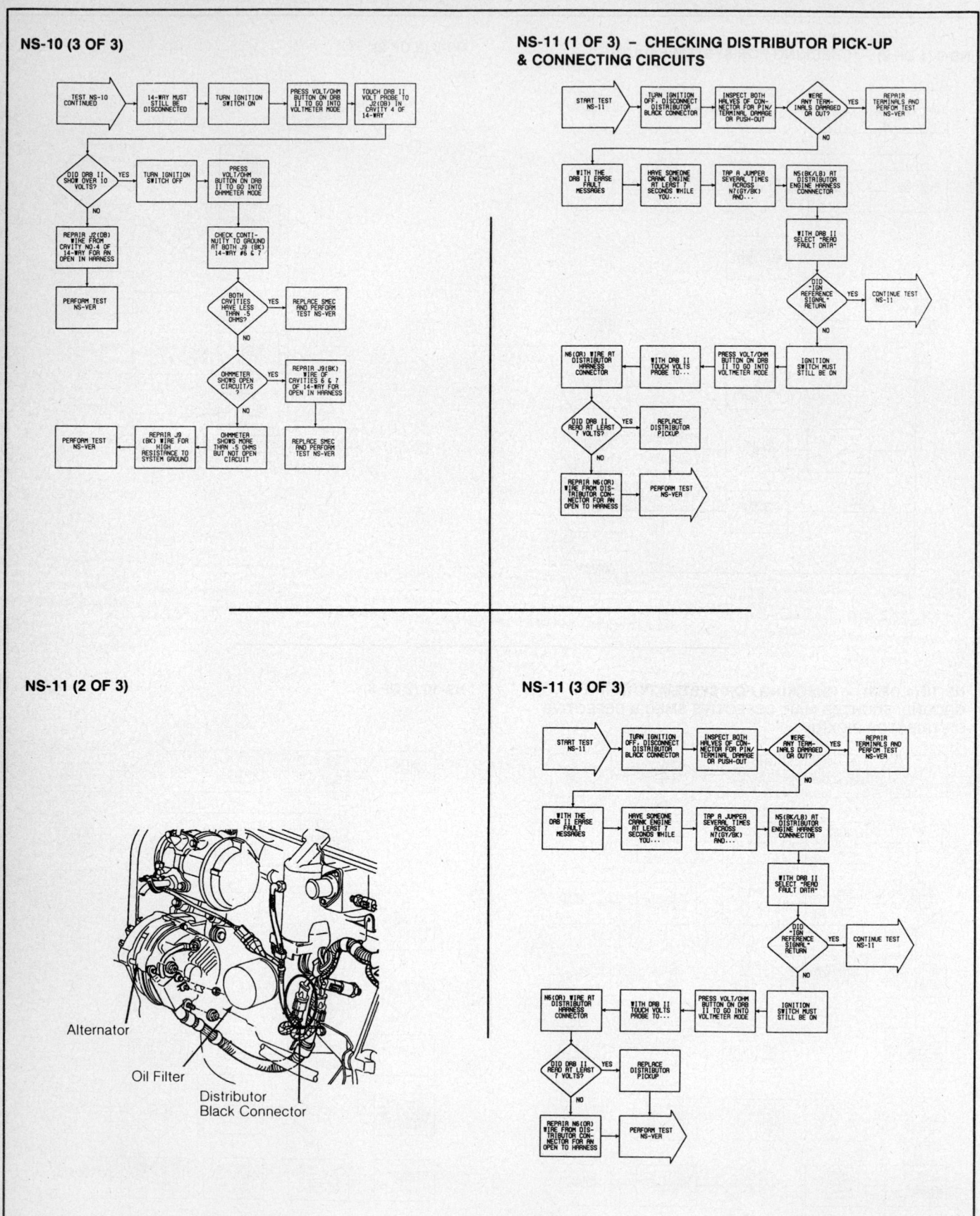

NS-10 (3 OF 3)

TEST NS-10 CONTINUED → 14-WAY MUST STILL BE DISCONNECTED → TURN IGNITION SWITCH ON → PRESS VOLT/OHM BUTTON ON DRB II TO GO INTO VOLTMETER MODE → TOUCH DRB II VOLT PROBE TO J2(DB) IN CAVITY 4 OF 14-WAY

DID DRB II SHOW OVER 10 VOLTS?
- YES → TURN IGNITION SWITCH OFF → PRESS VOLT/OHM BUTTON ON DRB II TO GO INTO OHMMETER MODE → CHECK CONTINUITY TO GROUND AT BOTH J9 (BK) 14-WAY #6 & 7
- NO → REPAIR J2(DB) WIRE FROM CAVITY NO. 4 OF 14-WAY FOR AN OPEN IN HARNESS → PERFORM TEST NS-VER

BOTH CAVITIES HAVE LESS THAN .5 OHMS?
- YES → REPLACE SMEC AND PERFORM TEST NS-VER
- NO → OHMMETER SHOWS OPEN CIRCUIT/S?
  - YES → REPAIR J9 (BK) WIRE OF CAVITIES 6 & 7 OF 14-WAY FOR OPEN IN HARNESS
  - NO → OHMMETER SHOWS MORE THAN .5 OHMS BUT NOT OPEN CIRCUIT → REPAIR J9 (BK) WIRE FOR HIGH RESISTANCE TO SYSTEM GROUND → PERFORM TEST NS-VER
    → REPLACE SMEC AND PERFORM TEST NS-VER

NS-11 (1 OF 3) – CHECKING DISTRIBUTOR PICK-UP & CONNECTING CIRCUITS

START TEST NS-11 → TURN IGNITION OFF, DISCONNECT DISTRIBUTOR BLACK CONNECTOR → INSPECT BOTH HALVES OF CONNECTOR FOR PIN/TERMINAL DAMAGE OR PUSH-OUT → WERE ANY TERMINALS DAMAGED OR OUT?
- YES → REPAIR TERMINALS AND PERFORM TEST NS-VER
- NO → WITH THE DRB II ERASE FAULT MESSAGES → HAVE SOMEONE CRANK ENGINE AT LEAST 7 SECONDS WHILE YOU... → TAP A JUMPER SEVERAL TIMES ACROSS N7(GY/BK) AND... → N5(BK/LB) AT DISTRIBUTOR ENGINE HARNESS CONNNECTOR → WITH DRB II SELECT "READ FAULT DATA"

DID "IGN REFERENCE SIGNAL" RETURN
- YES → CONTINUE TEST NS-11
- NO → IGNITION SWITCH MUST STILL BE ON → PRESS VOLT/OHM BUTTON ON DRB II TO GO INTO VOLTMETER MODE → WITH DRB II TOUCH VOLTS PROBE TO... → N6(OR) WIRE AT DISTRIBUTOR HARNESS CONNECTOR

DID DRB II READ AT LEAST 7 VOLTS?
- YES → REPLACE DISTRIBUTOR PICKUP
- NO → REPAIR N6(OR) WIRE FROM DISTRIBUTOR CONNECTOR FOR AN OPEN TO HARNESS → PERFORM TEST NS-VER

NS-11 (2 OF 3)

Alternator

Oil Filter

Distributor Black Connector

NS-11 (3 OF 3)

START TEST NS-11 → TURN IGNITION OFF, DISCONNECT DISTRIBUTOR BLACK CONNECTOR → INSPECT BOTH HALVES OF CONNECTOR FOR PIN/TERMINAL DAMAGE OR PUSH-OUT → WERE ANY TERMINALS DAMAGED OR OUT?
- YES → REPAIR TERMINALS AND PERFORM TEST NS-VER
- NO → WITH THE DRB II ERASE FAULT MESSAGES → HAVE SOMEONE CRANK ENGINE AT LEAST 7 SECONDS WHILE YOU... → TAP A JUMPER SEVERAL TIMES ACROSS N7(GY/BK) AND... → N5(BK/LB) AT DISTRIBUTOR ENGINE HARNESS CONNNECTOR → WITH DRB II SELECT "READ FAULT DATA"

DID IGN REFERENCE SIGNAL" RETURN
- YES → CONTINUE TEST NS-11
- NO → IGNITION SWITCH MUST STILL BE ON → PRESS VOLT/OHM BUTTON ON DRB II TO GO INTO VOLTMETER MODE → WITH DRB II TOUCH VOLTS PROBE TO... → N6(OR) WIRE AT DISTRIBUTOR HARNESS CONNECTOR

DID DRB II READ AT LEAST 7 VOLTS?
- YES → REPLACE DISTRIBUTOR PICKUP
- NO → REPAIR N6(OR) WIRE FROM DISTRIBUTOR CONNECTOR FOR AN OPEN TO HARNESS → PERFORM TEST NS-VER

1989 COMPUTERIZED ENGINE CONTROLS
Chrysler Motors 2.5L Turbo I MPFI (Cont.)

1a-95

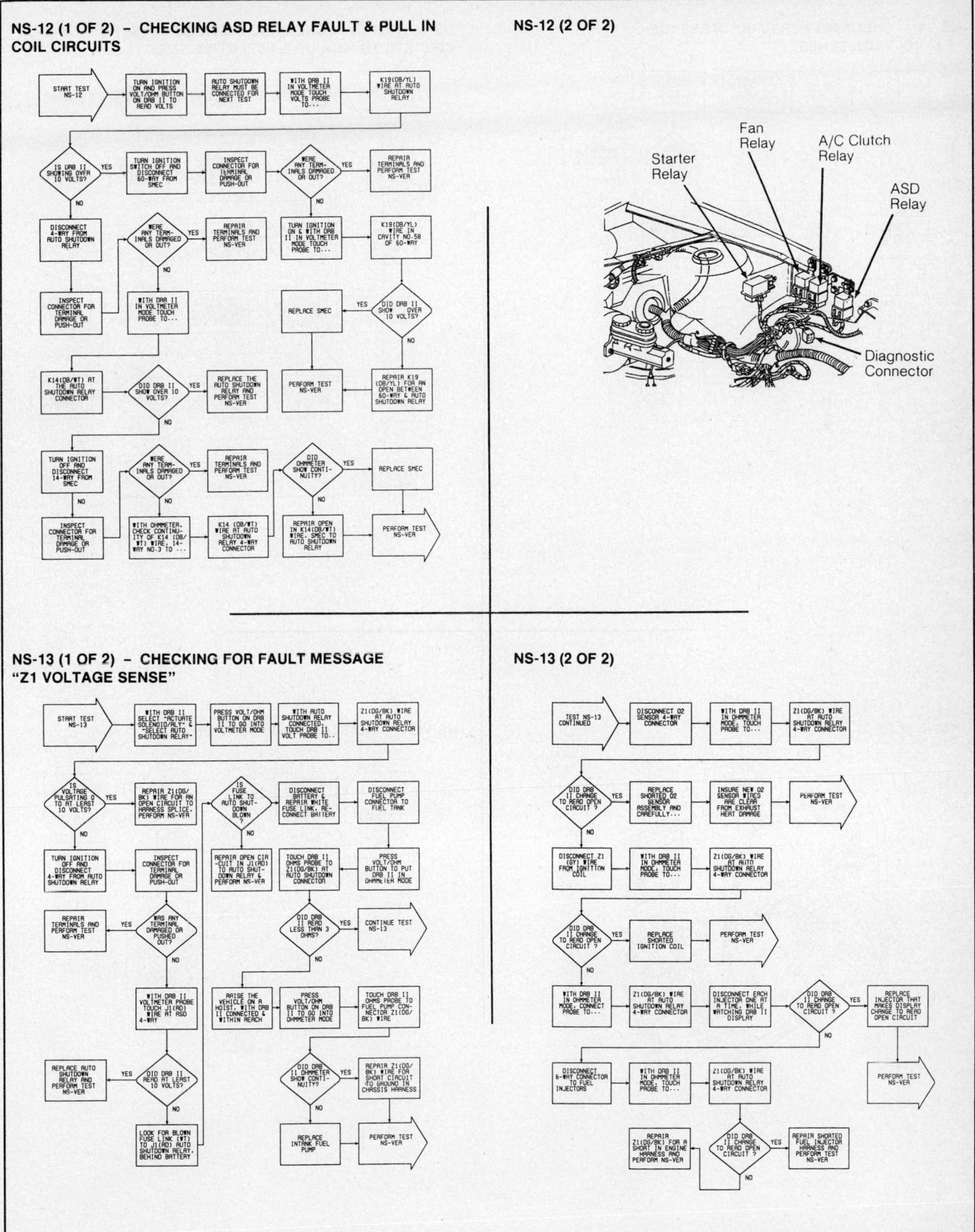

NS-12 (1 OF 2) – CHECKING ASD RELAY FAULT & PULL IN COIL CIRCUITS

NS-12 (2 OF 2)

Starter Relay
Fan Relay
A/C Clutch Relay
ASD Relay
Diagnostic Connector

NS-13 (1 OF 2) – CHECKING FOR FAULT MESSAGE "Z1 VOLTAGE SENSE"

NS-13 (2 OF 2)

1a-96

1989 COMPUTERIZED ENGINE CONTROLS
Chrysler Motors 2.5L Turbo I MPFI (Cont.)

NS-14 – CHECKING FOR FAULT MESSAGE "FJ2 VOLTAGE SENSE"

NS-15 (1 OF 2) – CHECKING DISTRIBUTOR SYNC PICK-UP, CIRCUITS TO PICK-UP & DEFECTIVE SMEC

NS-15 (2 OF 2)

NS-VER – NO START VERIFICATION

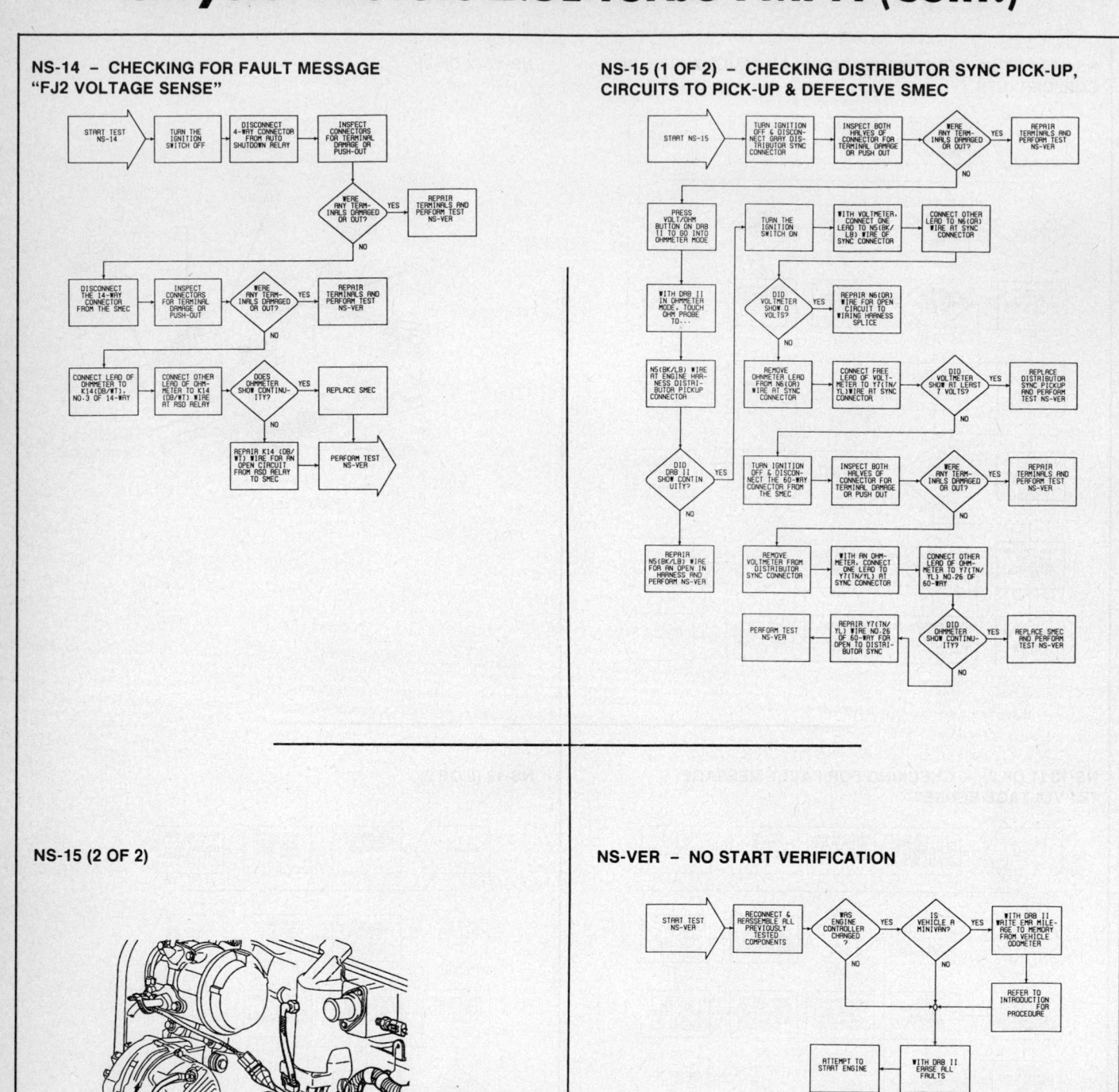

Alternator

Oil Filter

Distributor Gray Connector

1989 COMPUTERIZED ENGINE CONTROLS
Chrysler Motors 2.5L Turbo I MPFI (Cont.)

1a-97

DR-1 (1 OF 12) – CHECKING SYSTEM FOR FAULTS

DR-1 (2 OF 12)

DR-1 (3 OF 12)

DR-1 (4 OF 12)

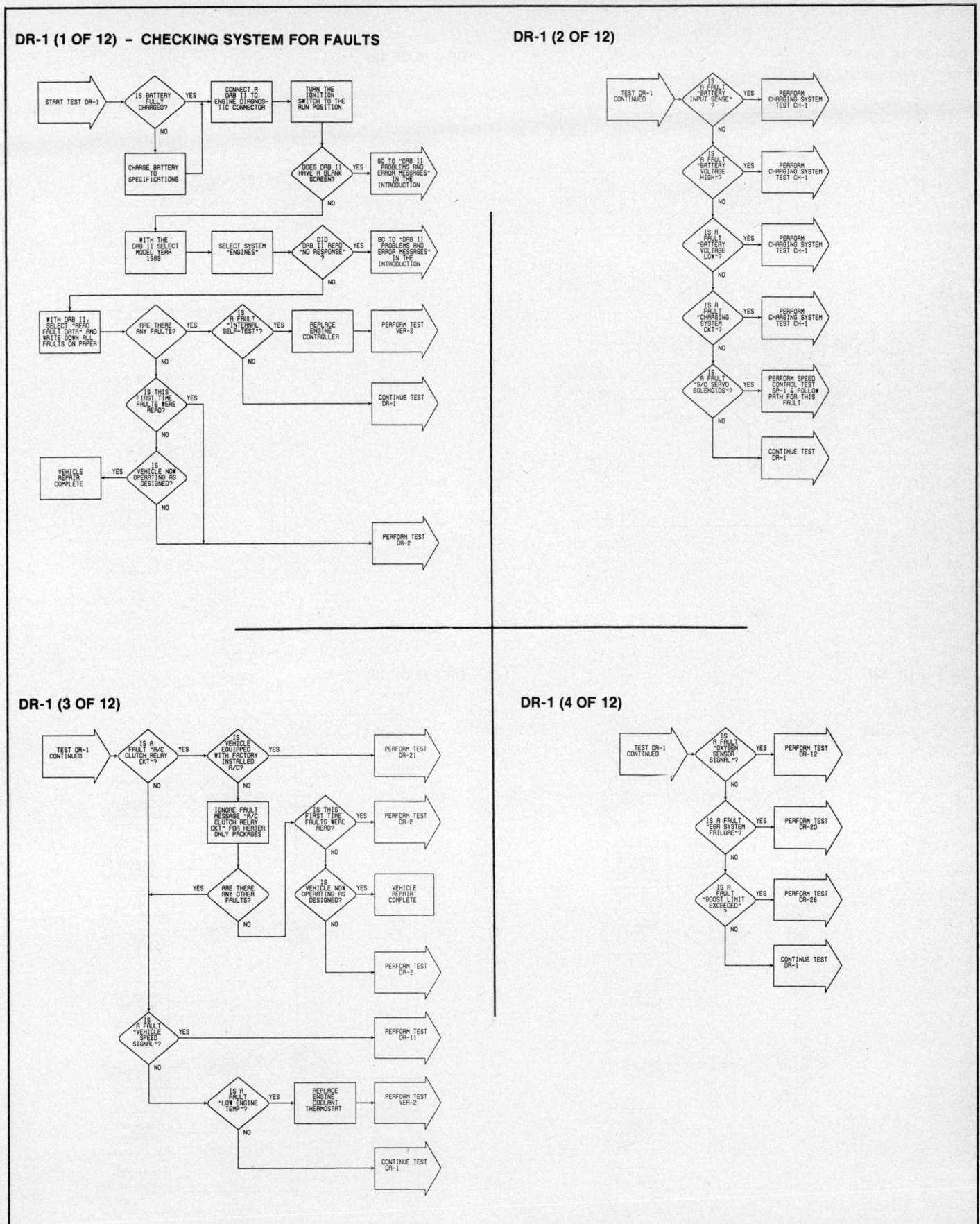

1a-98

1989 COMPUTERIZED ENGINE CONTROLS
Chrysler Motors 2.5L Turbo I MPFI (Cont.)

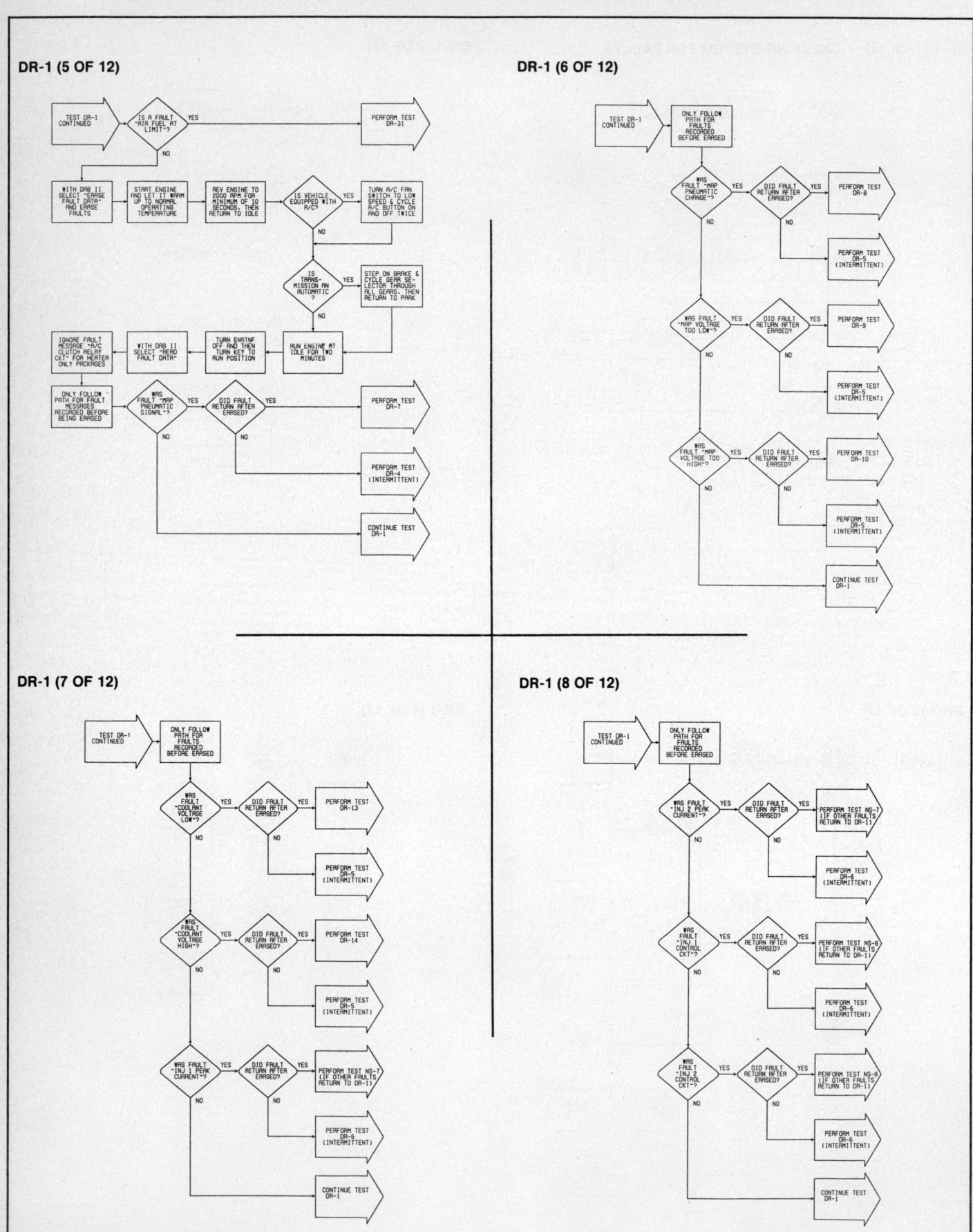

1989 COMPUTERIZED ENGINE CONTROLS
Chrysler Motors 2.5L Turbo I MPFI (Cont.)

1a-99

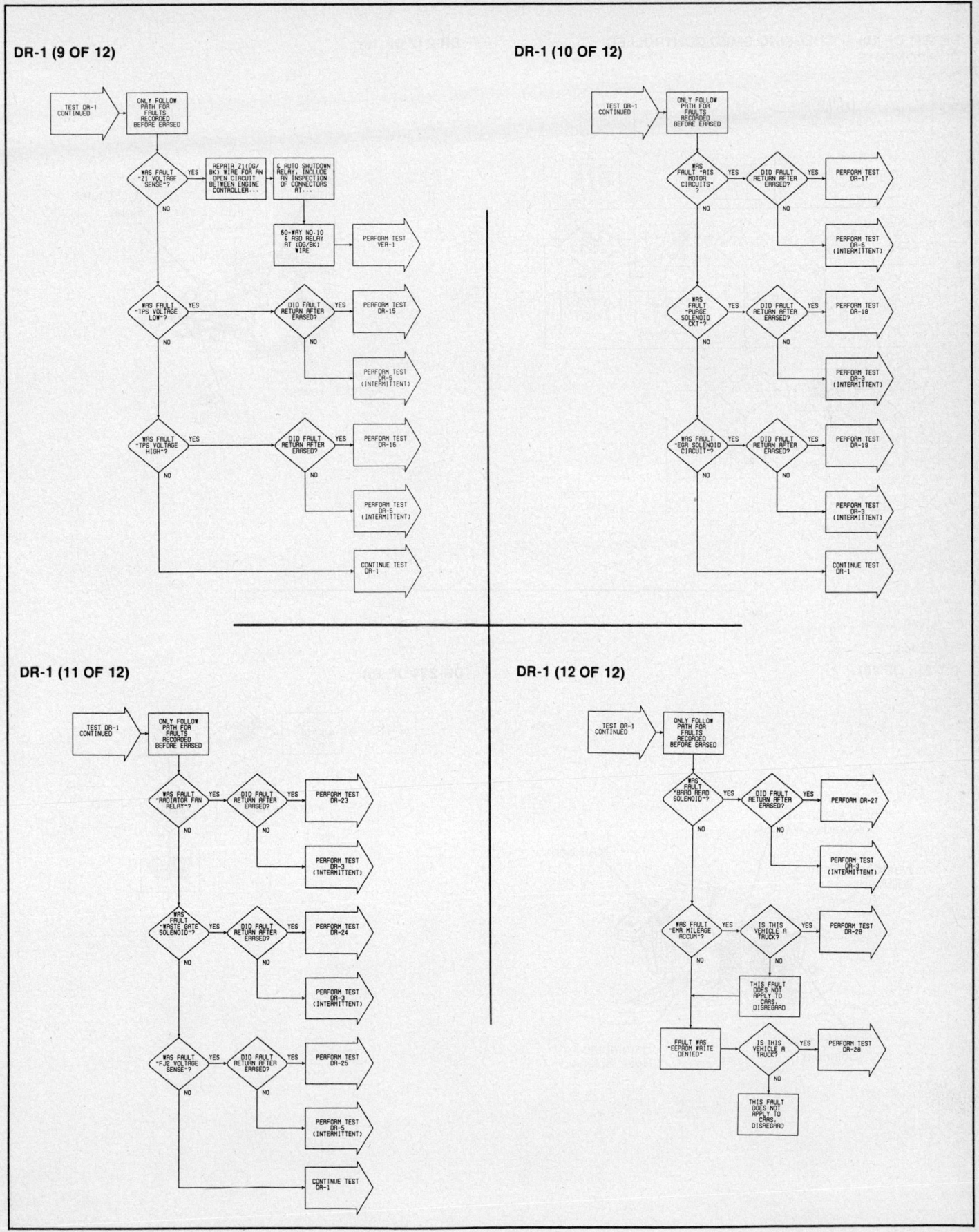

1a-100

1989 COMPUTERIZED ENGINE CONTROLS
Chrysler Motors 2.5L Turbo I MPFI (Cont.)

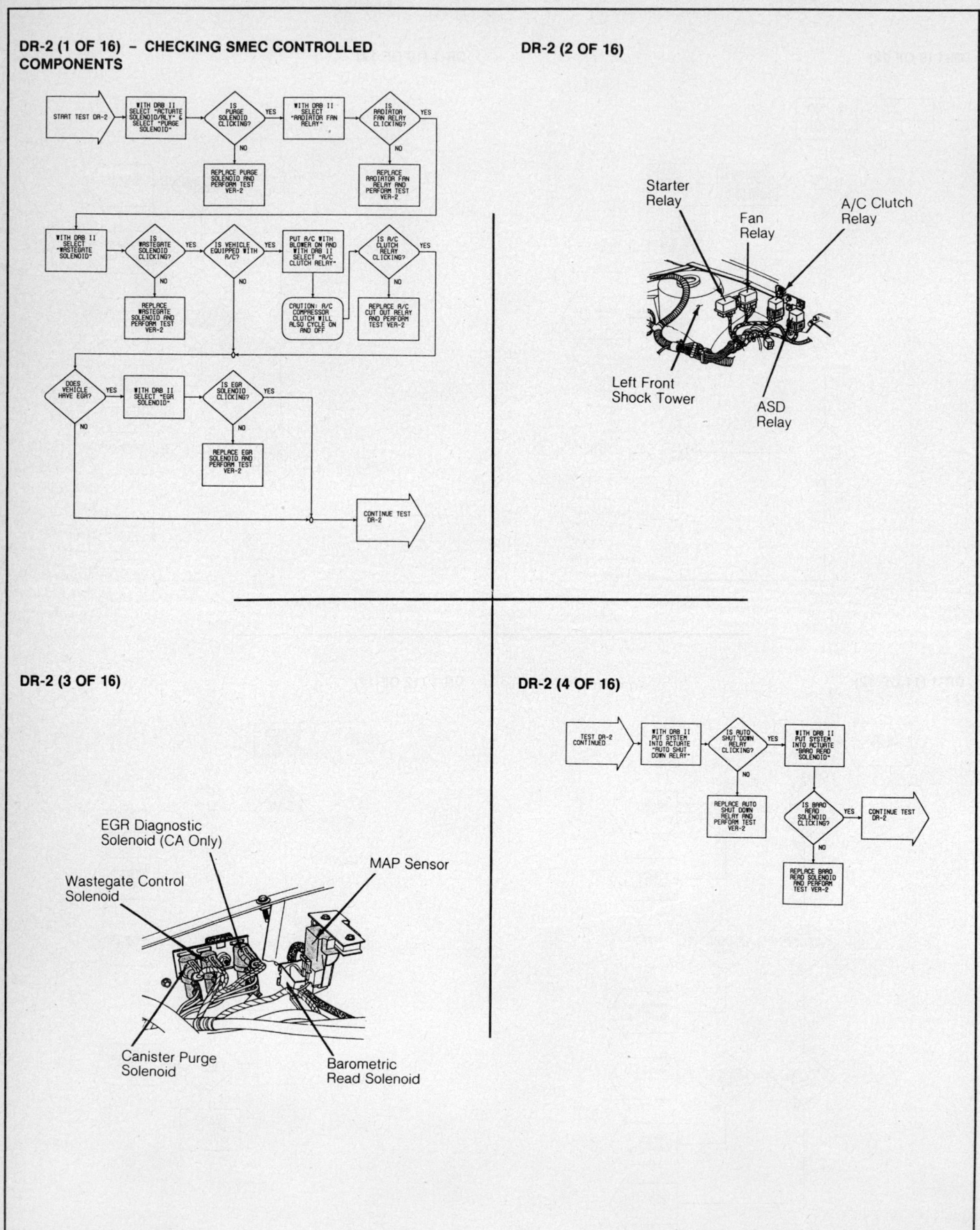

DR-2 (1 OF 16) – CHECKING SMEC CONTROLLED COMPONENTS

DR-2 (2 OF 16)

Starter Relay

Fan Relay

A/C Clutch Relay

Left Front Shock Tower

ASD Relay

DR-2 (3 OF 16)

EGR Diagnostic Solenoid (CA Only)

Wastegate Control Solenoid

MAP Sensor

Canister Purge Solenoid

Barometric Read Solenoid

DR-2 (4 OF 16)

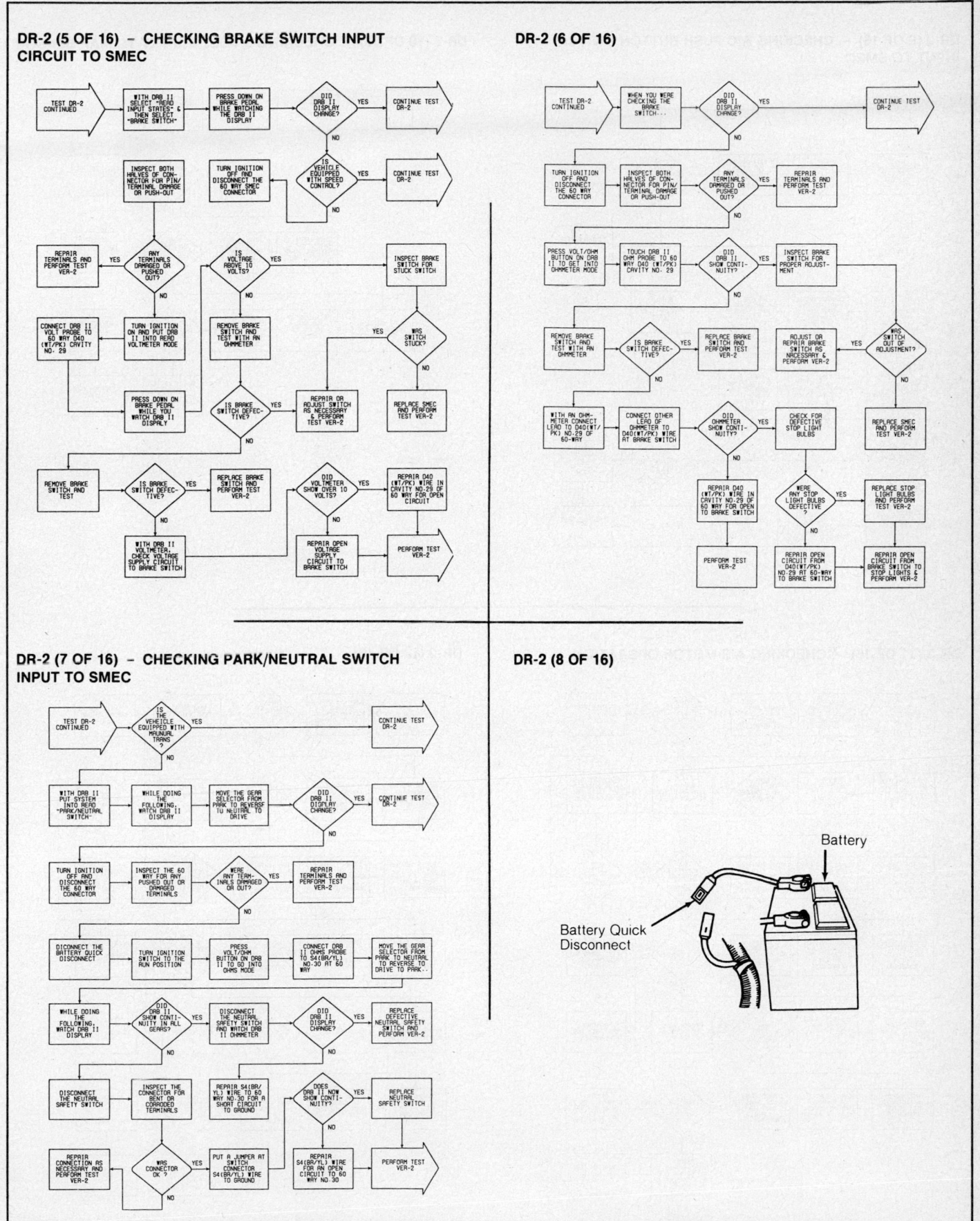

DR-2 (5 OF 16) – CHECKING BRAKE SWITCH INPUT CIRCUIT TO SMEC

DR-2 (6 OF 16)

DR-2 (7 OF 16) – CHECKING PARK/NEUTRAL SWITCH INPUT TO SMEC

DR-2 (8 OF 16)

Battery

Battery Quick Disconnect

1a-102

1989 COMPUTERIZED ENGINE CONTROLS
Chrysler Motors 2.5L Turbo I MPFI (Cont.)

DR-2 (9 OF 16) – CHECKING A/C PUSH BUTTON SWITCH INPUT TO SMEC

DR-2 (10 OF 16) – CHECKING 5 VOLT SUPPLY TO MAP SENSOR

DR-2 (11 OF 16) – CHECKING AIS MOTOR OPERATION

DR-2 (12 OF 16)

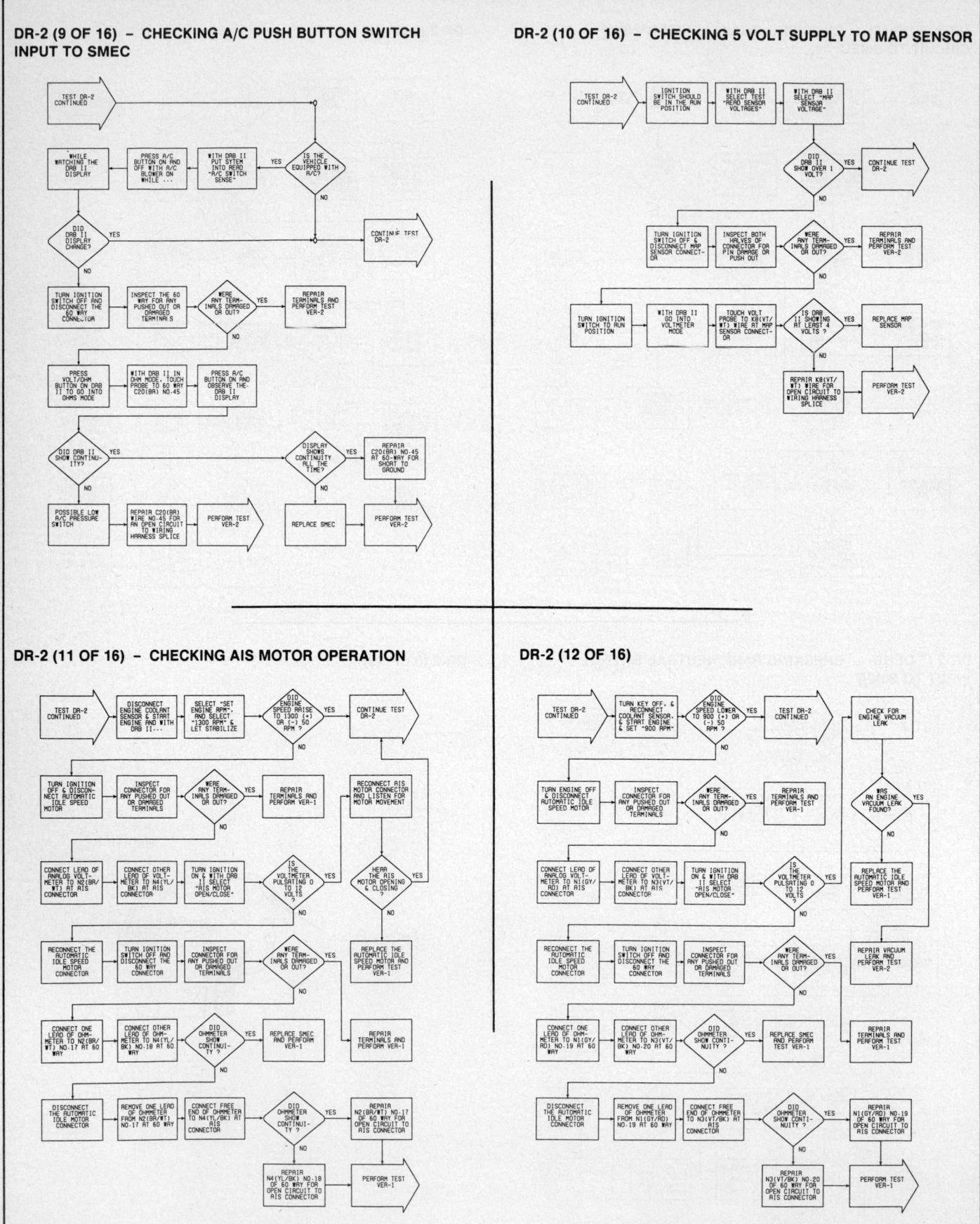

1989 COMPUTERIZED ENGINE CONTROLS
Chrysler Motors 2.5L Turbo I MPFI (Cont.)

1a-103

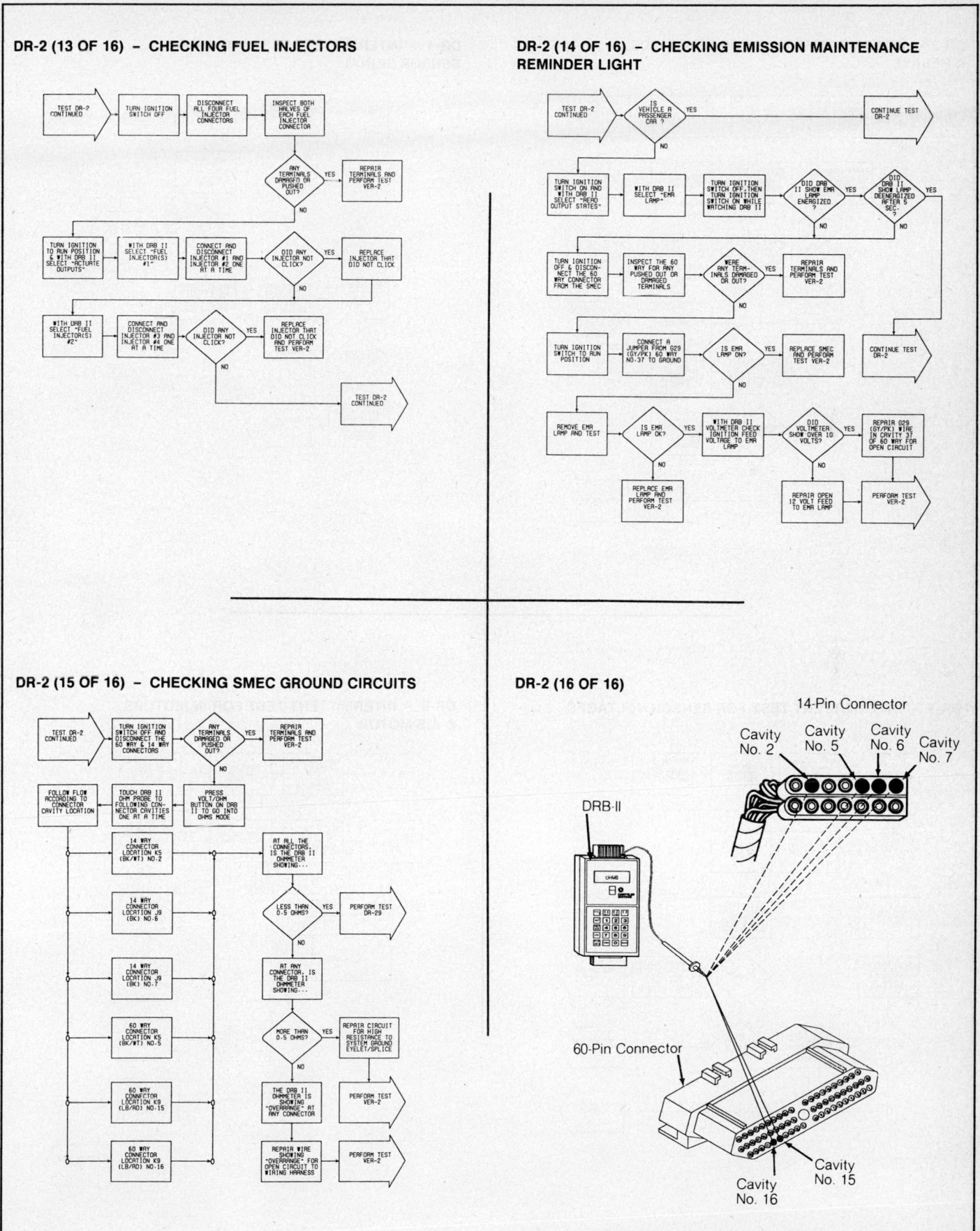

DR-2 (13 OF 16) – CHECKING FUEL INJECTORS

DR-2 (14 OF 16) – CHECKING EMISSION MAINTENANCE REMINDER LIGHT

DR-2 (15 OF 16) – CHECKING SMEC GROUND CIRCUITS

DR-2 (16 OF 16)

DRB-II

14-Pin Connector

Cavity No. 2

Cavity No. 5

Cavity No. 6

Cavity No. 7

60-Pin Connector

Cavity No. 16

Cavity No. 15

DR-3 – INTERMITTENT TEST FOR SOLENOIDS & RELAYS

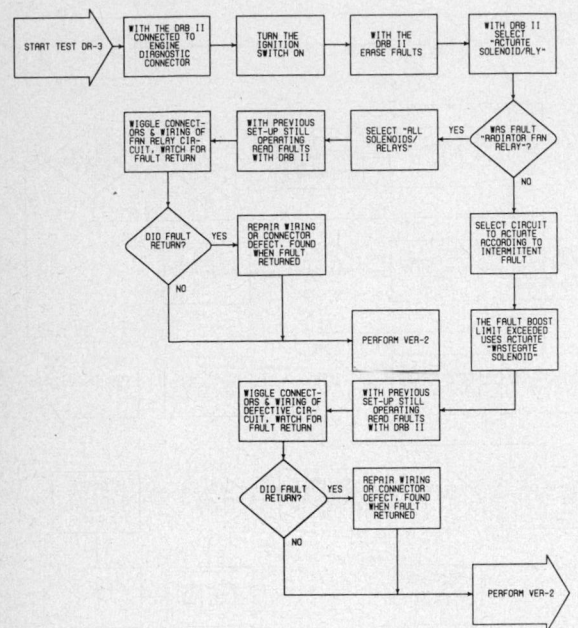

DR-4 – INTERMITTENT TEST FOR MAP SENSOR SIGNAL

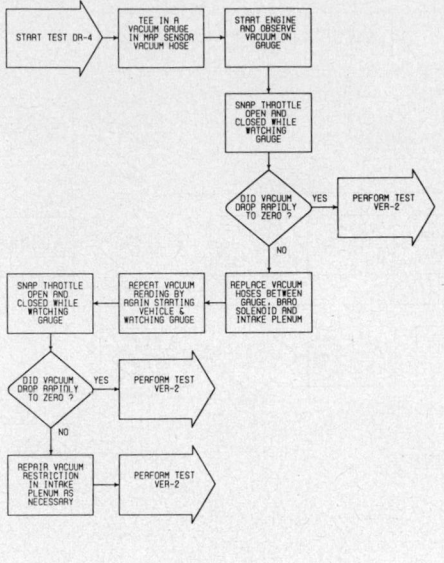

DR-5 – INTERMITTENT TEST FOR SENSOR VOLTAGES

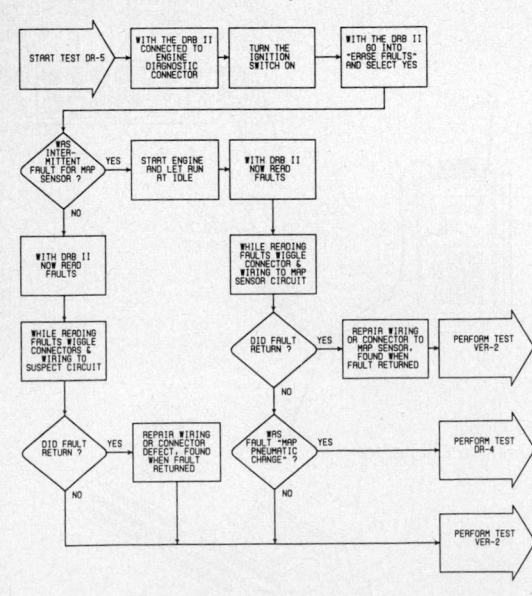

DR-6 – INTERMITTENT TEST FOR INJECTORS & AIS MOTOR

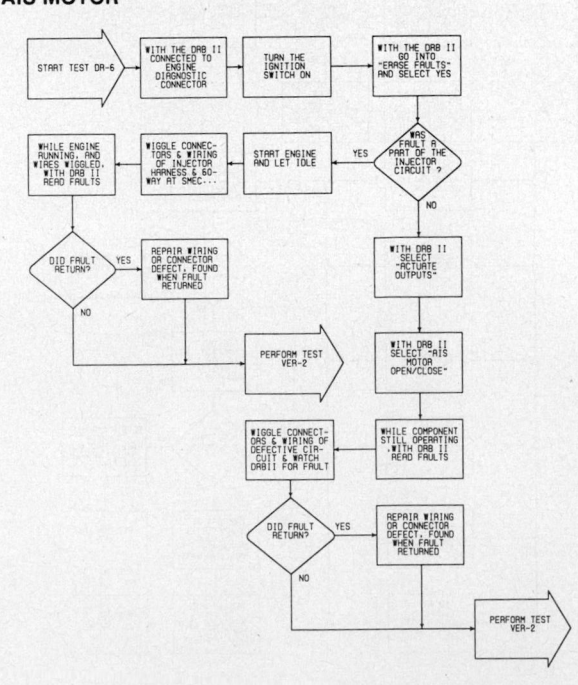

1989 COMPUTERIZED ENGINE CONTROLS
Chrysler Motors 2.5L Turbo I MPFI (Cont.)

1a-105

DR-7 (1 OF 2) – CHECKING FOR FAULT MESSAGE "MAP PNEUMATIC SIGNAL"

DR-7 (2 OF 2)

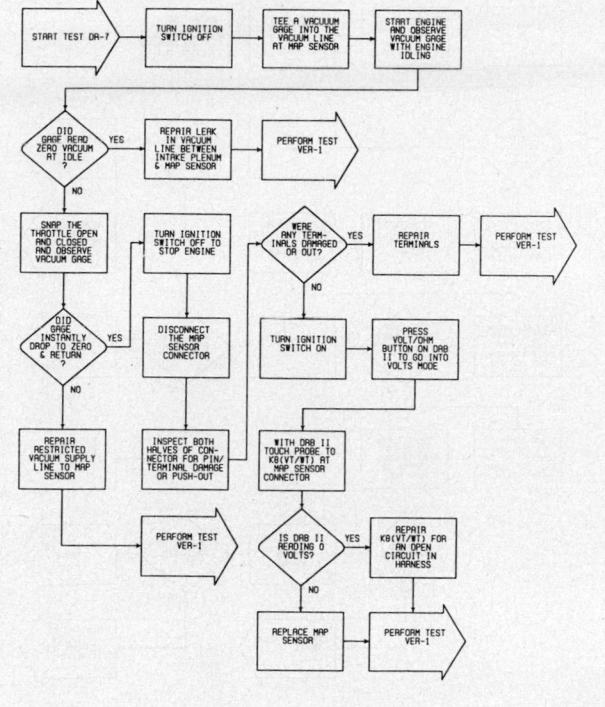

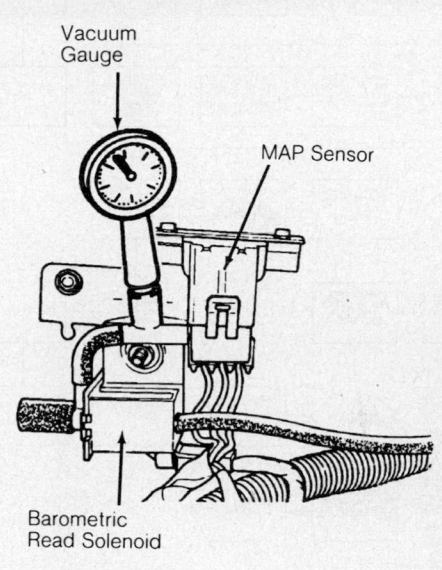

Vacuum Gauge

MAP Sensor

Barometric Read Solenoid

DR-8 – CHECKING FOR FAULT MESSAGE "MAP PNEUMATIC CHANGE"

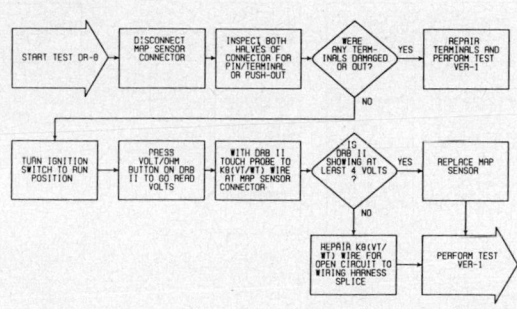

DR-9 – CHECKING FOR FAULT MESSAGE "MAP VOLTAGE TOO LOW"

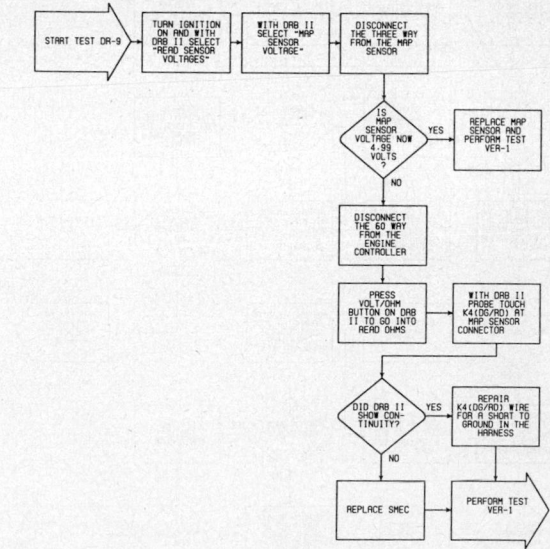

DR-10 – CHECKING FOR FAULT MESSAGE "MAP VOLTAGE TOO HIGH"

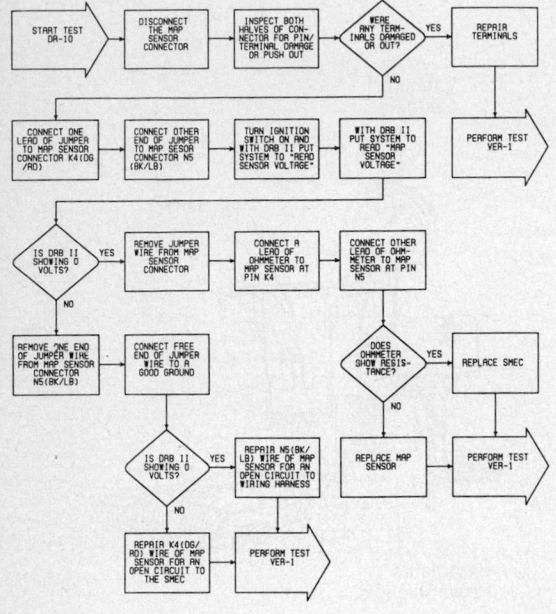

DR-11 (1 OF 2) – CHECKING FOR FAULT MESSAGE "VEHICLE SPEED SIGNAL"

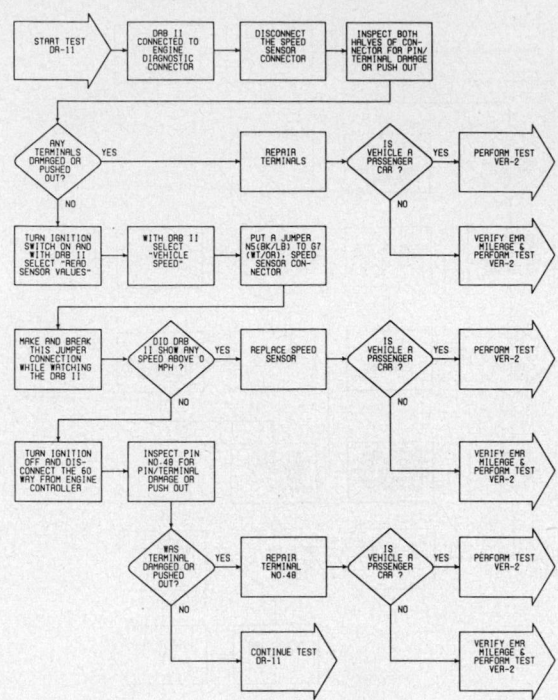

DR-11 (2 OF 2)

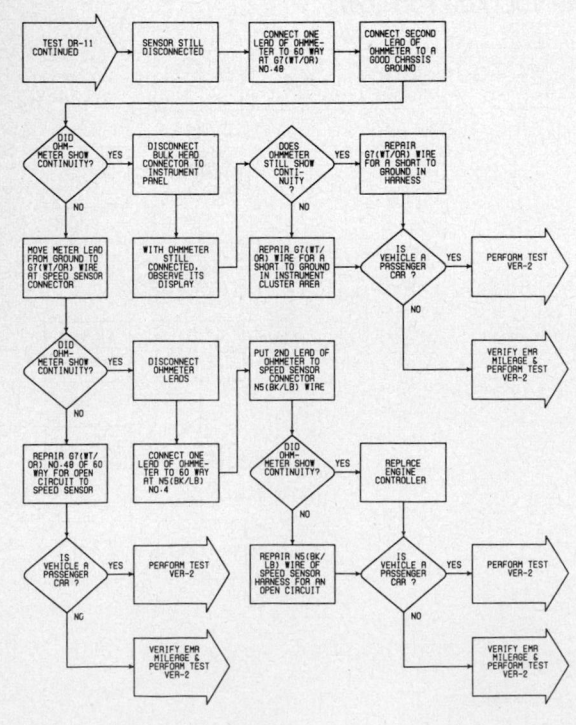

DR-12 (1 OF 2) – CHECKING FOR FAULT MESSAGE "OXYGEN SENSOR SIGNAL"

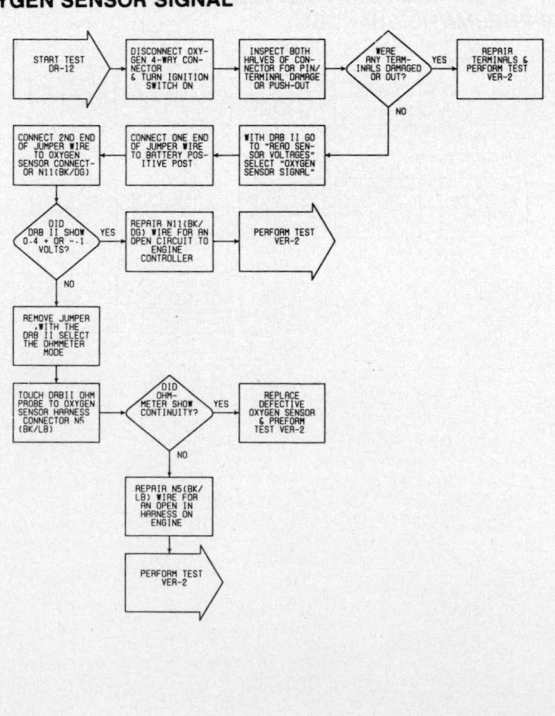

1989 COMPUTERIZED ENGINE CONTROLS
Chrysler Motors 2.5L Turbo I MPFI (Cont.)

1a-107

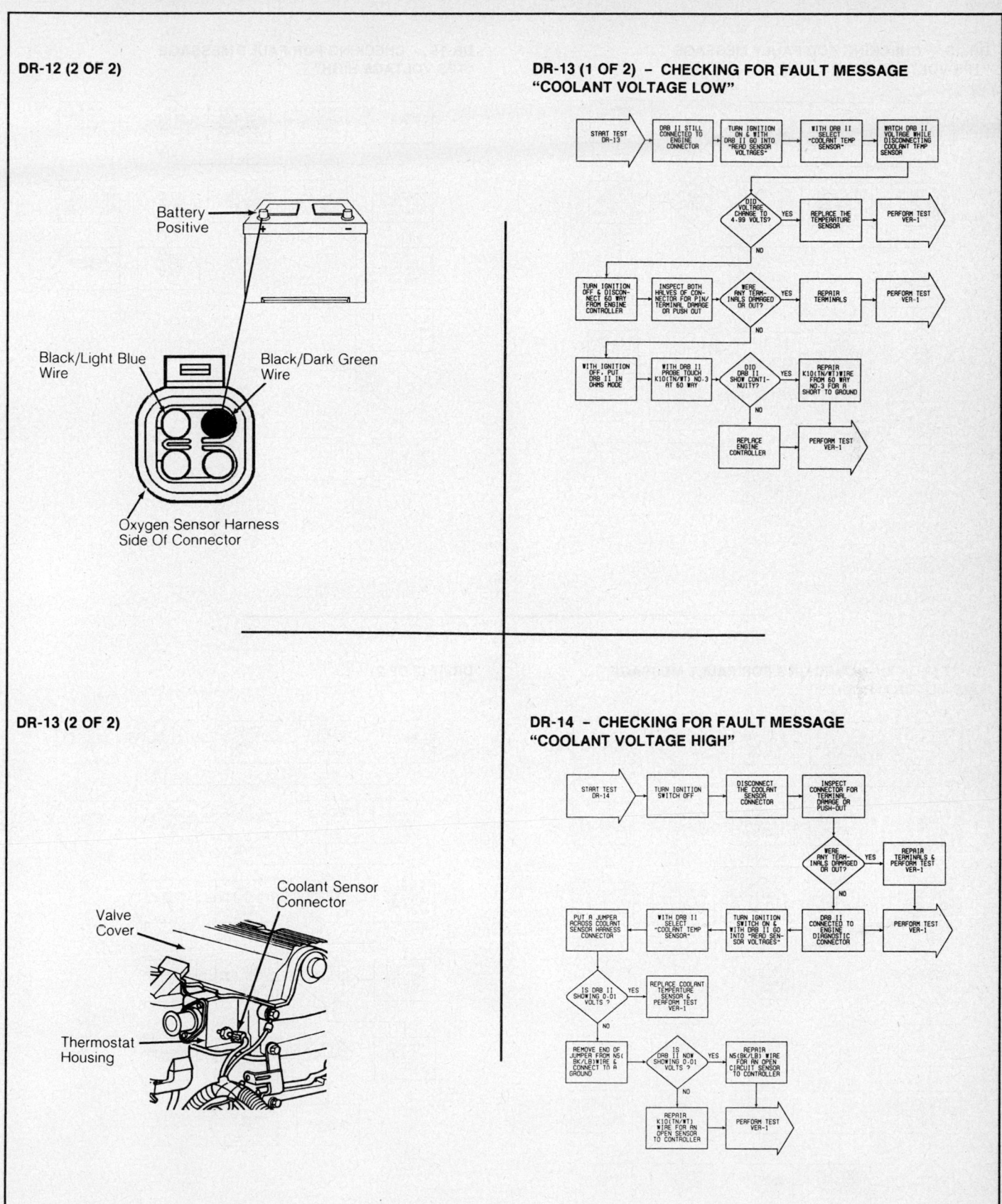

DR-12 (2 OF 2)

Battery Positive

Black/Light Blue Wire

Black/Dark Green Wire

Oxygen Sensor Harness Side Of Connector

DR-13 (1 OF 2) – CHECKING FOR FAULT MESSAGE "COOLANT VOLTAGE LOW"

DR-13 (2 OF 2)

Coolant Sensor Connector

Valve Cover

Thermostat Housing

DR-14 – CHECKING FOR FAULT MESSAGE "COOLANT VOLTAGE HIGH"

1989 COMPUTERIZED ENGINE CONTROLS
Chrysler Motors 2.5L Turbo I MPFI (Cont.)

DR-15 – CHECKING FOR FAULT MESSAGE
"TPS VOLTAGE LOW"

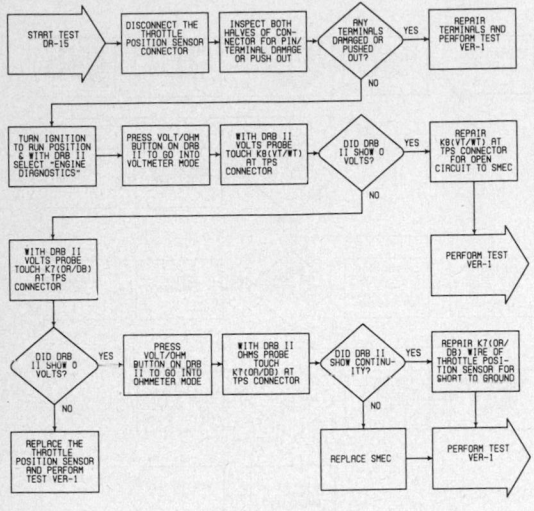

DR-16 – CHECKING FOR FAULT MESSAGE
"TPS VOLTAGE HIGH"

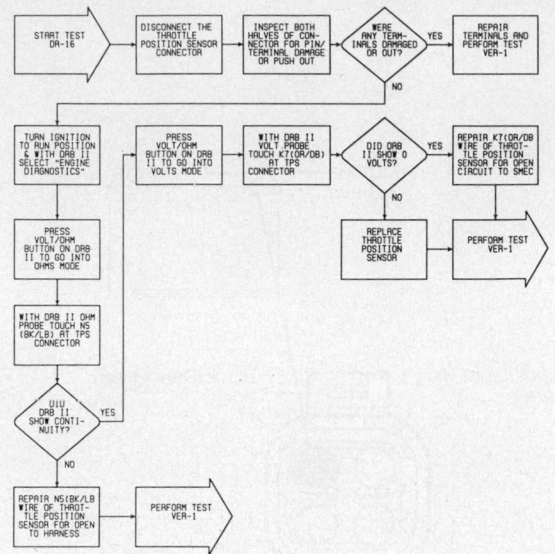

DR-17 (1 OF 2) – CHECKING FOR FAULT MESSAGE
"AIS MOTOR CIRCUITS"

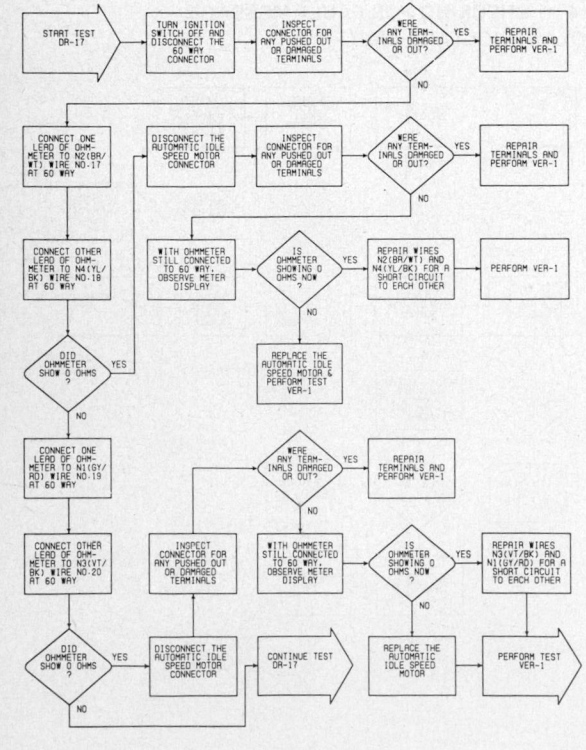

DR-17 (2 OF 2)

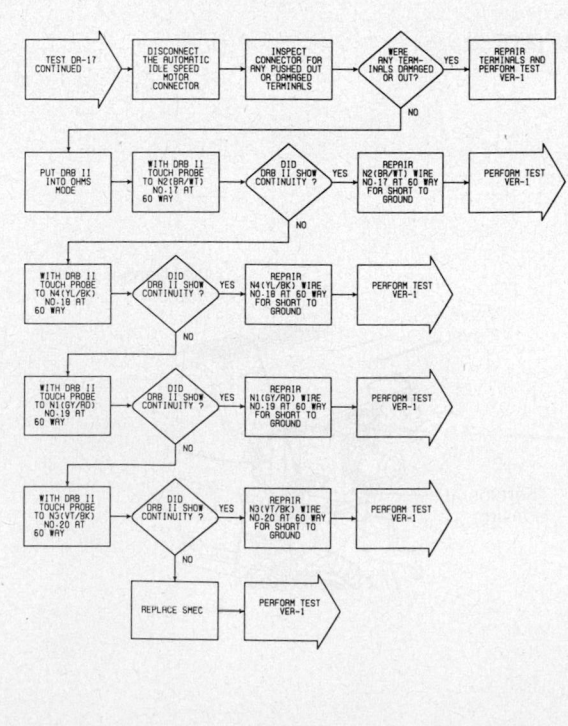

DR-18 (1 OF 2) – CHECKING FOR FAULT MESSAGE "PURGE SOLENOID CIRCUIT"

DR-18 (2 OF 2)

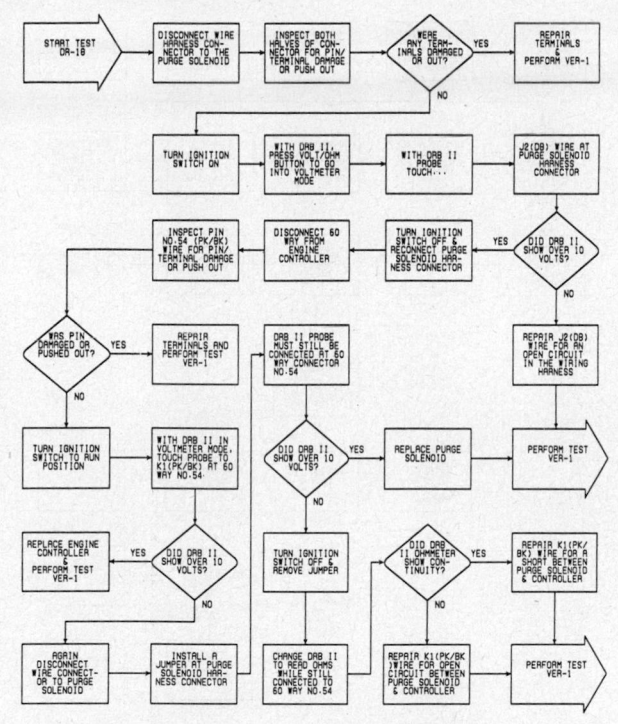

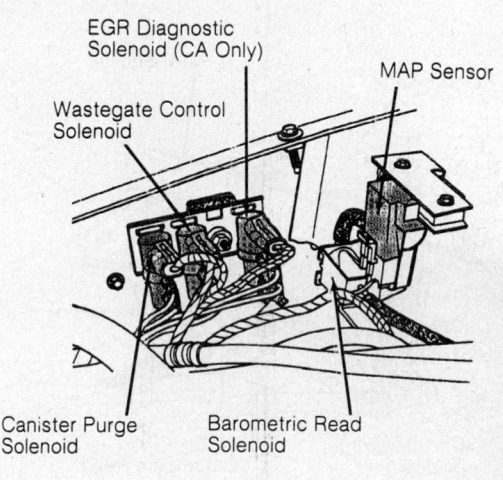

EGR Diagnostic Solenoid (CA Only)

Wastegate Control Solenoid

MAP Sensor

Canister Purge Solenoid

Barometric Read Solenoid

DR-19 – CHECKING FOR FAULT MESSAGE "EGR SOLENOID CIRCUIT"

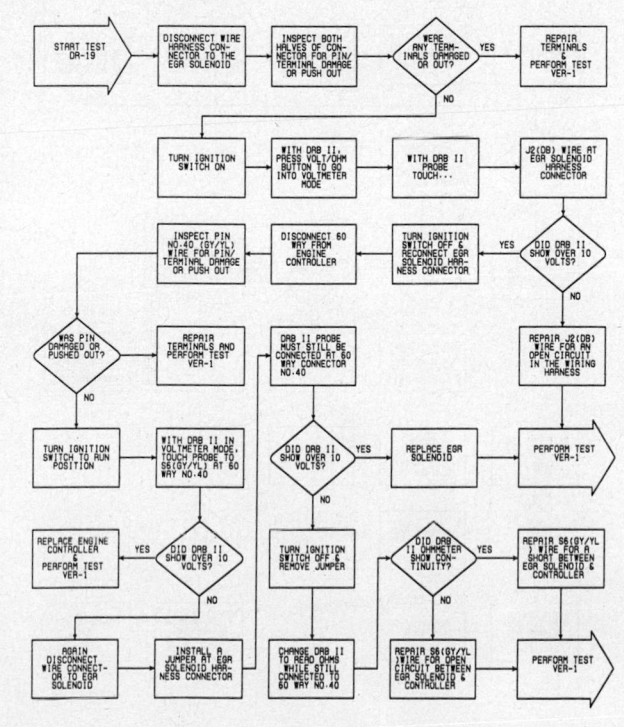

DR-20 (1 OF 3) – CHECKING FOR FAULT MESSAGE "EGR SYSTEM FAILURE"

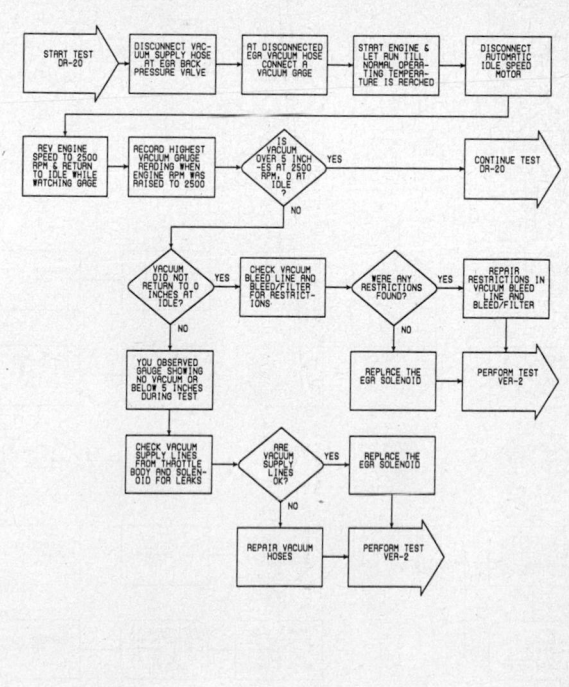

1a-110

1989 COMPUTERIZED ENGINE CONTROLS
Chrysler Motors 2.5L Turbo I MPFI (Cont.)

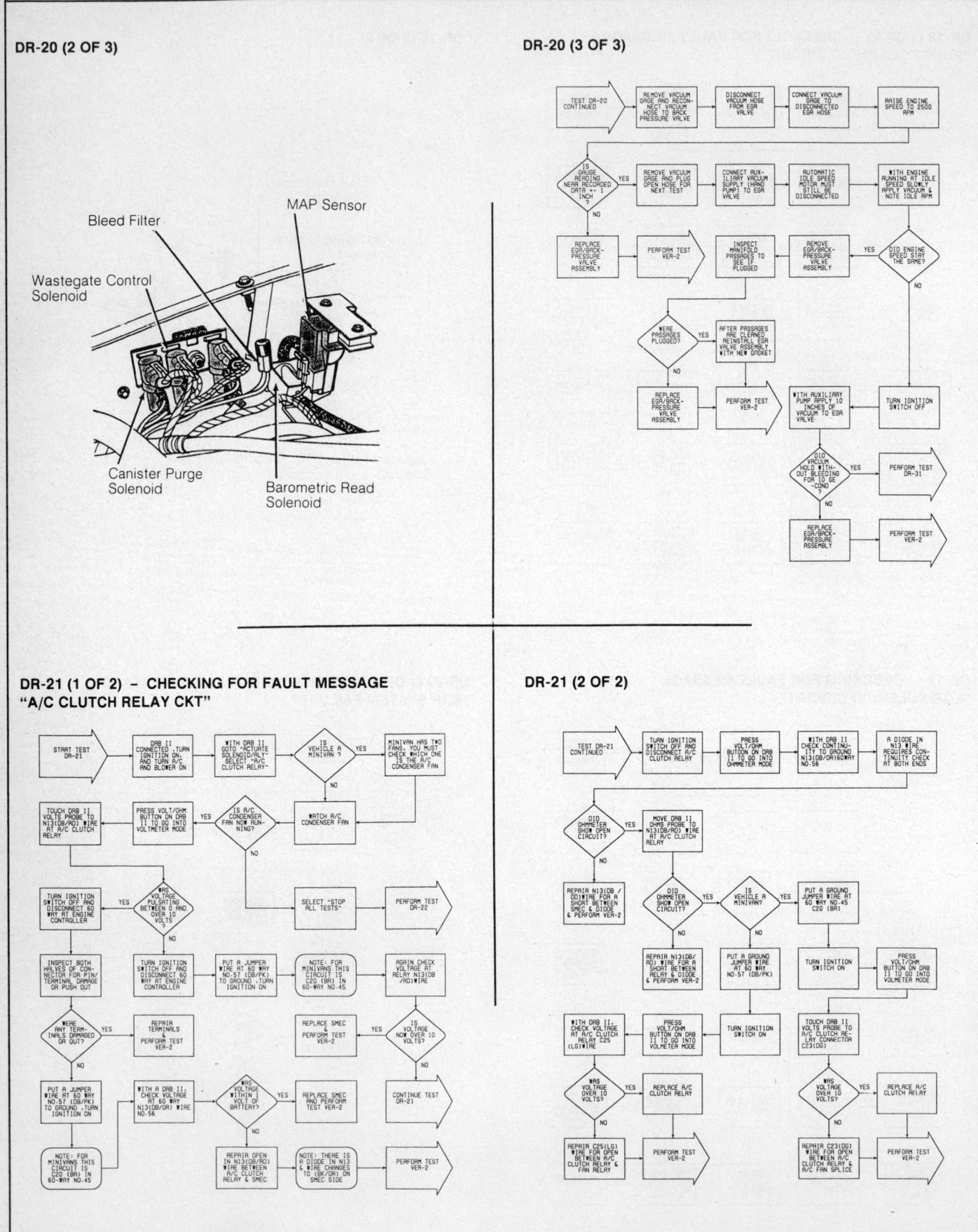

DR-20 (2 OF 3)

MAP Sensor

Bleed Filter

Wastegate Control Solenoid

Canister Purge Solenoid

Barometric Read Solenoid

DR-20 (3 OF 3)

DR-21 (1 OF 2) – CHECKING FOR FAULT MESSAGE "A/C CLUTCH RELAY CKT"

DR-21 (2 OF 2)

1989 COMPUTERIZED ENGINE CONTROLS
Chrysler Motors 2.5L Turbo I MPFI (Cont.)

1a-111

DR-22 – CHECKING A/C CONDENSER FAN OPERATION

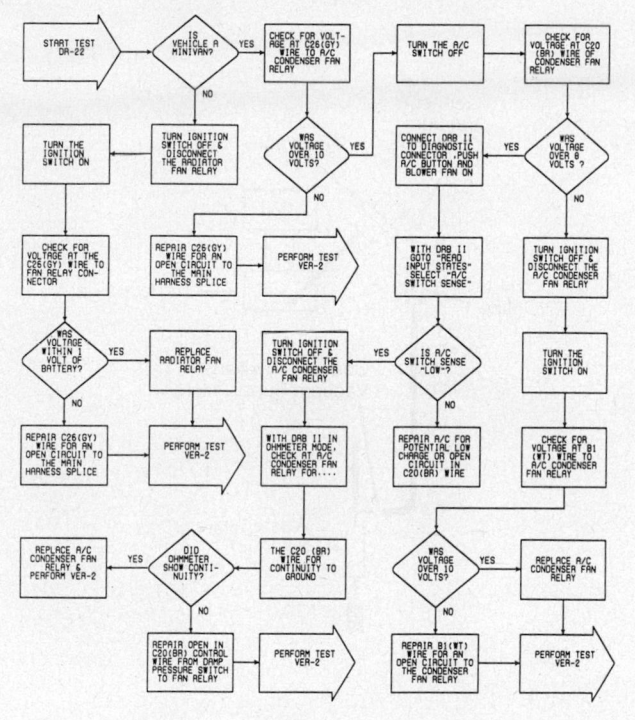

DR-23 – CHECKING FOR FAULT MESSAGE "RADIATOR FAN RELAY"

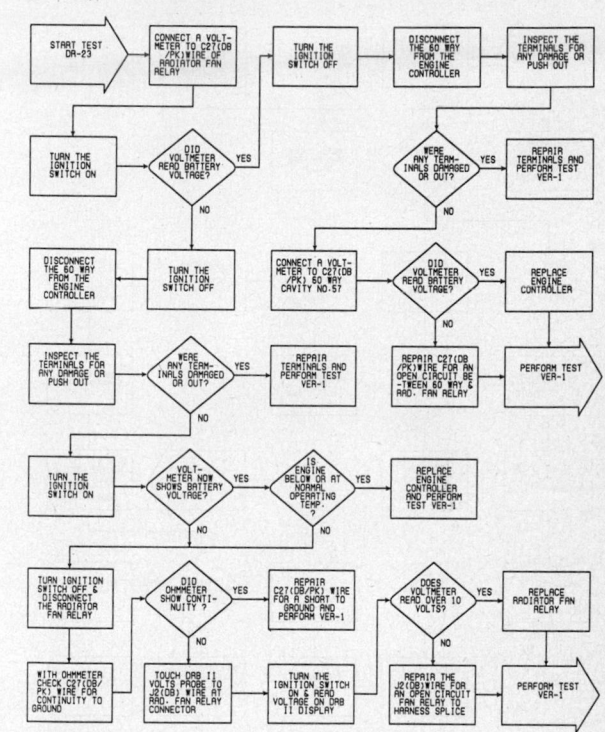

DR-24 – CHECKING FOR FAULT MESSAGE "WASTEGATE SOLENOID"

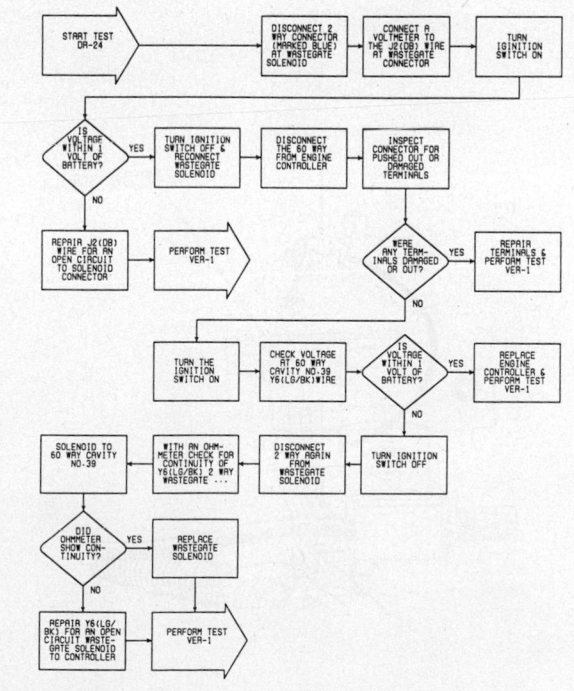

DR-25 – CHECKING FOR FAULT MESSAGE "FJ2 VOLTAGE SENSE"

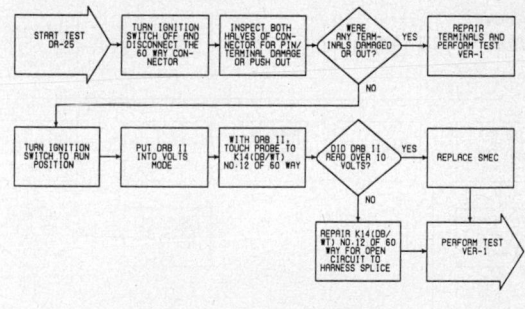

1a-112

1989 COMPUTERIZED ENGINE CONTROLS
Chrysler Motors 2.5L Turbo I MPFI (Cont.)

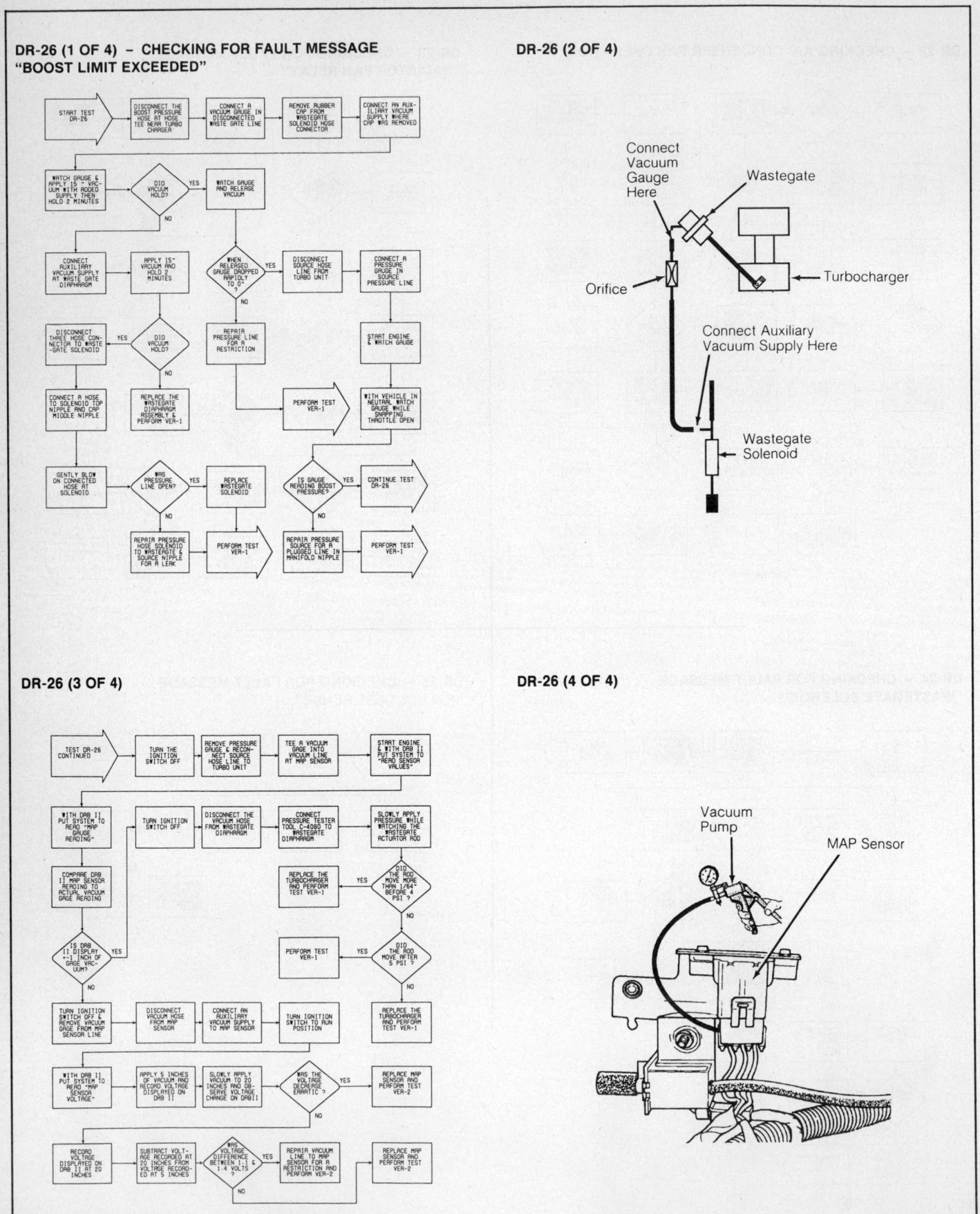

DR-26 (1 OF 4) – CHECKING FOR FAULT MESSAGE "BOOST LIMIT EXCEEDED"

DR-26 (2 OF 4)

DR-26 (3 OF 4)

DR-26 (4 OF 4)

1989 COMPUTERIZED ENGINE CONTROLS
Chrysler Motors 2.5L Turbo I MPFI (Cont.)

1a-113

**DR-27 – CHECKING FOR FAULT MESSAGE
"BAROMETRIC READ SOLENOID"**

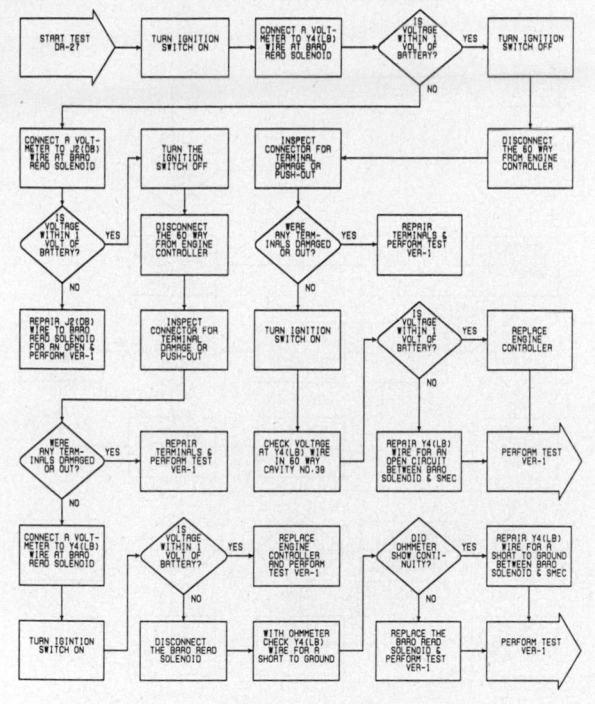

**DR-28 – CHECKING FOR FAULT MESSAGE
"EMR MILEAGE ACCUM" & "EEPROM WRITE DENIED"**

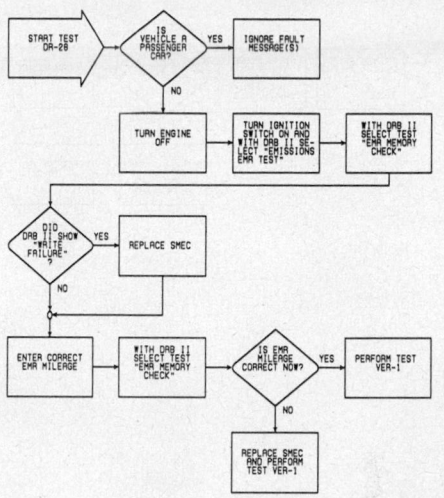

**DR-29 (1 OF 2) – CHECKING SENSOR CALIBRATIONS
(BEGIN WITH COLD ENGINE)**

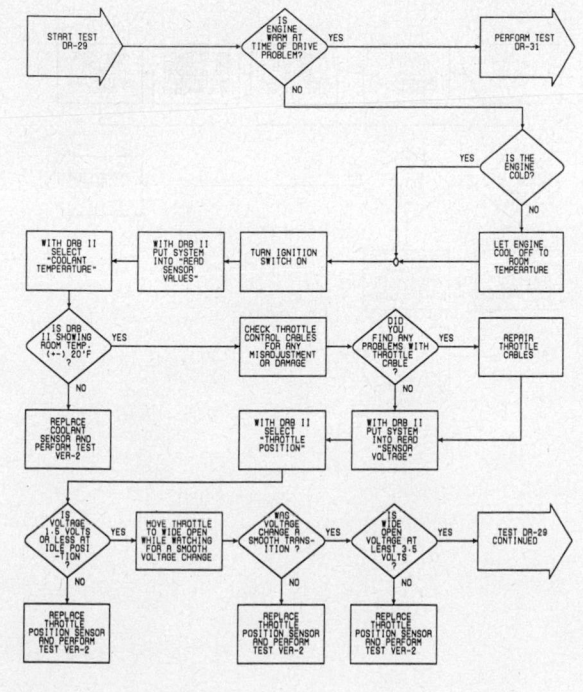

DR-29 (2 OF 2)

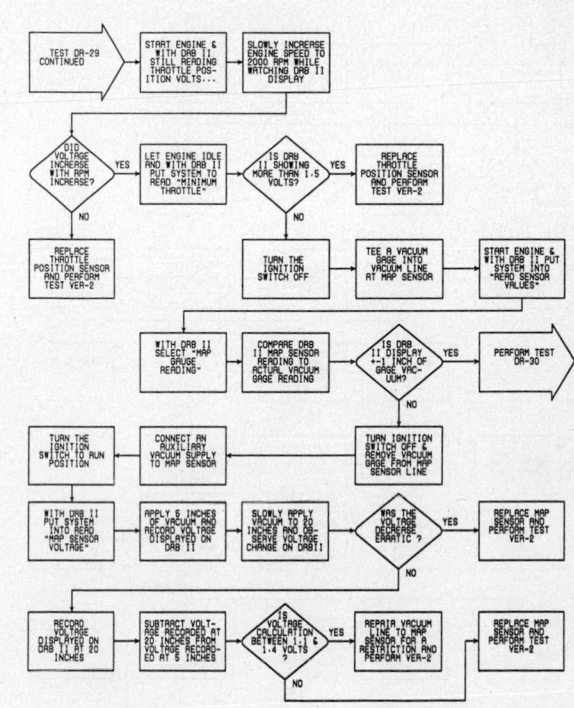

1a-114

1989 COMPUTERIZED ENGINE CONTROLS
Chrysler Motors 2.5L Turbo I MPFI (Cont.)

DR-30 – CHECKING SPARK PLUGS

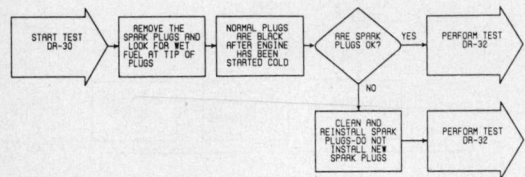

DR-31 (1 OF 2) – CHECKING SENSOR CALIBRATIONS (BEGIN WITH WARM ENGINE)

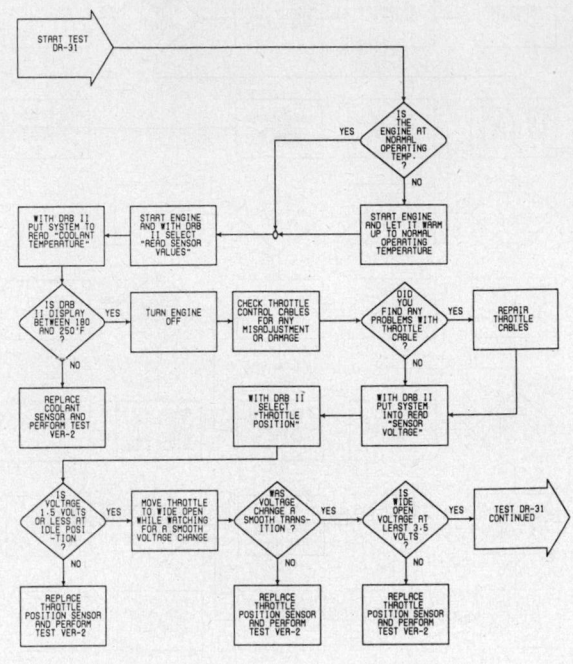

DR-31 (2 OF 2)

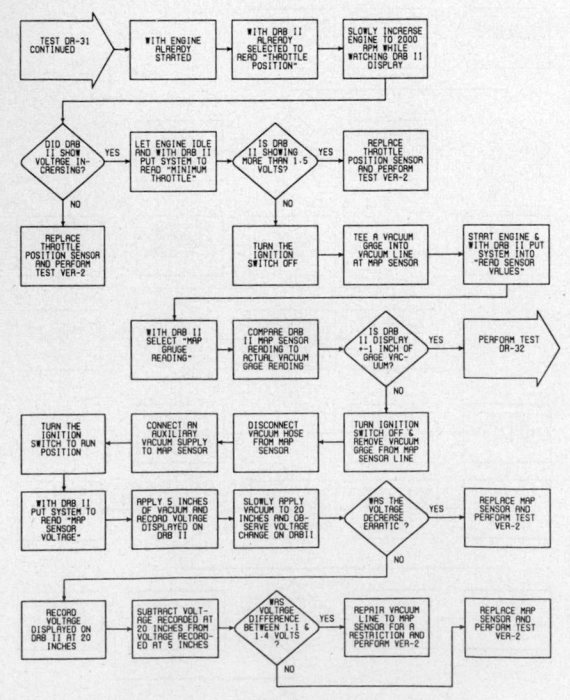

DR-32 – CHECKING SECONDARY IGNITION SYSTEM

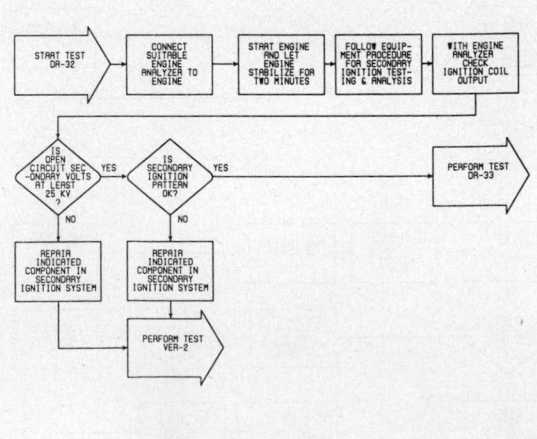

1989 COMPUTERIZED ENGINE CONTROLS
Chrysler Motors 2.5L Turbo I MPFI (Cont.)

1a-115

DR-33 (1 OF 5) – CHECKING BASIC TIMING & FUEL SYSTEM

DR-33 (2 OF 5)

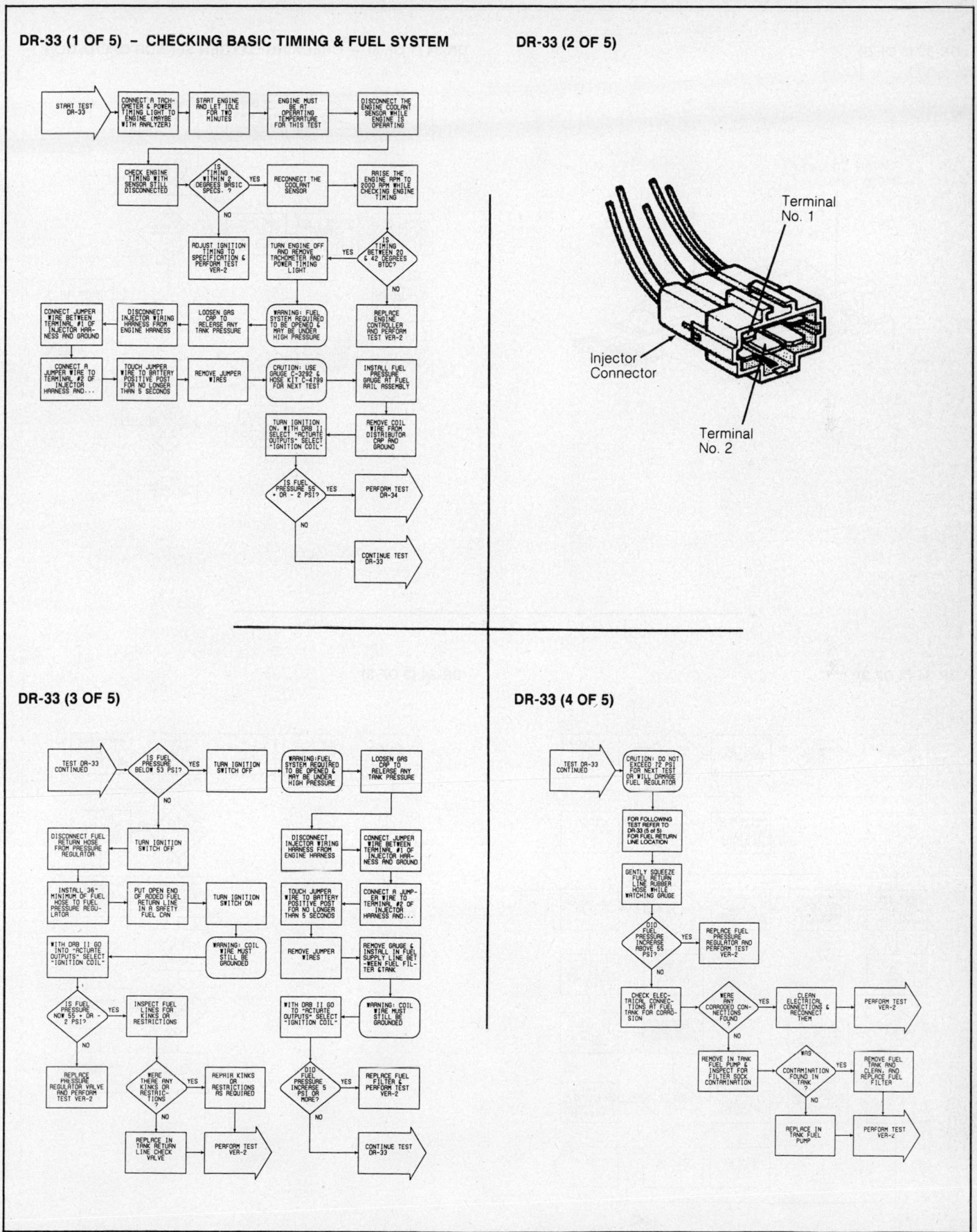

DR-33 (3 OF 5)

DR-33 (4 OF 5)

1989 COMPUTERIZED ENGINE CONTROLS
Chrysler Motors 2.5L Turbo I MPFI (Cont.)

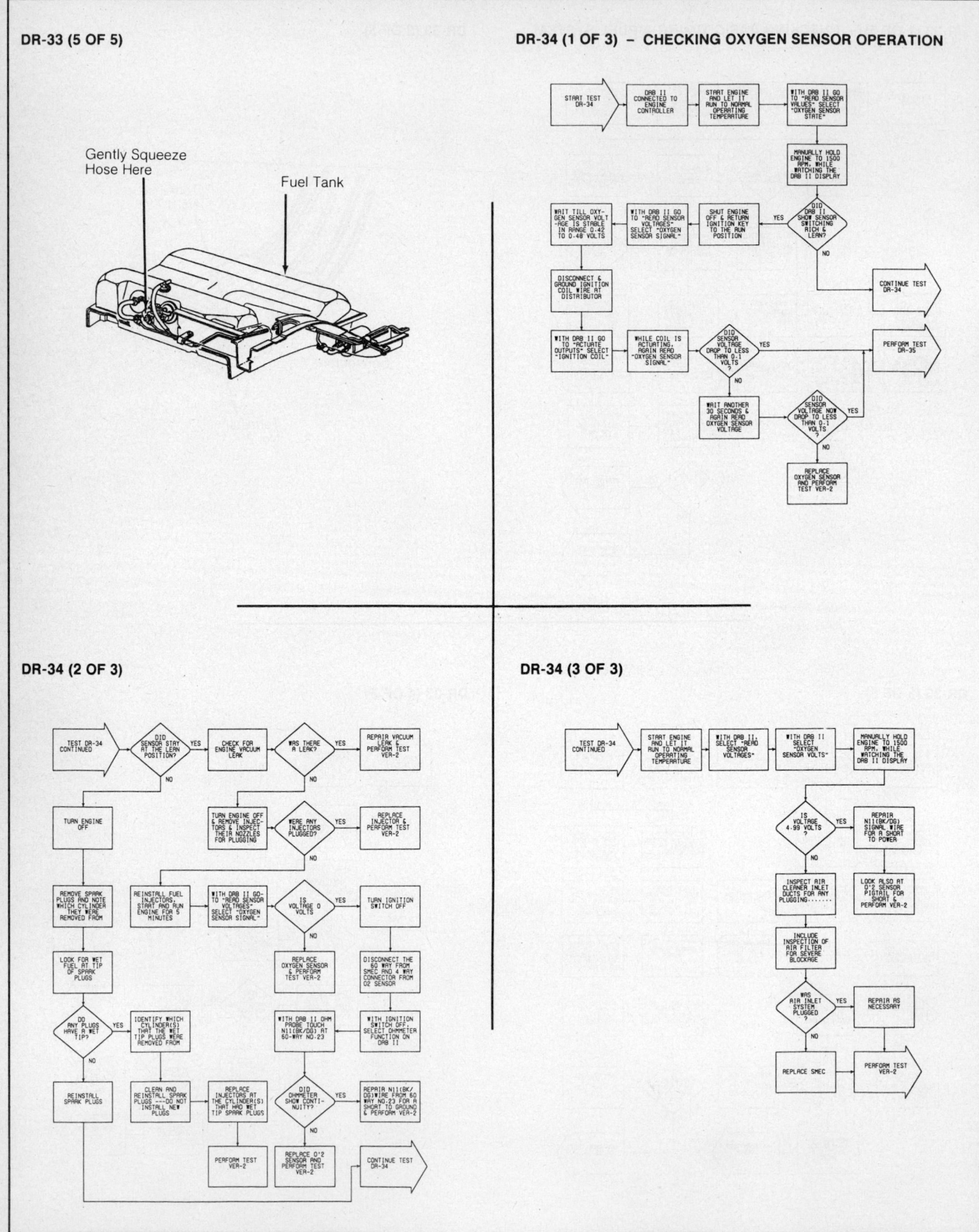

DR-33 (5 OF 5)

Gently Squeeze Hose Here

Fuel Tank

DR-34 (1 OF 3) – CHECKING OXYGEN SENSOR OPERATION

DR-34 (2 OF 3)

DR-34 (3 OF 3)

1989 COMPUTERIZED ENGINE CONTROLS
Chrysler Motors 2.5L Turbo I MPFI (Cont.)

1a-117

DR-35 – CHECKING THROTTLE BODY MINIMUM AIRFLOW

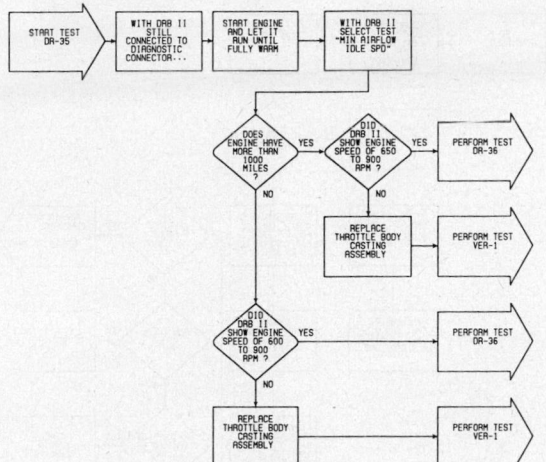

DR-36 – OTHER POSSIBLE CAUSES OF DRIVEABILITY RELATED PROBLEMS

AT THIS POINT IN THE DRIVEABILITY TEST PROCEDURE YOU HAVE DETERMINED THAT ALL OF THE ENGINE CONTROL SYSTEMS ARE OPERATING AS THEY WERE DESIGNED. THEREFORE, THEY ARE **NOT THE CAUSE OF THE DRIVEABILITY PROBLEM.**

THE FOLLOWING ADDITIONAL ITEMS SHOULD BE CHECKED AS POSSIBLE CAUSES:

1. **ENGINE VACUUM** - MUST BE AT LEAST 13 INCHES IN NEUTRAL.
2. **ENGINE VALVE TIMING** - TO SPECIFICATIONS.
3. **ENGINE COMPRESSION** - TO SPECIFICATIONS.
4. **ENGINE EXHAUST SYSTEM** - MUST BE FREE OF ANY RESTRICTIONS.
5. **ENGINE PCV SYSTEM** - MUST FLOW FREELY.
6. **ENGINE DRIVE SPROCKETS** - CAM, CRANK AND INTERMEDIATE SHAFTS.
7. **TORQUE CONVERTOR STALL SPEED** - TO SPECIFICATIONS.
8. **POWER BRAKE BOOSTER** - NO INTERNAL VACUUM LEAKS.
9. **FUEL CONTAMINATION** - HIGH ALCOHOL AND WATER CONTENT.
10. **TECHNICAL SERVICE BULLETINS** - ANY THAT MAY APPLY TO VEHICLE.

ANY ONE OR MORE OF THESE ITEMS CAN CREATE A DRIVEABILITY RELATED PROBLEM. THEY CAN NOT BE OVERLOOKED AS POSSIBLE CAUSES.

VER-1 (1 OF 2) – DRIVEABILITY VERIFICATION

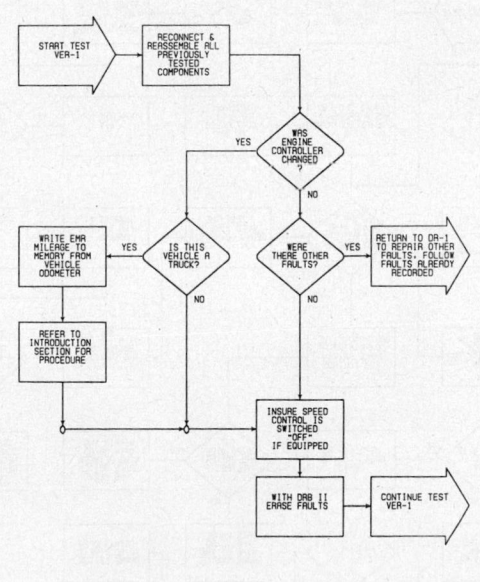

VER-1 (2 OF 2)

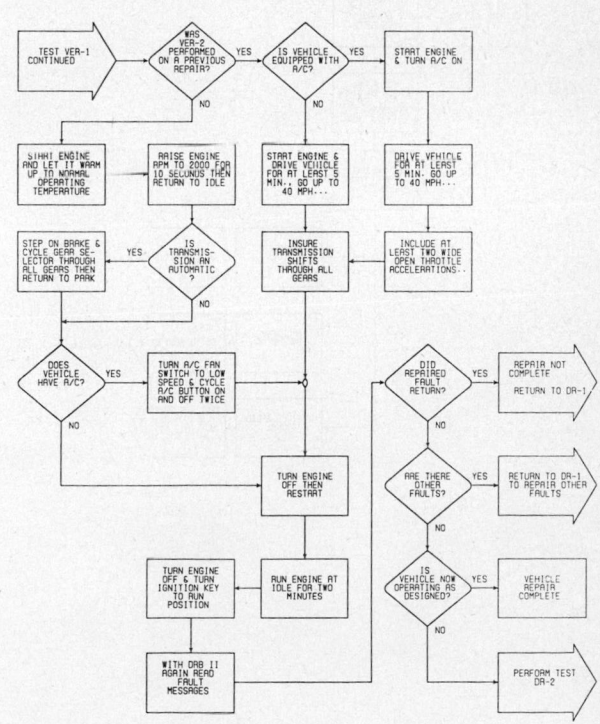

1989 COMPUTERIZED ENGINE CONTROLS
Chrysler Motors 2.5L Turbo I MPFI (Cont.)

VER-2 (1 OF 2) – DRIVEABILITY VERIFICATION

- START TEST VER-2
- RECONNECT & REASSEMBLE ALL PREVIOUSLY TESTED COMPONENTS
- WAS ENGINE CONTROLLER CHANGED?
  - YES
  - NO
- IS THIS VEHICLE A TRUCK?
  - YES → WRITE EMR MILEAGE TO MEMORY FROM VEHICLE ODOMETER
  - NO → REFER TO INTRODUCTION SECTION FOR PROCEDURE
- WERE THERE OTHER FAULTS?
  - YES → RETURN TO DR-1 TO REPAIR OTHER FAULTS. FOLLOW FAULTS ALREADY RECORDED
  - NO
- CONTINUE TEST VER-2

VER-2 (2 OF 2)

- VER-2 CONTINUED
- INSURE SPEED CONTROL IS SWITCHED "OFF" IF EQUIPPED
- WITH DRB II ERASE FAULTS
- IS VEHICLE EQUIPPED WITH A/C?
  - YES → START ENGINE & TURN A/C ON
- DRIVE VEHICLE FOR AT LEAST 5 MIN. GO UP TO 40 MPH...
- START ENGINE & DRIVE VEHICLE FOR AT LEAST 5 MIN. GO UP TO 40 MPH...
- INCLUDE AT LEAST TWO WIDE OPEN THROTTLE ACCELERATIONS..
- INSURE TRANSMISSION SHIFTS THROUGH ALL GEARS
- DID REPAIRED FAULT RETURN?
  - YES → REPAIR NOT COMPLETE RETURN TO DR-1
  - NO
- ARE THERE OTHER FAULTS?
  - YES → RETURN TO DR-1 TO REPAIR OTHER FAULTS
  - NO
- AT END OF ROAD TEST TURN ENGINE OFF & TURN IGNITION KEY TO RUN POSITION
- IS VEHICLE NOW OPERATING AS DESIGNED?
  - YES → VEHICLE REPAIR COMPLETE
  - NO
- WITH DRB II AGAIN READ FAULT MESSAGES
- PERFORM TEST DR-2

SP-1 – CHECKING SPEED CONTROL SYSTEM FOR FAULT CODES

- START TEST SP-1
- CONNECT THE DRB11 TO THE SC1 DIAGNOSTIC CONNECTOR
- FOR BLANK SCREEN OR OTHER DRB11 ERROR MESSAGES– SEE INTRODUCTION
- USE THE DRB11 TO READ FAULT CODES
  - NO FAULT CODES → GO TO TEST SP-3
  - S/C SERVO SOLENOIDS → GO TO TEST SP-2
  - VEHICLE SPEED SIGNAL → TEST THE SPEED SENSOR AS OUTLINED IN DRIVEABILITY

SP-2 (1 OF 3) – CHECKING FOR FAULT CODE 34

- START TEST SP-2
- PLACE THE KEY IN THE RUN POSITION
- LISTEN FOR THE SERVO TO CLICK AS YOU......
- ....MOVE THE SPEED CONTROL SWITCH FROM OFF TO ON SEVERAL TIMES
- THE SERVO CLICKED?
  - YES → TURN THE KEY OFF → DISCONNECT THE ENGINE CONTROLLER 60-WAY → INSURE SLOT 53 HAS A PROPERLY INSTALLED TN/RD WIRE → CAVITY 53 IS OK?
    - YES → REPAIR THE CONNECTOR AS NECESSARY AND RE-TEST THE SPEED CONTROL
    - NO
  - NO → DISCONNECT THE SERVO 4-WAY → INSPECT IT FOR CORRECT ASSEMBLY → ...TEST THE DB/RD WIRE AT SERVO CONNECTOR FOR VOLTAGE
- THE DB/RD WIRE HAS BATTERY VOLTAGE?
  - YES → REPAIR THE CONNECTOR AS NECESSARY AND RE-TEST THE SPEED CONTROL
  - NO → BACK PROBE THE DB/RD WIRE AT BRAKE SWITCH FOR VOLTAGE
- TEST THE BK WIRE FOR CONTINUITY TO GROUND
- THE BK WIRE HAS UNDER 10 OHMS?
  - YES → REPLACE THE SPEED CONTROL SERVO
  - NO → REPAIR THE OPEN BK GROUND WIRE
- THE DB/RD WIRE HAS BATTERY VOLTAGE?
  - YES → REPAIR THE OPEN DB/RD WIRE BETWEEN BRAKE SWITCH AND SERVO
  - NO
- WITH THE S/C SWITCH AND THE IGNITION SWITCH ON...
- THE SERVO 4-WAY IS OK?
  - YES
  - NO → REPAIR THE CONNECTOR AS NECESSARY AND RE-TEST SPEED CONTROL
- IS BRAKE SWITCH PROPERLY ADJUSTED?
  - YES → ADJUST THE SWITCH AND RE-TEST SPEED CONTROL
  - NO → REPLACE THE BRAKE LAMP SWITCH AND RE-TEST THE SPEED CONTROL
- BACK PROBE THE YL/RD WIRE AT THE BRAKE SWITCH
- THE YL/RD WIRE HAS BATTERY VOLTAGE?
  - YES → REPAIR OPEN YL/RD WIRE TO BRAKE SWITCH
  - NO
- TEST SP-2 CONTINUED

1989 COMPUTERIZED ENGINE CONTROLS
Chrysler Motors 2.5L Turbo I MPFI (Cont.)

1a-119

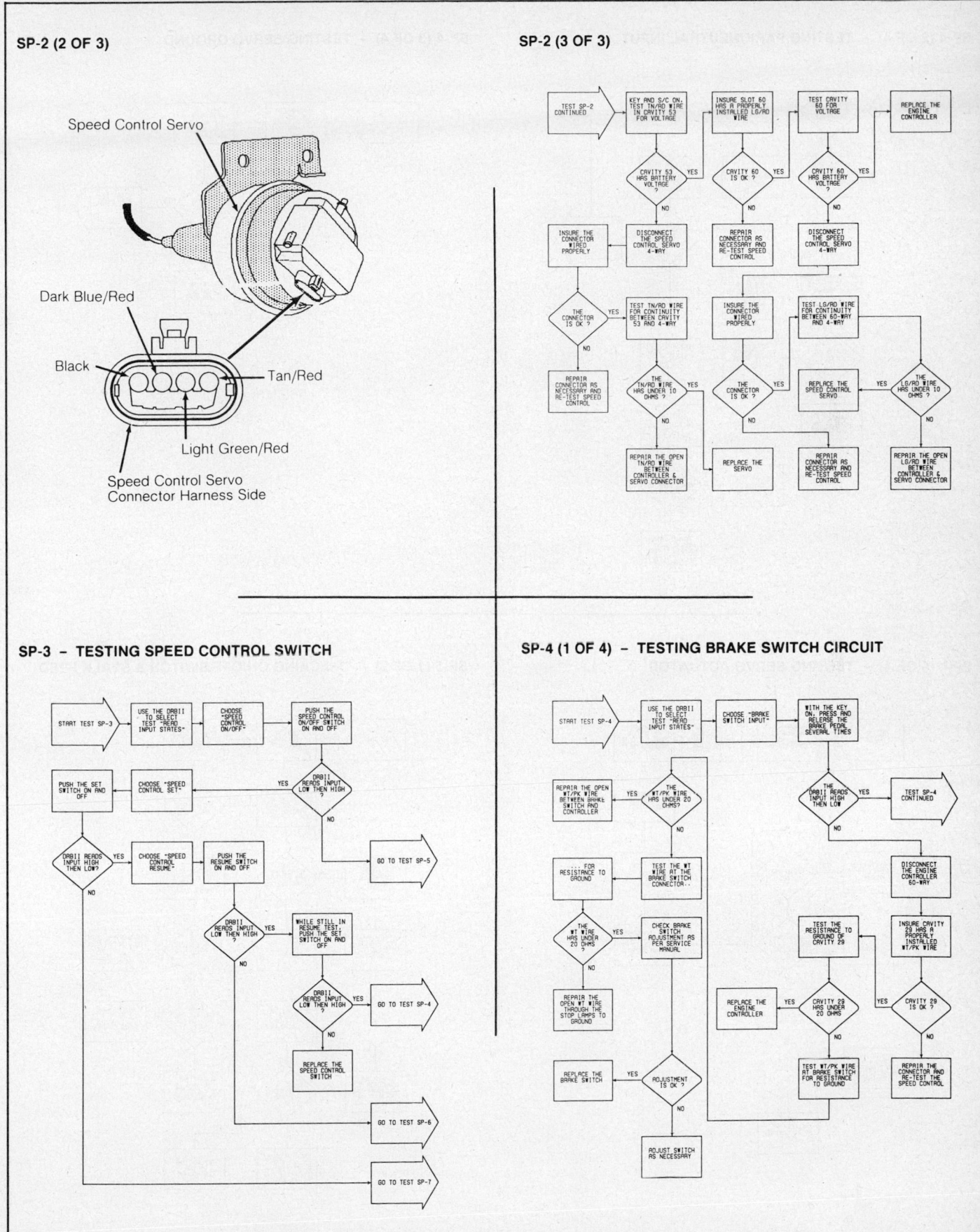

SP-2 (2 OF 3)

Speed Control Servo

Dark Blue/Red

Black

Tan/Red

Light Green/Red

Speed Control Servo
Connector Harness Side

SP-2 (3 OF 3)

SP-3 – TESTING SPEED CONTROL SWITCH

SP-4 (1 OF 4) – TESTING BRAKE SWITCH CIRCUIT

1a-120

1989 COMPUTERIZED ENGINE CONTROLS
Chrysler Motors 2.5L Turbo I MPFI (Cont.)

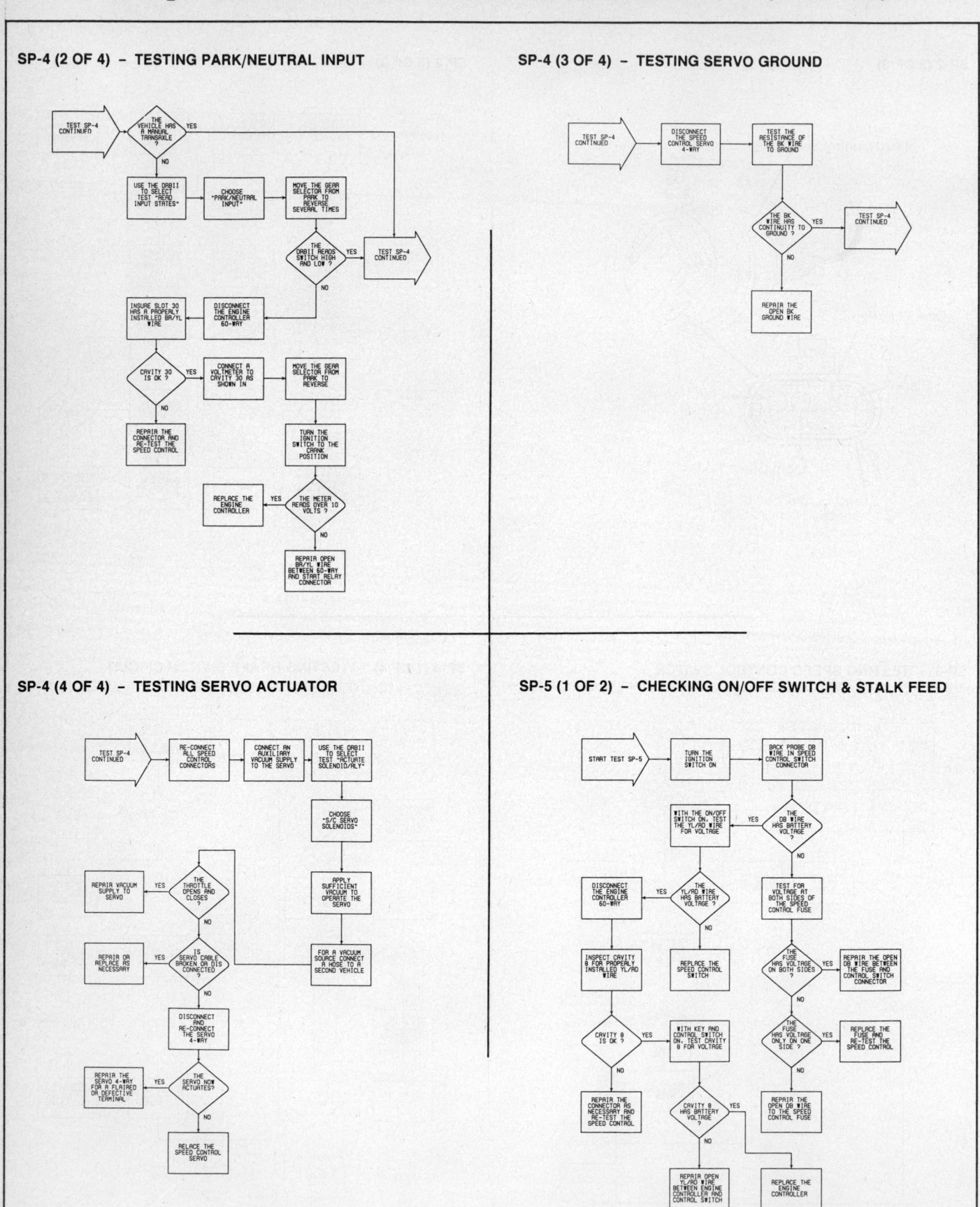

SP-4 (2 OF 4) – TESTING PARK/NEUTRAL INPUT

SP-4 (3 OF 4) – TESTING SERVO GROUND

SP-4 (4 OF 4) – TESTING SERVO ACTUATOR

SP-5 (1 OF 2) – CHECKING ON/OFF SWITCH & STALK FEED

1989 COMPUTERIZED ENGINE CONTROLS
Chrysler Motors 2.5L Turbo I MPFI (Cont.)

1a-121

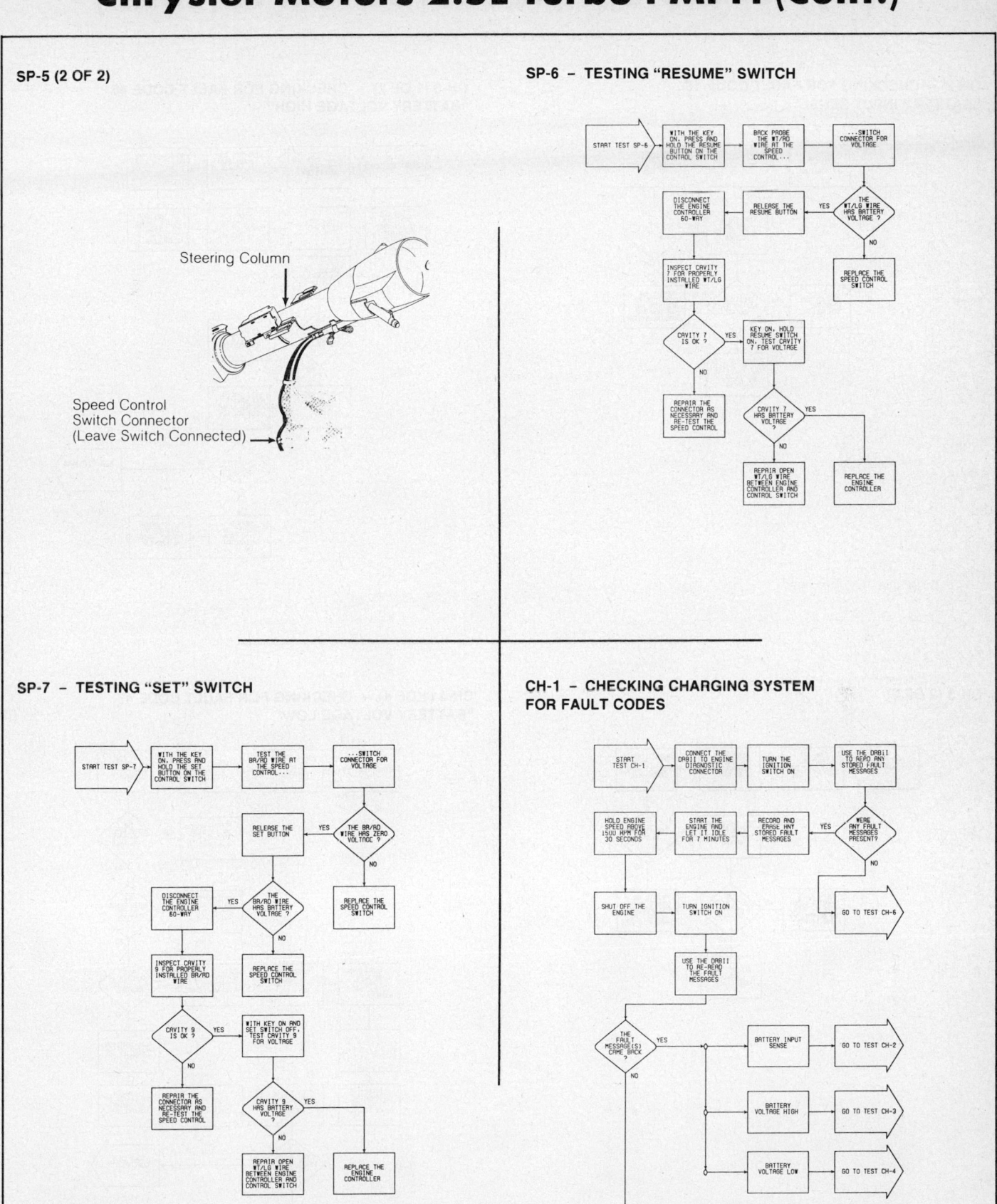

SP-5 (2 OF 2)

Steering Column

Speed Control
Switch Connector
(Leave Switch Connected)

SP-6 – TESTING "RESUME" SWITCH

SP-7 – TESTING "SET" SWITCH

CH-1 – CHECKING CHARGING SYSTEM FOR FAULT CODES

**CH-2 – CHECKING FOR FAULT CODE 16
"BATTERY INPUT SENSE"**

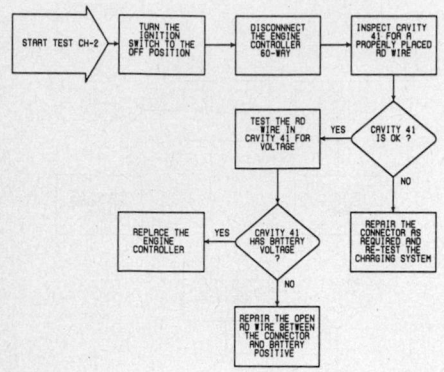

**CH-3 (1 OF 2) – CHECKING FOR FAULT CODE 46
"BATTERY VOLTAGE HIGH"**

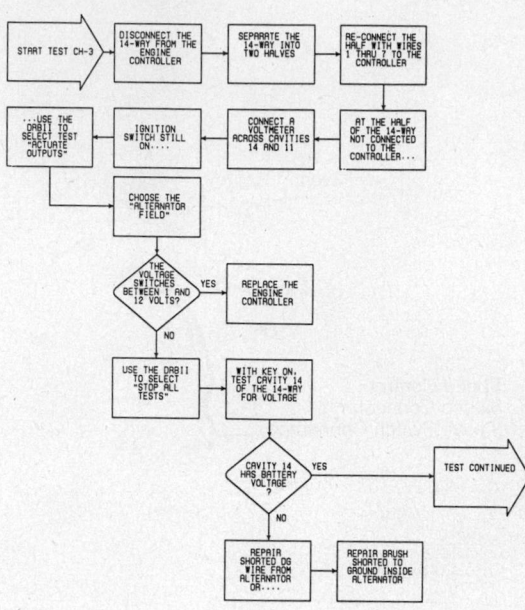

CH-3 (2 OF 2)

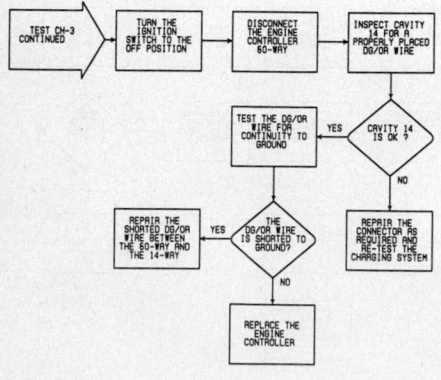

**CH-4 (1 OF 4) – CHECKING FOR FAULT CODE 47
"BATTERY VOLTAGE LOW"**

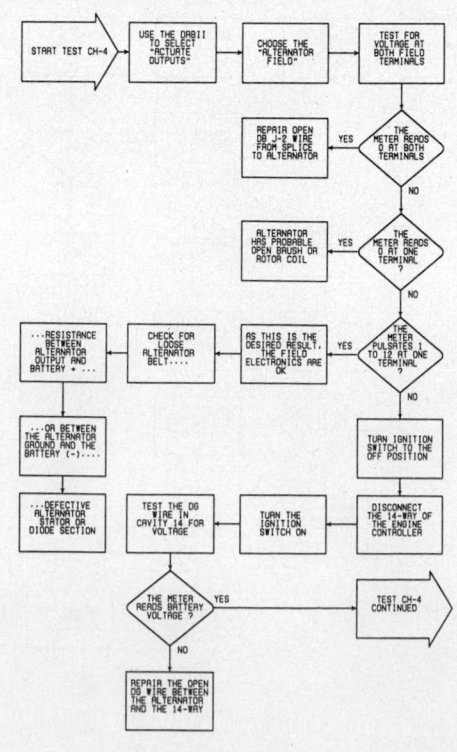

1989 COMPUTERIZED ENGINE CONTROLS
Chrysler Motors 2.5L Turbo I MPFI (Cont.)

1a-123

CH-4 (2 OF 4)

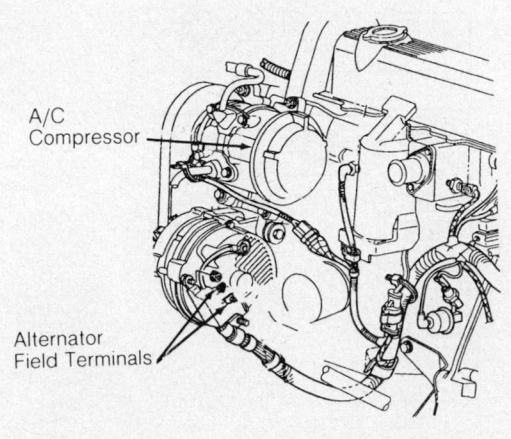

A/C Compressor

Alternator Field Terminals

CH-4 (3 OF 4)

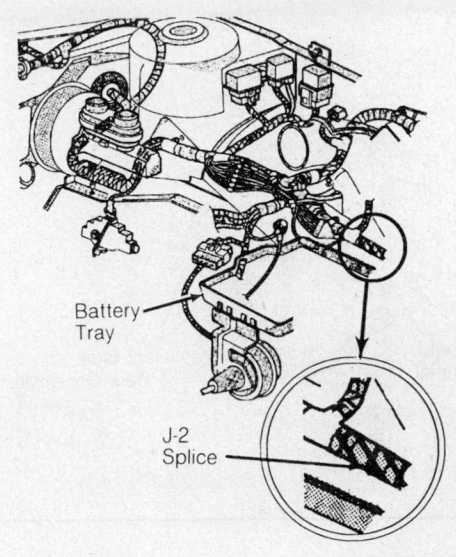

Battery Tray

J-2 Splice

CH-4 (4 OF 4)

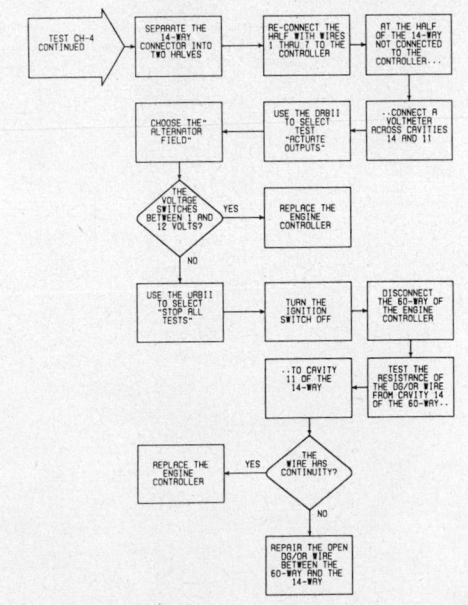

CH-5 (1 OF 2) – CHECKING FOR INTERMITTENT FAULT CODES

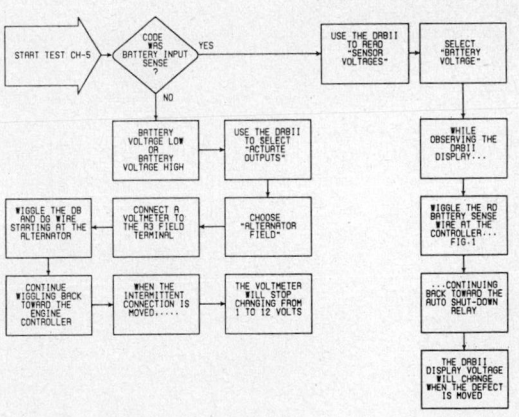

1a-124

1989 COMPUTERIZED ENGINE CONTROLS
Chrysler Motors 2.5L Turbo I MPFI (Cont.)

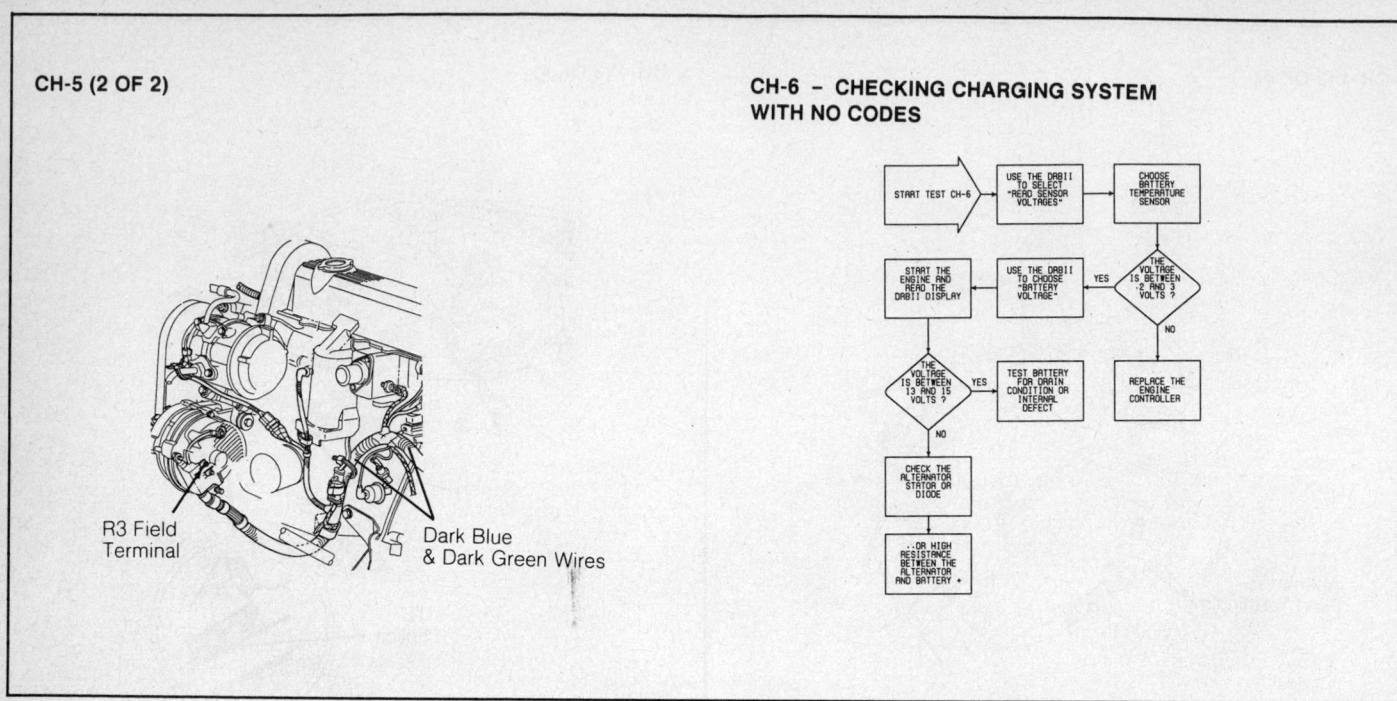

CH-5 (2 OF 2)

R3 Field Terminal

Dark Blue & Dark Green Wires

CH-6 – CHECKING CHARGING SYSTEM WITH NO CODES

1989 Computerized ENGINE CONTROLS
Chrysler Motors 2.5L Turbo I MPFI (Cont.)

1a-125

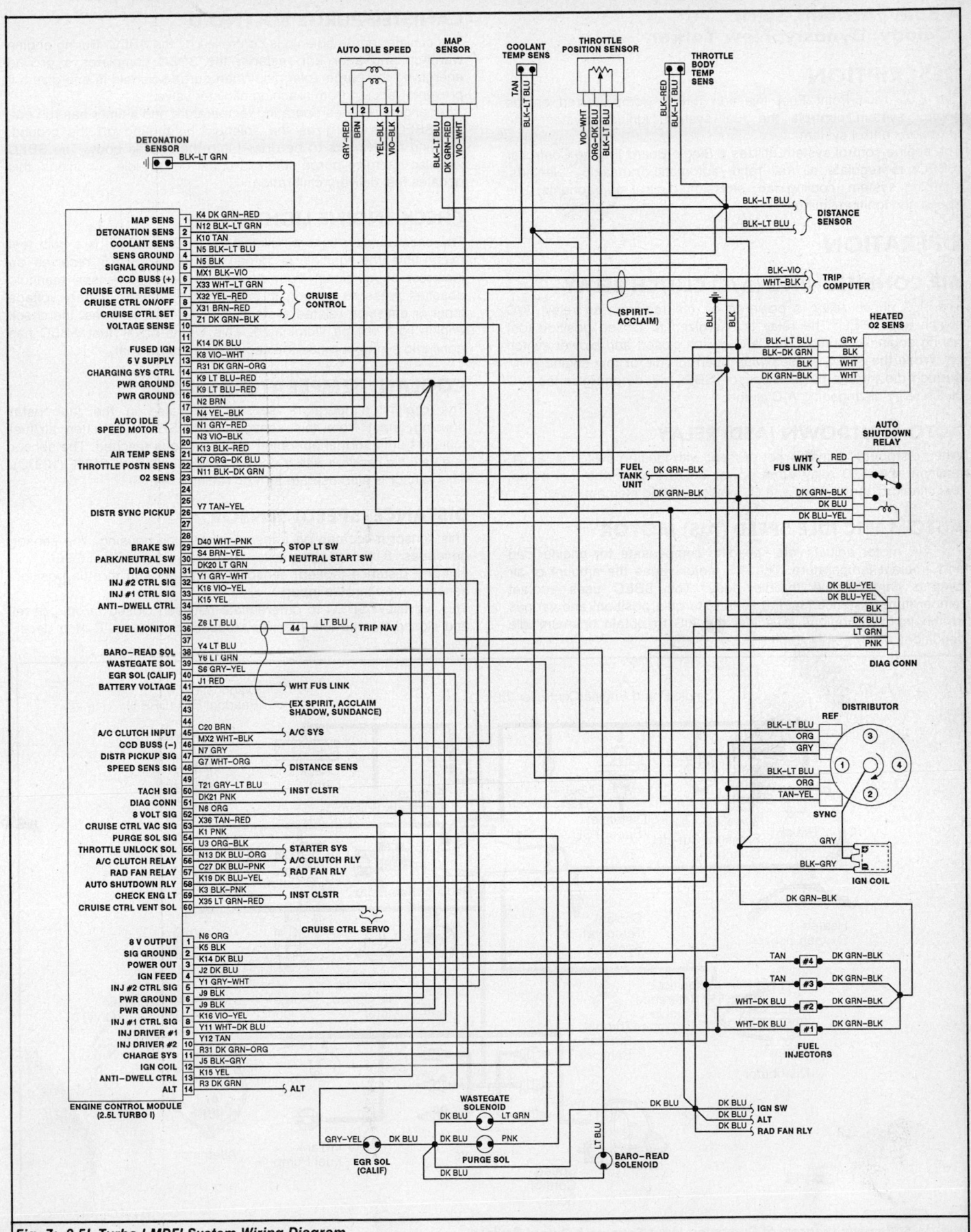

Fig. 7: *2.5L Turbo I MPFI System Wiring Diagram*

1989 COMPUTERIZED ENGINE CONTROLS
Chrysler Motors 3.0L MPFI

A Body: Acclaim, Spirit
C Body: Dynasty, New Yorker

DESCRIPTION

The 3.0L Multi-Point Fuel Injection (MPFI) computerized engine control system controls the fuel system, ignition system and emission control system.

The engine control system utilizes a Single Board Engine Controller (SBEC) to regulate air/fuel ratio, automatic transaxle solenoids, charging system, cooling fan, emission control components, idle speed and ignition timing.

OPERATION

AIR CONDITIONING (A/C) CLUTCH RELAY

The A/C clutch relay is powered by the radiator fan relay, A/C switch and SBEC. The relay is energized to closed position (on) during engine operation with A/C switch closed and blower switch on. When the SBEC senses wide open throttle or low engine RPM through the throttle position sensor, SBEC will de-energize the A/C clutch relay disengaging A/C clutch.

AUTO SHUTDOWN (ASD) RELAY

When distributor signal is not present with ignition switch in "RUN" position, the ASD relay turns power off to the electric fuel pump, fuel injectors, ignition coil and O$_2$ sensor heating element.

AUTOMATIC IDLE SPEED (AIS) MOTOR

The AIS motor adjusts idle speed to compensate for engine load and ambient temperature. The AIS motor varies the amount of air by-pass through the throttle body. The SBEC uses coolant temperature, distance (speed) sensor, throttle position, and various switch input operations to adjust the AIS to obtain optimum idle conditions.

CANISTER PURGE SOLENOID

The canister purge solenid is controlled by the SBEC. During engine warm-up and after hot restarts, the SBEC completes a ground energizing the purge solenoid. When purge solenoid is energized, it prevents vacuum from reaching canister valve.

After engine reaches operating temperature and a timer has run out, the SBEC de-energizes the solenoid by turning off the ground, allowing fuel vapors to be drawn into the throttle body. The SBEC will also energize purge solenoid under certain idle conditions, this updates fuel delivery calibration.

CHECK ENGINE LIGHT

The check engine light will illuminate for 3 seconds as a bulb test every time the ignition is turned on. If the SBEC receives an incorrect or no signal from coolant temperature sensor, manifold absolute pressure sensor, throttle position sensor, battery voltage input or emission related systems on California vehicles, the check engine light will be illuminated. This warns driver that SBEC has gone into a limp-in mode to keep system operational.

COOLANT TEMPERATURE SENSOR

The coolant temperature sensor is located in the thermostat housing. Input from this sensor allows SBEC to richen air/fuel mixtures until normal operating temperature is reached. The sensor is a variable resistor with a range of -40°F (-40°C) to 265°F (129°C). This sensor is also used to turn on radiator fan.

DISTANCE (SPEED) SENSOR

This sensor is located on transaxle extension housing. The sensor generates 8 pulses per axle shaft revolution. The SBEC will interpret distance (speed) sensor input along with throttle position sensor closed throttle input.

This will allow SBEC to differentiate between closed throttle decel and closed throttle idle (vehicle stopped) conditions. During decel,

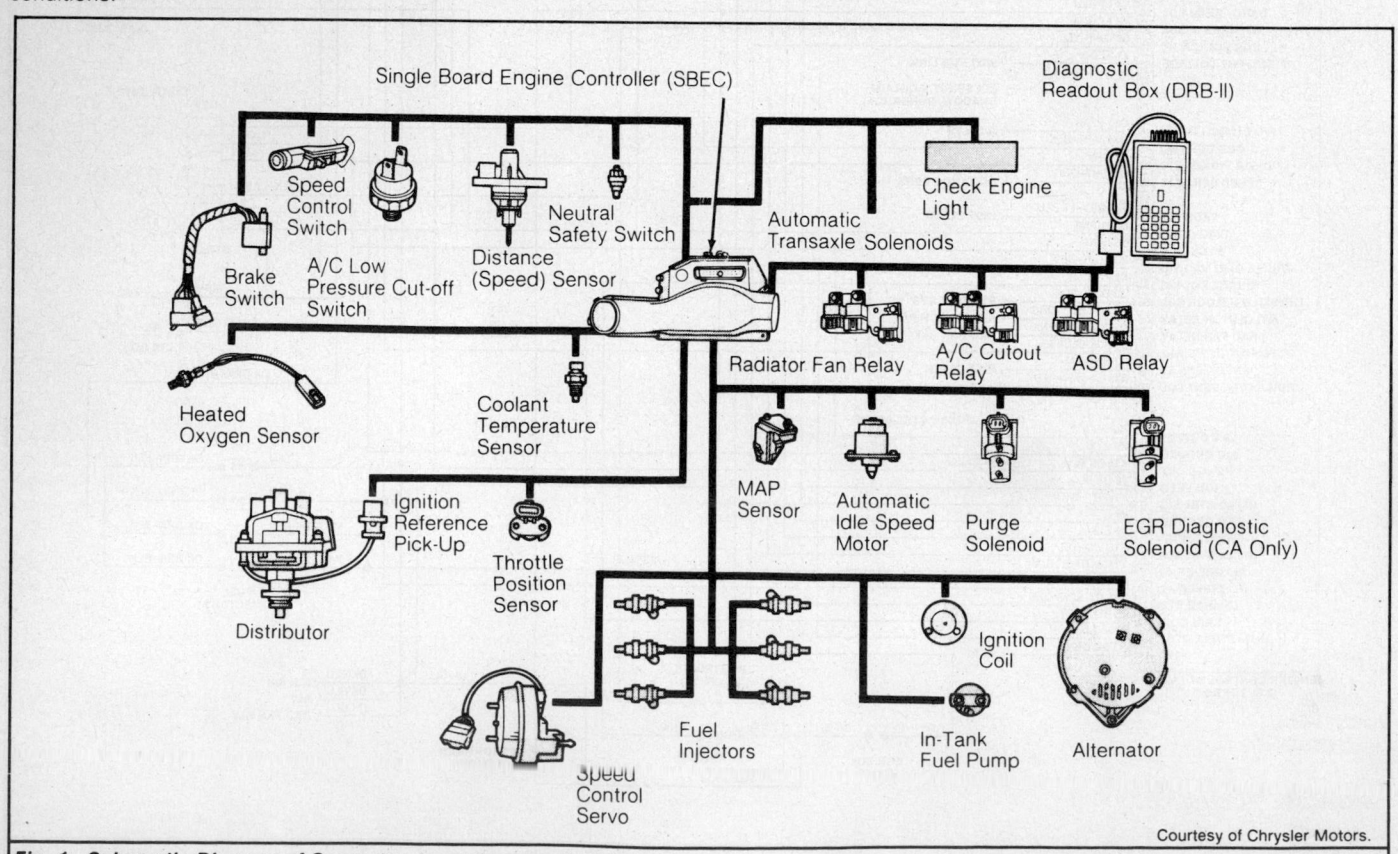

Courtesy of Chrysler Motors.

Fig. 1: _Schematic Diagram of Computer, Input Sensors & Output Devices_

1989 COMPUTERIZED ENGINE CONTROLS
Chrysler Motors 3.0L MPFI (Cont.)

1a-127

the SBEC controls Automatic Idle Speed (AIS) motor to maintain a desired manifold absolute pressure value. During idle (vehicle stopped), the SBEC controls AIS motor to maintain a desired idle speed.

LIMP-IN MODE

If SBEC senses incorrect data or no data from battery voltage sensor, coolant temperature sensor, Manifold Absolute Pressure (MAP) sensor or Throttle Position Sensor (TPS), SBEC will put system in limp-in mode and illuminate check engine light.

MANIFOLD ABSOLUTE PRESSURE (MAP) SENSOR

The MAP sensor is connected to the intake manifold with a vacuum hose. MAP sensor is electrically connected to SBEC. The SBEC uses MAP sensor to monitor manifold pressure and other sensors to calibrate the air/fuel mixture.

OXYGEN SENSOR

The O_2 sensor is used by SBEC to measure oxygen content in the exhaust gases. The sensor is electrically heated for faster switching during engine operation. If O_2 sensor measures a lean mixture, sensor will produce a low voltage. If O_2 sensor measures a rich mixture, sensor will produce a high voltage.

SINGLE BOARD ENGINE CONTROLLER (SBEC)

The SBEC is a digital computer containing a microprocessor. The SBEC receives input from the following sensors: coolant temperature sensor, Manifold Absolute Pressure (MAP) sensor, oxygen sensor, Throttle Position Sensor (TPS), and Vehicle Speed Sensor (VSS).

The SBEC also receives input from the following switches: air conditioning clutch switch, brake switch, speed control switches, and neutral safety switch. During operation, the SBEC monitors many of its own input and output circuits. If a fault is detected, the computer will go into limp-in mode and store a trouble code to help in diagnosis of the system.

THROTTLE POSITION SENSOR (TPS)

The TPS is an electronic variable resistor. The SBEC uses TPS input and input from other sensors to adjust air/fuel ratio for varying driveability conditions.

REMOVAL & INSTALLATION

AIS MOTOR

Removal & Installation – Disconnect negative battery cable. Disconnect 4-pin connector on AIS. Remove 2 screws and AIS motor from throttle body. Ensure "O" ring is removed with AIS motor. To install, reverse removal procedure. Ensure that pintle is in retracted position. Length of pintle must be 1" (25 mm) or less.

ASD RELAY

Removal & Installation – Located on left fenderwell near the SBEC. Disconnect wiring harness from relay. Remove attaching screws and component. To install, reverse removal procedure.

MAP SENSOR

Removal & Installation – Remove vacuum hose and screws from sensor. Remove sensor from alternator bracket. Remove electrical harness. To install, reverse removal procedure.

OXYGEN SENSOR

Removal & Installation – The oxygen sensor is located in exhaust manifold. Use Wrench (C-4907) to remove sensor. Threads in exhaust manifold must be cleaned with a tap prior to installation of sensor. If old sensor is being reinstalled, threads on sensor must be coated with anti-seize compound. Tighten sensor to 20 ft. lbs. (27 N.m).

SINGLE BOARD ENGINE CONTROLLER (SBEC)

Removal & Installation – Remove air cleaner duct from SBEC. Remove battery and 2 module mounting bolts. Remove 60-pin wiring connector from module. Remove module. To install, reverse removal procedure.

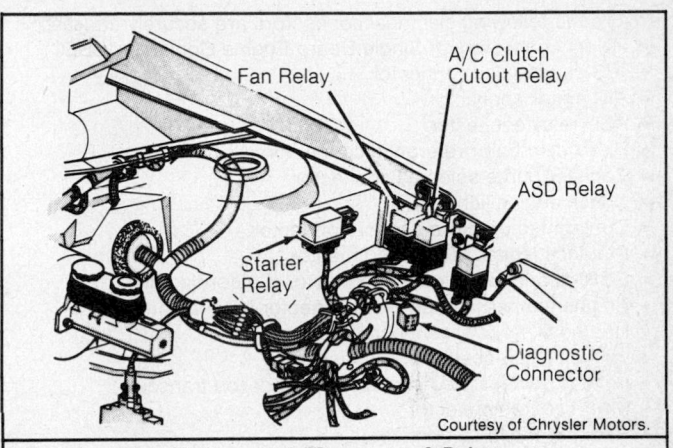

Fan Relay
A/C Clutch Cutout Relay
ASD Relay
Starter Relay
Diagnostic Connector
Courtesy of Chrysler Motors.

Fig. 2: Location Of Diagnostic Connector & Relays

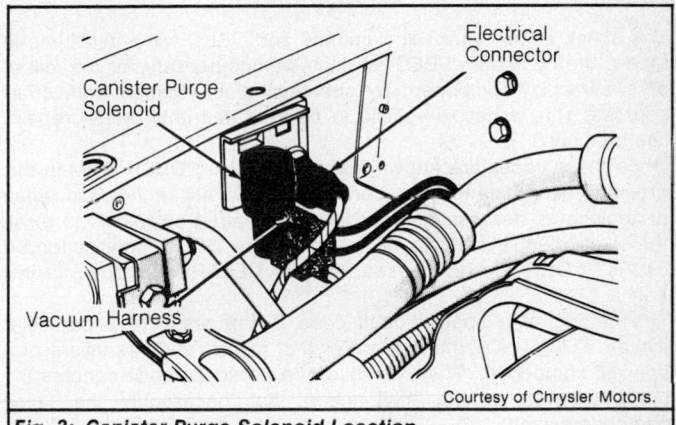

Electrical Connector
Canister Purge Solenoid
Vacuum Harness
Courtesy of Chrysler Motors.

Fig. 3: Canister Purge Solenoid Location

THROTTLE POSITION SENSOR (TPS)

Removal & Installation – Disconnect negative battery cable and remove air cleaner. Disconnect 3-pin connector at throttle position sensor. Remove 2 screws mounting throttle position sensor to throttle body. Lift throttle position sensor from throttle shaft. To install, reverse removal procedure.

TESTING & DIAGNOSIS

PRELIMINARY CHECKS

Most driveability problems in the engine control system result from faulty wiring or leaking hose connections. To avoid unnecessary component testing, a visual check should be performed before beginning trouble shooting procedures to help spot these common faults. A preliminary visual check should include:

- Air ducts to air cleaner and from air cleaner to throttle body.
- Electrical connections at all components. Clean, tight and unbroken.

Check vacuum lines for secure, leak-free connections in these areas:

- Canister purge hose (this hose has a check valve and tee connector in it.)

1a-128

1989 COMPUTERIZED ENGINE CONTROLS
Chrysler Motors 3.0L MPFI (Cont.)

- EGR vacuum line on EGR valve and EGR solenoid. Check hose between backpressure valve and exhaust supply tube on EGR.
- Evaporative control system.
- MAP sensor.
- PCV valve hose and correct PCV valve.
- Power brake, speed control, heater and A/C system vacuum hoses.
- Throttle body.

Ensure the following electrical connectors are securely attached:
- 60-pin connectors at Single Board Engine Controller (SBEC).
- A/C clutch relay connector.
- AIS motor connector.
- ASD relay connector.
- Black distributor reference connector.
- Canister purge solenoid connector.
- Check engine light.
- Coolant temperature sensor connector.
- Distance (speed) sensor connector.
- EGR diagnostic solenoid connector (California only).
- Engine temperature sensor connector (1-wire connector).
- Heated O$_2$ sensor connector.
- Ignition reference pick-up connector.
- Input (turbine) speed sensor connector (on transaxle).
- MAP sensor connector.
- Radiator fan relay connector.
- TPS connector.
- Transmission solenoids connector.

The check engine light will illuminate and SBEC will enter "Limp-In Mode". In this mode, SBEC attempts to compensate for the failure of a particular component by substituting information from other sources. This will allow vehicle to be operated until proper repairs can be made.

Once these codes are known, refer to FAULT CODES listed in this article to determine the questionable circuit. Test circuits and repair or replace as necessary. If problem is repaired or ceases to exist, the logic module cancels fault codes after 50-100 ignition on/off cycles. If DRB-II is being used, refer to CLEARING CODES in this article.

The setting of a specific fault code is the result of a particular system failure, NOT the reason for that failure, such as failure of a specific component. The existence of a particular code denotes the probable area of the malfunction, not necessarily the failed component itself.

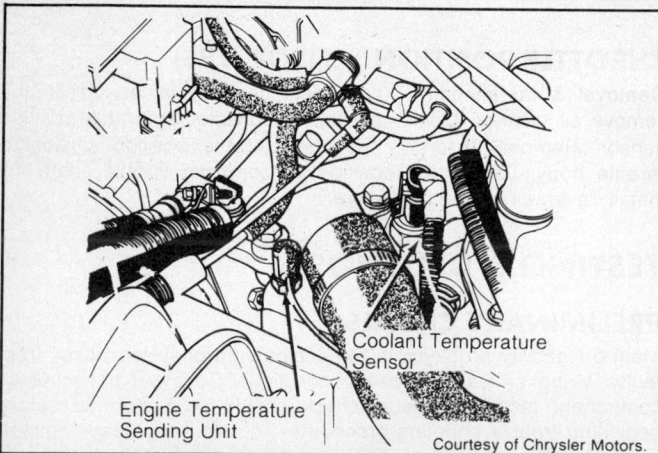

Fig. 4: Location of Temperature Sensors

SYSTEM DIAGNOSIS

The self-diagnostic capabilities of this system, if properly utilized, can greatly simplify testing. The SBEC has been programmed to monitor several different circuits of the engine control system. If a problem is sensed with a monitored circuit, a fault code is stored in the SBEC.

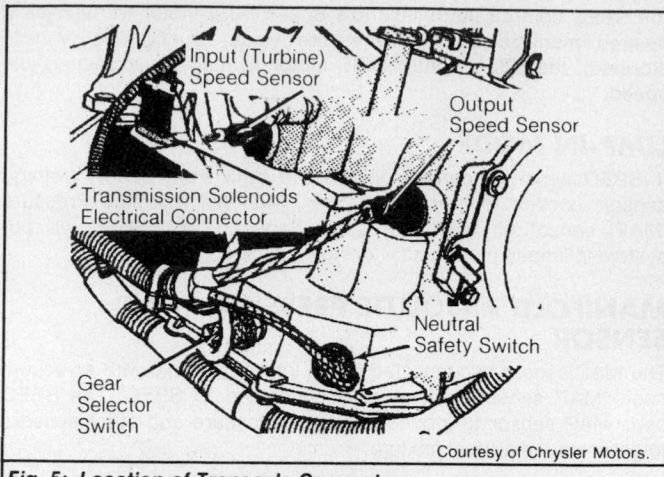

Fig. 5: Location of Transaxle Connectors

DIAGNOSTIC PROCEDURE

Refer to ENTERING ON-BOARD DIAGNOSTICS to retrieve fault codes. When using check engine light to retrieve fault codes, refer to description of DRB-II display under FAULT CODES for an explanation of fault code. Once description of fault code is obtained, refer to appropriate trouble shooting chart to diagnose problem. Use trouble shooting chart titles to find appropriate chart.

If no fault codes are present, but vehicle still displays one of the following conditions, go to appropriate test.
- No start condition. Go to NS-1.
- Cold driveability problem. Go to DR-1.
- Warm driveability problem. Go to DR-1.
- Check engine light is illuminated. Go to DR-1.
- Charging system problem. Go to CH-1.
- Speed control system problem. Go to SP-1.

NOTE: When using trouble shooting charts for diagnosis, DO NOT skip any steps in chart as incorrect diagnosis will result.

Before proceeding with diagnosis, the following precautions must be followed:
- Vehicle must have a fully charged battery.
- When performing a cold driveability test, engine must not have been started for at least 7 hours.
- When performing a warm driveability test, engine must be at normal operating temperature.
- When probing SBEC connector, probe connector from pin side DO NOT backprobe connector.
- When performing electrical tests, be careful to not cause any short circuits. This will set more fault codes, making diagnosis of original problem more difficult.
- DO NOT use a test light in place of a voltmeter.
- When checking for spark, ensure coil wire is no more than 1/4" from ground. If wire is farther away from ground, damage to SBEC may result.
- DO NOT prolong testing of fuel injectors as engine may hydrostatically lock.
- Always repair lowest fault number (check engine light) or first fault displayed (DRB-II), first.
- Always perform indicated verification test after repairs are made.

ENTERING ON-BOARD DIAGNOSTICS

Check Engine Light Diagnostic Mode – 1) Start engine (if possible). Move transmission shift lever through all positions, ending in Park. Turn A/C switch on, then off (if equipped).
2) Turn engine off. Without starting engine again, turn ignition on, off, on, off and on. Record 2-digit fault codes as displayed by flashing check engine light.

1989 COMPUTERIZED ENGINE CONTROLS
Chrysler Motors 3.0L MPFI (Cont.)

1a-129

3) For example, Code 23 is displayed as flash, flash, 4 second pause, flash, flash, flash. After a slightly longer pause, any other codes stored are displayed in numerical order.

4) Once check engine light begins to flash fault codes, it cannot be stopped. If you loose count, it will be necessary to start over. Code 55 indicates end of fault code display. Refer to FAULT CODES in this article.

DRB-II Diagnostic Mode – 1) Attach DRB-II Tester (C-4805) to self-test connector. Connector is located in engine compartment near left shock tower.

2) Start engine (if possible). Move transmission shift lever through all positions, ending in Park. Turn A/C switch on, then off (if equipped).

3) Turn engine off. Without starting engine again, turn ignition on. Enter vehicle model year and engine size. Read fault data on DRB-II. Refer to FAULT CODES in this article.

DRB-II Switch Test Mode – The SBEC can only recognize high and low states on switch circuits. SBEC cannot tell the difference between an open or short circuit or a defective switch.

The DRB-II display must change between "00" and "88" and flashing check engine light when brake switch, gear shift selector and A/C switch (if equipped) are activated and released.

DRB-II Read Input States – This state on DRB-II allows technician to read input states of Z1 voltage sense, park/neutral switch, brake switch, A/C switch, speed control resume, on/off and set switches. DRB-II will display "INPUT LOW" or "INPUT HIGH" as SBEC senses component status changing.

DRB-II Read Output States – This state on DRB-II allows technician to read output states of speed control vacuum solenoid, purge solenoid, A/C clutch relay, radiator fan relay, ASD relay, check engine light, speed control vent solenoid and EGR solenoid. DRB-II will display "ENERGIZED" OR "DE-ENERGIZED" as SBEC senses component status changing.

DRB-II Actuate Solenoids & Relays – This state on DRB-II allows SBEC to actuate radiator fan relay, A/C clutch relay, ASD relay, purge solenoid, speed control servo solenoids and EGR solenoid. With tester in this state, SBEC can also actuate all solenoids and relays simultaneously. This test allows technician to visually and physically observe components under operation.

DRB-II Actuate Outputs – This state on DRB-II allows SBEC to actuate ignition coil, fuel injectors (#1), fuel injectors (#2), fuel injectors (#3), AIS motor open and close, alternator field, tachometer output (tach should read 1364 RPM) and fuel monitor signal. During this test DRB-II will read "ACTUATING".

DRB-II Read Sensor Voltages – This state on DRB-II allows technician to read battery temperature sensor, oxygen sensor, coolant temperature sensor, TPS sensor, minimum throttle in volts, knock sensor, battery voltage and MAP sensor.

DRB-II Read Sensor Values – This state on DRB-II allows technician to read coolant temperature in degrees fahrenheit or centigrade, manifold pressure in inches of vacuum or kilopascals, AIS motor in steps, adaptive fuel factor in percent, barometric pressure in inches of mercury or or kilopascals, engine speed in RPM, SBEC spark advance in degrees, vehicle speed given in MPH and oxygen sensor state given as center, rich or lean.

DRB-II Set Engine RPM – This state on DRB-II allows technician to set engine RPM at a fixed speed from 900-2000 in 100 RPM increments. This allows for accuracy of AIS motor control to be checked.

DRB-II Minimum Airflow Speed – This state on DRB-II allows technician to completely close AIS motor to check minimum idle speed.

DRB-II Emissions EMR Tests – This state on DRB-II allows technician to reset emission reminder light and mileage. This is only used on trucks.

DRB-II Read Module Information – This state on DRB-II allows technician to read SBEC part number and application.

DRB-II PROBLEMS & ERROR MESSAGES

Blank Message Screen – 1) Connect DRB-II to a different vehicle. If message screen is still blank, DRB-II or cable adapter are faulty. Substitute to find faulty component. If message screen is not blank, DRB-II and cable adapter are functioning properly.

2) Inspect diagnostic connector for proper wire placement, damaged terminals or pushed out pins. Repair as necessary. If connector is okay, using an ohmmeter, check Black/White ground wire of diagnostic connector for continuity to ground. Repair as necessary.

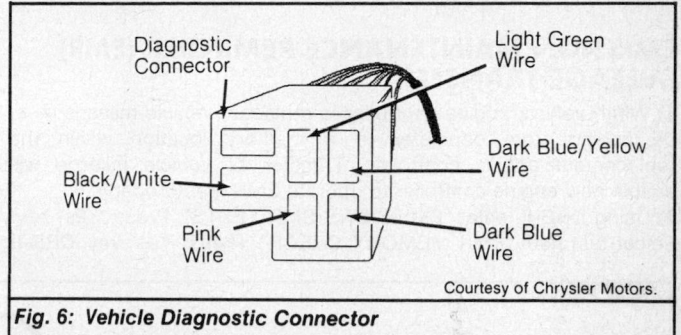

Fig. 6: Vehicle Diagnostic Connector

Courtesy of Chrysler Motors.

"NO RESPONSE" Message – 1) Ensure ignition is turned on. Disconnect SBEC 60-pin connector. Using an ohmmeter, check Pink wire of diagnostic connector for continuity to SBEC 60-pin connector cavity No. 25.

2) Check Light Green wire of diagnostic connector for continuity to SBEC 60-pin connector cavity No. 45. If continuity is not present, repair circuit as necessary. If continuity is present, replace SBEC. Attempt retest.

"RAM TEST FAILURE" Message – Replace DRB-II.

"CARTRIDGE ERROR" Message – Replace DRB-II cartridge.

"KEY PAD TEST FAILURE" Message – Power up DRB-II again with fingers off the keypad. If error message returns, replace DRB-II.

"HIGH OR LOW BATTERY" Message – Correct condition of vehicle battery and reconnect DRB-II.

CLEARING CODES

Using DRB-II, select test "ERASE FAULT DATA". Press "YES" key on DRB-II. DRB-II will display "ARE YOU SURE? YES/NO". Press "YES" key on tester. Tester will display "ERASING FAULT DATA X". When DRB-II is finished erasing fault codes, it will display "FAULT DATA ERASED".

If DRB-II is not available, fault codes may be cleared by allowing 50-100 key on/off cycles to occur. This will allow SBEC to clear fault codes.

VEHICLE SECURITY SYSTEM DIAGNOSIS

1) Cycle ignition switch to "ACCESSORY" position 3 times, leaving ignition in "ACCESSORY" position. Security system is now in diagnostic mode. Park and tail lights will begin flashing verifying their operation. The horn will sound twice verifying that trunk key cylinder is in proper position.

2) Return ignition switch to "OFF" position. Turning ignition off will stop lights from flashing, but keep security system in diagnostic mode. With security system in diagnostic mode, vehicle horn will sound when switches are activated verifying proper operation of switches.

3) Begin diagnosis with all doors, hood and trunk closed. Open and close each door with a one second delay between opening and closing. Vehicle horn will sound when door switch opens and when door switch closes.

4) Open and close hood. Vehicle horn will sound when hood switch opens and when switch closes. Activate power door locks. Vehicle horn will sound when door locks are activated in "LOCK" position and again when door locks are activated to "UNLOCK" position.

5) Using door key, lock and unlock vehicle doors with a one second delay between locking and unlocking. Vehicle horn will sound when switch is locked and when switch is unlocked.

6) Cycle ignition switch to "RUN" position. Vehicle horn will sound once, indicating ignition input is operating properly. Cycling ignition switch to "RUN" position will also take security system out of diagnostic mode.

7) If horn does not sound during testing, this indicates no input from switch, faulty wiring, or defective security system module. If SBEC has been replaced recently, vehicle security system will not function until 20 engine cranks have occured.

EMISSION MAINTENANCE REMINDER (EMR) MILEAGE TRANSFER

1) When vehicle engine controller is replaced, vehicle mileage must be copied from odometer to a memory location within the replacement engine controller. Transfer of vehicle mileage will enable new engine controller to operate EMR light properly.

2) Using DRB-II, enter "EMISSIONS EMR TESTS". Press "Yes" key. Select test item "EMR MEMORY CHECK". Press "Yes" key. DRB-II display will read "EMR MEMORY CHECK ARE YOU SURE ? Yes,No". Press "Yes" key.

3) DRB-II will display "IS INSTRUMENT PANEL MILEAGE BETWEEN 9953 AND 10051 ?". If vehicle mileage is within specification, EMR memory check is complete. Press "Yes" key. If vehicle mileage is not within specification, go to next step.

4) Press "No" key. DRB-II will display "DO YOU WANT TO CORRECT EMR MILEAGE ?". Press "Yes" key. DRB-II will display "ENTER MILEAGE SHOWN ON INSTRUMENT PANEL USE ENTER KEY TO END".

5) Enter vehicle mileage. DO NOT enter tenths. When correct vehicle mileage is entered, press "Enter" key. DRB-II will ask for verification of mileage entry. If mileage entry was accurate, press "Enter" key. DRB-II will display "EMR MEMORY CHECK TEST COMPLETE". Vehicle must travel at least 8 miles for reset to occur.

NOTE: The following trouble shooting charts and illustrations are courtesy of Chrysler Motors.

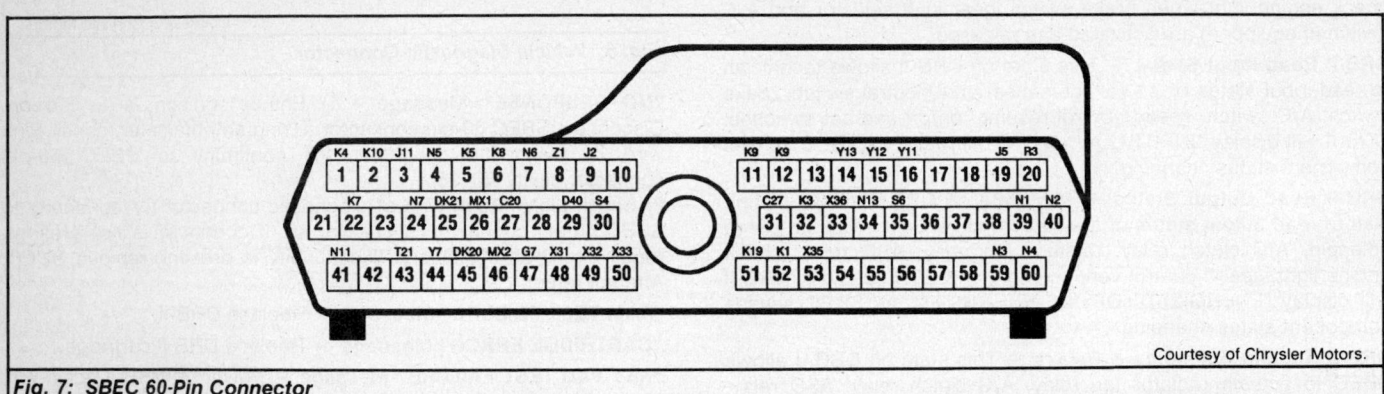

Courtesy of Chrysler Motors.

Fig. 7: SBEC 60-Pin Connector

FAULT CODES

CODE	DISPLAY ON DRB-II	FAULT CONDITION
11	IGN REFERENCE SIGNAL	No distributor reference signal picked up during cranking.
12	Number of key-ons since last fault or since faults were erased.	Direct battery input to SBEC was disconnected within last 50-100 ignition key-ons.
13	MAP PNEUMATIC SIGNAL OR MAP PNEUMATIC CHANGE	No difference in MAP sensor signal is detected. No difference is detected between MAP reading and stored barometric pressure reading.
14	MAP VOLTAGE TOO LOW OR MAP VOLTAGE TOO HIGH	MAP sensor input less than minimum acceptable voltage. MAP sensor input more than maximum acceptable voltage.
15	VEHICLE SPEED SIGNAL	No distance sensor signal detected with road load conditions.
16	BATTERY INPUT SENSE	Battery voltage sense input not detected with engine running.
17	LOW ENGINE TEMP	Coolant temperature stays below normal operating temperature during vehicle operation.
21	OXYGEN SENSOR SIGNAL	No rich or lean signal is detected from O_2 sensor input.
22	COOLANT VOLTAGE LOW OR COOLANT VOLTAGE HIGH	Coolant temp. sensor input below minimum acceptable voltage. Coolant temp. sensor input above maximum acceptable voltage.

1989 COMPUTERIZED ENGINE CONTROLS
Chrysler Motors 3.0L MPFI (Cont.)

1a-131

FAULT CODES (Cont.)

CODE	DISPLAY ON DRB-II	FAULT CONDITION
24	TPS VOLTAGE LOW OR TPS VOLTAGE HIGH	TPS sensor output less than minimum acceptable voltage. TPS sensor output more than maximum acceptable voltage.
25	AIS MOTOR CIRCUITS	Shorted condition detected in one or more AIS control circuits.
26	INJ 1 PEAK CURRENT OR INJ 2 PEAK CURRENT OR INJ 3 PEAK CURRENT	High resistance detected in INJ 1 injector bank circuit. High resistance detected in INJ 2 injector bank circuit. High resistance detected in INJ 3 injector bank circuit.
27	INJ 1 CONTROL CIRCUIT OR INJ 2 CONTROL CIRCUIT OR INJ 3 CONTROL CIRCUIT	INJ 1 injector bank output driver stage does not respond correctly to SBEC control signal. INJ 2 injector bank output driver stage does not respond correctly to SBEC control signal. INJ 3 injector bank output driver stage does not respond correctly to SBEC control signal.
31	PURGE SOLENOID CKT	Open or shorted condition is detected in purge solenoid circuit.
32	EGR SOLENOID CIRCUIT OR EGR SYSTEM FAILURE	Open or short is detected in EGR solenoid circuit (CA only). SBEC did not detect required air/fuel change during diagnostic test (CA only).
33	A/C CLUTCH RELAY CKT	Open or shorted condition detected in A/C clutch relay circuit.
34	S/C SERVO SOLENOIDS	Open or shorted condition detected in speed control vacuum or vent solenoid circuits.
35	RADIATOR FAN RELAY	Open or shorted condition detected in radiator fan relay circuit.
41	CHARGING SYSTEM CKT	Output driver stage does not respond correctly to voltage regulator control signal.
42	ASD RELAY CIRCUIT OR Z1 VOLTAGE SENSE	Open or shorted condition detected in ASD relay circuit. No battery voltage sensed when ASD relay is energized.
43	IGNITION CONTROL CIRCUIT	Output driver stage for ignition coil does not respond properly to dwell control signal.
46	BATTERY VOLTAGE HIGH	Battery voltage sense input more than target charging voltage during engine operation.
47	BATTERY VOLTAGE LOW	Battery voltage sense input less than target charging voltage during engine operation.
51	LEAN F/A CONDITION	Oxygen sensor input indicates lean air/fuel ratio during engine operation.
52	RICH F/A CONDITON	Oxygen sensor input indicates rich air/fuel ratio during engine operation.
53	INTERNAL SELF-TEST	SBEC detects internal failure.
54	SYNC PICK-UP SIGNAL	No high data rate detected during engine rotation.
55		Completion of fault code display by check engine light.
62	EMR MILEAGE ACCUM	Attempt is unsuccessful to update EMR mileage in SBEC EEPROM (trucks only).
63	EEPROM WRITE DENIED	Attempt is unsuccessful to write to an EEPROM location by SBEC.
N/A	FAULT CODE ERROR	DRB-II does not recognize fault identification.

1a-132

1989 COMPUTERIZED ENGINE CONTROLS
Chrysler Motors 3.0L MPFI (Cont.)

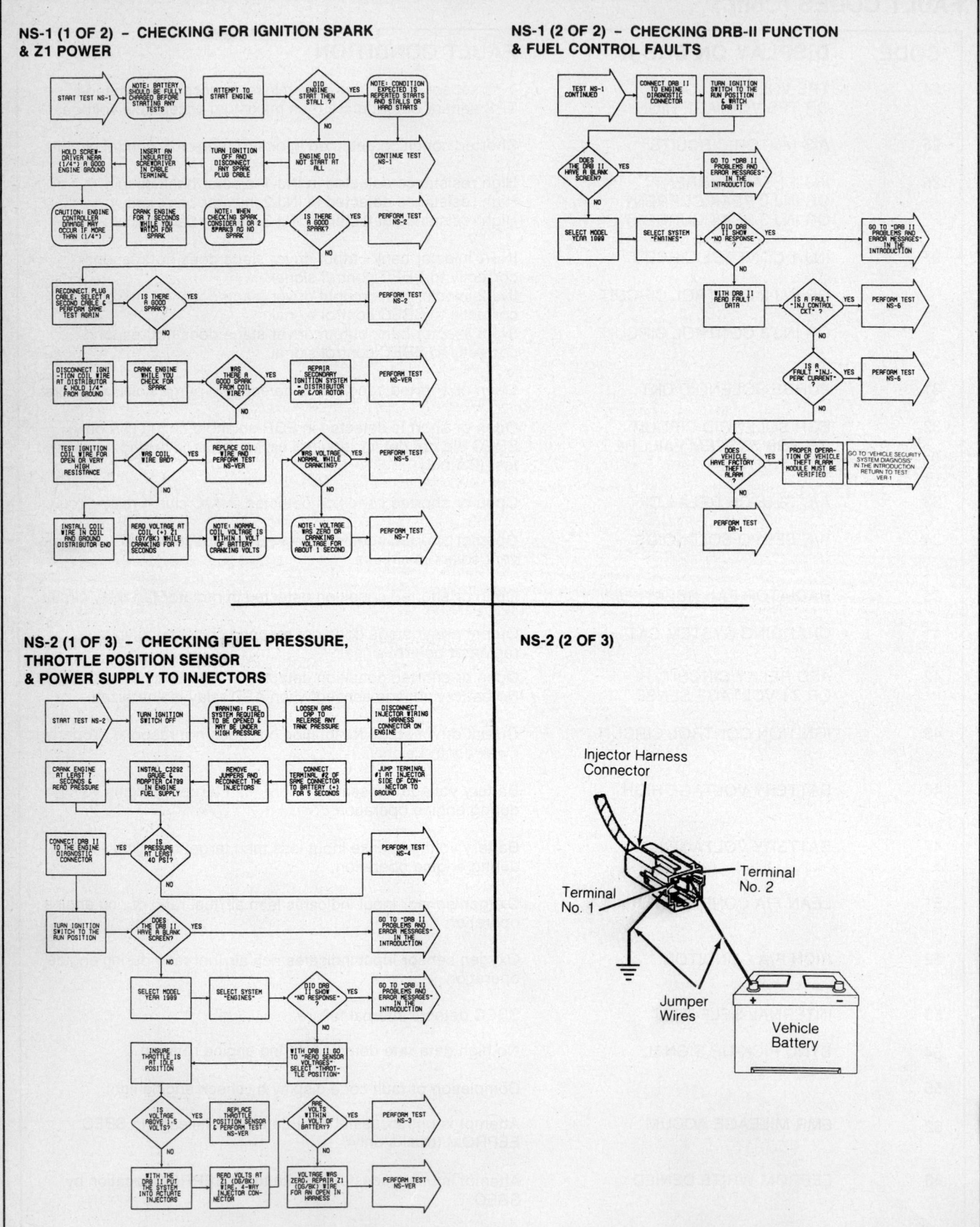

NS-1 (1 OF 2) – CHECKING FOR IGNITION SPARK & Z1 POWER

NS-1 (2 OF 2) – CHECKING DRB-II FUNCTION & FUEL CONTROL FAULTS

NS-2 (1 OF 3) – CHECKING FUEL PRESSURE, THROTTLE POSITION SENSOR & POWER SUPPLY TO INJECTORS

NS-2 (2 OF 3)

Injector Harness Connector

Terminal No. 2

Terminal No. 1

Jumper Wires

Vehicle Battery

1989 COMPUTERIZED ENGINE CONTROLS
Chrysler Motors 3.0L MPFI (Cont.)

1a-133

NS-2 (3 OF 3)

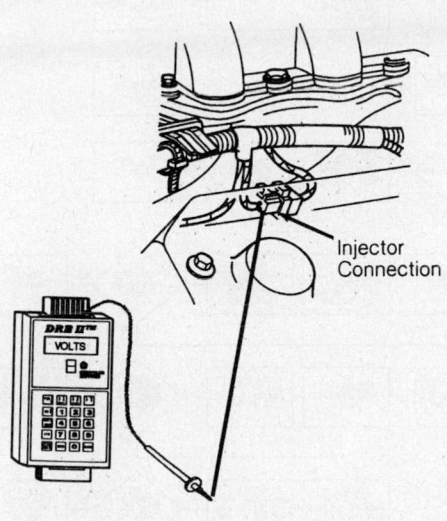

Injector Connection

NS-3 – CHECKING FOR WET PLUGS, VALVE & IGNITION TIMING

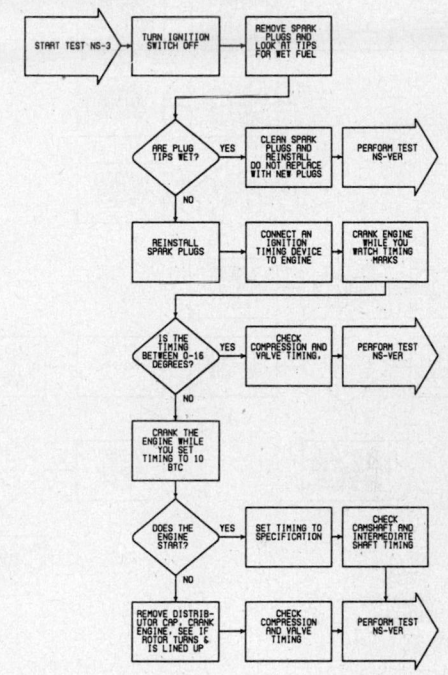

START TEST NS-3 → TURN IGNITION SWITCH OFF → REMOVE SPARK PLUGS AND LOOK AT TIPS FOR WET FUEL

ARE PLUG TIPS WET? — YES → CLEAN SPARK PLUGS AND REINSTALL. DO NOT REPLACE WITH NEW PLUGS → PERFORM TEST NS-VER

NO ↓

REINSTALL SPARK PLUGS → CONNECT AN IGNITION TIMING DEVICE TO ENGINE → CRANK ENGINE WHILE YOU WATCH TIMING MARKS

IS THE TIMING BETWEEN 0-16 DEGREES? — YES → CHECK COMPRESSION AND VALVE TIMING. → PERFORM TEST NS-VER

NO ↓

CRANK THE ENGINE WHILE YOU SET TIMING TO 10 BTC

DOES THE ENGINE START? — YES → SET TIMING TO SPECIFICATION → CHECK CAMSHAFT AND INTERMEDIATE SHAFT TIMING

NO ↓

REMOVE DISTRIBUTOR CAP. CRANK ENGINE. SEE IF ROTOR TURNS & IS LINED UP → CHECK COMPRESSION AND VALVE TIMING → PERFORM TEST NS-VER

NS-4 (1 OF 3) – CHECKING DRB-II, Z1 POWER & FUEL FILTERS

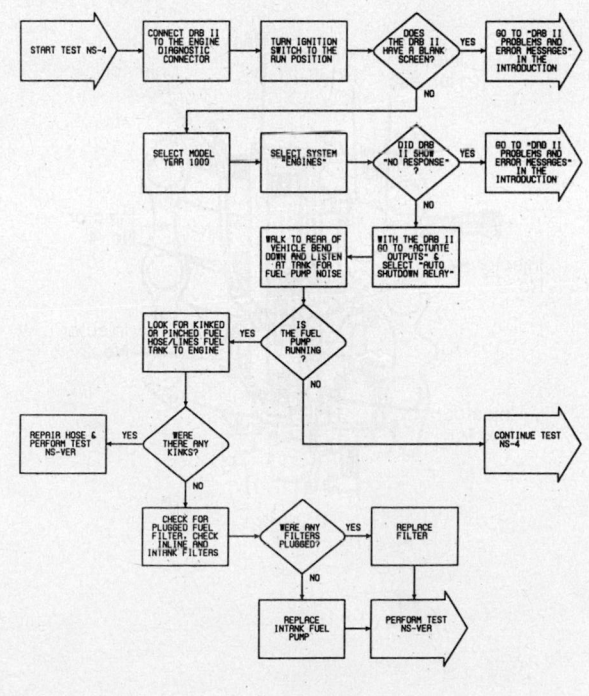

START TEST NS-4 → CONNECT DRB II TO THE ENGINE DIAGNOSTIC CONNECTOR → TURN IGNITION SWITCH TO THE RUN POSITION → DOES THE DRB II HAVE A BLANK SCREEN? — YES → GO TO "DRB II PROBLEMS AND ERROR MESSAGES" IN THE INTRODUCTION

NO ↓

SELECT MODEL YEAR 1989 → SELECT SYSTEM "ENGINES" → DID DRB II SHOW "NO RESPONSE"? — YES → GO TO "DRB II PROBLEMS AND ERROR MESSAGES" IN THE INTRODUCTION

NO ↓

WITH THE DRB II GO TO "ACTUATE OUTPUTS" & SELECT "AUTO SHUTDOWN RELAY" → WALK TO REAR OF VEHICLE BEND DOWN AND LISTEN AT TANK FOR FUEL PUMP NOISE

IS THE FUEL PUMP RUNNING? — YES → LOOK FOR KINKED OR PINCHED FUEL HOSE/LINES FUEL TANK TO ENGINE

NO ↓

WERE THERE ANY KINKS? — YES → REPAIR HOSE & PERFORM TEST NS-VER

NO ↓ ; → CONTINUE TEST NS-4

CHECK FOR PLUGGED FUEL FILTER. CHECK INLINE AND INTANK FILTERS → WERE ANY FILTERS PLUGGED? — YES → REPLACE FILTER

NO ↓

REPLACE INTANK FUEL PUMP → PERFORM TEST NS-VER

NS-4 (2 OF 3)

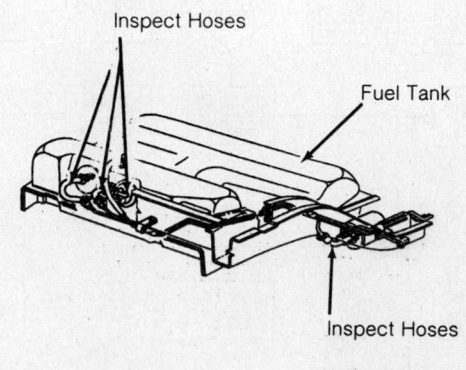

Inspect Hoses

Fuel Tank

Inspect Hoses

NS-4 (3 OF 3) – CHECKING FUEL PUMP CIRCUITS

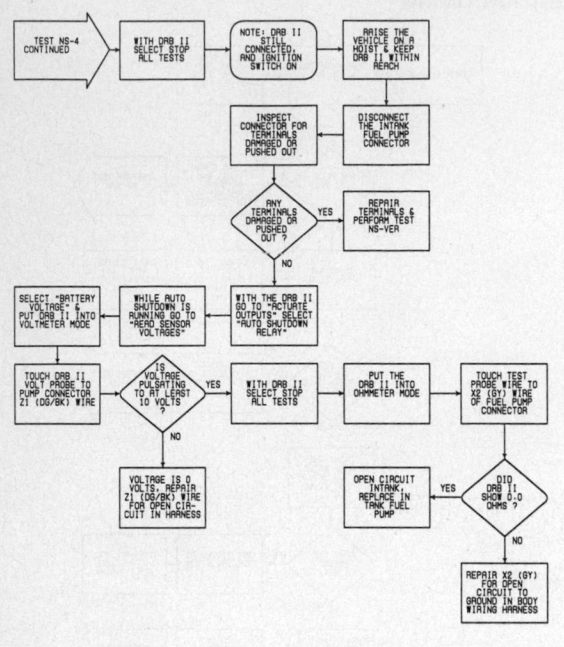

NS-5 – CHECKING FOR DEFECTIVE COIL OR CONTROL CIRCUITRY

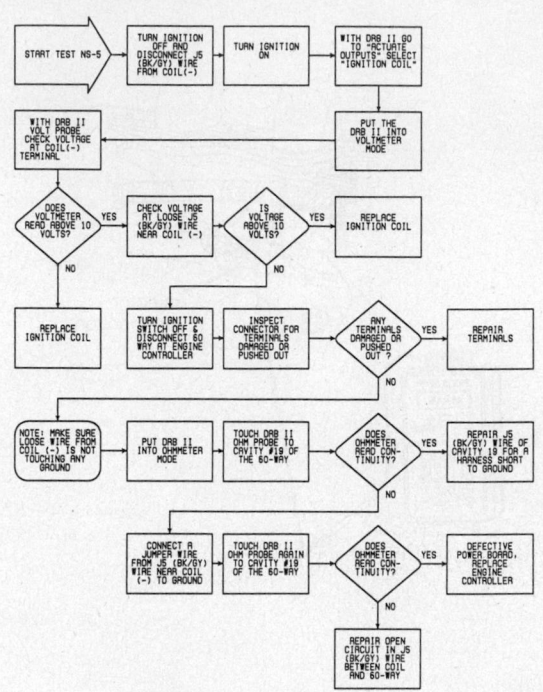

NS-6 (1 OF 4) – CHECKING INJECTOR CONTROL CIRCUIT & CONTROLLER

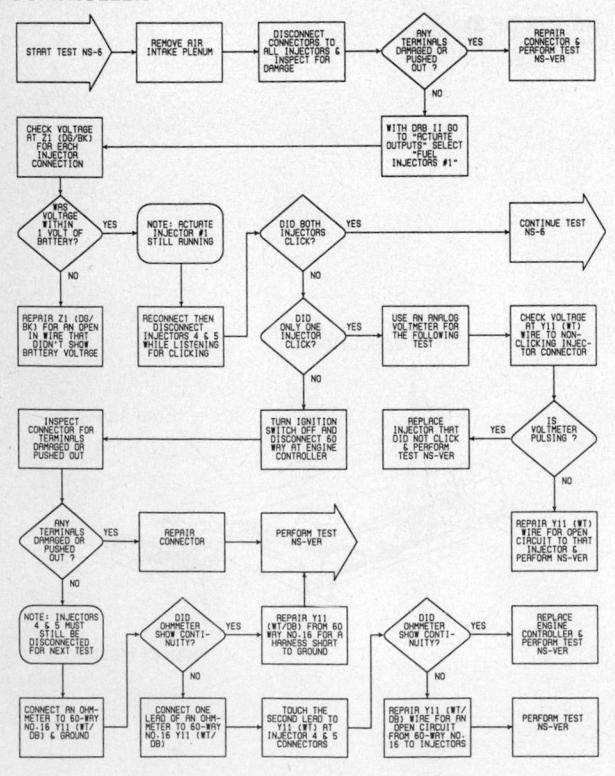

NS-6 (2 OF 4)

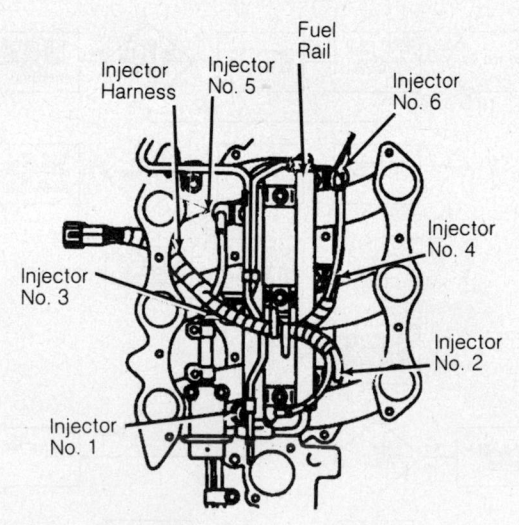

Injector Harness
Injector No. 5
Fuel Rail
Injector No. 6
Injector No. 4
Injector No. 3
Injector No. 2
Injector No. 1

1989 COMPUTERIZED ENGINE CONTROLS
Chrysler Motors 3.0L MPFI (Cont.)

1a-135

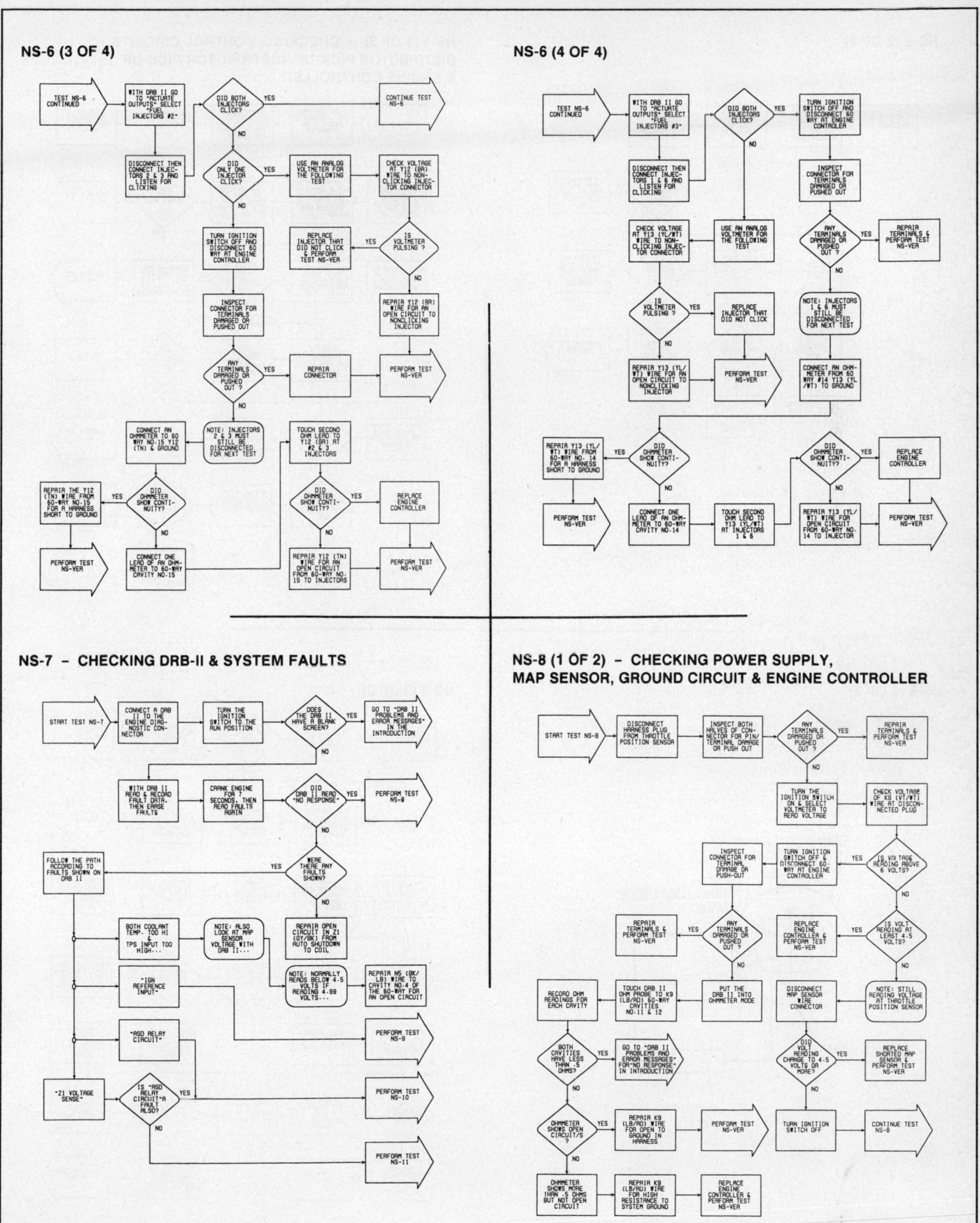

NS-6 (3 OF 4)

NS-6 (4 OF 4)

NS-7 – CHECKING DRB-II & SYSTEM FAULTS

NS-8 (1 OF 2) – CHECKING POWER SUPPLY, MAP SENSOR, GROUND CIRCUIT & ENGINE CONTROLLER

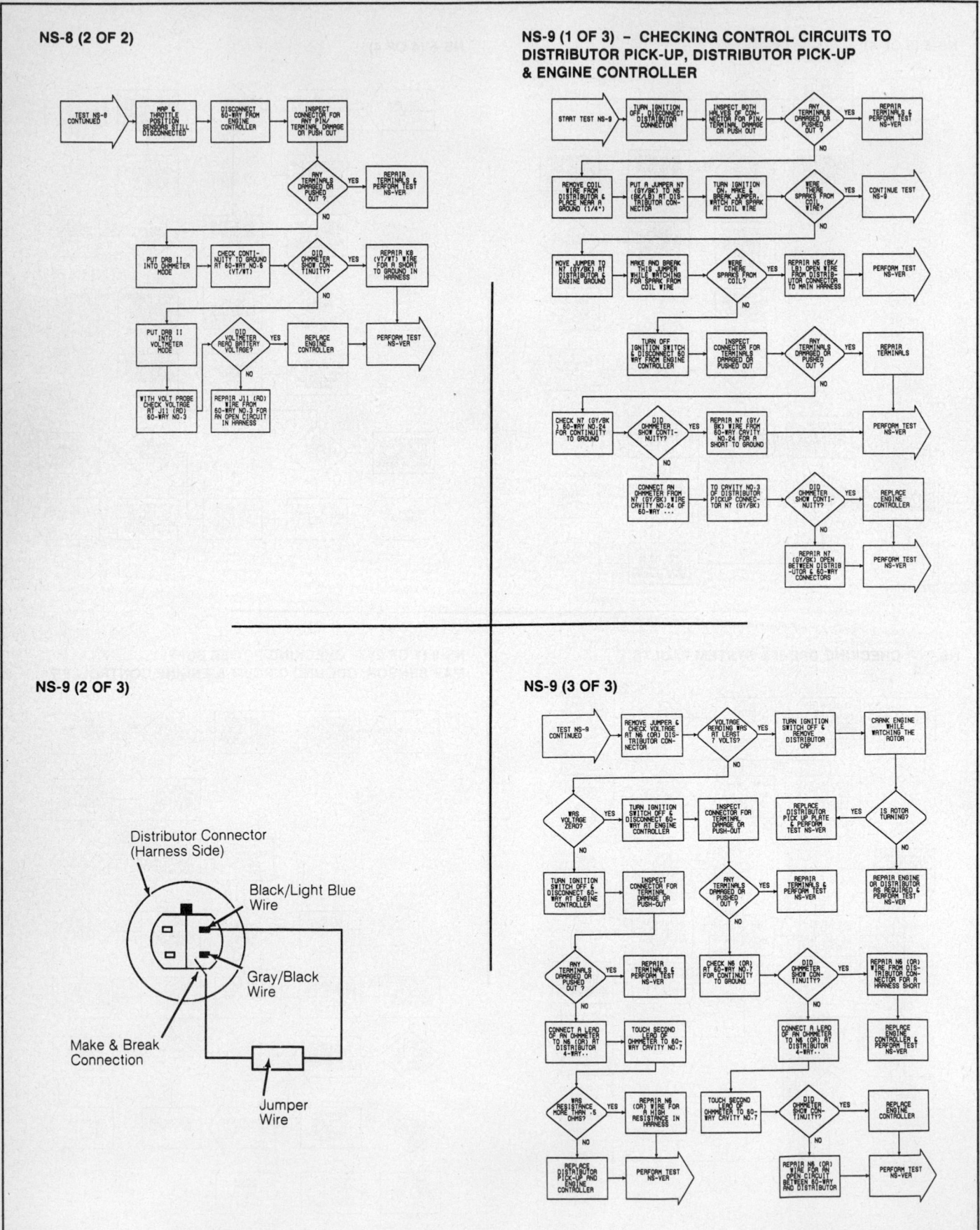

NS-8 (2 OF 2)

NS-9 (1 OF 3) – CHECKING CONTROL CIRCUITS TO DISTRIBUTOR PICK-UP, DISTRIBUTOR PICK-UP & ENGINE CONTROLLER

NS-9 (2 OF 3)

Distributor Connector (Harness Side)

Black/Light Blue Wire

Gray/Black Wire

Make & Break Connection

Jumper Wire

NS-9 (3 OF 3)

1989 COMPUTERIZED ENGINE CONTROLS
Chrysler Motors 3.0L MPFI (Cont.)

1a-137

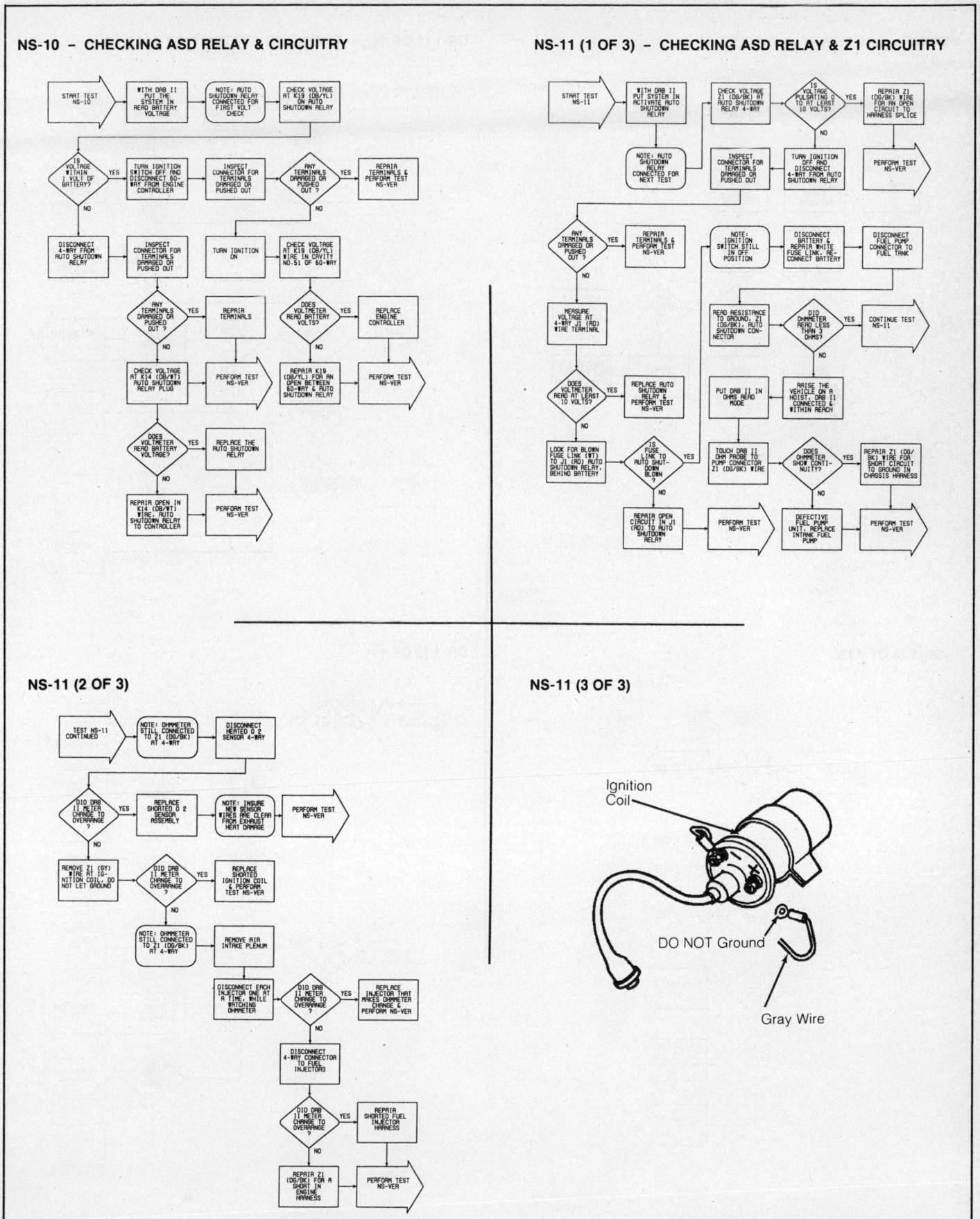

NS-10 – CHECKING ASD RELAY & CIRCUITRY

NS-11 (1 OF 3) – CHECKING ASD RELAY & Z1 CIRCUITRY

NS-11 (2 OF 3)

NS-11 (3 OF 3)

Ignition Coil

DO NOT Ground

Gray Wire

1a-138

1989 COMPUTERIZED ENGINE CONTROLS
Chrysler Motors 3.0L MPFI (Cont.)

NS-VER – NO START VERIFICATION

DR-1 (1 OF 11) – CHECKING SYSTEM FOR FAULTS

DR-1 (2 OF 11)

DR-1 (3 OF 11)

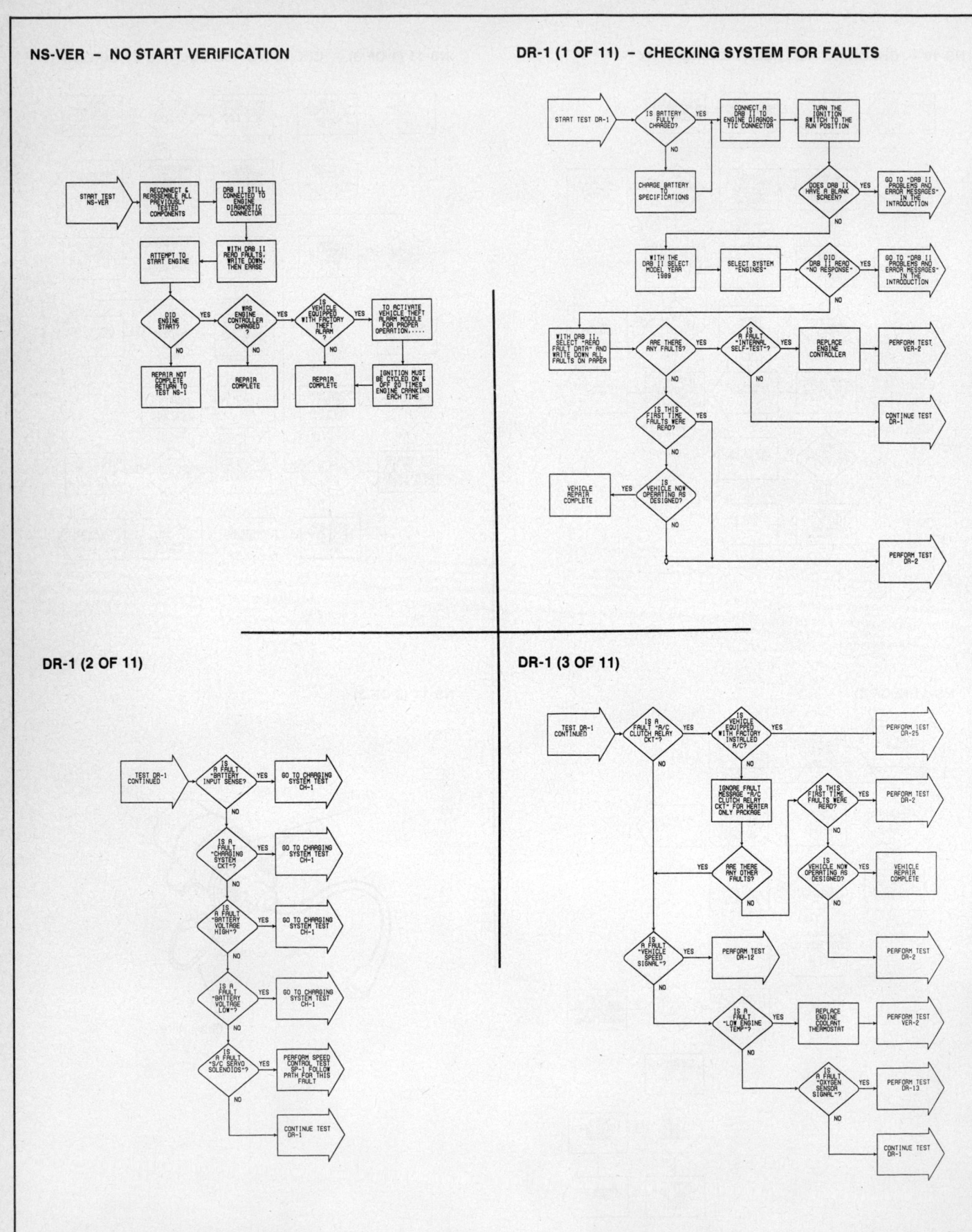

1989 COMPUTERIZED ENGINE CONTROLS
Chrysler Motors 3.0L MPFI (Cont.)

1a-139

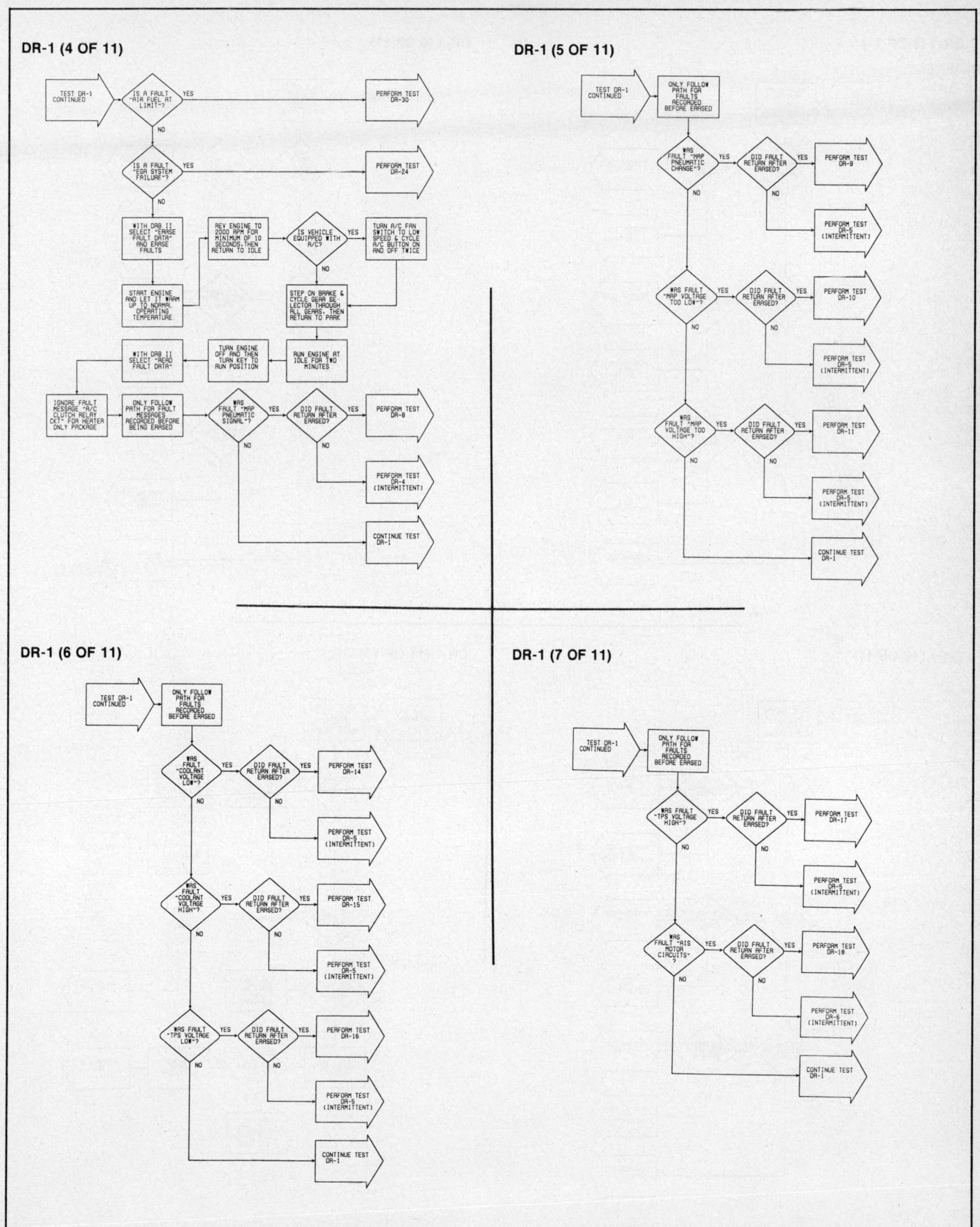

1989 COMPUTERIZED ENGINE CONTROLS
Chrysler Motors 3.0L MPFI (Cont.)

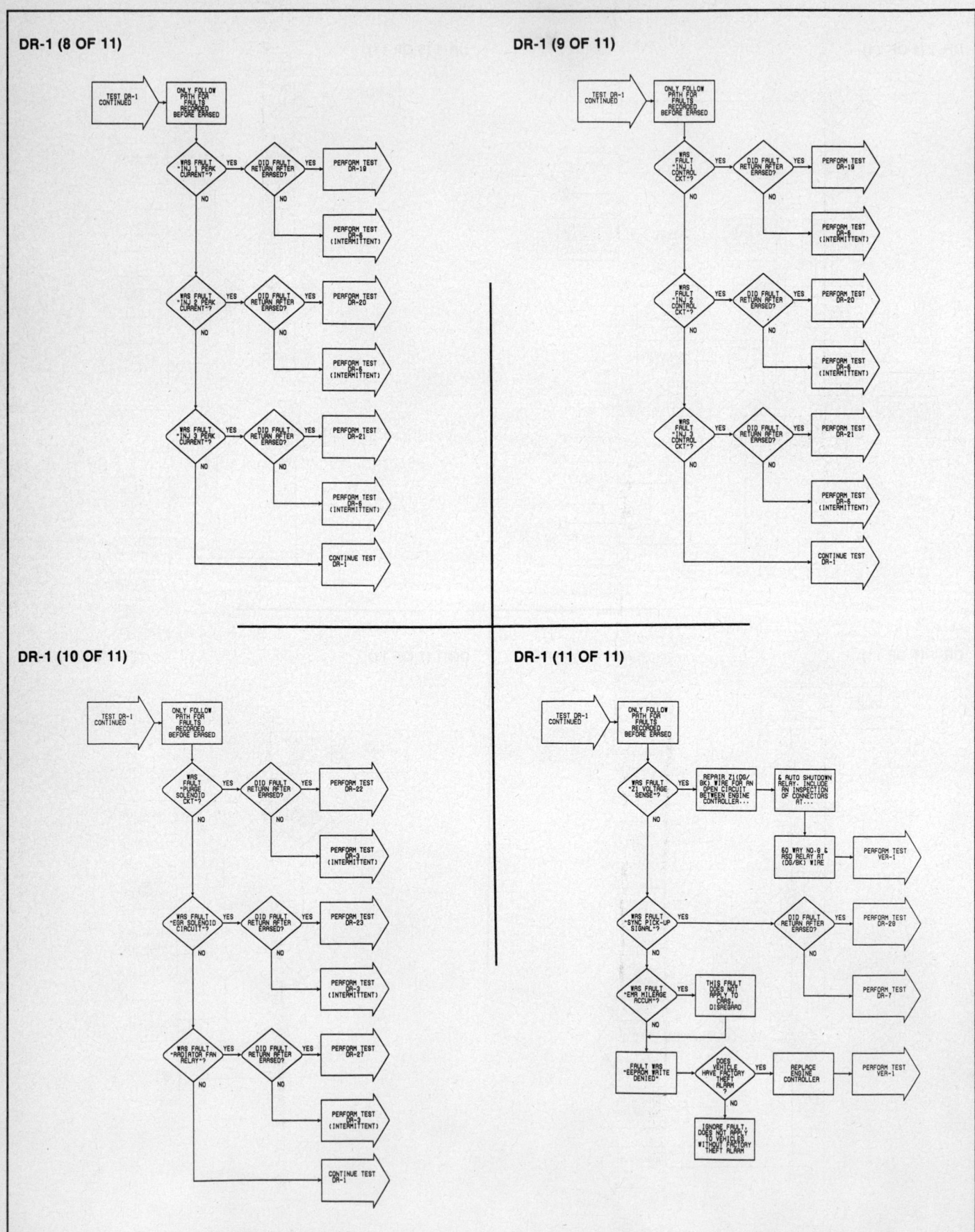

1989 COMPUTERIZED ENGINE CONTROLS
Chrysler Motors 3.0L MPFI (Cont.)

1a-141

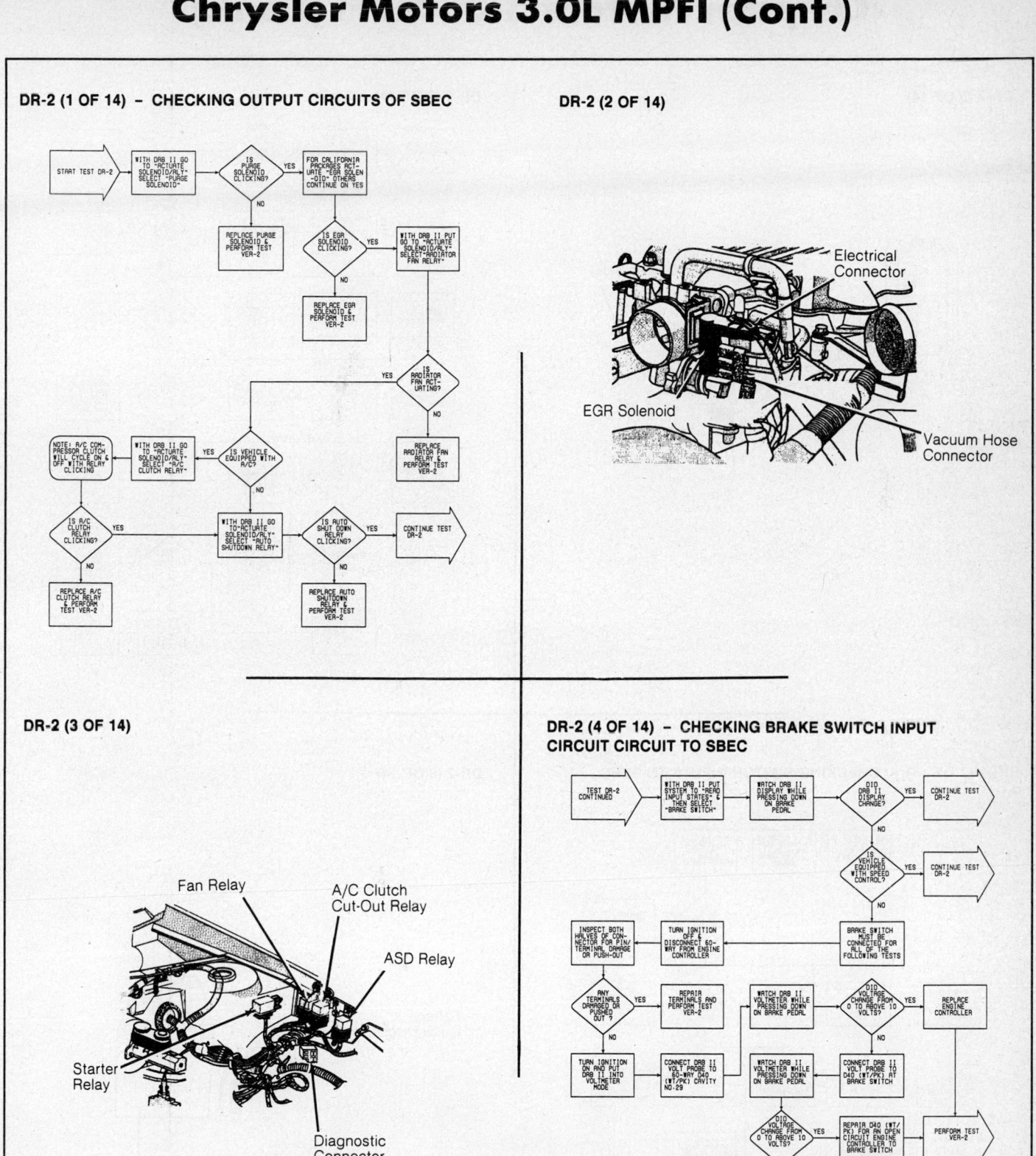

DR-2 (1 OF 14) – CHECKING OUTPUT CIRCUITS OF SBEC

DR-2 (2 OF 14)

Electrical Connector

EGR Solenoid

Vacuum Hose Connector

DR-2 (3 OF 14)

Fan Relay

A/C Clutch Cut-Out Relay

ASD Relay

Starter Relay

Diagnostic Connector

DR-2 (4 OF 14) – CHECKING BRAKE SWITCH INPUT CIRCUIT CIRCUIT TO SBEC

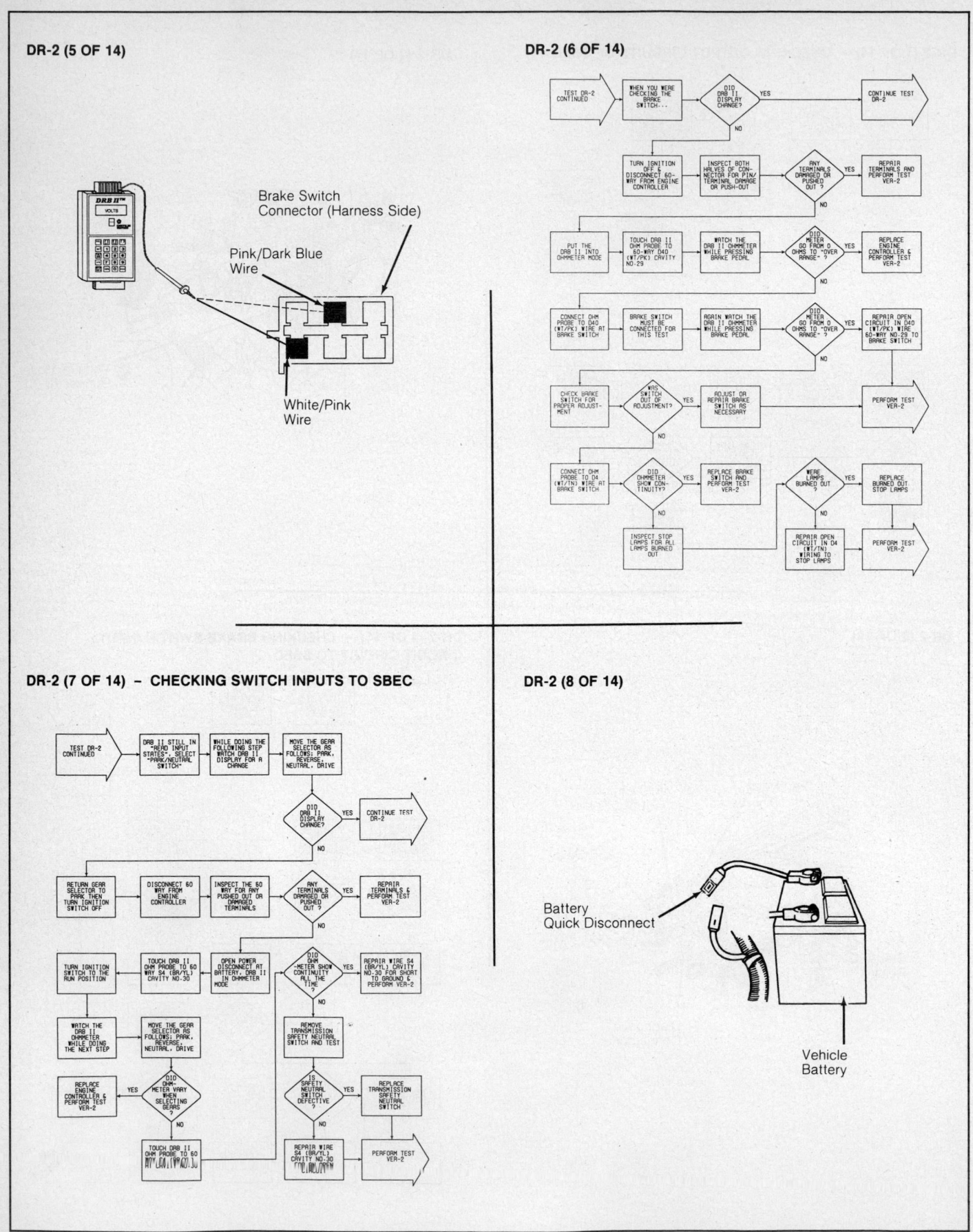

1989 COMPUTERIZED ENGINE CONTROLS
Chrysler Motors 3.0L MPFI (Cont.)

1a-143

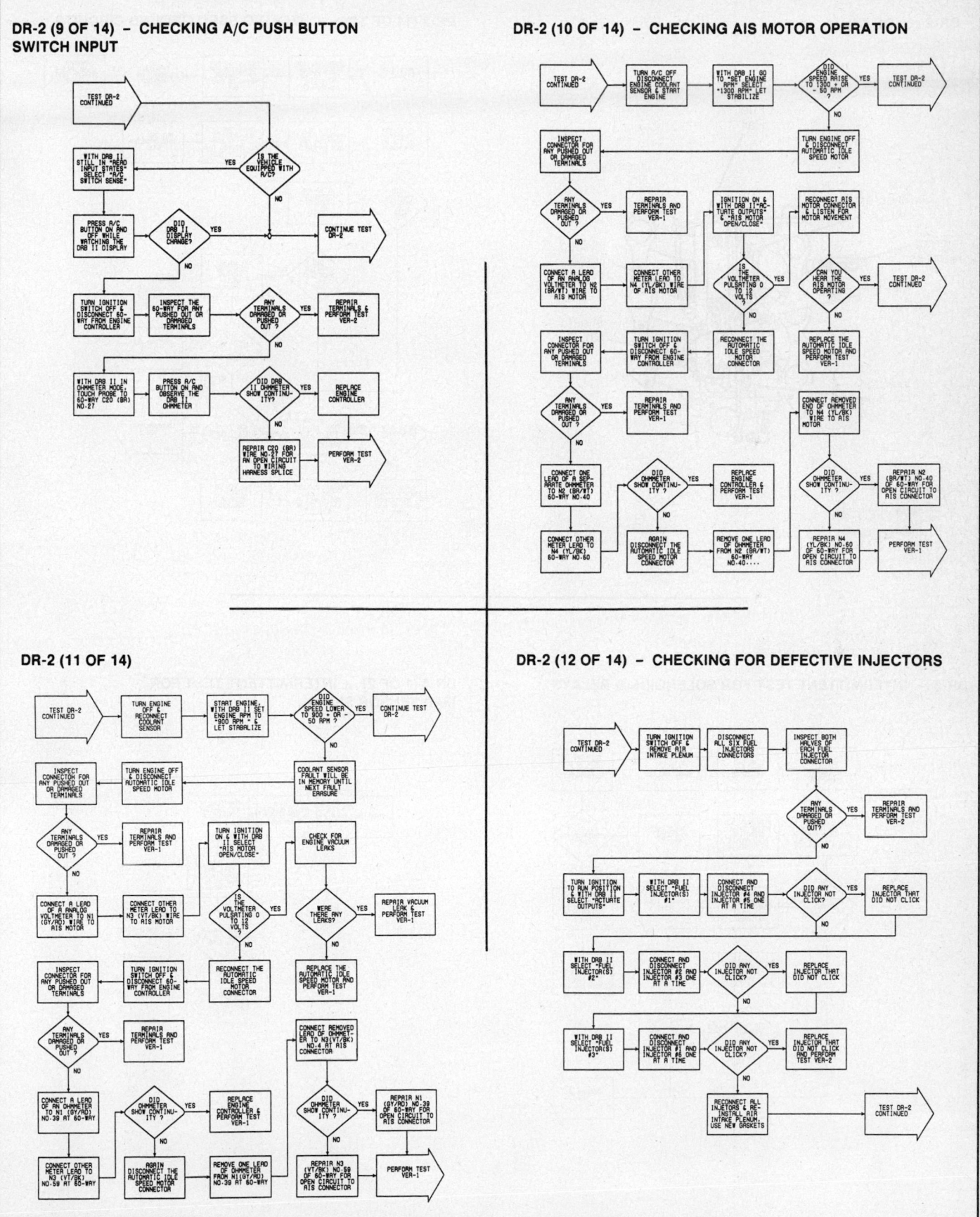

DR-2 (9 OF 14) – CHECKING A/C PUSH BUTTON SWITCH INPUT

DR-2 (10 OF 14) – CHECKING AIS MOTOR OPERATION

DR-2 (11 OF 14)

DR-2 (12 OF 14) – CHECKING FOR DEFECTIVE INJECTORS

DR-2 (13 OF 14)

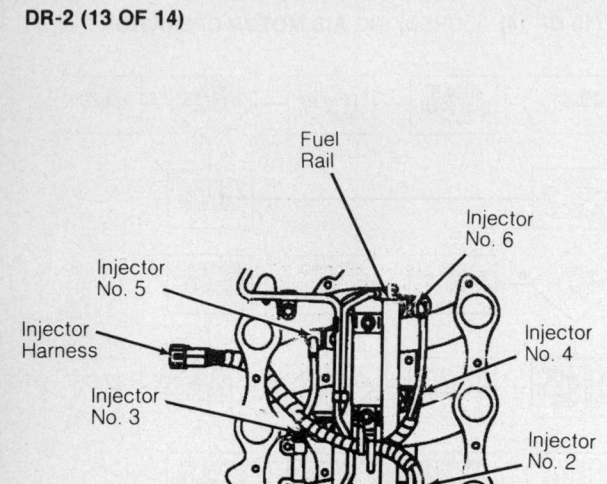

- Fuel Rail
- Injector No. 6
- Injector No. 5
- Injector Harness
- Injector No. 4
- Injector No. 3
- Injector No. 2
- Injector No. 1

DR-2 (14 OF 14) – CHECKING SBEC GROUND CIRCUITS

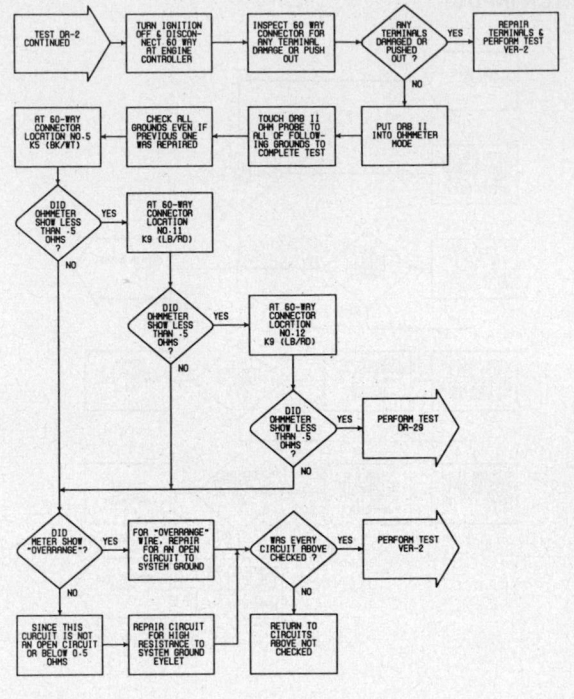

DR-3 – INTERMITTENT TEST FOR SOLENOIDS & RELAYS

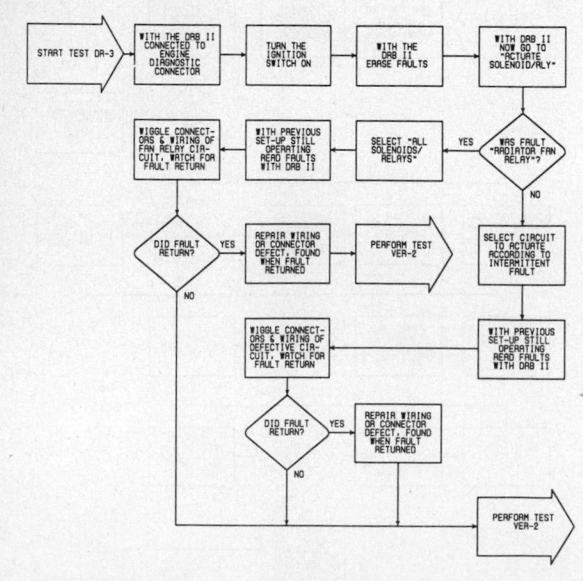

DR-4 (1 OF 2) – INTERMITTENT TEST FOR MAP SENSOR SIGNAL

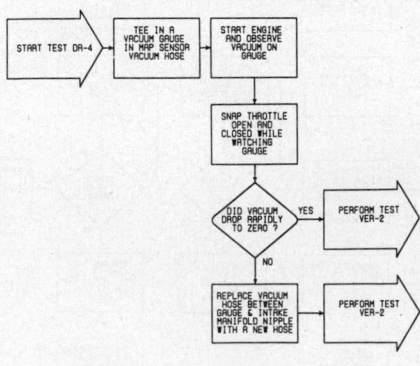

1989 COMPUTERIZED ENGINE CONTROLS
Chrysler Motors 3.0L MPFI (Cont.)

1a-145

DR-4 (2 OF 2)

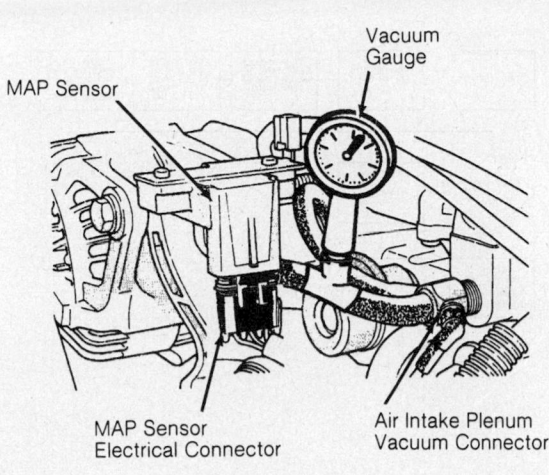

Vacuum Gauge

MAP Sensor

MAP Sensor Electrical Connector

Air Intake Plenum Vacuum Connector

DR-5 – INTERMITTENT TEST FOR SENSOR VOLTAGES

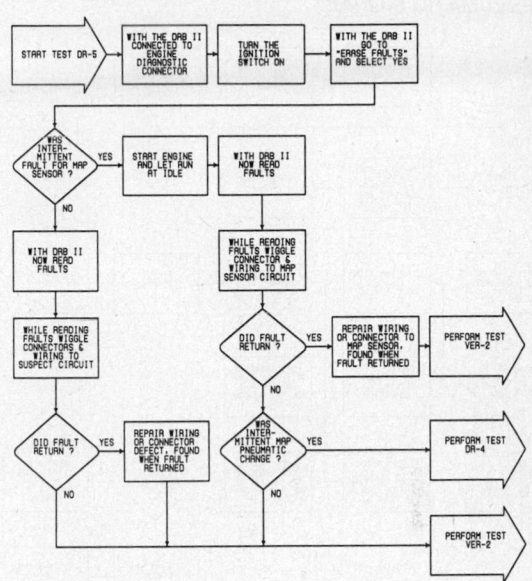

DR-6 – INTERMITTENT TEST FOR INJECTORS & AIS MOTOR

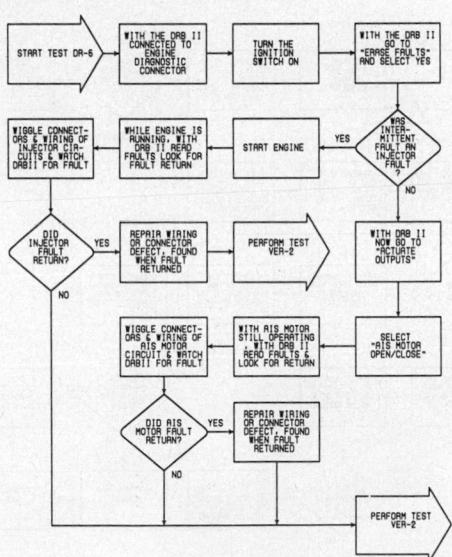

DR-7 – INTERMITTENT TEST FOR DISTRIBUTOR SYNC PICK-UP

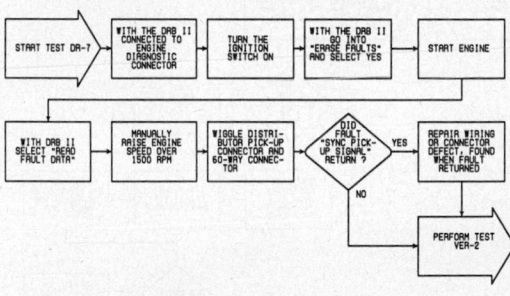

DR-8 – CHECKING FOR FAULT MESSAGE "MAP PNEUMATIC SIGNAL"

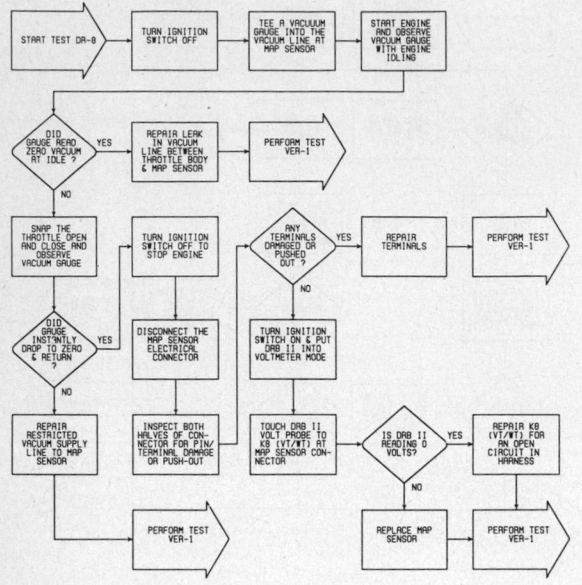

DR-9 – CHECKING FOR FAULT MESSAGE "MAP PNEUMATIC CHANGE"

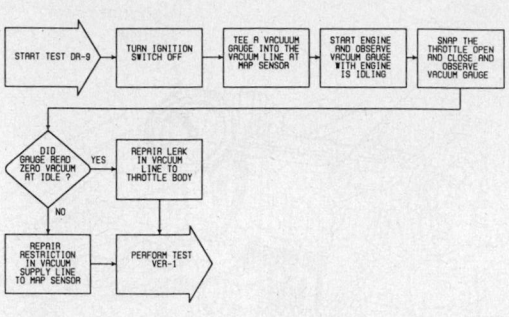

DR-10 – CHECKING FOR FAULT MESSAGE "MAP VOLTAGE TOO LOW"

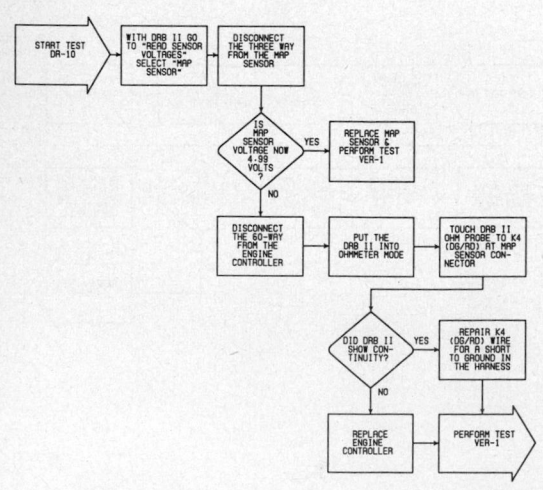

DR-11 – CHECKING FOR FAULT MESSAGE "MAP VOLTAGE TOO HIGH"

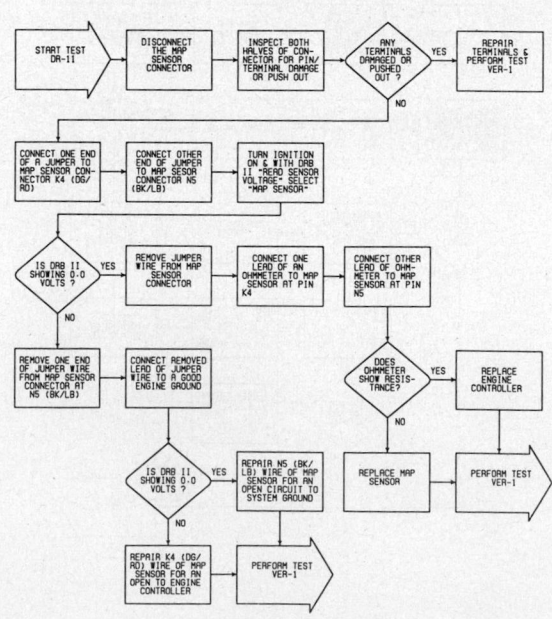

1989 COMPUTERIZED ENGINE CONTROLS
Chrysler Motors 3.0L MPFI (Cont.)

1a-147

**DR-12 (1 OF 4) – CHECKING FOR FAULT MESSAGE
"VEHICLE SPEED SIGNAL"**

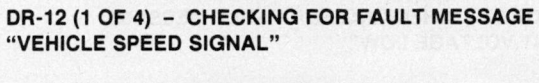

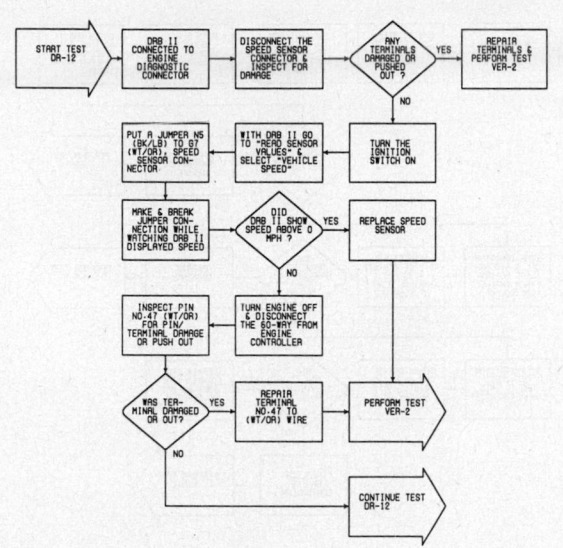

DR-12 (2 OF 4)

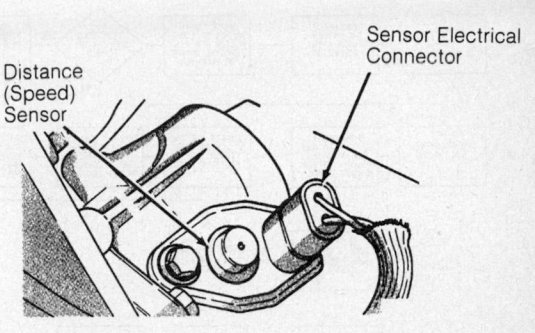

Distance (Speed) Sensor

Sensor Electrical Connector

DR-12 (3 OF 4)

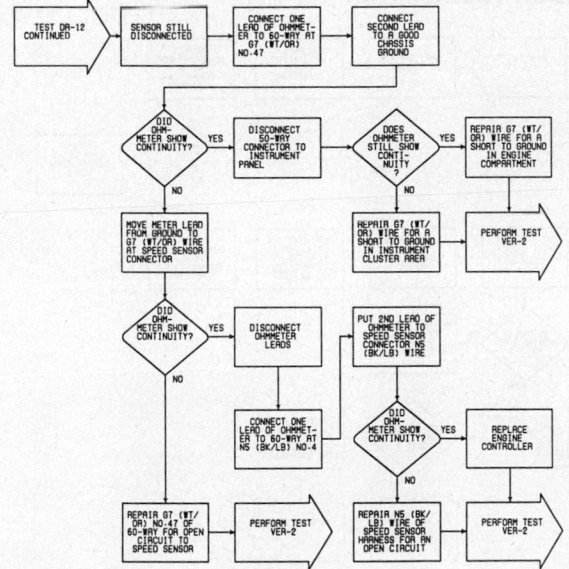

DR-12 (4 OF 4)

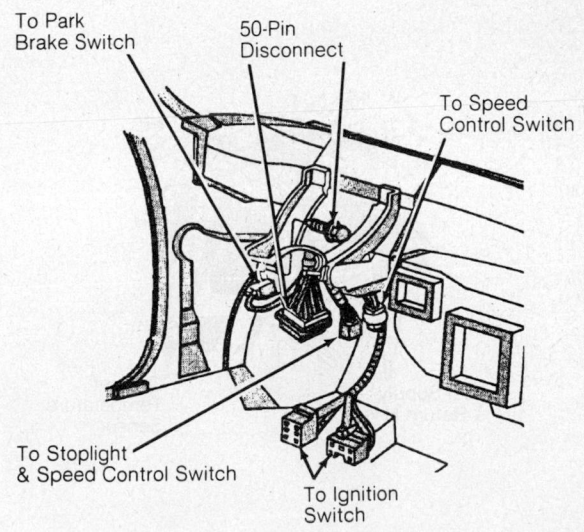

To Park Brake Switch

50-Pin Disconnect

To Speed Control Switch

To Stoplight & Speed Control Switch

To Ignition Switch

1a-148

1989 COMPUTERIZED ENGINE CONTROLS
Chrysler Motors 3.0L MPFI (Cont.)

DR-13 – CHECKING FOR FAULT MESSAGE "OXYGEN SENSOR SIGNAL"

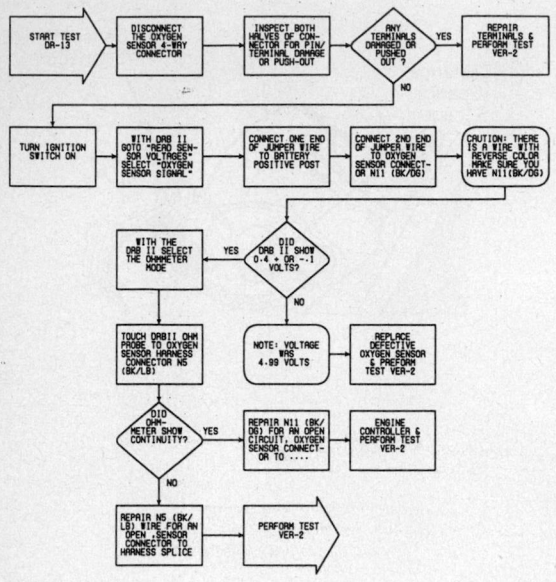

DR-14 (1 OF 2) – CHECKING FOR FAULT MESSAGE "COOLANT VOLTAGE LOW"

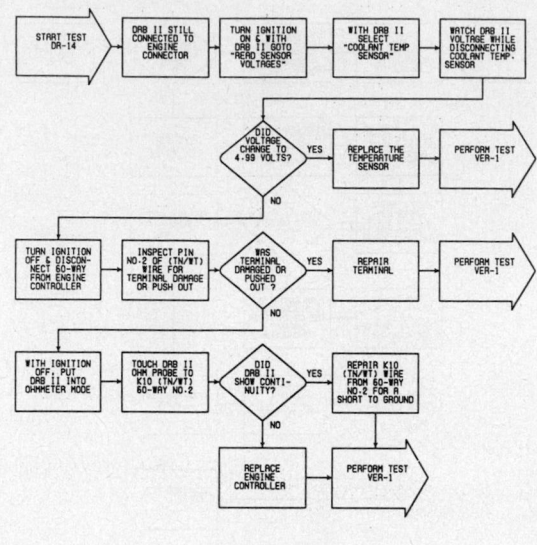

DR-14 (2 OF 2)

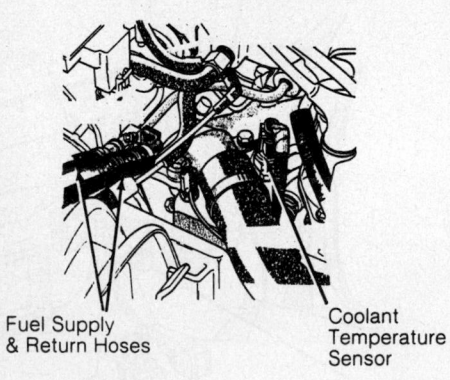

Fuel Supply & Return Hoses

Coolant Temperature Sensor

DR-15 – CHECKING FOR FAULT MESSAGE "COOLANT VOLTAGE HIGH"

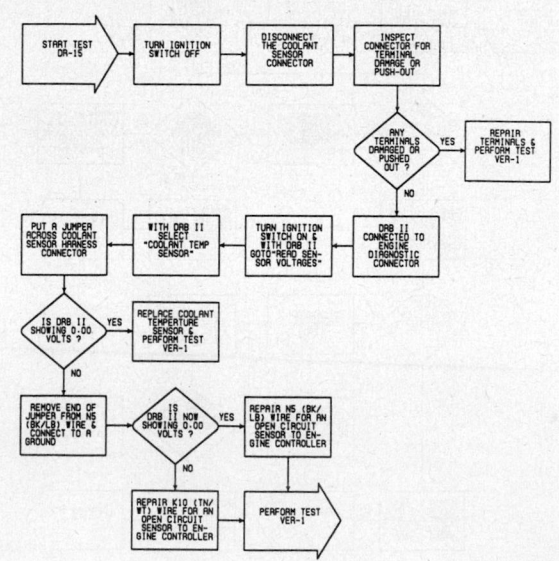

1989 COMPUTERIZED ENGINE CONTROLS
Chrysler Motors 3.0L MPFI (Cont.)

1a-149

**DR-16 – CHECKING FOR FAULT MESSAGE
"TPS VOLTAGE LOW"**

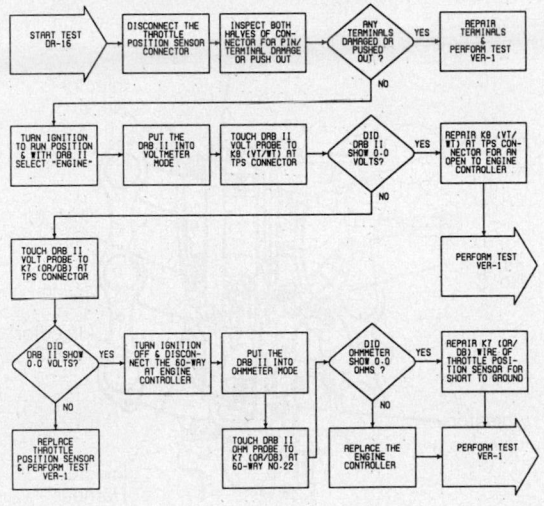

**DR-17 – CHECKING FOR FAULT MESSAGE
"TPS VOLTAGE HIGH"**

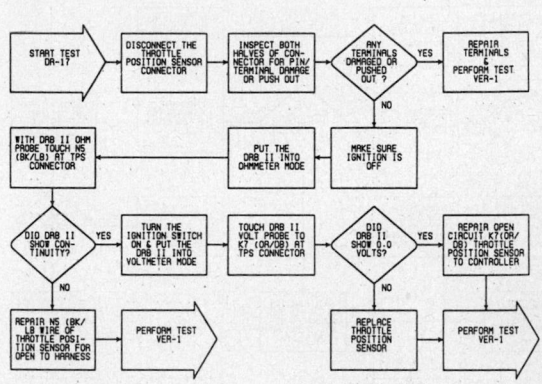

**DR-18 (1 OF 2) – CHECKING FOR FAULT MESSAGE
"AIS MOTOR CIRCUITS"**

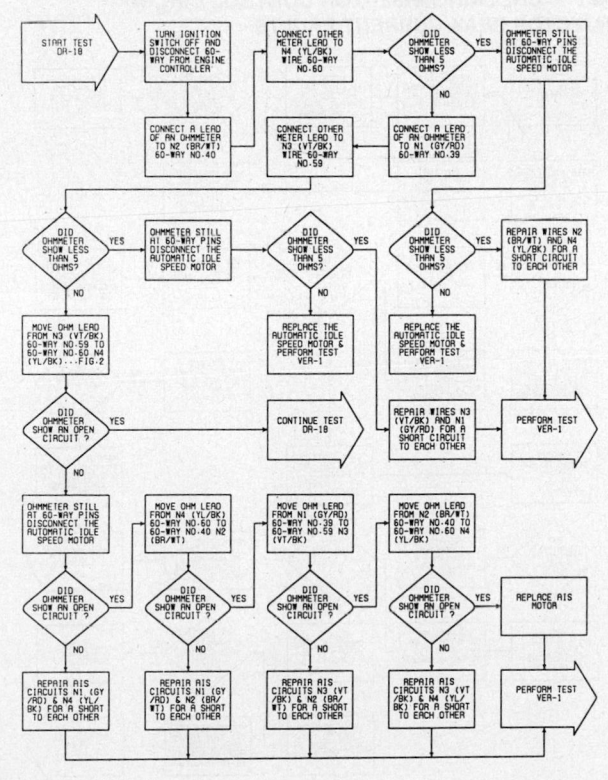

DR-18 (2 OF 2)

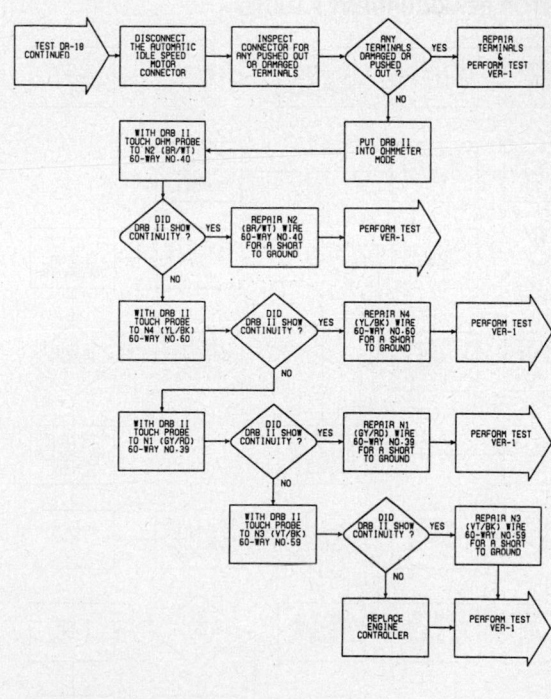

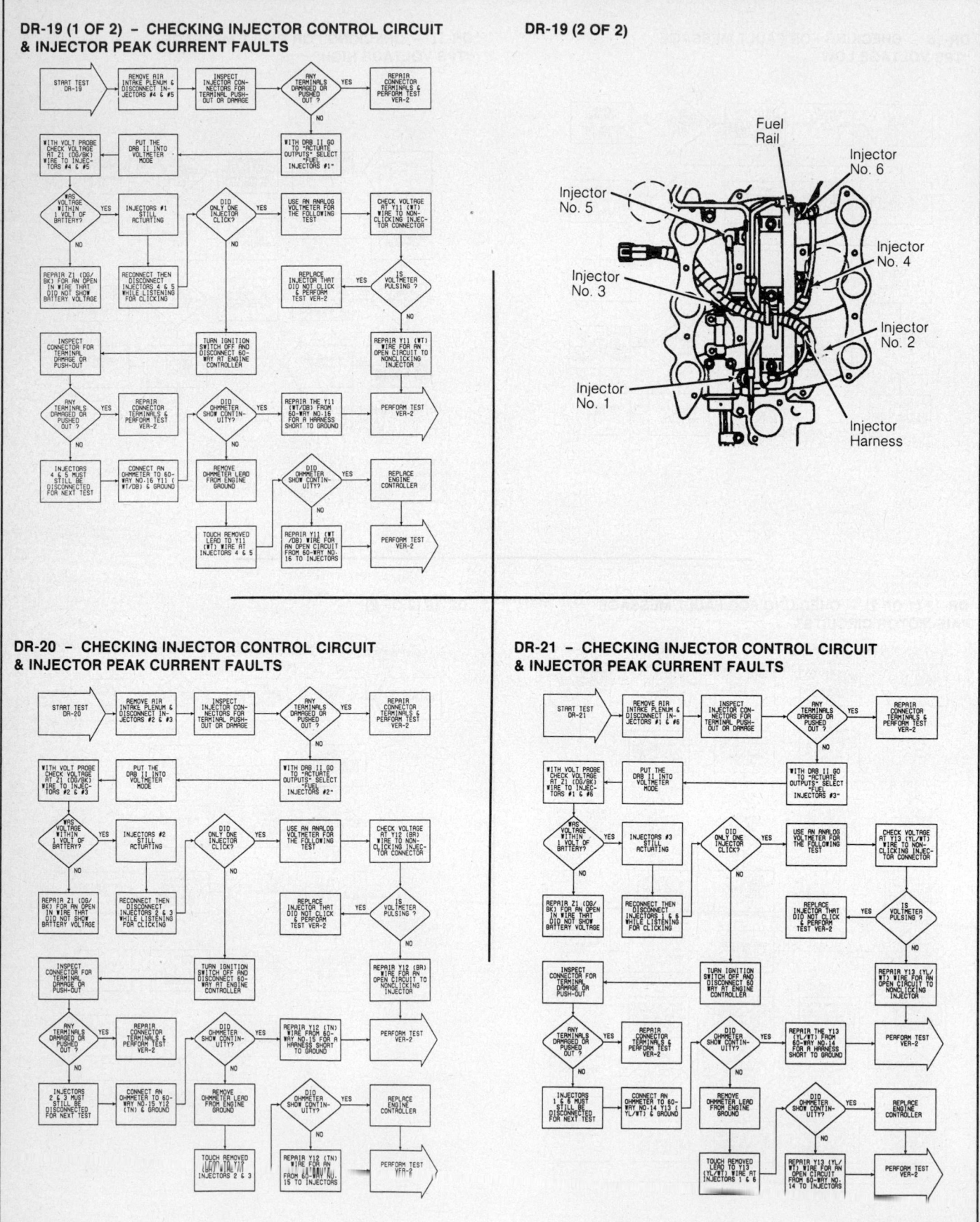

DR-19 (1 OF 2) – CHECKING INJECTOR CONTROL CIRCUIT & INJECTOR PEAK CURRENT FAULTS

DR-19 (2 OF 2)

DR-20 – CHECKING INJECTOR CONTROL CIRCUIT & INJECTOR PEAK CURRENT FAULTS

DR-21 – CHECKING INJECTOR CONTROL CIRCUIT & INJECTOR PEAK CURRENT FAULTS

1989 COMPUTERIZED ENGINE CONTROLS
Chrysler Motors 3.0L MPFI (Cont.)

1a-151

DR-22 (1 OF 2) – CHECKING FOR FAULT MESSAGE "PURGE SOLENOID CKT"

DR-22 (2 OF 2)

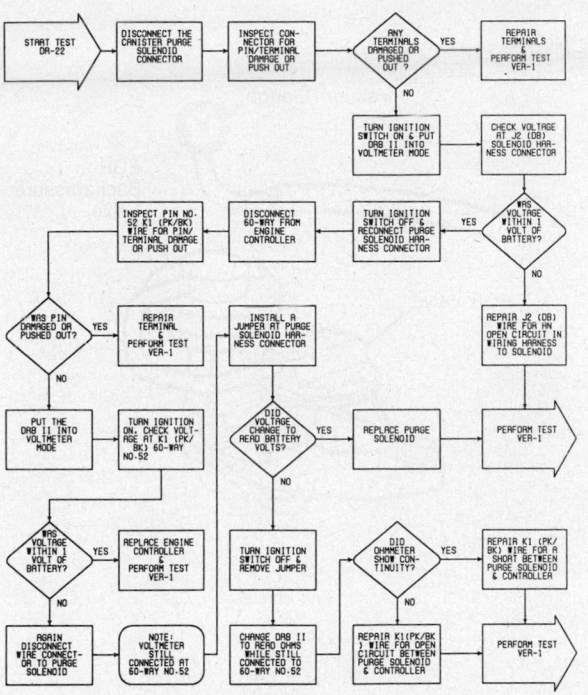

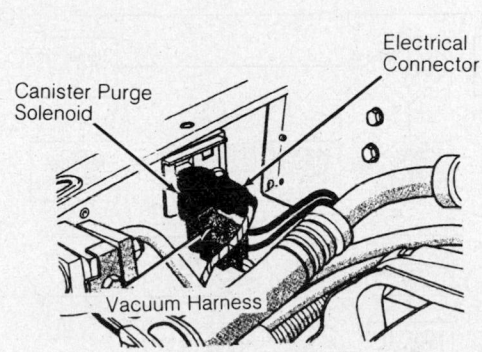

Canister Purge Solenoid

Electrical Connector

Vacuum Harness

DR-23 (1 OF 2) – CHECKING FOR FAULT MESSAGE "EGR SOLENOID CIRCUIT"

DR-23 (2 OF 2)

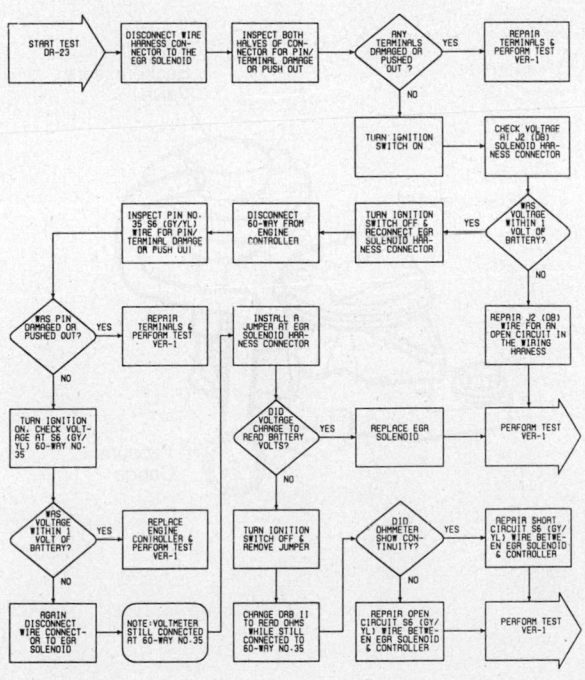

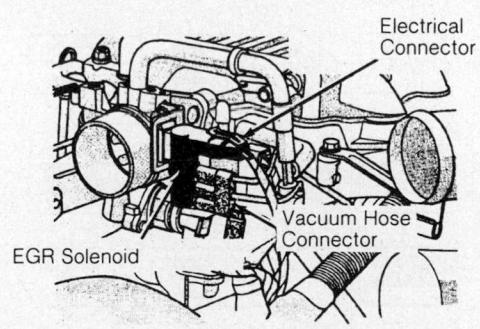

Electrical Connector

EGR Solenoid

Vacuum Hose Connector

DR-24 (1 OF 4) – CHECKING FOR FAULT MESSAGE "EGR SYSTEM FAILURE"

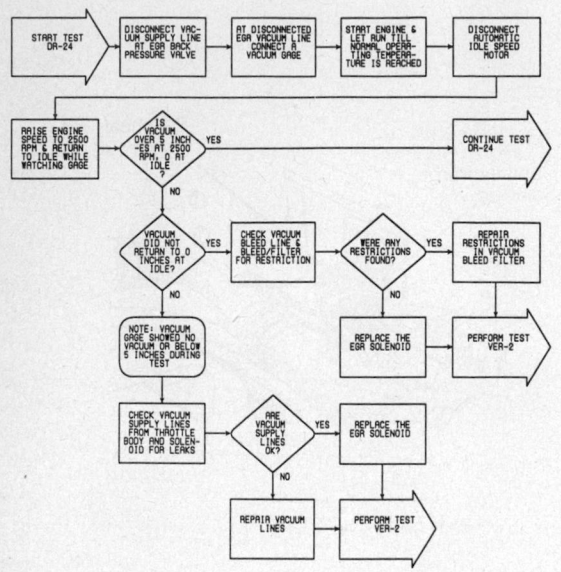

DR-24 (2 OF 4)

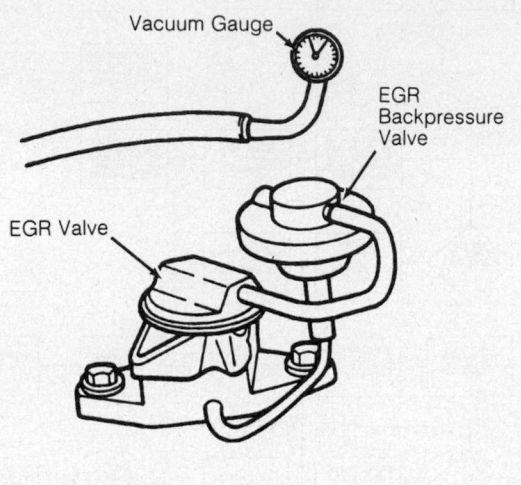

DR-24 (3 OF 4)

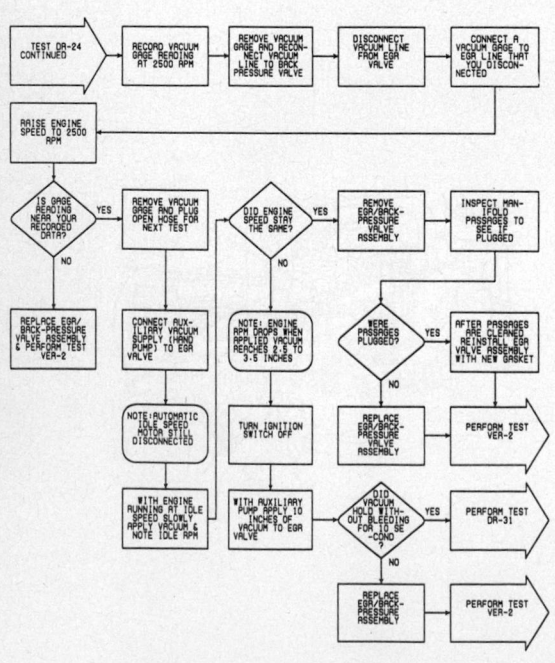

DR-24 (4 OF 4)

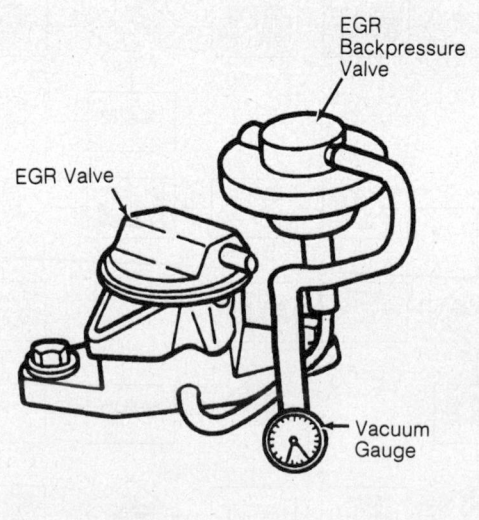

1989 COMPUTERIZED ENGINE CONTROLS
Chrysler Motors 3.0L MPFI (Cont.)

1a-153

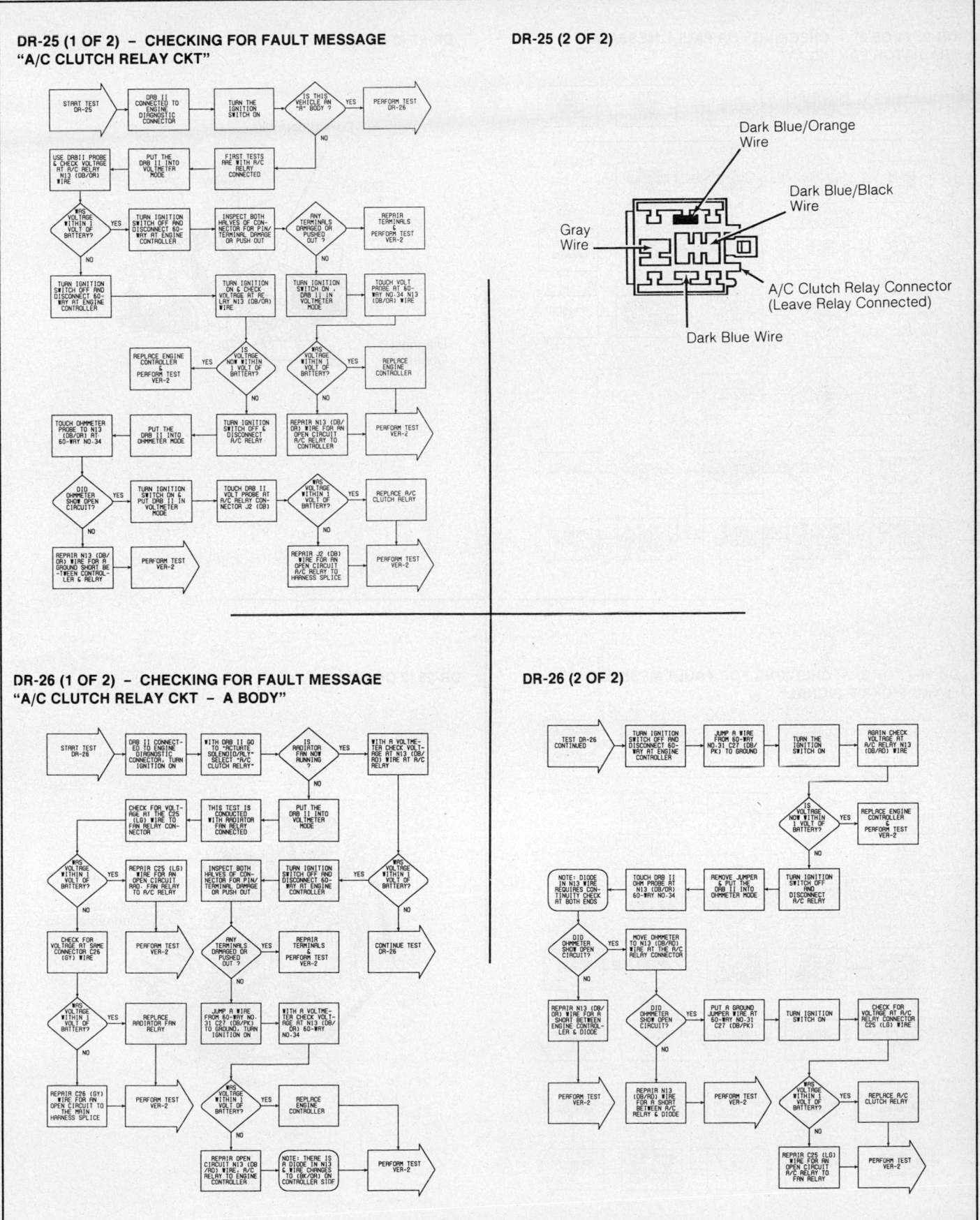

DR-25 (1 OF 2) – CHECKING FOR FAULT MESSAGE "A/C CLUTCH RELAY CKT"

DR-25 (2 OF 2)

Dark Blue/Orange Wire

Dark Blue/Black Wire

Gray Wire

A/C Clutch Relay Connector (Leave Relay Connected)

Dark Blue Wire

DR-26 (1 OF 2) – CHECKING FOR FAULT MESSAGE "A/C CLUTCH RELAY CKT – A BODY"

DR-26 (2 OF 2)

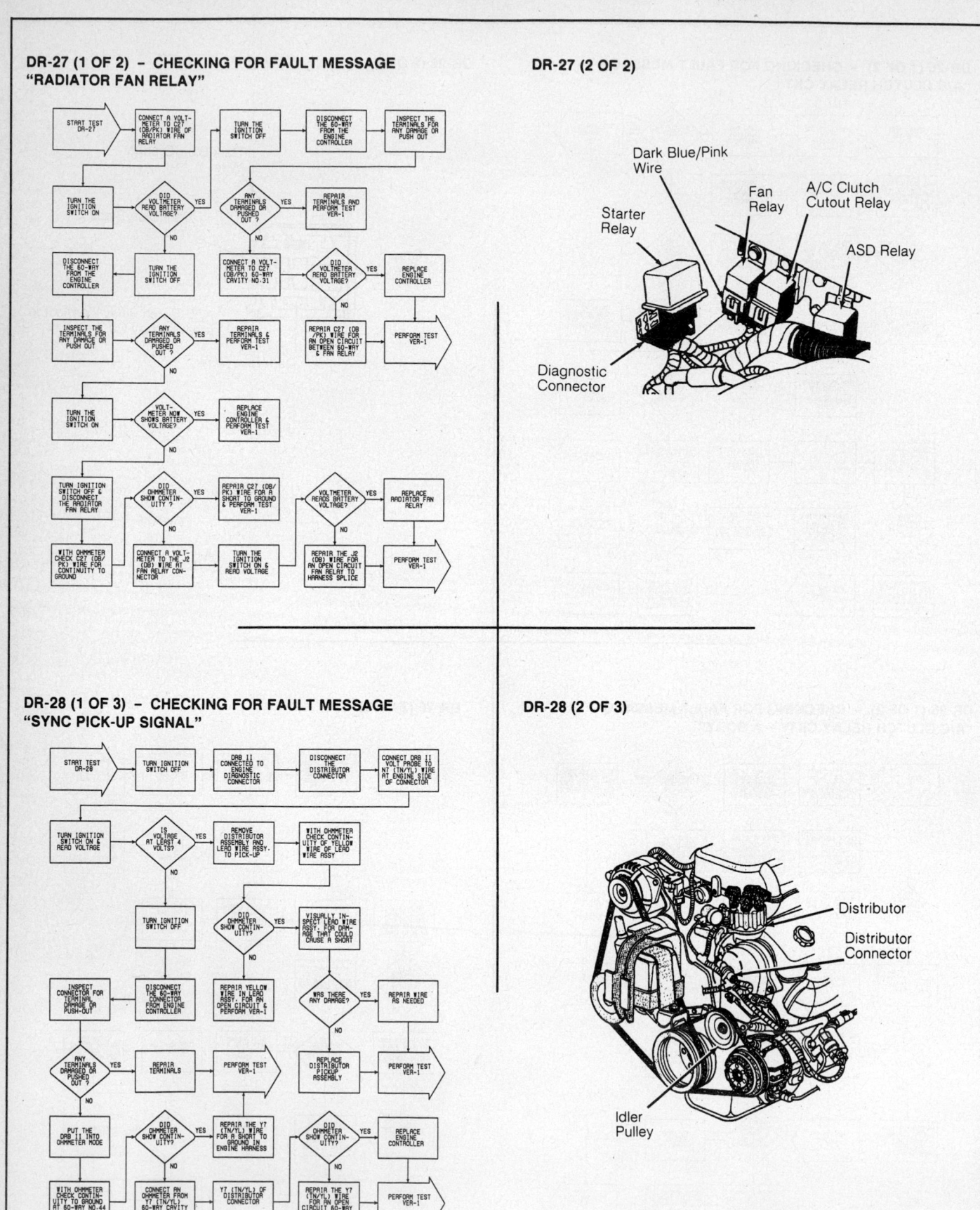

DR-27 (1 OF 2) – CHECKING FOR FAULT MESSAGE "RADIATOR FAN RELAY"

DR-27 (2 OF 2)

Dark Blue/Pink Wire

Fan Relay

A/C Clutch Cutout Relay

Starter Relay

ASD Relay

Diagnostic Connector

DR-28 (1 OF 3) – CHECKING FOR FAULT MESSAGE "SYNC PICK-UP SIGNAL"

DR-28 (2 OF 3)

Distributor

Distributor Connector

Idler Pulley

1989 COMPUTERIZED ENGINE CONTROLS
Chrysler Motors 3.0L MPFI (Cont.)

1a-155

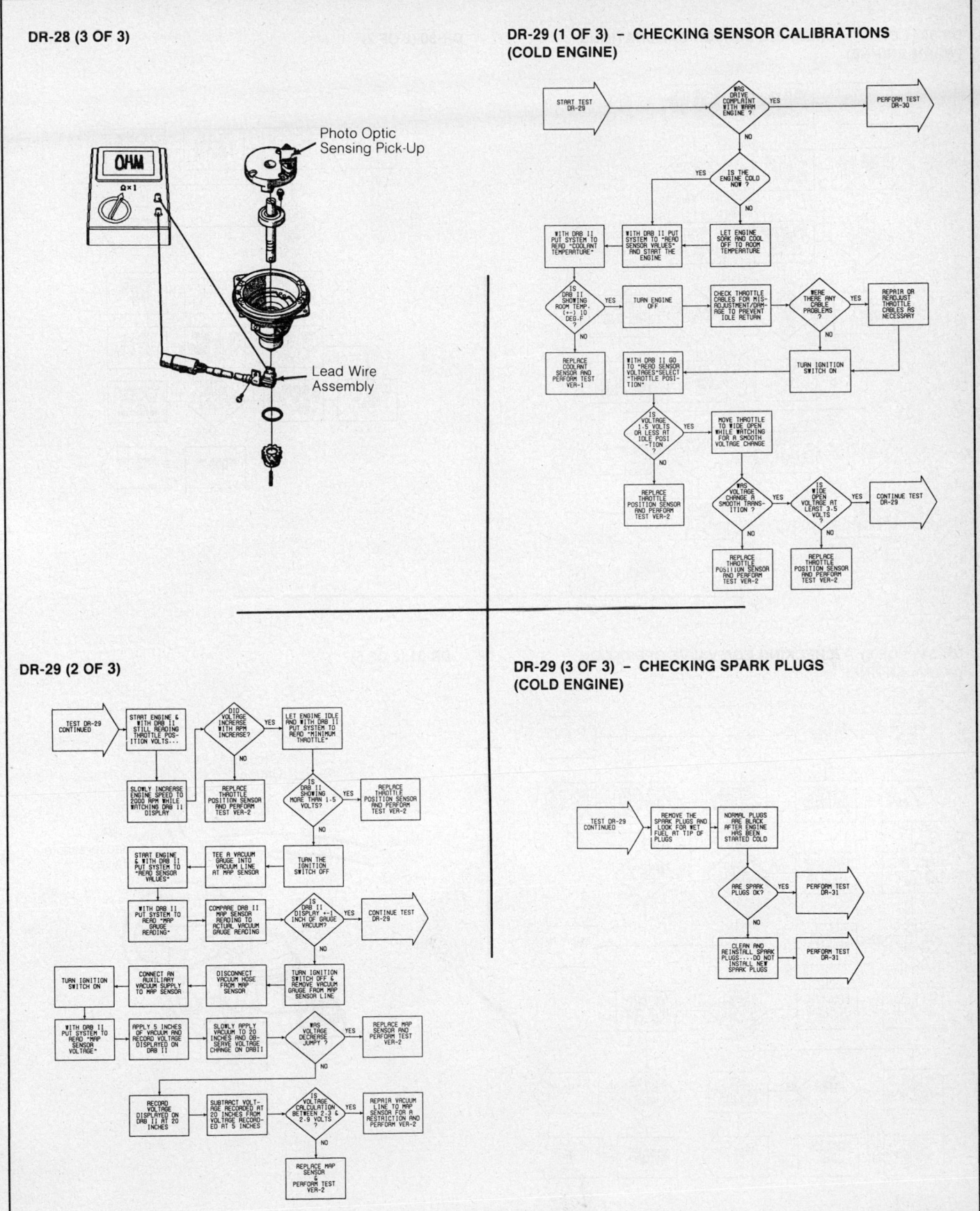

DR-28 (3 OF 3)

Photo Optic
Sensing Pick-Up

Lead Wire
Assembly

**DR-29 (1 OF 3) – CHECKING SENSOR CALIBRATIONS
(COLD ENGINE)**

DR-29 (2 OF 3)

**DR-29 (3 OF 3) – CHECKING SPARK PLUGS
(COLD ENGINE)**

DR-30 (1 OF 2) – CHECKING SENSOR CALIBRATIONS (WARM ENGINE)

DR-30 (2 OF 2)

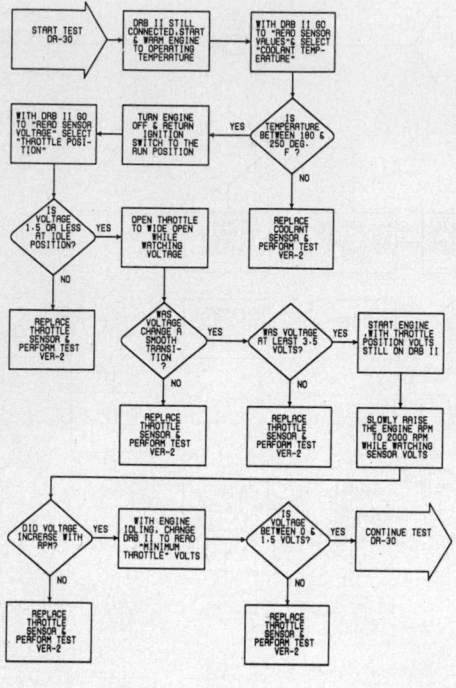

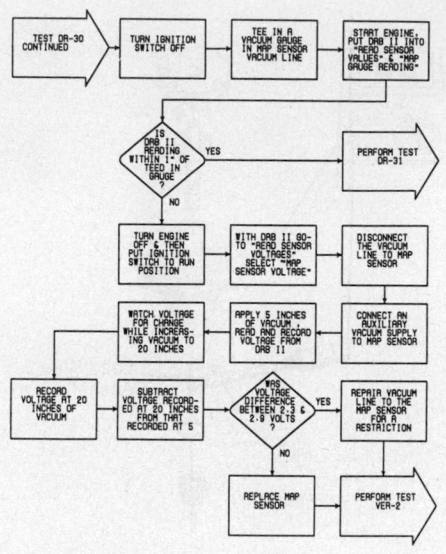

DR-31 (1 OF 5) – CHECKING EGR VALVE OPERATION (WARM ENGINE)

DR-31 (2 OF 5)

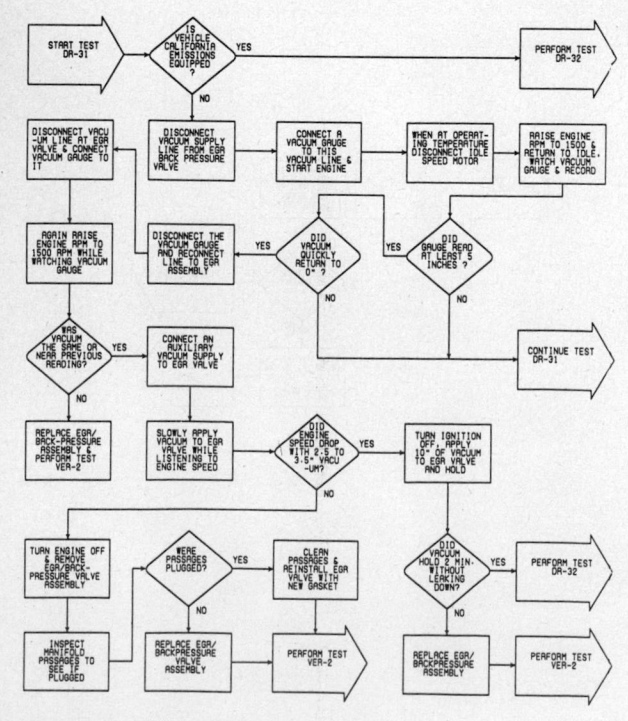

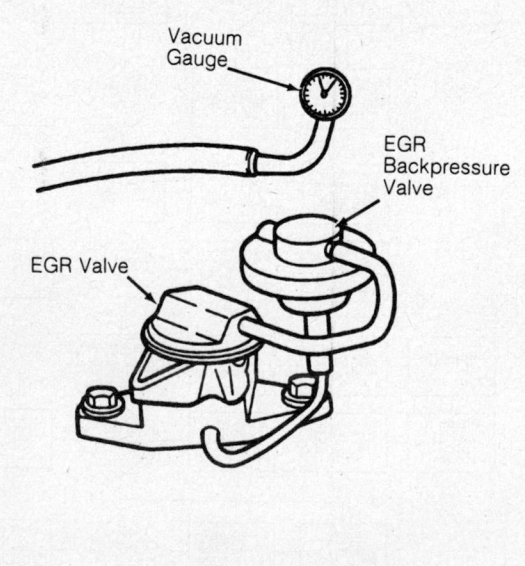

Vacuum Gauge

EGR Backpressure Valve

EGR Valve

1989 COMPUTERIZED ENGINE CONTROLS
Chrysler Motors 3.0L MPFI (Cont.)

1a-157

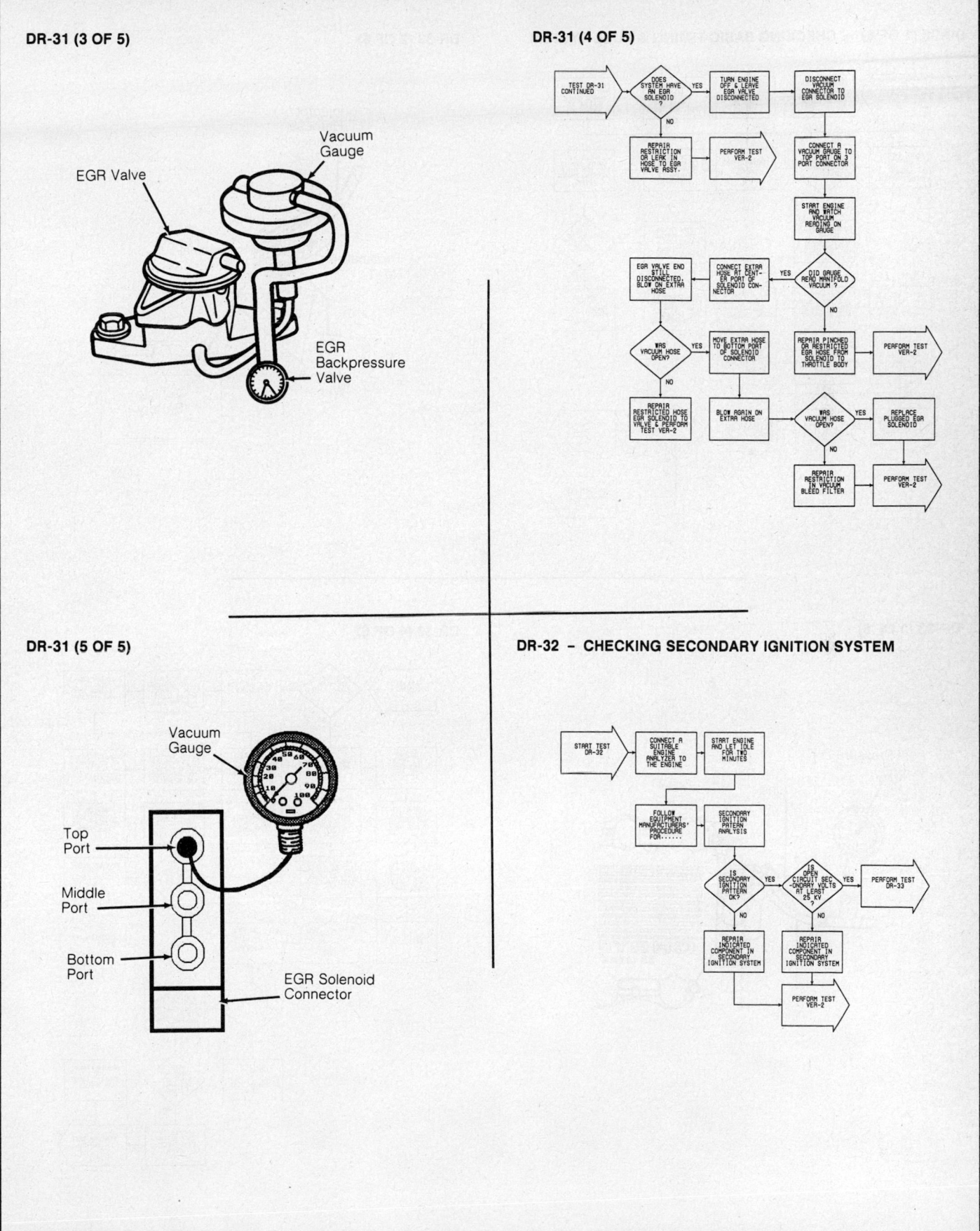

DR-31 (3 OF 5)

EGR Valve

Vacuum Gauge

EGR Backpressure Valve

DR-31 (4 OF 5)

TEST DR-31 CONTINUED

DOES SYSTEM HAVE AN EGR SOLENOID ?

YES — TURN ENGINE OFF & LEAVE EGR VALVE DISCONNECTED

DISCONNECT VACUUM CONNECTOR TO EGR SOLENOID

NO — REPAIR RESTRICTION OR LEAK IN HOSE TO EGR VALVE ASSY. — PERFORM TEST VER-2

CONNECT A VACUUM GAUGE TO TOP PORT ON 3 PORT CONNECTOR

START ENGINE AND WATCH VACUUM READING ON GAUGE

DID GAUGE READ MANIFOLD VACUUM ?

YES — CONNECT EXTRA HOSE AT CENTER PORT OF SOLENOID CONNECTOR — EGR VALVE END STILL DISCONNECTED, BLOW ON EXTRA HOSE

NO — REPAIR PINCHED OR RESTRICTED EGR HOSE FROM SOLENOID TO THROTTLE BODY — PERFORM TEST VER-2

WAS VACUUM HOSE OPEN?

YES — MOVE EXTRA HOSE TO BOTTOM PORT OF SOLENOID CONNECTOR

NO — REPAIR RESTRICTED HOSE EGR SOLENOID TO VALVE & PERFORM TEST VER-2

BLOW AGAIN ON EXTRA HOSE

WAS VACUUM HOSE OPEN?

YES — REPLACE PLUGGED EGR SOLENOID

NO — REPAIR RESTRICTION IN VACUUM BLEED FILTER — PERFORM TEST VER-2

DR-31 (5 OF 5)

Vacuum Gauge

Top Port

Middle Port

Bottom Port

EGR Solenoid Connector

DR-32 – CHECKING SECONDARY IGNITION SYSTEM

START TEST DR-32

CONNECT A SUITABLE ENGINE ANALYZER TO THE ENGINE

START ENGINE AND LET IDLE FOR TWO MINUTES

FOLLOW EQUIPMENT MANUFACTURERS' PROCEDURE FOR......

SECONDARY IGNITION PATTERN ANALYSIS

IS SECONDARY IGNITION PATTERN OK?

YES — IS OPEN CIRCUIT SECONDARY VOLTS AT LEAST 25 KV ?

YES — PERFORM TEST DR-33

NO — REPAIR INDICATED COMPONENT IN SECONDARY IGNITION SYSTEM

NO — REPAIR INDICATED COMPONENT IN SECONDARY IGNITION SYSTEM — PERFORM TEST VER-2

1a-158

1989 COMPUTERIZED ENGINE CONTROLS
Chrysler Motors 3.0L MPFI (Cont.)

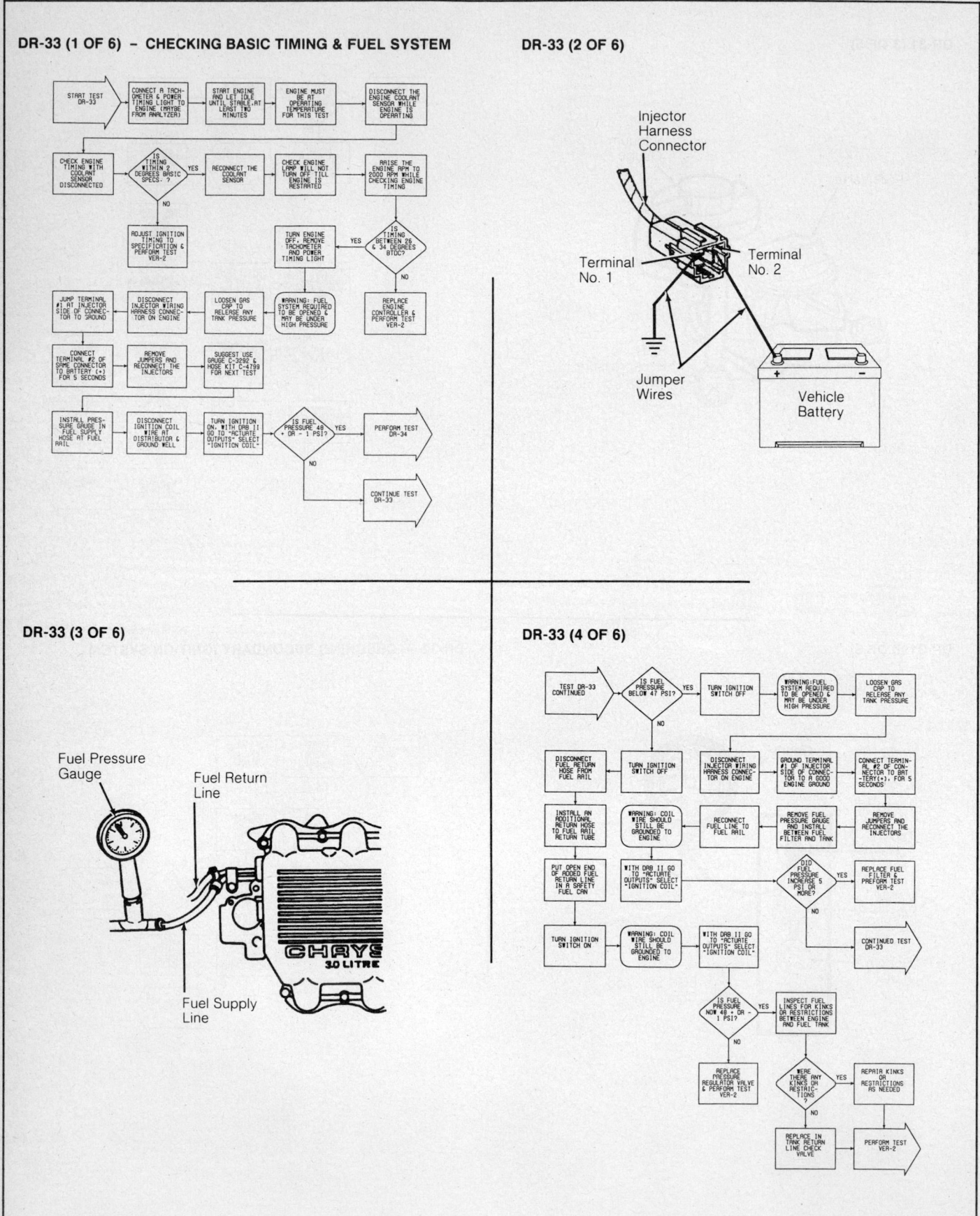

DR-33 (1 OF 6) – CHECKING BASIC TIMING & FUEL SYSTEM

DR-33 (2 OF 6)

DR-33 (3 OF 6)

DR-33 (4 OF 6)

1989 COMPUTERIZED ENGINE CONTROLS
Chrysler Motors 3.0L MPFI (Cont.)

1a-159

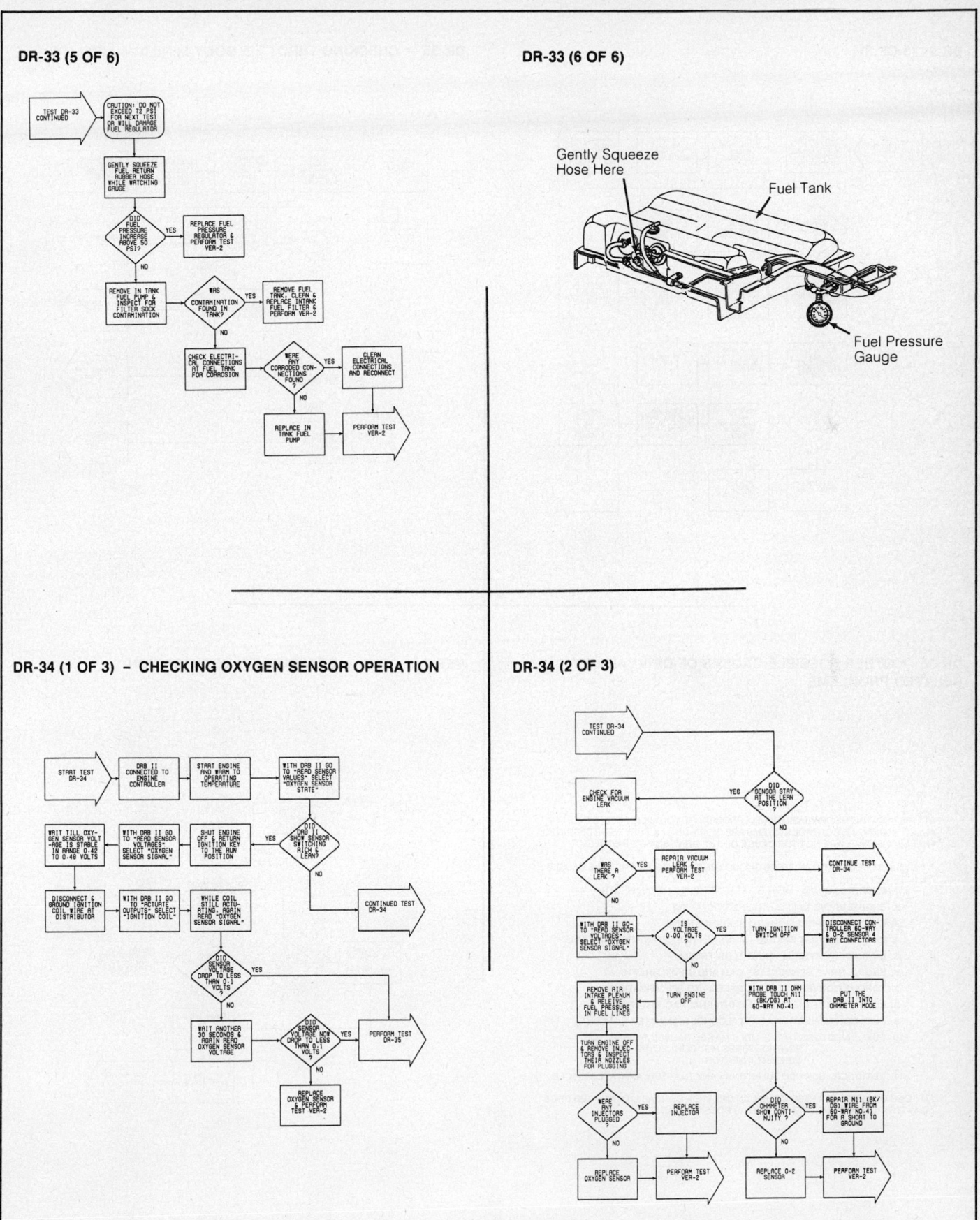

DR-33 (5 OF 6)

DR-33 (6 OF 6)

Gently Squeeze Hose Here

Fuel Tank

Fuel Pressure Gauge

DR-34 (1 OF 3) – CHECKING OXYGEN SENSOR OPERATION

DR-34 (2 OF 3)

1a-160

1989 COMPUTERIZED ENGINE CONTROLS
Chrysler Motors 3.0L MPFI (Cont.)

DR-34 (3 OF 3)

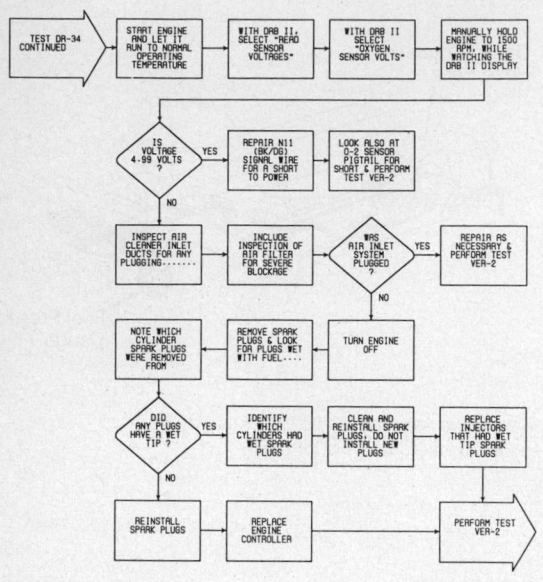

DR-35 – CHECKING THROTTLE BODY MINIMUM AIRFLOW

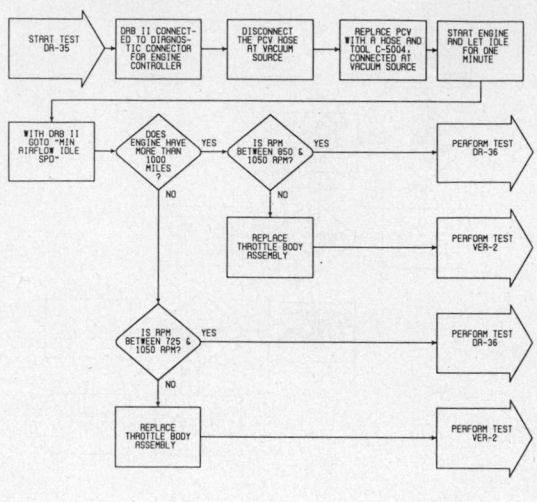

DR-36 – OTHER POSSIBLE CAUSES OF DRIVEABILITY RELATED PROBLEMS

AT THIS POINT IN THE DRIVEABILITY TEST PROCEDURE YOU HAVE DETERMINED THAT ALL OF THE ENGINE CONTROL SYSTEMS ARE OPERATING AS THEY WERE DESIGNED. THEREFORE, THEY ARE **NOT THE CAUSE OF THE DRIVEABILITY PROBLEM.**

THE FOLLOWING ADDITIONAL ITEMS SHOULD BE CHECKED AS POSSIBLE CAUSES:

1. **ENGINE VACUUM** - MUST BE AT LEAST 13 INCHES IN NEUTRAL.
2. **ENGINE VALVE TIMING** - TO SPECIFICATIONS.
3. **ENGINE COMPRESSION** - TO SPECIFICATIONS.
4. **ENGINE EXHAUST SYSTEM** - MUST BE FREE OF ANY RESTRICTIONS.
5. **ENGINE PCV SYSTEM** - MUST FLOW FREELY.
6. **ENGINE DRIVE SPROCKETS** - CAM AND CRANK SHAFTS.
7. **TORQUE CONVERTOR STALL SPEED** - TO SPECIFICATIONS.
8. **POWER BRAKE BOOSTER** - NO INTERNAL VACUUM LEAKS.
9. **FUEL CONTAMINATION** - HIGH ALCOHOL AND WATER CONTENT.
10. **FUEL INJECTORS** - ROUGH IDLE MAY BE CAUSED BY INJECTOR CONTROL WIRES NOT CONNECTED TO THE CORRENT INJECTOR.
11. **TECHNICAL SERVICE BULLETINS** - ANY THAT MAY APPLY TO VEHICLE.

ANY ONE OR MORE OF THESE ITEMS CAN CREATE A DRIVEABILITY RELATED PROBLEM. THEY CAN NOT BE OVERLOOKED AS POSSIBLE CAUSES.

VER-1 (1 OF 2) – DRIVEABILITY VERIFICATION

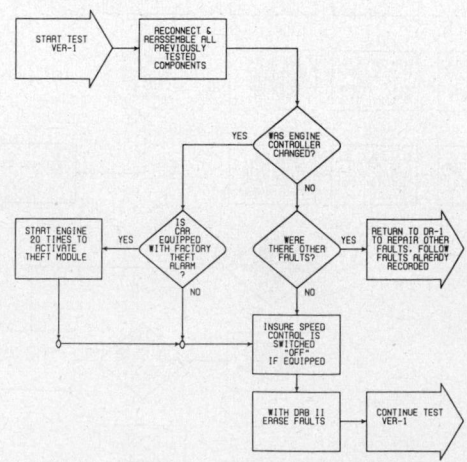

1989 COMPUTERIZED ENGINE CONTROLS
Chrysler Motors 3.0L MPFI (Cont.)

1a-161

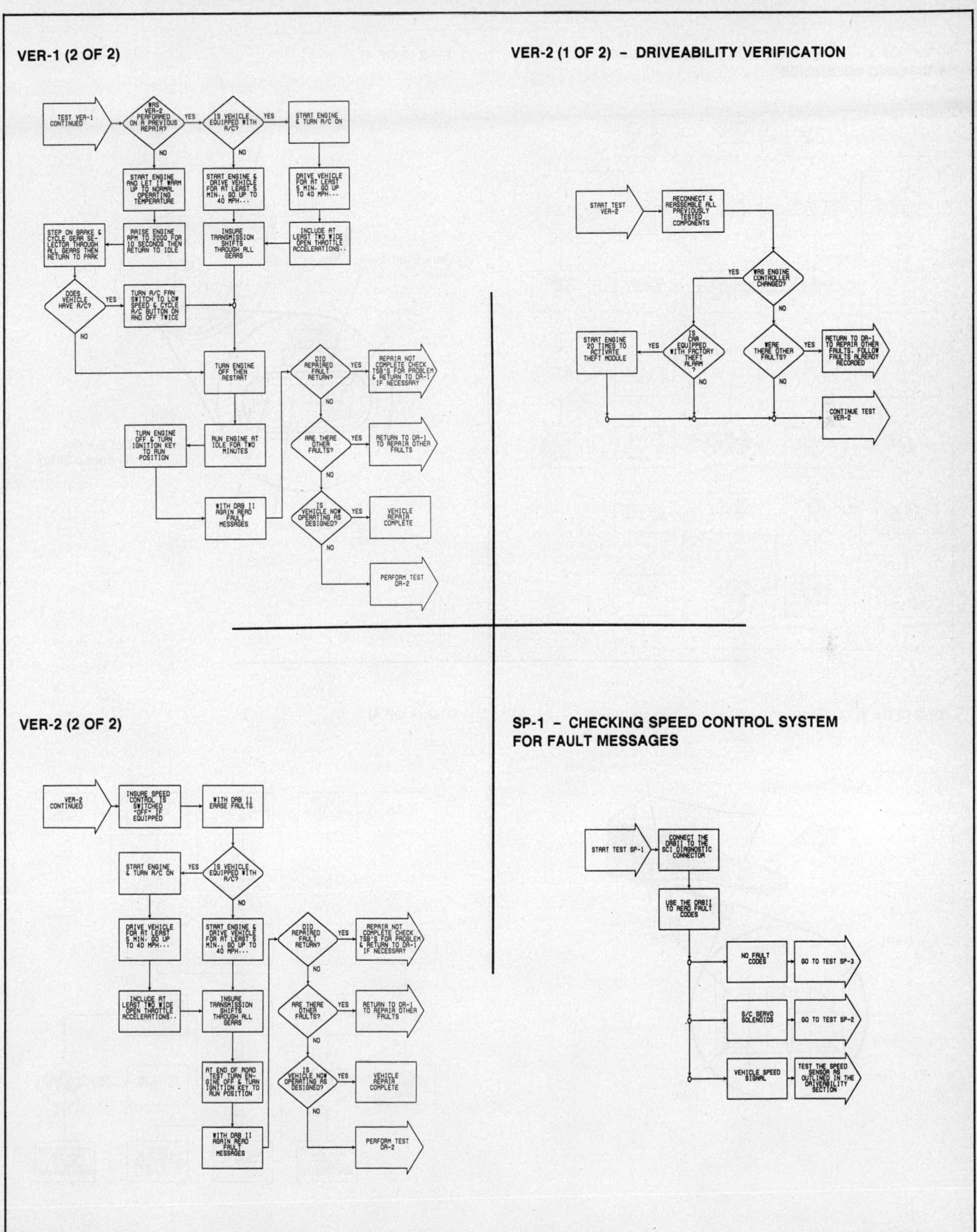

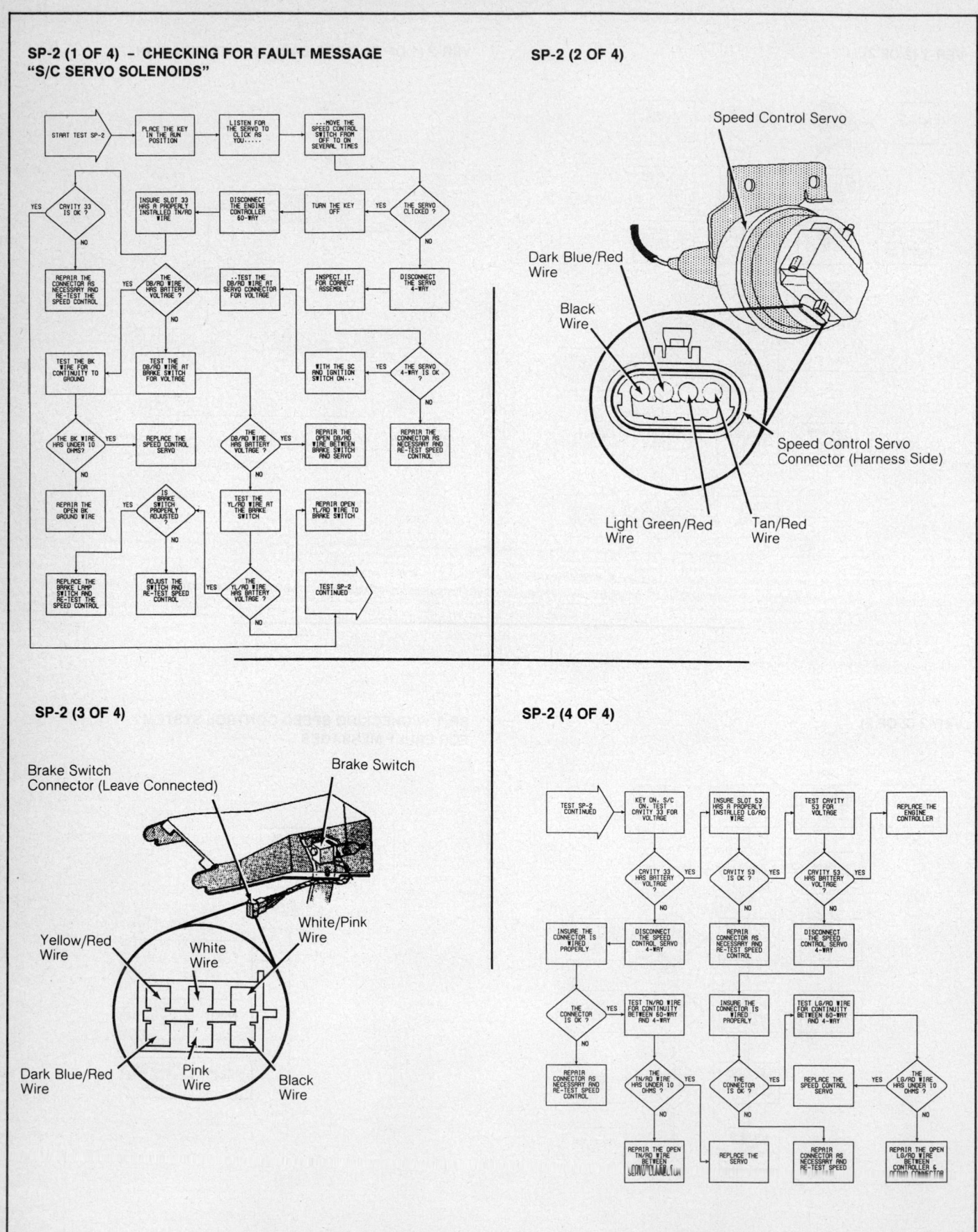

SP-2 (1 OF 4) – CHECKING FOR FAULT MESSAGE "S/C SERVO SOLENOIDS"

SP-2 (2 OF 4)

Speed Control Servo

Dark Blue/Red Wire

Black Wire

Light Green/Red Wire

Tan/Red Wire

Speed Control Servo Connector (Harness Side)

SP-2 (3 OF 4)

Brake Switch Connector (Leave Connected)

Brake Switch

Yellow/Red Wire

White Wire

White/Pink Wire

Dark Blue/Red Wire

Pink Wire

Black Wire

SP-2 (4 OF 4)

1989 COMPUTERIZED ENGINE CONTROLS
Chrysler Motors 3.0L MPFI (Cont.)

1a-163

SP-3 – TESTING SPEED CONTROL SWITCH

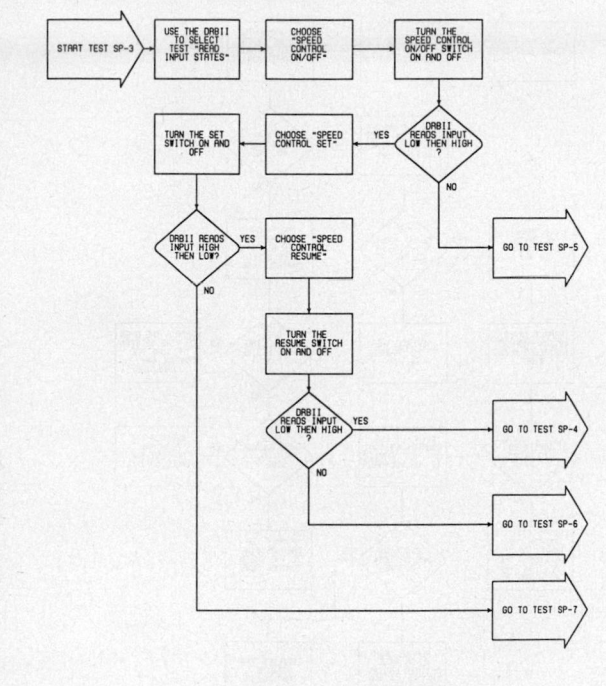

SP-4 (1 OF 4) – TESTING BRAKE SWITCH CIRCUIT

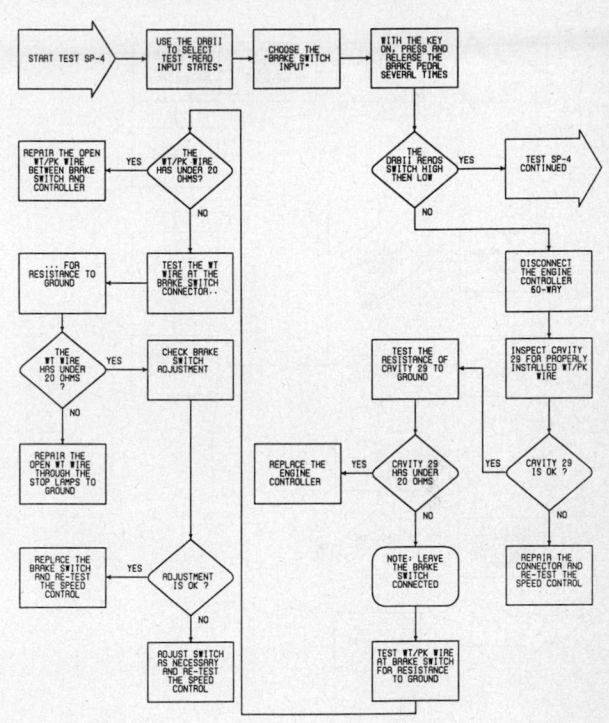

SP-4 (2 OF 4) – TESTING PARK/NEUTRAL INPUT

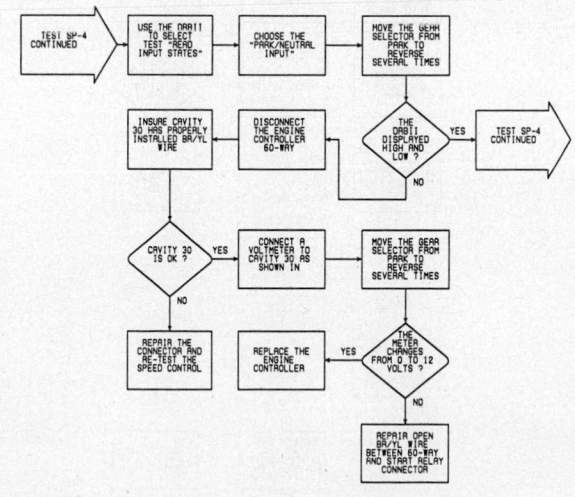

SP-4 (3 OF 4) – TESTING SERVO GROUND

1989 COMPUTERIZED ENGINE CONTROLS
Chrysler Motors 3.0L MPFI (Cont.)

SP-4 (4 OF 4) – SERVO ACTUATOR TEST

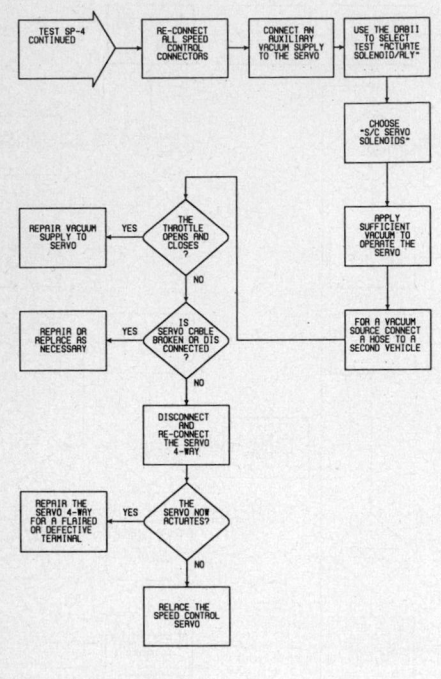

SP-5 (1 OF 2) – CHECK ON/OFF SWITCH & STALK FEED

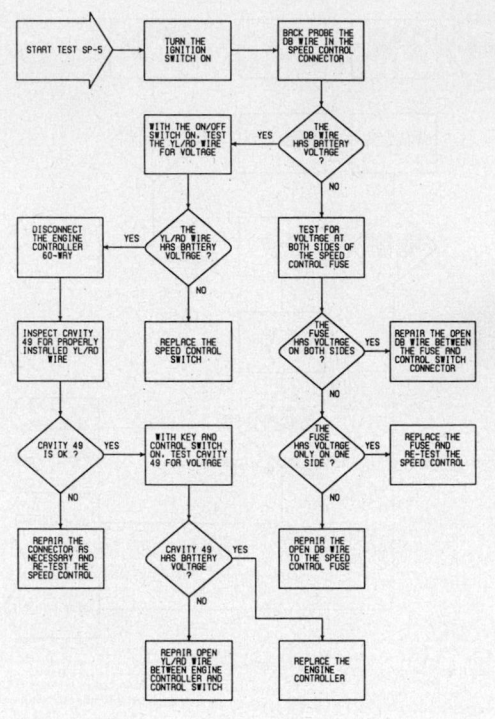

SP-5 (2 OF 2)

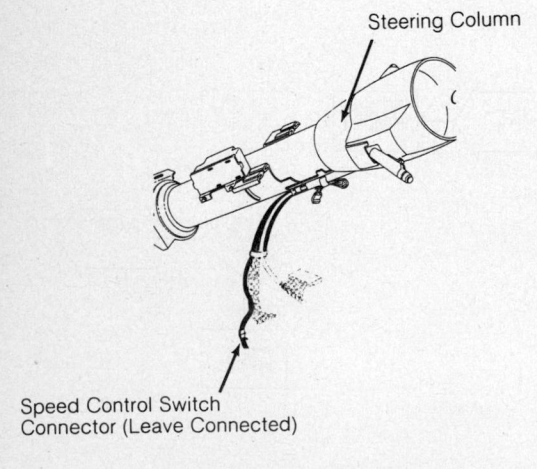

Steering Column

Speed Control Switch
Connector (Leave Connected)

SP-6 – TESTING "RESUME" SWITCH

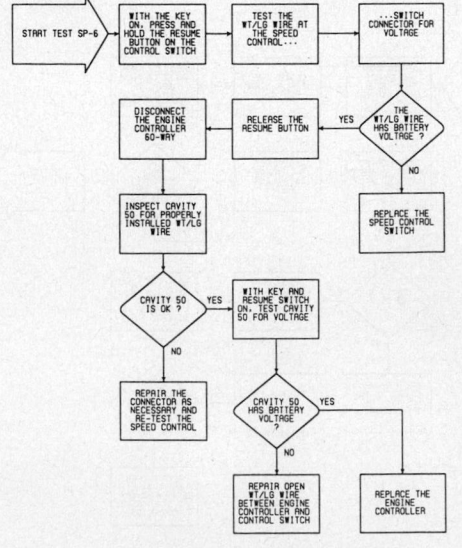

1989 COMPUTERIZED ENGINE CONTROLS
Chrysler Motors 3.0L MPFI (Cont.)

1a-165

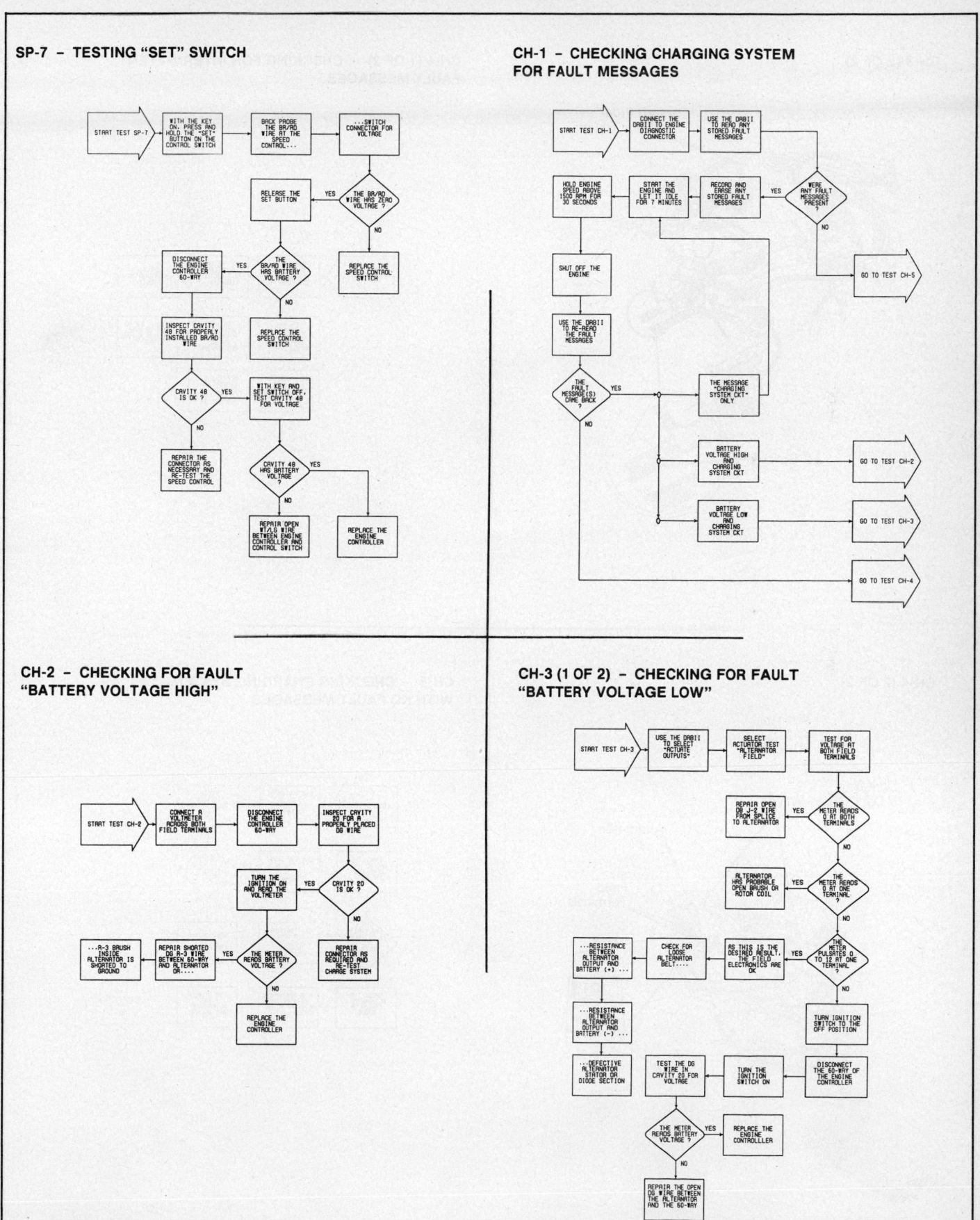

SP-7 – TESTING "SET" SWITCH

CH-1 – CHECKING CHARGING SYSTEM FOR FAULT MESSAGES

CH-2 – CHECKING FOR FAULT "BATTERY VOLTAGE HIGH"

CH-3 (1 OF 2) – CHECKING FOR FAULT "BATTERY VOLTAGE LOW"

1989 COMPUTERIZED ENGINE CONTROLS
Chrysler Motors 3.0L MPFI (Cont.)

CH-3 (2 OF 2)

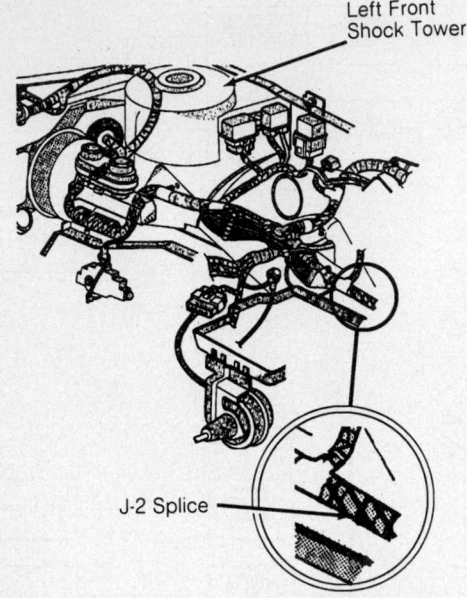

Left Front
Shock Tower

J-2 Splice

**CH-4 (1 OF 2) – CHECKING FOR INTERMITTENT
FAULT MESSAGES**

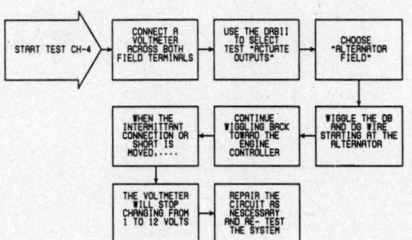

CH-4 (2 OF 2)

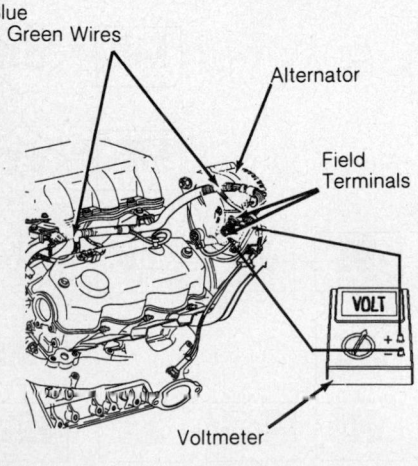

Dark Blue
& Dark Green Wires

Alternator

Field
Terminals

VOLT

Voltmeter

**CH-5 – CHECKING CHARGING SYSTEM
WITH NO FAULT MESSAGES**

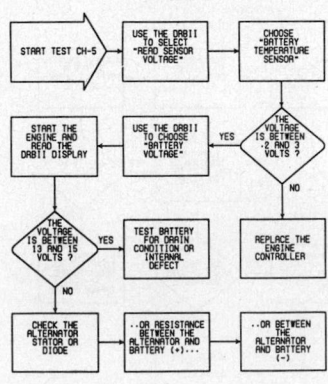

1989 Computerized Engine Controls
Chrysler Motors 3.0L MPFI (Cont.)

1a-167

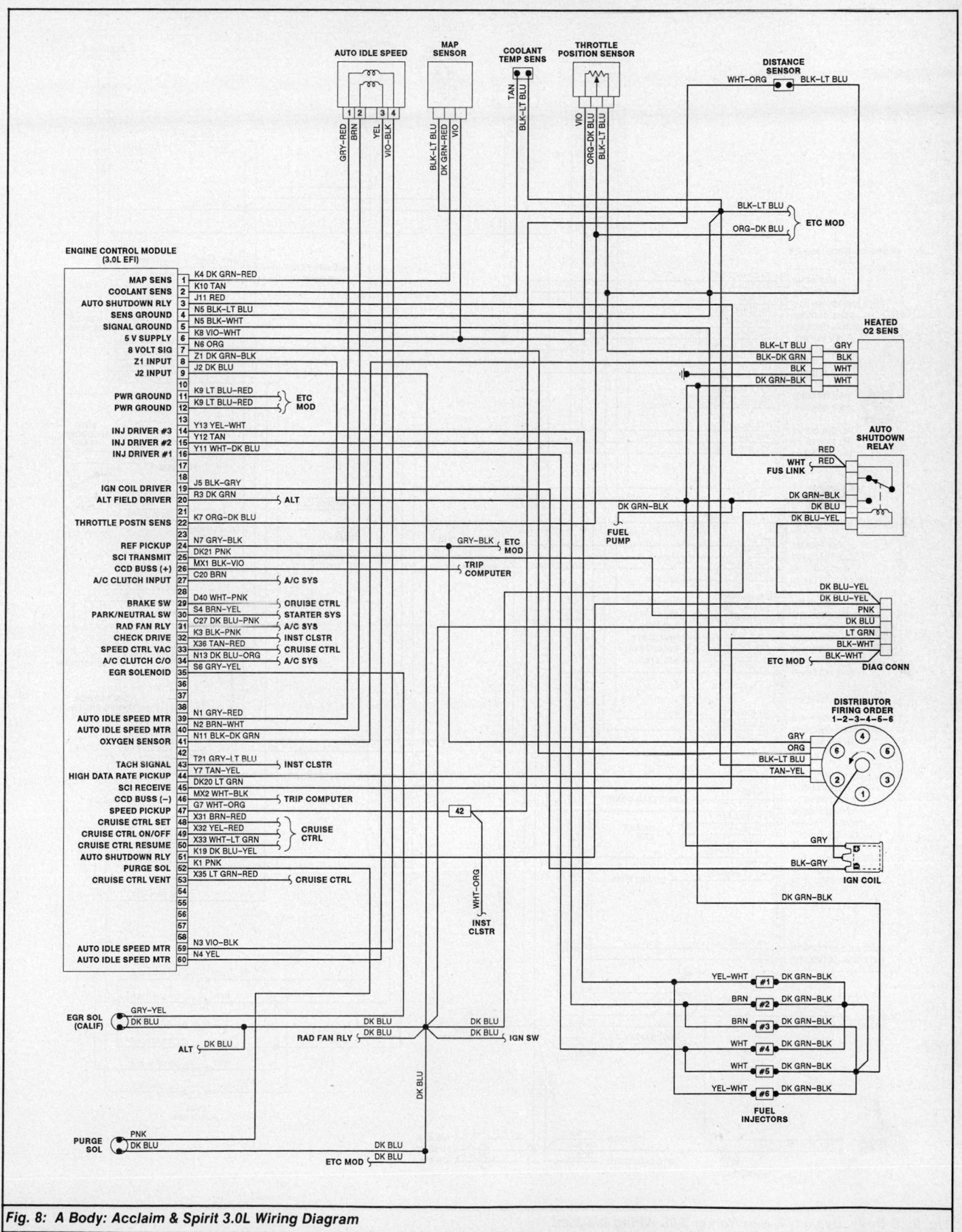

1989 Computerized ENGINE CONTROLS
Chrysler Motors 3.0L MPFI (Cont.)

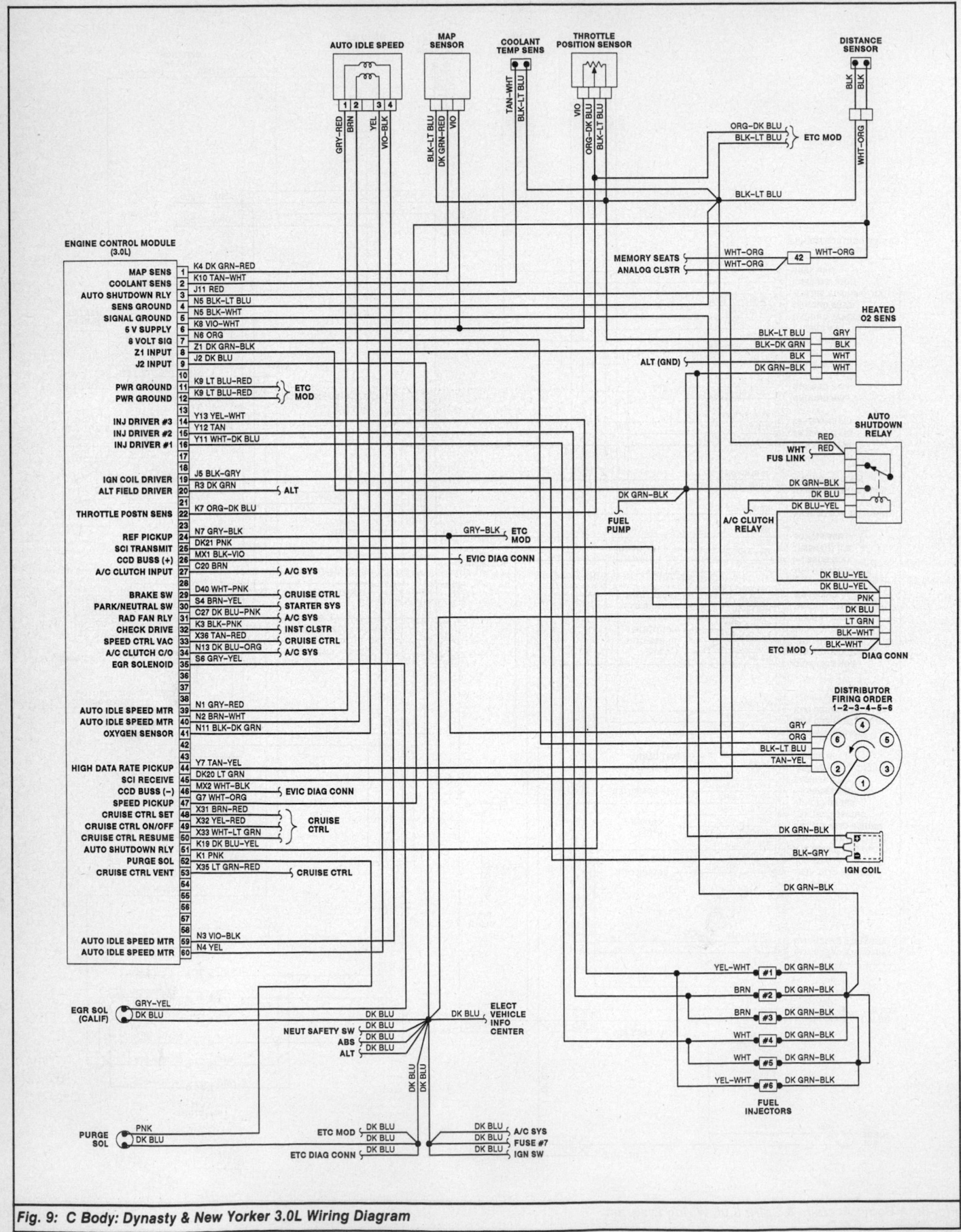

Fig. 9: C Body: Dynasty & New Yorker 3.0L Wiring Diagram

RWD Models

DESCRIPTION

The Electronic Fuel Control System (EFC) is used on all models. System consists of a Spark Control Computer (SCC), various engine sensors, a specially calibrated carburetor and a dual pick-up distributor. The purpose of the system is to maintain the ideal air/fuel ratio of 14.7:1 in almost all operating conditions.

SPARK CONTROL COMPUTER (SCC)

The SCC controls the entire ignition system. It is capable of igniting the fuel mixture according to different engine operating conditions during a run-drive period by delivering an infinite amount of variable electronic spark advance curves.

The SCC has a built-in microprocessor that continually receives input from different engine sensors to enable the computer to electronically retard or advance the ignition timing and adjust the air/fuel mixture to assure the most efficient fuel burn possible.

SENSORS

Engine control sensors supply the Spark Control Computer (SCC) with information needed to fire the spark plugs at the right time and change the air/fuel mixture. Spark advance provided by computer is determined by input factors from coolant temperature, engine RPM, and available manifold vacuum. Air/fuel mixture information comes from the oxygen sensor and carburetor idle stop switch.

Other sensors include, magnetic pick-up assembly, charge temperature sensor, vacuum transducer, distance/speed sensor, and detonation sensor.

FUEL CONTROL

Carburetors used include the Holley 6280 2-Barrel and the Rochester Quadrajet 4-Barrel used on police models only. Both models are equipped with an electronically-operated oxygen feedback solenoid. This solenoid meters the main fuel system of the carburetor and operates in parallel with the conventional fixed main metering jets. The computer controls the operation of the solenoid with electrical signals, in response to input from data sensors. *See Figs. 1 and 2.*

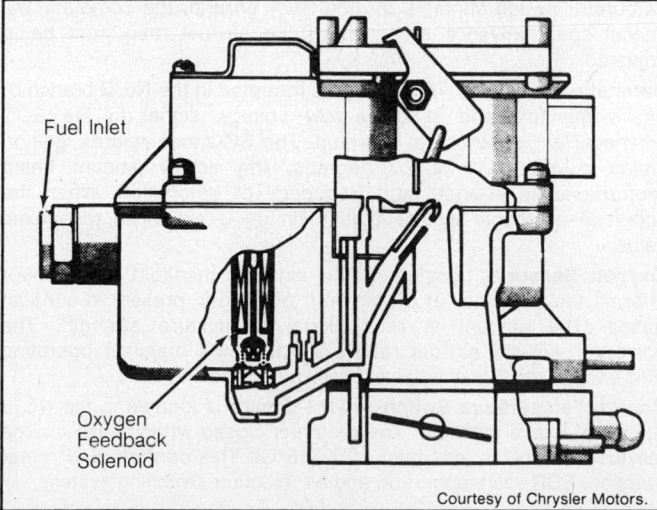

Fig. 1: Sectional View of Holley 6280 2-Bbl. Feedback Carburetor

When de-energized, the solenoid main metering orifice is fully uncovered, providing the richest mixture for any given airflow.

When the solenoid is energized by the computer, the solenoid main metering orifice is fully sealed. This solenoid position offers the leanest mixture within the carburetor for any given airflow.

Main system fuel is regulated between rich and lean mixture

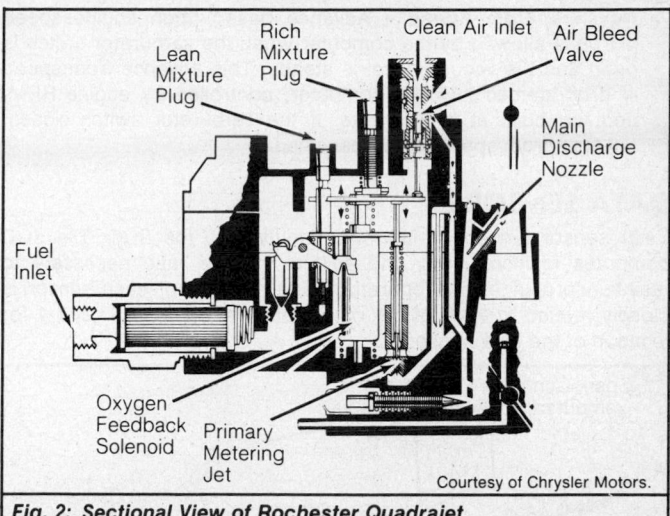

Fig. 2: Sectional View of Rochester Quadrajet 4-Bbl. Feedback Carburetor

conditions by controlling the amount of time that the solenoid is energized and de-energized. The computer controls the duration of time that solenoid is energized in comparison to total time of solenoid operation.

This duration of time is determined by engine operating conditions and/or oxygen sensor signals. In this manner, the ideal air/fuel ratio can be constantly maintained.

ELECTRONIC THROTTLE CONTROL

The Electronic Throttle Control system and 2 electric timers are incorporated within the SCC. A solenoid, mounted on the carburetor, is energized whenever the air conditioning, rear window defogger or electric timers are activated. The 2 timers operate when the throttle is closed, providing a 2-second time delay, or after engine is started.

SPARK CONTROL

Spark control allows the computer to determine the exact instant that ignition is required. The computer eliminates the need for a vacuum advance unit or centrifugal advance weights. Spark control operates in one of the following modes:

Start Mode (4-Bbl.) – During cranking, an electrical signal from the distributor "Start" pick-up coil is fed into the computer. This signal causes the computer to fire the spark plugs at a fixed amount of advance during engine cranking only. The amount of advance is determined by distributor position.

Run Mode (2-Bbl. & 4-Bbl.) – On 2-Bbl. models, the "Run" pick-up coil is the only pick-up coil used. This pick-up coil starts and runs the engine. The pick-up coil sends a reference signal to the computer. Timing is controlled by the computer, based upon information received by the data sensors. If this component fails, the vehicle will not run.

On 4-Bbl. models, once the engine starts, the "Run" pick-up coil sends a reference signal to the computer. Timing, however, is controlled by the computer, based upon information received by the data sensors. *See Figs. 3 and 4.*

Spark timing and dwell cannot be adjusted in the run mode. If the computer fails, the system will go into the start mode. This enables the vehicle to be driven in for repair; but performance and fuel economy will be poor. If the start mode fails, the engine will not start or run.

On all models, the amount of spark advance is determined by engine speed and engine vacuum. However, when it happens depends upon the following conditions:

- **Advance From Vacuum** – Advance based upon engine vacuum is allowed by the computer when the carburetor switch is open. The amount of advance is programmed into the computer and is proportionate to the amount of vacuum and engine RPM.

- **Advance From Speed** – Advance based upon engine speed (RPM) is allowed by the computer when the carburetor switch is open and the vacuum level is steady. This advance from speed is programmed into the computer, controlled by engine RPM, and will build at a slow rate. If the carburetor switch closes, advance from speed will be canceled.

DATA SENSORS

Each sensor furnishes electronic impulses to the SCC. The SCC computes ignition timing and air/fuel mixture ratio necessary to maintain proper engine operation. The function of each sensor is closely related to each of the other sensors. *See Figs. 3 and 4 for* location of the data sensors.

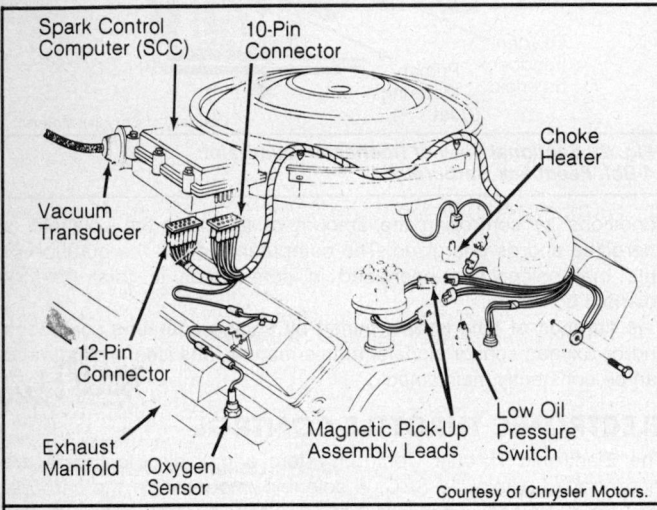

Fig. 3: *Location of Data Sensors (Rear View)*

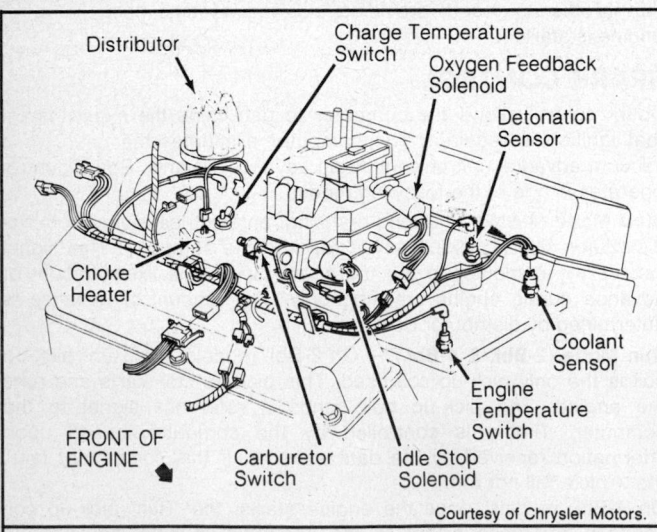

Fig. 4: *Location of Data Sensors (Front View)*

Magnetic Pick-Up Assembly – The magnetic pick-up assemblies are located inside the distributor. All 2-Bbl. models use one pick-up coil assembly, a run pick-up coil assembly. All models with 4-Bbl. carburetor use 2 pick-up coils, a start pick-up coil and a run pick-up coil. The dual pick-up coils operate as follows:

- **"Start" Pick-Up Coil (4-Bbl.)** – Supplies a signal to SCC which will cause the spark plugs to fire at a fixed amount of advance during cranking only. This coil is permanently positioned in distributor and the amount of advance will be determined by distributor position. *See Fig. 5.*
- **"Run" Pick-Up Coil (2-Bbl. & 4-Bbl.)** – On 2-Bbl. models, the "Run" pick-up coil is the only pick-up coil used. This pick-up coil starts and runs the engine. Timing is controlled by the computer,

based upon information received by the data sensors.
On 4-Bbl. models, once engine begins to run, the start pick-up coil signal is by-passed and the run pick-up coil supplies advance information to SCC. *See Fig. 5.* The SCC then modifies ignition timing advance to reflect engine operating conditions reported by the other sensors.

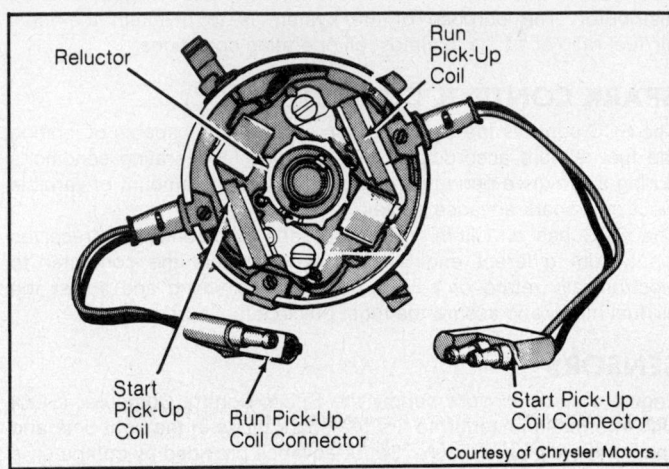

Fig. 5: *Location of Magnetic Pick-Up Assemblies (4-Bbl. Shown)*

Coolant Temperature Sensor/Switch – The coolant temperature sensor/switch is located in the intake manifold. It informs the SCC when the engine has reached normal operating temperature. It prevents any changes from being made until such temperature is reached, permitting proper adjustment of the air/fuel ratio. The coolant temperature sensor/switch also controls the amount of ignition timing advance or retard when the engine is cold.

Vacuum Transducer – This sensor is mounted on the computer and provides the computer with a signal indicating the amount of engine vacuum. Engine vacuum is used by the computer to determine how much to advance or retard ignition timing and to change air/fuel mixture.

Carburetor Switch – Located on the end of idle stop, the carburetor switch informs the computer when the engine is at idle. When carburetor switch contacts throttle lever ground, the computer will cancel spark advance and prevent the air/fuel ratio from being adjusted.

Detonation Sensor – This sensor is mounted in the No. 2 branch of intake manifold and sends a low voltage signal to the SCC whenever engine knock is detected. The SCC then retards ignition timing a maximum of 20 degrees, the actual amount being proportional to strength and frequency of detonation. When the condition no longer exists, ignition timing is advanced to original value.

Oxygen Sensor – Located in the exhaust manifold, this sensor informs the computer of the amount of oxygen present in exhaust gases. The amount is proportional to mixture strength. The computer adjusts air/fuel ratio so that it will maintain operating efficiency of the 3-way catalyst system and the engine.

Charge Temperature Switch – This sensor is located in the No. 8 runner of intake manifold. The switch is closed when intake charge (air/fuel mixture) is less than 60°F (16°C). This controls EGR timer function, EGR valve operation and air injection switching system.

SPARK CONTROL COMPUTER

The computer is mounted on the air cleaner housing. It consists of a printed circuit board, which simultaneously receives signals from all data sensors and analyzes these signals to determine spark advance and air/fuel mixture. *See Fig. 6.* Incorporated within the computer are the electronics for the throttle control, EGR and air switching systems. After determining spark advance, the computer will operate the engine in one of the following modes:

Open Loop Mode – During cold engine operation, the air/fuel ratio is controlled by information programmed into the computer by the manufacturer. Until normal operating temperature is reached, the air/fuel mixture will be fixed at a rich level to allow proper engine warm-up. During this mode of operation, air from the air pump is injected "upstream" in the exhaust manifold to assist in heating-up the oxygen sensor.

Closed Loop Mode – Once normal engine operating temperature is achieved, the air/fuel ratio is controlled by the computer based upon information received from the oxygen sensor. During this mode of operation, air from the air pump is injected "downstream" into the catalytic converter.

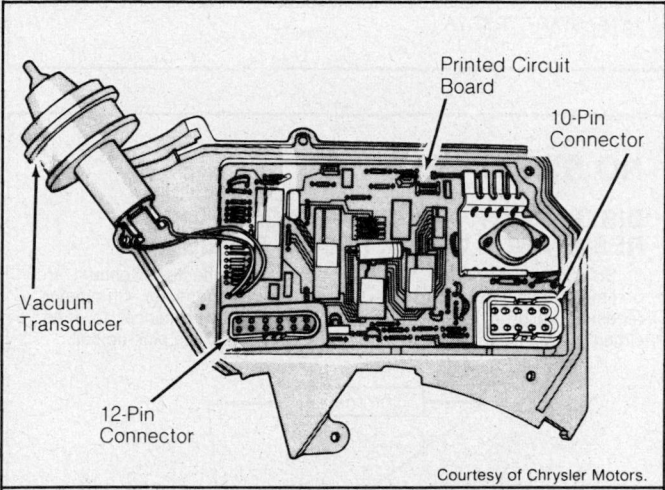

Courtesy of Chrysler Motors.

Fig. 6: Internal View of Spark Control Computer

EXHAUST GAS RECIRCULATION (EGR)

The electronic EGR system is incorporated within the SCC. This system prevents EGR flow until engine has reached normal operating temperature (after a predetermined length of time).

ELECTRONIC AIR SWITCHING

The electronic air switching system is incorporated within the SCC. This system directs the flow of air from the air pump either "upstream" (cold engine) or "downstream" after engine has reached operating temperature and a specified period of time has elapsed.

ADJUSTMENTS

CARBURETOR SWITCH

Carburetor switch is located on the end of the idle stop. It cancels spark advance and changes air/fuel ratio. Ensure carburetor switch contacts throttle lever ground when throttle is in closed or idle position only.

REMOVAL & INSTALLATION

SPARK CONTROL COMPUTER

NOTE: Do not remove grease from either harness connectors or connector cavities in computer. The grease is used to prevent moisture from corroding the terminals. If there is not at least 1/8" of grease on bottom of computer connector cavities, apply a liberal amount of Mopar Multipurpose Grease (2932524) over entire end of plug before reinstalling.

Removal & Installation – Disconnect negative battery terminal. Disconnect 10-wire and 12-wire connectors from computer. Remove vacuum hose from vacuum transducer. Remove mounting screws from inside air cleaner and remove computer. To install, reverse removal procedure.

NOTE: Computer is not serviceable. Do not attempt to take it apart for any reason. Also, if the vacuum transducer becomes defective, entire computer must be replaced.

CARBURETOR SWITCH

Removal & Installation – Remove bracket and switch assembly from carburetor. Disconnect electrical connector. To install, reverse removal procedure and adjust as necessary.

OXYGEN FEEDBACK SOLENOID

Removal & Installation – Disconnect electrical connector. Remove retaining screw, oxygen feedback solenoid and gasket. To install, reverse removal procedure.

OXYGEN SENSOR

Removal & Installation – Disconnect battery cable. Without pulling on wire, remove electrical lead at sensor. Using O₂ Sensor Socket (C-4589), remove sensor. To install, coat threads of new sensor with nickel-based anti-seize compound. Do not use graphite or other compounds. Install sensor and tighten to 20 ft. lbs. (27 N.m). Connect electrical connector and battery cable.

TESTING

A malfunction in the EFC system may result in engine surge, hesitation, rough idle and/or poor fuel economy. Before performing any tests, check all vacuum hoses and electrical wiring for proper routing and connections and check for exhaust and intake manifold leaks. If these are in order, proceed with testing.

NO START TEST 1

CHECKING FOR SPARK AT PLUG WIRES

1) Disconnect any spark plug wire and insert spark tester or an insulated screwdriver into terminal. If using screwdriver, hold screwdriver shaft about 1/4" from ground. Have an assistant crank engine.

2) There should be a good spark between screwdriver and ground. If there is spark, proceed to NO START TEST 2. If no spark, proceed to NO START TEST 5.

NO START TEST 2

CHECKING FOR FUEL IN CARBURETOR

1) Remove air cleaner cover. Open throttle several times by hand. Look for fuel spray from accelerator pump nozzle in carburetor throat. There should be fuel spraying from the accelerator pump nozzle while opening throttle.

2) If fuel spray tests okay, proceed to NO START TEST 3. If there is no fuel spray, proceed to NO START TEST 9.

NO START TEST 3

CHECKING FOR FUEL FOULED SPARK PLUGS

Remove spark plugs. Inspect spark plug tips for wet fuel. Spark plugs should be dry. If spark plugs are dry, proceed to NO START TEST 4. If spark plugs are wet with fuel, clean and reinstall.

NO START TEST 4

ENGINE TIMING CHECK

1) Connect timing light to engine. Have an assistant crank engine while you watch timing marks. Timing should be between 0-16 degrees BTDC. If timing is okay, check valve timing and compression.

2) If timing is not okay, set timing to 10 degrees BTDC while cranking. Engine should start. If engine starts, set timing to specification. If engine does not start, check valve timing and compression.

NO START TEST 5

IGNITION COIL SPARK CHECK

1) Disconnect secondary coil wire from distributor cap. Hold coil wire 1/4" from ground. Crank engine. There should be spark between coil wire and ground.

2) If there is spark, check for problem in distributor cap, rotor or secondary wires. Repair or replace as necessary. If no spark, check coil wire resistance. Resistance should be 250-600 ohms per INCH or 3000-7500 ohms per foot. If resistance is within specifications, proceed to NO START TEST 6. If resistance exceeds specifications, replace coil wire.

NO START TEST 6

IGNITION COIL PRIMARY WINDINGS RESISTANCE CHECK

1) Ensure ignition is off. Connect an ohmmeter between ignition coil positive and negative terminals. Ohmmeter reading should be 1-2 ohms. If resistance is not within specifications, replace ignition coil.

2) If resistance is within specifications, disconnect coil secondary wire from coil. Connect ohmmeter to the coil negative terminal and the secondary terminal. Ohmmeter reading should be 9400-11,700 ohms.

3) If resistance is not within specifications, replace ignition coil. If resistance is okay, check coil with a load test. If coil is okay, proceed to NO START TEST 7A.

NO START TEST 7A

DISTRIBUTOR RUN PICK-UP COIL RESISTANCE CHECK (2-BBL. & 4-BBL.)

1) Disconnect distributor "Run" pick-up coil connector. Connect an ohmmeter between terminals of the pick-up coil connector. Ohmmeter reading should be 150-900 ohms. If there is zero resistance, an open circuit or resistance is not within specifications, replace pick-up coil.

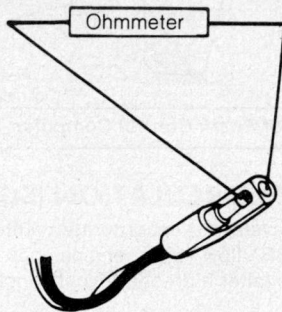

Ohmmeter

2) If resistance is okay, reconnect distributor "Run" pick-up coil connector. Disconnect the computer 10-pin connector. Connect an ohmmeter between 10-pin connector cavities No. 5 and 9. Ohmmeter reading should be 150-900 ohms.

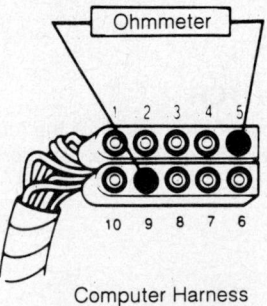

Computer Harness
10-Pin Connector

3) If there is zero resistance, open circuit or not within specifications, replace pick-up coil. If resistance is okay, check distributor "Run" pick-up coil air gap. If okay, proceed to NO START TEST 7B.

NO START TEST 7B

DISTRIBUTOR START PICK-UP COIL RESISTANCE CHECK (4-BBL. ONLY)

1) Disconnect distributor start pick-up coil connector (large connector). Connect an ohmmeter between pick-up coil connector terminals. Ohmmeter reading should be 150-900 ohms.

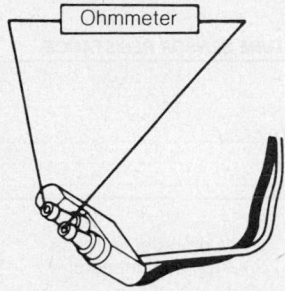

Ohmmeter

2) If there is zero resistance, open circuit or resistance not within specifications, replace pick-up coil. If resistance is okay, reconnect distributor start pick-up coil connector. Disconnect the computer 10-pin connector. Connect ohmmeter between 10-pin connector cavities No. 3 and 5.

3) Ohmmeter reading should be 150-900 ohms. If there is zero resistance, an open circuit or resistance not within specifications, replace pick-up coil. If resistance is okay, check distributor pick-up coil air gap. If okay, proceed to NO START TEST 8.

NO START TEST 8

IGNITION SWITCH VOLTAGE SUPPLY TO COMPUTER CHECK

1) Turn ignition off. Disconnect computer 10-pin connector. Connect a voltmeter between 10-pin connector terminal No. 2 and ground. Turn ignition switch to the "RUN" position. Voltage reading should be within one volt of battery voltage.

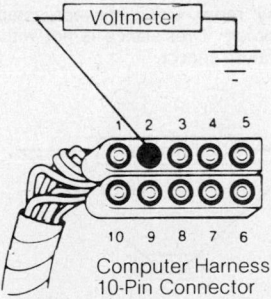

Voltmeter

Computer Harness
10-Pin Connector

2) If voltage is not as specified, repair open circuit in wire from ignition switch to cavity No. 2. If voltage is okay, turn ignition off. Connect ohmmeter to 10-pin connector cavity No. 10 and ground. Ohmmeter should show continuity.

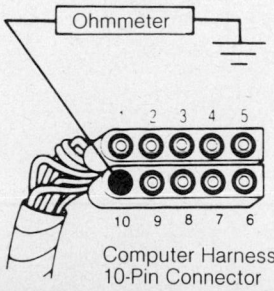

Ohmmeter

Computer Harness
10-Pin Connector

NO START TEST 8 (Cont.)

3) If no continuity, repair open circuit. If there is continuity, check terminals No. 2 and 10 to ensure they are not spread apart causing a poor connection. If connections are okay, replace computer.

NO START TEST 9

FUEL PUMP PRESSURE CHECK

1) Connect fuel pump pressure gauge to fuel line at carburetor. Plug fuel return line at fuel filter. Crank engine for at least 10 seconds. Fuel pump pressure should be at least 2-6 psi.

2) If fuel pump pressure is okay, replace fuel filter. If fuel pressure is not within specifications, connect a vacuum gauge to fuel pump inlet line. With fuel line disconnected from carburetor, crank engine for at least 10 seconds. Vacuum gauge should read a minimum of 10 in. Hg vacuum.

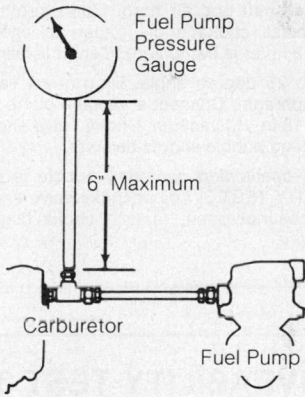

Fuel Pump
Pressure
Gauge

6" Maximum

Carburetor

Fuel Pump

3) If vacuum is not within specifications, replace fuel pump. If vacuum is okay, check for restricted or plugged fuel lines, fuel tank vent or in-tank filter.

COLD DRIVEABILITY TEST 1

CHOKE POSITION CHECK

1) Depress gas pedal to set choke. Remove air cleaner cover. Check choke plate and fast idle cam position. Choke plate should be fully closed and fast idle cam set to highest step.

2) If choke plate is not fully closed or cam not in position, check choke plate for binding or sticking. Repair choke plate or linkage as necessary. If choke plate position and cam are okay, proceed to COLD DRIVEABILITY TEST 2A (2-BBL.) or COLD DRIVEBILITY TEST 2B (4-BBL.).

COLD DRIVEABILITY TEST 2A

CHOKE VACUUM KICK CHECK (2-BBL.)

1) Remove air cleaner assembly. Position fast idle screw on highest step of fast idle cam. Remove vacuum hose from choke vacuum kick diaphragm. Connect a vacuum pump and apply 15 in. Hg vacuum to the diaphragm. Measure clearance between top of choke plate and air horn.

2) Vacuum should remain at 15 in. Hg and choke plate should be set to .130". If vacuum does not remain at 15 in. Hg, replace vacuum kick diaphragm. Adjust vacuum kick as necessary. If vacuum remains constant, proceed to COLD DRIVEABILITY TEST 3.

COLD DRIVEABILITY TEST 2B

CHOKE VALVE ANGLE CHECK (4-BBL.)

1) Remove air cleaner assembly. Attach a rubber band between the intermediate choke shaft and air horn. Open throttle to allow choke valve to close. Install choke angle gauge to choke plate. Rotate degree scale until pointer is set to zero. Center leveling bubble.

2) Rotate scale to 25 degree angle. Disconnect vacuum hose from choke vacuum diaphragm. Connect a vacuum pump to choke vacuum diaphragm. Apply 18 in. Hg vacuum. Choke valve should open and the angle gauge centering bubble should be level.

3) If choke valve opens and centering bubble is level, proceed to COLD DRIVEABILITY TEST 3. Adjust choke valve angle as necessary. If choke valve does not open, replace choke diaphragm or repair linkage as necessary.

COLD DRIVEABILITY TEST 3

AIR CLEANER HEATED AIR INTAKE SYSTEM

1) Disconnect air duct from air cleaner snorkel. Disconnect vacuum supply hose to heated air intake system air temperature sensor. Connect vacuum pump to the air temperature sensor and apply 15 in. Hg vacuum to the sensor. Vacuum should build up to 15 in. Hg and close the heated air door when air temperature is below 70°F (21°C). Vacuum should bleed down slowly, opening the heated air door.

NOTE: Models equipped with 2-Bbl. carburetors use a vacuum delay valve at the heated air door vacuum diaphragm. This delays opening of the door when vacuum bleeds off.

2) If vacuum builds up, but heated air door does not close, repair or replace door as necessary. If vacuum does not build up or bleed down, replace the air temperature sensor. If vacuum builds up and bleeds down, but heated air door does not open, repair or replace door as necessary.

3) If vacuum builds up, closes the heated air door and then bleeds down, proceed to COLD DRIVEABILITY TEST 4 on 2-Bbl. models. On 4-Bbl. models, remove vacuum hose from vapor containment door diaphragm. Connect a vacuum pump to the diaphragm and apply 15 in. Hg vacuum. Vacuum should hold and door should be open.

4) If vacuum does not hold or door is not open, repair or replace as necessary. If vacuum holds and door is open, reconnect hose to vapor containment door diaphragm. Remove vacuum supply hose from vapor containment door vacuum delay valve. Connect vacuum pump to delay valve and apply 15 in. Hg vacuum. Release vacuum.

5) Vapor containment door should open when vacuum is applied and close within 40 seconds after vacuum is released. If door does not close or open, replace vacuum delay valve. If door closes and opens okay, proceed to COLD DRIVEABILITY TEST 4.

COLD DRIVEABILITY TEST 4

CHARGE TEMPERATURE SENSOR CIRCUIT CHECK

1) Disconnect both connectors from the computer. Connect an ohmmeter between 10-pin connector cavity No. 9 and 12-pin connector cavity No. 10. Ohmmeter reading should be as shown in CHARGE TEMPERATURE SENSOR RESISTANCE table.

CHARGE TEMPERATURE SENSOR RESISTANCE

Temperature °F (°C)	Ohms
-40 to 20 (-40 to -7)	382,000-22,000
50-100 (10-38)	36,000-3300
140-245 (60-118)	3900-176

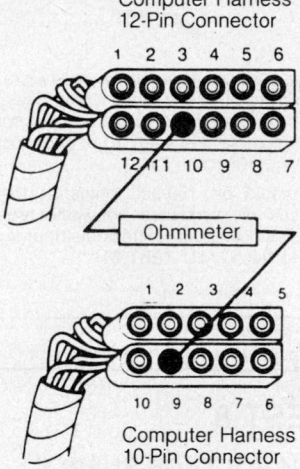

Computer Harness 12-Pin Connector

Ohmmeter

Computer Harness 10-Pin Connector

2) If resistance checks okay, proceed to COLD DRIVEABILITY TEST 5. If resistance is not within specifications, disconnect charge temperature sensor connector. Connect an ohmmeter between charge temperature sensor terminals. Resistance should be as shown in CHARGE TEMPERATURE SENSOR RESISTANCE table.

3) If resistance is okay, repair wiring between computer and sensor for a short or open circuit. If resistance is not within specifications, replace charge temperature sensor.

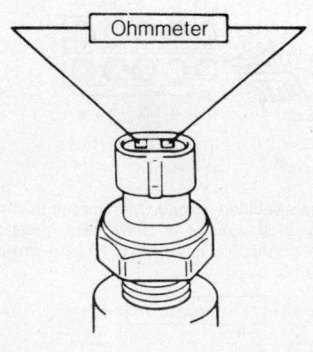

Ohmmeter

COLD DRIVEABILITY TEST 5

CHOKE PLATE POSITION WITH ENGINE RUNNING CHECK

1) Remove air cleaner lid. Set choke. Start engine and observe choke plate position. Choke plate should open part way. If choke plate is not opening properly, check vacuum supply to choke vacuum kick. If choke plate opened properly, connect a voltmeter between the choke heater wire at choke control switch and ground.

2) If air temperature is less than 55°F (13°C), voltage reading should be 5-9 volts. If air temperature is greater than 80°F (27°C), voltage reading should be within one volt of battery voltage. If voltage is not within specification, go to step **5)**. On 2-Bbl. models, if voltage reading is within specifications, turn ignition off. Disconnect wire from choke control that goes to electric choke heater.

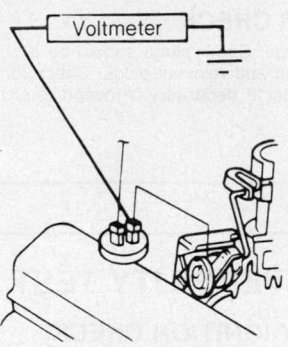

3) Connect an ohmmeter between choke heater wire and choke heating element retaining screw. Reading should be 4-12 ohms. If resistance is not within specification, replace choke heating element. If resistance is okay, proceed to COLD DRIVEABILITY TEST 6.

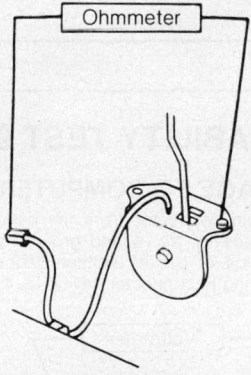

4) On 4-Bbl. models, if voltage reading is okay, connect voltmeter to choke heating element harness connector and ground. There should be voltage present. If there is voltage at heater, proceed to COLD DRIVEABILITY TEST 6. If voltage reading is not okay, repair choke control switch wiring for an open circuit.

COLD DRIVEABILITY TEST 5 (Cont.)

5) If voltage reading in step **2)** was not as specified, connect voltmeter to choke control switch ignition feed wire and ground. Voltage reading should be within one volt of battery voltage. If voltage reading is okay, replace choke control switch.

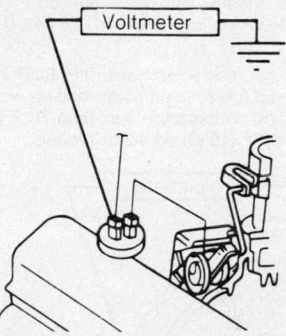

6) If voltage is not within specification, turn ignition off. Disconnect oil pressure switch connector. Connect voltmeter to engine harness connector at oil pressure switch terminal "C" and ground. Turn ignition switch to the "RUN" position. Voltage should be within one volt of battery voltage.

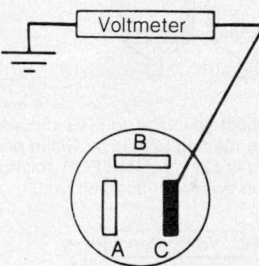

7) If voltage is not within specification, repair harness to ignition switch for an open circuit. If voltage is within specification, turn ignition off. Disconnect ignition feed wire from choke control switch. Connect an ohmmeter between engine harness connector at the oil pressure switch terminal "A" and choke control switch wire.

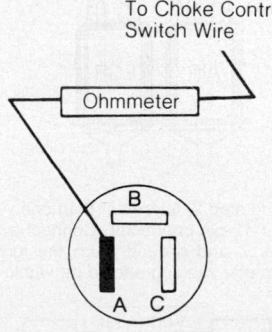

8) Ohmmeter should show continuity. If there is continuity, replace oil pressure switch. If no continuity, repair harness for an open circuit.

COLD DRIVEABILITY TEST 6

EGR SYSTEM CHECK

1) Disconnect vacuum hose from EGR valve. Connect vacuum gauge to the vacuum hose. Start engine. Slowly increase engine speed. Vacuum reading should be zero with the engine temperature less than 70°F (21°C) on 2-Bbl. models and less than 50°F (10°C) on 4-Bbl. models. If there is NO vacuum, proceed to COLD DRIVEABILITY TEST 7.

2) If there is vacuum, connect voltmeter to the EGR vacuum solenoid (Gray wire) and ground. Observe voltmeter reading. Voltage should be 0-1 volts with the engine temperature less than 70°F (21°C) on 2-Bbl. models and less than 50°F (10°C) on 4-Bbl. models.

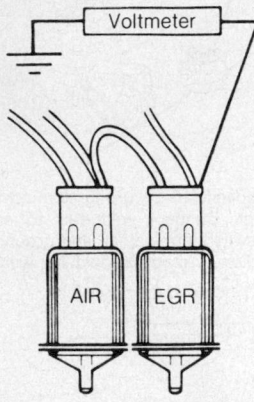

3) If voltage is okay, connect voltmeter to EGR vacuum solenoid (Blue wire) and ground. Voltage reading should be within one volt of battery voltage. If voltage reading is okay, replace EGR solenoid. If zero volts, repair wiring to the ignition switch for an open circuit.

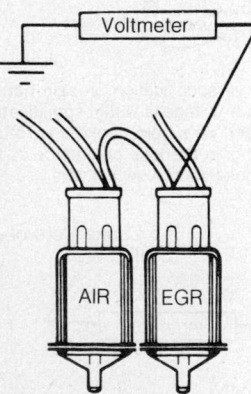

4) If voltage reading in step **2)** is greater than one volt, turn ignition off. Disconnect computer 12-pin connector. Connect a voltmeter to 12-pin connector cavity No. 7 and ground. Turn the ignition switch to the "RUN" position. Voltmeter reading should be within one volt of battery voltage.

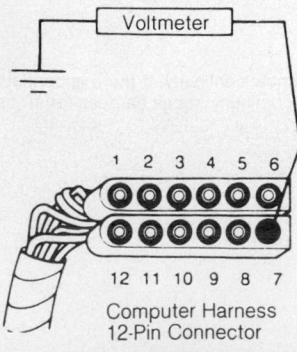

Computer Harness
12-Pin Connector

COLD DRIVEABILITY TEST 6 (Cont.)

5) If voltage is within specifications, check terminal in 12-pin connector cavity No. 7 to ensure it is not spread apart causing a poor connection. If connections are okay, replace computer. If there is zero volts, repair wiring to cavity No. 7 for an open circuit to the EGR vacuum solenoid.

COLD DRIVEABILITY TEST 7

SPARK PLUG CHECK

Remove spark plugs. Spark plugs should be dry. If spark plugs are wet with fuel, clean and reinstall plugs. Check for fuel in crankcase. Change oil and filter if necessary. Proceed to COLD DRIVEABILITY TEST 8.

COLD DRIVEABILITY TEST 8

SECONDARY IGNITION CHECK

Turn all lights and accessories off. Connect a suitable engine analyzer to the engine. Start engine. Check secondary ignition pattern. Check ignition coil output. Open circuit secondary ignition voltage should be at least 25,000 volts. If scope pattern is okay, proceed to COLD DRIVEABILITY TEST 9. If scope pattern is not okay, repair secondary ignition as necessary.

COLD DRIVEABILITY TEST 9

BATTERY VOLTAGE TO COMPUTER CHECK

1) Disconnect the 12-pin connector from the computer. Connect a voltmeter to connector cavity No. 4 and ground. Voltmeter reading should be within one volt of battery voltage. If there is zero volts, repair open circuit in wiring to connector cavity No. 4.

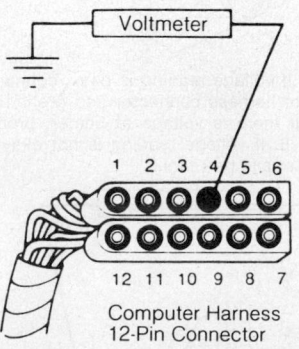

Computer Harness
12-Pin Connector

2) If voltage is okay, check terminal in connector cavity No. 4 to ensure it is not spread apart causing a poor connection. Connect a voltmeter to oxygen solenoid connector (Green wire) and ground. Connect a tachometer and start engine. Voltage reading should be a steady 7-14 volts.

COLD DRIVEABILITY TEST 9 (Cont.)

3) If voltage reading is greater than zero volts, but less than 7 volts, replace the computer. If voltage is 0-1 volt, turn the ignition off. Disconnect the computer 12-pin connector. Turn the ignition switch to the "RUN" position. Voltage reading should be within one volt of battery voltage.

4) If voltage is okay, replace the computer. If there is still zero volts, connect a voltmeter to the O_2 solenoid connector Blue or Tan wire and ground. Voltmeter reading should be within one volt of battery voltage. If voltage is okay, replace the O_2 solenoid. If voltage is still zero, repair Blue or Tan wire for an open circuit to the ignition switch.

5) If voltage in step **2)** is okay, ground O_2 solenoid (Green wire) using a jumper lead. Engine speed should drop. If engine speed does not drop, replace O_2 solenoid. If engine speed drops, proceed to COLD DRIVEABILITY TEST 10.

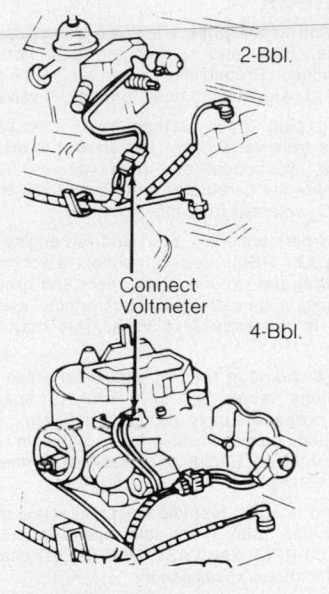

2-Bbl.

Connect
Voltmeter

4-Bbl.

COLD DRIVEABILITY TEST 10

BOWL VENT VALVE CHECK
1) Disconnect bowl vent hose from the vapor canister. Blow lightly into hose. Air should flow through hose. If air does not flow through the hose, check for a restricted/plugged hose or repair bowl vent.

Bowl Vent Hose

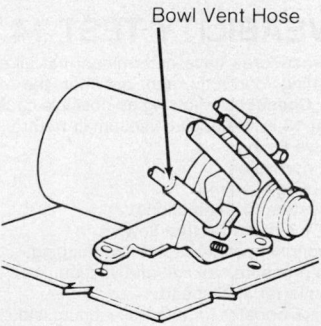

COLD DRIVEABILITY TEST 10 (Cont.)

2) If airflow is okay, start engine. Blow lightly into hose. Air should not flow through hose. If air flows through hose, repair bowl vent valve. If air does not flow through hose, proceed to COLD DRIVEABILITY TEST 11 (4-Bbl. models) or COLD DRIVEABILITY TEST 12 (2-Bbl. models).

NOTE: Models equipped with 2-Bbl. carburetors use an electric valve. Models equipped with 4-Bbl. carburetors use an external valve that closes with air pump pressure.

COLD DRIVEABILITY TEST 11

START-TO-RUN PICK-UP COIL
TRANSFER CIRCUIT CHECK (4-BBL. ONLY)
1) Start and run engine until normal operating temperature is reached. Raise engine speed to 1100 RPM. Disconnect "Start" pick-up coil connector at the distributor (larger connector). Engine should stay running. If engine stays running, proceed to COLD DRIVEABILITY TEST 12.

Start Pick-Up
Connector

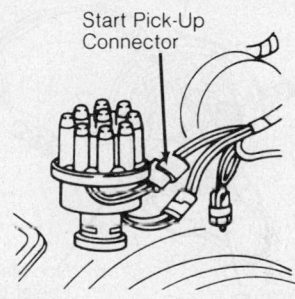

2) If engine stalls, disconnect the "Run" pick-up coil. Connect an ohmmeter between the connector terminals. Ohmmeter reading should be 150-900 ohms. If resistance is within specifications, reconnect the distributor pick-up coil connector. Disconnect the computer 10-pin connector.

Ohmmeter

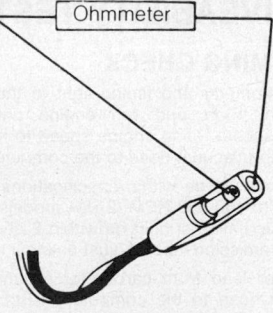

3) Connect an ohmmeter between 10-pin connector cavities No. 5 and 9. Ohmmeter reading should be 150-900 ohms. If resistance is okay, remove distributor cap. Measure "Run" pick-up coil air gap. Air gap should be .012" (.3 mm). Adjust air gap as necessary.

COLD DRIVEABILITY TEST 11 (Cont.)

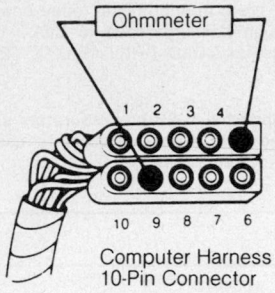

Computer Harness
10-Pin Connector

4) If air gap is okay, check terminals in cavities No. 5 and 9 to ensure they are not spread apart causing a poor connection. If connections are okay, replace computer. If resistance in step **2)** is not to specifications, replace the "Run" pick-up coil.

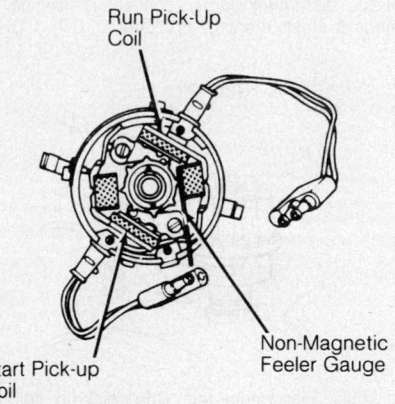

Run Pick-Up Coil

Non-Magnetic Feeler Gauge

Start Pick-up Coil

COLD DRIVEABILITY TEST 12

IGNITION TIMING CHECK

1) Connect a tachometer and timing light to the engine. Ground the carburetor switch. Start and run engine until normal operating temperature is reached. Raise engine speed to more than 1100 RPM. Disconnect and plug vacuum hose to the computer (2-Bbl. models).

2) Engine speed should be within specifications when setting timing. Adjust idle speed to 450-650 RPM (2-Bbl. models) or 550-750 RPM (4-Bbl. models). Basic timing should be within 2 degrees of specification shown on vehicle emission label. Adjust timing if necessary.

3) Remove jumper lead from carburetor ground switch. Disconnect and plug vacuum hose to the computer (4-Bbl. models). Connect a vacuum pump to the computer. Apply 16 in. Hg vacuum. Raise engine speed to 2000 RPM. Timing should be within 4 degrees of specification. See SPARK ADVANCE TEST SPECIFICATIONS chart.

SPARK ADVANCE SPECIFICATIONS [1]

Application	Computer No.	Spark Advance
5.2L (2-Bbl.)	4379484	46°BTDC
5.2L (2-Bbl.)	4379682	46°BTDC
5.2L (4-Bbl.)	4379226	38°BTDC
5.2L (4-Bbl.)	4379228	38°BTDC

[1] - Specifications are ± 4 degrees.

COLD DRIVEABILITY TEST 12 (Cont.)

4) If spark advance is not within specifications, replace the computer. If spark advance is okay, return engine to idle. Disconnect vacuum pump from the computer. Connect a vacuum gauge to the computer vacuum supply hose. Gauge should read manifold vacuum. If vacuum reading is not okay, check and repair vacuum supply from carburetor. If vacuum reading is okay, proceed to COLD DRIVEABILITY TEST 13.

COLD DRIVEABILITY TEST 13

IDLE RPM CHECK

1) Turn all lights and accessories off. Place transmission in Neutral. Set parking brake. Start and run engine until normal operating temperature is reached. Ground the carburetor switch with a jumper lead. Disconnect and plug vacuum hose to the EGR valve.

2) Disconnect and plug 3/16" vacuum hose from vapor canister. Remove PCV valve from valve cover and allow it to draw outside air. On 2-Bbl. models, disconnect and plug vacuum hose from the computer. Disconnect the carburetor 4-pin connector and remove the Green wire to the O_2 solenoid from the connector.

3) Reconnect the 4-pin connector. Start and run engine for 4 minutes before proceeding. On 4-Bbl. models, connect a voltmeter to the O_2 solenoid (Green wire) and ground. Disconnect and ground wire from the O_2 sensor using a jumper lead. Start engine and let idle until voltmeter reading is a steady 7-13 volts. This may take up to 4 minutes.

4) On all engines, tachometer reading should be within specifications shown on emissions label. Set idle RPM to specifications as necessary. Tee in propane supply into heated air temperature sensor vacuum hose. Open propane valve and meter in propane until maximum RPM is obtained. Engine speed should increase 60 RPM (2-Bbl. models) or 50 RPM (4-Bbl. models) ±50 RPM.

5) Open throttle and position fast idle adjusting screw on 2nd highest step of the fast idle cam. Fast idle speed should be set to specifications ± 100 RPM. See FAST IDLE SPEED chart. Adjust fast idle speed to specifications as necessary.

FAST IDLE SPEED

Carb. No.	Specification
4306441	1700
4306433	1450

COLD DRIVEABILITY TEST 14

At this point, test procedures have determined that all engine control systems are operating correctly and are not the cause of the driveability problem. Check the following as possible causes:
- Check for at least 13 in. Hg engine vacuum in Neutral.
- Check engine valve timing.
- Check engine compression.
- Check engine cooling system.
- Check exhaust system for restrictions.
- Check engine PCV system for free flow.
- Check intake manifold heat crossover for plugging.
- Check fuel pump pressure, volume and vacuum.
- Check torque converter stall speed.
- Check power brake booster for internal vacuum leaks.
- Check for fuel contamination.
- Check carburetor for circuit contamination and proper calibration.
- Check Technical Service Bulletins that may apply to vehicle.

WARM DRIVEABILITY TEST 1

CARBURETOR SWITCH CHECK

1) With engine at normal operating temperature, disconnect computer 10-pin connector. Connect an ohmmeter between 10-pin connector cavity No. 7 and ground. Open and close the throttle while watching ohmmeter. Ohmmeter reading should show continuity, with no resistance, when the throttle is closed and no continuity when the throttle is open.

2) If there is continuity when the throttle is open, repair wire to connector cavity No. 7 for a short to ground. If there is continuity with resistance when the throttle is closed, check carburetor switch for corrosion. Clean as necessary.

3) If there is no continuity when the throttle is closed, repair wire to connector cavity No. 7 for an open circuit to the carburetor switch. If continuity checks okay, proceed to WARM DRIVEABILITY TEST 2.

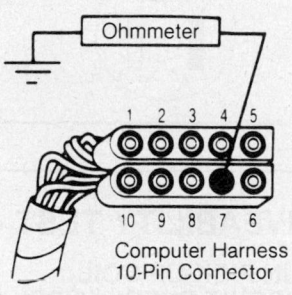

Computer Harness
10-Pin Connector

WARM DRIVEABILITY TEST 2

CHARGE TEMPERATURE SWITCH CIRCUIT CHECK

1) Disconnect both connectors from computer. Connect an ohmmeter between 10-pin connector cavity No. 9 and 12-pin connector cavity No. 10. Ohmmeter reading should be 176-3900 ohms. If resistance is okay, proceed to WARM DRIVEABILITY TEST 3. If resistance is not okay, disconnect charge temperature sensor connector.

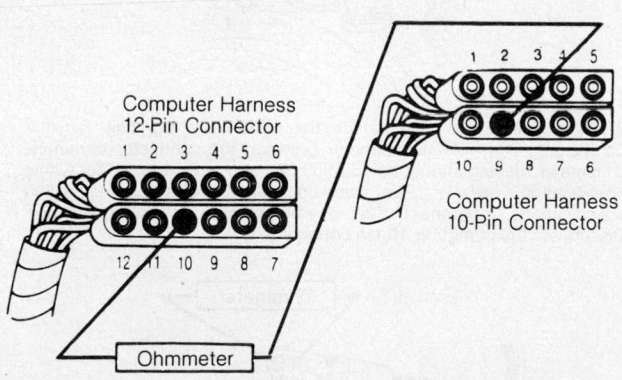

Computer Harness
12-Pin Connector

Computer Harness
10-Pin Connector

Ohmmeter

2) Connect an ohmmeter between charge temperature switch terminals. Ohmmeter reading should be 176-3900 ohms. If resistance is okay, repair wiring between computer and sensor for an open/short circuit. If resistance is not within specifications, replace charge temperature switch.

WARM DRIVEABILITY TEST 2 (Cont.)

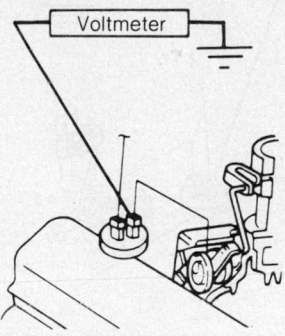

Ohmmeter

WARM DRIVEABILITY TEST 3

CHOKE POSITION WITH ENGINE RUNNING CHECK

1) Remove air cleaner lid. Start engine. Observe choke plate position. Choke plate should be fully open. If choke position is okay, proceed to WARM DRIVEABILITY TEST 4 (4-Bbl.) or WARM DRIVEABILITY TEST 5 (2-Bbl.). If choke position is not okay, connect a voltmeter to choke heater wire at choke control switch terminal and ground. Voltage reading should be within one volt of battery voltage.

Voltmeter

2) On 2-Bbl. models, if voltage reading is within specifications, turn ignition off. Disconnect wire from choke control that goes to electric choke heater. Connect an ohmmeter between choke heater wire and choke heating element retaining screw. Ohmmeter reading should be 4-12 ohms. If resistance is not within specification, replace choke heating element. If resistance is okay, check and repair choke linkage for sticking or binding. If voltage reading is not within specification, go to step **4)**.

Voltmeter

WARM DRIVEABILITY TEST 3 (Cont.)

3) On 4-Bbl. models, if voltage reading is within specification, connect voltmeter to choke heating element harness connector and ground. Voltage reading should be within one volt of battery voltage. If voltage is okay, check choke linkage for binding. If choke linkage is okay, replace the choke heating element. If voltage is not okay, repair open circuit in wiring to the choke control switch. If voltage reading is not within specification, go to next step.

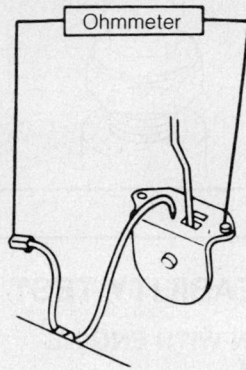

4) Connect voltmeter to ignition feed wire connector of choke control switch and ground. Voltage reading should be within one volt of battery voltage.

5) If voltage is within specifications, replace choke control switch. If voltage is not within specifications, turn ignition off. Disconnect oil pressure switch connector. Connect voltmeter to engine harness connector at oil pressure switch terminal "C" and ground.

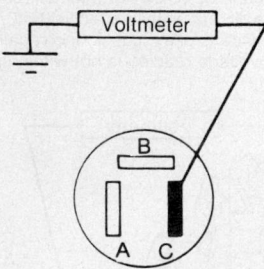

6) Turn ignition switch to the "RUN" position. Voltage should be within one volt of battery voltage. If voltage is not within specification, repair harness to ignition switch for an open circuit. If voltage is within specification, disconnect ignition feed wire from choke control switch.

WARM DRIVEABILITY TEST 3 (Cont.)

7) Connect an ohmmeter between engine harness connector at oil pressure switch terminal "A" and choke control switch wire. Ohmmeter should show continuity. If there is continuity, replace oil pressure switch. If there is no continuity, repair harness for an open circuit.

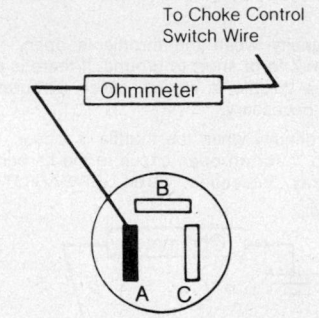

WARM DRIVEABILITY TEST 4

START-TO-RUN PICK-UP COIL TRANSFER CIRCUIT CHECK (4-BBL. ONLY)

1) Start engine. Raise engine speed to 1100 RPM. Disconnect "Start" pick-up coil connector at distributor (larger connector). Engine should stay running. If engine stays running, proceed to WARM DRIVEABILITY TEST 5.

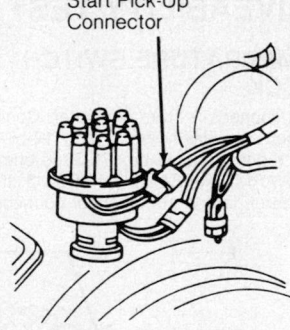

2) If engine stalls, disconnect the "Run" pick-up coil (smaller connector). Connect an ohmmeter between the connector terminals. Ohmmeter reading should be 150-900 ohms. If resistance is not within specification, replace "Run" pick-up coil. If resistance is within specifications, reconnect the distributor pick-up coil connector. Disconnect the computer 10-pin connector.

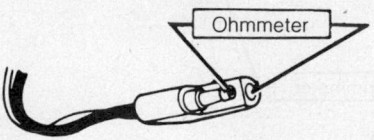

3) Connect an ohmmeter between 10-pin connector cavities No. 5 and 9. Ohmmeter reading should be 150-900 ohms. If resistance is okay, remove distributor cap. Measure "Run" pick-up coil air gap. Air gap should be .012" (.3 mm). Adjust air gap as necessary.

WARM DRIVEABILITY TEST 4 (Cont.)

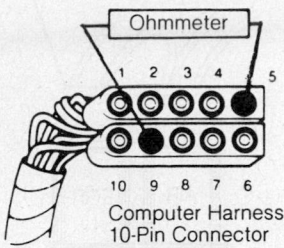

Ohmmeter

Computer Harness 10-Pin Connector

4) If air gap is okay, check terminals in cavities No. 5 and 9 to ensure they are not spread apart causing a poor connection. If connections are okay, replace computer.

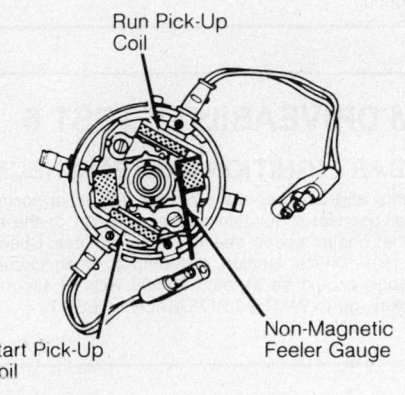

Run Pick-Up Coil

Start Pick-Up Coil

Non-Magnetic Feeler Gauge

WARM DRIVEABILITY TEST 5

EGR SYSTEM CHECK

1) With engine at normal operating temperature, let engine idle for one minute. While observivg EGR valve stem, raise engine speed to more than 2500 RPM for more than 5 seconds. As engine speed increases, EGR valve stem should move upward. If EGR valve stem moves upward, go to next step. If EGR valve stem does not move, go to step **4)**.

2) Connect a tachometer to engine. Disconnect EGR vacuum line. Connect a vacuum pump to EGR valve. Slowly apply vacuum to EGR valve. Engine speed should decrease with 3-5 in. Hg vacuum applied and continue to drop as more vacuum is applied to EGR valve. If engine speed decreases, on 4-Bbl. models, go to WARM DRIVEABILITY TEST NO. 6, on 2-Bbl. models, go to next step. If engine speed does not decrease until 5 in. Hg vacuum or more is applied to EGR valve, replace EGR valve.

3) With engine running, disconnect manifold vacuum line from vacuum bleed-off valve and plug hose. Connect a vacuum pump to bleed-off valve nipple. Apply 25 in. Hg vacuum. Raise engine speed to 2500 RPM for 5 seconds. As engine speed is increased, EGR valve stem should not move. If EGR valve stem does not move, go to WARM DRIVEABILITY TEST NO. 6. If EGR valve stem moves upward, replace vacuum bleed-off valve.

WARM DRIVEABILITY TEST 5 (Cont.)

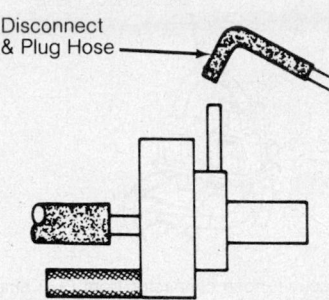

Disconnect & Plug Hose

4) Disconnect vacuum hose from EGR valve. Connect a vacuum gauge to EGR vacuum hose. Raise engine speed to 2500 RPM for 5 seconds. As engine speed is increased, vacuum gauge reading should increase. If vacuum gauge reading increases, replace EGR valve. If vacuum gauge reading does not increase, on 2-Bbl. models, go to next step, on 4-Bbl. models go to step **7)**.

5) Disconnect EGR signal hose from vacuum bleed-off valve. Plug vacuum hose. Reconnect vacuum hose to EGR valve. Raise engine speed to 2500 RPM for 5 seconds. As engine speed is increased, EGR valve stem should move upward. If EGR valve stem moves upward, replace vacuum bleed-off valve. If EGR valve stem does not move upward, on California models, go to step **7)**, on Federal models, go to next step.

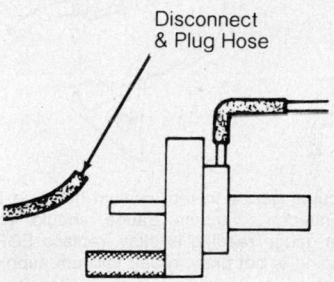

Disconnect & Plug Hose

6) Disconnect vacuum hose from White side of EGR vacuum delay valve. Connect a vacuum gauge to vacuum delay valve vacuum hose. Raise engine speed to 2500 RPM. As engine speed is increased, reading on vacuum gauge should increase. If vacuum gauge reading increased, replace EGR vacuum delay valve. If vacuum gauge reading did not increase, go to next step.

7) Disconnect bottom hose from EGR vacuum solenoid. Connect a vacuum gauge to EGR vacuum solenoid. Raise engine speed to 2500 RPM. As engine speed is increased, reading on vacuum gauge should increase. If vacuum gauge reading increases, repair vacuum hose to EGR valve. If vacuum gauge reading did not increase, go to next step.

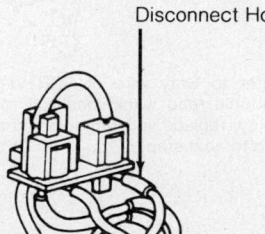

Disconnect Hose

8) Remove top hose from EGR vacuum solenoid. Connect a vacuum gauge to EGR vacuum solenoid. Raise engine speed to 2500 RPM. As engine speed is increased, reading on vacuum gauge should increase. If vacuum gauge reading increases, go to step **11)**. If vacuum gauge reading does not increase, on 2-Bbl. models, repair vacuum supply from carburetor, on 4-Bbl. models, go to next step.

WARM DRIVEABILITY TEST 5 (Cont.)

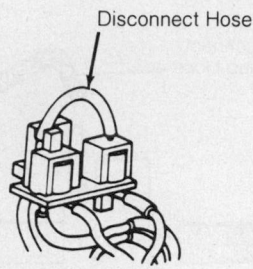

Disconnect Hose

9) Disconnect vacuum hose connector from EGR amplifer. Connect a vacuum gauge to middle vacuum hose on connector. Slowly increase engine speed. As engine speed increases, vacuum gauge reading should increase. If vacuum gauge reading increased, go to next step. If vacuum gauge reading does not increase, repair vacuum supply from carburetor.

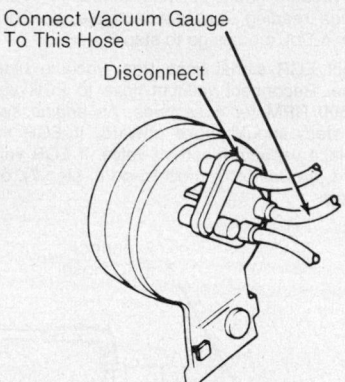

Connect Vacuum Gauge To This Hose

Disconnect

10) Connect a vacuum gauge to top vacuum hose on EGR amplifer vacuum hose connector. Vacuum gauge should read manifold vacuum. If vacuum gauge reading is okay, replace EGR amplifier. If vacuum gauge reading is not okay, repair vacuum supply from intake manifold.

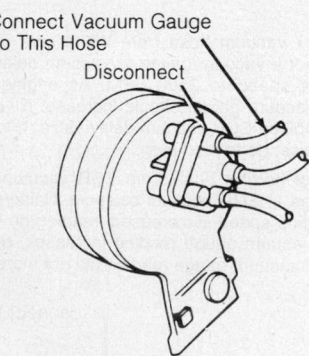

Connect Vacuum Gauge To This Hose

Disconnect

11) Connect voltmeter to Gray wire of EGR vacuum solenoid and ground. Voltmeter should read within one volt of battery voltage. If voltage reading is okay, replace vacuum solenoid assembly. If voltage reading is 0-1 volt, go to next step.

WARM DRIVEABILITY TEST 5 (Cont.)

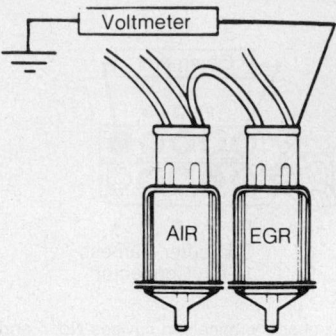

Voltmeter

AIR   EGR

12) Turn engine off. Disconnect computer 12-pin connector. Turn ignition switch to "RUN" position. Voltmeter reading should be within one volt of battery voltage. If voltmeter reading is okay, replace computer. If voltmeter reading is still 0-1 volt, repair Gray wire for a short to ground.

WARM DRIVEABILITY TEST 6

SECONDARY IGNITION SYSTEM CHECK

Turn all lights and accessories off. With engine at normal operating temperature, connect a suitable engine analyzer to the engine. Start engine and let engine speed stabilize for 2 minutes. Check secondary ignition pattern. Check ignition coil output. Open circuit secondary ignition voltage should be at least 25,000 volts. If secondary ignition voltage is okay, go to WARM DRIVEABILITY TEST 7.

WARM DRIVEABILITY TEST 7

AIR SWITCHING SYSTEM CHECK

1) Disconnect downstream air hose from air switching valve. Start engine and wait 4 minutes. There should be air coming out of air switching valve downstream air port. If there is air flowing from port, proceed to WARM DRIVEABILITY TEST 8.

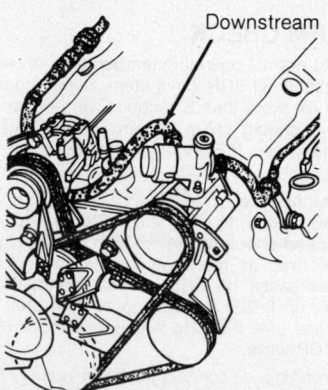

Downstream

2) If there is no air flowing from the port, disconnect upstream air hose from the air switching valve. There should be air flowing from the air switching valve upstream port. If there is no air flowing from the port, repair or replace the air pump.

WARM DRIVEABILITY TEST 7 (Cont.)

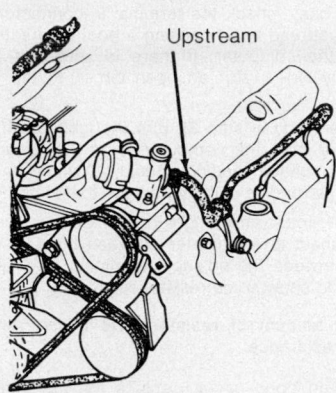

Upstream

3) If there is air flowing from the port, disconnect vacuum hose from air switching valve and connect a vacuum gauge to the hose. Vacuum reading should be zero in. Hg vacuum. If vacuum reading is as specified, replace air switching valve. If there is vacuum, connect a voltmeter to air switching solenoid (Green wire) and ground.

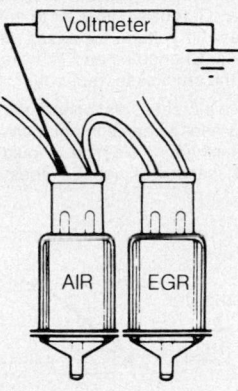

Voltmeter

AIR EGR

4) Voltage reading should be within one volt of battery voltage. If voltage reading is okay, replace vacuum solenoid assembly. If there is 0-1 volt, turn the ignition off. Disconnect computer 12-pin connector. Connect voltmeter to connector cavity No. 12 and ground. Turn ignition switch to the "RUN" position.

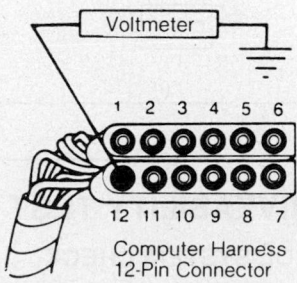

Voltmeter

1 2 3 4 5 6
12 11 10 9 8 7

Computer Harness
12-Pin Connector

5) Voltage reading should be within one volt of battery voltage. If voltage is okay, replace computer. If there is still 0-1 volt, repair the Green wire for a short to ground.

WARM DRIVEABILITY TEST 8

BOWL VENT VALVE CHECK

1) Disconnect bowl vent hose from canister. Blow lightly into hose. Air should flow through hose. If air does not flow through hose, check for a restricted hose and/or repair the bowl vent.

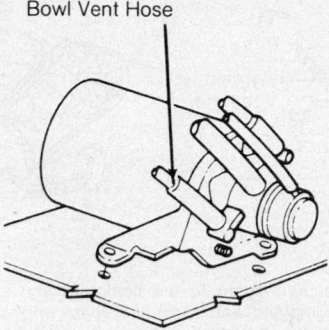

Bowl Vent Hose

2) If air flows through hose, start the engine. Blow lightly into hose. Air should not flow through hose. If air does not flow through hose, proceed to WARM DRIVEABILITY TEST 9. If air flows through hose, repair bowl vent.

NOTE: Models equipped with 2-Bbl. carburetors use an electric bowl vent valve. Models equipped with 4-Bbl. carburetors use an external valve that closes with air pump pressure.

WARM DRIVEABILITY TEST 9

O$_2$ FEEDBACK SYSTEM CHECK

1) Disconnect 12-pin connector from computer. Connect a voltmeter to connector cavity No. 4 and ground. Voltage reading should be within one volt of battery voltage. If there is zero volts, repair wiring to connector cavity No. 4 for an open circuit to the battery.

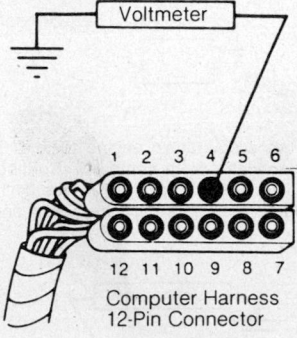

Voltmeter

1 2 3 4 5 6
12 11 10 9 8 7

Computer Harness
12-Pin Connector

2) If voltage reading is okay, check terminal in connector cavity No. 4 to ensure it is not spread apart causing a poor connection. Connect voltmeter to the O$_2$ solenoid connector (Green wire) and ground. Disconnect and plug the vacuum hose from the computer.

WARM DRIVEABILITY TEST 9 (Cont.)

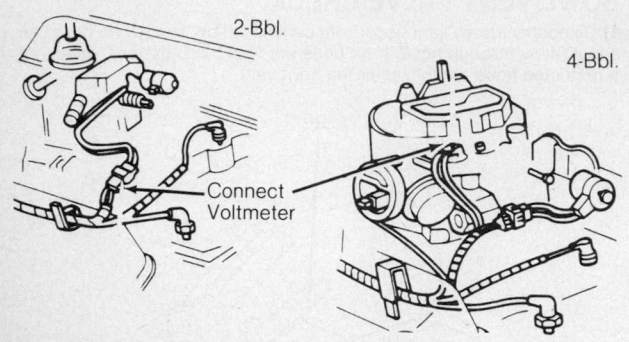

2-Bbl.

4-Bbl.

Connect Voltmeter

3) Connect a vacuum pump to the computer and apply 14 in. Hg vacuum. Start engine and wait 4 minutes. Raise engine speed to 2000 RPM. Voltage reading should be varying between 4-14 volts. If voltage reading is okay, remove air cleaner lid. Close choke plate. Voltage reading should drop toward zero. If voltage reading is zero volts, go to next step. If voltage reading is 1-3 volts, go to step **12)**.

4) If voltage drops, connect a tachometer to engine. Connect a jumper lead to O_2 solenoid (Green wire) and ground. Engine speed should drop. If engine speed drops, proceed to WARM DRIVEABILITY TEST 10. If engine speed did not drop, replace O_2 solenoid.

5) If voltage reading in step **3)** does not drop, disconnect O_2 sensor connector. Hold O_2 sensor harness terminal in one hand and touch battery positive with the other hand. Voltage should drop. If voltage drops, replace O_2 sensor.

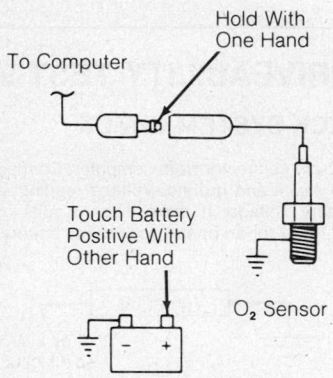

Hold With One Hand

To Computer

Touch Battery Positive With Other Hand

O_2 Sensor

6) If voltage does not drop, return engine to idle. Turn ignition off. Disconnect 12-pin connector from computer. Connect a voltmeter to the connector cavity No. 11 and ground. Turn the ignition switch to the "RUN" position. Voltage reading should be within one volt of battery voltage.

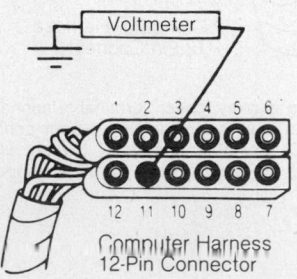

Voltmeter

2 3 4 5 6

12 11 10 9 8 7

Computer Harness 12-Pin Connector

WARM DRIVEABILITY TEST 9 (Cont.)

7) If voltage is okay, check the terminal in connector cavity No. 4 to ensure it is not spread apart causing a poor connection. If terminal is okay, replace the computer. If there is zero volt, repair wiring in connector cavity No. 11 for an open circuit to the carburetor 4-pin connector.

8) If there is zero volt in step **3)**, turn the ignition off. Disconnect the 12-pin connector from the computer. Turn the ignition switch to the "RUN" position. Voltage reading should be within one volt of battery voltage. If voltage reading is okay, replace the computer.

9) If there is 0-1 volt, turn the ignition off. Disconnect the O_2 solenoid connector. Connect an ohmmeter between the O_2 solenoid Tan and Green wires (between the solenoid terminals on 4-Bbl. models). The ohmmeter should show some resistance.

NOTE: The amount of resistance is unimportant. Just ensure there is some resistance.

10) If there is an open circuit, replace the O_2 solenoid. If there is resistance, connect a voltmeter to the O_2 solenoid connector (Blue wire) and ground. Turn the ignition switch to the "RUN" position. Voltage reading should be within one volt of battery voltage.

11) If voltage reading is okay, repair the Green wire to the computer for a short to ground. If voltage reading is not okay, repair the Blue wire for an open circuit to the ignition switch.

12) If there is 1-3 volts in step **3)**, disconnect the PCV valve hose and plug it with your finger. Gradually allow air to enter PCV hose. Voltage reading should increase. If voltage increases, check for fuel contamination in the crankcase. Change oil and filter as necessary. If there is fuel contamination in the crankcase, repair the carburetor.

13) If voltage does not increase, disconnect the O_2 sensor connector. Hold the O_2 sensor harness terminal in one hand and touch the battery positive with the other hand. Voltage should increase. If voltage increases, replace O_2 sensor. If voltage does not increase, replace computer.

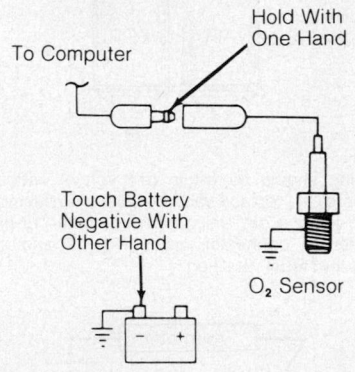

Hold With One Hand

To Computer

Touch Battery Negative With Other Hand

O_2 Sensor

WARM DRIVEABILITY TEST 10

IDLE CONTROL SYSTEM CHECK

1) Turn all lights and accessories off. Position air cleaner aside so that idle control solenoid is visible. Have an assistant start the engine while you observe the solenoid plunger. Open and close the throttle if necessary to activate the solenoid.

2) Solenoid plunger should move out and hold the throttle open for a specified length of time. See ELECTRONIC THROTTLE CONTROL chart. After specified length of time, solenoid should allow throttle to return to curb idle position. If plunger extends, but does not retract as specified, go to step **7)**. If plunger does not operate, go to step **3)**. If plunger operation is okay, go to step **8)**, **13)** or **17)** as equipped.

WARM DRIVEABILITY TEST 10 (Cont.)

ELECTRONIC THROTTLE CONTROL

Computer No.	¹ Throttle Control
4379484 & 4379682	120 Seconds
4379226 & 4379228	200 Seconds

¹ – After hot restart.

3) If plunger does not operate, turn ignition off. Connect a voltmeter to the idle solenoid (Blue wire) at the carburetor connector and ground. Start the engine. Voltage reading should be within one volt of battery voltage for the length of time specified in the ELECTRONIC THROTTLE CONTROL table. If voltage reading is not okay, go to step **6)**. If voltage reading is okay, go to next step.

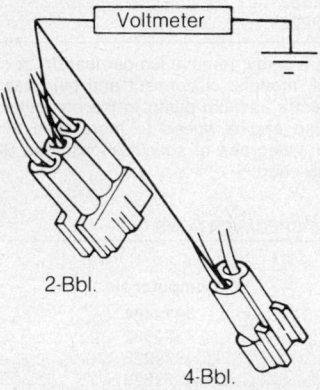

4) After specified length of time, voltage reading should drop to zero volt. If voltage reading is okay, turn ignition off. Disconnect the computer 12-pin connector. Back off adjusting screw on idle solenoid 3 turns. Set throttle on highest step of the fast idle cam.

5) Connect a jumper wire to the solenoid (Blue wire) at the carburetor connector. Touch other end of jumper lead to battery positive terminal while observing solenoid plunger. Plunger should extend when voltage is applied. If plunger extends, set idle speed to specifications. If solenoid does not extend, replace the solenoid.

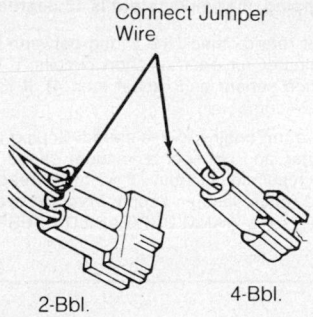

6) If voltage reading in step **3)** is not okay, disconnect the computer 12-pin connector. Connect an ohmmeter between the connector cavity No. 5 and the idle solenoid (Blue wire) at the carburetor connector. Ohmmeter should show continuity. If there is no continuity, repair wiring to connector cavity No. 5 for an open circuit to the carburetor connector.

WARM DRIVEABILITY TEST 10 (Cont.)

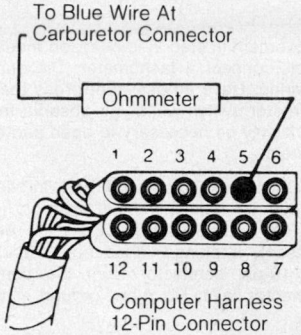

7) If there is continuity, check the terminal in connector cavity No. 5 to ensure it is not spread apart causing a poor connection. If terminal is okay, replace the computer. If solenoid plunger in step **2)** extends, but does not retract after specified length of time, replace the computer.

NOTE: On models equipped with A/C or rear window defroster, ensure they are turned off before diagnosing the computer as defective.

8) If plunger movement in step **2)** is okay, on models without A/C or rear window defroster, connect a tachometer. Connect a jumper lead between idle solenoid (Blue wire) at the carburetor connector and the positive battery terminal. Open throttle slightly and release. Tachometer reading should be within 100 RPM of specifications.

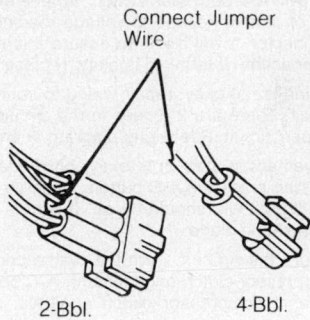

9) If solenoid idle speed is okay, proceed to WARM DRIVEABILITY TEST 11. If solenoid idle speed is not to specifications, set idle to specifications using the following procedure. Disconnect and plug vacuum hose to the EGR valve. Ground the carburetor switch using a jumper lead. Disconnect and plug 3/16" vacuum hose at the vapor canister.

10) Remove the PCV valve from the valve cover and allow it to draw outside air. Connect a tachometer. Start the engine and let the idle speed stabilize for 2 minutes. Energize the solenoid. Open throttle slightly to allow solenoid plunger to extend. Remove the solenoid adjusting screw and spring.

11) Insert a 1/8" Allen wrench into the solenoid and rotate to adjust solenoid to specifications. Reinstall solenoid adjusting screw and spring until it lightly bottoms out. De-energize the solenoid. Disconnect the engine harness connector from the O₂ sensor and ground the engine harness lead using a jumper wire.

12) Allow the engine to run for 4 minutes to stabilize O₂ sensor circuit. Rotate the solenoid adjusting screw to adjust the speed to specification listed on emission label. Reconnect the O₂ sensor wire. Reinstall PCV valve and install hoses that were disconnected. Remove ground wire from carburetor switch.

NOTE: Engine RPM in normal operating condition (everything connected) may vary from set speeds. DO NOT readjust.

WARM DRIVEABILITY TEST 10 (Cont.)

13) If plunger movement in step **2)** is okay, on models with A/C or rear window defroster, connect a tachometer. Disconnect the A/C compressor clutch wiring. Have an assistant press the A/C button or the rear window defroster switch while you observe the solenoid plunger and tachometer. It may be necessary to open and close the throttle to activate the solenoid.

14) Solenoid plunger should extend and increase idle speed to specification. If plunger movement and solenoid idle speed is okay, proceed to WARM DRIVEABILITY TEST 11. Adjust solenoid idle speed as necessary. If plunger does not extend, turn ignition off. Disconnect the 10-pin connector from the computer. Connect a voltmeter to connector cavity No. 4 and ground.

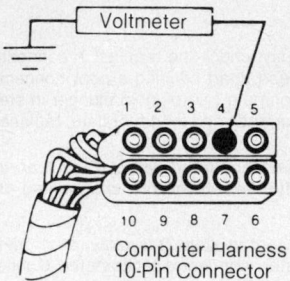

Computer Harness
10-Pin Connector

15) Turn the ignition switch to the "RUN" position. Press the A/C button or the rear window defroster switch. Voltmeter reading should be within one volt of battery voltage. If voltage reading is okay, check the terminal in connector cavity No. 4 to ensure it is not spread apart causing a poor connection. If terminal is okay, replace the computer.

16) If voltage reading is not okay, repair wiring to connector cavity No. 4 for an open circuit. There are 2 diodes in the circuit which could be the cause of the open circuit. See wiring diagram at end of this article.

17) If plunger movement in step **2)** is okay, on models with A/C and rear window defroster, press the A/C button. Observe the rear window defroster indicator light. Light should be off. If light is on, replace rear window defroster isolation diode.

18) If light is off, turn the A/C off. Turn the rear window defroster on. Listen for A/C compressor clutch engagement. A/C compressor clutch should not engage. If compressor clutch engages, replace the A/C isolation diode.

19) If clutch does not engage, turn rear window defroster off. Connect a tachometer. Disconnect A/C compressor clutch wiring. Have an assistant press the A/C button while you observe the solenoid plunger and the tachometer.

20) Open and close throttle to activate solenoid if necessary. Solenoid plunger should extend and increase solenoid idle speed to specifications. If plunger movement and idle speed are okay, turn A/C off and turn rear window defroster on.

21) Repeat steps **19)** and **20)**. If plunger movement and idle speed are okay, proceed to WARM DRIVEABILITY TEST 11. Adjust solenoid idle speed as necessary. If there is no plunger movement when A/C is turned on, replace A/C isolation diode.

22) If there is no plunger movement when the rear window defroster is turned on, replace the rear window defroster isolation diode. If there is no plunger movement when either A/C or rear window defroster is turned on, turn the ignition off. Disconnect the computer 10-pin connector. Connect a voltmeter to connector cavity No. 4 and ground.

23) Turn the ignition switch to the "RUN" position. Turn the A/C or rear window defroster on. Voltage reading should be within one volt of battery voltage. If voltage reading is okay, check the terminal in connector cavity No. 4 to ensure it is not spread apart causing a poor connection. If terminal is okay, replace the computer.

24) If voltage reading is not okay, repair wiring to 10-pin connector cavity No. 4 for an open circuit. There is a diode in the A/C circuit which could be the cause of the open circuit.

WARM DRIVEABILITY TEST 11

IGNITION TIMING SYSTEM CHECK

1) Connect a tachometer and timing light. Ground the carburetor switch. Start the engine. Raise engine speed to more than 1100 RPM until engine reaches normal operating temperature. On 2-Bbl. models, disconnect and plug the vacuum hose to the computer.

2) Engine speed should be 450-650 RPM on 2-Bbl. models and 550-750 RPM on 4-Bbl. models. Adjust idle speed as necessary. Basic timing should be within 2 degrees of specifications. See BASIC TIMING SPECIFICATIONS chart. Adjust timing as necessary.

BASIC TIMING SPECIFICATIONS

Computer No.	Specification
4379484 & 4379682	7°BTDC
4379226 & 4379228	16°BTDC

3) If basic timing is okay, remove jumper lead from carburetor ground switch. On 4-Bbl. models, disconnect and plug vacuum hose to the computer. Connect a vacuum pump to the computer and apply 16 in. Hg vacuum. Raise engine speed to more than 2000 RPM. Timing should be within 4 degrees of specifications. See SPARK ADVANCE SPECIFICATIONS chart.

SPARK ADVANCE SPECIFICATIONS [1]

Application	Computer No.	Spark Advance
5.2L (2-Bbl.)	4379484	46°BTDC
5.2L (2-Bbl.)	4379682	46°BTDC
5.2L (4-Bbl.)	4379226	38°BTDC
5.2L (4-Bbl.)	4379228	38°BTDC

[1] – Specifications are ± 4 degrees.

4) If spark advance is not within specifications, replace the computer. If spark advance is okay, apply 16 in. Hg vacuum (2-Bbl. models) and 2 in. Hg vacuum (4-Bbl. models) to the computer. Position fast idle speed screw on the 2nd highest step of the fast idle cam. Tap lightly on the intake manifold near the detonation sensor while watching the timing. Timing should retard as you tap on the intake manifold.

NOTE: The amount of timing retard is directly proportional to the frequency of the tapping. Maximum retard is 16 degrees.

5) If timing does not retard, check the wiring between the detonation sensor and the computer for open or short circuits. If wiring is okay, replace the detonation sensor and repeat step **4)**. If timing still does not retard, replace the computer.

6) If timing retards, return engine to idle speed. Unplug vacuum supply hose to the computer and connect a vacuum gauge to it. Vacuum reading should be manifold vacuum. If vacuum reading is not as specified, check and repair vacuum supply from carburetor. If vacuum reading is okay, proceed to WARM DRIVEABILITY TEST 12.

WARM DRIVEABILITY TEST 12

IDLE RPM CHECK

1) Set parking brake. Place transmission in Neutral. Turn all lights and accessories off. Connect a tachometer. Ground carburetor switch using a jumper lead. Disconnect and plug vacuum hose to the EGR valve. Remove PCV valve from valve cover and allow it to draw outside air.

2) Disconnect and plug 3/16" hose from vapor canister. On 2-Bbl. models, disconnect and plug vacuum hose to the computer. Disconnect the carburetor 4-pin connector and remove the O₂ solenoid (Green wire) from the carburetor connector. Reconnect carburetor connector. Start the engine and let stabilize for 4 minutes.

WARM DRIVEABILITY TEST 12 (Cont.)

3) On 4-Bbl. models, connect a voltmeter to O_2 solenoid (Green wire) and ground. Disconnect O_2 sensor wiring and ground O_2 sensor harness connector using a jumper lead. Start the engine and let run until voltmeter reading is a steady 7-13 volts. This may take up to 4 minutes. Tachometer reading should be at specification shown on emission label.

4) Adjust idle RPM as necessary. Tee in propane supply into heated air temperature vacuum supply hose. Slowly meter propane supply into hose until maximum RPM is obtained. Engine speed should increase 10-110 RPM (2-Bbl. models) and 0-100 RPM (4-Bbl. models). Adjust propane idle speed as necessary. Proceed to WARM DRIVEABILITY TEST 13.

WARM DRIVEABILITY TEST 14

At this point, test procedures have determined that all engine control systems are operating correctly and are not the cause of the driveability problem. Check the following as possible causes:

- Check for at least 13 in. Hg engine vacuum in Neutral.
- Check engine valve timing.
- Check engine compression.
- Check engine cooling system.
- Check exhaust system for restrictions.
- Check engine PCV system for free flow.
- Check intake manifold heat crossover for plugging.
- Check torque converter stall speed.
- Check power brake booster for internal vacuum leaks.
- Check for fuel contamination.
- Check carburetor for circuit contamination and proper calibration.
- Check Technical Service Bulletins that may apply to vehicle.

WARM DRIVEABILITY TEST 13

HEATED AIR INTAKE SYSTEM CHECK

1) Remove outside air duct from the air cleaner. Start the engine. The heated air door should be laying flat in snorkel. If heated air door is not in proper position, disconnect vacuum supply hose from temperature sensor. Connect a vacuum pump to the sensor and apply 10 in. Hg vacuum.

2) Vacuum should bleed down. If vacuum bleeds down, check for sticking heated air door or a faulty vacuum delay valve (if equipped). If vacuum does not bleed down, replace temperature sensor. If heated air door is in proper position in step **1)**, on 2-Bbl. models, proceed to WARM DRIVEABILITY TEST 14.

3) On 4-Bbl. models, watch vapor containment door. Vapor containment door should be open. If vapor containment door is not open, check for sticking door or faulty vacuum delay valve. If door is open, proceed to WARM DRIVEABILITY TEST 14.

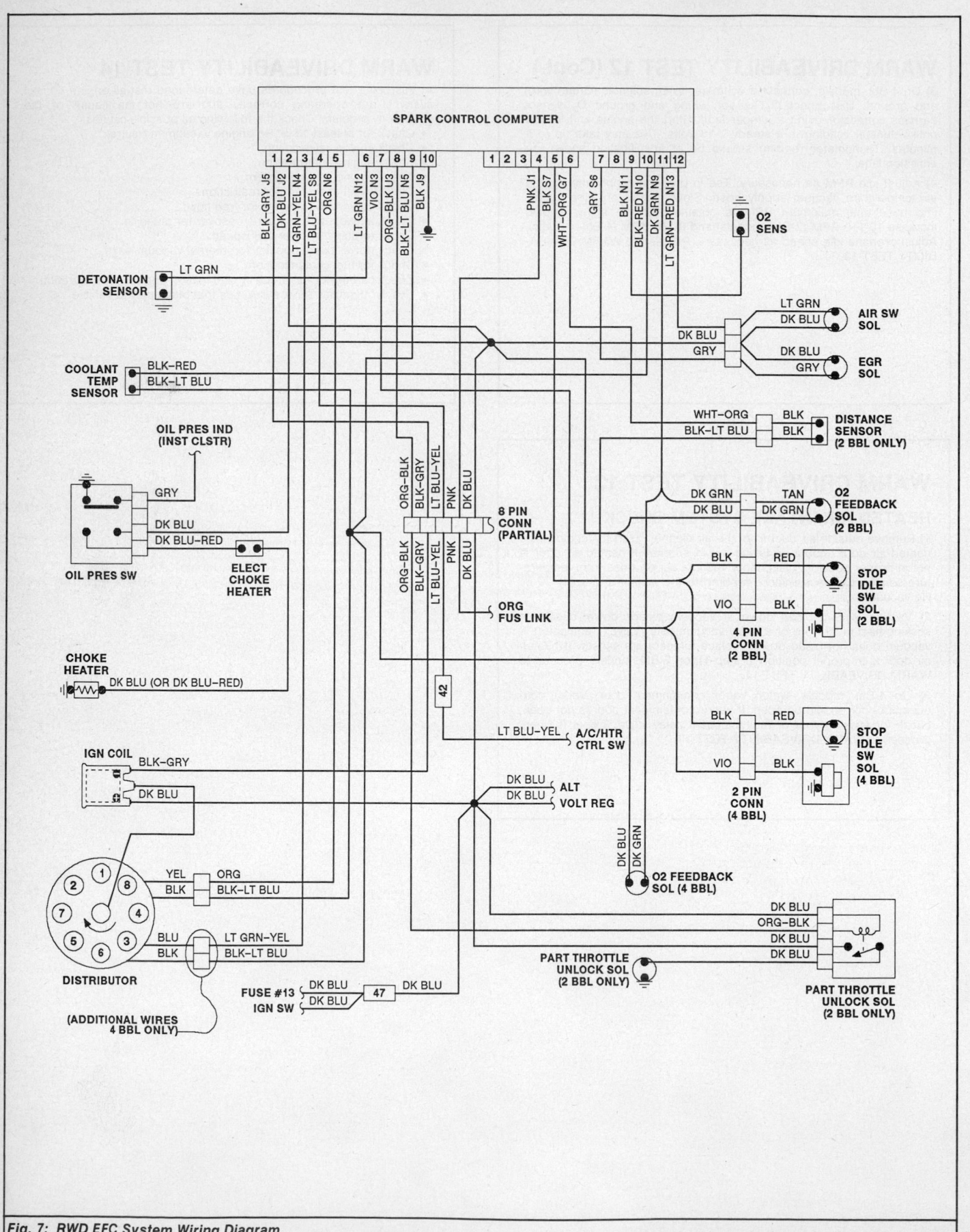

Fig. 7: RWD EFC System Wiring Diagram

Dynasty, New Yorker

DESCRIPTION

All Dynasty and New Yorker models are equipped with an On-Board Diagnostic System (OBDS) which links together body and chassis electronic components. The diagnostic test procedure is designed to find problems quickly using all system features.

The OBDS monitors Single Board Engine Controller (SBEC)/Single Module Engine Controller (SMEC), Electronic Vehicle Information Center (EVIC), traveler, instrument cluster, vehicle theft alarm and automatic load leveling functions. It also monitors fluid level sensors, temperature sensors, brake sensors and lighting system functions.

OPERATION

Diagnostic test procedures are designed to detect system faults as quickly as possible. Body and chassis fault codes are accessed through diagnostic test connector, under middle of dashboard. Chrysler's Diagnostic Readout Box II (DRB-II) tester is used to access information from Chrysler Collision Detection multiplex system (C²D bus).

C²D BUS

C²D Bus is a twisted pair of wires traveling from module-to-module receiving and delivering coded information. The code identifies the message and its importance. When multiple messages attempt to access C²D bus at once, the code assigns priority ranking.

The 2 twisted wires used by C²D bus system are called Bus "+" and Bus "−". Both wires carry approximately 2.5 volts.

AUTOMATIC AIR LOAD LEVELING

The automatic air load leveling system consists of control module, height sensing right shock absorber and compressor assembly, including air exhaust solenoid and compressor relay. The module controls ground circuits for compressor relay and air exhaust solenoid. A microprocessor within module controls compressor pump operation from 140-160 seconds.

BODY CONTROLLER

The body controller, behind right kick panel, receives information from engine node and lamp outage module. It also stores odometer information for instrument cluster display. See ODOMETER READING TRANSFER under REMOVAL & INSTALLATION in this article.

The body controller also provides power or ground for a variety of systems. It monitors system through voltage drops.

The engine node sends body controller information regarding brake fluid level, brake pad condition, engine coolant level and engine oil level. Exterior lamps are monitored by lamp outage module. If a headlight, side marker lamp or taillight fails, lamp outage module senses discrepancy and reports it to body controller.

ELECTRONIC INSTRUMENT CLUSTER

The electronic instrument cluster consists of digital and linear displays. The electronic cluster receives its display information from body controller and engine controller via C²D multiplex system. The electronic cluster includes gauges for oil pressure, coolant temperature, fuel, voltage and a series of warning lights. Odometer information is stored in body controller.

The electronic cluster has 2 forms of diagnostic routines used for self-diagnostics. It uses trip and trip rest buttons for access and C²D bus diagnostic routines which require use of DRB-II tester. Successful completion of cluster self-diagnostic test indicates a problem in C²D bus, interfacing module, connectors, wiring harnesses or sensors. See ELECTRONIC CLUSTER FAULT CODES in TEST 41 in this article.

ENGINE NODE

The engine node, located behind front grille and mounted to radiator support, is used in conjunction with EVIC head. It collects data from various switches and sensors in front of vehicle and relays information to body controller through C²D bus wires. It also contains compass and outside air temperature sensor.

EVIC HEAD

The Electronic Vehicle Information Center (EVIC) module, located in overhead console, is a computer controlled warning system which monitors various sensors. The system supplements instrument cluster warning indicators with digital warning messages. When a warning message is activated, a tone will alert driver. Messages relate to safety, vehicle operation, convenience and maintenance.

The EVIC head provides navigational information, such as time, outside temperature, compass direction and fuel economy. The EVIC head also receives information from other modules on C²D bus regarding status of systems and components. Any failure of a monitored system results in a warning message on EVIC screen.

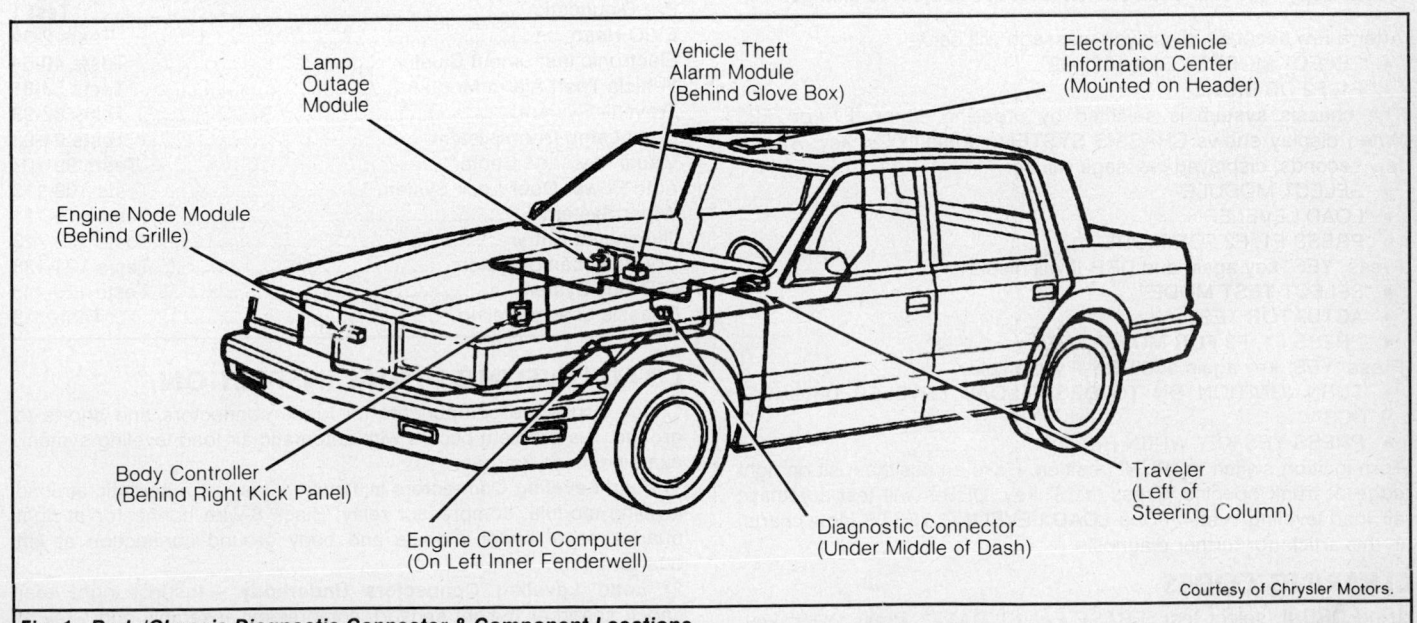

Lamp Outage Module

Vehicle Theft Alarm Module (Behind Glove Box)

Electronic Vehicle Information Center (Mounted on Header)

Engine Node Module (Behind Grille)

Body Controller (Behind Right Kick Panel)

Engine Control Computer (On Left Inner Fenderwell)

Diagnostic Connector (Under Middle of Dash)

Traveler (Left of Steering Column)

Courtesy of Chrysler Motors.

Fig. 1: Body/Chassis Diagnostic Connector & Component Locations

1989 COMPUTERIZED ENGINE CONTROLS
Chrysler Motors Body Control Computer (Cont.)

MESSAGE CENTER

The message center, left of steering column, operates with ignition switch in "ON" or "START" positions. It provides graphic indication of washer fluid level, trunk ajar and door ajar conditions.

TRAVELER MODULE

The traveler module, located to left of steering column, provides navigational information such as average fuel economy, instant fuel economy, distance to empty, elapsed time and trip odometer. Traveler information regarding fuel and odometer comes from body controller and engine controller via C²D bus. The traveler is not used when vehicle is equipped with EVIC head.

VEHICLE THEFT ALARM SYSTEM

The vehicle theft alarm system is a logic controlled system, using an electronic module. The module monitors vehicle doors, hood, trunk key cylinder and ignition for unauthorized operation. The system is composed of security control module, 4 door ajar switches, hood ajar switch, trunk key sensing switch, 2 door key cylinder disarming switches, instrument panel set lamp, engine controller, horn and horn relay, park lamps and tail lights, power door lock circuits and ignition switch.

TESTING & DIAGNOSIS

Perform a thorough visual inspection of all connectors and pins of suspected components before replacing any components. Also, battery must be fully charged before any testing. Chrysler's DRB-II (C-4805), jumper wires, analog volt/ohmmeter and circuit tester will be needed for testing.

ENTERING ON-BOARD DIAGNOSTICS

Choose cartridge and plug DRB-II into diagnostic connector. The DRB-II will now perform a self-test. Display should turn on, including Red and Green indicator lamps. A beeping sound should be heard. If any of these functions fail to occur, or "HARDWARE FAILURE" appears on display, the DRB-II has malfunctioned and must be repaired. DO NOT press any key during self-test.
After a few seconds, displayed message will be:
- "CHRYSLER MOTORS"
- "DRB-II"
- "COPYRIGHT 1987"
- "REVISION 0.0"

NOTE: Copyright year and revision level are subject to change.

After a few seconds, displayed message will be:
- "SELECT MODEL YEAR 1983-89"
- "F1, F2 OR MORE"

The chassis system is selected by pressing either "F1" or "F2." When display shows CHASSIS SYSTEM, press "YES" key. After a few seconds, displayed message will be:
- "SELECT MODULE"
- "LOAD LEVELER"
- "PRESS F1, F2 FOR MORE"

Press "YES" key again and DRB-II will display:
- "SELECT TEST MODE"
- "ACTUATOR TEST"
- "PRESS F1, F2 FOR MORE"

Press "YES" key again and DRB-II will display:
- "TURN IGNITION ON TO BEGIN LOAD LEVELER DIAGNOS-TICS"
- "PRESS YES KEY WHEN READY"

Turn ignition switch to "RUN" position. Have an assistant sit on right edge of trunk opening. Press "YES" key. DRB-II will test automatic air load leveling system. See LOAD LEVELING TESTS (flow charts) in this article for further diagnosis.

CLEARING CODES

Using DRB-II, select test "ERASE FAULT DATA". Press "YES" key on DRB-II. DRB-II will display "ARE YOU SURE? YES/NO". Press

"YES" key on tester. Tester will display "ERASING FAULT DATA X". When DRB-II is finished erasing fault codes, it will display "FAULT DATA ERASED".
If DRB-II is not available, fault codes may be cleared by allowing 50-100 key on/off cycles to occur. This allows SBEC/SMEC to clear fault codes.

DIAGNOSTIC TEST PROCEDURE

The diagnostic test procedure is comprised of 3 categories:
- Visual inspection
- Body diagnostics
- Chassis diagnostics

It is NOT necessary to perform all 3 test procedures for each problem. The category used will be determined by the customer's complaint. Always perform a thorough visual inspection before any chassis diagnosis. Body system problems require no visual inspection. Due to the complexity of the system, test procedures will cover all visual inspections as required.
Once problem has been determined, perform test procedures using following guidelines:

1) Always start at the first test in each category or incorrect results may occur.
2) Only perform test steps indicated. It is NOT necessary to perform all steps in a test.
3) At the end of each test step, reconnect all wires and install any components removed for testing.
4) Vehicle battery must be fully charged.
5) When checking for voltage or continuity at SBEC/SMEC 60-wire connector, probe at terminal side of connector, not wire side. Probing wire will give inaccurate results, damage female terminals and cause failures. See *Figs. 3 and 4* for cavity identification of terminals.
6) Use extreme care when connecting or disconnecting wiring during testing to prevent accidental grounding, shorting or energizing SBEC/SMEC terminals or damage can occur.
7) DO NOT use a test light in place of a voltmeter. Damage to electronic components may occur.

DIAGNOSTIC TEST OUTLINE

Diagnostic tests come in flow chart form and will be broken into 12 separate categories. See DIAGNOSTIC TEST OUTLINE table in this article.

DIAGNOSTIC TEST OUTLINE

Test Name	Test Nos.
Pre-Diagnostic	Test 1
EVIC Head	Tests 2-39
Electronic Instrument Cluster	Tests 40-54
Vehicle Theft Alarm Module	Tests 55-81
Traveler System	Tests 82-93
Head Lamp Door System	Tests 94-98
Visual Message Center	Tests 99-107
Auto Power Door Lock System	Tests 108-118
Wiper System	Tests 119-121
Illuminated Entry	Tests 122-123
Courtesy Lamp System	Tests 124-128
C²D Bus System	Tests 129-145
Chassis Load Leveling	Tests 1-9

LOAD LEVELING VISUAL INSPECTION

Check suspected components for loose connectors and shorts to ground. If a problem occurs with automatic air load leveling system, examine these 3 areas:

1) **Load Leveling Connectors in Trunk** – Inspect automatic air load leveling module, compressor relay, Black 8-wire connector at right quarter panel under module and body ground connection at left quarter panel.

2) **Load Leveling Connectors Underbody** – Inspect right rear shock absorber (height sensor), compressor assembly and Gray 4-wire connector, below right quarter panel.

3) Pressure Line Connectors – Ensure all pressure line connectors are fully and firmly seated at connections and are not pinched.

C²D BUS TESTING

Using Chrysler Tester DRB-II, a bus problem will show up in one of 3 ways. Despite passing automatic bus test, a "NO RESPONSE" message appears rather than an expected value. It is impossible to use DRB-II until reason for "NO RESPONSE" message is found and corrected.

These problems can cause a "NO RESPONSE" message:
- A bus wire is open or poorly connected at a module.
- If ground or power supply is missing at certain modules.
- When body controller has timed out.

There are 4 major bus failures:
- "SHORT TO GROUND"
- "SHORT TO BATTERY"
- "SHORT TO 5 VOLTS"
- "BUS "+" & BUS "–" SHORTED TOGETHER"

These can cause anything from a "ENGINE NO START" to a blank message screen on EVIC head. The automatic bus test will not complete or allow access to further system tests at this point and red light on DRB-II will come on.

There are 8 critical bus messages which may prevent proper operation:
- "NO TERMINATION"
- "BIAS LEVEL TOO HIGH"
- "BIAS LEVEL TOO LOW"
- "NO BUS BIAS"
- "BUS – OPEN"
- "BUS + OPEN"
- "BUS + & BUS – OPEN"
- "NOT RECEIVING BUS MESSAGES CORRECTLY"

These messages will prevent DRB-II from operating properly but will allow test to continue without Red light coming on. The only interference will come when trying to access a module directly related to or causing bus failure.

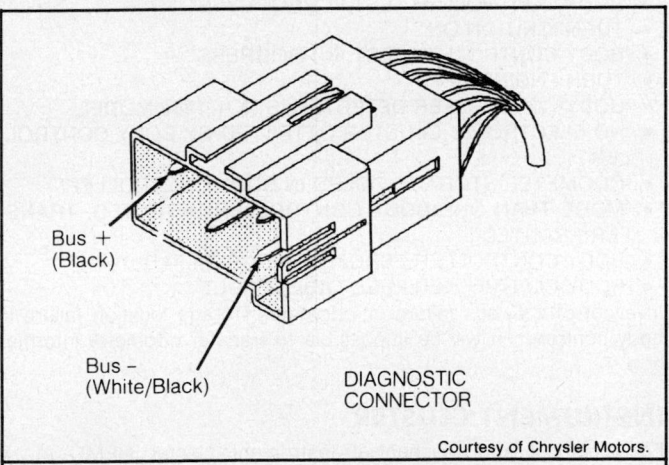

Bus +
(Black)

Bus –
(White/Black)

DIAGNOSTIC
CONNECTOR

Courtesy of Chrysler Motors.

Fig. 2: Diagnostic Connector (Under Middle of Dash)

BODY CONTROLLER TESTING

NOTE: In early 1989 models, a change in windshield wiper circuit wiring may cause the intermittent wipers to run continuously. This is caused by a voltage spike that would cause the body controller contacts to stick closed. Wiring in later 1989 vehicles was returned to that used in 1988. The early 1989 circuitry can be identified by a missing wire in cavity No. 18 of the 25-way instrument panel-to-steering column connector.

Wipers Run Continuously In "OFF" Position – **1)** If windshield wipers operate continuously on low speed with switch in "OFF" position, the problem may be caused by a stuck relay in the body

controller module. The relay can NOT be serviced separately. If a light tap on the module fails to break loose the stuck relay, the body controller module must be replaced.

2) To prevent relay in body controller module from sticking again, the vehicle instrument panel wiring harness must be modified. A new wire must be run from the steering column connector to the body controller module connector to correct this condition. The following steps outline the repair procedure:

3) Disconnect negative battery cable. Disconnect 2 body controller module connectors.

4) Remove and retain body controller connector wedge lock. Remove Dark Blue wire from cavity No. 22 of the Black connector. *See Fig. 3.* Insulate and tape this terminal to main wiring harness. The wire will not be used again.

5) Locate steering column connector and remove wiper switch connector from the 25-way steering column-to-instrument panel wiring harness. Cut a piece of 18-gauge wire long enough to reach from the steering column connector to the body controller connector. Add appropriate terminal connectors.

6) Install new wire terminal into Black connector. Insert locking wedge. Connect Black connector to body controller module. Route new wire under instrument panel, along steering column base. Allow enough slack in wire for future servicing.

7) Remove locking wedge from steering column connector and install new wire into empty cavity No. 18. Install locking wedge. Reconnect steering column connector to instrument panel wiring harness.

8) Reconnect negative battery cable. Check for normal operation of windshield wiper system. Depress washer button while wipers are operating on the highest speed. The wipers should NOT slow down. Check that intermittent wiper mode works properly.

REMOVAL & INSTALLATION

BODY CONTROLLER

NOTE: When replacing body controller, odometer reading must be transferred from original to new body controller using DRB-II.

Removal & Installation – Disconnect negative battery cable. Remove right kick panel. Remove body controller connectors. Remove mounting screws. Remove body controller. To install, reverse removal procedure. To transfer odometer reading to new body controller, see BODY CONTROLLER & ODOMETER READING TRANSFER under REMOVAL & INSTALLATION in this article.

BODY CONTROLLER & ODOMETER READING TRANSFER

Whenever a new body controller is installed on vehicles with electronic instrument cluster, odometer reading must be transferred to the new body controller's memory. The odometer reading is NOT stored in instrument cluster. The following is a step-by-step odometer transfer procedure.

1) DRB-II tester must be connected to diagnostic connector with ignition switch in "RUN" position.

2) Regardless of test mode being used, press "NO" key and following message appears on DRB-II screen:
- "SELECT MODULE XXXXX"
- "VERSION XX"
- "PRESS F1, F2 FOR MORE"

At this point press, "F1" or "F2" and following message appears:
- "SELECT MODULE"
- "BODY CONTROLLER"
- "VERSION XX"
- "PRESS F1, F2 FOR MORE"

Press "YES" key and following message appears:
- "SELECT TEST"
- "DISPLAY FAULT CODES"

- "BODY CONTROLLER"
- "PRESS F1, F2 FOR MORE"

Press "F1" OR "F2" key and following message appears:
- "SELECT TEST"
- "ODOMETER TRANSFER"
- "BODY CONTROLLER"
- "PRESS F1, F2 FOR MORE"

Press "YES" key and following message appears:
- THIS TEST HAS RESTRICTED ACCESS, ENTER CODE OR PRESS NO TO EXIT

Type 0843 and press "ENTER" and following message appears:
- "SELECT TEST"
- "RECEIVE ODOMETER"
- "BODY CONTROLLER"
- "PRESS F1, F2 FOR MORE"

Press "YES" key. If DRB-II has previously received an odometer reading which has not been transferred to a new body controller, the user will be notified, as shown below. The transfer will abort. Press "NO" key to exit.
- "RECEIVED ODOMETER"
- "MUST BE TRANSFERRED TO A REPLACEMENT BODY COMPUTER"

If DRB-II has not previously received an odometer reading, following message appears:
- "WARNING – ODOMETER WILL BE ERASED FROM BODY CONTROLLER"
- "(ENTER) TO CONTINUE"

DRB-II will warn user the odometer reading will be erased from body controller as a result of transfer shown above. Press "NO" key to abort, or press "ENTER" key to continue with odometer reception. If "ENTER" key is pressed now, following message appears:
- "BODY CONTROLLER TEST IN PROGRESS"

During "TEST IN PROGRESS," DRB-II will automatically verify body controller and engine controller for following conditions:
1) Ignition on.
2) Engine not running.
3) One 1989 MY body controller on C²D bus.
4) An electronic cluster detected by body controller.
5) No odometer fault.

If all required conditions are met, odometer will be requested from body controller and DRB-II will automatically show following:
- "BODY CONTROLLER TEST COMPLETE"
Followed by:
- "REQUESTING ODOMETER FROM BODY CONTROLLER"
Followed by:
- "RECEIVED ODOMETER SUCCESSFULLY (MILEAGE) * MILES"

If odometer reading transfer was successful, mileage will be displayed on DRB-II followed by an asterisk. The odometer reading on DRB-II will be within one mile or kilometer of reading before transfer. After a successful retrieval, instrument cluster will display an arbitrarily high odometer reading of approximately 136823 miles.

If transfer request is unsuccessful, DRB-II will read "NO RESPONSE." If any of required conditions are not met, the receive procedure is halted. The user will be prompted with a possible problem (shown below as they would appear on DRB-II):
- "BODY CONTROLLER TEST IN PROGRESS"
- "TURN IGNITION ON"
- "BODY CONTROLLER TEST IN PROGRESS"
- "TURN ENGINE OFF"
- "BODY CONTROLLER DETECTED IS NOT 1989 MODEL"
- "NO ELECTRONIC CLUSTER DETECTED BY BODY CONTROLLER"
- "ODOMETER STORAGE FAILED IN BODY CONTROLLER"
- "MORE THAN 1 BODY CONTROLLER DETECTED TRANSFER ABORTED"

Transmit Odometer to New Body Controller – Press "NO" key and following message will appear:
- "SELECT TEST"
- "RECEIVE ODOMETER"
- "BODY CONTROLLER"
- "PRESS F1, F2 FOR MORE"

The following message will appear:
- "SELECT TEST"
- "TRANSMIT ODOMETER"
- "BODY CONTROLLER"
- "PRESS F1, F2 FOR MORE"

Press "YES" key and if DRB-II has a previously received odometer following message appears:
- "BODY CONTROLLER TEST IN PROGRESS"

If DRB-II has no previously received odometer reading, transfer process is halted. The user is warned there is nothing to transfer. The following message appears:
- NO PREVIOUSLY RECEIVED ODOMETER FOUND TO TRANSFER

During "TEST IN PROGRESS," DRB-II will begin to automatically verify body controller and engine controller for following conditions:
1) Ignition on.
2) Engine not running.
3) One 1989 MY body controller on C²D bus.
4) An electronic cluster detected by body controller.
5) No odometer fault.
6) No EEROM check sum fault.
7) No fuel table check sum fault.

If all required conditions are met, odometer will be transmitted to body controller and DRB-II will show following:
- "BODY CONTROLLER TEST COMPLETE"
Followed by:
- "SENDING ODOMETER TO BODY CONTROLLER"
Followed by:
- "ODOMETER TRANSFER COMPLETE"

Unsuccessful Transfer of Odometer Reading – DRB-II will display "ODOMETER TRANSFER FAILED" instead of "ODOMETER TRANSFER COMPLETE." A failure here indicates the replacement body controller has been used for more than 10 miles and will not accept the odometer reading. If any of the following conditions are not met, the receive procedure is halted. The user is alerted and the following will appear:
- "BODY CONTROLLER TEST IN PROGRESS"
- "TURN IGNITION ON"
- "BODY CONTROLLER TEST IN PROGRESS"
- "TURN ENGINE OFF"
- "BODY CONTROLLER DETECTED IS NOT 1989 MODEL"
- "NO ELECTRONIC CLUSTER DETECTED BY BODY CONTROLLER"
- "ODOMETER STORAGE FAILED IN BODY CONTROLLER"
- "MORE THAN ONE BODY CONTROLLER DETECTED, TRANSFER ABORTED"
- "BODY CONTROLLER EEROM CHECK SUM FAULT"
- "BODY CONTROLLER FUEL TABLE FAULT"

In event of C²D bus failure or odometer storage location failure in body controller, it will be impossible to transfer odometer information.

INSTRUMENT CLUSTER

For electrical and mechanical instrument cluster REMOVAL & INSTALLATION, see CHRYSLER ELECTRONIC INSTRUMENT CLUSTER in ACCESSORIES & EQUIPMENT section.

WIRING DIAGRAMS

For wiring diagrams, refer to appropriate chassis wiring diagram in WIRING DIAGRAMS section.

CONNECTORS VIEWED FROM WIRE END

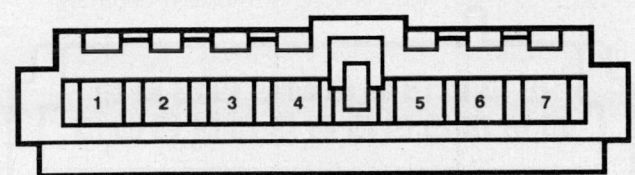

TRAVELER CONNECTOR (BLACK)

1) White/Black	5) Orange
2) Black	6) Black/Lt. Green (Ground)
3) Not Used	7) Dk. Blue
4) Not Used	

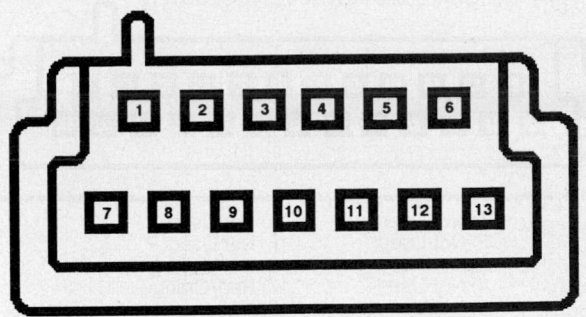

ELECTRONIC INSTRUMENT CLUSTER
CONNECTOR (RED)

1) Gray/Lt. Blue	8) Gray
2) Pink	9) White/Black
3) Red/Orange	10) Black
4) Gray/Black	11) Dk. Blue
5) Lt. Green	12) Black/Pink
6) Orange	13) Tan
7) Black/Lt. Green	

BODY CONTROLLER CONNECTOR (RED)
(ELECTRONIC INSTRUMENT CLUSTER)

1) Tan/Orange	14) Not Used
2) Tan/Red	15) Not Used
3) Tan/Yellow	16) Not Used
4) Tan/Black	17) Red/Orange
5) Lt. Blue/Black	18) Violet
6) Brown/Yellow	19) Not Used
7) Orange/Lt. Green	20) Orange/Violet
8) Gray/Black	21) Gray
9) Black/Lt. Blue	22) Gray/Yellow
10) Dk. Blue	23) Violet/Yellow
11) Dk. Blue	24) Gray/Red
12) Dk. Blue	25) Gray/Pink
13) Red	

BODY CONTROLLER CONNECTOR (BLACK)
(ELECTRONIC INSTRUMENT CLUSTER)

1) Black/Lt. Blue	14) Black
2) Tan	15) White/Black
3) Lt. Green	16) Pink
4) Lt. Blue	17) Orange/White
5) Black/Tan	18) Not Used
6) Yellow/Orange	19) Yellow/Red
7) Yellow/Black	20) Black
8) Orange	21) Not Used
9) White	22) Dk. Blue
10) Brown	23) Not Used
11) Dk. Blue/Yellow	24) Brown
12) Dk. Blue	25) Yellow
13) Black/Lt. Green	

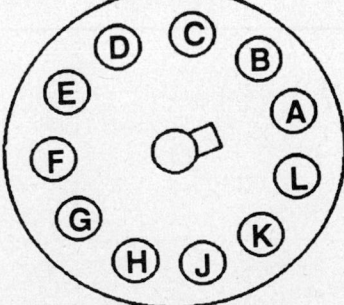

EVIC
HEAD
CONNECTOR
(GRAY)

A) Black/Tan	G) Orange
B) Dk. Blue	H) Black
C) Tan	J) Tan/White
D) Tan/Orange	K) Tan/Yellow
E) Tan/Black	L) Tan/Red
F) Not Used	

ENGINE NODE CONNECTOR

1) Black/Lt. Green	7) Black
2) Not Used	8) White/Black
3) Brown/Lt. Blue	9) Not Used
4) Not Used	10) Lt. Green/Lt. Blue
5) Dk. Green/Gray	11) Dk. Blue
6) Pink	12) Not Used

Courtesy of Chrysler Motors.

Fig. 3: Electrical Connectors For Body Control Computer System Diagnostic Testing (Part I)

1989 COMPUTERIZED ENGINE CONTROLS
Chrysler Motors Body Control Computer (Cont.)

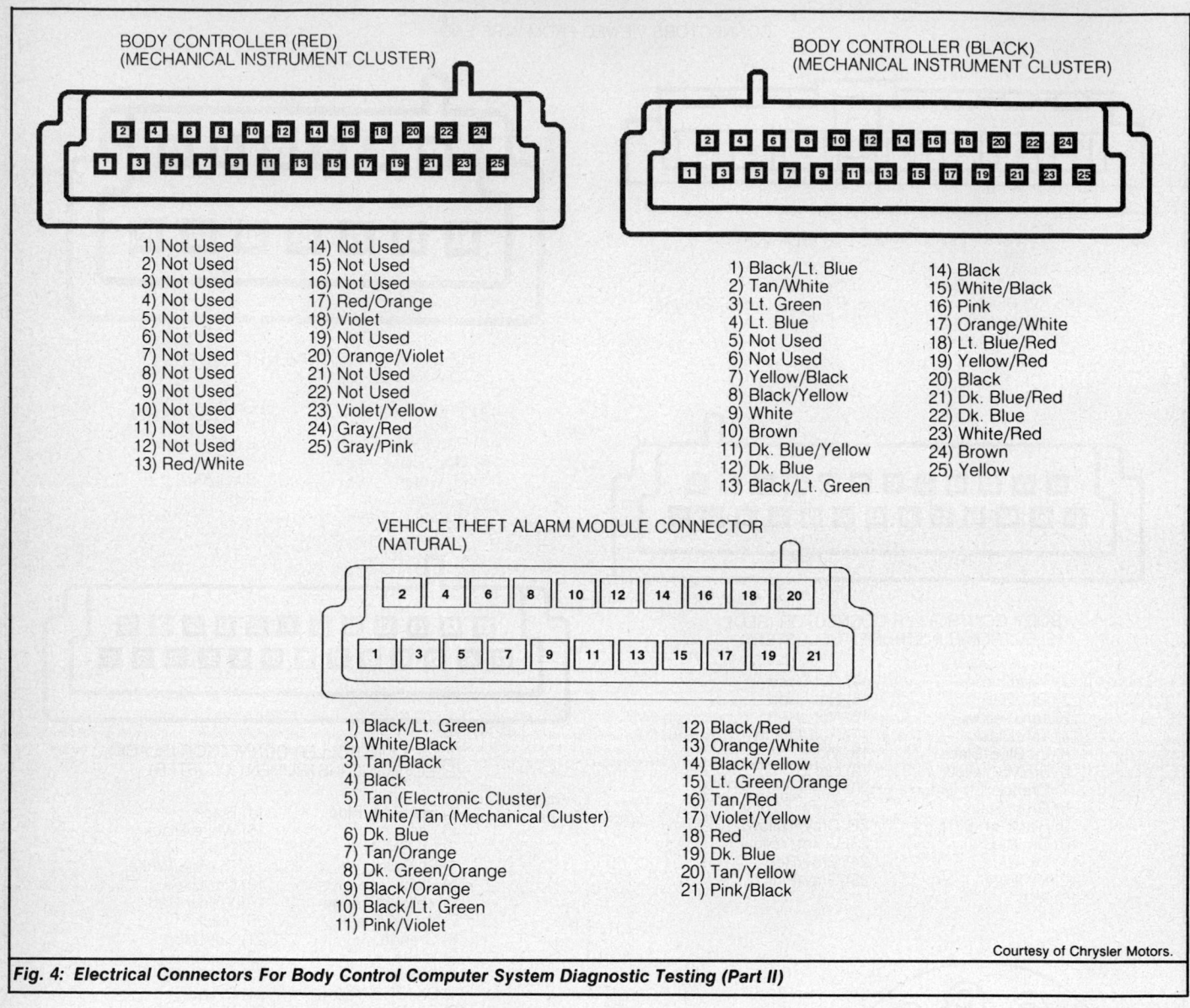

Fig. 4: Electrical Connectors For Body Control Computer System Diagnostic Testing (Part II)

1989 COMPUTERIZED ENGINE CONTROLS
Chrysler Motors Body Control Computer (Cont.)

1a-195

TEST 1 – IDENTIFYING VEHICLE EQUIPMENT & SYSTEM PROBLEMS (1 OF 3)

TEST 1 – IDENTIFYING VEHICLE EQUIPMENT & SYSTEM PROBLEMS (2 OF 3)

TEST 1 – IDENTIFYING VEHICLE EQUIPMENT & SYSTEM PROBLEMS (3 OF 3)

TEST 2 – BLANK MESSAGE SCREEN (1 OF 6)

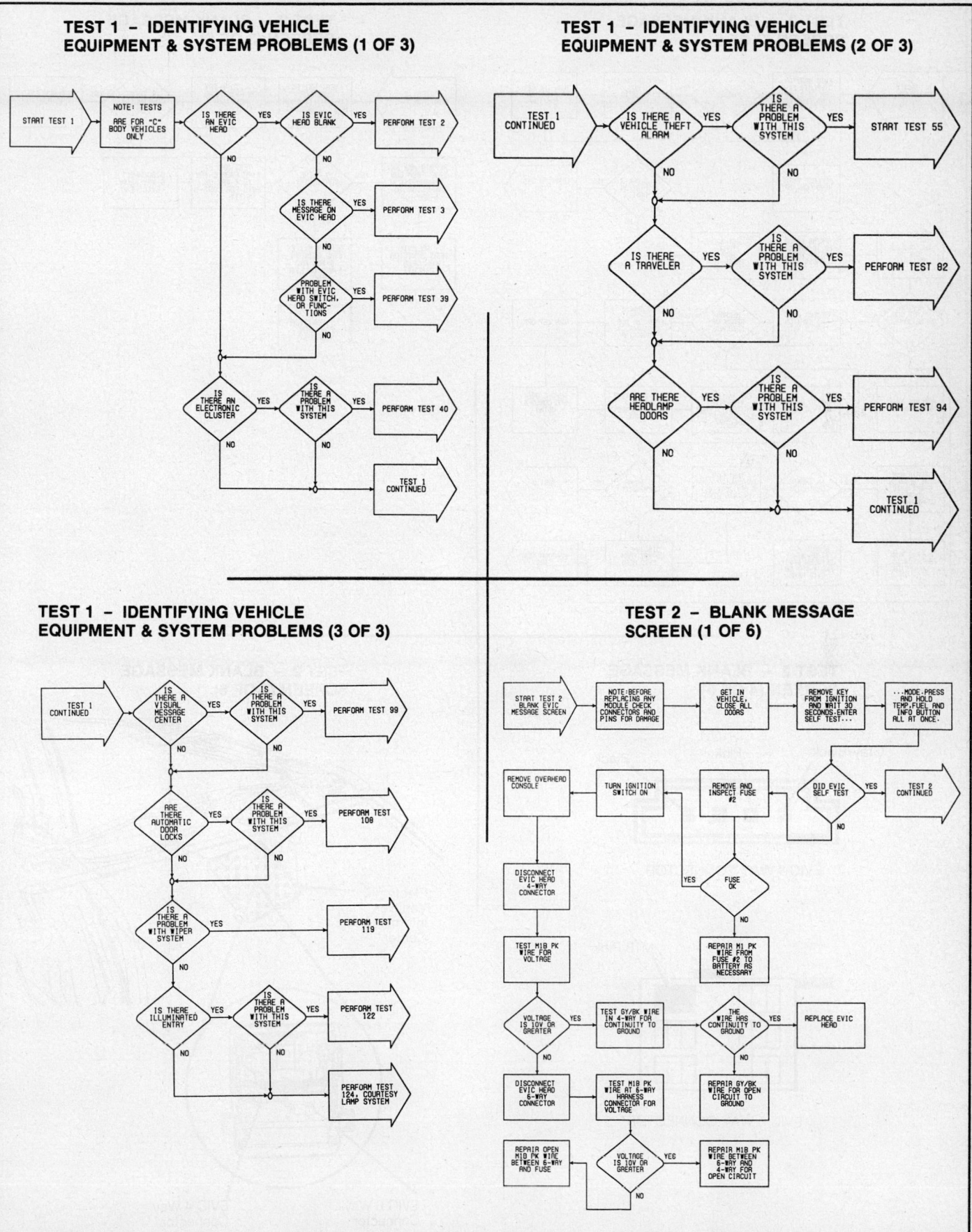

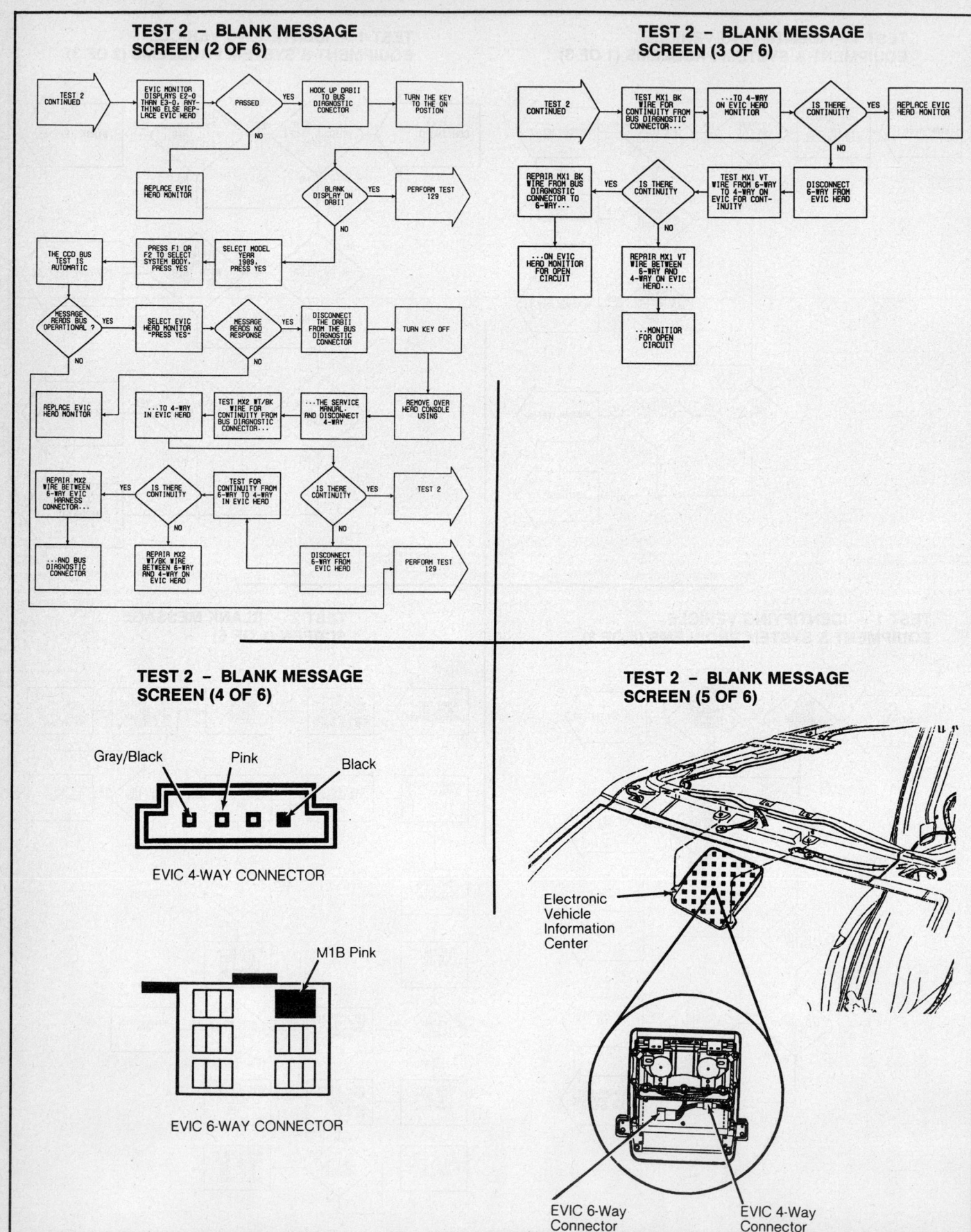

TEST 2 – BLANK MESSAGE SCREEN (2 OF 6)

TEST 2 – BLANK MESSAGE SCREEN (3 OF 6)

TEST 2 – BLANK MESSAGE SCREEN (4 OF 6)

Gray/Black   Pink   Black

EVIC 4-WAY CONNECTOR

M1B Pink

EVIC 6-WAY CONNECTOR

TEST 2 – BLANK MESSAGE SCREEN (5 OF 6)

Electronic Vehicle Information Center

EVIC 6-Way Connector

EVIC 4-Way Connector

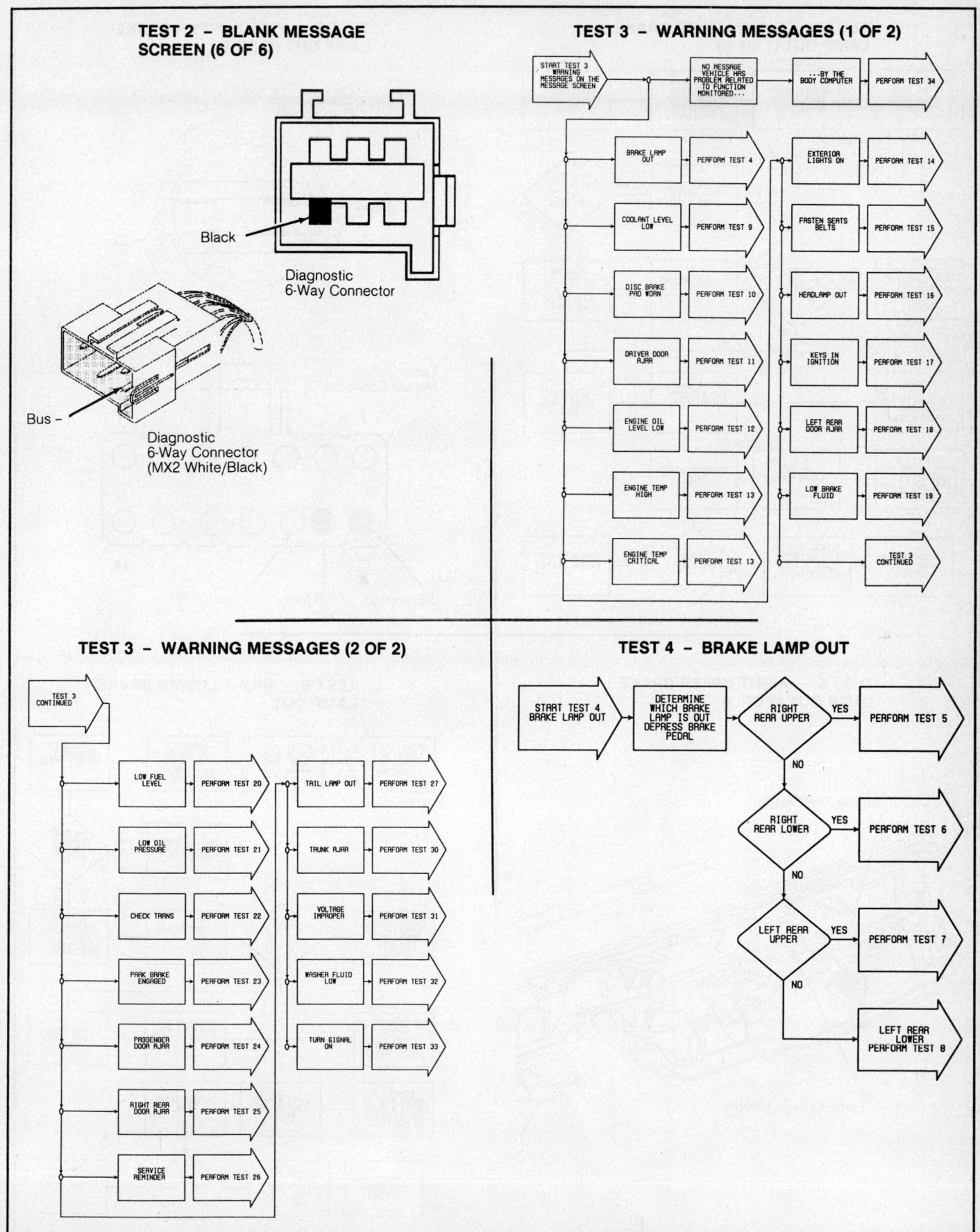

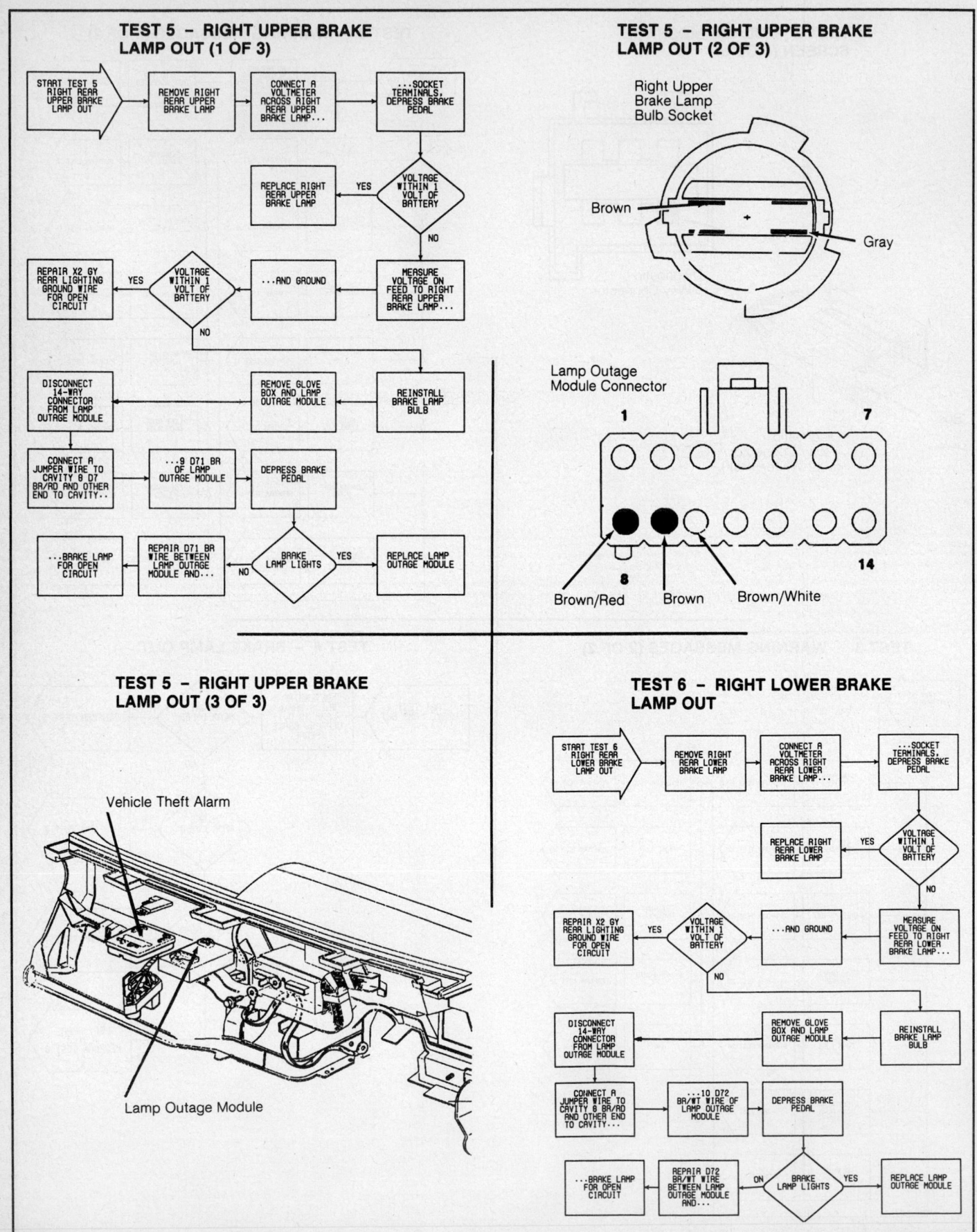

TEST 5 – RIGHT UPPER BRAKE LAMP OUT (1 OF 3)

START TEST 5 RIGHT REAR UPPER BRAKE LAMP OUT → REMOVE RIGHT REAR UPPER BRAKE LAMP → CONNECT A VOLTMETER ACROSS RIGHT REAR UPPER BRAKE LAMP... → ...SOCKET TERMINALS, DEPRESS BRAKE PEDAL

VOLTAGE WITHIN 1 VOLT OF BATTERY — YES → REPLACE RIGHT REAR UPPER BRAKE LAMP
NO ↓

MEASURE VOLTAGE ON FEED TO RIGHT REAR UPPER BRAKE LAMP... → ...AND GROUND → VOLTAGE WITHIN 1 VOLT OF BATTERY — YES → REPAIR X2 GY REAR LIGHTING GROUND WIRE FOR OPEN CIRCUIT
NO ↓

REINSTALL BRAKE LAMP BULB → REMOVE GLOVE BOX AND LAMP OUTAGE MODULE → DISCONNECT 14-WAY CONNECTOR FROM LAMP OUTAGE MODULE

CONNECT A JUMPER WIRE TO CAVITY 8 D7 BR/RD AND OTHER END TO CAVITY.. → ...9 D71 BR OF LAMP OUTAGE MODULE → DEPRESS BRAKE PEDAL

BRAKE LAMP LIGHTS — YES → REPLACE LAMP OUTAGE MODULE
NO → REPAIR D71 BR WIRE BETWEEN LAMP OUTAGE MODULE AND... → ...BRAKE LAMP FOR OPEN CIRCUIT

TEST 5 – RIGHT UPPER BRAKE LAMP OUT (2 OF 3)

Right Upper Brake Lamp Bulb Socket

Brown — Gray

Lamp Outage Module Connector

1 ... 7

8

14

Brown/Red   Brown   Brown/White

TEST 5 – RIGHT UPPER BRAKE LAMP OUT (3 OF 3)

Vehicle Theft Alarm

Lamp Outage Module

TEST 6 – RIGHT LOWER BRAKE LAMP OUT

START TEST 6 RIGHT REAR LOWER BRAKE LAMP OUT → REMOVE RIGHT REAR LOWER BRAKE LAMP → CONNECT A VOLTMETER ACROSS RIGHT REAR LOWER BRAKE LAMP... → ...SOCKET TERMINALS, DEPRESS BRAKE PEDAL

VOLTAGE WITHIN 1 VOLT OF BATTERY — YES → REPLACE RIGHT REAR LOWER BRAKE LAMP
NO ↓

MEASURE VOLTAGE ON FEED TO RIGHT REAR LOWER BRAKE LAMP... → ...AND GROUND → VOLTAGE WITHIN 1 VOLT OF BATTERY — YES → REPAIR X2 GY REAR LIGHTING GROUND WIRE FOR OPEN CIRCUIT
NO ↓

REINSTALL BRAKE LAMP BULB → REMOVE GLOVE BOX AND LAMP OUTAGE MODULE → DISCONNECT 14-WAY CONNECTOR FROM LAMP OUTAGE MODULE

CONNECT A JUMPER WIRE TO CAVITY 8 BR/RD AND OTHER END TO CAVITY... → ...10 D72 BR/WT WIRE OF LAMP OUTAGE MODULE → DEPRESS BRAKE PEDAL

BRAKE LAMP LIGHTS — YES → REPLACE LAMP OUTAGE MODULE
ON → REPAIR D72 BR/WT WIRE BETWEEN LAMP OUTAGE MODULE AND... → ...BRAKE LAMP FOR OPEN CIRCUIT

1989 COMPUTERIZED ENGINE CONTROLS
Chrysler Motors Body Control Computer (Cont.)

1a-199

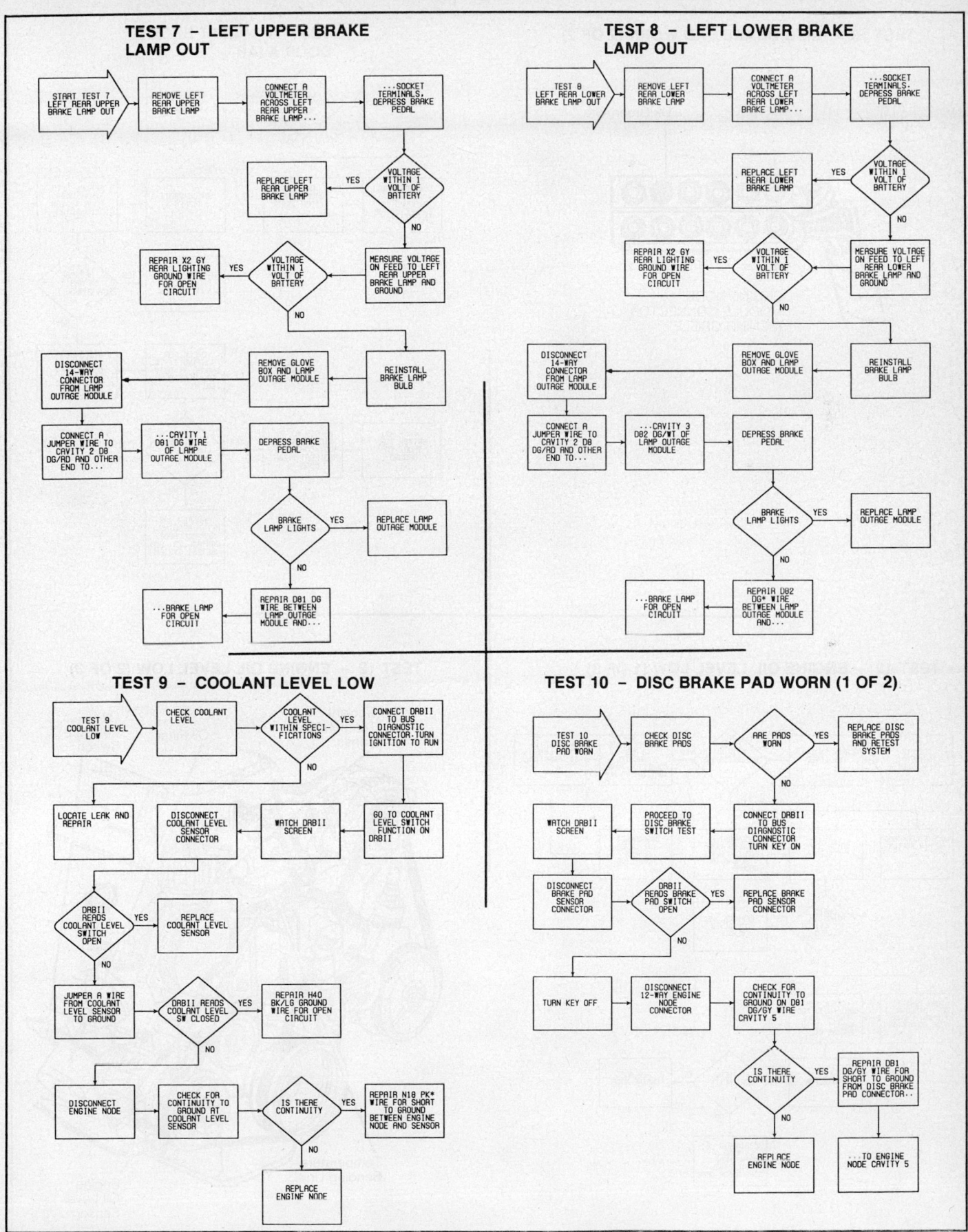

TEST 7 – LEFT UPPER BRAKE LAMP OUT

TEST 8 – LEFT LOWER BRAKE LAMP OUT

TEST 9 – COOLANT LEVEL LOW

TEST 10 – DISC BRAKE PAD WORN (1 OF 2)

TEST 10 – DISC BRAKE PAD WORN (2 OF 2)

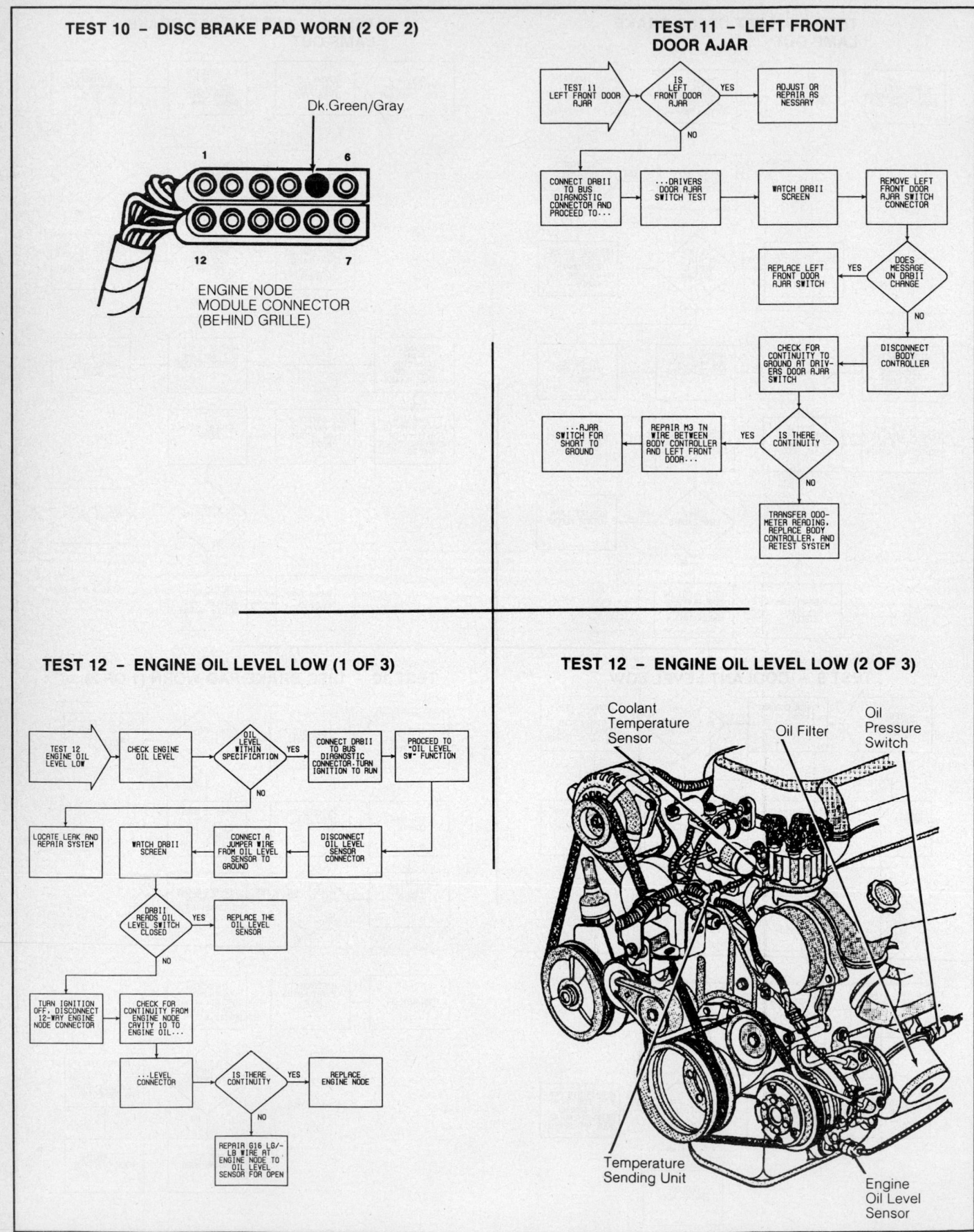

Dk.Green/Gray

1   6
12   7

ENGINE NODE
MODULE CONNECTOR
(BEHIND GRILLE)

TEST 11 – LEFT FRONT DOOR AJAR

TEST 11
LEFT FRONT DOOR
AJAR

IS LEFT FRONT DOOR AJAR — YES → ADJUST OR REPAIR AS NESSARY

NO

CONNECT DRBII TO BUS DIAGNOSTIC CONNECTOR AND PROCEED TO... → ...DRIVERS DOOR AJAR SWITCH TEST → WATCH DRBII SCREEN → REMOVE LEFT FRONT DOOR AJAR SWITCH CONNECTOR

REPLACE LEFT FRONT DOOR AJAR SWITCH ← YES — DOES MESSAGE ON DRBII CHANGE

NO

CHECK FOR CONTINUITY TO GROUND AT DRIVERS DOOR AJAR SWITCH ← DISCONNECT BODY CONTROLLER

...AJAR SWITCH FOR SHORT TO GROUND ← REPAIR M3 TN WIRE BETWEEN BODY CONTROLLER AND LEFT FRONT DOOR... ← YES — IS THERE CONTINUITY

NO

TRANSFER ODO-METER READING, REPLACE BODY CONTROLLER, AND RETEST SYSTEM

TEST 12 – ENGINE OIL LEVEL LOW (1 OF 3)

TEST 12 ENGINE OIL LEVEL LOW → CHECK ENGINE OIL LEVEL → OIL LEVEL WITHIN SPECIFICATION — YES → CONNECT DRBII TO BUS DIAGNOSTIC CONNECTOR. TURN IGNITION TO RUN → PROCEED TO "OIL LEVEL SW" FUNCTION

NO

LOCATE LEAK AND REPAIR SYSTEM ← WATCH DRBII SCREEN ← CONNECT A JUMPER WIRE FROM OIL LEVEL SENSOR TO GROUND ← DISCONNECT OIL LEVEL SENSOR CONNECTOR

DRBII READS OIL LEVEL SWITCH CLOSED — YES → REPLACE THE OIL LEVEL SENSOR

NO

TURN IGNITION OFF, DISCONNECT 12-WAY ENGINE NODE CONNECTOR → CHECK FOR CONTINUITY FROM ENGINE NODE CAVITY 10 TO ENGINE OIL...

...LEVEL CONNECTOR → IS THERE CONTINUITY — YES → REPLACE ENGINE NODE

NO

REPAIR G16 LG/-LB WIRE AT ENGINE NODE TO OIL LEVEL SENSOR FOR OPEN

TEST 12 – ENGINE OIL LEVEL LOW (2 OF 3)

Coolant Temperature Sensor

Oil Filter

Oil Pressure Switch

Temperature Sending Unit

Engine Oil Level Sensor

1989 COMPUTERIZED ENGINE CONTROLS
Chrysler Motors Body Control Computer (Cont.)

1a-201

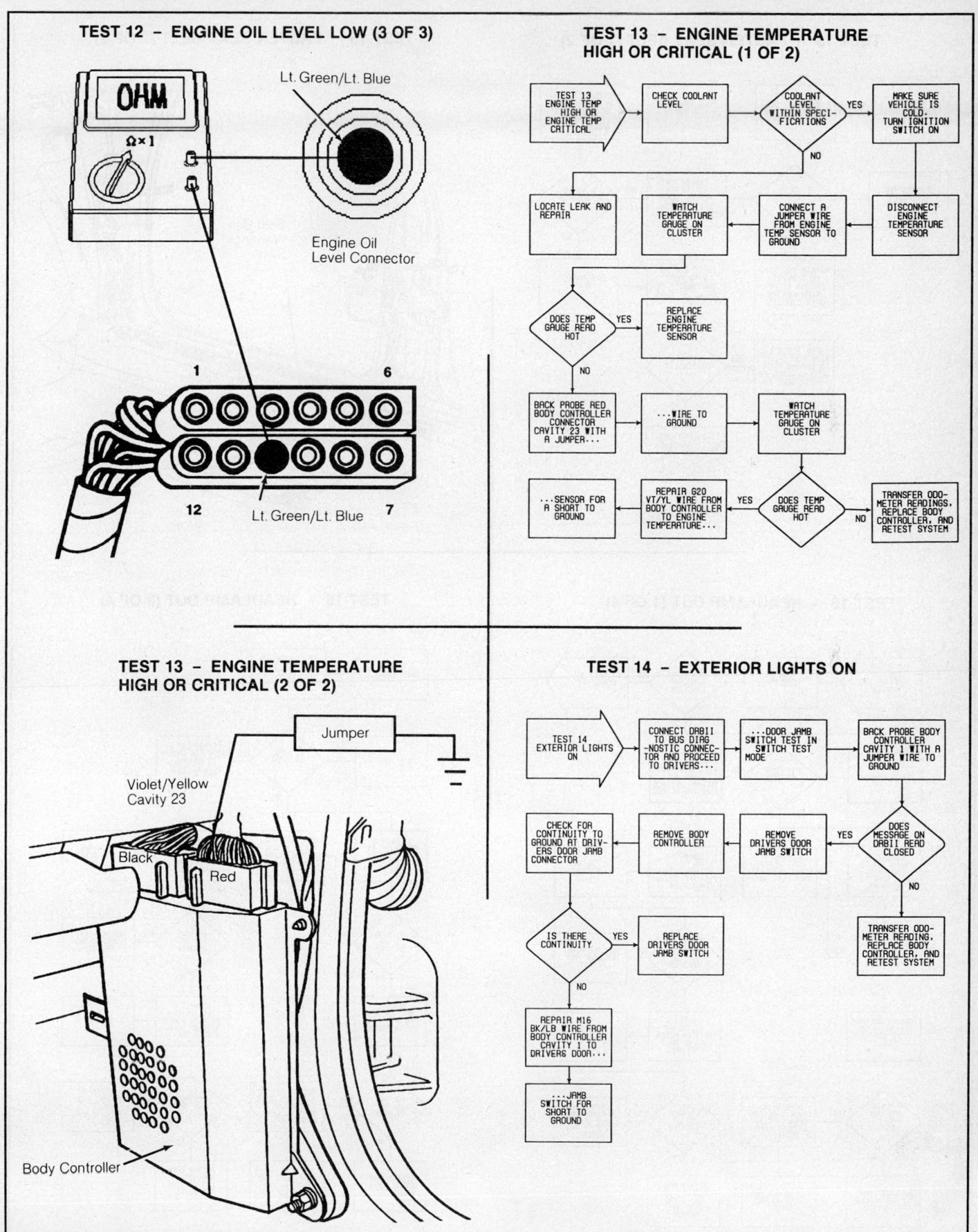

TEST 12 - ENGINE OIL LEVEL LOW (3 OF 3)

OHM

Ω × 1

Lt. Green/Lt. Blue

Engine Oil
Level Connector

1   6

12   7

Lt. Green/Lt. Blue

**TEST 13 - ENGINE TEMPERATURE
HIGH OR CRITICAL (1 OF 2)**

TEST 13 ENGINE TEMP HIGH OR ENGINE TEMP CRITICAL → CHECK COOLANT LEVEL → COOLANT LEVEL WITHIN SPECIFICATIONS → YES → MAKE SURE VEHICLE IS COLD. TURN IGNITION SWITCH ON

NO

LOCATE LEAK AND REPAIR ← WATCH TEMPERATURE GAUGE ON CLUSTER ← CONNECT A JUMPER WIRE FROM ENGINE TEMP SENSOR TO GROUND ← DISCONNECT ENGINE TEMPERATURE SENSOR

DOES TEMP GAUGE READ HOT → YES → REPLACE ENGINE TEMPERATURE SENSOR

NO

BACK PROBE RED BODY CONTROLLER CONNECTOR CAVITY 23 WITH A JUMPER... → ...WIRE TO GROUND → WATCH TEMPERATURE GAUGE ON CLUSTER

...SENSOR FOR A SHORT TO GROUND ← REPAIR G20 VT/YL WIRE FROM BODY CONTROLLER TO ENGINE TEMPERATURE... ← YES ← DOES TEMP GAUGE READ HOT ← NO ← TRANSFER ODOMETER READINGS, REPLACE BODY CONTROLLER, AND RETEST SYSTEM

**TEST 13 - ENGINE TEMPERATURE
HIGH OR CRITICAL (2 OF 2)**

Jumper

Violet/Yellow
Cavity 23

Black

Red

Body Controller

TEST 14 - EXTERIOR LIGHTS ON

TEST 14 EXTERIOR LIGHTS ON → CONNECT DRBII TO BUS DIAGNOSTIC CONNECTOR AND PROCEED TO DRIVERS... → ...DOOR JAMB SWITCH TEST IN SWITCH TEST MODE → BACK PROBE BODY CONTROLLER CAVITY 1 WITH A JUMPER WIRE TO GROUND

CHECK FOR CONTINUITY TO GROUND AT DRIVERS DOOR JAMB CONNECTOR ← REMOVE BODY CONTROLLER ← REMOVE DRIVERS DOOR JAMB SWITCH ← YES ← DOES MESSAGE ON DRBII READ CLOSED

NO

IS THERE CONTINUITY → YES → REPLACE DRIVERS DOOR JAMB SWITCH

NO

REPAIR M16 BK/LB WIRE FROM BODY CONTROLLER CAVITY 1 TO DRIVERS DOOR...

...JAMB SWITCH FOR SHORT TO GROUND

TRANSFER ODOMETER READING, REPLACE BODY CONTROLLER, AND RETEST SYSTEM

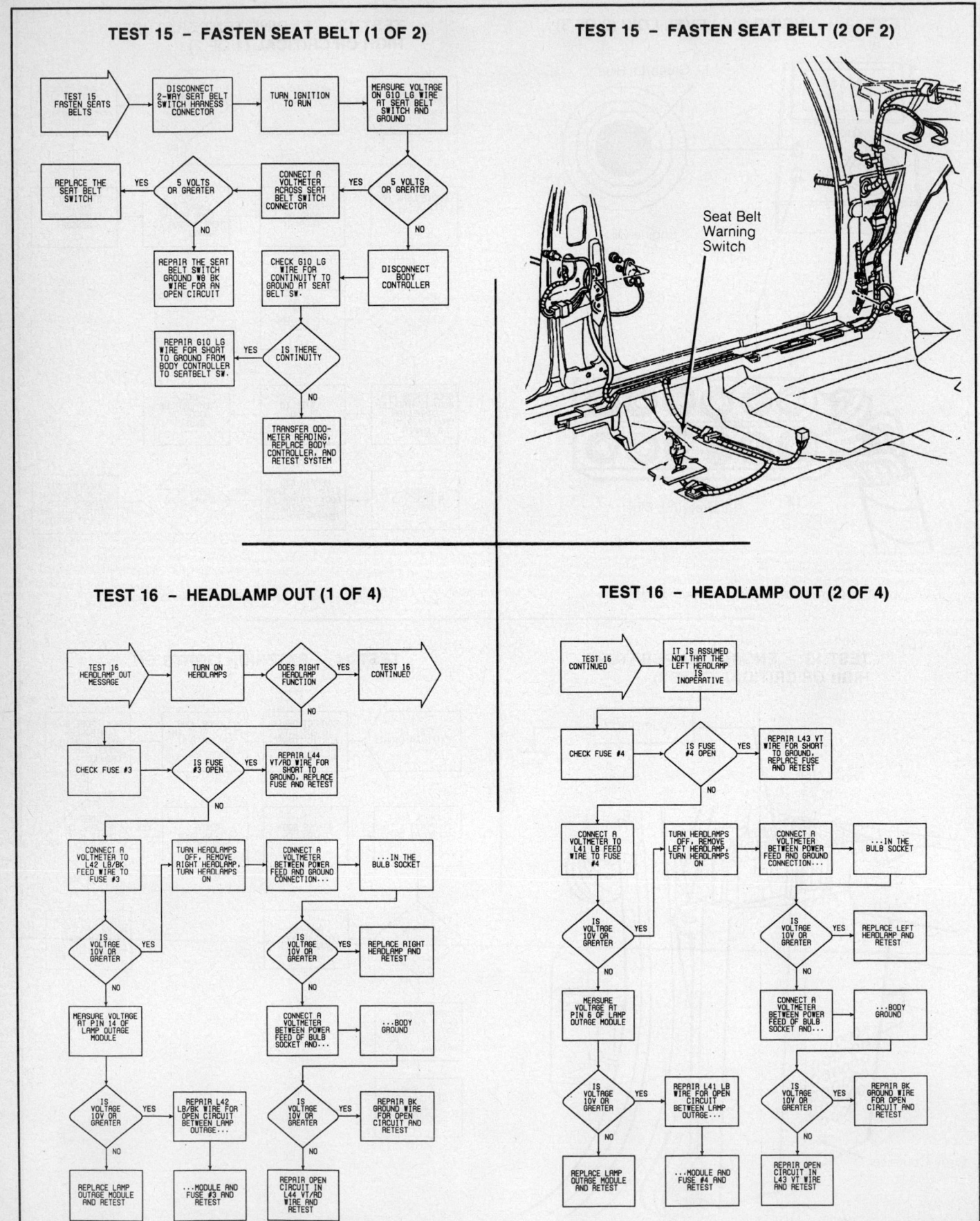

TEST 15 — FASTEN SEAT BELT (1 OF 2)

TEST 15 — FASTEN SEAT BELT (2 OF 2)

Seat Belt Warning Switch

TEST 16 — HEADLAMP OUT (1 OF 4)

TEST 16 — HEADLAMP OUT (2 OF 4)

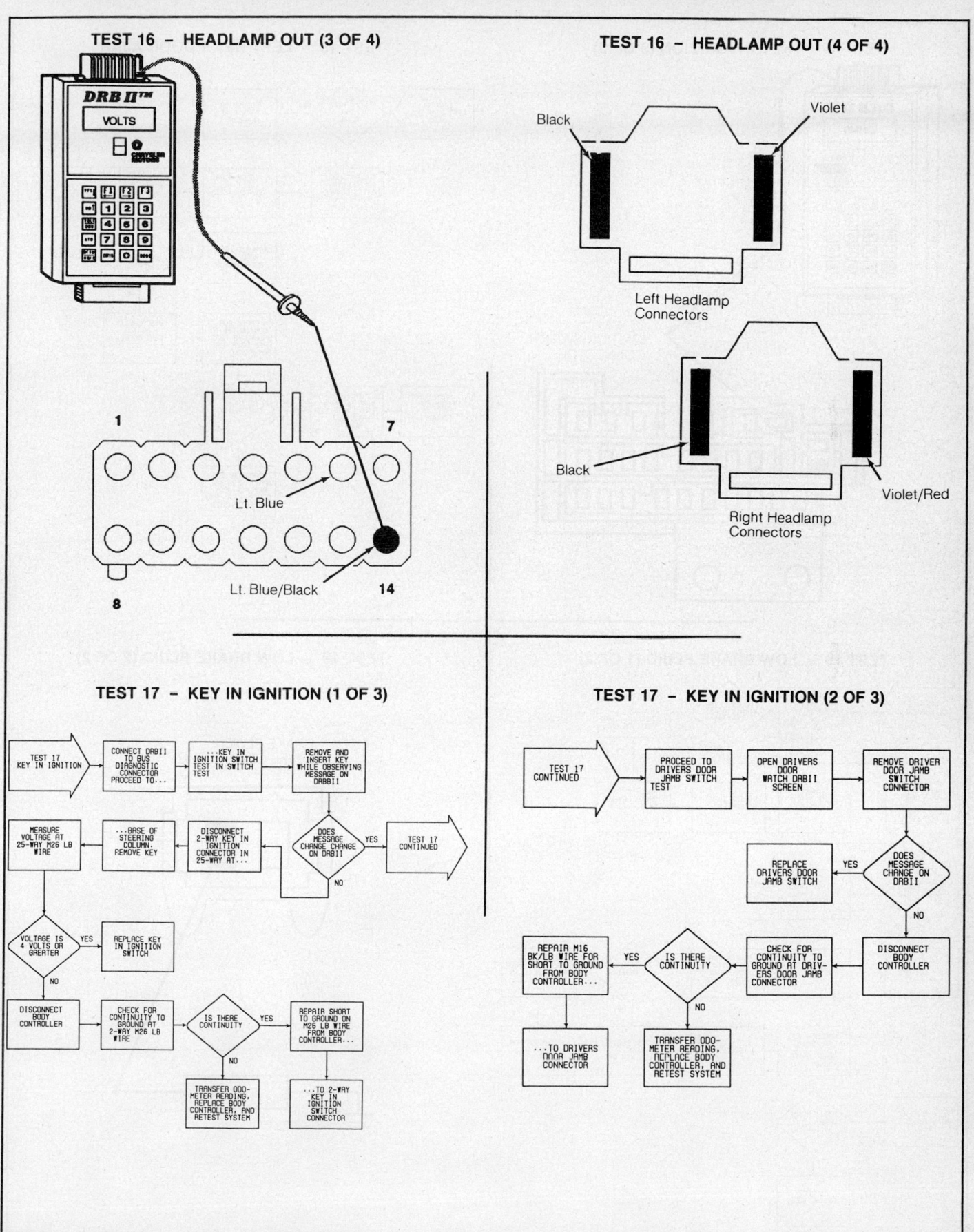

TEST 16 – HEADLAMP OUT (3 OF 4)

DRB II™
VOLTS

1
7
Lt. Blue
Lt. Blue/Black
8
14

TEST 16 – HEADLAMP OUT (4 OF 4)

Black
Violet
Left Headlamp Connectors

Black
Violet/Red
Right Headlamp Connectors

TEST 17 – KEY IN IGNITION (1 OF 3)

TEST 17 KEY IN IGNITION →
CONNECT DRBII TO BUS DIAGNOSTIC CONNECTOR PROCEED TO...
...KEY IN IGNITION SWITCH TEST IN SWITCH TEST
REMOVE AND INSERT KEY WHILE OBSERVING MESSAGE ON DRBBII

MEASURE VOLTAGE AT 25-WAY M26 LB WIRE
...BASE OF STEERING COLUMN. REMOVE KEY
DISCONNECT 2-WAY KEY IN IGNITION CONNECTOR IN 25-WAY AT...
DOES MESSAGE CHANGE ON DRBII → YES → TEST 17 CONTINUED
NO

VOLTAGE IS 4 VOLTS OR GREATER → YES → REPLACE KEY IN IGNITION SWITCH
NO

DISCONNECT BODY CONTROLLER
CHECK FOR CONTINUITY TO GROUND AT 2-WAY M26 LB WIRE
IS THERE CONTINUITY → YES → REPAIR SHORT TO GROUND ON M26 LB WIRE FROM BODY CONTROLLER...
NO
TRANSFER ODO-METER READING, REPLACE BODY CONTROLLER, AND RETEST SYSTEM
...TO 2-WAY KEY IN IGNITION SWITCH CONNECTOR

TEST 17 – KEY IN IGNITION (2 OF 3)

TEST 17 CONTINUED →
PROCEED TO DRIVERS DOOR JAMB SWITCH TEST
OPEN DRIVERS DOOR WATCH DRBII SCREEN
REMOVE DRIVER DOOR JAMB SWITCH CONNECTOR

REPLACE DRIVERS DOOR JAMB SWITCH ← YES ← DOES MESSAGE CHANGE ON DRBII
NO

REPAIR M16 BK/LB WIRE FOR SHORT TO GROUND FROM BODY CONTROLLER... ← YES ← IS THERE CONTINUITY ← CHECK FOR CONTINUITY TO GROUND AT DRIVERS DOOR JAMB CONNECTOR ← DISCONNECT BODY CONTROLLER
NO
...TO DRIVERS DOOR JAMB CONNECTOR
TRANSFER ODO-METER READING, REPLACE BODY CONTROLLER, AND RETEST SYSTEM

1a-204

1989 COMPUTERIZED ENGINE CONTROLS
Chrysler Motors Body Control Computer (Cont.)

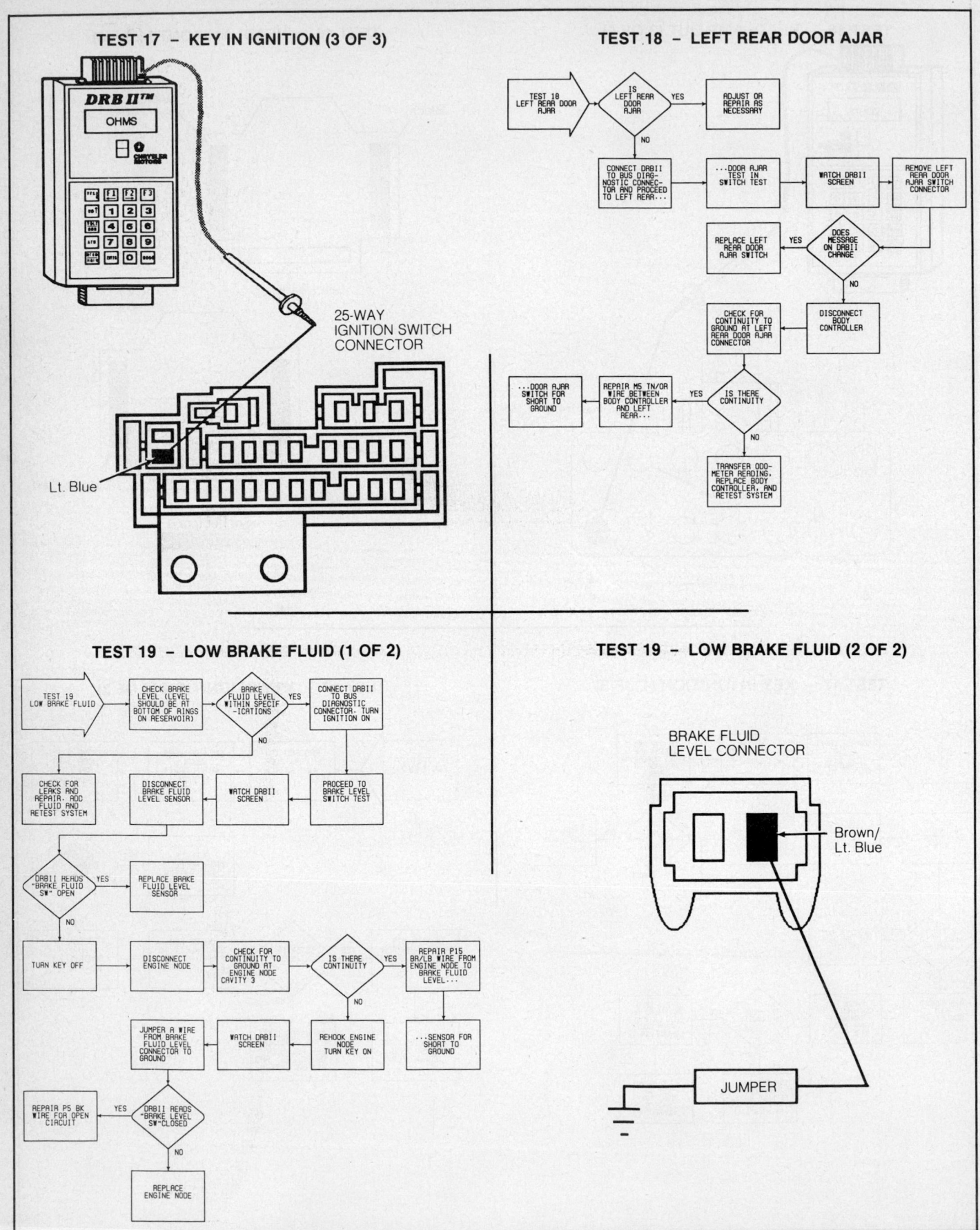

TEST 17 – KEY IN IGNITION (3 OF 3)

DRB II™

OHMS

CHRYSLER MOTORS

25-WAY IGNITION SWITCH CONNECTOR

Lt. Blue

TEST 18 – LEFT REAR DOOR AJAR

TEST 18 LEFT REAR DOOR AJAR → IS LEFT REAR DOOR AJAR → YES → ADJUST OR REPAIR AS NECESSARY

NO ↓

CONNECT DRBII TO BUS DIAGNOSTIC CONNECTOR AND PROCEED TO LEFT REAR... → ...DOOR AJAR TEST IN SWITCH TEST → WATCH DRBII SCREEN → REMOVE LEFT REAR DOOR AJAR SWITCH CONNECTOR

REPLACE LEFT REAR DOOR AJAR SWITCH ← YES ← DOES MESSAGE ON DRBII CHANGE

NO ↓

CHECK FOR CONTINUITY TO GROUND AT LEFT REAR DOOR AJAR CONNECTOR ← DISCONNECT BODY CONTROLLER

...DOOR AJAR SWITCH FOR SHORT TO GROUND ← REPAIR M5 TN/OR WIRE BETWEEN BODY CONTROLLER AND LEFT REAR... ← YES ← IS THERE CONTINUITY

NO ↓

TRANSFER ODOMETER READING, REPLACE BODY CONTROLLER, AND RETEST SYSTEM

TEST 19 – LOW BRAKE FLUID (1 OF 2)

TEST 19 LOW BRAKE FLUID → CHECK BRAKE LEVEL (LEVEL SHOULD BE AT BOTTOM OF RINGS ON RESERVOIR) → BRAKE FLUID LEVEL WITHIN SPECIFICATIONS → YES → CONNECT DRBII TO BUS DIAGNOSTIC CONNECTOR. TURN IGNITION ON

NO ↓

CHECK FOR LEAKS AND REPAIR. ADD FLUID AND RETEST SYSTEM ← DISCONNECT BRAKE FLUID LEVEL SENSOR ← WATCH DRBII SCREEN ← PROCEED TO BRAKE LEVEL SWITCH TEST

↓

DRBII READS "BRAKE FLUID SW" OPEN → YES → REPLACE BRAKE FLUID LEVEL SENSOR

NO ↓

TURN KEY OFF → DISCONNECT ENGINE NODE → CHECK FOR CONTINUITY TO GROUND AT ENGINE NODE CAVITY 3 → IS THERE CONTINUITY → YES → REPAIR P15 BR/LB WIRE FROM ENGINE NODE TO BRAKE FLUID LEVEL...

NO ↓

JUMPER A WIRE FROM BRAKE FLUID LEVEL CONNECTOR TO GROUND ← WATCH DRBII SCREEN ← REHOOK ENGINE NODE TURN KEY ON → ...SENSOR FOR SHORT TO GROUND

↓

REPAIR P5 BK WIRE FOR OPEN CIRCUIT ← YES ← DRBII READS "BRAKE LEVEL SW" CLOSED

NO ↓

REPLACE ENGINE NODE

TEST 19 – LOW BRAKE FLUID (2 OF 2)

BRAKE FLUID LEVEL CONNECTOR

Brown/ Lt. Blue

JUMPER

1989 COMPUTERIZED ENGINE CONTROLS
Chrysler Motors Body Control Computer (Cont.)

1a-205

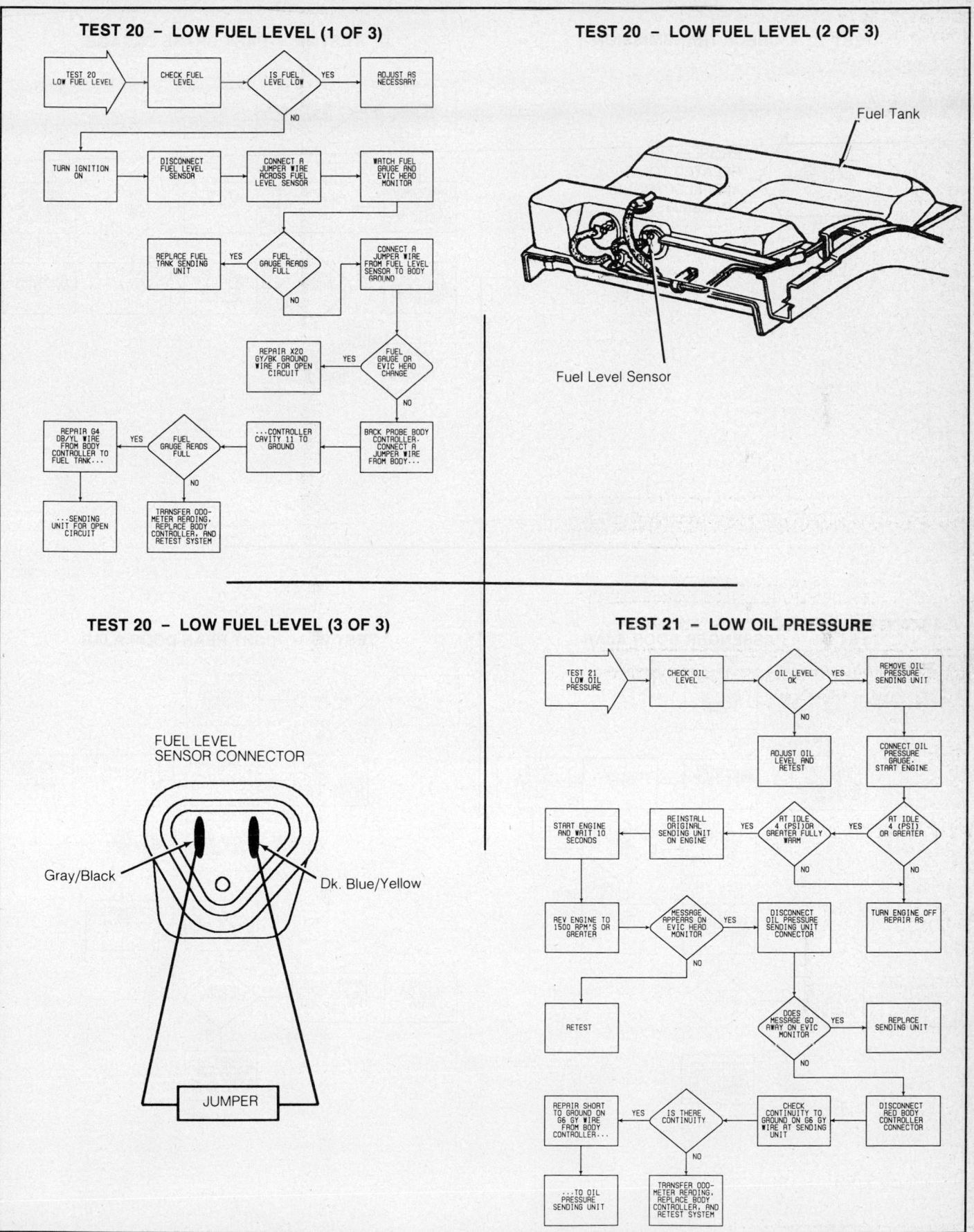

TEST 20 – LOW FUEL LEVEL (1 OF 3)

TEST 20 LOW FUEL LEVEL → CHECK FUEL LEVEL → IS FUEL LEVEL LOW → YES → ADJUST AS NECESSARY

NO → TURN IGNITION ON → DISCONNECT FUEL LEVEL SENSOR → CONNECT A JUMPER WIRE ACROSS FUEL LEVEL SENSOR → WATCH FUEL GAUGE AND EVIC HEAD MONITOR

REPLACE FUEL TANK SENDING UNIT ← YES ← FUEL GAUGE READS FULL ← CONNECT A JUMPER WIRE FROM FUEL LEVEL SENSOR TO BODY GROUND

NO → REPAIR X20 GY/BK GROUND WIRE FOR OPEN CIRCUIT ← YES ← FUEL GAUGE OR EVIC HEAD CHANGE

NO → REPAIR G4 DB/YL WIRE FROM BODY CONTROLLER TO FUEL TANK... ← YES ← FUEL GAUGE READS FULL ← ...CONTROLLER CAVITY 11 TO GROUND ← BACK PROBE BODY CONTROLLER. CONNECT A JUMPER WIRE FROM BODY...

...SENDING UNIT FOR OPEN CIRCUIT

NO → TRANSFER ODD-OMETER READING, REPLACE BODY CONTROLLER, AND RETEST SYSTEM

TEST 20 – LOW FUEL LEVEL (2 OF 3)

Fuel Tank

Fuel Level Sensor

TEST 20 – LOW FUEL LEVEL (3 OF 3)

FUEL LEVEL SENSOR CONNECTOR

Gray/Black

Dk. Blue/Yellow

JUMPER

TEST 21 – LOW OIL PRESSURE

TEST 21 LOW OIL PRESSURE → CHECK OIL LEVEL → OIL LEVEL OK → YES → REMOVE OIL PRESSURE SENDING UNIT

NO → ADJUST OIL LEVEL AND RETEST

CONNECT OIL PRESSURE GAUGE. START ENGINE

START ENGINE AND WAIT 10 SECONDS ← REINSTALL ORIGINAL SENDING UNIT ON ENGINE ← YES ← AT IDLE 4 (PSI) OR GREATER FULLY WARM ← YES ← AT IDLE 4 (PSI) OR GREATER

NO → REV ENGINE TO 1500 RPM'S OR GREATER → MESSAGE APPEARS ON EVIC HEAD MONITOR → YES → DISCONNECT OIL PRESSURE SENDING UNIT CONNECTOR

NO → TURN ENGINE OFF REPAIR AS

NO → RETEST

DOES MESSAGE GO AWAY ON EVIC MONITOR → YES → REPLACE SENDING UNIT

NO → CHECK CONTINUITY TO GROUND ON G6 GY WIRE AT SENDING UNIT ← DISCONNECT RED BODY CONTROLLER CONNECTOR

REPAIR SHORT TO GROUND ON G6 GY WIRE FROM BODY CONTROLLER... ← YES ← IS THERE CONTINUITY

NO → ...TO OIL PRESSURE SENDING UNIT

TRANSFER ODD-OMETER READING, REPLACE BODY CONTROLLER, AND RETEST SYSTEM

1a-206

1989 COMPUTERIZED ENGINE CONTROLS
Chrysler Motors Body Control Computer (Cont.)

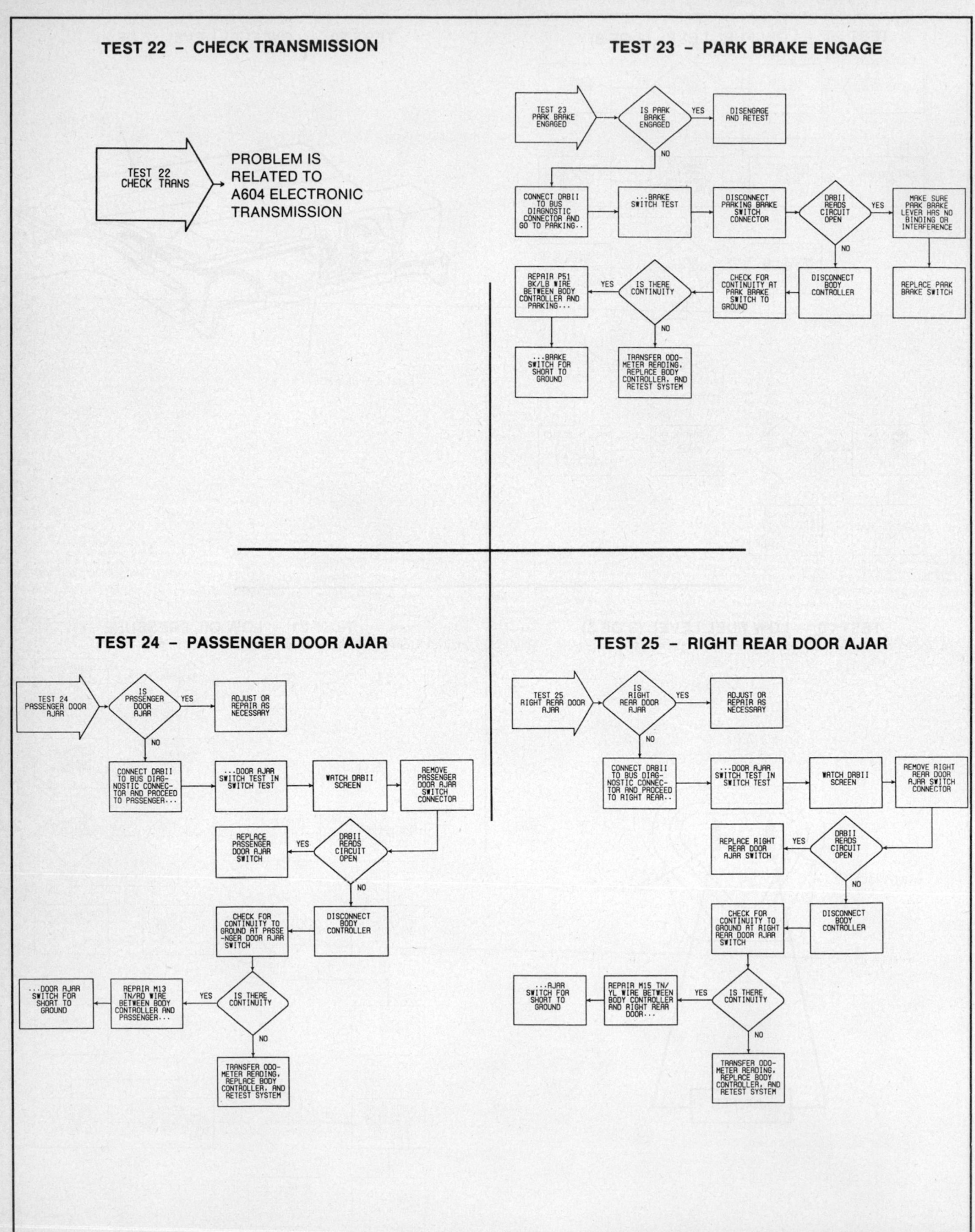

TEST 22 – CHECK TRANSMISSION

TEST 22 CHECK TRANS → PROBLEM IS RELATED TO A604 ELECTRONIC TRANSMISSION

TEST 23 – PARK BRAKE ENGAGE

TEST 23 PARK BRAKE ENGAGED → IS PARK BRAKE ENGAGED → (YES) DISENGAGE AND RETEST

(NO) → CONNECT DRBII TO BUS DIAGNOSTIC CONNECTOR AND GO TO PARKING... → ...BRAKE SWITCH TEST → DISCONNECT PARKING BRAKE SWITCH CONNECTOR → DRBII READS CIRCUIT OPEN → (YES) MAKE SURE PARK BRAKE LEVER HAS NO BINDING OR INTERFERENCE → REPLACE PARK BRAKE SWITCH

(NO) → DISCONNECT BODY CONTROLLER → CHECK FOR CONTINUITY AT PARK BRAKE SWITCH TO GROUND → IS THERE CONTINUITY → (YES) REPAIR P51 BK/LB WIRE BETWEEN BODY CONTROLLER AND PARKING... → ...BRAKE SWITCH FOR SHORT TO GROUND

(NO) TRANSFER ODOMETER READING, REPLACE BODY CONTROLLER, AND RETEST SYSTEM

TEST 24 – PASSENGER DOOR AJAR

TEST 24 PASSENGER DOOR AJAR → IS PASSENGER DOOR AJAR → (YES) ADJUST OR REPAIR AS NECESSARY

(NO) → CONNECT DRBII TO BUS DIAGNOSTIC CONNECTOR AND PROCEED TO PASSENGER... → ...DOOR AJAR SWITCH TEST IN SWITCH TEST → WATCH DRBII SCREEN → REMOVE PASSENGER DOOR AJAR SWITCH CONNECTOR → DRBII READS CIRCUIT OPEN → (YES) REPLACE PASSENGER DOOR AJAR SWITCH

(NO) → DISCONNECT BODY CONTROLLER → CHECK FOR CONTINUITY TO GROUND AT PASSENGER DOOR AJAR SWITCH → IS THERE CONTINUITY → (YES) REPAIR M13 TN/RD WIRE BETWEEN BODY CONTROLLER AND PASSENGER... → ...DOOR AJAR SWITCH FOR SHORT TO GROUND

(NO) TRANSFER ODOMETER READING, REPLACE BODY CONTROLLER, AND RETEST SYSTEM

TEST 25 – RIGHT REAR DOOR AJAR

TEST 25 RIGHT REAR DOOR AJAR → IS RIGHT REAR DOOR AJAR → (YES) ADJUST OR REPAIR AS NECESSARY

(NO) → CONNECT DRBII TO BUS DIAGNOSTIC CONNECTOR AND PROCEED TO RIGHT REAR... → ...DOOR AJAR SWITCH TEST IN SWITCH TEST → WATCH DRBII SCREEN → REMOVE RIGHT REAR DOOR AJAR SWITCH CONNECTOR → DRBII READS CIRCUIT OPEN → (YES) REPLACE RIGHT REAR DOOR AJAR SWITCH

(NO) → DISCONNECT BODY CONTROLLER → CHECK FOR CONTINUITY TO GROUND AT RIGHT REAR DOOR AJAR SWITCH → IS THERE CONTINUITY → (YES) REPAIR M15 TN/YL WIRE BETWEEN BODY CONTROLLER AND RIGHT REAR DOOR... → ...AJAR SWITCH FOR SHORT TO GROUND

(NO) TRANSFER ODOMETER READING, REPLACE BODY CONTROLLER, AND RETEST SYSTEM

1989 COMPUTERIZED ENGINE CONTROLS
Chrysler Motors Body Control Computer (Cont.)

1a-207

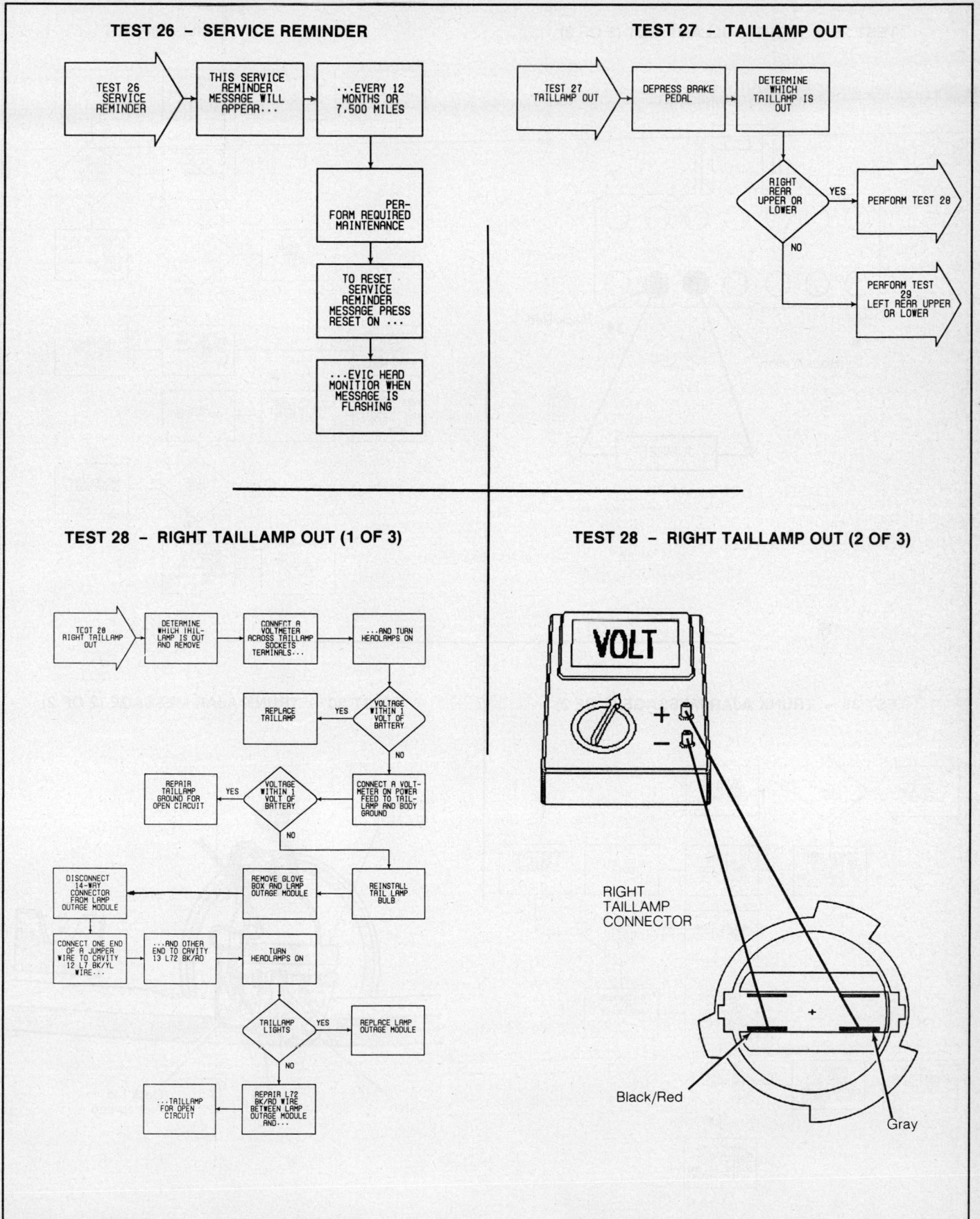

TEST 26 – SERVICE REMINDER

TEST 26 SERVICE REMINDER → THIS SERVICE REMINDER MESSAGE WILL APPEAR... → ...EVERY 12 MONTHS OR 7,500 MILES → PER-FORM REQUIRED MAINTENANCE → TO RESET SERVICE REMINDER MESSAGE PRESS RESET ON ... → ...EVIC HEAD MONITIOR WHEN MESSAGE IS FLASHING

TEST 27 – TAILLAMP OUT

TEST 27 TAILLAMP OUT → DEPRESS BRAKE PEDAL → DETERMINE WHICH TAILLAMP IS OUT → RIGHT REAR UPPER OR LOWER

YES → PERFORM TEST 28

NO → PERFORM TEST 29 LEFT REAR UPPER OR LOWER

TEST 28 – RIGHT TAILLAMP OUT (1 OF 3)

TEST 28 RIGHT TAILLAMP OUT → DETERMINE WHICH TAIL-LAMP IS OUT AND REMOVE → CONNECT A VOLTMETER ACROSS TAILLAMP SOCKETS TERMINALS... → ...AND TURN HEADLAMPS ON → VOLTAGE WITHIN 1 VOLT OF BATTERY

YES → REPLACE TAILLAMP

NO → CONNECT A VOLT-METER ON POWER FEED TO TAIL-LAMP AND BODY GROUND → VOLTAGE WITHIN 1 VOLT OF BATTERY

YES → REPAIR TAILLAMP GROUND FOR OPEN CIRCUIT

NO → REINSTALL TAIL LAMP BULB → REMOVE GLOVE BOX AND LAMP OUTAGE MODULE → DISCONNECT 14-WAY CONNECTOR FROM LAMP OUTAGE MODULE → CONNECT ONE END OF A JUMPER WIRE TO CAVITY 12 L7 BK/YL WIRE... → ...AND OTHER END TO CAVITY 13 L72 BK/RD → TURN HEADLAMPS ON → TAILLAMP LIGHTS

YES → REPLACE LAMP OUTAGE MODULE

NO → REPAIR L72 BK/RD WIRE BETWEEN LAMP OUTAGE MODULE AND... → ...TAILLAMP FOR OPEN CIRCUIT

TEST 28 – RIGHT TAILLAMP OUT (2 OF 3)

VOLT

RIGHT TAILLAMP CONNECTOR

Black/Red

Gray

1989 COMPUTERIZED ENGINE CONTROLS
Chrysler Motors Body Control Computer (Cont.)

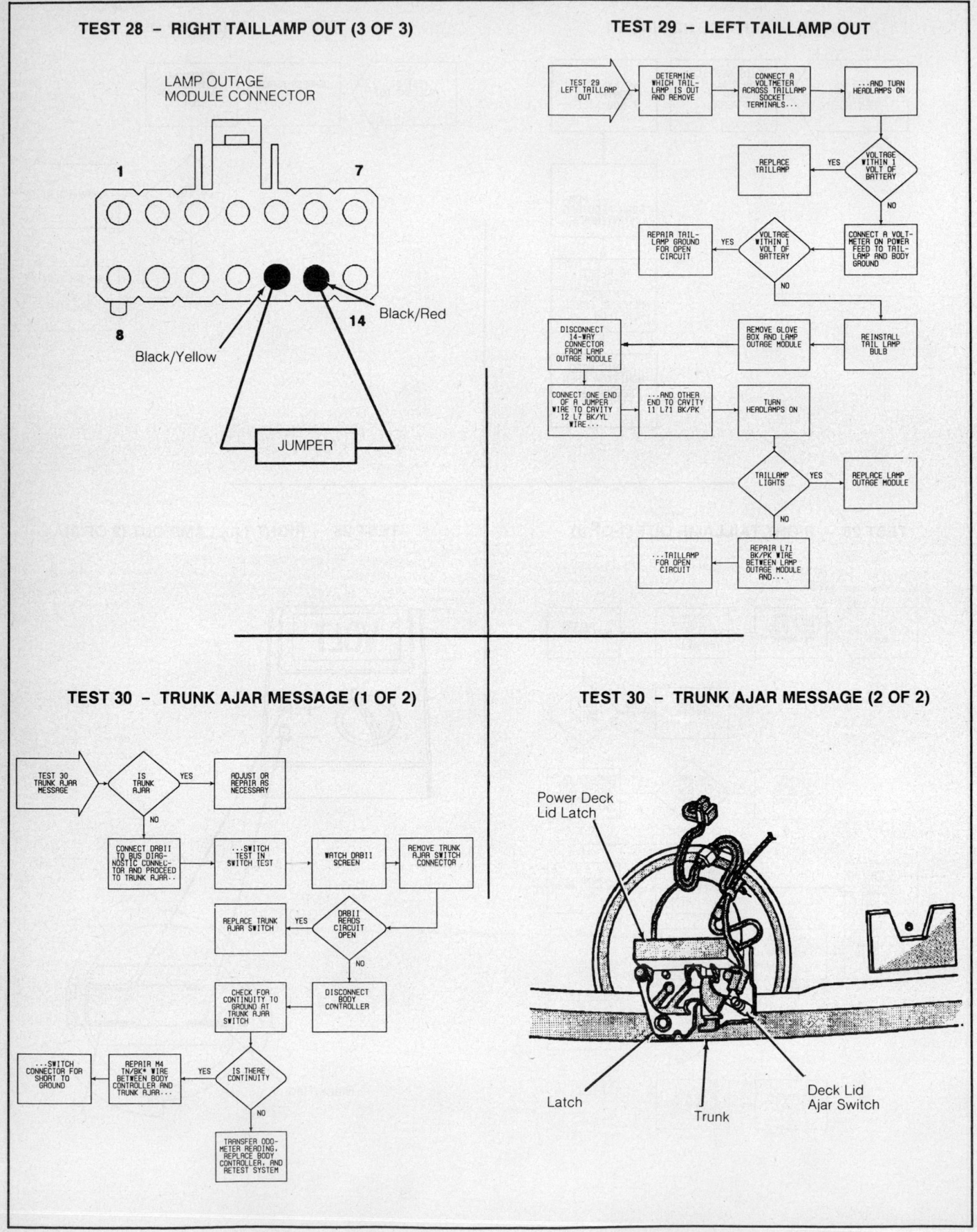

TEST 28 – RIGHT TAILLAMP OUT (3 OF 3)

LAMP OUTAGE
MODULE CONNECTOR

1

7

8

14

Black/Red

Black/Yellow

JUMPER

TEST 29 – LEFT TAILLAMP OUT

TEST 29 LEFT TAILLAMP OUT

DETERMINE WHICH TAILLAMP IS OUT AND REMOVE

CONNECT A VOLTMETER ACROSS TAILLAMP SOCKET TERMINALS...

...AND TURN HEADLAMPS ON

VOLTAGE WITHIN 1 VOLT OF BATTERY — YES → REPLACE TAILLAMP

NO

CONNECT A VOLTMETER ON POWER FEED TO TAILLAMP AND BODY GROUND

VOLTAGE WITHIN 1 VOLT OF BATTERY — YES → REPAIR TAILLAMP GROUND FOR OPEN CIRCUIT

NO

REINSTALL TAIL LAMP BULB

REMOVE GLOVE BOX AND LAMP OUTAGE MODULE

DISCONNECT 14-WAY CONNECTOR FROM LAMP OUTAGE MODULE

CONNECT ONE END OF A JUMPER WIRE TO CAVITY 12 L7 BK/YL WIRE...

...AND OTHER END TO CAVITY 11 L71 BK/PK WIRE...

TURN HEADLAMPS ON

TAILLAMP LIGHTS — YES → REPLACE LAMP OUTAGE MODULE

NO

REPAIR L71 BK/PK WIRE BETWEEN LAMP OUTAGE MODULE AND...

...TAILLAMP FOR OPEN CIRCUIT

TEST 30 – TRUNK AJAR MESSAGE (1 OF 2)

TEST 30 TRUNK AJAR MESSAGE

IS TRUNK AJAR — YES → ADJUST OR REPAIR AS NECESSARY

NO

CONNECT DRBII TO BUS DIAGNOSTIC CONNECTOR AND PROCEED TO TRUNK AJAR...

...SWITCH TEST IN SWITCH TEST

WATCH DRBII SCREEN

REMOVE TRUNK AJAR SWITCH CONNECTOR

DRBII READS CIRCUIT OPEN — YES → REPLACE TRUNK AJAR SWITCH

NO

DISCONNECT BODY CONTROLLER

CHECK FOR CONTINUITY TO GROUND AT TRUNK AJAR SWITCH

IS THERE CONTINUITY — YES → REPAIR M4 TN/BK* WIRE BETWEEN BODY CONTROLLER AND TRUNK AJAR... → ...SWITCH CONNECTOR FOR SHORT TO GROUND

NO

TRANSFER ODOMETER READING, REPLACE BODY CONTROLLER, AND RETEST SYSTEM

TEST 30 – TRUNK AJAR MESSAGE (2 OF 2)

Power Deck Lid Latch

Latch

Trunk

Deck Lid Ajar Switch

1989 COMPUTERIZED ENGINE CONTROLS
Chrysler Motors Body Control Computer (Cont.)

1a-209

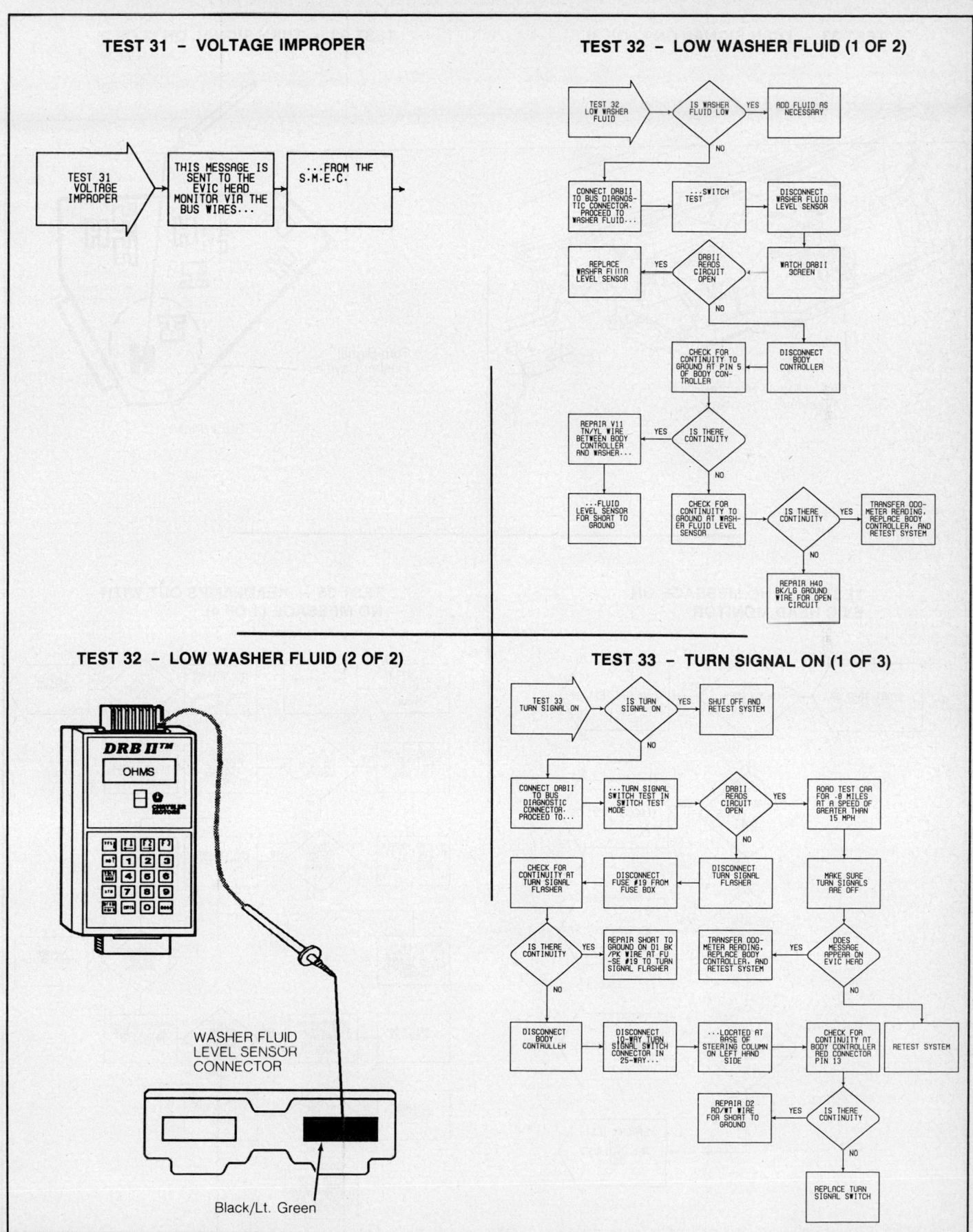

TEST 31 – VOLTAGE IMPROPER

TEST 31 VOLTAGE IMPROPER → THIS MESSAGE IS SENT TO THE EVIC HEAD MONITOR VIA THE BUS WIRES... → ...FROM THE S.M.E.C. →

TEST 32 – LOW WASHER FLUID (1 OF 2)

TEST 32 LOW WASHER FLUID → IS WASHER FLUID LOW → YES → ADD FLUID AS NECESSARY

NO

CONNECT DRBII TO BUS DIAGNOSTIC CONNECTOR. PROCEED TO WASHER FLUID... → ...SWITCH TEST → DISCONNECT WASHER FLUID LEVEL SENSOR

REPLACE WASHER FLUID LEVEL SENSOR ← YES ← DRBII READS CIRCUIT OPEN ← WATCH DRBII SCREEN

NO

CHECK FOR CONTINUITY TO GROUND AT PIN 5 OF BODY CONTROLLER ← DISCONNECT BODY CONTROLLER

REPAIR Y11 TN/YL WIRE BETWEEN BODY CONTROLLER AND WASHER... ← YES ← IS THERE CONTINUITY

NO

...FLUID LEVEL SENSOR FOR SHORT TO GROUND   CHECK FOR CONTINUITY TO GROUND AT WASHER FLUID LEVEL SENSOR → IS THERE CONTINUITY → YES → TRANSFER ODOMETER READING, REPLACE BODY CONTROLLER, AND RETEST SYSTEM

NO

REPAIR H40 BK/LG GROUND WIRE FOR OPEN CIRCUIT

TEST 32 – LOW WASHER FLUID (2 OF 2)

DRB II™ OHMS

WASHER FLUID LEVEL SENSOR CONNECTOR

Black/Lt. Green

TEST 33 – TURN SIGNAL ON (1 OF 3)

TEST 33 TURN SIGNAL ON → IS TURN SIGNAL ON → YES → SHUT OFF AND RETEST SYSTEM

NO

CONNECT DRBII TO BUS DIAGNOSTIC CONNECTOR. PROCEED TO... → ...TURN SIGNAL SWITCH TEST IN SWITCH TEST MODE → DRBII READS CIRCUIT OPEN → YES → ROAD TEST CAR FOR .0 MILES AT A SPEED OF GREATER THAN 15 MPH

NO

CHECK FOR CONTINUITY AT TURN SIGNAL FLASHER ← DISCONNECT FUSE #19 FROM FUSE BOX ← DISCONNECT TURN SIGNAL FLASHER   MAKE SURE TURN SIGNALS ARE OFF

IS THERE CONTINUITY → YES → REPAIR SHORT TO GROUND ON D1 BK/PK WIRE AT FUSE #19 TO TURN SIGNAL FLASHER → TRANSFER ODOMETER READING, REPLACE BODY CONTROLLER, AND RETEST SYSTEM ← YES ← DOES MESSAGE APPEAR ON EVIC HEAD

NO   NO

DISCONNECT BODY CONTROLLER → DISCONNECT 10-WAY TURN SIGNAL SWITCH CONNECTOR IN 25-WAY... → ...LOCATED AT BASE OF STEERING COLUMN ON LEFT HAND SIDE → CHECK FOR CONTINUITY AT BODY CONTROLLER RED CONNECTOR PIN 13 → RETEST SYSTEM

REPAIR D2 RD/WT WIRE FOR SHORT TO GROUND ← YES ← IS THERE CONTINUITY

NO

REPLACE TURN SIGNAL SWITCH

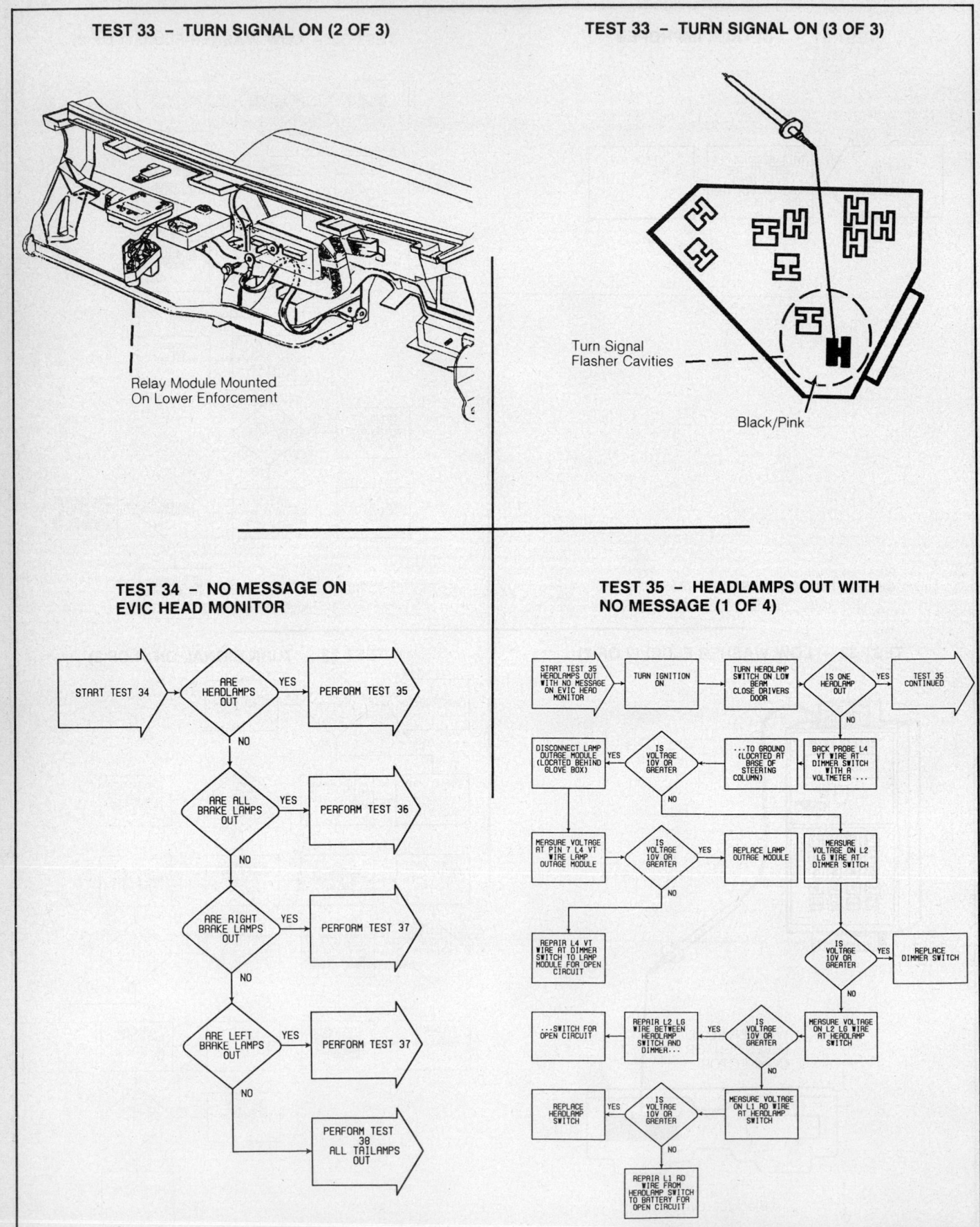

TEST 33 – TURN SIGNAL ON (2 OF 3)

Relay Module Mounted
On Lower Enforcement

TEST 33 – TURN SIGNAL ON (3 OF 3)

Turn Signal
Flasher Cavities

Black/Pink

TEST 34 – NO MESSAGE ON
EVIC HEAD MONITOR

START TEST 34 → ARE HEADLAMPS OUT → YES → PERFORM TEST 35

NO

ARE ALL BRAKE LAMPS OUT → YES → PERFORM TEST 36

NO

ARE RIGHT BRAKE LAMPS OUT → YES → PERFORM TEST 37

NO

ARE LEFT BRAKE LAMPS OUT → YES → PERFORM TEST 37

NO

PERFORM TEST 38 ALL TAILAMPS OUT

TEST 35 – HEADLAMPS OUT WITH
NO MESSAGE (1 OF 4)

START TEST 35 HEADLAMPS OUT WITH NO MESSAGE ON EVIC HEAD MONITOR → TURN IGNITION ON → TURN HEADLAMP SWITCH ON LOW BEAM CLOSE DRIVERS DOOR → IS ONE HEADLAMP OUT → YES → TEST 35 CONTINUED

NO

DISCONNECT LAMP OUTAGE MODULE (LOCATED BEHIND GLOVE BOX) ← YES ← IS VOLTAGE 10V OR GREATER ← ...TO GROUND (LOCATED AT BASE OF STEERING COLUMN) ← BACK PROBE L4 VT WIRE AT DIMMER SWITCH WITH A VOLTMETER ...

NO

MEASURE VOLTAGE AT PIN 7 L4 VT WIRE LAMP OUTAGE MODULE → IS VOLTAGE 10V OR GREATER → YES → REPLACE LAMP OUTAGE MODULE → MEASURE VOLTAGE ON L2 LG WIRE AT DIMMER SWITCH

NO

REPAIR L4 VT WIRE AT DIMMER SWITCH TO LAMP MODULE FOR OPEN CIRCUIT

IS VOLTAGE 10V OR GREATER → YES → REPLACE DIMMER SWITCH

NO

...SWITCH FOR OPEN CIRCUIT ← REPAIR L2 LG WIRE BETWEEN HEADLAMP SWITCH AND DIMMER... ← YES ← IS VOLTAGE 10V OR GREATER ← MEASURE VOLTAGE ON L2 LG WIRE AT HEADLAMP SWITCH

NO

REPLACE HEADLAMP SWITCH ← YES ← IS VOLTAGE 10V OR GREATER ← MEASURE VOLTAGE ON L1 RD WIRE AT HEADLAMP SWITCH

NO

REPAIR L1 RD WIRE FROM HEADLAMP SWITCH TO BATTERY FOR OPEN CIRCUIT

1989 COMPUTERIZED ENGINE CONTROLS
Chrysler Motors Body Control Computer (Cont.)

1a-211

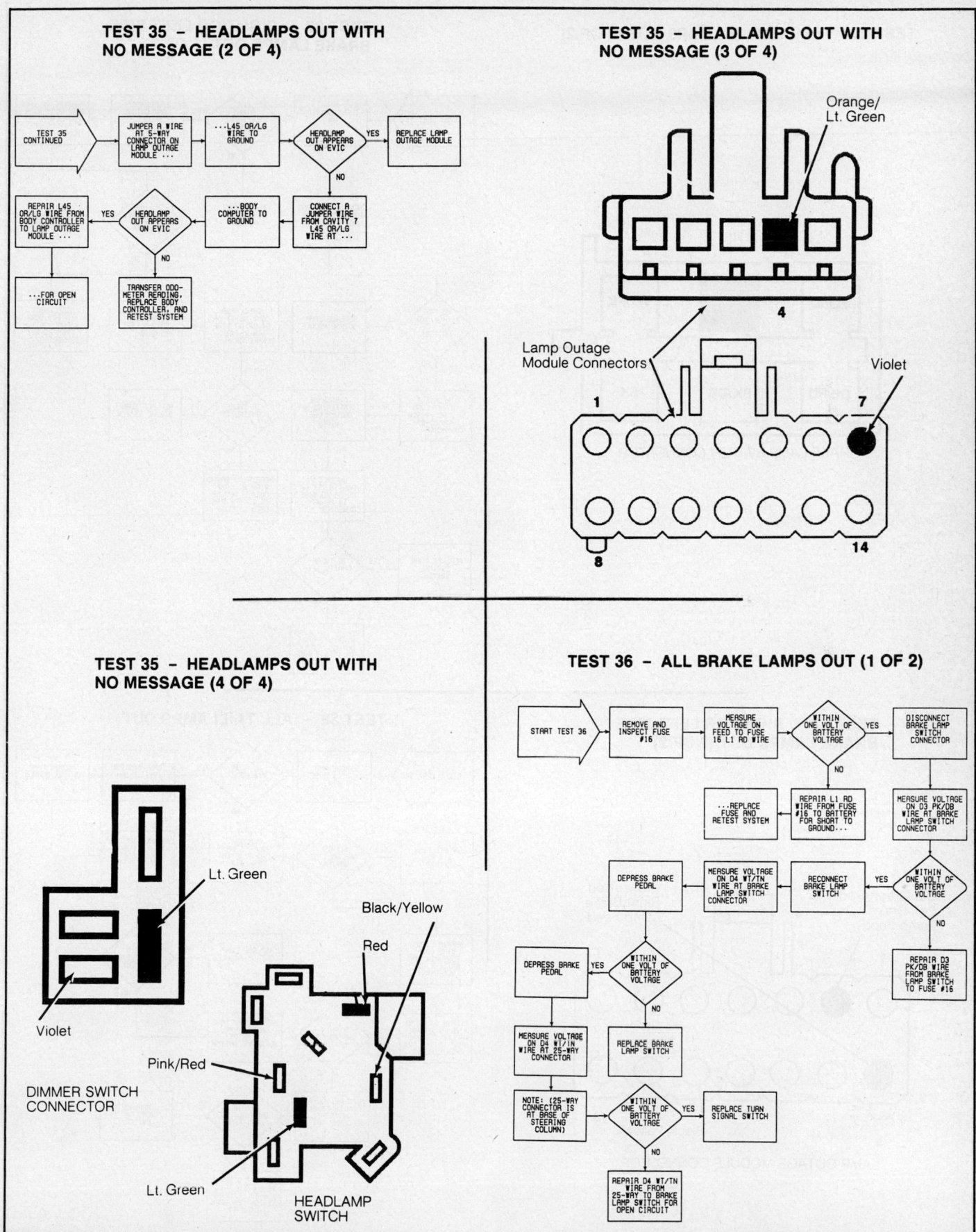

TEST 35 – HEADLAMPS OUT WITH
NO MESSAGE (2 OF 4)

TEST 35 – HEADLAMPS OUT WITH
NO MESSAGE (3 OF 4)

Orange/
Lt. Green

Lamp Outage
Module Connectors

Violet

1

7

8

14

4

TEST 35 – HEADLAMPS OUT WITH
NO MESSAGE (4 OF 4)

TEST 36 – ALL BRAKE LAMPS OUT (1 OF 2)

Lt. Green

Violet

DIMMER SWITCH
CONNECTOR

Black/Yellow

Red

Pink/Red

Lt. Green

HEADLAMP
SWITCH

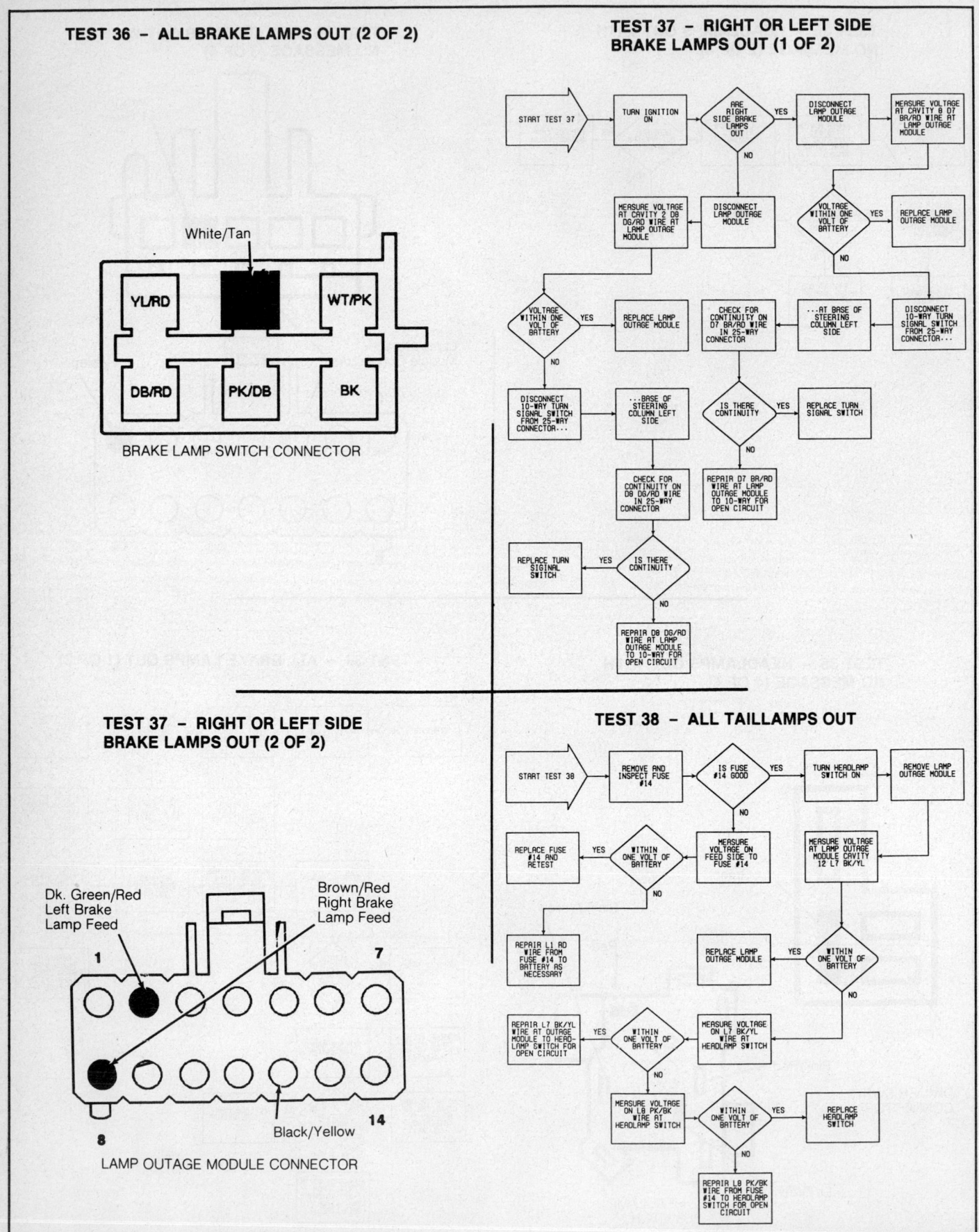

TEST 36 – ALL BRAKE LAMPS OUT (2 OF 2)

White/Tan

| YL/RD | | WT/PK |
| DB/RD | PK/DB | BK |

BRAKE LAMP SWITCH CONNECTOR

TEST 37 – RIGHT OR LEFT SIDE BRAKE LAMPS OUT (1 OF 2)

START TEST 37 → TURN IGNITION ON → ARE RIGHT SIDE BRAKE LAMPS OUT → YES → DISCONNECT LAMP OUTAGE MODULE → MEASURE VOLTAGE AT CAVITY 8 D7 BR/RD WIRE AT LAMP OUTAGE MODULE

NO ↓

MEASURE VOLTAGE AT CAVITY 2 D8 DG/RD WIRE AT LAMP OUTAGE MODULE ← DISCONNECT LAMP OUTAGE MODULE

VOLTAGE WITHIN ONE VOLT OF BATTERY → YES → REPLACE LAMP OUTAGE MODULE

NO ↓

VOLTAGE WITHIN ONE VOLT OF BATTERY → YES → REPLACE LAMP OUTAGE MODULE

CHECK FOR CONTINUITY ON D7 BR/RD WIRE IN 25-WAY CONNECTOR ← ...AT BASE OF STEERING COLUMN LEFT SIDE ← DISCONNECT 10-WAY TURN SIGNAL SWITCH FROM 25-WAY CONNECTOR...

NO ↓

DISCONNECT 10-WAY TURN SIGNAL SWITCH FROM 25-WAY CONNECTOR... → ...BASE OF STEERING COLUMN LEFT SIDE → IS THERE CONTINUITY → YES → REPLACE TURN SIGNAL SWITCH

NO ↓

CHECK FOR CONTINUITY ON D8 DG/RD WIRE IN 25-WAY CONNECTOR / REPAIR D7 BR/RD WIRE AT LAMP OUTAGE MODULE TO 10-WAY FOR OPEN CIRCUIT

REPLACE TURN SIGNAL SWITCH ← YES ← IS THERE CONTINUITY

NO ↓

REPAIR D8 DG/RD WIRE AT LAMP OUTAGE MODULE TO 10-WAY FOR OPEN CIRCUIT

TEST 37 – RIGHT OR LEFT SIDE BRAKE LAMPS OUT (2 OF 2)

Dk. Green/Red
Left Brake
Lamp Feed

Brown/Red
Right Brake
Lamp Feed

1   7

8   14

Black/Yellow

LAMP OUTAGE MODULE CONNECTOR

TEST 38 – ALL TAILLAMPS OUT

START TEST 38 → REMOVE AND INSPECT FUSE #14 → IS FUSE #14 GOOD → YES → TURN HEADLAMP SWITCH ON → REMOVE LAMP OUTAGE MODULE

NO ↓

REPLACE FUSE #14 AND RETEST ← YES ← WITHIN ONE VOLT OF BATTERY ← MEASURE VOLTAGE ON FEED SIDE TO FUSE #14 / MEASURE VOLTAGE AT LAMP OUTAGE MODULE CAVITY 12 L7 BK/YL

NO ↓

REPAIR L1 RD WIRE FROM FUSE #14 TO BATTERY AS NECESSARY / REPLACE LAMP OUTAGE MODULE ← YES ← WITHIN ONE VOLT OF BATTERY

NO ↓

REPAIR L7 BK/YL WIRE AT OUTAGE MODULE TO HEADLAMP SWITCH FOR OPEN CIRCUIT ← YES ← WITHIN ONE VOLT OF BATTERY ← MEASURE VOLTAGE ON L7 BK/YL WIRE AT HEADLAMP SWITCH

NO ↓

MEASURE VOLTAGE ON L8 PK/BK WIRE AT HEADLAMP SWITCH → WITHIN ONE VOLT OF BATTERY → YES → REPLACE HEADLAMP SWITCH

NO ↓

REPAIR L8 PK/BK WIRE FROM FUSE #14 TO HEADLAMP SWITCH FOR OPEN CIRCUIT

1989 COMPUTERIZED ENGINE CONTROLS
Chrysler Motors Body Control Computer (Cont.)

1a-213

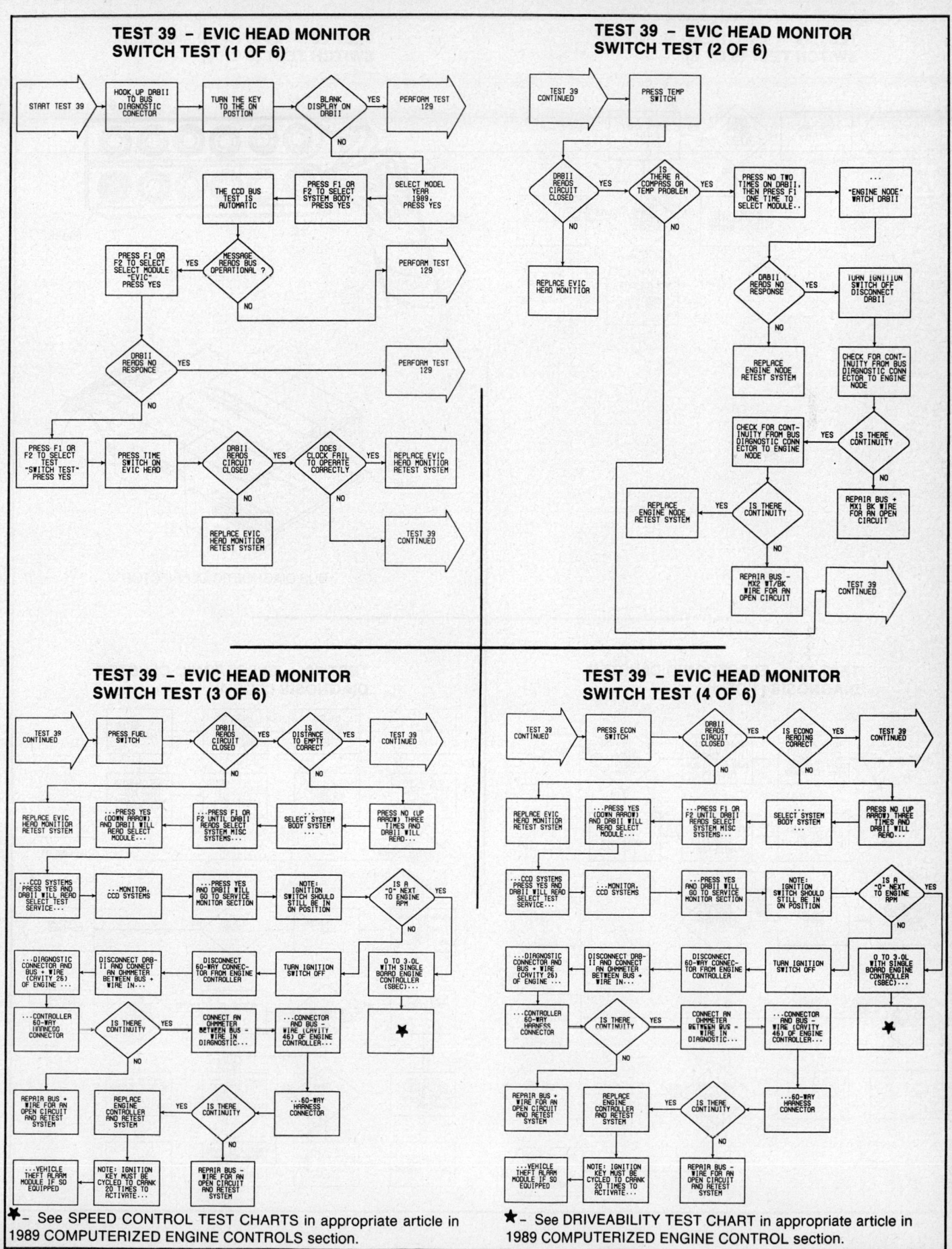

TEST 39 - EVIC HEAD MONITOR SWITCH TEST (1 OF 6)

TEST 39 - EVIC HEAD MONITOR SWITCH TEST (2 OF 6)

TEST 39 - EVIC HEAD MONITOR SWITCH TEST (3 OF 6)

TEST 39 - EVIC HEAD MONITOR SWITCH TEST (4 OF 6)

�star - See SPEED CONTROL TEST CHARTS in appropriate article in 1989 COMPUTERIZED ENGINE CONTROLS section.

�star - See DRIVEABILITY TEST CHART in appropriate article in 1989 COMPUTERIZED ENGINE CONTROL section.

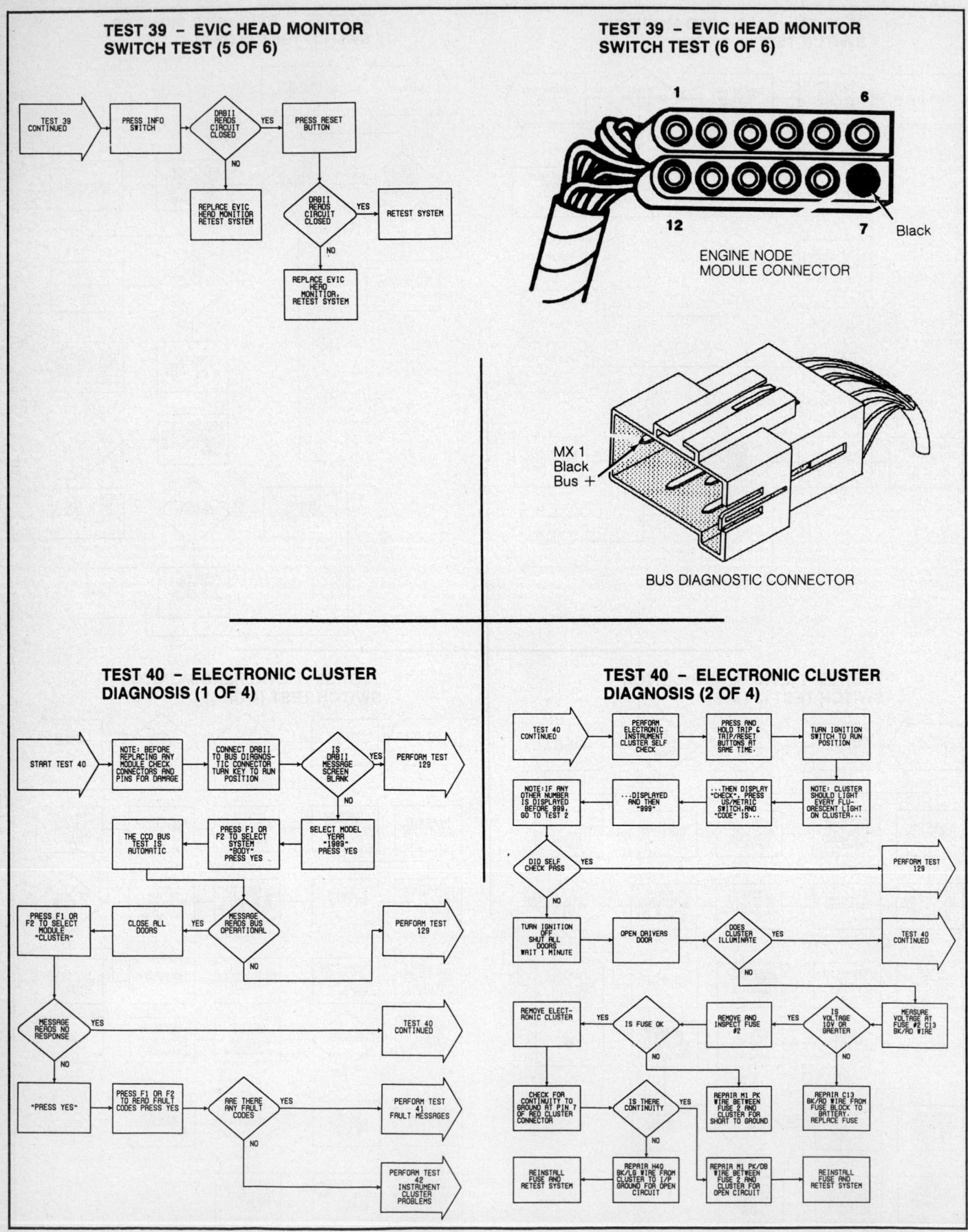

TEST 39 – EVIC HEAD MONITOR SWITCH TEST (5 OF 6)

TEST 39 – EVIC HEAD MONITOR SWITCH TEST (6 OF 6)

ENGINE NODE MODULE CONNECTOR

Black

BUS DIAGNOSTIC CONNECTOR

MX 1 Black Bus +

TEST 40 – ELECTRONIC CLUSTER DIAGNOSIS (1 OF 4)

TEST 40 – ELECTRONIC CLUSTER DIAGNOSIS (2 OF 4)

1989 COMPUTERIZED ENGINE CONTROLS
Chrysler Motors Body Control Computer (Cont.)

1a-215

TEST 40 – ELECTRONIC CLUSTER DIAGNOSIS (3 OF 4)

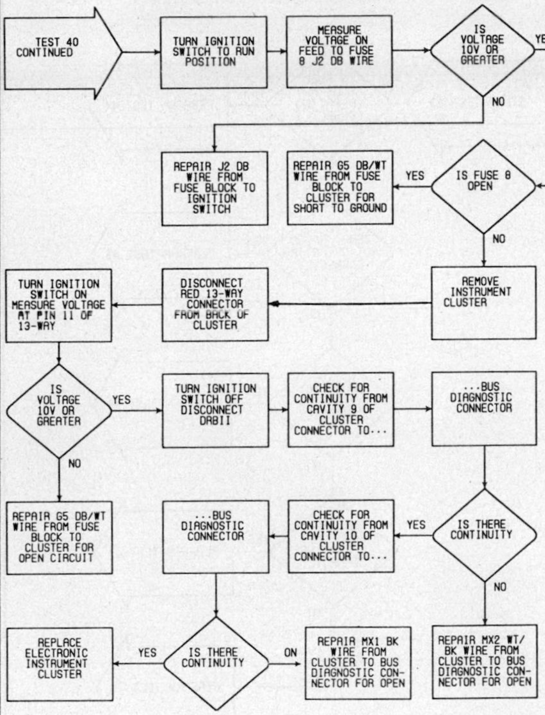

```
TEST 40 CONTINUED → TURN IGNITION SWITCH TO RUN POSITION → MEASURE VOLTAGE ON FEED TO FUSE 8 J2 DB WIRE → IS VOLTAGE 10V OR GREATER
```

IS VOLTAGE 10V OR GREATER — YES → REMOVE AND INSPECT FUSE #8

NO ↓

REPAIR J2 DB WIRE FROM FUSE BLOCK TO IGNITION SWITCH ← REPAIR G5 DB/WT WIRE FROM FUSE BLOCK TO CLUSTER FOR SHORT TO GROUND ← YES — IS FUSE 8 OPEN

NO ↓

REMOVE INSTRUMENT CLUSTER

TURN IGNITION SWITCH ON MEASURE VOLTAGE AT PIN 11 OF 13-WAY ← DISCONNECT RED 13-WAY CONNECTOR FROM BACK OF CLUSTER

IS VOLTAGE 10V OR GREATER — YES → TURN IGNITION SWITCH OFF DISCONNECT DRBII → CHECK FOR CONTINUITY FROM CAVITY 9 OF CLUSTER CONNECTOR TO... → ...BUS DIAGNOSTIC CONNECTOR

NO ↓

REPAIR G5 DB/WT WIRE FROM FUSE BLOCK TO CLUSTER FOR OPEN CIRCUIT ← ...BUS DIAGNOSTIC CONNECTOR ← CHECK FOR CONTINUITY FROM CAVITY 10 OF CLUSTER CONNECTOR TO... — YES — IS THERE CONTINUITY

NO ↓

REPLACE ELECTRONIC INSTRUMENT CLUSTER — YES — IS THERE CONTINUITY — ON → REPAIR MX1 BK WIRE FROM CLUSTER TO BUS DIAGNOSTIC CONNECTOR FOR OPEN | REPAIR MX2 WT/BK WIRE FROM CLUSTER TO BUS DIAGNOSTIC CONNECTOR FOR OPEN

TEST 40 – ELECTRONIC CLUSTER DIAGNOSIS (4 OF 4)

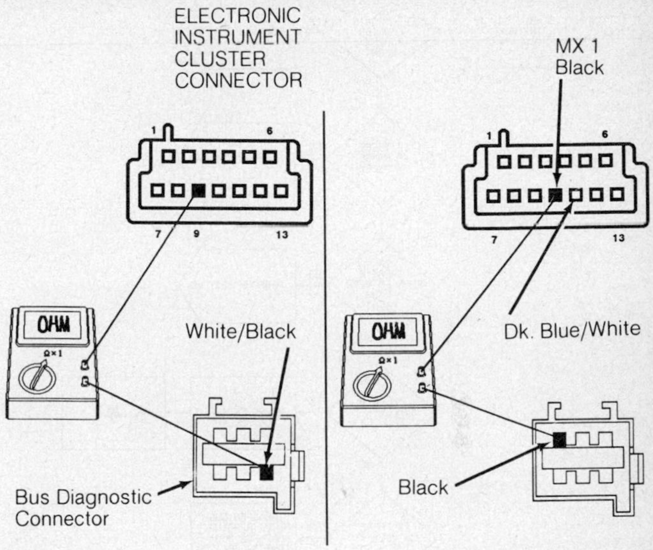

ELECTRONIC INSTRUMENT CLUSTER CONNECTOR

MX 1 Black

OHM Ω×1 — White/Black — Bus Diagnostic Connector

OHM Ω×1 — Dk. Blue/White — Black

TEST 41 – FAULT MESSAGES

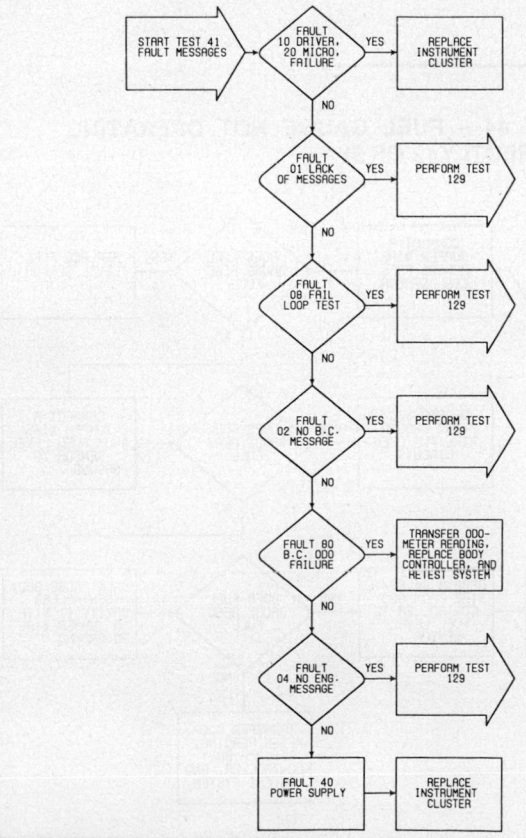

START TEST 41 FAULT MESSAGES → FAULT 10 DRIVER, 20 MICRO FAILURE — YES → REPLACE INSTRUMENT CLUSTER

NO ↓

FAULT 01 LACK OF MESSAGES — YES → PERFORM TEST 129

NO ↓

FAULT DB FAIL LOOP TEST — YES → PERFORM TEST 129

NO ↓

FAULT 02 NO B.C. MESSAGE — YES → PERFORM TEST 129

NO ↓

FAULT 80 B.C. ODO FAILURE — YES → TRANSFER ODOMETER READING, REPLACE BODY CONTROLLER, AND RETEST SYSTEM

NO ↓

FAULT 04 NO ENG. MESSAGE — YES → PERFORM TEST 129

NO ↓

FAULT 40 POWER SUPPLY → REPLACE INSTRUMENT CLUSTER

ELECTRONIC CLUSTER FAULT CODES

Electronic Cluster Fault Codes Using Self-Check Routine – Proceed to appropriate test as follows:

900 – Perform Test 129.

905 – Replace Electronic Instrument Cluster.

920 – Perform Test 129.

921 – Transfer odometer reading, replace body controller and retest system.

940 – Perform Test 129.

999 – End of Codes.

TEST 42 - IDENTIFYING PROBLEMS WITH ELECTRONIC CLUSTER NOT COVERED BY FAULT CODES

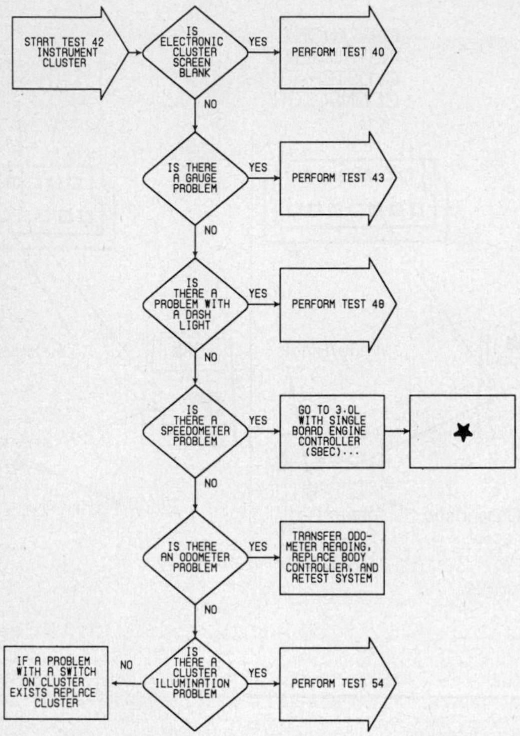
START TEST 42 INSTRUMENT CLUSTER
IS ELECTRONIC CLUSTER SCREEN BLANK
YES
PERFORM TEST 40
NO
IS THERE A GAUGE PROBLEM
YES
PERFORM TEST 43
NO
IS THERE A PROBLEM WITH A DASH LIGHT
YES
PERFORM TEST 48
NO
IS THERE A SPEEDOMETER PROBLEM
YES
GO TO 3.0L WITH SINGLE BOARD ENGINE CONTROLLER (SBEC)...
★
NO
IS THERE AN ODOMETER PROBLEM
YES
TRANSFER ODOMETER READING, REPLACE BODY CONTROLLER, AND RETEST SYSTEM
NO
IS THERE A CLUSTER ILLUMINATION PROBLEM
YES
PERFORM TEST 54
NO
IF A PROBLEM WITH A SWITCH ON CLUSTER EXISTS REPLACE CLUSTER

★ - See SPEED CONTROL TEST CHARTS in appropriate article in 1989 COMPUTERIZED ENGINE CONTROLS section.

TEST 43 - IDENTIFYING GAUGE PROBLEM WITH ELECTRONIC CLUSTER

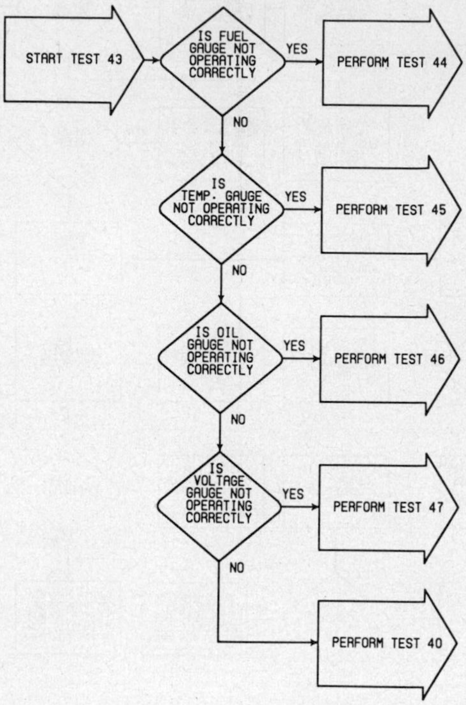
START TEST 43
IS FUEL GAUGE NOT OPERATING CORRECTLY
YES
PERFORM TEST 44
NO
IS TEMP. GAUGE NOT OPERATING CORRECTLY
YES
PERFORM TEST 45
NO
IS OIL GAUGE NOT OPERATING CORRECTLY
YES
PERFORM TEST 46
NO
IS VOLTAGE GAUGE NOT OPERATING CORRECTLY
YES
PERFORM TEST 47
NO
PERFORM TEST 40

TEST 44 - FUEL GAUGE NOT OPERATING CORRECTLY (1 OF 3)

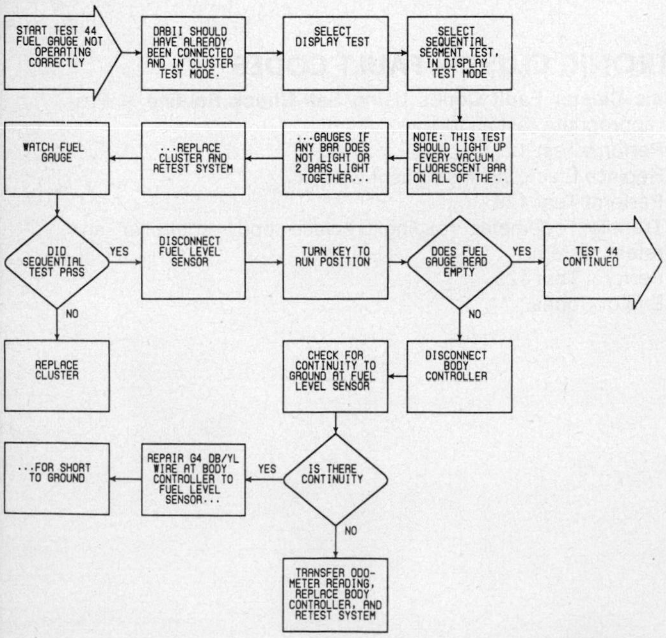
START TEST 44 FUEL GAUGE NOT OPERATING CORRECTLY
DRBII SHOULD HAVE ALREADY BEEN CONNECTED AND IN CLUSTER TEST MODE.
SELECT DISPLAY TEST
SELECT SEQUENTIAL SEGMENT TEST, IN DISPLAY TEST MODE
NOTE: THIS TEST SHOULD LIGHT UP EVERY VACUUM FLUORESCENT BAR ON ALL OF THE..
...GAUGES IF ANY BAR DOES NOT LIGHT OR 2 BARS LIGHT TOGETHER...
...REPLACE CLUSTER AND RETEST SYSTEM
WATCH FUEL GAUGE
DID SEQUENTIAL TEST PASS
YES
DISCONNECT FUEL LEVEL SENSOR
TURN KEY TO RUN POSITION
DOES FUEL GAUGE READ EMPTY
YES
TEST 44 CONTINUED
NO
REPLACE CLUSTER
NO
DISCONNECT BODY CONTROLLER
CHECK FOR CONTINUITY TO GROUND AT FUEL LEVEL SENSOR
IS THERE CONTINUITY
YES
REPAIR G4 DB/YL WIRE AT BODY CONTROLLER TO FUEL LEVEL SENSOR...
...FOR SHORT TO GROUND
NO
TRANSFER ODOMETER READING, REPLACE BODY CONTROLLER, AND RETEST SYSTEM

TEST 44 - FUEL GAUGE NOT OPERATING CORRECTLY (2 OF 3)

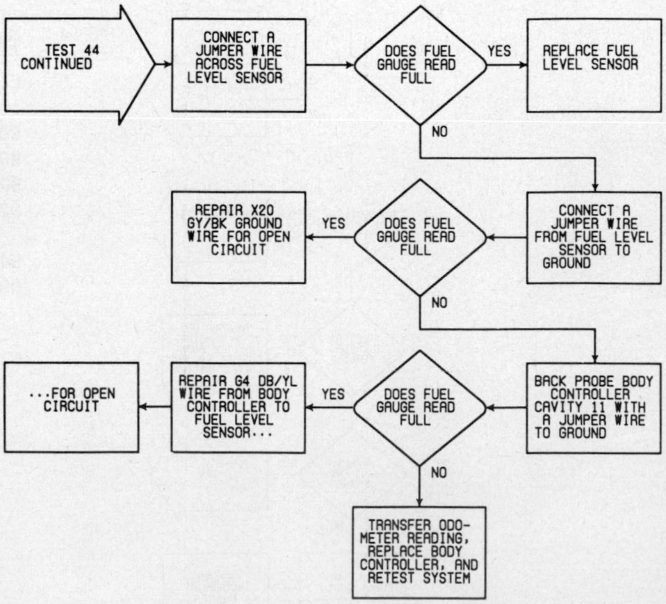
TEST 44 CONTINUED
CONNECT A JUMPER WIRE ACROSS FUEL LEVEL SENSOR
DOES FUEL GAUGE READ FULL
YES
REPLACE FUEL LEVEL SENSOR
NO
CONNECT A JUMPER WIRE FROM FUEL LEVEL SENSOR TO GROUND
DOES FUEL GAUGE READ FULL
YES
REPAIR X20 GY/BK GROUND WIRE FOR OPEN CIRCUIT
NO
BACK PROBE BODY CONTROLLER CAVITY 11 WITH A JUMPER WIRE TO GROUND
DOES FUEL GAUGE READ FULL
YES
REPAIR G4 DB/YL WIRE FROM BODY CONTROLLER TO FUEL LEVEL SENSOR...
...FOR OPEN CIRCUIT
NO
TRANSFER ODOMETER READING, REPLACE BODY CONTROLLER, AND RETEST SYSTEM

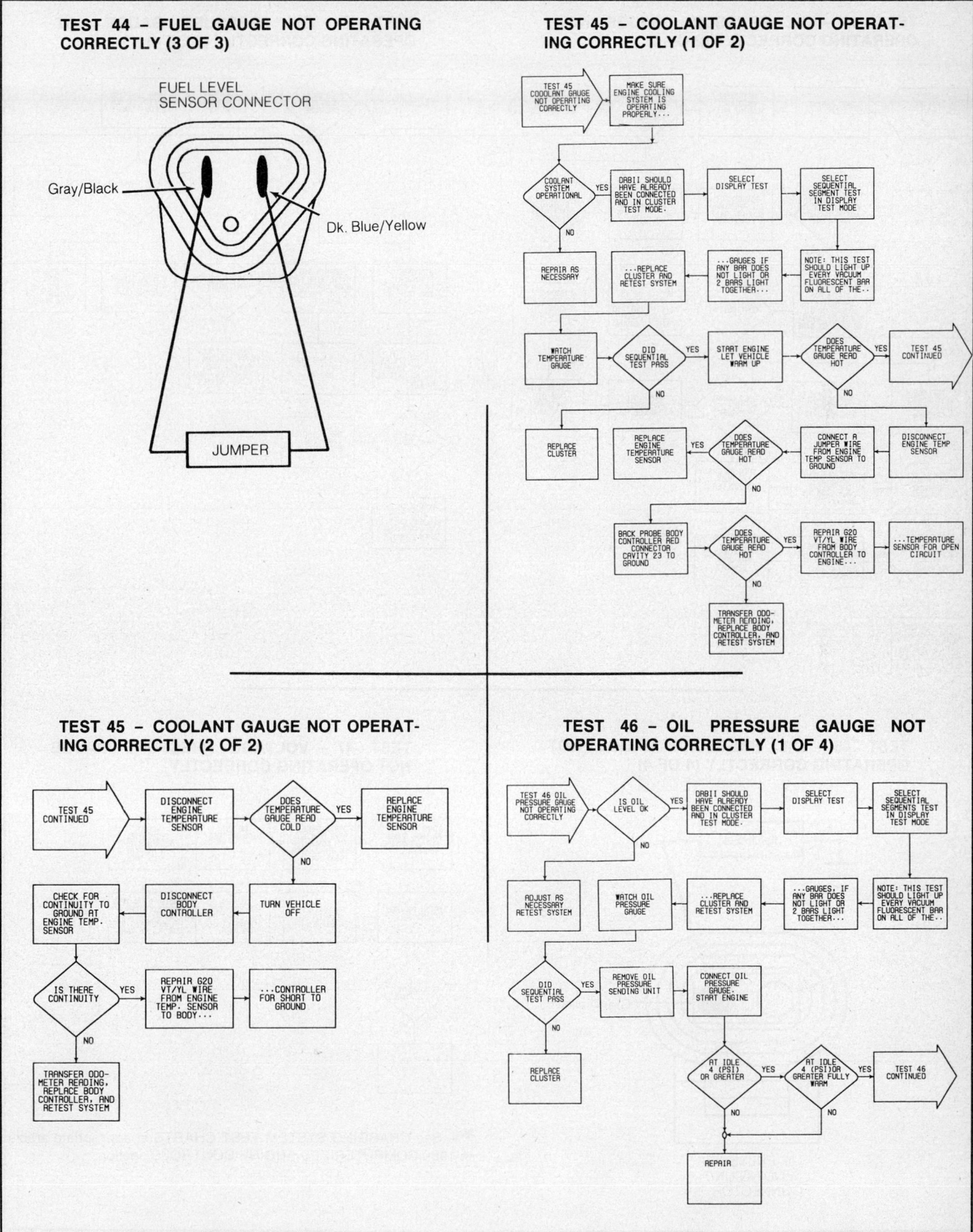

TEST 44 – FUEL GAUGE NOT OPERATING CORRECTLY (3 OF 3)

FUEL LEVEL SENSOR CONNECTOR

Gray/Black

Dk. Blue/Yellow

JUMPER

TEST 45 – COOLANT GAUGE NOT OPERATING CORRECTLY (1 OF 2)

TEST 45 – COOLANT GAUGE NOT OPERATING CORRECTLY (2 OF 2)

TEST 46 – OIL PRESSURE GAUGE NOT OPERATING CORRECTLY (1 OF 4)

TEST 46 – OIL PRESSURE GAUGE NOT OPERATING CORRECTLY (2 OF 4)

TEST 46 – OIL PRESSURE GAUGE NOT OPERATING CORRECTLY (3 OF 4)

TEST 46 – OIL PRESSURE GAUGE NOT OPERATING CORRECTLY (4 OF 4)

TEST 47 – VOLTAGE PRESSURE GAUGE NOT OPERATING CORRECTLY

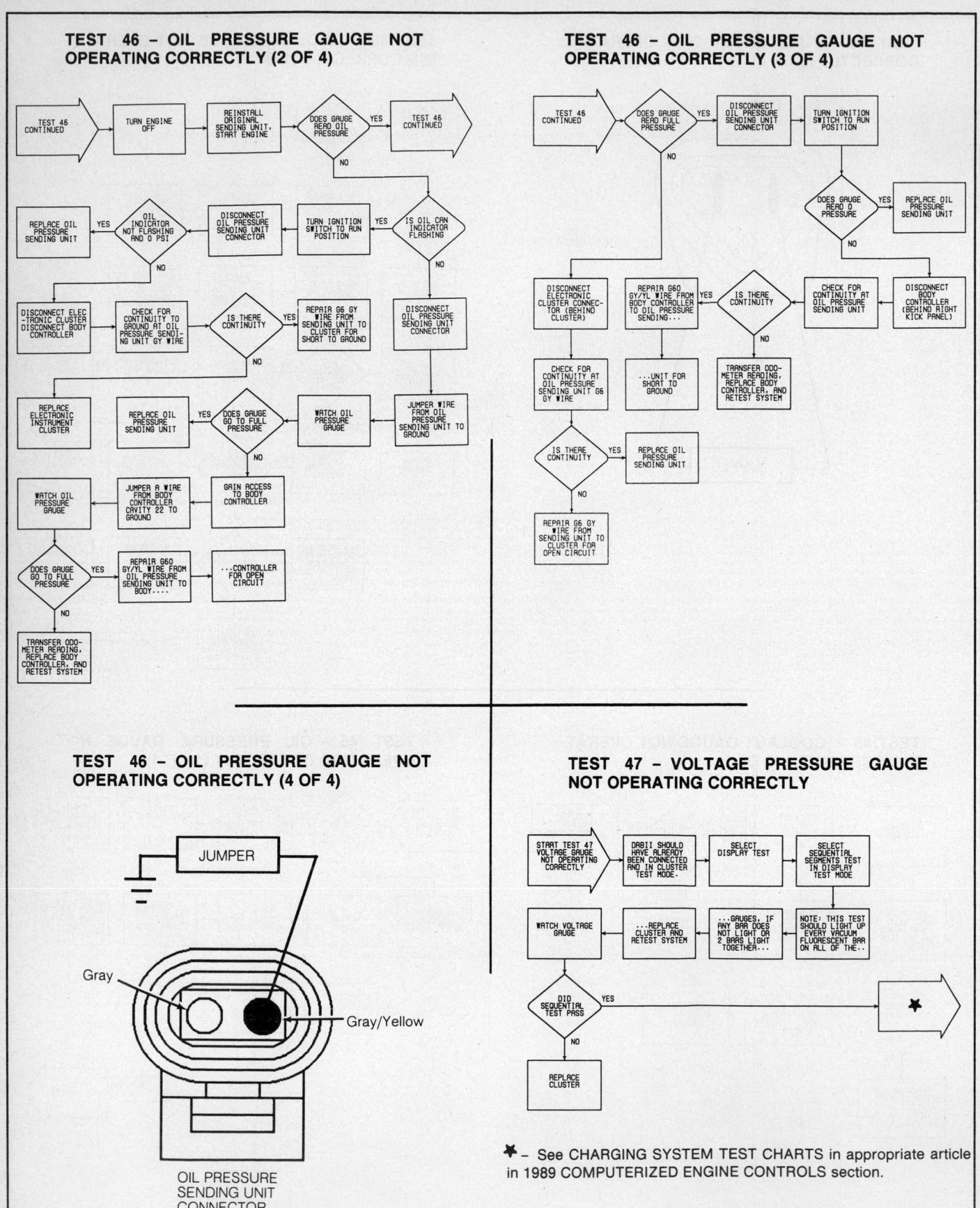

Gray

Gray/Yellow

JUMPER

OIL PRESSURE SENDING UNIT CONNECTOR

★ – See CHARGING SYSTEM TEST CHARTS in appropriate article in 1989 COMPUTERIZED ENGINE CONTROLS section.

1989 COMPUTERIZED ENGINE CONTROLS
Chrysler Motors Body Control Computer (Cont.)

1a-219

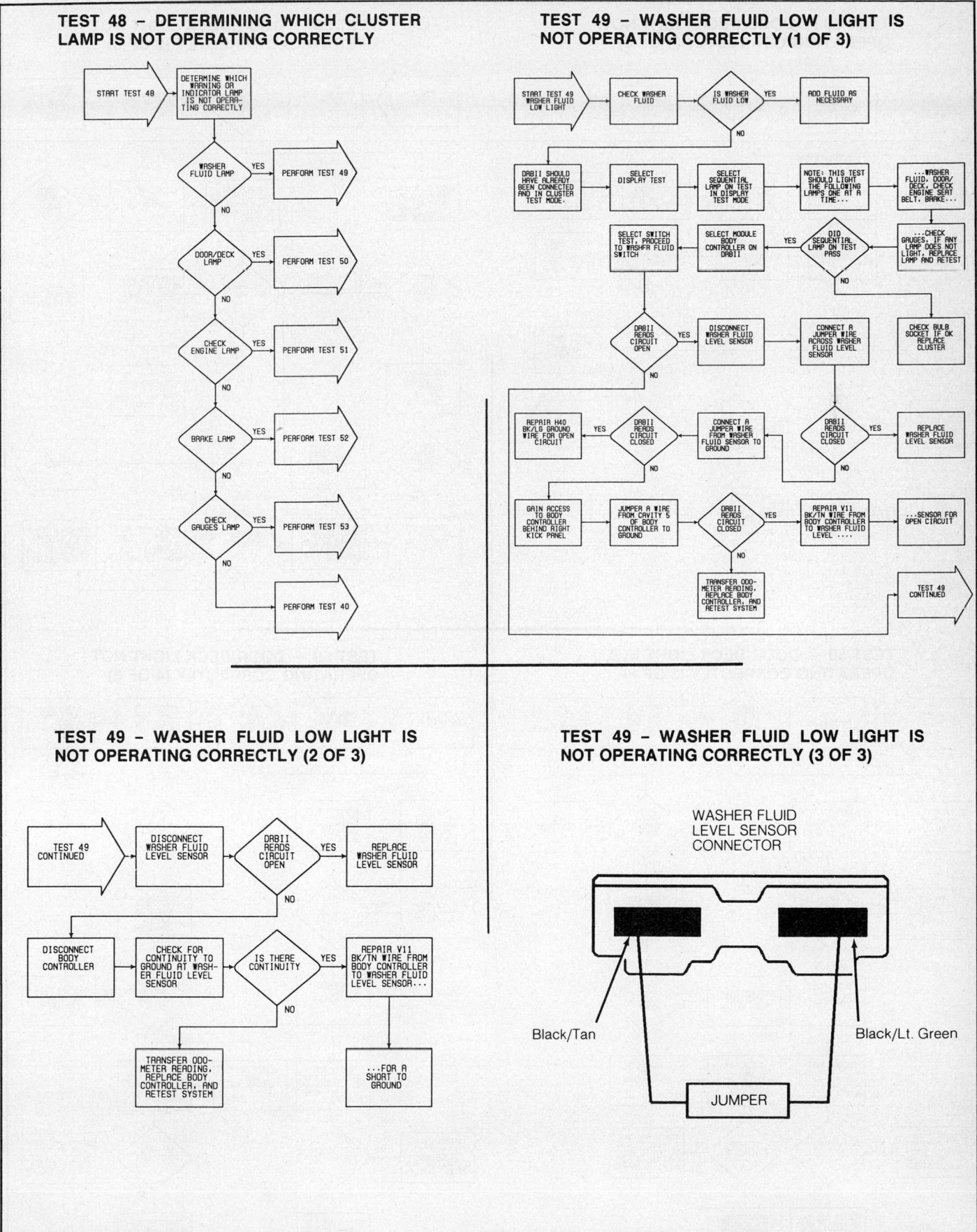

TEST 48 – DETERMINING WHICH CLUSTER LAMP IS NOT OPERATING CORRECTLY

TEST 49 – WASHER FLUID LOW LIGHT IS NOT OPERATING CORRECTLY (1 OF 3)

TEST 49 – WASHER FLUID LOW LIGHT IS NOT OPERATING CORRECTLY (2 OF 3)

TEST 49 – WASHER FLUID LOW LIGHT IS NOT OPERATING CORRECTLY (3 OF 3)

WASHER FLUID LEVEL SENSOR CONNECTOR

Black/Tan

Black/Lt. Green

JUMPER

TEST 50 – DOOR/DECK LIGHT NOT OPERATING CORRECTLY (1 OF 6)

TEST 50 – DOOR/DECK LIGHT NOT OPERATING CORRECTLY (2 OF 6)

TEST 50 – DOOR/DECK LIGHT NOT OPERATING CORRECTLY (3 OF 6)

TEST 50 – DOOR/DECK LIGHT NOT OPERATING CORRECTLY (4 OF 6)

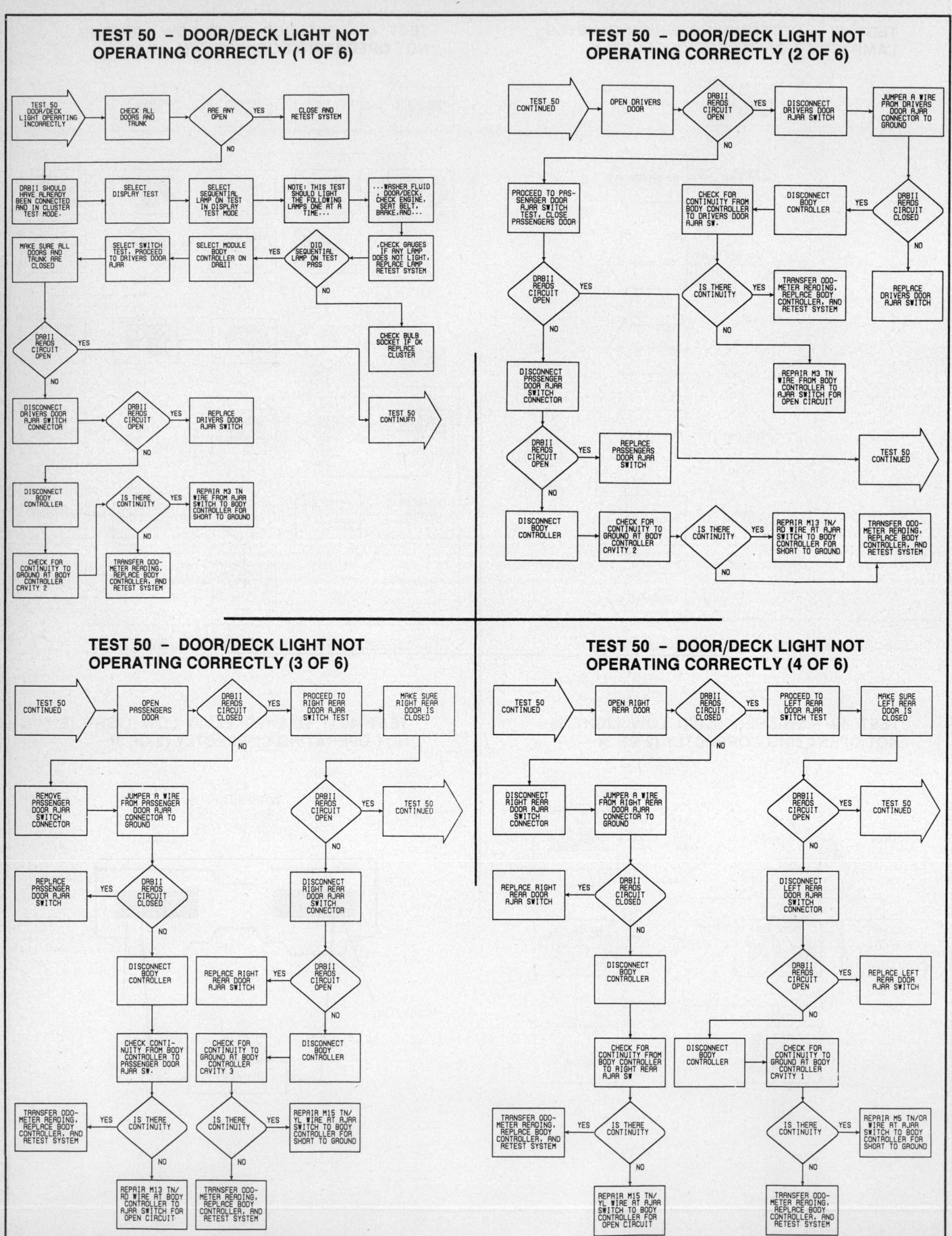

1989 COMPUTERIZED ENGINE CONTROLS
Chrysler Motors Body Control Computer (Cont.)

1a-221

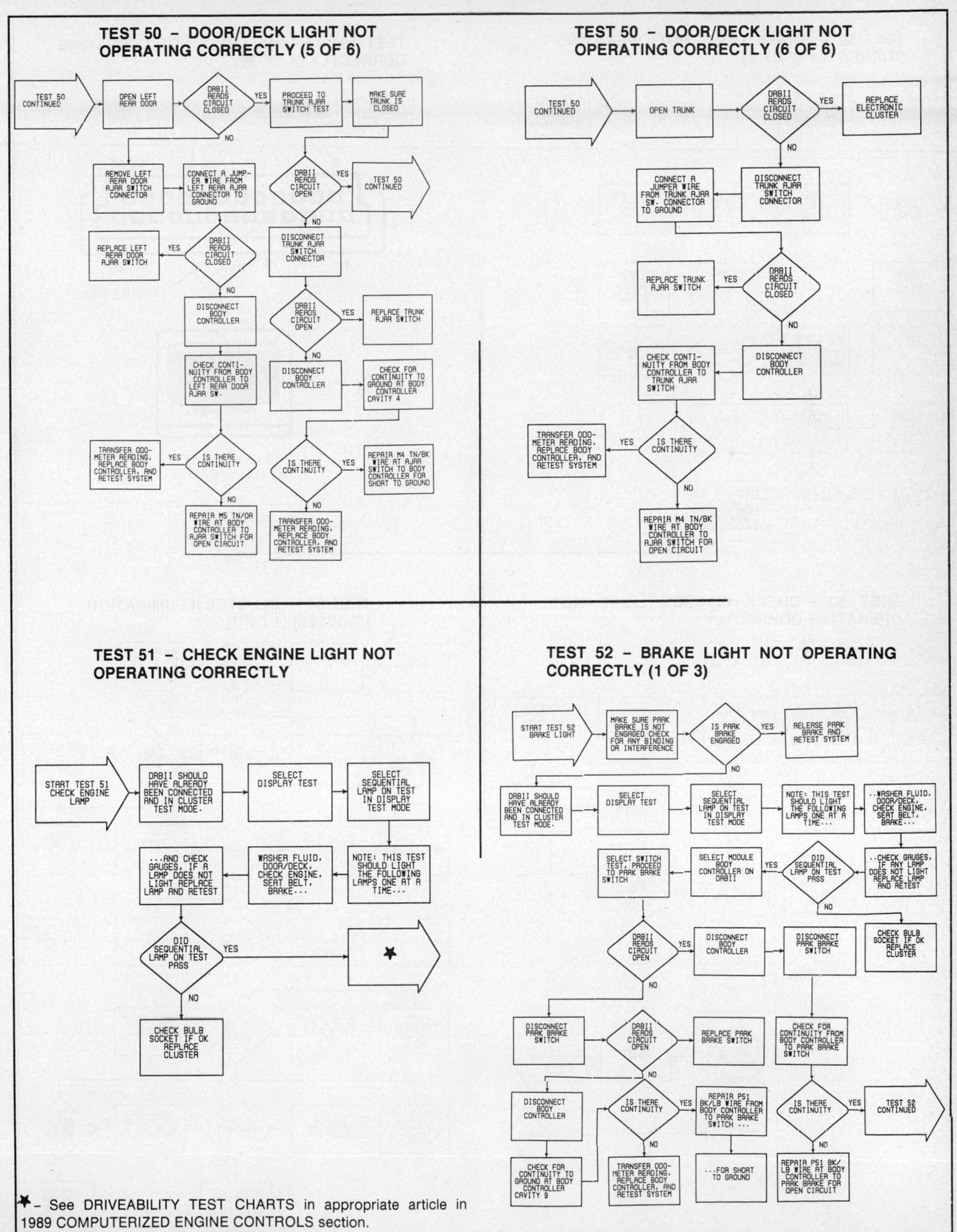

TEST 50 - DOOR/DECK LIGHT NOT OPERATING CORRECTLY (5 OF 6)

TEST 50 - DOOR/DECK LIGHT NOT OPERATING CORRECTLY (6 OF 6)

TEST 51 - CHECK ENGINE LIGHT NOT OPERATING CORRECTLY

TEST 52 - BRAKE LIGHT NOT OPERATING CORRECTLY (1 OF 3)

★ - See DRIVEABILITY TEST CHARTS in appropriate article in 1989 COMPUTERIZED ENGINE CONTROLS section.

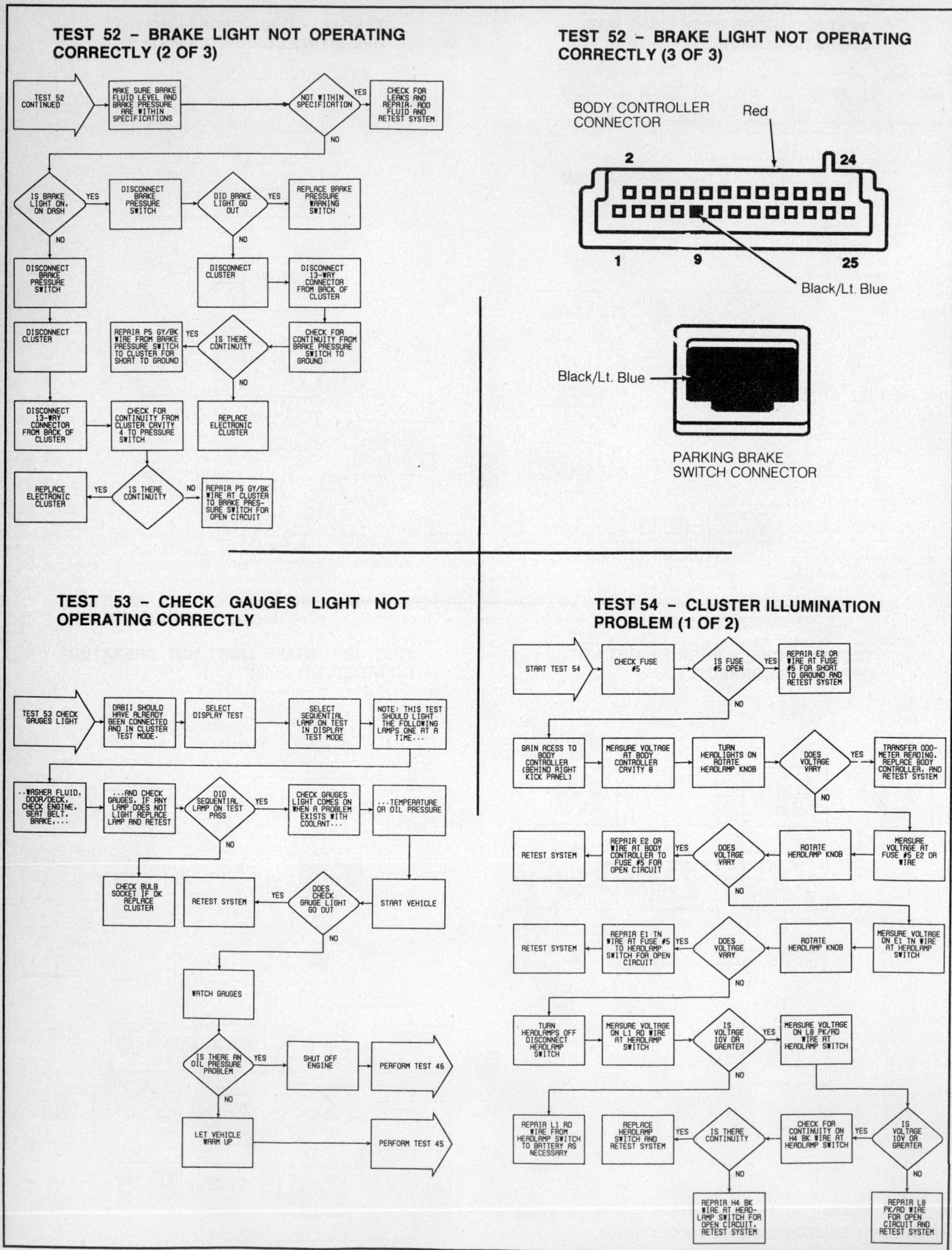

TEST 52 – BRAKE LIGHT NOT OPERATING CORRECTLY (2 OF 3)

TEST 52 – BRAKE LIGHT NOT OPERATING CORRECTLY (3 OF 3)

BODY CONTROLLER CONNECTOR — Red

Black/Lt. Blue

PARKING BRAKE SWITCH CONNECTOR

TEST 53 – CHECK GAUGES LIGHT NOT OPERATING CORRECTLY

TEST 54 – CLUSTER ILLUMINATION PROBLEM (1 OF 2)

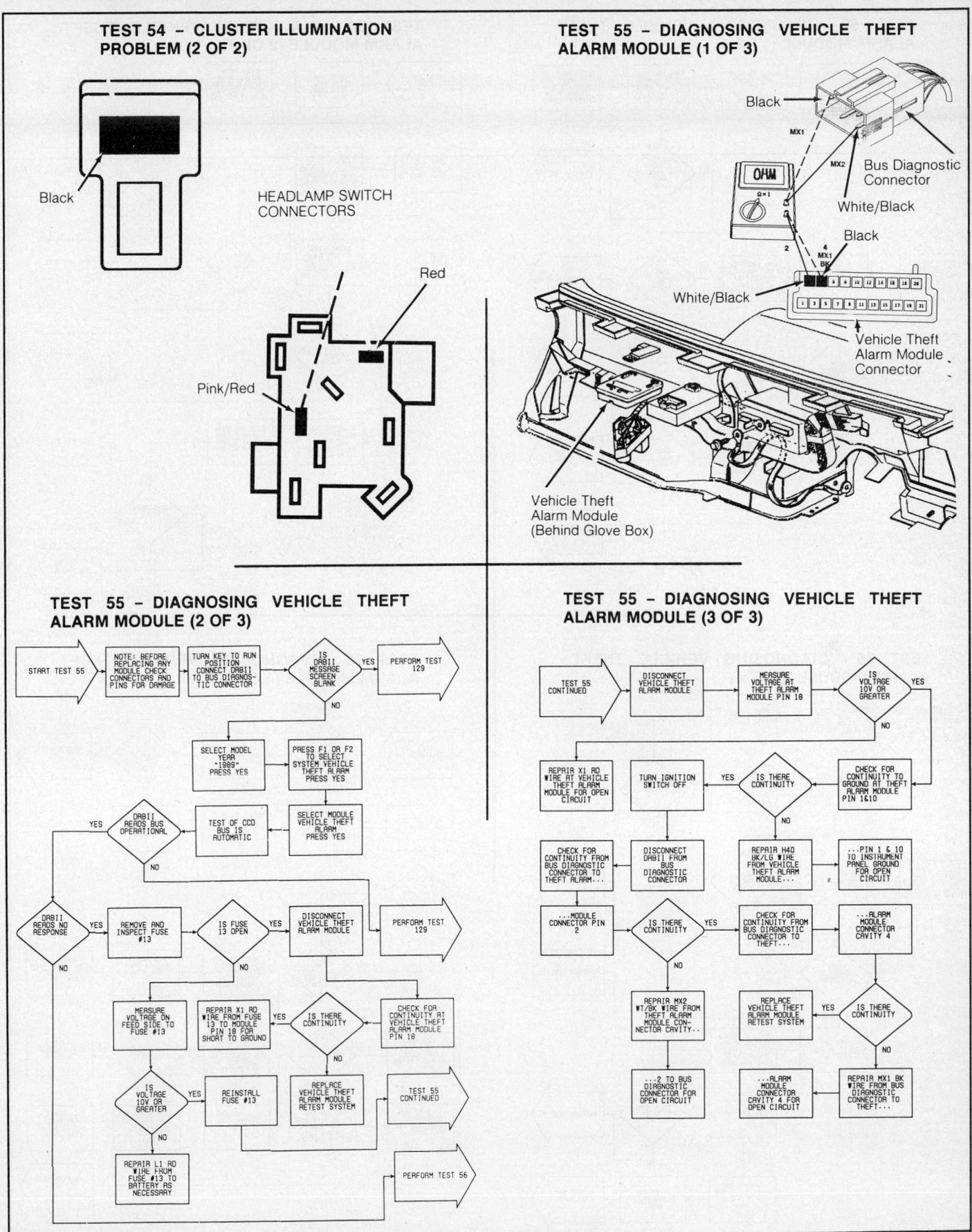

TEST 54 – CLUSTER ILLUMINATION PROBLEM (2 OF 2)

Black

HEADLAMP SWITCH CONNECTORS

Red

Pink/Red

TEST 55 – DIAGNOSING VEHICLE THEFT ALARM MODULE (1 OF 3)

Black

MX1

MX2

Bus Diagnostic Connector

White/Black

Black

4 MX1 BK

2

White/Black

Vehicle Theft Alarm Module Connector

Vehicle Theft Alarm Module (Behind Glove Box)

TEST 55 – DIAGNOSING VEHICLE THEFT ALARM MODULE (2 OF 3)

TEST 55 – DIAGNOSING VEHICLE THEFT ALARM MODULE (3 OF 3)

1a-224

1989 COMPUTERIZED ENGINE CONTROLS
Chrysler Motors Body Control Computer (Cont.)

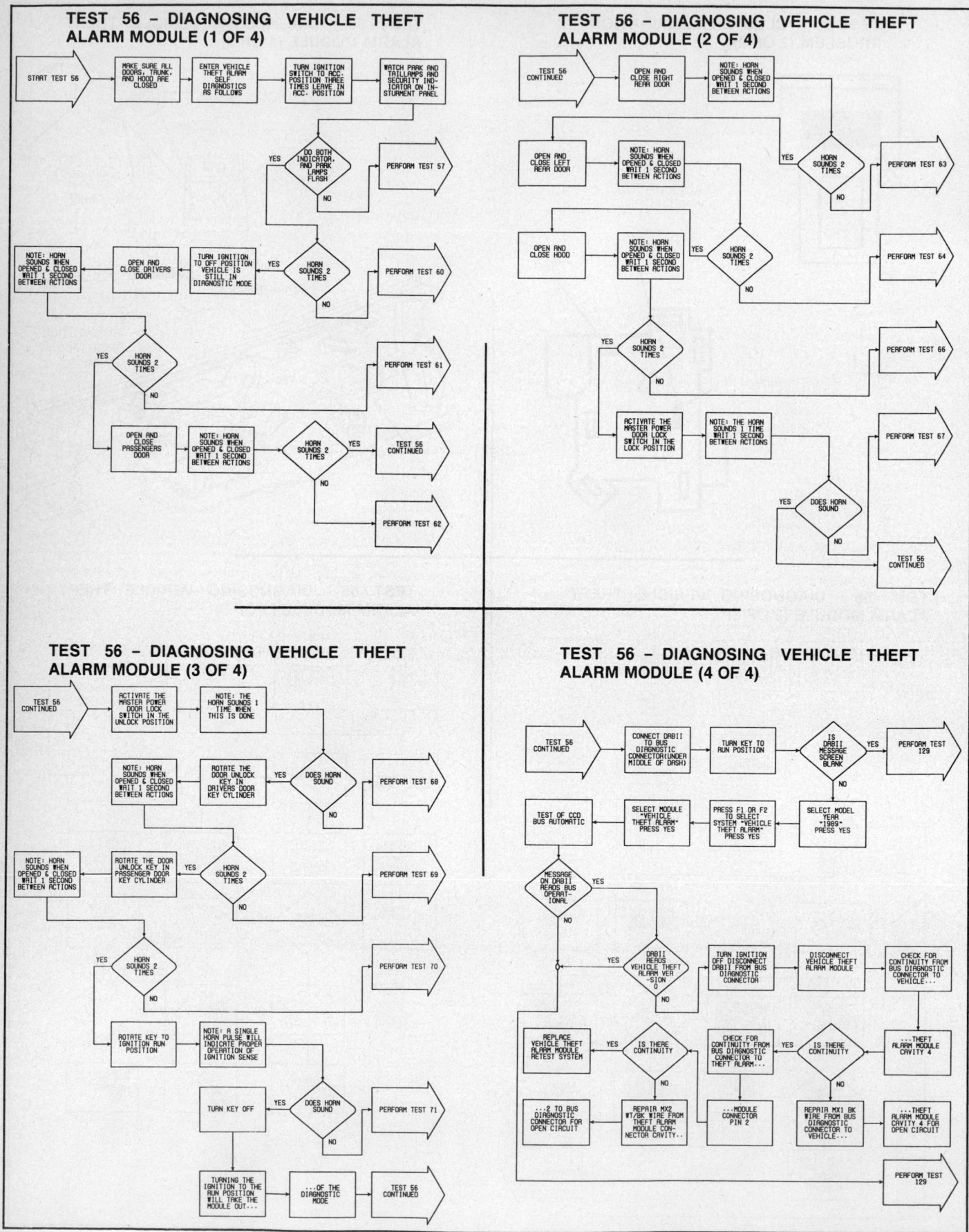

TEST 56 – DIAGNOSING VEHICLE THEFT ALARM MODULE (1 OF 4)

TEST 56 – DIAGNOSING VEHICLE THEFT ALARM MODULE (2 OF 4)

TEST 56 – DIAGNOSING VEHICLE THEFT ALARM MODULE (3 OF 4)

TEST 56 – DIAGNOSING VEHICLE THEFT ALARM MODULE (4 OF 4)

TEST 57 – DIAGNOSING VEHICLE THEFT ALARM MODULE

TEST 58 – THEFT ALARM INDICATOR LAMP

TEST 59 – DIAGNOSING VEHICLE THEFT ALARM MODULE (1 OF 2)

TEST 59 – DIAGNOSING VEHICLE THEFT ALARM MODULE (2 OF 2)

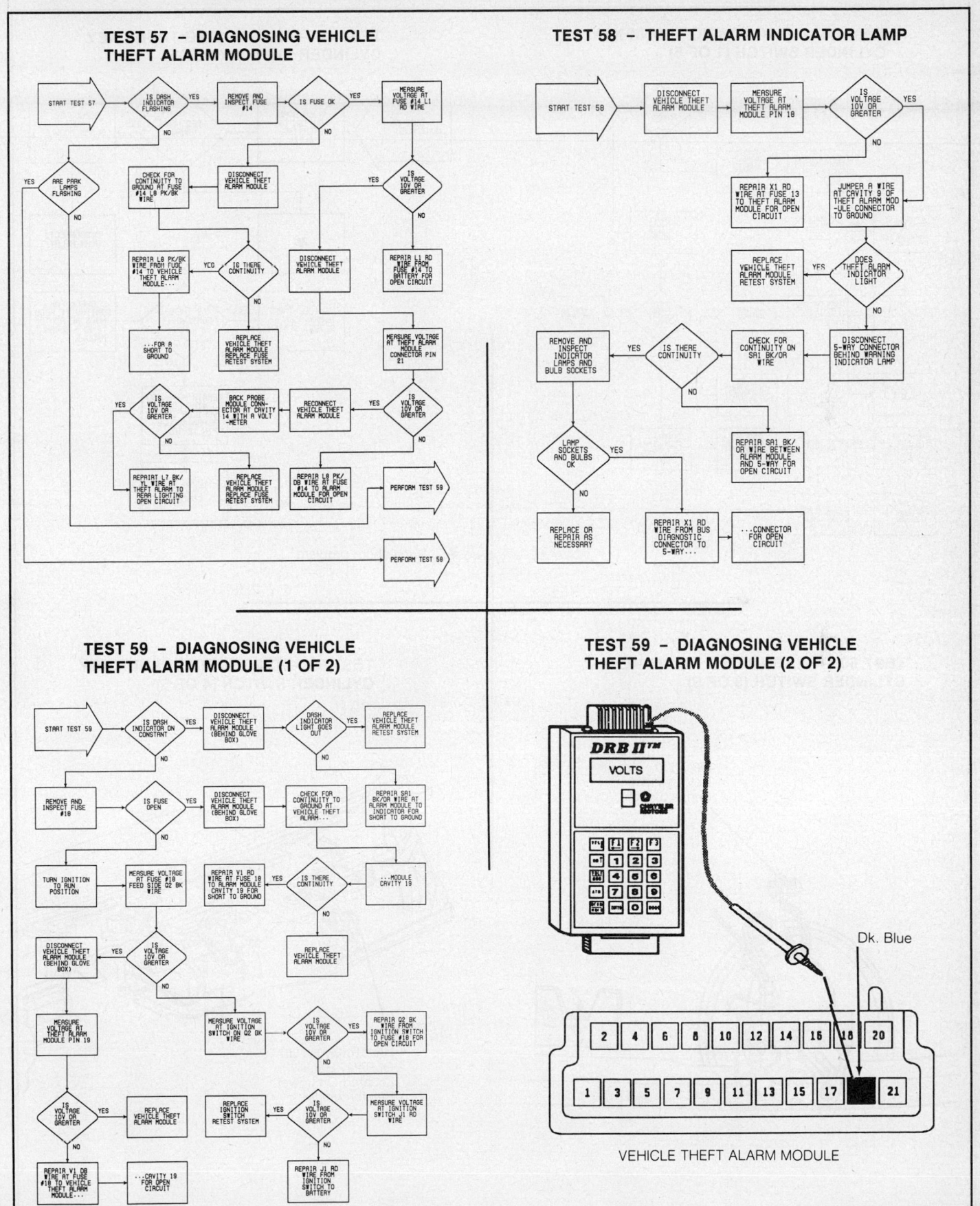

VEHICLE THEFT ALARM MODULE

Dk. Blue

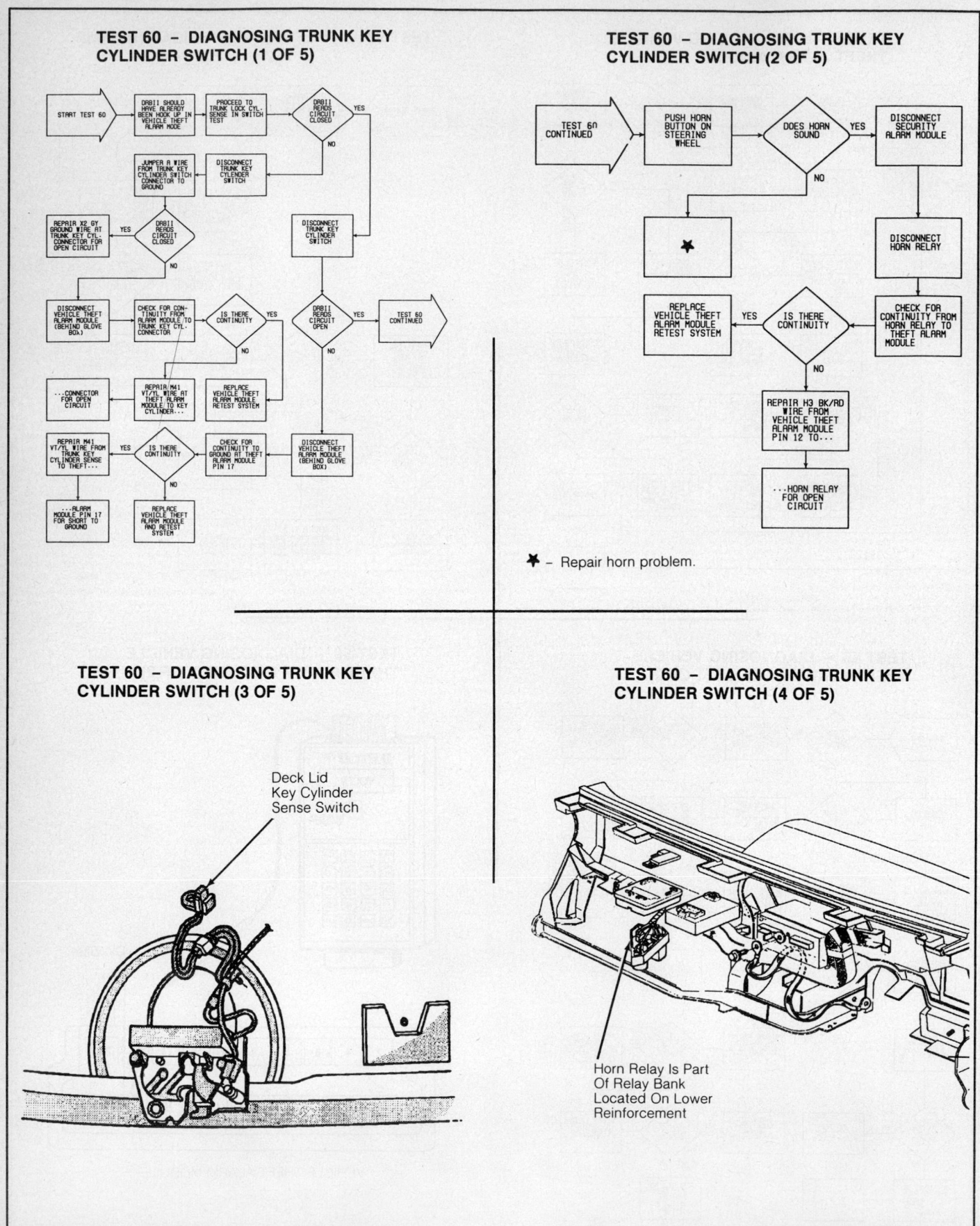

TEST 60 – DIAGNOSING TRUNK KEY CYLINDER SWITCH (1 OF 5)

TEST 60 – DIAGNOSING TRUNK KEY CYLINDER SWITCH (2 OF 5)

★ – Repair horn problem.

TEST 60 – DIAGNOSING TRUNK KEY CYLINDER SWITCH (3 OF 5)

Deck Lid Key Cylinder Sense Switch

TEST 60 – DIAGNOSING TRUNK KEY CYLINDER SWITCH (4 OF 5)

Horn Relay Is Part Of Relay Bank Located On Lower Reinforcement

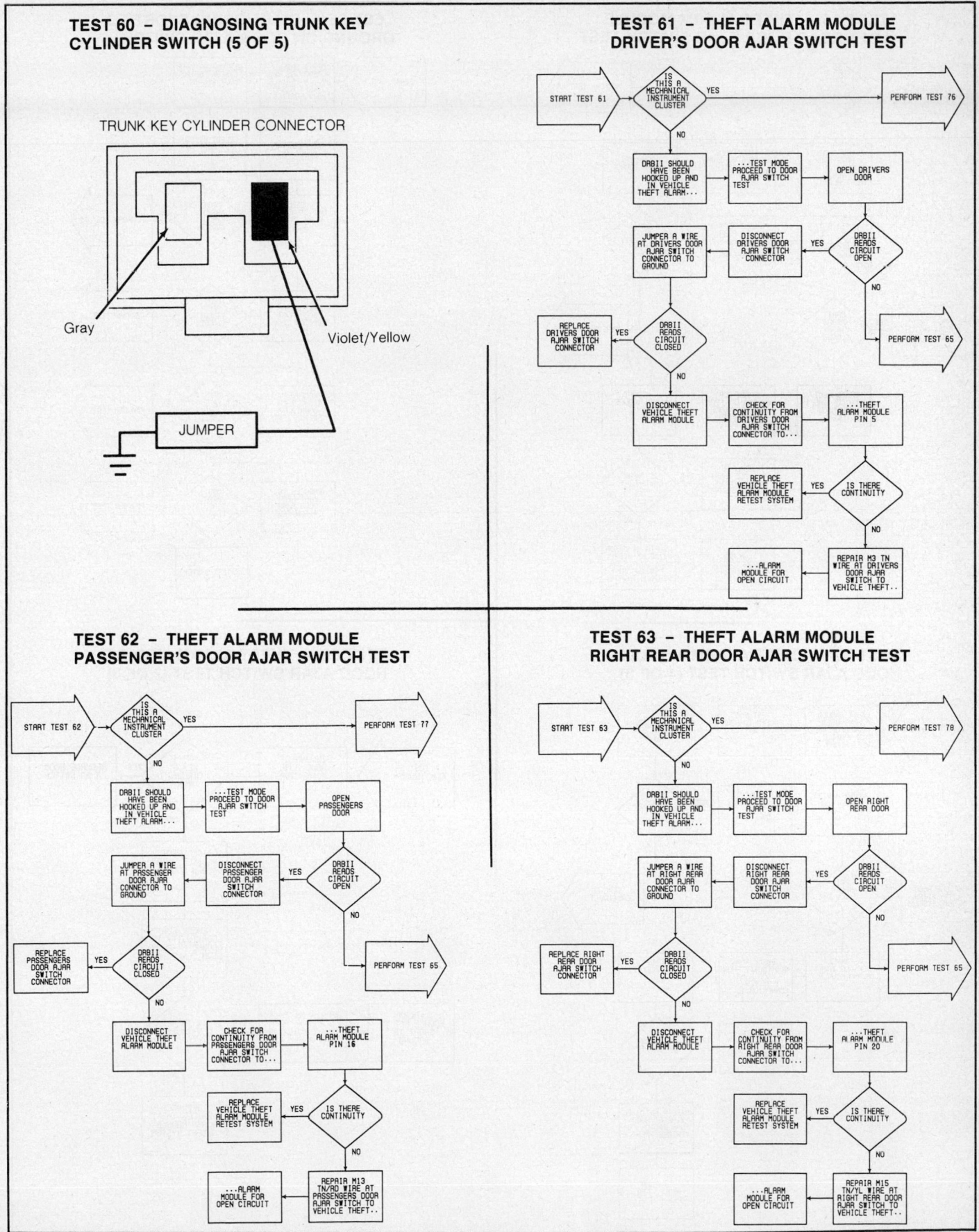

TEST 60 – DIAGNOSING TRUNK KEY CYLINDER SWITCH (5 OF 5)

TRUNK KEY CYLINDER CONNECTOR

Gray

Violet/Yellow

JUMPER

TEST 61 – THEFT ALARM MODULE DRIVER'S DOOR AJAR SWITCH TEST

TEST 62 – THEFT ALARM MODULE PASSENGER'S DOOR AJAR SWITCH TEST

TEST 63 – THEFT ALARM MODULE RIGHT REAR DOOR AJAR SWITCH TEST

1989 COMPUTERIZED ENGINE CONTROLS
Chrysler Motors Body Control Computer (Cont.)

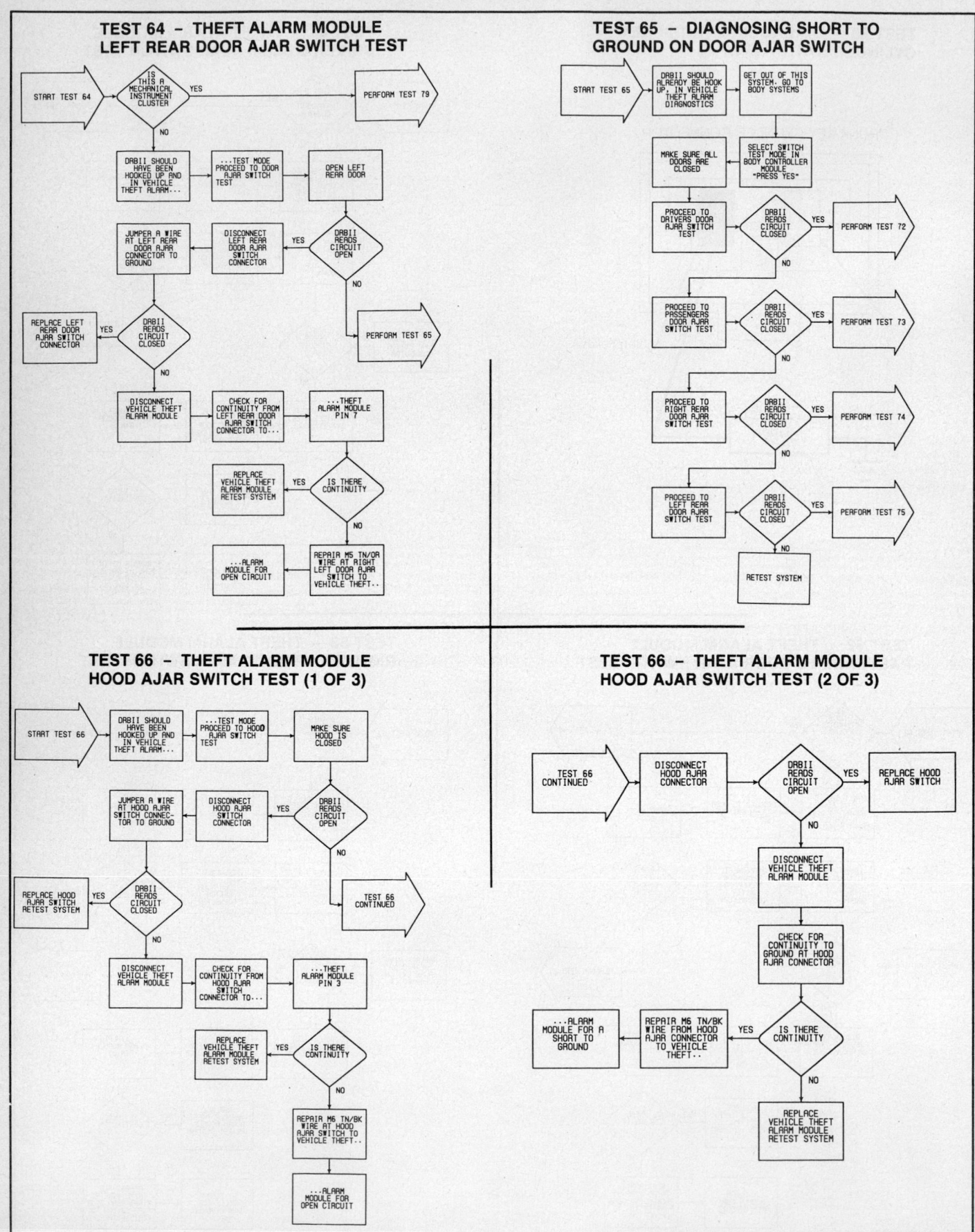

TEST 64 – THEFT ALARM MODULE LEFT REAR DOOR AJAR SWITCH TEST

START TEST 64 → IS THIS A MECHANICAL INSTRUMENT CLUSTER — YES → PERFORM TEST 79

NO ↓

DRBII SHOULD HAVE BEEN HOOKED UP AND IN VEHICLE THEFT ALARM... → ...TEST MODE PROCEED TO DOOR AJAR SWITCH TEST → OPEN LEFT REAR DOOR

↓

JUMPER A WIRE AT LEFT REAR DOOR AJAR CONNECTOR TO GROUND ← DISCONNECT LEFT REAR DOOR AJAR SWITCH CONNECTOR ← YES ← DRBII READS CIRCUIT OPEN

NO → PERFORM TEST 65

REPLACE LEFT REAR DOOR AJAR SWITCH CONNECTOR ← YES ← DRBII READS CIRCUIT CLOSED

NO ↓

DISCONNECT VEHICLE THEFT ALARM MODULE → CHECK FOR CONTINUITY FROM LEFT REAR DOOR AJAR SWITCH CONNECTOR TO... → ...THEFT ALARM MODULE PIN 7

↓

REPLACE VEHICLE THEFT ALARM MODULE RETEST SYSTEM ← YES ← IS THERE CONTINUITY

NO ↓

...ALARM MODULE FOR OPEN CIRCUIT ← REPAIR M5 TN/OR WIRE AT RIGHT LEFT DOOR AJAR SWITCH TO VEHICLE THEFT...

TEST 65 – DIAGNOSING SHORT TO GROUND ON DOOR AJAR SWITCH

START TEST 65 → DRBII SHOULD ALREADY BE HOOK UP, IN VEHICLE THEFT ALARM DIAGNOSTICS → GET OUT OF THIS SYSTEM. GO TO BODY SYSTEMS

↓

MAKE SURE ALL DOORS ARE CLOSED ← SELECT SWITCH TEST MODE IN BODY CONTROLLER MODULE "PRESS YES"

↓

PROCEED TO DRIVERS DOOR AJAR SWITCH TEST → DRBII READS CIRCUIT CLOSED — YES → PERFORM TEST 72

NO ↓

PROCEED TO PASSENGERS DOOR AJAR SWITCH TEST → DRBII READS CIRCUIT CLOSED — YES → PERFORM TEST 73

NO ↓

PROCEED TO RIGHT REAR DOOR AJAR SWITCH TEST → DRBII READS CIRCUIT CLOSED — YES → PERFORM TEST 74

NO ↓

PROCEED TO LEFT REAR DOOR AJAR SWITCH TEST → DRBII READS CIRCUIT CLOSED — YES → PERFORM TEST 75

NO ↓

RETEST SYSTEM

TEST 66 – THEFT ALARM MODULE HOOD AJAR SWITCH TEST (1 OF 3)

START TEST 66 → DRBII SHOULD HAVE BEEN HOOKED UP AND IN VEHICLE THEFT ALARM... → ...TEST MODE PROCEED TO HOOD AJAR SWITCH TEST → MAKE SURE HOOD IS CLOSED

↓

JUMPER A WIRE AT HOOD AJAR SWITCH CONNECTOR TO GROUND ← DISCONNECT HOOD AJAR SWITCH CONNECTOR ← YES ← DRBII READS CIRCUIT OPEN

NO → TEST 66 CONTINUED

REPLACE HOOD AJAR SWITCH RETEST SYSTEM ← YES ← DRBII READS CIRCUIT CLOSED

NO ↓

DISCONNECT VEHICLE THEFT ALARM MODULE → CHECK FOR CONTINUITY FROM HOOD AJAR SWITCH CONNECTOR TO... → ...THEFT ALARM MODULE PIN 3

↓

REPLACE VEHICLE THEFT ALARM MODULE RETEST SYSTEM ← YES ← IS THERE CONTINUITY

NO ↓

REPAIR M6 TN/BK WIRE AT HOOD AJAR SWITCH TO VEHICLE THEFT...

↓

...ALARM MODULE FOR OPEN CIRCUIT

TEST 66 – THEFT ALARM MODULE HOOD AJAR SWITCH TEST (2 OF 3)

TEST 66 CONTINUED → DISCONNECT HOOD AJAR CONNECTOR → DRBII READS CIRCUIT OPEN — YES → REPLACE HOOD AJAR SWITCH

NO ↓

DISCONNECT VEHICLE THEFT ALARM MODULE

↓

CHECK FOR CONTINUITY TO GROUND AT HOOD AJAR CONNECTOR

↓

...ALARM MODULE FOR A SHORT TO GROUND ← REPAIR M6 TN/BK WIRE FROM HOOD AJAR CONNECTOR TO VEHICLE THEFT... ← YES ← IS THERE CONTINUITY

NO ↓

REPLACE VEHICLE THEFT ALARM MODULE RETEST SYSTEM

1989 COMPUTERIZED ENGINE CONTROLS
Chrysler Motors Body Control Computer (Cont.)

1a-229

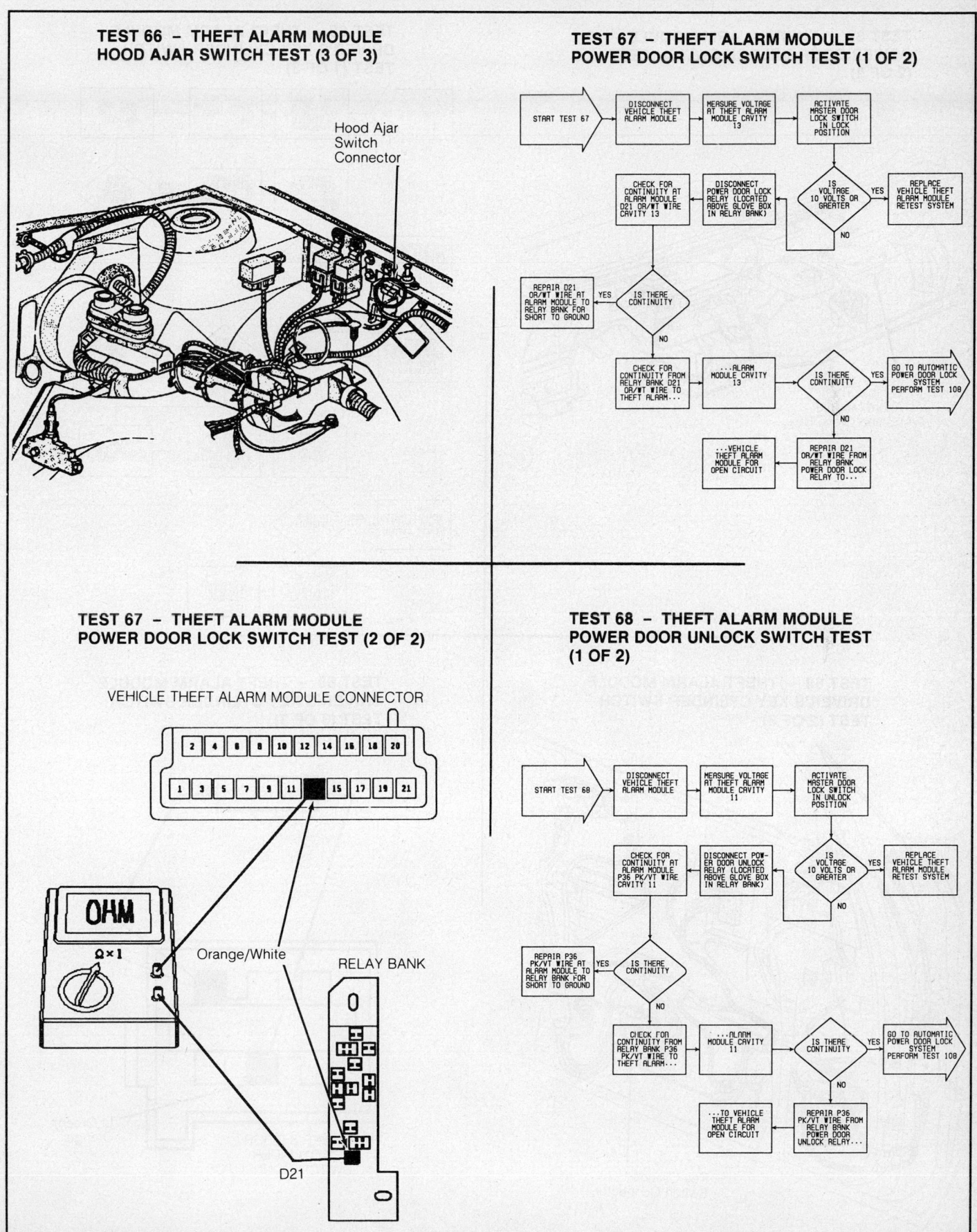

TEST 66 – THEFT ALARM MODULE HOOD AJAR SWITCH TEST (3 OF 3)

Hood Ajar Switch Connector

TEST 67 – THEFT ALARM MODULE POWER DOOR LOCK SWITCH TEST (1 OF 2)

START TEST 67 → DISCONNECT VEHICLE THEFT ALARM MODULE → MEASURE VOLTAGE AT THEFT ALARM MODULE CAVITY 13 → ACTIVATE MASTER DOOR LOCK SWITCH IN LOCK POSITION

IS VOLTAGE 10 VOLTS OR GREATER — YES → REPLACE VEHICLE THEFT ALARM MODULE RETEST SYSTEM

NO → DISCONNECT POWER DOOR LOCK RELAY (LOCATED ABOVE GLOVE BOX IN RELAY BANK) → CHECK FOR CONTINUITY AT ALARM MODULE D21 OR/WT WIRE CAVITY 13

IS THERE CONTINUITY — YES → REPAIR D21 OR/WT WIRE AT ALARM MODULE TO RELAY BANK FOR SHORT TO GROUND

NO → CHECK FOR CONTINUITY FROM RELAY BANK D21 OR/WT WIRE TO THEFT ALARM... → ...ALARM MODULE CAVITY 13

IS THERE CONTINUITY — YES → GO TO AUTOMATIC POWER DOOR LOCK SYSTEM PERFORM TEST 108

NO → REPAIR D21 OR/WT WIRE FROM RELAY BANK POWER DOOR LOCK RELAY TO... → ...VEHICLE THEFT ALARM MODULE FOR OPEN CIRCUIT

TEST 67 – THEFT ALARM MODULE POWER DOOR LOCK SWITCH TEST (2 OF 2)

VEHICLE THEFT ALARM MODULE CONNECTOR

2 4 6 8 10 12 14 16 18 20
1 3 5 7 9 11 13 15 17 19 21

OHM
Ω × 1

Orange/White

RELAY BANK

D21

TEST 68 – THEFT ALARM MODULE POWER DOOR UNLOCK SWITCH TEST (1 OF 2)

START TEST 68 → DISCONNECT VEHICLE THEFT ALARM MODULE → MEASURE VOLTAGE AT THEFT ALARM MODULE CAVITY 11 → ACTIVATE MASTER DOOR LOCK SWITCH IN UNLOCK POSITION

IS VOLTAGE 10 VOLTS OR GREATER — YES → REPLACE VEHICLE THEFT ALARM MODULE RETEST SYSTEM

NO → DISCONNECT POWER DOOR UNLOCK RELAY (LOCATED ABOVE GLOVE BOX IN RELAY BANK) → CHECK FOR CONTINUITY AT ALARM MODULE P36 PK/VT WIRE CAVITY 11

IS THERE CONTINUITY — YES → REPAIR P36 PK/VT WIRE AT ALARM MODULE TO RELAY BANK FOR SHORT TO GROUND

NO → CHECK FOR CONTINUITY FROM RELAY BANK P36 PK/VT WIRE TO THEFT ALARM... → ...ALARM MODULE CAVITY 11

IS THERE CONTINUITY — YES → GO TO AUTOMATIC POWER DOOR LOCK SYSTEM PERFORM TEST 108

NO → REPAIR P36 PK/VT WIRE FROM RELAY BANK POWER DOOR UNLOCK RELAY... → ...TO VEHICLE THEFT ALARM MODULE FOR OPEN CIRCUIT

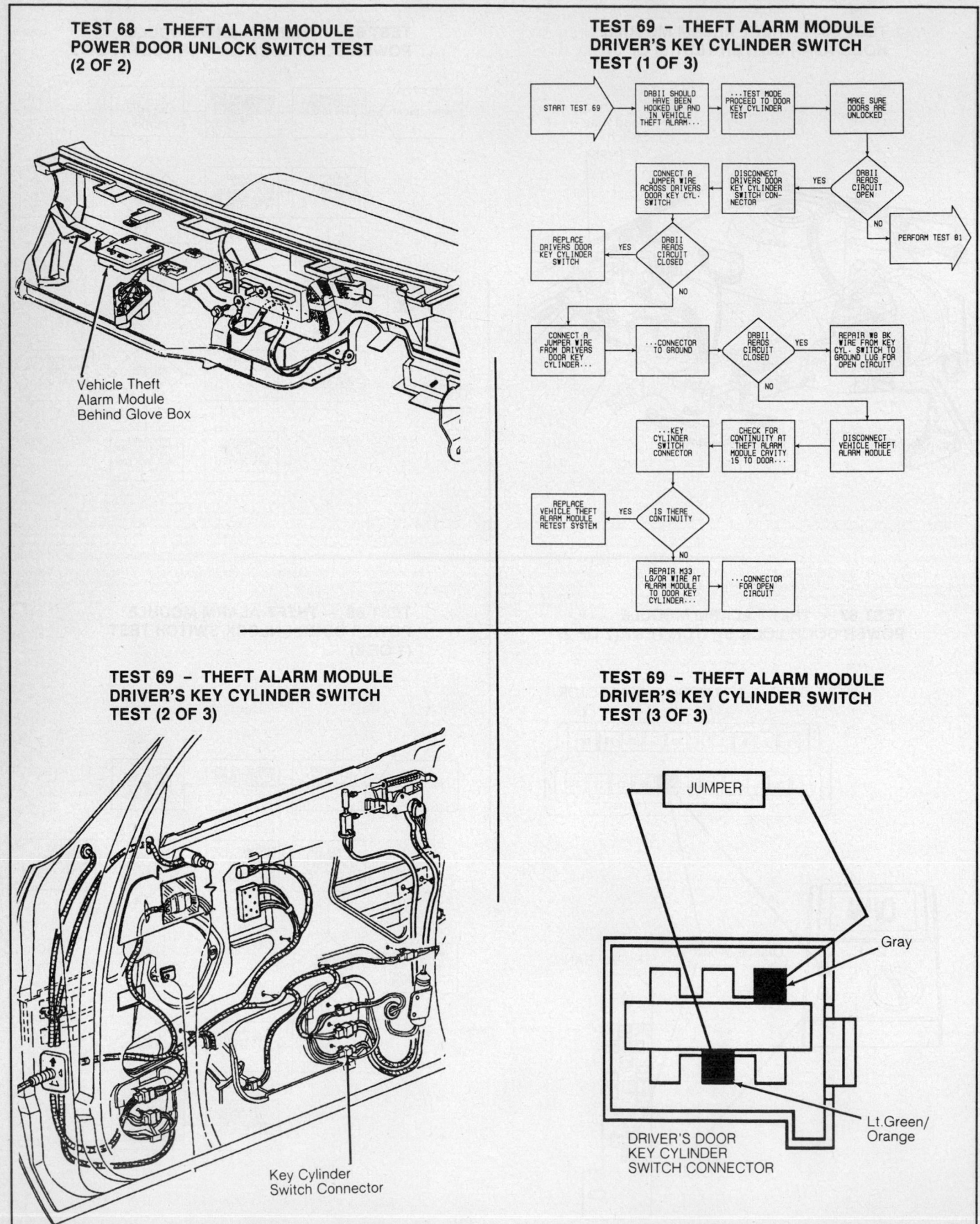

TEST 68 – THEFT ALARM MODULE POWER DOOR UNLOCK SWITCH TEST (2 OF 2)

Vehicle Theft Alarm Module Behind Glove Box

TEST 69 – THEFT ALARM MODULE DRIVER'S KEY CYLINDER SWITCH TEST (1 OF 3)

START TEST 69 → DRBII SHOULD HAVE BEEN HOOKED UP AND IN VEHICLE THEFT ALARM... → ...TEST MODE PROCEED TO DOOR KEY CYLINDER TEST → MAKE SURE DOORS ARE UNLOCKED

DRBII READS CIRCUIT OPEN — YES → DISCONNECT DRIVERS DOOR KEY CYLINDER SWITCH CONNECTOR → CONNECT A JUMPER WIRE ACROSS DRIVERS DOOR KEY CYL. SWITCH

NO → PERFORM TEST 81

DRBII READS CIRCUIT CLOSED — YES → REPLACE DRIVERS DOOR KEY CYLINDER SWITCH

NO

CONNECT A JUMPER WIRE FROM DRIVERS DOOR KEY CYLINDER... → ...CONNECTOR TO GROUND → DRBII READS CIRCUIT CLOSED — YES → REPAIR WB BK WIRE FROM KEY CYL. SWITCH TO GROUND LUG FOR OPEN CIRCUIT

NO → DISCONNECT VEHICLE THEFT ALARM MODULE → CHECK FOR CONTINUITY AT THEFT ALARM MODULE CAVITY 15 TO DOOR... → ...KEY CYLINDER SWITCH CONNECTOR

IS THERE CONTINUITY — YES → REPLACE VEHICLE THEFT ALARM MODULE RETEST SYSTEM

NO → REPAIR M33 LG/OR WIRE AT ALARM MODULE TO DOOR KEY CYLINDER... → ...CONNECTOR FOR OPEN CIRCUIT

TEST 69 – THEFT ALARM MODULE DRIVER'S KEY CYLINDER SWITCH TEST (2 OF 3)

Key Cylinder Switch Connector

TEST 69 – THEFT ALARM MODULE DRIVER'S KEY CYLINDER SWITCH TEST (3 OF 3)

JUMPER

Gray

Lt.Green/Orange

DRIVER'S DOOR KEY CYLINDER SWITCH CONNECTOR

1989 COMPUTERIZED ENGINE CONTROLS
Chrysler Motors Body Control Computer (Cont.)

1a-231

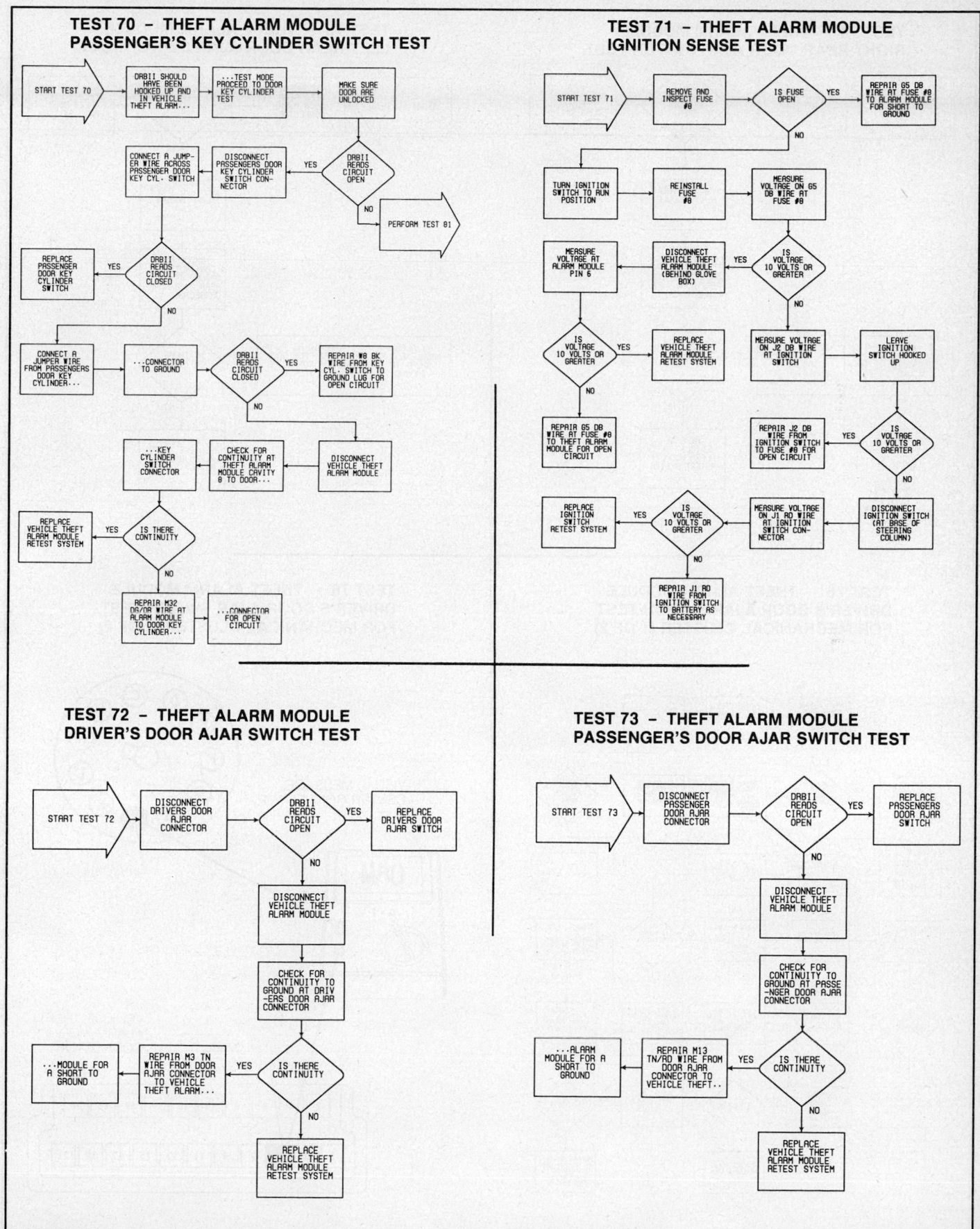

TEST 70 – THEFT ALARM MODULE PASSENGER'S KEY CYLINDER SWITCH TEST

TEST 71 – THEFT ALARM MODULE IGNITION SENSE TEST

TEST 72 – THEFT ALARM MODULE DRIVER'S DOOR AJAR SWITCH TEST

TEST 73 – THEFT ALARM MODULE PASSENGER'S DOOR AJAR SWITCH TEST

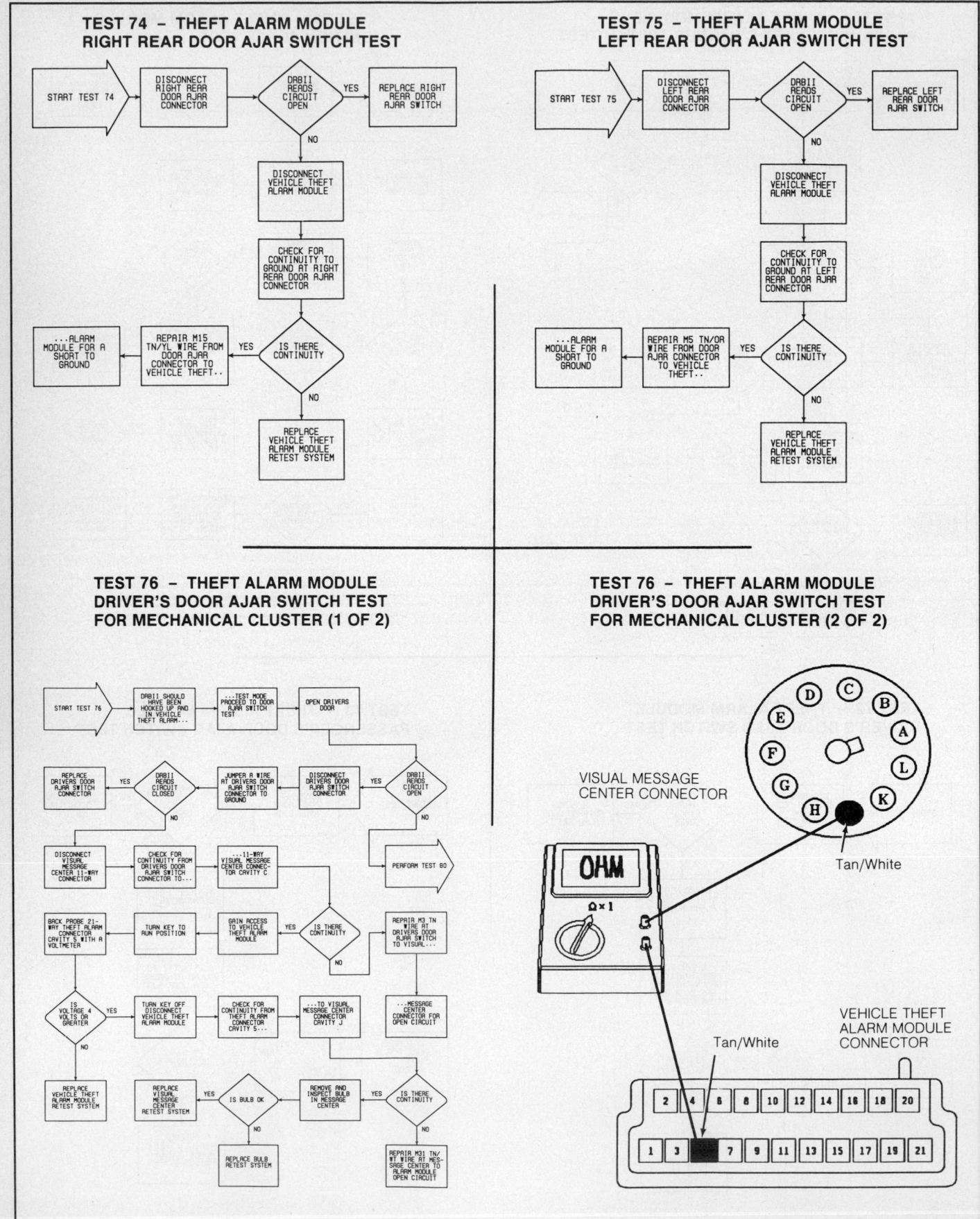

TEST 74 – THEFT ALARM MODULE RIGHT REAR DOOR AJAR SWITCH TEST

START TEST 74 → DISCONNECT RIGHT REAR DOOR AJAR CONNECTOR → DRBII READS CIRCUIT OPEN — YES → REPLACE RIGHT REAR DOOR AJAR SWITCH

NO → DISCONNECT VEHICLE THEFT ALARM MODULE → CHECK FOR CONTINUITY TO GROUND AT RIGHT REAR DOOR AJAR CONNECTOR → IS THERE CONTINUITY — YES → REPAIR M15 TN/YL WIRE FROM DOOR AJAR CONNECTOR TO VEHICLE THEFT... → ...ALARM MODULE FOR A SHORT TO GROUND

NO → REPLACE VEHICLE THEFT ALARM MODULE RETEST SYSTEM

TEST 75 – THEFT ALARM MODULE LEFT REAR DOOR AJAR SWITCH TEST

START TEST 75 → DISCONNECT LEFT REAR DOOR AJAR CONNECTOR → DRBII READS CIRCUIT OPEN — YES → REPLACE LEFT REAR DOOR AJAR SWITCH

NO → DISCONNECT VEHICLE THEFT ALARM MODULE → CHECK FOR CONTINUITY TO GROUND AT LEFT REAR DOOR AJAR CONNECTOR → IS THERE CONTINUITY — YES → REPAIR M5 TN/OR WIRE FROM DOOR AJAR CONNECTOR TO VEHICLE THEFT... → ...ALARM MODULE FOR A SHORT TO GROUND

NO → REPLACE VEHICLE THEFT ALARM MODULE RETEST SYSTEM

TEST 76 – THEFT ALARM MODULE DRIVER'S DOOR AJAR SWITCH TEST FOR MECHANICAL CLUSTER (1 OF 2)

START TEST 76 → DRBII SHOULD HAVE BEEN HOOKED UP AND IN VEHICLE THEFT ALARM... → ...TEST MODE PROCEED TO DOOR AJAR SWITCH TEST → OPEN DRIVERS DOOR

REPLACE DRIVERS DOOR AJAR SWITCH CONNECTOR ← YES — DRBII READS CIRCUIT CLOSED ← JUMPER A WIRE AT DRIVERS DOOR AJAR SWITCH CONNECTOR TO GROUND ← DISCONNECT DRIVERS DOOR AJAR SWITCH CONNECTOR ← YES — DRBII READS CIRCUIT OPEN

NO ↓ (from DRBII READS CIRCUIT CLOSED)
NO → PERFORM TEST 80 (from DRBII READS CIRCUIT OPEN)

DISCONNECT VISUAL MESSAGE CENTER 11-WAY CONNECTOR → CHECK FOR CONTINUITY FROM DRIVERS DOOR AJAR SWITCH CONNECTOR TO... → ...11-WAY VISUAL MESSAGE CENTER CONNECTOR CAVITY C

BACK PROBE 21-WAY THEFT ALARM CONNECTOR CAVITY 5 WITH A VOLTMETER ← TURN KEY TO RUN POSITION ← GAIN ACCESS TO VEHICLE THEFT ALARM MODULE ← YES — IS THERE CONTINUITY → REPAIR M3 TN WIRE AT DRIVERS DOOR AJAR SWITCH TO VISUAL...

NO ↓

IS VOLTAGE 4 VOLTS OR GREATER — YES → TURN KEY OFF DISCONNECT VEHICLE THEFT ALARM MODULE → CHECK FOR CONTINUITY FROM THEFT ALARM CONNECTOR CAVITY 5... → ...TO VISUAL MESSAGE CENTER CONNECTOR CAVITY J → ...MESSAGE CENTER CONNECTOR FOR OPEN CIRCUIT

NO ↓

REPLACE VEHICLE THEFT ALARM MODULE RETEST SYSTEM

REPLACE VISUAL MESSAGE CENTER RETEST SYSTEM ← YES — IS BULB OK ← REMOVE AND INSPECT BULB IN MESSAGE CENTER ← YES — IS THERE CONTINUITY

NO (IS BULB OK) ↓ REPLACE BULB RETEST SYSTEM

NO (IS THERE CONTINUITY) ↓ REPAIR M31 TN/WT WIRE AT MESSAGE CENTER TO ALARM MODULE OPEN CIRCUIT

TEST 76 – THEFT ALARM MODULE DRIVER'S DOOR AJAR SWITCH TEST FOR MECHANICAL CLUSTER (2 OF 2)

VISUAL MESSAGE CENTER CONNECTOR

Connector cavities: D C B A L K H G F E (with center)

Tan/White

OHM Ω × 1

Tan/White

VEHICLE THEFT ALARM MODULE CONNECTOR

2 4 6 8 10 12 14 16 18 20
1 3 5 7 9 11 13 15 17 19 21

1989 COMPUTERIZED ENGINE CONTROLS
Chrysler Motors Body Control Computer (Cont.)

1a-233

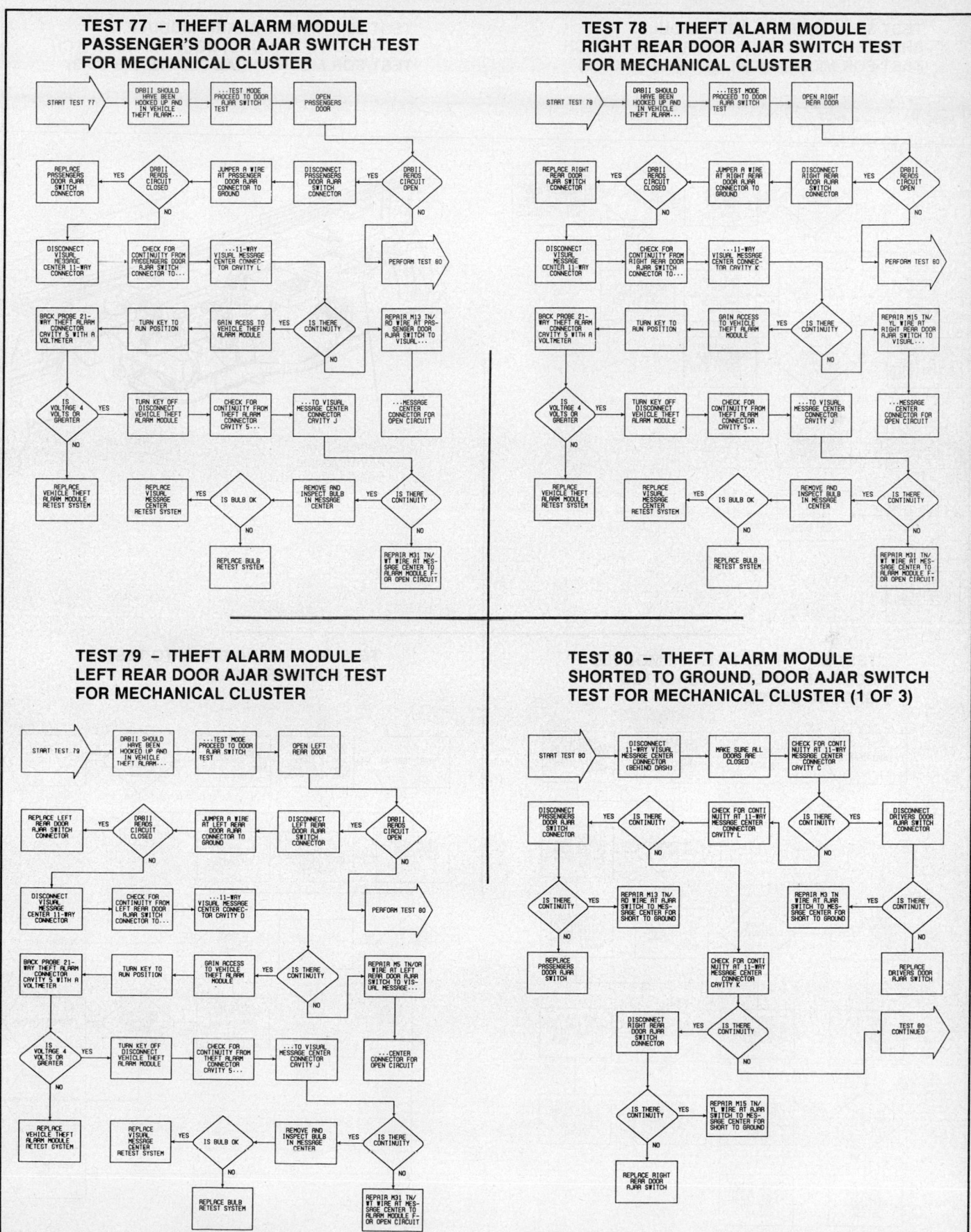

TEST 77 – THEFT ALARM MODULE PASSENGER'S DOOR AJAR SWITCH TEST FOR MECHANICAL CLUSTER

TEST 78 – THEFT ALARM MODULE RIGHT REAR DOOR AJAR SWITCH TEST FOR MECHANICAL CLUSTER

TEST 79 – THEFT ALARM MODULE LEFT REAR DOOR AJAR SWITCH TEST FOR MECHANICAL CLUSTER

TEST 80 – THEFT ALARM MODULE SHORTED TO GROUND, DOOR AJAR SWITCH TEST FOR MECHANICAL CLUSTER (1 OF 3)

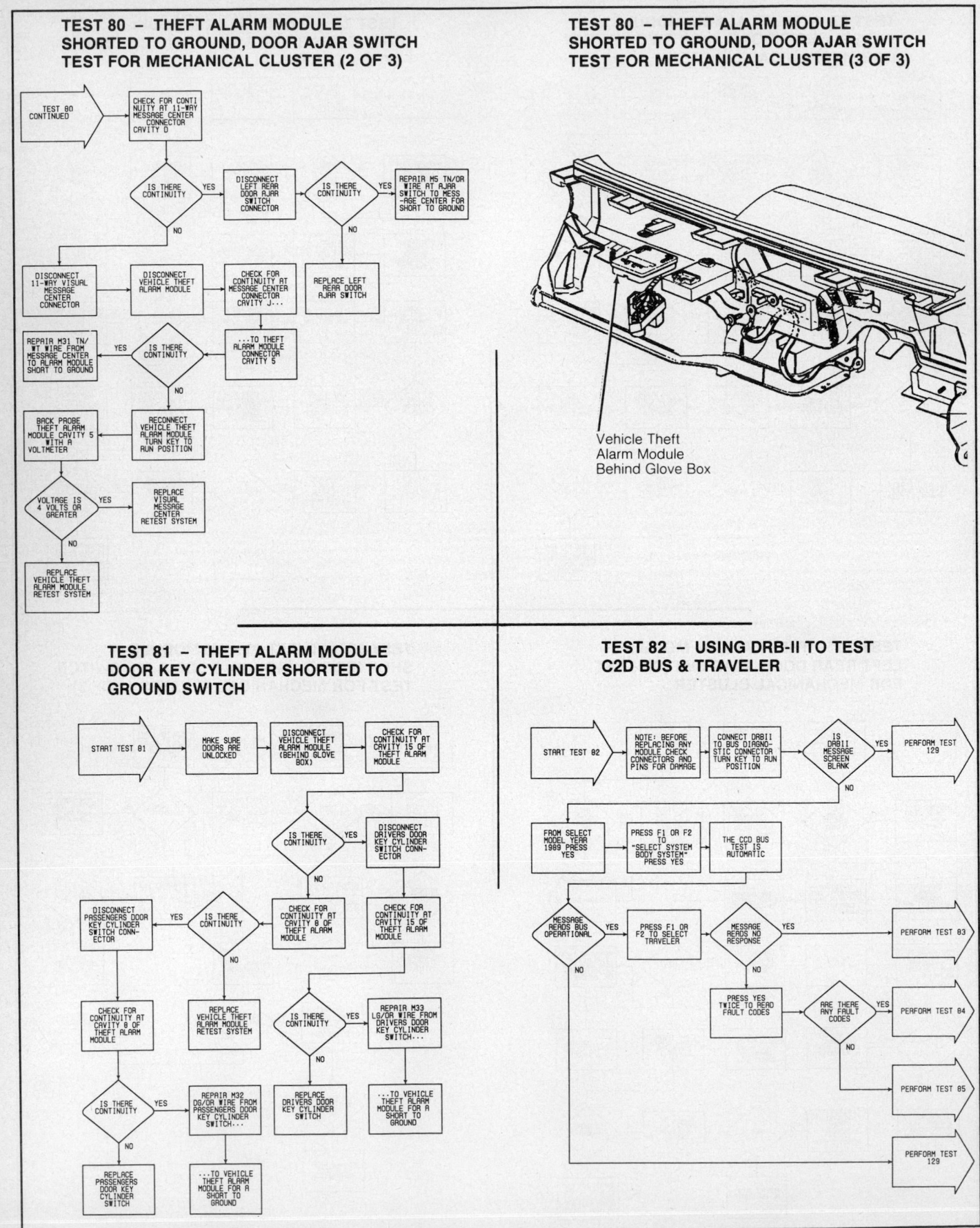

TEST 80 – THEFT ALARM MODULE SHORTED TO GROUND, DOOR AJAR SWITCH TEST FOR MECHANICAL CLUSTER (2 OF 3)

TEST 80 – THEFT ALARM MODULE SHORTED TO GROUND, DOOR AJAR SWITCH TEST FOR MECHANICAL CLUSTER (3 OF 3)

Vehicle Theft Alarm Module Behind Glove Box

TEST 81 – THEFT ALARM MODULE DOOR KEY CYLINDER SHORTED TO GROUND SWITCH

TEST 82 – USING DRB-II TO TEST C2D BUS & TRAVELER

TEST 83 – CHECKING FUSE NO. 8, J2 (DB) CIRCUIT & G5 (DB) CIRCUIT FOR OPEN & SHORT (1 OF 3)

TEST 83 – CHECKING FUSE NO. 8, J2 (DB) CIRCUIT & G5 (DB) CIRCUIT FOR OPEN & SHORT (2 OF 3)

TEST 83 – CHECKING FUSE NO. 8, J2 (DB) CIRCUIT & G5 (DB) CIRCUIT FOR OPEN & SHORT (3 OF 3)

TEST 84 – CHECKING FOR FAULT MESSAGES

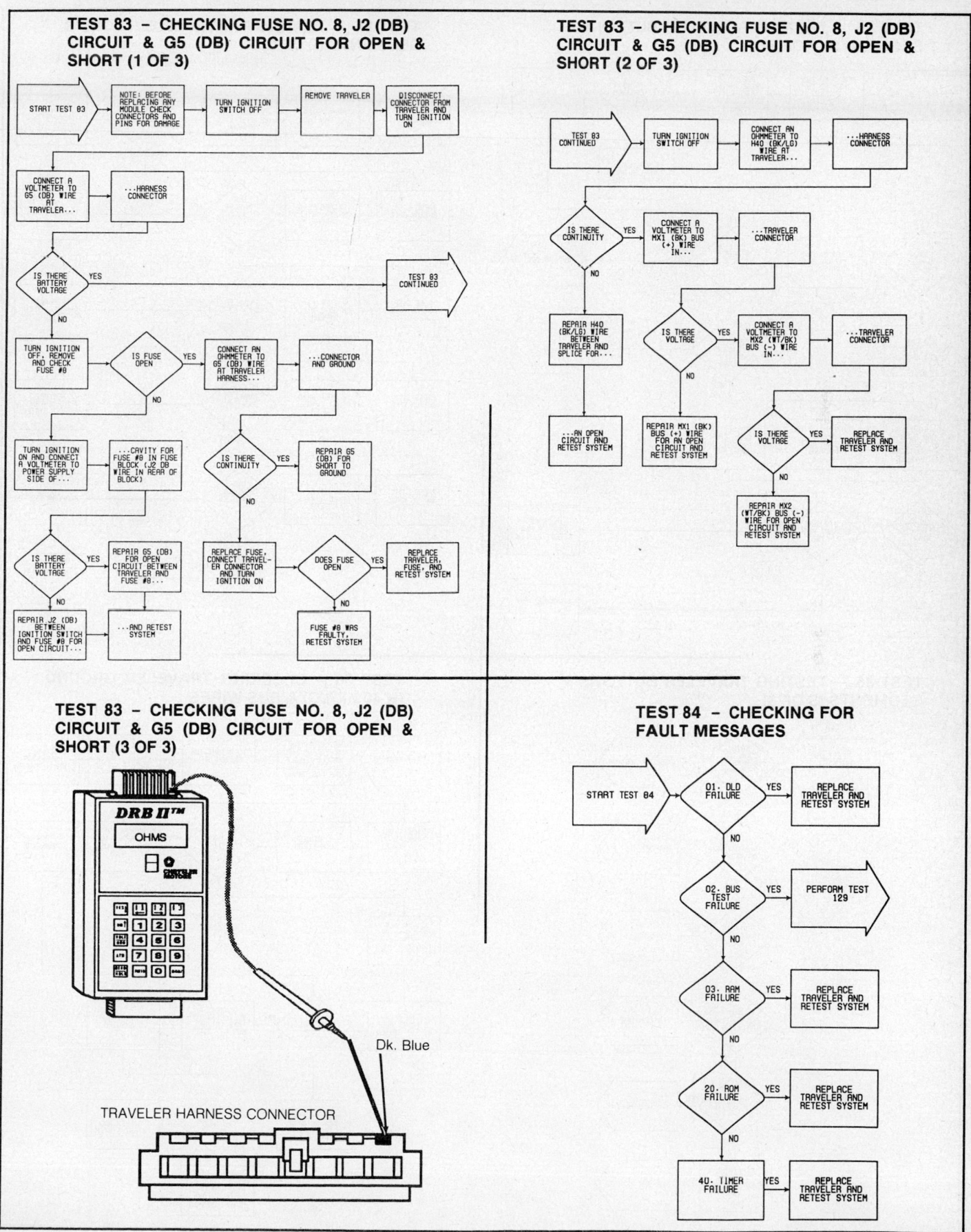

1a-236

1989 COMPUTERIZED ENGINE CONTROLS
Chrysler Motors Body Control Computer (Cont.)

TEST 85 – TESTING TRAVELER BUTTONS & SEGMENTS (1 OF 3)

TEST 85 – TESTING TRAVELER BUTTONS & SEGMENTS (2 OF 3)

TEST 85 – TESTING TRAVELER BUTTONS & SEGMENTS (3 OF 3)

TEST 86 – CHECKING TRAVELER GROUND (H 40 BK/LG) & BUS WIRES

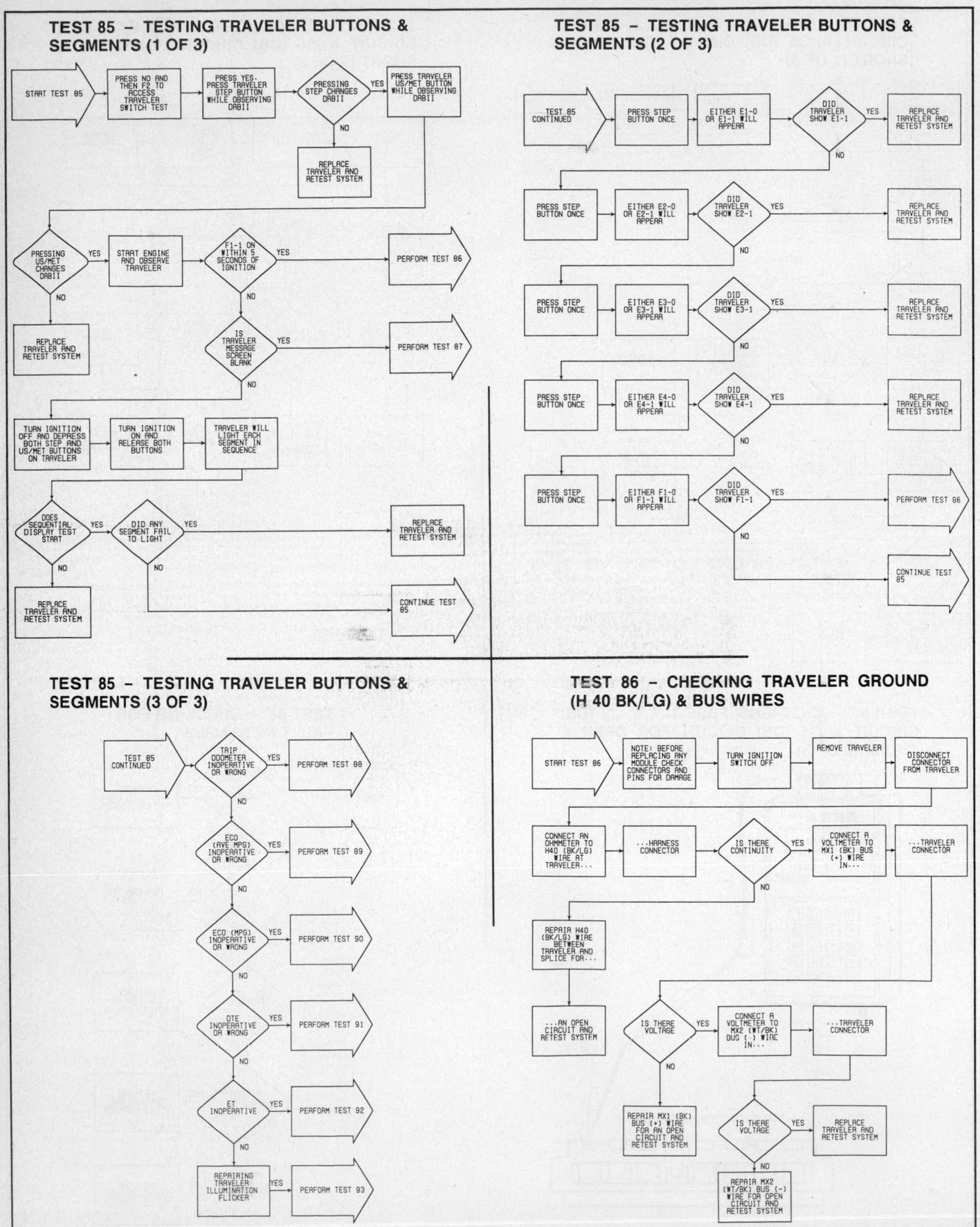

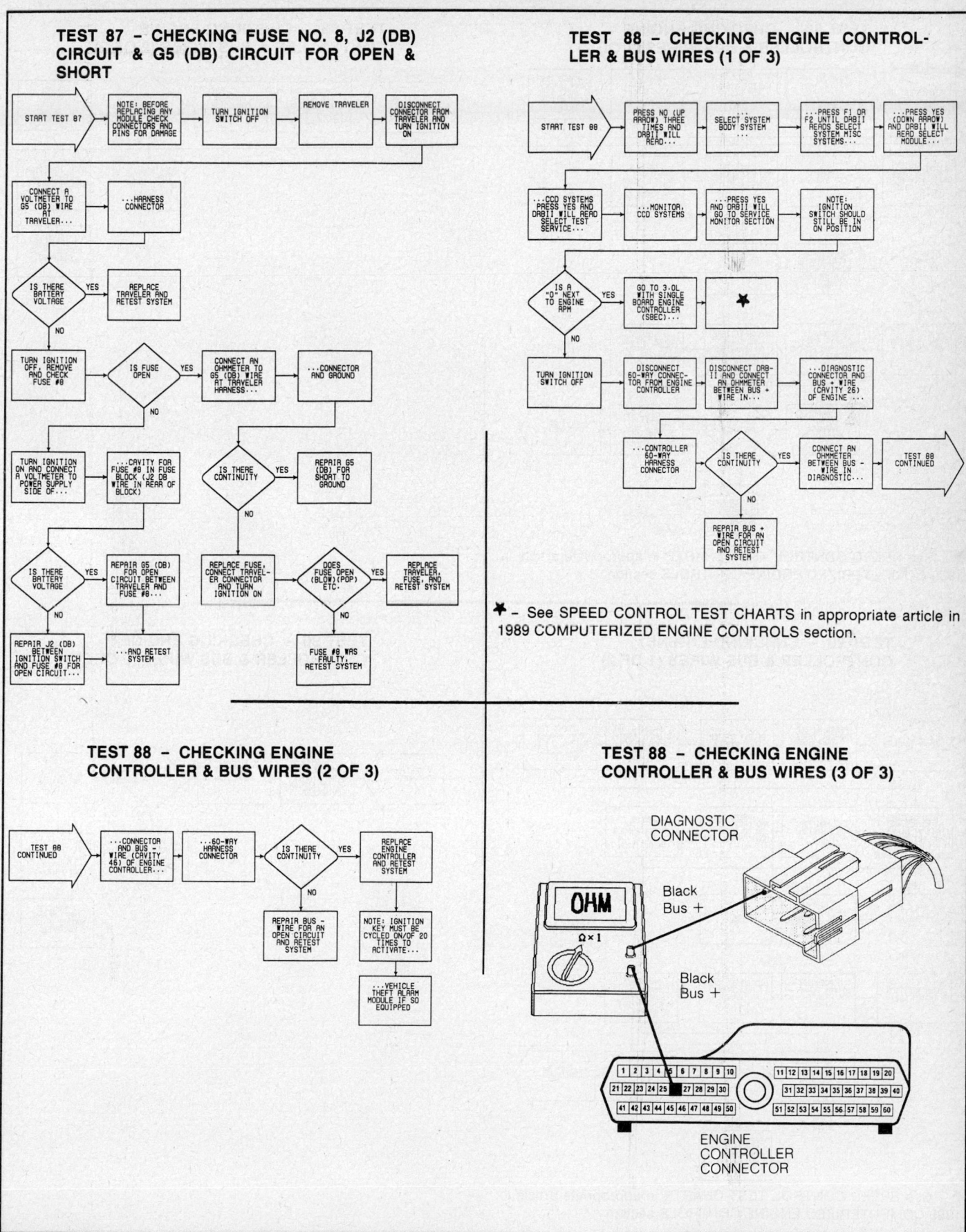

TEST 87 - CHECKING FUSE NO. 8, J2 (DB) CIRCUIT & G5 (DB) CIRCUIT FOR OPEN & SHORT

TEST 88 - CHECKING ENGINE CONTROLLER & BUS WIRES (1 OF 3)

✹ - See SPEED CONTROL TEST CHARTS in appropriate article in 1989 COMPUTERIZED ENGINE CONTROLS section.

TEST 88 - CHECKING ENGINE CONTROLLER & BUS WIRES (2 OF 3)

TEST 88 - CHECKING ENGINE CONTROLLER & BUS WIRES (3 OF 3)

1989 COMPUTERIZED ENGINE CONTROLS
Chrysler Motors Body Control Computer (Cont.)

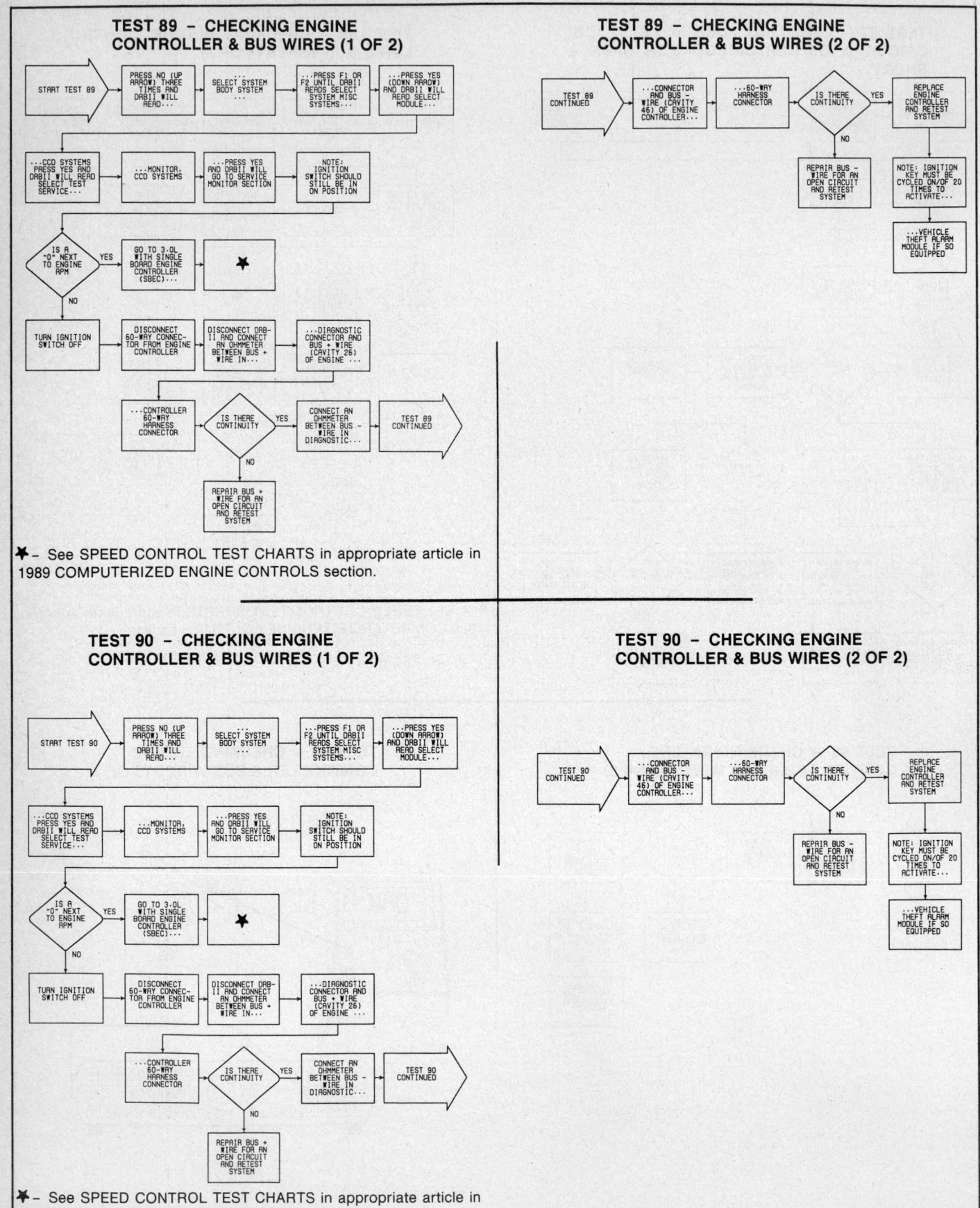

TEST 89 – CHECKING ENGINE CONTROLLER & BUS WIRES (1 OF 2)

✦ – See SPEED CONTROL TEST CHARTS in appropriate article in 1989 COMPUTERIZED ENGINE CONTROLS section.

TEST 89 – CHECKING ENGINE CONTROLLER & BUS WIRES (2 OF 2)

TEST 90 – CHECKING ENGINE CONTROLLER & BUS WIRES (1 OF 2)

✦ – See SPEED CONTROL TEST CHARTS in appropriate article in 1989 COMPUTERIZED ENGINE CONTROLS section.

TEST 90 – CHECKING ENGINE CONTROLLER & BUS WIRES (2 OF 2)

1989 COMPUTERIZED ENGINE CONTROLS
Chrysler Motors Body Control Computer (Cont.)

1a-239

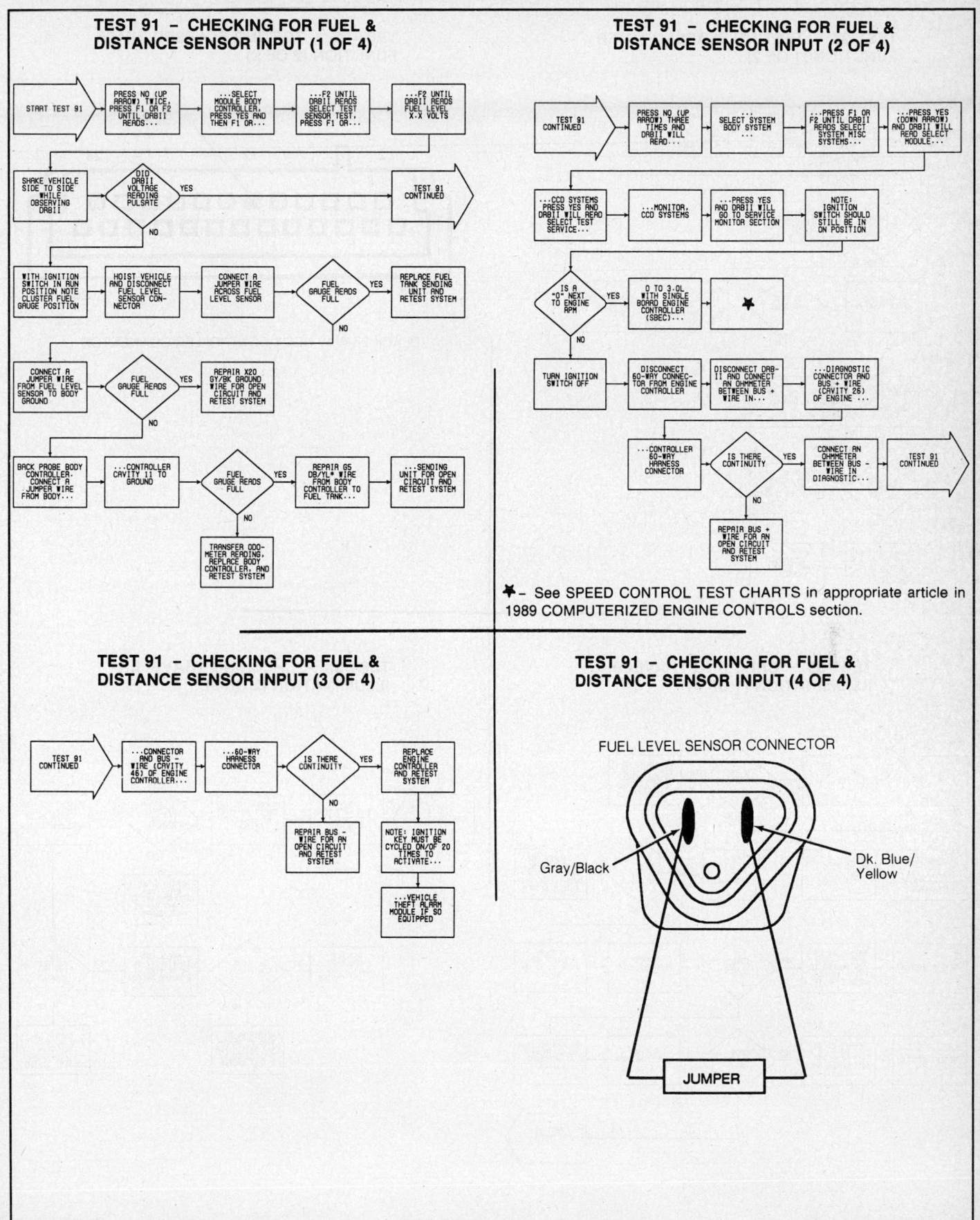

TEST 91 – CHECKING FOR FUEL & DISTANCE SENSOR INPUT (1 OF 4)

TEST 91 – CHECKING FOR FUEL & DISTANCE SENSOR INPUT (2 OF 4)

✱ – See SPEED CONTROL TEST CHARTS in appropriate article in 1989 COMPUTERIZED ENGINE CONTROLS section.

TEST 91 – CHECKING FOR FUEL & DISTANCE SENSOR INPUT (3 OF 4)

TEST 91 – CHECKING FOR FUEL & DISTANCE SENSOR INPUT (4 OF 4)

FUEL LEVEL SENSOR CONNECTOR

Gray/Black

Dk. Blue/ Yellow

JUMPER

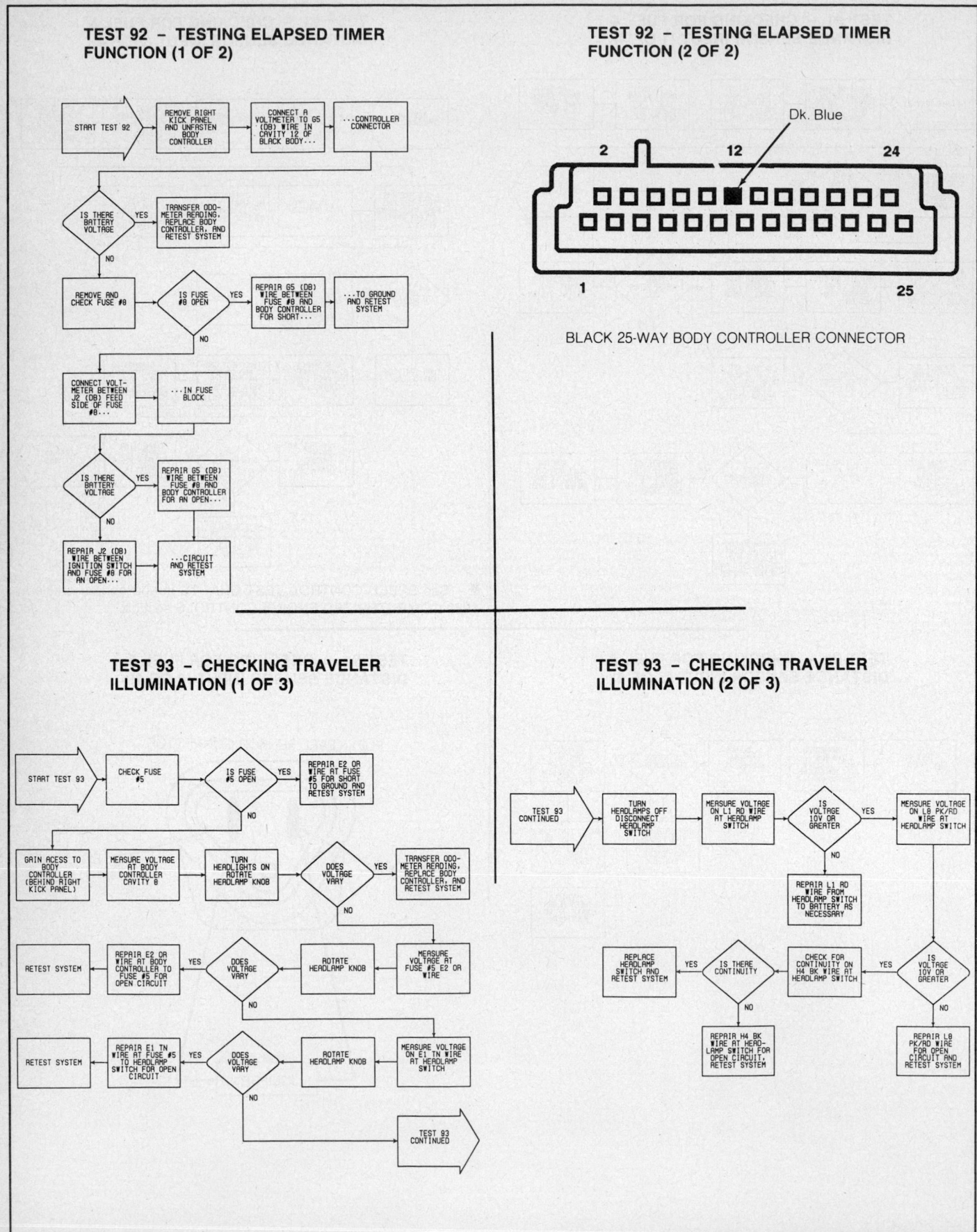

TEST 92 – TESTING ELAPSED TIMER FUNCTION (1 OF 2)

START TEST 92 → REMOVE RIGHT KICK PANEL AND UNFASTEN BODY CONTROLLER → CONNECT A VOLTMETER TO G5 (DB) WIRE IN CAVITY 12 OF BLACK BODY... → ...CONTROLLER CONNECTOR

IS THERE BATTERY VOLTAGE — YES → TRANSFER ODOMETER READING, REPLACE BODY CONTROLLER, AND RETEST SYSTEM

NO ↓

REMOVE AND CHECK FUSE #8 → IS FUSE #8 OPEN — YES → REPAIR G5 (DB) WIRE BETWEEN FUSE #8 AND BODY CONTROLLER FOR SHORT... → ...TO GROUND AND RETEST SYSTEM

NO ↓

CONNECT VOLT-METER BETWEEN J2 (DB) FEED SIDE OF FUSE #8... → ...IN FUSE BLOCK

IS THERE BATTERY VOLTAGE — YES → REPAIR G5 (DB) WIRE BETWEEN FUSE #8 AND BODY CONTROLLER FOR AN OPEN...

NO ↓

REPAIR J2 (DB) WIRE BETWEEN IGNITION SWITCH AND FUSE #8 FOR AN OPEN... → ...CIRCUIT AND RETEST SYSTEM

TEST 92 – TESTING ELAPSED TIMER FUNCTION (2 OF 2)

Dk. Blue

2   12   24

1   25

BLACK 25-WAY BODY CONTROLLER CONNECTOR

TEST 93 – CHECKING TRAVELER ILLUMINATION (1 OF 3)

START TEST 93 → CHECK FUSE #5 → IS FUSE #5 OPEN — YES → REPAIR E2 OR WIRE AT FUSE #5 FOR SHORT TO GROUND AND RETEST SYSTEM

NO ↓

GAIN ACESS TO BODY CONTROLLER (BEHIND RIGHT KICK PANEL) → MEASURE VOLTAGE AT BODY CONTROLLER CAVITY 8 → TURN HEADLIGHTS ON ROTATE HEADLAMP KNOB → DOES VOLTAGE VARY — YES → TRANSFER ODOMETER READING, REPLACE BODY CONTROLLER, AND RETEST SYSTEM

NO ↓

RETEST SYSTEM ← REPAIR E2 OR WIRE AT BODY CONTROLLER TO FUSE #5 FOR OPEN CIRCUIT — YES ← DOES VOLTAGE VARY ← ROTATE HEADLAMP KNOB ← MEASURE VOLTAGE AT FUSE #5 E2 OR WIRE

NO ↓

RETEST SYSTEM ← REPAIR E1 TN AT FUSE #5 TO HEADLAMP SWITCH FOR OPEN CIRCUIT — YES ← DOES VOLTAGE VARY ← ROTATE HEADLAMP KNOB ← MEASURE VOLTAGE ON E1 IN WIRE AT HEADLAMP SWITCH

NO ↓

TEST 93 CONTINUED

TEST 93 – CHECKING TRAVELER ILLUMINATION (2 OF 3)

TEST 93 CONTINUED → TURN HEADLAMPS OFF DISCONNECT HEADLAMP SWITCH → MEASURE VOLTAGE ON L1 RD WIRE AT HEADLAMP SWITCH → IS VOLTAGE 10V OR GREATER — YES → MEASURE VOLTAGE ON L8 PK/RD WIRE AT HEADLAMP SWITCH

NO ↓

REPAIR L1 RD WIRE FROM HEADLAMP SWITCH TO BATTERY AS NECESSARY

REPLACE HEADLAMP SWITCH AND RETEST SYSTEM ← IS THERE CONTINUITY — YES ← CHECK FOR CONTINUITY ON H4 BK WIRE AT HEADLAMP SWITCH — YES ← IS VOLTAGE 10V OR GREATER

NO ↓   NO ↓

REPAIR H4 BK WIRE AT HEAD-LAMP SWITCH FOR OPEN CIRCUIT, RETEST SYSTEM

REPAIR L8 PK/RD WIRE FOR OPEN CIRCUIT AND RETEST SYSTEM

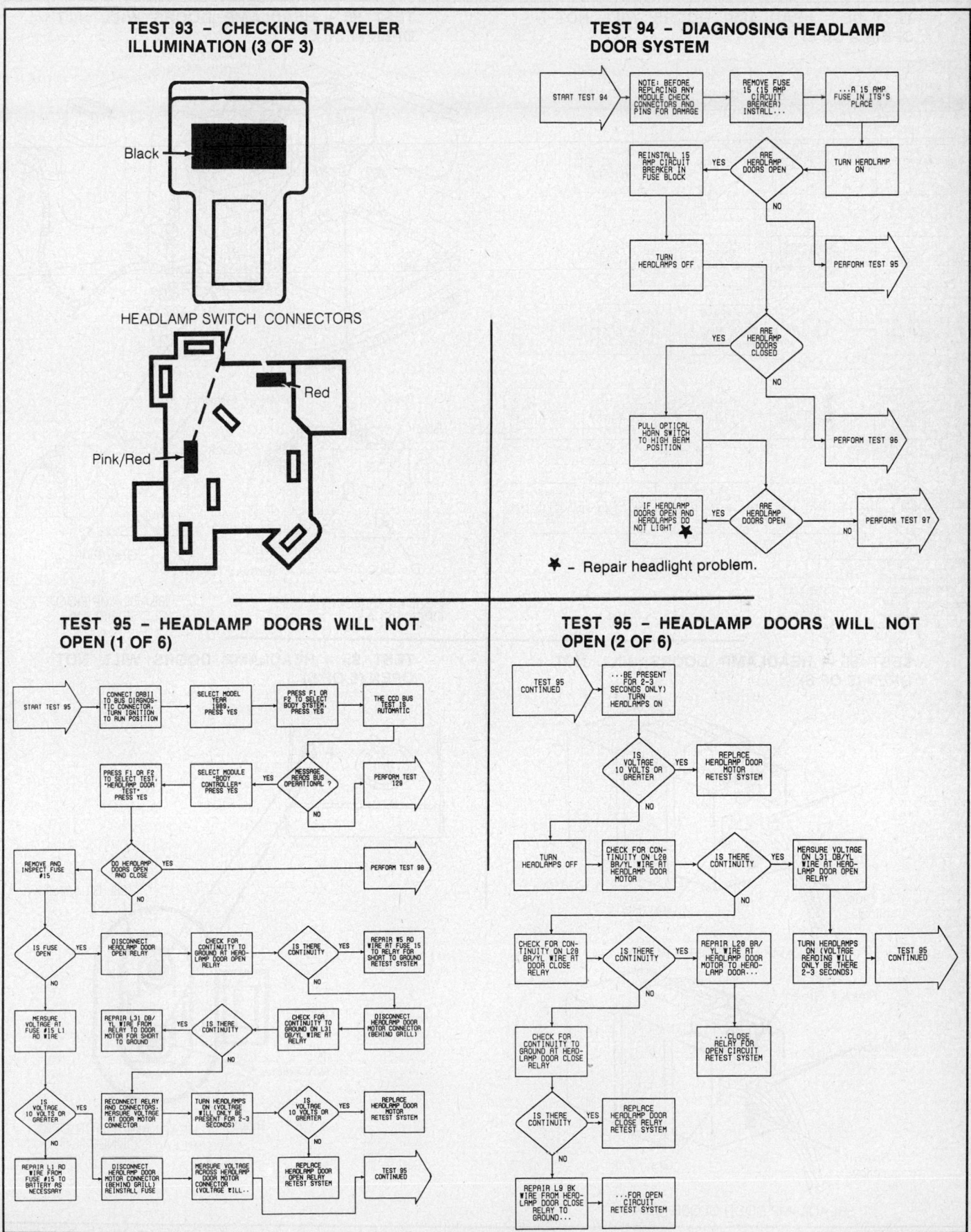

TEST 93 – CHECKING TRAVELER ILLUMINATION (3 OF 3)

Black

HEADLAMP SWITCH CONNECTORS

Red

Pink/Red

TEST 94 – DIAGNOSING HEADLAMP DOOR SYSTEM

★ – Repair headlight problem.

TEST 95 – HEADLAMP DOORS WILL NOT OPEN (1 OF 6)

TEST 95 – HEADLAMP DOORS WILL NOT OPEN (2 OF 6)

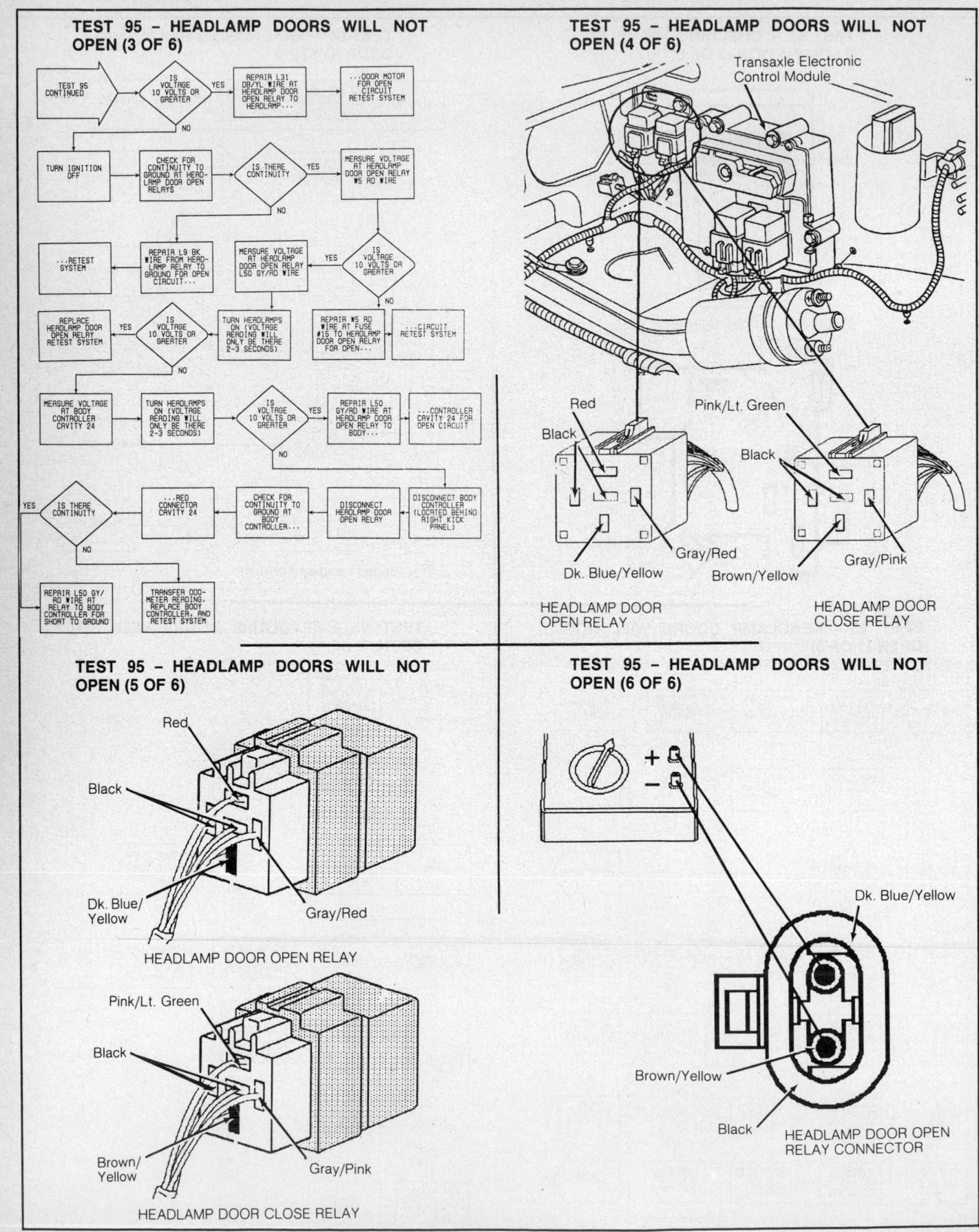

TEST 95 – HEADLAMP DOORS WILL NOT OPEN (3 OF 6)

TEST 95 – HEADLAMP DOORS WILL NOT OPEN (4 OF 6)

HEADLAMP DOOR OPEN RELAY

HEADLAMP DOOR CLOSE RELAY

TEST 95 – HEADLAMP DOORS WILL NOT OPEN (5 OF 6)

HEADLAMP DOOR OPEN RELAY

HEADLAMP DOOR CLOSE RELAY

TEST 95 – HEADLAMP DOORS WILL NOT OPEN (6 OF 6)

HEADLAMP DOOR OPEN RELAY CONNECTOR

1989 COMPUTERIZED ENGINE CONTROLS
Chrysler Motors Body Control Computer (Cont.)

1a-243

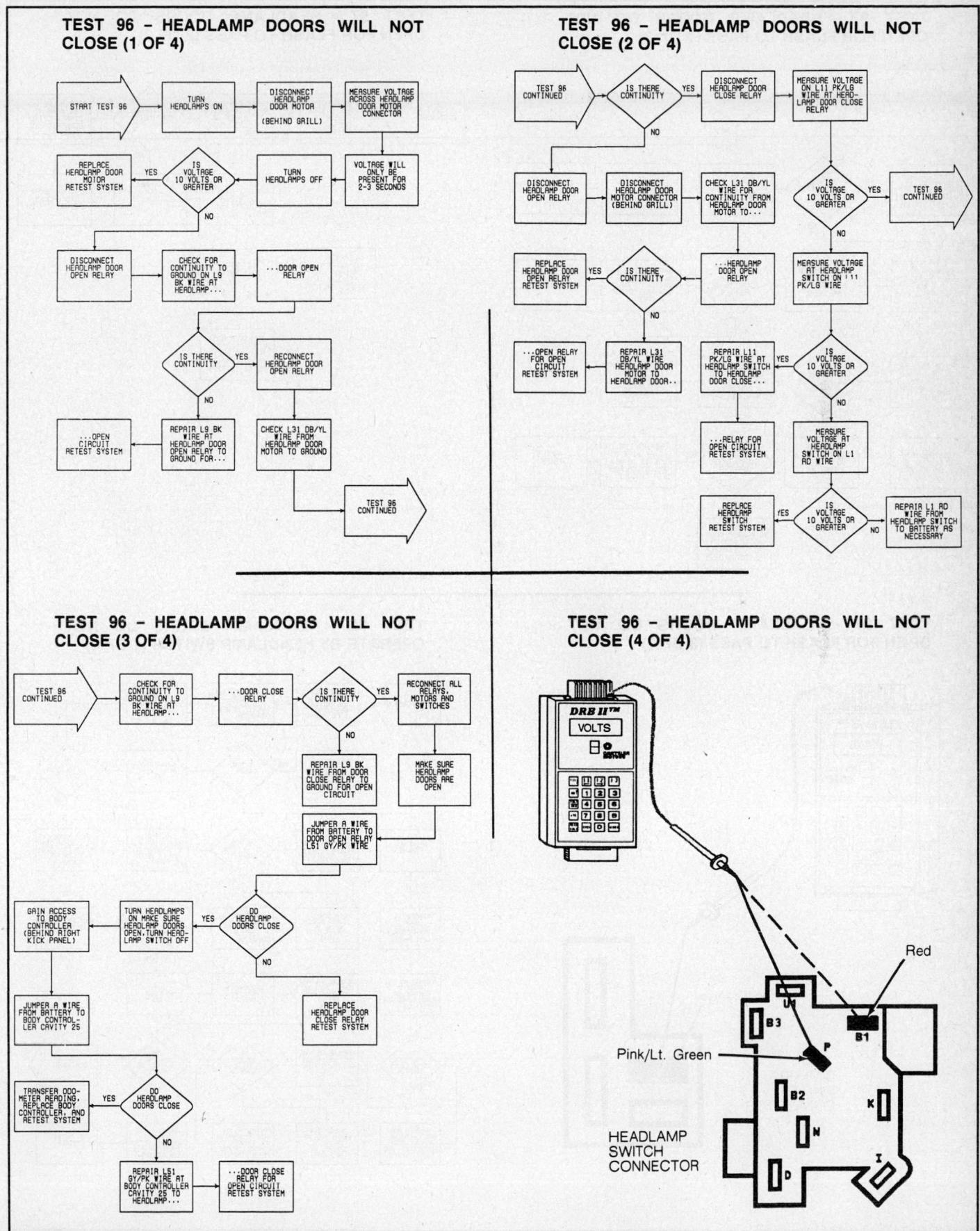

TEST 96 – HEADLAMP DOORS WILL NOT CLOSE (1 OF 4)

START TEST 96 → TURN HEADLAMPS ON → DISCONNECT HEADLAMP DOOR MOTOR (BEHIND GRILL) → MEASURE VOLTAGE ACROSS HEADLAMP DOOR MOTOR CONNECTOR

VOLTAGE WILL ONLY BE PRESENT FOR 2-3 SECONDS

TURN HEADLAMPS OFF

IS VOLTAGE 10 VOLTS OR GREATER — YES → REPLACE HEADLAMP DOOR MOTOR RETEST SYSTEM
— NO →

DISCONNECT HEADLAMP DOOR OPEN RELAY → CHECK FOR CONTINUITY TO GROUND ON L9 BK WIRE AT HEADLAMP... → ...DOOR OPEN RELAY

IS THERE CONTINUITY — YES → RECONNECT HEADLAMP DOOR OPEN RELAY
— NO →

...OPEN CIRCUIT RETEST SYSTEM ← REPAIR L9 BK WIRE AT HEADLAMP DOOR OPEN RELAY TO GROUND FOR...

CHECK L31 DB/YL WIRE FROM HEADLAMP DOOR MOTOR TO GROUND

TEST 96 CONTINUED

TEST 96 – HEADLAMP DOORS WILL NOT CLOSE (2 OF 4)

TEST 96 CONTINUED → IS THERE CONTINUITY — YES → DISCONNECT HEADLAMP DOOR CLOSE RELAY → MEASURE VOLTAGE ON L11 PK/LG WIRE AT HEADLAMP DOOR CLOSE RELAY
— NO →

DISCONNECT HEADLAMP DOOR OPEN RELAY → DISCONNECT HEADLAMP DOOR MOTOR CONNECTOR (BEHIND GRILL) → CHECK L31 DB/YL WIRE FOR CONTINUITY FROM HEADLAMP DOOR MOTOR TO...

IS VOLTAGE 10 VOLTS OR GREATER — YES → TEST 96 CONTINUED
— NO →

REPLACE HEADLAMP DOOR OPEN RELAY RETEST SYSTEM ← IS THERE CONTINUITY — YES
— NO → ...HEADLAMP DOOR OPEN RELAY

MEASURE VOLTAGE AT HEADLAMP SWITCH ON '11 PK/LG WIRE

...OPEN RELAY FOR OPEN CIRCUIT RETEST SYSTEM ← REPAIR L31 DB/YL WIRE HEADLAMP DOOR MOTOR TO HEADLAMP DOOR.. ← REPAIR L11 PK/LG WIRE AT HEADLAMP SWITCH TO HEADLAMP DOOR CLOSE...

IS VOLTAGE 10 VOLTS OR GREATER — YES
— NO →

...RELAY FOR OPEN CIRCUIT RETEST SYSTEM

MEASURE VOLTAGE AT HEADLAMP SWITCH ON L1 RD WIRE

REPLACE HEADLAMP SWITCH RETEST SYSTEM ← IS VOLTAGE 10 VOLTS OR GREATER — YES
— NO → REPAIR L1 RD WIRE FROM HEADLAMP SWITCH TO BATTERY AS NECESSARY

TEST 96 – HEADLAMP DOORS WILL NOT CLOSE (3 OF 4)

TEST 96 CONTINUED → CHECK FOR CONTINUITY TO GROUND ON L9 BK WIRE AT HEADLAMP... → ...DOOR CLOSE RELAY → IS THERE CONTINUITY — YES → RECONNECT ALL RELAYS, MOTORS AND SWITCHES
— NO →

REPAIR L9 BK WIRE FROM DOOR CLOSE RELAY TO GROUND FOR OPEN CIRCUIT

MAKE SURE HEADLAMP DOORS ARE OPEN

JUMPER A WIRE FROM BATTERY TO DOOR OPEN RELAY L51 GY/PK WIRE

GAIN ACCESS TO BODY CONTROLLER (BEHIND RIGHT KICK PANEL) ← TURN HEADLAMPS ON MAKE SURE HEADLAMP DOORS OPEN. TURN HEADLAMP SWITCH OFF ← YES — DO HEADLAMP DOORS CLOSE
— NO → REPLACE HEADLAMP DOOR CLOSE RELAY RETEST SYSTEM

JUMPER A WIRE FROM BATTERY TO BODY CONTROLLER CAVITY 25

TRANSFER ODOMETER READING, REPLACE BODY CONTROLLER, AND RETEST SYSTEM ← YES — DO HEADLAMP DOORS CLOSE
— NO →

REPAIR L51 GY/PK WIRE AT BODY CONTROLLER CAVITY 25 TO HEADLAMP... → ...DOOR CLOSE RELAY FOR OPEN CIRCUIT RETEST SYSTEM

TEST 96 – HEADLAMP DOORS WILL NOT CLOSE (4 OF 4)

DRB II™ VOLTS

Red

Pink/Lt. Green

HEADLAMP SWITCH CONNECTOR

1a-244

1989 COMPUTERIZED ENGINE CONTROLS
Chrysler Motors Body Control Computer (Cont.)

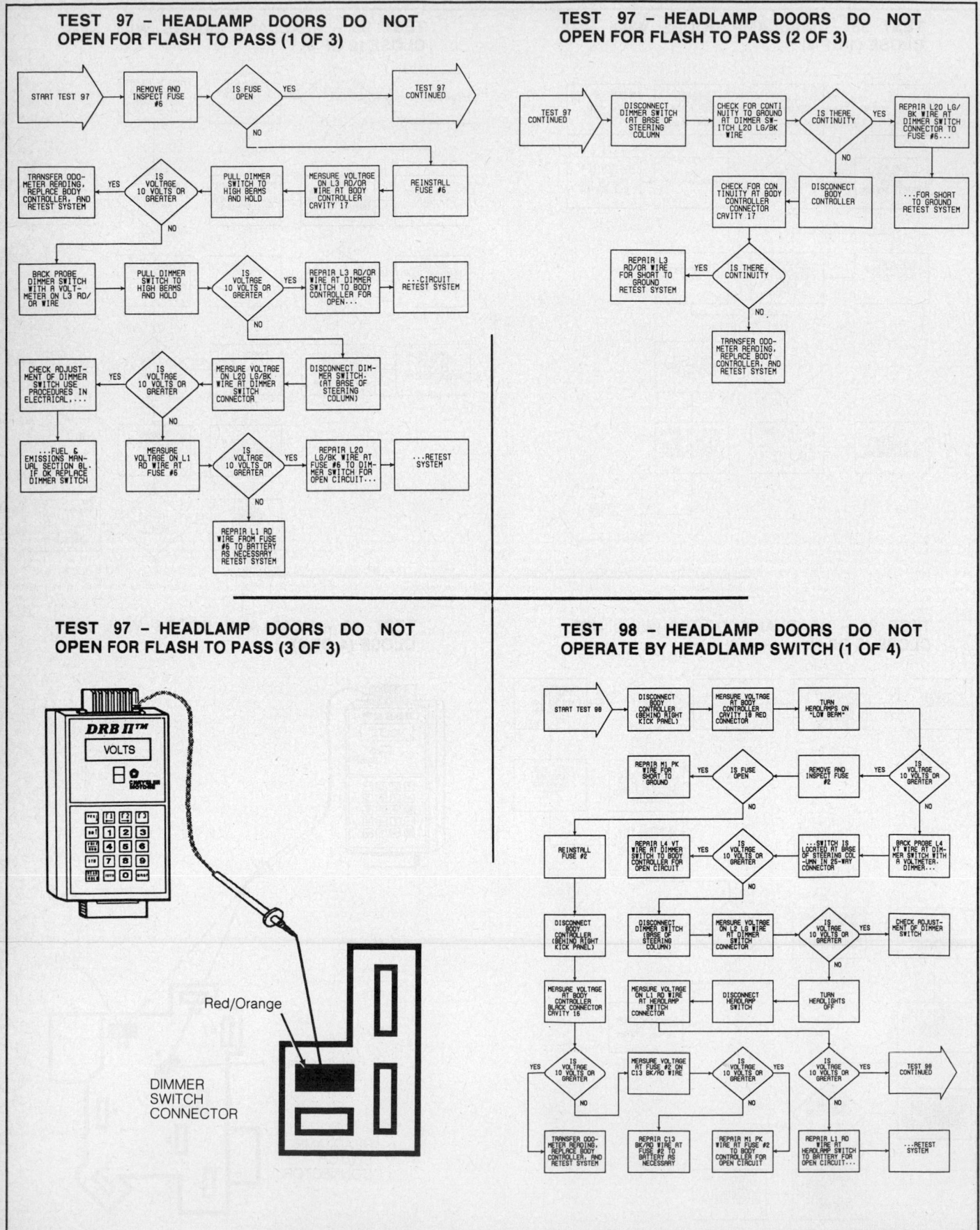

TEST 97 – HEADLAMP DOORS DO NOT OPEN FOR FLASH TO PASS (1 OF 3)

TEST 97 – HEADLAMP DOORS DO NOT OPEN FOR FLASH TO PASS (2 OF 3)

TEST 97 – HEADLAMP DOORS DO NOT OPEN FOR FLASH TO PASS (3 OF 3)

TEST 98 – HEADLAMP DOORS DO NOT OPERATE BY HEADLAMP SWITCH (1 OF 4)

1989 COMPUTERIZED ENGINE CONTROLS
Chrysler Motors Body Control Computer (Cont.)

1a-245

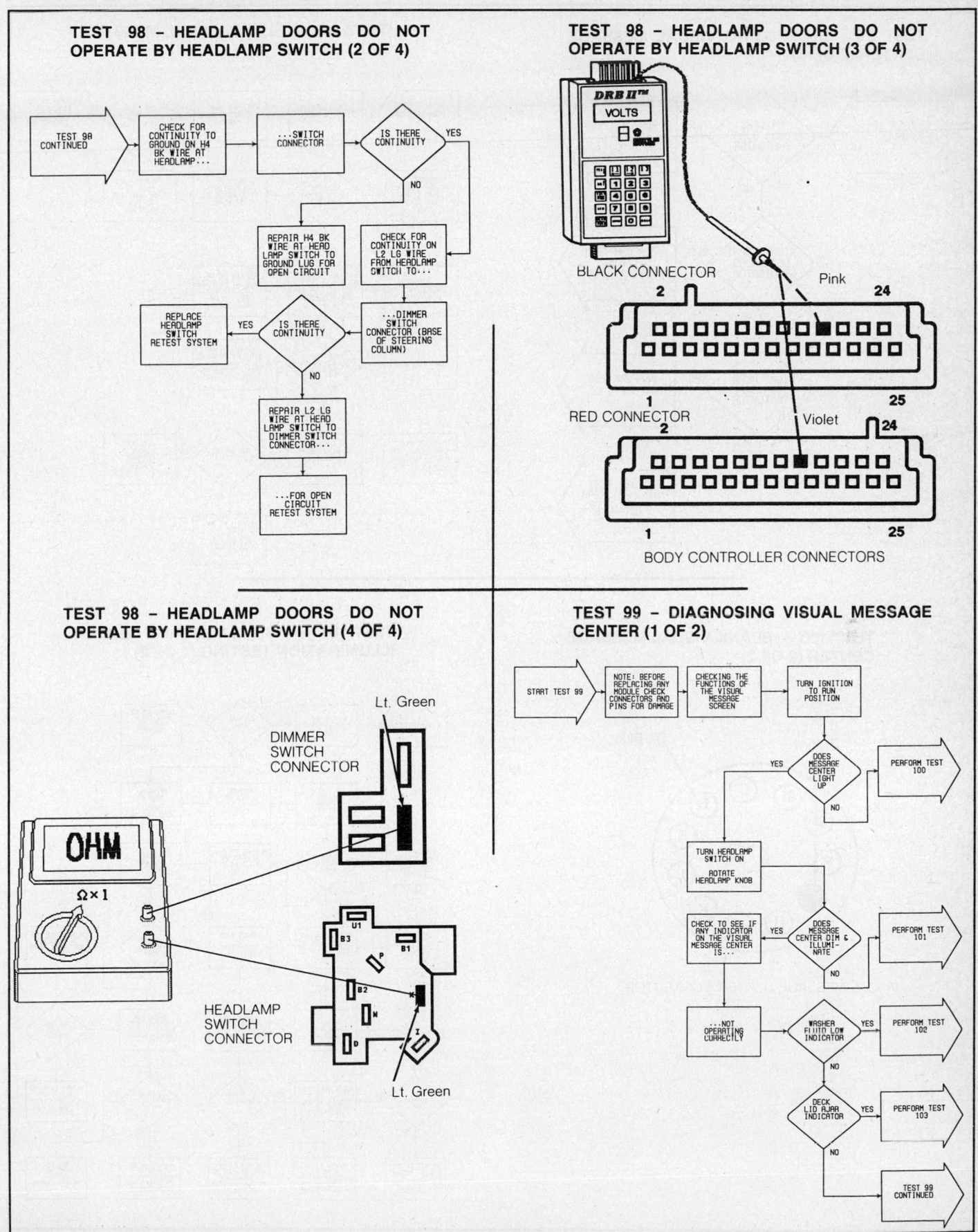

TEST 98 – HEADLAMP DOORS DO NOT OPERATE BY HEADLAMP SWITCH (2 OF 4)

TEST 98 CONTINUED → CHECK FOR CONTINUITY TO GROUND ON H4 BK WIRE AT HEADLAMP... → ...SWITCH CONNECTOR → IS THERE CONTINUITY → YES

NO ↓

REPAIR H4 BK WIRE AT HEAD LAMP SWITCH TO GROUND LUG FOR OPEN CIRCUIT ← CHECK FOR CONTINUITY ON L2 LG WIRE FROM HEADLAMP SWITCH TO...

REPLACE HEADLAMP SWITCH RETEST SYSTEM ← YES ← IS THERE CONTINUITY ← ...DIMMER SWITCH CONNECTOR (BASE OF STEERING COLUMN)

NO ↓

REPAIR L2 LG WIRE AT HEAD LAMP SWITCH TO DIMMER SWITCH CONNECTOR...

...FOR OPEN CIRCUIT RETEST SYSTEM

TEST 98 – HEADLAMP DOORS DO NOT OPERATE BY HEADLAMP SWITCH (3 OF 4)

DRB II™ VOLTS

BLACK CONNECTOR

Pink

2 ... 24

1 ... 25

RED CONNECTOR

Violet

2 ... 24

1 ... 25

BODY CONTROLLER CONNECTORS

TEST 98 – HEADLAMP DOORS DO NOT OPERATE BY HEADLAMP SWITCH (4 OF 4)

OHM
Ω × 1

Lt. Green

DIMMER SWITCH CONNECTOR

HEADLAMP SWITCH CONNECTOR

U1
B3
B1
P
B2
M
D
I

Lt. Green

TEST 99 – DIAGNOSING VISUAL MESSAGE CENTER (1 OF 2)

START TEST 99 → NOTE: BEFORE REPLACING ANY MODULE CHECK CONNECTORS AND PINS FOR DAMAGE → CHECKING THE FUNCTIONS OF THE VISUAL MESSAGE SCREEN → TURN IGNITION TO RUN POSITION

YES ← DOES MESSAGE CENTER LIGHT UP → PERFORM TEST 100

NO ↓

TURN HEADLAMP SWITCH ON

ROTATE HEADLAMP KNOB

CHECK TO SEE IF ANY INDICATOR ON THE VISUAL MESSAGE CENTER IS... ← YES ← DOES MESSAGE CENTER DIM & ILLUMINATE → PERFORM TEST 101

NO ↓

...NOT OPERATING CORRECTLY → WASHER FLUID LOW INDICATOR → YES → PERFORM TEST 102

NO ↓

DECK LID AJAR INDICATOR → YES → PERFORM TEST 103

NO ↓

TEST 99 CONTINUED

TEST 99 – DIAGNOSING VISUAL MESSAGE CENTER (2 OF 2)

TEST 100 – BLANK VISUAL MESSAGE CENTER (1 OF 2)

TEST 100 – BLANK VISUAL MESSAGE CENTER (2 OF 2)

TEST 101 – VISUAL MESSAGE CENTER ILLUMINATION TESTING (1 OF 2)

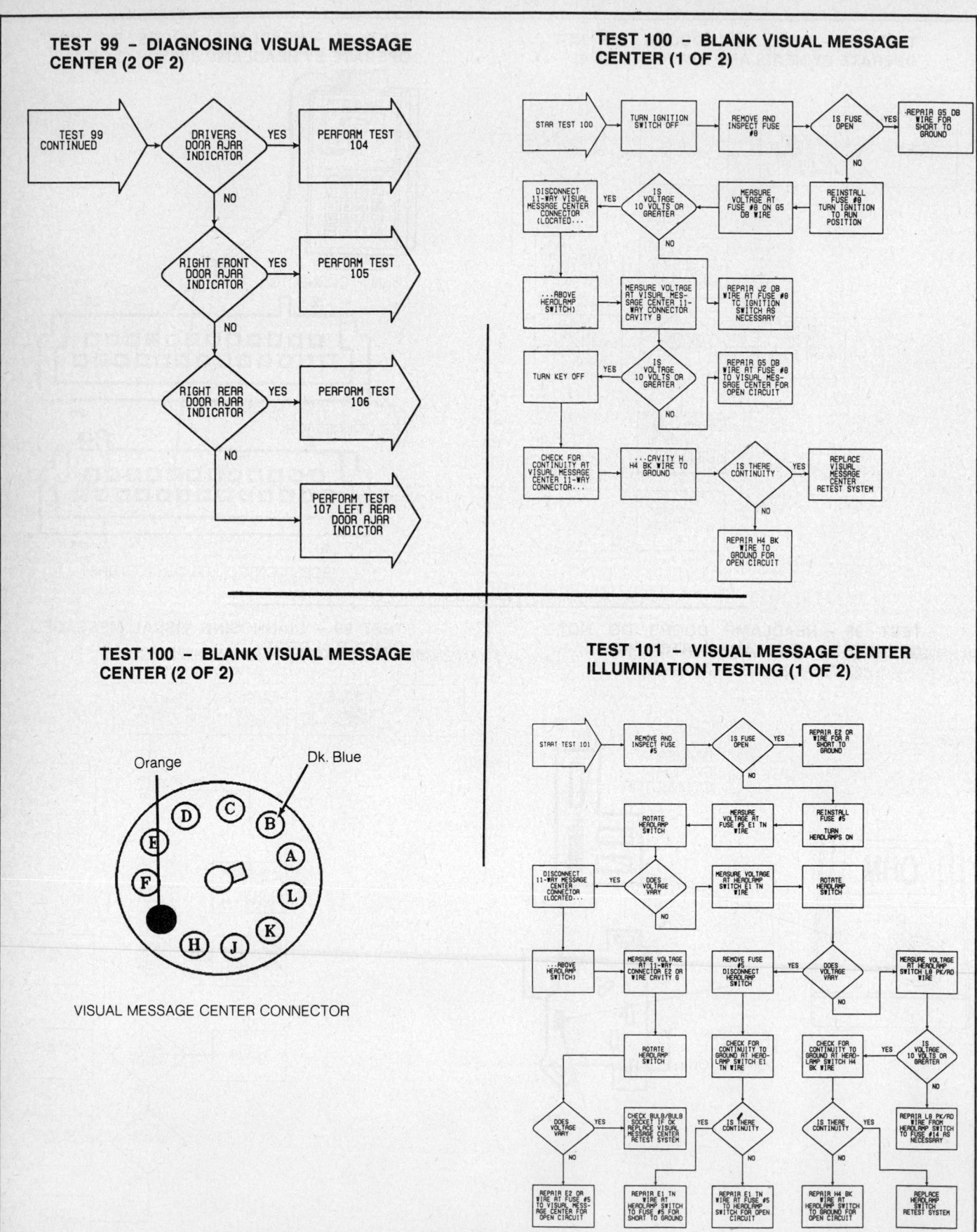

VISUAL MESSAGE CENTER CONNECTOR

1989 COMPUTERIZED ENGINE CONTROLS
Chrysler Motors Body Control Computer (Cont.)

1a-247

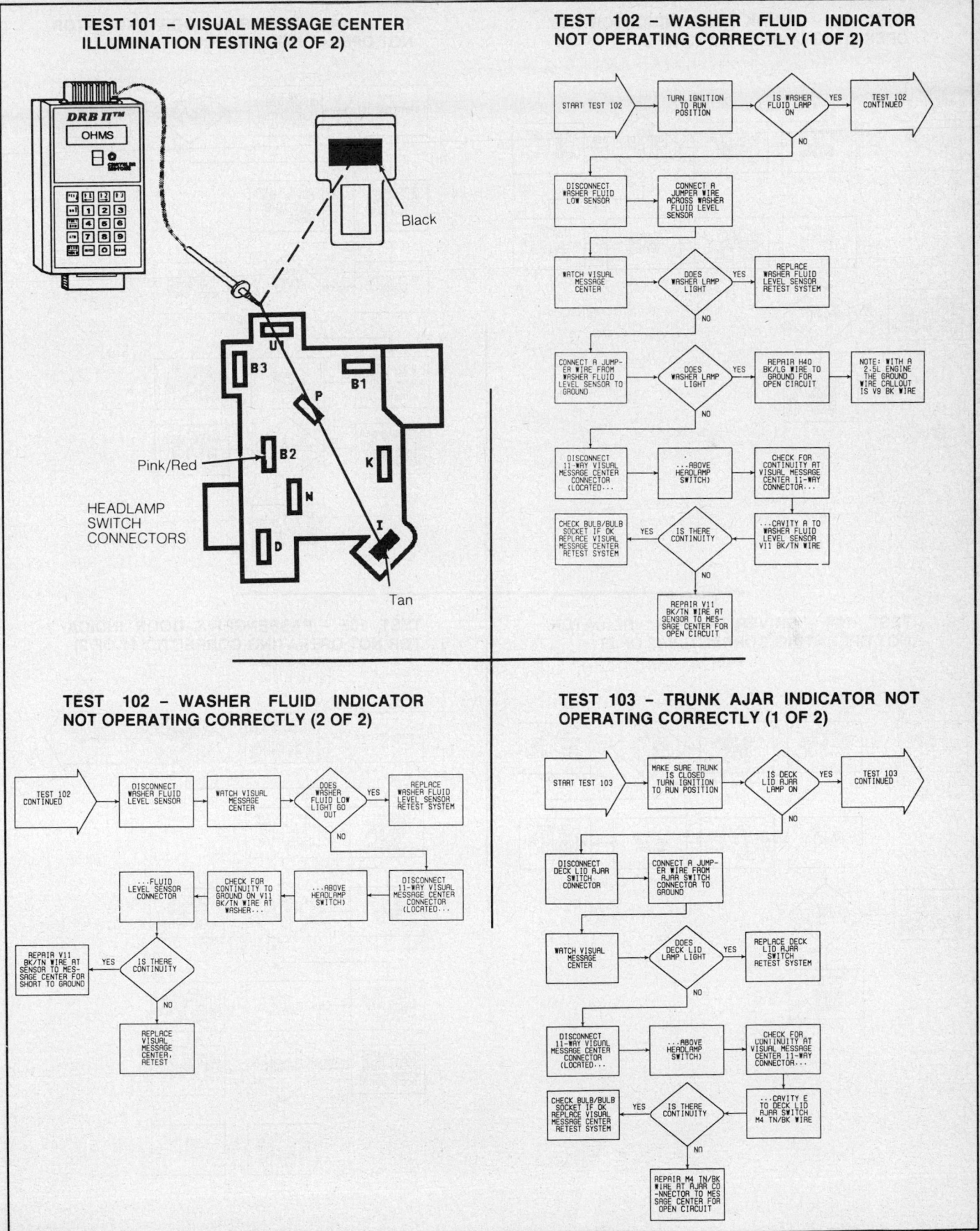

TEST 101 – VISUAL MESSAGE CENTER ILLUMINATION TESTING (2 OF 2)

DRB II™
OHMS

Black

U
B3
P
B1
Pink/Red — B2
K
N
HEADLAMP SWITCH CONNECTORS
D
I

Tan

TEST 102 – WASHER FLUID INDICATOR NOT OPERATING CORRECTLY (1 OF 2)

START TEST 102 → TURN IGNITION TO RUN POSITION → IS WASHER FLUID LAMP ON → YES → TEST 102 CONTINUED

NO ↓

DISCONNECT WASHER FLUID LOW SENSOR → CONNECT A JUMPER WIRE ACROSS WASHER FLUID LEVEL SENSOR

WATCH VISUAL MESSAGE CENTER → DOES WASHER LAMP LIGHT → YES → REPLACE WASHER FLUID LEVEL SENSOR RETEST SYSTEM

NO ↓

CONNECT A JUMPER WIRE FROM WASHER FLUID LEVEL SENSOR TO GROUND → DOES WASHER LAMP LIGHT → YES → REPAIR H40 BK/LG WIRE TO GROUND FOR OPEN CIRCUIT → NOTE: WITH A 2.5L ENGINE THE GROUND WIRE CALLOUT IS V9 BK WIRE

NO ↓

DISCONNECT 11-WAY VISUAL MESSAGE CENTER CONNECTOR (LOCATED... → ...ABOVE HEADLAMP SWITCH) → CHECK FOR CONTINUITY AT VISUAL MESSAGE CENTER 11-WAY CONNECTOR...

CHECK BULB/BULB SOCKET IF OK REPLACE VISUAL MESSAGE CENTER RETEST SYSTEM ← YES ← IS THERE CONTINUITY ← ...CAVITY A TO WASHER FLUID LEVEL SENSOR V11 BK/TN WIRE

NO ↓

REPAIR V11 BK/TN WIRE AT SENSOR TO MESSAGE CENTER FOR OPEN CIRCUIT

TEST 102 – WASHER FLUID INDICATOR NOT OPERATING CORRECTLY (2 OF 2)

TEST 102 CONTINUED → DISCONNECT WASHER FLUID LEVEL SENSOR → WATCH VISUAL MESSAGE CENTER → DOES WASHER FLUID LOW LIGHT GO OUT → YES → REPLACE WASHER FLUID LEVEL SENSOR RETEST SYSTEM

NO ↓

...FLUID LEVEL SENSOR CONNECTOR ← CHECK FOR CONTINUITY TO GROUND ON V11 BK/TN WIRE AT WASHER... ← ...ABOVE HEADLAMP SWITCH) ← DISCONNECT 11-WAY VISUAL MESSAGE CENTER CONNECTOR (LOCATED...

↓

REPAIR V11 BK/TN WIRE AT SENSOR TO MESSAGE CENTER FOR SHORT TO GROUND ← YES ← IS THERE CONTINUITY

NO ↓

REPLACE VISUAL MESSAGE CENTER, RETEST

TEST 103 – TRUNK AJAR INDICATOR NOT OPERATING CORRECTLY (1 OF 2)

START TEST 103 → MAKE SURE TRUNK IS CLOSED TURN IGNITION TO RUN POSITION → IS DECK LID AJAR LAMP ON → YES → TEST 103 CONTINUED

NO ↓

DISCONNECT DECK LID AJAR SWITCH CONNECTOR → CONNECT A JUMPER WIRE FROM AJAR SWITCH CONNECTOR TO GROUND

WATCH VISUAL MESSAGE CENTER → DOES DECK LID LAMP LIGHT → YES → REPLACE DECK LID AJAR SWITCH RETEST SYSTEM

NO ↓

DISCONNECT 11-WAY VISUAL MESSAGE CENTER CONNECTOR (LOCATED... → ...ABOVE HEADLAMP SWITCH) → CHECK FOR CONTINUITY AT VISUAL MESSAGE CENTER 11-WAY CONNECTOR...

CHECK BULB/BULB SOCKET IF OK REPLACE VISUAL MESSAGE CENTER RETEST SYSTEM ← YES ← IS THERE CONTINUITY ← ...CAVITY E TO DECK LID AJAR SWITCH M4 TN/BK WIRE

NO ↓

REPAIR M4 TN/BK WIRE AT AJAR CONNECTOR TO MESSAGE CENTER FOR OPEN CIRCUIT

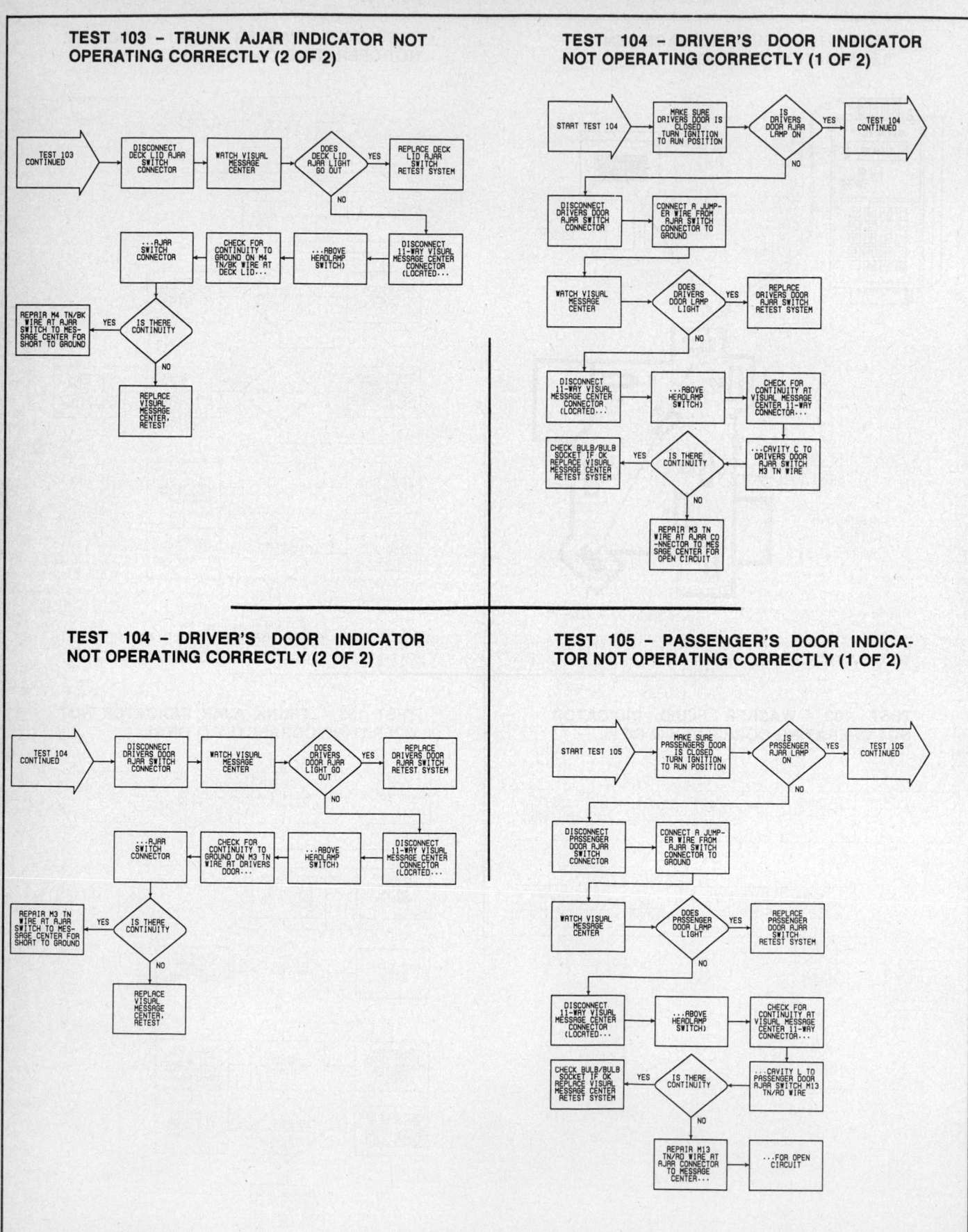

TEST 103 – TRUNK AJAR INDICATOR NOT OPERATING CORRECTLY (2 OF 2)

TEST 104 – DRIVER'S DOOR INDICATOR NOT OPERATING CORRECTLY (1 OF 2)

TEST 104 – DRIVER'S DOOR INDICATOR NOT OPERATING CORRECTLY (2 OF 2)

TEST 105 – PASSENGER'S DOOR INDICATOR NOT OPERATING CORRECTLY (1 OF 2)

1989 COMPUTERIZED ENGINE CONTROLS
Chrysler Motors Body Control Computer (Cont.)

1a-249

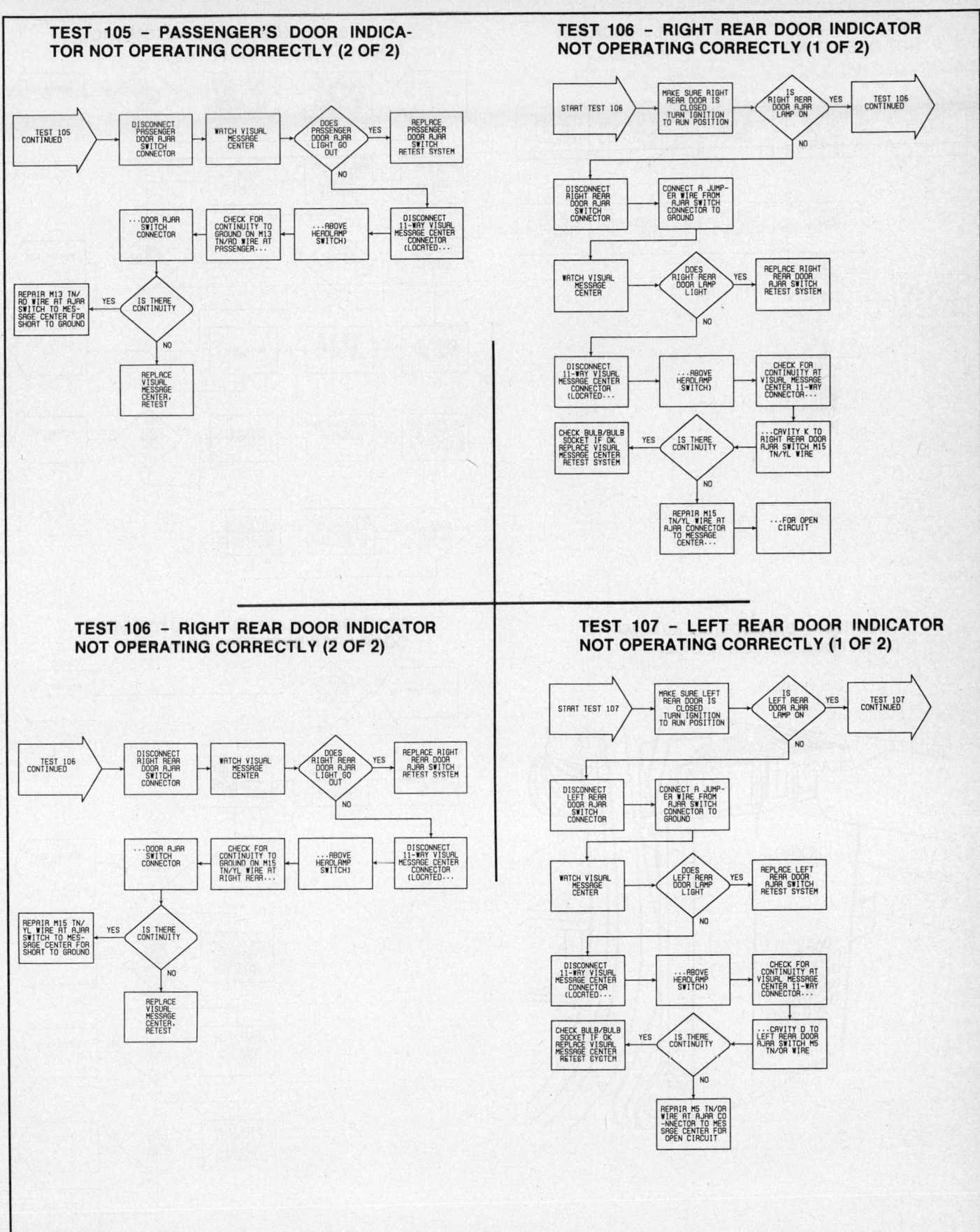

TEST 105 – PASSENGER'S DOOR INDICATOR NOT OPERATING CORRECTLY (2 OF 2)

TEST 106 – RIGHT REAR DOOR INDICATOR NOT OPERATING CORRECTLY (1 OF 2)

TEST 106 – RIGHT REAR DOOR INDICATOR NOT OPERATING CORRECTLY (2 OF 2)

TEST 107 – LEFT REAR DOOR INDICATOR NOT OPERATING CORRECTLY (1 OF 2)

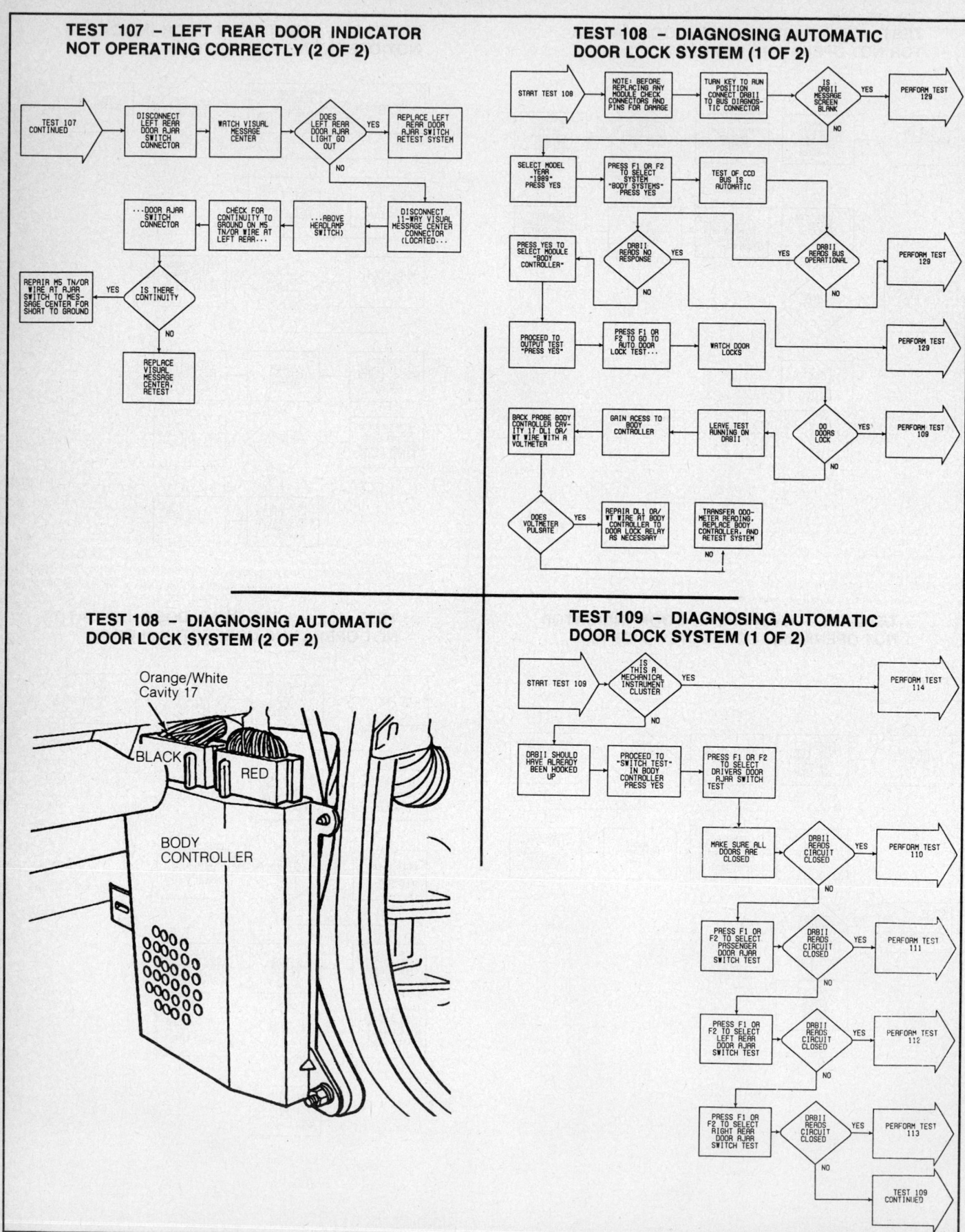

TEST 107 – LEFT REAR DOOR INDICATOR NOT OPERATING CORRECTLY (2 OF 2)

TEST 108 – DIAGNOSING AUTOMATIC DOOR LOCK SYSTEM (1 OF 2)

TEST 108 – DIAGNOSING AUTOMATIC DOOR LOCK SYSTEM (2 OF 2)

Orange/White
Cavity 17

BLACK

RED

BODY CONTROLLER

TEST 109 – DIAGNOSING AUTOMATIC DOOR LOCK SYSTEM (1 OF 2)

1989 COMPUTERIZED ENGINE CONTROLS
Chrysler Motors Body Control Computer (Cont.)

1a-251

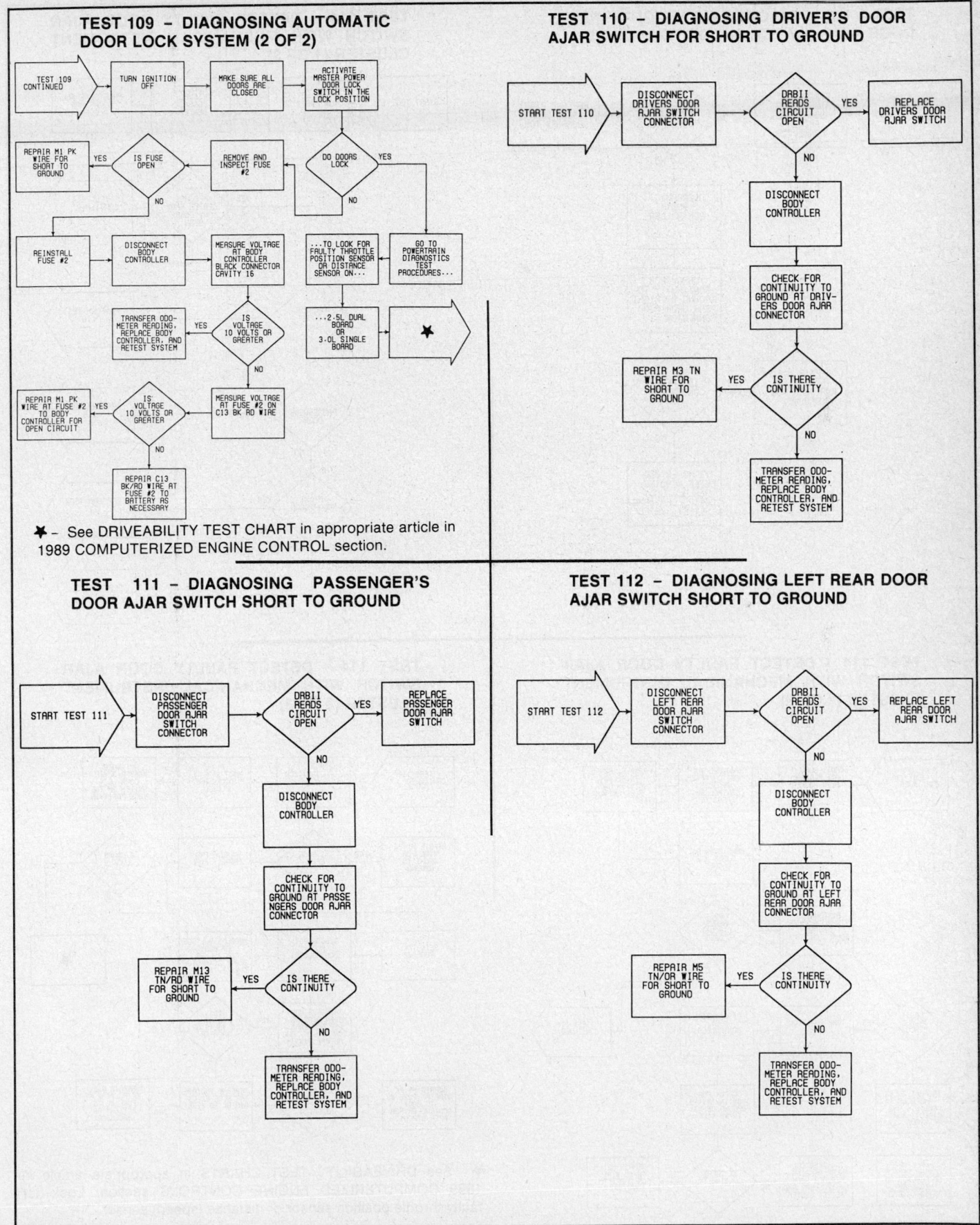

TEST 109 – DIAGNOSING AUTOMATIC DOOR LOCK SYSTEM (2 OF 2)

TEST 109 CONTINUED → TURN IGNITION OFF → MAKE SURE ALL DOORS ARE CLOSED → ACTIVATE MASTER POWER DOOR LOCK SWITCH IN THE LOCK POSITION

DO DOORS LOCK — YES → GO TO POWERTRAIN DIAGNOSTICS TEST PROCEDURES... / ...TO LOOK FOR FAULTY THROTTLE POSITION SENSOR OR DISTANCE SENSOR ON...

DO DOORS LOCK — NO → REMOVE AND INSPECT FUSE #2

IS FUSE OPEN — YES → REPAIR M1 PK WIRE FOR SHORT TO GROUND

IS FUSE OPEN — NO → REINSTALL FUSE #2 → DISCONNECT BODY CONTROLLER → MEASURE VOLTAGE AT BODY CONTROLLER BLACK CONNECTOR CAVITY 16

IS VOLTAGE 10 VOLTS OR GREATER — YES → TRANSFER ODOMETER READING, REPLACE BODY CONTROLLER, AND RETEST SYSTEM

...2.5L DUAL BOARD OR 3.0L SINGLE BOARD → ★

IS VOLTAGE 10 VOLTS OR GREATER — NO → MEASURE VOLTAGE AT FUSE #2 ON C13 BK RD WIRE

IS VOLTAGE 10 VOLTS OR GREATER — YES → REPAIR M1 PK WIRE AT FUSE #2 TO BODY CONTROLLER FOR OPEN CIRCUIT

IS VOLTAGE 10 VOLTS OR GREATER — NO → REPAIR C13 BK/RD WIRE AT FUSE #2 TO BATTERY AS NECESSARY

★ – See DRIVEABILITY TEST CHART in appropriate article in 1989 COMPUTERIZED ENGINE CONTROL section.

TEST 110 – DIAGNOSING DRIVER'S DOOR AJAR SWITCH FOR SHORT TO GROUND

START TEST 110 → DISCONNECT DRIVERS DOOR AJAR SWITCH CONNECTOR → DRBII READS CIRCUIT OPEN

DRBII READS CIRCUIT OPEN — YES → REPLACE DRIVERS DOOR AJAR SWITCH

DRBII READS CIRCUIT OPEN — NO → DISCONNECT BODY CONTROLLER → CHECK FOR CONTINUITY TO GROUND AT DRIVERS DOOR AJAR CONNECTOR

IS THERE CONTINUITY — YES → REPAIR M3 TN WIRE FOR SHORT TO GROUND

IS THERE CONTINUITY — NO → TRANSFER ODOMETER READING, REPLACE BODY CONTROLLER, AND RETEST SYSTEM

TEST 111 – DIAGNOSING PASSENGER'S DOOR AJAR SWITCH SHORT TO GROUND

START TEST 111 → DISCONNECT PASSENGER DOOR AJAR SWITCH CONNECTOR → DRBII READS CIRCUIT OPEN

DRBII READS CIRCUIT OPEN — YES → REPLACE PASSENGER DOOR AJAR SWITCH

DRBII READS CIRCUIT OPEN — NO → DISCONNECT BODY CONTROLLER → CHECK FOR CONTINUITY TO GROUND AT PASSENGERS DOOR AJAR CONNECTOR

IS THERE CONTINUITY — YES → REPAIR M13 TN/RD WIRE FOR SHORT TO GROUND

IS THERE CONTINUITY — NO → TRANSFER ODOMETER READING, REPLACE BODY CONTROLLER, AND RETEST SYSTEM

TEST 112 – DIAGNOSING LEFT REAR DOOR AJAR SWITCH SHORT TO GROUND

START TEST 112 → DISCONNECT LEFT REAR DOOR AJAR SWITCH CONNECTOR → DRBII READS CIRCUIT OPEN

DRBII READS CIRCUIT OPEN — YES → REPLACE LEFT REAR DOOR AJAR SWITCH

DRBII READS CIRCUIT OPEN — NO → DISCONNECT BODY CONTROLLER → CHECK FOR CONTINUITY TO GROUND AT LEFT REAR DOOR AJAR CONNECTOR

IS THERE CONTINUITY — YES → REPAIR M5 TN/OR WIRE FOR SHORT TO GROUND

IS THERE CONTINUITY — NO → TRANSFER ODOMETER READING, REPLACE BODY CONTROLLER, AND RETEST SYSTEM

1a-252

1989 COMPUTERIZED ENGINE CONTROLS
Chrysler Motors Body Control Computer (Cont.)

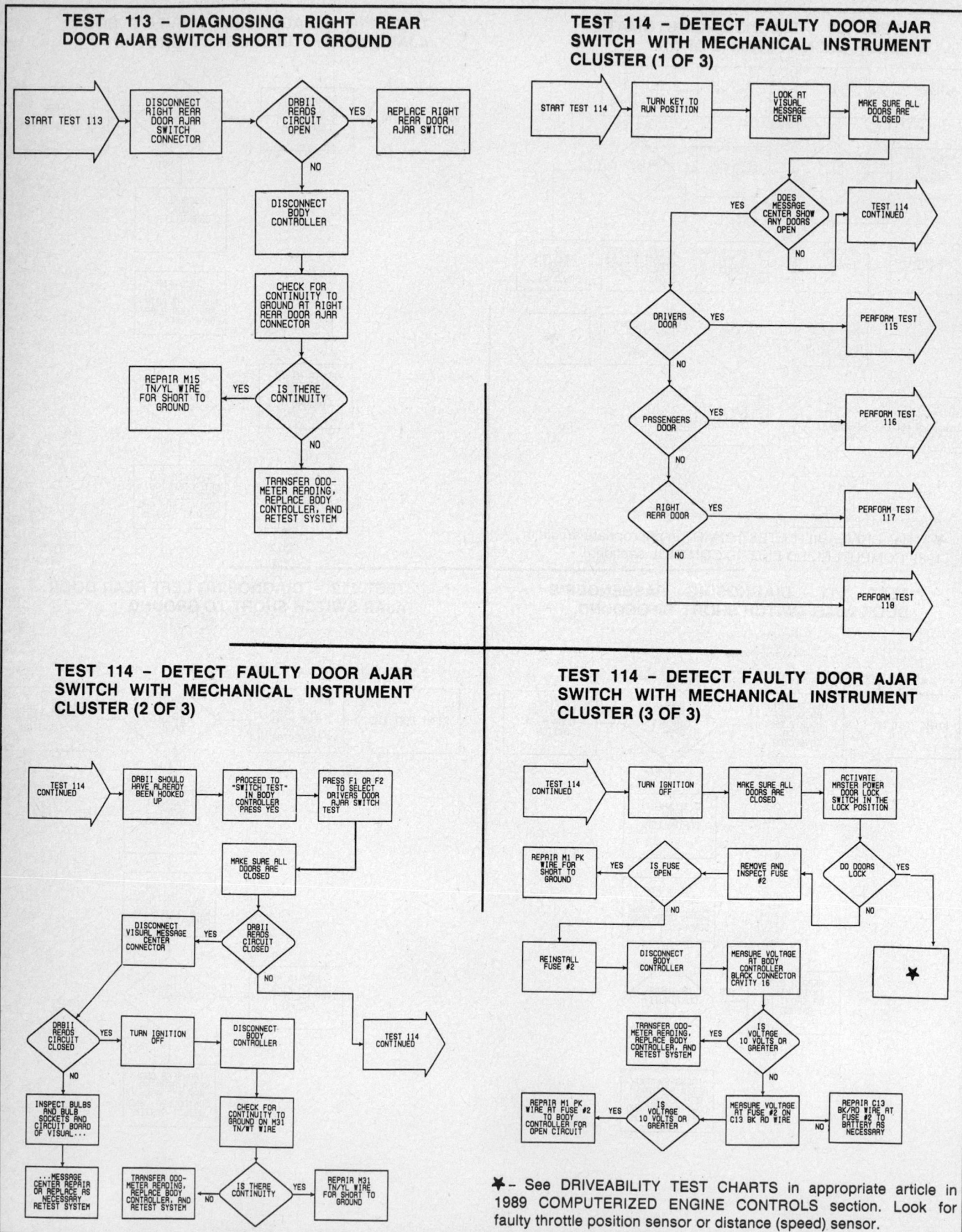

TEST 113 – DIAGNOSING RIGHT REAR DOOR AJAR SWITCH SHORT TO GROUND

TEST 114 – DETECT FAULTY DOOR AJAR SWITCH WITH MECHANICAL INSTRUMENT CLUSTER (1 OF 3)

TEST 114 – DETECT FAULTY DOOR AJAR SWITCH WITH MECHANICAL INSTRUMENT CLUSTER (2 OF 3)

TEST 114 – DETECT FAULTY DOOR AJAR SWITCH WITH MECHANICAL INSTRUMENT CLUSTER (3 OF 3)

✶ – See DRIVEABILITY TEST CHARTS in appropriate article in 1989 COMPUTERIZED ENGINE CONTROLS section. Look for faulty throttle position sensor or distance (speed) sensor.

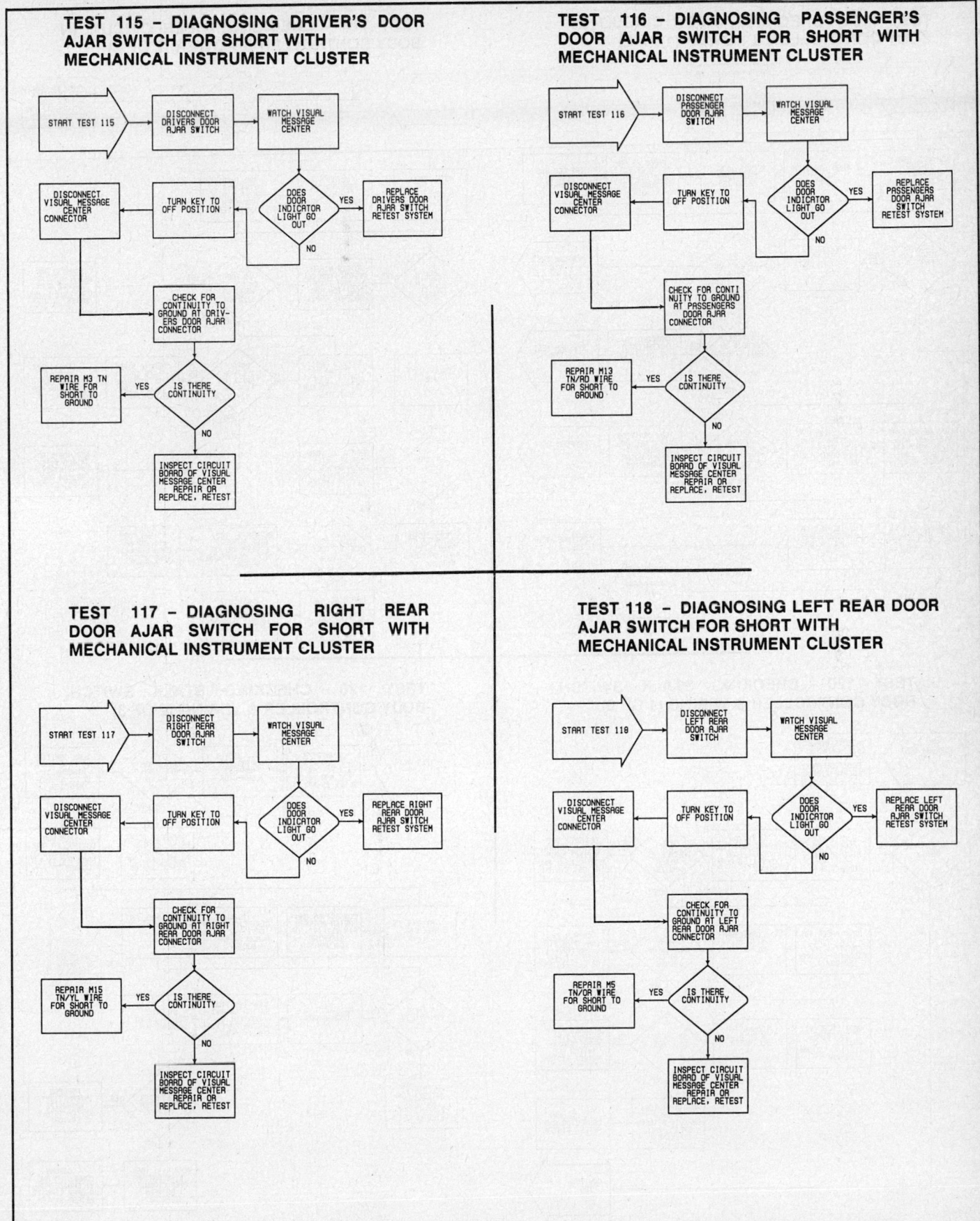

TEST 115 – DIAGNOSING DRIVER'S DOOR AJAR SWITCH FOR SHORT WITH MECHANICAL INSTRUMENT CLUSTER

START TEST 115 → DISCONNECT DRIVERS DOOR AJAR SWITCH → WATCH VISUAL MESSAGE CENTER

DOES DOOR INDICATOR LIGHT GO OUT — YES → REPLACE DRIVERS DOOR AJAR SWITCH RETEST SYSTEM

NO → TURN KEY TO OFF POSITION → DISCONNECT VISUAL MESSAGE CENTER CONNECTOR → CHECK FOR CONTINUITY TO GROUND AT DRIVERS DOOR AJAR CONNECTOR

IS THERE CONTINUITY — YES → REPAIR M3 TN WIRE FOR SHORT TO GROUND

NO → INSPECT CIRCUIT BOARD OF VISUAL MESSAGE CENTER REPAIR OR REPLACE, RETEST

TEST 116 – DIAGNOSING PASSENGER'S DOOR AJAR SWITCH FOR SHORT WITH MECHANICAL INSTRUMENT CLUSTER

START TEST 116 → DISCONNECT PASSENGER DOOR AJAR SWITCH → WATCH VISUAL MESSAGE CENTER

DOES DOOR INDICATOR LIGHT GO OUT — YES → REPLACE PASSENGERS DOOR AJAR SWITCH RETEST SYSTEM

NO → TURN KEY TO OFF POSITION → DISCONNECT VISUAL MESSAGE CENTER CONNECTOR → CHECK FOR CONTINUITY TO GROUND AT PASSENGERS DOOR AJAR CONNECTOR

IS THERE CONTINUITY — YES → REPAIR M13 TN/RD WIRE FOR SHORT TO GROUND

NO → INSPECT CIRCUIT BOARD OF VISUAL MESSAGE CENTER REPAIR OR REPLACE, RETEST

TEST 117 – DIAGNOSING RIGHT REAR DOOR AJAR SWITCH FOR SHORT WITH MECHANICAL INSTRUMENT CLUSTER

START TEST 117 → DISCONNECT RIGHT REAR DOOR AJAR SWITCH → WATCH VISUAL MESSAGE CENTER

DOES DOOR INDICATOR LIGHT GO OUT — YES → REPLACE RIGHT REAR DOOR AJAR SWITCH RETEST SYSTEM

NO → TURN KEY TO OFF POSITION → DISCONNECT VISUAL MESSAGE CENTER CONNECTOR → CHECK FOR CONTINUITY TO GROUND AT RIGHT REAR DOOR AJAR CONNECTOR

IS THERE CONTINUITY — YES → REPAIR M15 TN/YL WIRE FOR SHORT TO GROUND

NO → INSPECT CIRCUIT BOARD OF VISUAL MESSAGE CENTER REPAIR OR REPLACE, RETEST

TEST 118 – DIAGNOSING LEFT REAR DOOR AJAR SWITCH FOR SHORT WITH MECHANICAL INSTRUMENT CLUSTER

START TEST 118 → DISCONNECT LEFT REAR DOOR AJAR SWITCH → WATCH VISUAL MESSAGE CENTER

DOES DOOR INDICATOR LIGHT GO OUT — YES → REPLACE LEFT REAR DOOR AJAR SWITCH RETEST SYSTEM

NO → TURN KEY TO OFF POSITION → DISCONNECT VISUAL MESSAGE CENTER CONNECTOR → CHECK FOR CONTINUITY TO GROUND AT LEFT REAR DOOR AJAR CONNECTOR

IS THERE CONTINUITY — YES → REPAIR M5 TN/OR WIRE FOR SHORT TO GROUND

NO → INSPECT CIRCUIT BOARD OF VISUAL MESSAGE CENTER REPAIR OR REPLACE, RETEST

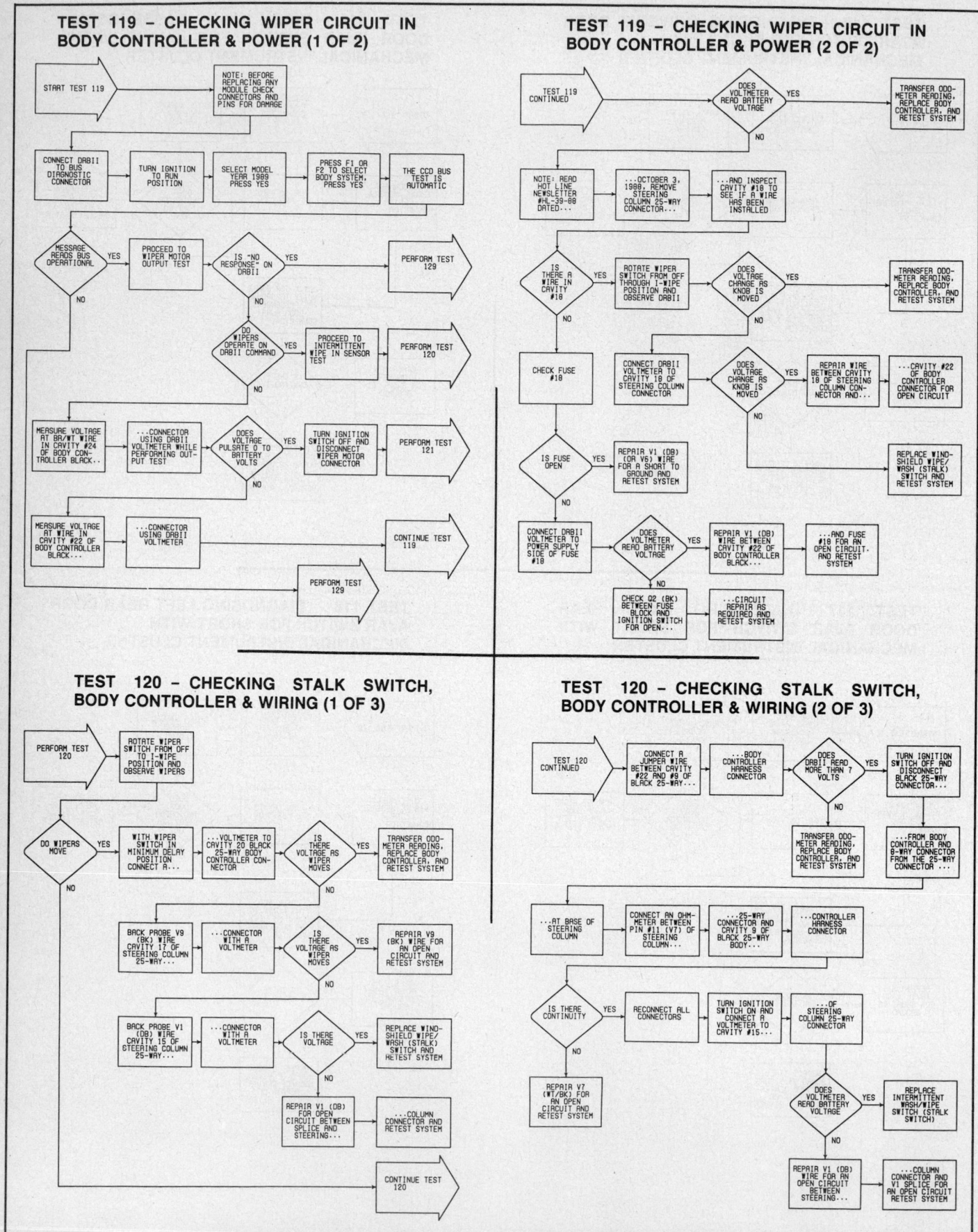

TEST 119 – CHECKING WIPER CIRCUIT IN BODY CONTROLLER & POWER (1 OF 2)

TEST 119 – CHECKING WIPER CIRCUIT IN BODY CONTROLLER & POWER (2 OF 2)

TEST 120 – CHECKING STALK SWITCH, BODY CONTROLLER & WIRING (1 OF 3)

TEST 120 – CHECKING STALK SWITCH, BODY CONTROLLER & WIRING (2 OF 3)

1989 COMPUTERIZED ENGINE CONTROLS
Chrysler Motors Body Control Computer (Cont.)

1a-255

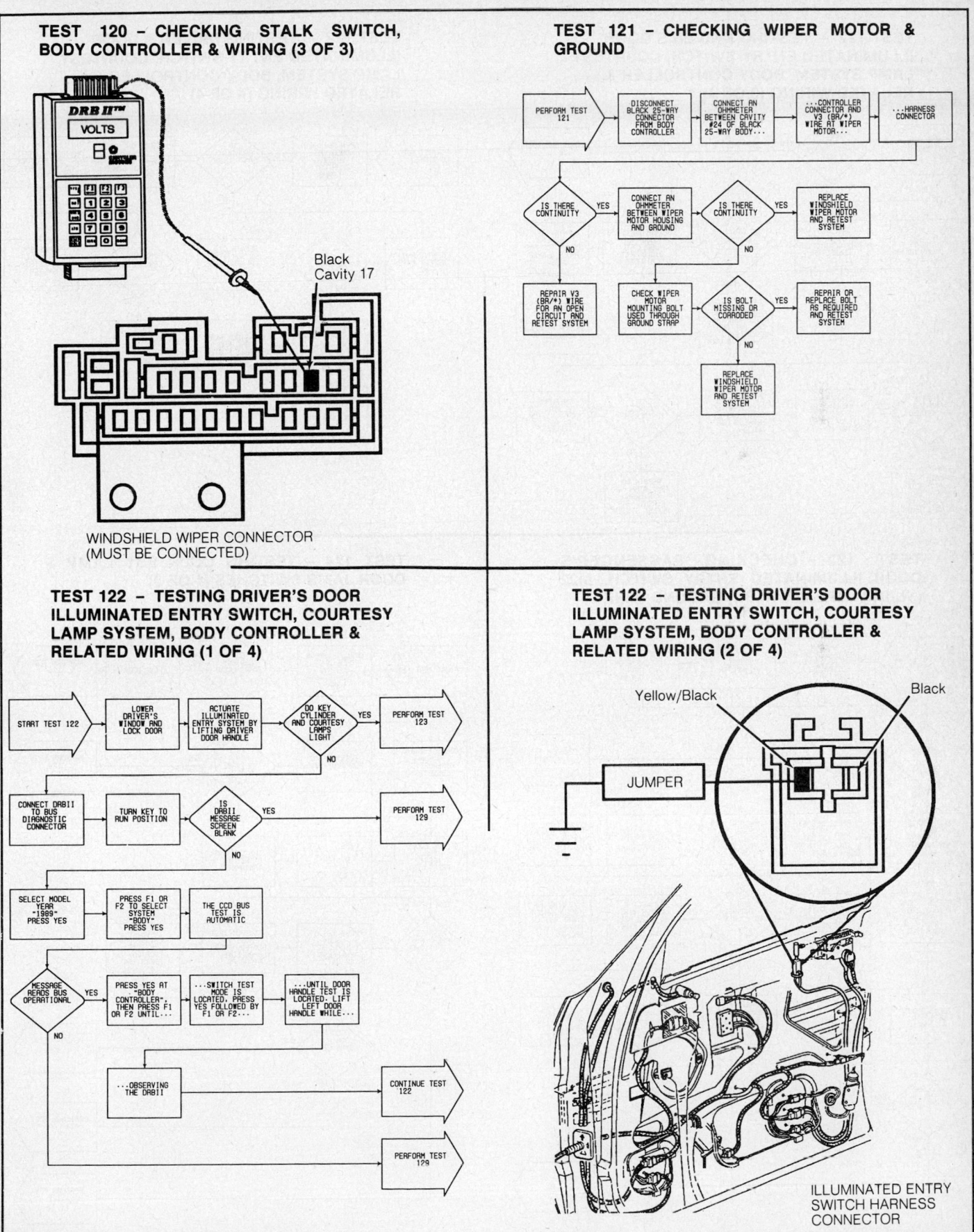

TEST 120 – CHECKING STALK SWITCH, BODY CONTROLLER & WIRING (3 OF 3)

Black Cavity 17

WINDSHIELD WIPER CONNECTOR
(MUST BE CONNECTED)

TEST 121 – CHECKING WIPER MOTOR & GROUND

PERFORM TEST 121 → DISCONNECT BLACK 25-WAY CONNECTOR FROM BODY CONTROLLER → CONNECT AN OHMMETER BETWEEN CAVITY #24 OF BLACK 25-WAY BODY... → ...CONTROLLER CONNECTOR AND V3 (BR/*) WIRE AT WIPER MOTOR... → ...HARNESS CONNECTOR

IS THERE CONTINUITY — YES → CONNECT AN OHMMETER BETWEEN WIPER MOTOR HOUSING AND GROUND → IS THERE CONTINUITY — YES → REPLACE WINDSHIELD WIPER MOTOR AND RETEST SYSTEM

NO

REPAIR V3 (BR/*) WIRE FOR AN OPEN CIRCUIT AND RETEST SYSTEM

NO

CHECK WIPER MOTOR MOUNTING BOLT USED THROUGH GROUND STRAP → IS BOLT MISSING OR CORRODED — YES → REPAIR OR REPLACE BOLT AS REQUIRED AND RETEST SYSTEM

NO

REPLACE WINDSHIELD WIPER MOTOR AND RETEST SYSTEM

TEST 122 – TESTING DRIVER'S DOOR ILLUMINATED ENTRY SWITCH, COURTESY LAMP SYSTEM, BODY CONTROLLER & RELATED WIRING (1 OF 4)

START TEST 122 → LOWER DRIVER'S WINDOW AND LOCK DOOR → ACTUATE ILLUMINATED ENTRY SYSTEM BY LIFTING DRIVER DOOR HANDLE → DO KEY CYLINDER AND COURTESY LAMPS LIGHT — YES → PERFORM TEST 123

NO

CONNECT DRBII TO BUS DIAGNOSTIC CONNECTOR → TURN KEY TO RUN POSITION → IS DRBII MESSAGE SCREEN BLANK — YES → PERFORM TEST 129

NO

SELECT MODEL YEAR "1989" PRESS YES → PRESS F1 OR F2 TO SELECT SYSTEM "BODY" PRESS YES → THE CCD BUS TEST IS AUTOMATIC

MESSAGE READS BUS OPERATIONAL — YES → PRESS YES AT "BODY CONTROLLER", THEN PRESS F1 OR F2 UNTIL... → ...SWITCH TEST MODE IS LOCATED. PRESS YES FOLLOWED BY F1 OR F2... → ...UNTIL DOOR HANDLE TEST IS LOCATED. LIFT LEFT DOOR HANDLE WHILE...

NO

...OBSERVING THE DRBII → CONTINUE TEST 122

PERFORM TEST 129

TEST 122 – TESTING DRIVER'S DOOR ILLUMINATED ENTRY SWITCH, COURTESY LAMP SYSTEM, BODY CONTROLLER & RELATED WIRING (2 OF 4)

Yellow/Black   Black

JUMPER

ILLUMINATED ENTRY SWITCH HARNESS CONNECTOR

1989 COMPUTERIZED ENGINE CONTROLS
Chrysler Motors Body Control Computer (Cont.)

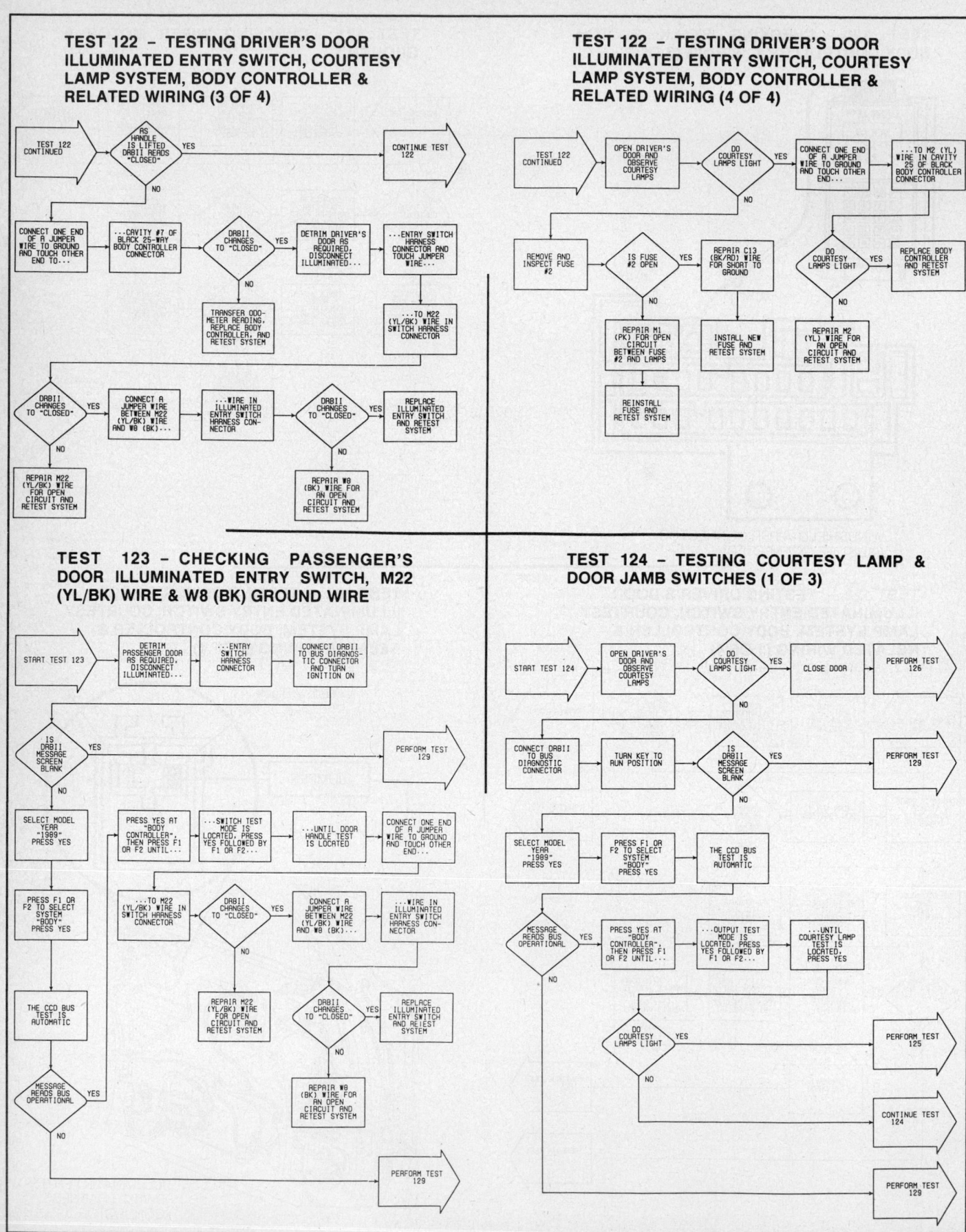

TEST 122 – TESTING DRIVER'S DOOR ILLUMINATED ENTRY SWITCH, COURTESY LAMP SYSTEM, BODY CONTROLLER & RELATED WIRING (3 OF 4)

TEST 122 – TESTING DRIVER'S DOOR ILLUMINATED ENTRY SWITCH, COURTESY LAMP SYSTEM, BODY CONTROLLER & RELATED WIRING (4 OF 4)

TEST 123 – CHECKING PASSENGER'S DOOR ILLUMINATED ENTRY SWITCH, M22 (YL/BK) WIRE & W8 (BK) GROUND WIRE

TEST 124 – TESTING COURTESY LAMP & DOOR JAMB SWITCHES (1 OF 3)

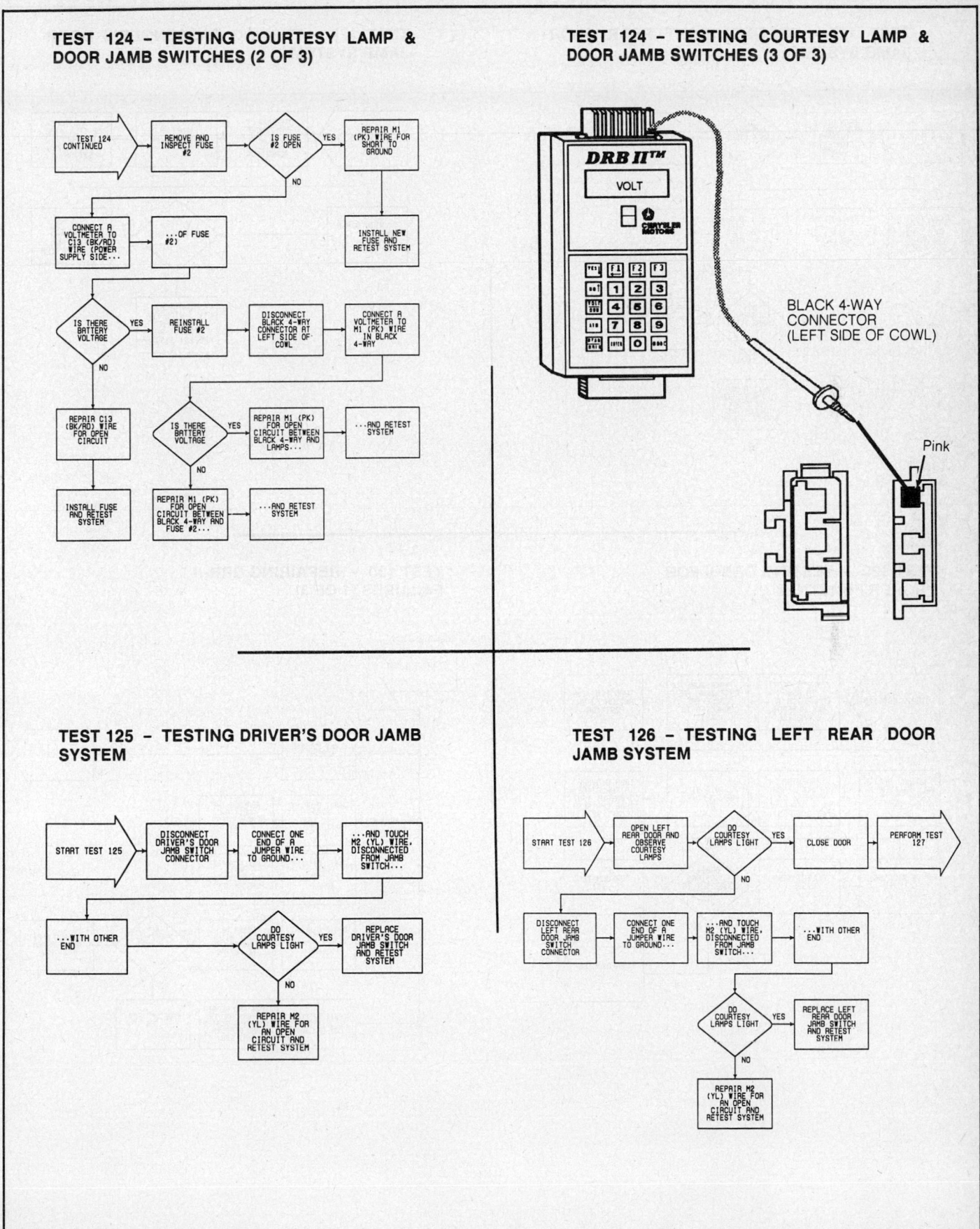

TEST 124 – TESTING COURTESY LAMP & DOOR JAMB SWITCHES (2 OF 3)

TEST 124 – TESTING COURTESY LAMP & DOOR JAMB SWITCHES (3 OF 3)

DRB II™

VOLT

CHRYSLER MOTORS

BLACK 4-WAY CONNECTOR (LEFT SIDE OF COWL)

Pink

TEST 125 – TESTING DRIVER'S DOOR JAMB SYSTEM

TEST 126 – TESTING LEFT REAR DOOR JAMB SYSTEM

1989 COMPUTERIZED ENGINE CONTROLS
Chrysler Motors Body Control Computer (Cont.)

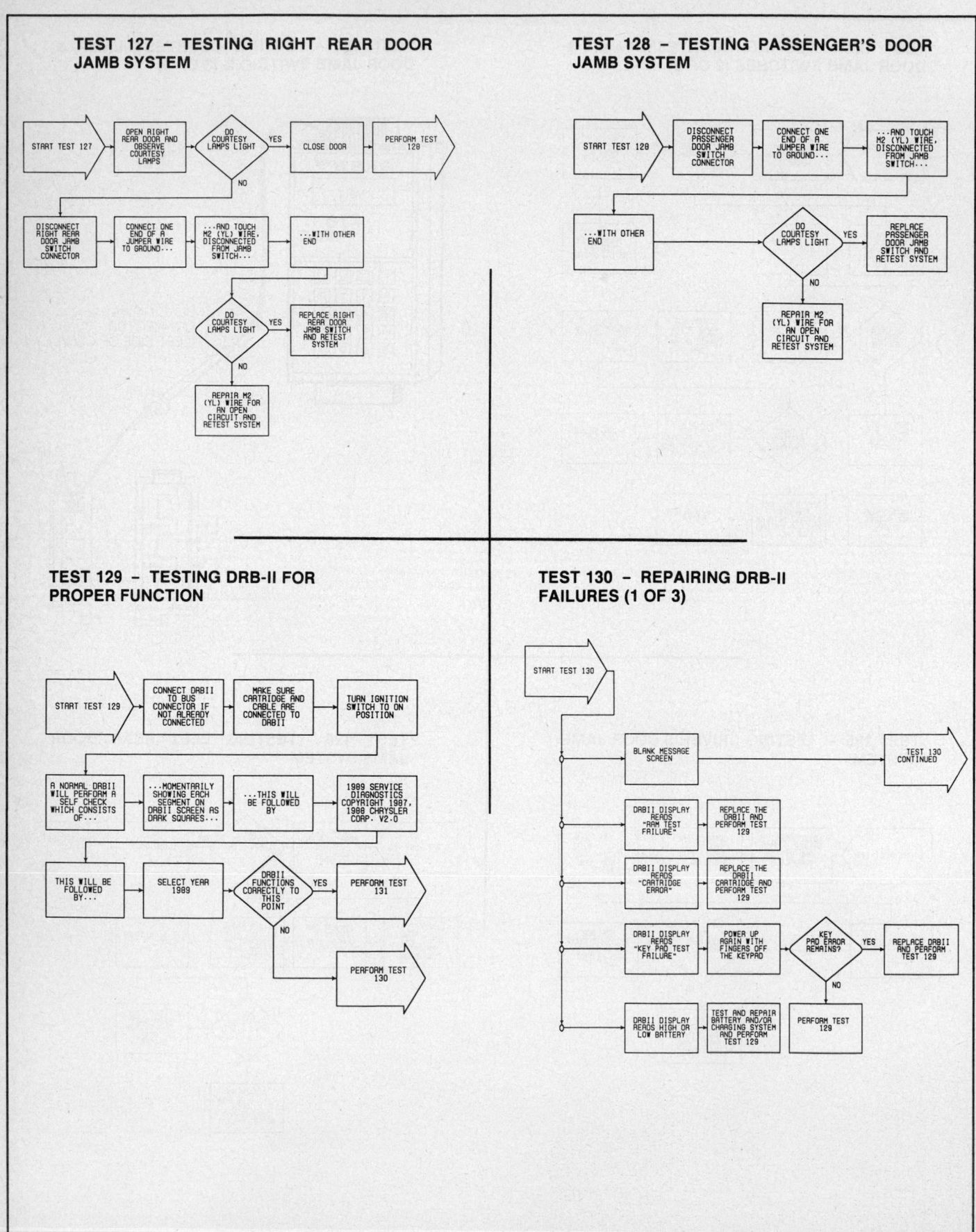

TEST 127 – TESTING RIGHT REAR DOOR JAMB SYSTEM

START TEST 127 → OPEN RIGHT REAR DOOR AND OBSERVE COURTESY LAMPS → DO COURTESY LAMPS LIGHT → YES → CLOSE DOOR → PERFORM TEST 128

DO COURTESY LAMPS LIGHT → NO → DISCONNECT RIGHT REAR DOOR JAMB SWITCH CONNECTOR → CONNECT ONE END OF A JUMPER WIRE TO GROUND... → ...AND TOUCH M2 (YL) WIRE, DISCONNECTED FROM JAMB SWITCH... → ...WITH OTHER END

...WITH OTHER END → DO COURTESY LAMPS LIGHT → YES → REPLACE RIGHT REAR DOOR JAMB SWITCH AND RETEST SYSTEM

DO COURTESY LAMPS LIGHT → NO → REPAIR M2 (YL) WIRE FOR AN OPEN CIRCUIT AND RETEST SYSTEM

TEST 128 – TESTING PASSENGER'S DOOR JAMB SYSTEM

START TEST 128 → DISCONNECT PASSENGER DOOR JAMB SWITCH CONNECTOR → CONNECT ONE END OF A JUMPER WIRE TO GROUND... → ...AND TOUCH M2 (YL) WIRE, DISCONNECTED FROM JAMB SWITCH...

...WITH OTHER END → DO COURTESY LAMPS LIGHT → YES → REPLACE PASSENGER DOOR JAMB SWITCH AND RETEST SYSTEM

DO COURTESY LAMPS LIGHT → NO → REPAIR M2 (YL) WIRE FOR AN OPEN CIRCUIT AND RETEST SYSTEM

TEST 129 – TESTING DRB-II FOR PROPER FUNCTION

START TEST 129 → CONNECT DRBII TO BUS CONNECTOR IF NOT ALREADY CONNECTED → MAKE SURE CARTRIDGE AND CABLE ARE CONNECTED TO DRBII → TURN IGNITION SWITCH TO ON POSITION

A NORMAL DRBII WILL PERFORM A SELF CHECK WHICH CONSISTS OF... → ...MOMENTARILY SHOWING EACH SEGMENT ON DRBII SCREEN AS DARK SQUARES... → ...THIS WILL BE FOLLOWED BY → 1989 SERVICE DIAGNOSTICS COPYRIGHT 1987, 1988 CHRYSLER CORP. V2-0

THIS WILL BE FOLLOWED BY... → SELECT YEAR 1989 → DRBII FUNCTIONS CORRECTLY TO THIS POINT → YES → PERFORM TEST 131

DRBII FUNCTIONS CORRECTLY TO THIS POINT → NO → PERFORM TEST 130

TEST 130 – REPAIRING DRB-II FAILURES (1 OF 3)

START TEST 130

BLANK MESSAGE SCREEN → TEST 130 CONTINUED

DRBII DISPLAY READS "RAM TEST FAILURE" → REPLACE THE DRBII AND PERFORM TEST 129

DRBII DISPLAY READS "CARTRIDGE ERROR" → REPLACE THE DRBII CARTRIDGE AND PERFORM TEST 129

DRBII DISPLAY READS "KEY PAD TEST FAILURE" → POWER UP AGAIN WITH FINGERS OFF THE KEYPAD → KEY PAD ERROR REMAINS? → YES → REPLACE DRBII AND PERFORM TEST 129

KEY PAD ERROR REMAINS? → NO → PERFORM TEST 129

DRBII DISPLAY READS HIGH OR LOW BATTERY → TEST AND REPAIR BATTERY AND/OR CHARGING SYSTEM AND PERFORM TEST 129

1989 COMPUTERIZED ENGINE CONTROLS
Chrysler Motors Body Control Computer (Cont.)

1a-259

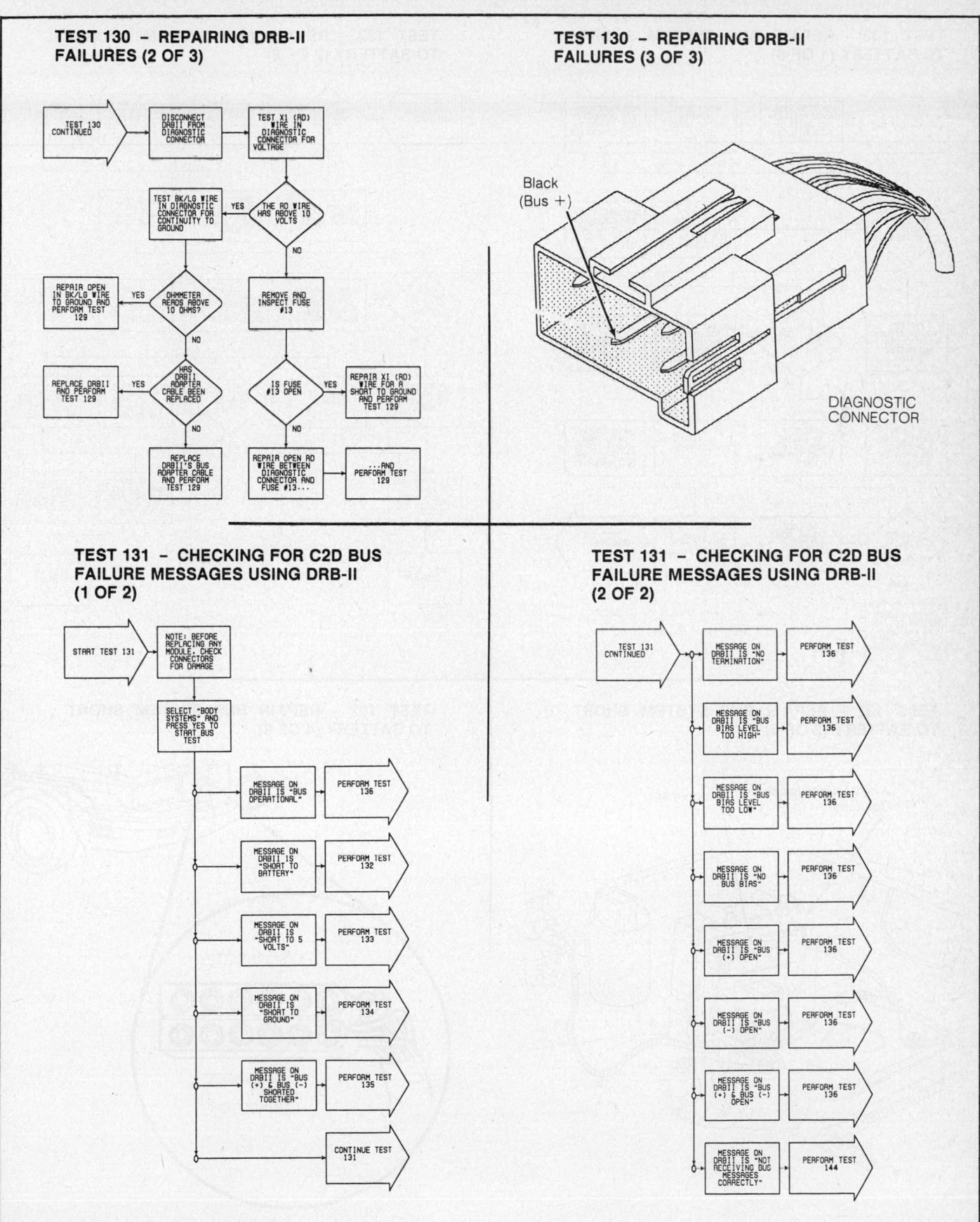

TEST 130 – REPAIRING DRB-II FAILURES (2 OF 3)

TEST 130 CONTINUED → DISCONNECT DRBII FROM DIAGNOSTIC CONNECTOR → TEST X1 (RD) WIRE IN DIAGNOSTIC CONNECTOR FOR VOLTAGE → THE RD WIRE HAS ABOVE 10 VOLTS

YES → TEST BK/LG WIRE IN DIAGNOSTIC CONNECTOR FOR CONTINUITY TO GROUND → OHMMETER READS ABOVE 10 OHMS?

YES → REPAIR OPEN IN BK/LG WIRE TO GROUND AND PERFORM TEST 129

NO → HAS DRBII ADAPTER CABLE BEEN REPLACED

YES → REPLACE DRBII ADAPTER AND PERFORM TEST 129

NO → REPLACE DRBII'S BUS ADAPTER CABLE AND PERFORM TEST 129

NO → REMOVE AND INSPECT FUSE #13 → IS FUSE #13 OPEN

YES → REPAIR X1 (RD) WIRE FOR A SHORT TO GROUND AND PERFORM TEST 129

NO → REPAIR OPEN RD WIRE BETWEEN DIAGNOSTIC CONNECTOR AND FUSE #13... → ...AND PERFORM TEST 129

TEST 130 – REPAIRING DRB-II FAILURES (3 OF 3)

Black (Bus +)

DIAGNOSTIC CONNECTOR

TEST 131 – CHECKING FOR C2D BUS FAILURE MESSAGES USING DRB-II (1 OF 2)

START TEST 131 → NOTE: BEFORE REPLACING ANY MODULE, CHECK CONNECTORS FOR DAMAGE → SELECT "BODY SYSTEMS" AND PRESS YES TO START BUS TEST

MESSAGE ON DRBII IS "BUS OPERATIONAL" → PERFORM TEST 136

MESSAGE ON DRBII IS "SHORT TO BATTERY" → PERFORM TEST 132

MESSAGE ON DRBII IS "SHORT TO 5 VOLTS" → PERFORM TEST 133

MESSAGE ON DRBII IS "SHORT TO GROUND" → PERFORM TEST 134

MESSAGE ON DRBII IS "BUS (+) & BUS (-) SHORTED TOGETHER" → PERFORM TEST 135

CONTINUE TEST 131

TEST 131 – CHECKING FOR C2D BUS FAILURE MESSAGES USING DRB-II (2 OF 2)

TEST 131 CONTINUED →

MESSAGE ON DRBII IS "NO TERMINATION" → PERFORM TEST 136

MESSAGE ON DRBII IS "BUS BIAS LEVEL TOO HIGH" → PERFORM TEST 136

MESSAGE ON DRBII IS "BUS BIAS LEVEL TOO LOW" → PERFORM TEST 136

MESSAGE ON DRBII IS "NO BUS BIAS" → PERFORM TEST 136

MESSAGE ON DRBII IS "BUS (+) OPEN" → PERFORM TEST 136

MESSAGE ON DRBII IS "BUS (-) OPEN" → PERFORM TEST 136

MESSAGE ON DRBII IS "BUS (+) & BUS (-) OPEN" → PERFORM TEST 136

MESSAGE ON DRBII IS "NOT RECEIVING BUS MESSAGES CORRECTLY" → PERFORM TEST 144

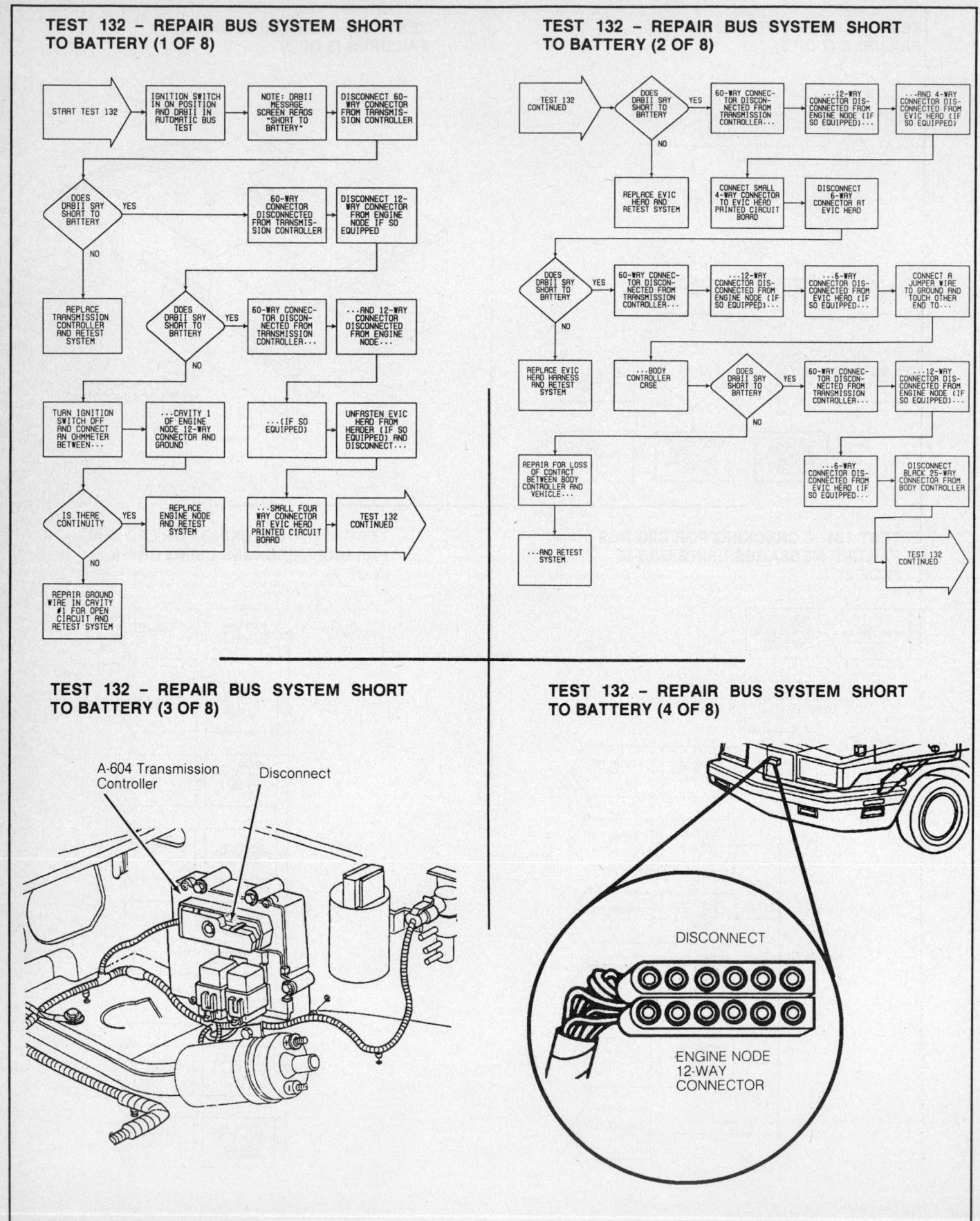

TEST 132 – REPAIR BUS SYSTEM SHORT TO BATTERY (1 OF 8)

TEST 132 – REPAIR BUS SYSTEM SHORT TO BATTERY (2 OF 8)

TEST 132 – REPAIR BUS SYSTEM SHORT TO BATTERY (3 OF 8)

A-604 Transmission Controller

Disconnect

TEST 132 – REPAIR BUS SYSTEM SHORT TO BATTERY (4 OF 8)

DISCONNECT

ENGINE NODE 12-WAY CONNECTOR

1989 COMPUTERIZED ENGINE CONTROLS
Chrysler Motors Body Control Computer (Cont.)

1a-261

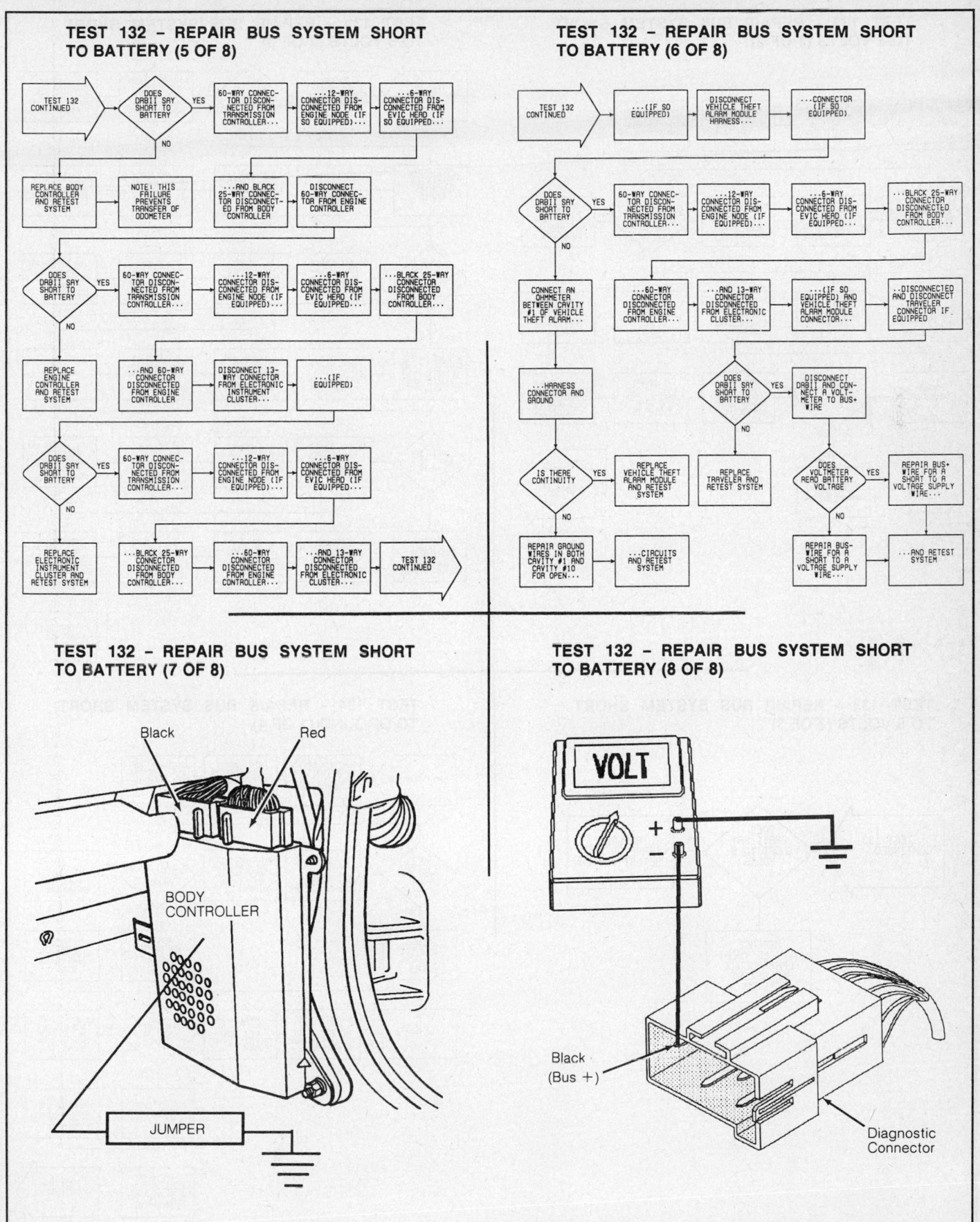

TEST 132 – REPAIR BUS SYSTEM SHORT TO BATTERY (5 OF 8)

TEST 132 – REPAIR BUS SYSTEM SHORT TO BATTERY (6 OF 8)

TEST 132 – REPAIR BUS SYSTEM SHORT TO BATTERY (7 OF 8)

Black   Red

BODY CONTROLLER

JUMPER

TEST 132 – REPAIR BUS SYSTEM SHORT TO BATTERY (8 OF 8)

VOLT

Black (Bus +)

Diagnostic Connector

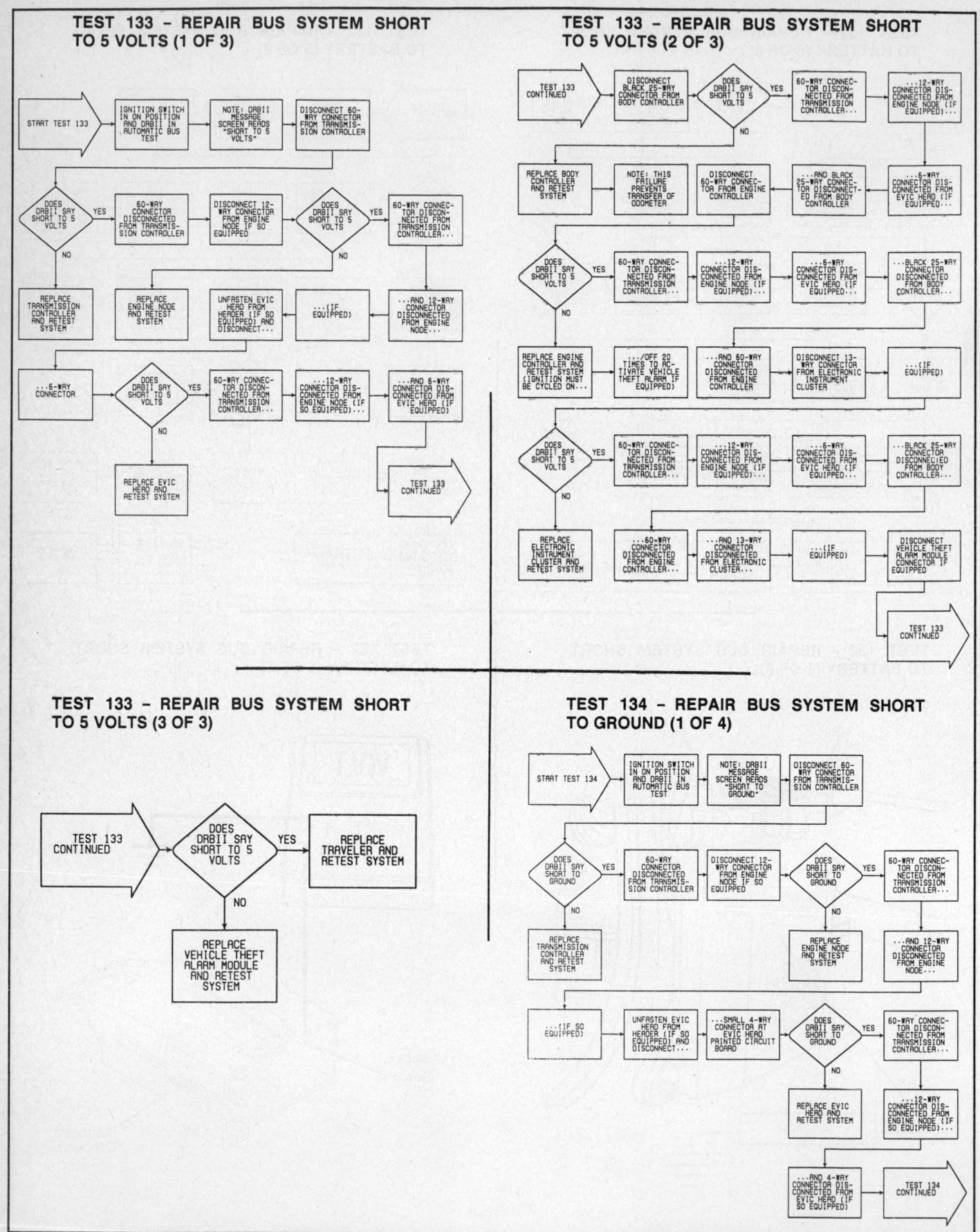

1989 COMPUTERIZED ENGINE CONTROLS
Chrysler Motors Body Control Computer (Cont.)

1a-263

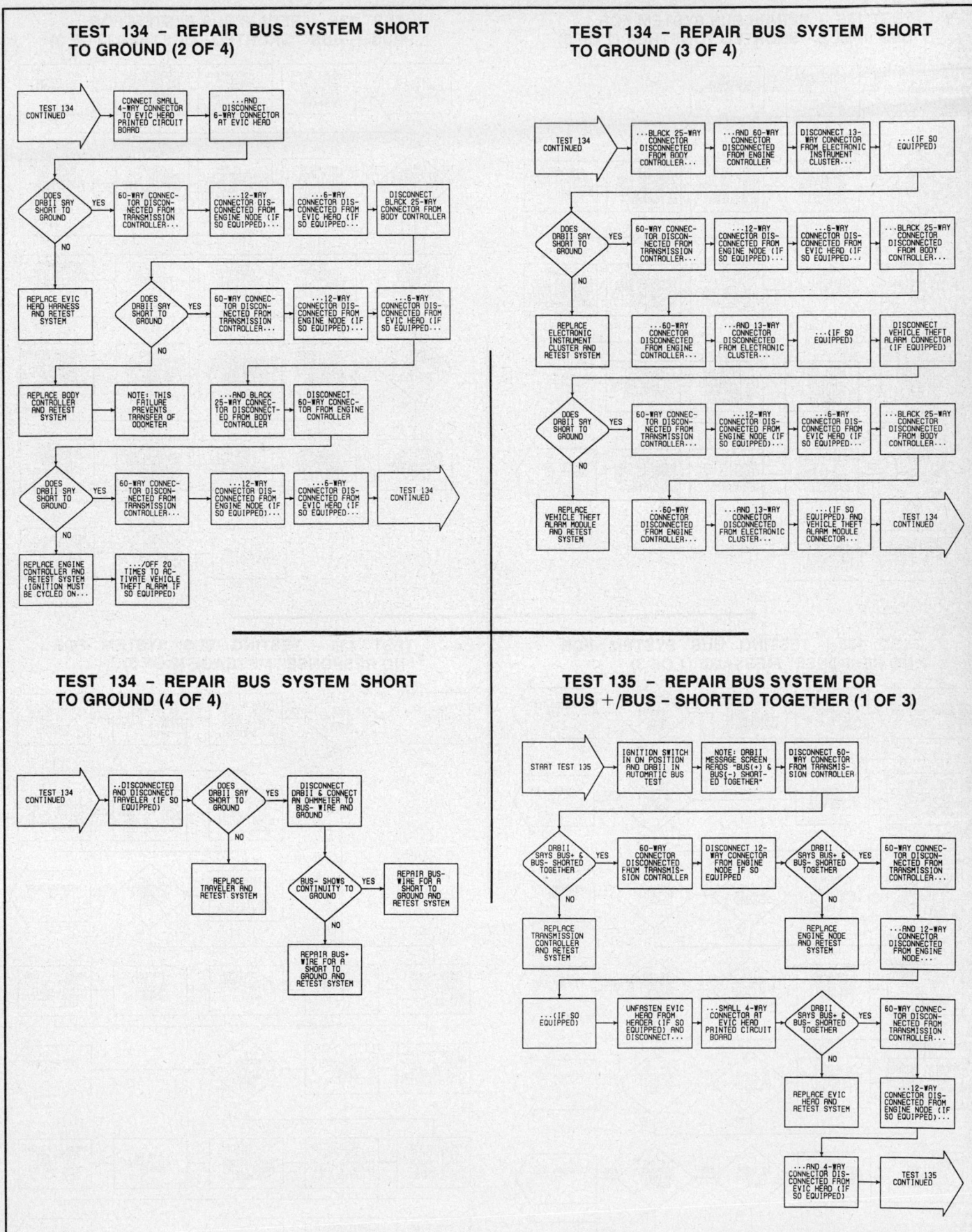

TEST 134 – REPAIR BUS SYSTEM SHORT TO GROUND (2 OF 4)

TEST 134 – REPAIR BUS SYSTEM SHORT TO GROUND (3 OF 4)

TEST 134 – REPAIR BUS SYSTEM SHORT TO GROUND (4 OF 4)

TEST 135 – REPAIR BUS SYSTEM FOR BUS +/BUS – SHORTED TOGETHER (1 OF 3)

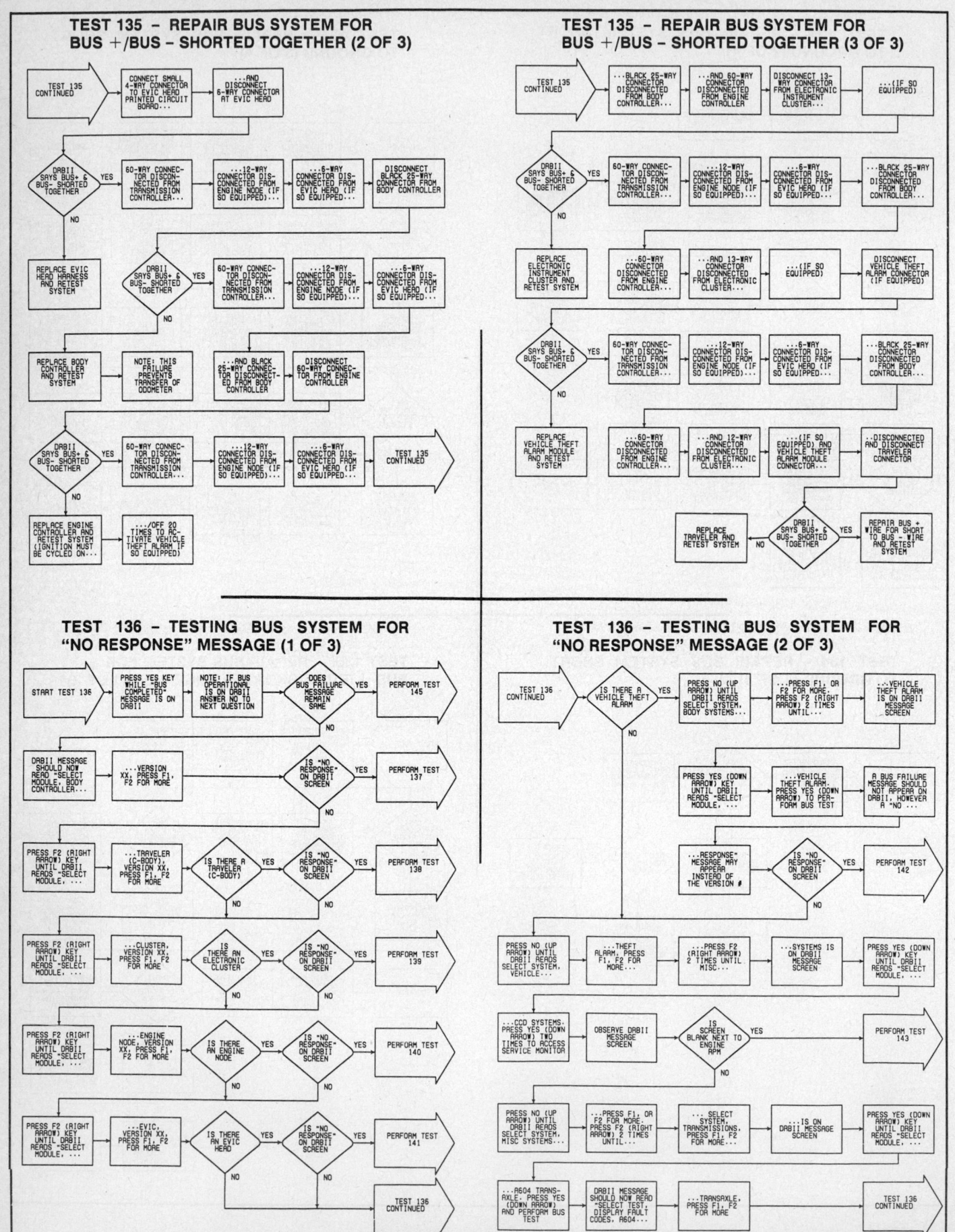

TEST 135 – REPAIR BUS SYSTEM FOR BUS +/BUS – SHORTED TOGETHER (2 OF 3)

TEST 135 – REPAIR BUS SYSTEM FOR BUS +/BUS – SHORTED TOGETHER (3 OF 3)

TEST 136 – TESTING BUS SYSTEM FOR "NO RESPONSE" MESSAGE (1 OF 3)

TEST 136 – TESTING BUS SYSTEM FOR "NO RESPONSE" MESSAGE (2 OF 3)

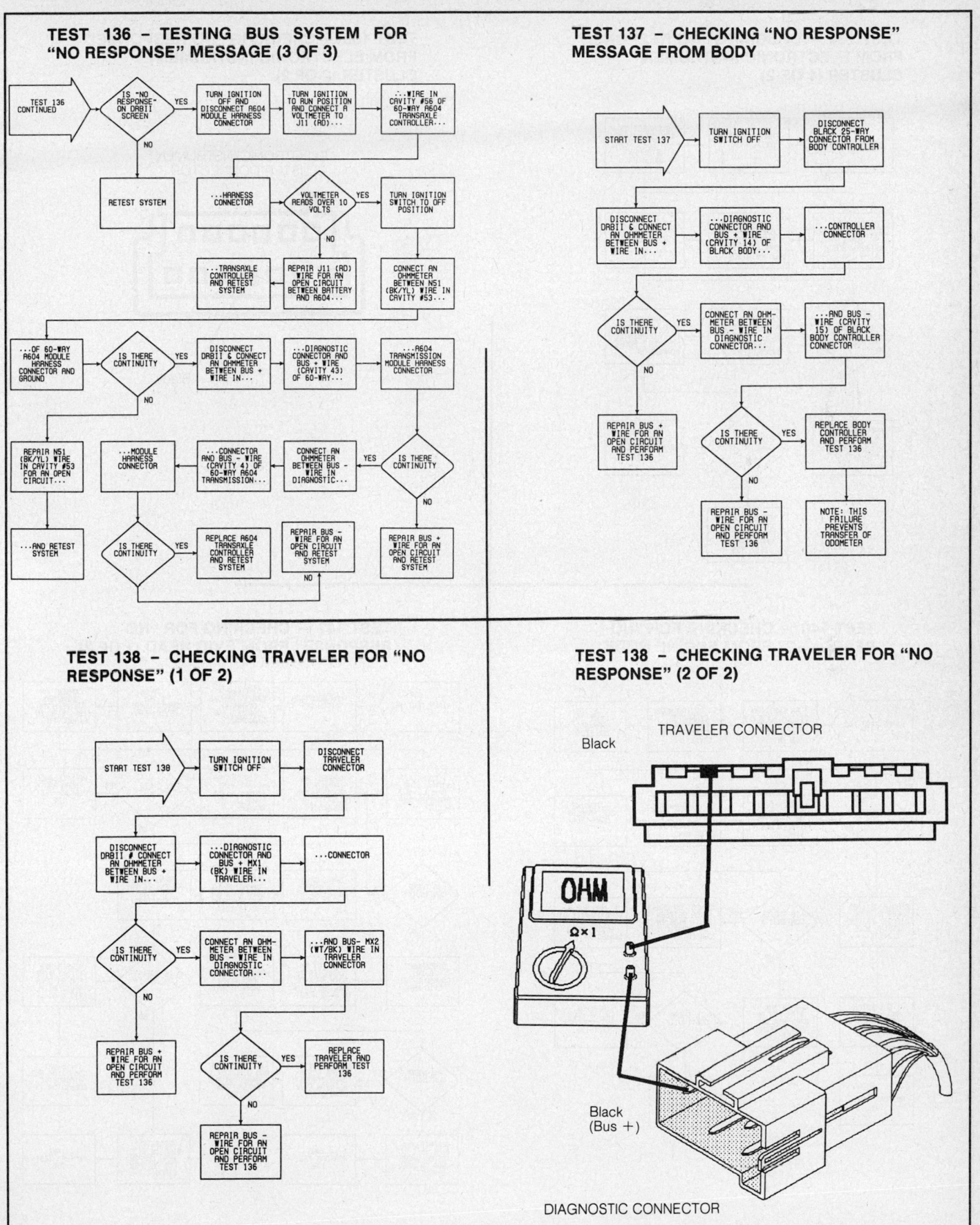

TEST 136 – TESTING BUS SYSTEM FOR "NO RESPONSE" MESSAGE (3 OF 3)

TEST 137 – CHECKING "NO RESPONSE" MESSAGE FROM BODY

TEST 138 – CHECKING TRAVELER FOR "NO RESPONSE" (1 OF 2)

TEST 138 – CHECKING TRAVELER FOR "NO RESPONSE" (2 OF 2)

TRAVELER CONNECTOR

Black

OHM

Ω × 1

Black
(Bus +)

DIAGNOSTIC CONNECTOR

1989 COMPUTERIZED ENGINE CONTROLS
Chrysler Motors Body Control Computer (Cont.)

TEST 139 – CHECKING "NO RESPONSE" FROM ELECTRONIC INSTRUMENT CLUSTER (1 OF 2)

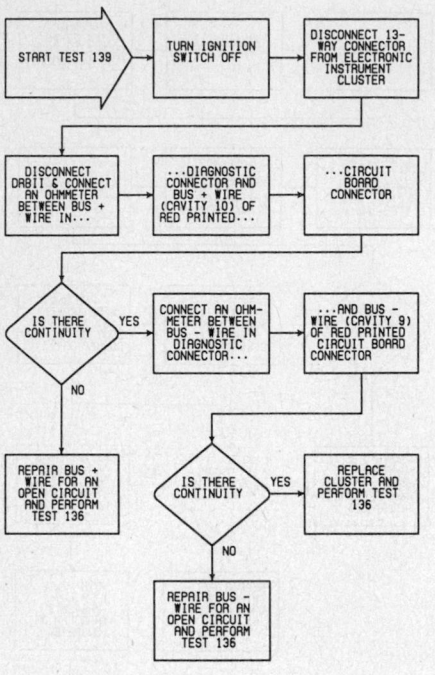

TEST 139 – CHECKING "NO RESPONSE" FROM ELECTRONIC INSTRUMENT CLUSTER (2 OF 2)

ELECTRONIC INSTRUMENT CLUSTER CONNECTOR

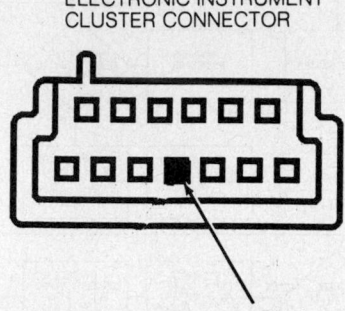

Black

TEST 140 – CHECKING FOR "NO RESPONSE" FROM ENGINE NODE

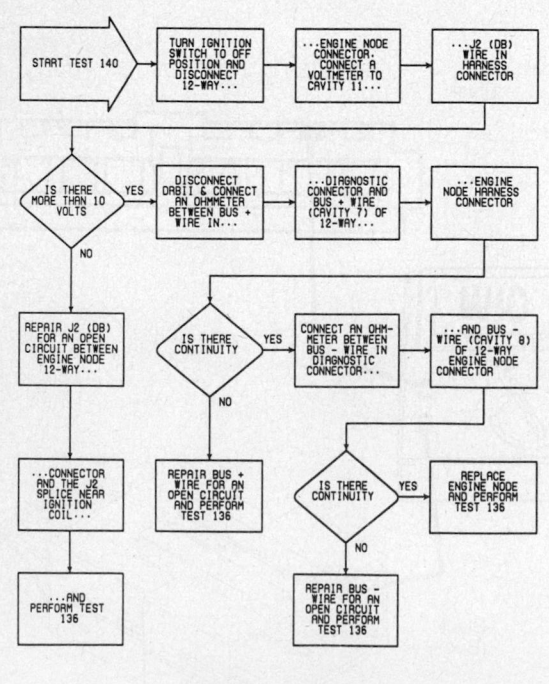

TEST 141 – CHECKING FOR "NO RESPONSE" FROM EVIC HEAD (1 OF 2)

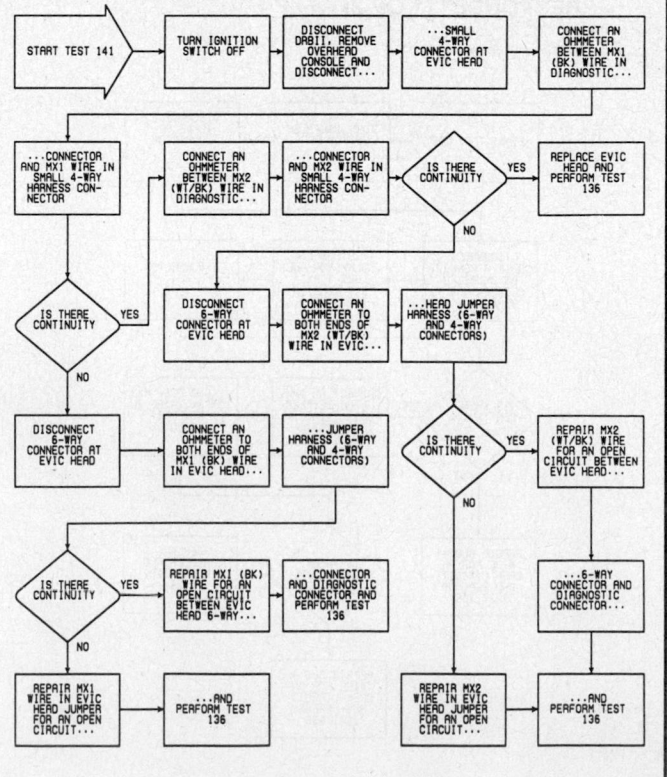

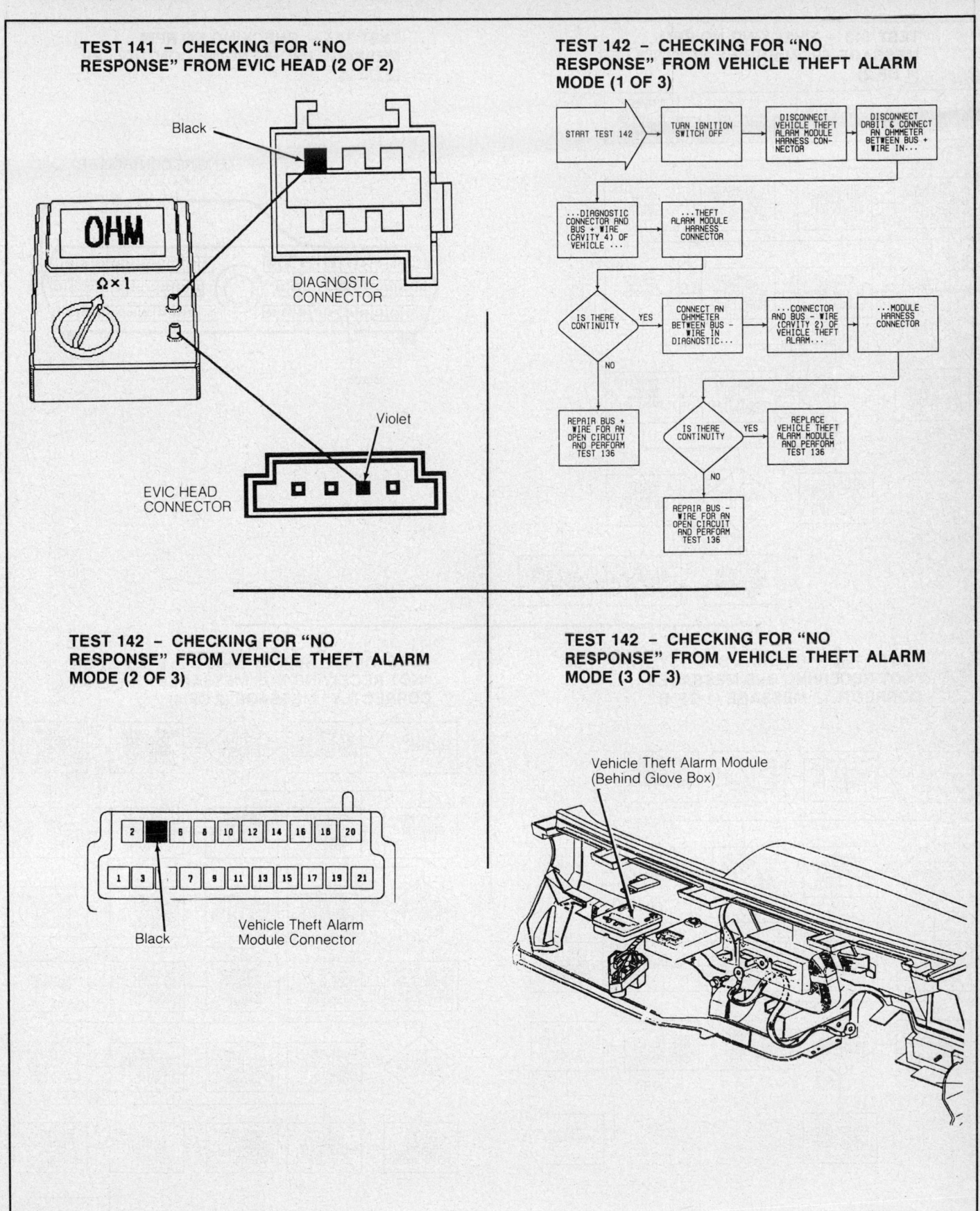

TEST 141 – CHECKING FOR "NO RESPONSE" FROM EVIC HEAD (2 OF 2)

Black

OHM

Ω × 1

DIAGNOSTIC CONNECTOR

Violet

EVIC HEAD CONNECTOR

TEST 142 – CHECKING FOR "NO RESPONSE" FROM VEHICLE THEFT ALARM MODE (1 OF 3)

START TEST 142 → TURN IGNITION SWITCH OFF → DISCONNECT VEHICLE THEFT ALARM MODULE HARNESS CONNECTOR → DISCONNECT DRBII & CONNECT AN OHMMETER BETWEEN BUS + WIRE IN...

...DIAGNOSTIC CONNECTOR AND BUS + WIRE (CAVITY 4) OF VEHICLE... → ...THEFT ALARM MODULE HARNESS CONNECTOR

IS THERE CONTINUITY — YES → CONNECT AN OHMMETER BETWEEN BUS - WIRE IN DIAGNOSTIC... → ...CONNECTOR AND BUS - WIRE (CAVITY 2) OF VEHICLE THEFT ALARM... → ...MODULE HARNESS CONNECTOR

NO

REPAIR BUS + WIRE FOR AN OPEN CIRCUIT AND PERFORM TEST 136

IS THERE CONTINUITY — YES → REPLACE VEHICLE THEFT ALARM MODULE AND PERFORM TEST 136

NO

REPAIR BUS - WIRE FOR AN OPEN CIRCUIT AND PERFORM TEST 136

TEST 142 – CHECKING FOR "NO RESPONSE" FROM VEHICLE THEFT ALARM MODE (2 OF 3)

| 2 | | 6 | 8 | 10 | 12 | 14 | 16 | 18 | 20 |
| 1 | 3 | | 7 | 9 | 11 | 13 | 15 | 17 | 19 | 21 |

Black

Vehicle Theft Alarm Module Connector

TEST 142 – CHECKING FOR "NO RESPONSE" FROM VEHICLE THEFT ALARM MODE (3 OF 3)

Vehicle Theft Alarm Module (Behind Glove Box)

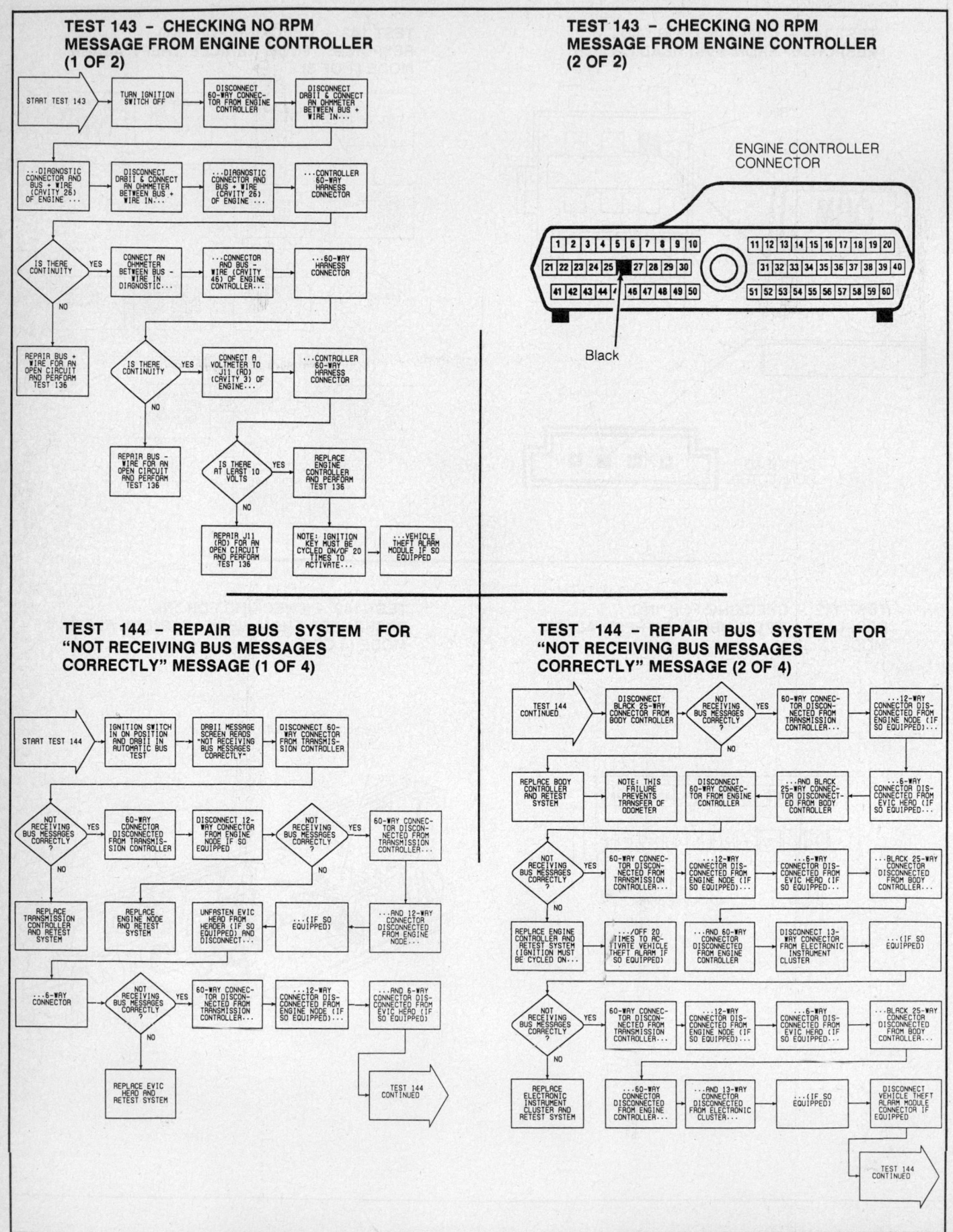

1989 COMPUTERIZED ENGINE CONTROLS
Chrysler Motors Body Control Computer (Cont.)

1a-269

TEST 144 – REPAIR BUS SYSTEM FOR "NOT RECEIVING BUS MESSAGES CORRECTLY" MESSAGE (3 OF 4)

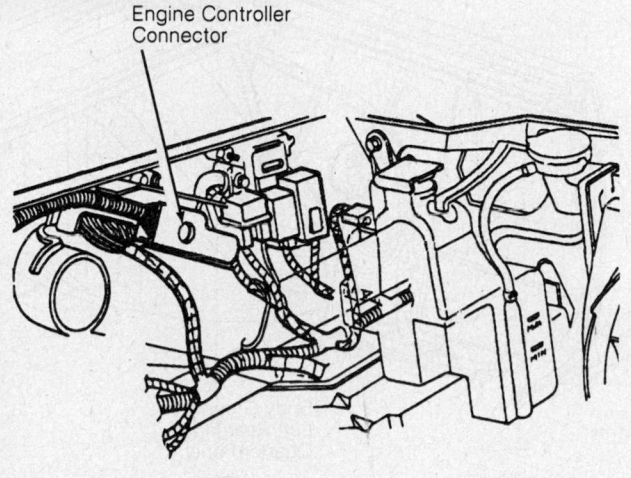

Engine Controller Connector

TEST 144 – REPAIR BUS SYSTEM FOR "NOT RECEIVING BUS MESSAGES CORRECTLY" MESSAGE (4 OF 4)

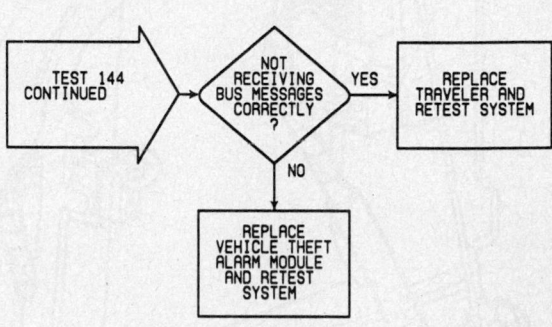

TEST 145 – CHECKING ENGINE CONTROLLER FOR OPEN BUS MESSAGE

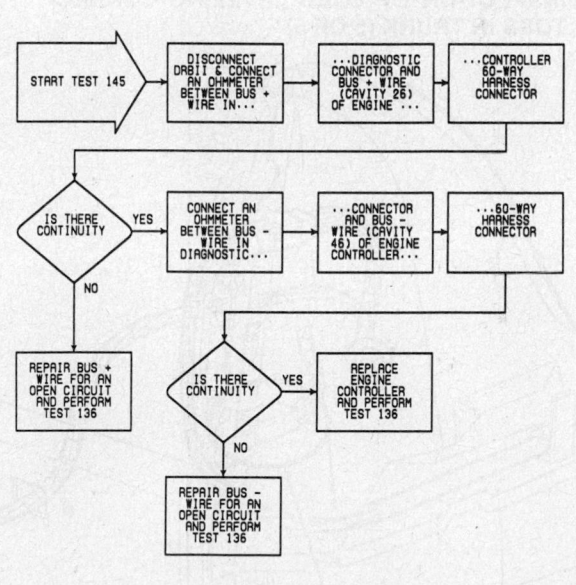

LOAD LEVELING TEST 1 – VISUAL INSPECTION OF LOAD LEVELING CONNECTORS IN TRUNK (1 OF 5)

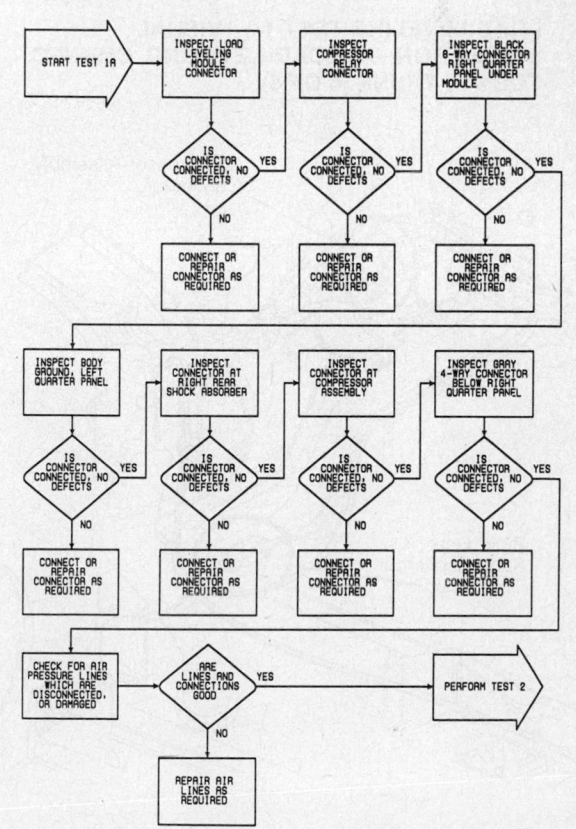

LOAD LEVELING TEST 1 – VISUAL INSPECTION OF LOAD LEVELING CONNECTORS IN TRUNK (2 OF 5)

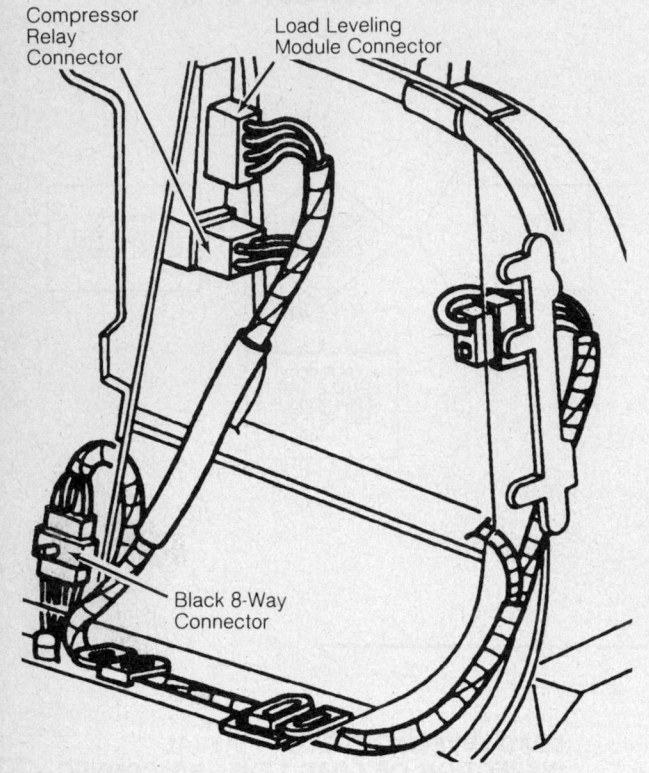

Compressor Relay Connector

Load Leveling Module Connector

Black 8-Way Connector

LOAD LEVELING TEST 1 – VISUAL INSPECTION OF LOAD LEVELING CONNECTORS IN TRUNK (3 OF 5)

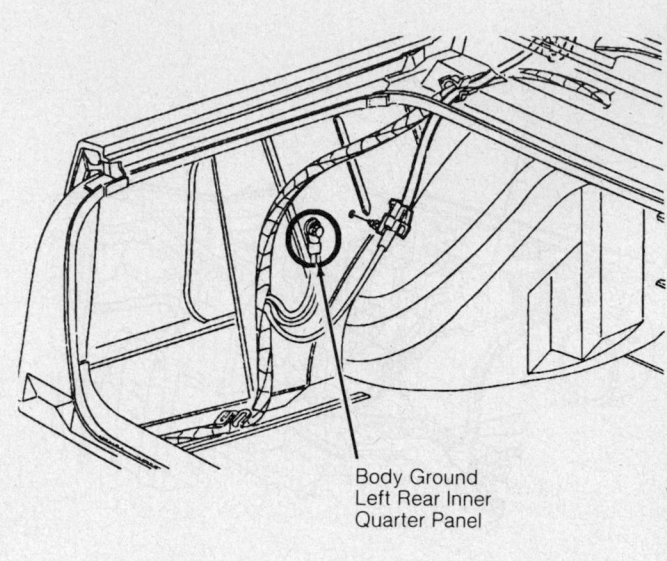

Body Ground Left Rear Inner Quarter Panel

LOAD LEVELING TEST 1 – VISUAL INSPECTION OF LOAD LEVELING CONNECTORS IN TRUNK (4 OF 5)

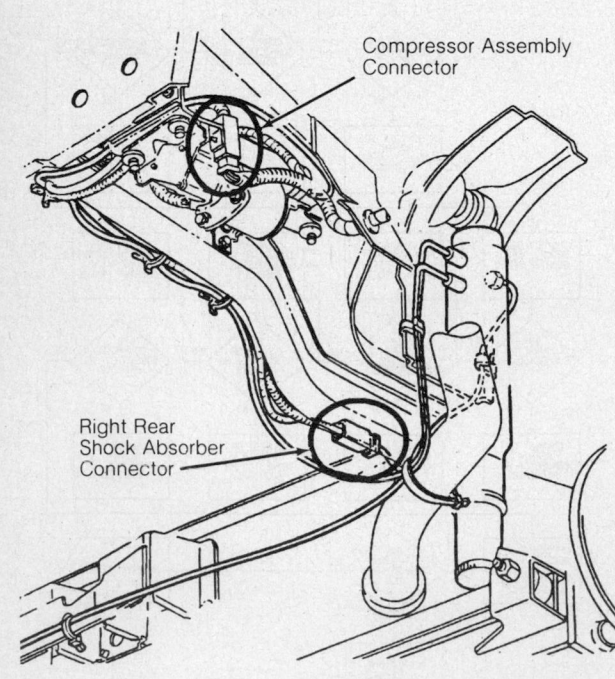

Compressor Assembly Connector

Right Rear Shock Absorber Connector

LOAD LEVELING TEST 1 – VISUAL INSPECTION OF LOAD LEVELING CONNECTORS IN TRUNK (5 OF 5)

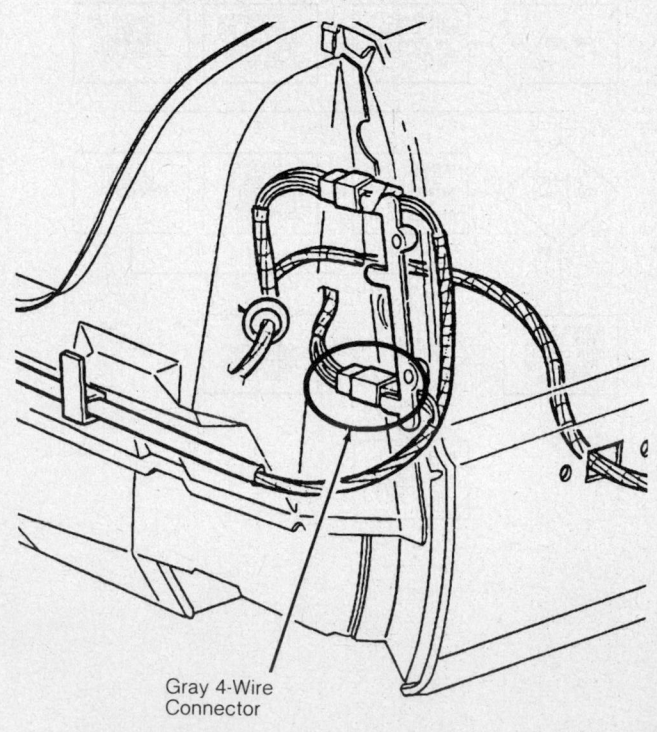

Gray 4-Wire Connector

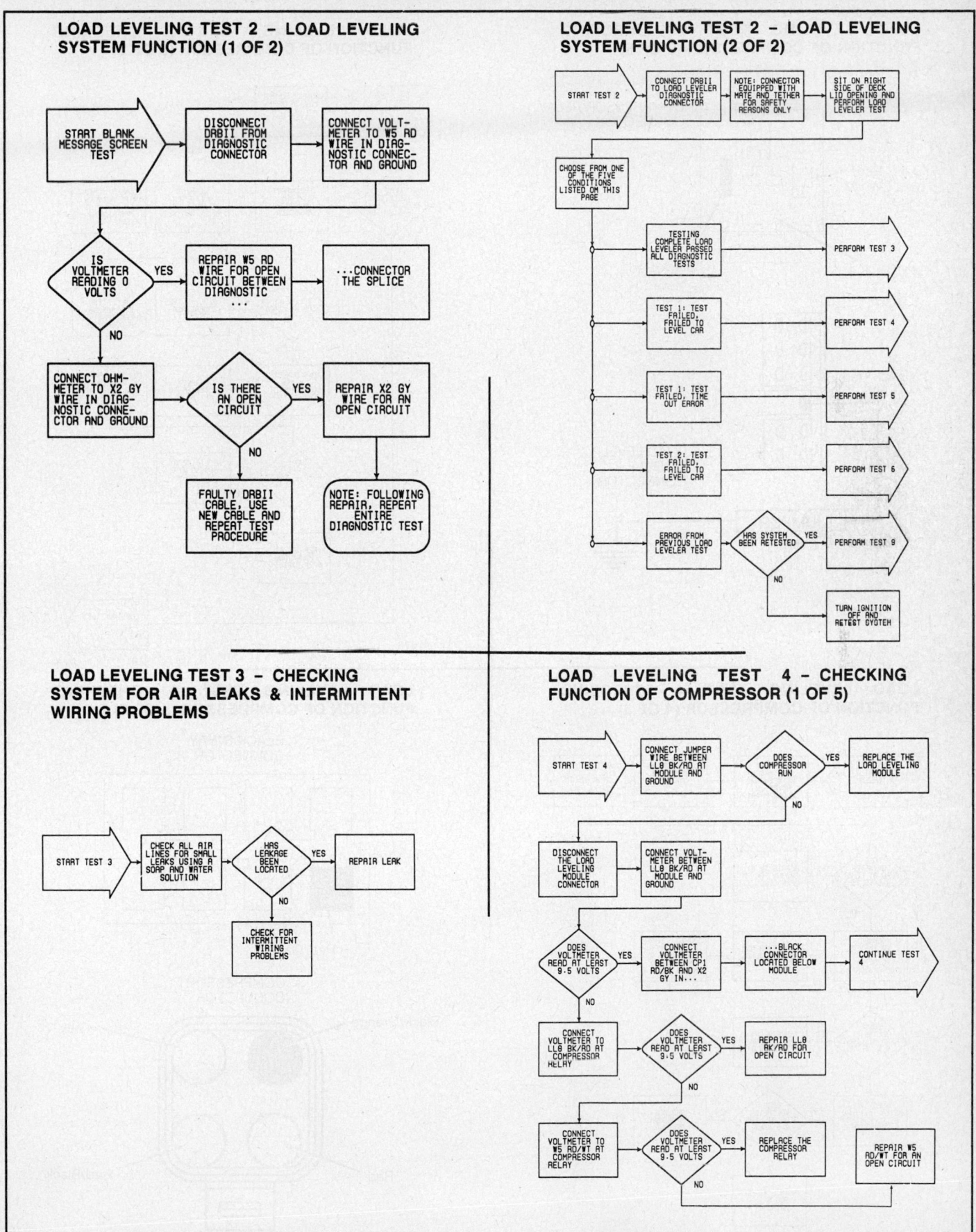

LOAD LEVELING TEST 2 – LOAD LEVELING SYSTEM FUNCTION (1 OF 2)

LOAD LEVELING TEST 2 – LOAD LEVELING SYSTEM FUNCTION (2 OF 2)

LOAD LEVELING TEST 3 – CHECKING SYSTEM FOR AIR LEAKS & INTERMITTENT WIRING PROBLEMS

LOAD LEVELING TEST 4 – CHECKING FUNCTION OF COMPRESSOR (1 OF 5)

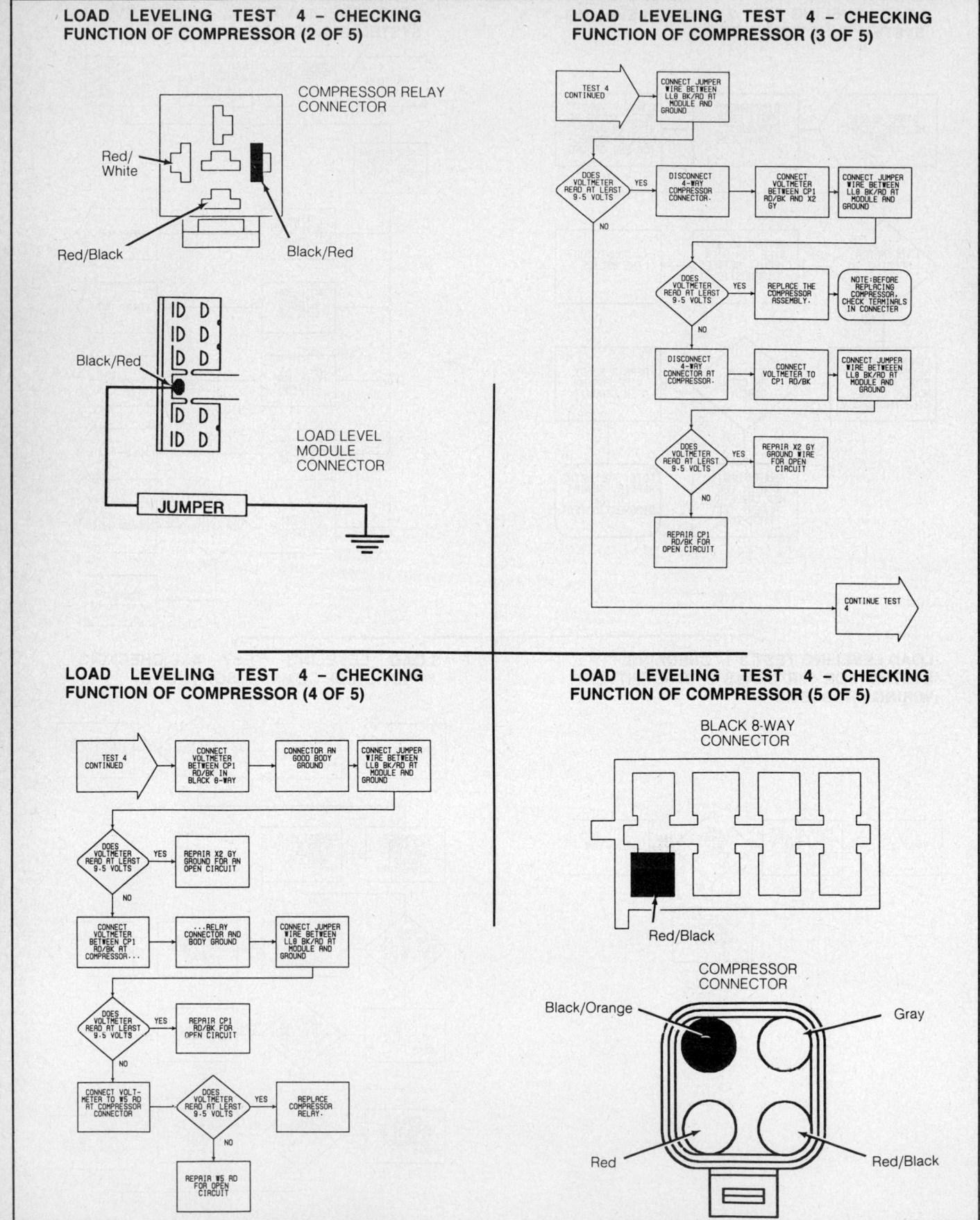

LOAD LEVELING TEST 4 – CHECKING FUNCTION OF COMPRESSOR (2 OF 5)

COMPRESSOR RELAY CONNECTOR

Red/White

Red/Black

Black/Red

Black/Red

LOAD LEVEL MODULE CONNECTOR

JUMPER

LOAD LEVELING TEST 4 – CHECKING FUNCTION OF COMPRESSOR (3 OF 5)

TEST 4 CONTINUED

CONNECT JUMPER WIRE BETWEEN LL8 BK/RD AT MODULE AND GROUND

DOES VOLTMETER READ AT LEAST 9.5 VOLTS — YES → DISCONNECT 4-WAY COMPRESSOR CONNECTOR. → CONNECT VOLTMETER BETWEEN CP1 RD/BK AND X2 GY → CONNECT JUMPER WIRE BETWEEN LL8 BK/RD AT MODULE AND GROUND

NO

DOES VOLTMETER READ AT LEAST 9.5 VOLTS — YES → REPLACE THE COMPRESSOR ASSEMBLY. → NOTE: BEFORE REPLACING COMPRESSOR, CHECK TERMINALS IN CONNECTER

NO

DISCONNECT 4-WAY CONNECTOR AT COMPRESSOR. → CONNECT VOLTMETER TO CP1 RD/BK → CONNECT JUMPER WIRE BETWEEN LL8 BK/RD AT MODULE AND GROUND

DOES VOLTMETER READ AT LEAST 9.5 VOLTS — YES → REPAIR X2 GY GROUND WIRE FOR OPEN CIRCUIT

NO

REPAIR CP1 RD/BK FOR OPEN CIRCUIT

CONTINUE TEST 4

LOAD LEVELING TEST 4 – CHECKING FUNCTION OF COMPRESSOR (4 OF 5)

TEST 4 CONTINUED → CONNECT VOLTMETER BETWEEN CP1 RD/BK IN BLACK 8-WAY → CONNECTOR AN GOOD BODY GROUND → CONNECT JUMPER WIRE BETWEEN LL8 BK/RD AT MODULE AND GROUND

DOES VOLTMETER READ AT LEAST 9.5 VOLTS — YES → REPAIR X2 GY GROUND FOR AN OPEN CIRCUIT

NO

CONNECT VOLTMETER BETWEEN CP1 RD/BK AT COMPRESSOR... → ...RELAY CONNECTOR AND BODY GROUND → CONNECT JUMPER WIRE BETWEEN LL8 BK/RD AT MODULE AND GROUND

DOES VOLTMETER READ AT LEAST 9.5 VOLTS — YES → REPAIR CP1 RD/BK FOR OPEN CIRCUIT

NO

CONNECT VOLT-METER TO W5 RD AT COMPRESSOR CONNECTOR → DOES VOLTMETER READ AT LEAST 9.5 VOLTS — YES → REPLACE COMPRESSOR RELAY.

NO

REPAIR W5 RD FOR OPEN CIRCUIT

LOAD LEVELING TEST 4 – CHECKING FUNCTION OF COMPRESSOR (5 OF 5)

BLACK 8-WAY CONNECTOR

Red/Black

COMPRESSOR CONNECTOR

Black/Orange

Gray

Red

Red/Black

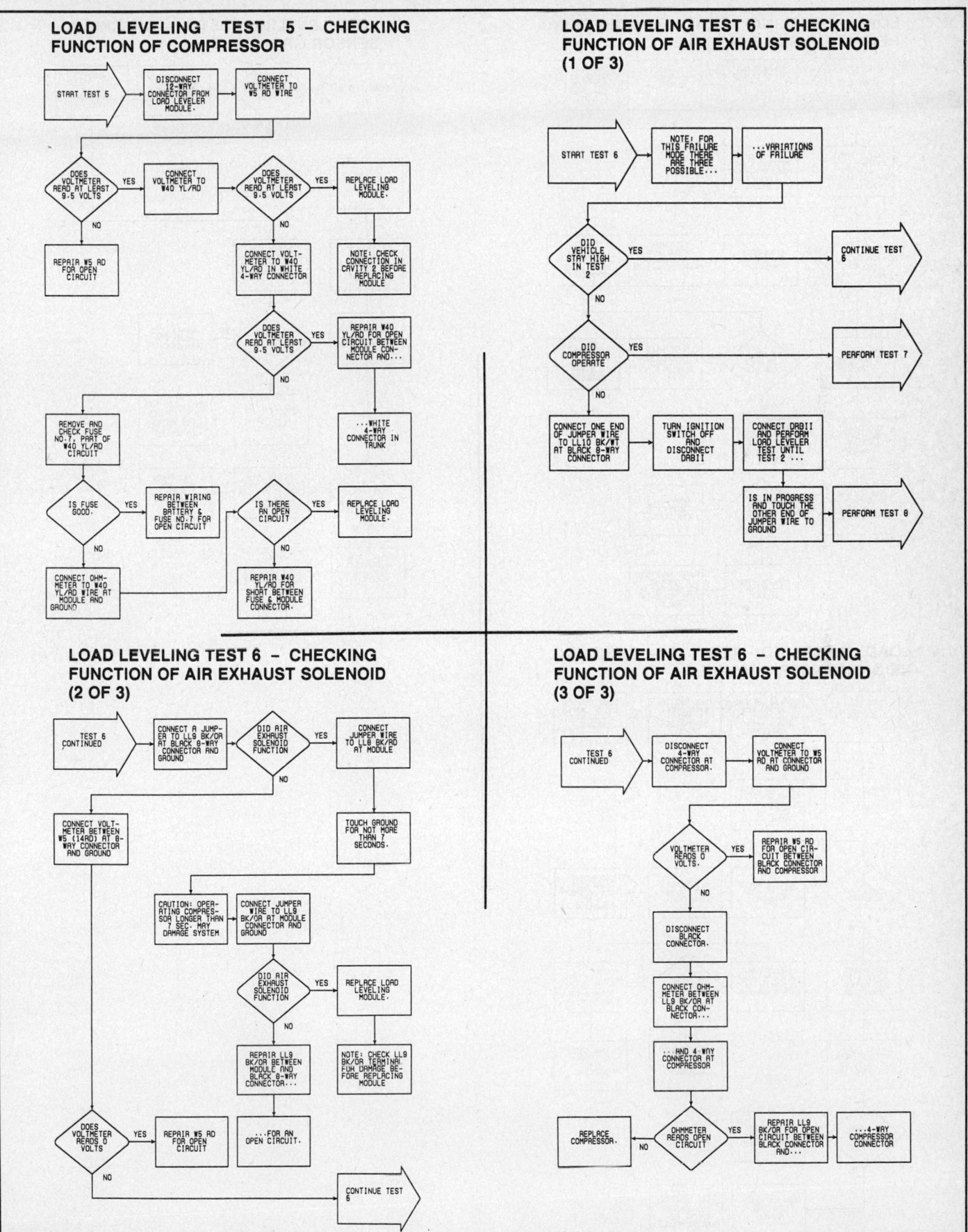

LOAD LEVELING TEST 5 - CHECKING FUNCTION OF COMPRESSOR

LOAD LEVELING TEST 6 - CHECKING FUNCTION OF AIR EXHAUST SOLENOID (1 OF 3)

LOAD LEVELING TEST 6 - CHECKING FUNCTION OF AIR EXHAUST SOLENOID (2 OF 3)

LOAD LEVELING TEST 6 - CHECKING FUNCTION OF AIR EXHAUST SOLENOID (3 OF 3)

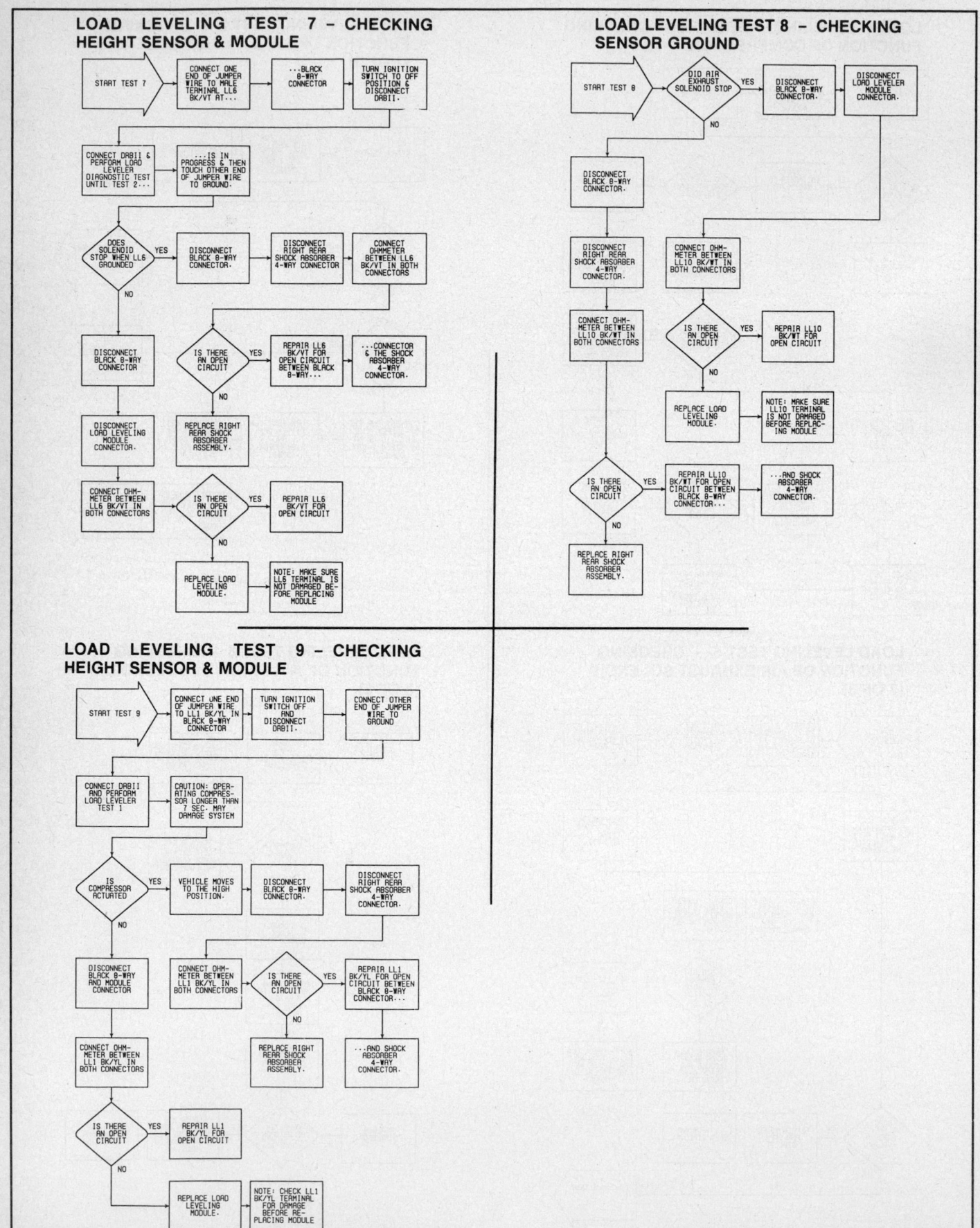

LOAD LEVELING TEST 7 – CHECKING HEIGHT SENSOR & MODULE

LOAD LEVELING TEST 8 – CHECKING SENSOR GROUND

LOAD LEVELING TEST 9 – CHECKING HEIGHT SENSOR & MODULE

Premier

DESCRIPTION

The 2.5L engine uses a single-point throttle body fuel injection system. An injector mounted within the throttle body is controlled by the Electronic Control Unit (ECU). The ECU controls the duration of the injection and meters fuel to the engine.

OPERATION

A/C CONTROLS

The A/C controls indicate to the ECU when the A/C switch is turned on and when A/C compressor is engaged. The ECU changes engine idle speed to compensate for increased engine load during A/C operation through the A/C select circuit. The ECU will also change fuel injector pulse width through A/C predict circuit.

BATTERY VOLTAGE

The battery voltage input to the ECU is used to ensure proper voltage is supplied to the fuel injector. The ECU can vary voltage applied to the injector to compensate for voltage fluctuations.

B+ LATCH RELAY

The B+ latch relay is initially energized during engine start-up and remains energized for 3-5 seconds after engine is stopped. This relay supplies current to Idle Speed Actuator (ISA)/Idle Speed Control (ISC) motor after engine shutdown, enabling the ECU to extend ISA/ISC for next engine start-up.

CLOSED THROTTLE SWITCH

The closed throttle switch is integral with the ISA/ISC motor. This switch provides an input voltage to the ECU. When throttle is closed, the closed throttle switch provides a ground circuit from the ECU. This signal tells the ECU to control idle speed through the ISA/ISC motor.

COOLANT TEMPERATURE SENSOR

The coolant temperature sensor provides an input voltage to the ECU. As coolant temperature varies, the resistance of the sensor will change, resulting in a different input voltage to the ECU.

CRANKSHAFT POSITION/ENGINE SPEED SENSOR

This sensor detects flywheel/drive plate teeth as they pass by during engine operation. This sensor provides ECU with engine speed and crankshaft angle position.

The flywheel/drive plate has a larger trigger tooth and notch located 90 degrees before each Top Dead Center (TDC) position. There are 12 small teeth between the notch and TDC.

When a small tooth and notch pass under the magnet in the sensor, the concentration and then collapse of magnetic flux induces a small voltage spike into the sensor pick-up coil winding. These small voltage spikes enable the ECU to count the teeth as they pass the sensor.

When a large trigger tooth and notch pass under the sensor, the increased concentration and then collapse of the magnetic flux induces a higher voltage spike into the sensor pick-up coil winding. The higher voltage spike indicates to the ECU that a piston will be at TDC position 12 teeth later. The ECU can advance or retard ignition timing as necessary according to sensor inputs.

EGR VALVE VACUUM SOLENOID

This solenoid is controlled by the ECU. When engerized, the solenoid prevents vacuum from reaching the EGR valve. When de-energized, the solenoid allows vacuum to the EGR valve.

The solenoid is engerized during engine warm-up, closed throttle, wide open throttle and rapid acceleration/deceleration. If the solenoid wire connector is disconnected, the EGR valve will be operational at all times, resulting in poor engine performance.

ELECTRONIC CONTROL UNIT (ECU)

The ECU is powered by vehicle battery. With ignition switch in "ON" or "START" position, the following inputs are supplied to the ECU: start signal, engine coolant temperature, intake manifold air temperature, intake manifold absolute pressure, crankshaft position/engine speed, throttle position, exhaust gas oxygen content, engine knock, battery voltage, A/C select and request, closed throttle switch and neutral safety switch.

The following ECU outputs are controlled by the ECU: fuel pump relay, B+ latch relay, A/C compressor clutch relay, ISA/ISC motor, ignition power module, fuel injector, EGR valve vacuum solenoid and shift indicator light (man. trans. only).

FUEL PUMP CONTROL RELAY

Battery voltage is supplied through the ignition switch to the relay. The relay is energized when ground is provided by the ECU, applying voltage to the fuel pump.

HEATED OXYGEN (O$_2$) SENSOR

The O$_2$ sensor supplies an input voltage to the ECU. The ECU uses this information to vary air/fuel ratio. Voltage is supplied to the O$_2$ sensor through the ignition switch.

IDLE SPEED ACTUATOR (ISA)/ IDLE SPEED CONTROL (ISC) MOTOR

The ISA/ISC motor plunger extends or retracts to control engine idle speed and to set throttle angle stop during deceleration. The ECU, using inputs from various sensors, supplies current to ISA/ISC motor to adjust plunger position.

When engine is shutoff, current is momentarily supplied to ISA/ISC motor through B+ latch relay causing ISA/ISC to extend plunger for next engine start-up. When engine is started, it will run on fast idle until ECU senses engine has reached normal operating temperature.

IGNITION CONTROL MODULE

The ECU triggers the ignition coil using the ignition control module. The ECU can advance or retard ignition timing by controlling the ignition coil through the ignition control module.

KNOCK SENSOR

The knock sensor provides an input to ECU that indicates detonation during engine operation. When detonation occurs, the ECU retards ignition timing to eliminate detonation at the applicable cylinder.

MANIFOLD ABSOLUTE PRESSURE (MAP) SENSOR

The MAP sensor responds to absolute pressure in the intake manifold and sends input voltage to the ECU. As engine load changes, intake manifold pressure changes, causing the MAP sensor resistance to change.

When resistance in the MAP sensor changes, this causes voltage signal to the ECU to change. The change in input voltage allows the ECU to adjust air/fuel ratio as necessary. During engine start-up, the MAP sensor input voltage signal supplies the ECU with ambient barometric pressure.

MANIFOLD AIR TEMPERATURE (MAT) SENSOR

The MAT sensor extends into the air/fuel stream. As air/fuel mixture temperature changes, MAT sensor resistance changes, causing the input voltage to the ECU to change.

THROTTLE POSITION SENSOR (TPS)

The TPS is a variable resistor that represents throttle valve position. Input voltage to the ECU from the TPS varies from 1-5 volts. The TPS used on auto. trans. vehicles has 2 integral wire harness connectors (one 4-pin connector and one 3-pin connector) which plug into the engine wire harness. The 4-pin connector supplies input to the ECU, while the 3-pin connector supplies input to the transmission control unit.

REMOVAL & INSTALLATION

COOLANT TEMPERATURE SENSOR (CTS)

Removal & Installation – Coolant temperature sensor is located on the side of the intake manifold behind the throttle body. Disconnect coolant temperature sensor wire connector. Remove sensor from water jacket. To install, reverse removal procedure.

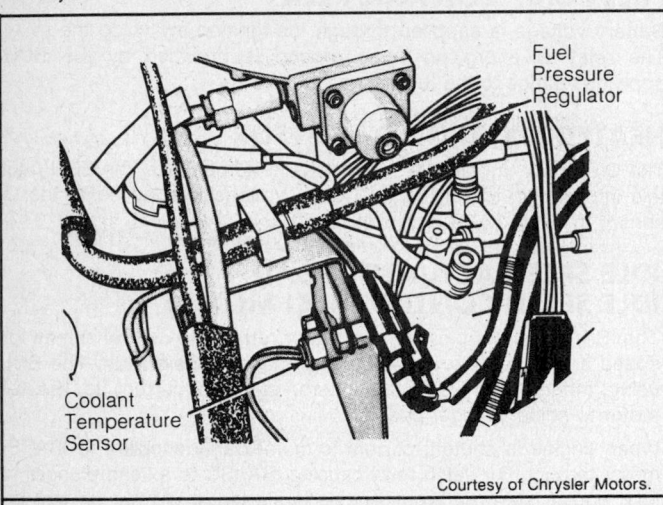

Fig. 1: Location of Coolant Temperature Sensor

CRANKSHAFT POSITION/ENGINE SPEED SENSOR

The crankshaft position/engine speed sensor is located on the converter housing behind the rear face of the engine on the left side. Remove sensor mounting screws. Disconnect sensor electrical connector. Remove sensor. To install, reverse removal procedure.

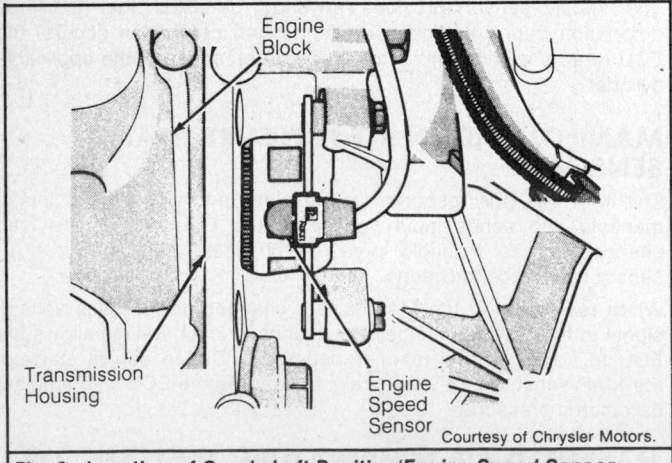

Fig. 2: Location of Crankshaft Position/Engine Speed Sensor

ELECTRONIC CONTROL UNIT

The ECU is located under the instrument panel on the passenger side of vehicle. Disconnect negative battery cable. Remove ECU

mounting nuts and disconnect ground wire. Remove harness connectors from ECU. To install, reverse removal procedure.

IDLE SPEED ACTUATOR (ISA)/ IDLE SPEED CONTROL (ISC) MOTOR

The ISA/ISC motor is located on the side of the throttle body. Remove air cleaner top. Remove 2 motor mounting screws. Remove motor from bracket and disconnect electrical connector. To install, reverse removal procedure.

IGNITION CONTROL MODULE

Disconnect coil wire from coil. Disconnect electrical connectors from ignition control module. Remove ignition control module mounting nuts. Remove ignition control module. To install, reverse removal procedure.

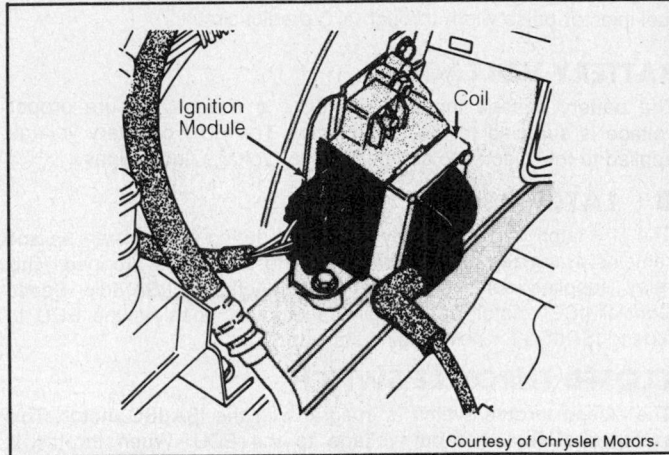

Fig. 3: Location of Ignition Control Module

KNOCK SENSOR

Disconnect knock sensor electrical connector. Remove knock sensor from connector on engine mount. To install, reverse removal procedure. Tightening torque is critical to sensor operation. Tighten sensor to 89 INCH lbs. (10 N.m).

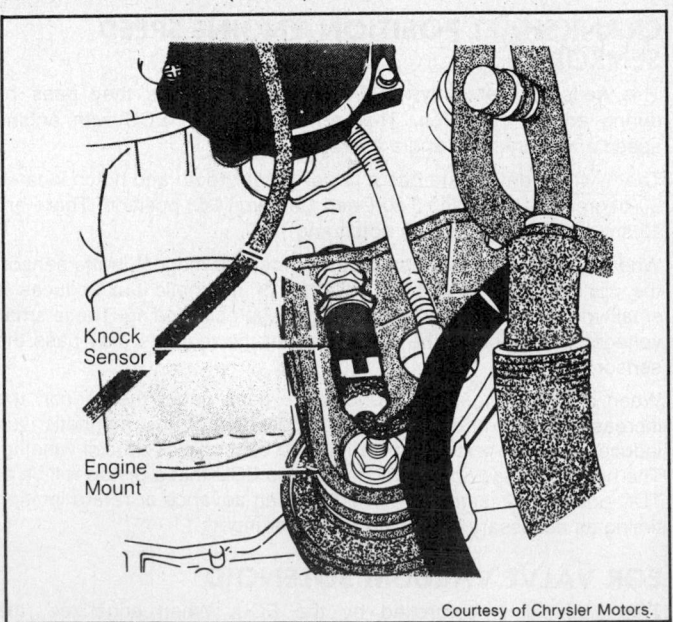

Fig. 4: Location of Knock Sensor

MANIFOLD ABSOLUTE PRESSURE (MAP) SENSOR

The MAP sensor is located next to power brake booster. Disconnect electrical connector and vacuum hose. Remove MAP sensor mounting screws. Remove MAP sensor. To install, reverse removal procedure.

MANIFOLD AIR TEMPERATURE (MAT) SENSOR

The MAT sensor is located in the intake manifold between No. 3 and No. 4 intake runners. Disconnect electrical connector. Unscrew sensor from intake manifold. To install, reverse removal procedure.

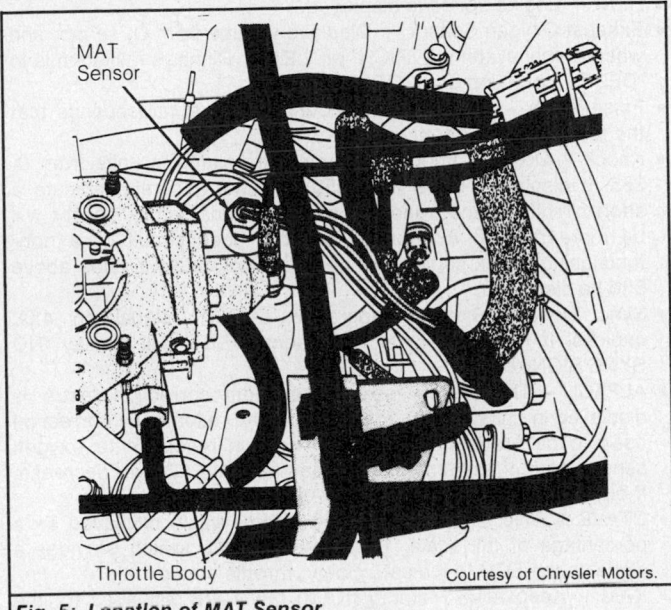

Fig. 5: Location of MAT Sensor

THROTTLE POSITION SENSOR (TPS)

Disconnect TPS electrical connectors. Remove TPS mounting screws. Remove electrical wire harness mounting bracket screws. Remove TPS. To install, reverse removal procedure.

TESTING & DIAGNOSIS

PRELIMINARY CHECKS

Most driveability problems in the engine control system result from faulty wiring or leaking hose connections. To avoid unnecessary component testing, a visual check should be performed before beginning trouble shooting procedures to help spot these common faults.

SYSTEM DIAGNOSIS

The self-diagnostic capabilities of this system, if properly utilized, can greatly simplify testing. The ECU has been programmed to monitor several different circuits of the engine control system. If a problem is sensed with a monitored circuit, a fault code is stored in the ECU.

The setting of a specific fault code is the result of a particular system failure, NOT the reason for that failure, such as failure of a specific component. The existence of a particular code denotes the probable area of the malfunction, not necessarily the failed component itself.

ECU/TCU CHECKOUT PROCEDURE

1) If during testing the Electronic Control Unit (ECU) or Transmission Control Unit (TCU) is found to be faulty, perform the following steps to ensure control unit is faulty. Most components are incorrectly diagnosed due to faulty electrical connectors or a poor mechanical connection between component and vehicle.

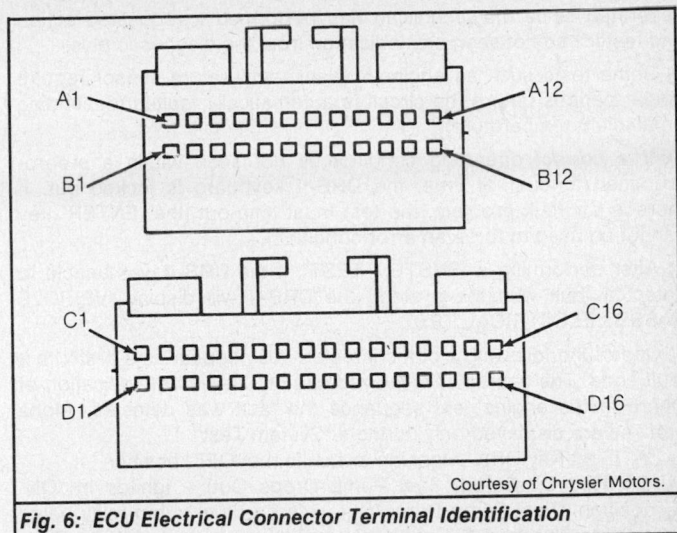

Fig. 6: ECU Electrical Connector Terminal Identification

2) Sometimes simply disconnecting and connecting an electrical component will provide a good electrical connection. Before replacing a control unit, check all components in the suspect circuit. If other components are okay, carefully disconnect control unit from vehicle harness.

3) Inspect control unit harness connector and control unit contact pins for corrosion. Clean harness connector and control unit contact pins with contact cleaner. Inspect control unit harness connector for bent pins, missing pins and broken wires. Repair or replace as necessary.

4) Connect control unit harness connector to control unit and retest system with DRB-II and adapter. If vehicle does not pass test and fails with the same message, replace control unit.

DIAGNOSING WITH DRB-II & JEEP/EAGLE ADAPTER

1) With DRB-II connected to Jeep/Eagle adapter and Jeep/Eagle adapter connected to both vehicle diagnostic connectors, all character positions will illuminate and copyright information will appear on screen. The DRB-II will offer 3 menus, "VEHICLES TESTED", "HOW TO USE" and "SELECT VEHICLE".

Vehicles Tested – Press "1" key or "Enter" key when "VEHICLES TESTED" appears on DRB-II display. DRB-II will show vehicles supported with cartridge used. This screen will display for 5 seconds and return to DRB-II menu. To return to DRB-II menu sooner, press "ATM" key.

How To Use – Press "2" key or press downward facing arrow button to display "HOW TO USE" option. Press "Enter" key. DRB-II will display instructions for use of DRB-II with cartridge being used.

Select Vehicle – **1)** This option provides a means which the user may enter information about vehicle being tested. Usually this option will have more than one display screen. Use "Enter" key to enter vehicle information. If an option is not available for vehicle being tested, DRB-II will not display that option.

2) When all information about the vehicle is entered, DRB-II will display a summary of information technician entered as a confirming menu. DRB-II will show an additional option marked "CONFIRM". If information is correct, press "CONFIRM". DRB-II will display "MAIN MENU".

Main Menu – The "MAIN MENU" will present all diagnostic functions available for vehicle selected. Functions are "SYSTEM TESTS", "STATE DISPLAYS" and "ADJUSTMENTS".

System Tests – **1)** This is an interactive functional test of a particular system. During testing, DRB-II will provide instructions to technician. After task is performed, press "Enter" key. A fault will be generated since the technician has performed a requested action and tester had not seen any indication from the diagnostic pins.

2) Some tests such as engine coolant temperature sensor require longer periods before the circuit is automatically faulted (depending on ambient temperature).

3) If a correct operating condition is not seen within a prepro-grammed amount of time, the DRB-II keyboard is locked out. If there is a circuit problem, the test must time-out (the "ENTER" key cannot be used to force an error condition).

4) After performing a "SYSTEM TEST", if the DRB-II was unable to detect a fault with the system, the DRB-II will display "VEHICLE PASSES ELECTRICAL TEST".

5) One of the following alpha characters may appear as a prefix to a fault code. The character displayed can be used as an indication of where in the engine test sequence the fault was detected. Alpha prefixes are displayed only during a "System Test".

- "A" (First Key Off) – Ignition switch in the "OFF" position.
- "B" (Key On Before Fuel Pump Drops Out) – Igniton in "ON" position. "Fuel Pump Drops Out" refers to fuel pump relay being activated by the ECU and fuel pump being activated. If the ECU does not detect a crank signal within a few seconds after ignition is turned on, the ECU will automatically open ground circuit to fuel pump relay. This will disable fuel pump.
- "C" (Key On After Fuel Pump Drops Out) – Ignition is in "ON" position after fuel pump relay has timed out (fuel pump off).
- "D" (First Crank) – The engine is cranking but not running.
- "E" (First Engine Start) – Engine idling.
- "F" (Second Key Off Before Fuel Pump Drops Out) – Ignition is in "OFF" position for the second time before fuel pump relay has timed out.
- "G" (Second Key Off After Fuel Pump Drops Out) – Ignition is in "OFF" position for the second time before fuel pump relay has timed out.
- "G" (Second Key On) – No text.
- "I" (Second Engine Start) – No text.
- "J" (Last Key Off) – No text.
- "X" (ECU Defined Faults) – Faults detected by ECU on-board diagnostics.

State Displays – 1) This display enables technician to view conditions at the signal level. The 2 types of signals used are analog and digital. Analog signals are monitored at pins corresponding to vehicle harness splices (e.g. fuel pump relay). Digital signals correspond to data transmitted by the system contollers. Both signals are displayed in common units (e.g. temperature), this information is not relative to diagnostic intent.

2) Use up and down arrow keys on DRB-II to scroll through displays available. When "State Display" is selected, a menu showing systems for which state displays are supported is displayed. If "Engine" state display is selected, technician has the option to view either static state displays or "Max/Current/Min" value display.

3) The "Static" display shows conditions as they exist at the time the user is viewing the display. The "Min/Current/Max" display shows a history of conditions for specific sensor. When this option is selected, maximum, current (static) and minimum value can be displayed for a specific sensor. To reset sensors to a zero value, simply press "Enter" key. This display may be used to isolate intermittent faults.

4) The following "Engine" state displays are available on the DRB-II.

- Vehicle Program and Calibration Code – Program numbers indicate the ECU is programmed for a specific engine. Calibration code applies to manual or automatic transmission.
- Battery – Displays battery voltage.
- H_2O – Engine coolant temperature is displayed in degrees Fahrenheit and Celsius.
- Air – Air temperature is displayed in degrees Fahrenheit and Celsius.
- TPS – Throttle Position Sensor (TPS) is displayed as "WIDE OPEN", "CLOSED" or "PARTIAL" and percentage of opening from closed throttle to Wide Open Throttle (WOT).

- A/C Status – If any of the A/C signals are active, an abbreviated display showing A/C state will be dislayed as select "SEL", predict "PRE", clutch "CL" and cut-out "CO". If A/C signals are inactive, "A/C OFF" will be displayed.
- Relay Status – Displays EGR solenoid, B+ latch relay and fuel pump relay as on "+" or off "0". When EGR solenoid is off, vacuum is present. When EGR solenoid is on, vacuum is absent.
- Barometric Pressure Reading – Barometric pressure value can be used to test MAP sensor. A good MAP sensor will read within .60 in. Hg of current barometric pressure at sea level. Subtract .1 in. Hg for every 100 feet above sea level. Current barometric pressure may be obtained from your local weather bureau.
- RPM – Engine speed is displayed.
- Exhaust Oxygen Sensor – Displays voltage from O_2 sensor and whether fuel system is "RICH" or "LEAN". Displays if system is in "DECEL" condition or in "OPEN LOOP".
- Pulse Width – Displays the amount of time in milliseconds that the fuel injector is open.
- Knock – Displays knock sensor noise volume in units from 0-255. If display is more than 250, this will generally indicate a short circuit. Normal readings of a functional knock sensor will be more than 5. A short to ground, open circuit or a non-functioning knock sensor will generally not cause a value above 5 to be displayed.
- Sync Signal – Displays operation of sync signal on 4.0L engines. If no sync signal is present, DRB-II will display "NO SYNC SIGNAL".
- ALFACL – The closed loop pulse width correction factor is displayed in units from 0-255. ALFACL represents the correction used to calculate injector pulse width in response to oxygen sensor input. If oxygen sensor reads rich, ALFACL will decrease. If oxygen sensor reads lean, ALFACL will increase.
- CTAVE – This is average closed throttle value displayed as a percentage of full scale. The closed throttle switch provides a signal to the ECU to indicate closed throttle status.
- KAM – Keep Alive Memory (KAM) faults are displayed for the O_2 sensor, MAP sensor, TPS, air temperature sensor and coolant temperature sensor. Next to sensor display, a pair of numbers is displayed. Each number reflects a period since the ECU has detected a fault. The first number corresponds to a sensed "low" condition failure and the second number corresponds to a sensed "high" condition failure. When ECU detects a "low" or "high" condition failure, then number "15" will be stored for the respective sensor. If the engine is started and closed loop is attempted and fault is no longer present, the counter will be decreased by one. If the fault is still present, counter will remain at 15. Values of "0" (zero) are an indication that a "low" or "high" fault condition does not exist for the sensor displayed. Values less than 15 and greater than zero are an indication that the ECU has detected a fault at some time, but fault is not present during the current start cycle (possible intermittent).
- Warranty – A 6 digit code for warranty reporting.

5) The "Min/Current/Max" display allows technician to observe operation of 6 different sensor values. Information is displayed as a 3 digit number. The first value displayed is the minumum reading, second number displayed is current reading and third value displayed is the maximum reading. The sensors that are monitored are: MAP sensor, O_2 sensor, Throttle Position Sensor (TPS), Coolant Temperature Sensor (CTS), Manifold Air Temperature (MAT) sensor and CTAVG (average learned closed throttle value).

6) Typically sensors range between 2-252. Values less than 2 or greater than 252 will usually indicate that a sensor is shorted or disconnected. Watch minimum and maximum values to help diagnose intermittent problems.

Adjustments – The "Adjustments" option provides TPS adjustment or erasing stored information in system controller. Follow DRB-II instructions to accomplish desired task.

CLEARING CODES
Refer to ADJUSTMENTS in this article.

FAULT CODES

FAULT CODE IDENTIFICATION

Fault Code	Fault Condition
1000	Ignition line low
1001	Ignition line high
1004	Battery voltage low
1005	Sensor ground line out of limits
1010	Diagnostic enable line low
1011	Diagnostic enable line high
1012	Ignition control module line low
1013	Ignition control module line high
1014	Fuel pump line low
1015	Fuel pump line high
1016	Manifold Air Temperature (MAT) sensor line low
1017	Manifold Air Temperature (MAT) sensor line high
1018	No serial data from ECU
1021	Engine failed to start due to mechanical, fuel or ignition problem
1022	Start line low
1024	ECU does not see start signal
1027	ECU sees Wide Open Throttle (WOT)
1028	ECU does not see Wide Open Throttle (WOT)
1031	ECU sees closed throttle
1032	ECU does not see closed throttle
1033	Idle speed increase line low
1034	Idle speed increase line high
1035	Idle speed decrease line low
1036	Idle speed decrease line high
1037	Throttle Position Sensor (TPS) reads low
1038	Park/Neutral line high
1040	Latched B+ line low
1041	Latched B+ line high
1042	No latched B+ .5 volt drop
1047	Wrong ECU
1048	Manual vehicle equipped with automatic ECU
1049	Automatic vehicle equipped with manual ECU
1050	Idle speed less than 500 RPM
1051	Idle speed greater than 2000 RPM
1052	MAP sensor out of limits
1053	Change in MAP reading out of limits
1054	Coolant temperature sensor line low
1055	Coolant temperature sensor line high
1056	Inactive coolant temperature sensor
1057	Knock circuit shorted
1058	Knock value out of limits
1059	A/C request line low
1060	A/C request line high
1061	A/C select line low
1062	A/C select line high
1063	A/C clutch line low
1064	A/C clutch line high
1065	O₂ sensor reads rich
1066	O₂ sensor reads lean
1067	Latch relay line low
1068	Latch relay line high
1069	No tach
1070	A/C cut-out line low
1071	A/C cut-out line line high
1073	ECU does not see crankshaft position/ engine speed sensor signal
1200	ECU defective
1202	Injector shorted to ground
1209	Injector open
1218	No voltage at ECU from power latch relay
1219	No voltage at ECU from shift light
1220	No voltage at ECU from EGR solenoid
1221	No injector voltage
1222	Ignition control module not grounded
1223	No ECU tests run

COMPONENT TESTING

NOTE: Testing information for fuel injector and knock sensor is not available.

A/C Clutch Relay – With ignition switch in "RUN" position, leave A/C clutch relay connected. Connect a voltmeter between, relay terminal No. 86 and ground. *See Fig. 7.* Voltmeter should read battery voltage. If battery voltage is present, go to next step. If battery voltage is not present, check fuse No. 8. If fuse No. 8 is okay, check for an open circuit to fuse No. 8.

2) Connect voltmeter between relay terminal No. 30 and ground. *See Fig. 7.* Voltmeter should read battery voltage. If battery voltage is present, go to next step. If battery voltage is not present, check fusible link in circuit. If fusible link is okay, check for an open circuit to fusible link.

3) Connect voltmeter between relay terminals No. 86 and 85. *See Fig. 7.* Voltmeter should read battery voltage. If battery voltage is present, go to next step. If battery voltage is not present, check for an open circuit to Air Control Module (ACM) connecter terminal "C5". If circuit is okay, replace Air Control Module (ACM).

4) Connect voltmeter between relay terminals No. 30 and 87. *See Fig. 7.* A/C compressor clutch should engage. If A/C compressor clutch engages, replace A/C clutch relay.

B+ (Power) Latch, Fuel Pump & Ignition Relays – **1)** With relay in de-energized position, relay should have continuity between relay terminals No. 87A and 30. *See Fig. 7.* Measure resistance between relay terminals No. 85 and 86.

2) Ohmmeter should read 70-80 ohms for resistor relays and 81-91 ohms for diode relays. Replace relay if not within specification. Not all relays have battery voltage connected to terminal No. 30. Some relays have battery voltage connected to terminals No. 87 or 87A.

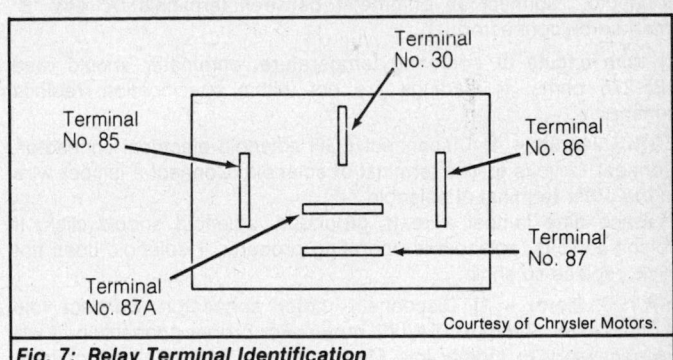

Fig. 7: Relay Terminal Identification

Courtesy of Chrysler Motors.

Closed Throttle Switch – **1)** Ensure all testing is done with ISA/ISC plunger fully extended (as it would be after engine shutdown). If it is necessary to extend ISA/ISC plunger with a test switch, an ISA/ISC motor failure can be suspected.

2) Turn ignition on. Connect a voltmeter between terminals "A" and "B" of ISA/ISC motor. Voltmeter reading should be close to zero at closed throttle and greater than 2 volts with throttle partially open.

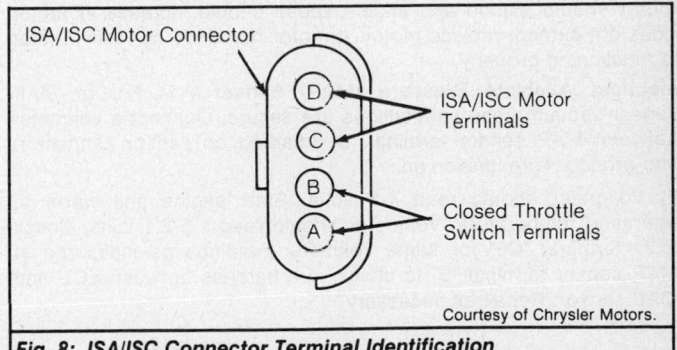

Courtesy of Chrysler Motors.

Fig. 8: ISA/ISC Connector Terminal Identification

3) If voltage is not present in either position, check for a short circuit to ground in wiring harness or switch and check for an open circuit between ECU connector terminal "D5" and closed throttle switch.

4) If voltage is always more than 2 volts, check for an open circuit between ECU and switch connector (ISA/ISC connector) and between switch connector and ground. Repair or replace as necessary.

Coolant Temperature Sensor (CTS) – 1) Disconnect electrical connector from coolant temperature sensor. Using a DVOM, check resistance between ECU connector terminal "C10" to sensor connector and ECU connector terminal "D3" to sensor connector. See Fig. 6.

2) If resistance is greater than one ohm, repair wiring harness. Measure resistance of sensor between sensor terminals. Refer to COOLANT TEMPERATURE SENSOR RESISTANCE table for specifications on coolant temperature sensor resistance.

COOLANT TEMPERATURE SENSOR RESISTANCE [1]

°F (°C)	Ohms
212 (100)	185
160 (70)	450
100 (38)	1600
70 (20)	3400
40 (4)	7500
20 (-7)	13,500
0 (-18)	25,500
-40 (-40)	100,700

[1] – Values given are approximate.

Crankshaft Position/Engine Speed Sensor – 1) Disconnect sensor connector. Connect an ohmmeter between terminals "A" and "B" (marked on connector).

2) With engine at operating temperature, ohmmeter should read 125-275 ohms. If readings are not within specification, replace sensor.

EGR Solenoid – 1) Disconnect EGR solenoid electrical connector. Connect 12 volts to one terminal of solenoid. Connect a jumper wire to the other terminal of solenoid.

2) Each time jumper wire is grounded, solenoid should click. If solenoid clicks, solenoid is operating properly. If solenoid does not click, replace solenoid.

ISA/ISC Motor – 1) Disconnect motor connector. Connect Idle Motor Tester (7088) to ISA/ISC motor. For proper connection, it will be necessary to modify Idle Motor Tester (7088). Cut a groove in terminal "A" the same size and shape as grooves in teminals "B" and "D".

2) Connect Idle Motor Tester (7088) to vehicle battery. Start engine. Put Idle Motor Tester's switch in "RETRACT" position. ISA/ISC motor should retract and engine idle speed should decrease. If ISA/ISC motor retracts and engine speed decreases, go to next step. If ISC motor does not retract, replace ISA/ISC motor.

3) Put idle motor tester's switch in "EXTEND" position. ISA/ISC motor should extend and engine speed should increase. If motor does not extend, replace motor. If motor responds correctly, motor is functioning properly.

Manifold Absolute Pressure (MAP) Sensor – 1) Ensure MAP sensor vacuum hose connections are secure. Connect a voltmeter between MAP sensor terminal "B" (marked on sensor connector) and ground. Turn ignition on.

2) Voltmeter should read 4-5 volts. Start engine and warm to operating temperature. Voltmeter should read 1.5-2.1 volts. Check ECU terminal "C6" for same voltmeter readings as measured at MAP sensor terminal "B" to check wire harness between ECU and MAP sensor. Repair as necessary.

3) Turn ignition off. Connect voltmeter between MAP sensor terminal C and ground. Turn ignition on. Voltmeter should read 4.5-5.5 volts. Check for same voltmeter reading at ECU terminal "C14". See Fig. 6. Repair wiring harness as necessary.

4) Turn ignition off. Check for continuity between MAP sensor terminal "A" and ECU terminal "D3". Repair wire harness as necessary.

Manifold Air Temperature (MAT) Sensor – 1) Disconnect wire harness connector from MAT sensor. Using a DVOM, sensor resistance should be less than 1000 ohms with engine at operating temperature.

2) Check resistance between ECU terminal "C8" and sensor connector and ECU terminal "D3" and sensor connector. See Fig. 6. Repair wire harness if resistance is more than one ohm. Refer to MANIFOLD AIR TEMPERATURE SENSOR RESISTANCE table. Replace sensor if not within specification.

MANIFOLD AIR TEMPERATURE SENSOR RESISTANCE [1]

°F (°C)	Ohms
212 (100)	185
160 (70)	450
100 (38)	1600
70 (20)	3400
40 (4)	7500
20 (-7)	13,500
0 (-18)	25,500
-40 (-40)	100,700

[1] – Values given are approximate.

Oxygen Sensor Heating Element – Disconnect O₂ sensor connector. Connect an ohmmeter between sensor terminals "A" and "B". Ohmmeter should read less than 10 ohms. Replace sensor if ohmmeter reads infinity.

Starter Relay – 1) Turn ignition on. Starter relay is connected to vehicle during testing. Connect a voltmeter between Black/White wire and ground. Turn ignition switch to "START" position. Voltmeter should read battery voltage. If voltmeter does not read battery voltage, replace defective starter relay or repair open circuit from ignition switch.

2) Connect voltmeter between 2 Green wires and ground one at a time on starter relay. Turn ignition switch to "START" position. Voltmeter should read battery voltage. If voltmeter does not read battery voltage, repair ground circuit.

3) Connect voltmeter between Green/White wire and ground. Turn ignition switch to "START" position. Voltmeter should read battery voltage. If voltmeter does not read battery voltage, replace starter relay.

Throttle Position Sensor (TPS) – 1) Turn ignition off. Disconnect TPS electrical connector. Turn ignition on. Using a DVOM, check voltage between terminals "B" and "C". If voltage is 5 volts, go to next step. If voltage is not 5 volts, go to step **3)**.

2) Connect TPS electrical connector. Open throttle to wide open throttle. Measure voltage between terminals "A" and "B". If voltage is 4.6-4.7 volts, TPS is okay. If voltage is not 4.6-4.7 volts, adjust TPS to obtain correct voltage reading. If TPS cannot be adjusted within specification, replace TPS.

3) Turn ignition off. Check for continuity between ECU connector terminal "C15" and TPS harness terminal "C". See Fig. 6. If continiuty is present, go to next step. If continuity is not present, repair wire harness and retest.

4) Check for continuity between ECU connector terminal "D3" and TPS harness terminal "B". If continuity is not present, go to next step. If continuity is present, repair TPS wire harness ground circuit.

5) Check for continuity between ECU terminal "C7" and TPS harness terminal "A". If continuity is present, replace ECU and retest. If continiuty is not present repair wire between ECU and TPS.

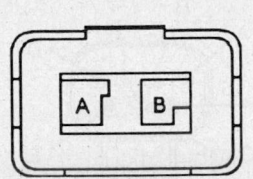

KNOCK SENSOR (C519)

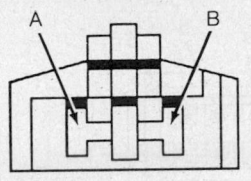

EGR SOLENOID (C510)

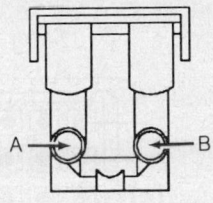

AIR INJECTOR (C511)

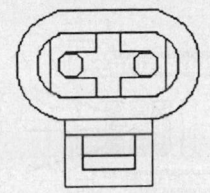

LEFT FRONT ENGINE COMPARTMENT CONNECTOR (C133)

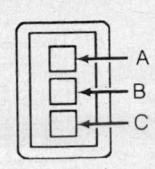

COOLANT FAN ASSEMBLY (C619)

IGNITION MODULE (C506), OXYGEN SENSOR (C502), & TPS SENSOR (C514)

IGNITION MODULE (C507) & MAT SENSOR (C568)

CRANKSHAFT POSITION/ ENGINE SPEED SENSOR (C512) & MAP SENSOR (C513)

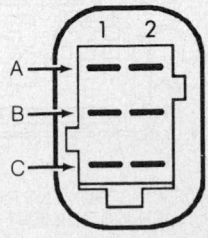

TRANSMISSION CONTROL UNIT (C677)

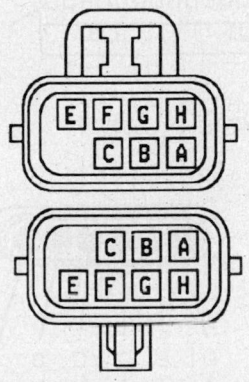

CENTER REAR ENGINE COMPARTMENT CONNECTOR (C106)

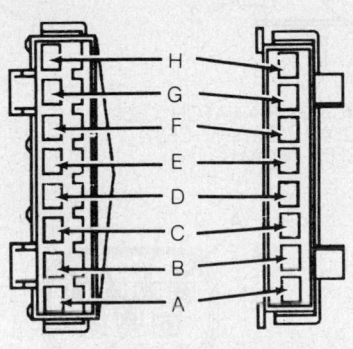

UNDER RIGHT SIDE INSTRUMENT PANEL (C114)

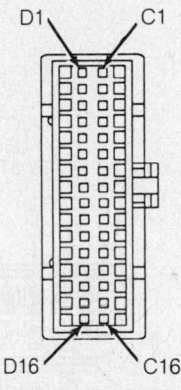

ELECTRONIC CONTROL UNIT (C505)

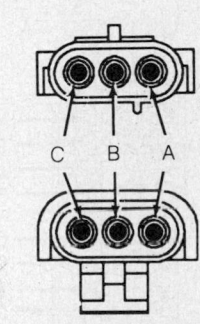

LEFT FRONT CORNER ENGINE COMPARTMENT (C107)

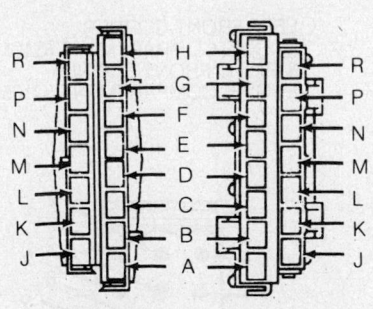

UNDER INSTRUMENT PANEL LEFT SIDE (C109)

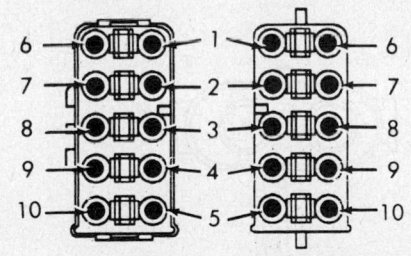

UNDER INSTRUMENT PANEL RIGHT SIDE (C108)

CENTER REAR ENGINE COMPARTMENT (C106)

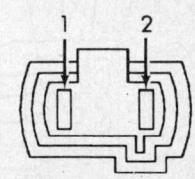

A/C LOW PRESSURE SWITCH (C617)

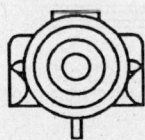

A/C COMPRESSOR CLUTCH (C622)

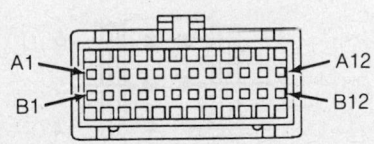

ELECTRONIC CONTROL UNIT (C504)

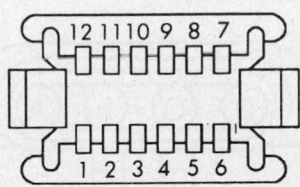

BEHIND INSTRUMENT CLUSTER (C542)

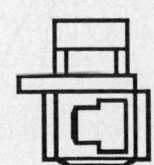

UNDER LEFT SIDE INSTRUMENT PANEL (C143)

Courtesy of Chrysler Motors.

Fig. 9: Connector Identification

1989 COMPUTERIZED ENGINE CONTROLS
Eagle 2.5L TBI (Cont.)

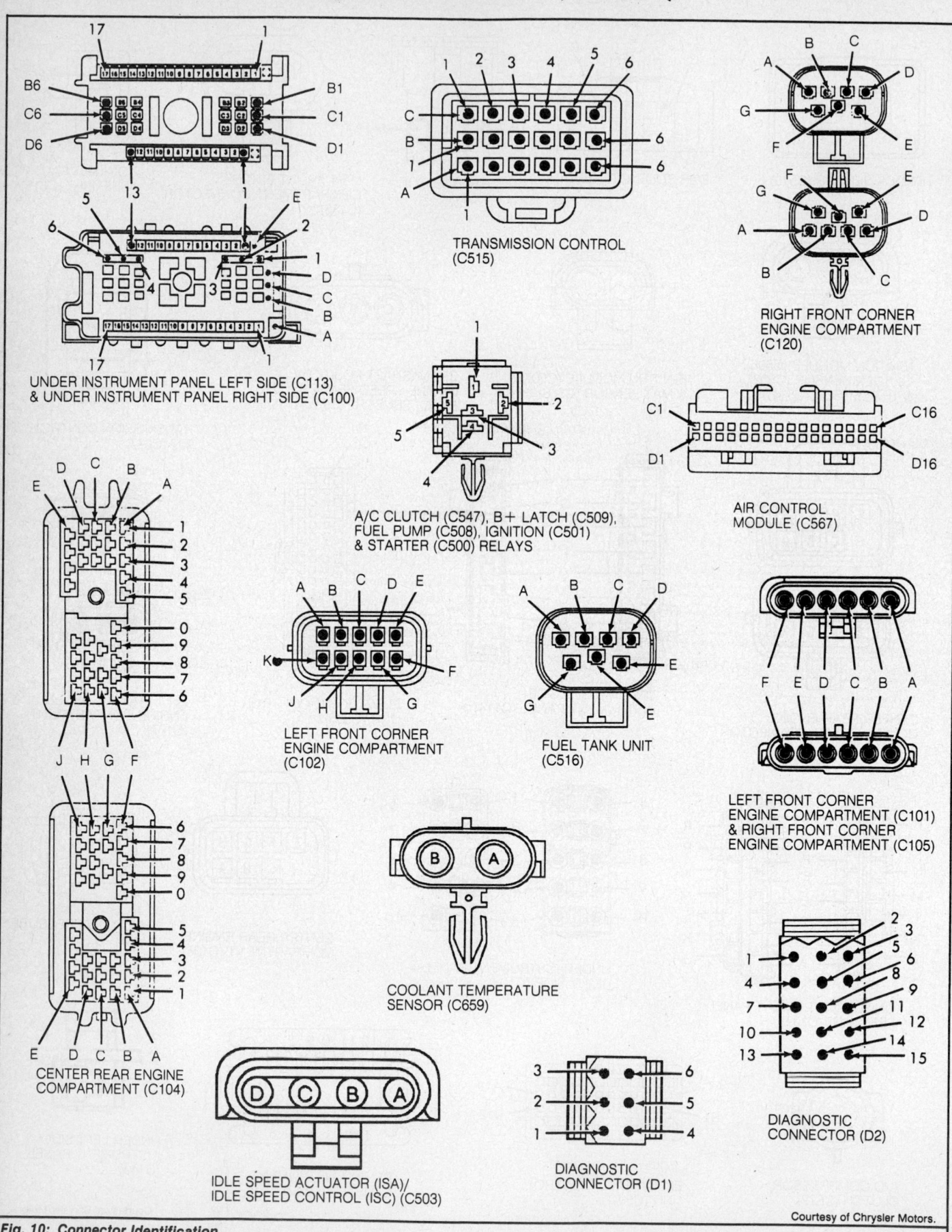

UNDER INSTRUMENT PANEL LEFT SIDE (C113)
& UNDER INSTRUMENT PANEL RIGHT SIDE (C100)

TRANSMISSION CONTROL (C515)

RIGHT FRONT CORNER ENGINE COMPARTMENT (C120)

A/C CLUTCH (C547), B+ LATCH (C509), FUEL PUMP (C508), IGNITION (C501) & STARTER (C500) RELAYS

AIR CONTROL MODULE (C567)

LEFT FRONT CORNER ENGINE COMPARTMENT (C102)

FUEL TANK UNIT (C516)

LEFT FRONT CORNER ENGINE COMPARTMENT (C101) & RIGHT FRONT CORNER ENGINE COMPARTMENT (C105)

CENTER REAR ENGINE COMPARTMENT (C104)

COOLANT TEMPERATURE SENSOR (C659)

DIAGNOSTIC CONNECTOR (D2)

IDLE SPEED ACTUATOR (ISA)/ IDLE SPEED CONTROL (ISC) (C503)

DIAGNOSTIC CONNECTOR (D1)

Courtesy of Chrysler Motors.

Fig. 10: Connector Identification

NOTE: *The following trouble shooting charts and illustrations are courtesy of Chrysler Motors.*

FAULT 1000 (1 OF 3) – IGNITION LINE LOW

FAULT 1000 (2 OF 3)

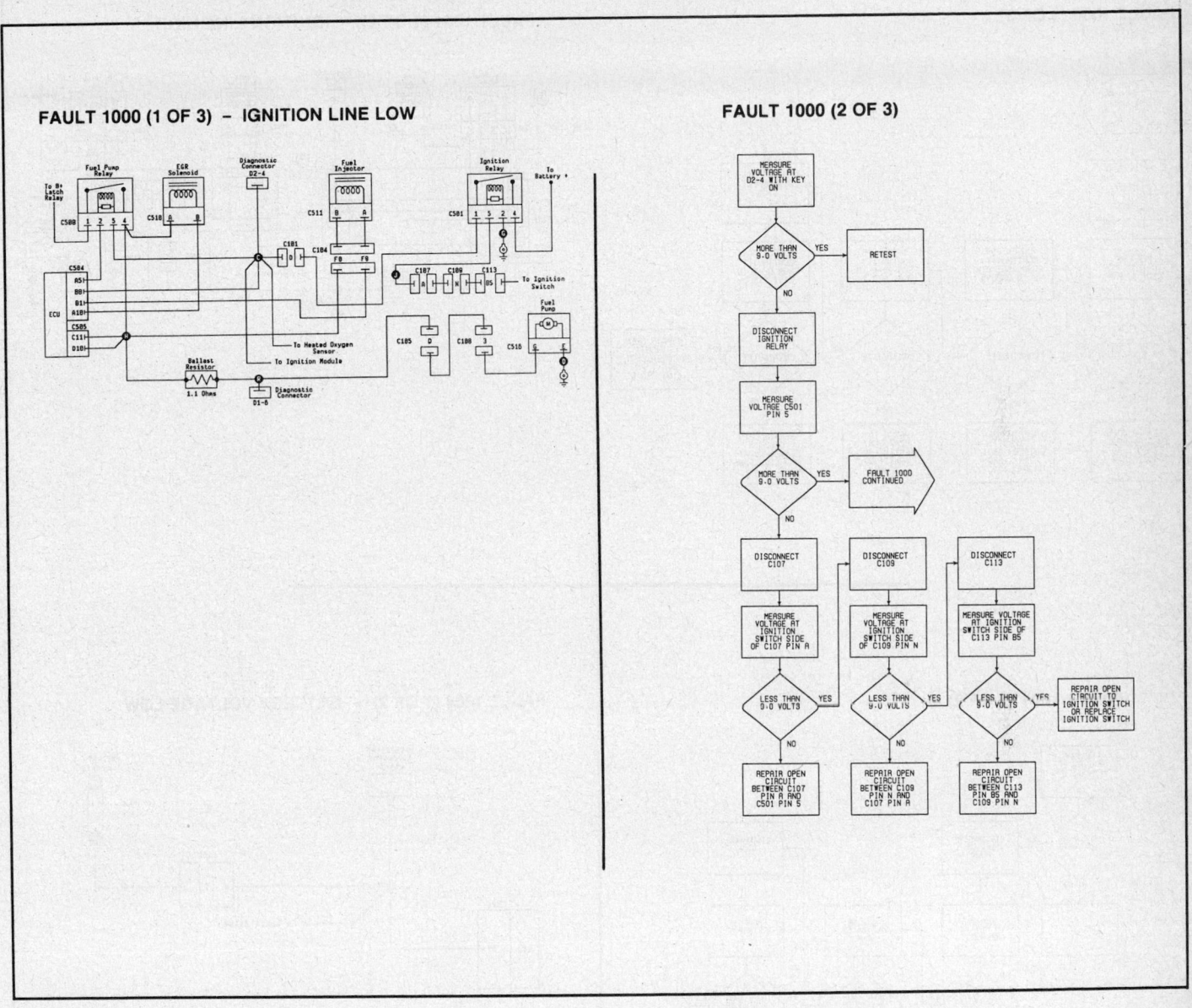

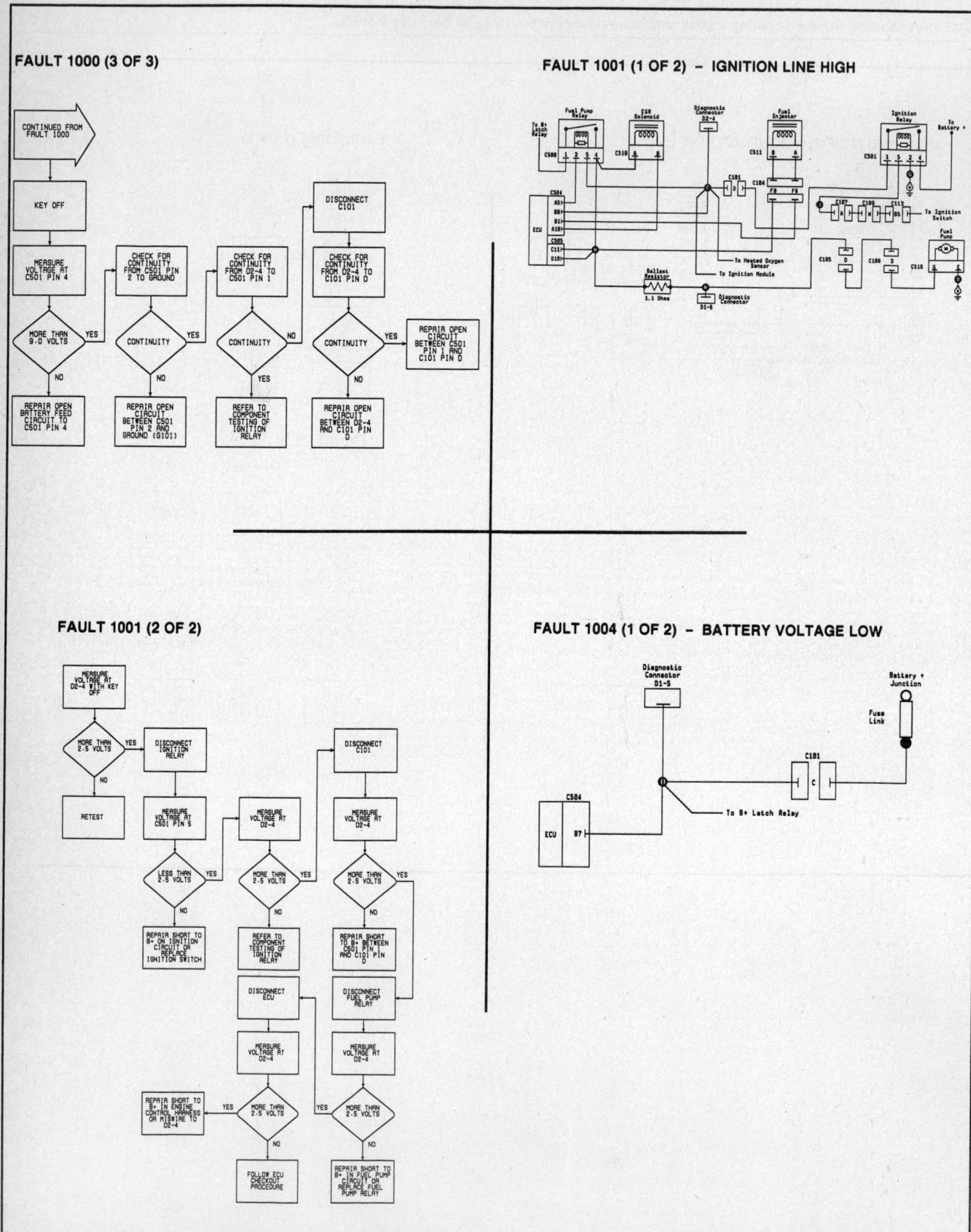

FAULT 1000 (3 OF 3)

FAULT 1001 (1 OF 2) – IGNITION LINE HIGH

FAULT 1001 (2 OF 2)

FAULT 1004 (1 OF 2) – BATTERY VOLTAGE LOW

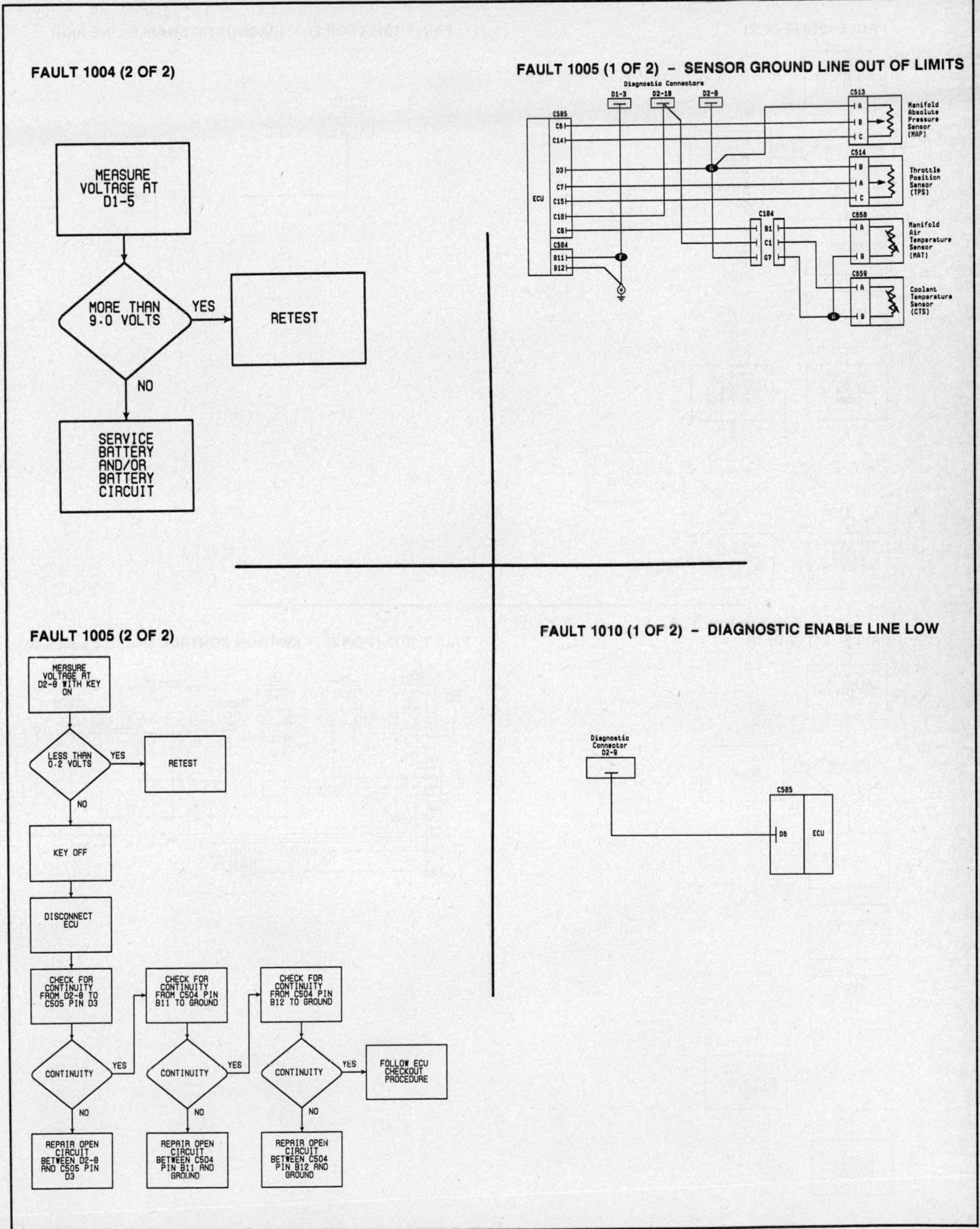

FAULT 1004 (2 OF 2)

MEASURE VOLTAGE AT D1-5

MORE THAN 9.0 VOLTS

YES → RETEST

NO → SERVICE BATTERY AND/OR BATTERY CIRCUIT

FAULT 1005 (1 OF 2) – SENSOR GROUND LINE OUT OF LIMITS

Diagnostic Connectors

Manifold Absolute Pressure Sensor (MAP)
Throttle Position Sensor (TPS)
Manifold Air Temperature Sensor (MAT)
Coolant Temperature Sensor (CTS)

FAULT 1005 (2 OF 2)

MEASURE VOLTAGE AT D2-8 WITH KEY ON

LESS THAN 0.2 VOLTS

YES → RETEST

NO → KEY OFF → DISCONNECT ECU → CHECK FOR CONTINUITY FROM D2-8 TO C505 PIN D3

CONTINUITY
YES → CHECK FOR CONTINUITY FROM C504 PIN B11 TO GROUND
NO → REPAIR OPEN CIRCUIT BETWEEN D2-8 AND C505 PIN D3

CONTINUITY
YES → CHECK FOR CONTINUITY FROM C504 PIN B12 TO GROUND
NO → REPAIR OPEN CIRCUIT BETWEEN C504 PIN B11 AND GROUND

CONTINUITY
YES → FOLLOW ECU CHECKOUT PROCEDURE
NO → REPAIR OPEN CIRCUIT BETWEEN C504 PIN B12 AND GROUND

FAULT 1010 (1 OF 2) – DIAGNOSTIC ENABLE LINE LOW

Diagnostic Connector D2-8

C505 D8 ECU

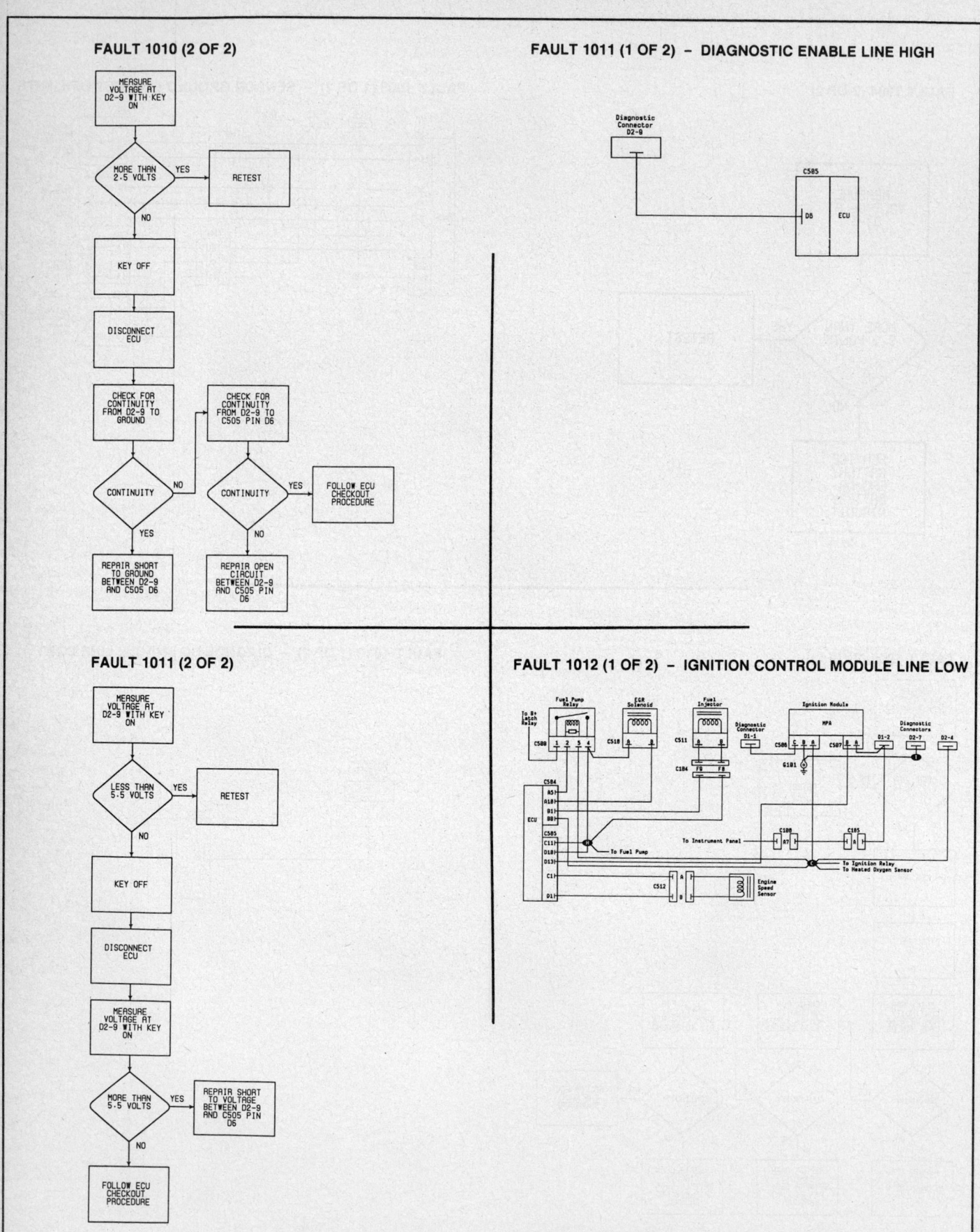

FAULT 1010 (2 OF 2)

FAULT 1011 (1 OF 2) – DIAGNOSTIC ENABLE LINE HIGH

FAULT 1011 (2 OF 2)

FAULT 1012 (1 OF 2) – IGNITION CONTROL MODULE LINE LOW

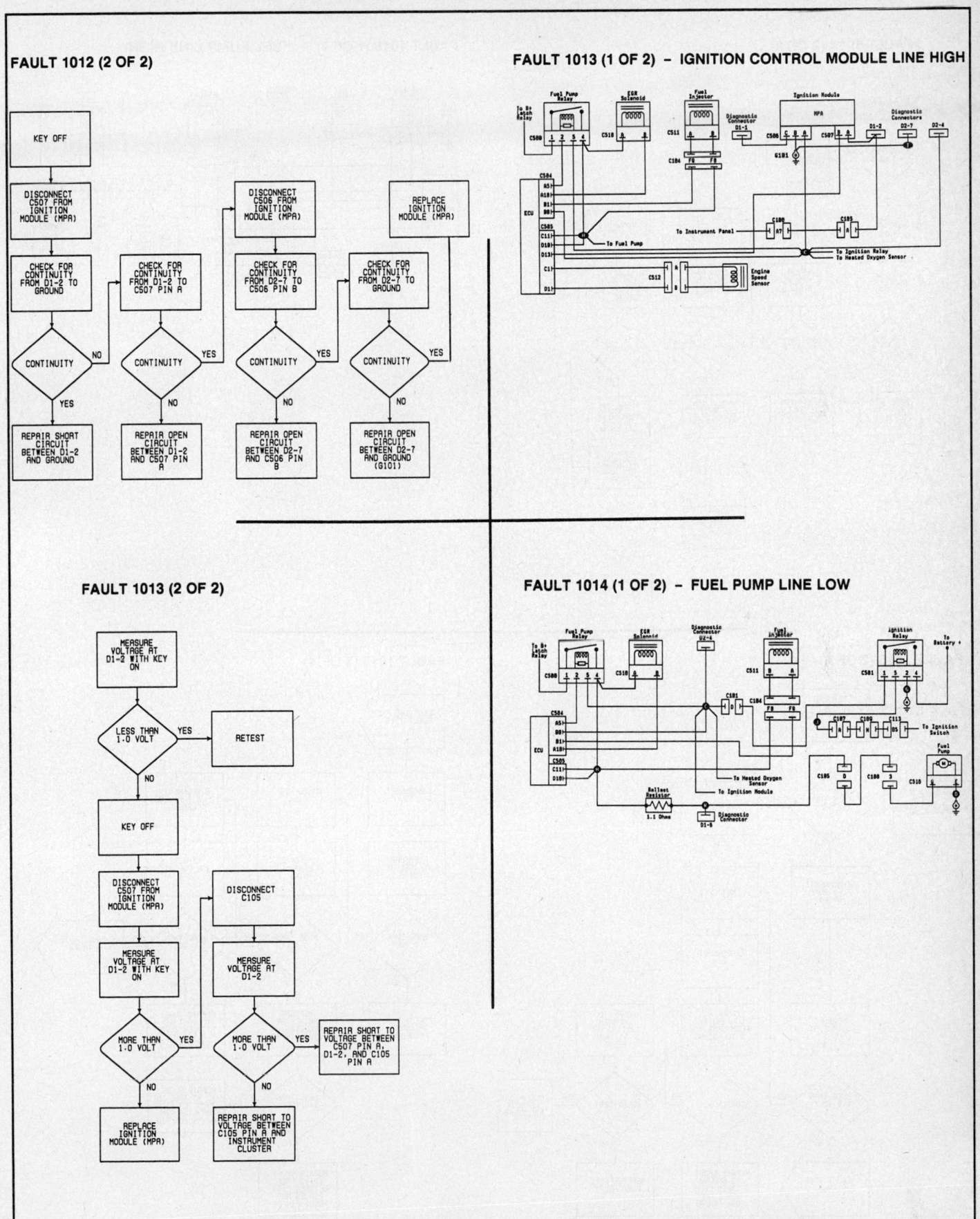

FAULT 1012 (2 OF 2)

FAULT 1013 (1 OF 2) – IGNITION CONTROL MODULE LINE HIGH

FAULT 1013 (2 OF 2)

FAULT 1014 (1 OF 2) – FUEL PUMP LINE LOW

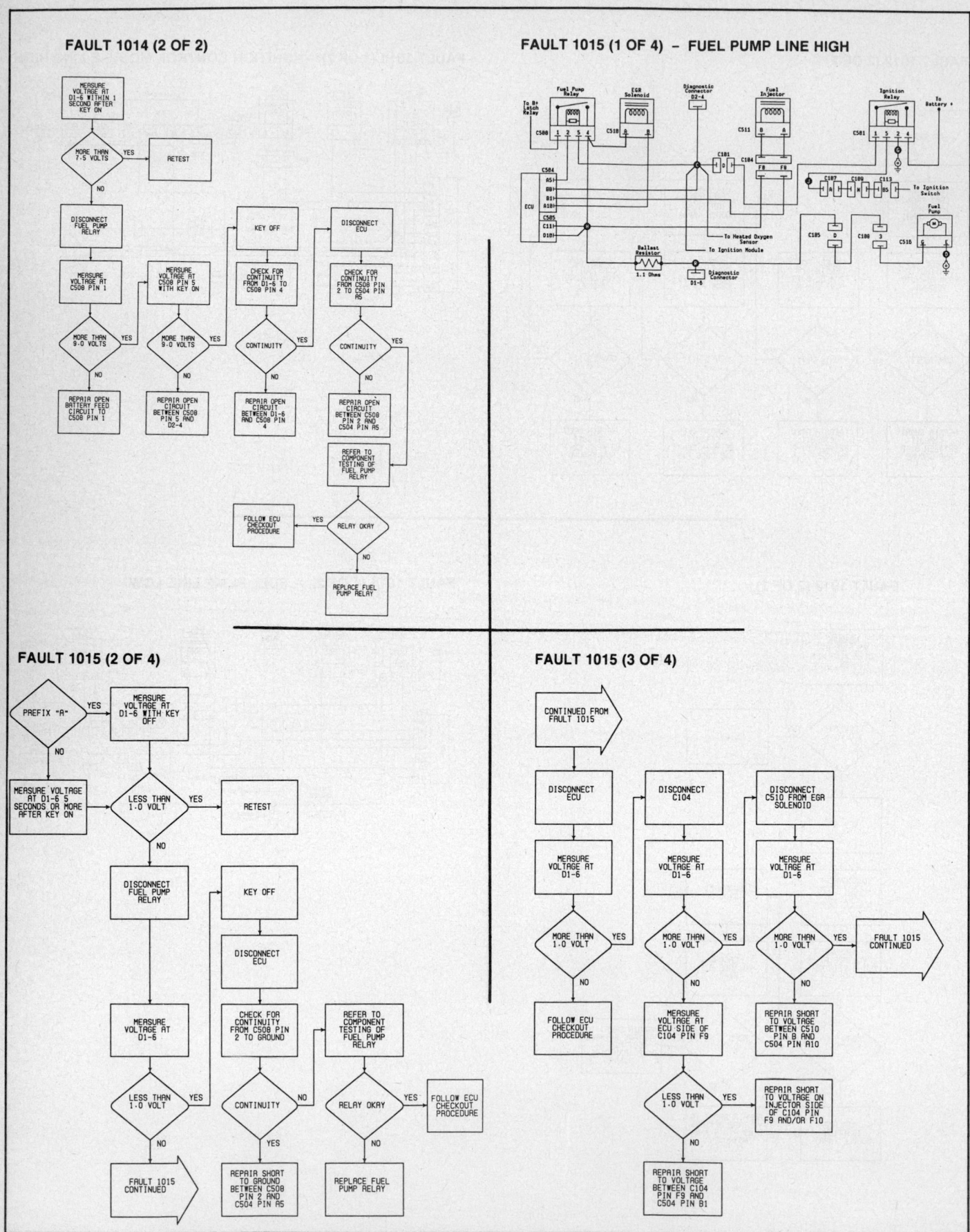

FAULT 1014 (2 OF 2)

FAULT 1015 (1 OF 4) – FUEL PUMP LINE HIGH

FAULT 1015 (2 OF 4)

FAULT 1015 (3 OF 4)

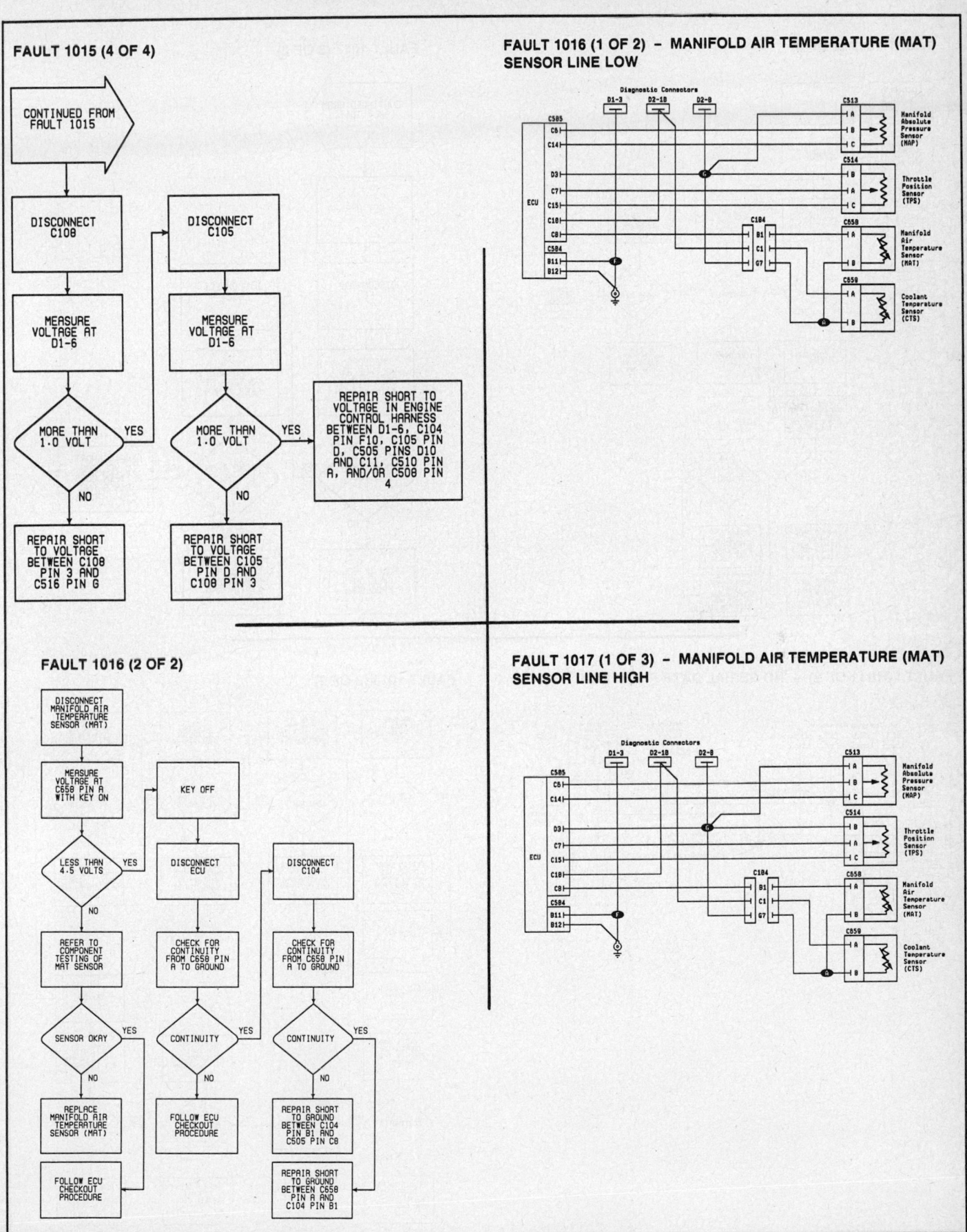

FAULT 1015 (4 OF 4)

CONTINUED FROM FAULT 1015

DISCONNECT C108 → MEASURE VOLTAGE AT D1-6 → MORE THAN 1.0 VOLT
- YES →
- NO → REPAIR SHORT TO VOLTAGE BETWEEN C108 PIN 3 AND C516 PIN G

DISCONNECT C105 → MEASURE VOLTAGE AT D1-6 → MORE THAN 1.0 VOLT
- YES → REPAIR SHORT TO VOLTAGE IN ENGINE CONTROL HARNESS BETWEEN D1-6, C104 PIN F10, C105 PIN D, C505 PINS D10 AND C11, C510 PIN A, AND/OR C508 PIN 4
- NO → REPAIR SHORT TO VOLTAGE BETWEEN C105 PIN D AND C108 PIN 3

FAULT 1016 (1 OF 2) – MANIFOLD AIR TEMPERATURE (MAT) SENSOR LINE LOW

FAULT 1016 (2 OF 2)

DISCONNECT MANIFOLD AIR TEMPERATURE SENSOR (MAT) → MEASURE VOLTAGE AT C658 PIN A WITH KEY ON → LESS THAN 4.5 VOLTS
- YES → KEY OFF → DISCONNECT ECU → CHECK FOR CONTINUITY FROM C658 PIN A TO GROUND → CONTINUITY
  - YES → DISCONNECT C104 → CHECK FOR CONTINUITY FROM C658 PIN A TO GROUND → CONTINUITY
    - YES → REPAIR SHORT TO GROUND BETWEEN C104 PIN B1 AND C505 PIN C8
    - NO → REPAIR SHORT TO GROUND BETWEEN C658 PIN A AND C104 PIN B1
  - NO → FOLLOW ECU CHECKOUT PROCEDURE
- NO → REFER TO COMPONENT TESTING OF MAT SENSOR → SENSOR OKAY
  - YES →
  - NO → REPLACE MANIFOLD AIR TEMPERATURE SENSOR (MAT) → FOLLOW ECU CHECKOUT PROCEDURE

FAULT 1017 (1 OF 3) – MANIFOLD AIR TEMPERATURE (MAT) SENSOR LINE HIGH

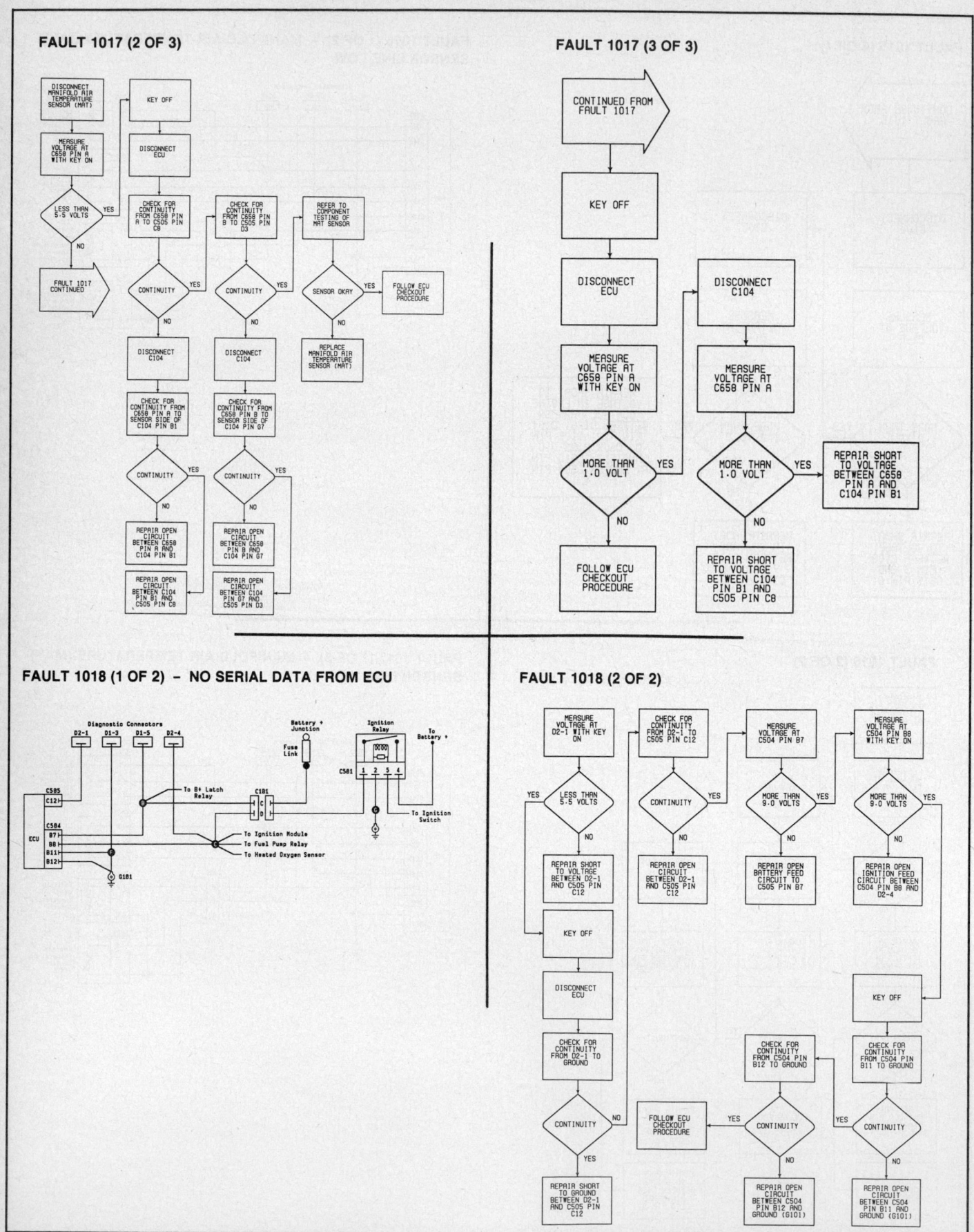

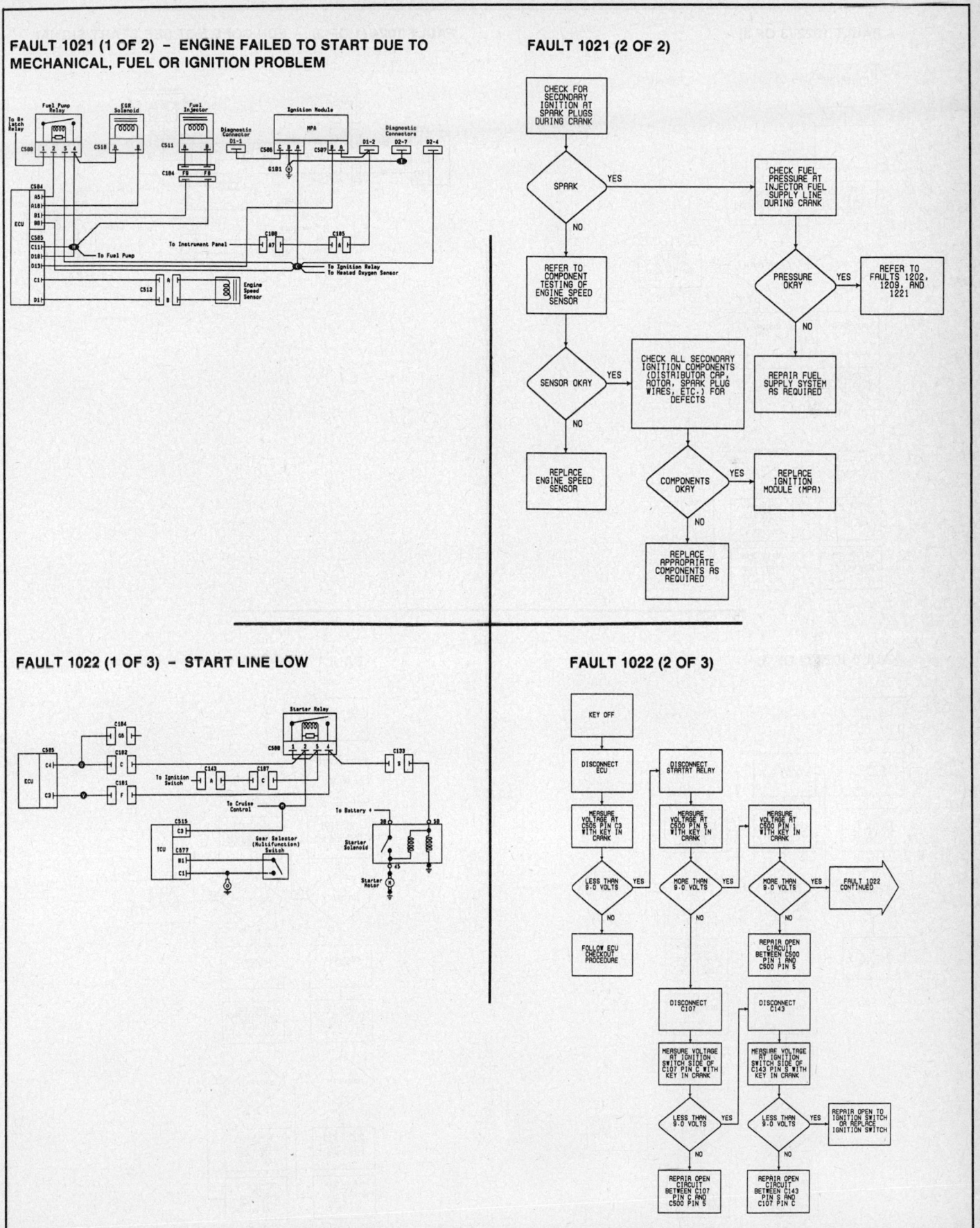

FAULT 1021 (1 OF 2) — ENGINE FAILED TO START DUE TO MECHANICAL, FUEL OR IGNITION PROBLEM

FAULT 1021 (2 OF 2)

FAULT 1022 (1 OF 3) — START LINE LOW

FAULT 1022 (2 OF 3)

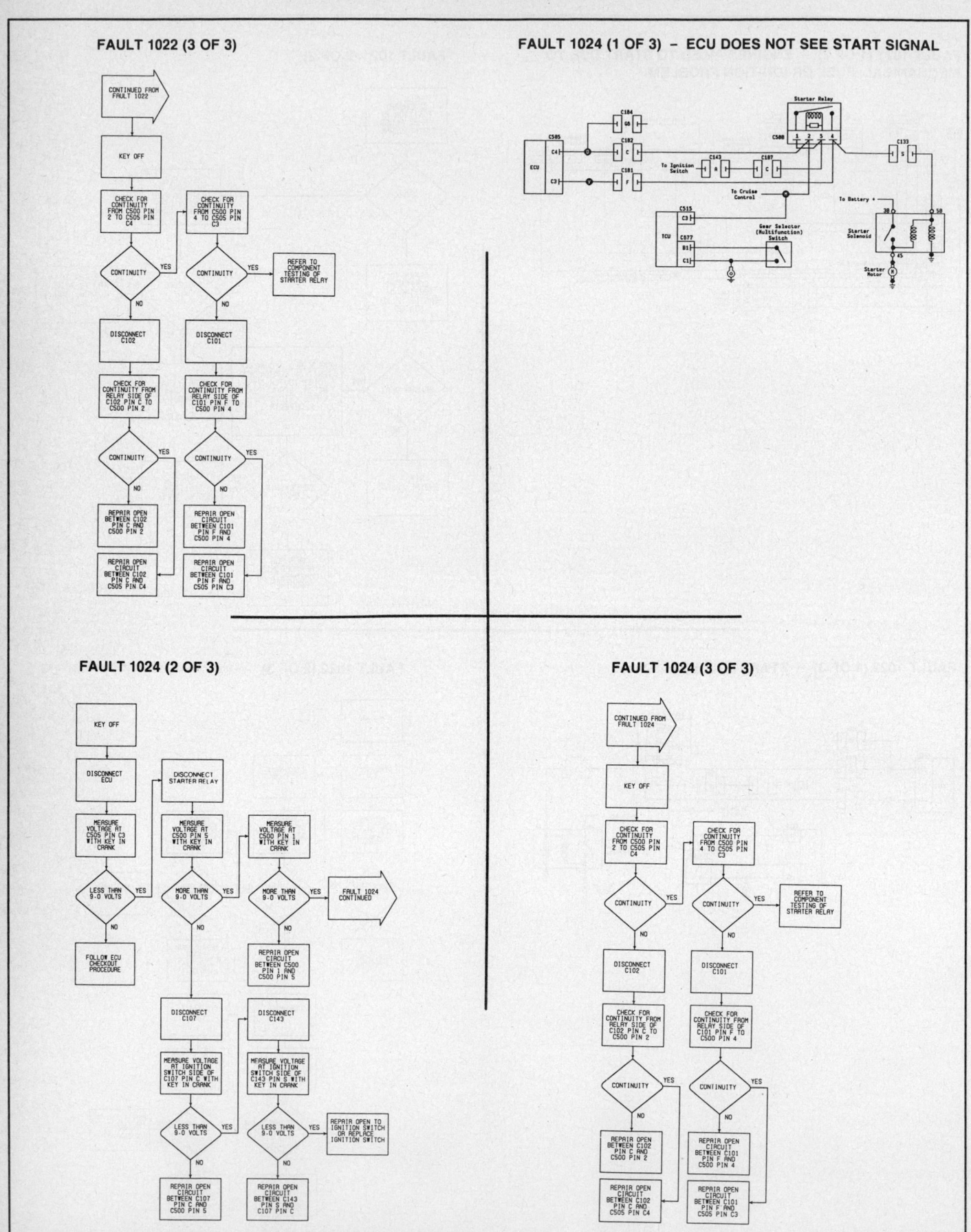

FAULT 1022 (3 OF 3)

FAULT 1024 (1 OF 3) – ECU DOES NOT SEE START SIGNAL

FAULT 1024 (2 OF 3)

FAULT 1024 (3 OF 3)

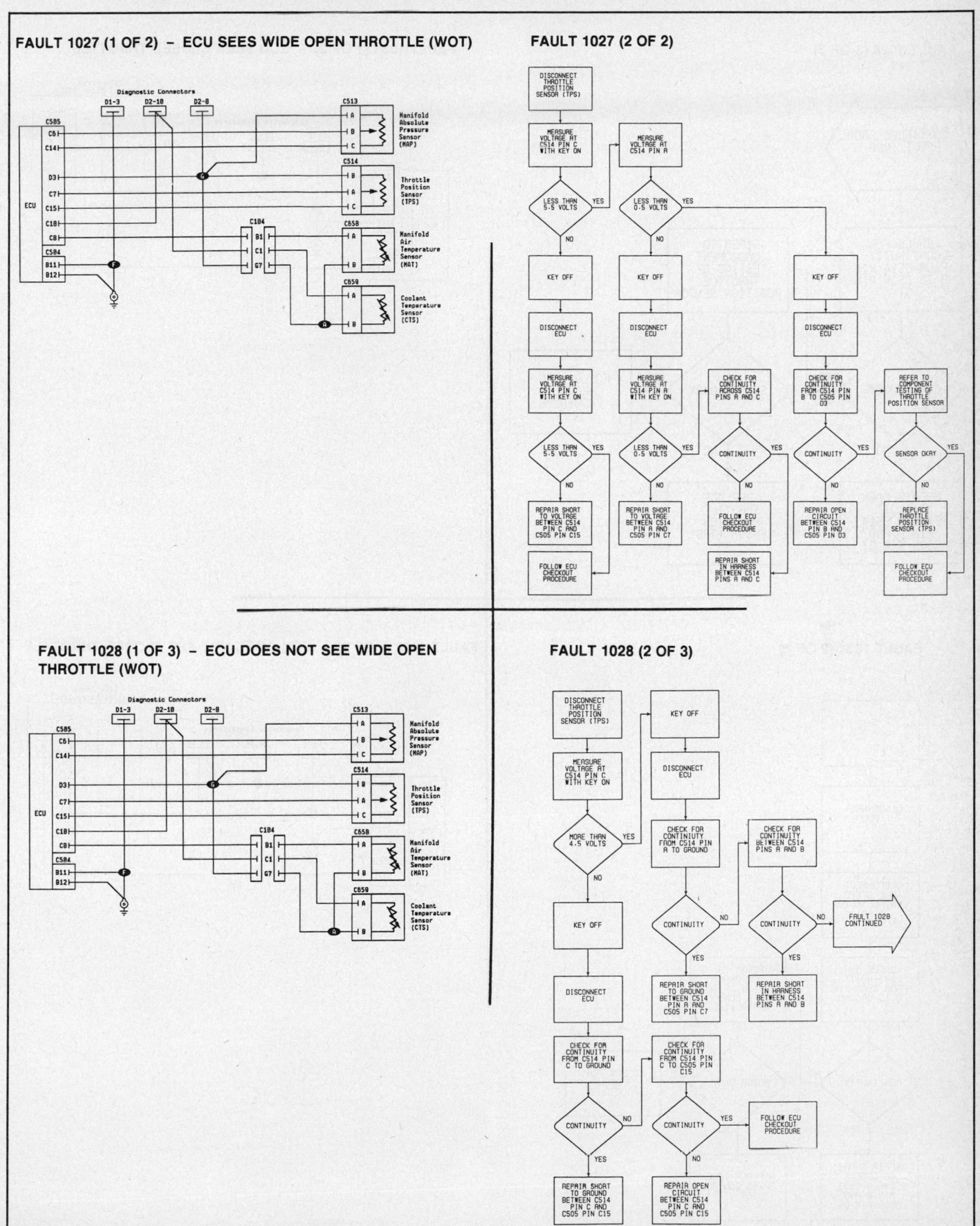

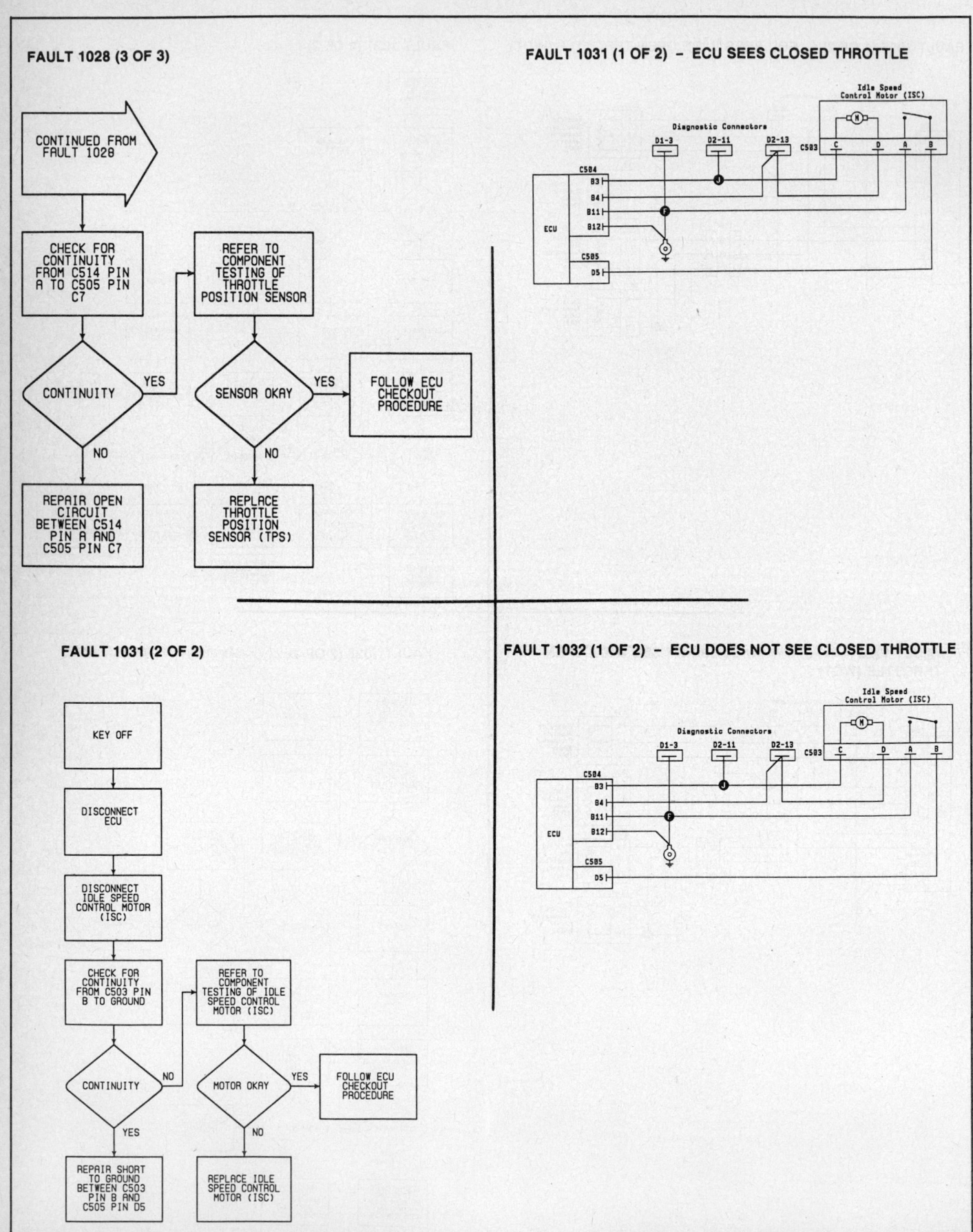

FAULT 1028 (3 OF 3)

CONTINUED FROM
FAULT 1028

CHECK FOR
CONTINUITY
FROM C514 PIN
A TO C505 PIN
C7

REFER TO
COMPONENT
TESTING OF
THROTTLE
POSITION SENSOR

CONTINUITY — YES → SENSOR OKAY — YES → FOLLOW ECU
CHECKOUT
PROCEDURE

NO

REPAIR OPEN
CIRCUIT
BETWEEN C514
PIN A AND
C505 PIN C7

NO

REPLACE
THROTTLE
POSITION
SENSOR (TPS)

FAULT 1031 (1 OF 2) – ECU SEES CLOSED THROTTLE

FAULT 1031 (2 OF 2)

KEY OFF

DISCONNECT
ECU

DISCONNECT
IDLE SPEED
CONTROL MOTOR
(ISC)

CHECK FOR
CONTINUITY
FROM C503 PIN
B TO GROUND

REFER TO
COMPONENT
TESTING OF IDLE
SPEED CONTROL
MOTOR (ISC)

CONTINUITY — NO → MOTOR OKAY — YES → FOLLOW ECU
CHECKOUT
PROCEDURE

YES

REPAIR SHORT
TO GROUND
BETWEEN C503
PIN B AND
C505 PIN D5

NO

REPLACE IDLE
SPEED CONTROL
MOTOR (ISC)

FAULT 1032 (1 OF 2) – ECU DOES NOT SEE CLOSED THROTTLE

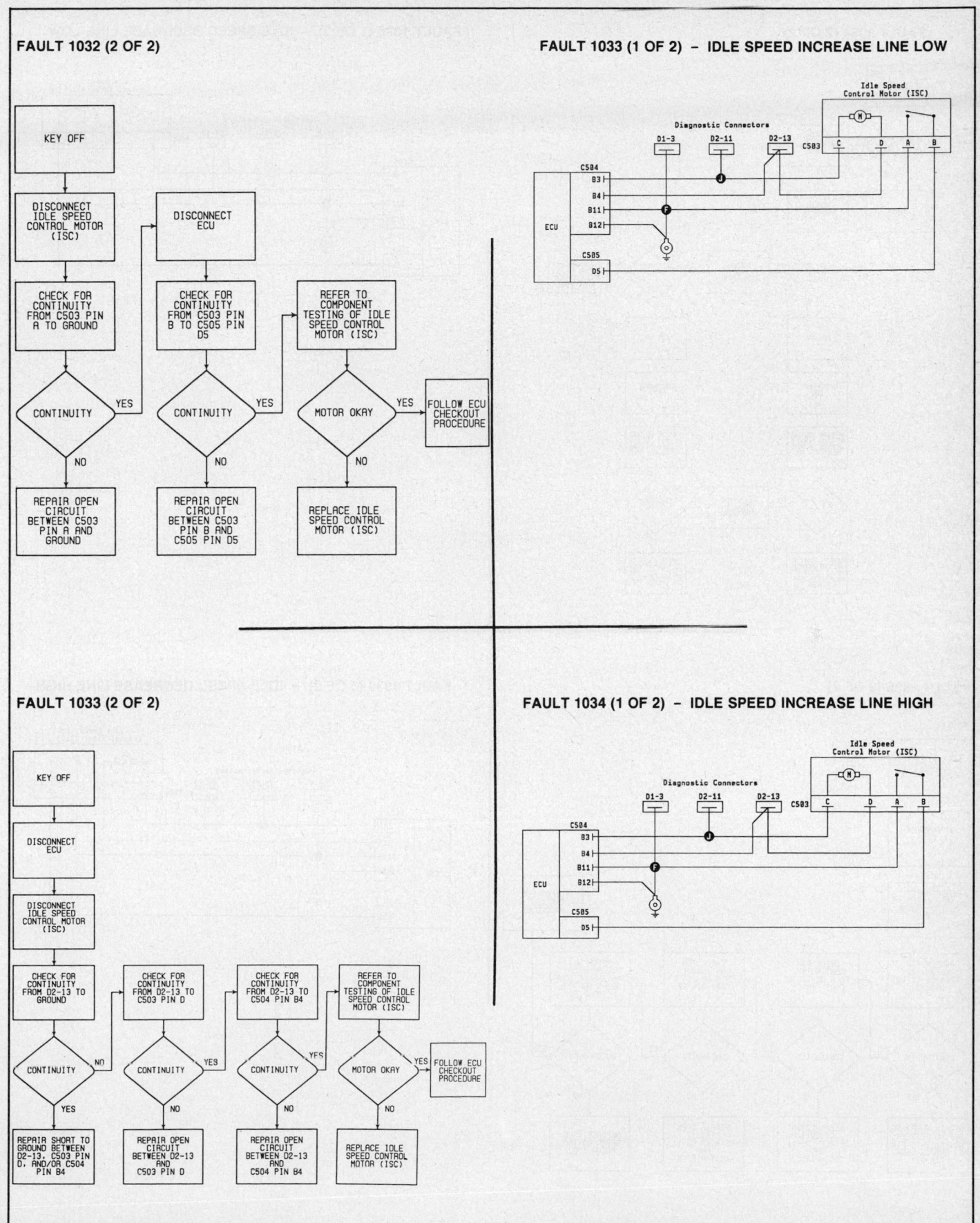

FAULT 1032 (2 OF 2)

FAULT 1033 (1 OF 2) – IDLE SPEED INCREASE LINE LOW

FAULT 1033 (2 OF 2)

FAULT 1034 (1 OF 2) – IDLE SPEED INCREASE LINE HIGH

KEY OFF

DISCONNECT IDLE SPEED CONTROL MOTOR (ISC)

DISCONNECT ECU

CHECK FOR CONTINUITY FROM C503 PIN A TO GROUND

CHECK FOR CONTINUITY FROM C503 PIN B TO C505 PIN D5

REFER TO COMPONENT TESTING OF IDLE SPEED CONTROL MOTOR (ISC)

CONTINUITY — YES

CONTINUITY — YES

MOTOR OKAY — YES

FOLLOW ECU CHECKOUT PROCEDURE

NO

REPAIR OPEN CIRCUIT BETWEEN C503 PIN A AND GROUND

REPAIR OPEN CIRCUIT BETWEEN C503 PIN B AND C505 PIN D5

REPLACE IDLE SPEED CONTROL MOTOR (ISC)

KEY OFF

DISCONNECT ECU

DISCONNECT IDLE SPEED CONTROL MOTOR (ISC)

CHECK FOR CONTINUITY FROM D2-13 TO GROUND

CHECK FOR CONTINUITY FROM D2-13 TO C503 PIN D

CHECK FOR CONTINUITY FROM D2-13 TO C504 PIN B4

REFER TO COMPONENT TESTING OF IDLE SPEED CONTROL MOTOR (ISC)

CONTINUITY — NO

CONTINUITY — YES

CONTINUITY — YES

MOTOR OKAY — YES

FOLLOW ECU CHECKOUT PROCEDURE

YES / NO / NO / NO

REPAIR SHORT TO GROUND BETWEEN D2-13, C503 PIN D, AND/OR C504 PIN B4

REPAIR OPEN CIRCUIT BETWEEN D2-13 AND C503 PIN D

REPAIR OPEN CIRCUIT BETWEEN D2-13 AND C504 PIN B4

REPLACE IDLE SPEED CONTROL MOTOR (ISC)

Idle Speed Control Motor (ISC)

Diagnostic Connectors

D1-3   D2-11   D2-13   C503   C   D   A   B

C504   B3   B4   B11   B12

ECU

C505   D5

1989 COMPUTERIZED ENGINE CONTROLS
Eagle 2.5L TBI (Cont.)

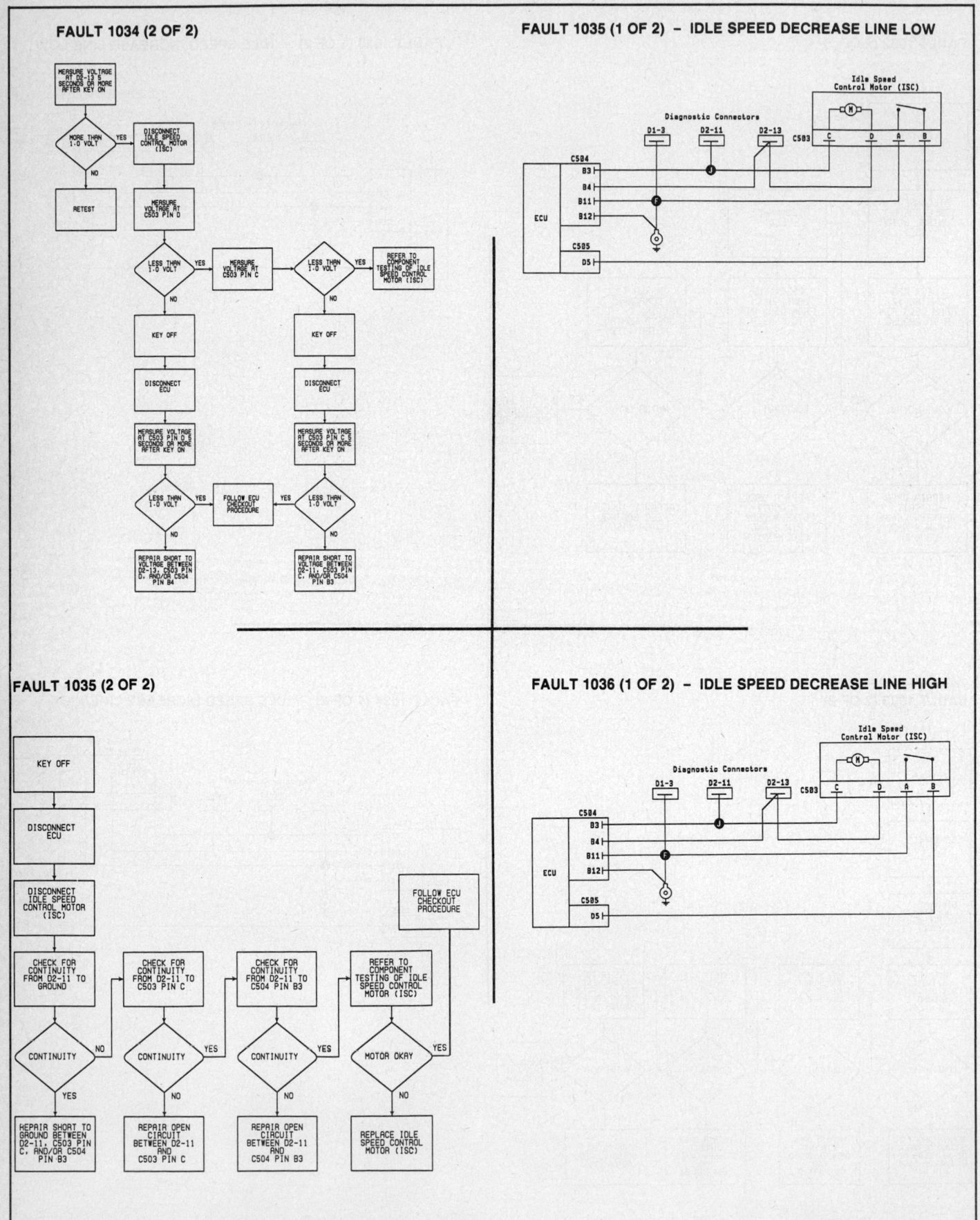

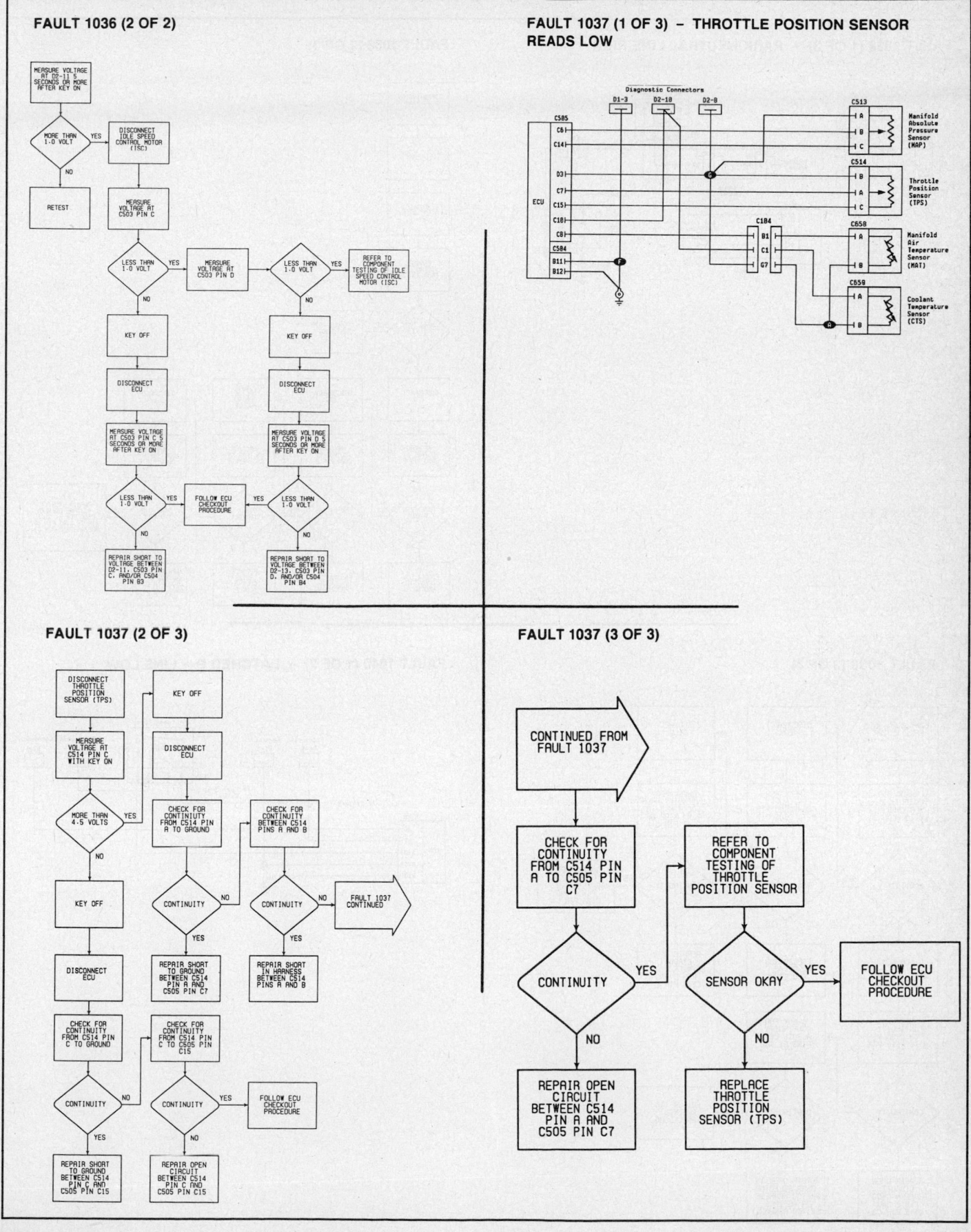

FAULT 1036 (2 OF 2)

FAULT 1037 (1 OF 3) – THROTTLE POSITION SENSOR READS LOW

FAULT 1037 (2 OF 3)

FAULT 1037 (3 OF 3)

1989 COMPUTERIZED ENGINE CONTROLS
Eagle 2.5L TBI (Cont.)

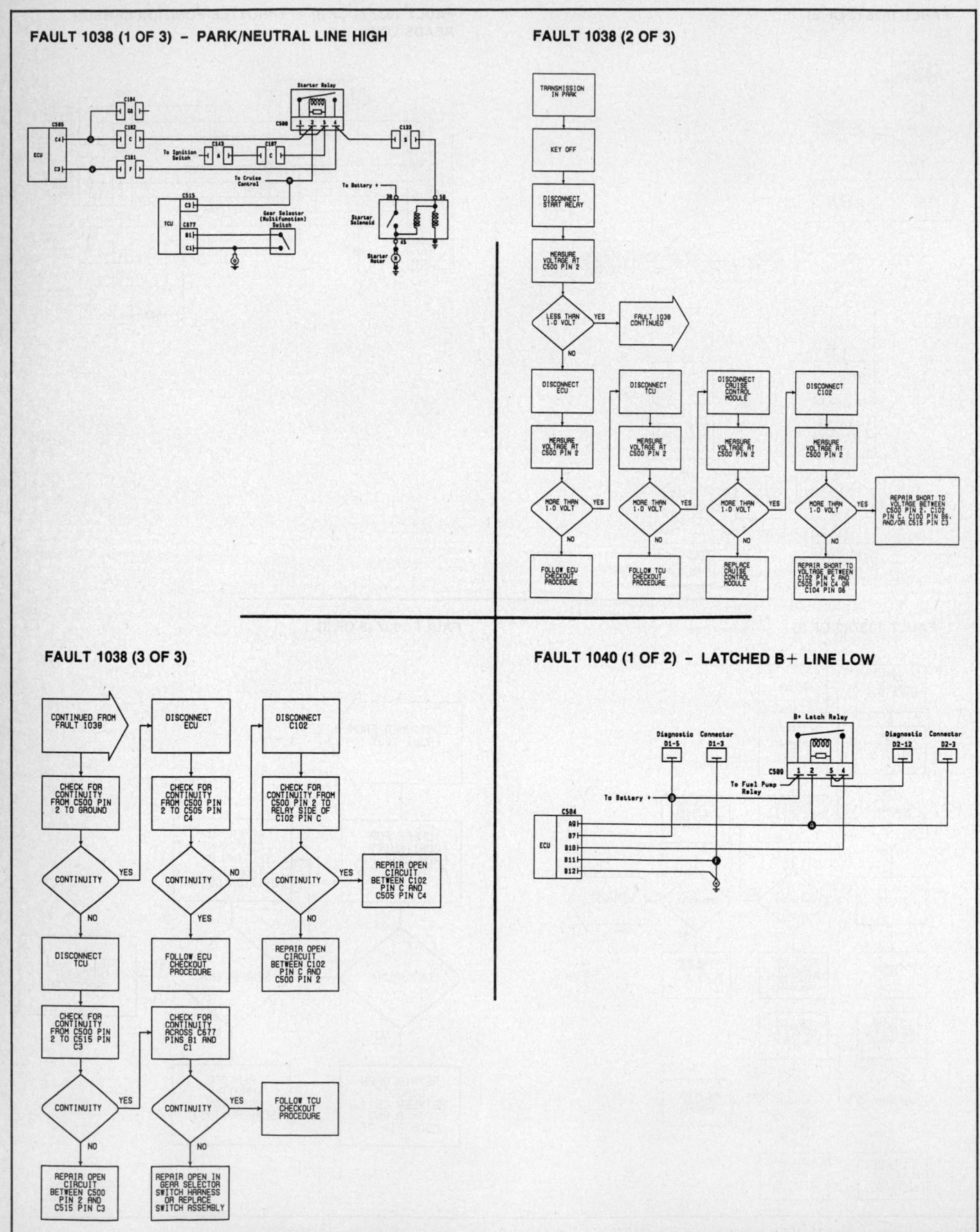

FAULT 1038 (1 OF 3) - PARK/NEUTRAL LINE HIGH

FAULT 1038 (2 OF 3)

FAULT 1038 (3 OF 3)

FAULT 1040 (1 OF 2) - LATCHED B+ LINE LOW

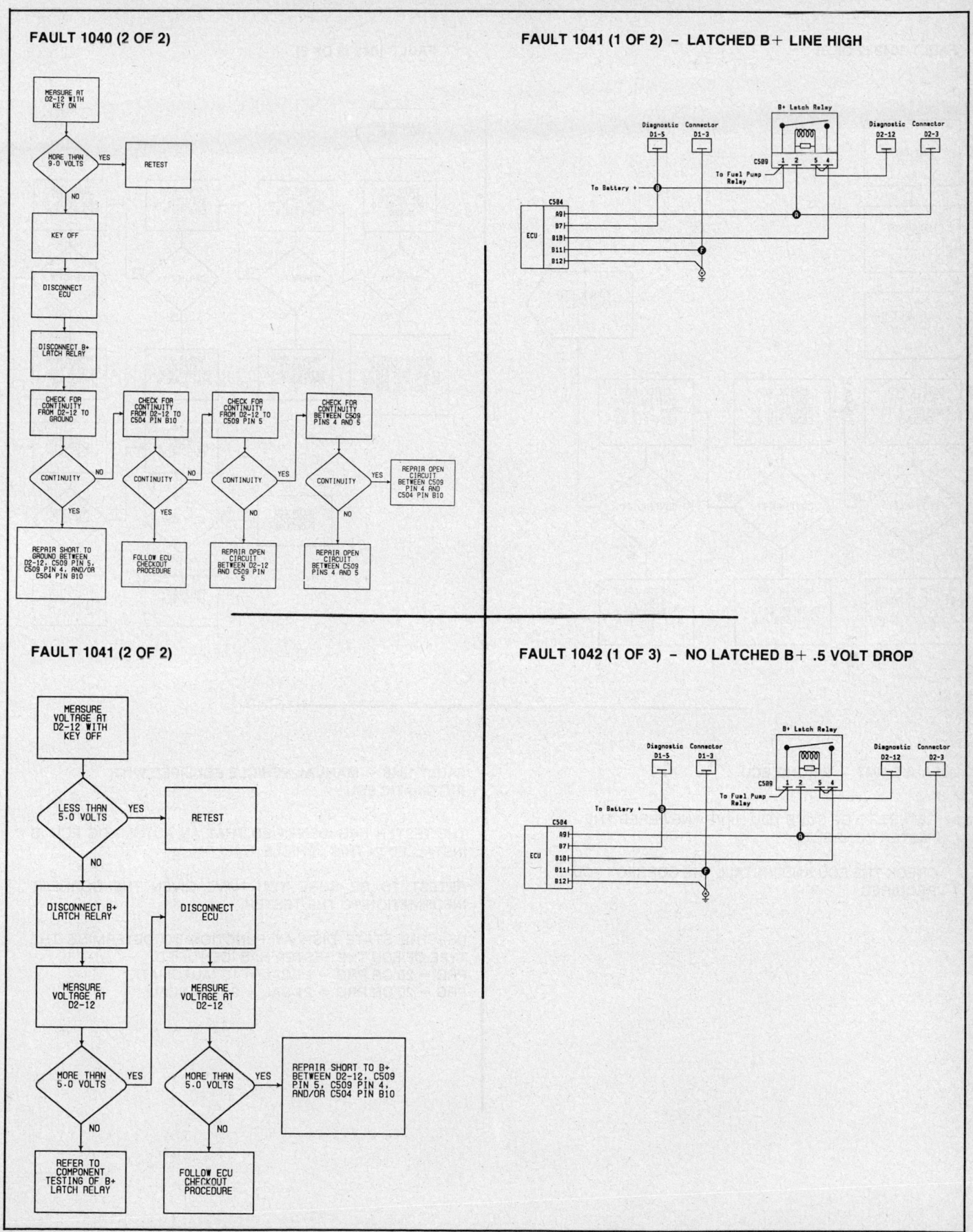

FAULT 1040 (2 OF 2)

FAULT 1041 (1 OF 2) – LATCHED B+ LINE HIGH

FAULT 1041 (2 OF 2)

FAULT 1042 (1 OF 3) – NO LATCHED B+ .5 VOLT DROP

FAULT 1042 (2 OF 3)

FAULT 1042 (3 OF 3)

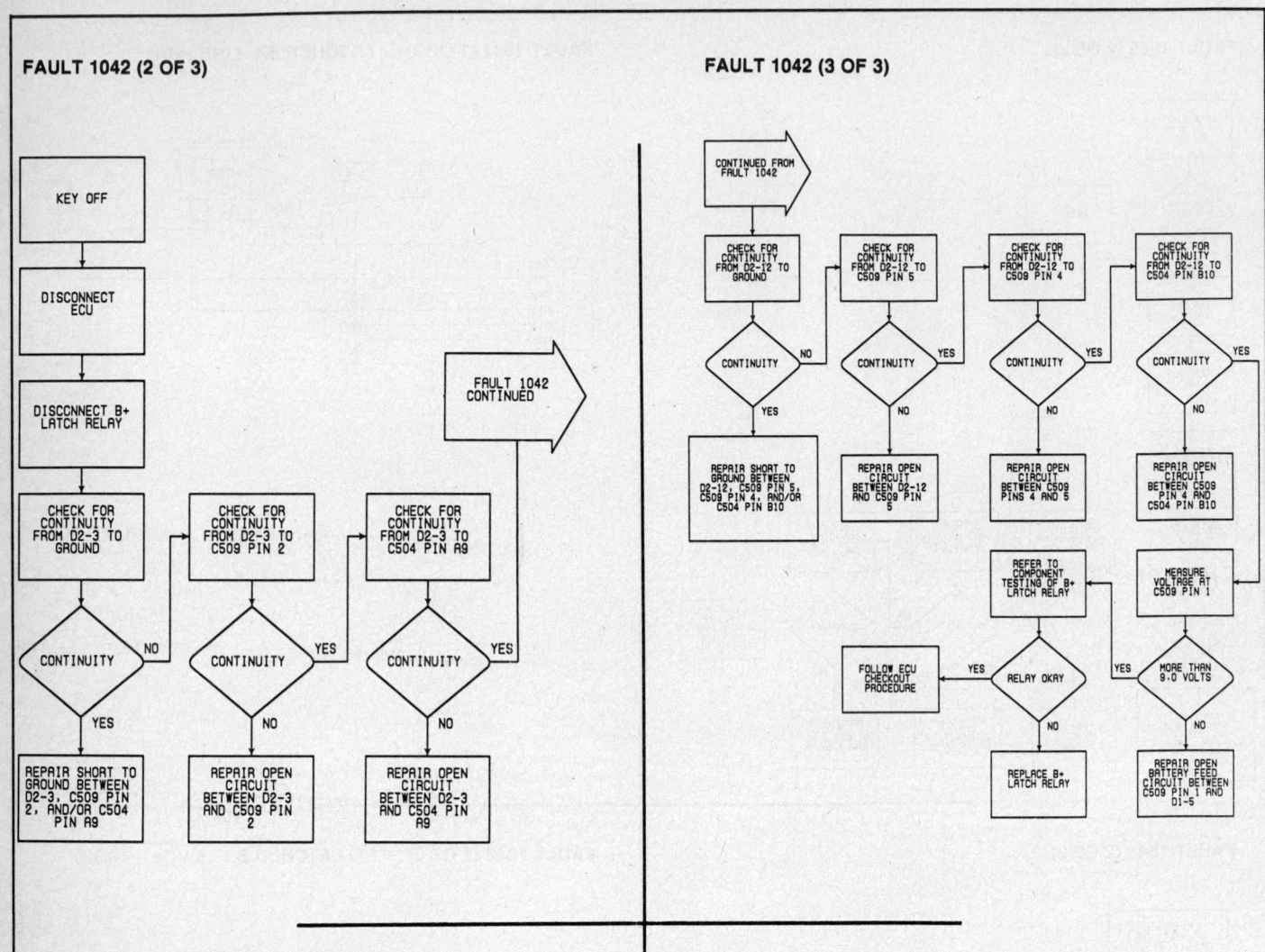

FAULT 1047 - WRONG ECU

RETEST TO BE SURE YOU HAVE ANSWERED THE TESTER CORRECTLY.

CHECK THE ECU AND INSTALL THE CORRECT ECU IF REQUIRED.

FAULT 1048 - MANUAL VEHICLE EQUIPPED WITH AUTOMATIC ECU

THE TESTER HAS IDENTIFIED THAT AN AUTOMATIC ECU IS INSTALLED IN THIS VEHICLE.

RETEST TO BE SURE YOU HAVE GIVEN THE CORRECT INFORMATION TO THE TESTER.

USE THE STATE DISPLAY FUNCTION TO DETERMINE THE TYPE OF ECU THE TESTER HAS IDENTIFIED.
PRG = 20 OR PRG = 21 CAL = 1C (AUTOMATIC)
PRG = 20 OR PRG = 21 CAL = 9C (MANUAL)

FAULT 1049 – AUTOMATIC VEHICLE EQUIPPED WITH MANUAL ECU

THE TESTER HAS IDENTIFIED THAT A MANUAL ECU IS INSTALLED IN THIS VEHICLE.

RETEST TO BE SURE YOU HAVE GIVEN THE CORRECT INFORMATION TO THE TESTER.

USE THE STATE DISPLAY FUNCTION TO DETERMINE THE TYPE OF ECU THE TESTER HAS IDENTIFIED.
PRG = 20 OR PRG = 21 CAL = 1C (AUTOMATIC)
PRG = 20 OR PRG = 21 CAL = 9C (MANUAL)

FAULT 1050 (1 OF 2) – IDLE SPEED LESS THAN 500 RPM

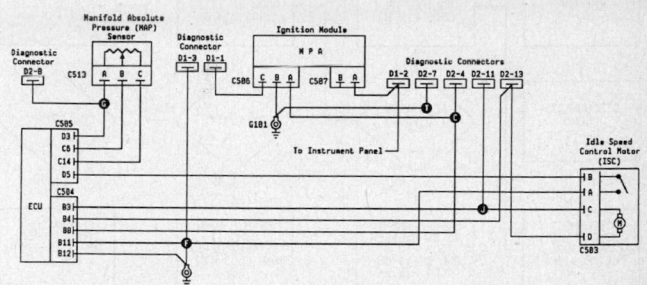

FAULT 1050 (2 OF 2)

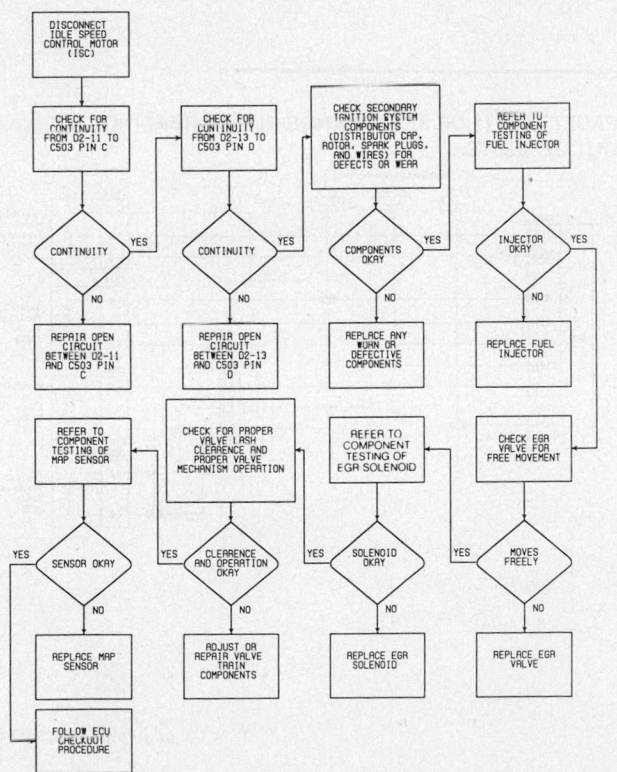

FAULT 1051 (1 OF 2) – IDLE SPEED GREATER THAN 2000 RPM

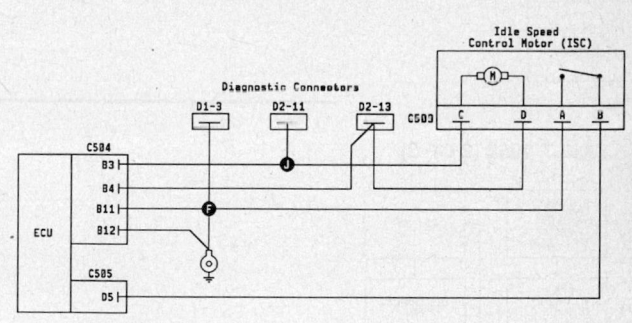

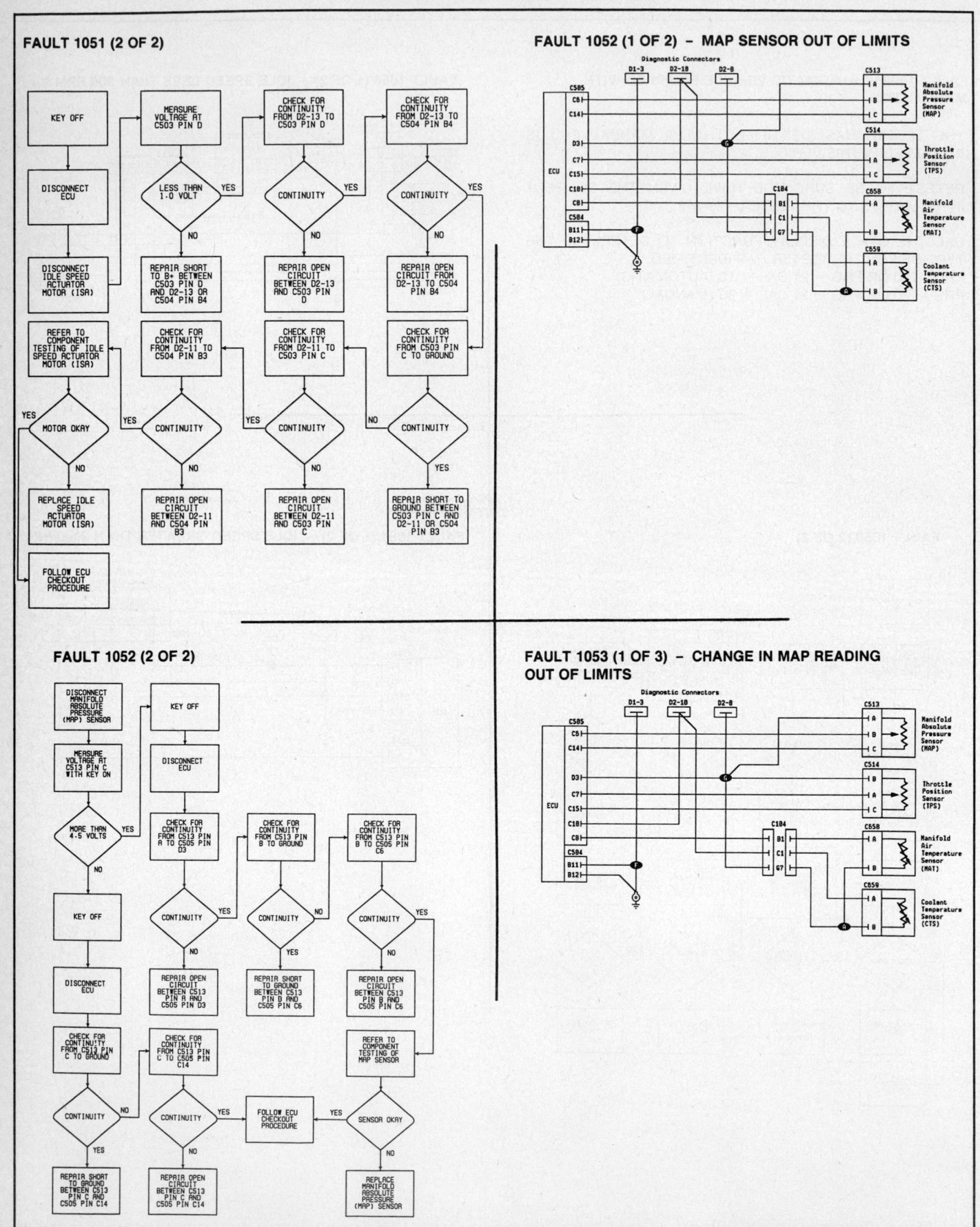

FAULT 1051 (2 OF 2)

FAULT 1052 (1 OF 2) – MAP SENSOR OUT OF LIMITS

FAULT 1052 (2 OF 2)

FAULT 1053 (1 OF 3) – CHANGE IN MAP READING OUT OF LIMITS

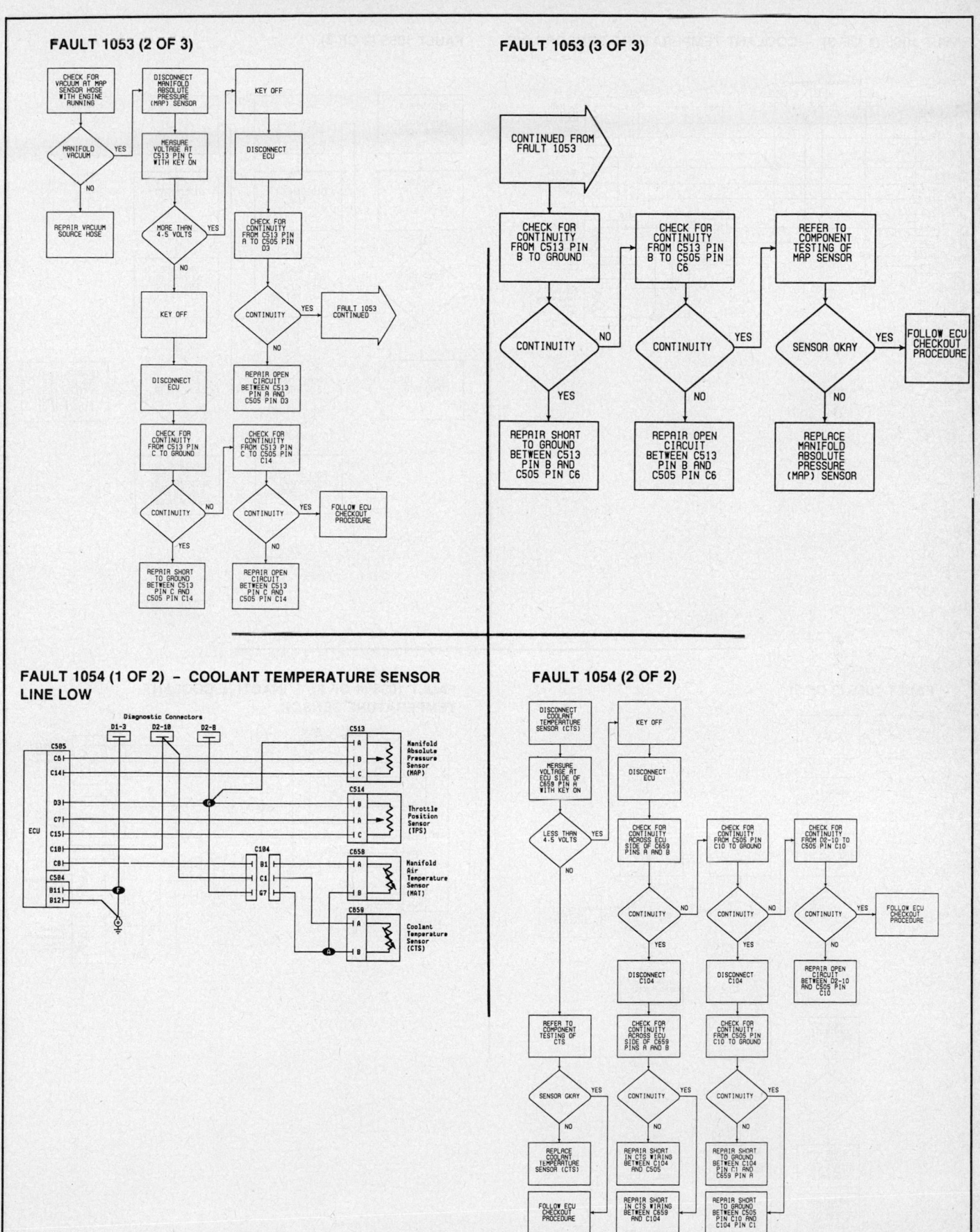

FAULT 1053 (2 OF 3)

FAULT 1053 (3 OF 3)

FAULT 1054 (1 OF 2) – COOLANT TEMPERATURE SENSOR LINE LOW

FAULT 1054 (2 OF 2)

1989 COMPUTERIZED ENGINE CONTROLS
Eagle 2.5L TBI (Cont.)

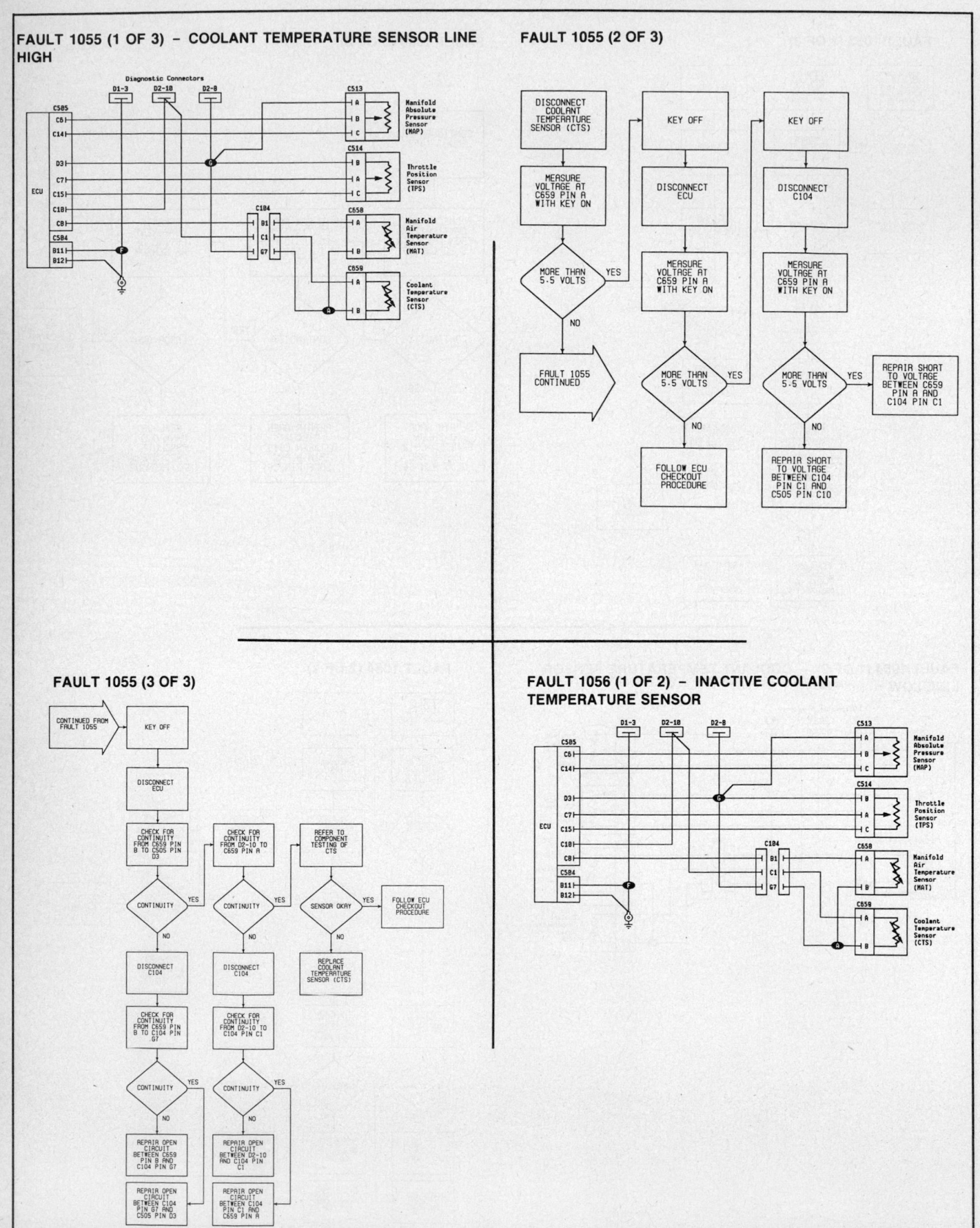

FAULT 1055 (1 OF 3) – COOLANT TEMPERATURE SENSOR LINE HIGH

FAULT 1055 (2 OF 3)

FAULT 1055 (3 OF 3)

FAULT 1056 (1 OF 2) – INACTIVE COOLANT TEMPERATURE SENSOR

FAULT 1056 (2 OF 2)

REFER TO COMPONENT TESTING OF COOLANT
TEMPERATURE SENSOR (CTS).

FAULT 1057 (1 OF 2) – KNOCK CIRCUIT SHORTED

FAULT 1057 (2 OF 2)

FAULT 1058 (1 OF 3) – KNOCK VALUE OUT OF LIMITS

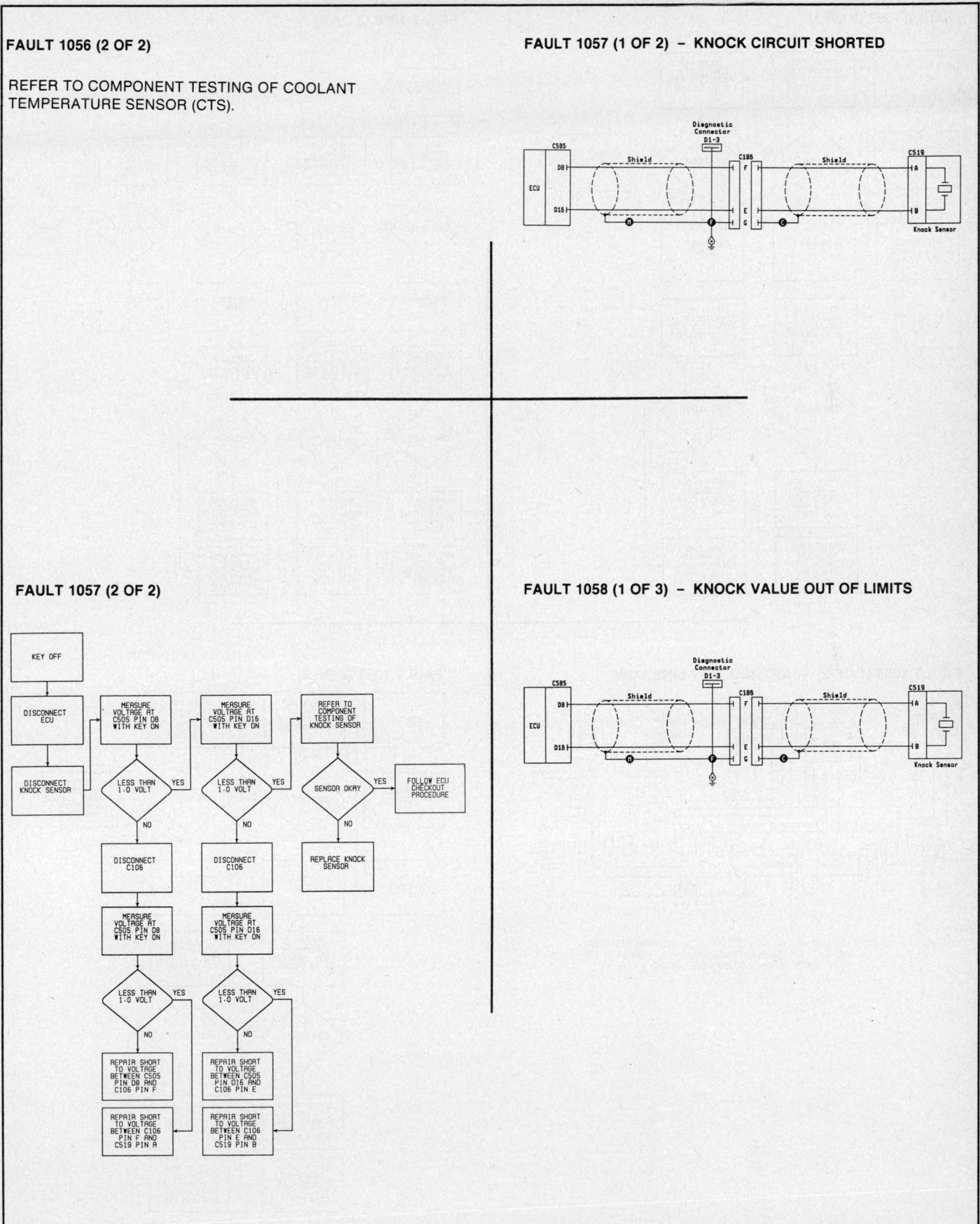

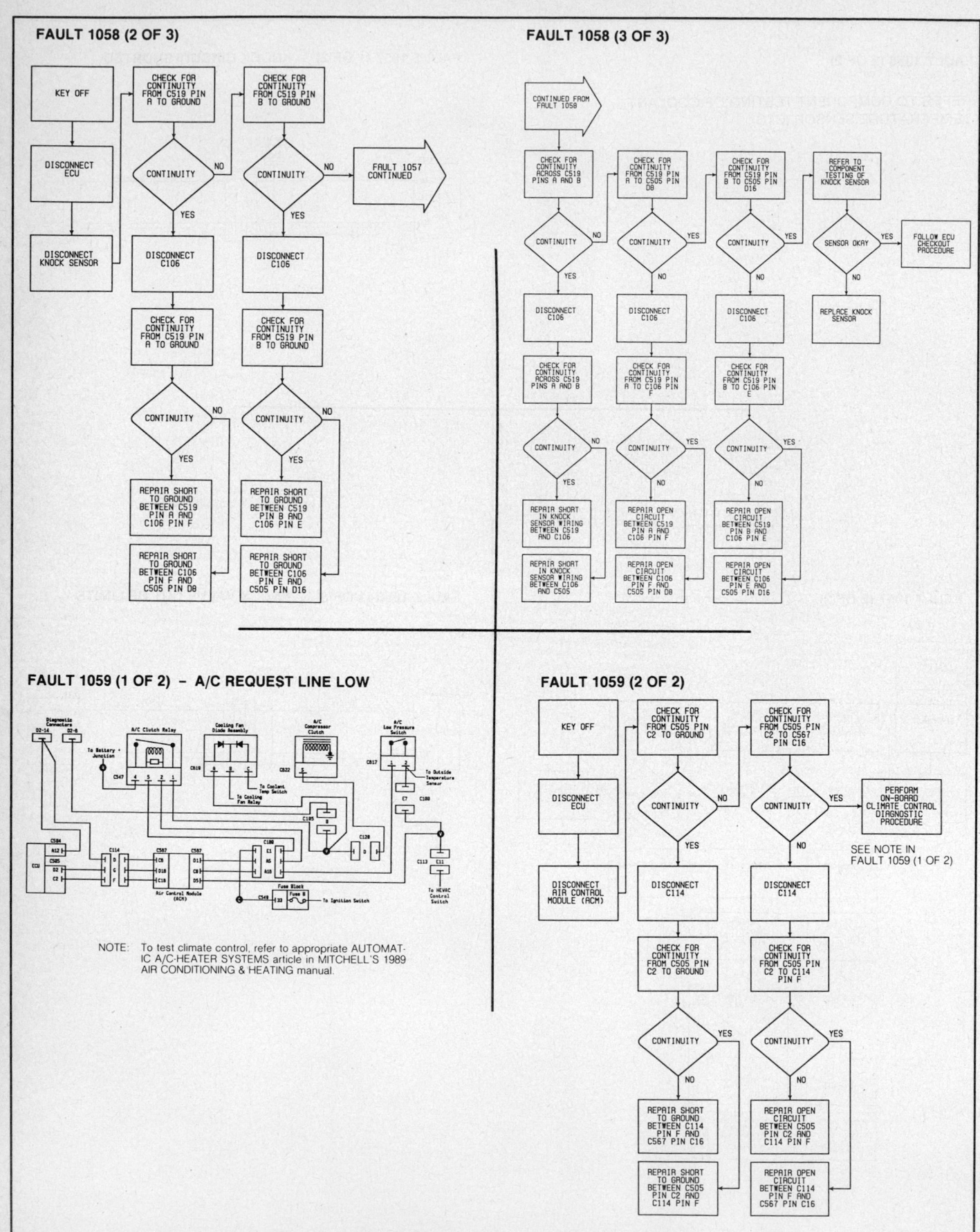

FAULT 1058 (2 OF 3)

FAULT 1058 (3 OF 3)

FAULT 1059 (1 OF 2) – A/C REQUEST LINE LOW

NOTE: To test climate control, refer to appropriate AUTOMATIC A/C-HEATER SYSTEMS article in MITCHELL'S 1989 AIR CONDITIONING & HEATING manual.

FAULT 1059 (2 OF 2)

SEE NOTE IN FAULT 1059 (1 OF 2)

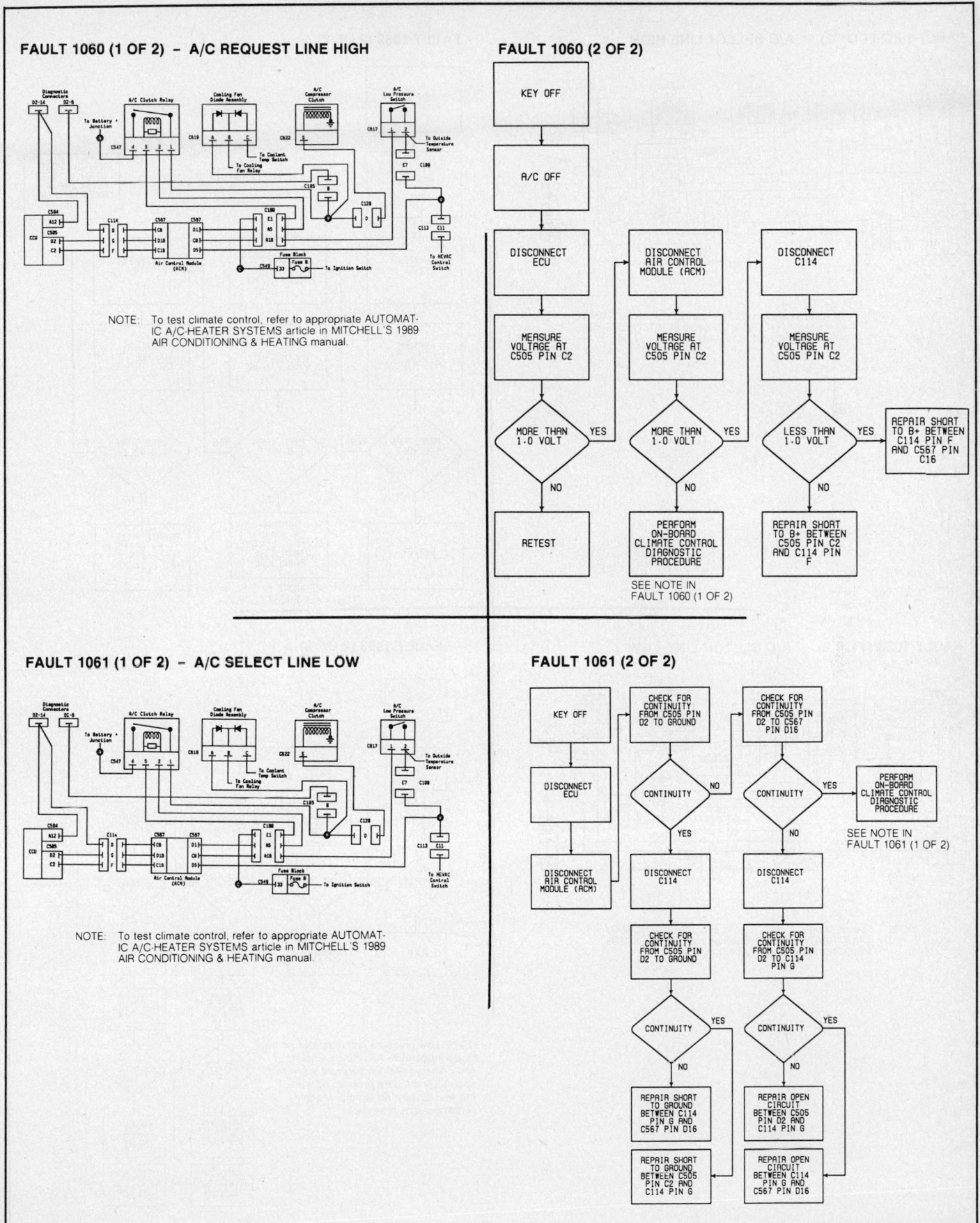

1989 COMPUTERIZED ENGINE CONTROLS
Eagle 2.5L TBI (Cont.)

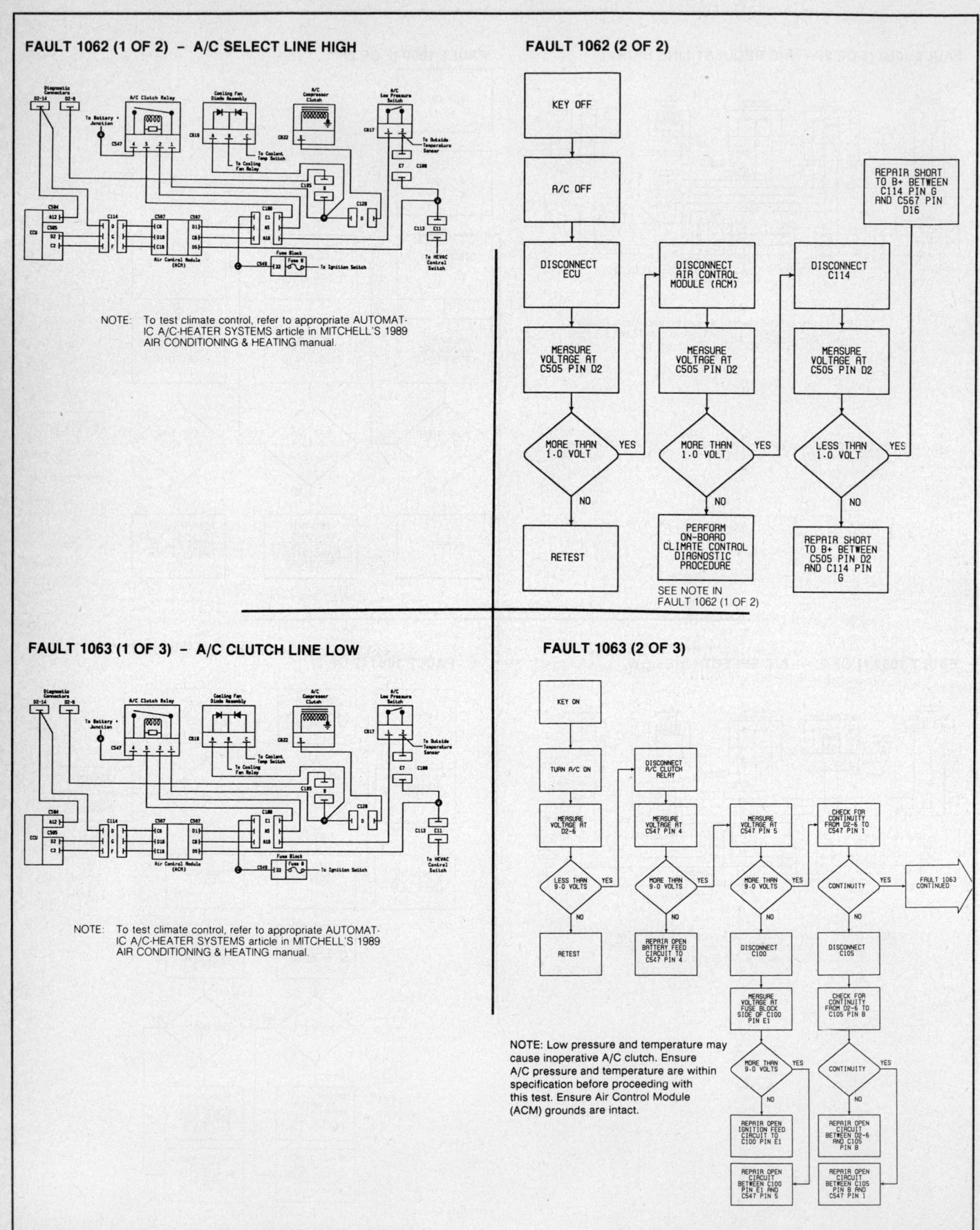

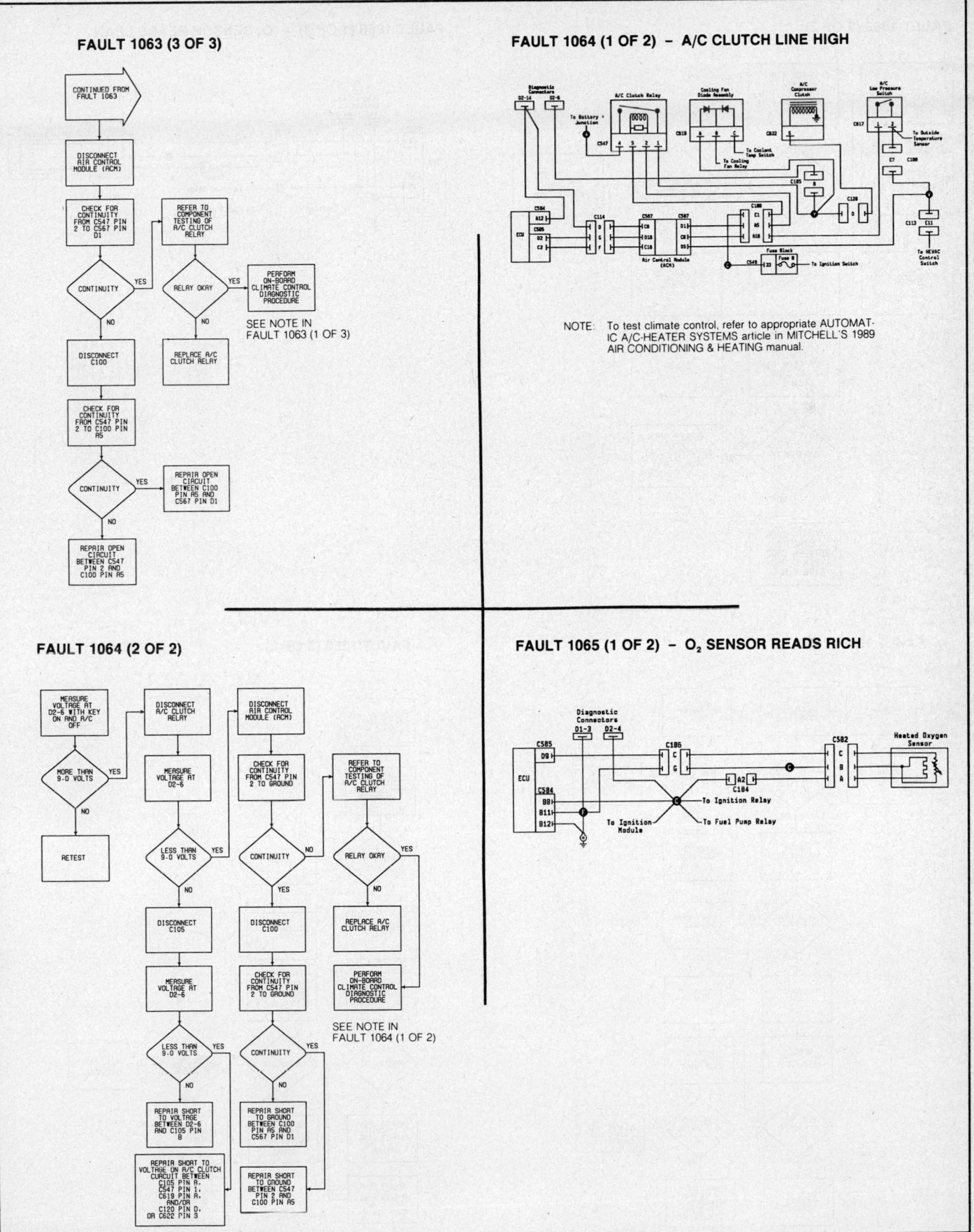

FAULT 1063 (3 OF 3)

FAULT 1064 (1 OF 2) – A/C CLUTCH LINE HIGH

NOTE: To test climate control, refer to appropriate AUTOMATIC A/C-HEATER SYSTEMS article in MITCHELL'S 1989 AIR CONDITIONING & HEATING manual.

FAULT 1064 (2 OF 2)

FAULT 1065 (1 OF 2) – O₂ SENSOR READS RICH

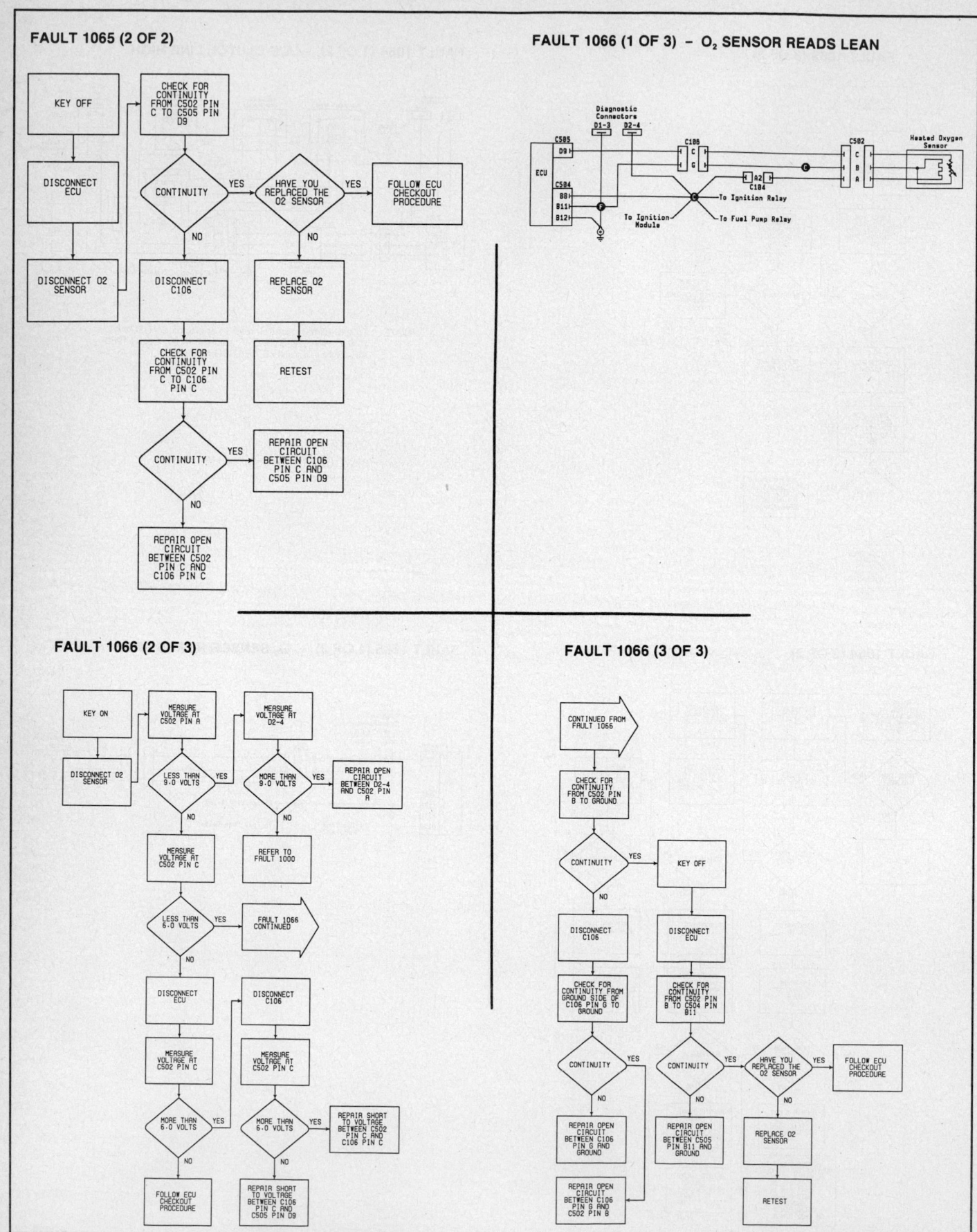

FAULT 1065 (2 OF 2)

FAULT 1066 (1 OF 3) – O₂ SENSOR READS LEAN

FAULT 1066 (2 OF 3)

FAULT 1066 (3 OF 3)

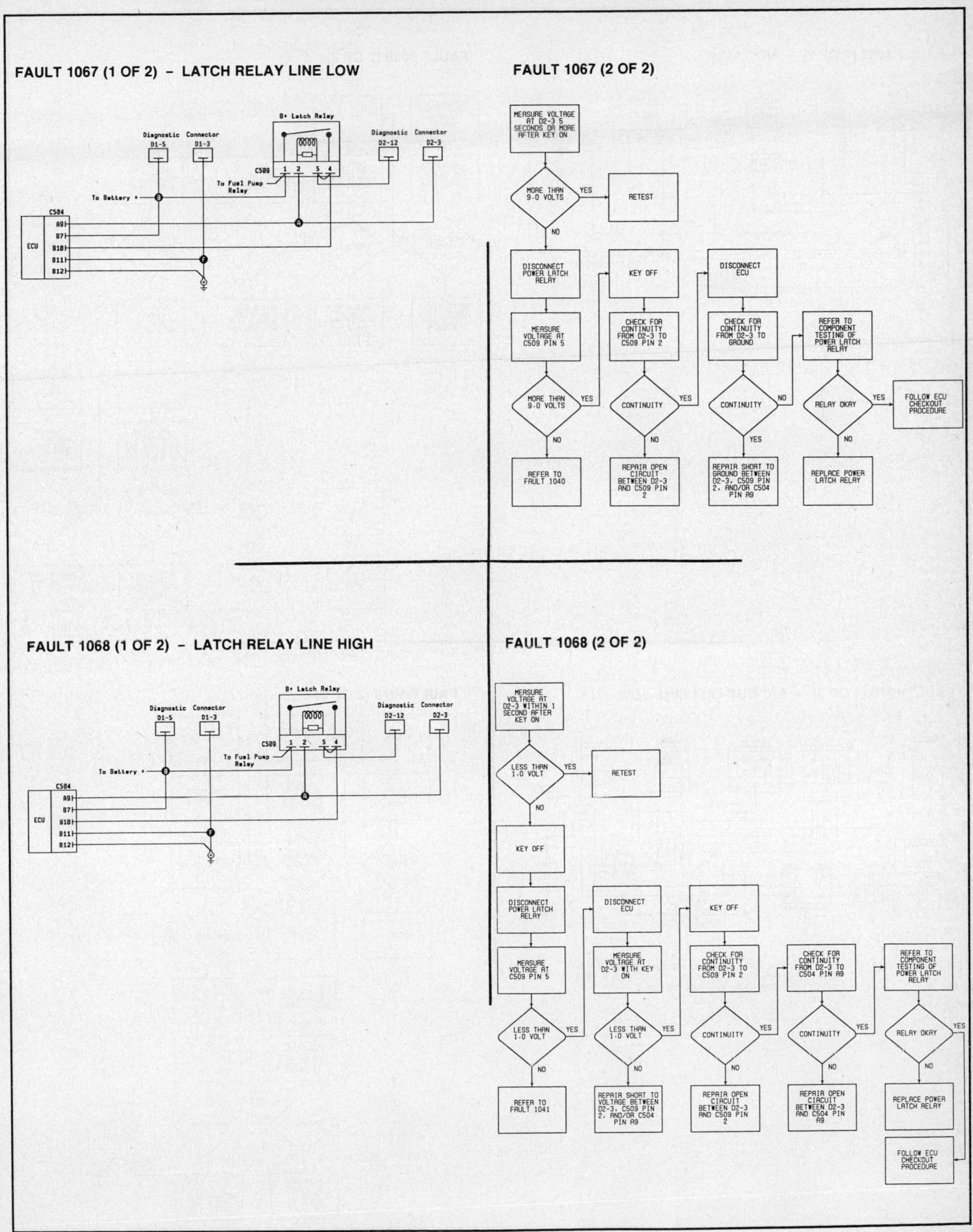

FAULT 1067 (1 OF 2) – LATCH RELAY LINE LOW

FAULT 1067 (2 OF 2)

FAULT 1068 (1 OF 2) – LATCH RELAY LINE HIGH

FAULT 1068 (2 OF 2)

1989 COMPUTERIZED ENGINE CONTROLS
Eagle 2.5L TBI (Cont.)

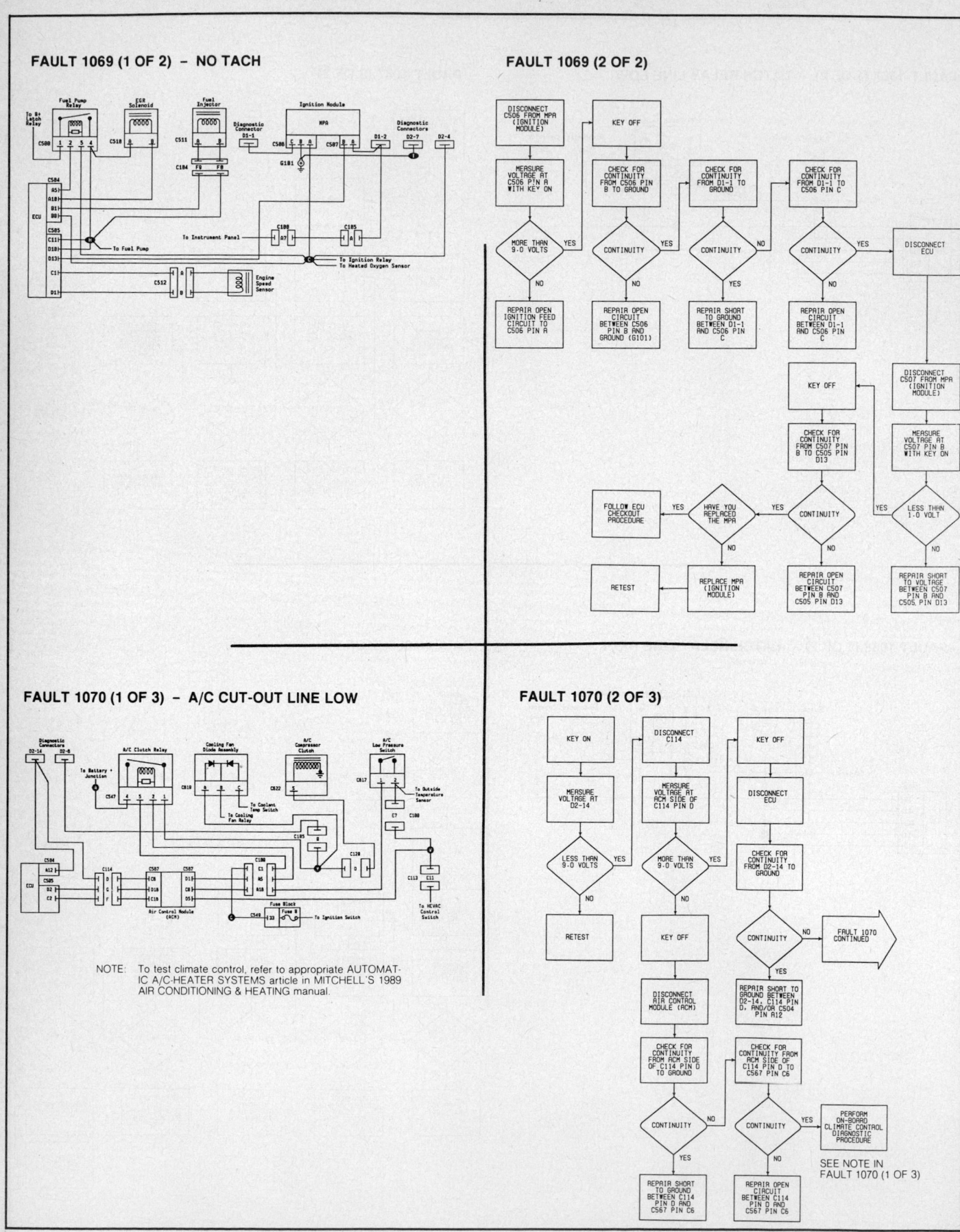

FAULT 1069 (1 OF 2) – NO TACH

FAULT 1069 (2 OF 2)

FAULT 1070 (1 OF 3) – A/C CUT-OUT LINE LOW

NOTE: To test climate control, refer to appropriate AUTOMATIC A/C-HEATER SYSTEMS article in MITCHELL'S 1989 AIR CONDITIONING & HEATING manual.

FAULT 1070 (2 OF 3)

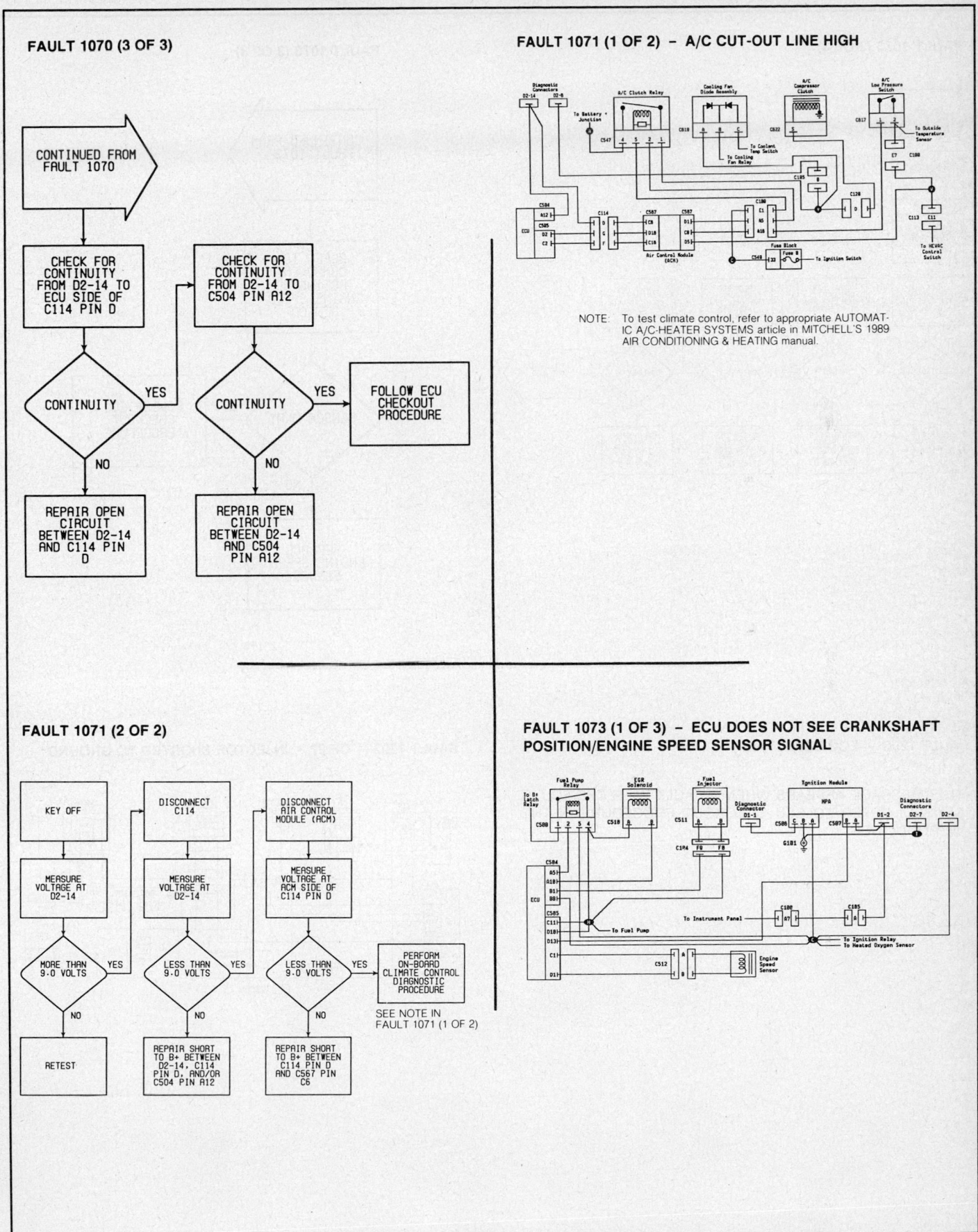

FAULT 1070 (3 OF 3)

FAULT 1071 (1 OF 2) – A/C CUT-OUT LINE HIGH

NOTE: To test climate control, refer to appropriate AUTOMATIC A/C-HEATER SYSTEMS article in MITCHELL'S 1989 AIR CONDITIONING & HEATING manual.

FAULT 1071 (2 OF 2)

FAULT 1073 (1 OF 3) – ECU DOES NOT SEE CRANKSHAFT POSITION/ENGINE SPEED SENSOR SIGNAL

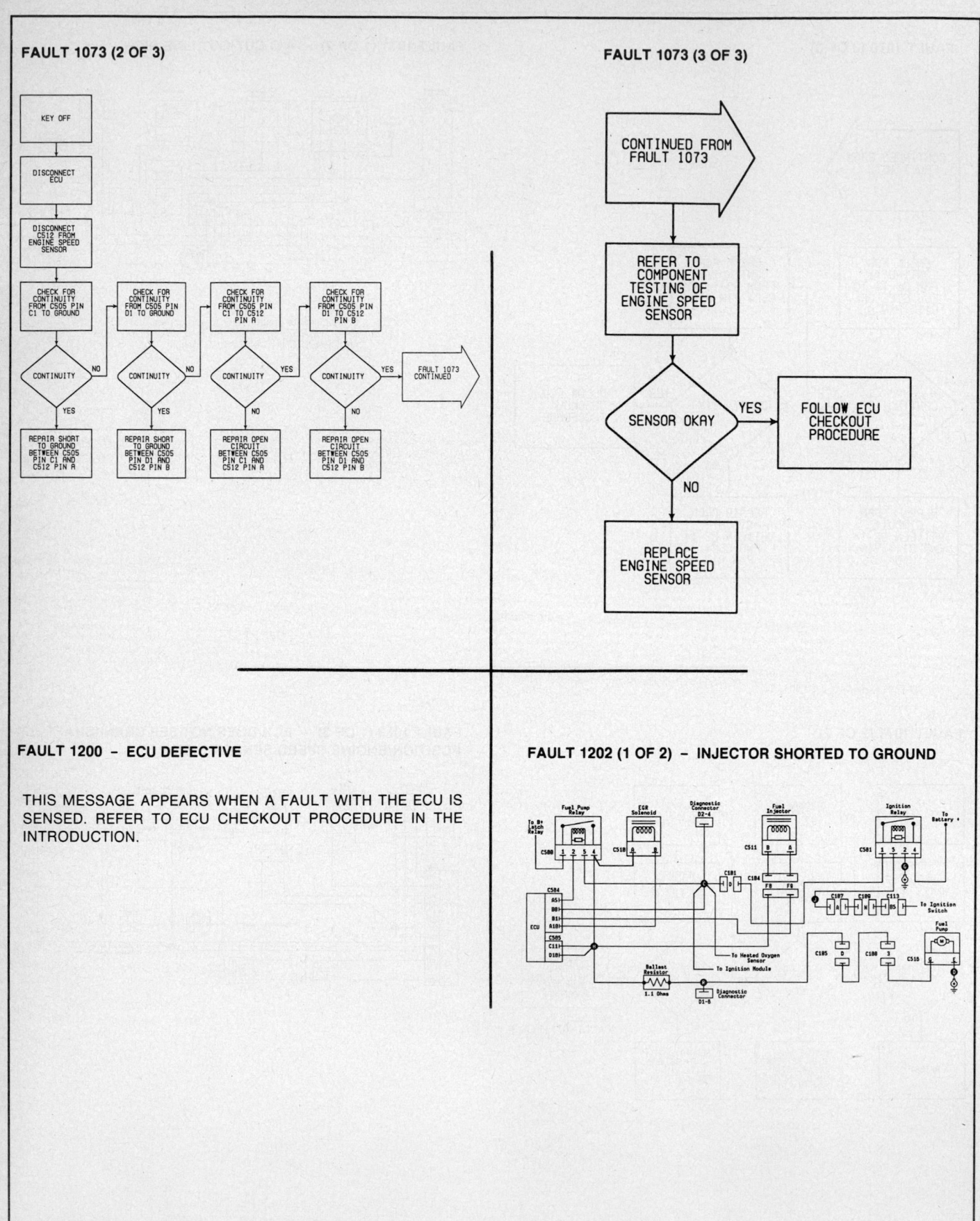

FAULT 1073 (2 OF 3)

FAULT 1073 (3 OF 3)

FAULT 1200 – ECU DEFECTIVE

THIS MESSAGE APPEARS WHEN A FAULT WITH THE ECU IS SENSED. REFER TO ECU CHECKOUT PROCEDURE IN THE INTRODUCTION.

FAULT 1202 (1 OF 2) – INJECTOR SHORTED TO GROUND

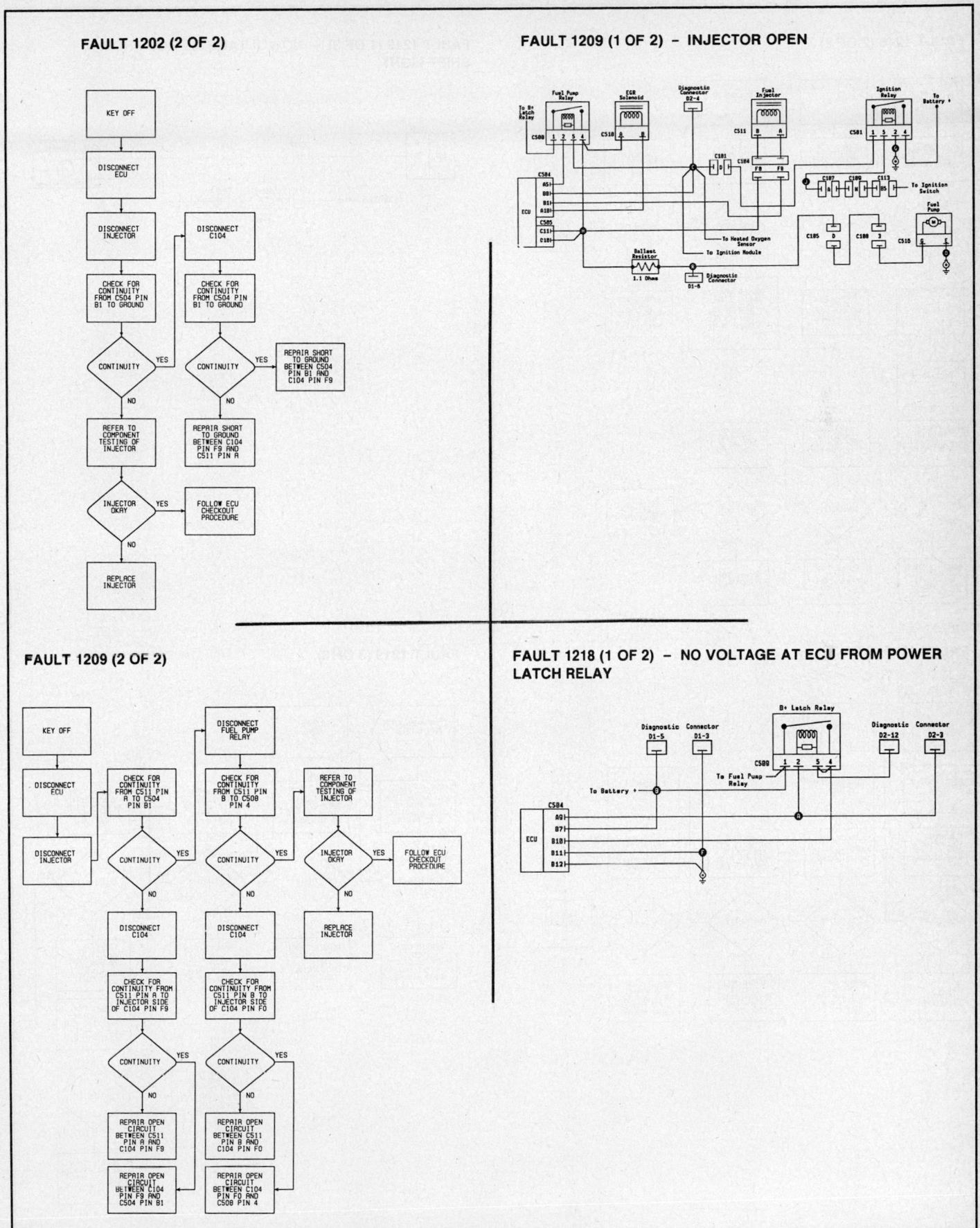

FAULT 1202 (2 OF 2)

FAULT 1209 (1 OF 2) – INJECTOR OPEN

FAULT 1209 (2 OF 2)

FAULT 1218 (1 OF 2) – NO VOLTAGE AT ECU FROM POWER LATCH RELAY

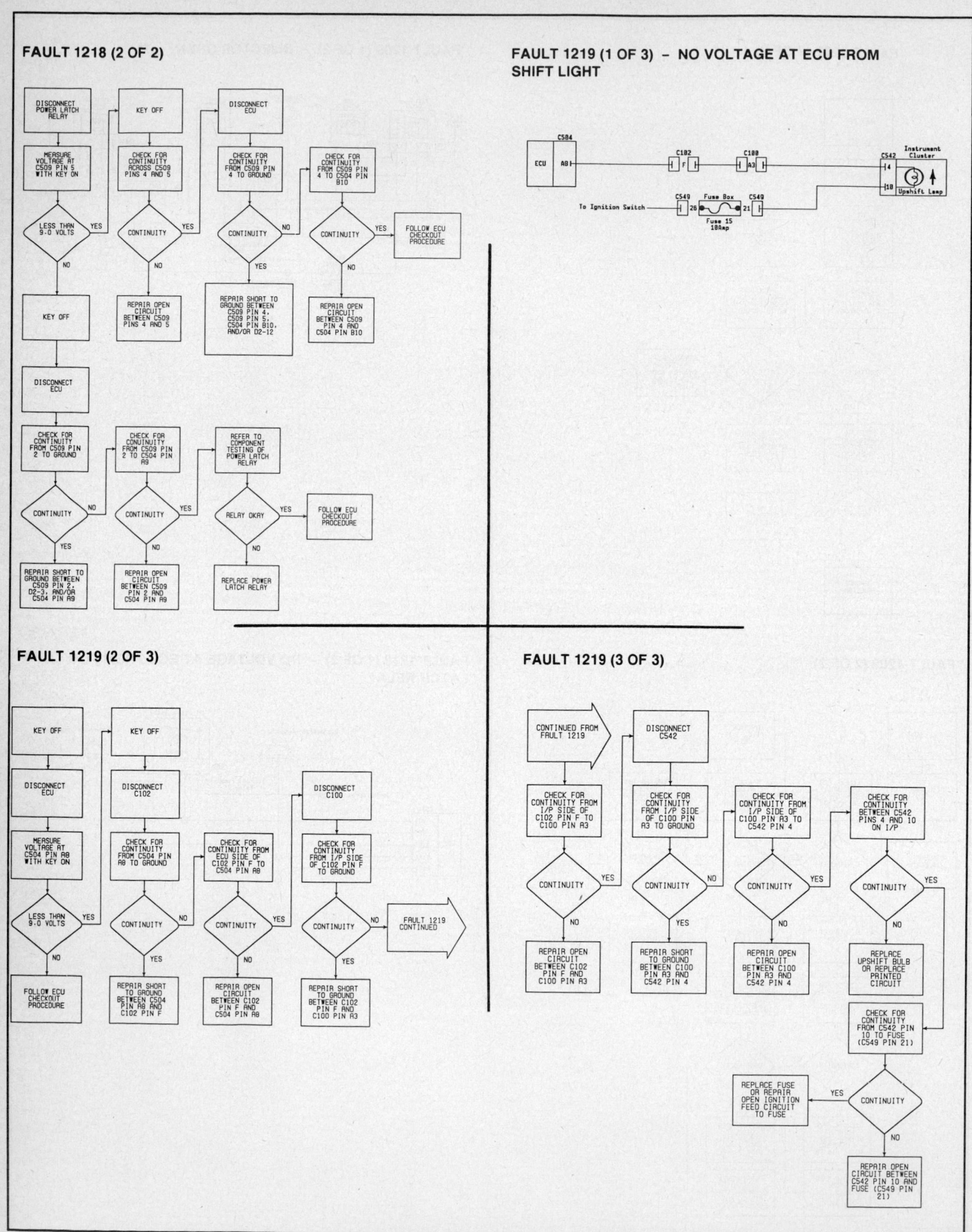

FAULT 1218 (2 OF 2)

FAULT 1219 (1 OF 3) – NO VOLTAGE AT ECU FROM SHIFT LIGHT

FAULT 1219 (2 OF 3)

FAULT 1219 (3 OF 3)

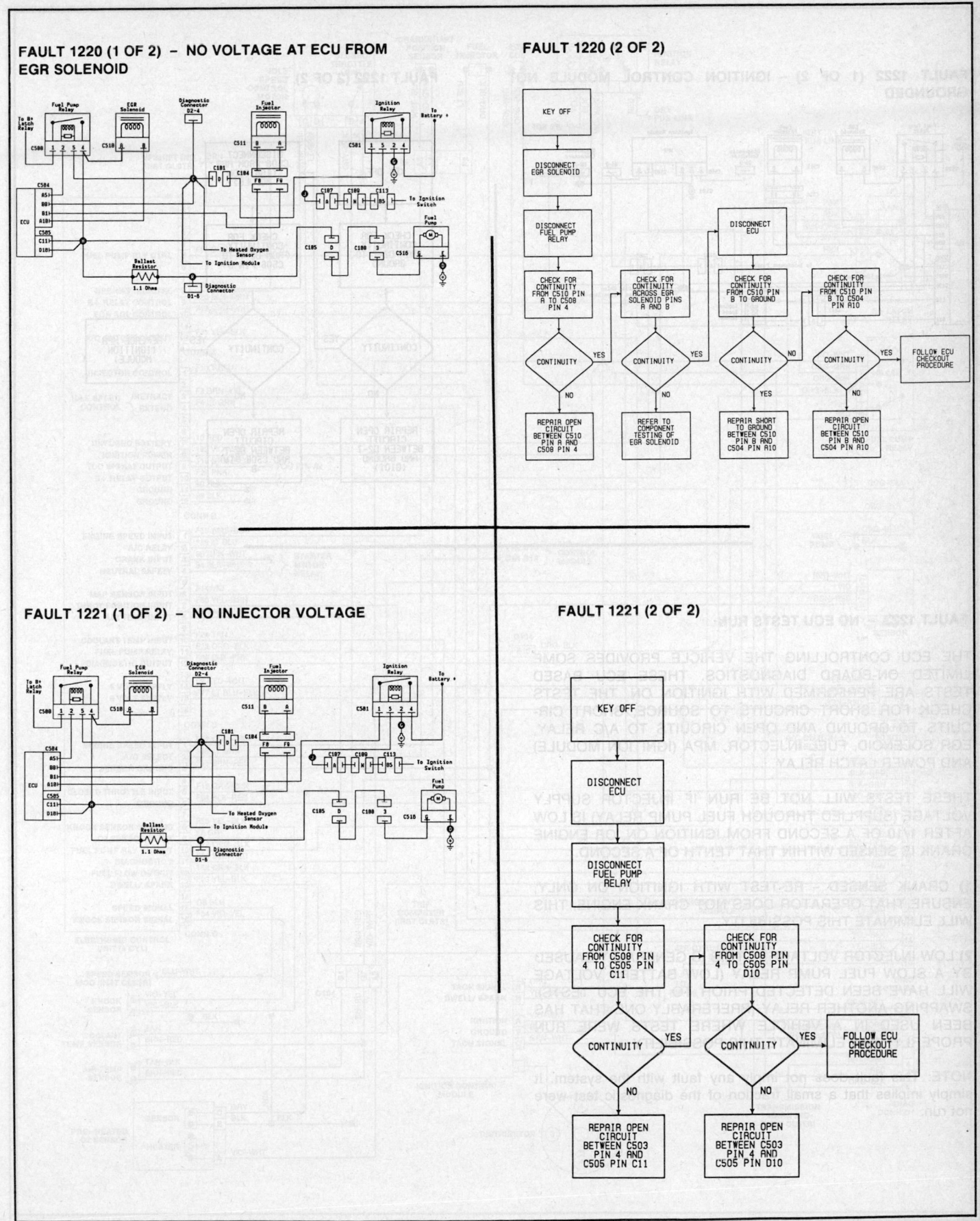

FAULT 1220 (1 OF 2) – NO VOLTAGE AT ECU FROM EGR SOLENOID

FAULT 1220 (2 OF 2)

FAULT 1221 (1 OF 2) – NO INJECTOR VOLTAGE

FAULT 1221 (2 OF 2)

be decreased by one. If the fault is still present, counter will remain at 15. Values of "0" (zero) are an indication that a "low" or "high" fault condition does not exist for the sensor displayed. Values less than 15 and greater than zero are an indication that the ECU has detected a fault at some time, but fault is not present during the current start cycle (possible intermittent).

- Warranty – A 6 digit code for warranty reporting.

5) The "Min/Current/Max" display allows technician to observe operation of 6 different sensor values. Information is displayed as a 3 digit number. The first value displayed is the minumum reading, second number displayed is current reading and third value displayed is the maximum reading. The sensors that are monitored are: MAP sensor, O_2 sensor, Throttle Position Sensor (TPS), Coolant Temperature Sensor (CTS), Manifold Air Temperature (MAT) sensor and CTAVG (average learned closed throttle value).

6) Typically sensors range between 2-252. Values less than 2 or greater than 252 will usually indicate that a sensor is shorted or disconnected. Watch minimum and maximum values to help diagnose intermittent problems.

Adjustments – The "Adjustments" option provides TPS adjustment or erasing stored information in system controller. Follow DRB-II instructions to accomplish desired task.

CLEARING CODES

Refer to ADJUSTMENTS in this article.

FAULT CODES

FAULT CODE IDENTIFICATION

Fault Code	Fault Condition
1000	Ignition line low
1001	Ignition line high
1004	Battery voltage low
1005	Sensor ground line out of limits
1010	Diagnostic enable line low
1011	Diagnostic enable line high
1012	Ignition control module low
1013	Ignition control module line high
1014	Fuel pump line low
1015	Fuel pump line high
1016	Manifold Air Temperature (MAT) sensor line low
1017	Manifold Air Temperature (MAT) sensor line high
1018	No serial data from ECU
1021	Engine failed to start due to mechanical, fuel or ignition problem
1022	Start line low
1024	ECU does not see start signal
1027	ECU sees Wide Open Throttle (WOT)
1028	ECU does not see Wide Open Throttle (WOT)
1031	ECU sees closed throttle
1032	ECU does not see closed throttle
1033	Idle speed increase line low
1034	Idle speed increase line high
1035	Idle speed decrease line low
1036	Idle speed decrease line high
1037	Throttle Position Sensor (TPS) reads low
1038	Park/Neutral line high
1040	Latched B+ line low
1041	Latched B+ line high
1042	No latched B+ .5 volt drop
1047	Wrong ECU
1048	Manual vehicle equipped with automatic ECU
1049	Automatic vehicle equipped with manual ECU
1050	Idle speed less than 500 RPM
1051	Idle speed greater than 2000 RPM
1052	MAP sensor out of limits
1053	Change in MAP reading out of limits
1054	Coolant temperature sensor line low
1055	Coolant temperature sensor line high

FAULT CODE IDENTIFICATION (Cont.)

Fault Code	Fault Condition
1056	Inactive coolant temperature sensor
1057	Knock circuit shorted
1058	Knock value out of limits
1059	A/C request line low
1060	A/C request line high
1061	A/C select line low
1062	A/C select line high
1063	A/C clutch line low
1064	A/C clutch line high
1065	O_2 sensor reads rich
1066	O_2 sensor reads lean
1067	Latch relay line low
1068	Latch relay line high
1069	No tach
1070	A/C cut-out line low
1071	A/C cut-out line line high
1073	ECU does not see crankshaft position/ engine speed sensor signal
1200	ECU defective
1202	Injector shorted to ground
1209	Injector open
1218	No voltage at ECU from power latch relay
1220	No voltage at ECU from EGR solenoid
1221	No injector voltage
1222	Ignition control module not grounded
1223	No ECU tests run

COMPONENT TESTING

NOTE: Testing information for fuel injector and knock sensor is not available.

A/C Clutch Relay – 1) With ignition switch in "RUN" position, leave A/C clutch relay connected. Connect a voltmeter between, relay terminal No. 86 and ground. See Fig. 7. Voltmeter should read battery voltage. If battery voltage is present, go to next step. If battery voltage is not present, check fuse No. 8. If fuse No. 8 is okay, check for an open circuit to fuse No. 8.

2) Connect voltmeter between relay terminal No. 30 and ground. See Fig. 7. Voltmeter should read battery voltage. If battery voltage is present, go to next step. If battery voltage is not present, check fusible link in circuit. If fusible link is okay, check for an open circuit to fusible link.

3) Connect voltmeter between relay terminals No. 86 and 85. See Fig. 7. Voltmeter should read battery voltage. If battery voltage is present, go to next step. If battery voltage is not present, check for an open circuit to Air Control Module (ACM) connector terminal "C5". If circuit is okay, replace Air Control Module (ACM).

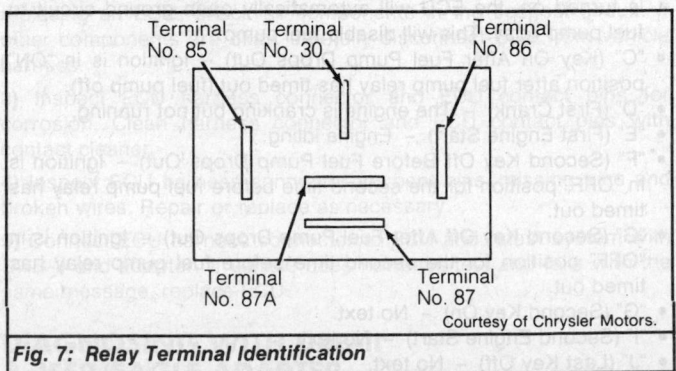

Terminal No. 85 Terminal No. 30 Terminal No. 86

Terminal No. 87A Terminal No. 87

Courtesy of Chrysler Motors.

Fig. 7: Relay Terminal Identification

4) Connect voltmeter between relay terminals No. 30 and 87. See Fig. 7. A/C compressor clutch should engage. If A/C compressor clutch engages, replace A/C clutch relay.

B+ (Power) Latch, Fuel Pump & Ignition Relays – 1) With relay in de-energized position, relay should have continuity between relay terminals No. 87A and 30. *See Fig. 7.* Measure resistance between relay terminals No. 85 and 86.

2) Ohmmeter should read 70-80 ohms for resistor relays and 81-91 ohms for diode relays. Replace relay if not within specification. Not all relays have battery voltage connected to terminal No. 30. Some relays have battery voltage connected to terminals No. 87 or 87A.

Coolant Temperature Sensor – 1) Disconnect electrical connector from coolant temperature sensor. Using a DVOM, check resistance between ECU connector terminal "C10" to sensor connector and ECU connector terminal "D3" to sensor connector. *See Fig. 6.*

2) If resistance is greater than one ohm, repair wiring harness. Measure resistance of sensor between sensor terminals. Refer to COOLANT TEMPERATURE SENSOR RESISTANCE table for specifications on coolant temperature sensor resistance.

COOLANT TEMPERATURE SENSOR RESISTANCE [1]

°F (°C)	Ohms
212 (100)	185
160 (70)	450
100 (38)	1600
70 (20)	3400
40 (4)	7500
20 (-7)	13,500
0 (-18)	25,500
-40 (-40)	100,700

[1] – Values given are approximate.

Crankshaft Position/Engine Speed Sensor – 1) Disconnect sensor connector. Connect an ohmmeter between terminals "A" and "B" (marked on connector).

2) With engine at operating temperature, ohmmeter should read 125-275 ohms. If readings are not within specification, replace sensor.

EGR Solenoid – 1) Disconnect EGR solenoid electrical connector. Connect 12 volts to one terminal of solenoid. Connect a jumper wire to the other terminal of solenoid.

2) Each time jumper wire is grounded, solenoid should click. If solenoid clicks, solenoid is operating properly. If solenoid does not click, replace solenoid.

Idle Speed Regulator – 1) Attach harness Adapter (7195) to Idle Speed Tester (7088). Connect harness adapter and idle speed tester to idle speed regulator harness connector.

2) Connect idle speed tester (7088) to vehicle battery. Start engine. Put Idle Speed Tester's switch in "RETRACT" position, then in "EXTEND" position. Idle speed regulator should increase and decrease idle speed.

3) If idle speed changes, regulator is functioning properly. If idle speed does not change, disconnect air hoses from idle speed regulator. Watch for valve to open and close while activating idle speed regulator. If idle speed regulator valve does not move while activating regulator, replace idle speed regulator.

Manifold Absolute Pressure (MAP) Sensor – 1) Ensure MAP sensor vacuum hose connections are secure. Connect a voltmeter between MAP sensor terminal "B" (marked on sensor connector) and ground. Turn ignition on.

2) Voltmeter should read 4-5 volts. Start engine and warm to operating temperature. Voltmeter should read 1.5-2.1 volts. Check ECU terminal "C6" for same voltmeter readings as measured at MAP sensor terminal "B" to check wiring harness between ECU and MAP sensor. Repair as necessary.

3) Turn ignition off. Connect voltmeter between MAP sensor terminal "C" and ground. Turn ignition on. Voltmeter should read 4.5-5.5 volts. Check for same voltmeter reading at ECU terminal "C14". *See Fig. 6.* Repair wiring harness as necessary.

4) Turn ignition off. Check for continuity between MAP sensor terminal "A" and ECU terminal "D3". Repair wire harness as necessary.

Manifold Air Temperature (MAT) Sensor – 1) Disconnect wire harness connector from MAT sensor. Using a DVOM, sensor resistance should be less than 1000 ohms with engine at operating temperature.

2) Check resistance between ECU terminal "C8" and sensor connector and ECU terminal "D3" and sensor connector. *See Fig. 6.* Repair wiring harness if resistance is more than one ohm. Refer to MANIFOLD AIR TEMPERATURE SENSOR RESISTANCE table. Replace sensor if not within specification.

MANIFOLD AIR TEMPERATURE SENSOR RESISTANCE [1]

°F (°C)	Ohms
212 (100)	185
160 (70)	450
100 (38)	1600
70 (20)	3400
40 (4)	7500
20 (-7)	13,500
0 (-18)	25,500
-40 (-40)	100,700

[1] – Values given are approximate.

Oxygen Sensor Heating Element – Disconnect O_2 sensor connector. Connect an ohmmeter between sensor terminals "A" and "B". Ohmmeter should read less than 10 ohms. Replace sensor if ohmmeter reads infinity.

Starter Relay – 1) Turn ignition on. Starter relay is connected to vehicle during testing. Connect a voltmeter between Black/White wire and ground. Turn ignition switch to "START" position. Voltmeter should read battery voltage. If voltmeter does not read battery voltage, replace defective starter relay or repair open circuit from ignition switch.

2) Connect voltmeter between 2 Green wires and ground one at a time on starter relay. Turn ignition switch to "START" position. Voltmeter should read battery voltage. If voltmeter does not read battery voltage, repair ground circuit.

3) Connect voltmeter between Green/White wire and ground. Turn ignition switch to "START" position. Voltmeter should read battery voltage. If voltmeter does not read battery voltage, replace starter relay.

Throttle Position Sensor (TPS) – 1) Disconnect TPS electrical connector. Turn ignition on. Using a DVOM, backprobe TPS harness connector between terminals "B" and "C".

2) Voltmeter should read approximately 5 volts. If voltmeter reading is incorrect, test vehicle with DRB-II (C-4805). If voltmeter reading is correct, go to next step.

3) Turn ignition off. Check for continuity between TPS terminal "B" and ground. If circuit is open, test vehicle with DRB-II (C-4805). If continuity is present, go to next step.

4) Reconnect TPS electrical connector. Turn ignition on. Measure voltage between TPS terminal "A" and ground. Voltmeter should read approximately .5-1.0 volt.

5) If voltmeter reading is correct, TPS is okay. If voltmeter reading is incorrect, attempt to adjust TPS. If TPS cannot be adjusted within specification, replace TPS.

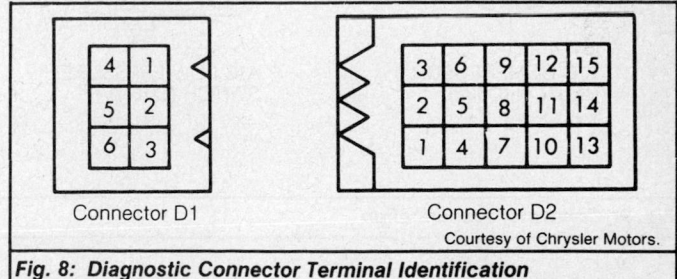

Connector D1   Connector D2

Courtesy of Chrysler Motors.

Fig. 8: Diagnostic Connector Terminal Identification

1989 COMPUTERIZED ENGINE CONTROLS
Eagle 3.0L MPFI (Cont.)

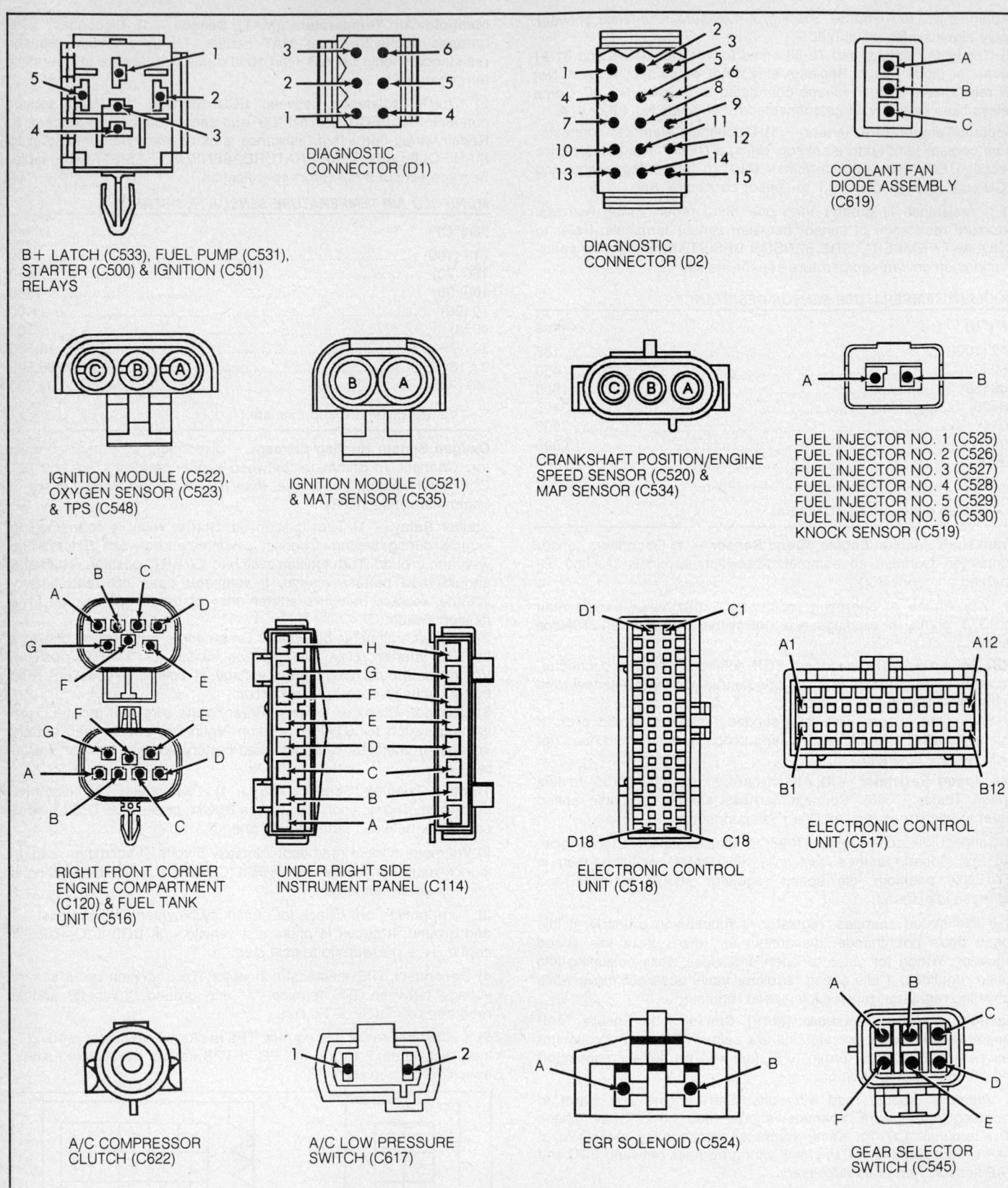

B+ LATCH (C533), FUEL PUMP (C531), STARTER (C500) & IGNITION (C501) RELAYS

DIAGNOSTIC CONNECTOR (D1)

DIAGNOSTIC CONNECTOR (D2)

COOLANT FAN DIODE ASSEMBLY (C619)

IGNITION MODULE (C522), OXYGEN SENSOR (C523) & TPS (C548)

IGNITION MODULE (C521) & MAT SENSOR (C535)

CRANKSHAFT POSITION/ENGINE SPEED SENSOR (C520) & MAP SENSOR (C534)

FUEL INJECTOR NO. 1 (C525)
FUEL INJECTOR NO. 2 (C526)
FUEL INJECTOR NO. 3 (C527)
FUEL INJECTOR NO. 4 (C528)
FUEL INJECTOR NO. 5 (C529)
FUEL INJECTOR NO. 6 (C530)
KNOCK SENSOR (C519)

RIGHT FRONT CORNER ENGINE COMPARTMENT (C120) & FUEL TANK UNIT (C516)

UNDER RIGHT SIDE INSTRUMENT PANEL (C114)

ELECTRONIC CONTROL UNIT (C518)

ELECTRONIC CONTROL UNIT (C517)

A/C COMPRESSOR CLUTCH (C622)

A/C LOW PRESSURE SWITCH (C617)

EGR SOLENOID (C524)

GEAR SELECTOR SWTICH (C545)

Courtesy of Chrysler Motors.

Fig. 9: Connector Identification

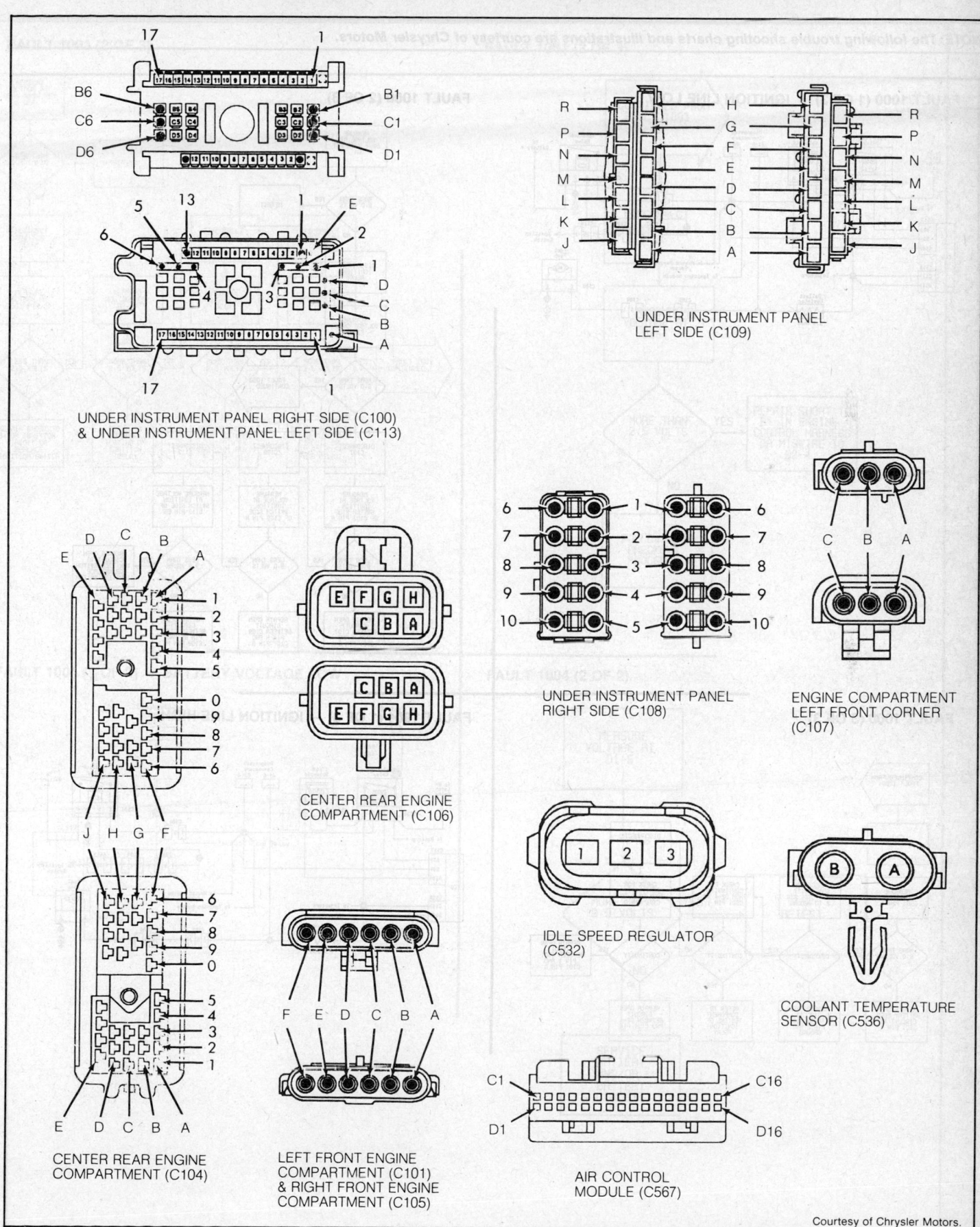

UNDER INSTRUMENT PANEL
LEFT SIDE (C109)

UNDER INSTRUMENT PANEL RIGHT SIDE (C100)
& UNDER INSTRUMENT PANEL LEFT SIDE (C113)

UNDER INSTRUMENT PANEL
RIGHT SIDE (C108)

ENGINE COMPARTMENT
LEFT FRONT CORNER
(C107)

CENTER REAR ENGINE
COMPARTMENT (C106)

IDLE SPEED REGULATOR
(C532)

COOLANT TEMPERATURE
SENSOR (C536)

CENTER REAR ENGINE
COMPARTMENT (C104)

LEFT FRONT ENGINE
COMPARTMENT (C101)
& RIGHT FRONT ENGINE
COMPARTMENT (C105)

AIR CONTROL
MODULE (C567)

Courtesy of Chrysler Motors.

Fig. 10: Connector Identification

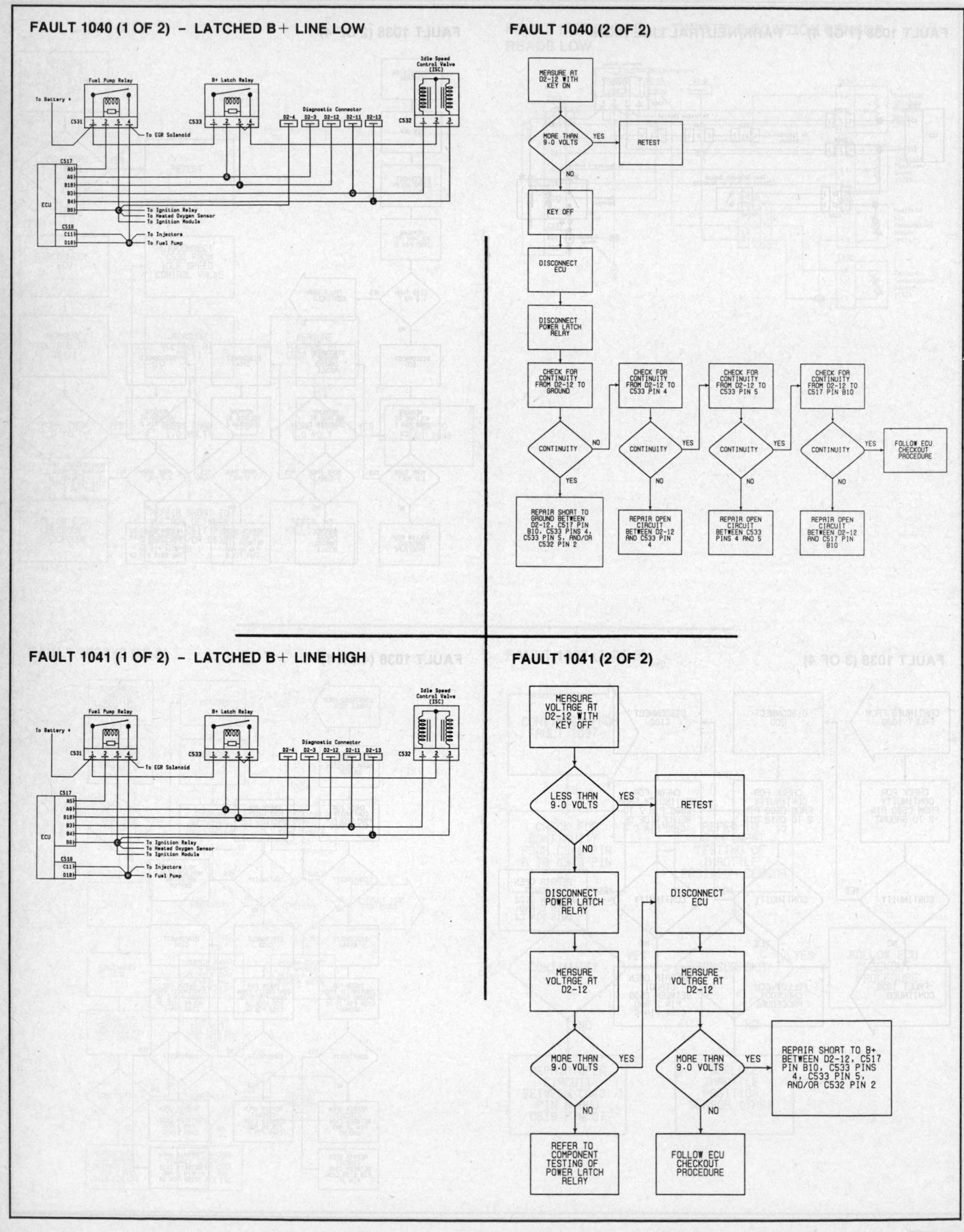

FAULT 1040 (1 OF 2) – LATCHED B+ LINE LOW

FAULT 1040 (2 OF 2)

FAULT 1041 (1 OF 2) – LATCHED B+ LINE HIGH

FAULT 1041 (2 OF 2)

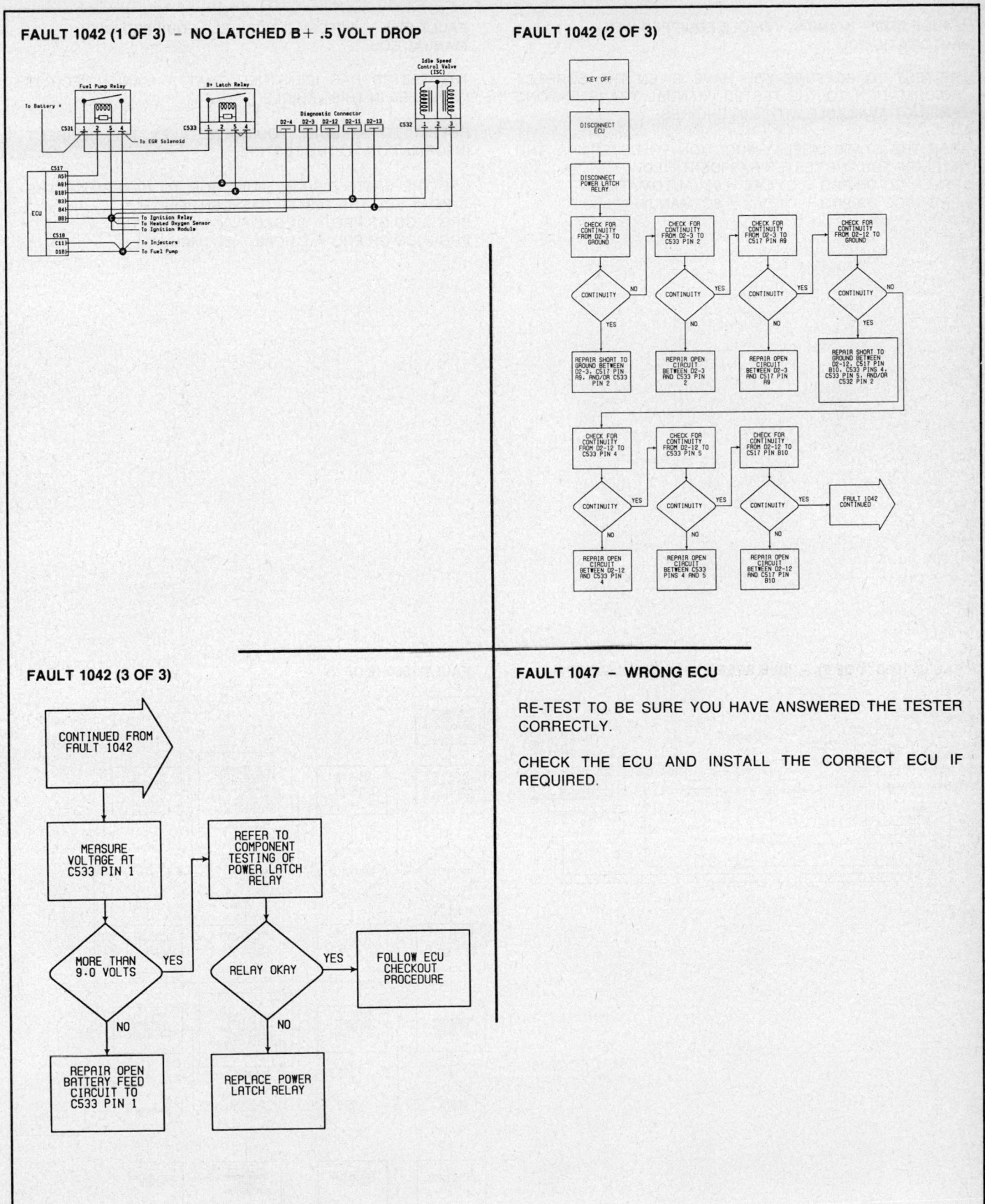

FAULT 1042 (1 OF 3) — NO LATCHED B+ .5 VOLT DROP

FAULT 1042 (2 OF 3)

FAULT 1042 (3 OF 3)

FAULT 1047 — WRONG ECU

RE-TEST TO BE SURE YOU HAVE ANSWERED THE TESTER CORRECTLY.

CHECK THE ECU AND INSTALL THE CORRECT ECU IF REQUIRED.

1989 COMPUTERIZED ENGINE CONTROLS
Eagle 3.0L MPFI (Cont.)

FAULT 1048 – MANUAL VEHICLE EQUIPPED WITH AUTOMATIC ECU

RE-TEST TO BE SURE YOU HAVE GIVEN THE CORRECT INFORMATION TO THE TESTER. MANUAL TRANSMISSIONS ARE NOT AVAILABLE WITH 3.0L ENGINES.

USE THE STATE DISPLAY FUNCTION TO DETERMINE THE TYPE OF ECU THE TESTER HAS IDENTIFIED.
PRG = CO OR PRG = C1 CAL = 0C (AUTOMATIC)
PRG = CO OR PRG = C1 CAL = 8C (MANUAL)

FAULT 1049 – AUTOMATIC VEHICLE EQUIPPED WITH MANUAL ECU

THE TESTER HAS IDENTIFIED THAT A MANUAL ECU IS INSTALLED IN THIS VEHICLE.

RETEST TO BE SURE YOU HAVE GIVEN THE CORRECT INFORMATION TO THE TESTER.

USE THE STATE DISPLAY FUNCTION TO DETERMINE THE TYPE OF ECU THE TESTER HAS IDENTIFIED.
PRG = CO OR PRG = C1 CAL = 0C (AUTOMATIC)
PRG = CO OR PRG = C1 CAL = 8C (MANUAL)

FAULT 1050 (1 OF 2) – IDLE SPEED LESS THAN 500 RPM

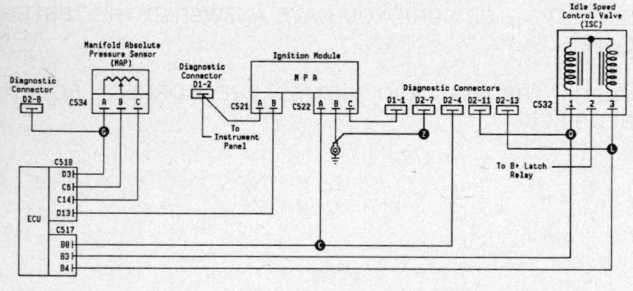

FAULT 1050 (2 OF 2)

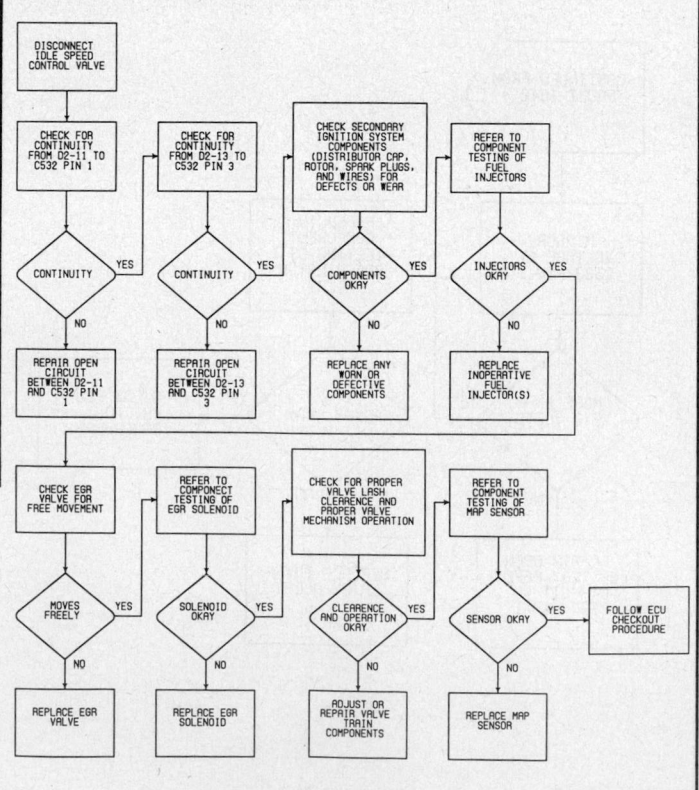

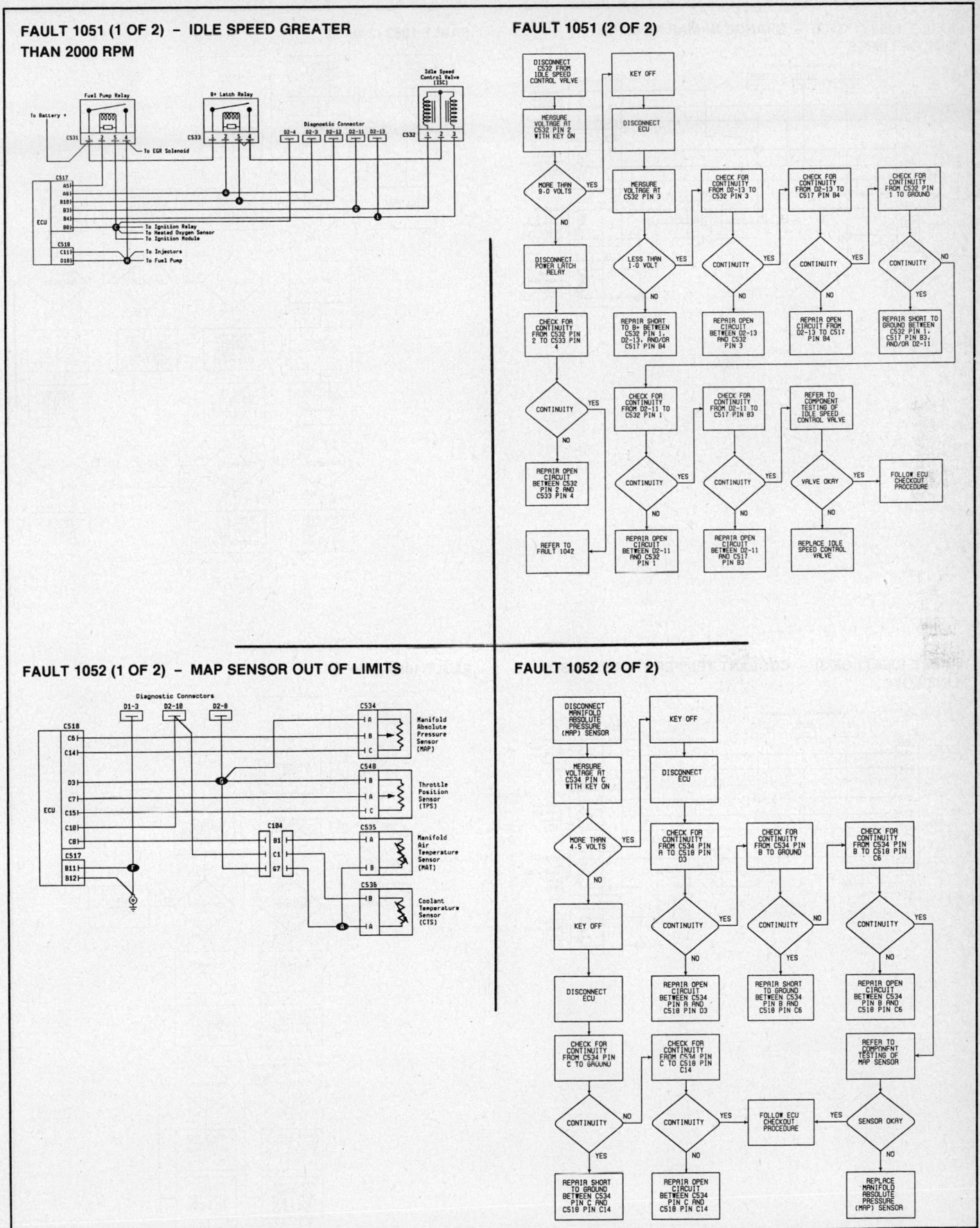

FAULT 1051 (1 OF 2) – IDLE SPEED GREATER THAN 2000 RPM

FAULT 1051 (2 OF 2)

FAULT 1052 (1 OF 2) – MAP SENSOR OUT OF LIMITS

FAULT 1052 (2 OF 2)

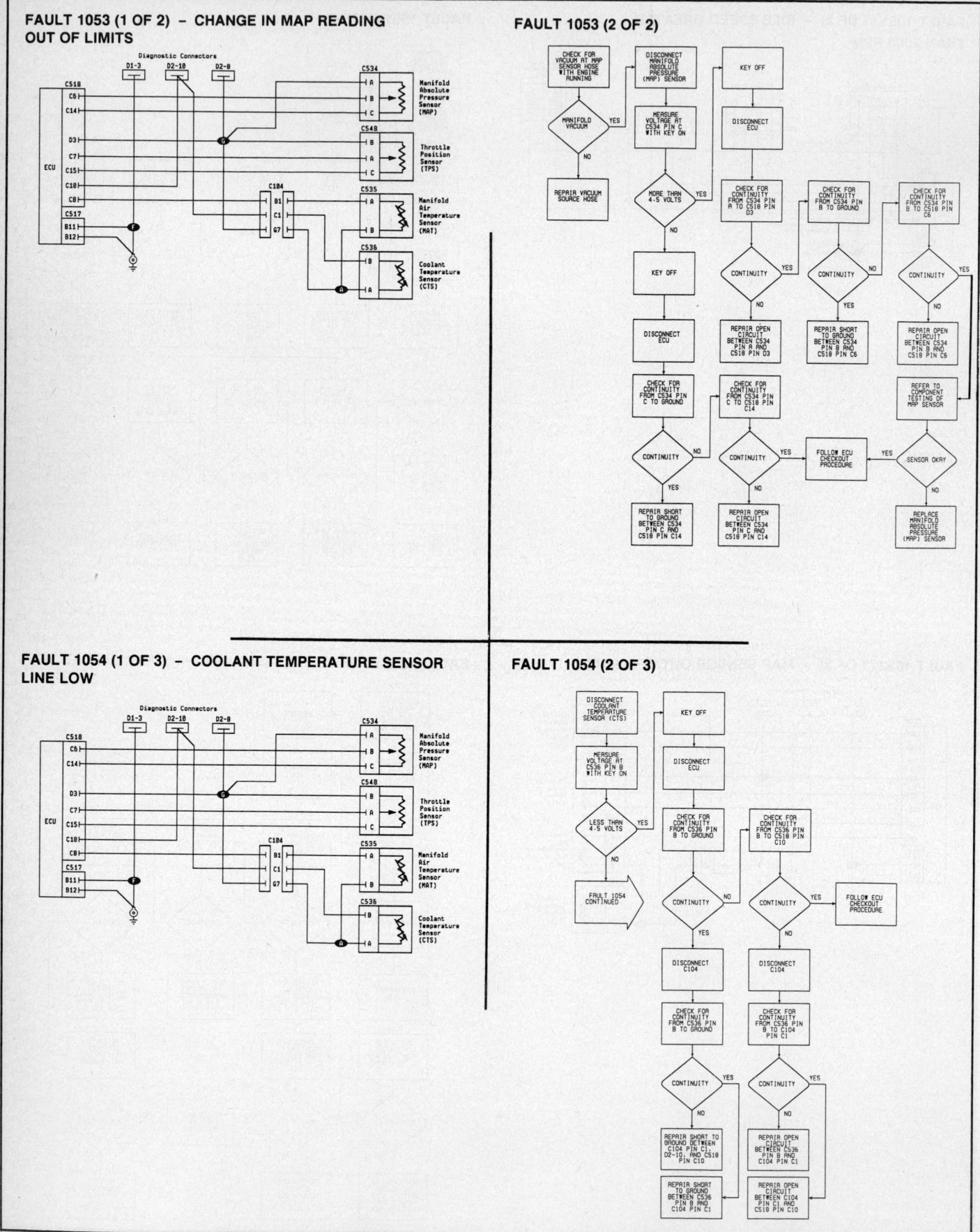

FAULT 1053 (1 OF 2) – CHANGE IN MAP READING OUT OF LIMITS

FAULT 1053 (2 OF 2)

FAULT 1054 (1 OF 3) – COOLANT TEMPERATURE SENSOR LINE LOW

FAULT 1054 (2 OF 3)

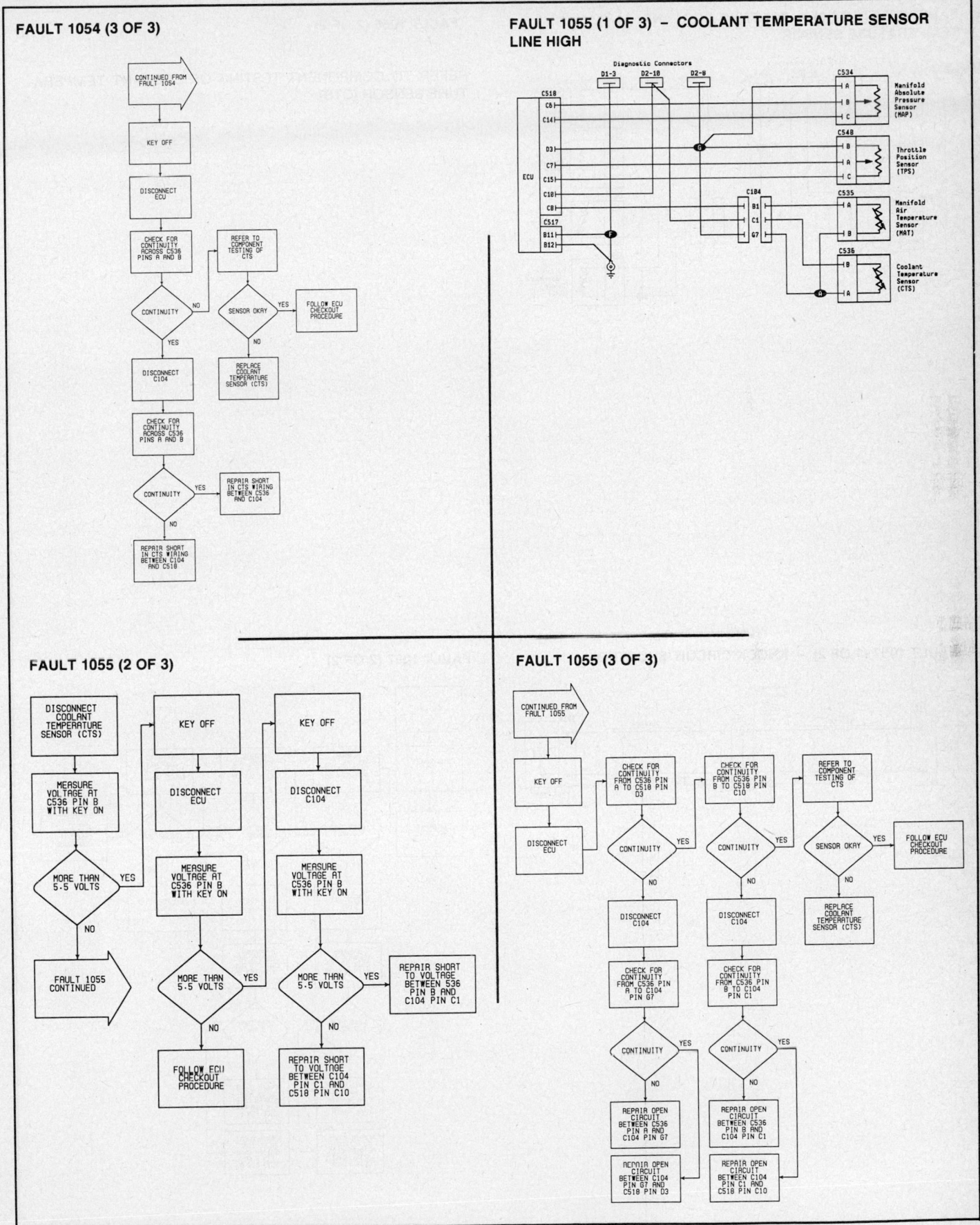

FAULT 1054 (3 OF 3)

FAULT 1055 (1 OF 3) — COOLANT TEMPERATURE SENSOR LINE HIGH

FAULT 1055 (2 OF 3)

FAULT 1055 (3 OF 3)

FAULT 1056 (1 OF 2) – INACTIVE COOLANT TEMPERATURE SENSOR

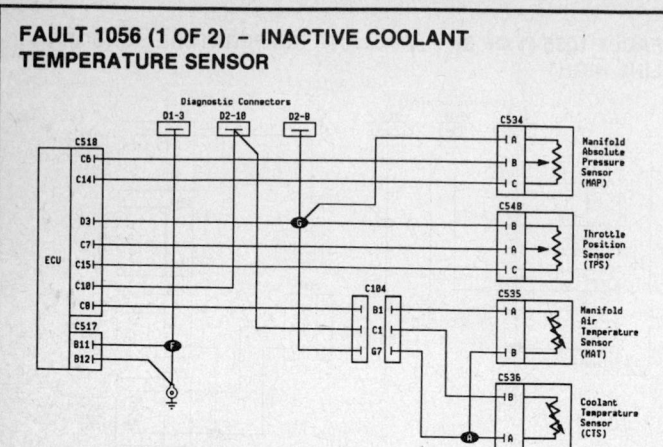

FAULT 1056 (2 OF 2)

REFER TO COMPONENT TESTING OF COOLANT TEMPERATURE SENSOR (CTS).

FAULT 1057 (1 OF 2) – KNOCK CIRCUIT SHORTED

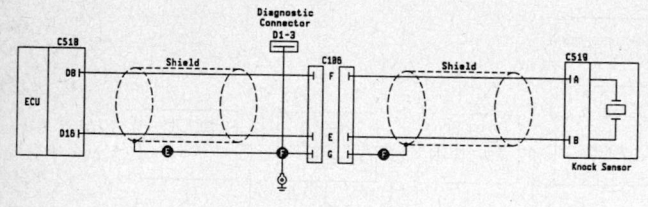

FAULT 1057 (2 OF 2)

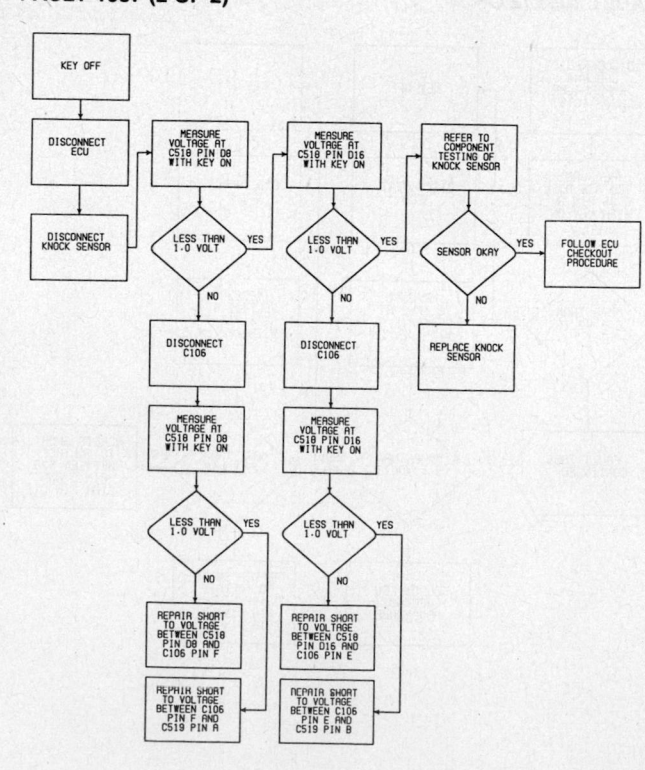

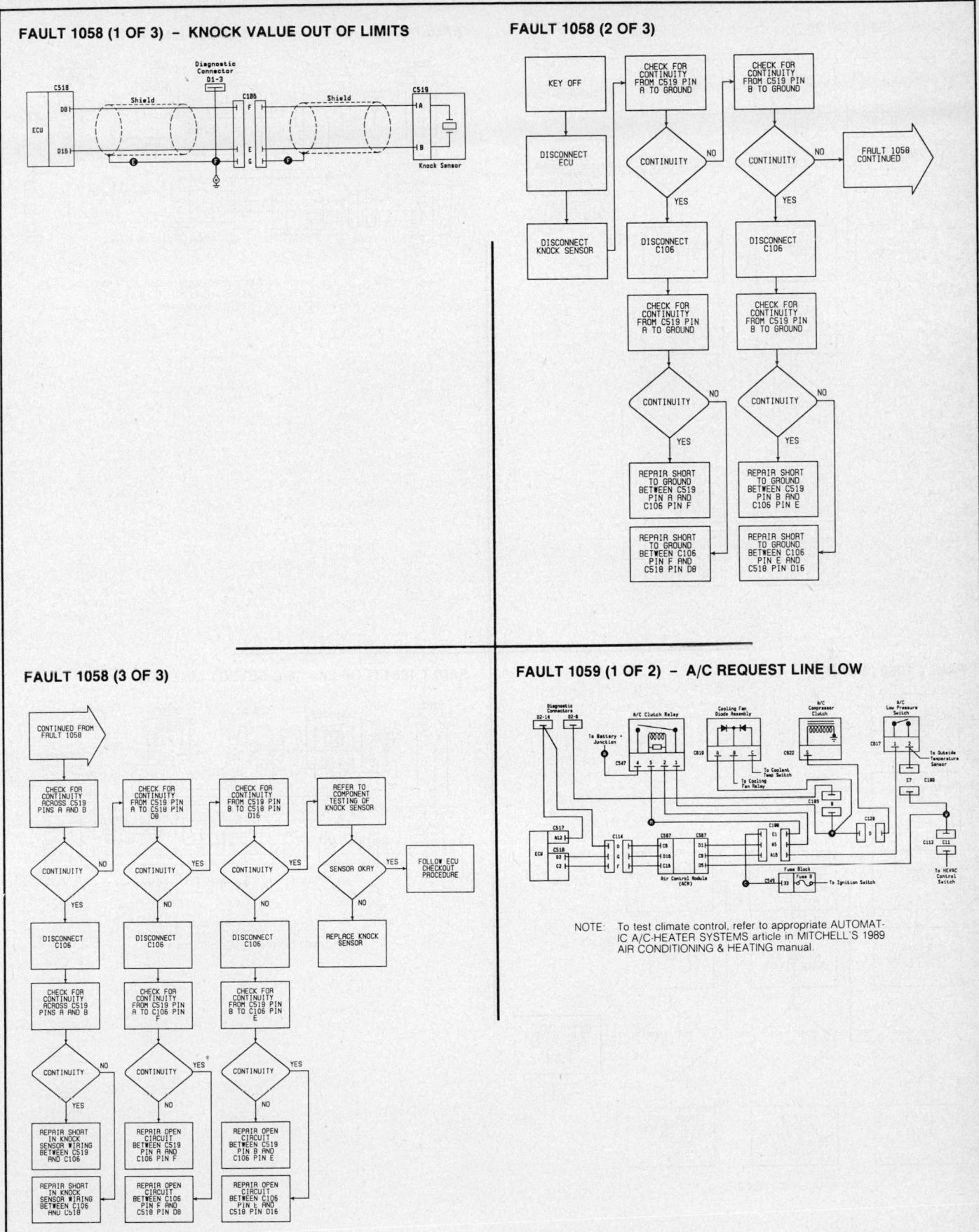

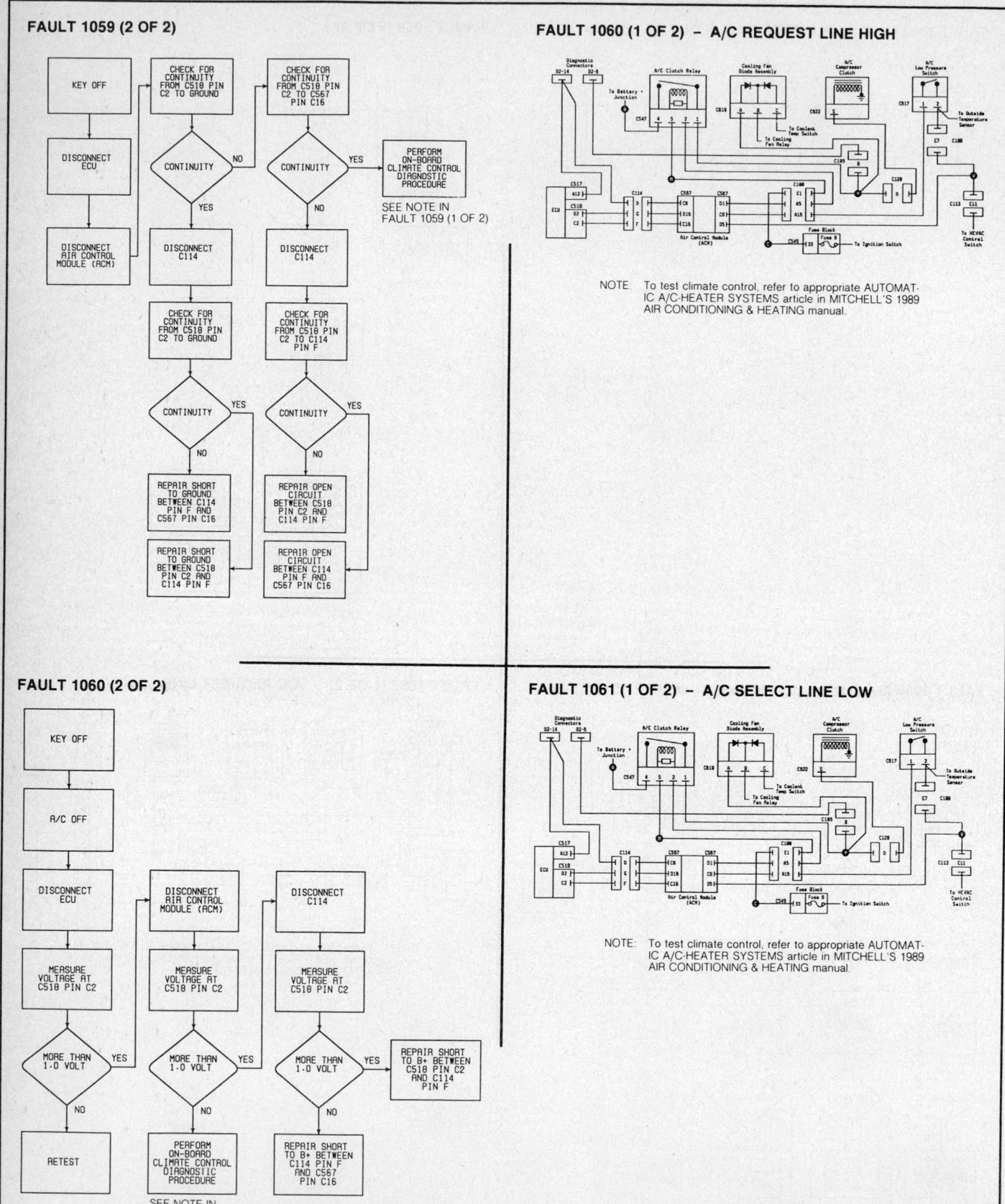

FAULT 1059 (2 OF 2)

FAULT 1060 (1 OF 2) – A/C REQUEST LINE HIGH

NOTE: To test climate control, refer to appropriate AUTOMAT-
IC A/C-HEATER SYSTEMS article in MITCHELL'S 1989
AIR CONDITIONING & HEATING manual.

FAULT 1060 (2 OF 2)

FAULT 1061 (1 OF 2) – A/C SELECT LINE LOW

NOTE: To test climate control, refer to appropriate AUTOMAT-
IC A/C-HEATER SYSTEMS article in MITCHELL'S 1989
AIR CONDITIONING & HEATING manual.

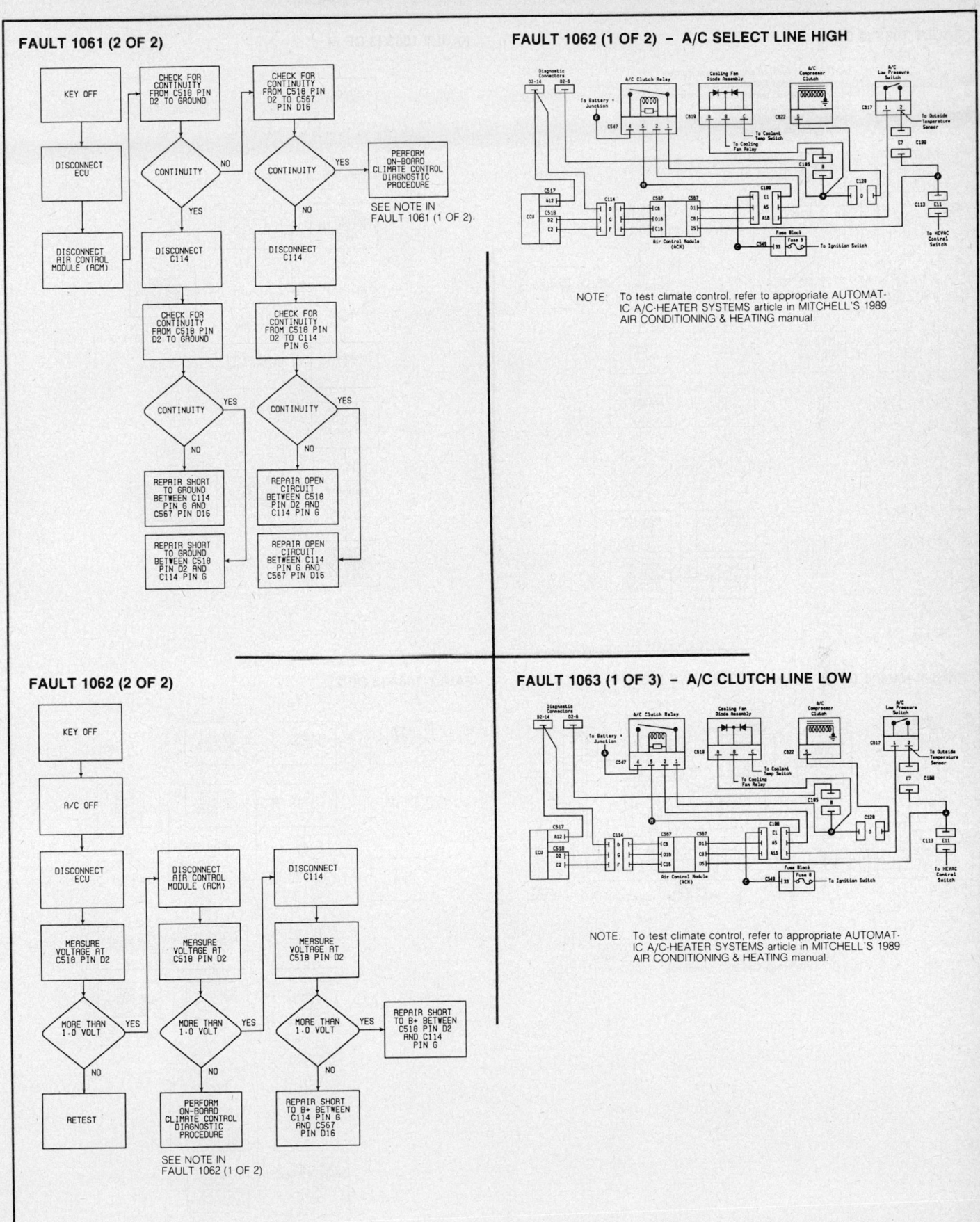

FAULT 1061 (2 OF 2)

FAULT 1062 (1 OF 2) – A/C SELECT LINE HIGH

NOTE: To test climate control, refer to appropriate AUTOMATIC A/C-HEATER SYSTEMS article in MITCHELL'S 1989 AIR CONDITIONING & HEATING manual.

FAULT 1062 (2 OF 2)

FAULT 1063 (1 OF 3) – A/C CLUTCH LINE LOW

NOTE: To test climate control, refer to appropriate AUTOMATIC A/C-HEATER SYSTEMS article in MITCHELL'S 1989 AIR CONDITIONING & HEATING manual.

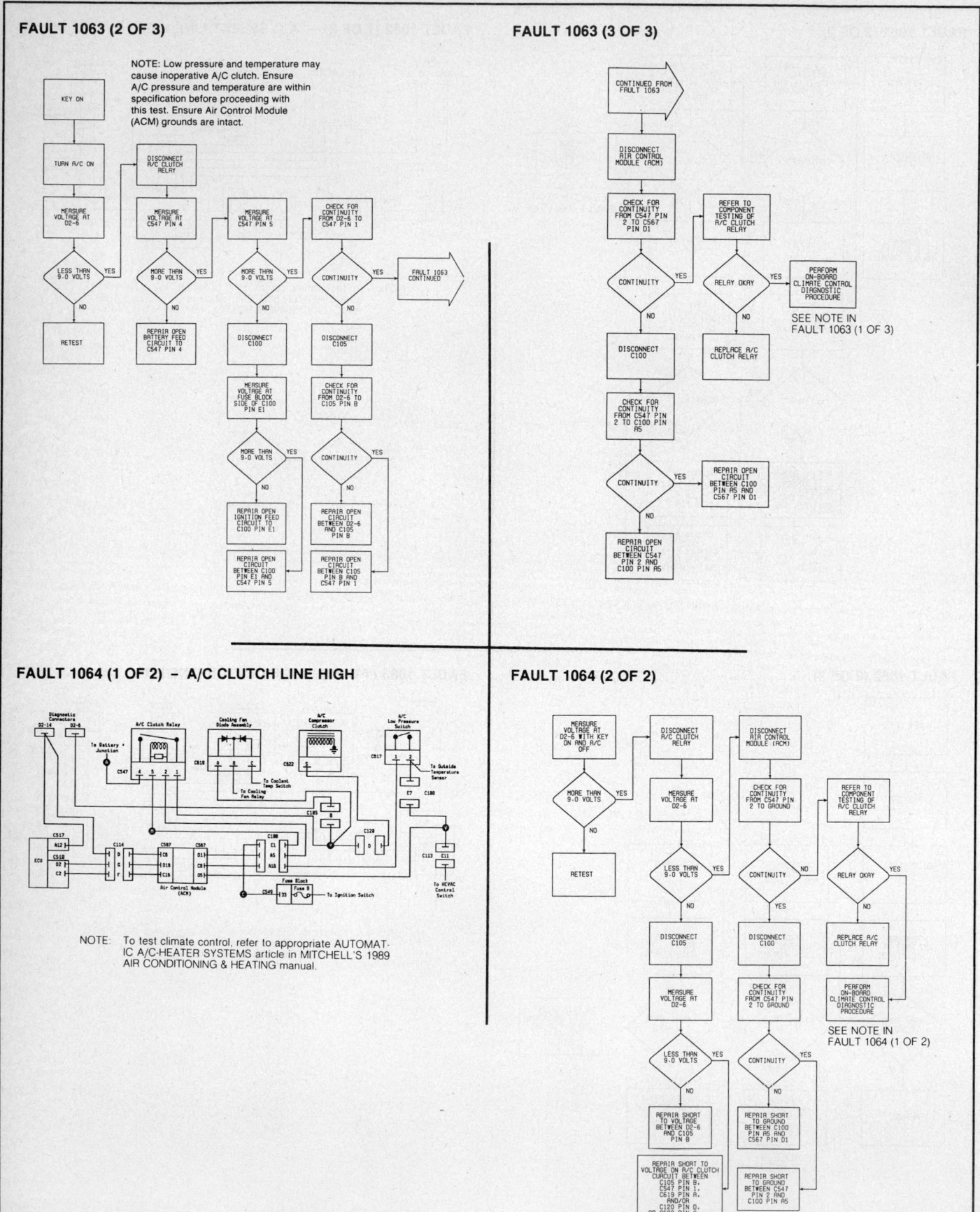

FAULT 1063 (2 OF 3)

NOTE: Low pressure and temperature may cause inoperative A/C clutch. Ensure A/C pressure and temperature are within specification before proceeding with this test. Ensure Air Control Module (ACM) grounds are intact.

FAULT 1063 (3 OF 3)

SEE NOTE IN FAULT 1063 (1 OF 3)

FAULT 1064 (1 OF 2) – A/C CLUTCH LINE HIGH

NOTE: To test climate control, refer to appropriate AUTOMATIC A/C-HEATER SYSTEMS article in MITCHELL'S 1989 AIR CONDITIONING & HEATING manual.

FAULT 1064 (2 OF 2)

SEE NOTE IN FAULT 1064 (1 OF 2)

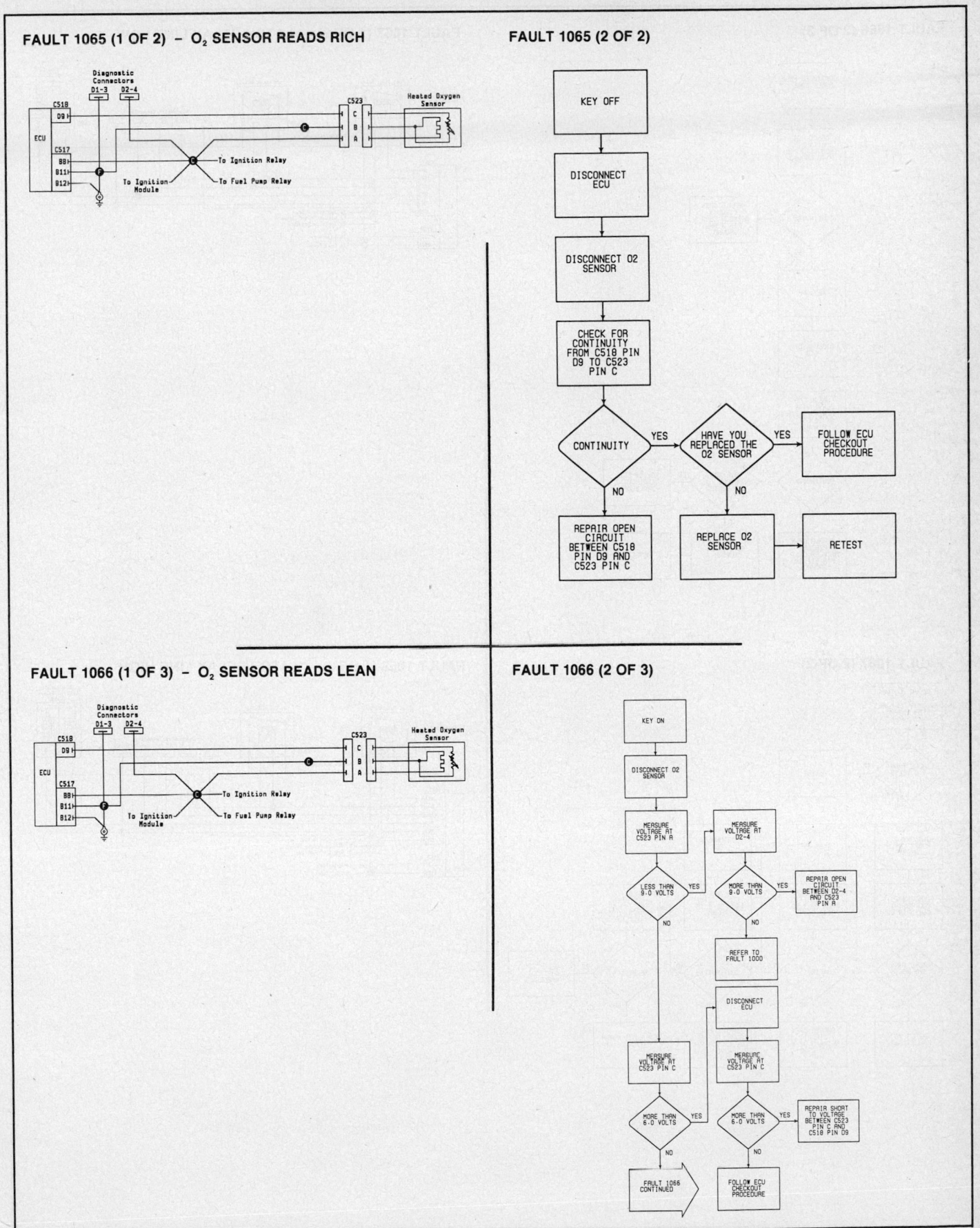

FAULT 1065 (1 OF 2) – O₂ SENSOR READS RICH

FAULT 1065 (2 OF 2)

FAULT 1066 (1 OF 3) – O₂ SENSOR READS LEAN

FAULT 1066 (2 OF 3)

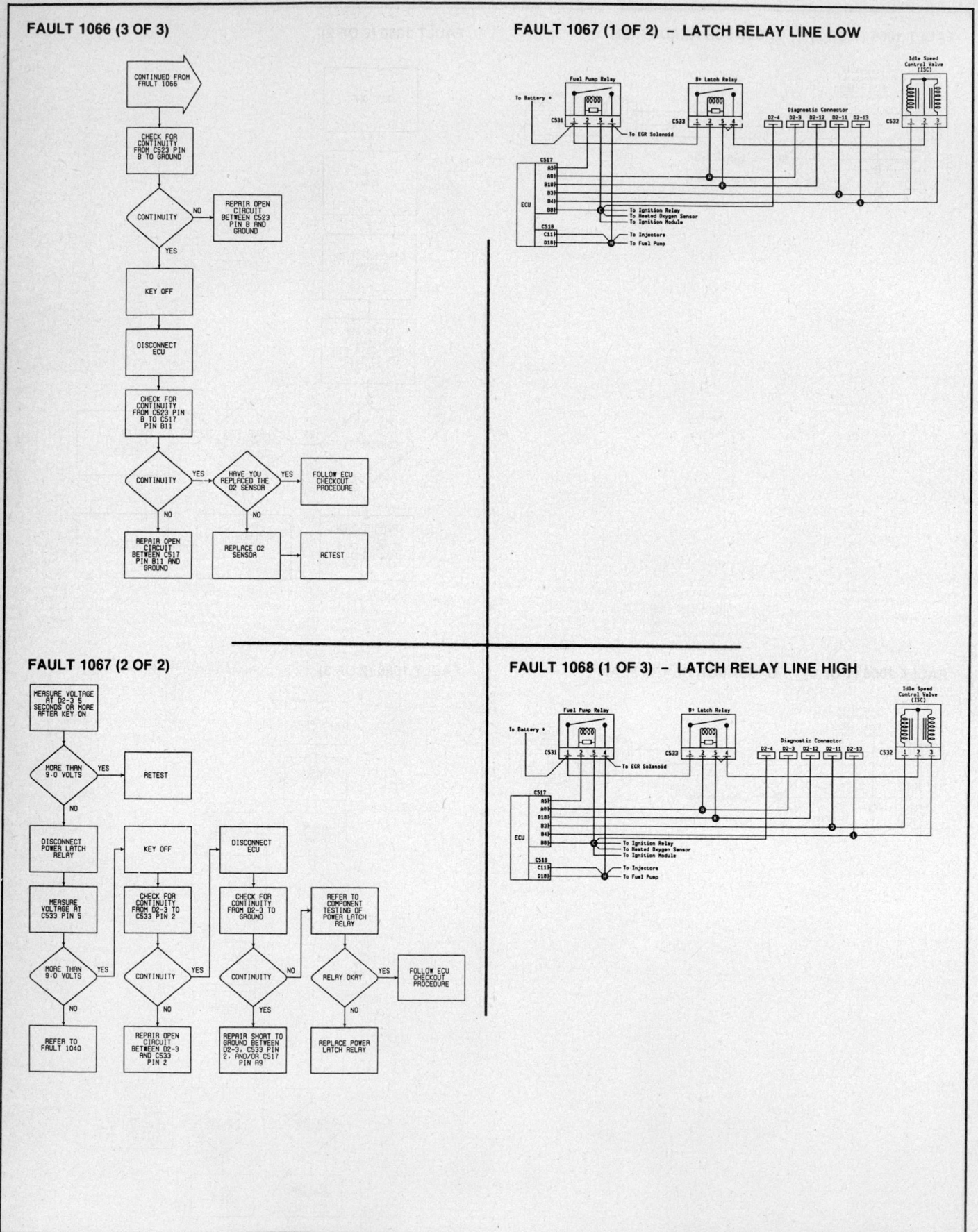

FAULT 1066 (3 OF 3)

CONTINUED FROM FAULT 1066

CHECK FOR CONTINUITY FROM C523 PIN B TO GROUND

CONTINUITY — NO → REPAIR OPEN CIRCUIT BETWEEN C523 PIN B AND GROUND

YES

KEY OFF

DISCONNECT ECU

CHECK FOR CONTINUITY FROM C523 PIN B TO C517 PIN B11

CONTINUITY — YES → HAVE YOU REPLACED THE O2 SENSOR — YES → FOLLOW ECU CHECKOUT PROCEDURE

NO (CONTINUITY) → REPAIR OPEN CIRCUIT BETWEEN C517 PIN B11 AND GROUND

NO (O2 SENSOR) → REPLACE O2 SENSOR → RETEST

FAULT 1067 (1 OF 2) – LATCH RELAY LINE LOW

FAULT 1067 (2 OF 2)

MEASURE VOLTAGE AT D2-3 5 SECONDS OR MORE AFTER KEY ON

MORE THAN 9.0 VOLTS — YES → RETEST

NO

DISCONNECT POWER LATCH RELAY

MEASURE VOLTAGE AT C533 PIN 5

MORE THAN 9.0 VOLTS — NO → REFER TO FAULT 1040

YES → KEY OFF → CHECK FOR CONTINUITY FROM D2-3 TO C533 PIN 2

CONTINUITY — NO → REPAIR OPEN CIRCUIT BETWEEN D2-3 AND C533 PIN 2

CONTINUITY — YES → DISCONNECT ECU → CHECK FOR CONTINUITY FROM D2-3 TO GROUND

CONTINUITY — YES → REPAIR SHORT TO GROUND BETWEEN D2-3, C533 PIN 2, AND/OR C517 PIN A9

CONTINUITY — NO → REFER TO COMPONENT TESTING OF POWER LATCH RELAY

RELAY OKAY — YES → FOLLOW ECU CHECKOUT PROCEDURE

RELAY OKAY — NO → REPLACE POWER LATCH RELAY

FAULT 1068 (1 OF 3) – LATCH RELAY LINE HIGH

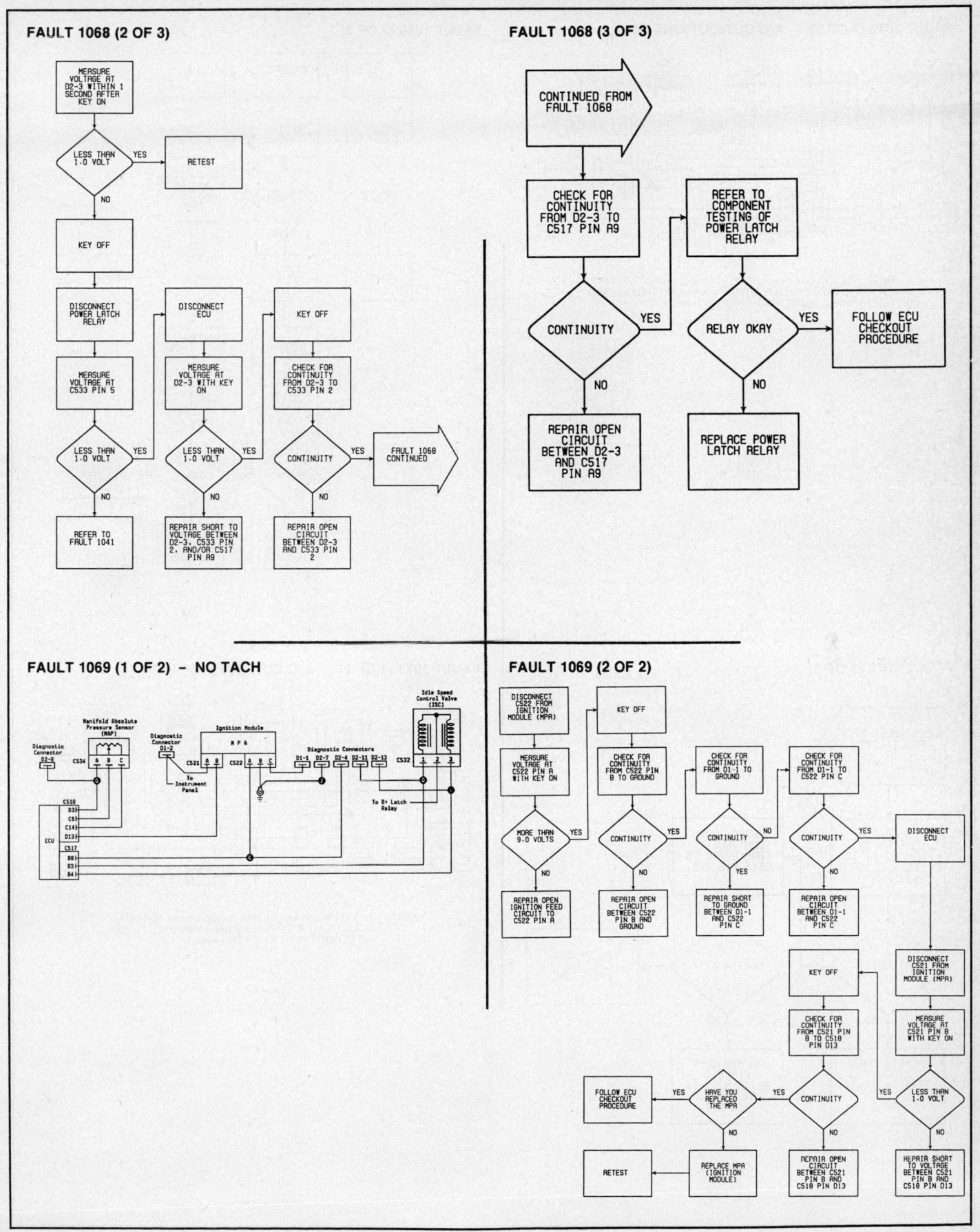

FAULT 1070 (1 OF 3) – A/C CUT-OUT LINE LOW

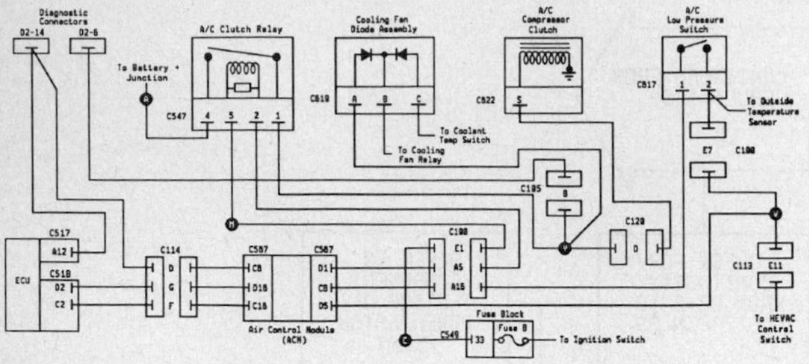

NOTE: To test climate control, refer to appropriate AUTOMATIC A/C-HEATER SYSTEMS article in MITCHELL'S 1989 AIR CONDITIONING & HEATING manual.

FAULT 1070 (2 OF 3)

SEE NOTE IN FAULT 1070 (1 OF 3)

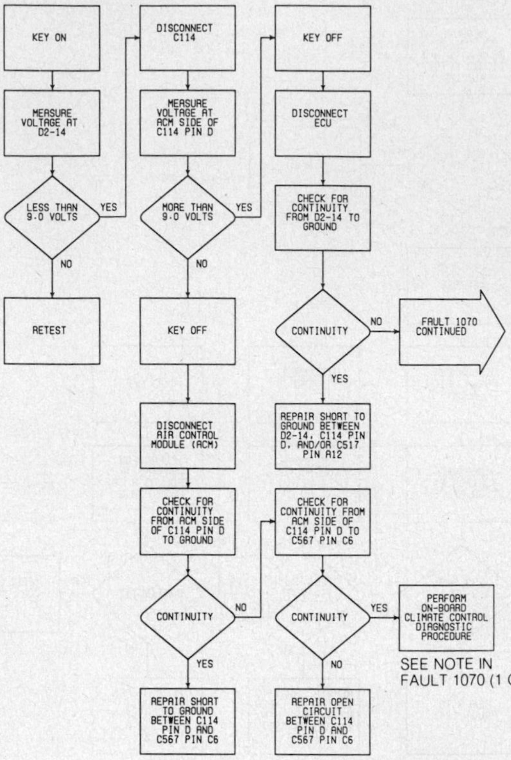

FAULT 1070 (3 OF 3)

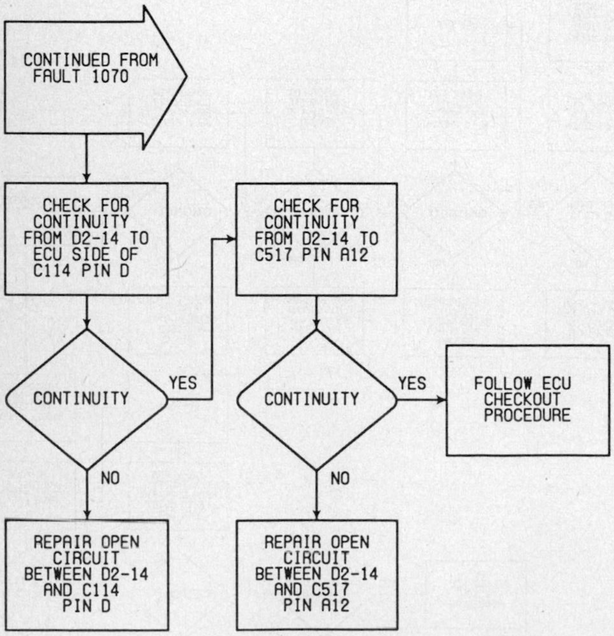

FAULT 1071 (1 OF 2) – A/C CUT-OUT LINE HIGH

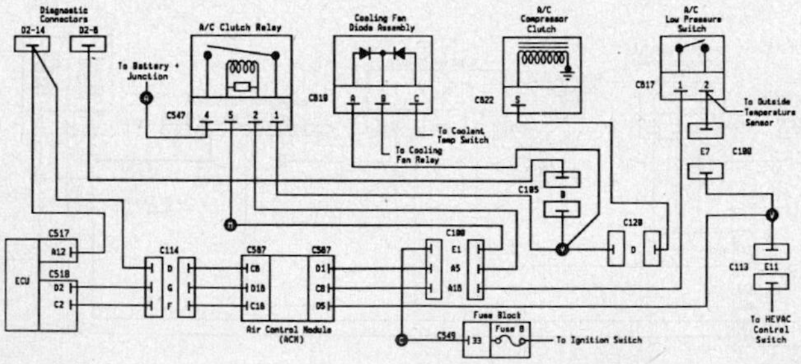

NOTE: To test climate control, refer to appropriate AUTOMATIC A/C-HEATER SYSTEMS article in MITCHELL'S 1989 AIR CONDITIONING & HEATING manual.

FAULT 1071 (2 OF 2)

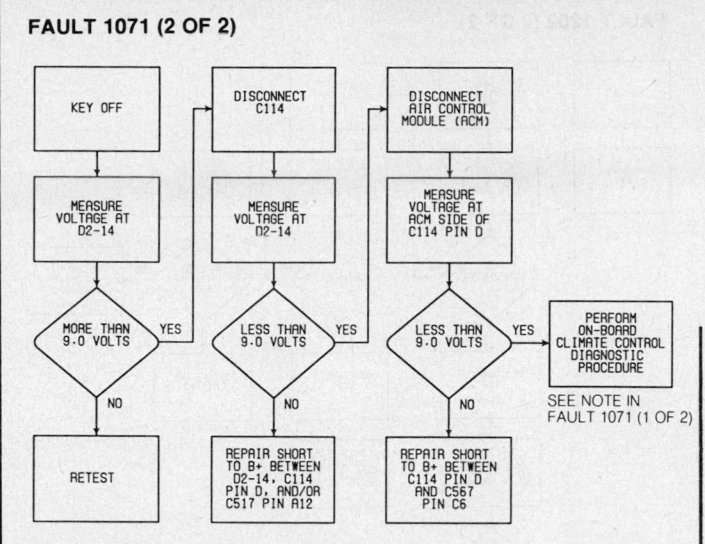

FAULT 1073 (1 OF 2) – ECU DOES NOT SEE CRANKSHAFT POSITION/ENGINE SPEED SENSOR SIGNAL

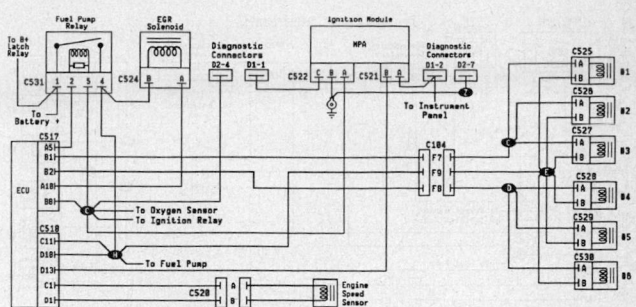

FAULT 1073 (2 OF 2)

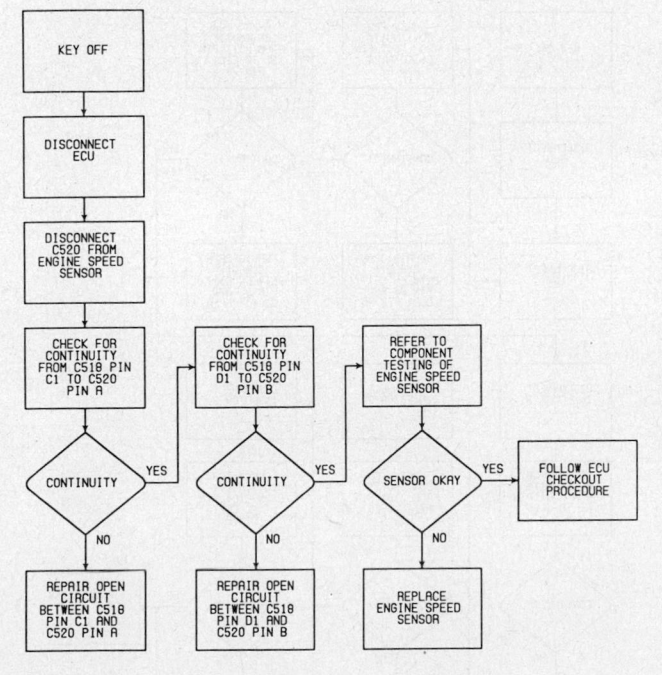

FAULT 1200 – ECU DEFECTIVE

THIS MESSAGE APPEARS WHEN A FAULT WITH THE ECU IS SENSED. REFER TO ECU CHECKOUT PROCEDURE IN THE INTRODUCTION.

1989 COMPUTERIZED ENGINE CONTROLS
Eagle 3.0L MPFI (Cont.)

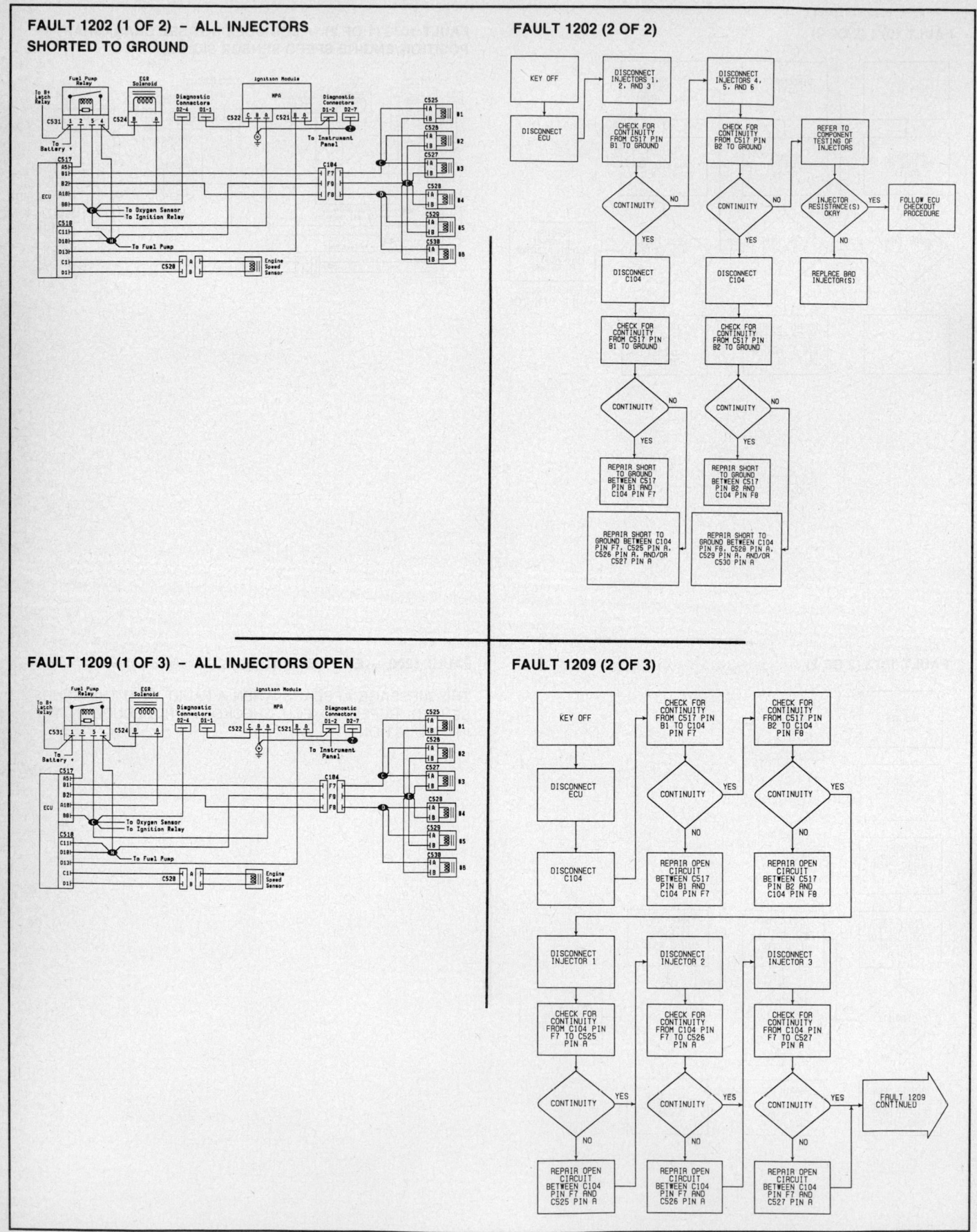

FAULT 1202 (1 OF 2) – ALL INJECTORS SHORTED TO GROUND

FAULT 1202 (2 OF 2)

FAULT 1209 (1 OF 3) – ALL INJECTORS OPEN

FAULT 1209 (2 OF 3)

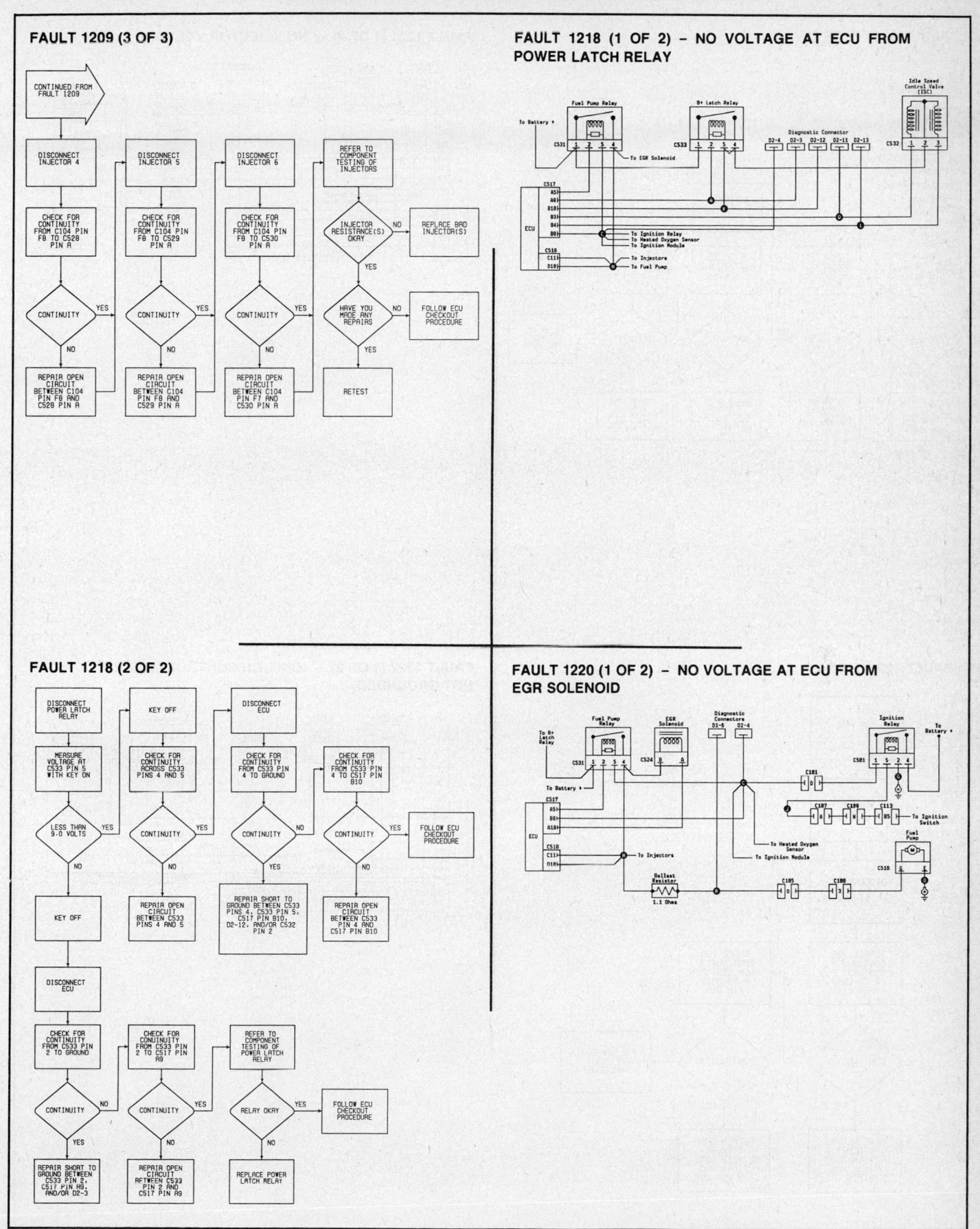

FAULT 1209 (3 OF 3)

FAULT 1218 (1 OF 2) – NO VOLTAGE AT ECU FROM POWER LATCH RELAY

FAULT 1218 (2 OF 2)

FAULT 1220 (1 OF 2) – NO VOLTAGE AT ECU FROM EGR SOLENOID

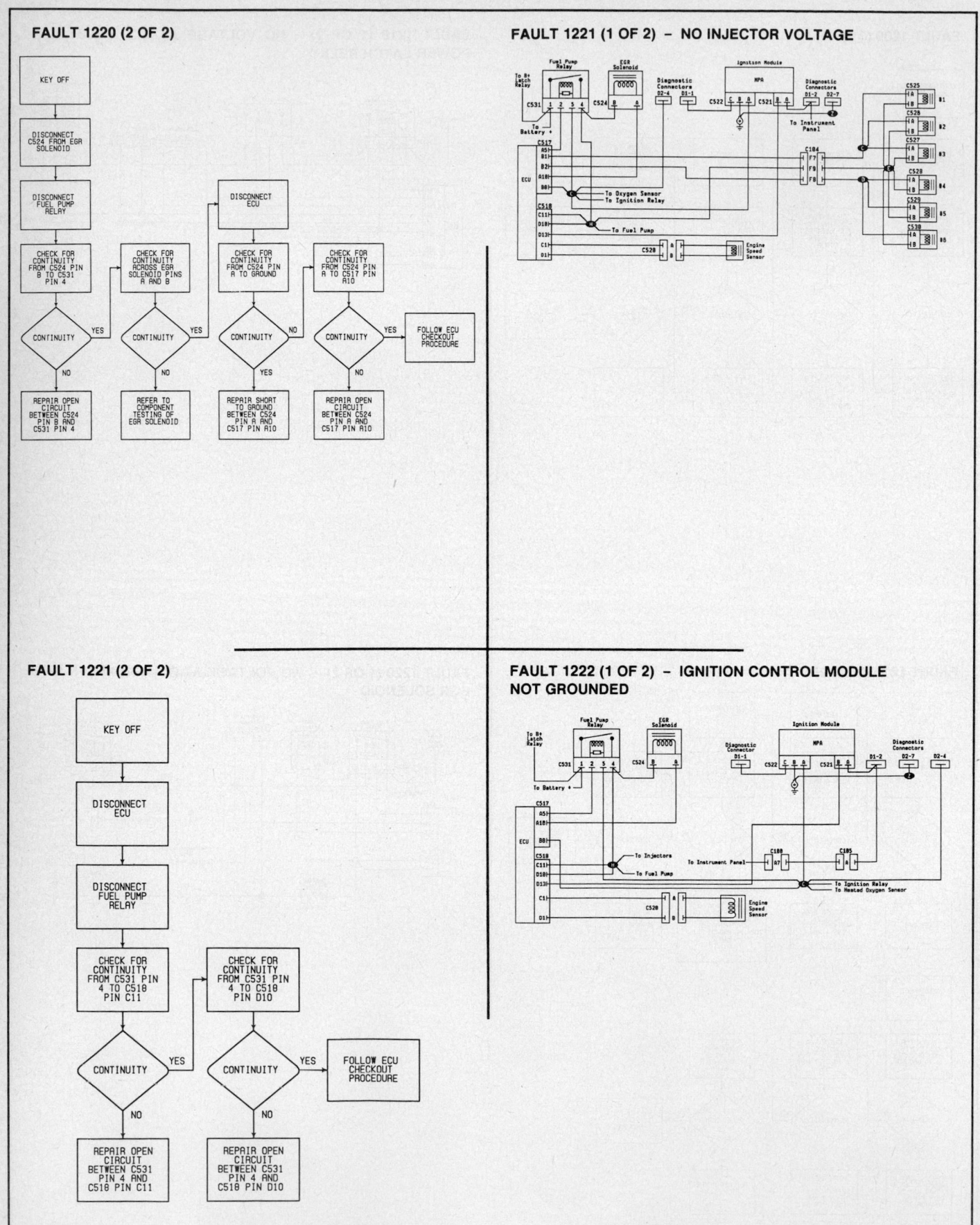

FAULT 1220 (2 OF 2)

FAULT 1221 (1 OF 2) – NO INJECTOR VOLTAGE

FAULT 1221 (2 OF 2)

FAULT 1222 (1 OF 2) – IGNITION CONTROL MODULE NOT GROUNDED

FAULT 1222 (2 OF 2)

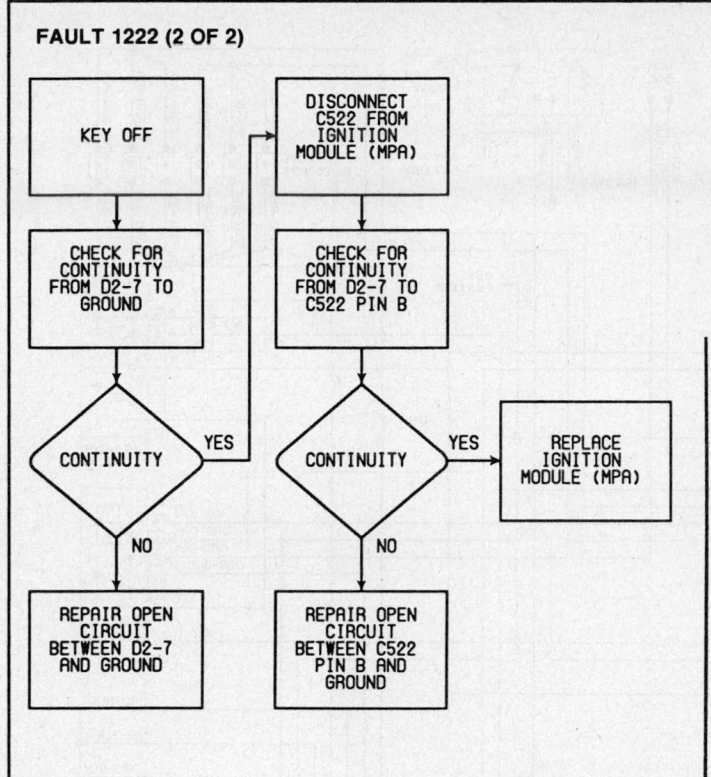

FAULT 1223 – NO ECU TESTS RUN

THE ECU CONTROLLING THE VEHICLE PROVIDES SOME LIMITED ON-BOARD DIAGNOSTICS. THESE ECU BASED TESTS ARE PERFORMED WITH IGNITION ON. THE TESTS CHECK FOR SHORT CIRCUITS TO SOURCE, SHORT CIRCUITS TO GROUND AND OPEN CIRCUITS TO A/C RELAY, EGR SOLENOID, FUEL INJECTORS, MPA (IGNITION MODULE) AND POWER LATCH RELAY.

THESE TESTS WILL NOT BE RUN IF INJECTOR SUPPLY VOLTAGE (SUPPLIED THROUGH FUEL PUMP RELAY) IS LOW AFTER 1/10 OF A SECOND FROM IGNITION ON, OR ENGINE CRANK IS SENSED WITHIN THAT TENTH OF A SECOND.

1) CRANK SENSED – RE-TEST WITH IGNITION ON ONLY, ENSURE THAT OPERATOR DOES NOT CRANK ENGINE, THIS WILL ELIMINATE THIS POSSIBILITY.

2) LOW INJECTOR VOLTAGE – THIS IS GENERALLY CAUSED BY A SLOW FUEL PUMP RELAY (LOW BATTERY VOLTAGE WILL HAVE BEEN DETECTED PRIOR TO THE ECU TESTS). SWAPPING ANOTHER RELAY (PREFERABLY ONE THAT HAS BEEN USED IN A VEHICLE WHERE TESTS WERE RUN PROPERLY) WILL ELIMINATE THIS POSSIBILITY.

NOTE: This fault does not imply any fault with the system. It simply implies that a small fraction of the diagnostic test were not run.

1989 Computerized Engine Controls
Eagle 3.0L MPFI (Cont.)

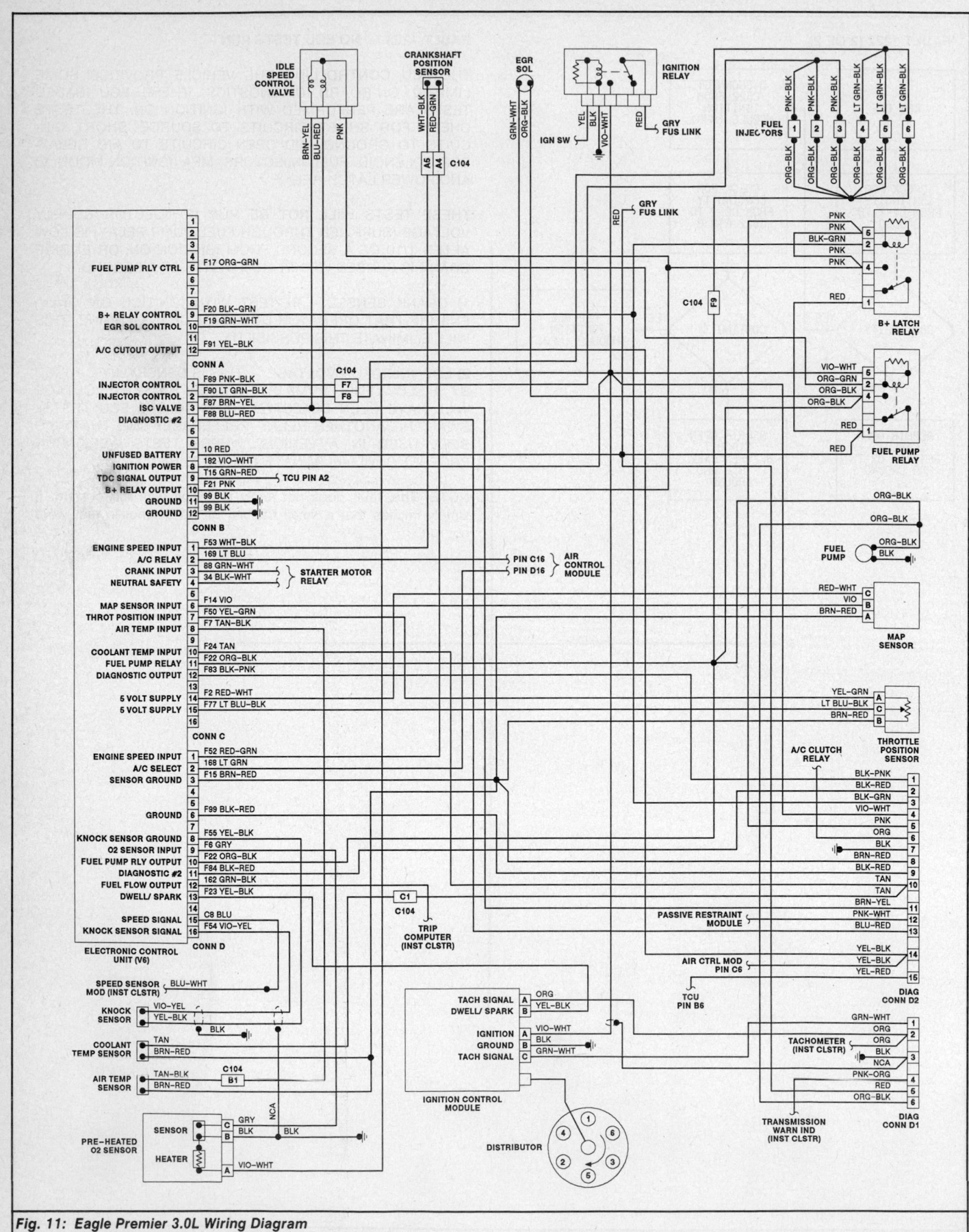

Fig. 11: Eagle Premier 3.0L Wiring Diagram

DESCRIPTION

The heart of the Electronic Engine Control (EEC) system is a microprocessor called the Electronic Control Assembly (ECA). The ECA monitors engine operating conditions by receiving inputs from a series of engine switches and sensors. The ECA output actuators control fuel mixture and idle speed. On models equipped with turbochargers, the ECA also controls the ignition output signal. The ECA is mounted to the floor panel, behind the front of the center console.

OPERATION

The engine control system consists of the ECA, sensors, switches, and actuators. In order for the ECA to perform properly, it must be kept constantly informed of engine operating conditions.

It is the task of the engine sensors to supply the ECA with specific information, in the form of electrical signals, required to determine engine operating conditions. The ECA sends out electrical signals to control air/fuel ratio, emission controls, idle speed and ignition timing. In the event of a sensor or actuator failure, the ECA initiates an alternative strategy to allow the vehicle to maintain driveability. This strategy is called Failure Mode Effects Management (FMEM). It substitutes a fixed sensor signal and continues to monitor the failed sensor. If the failed sensor signals return within operating limits the ECA will again use the sensor's signal. The "Check Engine" light will remain on when FMEM is in operation. The FMEM strategy is listed in the SERVICE CODE DEFINITIONS CHART. Individual component operation is as follows:

ECA INPUT SENSORS

Barometric Pressure (BP) Sensor – Senses changes in barometric pressure to allow ECA to adjust for changes in altitude. The BP sensor affects the air/fuel ratio and idle speed. The BP sensor is mounted on the firewall near the main power relays.

Brake On-Off (BOO) Switch – The BOO switch signals deceleration conditions and affects the air/fuel ratio. It is mounted on the brake pedal.

Clutch Engage Switch – This switch is mounted at the clutch pedal. It signals the ECA when the transmission is in gear. This signal to the ECA affects air/fuel ratio, idle speed, and ignition timing (turbo engine).

Crankshaft Position Sensor (CPS) – This sensor is used on turbo engines only and is located in the base of the distributor. This sensor detects crankshaft angle at equally spaced intervals and signals the ECA, which uses the signal to determine engine RPM. This signal affects, air/fuel ratio, injector timing, idle sped, EGR flow, canister purge flow, fuel pressure, turbo boost pressure and ignition timing.

Cylinder Identification (CID) Sensors – CID sensors are used on turbo engines only. They detect TDC position for cylinders No. 1 and 4. This signal affects injector timing and ignition timing.

Exhaust Gas Oxygen (EGO) Sensor – The voltage signal produced by the EGO sensor indicates to the ECA a rich or lean condition. The EGO sensor is threaded into the exhaust manifold.

EGR Valve Position (EVP) Sensor – The EVP sensor detects EGR valve position and sends a signal to the ECA. The sensor is mounted on the EGR valve. The EVP signal affects EGR flow and ignition timing.

Electrical Load (E/L) Control Unit – The E/L control unit monitors the electrical load placed on the alternator and electrical system. It is mounted beneath the ECA on the floor panel, behind the front of the center console. The E/L control unit signal affects idle speed.

Engine Coolant Temperature (ECT) Sensor – This sensor inputs the coolant temperature to the ECA. It is threaded into an engine water passage near the thermostat housing. The signal from the ECT affects the following:

- Air/Fuel Ratio
- Idle Speed
- EGR Flow
- Purge Flow
- Fuel Pressure
- Injector Timing (Turbo Engine)
- Boost Pressure (Turbo Engine)
- Ignition Timing (Turbo Engine)

Engine Coolant Temperature (ECT) Switch – ECT monitors radiator coolant temperature and signals the ECA. The switch is threaded into the lower part of the radiator. The ECT signal affects the air/fuel ratio, EGR flow and ignition timing (turbo engine).

Idle Switch – The idle switch signals the ECA when the throttle valve is fully closed. It is threaded into the throttle body and contacts the throttle linkage. The switch signal affects air/fuel ratio, injector timing, idle speed, EGR flow and ignition timing (turbo engine).

Knock Control Unit – This control unit is used on turbocharged engines only. It determines if signals produced by the knock sensor are due to pre-ignition or vibration. It filters the signal that is sent to the ECA. The ECA uses the signal to retard ignition timing. It is mounted on the firewall next to the BP sensor.

Knock Sensor (KS) – The KS measures vibrations and converts it into an electrical signal. The signal is sent to the Knock Control Unit (KCU) where it is filtered and sent to the ECA. The KS is threaded into the engine block near the oil pressure switch.

Neutral Gear Switch (NGS) – The NGS monitors in-gear conditions and signals the ECA. This signal affects, air/fuel ratio, idle speed, and ignition timing (turbo engine).

Neutral Safety Switch – The switch monitors gear position on automatic transmission vehicles. It sends a gear position to the 4EAT control unit. The signal affects air/fuel ratio, idle speed and EGR flow. The switch is mounted on side of transmission case.

Power Steering (P/S) Pressure Switch – The P/S switch monitors power steering pressure. When the power steering is in operation, the switch signals the ECA. The switch is located in the high pressure line from the P/S pump to the steering rack assembly. The P/S signal affects the idle speed.

Self-Test Output/Self-Test Input (STO/STI) Connectors – The STO connector is a 6-pin connector that is used to perform the Quick Test diagnostic procedure. The STI is a single-pin connector located next to the STO. When the STI is grounded, it activates the ECA fault code output function. Codes are retrieved through the STO connector. Both connectors are located in the engine compartment, behind the driver's side strut tower.

Throttle Position (TP) Sensor – The TP sensor monitors throttle plate opening. Its signal to the ECA is proportional to opening angle. It is mounted on the throttle body at throttle plate rod. The TP signal affects air/fuel ratio, injector timing, idle speed, EGR flow, fuel pressure, and ignition timing (turbo engine).

Vane Airflow Meter (VAF) – The VAF is mounted in the air inlet between the air cleaner and the throttle body. It measures the volume of air flowing into the engine. A movable door, attached to a potentiometer, signals the ECA as to door position. The ECA translates this to air volume. The Vane Air Temperature (VAT) sensor is mounted in the VAF. The VAF potentiometer also contains a fuel pump switching circuit which supplies a signal to cut fuel pump operation when the engine is off.

Vane Air Temperature (VAT) Sensor – The VAT is an integral part of the VAF. It senses the temperature of incoming air and inputs a signal to the ECA. This signal affects air/fuel ratio, idle speed, fuel pressure, and turbo boost pressure (turbo engine).

ECA OUTPUT ACTUATORS

A/C Clutch Relay – During Wide Open Throttle (WOT) operation a signal is sent from the ECA to the A/C clutch relay to interrupt power to the A/C clutch.

By-Pass Air Control (BAC) Valve – The BAC valve is mounted on the throttle body. It controls idle smoothness by regulating throttle plate by-pass air. The BAC valve consists of the air by-pass valve which functions during cold engine conditions below 122°F (50°C) and the idle speed control solenoid valve which works throughout the entire temperature range. The air by-pass valve is controlled by the engine coolant temperature. The idle speed control solenoid is controlled by the ECA. The BAC controls, cold engine fast idle, no touch starting, dashpot, hot engine idle and engine idle load correction.

1a-382

1989 COMPUTERIZED ENGINE CONTROLS
Ford Motor Co. Probe — EEC (Cont.)

DIAGNOSTIC ROUTINE CHARTS (Cont.)

DIAGNOSTIC ROUTINE NO. 18 (Cont.)

Fails Emission Test

System	Component	Reference
Fuel Delivery	Fuel (Contaminated) Lines Filter Pump Sender Filter Injectors	Fuel System Mechanical Components
Ignition Timing	Base plus Advance and Retard Functions	Ignition Mechanical Components
EGR	Components	QUICK TEST Procedures

DIAGNOSTIC ROUTINE NO. 19

Unusual Noises

System	Component	Reference
Squeal, Click, or Chirp	Oil Level (Low) Valve Train Drive Belts (Loose) Belt Driven Components	Visual & Mechanical Components
	EEC Solenoids	Audible & QUICK TEST Procedures
	Turbocharger	Fuel System Mechanical Components
Rumble, Grind	Belt Driven Components	Mechanical Engine Components
Rattle	Components (Loose)	Visual and Audible
Hiss	Vacuum Distribution (Leak) Induction System (Leak) Spark Plug (Loose)	Visual and Audible
	Turbocharger	Fuel System Mechanical Components
	Cooling System (Leak)	Visual, Audible and Group 27
	EVAP System (Leak)	Visual & QUICK TEST Procedures
Snap	Secondary Ignition	Visual, Audible & QUICK TEST Procedures
Rap, Roar	Exhaust System (Leak)	Visual, Audible and Group 26
	EGR System (Leak)	Visual, Audible & QUICK TEST Procedures
Whine	Turbocharger (Some Whine is Normal)	Visual, Audible and Group 2
Knock	Connecting Rod Bearings (Worn) Main Bearings (Worn) Piston Pins (Loose) Piston to Bore Clearance (Cold Engine)	Mechanical Engine Components
	Detonation	DIAGNOSTIC ROUTINE NO. 4

DIAGNOSTIC ROUTINE NO. 20

"Check Engine" Light Always or Never On

System	Component	Reference
EEC	Pinpoint Test ML	QUICK TEST Procedures

The "Check Engine" light alerts the driver to a malfunction in the engine control system.

1989 COMPUTERIZED ENGINE CONTROLS
Ford Motor Co. Probe — EEC (Cont.)

1a-383

CIRCUIT TESTS

HOW TO USE CIRCUIT TESTS

1) DO NOT perform any CIRCUIT TEST unless directed to do so by a QUICK TEST procedure. Ensure all non-EEC related faults are corrected. FOLLOW EACH TEST STEP IN ORDER UNTIL FAULT IS FOUND. Do not replace any part unless directed to do so. When more than one service code is received, start with the first code displayed.

2) CIRCUIT TESTS require that you prove the electrical circuits are okay before you replace sensors or any other components. Always test circuits for continuity between the sensor and the ECA. Test all circuits for shorts to power, opens, or shorts to ground. Voltage Reference (VREF) and Voltage Power (VPWR) circuits should be tested with KOEO or as specified in CIRCUIT TESTS.

3) DO NOT measure voltage or resistance at ECA or connect any test light, unless specified in testing procedure. DO NOT pierce wiring. If backprobing is specified, always backprobe harness side of connector, never the connector side. Isolate both ends of a circuit and turn key off whenever checking for shorts or continuity, unless specified.

4) An open circuit is defined as a circuit which has a resistance of greater than 5 ohms, unless otherwise specified. Disconnect solenoids and switches before checking circuit continuity or energizing solenoids.

5) A short is defined as any resistance to ground of less than 10,000 ohms, unless otherwise specified.

NOTE: CIRCUIT TESTS are grouped in the following catagories.
- *A1-A3 Preliminary Tests*
- *B1-B16 Input Sensor Tests*
- *C1-C3 Fuel Control Systems*
- *D1-D11 ECA Output Tests*

NOTE: In the following tests, circuits and illustrations are supplied courtesy of Ford Motor Co. Complete EEC system wiring diagrams may be found at the end of this article. The abbreviations for wire colors used in the individual CIRCUIT TEST diagrams are as follows:

- *"BK" Black*
- *"BL" Blue*
- *"BR" Brown*
- *"DB" Dark Blue*
- *"DG" Dark Green*
- *"GY" Gray*
- *"GN" Green*
- *"LB" Light Blue*
- *"LG" Light Green*
- *"N" Natural*
- *"O" Orange*
- *"PK" Pink*
- *"P" Purple*
- *"R" Red*
- *"T" Tan*
- *"W" White*
- *"Y" Yellow*

SERVICE CODE TO CIRCUIT TEST REFERENCE CHART

Diagnostic Service Code	Circuit Test Non-Turbo Engine	Circuit Test Turbo Engine
No Codes or "00"	Go To Next Quick Test	Go To Next Quick Test
"01"	A1	A1
"02"	.....	.....
"03"	.....	......
"04"	.....	.....
"05"	.....	B4
"08"	B6	B6
"09"	B2	B2
"10"	B1	B1
"12"	B5	B5
"14"	B3	B3
"15"	D3	D3
"16"	B9	B9
"17"	D3	C1
"25"	D7	D7
"26"	D2	D2
"28"	D1	D1
"29"	.....	D7
"34"	D3	D3
"42"	.....	D5
No Codes With "Check Engine" Light On or Low Voltage at STO Terminal	D9	D9
Codes Not Listed	D10	D10

1a-384

1989 COMPUTERIZED ENGINE CONTROLS
Ford Motor Co. Probe — EEC (Cont.)

CIRCUIT TEST A1

IGNITION PULSE

Ignition Circuits

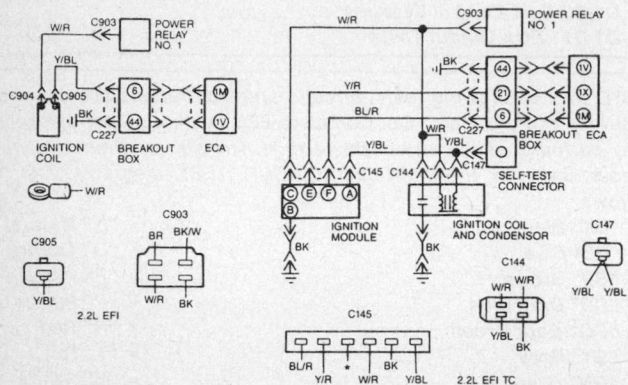

NOTE: Enter this test only when Code 01 is displayed during QUICK TEST procedures. This test will not diagnose ignition problems. This test is intended to diagnose only the following: spark (EEC controlled), and electrical circuits (PIP, ignition ground and VPWR). To prevent replacement of good components, be aware that the following non-EEC components may be faulty: fuel quality and quantity, ignition mechanical components and engine mechanical components.

NOTE: Turbo engines start at step 1), non-turbo engines start at step 14).

1) Checking System Integrity (Turbo Engines) – Visually check all wiring, harnesses, connectors and components for evidence of damage, overheating, shorting or looseness. If a fault is found, repair as necessary. If no faults are found, go to next step for Turbo engines or step **14)** for non-turbo engines.

2) Checking Coil Spark – Connect a spark tester between coil secondary wire and ground. Crank engine. If spark jumps spark tester, check for spark at plugs and return to DIAGNOSTIC ROUTIUNES. If spark does not jump tester air gap, go to next step.

3) Coil Pulse Check – DO NOT disconnect coil or pierce wire. Connect test light between coil Yellow/Blue wire and ground. Crank engine. If test lamp flashes, go to step **12)**. If test light stays on, go to step **7)**. If test light stays off, go to next step.

4) Check Power to Coil – With KOEO and DVOM set on 20-volt scale, measure voltage between coil White/Red wire and ground. If voltage is 10 volts or more, go to next step. If voltage is less than 10 volts, go to step **6)**.

5) Coil Ground Check – With key off, set DVOM on 200-ohm scale. Measure resistance between coil ground "BK" wire and ground. If resistance is less than 5 ohms, return to DIAGNOSTIC ROUTINES. If resistance is not less than 5 ohms, repair open in "BK" wire to ground.

6) Checking Power to Power Relay No. 1 – DO NOT disconnect relay or pierce wire. Set DVOM on 20-volt scale and turn key on. Measure voltage between No. 1 power relay "W/R" wire and ground. If voltage is greater than 10 volts, repair "W/R" wire from coil to relay. If voltage is 10 volts or less, go to CIRCUIT TEST B12, step **1)**.

7) Checking Tach Connector Pulse – Connect test light between TACH connector and ground. Crank engine. If test light flashes, repair "Y/BL" wire from tach connector to coil. If test light does not flash, go to next step.

8) Ignition Module Pulse Check – DO NOT disconnect module or pierce wire. Connect test light between ignition module terminal "A" ("Y/BL" wire) and ground. Crank engine. If test light flashes, repair "Y/BL" wire between ignition module and TACH test connector. If test light does not flash, go to next step.

9) Checking Power to Ignition Module – Set DVOM on 20-volt scale and turn ignition on. Measure voltage between ignition module terminal "C" ("W/R" wire) and ground. If voltage is greater than 10 volts, go to next step. If voltage is 10 volts or less, go back to step **6)**.

10) Checking Ignition Module Ground Circuit – Turn key off, set DVOM on 200-ohm scale. Measure resistance between ignition module terminal "B" ("BK" wire) and ground. If resistance is less than 5

CIRCUIT TEST A1 (Cont.)

ohms, go to next step. If resistance is greater than 5 ohms, repair "BK" wire from ignition module to ground.

TACH Test Connector Location (Turbo Engines)

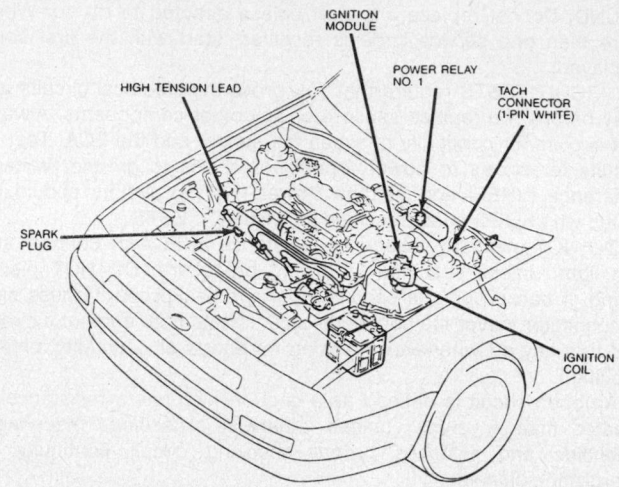

CAUTION: Ensure correct test connector is used. Tach connector has Yellow/Blue wires. The STI and Fuel Pump test connectors are located in the same area.

11) Checking Ignition Module Pulse – DO NOT disconnect module or pierce wire. Set DVOM on 5-volt scale. Crank engine. Measure voltage between ignition module terminal "E" ("Y/R" wire) and ground. If voltage is 0.6-1.0 volt, return to DIAGNOSTIC ROUTINES. If voltage is not 0.6-1.0 volt, go to next step.

12) Checking SPOUT Signal – Install breakout box. Set DVOM on 5-volt scale. Turn key on and crank engine. Measure voltage between test pins No. 21 and 44 (ground) at breakout box. If voltage is about zero volts with key on and 0.6-0.8 volt while cranking, repair "Y/R" wire from ECA to ignition module. If voltage is not as specified, go to next step.

13) Checking PIP Circuit Continuity – Turn key off and install breakout box. Set DVOM on 200-ohm scale. Turn key off and install breakout box. Set DVOM on 200-ohm scale. Measure resistance between test pin No. 6 and ignition module terminal "F" ("BL/R" wire). Measure resistance between test pins No. 6 and 44 (ground). If resistance between test pin No. 6 and ignition module is less than 5 ohms and the resistance between test pins No. 6 and 44 (ground) is greater than 5 ohms, replace ECA. If resistance is not as specified, repair "BL/R" wire from ECA to ignition module.

14) Checking System Integrity (Non-Tubo Engines) – Visually check all wiring, harnesses, connectors and components for evidence of damage, overheating, shorting or looseness. If a fault is found, repair as necessary. If no faults are found, go to next step.

15) Checking Coil (Negative) Pulse – Connect test light between ignition coil (–) "Y/BL" wire and ground. Crank engine. If test light flashes, go to step **17)**. If test light does not flash, go to next step.

16) Checking Voltage at Coil Positive (+) – Set DVOM on 20-volt scale and turn key on. Measure voltage between ignition coil positive (+) "W/R" wire and ground. If voltage is greater than 10 volts, ensure there is 6 volts at coil negative (–) and go to step **18)**. If coil positive (–) is 10 volts or less, go back to step **6)**.

17) Checking PIP Signal – Install breakout box. Connect test light between test pins No. 6 and 20 (ground). Crank engine. If test light flashes, go to step **19)**. If light does not flash, repair "Y/BL" wire from ECA to coil.

18) Checking Distributor Pulse – Ensure distributor is connected. DO NOT pierce wire. Connect test light between distributor "Y/BL" wire and ground. Crank engine. If test light flashes, repair "Y/BL" wire from distributor to coil. If test light does not flash, go to DIAGNOSTIC ROUTINES.

19) Check Spark at Plugs – Connect spark tester between plug wire (at each plug) and ground. Crank engine. If spark jumps tester air gap, ensure ignition timing is within specification. If not, adjust and rerun QUICK TEST. If timing cannot be adjusted to specification, replace ECA. If spark does not jump tester, go to DIAGNOSTIC ROUTINES.

1989 COMPUTERIZED ENGINE CONTROLS
Ford Motor Co. Probe — EEC (Cont.)

1a-385

CIRCUIT TEST A2

VEHICLE BATTERY

Battery Circuit Component Locations

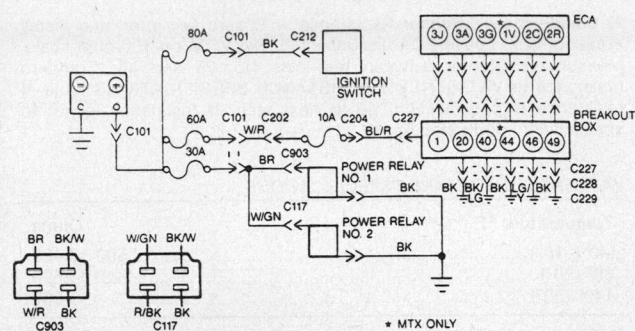

NOTE: Enter this test only when directed here from CIRCUIT TESTS A3, B4, D9, C1, C2 or C3. To prevent replacement of good components, be aware that the following non-EEC components may be faulty: ignition switch, alternator, battery cables, ground straps or voltage regulator. This test is intended to diagnose only the following: ECA, wiring harness circuits (KAPWR and ground), and battery voltage.

1) Checking Battery Circuit Integrity – Visually check all wiring, harnesses, connectors and components for evidence of damage, overheating, shorting or looseness. If a fault is found, repair as necessary. If no faults are found, go to next step.

2) Check Battery Charge – Check battery voltage and charge condition. Service if necessary and go to next step.

3) Power Check – Turn key off and install breakout box. Set DVOM on 20-volt scale. Measure voltage betweeen the followings points:
- Test pin No.1 and ground.
- Ignition switch "BK" and battery ground.
- Power Relay No. 1, "BR" wire and battery ground.
- Power Relay No. 2, "W/GN" wire and battery ground.

If all voltages are greater than 10 volts, go to step **5)**. If all voltages are not greater than 10 volts, go to next step.

4) Checking For Open Circuits – Turn key off and install breakout box. Set DVOM on 200-ohm scale. Measure the following resistances:
- 80A fuse to ignition switch "BK" wire.
- 60A fuse to 10A fuse.
- 30A fuse to Power Relay No. 1, "BR" wire.
- 30A fuse to Power Relay No. 2, "W/GN" wire.
- 10A fuse to test pin No. 1.
- Battery positive (+) to fuses (30A, 60A and 80A).

If all resistances are less than 5 ohms, go to next step. If resistances are greater than 5 ohms, repair circuits as necessary.

5) Checking Relay Ground Circuit – Turn key off and set DVOM on 200-ohm scale. Measure resistance between Power Relay No. 1 ("BK" wire) and battery negative (–). Measure resistance between Power Relay No. 2 and battery negative (–). If both resistances are less than 5 ohms, go to next step. If not, repair open in Power Relay(s) ground wire.

6) Checking ECA Ground – Turn key off and set DVOM on 200-ohm scale. Measure the following resistances:
- ECA case and battery negative (–).
- Test Pin No. 44 and battery negative (–), (manual transmission only).
- Test pin No. 49 and battery negative (–).
- Test pin No. 20 and battery negative (–).
- Test pin No. 46 and battery negative (–).

If all resistances are less than 5 ohms, go to next step. If any resistance is greater than 5 ohms, repair circuit as necessary.

7) Isolating ECA Ground Fault – Turn key off and install breakout box. Disconnect vehicle harness from breakout box. Set DVOM on 200-ohm scale. To isolate ECA ground faults, measure the resistances at the breakout box, between the following test pins:
- Test pin No. 46 and 44 (manual transmission only).
- Test pins No. 46 and 49.
- Test pins No. 46 and 20.
- Test pins No. 46 and 40.

If all resistances are less than 5 ohms, ECA is okay, return to DIAGNOSTIC ROUTINES. If any resistance is greater than 5 ohms, replace ECA.

CIRCUIT TEST A3

REFERENCE VOLTAGE & SIGNAL RETURN

NOTE: You should perform this test when a check for VREF has failed in the sensor input CIRCUIT TESTS or directed here from CIRCUIT TEST D10. This test is intended to diagnose the following circuits only: sensor harness circuits, signal return, ground, VPWR, KAPWR, VREF, and the ECA.

Signal Return Circuits

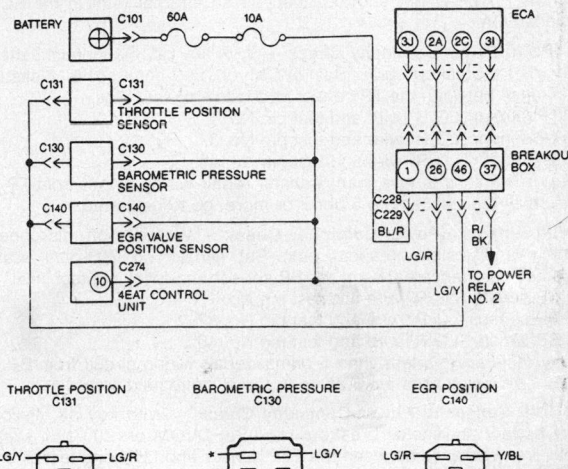

1) Checking System Integrity – Visually check all wiring, harnesses, connectors and components for evidence of damage, overheating, shorting or looseness. If a fault is found, repair as necessary. If no faults are found, go to next step.

2) Checking KAPWR At ECA – Install breakout box and set DVOM on 20-volt scale. With KOEO, measure voltage between test pins No. 1 and 20 (ground). If voltage is greater than 10 volts, go to next step. If voltage is 10 volts or less, go to CIRCUIT TEST A2, step 1).

3) Checking Reference Voltage – Install breakout box and set DVOM on 20-volt scale. With KOEO, measure voltage between test pins No. 26 (VREF) and 46 (Signal Return). If voltage is 4-6 volts, go to next step. If voltage is less than 4 volts, go to step 5). If voltage is greater than 6 volts, go to step 7).

4) Checking Continuity of Sensors to ECA – With key off and breakout box installed, set DVOM on 200-ohm scale. Measure resistance between the following test pins, at the breakout box, and the sensor circuit wires, at the sensors:
- Test pin No. 26 and TP sensor "LG/R" wire.
- Test pin No. 26 and BP sensor "LG/R" wire.
- Test pin No. 26 and EVP sensor "LG/R" wire.
- Test pin No. 26 and 4EAT connector terminal pin No. 10.
- Test pin No. 46 and TP sensor "LG/Y" wire.
- Test pin No. 46 and BP sensor "LG/Y" wire.
- Test pin No. 46 and EVP sensor "LG/Y" wire.

If all resistances are less than 5 ohms, return to DIAGNOSTIC ROUTINES. If any resistance is greater than 5 ohms, repair circuits as necessary.

5) Checking Signal Return Continuity to Ground – With key off and breakout box installed, set DVOM on 200-ohm scale. Measure resistance between test pin No. 46 (Signal Return) and ground. If resistance is less than 5 ohms, go to step 8). If resistance is 5 ohms or more, go to next step.

6) Checking ECA to Sensor Circuits – With key off and breakout box installed, set DVOM on 200-ohm scale. Measure resistance between the following test pins, at the breakout box, and the sensor circuit wires:
- Test pin No. 26 and TP sensor "LG/R" wire.
- Test pin No. 26 and BP sensor "LG/R" wire.
- Test pin No. 26 and EVP sensor "LG/R" wire.
- Test pin No. 26 and 4EAT connector terminal pin No. 10.
- Test pin No. 46 and TP sensor "LG/Y" wire.
- Test pin No. 46 and BP sensor "LG/Y" wire.
- Test pin No. 46 and EVP sensor "LG/Y" wire.

CIRCUIT TEST A3 (Cont.)

If all resistances are less than 5 ohms, there is an internal fault in the ECA, replace the ECA. If any resistance is greater than 5 ohms, repair circuits as necessary.

7) Checking For a Shorted VREF Circuit – With key off and breakout box installed, set DVOM on 200-ohm scale. Leave ECA disconnected from vehicle harness and breakout box. Measure resistance between test pins No. 26 (VREF) and No. 1 (KAPWR). Measure resistance between test pins No. 26 (VREF) and No. 37 (VPWR). If both resistances are less than 5 ohms, there is a short between VREF and KAPWR or VPWR, go to next step. If both resistances are greater than 5 ohms, VREF is not shorted, there is an internal fault in the ECA, replace ECA.

8) TPS to Power Continuity Check – With key off, disconnect battery and install breakout box. Set DVOM on 200-ohm scale. Measure resistance between the TP sensor and following test pins:
- TP sensor "LG/R" wire and test pin No. 1.
- TP sensor "LG/R" wire and test pin No. 37.
- TP sensor "LG/R" wire and test pin No. 46.

If any resistance is less than 5 ohms, repair wiring circuit from TP to ECA. If all resistances are 5 ohms or more, go to next step.

9) BP Sensor to Power Continuity Check – With key off, disconnect battery and install breakout box. Set DVOM on 200-ohm scale. Measure resistance between the BP sensor and following test pins:
- BP sensor "LG/R" wire and test pin No. 1.
- BP sensor "LG/R" wire and test pin No. 37.
- BP sensor "LG/R" wire and test pin No. 46.

If any resistance is less than 5 ohms, repair wiring circuit from BP to ECA. If all resistances are 5 ohms or more, go to next step.

10) EVP Sensor to Power Continuity Check – With key off, disconnect battery and install breakout box. Set DVOM on 200-ohm scale. Measure resistance between the EVP sensor and following test pins:
- EVP sensor "LG/R" wire and test pin No. 1.
- EVP sensor "LG/R" wire and test pin No. 37.
- EVP sensor "LG/R" wire and test pin No. 46.

If any resistance is less than 5 ohms, repair wiring circuit from EVP to ECA. If all resistances are 5 ohms or more, go to next step.

11) 4EAT to Power Continuity Check – With key off, disconnect battery and install breakout box. Set DVOM on 200-ohm scale. Measure resistance between the TP sensor and following test pins:
- 4EAT connector "LG/R" wire and test pin No. 1.
- 4EAT connector "LG/R" wire and test pin No. 37.
- 4EAT connector "LG/R" wire and test pin No. 46.

If any resistance is less than 5 ohms, repair wiring circuit from 4EAT connector terminal No. 10 to ECA. If any resistance is 5 ohms or more, replace ECA.

CIRCUIT TEST B1
VANE AIR TEMPERATURE (VAT)

VAT Circuits

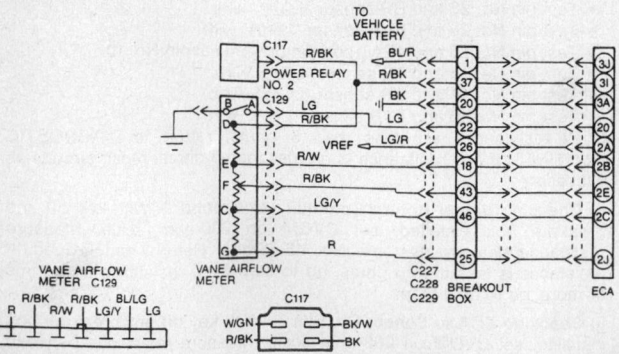

NOTE: Enter this test only when a Code 10 is displayed during the QUICK TEST procedure or when directed here from another CIRCUIT TEST. To prevent replacement of good components, be aware that the following non-EEC items may be faulty: ambient temperature too low or too high. Ambient temperature must be greater than 50°F (10°C) for this test. This test is intended to diagnose only the following: VAT sensor, VAT and Signal Return circuits, vehicle harness and ECA.

CIRCUIT TEST B1 (Cont.)

1) Checking System Integrity – Visually check all wiring, harnesses, connectors and components for evidence of damage, overheating, shorting or looseness. If a fault is found, repair as necessary. If no faults are found, go to next step.

2) Checking VAT Sensor Resistance – Ensure key is off and install breakout box. Leave ECA disconnected. Set VOM on 100-ohm scale. Measure resistance between test pins No. 25 and 46. Compare resistance to VAT SENSOR RESISTANCE SPECIFICATIONS table. If resistance is specification, go to next step. If resistance is not to specification, go to step 6).

VAT SENSOR RESISTANCE SPECIFICATIONS

Temperature °F (°C)	Ohms
–4° (–15°)	13,600-18,400
68° (20°)	2210-2690
140° (60°)	493-667

3) Checking VAT Sensor Voltage – With breakout box installed, set VOM on 10-volt scale. Turn key on and measure voltage between test pins No. 25 and 20. At 68°F (20°C), voltage should be 2.5 volts. Measure the voltage between test pins No. 46 and 20 (ground). At 68°F (20°C), voltage should be zero volts. Voltage will decrease if ambient temperature increases. If both voltages are as specified, there is an internal fault in the ECA, replace ECA. If voltage readings were not, as specified, go to next step.

4) Checking For Short Between VAT & ECA – Ensure key is off. Disconnect battery negative (–) cable. Install breakout box and leave ECA disconnected. Set VOM on 200-ohm scale. Measure resistance between the following test pins:
- Test pins No. 25 and 26
- Test pins No. 25 and 1
- Test pins No. 25 and 37
- Test pins No. 25 and 20 (ground)
- Test pins No. 46 and 26
- Test pins No. 46 and 1
- Test pins No. 46 and 37

If any resistance is less than 5 ohms, repair shorted circuit. If all circuits have a resistance of 5 ohms or more, go to next step.

5) Checking Signal Return – With key off, install breakout box and set VOM on 200-ohm scale. Measure resistance between test pins No. 46 and 20 (ground). If resistance is less than 5 ohms, replace ECA. If resistance is 5 ohms or more, go to CIRCUIT TEST A3, step 1).

6) Checking Open Circuits Between ECA & VAT – With key off, install breakout box and leave ECA disconnected. Set VOM on 200-ohm scale. Measure resistance between test pin No. 25 and "R" wire at VAF sensor. Measure resistance between test pin No. 46 and "GN/Y" wire at VAF sensor. If both resistances are less than 5 ohms, go to next step. If either resistance is 5 ohms or more, repair open circuit as necessary.

7) Checking VAT Sensor Resistance – With key off, disconnect VAT sensor and set VOM on 10k-ohm scale. Ensure temperature is approximately 68°F (20°C). Measure resistance between sensor terminals "D" and "G". Measure resistance between sensor terminals "C" and "G". If both resistances are 2000-2700 ohms, repair short in "R" wire. If resistances are not as specified, replace VAF sensor.

CIRCUIT TEST B2
ENGINE COOLANT TEMPERATURE SENSOR

ECT Sensor Circuits

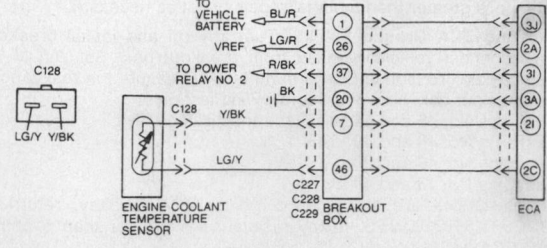

1989 COMPUTERIZED ENGINE CONTROLS
Ford Motor Co. Probe — EEC (Cont.)

1a-387

CIRCUIT TEST B2 (Cont.)

NOTE: Enter this test only when a Code 09 is displayed during the QUICK TEST procedure or when directed here from another CIRCUIT TEST. To prevent replacement of good components, be aware that the following non-EEC components may be at fault: coolant level, oil level, obstructed airflow to radiator, engine not at normal operating temperature, cooling fan, and thermostat. This test is intended to diagnose only the following ECT components: ECT sensor, ECT and Signal Return circuits, vehicle harness and ECA.

1) Checking System Integrity – Visually check all wiring, harnesses, connectors and components for evidence of damage, overheating, shorting or looseness. If a fault is found, repair as necessary. If no faults are found, go to next step.

2) Checking ECT Resistance – With key off, install breakout box and set VOM on 200k-ohm scale. Leave ECA disconected. Measure resistance between test pins No. 7 and 46. Compare resistance to specifications shown in ECT SENSOR RESISTANCE table. If resistance is within specification, go to next step. If resistance is not to specification, go to step 6).

ECT SENSOR RESISTANCE

Temperature: °F (°C)	Ohms
–4° (–15°)	14,500-17,800
68° (20°)	2200-2700
140° (60°)	500-640
176° (80°)	280-350

3) Checking ECT Voltage – Install breakout box, set VOM on 20-volt scale and turn key on. Measure voltage between test pins No. 7 and 46. Compare voltage to specifications shown in ECT VOLTAGE CHECK table. If both voltage readings are within specification, ECT signal is okay. Replace ECA. If ECT does not meet specification, go to next step.

ECT VOLTAGE CHECK

Temperature °F (°C)	Volts
Normal Operating Temperature	0.3-0.6
68° (20°)	2.5

4) Checking For Short Between ECT & ECA – Ensure key is off. Disconnect battery negative (–) cable and install breakout box. Set VOM on 200-ohm scale. Measure resistance between the following test pins:
- Test pins No. 7 and 1
- Test pins No. 7 and 26
- Test pins No. 7 and 37
- Test pins No. 7 and 20 (ground)
- Test pins No. 46 and 1
- Test pins No. 46 and 26
- Test pins No. 46 and 37

If any resistance is less than 5 ohms, repair shorted circuit. If all circuits have a resistance of 5 ohms or more, go to next step.

5) Checking Signal Return – With key off, install breakout box and set VOM on 200-ohm scale. Measure resistance between test pins No. 46 and 20 (ground). If resistance is less than 5 ohms, replace ECA. If resistance is 5 ohms or more, go to next step.

6) Checking Open Circuits Between ECA & ECT – With key off, install breakout box. Set VOM on 200-ohm scale. Measure resistance between test pin No. 7 and "Y/BK" wire at ECT sensor. Measure resistance between test pin No. 46 and "LG/Y" wire at ECT sensor. If both resistances are less than 5 ohms, go to next step. If either resistance is 5 ohms or more, repair open circuit as necessary.

7) Checking ECT Sensor Resistance – With key off, disconnect sensor. Set VOM on 200k-ohm scale. Measure resistance across ECT sensor. If resistance is within specification, repair short in wires. If resistance is not to specification, replace ECT.

ECT SENSOR RESISTANCE

Temperature °F (°C)	Ohms
–4° (–15°)	14,500-17,800
68° (20°)	2200-2700
140° (60°)	500-640
176° (80°)	280-350

CIRCUIT TEST B3

BAROMETRIC PRESSURE (BP) SENSOR

BP Sensor Circuits

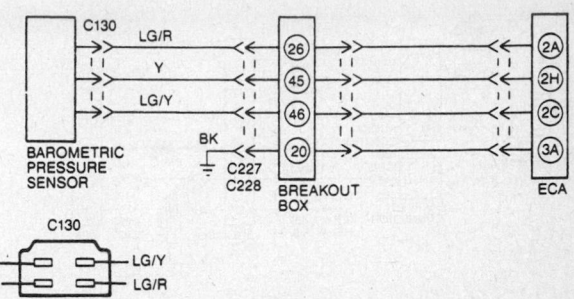

NOTE: Enter this test only when a Code 14 is displayed during the QUICK TEST procedure or when directed here from another CIRCUIT TEST. To prevent replacement of good components, be aware that the following non-EEC items may be at fault: unusually high or low atmospheric barometer reading, blocked vacuum lines and basic mechanical engine components. This test is intended to diagnose only the following components: BP sensor, VREF, BP Signal and Signal Return harness circuits, and ECA.

1) Checking System Integrity – Visually check all wiring, harnesses, connectors and components for evidence of damage, overheating, shorting or looseness. If a fault is found, repair as necessary. If no faults are found, go to next step.

2) Checking VREF & Signal Return Circuits – Install breakout box and set VOM on 20-volt scale. Turn key on and measure voltage between test pins shown in VREF & SIGNAL RETURN VOLTAGE CHECKS table. If all voltage readings are within specifications, go to next step. If readings are not within specifications, go to CIRCUIT TEST A3, step 1).

VREF & SIGNAL RETURN VOLTAGE CHECKS

Test Pins No.	Voltage
26 & 20	4-6
26 & 46	4-6
20 & 46	0

3) Checking BP Voltage Supply – Install breakout box and set VOM on 20-volt scale. Turn key on and measure voltage between test pins No. 45 and 46. At sea level, voltage should be 3.5-4.5 volts. At high altitude (6500 ft.), voltage should be 2.5-3.5 volts. Connect a vacuum pump to BP sensor vent nipple, with 0 in. Hg (low vacuum), voltage should be 3.5-4.5 volts. With 30 in. Hg (high vacuum), voltage should be zero volts. If voltage is within specifications, BP sensor is okay, replace ECA. If voltage is not within specifications, go to next step.

4) Checking Power at BP Sensor – Set VOM on 20-volt scale. Turn key on. Perform and record the following voltage checks at the sensor connector. If all voltage readings are within specifications, go to next step. If not, repair wiring from BP sensor to ECA as necessary.

BP SENSOR VOLTAGE CHECKS

Test Circuits	Volts
"LG/R" wire to ground	4-6
"LG/R" to "LG/Y" wire	4-6
"LG/Y" wire to ground	0

5) Checking Voltage at BP Sensor – Set VOM on 20-volt scale and turn key on. Leave BP sensor connected and test by backprobing connector at sensor. Measure voltage between "Y" wire and ground. At sea level, voltage should be 3.5-4.5 volts. At high altitude (6500 ft.), voltage should be 2.5-3.5 volts. Connect a vacuum pump to BP sensor vent nipple, with zero in. Hg (low vacuum), voltage should be 3.5-4.5 volts. With 30 in. Hg (high vacuum), voltage should be zero volts. If voltage is within specifications, repair open circuit in "Y" wire between BP sensor and ECA. If voltage is not within specifications, replace BP sensor.

1a-388

1989 COMPUTERIZED ENGINE CONTROLS
Ford Motor Co. Probe — EEC (Cont.)

CIRCUIT TEST B4

KNOCK SENSOR (KS) & KNOCK CONTROL UNIT (KCU)

KS Sensor Circuits

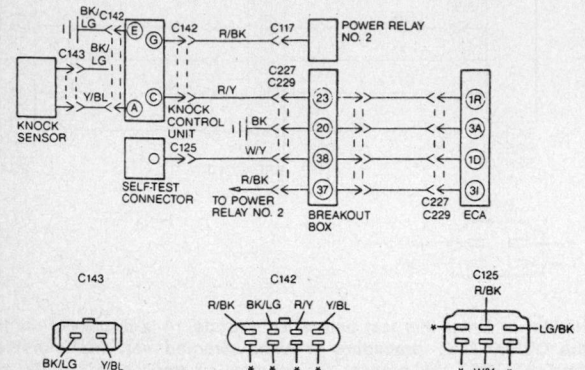

NOTE: Enter this test only when a Code 05 is displayed during the QUICK TEST procedure or when directed here from another CIRCUIT TEST. To prevent replacement of good components, be aware that the following non-EEC areas may be at fault: fuel quality, basic mechanical engine components and spark timing. This test is intended to diagnose only the following components: knock sensor, ECA, and wiring harness circuits (KA and signal return).

1) Checking System Integrity – Visually check all wiring, harnesses, connectors and components for evidence of damage, overheating, shorting or looseness. If a fault is found, repair as necessary. If no faults are found, go to next step.

2) Checking KCU Voltage – Install breakout box. Leave ECA disconnected and set VOM on 20-volt scale. With key on, measure voltage between test pins No. 23 and 20 (ground). Tap lightly on engine lifting "eye" bracket with a small (4 oz.) hammer while varying engine speed between 2500 and 4000 RPM. Voltage should be 3.3-5.0 volts and decrease when engine is tapped with hammer. If test is to specification, go to step **8)**. If not, go to next step.

3) Checking KCU Power – Set VOM on 20-volt scale. Turn key on and measure voltage between the "R/BK" wire at the KCU and ground. If voltage is greater than 10.0 volts, go to step **5)**. If voltage is 10.0 volts or less, go to next step.

4) Checking Power at Relay No. 2 – Do not disconnect relay or pierce wire. Set VOM on 20-volt scale. Turn key on. Measure voltage between "BK/LG" wire at power relay and ground. If voltage is greater than 10.0 volts, repair "BK/LG" wire from relay to KCU. If voltage is less than 10.0 volts, go to CIRCUIT TEST A2.

5) Checking KCU Ground Circuit – Set VOM on 200-ohm scale. Turn key on. Measure resistance between "BK/LG" wire at KCU and ground. If resistance is greater than 5 ohms, repair ground connection or open in "BK/LG" wire. If resistance is less than 5 ohms, go to next step.

6) Checking Voltage to "C" Terminal at KCU – Leave KCU connected, do not pierce wire. Turn key on and set VOM on 20-volt scale. Measure voltage between "R/Y" wire at KCU and ground. Tap lightly on engine lifting "eye" bracket with a small (4 oz.) hammer while varying engine speed between 2500 and 4000 RPM. Voltage should be 3.3-5.0 volts and decrease when engine is tapped with hammer. If test is to specification, repair open or short to VPWR in "R/Y" wire from KCU to ECA. If voltage does not test to specification, go to next step.

7) Checking KS Voltage – Disconnect KS. Set VOM on 1-volt AC scale. Measure voltage at KS between "Y/BL" wire and "BK" wire. Tap lightly on engine lifting "eye" bracket with a small (4 oz.) hammer. If voltage reads zero volts normally and about .03 volt while tapping, replace KCU. If not, replace KS.

8) Checking KCU Voltage at Self-Test Output (STO) – Install breakout box and set VOM on 20-volt scale. Ensure all accessories are turned off. Ground STI connector. Turn key on. Measure voltage between test pins No. 37 and 38. Tap lightly on engine lifting "eye" bracket with a small (4 oz.) hammer. If voltage reads zero volts normally and about 10.0 volts while tapping, the system is okay, return to DIAGNOSTIC ROUTINES. If voltage readings are not as specified, replace ECA.

CIRCUIT TEST B5

THROTTLE POSITION (TP) SENSOR

TP Sensor Circuits

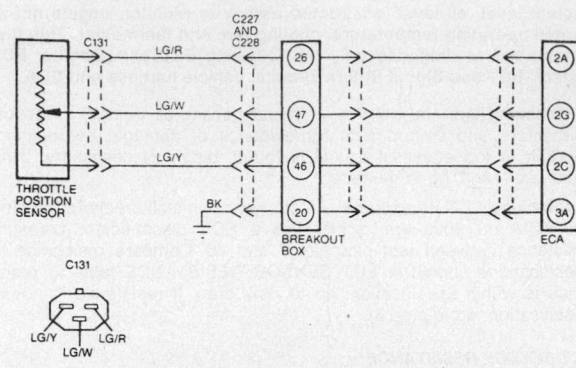

NOTE: Enter this test only when a Code 12 is displayed during the QUICK TEST procedure or when directed here from another CIRCUIT TEST. To prevent replacement of good components, be aware that the following non-EEC components may be at fault: idle speed or throttle stop adjustments. Binding throttle shaft or linkage. Binding cruise control linkage. This test is intended to diagnose only the following components: TP sensor, ECA, and wiring harness circuits (VREF, TP signal and signal return).

1) Checking System Integrity – Visually check all wiring, harnesses, connectors and components for evidence of damage, overheating, shorting or looseness. If a fault is found, repair as necessary. If no faults are found, go to next step.

2) Checking VREF & Signal Return – Install breakout box and set VOM on 20-volt scale. Turn key on. Measure voltages between pins as shown in VREF & SIGNAL RETURN CHECKS table. If all voltage readings are within specifications, go to step **3)**. If readings are not to specifications, go to CIRCUIT TEST A3, step **1)**.

VREF & SIGNAL RETURN CHECKS

Test Pins at Breakout Box	Volts
Between Pins No. 26 & 20	4-6
Between Pins No. 26 & 46	4-6
Between Pins No. 20 & 46	4

3) Checking TP Voltage – Install breakout box. Set VOM on 20-volt scale and turn key on. Measure voltage between test pins No. 46 and 47. With throttle closed, voltage should be 0.36-0.66 volt. At Wide Open Throttle (WOT), voltage should be approximately 4.3 volts. If both readings are within specifications, replace ECA. If not, go to next step.

4) Checking Power at TP Sensor – Set VOM on 20-volt scale. Turn key on. Measure voltage at the TP sensor for circuits shown in VOLTAGE CHECKS AT TP SENSOR table. If all readings are to specifications, go to next step. If voltage readings are not to specifications, repair "LG/R" and/or "LG/Y" wire(s) from TP sensor to ECA.

VOLTAGE CHECKS AT TP SENSOR

TP Circuits	Volts
"LG/R" wire to ground	4-6
"LG/R" to "LG/Y" wire	4-6
"LG/Y" wire to ground	0

5) Checking TP Sensor Voltage – Leave TP sensor connected for this test. Do not pierce wire, backprobe at harness connector. Set VOM on 20-volt scale. Turn key on. Measure voltage at TP sensor between "LG/W" wire and ground. With throttle closed, voltage should be 0.36-0.66 volt. At Wide Open Throttle (WOT), voltage should be approximately 4.3 volts. If both readings are within specifications, repair open in "LG/W" wire between TP sensor and ECA. If not, adjust or replace TP sensor.

1989 COMPUTERIZED ENGINE CONTROLS
Ford Motor Co. Probe — EEC (Cont.)

1a-389

CIRCUIT TEST B6

VANE AIRFLOW (VAF) METER

VAF Meter Circuits

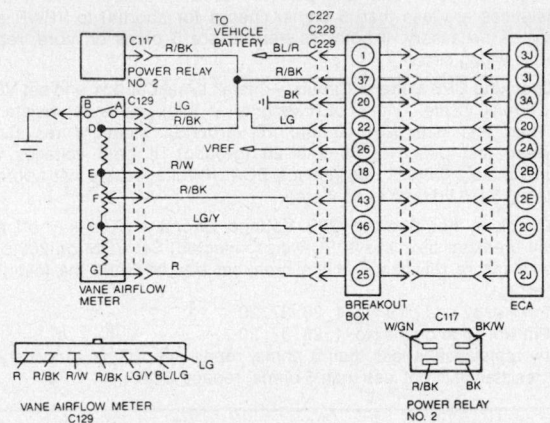

VANE AIRFLOW METER

VANE AIRFLOW METER C129

BREAKOUT BOX

POWER RELAY NO. 2

ECA

NOTE: Enter this test only when a Code 08 is displayed during the QUICK TEST procedure or when directed here from another CIRCUIT TEST. To prevent replacement of good components, be aware that the following non-EEC items may be at fault: unmetered air leaks between VAF meter and throttle body. Vacuum leaks. Engine seals (PCV seals, valve cover, dipstick). This test is intended to diagnose only the following components: VAF meter, ECA, and wiring harness circuits (VREF, VAF signal and signal return).

1) Checking System Integrity – Visually check all wiring, harnesses, connectors and components for evidence of damage, overheating, shorting or looseness. If a fault is found, repair as necessary. If no faults are found, go to next step.

2) Checking Voltage to VAF Meter – Install breakout box and set VOM on 20-volt scale. Leave ECA disconnected. Turn key on. Measure voltage between test pins No. 18 and 20 (ground). If voltage is 7-9 volts, go to step **6)**. If not, go to next step.

3) Checking Voltage at VAF Meter – Leave VAF meter connected. Do not pierce wire, carefully backprobe harness connector. Set VOM on 20-volt scale. Turn key on. Measure voltage between terminal "E" at VAF meter ("R/W" wire) and ground. If voltage is 7-9 volts, repair open or short in "R/W" wire between VAF meter and ECA. If voltage is not 7-9 volts, go to next step.

4) Checking Voltage at VAF Meter – Leave VAF meter connected. Do not pierce wire, carefully backprobe harness connector. Set VOM on 20-volt scale. Turn key on. Measure voltage between terminal "D" at VAF meter ("R/BK" wire) and ground. If voltage is greater than 10 volts, replace VAF meter. If voltage is less than 10 volts, go to next step.

5) Checking Power to Relay No. 2 – Do not disconnect relay or pierce wire. Set VOM on 20-volt scale. Turn key on. Measure voltage between "R/BK" wire at relay No. 2, and ground. If voltage is greater than 10.0 volts, repair open or short in "R/BK" wire from relay to VAF meter. If voltage is 10.0 or less, go to CIRCUIT TEST B12, step **1)**.

6) Checking Signal Return Circuit – Turn key off, and install breakout box. Set VOM on 200-ohm scale. Measure resistance between test pins No. 46 and 20 (ground). If resistance is less than 5 ohms, go to next step. If resistance is 5 ohms or more, go to CIRCUIT TEST A3, step **1)**.

7) Checking Signal Return at VAF Meter – Turn key off, and install breakout box. Set VOM on 200-ohm scale. Measure resistance between "LG/Y" wire at VAF meter terminal "C" and test pin No. 46. If resistance is less than 5 ohms, go to next step. If not, repair open in "LG/Y" wire between VAF meter and ECA.

8) Checking VAF Meter Voltage – Install breakout box and set VOM on 20-volt scale. Perform the following KOEO and KOER (engine at idle) checks:

VAF VOLTAGE at BREAKOUT BOX

Circuit	KOEO	KOER (Idle)
Test pins No. 43 & 20	1.7 volts	4-6 volts
Test pins No. 43 & 46	1.7 volts	4-6 volts
Test pins No. 20 & 46	0 volts	0 volts

CIRCUIT TEST B6 (Cont.)

9) Checking VAF Meter Signal – Leave breakout box connected. Do not pierce wire. Set VOM on 20-volt scale. Perform the following KOEO and KOER (engine at idle) checks. If all readings are within specifications repair "R/BK" wire from VAF meter to ECA. If readings are not within specifications, replace VAF meter.

VAF METER VOLTAGE at METER

Circuit	KOEO	KOER (Idle)
Terminal "F" ("R/BK" wire) to ground	1.7 volts	4-6 volts
Terminal "C" ("LG/Y" wire) to ground	0 volts	0 volts
Terminals "C" to "F" and ground	1.7 volts	4-6 volts

CIRCUIT TEST B7

CYLINDER IDENTIFICATION SENSOR

CID Circuit

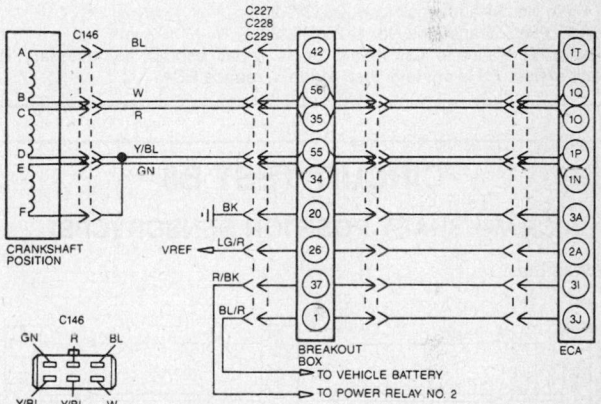

CRANKSHAFT POSITION

C146

BREAKOUT BOX

ECA

TO VEHICLE BATTERY

TO POWER RELAY NO. 2

NOTE: Enter this test only when Codes 03 or 04 are displayed during the QUICK TEST procedure or when directed here from another CIRCUIT TEST. To prevent replacement of good components, be aware that the following non-EEC components may be at fault: non-electronic components of ignition system. This test is intended to diagnose only the following components: cylinder identification sensor, ECA, wiring harness and CID circuit.

NOTE: The CID is incorporated with the Crankshaft Position (CPS), inside the distributor.

1) Checking System Integrity – Visually check all wiring, harnesses, connectors and components for evidence of damage, overheating, shorting or looseness. If a fault is found, repair as necessary. If no faults are found, go to next step.

2) Checking CID Circuit Resistance – Turn key off and install breakout box. Leave ECA disconnected. Set VOM on 1k-ohm scale. Check the following resistances. If all resistances are within specification, go to step **5)**. If not, go to next step.

CID CIRCUIT RESISTANCE

Breakout Box Test Pin	Ohms
No. 34 & 55	210-260
No. 35 & 55	210-260
No. 34 & 35	420-520

3) Checking CID Sensor Resistance – Turn key off and disconnect CID sensor. Set VOM on 1k-ohm scale. Measure resistance between the following terminals at the crankshaft position sensor harness connector.

- Terminals "C" (Red wire) and "D" (Yellow/Blue wire)
- Terminals "E" (Green wire) and "F" (Yellow/Blue wire)

If both resistances are 210-260 ohms, go to next step. If either resistance is not to specification, replace CID sensor.

1a-390

1989 COMPUTERIZED ENGINE CONTROLS
Ford Motor Co. Probe – EEC (Cont.)

CIRCUIT TEST B7 (Cont.)

4) Checking For Opens In Harness Between ECA & CID – Turn key off and install breakout box. Set VOM on 200-ohm scale. Measure resistance between the following wires at the sensor connector and the breakout box:

- Red wire and test pin No. 35
- Yellow/Blue wire(s) and test pin No. 55
- Green wire and test pin No. 34

If all resistances are less than 5 ohms, check for shorts to VPWR and repair as necessary. If resistances are not less than 5 ohms, repair open circuits as necessary.

5) Checking CID Voltage Circuit – Install breakout box and set VOM on 20-volt scale. With KOER (engine at idle), measure the following voltages at the breakout box:

- Test pins No. 34 and 20 (ground)
- Test pins No. 35 and 20 (ground)
- Test pins No. 55 and 20 (ground)

If all voltages are approximately 0.6-0.8 volt, replace ECA. If voltages are not approximately 0.6-0.8 volt, go to next step.

6) Checking For Shorted CID Voltage Circuit – Turn key off and install breakout box. Leave ECA disconnected. Set VOM on 200-ohm sale. Measure resistance at the breakout box between the following test pins:

- Pin No. 34 and pins No. 1, 26, 37, 20
- Pin No. 35 and pins No. 1, 26, 37, 20
- Pin No. 55 and pins No. 1, 26, 37, 20

If any resistance is less than 5 ohms, repair short(s) as necessary. If any resistance is not less than 5 ohms, repace ECA.

CIRCUIT TEST B8 (Cont.)

between "Blue wire" at CPS harness connector and test pin No. 42 at breakout box. Measure resistance between "White wire" at CPS harness connector and test pin No. 56 at breakout box. If both resistances are less than 5 ohms, checks for short(s) to VPWR and repair as necessary. If both resistances are 5 ohms or more, repair open in wiring circuit.

5) Checking CPS Voltage Circuit – Install breakout box and set VOM on 200-volt scale. With KOER (engine at idle), measure resistance between test pins No. 42 and 20 (ground). Measure resistance between test pins No. 56 and 20 (ground). If both voltages are approximately 0.6-0.8 volt, replace ECA. If voltages are not approximately 0.6-0.8 volt, go to next step.

6) Checking For Shorted CPS Voltage Circuit – Turn key off and install breakout box. Leave ECA disconnected. Set VOM on 200-ohm sale. Measure resistance at the breakout box between the following test pins:

- Pin No. 42 and pins No. 1, 26, 37, 20
- Pin No. 56 and pins No. 1, 26, 37, 20

If any resistance is less than 5 ohms, repair short(s) as necessary. If any resistance is not less than 5 ohms, repace ECA.

CIRCUIT TEST B8

CRANKSHAFT POSITION SENSOR (CPS)

CPS Circuit

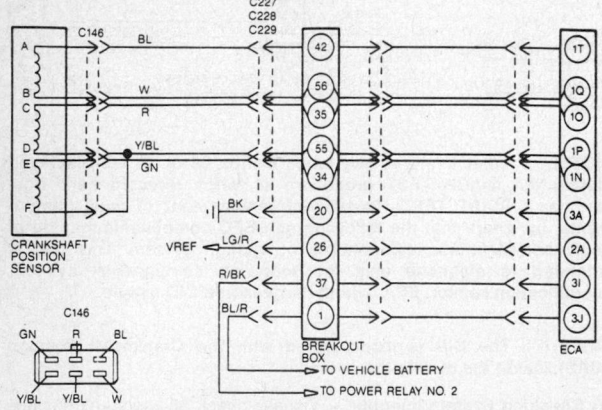

NOTE: Enter this test only when Code 02 is displayed during the QUICK TEST procedure or when directed here from another CIRCUIT TEST. To prevent replacement of good components, be aware that the following non-EEC components may be at fault: non-electronic components of ignition system. This test is intended to diagnose only the following components: crankshaft position sensors, ECA, wiring harness and CPS circuit.

1) Checking System Integrity – Visually check all wiring, harnesses, connectors and components for evidence of damage, overheating, shorting or looseness. If a fault is found, repair as necessary. If no faults are found, go to next step.

2) Checking Resistance of CPS Circuit – Turn key off and install breakout box. Leave ECA disconnected. Set VOM on 1k-ohm scale. Measure resistance between test pins No. 42 and 56. If resistance is 210-260 ohms, go to step **5)**. If not, go to next step.

3) Checking Resistance of CPS – Turn key off and disconnect CPS. set VOM on 1k-ohm scale. Measure resistance between terminals "A" (Blue wire) and "B" (White wire) at CPS connector. If resistance is 210-260 ohms, go to next step. If resistance is not 210-260 ohms, replace CPS.

4) Checking CPS to ECA Circuit For Opens – Turn key off and install breakout box. Set VOM on 200-ohm scale. Measure resistance

CIRCUIT TEST B9

EGR VALVE POSITION SENSOR (EVP)

EVP Sensor Circuit

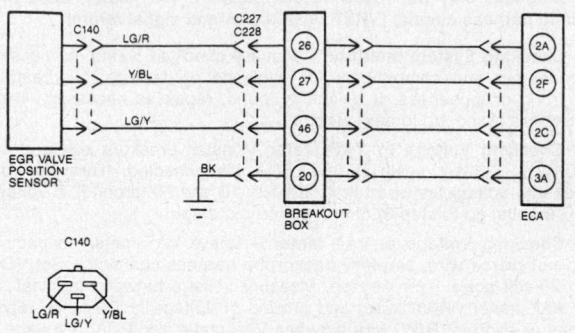

NOTE: Enter this test only when Code 16 is displayed during the QUICK TEST procedure or when directed here from another CIRCUIT TEST. To prevent replacement of good components, be aware that the following non-EEC components may be at fault: damaged EGR valve, and blocked or obstructed vacuum lines. This test is intended to diagnose only the following components: EVP sensor, ECA, wiring harness and VREF, EVP and Signal Return circuits.

1) Checking System Integrity – Visually check all wiring, harnesses, connectors and components for evidence of damage, overheating, shorting or looseness. If a fault is found, repair as necessary. If no faults are found, go to next step.

2) Checking VREF & Signal Return Circuits – Install breakout box and set VOM on 20-volt scale. Turn key on and measure VREF and Signal Return voltage at the breakout box. If all voltage readings are within specifications, go to next step. If voltage readings are not to specification, go to CIRCUIT TEST A3, step **1)**.

VREF & SIGNAL RETURN VOLTAGE

Test Pins	Volts
26 & 20	4-6
26 & 46	4-6
20 & 46	0

3) Checking EVP Voltage Circuit – Install breakout box and set VOM on 20-volt scale. Disconnect vacuum hose from EVP. Connect vacuum pump to EVP. Turn key on and measure voltage between test pins No. 27 and 46. With zero vacuum, voltage should be 0.25-0.95 volt. Increase vacuum to 4.7 in. Hg, voltage should be approximately 4.0 volts. If both readings are within specification, replace ECA. If voltage readings are not to specification, go to next step.

1989 COMPUTERIZED ENGINE CONTROLS
Ford Motor Co. Probe – EEC (Cont.)

1a-391

CIRCUIT TEST B9 (Cont.)

4) Checking Power At EVP Sensor – Set VOM on 20-volt scale. Turn key on and measure voltages at EVP sensor connector. See EVP SENSOR VOLTAGE table. If all voltages are within specification, go to next step. If not, repair "LG/R wire" or "LG/Y wire" between ECA and EVP sensor.

EVP SENSOR VOLTAGE

Circuit	Volts
LG/R wire to ground	4-6
LG/R wire to LG/Y wire	4-6
LG/Y wire to ground	
	0

5) Checking EVP Sensor Voltage – Set VOM on 20-volt scale. Disconnect vacuum hose from EVP. Leave EVP sensor connector. Connect vacuum pump to EVP. Do not pierce wire, backprobe sensor connect. Turn key on and measure voltage between "Y/BL wire" and ground. With zero vacuum, voltage should be 0.25-0.95 volt. Increase vacuum to 4.7 in. Hg, voltage should be approximately 4.0 volts. If both readings are within specification, repair open in "Y/BL wire" between EVP sensor and ECA. If voltage readings are not to specification, replace EVP sensor.

CIRCUIT TEST B10

NEUTRAL GEAR SWITCH (NGS) & CLUTCH ENGAGE SWITCH (CES)

NGS & CES Circuits

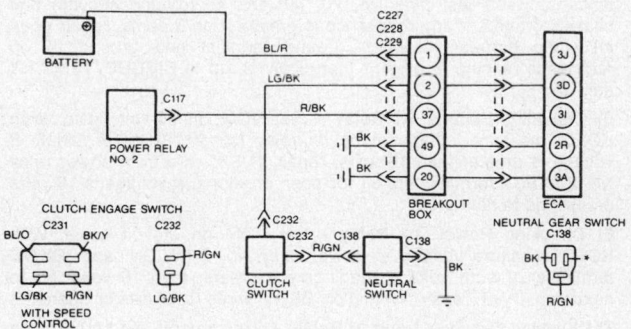

NOTE: Enter this test only when directed here from SWITCH MONITOR TEST procedure. To prevent replacement of good components, be aware that the following non-EEC items may be at fault: clutch switch adjustment, clutch pedal operation, transaxle operation and neutral switch installation. This test is intended to diagnose only the following: clutch or neutral switch, and wiring harness.

1) Checking System Integrity – Visually check all wiring, harnesses, connectors and components for evidence of damage, overheating, shorting or looseness. If a fault is found, repair as necessary. If no faults are found, go to next step.

2) Checking For Open Circuits – Install breakout box and leave ECA disconnected. Set VOM on 200-ohm scale. Using CIRCUIT RESISTANCE table, measure and record resistance between test pins No. 2 and 20 (ground). If all resistances are to specifications, go to step **5)**. If not, go to next step.

CIRCUIT RESISTANCE

Test Procedure	Ohms
Clutch released and in gear	Less than 5
Clutch depressed and in gear	Greater than 10k
Clutch released and in Neutral	Greater than 10k
Clutch depressed and in Neutral	Greater than 10k

CIRCUIT TEST B10 (Cont.)

3) Checking CES Operation – Disconnect 2-pin CES connector. Set VOM on 200-ohm scale. Measure resistance between terminals on clutch engage switch with pedal depressed and released. If resistance is greater than 5 ohms with pedal depressed and less than 5 ohms with pedal released, go to next step. If switch does not meet specifications, adjust or replace as necessary.

Measuring CES Resistance

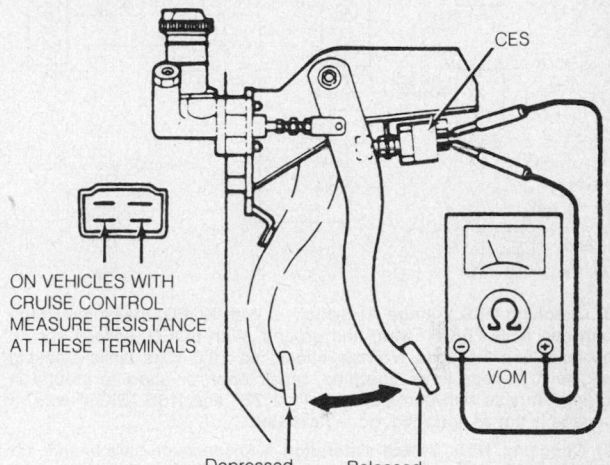

ON VEHICLES WITH CRUISE CONTROL MEASURE RESISTANCE AT THESE TERMINALS

Depressed   Released

4) Checking NGS Operation – Remove vehicle battery to access NGS connector. Disconnect NGS. Set VOM on 200-ohm range. Measure resistance between wire terminals "R/GN" and "BK" at the NGS connector. If resistance is less than 5 ohms in gear and greater than 5 ohms in Neutral, repair open harness circuit between ECA and CES ("LG/BK" wire); between CES and NGS ("R/GN" wire); or in ground wire (BK wire) between NGS and ground. If resistance IS NOT less than 5 ohms in gear and greater than 5 ohms in Neutral, replace NGS.

5) Check For Short to VPWR & KAPWR – Install breakout box and disconnect ECA. Set VOM on 20-volt scale. With KOEO, measure voltage between test pins No. 2 and 20 (ground), and between test pins No. 2 and 49. If any reading is greater than one volt, repair short in wiring harness to VPWR or KAPWR. If both readings are one volt or less, go to next step.

6) Checking Voltage At ECA – Install breakout box, leaving ECA connected. Set DVOM on 20-volt scale. With KOEO and transmission in gear, measure voltage between test pins No. 2 and 20 (ground) at breakout box. If readings are greater than 10 volts with clutch pedal depressed and less than 0.5 volt with clutch pedal released, replace ECA. If voltage is not as specified, repair short to ground in wiring harness between ECA terminal No. "3D" and "R/GN" wire terminal at NGS connector.

CIRCUIT TEST B11

NEUTRAL SAFETY SWITCH (NSS) (AUTOMATIC TRANSMISSION)

NOTE: Enter this test only when directed here from SWITCH MONITOR TEST procedure. To prevent replacement of good components, be aware that the following non-EEC areas may be at fault: transaxle operation, and Neutral Safety Switch (NSS) installation. This test is intended to diagnose only the following: Neutral Safety Switch (NSS).

1) Checking System Integrity – Visually check all wiring, harnesses, connectors and components for evidence of damage, overheating, shorting or looseness. If a fault is found, repair as necessary. If no faults are found, go to next step.

2) Checking NSS Voltage at ECA – Install breakout box and set VOM on 20-volt scale. Measure voltage between test pins No. 5 and 40 (ground) at breakout box. With KOEO, voltage should be less than 2.5 volts. Voltage should be 10.0 volts while cranking engine. If voltage is as specified, go to step **5)**. If not, go to next step.

1a-392

1989 COMPUTERIZED ENGINE CONTROLS
Ford Motor Co. Probe – EEC (Cont.)

CIRCUIT TEST B11 (Cont.)

NSS Circuits

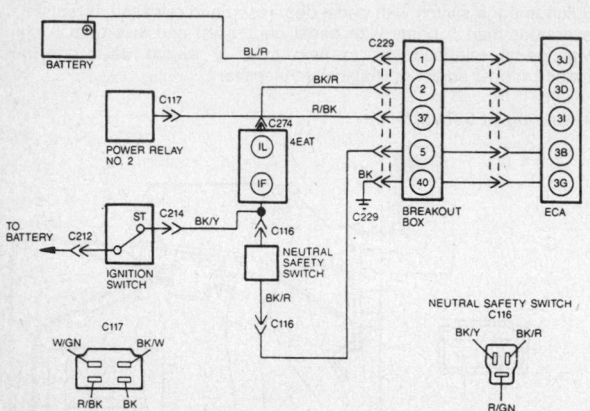

3) Checking NSS Voltage At Switch – With KOEO, measure voltage between NSS ("BK/R" wire) and ground. With KOEO, voltage should be less than 2.5 volts. Voltage should be 10.0 volts while cranking engine. If voltage is as specified, repair open or short to ground in wiring harness between ECA terminal "3B" and NSS "BK/R" wire. If voltage is not as specified, go to next step.

4) Checking NSS Switch Operation – Disconnect switch and set VOM on 200-ohm scale. Measure resistance between "BK/Y" wire and "BK/R" wire at switch connector. If resistance is greater than 5 ohms in "D" and "R" and less than 5 ohms in "N", go to next step. If resistance is less than specified, replace NSS switch.

5) Checking Voltage At ECA Pin No. 2 – Install breakout box and set VOM on 20-volt scale. Turn key on and measure voltage between test pins No. 2 and 40 (ground) at breakout box. In "N" and "P", voltage should be less than 2.5 volts. In other gear selector positions, voltage should be 7-9 volts. If voltage readings are to specifications, replace ECA. If voltage is not as specified, go to next step.

6) Checking Voltage From Transmission (4EAT) – DO NOT disconnect transmission connector or piece wire. Set VOM on 20-volt scale. Turn key on. Measure voltage between transmission connector terminal "2N" (LG/BK wire) and ground. In "P" and "N", voltage should be less than 2.5 volts. In other ranges, voltage should be 7-9 volts. If voltage readings are to specification, repair "LG/BK" wire from 4EAT to ECA. If voltage is not to specification, go to next step.

7) Checking Voltage To Transmission – Set VOM on 20-volt scale. Turn key on and crank engine. Measure voltage between transmission connector terminal "1F" ("BK/Y" wire) and ground. With key on, voltage should be less than 1.5 volt. When cranking, voltage should be 7-9 volts. If voltage readings are within specifications, fault is in the transmission, repair as necessary. If voltage is not within specifications, go to next step.

8) Checking Power At Ignition Switch – DO NOT disconnect transmission connector or pierce wire. Set VOM on 20-volt scale. Turn key on. Measure voltage between ignition switch ("BK/Y" wire) and ground. With KOEO, voltage should be less than 1.5 volts. When cranking, voltage should be 7-9 volts. If voltage readings are to specification, repair open circuit(s) to NSS or transmission. If voltage is not to specification, repair ignition switch as necessary.

CIRCUIT TEST B12
VEHICLE POWER

NOTE: Enter this test only when directed here by other CIRCUIT TESTS. To prevent replacement of good components, be aware that the following non-EEC components may be faulty: ignition switch, fuses, battery and charging system. This test is intended to diagnose only the following: power relay No. 2, wiring harness circuits Vehicle Power (VP), Keep Alive Power (KAPWR) and ECA grounds.

CIRCUIT TEST B12 (Cont.)

Vehicle Power Circuits

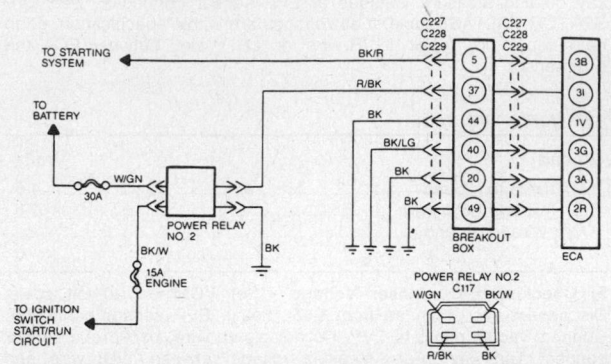

1) Checking System Integrity – Visually check all wiring, harnesses, connectors and components for evidence of damage, overheating, shorting or looseness. If a fault is found, repair as necessary. If no faults are found, go to next step.

2) Checking For VPWR To ECA – Install breakout box and set VOM on 20-volt scale. Leave ECA disconnected. With KOEO, measure voltage between test pins No. 37 and 40 at breakout box. If reading is greater than 10 volts, go to next step. If not, go to step 5).

3) Check For Cranking Power To ECA – Install breakout box and set VOM on 20-volt scale. Leave ECA disconnected. With KOEO, measure voltage between test pins No. 5 and 40 during cranking. If reading is greater than 10 volts during cranking, go to next step. If not, repair open in wiring harness between ground terminal and ground.

4) Checking ECA Ground Circuits – Install breakout box and set VOM on 200-ohm scale. Leave ECA disconnected. Measure resistance between test pins No. 20, 40, and 49 (ground circuits) and chassis ground. If any resistance is greater than 5 ohms, repair open in wiring harness between ground terminal and ground. If no resistance reading is greater than 5 ohms, go to CIRCUIT TEST A2, step 1).

5) Checking Voltage At Relay – Set VOM on 20-volt scale. With KOEO, measure voltage at power relay No. 2 ("R/BK" terminal). If voltage is greater than 10 volts, repair "R/BK" wire from power relay No. 2 to ECA terminal No. 31 for open or shorts. If voltage is 10 volts or less, go to next step.

6) Checking Power To Relay – Set VOM on 20-volt scale. With KOEO, measure voltage at power relay No. 2 ("W/GN" and "BK/W" terminals). If both voltage readings are greater than 10 volts, go to next step. If not, repair "W/GN" or "BK/W" wires for shorts or opens.

7) Checking Ground Circuit At Relay – Turn key off and set VOM on 200-ohm scale. Disconnect power relay No. 2. Measure resistance between relay "BK" wire terminal and ground. If resistance is less than 5 ohms, go to next step. If resistance is not less than 5 ohms, repair open in wiring harness between power relay No. 2 "BK" terminal and ground.

8) Checking Power Relay Operation – Turn key off and set VOM on 200-ohm scale. Disconnect power relay No. 2. Ground "BK" terminal (B) of power relay. Measure resistance between "W/GN" terminal (C) and "R/BK" terminal (D) of relay. Jump battery power to "BK/W" terminal (A) of power relay. If reading is less than 5 ohms with power applied and greater than 10,000 ohms with power removed, go to CIRCUIT TEST A2, step 1). If readings are not to specifications, replace relay.

Testing Power Relay No. 2

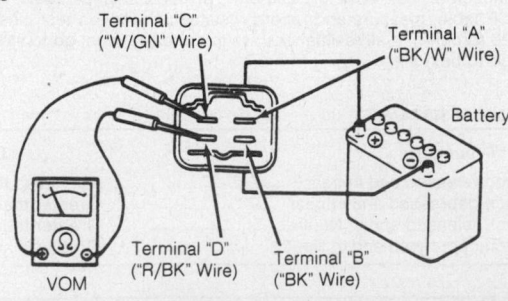

CIRCUIT TEST B13

BRAKE ON-OFF SWITCH (BOO)

BOO Circuits

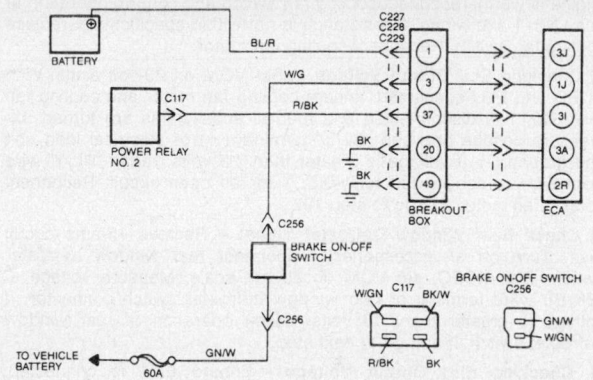

NOTE: Enter this test only when directed here from SWITCH MONITOR TEST procedure. To prevent replacement of good components, be aware that the following non-EEC components may be faulty: brake switch adjustment, brake pedal operation and brake light system. This test is intended to diagnose only the following: BOO switch and circuit.

1) **Checking System Integrity** – Visually check all wiring, harnesses, connectors and components for evidence of damage, overheating, shorting or looseness. If a fault is found, repair as necessary. If no faults are found, go to next step.

2) **Checking BOO Switch Signal At ECA** – With breakout box installed and ECA disconnected, set VOM on 20-volt scale. With KOEO and brake pedal depressed, measure voltage between test pins No. 3 and 20 (ground) and between test pins No. 3 and 49 (ground). If voltage is less than 4 volts with pedal released and greater than 10 volts with pedal depressed, replace ECA. If voltage is not within specifications, go to next step.

3) **Checking Voltage From BOO Switch** – With VOM on 20-volt scale, turn key on. Measure voltage between "W/GN" wire at BOO switch and ground. If voltage is less than 4 volts with pedal released and greater than 10 volts with pedal depressed, repair open or short to power in wiring harness between ECA terminal "1J" and BOO switch. If voltage is not to specification, go to next step.

4) **Check Power To Brake Switch** – Set VOM on 20-volt scale. With KOEO, measure voltage between vehicle battery and ground. If voltage reading is greater than 10 volts, repair faulty fuse or open in "GN/W" wire from battery to brake switch. If voltage is not greater than 10 volts, go to CIRCUIT TEST A2, step 1).

CIRCUIT TEST B14

IDLE SWITCH

Idle Switch Circuits

CIRCUIT TEST B14 (Cont.)

NOTE: Enter this test only when directed here from SWITCH MONITOR TEST procedure. To prevent replacement of good components, be aware that the following non-EEC items may be at fault: throttle linkage and operation and idle switch adjustment. This test is intended to diagnose only the following: idle switch and circuits.

1) **Checking System Integrity** – Visually check all wiring, harnesses, connectors and components for evidence of damage, overheating, shorting or looseness. If a fault is found, repair as necessary. If no faults are found, go to next step.

2) **Checking For Open Circuits** – With breakout box installed and ECA disconnected, set VOM on 20-volt scale. With throttle closed, measure resistance between test pins No. 28 and 20 (ground). Resistance should be less than 30 ohms. Open throttle and measure resistance. Resistance should be greater than 10k ohms with throttle open. If both resistances are within specifications, go to step 4). If not, go to next step.

3) **Checking Idle Switch Operation** – Disconnect idle switch at throttle body and set VOM on 200-ohm scale. With throttle closed, measure resistance between idle switch connector and ground. Resistance should be less than 30 ohms. Open throttle and measure resistance. Resistance should be greater than 10k ohms with throttle open. If both resistances are within specifications, repair open in wiring harness between ECA terminal "1E" and idle switch. If resistances are not within specifications, replace idle switch.

4) **Checking For Short To VPWR & KAPWR** – With breakout box installed and ECA disconnected, set VOM on 20-volt scale. With KOEO, measure voltage between test pins No. 28 and 20 (ground). Measure voltage between test pins No. 28 and 49 (ground). If any reading is greater than one volt, repair short in wiring harness to VPWR or KAPWR as necessary. If all readings are less than one volt, go to next step.

5) **Checking Voltage At ECA** – With breakout box installed and ECA connected, set VOM on 20-volt scale. With KOEO, measure voltage between test pins No. 28 and 20 (ground). If voltage is between one volt with throttle closed and 7.7 volts with throttle open, replace ECA. If voltage readings are not to specifications, repair short to ground in wiring harness between ECA terminal "1E" and idle switch.

CIRCUIT TEST B15

AIR CONDITIONING PRESSURE SWITCH (ACPS)

ACPS Circuits

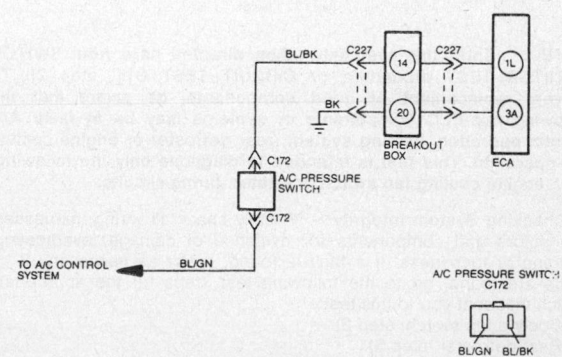

NOTE: Enter this test only when directed here from SWITCH MONITOR TEST procedure. To prevent replacement of good components, be aware that the following non-EEC components or systems may be faulty: A/C system, and A/C or blower motor controls. This test is intended to diagnose only the following: A/C pressure switch or circuits.

1) **Checking System Integrity** – Visually check all wiring, harnesses, connectors and components for evidence of damage, overheating, shorting or looseness. If a fault is found, repair as necessary. If no faults are found, go to next step.

CIRCUIT TEST B15 (Cont.)

2) Checking ECA Terminal Voltage – Install breakout box and disconect ECA. Turn on A/C and blower motor. With KOEO, set VOM on 20-volt scale. Measure voltage between test pins No. 14 and 20 (ground) at breakout box. If voltage is greater than 10 volts with A/C off and less than 2 volts with A/C on, go to CIRCUIT TEST D4, step 1). If voltage is not to specification, go to next step.

3) Checking ACPS Voltage – With ECA and ACPS disconnected, set VOM on 20-volt scale. With KOEO, ensure A/C is off and blower motor is on. Measure voltage at ACPS "BL/BK" terminal. If voltage is greater than 10 volts with A/C off and less than 2 volts with A/C on, repair "BL/BK" wire from ACPS to ECA terminal "1L". If voltage is not to specification, go to next step.

4) Checking ACPS Voltage Supply – Disconnect ACPS. Ensure A/C is off and blower motor is on. Set VOM on 20-volt scale. Measure voltage at "BL/GN" terminal wire at ACPS connector. If voltage is greater than 10 volts with A/C off and less than 2 volts with A/C on, replace ACPS. If voltage is not as specified, EEC system is not at fault, repair A/C components as necessary.

CIRCUIT TEST B16

ELECTRICAL LOAD UNIT (ELU)

ELU Circuits

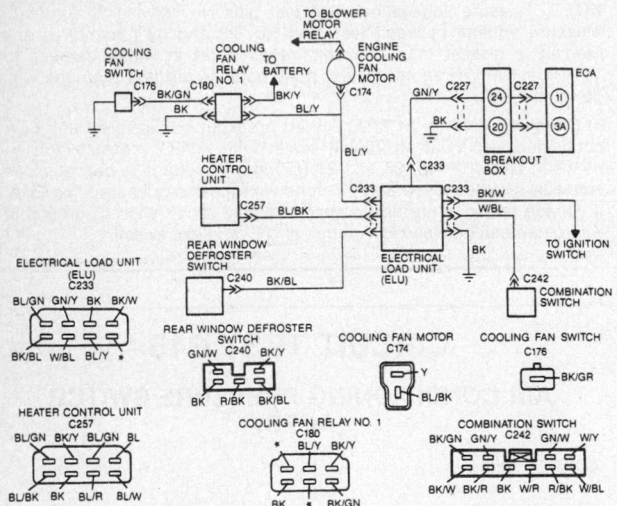

NOTE: Enter this test only when directed here from SWITCH MONITOR TEST procedure or CIRCUIT TEST B15, step 2). To prevent replacement of good components, be aware that the following non-EEC components or systems may be at fault: A/C system operation, lighting system, rear defroster or engine cooling fan operation. This test is intended to diagnose only the following: ELU, engine cooling fan switch or related wiring circuits.

1) Checking System Integrity – Visually check all wiring, harnesses, connectors and components for evidence of damage, overheating, shorting or looseness. If a fault is found, repair as necessary. If no faults are found, go to the following test steps for the appropriate switch that sent you to this test:
- Cooling fan switch, step 2).
- Rear defroster, step 5).
- Combination switch, step 7).
- Heater blower, step 8).

2) Checking Cooling Fan Signal – Set VOM on 20-volt scale. Disconnect cooling fan motor. With KOEO, ensure all accessories are off and disconnect cooling fan relay No. 1. Measure voltage between "BL/Y" wire terminal (+) of cooling fan relay No. 1 connector and ground (–). If voltage is greater than 7.3 volts, go to next step. If not, go to step 4).

CIRCUIT TEST B16 (Cont.)

3) Checking Cooling Fan Switch Operation – Disconnect cooling fan motor and cooling fan switch. Set VOM on 200-ohm scale. Measure resistance between cooling fan switch and ground. If resistance is less than 5 ohms when engine is cold and greater than 10k ohms when engine is warm, reconnect cooling fan switch and confirm operation of relay No. 1 and wiring. If resistance is not within specification, replace cooling fan switch. Reconnect cooling fan motor.

4) Checking ELU Output Voltage – Set VOM on 20-volt scale. With KOEO and ELU connected, ensure cooling fan motor and cooling fan relay No. 1 is disconnected and that all accessories are turned off. Measure voltage between "BL/Y" terminal (+) of electrical load unit and ground (–). If voltage is greater than 7.3 volts, repair "BL/Y" wire from ECU to cooling fan relay No. 1 for an open circuit. Reconnect cooling fan motor and go to step 10).

5) Check Rear Window Defroster Signal – Remove 15-amp circuit fuse. Turn off all accessories. Disconnect rear window defroster switch. With KOEO, set VOM on 20-volt scale. Measure voltage at "BK/BL" wire terminal of rear window defroster switch connector. If voltage is greater than 7.3 volts, check operation of rear window defroster switch. If not, go to next step.

6) Checking ELU Output Voltage – Ensure ELU is connected. Remove 15-amp circuit fuse. Turn off all accessories. Disconnect rear window defroster switch. With KOEO, set VOM on 20-volt scale. Measure voltage between ELU "BK/BL" wire terminal (+) and ground (–). If voltage is greater than 7.3 volts, repair "BK/BL" wire between ELU and rear window defroster switch for opens. If voltage is 7.3 volts or less, replace fuse and reconnect rear window defroster switch. Go to step 10).

7) Checking Combination Switch Signal – Disconnect ELU. With KOEO, ensure all accessories are turned off. Set VOM on 20-volt scale. Turn headlamps on. Measure voltage between "W/BL" wire terminal (+) at ELU and ground (–). If voltage is greater than 6 volts, go to step 10). If not, repair "W/BL" wire from combination switch to ELU for open or shorts. If all circuits are okay, repair combination switch as necessary.

8) Checking Heater Blower Signal – Set VOM on 20-volt scale. Disconnect heater control unit. Ensure all accessories are turned off. With KOEO, measure voltage between "BL/BK" wire terminal at heater control unit connector and ground (–). If voltage is greater than 5 volts, repair heater control unit as necessary. If voltage is 5 volts or less, go to next step.

9) Checking ELU Output Voltage – Disconnect heater control unit. Ensure all accessories are turned off and ELU is connected. Set VOM on 20-volt scale. Measure voltage between "BL/BK" wire terminal (+) at ELU and ground (–). If voltage is greater than 5 volts, repair "BL/BK" wire for open between ELU and heater control unit. If voltage is not greater than 5 volts, go to next step.

10) Check For Shorts To Ground – Disconnect ELU and cooling fan relay No. 1. Ensure all accessories are turned off. Set VOM on 20k-ohm scale. Measure resistance between ground and the following wire terminals at the ELU connector: "BL/GN", "BL/Y", "BK/BL", and "W/BL". If any resistance is less than 10k ohms, repair short(s) to ground. If there are no resistance readings less than 10k ohms, reconnect cooling fan relay No. 1 and go to next step.

11) Checking For Power At ELU – Disconnect ELU and set VOM on 20-volt scale. With KOEO, measure voltage between "BK/W" wire terminal (+) at ELU connector and ground (–). If voltage is greater than 10 volts, go to next step. If voltage is 10 volts or less, repair "BK/W" wire between ELU and ignition switch for shorts or opens. Ensure ignition switch is okay.

12) Checking ELU Ground – Disconnect ELU and set VOM on 200-ohm scale. Measure resistance between "BK" wire terminal of ELU connector and ground. If resistance is less than 5 ohms, go to next step. If not, repair open in "BK" wire from ELU to ground.

13) Checking ECA Pin Voltage – Install breakout box. Ensure all accessories are turned off. With KOEO, set VOM on 20-volt scale. Measure voltage between test pins No. 24 (+) and 20 (ground). If voltage is greater than 7 volts with all accessories off and less than 1.5 volts with headlights and rear defroster on, replace ECA. If voltage is not as specified, repair open or short in "GN/Y" wire from ECA terminal "1F" to ELU. If wire circuit is okay, replace ELU.

1989 COMPUTERIZED ENGINE CONTROLS
Ford Motor Co. Probe — EEC (Cont.)

1a-395

CIRCUIT TEST C1

FUEL CONTROL

Fuel Control Circuits

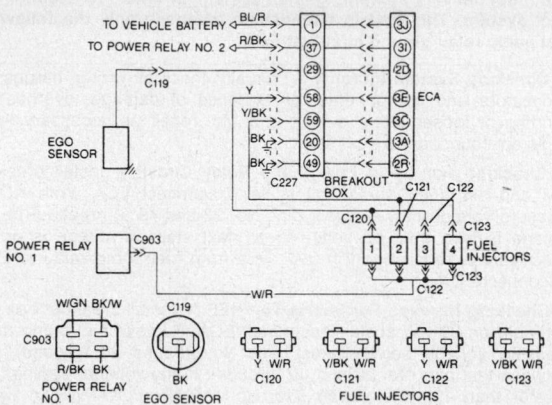

NOTE: Enter this test only when a Code 17 is displayed during the QUICK TEST procedure or when directed here from another CIRCUIT TEST. To prevent replacement of good components, be aware that the following non-EEC items may be faulty: fuel quantity and quality, fuel lines, intake air cleaner and duct, intercooler (turbo models), ignition components or intake manifold and gaskets. This test is intended to diagnose only the following: injector circuits, injector drivers (internal ECA) and EGO sensor circuits.

1) Checking System Integrity – Visually check all wiring, harnesses, connectors and components for evidence of damage, overheating, shorting or looseness. If a fault is found, repair as necessary. If no faults are found, go to next step.

2) Checking EGO Sensor Sensitivity – This step requires Ford Motor Co. SUPER STAR II Tester and Adapter Cable (007-00036). Connect adapter cable to Self-Test (STO) connector and ground. Leave STI connector open (not grounded). Warm up engine and run at idle. Increase engine speed to 2500 RPM. If monitor light on tester flashes 8 times in 10 seconds, go to step 5). If not, go to next step.

3) Check For Air Leaks – Inspect inlet air system for leaks. If any leaks are present in the inlet tract, service or repair as necessary. If not, go to next step.

4) Check EGO Sensor – With key off, inspect EGO sensor circuit for damage, broken wire or faulty connectors. Remove EGO sensor and inspect for contamination. If EGO sensor or circuit is okay, go to next step. If not, service or replace as necessary.

5) Inspect Spark Plugs – With key off, remove spark plugs and inspect for excessive carbon build-up or damage. If sparks plugs are okay, go to next step. If not, service or replace as necessary.

6) Checking EGO Sensor Output – Warm up engine and run at idle. Set VOM on 5-volt scale. Disconnect EGO sensor. Measure voltage between EGO sensor connector (sensor side) and ground. Increase engine speed to 4000-4500 RPM until voltmeter reads 0.7 volt. Rapidly decrease and increase engine speed while reading voltmeter. When engine speed is decreasing, voltage should be 0-0.4 volt. When engine speed is increasing, voltage should be 0.5-1.0 volt. If both voltages are okay, go to next step. If voltage does not meet specifications, go to CIRCUIT TEST D3, step 1).

7) Check EGO Switching Voltage – With EGO sensor connected, install breakout box. Warm up engine and run at idle. Set VOM on 5-volt scale. Measure voltage between test pins No. 29 and 49 at breakout box. Increase engine speed to 4000-4500 RPM until voltmeter reads 0.7 volt. Rapidly decrease and increase engine speed while reading voltmeter. When engine speed is decreasing, voltage should be 0-0.4 volt. When engine speed is increasing, voltage should be 0.5-1.0 volt. If both voltages are okay, go to next step. If voltage does not meet specifications, repair EGO sensor wire harness.

8) Checking Injector Drive Signal – With breakout box installed, connect standard 12-volt non-powered test light between test pins No. 58 and 37 at the breakout box. Crank or start engine. Repeat test between test pins No. 37 and 59 at the breakout box. Observe the following test results:
- Dim glow in both tests. Go to step **11)**.
- No light in either test. Go to next step.
- Bright light in one or both tests. Go to step **10)**.

CIRCUIT TEST C1 (Cont.)

9) Check ECA Power – Connect breakout box and set VOM on 20-volt scale. Disconnect ECA. With KOEO, measure voltage between test pins No. 1 and 20 (ground), and between test pins No. 37 and 20 (ground). If all readings are greater than 10 volts, replace ECA. If not, go to CIRCUIT TEST B12, step 1).

10) Checking Injector Circuit For Shorts – Install breakout box. Disconnect battery and ECA. Set VOM on 200k-ohm scale. At breakout box, measure resistance between test pin No. 59 and test pins No. 37, 20, 40, 1, and 49. Measure resistance between test pin No. 58 and test pins No. 37, 20, 40, 1, and 49. If any resistance is less than 10k ohms, repair shorts to ground or VPWR in harness, as necessary. If no resistance readings are less than 10k ohms, replace ECA.

11) Checking Injector Balance – Connect test tachometer. Disconnect ISC at connector. Run engine at 2000 RPM. Disconnect and reconnect injectors one at a time. Note RPM drop for each injector. If each injector produces an RPM drop of at least 150 RPM, go to next step. If not, replace faulty injector.

12) Checking Deceleration Fuel Cut-Off – Install breakout box, leave ECA connected. With engine at idle, connect a non-powered 12-volt test light between test pins No. 58 and 37. Increase engine speed to 4000 RPM. Decrease engine speed rapidly. Repeat test between test pins No. 59 and 37. If light flashes at idle but is off during deceleration between 2000 and 4000 RPM, system is okay, return to DIAGNOSTIC ROUTINES. If test light does not flash as specified, replace ECA.

CIRCUIT TEST C2

EXHAUST GAS/OXYGEN (EGO) SENSOR

EGO Sensor Circuits

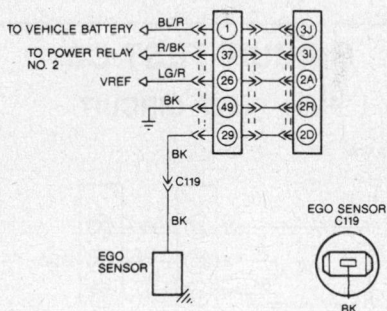

NOTE: Enter this test only when a Code 15 is displayed during the QUICK TEST procedure. This test will not diagnose fuel system problems. To prevent replacement of good components, be aware that the following non-EEC items may be faulty: fuel quality, intake air cleaner and duct, fuel delivery system or ignition system. This test is intended to diagnose only the following: EGO sensor, EGO circuits or ECA.

1) Checking System Integrity – Visually check all wiring, harnesses, connectors and components for evidence of damage, overheating, shorting or looseness. If a fault is found, repair as necessary. If no faults are found, go to next step.

2) Checking EGO Sensor Output Voltage – Warm up engine and run at idle. Set VOM on 5-volt scale. Disconnect EGO sensor. Measure voltage between EGO sensor connector (sensor side) and ground. Increase engine speed to 4000-4500 RPM until voltmeter reads 0.7 volt. Rapidly decrease and increase engine speed while reading voltmeter. When engine speed is decreasing, voltage should be 0-0.4 volt. When engine speed is increasing, voltage should be 0.5-1.0 volt. If voltage is within specification, go to step 5). If voltage is not to specification, go to next step.

3) Isolating Open Circuit In EGO Sensor – With key off, disconnect EGO sensor. Inspect "BK" wire from EGO sensor connector for possible opens. If EGO sensor wire is okay, go to next step. If not, repair wire or replace sensor as necessary.

CIRCUIT TEST C2 (Cont.)

4) Isolating Short In EGO Circuit – With key off, disconnect EGO sensor. Set VOM on 200k-ohm scale. Connect VOM between EGO sensor connector (sensor side) and ground. If resistance is greater than 10k ohms, replace EGO sensor. If resistance is not greater than 10k ohms, repair short in EGO sensor wire or replace EGO sensor as required.

5) Checking EGO Sensor Sensitivity – Ensure EGO sensor is connected. Start engine. This step requires Ford Motor Co. SUPER STAR II Tester and Adapter Cable (007-00036). Connect adapter cable to Self-Test Output (STO) connector and ground. Leave Self-Test Input (STI) connector open (not grounded). Warm up engine and run at idle. Increase engine speed to 2500 RPM. If monitor light on tester flashes 8 times in 10 seconds, go to step **8)**. If not, go to next step.

6) Checking EGO Sensor Circuit – With key off, install breakout box. Leave ECA and EGO sensor disconnected. Set DVOM on 200-ohm scale. Measure resistance between EGO sensor connector (harness side) and test pin No. 29 at breakout box. If resistance is greater than 10 ohms, repair open circuit and reconnect EGO sensor. If resistance is 10 ohms or less, go to next step.

7) Checking EGO Sensor Circuit – With key off, install breakout box. Leave ECA and EGO sensor disconnected. Set VOM on 200k-ohm scale. Measure resistance between test pin No. 29 and test pins No. 1, 26, 37 and 49. If any resistance is less than 10k ohms, repair short in EGO sensor circuit to VPWR, VREF, KAPWR or ground as necessary. If none of the resistance readings are 10k ohms or less, replace EGO sensor.

8) Checking ECA Input Voltage – Install breakout box, leave ECA connected. Set VOM 5-volt scale. Warm engine to normal operating temperature. Measure voltage between test pins No. 29 and 49 at breakout box wile increasing and decreasing engine speed between 1500 and 4000 RPM. If voltage changes between 0.5 volt and 1.0 volt, replace ECA. If voltage does not change as specified, inspect ECA and ECA No. 2 connector for damage, looseness or corrosion. Repair as necessary.

CIRCUIT TEST C3
FUEL PUMP CIRCUIT

Fuel Pump Circuits

CIRCUIT TEST C3 (Cont.)

NOTE: Enter this test only when directed here from CONTINUOUS SELF-TEST procedure. To prevent replacement of good components, be aware that the following non-EEC areas may be at fault: fuel delivery system, ignition system, or intake air cleaner and duct system. This test is intended to diagnose only the following: fuel pump relay ground circuit at ECA.

1) Checking System Integrity – Visually check all wiring, harnesses, connectors and components for evidence of damage, overheating, shorting or looseness. If a fault is found, repair as necessary. If no faults are found, go to next step.

2) Checking For Open Fuel Pump Relay Circuit – Install breakout box and set VOM on 20-volt scale. Disconnect ECA. With KOEO, measure voltage between test pins No. 22 and 49 at breakout box. If voltage is less than 10 volts, go to next step. If voltage is not to specification, repair open in "LG" wire from fuel pump relay to ECA. Reconnect ECA.

3) Checking Harness For Shorts To VREF – Install breakout box and set VOM on 20-volt scale. Disconnect ECA. Remove fuel pump relay. Measure voltage between test pins No. 22 and 20 (ground), and between test pins No. 22 and 49 (ground). If any voltage readings are greater than 10 volts, repair short to VAPWR or KAPWR in wiring harness. Reinstall fuel pump relay. If voltage is not as specified, go to next step.

4) Checking ECA Input Voltage – Install breakout box. Leave ECA connected and fuel pump relay installed. Measure voltage between test pins No. 22 and 49 at breakout box with KOEO and KOER (engine at idle). If voltage is greater than 10 volts with engine off, and less than 4 volts at idle, go to DIAGNOSTIC ROUTINES. If readings are not as specified, ensure fuel pump relay and related circuit are okay and replace ECA.

CIRCUIT TEST D1
EGR ON/OFF CONTROL & EGR CONTROL (EGRC)

EGR Control Circuits

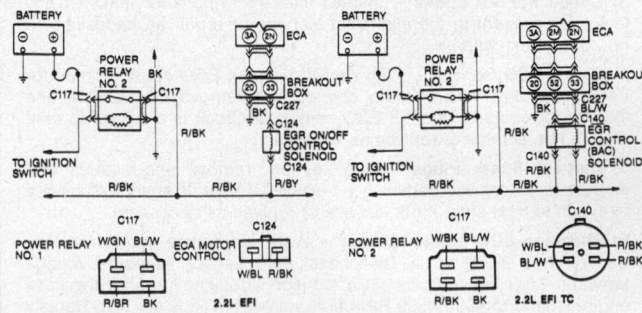

NOTE: Enter this test only when a Code 28 is displayed during the QUICK TEST procedure or when directed here from another CIRCUIT TEST. To prevent replacement of good components, be aware that the following non-EEC areas may be faulty: air or vacuum leaks, restricted EGR flow or EGR valve. This test is intended to diagnose only the following: harness circuits, ECA, or EGR solenoid.

1) Checking System Integrity – Visually check all wiring, harnesses, connectors and components for evidence of damage, overheating, shorting or looseness. If a fault is found, repair as necessary. If no faults are found, go to next step.

2) Checking Voltage At ECA – Install breakout box. Disconnect ECA. Set VOM on 20-volt scale. On turbo models, test with KOEO. On non-turbo models, test with KOER (engine above 1500 RPM). Measure voltage between test pins No. 33 and 20 (ground). If voltage is less than 10 volts, go to next step. If not, go to step **6)**.

3) Checking Voltage From EGR Solenoid – On turbo models, test with KOEO. On non-turbo models, test with KOER (engine above 1500 RPM). Disconnect ECA. Leave EGR solenoid connected. Set VOM on 20-volt scale. Do not pierce wires during testing. Measure voltage at "W/BL" wire terminal between EGR solenoid connector and ground. If

1989 COMPUTERIZED ENGINE CONTROLS
Ford Motor Co. Probe – EEC (Cont.)

1a-397

CIRCUIT TEST D1 (Cont.)

voltage reading is less than 10 volts, go to next step. If voltage is not to specification, repair "W/BL" wire between ECA and EGR solenoid.

4) Checking Voltage To EGR Solenoid – With KOEO and ECA disconnected, set VOM on 20-volt scale. Measure voltage at "R/BK" wire between EGR solenoid and ground. If voltage reading is less than 10 volts, go to next step. If voltage is not as specified, replace EGR solenoid.

5) Checking Voltage From Power Relay No. 2 – With KOEO, set VOM on 20-volt scale. Leave power relay disconnected. Do not pierce wires during testing. Measure voltage at "R/BK" wire between power relay No. 2 and ground. If voltage reading is 10 volts or less, go to CIRCUIT TEST B1, step 1). If voltage is not as specified, repair "R/BK" wire between EGR solenoid and power relay No. 2.

6) Checking EGR Circuit For Short To VPWR – Install breakout box. Leave ECA disconnected. Disconnect EGR solenoid at connector. Set VOM on 20-volt scale. With KOEO, measure voltage between test pins No. 33 and 20 (ground). If voltage is greater than zero, repair short to VPWR. If voltage is zero, replace ECA.

CIRCUIT TEST D2

CANISTER PURGE (CANP)

CANP Circuits

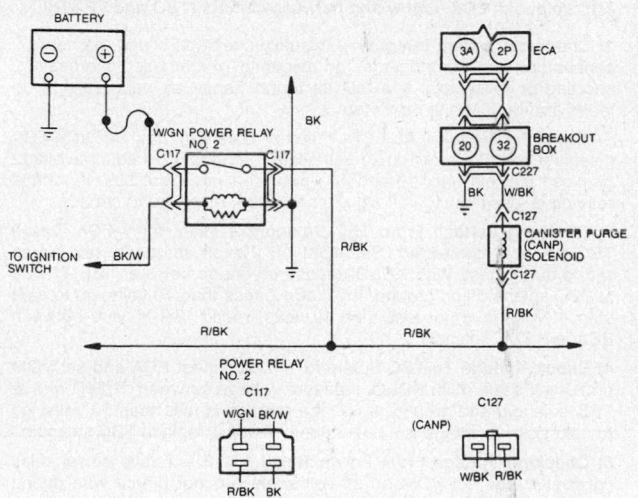

NOTE: Enter this test only when a Code 26 is displayed during the QUICK TEST procedure or when directed here from another CIRCUIT TEST. This test is intended to diagnose only the following: harness circuits (CANP and VPWR), ECA or CANP solenoid.

1) Checking System Integrity – Visually check all wiring, harnesses, connectors and components for evidence of damage, overheating, shorting or looseness. If a fault is found, repair as necessary. If no faults are found, go to next step.

2) Checking Voltage At ECA – Install breakout box. Leave ECA disconnected and set VOM on 20-volt scale. With KOEO, measure voltage between test pins No. 32 and 20 (ground). If voltage is 10 volts or less, go to next step. If not, go to step 6).

3) Check Voltage From CANP Solenoid – Disconnect ECA. Ensure CANP solenoid is connected. Set VOM on 20-volt scale. Do not pierce wire. With KOEO, measure voltage between "W/BK" wire at CANP solenoid and ground. If voltage reading is less than 10 volts, go to next step. If not, repair "W/BK" wire between ECA and CANP solenoid.

4) Check Voltage To CANP Solenoid – Ensure ECA is disconnected and set VOM on 20-volt scale. With KOEO, measure voltage between "R/BK" wire at CANP solenoid and ground. If voltage is less than 10 volts, go to next step. If not, replace CANP solenoid.

5) Check Voltage From Power Relay No. 2 – Ensure power relay No. 2 is connected and set VOM on 20-volt scale. Do not pierce wire to test. With KOEO, measure between "R/BK" wire at power relay No. 2

CIRCUIT TEST D2 (Cont.)

and ground. If voltage is less than 10 volts, go to CIRCUIT TEST B12, step 1). If voltage is not to specification, repair "R/BK" wire between CANP solenoid and power relay No. 2.

6) Check CANP Circuit For Short To VPWR – Install breakout box, leaving ECA disconnected. Disconnect CANP solenoid connector. With KOEO, set VOM on 20-volt scale. Measure voltage between test pins No. 32 and 20 (ground). If voltage is greater than zero, repair short to VPWR. If voltage is zero, replace ECA.

CIRCUIT TEST D3

IDLE SPEED CONTROL (ISC)
(BYPASS AIR)

ISC Circuits

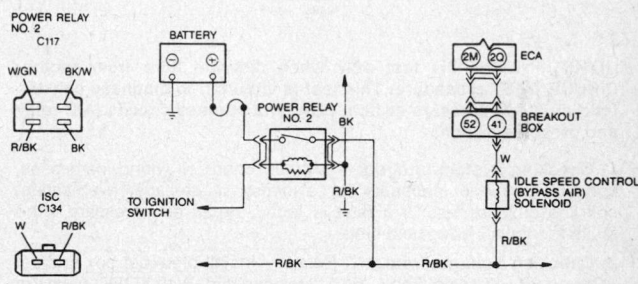

CAUTION: If engine runs or idles rough, correct these conditions before diagnosing Idle Speed Control (ISC) system. Rough running or misses may be caused by the following: ignition system, fuel system, or EGR system.

NOTE: Enter this test only when a Code 34 is displayed during the QUICK TEST procedure or when directed here from another CIRCUIT TEST. To prevent replacement of good components, be aware that the following non-EEC areas may be at fault: engine not up to operating temperature, engine hotter than maximum operating temperature, incorrect air adjust screw adjustment, faulty electrical load input signal, or sticking throttle linkage. This test is intended to diagnose only the following: ISC solenoid, ECA, and harness circuits (ISC and VPWR).

1) Checking System Integrity – Visually check all wiring, harnesses, connectors and components for evidence of damage, overheating, shorting or looseness. If a fault is found, repair as necessary. If no faults are found, go to next step.

2) Check Voltage At ECA – Install breakout box and leave ECA disconnected. Set DVOM on 20-volt scale. With KOEO, measure voltage between test pins No. 41 and 20 (ground). If voltage is less than one volt, go to next step. If not, go to step 6).

3) Check Voltage From ISC Solenoid – Disconnect ECA. Leave ISC solenoid connected. Set VOM on 20-volt scale. Do not pierce wire to test. With KOEO, measure voltage between "W" wire at ISC solenoid and ground. If voltage is less than one volt, go to next step. If not, repair "W" wire between ECA and ISC solenoid.

4) Checking Voltage To ISC Solenoid – Disconnect ECA and set VOM on 20-volt scale. With KOEO, measure voltage between "R/BK" wire at ISC solenoid and ground. If voltage is less than 10 volts, go to next step. If not, replace ISC solenoid.

5) Checking Voltage From Power Relay No. 2 – Ensure power relay is connected. Set VOM on 20-volt scale. Do not pierce wire to test. With KOEO, measure voltage between "R/BK" wire at power relay No. 2 and ground. If voltage is less than 10 volts, go to CIRCUIT TEST B12, step 1). If voltage is not as specified, repair "R/BK" wire between ISC solenoid and power relay No. 2.

6) Checking ISC Circuit For Short To VPWR – Install breakout box, leaving ECA disconnected. Disconnect ISC solenoid connector. Set VOM on 20-volt scale. With KOEO, measure voltage between test pins No. 41 and 20 (ground). If voltage is greater than zero volts, repair short to VPWR. If voltage is zero volts, replace ECA.

1a-398

1989 COMPUTERIZED ENGINE CONTROLS
Ford Motor Co. Probe — EEC (Cont.)

CIRCUIT TEST D4

WOT A/C CUT-OFF (ACC)

ACC Circuits

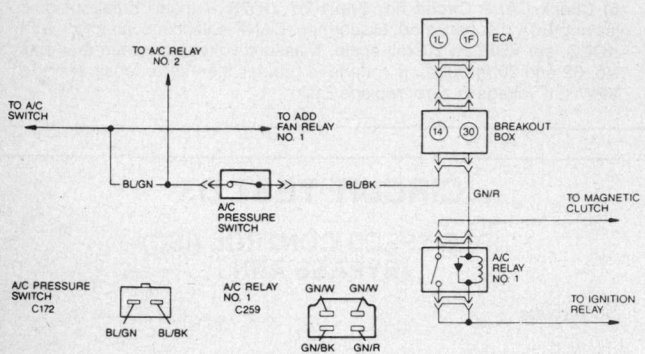

NOTE: Enter this test only when directed here from another CIRCUIT TEST procedure. This test is intended to diagnose only the following: A/C pressure switch, ECA, and harness circuits (A/C relay and pressure switch)

1) Checking System Integrity – Visually check all wiring, harnesses, connectors and components for evidence of damage, overheating, shorting or looseness. If a fault is found, repair as necessary. If no faults are found, go to next step.

2) Checking Voltage From A/C Relay – Install breakout box and set VOM on 20-volt scale. Leave ECA disconnected. With KOEO, measure voltage between test pins No. 30 and 20 (ground). If voltage is less than 10 volts, go to step **3)**. If not, go to step **4)**.

3) Measure Voltage At A/C Relay No. 1 – Set VOM on 20-volt scale. Leave ECA disconnected. Ensure A/C relay No. 1 is connected. Do not pierce wire during test. With KOEO, measure voltage between "GN/R" wire at A/C relay No. 1 and ground. If voltage is less than 10 volts, repair or replace A/C switch or relay. If not, repair "GN/R" wire between ECA and A/C relay No. 1.

4) Checking A/C Circuit For Short To VPWR – Install breakout box and set VOM on 20-volt scale. Leave ECA disconnected. Disconnect A/C relay No. 1. With KOEO, measure voltage between test pins No. 30 and 20 (ground). If voltage is greater than zero volts, repair short to VPWR. If voltage is zero volts, go to next step.

5) Checking Voltage From A/C Pressure Switch (ACPS) – Install breakout box and set VOM on 20-volt scale. Leave ECA disconnected. With KOEO, measure voltage between test pins No. 14 and 20 (ground). If voltage is less than 10 volts, go to step **6)**. If not, go to next step.

6) Checking Voltage At ACPS – Disconnect ECA and set VOM on 20-volt scale. Leave ACPS connected. Do not pierce wires during test. With KOEO, measure voltage between "BL/BK" wire at ACPS and ground. If voltage is less than 10 volts, go to step **8)**. If not, repair "BL/BK" wire between ECA and ACPS.

7) Checking ACPS Circuit For Short To VPWR – Install breakout box and set VOM on 20-volt scale. Leave ECA disconnected. Disconnect A/C relay No. 1. With KOEO, measure voltage between test pins No. 14 and 20 (ground). If voltage is greater than zero volts, repair short to VPWR. If voltage is zero volts, replace ECA.

8) Checking Voltage To ACPS – Disconnect ECA and set VOM on 20-volt scale. Leave ECA disconnected. With KOEO, measure voltage between "BL/GN" wire at ACPS and ground. If voltage is less than 10 volts, repair or replace A/C switch or relay. If not, replace ACPS.

CIRCUIT TEST D5

TURBOCHARGER BOOST CONTROL SOLENOID VALVE (TBC)

TBC Circuits

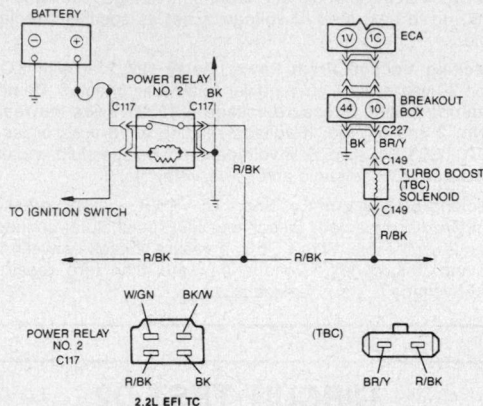

NOTE: Enter this test only when a Code 42 is displayed during the QUICK TEST procedure or when directed here from another CIRCUIT TEST. This test is intended to diagnose only the following: TBC solenoid, ECA, and wiring harness circuits (TBC and VPWR).

1) Checking System Integrity – Visually check all wiring, harnesses, connectors and components for evidence of damage, overheating, shorting or looseness. If a fault is found, repair as necessary. If no faults are found, go to next step.

2) Checking Voltage At ECA – Install breakout box, leaving ECA disconnected. Set VOM on 20-volt scale. With KOEO, measure voltage between test pins No. 10 and 44 (ground) at breakout box. If voltage reading is less than 10 volts, go to next step. If not, go to step **6)**.

3) Checking Voltage From TBC Solenoid – Disconnect ECA. Leave TBC solenoid connected. Set VOM on 20-volt scale. Do not pierce wiring during test. With KOEO, measure voltage between "BR/Y" wire at TBC solenoid and ground. If voltage is less than 10 volts, go to next step. If voltage is not less than 10 volts, repair "BR/Y" wire between ECA and TBC solenoid.

4) Check Voltage To TBC Solenoid – Disconnect ECA and set VOM on 20-volt scale. With KOEO, measure voltage between "R/BK" wire at TBC solenoid and ground. If voltage reading is less than 10 volts, go to next step. If voltage is not less than 10 volts, replace TBC solenoid.

5) Checking Voltage From Power Relay No. 2 – Leave power relay connected and set VOM on 20-volt scale. Do not pierce wire during testing. With KOEO, measure voltage between "R/BK" wire at power relay No. 2 and ground. If voltage is less than 10 volts, go to CIRCUIT TEST B12, step **1)**.

6) Checking TBC Circuit For Shorts To VPWR – Install breakout box, leaving ECA disconnected. Disconnect TBC solenoid connector. Set VOM on 20-volt scale. With KOEO, measure voltage between test pins No. 10 and 44 (ground). If voltage reading is above zero volts, repair short to VPWR. If voltage reading is zero volts, replace ECA.

CIRCUIT TEST D6

EGR VENT (EGRV) SOLENOID

NOTE: Enter this test only when a Code 29 is displayed during the QUICK TEST procedure or when directed here from another CIRCUIT TEST. To prevent replacement of good components, be aware that the following non-EEC areas may be at fault: air or vacuum leaks, EGR flow restrictions, or EGR valve. This test is intended to diagnose only the following: EGR solenoid, ECA and harness circuits (EGRV and VPWR).

1) Checking System Integrity – Visually check all wiring, harnesses, connectors and components for evidence of damage, overheating, shorting or looseness. If a fault is found, repair as necessary. If no faults are found, go to next step.

1989 COMPUTERIZED ENGINE CONTROLS
Ford Motor Co. Probe — EEC (Cont.)

1a-399

CIRCUIT TEST D6 (Cont.)

EGRV Circuits

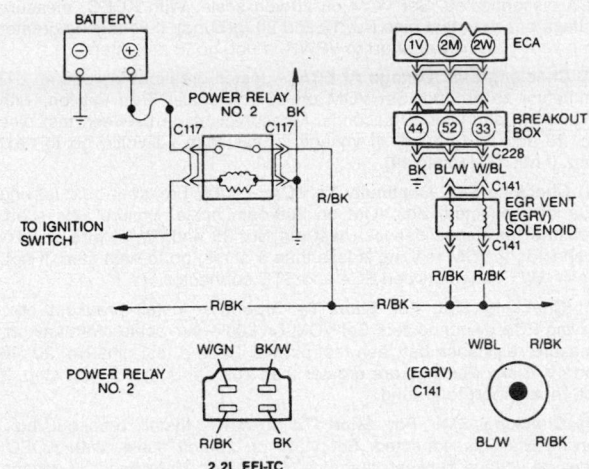

2) Checking Voltage At ECA – Install breakout box and disconnect ECA. Set DVOM on 20-volt scale. With KOEO, measure voltage between test pins No. 52 and 44 (ground) at breakout box. If voltage reading is less than 10 volts, go to next step. If not, go to step **6)**.

3) Checking Voltage From EGR Solenoid – Ensure EGR solenoid is connected and ECA is disconnected. Set VOM on 20-volt scale. Do not pierce wire during testing. With KOEO, measure voltage between "BL/W" wire at EGR solenoid and ground. If voltage reading is less than 10 volts, go to next step. If not, repair "BL/W" wire between ECA and EGR solenoid.

4) Checking Voltage To EGR Solenoid – With ECA disconnected, set VOM on 20-volt scale. With KOEO, measure voltage between "R/BK" wire at EGR solenoid and ground. If voltage reading is less than 10 volts, go to next step. If voltage is not less than 10 volts, replace EGR solenoid.

5) Checking Voltage From Power Relay No. 2 – Ensure power relay is connected. Set VOM on 20-volt scale. Do not pierce wire during testing. With KOEO, measure voltage between "R/BK" wire between power relay No. 2 and ground. If voltage is less than 10 volts, go to CIRCUIT TEST B12, step **1)**. If voltage is not less than 10 volts, repair "R/BK" wire between EGR solenoid and power relay No. 2.

6) Checking EGR Circuit For Short To VPWR – Install breakout box, leaving ECA disconnected. Disconnect EGRV solenoid connector. Set VOM on 20-volt scale. With KOEO, measure voltage between test pins No. 52 and 44 (ground) at breakout box. If voltage is greater than zero volts. Repair short to VPWR. If voltage is zero volts, replace ECA.

CIRCUIT TEST D7

PRESSURE REGULATOR CONTROL (PRC)

PRC Circuits

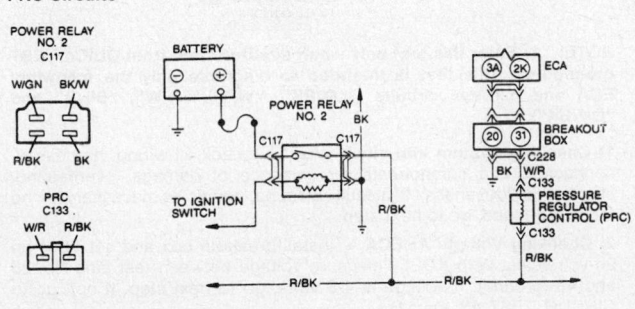

CIRCUIT TEST D7 (Cont.)

NOTE: Enter this test only when a Code 25 is displayed during the QUICK TEST procedure. To prevent replacement of good components, be aware that the following non-EEC areas may be at fault: vacuum leaks or fuel pressure regulator. This test is intended to diagnose only the following: PRC solenoid, ECA and wiring harness circuits (PRC and VPWR).

1) Checking System Integrity – Visually check all wiring, harnesses, connectors and components for evidence of damage, overheating, shorting or looseness. If a fault is found, repair as necessary. If no faults are found, go to next step.

2) Checking Voltage At ECA – Install breakout box and disconnect ECA. Set VOM on 20-volt scale. Turn key on and wait 2 minutes. Measure voltage between test pins No. 31 and 20 (ground). If voltage is less than 10 volts, go to next step. If not, go to step **6)**.

3) Checking Voltage From PRC Solenoid – Disconnect ECA. Leave PRC solenoid connected and set VOM on 20-volt scale. Do not pierce wire during testing. Turn key on and wait 2 minutes. Measure voltage at "W/R" wire between PRC solenoid and ground. If voltage is less than 10 volts, go to next step. If not, repair "W/R" wire between ECA and PRC solenoid.

4) Checking Voltage To PRC Solenoid – Disconnect ECA and set VOM on 20-volt scale. With KOEO, measure voltage between "R/BK" wire at PRC solenoid and ground. If voltage is less than 10 volts, go to next step. If not, repace PRC solenoid.

5) Checking Voltage From Power Relay No. 2 – Ensure power relay is connected. Set VOM on 20-volt scale. Do not pierce wire during testing. With KOEO, measure voltage between "R/BK" wire at power relay No. 2 and ground. If voltage is less than 10 volts, go to CIRCUIT TEST B12, step **1)**. If voltage is greater than 10 volts, repair "R/BK" wire between EGR solenoid and power relay No. 2.

6) Checking PRC Circuit For Shorts To VPWR – Install breakout box. Disconnect PRC solenoid at harness connector. Disconnect ECA and set VOM on 20-volt scale. With KOEO, measure voltage between test pins No. 31 and 20 (ground). If voltage reading is above zero volts, repair short to VPWR. If not, replace ECA.

CIRCUIT TEST D8

"CHECK ENGINE" MALFUNCTION INDICATOR LIGHT (MIL)

MIL Circuit

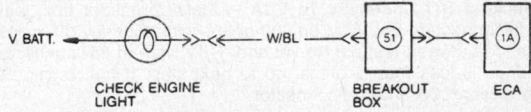

NOTE: Enter this test only when directed here from DIAGNOS-TIC ROUTINES or other test procedure. To prevent replacement of good components, be aware that the following non-EEC areas may be at fault: fuse, bulb or socket. This test is intended to diagnose only the following: ECA and harness circuit (MIL).

1) Checking System Integrity – Visually check all wiring, harnesses, connectors and components for evidence of damage, overheating, shorting or looseness. If a fault is found, repair as necessary. If no faults are found, go to next step.

2) Checking ECA Ground – Install breakout box, leaving ECA disconnected. With KOEO, jumper test pin No. 51 to test pin No. 20 (ground). If "CHECK ENGINE" light is on, go to CIRCUIT TEST B12, step **1)**. If light is off, go to next step.

3) Checking MIL Circuit For Power – Ensure MIL is connected. Do not pierce wire during test procedure. With KOEO, ground "W/BL" wire with jumper at connector "C235" (located at rear of instrument panel). If "CHECK ENGINE" light is on, repair "W/BL" wire between MIL light and ECA. If not, repair power circuit to "CHECK ENGINE" light or replace bulb as necessary.

1a-400

1989 COMPUTERIZED ENGINE CONTROLS
Ford Motor Co. Probe – EEC (Cont.)

CIRCUIT TEST D8 (Cont.)

Dash Connector "C235"

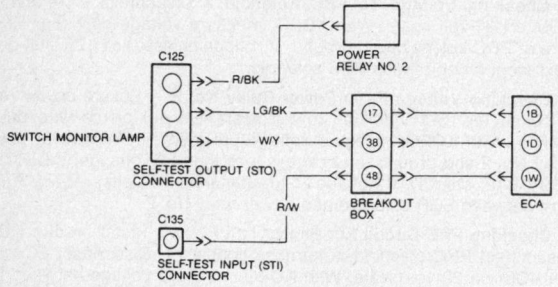

CONNECTOR IS SHOWN
LOOKING INTO HARNESS
C235

W/BL

CIRCUIT TEST D9

CODE "88" CONTINUOUSLY FLASHING

STI Circuits

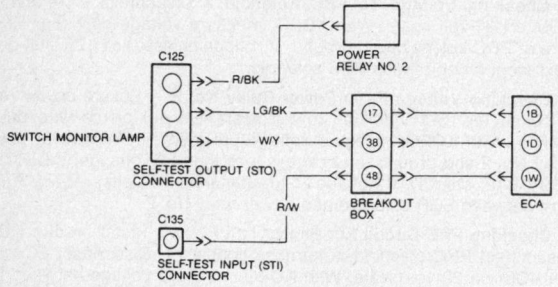

POWER RELAY NO. 2

C125
R/BK
LG/BK
W/Y

SWITCH MONITOR LAMP

SELF-TEST OUTPUT (STO) CONNECTOR

17
38
48

BREAKOUT BOX

1B
1D
1W

ECA

C135
R/W

SELF-TEST INPUT (STI) CONNECTOR

NOTE: Enter this test only when Code 88 is received in QUICK TEST PROCEDURE. This test is intended to diagnose only the following: ECA and harness circuits (STO, SML, STI, and VPWR.)

1) Checking System Integrity – Visually check all wiring, harnesses, connectors and components for evidence of damage, overheating, shorting or looseness. If a fault is found, repair as necessary. If no faults are found, go to next step.

2) Checking STI Voltage At ECA – Install breakout box. Set VOM on 20-volt scale. With KOEO, measure voltage between test pins No. 48 and 20 (ground). If voltage is less than 10 volts, go to next step. If not, go to step **6)**.

3) Checking STI Continuity To ECA – Install breakout box, leaving ECA disconnected. Set VOM on 200-ohm scale. With key off, measure resistance between test pin No. 48 and "R/W" wire at STI connector. If resistance is less than 5 ohms, go to next step. If not, repair "R/W" wire between ECA and STI connector.

4) Checking STI For Short To Ground – Install breakout box, leaving ECA disconnected. Set VOM on 200k-ohm scale. With key off, measure resistance between test pin No. 48 and test pins No. 20, 40 and 49. If any readings are greater than 10k ohms, go to next step. If not, repair short to ground.

5) Checking STI For Short To VPWR – Install breakout box, leaving ECA disconnected. Set VOM on 20-volt scale. With KOEO, measure voltage between test pins No. 48 and 20 (ground). If voltage is greater than zero volts, repair short to VPWR. If voltage is zero volts, go to next step.

6) Checking STO Voltage At ECA – Install breakout box. Jump STI connector to ground. Set VOM on 20-volt scale. Turn key on, with engine off, and wait 10 seconds. Measure voltage between test pins No. 17 and 20 (ground). If voltage is less than 10 volts, go to next step. If not, go to step **10)**.

7) Checking For Continuity To ECA – Install breakout box, leaving ECA disconnected. Set VOM on 200-ohm scale. Ensure key is off. Measure resistance between test pin No. 17 and "LG/BK" wire at STO connector. If VOM reading is less than 5 ohms, go to next step. If not, repair "LG/BK" wire between ECA and STO connector.

8) Checking STO For Short to Ground – Install breakout box, leaving ECA disconnected. Set VOM on 200k-ohm scale. With key off, measure resistance between test pin No. 17 and test pins No. 20, 40 and 49. If any readings are greater than 10k ohms, go to next step. If not, repair short to ground.

CIRCUIT TEST D9 (Cont.)

9) Checking STO For Short To VPWR – Install breakout box, leaving ECA disconnected. Set VOM on 20-volt scale. With KOEO, measure voltage between test pins No. 17 and 20 (ground). If voltage is greater than zero volts, repair short to VPWR. If not, go to next step.

10) Checking SML Voltage At ECA – Install breakout box. Jump STI connector to ground. Set VOM on 20-volt scale. Turn key on, with engine off, and wait 10 seconds. Measure voltage between test pins No. 38 and 20 (ground). If voltage is less than 10 volts, go to next step. If not, go to step **14)**.

11) Checking SML Continuity To ECA – Intall breakout box, leaving ECA disconnected. Set VOM on 200-ohm scale. Ensure key is off. Measure resistance between test pin No. 38 and "W/Y" wire at STO connector. If VOM reading is less than 5 ohms, go to next step. If not, repair "W/Y" wire between ECA and STO connector.

12) Checking SML For Short To Ground – Install breakout box, leaving ECA disconnected. Set VOM on 200k-ohm scale. With key off, measure resistance between test pin No. 38 and test pins No. 20, 40 and 49. If any readings are greater than 10k ohms, go to next step. If not, repair short to ground.

13) Checking SML For Short To VPWR – Install breakout box, leaving ECA disconnected. Set VOM on 20-volt scale. With KOEO, measure voltage between test pins No. 38 and 20 (ground). If voltage is less than 10 volts, repair short to VPWR. If not, go to step **14)**.

14) Checking Voltage At STO Connector – Set VOM on 20-volt scale. With KOEO, measure voltage between "R/BK" wire at STO connector and ground. If voltage is less than 10 volts, go to next step. If not, go to CIRCUIT TEST A2, step **1)**.

15) Checking Voltage From Power Relay – Do not pierce wire during test. Ensure power relay No. 2 is connected. Set VOM on 20-volt scale. With KOEO, measure voltage between "R/BK" wire at power relay No. 2 and ground. If voltage reading is less than 10 volts, go to CIRCUIT TEST B12, step **1)**. If voltage reading is greater than 10 volts, repair "R/BK" wire between STO connecter and power relay No. 2.

CIRCUIT TEST D10

NO CODES/CODES NOT LISTED

ECA Harness Circuits

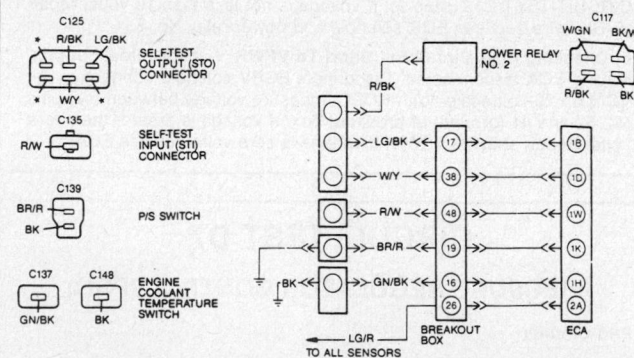

C125
R/BK LG/BK
SELF-TEST OUTPUT (STO) CONNECTOR
W/Y

C135
R/W
SELF-TEST INPUT (STI) CONNECTOR

C139
BR/R
BK
P/S SWITCH

C137 C148
GN/BK BK
ENGINE COOLANT TEMPERATURE SWITCH

R/BK

LG/BK 17 1B
W/Y 38 1D
R/W 48 1W
BR/R 19 1K
GN/BK 16 1H
26 2A

BREAKOUT BOX   ECA

POWER RELAY NO. 2

C117
W/GN BK/W
R/BK BK

LG/R
TO ALL SENSORS

NOTE: Enter this test only when directed here from QUICK TEST procedures. This test is intended to diagnose only the following: ECA and harness circuits ("LG/BK", "W/Y", "R/W", "BR/R" and "GN/BK").

1) Checking System Integrity – Visually check all wiring, harnesses, connectors and components for evidence of damage, overheating, shorting or looseness. If a fault is found, repair as necessary. If no faults are found, go to next step.

2) Checking Voltage At ECA – Install breakout box and set VOM on 20-volt scale. With KOEO, measure voltage between test pins No. 26 and 49 (ground). If voltage is 4-6 volts, go to next step. If not, go to CIRCUIT TEST A3, step **1)**.

3) Checking Voltage At ECA – Install breakout box. Set VOM on 20-volt scale. With KOEO, measure and record the following voltages. If all voltages are within specification, go to step **6)**. If not, go to next step.

1989 COMPUTERIZED ENGINE CONTROLS
Ford Motor Co. Probe — EEC (Cont.)

1a-401

CIRCUIT TEST D10 (Cont.)

ECA VOLTAGE

Test Pins No.	Volts
16 & 20	
Radiator Temp. Below 63°F (17°C)	7.3+
Radiator Temp. Above 63°F (17°C)	1.5
17 & 20 (w/STO Grounded)	10+
19 & 20 (Front Wheels Straight)	10+
38 & 20 (w/STO Grounded)	10+
48 & 20	10+

4) Checking Circuit Continuity – Install breakout box, leaving ECA disconnected. Set VOM on 200-ohm scale. With key off, measure and record the following resistances. If all resistances are less than 5 ohms, go to next step. If not, repair circuits in question as necessary.

CIRCUIT CONTINUITY

Test Pin No. & Circuit	Wire Colors
16 & ECT Switch	"GN/BK"
17 & STO Connector	"LG/BK"
19 & P/S Switch	"BR/R"
38 & STO Connector	"W/Y"
48 & STI Connector	"R/W"

5) Checking Circuits For Shorts To Ground – Install breakout box. Ensure engine is cold and ECA is disconnected. Set VOM on 200k-ohm scale. Measure and record the resistance between the following test pins at the breakout box:
- No. 16 and ground pins 20, 40, 44 (man. trans. only), 46, and 49.
- No. 17 and ground pins 20, 40, 44 (man. trans. only), 46, and 49.
- No. 19 and ground pins 20, 40, 44 (man. trans. only), 46, and 49.
- No. 38 and ground pins 20, 40, 44 (man. trans. only), 46, and 49.
- No. 48 and ground pins 20, 40, 44 (man. trans. only), 46, and 49.

If all resistances are greater than 10k ohms, go to CIRCUIT TEST B12, step 1). If not, repair shorted circuits as necessary. Refer to table in step 4) for wiring color.

6) Checking Voltage At Self-Test Connector – Set VOM on 20-volt scale. With KOEO, measure voltage between "R/BK" wire at Self-Test connector and ground. If voltage reading is less than 10 volts, go to next step. If not, return to DIAGNOSTIC ROUTINES.

7) Checking Voltage At Power Supply – Do not pierce wire during test. Leave power relay No. 2 connected. Set VOM on 20-volt scale. With KOEO, measure voltage between "R/BK" wire at power relay No. 2 and ground. If voltage reading is less than 10 volts, go to CIRCUIT TEST B12, step 1). If not, repair "R/BK" wire between Self-Test connector and power relay No. 2.

CIRCUIT TEST D11
TURBO OVERBOOST WARNING BUZZER

ECA to CPU Circuits

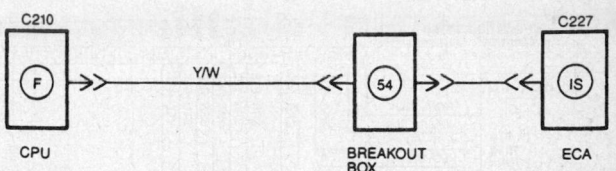

NOTE: Enter this test only when directed here from other test procedure. This test is intended to diagnose only the following: overboost harness circuit wiring.

1) Checking System Integrity – Visually check all wiring, harnesses, connectors and components for evidence of damage, overheating, shorting or looseness. If a fault is found, repair as necessary. If no faults are found, go to next step.

2) Checking ECA Ground Function – Install breakout box, leaving ECA disconnected. With KOEO, jumper test pins No. 54 to 44 (ground). If CPU unit "Chimes", go to CIRCUIT TEST B12, step 1). If not, go to next step.

3) Checking Overboost Circuit For Power – Do not pierce wire during this test. Leave CPU unit disconnected. With KOEO, ground "Y/W" wire at connector "C210" with jumper. If CPU unit "Chimes", repair "Y/W" wire between CPU unit and ECA. If CPU unit does not chime, repair or replace dash CPU unit as necessary.

CPU Harness Connector "C210"

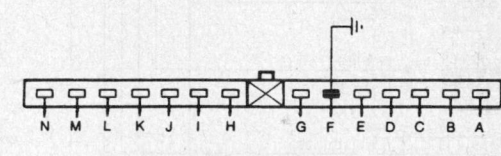

C210 CONNECTOR IS SHOWN LOOKING INTO HARNESS

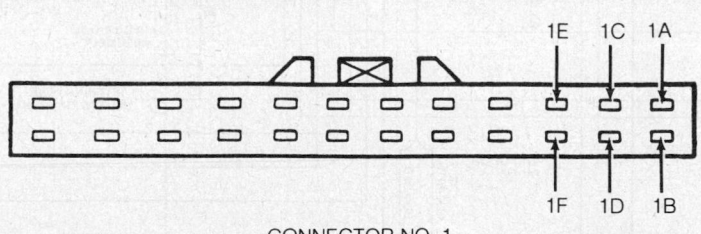

CONNECTOR NO. 1

CONNECTOR NO. 2

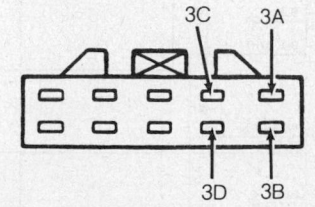

CONNECTOR NO. 3

Always use breakout box to test connectors. Never probe connector terminals or permanent damage will result. Pin locations given are for reference only, view is from connector side.

Courtesy of Ford Motor Co.

Fig. 4: *ECA Electrical Connector Diagrams & Numbering Sequence*

1989 **COMPUTERIZED ENGINE CONTROLS**
Ford Motor Co. Probe — EEC (Cont.)

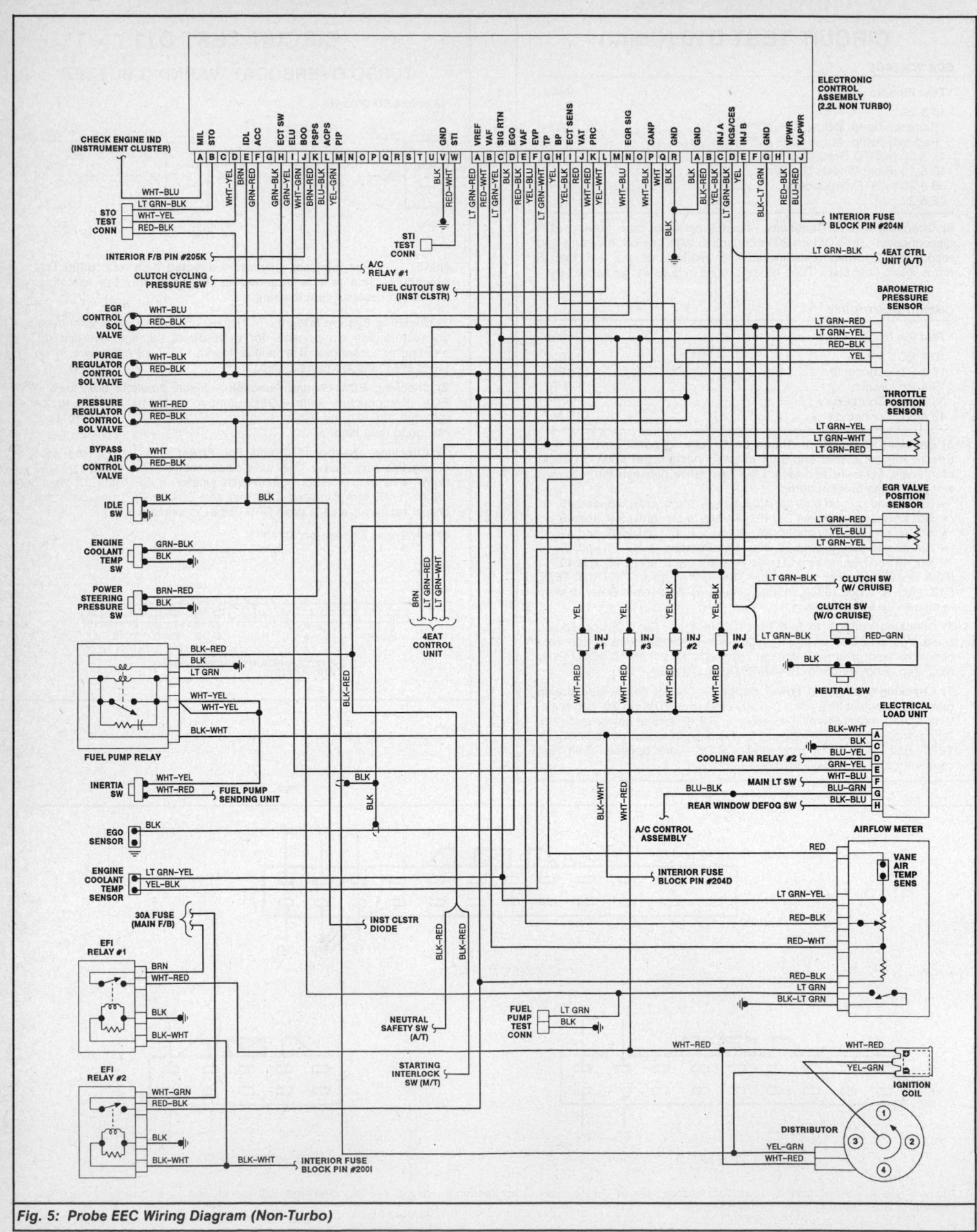

Fig. 5: Probe EEC Wiring Diagram (Non-Turbo)

1989 Computerized Engine Controls
Ford Motor Co. Probe — EEC (Cont.)

1a-403

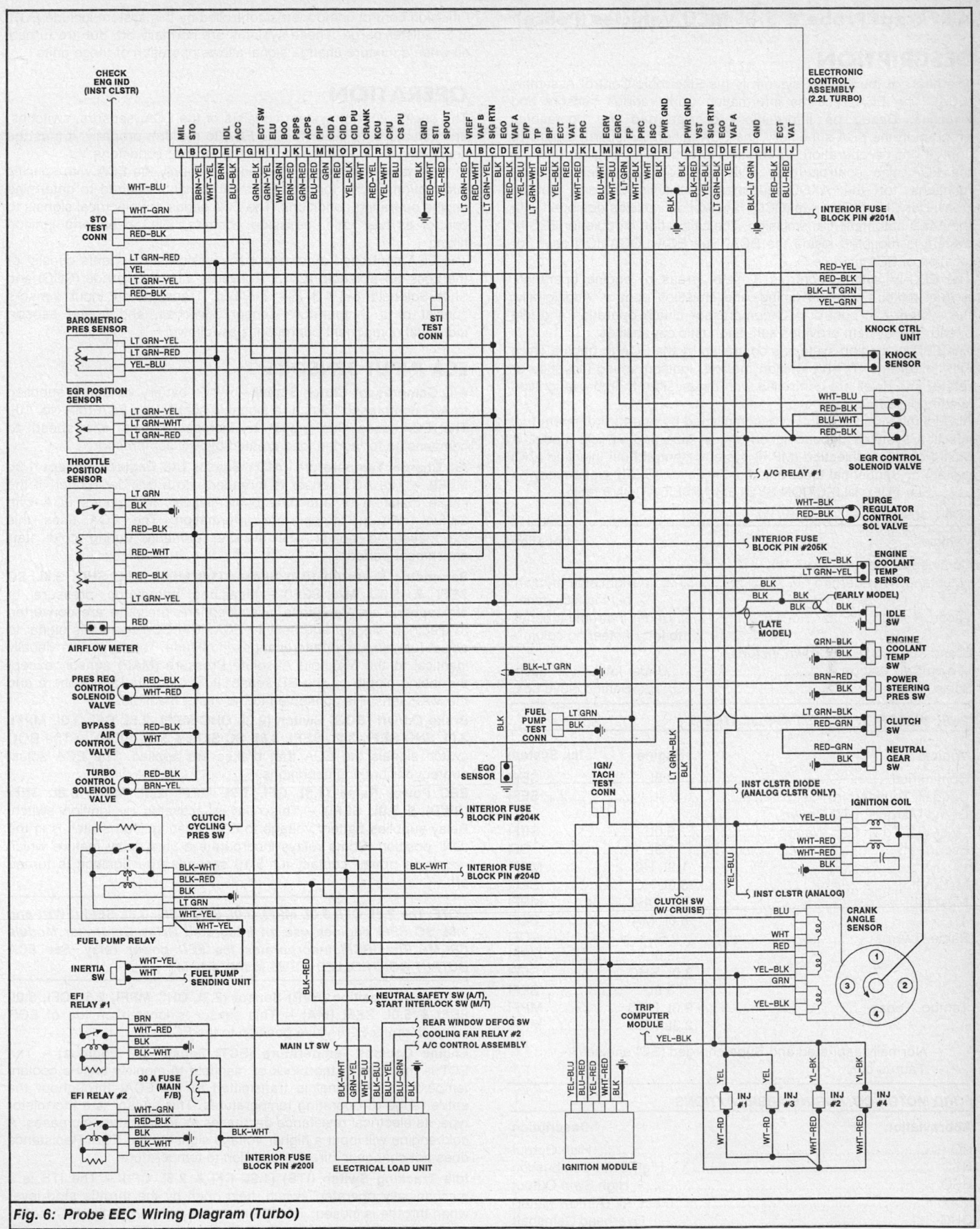

Fig. 6: Probe EEC Wiring Diagram (Turbo)

1989 COMPUTERIZED ENGINE CONTROLS
Ford Motor Co. EEC-IV

All Except Probe & 5.8L MCU Vehicles (Police)

DESCRIPTION

The heart of the EEC-IV system is the Electronic Control Assembly (ECA). The ECA receives information from various sensors and switches. Based on information received and the operational program in the ECA's memory, the ECA generates output signals to control engine operation. In addition to controlling engine function, the ECA also controls gear shift and Lock-Up Solenoid (LUS) functions for the AXOD automatic transmission and Torque Converter Clutch Override (CCO) function on vehicles equipped with the A4LD automatic transmission. The calibration module for EEC-IV system is mounted inside the ECA. See ECA LOCATION table for location of ECA module.

The EEC-IV system controls 3 major areas of engine operation: air/fuel mixture, ignition timing, and emission control. Additionally, the system can control A/C compressor clutch operation and idle speed. The system provides self-diagnostic capabilities.

The EEC-IV ignition system is controlled by the ECA through a Thick Film Integrated (TFI-IV) ignition module. Ignition timing (advance or retard) and dwell are controlled with this system to improve ignition system performance.

Air/fuel mixture operation is accomplished by one of 3 different fuel injection systems depending on engine size and vehicle model. A Multi-Point Fuel Injection (MPFI) system, Central Fuel Injection (CFI) system or Sequential Electronic Fuel Injection (SEFI) system may be used. See FUEL INJECTION SYSTEM APPLICATIONS table.

ECA LOCATION

Vehicle	Location
Continental, Cougar, Mark VII, Mustang, Thunderbird	Right side of dash, behind kick panel.
Escort, Tempo, Topaz	Under instrument panel, to left of steering column.
Grand Marquis, LTD Crown Victoria Town Car, Wagon	Under left side of dash.
Sable, Taurus	Behind glove box.

FUEL INJECTION SYSTEM APPLICATIONS

Vehicle	Engine	Inj. System
Continental	3.8L	SEFI
Cougar, Thunderbird	3.8L [1]	SEFI
Grand Marquis, LTD Crown Victoria, Town Car, Wagon	5.0L	SEFI
Escort	1.9L	CFI
	1.9L HO	MPFI
Mark VII	5.0L HO	SEFI
Mustang	2.3L OHC	MPFI
	5.0L MA	SEFI
Sable, Taurus	2.5L [2]	CFI
	3.0L	MPFI
	3.0L SHO	SEFI
	3.8L	SEFI
Tempo, Topaz	2.3L HSC	MPFI
	2.3L HSO	MPFI

[1] – Normally aspirated and Supercharged (SC) engines.
[2] – Taurus only.

FORD MOTOR CO. ENGINE ABBREVIATIONS

Abbreviation	Description
HO	High Output
HSC	High Swirl Combustion
HSO	High Swirl Output
MA	Mass Air (Airflow Meter)
OHC	Overhead Camshaft
SC	Supercharged
SHO	Super High Output

Emission control components controlled by this system include EGR and canister purge. These systems are normally off, but are turned on when a mixture change signal allows operation of these units.

OPERATION

The engine control system consists of the ECA, sensors, switches, and actuators. In order for the ECA to perform properly, it must be kept constantly informed of engine operating conditions.

It is the task of the engine sensors to supply the ECA with specific information, in the form of electrical signals, required to determine engine operating conditions. The ECA sends out electrical signals to control air/fuel ratio, emission controls, idle speed and ignition timing.

The ECA controlled automatic transmission components consist of the Lock-Up Solenoid (LUS), Converter Clutch Override (CCO) and Shift Solenoid 3-4/4-3 (SS 3-4/4-3). Transmission input sensors consist of a temperature sensor, switches, and speed sensor. Individual component operation is as follows:

ECA INPUT SENSORS

A/C Compressor Clutch Signal – When battery voltage is supplied to A/C compressor clutch, a signal is sent to the ECA (pin No. 10). The ECA uses this signal to increase engine idle speed to compensate for added load created by A/C compressor.

Air Charge Temperature (ACT) Sensor (All Engines Except 1.9L MPFI) – The ACT sensor is threaded into a cylinder runner of the intake manifold or attached to air cleaner. It provides ECA with air/fuel mixture temperature information. The ECA uses this information to adjust fuel mixture, primarily during cold start enrichment periods.

Barometric Pressure (BP) Sensor (1.9 MPFI, 3.0L SHO, 3.8L SC SEFI & 5.0L MA SEFI) – Measures barometric pressure of atmospheric air. Variations in atmospheric pressure are converted to electrical signals and sent to ECA. The ECA uses this signal to adjust fuel mixture due to changes in altitude. This sensor is visually identical to the Manifold Absolute Pressure (MAP) sensor, except the tubing nipple on the BP sensor is open to the atmosphere and the MAP sensor is connected to the intake manifold.

Brake On/Off (BOO) Switch (2.3L OHC MPFI, 2.5L CFI, 3.0L MPFI, 3.0L SHO SEFI, 3.8L SEFI, 3.8L SC SEFI & 5.0L SEFI) – The BOO switch signals the ECA that brakes are applied. The ECA adjust strategy for braking conditions.

EEC Power Relay (1.9L CFI, 1.9L MPFI, 2.3L MPFI, 3.8L SEFI (RWD) & 5.0L SEFI) – This relay is activated by ignition switch. Relay supplies battery voltage to ECA when ignition switch is in the "ON" position. Some relays incorporate a time delay feature which maintains power contact for 5-10 seconds after ignition is turned off.

NOTE: The 2.5L CFI, 3.0L MPFI, 3.0L SHO SEFI, 3.8L SEFI (FWD) and 3.8L SC SEFI engines use an Integrated Relay Controller Module (IRCM). The IRCM incorporates the EEC power relay. See ECA OUTPUT CONTROLLED ITEMS in this article.

EGR Valve Position (EVP) Sensor (2.3L OHC MPFI, 2.5L CFI, 5.0L SEFI & 5.0L SEFI (MA) – This sensor is located on top of EGR valve. It inputs EGR valve position to the ECA.

Engine Coolant Temperature (ECT) Sensor (All Engines) – The ECT is mounted in the block or manifold to monitor engine coolant temperature. A signal is transmitted to the ECA, throughout the entire range of operating temperatures. This sensor is a thermistor type, its electrical resistance decreases as temperature increases. A cold engine will input a higher voltage signal to the ECA. Resistance does not change in direct proportion to temperature.

Idle Tracking Switch (ITS) (1.9L CFI & 2.5L CFI) – The ITS is a mechanically operated switch, held open by the throttle stop lever when throttle is closed. The ITS is an integral part of the ISC motor. A signal is transmitted to the ECA that the ISC motor plunger is touching throttle.

1989 COMPUTERIZED ENGINE CONTROLS
Ford Motor Co. EEC-IV (Cont.)

1a-405

Knock Sensor (2.3L OHC MPFI, 3.0L MPFI, 3.0L SHO SEFI & 3.8L SC SEFI) – The knock sensor is a piezoelectric device designed to resonate at approximately the same frequency as engine knock. This unit senses and amplifies engine detonation (knock) and signals ECA to retard timing. The 3.0L MPFI engine does not use a knock sensor on vehicles sold in California.

Manifold Absolute Pressure (MAP) Sensor (1.9L CFI, 2.3L OHC MPFI, 2.3L HSC MPFI, 2.5L CFI, 3.0L MPFI, 3.8L SEFI & 5.0L SEFI) – MAP sensor measures absolute pressure of mixture in intake manifold and sends a proportional signal to the ECA. It is mounted on right inner fender for 5.0L engine and left inner fender for all others. A vacuum hose is connected between the sensor and the intake manifold.

Mass Airflow (MAF) Sensor (5.0L MA SEFI) – Measures airflow by measuring temperature differential. Incoming air is heated by a heated platinum wire ("Hot Wire") as it enters the sensor and remeasured again as it passes over a cold wire sensor. The ECA uses the temperature differential to compute the quantity of air flowing across the sensor and into the engine.

Neutral Drive Switch (NDS) & Neutral Gear Switch (NGS) – The NDS is used on Automatic Transmission (A/T) equipped vehicles to adjust idle speed due to increased load of engaged transaxle/transmission. Vehicles equipped with manual transaxle/transmission use a NGS switch to notify the ECA when transaxle/transmission is in gear.

Heated Oxygen (HEGO) Sensor (All Engines) – This sensor monitors oxygen content of exhaust gases. When it is at operating temperature, a voltage signal is produced which varies according to oxygen content of exhaust gases. The signal is transmitted to the ECA and is translated into a rich or lean mixture signal. A heating circuit in the sensor is used to bring the sensor to operating temperature. With the exception of the 3.0L MPFI engine, all V6 and V8 engines are equipped with 2 sensors. One for each exhaust bank.

Profile Ignition Pick-Up (PIP) (All Engines) – The PIP signal is generated by the ignition system. It informs the ECA of crankshaft position and engine speed. The PIP assembly is integral with distributor on all models. It has an armature with windows and metal tabs, that rotate past a stator assembly (Hall Effect switch). Ignition distributor does not have any mechanical or vacuum advance.

Power Steering Pressure Switch (PSPS) (2.3L OHC MPFI, 2.3L HSC MPFI, 2.5L CFI, 3.0L MPFI & 3.0L SHO SEFI) – The PSPS signals the ECA when power steering pressure exceeds 400-600 psi. The ECA uses this signal to raise engine rpm to compensate for power steering pump load when engine is at idle. Switch may be located on power steering rack or on power steering pump.

Pressure Feedback Electronic (PFE) EGR Valve (1.9L CFI, 2.3L HSC MPFI, 3.0L MPFI, 3.0L SHO SEFI, 3.8L MPFI & 3.8L SC SEFI) – The PFE exhaust gas recirculation valve is a conventional ported EGR valve with a backpressure sensing element attached. The valve is used in conjunction with the backpressure transducer, to inform ECA of EGR valve position. The PFE transducer converts varying exhaust pressure signals into a proportional analog voltage, which is used by the ECA to regulate EGR flow.

Self-Test Input (STI) (All Engines) – Self-Test Input (STI) is a circuit in the EEC system which is used to initiate the Self-Test procedures. The STI connector (pigtail) near the Self-Test connector is used to complete a circuit to activate this procedure. Self-Test functions are built into EEC-IV control module so system can display service codes for diagnosis of existing or intermittent problems.

Throttle Position (TP) Sensor (All Engines) – The rotary TP sensor is mounted on side of throttle body and connected directly to throttle plate shaft. The TP sensor senses throttle movement and position, and transmits a proportional electrical signal to ECA.

Vane Airflow (VAF) Meter (1.9L MPFI) – The airflow meter housing incorporates a sensor to measure air temperature and a movable vane (flapper door) potentiometer to measure airflow. It is mounted

between the air cleaner and the throttle body. VAF information is transmitted to the ECA.

Vane Air Temperature (VAT) – VAT sensor is incorporated in the VAF or MAF. It measures the temperature of air flowing through the inlet manifold and sends a signal to the ECA.

Vehicle Speed Sensor (VSS) – Sensor is transmission mounted, and sends a constant pulse signal to the ECA when the vehicle is in motion.

ECA OUTPUT CONTROLLED COMPONENTS

Wide Open Throttle A/C (WAC) Cut-Off (All Engines With A/C) – During Wide Open Throttle (WOT) operation, the WAC circuit interrupts power to the A/C compressor clutch. The A/C remains off for about 3 seconds after returning from WOT.

Canister Purge Solenoid (CANP) (All Except 2.3L OHC MPFI) – This solenoid switches manifold vacuum to operate canister purge valve when a signal is received from ECA. Vacuum opens purge valve when solenoid is energized by ECA and fuel in charcoal emission canister is purged into intake system.

EGR Control (EGRC) Solenoid (2.3L OHC MPFI) – Solenoid switches manifold vacuum to operate EGR valve on command from ECA. Vacuum opens the EGR valve when the solenoid is energized.

EGR Shut-Off (EGRSO) Solenoid (1.9L MPFI) – The EGR shut-off solenoid is an electrically-operated vacuum valve located between manifold vacuum source and EGR valve. A controlled vacuum bleed is located between solenoid and EGR valve. Vacuum bleed is a backpressure variable transducer. These 2 devices operate EGR valve. Solenoid switched vacuum is also supplied to canister purge valve.

EGR Vent (EGRV) Solenoid (2.3L OHC MPFI) – Solenoid vents EGR control solenoid vacuum line. Valve is normally open. When energized, vacuum is supplied to EGR valve.

EGR Vacuum Regulator (EVR) (All Engines Except 1.9L MPFI & 2.3L OHC MPFI) – Controlled by a signal from the ECA. Regulates the amount of vacuum supplied to the EGR valve.

Fuel Injectors (All Engines) – On MPFI and SEFI engines, each cylinder has a solenoid-operated injector which sprays fuel toward back of each intake valve. Each injector receives battery voltage through an ignition switch circuit. The ECA controlled ground circuit is used to complete the circuit and energize the injector. On CFI engines, one injector is mounted in the throttle body. On all fuel injected models, the ECA controls length of time each injector is "on" or energized. The "on" time governs the amount of fuel delivered.

Fuel Pump Relay (All Engines) – Fuel pump relay and ignition is activated by ECA when the ignition switch is in the "ON" or "START" positions. When ignition is turned on, the relay is activated to supply initial fuel line pressure to system. Some models use an Integrated Relay Controller Module (IRCM) which incorporates the fuel pump relay.

Idle Speed Control (ISC) Motor (1.9L CFI & 2.5L CFI) – This DC motor controls idle speed according to signals from ECA. Idle speed motor also controls high cam RPM, anti-diesel shutoff, dashpot, and pre-positioning for next vehicle start up. The ISC includes an integral Idle Tracking Switch (ITS) which sends a signal to the ECA that the throttle is at idle position.

Idle Speed Control By-Pass Air (All Engines Except 1.9L CFI & 2.5L CFI) – The throttle air by-pass valve is a solenoid-operated valve controlled by ECA. The valve allows air to by-pass around throttle plates to control cold engine fast idle, no-touch start, dashpot, overtemperature idle boost, and engine load idle correction.

Integrated Relay Controller Module (IRCM) (2.5L CFI, 3.0L MPFI, 3.0L SHO SEFI, 3.8L FWD SEFI & 3.8L SC SEFI) – The IRCM incorporates relays to provide control of the cooling fan, A/C compressor clutch, and fuel pump. The module incorporates the EEC power and fuel pump relays.

Self-Test Output (STO) (All Engines) – STO is a circuit in the ECA which transmits timed electrical pulse signals. These pulses

1a-406

1989 COMPUTERIZED ENGINE CONTROLS
Ford Motor Co. EEC-IV (Cont.)

correspond to self diagnostic service codes. They may be recorded using any of the following test equipment:

- Voltmeter (Digital or Analog)
- The "Check Engine" Light or Malfunction Indicator Light (MIL) on the dash.
- Ford Motor Co. Testers (STAR, SUPER STAR II, EEC-IV Monitor).
- Aftermarket specialized testers.

Shift Indicator Light (SIL) (1.9L CFI, 1.9L MPFI, 2.3L HSC MPFI, 2.5L CFI (M/T) & 3.8L SC SEFI) – Shift indicator light indicates when to shift gears for optimum fuel economy. ECA activates light based on engine speed and manifold vacuum or pressure levels.

Spark Output (SPOUT) (All Engines) – SPOUT information is transmitted from the ECA to the distributor. The SPOUT signal is the ECA generated ignition signal to the ignition module. A SPOUT connector is located in the SPOUT wire from the TFI module. If this connector is disconnected, ECA signal is interrupted and basic ignition function is controlled by the ignition module.

Thermactor Air By-Pass (TAB) Solenoid (5.0L SEFI) – Solenoid provides a vacuum signal to by-pass valve in response to ECA signals. The TAB solenoid by-passes thermactor pump air to atmosphere.

Thermactor Air Diverter (TAD) Solenoid (5.0L SEFI) – Solenoid provides a vacuum signal to diverter valve in response to ECA signals. The TAD valve diverts thermactor pump air to either exhaust manifold or catalytic converter.

DIAGNOSIS & TESTING

DIAGNOSTIC FORMATS

There are 2 diagnostic formats used to test and service the EEC-IV system: QUICK TEST and CIRCUIT TESTS. A DIAGNOSIS BY SYMPTOM chart is available to identify specific problems and reference specific CIRCUIT TESTS, if no Key On Engine Off (KOEO) or Key On Engine Running (KOER) fault code is identified.

Always start with the QUICK TEST procedures before attempting any CIRCUITS TESTS. The QUICK TEST procedure is designed to allow the technician to identify problems and retrieve service codes. The CIRCUIT TESTS give procedures for testing circuits and checking sensors and actuators. If a vehicle passes the QUICK TEST procedures, and there are no driveability problems, the EEC-IV system is okay. Problem exists somewhere else besides the EEC-IV system. If an intermittent driveability problem exists, use the KOER "Wiggle" Test procedure to set a code or identify the problem.

RETRIEVING & CLEARING CODES

Service codes are retrieved from the EEC-IV system through the Self-Test connector by using various test equipment. The KOEO and KOER SELF-TESTS are used for this purpose. After these codes have been recorded or repaired, they may be cleared from the ECA memory.

To clear continuous memory codes, run the KOEO SELF-TEST, when service codes begin to appear on your test equipment or "Check Engine" light, disconnect the the jumper wire from the STI connector. If using a STAR tester, unlatch the center button. This will erase continuous memory codes from the processor's memory. If a problem has not been corrected, or the fault is still present, the code will be immediately reset into the ECA memory.

CAUTION: DO NOT disconnect the vehicle battery to clear codes. This will erase stored operating information from the Keep Alive Memory (KAM). To clear the KAM, disconnect the negative battery terminal for a minimum of 5 minutes. If the KAM has been cleared, the vehicle must be driven 10 or more miles to allow the ECA to relearn the vehicle operating conditions. Driveability concerns may be noticed during this relearning drive cycle.

TEST EQUIPMENT

The following equipment is recommended to diagnose and test EEC-IV system. Some equipment is REQUIRED to perform tests. DO NOT attempt to test this system without proper equipment. Damage to vehicle components may result if improper equipment is used.

- The Self-Test Automatic Read-Out (STAR) Diagnostic Tester (Rotunda 007 00004) or SUPER STAR II (Rotunda 007-00028) is recommended but not required. It is specially built for the EEC-IV system and is used to display the 2-digit (numeric) service codes that are programmed into the control module. There are also a number of aftermarket scan tool testers available.
- Analog Volt/Ohmmeter (VOM) with 0-20V DC range. This can be used as an alternate to diagnostic tester, to read codes only.
- Digital Volt/Ohmmeter (DVOM) with minimum 10-megohm input impedance.
- Breakout Box (Rotunda 014-00322). This is a jumper wire assembly which connects between the vehicle harness and the ECA. The breakout box is REQUIRED to perform certain tests on the system. Ford Motor Co. specifically states that back-probing will cause PERMANENT DAMAGE to the ECA 60-pin connector. The "test pin No." called out in CIRCUIT TESTS refers to Test Pin numbers on breakout box. Once the breakout box has been installed during a test sequence, it may remain connected for the remainder of that test unless otherwise specified. Aftermarket breakout boxes are available.
- Vacuum gauge with 0-30 in. Hg range and resolution (units on scale) of 1 in. Hg.
- Tachometer with 0-6000 RPM range, accuracy ± 40 RPM, and a resolution of 20 RPM.
- Vacuum pump with 0-30 in. Hg range.
- Timing light.
- Spark Tester (D81P-6666-A or ST-125). A modified side electrode spark plug IS NOT sufficient for these testing procedures.
- Fuel Injection Pressure Gauge (T80L-9974-A).
- 12-volt test light (non-powered type).
- Jumper wire, about 15" long.
- MAP/BP Tester. This unit plugs into MAP/BP sensor circuit and DVOM to check input and output signals. The MAP sensor produces a frequency signal which may be checked using a scope with a millivolt scale or a DVOM that measures frequency.

READING DIAGNOSTIC CODES

KOEO and KOER SELF-TEST Codes – All service codes are 2 digit numbers which are generated one digit at a time. These codes indicate a current fault in the system. They should be serviced in the order in which they appear. Use the appropriate code chart to find the correct CIRCUIT TEST. Codes are shown as voltage pulses (needle sweeps) on an analog Volt/Ohmmeter (VOM).

If a VOM is being used, pay careful attention to the length of the pauses in order to read the codes correctly. There will be a 1/2 second pause between the number of sweeps indicating a digit and a 2 second pause between each digit in a code. There will be a 4 second pause between each code. The KOEO SELF-TEST memory codes are separated from the Continuous Memory codes by a 6 second delay, a single 1/2 second sweep (Separator), and another 6 second delay. Always record the codes in the order received.

If a scan tool diagnostic tester is used, it will count the pulses and display them as a digital code. The STAR tester will add a zero (0) to single digit Separator (10) and Dynamic Response (10) codes. The Dynamic Response code is displayed in the KOER SELF-TEST. *See Fig. 1.*

If the "CHECK ENGINE" light is used, service codes will be displayed as flashes. On Continental models, the "MESSAGE CENTER" may be used to display codes. *See Fig. 2.*

Separator Pulse – A single 1/2 second separator pulse is issued 6-9 seconds after last functional KOEO Self-Test code. Then 6-9 seconds after the single 1/2 second separator pulse, the continuous memory codes will be displayed.

1989 COMPUTERIZED ENGINE CONTROLS
Ford Motor Co. EEC-IV (Cont.)

1a-407

Continuous Memory Codes – These codes are issued as a result of information stored by the ECA during continuous self test monitoring. These codes are displayed during the KOEO SELF-TEST after the separator pulse code. These codes should be used for diagnosis, ONLY when KOEO and KOER SELF-TEST results in a Code 11 (pass code) and all QUICK TEST steps have been successfully completed. There are a few exceptions which may be checked after the KOEO SELF-TEST codes have been repaired.

These codes indicate a fault that has been recored within the last 40 key starts. The fault may or may not be currently present.

Fast Codes – At the start of the KOEO testing and after the WOT request in the KOER test there is an output from the ECA known as "Fast Codes". These are short bursts of information that are used by the manufacturer during assembly. With most equipment these code bursts are not visible as the whole code sequence lasts less than 1/2 second. Ignore this fluctuation if noticed with your test equipment.

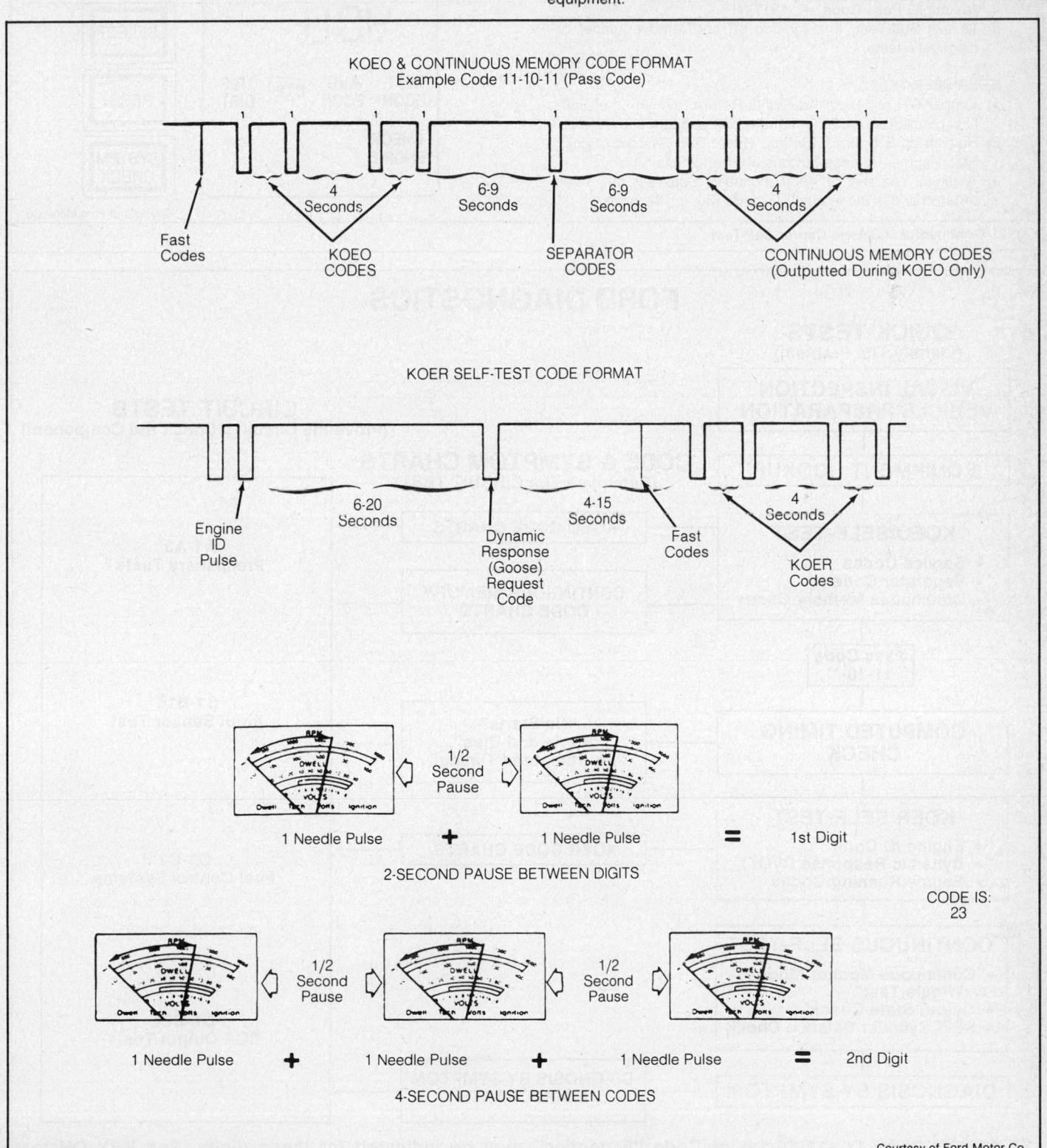

Courtesy of Ford Motor Co.

Fig. 1: Code Format Diagrams

KOEO SELF-TEST

1) Jumper STI connector to Signal Return (pin No. 2) of Self-Test connector or connect and activate diagnostic tester.
2) Hold in all 3 buttons (Select, Reset and System Check). Turn ignition switch to the "ON" position.
3) A digital readout of 4255 indicates Self-Test has been entered.
4) Service codes will be displayed as the right 3 digits (example: Pass Code = 4011).
5) To exit Self-Test, turn ignition off and remove jumper or diagnostic tester.

KOER SELF-TEST

1) Jumper STI connector to Signal Return (pin No. 2) of Self-Test connector or connect and activate diagnostic tester.
2) Hold in all 3 buttons (Select, Reset and System Check). Start engine. Release buttons after engine is running.
3) A digital readout of 4030 indicates Self-Test has been entered and is the engine I.D. code (30 = 6-cylinders).
4) Service codes will be displayed as the right 3 digits (example: Pass Code = 4011).
5) To exit Self-Test turn ignition off and remove jumper or diagnostic tester.

MESSAGE DISPLAY
4011
INST ECON
AVG ECON
DTE
TRIP DIST
CHECK ENGINE
SELECT
RESET
SYSTEM CHECK

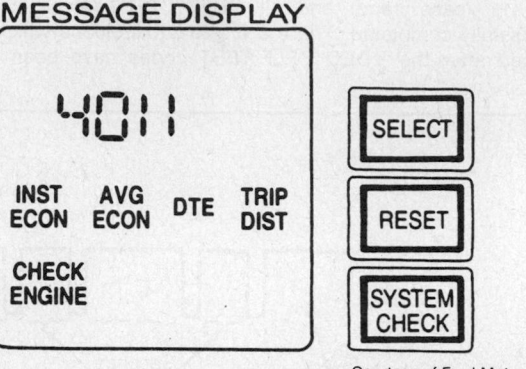

Courtesy of Ford Motor Co.

Fig. 2: Continental Message Center Self-Test

FORD DIAGNOSTICS

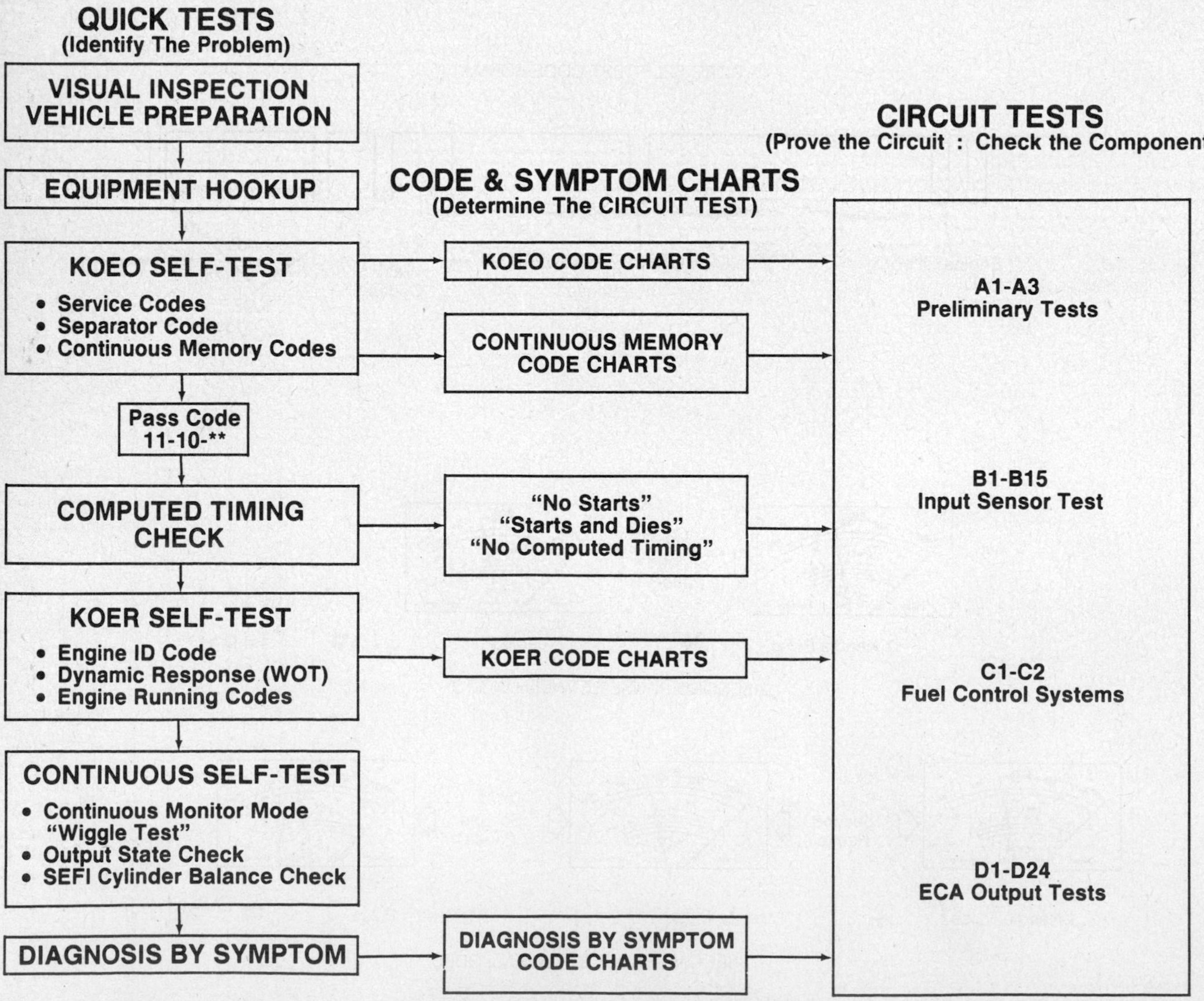

QUICK TESTS
(Identify The Problem)
VISUAL INSPECTION VEHICLE PREPARATION
EQUIPMENT HOOKUP
KOEO SELF-TEST
• Service Codes
• Separator Code
• Continuous Memory Codes
Pass Code 11-10-**
COMPUTED TIMING CHECK
KOER SELF-TEST
• Engine ID Code
• Dynamic Response (WOT)
• Engine Running Codes
CONTINUOUS SELF-TEST
• Continuous Monitor Mode "Wiggle Test"
• Output State Check
• SEFI Cylinder Balance Check
DIAGNOSIS BY SYMPTOM
CODE & SYMPTOM CHARTS
(Determine The CIRCUIT TEST)
KOEO CODE CHARTS
CONTINUOUS MEMORY CODE CHARTS
"No Starts"
"Starts and Dies"
"No Computed Timing"
KOER CODE CHARTS
DIAGNOSIS BY SYMPTOM CODE CHARTS
CIRCUIT TESTS
(Prove the Circuit : Check the Component)
A1-A3 Preliminary Tests
B1-B15 Input Sensor Test
C1-C2 Fuel Control Systems
D1-D24 ECA Output Tests

** – A Code 11 (11-10-11) or Code "Exception" may be indicated for these digits. See KEY ON ENGINE OFF (KOEO) SELF-TEST and KOEO CONTINUOUS MEMORY CODE EXCEPTIONS table.

1989 COMPUTERIZED ENGINE CONTROLS
Ford Motor Co. EEC-IV (Cont.)

1a-409

QUICK TEST

Description – The QUICK TEST diagnostic procedure is a functional test of the EEC-IV system. It consists of 7 basic test steps. These basic steps must be carefully followed in sequence, otherwise misdiagnosis, or replacement of non-faulty components may result.

- VISUAL CHECK & VEHICLE PREPARATION
- EQUIPMENT HOOK-UP
- KEY ON ENGINE OFF (KOEO) SELF-TEST
- COMPUTED TIMING CHECK
- KEY ON ENGINE RUNNING (KOER) SELF-TEST
- CONTINUOUS MONITOR MODE (WIGGLE TEST)
- DIAGNOSIS BY SYMPTOM

After all tests, servicing, or repairs have been completed, repeat QUICK TEST to ensure all EEC-IV systems work properly.

The KOEO and KOER SELF-TESTS are intended to detect faults present at the time of testing, not intermittent faults. Intermittent faults are recorded and stored as Continuous Memory Codes, or may be detected by CONTINUOUS MONITOR MODE "WIGGLE" TEST, which is entered after the KOER SELF-TEST. A fault discovered during the "Wiggle" Test, may or may not set a code in the Continuous Memory, but the "Wiggle" Test is always circuit specific as directed in the CIRCUIT TESTS.

NOTE: Correct test results for system are dependent on the correct operation of several related non-EEC components and systems. All non-EEC problems in the engine, ignition or fuel system should be corrected before attempting to diagnose the EEC system.

VISUAL CHECK & VEHICLE PREPARATION

Before hooking up any equipment to diagnose the EEC system, make the following visual checks and perform the preparation procedures:

- Verify condition of air cleaner and air ducting.
- Check all vacuum hoses for leaks, restrictions, and proper routing.
- Check the EEC-IV system wiring harness electrical connections for corrosion, bent or broken pins, loose wires or terminals, and proper routing.
- Check the ECA, sensors and actuators for physical damage.
- Check engine coolant level.
- Perform all necessary safety precautions to prevent personal injury or vehicle damage.
- Set parking brake and place shift lever in "P" for automatic transmissions, and Neutral for manual transmissions. DO NOT move shift lever during test unless specifically directed to do so.

- Turn off all lights and accessories. Ensure vehicle doors are closed when making voltage or resistance readings.
- Start engine and idle until upper radiator hose is hot and pressurized, and throttle is off fast idle. Check for leaks around exhaust manifold, exhaust gas oxygen sensor, and vacuum hose connections.
- Turn ignition off. Service items as required, then go to EQUIPMENT HOOK-UP.

SELF-TEST CONNECTOR LOCATIONS

Application	Location
Continental & Mark VII	Right rear of engine compartment
Cougar & Thunderbird	In front of left shock tower
Escort	Right rear of engine compartment near cowl
Grand Marquis, LTD Crown Victoria Town Car & Wagon	Left inner fender above wheelwell
Mustang	Left shock tower near ignition coil
Taurus & Sable 2.5L CFI (Taurus Only)	Right rear of engine
3.0L & 3.8L	Right rear of engine compartment below MAP sensor
Tempo & Topaz	Right rear of engine compartment near cowl

EQUIPMENT HOOK-UP

Analog Volt/Ohmmeter (VOM) – 1) Turn ignition switch to "OFF" position. Set VOM at 0-15V DC range and connect positive lead of VOM to positive battery terminal.

2) Connect negative VOM lead to pin No. 4 (STO) on Self-Test connector. *See Fig. 3.* Connect timing light, and go to KOEO SELF-TEST. KOEO SELF-TEST is activated by connecting jumper wire from Self-Test Input (STI) pigtail to pin No. 2 (Signal Return) on Self-Test connector with the ignition on.

STAR Tester – Turn ignition switch to "OFF" position. Connect color coded adapter cable leads to diagnostic tester. Connect adapter cable's 2 service connectors to vehicle Self-Test and STI connectors. Connect timing light. Go to KOEO SELF-TEST.

"CHECK ENGINE" Light (MIL) & "MESSAGE CENTER" (Lincoln Continental) – With ignition on, connect a jumper wire between STI and pin No. 2 of Self-Test connector. No additional special equipment hookup is required. *See Fig. 2.*

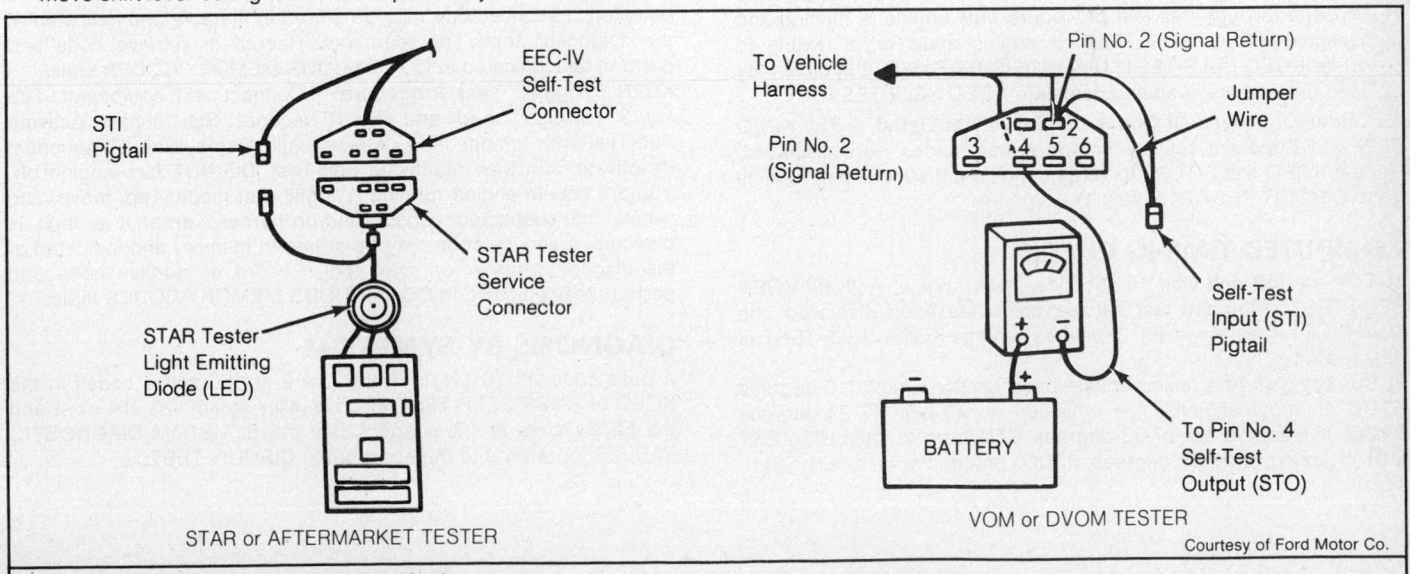

STAR or AFTERMARKET TESTER

VOM or DVOM TESTER

Courtesy of Ford Motor Co.

Fig. 3: Self-Test Connector Equipment Hookup

1989 COMPUTERIZED ENGINE CONTROLS
Ford Motor Co. EEC-IV (Cont.)

KEY ON ENGINE OFF (KOEO) SELF-TEST

Test Procedure – 1) Turn ignition switch to "OFF" position. Ensure all procedures of PREPARATION & EQUIPMENT HOOK-UP have been followed. Engine should be at normal operating temperature.

2) Turn ignition on. If using an analog VOM or the "Check Engine" (MIL) light, connect a jumper wire from Self-Test Input (STI) pigtail to pin No. 2 (Signal Return) on Self-Test connector, this will activate the KOEO Self-Test. If Star Tester is being used latch center button in down position at this time. The "MESSAGE CENTER" on Continental models may be used instead of test equipment. *See Fig. 2.*

3) The ECA will run through a test cycle, opening and closing various solenoids and switches. After the completion of the test cycle the codes will appear. Record all codes.

NOTE: DO NOT depress the throttle during the KOEO SELF-TEST. Ensure ignition switch is in the "ON" position before jumping STI connector to pin No. 2 of the Self-Test connector.

4) The first set of codes to appear are the KOEO SELF-TEST codes, they will be repeated twice, followed by the Separator Pulse signal and then the CONTINUOUS MEMORY codes. These codes will also be repeated twice.

5) A KOEO Code 11 indicates the system has passed the self-test. A Code 11 must be present before continuing. Disregard any Continuous Memory Codes at this time. Service KOEO codes in the order they appear. Refer to the KOEO SELF-TEST CODES table to find the appropriate CIRCUIT TEST. After each repair, repeat KOEO SELF-TEST until a Code 11 is displayed.

6) If no KOEO codes are displayed, a Code 11 (pass code) and a Code 10 (separator pulse) are present, record the Continuous Memory Codes. Service only the KOEO CONTINUOUS MEMORY CODE EXCEPTIONS at this time. All other Continuous Memory Codes will be serviced after a Code 11 is displayed during the KOER SELF-TEST.

KOEO CONTINUOUS MEMORY CODE EXCEPTIONS

Application/Code	Circuit Test & Step
All Engines	
11-10-15	D15 **1)**
5.0L MA, 3.0L SHO, 3.8L SC	
11-10-56	B3 **10)**
11-10-66	B3 **4)**
3.0L SHO, 3.8L SC	
11-10-19	D12 **9)**
11-10-45, 46 or 48	D12 **12)**

No Starts – If engine does not start, go to CIRCUIT TEST A1, step **1)**. Proceed through this test procedure until engine is running and then repeat KOEO SELF-TEST. If engine stalls or is unable to complete KOEO SELF-TEST, DIAGNOSIS BY SYMPTOM table may be used until engine is able to complete KOEO SELF-TEST.

No Codes Displayed Or Codes Displayed Not Listed – The KOEO SELF-TEST did not activate or non-system codes were displayed. Repeat KOEO SELF-TEST to verify condition. If condition still exists go to CIRCUIT TEST D14, step **1)**.

COMPUTED TIMING CHECK

1) Turn key off and wait 10 seconds. Start engine. Activate KOER SELF-TEST. After the last service code has been displayed, the timing will remain fixed for 2 minutes, unless KOER SELF-TEST is deactivated.

2) Correct Self-Test timing equals base ignition timing (10 degrees BTDC on most engines, see emission decal) plus 17-23 degrees BTDC. If timing is not 27-33 degrees BTDC, go to CIRCUIT TEST D13. If timing is 27-33 degrees BTDC, proceed with KOER SELF-TEST.

KEY ON ENGINE RUNNING (KOER) SELF-TEST

Description – This test checks engine sensors under actual operating conditions and at operating temperature. The ECA operates and tests actuators and sensors during this test. A number of special test procedures may be requested by the ECA during this test, depending on vehicle equipment. These tests allow the ECA to test the following sensors.

Engine ID Codes – The first code displayed during the KOER SELF-TEST is an engine identification code. They indicate the number of cylinders in the engine. An engine ID Code of 2 (20), 3 (30), or 4 (40) indicates 4, 6, or 8 cylinder engines, repectively.

Dynamic Response or Wide Open Throttle (WOT) Check – Allows the ECA to check the TP, VAF and MAP sensors. This test is accomplished by a brief opening of the throttle to the full open position. It is also called the "Goose" test. It is requested by a single pulse or Code 10 approximately 6-20 seconds after the engine identification codes are displayed.

Test Procedure – 1) Deactivate Self-Test by disconnecting STI jumper wire. Start and run engine at 2000 RPM for 2 minutes to warm up HEGO sensor. Turn engine off and wait 10 seconds

2) Start engine. Insert jumper to activate Self-Test. The engine ID code will be displayed. On vehicles equipped with Brake On/Off switch (BOO), the brake pedal MUST be depressed and released AFTER the ID code (within 1-2 seconds). On vehicles equipped with Power Steering Pressure Switch (PSPS), the steering wheel MUST be turned one-half turn and released AFTER the ID code. On vehicles equipped with an Overdrive Cancel Switch (OCS) the switch must be cycled AFTER the ID code.

3) If a Dynamic Response code occurs, briefly depress accelerator pedal to Wide Open Throttle (WOT). A Dynamic Response code is a Code 1 or 10 displayed after the Engine ID code and before the Engine Running codes. DO NOT depress throttle during test unless a Dynamic Response code occurs. The KOER SELF-TEST service codes will then be displayed. Observe and record all codes.

CONTINUOUS MONITOR MODE (WIGGLE TEST)

The Continuous Monitor Mode allows a technician to attempt to recreate an intermittent fault while monitoring the system. This mode, also called the "Wiggle" test, may be used in both KOEO and KOER modes. The CIRCUIT TESTS specify the use of this procedure to identify intermittent faults in specific circuits or components.

KOEO "Wiggle" Test Procedure – Connect test equipment. See Fig. 3. Turn ignition on and activate Self-Test with jumper lead or diagnostic tester. Wait 10 seconds, deactivate, and then reactivate Self-Test. You are now in "Wiggle" test mode. Tap, move, and wiggle the suspected sensor and/or harness area. If a fault is detected, a service code may be stored in memory and indicated at the diagnostic tester or scan tool. Record or retrieve code and perform test indicated in CONTINUOUS MEMORY CODES table.

KOER "Wiggle" Test Procedure – Connect test equipment. *See Fig. 3.* Turn ignition off and wait 10 seconds. Start engine. Activate Self-Test with jumper lead or diagnostic tester. Wait 10 seconds, deactivate, and then reactivate Self-Test. DO NOT turn engine off. You are now in engine running "Wiggle" test mode. Tap, move, and wiggle the suspected sensor and/or harness area. If a fault is detected, a service code may be stored in memory and indicated at the diagnostic tester or scan tool. Record or retrieve code and perform test indicated in CONTINUOUS MEMORY CODES table.

DIAGNOSIS BY SYMPTOM

A pass code (11-10-11), indicates there are no active codes in the KOEO or KOER SELF-TEST. If driveability symptoms still exist and the EEC system is still suspect, use the SYMPTOM DIAGNOSTIC TABLES for referral to the appropriate CIRCUIT TEST.

1989 COMPUTERIZED ENGINE CONTROLS
Ford Motor Co. EEC-IV (Cont.)

1a-411

DIAGNOSTIC AIDS

A number of additional diagnostic test features are available to aid in diagnosis of driveability problems.

Output State Check – The Output State Check is used as an aid in servicing output actuators associated with the EEC-IV system. It allows you to energize and de-energize most of the system output actuators on command. This mode is entered from the KOEO SELF-TEST after all codes have been received. At this time, leave SELF-TEST activated and depress throttle to initiate the test sequence. Each time throttle is depressed and released, the output actuators will change state (go from on to off, or off to on).

Failure Mode Effects Management (FMEM), Code 98 – The FMEM mode allows system operation when one or more sensors fail or transmit signals which are out of their normal operating range. The ECA will substitute a mid-range signal for the defective sensor and continue to monitor the sensor. If the faulty sensor signals return to within the normal operating range the ECA will use those signals. A Code 98 will be displayed when the FMEM mode is in effect.

Cylinder Balance Test – The cylinder balance test is an aid in finding a weak or noncontributing cylinder in engines equipped with SEFI fuel systems. The ECA shuts off the fuel supply to each injector and measures the RPM drop. It computes the variation between the cylinders and identifies any weak ones. This test mode is entered during the KOER SELF-TEST after all codes have been displayed. Within 2 minutes after the codes have been displayed lightly depress throttle (a 2-3 degree throttle angle is required, NOT a wide open throttle). After a brief stabilizing period the ECA will activate the test procedure. The test will be repeated if the throttle is depressed within 2 minutes of the final code output. During the 2nd and 3rd test sequence the percentage of allowable variation between cylinders will be reduced. Service codes displayed during this test correspond to cylinder number and indicate a weak or non-contributing cylinder. If Code 90 is displayed during this test it indicates a pass. If Code 77 is displayed, repeat cylinder balance test. If throttle is moved during this test, Code 77 will appear, indicating that test was not completed. Total test time is about 3 minutes.

CYLINDER BALANCE TEST SERVICE CODES

Service Code	Application
90	Pass
10	Cylinder No. 1
20	No. 2
30	No. 3
40	No. 4
50	No. 5
60	No. 6
70	No. 7
80	No. 8
77	Retest

ECA PIN VOLTAGE & RESISTANCE CHECKS

The ECA pin voltage chart may be helpful when diagnosing hard-to-find problems. It must be used with a EEC-IV breakout box and a high impedance DVOM. The voltages and resistances shown are typical component values. Actual measured values may differ slightly from those shown. Always check wiring diagrams for actual pin callouts as some models may vary slightly, depending on equipment. Components shown may not be on all vehicles. The engine should be at normal operating temperature and run at 2000 RPM for about 2 minutes and returned to idle. Always refer to the appropriate CIRCUIT TEST to diagnose a suspected faulty component.

ECA SENSOR RESISTANCE & PIN VOLTAGE REFERENCE CHART

Application	Breakout Box Pin No. + / –	KOEO [1] Ohms	KOEO Volts	KOER Volts
Inputs				
Engine Coolant Temperature (ECT)	7/46	1700-3600	.....	0.74-0.31
Throttle Position Sensor (TPS)	47/46	500-1200	0.7-1.3	0.7-1.3
Pressure Feedback EGR (PFE)	27/46	.....	3.0-3.5	3.0-3.5
EGR Valve Position (EVP)	27/46	480-650	0.30-0.45	0.30-0.45
Heated Exhaust Gas Oxygen (HEGO)	29/46	1.5 Milliohms	0.4 (Maximum)	0-0.9
Coil Tach Signal (IDM)	4/16	21,800	8.0-10.0	8.0-12.0
Distributor Position (PIP)	56/16	1100-2100	.....	3.0-7.0
Reference Voltage (VREF)	26/46	.....	5.0	5.0
Vehicle Speed Sensor (VSS)	3/6	190-240	.....	.....
Knock Sensor (KS)	23/46	4500-6500	.....	.....
Outputs				
Idle Speed Control Motor (ISC)	37/21	10.3	0.0	3.0-5.0
Fuel Pump Relay (FP)	37/22	.....	0.0	Battery +
Computed Spark Advance (DIS)	36/16	.....	9.0-12.5	8.5-9.5
Computed Spark Advance (TFI)	36/16	.....	0.0	5.0-7.0
EGR Valve Regulator (EVR)	37/33	40-50	0.0 (Off)	0.0 (Off)

A/C: Air Conditioning
ACCS: A/C Cycling Switch
ACC: A/C Clutch Compressor
ACT: Air Charge Temperature sensor
ACV: Thermactor Air Control Valve
AXOD: Automatic Transaxle Overdrive

BOO: Brake On/Off switch
BP: Barometric Pressure sensor

CANP: Canister Purge solenoid
CCO: Converter Clutch Override
CFI: Central Fuel Injection
CID: Cylinder Identification sensor

DIS: Direct Ignition System
DVOM: Digital Volt/Ohm Meter (see VOM)

ECA: Electronic Control Assembly, processor, computer
ECT: Engine Coolant Temperature sensor
EDF: Electric Drive Fan relay assembly
EEC: Electronic Engine Control
EGO: Exhaust Gas Oxygen sensor (see HEGO)
EGR: Exhaust Gas Recirculation system
EGRC: EGR Control solenoid or system
EGRV: EGR Vent solenoid or system
EVP: EGR Position sensor
EVR: EGR Valve Regulator

FI: Fuel Injector or Fuel Injection
FP: Fuel Pump
FPM: Fuel Pump Monitor
FWD: Front Wheel Drive

GND or GRND: Ground

HEDF: High Speed Electro Drive Fan relay or circuit
HEGO: Heated EGO sensor
HEGOG: HEGO Ground circuit
HO: High Output
HSC: High Swirl Combustion, engine type

IDM: Ignition Diagnostic Module
IGN: Ignition system or circuit
INJ: Injector or Injection
ISC: Idle Speed Control
ITS: Idle Tracking Switch

KAM: Keep Alive Memory
KAPWR: Keep Alive Power
KOEO: Key On Engine Off
KOER: Key On Engine Running
KS: Knock Sensor

L: Liter(s)
LOS: Limited Operation Strategy, computer function
LUS: Lock-Up Solenoid

MAF: Mass Air Flow sensor, meter or circuit
MAP: Manifold Absolute Pressure sensor
MA SEFI: Mass Air Sequential Fuel Injection system
MCU: Microprocessor Control Unit
MIL: Malfunction Indicator Light
MPFI: Multi Point Fuel Injection

NDS: Neutral Drive Switch
NGS: Neutral Gear Switch
NPS: Neutral Pressure Switch

OCC: Output Circuit Check
OHC: Overhead Camshaft, engine type
OSC: Output State Check

PFE: Pressure Feedback EGR sensor or circuit
PIP: Profile Ignition Pickup
PSPS: Power Steering Pressure Switch
PWR GND: Power Ground circuit

RWD: Rear Wheel Drive

SEFI: Sequential Fuel Injection (see MA SEFI)
SIG RTN: Signal Return circuit
SIL: Shift Indicator Light
SPOUT: Spark Output Signal, from ECA
SS 3/4-4/3: Shift Solenoid circuit
STAR: Self Test Automatic Readout, test equipment
STI: Self Test Input circuit
STO: Self Test Output circuit

TAB/TAD: Thermactor Air Bypass/Thermactor Air Diverter Tandem solenoid valves operated by separate circuits.
TFI: Thick Film Ignition system
TGS: Top Gear Switch (cancels SIL operation in top gear)
THS: Transmission Hydraulic Switch
TP or TPS: Throttle Position Sensor
TTS: Transmission Temperature Switch

VAF: Vane Air Flow sensor or circuit
VAT: Vane Air Temperature
VBATT: Vehicle Battery Voltage
VM: Vane Meter
VOM: Analog Volt/Ohm Meter (see DVOM)
VPWR: Vehicle Power supply voltage (regulated 10-14 volts)
VREF: Voltage Reference (ECA supplied reference voltage, 4-6 volts)
VSC: Vehicle Speed Control sensor or signal
VSS: Vehicle Speed Sensor or signal

WAC: WOT A/C Cut-off switch or circuit
WOT: Wide Open Throttle

Fig. 4: Frequently Used EEC-IV Abbreviations

1989 COMPUTERIZED ENGINE CONTROLS
Ford Motor Co. EEC-IV (Cont.)

KOEO SELF-TEST CODES, CIRCUIT TEST & STEP (4-CYLINDER ENGINES)

Service Codes	1.9L MPFI	1.9L CFI	2.3L OHC MPFI	2.3L Turbo MPFI	2.3L HSC MPFI	2.5L CFI
13	.....	D2, Step 1)	.....	.....	.....	D2, Step 1)
15	D15, Step 3)	D15, Step 3)	D15, Step 3)	D15, Step 3)	D15, Step 3)	D15, Step 3)
19	.....	.....	D17, Step 1)	.....	D17, Step 1)	.....
21	B5, Step 1)	B5, Step 1)	B5, Step 1)	B5, Step 1)	B5, Step 1)	B5, Step 1)
22	B6, Step 1)	B6, Step 1)	B6, Step 1)	B6, Step 1)	B6, Step 1)	B6, Step 1)
23	B8, Step 1)	D2, Step 12)	B8, Step 1)	B8, Step 1)	B8, Step 1)	D2, Step 12)
24	.....	B2, Step 1)	B2, Step 1)	B1, Step 1)	B2, Step 1)	B2, Step 1)
26	B9, Step 1)	.....	.....	B9, Step 1)	.....	.....
28	B1, Step 1)	.....	.....	B1, Step 1)	.....	.....
31	.....	B10, Step 1)	B4, Step 2)	.....	B10, Step 1)	B11, Step 1)
32	.....	.....	.....	.....	.....	B11, Step 15)
34	.....	B10, Step 8)	.....	.....	B10, Step 8)	B11, Step 12)
35	.....	B10, Step 5)	.....	.....	B10, Step 5)	B11, Step 5)
51	B5, Step 5)	B5, Step 5)	B5, Step 5)	B5, Step 5)	B5, Step 5)	B5, Step 5)
52	.....	.....	B15, Step 1)	.....	B15, Step 1)	B15, Step 1)
53	B8, Step 3)	D2, Step 15)	B8, Step 3)	B8, Step 3)	B8, Step 3)	D2, Step 15)
54	.....	B2, Step 5)	B2, Step 5)	B1, Step 4)	B2, Step 5)	B2, Step 5)
56	B9, Step 3)	.....	.....	B9, Step 3)	.....	.....
58	B1, Step 4)	D2, Step 5)	.....	B1, Step 4)	.....	D2, Step 5)
61	B5, Step 7)	B5, Step 7)	B5, Step 7)	B5, Step 7)	B5, Step 7)	B5, Step 7)
63	B8, Step 6)	D2, Step 18)	B8, Step 6)	B8, Step 6)	B8, Step 6)	D2, Step 18)
64	.....	B2, Step 7)	B2, Step 7)	B1, Step 6)	B2, Step 7)	B2, Step 7)
66	B9, Step 6)	.....	.....	B9, Step 6)	.....	....
67	B13, Step 1)	B13, Step 1)	B13, Step 1)	B13, Step 1)	B13, Step 1)	B13, Step 1)
68	B1, Step 6)	D2, Step 9)	.....	.....	.....	D2, Step 9)
73	.....	D2, Step 22)	.....	.....	.....	D2, Step 22)
83	.....	.....	B4, Step 12)	.....	.....	D23, Step 26)
84	.....	B10, Step 11)	B4, Step 12)	.....	B10, Step 11)	B11, Step 8)
85	.....	D4, Step 6)	.....	.....	D4, Step 6)	D4, Step 6)
87	.....	C2, Step 7)	C2, Step 7)	.....	C2, Step 7)	D23, Step 14)
88	.....	.....	.....	.....	.....	D23, Step 53)
89	.....	.....	D22, Step 1)	.....	.....	.....
93	.....	D2, Step 11)	.....	.....	.....	D2, Step 11)
95	C2, Step 12)	C2, Step 12)	.....	.....	C2, Step 12)	D23, Step 58)
96	C2, Step 6)	C2, Step 18)	.....	.....	C2, Step 18)	D23, Step 63)

1989 COMPUTERIZED ENGINE CONTROLS
Ford Motor Co. EEC-IV (Cont.)

KOEO SELF-TEST CODES, CIRCUIT TEST & STEP (V6 & V8 ENGINES)

Service Codes	3.0L MPFI	3.0L SHO/SEFI	3.8L SEFI (FWD)	3.8L SEFI (RWD)	3.8L SC/SEFI	5.0L SEFI	5.0L MA SEFI
15	D15, Step 3)	D15, Step 3)	D15, Step 3)	D15, Step 3)	D15, Step 3)	D15, Step 3)	D15, Step 3)
19	D17, Step 1)	D17, Step 1)	D17, Step 1)	D17, Step 1)	D17, Step 1)	D17, Step 1)	
21	B5, Step 1)	B5, Step 1)	B5, Step 1)	B5, Step 1)	B5, Step 1)	B5, Step 1)	B5, Step 1)
22	B6, Step 1)	B6, Step 1)	B6, Step 1)	B6, Step 1)	B6, Step 1)	B6, Step 1)	B6, Step 1)
23	B8, Step 1)	B8, Step 1)	B8, Step 1)	B8, Step 1)	B8, Step 1)	B8, Step 1)	B8, Step 1)
24	B2, Step 1)	B2, Step 1)	B2, Step 1)	B2, Step 1)	B2, Step 1)	B2, Step 1)	B2, Step 1)
26	.....	B3, Step 2)	.....	.....	B3, Step 2)	.....	B3, Step 1)
31	B10, Step 1)	B10, Step 1)	B10, Step 1)	B10, Step 1)	B10, Step 1)	B11, Step 1)	B11, Step 1)
32	.....	.....	.....	.....	.....	B11, Step 15)	B11, Step 15)
34	B10, Step 8)	B10, Step 8)	B10, Step 8)	B10, Step 8)	B10, Step 8)	B11, Step 12)	B11, Step 12)
35	B10, Step 5)	B10, Step 5)	B10, Step 5)	B10, Step 5)	B10, Step 5)	B10, Step 5)	B10, Step 5)
51	B5, Step 5)	B5, Step 5)	B5, Step 5)	B5, Step 5)	B5, Step 5)	B5, Step 5)	B5, Step 5)
52	B15, Step 1)	B15, Step 1)	B15, Step 1)	.....	.....	.....	.....
53	B8, Step 3)	B8, Step 3)	B8, Step 3)	B8, Step 3)	B8, Step 3)	B8, Step 3)	B8, Step 3)
54	B2, Step 10)	B2, Step 10)	B2, Step 10)	B2, Step 10)	B2, Step 10)	B2, Step 10)	
56	.....	B3, Step 10)	.....	.....	B3, Step 10)	.....	B3, Step 10)
59	.....	D23, Step 63)	D21, Step 24)	.....	.....	.....	.....
61	B5, Step 7)	B5, Step 7)	B5, Step 7)	B5, Step 7)	B5, Step 7)	B5, Step 7)	B5, Step 7)
62	D21, Step 22)	.....	.....	.....	.....	.....	.....
63	B8, Step 6)	B8, Step 6)	B8, Step 6)	B8, Step 6)	B8, Step 6)	B8, Step 6)	B8, Step 6)
64	B2, Step 7)	B2, Step 7)	B2, Step 7)	B2, Step 7)	B2, Step 7)	B2, Step 7)	B2, Step 7)
66	.....	B3, Step 4)	.....	.....	B3, Step 4)	.....	B3, Step 6)
67	D21, Step 28)	B13, Step 1)	D21, Step 29)	B13, Step 1)	B13, Step 1)	B13, Step 1)	B13, Step 1)
68	.....	.....	D21, Step 31)	.....	.....	.....	.....
69	.....	.....	D21, Step 26)	.....	.....	.....	.....
79	.....	B13, Step 9)	B13, Step 9)	B13, Step 9)	B13, Step 9)	B13, Step 9)	B13, Step 9)
81	.....	D20, Step 1)	.....	.....	.....	D3, Step 8)	D3, Step 8)
82	.....	.....	.....	.....	D9, Step 1)	D3, Step 8)	D3, Step 8)
83	D23, Step 26)	D23, Step 14)	D23, Step 26)	.....	D23, Step 26)	.....	.....
84	B10, Step 11)	B10, Step 11)	B10, Step 11)	B10, Step 11)	B10, Step 11)	B11, Step 8)	B11, Step 8)
85	D4, Step 6)	D4, Step 6)	D4, Step 6)	D4, Step 6)	D4, Step 6)	D4, Step 6)	D4, Step 6)
87	D23, Step 14)	D23, Step 14)	D23, Step 14)	C2, Step 7)	C2, Step 7)	C2, Step 7)	C2, Step 7)
88	D23, Step 53)	D23, Step 53)	D23, Step 53)	.....	D23, Step 53)	.....	.....
89	D21, Step 18)	.....	D21, Step 18)	.....	.....	.....	.....
95	D23, Step 58)	D23, Step 58)	D23, Step 58)	C2, Step 12)	C2, Step 12)	.....	C2, Step 12)
96	D23, Step 63)	D23, Step 63)	D23, Step 63)	C2, Step 18)	C2, Step 18)	.....	C2, Step 18)

1989 COMPUTERIZED ENGINE CONTROLS
Ford Motor Co. EEC-IV (Cont.)

1a-415

KOER SELF-TEST CODES, CIRCUIT TEST & STEP (4-CYLINDER ENGINES)

Service Codes	1.9L MPFI	1.9L CFI	2.3L OHC MPFI	2.3L Turbo MPFI	2.3L HSC MPFI	2.5L CFI
12	D5, Step 1)	D2, Step 23)	D5, Step 1)	D5, Step 1)	D5, Step 1)	D2, Step 23)
13	D5, Step 13)	D2, Step 1)	D5, Step 13)	D5, Step 13)	D5, Step 13)	D2, Step 1)
16	D5, Step 20)	D2, Step 30)	D5, Step 1)	.....		D2, Step 30)
17	D5, Step 22)	D2, Step 30)	.....	D5, Step 22)		D2, Step 30)
18	D13, Step 1)	D13, Step 1)	.....	.....	D13, Step 1)	.....
19	D5, Step 21)	D2, Step 26)	.....	.....	.....	.....
21	B5, Step 1)	B5, Step 1)	B5, Step 1)	B5, Step 1)	B5, Step 1)	B5, Step 1)
22	B6, Step 1)	B6, Step 7)	B6, Step 7)	B6, Step 1)	B6, Step 7)	B6, Step 7)
23	B8, Step 1)	D2, Step 12)	B8, Step 1)	B8, Step 1)	B8, Step 1)	D2, Step 12)
24	.....	B2, Step 1)	B2, Step 1)	B1, Step 1)	B2, Step 1)	B2, Step 1)
25	.....	.....	B7, Step 1)	B7, Step 1)	.....	.....
26	B9, Step 1)	.....	.....	B9, Step 1)	.....	.....
28	B1, Step 1)	.....	.....	B1, Step 1)	.....	.....
31	.....	B10, Step 16)	B4, Step 1)	.....	B10, Step 16)	B11, Step 1)
32	.....	B10, Step 15)	B4, Step 8)	.....	B10, Step 15)	B11, Step 15)
33	.....	B10, Step 20)	B4, Step 8)	.....	B10, Step 20)	B11, Step 17)
34	.....	B10, Step 19)	B4, Step 8)	D1, Step 1)	B10, Step 19)	B11, Step 23)
35	.....	B10, Step 19)	B4, Step 17)	.....	B10, Step 19)	B11, Step 5)
41	C1, Step 10)	C1, Step 10)	C1, Step 10)	C1, Step 10)	C1, Step 10)	C1, Step 10)
42	C1, Step 22)	C1, Step 22)	C1, Step 22)	C1, Step 22)	C1, Step 22)	C1, Step 22)
47	D5, Step 18)	.....	.....	.....	.....	.....
48	D5, Step 19)	.....	.....	.....	.....	.....
52	.....	.....	.....	.....	B15, Step 5)	B15, Step 5)
55	.....	D18, Step 1)	.....	.....	.....	D18, Step 1)
58	.....	D2, Step 5)	.....	.....	.....	D2, Step 5)
67	.....	B13, Step 1)	.....	.....	.....	....
68	.....	D2, Step 9)	.....	.....	.....	D2, Step 9)
72	.....	.....	B6, Step 10)	.....	B6, Step 10)	.....
73	B8, Step 10)	.....	B8, Step 10)	B8, Step 10)	B8, Step 10)	.....
74	.....	.....	B14, Step 1)	.....	.....	B14, Step 7)
75	.....	.....	B14, Step 4)	.....	.....	.....
76	B9, Step 10)	.....	.....	B9, Step 10)	.....	.....
77	D10, Step 1)	.....	D10, Step 1)	D10, Step 1)	D10, Step 1)	.....
84	.....	B10, Step 11)	.....	.....	.....	.....
85	.....	D4, Step 6)	.....	.....	.....	.....
87	.....	C2, Step 7)	.....	.....	.....	.....
98	[1]	[1]	[1]	[1]	[1]	[1]
99	.....	D2, Step 29)	.....	.....	.....	D2, Step 29)

[1] – If Code 98 is displayed, go back and perform KEY ON/ENGINE OFF (KOEO) SELF-TEST and obtain a Code 11 for KEY ON/ENGINE OFF SELF-TEST portion QUICK TEST.

1989 COMPUTERIZED ENGINE CONTROLS
Ford Motor Co. EEC-IV (Cont.)

KOER SELF-TEST CODES, CIRCUIT TEST & STEP (V6 & V8 ENGINES)

Service Codes	3.0L MPFI	3.0L SHO/SEFI	3.8L SEFI (FWD)	3.8L SEFI (RWD)	3.8L SC/SEFI	5.0L SEFI	5.0L MA SEFI
12	D5, Step 1)	D5, Step 1)	D5, Step 1)	D5, Step 1)	D5, Step 1)	D5, Step 1)	D5, Step 1)
13	D5, Step 13)	D5, Step 13)	D5, Step 13)	D5, Step 13)	D5, Step 13)	D5, Step 13)	D5, Step 13)
16	.....	.....	.....	.....	.....	D5, Step 1)	D5, Step 1)
18	D13, Step 1)	D13, Step 1)	D13, Step 1)	D13, Step 1)	D13, Step 1)	D13, Step 1)	D13, Step 1)
21	B5, Step 1)	B5, Step 1)	B5, Step 1)	B5, Step 1)	B5, Step 1)	B5, Step 1)	B5, Step 1)
22	B6, Step 7)	B6, Step 1)	B6, Step 7)	B6, Step 7)	B6, Step 1)	B6, Step 7)	B6, Step 1)
23	B8, Step 1)	B8, Step 1)	B8, Step 1)	B8, Step 1)	B8, Step 1)	B8, Step 1)	B8, Step 1)
24	B2, Step 1)	B2, Step 1)	B2, Step 1)	B2, Step 1)	B2, Step 1)	B2, Step 1)	B2, Step 1)
25	B7, Step 1)	B7, Step 1)	.....	.....	B7, Step 1)	.....	.....
26	.....	B3, Step 1)	.....	.....	B3, Step 1)	.....	B3, Step 1)
31	B10, Step 16)	B10, Step 16)	B10, Step 16)	B10, Step 16)	B10, Step 16)	B11, Step 1)	B11, Step 1)
32	B10, Step 15)	B10, Step 15)	B10, Step 15)	B10, Step 15)	B10, Step 15)	B11, Step 15)	B11, Step 15)
33	B10, Step 20)	B10, Step 20)	B10, Step 20)	B10, Step 20)	B10, Step 20)	B11, Step 17)	B11, Step 17)
34	B10, Step 19)	B10, Step 19)	B10, Step 19)	B10, Step 19)	B10, Step 19)	B11, Step 23)	B11, Step 23)
35	B10, Step 19)	B10, Step 19)	B10, Step 19)	B10, Step 19)	B10, Step 19)	B11, Step 5)	B11, Step 5)
41	C1, Step 10)	C1, Step 10)	C1, Step 10)	C1, Step 10)	C1, Step 10)	C1, Step 10)	C1, Step 10)
42	C1, Step 22)	C1, Step 1)	C1, Step 22)	C1, Step 22)	C1, Step 1)	C1, Step 22)	C1, Step 1)
44	.....	.....	.....	.....	.....	D3, Step 1)	D3, Step 1)
45	.....	.....	.....	.....	.....	D3, Step 1)	D3, Step 1)
46	.....	.....	.....	.....	D3, Step 1)	D3, Step 1)	.....
52	B15, Step 5)	B15, Step 5)	B15, Step 5)	.....	B15, Step 5)	.....	.....
56	.....	B3, Step 10)	.....	.....	B3, Step 10)	.....	B3, Step 10)
66	.....	B3, Step 4)	.....	.....	B3, Step 4)	.....	B3, Step 4)
68	.....	.....	D21, Step 31)	.....	.....	.....	.....
72	B6, Step 10)	D23, Step 10)	.....	.....	D23, Step 10)	.....	.....
73	B8, Step 10)	B8, Step 10)	.....	.....	B8, Step 10)	.....	.....
74	B14, Step 7)	B14, Step 7)	B14, Step 7)	B14, Step 7)	B14, Step 7)	B14, Step 1)	.....
75	.....	.....	.....	.....	.....	B14, Step 4)	.....
77	D10, Step 1)	D10, Step 1)	.....	.....	D10, Step 1)	.....	D10, Step 1)
91	.....	C1, Step 1)	C1, Step 10)	C1, Step 10)	C1, Step 1)	C1, Step 10)	C1, Step 1)
92	.....	C1, Step 1)	C1, Step 22)	C1, Step 22)	C1, Step 1)	C1, Step 22)	C1, Step 1)
94	.....	.....	.....	.....	.....	D3, Step 1)	D3, Step 1)
98	[1]	[1]	[1]	[1]	[1]		

[1] – If Code 98 is displayed, go back and perform KOEO SELF-TEST and obtain a Code 11 (Pass Code) for KOEO SELF-TEST portion of QUICK TEST.

1989 COMPUTERIZED ENGINE CONTROLS
Ford Motor Co. EEC-IV (Cont.)

1a-417

CONTINUOUS MEMORY CODES – CIRCUIT TEST & STEP, (4-CYLINDER ENGINES)

Service Codes	1.9L MPFI	1.9L CFI	2.3L OHC MPFI	2.3L Turbo MPFI	2.3L HSC MPFI	2.5L CFI
13	.....	D2, Step 31)	.....	.....	.....	D2, Step 31)
14	D12, Step 1)	D12, Step 1)	D12, Step 1)	D12, Step 1)	D12, Step 1)	D12, Step 1)
15	D15, Step 1)	D15, Step 1)	D15, Step 1)	D15, Step 1)	D15, Step 1)	D15, Step 1)
18	D12, Step 3)	D12, Step 3)	D12, Step 3)	D12, Step 3)	D12, Step 3)	D12, Step 3)
22	B6, Step 13)	B6, Step 13)	B6, Step 13)	B6, Step 13)	B6, Step 13)	B6, Step 13)
23	.....	D2, Step 38)	.....	.....	.....	D2, Step 38)
29	.....	.....	.....	.....	B12, Step 1)	B12, Step 1)
31	.....	B10, Step 28)	B4, Step 19)	.....	B10, Step 28)	B11, Step 26)
32	.....	B10, Step 32)	.....	.....	B10, Step 32)	B11, Step 25)
33	.....	B10, Step 35)	.....	.....	B10, Step 35)	B11, Step 28)
34	.....	B10, Step 31)	.....	.....	B10, Step 31)	B11, Step 30)
35	.....	B10, Step 28)	.....	.....	B10, Step 28)	B11, Step 26)
38	.....	D2, Step 32)	.....	.....	.....	D2, Step 32)
41	C1, Step 29)	C1, Step 28)	C1, Step 28)	C1, Step 29)	C1, Step 28)	C1, Step 28)
42	C1, Step 29)	.....	.....	C1, Step 29)	.....	.....
43	C1, Step 29)	.....	.....	.....	.....	.....
51	B5, Step 10)	B5, Step 10)	B5, Step 10)	B5, Step 10)	B5, Step 10)	B5, Step 10)
53	B8, Step 11)	D2, Step 34)	B8, Step 11)	B8, Step 11)	B8, Step 11)	D2, Step 34)
54	.....	B2, Step 10)	B2, Step 10)	B1, Step 9)	B2, Step 10)	B2, Step 10)
56	B9, Step 15)	.....	.....	B9, Step 15)	.....	.....
58	B1, Step 9)	.....	.....	.....	.....	.....
61	B5, Step 13)	B5, Step 13)	B5, Step 13)	B5, Step 13)	B5, Step 13)	B5, Step 13)
63	B8, Step 15)	D2, Step 38	B8, Step 15)	B8, Step 15)	B8, Step 15)	D2, Step 38
64	.....	B2, Step 13)	B2, Step 13)	B1, Step 12)	B2, Step 13)	B2, Step 13)
65	C1, Step 29)	.....	.....	.....	.....	.....
66	B9, Step 15)	.....	.....	B9, Step 15)	.....	.....
67	B13, Step 1)	.....	.....	B13, Step 1)	.....	.....
68	B1, Step 12)	.....	.....	B1, Step 12)	.....	.....
71	D18, Step 1)	D2, Step 33)	.....	.....	.....	D2, Step 33)
72	D18, Step 4)	.....	.....	.....	.....	.....
85	C1, Step 29)	.....	.....	.....	.....	.....
86	C1, Step 29)	.....	.....	.....	.....	.....
87	.....	C2, Step 26)	.....	.....	C2, Step 24)	D23, Step 69)
95	C2, Step 21)	C2, Step 21)	.....	.....	C2, Step 21)	D23, Step 65)
96	C2, Step 24)	C2, Step 24)	.....	.....	C2, Step 24)	D23, Step 67)

1989 COMPUTERIZED ENGINE CONTROLS
Ford Motor Co. EEC-IV (Cont.)

CONTINUOUS MEMORY CODES − CIRCUIT TEST & STEP (V6 & V8 ENGINES)

Service Codes	3.0L MPFI	3.0L SHO/SEFI	3.8L SEFI (FWD)	3.8L SEFI (RWD)	3.8L SC/SEFI	5.0L SEFI	5.0L MA SEFI
14	D12, Step 1)	D12, Step 1)	D12, Step 1)	D12, Step 1)	D12, Step 1)	D12, Step 1)	D12, Step 1)
15	D15, Step 1)	D15, Step 1)	D15, Step 1)	D15, Step 1)	D15, Step 1)	D15, Step 1)	D15, Step 1)
18	D12, Step 3)	D12, Step 2)	D12, Step 3)	D12, Step 3)	D12, Step 2)	D12, Step 3)	D12, Step 3)
22	B6, Step 13)	B6, Step 13)	B6, Step 13)	B6, Step 13)	B6, Step 13)	B6, Step 13)	B6, Step 13)
29	D21, Step 1)	B12, Step 1)	D21, Step 1)	B12, Step 1)	B12, Step 1)	B12, Step 1)	B12, Step 1)
31	B10, Step 28)	B10, Step 28)	B10, Step 28)	B10, Step 28)	B10, Step 28)	B11, Step 26)	B11, Step 26)
32	B10, Step 32)	B10, Step 32)	B10, Step 32)	B10, Step 32)	B10, Step 32)	B11, Step 25)	B11, Step 25)
33	B10, Step 35)	B10, Step 35)	B10, Step 35)	B10, Step 35)	B10, Step 35)	B11, Step 28)	B11, Step 28)
34	B10, Step 31)	B10, Step 31)	B10, Step 31)	B10, Step 31)	B10, Step 31)	B11, Step 40)	B11, Step 40)
35	B10, Step 28)	B10, Step 28)	B10, Step 28)	B10, Step 28)	B10, Step 28)	B11, Step 26)	B11, Step 26)
39	D21, Step 13)	.....	D21, Step 13)	.....	.....	.....	.....
41	C1, Step 28)	C1, Step 28)	C1, Step 28)	C1, Step 28)	C1, Step 28)	C1, Step 28)	C1, Step 28)
45	.....	D12, Step 12)	.....	.....	D12, Step 12)	.....	.....
46	.....	D12, Step 12)	.....	.....	D12, Step 12)	.....	.....
48	.....	D12, Step 12)	.....	.....	D12, Step 12)	.....	.....
49	.....	D13, Step 7)	.....	.....	D13, Step 7)	.....	.....
51	B5, Step 10)	B5, Step 10)	B5, Step 10)	B5, Step 10)	B5, Step 10)	B5, Step 10)	B5, Step 10)
53	B8, Step 11)	B8, Step 11)	B8, Step 11)	B8, Step 11)	B8, Step 11)	B8, Step 11)	B8, Step 11)
54	B2, Step 10)	B2, Step 10)	B2, Step 10)	B2, Step 10)	B2, Step 10)	B2, Step 10)	B2, Step 10)
56	.....	B3, Step 10)	.....	.....	B3, Step 10)	.....	B3, Step 10)
57	D21, Step 14)	.....	D21, Step 14)	.....	.....	.....	.....
59	D21, Step 9)	D23, Step 63)	D21, Step 9)	.....	.....	.....	.....
61	B5, Step 13)	B5, Step 13)	B5, Step 13)	B5, Step 13)	B5, Step 13)	B5, Step 13)	.....
63	D2, Step 39)	B8, Step 15)	B8, Step 15)	B8, Step 15)	B8, Step 15)	B8, Step 15)	.....
64	B2, Step 13)	B2, Step 13)	B2, Step 13)	B2, Step 13)	B2, Step 13)	B2, Step 13)	B2, Step 13)
66	.....	B3, Step 4)	.....	.....	B3, Step 4)	.....	B3, Step 4)
67	.....	.....	.....	.....	B13, Step 1)	.....	.....
68	.....	.....	.....	D21, Step 31)	.....	.....	.....
69	D21, Step 5)	.....	D21, Step 5)	.....	.....	.....	.....
70	.....	.....	D11, Step 8)	.....	.....	.....	.....
71	.....	.....	D11, Step 8)	.....	.....	.....	.....
72	.....	.....	D11, Step 8)	.....	.....	.....	.....
83	.....	D23, Step 14)	.....	.....	.....	.....	.....
87	D23, Step 69)	D23, Step 69)	D23, Step 69)	C2, Step 26)	C2, Step 26)	C2, Step 26)	C2, Step 26)
91	.....	C1, Step 28)	C1, Step 28)	C1, Step 28)	C1, Step 28)	C1, Step 28)	C1, Step 28)
95	D23, Step 65)	D23, Step 65)	D23, Step 65)	C2, Step 21)	C2, Step 21)	.....	C2, Step 21)
96	D23, Step 67)	D23, Step 67)	D23, Step 67)	C2, Step 24)	C2, Step 24)	.....	C2, Step 24)

1989 COMPUTERIZED ENGINE CONTROLS
Ford Motor Co. EEC-IV (Cont.)

1a-419

DIAGNOSIS BY SYMPTOM TEST – CIRCUIT TEST & STEP (4-CYLINDER ENGINES)

Symptom	1.9L EFI	1.9L CFI	2.3L OHC EFI	2.3L Turbo EFI	2.3L HSC EFI	2.5L CFI
Runs Rough, Misses, Lacks Power, Rough Idle, Surges.	D20, 2)	D20, 2)	D20, 2)	D20, 2)	D20, 2)	D20, 2)
Stalls At Idle Or During Self-Test.	D20, 1)	D20, 2)	D20, 1)	D20, 1)	D20, 1)	D20, 2)
Stalls When Parking.	.....	B15, 3)	B15, 3)	.....	.....	B15, 3)
Surges With A/C On At Idle.	....	.....	D7, 16)	....	D7, 16)	....
A/C Stays On During WOT.	D7, 11)	D7, 11)	D7, 11)	D7, 11)	D7, 11)	D23, 44)
A/C Not Functioning.	D7, 11)	D7, 11)	D7, 11)	D7, 11)	D7, 11)	D23, 42)
A/C Compressor Always Runs.	....	....	D7, 1)	....	....	....
High Idle Speed After Restart. May Have Spark Knock For 3-5 Minutes After Restart.	D1, 1)	....	....	B7, 1)	....	....
Low Idle With A/C On.	B13, 1)	B13, 10)	B13, 10)	B13, 10)	B13, 10)	B13, 10)
High Idle In "Drive" (A/T Only)	....	....	....	....	....	B13, 15)
Shift Indicator Light Always On Or Never On.	D6, 1)	D6, 1)	....	....	D6, 1)	D6, 1)
"CHECK ENGINE" Light Always On.	D11, 1)	D11, 1)	D11, 1)	D11, 1)	D11, 1)	D11, 1)
"CHECK ENGINE" Light Never On.	D11, 2)	D11, 2)	D11, 2)	D11, 2)	D11, 2)	D11, 2)
"CHECK ENGINE" Light On Intermittently.	D11, 5)	D11, 5)	D11, 5)	D11, 5)	D11, 5)	D11, 5)
"CHECK ENGINE" Light Flashes With Erratic Idle.	D11, 6)	D11, 6)	D11, 6)	D11, 6)	D11, 6)	D11, 6)
No Cruise Control And Stalls On Decel.	....	....	....	....	....	B12, 1)
Stumble After Hot Restart.	C1, 19)	C1, 19)	C1, 19)	C1, 19)	C1, 19)	C1, 19)
Engine Will Not Restart.	....	D18, 1)	.....	.....	.....	D18, 1)
Fuel Pump Runs With Engine Off.	.....	....	C2, 14)	C2, 14)	....	D23, 13)
Gasoline Fumes In Engine Compartment.	D4, 1)	D4, 1)	.....	D4, 1)	D4, 1)	D4, 1)
Detonation/Spark Knock.	D1, 1)	....	B7, 1)	B7, 2)	.....	.....
Engine Cooling Fan Inoperative (Single Speed Fan).	.....	.....	.....	.....	.....	D23, 35)
Engine Cooling Fan Inoperative (Dual Speed Fan).	.....	.....	.....	.....	.....	D23, 17)
Cooling Fan Always On.	.....	.....	.....	.....	.....	D23, 30)

1989 COMPUTERIZED ENGINE CONTROLS
Ford Motor Co. EEC-IV (Cont.)

DIAGNOSIS BY SYMPTOM TEST — CIRCUIT TEST & STEP (V6 & V8 ENGINES)

Symptom	3.0L MPFI	3.0L SHO SEFI	3.8L AXOD SEFI	3.8L RWD SEFI	3.8L SC SEFI	5.0L SEFI	5.0L MA SEFI
Runs Rough, Misses, Stalls, Lacks Power, Rough Idle, Surges, Stalls in Self-Test.	D20, 2)	[1] D20, 2)	D20, 2)	D20, 2)	[1] D20, 2)	D20, 2)	[1] D20, 2)
Stalls At Idle Or During Self-Test.	D20, 1)	D20, 1)	D20, 1)	D20, 1)	D20, 1)	D20, 1)	D20, 1)
Stalls When Parking.	B15, 3)	B15, 3)	B15, 3)	.....	.....	.....	.....
A/C Stays On During WOT.	D23, 44)	D23, 44)	D23, 44)	D7, 11)	D23, 44)	D7, 11)	D7, 11)
A/C Not Functioning.	D23, 42)	D23, 42)	D23, 42)	D7, 11)	D23, 42)	D7, 11)	D7, 11)
Low Idle With A/C On.	B13, 10)	B13, 10)	B13, 10)	B13, 10)	B13, 10)	B13, 10)	B13, 10)
High Idle In "Drive" (A/T Only)	....	....	....	B13, 15)	....	....	....
Shift Indicator Light Always On Or Never On.	....	....	....	....	D6, 1)	....	D6, 1)
"CHECK ENGINE" Light Always On.	D11, 1)	D11, 1)	D11, 1)	D11, 1)	D11, 1)	D11, 1)	D11, 1)
"CHECK ENGINE" Light Never On.	D11, 2)	D11, 2)	D11, 2)	D11, 2)	D11, 2)	D11, 2)	D11, 2)
"CHECK ENGINE"/"CHECK DCL" Message On.	....	....	D11, 8)	....	....	....	....
"CHECK ENGINE" Message On.	....	....	D11, 7)	....	....	....	....
"CHECK ENGINE" Light On Intermittently.	D11, 5)	D11, 5)	D11, 5)	D11, 5)	D11, 5)	D11, 5)	D11, 5)
"CHECK ENGINE" Light Flashes With Erratic Idle.	D11, 6)	D11, 6)	D11, 6)	D11, 6)	D11, 6)	D11, 6)	D11, 6)
Lack Of Power At WOT.	....	D20, 6)	....	....	....	....	....
Tachometer Inoperative.	....	D12, 3)	....	....	....	....	....
Stumble After Hot Restart.	C1, 19)	C1, 19)	C1, 19)	C1, 19)	C1, 19)	C1, 19)	C1, 19)
Fuel Pump Runs With Engine Off.	D23, 13)	D23, 13)	....	....	C2, 14)	C2, 14)	....
Gasoline Fumes In Engine Compartment.	D4, 1)	D4, 1)	D4, 1)	D4, 1)	D4, 1)	D4, 1)	D4, 1)
Detonation/Spark Knock.	B7, 1)	D8, 1)	....	....	D8, 1)	....	.....
Poor Performance, Low Or High Supercharger Pressure.	....	....	....	....	D9, 6)	....	....
Engine Cooling Fan Inoperative (Single Speed Fan).	.....	D23, 35)	.....	.....	.....	.....	.....
Engine Cooling Fan Inoperative (Dual Speed Fan).	D23, 17)	.....	D23, 17)	.....	D23, 17)	.....	.....
Cooling Fan Always On.	D23, 30)	D23, 30)	D23, 30)	.....	D23, 33)	.....	.....

[1] – Ensure MAF sensor is operating correctly.

1989 COMPUTERIZED ENGINE CONTROLS
Ford Motor Co. EEC-IV (Cont.)

1a-421

SERVICE CODE DEFINITIONS – 1.9L MPFI

SERVICE CODE			SERVICE CODE DEFINITION
11	orc	▶	System PASS
12	r	▶	Rpm unable to achieve Self-Test upper limit
13	r	▶	Rpm unable to achieve Self-Test lower limit
14	c	▶	PIP circuit failure
15	o	▶	ROM test failure
15	c	▶	Power interruption to Keep Alive Memory (KAM)
16	r	▶	Rpm above Self-Test limit with ISC off
17	r	▶	Rpm below Self-Test limit with ISC off
18	r	▶	SPOUT circuit open
18	c	▶	Loss of tach input to Processor/SPOUT circuit grounded
19	r	▶	Rpm dropped too low during ISC off test
21	or	▶	ECT sensor input is out of Self-Test range
22	orc	▶	BP sensor input is out of Self-Test range
23	or	▶	TP sensor input is out of Self-Test range
26	or	▶	VAF sensor input is out of Self-Test range
28	or	▶	VAT sensor input is out of Self-Test range
41	r	▶	HEGO sensor circuit indicates system lean
41	c	▶	No HEGO switching detected — always lean
42	r	▶	HEGO sensor circuit indicates system rich
42	c	▶	No HEGO switching detected — always rich
43	c	▶	HEGO lean at wide open throttle
47	r	▶	Measured airflow low at base idle
48	r	▶	Measured airflow high at base idle
51	oc	▶	ECT sensor input is greater than Self-Test maximum
53	oc	▶	TP sensor input is greater than Self-Test maximum
56	oc	▶	VAF sensor input is greater than Self-Test maximum
58	oc	▶	VAT sensor input is greater than Self-Test maximum
61	oc	▶	ECT sensor input is less than Self-Test minimum
63	oc	▶	TP sensor input is less than Self-Test minimum
65	c	▶	Never went to closed loop fuel
66	oc	▶	VAF sensor input is less than Self-Test minimum
67	o	▶	Neutral Drive Switch (NDS) circuit open; A/C input high
67	c	▶	Clutch switch circuit failure
68	oc	▶	VAT sensor input is less than Self-Test minimum
71	c	▶	Software reinitialization detected
72	c	▶	Power interrupt detected
73	r	▶	Insufficient TP output change during Dynamic Response Test
76	r	▶	Insufficient VAF output change during Dynamic Response Test
77	r	▶	Brief WOT not sensed during Self-Test/Operator error
85	c	▶	Adaptive fuel lean limit reached
86	c	▶	Adaptive fuel rich limit reached
95	oc	▶	Fuel pump secondary circuit failure
96	oc	▶	Fuel pump secondary circuit failure
NO CODES		▶	Unable to initiate Self-Test or unable to output Self-Test codes
CODES NOT LISTED		▶	Service codes displayed are not applicable to the vehicle being tested

KEY: o = Key On Engine Off (KOEO)   r = Engine Running (ER)   c = Continuous Memory

1989 COMPUTERIZED ENGINE CONTROLS
Ford Motor Co. EEC-IV (Cont.)

SERVICE CODE DEFINITIONS — 1.9L CFI

SERVICE CODE			SERVICE CODE DEFINITION
11	orc	▶	System PASS
12	r	▶	Rpm below Self-Test limit
13	o	▶	D.C. motor did not move
13	r	▶	Rpm above Self-Test limit
13	c	▶	D.C. motor did not follow dashpot
14	c	▶	PIP circuit failure
15	o	▶	ROM test failure
15	c	▶	Power interruption to Keep Alive Memory (KAM)
16	r	▶	Idle hard set high
17	r	▶	Idle hard set low
18	r	▶	SPOUT circuit open
18	c	▶	Loss of tach input to Processor/SPOUT circuit grounded
19	r	▶	Erratic rpm during hard idle set test
21	or	▶	ECT sensor input is out of Self-Test range
22	orc	▶	MAP sensor input is out of Self-Test range
23	orc	▶	TP sensor input is out of Self-Test range
24	or	▶	ACT sensor input is out of Self-Test range
31	orc	▶	PFE circuit is below minimum voltage
32	rc	▶	EGR valve not seated
33	rc	▶	EGR valve is not opening (PFE)
34	o	▶	Defective PFE sensor
34	rc	▶	Excessive exhaust back pressure
35	orc	▶	PFE circuit is above maximum voltage
38	c	▶	Idle Tracking Switch (ITS) circuit open
41	r	▶	HEGO sensor circuit indicates system lean
41	c	▶	No HEGO switching detected
42	r	▶	HEGO sensor circuit indicates system rich
51	oc	▶	ECT sensor input is greater than Self-Test maximum
53	oc	▶	TP sensor input is greater than Self-Test maximum
54	oc	▶	ACT sensor input is greater than Self-Test maximum
55	r	▶	Keypower input to processor is open
58	o	▶	Idle Tracking Switch (ITS) circuit open
58	r	▶	Idle Tracking Switch (ITS) closed
61	oc	▶	ECT sensor input is less than Self-Test minimum
63	oc	▶	TP sensor input is less than Self-Test minimum
64	oc	▶	ACT sensor input is less than Self-Test minimum
67	or	▶	Neutral Drive Switch (NDS) circuit open; A/C input high
68	o	▶	Idle Tracking Switch (ITS) closed
68	r	▶	Idle Tracking Switch (ITS) circuit open
71	c	▶	Idle Tracking Switch (ITS) closed on pre-position
73	o	▶	Insufficient throttle position change
84	or	▶	EGR Vacuum Regulator (EVR) circuit failure
85	or	▶	Canister Purge (CANP) circuit failure
87	orc	▶	Fuel pump primary circuit failure
93	o	▶	TP sensor input low at maximum D.C. motor extension
95	oc	▶	Fuel pump secondary circuit failure
96	oc	▶	Fuel pump secondary circuit failure
98	r	▶	Hard fault is present
99	r	▶	EEC system has not learned to control idle
NO CODES		▶	Unable to initiate Self-Test or unable to output Self-Test codes
CODES NOT LISTED		▶	Service codes displayed are not applicable to the vehicle being tested

KEY: o = Key On Engine Off (KOEO)   r = Engine Running (ER)   c = Continuous Memory

1989 COMPUTERIZED ENGINE CONTROLS
Ford Motor Co. EEC-IV (Cont.)

1a-423

SERVICE CODE DEFINITIONS – 2.3L OHC MPFI

SERVICE CODE			SERVICE CODE DEFINITION
11	orc	▶	System PASS
12	r	▶	Unable to control rpm to Self-Test upper limit band
13	r	▶	Unable to control rpm to Self-Test lower limit band
14	c	▶	PIP circuit failure
15	o	▶	ROM test failure
15	c	▶	Power interruption to Keep Alive Memory (KAM)
16	r	▶	Rpm too low to perform fuel test
18	c	▶	Loss of tach input to Processor/SPOUT circuit grounded
19	o	▶	Failure of EEC power supply
21	or	▶	ECT sensor input is out of Self-Test range
22	orc	▶	MAP sensor input is out of Self-Test range
23	or	▶	TP sensor input is out of Self-Test range
24	or	▶	ACT sensor input is out of Self-Test range
25	r	▶	KS sensor signal is not sensed in Dynamic Response Test
31	orc	▶	EVP circuit is below minimum voltage
32	r	▶	EGR not controlling
33	r	▶	EVP not closing in limits
34	r	▶	Insufficient EGR flow
35	r	▶	Rpm too low for EGR test
41	r	▶	HEGO sensor circuit indicates system lean
41	c	▶	No HEGO switching detected
42	r	▶	HEGO sensor circuit indicates system rich
51	oc	▶	ECT sensor input is greater than Self-Test maximum
52	o	▶	PSPS circuit is open
53	oc	▶	TP sensor input is greater than Self-Test maximum
54	oc	▶	ACT sensor input is greater than Self-Test maximum
61	oc	▶	ECT sensor input is less than Self-Test minimum
63	oc	▶	TP sensor input is less than Self-Test minimum
64	oc	▶	ACT sensor input is less than Self-Test minimum
67	o	▶	Neutral Drive Switch (NDS) circuit open; A/C input high
72	r	▶	Insufficient MAP output change during Dynamic Response Test
73	r	▶	Insufficient TP output change during Dynamic Response Test
74	r	▶	Brake On/Off (BOO) circuit open — not actuated during test
75	r	▶	Brake On/Off (BOO) circuit closed — always high
77	r	▶	Brief WOT not sensed during Self-Test/Operator error
83	o	▶	EGRC solenoid circuit failure
84	o	▶	EGRV solenoid circuit failure
87	o	▶	Fuel pump primary circuit failure
89	o	▶	Clutch Converter Override (CCO) circuit failure
98	r	▶	Hard fault is present
NO CODES		▶	Unable to initiate Self-Test or unable to output Self-Test codes
CODES NOT LISTED		▶	Service codes displayed are not applicable to the vehicle being tested

KEY: o = Key On Engine Off (KOEO)   r = Engine Running (ER)   c = Continuous Memory

1989 COMPUTERIZED ENGINE CONTROLS
Ford Motor Co. EEC-IV (Cont.)

SERVICE CODE DEFINITIONS – 2.3L HSC MPFI

SERVICE CODE		SERVICE CODE DEFINITION
11 orc ▶		System PASS
12 r ▶		Unable to control rpm to Self-Test upper limit band
13 r ▶		Unable to control rpm to Self-Test lower limit band
14 c ▶		PIP circuit failure
15 o ▶		ROM test failure
15 c ▶		Power interruption to Keep Alive Memory (KAM)
18 r ▶		SPOUT circuit open
18 c ▶		Loss of tach input to Processor/SPOUT circuit grounded
19 o ▶		Failure of EEC power supply
21 or ▶		ECT sensor input is out of Self-Test range
22 orc ▶		MAP sensor input is out of Self-Test range
23 or ▶		TP sensor input is out of Self-Test range
24 or ▶		ACT sensor input is out of Self-Test range
29 c ▶		Insufficient input from the Vehicle Speed Sensor (VSS)
31 orc ▶		PFE circuit is below minimum voltage
32 rc ▶		EGR valve not seated
33 rc ▶		EGR valve is not opening (PFE)
34 o ▶		Defective PFE sensor
34 rc ▶		Excessive exhaust back pressure
35 orc ▶		PFE circuit is above maximum voltage
41 r ▶		HEGO sensor circuit indicates system lean
41 c ▶		No HEGO switching detected
42 r ▶		HEGO sensor circuit indicates system rich
51 oc ▶		ECT sensor input is greater than Self-Test maximum
52 o ▶		PSPS circuit is open
52 r ▶		PSPS always staying open or closed
53 oc ▶		TP sensor input is greater than Self-Test maximum
54 oc ▶		ACT sensor input is greater than Self-Test maximum
61 oc ▶		ECT sensor input is less than Self-Test minimum
63 oc ▶		TP sensor input is less than Self-Test minimum
64 oc ▶		ACT sensor input is less than Self-Test minimum
67 o ▶		Neutral Drive Switch (NDS) circuit open; A/C input high
72 r ▶		Insufficient MAP output change during Dynamic Response Test
73 r ▶		Insufficient TP output change during Dynamic Response Test
77 r ▶		Brief WOT not sensed during Self-Test/Operator error
84 o ▶		EGR Vacuum Regulator (EVR) circuit failure
85 o ▶		Canister Purge (CANP) circuit failure
87 oc ▶		Fuel pump primary circuit failure
95 oc ▶		Fuel pump secondary circuit failure
96 oc ▶		Fuel pump secondary circuit failure
98 r ▶		Hard fault is present
NO CODES ▶		Unable to initiate Self-Test or unable to output Self-Test codes
CODES NOT LISTED ▶		Service codes displayed are not applicable to the vehicle being tested

KEY: o = Key On Engine Off (KOEO)   r = Engine Running (ER)   c = Continuous Memory

1989 COMPUTERIZED ENGINE CONTROLS
Ford Motor Co. EEC-IV (Cont.)

1a-425

SERVICE CODE DEFINITIONS – 2.3L TC MPFI

SERVICE CODE			SERVICE CODE DEFINITION
11	orc	▶	System PASS
12	r	▶	Unable to control rpm to Self-Test upper limit band
13	r	▶	Unable to control rpm to Self-Test lower limit band
14	c	▶	PIP circuit failure
15	o	▶	ROM test failure
15	c	▶	Power interruption to Keep Alive Memory (KAM)
18	c	▶	Loss of tach input to Processor/SPOUT circuit grounded
21	or	▶	ECT sensor input is out of Self-Test range
22	orc	▶	BP sensor input is out of Self-Test range
23	or	▶	TP sensor input is out of Self-Test range
24	or	▶	VAT sensor input is out of Self-Test range
25	r	▶	KS sensor signal is not sensed in Dynamic Response Test
26	or	▶	VAF sensor input is out of Self-Test range
34	r	▶	Insufficient EGR flow
41	r	▶	EGO sensor circuit indicates system lean
41	c	▶	No EGO switching detected — system always lean
42	r	▶	EGO sensor circuit indicates system rich
42	c	▶	No EGO switch detected — always rich
51	oc	▶	ECT sensor input is greater than Self-Test maximum
53	oc	▶	TP sensor input is greater than Self-Test maximum
54	oc	▶	VAT sensor input is greater than Self-Test maximum
61	oc	▶	ECT sensor input is less than Self-Test minimum
63	oc	▶	TP sensor input is less than Self-Test minimum
64	oc	▶	VAT sensor input is less than Self-Test minimum
66	oc	▶	VAF sensor input is less than Self-Test minimum
67	o	▶	Neutral Drive Switch (NDS) circuit open; A/C input high
67	c	▶	Clutch switch circuit failure
71	c	▶	Software reinitialization detected
72	c	▶	Power interrupt detected
73	r	▶	Insufficient TP output change during Dynamic Response Test
76	r	▶	Insufficient VAF output change during Dynamic Response Test
77	r	▶	Brief WOT not sensed during Self-Test/Operator error
NO CODES		▶	Unable to initiate Self-Test or unable to output Self-Test codes
CODES NOT LISTED		▶	Service codes displayed are not applicable to the vehicle being tested

KEY: o = Key On Engine Off (KOEO)   r = Engine Running (ER)   c = Continuous Memory

1989 COMPUTERIZED ENGINE CONTROLS
Ford Motor Co. EEC-IV (Cont.)

SERVICE CODE DEFINITIONS – 2.5L CFI (AUTOMATIC TRANSMISSION)

SERVICE CODE		SERVICE CODE DEFINITION
11 orc	▶	System PASS
12 r	▶	Rpm below Self-Test limit
13 o	▶	D.C. motor did not move
13 r	▶	Rpm above Self-Test limit
13 c	▶	D.C. motor did not follow dashpot
14 c	▶	PIP circuit failure
15 o	▶	ROM test failure
15 c	▶	Power interruption to Keep Alive Memory (KAM)
16 r	▶	Idle hard set high
17 r	▶	Idle hard set low
18 r	▶	SPOUT circuit open
18 c	▶	Loss of tach input to Processor/SPOUT circuit grounded
21 or	▶	ECT sensor input is out of Self-Test range
22 orc	▶	MAP sensor input is out of Self-Test range
23 orc	▶	TP sensor input is out of Self-Test range
24 or	▶	ACT sensor input is out of Self-Test range
29 c	▶	Insufficient input from the Vehicle Speed Sensor (VSS)
31 orc	▶	EVP circuit is below minimum voltage
32 orc	▶	EVP voltage is below closed limit (SONIC)
33 rc	▶	EGR valve is not opening (SONIC)
34 orc	▶	EVP voltage is above closed limit (SONIC)
35 orc	▶	EVP circuit is above maximum voltage
38 c	▶	Idle Tracking Switch (ITS) circuit open
41 r	▶	HEGO sensor circuit indicates system lean
41 c	▶	No HEGO switching detected
42 r	▶	HEGO sensor circuit indicates system rich
51 oc	▶	ECT sensor input is greater than Self-Test maximum
52 o	▶	PSPS circuit is open
52 r	▶	PSPS always staying open or closed
53 oc	▶	TP sensor input is greater than Self-Test maximum
54 oc	▶	ACT sensor input is greater than Self-Test maximum
55 r	▶	Keypower input to processor is open
58 o	▶	Idle Tracking Switch circuit open
58 r	▶	Idle Tracking Switch closed
61 oc	▶	ECT sensor input is less than Self-Test minimum
63 oc	▶	TP sensor input is less than Self-Test minimum
64 oc	▶	ACT sensor input is less than Self-Test minimum
67 o	▶	Neutral Drive Switch (NDS) circuit open; A/C input high
67 c	▶	Clutch switch circuit failure
68 o	▶	Idle Tracking Switch (ITS) closed
68 r	▶	Idle Tracking Switch (ITS) circuit open
71 c	▶	Idle Tracking Switch (ITS) closed on pre-position
72 c	▶	Power interrupt detected
73 o	▶	Insufficient throttle position change
74 r	▶	Brake On/Off (BOO) circuit failure — not actuated during test
83 o	▶	High speed electro drive fan (HEDF) circuit failure
84 o	▶	EGR Vacuum Regulator (EVR) circuit failure
85 o	▶	Canister Purge (CANP) circuit failure
87 oc	▶	Fuel pump primary circuit failure
88 o	▶	Electro-drive fan (EDF) circuit failure
93 o	▶	TP sensor input low at maximum D.C. motor extension
95 oc	▶	Fuel pump secondary circuit failure
96 oc	▶	Fuel pump secondary circuit failure
99 r	▶	EEC system has not learned to control idle
NO CODES	▶	Unable to initiate Self-Test or unable to output Self-Test codes
CODES NOT LISTED	▶	Service codes displayed are not applicable to the vehicle being tested

KEY: o = Key On Engine Off (KOEO)   r = Engine Running (ER)   c = Continuous Memory

1989 COMPUTERIZED ENGINE CONTROLS
Ford Motor Co. EEC-IV (Cont.)

1a-427

SERVICE CODE DEFINITIONS – 2.5L CFI (MANUAL TRANSMISSION)

SERVICE CODE			SERVICE CODE DEFINITION
11	orc	▶	System PASS
12	r	▶	Rpm below Self-Test limit
13	o	▶	D.C. motor did not move
13	r	▶	Rpm above Self-Test limit
13	c	▶	D.C. motor did not follow dashpot
14	c	▶	PIP circuit failure
15	o	▶	ROM test failure
15	c	▶	Power interruption to Keep Alive Memory (KAM)
16	r	▶	Idle hard set high
17	r	▶	Idle hard set low
18	r	▶	SPOUT circuit open
18	c	▶	Loss of tach input to Processor/SPOUT circuit grounded
21	or	▶	ECT sensor input is out of Self-Test range
22	orc	▶	MAP sensor input is out of Self-Test range
23	orc	▶	TP sensor input is out of Self-Test range
24	or	▶	ACT sensor input is out of Self-Test range
29	c	▶	Insufficient input from the Vehicle Speed Sensor (VSS)
31	orc	▶	EVP circuit is below minimum voltage
32	orc	▶	EVP voltage is below closed limit (SONIC)
33	rc	▶	EGR valve is not opening (SONIC)
34	orc	▶	EVP voltage is above closed limit (SONIC)
35	orc	▶	EVP circuit is above maximum voltage
38	c	▶	Idle Tracking Switch (ITS) circuit open
41	r	▶	HEGO sensor circuit indicates system lean
41	c	▶	No HEGO switching detected
42	r	▶	HEGO sensor circuit indicates system rich
51	oc	▶	ECT sensor input is greater than Self-Test maximum
52	o	▶	PSPS circuit is open
52	r	▶	PSPS always staying open or closed
53	oc	▶	TP sensor input is greater than Self-Test maximum
54	oc	▶	ACT sensor input is greater than Self-Test maximum
55	r	▶	Keypower input to processor is open
58	o	▶	Idle Tracking Switch circuit open
58	r	▶	Idle Tracking Switch closed
61	oc	▶	ECT sensor input is less than Self-Test minimum
63	oc	▶	TP sensor input is less than Self-Test minimum
64	oc	▶	ACT sensor input is less than Self-Test minimum
67	o	▶	A/C input high
67	c	▶	Clutch switch circuit failure
68	o	▶	Idle Tracking Switch (ITS) closed
68	r	▶	Idle Tracking Switch (ITS) circuit open
71	c	▶	Idle Tracking Switch (ITS) closed on pre-position
72	c	▶	Power interrupt detected
73	o	▶	Insufficient throttle position change
74	r	▶	Brake On/Off (BOO) circuit failure — not actuated during test
83	o	▶	High speed electro drive fan (HEDF) circuit failure
84	o	▶	EGR Vacuum Regulator (EVR) circuit failure
85	o	▶	Canister Purge (CANP) circuit failure
87	oc	▶	Fuel pump primary circuit failure
88	o	▶	Electro-drive fan (EDF) circuit failure
93	o	▶	TP sensor input low at maximum D.C. motor extension
95	oc	▶	Fuel pump secondary circuit failure
96	oc	▶	Fuel pump secondary circuit failure
99	r	▶	EEC system has not learned to control idle
NO CODES		▶	Unable to initiate Self-Test or unable to output Self-Test codes
CODES NOT LISTED		▶	Service codes displayed are not applicable to the vehicle being tested

KEY: o = Key On Engine Off (KOEO) r = Engine Running (ER) c = Continuous Memory

1989 COMPUTERIZED ENGINE CONTROLS
Ford Motor Co. EEC-IV (Cont.)

SERVICE CODE DEFINITIONS – 3.0L MPFI

SERVICE CODE		SERVICE CODE DEFINITION
11	orc ▶	System PASS
12	r ▶	Unable to control rpm to Self-Test upper limit band
13	r ▶	Unable to control rpm to Self-Test lower limit band
14	c ▶	PIP circuit failure
15	o ▶	ROM test failure
15	c ▶	Power interruption to Keep Alive Memory (KAM)
18	r ▶	SPOUT circuit open
18	c ▶	Loss of tach input to Processor/SPOUT circuit grounded
19	o ▶	Failure of EEC power supply
21	or ▶	ECT sensor input is out of Self-Test range
22	orc ▶	MAP sensor input is out of Self-Test range
23	or ▶	TP sensor input is out of Self-Test range
24	or ▶	ACT sensor input is out of Self-Test range
25	r ▶	KS sensor signal is not sensed in Dynamic Response Test
29	c ▶	Insufficient input from the Vehicle Speed Sensor (VSS)
31	orc ▶	PFE circuit is below minimum voltage
32	rc ▶	EGR valve not seated
33	rc ▶	EGR valve is not opening (PFE)
34	o ▶	Defective PFE sensor
34	rc ▶	Excessive exhaust back pressure
35	orc ▶	PFE circuit is above maximum voltage
39	c ▶	AXOD converter bypass clutch not applying properly
41	r ▶	HEGO sensor circuit indicates system lean
41	c ▶	No HEGO switching detected
42	r ▶	HEGO sensor circuit indicates system rich
51	oc ▶	ECT sensor input is greater than Self-Test maximum
52	o ▶	PSPS circuit is open
52	r ▶	PSPS always staying open or closed
53	oc ▶	TP sensor input is greater than Self-Test maximum
54	oc ▶	ACT sensor input is greater than Self-Test maximum
57	c ▶	AXOD Neutral Pressure Switch (NPS) circuit failed open
59	c ▶	AXOD 4/3 pressure switch circuit failed open
61	oc ▶	ECT sensor input is less than Self-Test minimum
62	o ▶	AXOD 4/3 or 3/2 pressure switch circuit failed closed
63	oc ▶	TP sensor input is less than Self-Test minimum
64	oc ▶	ACT sensor input is less than Self-Test minimum
67	o ▶	Neutral Pressure Switch (NPS) circuit open; A/C input high
69	c ▶	AXOD 3/4 pressure switch circuit failed open
72	r ▶	Insufficient MAP output change during Dynamic Response Test
73	r ▶	Insufficient TP output change during Dynamic Response Test
74	r ▶	Brake On/Off (BOO) circuit failure — not actuated during test
77	r ▶	Brief WOT not sensed during Self-Test/Operator error
83	o ▶	High speed electro drive fan (HEDF) circuit failure
84	o ▶	EGR Vacuum Regulator (EVR) circuit failure
85	o ▶	Canister Purge (CANP) circuit failure
87	oc ▶	Fuel pump primary circuit failure
88	o ▶	Electro-drive fan (EDF) circuit failure
89	o ▶	AXOD Lock-Up Solenoid (LUS) circuit failed
95	oc ▶	Fuel pump secondary circuit failure
96	oc ▶	Fuel pump secondary circuit failure
98	r ▶	Hard fault is present
NO CODES	▶	Unable to initiate Self-Test or unable to output Self-Test codes
CODES NOT LISTED	▶	Service codes displayed are not applicable to the vehicle being tested

KEY: o = Key On Engine Off (KOEO)   r = Engine Running (ER)   c = Continuous Memory

1989 COMPUTERIZED ENGINE CONTROLS
Ford Motor Co. EEC-IV (Cont.)

1a-429

SERVICE CODE DEFINITIONS – 3.0L SHO MPFI

SERVICE CODE		SERVICE CODE DEFINITION
11 orc	▶	System PASS
12 r	▶	Unable to control rpm to Self-Test upper limit band
13 r	▶	Unable to control rpm to Self-Test lower limit band
14 c	▶	PIP circuit failure
15 o	▶	ROM test failure
15 c	▶	Power interruption to Keep Alive Memory (KAM)
18 r	▶	SPOUT circuit open
18 c	▶	Loss of tach input to Processor, SPOUT circuit grounded
19 c	▶	CID sensor input failed
21 or	▶	ECT sensor input is out of Self-Test range
22 oc	▶	BP sensor input is out of Self-Test range
23 or	▶	TP sensor input is out of Self-Test range
24 or	▶	ACT sensor input is out of Self-Test range
25 r	▶	KS sensor signal is not sensed in Dynamic Response Test
26 or	▶	MAF sensor input is out of Self-Test range
29 c	▶	Insufficient input from the Vehicle Speed Sensor (VSS)
31 orc	▶	PFE circuit is below minimum voltage
32 rc	▶	EGR valve not seated
33 rc	▶	EGR valve is not opening (PFE)
34 o	▶	Defective PFE sensor
34 rc	▶	Excessive exhaust back pressure
35 orc	▶	PFE circuit is above maximum voltage
41 r	▶	HEGO sensor circuit indicates system lean (right HEGO)
41 c	▶	No HEGO switching detected (right HEGO)
42 r	▶	HEGO sensor circuit indicates system rich (right HEGO)
45 c	▶	DIS Coil pack 3 circuit failure
46 c	▶	DIS Coil pack 1 circuit failure
48 c	▶	DIS Coil pack 2 circuit failure
49 c	▶	SPOUT signal defaulted to 10 degrees BTDC
51 oc	▶	ECT sensor input is greater than Self-Test maximum
52 o	▶	PSPS circuit is open
52 r	▶	PSPS always staying open or closed
53 oc	▶	TP sensor input is greater than Self-Test maximum
54 oc	▶	ACT sensor input is greater than Self-Test maximum
56 oc	▶	MAF sensor input is greater than Self-Test maximum
59 oc	▶	Low speed fuel pump circuit failure
61 oc	▶	ECT sensor input is less than Self-Test minimum
63 oc	▶	TP sensor input is less than Self-Test minimum
64 oc	▶	ACT sensor input is less than Self-Test minimum
66 c	▶	MAF sensor input is less than Self-Test minimum
67 o	▶	Neutral Pressure Switch (NPS) circuit open; A/C input high
72 r	▶	Insufficient BP output change during Dynamic Response Test
73 r	▶	Insufficient TP output change during Dynamic Response Test
74 r	▶	Brake On/Off (BOO) circuit failure — not actuated during test
77 r	▶	Brief WOT not sensed during Self-Test/Operator error
79 o	▶	A/C on during Self-Test
81 o	▶	Insufficient IAS output voltage change when solenoid activate
83 oc	▶	Low speed fuel pump relay circuit open
84 o	▶	EGR Vacuum Regulator (EVR) circuit failure
85 o	▶	Canister Purge (CANP) circuit failure
87 oc	▶	Fuel pump primary circuit failure
88 o	▶	Electro-Drive Fan (EDF) circuit failure
91 r	▶	HEGO sensor circuit indicates system lean (left HEGO)
91 c	▶	No HEGO switching detected (left HEGO)
92 r	▶	HEGO sensor circuit indicates system rich (left HEGO)
95 oc	▶	Fuel pump secondary circuit failure
96 oc	▶	High speed fuel pump relay circuit open
98 r	▶	Hard fault is present
NO CODES	▶	Unable to initiate Self-Test or unable to output Self-Test codes
CODES NOT LISTED	▶	Service codes displayed are not applicable to the vehicle being tested

KEY: o = Key On Engine Off (KOEO)   r = Engine Running (ER)   c = Continuous Memory

1989 COMPUTERIZED ENGINE CONTROLS
Ford Motor Co. EEC-IV (Cont.)

SERVICE CODE DEFINITIONS – 3.8L SEFI (FRONT WHEEL DRIVE)

SERVICE CODE			SERVICE CODE DEFINITION
11	orc	▶	System PASS
12	r	▶	Unable to control rpm to Self-Test upper limit band
13	r	▶	Unable to control rpm to Self-Test lower limit band
14	c	▶	PIP circuit failure
15	o	▶	ROM test failure
15	c	▶	Power interruption to Keep Alive Memory (KAM)
18	r	▶	SPOUT circuit open
18	c	▶	Loss of tach input to Processor/SPOUT circuit grounded
19	o	▶	Failure of EEC power supply
21	or	▶	ECT sensor input is out of Self-Test range
22	orc	▶	MAP sensor input is out of Self-Test range
23	or	▶	TP sensor input is out of Self-Test range
24	or	▶	ACT sensor input is out of Self-Test range
29	c	▶	Insufficient input from the Vehicle Speed Sensor (VSS)
31	orc	▶	PFE circuit is below minimum voltage
32	rc	▶	EGR valve not seated
33	rc	▶	EGR valve is not opening (PFE)
34	o	▶	Defective PFE sensor
34	rc	▶	Excessive exhaust back pressure
35	orc	▶	PFE circuit is above maximum voltage
39	c	▶	AXOD converter bypass clutch not applying properly
41	r	▶	HEGO sensor circuit indicates system lean (right HEGO)
41	c	▶	No HEGO switching detected (right HEGO)
42	r	▶	HEGO sensor circuit indicates system rich (right HEGO)
51	oc	▶	ECT sensor input is greater than Self-Test maximum
52	o	▶	PSPS circuit is open
52	r	▶	PSPS always staying open or closed
53	oc	▶	TP sensor input is greater than Self-Test maximum
54	oc	▶	ACT sensor input is greater than Self-Test maximum
57	c	▶	AXOD Neutral Pressure Switch (NPS) circuit failed open
59	o	▶	AXOD 4/3 pressure switch circuit failed closed
59	c	▶	AXOD 4/3 pressure switch circuit failed open
61	oc	▶	ECT sensor input is less than Self-Test minimum
63	oc	▶	TP sensor input is less than Self-Test minimum
64	oc	▶	ACT sensor input is less than Self-Test minimum
67	o	▶	AXOD Neutral Pressure Switch (NPS) circuit failed closed
68	orc	▶	AXOD Transmission Temperature Switch (TTS) failed open
69	o	▶	AXOD 3/2 pressure switch circuit failed closed
69	c	▶	AXOD 3/4 pressure switch circuit failed open
70	c	▶	EEC IV data transmission circuit failed (DCL)
71	c	▶	Cluster Control Assembly (CCA) circuit failed (DCL)
72	c	▶	Message Center Control Assembly (MCCA) circuit failed (DCL)
74	r	▶	Brake On/Off (BOO) circuit failure — not actuated during test
79	o	▶	A/C on during Self-Test
83	o	▶	High speed electro drive fan (HEDF) circuit failure
84	o	▶	EGR Vacuum Regulator (EVR) circuit failure
85	o	▶	Canister Purge (CANP) circuit failure
87	oc	▶	Fuel pump primary circuit failure
88	o	▶	Electro-Drive Fan (EDF) circuit failure
89	o	▶	AXOD Lock-Up Solenoid (LUS) circuit failed
91	r	▶	HEGO sensor circuit indicates system lean (left HEGO)
91	c	▶	No HEGO switching detected (left HEGO)
92	r	▶	HEGO sensor circuit indicates system rich (left HEGO)
95	oc	▶	Fuel pump secondary circuit failure
96	oc	▶	Fuel pump secondary circuit failure
98	r	▶	Hard fault present
NO CODES		▶	Unable to initiate Self-Test or unable to output Self-Test codes
CODES NOT LISTED		▶	Service codes displayed are not applicable to the vehicle being tested

KEY: o = Key On Engine Off (KOEO)   r = Engine Running (ER)   c = Continuous Memory

1989 COMPUTERIZED ENGINE CONTROLS
Ford Motor Co. EEC-IV (Cont.)

1a-431

SERVICE CODE DEFINITIONS – 3.8L SEFI (REAR WHEEL DRIVE / EXCEPT SC)

SERVICE CODE			SERVICE CODE DEFINITION
11	orc	▶	System PASS
12	r	▶	Unable to control rpm to Self-Test upper limit band
13	r	▶	Unable to control rpm to Self-Test lower limit band
14	c	▶	PIP circuit failure
15	o	▶	ROM test failure
15	c	▶	Power interruption to Keep Alive Memory (KAM)
18	r	▶	SPOUT circuit open
18	c	▶	Loss of tach input to Processor/SPOUT circuit grounded
19	o	▶	Failure of EEC power supply
21	or	▶	ECT sensor input is out of Self-Test range
22	orc	▶	MAP sensor input is out of Self-Test range
23	or	▶	TP sensor input is out of Self-Test range
24	or	▶	ACT sensor input is out of Self-Test range
29	c	▶	Insufficient input from the Vehicle Speed Sensor (VSS)
31	orc	▶	PFE circuit is below minimum voltage
32	rc	▶	EGR valve not seated
33	rc	▶	EGR valve is not opening (PFE)
34	o	▶	Defective PFE sensor
34	rc	▶	Excessive exhaust back pressure
35	orc	▶	PFE circuit is above maximum voltage
41	r	▶	HEGO sensor circuit indicates system lean (right HEGO)
41	c	▶	No HEGO switching detected (right HEGO)
42	r	▶	HEGO sensor circuit indicates system rich (right HEGO)
51	oc	▶	ECT sensor input is greater than Self-Test maximum
53	oc	▶	TP sensor input is greater than Self-Test maximum
54	oc	▶	ACT sensor input is greater than Self-Test maximum
61	oc	▶	ECT sensor input is less than Self-Test minimum
63	oc	▶	TP sensor input is less than Self-Test minimum
64	oc	▶	ACT sensor input is less than Self-Test minimum
67	o	▶	Neutral Drive Switch (NDS) circuit open
74	r	▶	Brake On/Off (BOO) circuit failure — not actuated during test
79	o	▶	A/C on during Self-Test
84	o	▶	EGR Vacuum Regulator (EVR) circuit failure
85	o	▶	Canister Purge (CANP) circuit failure
87	oc	▶	Fuel pump primary circuit failure
91	r	▶	HEGO sensor circuit indicates system lean (left HEGO)
91	c	▶	No HEGO switching detected (left HEGO)
92	r	▶	HEGO sensor circuit indicates system rich (left HEGO)
95	oc	▶	Fuel pump secondary circuit failure
96	oc	▶	Fuel pump secondary circuit failure
98	r	▶	Hard fault is present
NO CODES		▶	Unable to initiate Self-Test or unable to output Self-Test codes
CODES NOT LISTED		▶	Service codes displayed are not applicable to the vehicle being tested

KEY: o = Key On Engine Off (KOEO)   r = Engine Running (ER)   c = Continuous Memory

1989 COMPUTERIZED ENGINE CONTROLS
Ford Motor Co. EEC-IV (Cont.)

SERVICE CODE DEFINITIONS – 3.8L SC SEFI

SERVICE CODE			SERVICE CODE DEFINITION
11	orc	▶	System PASS
12	r	▶	Unable to control rpm to Self-Test upper limit band
13	r	▶	Unable to control rpm to Self-Test lower limit band
14	c	▶	PIP circuit failure
15	o	▶	ROM test failure
15	c	▶	Power interruption to Keep Alive Memory (KAM)
18	r	▶	SPOUT circuit open
18	c	▶	Loss of tach input to Processor/SPOUT circuit grounded
19	c	▶	CID sensor input failed
21	or	▶	ECT sensor input is out of Self-Test range
22	oc	▶	BP sensor input is out of Self-Test range
23	or	▶	TP sensor input is out of Self-Test range
24	or	▶	ACT sensor input is out of Self-Test range
25	r	▶	KS sensor signal is not sensed in Dynamic Response Test
26	or	▶	MAF sensor input is out of Self-Test range
29	c	▶	Insufficient input from the Vehicle Speed Sensor (VSS)
31	orc	▶	PFE circuit is below minimum voltage
32	rc	▶	EGR valve not seated
33	rc	▶	EGR valve is not opening (PFE)
34	o	▶	Defective PFE sensor
34	rc	▶	Excessive exhaust back pressure
35	orc	▶	PFE circuit is above maximum voltage
41	r	▶	HEGO sensor circuit indicates system lean (right HEGO)
41	c	▶	No HEGO switching detected (right HEGO)
42	r	▶	HEGO sensor circuit indicates system rich (right HEGO)
45	c	▶	DIS Coil pack 3 circuit failure
46	c	▶	DIS Coil pack 1 circuit failure
48	c	▶	DIS Coil pack 2 circuit failure
49	c	▶	SPOUT signal defaulted to 10 degrees BTDC
51	oc	▶	ECT sensor input is greater than Self-Test maximum
52	o	▶	PSPS circuit is open
52	r	▶	PSPS always staying open or closed
53	oc	▶	TP sensor input is greater than Self-Test maximum
54	oc	▶	ACT sensor input is greater than Self-Test maximum
56	oc	▶	MAF sensor input is greater than Self-Test maximum
61	oc	▶	ECT sensor input is less than Self-Test minimum
63	oc	▶	TP sensor input is less than Self-Test minimum
64	oc	▶	ACT sensor input is less than Self-Test minimum
66	c	▶	MAF sensor input is less than Self-Test minimum
67	o	▶	Neutral Drive Switch (NDS) circuit open; A/C input high
67	c	▶	Clutch switch circuit failure
72	r	▶	Insufficient BP output change during Dynamic Response Test
73	r	▶	Insufficient TP output change during Dynamic Response Test
74	r	▶	Brake On/Off (BOO) circuit failure — not actuated during test
77	r	▶	Brief WOT not sensed during Self-Test/Operator error
79	o	▶	A/C on during Self-Test
82	o	▶	Supercharger bypass circuit failure
83	o	▶	High speed electro-drive fan circuit failure
84	o	▶	EGR Vacuum Regulator (EVR) circuit failure
85	o	▶	Canister Purge (CANP) circuit failure
87	oc	▶	Fuel pump primary circuit failure
88	o	▶	Electro-Drive Fan (EDF) circuit failure
91	r	▶	HEGO sensor circuit indicates system lean (left HEGO)
91	c	▶	No HEGO switching detected (left HEGO)
92	r	▶	HEGO sensor circuit indicates system rich (left HEGO)
95	oc	▶	Fuel pump secondary circuit failure
96	oc	▶	Fuel pump secondary circuit failure
98	r	▶	Hard fault is present
NO CODES		▶	Unable to initiate Self-Test or unable to output Self-Test codes
CODES NOT LISTED		▶	Service codes displayed are not applicable to the vehicle being tested

KEY: o = Key On Engine Off (KOEO) r = Engine Running (ER) c = Continuous Memory

SERVICE CODE DEFINITIONS – 5.0L SEFI (EXCEPT MA)

SERVICE CODE			SERVICE CODE DEFINITION
11	orc	▶	System PASS
12	r	▶	Unable to control rpm to Self-Test upper limit band
13	r	▶	Unable to control rpm to Self-Test lower limit band
14	c	▶	PIP circuit failure
15	o	▶	ROM test failure
15	c	▶	Power interruption to Keep Alive Memory (KAM)
16	r	▶	RPM too low to perform fuel test
18	r	▶	SPOUT circuit open
18	c	▶	Loss of tach input to Processor/SPOUT circuit grounded
19	o	▶	Failure of EEC power supply
21	or	▶	ECT sensor input is out of Self-Test range
22	orc	▶	MAP sensor input is out of Self-Test range
23	or	▶	TP sensor input is out of Self-Test range
24	or	▶	ACT sensor input is out of Self-Test range
29	c	▶	Insufficient input from the Vehicle Speed Sensor (VSS)
31	orc	▶	EVP circuit is below minimum voltage
32	orc	▶	EVP voltage is below closed limit (SONIC)
33	rc	▶	EGR valve is not opening (SONIC)
34	orc	▶	EVP voltage is above closed limit (SONIC)
35	orc	▶	EVP circuit is above maximum voltage
41	r	▶	HEGO sensor circuit indicates system lean (right HEGO)
41	c	▶	No HEGO switching detected (right HEGO)
42	r	▶	HEGO sensor circuit indicates system rich (right HEGO)
44	r	▶	Thermactor air system inoperative (cyl. 1-4)
45	r	▶	Thermactor air upstream during Self-Test
46	r	▶	Thermactor air not bypassed during Self-Test
51	oc	▶	ECT sensor input is greater than Self-Test maximum
53	oc	▶	TP sensor input is greater than Self-Test maximum
54	oc	▶	ACT sensor input is greater than Self-Test maximum
61	oc	▶	ECT sensor input is less than Self-Test minimum
63	oc	▶	TP sensor input is less than Self-Test minimum
64	oc	▶	ACT sensor input is less than Self-Test minimum
67	o	▶	Neutral Drive Switch (NDS) circuit open
74	r	▶	Brake On/Off (BOO) circuit open — not actuated during test
75	r	▶	Brake On/Off (BOO) circuit closed - always high
79	o	▶	A/C on during Self-Test
81	o	▶	Air Management 2 (AM2) circuit failure
82	o	▶	Air Management 1 (AM1) circuit failure
84	o	▶	EGR Vacuum Regulator (EVR) circuit failure
85	o	▶	Canister Purge (CANP) circuit failure
87	oc	▶	Fuel pump primary circuit failure
91	r	▶	HEGO sensor circuit indicates system lean (left HEGO)
91	c	▶	No HEGO switching detected (left HEGO)
92	r	▶	HEGO sensor circuit indicates system rich (left HEGO)
94	r	▶	Thermactor air system inoperative (cyl. 5-8)
98	r	▶	Hard fault is present
NO CODES		▶	Unable to initiate Self-Test or unable to output Self-Test codes
CODES NOT LISTED		▶	Service codes displayed are not applicable to the vehicle being tested

KEY: o = Key On Engine Off (KOEO)   r = Engine Running (ER)   c = Continuous Memory

1989 COMPUTERIZED ENGINE CONTROLS
Ford Motor Co. EEC-IV (Cont.)

SERVICE CODE DEFINITIONS – 5.0L MA SEFI

SERVICE CODE	SERVICE CODE DEFINITION
11 orc ▶	System PASS
12 r ▶	Unable to control rpm to Self-Test upper limit band
13 r ▶	Unable to control rpm to Self-Test lower limit band
14 c ▶	PIP circuit failure
15 o ▶	ROM test failure
15 c ▶	Power interruption to Keep Alive Memory (KAM)
18 r ▶	SPOUT circuit open
18 c ▶	Loss of tach input to Processor/SPOUT circuit grounded
19 o ▶	Failure of EEC power supply
21 or ▶	ECT sensor input is out of Self-Test range
22 oc ▶	BP sensor input is out of Self-Test range
23 or ▶	TP sensor input is out of Self-Test range
24 or ▶	ACT sensor input is out of Self-Test range
26 or ▶	MAF sensor input is out of Self-Test range
29 c ▶	Insufficient input from the Vehicle Speed Sensor (VSS)
31 orc ▶	EVP circuit is below minimum voltage
32 orc ▶	EVP voltage is below closed limit (SONIC)
33 rc ▶	EGR valve not opening (SONIC)
34 orc ▶	EVP voltage is above closed limit (SONIC)
35 orc ▶	EVP circuit is above maximum voltage
41 r ▶	HEGO sensor circuit indicates system lean (right HEGO)
41 c ▶	No HEGO switching detected (right HEGO)
42 r ▶	HEGO sensor circuit indicates system rich (right HEGO)
44 r ▶	Thermactor air system inoperative (cylinders 1-4)
45 r ▶	Thermactor air upstream during Self-Test
46 r ▶	Thermactor air not bypassed during Self-Test
51 oc ▶	ECT sensor input is greater than Self-Test maximum
53 oc ▶	TP sensor input is greater than Self-Test maximum
54 oc ▶	ACT sensor input is greater than Self-Test maximum
56 oc ▶	MAF sensor input is greater than Self-Test maximum
61 oc ▶	ECT sensor input is less than Self-Test minimum
63 oc ▶	TP sensor input is less than Self-Test minimum
64 oc ▶	ACT sensor input is less than Self-Test minimum
66 c ▶	MAF sensor input is less than Self-Test minimum
67 o ▶	Neutral Drive Switch (NDS) circuit open; A/C input high
77 r ▶	Brief WOT not sensed during Self-Test/Operator error
79 o ▶	A/C on during Self-Test
81 o ▶	Air Management 2 (AM2) circuit failure
82 o ▶	Air Management 1 (AM1) circuit failure
84 o ▶	EGR Vacuum Regulator (EVR) circuit failure
85 o ▶	Canister Purge (CANP) circuit failure
87 oc ▶	Fuel pump primary circuit failure
91 r ▶	HEGO sensor circuit indicates system lean (left HEGO)
91 c ▶	No HEGO switching detected (left HEGO)
92 r ▶	HEGO sensor circuit indicates system rich (left HEGO)
94 r ▶	Thermactor air system inoperative (cylinders 5-8)
95 oc ▶	Fuel pump secondary circuit failure
96 oc ▶	Fuel pump secondary circuit failure
98 r ▶	Hard fault is present
NO CODES ▶	Unable to initiate Self-Test or unable to output Self-Test codes
CODES NOT LISTED ▶	Service codes displayed are not applicable to the vehicle being tested

KEY: o = Key On Engine Off (KOEO) r = Engine Running (ER) c = Continuous Memory

CIRCUIT TESTS

HOW TO USE CIRCUIT TESTS

1) DO NOT perform any CIRCUIT TEST unless directed to do so by a QUICK TEST procedure. Ensure all non-EEC related faults are corrected. FOLLOW EACH TEST STEP IN ORDER UNTIL FAULT IS FOUND. Do not replace any part unless directed to do so. When more than one service code is received, start with the first code displayed.

2) CIRCUIT TESTS require that you prove the electrical circuits are okay before you replace sensors or any other components. Always test circuits for continuity between the sensor and the ECA. Test all circuits for shorts to power, opens, or shorts to ground. Voltage Reference (VREF) and Voltage Power (VPWR) circuits should be tested with KOEO or as specified in CIRCUIT TESTS.

3) DO NOT measure voltage or resistance at ECA or connect any test light, unless specified in testing procedure. All measurements are made by probing REAR of connector. Isolate both ends of a circuit and turn key off whenever checking for shorts or continuity, unless specified.

NOTE: When directed in testing procedure to service or repair TFI ignition system, see MOTORCRAFT TFI-IV IGNITION article in DISTRIBUTORS & IGNITION SYSTEMS section.

---

4) Disconnect solenoids and switches from harness before measuring continuity, resistance, or applying voltage. After each repair, check all component connections and repeat CIRCUIT TEST.

5) An "open" is defined as any resistance reading greater than 5 ohms. This specification tolerance may be too high for some items in the EEC-IV system. If resistance approaches 5 ohms, always clean the suspected connector and coat with protective dielectric silicone grease. A "short" is defined as any resistance reading less than 10K ohms to ground, unless otherwise specified in CIRCUIT TEST.

6) On FUEL CONTROL CIRCUIT TESTS C1, and C2, to prevent replacement of good components, be aware that the following non-EEC related areas may also be at fault. These areas include ignition coil, distributor cap and rotor, spark plug wires, fouled spark plugs, canister purge problems, EGR valve and gasket, air filter, poor power and ground circuits, fuel pressure, intake and exhaust manifold leaks, engine not at normal operating temperature, and problems with PCV valves or fuel contaminated engine oil.

NOTE: Fuel contaminated engine oil may affect some service codes. If this is suspected, remove PCV valve from valve cover and repeat QUICK TEST. If problem is corrected, change engine oil and filter.

---

7) On FUEL CONTROL CIRCUIT TESTS C1, and C2, vacuum leaks in non-EEC related areas may also cause code 41 or 91 to be displayed. Check for unmetered air leaks between airflow meter and throttle body, leaking vacuum motors, engine seals, EGR system, PCV system, Canister Purge (CANP) problems, or contaminated HEGO sensor. Code 42 or 92 may be caused by fuel contaminated engine oil, ignition misfire, EGR system, or CANP problems.

NOTE: In the following tests, circuits and illustrations are supplied courtesy of Ford Motor Co.

NOTE: CIRCUIT TESTS are grouped in the following categories.
- *A1-A3 Preliminary Tests*
- *B1-B15 Input Sensor Tests*
- *C1-C2 Fuel Control Systems*
- *D1-D24 ECA Output Tests*

CIRCUIT TEST A1
NO START

TFI Module Circuits

APPLICATIONS: 3.8L SEFI AXOD, 3.8L SEFI RWD, 7.5L EFI TRK

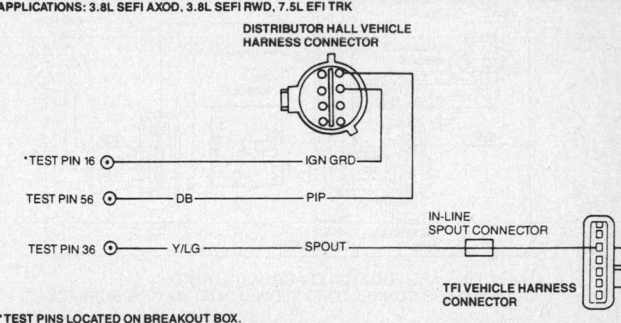

*TEST PINS LOCATED ON BREAKOUT BOX.
ALL HARNESS CONNECTORS VIEWED INTO MATING SURFACE.

Test Pin 16	IGN. GND
Application	**Wire Color**
3.8L SEFI AXOD	GY
3.8L SEFI RWD 7.5L EFI TRK	BK/O

TFI Location	
Application	**Location**
3.8L SEFI AXOD	Cowl
3.8L SEFI RWD	Radiator Support
7.5L EFI TRK	Distributor

ALL OTHER TFI APPLICATIONS

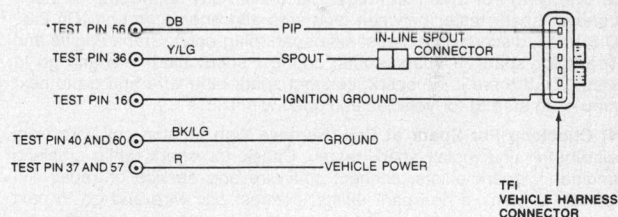

*TEST PINS LOCATED ON BREAKOUT BOX.
ALL HARNESS CONNECTORS VIEWED INTO MATING SURFACE.
NOTE: WHEN BREAKOUT BOX IS INSTALLED, ENSURE THAT TIMING SWITCH IS IN "COMPUTED" POSITION UNLESS OTHERWISE NOTED.

Test Pin 16	IGN. GND
3.0L, 3.8L AXOD	GY
2.9L TK 2.3L TK	BK
2.3L Merkur XR4Ti	R/O
All Others	BK/O

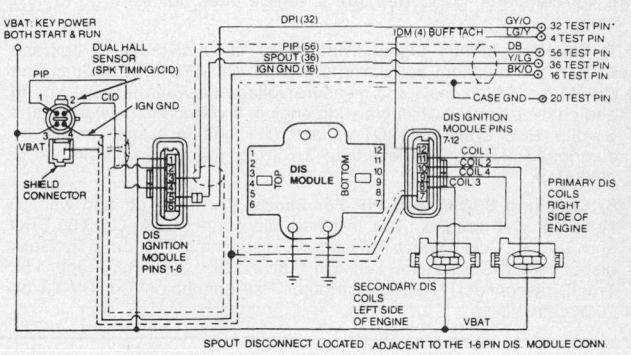

SPOUT DISCONNECT LOCATED ADJACENT TO THE 1-6 PIN DIS. MODULE CONN.

1a-436

1989 COMPUTERIZED ENGINE CONTROLS
Ford Motor Co. EEC-IV (Cont.)

CIRCUIT TEST A1 (Cont.)

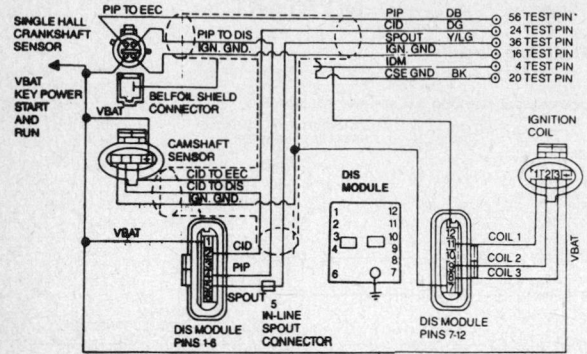

*TEST PINS ARE LOCATED ON BREAKOUT BOX.
ALL HARNESS CONNECTORS VIEWED INTO MATING SURFACE.

To prevent replacement of good components, be aware that the following non-EEC related areas may be at fault: fuel quantity and quality, ignition system damage, cracks, moisture, etc., engine mechanical conditions such as bad valves, timing belt, etc. Also included are starter and battery circuit problems.

1) Starting System. Try to start engine. If engine does not crank, check vehicle starting and charging systems. Ensure fuel pump inertia switch is set (button pushed in). If engine cranks, but does not start or stalls after starting, go to next step.

2) Checking VREF Signal at TPS. Turn key off and wait 10 seconds. Set DVOM on 20-volt scale and disconnect Throttle Position Sensor (TPS). Turn key on, leaving engine off (KOEO). Measure voltage at TPS harness connector between (VREF) and SIGNAL RETURN. If reading is less than 4 volts or more than 6 volts, go to CIRCUIT TEST A3, step 1). If reading is between 4 and 6 volts, reconnect TPS and go to next step.

3) Checking For Spark At Plugs. Disconnect any spark plug wire and connect spark tester between plug wire and engine ground (On 2.3L DIS truck, disconnect exhaust side spark plug only). Crank engine and check for spark. If spark exists, connect spark plug wire and go to step 12). If there is no spark, connect spark plug wire and go to next step or to step 5) for vehicles equipped with DIS.

4) Checking For Spark at Coil. Remove high tension coil wire from distributor and install spark tester. Check for spark while cranking engine. If spark exists, connect coil wire and service or repair TFI ignition system. If no spark exists, connect coil wire and go to next step.

5) Ignition Ground Continuity. Turn key off and wait 10 seconds. Install breakout box, leaving ECA disconnected. Set DVOM on 200-ohm scale and disconnect TFI or DIS (pins No. 7-12). Disconnect Hall sensor on 3.8L Measure resistance between test pin No. 16 and TFI harness connector ignition ground. If reading is more than 5 ohms, repair harness and repeat QUICK TEST. If reading is less than 5 ohms, go to next step.

6) Isolating SPOUT Circuit Fault. Install breakout box. Connect TFI or DIS (pins No. 7-12). For 3.8L AXOD, 3.8L RWD and 7.5L Truck, connect distributor hall connector. Connect ECA to breakout box. Set breakout box switch to "DISTRIBUTOR" position. Try to start vehicle. If vehicle starts, go to step 10). If vehicle does not start, go to next step.

7) Checking SPOUT Signal. With KOEO, connect breakout box and ECA. Move breakout box timing switch to "COMPUTED" position. Set DVOM on 20-volt scale and measure voltage between test pin No. 36 and chassis ground while cranking engine. If voltage is between 3 and 6 volts, EEC system is NOT at fault. TFI ignition system should be diagnosed. If voltage is less than 3 volts or more than 6 volts, go to next step.

8) Checking SPOUT and PIP For Shorts. Turn key off and wait 10 seconds. With breakout box installed, disconnect ECA. On 3.0L SHO and 3.8L SC, disconnect PIP sensor. Disconnect TFI (on 2.3L Truck disconnect DIS pins No. 1-6). On 3.8L AXOD, 3.8L RWD and 7.5L Truck, disconnect TFI and distributor Hall connector. Set DVOM on 200K-ohm scale.

CIRCUIT TEST A1 (Cont.)

On SPOUT circuit, measure resistance between test pin No. 36 (SPOUT) and test pins No. 16, 20, 40, 46, and 60 for short to ground. Measure resistance between test pin No. 36 and test pins No. 26, 37 and 57 for short to power. Measure resistance between test pins No. 36 and 56 for short to PIP.

On PIP circuit, measure resistance between test pin No. 56 and test pins No. 16, 20, 40, 46, and 60 for short to ground. Measure resistance between test pin No. 56 and test pins No. 26, 37 and 57 for short to power. Measure resistance between test pins No. 56 and 36 for short to SPOUT.

If any reading is less than 10K ohms, repair short in harness and repeat QUICK TEST. If engine still does not start, go to next step. If all readings are 10K ohms or more, go to next step.

9) Isolating Shorts In Processor. Turn key off and wait 10 seconds. With breakout box installed, connect ECA, but leave TFI or DIS disconnected. On 3.8L & 7.5L (Truck), disconnect TFI and distributor Hall connector. Set DVOM on 200K ohm scale.

On SPOUT circuit, measure resistance between test pin No. 36 (SPOUT) and test pins No. 37 and 57 for short to power. Measure resistance between test pin No. 36 and test pins No. 40 and 60 for short to ground.

On PIP circuit, measure resistance between test pin No. 56 (PIP) and test pins No. 37 and 57 for short to power. Measure resistance between test pin No. 56 and test pins No. 40 and 60 for short to ground.

If any reading is less than 500 ohms, replace ECA and repeat QUICK TEST. If all readings are greater than 500 ohms, connect TFI and go to next step.

10) Checking PIP Signal. With key off, install breakout box. Set DVOM on 20-volt scale. On 2.3L Truck with DIS, switch timing switch to "DIST" on breakout box. Measure voltage between test pins No. 56 and 16, while cranking engine. If reading is between 3 and 7 volts, remove breakout box. Replace ECA and repeat QUICK TEST. If reading is less than 3 volts or more than 7 volts, go to next step (on 2.3L DIS Truck, switch timing switch on breakout box to "COMPUTED" position).

11) Continuity of PIP Circuit. Install breakout box, turn key off and wait 10 seconds. Set DVOM on 200-ohm scale. Disconnect ECA and TFI (on 2.3L Truck, disconnect DIS pins No. 1-6). On 3.8L SC or 3.0L SHO, disconnect PIP sensor. On 3.8L and 7.5L (Truck), disconnect distributor Hall sensor. Measure resistance between test pin No. 56 and TFI connector PIP circuit. If reading is 5 ohms or more, repair open PIP circuit and repeat QUICK TEST. If readings is less than 5 ohms, go to next step.

12) Verifying SPOUT Signal. Turn key off and wait 10 seconds. Disconnect ECA 60-pin connector and inspect for damaged pins, corrosion, or loose wires. Repair as necessary. Install breakout box and connect ECA. Ensure breakout box timing switch is in "COMPU-TED" position. Set DVOM on 20-volt scale and measure voltage between test pin No. 36 and test pins No. 40 and 60 while cranking engine. If reading is between 3 and 6 volts, go to step 20). If reading is less than 3 volts or more than 6 volts, go to step 8).

CAUTION: Use safety precautions when working on fuel system. No smoking or open flame. If fuel starts leaking, immediately turn key off.

13) Fuel Pump Check. Connect pressure gauge to vehicle. Note initial pressure reading. Pressurize fuel system by turning key on for one second and observe pressure gauge. Turn key off, and wait 10 seconds. Repeat sequence 5 times. If pressure increased, go to CIRCUIT TEST D19, step 1) for MPFI and SEFI fuel injected engines. Go to CIRCUIT TEST D19, step 2) for CFI fuel injected engines. If pressure did not increase, go to next step.

14) Inertia Switch Check. Turn key off. Locate fuel pump inertia switch and ensure push button on switch is pushed down in the "ON" position. Set DVOM on 200-ohm scale. Measure resistance of switch. If resistance is greater than 5 ohms, replace switch. If resistance is less than 5 ohms, go to CIRCUIT TEST D22, step 11) for 2.5L CFI, 3.0L MPFI, and 3.8L MPFI (FWD) engines. Go to CIRCUIT TEST C, step 1) for all other engines.

1989 COMPUTERIZED ENGINE CONTROLS
Ford Motor Co. EEC-IV (Cont.)

1a-437

CIRCUIT TEST A2

VEHICLE BATTERY

NOTE: Perform this test when directed here by CIRCUIT TEST A3, C2, or D13 test procedures.

Vehicle Battery Circuits

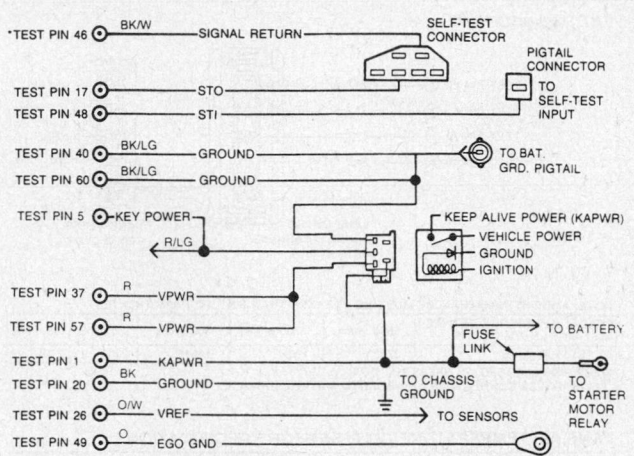

*TEST PINS LOCATED ON BREAKOUT BOX.
ALL HARNESS CONNECTORS VIEWED INTO MATING SURFACE.

Test Pin 17	STO
Application	Wire Color
Car:	
1.9L EFI	T/LB
2.3L TC 3.8L RWD-SEFI 3.8L SEFI SC 5.0L SEFI, Mark VII	Y/BK
2.3L OHC EFI 5.0L MA	T
Truck: F-Series	PK/LG
All Others	T/R

Test Pin 1	KAPWR
Application	Wire Color
Car: 2.3 OHC, EFI 5.0L SEFI, Mark VII 5.0L SEFI-MA Truck: 5.0L EFI, E-Series	BK/O
All Others	Y

Test Pin 48	STI
Application	Wire Color
Car: 2.5L CFI CLC 2.5L CFI MTX 3.0L EFI 3.8L SEFI MA 5.0L SEFI, Crown Victoria and Grand Marquis Town Car	W/BK
All Others	W/R

To prevent replacement of good components, be aware that the following non-EEC related areas may be at fault: battery cables and ground straps, voltage regulator, alternator, or ignition switch. This test is intended to diagnose the ECA, power relay, battery voltage and the following harness circuits:
* Signal Return
* STO
* STI
* Ground
* VPWR
* KAPWR
* VREF
* Ignition

CIRCUIT TEST A2 (Cont.)

1) Battery Voltage Check. Turn key on, leaving engine off. Set DVOM on 20-volt scale and measure voltage across battery terminals. If reading is less than 10.5 volts, service or replace discharged battery. If reading is 10.5 volts or more, go to next step.

2) Checking EEC Ground Circuit. Turn key off and wait 10 seconds. Inspect ECA connector and pins. Install breakout box, leave ECA connected. Set DVOM on 200-ohm scale and measure resistance between test pin No. 40 and negative post on battery. Also measure resistance between test pin No. 60 and negative post on battery. If readings are greater than 5 ohms, repair cause of resistance in circuit(s). Repeat QUICK TEST. If both readings are less than 5 ohms, go to next step.

3) Checking ECA Ground Insolation. With breakout box installed and ECA connected, turn key off and wait 10 seconds. Set DVOM on 200-ohm scale. Measure resistance between test pins No. 46 and 40 and between test pins No. 46 and 60 at breakout box. If both readings are less than 5 ohms, go to next step. If readings are greater than 5 ohms, disconnect ECA connector and inspect for corrosion or damaged pins. Repair if necessary. If fault is still present, replace ECA and repeat QUICK TEST.

4) Continuity of Signal Return Circuit. With breakout box installed and ECA connected, turn key off and wait 10 seconds. Set DVOM on 200-ohm scale. Measure resistance between test pin No. 46 at breakout box and signal return circuit in SELF-TEST connector. If reading is greater than 5 ohms, repair cause of resistance in signal return circuit. Repeat QUICK TEST. If readings is less than 5 ohms, go to next step.

5) Checking KAPWR Circuit. Turn key on, leaving engine off. With ECA connected, set DVOM on 20-volt scale. Measure voltage between battery negative post and test pin No. 1 (KAPWR circuit at EEC power relay). If reading is less than 10.5 volts, check KAPWR and Vehicle Power (VPWR) circuits for shorts to ground. Also check KAPWR circuit from EEC power relay to battery positive post for open circuit. If reading is 10.5 volts or more, go to next step.

6) Ignition Circuit Voltage. Turn key on, leaving engine off. With breakout box and ECA connected, set DVOM on 20-volt scale. Measure voltage between battery negative post and ignition circuit at EEC power relay. If reading is less than 10.5 volts, check for open ignition switch circuits. Repair wiring and repeat QUICK TEST. If reading is 10.5 volts or more, go to next step.

7) Checking Power Relay Ground Circuit Continuity. Turn key off and wait 10 seconds. With ECA connected and DVOM on 200-ohm scale, measure voltage between battery negative post and EEC relay ground. If reading is greater than 5 ohms, repair wiring in ground circuit. Repeat QUICK TEST. If reading is less than 5 ohms, go to next step.

8) Checking Power Circuit (VPWR) at Relay. Turn key on, leaving engine off. With ECA connected and DVOM on 20-volt scale, measure voltage between battery negative post and VPWR circuit at EEC power relay. If reading is 10.5 volts or greater, repair open in VPWR circuit. If okay, repair short to ground in VPWR circuit. If reading is less than 10.5 volts, replace EEC power relay. Repeat QUICK TEST.

CIRCUIT TEST A3

REFERENCE VOLTAGE

NOTE: Perform this test when check of VREF circuit has failed, or directed here by a sensor test or other CIRCUIT TEST.

Reference Voltage Circuits

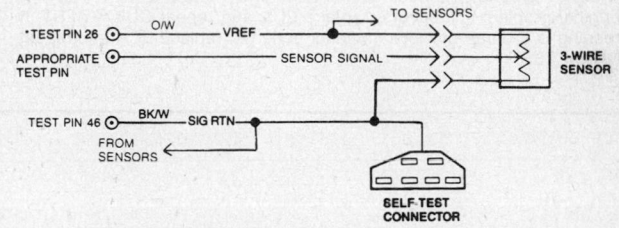

*TEST PINS LOCATED ON BREAKOUT BOX.
ALL HARNESS CONNECTORS VIEWED INTO MATING SURFACE.

1a-438

1989 COMPUTERIZED ENGINE CONTROLS
Ford Motor Co. EEC-IV (Cont.)

CIRCUIT TEST A3 (Cont.)

1) Checking Battery Power Circuit. Disconnect ECA 60-pin connector. Inspect connector for damaged pins, corrosion, or loose wires. Repair if necessary. Install breakout box, leaving ECA connected. Turn key on, leaving engine off. Set DVOM on 20-volt scale and measure voltage between test pin No. 37 and SIGNAL RETURN in SELF-TEST connector. If reading is less than 10.5 volts, go to CIRCUIT TEST D22, step 1) for 2.5L HSC CFI, 3.0L MPFI, 3.0L SHO SEFI, 3.8L FWD SEFI and 3.8L SC SEFI engines. If reading is less than 10.5 volts, go to CIRCUIT TEST A2, step 1) for all other engines. If reading is 10.5 volts or more, go to next step.

2) Checking VREF Voltage. With breakout box installed and ECA connected, turn key on, leaving engine off. Set DVOM on 20-volt scale and measure voltage between test pins No. 26 and 46. If reading is 6 volts or more, go to step 4). If reading is 4 volts or less, go to step 5). If reading is between 4 and 6 volts, go to next step.

3) VREF and Signal Return Continuity. With breakout box installed and ECA disconnected, turn key off. If directed here by a sensor test, ensure that sensor is disconnected. Set DVOM on 200-ohm scale. Measure resistance from test pins No. 26 and 46 to suspect VREF sensor harness connector. If both readings are less than 5 ohms, VREF voltage is okay. Connect all sensors and repeat QUICK TEST. If any reading is 5 ohms or more, repair open circuit in VREF or signal return and then repeat QUICK TEST.

4) Checking For Excess VREF Circuit Voltage. Turn key off and wait 10 seconds. With breakout box installed and ECA disconnected, turn key on, leaving engine off. Set DVOM on 20-volt scale and measure voltage between test pin No. 26 and battery ground. If reading is less than 0.5 volt, replace ECA and repeat QUICK TEST. If reading is 0.5 volt or more, repair short to battery power in EEC harness. Repeat QUICK TEST. Replace ECA if fault still occurs.

5) Shorted TPS Sensor. Turn key off and wait for 10 seconds. With breakout box installed and ECA connected, disconnect Throttle Position Sensor (TPS) from vehicle harness. Turn key on, leaving engine off. Set DVOM on 20-volt scale and measure voltage between test pins No. 26 and 46. If reading is 4 volts or more, replace TPS and repeat QUICK TEST. If less than 4 volts on models with EVP/PFE sensor, go to next step. If reading is less than 4 volts on all other models, go to step 7).

6) Shorted EVP/PFE Sensor. Turn key off and wait 10 seconds. With breakout box installed and ECA connected, disconnect EVP/PFE sensor. Turn key on, leaving engine off. Set DVOM on 20-volt scale. Measure voltage between test pins No. 26 and 46. If reading is 4 volts or more, replace EVP/PFE sensor and repeat QUICK TEST. If reading is less than 4 volts, go to next step.

7) Shorted MAP/BP Sensor. Turn key off and wait 10 seconds. With breakout box installed and ECA connected, disconnect MAP/BP sensor. Turn key on, leaving engine off. Set DVOM on 20-volt scale. Measure voltage between test pins No. 26 and 46. If reading is 4 volts or more, replace MAP/BP sensor and repeat QUICK TEST. If reading is less than 4 volts on models without Vane Airflow (VAF) sensor, go to step 9). If reading is less than 4 volts on models with VAF sensor, go to next step.

8) Shorted VAF Sensor. Turn key off and wait 10 seconds. With breakout box installed and ECA connected, disconnect VAF sensor. Turn key on, leaving engine off. Set DVOM on 20-volt scale. Measure voltage between test pins No. 26 and 46. If reading is 4 volts or more, replace VAF sensor and repeat QUICK TEST. If reading is less than 4 volts, go to next step.

9) VREF Shorted to Ground. With breakout box installed and ECA disconnected, turn key off and wait 10 seconds. Disconnect TPS, MAP/BP, EVP/PFE, and VAF sensor (if equipped). Set DVOM on 200-ohm scale. Measure resistance between test pin No. 26 and test pins No. 20, 40, 46, and 60. If any resistance is less than 5 ohms, repair short to ground, connect all sensors and repeat QUICK TEST. If original problem still occurs, replace ECA and repeat QUICK TEST. If reading is 5 ohms or more, connect sensors, replace ECA and repeat QUICK TEST.

CIRCUIT TEST B1

VANE AIR TEMPERATURE (VAT) SENSOR

NOTE: Perform this test only when service code 24, 28, 54, 58, 64, or 68 is received in QUICK TEST. Ambient air temperature must be at least 50°F (10°C) for test results to be valid. Avoid performing test in unusually hot or cold conditions.

VAT Sensor Circuit

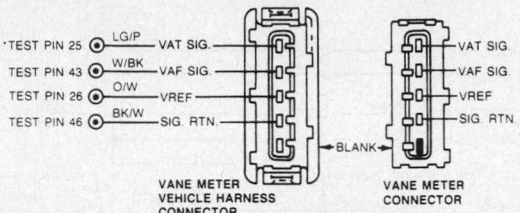

NOTE: AMBIENT TEMPERATURE MUST BE GREATER THAN 50°F TO PASS THIS TEST.

TYPICAL RESISTANCE BETWEEN TEST PINS 25 (OR 43) & 46	5800 ohms	2700 ohms	300 ohms	180 ohms	125 ohms
AT TEMPERATURE	32°F	65°F	185°F	220°F	240°F

*TEST PINS LOCATED ON BREAKOUT BOX.
ALL HARNESS CONNECTORS VIEWED INTO MATING SURFACE.

VANE AIR TEMPERATURE (VAT) SENSOR SPECIFICATIONS

Temperature: F° (C°)	Volts	K Ohms
50 (10)	3.46	3.77
68 (20)	3.07	2.50
86 (30)	2.65	1.70
104 (40)	2.23	1.18
122 (50)	1.84	0.83
140 (60)	1.49	0.60
158 (70)	1.19	0.44
176 (80)	0.95	0.33
194 (90)	0.76	0.25
212 (100)	0.56	0.19
230 (110)	0.46	0.14
248 (120)	0.38	0.11

1) Code 24 or 28: Check Ambient Temperature. Codes 24 and 28 indicate that the VAT sensor is out of Self-Test range. Correct range for measurement is .35-3.5 volts. Possible causes are; low ambient temperature, Faulty VAF meter, faulty ECA, faulty wiring or connector. Ensure ambient air temperature is at least 50°F (10°C). If not, repeat QUICK TEST. If temperature is at least 50°F (10°C), go to next step.

2) Voltage Reference at TPS. Turn key off and wait 10 seconds. Set DVOM on 20-volt scale. Disconnect Throttle Position Sensor (TPS). Turn key on, leaving engine off. Measure voltage at TPS harness connector between VREF and SIG RTN. If reading is less than 4 volts or more than 6 volts, go to CIRCUIT TEST A3, step 1). If reading is between 4 and 6 volts, connect TPS and go to next step.

3) Checking VAT Sensor. Turn key off and wait 10 seconds. Disconnect harness from airflow meter. Set DVOM on 200K-ohm scale. Measure resistance at VAT sensor between VAT and SIG RTN. If resistance is 125 ohms at 240°F (116°C) to 3700 ohms at 50°F (10°C), replace ECA. Connect airflow meter and repeat QUICK TEST. If reading is out of range, repair or replace VAF meter and repeat QUICK TEST.

4) Code 54 or 58: Induce Opposite Code. Service Code 54 and 58 indicate VAT sensor signal is greater than the Self-Test maximum of 3.5 volts (temperature is too low). Possible causes are a lack of continuity between the VAF harness connector and the ECA, a faulty VAF, or a faulty ECA. Turn key off and wait 10 seconds. Disconnect harness from airflow meter. Inspect for and repair any damaged wiring. Install a jumper wire between VAT SIG and SIG RTN at VAF meter connector. Perform KOEO SELF-TEST. If Code 64 or 68 is displayed, replace VAF meter. Remove jumper wire, connect airflow meter, and repeat QUICK TEST. If code 64 or 68 is not displayed, remove jumper wire and go to next step.

5) Checking VAT Signal and Signal Return. Turn key off and wait 10 seconds. With jumper wire removed, leave airflow meter disconnected. Disconnect ECA 60-pin connector. Inspect for and repair any damaged wiring. Install breakout box, leaving ECA disconnected. Set DVOM on 200-ohm scale. Measure resistance between test pin No. 25, at the breakout box and VAT SIG at VAF meter connector. Also measure

1989 COMPUTERIZED ENGINE CONTROLS
Ford Motor Co. EEC-IV (Cont.)

1a-439

CIRCUIT TEST B1 (Cont.)

resistance between test pin No. 46 and signal return at connector. If both readings are less than 5 ohms, replace ECA. Remove breakout box and connect wiring to ECA and airflow meter. Repeat QUICK TEST. If either reading is 5 ohms or more, repair open circuit. Remove breakout box, connect wiring to ECA and airflow meter. Repeat QUICK TEST.

6) Code 64 or 68: Opposite Code Test. Service Code 64 or 68 indicates VAT sensor signal is less than Self-Test minimum value of 0.35 volts. Possible causes of this fault is, VAT signal shorted to signal return, ground, or VREF. A faulty VAF meter or a faulty ECA. Turn key off and wait 10 seconds. Disconnect harness from airflow meter. Inspect for and repair any damaged wiring. Perform KOEO SELF-TEST. If Code 54 or 58 is displayed, replace VAF meter and connect harness. Repeat QUICK TEST. If Code 54 or 58 is not displayed, go to next step.

7) Checking VREF at TPS. Turn key off and wait 10 seconds. Set DVOM on 20-volt scale. Disconnect TPS. Turn key on, leaving engine off. Measure voltage between VREF and SIG RTN at connector. If reading is less than 4 volts or more than 6 volts, go to CIRCUIT TEST A3, step **1)**. If reading is between 4 and 6 volts, connect TPS and go to next step.

8) Checking VAT Signal For Shorts. Turn key off and wait 10 seconds. Leave airflow meter disconnected. Disconnect ECA 60-pin connector. Inspect for and repair any damaged wiring. Install breakout box, leaving ECA disconnected. Set DVOM on 200K-ohm scale. Measure resistance between test pin No. 25 and test pins No. 40, 46, and 60. If any reading is less than 10K ohms, repair shorts. Remove breakout box, connect ECA and airflow meter. Repeat QUICK TEST. If all readings are 10K ohms or more, replace ECA. Remove breakout box and connect ECA. Repeat QUICK TEST.

9) Continuous Code 54 or 58. A Continuous Memory Code 54 or 58 indicates that the VAT signal was greater than the Self-Test maximum of 4.5 volts. The code was set during normal driving conditions. Possible causes for this fault: faulty harness or connectors, ECA or VAF meter. Enter KOEO CONTINUOUS MONITOR (WIGGLE) TEST, observe VOM or diagnostic tester for indication of fault while tapping VAT sensor lightly and wiggling connector. If fault is indicated, inspect connector and terminals. If connector and terminals are good, replace VAT sensor and repeat QUICK TEST. If a fault is not indicated, go to next step.

10) Wiggle Testing Harness. While in CONTINUOUS MONITOR (WIGGLE) TEST, wiggle and bend EEC-IV harness from VAT sensor to cowl, a small section at a time. Also check harness from cowl to ECA. If fault is indicated, isolate fault and repair as necessary. Repeat QUICK TEST. If no fault is found, go to next step.

11) Inspecting ECA Connectors and Terminals. Turn key off and wait 10 seconds. Disconnect ECA 60-pin connector. Inspect both connector and connector terminals for obvious damage. If connectors and terminals are damaged, repair as necessary and repeat QUICK TEST. If connectors and terminals are okay, and you are unable to duplicate fault at this time, clear codes and repeat QUICK TEST.

12) Continuous Codes 64 or 68. A Code 64 or 68 indicates that the VAT signal was less than the Self-Test minimum of 0.3 volt. The code was set during normal driving conditions. Possible causes for this fault: faulty harness or connectors, ECA or VAF meter. Enter KOEO CONTINUOUS MONITOR (WIGGLE) TEST, observe VOM or diagnostic tester for indication of fault while tapping VAT sensor lightly and wiggling connector. If fault is indicated, inspect connector and terminals. If connector and terminals are good, replace VAF meter and repeat QUICK TEST. If no fault is indicated, go back and repeat steps **10)** and **11)**.

CIRCUIT TEST B2

AIR CHARGE TEMPERATURE (ACT) SENSOR

NOTE: Perform this test when Service Code 24, 54, or 64 is displayed during QUICK TESTS or when directed here by other test procedures.

CIRCUIT TEST B2 (Cont.)

Air Charge Temperature (ACT) Sensor Circuit

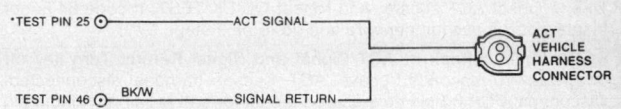

*TEST PINS LOCATED ON BREAKOUT BOX.
ALL HARNESS CONNECTORS VIEWED INTO MATING SURFACE.

Test Pin 25	ACT Signal
Application	**Wire Color**
Truck: 2.3L, 4.9L, 5.0L 5.8L, 7.5L	Y/R
2.3L OHC EFI	LG/R
All Others	LG/P

To prevent replacement of good components, be aware that the following non-EEC related areas may be at fault: cooling system, improper engine oil level, or air cleaner duct problems. Ambient air temperature must be at least 50°F (10°C) for test results to be valid. Avoid performing test in unusually hot or cold conditions.

AIR CHARGE TEMPERATURE (ACT) SENSOR SPECIFICATIONS

Temperature: F° (C°)	Volts	K Ohms
50 (10)	3.51	58.75
68 (20)	3.07	37.30
86 (30)	2.60	24.27
104 (40)	2.13	16.15
122 (50)	1.70	10.97
140 (60)	1.33	7.70
158 (70)	1.02	5.37
176 (80)	0.78	3.84
194 (90)	0.60	2.80
212 (100)	0.46	2.07
230 (110)	0.35	1.55
248 (120)	0.27	1.18

1) Code 24: Checking ACT Sensor. Code 24 indicates that the ACT is out of the Self-Test limit range. Correct range for Self-Test measurement is 0.3-3.7 volts. Possible causes for this code are: ACT resistance out of limits or a faulty ECA. For vehicles with ACT sensor mounted in intake manifold, go to next step. If sensor is properly mounted in air cleaner on all other models, go to next step. If sensor is not properly mounted, install ACT sensor properly and repeat QUICK TEST.

2) Checking VREF at TPS. Turn key off and wait 10 seconds. Set DVOM on 20-volt scale and disconnect TPS. With KOEO, measure voltage between VREF and SIGNAL RETURN at TPS harness connector. If reading is less than 4 volts or more than 6 volts, go to CIRCUIT TEST A3, step **1)**. If reading is between 4 and 6 volts, connect TPS and go to next step.

3) Checking ACT With Engine Off. Start engine and ensure engine reaches normal operating temperature. Turn key off and wait 10 seconds. Disconnect ACT sensor, set DVOM on 200K-ohm scale, and measure ACT sensor resistance. If reading is less than 1100 ohms or more than 58K ohms, check function of heat stove duct valve. If valve is operating correctly, replace ACT sensor. Connect ACT sensor, and repeat QUICK TEST. If reading is between 1100 and 58K ohms, go to next step.

4) Checking ACT With Engine Running. Turn key off. Disconnect ACT sensor harness. Set DVOM on 200K-ohm scale and run engine for 2 minutes. While engine is running, measure ACT sensor resistance. If reading is between 2400 and 29K ohms, replace ECA. Connect ACT harness, and repeat QUICK TEST. If reading is less than 2400 ohms or more than 29K ohms, check function of heat stove duct valve. If valve works properly, replace ACT sensor. Repeat QUICK TEST.

5) Code 54: Generate Code 64. Code 54 indicates the ACT signal is greater than the Self-Test maximum value of 4.6 volts, which could also indicate an open circuit. Possible causes for this code are, open in harness wiring, faulty ACT sensor or faulty ECA. Turn key off and wait 10 seconds. Disconnect ACT sensor harness. Inspect for and repair any damaged wiring. Install a jumper wire between ACT

1a-440

1989 COMPUTERIZED ENGINE CONTROLS
Ford Motor Co. EEC-IV (Cont.)

CIRCUIT TEST B2 (Cont.)

SIGNAL and SIGNAL RETURN at connector. Perform KOEO SELF-TEST. If code 64 is displayed, replace ACT sensor. Remove jumper wire, connect ACT sensor, and repeat QUICK TEST. If code 64 is not displayed, remove jumper wire and go to next step.

6) Continuity Check of ACT Signal and Signal Return. Turn key off and wait 10 seconds. Leave ACT sensor harness disconnected. Disconnect ECA 60-pin connector. Inspect for and repair any damaged wiring. Install breakout box, leaving ECA disconnected. Set DVOM on 200-ohm scale. Measure resistance between test pin No. 25 and ACT SIGNAL at ACT connector, and between test pin No. 46 and SIGNAL RETURN at ACT connector. If both readings are less than 5 ohms, replace ECA and remove breakout box. Connect ECA and ACT sensor, and repeat QUICK TEST. If either reading is 5 ohms or more, repair opens in circuit. Remove breakout box, and connect ECA and ACT sensor. Repeat QUICK TEST.

7) Code 64: Generate Code 54. Code 64 indicates that the ACT signal is less than the Self-Test minimum value of 0.2 volt (grounded circuit). Possible cause for this fault are, faulty ACT sensor, short to ground in harness, faulty ECA. Turn key off and wait 10 seconds. Disconnect ACT sensor. Inspect for and repair any damaged wiring. Perform KOEO SELF-TEST. If code 54 is displayed, replace ACT sensor. Connect harness, and repeat QUICK TEST. If code 54 is not displayed, go to next step.

8) Checking VREF at TPS. Turn key off and wait 10 seconds. Set DVOM on 20-volt scale and disconnect TPS. Turn key on, leaving engine off. Measure voltage at TPS harness connector between VREF and SIGNAL RETURN at TPS connector (refer to wiring diagram for CIRCUIT TEST B8). If reading is less than 4 volts or more than 6 volts, go to CIRCUIT TEST A3, step **1)**. If reading is between 4 and 6 volts, connect TPS and go to next step.

9) Checking ACT Signal for Ground Short. Turn key off and wait 10 seconds. Disconnect harness at ACT sensor. Disconnect ECA 60-pin connector. Inspect for and repair any damaged wiring. Install breakout box and set DVOM on 200K-ohm scale. Measure resistance between test pin No. 25 and test pins No. 40, 46, and 60. If any reading is less than 10K ohms, repair shorts. Remove breakout box, and connect ECA and ACT sensor. Repeat QUICK TEST. If all readings are 10K ohms or more, replace ECA. Remove breakout box, and connect ECA and ACT sensor. Repeat QUICK TEST.

10) Continuous Code 54 Displayed. Code 54 indicates that the ACT signal was greater then the Self-Test maximum value sometime during vehicle operation. Possible causes for this fault are; faulty ACT sensor, open in harness or faulty ECA. Using KOEO CONTINUOUS MONITOR (WIGGLE) TEST, observe VOM or diagnostic tester for indication of fault while tapping ACT sensor lightly and wiggling connector. If fault is indicated, inspect connector and terminals. If connector and terminals are good, replace ACT sensor and repeat QUICK TEST. If no fault is indicated, go to next step.

11) Wiggle Testing ACT Harness. While in CONTINUOUS MONITOR (WIGGLE) TEST, wiggle and bend small sections of harness from ACT sensor to firewall. Repeat action from firewall to ECA. If fault is indicated, isolate fault and repair as necessary. Clear continuous memory codes and repeat QUICK TEST. If no fault is indicated, go to next step.

12) Inspecting Connectors and Terminals. Turn key off and wait 10 seconds. Disconnect ECA 60-pin connector. Inspect both connector and connector terminals for obvious damage. If connectors and terminals are not okay, repair as necessary and repeat QUICK TEST. If connectors and terminals are okay, and you are unable to duplicate fault at this time, clear memory codes and repeat QUICK TEST.

13) Continuous Code 64, Check ACT Sensor. Code 64 indicates that the ACT sensor signal was less than the Self-Test minimum value of 0.2 volt sometime during vehicle operation. Possible causes of this fault are; faulty ACT sensor, open in harness or faulty ECA. Using KOEO CONTINUOUS MONITOR (WIGGLE) TEST, observe VOM or diagnostic tester for indication of fault while tapping ACT sensor lightly and wiggling connector. If fault is indicated, inspect connector and terminals. If connector and terminals are good, replace ACT sensor and repeat QUICK TEST. If no fault is indicated, repeat step **11)**.

CIRCUIT TEST B3

MASS AIRFLOW SENSOR (MAF)

NOTE: Perform this test when Service Code 26, 56, or 66 in displayed in the QUICK TESTS or when directed here by test charts. This test procedure is intended to diagnose only MAF and ECA.

Mass Airflow Sensor (MAF) Circuits

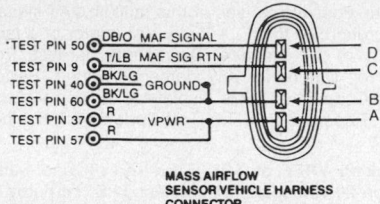

```
•TEST PIN 50    DB/O  MAF SIGNAL         D
TEST PIN 9      T/LB  MAF SIG RTN        C
TEST PIN 40     BK/LG GROUND            B
TEST PIN 60     BK/LG                    A
TEST PIN 37     R     VPWR
TEST PIN 57     R
```

MASS AIRFLOW SENSOR VEHICLE HARNESS CONNECTOR

*TEST PINS LOCATED ON THE BREAKOUT BOX.
NOTE: ALL HARNESS CONNECTORS VIEWED INTO MATING SURFACE.

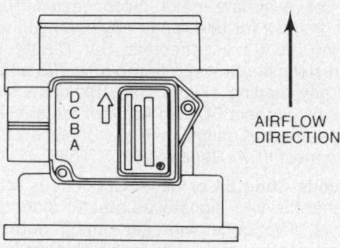

AIRFLOW DIRECTION

MASS AIRFLOW SENSOR

MAF SIGNAL VOLTAGE

Application	Volts
Idle	.80
20 MPH	1.10
40 MPH	1.70
60 MPH	2.10

NOTE: MAF signal voltage is typical for an A/T equipped vehicle at normal operating temperature. Voltage signal may vary do to load and temperature.

To prevent replacement of good components, be aware that the following non-EEC related areas may be at fault: air cleaner element, inlet air duct, or throttle body.

1) KOER Code 26: Out of Range. Code 26 indicates MAF sensor voltage is not in range of .20-1.50 DC volts, and a KOEO or Continuous memory code has been set. Service Code 26 first and then the Continuous memory code (56 or 66). For Code 26, go to next step. For Code 56, go to step **10)**. For Code 66, go to step **4)**.

2) Voltage Check at VPWR Circuit. Turn key off and disconnect MAF sensor from vehicle harness. Set DVOM on 20-volt scale. Measure voltage between VPWR circuit at the MAF sensor connector and the negative battery post. If voltage is greater than 10.5 volts, go to next step. If voltage is less than 10.5 volts, go to CIRCUIT TEST A2, step **1)**.

3) Checking MAF Sensor Ground. With KOEO and MAF sensor disconnected, set DVOM on 20-volt scale. Measure voltage between VPWR circuit and PWR GND circuit at the MAF sensor connector. If voltage is greater than 10.5 volts, go to next step. If voltage is less than 10.5 volts repair open PWR GND circuit, reconnect MAF and rerun QUICK TEST.

4) Code 66: Continuity of MAF Signal and VPWR Circuits. Code 66 indicates that MAF signal was less than .40 volt during engine operation or KOER SELF-TEST. Possible causes for this fault are: open MAF signal circuit, open VPWR circuit to MAF, open PWR GND circuit to MAF, MAF SIGNAL shorted to ground, Faulty ECA or MAF sensor, air leak before or after MAF sensor, or MAF sensor disconnected.

With KOEO and MAF sensor disconnected, disconnect and inspect 60-pin connector. Install breakout box, leaving ECA disconnected. Set DVOM on 200-ohm scale. Measure resistance between MAF SIGNAL

1989 COMPUTERIZED ENGINE CONTROLS
Ford Motor Co. EEC-IV (Cont.)

1a-441

CIRCUIT TEST B3 (Cont.)

at the MAF sensor connector and test pin No. 50 at the breakout box. Measure resistance between VPWR at the MAF sensor connector and test pins No. 37 and 57 at the breakout box. If both resistances are less than 5 ohms, do to next step. If either resistance is greater than 5 ohms, remove breakout box, repair open circuit, reconnect all components and rerun QUICK TEST.

5) Checking MAF Signal Circuit For Shorts. With key off and MAF sensor disconnected, set DVOM on 200K-ohm scale. Disconnect ECA 60-pin connector, inspect connector and terminals. Install breakout box leaving ECA disconnected. Measure resistance between test pin No. 50 and test pins No. 40, 9 and 60, at the breakout box. If all resistances are greater than 10K ohms, go to next step. If resistance in any circuit is below 10K ohms, repair short circuit and rerun QUICK TEST.

6) Checking Continuity of PWR GND Circuit. With key off disconnect MAF sensor. Set DVOM on 200-ohm scale. Measure resistance between PWR GND circuit at MAF sensor connector and battery negative post. If resistance is less than 5 ohms, go to next step. If resistance is greater than 5 ohms, repair open circuit, reconnect MAF sensor and rerun QUICK TEST. If resistance is 5 ohms or less, go to next step.

7) Checking MAF SIG RTN Circuit Continuity. With key off and MAF sensor disconnected, set DVOM on 200-ohm scale. Disconnect ECA 60-pin connector, inspect pins and install breakout box, leave ECA disconnected. Measure resistance between MAF SIG RTN, at sensor connector, and test pin No. 9 at breakout box. If resistance is less than 5 ohms, go to next step. If resistance is more than 5 ohms, remove breakout box. Service open circuit an rerun QUICK TEST.

8) Checking MAF Signal for Short to Ground. With key off, breakout box installed, and ECA connected, disconnect MAF sensor. Set DVOM on 20K-ohm scale. Measure resistance between test pin No. 50 and pins No. 9, 40, and 60 at the breakout box. If all resistances are less than 10K ohms, remove breakout box. Replace ECA and rerun QUICK TEST. If resistances are greater than 10K ohms, go to next step.

9) Checking MAF Output. With key off, install breakout box. Ensure ECA and MAF are connected. Set DVOM on 20 volt scale. Measure voltage between test pin No. 50 and the battery negative post. Start engine. If voltage is .20-1.50 volts replace ECA. If voltage is not .20-1.5, replace MAF sensor.

10) Code 56: Rerun SELF-TEST With MAF Disconnected. With key off, disconnect MAF sensor from vehicle harness. Start engine and allow to idle for one minute. Turn key off. Rerun KOEO SELF-TEST. If Code 66 is present, replace MAF sensor and rerun QUICK TEST. If Code 66 is not present, go to next step.

11) Checking MAF Signal for Short to VPWR. With key off, install breakout box and disconnect MAF sensor and ECA. Set DVOM on 200K-ohm scale. Measure resistance between MAF SIGNAL and VPWR at MAF sensor connector. If resistance is greater than 10K ohms, remove breakout box. Reconnect MAF sensor, replace ECA, and rerun QUICK TEST. If resistance is less than 10K ohms, repair circuit short and rerun QUICK TEST.

CIRCUIT TEST B4

EGR VALVE POSITION (EVP) SENSOR
EGR CONTROL (EGRC) SOLENOID &
EGR VENT (EGRV) SOLENOID

NOTE: Perform this test when Service Code 31, 32, 33, 34, 35, 83, or 84 is displayed during QUICK TESTS or when directed here by other test procedures.

To prevent replacement of good components, be aware that the following non-EEC related area may be at fault: damaged EGR valve.

1) KOER Code 31. Code 31 indicates that during the KOER SELF-TEST the EVP sensor signal was out of range with the EGR valve in the closed position. Possible causes for this code are a faulty EGRC/EGRV solenoids or a clogged EGRV filter. Turn key off and wait 10 seconds. Disconnect and plug vacuum line at EGR valve. Perform KOER SELF-TEST. If Code 31 is not displayed, reconnect vacuum and go to step **8)**. If Code 31 is displayed, go to next step. Ignore all other service codes at this time.

CIRCUIT TEST B4 (Cont.)

EVP, EGRC & EGRV Solenoid Circuits

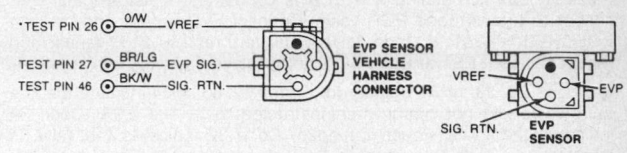

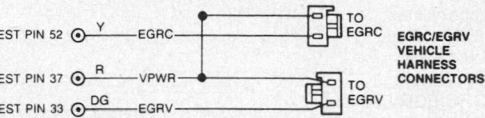

*TEST PINS LOCATED ON BREAKOUT BOX.
ALL HARNESS CONNECTORS VIEWED INTO MATING SURFACE.

EVP SENSOR SPECIFICATIONS

EGR Valve Opening (%)	EVP Sensor Voltage
0	0.40
10	0.75
20	1.10
30	1.45
40	1.80
50	2.15
60	2.50
70	2.85
80	3.20
90	3.55
100	3.90

2) KOEO Code 31: Checking EVP Resistance With Vacuum Applied. Code 31 displayed during the KOEO SELF-TEST indicates that the EVP sensor signal was out of range with the EGR valve in the closed position. Possible causes for this code are, an open or shorted circuit, faulty EGR valve, faulty EVP sensor, or a faulty ECA. Turn key off and wait 10 seconds. Leave EGR vacuum line disconnected and plugged. Disconnect EVP sensor harness. Set DVOM on 200K-ohm scale and connect vacuum pump to EGR valve. Measure resistance between EVP SIG and VREF at EVP connector while vacuum is slowly increased to 10 in. Hg. If reading is less than 100 ohms or more than 5500 ohms, replace EVP sensor. Connect vacuum line and harness. Repeat QUICK TEST. If reading does not decrease or valve does not hold vacuum, go to step **11)**. If reading gradually decreases from a maximum of 5500 ohms to a minimum of 100 ohms, go to next step.

3) Checking EVP Signal for Shorts to VREF and SIG RTN. With KOEO, disconnect harness from EVP sensor. Set DVOM on 20-volt scale. Measure voltage between VREF and SIG RTN at EVP connector. If reading is less than 4 volts or more than 6 volts, go to CIRCUIT TEST A3, step **1)**. If reading is between 4 and 6 volts, go to next step.

4) Checking EVP Signal Continuity. Turn key off and wait 10 seconds. Disconnect harness at EVP sensor and ECA 60-pin connector. Inspect for and repair any damaged wiring. Install breakout box, leaving ECA disconnected. Set DVOM on 200-ohm scale. Measure resistance between test pin No. 27 and EVP SIG at EVP connector. If reading is 5 ohms or more, repair open in circuit. Remove breakout box, connect ECA and EVP sensor, and repeat QUICK TEST. If reading is less than 5 ohms, go to next step.

5) Checking EVP Signal Circuit for Shorts. Turn key off and disconnect harness at EVP sensor. Install breakout box, leaving ECA disconnected. Set DVOM on 200K-ohm scale. Measure resistance between test pin No. 27 and test pins No. 26, 40, 46, and 60. If any reading is less than 10K ohms, repair short circuit. Remove breakout box, connect ECA and EVP sensor. Repeat QUICK TEST. If all readings are 10K ohms or more, go to next step.

6) EVP Sensor and EGR Valve Substitution Test. Turn key off and wait 10 seconds. Connect known good EVP sensor and EGR valve assembly to harness and vacuum lines. Connect ECA to breakout box. Perform KOEO SELF-TEST. If code 31 is displayed, replace ECA. Connect original EVP sensor and EGR valve assembly. Repeat QUICK TEST. If Code 31 is not displayed, go to next step.

1a-442

1989 COMPUTERIZED ENGINE CONTROLS
Ford Motor Co. EEC-IV (Cont.)

CIRCUIT TEST B4 (Cont.)

7) Testing EVP Sensor. Turn key off and wait 10 seconds. Ensure breakout box is installed and ECA is connected. Install original EVP sensor to known good EGR valve. Connect EVP sensor and perform KOEO SELF-TEST. If Code 31 is displayed, replace EVP sensor and repeat QUICK TEST. If Code 31 is not displayed, service EGR system.

8) Codes 32, 33, or 34 Displayed. Codes 32, 33 or 34 indicate that the EGR valve did not open when instructed to by the ECA. Code 34 indicates the valve would not open. Code 32 indicates the valve is stuck open. Code 33 indicates the valve would not close correctly. Possible causes for these faults are as follows:
- Faulty vacuum lines.
- Clogged EGRV filter.
- Faulty EVP sensor.
- Faulty EGR valve.
- Faulty EGRC/EGRV solenoid.
- Faulty ECA.

With key off, disconnect vacuum line at the EGR valve. Connect a vacuum gauge to the vacuum line, leaving the EGR valve disconnected. Observe vacuum gauge while running KOER SELF-TEST. Disregard all other codes produced during this test. If vacuum reading increased from less than one in. Hg to greater than 5 in. Hg and, within 10 seconds, returned to less than one in. Hg go to step **10)**. If vacuum did not increase, go to next step. If vacuum increased but did not return to less than one in. Hg, check EGRV filter for obstructions, replace filter or solenoid as necessary. Reconnect all vacuum lines and rerun QUICK TEST.

9) Checking Vacuum Supply to EGRC/EGRV Solenoids. With key off, disconnect vacuum scource to EGRC/EGRV solenoids. Install a vacuum gauge at the source vacuum line. Start engine and check vacuum. If vacuum is greater than 10 in. Hg, check vacuum line from EGRC/EGRV solenoids to EGR valve for blockage, leaks or damage, replace as necessary. If supply line is okay, replace solenoid assembly and rerun QUICK TEST. If vacuum was below specification, check vacuum source and repair as necessary.

10) Checking EVP Resistance. With key off, disconnect EVP sensor harness. Inspect for and repair any damaged wiring. Set DVOM on 200K-ohm scale. Disconnect vacuum line at EGR valve and connect vacuum pump to valve. Measure resistance of EVP sensor between EVP signal and VREF terminals while increasing vacuum to 10 in. Hg If reading slowly decreases from maximum of 5500 ohms to minimum of 100 ohms, replace ECA. Connect EVP sensor and EGR vacuum line. Repeat QUICK TEST. If reading does not slowly decrease, go to next step.

11) Manual Test of EVP Sensor. With key off, disconnect EVP sensor harness. Remove EVP sensor and vacuum line from EGR valve. Measure resistance of EVP SIG and VREF at the connector while sensor shaft is slowly pushed in and slowly released. If reading increases and decreases smoothly in range of 100-5500 ohms, service or replace EGR valve assembly. Connect EVP sensor and EGR vacuum line. Repeat QUICK TEST. If either reading changes abruptly during range of 100-5500 ohms, replace EVP sensor. Reconnect harness and EGR vacuum line. Repeat QUICK TEST.

NOTE: It is normal for EVP sensor total resistance to drop to less than 100 ohms when disconnected from EGR valve. A defective sensor will change resistance suddenly between 5500 and 100 ohms.

12) Code 83 or 84 Displayed: Checking EGRV/EGRC Solenoid Resistance. A Code 83 indicates an EGRC circuit failure. A Code 84 indicates an EGRV circuit failure. Possible causes for these faults are an open or shorted circuit, a faulty EGRC/EGRV solenoid or a faulty ECA.
Turn key off and wait 10 seconds. Set DVOM on 200-ohm scale. Disconnect EGRC and EGRV solenoids from harness. Inspect for and repair any damaged wiring. Measure resistance of both solenoids. If either reading is less than 30 ohms or more than 70 ohms, replace EGRC/EGRV solenoid assembly. Repeat QUICK TEST. If both readings are between 30 and 70 ohms, reconnect solenoids and go to next step.

13) Checking VPWR at EGRC/EGRV Solenoids. Disconnect EGRC and EGRV solenoids from harness. Turn key on, leaving engine off. Set DVOM on 20-volt scale. Measure voltage between battery negative terminal and VPWR circuit for both solenoids. If either reading is less than 10.5 volts, repair open circuit and repeat QUICK TEST. If both readings are 10.5 volts or more, go to next step.

CIRCUIT TEST B4 (Cont.)

14) Continuity Check. Turn key off and wait 10 seconds. Leave EGRC and EGRV solenoids disconnected. Disconnect ECA 60-pin connector. Inspect for and repair any damaged wiring. Install breakout box, leaving ECA disconnected. Set DVOM on 200-ohm scale. Measure resistance between test pin No. 33 and EGRV signal at EGRV solenoid connector. Measure resistance between test pin No. 52 and EGRC signal at EGRC solenoid connector. If either reading is 5 ohms or more, repair open circuit. Remove breakout box, connect ECA solenoids, and repeat QUICK TEST. If both readings are less than 5 ohms, go to next step.

15) Checking For Shorts To Ground. Turn key off and wait 10 seconds. Set DVOM on 200K-ohm scale. Install breakout box, leaving ECA disconnected. Disconnect EGRC and EGRV solenoids. Measure resistance between test pin No. 33 and test pins No. 40, 46, and 60. Measure resistance between test pin No. 52 and test pins No. 40, 46, and 60. If readings are less than 10K ohms, repair short to ground. Repeat QUICK TEST. If readings are 10K ohms or more, go to next step.

16) Checking For Shorts To Power. With key off, disconnect EGRC and EGRV solenoids from harness. Install breakout box, leaving ECA disconnected. Set DVOM on 200K-ohm scale. Measure resistance between test pin No. 33 and test pins No. 37 and 57. Measure resistance between test pin No. 52 and test pins No. 37 and 57. If any reading is less than 10K ohms, repair short in circuit. Remove breakout box and connect ECA. Repeat QUICK TEST. If all resistances are greater than 10K ohms, replace ECA. Remove breakout box and connect ECA. Repeat QUICK TEST.

17) Code 35: RPM To Low For EGR Test. This code indicates that engine RPM is too low for correct EGR testing. Possible causes for this fault are a faulty ISC system or a faulty ECA.
If Code 12 is also displayed go to CIRCUIT TEST D5, step **1)**. If Code 12 is not displayed with Code 35, go to next step.

18) Retest at 1500 RPM. Turn key off and wait 10 seconds. Install tachometer. Perform KOER SELF-TEST at 1500 RPM. Ignore all other codes at this time. Record KOER service codes. If code 35 is displayed, replace ECA. Clear codes and repeat QUICK TEST. If code 35 is not displayed, clear codes and repeat QUICK TEST and repair codes as necessary.

19) Continuous Code 31 Displayed. Continuous Code 31 indicates that sometime during vehicle operation the EVP signal was out of the Self-Test range. Possible causes for this fault are an open or shorted circuit or a faulty EVP sensor.
Using KOEO CONTINUOUS MONITOR (WIGGLE) TEST, observe VOM or diagnostic tester for indication of fault while doing the following: connect vacuum pump to EGR valve. Very slowly apply 6 in. Hg vacuum to EGR valve. Bleed vacuum slowly and lightly tap on EVP sensor. Wiggle EVP sensor connector. If fault is indicated, go to next step. If no fault is indicated, go to step **21)**.

20) EVP Signal Voltage During Operation. Turn key off and wait 10 seconds. Disconnect ECA 60-pin connector. Inspect for and repair any damaged wiring. Install breakout box and connect ECA. Stay in KOEO CONTINUOUS MONITOR (WIGGLE) TEST. Connect DVOM between test pins No. 27 and 46. Set DVOM on 20-volt scale. Turn key on, leaving engine off. Repeat step **19)** while watching voltage. If fault occurs below 4.25 volts, disconnect EVP sensor from harness. Inspect for and repair any damaged wiring. If wiring is okay, replace EVP sensor. Clear codes and repeat QUICK TEST. If fault does not occur below 4.25 volts, EGR valve overshoot may have caused Continuous Memory Code 31. Sensor test is complete. Go to next step for harness test.

21) Checking Harness. While in KOEO CONTINUOUS MONITOR (WIGGLE) TEST, bend, shake, and wiggle small sections of EEC-IV harness from sensor to firewall and from firewall to ECA. If fault is indicated, isolate fault and repair as necessary. Clear codes and repeat QUICK TEST. If no fault is indicated, go to next step.

22) Checking ECA and Harness Connectors. Turn key off and wait 10 seconds. Disconnect ECA 60-pin connector. Inspect both connector and terminals for obvious damage. If connector and terminals are damaged, repair as necessary and repeat QUICK TEST. If connector and terminals are okay, fault cannot be duplicated at this time. Continuous Code 31 testing is complete.

1989 COMPUTERIZED ENGINE CONTROLS
Ford Motor Co. EEC-IV (Cont.)

1a-443

CIRCUIT TEST B5

ENGINE COOLANT TEMPERATURE (ECT) SENSOR

NOTE: Perform this test when directed to by a Code 21, 51, or 61 during QUICK TEST procedure. For purposes of this test, a "warmed up" engine has a coolant temperature of 50-240°F (10-116°C) for KOEO SELF-TEST and 180-240°F (82-116°C) for KOER SELF-TEST. The test procedure will be invalid outside these ranges.

Engine Coolant Temperature (ECT) Sensor Circuit

*TEST PIN 7 — LG/Y — ECT SIGNAL

TEST PIN 46 — BK/W — SIGNAL RETURN

ECT VEHICLE HARNESS CONNECTOR

*TEST PINS LOCATED ON BREAKOUT BOX.
ALL HARNESS CONNECTORS VIEWED INTO MATING SURFACE.

ECT SENSOR SPECIFICATIONS

Temperature F° (C°)	Voltage	Resistance K-Ohms
248 (120)	.27	1.18
230 (110)	.35	1.55
212 (100)	.46	2.07
194 (90)	.60	2.80
176 (80)	.78	3.84
158 (70)	1.02	5.37
140 (60)	1.33	7.70
122 (50)	1.70	10.97
104 (40)	2.13	16.15
86 (30)	2.60	24.27
68 (20)	3.07	37.30
50 (10)	3.51	58.75

To prevent replacement of good components, be aware that the following non-EEC related areas may be at fault: coolant or oil level, blocked or obstructed airflow, engine not at normal operating temperature, or cooling fan.

1) Code 21: Check Engine Temperature. Code 21 indicates that the ECT is out of the 0.3-3.5 volt Self-Test range. Possible causes for this fault are ECT resistance out of limits or a faulty ECA. If engine will not start, go to step **4)**. Start engine and run at 2000 RPM for 2 minutes. Check that upper radiator hose is hot and pressurized. Repeat QUICK TEST before continuing. If vehicle stalls, DO NOT service code 21 at this time, go directly to DIAGNOSIS BY SYMPTOM TEST. If code 21 is not displayed, service other codes as necessary (if displayed). If code 21 appears, go to next step.

2) Checking for VREF at TPS. Refer to wiring diagram in CIRCUIT TEST B8. Turn key off and wait 10 seconds. Disconnect TPS. Set DVOM on 20-volt scale. With KOEO measure voltage at TPS harness connector between VREF and SIGNAL RETURN. If voltage is less than 4 volts or more than 6 volts, go to CIRCUIT TEST A3, step 1). If voltage is between 4 and 6 volts, reconnect TPS and go to next step.

3) ECT Sensor Resistance. Ensure engine is fully warmed up for this step. Turn key off and wait 10 seconds. Disconnect wiring harness at ECT sensor. Set DVOM on 200K-ohm scale and measure resistance of ECT sensor. If reading is 1300-7700 ohms at engine coolant temperature of 140-240°F (60-116°C) with engine off and 1550-4550 ohms at 180-230°F (82-110°C) with engine running, replace ECA, connect ECT sensor and repeat QUICK TEST. If readings are not correct for coolant temperature, replace ECT sensor, connect harness, and repeat QUICK TEST.

4) Checking ECT Resistance: No Start Condition. With key off, disconnect ECT sensor and set DVOM on 200K-ohm scale. Measure resistance of ECT sensor. If resistance is within specifications, DO NOT service Code 21 at this time. Go to CIRCUIT TEST A1. If resistance is not within specification, replace ECT sensor.

5) Code 51: Generate Code 61. Code 51 indicates that the ECT signal was greater than the Self-Test maximum value of 4.6 volts (open circuit). Possible causes for this fault are a faulty ECT sensor, open circuit or faulty ECA.

CIRCUIT TEST B5 (Cont.)

Turn key off and wait 10 seconds. Disconnect ECT sensor at wiring harness and inspect wiring for damage or corrosion. Connect a jumper wire between ECT SIGNAL and SIGNAL RETURN terminals in sensor harness connector. Repeat KOEO SELF-TEST. If Code 61 is displayed, replace ECT sensor and remove jumper wire. Reconnect harness to ECT sensor and repeat QUICK TEST. If Code 61 is not displayed, remove jumper wire and go to next step.

6) ECT Signal and Return Continuity Check. Turn key off and wait 10 seconds. With harness disconnected at ECT sensor and jumper removed from harness connector, disconnect ECA 60-pin connector. Inspect for and repair any damaged wiring. Install breakout box, leaving ECA disconnected. Set DVOM on 200-ohm scale. Measure resistance between ECT SIGNAL at ECT connector and test pin No. 7. Measure resistance between SIGNAL RETURN at ECT connector and test pin No. 46. If both readings are less than 5 ohms, replace ECA. Remove breakout box and connect ECA and ECT sensor. Repeat QUICK TEST. If either reading is 5 ohms or more, repair open circuits. Remove breakout box, and connect ECA and ECT sensor. Repeat QUICK TEST.

7) Code 61: Generate Code 51. Code 61 indicates that the ECT signal is less than the 0.2 volt Self-Test minimum value (grounded circuit). Possible causes of this fault are a faulty ECT, grounded circuit or faulty ECA. Turn key off and wait 10 seconds. Disconnect ECT sensor and inspect connector for damage or corrosion. Repair wiring and repeat KOEO SELF-TEST. If Code 51 is displayed, replace ECT sensor, connect sensor, and repeat QUICK TEST. If Code 51 is not displayed, go to next step.

8) Checking VREF at TPS. Refer to wiring diagram in CIRCUIT TEST B8. Turn key off and wait 10 seconds. Set DVOM on 20-volt scale. Disconnect TPS. Turn key on, leaving engine off. Measure voltage between VREF and SIGNAL RETURN at TPS connector. If reading is less than 4 volts or more than 6 volts, go to CIRCUIT TEST A3, step 1). If voltage is between 4 and 6 volts, connect TPS and go to next step.

9) Checking ECT Signal for Short to Ground. Turn key off and wait 10 seconds. Disconnect harness from ECT sensor. Disconnect ECA 60-pin connector. Inspect for and repair any damaged wiring. Install breakout box, leaving ECA disconnected. Set DVOM on 200K-ohm scale. Measure resistance between test pin No. 7 and test pins No. 40, 46, and 60. If any reading is less than 10K ohms, repair short circuits. Remove breakout box, connect ECA and ECT sensor, and repeat QUICK TEST. If all readings are 10K ohms or more, replace ECA. Remove breakout box, connect ECA and ECT sensor. Repeat QUICK TEST.

10) Continuous Code 51: Check ECT Sensor. Code 51 indicates that the ECT signal was greater than the Self-Test maximum voltage of 4.6 volts sometime during vehicle operation.
Using KOEO CONTINUOUS MONITOR (WIGGLE) TEST, observe VOM or diagnostic tester for indication of fault while tapping ECT sensor and wiggling ECT connector. If fault is indicated, disconnect and inspect ECT connector and terminals. If connector and terminals are okay, replace ECT sensor. Clear codes and repeat QUICK TEST. If no fault is indicated, go to next step.

11) Checking Harness. While in KOEO CONTINUOUS MONITOR (WIGGLE) TEST, observe VOM or diagnostic tester for indication of fault as you bend, shake or wiggle EEC-IV harness. Start at sensor connector and work toward firewall. Also test harness from firewall to ECA in same manner. If fault is indicated, isolate fault in wiring and repair as necessary. Clear codes and repeat QUICK TEST. If fault is not indicated, go to next step.

12) Checking ECA and Harness Connectors. Turn key off and wait 10 seconds. Disconnect ECA 60-pin connector. Inspect both connectors and terminals for obvious damage. If connectors and terminals are damaged, repair as necessary and repeat QUICK TEST. If connectors and terminals are okay, fault cannot be duplicated at this time. Go to next step.

13) Continuous Code 61: Check ECT Sensor. Code 61 indicates that the ECT signal was less than the 0.2 volt Self-Test minimum value (grounded circuit) sometime during vehicle operation. Possible causes of this fault are; faulty ECT, grounded circuit or faulty ECA. Using KOEO CONTINUOUS MONITOR (WIGGLE) TEST, observe VOM or diagnostic tester for indication of fault while tapping ECT sensor and wiggling ECT connector. If fault is indicated, disconnect and inspect ECT connector and terminals. If connector and terminals are okay, replace ECT sensor and repeat QUICK TEST. If no fault is indicated, repeat steps 10) and 11).

1a-444

1989 COMPUTERIZED ENGINE CONTROLS
Ford Motor Co. EEC-IV (Cont.)

CIRCUIT TEST B6

MANIFOLD ABSOLUTE PRESSURE (MAP)/ BAROMETRIC PRESSURE (BP) SENSOR

NOTE: This test should be performed when Service Code 22 or 72 is displayed in QUICK TEST procedures, or when directed here by CIRCUIT TEST D20 or other symptom. Barometric pressure sensor output is digital and must be measured with an oscilloscope or MAP/BP tester.

MAP/BP Tester Hook-Up

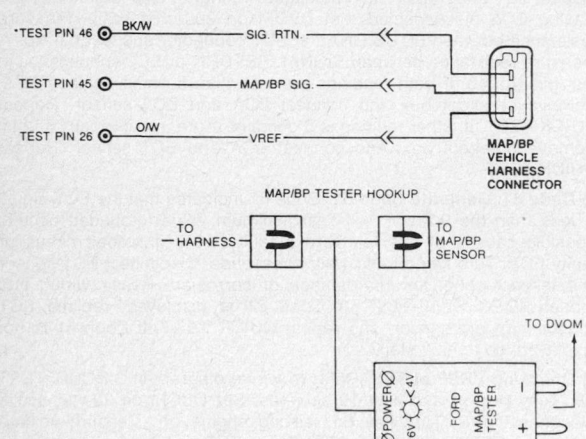

* TEST PINS LOCATED ON BREAKOUT BOX.
ALL HARNESS CONNECTORS VIEWED INTO MATING SURFACE.

Test Pin 45 Manifold Absolute/Barometric Pressure	
Application	Wire Colors
3.8L RWD SEFI 5.0L SEFI All Trucks	DB/LG
All Other Passenger Cars	LG/BK

MAP SENSOR SPECIFICATIONS

Manifold Vacuum In. Hg	Frequency Hz
0	80
3	88
6	95
9	102
12	109
15	117
18	125
21	133
24	141
27	150
30	159

MAP/BP SENSOR SPECIFICATIONS

Barometric Pressure In. Hg	Frequency Hz
17.1	122.4
18.3	125.5
19.5	128.7
20.7	131.9
21.8	135.1
23.0	138.3
24.2	141.8
25.4	145.4
26.6	148.9
27.7	152.5
28.9	156.1
30.1	159.6
31.0	162.4

CIRCUIT TEST B6 (Cont.)

To prevent replacement of good components, be aware that the following non-EEC related areas may be at fault: unusually high/low atmospheric barometer reading, kinked or blocked vacuum lines, or engine condition (valves, vacuum leaks, valve timing, EGR valve, etc.).

1) KOEO Code 22. Code 22 indicates that the MAP/BP sensor is out of Self-Test voltage range (1.4-1.6 volts). Possible causes of this code are:
- MAP/BP signal circuit open between sensor and ECA.
- MAP/BP signal circuit shorted to VREF, SIG RTN or ground.
- Faulty MAP/BP sensor.
- High atmospheric pressure.
- Faulty ECA.
- VREF circuit open at sensor.
- SIG RTN open at sensor.

Turn key off. Disconnect MAP/BP sensor from harness. Connect MAP/BP tester between wiring harness and MAP/BP sensor. Connect banana plugs of tester into DVOM and set DVOM on 20-volt scale. See MAP/BP TESTER HOOK-UP illustration. Go to next step.

2) Checking Power to Sensor. With MAP/BP tester connected, turn key on. If only Green light on tester is lit, VREF is correct, go to step **4)**. If "LESS THAN 4 VOLTS" Red light or no lights come on, VREF is too low. If "MORE THAN 6 VOLTS" Red light comes on, VREF is too high. If VREF is too high or too low, go to next step.

3) VREF Testing. With MAP/BP tester connected, turn key on. Disconnect MAP/BP sensor and repeat step **2)**. If only Green light comes on, VREF is correct. Replace MAP/BP sensor and repeat QUICK TEST. If "LESS THAN 4 VOLTS" Red light or no lights come on, VREF is too low. If "MORE THAN 6 VOLTS" Red light comes on, VREF is too high. If VREF is too high or too low, remove MAP/BP tester, connect sensor, then go to CIRCUIT TEST A3, step **1)**.

4) Tester Output Reading. With MAP/BP tester connected and key on, measure sensor output voltage. If voltage output is in correct range for altitude of vehicle being tested, remove MAP/BP tester and go to next step. If output reading is outside range, remove MAP/BP tester and go to step **6)**.

NOTE: Measure several known good MAP/BP sensors on available vehicles. Average voltage reading will be typical for your location on date of testing.

MAP SENSOR VOLTAGE OUTPUT

Elevation (Ft.)	Volts
0	1.55-1.63
1000	1.52-1.60
2000	1.49-1.57
3000	1.46-1.54
4000	1.43-1.51
5000	1.40-1.48
6000	1.37-1.45
7000	1.35-1.43

5) Checking Signal Continuity. Turn key off and wait 10 seconds. Disconnect MAP/BP sensor from harness. Disconnect ECA 60-pin connector. Inspect for and repair any damaged wiring. Install breakout box, leaving ECA disconnected. Set DVOM on 200-ohm scale. Measure resistance between MAP/BP signal at sensor connector and test pin No. 45. If reading is less than 5 ohms, replace ECA. Connect ECA and MAP/BP sensor and repeat QUICK TEST. If reading is 5 ohms or higher, repair opens in wiring. Remove breakout box, connect ECA and MAP/BP sensor. Repeat QUICK TEST.

6) Checking MAP/BP Signal For Shorts. Turn key off and wait 10 seconds. Disconnect ECA 60-pin connector. Inspect for and repair any damaged wiring. Install breakout box, leaving ECA disconnected. Disconnect harness at MAP/BP sensor. Set DVOM on 200K-ohm scale. Measure resistance between test pin No. 45 and test pins No. 26, 46, 40, and 60. If any reading is less than 10K ohms, repair shorts in wiring. Remove breakout box and connect ECA and MAP/BP sensor. Repeat QUICK TEST. If all readings are 10K ohms or more, replace MAP/BP sensor. Remove breakout box and connect all wiring. Repeat QUICK TEST.

7) Code 22: Check for EGR Codes. Check to see if Service Codes 31, 32, 33, 34 or 35 are present. If so, go to KOER SELF-TEST table and perform appropriate CIRCUIT TEST. If not, go to next step.

8) Checking MAP Sensor. Turn key off and wait 10 seconds. Disconnect vacuum hose from MAP sensor. Connect vacuum pump to

1989 COMPUTERIZED ENGINE CONTROLS
Ford Motor Co. EEC-IV (Cont.)

1a-445

CIRCUIT TEST B6 (Cont.)

MAP sensor and apply 18 in. Hg vacuum to sensor. If sensor does not hold vacuum, replace sensor, connect vacuum line and repeat QUICK TEST. If MAP sensor does hold vacuum, release vacuum and go to next step.

9) Eliminating Code 22. Turn key off and wait 10 seconds. Plug vacuum hose going to MAP sensor. Start engine and run at 1400-1600 RPM. Slowly apply 15 in. Hg. vacuum to MAP sensor. With engine under these operating conditions, perform KOER SELF-TEST. Check for Code 22, disregard any other codes at this time. If Code 22 is still present, replace MAP sensor. If Code 22 is no longer displayed, inspect vacuum hose going to MAP sensor. If okay, service other codes at this time. If there are none, check engine for cause of low vacuum.

10) Code 72: Check Vacuum Lines. Code 72 indicates that MAP sensor output did not change enough during dynamic response ("Goose") test. Possible causes for this code are an incorrect MAP sensor vacuum line routing or a faulty MAP sensor.

With key on, check vacuum lines for correct routing. Check for dis connections, kinks or blockage. Repair vacuum lines as necessary. If vacuum lines are okay, go to next step.

11) Checking MAP Sensor. Test MAP sensor as described in step **8)**. If MAP sensor does hold vacuum, release vacuum and go to next step.

12) Checking Vacuum Supply During "Goose" Test. Turn key off, wait 10 seconds. Use a "T" fitting to install a vacuum gauge in the intake manifold MAP sensor supply line. Run the KOER SELF-TEST while observing the vacuum gauge. If vacuum decreased by more than 10 in. Hg during dynamic response ("Goose") test, remove gauge, replace MAP sensor and rerun QUICK TEST. If vacuum did not decrease by 10 in. Hg or more, repair engine mechanical components as necessary to increase engine vacuum.

13) Continuous Code 22: Operating MAP/BP Sensor. Continuous Code 22 indicates the MAP/BP sensor was out of Self-Test range (1.4-1.6 volts) during normal driving conditions. Possible causes for this code are a faulty MAP/BP sensor, faulty wiring harness or connectors, and unusually high or low barometric pressure.

In KOEO CONTINUOUS MONITOR TEST mode, observe test equip-ment while performing the following:
- Connect a vacuum pump to the MAP/BP sensor.
- Slowly apply 25 in. Hg vacuum to sensor.
- Slowly bleed off vacuum from sensor.
- Lightly tap on sensor (to simulate road shock).
- "Wiggle" sensor connector.

If a fault is indicated disconnect sensor and inspect connectors. Repair as necessary. If connectors are okay, replace MAP/BP sensor. If a fault is not indicated, go to next step.

14) Checking Harness. Stay in KOEO CONTINUOUS MONITOR (WIGGLE) TEST. Observe VOM or diagnostic tester for indication of fault while shaking, bending or wiggling small sections of harness from sensor connector to firewall. Check harness from firewall to ECA in same manner. If fault is indicated, isolate fault in harness and repair as necessary. Clear codes and repeat QUICK TEST. If no fault is indicated, go to next step.

15) Checking ECA Connector and Harness. Turn key off and wait 10 seconds. Disconnect ECA 60-pin connector. Inspect both connectors and terminals for obvious damage. If connectors and terminals are not okay, repair as necessary. Repeat QUICK TEST. If connectors and terminals are okay, fault cannot be duplicated at this time. Continuous Code 22 testing is complete.

CIRCUIT TEST B7

KNOCK SENSOR (KS)

NOTE: Perform this test when Service Code 25 is received during QUICK TEST procedure or you are directed here by other diagnostic tests. Use DYNAMIC RESPONSE CHECK as specified in steps 1) and 6). There is no need to perform WOT during this test. For additional information see QUICK TEST DIAGNOSTIC AIDS, DYNAMIC RESPONSE CHECK in front of this article.

CIRCUIT TEST B7 (Cont.)

Knock (Detonation) Sensor Circuit

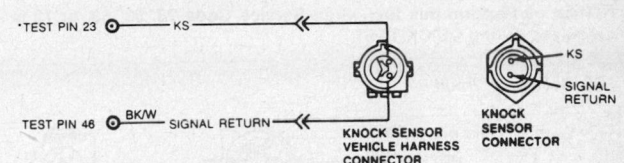

*TEST PINS LOCATED ON BREAKOUT BOX.
ALL HARNESS CONNECTORS VIEWED INTO MATING SURFACE.

Test Pin 23	KS Signal
Application	Wire Color
Car: 2.3L OHC 2.3L TC 3.0L SHO-MA 3.8L SUP-CHG	Y/R
Truck: 4.9L/5.0L	LG/BK

To prevent replacement of good components, be aware that the following non-EEC related areas may be at fault: fuel quality, engine condition (valves, vacuum leaks, valve timing, EGR valve, etc.) and spark timing.

1) Code 25: Generate Knock Manually. Code 25 indicates that the Knock Sensor (KS) signal was not sensed during the dynamic response ("Goose") test after the engine ID code in the KOER SELF-TEST. Possible causes for this fault are a faulty KS, open or shorted harness or faulty ECA. Have 4 oz. hammer ready. Ensure engine is at normal operating temperature. Perform KOER SELF-TEST. When DYNAMIC RESPONSE CHECK signal appears, lightly tap above knock sensor with 4 oz. hammer. Do Not "Goose" throttle. After 15 seconds, check for Code 25. Ignore all other codes at this time. If code 25 is displayed, go to next step. If Code 25 is not displayed, knock system is okay. Repeat KOER SELF-TEST and service other codes.

2) Circuit Voltage Check. Turn key off and wait 10 seconds. Disconnect knock sensor. Inspect for and repair any damaged wiring. Set DVOM on 20-volt scale. With KOEO measure voltage at knock sensor connector between KS and SIGNAL RETURN. If reading is greater than 4 volts, go to step 5). If voltage is 1-4 volts, go to step 6). If reading is less than one volt, go to next step.

3) Check Continuity of KS and Signal Return Circuit. Turn key off and wait 10 seconds. Disconnect ECA 60-pin connector. Inspect for and repair any damaged wiring. Install breakout box, leaving ECA and knock sensor disconnected. With DVOM on 200-ohm scale, measure resistance between SIGNAL RETURN at sensor harness connector and test pin No. 46, and between knock sensor connector KS signal and test pin No. 23. If either reading is 5 ohms or more, service open circuit and repeat QUICK TEST. If both readings are less than 5 ohms, go to next step.

4) Checking KS Circuit for Short to Ground. Turn key off and wait 10 seconds. With breakout box installed, ECA and knock sensor disconnected, set DVOM on 200K-ohm scale. Measure resistance between knock sensor connector KS signal and test pins No. 40, 46 and 60. If all readings are 10K ohms or more, go to step 6). If any reading is less than 10K ohms, repair shorts in harness and repeat QUICK TEST.

5) Checking KS Circuit fo Short to Power. Turn key off and wait 10 seconds. With breakout box installed, ECA and sensor disconnected, set DVOM on 20-volt scale. Turn key on, leaving engine off. Measure voltage between test pins No. 23 and 40. If reading is 0.5 volt or more, repair knock sensor harness short to power, and repeat QUICK TEST. If reading is less than 0.5 volt, go to next step.

6) Test ECA By Sensor Substitution. Turn key off and wait 10 seconds. Remove breakout box and connect ECA. Connect substitute knock sensor into harness but do not install in engine. Substitute should be a known good unit with the same part number. Ensure engine is at normal operating temperature. Perform KOER SELF-TEST. When DYNAMIC RESPONSE CHECK signal appears, lightly tap knock sensor with 4 oz. hammer. Do Not "Goose" throttle. If Code 25 is displayed replace ECA, reconnect original knock sensor and rerun QUICK TEST. Ignore all other codes at this time. If Code 25 does not appear, install new knock sensor and repeat QUICK TEST.

1a-446

1989 COMPUTERIZED ENGINE CONTROLS
Ford Motor Co. EEC-IV (Cont.)

CIRCUIT TEST B8

THROTTLE POSITION SENSOR (TPS)

NOTE: Perform this test when Service Code 23, 53, 63, or 73 is displayed during QUICK TEST.

TPS Electrical Circuit

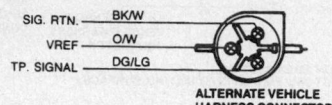

SIG. RTN. — BK/W
VREF — O/W
TP. SIGNAL — DG/LG

ALTERNATE VEHICLE HARNESS CONNECTOR

ALTERNATE SENSOR CONNECTOR

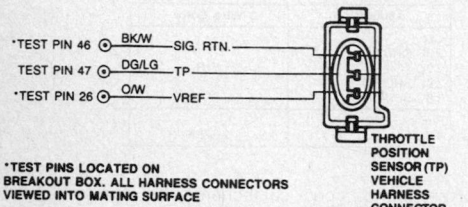

*TEST PIN 46 — BK/W — SIG. RTN.
TEST PIN 47 — DG/LG — TP
*TEST PIN 26 — O/W — VREF

*TEST PINS LOCATED ON BREAKOUT BOX. ALL HARNESS CONNECTORS VIEWED INTO MATING SURFACE

THROTTLE POSITION SENSOR (TP) VEHICLE HARNESS CONNECTOR

THROTTLE POSITION SENSOR (TP) CONNECTOR

TPS Specification Table

Throttle Position Sensor Setting (K.O.E.O. and K.O.E.R.)			TP Circuit (Signal) Operating Voltage Range (K.O.E.O.)	
Engine Application	Rotational Degree Range	Voltage Range	Minimum	Maximum
Passenger Car:				
1.9L EFI	4° - 13°	0.80 - 1.20	0.24	4.84
1.9L CFI	0° - 12° (off) 2.5° - 14° (run)	0.49 - 1.15 0.71 - 1.25	0.39	4.84
2.3L OHC-EFI	0° - 13.5°	0.59 - 1.22	0.20	4.84
2.3L TC-EFI	2.5° - 15°	0.71 - 1.30	0.20	4.84
2.3L HSC-EFI	3° - 13.5°	0.73 - 1.22	0.20	4.84
2.5L HSC-CFI	1° - 15° (off) 3.5° - 25° (run)	0.66 - 1.30 0.76 - 1.78	0.39	4.84
3.0L EFI	0° - 13.5°	0.59 - 1.22	0.34	4.84
3.0L SHO-MA SEFI	0° - 4.5°	0.38 - 0.82	0.23	4.89
3.8L FWD/RWD 3.8L/5.0L SEFI	3° - 13.5°	0.73 - 1.22	0.39	4.84
3.8L SC MA 5.0L MA-SEFI	0° - 13.5°	0.49 - 1.22	0.39	4.84
Truck:				
2.3L DIS-EFI	0° - 13.5°	0.59 - 1.22	0.34	4.84
2.9L EFI	0° - 13.5°	0.59 - 1.22	0.34	4.84
3.0L EFI	0° - 13.5°	0.59 - 1.22	0.34	4.84
4.9L EFI	3° - 13.5°	0.73 - 1.22	0.20	4.84
5.0L EFI	3° - 13.5°	0.73 - 1.22	0.20	4.84
5.8L EFI	3° - 13.5°	0.73 - 1.22	0.20	4.84
7.5L EFI	3° - 13.5°	0.73 - 1.22	0.20	4.84
5.8L/7.5L EFI E4OD	3° - 13.5°	0.73 - 1.22	0.34	4.84

To prevent replacement of good components, be aware that the following non-EEC related areas may be at fault: idle speed/throttle stop adjustment, binding throttle shaft/linkage or cruise control linkage.

1) Code 23. Code 23 indicates that the TPS rotational setting may be out of the Self-Test range. See TPS SPECIFICATION TABLE. If KOEO SELF-TEST Code 68 or KOER SELF-TEST Codes 31, 41, or 58 are displayed, service these codes first. Disregard Code 23 at this time. If these codes have been serviced or are not displayed, go to next step.

2) Check for Stuck Throttle Plate. Inspect throttle body and linkage for binding or sticking. Ensure linkage is set with throttle in closed position. If throttle plate or linkage is binding, check for binding throttle or cruise control linkage, vacuum line or harness interference, etc. Repair any problem and repeat QUICK TEST. If no mechanical problem is found, go to next step.

3) Code 53: Generate Code 63. Code 53 indicates that TPS signal is greater than Self-Test maximum value. Turn key off and wait 10 seconds. Disconnect TPS from harness at throttle body. Inspect for and repair any damaged wiring. Perform KOEO SELF-TEST. Check for Code 63. Ignore all other codes at this time. If Code 63 is not displayed, go to step **5)**. If Code 63 is displayed, go to next step.

CIRCUIT TEST B8 (Cont.)

4) Check VREF to Signal Return. Turn key off and wait 10 seconds. Set DVOM on 20-volt scale and disconnect TPS from harness. Inspect for and repair any damaged wiring. With KOEO, measure voltage at TPS connector between VREF and SIG RTN If reading is less than 4 volts or more than 6 volts, go to CIRCUIT TEST A3, step **1)**. If reading is between 4 and 6 volts, replace TPS and repeat QUICK TEST.

5) Checking TP Signal For Short to Power. Turn key off and wait 10 seconds. Disconnect TPS from harness. Set DVOM on 200K-ohm scale. Disconnect ECA 60-pin connector. Inspect for and repair any damaged wiring. Install breakout box, leaving ECA disconnected. Measure resistance between test pin No. 47 and test pins No. 26 and 57. If either reading is less than 10K ohms, repair short in harness and repeat QUICK TEST. If both readings are 10K ohms or more, replace ECA and repeat QUICK TEST.

6) Code 63: Generate Code 53. Code 63 indicates that TP signal is less than minimum Self-Test value. Turn key off and wait 10 seconds. Disconnect TPS from harness. Install a jumper wire between VREF and TP signal at connector. Perform KOEO SELF-TEST. Check for Codes 53 or 23. Ignore all other codes at this time. If no codes are displayed, immediately remove jumper wire, and go to step **9)**. If either Code 53 or 23 is displayed, replace TPS and repeat QUICK TEST. If neither Code 53 or 23 is displayed, go to next step.

7) Code 63: Check Voltage VREF to SIG RTN. Turn key off and wait 10 seconds. Disconnect TPS from harness. Inspect for and repair any damaged wiring. Set DVOM on 20-volt scale. With KOEO, measure voltage between VREF and SIG RTN at TP connector. If reading is less than 4 volts or more than 6 volts, go to CIRCUIT TEST A3, step **1)**. If reading is between 4 and 6 volts, go to next step.

8) Checking TPS Circuit Continuity. Turn key off and wait 10 seconds. Leave TPS disconnected. Set DVOM on 200-ohm scale and disconnect ECA 60-pin connector. Inspect for and repair any damaged wiring. Install breakout box and connect ECA. Measure resistance between TP signal at connector and test pin No. 47. If reading is 5 ohms or more, repair faulty circuit. Remove breakout box, connect ECA and TPS, and repeat QUICK TEST. If reading is less than 5 ohms, go to next step.

9) Checking Resistance Between Ground and Signal Return. Turn key off and wait 10 seconds. Leave TPS disconnected. Disconnect ECA 60-pin connector. Inspect for and repair any damaged wiring. Install breakout box and set DVOM on 200K-ohm scale. Measure resistance at connector between TPS signal and ground, and between TPS signal and test pin No. 46. If either reading is less than 10K ohms, repair short circuit and repeat QUICK TEST. If both readings are 10K ohms or more, replace ECA. Remove breakout box, connect TPS, and repeat QUICK TEST.

NOTE: Code 73 in step 10) indicates that TPS did not exceed 25% of its rotation during DYNAMIC RESPONSE ("Goose") CHECK. For additional information see KOER SELF-TEST, DYNAMIC RESPONSE CHECK in this article.

10) Code 73: TPS Movement. Turn key off. Install breakout box and connect ECA. Set DVOM on 20-volt scale. Connect DVOM to test pins No. 46 and 47. Perform KOER SELF-TEST. Verify that DVOM reading exceeds 3.5 volts during "Goose" check. If reading exceeds 3.5 volts, replace ECA. Clear codes and repeat QUICK TEST. If reading does not exceed 3.5 volts, ensure TPS is correctly installed and adjusted. If okay, replace TPS, clear codes and repeat QUICK TEST.

11) Code 53: TPS Movement. Using KOEO CONTINUOUS MONITOR (WIGGLE) TEST, observe VOM or diagnostic tester for indication of fault while slowly opening throttle to WOT. Slowly bring throttle to closed position, lightly tap TPS and wiggle connector. If no fault is indicated, go to step **13)**. If fault is indicated, go to next step.

12) TPS Voltage Measurement. Turn key off and wait 10 seconds. Disconnect ECA 60-pin connector. Inspect for and repair any damaged wiring. Install breakout box, leaving ECA connected. Stay in KOEO CONTINUOUS MONITOR (WIGGLE) TEST as in previous step **11)**. Connect DVOM between test pins No. 47 and 46. Set DVOM on 20-volt scale. Turn key on, leaving engine off. Observe DVOM and repeat step **11)**. If fault occurs at less than 4.25 volts, inspect TPS connectors and terminals. If okay, replace TPS, clear codes and repeat QUICK TEST. If fault does not occur at less than 4.25 volts, TPS over-travel may have caused Continuous Code 53. TPS is okay, go to next step to check harness.

13) Checking Harness. While in KOEO CONTINUOUS MONITOR (WIGGLE) TEST, shake, bend and wiggle small sections of EEC-IV harness from TPS to firewall, and from firewall to ECA. If fault is indicated, isolate fault in wiring and repair as necessary. Clear codes and repeat QUICK TEST. If no fault is indicated, go to next step.

1989 COMPUTERIZED ENGINE CONTROLS
Ford Motor Co. EEC-IV (Cont.)

1a-447

CIRCUIT TEST B8 (Cont.)

14) Checking Harness Connectors. Turn key off and wait 10 seconds. Disconnect ECA 60-pin connector. Inspect both connectors and terminals for obvious damage. If connectors and teminals are damaged, repair as necessary. Clear codes and repeat QUICK TEST. If connectors and terminals are okay, fault cannot be duplicated at this time. Continuous Code 53 testing is complete.

15) Continuous Code 63 Displayed. Using KOEO CONTINUOUS MONITOR (WIGGLE) TEST, observe VOM or diagnostic tester for indication of fault while slowly opening throttle to WOT. Slowly bring throttle to closed position and lightly tap TPS and wiggle connector. If fault is indicated, disconnect TPS. Inspect connectors and terminals. If connectors and terminals are okay, replace TPS. Clear codes and repeat QUICK TEST. If no fault is indicated, go to next step.

16) Harness Test. While in KOEO CONTINUOUS MONITOR (WIGGLE) TEST, shake, bend and wiggle small sections of EEC-IV harness from TPS sensor to firewall, and from firewall to ECA. If fault is indicated, isolate fault in wiring and repair as necessary. Clear codes and repeat QUICK TEST. If no fault is indicated, go to next step.

17) ECA Connector Test. Turn key off and wait 10 seconds. Disconnect ECA 60-pin connector. Inspect both connectors and terminals for obvious damage. If connectors and teminals are damaged, repair as necessary. Clear codes and repeat QUICK TEST. If connectors and terminals are okay, fault cannot be duplicated at this time. Continuous Code 63 testing is complete.

CIRCUIT TEST B9

VANE AIRFLOW (VAF) SENSOR

NOTE: Perform this test when Service Code 26, 56, 66, or 76 is displayed during QUICK TESTS or when directed here by other test procedures.

VAF Sensor Circuit

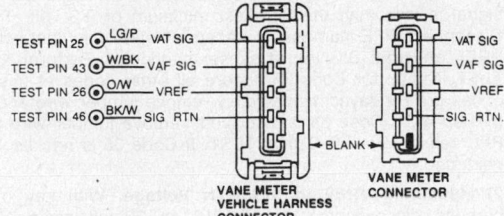

TEST PIN 25 — LG/P — VAT SIG
TEST PIN 43 — W/BK — VAF SIG
TEST PIN 26 — O/W — VREF
TEST PIN 46 — BK/W — SIG RTN

VAT SIG
VAF SIG
VREF
SIG. RTN.

BLANK

VANE METER VEHICLE HARNESS CONNECTOR

VANE METER CONNECTOR

*TEST PINS LOCATED ON BREAKOUT BOX. ALL HARNESS CONNECTORS VIEWED INTO MATING SURFACE.

VAF SENSOR SPECIFICATIONS

Airflow m³/hr ¹	Output Voltage
1.9L MPFI	
9	0.80
16	1.35
26	1.85
40	2.25
60	2.65
100	3.15
160	3.60
240	4.00
380	4.50

¹ – m³/hr equals cubic meters per hour.

To prevent replacement of good components, be aware that the following non-EEC related areas may be at fault: check for air leaks between VAF sensor and throttle body. Check for vacuum leaks. Check engine sealing at PCV, CANP, valve cover(s), and at dipstick seal.

1) Code 26: VAF Movement Obstructed. Code 26 indicates VAF sensor signal is out of Self-Test range. Self-Test range is 0.17-0.50 volts with KOEO or 1.10-1.70 volts with KOER. Possible causes for this fault are a faulty vane meter, faulty ECA or wiring harness. Turn key off and wait 10 seconds. Remove air filter and check for

CIRCUIT TEST B9 (Cont.)

contamination (oil residue or foreign matter). If Code 26 appears in KOEO SELF-TEST, replace or service VAF sensor. Install air cleaner and repeat QUICK TEST. If Code 26 is not displayed, go to next step.

2) Checking VAF Sensor. With key off, check for air leaks allowing unmetered air into system between VAF sensor and throttle body. Disconnect ECA 60-pin connector. Inspect for and repair any damaged wiring. Install breakout box and connect ECA to box. Set DVOM on 20-volt scale. Turn key on, leaving engine off. Place new, unsharpened pencil through air inlet opening of VAF sensor. See VAF SENSOR CHECK illustration. Measure voltage between test pins No. 43 and 46. If reading is between 2.8 and 3.7 volts, VAF sensor is okay. Code 26 may be caused by incorrect engine speed or vacuum leak. Go to CIRCUIT TEST D4, step **11)** and ensure Code 26 has not been caused by canister purge function. Repair problem, remove breakout box and repeat QUICK TEST. If reading is not between 2.8 and 3.7 volts, inspect VAF connector pins and repeat QUICK TEST. Replace VAF if problem still exists.

VAF Sensor Check

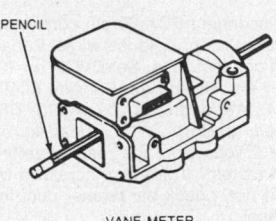 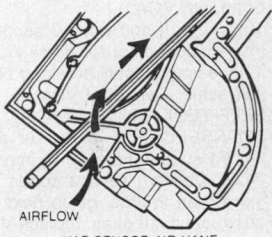

PENCIL

VANE METER

AIRFLOW

VAF SENSOR AIR VANE

3) Code 56: Generate Code 66. Code 56 indicates that the VAF signal is greater than the Self-Test maximum of 4.89 volts. Possible causes for this fault are a faulty VAF, faulty ECA, VAF SIG circuit shorted to power or a faulty wiring harness.
Turn key off and wait 10 seconds. Disconnect harness from VAF. Inspect for and repair any damaged wiring. Rerun KOEO SELF-TEST. If Code 66 is not displayed, go to step **5)**. If Code 66 is displayed, go to next step.

4) Checking VAF Signal Return Voltage. Turn key off and wait 10 seconds. Leave harness disconnected from VAF sensor. Set DVOM on 20-volt scale. With KOEO measure voltage at VAF harness connector between VREF and SIG RTN. If reading is between 4 and 6 volts, replace VAF sensor. Connect harness and repeat QUICK TEST. If reading is less than 4 or more than 6 volts, go to CIRCUIT TEST A3, step **1)**.

5) Checking VAF Signal For Shorts to Power. Turn key off and wait 10 seconds. Leave VAF sensor disconnected. Disconnect 60-pin connector from ECA. Inspect for and repair any damaged wiring. Install breakout box, leaving ECA disconnected. Set DVOM on 200K-ohm scale. Measure resistance between test pin No. 43 and test pins No. 26 and 57. If either reading is less than 10K ohms, repair short in wiring. Remove breakout box. Connect ECA and VAF sensor and then repeat QUICK TEST. If both readings are 10K ohms or more, replace ECA. Remove breakout box. Connect ECA and VAF sensor. Repeat QUICK TEST.

6) KOEO Code 66: Generate Code 56. Code 66 indicates that the VAF signal is less than the Self-Test minimum of 0.17 volt during the KOEO SELF-TEST. Possible causes for this fault are a faulty VAF, faulty ECA, VAF SIG circuit shorted to ground or a faulty wiring harness.
Turn key off and wait 10 seconds. Disconnect harness from VAF sensor. Install jumper wire between VREF and VAF SIG at connector. Perform KOEO SELF-TEST. Ignore all codes except VAF codes at this time. If no codes are displayed, immediately remove jumper wire and go directly to step **9)**. If Code 56 is displayed, replace VAF sensor. Remove jumper wire, connect VAF sensor, and repeat QUICK TEST. If Code 56 is not displayed, remove jumper wire and go to next step.

7) Checking VREF at VAF Sensor. Turn key off and wait 10 seconds. Leave VAF sensor disconnected. Turn key on, leaving engine off. Set DVOM on 20-volt scale. Measure voltage between VREF and SIG RTN return at VAF sensor harness connector. If reading is less than 4 volts or more than 6 volts, go to CIRCUIT TEST A3, step **1)**. If reading is between 4 and 6 volts, go to next step.

8) Checking Continuity of VAF SIG. With key off and VAF sensor disconnected, disconnect ECA 60-pin connector. Inspect for and repair any damaged wiring. Install breakout box, leaving ECA disconnected. Set DVOM on 200-ohm scale. Measure resistance between VAF SIG at sensor connector and test pin No. 43. If reading is 5 ohms or more, repair open circuit. Remove breakout box, connect

1a-448

1989 COMPUTERIZED ENGINE CONTROLS
Ford Motor Co. EEC-IV (Cont.)

CIRCUIT TEST B9 (Cont.)

ECA and VAF sensor. Repeat QUICK TEST. If reading is less than 5 ohms, go to next step.

9) Checking VAF Signal For Short to Ground. Turn key off and wait 10 seconds. Leave ECA and VAF sensor disconnected. Set DVOM on 200K-ohm scale. Measure resistance between VAF SIG and SIG RTN at harness connector. Also measure resistance between VAF SIG and negative battery terminal. If either reading is less than 10K ohms, repair shorts. Connect VAF sensor and repeat QUICK TEST. If both readings are 10K ohms or more, replace ECA. Remove breakout box, and connect ECA and VAF sensor. Repeat QUICK TEST.

NOTE: A quick "Goose" test may not be sufficient to pass step 10). Be sure to move throttle to WOT. For additional information, see KOER SELF-TEST, DYNAMIC RESPONSE CHECK in front of this article.

10) KOER Code 76 Displayed. Code 76 indicates that VAF output voltage did not change during the WOT "Goose" test. Possible causes for this fault are an obstructed air cleaner or duct, a faulty vane meter or a faulty ECA.
Turn key off and wait 10 seconds. Disconnect ECA 60-pin connector. Inspect connector for damaged pins, corrosion, or loose wires. Repair if necessary. Install breakout box and connect ECA. Set DVOM on 20-volt scale. Connect DVOM to test pin No. 43 and 46. Perform KOER SELF-TEST while observing DVOM. As soon as DYNAMIC RESPONSE CHECK signal is displayed, perform WOT. Reading on DVOM should increase by more than 2 volts from the reading before WOT. Observe service codes at end of test. If reading increased by more than 2 volts, go to next step. If not, check air cleaner duct for obstructions. If okay, replace VAF sensor.

11) Checking Service Codes. Observe KOEO SELF-TEST service codes at end of step 10). If Code 76 is still displayed, replace ECA. Remove breakout box and repeat QUICK TEST. If Code 76 is not displayed, VAF sensor is okay. Service other codes as necessary.

12) Continuous Memory Code 56. Code 56 indicates that the VAF sensor signal was greater than the Self-Test maximum value of 4.89 volts. The code was set during normal driving conditions. Possible causes for this fault are a faulty vane meter, Using KOEO CONTINUOUS MONITOR (WIGGLE) TEST, observe VOM or diagnostic tester for indication of fault while lightly tapping VAF sensor and wiggling connector. If a fault is indicated, disconnect connector. Inspect connector and terminals for damage. If connector and terminals are okay, replace VAF sensor and repeat QUICK TEST. If no fault is indicated, go to next step.

13) Checking Harness. While in KOEO CONTINUOUS MONITOR (WIGGLE) TEST, shake, bend and wiggle small sections of EEC-IV harness from VAF sensor connector to firewall and from firewall to ECA. If fault is indicated, isolate and repair damaged wiring. Repeat QUICK TEST. If no fault is indicated, go to next step.

14) Checking Harness Connectors. Turn key off and wait 10 seconds. Disconnect ECA 60-pin connector. Inspect both connectors and terminals for obvious damage. If connectors and terminals are damaged, repair as necessary and repeat QUICK TEST. If connectors and terminals are okay, fault cannot be duplicated at this time. Clear codes and rerun QUICK TEST.

15) KOER Code 66. KOER Code 66 indicates that the VAF sensor signal was less than the Self-Test minimum of 0.17 volts. The code was set during normal driving conditions. Possible causes for this fault are a faulty VAF harness or connector, faulty VAF sensor, or a fault ECA.
Enter KOEO Continuous Monitor mode. Observe DVOM while tapping lightly on VAF sensor to simulate road shock. Wiggle VAF connector. If a fault is indicated repair wiring or connectors as necessary. If connectors and wiring are okay, replace VAF sensor. If a fault is not indicated, check harness and connectors as described in steps 13) and 14).

CIRCUIT TEST B10

PRESSURE FEEDBACK EGR (PFE) VALVE & EGR VACUUM REGULATOR (EVR) SOLENOID

NOTE: Perform this test when Service Code 31, 32, 33, 34, 35, or 84 is displayed during QUICK TESTS or when directed here by other test procedures.

CIRCUIT TEST B10 (Cont.)

Pressure Feedback EGR (PFE)
& EGR Valve Regulator (EVR) Circuits

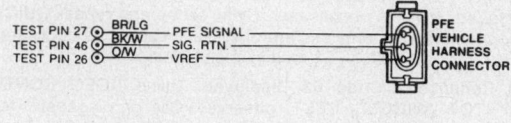

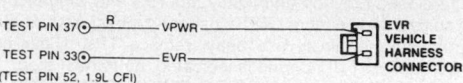

*TEST PINS LOCATED ON BREAKOUT BOX.
ALL HARNESS CONNECTORS VIEWED INTO MATING SURFACE.

Test Pin 33 (52)	EVR
Application	**Wire Color**
1.9L CFI 2.3L HSC EFI	Y
3.0L EFI 3.8L AXOD SEFI 3.8L RWD SEFI	DG

PFE SENSOR SPECIFICATIONS

Pressure psi/in. Hg (kPa)	Voltage
1.82 PSI (12.5)	4.75
1.36 psi (9.42)	4.38
0.91 psi (6.25)	4.00
0.46 psi (3.17)	3.63
0 (0)	3.25
5 in. Hg (-17)	1.22
7.4 in. Hg (-25)	0.25

1) Code 31: Generate Code 35. Code 31 indicates the PFE sensor signal is less than the Self-Test minimum of 0.2 volt. Turn key off. Disconnect PFE harness at sensor. Install a jumper wire between VREF and PFE SIGNAL at sensor connector. Perform KOEO SELF-TEST. Check for Code 35. Ignore all other codes at this time. If no codes are displayed, immediately remove jumper wire and go directly to step 4). If Code 35 is displayed, remove jumper wire and replace PFE sensor. Repeat QUICK TEST. If Code 35 is not displayed, go to next step.

2) Measuring VREF to SIG RTN Voltage. With key off and PFE harness disconnected, set DVOM on 20-volt scale. With KOEO, measure voltage at PFE connector between VREF and SIG RTN. If reading is less than 4 volts or more than 6 volts, go to CIRCUIT TEST A3, step 1). If reading is between 4 and 6 volts, go to next step.

3) PFE Signal Continuity. With key off and PFE harness disconnected, set DVOM on 200-ohm scale. Disconnect ECA 60-pin connector. Inspect for and repair any damaged wiring. Install breakout box, leaving ECA disconnected. Measure resistance between PFE SIGNAL at connector and test pin No. 27. If reading is 5 ohms or more, repair faulty circuit. Connect PFE sensor and remove breakout box. Repeat QUICK TEST. If reading is less than 5 ohms, go to next step.

4) PFE Signal Circuit Resistance. With key off and PFE harness disconnected, install breakout box leaving ECA disconnected. Set DVOM on 200K-ohm scale. Measure resistance between ground and PFE signal at connector. Measure resistance between PFE signal at connector and test pin No. 46. If either reading is less than 10K ohms, repair short circuit. Connect PFE and remove breakout box. Repeat QUICK TEST. If both readings are 10K ohms or more, replace ECA. Connect PFE and remove breakout box. Repeat QUICK TEST.

5) Code 35: Generate Code 31. Code 35 indicates the PFE sensor signal is greater than the Self-Test maximum of 4.8 volts. Turn key off and disconnect PFE harness at sensor. Inspect for and repair any damaged wiring. Perform KOEO SELF-TEST. Check for Code 31. Ignore all other codes at this time. If Code 31 is not displayed, go to step 7). If Code 31 is displayed, go to next step.

6) Measuring VREF to SIG RTN Voltage. Refer to wiring diagram in CIRCUIT TEST B10. With key off and PFE harness disconnected, set DVOM on 20-volt scale. Turn key on, leaving engine off. Measure voltage at PFE connector between VREF and SIG RTN. If reading is

1989 COMPUTERIZED ENGINE CONTROLS
Ford Motor Co. EEC-IV (Cont.)

1a-449

CIRCUIT TEST B10 (Cont.)

between 4 and 6 volts, replace PFE sensor. Repeat QUICK TEST. If reading is less than 4 volts or more than 6 volts, go to CIRCUIT TEST A3, step 1).

7) Checking PFE Circuit For Shorts. With key off and PFE harness disconnected, disconnect ECA 60-pin connector. Inspect for and repair any damaged wiring. Install breakout box, leaving ECA disconnected. Set DVOM on 200K-ohm scale. Measure resistance between test pin No. 27 and test pins No. 26, 37 and 57. If either reading is less than 10K ohms, repair short. Connect PFE and remove breakout box. Repeat QUICK TEST. If both readings are 10K ohms or more, replace ECA. Connect PFE and remove breakout box. Repeat QUICK TEST.

8) Code 34: PFE Sensor Out Of Range. Code 34 indicates that PFE sensor is out of Self-Test range of 2.6-4.2 volts and that PFE sensor is probably faulty. The PFE system can detect lack of pressure in exhaust system. An efficient garage exhaust ventilation system, installed during KOEO SELF-TEST may cause PFE sensor to generate Code 34. Remove exhaust ventilation system and retest. If Code 34 is not displayed, service other codes displayed during KOEO SELF-TEST. If none are displayed, continue with QUICK TEST. If Code 34 is displayed, go to next step.

9) Inspecting Supply to PFE Sensor. Remove pressure feed tube from PFE sensor. Inspect complete tube, including PFE inlet for blockage. If blockage is found, repair as necessary. Repeat QUICK TEST. If no blockage is found, go to next step.

10) Measuring VREF to SIG RTN Voltage. Turn key off and disconnect PFE sensor. Inspect for and repair any damaged wiring. Set DVOM on 20-volt scale. Turn key on, leaving engine off. Measure voltage at PFE connector between VREF and SIG RTN. If reading is between 4 and 6 volts, replace PFE sensor. Repeat QUICK TEST. If reading is less than 4 volts or more than 6 volts, go to CIRCUIT TEST A3, step 1).

11) Code 84: Measure EVR Solenoid Resistance. Code 84 indicates a failure in EVR solenoid circuit. Turn key off. Set DVOM on 200-ohm scale. Disconnect EVR solenoid connector and measure solenoid resistance. If reading is less than 30 ohms or more than 70 ohms, replace EVR solenoid assembly. Repeat QUICK TEST. If reading is between 30 and 70 ohms, go to next step.

12) Checking VPWR at EVR Solenoid. With KOEO and EVR solenoid disconnected from harness, set DVOM on 20-volt scale. Turn key on, leaving engine off. Measure voltage between negative battery terminal and VPWR circuit at EVR solenoid connector. If reading is less than 10.5 volts, repair VPWR open circuit. Repeat QUICK TEST. If reading is 10.5 volts or more, go to next step.

13) Checking Continuity of EVR Circuit. Turn key off and disconnect EVR solenoid from harness. Disconnect ECA 60-pin connector. Inspect for and repair any damaged wiring. Install breakout box, leaving ECA disconnected. Set DVOM on 200-ohm scale. Measure resistance between test pin No. 33 (test pin No. 52 on 1.9L CFI) at the breakout box and EVR signal at the EVR solenoid harness. If reading is 5 ohms or more, repair open circuit. Connect EVR solenoid and remove breakout box. Repeat QUICK TEST. If reading is less than 5 ohms, go to next step.

14) Checking EVR Circuit For Ground Shorts. Turn key off. Install breakout box, leaving ECA disconnected. Disconnect EVR solenoid. Set DVOM on 200K-ohm scale. Measure resistance between test pin No. 33 (test pin No. 52 on 1.9L CFI) and test pins No. 37, 57, 40, and 60 at the breakout box. If any reading is less than 10K ohms, repair short circuit. Remove breakout box. Connect ECA and EVR solenoid. Repeat QUICK TEST. If code is repeated, replace ECA. If all readings are 10K ohms or more, replace ECA. Remove breakout box. Connect ECA and EVR solenoid. Repeat QUICK TEST.

15) Code 32: Verify Engine Running Codes. Code 32 indicates EGR valve is not fully seated. Possible causes for this fault are obstructed vacuum line, contaminated EVR filter, faulty EGR valve or faulty EVR solenoid. The PFE system can detect a lack of pressure in exhaust system. An efficient garage exhaust ventilation system, installed during KOER SELF-TEST may cause PFE sensor to generate Code 32. Temporarily remove exhaust ventilation system and retest. If Code 32 is not displayed, service other codes displayed during KOER SELF-TEST. If none, continue with QUICK TEST. If Code 32 is displayed, go to next step.

16) Code 31: Separating EVR From PFE. Code 31 indicates PFE sensor signal is less than Self-Test minimum. Turn key off. Disconnect and plug EGR valve vacuum hose. Perform KOER SELF-TEST. If Codes 31 or 32 are present, go to next step. If not, go to step 18).

17) Checking PFE Supply Tube for Blockage. With key off, check PFE sensor supply tube for blockage or leaks. If these faults are found,

CIRCUIT TEST B10 (Cont.)

repair as necessary. Connect all lines and repeat QUICK TEST. If no faults are found, service exhaust gas recirculation system.

18) EVR Filter Inspection. Turn key off. Remove and inspect EVR filter for contamination. A blocked filter will cause vacuum to be applied to EGR valve prematurely. If filter is contaminated, replace filter. Connect all lines and repeat QUICK TEST. If filter is not contaminated, replace EVR solenoid. Repeat QUICK TEST.

19) Codes 34 or 35: Check for Excessive Backpressure. Codes 34 and 35 in KOER SELF-TEST indicate excessive exhaust backpressure. There are 2 possible causes: the exhaust system is blocked, or faulty PFE sensor. Turn key off. Susbtitute known good PFE sensor in place of original. Repeat KOER SELF-TEST. If Code 34 or 35 is not displayed, replace PFE sensor. Repeat QUICK TEST. If Code 34 or 35 is displayed, check exhaust system for restrictions.

20) Code 33: Verify Vacuum at EGR Valve. Code 33 indicates PFE sensor input did not change after EVR solenoid received signal from ECA to open the EGR valve. Possible causes for this fault are as follows:

- Vacuum hose leaks.
- Obstructed vacuum hose.
- Faulty EVR solenoid.
- Faulty PFE sensor.
- Faulty EGR valve.
- Paulty PCV valve (1.9L CFI only).

Turn key off and wait 10 seconds. Using a vacuum "T", connect vacuum gauge at EGR valve. Perform KOER SELF-TEST while observing vacuum gauge. Disregard code output. If vacuum reading is greater than one in. Hg, go to step 26). If vacuum reading is one in. Hg or less, go to next step.

21) Vacuum Supply Hose Inspection. With key off, check vacuum hose from EVR solenoid to EGR valve and from vacuum source to EVR solenoid for loose connections, obstructions, cracks, etc. If vacuum hoses are damaged, repair or replace as necessary. Repeat QUICK TEST. If hoses are okay, go to next step (1.9L CFI) or step No. 24 (all others).

22) Supply Hose to EVR Verification. Turn key off and wait 10 seconds. Attach vacuum gauge to supply line between throttle body and EVR solenoid. Start and run engine at 2000 RPM. If vacuum reading is greater than 10 in. Hg, go to next step. If vacuum reading is less than 10 in. Hg, replace vacuum line to EVR, remove vacuum gauge and rerun QUICK TEST.

23) Checking PCV Valve for Operation. With key off, disconnect vacuum hose at PCV valve from EVR solenoid. Connect vacuum pump to PCV valve. Slowly apply 10 in. Hg vacuum. If PCV valve opens and does not leak down, remove vacuum gauge, reconnect valve and go to step 25). If PCV valve does not open, service or replace PCV valve.

24) Vacuum Supply to EVR Verification. Turn key off and wait 10 seconds. Attach vacuum gauge to source line from manifold. Start engine and run at idle. If vacuum is present, go to step 35). If no vacuum is present, replace vacuum hose to EVR solenoid and repeat QUICK TEST.

25) Checking EGR Valve Operation. With KOEO, disconnect vacuum hose at EGR valve. Connect vacuum pump to EGR valve. While observing EGR valve, slowly apply 10 in. Hg vacuum. The EGR valve should begin to open with a very small amount of vacuum (1-1.5 in. Hg) and be fully open with about 4 in. Hg. If EGR opens freely and smoothly, check EVR solenoid filter for obstructions. If filter is okay, replace EVR solenoid and rerun QUICK TEST. If EGR valve does not open freely and smoothly, service or replace EGR valve.

26) Checking PFE Sensor Supply Tube. With key off, check control pressure input tube to PFE sensor for cracks, obstructions or faulty connections. If supply tube is faulty, repair as necessary. If supply tube is okay, go to next step.

27) Substitute Known Good PFE Sensor. Turn key off and wait 10 seconds. Substitute known good PFE sensor in place of original. Rerun KOER SELF-TEST. If Code 33 is present, service or replace EGR valve as necessary. If Code 33 is not present, original PFE sensor was the cause of the original Code 33. Replace PFE sensor and rerun QUICK-TEST.

28) Continuous Memory Code 31 or 35: Testing PFE Sensor. Code 31 or 35 indicates that PFE sensor signal was less than (Code 31) or greater than (Code 35) the Self-Test voltage sometime during vehicle operation.

Using KOEO CONTINUOUS MONITOR (WIGGLE) TEST, observe VOM or diagnostic tester for indication of fault while performing the following steps. Connect a vacuum pump to PFE sensor and slowly apply 5 in. Hg vacuum to sensor. Slowly bleed vacuum off PFE

1a-450

1989 COMPUTERIZED ENGINE CONTROLS
Ford Motor Co. EEC-IV (Cont.)

CIRCUIT TEST B10 (Cont.)

sensor. Lightly tap on PFE sensor and wiggle PFE connector. If fault is indicated, disconnect harness and inspect connector. If connector and terminals are okay, replace PFE sensor. Repeat QUICK TEST. If no fault is indicated, go to next step.

29) Checking Harness. Observe VOM or diagnostic tester for fault indication while grasping harness close to sensor connector, then wiggling, shaking or bending small sections of harness while working your way to firewall. Also wiggle, shake or bend harness from firewall to ECA. If fault is indicated, isolate fault and repair as necessary. Repeat QUICK TEST. If fault is not indicated, go to next step.

30) Checking ECA and Harness Connectors. Turn key off and wait 10 seconds. Disconnect ECA 60-pin connector. Inspect both connector and terminals for damage. If connector and terminals are damaged, repair as necessary. Repeat QUICK TEST. If connector and terminals are okay, fault is intermittent and cannot be duplicated at this time.

31) Continuous Memory Code 34: Checking PFE Supply Tube for Blockage. Code 34 indicates that the PFE sensor was restricted sometime during vehicle operation. Turn key off. Remove PFE sensor and inspect sensor supply inlet for liquids or any type of blockage. Inspect PFE supply tube at EGR valve base for liquids or blockage. If supply tube is blocked, clean or service as necessary. Repeat QUICK TEST. If supply tube is not blocked, fault is intermittent and cannot be duplicated at this time.

32) Continuous Memory Code 32: Check EGR Valve Operation. Code 32 indicates that the EGR valve did not seat itself fully sometime during vehicle operation. Turn key off. Connect vacuum pump to EGR valve and apply 10 in. Hg of vacuum. While observing EGR valve, release vacuum, and repeat step if necessary. If EGR valve does not operate smoothly, service or replace EGR valve. If EGR valve works smoothly, go to next step.

33) Vacuum Line Inspection. Inspect EGR valve vacuum supply line, from EVR solenoid to EGR valve for kinks or obstructions. If vacuum supply line is blocked, repair as necessary. Repeat QUICK TEST. If vacuum supply line is okay, go to next step.

34) EVR Solenoid Filter Inspection. Carefully check EVR filter for contamination or obstructions. If EVR filter is contaminated, replace filter and repeat QUICK TEST. If EVR filter is not contaminated, fault is intermittent and cannot be duplicated at this time. Continuous Memory Code 32 testing is complete.

35) Continuous Memory Code 33: Checking EGR Valve Operation. Code 33 indicates that EGR valve intermittently did not open during vehicle operation. Turn key off. Connect a vacuum pump to EGR valve. While observing EGR valve, slowly apply 10 in. Hg of vacuum. EGR valve should begin to open at 1-1.5 in. Hg and be fully open at 4 in. Hg of vacuum. If EGR valve does not move freely and smoothly, service exhaust gas recirculation system. If EGR valve moves freely and smoothly, go to next step.

36) EVR Harness Test. With key off, disconnect ECA 60-pin connector. Inspect for and repair any damaged wiring. Install breakout box and connect ECA to box. Enter OUTPUT STATE CHECK. Set DVOM on 20-volt scale. Connect DVOM negative test lead to test pin No. 40 at breakout box and DVOM positive test lead on test pin No. 33 (test pin No. 52 on 1.9L CFI). Move throttle valve to indicate 10.5 volts or more and maintain position. While observing DVOM, grasp harness closest to EVR connector. Wiggle, shake or bend small sections of harness while working your way to firewall. Lightly tap EVR solenoid to simulate road vibration. If DVOM reads 10.5 volts or less, isolate fault and repair as necessary. Repeat QUICK TEST. If DVOM reads 10.5 volts or more, fault cannot be duplicated at this time. Continuous Memory Code 33 testing is complete.

CIRCUIT TEST B11

EGR VALVE POSITION (EVP) SENSOR & EGR VALVE REGULATOR (EVR) SOLENOID

NOTE: Perform this test when Service Code 31, 32, 33, 34, 35, 38 or 84 is displayed during QUICK TESTS or when directed here by other test procedures.

1) Code 31: Generate Code 35. Code 31 indicates that EVP signal is less than the Self-Test minimum of 0.2 volt. Turn key off and wait 10 seconds. Disconnect EVP harness at sensor. Install a jumper wire between VREF and EVP SIGNAL at sensor harness connector. Perform KOEO SELF-TEST. Check for code 35. Ignore all other codes

CIRCUIT TEST B11 (Cont.)

EGR Valve Position (EVP) Sensor & EGR Valve Regulator (EVR) Solenoid Circuits

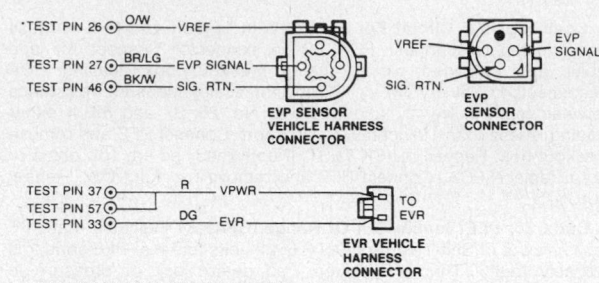

*TEST PINS LOCATED ON BREAKOUT BOX.
ALL HARNESS CONNECTORS VIEWED INTO MATING SURFACE.

at this time. If Code 35 is displayed, remove jumper and replace EVP sensor. Repeat QUICK TEST. If Code 35 is not displayed, remove jumper wire and go to next step.

2) Checking VREF to SIG RTN Voltage. With KOEO and EVP disconnected, set DVOM on 20-volt scale. Measure voltage at EVP connector between VREF and SIG RTN. If reading is less than 4 or more than 6 volts, go to CIRCUIT TEST A3, step **1)**. If reading is between 4 and 6 volts, go to next step.

3) Checking EVP SIGNAL Continuity. With key off, wait 10 seconds. Disconnect EVP sensor, set DVOM on 200-ohm scale. Disconnect ECA 60-pin connector. Inspect for and repair any damaged wiring. Install breakout box, and connect ECA to box. Measure resistance between EVP SIGNAL at connector and test pin No. 27. If reading is 5 ohms or more, open circuit. Connect EVP sensor and remove breakout box. Repeat QUICK TEST. If reading is less than 5 ohms, go to next step.

4) Checking EVP SIGNAL For Shorts To Ground. With key off and EVP harness disconnected, leave breakout box installed and ECA disconnected. Set DVOM on 200K-ohm scale. Measure resistance between EVP signal at EVP connector and ground. Measure resistance between test pin No. 27 and test pins No. 40, 46 and 60. If any reading is less than 10K ohms, repair short circuit. Connect EVP and remove breakout box. Repeat QUICK TEST. If both readings are 10K ohms or more, replace ECA. Connect EVP and remove breakout box. Repeat QUICK TEST.

5) Code 35: Generate Code 31. Code 35 indicates EVP signal is greater than the Self-Test maximum of 4.81 volts. Turn key off and wait 10 seconds. Disconnect EVP sensor. Inspect for and repair any damaged wiring. Perform KOEO SELF-TEST. Check for Code 31. Ignore all other codes at this time. If code 31 is not displayed, go to step **7)**. If Code 31 is displayed, go to next step.

6) Checking VREF To SIG RTN Voltage. With EVP harness disconnected, set DVOM on 20-volt scale. With KOEO, measure voltage at EVP harness connector VREF and SIG RTN. If reading is between 4 and 6 volts, replace EVP sensor. Repeat QUICK TEST. If reading is less than 4 volts or more than 6 volts, go to CIRCUIT TEST A3, step **1)**.

7) Checking EVP SIGNAL For Short To Power. Turn key off and disconnect EVP from harness. Disconnect ECA 60-pin connector. Inspect for and repair any damaged wiring. Install breakout box, leaving ECA disconnected. Set DVOM on 200K-ohm scale. Measure resistance between test pin No. 27 and test pins No. 26 and 57. If either reading is less than 10K ohms, repair short in harness. Connect EVP sensor and remove breakout box. Repeat QUICK TEST. If both readings are 10K ohms or more, replace ECA. Connect EVP sensor and remove breakout box. Repeat QUICK TEST.

8) Code 84: EVR Solenoid Resistance. Code 84 indicates a faulty EVR circuit. Turn key off. Set DVOM on 200-ohm scale. Disconnect EVR solenoid connector and measure solenoid resistance. If reading is less than 30 ohms or more than 70 ohms, replace EVR solenoid assembly. Repeat QUICK TEST. If reading is between 30 and 70 ohms, go to next step.

9) Checking VPWR at EVR Solenoid. Leave EVR solenoid disconnected and set DVOM on 20-volt scale. Turn key on, leaving engine off. Measure voltage between negative battery terminal and VPWR circuit at EVR solenoid harness connector. If reading is less than 10.5 volts, repair VPWR open circuit. Repeat QUICK TEST. If reading is 10.5 volts or more, go to next step.

10) EVR Circuit Continuity. With key off and EVR solenoid disconnected, disconnect ECA 60-pin connector. Inspect for and repair any

1989 COMPUTERIZED ENGINE CONTROLS
Ford Motor Co. EEC-IV (Cont.)

1a-451

CIRCUIT TEST B11 (Cont.)

damaged wiring. Install breakout box, leaving ECA disconnected. Set DVOM on 200-ohm scale. Measure resistance between test pin No. 33 and EVR SIGNAL at EVR solenoid connector. If reading is 5 ohms or more, repair open circuit. Connect EVR solenoid and remove breakout box. Repeat QUICK TEST. If reading is less than 5 ohms, go to next step.

11) Checking EVR Circuit Shorts. With key off, breakout box installed, and ECA and EVR solenoid disconnected, set DVOM on 200K-ohm scale. Measure resistance between test pin No. 33 and test pins No. 37 and 57, 40, 60, and 46 at breakout box. If any reading is less than 10K ohms, repair short circuit. Remove breakout box, and connect ECA and EVR solenoid. Repeat QUICK TEST. If code is repeated, replace ECA. If all readings are 10K ohms or more, replace ECA. Remove breakout box, and connect ECA and EVR solenoid. Repeat QUICK TEST.

12) KOEO Code 34: Check For Code 84. KOEO Code 34 indicates EGR valve and/or EVP is not fully seated in the closed position. EVP voltage signal, in the closed position, is greater than the Self-Test maximum of 0.67 volt. Because of the preload on the installed EVP sensor it is very difficult to determine if the EGR valve is seated or the EVP sensor is in contact with the EGR valve. Turn key off and wait 10 seconds. Check for Code 84 in KOEO SELF-TEST. If Code 84 is present, go to step **8)**. If Code 84 is not displayed, go to next step.

13) Functional Test of EVP Sensor and EGR Valve. Turn key off and wait 10 seconds. Disconnect EVP sensor. Inspect harness and connector, service as necessary. Remove vacuum line from EGR valve. Test EGR valve operation by applying and releasing vacuum to valve, using a vacuum pump. Reconnect vacuum line. Repeat KOEO and KOER SELF-TEST. If Code 34 is still displayed, go to next step. If Code 34 is not displayed, the original code was set by a faulty connection or a sticking EGR valve. Testing of EGR valve is complete.

14) Substitute EVP Sensor on Original EGR Valve. Turn key off and wait 10 seconds. Install a good known EVP sensor on original EGR valve. Perform KOEO SELF-TEST. If Code 34 is present, check EGR valve for mechanical malfunction. If Code 34 is not present, replace original EVP sensor. Repeat QUICK TEST.

15) KOEO and KOER Code 32 Checking EVP and EGR. Code 32 indicates that EGR valve and/or EVP sensor signal voltage is less than closed position minimum of 0.29 volt. Preload on EVP sensor makes it difficult to determine whether the EGR valve has malfunctioned or if the EVP sensor has abnormally high resistance. Possible causes for this fault are: poor continuity at EVP sensor connector, non-seated or faulty EGR valve or faulty EVP sensor.

Turn key off and wait 10 seconds. Inspect connector and harness for damage and service as necessary. Remove vacuum line from EGR valve. Test EGR valve operation by applying and releasing vacuum to valve, using a vacuum pump. Reconnect vacuum line. If Code 32 is still present, go to next step. If Code 34 is not displayed, the original code was set by a faulty connection or a sticking EGR valve. Testing of EGR valve is complete.

16) Substitute EVP Sensor On Original EGR Valve. Turn key off and wait 10 seconds. Install a known good EVP sensor on original EGR valve. Perform KOEO SELF-TEST. If Code 32 is present, check EGR valve for mechanical malfunction. If Code 32 is not present, replace original EVP sensor. Repeat QUICK TEST.

17) KOER Code 33: Checking Vacuum at EGR. KOER Code 33 indicates that EVP sensor input did not change after ECA signaled EGR operation. Because a Code 84 was not received in the KOEO SELF-TEST, the EVR solenoid electrical function is okay. The lack of Code 32 or 34 indicate the EVP sensor is within the closed position specifications. Possible causes for this fault are; leaking vacuum hose, restricted vacuum hose, restricted EVR solenoid filter, or a faulty EGR valve.

Turn key off. Using vacuum "T", connect vacuum gauge at EGR valve. Perform KOER SELF-TEST and observe vacuum gauge. If reading is 1.5 in. Hg or greater, go to step **20)**. If reading is less than 1.5 in. Hg, remove vacuum gauge and reconnect EGR valve, or go to next step.

18) Checking Vacuum Supply to EVR Solenoid. Turn key off. Disconnect vacuum source to EVR solenoid. Install vacuum gauge at source vacuum hose. Start engine. If reading is 10 in. Hg or more, go to next step. If reading is less than 10 in. Hg, check vacuum hose to EVR solenoid. Replace if necessary. Repeat QUICK TEST.

19) Checking Vacuum Hoses. Carefully check vacuum line for cracks, loose connections, blockage, kinks, and leaks. If vacuum hose is not okay, replace hose. Connect new vacuum hose and repeat QUICK TEST. If vacuum hose is okay, check EVR solenoid filter for obstructions. Replace if necessary. If filter is okay, replace EVR solenoid. Connect all vacuum hoses and repeat QUICK TEST.

CIRCUIT TEST B11 (Cont.)

20) Checking EVP Sensor and EGR Valve. Turn key off and wait 10 seconds. Disconnect EVP sensor. Inspect connector and harness or damage and service as necessary. Remove vacuum line from EGR valve. Test EGR valve operation by manually depressing and releasing the diaphragm. Reconnect vacuum line to EGR valve and connector to EVP sensor. Repeat KOEO and KOER SELF-TEST. If Code 33 is still present, go to next step. If Code 33 is not displayed, the original code was set by poor continuity or a sticking EGR valve. Testing of EGR valve is complete.

21) Checking EGR Valve Vacuum Control. With key off, disconnect EGR valve vacuum supply. Connecty a vacuum gauge to EGR valve and apply 2-3 in. Hg for 2 minutes. If EGR holds vacuum, reconnect supply line and go to next step. If EGR valve will not hold vacuum, service or replace EGR valve.

22) Substitute Known Good EVP Sensor. Turn key off and wait 10 seconds. Install a known good EVP sensor on original EGR valve. Perform KOER SELF-TEST. If Code 33 is present, check EGR valve and/or system for mechanical malfunction. If Code 33 is not present, service or replace original EVP sensor. Repeat QUICK TEST.

23) Code 34: EGR Valve Operation. Code 34 indicates that EVP voltage is greater than closed position Self-Test minimum of 0.67 volts. Turn key off. Disconnect and plug EGR valve vacuum hose. Perform KOER SELF-TEST. If Code 34 is not present, check EVR filter for obstructions. Replace if necessary. If filter is okay, replace EVR solenoid. Connect all vacuum hoses and repeat QUICK TEST. If Code 34 is present, go to next step.

24) Checking EVP Resistance, While Applying Vacuum to EGR. Turn key off and wait 10 seconds. Disconnect harness from EVP sensor. Inspect connectors for damaged pins or corrosion. Repair if necessary. Set DVOM on 200K-ohm scale. Disconnect vacuum hose to EGR valve and connect vacuum pump to valve. Measure resistance at EVP sensor between EVP SIGNAL and VREF while gradually increasing vacuum to 10 in. Hg. If reading decreases from no more than 5500 ohms to no less than 100 ohms, check EGR valve for mechanical malfunction and service or replacve as necessary. If reading does not change as indicated, replace EVP sensor. Reconnect vacuum hose and rerun QUICK TEST.

25) Continuous Memory Code 32: Check EVP Signal Voltage While Operating EGR. Code 32 indicates that EGR valve closed further than normal with engine at idle and at normal operating temperature. Turn key off and wait 10 seconds. Disconnect ECA 60-pin connector. Inspect for and repair any damaged wiring. Install breakout box and connect ECA. Connect vacuum pump to EGR valve. Place DVOM on 20-volt scale and connect between test pins No. 27 and 46. With KOEO, observe DVOM readings. Slowly apply 6 in. Hg vacuum to EGR valve. Slowly bleed vacuum off EGR valve and lightly tap on EVP sensor to simulate road shock. If voltage drops to less than .29 volt, the EGR valve may have caused Code 32. Clear Continuous Memory Codes. Check EGR valve for mechanical malfunction. If all readings are more than .29 volt, Code 32 fault cannot be duplicated at this time. Testing is complete.

26) Continuous Memory Code 31 and/or 35: Check Harness. Code 31 indicates an open in the EVP SIGNAL or VREF, or a short to SIG RTN with the engine at idle and at normal operating temperature.
Code 35 indicates a short to VREF and/or VPWR, or an open in SIGNAL RETURN with the engine at idle and at normal operating temperature.
Using KOEO CONTINUOUS MONITOR (WIGGLE) TEST, observe VOM or diagnostic tester for fault indication while grasping harness close to sensor and wiggling, shaking, or bending a small section of EEC-IV harness while working toward dash panel. Wiggle, shake or bend harness from firewall to ECA. If fault is indicated, isolate fault and repair wiring harness as required. Repeat QUICK TEST. If fault is not found, go to next step.

27) Checking ECA and Harness Connectors. Turn key off and wait 10 seconds. Disconnect ECA 60-pin connector. Inspect connector and terminals for obvious damage. If connector and terminals are damaged, repair as necessary. Repeat QUICK TEST. If connector and terminals are okay, fault cannot be duplicated at this time. Test is completed.

28) Continuous Memory Code 33: Leak Test. Code 33 indicates that EGR valve did not open with the engine at normal operating temperature and with the EVR solenoid signal present. Turn key off and wait 10 seconds. Connect vacuum pump to EGR valve. Apply 20 in. Hg to EGR valve. If EGR valve opens and holds vacuum, go to next step. If not, service or replace EGR valve as necessary, clear codes and repeat QUICK TEST.

1989 COMPUTERIZED ENGINE CONTROLS
Ford Motor Co. EEC-IV (Cont.)

CIRCUIT TEST B11 (Cont.)

29) EVR Check. Using CONTINUOUS MONITOR (WIGGLE) TEST, observe VOM or diagnostic tester for fault indication. Grasp harness close to EVR solenoid connector and wiggle, shake, or bend a small section of harness while working toward ECA. Inspect connectors and terminals for obvious damage. If fault is indicated, isolate fault and repair as necessary. Repeat QUICK TEST. If no fault is indicated, fault cannot be duplicated at this time. Testing is complete.

30) Continuous Memory Code 34: EVP Resistance Check While Operating EGR Valve. Code 34 indicates EGR valve was open with the engine idling at normal operating temperature.
Turn key off. Disconnect harness from EVP sensor. Inspect connector for obvious damage. Place DVOM on 200K-ohm scale. Disconnect vacuum hose to EGR valve and connect vacuum pump to valve. Measure resistance at EVP sensor between EVP SIGNAL and VREF at the sensor while increasing vacuum to 10 in. Hg. If reading does not decrease gradually from up to 5500 ohms to not less than 100 ohms, check EGR valve for mechanical malfunction. If reading gradually decreases from no more than 5500 ohms to no less than 100 ohms, go to next step.

31) EVR Check. Turn key off. Disconnect vacuum hose from EGR valve and plug hose. Perform KOER SELF-TEST. If Code 34 is present, check EVR filter for obstructions. Replace if necessary. If filter is okay, replace EVR solenoid. Connect all vacuum hoses and repeat QUICK TEST. If Code 34 is not present, fault cannot be duplicated at this time. Testing is completed.

CIRCUIT TEST B12

VEHICLE SPEED SENSOR (VSS)

NOTE: Perform this test when Service Code 29 is displayed during QUICK TESTS or when directed here by other test procedures.

Vehicle Speed Sensor Circuit

Test Pin 6	VSS DIF -
Application	**Wire Color**
2.3L HSC EFI 2.5L CFI 3.0L SHO SEFI 5.0L SEFI-MA E-Series: 4.9L, 5.0L, 5.8L, 7.3L, 7.5L E4OD	O/Y
2.3L EFI Ranger 2.9L EFI Ranger/Bronco II 3.8L RWD SEFI 3.8L SC SEFI 5.0L SEFI-Crown Victoria, Grand Marquis and Town Car	BK/W
3.0L EFI Aerostar	BK/Y
5.0L SEFI-Mark VII	P/LB
F-Series/Bronco 4.9L, 5.0L, 5.8L, 7.3L, 7.5L E4OD	BK

* TEST PINS LOCATED ON BREAKOUT BOX.
ALL HARNESS CONNECTORS VIEWED INTO MATING SURFACE.

To prevent replacement of good components, be aware that the following circuit test is to be used only when Continuous Memory Code 29 is displayed. This test checks vehicle speed sensor, wiring harness, and ECA. Before testing the VSS perform the following drive cycle procedure on all vehicles except, 2.5L CFI and 3.0L MPFI Aerostar:
Automatic Transmission Equipped Vehicles. Record and clear CONTINUOUS SELF-TEST codes. Warm engine to normal operating temperature. In Low gear, accelerate moderately to 25 MPH and coast down to idle and stop. Shut off engine. Perform KOEO SELF-TEST. If Code 29 is present, go to step 1). If not, fault cannot be duplicated at this time. If any other codes are present, return to QUICK TEST. If codes are not present, test is completed.

CIRCUIT TEST B12 (Cont.)

Manual Transmission Equipped Vehicles. Record and clear CONTINUOUS SELF-TEST codes. Warm engine to normal operating temperature. Start in first gear, shift to second gear, and accelerate moderately to 40 MPH. Coast down to idle and stop. Shut engine off. Perform KOEO SELF-TEST. If Code 29 is present, go to next step. If not, fault cannot be duplicated at this time. If any other codes are present, return to QUICK TEST. If codes are not present, test is completed.

1) Continuous Memory Code 29. Code 29 indicates there is insufficient input to the ECA from the VSS. Possible causes for this code are a faulty VSS, open or shorted circuit or a faulty ECA. Perform drive cycle procedure. If Code 29 is displayed or driveability complaint can be verified (2.5L CFI and 3.0L MPFI Aerostar), go to next step. If not, fault cannot be duplicated at this time.

2) Checking VSS Sensor. Turn key off and wait 10 seconds. Disconnect vehicle speed sensor. Set DVOM on 200K-ohm scale. Measure resistance across vehicle speed sensor. If reading is between 190-240 ohms, go to next step. If reading is incorrect, replace vehicle speed sensor and repeat drive cycle procedure.

3) VSS Harness Continuity. Turn key off and wait 10 seconds. Remove ECA 60-pin connector and inspect for damaged pins, corrosion, or loose wires. Repair as necessary. Install breakout box. With ECA and VSS disconnected, set DVOM on 200-ohm scale. Measure resistance between test pin No. 3 at breakout box and VSS harness connector. Also measure resistance between test pin No. 6 at breakout box and VSS harness connector. If both readings are 5 ohms or less, go to next step. If readings are 5 ohms or more, service open circuit in VSS wiring harness. After repairs, repeat step 1).

4) Checking VSS Harness For Shorts. Turn key off. With ECA and VSS disconnected, set DVOM on 200K-ohm scale. Measure resistance between test pin No. 3 and test pins No. 37, 40 and 6 at breakout box. Also measure resistance between test pin No. 6 and test pin No. 37. If all readings are greater than 10K ohms, go to next step. If any reading is less than 10K ohms, repair short(s) in VSS wiring harness. After repairs, repeat step 1).

5) Test By Substitution. Substitute VSS with known good sensor and repeat drive cycle procedure (except 2.5L CFI and 3.0L MPFI Aerostar). Connect ECA and VSS. Repeat step 1), and return to this step. If Code 29 is present, replace ECA and repeat step 1). If no code is present, replace original vehicle speed sensor.

CIRCUIT TEST B13

NEUTRAL DRIVE SWITCH (NDS) A/C INPUT

NOTE: Perform this test when Service Code 67 or 79 is displayed during QUICK TESTS or when directed here by other test procedures. This test is designed to diagnose the following:
- A/C input to ECA.
- Clutch engagement switch.
- Neutral cutch switch.
- Neutral drive switch.
- ECA
- Harness connector and electrical circuits.

1) Code 67 System Identification. Code 67 indicates that during engine cranking or KOEO SELF-TEST, signal voltage was greater than specification at test pin No. 10 (A/C input) or test pin No. 30 (NDS). Possible causes for this fault are: A/C circuit shorted to power, Neutral clutch/drive circuits open, Neutral clutch/drive switch open, or a faulty ECA. See TEST STEP APPLICATION REFERENCE table to enter this test at the correct step.

TEST STEP APPLICATION REFERENCE

Engine/Transmission Application	Go To Step Number
1.9L CFI M/T, 2.5L M/T, 5.0L MPFI Truck 5.8L MPFI, 7.5L MPFI, 7.3L Diesel	9)
2.9L M/T Truck, 5.0L SEFI M/T	2)
1.9L MPFI M/T, 2.3L OHC MPFI M/T	2)
2.3L T/C M/T	6)
3.0L SHO SEFI, 3.8L SC SEFI M/T, 4.9L M/T Truck	5)
All Others	7)

1989 COMPUTERIZED ENGINE CONTROLS
Ford Motor Co. EEC-IV (Cont.)

1a-453

CIRCUIT TEST B13 (Cont.)

Neutral Gear/Clutch Circuit Diagram

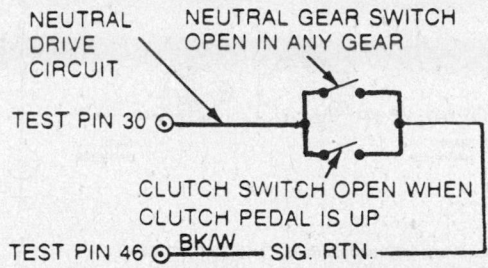

2) Checking Neutral Gear/Clutch Input. Turn key off and wait 10 seconds. Ensure A/C control is in "OFF" position. Disconnect ECA 60-pin connector. Inspect for and repair any damaged wiring. Install breakout box, leave ECA disconnected. Set DVOM on 200-ohm scale. Measure resistance between test pins No. 30 and 46 with transmission in Neutral and clutch pedal in the up position. Measure resistance with transmission in gear and clutch pedal depressed. If both resistances are less than 5 ohms. On vehicles with A/C go to step 9). If vehicle is not equipped with A/C, replace ECA. If reading is more than 5 ohms, go to next step.

3) Checking Neutral Gear/Clutch Switch. Turn key off and wait 10 seconds. Leave breakout box installed and ECA disconnected. Locate Neutral Gear Switch (NGS) on transmission and clutch switch at clutch pedal linkage. Disconnect harness at both switches and inspect connector pins. Set DVOM on 200-ohm scale and measure resistance across NGS with transmission in Neutral, and across clutch switch terminals with clutch pedal depressed. If both resistances are less than 5 ohms, go to next step. If all resistances are more than 5 ohms, replace open switches, remove test equipment, reconnect components and repeat QUICK TEST.

4) Checking Neutral Gear/Clutch Switch Harness. Turn key off and wait 10 seconds. Install breakout box, leave ECA disconnected and set DVOM to 200-ohm scale. Disconnect harness at NGS and clutch switch. Measure resistance between test pin No. 30 and NGS harness connector and, between test pin No. 30 and clutch switch harness connector. Measure resistance between test pin No. 46 and NGS harness connector, and between test pin No. 46 and clutch switch harness connector. If all resistances are less than 5 ohms, on vehicles equipped with A/C, go to step 9). If not equipped with A/C, replace ECA. If any reading is greater than 5 ohms, repair open in harness or connector. Repeat QUICK TEST.

Clutch Engage Switch Circuit Diagram

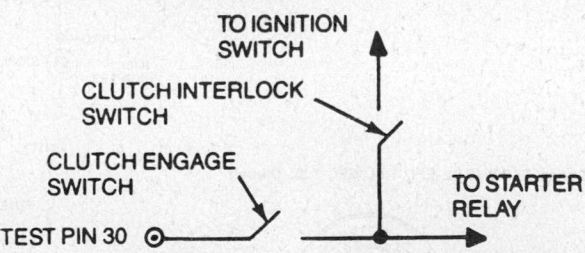

NOTE: If clutch pedal is not depressed during KOEO test, a Code 67 will be displayed.

5) Checking Clutch Engage Switch. Turn key off. Disconnect ECA 60-pin connector. Inspect for and repair any damaged wiring. Install breakout box and leave ECA disconnected. Set DVOM on 200-ohm scale. Depress clutch pedal. Measure resistance between test pin No. 30 and test pin No. 46. If both readings are less than 5 ohms, on vehicles equipped with A/C, go to step 9). If not equipped with A/C, replace ECA. If any reading is 5 ohms or more, repair open circuit.

Neutral Input Circuit Diagram (2.3L Turbo M/T)

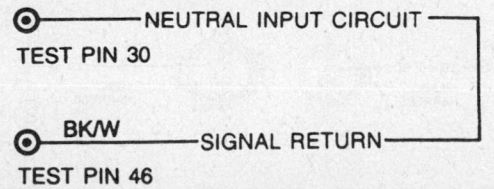

CIRCUIT TEST B13 (Cont.)

6) Checking Neutral Input Circuit: 2.3L Turbo MPFI With M/T. Turn key off, wait 10 seconds. Ensure A/C is turned off. Disconnect ECA 60-pin connector. Inspect for and repair any damaged wiring. Install breakout box. Leave ECA disconnected. Set DVOM on 200-ohm scale. Measure resistance between test pins No. 30 and 46. If resistance is less than 5 ohms, on vehicles equipped with A/C, go to step 9). If vehicle is not equipped with A/C, replace ECA. If reading is more than 5 ohms, repair open circuit. Rerun QUICK TEST.

Neutral Drive Input Circuit Diagram

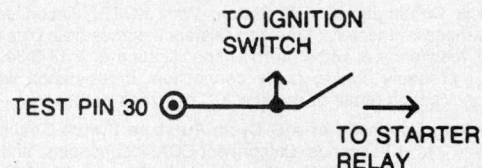

NEUTRAL DRIVE CIRCUIT
(CLOSED IN PARK & NEUTRAL)

7) Checking Neutral Drive Input. Turn key off and wait 10 seconds. Ensure heater control is in "OFF" position. Ensure transmission is in Neutral or Park position. Disconnect ECA 60-pin connector. Inspect for and repair any damaged wiring. Install breakout box and leave ECA disconnected. Set DVOM to 20-volt scale. Connect ECA to breakout box. With KOEO, measure voltage between test pin No. 30 at the breakout box and chassis ground. If voltage is less than one volt, on vehicles equipped with A/C, go to step 9). If not equipped with A/C, replace ECA. If reading is more than one volt, go to next step.

8) Checking Neutral Drive Switch. Turn key off and wait 10 seconds. Install breakout box, leave ECA disconnected. Set DVOM on 200-ohm scale. Disconnect vehicle harness from NDS at transmission and measure resistance across switch. If resistance is less than 5 ohms, remove breakout box. Reconnect all components and service open in NDS circuit. If resistance is more than 5 ohms, replace NDS and rerun QUICK TEST.

A/C Input Circuit Diagram

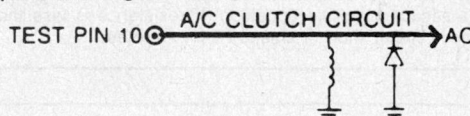

9) Checking A/C Input Voltage. Ensure A/C is switched "OFF". If A/C was on, rerun QUICK TEST. If Code 67 or 79 is displayed, continue with this test. Install breakout box and leave ECA disconnected. With KOEO, set DVOM on 20-volt scale. Measure voltage at test pin No. 10 at the breakout box and chassis ground. If reading is greater than one volt, remove breakout box and repair short in A/C clutch power circuit. If voltage is less than one volt replace ECA, except on vehicles equipped with E4OD transmissions. Vehicles equipped with E4OD transmissions, go to CIRCUIT TEST D25, step 1). Reconnect all components and rerun QUICK TEST.

10) Checking A/C Input Circuit. A low idle with A/C switched "ON" could result in the ECA not receiving or recognizing A/C input on pin No. 10. Turn key off and wait 10 seconds. Disconnect ECA, inspect pins, and install breakout box. Leave ECA disconnected. Set DVOM on 20-volt scale. With KOEO, and A/C on, measure voltage between test pins No. 10 and 40. If voltage is greater than 10.5 volts, replace ECA. Reconnect all components and rerun QUICK TEST. If voltage is less than 10.5 volts, service open in A/C circuit and rerun QUICK TEST.

A/C Clutch Circuit Diagram

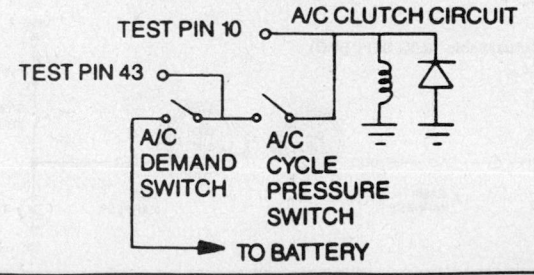

1a-454

1989 COMPUTERIZED ENGINE CONTROLS
Ford Motor Co. EEC-IV (Cont.)

CIRCUIT TEST B13 (Cont.)

11) Checking Inoperative A/C With High Idle. A high idle condition with the A/C dash switch in the "ON" position may be the result of a lack of signal reaching the A/C clutch. Turn key off and wait 10 seconds. Disconnect ECA, inspect pins, and install breakout box. Leave ECA disconnected. Disconnect A/C clutch connector. Set DVOM on 20-volt scale. With KOEO, turn on A/C. Measure voltage between input pin on fan connector and test pin No. 40 at the breakout box. If voltage is greater than 10.5 volts, go to next step. If voltage is less than 10.5 volts, repair open circuit and rerun QUICK TEST.

12) Check Continuity of A/C Clutch. With KOEO, disconnect A/C clutch harness connector. Measure resistance across both pins of A/C clutch. If resistance is within normal specification of 2.14-3.34 ohms, fault was probably due to faulty connection. If resistance was not within specification repair or replace A/C clutch as necessary.

13) Checking Continuity of A/C Cycle Pressure Switch Circuit. Turn key off and wait 10 seconds. Disconnect ECA, inspect pins, and install breakout box. Leave ECA disconnected. Disconnect A/C cycle pressure switch. Turn on A/C switch. Set DVOM on 200-ohm scale. Measure resistance between test pin No. 43 at the breakout box and battery positive side of the A/C cycle pressure switch. Measure resistance between test pin No. 10 at the breakout box and negative side of the A/C cycle pressure switch connector. If both resistances are less than 5 ohms, EEC-IV system is not at fault. Repair or replace cycle pressure switch. If resistances are greater than 5 ohms, repair open circuit and rerun QUICK TEST.

14) Check A/C Demand and A/C Cycle Pressure Switch For Short to Power. Turn key off. Disconnect ECA, inspect pins, and install breakout box. Leave ECA disconnected. Ensure A/C switch is off. Set DVOM on 20-volt scale. With KOEO, measure voltage between test pin No. 43 and chassis ground. If voltage is greater than 1.0 volt, EEC-IV is not at fault. Repair or replace A/C switches or electrical circuit. If voltage is less than 1.0 volt, reconnect components and check switch operation. If switches are okay, repair short in circuit wiring and rerun QUICK TEST.

15) Checking NDS Circuit For Short to Ground or Closed NDS. Turn key off and wait 10 seconds. Disconnect ECA 60-pin connector, inspect pins, and install breakout box. Place transmission in Drive. Set DVOM on 200K-scale. Measure resistance between test pin No. 30 and test pin No. 40 or 60 at breakout box. If resistance is greater than 10K ohms service high idle condition. If resistance is less than 10K ohms, service circuit short or closed NDS and retest.

CIRCUIT TEST B14
BRAKE ON/OFF SWITCH (BOO)

NOTE: Perform this test when Service Code 74 or 75 is displayed during QUICK TESTS or when directed here by other test procedures.

Brake ON/OFF (BOO) Circuit

Mustang (2.3L OHC EFI)

Taurus/Sable (3.0L SEFI SHO)

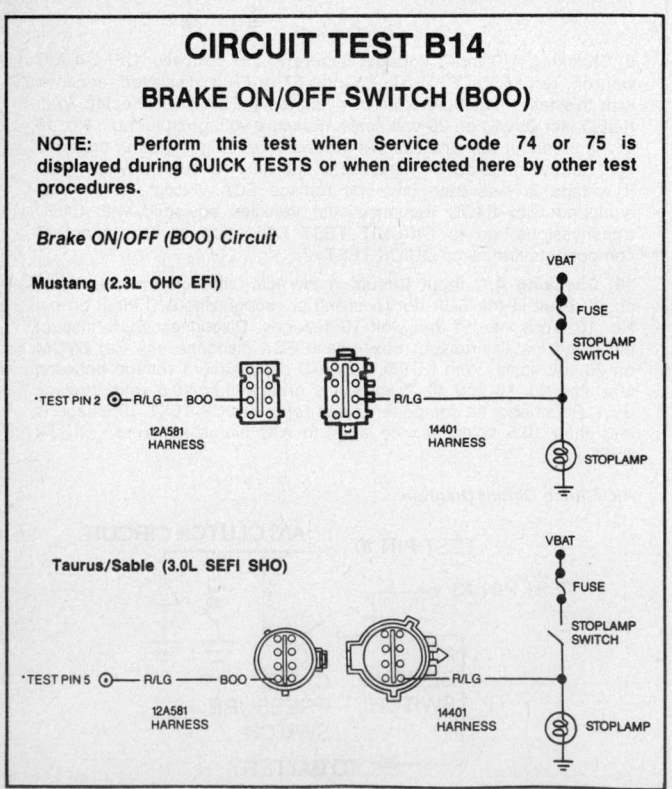

CIRCUIT TEST B14 (Cont.)

Continental (3.8L SEFI AXOD)

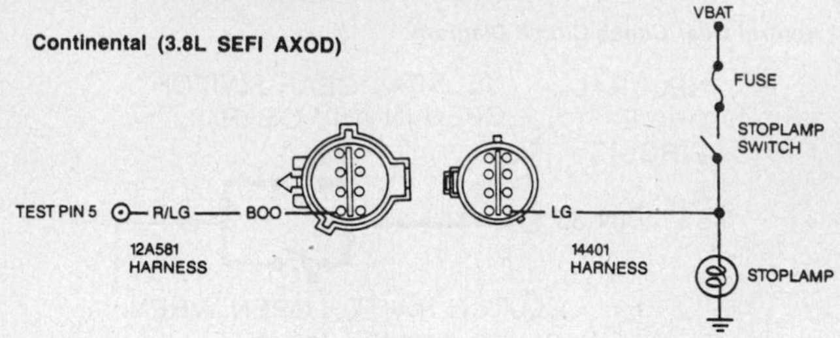

LTD Crown Victoria/Grand Marquis, Town Car (5.0L SEFI)

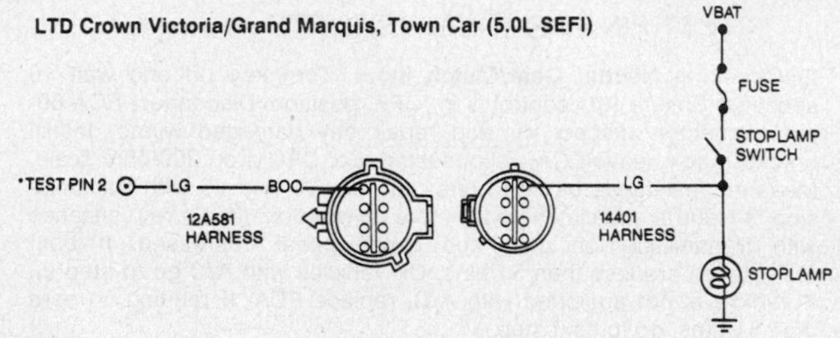

Mark VII (5.0L SEFI)

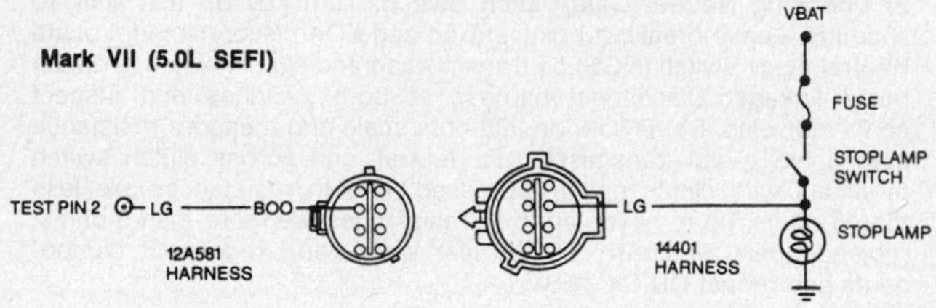

89 1/4 Aerostar (3.0L EFI)

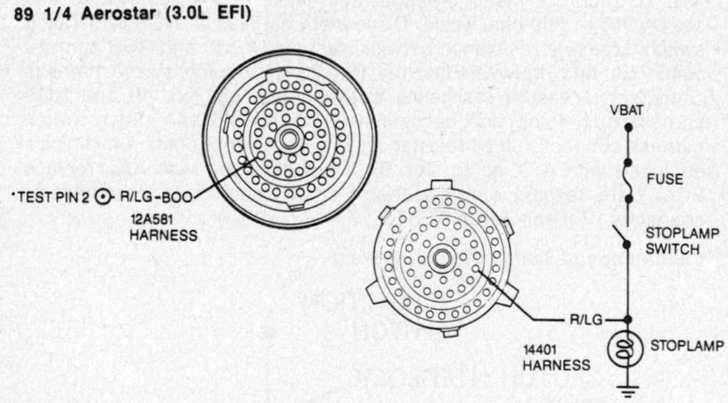

E-Series E4OD (5.8L EFI, 7.5L EFI, 7.3L Diesel)

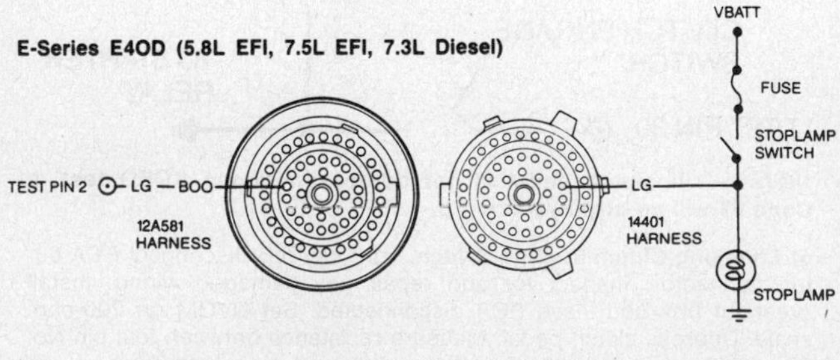

Bronco II/Ranger (2.3L EFI, 2.9L EFI)

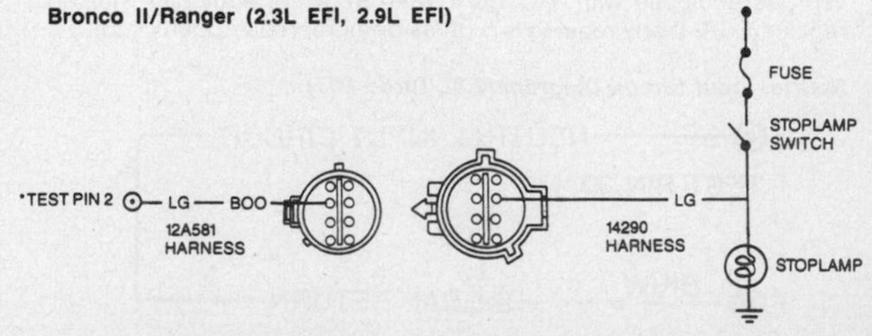

1989 COMPUTERIZED ENGINE CONTROLS
Ford Motor Co. EEC-IV (Cont.)

1a-455

CIRCUIT TEST B14 (Cont.)

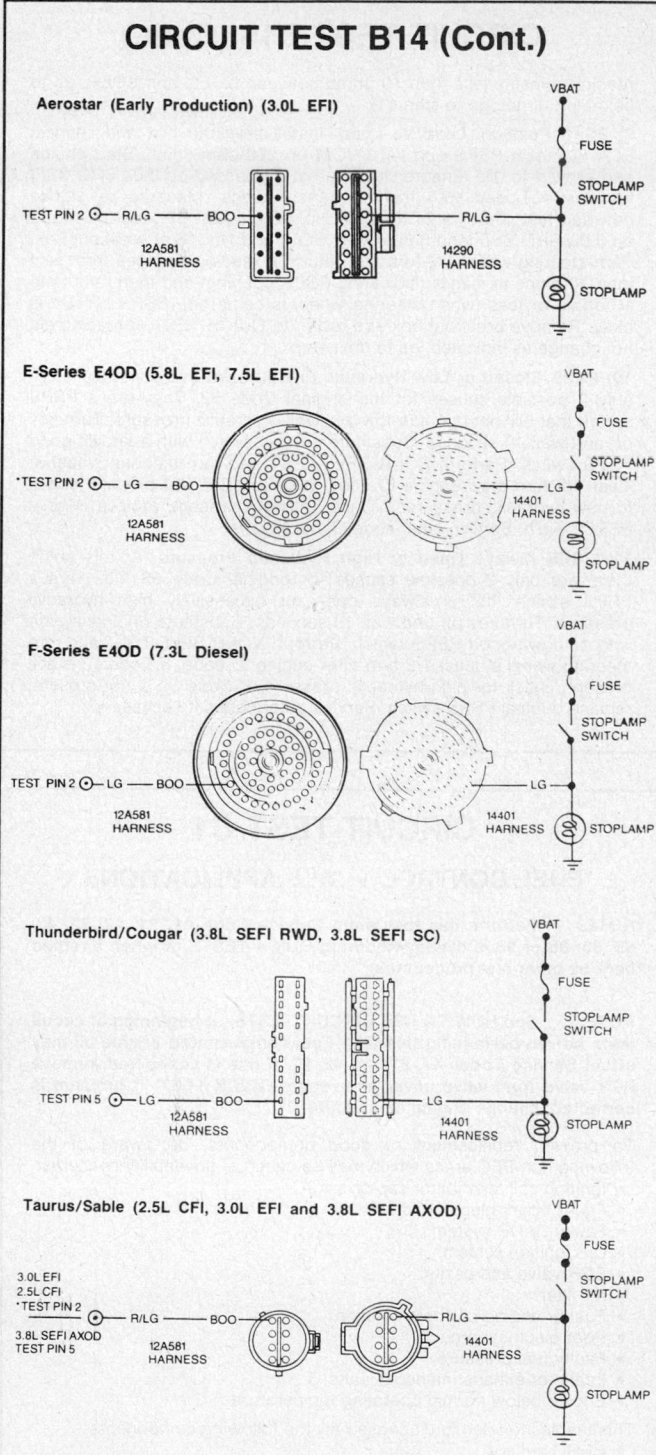

Aerostar (Early Production) (3.0L EFI)

TEST PIN 2 — R/LG — BOO
12A581 HARNESS
14290 HARNESS
R/LG
VBAT
FUSE
STOPLAMP SWITCH
STOPLAMP

E-Series E4OD (5.8L EFI, 7.5L EFI)

*TEST PIN 2 — LG — BOO
12A581 HARNESS
14401 HARNESS
LG
VBAT
FUSE
STOPLAMP SWITCH
STOPLAMP

F-Series E4OD (7.3L Diesel)

TEST PIN 2 — LG — BOO
12A581 HARNESS
14401 HARNESS
LG
VBAT
FUSE
STOPLAMP SWITCH
STOPLAMP

Thunderbird/Cougar (3.8L SEFI RWD, 3.8L SEFI SC)

TEST PIN 5 — LG — BOO
12A581 HARNESS
14401 HARNESS
LG
VBAT
FUSE
STOPLAMP SWITCH
STOPLAMP

Taurus/Sable (2.5L CFI, 3.0L EFI and 3.8L SEFI AXOD)

3.0L EFI
2.5L CFI
*TEST PIN 2 — R/LG — BOO
3.8L SEFI AXOD TEST PIN 5
12A581 HARNESS
14401 HARNESS
R/LG
VBAT
FUSE
STOPLAMP SWITCH
STOPLAMP

To prevent replacement of good components, be aware that the following non-EEC related areas may be at fault: brake light bulb, brake light switch, or brake light fuse. This test is intended to diagnose a faulty BOO circuit or ECA.

1) Code 74: Verify Brake Pedal Was Depressed. If brake was NOT depressed during KOER SELF-TEST, repeat test and depress brake pedal ONLY once during test. Depress and release brake pedal AFTER dynamic response code but before brief WOT. If pedal was depressed, go to next step.

2) Checking Power Circuit. Turn key off and wait 10 seconds. Disconnect ECA 60-pin connector. Inspect connector for damaged pins, corrosion, and loose wires. Install breakout box, leaving ECA

CIRCUIT TEST B14 (Cont.)

disconnected. Set DVOM on 20-volt scale. Measure voltage between test pins No. 2 and 40 while applying and releasing brake. If voltage cycles, switch circuit is okay, replace ECA and repeat QUICK TEST. If voltage does not cycle, go to next step.

3) Checking For Shorts To Ground. Turn key off. Leave breakout box installed and ECA disconnected. Set DVOM on 200K-ohm scale. Disconnect BOO circuit at 12-pin connector (14290 Harness). Measure resistance between test pins No. 2 and 40 at the breakout box. If resistance is greater than 10K ohms, repair stoplamp circuit as necessary. If resistance is less than 10K ohms remove breakout box repair short, and repeat KOER SELF-TEST.

4) Code 75 Displayed. Turn key off and wait 10 seconds. Disconnect ECA 60-pin connector. Inspect for and repair any damaged wiring. Install breakout box, leaving ECA disconnected. Set DVOM on 200-ohm scale. Disconnect BOO from Transmission Hydraulic Switch 12-pin connector (14290 Harness). Measure resistance between test pin No. 2 and BOO circuit at the 12-pin connector (14290 Harness). If resistance is greater than 5 ohms, remove breakout box. Reconnect ECA, repair open circuit, and rerun SELF-TEST.

5) Code 75: Cycle BOO Circuit. Turn key off. With breakout box installed and ECA disconnected, set DVOM on 20-volt scale. Measure voltage between test pins No. 2 and 40 at the breakout box while depressing and releasing the brake pedal. If voltage cycles, remove breakout box. Replace ECA, and rerun QUICK TEST. If voltage does not cycle, go to next step.

6) Checking BOO Circuit For Short To Power. Turn key off. Install breakout box, leaving ECA disconnected. Set DVOM on 20-volt scale. Disconnect BOO circuit at 12-pin connector. Measure voltage between test pin No. 2 at the breakout box and engine block ground. If voltage is greater than 10.5 volts, BOO circuit is okay. Check and repair brake light circuit as necessary. If voltage is less than 10.5 volts, remove breakout box. Reconnect ECA, repair circuit short and rerun QUICK TEST.

7) Code 74: Verify Brake Pedal Was Depressed. Code 74 incdicates that brake was NOT depressed during KOER SELF-TEST, the BOO signal did not cycle during test. Repeat test and depress brake pedal ONLY once during test. Depress and release brake pedal AFTER dynamic response code, but before brief WOT If pedal was depressed, go to next step. If voltage did not cycle, repeat KOER SELF-TEST and depress brake pedal once during test.

8) Checking BOO Circuit Cycling. Turn key off and wait 10 seconds. Disconnect ECA 60-pin connector. Inspect connector for damaged pins, corrosion, and loose wires. Install breakout box, leaving ECA disconnected. Set DVOM on 20-volt scale. Measure voltage between test pins No. 2 (pin No. 5 on 3.8L SEFI and 3.0L SHO SEFI) and 40 while applying and releasing brake. If voltage cycles, switch circuit is okay, replace ECA and repeat QUICK TEST. If voltage does not cycle, go to next step.

9) Checking Continuity of BOO Circuit. Turn key off. Leave breakout box installed and ECA disconnected. Set DVOM on 200-ohm scale. Disconnect BOO circuit at 12-pin connector (12A581 to 14290 or 14401 Harness Connector). Measure resistance between test pins No. 2 (pin No. 5 on 3.8L SEFI and 3.0L SHO SEFI) and 40 at the breakout box. If resistance is less than 5 ohms, go to next step. If resistance is greater than 5 ohms remove breakout box repair open circuit, and repeat KOER SELF-TEST.

10) Checking BOO Circuit For Short to Power. Turn key off and wait 10 seconds. Disconnect ECA 60-pin connector. Inspect for and repair any damaged wiring. Install breakout box, leaving ECA disconnected. Set DVOM on 20-volt scale. Disconnect BOO from Transmission Hydraulic Switch 12-pin connector (12A581 to 14290 or 14401 Harness). Measure voltage between test pin No. 2 (pin No. 5 on 3.8L SEFI and 3.0L SHO SEFI) at the breakout box and engine block ground. If voltage is greater than 1.0 volt, remove breakout box. Reconnect ECA, repair short circuit, and rerun SELF-TEST. If voltage is less than 1.0 volt, go to next step.

11) Check BOO Circuit For Short to Ground. Turn key off. Leave breakout box installed and ECA disconnected. Set DVOM on 200K-ohm scale. Disconnect BOO circuit at 12-pin connector (12A581 to 14290 or 14401 Harness Connector). Measure resistance between test pin No. 2 (pin No. 5 on 3.8L SEFI and 3.0L SHO SEFI) and test pin No. 40 at the breakout box. If resistance is greater than 10K ohms, repair stoplamp circuit as necessary. If resistance is less than 10K ohms remove breakout box repair short, and repeat KOER SELF-TEST.

1a-456

1989 COMPUTERIZED ENGINE CONTROLS
Ford Motor Co. EEC-IV (Cont.)

CIRCUIT TEST B15

POWER STEERING PRESSURE SWITCH (PSPS)

NOTE: Perform this test when Service Code 52 is displayed during QUICK TESTS or when directed here by other test procedures. Some vehicles ECA's may be equipped with PSPS software strategy but do not have power steering. If a KOEO Code 52 is displayed, check to see that vehicle is equipped with power steering. If not, disregard Code 52.

Power Steering Pressure Switch (PSPS) Circuit

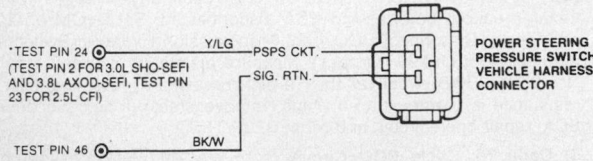

*TEST PINS LOCATED ON BREAKOUT BOX.
ALL HARNESS CONNECTORS VIEWED INTO MATING SURFACE.

To prevent replacement of good components, be aware that the following non-EEC related areas may be at fault: idle speed/throttle stop adjustment, binding throttle shaft/linkage or cruise control linkage.

1) Code 52 Elimination. Code 52 indicates that PSPS circuit is open. Turn key off and wait 10 seconds. Disconnect PSPS. Install a jumper wire between PSPS circuit and SIG RTN at harness connector. Repeat KOEO SELF-TEST. If Code 52 is not displayed, replace PSPS and repeat QUICK TEST. If Code 52 is still displayed, go to next step.

2) PSPS Harness Check. Turn key off and wait 10 seconds. Disconnect PSPS and ECA 60-pin connector. Inspect for and repair any damaged wiring. Install breakout box, leaving ECA disconnected. Set DVOM on 200-ohm scale and measure resistance between test pin No. 46 and SIG RTN at the PSPS harness connector. Also measure resistance between PSPS CKT. at the harness connector and test pin No. 24 (test pin No. 23 on 2.5L CFI, test pin No. 2 on 3.0L SHO SEFI and 3.8L AXOD SEFI). If both readings are less than 5 ohms, replace ECA. Repeat QUICK TEST. If readings are greater than 5 ohms, repair open in circuit. Repeat QUICK TEST.

3) Checking Switch Integrity. Connect tachometer and start engine. Allow engine to idle in Park or Neutral. Disconnect PSPS at switch. If RPM increases, replace PSPS. If RPM does not increase, go to next step.

4) Checking PSPS Harness. Turn key off and wait 10 seconds. Disconnect PSPS and ECA 60-pin connector. Inspect for and repair any damaged wiring. Install breakout box, leaving ECA disconnected. Set DVOM on 200K-ohm scale. Measure resistance between test pin No. 24 (test pin No. 23 on 2.5L CFI, test pin No. 2 on 3.0L SHO SEFI and 3.8L AXOD SEFI) and test pin No. 46 at the breakout box. If resistance is 10K ohms or less, repair short in harness. If reading is greater than 10K ohms, replace ECA. Repeat QUICK TEST.

5) KOER SELF-TEST Code 52 Displayed. If you turned steering wheel 1/2 turn within 1-2 seconds AFTER engine ID code, but BEFORE dynamic response code, go to next step. If steering wheel was not turned, ensure front wheels are centered (no load condition). Repeat QUICK TEST.

6) Checking ECA Open Circuit Identifying Capabilities. Turn key off and wait 10 seconds. Disconnect PSPS. Perform KOEO SELF-TEST. If Code 52 is present, go to step **8)**. If Code 52 is not present, go to next step.

7) PSPS Harness Check. Turn key off and wait 10 seconds. Disconnect PSPS and ECA 60-pin connector. Inspect connector for damaged pins, corrosion, or loose wires. Install breakout box, leaving ECA disconnected, and set DVOM on 200K-ohm scale. Measure resistance between test pins No. 46 and 24 (test pin No. 23 on 2.5L CFI, test pin No. 2 on 3.0L SHO SEFI and 3.8L AXOD SEFI) at breakout box. If reading is 10K ohms or less, repair short to SIG RTN in PSPS circuit. Repeat QUICK TEST. If reading is 10K ohms or more, replace ECA and repeat QUICK TEST.

8) PSPS Position Comparison. Turn key off and wait 10 seconds. Install breakout box, leaving ECA connected. With PSPS connected, set DVOM on 200-ohm scale. Turn key on and measure resistance between test pins No. 24 (test pin No. 23 on 2.5L CFI, test pin No. 2 on 3.0L SHO SEFI and 3.8L AXOD SEFI) and No. 46. Start engine. If

CIRCUIT TEST B15 (Cont.)

reading remains less than 10 ohms between KOEO and KOER, go to next step. If not, go to step **11)**.

9) PSPS Position: Load/No Load. Install breakout box and connect ECA. Connect PSPS and set DVOM on 200-ohm scale. Start engine and allow it to idle. Ensure clutch is not depressed on 3.0L SHO SEFI vehicles equipped with manual transmissions. Measure resistance between test pins No. 24 (test pin No. 23 on 2.5L CFI, test pin No. 2 on 3.0L SHO SEFI and 3.8L AXOD SEFI) and No. 46 at breakout box. Turn steering wheel 1/2 turn and return. If reading changes from less than 10 ohms to infinity (indicating PSPS opening) and then returns to 10 ohms or less (when steering wheel is centered), PSPS system is okay. Remove breakout box and return to QUICK TEST. If reading did not change as indicated, go to next step.

10) PSPS Closed or Low Hydraulic Pressure. At this point, there are only 2 possible causes for the original Code 52. They are a PSPS switch that will not open, or low available hydraulic pressure. Turn key off and wait 10 seconds. Substitute original switch with a known good PSPS switch. Perform KOER SELF-TEST and turn steering wheel at least 1/2 turn after engine ID code. If Code 52 is still present, check for low hydraulic pressure. If Code 52 is not present, replace original PSPS switch. Service other codes if necessary.

11) PSPS Always Open or High Hydraulic Pressure. At this point, there are only 2 possible causes for original Code 52. They are a PSPS switch that is always open, or excessively high hydraulic pressure. Turn key off and wait 10 seconds. Substitute original switch with a known good PSPS switch. Perform KOER SELF-TEST and turn steering wheel at least 1/2 turn after engine ID code. If Code 52 is still present, check for high hydraulic pressure. If Code 52 is not present, replace original PSPS switch. Service other codes if necessary.

CIRCUIT TEST C1

FUEL CONTROL – ALL APPLICATIONS

NOTE: Perform this test when Service Code 41, 91, 42, 92, 43, 65, 85, 86 or 93 is displayed during QUICK TESTS or when directed here by other test procedures.

NOTE: See HOW TO USE CIRCUIT TESTS, at beginning of circuit tests before performing this test. Fuel contaminated engine oil may affect Service Codes 41, 91 and 42, 92. If this is suspected, remove PCV valve from valve cover and repeat QUICK TEST. If problem is corrected, change engine oil and filter.

To prevent replacement of good components, be aware of the following non-EEC areas which may be cause of driveability concerns:
* Ignition coil, distributor cap or rotor
* Faulty spark plugs or wires
* Faulty CANP system
* DIS ignition system
* EGR valve and gasket
* Air filter
* Fuel or engine oil contamination
* Poor electrical ground
* Faulty fuel pressure
* Intake or exhaust manifold leaks
* Engine below normal operating temperature

This test is intended to diagnose only the following components:
* HEGO sensor
* HEGO signal and ground circuit
* HEGO sensor connection
* Vacuum systems
* Fuel injector
* ECA
* Electrical circuits HEGO GRD, HEGO, INJ 1-8, and VPWR

CAR – INJECTOR BANK RESISTANCE

Engine	Ohms (Ω)
1.9L MPFI	1.2-1.8
2.3L OHC MPFI	7.0-9.5
2.3L Turbo MPFI	1.2-1.8
2.3L HSC MPFI	7.0-9.5
3.0L MPFI	5.0-6.5

1989 COMPUTERIZED ENGINE CONTROLS
Ford Motor Co. EEC-IV (Cont.)

1a-457

CIRCUIT TEST C1 (Cont.)

CAR – INDIVIDUAL INJECTOR RESISTANCE [1]

Engine	Ohms (Ω)
1.9L MPFI	2.0-2.7
1.9L CFI	1.0-2.0
2.3L OHC MPFI	15.0-19.0
2.3L Turbo MPFI	2.0-3.0
2.3L HSC MPFI	13.5-16.0
2.5L CFI	1.0-2.0
3.0L MPFI	15.0-18.0
3.0L SHO SEFI	13.5-16.0
3.8L MPFI (FWD)	13.5-16.0
3.8L MPFI (RWD)	13.5-16.0
3.8L SC SEFI	13.5-16.0
5.0L SEFI	13.5-19.0
5.0L MA SEFI	13.5-19.0

[1] – Resistance values are for a single injector.

TRUCK – INDIVIDUAL INJECTOR RESISTANCE [1]

Engine	Ohms (Ω)
2.3L MPFI	13.5-18.0
2.9L MPFI	13.5-18.0
3.0L MPFI	15.0-18.0
4.9L MPFI	13.5-18.0
5.0L MPFI	13.5-18.0
5.8L MPFI	13.5-18.0
7.5L MPFI	13.5-19.0

[1] – Resistance values are for a single injector.

TRUCK INJECTOR BANK RESISTANCE

Engine	Ohms (Ω)
2.3L MPFI	7.0-9.5
2.9L MPFI	5.0-6.5
3.0L MPFI	5.0-6.5
4.9L MPFI	5.0-6.5
5.0L MPFI	3.5-5.0
5.8L MPFI	2.5-5.0
7.5L MPFI	2.5-5.0

CAR – FUEL PRESSURE SPECIFICATIONS: psi (kg/cm²)

Engine	Pressure KOER	Pressure KOEO
1.9L MPFI	30-45 (2.11-3.16)	35-45 (2.46-3.16)
1.9L CFI	13-17 (.91-1.12)	13-17 (.91-1.12)
2.3L OHC MPFI	30-45 (2.11-3.16)	35-45 (2.46-3.16)
2.3L Turbo MPFI	30-55 (2.11-3.87)	35-45 (2.46-3.16)
2.3L HSC MPFI	45-60 (3.16-4.22)	50-60 (3.52-4.22)
2.5L CFI	39.2 (2.7)	39.2 (2.7)
3.0L MPFI	30-45 (2.11-3.16)	35-45 (2.46-3.16)
3.0L SHO SEFI	28-33 (1.97-2.32)	30-45 (2.11-3.16)
3.8L SEFI (FWD)	30-45 (2.11-3.16)	35-45 (2.46-3.16)
3.8L SEFI (RWD)	30-45 (2.11-3.16)	35-45 (2.46-3.16)
3.8L SC SEFI	30-40 (2.11-2.81)	35-40 (2.46-2.81)
5.0L SEFI	30-45 (2.11-3.16)	35-45 (2.46-3.16)
5.0L MA SEFI	30-45 (2.11-3.16)	35-45 (2.46-3.16)

CIRCUIT TEST C1 (Cont.)

TRUCK – FUEL PRESSURE SPECIFICATIONS: psi (kg/cm²)

Engine	Pressure KOER	Pressure KOEO
2.3L MPFI	30-45 (2.11-3.16)	35-45 (2.46-3.16)
2.9L MPFI	30-45 (2.11-3.16)	35-45 (2.46-3.16)
3.0L MPFI	30-45 (2.11-3.16)	35-45 (2.46-3.16)
4.9L MPFI	45-60 (3.16-4.22)	50-60 (3.52-4.22)
5.0L MPFI	30-45 (2.11-3.16)	35-45 (2.46-3.16)
5.8L MPFI	30-45 (2.11-3.16)	35-45 (2.46-3.16)
7.5L MPFI	30-45 (2.11-3.16)	35-45 (2.46-3.16)

1.9L & 2.5L CFI Test Schematic

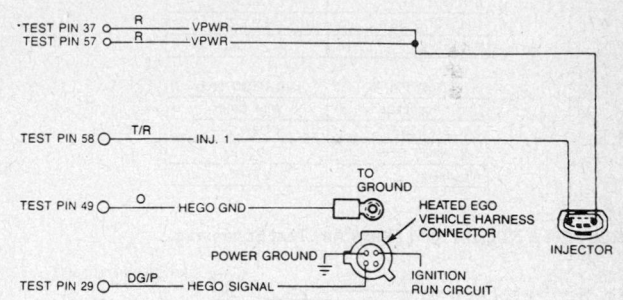

All MPFI (Except 2.3L MPFI Turbo) Test Schematic

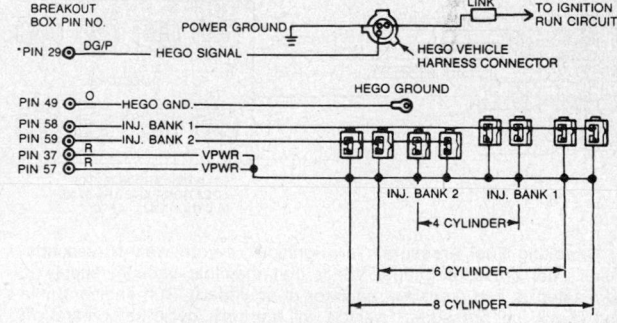

Test Pin 58	INJ BANK 1
Application	**Wire Color**
2.3L DIS Truck 2.9L Truck	LG/W
1.9L EFI	T/R
All Others	T/O

Test Pin 59	INJ BANK 2
Application	**Wire Color**
1.9L EFI	T/O
All Others	T/R

2.3L MPFI Turbo Test Schematic

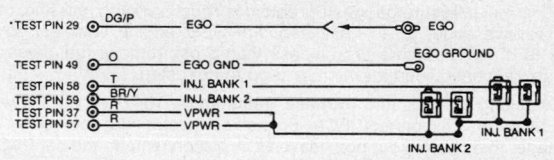

1a-458

1989 COMPUTERIZED ENGINE CONTROLS
Ford Motor Co. EEC-IV (Cont.)

CIRCUIT TEST C1 (Cont.)

All V6 SEFI Test Schematic

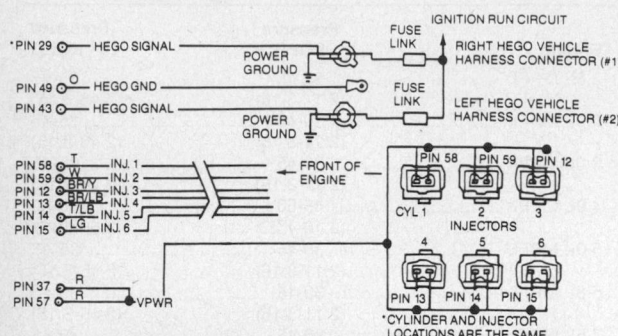

Test Pin 29	Right HEGO (#1)
Application	**Wire Color**
3.0L SHO SEFI	DG/P
3.8L AXOD SEFI	DB/LG
All Others	T/O

Test Pin 43	Left HEGO (#2)
Application	**Wire Color**
3.0L SHO SEFI	DB/LG
3.8L AXOD SEFI	DG/P
All Others	T/R

5.0L SEFI & 5.0L MA SEFI (Mass Air) Test Schematic

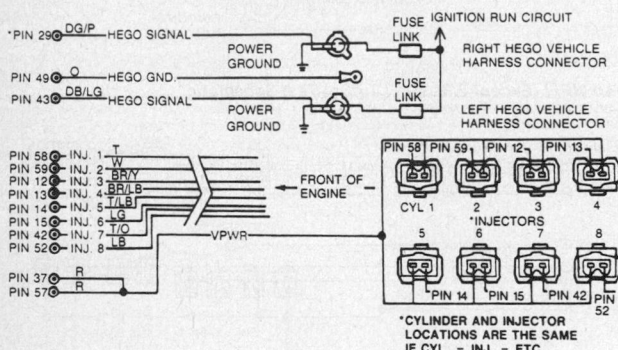

1) Checking Fuel Pressure. Turn ignition key off, wait 10 seconds. Install fuel pressure gauge. Verify that manifold vacuum supply is connected to fuel pressure regulator (if equipped). Run engine at idle and check fuel pressure. If vehicle will not start, cycle key on and off several times. See FUEL PRESSURE SPECIFICATIONS table. If fuel pressure is within specification, go to next step. If pressure is not to specification, remove fuel pressure gauge. Repair electric fuel pump or fuel pressure regulator.

2) Checking Fuel Pressure Check Valve. With KOEO, check that fuel pressure remains to specification for approximately 60 seconds. If system holds pressure, go to next step. If system does not hold pressure, go to step **6)** for all engine applications except SEFI. For SEFI engines, go to step **9)**.

3) Fuel Delivery Test. Ensure fuel is of good quality. With key off, install fuel pressure gauge and pressurize fuel system as in step **1)**. Disconnect inertia switch. Crank engine for 5 seconds. If fuel pressure drop is greater than 5 psi after 5 seconds of cranking, the EEC-IV system is not the cause of the no start condition. Check additional DIAGNOSIS BY SYMPTOM tests. Reconnect inertia switch and remove fuel pressure gauge. If problem is rough running, missing, or a fuel service code, go to next step. For SEFI engine vehicles, go to step **9)**. If fuel pressure drop is less than 5 psi, remove fuel pressure gauge, reconnect inertia switch, and go to next step.

4) Checking Injector and Harness Resistance. Turn key off and wait 10 seconds. Disconnect ECA 60-pin connector. Inspect pins for damage. Install breakout box, leave ECA disconnected, and set DVOM on 200-ohm scale.

CIRCUIT TEST C1 (Cont.)

MPFI Engines:
Measure resistance of injector banks between test pins No. 37 and 58 (bank No. 1) or 59 (bank No. 2) at breakout box. Record resistance. Refer to INJECTOR BANK RESISTANCE table.

SEFI Engines:
Measure resistance between suspect cylinder test pin (from Cylinder Balance Test) and test pin No. 37, at the breakout box. Refer to INJECTOR BANK RESISTANCE table.

For No Starts: Choose any injector and measure resistance between that injector circuit test pin and test pin No. 37, at breakout box. Record resistance.

CFI Engines:
Measure resistance of injector circuit between test pins No. 37 and 58, at the breakout box. Record resistance.

Compare resistance with appropriate specification in INJECTOR BANK RESISTANCE table. If injector is within specification, go to step **6)**. If injector is not within specification, do the following:

MPFI Engines:
Go to next step.

SEFI Engines:
Remove breakout box and reconnect ECA. Service open/short in harness/connector. If okay, replace injector. Rerun QUICK TEST and Cylinder Balance Test.

For No Start: Service open in VPWR circuit.

CFI Engines:
Remove breakout box and reconnect ECA. Repair open/short in harness/connector. If okay, replace injector. Rerun QUICK TEST.

5) Isolating Faulty Injector Circuit. Turn key off. Install breakout box and disconnect ECA. Disconnect all injectors on suspect bank. With DVOM set on 200-ohm scale, connect one injector and measure resistance between test pins No. 37 and 58 or 59. Disconnect injector and repeat process for all other injectors. See INDIVIDUAL INJECTOR RESISTANCE table for specifications. If injectors are within specifications, go to step **6)**. If injectors are not to specification, remove breakout box, reconnect ECA and injectors. Repair open/short in injector harness. If okay, replace injector. Rerun QUICK TEST.

6) Checking Injector Drive Signal. With key off and breakout box installed, connect ECA to breakout box. Use a non-powered 12-volt test light and the following connection procedure:

MPFI Engines:
Connect test light between test pins No. 37 and 58 at the breakout box. Connect light between test pins No. 37 and 59 at the breakout box.

SEFI Engines:
Connect test light between test pin No. 37 and the suspect injector(s) test pin at the breakout box.

CFI Engines:
Connect test light between test pins No. 37 and 58, at the breakout box.

Crank or start engine. A properly operating system is indicated by a test light that glows dimly. If light glows dim, go to next step; except on SEFI engines. On SEFI engine, remove breakout box and reconnect ECA. Clean and test injectors. Rerun QUICK TEST and CYLINDER BALANCE TEST. If test light does not glow dimly, perform the following procedure.

No Light:
Check for 12 volts at test pins No. 37 and 57.

Bright Light:
Check injector circuit for shorts to ground. If okay, remove breakout box and replace ECA. Rerun QUICK TEST.

7) Fuel Pressure Problems: External Sources. Pressurize fuel system as per step **1)**. Examine fuel system in the following manner.

MPFI Engines:
Visually inspect, fuel injector "O" rings, fuel pressure regulator, and fuel rails.

CFI Engines:
Remove air inlet duct at fuel charging assembly injection inlet. Visually inspect, fuel injector "O" rings, fuel pressure regulator, and fuel line connections.

If there is a visible leak, remove pressure gauge. Repair leak as necessary. Rerun QUICK TEST. If there is no leak, go to next step for MPFI engines. For CFI engines, remove pressure gauge. Fuel delivery system is okay. Problem is in common area for all cylinders, such as, vacuum leak, fuel contamination, or EGR leak.

8) Injector Balance Test. Connect tachometer to engine. Start and run engine at idle. Disconnect and reconnect injectors one at a time. Note

1989 COMPUTERIZED ENGINE CONTROLS
Ford Motor Co. EEC-IV (Cont.)

1a-459

CIRCUIT TEST C1 (Cont.)

RPM drop for each injector. Each injector should produce a momentary RPM drop of about 100 RPM drop. Note that ISC will attempt to re-establish correct RPM. If each injector does not produce at least 100 RPM drop when disconnected, service or replace faulty injector(s) and repeat QUICK TEST. If RPM drop is correct for all injectors, fuel delivery is okay. Problem is in area common to all cylinders such as a vacuum leak, fuel contamination, EGR, etc.

9) Cylinder Balance Test: SEFI Engines ONLY. Perform KOER SELF-TEST. After last code is displayed, wait 5-10 seconds. Enter CYLINDER BALANCE TEST by briefly opening throttle for one second (not WOT). Test time is approximately 2-3 minutes. A Code 77 indicates that the throttle was touched when the test was running and that the test was not completed. Use table to interpret codes received from test. If balance test does not display code 90, go to step **4)**. If balance test displays Code 90 (Pass), fuel delivery is okay, fault is in an area common to all cylinders (except SEFI MA vehicles). Vehicles with 5.0 SEFI MA engines, and Code 41 or 91 displayed, go to next step. If a Code 42 or 92 is displayed, go to step **22)**

CYLINDER BALANCE TEST SERVICE CODES

Service Code	Cylinder or Injector No.	Breakout Box Test Pin No.
90	(Pass)	(Pass)
10	1	58
20	2	59
30	3	12
40	4	13
50	5	14
60	6	15
70	7	42
80	8	52
77	(Retest)	(Retest)

NOTE: A Code 90 received in the initial stage of the cylinder balance test indicates that the injector harness is not open or shorted, and a signal is being sent to all injectors.

10) Code 41 or 91: Fuel Control Always Lean. If vehicle is equipped with dual HEGO's, Code 41 refers to the Right, or No. 1 HEGO and Code 91 refers to the Left, or No. 2 HEGO. Run engine at 2000 RPM for 2 minutes. Turn key off and wait 10 seconds. Rerun KOER SELF-TEST. Check for Code 41 or 91. If Code 41 or 91 is not displayed, go to step **19)**. If Code 41 and 91 is displayed, go to appropriate step number as listed below.

Engines equipped with MAP sensors: Go to next step.
Engines equipped with VAF meters: Go to step **12)**.
Engines equipped with MA meters: Go to step **13)**.

11) Checking HEGO Sensor on Engines With MAP Sensors. Turn key off and set DVOM on 20-volt scale. Disconnect appropriate HEGO sensor from vehicle harness. Connect DVOM to HEGO SIGNAL lead at sensor and engine ground. Apply 10-14 in. Hg vacuum to Manifold Absolute Pressure (MAP) sensor and start engine. Run engine at 2000 RPM for 2 minutes. If reading is less than 0.5 volt, replace HEGO sensor(s) and then repeat QUICK TEST. If reading is greater than 0.5 volt, go to step **14)**. If reading is less than 0.5 volt, replace HEGO sensor, reconnect MAP, and rerun QUICK CHECK.

NOTE: Vacuum or air leaks in non-EEC-IV related areas may cause Code 41 or 91. Check the following areas: A/C control motor, engine seals, EGR system, PVC system and lead contamination of HEGO sensor.

12) Checking HEGO Sensor on Engines With VAF meters. With key off and DVOM set on 20-volt scale, disconnect HEGO sensor from harness. Connect DVOM between HEGO sensor and engine ground. Remove air cleaner in order to reach airflow meter inlet. Use a pencil to prop airflow meter door in partially open position. Start and run engine at 2000 RPM for 2 minutes. If reading is not greater than 0.5 volt after one minute, replace HEGO sensor and repeat QUICK TEST. If reading is greater than 0.5 volt after one minute, go to step **14)**.

13) Checking HEGO Sensor on Engines With MA Sensor. The purpose of this test is to verify HEGO sensor can generate a voltage signal of greater than 0.5 volt during KOER SELF-TEST. With key off and DVOM set on 20-volt scale, disconnect HEGO sensor from harness. Connect DVOM between HEGO SIGNAL and battery negative post. Rerun KOER SELF-TEST and monitor HEGO sensor voltage. If voltage is greater than 0.5 volt, go to next step. If voltage is less than 0.5 volt, replace HEGO sensor and rerun QUICK TEST.

CIRCUIT TEST C1 (Cont.)

14) Checking Continuity of HEGO Signal and Ground Circuits. Turn key off. Install breakout box, leaving ECA and HEGO disconnected. Set DVOM on 200-ohm scale and measure resistance between test pin No. 49 and battery negative post. Measure resistance between test pin No. 29 and HEGO SIGNAL at vehicle harness connector. For vehicles with dual HEGO sensors, measure resistance between test pin No. 43 and HEGO SIGNAL at vehicle harness connector. If all readings are greater than 5 ohms, repair open in appropriate circuit, connect HEGO sensor and ECA, and repeat QUICK TEST. If all readings are less than 5 ohms, go to next step.

15) Checking HEGO Circuit For Short to Ground. Turn key off. Leave breakout box installed and ECA disconnected. Disconnect HEGO sensor and set DVOM on 200K-ohm scale. Measure resistance between test pin No. 29 and test pin No. 40 at the breakout box. For vehicles with dual sensors measure resistance between test pin No. 43 and test pin No. 40. If any reading is less than 10K ohms, repair short to ground. Repeat QUICK TEST. If reading is 10K ohms or more, go to next step. On models with 2.3L TC MPFI, go to step **18)**.

16) Checking HEGO Sensor For Short to Ground. With key off, breakout box installed, and ECA disconnected, set DVOM to 200K-ohm scale. Disconnect HEGO sensor. Measure resistance between PWR GND and HEGO SIGNAL at the HEGO sensor connector. If resistance is less than 10K ohms, replace HEGO sensor and rerun QUICK TEST. If resistance is greater than 10K ohms, do the appropriate following procedure.
Engines equipped with MAP sensor: Go to next step.
Engines equipped with VAF meter: Go to step **18)**.
Engines equipped with MA (Mass Air Sensor): Remove breakout box, reconnect HEGO sensor, replace ECA and rerun QUICK TEST.

17) Eliminating Code 41: Engines With MAP Sensor. Turn key off. Install breakout box and connect ECA and HEGO sensor. Ensure MAP sensor vacuum hose is disconnected and plugged. Apply 10-14 in. Hg to MAP sensor. Start and run engine at 2000 RPM for 2 minutes. Allow engine to return to idle. Perform KOER SELF-TEST. If Code 41 is still present, check ECA connector for corroded or damaged pins. If connector is okay, replace ECA. Connect MAP sensor vacuum hose and repeat QUICK TEST. If Code 41 is not present, connect MAP sensor vacuum hose. HEGO input circuit is okay. Return to step **1)**.

18) Eliminating Code 41: Engines With VAF Meter. With key off, install breakout box and connect ECA. Reconnect HEGO sensor. Remove air filter and insert a pencil in VAF meter inlet. Start engine and run at 2000 RPM for approximately 2 minutes. Rerun SELF-TEST. If Code 41 is not present, the HEGO circuit is okay. Remove breakout box, reconnect ECA and go to step **1)** of this test. If Code 41 is displayed, remove test set-up, replace ECA, and rerun QUICK TEST.

19) Checking Resistance of HEGO Heating Element. Turn key off, disconnect HEGO sensor, and set DVOM on 200-ohm scale. Measure resistance between KEY POWER circuit and POWER GROUND circuit at HEGO connector. Hot to warm resistance should be 5-20 ohms. Room temperature resistance is 2-5 ohms. If resistance is within specification, go to next step. If resistance is not within specifications, replace HEGO sensor and rerun QUICK TEST.

20) Checking Power at HEGO Harness Connector. With KOEO, and HEGO disconnected, set DVOM on 20-volt scale. Measure voltage between KEY POWER circuit and POWER GROUND circuit at HEGO harness connector. If voltage is greater than 10.5 volts, HEGO system is okay, go to step **1)** of this test. If voltage is less than 10.5 volts, go to next step.

21) Checking Continuity of Power Ground Circuit. Turn key off and wait 10 seconds. Disconnect HEGO sensor and set DVOM on 200-ohm scale. Measure resistance between POWER GROUND circuit at HEGO vehicle harness connector and battery negative post. If resistance is less than 5 ohms, repair open in KEY POWER circuit and rerun QUICK TEST. If resistance is more than 5 ohms, reconnect HEGO sensor and repair open in POWER GROUND circuit. Rerun QUICK TEST.

22) Code 42 or 92: Fuel Control Rich, Check HEGO SIGNAL For Short To Power. On dual HEGO systems, Code 42 refers to right side HEGO, Code 92 refers to left side HEGO. Turn key off and wait 10 seconds. Disconnect appropriate HEGO sensor. Set DVOM on 20-volt scale. With KOEO, measure voltage between HEGO SIGNAL and POWER GROUND at HEGO harness connector. If reading is more than .5 volt, repair short to power in HEGO circuit. Repeat QUICK TEST. If reading is less than 0.5 volt, go to next step.

23) Checking HEGO Sensor For Short to Key Power Circuit. Turn key off and leave HEGO disconnected. Set DVOM on 200K-ohm scale. Measure resistance from KEY POWER circuit to HEGO SIGNAL circuit at HEGO sensor connector. If reading is 10K ohms or less, replace

CIRCUIT TEST C1 (Cont.)

HEGO sensor and repeat QUICK TEST. If reading is greater than 10K ohms, go to next step.

24) Attempt to Generate Code 41 or 91. The following non-EEC areas may cause these codes: fuel contaminated engine oil, ignition misfire and faulty CANP system. Turn key off and wait 10 seconds. Disconnect appropriate HEGO sensor. Using jumper wire, connect HEGO SIGNAL circuit at HEGO harness connector to battery negative terminal. Repeat KOER SELF-TEST. If Codes 41 or 91 are present, remove jumper wire and go to next step for engines with MAP. All others, go to step **27)**. If codes 41 or 91 are not present, remove jumper wire. Disconnect ECA connector and inspect for damage. If connector is okay, replace ECA. Repeat QUICK TEST.

NOTE: Because the MAP sensor has a large influence on fuel control, a Code 42 or 92 may be the result of a faulty MAP sensor, even thogh a Code 22 has not been set. The next 2 test steps will verify the MAP vacuum circuit.

25) Checking MAP Sensor For Vacuum Leaks. Turn key off and wait 10 seconds. Disconnect vacuum hose from MAP sensor and connect vacuum pump to sensor. Apply 18 in. Hg of vacuum to MAP sensor. If sensor does not hold vacuum, replace MAP sensor. Connect vacuum hose and repeat QUICK TEST. If MAP holds vacuum, release vacuum and go to next step.

26) Checking For Loss of Vacuum to MAP Sensor. Using vacuum "T", connect vacuum gauge in intake manifold vacuum hose at MAP sensor. Start engine and note vacuum reading. Turn key off and wait 10 seconds. Remove "T" and vacuum gauge. Reconnect hose to MAP sensor. Connect vacuum gauge at a different intake manifold location. Start engine and note vacuum reading. If readings differ by more than one in. Hg, inspect vacuum hoses for leaks, kinks, or blockage. Repair as required. If readings are within one in. Hg of each other, go to next step.

27) HEGO Sensor Check. Turn key off and wait 10 seconds. Disconnect HEGO sensor. Set DVOM on 20-volt scale and connect to HEGO SIGNAL at HEGO sensor connector. Remove a vacuum hose to create a vacuum leak, which will cause the HEGO sensor to go lean. Start engine and run at 2000 RPM. The DVOM should indicate 0.4 volt within 30 seconds. If voltage is within specification, HEGO is okay, go to step **1)** of this test. If voltage is not within specification, replace HEGO sensor and rerun QUICK TEST.

Create a vacuum leak in the following manner:
1.9L MPFI and 2.3L Turbo MPFI Engines: Disconnect the manifold vacuum hose as illustrated.

MA SEFI Engines: Disconnect any vacuum hose from the manifold vacuum "T".

All Other Engines: Disconnect the PCV valve hose from the PCV valve.

1.9L MPFI & 2.3L Turbo MPFI Engines: Induced Vacuum Leaks.

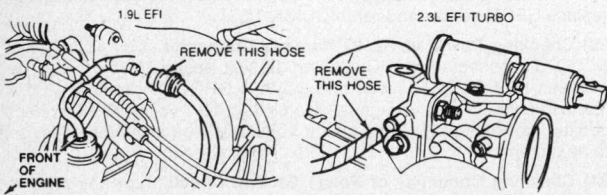

28) Continuous Memory Code 41 or 91. Indicates that a HEGO circuit has not switched during closed loop fuel control. In this situation a Code 41 or 91 may not indicate a lean condition. Diagnose all other driveability complaints in the DIAGNOSIS BY SYMPTOM test before attempting to service a Continuous Memory Code 41 or 91. Check the following areas.

Unmetered Air/Vacuum Leaks
- Canister Purge System
- PVC System
- Engine Sealing
- Crimped Fuel Lines
- Plugged Fuel Filter
- Fouled Injectors

HEGO Fuel Fouled
- If an over-rich condition is suspected of fouling the HEGO sensor, run the vehicle at sustained high (legal) speeds followed by a few hard acceleration runs. This will allow the HEGO contamination to be burned off.

CIRCUIT TEST C1 (Cont.)

Ignition System
- Check for DEFAULT base timing in QUICK TEST procedure.

Improper Fuel Used
- Lead Fouled HEGO Sensor.

Fuel Pressure
- Check Pressure Using Steps **1)** and **2)**.

TP Sensor
- With KOEO, move throttle slowly to WOT. Measure voltage between test pins No. 47 and 46 at breakout box. If voltage does not increase with throttle opening, replace TP sensor or linkage as necessary.

If vehicle still has driveability problems, perform test steps **3)** through **6)**.

29) Continuous Memory Codes 41, 42, 43, 65, 85 or 86. Diagnose all other driveability complaints before servicing these codes.

Code 41:
- HEGO indication that the fuel system was lean for more than 15 seconds when the fuel system should have been in closed loop fuel control.

Code 42:
- HEGO indication that the fuel system was rich for more than 15 seconds when the fuel system should have been in closed loop fuel control.

Code 43:
- HEGO indicated that the fuel system was lean during WOT for more than 3 seconds.

Code 65:
- Closed loop not activated on HEGO switching.

Code 85:
- Excessive rich mixture condition corrected by adaptive fuel strategy.

Code 86:
- Excessive lean fuel mixture condition corrected by adaptive fuel strategy.

If an over-rich fuel condition is suspected or experienced, check ignition system. Burn off fuel deposits on HEGO by operating the vehicle at sustained high (legal) speeds followed by a few hard acceleration runs. This will allow the HEGO contamination to be burned off. Check the following areas:

Code 41:
- Intermittent HEGO signal (Signal or Ground circuit).
- If Code 65 also present, repair faulty HEGO circuit (Signal or Ground circuit).
- If Code 43 also present, service Code 43 first.
- Check VAF for leaks or sticking (caused by contamination or frost).
- Low fuel pressure at WOT, check fuel supply.
- Low fuel flow at WOT (pressure okay), check clogged injectors or low battery voltage.

Code 42:
- Intermittent HEGO signal (Signal or Ground circuit).
- Airflow meter indicating incorrect airflow, check for high voltage output due to sticking air vane ("flapper door").
- Excessive fuel flow, pressure regulator vacuum supply disconnected or blocked fuel return line.
- Excessive fuel flow, damaged or stuck open injector(s).

Codes 41 and 42:
- Intermittent HEGO signal (Signal or Ground circuit).
- Sticking air vane ("flapper door"), due to contamination.
- Contaminated HEGO sensor, lead or silicone fouled.

Code 43:
- Low fuel pressure at WOT, fuel pump or restricted supply.
- Low fuel flow at WOT, injectors plugged or low battery voltage (less than 11 volts).

Code 65:
- Check for faulty HEGO signal (Signal or Ground circuit).

Code 85:
- If Code 42 also displayed, service it first.
- Excessive fuel pressure, check regulator vacuum line and fuel supply line.
- Excessive fuel flow, check for damaged injector pintles or injector stuck open.

Code 86:
- If Code 41 also displayed, service it first.
- Low fuel pressure, low pressure pump or restricted fuel supply.
- Low fuel flow, clogged injectors or low battery voltage.

1989 Computerized ENGINE CONTROLS
Ford Motor Co. EEC-IV (Cont.)

1a-461

CIRCUIT TEST C2

FUEL PUMP CIRCUIT (INERTIA SWITCH)

NOTE: Perform this test when Service Code 87, 95, or 96 is displayed during QUICK TESTS or when directed here by other test procedures.

Fuel Pump Circuit Wiring Diagrams

1.9L CFI, 1.9L EFI, 2.3L HSC

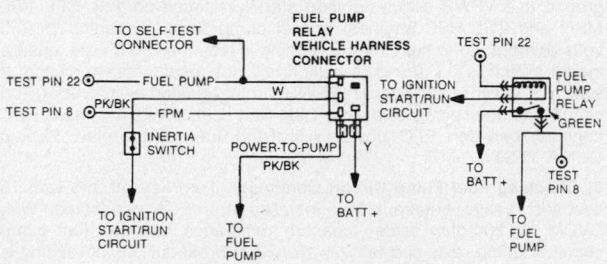

Test Pin 22

Application	Wire Color
1.9L CFI 1.9L EFI	T/LG
2.3L HSC	O/LB

5.0L SEFI MA, 2.3L EFI TRUCK, 2.9L EFI TRUCK, 3.0L EFI TRUCK

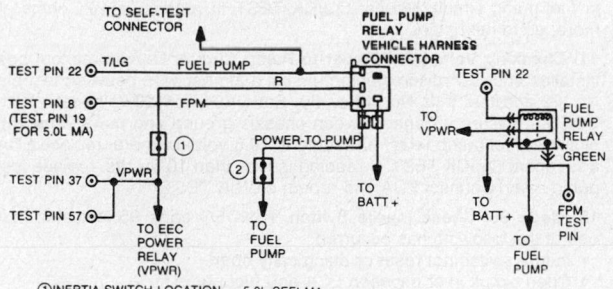

① INERTIA SWITCH LOCATION — 5.0L SEFI MA
② INERTIA SWITCH LOCATION — ALL OTHERS

POWER-TO-PUMP Circuit

Application	Wire Color
2.3L EFI Truck 3.0L EFI Truck	O/LB
2.9L EFI Truck 5.0L SEFI MA	PK/BK

Test Pin 8 (19)

Application	FPM Wire Color
2.3L EFI Truck 2.9L EFI Truck 3.0L EFI Truck	O/LB
5.0L SEFI MA	PK/BK

BATT+

Application	Wire Color
2.3L EFI Truck 2.9L EFI Truck	BK/Y
3.0L EFI Truck	Y
5.0L SEFI MA	O/LB

CIRCUIT TEST C2 (Cont.)

Fuel Pump Circuit Wiring Diagrams (Cont.)

2.3L OHC EFI CAR, 5.0L SEFI

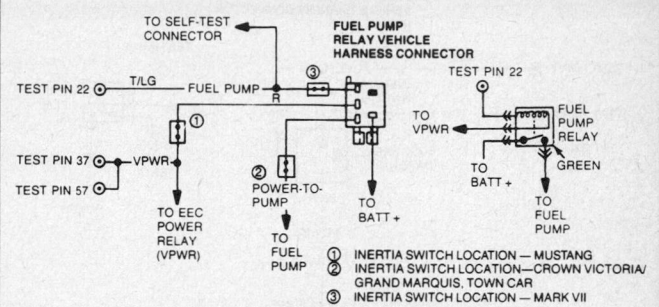

① INERTIA SWITCH LOCATION — MUSTANG
② INERTIA SWITCH LOCATION—CROWN VICTORIA/GRAND MARQUIS, TOWN CAR
③ INERTIA SWITCH LOCATION — MARK VII

POWER-TO-PUMP Circuit

Application	Wire Color
Crown Victoria/Grand Marquis, Town Car	O
Mustang Mark VII	PK/BK

BATT+ At Relay

Application	Wire Color
Crown Victoria/Grand Marquis, Town Car	Y
Mustang	O/LB
Mark VII	R

3.8L SEFI RWD, 3.8L SEFI SC, 4.9L EFI, 5.0L EFI, 5.8L EFI, 7.5L EFI, TRUCKS

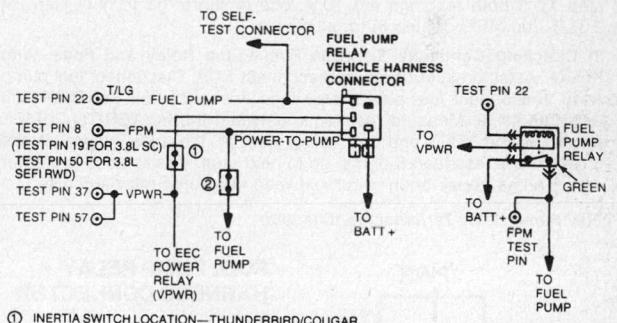

① INERTIA SWITCH LOCATION—THUNDERBIRD/COUGAR
② INERTIA SWITCH LOCATION—F-SERIES, E-SERIES, BRONCO

TEST PIN 8 (19, 50) POWER-TO-PUMP Circuit

Application	Wire Color
F-Series Bronco	BR
E-Series	O/LB
Thunderbird/Cougar	PK/BK

BATT+ At Relay

Application	Wire Color
F-Series E-Series Bronco	Y
Thunderbird/Cougar	BK/Y

VPWR At Relay

Application	Wire Color
F-Series E-Series Bronco	R
Thunderbird/Cougar	W

CIRCUIT TEST C2 (Cont.)

Fuel Pump Circuit Wiring Diagrams (Cont.)

2.3L EFI TC

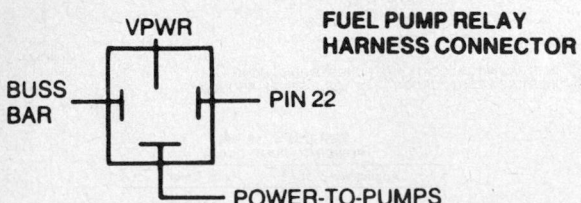

To prevent replacement of good components, be aware that the following non-EEC related areas may be at fault: fuel lines, fuel filters, throttle body, fuel pump or contaminated fuel.

1) No Fuel Pressure: Electrical Check. Install fuel pressure gauge. Cycle key from off to on several times to check if fuel pump runs. DO NOT crank engine. Pump should operate briefly each time key is on. If pump runs as indicated, service or replace fuel pump as necessary. If pump does not run as indicated, go to next step.

2) Checking For VPWR to ECA. Turn key off and wait 10 seconds. Disconnect ECA 60-pin connector. Inspect connector for damaged pins, corrosion, or loose wires. Install breakout box and reconnect ECA. With KOEO, set DVOM on 20-volt scale and measure voltage between test pins No. 37 and 40, and between test pins No. 57 and 60. If either reading is less than 10.5 volts, go to CIRCUIT TEST A2, step 1). If both readings are 10.5 volts or more, go to next step for 2.3L Turbo MPFI or step 5) for all others.

3) Checking Continuity Between Fuel Pump Relay and Fuse. With KOEO, install breakout box and reconnect ECA. Disconnect fuel pump relay. Disconnect fuel pump relay fuse (fuse No. 20). Set DVOM on 200-ohm scale. Measure resistance between the POWER-TO-PUMPS circuit of the relay and the relay side of the fuse holder. If the resistance is less than 5 ohms, go to next step. If resistance is greater than 5 ohms, repair open circuit between fuel pump relay and fuse.

Fuel Pump Relay Terminal Identification

FUEL PUMP RELAY
HARNESS CONNECTOR

VPWR

BUSS BAR — PIN 22

POWER-TO-PUMPS

4) Check Voltage to Power-to-Pumps Circuit (2.3L Turbo MPFI). With KOEO, breakout box installed and ECA connected. Disconnect fuel pump circuit fuse (fuse No. 20). Reconnnect fuel pump relay. Set DVOM on 20-volt scale. Measure voltage between chassis ground and power-to-pump circuit at fuel pump relay while cranking engine. If reading is less than 8 volts, go to step 6). If reading is 8 volts or more, check the following: open in power-to-pump circuit, open in fuel pump and open in fuel pump ground circuit.

5) Check Voltage to Power-to-Pump Circuit. With KOEO, breakout box installed and ECA connected. Disconnect fuel pump circuit fuse (fuse No. 20). Reconnnect fuel pump relay. Set DVOM on 20-volt scale. Measure voltage between chassis ground and power-to-pump circuit at fuel pump relay while cranking engine. If reading is less than 8 volts, go to step 6). If reading is 8 volts or more, check the following: open in power-to-pump circuit, open in fuel pump and open in fuel pump ground circuit.

6) Checking BATT+ Circuit to Fuel Pump Relay. Turn key on, leaving engine off. Leave breakout box installed and ECA connected, locate

CIRCUIT TEST C2 (Cont.)

fuel pump relay. Set DVOM on 20-volt scale. Measure voltage between chassis ground and BATT+ circuit at fuel pump relay. If reading is less than 10.5 volts, repair open in BATT+ circuit between fuel pump relay and battery positive post. Repeat QUICK TEST. If reading is 10.5 volts or greater, go to next step for 1.9L MPFI and 2.3L Turbo MPFI. All others, go to step 11).

7) Code 87: Checking VPWR Circuit to Fuel Pump Relay. Code 87 indicates a fuel pump primary circuit failure. Possible causes for this fault are: inertia switch not reset or electrically open, faulty fuel pump relay, ECA or, open or shorted circuit. Turn key on, leaving engine off. Leave breakout box installed and ECA connected. Locate fuel pump relay. Set DVOM on 20-volt scale. Measure voltage between chassis ground and VPWR circuit (ignition start/run circuit on 1.9L CFI, 1.9L MPFI and 2.3L HSC engines) at fuel pump relay. If reading is 10.5 volts or more, go to next step. If reading is less than 10.5 volts, ensure inertia switch is on. If inertia switch will not reset, replace switch. If switch is okay, repair open in VPWR circuit (ignition switch Start/Run circuit and fuel pump relay on 1.9L CFI, 1.9L MPFI and 2.3L HSC engines) between EEC power relay and fuel pump relay. Repeat QUICK TEST.

8) Checking Fuel Pump Circuit Continuity. Turn key off and wait 10 seconds. Leave breakout box installed and ECA connected. With DVOM on 200-ohm scale, measure resistance between fuel pump circuit at pump relay and test pin No. 22 at breakout box. If reading is 5 ohms or more, repair open in fuel pump circuit. Repeat QUICK TEST. If reading is less than 5 ohms, go to next step.

9) Checking For Short to Power. Disconnect ECA and fuel pump relay. With key on, and breakout box installed, set DVOM on 20-volt scale. Measure voltage between test pin No. 22 and battery negative terminal. If voltage is less than one volt, go to next step. If voltage is more than one volt, repair short circuit. Reconnect ECA and attempt to start vehicle. If vehicle fails to start, replace ECA. Rerun QUICK TEST.

10) Checking For Shorts to Ground. Turn key off. Leave breakout box installed and disconnect ECA. Disconnect fuel pump relay. With DVOM on 200K-ohm scale, measure resistance between test pin No. 22 and test pins No. 40 and 60. If reading is less than 10K ohms, repair short in fuel pump circuit. Repeat QUICK TEST. If reading is 10K ohms or more, go to next step.

11) Checking Voltage at Power-to-Pump Circuit. Leave breakout box installed and ECA disconnected. Install a jumper wire between test pin No. 22 and test pins No. 40 or 60. Set DVOM on 20-volt scale. With KOEO, measure voltage between chassis ground and power-to-pump circuit at fuel pump relay. If reading is 10.5 volts or more, replace ECA and repeat QUICK TEST. If reading is less than 10.5 volts, replace fuel pump relay. Connect ECA and repeat QUICK TEST.

12) Code 95: Check Inertia Switch. A KOEO code 95 indicates that one of the following has occurred:

- Inertia switch not reset or electrically open.
- Open circuit in or between ECA and fuel pump.
- Faulty ground connection at fuel pump.
- Fuel pump secondary circuit shorted to power.
- Fuel pump relay contacts always closed.
- Faulty ECA.

Turn key off and wait 10 seconds. Locate and disconnect inertia switch. Set DVOM on 200-ohm scale. Measure resistance of inertia switch. If resistance is less than 5 ohms, reconnect inertia switch and go to next step. If resistance is more than 5 ohms, replace or reset inertia switch and rerun QUICK TEST.

13) Verifying Fuel Pump is Off. With key off, listen for fuel pump noise. If fuel pump is off, go to step 15). If fuel pump is on, go to next step.

14) Fuel Pump Relay Check. Turn key off. Remove fuel pump relay. If fuel pump turns off, replace fuel pump relay. Repeat QUICK TEST. If fuel pump does not turn off, repair short to power-to-pump circuit. Repeat QUICK TEST.

15) Checking Continuity of Fuel Pump Monitor (FPM) Circuit. Turn key off and wait 10 seconds. Disconnect ECA 60-pin connector. Inspect connector for damaged pins, corrosion, or loose wires. Install breakout box and leave ECA disconnected. Disconnect fuel pump relay. Set DVOM on 200-ohm scale and measure resistance between test pin No. 8 (No. 19 on 5.0L MA SEFI, 3.8L SC SEFI and No. 50 on 3.8L RWD SEFI engines) at the breakout box and power-to-pump circuit at the fuel pump relay harness. If resistance is less than 5 ohms, go to next step. If resistance is greater than 5 ohms, repair open circuit and rerun QUICK TEST.

1989 COMPUTERIZED ENGINE CONTROLS
Ford Motor Co. EEC-IV (Cont.)

1a-463

CIRCUIT TEST C2 (Cont.)

Fuel Pump Relay Vehicle Harness Connector

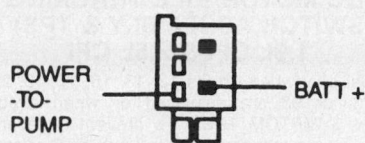

POWER -TO- PUMP   BATT +

FUEL PUMP RELAY
VEHICLE HARNESS CONNECTOR

16) Checking Continuity Between FPM Circuit and Ground. Turn key off. Install breakout box and disconnect ECA. Disconnect fuel pump relay. Set DVOM on 200-ohm scale and measure resistance between test pin No. 8 (No. 19 on 5.0L MA SEFI, 3.8 SC SEFI and No. 50 on 3.8L RWD SEFI Engines) at the breakout box and battery negative terminal. If resistance is less than 10 ohms, go to next step for 1.9L MPFI engines. On all others, remove test set-up, reconnect fuel pump relay, replace ECA and rerun QUICK TEST. If resistance is more than 10 ohms, remove test set-up and check the following: open circuit in fuel pump, poor ground connection at fuel pump, or an open in power-to-pump circuit.

17) Checking Fuel Pump Primary Circuit For Short to Ground. Turn key off and wait 10 seconds. Install breakout box and disconnect ECA. Disconnect fuel pump relay and set DVOM on 200K-ohm scale. Measure resistance between test pins No. 22 and 40 at the breakout box. If resistance is greater than 10K ohms, remove test set-up. Replace ECA, and rerun QUICK TEST. If resistance is less than 10K ohms, remove test set-up. Repair short circuit and rerun QUICK TEST.

18) Code 96: Checking BATT+ to Fuel Pump Relay. Service code 96 indicates a fuel pump secondary circuit failure between the BATT+ supply and the FPM connection to the POWER-to-PUMP connection. Possible causes for this fault are; faulty fuel pump relay or ECA, open circuit.
Turn key off and wait 10 seconds. Locate fuel pump relay. With the DVOM on 20-volt scale, measure voltage between BATT+ circuit at fuel pump relay and battery negative. If voltage is greater than 10.5 volts, go to next step. If voltage is less than 10.5 volts, repair open circuit and rerun QUICK TEST.

19) Verifying Fuel Pump Operation. With key off, set DVOM on 20-volt scale. Connect DVOM between POWER-to-PUMP circuit at fuel pump relay and battery negative post. Check voltage while turning key to ON position (one second) and OFF position (10 seconds). Repeat cycle at least 5 times. If voltage is greater than 10.5 volts for approximately one second after key is turned to ON position, go to next step (3.8L SC & RWD SEFI cars, 4.9 MPFI, 5.0L MPFI, 5.8L MPFI and 7.5L MPFI Trucks) or replace ECA (all other models) and rerun QUICK TEST. If voltage is not to specification, inspect relay harness connector and if okay, replace fuel pump relay.

20) Checking Continuity of Power-to-Pump Circuit. Turn key off and disconnect ECA 60-pin connector. Inspect connector for damaged pins, corrosion, or loose wires. Install breakout box and leave ECA disconnected. With DVOM on 200-ohm scale, measure resistance between test pin No. 8 (No. 19 on 3.8L SC SEFI and No. 50 on 3.8L RWD SEFI) at breakout box and POWER-to-PUMP circuit at relay harness connector. If resistance is less than 5 ohms, remove test set-up, replace ECA, and rerun QUICK TEST. If resistance is more than 5 ohms, repair open circuit between FPM connecting splice and relay. Rerun QUICK TEST.

21) Continuous Code 95: Checking EEC-IV Harness. A continuous code 95 indicates that one of the following conditions has occurred intermittently:
Open circuit in or between the fuel pump and FPM circuit at the ECA. Faulty ground circuit at the fuel pump. Start engine and perform WIGGLE TEST on harness assembly to fuel pump, and to pump ground circuit harness. Lightly tap inertia switch and pump to simulate road shock. Check for engine miss or stumble while performing test. With key off, check harness connectors for corrosion or damage. Isolate and repair any faults that are found, clear Code 95 and rerun QUICK TEST. If no fault is found, go to next step.

22) Checking FPM Circuit. Turn key off. Disconnect ECA 60-pin connector. Inspect connector for damaged pins, corrosion, or loose wires. Install breakout box and leave ECA disconnected. With KOEO,

CIRCUIT TEST C2 (Cont.)

connect a test light between test pin No. 8 (No. 19 on 5.0L MA SEFI, 3.8L SC SEFI and No. 50 on 3.8L RWD SEFI) and test pin No. 37. With test light lit, perform WIGGLE test on FPM circuit between pump and monitor. Light should go out if fault is found during WIGGLE TEST. Isolate and repair any found faults, remove test set-up and rerun QUICK TEST. If no faults are found, go to next step.

23) Check For Short to Power. With KOEO, breakout box installed and ECA disconnected. Connect a test light between test pin No. 8 (No. 19 on 5.0L MA SEFI, 3.8L SC SEFI and No. 50 on 3.8L RWD SEFI) and test pin No. 40. Observe test light, perform WIGGLE test on FPM circuit and POWER-to-PUMP circuit. Lightly tap the fuel pump relay to simulate road shock. Light should go on when fault is found during WIGGLE TEST, indicating a short to power. Listen for sound of fuel pump turning on. Isolate and repair any found faults, remove test set-up and rerun QUICK TEST. If no faults are found, fault is intermittent and cannot be duplicated at this time.

24) Continuous Code 96: Check For Code 87. If Code 87 is also present with Code 96, go to step **26)**. If code 87 is not displayed, go to next step.

25) Checking EEC-IV Harness. A continuous code 96 without an accompanying code 87 indicates one of the following occurred during vehicle operation: An open in the BATT+ circuit between the BATT+ and the fuel pump relay, relay contacts opened or open in the POWER-to-PUMP circuit from the fuel pump relay to the FPM splice. With engine running attempt to cause a miss or stumble while performing WIGGLE TEST on pump harness and connectors. With engine off, inspect all connectors for damage or corrosion. If a fault is found, isolate and repair it. Clear codes and rerun QUICK TEST. If no fault is found on 1.9L MPFI engines, go to next step. If no fault is found on all other models, fault may not be duplicated at this time. Clear memory codes, code 96 testing is complete.

26) Continuous Code 87: Checking EEC-IV Harness. A continuous Code 87 indicates the primary fuel pump circuit has failed during vehicle operation. Possible causes for this fault are; An open in the VPWR circuit between the EEC power relay and the fuel pump relay, open coil in fuel pump relay or open in fuel pump circuit. Faulty inertia switch.

With engine running, attempt to cause a miss or stumble while performing WIGGLE TEST on VPWR circuit between EEC power relay and fuel pump relay. Wiggle fuel pump circuit harness (test pin No. 22) between ECA and the fuel pump relay. Lightly tap fuel pump relay to simulate road shock. With key off, inspect ECA 60-pin connector for damage or corrosion. If a fault is found, isolate and repair it. Rerun QUICK TEST. If no fault is found, fault may not be duplicated at this time.

CIRCUIT TEST D1

EGR ON/OFF CONTROL

NOTE: Perform this test when Service Code 34 is displayed during QUICK TESTS or when directed here by other test procedures. Code 34 may be result of high volume exhaust vent system reducing backpressure. If this is suspected, perform test in well-ventilated area without exhaust vent connected.

EGR On/Off Circuit

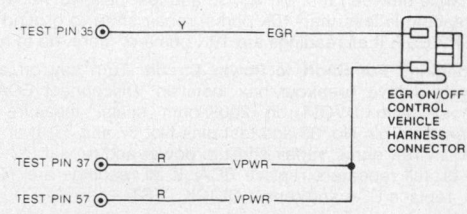

TEST PIN 35 — Y — EGR

EGR ON/OFF CONTROL VEHICLE HARNESS CONNECTOR

TEST PIN 37 — R — VPWR

TEST PIN 57 — R — VPWR

*TEST PINS LOCATED ON BREAKOUT BOX.
ALL HARNESS CONNECTORS VIEWED INTO MATING SURFACE.

To prevent replacement of good components, be aware that the following non-EEC related areas may be at fault: air or vacuum leaks, EGR flow restrictions or EGR valve.

CIRCUIT TEST D1 (Cont.)

1) Code 34: Enter Output State Check. KOER Code 34 indicates that with engine RPM above idle and stable, a specified RPM drop did not occur when EGR was cycled. Possible causes for this fault are:

- Faulty EGR On/Off control solenoid
- Faulty EGR solenoid
- Faulty EGR vent solenoid
- Faulty EVP sensor
- Faulty wiring harness
- Faulty ECA
- Manifold vacuum line blocked or leaking

Use only VOM/DVOM, not diagnostic tester, for this step. Turn key off and wait 10 seconds. Set DVOM on 20-volt scale. Connect negative DVOM lead to STO at SELF-TEST connector and positive lead to positive battery terminal. Jumper STI to SIGNAL RETURN at SELF-TEST connector. Rerun KOEO SELF-TEST until end of CONTINUOUS SELF-TEST code display (DVOM will read zero volts). Depress and release throttle and observe DVOM reading. If DVOM reading changes to a higher voltage, stay in OUTPUT STATE CHECK and go to next step. If DVOM did not show high voltage, depress throttle to WOT and release. If STO voltage does not go high, go to CIRCUIT TEST D16, step 1). Leave test equipment hooked up.

2) Checking Solenoid Electrical Operation. Set DVOM on 20-volt scale. Connect DVOM positive lead to VPWR circuit at EGR solenoid and negative lead to EGR output circuit. Depress and release throttle several times to cycle EGR solenoid output on and off. If output does not cycle on and off, remove STI jumper wire and go to step 5). If output cycles on and off, go to next step.

3) Checking Solenoid For Vacuum Cycling. Connect vacuum pump to solenoid vacuum supply port and vacuum gauge to output port of solenoid. Apply minimum vacuum of 6 in. Hg. Depress and release throttle several times to cycle EGR solenoid output while maintaining vacuum at supply port. Note gauge reading. If vacuum output does not cycle, replace EGR solenoid and repeat QUICK TEST. If vacuum output cycles, go to next step.

4) Checking Manifold Vacuum Lines. With vacuum lines disconnected at EGR solenoid, start engine. If vacuum is present, EEC system is not cause of problem. Check exhaust gas recirculation system. If vacuum is not present, correct vacuum source blockage or leak and repeat QUICK TEST.

5) Measuring Solenoid Resistance. Turn key off and wait 10 seconds. Disconnect EGR solenoid. Set DVOM on 200-ohm scale and measure solenoid resistance. If reading is less than 65 ohms or more than 110 ohms, replace EGR solenoid and repeat QUICK TEST. If reading is between 65 and 110 ohms, go to next step.

6) Checking VPWR Circuit. With KOEO, set DVOM on 20-volt scale. Measure voltage between VPWR circuit at EGR solenoid harness connector and battery ground. If reading is less than 10.5 volts, repair open in harness and repeat QUICK TEST. If reading is 10.5 volts or more, go to next step.

7) Checking Continuity of EGR Circuit. Turn key off and wait 10 seconds. Disconnect ECA 60-pin connector. Inspect connector for damaged pins, corrosion, or loose wires. Repair if necessary. Install breakout box, leaving ECA disconnected. Set DVOM on 200-ohm scale. Measure resistance between test pin No. 35 at the breakout box and EGR circuit at harness connector. If reading is 5 ohms or more, repair open circuit and repeat QUICK TEST. If reading is less than 5 ohms, go to next step.

8) Checking Circuit For Short to Ground. Turn key off and wait 10 seconds. Leave breakout box installed and ECA disconnected. Disconnect EGR solenoid. Set DVOM on 200K-ohm scale. Measure resistance between test pin No. 35 and test pins No. 40, 46, and 60. If any reading is less than 10K ohms, repair short to ground and repeat QUICK TEST. If all readings are 10K ohms or more, go to next step.

9) Checking For Short to Power Circuit. Turn key off and wait 10 seconds. Leave breakout box installed. Disconnect ECA and EGR solenoid. With DVOM on 200K-ohm scale, measure resistance between test pin No. 35 and test pins No. 37 and 57. If any reading is less than 10K ohms, repair short to power and repeat QUICK TEST. If code is still repeated, replace ECA. If all readings are 10K ohms or more, replace ECA and repeat QUICK TEST.

CIRCUIT TEST D2

IDLE SPEED CONTROL (DC MOTOR/IDLE TRACKING SWITCH ASSEMBLY & TPS) 1.9L CFI & 2.5L CFI

Perform this test only when Codes 12, 13, 16, 17, 19, 23, 38, 53, 58, 63, 68, 71, 73, or 93 are displayed or when directed here by DIAGNOSIS BY SYMPTOM TEST. To prevent replacement of good components be aware that the following non-EEC related areas may be at fault: throttle stop screw out of adjustment, vacuum leaks, sticking throttle, or basic engine (valves, timing, etc.).

DC Motor/Idle Tracking Switch (ITS) & TPS Circuit

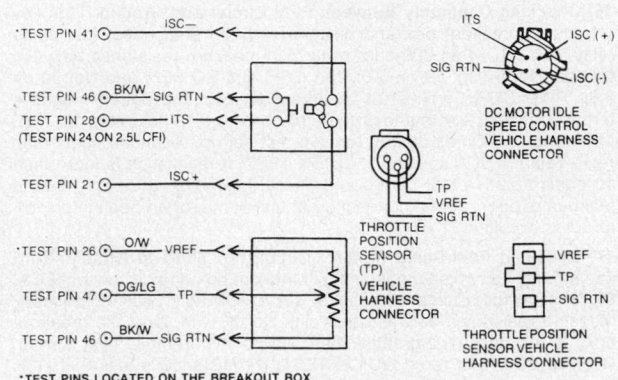

TEST PINS LOCATED ON THE BREAKOUT BOX.
ALL HARNESS CONNECTORS VIEWED INTO MATING SURFACE.

Test Pin 41		ISC –
1.9L CFI		W/LB
2.5L CFI		W

Idle Tracking Switch Circuit		
1.9L CFI	Pin 28	LG/W
2.5L CFI	Pin 24	W/R

Test Pin 21		ISC+
1.9L CFI		BR/W
2.5L CFI		Y/BK

DC Motor Shaft Measurements

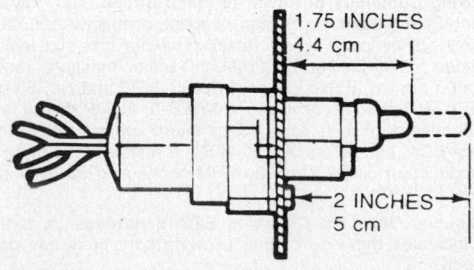

1) Code 13: Checking DC Motor Operation. Code 13 indicates and error in idle speed control management. Engine did not return to a specified lower RPM prior to "Goose" test portion of Self-Test. Possible causes for this fault are; faulty DC motor, open or shorted ISC circuit, faulty ECA.
Turn key off and wait 10 seconds. Disconnect harness from DC motor. Using jumper wires, connect ISC positive (+) circuit of DC motor to battery positive (+) terminal and ISC negative (–) circuit of DC motor to battery negative terminal for 4 seconds. DC motor shaft should extend more than 2" (50 mm). See DC MOTOR SHAFT MEASUREMENTS illustration. Now connect ISC + circuit of DC motor to battery negative terminal and ISC– circuit of DC motor to battery positive terminal for 4 seconds. DC motor shaft should retract to less

1989 COMPUTERIZED ENGINE CONTROLS
Ford Motor Co. EEC-IV (Cont.)

1a-465

CIRCUIT TEST D2 (Cont.)

than 1 3/4" (44 mm). If DC motor shaft moves in and out as indicated, go to next step. If not, replace DC motor and repeat QUICK TEST.

2) Checking Continuity of ISC+ and ISC– Circuits. Turn key off and wait 10 seconds. Leave harness disconnected from DC motor. Disconnect ECA 60-pin connector. Inspect connector for damaged pins, corrosion, or loose wires. Repair if necessary. Connect breakout box, leaving ECA disconnected. Set DVOM on 200-ohm scale. Measure resistance between test pin No. 41 and ISC– circuit at harness connector and between test pin No. 21 and ISC+ circuit at harness connector. If both readings are less than 5 ohms, go to next step. If readings are 5 ohms or more, repair circuit(s) and repeat QUICK TEST.

3) Checking ISC+ and ISC– Circuits For Shorts To Ground. Turn key off and wait 10 seconds. Leave breakout box and ECA disconnected. Set DVOM on 200K-ohm scale. Measure resistance between test pin No. 41 and test pins No. 40, 46 and 60. Also measure resistance between test pin No. 21 and test pins No. 40, 46 and 60. If all readings are greater than 10K ohms, go to next step. If any reading is less than 10K ohms, repair faulty circuit(s) and repeat QUICK TEST.

4) Checking ISC+ and ISC– For Shorts to PWR. Turn key off and wait 10 seconds. Leave breakout box installed and ECA disconnected. Disconnect DC motor from harness. Set DVOM to 20 volt scale. Measure voltage between test pin No. 41 and test pins No. 40 and 60. Also measure voltage between test pin No. 21 and test pins No. 40 and 60. If all readings are less than one volt, replace ECA and repeat QUICK TEST. If any reading is more than one volt, repair faulty circuit(s) and repeat QUICK TEST.

5) Code 58: Check For Full Motor Retraction. Turn key off and wait 10 seconds. Disconnect DC motor from harness. Using jumper wires, connect DC motor ISC - circuit to battery positive (+) terminal and ISC positive (+) circuit to battery negative (–) terminal for 4 seconds. DC motor shaft should be fully retracted, away from throttle lever. If shaft is retracted, go to step **7)**. If shaft does not retract, go to next step.

6) Measuring Motor Retraction. Turn key off and wait 10 seconds. Disconnect DC motor from harness. Ensure DC motor is fully retracted. Measure distance from DC motor mounting bracket to tip of motor shaft. See DC MOTOR SHAFT MEASUREMENTS. If DC motor shaft is retracted to less than 1 3/4" (44 mm), reconnect DC motor. Check throttle stop adjustment. If DC motor shaft does not retract, replace DC motor and repeat quick test.

7) Checking Idle Tracking Switch (ITS). Turn key off and wait 10 seconds. Disconnect DC motor from harness. Ensure DC motor is fully retracted and not touching throttle lever. Set DVOM on 200-ohm scale. Measure resistance between ITS circuit and SIG RTN at DC motor connector. If reading is less than 5 ohms, go to next step. If not, replace DC motor and repeat QUICK TEST.

8) Checking Continuity of ITS & SIG RTN Circuits. Turn key off and wait 10 seconds. Disconnect DC motor from harness. Disconnect ECA 60-pin connector. Inspect connector for damaged pins, corrosion, or loose wires. Repair if necessary. Connect breakout box, leaving ECA disconnected. Set DVOM on 200-ohm scale. Measure resistance between test pin No. 46 and SIG RTN circuit at DC motor harness connector. Also measure resistance between test pin No. 28 (No. 24 on 2.5L CFI) at the breakout box and ITS circuit at DC motor harness connector. If both readings are less than 5 ohms, reconnect DC motor. Replace ECA and repeat QUICK TEST. If any reading is 5 ohms or more, reconnect DC motor. Repair open circuit(s) and repeat QUICK TEST.

9) Code 68: Checking Idle Tracking Switch. Code 68 indicates DC motor shaft is in contact with throttle lever when DC motor signal was produced to retract shaft. Possible causes for this fault are: faulty DC motor, short to ground in ITS circuit or faulty ECA.
Turn key off and wait 10 seconds. Disconnect DC motor from harness. Set DVOM on 200-ohm scale. Measure resistance between ITS circuit and SIG RTN circuit at DC motor connector. If all readings are greater than 5 ohms, go to next step. If any reading is 5 ohms or less, replace DC motor and repeat QUICK TEST.

10) Checking ITS For Shorts To Ground. Turn key off and wait 10 seconds. Disconnect DC motor from harness. Disconnect ECA 60-pin connector. Inspect connector for damaged pins, corrosion, or loose wires. Repair if necessary. Connect breakout box, leaving ECA disconnected. Set DVOM on 200K-ohm scale. Measure resistance between test pin No. 28 (No. 24 on 2.5L CFI) and test pins No. 40, 46, and 60. If all readings are greater than 10K ohms, reconnect DC motor. Replace ECA and repeat QUICK TEST. If any reading is 10K ohms or less, reconnect DC motor. Repair faulty circuit(s) and repeat QUICK TEST.

CIRCUIT TEST D2 (Cont.)

11) Code 93: Checking Throttle Linkage. Code 93 indicates a fault between DC motor a throttle linkage. Turn key off and wait 10 seconds. Inspect throttle for freedom of movement to wide open throttle and for damaged or bent throttle lever. If throttle lever and linkage are okay, replace DC motor and repeat QUICK TEST. If throttle lever and/or linkage are damaged, repair as necessary and repeat QUICK TEST.

12) Code 23: Checking Throttle Plate Closing. Code 23 indicates throttle plate is not in correct position during Self-Test. Possible causes for this fault are: a faulty TPS, open in TPS circuit, or a faulty ECA.
Perform KOEO SELF-TEST. Disconnect DC motor when shaft is fully retracted. Turn key off and wait 10 seconds. Remove air cleaner from throttle body. Inspect throttle for freedom of movement and for proper closing of throttle valves. If throttle moves freely and closes without obstructions, reconnect DC motor and go to next step. If throttle binds or does not close properly, repair as necessary and repeat QUICK TEST.

13) Checking Voltage Of VREF to SIG RTN. Turn key off and wait 10 seconds. Disconnect TPS harness connector at throttle body. Inspect connector for damaged pins, corrosion, or loose wires. Repair if necessary. Set DVOM on 20-volt scale. Turn key on, leaving engine off. Measure voltage between VREF and SIG RTN at TPS harness connector. If reading is between 4-6 volts, reconnect TPS and go to next step. If reading is incorrect, go to CIRCUIT TEST A3, step **1)**.

14) Checking Throttle Stop RPM. Perform KOEO SELF-TEST. Disconnect DC motor after shaft has fully retracted and exit SELF-TEST. Start engine and verify that throttle stop RPM is less than curb idle speed. If throttle stop RPM is set to less than curb idle speed, replace TPS. Connect DC motor and repeat QUICK TEST. If throttle stop RPM is not less than curb idle speed, adjust throttle stop RPM. Connect DC motor and repeat QUICK TEST.

15) Code 53: Generate Code 63. Code 53 indicates TPS output signal is greater than the Self-Test maximum of 4.7 volts. Possible causes for this fault are: faulty TPS, faulty ECA or short to power in TPS circuit. Turn key off and wait 10 seconds. Disconnect harness from TPS at throttle body. Inspect connector for damaged pins, corrosion, or loose wires. Repair if necessary. Perform KOEO SELF-TEST and record codes. If Code 63 is displayed, go to next step. If Code 63 is not displayed, go to step **17)**. Ignore all other codes.

16) Check Voltage at VREF to SIG RTN. Turn key off and wait 10 seconds. Disconnect TPS harness at throttle body. Set DVOM on 20-volt scale. Turn key on, leaving engine off. Measure voltage between VREF and SIG RTN at TPS harness connector. If reading is 4-6 volts, replace TPS and repeat QUICK TEST. If not, go to CIRCUIT TEST A3, step **1)**.

17) Check TP Signal For Short To Power. Turn key off and wait 10 seconds. Disconnect TPS harness at throttle body. Set DVOM on 200K-ohm scale. Disconnect ECA 60-pin connector. Inspect connector for damaged pins, corrosion, or loose wires. Repair if necessary. Install breakout box, leaving ECA disconnected. Measure resistance between test pin No. 47 and test pins No. 26 and 57 at breakout box. If both readings are 10K ohms or greater, replace ECA and repeat QUICK TEST. If any reading is less than 10K ohms, repair faulty circuit(s) and repeat QUICK TEST.

18) Code 63: Generate Service Code 53. Code 63 indicates TP signal is less than Self-Test minimum of 0.2 volt. A failure mode signal indicates a closed throttle to the ECA. Possible causes for this fault are: a faulty TPS or ECA, open in TPS circuit or short to ground in TPS.
Turn key off and wait 10 seconds. Disconnect TPS harness at throttle body. Inspect connector for damaged pins, corrosion, or loose wires. Repair if necessary. Using jumper wire, connect VREF to TP signal at TPS harness connector. Perform KOEO SELF-TEST. If no codes are displayed, immediately remove jumper wire and go directly to step **21)**. If Code 53 is displayed, replace TPS sensor and repeat QUICK TEST. If Code 53 is not displayed, go to next step. Ignore all other codes at this time.

19) Voltage Check: VREF to SIG RTN. Turn key off and wait 10 seconds. Disconnect TPS harness at throttle body. Set DVOM on 20-volt scale. Turn key on, leaving engine off. Measure voltage between VREF and SIG RTN at TPS harness connector. If reading is between 4-6 volts, go to next step. If not, go to CIRCUIT TEST A3, step **1)**.

20) Checking Continuity of TP Signal Circuit. Turn key off and wait 10 seconds. Disconnect TPS harness at throttle body. Set DVOM on 200-ohm scale. Disconnect ECA 60-pin connector. Inspect connector for damaged pins, corrosion, or loose wires. Repair if necessary. Install

1a-466

1989 COMPUTERIZED ENGINE CONTROLS
Ford Motor Co. EEC-IV (Cont.)

CIRCUIT TEST D2 (Cont.)

breakout box, leaving ECA disconnected. Measure resistance between TPS signal at harness connector and test pin No. 47 at breakout box. If reading is less than 5 ohms, go to next step. If not, repair circuit. Reconnect TPS harness and repeat QUICK TEST.

21) Checking TP Signal For Short To Ground. Turn key off and wait 10 seconds. Disconnect TPS harness at throttle body. With breakout box installed and ECA disconnected, set DVOM on 200K-ohm scale. Measure resistance between TP signal at harness connector and test pins No. 40, 46, and 60 at breakout box. If all readings are greater than 10K ohms, replace ECA. Connect TPS and repeat QUICK TEST. If any reading is less than 10K ohms, repair faulty circuit(s) and repeat QUICK TEST.

22) Code 73: Displayed. Code 73 indicates ECA did not detect sufficient change in throttle position during "Goose" test. Possible causes for this fault are: faulty TPS or sensor circuit, faulty EGR system, faulty EGO sensor or sensor circuit or faulty ITS circuit. Perform KOEO SELF-TEST. If Code 73 is still displayed in KOEO SELF-TEST, replace TPS and repeat QUICK TEST. If Code 73 is not displayed, repair other codes.

23) Code 12: Check For Codes That Could Cause Code 12. Code 12 indicates system is not capable of raising engine speed above curb idle. Perform KOER SELF-TEST. If Codes 31, 32, 34, 35, 41, or 58 are displayed, repair these codes first. See KOER SELF-TEST table for instructions. If these codes are not displayed, go to next step.

24) Check For Sticking Throttle Linkage. Check throttle plates and linkage for binding. Check cruise control linkage for proper adjustment. If throttle opens and closes properly, go to next step. If throttle does not operate properly, repair throttle as required and repeat QUICK TEST.

25) Checking DC Motor Operation. Turn key off and wait 10 seconds. Disconnect harness from DC motor. Ensure other pins are not shorted when connecting jumper to ISC connector. Using jumper wires, carefully connect ISC positive (+) circuit of DC motor to battery positive (+) terminal and ISC negative (–) circuit of DC motor to battery negative terminal for 4 seconds. DC motor shaft should extend more than 2" (50 mm). See DC MOTOR SHAFT MEASUREMENTS illustration. Now connect ISC positive (+) circuit of DC motor to battery negative (–) terminal and ISC negative (–) circuit of DC motor to battery positive (+) terminal for 4 seconds. DC motor shaft should retract to less than 1 3/4" (44 mm). If DC motor shaft moves in and out as indicated, replace ECA and repeat QUICK TEST. If not, replace DC motor and repeat QUICK TEST.

26) Code 13 or 19: Erratic Idle Check. Code 13 or 19 indicates that the engine does not remain at a specified lower RPM prior to entering the "Goose" test portion of the Self-Test. Possible causes for this fault are; faulty MAP/BP sensor, faulty EGR sensor or circuit, faulty EGO sensor or circuit, faulty ITS.
Ensure engine is at normal operating temperature. Deactivate SELF-TEST. Ensure A/C is off (if equipped). Start and run engine for 3 minutes, alternating between 30 second idle and 5 second part throttle operation. If idle is erratic, go to next step. If idle is not erratic at end of 3 minute idle/part throttle test, go to step 28).

27) Check For Additional Codes During KOER SELF-TEST. Check for vacuum leaks, and Codes 22, 31, 32, 34, 35, 41, or 58. Repair these codes before going on to next step.

28) Checking Throttle Plates and Linkage. Inspect throttle plates and/or linkage for binding. If throttle opens and closes properly, replace DC motor and repeat QUICK TEST. If throttle binds, repair throttle as required and repeat QUICK TEST.

29) Continuous Memory Code 99: Check ECA Operation. Code 99 indicates the ECA has not received enough information to control engine idle speed. Deactivate SELF-TEST and start engine. DO NOT touch the throttle. Allow engine to idle for 2 minutes and shut engine off. When key has been off 10 seconds, run KOEO SELF-TEST. After service codes are displayed, deactivate SELF-TEST. Turn key off and wait 10 seconds. Rerun KOER SELF-TEST. If Code 99 is displayed, replace ECA. If Code 99 is not displayed, service other service codes.

30) Code 16 or 17: Related Mechanical Problems. Code 16 may indicate that the accelerator pedal was touched during KOER SELF-TEST. Code 17 indicates an electrical load such as as engine cooling fan or A/C compressor was activated during the SELF-TEST. Check engine for vacuum leaks, binding throttle linkage, base ignition timing, and throttle stop screw adjustment. If these items are okay, service other codes as necessary and rerun QUICK TEST. If a faulty item is found, service as necessary and rerun QUICK TEST.

CIRCUIT TEST D2 (Cont.)

31) Continuous Code 13 Displayed. Code 13 indicates that in the last 40 engine warm-up cycles, the Throttle Position Sensor (TPS) rotation did not follow the reaction of DC motor when idle speed control was in dashpot mode. This condition may be caused by the following:
- DC motor sticking at part throttle.
- An open in ITS circuit which, when coupled with other inputs to ECA, causes EEC system to falsely enter dashpot mode.
- TPS sticking at part throttle.

Each of these areas may generate KOEO SELF-TEST Codes or Continuous Memory Codes. If repairs have been made for KOEO SELF-TEST Codes 13 or 58, Continuous Memory Code 13 can be considered serviced and erased from memory. If Continuous Memory Codes 13 and 38 are present, service Code 38 first. If these codes are not present, make the following checks:

- Go to step **1)** of this test and check for FULL travel of DC motor shaft. Replace DC motor if travel is not obtained. Leave motor in FULL retract position. See DC MOTOR SHAFT MEASUREMENTS illustrationrb.
- With motor in full retract position, and with ITS not touching throttle lever check for an open in ITS circuit. Turn key off and install breakout box. Make necessary connector/pin inspections. With DVOM on 200-ohm scale, monitor resistance between test pins No. 28 (No. 24 on 2.5L CFI) and 46 while tapping, wiggling, and bending DC motor connector and harness. DO NOT push in idle tracking switch. If DVOM reading changes from less than 5 ohms to more than 5 ohms, an open circuit exists in wiring. Repair as necessary.
- Check for binding TPS by monitoring TPS voltage while moving throttle from a wide open position to a closed throttle position. Install breakout box and make all necessary connector/pin inspections. Fully retract DC motor shaft by placing a jumper wire between test pins No. 41 and 57. When motor is fully retracted, disconnect it at harness and remove jumper wire from breakout box. Turn key on and set DVOM on 20-volt scale. Slowly move throttle to wide open and closed throttle positions. Readings should move from more than 4 volts to less than 1.5 volts. If voltage readings hang up in mid-range, showing zero to 1.5 volts, replace TPS. If readings are correct, TPS is okay, do not service.

32) Continuous Code 38 Displayed. Code 38 indicates that in the last 40 engine warm-up cycles the idle tracking switch was open (ITS touching throttle) when throttle angle was greater than the maximum extension of DC motor shaft. This condition could be caused by the following conditions:
- An open in ITS circuit.
- Idle tracking switch stuck in open (pushed in) position.

These conditions may cause a Code 58 to appear in KOEO SELF-TEST. If repair has been made for Code 58, Continuous Memory Code 38 can be considered serviced, and erased from memory. If KOEO SELF-TEST Code 58 was not displayed, check the following:

- With DC motor fully retracted and ITS not touching throttle lever, check for an intermittent in ITS circuit. Turn ignition off and install breakout box. Make the necessary connector/pin inspections. With DVOM on 200-ohm scale, measure resistance between test pins No. 28 (No. 24 on 2.5L CFI) and 46 while tapping, wiggling, or bending DC motor connector and harness. DO NOT push in idle tracking switch. If DVOM reading changes from less than 5 ohms to more than 5 ohms, an open circuit exists in wiring. Repair as necessary.

33) Continuous Code 71 Displayed. This code indicates that in the last 40 engine warm-up cycles the idle tracking switch was closed (ITS not touching throttle lever) when DC motor was in preset position. This condition can be caused by the following:

- ITS circuit shorted to ground or SIG RTN.
- ITS stuck in closed position (NOT in pushed in position).

Either of these conditions may cause KOEO SELF-TEST Code 68. If repairs have been made for Code 68, Continuous Memory Code 71 can be considered serviced and erased from memory. If Code 68 was not displayed, check the following:

- Check ITS circuit for an intermittent short to ground or SIG RTN. Turn key off. Enter KOEO CONTINUOUS MONITOR (WIGGLE) TEST and systematically tap, wiggle, or bend harness while looking for indication of fault. If fault is created, repair as necessary. Due to nature of this test step, Code 71 will NOT reappear in memory if fault is found.

1989 COMPUTERIZED ENGINE CONTROLS
Ford Motor Co. EEC-IV (Cont.)

1a-467

CIRCUIT TEST D2 (Cont.)

34) Continuous Code 53 Displayed. Code 53 indicates TPS sensor output signal was greater than the 4.7 volt Self-Test maximum. The failure mode sends a WOT signal to the ECA. Possible causes for this fault are: faulty TPS or faulty ECA, short to power in TPS circuit. Using KOEO CONTINUOUS MONITOR (WIGGLE) TEST, observe VOM or diagnostic tester for indication of fault, while slowly moving throttle slowly to WOT. Slowly release throttle to closed position and lightly tap on TPS to simulate road shock and lightly wiggle TPS harness connector. If fault is indicated, go to next step. If not, go to step 36).

35) Throttle Position Signal Voltage. Turn key off and wait 10 seconds. Disconnect ECA 60-pin connector. Inspect connector for damaged pins, corrosion, or loose wires. Repair if necessary. Install breakout box and connect ECA. Set DVOM on 20-volt scale. Connect DVOM from test pin No. 47 to test pin No. 46. Turn key on, leaving engine off. While observing DVOM, move throttle slowly to closed position and lightly tap on TPS. Wiggle TPS harness and connector. If fault occurs at less than 4.25 volts, disconnect and inspect connectors. If okay, replace TPS and repeat QUICK TEST. If fault occurs at greater than 4.25 volts, TPS overtravel may have caused Code 53. Go to next step.

36) Checking EEC-IV Harness. Observe VOM or diagnostic tester for fault indication while grasping harness close to sensor connector. Wiggle, shake, or bend a small section of harness while working toward firewall. Repeat procedure from firewall to ECA. If fault is indicated, isolate fault and repair as necessary. After repairs repeat QUICK TEST. If no fault occurs, go to next step.

37) Checking ECA and Harness Connectors. Turn key off and wait 10 seconds. Disconnect ECA 60-pin connector. Inspect both connector and connector terminals for obvious fault or damage. If connector and terminals are okay, fault cannot be duplicated at this time. Testing is complete. If connector or terminals are damaged, repair as necessary. After repairs, repeat QUICK TEST.

38) Checking Continuous Codes 23 or 63: Operate TPS. Code 23 or 63 indicates TPS output signal is less than the Self-Test minimum of 0.2 volt. Failure mode indicates closed throttle to the ECA. Possible causes for this fault are: faulty TPS, open or short to ground in TPS harness circuit or faulty ECA. Using KOEO CONTINUOUS MONITOR (WIGGLE) TEST, observe VOM or diagnostic tester for indication of fault while slowly moving throttle to WOT. Slowly release throttle to closed position, lightly tap on TPS to simulate road shock and lighty wiggle TPS harness connector. If fault is indicated, disconnect and inspect connectors. If connectors and terminals are okay, replace TPS and repeat QUICK TEST. If no fault is indicated, repeat test steps 36) and 37).

CIRCUIT TEST D3

AIR MANAGEMENT SYSTEM (AM1/AM2)

NOTE: Perform this test when Service Codes 44, 45, 46, 81, 82 or 94 is displayed during QUICK TESTS or when directed here by other test procedures.

To prevent replacement of good components, be aware that the following non-EEC related areas may be at fault: thermactor air system drive belt, air pump or valve.

1) Codes 44 (94), 45 & 46: Verify Vacuum Line Routing. Code 44 or 94 indicates thermactor system is inoperative. Code 45 indicates thermactor air not flowing upstream when signaled to do so by ECA. Code 46 indicates thermactor air not by-passed when directed. Possible causes for these faults are: vacuum hoses leaking, blocked or kinked, diverter valve or thermactor pump inoperative or AM solenoid defective or blocked.
Check for correct vacuum hose routing to AM1/AM2 solenoids and by-pass diverter valve. Use vehicle emissions label as a guide. Check for kinked or blocked vacuum hoses. Check for kinked or blocked air hoses. Check for disconnected vacuum hoses. If problems are detected, correct hose routing, repair faults and repeat QUICK TEST. If vacuum routing is okay, and Code 44 (94) is displayed, go to step 4). If Code 46 is displayed, go to step 3). If Code 45 is displayed, go to next step.

2) Eliminating Displayed Code 45 (AM2). This step checks AM2 solenoid only. Disconnect and plug vacuum hose at diverter valve. Turn key off and wait 10 seconds. Repeat KOER SELF-TEST and record codes. If Code 45 is displayed, EEC system is okay. Check

CIRCUIT TEST D3 (Cont.)

Air Management Circuits

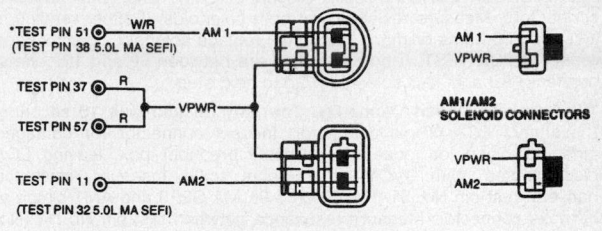

*TEST PINS LOCATED ON BREAKOUT BOX.
ALL HARNESS CONNECTORS VIEWED INTO MATING SURFACE.

Test Pin 11 or 32	AM2
Application	**Wire Color**
Car: 5.0L SEFI 5.0L SEFI MA	LG/BK
Truck: 4.9L, 5.0L, 5.8L, 7.5L	W/BK

diverter valve and/or check valve for problem. If Code 45 is not displayed, go to step 4).

3) Eliminating Displayed Code 46 (AM1). This step checks AM1 solenoid only. Disconnect and plug vacuum hose at by-pass valve. Turn key off and wait 10 seconds. Repeat KOER SELF-TEST and record codes. If Code 46 is displayed, EEC system is okay. Check by-pass valve for problem. If Code 46 is not displayed, go to next step.

4) Output Check. Enter OUTPUT STATE CHECK, see OUTPUT STATE CHECK, under DIAGNOSTIC AIDS. Use only DVOM, not diagnostic tester, for this step. Turn key off and wait 10 seconds. With DVOM on 20-volt scale, connect DVOM negative test lead to STO circuit at SELF-TEST connector and positive test lead to battery positive terminal. Using jumper wire, connect STI to SIG RTN at SELF-TEST connector. Perform KOEO SELF-TEST until end of CONTINUOUS SELF-TEST codes (DVOM reads zero volts). Depress and release throttle. DVOM should change to a high voltage reading. If reading changed, remain in OUTPUT STATE CHECK and go to next step. If reading did not change, depress throttle to WOT and release. If STO voltage does not go high, go to CIRCUIT TEST D16, step 1). Leave test equipment hooked up.

5) Checking AM1/AM2 Solenoid Operation. Set DVOM on 20-volt scale. Connect DVOM positive test lead to VPWR circuit and negative test lead to AM1 circuit at AM1 solenoid. While observing DVOM, depress and release throttle several times to cycle output on and off. Repeat for AM2 solenoid. Connect positive test lead to VPWR circuit and negative test lead to AM2 circuit at AM2 solenoid. Cycle AM2 solenoid on and off. If either solenoid does not cycle on and off, remove jumper and go to step 9). If both solenoids cycle on and off, go to next step.

6) Checking Solenoids For Vacuum Cycling. Connect vacuum pump to AM1 solenoid vacuum supply port. Connect vacuum gauge to output port. Maintain vacuum at source while depressing and releasing throttle to cycle output on and off. Observe vacuum gauge. Repeat for AM2 solenoid. If either output does not cycle on and off, replace solenoid assembly and repeat QUICK TEST. If both outputs cycle on and off, go to next step.

7) Checking Manifold Vacuum Lines. With vacuum hoses disconnected at AM1/AM2 solenoid assembly, start engine and check for vacuum. If vacuum is present, EEC system is okay. Check thermactor valve and air pump for problems. If no vacuum is present, repair blockage as required and repeat QUICK TEST.

8) Codes 81 and 82: Checking Voltage to VPWR Circuit. Code 81 and 82 indicates voltage output for thermactor air solenoid did not change when activated. Possible causes for this fault are: shorted or open circuits, solenoid resistance out of range or faulty ECA. Turn key on, leaving engine off. Set DVOM on 20-volt scale. Measure voltage between AM1 solenoid VPWR circuit and battery ground. Repeat test for AM2 solenoid. If either voltage reading is less than 10.5 volts, repair harness circuit open and repeat QUICK TEST. If both readings are greater than 10.5 volts, go to next step.

1a-468

1989 COMPUTERIZED ENGINE CONTROLS
Ford Motor Co. EEC-IV (Cont.)

CIRCUIT TEST D3 (Cont.)

9) Measuring Solenoid Resistance. Turn key off and wait 10 seconds. Set DVOM on 200-ohm scale. Disconnect AM1 and AM2 solenoid connectors. Measure resistance of both solenoids. If either reading is less than 50 ohms or more than 100 ohms, replace solenoid assembly and repeat QUICK TEST. If both readings are between 50 and 100 ohms, connect TAB and TAD solenoids. Go to next step.

10) Checking Circuit Continuity. Turn key off and wait 10 seconds. Disconnect ECA 60-pin connector. Inspect connector for damaged pins, corrosion, or loose wires. Install breakout box, leaving ECA disconnected. With DVOM on 200-ohm scale, measure resistance between test pin No. 51 (No. 38 on 5.0L MA SEFI) and AM1 circuit at harness connector. Measure resistance between test pin No. 11 (No. 32 on 5.0L MA SEFI) and AM2 circuit at harness connector. If either reading is 5 ohms or more, repair harness open circuit and repeat QUICK TEST. If both readings are less than 5 ohms, go to next step.

11) Checking For Shorts to Ground. Turn key off and wait 10 seconds. Set DVOM on 200K-scale. Leave breakout box installed and ECA disconnected. Disconnect AM1/AM2 solenoids. Measure resistance between test pin No. 51 (No. 38 on 5.0L MA SEFI) and test pins No. 40, 46 and 60, and between test pin No. 11 (No. 32 on 5.0L MA SEFI) and test pins No. 40, 46 and 60. If any reading is less than 10K ohms, repair short to power. Remove breakout box, connect harness to ECA and repeat QUICK TEST. If all readings are 10K ohms or more, go to next step.

12) Checking For Shorts to Power Circuit. Turn key off and wait 10 seconds. Set DVOM on 200K-ohm scale. Leave breakout box installed with ECA and solenoids disconnected. Measure resistance between test pin No. 51 (No. 38 on 5.0L MA SEFI) and test pins No. 37 and 57 and between test pin No. 11 (No. 32 on 5.0L MA SEFI) and test pins No. 37 and 57. If any reading is less than 10K ohms, repair short to power. Remove breakout box, connect harness to ECA and repeat QUICK TEST. If code is repeated, replace ECA. If all readings are 10K ohms or more, replace ECA and repeat QUICK TEST.

CIRCUIT TEST D4

CANISTER PURGE (CANP)

NOTE: Perform this test when Service Code 85 is displayed during QUICK TESTS or when directed here by other test procedures.

Canister Purge (CANP) Circuit

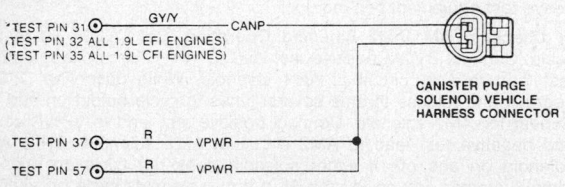

*TEST PINS LOCATED ON BREAKOUT BOX.
ALL HARNESS CONNECTORS VIEWED INTO MATING SURFACE.

1) Checking System Function. Enter OUTPUT STATE CHECK see OUTPUT STATE CHECK, under QUICK TEST DIAGNOSTIC AIDS. Use only DVOM, not diagnostic tester, for this step. Turn key off and wait 10 seconds. Set DVOM on 20-volt scale. Connect DVOM negative test lead to STO and positive test lead to positive battery terminal. Using jumper wire, connect STI circuit to SIGNAL RETURN at SELF-TEST connector. Perform KOEO SELF-TEST until end of Continuous Memory Codes (DVOM reads zero volts). Depress and release throttle. DVOM should change to a high voltage reading. If reading did not change, depress throttle to WOT and release. If STO voltage does not go high, go to CIRCUIT TEST D16, step 1). Leave test equipment hooked up. If reading changed, remain in OUTPUT STATE CHECK and go to next step.

CIRCUIT TEST D4 (Cont.)

2) Checking Solenoid Electrical Function. With KOEO, set DVOM on 20-volt scale. Disconnect CANP solenoid. Connect DVOM positive test lead to VPWR circuit and negative test lead to CANP output circuit on harness connector. While observing DVOM, depress and release throttle several times to cycle output on and off. If CANP circuit does not cycle on and off, remove jumper wire and go to step 6). If CANP circuit cycles, go to next step.

3) Checking Solenoid For Vacuum Leaks. Turn key on. Leave CANP solenoid disconnected. Disconnect vacuum hose at canister purge solenoid from manifold vacuum side of engine. Apply 16 in. Hg vacuum to manifold vacuum side of CANP solenoid. If CANP solenoid does not hold vacuum for 20 seconds, replace it and repeat QUICK TEST. If fault is still present, service fuel evaporation canister. If CANP holds vacuum for 20 seconds, leave vacuum pump attached and go to next step.

4) Checking Solenoid Mechanical Operation. While still in OUTPUT STATE CHECK, cycle CANP circuit off (no voltage). Reconnect CANP solenoid connector. Apply 16 in. Hg. vacuum to CANP solenoid as in step 3). Depress and release throttle. If vacuum is released, check hose from solenoid to canister for leaks or cracks, if okay, remove jumper wire from STI and go to next step. If vacuum is not released, replace CANP solenoid and repeat QUICK TEST.

5) Checking Vacuum Supply. Disconnect vacuum hose from canister purge solenoid on manifold vacuum (PVC) side. Start engine. If vacuum is present at vacuum hose, EEC system is okay. If vacuum is not present at hose, check vacuum hose for proper routing, kinks, or blockage, If okay, check engine for cause of low vacuum.

6) Measuring CANP Solenoid Resistance. Code 85 indicates a fault in the CANP solenoid circuit. Turn key off and wait 10 seconds. Set DVOM on 200-ohm scale. Disconnect CANP solenoid connector and measure solenoid resistance. If reading is between 40-90 ohms, go to next step. If reading is incorrect, replace CANP solenoid and repeat QUICK TEST.

7) Checking Voltage of VPWR Circuit. With KOEO, and CANP solenoid disconnected, set DVOM on 20-volt scale. Measure voltage between VPWR circuit at CANP solenoid harness connector and battery negative terminal. If reading is 10.5 volts or greater, go to next step. If reading is less than 10.5 volts, repair open in circuit and repeat QUICK TEST.

8) Checking Continuity of CANP Circuit. Turn key off and wait 10 seconds. Disconnect CANP solenoid and ECA 60-pin connector. Inspect connector for damaged pins, corrosion, or loose wires. Repair if necessary. Connect breakout box, leaving ECA disconnected. Set DVOM on 200-ohm scale. Measure resistance between test pin No. 31 (No. 35 for 1.9L CFI, No. 32 for 1.9L MPFI engines) and CANP harness connector. If reading is less than 5 ohms, go to next step. If reading is 5 ohms or more, repair open circuit and repeat QUICK TEST.

9) Checking For Short to Ground. Turn key off and wait 10 seconds. Install breakout box, leaving ECA disconnected. Set DVOM on 200K-ohm scale and disconnect CANP solenoid. Measure resistance between test pin No. 31 (No. 35 for 1.9L CFI, No. 32 for 1.9L MPFI engines) and test pins No. 40, 46, and 60. If all readings are 10K ohms or more, go to next step. If any reading is less than 10K ohms, repair short to ground and repeat QUICK TEST.

10) Checking For Short to Power. Turn key off and wait 10 seconds. Disconect CANP solenoid. Install breakout box, leaving ECA disconnected. Set DVOM on 200K-ohm scale and disconnect CANP solenoid. Measure resistance between test pin No. 31 (No. 35 for 1.9L CFI, No. 32 for 1.9L MPFI engines) and test pins No. 37 and 57. If all reading are 10K ohms or more, remove breakout box. Replace ECA and repeat QUICK TEST. If any reading is less than 10K ohms, repair short to power and repeat QUICK TEST. If code is repeated, replace ECA and repeat QUICK TEST.

11) Check If CANP Caused Codes 16 or 26. With key off, disconnect vacuum hose at canister purge solenoid on canister side. Start engine and allow to idle. If vacuum is present on canister side of canister purge solenoid, go to step 1), in this test. If vacuum is not present, and a Code 26 is displayed, check for vacuum leaks or lack of vacuum. If Code 16 is present, check for vacuum leaks at injector "O" rings, vacuum lines and fittings, or between air meter and throttle body. Service as necessary and rerun QUICK TEST.

1989 COMPUTERIZED ENGINE CONTROLS
Ford Motor Co. EEC-IV (Cont.)

1a-469

CIRCUIT TEST D5

IDLE SPEED CONTROL (AIR BY-PASS)

NOTE: Perform this test when Service Code 12, 13, 16, 17, 19, 47 or 48 displayed during QUICK TESTS or when directed here by other test procedures. If engine is running rough or has rough idle, correct these conditions before performing test. Causes may be in ignition system, fuel system or EGR system.

Idle Speed Control (Air By-Pass) Circuit

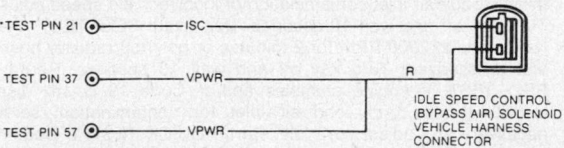

```
*TEST PIN 21 ——————— ISC ———————
TEST PIN 37 ——————— VPWR ———————  R
TEST PIN 57 ——————— VPWR ———————
                                    IDLE SPEED CONTROL
                                    (BYPASS AIR) SOLENOID
                                    VEHICLE HARNESS
                                    CONNECTOR
```

*TEST PINS LOCATED ON BREAKOUT BOX.
ALL HARNESS CONNECTORS VIEWED INTO MATING SURFACE.

TEST PIN 21	ISC
APPLICATION	**COLOR**
1.9L EFI 3.0L EFI CAR/TRK 3.0L SHO 3.8L SEFI AXOD	O/BK
2.3L EFI HSC	BR/W
2.3L EFI OHC 5.0L SEFI 5.0L SEFI MA	W/LB
3.8L SEFI RWD 3.8L SEFI SC	R/LG
2.3L EFI TC 2.3L EFI TRK 2.9L EFI TRK 4.9L EFI TRK 5.0L EFI TRK 5.8L EFI TRK 7.5L EFI TRK	GY/W

To prevent replacement of good components, be aware that the following non-EEC related areas may be at fault: engine temperature not up to operating temperature, engine over operating temperature, A/C input (electrical problem), improper idle speed/throttle stop adjustment or cruise control linkage.

1) Code 12: Check For RPM Drop. On 1.9 MPFI engine, Code 12 indicates that during KOER SELF-TEST, engine was unable to reach maximum Self-Test RPM.

On all other models, Code 12 indicates that during KOER Self-Test engine RPM could not be controlled within Self-Test minimum RPM. Possible causes for this fault are:
- Open or shorted circuit.
- Sticking or binding throttle linkage.
- Incorrect idle adjustment.
- Throttle body or ISC solenoid contamination.
- Faulty ISC solenoid.
- Faulty ECA.
- Non-ECC mechanical faults.

Turn key off. Connect engine tachometer and start engine. Disconnect Idle Speed Control (ISC) harness. If RPM drops or if engine stalls, go to next step. If not, go to step **3)**.

2) Checking For EGR Codes. If EGR service codes 31, 32, 33 or 34 are displayed, reconnect ISC solenoid and go to ENGINE RUNNING SELF-TEST table and perform appropriate CIRCUIT TEST. If these codes are not displayed, go to next step.

3) Checking Other Codes. If Codes 22, 41, 42, 91, or 92 are displayed, reconnect ISC solenoid, go to ENGINE RUNNING SELF-TEST table and perform appropriate CIRCUIT TEST (except 1.9L MPFI, go to next step). If these codes are not displayed, go to next step.

CIRCUIT TEST D5 (Cont.)

4) Measuring ISC Solenoid Resistance. Turn key off. Disconnect ISC solenoid. Set DVOM on 200-ohm scale, and measure resistance of ISC solenoid. If resistance is between 7 and 13 ohms, go to next step. If resistance is less than 7 ohms or more than 13 ohms, replace ISC solenoid and repeat QUICK TEST.

ISC Solenoid Connector

NOTE: Due to diode in solenoid, place DVOM + lead on VPWR pin and – lead on ISC pin

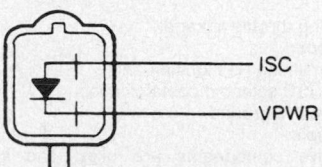

```
                    ——— ISC
                    ——— VPWR
```

ISC SOLENOID CONNECTOR

5) Checking For Internal Short to ISC Solenoid Case. With key off and ISC solenoid disconnected, set DVOM on 200K-ohm scale. Measure resistance from either ISC terminal pin to ISC solenoid housing. If reading is greater than 10K ohms, go to next step. If reading is 10K ohms or less, replace ISC solenoid. Repeat QUICK TEST.

6) Checking VPWR Circuit. Leave ISC harness disconnected. With KOEO, set DVOM on 20-volt scale. Measure voltage between VPWR circuit at ISC harness connector and battery ground terminal. If reading is less than 10.5 volts, repair open in circuit and repeat QUICK TEST. If reading is 10.5 volts or more, go to next step.

7) Checking ISC Circuit Continuity. Turn key off and wait 10 seconds. Leave ISC solenoid disconnected. Disconnect ECA 60-pin connector. Inspect connector for damaged pins, corrosion, or loose wires. Repair if necessary. Install breakout box, leaving ECA disconnected. With DVOM on 200-ohm scale, measure resistance between test pin No. 21 and ISC circuit at ISC harness connector. If reading is greater than 5 ohms, repair open circuit and repeat QUICK TEST. If reading is less than 5 ohms, go to next step.

8) Checking For Circuit Short to Ground. Turn key off and wait 10 seconds. Leave ISC solenoid disconnected. Install breakout box, leaving ECA disconnected. Set DVOM on 200K-ohm scale. Measure resistance between test pin No. 21 and test pins No. 40, 46, and 60. If any reading is less than 10K ohms, repair short to ground and repeat QUICK TEST. If all readings are 10K ohms or more, go to next step.

9) Checking For Short to Power. Turn key off and wait 10 seconds. Leave breakout box installed. Leave ECA and ISC solenoid disconnected. Set DVOM on 200K-ohm scale. Measure resistance by connecting DVOM negative lead to test pin No. 21 and positive lead to test pin No. 37. If reading is greater than 10K ohms, go to next step. If reading is 10K ohms or less, repair short to power and repeat QUICK TEST. If code or symptom is still present, replace ECA.

10) Checking ISC Signal From ECA. With key off, connect ECA and ISC. Leave breakout box installed and set DVOM on 20-volt scale. Connect DVOM between test pins No. 21 and 40. Start engine and observe DVOM while slowly increasing and decreasing engine RPM. If DVOM reading varies, go to next step. If DVOM reading does not vary, replace ECA and repeat QUICK TEST.

11) Checking Base/Curb Idle. Verify base/curb idle speed. If base/curb idle speed is within specifications, on 3.8L SEFI engines, replace ISC and repeat QUICK TEST. On all other engines, remove ISC solenoid and inspect for contamination, service as necessary. Rerun QUICK TEST, if code or symptom is still present, replace ISC solenoid.

If curb idle speed is incorrect, reset idle speed to specification. Rerun QUICK TEST. If unable to set idle to specification, go to next step.

12) Check Faults Which Affect Idle Speed. Check the following mechanical items for faults:
- Throttle linkage and/or cruise control linkage for sticking or binding.
- Throttle body for contamination.
- Vacuum hoses (check emission decal).

1a-470

1989 COMPUTERIZED ENGINE CONTROLS
Ford Motor Co. EEC-IV (Cont.)

CIRCUIT TEST D5 (Cont.)

If all of the above items are okay, on 3.8L SEFI engines replace ISC solenoid and rerun QUICK TEST. On all other engines, remove ISC solenoid and inspect for contamination. Service as necessary and rerun QUICK TEST. If code or symptom is still present, replace ISC. If any of the above items are faulty, service as necessary and rerun QUICK TEST.

13) Code 13: Verify Idle Speed is Within Specification. On 1.9L MPFI or 2.3L Turbo MPFI engines, Code 13 indicates that during KOER SELF-TEST, engine RPM did not reach lower limit in Self-Test. On all other engines, Code 13 indicates engine could not be controlled within lower RPM range. Possible causes for this fault are as follows:
- Incorrect idle setting.
- Vacuum leaks.
- Sticking or binding throttle linkage.
- Throttle plates open.
- Incorrect ignition timing (TFI ignition only).
- Throttle body or ISC solenoid contamination.
- ISC circuit shorted to ground.
- Faulty ISC solenoid.

If all of the above components are okay, and idle is set to specification, replace the ISC solenoid on 3.8L SEFI engines. On all other engines, remove ISC solenoid and inspect for contamination. Service as necessary and rerun QUICK TEST. If code or symptom is still present, replace ISC solenoid. If idle speed is not set to specification, reset and rerun QUICK TEST. If idle speed cannot be reset to specification, go to step **6)** of this test.

14) Check For Conditions Affecting Idle Speed. Check the following mechanical components for faults:
- Engine vacuum hoses (refer to emission decal).
- Throttle linkage and/or cruise control linkage for sticking or binding.
- Check throttle plates are fully closed.
- Check for vacuum leaks in induction system.
- Check throttle body for contamination.
- Ensure base ignition timing is to specification on emission decal (TFI vehicles only).

If all above checks are okay, go to next step. If a fault has been found, service as necessary and rerun QUICK-TEST.

15) Checking For Internal Short to ISC Solenoid Case. With key off and ISC solenoid disconnected, set DVOM on 200K-ohm scale. Measure resistance from either ISC terminal pin to ISC solenoid housing. If reading is greater than 10K ohms, go to next step. If reading is 10K ohms or less, replace ISC solenoid. Repeat QUICK TEST.

16) Checking For Circuit Short to Ground. Turn key off and wait 10 seconds. Leave ISC solenoid disconnected. Install breakout box, leaving ECA disconnected. Set DVOM on 200K-ohm scale. Measure resistance between test pin No. 21 and test pins No. 40, 46, and 60. If any reading is less than 10K ohms, repair short to ground and repeat QUICK TEST. If all readings are 10K ohms or more, go to next step.

17) Checking ISC Signal From ECA. With key off, connect ECA and ISC. Leave breakout box installed and set DVOM on 20-volt scale. Connect DVOM between test pins No. 21 and 40. Start engine and observe DVOM while slowly increasing and decreasing engine RPM. If DVOM voltage reading varies on 3.8L SEFI engines, replace ISC solenoid and rerun QUICK TEST. On all other engines, remove ISC solenoid and inspect for contamination, service as necessary. Rerun QUICK TEST, if code or symptom is still present, replace ISC solenoid. If DVOM voltage does not vary, replace ECA and rerun QUICK TEST.

18) Code 47: Check For Low Flow of Unmetered Air. Code 47 indicates that measured airflow at base idle was lower than ECA specification. Possible causes for this fault are: air/vacuum leaks in fuel charging system or faulty or leaking purge solenoid and/or injector "O" rings. Service any faults as necessary and rerun QUICK TEST. If no faults are present, EEC-IV system is okay, service other codes as necessary.

19) Code 48: Check For High Flow of Unmetered Air. Code 48 indicates that measured airflow at base idle was higher than ECA specification. Possible causes for this fault are: air/vacuum leaks in fuel charging system or loss of ignition or fuel.

Check for and repair holes, cracks, and/or bad connections at air cleaner outlet tube (between vane airflow meter and fuel charging assembly). Check for loss of ignition or injection on one or more cylinders. If any faults are found, service as necessary. Rerun QUICK TEST. If no faults are found, EEC-IV system is okay for metered air.

CIRCUIT TEST D5 (Cont.)

20) Code 16: High ISC RPM. Code 16 indicates that with ISC off, engine RPM was above Self-Test specification limit. Possible causes for this fault are: incorrect idle adjustment, faulty purge solenoid, air/vacuum leaks.

If Code 48 is also present, reset throttle plate. Refer to Vehicle Emission Control Decal for curb idle set procedure. Rerun QUICK TEST. If Code 48 is still present, go to step **19)** of this test. If Code 48 is not present, go to step **13)** of this test.

21) Code 19: ISC RPM Low. Code 19 indicates that with ISC off, engine RPM dropped below Self-Test limit (about 600 RPM). Possible causes for this fault are: engine below normal operating temperature, throttle body/air inlet contamination or incorrect idle speed adjustment. Turn key off and wait 10 seconds. Deactivate SELF-TEST. Start and run engine at 2000 RPM for 2 minutes or until top radiator hose is hot and pressurized. Turn key off and wait 10 seconds. Rerun KOER SELF-TEST. If engine stumbles and/or Code 19 is still displayed, inspect throttle body and air inlet for contamination, service as necessary and adjust curb idle. Rerun QUICK TEST. If Code 19 has been cleared, service other codes as necessary.

22) Code 17: ISC RPM Low. Code 17 indicates that with the ISC off, engine RPM was below Self-Test limit. Possible causes for this fault are: excessive engine accessory load, engine temperature below normal operating temperature, throttle body/air inlet contamination or incorrect idle adjustment.

Check and correct excessive engine load conditions, cooling fans, lights, etc. Run engine at 2000 RPM for 2 minutes. Turn key off and wait 10 seconds. Rerun KOER SELF-TEST. If Code 17 is displayed, inspect throttle body and air inlet for contamination and clean as necessary. If okay, adjust base/curb idle speed and repeat QUICK TEST. If Code 17 is not displayed, service other codes as necessary.

CIRCUIT TEST D6
SHIFT INDICATOR LIGHT (SIL)

1.9L MPFI Shift Indicator Light (SIL) Circuits

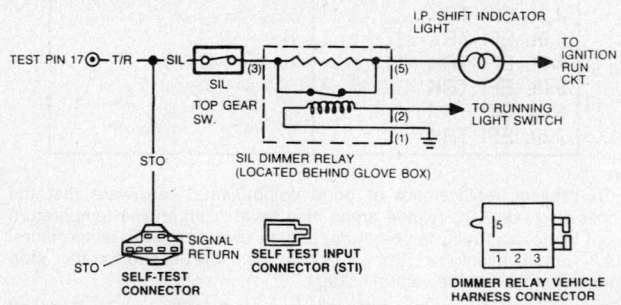

All Other Shift Indicator Light (SIL) Circuits

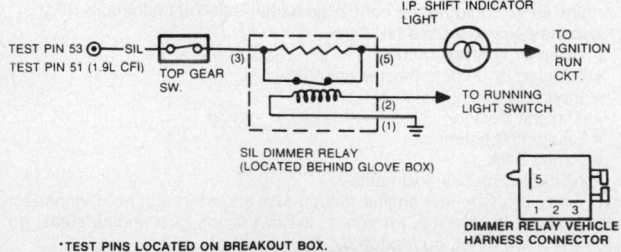

*TEST PINS LOCATED ON BREAKOUT BOX.
ALL HARNESS CONNECTORS VIEWED INTO MATING SURFACE.

1) Checking SIL Operation. Inspect SIL while driving vehicle. SIL should turn on when optimum shift RPM is reached in each gear. Light should be off in highest gear. If SIL light is always on, check for a short in SIL circuit. If light is always off, check for an open in SIL circuit. If light is always on, go to step **6)**. If light is always off, go to next step.

1989 COMPUTERIZED ENGINE CONTROLS
Ford Motor Co. EEC-IV (Cont.)

1a-471

CIRCUIT TEST D6 (Cont.)

2) Check SIL Circuit Fuse. Turn key off and wait 10 seconds. Remove and inspect SIL fuse (No. 18). If fuse is okay, reconnect and go to next step. If fuse is blown, repair short to ground between fuse and SIL bulb. Replace fuse and check SIL operation.

3) Check SIL Bulb. With key off, remove and inspect SIL bulb. If bulb is okay, go to next step. If bulb has failed, relace and check SIL operation.

4) Check Continuity of SIL Dimmer Relay. With key off, disconnect SIL dimmer relay. Set DVOM on 200-ohm scale. Measure resistance between pins No. 3 and 5 on SIL dimmer relay. If resistance is less than 5 ohms, go to next step. If resistance is more than 5 ohms, replace SIL dimmer relay and check operation.

5) Check SIL Dimmer Relay Function. With key off, disconnect SIL dimmer relay. Apply 12 volts across pins No. 1 and 2 of SIL dimmer relay. With DVOM on 200-ohm scale, measure resistance between pins No. 3 and 5 on SIL dimmer relay. If resistance is between 40 and 55 ohms, go to next step. If resistance is not 40-55 ohms, replace SIL dimmer relay and retest operation.

6) Check Voltage at SIL Dimmer Relay. With KOEO, disconnect SIL dimmer relay. Set DVOM on 20-volt scale. Measure voltage between test pin No. 5 of the SIL dimmer relay harness connector and the battery negative post. If voltage is greater than 5 volts, reconnect relay and go to next step. If voltage is less than 5 volts repair circuit between top gear switch and SIL dimmer relay. Recheck SIL operation.

7) Check Voltage at Top Gear Switch. With KOEO, disconnect top gear switch. Set DVOM on 20-volt scale. Measure voltage between the SIL dimmer relay side of the top gear switch harness connector and battery negative post. If voltage is greater than 5 volts, go to next step. If voltage is less than 5 volts, repair circuit between high gear switch and dimmer relay. Check SIL operation.

8) Checking Operation of Top Gear Switch. Turn key off and wait 10 seconds. Disconnect high gear switch. Set DVOM on 200-ohm scale. Measure resistance of top gear switch while shifting transmission from top gear to the next lower gear. If switch opens and closes, go to next step. If circuit does not open and close, replace switch and check operation.

9) Checking Continuity of SIL Circuit. Turn key off, and disconnect high gear switch. Install breakout box and leave ECA disconnected. Set DVOM on 200-ohm scale, and measure resistance between test pin No. 53 (No. 51 on 1.9L CFI and No. 17 on 1.9L MPFI) and the ECA side of the high gear switch. If resistance is less than 5 ohms, reconnect high gear switch, shift transmission into high gear and go to next step. If resistance is more than 5 ohms, repair circuit between high gear switch and ECA.

10) Checking SIL Circuit For Short to Ground. Turn key off, and place transmission in highest gear. Set DVOM on 200-ohm scale, and install breakout box, leaving ECA disconnected. Measure resistance between test pin No. 53 (No. 51 on 1.9L CFI, and No. 17 on 1.9L MPFI) and test pin No. 60. If resistance is less than 100K ohms, repair short between high gear switch and ECA. On 1.9L MPFI, also check STO circuit for short to ground. If resistance is greater than 10K ohms, repace ECA and rerun QUICK TEST.

CIRCUIT TEST D7

WIDE OPEN THROTTLE A/C CUT-OUT (WAC) & A/C DEMAND SWITCH

3.8L RWD SEFI, 5.0L SEFI & 5.0L MA SEFI Car Engines, 2.9L MPFI & 3.0L MPFI Truck Engines, WOT A/C Cut-Out Circuits

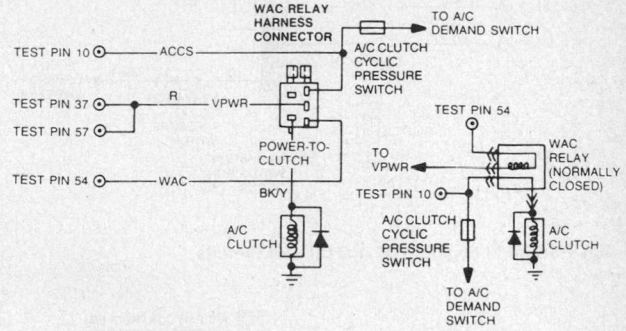

| Test Pin 10 | ACCS |
Application	Color
3.8L SEFI RWD 5.0L SEFI MA 5.0L SEFI Except Mark VII	PK/LB
2.9L EFI Truck	T/Y
3.0L EFI Truck	BK/Y
5.0L SEFI Mark VII	LG/P

| Test Pin 54 | WAC |
Application	Color
3.8L SEFI RWD 5.0L SEFI 5.0L SEFI MA	O/LB
2.9L EFI Truck	P
3.0L EFI Truck	R

2.3L MPFI Truck Engine WOT A/C Cut-Out Circuits

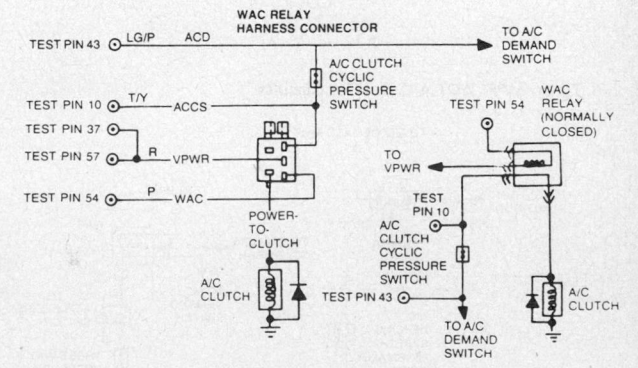

1989 COMPUTERIZED ENGINE CONTROLS
Ford Motor Co. EEC-IV (Cont.)

CIRCUIT TEST D7 (Cont.)

1.9L CFI & 1.9L MPFI Engine WOT A/C Cut-Out Circuits

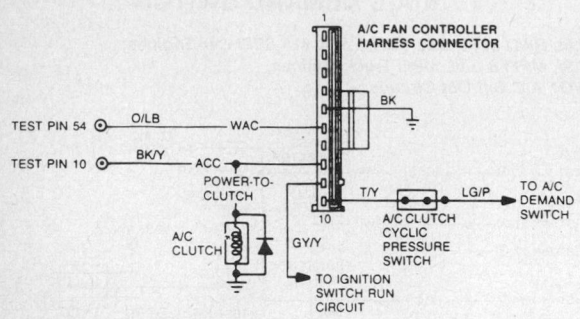

2.3L HSC MPFI Engine WOT A/C Cut-Out Circuits

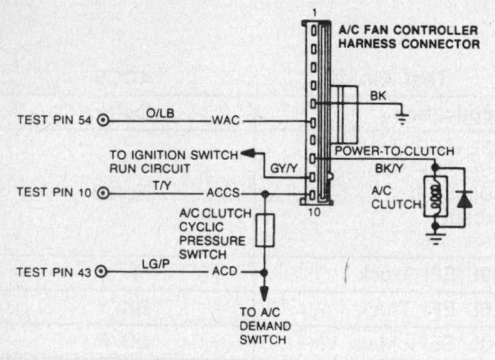

2.3L OHC MPFI Engine WOT A/C Cut-Out Circuits

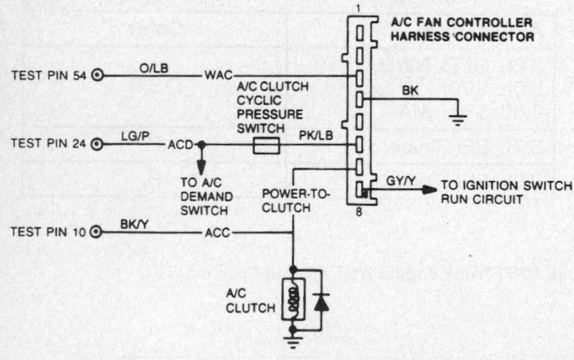

2.3L Turbo MPFI WOT A/C Cut-Out Circuits

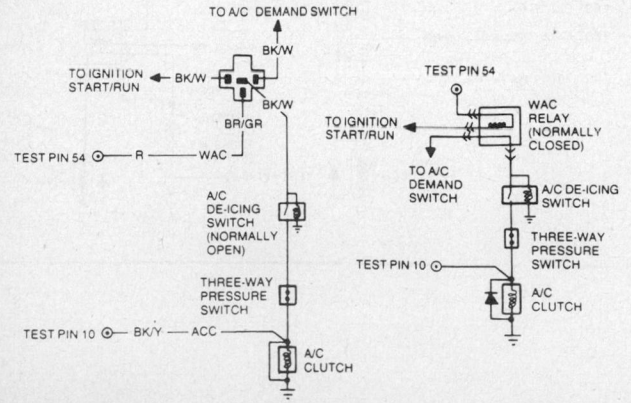

CIRCUIT TEST D7 (Cont.)

1) No A/C: Check For Voltage at A/C Clutch. Check all A/C related fuses in fuse panel before proceeding with this test. Use only DVOM, not diagnostic tester, for this step. Disconnect A/C clutch harness connector. Turn A/C switch to "A/C" position. Set DVOM on 20-volt scale. Start engine and wait 10 bseconds. Measure voltage between the power side of the A/C clutch harness connector and negative battery terminal. If voltage is greater than 10.5 volts, EEC-IV system is okay, diagnose A/C clutch system. If voltage is less than 10.5 volts, go to next step for 2.3L Turbo MPFI. Go to step **5)** for all other models.

2) Check Voltage at A/C De-Icing Switch. With key off, disconnect A/C clutch harness. Disconnect A/C de-icing switch. Turn A/C switch to ON position. Set DVOM to 20-volt scale. Start engine and wait 10 seconds. Measure voltage between both Power-from-WAC relay circuits at the A/C de-icing switch harness connector to chassis ground. If both voltages are greater than 10.5 volts, turn key off and go to step **4)**. If both voltages are not greater than 10.5 volts, reconnect A/C clutch harness and go to next step.

A/C De-Icing Switch

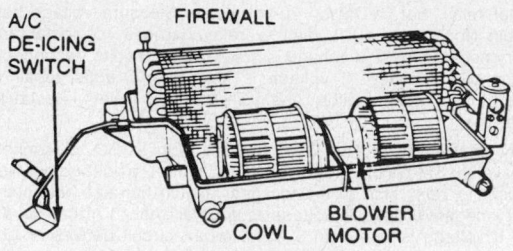

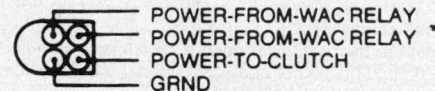

A/C DE-ICING SWITCH HARNESS CONNECTOR

NOTE: THE A/C DE-ICING SWITCH IS A NORMALLY OPEN RELAY

3) Check Continuity From WAC Relay to De-Icing Switch. Turn key off, and disconnect A/C de-icing switch. Set DVOM on 200-ohm scale. Measure resistance between the Power-to-Clutch circuit on the WAC relay harness connector and both Power-from-WAC relay circuits on the A/C de-icing switch harness connector. If both resistances are less than 5 ohms, go to step **6)**. If both resistances are not less than 5 ohms, repair open circuit, reconnect components and retest system.

WAC Relay Harness Connector

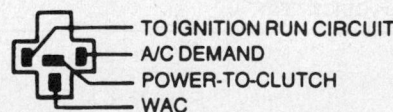

WIDE OPEN THROTTLE A/C CUTOUT (WAC) RELAY HARNESS CONNECTOR

4) Check Continuity From A/C De-Icing Switch to A/C Clutch. With key off, disconnect A/C clutch harness. Set DVOM on 200-ohm scale. Measure resistance between power side of A/C clutch harness connector and Power-to-Clutch terminal at A/C de-icing switch. If resistance is less than 5 ohms, check ground circuit to A/C de-icing switch. If circuit is okay, problem is not EEC-IV related. Service or replace A/C de-icing switch. If resistance is greater than 5 ohms, check operation of 3-way pressure switch. If 3-way pressure switch is okay, repair open circuit and retest system.

5) Checking Continuity of Power-to-Clutch Circuit. Turn key off and wait 10 seconds. Set DVOM on 200-ohm scale. Disconnect A/C clutch harness and harness from WAC relay or A/C fan controller. Measure resistance between power side of A/C clutch harness connector and Power-to-Clutch terminal pin at WAC relay or A/C fan controller. If resistance is less than 5 ohms, reconnect A/C clutch and go to next

1989 COMPUTERIZED ENGINE CONTROLS
Ford Motor Co. EEC-IV (Cont.)

1a-473

CIRCUIT TEST D7 (Cont.)

step. If resistance is more than 5 ohms, service open circuit and re-test system. System application is as follows:

WAC Relay
2.3L Turbo MPFI
3.8L RWD SEFI
5.0L SEFI & MA SEFI
2.3L MPFI Truck
2.9L MPFI Truck
3.0L MPFI Truck

A/C Fan Controller
1.9L CFI
1.9L MPFI
2.3L HSC MPFI
2.3L OHC MPFI

6) Checking Power on A/C Demand Circuit. With KOEO and WAC relay or A/C fan controller disconnected, turn on A/C switch. Set DVOM to 20-volt scale. Measure voltage between A/C demand input terminal pin at WAC relay or A/C fan controller harness connector and ground. If voltage is greater than 10.5 volts, go to next step. If voltage is less than 10.5 volts, check switch operation, repair open circuit and retest system.

7) Checking WAC Circuit For Short to Ground. Turn key off and wait 10 seconds. Disconnect ECA 60-pin connector and WAC relay or A/C fan controller. Inspect for and repair any damaged wiring. Install breakout box, leaving ECA disconnected. Set DVOM on 200K-ohm scale. Measure resistance between WAC circuit at WAC relay or A/C fan controller and chassis ground. If resistance is greater than 10K ohms, go to next step for A/C fan controller systems or step 10) for WAC relay systems. If resistance is less than 10K ohms, repair short and retest system.

8) Checking A/C Fan Controller Ground Circuit. With key off and A/C fan controller disconnected, set DVOM on 200-ohm scale. Disconnect ECA. Measure resistance between ground circuit at A/C fan controller harness connector and chassis ground. If resistance is less than 5 ohms, go to next step. If resistance is more than 5 ohms, repair open circuit and retest system.

9) Checking For Voltage to A/C Fan Controller. With key on, ECA and A/C fan controller disconnected, set DVOM on 20-volt scale. Measure voltage between ignition switch RUN circuit at the A/C fan controller harness connector and chassis ground. If voltage is greater than 10.5 volts, go to next step. If voltage is less than 10.5 volts, repair open circuit, reconnect ECA and A/C controller and re-test system.

10) Checking WAC Relay or A/C Fan Controller. Turn key off and wait 10 seconds. Leave ECA disconnected and reconnect WAC relay or fan controller. Set DVOM on 20-volt scale. With KOEO and A/C on, measure voltage between power side of A/C clutch harness connector and battery negative terminal. If voltage is greater than 10.5 volts, replace ECA, reconnect A/C clutch and retest system. If voltage is less than 10.5 volts, replace WAC relay or fan controller. Retest system.

11) Checking A/C Output at WOT. Enter OUTPUT STATE CHECK, see OUTPUT STATE CHECK under DIAGNOSTIC AIDS. Use a VOM or DVOM meter for this test. Turn key off and wait 10 seconds. Set DVOM on 20-volt scale. Connect DVOM negative (–) lead to STO at Self-Test connector and positive lead to positive (+) battery terminal. Jumper STI to SIG RTN at Self-Test connector. Perform KOEO SELF-TEST until completion of Continuous Memory Code sequence. Meter will indicate less than one volt when test is complete. Depress and release throttle. If voltage increases to 10.5 volts or more, remain in OUTPUT STATE CHECK and go to next step. If voltage does not increase to 10.5 volts, leave test equipment connected and go to test D16, step **2)**.

12) System Identification. If vehicle is equipped with WAC relay, go to step **17)**. If vehicle is equipped with A/C fan controller, go to step **22)**.

WAC Relay
2.3L Turbo MPFI
3.8L RWD SEFI
5.0L SEFI & MA SEFI
2.3L MPFI Truck
2.9L MPFI Truck
3.0L MPFI Truck

A/C Fan Controller
1.9L CFI
1.9L MPFI
2.3L HSC MPFI
2.3L OHC MPFI

CIRCUIT TEST D7 (Cont.)

13) Checking VPWR to Relay. With vehicle in OUTPUT STATE CHECK, disconnect harness from WAC relay and set DVOM on 20-volt scale. Measure voltage between VPWR circuit (START/RUN circuit for 2.3L Turbo MPFI) at the WAC relay harness connector and chassis ground. If voltage is greater than 10.5 volts, go to next step. If voltage is less than 10.5 volts, repair open circuit, remove test equipment, and retest system.

14) Checking WAC System For Cycling. With vehicle in OUTPUT STATE CHECK, disconnect harness from WAC relay and set DVOM on 20-volt scale. Connect positive test lead to VPWR circuit (START/RUN circuit for 2.3L Turbo MPFI) and negative test lead to WAC circuit at WAC relay harness connector. Check DVOM while depressing and releasing throttle several times, to cycle system. If voltage cycles from high to low, replace WAC relay and retest system. If voltage does not cycle, remove test leads and go to next step.

15) Checking Continuity of WAC Circuit. Turn key off and wait 10 seconds. Disconnect ECA 60-pin connector. Inspect for and repair any damaged wiring. Install breakout box, leaving ECA and WAC relay disconnected. Set DVOM on 200-ohm scale. Measure resistance between test pin No. 54 and WAC circuit at relay connector. If reading is 5 ohms or more, repair open circuit and repeat QUICK TEST. If reading is less than 5 ohms, go to next step.

16) Checking For Short to Power. Turn key off and wait 10 seconds. Leave breakout box installed, ECA and WAC relay disconnected. Set DVOM on 200K-ohm scale. Measure resistance between test pin No. 54 and test pins No. 37 and 57. If any reading is less than 10K ohms, repair short circuit and repeat QUICK TEST. If all readings are 10K ohms or more, replace ECA and retest system.

17) Check WAC Cycling. With vehicle in OUTPUT STATE CHECK, disconnect A/C fan controller and set DVOM on 20-volt scale. Connect DVOM positive test lead to ignition run circuit and negative test lead to WAC circuit at A/C fan controller harness connector. Check DVOM while depressing and releasing throttle several times, to cycle system. If voltage cycles from high to low, replace A/C fan controller and retest system. If voltage does not cycle, remove jumper and go to next step.

18) Checking Continuity of WAC Circuit. Turn key off and wait 10 seconds. Disconnect ECA 60-pin connector. Inspect for and repair any damaged wiring. Install breakout box, leaving ECA and fan controller disconnected. Set DVOM on 200-ohm scale. Measure resistance between test pin No. 54 and WAC circuit at WAC relay harness connector. If reading is 5 ohms or more, repair open in harness and repeat QUICK TEST. If reading is less than 5 ohms, go to next step.

19) Checking For Short to Power. Turn key off and wait 10 seconds. Install breakout box, ECA and A/C fan controller disconnected. Set DVOM on 200K-ohm scale. Measure resistance between test pin No. 54 and test pins No. 37 and 57 at the breakout box. If all readings are greater than 10K ohms, replace ECA, reconnect A/C fan controller and retest system. If any reading is 10K ohms or less, repair short to power and repeat QUICK TEST. If symptom is still present, replace ECA.

20) Cycle A/C Demand Switch. Turn key off and wait 10 seconds. Install breakout box, leaving ECA disconnected. Set DVOM on 20-volt scale. With KOEO, connect DVOM positive test lead to test pin No. 43 (No. 24 on 2.3L OHC MPFI) and negative test lead to test pin No. 40. If voltage goes high and low as switch is cycled, replace ECA and retest system. If voltage does not cycle, go to next step.

21) Checking Continuity of A/C Demand (ACD) Circuit. Turn key off and wait 10 seconds. Set DVOM on 200-ohm scale. Measure resistance between test pin No. 43 (No. 24 on 2.3L OHC MPFI) at the breakout box and A/C demand switch. If resistance is greater than 5 ohms, repair open in A/C demand circuit and rerun QUICK TEST. If resistance is less than 5 ohms, EEC-IV system is okay.

22) Checking A/C Demand (ACD) Circuit For Short to Power. Disconnect WAC relay or A/C fan controller. Disconnect ECA and install breakout box. With A/C demand switch "OFF", set DVOM on 20-volt scale. Turn key on. Measure voltage between test pin No. 24 (No. 43 on 2.3L Turbo MPFI) at breakout box and chassis ground. If voltage is less than one volt EEC-IV system is okay. If voltage is more than one volt, check operation of A/C demand switch, repair short circuit and retest system.

1a-474

1989 COMPUTERIZED ENGINE CONTROLS
Ford Motor Co. EEC-IV (Cont.)

CIRCUIT TEST D8

OCTANE ADJUST

NOTE: Enter this test when directed here by Diagnosis By Symptom Test in QUICK TEST procedure.

Octane Adjust Circuit

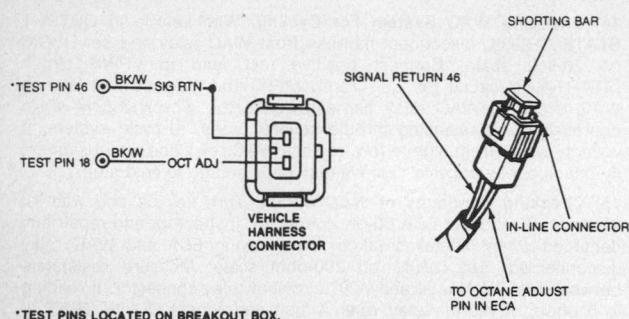

*TEST PINS LOCATED ON BREAKOUT BOX.
ALL HARNESS CONNECTORS VIEWED INTO MATING SURFACE.

NOTE: This test is intended to diagnose the following:
- Harness circuits, VPWR and OCTANE ADJUST
- Octane Adjust Shorting Bar connector

OCTANE ADJUST SHORTING BAR LOCATIONS

Application	Location
2.3L MPFI Truck	Passenger side inner fender, taped to self test connector.
3.0L SHO SEFI	Driver side of engine, Tie wrapped to transmission bracket.
3.8L SC SEFI	Passenger side of engine, next to Self-Test connector.

The purpose of the Octane Adjust Shorting Bar is to provide optimum spark advance for the fuel being used. If the vehicle engine detonates (spark knock), REMOVE the Octane Shorting Bar. This retards spark advance about 3 to 4 degrees. If the vehicle continues to detonate, use fuel with a higher octane rating.

CIRCUIT TEST D9

SUPERCHARGER BY-PASS SOLENOID (SBS)

NOTE: Perform this test when Service Code 82 is displayed or when directed here by other test procedures.

SBS Circuit

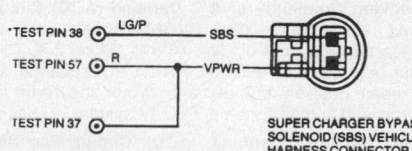

*TEST PINS LOCATED ON BREAKOUT BOX.
ALL HARNESS CONNECTORS VIEWED INTO MATING SURFACE.

1) Code 82: Check Solenoid Resistance. Code 82 indicates that voltage output for the SBS did not change when activated by the ECA during KOEO SELF-TEST. Possible causes for this fault are: open or shorted SBS circuit, open or grounded ECA driver or disconnected or open solenoid.
With key off, set DVOM on 20-volt scale. Disconnect SBS solenoid and measure solenoid resistance. If resistance is between 50 and 100 ohms, go to next step. If resistance is not 50-100 ohms, replace SBS and rerun QUICK TEST.

CIRCUIT TEST D9 (Cont.)

2) Check Voltage On VPWR Circuit. With KOEO, set DVOM on 20-volt scale. Measure voltage between SBS VPWR circuit and battery ground. If voltage is greater than 10.5 volts, go to next step. If voltage was less than 10.5 volts, repair open circuit and rerun QUICK TEST.

3) Check Continuity of SBS Circuit. Turn key off, disconnect ECA 60-pin connector. Inspect for and repair any damaged wiring. Install breakout box, leaving ECA disconnected. Set DVOM on 200-ohm scale. Measure resistance between test pin No. 38 at the breakout box and SBS circuit at the vehicle harness. If resistance is less than 5 ohms, go to next step. If resistance is greater than 5 ohms, repair open circuit, reconnect ECA and rerun QUICK TEST.

4) Check For Short to Ground. Set DVOM on 200K-ohm scale. Install breakout box, leave ECA disconnected. Disconnect SBS. Measure resistance between test pin No. 38 and test pins No. 40, 46 and 60, at the breakout box. If resistance is greater than 10K ohms, go to next step. If resistance is less than 10K ohms, repair short to ground and rerun QUICK TEST.

5) Check For Shorts to Power. With key off and DVOM on 200K-ohm scale, Install breakout box and leave ECA and SBS disconnected. Measure resistance between test pin No. 38 and test pin No. 1 at the breakout box. If resistance is greater than 10K ohms, remove breakout box and reconnect SBS, replace ECA and rerun QUICK TEST. If resistance is less than 10K ohms, repair short to power, rerun QUICK TEST. If Code 82 is still present, replace ECA.

NOTE: You should have been directed to test step 6) by the Diagnosis By Symptom chart.

6) Check Supercharger By-pass Valve. With key off, disconnect vacuum line from supercharger by-pass valve. Apply 16 in. Hg to valve. If valve holds vacuum, go to next step. If valve does not hold vacuum, replace it and retest.

7) Check By-pass System. With key off, apply vacuum to valve and visually observe valve and linkage. If valve operates linkage correctly, go to next step. If linkage does not operate correctly, repair as necessary and retest.

8) Check Vacuum Supply to By-pass Valve. With key off, check vacuum hose between supercharger valve and SBS for damage or blockage. If hose and connections are okay, go to next step. If hose is faulty, replace as necessary and rerun QUICK TEST.

9) Check Vacuum Supply. Disconnect source vacuum hose from SBS. Start engine and check vacuum. If vacuum is present at hose replace SBS and rerun QUICK TEST. If vacuum is not present, service or repair vacuum source blockage and rerun QUICK TEST.

CIRCUIT TEST D10

DYNAMIC RESPONSE TEST

To prevent replacement of good components, be aware that the following non-EEC related areas may be at fault: person testing EEC system did not perform brief Wide Open Throttle (WOT) after Dynamic Response code, mechanical engine problems, or engine did not go over 2000 RPM. This test is intended to diagnose the following:
- Throttle movement (Minimum 3/4 throttle).
- Vane Airflow Meter (VAF) open at least 50%.
- RPM increase greater than 2000 RPM.

NOTE: If throttle is snapped open briefly it may not pass the WOT test. Ensure that the throttle is depressed fully to WOT and that engine exceeds 2000 RPM.

Code 77 Displayed: System Failed to Recognize WOT Test. Rerun KOER SELF TEST as follows:
- Start engine.
- Activate KOER SELF-TEST.
- Observe ID code 2 (0 with STAR tester).
- Observe Dynamic Response Code 1 (0 with STAR tester).
- Perform brief WOT.
- Testing complete, service code output begins.

If Code 77 is still displayed, replace ECA and rerun QUICK TEST. If Code 77 is no longer present, vehicle has passed Dynamic Response test, service other codes as necessary.

1989 COMPUTERIZED ENGINE CONTROLS
Ford Motor Co. EEC-IV (Cont.)

1a-475

CIRCUIT TEST D11

"CHECK ENGINE" LIGHT/MESSAGE
(MALFUNCTION INDICATOR)

NOTE: To prevent replacement of good components, be aware that the following non-EEC related areas may be at fault: fuses, bulb, or socket. This circuit test checks STO-MIL circuit and ECA. You should perform this test when Codes 70, 71 or 72 is displayed, or when directed here by other test procedure.

"CHECK ENGINE" Light (Malfunction Indicator) Circuit

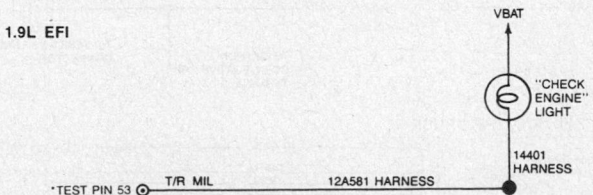

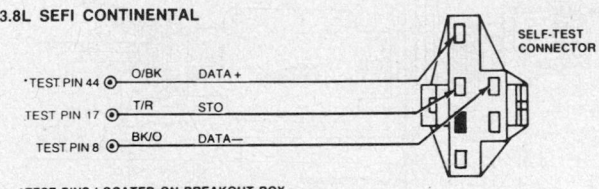

* TEST PINS LOCATED ON BREAKOUT BOX.
HARNESS CONNECTOR VIEWED INTO MATING SURFACE.

ALL EXCEPT 1.9L EFI AND 3.8L SEFI CONTINENTAL

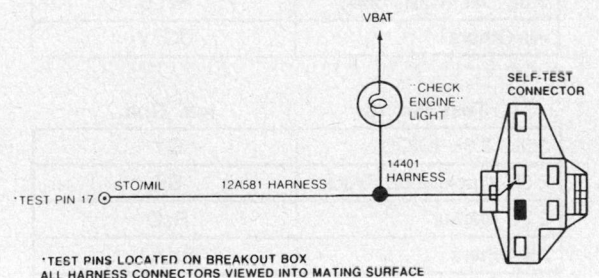

* TEST PINS LOCATED ON BREAKOUT BOX.
ALL HARNESS CONNECTORS VIEWED INTO MATING SURFACE

Test Pin 17   STO/MIL

Application	Wire Colors
3.8L RWD SEFI 3.8L SC SEFI 5.0L SEFI Mark VII	Y/BK
2.3L OHC EFI 5.0L SEFI-MA	T
F-Series/Bronco: 4.9L EFI, 5.0L EFI, 5.8L EFI 7.5L EFI 7.3L Diesel F-Series	PK/LG
All Others	T/R

CIRCUIT TEST D11 (Cont.)

NOTE: All service codes, except a Code 11 (pass), must be cleared before continuing.

1) "CHECK ENGINE" Light Always On: Checking Short to Ground. If vehicle will not start, go to CIRCUIT TEST A1, step **1).** Turn key off. Disconnect ECA 60-pin connector. Inspect connector for damaged pins, corrosion, or loose wires. Install breakout box, leaving ECA disconnected. Set DVOM on 200K-ohm scale. Connect DVOM between test pins No. 17 (No. 53 on 1.9L MPFI) and No. 40 at the breakout box. If resistance is greater than 10K ohms, replace ECA. If reading is less than 10K ohms, repair short between test pin No. 17 (No. 53 on 1.9L MPFI) and SELF-TEST connector or "CHECK ENGINE" light.

2) "CHECK ENGINE" Light Never On: Check Continuity of STO/MIL Circuit. If vehicle will not start, go to CIRCUIT TEST A1, step **1).** Turn key off. Disconnect ECA 60-pin connector. Inspect connector for damaged pins, corrosion, or loose wires. Repair if necessary. Install breakout box, leaving ECA disconnected. Set DVOM on 200-ohm scale. Measure resistance between test pin No. 17 (No. 53 on 1.9L MPFI) and "CHECK ENGINE" light. If resistance is less than 5 ohms, go to next step. If not, repair open circuit in wiring harness and rerun QUICK TEST.

3) Checking For Power to "CHECK ENGINE" Light Bulb. If power exists at bulb, replace bulb or socket and go to next step. If no power exists at socket, check fuse and input circuit, and then go to next step.

4) Confirming Circuit Repair. Remove breakout box and reconnect ECA to harness. Turn key to "RUN" position. See if "CHECK ENGINE" light is on. If light is on, malfunction indicator system is okay. If light does not come on, replace ECA.

5) "CHECK ENGINE" Intermittent, Check Short From STO to Ground. If vehicle does not start, go to CIRCUIT TEST A1, step **1).** Service all Continuous Memory Codes before proceeding. If no codes are outputted, proceed with this test.
Enter KOEO CONTINUOUS MONITOR MODE ("WIGGLE TEST"). Observe DVOM for indication of fault while performing "Wiggle" test on the harness in the following areas.
• From Self-Test connector to dash panel.
• Dash panel to ECA.
• Dash panel to "CHECK ENGINE" light.
If a fault is indicated, repair as necessary and rerun QUICK TEST. If a fault is not indicated, fault cannot be duplicated at this time.

6) "CHECK ENGINE" Light Flashes With Erratic Idle: Check STI Short to Ground. Vehicle symptoms indicate STI is grounded and ECA is performing Self-Test without tester installed. With key off, disconnect ECA 60-pin connector. Inspect connector for damaged pins, corrosion, or loose wires. Repair if necessary. Set DVOM on 200K-ohm scale. Measure resistance between STI connector and engine block ground. If resistance is less than 10K ohms, repair short circuit. Reconnect ECA and retest. If reconnect ECA and test for other rough idle symptoms.

7) "CHECK ENGINE" Message Displayed. If vehicle will not start, go to CIRCUIT TEST A, step **1).** Perform KOEO SELF-TEST, if the result is a pass code (11-10-11), repair fault in electronic message center Data Communications Link (DCL). If Pass Code is not displayed, service codes as described in Self-Test procedures.

8) Continuous Memory Code 70, 71 and 72: "CHECK ENGINE" Light On. Codes 70, 71 and 72 indicate a circuit failure has occurred on the Data Communications Link (DCL). These codes can occur alone or together. "CHECK ENGINE" message will be on.
• Code 70 indicates ECA is unable to transmit data.
• Code 71 indicates Cluster Control Assembly (CCA) is unable to transmit data.
• Code 72 indicates that Message Center Control Assembly (MCCA) is unable to transmit data.
Perform KOEO SELF-TEST, if the result is a Pass Code (11-10-11), repair fault in electronic message center Data Communications Link (DCL). If pass code is not displayed, service codes as described in Self-Test procedures.

1a-476

1989 COMPUTERIZED ENGINE CONTROLS
Ford Motor Co. EEC-IV (Cont.)

CIRCUIT TEST D12

IGNITION DIAGNOSTIC MONITOR (IDM)

IDM Circuit

ALL OTHER TFI APPLICATIONS

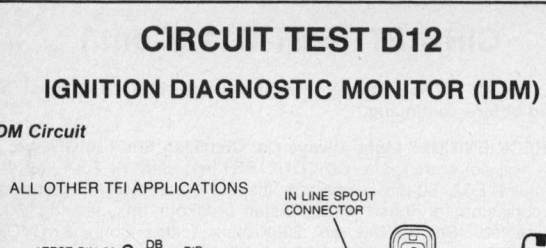

* TEST PINS LOCATED ON BREAKOUT BOX.
ALL HARNESS CONNECTORS VIEWED INTO MATING SURFACE.
** NO 22K OHM RESISTOR FOR 3.0L CALIFORNIA CAR

Test Pin 16	Ignition Ground
Application	**Wire Color**
3.8L SEFI AXOD	GY
3.8L SEFI RWD 7.5L EFI TRK	BK/O

TFI Location	
Application	**Location**
3.8L SEFI AXOD	Cowl
3.8L SEFI RWD	Radiator Support
7.5L EFI TRK	Distributor

3.0L SHO SEFI MA & 3.8L SEFI SC

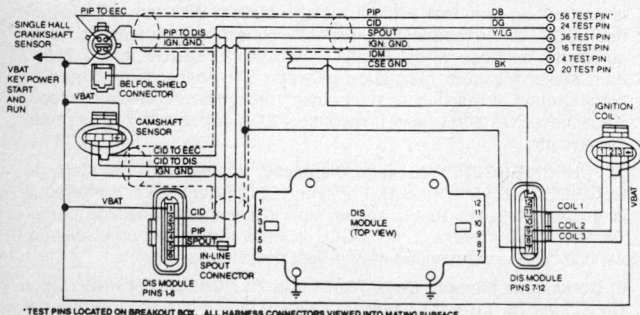

*TEST PINS LOCATED ON BREAKOUT BOX. ALL HARNESS CONNECTORS VIEWED INTO MATING SURFACE.

Test Pin 4	IDM
3.0L SHO MA	GY/O
3.8L SC. MA	DG/Y

Test Pin 16	Ign. Gnd.
3.0L SHO MA	BK/O
3.8L SC MA	LB

CIRCUIT TEST D12 (Cont.)

3.8L SEFI (EXCEPT SC) & 7.5L MPFI TRUCK

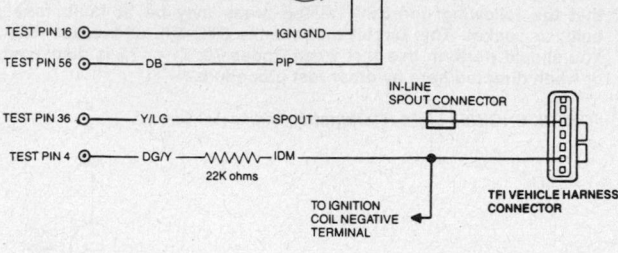

2.3L OHC MPFI TRUCK

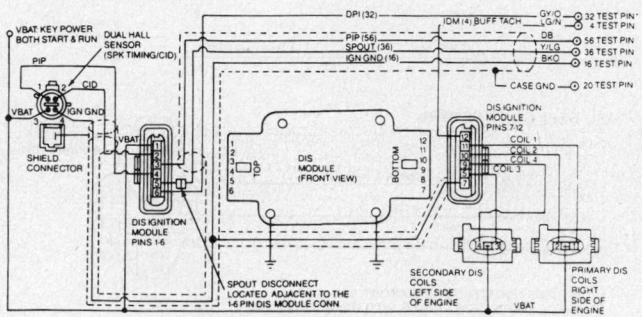

Test Pin 4	Ign. Gnd.
3.0L Car (Calif. only)	R/LB
All Others	DG/Y

Test Pin 16	Ign. Gnd.
3.0L, 3.8L AXOD	GY
2.3L Truck, 2.9L Truck	BK
2.3L Merkur	R/O
All Others	BK/O

NOTE: Perform this test when Service Code 14, 18, 19, 28, 45, 46, 48 or 88 is displayed during QUICK TESTS or when directed here by other test procedures.

To prevent replacement of good components, be aware that the following non-EEC related areas may be at fault:
- TFI or DIS ignition module.
- Ignition coil or DIS coil packs.
- Spark plugs and/or high tension cables.
- Distributor and PIP sensor.
- Secondary ignition component arcing.

This test is intended to diagnose the following circuits and components.
- Harness circuits: IGNITION GROUND, SPOUT, PIP, IDM & DPI
- ECA assembly

There are 3 types of ignition system connections used with EEC-IV. They are configured as follows:

Distributorless Ignition System (DIS)
Two 6-pin connectors located at top and bottom of DIS module. Pins No. 1-6 are located on the top of the module. Pins No. 7-12 are located in the connector on the bottom of the module.

Closed Bowl Distributor (CBD)
TFI module is located on the cowl, away from the distributor. The previous mounting window in the bowl of the distributor is closed. Two connectors are used, one connecting the harness to the vehicle Hall sensor, located in the distributor, and another connecting the harness to the TFI module.

TFI Module Distributor
This is the most common system. The TFI module is mounted in the distributor and a single module connector is used.

1989 COMPUTERIZED ENGINE CONTROLS
Ford Motor Co. EEC-IV (Cont.)

1a-477

CIRCUIT TEST D12 (Cont.)

IGNITION SYSTEM APPLICATIONS

Vehicle	Application
2.3L OHC MPFI, 3.0L SHO SEFI & 3.8L SC SEFI	DIS
3.8L RWD SEFI, 3.8L AXOD SEFI & 7.5L Truck	CBD
All Others	TFI

1) Code 14: Erratic Ignition. Code 14 indicates two successive erratic Profile Ignition Pickup (PIP) pulses occurred, resulting in a possible engine miss or stall. Possible causes for this fault are: loose wires or connectors, arcing secondary ignition components or on-board transmitter equipment (2-way radio). If any of the above are present, service as necessary, clear code and rerun QUICK TEST. If the items listed are not present, go to step **4)**.

2) Check For Other Codes. If Codes 45, 46 or 48 are present, go to step **12)**. If Codes 45, 46 or 48 are not present, go to next step.

3) Continuous Memory Codes 18, 28 or 48: Check IDM Circuit Continuity. Code 18 indicates a loss of IDM input signal. Possible causes:
- Open harness circuit
- Shorted harness
- Faulty TFI or DIS module
- Faulty ECA

Code 28 indicates IDM input signal always low. Possible causes:
- Open or shorted harness
- Faulty CID sensor
- VBAT (battery voltage) low at DIS
- Faulty DIS module
- Faulty ECA

Code 48 indicates IDM input signal always high. Possible causes:
- Open signal in harness
- VBAT open at secondary coil
- VBAT low at secondary coil

NOTE: On TFI vehicles the IDM circuit has a 22K-ohm resistor between test pin No. 4 and the ignition coil negative terminal (except 3.0L CALIFORNIA vehicles).

Turn key off an wait 10 seconds. Disconect E core ignition coil on TFI vehicles and DIS module connector (pins No. 7-12) on DIS equipped vehicles. Disconnect ECA 60-pin connector. Inspect connector for damaged pins, corrosion, or loose wires. Repair if necessary. Install breakout box, leave ECA connected and set DVOM on 200K-ohm scale.

On TFI equipped vehicles, measure resistance between test pin No. 4 at the breakout box and negative terminal of ignition coil harness connector.

On DIS equipped vehicles, measure resistance between test pin No. 4 at the breakout box and DIS module harness connector pin No. 12.

If resistance is between 20K and 24K ohms (on DIS and 3.0L CALIFORNIA vehicles, resistance should be less than 5 ohms), go to next step. If resistance is not to specification, repair open circuit, clear codes, retest and reconnect E-core coil.

4) Checking IDM Circuit For Short to Ground. Turn key off and wait 10 seconds. Disconect E-core ignition coil on TFI vehicles and DIS module connector (pins No. 7-12) on DIS equipped vehicles. Install breakout box and ECA disconnected. With DVOM on 200K-ohm scale, measure resistance between test pin No. 4 and test pins No. 40, 46, and 60. If any reading is less than 10K ohms, repair short to ground in IDM circuit, reconnect all components and rerun QUICK TEST. If all readings are 10K ohms or more, reconnect components and go to next step.

5) Checking ECA For Short to Ground. Turn key off and wait 10 seconds. Disconect E-core ignition coil on TFI vehicles and DIS module connector (pins No. 7-12) on DIS equipped vehicles. Install breakout box and connect ECA. With DVOM on 200K-ohm scale, measure resistance between test pin No. 4 and test pins No. 40, 46, and 60. If any reading is less than 10K ohms, replace ECA, reconnect all components and rerun QUICK TEST. If all readings are 10K ohms or more, reconnect components and go to next step.

6) Checking Ignition Module. Turn key off and wait 10 seconds. Deactivate SELF-TEST. Using CONTINUOUS MONITOR (WIGGLE) TEST, observe VOM or diagnostic tester for indication of fault while lightly tapping on TFI or DIS module to simulate road shock. Wiggle TFI or DIS harness connectors. On Closed Bowl Distributor (CBD) models, wiggle TFI and distributor hall connectors. If fault is indicated, disconnect and inspect TFI harness connectors and terminals for damage. If connector and terminals are okay, check TFI ignition system, if ignition is okay, replace ECA. If no fault is indicated, go to next step.

CIRCUIT TEST D12 (Cont.)

7) Checking EEC-IV Harness. While in CONTINUOUS MONITOR (WIGGLE) TEST, observe VOM or diagnostic tester for indication of fault while wiggling, shaking, or bending small sections of harness while working from TFI or DIS connector toward firewall. Repeat process from firewall to ECA. On CBD systems also test distributor Hall connector. Perform this test to check for faults in the following circuits:

- PIP Open/Shorted to Ground .... Check circuit at test pin No. 56.
- SPOUT Shorted to Ground .... Check circuit at test pin No. 36.
- Ignition Ground Open .... Check circuit at test pin No. 16.
- IDM Open to Ground .... Check circuit at test pin No. 4.
- IDM Shorted to Power .... Check circuit at test pin No. 4.

Perform CONTINUOUS MONITOR (WIGGLE) TEST on these circuits one at a time in order to isolate fault. If fault is indicated, isolate fault and repair harness. Repeat QUICK TEST. If no fault is indicated, go to next step.

8) Checking ECA and Harness Connectors. Turn key off and wait 10 seconds. Disconnect ECA 60-pin connector. Inspect connector for damaged pins, corrosion or loose wires. If connector is damaged, repair as necessary, clear codes and repeat QUICK TEST. If connector is okay, perform the following procedure based on the Continuous Memory Code displayed:
- **Code 14:** Unable to duplicate erratic ignition fault in EEC system. Remove breakout box, reconnect all components. Diagnosis DIS ignition system.
- **Code 18:** Replace ECA, remove breakout box and reconnect all components. Start and run engine for about one minute and rerun QUICK TEST.
- **Codes 28 and 48:** Remove breakout box and reconnect all components. Diagnose ignition system. If ignition system is okay, replace ECA.

9) Continuous Memory Code 19: Check Camshaft Sensor Output. Code 19 indicates one of the 2 Cylinder Identification (CID) sensor output signals has failed. One of the outputs is a signal sent to the DIS and the second output is the signal to the ECA. Both outputs have a 50% duty cycle of 0.4 volt to battery voltage (VBAT). Possible causes for this fault are; open or short in CID-to-ECA circuit.

With key off, disconnect ECA 60-pin connector. Inspect connector for damaged pins, corrosion or loose wires. If connector is damaged, repair as necessary. Install breakout box and connect ECA. With KOER, and DVOM set on AC scale, measure voltage between test pin No. 24 and GROUND. If voltage varies, replace ECA, remove breakout box, reconnect all components and rerun QUICK TEST. If voltage does not vary, go to next step.

10) Check CID Harness For Continuity. With key off and breakout box installed, disconnect ECA. Disconnect DIS module. Set DVOM on 200-ohm scale. Measure resistance between test pin No. 24 at the breakout box and Pin No. 2 (CID signal) at the DIS module connector. If resistance is less than 5 ohms, go to next step. If resistance is greater than 5 ohms, repair open circuit, remove breakout box, reconnect all components and rerun QUICK TEST.

11) Check CID Circuit For Shorts. Turn key off, Install breakout box and disconnect ECA and DIS module. Set DVOM on 200K-ohm scale. Measure resistance between test pin No. 24 and test pins No. 16, 37 and 40 at the breakout box. If all resistances are not greater than 10K ohms, repair CID circuit to GROUND or POWER. Remove breakout box, reconnect all components and rerun QUICK TEST. If all resistances are greater than 10K ohms, remove breakout box, reconnect all components and diagnose TFI or DIS system.

12) Continuous Memory Codes 45, 46 or 48: Check Continuity of Coil Circuits From DIS to Coil Pack. Codes 45, 46 and 48 indicate a fault has been detected by the ECA in one of the 3 coils contained in the ignition pack. Possible causes for this fault are: an open in coil circuit from DIS module to coil pack or short to coil circuit GROUND or POWER in DIS module.

NOTE: Codes 45, 46 and 48 refer to faults related to coils No. 3, 1, or 2 respectively. Coil No. 1 provides voltage to cylinders No. 3 and 4 spark plugs. Coil No. 2 provides voltage to cylinders No. 2 and 6 spark plugs. Coil No. 3 provides voltage to cylinders No. 1 and 5 spark plugs. The IDM input contains a pulse signal for each operating coil. If that coil fails, the corresponding pulse will be missing from the IDM input pulse signal.

Turn key off and wait 10 seconds. Disconnect DIS module and set DVOM on 200-ohm scale. Measure resistance as described for appropriate service code:
- **Code 45:** Measure resistance between pin No. 8 at the DIS module and coil pin No. 3 at coil pack.

1a-478

1989 COMPUTERIZED ENGINE CONTROLS
Ford Motor Co. EEC-IV (Cont.)

CIRCUIT TEST D12 (Cont.)

- **Code 46:** Measure resistance between pin No. 11 at the DIS module and coil pin No. 1 at coil pack.
- **Code 48:** Measure resistance between pin No. 9 at the DIS module and coil pin No. 2 at coil pack.

If all resistances are less than 5 ohms, go to next step. If resistances are greater than 5 ohms, repair open circuit and reconnect all components. Rerun QUICK TEST.

13) Checking Coil Pack For Shorts to Ground and Power. With key off, disconnect coil pack and DIS module connector (pins No. 7-12). Set DVOM on 200K-ohm scale. Measure resistance between pin No. 7 and pins No. 8, 9 and 11 at the DIS module connector. Measure resistance between pin No. 1 and pins No. 8, 9 and 11 at the DIS module connector. If all resistances are greater than 10K ohms, diagnose DIS ignition system. If all resistances are not greater than 10K ohms, repair short circuit, reconnect all components, and rerun QUICK TEST.

14) Continuous Memory Code 88: Check Continuity of DPI Circuit. Code 88 indicates an open in the Dual Plug Inhibit (DPI) circuit or an open or short to ground in coil No. 4. Possible causes for this fault are: open or short circuit in harness, Faulty ECA or DIS module or faulty coil No. 4.
Turn key off and wait 10 seconds. Disconnect DIS connector (pins No. 7-12). Disconnect ECA 60-pin connector. Inspect connector for damaged pins, corrosion or loose wires. If connector is damaged, repair as necessary. Install breakout box and leave ECA disconnected. Set DVOM on 200K-ohm scale. Measure resistance between pin No. 6 at the DIS vehicle harness connector and test pin No. 32 at the breakout box. If resistance is less than 5 ohms, remove breakout box, reconnect all components. Diagnose DIS ignition system. If system is okay, replace ECA. If resistance is not less than 5 ohms, repair open circuit, remove breakout box, reconnect all components and rerun QUICK TEST.

15) Symptom: Hard Start, Check DPI Circuit For Short to Ground. Turn key off and wait 10 seconds. Disconnect DIS connector (pins No. 7-12). Disconnect ECA 60-pin connector. Inspect connector for damaged pins, corrosion or loose wires. If connector is damaged, repair as necessary. Install breakout box and leave ECA disconnected. Set DVOM on 200K-ohm scale. Measure resistance between test pin No. 32 and test pins No. 40 and 60 at the breakout box. If resistance is greater than 100K ohms, go to next step. If resistance is less than 100K ohms, repair short circuit, remove breakout box, reconnect all components and rerun QUICK TEST.

16) Check ECA For Short to Ground. Turn key off and wait 10 seconds. Disconnect DIS connector (pins No. 7-12). Install breakout box and connect ECA. Set DVOM on 200K-ohm scale. Measure resistance between test pin No. 32 and test pins No. 40 and 60 at the breakout box. If resistance is greater than 500 ohms, remove breakout box, reconnect all components. Diagnose DIS ignition system. If resistance is less than 500 ohms, replace ECA, remove breakout box, reconnect all components and rerun QUICK TEST.

CIRCUIT TEST D13
SPARK TIMING CHECK

NOTE: Perform this test when Service Code 18 or 49 is displayed during QUICK TESTS or when directed here by other test procedures.

To prevent replacement of good components, be aware that the following non-EEC related areas may be at fault: engine condition (valves, vacuum leaks, valve timing, EGR valve, etc.), PIP sensor, and TFI ignition module. This test is intended to diagnose the SPOUT circuit in the harness, base timing and the ECA.

1) KOER Code 18: Check Computed Spark Timing. On TFI vehicles, Code 18 indicates SPOUT circuit is open. Possible causes for this fault are: open harness circuit or faulty ECA or TFI module. On DIS vehicles, Code 18 indicates: SPOUT circuit is open or shorted to ground. Possible causes are; an open or shorted harness or faulty ECA or DIS module.
Perform KOER SELF-TEST and verify that SELF-TEST is activated. Check and record timing while in KOER SELF-TEST. System locks timing for a period of 2 minutes after last service code is displayed. Computed timing during these 2 minutes is equal to base timing plus 20 degrees (±3 degrees). On 2.3L DIS Trucks, use exhaust side spark plug. If computed timing is correct, go to KOER SELF-TEST. If timing is not to specification, go to next step.

CIRCUIT TEST D13 (Cont.)

Spark Timing Check Circuit

2.3L OHC MPFI TRUCK

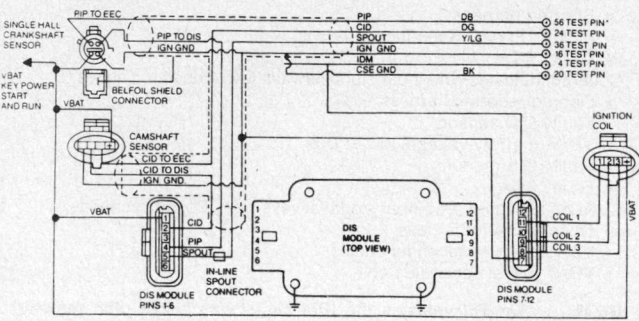

3.0L SHO SEFI MA & 3.8L SEFI SC

ALL TFI APPLICATIONS

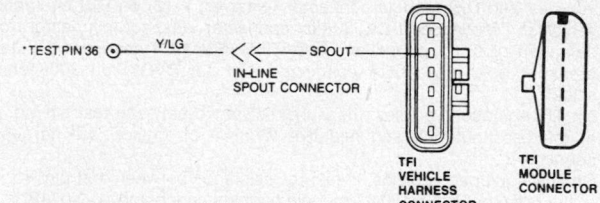

*TEST PINS LOCATED ON BREAKOUT BOX.
ALL HARNESS CONNECTORS VIEWED INTO MATING SURFACE.

2) Checking Base Timing. Locate Spark Output (SPOUT) connector and open the connection. Start engine and check for 10 degrees BTDC base timing ± 3 degrees. If base timing is correct, go to next step. If base timing is incorrect, on TFI equipped vehicles adjust base timing as necessary. After timing is reset, reconnect SPOUT and perform COMPUTED TIMING CHECK. On DIS equipped vehicles, base timing is not adjustable. diagnose DIS ignition system.

3) Checking For Power to ECA. Turn key off and wait 10 seconds. Disconnect ECA 60-pin connector. Inspect connector for damaged pins, corrosion, or loose wires. Repair if necessary. Install breakout box. With KOEO, and DVOM set on 20-volt scale, measure voltage between test pins No. 37 and 40, and between test pins No. 57 and 60 at the breakout box. If either reading is less than 10.5 volts, go to CIRCUIT TEST D22, step 1) on 2.5L HSC CFI, 3.0L MPFI, 3.0L SHO MPFI or 3.8L AXOD MPFI engine. If either reading is less than 10.5 volts, go to CIRCUIT TEST A2, step 1) for all other engines. If both readings are 10.5 volts or more, go to next step.

4) Checking SPOUT Circuit For Continuity. Turn key off and wait 10 seconds. Install breakout box. Disconnect ECA and TFI or DIS module. With DVOM set on 200-ohm scale, measure resistance between test pin No. 36 (SPOUT) at breakout box SPOUT pin at TFI or DIS harness connector. If reading is greater than 5 ohms, repair open circuit. Connect SPOUT connector and check timing as described in step 1). If reading is 5 ohms or less, go to next step for DIS vehicles, or step 6) for all others.

CIRCUIT TEST D13 (Cont.)

Module Connectors

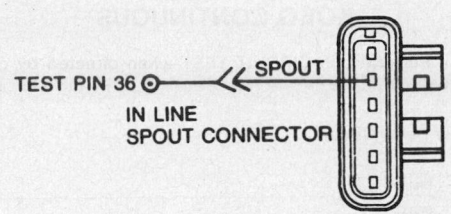

TFI VEHICLE HARNESS CONNECTOR

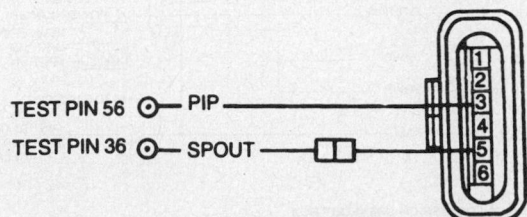

DIS VEHICLE HARNESS CONNECTOR (PINS NO. 1-6)

5) Check SPOUT For Shorts. Turn key off and wait 10 seconds, Install breakout box and disconnect ECA. Set DVOM on 200K-ohm scale. Perform the following measurements:

- **Shorts to Ground.** Measure resistance between test pin No. 36 and test pins No. 16, 20, 40, 46 and 60.
- **Shorts to Power.** Measure resistance between test pin No. 36 and test pins No. 26, 37 and 57.
- **Shorts to PIP Circuit.** Measure resistance between test pin No. 36 and test pin No. 56.

If all resistances are greater than 10K ohms, go to next step. If resistances are not greater than 10K ohms, service short circuit, remove breakout box, reconnect components and rerun QUICK TEST.

6) Checking ECA. Turn key off and wait 10 seconds. Install breakout box. Ensure ECA and TFI or DIS are connected. Set breakout box timing switch to "DIST" position. Set DVOM on 20-volt scale. Measure voltage between test pin No. 36 at the breakout box and battery negative terminal during KOER SELF-TEST. If voltage is between 4 and 10 volts, EEC system is okay, remove breakout box and diagnose TFI ignition system. If voltage is not between 4 and 10 volts, remove breakout box, replace ECA and rerun QUICK TEST.

7) Continuous Memory Code 49: Check Harness Continuity. Code 49 indicates SPOUT signal has defaulted to 10 degrees BTDC. The SPOUT signal has a variable duty cycle with a n amplitude of 4 volts to battery voltage (VBAT). If the SPOUT signal fails, the DIS module generates a fixed dwell and constant spark signal based on CID and PIP signals. This is the Failure Management Effects Mode (FMEM). Possible causes for this fault are: faulty DIS module or faulty SPOUT signal circuit from ECA to DIS module.

Turn key off and wait 10 seconds. Install breakout box and leave ECA disconnected. Disconnect DIS module. Set DVOM on 200-ohm scale. Measure resistance between test pin No. 36 at the breakout box and pin No. 5 at the DIS module connector. If resistance is less than 5 ohms, go to next step. If resistance is greater than 5 ohms, ensure SPOUT connector is okay. If okay, repair open circuit, reconnect all components and rerun QUICK TEST.

8) Check Spout Circuit For Short to Power or Ground. Turn key off and wait 10 seconds. Install breakout box. Disconnect ECA and DIS module. Set DVOM on 200K-ohm scale. Measure resistance between test pin No. 36 at the breakout box and test pins No. 16, 40 and battery positive. If all resistances are greater than 10K ohms, diagnose TFI or DIS ignition system. If resistances are less than 10K ohms, service SPOUT circuit for shorts. Reconnect all components and rerun QUICK TEST.

CIRCUIT TEST D14

NO CODES/CODES NOT LISTED

NOTE: Perform this CIRCUIT TEST when directed by other test procedures.

No Codes/Codes Not Listed Circuits

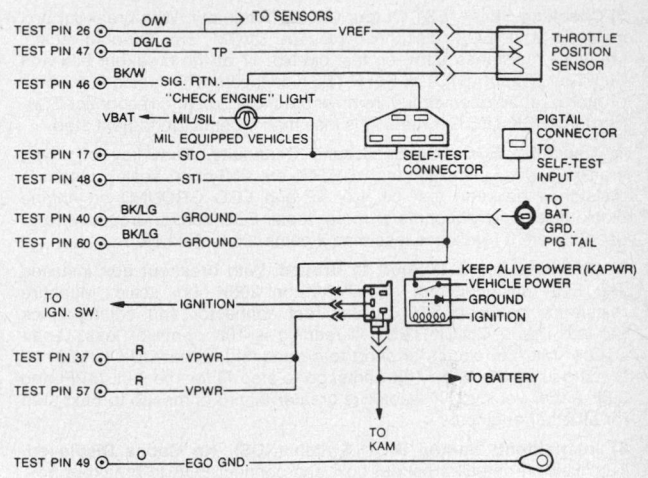

*TEST PINS LOCATED ON BREAKOUT BOX.
ALL HARNESS CONNECTORS VIEWED INTO MATING SURFACE.

	Self-Test Output and "Check Engine" Light
Test Pin 17	
Application	**Wire Color**
5.0L SEFI Mark VII 3.8L RWD SEFI 3.8L SC SEFI	Y/BK
5.0L SEFI MA 2.3L OHC EFI	T
1.9L EFI	T/LB
4.9L EFI F-Series Bronco 5.0L EFI F-Series, Bronco 5.8L EFI F-Series, Bronco 7.3L Diesel 7.5L F-Series Bronco	PK/LG
All Others	T/R

Test Pin 48	**Self-Test Input**
Application	**Wire Color**
3.0L EFI 3.8L EFI AXOD 2.5L CFI CLC 2.5L CFI MTX 5.0L SEFI Crown Victoria/Grand Marquis and Town Car	W/BK
All Others	W/R

1) Checking For VREF. Turn key off and wait 10 seconds. Disconnect ECA 60-pin connector. Inspect connector for damaged pins, corrosion, or loose wires. Repair if necessary. Install breakout box, and connect ECA. Set DVOM on 20-volt scale. With KOEO, measure voltage between test pin No. 26 and SIGNAL RETURN at Self-Test connector. If reading is less than 4 volts or more than 6 volts, go to CIRCUIT TEST A3, step **1).** If reading is between 4 and 6 volts, go to next step.

1a-480

1989 COMPUTERIZED ENGINE CONTROLS
Ford Motor Co. EEC-IV (Cont.)

CIRCUIT TEST D14 (Cont.)

2) Checking SELF-TEST Input Continuity. Turn key off and wait 10 seconds. With breakout box installed and ECA disconnected. Set DVOM on 200-ohm scale. Measure resistance between test pin No. 48 at the breakout box and Self-Test Input (STI) at SELF-TEST connector pigtail. If reading is 5 ohms or more, repair open in circuit, remove breakout box and reconnect ECA. Rerun QUICK TEST. If reading is less than 5 ohms, go to next step.

3) Checking SELF-TEST Output Circuit Continuity. With breakout box installed and ECA disconnected, set DVOM on 200-ohm scale. Measure resistance between test pin No. 17 at the breakout box and Self-Test Output (STO) at SELF-TEST connector. If reading is 5 ohms or more, repair open circuit, remove breakout box and reconnect ECA. Rerun QUICK TEST. If reading is less than 5 ohms, go to next step.

4) Checking EGO Sensor Ground Continuity. Turn key off. With breakout box installed and DVOM on 200-ohm scale, measure resistance between test pin No. 49 and EGO GROUND on engine block. If reading is 5 ohms or more, repair EGO sensor ground wire or open circuit. If reading is less than 5 ohms, go to next step.

5) Checking For STO Short to Ground. With breakout box installed and ECA disconnected, set DVOM on 200K-ohm scale. Measure resistance between STO at Self-Test connector and engine block ground. Rerun QUICK TEST. If reading is 10K ohms or less, repair STO or MIL/SIL circuit for short to ground and repeat QUICK TEST. If reading is greater than 10K ohms, go to step **7)** for the 3.0L MPFI and 3.8L AXOD vehicles. If reading is greater than 5 ohms, go to next step for all other engines.

6) Intermittent: Neutral Drive Switch (NDS), No Codes Displayed. Turn key off. Install breakout box, and connect ECA to breakout box. Set DVOM on 20-volt scale. Connect DVOM between test pin No. 30 and test pins No. 40 or 60 at the breakout box. Refer to the circuit diagram in CIRCUIT TEST B13 for this step. Perform KOER SELF-TEST. If reading is greater than one volt, repair intermittent open in NDS harness connector or switch. If okay, reconnect ECA and go to KOER SELF-TEST for appropriate service codes. If reading is less than one volt, go to next step.

7) Power Relay Always On. Leave key off and breakout box installed. Set DVOM on 20-volt scale. Connect DVOM between test pins No. 37 or 57 and pins No. 40 or 60. Turn key on and then off. Wait 10 seconds. If reading does not change from 10.5 volts (or more) to zero volts, go to next step. If reading changes from 10.5 volts (or more) to zero volts, go to step **9)** only if vehicle is equipped with Malfunction Indicator Light (MIL) or Shift Indicator Light (SIL). If vehicle is NOT equipped with either of these lights, replace ECA and repeat QUICK TEST.

NOTE: Malfunction Indicator Light (MIL) is displayed as "CHECK ENGINE" light on instrument cluster.

8) VPWR Harness Short to Power. With key off, breakout box installed and EEC power relay or Integrated Relay Controller Module (IRCM) disconnected, set DVOM on 20-volt scale. Connect DVOM to test pin No. 37 or 57 and to test pin No. 40 or 46 at the breakout box. If voltage is greater than 10.5 volts, repair short to VPWR circuit and rerun QUICK TEST. If voltage is less than 10.5 volts, replace EEC-IV power relay or IRCM and rerun QUICK TEST.

9) Malfunction Indicator Light (MIL) or Shift Indicator Light (SIL). If shift indicator light is always on or off, go to CIRCUIT TEST D6, step **1)**. If malfunction indicator light is always on, go to CIRCUIT TEST D11, step **1)**. If malfunction indicator light is always off, go to CIRCUIT TEST D11, step **5)**. If MIL or SIL is working normally, replace ECA and repeat QUICK TEST.

CIRCUIT TEST D15

CODE 15
KOEO CONTINUOUS

NOTE: Perform this CIRCUIT TEST when directed by other test procedures.

EEC Power Relay Circuit

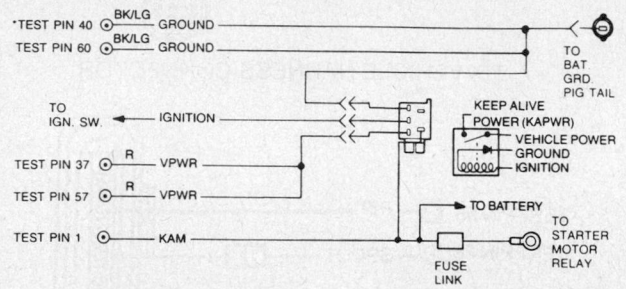

*TEST PINS LOCATED ON BREAKOUT BOX
ALL HARNESS CONNECTORS VIEWED INTO MATING SURFACE

Test Pin 1	Keep Alive Power
Application	**Wire Color**
2.3L OHC, EFI	
5.0L SEFI Mark VII	
5.0L SEFI-MA	BK/O
5.0L EFI, E-Series	
7.5L EFI, E-Series	
All Others	Y

1) Continuous Memory Code 15 Displayed. Clear Continuous Memory Codes using procedure outlined in DIAGNOSIS & TESTING. Repeat KOEO SELF-TEST through Continuous Memory Code output. If continuous Code 15 is not displayed, continuous Code 15 testing is complete. If Continuous Memory Code 15 is displayed during retest, go to next step.

NOTE: Continuous Memory Code 15 may be displayed when power to Keep Alive Memory (KAM) test pin No. 1 at ECA is interrupted. This code may be set when installing a breakout box. Code 15 may also be displayed the first time SELF-TEST is performed and power is restored to ECA. Repeat SELF-TEST to ensure correct diagnosis.

2) Engine Compartment Wire Routing. Ensure that EEC components and wiring are not close to high tension secondary voltage wires or ignition components. If EEC wiring is close to high tension wires, reroute EEC wiring. Repeat QUICK TEST. If Continuous Memory Code 15 is no longer displayed, Continuous Memory Code 15 testing is complete. If Continuous Memory Code 15 is still displayed, go to next step.

3) Checking Power Circuit For Keep Alive Memory (KAM). Turn key off and wait 10 seconds. Disconnect ECA 60-pin connector and inspect for damaged pins and loose wires. Service as necessary. Install breakout box, leaving ECA disconnected. Set DVOM on 20-volt scale. Connect DVOM positive test lead to test pin No. 1 and negative test lead to pins No. 40 or 60 at the breakout box. Turn key on and observe voltage reading. If reading is less than 10.5 volts, repair open circuit. Repeat QUICK TEST. If reading is 10.5 volts or more, replace ECA and repeat QUICK TEST.

1989 COMPUTERIZED ENGINE CONTROLS
Ford Motor Co. EEC-IV (Cont.)

1a-481

CIRCUIT TEST D16

OUTPUT STATE CHECK NOT FUNCTIONING

NOTE: Perform this CIRCUIT TEST when directed by other test procedures.

Output State Check Circuit

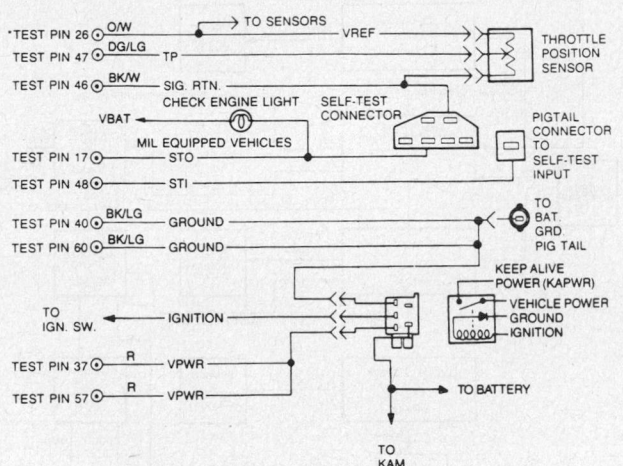

*TEST PINS LOCATED ON BREAKOUT BOX
ALL HARNESS CONNECTORS VIEWED INTO MATING SURFACE

Test Pin 17	Self-Test Output and "Check Engine" Light
Application	**Wire Color**
5.0L SEFI Mark VII 3.8L RWD SEFI 2.3L EFI Turbo	Y/BK
5.0L SEFI-MA 2.3L OHC EFI	T
1.9L EFI	T/LB
4.9L EFI 5.0L EFI F-Series, Bronco 5.8L EFI F-Series, Bronco	PK/LG
All Others	T/R

Test Pin 48	Self-Test Input
Application	**Wire Color**
3.0L EFI 3.8L SEFI AXOD 2.5L CFI CLC 2.5L CFI MTX 5.0L SEFI Crown Victoria/Grand Marquis and Town Car	W/BK
All Others	W/R

1) Checking Service Codes. Turn key off and wait 10 seconds. Perform KOEO SELF-TEST. If Codes 23, 53, 63 or 68 are displayed, go to KOEO SELF-TEST table and service code(s) as instructed. If no codes are displayed, go to CIRCUIT TEST D14, step **1)**. If Code 11 (Pass) is displayed, go to next step.

2) Checking Throttle Linkage. Check throttle and linkage for sticking or binding. If throttle and linkage are okay, replace TPS and repeat QUICK TEST. If throttle and linkage are binding, repair as necessary and repeat QUICK TEST.

CIRCUIT TEST D17

RE-INITIALIZATION CHECK

NOTE: Perform this CIRCUIT TEST when Codes 71, 72 or 78 is displayed or when directed by other test procedures.

NOTE: The electrical signatures of some aftermarket components may affect driveability of the vehicle.

EEC Power Relay Circuit

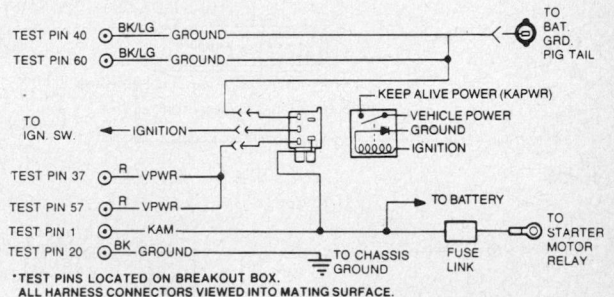

*TEST PINS LOCATED ON BREAKOUT BOX.
ALL HARNESS CONNECTORS VIEWED INTO MATING SURFACE.

Test Pin 1	Keep Alive Power
Application	**Wire Color**
2.3L OHC EFI 5.0L SEFI Mark VII 5.0L SEFI MA Mustang 5.0L EFI Econoline 7.5L EFI Econoline	BK/O
All Others	Y

1) Codes 71, 72 or 78: Checking For Electrical Noise Sources. Continuous Memory Code 72 or 78 indicates that power to the ECA was interrupted sometime during the last 40 warm-up cycle. A Continuous Code 71 indicates that sometime during the past 40 warm-up cycles, the ECA software requested a re-initialization or reveiw of previous drive sequence data. This process could result in a driveability complaint. Possible causes for this fault or complaint are:
* Vehicle power interrupted to ECA.
* Spark plug wires incorrectly routed too close to ignition.
* High tension wire shielding removed.
* Electrical, radio, or motor static noise.
* Test pin No. 20 (case ground) not grounded to chassis.
* Open diodes on A/C or ISC relay.

Turn key off. Ensure that EEC wiring and components are more than 2" (50 mm) away from secondary ignition wires. Make sure that EEC wiring and components are more than 4" (100 mm) away from distributor, ignition coil, and starter motor and its wiring. If these items are correct, go to next step. If not, correct as necessary and repeat QUICK TEST.

2) Checking Harness and Case Ground. Turn key off. Disconnect ECA 60-pin connector. Inspect connector for damaged pins, corrosion, or loose wires. Repair if necessary. Install breakout box, leaving ECA disconnected. Set DVOM on 200-ohm scale. Measure resistance between test pin No. 20 and chassis ground. If reading is less than 5 ohms, go to next step. If not, repair wiring harness and repeat QUICK TEST.

3) Case Ground Check With Harness Disconnected. Turn key off. Connect ECA to breakout box, but disconnect harness from breakout box. Set DVOM on 200-ohm scale. Measure resistance between test pin No. 20 and ECA metal case. If reading is less than 5 ohms, go to next step. On 2.5L CFI, go to D22, step **10)**. If reading is more than 5 ohms, replace ECA and repeat QUICK TEST.

4) "WIGGLE" Testing VPWR Circuit. With KOEO, connect DVOM to SELF TEST connector. Deactivate SELF-TEST. Using Continuous Monitor Mode, perform "WIGGLE" test on EEC-IV harness from ECA to power relay. If a fault is indicated or a Code 71 is displayed, repair intermittent in VPWR circuit. If no fault is indicated, inspect harness connections and pins. Replace power relay and rerun QUICK TEST.

5) Code 19: Internal Voltage. Code 19 indicates the ECA voltage regulator does not have the ability to maintain correct internal voltage. Run KOEO SELF-TEST, if Code 19-10-11 is present, replace ECA and rerun test. If Code 19-10-11 is not present, service other codes as indicated.

CIRCUIT TEST D18

KEY POWER CHECK

NOTE: Perform this test ONLY when a Code 55 is displayed in QUICK TEST.

Key Power Circuits

2.5L CFI WITH INTEGRATED CONTROLLER

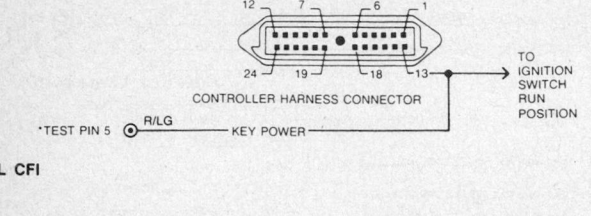

1.9L CFI

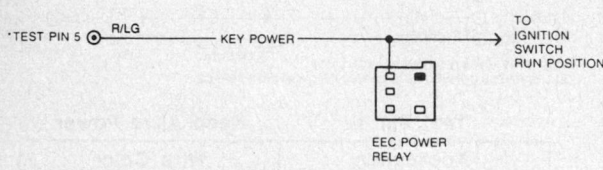

*TEST PINS LOCATED ON BREAKOUT BOX
ALL HARNESS CONNECTORS VIEWED INTO MATING SURFACE

To prevent replacement of good components, be aware that the following non-EEC related areas may be at fault: charging system overcharging, battery charger connected with engine running or jump starting vehicle.

1) Code 55: Checking Continuity of Key Power Circuit. Code 55 indicates key power circuit voltage is low. Possible causes for this fault are: circuit shorted to ground or faulty ECA.
Turn key off and wait 10 seconds. Install breakout box and connect ECA. Disconnect the EEC-IV power relay or IRCM. Set DVOM on 200-ohm scale. Measure the following resistances:
  1.9L CFI: Measure resistance between test pin No. 5 at the breakout box, and KEY POWER (KPWR) at the EEC-IV power relay.
  2.5L CFI: Measure resistance between test pin No. 5 at the breakout box and pin No. 5 at the IRCM harness connector.
If resistance is less than 5 ohms, go to next step. If resistance is greater than 5 ohms, repair open circuit, reconnect system components and rerun QUICK TEST.

2) Checking KEY POWER (KPWR) Circuit For Shorts to Ground. Turn key off, disconnect ECA and install breakout box. Disconnect power relay or IRCM. Set DVOM on 200K-ohm scale and measure resistance between test pin No. 5 and test pins No. 40, 46, and 60, at the breakout box. If resistance is greater than 10K ohms, replace ECA, reconnect components and retest system. If resistance is less than 10K ohms, repair short circuit and rerun QUICK TEST.

CIRCUIT TEST D19

SYSTEM CHECK

Perform this test ONLY after Code 11 is displayed in KOEO SELF-TEST and you have been directed here from CIRCUIT TEST A1 or by DIAGNOSIS BY SYMPTOM TEST.

1) ISC-BPA Check. For 1.9L CFI and 2.5L CFI engines, go directly to step **2)**. This step is for MPFI and SEFI vehicles with Stall or No Start faults.
If engine stalls or if it does not start, attempt to start engine at part throttle. If engine will start and run smoothly at part throttle, go to CIRCUIT TEST D5, step **4)**. If not, go to next step, except 1.9L MPFI and 2.3L Turbo MPFI and 5.0L MA SEFI engine equipped models, go to step **6)**.

2) Check Power to MAP/BP Sensor. Use Ford Motor Co. MAP/BP tester for this test. Turn key off and disconnect MAP/BP sensor. Connect MAP/BP tester between harness and MAP/BP sensor. Connect banana plugs of tester into DVOM and set DVOM on 20-volt scale. With tester connected, turn key on. If Green light is on, go to next step. If light is not on, repair open in VREF circuit, remove MAP/BP tester. Reconnect components and retest symptom.

CIRCUIT TEST D19 (Cont.)

System Check Diagram

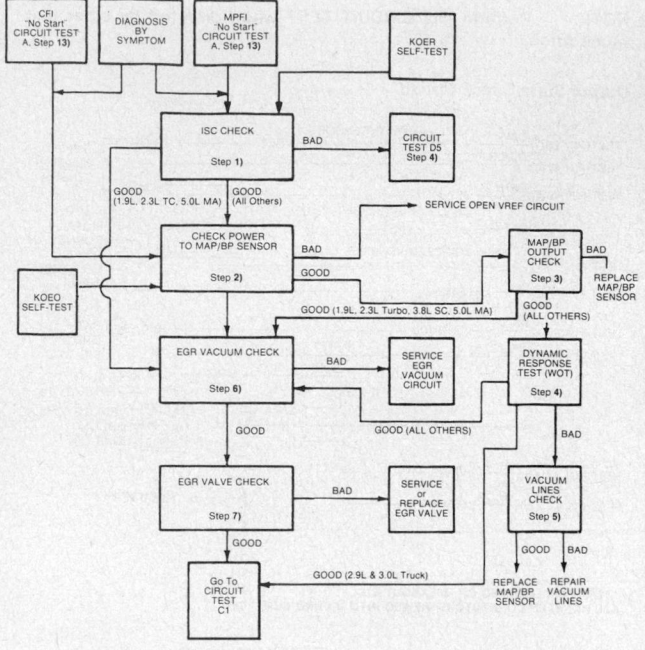

MAP/BP Tester & Circuit

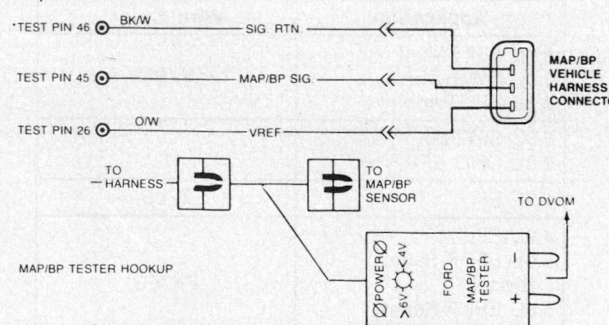

MAP/BP TESTER HOOKUP

3) MAP/BP Tester Output Reading. Measure several "known good" MAP sensors to obtain average measured voltage for specific location and date of testing. With MAP sensor connected and key on, measure SIGNAL voltage at MAP sensor. If voltage is in the correct range for your altitude, go to next step, except 1.9L MPFI and 2.3L Turbo MPFI and 5.0L MA SEFI engine equipped models, go to step **6)**. If voltage is not in the correct range for your altitude, replace MAP/BP sensor.

MAP VOLTAGE OUTPUT

Approx. Elevation (Ft.)	Voltage Output (Volts)
0	1.55-1.63
1000	1.52-1.60
2000	1.49-1.57
3000	1.46-1.54
4000	1.43-1.51
5000	1.40-1.48
6000	1.37-1.45
7000	1.35-1.43

4) MAP/BP Engine Running Response Test. With key on, crank engine. If MAP/BP output voltage changes while cranking engine, go to step **6)**, except 2.9L & 3.0 MPFI Trucks, go to CIRCUIT TEST C, step **1)**. If voltage does not change while cranking, go to next step.

5) Check Vacuum Lines. Check vacuum lines for correct routing, refer to Vehicle Emission Control Label. Checlk MAP sensor vacuum line for breaks, kinks or blockage. If vacuum lines are okay, replace MAP/BP sensor and retest. If vacuum lines are faulty, service as necessary and rerun QUICK TEST.

1989 COMPUTERIZED ENGINE CONTROLS
Ford Motor Co. EEC-IV (Cont.)

1a-483

CIRCUIT TEST D19 (Cont.)

6) EGR Vacuum Check. Disconnect vacuum hose at EGR valve. DO NOT plug vacuum line. Start or attempt to start engine. If symptom is driveability related, check to see if vacuum is present at vacuum line. If vehicle is a "No Start", does engine start? If results are negative, go to next step. If results are positive, go to the following tests, depending on engine application:

- CIRCUIT TEST D1, step **1)** for all 1.9L MPFI or 2.3L Turbo MPFI engine equipped models.
- CIRCUIT TEST B4, step **11)** for all 2.3L OHC MPFI engine equipped models.
- CIRCUIT TEST B11, step **42)** for all 2.5L HSC CFI, and 5.0L SEFI Car or, 2.3L OHC MPFI, 4.9L MPFI, 5.0L MPFI, 5.8L MPFI, and 7.5L MPFI Truck equipped models.
- CIRCUIT TEST B10, step **23)** for all 1.9L CFI, 2.3L HSC MPFI, 3.0L EFI or 3.8L SEFI engine equipped models.

7) Checking EGR Valve. Inspect EGR valve for leaking. If valve is fully closed, go to CIRCUIT TEST C1, step **1)**. If EGR valve is leaking or not fully seated, replace or repair valve.

CIRCUIT TEST D20

INTAKE AIR CONTROL VALVE (IAC) SYSTEM
TAURUS 3.0L SHO SEFI ONLY

NOTE: Perform this test only when service Code 81, is displayed during KOEO SELF-TEST or directed here by DIAGNOSIS BY SYMPTOM test.

IAC Circuit

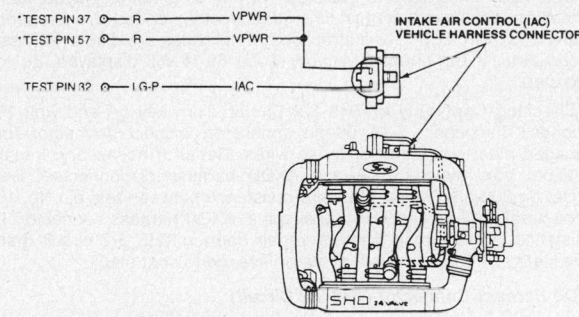

*TEST PINS LOCATED ON BREAKOUT BOX.
ALL HARNESS CONNECTORS VIEWED INTO MATING SURFACE.

1) Code 81: Check Solenoid Resistance. Code 81 indicates IAC solenoid output voltage did not change when IAC was activated during KOEO SELF-TEST. Possible causes for this fault are: IAC circuit open, shorted or disconnected or ECA output driver open or grounded. Turn key off and wait 10 seconds. Set DVOM on 200-ohm scale and disconnect IAC solenoid connector from harness. Measure resistance of solenoid. If resistance is 50-100 ohms, go to next step. If resistance is not 50-100 ohms, replace solenoid and rerun QUICK TEST.

IAC Solenoid

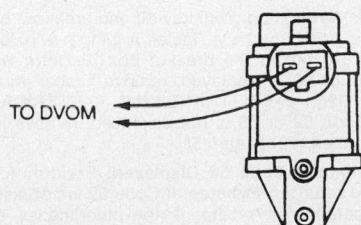

2) Check Voltage of VPWR Circuit. With KOEO, disconnect IAC solenoid. Set DVOM on 20-volt scale. Measure voltage between VPWR circuit of IAC solenoid harness connector and battery negative post. If voltage is greater than 10.5 volts, go to next step. If voltage is less than 10.5 volts, reconnect IAC solenoid, repair open circuit in harness and rerun QUICK TEST.

CIRCUIT TEST D20 (Cont.)

3) Check Continuity of IAC Solenoid Circuit. Turn key off and wait 10 seconds. Disconnect 60-pin ECA connector. Inspect pins for corrosion or damage and service as necessary. Install breakout box, leave ECA disconnected. Set DVOM on 200-ohm scale. Measure resistance between test pin No. 32 at the breakout box and IAC harness connector. If resistance is less than 5 ohms, go to next step. If resistance is greater than 5 ohms, repair open circuit and rerun QUICK TEST.

4) Check For Short to Ground. Turn key off and wait 10 seconds. With breakout box installed and ECA disconnected, set DVOM on 200K-ohm scale. Disconnect IAC solenoid. Measure resistance between test pin No. 32 and test pins No. 40, 46 and 60 at the breakout box. If resistance is greater than 100K ohms, go to next step. If resistance is less than 100K ohms, repair short circuit, reconnect components and retest.

5) Check For Short to Power. Turn key off and wait 10 seconds. With breakout box installed and ECA disconnected, set DVOM on 200K-ohm scale. Disconnect IAC solenoid. Measure resistance between test pin No. 32 and test pins No. 37 and 57 at the breakout box. If resistance is greater than 100K ohms, replace ECA, reconnect components and retest. If resistance is less than 100K ohms, repair short circuit, reconnect components and retest. If fault is still present, replace ECA.

6) Checking Front and Rear Intake Air Valves. With key off, disconnect vacuum lines from both intake air valves. Check each air valve with a vacuum pump. Apply 10 in. Hg vacuum. If both valves hold vacuum, go to next step. If not, replace valve(s) as necessary and rerun QUICK TEST.

Intake Air Valve Locations

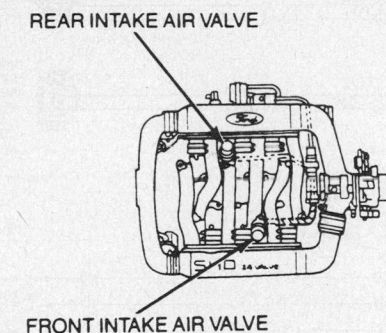

7) Checking Air Valve Systems. With key off, apply 10 in. Hg to each air valve. If both valves and mechanical linkage move in response to the applied vacuum, go to next step. If valves and linkage are faulty, service as necessary and rerun QUICK TEST.

8) Check Vacuum to Intake Air Valves. With key off, check the vacuum lines from air valves to IAC solenoid. Inspect for damage or blockage. If vacuum lines are okay, go to next step. If vacuum lines are faulty, service as necessary and retest.

Vacuum Line Routing

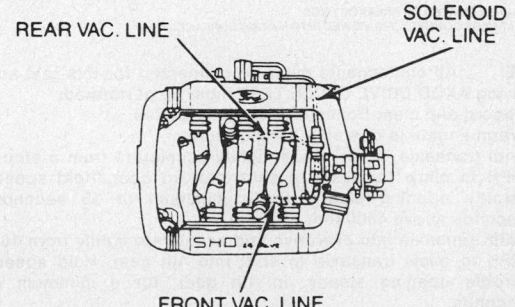

9) Check Vacuum Scource to IAC Solenoid. Disconnect IAC solenoid vacuum supply hose from intake manifold. Start engine and check vacuum at the disconnected manifold hose. If vacuum is present at hose, replace IAC solenoid and rerun QUICK TEST. If vacuum is not present, check supply hose to IAC solenoid. Service as necessary and rerun QUICK TEST.

1a-484

1989 COMPUTERIZED ENGINE CONTROLS
Ford Motor Co. EEC-IV (Cont.)

CIRCUIT TEST D20 (Cont.)

IAC Solenoid Vacuum Hose

SOLENOID VACUUM HOSE

VACUUM RESERVOIR TANK

CIRCUIT TEST D21

AXOD TRANSAXLE

NOTE: Perform this test only when service Codes 29, 39, 57, 59, 62, 67, 68, 69 or 89 are displayed.

AXOD Transaxle Circuits

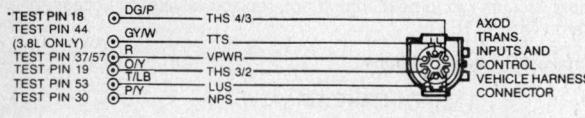

AXOD — HARNESS CONNECTIONS

*TEST PIN 18	DG/P	THS 4/3
TEST PIN 44 (3.8L ONLY)	GY/W	TTS
TEST PIN 37/57	R	VPWR
TEST PIN 19	O/Y	THS 3/2
TEST PIN 53	T/LB	LUS
TEST PIN 30	P/Y	NPS

AXOD TRANS. INPUTS AND CONTROL VEHICLE HARNESS CONNECTOR

TEST PIN 6 — O/Y — VSS DIF −
TEST PIN 3 — DG/W — VSS DIF +

VEHICLE SPEED SENSOR VEHICLE HARNESS CONNECTOR AT AXOD

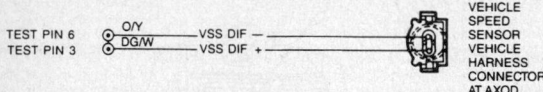

AXOD — FUNCTIONAL

TEST PIN 44 (3.8L ONLY) — TTS — TTS
TEST PIN 18 — THS 4/3 — 4/3 SWITCH
TEST PIN 19 — THS 3/2 — 3/2 SWITCH
TEST PIN 30 — NPS — NPS
TEST PIN 53 — LUS
TEST PIN 37/57 — VPWR

AXOD CASE GROUND
LOCK-UP SOLENOID

TEST PIN 6 — VSS DIF −
TEST PIN 3 — VSS DIF +

VEHICLE SPEED SENSOR

*TEST PINS LOCATED ON BREAKOUT BOX.
ALL HARNESS CONNECTORS VIEWED INTO MATING SURFACE.

NOTE: All components must be connected for this test and the following AXOD DRIVE CYCLE TEST must be performed:
- Record and clear Continuous Memory Codes.
- Warm engine to operating temperature.
- With transaxle in "D" range, lightly accelerate from a stop to 40 MPH to allow transaxle to shift into 3rd gear. Hold speed and throttle opening steady for a minimum of 15 seconds (30 seconds above 4000 feet altitude).
- Shift transaxle into overdrive and accelerate lightly from 40 to 50 MPH to allow transaxle to shift into 4th gear. Hold speed and throttle opening steady, in 4th gear, for a minimum of 15 seconds.
- With transaxle in 4th gear, throttle open and speed steady, lightly apply and release brakes (enough to turn on brake lights). Hold speed and throttle opening steady for an additional 15 seconds.
- Brake to a stop and remain stopped for a minimum of 20 seconds with transaxle in overdrive range. Perform KOEO SELF-TEST and record Continuous Memory Codes.

CIRCUIT TEST D21 (Cont.)

1) Continuous Memory Code 29 Displayed. Code 29 indicates insufficient input to the ECA from the Vehicle Speed Sensor (VSS). Possible causes for this fault are: faulty VSS, open or shorted circuit or faulty ECA.
Perform AXOD DRIVE CYCLE TEST and return to this step. If Continuous Memory Code 29 is not displayed, fault cannot be duplicated at this time. If any other codes are present, return to QUICK TEST for instructions. If there are none, test is complete. If Continuous Memory Code 29 is displayed, go to next step.

2) Checking Continuity of Vehicle Speed Sensor (VSS) Harness. Turn key off and wait 10 seconds. Disconnect ECA 60-pin connector. Inspect connector for damaged pins, corrosion, or loose wires. Repair if necessary. Install breakout box, leaving ECA and VSS disconnected. Set DVOM on 200-ohm scale. Measure resistance between test pin No. 3 at the breakout box and VSS positive (+) circuit at harness connector. Measure resistance between test pin No. 6 and VSS negative (−) circuit at harness connector. If both readings are 5 ohms or more, repair open circuit(s) in VSS harness, then repeat step **1)**. If both readings are less than 5 ohms, go to next step.

3) Checking VSS Harness For Shorts to Power or Ground. With key off, ECA and VSS disconnected, set DVOM on 200K-ohm scale. Measure resistance between test pin No. 3 and test pins No. 37, 40, and 6 at the breakout box. Measure resistance between test pin No. 6 and test pin No. 37 at the breakout box. If all readings are less than 10K ohms, repair short(s) in VSS harness, and repeat step **1)**. If all readings are more than 10K ohms, go to next step.

4) Repeat Drive Cycle With Substitute VSS Installed. Substitute original VSS with a good known VSS. With ECA and VSS connected, perform AXOD DRIVE CYCLE TEST and return to this step. If Continuous Memoryt Code 29 is displayed, replace ECA then repeat step **1)**. If Code 29 is not displayed, replace original VSS then repeat QUICK TEST.

5) Continuous Memory Code 69 Displayed. Perform AXOD DRIVE CYCLE TEST and return to this step. If Code 69 is not displayed, fault cannot be duplicated at this time. If any other codes are present, return to QUICK TEST for instructions. If no codes are displayed, test is complete. If Continuous Memory Code 69 is still displayed, go to next step.

6) Checking Continuity of THS 3/2 Circuit. Turn key off and wait 10 seconds. Disconnect ECA 60-pin connector. Inspect connector for damaged pins, corrosion, or loose wires. Repair if necessary. Install breakout box, leaving ECA and AXOD harness disconnected. Set DVOM on 200-ohm scale. Measure resistance between test pin No. 19 at the breakout box and THS 3/2 circuit at AXOD harness connector. If resistance is more than 5 ohms, repair open in THS 3/2 circuit then repeat step **5)**. If reading is 5 ohms or less, go to next step.

AXOD Harness Connector (THS 3/2 Circuit)

TEST PIN 19 — THS 3/2

7) Checking THS Circuit For Short to Power. With key off, breakout box installed, and ECA and AXOD harness disconnected, set DVOM on 200K-ohm scale. Measure resistance between test pin No. 19 and test pin No. 37. If reading is less than 10K ohms, repair short to power in THS 3/2 circuit, then repeat step **5)**. If reading is more than 10K ohms, go to next step.

8) Checking ECA Verification. With key off and breakout box installed, connect ECA and AXOD harness. Install a jumper wire between test pins No. 19 and No. 40 at the breakut box. Perform KOEO SELF-TEST. If Code 62 or 69 is displayed, remove jumper wire and go to CIRCUIT TEST D25, AXOD TRANSAXLE ELECTRICAL SYSTEM DIAGNOSIS. If Code 62 or 69 is not displayed, remove jumper wire, replace ECA, and then repeat step **5)**.

9) Continuous Memory Code 59 Displayed. Perform AXOD DRIVE CYCLE TEST and return to this step. If Code 59 is not displayed, fault cannot be duplicated at this time. If any other codes are present, return to QUICK TEST for instructions. If none, test is complete. If Code 59 is displayed, go to next step.

10) Checking Continuity of THS 4/3 Circuit. Turn key off and wait 10 seconds. Disconnect ECA 60-pin connector. Inspect connector for damaged pins, corrosion, or loose wires. Repair if necessary. Install breakout box, leaving ECA and AXOD harness disconnected. Set

1989 COMPUTERIZED ENGINE CONTROLS
Ford Motor Co. EEC-IV (Cont.)

1a-485

CIRCUIT TEST D21 (Cont.)

DVOM on 200-ohm scale. Measure resistance between test pin No. 18 and THS 4/3 circuit at AXOD harness connector. If reading is more than 5 ohms, repair open in THS 4/3 harness, then repeat step 9). If reading is 5 ohms or less, go to next step.

AXOD Harness Connector (THS 4/3 Circuit)

TEST PIN 18 ⊙——— THS 4/3 ———

11) Checking THS 4/3 Circuit For Short to Power. With key off, breakout box installed, and ECA and AXOD harness disconnected, set DVOM on 200K-ohm scale. Measure resistance between test pin No. 18 and test pin No. 37 at the breakout box. If reading is less than 10K ohms, repair short to power in THS 4/3 circuit, then repeat step 9). If reading is greater than 10K ohms, go to next step.

12) ECA Verification. With key off and breakout box installed, connect ECA and AXOD harness. Install a jumper wire between test pins No. 18 and 40. Perform KOEO SELF-TEST. If Code 62 or 59 is displayed, remove jumper wire and go to CIRCUIT TEST D25, AXOD TRANS-AXLE ELECTRICAL SYSTEM DIAGNOSIS. If Code 59 or 62 is not displayed, remove jumper wire, replace ECA, and then repeat step 10).

13) Continuous Memory Code 39 Displayed. Code 39 indicates AXOD converter by-pass clutch (lock-up) is not applying correctly. If Continuous Memory Code 59 is also present, go directly to step 9). Perform AXOD DRIVE CYCLE TEST then return to this step. If Continuous Memory Code 39 is still displayed, go to CIRCUIT TEST D25, AXOD TRANSAXLE ELECTRICAL SYSTEM DIAGNOSIS. If Continuous Memory Code 39 is not displayed, fault cannot be duplicated at this time. If any other codes are present, return to QUICK TEST for instructions. If no codes are displayed, test is completed.

14) Continuous Memory Code 57 Displayed. Code 57 indicates Neutral Pressure Switch (NPS) has failed in the open position. Possible causes for this fault are: open or short in NPS circuit, faulty ECA or faulty NPS.
Perform AXOD DRIVE CYCLE TEST and then return to this step. If Continuous Memory Code 57 is not displayed, fault cannot be duplicated at this time. If any other codes are present, return to QUICK TEST for instructions. If no codes are displayed, test is completed. If Continuous Memory Code 57 is still displayed, go to next step.

15) Checking Continuity of NPS Harness. Turn key off and wait 10 seconds. Disconnect ECA 60-pin connector. Inspect connector for damaged pins, corrosion, or loose wires. Repair if necessary. Install breakout box, leaving ECA and AXOD harness disconnected. Set DVOM on 200-ohm scale. Measure resistance between test pin No. 30 and NPS circuit at AXOD harness connector. If resistance is more than 5 ohms, repair open in NPS circuit, then repeat step 14). If reading is 5 ohms or less, go to next step.

AXOD Harness Connector (NPS Circuit)

TEST PIN 30 ⊙——— NPS ———

16) Check NPS Circuit For Short to Power. With key off, install breakout box and disconnect ECA. Disconnect AXOD harness connector and set DVOM on 200K-scale. Measure resistance between test pin No. 30 and test pin No. 37 at the breakout box. If resistance is greater than 10K ohms, go to next step. If resistance is less than 10K ohms, repair short to power in NPS circuit, reconnect components and retest.

17) ECA Verification. With key off, install breakout box and connect ECA. Ensure AXOD harness is connected. Jumper test pin No. 30 to test pin No. 40 at the breakout box. Run KOEO SELF-TEST. If Code 67 is present, remove breakout box and go to CIRCUIT TEST D25, AXOD TRANSAXLE ELECTRICAL SYSTEM DIAGNOSIS. If Code 67 is not present, replace ECA, reconnect components and repeat step 14).

CIRCUIT TEST D21 (Cont.)

18) Code 89 Displayed: Checking Continuity of VPWR Circuit. Code 89 indicates the Lock-Up Solenoid (LUS) signal indicates solenoid is always open or always closed. Possible causes for this fault are: open or shorted circuit, faulty ECA or faulty LUS.
Turn key off and wait 10 seconds. Disconnect ECA 60-pin connector. Inspect connector for damaged pins, corrosion, or loose wires. Repair if necessary. Install breakout box, leaving ECA and AXOD harness disconnected. Set DVOM on 200-ohm scale. Measure resistance between test pin No. 37 and VPWR circuit at AXOD harness connector. If reading is more than 5 ohms, repair open in VPWR cicuit then repeat QUICK TEST. If reading is 5 ohms or less, go to next step.

AXOD Harness Connector (VPWR Circuit)

TEST PIN 37 ⊙——— VPWR ———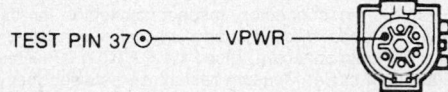

19) Check Continuity of LUS Circuit. With key off, breakout box installed, and ECA and AXOD harness disconnected, set DVOM on 200-ohm scale. Measure resistance between test pin No. 53 and LUS circuit at AXOD harness connector. If reading is more than 5 ohms, repair open in LUS circuit and then repeat QUICK TEST. If reading is 5 ohms or less, go to next step.

AXOD Harness Connector (LUS Circuit)

TEST PIN 53 ⊙——— LUS ———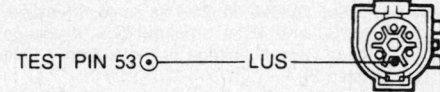

20) Checking LUS Circuit For Power to Ground. With key off, breakout box installed, and ECA and AXOD harness disconnected, set DVOM on 200K-ohm scale. Measure resistance between test pin No. 53 and test pins No. 37 and 40 at the breakout box. If both resistances are less than 10K ohms, repair shorts in LUS circuit. Repeat QUICK TEST. If Code 89 is still displayed, replace ECA and repeat QUICK TEST. If both readings are greater than 10K ohms, go to next step.

21) Checking Total Circuit Resistance. With key off, breakout box installed, and ECA disconnected, connect AXOD harness. Set DVOM on 200K-ohm scale. Measure resistance between test pin No. 53 and test pin No. 57. If resistance is between 20 and 40 ohms, replace ECA and repeat QUICK TEST. If resistance is not between 20 and 40 ohms, go to CIRCUIT TEST D25, AXOD TRANSAXLE ELECTRICAL SYSTEM DIAGNOSIS.

22) Code 62: AXOD Harness Verification. Code 62 indicates 4/3 or 3/2 pressure switch signal indicates switch has failed in the closed position. Possible causes for this fault are: short in THS 4/3 or THS 3/2 circuit, faulty ECA, faulty THS 4/3 or 3/2 pressure switch.
Turn key off and disconnect AXOD harness. Perform KOEO SELF-TEST and record codes. If Code 62 is still displayed, fault is in THS 4/3 circuit. Go to next step. If Code 62 is not displayed, remove test equipment and go to CIRCUIT TEST D25, AXOD TRANSAXLE ELECTRICAL SYSTEM DIAGNOSIS.

23) Checking THS 3/2 and 4/3 Circuits For Short to Ground. With key off, disconnect ECA 60-pin connector. Inspect connector for damaged pins, corrosion, or loose wires. Repair if necessary. Install breakout box and leave ECA disconnected. Leave AXOD harnesses disconnected. Set DVOM on 200K-ohm scale. Measure resistance between test pin No. 18 and test pins No. 40 and 60. Also measure resistance between test pin No. 19 and test pins No. 40 and 60. If all readings are less than 10K ohms, repair short(s) to ground. Repeat QUICK TEST. If all readings are greater than 10K ohms, replace ECA and repeat QUICK TEST.

24) Code 59: AXOD Harness Verification. Code 59 indicates THS 4/3 pressure switch circuit has failed in the closed position. Possible causes for this fault are: short in THS 4/3 circuit, faulty ECA or faulty THS 4/3 pressure switch.
Turn key off and disconnect AXOD Harness. Run KOEO SELF-TEST. If Code 59 is displayed, go to next step. If Code 59 is not displayed, go to CIRCUIT TEST D25, AXOD TRANSAXLE ELECTRICAL SYSTEM DIAGNOSIS.

25) Checking THS 4/3 Circuit For Short to Ground. With key off, disconnect ECA 60-pin connector. Inspect connector for damaged pins, corrosion, or loose wires. Repair if necessary. Install breakout

1a-486

1989 COMPUTERIZED ENGINE CONTROLS
Ford Motor Co. EEC-IV (Cont.)

CIRCUIT TEST D21 (Cont.)

box, leave ECA and AXOD harness connector disconnected. Set DVOM on 200-ohm scale. Measure resistance between test pin No. 18 and test pins No. 40 and 60. If readings are greater than 10K ohms, remove breakout box, replace ECA and rerun QUICK TEST. If reading is less than 10K ohms, repair short in ECA and rerun QUICK TEST.

26) Code 69: Checking AXOD Harness. Code 69 indicates THS 3/2 pressure switch circuit is failed in the closed position. Possible causes for this fault are: short in THS 3/2 circuit, faulty ECA or faulty 3/2 pressure switch.

With key off, disconnect AXOD harness. Perform KOEO SELF-TEST. If Code 69 is still displayed, go to next step. If Code 69 is not displayed, go to CIRCUIT TEST D25, AXOD TRANSAXLE ELECTRICAL SYSTEM DIAGNOSIS.

27) Checking THS 3/2 Circuit For Short to Ground. With key off, disconnect ECA 60-pin connector. Inspect connector for damaged pins, corrosion, or loose wires. Repair if necessary. Install breakout box and leave ECA disconnected. Disconnect AXOD harness and set DVOM on 200K-ohm scale. Measure resistance between test pin No. 19 and test pins No. 40 and 60 at the breakout box. If all readings are less than 10K ohms, repair short to ground and repeat QUICK TEST. If all readings are greater than 10K ohms, replace ECA and rerun QUICK TEST.

28) Code 67: Checking Voltage at NPS Input to ECA. Code 67 indicates that NPS circuit has failed closed or input to A/C clutch circuit is closed. Possible causes for this fault are: short in NPS circuit, short in A/C clutch circuit (3.0L MPFI only), A/C "ON" during Self-Test (3.0L MPFI only) or faulty ECA or NPS.

With KOEO, disconnect ECA and inspect connector for damaged pins, corrosion, or loose wires. Repair if necessary. Install breakout box and reconnect ECA. Set DVOM on 20-volt scale. Measure voltage between test pins No. 30 and 46 at breakout box. If voltage is less than 4 volts, go to next step. If voltage is more than 4 volts, go to CIRCUIT TEST B13, step **9)**.

29) Checking NPS Harness Circuit For Shorts to Ground. Turn key off. Install breakout box and disconnect ECA and AXOD harness. Set DVOM on 200K-ohm scale. Measure resistance between test pin No. 30 and test pins No. 40 and 60 at the breakout box. If resistances are greater than 10K ohms, go to next step. If resistances are less than 10K ohms, repair ground short in NPS circuit and rerun QUICK TEST.

30) Checking ECA. Turn key off and install breakout box. Reconnect ECA. Disconnect AXOD harness and run KOEO SELF-TEST. If Code 67 is displayed, replace ECA and rerun QUICK TEST. If Code 67 is not displayed, go to CIRCUIT TEST D25, AXOD TRANSAXLE ELECTRICAL SYSTEM DIAGNOSIS.

31) Code 68: Checking Continuity of TTS Harness Circuit. Code 68 indicates Transmission Temperature Switch (TTS) circuit is failed open. Possible causes for this fault are: open or shorted TTS circuit, faulty ECA or TTS.

Turn key off and wait 10 seconds. Disconnect AXOD harness. Disconnect ECA 60-pin connector. Inspect connector for damaged pins, corrosion, or loose wires. Repair if necessary. Install breakout box, leaving ECA disconnected. Set DVOM on 200-ohm scale. Measure resistance between test pin No. 44, at the breakout box, and TTS terminal of AXOD harness connector. If resistance is less than 5 ohms, go to next step. If resistance is more than 5 ohms, repair open circuit in TTS circuit and road test vehicle to verify complaint.

AXOD Harness Connector (TTS Circuit)

TEST PIN 44 ⊙———— TTS

32) Checking TTS Harness For Short to Power or Ground. Turn key off and wait 10 seconds. Disconnect ECA and AXOD harness. Install breakout box and set DVOM on 200K-ohm scale. Measure resistance between test pin No. 44 and test pin No. 37 at the breakout box. Measure resistance between test pins No. 44 and 40 at the breakout box. If resistance is greater than 10K ohms, go to next step. If resistance is less than 10K ohms, repair short in TTS circuit and rerun QUICK TEST.

33) Checking ECA Operation. With key off and breakout box installed, connect ECA and AXOD harness. Jumper between test pins No. 44 to No. 40 at the breakout box. Perform KOEO SELF-TEST. If Code 68 is still present, reconnect components and go to CIRCUIT TEST D25, AXOD TRANSAXLE ELECTRICAL SYSTEM DIAGNOSIS. If complaint is still present, replace ECA, reconnect components and retest.

CIRCUIT TEST D22

A4LD TRANSMISSION

NOTE: Perform this test only when Code 86 or 89 is displayed or referred here by other chart or test procedure. To prevent replacement of good components be aware that the following non-EEC areas may be at fault:
- Hydraulic or emergency brake system
- Transmission linkage
- Internal transmission components

A4LD Transmission Circuits

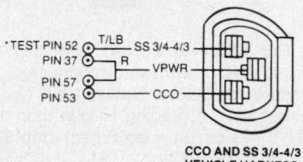

CCO AND SS 3/4-4/3
VEHICLE HARNESS
CONNECTOR

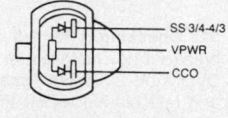

CCO AND SS 3/4-4/3
TRANSMISSION
BULKHEAD CONNECTOR

NOTE: SS 3/4-4/3 IS NOT USED ON 2.3L OHC MUSTANG

*TEST PINS LOCATED ON BREAKOUT BOX.
ALL HARNESS CONNECTORS VIEWED INTO MATING SURFACE.

Test Pin 53	CCO Solenoid
Application	**Wire Color**
Car: 2.3L OHC	O/Y
Truck: 2.3L, 2.9L, 3.0L	W

1) Code 86 or 89: Circuit Identification. Code 86 indicates ECA did not see a voltage drop when the Shift Solenoid (SS) was activated. Possible causes for this fault are: SS resistance out of limits, SS circuit open or grounded or faulty ECA.

Code 89 indicates ECA did not see a voltage drop when the CCO solenoid was activated. Possible causes for this fault are: Converter Clutch Override resistance is out of limits, CCO circuit open or grounded or faulty ECA.

Enter this test step for KOEO codes. Verify codes match appropriate transmission solenoid circuit.

TRANSMISSION SOLENOID CIRCUITS

Solenoid	ECA Signal Output Pin	KOEO Code
Converter Clutch Override (CCO)	53	89
Shift Solenoid (SS) 3/4-4/3	52	86

If any of the above codes are present, go to next step. If not, service other codes as necessary.

2) Checking Resistance of A4LD Solenoid. Turn key off and wait 10 seconds. Disconnect ECA 60-pin connector. Inspect connector for damaged pins, corrosion, or loose wires. Repair if necessary. Install breakout box, leaving ECA disconnected. Set DVOM on 200-ohm scale. Measure resistance between test pins No. 37 and 57 and ECA signal output pin at the breakout box. If the resistance is 26 to 40 ohms, go to step **5)**. If resistance is not 26-40 ohms, go to next step.

3) Check Continuity of Transmission Solenoid Harness. With key off, install breakout box. Leave ECA and transmission bulkhead connector (A4LD solenoids) disconnected. Set DVOM on 200-ohm scale. Measure resistance between test pins No. 37 and 57 at the breakout box and VPWR circuit pin of the harness connector at the transmission. Measure resistance between the ECA signal output pin No. 52 at the breakout box and SS pin of the harness connector at the transmission.

4) Check For Shorts to Power or Ground of A4LD Solenoid Harness. With key off, install breakout box, leaving ECA disconnected. Disconnect transmission bulkhead connector. Set DVOM on 200K-ohm scale. Measure resistance between the ECA signal output pin and test pins No. 37 and 57 at the breakout box. Measure resistance between the ECA signal output pin and test pins No. 40, 60 and 46 at the breakout box and at chassis ground. If all resistances are greater than 10K ohms, go to next step. If any resistance is less than 10K ohms, repair short circuit, reconnect components and rerun QUICK TEST.

1989 COMPUTERIZED ENGINE CONTROLS
Ford Motor Co. EEC-IV (Cont.)

1a-487

CIRCUIT TEST D22 (Cont.)

5) Check VPWR Voltage to Transmission Solenoids. With key off, breakout box installed and ECA connected, set DVOM on 20-volt scale. Disconnect transmission bulkhead connector. Turn key on, leaving engine off. Measure voltage between test pins No. 37 and 57 at the bulkhead connector and chassis ground. If voltage is greater than 10.5 volts, repair or replace transmission solenoid as necessary. If voltage is less than 10.5 volts, replace ECA, reconnect components and rerun QUICK TEST.

CIRCUIT TEST D23

INTEGRAL RELAY CONTROL MODULE (IRCM)

NOTE: Perform this test only when KOEO SELF-TEST Codes 72, 78, 82, 83, 87, 88, 95 or 96 are displayed, or when you are directed here by CIRCUIT TEST A1, CIRCUIT TEST A3, or by DIAGNOSIS BY SYMPTOM TEST.

2.5L CFI M/T

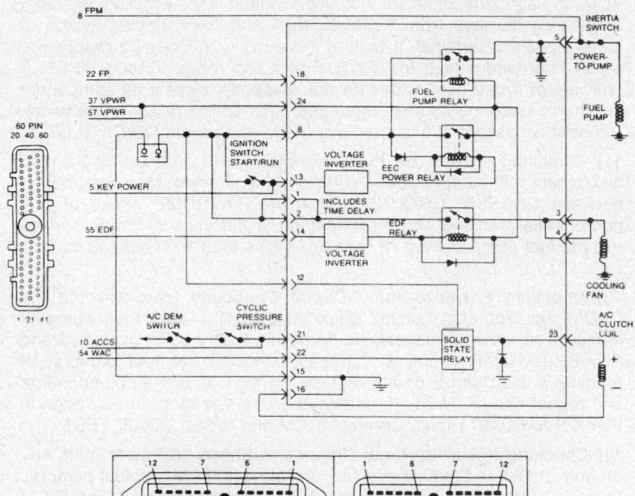

2.5L A/T & 3.0L AXOD MPFI

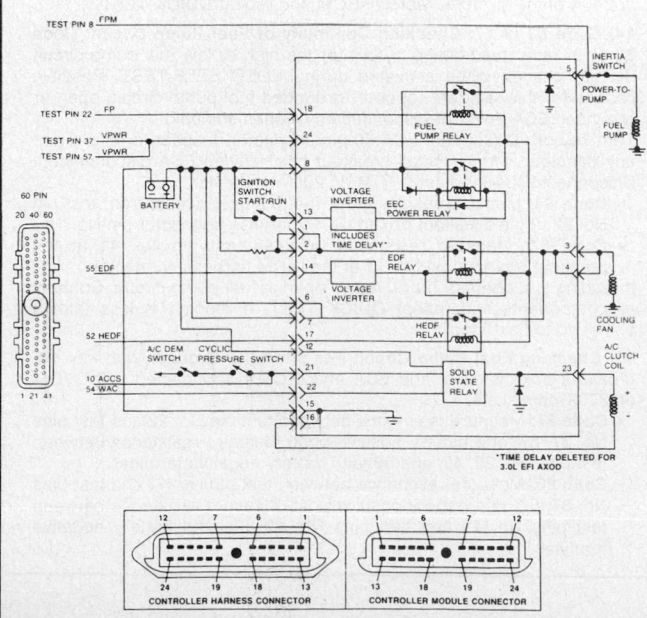

CIRCUIT TEST D23 (Cont.)

3.0L SHO SEFI

3.8L AXOD SEFI

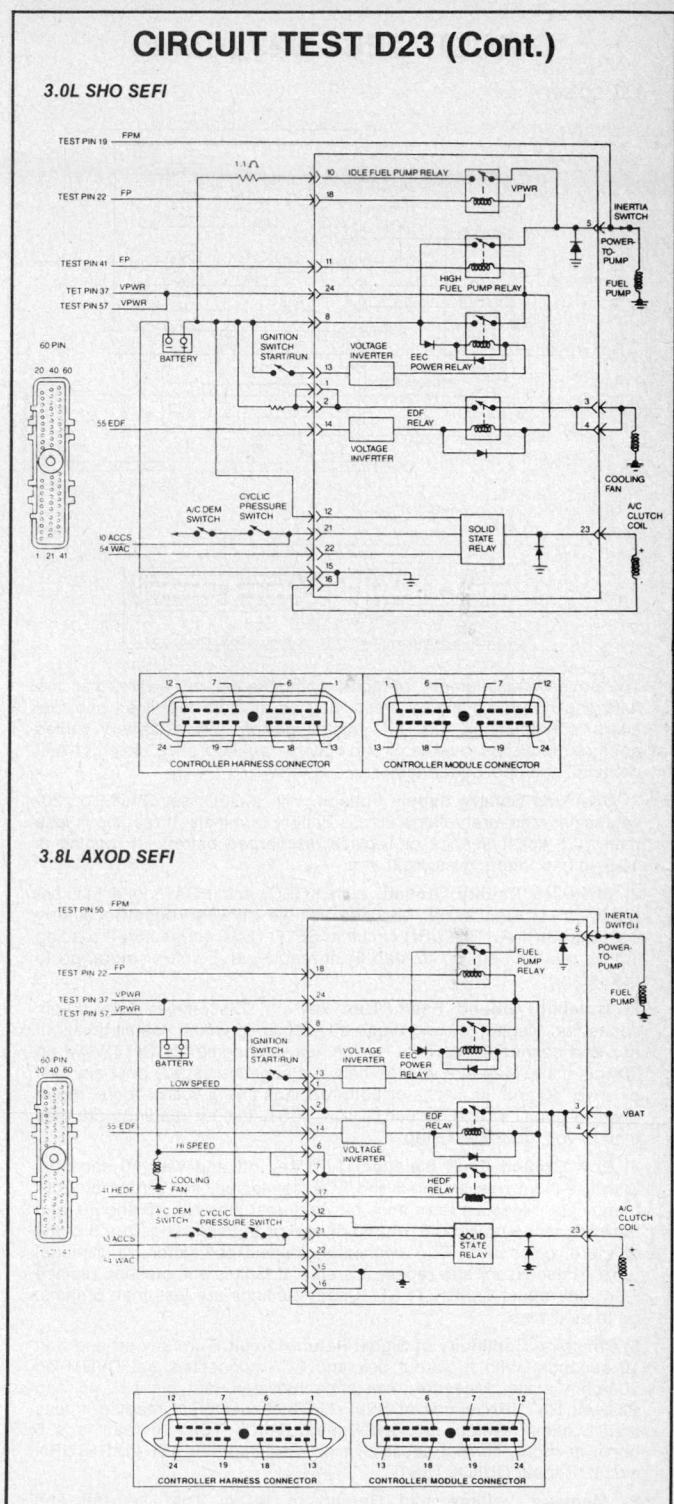

1a-488

1989 COMPUTERIZED ENGINE CONTROLS
Ford Motor Co. EEC-IV (Cont.)

CIRCUIT TEST D23 (Cont.)

3.8L SC SEFI

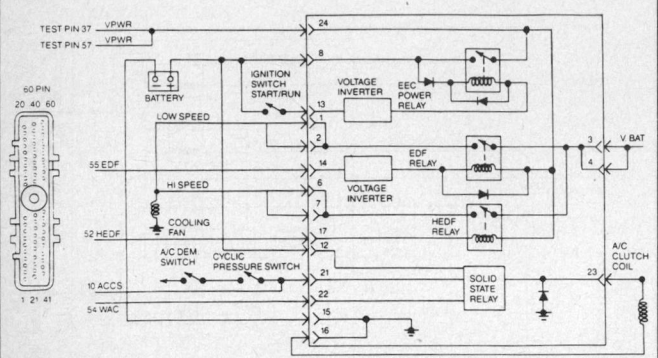

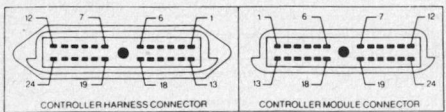

CONTROLLER HARNESS CONNECTOR   CONTROLLER MODULE CONNECTOR

To prevent replacement of good components, be aware that the following non-EEC related areas may be at fault: fuel lines and fuel filters, contaminated fuel, fuel pump, ignition switch, battery cables and ground straps, alternator and voltage regulator, A/C clutch or A/C demand, and cooling fan motor.

1) Checking Battery Supply Voltage. With KOEO, set DVOM on 20-volt scale. Measure voltage across battery terminals. If reading is less than 10.5 volts, service or replace discharged battery. If reading is 10.5 volts or more, go to next step.

2) Checking Battery Ground. With KOEO, and ECA connected, set DVOM on 20-volt scale. Measure voltage between negative battery post and SIGNAL RETURN circuit in SELF-TEST connector. If reading is less than .5 volt, go to step **6)**. If reading is .5 volt or more, go to next step.

3) Isolating Ground Fault. Turn key off. Disconnect ECA 60-pin connector. Inspect for and repair any damaged wiring. Install breakout box and connect ECA. Turn key on, leaving engine off. Set DVOM on 20-volt scale. Measure voltage between negative battery post and test pins No. 40 and 60. If one or both readings are .5 volt or more, repair open in circuit(s) and repeat QUICK TEST. If both readings are less than .5 volt, go to next step.

4) ECA Ground Fault Isolation. Turn key off and wait 10 seconds. With breakout box installed and ECA connected, set DVOM on 200-ohm scale. Measure resistance between test pins No. 46 and 40, and between test pins No. 46 and 60. If one or both readings are 5 ohms or more, disconnect ECA connector. Inspect connector for damage, repair if necessary and repeat this step. If fault is still present, replace ECA and repeat QUICK TEST. If both readings are less than 5 ohms, go to next step.

5) Checking Continuity of Signal Return Circuit. Turn key off and wait 10 seconds. With breakout box and ECA connected, set DVOM on 200-ohm scale. Measure resistance between test pin No. 46 and SIGNAL RETURN circuit at SELF-TEST connector. If reading is less than 5 ohms, system is okay. Repeat QUICK TEST. If reading is 5 ohms or more, correct cause of high resistance in SIGNAL RETURN circuit. Repeat QUICK TEST.

6) Measure Voltage and Ground to IRCM. Turn key off and disconnect Integral Relay Control Module (IRCM). Set DVOM on 20-volt scale. Measure voltage between IRCM harness connector pin No. 8 (battery positive) and pin No. 15 (ground). If reading is less than 10.5 volts, go to step **9)**. If reading is 10.5 volts or more, go to next step.

7) Key Power to IRCM. With key off, disconnect IRCM and set DVOM on 20-volt scale. Turn key on. Measure voltage between pins No. 13 (+) and 15 (–) at IRCM harness connector. If reading is less than 10.5 volts, repair open between pin No. 13 and ignition switch. Connect IRCM and repeat QUICK TEST. If reading is 10.5 volts or more, go to next step.

8) Checking Continuity of VPWR Circuit. Turn key off. Disconnect IRCM and ECA 60-pin connector. Inspect for and repair any damaged wiring. Install breakout box, leaving ECA disconnected. Set DVOM on

200-ohm scale. Measure resistance between test pins No. 37 and 57 at the breakout box to IRCM harness connector pin No. 24. If reading is 5 ohms or more, repair open in VPWR circuit. Connect IRCM and repeat QUICK TEST. If reading is less than 5 ohms, replace IRCM and repeat QUICK TEST.

9) Checking Continuity of Power Ground to IRCM. With key off and IRCM disconnected, set DVOM on 200-ohm scale. Measure resistance from negative battery post to IRCM harness connector pin No. 15. If reading is 5 ohms or more, repair open in ground circuit to IRCM harness connector pin No. 15. Repeat QUICK TEST. If reading is less than 5 ohms, repair open in battery positive to pin No. 8 of IRCM harness connector. Repeat QUICK TEST.

10) Code 72: Intermittent Open in VPWR Circuit. Code 72 indicates that while key power was present voltage to the IRCM was interrupted, or electrical noise caused the ECA to reset. Driveability problems such as, stalling, high idle, lack of power on acceleration or other drive symptoms could result. Possible causes for this fault are: intermittent open in VPWR circuit between IRCM and ECA, intermittent fault in EEC power relay, intermittent open in VBAT circuit of IRCM, intermittent open in KEY POWER circuit or EEC harness too close to spark plug wires.

Using CONTINUOUS MONITOR MODE (WIGGLE) TEST, observe VOM or diagnostic tester for indication of fault while wiggling, bending, or twisting harness from IRCM to ECA and from ignition switch to battery positive terminal. If fault is indicated or if Code 72 reappears, repair intermittent fault in VPWR circuit and repeat QUICK TEST. If fault is not found or if codes do not reappear, inspect all component and harness connectors for damaged pins, corrosion, or loose wires. Repair if necessary. If okay, replace IRCM and repeat QUICK TEST.

11) Checking Power to Fuel Pump(s). With KOEO, locate and disconnect fuel pump(s). Set DVOM on 20-volt scale. Measure voltage between CHASSIS GROUND and POWER-to-PUMP circuit at fuel pump while cranking engine. If reading is 8.0 volts or more, service electric fuel pump system. If reading is less than 8.0 volts, go to next step.

12) Checking Power-to-Pump Circuit Continuity. With key off and DVOM on 200-ohm scale, disconnect IRCM and fuel pump(s). Measure resistance between IRCM harness connector pin No. 5 and POWER-to-PUMP circuit at harness connector at fuel pump(s). If reading is less than 5 ohms, replace IRCM. Connect all components and repeat QUICK TEST. If reading is 5 ohms or more, repair open in POWER-to-PUMP circuit. Connect IRCM and repeat QUICK TEST.

13) Checking Power-to-Pump Circuit For Shorts to Power. With key off and DVOM on 200K-ohm scale, disconnect IRCM and fuel pump(s). Measure resistance between pin No. 5 and pin No. 24 at IRCM harness connector. Measure resistance between pin No. 5 at the IRCM harness connector and battery positive post. If any reading is less than 10K ohms, repair short circuit. Connect all components and attempt to start vehicle. If vehicle runs, repeat QUICK TEST. If vehicle does not run, replace IRCM and repeat QUICK TEST. If all readings are 10K ohms or more, replace IRCM and repeat QUICK TEST.

14) Code 83 or 87: Checking Continuity of Fuel Pump Circuit. Code 83 or 87 indicates voltage output for the high or low fuel pump circuit did not change when activated during KOEO SELF-TEST. Possible causes for this fault are: open or grounded fuel pump circuit, open or grounded ECA driver or disconnected or open solenoid.

Turn key off. Disconnect ECA 60-pin connector. Inspect for and repair any damaged wiring. Install breakout box, leaving ECA disconnected. Disconnect IRCM and set DVOM on 200-ohm scale.

- **Code 83:** Measure resistance of fuel pump(s) circuit, from test pin No. 22 at the breakout box to IRCM harness connector pin No. 18.
- **Code 87:** Measure resistance between test pin No. 41 at the breakout box and pin No. 11 at the IRCM harness connector.

If reading is 5 ohms or more, repair open in fuel pump circuit. Connect all components and repeat QUICK TEST. If reading is less than 5 ohms, go to next step.

15) Checking Fuel Pump Circuit For Shorts to Ground. With key off, breakout box installed, and ECA and IRCM disconnected, set DVOM on 200K-ohm scale.

- **Code 87:** Measure resistance between test pin No. 22 and test pins No. 37, 57, and battery positive post. Measure resistance between test pins No. 22, 40, and 60, and battery negative terminal.
- **Code 83:** Measure resistance between test pin No. 41 and test pins No. 37, 57, and battery positive post. Measure resistance between test pins No. 41 and test pins No. 40, 60, and battery negative terminal.

1989 COMPUTERIZED ENGINE CONTROLS
Ford Motor Co. EEC-IV (Cont.)

1a-489

CIRCUIT TEST D23 (Cont.)

If any reading is less than 10K ohms, repair fuel pump(s) circuit shorts to power or ground. Connect all components and repeat QUICK TEST. If Code 83 or 87 is still present, go to next step. If all readings are 10K ohms or more, go to next step.

16) **Checking Fuel Pump Relay Coil Resistance.** Turn key off. Disconnect IRCM and set DVOM on 200-ohm scale. Disconnect ECA and install breakout box. Measure resistance of IRCM between pins No. 18 and 24 or pins No. 11 and 24. If resistance is between 65 and 100 ohms, replace ECA. Connect all components and repeat QUICK TEST. If resistance is not between 65 and 100 ohms, replace IRCM. Connect all components and repeat QUICK TEST.

17) **No Fan Operation.** Turn key off. Disconnect IRCM and set DVOM on 20-volt scale. Measure voltage between battery negative post and IRCM harness connector pins No. 1, 2, 6, and 7 (pins No. 3 and 4 on 3.8L). If any reading is less than 10.5 volts, service open in power circuit. Re-evaluate symptom. If all readings are 10.5 volts or more, go to next step.

18) **Checking Fan Motor Operation.** Turn key off and disconnect IRCM connector. Install a jumper wire between IRCM harness connector pins No. 3 and 6. If cooling fan does not run, go to step 20). If cooling fan runs, go to next step.

19) **Checking Fan Low Speed.** Turn key off. Connect IRCM and disconnect ECA. Turn key on. If fan does not run at low speed, replace IRCM. Connect ECA and re-evaluate symptom. If fan runs at low speed, go to step 22).

20) **Measuring Voltage Supply at Fan.** With key off, disconnect cooling fan and IRCM. Install a jumper wire between IRCM harness connector pins No. 3 and 6. Set DVOM on 20-volt scale and measure voltage at cooling fan harness connector. If reading is 8.0 volts or more, replace cooling fan motor and re-evaluate symptom. If reading is less than 8.0 volts, go to next step.

21) **Checking Cooling Fan Ground Circuit.** Turn key off. Disconnect cooling fan and IRCM. Install a jumper wire between IRCM harness connector pins No. 3 and 6. Set DVOM on 20-volt scale. Measure voltage between positive terminal at cooling fan harness connector and battery negative post. If reading is 8 volts or more, repair open in ground circuit to tan. After repairs, connect IRCM and re-evaluate symptom. If reading is less than 8 volts, repair open in power-to-fan circuit from pins No. 3 and 4 of IRCM harness connector to cooling fan connector. After repairs, connect IRCM and re-evaluate symptom.

22) **Connecting High Speed Electric-Drive Fan Signal (HEDF) to Ground.** Turn key off. Disconnect ECA 60-pin connector. Inspect for and repair any damaged wiring. Install breakout box, leaving ECA disconnected. Turn key on. With IRCM connected, install a jumper wire between test pins No. 52 and 40. If fan does not run at high speed, replace IRCM. Connect ECA and re-evaluate symptom. If fan runs at high speed, go to next step.

23) **Checking ECT Sensor.** Connect ECA and check engine coolant level. Warm engine to normal operating temperature. Turn key off and wait 10 seconds. Disconnect Engine Coolant Temperature (ECT) sensor harness. Set DVOM on 200K-ohm scale. Measure resistance of ECT sensor. If reading is between 1500 and 2000 ohms, replace ECA. Connect all components and re-evaluate symptom. If reading is not between 1500 and 2000 ohms, replace ECT sensor. Connect all components and re-evaluate symptom.

24) **Checking A/C Pressure Switch Harness Continuity.** With key off, install breakout box and connect ECA. Disconnect A/C pressure switch. Set DVOM on 200K-ohm scale. Measure resistance between test pin No. 2 at the breakout box and A/C pressure switch circuit at the harness connector. Measure resistance between test pin No. 46 at the breakout box and SIGNAL RETURN at the A/C pressure switch harness connector. If both readings are less than 5 ohms, go to next step. If resistances are greater than 5 ohms, remove breakout box, repair open circuit and rerun QUICK TEST.

25) **Checking HEDF Operation.** With key off, disconnect A/C pressure switch. Jumper A/C pressure circuit to SIGNAL RETURN at the switch vehicle harness connector. Turn key on. If HEDF is on, replace A/C pressure switch. If HEDF is not on, replace ECA, reconnect components and rerun QUICK TEST.

26) **Code 83 Displayed: Check HEDF Circuit Resistance.** Code 83 indicates a failed HEDF circuit. Turn key off and disconnect IRCM. Set DVOM on 200-ohm scale. Measure resistance of IRCM between pins No. 17 and 24. If reading is not between 50 and 100 ohms, replace IRCM and repeat QUICK TEST. If reading is between 50 and 100 ohms, go to next step.

CIRCUIT TEST D23 (Cont.)

27) **Checking HEDF ECA Signal to IRCM For Open.** Turn key off. Disconnect ECA 60-pin connector. Inspect for and repair any damaged wiring. Install breakout box, leaving ECA disconnected. Disconnect IRCM connector. Set DVOM on 200-ohm scale and measure continuity between test pin No. 52 and IRCM harness connector pin No. 17. If reading is greater than 5 ohms, repair open in HEDF circuit. Connect all components and repeat QUICK TEST. If reading is 5 ohms or less, go to next step.

28) **Checking HEDF Circuit For Shorts to Ground.** With key off, breakout box installed, and ECA and IRCM disconnected, set DVOM on 200K-ohm scale. Measure resistance between test pins No. 52 and 40. If reading is 10K ohms or less, repair short to ground in HEDF circuit. Reconnect components and repeat QUICK TEST. If reading is greater than 10K ohms, go to next step.

29) **Checking HEDF Circuit For Short to Power.** With key off, breakout box installed, and ECA and IRCM disconnected, set DVOM on 200K-ohm scale. Measure resistance between test pins No. 52 and 37. If reading is more than 10K ohms, replace ECA. Connect all components and repeat QUICK TEST. If reading is 10K ohms or less, repair short to power. Connect all components and repeat QUICK TEST. If Code 83 is still present, replace ECA and repeat QUICK TEST.

30) **Low Speed Fan Always On.** Turn key off. Disconnect ECA 60-pin connector. Inspect for and repair any damaged wiring. Install breakout box, leaving ECA disconnected. Disconnect IRCM and set DVOM on 200-ohm scale. Measure resistance between test pin No. 55 and IRCM harness connector pin No. 14. If reading is more than 5 ohms, repair open in EDF circuit. Connect all components and re-evaluate symptom. If reading is 5 ohms or less, go to next step.

31) **Checking EDF Circuit For Shorts to Power.** With key off, breakout box installed, and ECA and IRCM disconnected, set DVOM on 200K-ohm scale. Measure resistance between test pins No. 55 and 37, and from test pin No. 55 to battery positive post. If reading is 10K ohms or less, repair short to power in EDF circuit, and then go to next step. If reading is more than 10K ohms, go to next step.

32) **Checking EDF Circuit For Short to Ground.** With key off, breakout box installed and ECA disconnected, connect IRCM. Install a jumper wire between test pin No. 55 and test pins No. 40 or 60 (ground). If cooling fan continues to run, replace IRCM, reconnect components and re-evaluate symptom. If cooling fan stops running, replace ECA. Re-evaluate symptom.

33) **Check A/C Pressure Switch Input.** With key off, disconnect vehicle harness at A/C pressure switch. Turn key on. If fan still runs, reconnect components and go to next step. If fan does not run, replace A/C pressure switch and re-evaluate symptom.

34) **Check A/C Pressure Switch For Short to Ground.** With key on, disconnect ECA 60-pin connector. Inspect for and repair any damaged wiring. Install breakout box, leaving ECA disconnected. Disconnect IRCM and set DVOM on 200K-ohm scale. Measure resistance between test pin No. 2 and test pins No. 40, 46, and 60. If resistance is less than 10K ohms, repair short circuit, remove breakout box and reconnect components. Re-evaluate system. If resistance is greater than 10K ohms, go back to step 30).

35) **Checking Fan Voltage.** Turn key off. Disconnect IRCM and set DVOM on 20-volt scale. Measure voltage between battery negative post and pins No. 1 and 2 at IRCM harness connector (3.8L engines check pins No. 3 and 4). If readings are less than 10.5 volts, repair open in power circuit and re-evaluate symptom. If reading is 10.5 volts or more, go to next step.

36) **Checking Fan Motor.** Turn key off and disconnect IRCM connector. Install a jumper wire between IRCM harness connector pins No. 1 and 3. If cooling fan does not run, go to step 38). If cooling fan runs, go to next step.

37) **Checking Fan Run Mode.** With key off and ECA disconnected, connect IRCM. Turn key on. If cooling fan does not run, go to step 39). If cooling fan runs, go to step 41).

38) **Measure Battery Voltage at Fan: By-Pass IRCM.** Turn key off. Disconnect cooling fan harness and IRCM connector. Install a jumper wire between IRCM harness connector pins No. 1 and 3. Set DVOM on 20-volt scale and measure voltage at cooling fan harness connector. If reading is 8.0 volts or more, replace cooling fan and re-evaluate symptom. If reading is less than 8.0 volts, go to step 40).

39) **Checking EDF Circuit For Short to Ground.** Turn key off. Disconnect ECA and IRCM. Set DVOM on 200K-ohm scale and measure resistance between IRCM harness connector pins No. 14

1a-490

1989 COMPUTERIZED ENGINE CONTROLS
Ford Motor Co. EEC-IV (Cont.)

CIRCUIT TEST D23 (Cont.)

and 15. If resistance is 10K ohms or more, replace IRCM. Connect all components and re-evaluate symptom. If reading is less than 10K ohms, repair short to ground in EDF circuit. Connect all components and re-evaluate symptom.

40) Checking Cooling Fan Ground Circuit. Turn key off and disconnect cooling fan. Disconnect IRCM connector. Install a jumper wire between IRCM harness connector pins No. 1 and 3. Set DVOM on 20-volt scale and measure voltage between cooling fan harness connector and battery negative terminal. If reading is 8.0 volts or more, repair open in fan ground circuit. Connect IRCM and re-evaluate symptom. If reading is less than 8.0 volts, repair open in power-to-fan circuit from IRCM harness connector pins No. 3 and 4 to cooling fan connector. Connect IRCM and re-evaluate symptom.

41) Checking ECT Sensor. Connect ECA and check engine coolant level. Warm engine to normal operating temperature. Turn key off and wait 10 seconds. Disconnect ECT sensor. Set DVOM on 200K-ohm scale and measure resistance of ECT sensor. If reading is between 1500 and 2000 ohms, replace ECA. Connect all components and re-evaluate symptom. If reading is not between 1500 and 2000 ohms, replace ECT sensor. Connect all components and re-evaluate symptom.

42) Checking Voltage at A/C Clutch. Turn key on, leaving engine off. Place A/C demand switch to A/C "ON" position. Set DVOM on 20-volt scale and check voltage at A/C clutch harness connector. If voltage reading is 10.5 volts or more, service A/C compressor and/or system. If voltage is less than 10.5 volts, go to next step.

43) Checking Continuity of IRCM to A/C Clutch Circuit. Turn key off and disconnect IRCM connector. Set DVOM on 200-ohm scale. Measure resistance between IRCM harness connector pin No. 23 and power circuit terminal pin at A/C clutch harness connector. Also measure resistance between IRCM harness connector pin No. 16 and ground circuit at A/C clutch harness connector. If readings are more than 5 ohms, repair open in power or ground A/C circuit(s) and re-evaluate symptom. If readings are 5 ohms or less, go to next step.

NOTE: Do not use diagnostic tester in step 44), use VOM/DVOM only. Enter OUTPUT STATE CHECK as specified in test. For additional information see DIAGNOSTIC AIDS, OUTPUT STATE CHECK in front of this article.

44) Turn key off and wait 10 seconds. Disconnect ECA 60-pin connector. Inspect for and repair any damaged wiring. After inspection, reconnect breakout box and ECA. Set DVOM on 20-volt scale. Connect DVOM negative test lead to Self-Test Output (STO) and positive lead to battery positive terminal. Using jumper wire, connect Self-Test Input (STI) to signal return at SELF-TEST connector. Perform KOEO SELF-TEST until completion of CONTINUOUS SELF-TEST codes (DVOM will read zero volts). DVOM should change to a high voltage reading. If DVOM did not change, depress throttle to WOT and release. If STO voltage still does not go high, go to CIRCUIT TEST D16, step 1). If DVOM changes, remain in OUTPUT STATE CHECK and go to next step.

45) Checking WAC Output Operation. With KOEO, place A/C demand switch to A/C "ON" position. Set DVOM on 20-volt scale. Connect DVOM positive test lead to pin No. 37 and negative test lead to test pin No. 54. While observing DVOM, depress and release throttle several times (to cycle output on and off). If voltage output does change, go to step 47). If voltage output changes, go to next step.

46) Checking Voltage at A/C Clutch Switch. With key on, engine off and A/C demand switch in A/C "ON" position, verify that breakout box is installed and that ECA and IRCM are connected. Set DVOM on 20-volt scale and measure voltage between test pins No. 10 and 40. If reading is less than 10.5 volts, go to step 48). If reading is 10.5 volts or more, go to next step.

47) Checking Continuity of ACCS to IRCM Circuit. Turn key off and wait 10 seconds. Disconnect ECA and IRCM connectors. Set DVOM on 200-ohm scale and measure resistance between test pin No. 10 and IRCM harness connector pin No. 21. If reading is more than 5 ohms, service open in ACCS circuit and re-evaluate symptom. If reading is 5 ohms or less, replace IRCM and re-evaluate symptom.

48) Checking ACCS Circuit Continuity. Turn key off and wait 10 seconds. Place A/C demand switch to A/C "ON" position. Set DVOM on 200-ohm scale and measure resistance between test pin No. 10 and A/C demand switch. If reading is 5 ohms or less, EEC system is okay. Service A/C system. If reading is more than 5 ohms, repair open in switch circuit. Repeat QUICK TEST.

CIRCUIT TEST D23 (Cont.)

49) Checking Continuity in WAC to IRCM Circuit. Turn key off and wait 10 seconds. Disconnect ECA 60-pin connector. Inspect for and repair any damaged wiring. Install breakout box, leaving ECA disconnected. Disconnect IRCM connector. Set DVOM on 200-ohm scale and measure resistance between test pin No. 54 and IRCM harness connector pin No. 22. If reading is more than 50 ohms, repair open in WAC circuit and re-evaluate symptom. If reading is 50 ohms or less, go to next step.

50) Checking WAC Circuit For Shorts to Ground. Turn key off and wait 10 seconds. Leave breakout box installed, and ECA disconnected. Disconnect IRCM connector. Set DVOM on 200-ohm scale. Measure resistance between test pins No. 54 and 40, and between test pins No. 54 and 46, and between test pin No. 54 and battery negative post. If any reading is less than 10K ohms, repair shorts to ground in WAC circuit and re-evaluate symptom. If all readings are 10K ohms or more, go to next step.

51) Checking WAC Circuit For Short to Power. Turn key off and wait 10 seconds. Leave breakout box installed, and ECA disconnected. Disconnect IRCM connector. Set DVOM on 200K-ohm scale. Measure resistance between test pins No. 54 and 37, and between test pin No. 54 and battery positive post. If any reading is less than 10K ohms, repair shorts to power in WAC circuit and then go to next step. If all readings are 10K ohms or more, go to next step.

52) Checking Voltage at A/C Clutch. Turn key off and wait 10 seconds. Leave breakout box installed, and ECA disconnected. Connect IRCM connector and disconnect A/C clutch harness. Place A/C demand switch to A/C "ON" position. With KOEO, set DVOM on 20-volt scale and measure voltage at A/C clutch harness connector. If reading is more than 10.5 volts, replace ECA and re-evaluate symptom. If reading is less than 10.5 volts, replace IRCM and re-evaluate symptom.

53) Code 88: Checking EDF Signal to IRCM For Short to Ground. If fan is always on with Code 88, go to step 55). With key off, disconnect ECA 60-pin connector. Inspect for and repair any damaged wiring. Install breakout box, leaving ECA disconnected. Disconnect IRCM connector. Set DVOM on 200K-ohm scale and measure resistance between test pins No. 40 and 55. If reading is 10K ohms or less, repair short to ground in EDF circuit. Connect all components and repeat QUICK TEST. If reading is more than 10K ohms, go to next step.

54) Check Fan Running Mode. With key off and breakout box installed, disconnect ECA and connect IRCM connector. Turn key on.

- On 2.5L CFI manual transmission equipped vehicles, cooling fan should run.
- On 2.5L CFI A/T, 3.0L and 3.8L MPFI AXOD vehicles, cooling fan should run at low speed.

If fan runs as indicated, replace ECA. Connect all components and repeat QUICK TEST. If fan does not run as indicated, replace IRCM. Connect all components and repeat QUICK TEST.

55) Code 88: Check EDF Signal to IRCM For Open Circuit. Turn key off. Disconnect ECA 60-pin connector. Inspect connector for damaged pins, corrosion, or loose wires. Repair if necessary. Install breakout box, leaving ECA disconnected. Disconnect IRCM connector. Set DVOM on 200-ohm scale and measure resistance between breakout box test pin No. 55 and pin No. 14 at IRCM harness connector. If reading is 5 ohms or less, go to next step. If not, repair open in EDF circuit. Connect all components and repeat QUICK TEST.

56) Checking EDF Circuit For Short to Power. Turn key off. Install breakout box, leaving ECA disconnected. Disconnect IRCM connector. Set DVOM on 200K-ohm scale. Measure resistance between test pins No. 55 and 37, and from test pin No. 55 to battery positive terminal. If readings are 10K ohms or less, repair short to power in EDF circuit. After repairs, go to next step. If readings are greater than 10K ohms, go to next step.

57) Checkng EDF For Shorts to Ground. Turn key off. Install breakout box, leaving ECA disconnected. Ensure IRCM is properly connected. Turn key on. Using jumper wire, connect test pin No. 55 to test pins No. 40 or 60. If fan continues to run, replace IRCM. Connect all components and repeat QUICK TEST. If fan does not run, replace ECA. Connect all components and repeat QUICK TEST.

58) Code 95: Check Inertia Switch. A KOEO SELF-TEST Code 95 indicates one of the following:
- Open circuit in fuel pump or between fuel pump and FPM circuit.
- Poor fuel pump ground connection.
- Short in fuel pump power circuit.
- Fuel pump relay contacts always closed.

1989 COMPUTERIZED ENGINE CONTROLS
Ford Motor Co. EEC-IV (Cont.)

1a-491

CIRCUIT TEST D23 (Cont.)

Turn key off and wait 10 seconds. Locate and disconnect fuel pump inertia switch. Set DVOM on 200-ohm scale. Measure resistance of fuel pump inertia switch. If resistance is less than 5 ohms, reconnect inertia switch and go to next step. If resistance is more than 5 ohms, replace or reset inertia switch, rerun QUICK TEST.

59) Checking That Fuel Pump is Off. Turn key off. Listen for fuel pump. If pump is still running go to next step. If pump is off, go to step **61).**

60) Checking For Closed Fuel Pump Relay. With key off, locate and disconnect IRCM. If fuel pump shuts off when controller is disconnected, replace IRCM and rerun QUICK TEST. If pump does not shut off, repair short in POWER-to-PUMP (FPM) circuit. Rerun QUICK TEST.

61) Checking Continuity of FPM Circuit. With key off, disconnect ECA 60-pin connector. Inspect connector for damaged pins, corrosion, or loose wires. Repair if necessary. Install breakout box, leaving ECA disconnected. Disconnect IRCM connector. Set DVOM on 200-ohm scale and measure resistance between FPM circuit at the breakout box and IRCM harness pin No. 5. If resistance is less than 5 ohms, go to next step. If resistance is greater than 5 ohms, repair open circuit and rerun QUICK TEST.

62) Checking FPM Circuit Ground Continuity. With key off, disconnect ECA 60-pin connector. Inspect connector for damaged pins, corrosion, or loose wires. Repair if necessary. Install breakout box, leaving ECA disconnected. Disconnect IRCM connector. Set DVOM on 200-ohm scale and measure resistance between FPM circuit at breakout box and battery negative terminal. If resistance is less than 5 ohms, replace ECA, reconnect and test system. If resistance is greater than 5 ohms, repair fuel pump circuit or replace fuel pump and rerun QUICK TEST.

63) Code 59 or 96: Fuel Pump Power Circuit Continuity. A Code 59 or 96 indicates that when fuel pump is activated, no power is supplied to pump. Turn key off and wait 10 seconds. Disconnect ECA 60-pin connector. Inspect connector for damaged pins, corrosion, or loose wires. Repair if necessary. Install breakout box, leaving ECA disconnected. Disconnect IRCM connector. Set DVOM on 200-ohm scale and measure resistance between FPM circuit at breakout box and IRCM harness connector pin No. 5. If resistance is less than 5 ohms, go to next step. If resistance is greater than 5 ohms, repair open in power to pump circuit between FPM splice and IRCM. Rerun QUICK TEST.

64) Checking Fuel Pump Operation. With key off, disconnect ECA 60-pin connector. Install breakout box, reconnect ECA and IRCM. Set DVOM on 20-volt scale. Connect DVOM between FPM circuit and test pin No. 40, at the breakout box. Observe DVOM and turn key to "ON" position. If voltage is 10.5 or more volts, for approximately one second after key is turned on, replace ECA and rerun QUICK TEST. If voltage does not increase to specification, replace IRCM and rerun QUICK TEST.

65) Continuous Memory Code 95: Checking EEC-IV Harness. A Code 95 indicates that there is an open circuit in the fuel pump or between the fuel pump and FPM circuit in the ECA. The fuel pump ground circuit is poor.

Start engine and test for stalling or stumble while performing "WIGGLE" test on fuel pump and ECA harness. Perform "WIGGLE" test on fuel pump ground circuit. Lightly tap on fuel pump to duplicate road shock. Turn key off and inspect connections for corrosion or damage. If no fault is found, go to next step. If fault is found, repair it, clear memory codes, and retest.

66) Checking FPM Circuit. Turn key off. Disconnect ECA 60-pin connector. Inspect connector for damaged pins, corrosion, or loose wires. Repair if necessary. Install breakout box, leaving ECA disconnected. With KOEO, connect a test light between FPM circuit and test pin No. 37. Observe test light while performing "WIGGLE" test on the monitor circuit (pin No. 8) between the ECA and the connection at the power to pump circuit. If a fault is found, isolate and repair. Clear memory codes and rerun QUICK TEST. If no fault is found, fault cannot be duplicated at this time. Clear memory codes for future testing.

67) Continuous Memory Code 59 or 96: Check For Code 83 or 87 Also Displayed. If Code 83 or 87 is also present, go to step **69).** If Code 83 or 87 is not present, go to next step.

68) Checking EEC-IV Harness. A Continuous Memory Code 59 or 96, without the presence of a Continuous Memory Code 83 or 87, indicates that during vehicle operation the fuel pump relay contacts have opened or that there is an open in the POWER-to-PUMP circuit from the IRCM pin No. 5 to the FPM splice. Start engine and listen for

CIRCUIT TEST D23 (Cont.)

fuel pump stopping, stall or stumble while performing "WIGGLE" test on fuel pump power circuit from IRCM. Inspect harness and connectors with key off. If a fault is found, isolate and repair, clear codes and retest. If no fault is found, problem cannot be duplicated at this time. Clear codes for future testing sequence.

69) Continuous Memory Code 83 or 87: Checking EEC-IV Harness. A Continuous Memory Code 83 or 87 indicates that during vehicle operation there has been an open condition in the VPWR circuit of the IRCM, an open coil in the fuel pump relay, or an open in the fuel pump primary circuit.

Start engine and listen for fuel pump stopping, stall or stumble while performing "WIGGLE" test on EEC-IV harness fuel pump circuit (pin No. 22 or 41) between the ECA and IRCM (pin No. 18 or 11). Inspect harness and connectors with key off. If a fault is found, isolate and repair, clear codes and retest. If no fault is found, problem cannot be duplicated at this time. Clear codes for future testing sequence.

CIRCUIT TEST D24

AXOD ELECTRICAL SYSTEM DIAGNOSIS

This test should be performed ONLY if a problem has been detected in transaxle. If any of these service codes appeared during SELF-TEST, the AXOD DRIVE CYCLE TEST should be performed. A jumper harness is used to connect to the transmission bulkhead connector and test electrical circuits. The following AXOD transaxle related items have malfunctioned or failed as indicated:

- **Code 39:** Transaxle converter by-pass clutch is not operating properly.
- **Code 59, 62, 68 and 69:** Refer to CIRCUIT TEST D21 for summary of these codes.
- **Code 89:** Transaxle converter by-pass clutch solenoid has stayed always open or closed.

The following service codes are not AXOD transaxle related, but can affect converter clutch by-pass operation. Service these components before servicing AXOD transaxle codes:

- **Code 21:** Engine Coolant Temperature (ECT) sensor out of range.
- **Code 22:** Manifold Absolute Pressure (MAP) sensor out of range.
- **Code 23:** Throttle Position Sensor (TPS) out of range.
- **Code 24:** Air Charge Temperature (ACT) sensor out of range.
- **Code 29:** Vehicle Speed Sensor (VSS) not functioning.
- **Code 74:** Brake ON/OFF (BOO) switch always open or brake not applied during KOER SELF-TEST.
- **Code 75:** Brake ON/OFF (BOO) switch always closed.

The following service code indicates that a transaxle component may have caused faulty engine idle speed control:

- **Code 57:** Neutral Pressure Switch (NPS) failed in Neutral (open) position. The NPS is normally open and closes with hydraulic pressure. Failure of transaxle to engage in "D" or "R" will cause Code 57 to be displayed. Check for proper hydraulic pressure before testing AXOD transaxle electrical components.
- **Code 67:** Neutral Pressure Switch (NPS) failed closed.

NOTE: Ensure that all components are connected before performing test. Perform AXOD DRIVE CYCLE TEST on a slight upgrade or flat terrain. If any other non-AXOD related codes appear, service those codes first as they could affect electrical operation of transaxle.

NOTE: All components must be connected for this test and the following AXOD DRIVE CYCLE TEST must be performed:

- Record and clear Continuous Memory Codes.
- Warm engine to operating temperature.
- With transaxle in "D" range, lightly accelerate from a stop to 40 MPH to allow transaxle to shift into 3rd gear. Hold speed and throttle opening steady for a minimum of 15 seconds (30 seconds above 4000 feet altitude).
- Shift transaxle into overdrive and accelerate lightly from 40 to 50 MPH to allow transaxle to shift into 4th gear. Hold speed and throttle opening steady, in 4th gear, for a minimum of 15 seconds.
- With transaxle in 4th gear, throttle open and speed steady, lightly apply and release brakes (enough to turn on brake lights). Hold speed and throttle opening steady for an additional 15 seconds.
- Brake to a stop and remain stopped for a minimum of 20 seconds with transaxle in overdrive range. Perform KOEO SELF-TEST and record Continuous Memory Codes.

1a-492

1989 COMPUTERIZED ENGINE CONTROLS
Ford Motor Co. EEC-IV (Cont.)

CIRCUIT TEST D24 (Cont.)

Jumper Harness

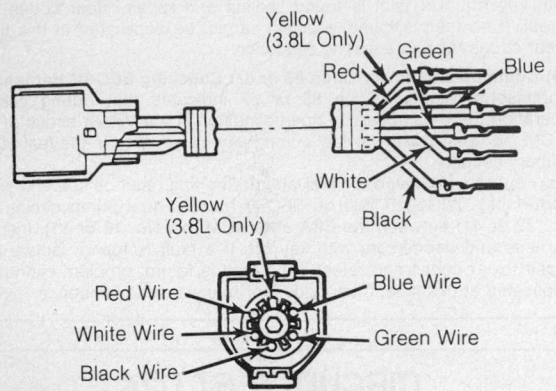

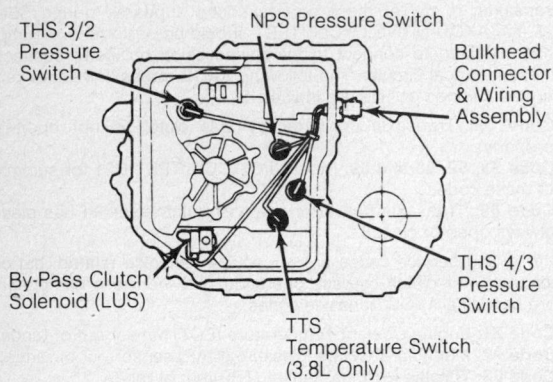

Transmission Component Locations

THS 3/2 Pressure Switch

NPS Pressure Switch

Bulkhead Connector & Wiring Assembly

By-Pass Clutch Solenoid (LUS)

TTS Temperature Switch (3.8L Only)

THS 4/3 Pressure Switch

1) Continuous Memory Code 39: Faulty Converter By-Pass Clutch (CBC), Check Harness Connections. Check that vehicle harness connector is fully attached to transaxle bulkhead connector and that vehicle harness connector terminals are fully seated in connector. If connector or terminals are not okay, repair as required and repeat QUICK TEST. If connector and terminals are okay, go to next step.

2) Checking Solenoid Resistance. Install jumper harness to transaxle bulkhead connector. Connect VOM positive test lead to Red wire and negative test lead to Black wire. Check resistance. If reading is between 20 and 40 ohms, go to QUICK TEST and service codes as required. If reading is not between 20 and 40 ohms, go to next step.

3) Check By-Pass Clutch Application. Connect jumper harness Red wire to battery positive post. With engine running and transaxle in 3rd gear, connect jumper harness Black wire to ground (to energize by-pass clutch solenoid). DO NOT connect with polarity reversed, otherwise solenoid diode will be damaged. If by-pass clutch is applied (engine RPM drops slightly), there is no electrical component failure. By-pass clutch is operating properly. Error code may be indicating a slipping by-pass clutch. Service transaxle for a no converter clutch apply condition and repeat QUICK TEST. If by-pass clutch is not applied (engine RPM does not drop), go to next step.

4) Check By-Pass Solenoid Valve. Check main control by-pass clutch control valve (in valve body) for sticking. If valve is sticking, service spool valve as necessary. If valve is okay, go to next step.

5) Check By-Pass Solenoid. Remove by-pass solenoid. Check condition of "O" ring. Also check for contamination in/on solenoid or small hole in valve. Shake solenoid vigorously to check for free armature. If solenoid is faulty, replace by-pass clutch solenoid and repeat QUICK TEST. If solenoid is okay, service transaxle for a no converter clutch apply condition and repeat QUICK TEST.

NOTE: The THS 4/3 and 3/2 pressure switches are normally open and close with hydraulic pressure. Failure of transaxle to engage in "D" will cause Code 59 to be displayed. Failure of transaxle to shift into 3rd gear will cause Code 69 to be displayed. Check for proper hydraulic operation before testing electrical components.

CIRCUIT TEST D24 (Cont.)

6) Code 59: THS 4/3 Switch Failed to Open, Check Wiring. Check that vehicle harness connector is fully engaged in transaxle bulkhead connector and that vehicle harness connector terminals are fully seated in connector. If connector or terminals are not okay, repair as required and repeat QUICK TEST. If connector and terminals are okay, go to next step.

7) Check Switch For Continuity. Install jumper harness to transaxle bulkhead connector. Using VOM, check for continuity between engine ground and Blue wire. With engine running and transaxle in Neutral, VOM should indicate no continuity (infinite resistance). Shift transaxle into "D". Switch should close and resistance should be less than 10 ohms. Switch should stay closed in 1st, 2nd and 3rd gears, and then open in 4th gear. If circuit is okay, go to QUICK TEST and service codes as required. If circuit is not okay, go to next step.

8) Checking Internal Connections. Remove transaxle side oil pan. Check that internal connector with Blue wire is firmly attached to THS 4/3 pressure switch. Connector should not pull off easily or fit loosely. If connector is not okay, replace bulkhead connector and wiring assembly. Repeat QUICK TEST. If connector is okay, go to next step.

9) Check Internal Wiring. Remove connector from pressure switch by pushing on end of connector, while pulling on wire end of connector. Check for continuity in bulkhead connector by measuring resistance between Blue wire and terminal inside connector just removed. If reading is more than 2 ohms, replace bulkhead connector and wiring assembly. Repeat QUICK TEST. If reading is less than 2 ohms, go to next step.

10) Check THS 4/3 Switch. Remove THS 4/3 pressure switch. Install a 1/8-27 pipe fitting that can be connected to LOW pressure air supply in order to pressure test leaks and switch closure. With 50 psi (3.5 kg/cm²) applied, check for ruptured diaphragm by submerging switch in clean transmission fluid. NEVER check in water. Check for bubbles coming out of small vent hole near switch terminal. If bubbles show, diaphragm has failed. Replace THS 4/3 pressure switch and repeat QUICK TEST. If no bubbles show, go to next step.

11) Check Switch Resistance. With 50 psi (3.5 kg/cm²) applied to switch, check resistance between switch terminal and switch case. If reading is less than 8 ohms, hydraulic pressure circuit to switch may have excessive leaks. Service transaxle as required. If reading is more than 8 ohms, replace switch. Repeat step **8)**, and then QUICK TEST. Codes 39, 59, 62, 69 and 89 should no longer be displayed.

NOTE: If Code 62 appears in KOEO SELF-TEST, THS 3/2 circuit has failed. If Code 62 appears in KOER SELF-TEST, THS 4/3 circuit has failed. If Code 62 appears in both SELF-TESTS, follow entire test procedure to determine which circuit has failed.

12) Code 62. Remove vehicle harness connector from transaxle bulkhead connector and install jumper harness. Using DVOM, measure continuity between engine ground and White wire (THS 3/2 circuit). With engine off, DVOM should indicate no continuity (infinite resistance). Measure continuity between engine ground and Blue wire (THS 4/3 circuit). With engine running and transaxle in Neutral, VOM should indicate no continuity (infinite resistance). If all readings show no continuity, go to QUICK TEST and service codes as required. If any reading indicates continuity, go to next step.

13) Check Internal Wiring. Remove transaxle side oil pan. Check for pinched, cut, or otherwise grounded wiring. If wiring is damaged, replace bulkhead connector and wiring assembly. After repairs, repeat QUICK TEST. If THS 4/3 pressure switch wiring is okay, go to step **15**. If THS 3/2 pressure switch wiring is okay, go to next step.

14) Checking 3/2 Switch. Remove wiring from THS 3/2 pressure switch. Using DVOM, check pressure switch for continuity to engine ground by connecting one lead to switch terminal and other lead to valve body. If there is no continuity (infinite resistance), go to step **16**. If there is continuity to ground, replace THS 3/2 pressure switch and repeat QUICK TEST.

15) Check 4/3 Switch. Remove wiring from THS 4/3 pressure switch. Using DVOM, check pressure switch for continuity to engine ground by connecting one lead to switch terminal and other lead to valve body. If there is continuity to ground, replace 4/3 pressure switch and repeat QUICK TEST. If there is no continuity (infinite resistance), go to next step.

16) Check Internal Wires. Using DVOM and with wiring removed from both pressure switches, check continuity to ground. Connect one test lead to White wire and other test lead to ground. Connect one test lead to Blue wire and other test lead to ground. Ensure internal

1989 COMPUTERIZED ENGINE CONTROLS
Ford Motor Co. EEC-IV (Cont.)

1a-493

CIRCUIT TEST D24 (Cont.)

terminals are not touching any metallic parts. If there is continuity to ground, replace bulkhead connector and wiring assembly. Repeat QUICK TEST. If there is no continuity (infinite resistance), go to QUICK TEST and service codes as required.

NOTE: The THS 4/3 and 3/2 pressure switches are normally open switches that close with hydraulic pressure. Failure of transaxle to engage in "D" will cause service Code 59 to be displayed. Failure of transaxle to shift into 3rd gear will cause Code 69 to be displayed. Check for proper hydraulic operation before testing electrical components.

17) Code 69: Check Wiring. Check that vehicle harness connector is fully attached to transaxle bulkhead connector and that terminals are fully seated in connector. If connector or terminals are faulty, repair as required and repeat QUICK TEST. If connector and terminals are okay, go to next step.

18) Check Switch For Continuity. Install jumper harness to transaxle bulkhead connector. Using DVOM, check for continuity between engine ground and White wire. With engine running and transaxle in Drive, 1st gear, or 2nd gear, VOM should indicate no continuity (infinite resistance). When transaxle shifts into 3rd or 4th gear, the switch should close and resistance should be less than 10 ohms between White wire and engine ground. If circuit is okay, go to QUICK TEST and service codes as required. If circuit is not okay, go to next step.

19) Checking Internal Connections. Remove transaxle side oil pan. Check that internal connector with White wire is firmly attached to THS 3/2 pressure switch. Connector should not pull off easily or fit loosely. If connector is faulty, replace bulkhead connector and wiring assembly. Repeat QUICK TEST. If connector is okay, go to next step.

20) Check Internal Wiring. Remove connector from pressure switch by pushing on end of connector, while pulling on wire end of connector. Check for continuity in bulkhead connector by measuring resistance between White wire and terminal inside connector just removed. If reading is more than 2 ohms, replace bulkhead connector and wiring assembly. Repeat QUICK TEST. If reading is less than 2 ohms, go to next step.

21) Check THS 2/3 Switch. Remove THS 3/2 pressure switch. Install a 1/8-27 pipe fitting that can be connected to LOW pressure air supply in order to pressure leak and test switch closure. With 50 psi (3.5 kg/cm²) applied, check for ruptured diaphragm by submerging switch in clean transmission fluid. NEVER use water to test switch. Check for bubbles coming out of small vent hole near switch terminal. If bubbles show, diaphragm has failed. Replace THS 3/2 pressure switch and repeat QUICK TEST. If no bubbles show, go to next step.

22) Check Switch Resistance. With 50 psi (3.5 kg/cm²) applied to switch, check resistance between switch terminal and switch case. If reading is less than 8 ohms, hydraulic pressure circuit to switch may have excessive leaks. Service transaxle as required. If reading is more than 8 ohms, replace switch. Repeat steps **21)** and **22)**, and then repeat QUICK TEST. Codes 39, 59, 62, 69 and 89 should no longer be displayed.

23) Code 89: LUS Circuit Failed. If Code 39 is also displayed, go to CIRCUIT TEST for that code. Check that vehicle harness connector is fully attached to transaxle bulkhead connector and that vehicle harness terminals are fully seated in connector. If connector or terminals are not okay, repair as required and repeat QUICK TEST. If connector and terminals are okay, go to next step.

24) Check Solenoid Resistance. Install jumper harness to transaxle bulkhead connector. Connect DVOM positive test lead to Red wire and negative test lead to Black wire. Check resistance. If reading is between 20 and 40 ohms, switch is okay, go to QUICK TEST and service codes as required. If reading is not between 20 and 40 ohms, go to next step.

25) Check Internal Connections. Remove transaxle side oil pan. Check that internal connector is fully attached to solenoid. If connector is okay, go to next step. If connector is not okay, fully engage connector and check continuity once more. If resistance is still not between 20 and 40 ohms, go to next step. If resistance is now okay, repeat QUICK TEST.

26) Check Solenoid Continuity. Remove connector from solenoid by pulling on wires at 2-way connector. Check solenoid continuity by connecting DVOM positive test lead to solenoid positive terminal and negative test lead to solenoid negative terminal (polarity symbols, + and –, are stamped on solenoid frame). If circuit is open (infinite resistance), replace solenoid and then repeat QUICK TEST. If solenoid

CIRCUIT TEST D24 (Cont.)

is okay (20 to 40 ohms resistance), replace bulkhead connector and wiring assembly. Connect all internal connectors and repeat step **24)**. If circuit tests okay, install oil pan. Repeat KOEO SELF-TEST. Code 89 should no longer be displayed.

NOTE: The NPS is normally open and closes with hydraulic pressure. Failure of transaxle to engage in "D" or "R" will cause Code 57 to be displayed. Check for correct hydraulic pressure before testing electrical components.

27) Code 57: NPS Failed Open, Check Wiring. Check that vehicle harness connector is fully attached to transaxle connector and that vehicle harness terminals are fully seated in connector. If connector or terminals are not okay, repair as required and repeat QUICK TEST. If connector and terminals are okay, go to next step.

28) Check Switch For Continuity. Install jumper harness to transaxle bulkhead connector. Using DVOM, check continuity between Green wire and engine ground. With engine running and transaxle in "P" or "N", DVOM should indicate no continuity (infinite resistance). Shift transaxle into "R" and "D" ranges, switch should close. Resistance should be less than 10 ohms in both ranges. If circuit is okay, go to QUICK TEST and service codes as required. If circuit is not okay, go to next step.

29) Check Internal Connections. Remove transaxle side oil pan. Check that terminal connector with Green wire is firmly attached to NPS. Connector should not pull off easily or fit loosely. If connector is not okay, replace bulkhead connector and wiring assembly. Repeat QUICK TEST. If connector is okay, go to next step.

30) Check Internal Wiring. Remove connector from NPS by pushing on end of connector while pulling on connector wire. Check for continuity in bulkhead connector by measuring resistance between service connector Green wire and terminal inside connector just removed. If resistance is greater than 2 ohms, replace bulkhead connector and wiring assembly. Repeat QUICK TEST. If reading is less than 2 ohms, go to next step.

31) Check THS NPS Switch. Remove NPS. Install a 1/8-27 pipe fitting that can be connected to LOW pressure air supply in order to pressure leak and test switch closure. With 50 psi (3.5 kg/cm²) applied, check for ruptured diaphragm by submerging switch in clean transmission fluid. NEVER use water to test switch. Check for bubbles coming out of small vent hole near switch terminal. If bubbles show, diaphragm has failed. Replace NPS and repeat QUICK TEST. If no bubbles show, go to next step.

32) Check Switch Resistance. With 50 psi (3.5 kg/cm²) applied to switch, check resistance between switch terminal and switch case. If reading is 8 ohms or less, hydraulic pressure circuit to switch may have excessive leaks. Service transaxle as required. If reading is more than 8 ohms, replace switch. Repeat step **28)**, and then repeat QUICK TEST. Codes 39, 59, 62, 69 and 89 should no longer be displayed.

NOTE: The Transmission Temperature Switch (TTS) is a normally closed switch that opens when transmission oil temperature reaches 270°F (132°C). Perform the following test ONLY on a cool transmission. If the circuit has failed open, the ECA assumes the transmission is hot and applies the converter clutch more frequently to allow the transmission to cool.

33) Check Wiring. Check that vehicle harness connector is fully attached to transaxle connector and that vehicle harness terminals are fully seated in connector. If connector or terminals are not okay, repair as required and repeat QUICK TEST. If connector and terminals are okay, go to next step.

34) Check Bulkhead Connector. Ensure that the correct bulkhead connector has been installed. The connector should be "Natural" color and have 6 pin terminals. If connector is incorrect, replace connector. If connector is correct, go to next step.

35) Check Switch Circuit Continuity. Install jumper harness on transmission bulkhead connector. Using a DVOM, check continuity between engine ground and Yellow wire. Since the TTS is a normally closed switch, the circuit should be closed when the transmission temperature is less than 270°F (132°C). Resistance should be less than 10 ohms between the Yellow wire and ground. If circuit is okay, go to QUICK TEST procedures and service other codes. If circuit is faulty, go to next step.

36) Check Internal Connectors. Remove transaxle side oil pan. Check that terminal connector with Yellow wire is firmly attached to TTS. Connector should not pull off easily or fit loosely. If connector is faulty,

1a-494

1989 COMPUTERIZED ENGINE CONTROLS
Ford Motor Co. EEC-IV (Cont.)

CIRCUIT TEST D24 (Cont.)

replace bulkhead connector and wiring assembly. Repeat QUICK TEST. If connector is okay, go to next step.

37) Check Internal Wiring. Remove connector from TTS by pushing on end of connector while pulling on connector wire. Check for continuity in bulkhead connector by measuring resistance between service connector Green wire and terminal inside connector just removed. If resistance is greater than 2 ohms, replace bulkhead connector and wiring assembly. Repeat QUICK TEST. If reading is less than 2 ohms, go to next step.

38) Check Temperature Switch. Disconnect internal connector from switch. Check for continuity between engine ground and "Nail Head" connecting pin on the switch. Resistance should be less than 8 ohms. Ensure switch terminal is not loose or an intermittent open circuit may result. If resistance and switch test okay, testing is complete. If switch is faulty, replace switch, reconnect internal wiring and verify continuity to ground.

39) Neutral Pressure Switch (NPS) Failed Closed, Check Wiring. Remove vehicle harness connector from transaxle bulkhead connector and install jumper harness. Check continuity between engine ground and Green wire (NPS circuit). With engine off, resistance should be infinite. If resistance is infinite, switch has not failed in closed posirion. Service other codes as required. If there is continuity between the Green wire and ground, go to next step.

40) Check Internal Wiring. Remove oil pan and check for pinched, cut or otherwise grounded wiring. If wiring is faulty, replace transaxle bulkhead connector. Repeat QUICK TEST. If wiring is okay, go to next step.

41) Check NPS Switch. Remove wiring from NPS. Measure the pressure switch for continuity to engine ground. Connect one test lead to switch connector and other to engine ground. If resistance is infinite, switch is open, go to next step. If there is continuity to ground, replace NPS and repeat QUICK TEST.

42) Check Internal Wires. Remove wire from NPS and check continuity to ground. Connect one test lead to Green wire and other lead to ground. Ensure internal terminals are not shorted to ground. If there is continuity to ground, replace bulkhead connector and repeat QUICK TEST. If there is infinite resistance, repeat QUICK TEST and service codes as required.

WIRING DIAGRAMS

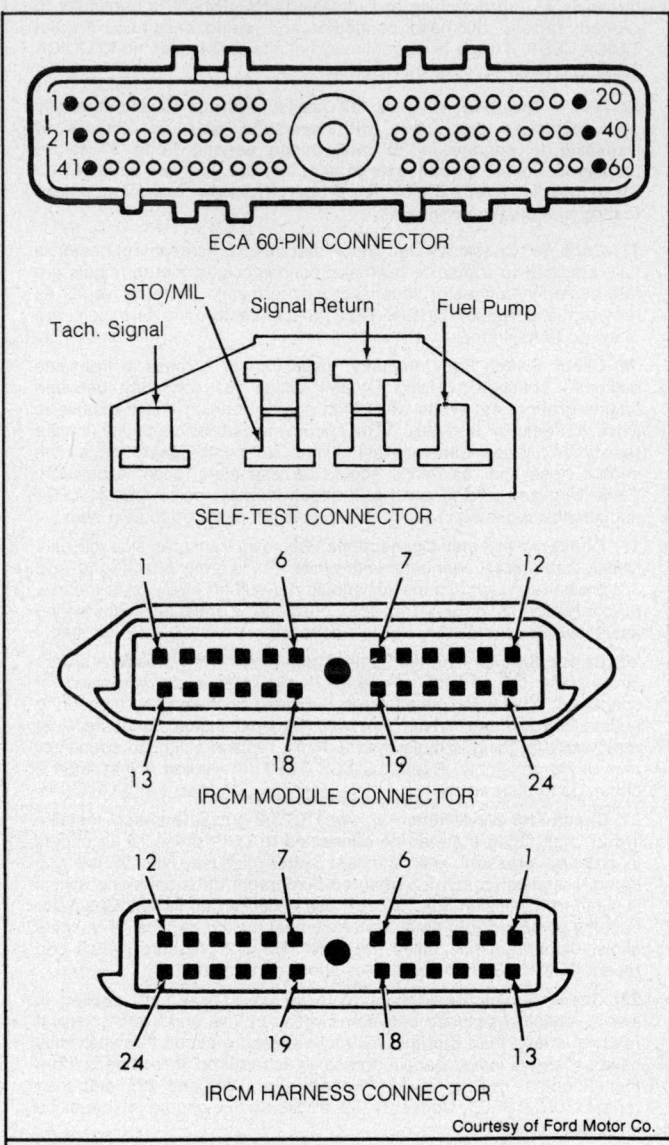

ECA 60-PIN CONNECTOR

SELF-TEST CONNECTOR

IRCM MODULE CONNECTOR

IRCM HARNESS CONNECTOR

Courtesy of Ford Motor Co.

Fig. 5:ECA Connector Pin Diagram

1989 Computerized Engine Controls
Ford Motor Co. EEC-IV (Cont.)

1a-495

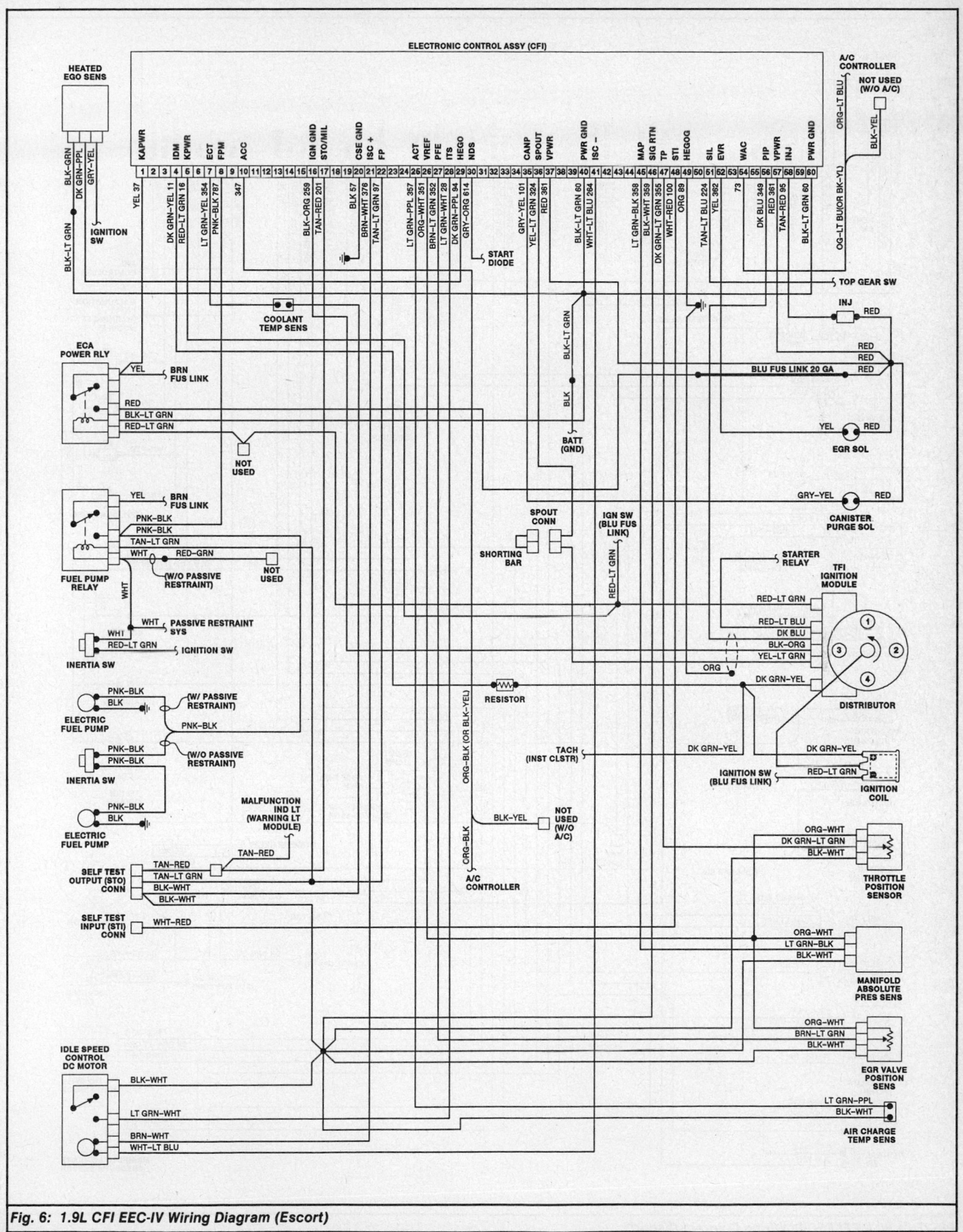

Fig. 6: 1.9L CFI EEC-IV Wiring Diagram (Escort)

1989 Computerized ENGINE CONTROLS
Ford Motor Co. EEC-IV (Cont.)

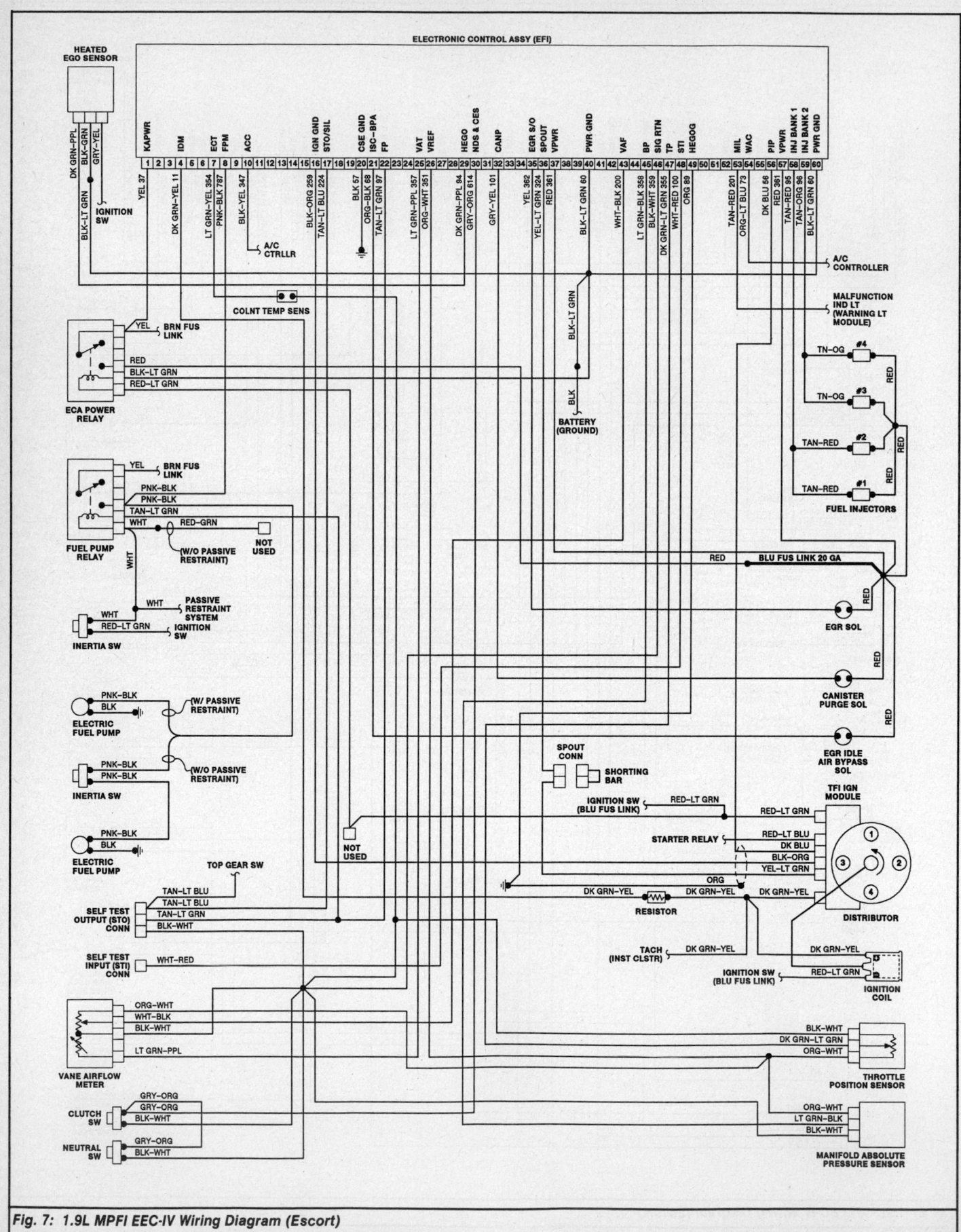

Fig. 7: 1.9L MPFI EEC-IV Wiring Diagram (Escort)

1989 COMPUTERIZED ENGINE CONTROLS
Ford Motor Co. EEC-IV (Cont.)

1a-497

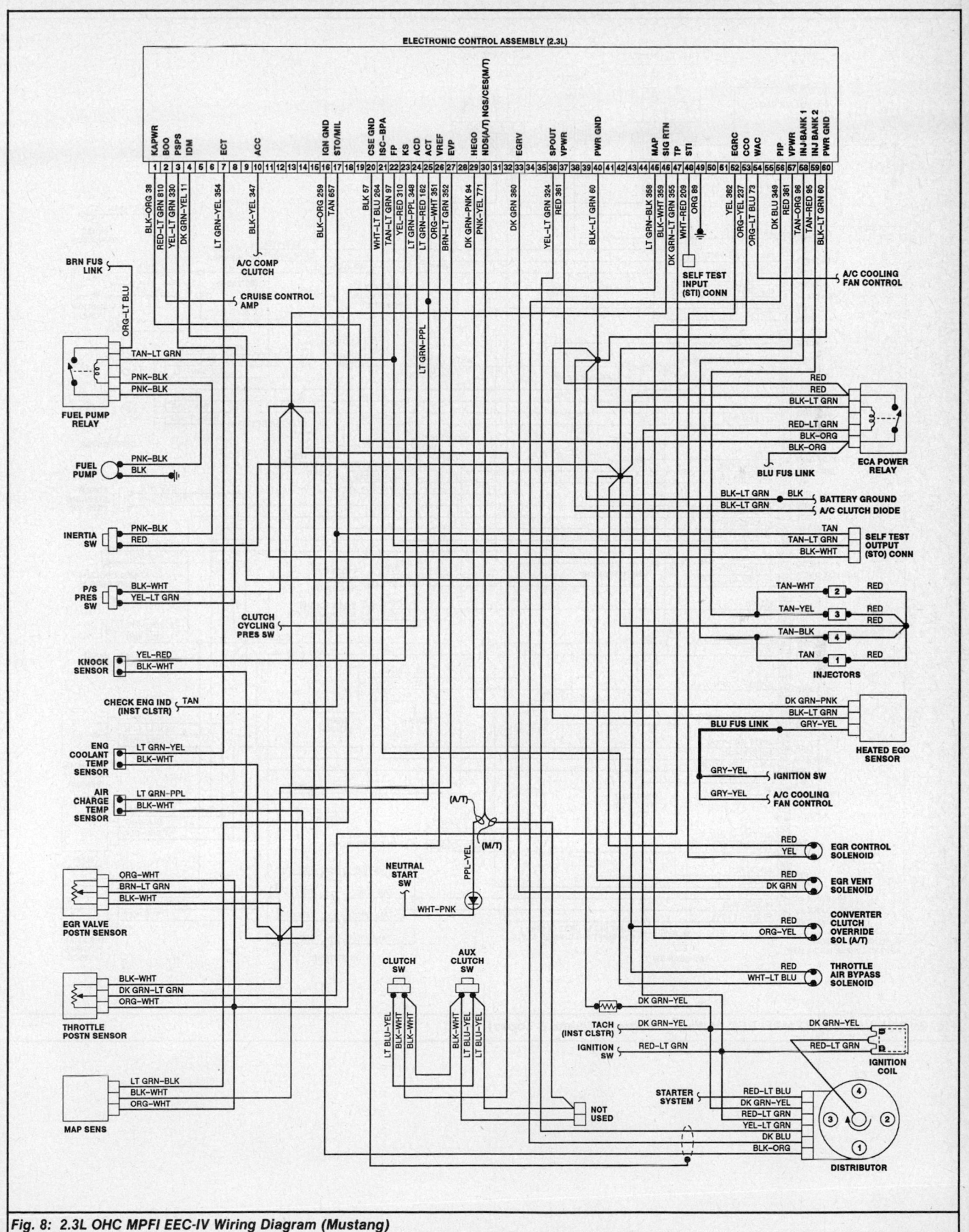

Fig. 8: 2.3L OHC MPFI EEC-IV Wiring Diagram (Mustang)

1989 Computerized Engine Controls
Ford Motor Co. EEC-IV (Cont.)

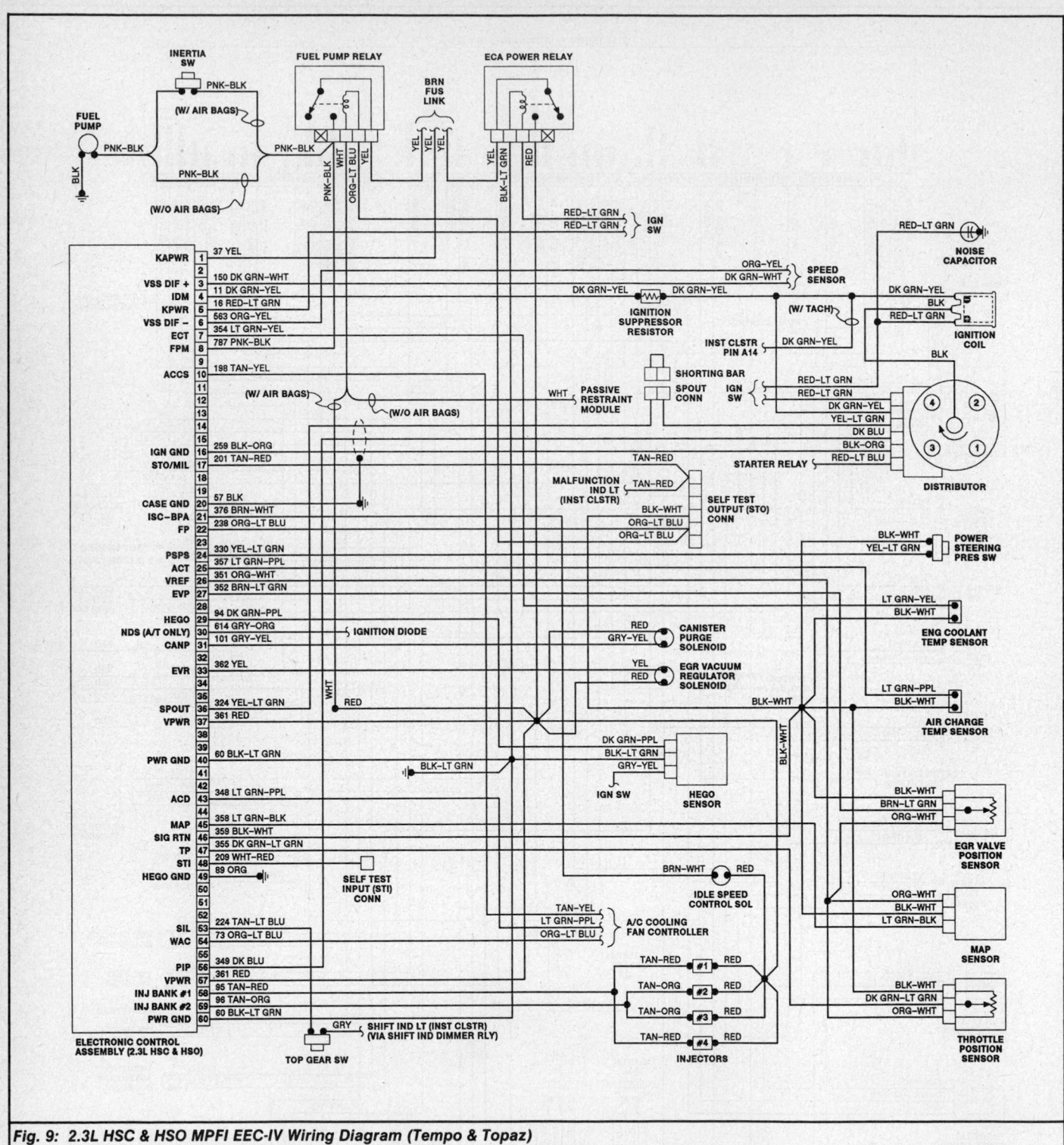

Fig. 9: 2.3L HSC & HSO MPFI EEC-IV Wiring Diagram (Tempo & Topaz)

1989 Computerized Engine Controls
Ford Motor Co. EEC-IV (Cont.)

1a-499

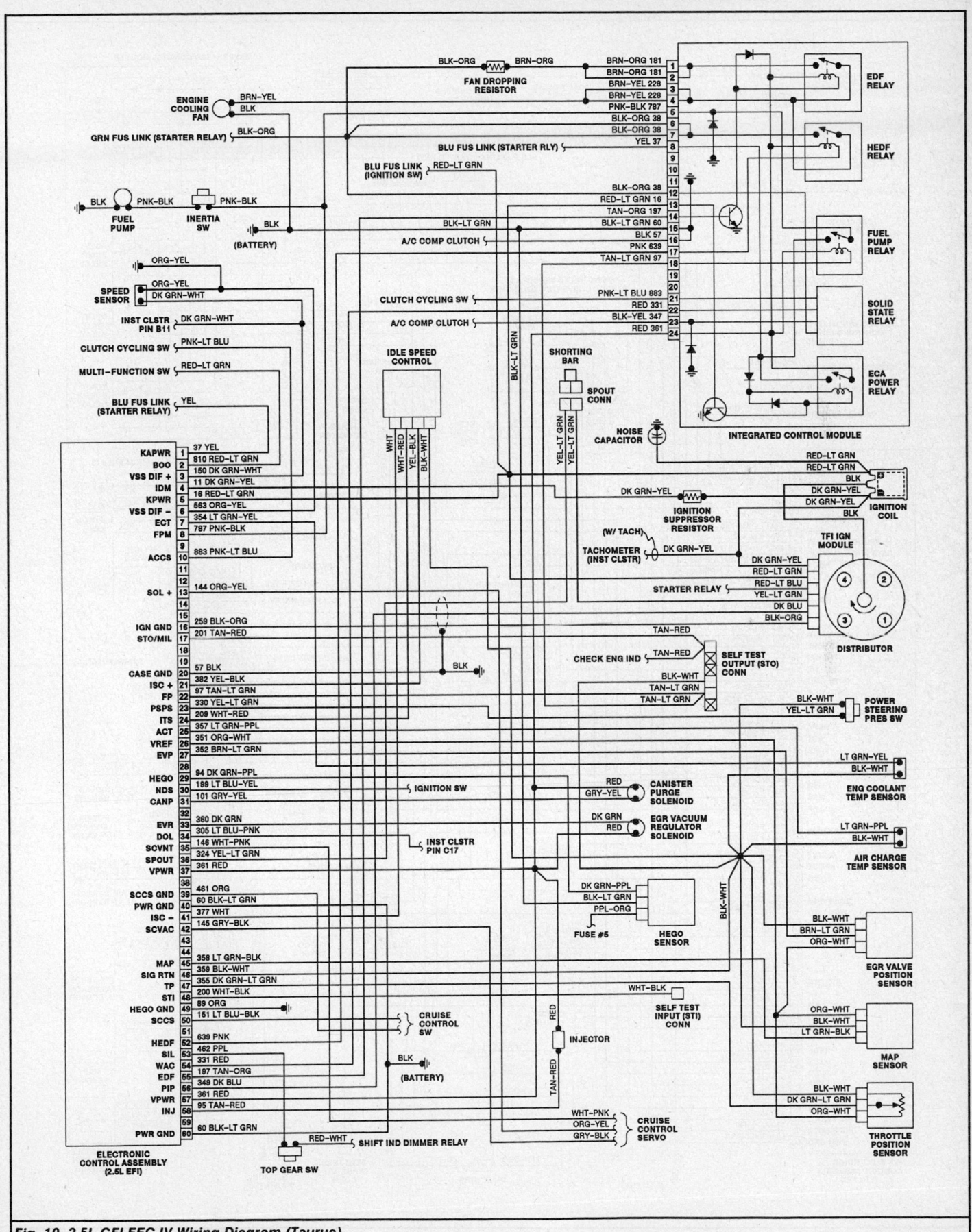

Fig. 10 2.5L CFI EEC-IV Wiring Diagram (Taurus)

1989 COMPUTERIZED ENGINE CONTROLS
Ford Motor Co. EEC-IV (Cont.)

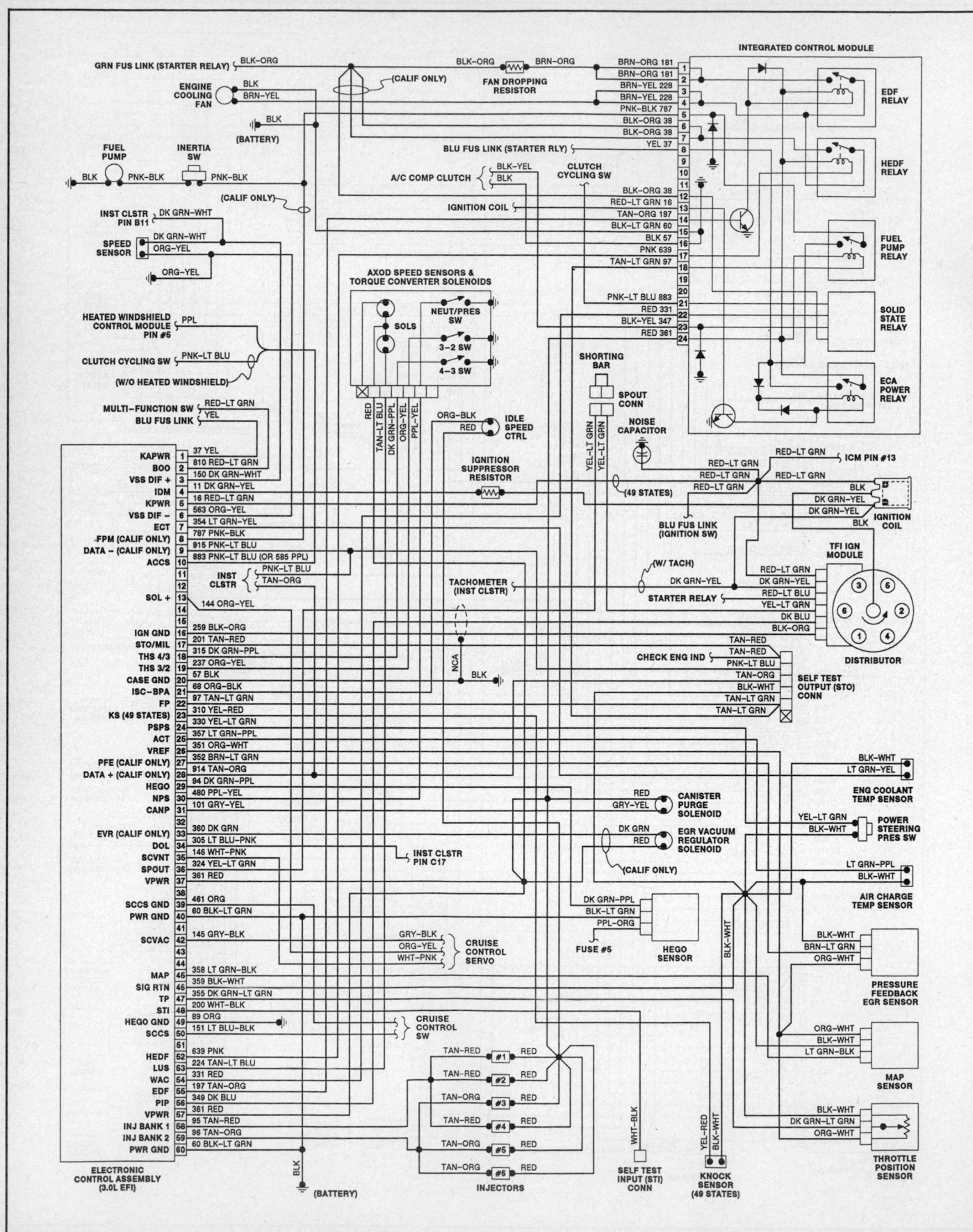

Fig. 11: 3.0L MPFI (FWD) EEC-IV Wiring Diagram (Sable & Taurus)

1989 COMPUTERIZED ENGINE CONTROLS
Ford Motor Co. EEC-IV (Cont.)

1a-501

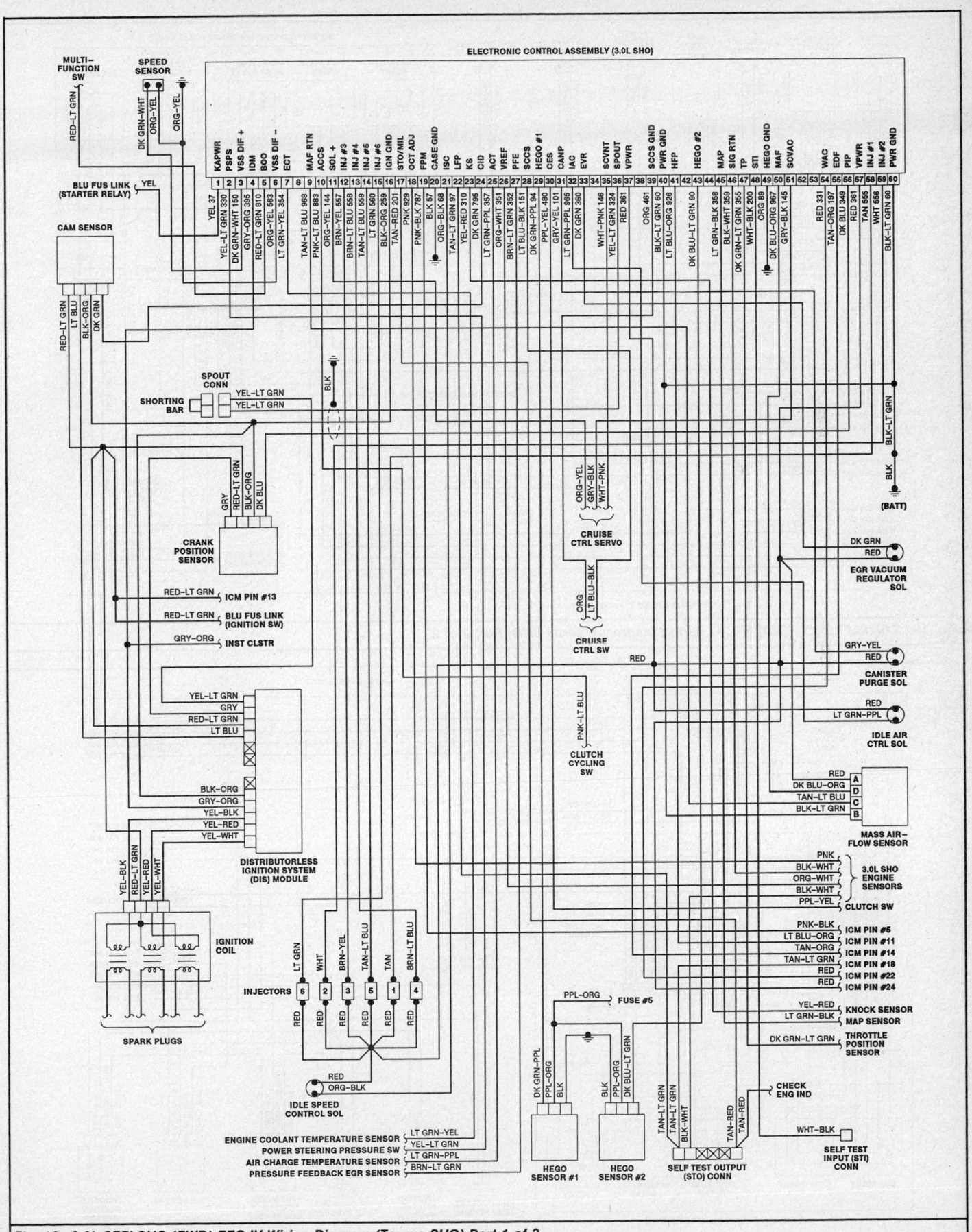

Fig. 12: 3.0L SEFI SHO (FWD) EEC-IV Wiring Diagram (Taurus SHO) Part 1 of 2

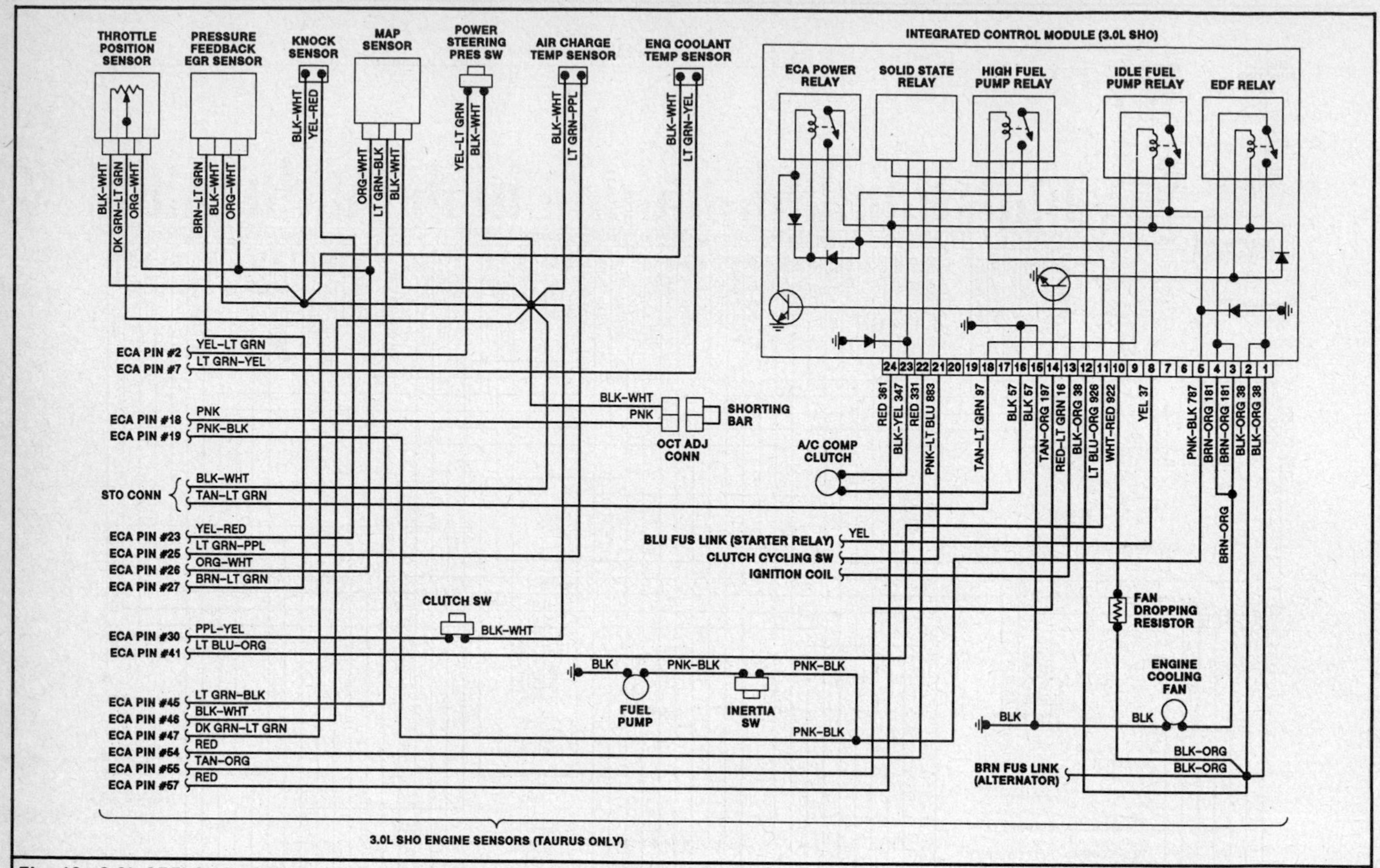

Fig. 13: 3.0L SEFI SHO (FWD) EEC-IV Wiring Diagram (Taurus SHO) Part 2 of 2

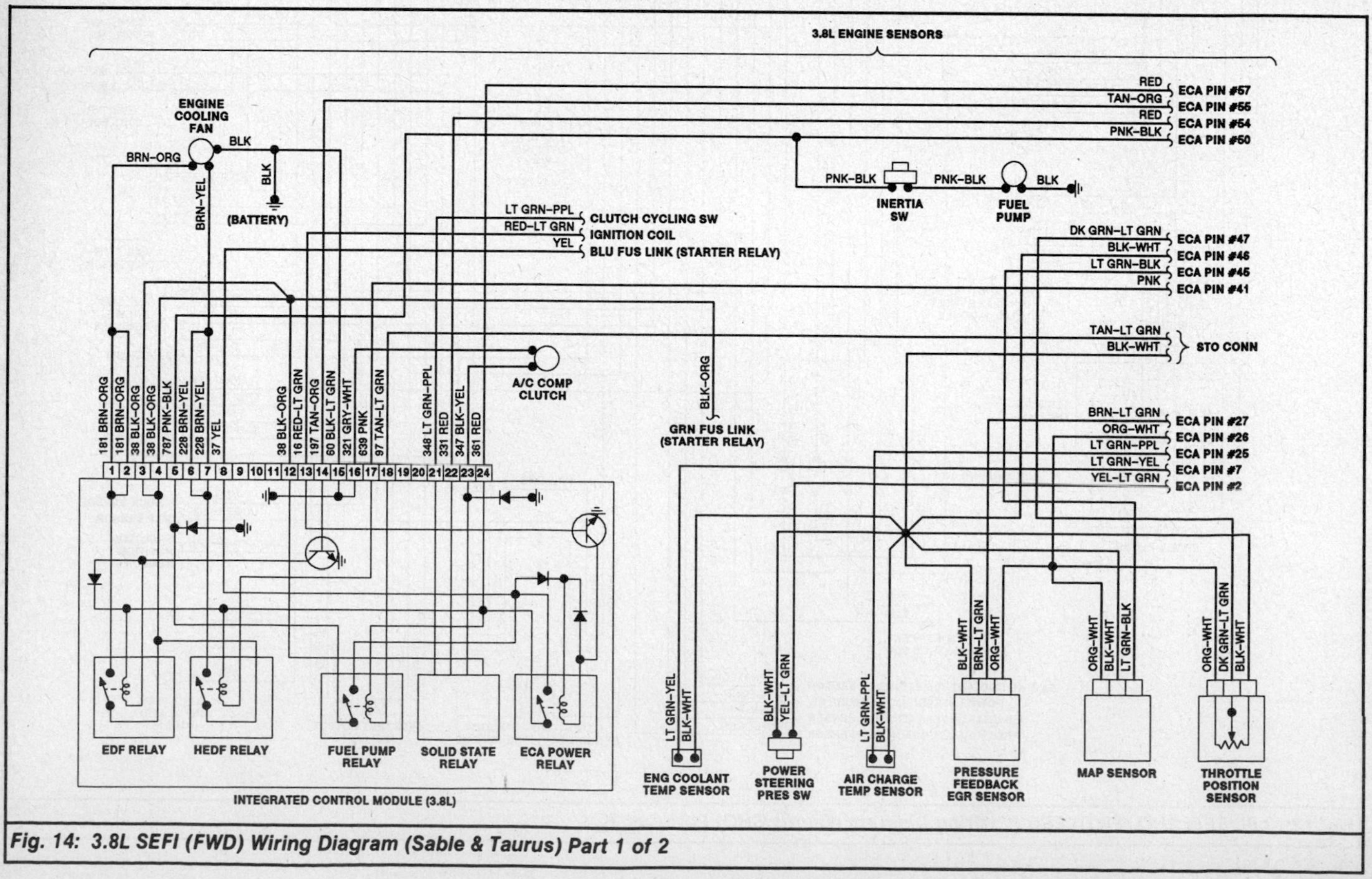

Fig. 14: 3.8L SEFI (FWD) Wiring Diagram (Sable & Taurus) Part 1 of 2

1989 Computerized ENGINE CONTROLS
Ford Motor Co. EEC-IV (Cont.)

1a-503

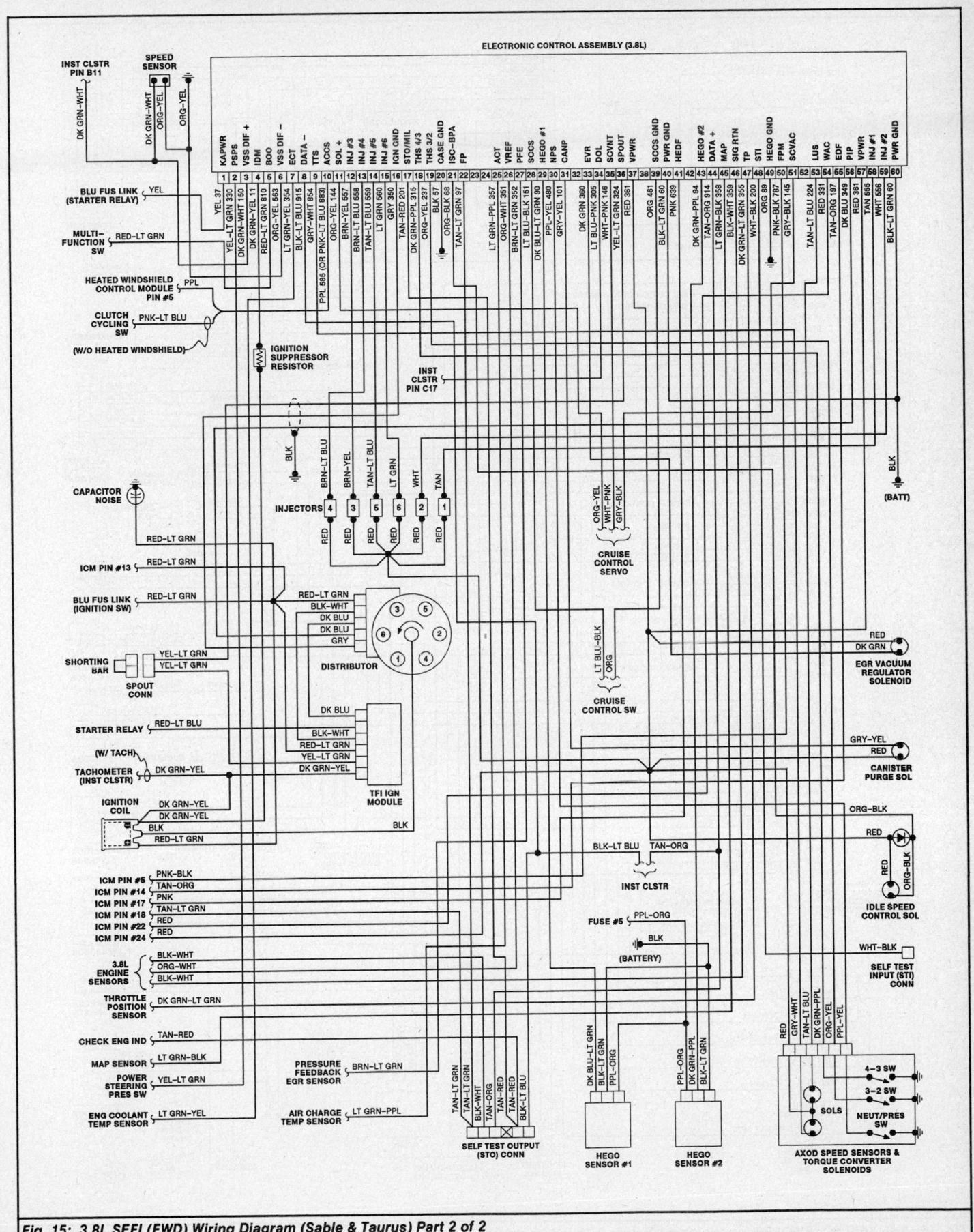

Fig. 15: 3.8L SEFI (FWD) Wiring Diagram (Sable & Taurus) Part 2 of 2

1a-504

1989 Computerized ENGINE CONTROLS
Ford Motor Co. EEC-IV (Cont.)

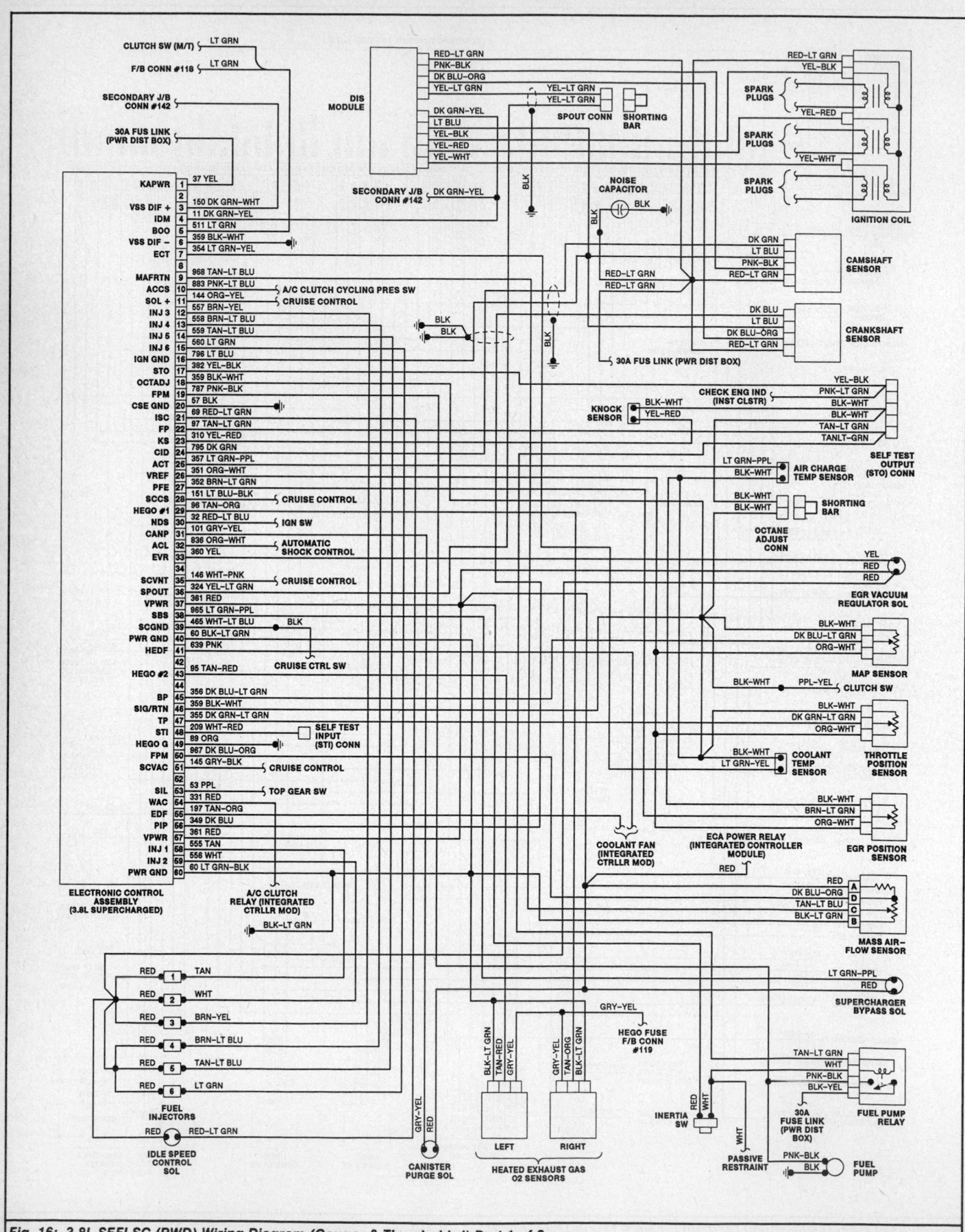

1989 Computerized ENGINE CONTROLS
Ford Motor Co. EEC-IV (Cont.)

1a-505

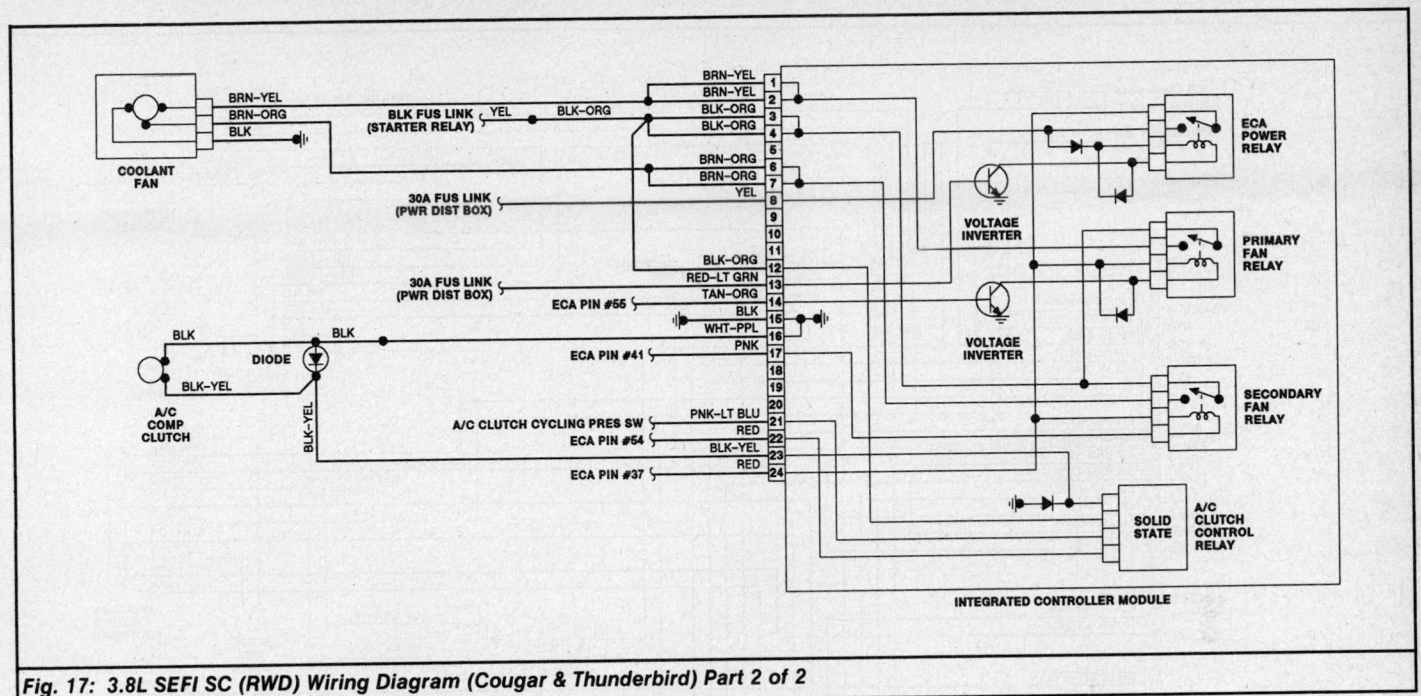

Fig. 17: 3.8L SEFI SC (RWD) Wiring Diagram (Cougar & Thunderbird) Part 2 of 2

1a-506

1989 Computerized Engine Controls
Ford Motor Co. EEC-IV (Cont.)

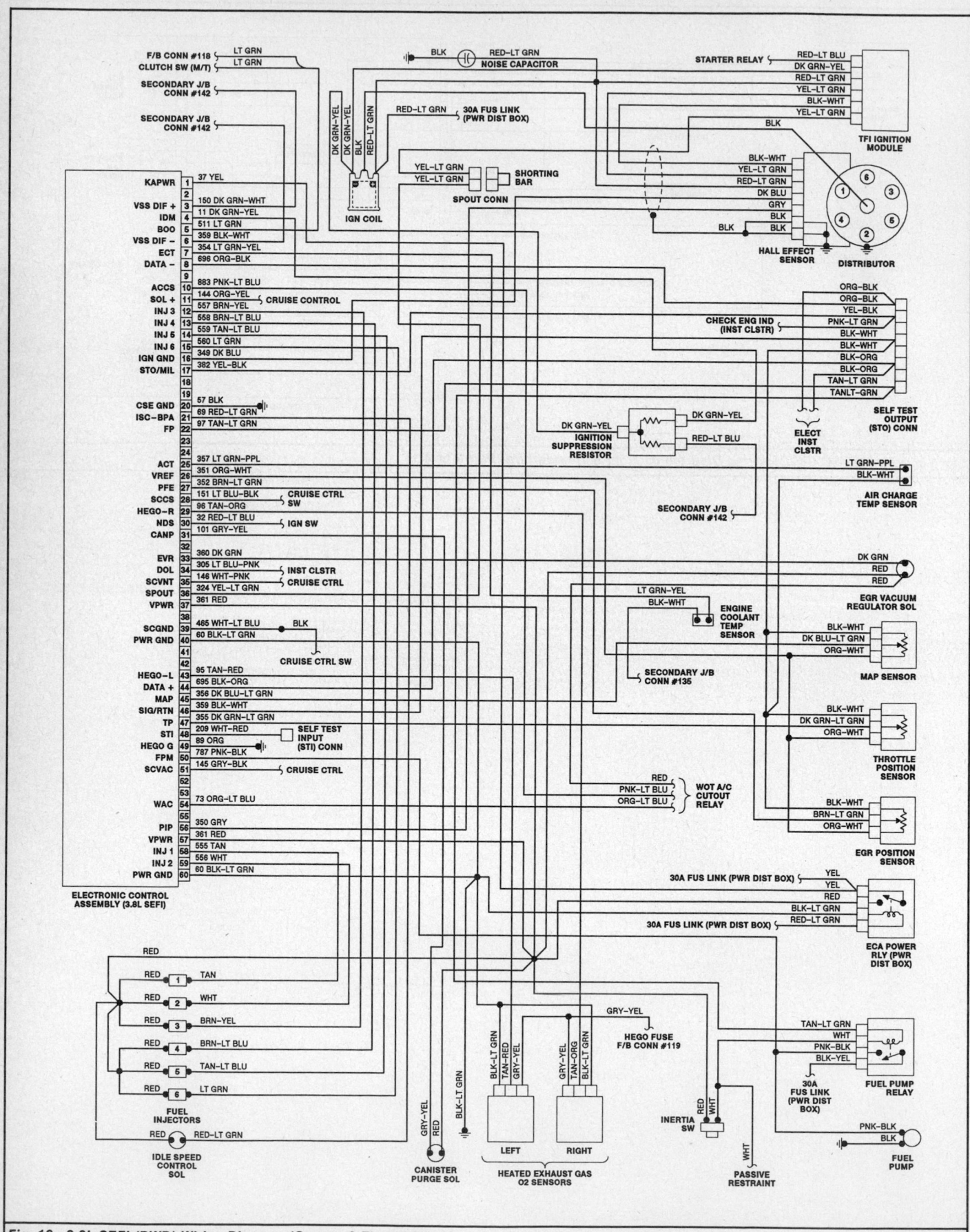

Fig. 18: 3.8L SEFI (RWD) Wiring Diagram (Cougar & Thunderbird)

1989 Computerized Engine Controls
Ford Motor Co. EEC-IV (Cont.)

1a-507

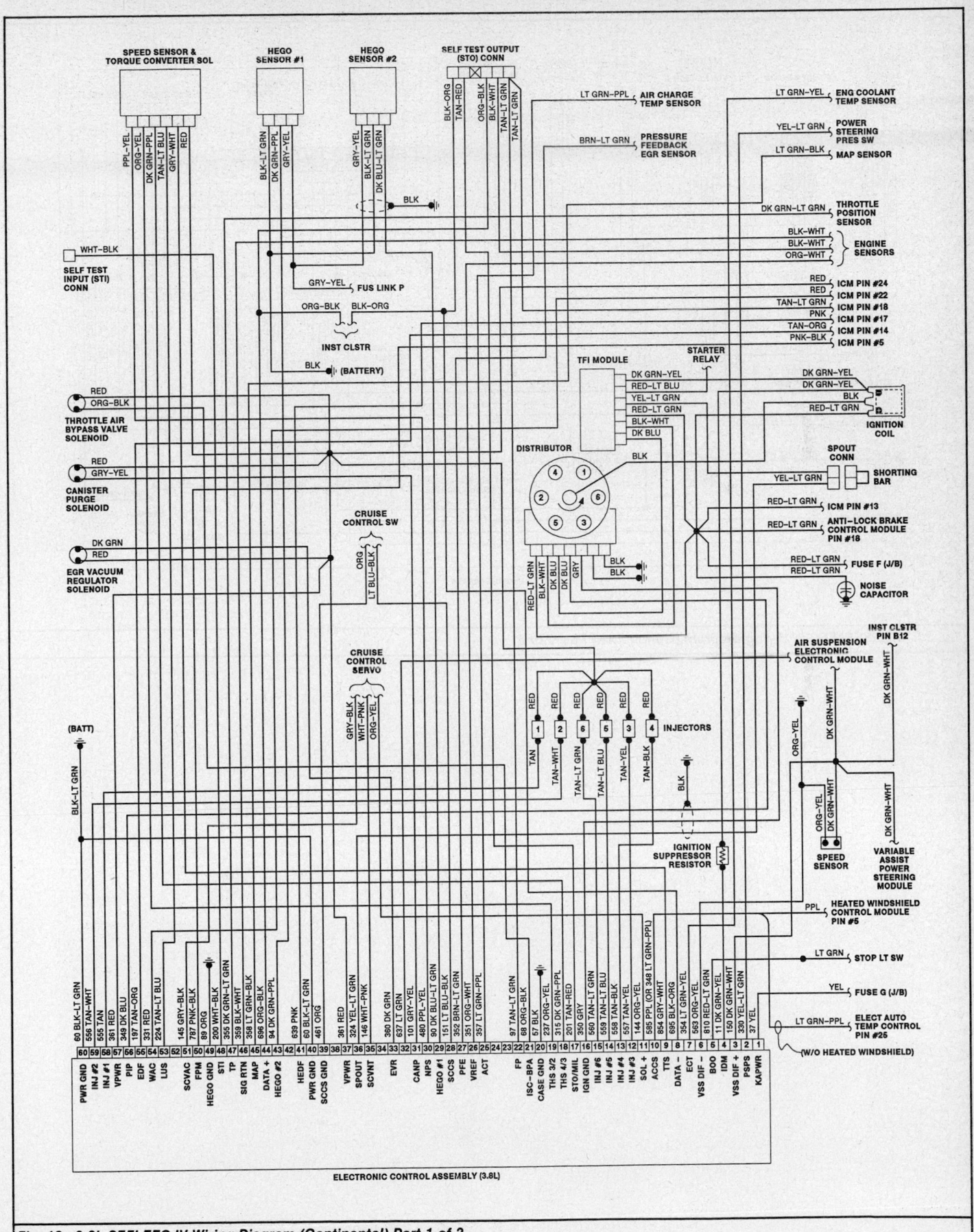

Fig. 19: 3.8L SEFI EEC-IV Wiring Diagram (Continental) Part 1 of 2

1989 COMPUTERIZED ENGINE CONTROLS
Ford Motor Co. EEC-IV (Cont.)

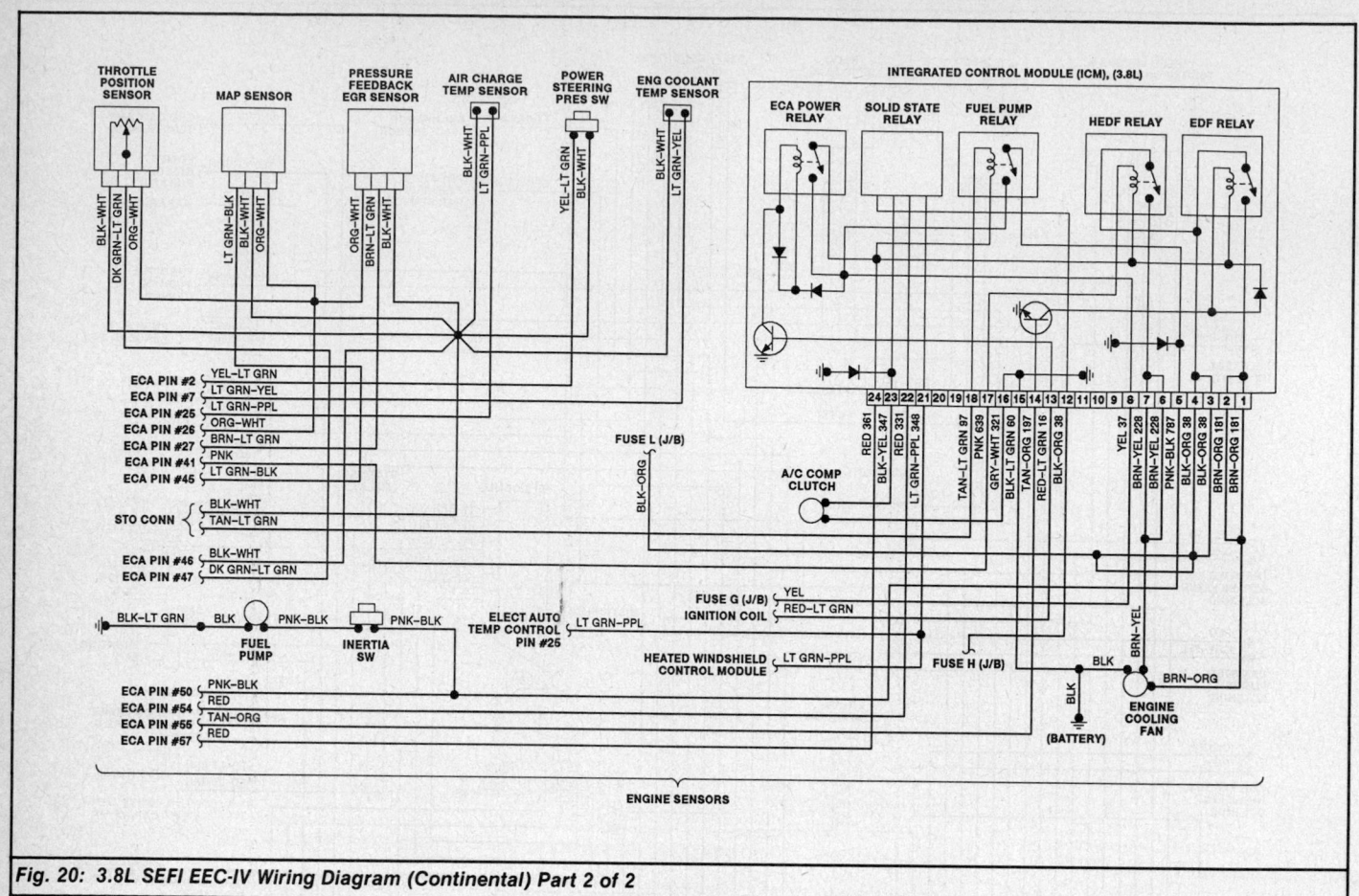

Fig. 20: 3.8L SEFI EEC-IV Wiring Diagram (Continental) Part 2 of 2

1989 Computerized Engine Controls
Ford Motor Co. EEC-IV (Cont.)

1a-509

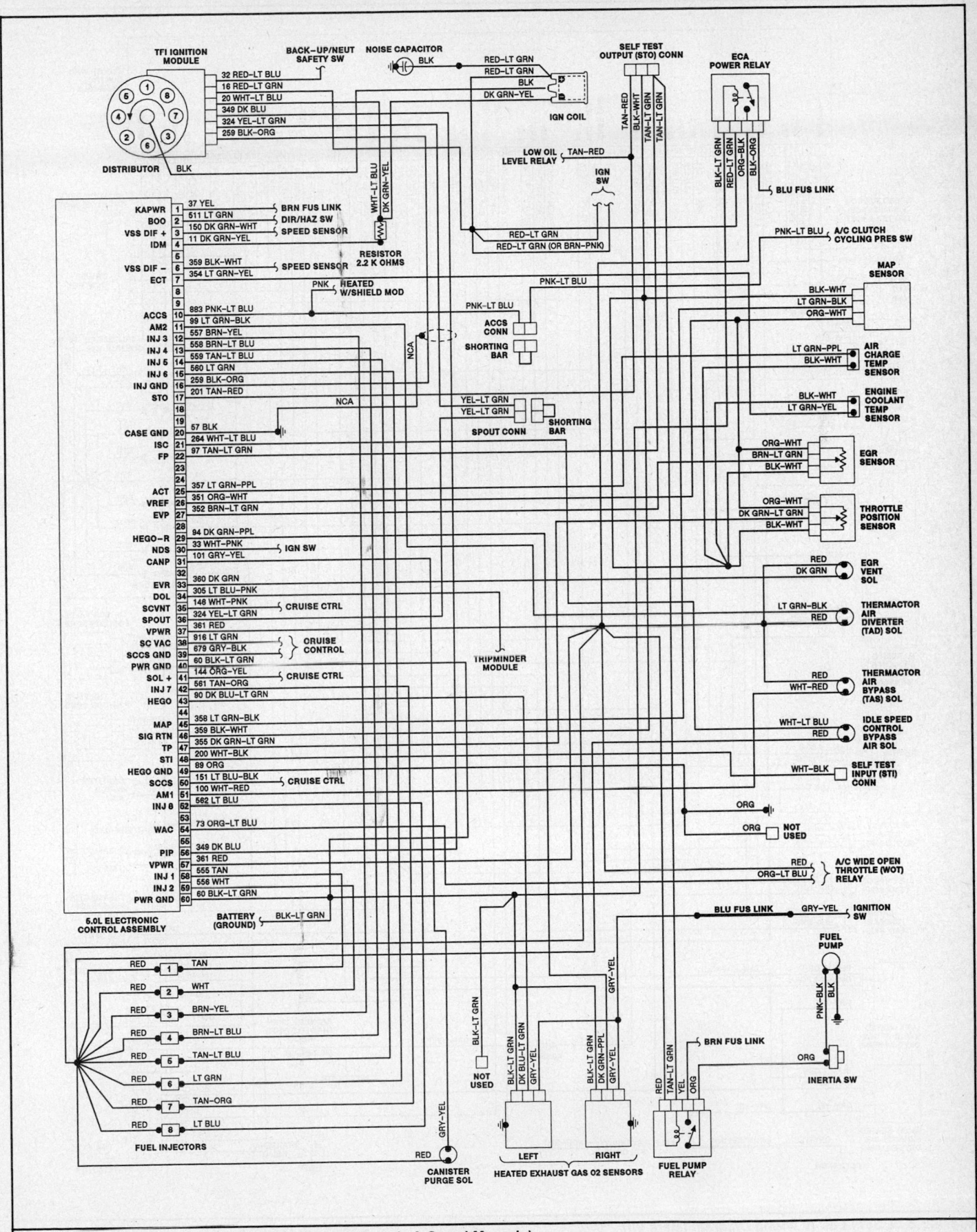

Fig. 21: 5.0L SEFI EEC-IV Wiring Diagram (Crown Victoria & Grand Marquis)

1989 COMPUTERIZED ENGINE CONTROLS
Ford Motor Co. EEC-IV (Cont.)

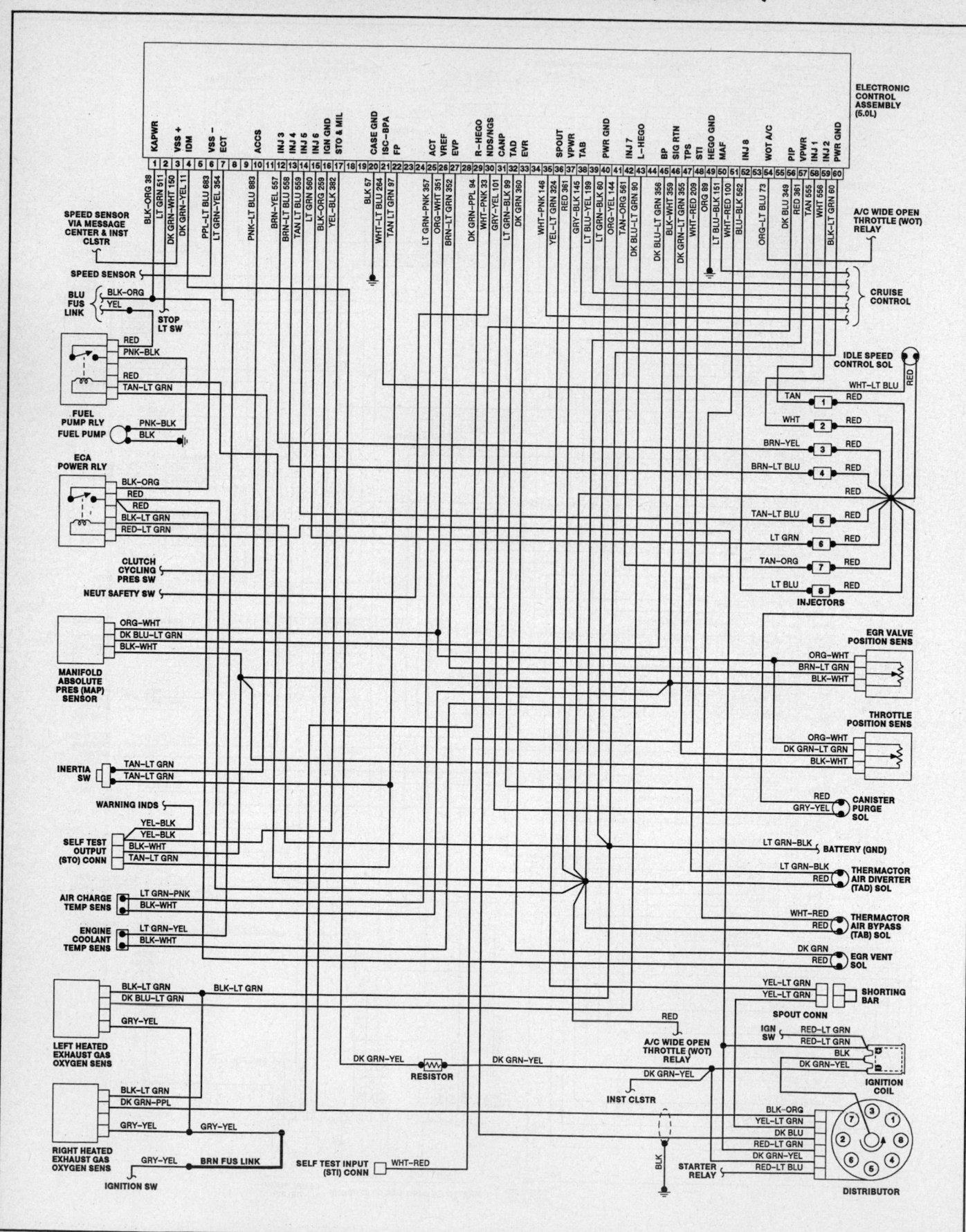

Fig. 22: 5.0L SEFI EEC-IV Wiring Diagram (Mark VII)

1989 Computerized Engine Controls
Ford Motor Co. EEC-IV (Cont.)

1a-511

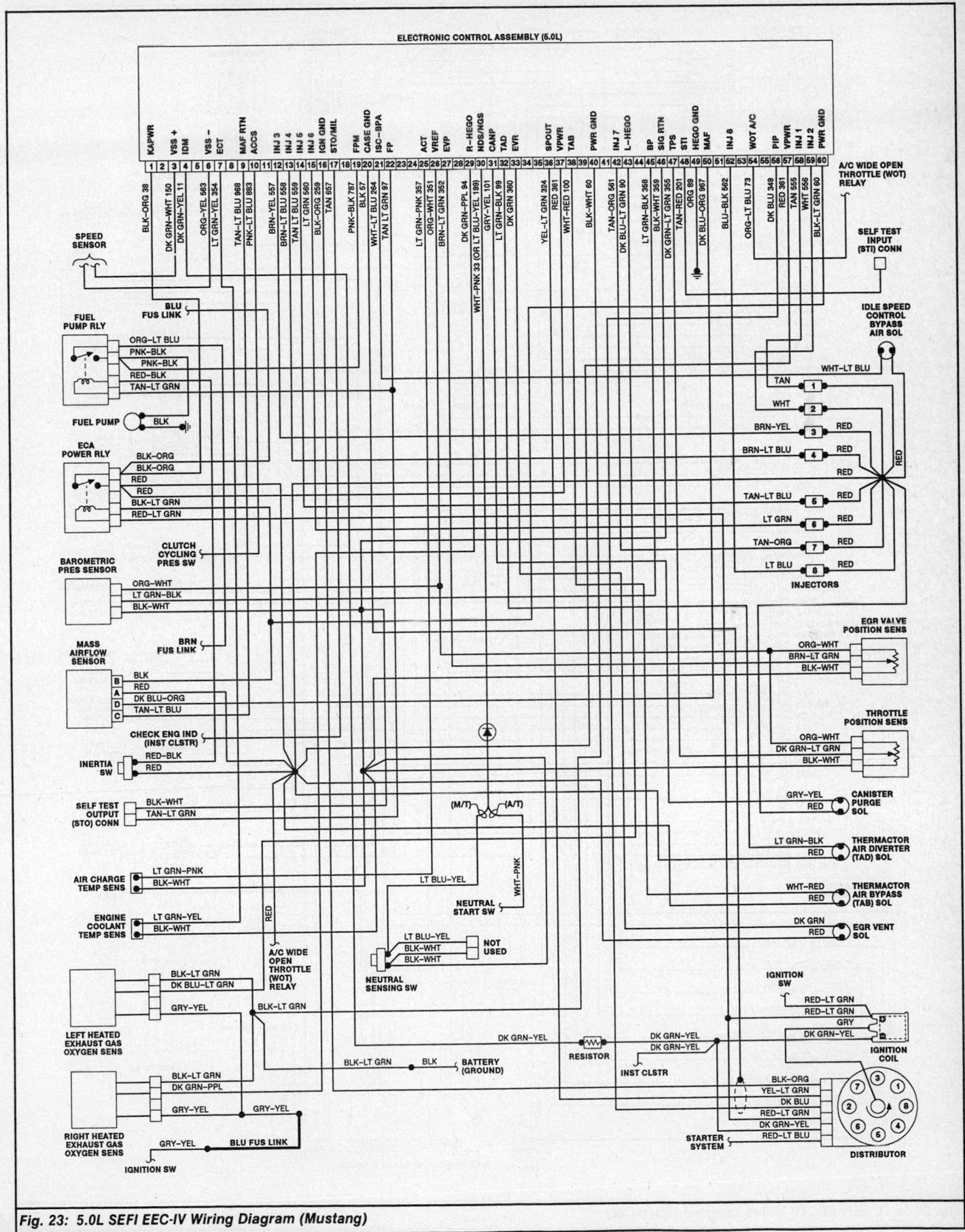

Fig. 23: 5.0L SEFI EEC-IV Wiring Diagram (Mustang)

1a-512

1989 Computerized Engine Controls
Ford Motor Co. EEC-IV (Cont.)

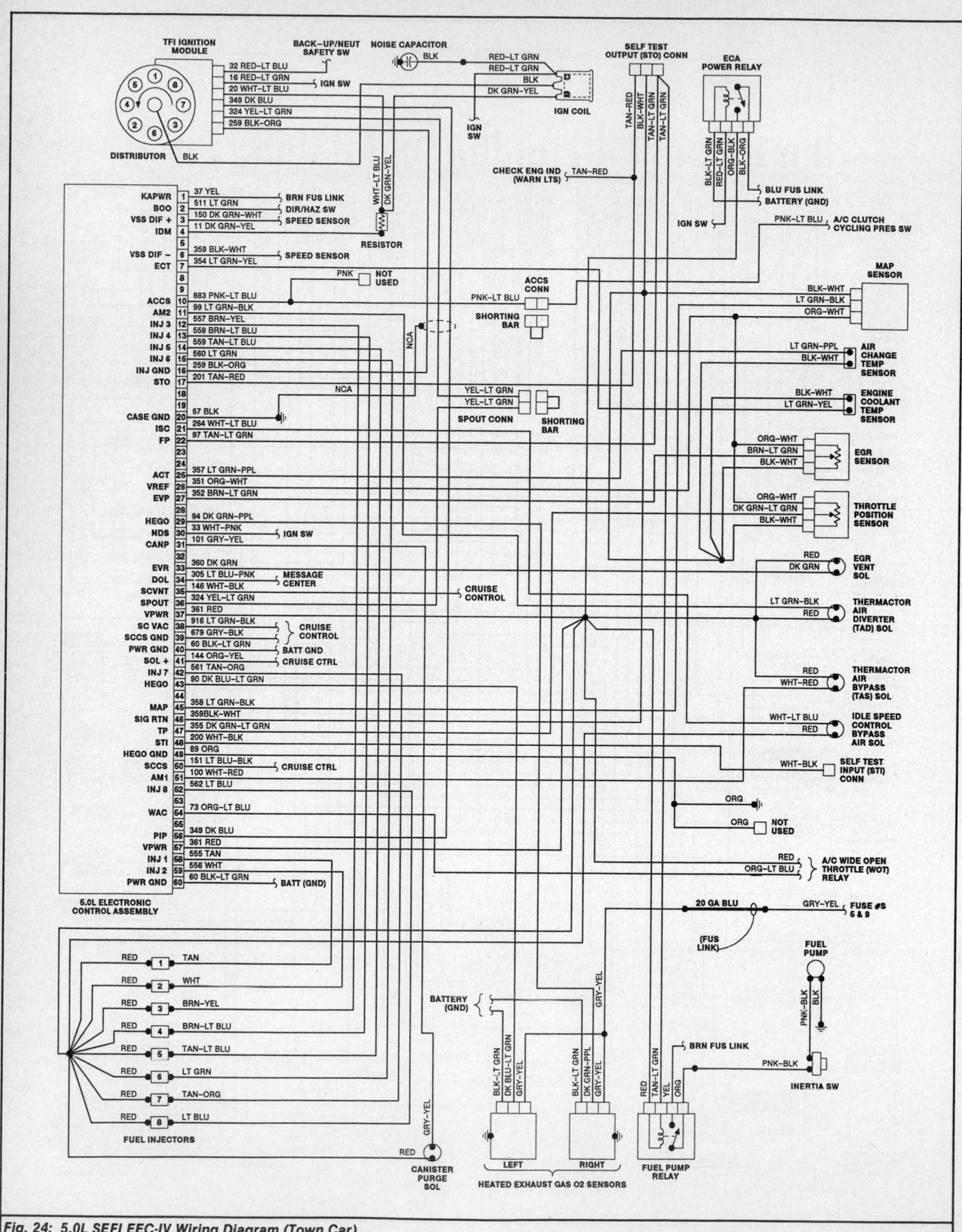

Fig. 24: 5.0L SEFI EEC-IV Wiring Diagram (Town Car)

5.8L Police

DESCRIPTION

The Microprocessor Control Unit (MCU) is located in the engine compartment and controls engine air/fuel ratios, air injection, canister purge, spark timing and idle speed.

The system consists of the MCU module, air/fuel control and air injection solenoids, engine sensors, feedback carburetor, and related circuitry.

OPERATION

MICROPROCESSOR CONTROL UNIT (MCU)

The MCU is a solid-state micro-computer located on the left fender panel. It is the "brain" of the system and receives inputs and sends signals through a 24-pin connector. The MCU is capable of operating in 3 modes: Initialization, Open loop and Closed loop.

Initialization mode occurs when the engine is started. In this mode the MCU richens the fuel mixture for easy starting. Open loop operation is controlled by MCU programming. Air/fuel ratio is fixed at a pre-determined level and allows good driveability at idle, moderate-to-heavy acceleration, and deceleration.

Closed loop operation occurs when the engine is warm and vehicle is operated at light load conditions. In closed loop, the MCU controls air/fuel mixture in response to signals from an oxygen sensor in the exhaust manifold.

ENGINE SENSORS

Coolant Temperature – There are 2 sensors used to signal temperature changes to the MCU. The sensors are mounted in coolant passages ahead of the carburetor. One sensor is open when the engine is warm; the other is open when the engine is cold and/or when it has overheated.

Vacuum Switches – Engine load is monitored by vacuum level. To measure vacuum level, 3 vacuum switches are used to signal the MCU of cruise, deceleration, and wide open throttle conditions.

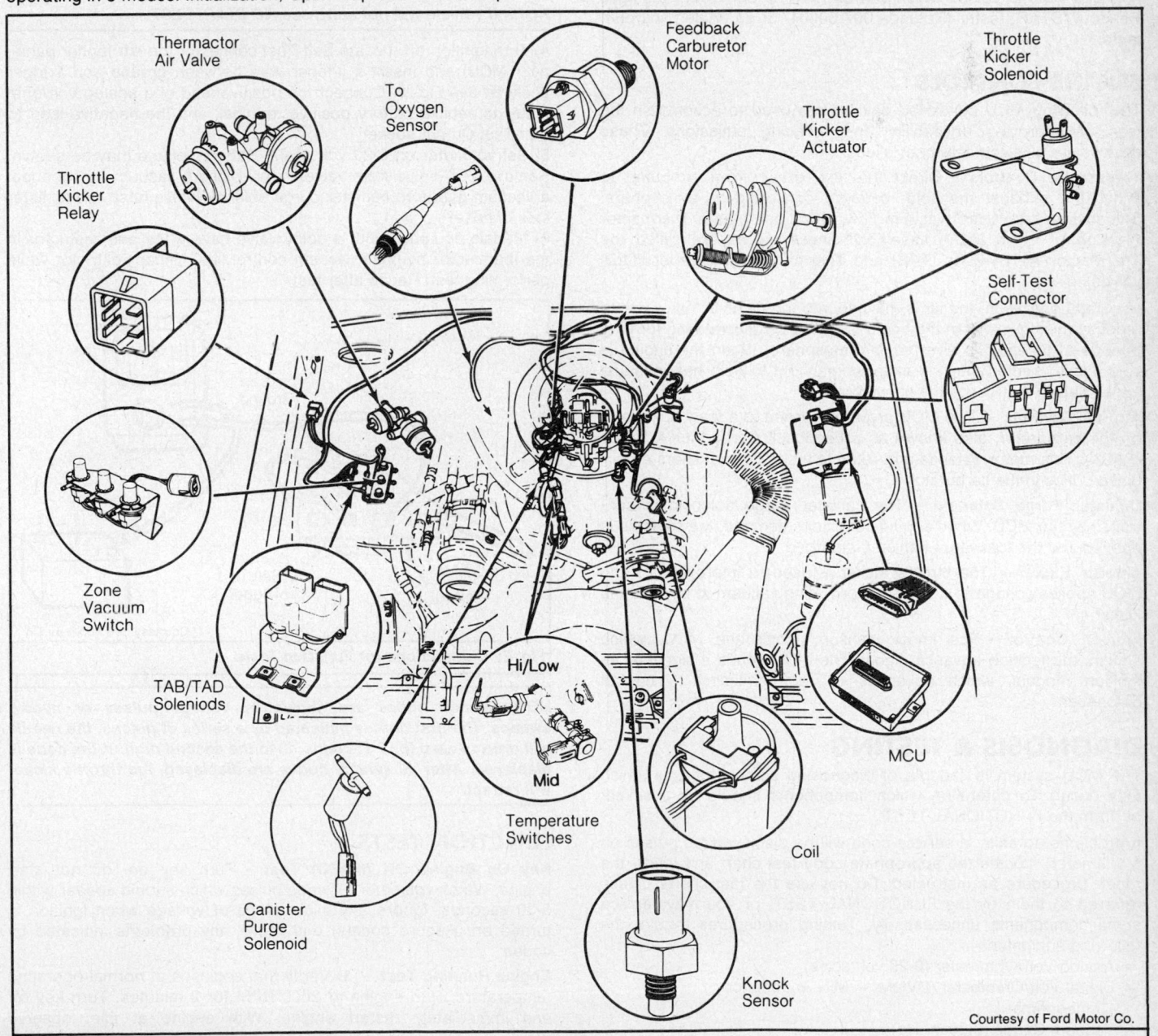

Fig. 1: 5.8L Police MCU System Layout

Courtesy of Ford Motor Co.

Oxygen Sensor – An electrically Heated Oxygen (HEGO) sensor is mounted in the rear of right exhaust manifold. This sensor sends a low voltage signal to the MCU to indicate rich or lean mixture. When mixture is lean, the signal is less than 0.2 volt. When mixture is rich, sensor voltage is slightly above 0.6 volt.

Engine Speed – The MCU receives a direct signal from the "Tach Test" terminal on the coil. It uses this signal to monitor engine speed and adjust the air/fuel ratio, based on this speed.

Knock Sensor – The knock sensor is used to help reduce detonation. It produces and transmits a voltage signal during detonation. The MCU uses this signal to adjust ignition timing. The MCU otherwise does not control ignition timing.

Barometric Pressure Sensor – The MCU uses a barometric pressure signal to adjust engine function in relation to altitude changes. The MCU modifies the air/fuel ratio to provide accurate mixture for all altitudes.

Self-Test Connector – The MCU can self-diagnose most common operating problems. In order to initiate and read the diagnostic program, connections are made to the Self-Test connector. It provides voltage pulses which can be read by Self-Test Automatic Readout (STAR) tester (Rotunda 007-00004) or an analog volt/ohm meter.

ENGINE CONTROLS

The following MCU controlled devices are used to accomplish the task of improving driveability and reducing emissions. These devices are all electrically controlled.

Thermactor Controls – Direct the flow of air from air pump to either the exhaust manifold, catalytic converter or atmosphere. Solenoid valves control vacuum flow which operates a Thermactor Air Control Valve (ACV) assembly. These valves are called the Thermactor Air By-Pass (TAB) and Thermactor Air Diverter (TAD) valves.

In normal operation, the air is injected into the catalytic converter to reduce emissions. When the engine is idling or decelerating for long periods of time, air is diverted to atmosphere. When the engine is cold, air is injected into the exhaust manifold to help heat exhaust gases before they reach the converter.

Air/Fuel Controls – The MCU provides current to a feedback motor on the carburetor, also known as a Feedback Carburetor Actuator (FBCA). This motor extends and retracts a shaft which alters an air-bleed orifice in the carburetor.

Canister Purge Solenoid – The canister purge solenoid is controlled by the MCU. When engine conditions demand, the solenoid is opened and the fuel vapor canister is purged.

Throttle Kicker – The throttle kicker is used to improve idle. The MCU applies voltage to a solenoid, providing vacuum to operate the kicker.

Ignition Control – The knock sensor signals the MCU, which adjusts the ignition advance signal. The MCU sends a signal to an ignition module, which advances or retards timing to control detonation.

DIAGNOSIS & TESTING

The MCU system is capable of diagnosing some problems which may occur. To determine which components should be checked, perform the FUNCTIONAL TEST.

If problems do exist, a service code will be displayed (as pulses on a voltmeter). Locate the appropriate code test chart and follow the repair procedure as instructed. Do not use the test charts unless referred to them by the FUNCTIONAL TEST, or you may replace some components unnecessarily. Testing procedures require the following equipment:

- Analog Volt/Ohmmeter (0-20 volt scale)
- Digital Volt/Ohmmeter (DVOM – Min. impedance 10 megohms)
- Vacuum Gauge (0-30 in. Hg)

- Vacuum Pump
- Tachometer
- Jumper Wire
- Timing Light
- Test Light (12-volt)
- Torque Wrench with deep 1 1/8" socket
- Steel Rod (socket extension) and 4 oz. Hammer
- Watch with second hand

PREPARATION FOR TESTING

1) Check vacuum hoses for leaks, cracks, or improper routing. Repair or replace as necessary. Check coolant level.
2) Check electrical connections. Repair any frayed or broken wires. Ensure that all connections are clean and tight.
3) Turn off all accessories. Place transmission in Neutral and set parking brake. Warm engine to normal operating temperature. If air cleaner must be moved, leave all vacuum hoses attached. Check to see that battery voltage is present at electric choke terminal while engine is running.

NOTE: If vehicle will not start, see NO START TEST.

4) Turn ignition off. Locate Self-Test connector (on left fender panel, near MCU) and insert a jumper wire between ground and Trigger sockets. *See Fig. 2.* Connect the positive lead of a analog volt/ohm meter to vehicle battery positive terminal, and the negative lead to Self-Test Output socket.
5) Set voltmeter on 0-20 volt scale. Battery voltage may be shown. Remove PCV valve from valve cover. Using a vacuum tee, connect a vacuum gauge to canister purge solenoid valve hose, on canister side of hose.
6) Models equipped with a delay valve have a tee and restrictor in the thermactor by-pass vacuum control line. Uncap restrictor while performing test. Recap after test.

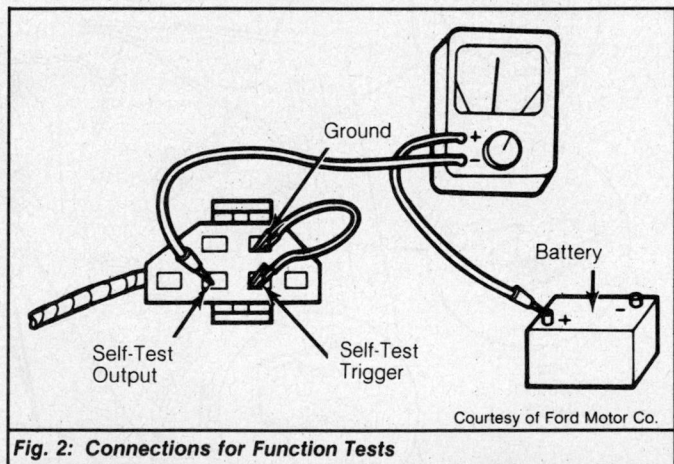

Ground

Battery

Self-Test Output

Self-Test Trigger

Courtesy of Ford Motor Co.

Fig. 2: Connections for Function Tests

NOTE: Service codes are shown by voltage pulses or needle sweeps. The first digit is indicated by a series of pulses, the needle will drop to zero for 2 seconds, then the second digit of the code is displayed. After all service codes are displayed, the throttle kicker will retract.

FUNCTION TESTS

Key On Engine Off (KOEO) Test – Turn key on, do not start engine. Watch voltmeter for code pulses which should appear within 5-30 seconds. Ignore any initial surge of voltage when ignition is turned on. Record code(s) and repair any problems indicated by codes.

Engine Running Test – **1)** Verify that engine is at normal operating temperature. Run engine at 2000 RPM for 2 minutes. Turn key off and immediately restart engine. With engine at idle, observe

1989 COMPUTERIZED ENGINE CONTROLS
Ford Motor Co. V8 MCU Control System (Cont.)

1a-515

voltmeter and vacuum gauge for initialization pulses after restarting engine. Throttle kicker should come on (engine speed increases) at this time and remain on throughout test.

2) To test knock sensor (if equipped), have steel bar (socket extension) and 4 oz. hammer ready. As soon as 4 initialization pulses appear, hold steel bar against manifold near knock sensor. Tap bar lightly with hammer for 15 seconds.

NOTE: If voltmeter and vacuum gauge do not pulse, or show steady high or low readings, see NO SELF-TEST OUTPUT.

NOTE: If more than 4 initialization pulses appear, check for open circuit between coil and MCU connector pin No. 8.

3) Observe and record service codes. When codes are complete (about 90 seconds), throttle kicker will retract. Stop engine, remove test equipment and reconnect PCV valve. Perform tests for codes in the order that codes were displayed.

NOTE: When Code 1-1 (Code 6-2 for vehicles above 4000 ft.) is displayed for vehicles with a drive complaint of detonation (at WOT only) and/or poor performance, and vehicle is equipped with a universal ignition module, perform SPARK KNOCK TEST. On all other vehicles, testing is complete and MCU is functioning.

MCU DIAGNOSTIC TEST CODES

Code	System Component
1-1	Continue QUICK TEST
1-1 & 6-2 [1]	Barometric Pressure Switch
1-2	RPM Out of Range
2-5	Knock Sensor
4-1	Lean Fuel Mixture
4-2	Rich Fuel Mixture
4-4	Thermactor System
4-5	Thermactor Air Upstream
4-6	Air Not By-passing
5-3 & 5-4	Temperature Switch Open
5-1 & 5-5	Open "Zone Vacuum" Switch
6-1 & 6-5	Closed "Zone Vacuum" Switch

[1] – Code 1-1 above 4000 ft. of elevation.
Code 6-2 below 4000 ft. of elevation.

NON-CODE TESTS

No Start Test – This test identifies faults in the MCU only, not other causes of No-Start condition.

1) Turn ignition off. Disconnect coil "horseshoe" shaped connector from coil, and vehicle harness from ignition module (4-wire connector). Check resistance between coil connector "Tach Test" terminal and ground. If resistance is less than 1K ohms, go to next step. If resistance is greater than 1K ohms, MCU is okay.

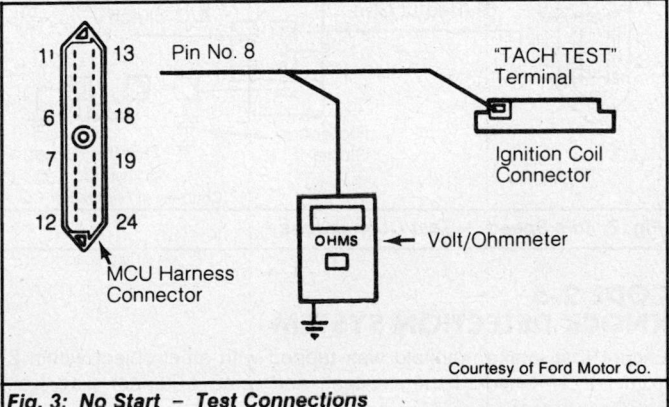

Fig. 3: No Start – Test Connections

Courtesy of Ford Motor Co.

2) Disconnect vehicle harness connector at MCU. Measure resistance between pin No. 8 of harness connector and ground. *See Fig. 3.* If greater than 1K ohms, replace MCU and re-test. If less than 1K ohms, repair circuit from MCU to ignition coil connector and re-test.

No Self-Test Output – Disconnect jumper wire from Self-Test Trigger in Self-Test connector.

1) Disconnect harness connector at MCU. Connect a voltmeter between pins No. 14 and 20 in harness connector. With ignition on, 10.5 volts or more should be present. If so, go to step **3)**. If not, go to next step.

2) Connect voltmeter between pin No. 20 and ground. If voltage reading is more than 10.5 volts, repair circuit from pin No. 14 to ground, and re-test. If voltage reading is not 10.5 volts, repair circuit from pin No. 20 to battery and re-test.

3) With ignition off, check continuity of circuit from Self-Test connector (Black/Light Green wire) to ground. If resistance is less than 1K ohms, go to next step. If resistance is greater than 1K ohms, repair circuit.

4) Check continuity between MCU harness connector Pin No. 19 and Self-Test Trigger socket (Tan/Red wire). If resistance is less than 5 ohms, go to next step. If resistance is greater than 5 ohms, repair circuit, and re-test.

5) Check continuity between harness connector Pin No. 8 and "Tach Test" lead at coil "horseshoe" connector (remove connector from coil). If resistance is 5 ohms or less, go to next step. If resistance is greater than 5 ohms, repair circuit and re-test.

6) Disconnect harness connector at canister purge solenoid. Check continuity between MCU connector Pin No. 9 and Gray/Yellow wire at canister purge connector. Also check between Pin No. 20 and Gray/Yellow wire. If resistance of each circuit is less than 5 ohms, go to next step. If resistance is greater than 5 ohms, repair circuit and re-test.

7) Connect ohmmeter across canister purge solenoid. Resistance should be 50-100 ohms. If not, replace solenoid. Retest. If no service code is present, replace MCU. If resistance is within specifications, go to next step.

8) Connect ohmmeter between engine ground and Gray/Yellow harness wire at canister purge solenoid. If resistance is less than 1K ohms, go to next step. If resistance is greater than 1K ohms, repair short circuit to ground, and re-test.

9) Check to ensure canister purge solenoid passes vacuum when energized with 12 volts, and blocks vacuum when de-energized. Check housing for leaks. If solenoid is okay, replace MCU, and re-test. If not, replace solenoid and re-test.

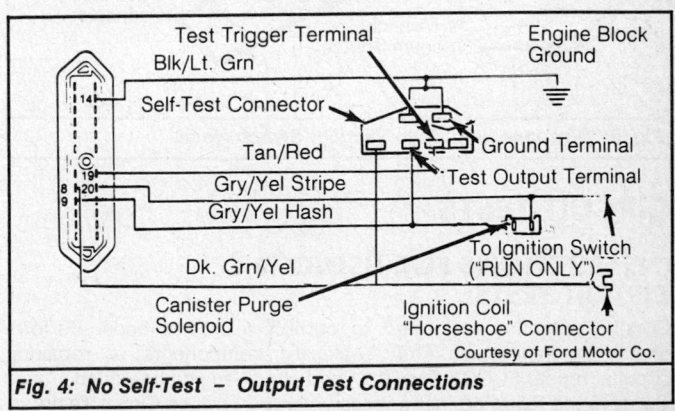

Fig. 4: No Self-Test – Output Test Connections

Courtesy of Ford Motor Co.

NOTE: Spark Knock Test should be performed if spark knock is detected only at wide open throttle, or engine exhibits poor performance or mileage.

Spark Knock Test – **1)** Disconnect knock sensor, check ignition timing and reset as necessary. With engine at normal operating temperature, disconnect 2-wire ignition module connector (Yellow and Black/White wires). Jumper wires together at module. *See Fig. 5.*

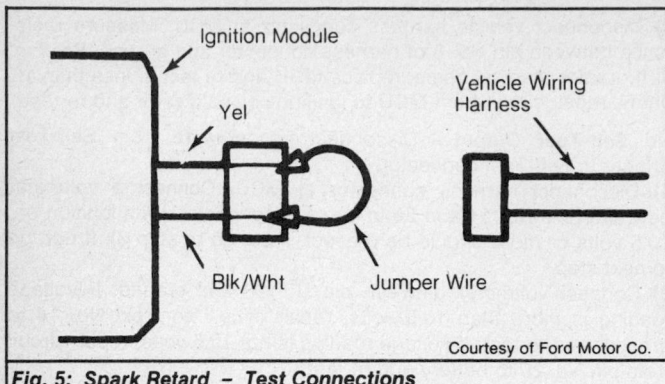

Fig. 5: Spark Retard – Test Connections

2) Check ignition timing. If timing retards 16-20 degrees, reconnect module and go to next step. If timing does not retard 16-20 degrees, replace module and repeat test.

3) With vehicle at normal operating temperature, set fast idle screw on cam step that will maintain engine speed above 2400 RPM. Read and record ignition timing.

4) Locate zone vacuum switch assembly, remove and plug vacuum supply hose. *See Fig. 6.* Recheck timing. If timing retards more than 5 degrees, go to step **6)**. If timing does not retard 5 degrees, go to next step.

5) With engine at 2400 RPM, disconnect 2-wire connector at ignition module. If timing retards, check Yellow wire for short to ground. If okay, replace MCU and re-test. If timing does not retard, check Yellow wire for open circuit. If okay, replace MCU and re-test.

6) Reconnect knock sensor. Repeat ENGINE RUNNING TEST under FUNCTION TESTS, but do not simulate knock by tapping rod on intake manifold. If service code 25 is obtained, MCU system is okay. If any other code is observed, replace knock sensor and re-test.

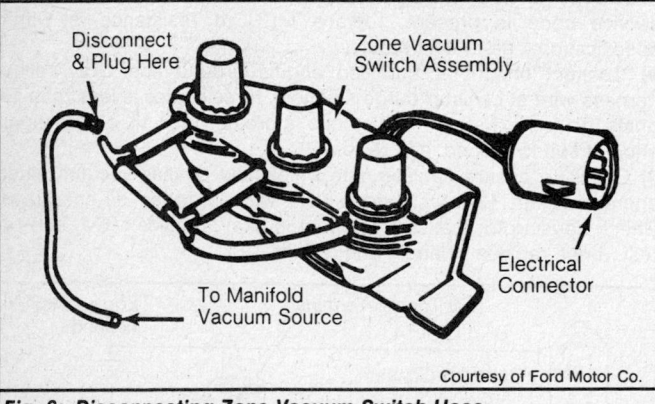

Fig. 6: Disconnecting Zone Vacuum Switch Hose

CIRCUIT TESTS

INSTRUCTIONS FOR USING THE CIRCUIT TESTS

Circuit Tests are performed to correct a service code. Perform check as instructed. After replacing components or repairing circuits, repeat FUNCTION TEST and check engine operation. Observe the following instructions when performing Circuit Tests:

- Do not measure voltage or resistance at MCU, or connect test lamps to it (unless specific instructions say to do so).
- Disconnect both ends of a circuit when checking for continuity or shorts. Ensure ignition is turned off.
- Disconnect solenoids and switches from harness before measuring resistance or continuity.
- When more than one service code is indicated, start service with the first code received.
- Use diagrams to locate pin locations and connectors.

NOTE: Partial wiring diagrams are provided for most CIRCUIT TESTS to aid in servicing. For complete system wiring diagram and connector terminal locations, see Fig. 17.

CODE 1-2
IDLE SPEED INCORRECT

Adjust carburetor idle speed and re-test. Check all connections to carburetor, throttle actuator, and throttle kicker solenoid. Repair if necessary, and repeat test.

1) Disconnect Self-Test input. Tee vacuum gauge to throttle kicker. Start engine and run at idle. Turn A/C on. Vacuum should be present. Turn A/C off. No vacuum should be present.

2) If vacuum switches, turn ignition off and continue test. If no vacuum is present or vacuum does not switch, check vacuum line for leaks, blockage and correct routing. If system is okay, go to step **4)**.

3) Turn ignition off and apply 10 in. Hg vacuum to throttle actuator. Arm should extend and hold position while vacuum is applied. If not, repair or replace actuator and re-test. If actuator operates properly, go to next step.

4) Disconnect wiring from throttle kicker solenoid and measure resistance of solenoid. If resistance is between 45-90 ohms, go to next step. If not, replace solenoid and re-test.

5) Check circuit resistance between throttle kicker relay connector and solenoid, and between solenoid and ground. If resistance is less than 5 ohms, go to next step. If greater than 5 ohms, repair circuit and and re-test.

6) Disconnect harness connector from MCU and throttle kicker relay. Check circuits for continuity between MCU connector Pin No. 12 (Red/Light Green wire) and throttle kicker relay connector, and Pin No. 20 and relay connector (Gray/Yellow wire). If resistance is more than 5 ohms, repair circuit and re-test. If less than 5 ohms, go to next step.

7) Connect ohmmeter between MCU connector pin No. 12 and ground. If resistance is less than 1K ohms, repair short to ground in the circuit and re-test. If more than 1K ohms, go to next step.

8) Reconnect throttle kicker relay and solenoid to harness. Leave MCU connector disconnected. Ensure A/C is off. Turn ignition on, leaving engine off. Connect voltmeter across solenoid terminals (with connector on solenoid). Ground pin No. 12 of MCU connector and observe voltmeter. If greater than 10 volts, verify that circuit No. 69 is not shorted to circuit No. 687. *See Fig. 7.* Repair harness if necessary, or replace MCU module. If less than 10 volts, replace relay and re-test.

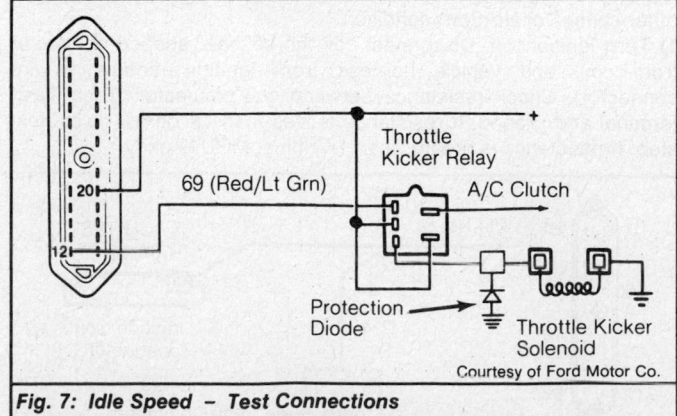

Fig. 7: Idle Speed – Test Connections

CODE 2-5
KNOCK DETECTION SYSTEM

Ensure that intake manifold was tapped with steel object within 2" from knock sensor. If not, re-test, and remove jumper wire from Self-Test trigger.

1) With ignition off, disconnect harness from knock sensor. Using 1 1/8" deep socket, loosen sensor and tighten to 12-18 ft. lbs. (16-24 N.m). Go to next step.

2) Disconnect MCU connector. Connect ohmmeter between engine ground and pin No. 13 of MCU connector. If resistance is less than 1K ohms, repair short circuit to ground, and re-test. If resistance is more than 1K ohms, go to next step.

3) Check continuity between pin No. 13 and knock sensor connector (Yellow/Red wire). If less than 5 ohms, go to next step. If more than 5 ohms, repair circuit, and re-test.

4) Check continuity between pin No. 14 and knock sensor connector (Black/Light Green wire). If less than 5 ohms, connect MCU and go to next step. If more than 5 ohms, repair circuit, and re-test.

5) Reconnect Self-Test trigger jumper on Self-Test connector. Connect a test light to battery positive terminal. Disconnect knock sensor. Perform steps 1) and 2) of ENGINE RUNNING TEST. Instead of tapping manifold with rod, tap test light to Yellow/Red wire contact in knock sensor connector for 5 seconds.

6) Observe voltmeter. If code 25 appears, replace MCU, and re-test. If any other code appears, replace knock sensor, and re-test.

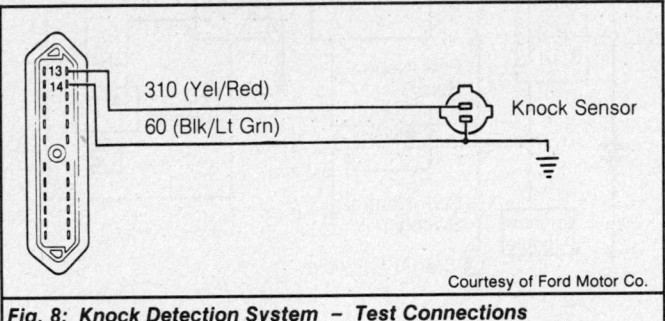

310 (Yel/Red)
60 (Blk/Lt Grn)
Knock Sensor

Courtesy of Ford Motor Co.

Fig. 8: Knock Detection System – Test Connections

CODE 4-1
FUEL ALWAYS LEAN

Run engine at 2000 RPM for one minute, and re-test. If code still appears, disconnect jumper wire from Self-Test connector and proceed.

CAUTION: To prevent damage to the oxygen sensor, never connect analog volt/ohmmeter to the sensor. Use digital volt/ohmmeter with 10 megohms (minimum) input impedance.

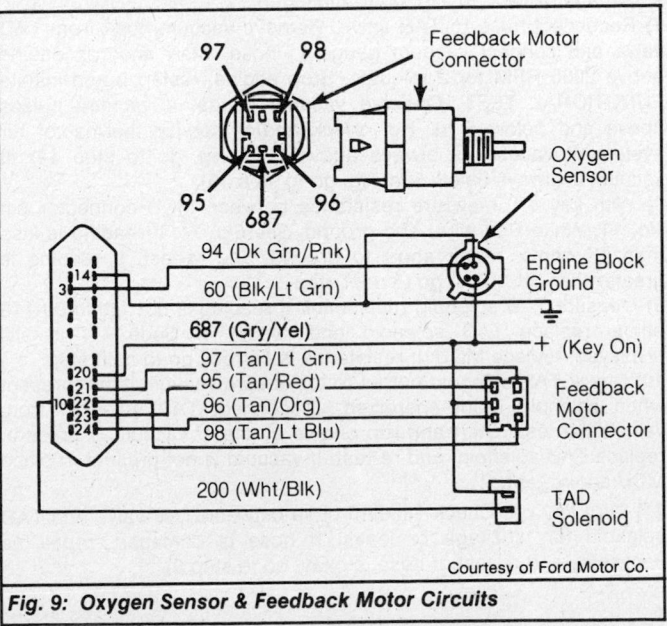

Feedback Motor Connector
97   98
95   96
687
Oxygen Sensor
94 (Dk Grn/Pnk)
60 (Blk/Lt Grn)
Engine Block Ground
687 (Gry/Yel)
+ (Key On)
97 (Tan/Lt Grn)
95 (Tan/Red)
96 (Tan/Org)
98 (Tan/Lt Blu)
Feedback Motor Connector
200 (Wht/Blk)
TAD Solenoid

Courtesy of Ford Motor Co.

Fig. 9: Oxygen Sensor & Feedback Motor Circuits

1) Turn ignition off. Disconnect oxygen sensor. Connect jumper wire from oxygen sensor (Dark Green/Pink wire) to harness. Connect DVOM between engine and jumper. Connect vacuum pump to zone vacuum switches.

2) Run engine at 2000-2300 RPM while applying 10-12 in. Hg to vacuum switch assembly. Wait 2 minutes, and check voltmeter. If voltage remains below 0.5 volt, go to next step. If voltage remains above 0.5 volt, go to step 8). If voltage alternates above and below 0.5 volt, go to step 17).

3) Turn engine off. Reconnect oxygen sensor. Disconnect thermactor air hose from air pump. Disconnect harness connector at MCU. Connect DVOM between MCU connector pin No. 3 and engine ground (pin No. 14). Run engine at idle.

4) Place carburetor on high idle cam. Depress CVR rod on top of carburetor to force system rich and observe voltmeter. If voltage is less than 0.5 volt, go to next step. If greater than 0.5 volt, go to step 8).

5) Turn engine off. Disconnect oxygen sensor (harness at MCU is still disconnected). Connect ohmmeter between MCU connector pin No. 14 and engine ground. If resistance is 5 ohms or less, go to next step. If resistance is more than 5 ohms, repair circuit, and re-test.

6) Check continuity of Dark Green/Pink wire. If resistance is 5 ohms or less, go to next step. If resistance is greater than 5 ohms, repair circuit.

7) Connect ohmmeter between engine ground and Dark Green/Pink wire. If resistance is less than 1K ohms, repair circuit, and re-test. If resistance is more than 1K ohms, replace oxygen sensor, and re-test.

8) Thermactor hose should still be disconnected from air pump. With ignition off, reconnect harness to MCU and oxygen sensor. Disconnect harness from feedback motor on carburetor. Using a known good feedback motor, connect harness to motor and fully depress shaft. Do not remove motor from carburetor. Apply 10-12 in. Hg vacuum to zone vacuum switches.

9) Start engine and set fast idle cam on low speed step. Observe feedback motor shaft and remove PCV hose from carburetor. Vehicle may run rough due to vacuum leak. If feedback motor shaft fully extends, reconnect PCV hose and thermactor hose, go to step 13). If shaft does not extend, reconnect PCV hose and go to next step. Disconnect substitute motor.

10) Turn ignition off. Disconnect harness connector at MCU and feedback motor. Check continuity of circuits from feedback connector to MCU connector. If resistance is more than 5 ohms in any circuit, repair circuit(s), and re-test. If less than 5 ohms in each circuit, go to next step.

11) With ignition off, connect ohmmeter lead to FBCA terminal No. 687 (Gray/Yellow wire) and to each of 4 outside FBCA terminals in turn. Measure resistance of each FBCA winding. If all resistances are 50-175 ohms at room temperature or above, go to next step. If any reading is not within 50-175 ohms, replace FBCA motor, and re-test.

12) Connect one ohmmeter lead to engine ground. Check all circuits in feedback harness connector (except Gray/Yellow wire) for continuity with ground. If resistance is more than 1K ohms in all circuits, replace MCU, and re-test. If less than 1K ohms, repair circuit, and re-test.

13) With ignition off, connect ohmmeter lead to feedback motor case and other lead to terminal 687 (Gry/Yel wire) of motor. If resistance is less than 190K ohms, replace motor, and re-test. If greater than 190K ohms, go to next step.

14) Remove feedback motor from carburetor. Check pintle shaft for binding or damage. Connect harness to motor and turn ignition on. Shaft should extend, then retract when ignition is turned off. If pintle binds, replace pintle and re-test. If motor is damaged or if pintle does not move, replace motor, and re-test. If motor is okay, reinstall motor in carburetor and reconnect harness.

15) Turn ignition off and disconnect vehicle harness from TAD solenoid. Connect an ohmmeter across terminals at TAD solenoid. If resistance is 50-100 ohms, go to next step. If resistance is less than

50 ohms or greater than 100 ohms, replace TAD solenoid, and re-test.

16) Disconnect harness connector at MCU. Measure resistance between ground and pin No. 10 (White/Black wire) in MCU connector. If resistance is less than 1K ohms, repair circuit, and re-test. If more than 1K ohms, reconnect harness at MCU and go to next step.

17) Check connections and operation of TAD solenoid and valve. If wiring and hoses are properly connected, check for carburetor leaks, hose routing errors, and operation of bowl vent solenoid.

CODE 4-2
FUEL ALWAYS RICH

1) Vehicle must be at normal operating temperature. Disconnect jumper wire between ground and Self-Test trigger. Ensure power is present at choke cap, cold enrichment circuit works, and that choke is off.

2) With ignition off, disconnect thermactor air hose at pump, and vehicle harness at oxygen sensor. Connect a voltmeter between oxygen sensor and ground. Disconnect PCV hose from carburetor. Run engine at 2400 RPM for 60 seconds, and observe voltmeter.

3) If voltage is greater than 0.5 volt, replace oxygen sensor and re-test. If voltage is less than 0.5 volt, reconnect PCV and oxygen sensor. Go to next step.

4) Turn ignition off. Disconnect vehicle harness from feedback motor on carburetor. Connect a known good motor (shaft fully depressed) to harness; leave original motor on carburetor. Turn ignition switch to "RUN" position. If shaft extends, then retracts slightly, go to next step. If motor does not extend, go to step 6).

5) Using a vacuum pump, apply 10-12 in. Hg vacuum to zone vacuum switches. Start engine and place on high step of fast idle cam. Let engine run for 2 minutes, force system rich by depressing CVR rod on top of carburetor. Observe test feedback motor. If shaft does not retract, disconnect motor and go to next step. If shaft retracts until flush, turn ignition off and reconnect thermactor hose. Go to step 8).

6) With ignition off, disconnect harness connector at MCU and feedback motor. Check continuity of all wires between feedback motor connector and MCU connector. If resistance in any circuit is more than 5 ohms, repair circuit, and re-test. If all are less than 5 ohms resistance, go to next step.

7) Connect one lead of ohmmeter to engine ground, and test pins from feedback motor connector (except Gray/Yellow wire). If resistance of each circuit is more than 1K ohms, go to next step. If resistance of any circuit is less than 1K ohms, repair circuit, and re-test.

8) Using ohmmeter, check resistance between feedback connector terminal No. 687 (Gray/Yellow wire) and each of 4 outside terminals. Measure resistance of each FBCA winding. If all resistances are 50-175 ohms at room temperature or above, replace feedback motor and re-test. If any winding is not 50-175 ohms, go to next step.

9) With ignition off, connect ohmmeter between feedback motor case and terminal No. 687 (Gray/Yellow wire) of motor. If resistance is less than 190K ohms, replace motor, and re-test. If resistance is greater than 190K ohms, go to next step.

10) Remove feedback motor from carburetor. Check pintle for binding or damage. Connect harness to motor and turn ignition on. Shaft should extend, then retract when ignition is turned off. If pintle binds, replace pintle and re-test. If motor is damaged or pintle does not move, replace motor, and re-test.

11) If motor is okay, check vacuum line routes, evaporative emission system, bowl vent solenoid, and crankcase for fuel contamination. If these items are okay, replace MCU and re-test.

CODE 4-4
THERMACTOR CHECK

1) Warm engine to normal operating temperature. Upper radiator hose should be hot and pressurized. Turn engine off. Restart engine at curb idle and immediately initiate FUNCTIONAL TEST within 10

seconds and record codes. If any other codes are displayed, go to appropriate tests. If Code 1-1 is displayed, continue with FUNC-TIONAL TEST. If Code 4-4 is displayed, go to next step.

2) Turn key off. Disconnect MCU from vehicle harness. Measure resistance from pin No. 11 (circuit No. 190) to dump relay pin No. 3, and from dump relay pin No. 4 to TAB solenoid. See Fig. 10. If both readings are less than 10K ohms, go to next step. If not, repair open in appropriate circuit.

3) With key off, measure resistance between dump relay pins No. 3 and 4. If reading is less than 5 ohms, replace dump relay and re-test. If reading is greater than 5 ohms, go to next step.

4) With MCU disconnected, measure resistance from pin No. 11 (circuit No. 190) to TAB solenoid. Turn key on to close dump relay contacts. If reading is less than 10K ohms, go to next step. If not, check MCU to TAB solenoid circuit and repair as necessary.

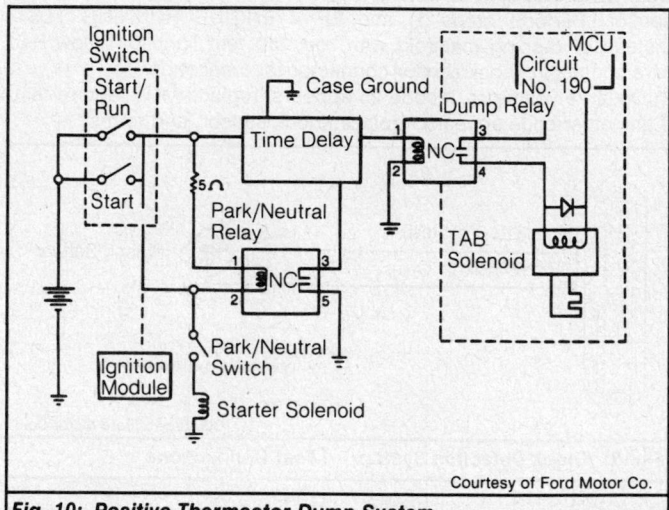

Courtesy of Ford Motor Co.

Fig. 10: Positive Thermactor Dump System

5) Reconnect all electrical and vacuum connections. Perform FUNCTIONAL TEST and record codes. If Code 4-4 is not displayed, service other codes as necessary. If Code 4-4 is still displayed, go to next step.

6) Remove vacuum hose from TAB valve and connect vacuum gauge to hose. Start and run engine above 2000 RPM for 2 minutes. Stop engine, restart it and initiate FUNCTIONAL TEST. Observe vacuum gauge. If vacuum is always above 5 in. Hg, go to step 8). If vacuum is always below 5 in. Hg, go to step 11). If vacuum pulses above and below 5 in. Hg, go to next step.

7) Reconnect hose to TAB valve. Remove vacuum hose from TAD valve and connect vacuum gauge to hose. Start and run engine above 2000 RPM for 2 minutes. Stop engine, restart it and initiate FUNCTIONAL TEST. Observe vacuum gauge. If vacuum pulses above and below 5 in. Hg, check and/or service thermactor air system. If vacuum is always above 5 in. Hg, go to step 14). If vacuum is always below 5 in. Hg, go to step 16).

8) With key off, measure resistance between MCU connector pin No. 11 (White/Red wire) and ground. See Fig. 11. If reading is less than 1K ohms, repair short to ground, and re-test. If reading is greater than 1K ohms, go to next step.

9) Measure TAB solenoid resistance. If reading is not within 50-110 ohms, replace TAB solenoid and re-test. If Code 4-4 is still displayed, replace MCU. If resistance is correct, go to next step.

10) Check TAB solenoid output to make sure vacuum is not present when solenoid is de-energized. Disconnect TAB solenoid from vehicle harness. Start and run engine at idle. If vacuum is present, replace TAB solenoid, and re-test. If vacuum is not present, replace MCU and re-test.

11) Turn key off. Check vacuum hose between TAB valve and TAB solenoid for blockage or leaks. If hose is damaged, repair as necessary and re-test. If hose is okay, go to step 9).

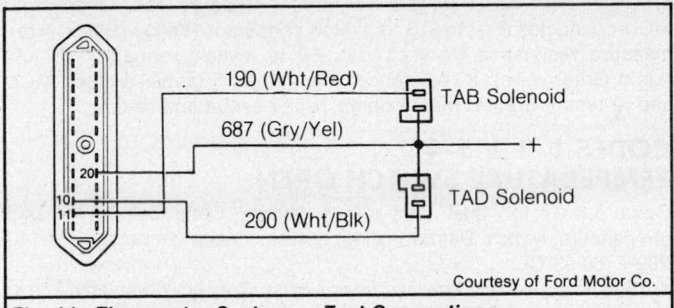

Fig. 11: Thermactor System – Test Connections

Courtesy of Ford Motor Co.

12) Check TAB solenoid output to ensure vacuum is present when solenoid is energized. Install a jumper wire from TAB solenoid circuit 190 to ground. Start and run engine at idle. If vacuum is not present, replace TAB solenoid and re-test. If Code 4-4 is still present, go to next step. If vacuum is present, go to next step.

13) Turn key off. Measure resistance between TAB solenoid and MCU (circuits No. 687 and No. 190). If reading is more than 5 ohms, repair circuit and re-test. If reading is 5 ohms or less, replace MCU and re-test.

14) With key off, measure resistance between circuit 200 and ground. If reading is less than 1K ohms, repair short to ground. If reading is more than 1K ohms, go to next step.

15) Check TAD solenoid output to make sure vacuum is not present when solenoid is de-energized. Disconnect TAD solenoid from vehicle harness. Start and run engine at idle. If vacuum is present, replace TAD solenoid, and re-test. If vacuum is not present, replace MCU and re-test.

16) Turn key off. Check vacuum hose between TAD valve and TAD solenoid for blockage or leaks. If hose is damaged, repair as necessary, and re-test. If hose is okay, go to next step.

17) With key off, measure TAD solenoid resistance. If reading is not within 50-100 ohms, replace solenoid and re-test. If Code 4-4 is still displayed, go to step **19)**. If resistance is correct, go to next step.

18) Check TAD solenoid output to make sure vacuum is present when solenoid is energized. Install a jumper wire from TAD solenoid circuit 200 to ground. Start and run engine at idle. If vacuum is not present, replace solenoid and re-test. If vacuum is present, go to next step.

19) Turn key off. Measure resistance between TAD solenoid and MCU (circuits No. 687 and 200). If reading is more than 5 ohms, repair circuit and re-test. If reading is 5 ohms or less, replace MCU and re-test.

CODE 4-5
THERMACTOR AIR DIVERTER

1) Ensure that TAD vacuum line restrictor was uncapped and free of obstruction. If plugged, clean out and re-test. If okay, go to next step.

2) Cap vacuum restrictor and remove vacuum delay valve from TAD vacuum control line. Reconnect system without delay valve and re-test. If Code 4-5 reappears, go to next step. If not, replace vacuum delay valve and re-test.

3) Remove vacuum hose from TAD valve and connect vacuum gauge to hose. Start and run engine above 2000 RPM for 2 minutes. Stop engine, restart it and initiate FUNCTIONAL TEST. Observe vacuum gauge. If vacuum pulses above and below 5 in. Hg, check and/or service thermactor air system. If vacuum is always above 5 in. Hg, go to step **8)**. If vacuum is always below 5 in. Hg, go to next step.

4) Check vacuum hoses between TAD valve and TAD solenoid, then between TAD solenoid and vacuum source for blockage, leaks, and proper routing. If hoses are damaged or improperly routed, repair as necessary, and re-test. If hoses are okay, go to next step.

5) With ignition off, remove TAD connector and measure TAD solenoid resistance. If between 50-110 ohms, go to next step. If not, replace solenoid and re-test.

6) Check TAD solenoid output to ensure vacuum is present when solenoid is energized. Using a jumper wire, jump circuit No. 200 (White/Black wire) to ground. Start and run engine at idle. If no vacuum is present, replace solenoid and re-test. If vacuum is present, go to next step.

7) With ignition off, disconnect harness connector from TAD solenoid and MCU. Measure resistance between MCU connector pin No. 20 and TAD solenoid Gray/Yellow wire, and between pin No. 10 and White/Black wire. If resistance is less than 5 ohms, replace MCU and re-test. If greater than 5 ohms, repair circuits and re-test.

8) Connect MCU. Leave TAD solenoid disconnected. Check that TAD solenoid output to make sure vacuum is not present when solenoid is de-energized. Start and run engine at idle. If vacuum is present, replace solenoid and re-test. If vacuum is not present, go to next step.

9) With ignition off, disconnect harness connector at MCU and TAD solenoid. Measure resistance between circuit No. 200 and ground. If reading is less than 1K ohms, repair short to ground and re-test. If reading is more than 1K ohms, replace MCU and re-test.

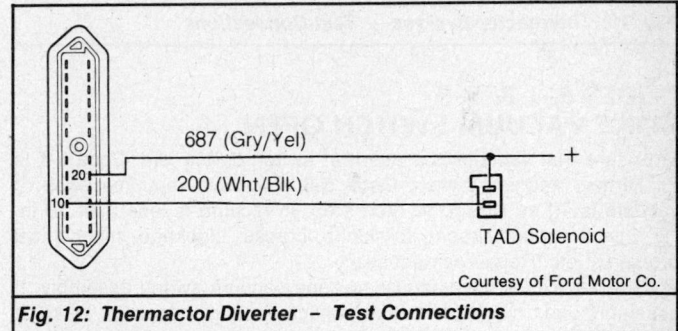

Fig. 12: Thermactor Diverter – Test Connections

Courtesy of Ford Motor Co.

CODE 4-6
THERMACTOR AIR BY-PASS

1) Ensure that TAB vacuum line restrictor was uncapped and free of obstruction. If plugged, clean out and re-test. If okay, go to next step.

2) Cap vacuum restrictor and remove vacuum delay valve from TAB vacuum control line. Reconnect system without delay valve and re-test. If Code 4-6 reappears, go to next step. If not, replace vacuum delay valve and re-test.

3) Start and warm engine to normal operating temperature. Ensure upper radiator hose is hot and pressurized. Stop engine and restart at curb idle. Immediately initiate FUNCTIONAL TEST within 10 seconds. Observe DVOM for codes. If any other code is displayed, go to appropriate test. If Code 1-1 is displayed, continue with FUNCTIONAL TEST. If Code 4-6 is displayed, go to next step.

4) Remove vacuum hose from TAB valve and connect vacuum gauge to hose. Start and run engine above 2000 RPM for 2 minutes. Stop engine, restart it, and initiate FUNCTIONAL TEST. Observe vacuum gauge. If vacuum pulses above and below 5 in. Hg, check and/or service thermactor air system. If vacuum is always above 5 in. Hg, go to step **8)**. If always below 5 in. Hg, go to next step.

5) Check vacuum hoses between TAB valve and TAB solenoid, and between TAB solenoid and vacuum source for blockage or leaks. If hoses are damaged, repair as necessary and re-test. If hoses are okay, go to next step.

6) Check TAB solenoid output to make sure vacuum is present when solenoid is energized. Jumper TAD solenoid circuit No. 190 (White/Red wire) to ground. Start and run engine at idle. If vacuum is not present, replace solenoid, and re-test. If vacuum is present, go to next step.

7) With ignition off, disconnect harness connectors at TAB solenoid and MCU. Measure resistance between MCU pin No. 11 (circuit No. 190) and TAB solenoid Wht/Red wire. If reading is more than 10 ohms, repair circuit and re-test. If reading is less than 10 ohms, replace MCU and re-test.

1a-520

1989 COMPUTERIZED ENGINE CONTROLS
Ford Motor Co. V8 MCU Control System (Cont.)

8) Connect harness connector at MCU. Leave TAB solenoid disconnected. Check TAB solenoid output to make sure vacuum is not present when solenoid is de-energized. Start and run engine at idle. If vacuum is present, replace solenoid and re-test. If vacuum is not present, go to next step.

9) Measure resistance between circuit No. 190 and ground. If reading is less than 1K ohms, repair short to ground and re-test. If reading is greater than 1K ohms, replace MCU and re-test.

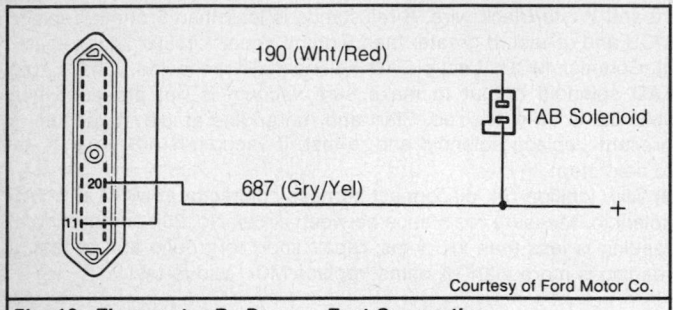

Fig. 13: Thermactor By-Pass – Test Connections

CODES 5-1 & 5-5
ZONE VACUUM SWITCH OPEN

1) Ensure that vacuum is present at switch during idle. Code 5-1 is for Hi/Low Vacuum switch, Code 5-5 is for mid-vacuum switch. If vacuum is 10 in. Hg, go to next step. If vacuum is less than 10 in. Hg, check vacuum hoses for kinks, cracks, blockage, mechanical problems, etc. Repair as necessary.

2) Turn key off. Apply vacuum to zone vacuum switch assembly. If assembly does not hold vacuum, check vacuum hoses for leaks. If no leaks are found, replace zone vacuum switch assembly, and re-test. If assembly holds vacuum, go to step **3)** for Code 5-1, and/or go to step **5)** for Code 5-5.

3) Turn key off. Disconnect hi/low vacuum switch from harness. Measure resistance across hi/low vacuum switch by inserting ohmmeter probes into switch connector. If resistance is less than 5 ohms, go to next step. If greater than 5 ohms, replace switch assembly, and re-test.

4) Disconnect MCU 24-pin connector. Measure resistance from MCU connector pin No. 5 to switch connector (Dark Green/Light Green wire), measure resistance from pin No. 14 to switch connector (Black/Light Green wire). If resistance is 5 ohms or less, replace MCU and re-test. If greater than 5 ohms, repair circuit and re-test.

5) Turn key off. Disconnect mid-vacuum switch from harness. Apply a minimum of 15 in. Hg vacuum to switch. Check resistance of switch (Yellow/Black-to-Black/Light Green wires). If resistance is greater than 5 ohms, replace switch assembly and re-test. If resistance is less than 5 ohms, reconnect hose and go to next step.

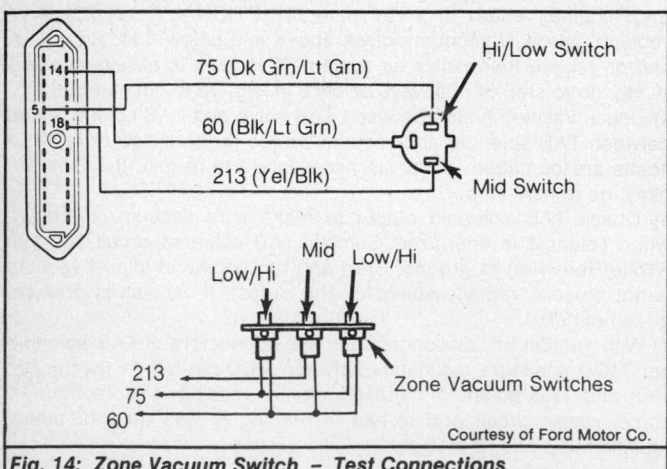

Fig. 14: Zone Vacuum Switch – Test Connections

6) Disconnect MCU 24-pin connector. Measure resistance from MCU connector Pin No. 18 to switch connector (Yellow/Black wire), measure resistance from pin No. 14 to switch connector (Black-/Light Green wire). If resistance is less than 5 ohms, replace MCU and re-test. If greater than 5 ohms, repair circuit and re-test.

CODES 5-3 & 5-4
TEMPERATURE SWITCH OPEN

Code 5-3 is for dual temperature switch, Code 5-4 is for mid-temperature. switch. Before testing, ensure coolant temperature is 140-200°F (60-93°C).

1) Disconnect vehicle harness from switch. Connect ohmmeter across switch terminals and measure resistance. If resistance is greater than 1K ohms, replace switch. If less than 5 ohms, go to next step.

2) Connect one lead of ohmmeter to Light Blue/Orange wire, then Orange/Red wire, and the other lead to ground. If resistance is 1K ohms or less in either location, repair circuit. If resistance is 1K ohms or more, go to next step.

3) Disconnect MCU harness connector. Check continuity of circuits from MCU side of connector to switch connector. (Pins No. 7 and 14 for dual temperature switch; pins No 14 and 17 for mid-temperature switch). If resistance is greater than 1K ohms, repair circuit and re-test. If less than 5 ohms, replace MCU module.

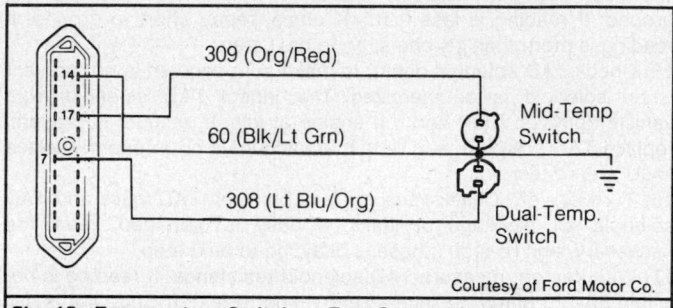

Fig. 15: Temperature Switch – Test Connections

CODE 6-2
BAROMETRIC PRESSURE SWITCH

1) Make sure that the barometric pressure switch connector is mated correctly with wiring harness connector. If not, reconnect and repeat FUNCTIONAL TEST.

2) Determine local altitude. Below 3500 ft., switch is normally open. Above 4000 ft., switch is normally closed. Do not test switch at altitudes between 3500 and 4000 ft., as switch may be in either condition. Disconnect harness connector from switch. Connect ohmmeter across switch terminals.

3) If resistance is greater than 10 ohms at altitudes above 4000 ft. or less than 1K ohms below 3500 ft., replace switch and repeat test. If resistance is less than 10 ohms at altitudes above 4000 ft. or more than 1K ohms below 3500 ft., go to next step.

4) Disconnect MCU harness connector. Check wires leading from MCU pins No. 14 and 6 to switch for continuity. If resistance of either wire is less than 10 ohms, replace MCU and re-test. If resistance is over 10 ohms in either wire, repair open circuit and re-test.

CODE 6-5
ZONE VACUUM SWITCH CLOSED

Ensure that engine is at normal operating temperature and that vacuum hoses are connected to zone vacuum switch assembly.

1) Turn key off. Disconnect zone vacuum switch from vehicle harness. Connect ohmmeter across mid-vacuum switch connector (Black/Light Green and Yellow/Black wires) and measure switch resistance. If reading is less than 1K ohms, replace switch assembly and re-test. If reading is greater than 1K ohms, reconnect vacuum hose and go to next step.

2) Disconnect vehicle harness from MCU. Connect ohmmeter between MCU connector pin No. 18 and engine ground. If resistance is greater than 1K ohms, replace MCU. If less than 1K ohms, repair circuits.

1989 Computerized Engine Controls
Ford Motor Co. V8 MCU Control System (Cont.)

1a-521

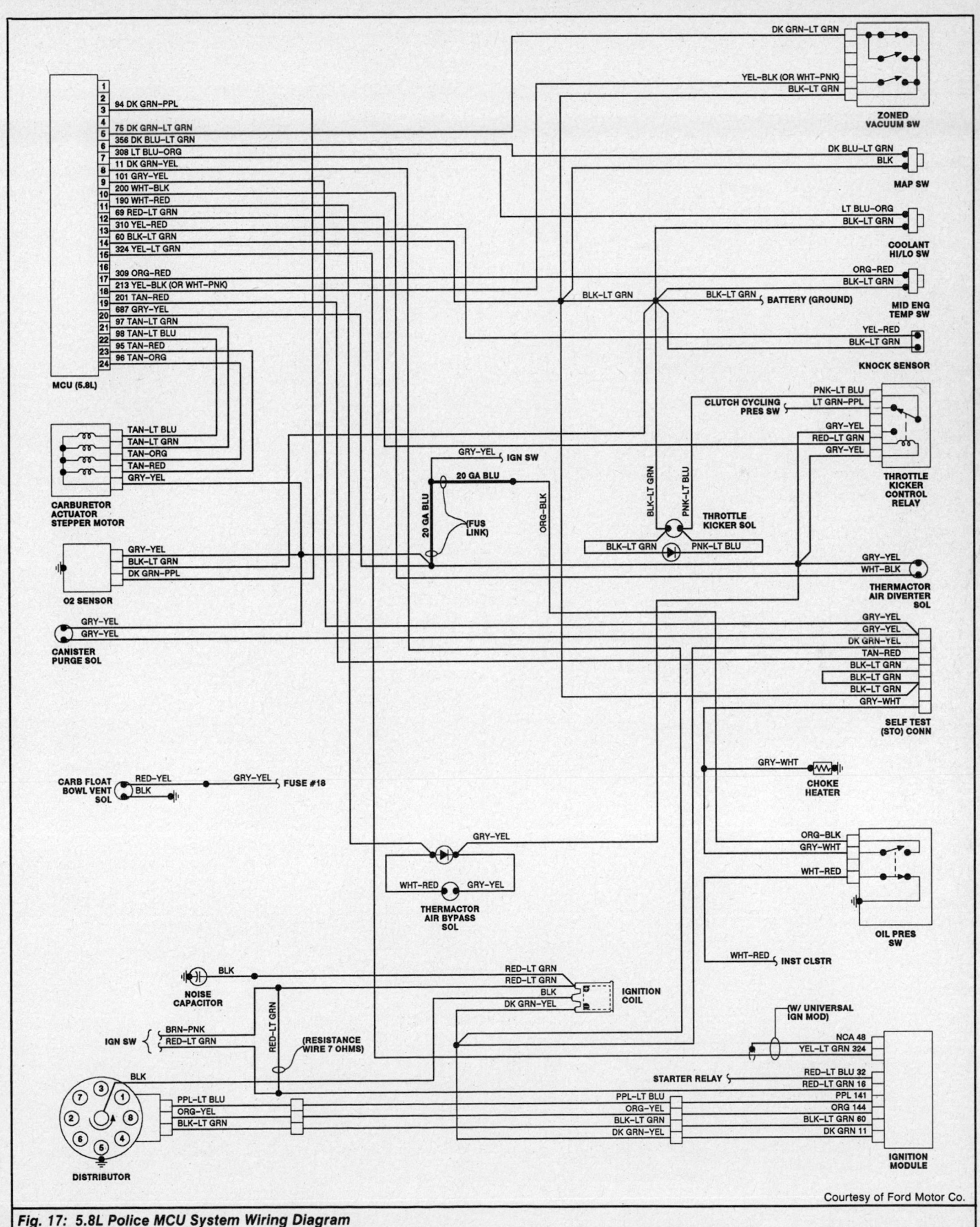

Fig. 17: 5.8L Police MCU System Wiring Diagram

Courtesy of Ford Motor Co.

Section 2

FUEL SYSTEMS

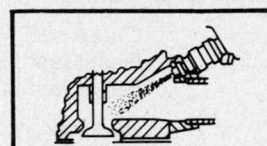

CONTENTS

TROUBLE SHOOTING   Page

Carburetor 2-2
Fuel Injection 2-3
Turbocharger 2-4
Supercharger 2-5

HOLLEY CARBURETORS

6280 2-Barrel
  Chrysler Motors 5.2L V8 2-6

MOTORCRAFT CARBURETORS

Model 7200 VV 2-Barrel
  Ford Motor Co. 5.8L V8 (Police Only) 2-9

ROCHESTER CARBURETORS   Page

Rochester E4ME 4-Barrel
  Chrysler Motors 5.2L (VIN 4 or S) V8 2-15

FUEL INJECTION

Chrysler Motors Multi-Point Fuel Injection
  2.2L Turbo, 2.5L Turbo & 3.0L 2-22
Chrysler Motors Throttle Body Injection
  2.2L & 2.5L (Non-Turbo) 2-26
Eagle Multi-Point Fuel Injection
  Premier 3.0L 2-29
Eagle Throttle Body Fuel Injection
  Premier 2.5L 2-32
Ford Motor Co. Central Fuel Injection
  Escort 1.9L, Sable & Taurus 2.5L HSC 2-36
Ford Motor Co. Multi-Point Fuel Injection
  1.9L, 2.2L, 2.2L Turbo, 2.3L,
    3.0L, 3.0L SHO, 3.8L & 5.0L 2-41

TURBOCHARGERS

Chrysler Motors
  2.2L Turbo II & 2.5L Turbo I 2-49
Ford Motor Co.
  2.2L Probe 2-51

SUPERCHARGERS

Ford Motor Co.
  3.8L Cougar XR7 &
    Thunderbird Super Coupe 2-53

FUEL PUMPS

Ford Motor Co. Inertia Switch 2-55

NOTE: ALSO SEE GENERAL INDEX

1989 FUEL SYSTEMS
Carburetor Trouble Shooting

CONDITION	POSSIBLE CAUSE	CORRECTION
Engine Won't Start	Choke not closing	Check choke operation, see FUEL SYSTEMS
	Choke linkage bent	Check linkage, see FUEL SYSTEMS
Engine Starts, Then Dies	Choke vacuum kick setting too wide	Check setting and adjust, see FUEL SYSTEMS
	Fast idle RPM too low	Reset RPM to specification, see TUNE-UP
	Fast idle cam index incorrect	Reset fast idle cam index, see FUEL SYSTEMS
	Vacuum leak	Inspect vacuum system for leaks
	Low fuel pump outlet	Repair or replace pump, see FUEL SYSTEMS
	Low carburetor fuel level	Check float setting, see FUEL SYSTEMS
Engine Quits Under Load	Choke vacuum kick setting incorrect	Check setting and adjust, see FUEL SYSTEMS
	Fast idle cam index incorrect	Reset fast idle cam index, see FUEL SYSTEMS
	Incorrect hot fast idle speed RPM	Reset fast idle RPM, see TUNE-UP
Engine Starts, Runs Up, Then Idles Slowly With Black Smoke	Choke vacuum kick set too narrow	Reset vacuum kick, see FUEL SYSTEMS
	Fast idle cam index incorrect	Reset fast idle cam index, see FUEL SYSTEMS
	Hot fast idle RPM too low	Reset fast idle RPM, see TUNE-UP

HOT STARTING SYMPTOMS

CONDITION	POSSIBLE CAUSE	CORRECTION
Engine Won't Start	Engine flooded	Allow fuel to evaporate

COLD ENGINE DRIVEABILITY SYMPTOMS

CONDITION	POSSIBLE CAUSE	CORRECTION
Engine Stalls in Gear	Choke vacuum kick setting incorrect	Check setting and adjust, see FUEL SYSTEMS
	Fast idle RPM incorrect	Reset fast idle RPM, see TUNE-UP
	Fast idle cam index incorrect	Reset fast idle cam index, see FUEL SYSTEMS
Acceleration Sag or Stall	Defective choke control switch	Replace choke control switch
	Choke vacuum kick setting incorrect	Adjust kick setting, see FUEL SYSTEMS
	Float level incorrect (too low)	Adjust float level, see FUEL SYSTEMS
	Accelerator pump defective	Repair or replace pump, see FUEL SYSTEMS
	Secondary throttle not closed	Inspect lock-out, see FUEL SYSTEMS
Sag or Stall After Warm-Up	Defective choke control switch	Replace control switch, see FUEL SYSTEMS
	Defective accelerator pump (low output)	Replace pump, see FUEL SYSTEMS
	Float level incorrect (too low)	Adjust float level, see FUEL SYSTEMS
Backfiring & Black Smoke	Plugged heat crossover system	Remove restriction

WARM ENGINE DRIVEABILITY SYMPTOM

CONDITION	POSSIBLE CAUSE	CORRECTION
Hesitation With Small Amount of Gas Pedal Movement	Vacuum leak	Inspect vacuum lines
	Accelerator pump weak or inoperable	Replace pump, see FUEL SYSTEMS
	Float level setting too low	Reset float level, see FUEL SYSTEMS
	Metering rods sticking or binding	Inspect and/or replace, see FUEL SYSTEMS
	Carburetor idle or transfer system plugged	Inspect system and remove restrictions
	Frozen or binding heated air inlet	Inspect heated air door for binding
Hesitation With Heavy Gas Pedal Movement	Defective accelerator pump	Replace pump, see FUEL SYSTEMS
	Metering rod carrier sticking or binding	Remove restriction
	Large vacuum leak	Inspect vacuum system and repair leak
	Float level setting too low	Reset float level, see FUEL SYSTEMS
	Defective fuel pump, lines or filter	Inspect pump, lines and filter
	Air door setting incorrect	Adjust air door setting, see FUEL SYSTEMS

NOTE: For additional carburetor trouble shooting information, see the appropriate article in COMPUTERIZED ENGINE CONTROLS section. Information is provided there for diagnosing fuel system problems on vehicles with feedback carburetors.

CONDITION	POSSIBLE CAUSE	CORRECTION
Engine Won't Start (Cranks Normally)	Cold start valve inoperative	Test valve and circuit
	Poor connection; vacuum or wiring	Check vacuum and electrical connections
	Contaminated fuel	Test fuel for water or alcohol
	Defective fuel pump relay or circuit	Test relay and wiring
	Battery too low	Charge and test battery
	Low fuel pressure	Test pressure regulator and fuel pump, check for restricted lines and filters
	No distributor reference pulses	Repair ignition system as necessary
	Open coolant temperature sensor circuit	Test sensor and wiring
	Shorted W.O.T. switch in T.P.S.	Disconnect W.O.T. switch, engine should start
	Defective ECM	Replace ECM
	Fuel tank residual pressure valve leaks	Test for fuel pressure drop after shut down
Hard Starting	Disconnected hot air tube to air cleaner	Reconnect tube and test control valve
	Defective Idle Air Control (IAC) valve	Test valve operation and circuit
	EGR valve open	Test EGR valve and control circuit
	Stalls when A/C is turned on	Check for A/C "On" signal at ECM, check for overcharged A/C system
	Restricted fuel lines	Test for restrictions
	Poor MAP sensor signal	Test MAP sensor, vacuum hose and wiring
	Engine stalls while parking	Test for excessive power steering pressure
	No power to injectors	Check injector fuse(s)
Rough Idle	Poor MAP sensor signal	Test MAP sensor, vacuum hose and wiring
	Intermittent injector operation	Loose injector harness connectors
	Erratic speed sensor inputs	Sensor harness too close to high tension wires
	Poor coolant temperature sensor signal	Test for shorted sensor or circuit
	Defective Idle Air Control (IAC) valve	Test valve operation and circuit
	Shorted, open or misadjusted T.P.S.	Test and adjust or replace T.P.S.
	EGR valve open	Test EGR valve and control circuit
	Poor Oxygen sensor signal	Test for shorted or open sensor or circuit
	Incorrect mixture from PCV system	Test PCV for flow, check sealing of oil filler cap
Poor High Speed Operation	Low fuel pump volume	Faulty pump or restricted fuel lines or filters
	Poor MAP sensor signal	Test MAP sensor, vacuum hose and wiring
	Poor Oxygen sensor signal	Test for shorted or open sensor or circuit
	Open coolant temperature sensor circuit	Test sensor and wiring
	Faulty ignition operation	Check wires for cracks or poor connections, test secondary voltage with ocilloscope
	Contaminated fuel	Test fuel for water or alcohol
	Intermittent ECM ground	Test ECM ground connection for resistance
	Restricted air cleaner	Replace air cleaner
	Restricted exhaust system	Test for exhaust manifold back pressure
	Poor MAF sensor signal	Check leakage between sensor and manifold
	Poor VSS signal	If tester for ALCL hook-up is available, check that VSS reading matches speedometer
Ping or Knock on Acceleration	Poor Knock sensor signal	Test for shorted or open sensor or circuit
	Poor Baro sensor signal	Test for shorted or open sensor or circuit
	Improper ignition timing	See VEHICLE EMISSION CONTROL LABEL
	Check for engine overheating problems	Low coolant, loose belts or electric cooling fan inoperative

NOTE: For additional fuel injection trouble shooting information, see appropriate article in COMPUTERIZED ENGINE CONTROLS section. Information is provided there for diagnosing fuel system problems on vehicles with electronic fuel injection.

1989 FUEL SYSTEMS
Turbocharger Trouble Shooting

CONDITION	POSSIBLE CAUSE	CORRECTION
Engine Detonation	Malfunction in ESC system	Check ESC system, see COMPUTERIZED ENGINE CONTROLS
	EGR system defect	Check EGR system, see COMPUTERIZED ENGINE CONTROLS
	Throttle body or turbocharger air inlet restrictions	Remove restrictions
	Actuator allows too much boost	Check boost pressure and adjust
	Defect in throttle body power system	Inspect and repair throttle body, see FUEL SYSTEMS
	Internal turbocharger defect	Replace turbocharger
Low Engine Power	Air inlet restriction	Remove restriction from inlet
	Exhaust system restriction	Remove restriction
	Malfunction in ESC system	Check ESC system, see COMPUTERIZED ENGINE CONTROLS
	EGR system defect	Check EGR system, see COMPUTERIZED ENGINE CONTROLS
Engine Noise	Loose exhaust system or leak	Check exhaust mounting and connections
	Restricted turbocharger oil supply	Check oil delivery system
Engine Surges	ESC malfunction	Check ESC system, see COMPUTERIZED ENGINE CONTROLS
	Engine vacuum leaks	Repair vacuum leaks
	EGR system defect	Check EGR system, see COMPUTERIZED ENGINE CONTROLS
	Loose turbocharger bolts on compressor side	Check mounting bolts and tighten
Excessive Oil Consumption (Blue Exhaust Smoke)	Leak at turbocharger oil inlet	Check fittings and repair
	Turbocharger oil drain hose leaks or restricted	Check drain hose for restrictions or loose fittings
	Turbocharger seals leaking	Replace turbocharger

CONDITION	POSSIBLE CAUSE	CORRECTION
Low Boost	Air leak at intercooler, flanges, ducts, supercharger housing or supercharger outlet	Locate and repair leak or replace damaged component
	Contamination in system or blockage	Remove obstruction
	Supercharger not turning	Check drive belt tension and condition
		Check coupling for damage
		Check for pulley slipping on shaft
	By-pass not closing	Check function of by-pass actuator
		Check stop adjustment
		Check vacuum hose condition and installation
	Insufficient flow from supercharger	Check supercharger for excessive clearance
		Check for correct pulley diameter
High Boost	Too much flow	Check for exhaust restrictions or damage
		Check catalyst for damage
		Check for correct pulley diameter
Vehicle Response Too "Touchy" and/or Poor Fuel Economy	By-pass not opening	Check function of by-pass actuator
		Check for stuck or restricted valve
		Check vacuum hose condition and installation
		Check actuator diaphragm for damage or leaks
Supercharger Noisy	Mechanical damage to supercharger	Replace supercharger
Noise in Air Handling Systems	Air leaks	Check all flanges for proper fit and position
		Check for proper installation of components
Oil on Outside of Supercharger	Leaking seals	Replace supercharger
	Loose fill plug	Tighten fill plug
	Input shaft damaged at seal	Replace supercharger

1989 HOLLEY CARBURETORS
6280 2-Barrel

APPLICATION

CHRYSLER MOTORS (HOLLEY) CARBURETOR NO.

Application	Chrysler Part No.	Holley Part No.
5.2L V8	4306441	R-40354A

IDENTIFICATION

Carburetor part number is stamped on main body flange. It is located in front of throttle position transducer lever, below choke vacuum diaphragm.

DESCRIPTION

The Holley 6280 dual venturi carburetor utilizes 4 basic metering systems: the idle, accelerator pump, main metering and power enrichment systems.

Basic idle system provides a fuel mixture during idle and low speeds. Main metering system provides fuel mixture during all other operating conditions. Accelerator pump system provides additional fuel during acceleration. Power enrichment system uses a power valve to provide a richer mixture during higher power output ranges.

ADJUSTMENTS

NOTE: For on-vehicle adjustments not covered in this article, see appropriate TUNE-UP article.

FLOAT LEVEL

1) With air horn removed, invert main body. Use caution, as pump intake check ball will fall from main body. Hold float hinge pin in place to fully seat float pin in cradle.
2) Using a "T" scale, measure float level clearance from air horn gasket surface on main body to toe of each float. *See Fig. 1.* Float level clearance should be 10/32-16/32".
3) Adjust float level by bending float tang. *See Fig. 1.* It may be necessary to bend either float arm to equalize both float positions.

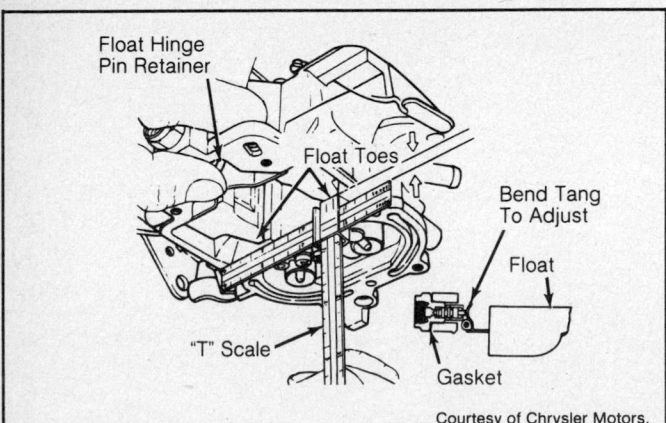

Fig. 1: Adjusting Float Level

CHOKE VACUUM KICK

1) Open throttle and close choke plate. Close throttle to position fast idle cam in proper position. Disconnect vacuum hose from choke vacuum diaphragm.
2) Connect vacuum pump to diaphragm and apply 15 in. Hg vacuum. Apply light finger pressure on choke shaft lever to compress spring in diaphragm stem. Diaphragm stem will reach a stop as spring is compressed. *See Fig. 2.*

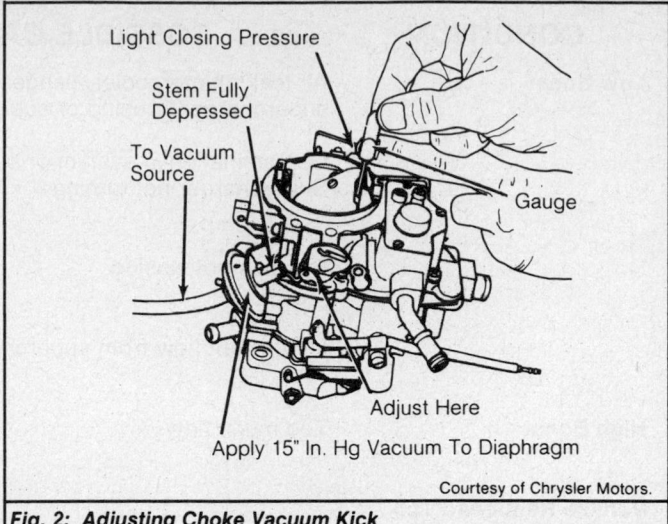

Fig. 2: Adjusting Choke Vacuum Kick

3) Using a specified drill or gauge, measure choke vacuum kick clearance between upper edge of choke valve and air horn wall. Clearance should be .130" (3.30 mm).
4) Adjust clearance by bending diaphragm link "U" bend area. *See Fig. 2.* Ensure linkage moves freely after adjustment. Remove vacuum pump and install vacuum hose.

FAST IDLE CAM POSITION

1) Position fast idle speed screw on 2nd highest step of fast idle cam. Apply light finger pressure on choke shaft lever to close choke valve. *See Fig. 3.*

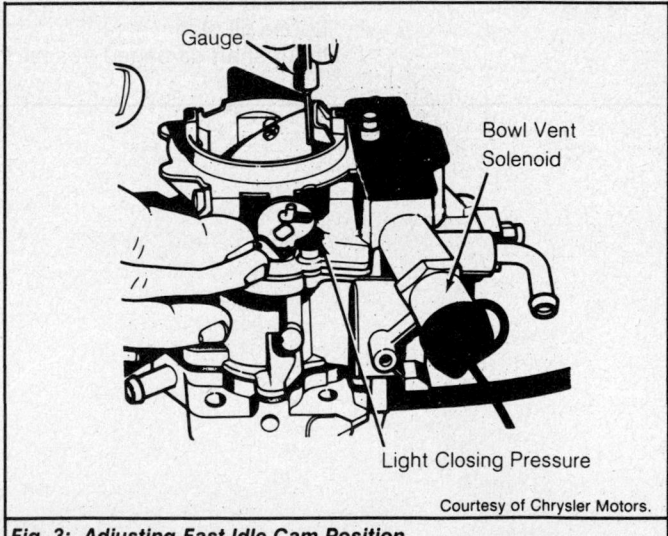

Fig. 3: Adjusting Fast Idle Cam Position

2) Using a specified drill bit or gauge, measure clearance between upper edge of choke valve and air horn wall. Clearance should be .060" (1.52 mm). Adjust clearance by bending fast idle rod at "U" bend area.

CHOKE UNLOADER

1) Hold throttle valves in wide open position. Apply light finger pressure on choke shaft lever to close choke valve. *See Fig. 4.*
2) Using a specified drill or gauge, check clearance between upper edge of choke valve and air horn wall. Clearance should be .280" (7.11 mm). Adjust clearance by bending accelerator pump lever tang.

ACCELERATOR PUMP STROKE

1) Remove bowl vent cover and gasket. *See Fig. 7.* With all linkages installed, adjust idle speed screw so throttle plates will fully close.

2) Using straightedge, check clearance from top of accelerator pump lever to bowl vent cover surface. Clearance should be .170-190" (4.31-4.83 mm). *See Fig. 5.*

3) Adjust clearance by bending pump link. Ensure wide open throttle can be obtained without linkage binding.

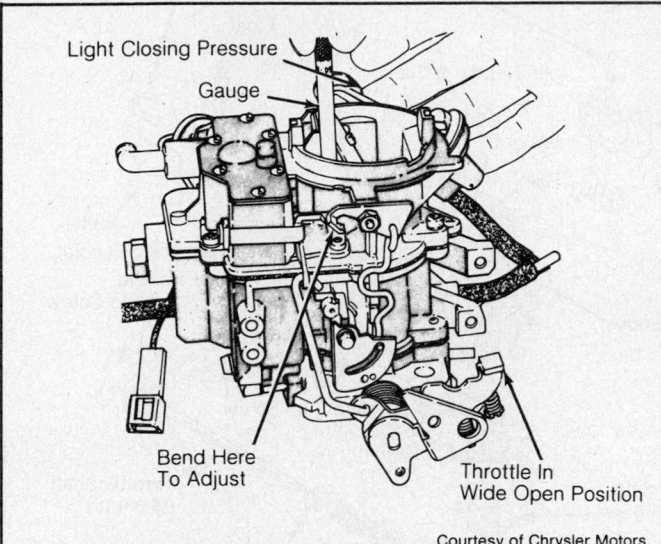

Light Closing Pressure

Gauge

Bend Here
To Adjust

Throttle In
Wide Open Position

Courtesy of Chrysler Motors.

Fig. 4: Adjusting Choke Unloader

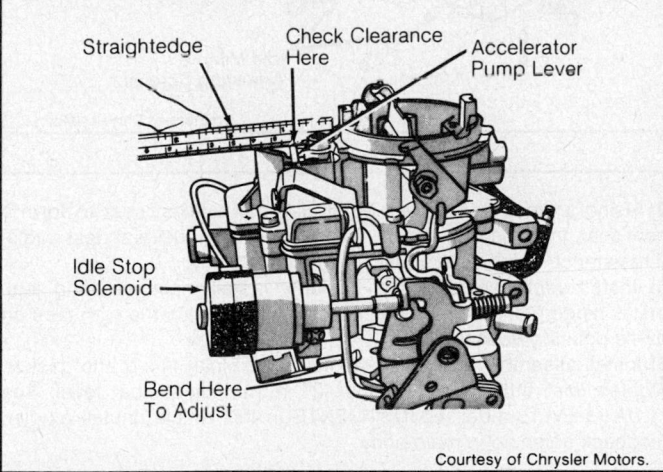

Straightedge

Check Clearance
Here

Accelerator
Pump Lever

Idle Stop
Solenoid

Bend Here
To Adjust

Courtesy of Chrysler Motors.

Fig. 5: Adjusting Accelerator Pump Stroke

OVERHAUL

DISASSEMBLY

1) Remove air cleaner bolt and bracket. Remove bowl vent cover and gasket. Remove idle stop solenoid.

2) Remove pump link. Remove bowl vent solenoid from air horn. Disconnect choke vacuum diaphragm hose from main body. Remove choke vacuum diaphragm and linkage.

3) Remove fast idle cam lever-to-choke shaft retaining nut and washer. Disengage fast idle linkage from lever and fast idle cam. Disconnect and remove accelerator pump operating lever.

4) Remove air horn-to-main body retaining screws. Separate air horn from main body. Remove "E" clip from pump operating shaft. Pull shaft from main body. Remove accelerator pump arm and pump operating lever. Remove accelerator pump cup only.

5) Power valve assembly retaining ring is staked in position. Remove staking with a sharp tool. Remove vacuum piston from air horn by depressing piston and allowing it to snap against retaining ring.

6) Remove fuel inlet fitting. Remove oxygen feedback solenoid from inside of main body. Remove float hinge pin, float baffle and float assembly. Remove main metering jets.

7) Using Valve Remover (C-4231), remove power valve from main body. Ensure blade is squarely seated in slot to prevent power valve needle damage.

8) Remove venturi cluster retaining screws. Remove venturi cluster. DO NOT remove idle well tubes. Invert main body and remove weight and check ball located below venturi cluster.

9) Remove throttle body-to-main body retaining screws. Separate throttle body from main body. Remove fast idle cam retaining clip. Remove fast idle cam from stub shaft.

10) If idle mixture screws are to be removed, plugs must be removed first (if equipped). Center punch locating point .250" (6.35 mm) from end of mixture screw housing. *See Fig. 6.*

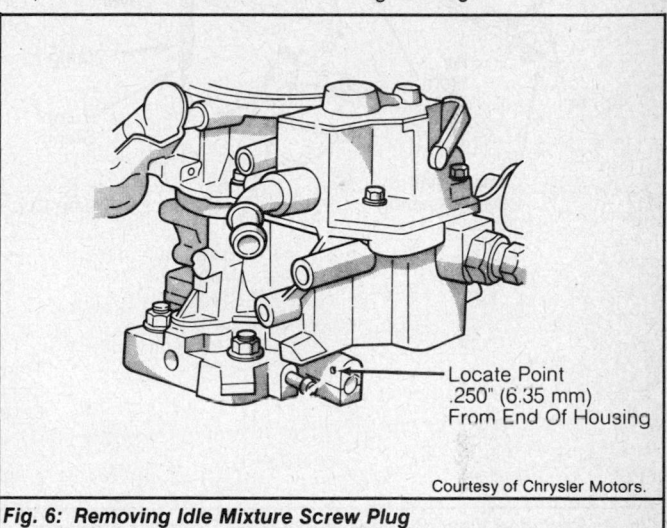

Locate Point
.250" (6.35 mm)
From End Of Housing

Courtesy of Chrysler Motors.

Fig. 6: Removing Idle Mixture Screw Plug

11) Drill a 3/16" hole at center punch point. Pry plugs from housing. Repeat procedure for remaining plug. Remove idle mixture screws and springs from throttle body.

CLEANING & INSPECTION

1) Clean parts thoroughly in carburetor cleaner. DO NOT soak choke diaphragm, plastic, or rubber parts in cleaner. Rinse all metal parts with HOT water. Blow dry with compressed air.

2) Check choke mechanism movement in air horn. Choke shaft must operate freely in air horn. Inspect idle mixture screws for grooves or nicks. Replace if damaged.

3) Inspect nitrophyl type float for fuel absorption by lightly squeezing float. Replace float if wetness appears when squeezed or float feels heavy compared to a new float.

REASSEMBLY

Throttle Body – Install idle mixture screws and springs in throttle body. For initial adjustment, turn idle mixture screws inward until they lightly contact seat areas. Turn screws one turn counterclockwise.

Main Body – 1) Install fast idle cam on stub shaft with step areas facing fast idle speed screw. Install retaining clip. Invert main body and install throttle body gasket. Ensure all holes align. Install throttle body on main body. Tighten retaining screws to 30 INCH lbs. (3 N.m).

2) Install accelerator pump discharge check ball and weight. Fill fuel bowl with clean fuel. Test check ball and seat for leakage. Using a small brass rod, hold check ball and weight downward. *See Fig. 8.*

1989 HOLLEY CARBURETORS
6280 2-Barrel (Cont.)

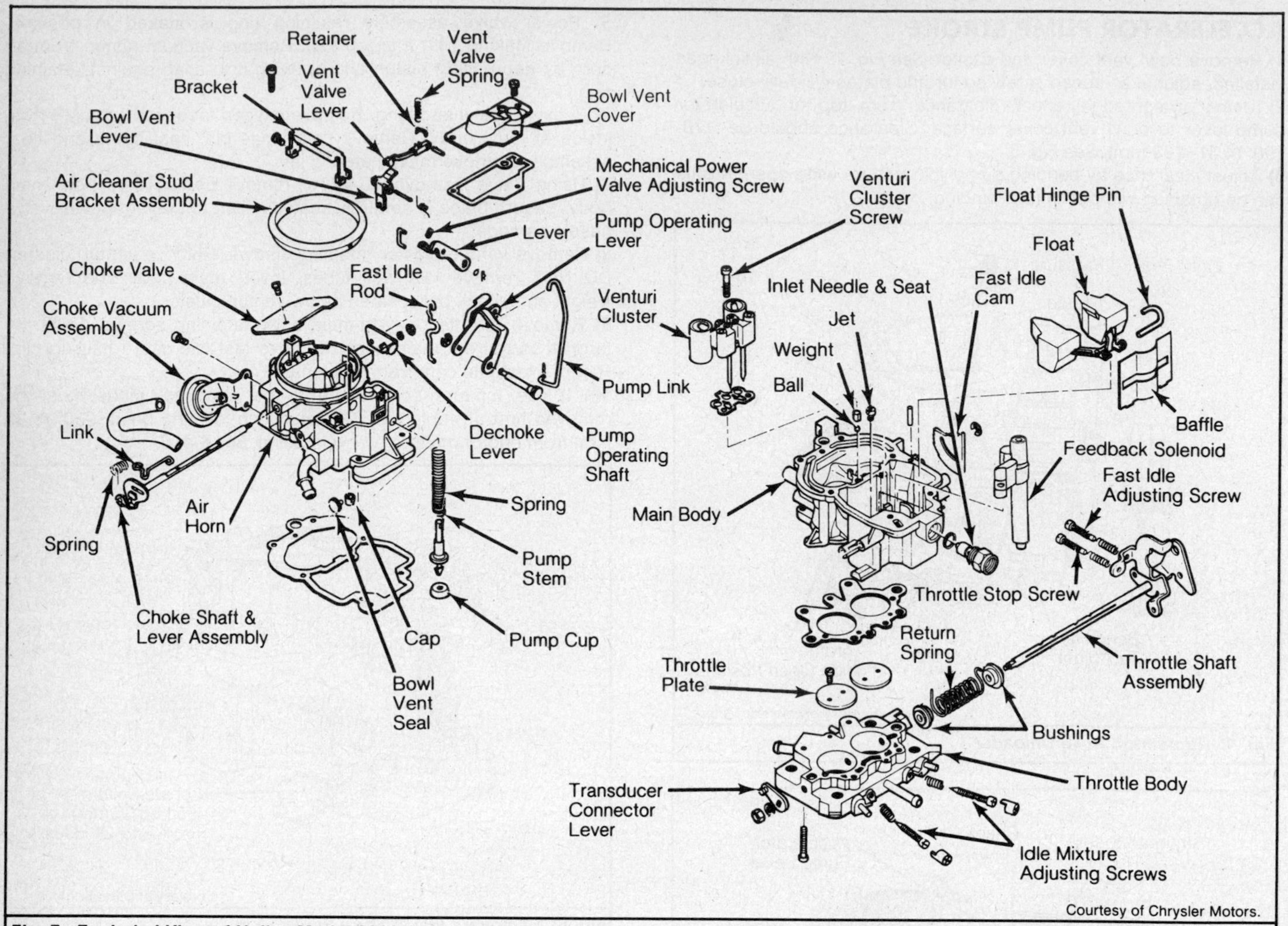

Retainer

Vent Valve Spring

Bracket

Vent Valve Lever

Bowl Vent Cover

Bowl Vent Lever

Mechanical Power Valve Adjusting Screw

Venturi Cluster Screw

Float Hinge Pin

Air Cleaner Stud Bracket Assembly

Lever

Pump Operating Lever

Float

Inlet Needle & Seat

Fast Idle Cam

Choke Valve

Fast Idle Rod

Venturi Cluster

Jet

Choke Vacuum Assembly

Weight

Baffle

Ball

Feedback Solenoid

Pump Link

Fast Idle Adjusting Screw

Link

Dechoke Lever

Main Body

Air Horn

Pump Operating Shaft

Spring

Spring

Choke Shaft & Lever Assembly

Pump Stem

Cap

Bowl Vent Seal

Pump Cup

Throttle Stop Screw

Return Spring

Throttle Plate

Throttle Shaft Assembly

Bushings

Throttle Body

Transducer Connector Lever

Idle Mixture Adjusting Screws

Courtesy of Chrysler Motors.

Fig. 7: Exploded View of Holley Model 6280 2-Barrel Carburetor

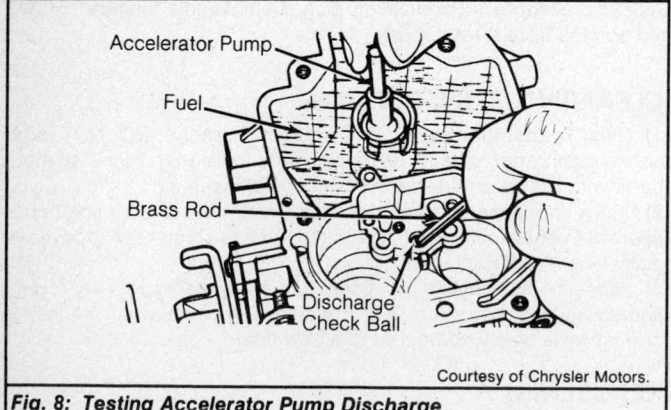

Accelerator Pump

Fuel

Brass Rod

Discharge Check Ball

Courtesy of Chrysler Motors.

Fig. 8: Testing Accelerator Pump Discharge

3) Place accelerator pump plunger in main body well. Operate accelerator pump by hand. If no resistance is felt against rod, check ball is leaking. Remove weight. Leave check ball in place.

4) Using a small drift punch, lightly tap ball against seat to form a new seat. Install a new ball and weight. Perform fuel leak test again. If resistance is felt, check ball is seating correctly.

5) Install venturi cluster and gaskets. Install main metering jets. Install hinge pin in float. Install assembly through baffle with tabs on baffle pointing downward.

6) Install assembly in main body. Install fuel inlet fitting and gasket. Tighten inlet fitting to 15 ft. lbs. (21 N.m). Adjust float level. See FLOAT LEVEL under ADJUSTMENTS in this article. Install oxygen feedback solenoid in main body.

Air Horn – 1) Ensure power valve bore is free of stake areas. Install spring and piston in vacuum cylinder. Install retainer and stake in air horn. Compress spring and check for binding. Replace piston if binding exists.

2) Install air horn and gasket on main body. Starting from the center and working outward, tighten retaining screws to 25 INCH lbs. (2.8 N.m).

3) Reverse removal procedure for remaining components and perform necessary adjustments. See ADJUSTMENTS in this article. Accelerator pump stroke must be adjusted prior to bowl vent cover and gasket installation.

CARBURETOR ADJUSTMENT SPECIFICATIONS

Carburetor Number	Float Level	Accel. Pump	Choke Unloader	Choke Vac. Kick	Fast Idle Cam
4306441 or R-40354A	10/32-16/32"	.170-.190"	.280"	.130"	.060"

APPLICATION

MOTORCRAFT CARBURETOR NO.

Application	Part No.
5.8L V8 (Police Only)	E2AE-9510-AJA

IDENTIFICATION

Carburetor part number is stamped on left side of upper throttle body or on metal identification tag. The upper line contains part number prefix and suffix. A design change code (if any) is included on the lower line. An assembly date code is also included on the lower line. *See Fig. 1.*

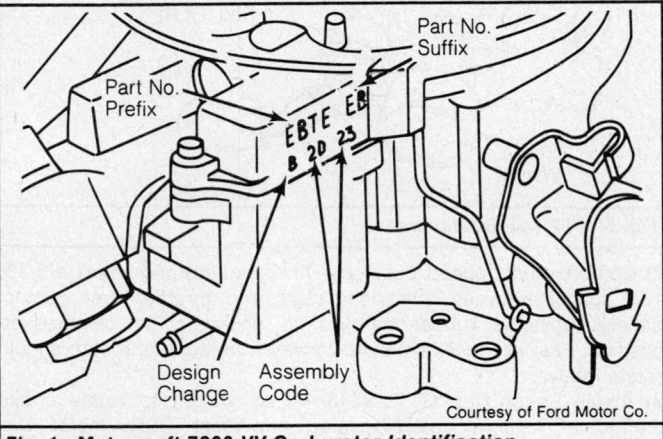

Fig. 1: Motorcraft 7200 VV Carburetor Identification

DESCRIPTION

The model 7200 VV (Variable Venturi) carburetor changes venturi opening size to allow for varying engine speed and load conditions. This is done by dual venturi valves which are controlled by engine vacuum and throttle position.

Depending upon engine demands, venturi valve positions change to determine amount of airflow through carburetor. Venturi valves are connected to 2 tapered main metering rods. As venturi valve position changes, metering rods adjust amount of fuel flow through main metering jets.

The carburetor changes air/fuel ratio in response to commands from MCU control module. The system uses a stepper motor to regulate amount of bleed air allowed into main metering fuel system. The greater amount of air entering the system, the leaner the air/fuel ratio.

TESTING

NOTE: Before performing continuity tests, disconnect stator terminal of alternator for alternator powered choke. Reconnect stator terminal after testing.

ELECTRIC CHOKE

Choke Cap Continuity – 1) With ignition off, connect a test light between battery positive terminal and choke cap terminal. Test light should light, indicating continuity. If test light is on, perform appropriate CIRCUIT CONTINUITY test.
2) If test light is not on, connect a jumper wire between choke cap clamp shroud and battery negative terminal. Connect test light between battery positive terminal and choke cap terminal. If test light is on, replace choke cap.
3) If test light is not on, connect a jumper wire directly to choke cap ground. If test light is on, correct poor contact between choke cap clamp shroud and choke cap ground.

Circuit Continuity (Alternator Powered Choke) – Connect test light between choke cap ground and battery negative terminal. Start engine. Test light should be on. If test light is not on, locate and repair open circuit between choke cap and alternator stator terminal. If no open in circuit is found, check alternator output.

Circuit Continuity (Battery Powered Choke) – 1) With engine and ignition off, disconnect oil pressure switch from harness. Using a jumper wire in place of switch, complete choke circuit. Connect test light between battery negative terminal and choke cap terminal.
2) Turn ignition on, but do not start engine. Test light should be on, indicating continuity. If test light is not on, locate and repair open circuit. Turn ignition off. Check fuse, fusible link, connectors, etc. in choke circuit.
3) Remove jumper wire and connect harness to oil pressure switch. Turn ignition on, but do not start engine. Test light is not on. If test light is not on, replace oil pressure switch. Start engine. Test light should be on. If test light is not on, replace oil pressure switch.

ADJUSTMENTS

NOTE: For on-vehicle adjustments not covered in this article, see appropriate article in TUNE-UP section.

NOTE: The model 7200 VV (Variable Venturi) carburetor is NOT sensitive to fuel float level. Adjusting only the float level will generally not correct starting or driveability problems.

FLOAT LEVEL

1) Remove upper body assembly. Remove upper body gasket. If necessary, construct a gauge to specified float level setting. Turn upper body assembly upside-down.
2) Using gauge, measure distance from surface of upper body to bottom of float. *See Fig. 2.* To adjust, bend fuel level adjustment tab away from inlet needle to decrease setting, and toward inlet needle to increase setting. See CARBURETOR ADJUSTMENT SPECIFICATIONS table at end of this article.

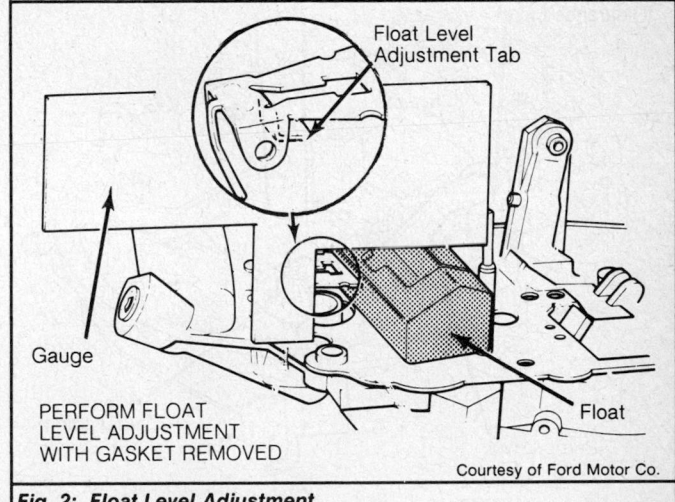

Fig. 2: Float Level Adjustment

FLOAT DROP

1) With upper body and gasket removed, hold upper body in upright position and allow float to hang. If necessary, construct a gauge to specified dimensions to measure float drop setting.
2) Use gauge to measure distance from surface of upper body to bottom of float. To adjust, bend float lever stop tab away from hinge pin to increase clearance and toward hinge pin to decrease clearance. See CARBURETOR ADJUSTMENT SPECIFICATIONS table at end of this article.

1989 MOTORCRAFT CARBURETORS
Model 7200 VV 2-Barrel (Cont.)

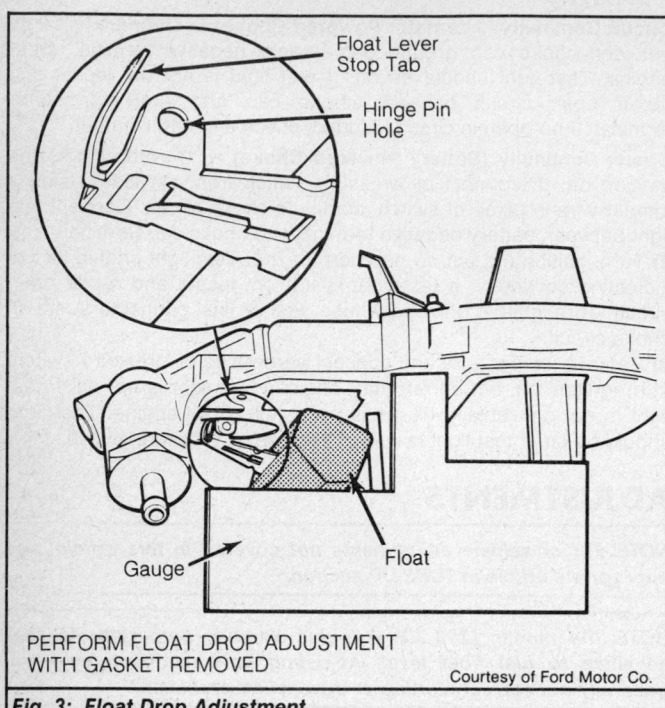

PERFORM FLOAT DROP ADJUSTMENT
WITH GASKET REMOVED

Courtesy of Ford Motor Co.

Fig. 3: Float Drop Adjustment

ACCELERATOR PUMP LEVER PRELOAD ADJUSTMENT

Adjust curb idle speed. Turn engine off. Push down lightly on top of nylon nut to remove freeplay from linkage. Use a feeler gauge to measure clearance between accelerator pump lever and stem. Adjust clearance to .010" ± .005". Remove feeler gauge and turn nylon nut one complete turn counterclockwise.

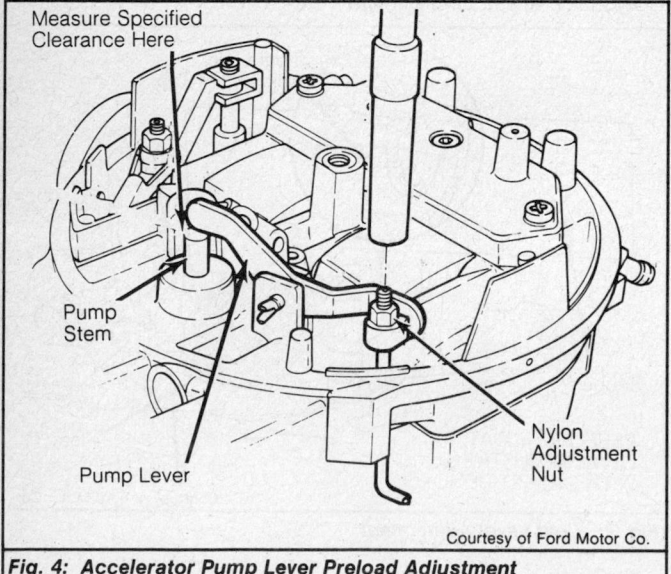

Courtesy of Ford Motor Co.

Fig. 4: Accelerator Pump Lever Preload Adjustment

COLD ENRICHMENT ROD (CER) & CONTROL VACUUM REGULATOR (CVR)

NOTE: The CER mechanism affects carburetor air/fuel mixture in all RPM ranges. Choke CER and CVR adjustment procedures must be performed in the following sequence.

CER Initial Adjustment – 1) Remove carburetor. Position dial indicator on carburetor, with indicator stem on top of cold enrichment rod. *See Fig. 5.* Remove choke diaphragm cover and

spring. Use a 1/4" drill bit to remove choke cap retaining screw heads. Carefully remove choke cap and remove remaining portion of screws.

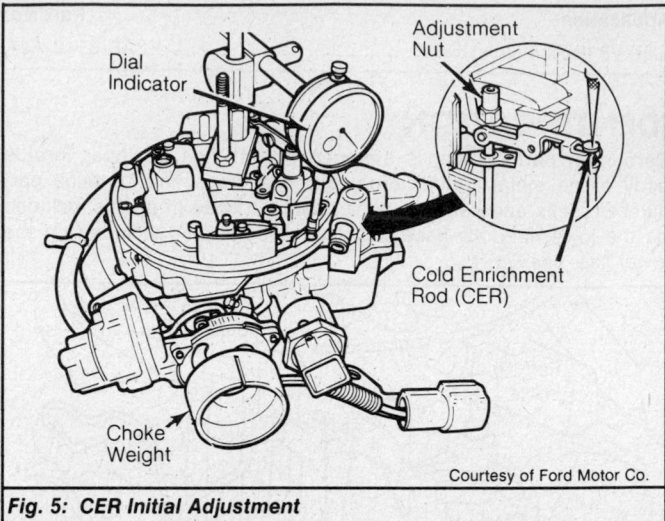

Courtesy of Ford Motor Co.

Fig. 5: CER Initial Adjustment

2) Compress idle speed positioner (if equipped) and insert a 5/16-1/2" spacer between positioner stem and throttle lever contact paddle. Using a rubber band, hold positioner in compressed position. Fast idle lever should be away from cam, and cam should rotate freely.

3) Install Stator Cap (T77L-9848-A7) as weight to rotate choke thermostat lever counterclockwise and seat CER. Install dial indicator on carburetor with tip on top of CER. Set dial indicator to zero and raise weight slightly to check zero setting.

CVR Swivel Assembly Replacement – 1) Remove "E" clip and hinge pin. Turn CER adjustment nut counterclockwise until nut disengages from rod. Remove CVR and swivel assembly. Replace with new assembly.

NOTE: Adjustment nut cavities are filled with epoxy after final adjustment. To adjust, the existing parts must be removed and new parts installed. Choke control rod is designed to break. If rod breaks during adjustment, a new rod must be installed.

---

2) With control rod in place, install swivel assembly and tighten CER adjustment nut to lower and align position. Connect lever to swivel. Install hinge pin and "E" clip. Perform CER RUN POSITION (75°F) ADJUSTMENT.

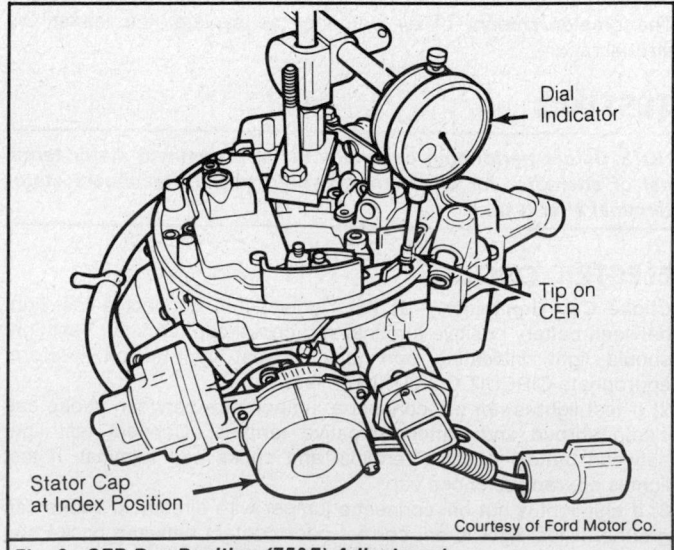

Courtesy of Ford Motor Co.

Fig. 6: CER Run Position (75°F) Adjustment

CER Run Position (75°F) Adjustment – Install stator cap and rotate clockwise to index position. Dial indicator reading should be 0.125" (3.18 mm) at 75°F (24°C). *See Fig. 6.* Adjust reading by turning choke adjustment nut clockwise to increase reading, or counterclockwise to decrease.

CER Start Position (0°F) Adjustment – Remove stator cap. Rotate choke thermostat lever clockwise until CER travel stop screw is bottomed on choke seal retainer (full travel). Dial indicator reading should be .490" (12.45 mm) at 0°F (-18°C). *See Fig. 7.* Adjust reading by turning screw with a 5/64" Allen wrench. Turn screw clockwise to decrease reading. Turn screw counterclockwise to increase reading.

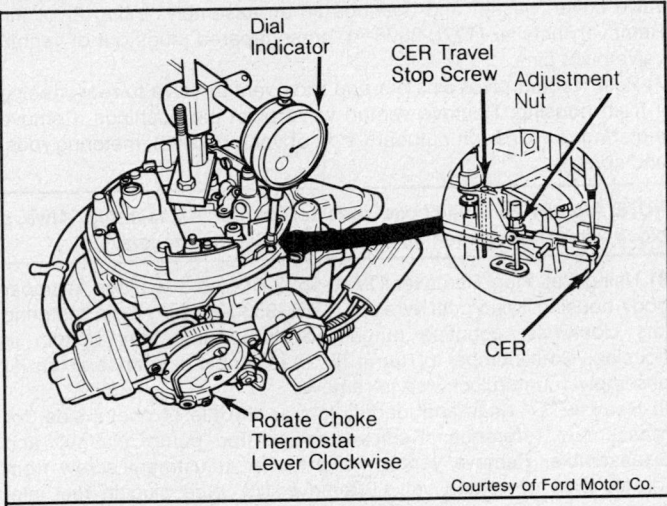

Fig. 7: CER Start Position (0°F) Adjustment

Choke Diaphragm Start Position (Warm Engine) – Push in diaphragm assembly. Dial indicator reading should be 0.460" (11.68 mm) at 75°F (24°C). Adjust reading by rotating diaphragm clockwise to decrease reading or counterclockwise to increase. *See Fig. 8.*

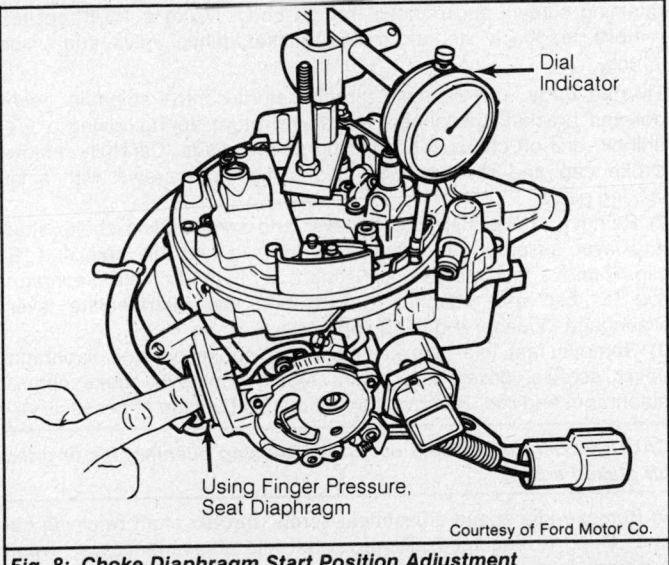

Fig. 8: Choke Diaphragm Start Position Adjustment

Control Vacuum Rod Position – **1)** Seat CER using stator cap weight and zero dial indicator. Remove stator cap weight. Depress CVR until seated. Dial indicator reading should be .250" (6.35 mm).
2) Adjust reading by holding CVR with 3/8" wrench and turning adjustment screw with a 3/32" Allen wrench. Turn screw clockwise to decrease reading or counterclockwise to increase. Install original choke diaphragm cover and spring. *See Fig. 9.*

Choke Diaphragm Run Position (Cold Engine) – **1)** Depress choke diaphragm rod until diaphragm bottoms out. Rotate choke thermostat lever clockwise until choke shaft lever pin contacts fast idle

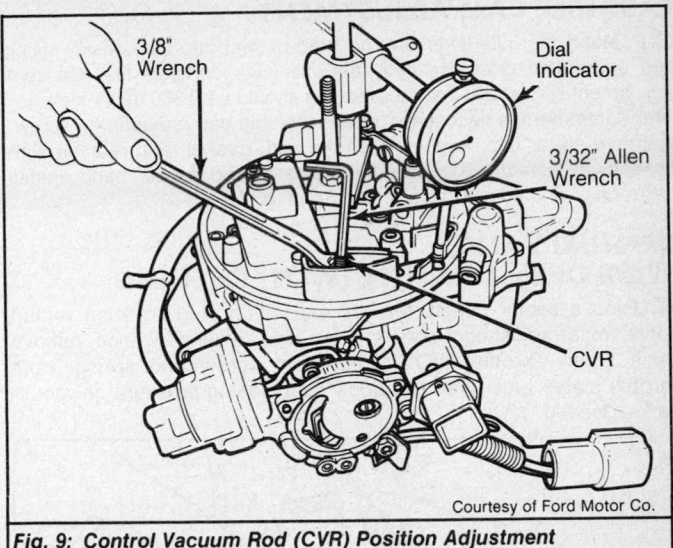

Fig. 9: Control Vacuum Rod (CVR) Position Adjustment

intermediate lever. Dial indicator reading should be .350" (8.89 mm) at 0°F (18°C). *See Fig. 10.*

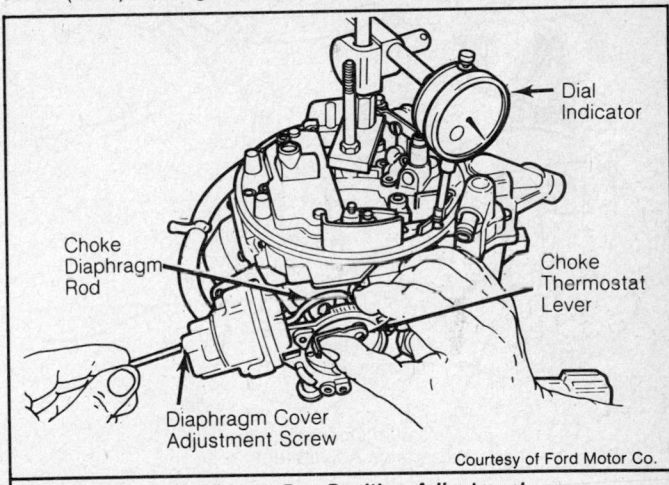

Fig. 10: Choke Diaphragm Run Position Adjustment

2) If reading is not to specification, remove choke diaphragm cover and install a new cover. Adjust reading by turning screw with a 5/64" Allen wrench. Turn screw clockwise to increase reading or counterclockwise to decrease. Apply Loctite on screw to secure adjustment. Install lead ball plug over adjustment screw.

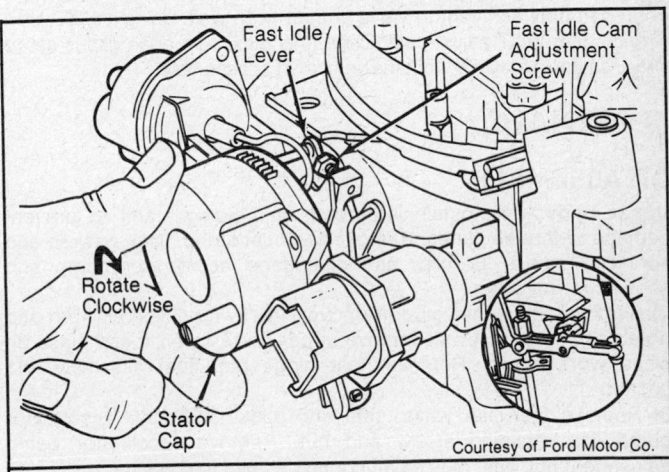

Fig. 11: Fast Idle Cam Adjustment

FAST IDLE CAM ADJUSTMENT

1) Position fast idle lever on 2nd step of fast idle cam. Install stator cap and rotate clockwise until fast idle lever contacts fast idle cam adjustment screw. Dial indicator reading should be 0.360" (9.14 mm).

2) If adjustment is necessary, rotate fast idle cam adjustment screw. Remove stator cap. Assemble choke cap, gasket, and retainer with breakaway screws. Remove dial indicator and rubber band. Install carburetor and adjust idle speeds. See Fig. 11.

VENTURI VALVE
WIDE OPEN THROTTLE (WOT) OPENING

1) Using a center punch, remove expansion plug covering venturi valve limiter adjustment screw. Using a 5/32" Allen wrench, remove Wide Open Throttle (WOT) adjustment screw and spring. Hold throttle plates wide open and apply light closing pressure on venturi valve. See Fig. 12.

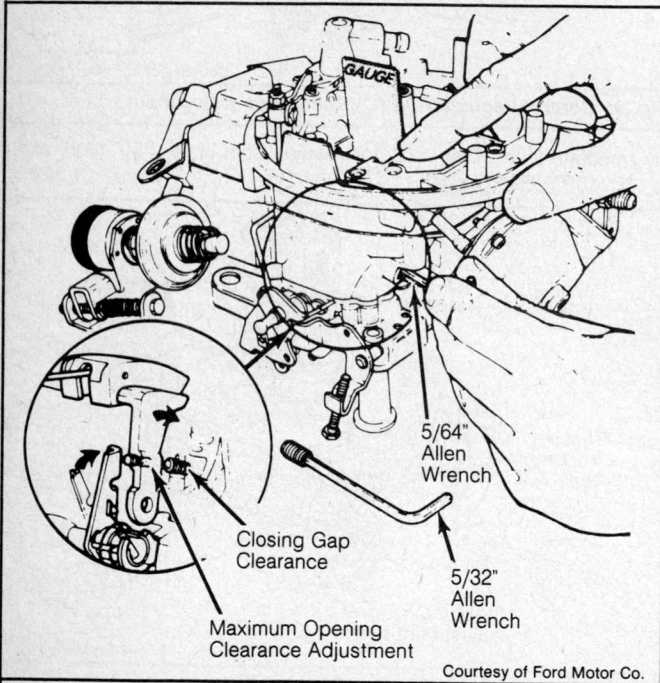

GAUGE

5/64" Allen Wrench

Closing Gap Clearance

5/32" Allen Wrench

Maximum Opening Clearance Adjustment

Courtesy of Ford Motor Co.

Fig. 12: Venturi Valve WOT Opening Adjustment

2) Measure gap between venturi valve and air horn wall. Using a 5/64" Allen wrench, turn venturi valve limiter adjustment screw on venturi valve arm to set closing gap. Using a 5/32" Allen wrench, install WOT adjustment screw and spring.

3) Apply light opening pressure on venturi valve. Measure maximum open gap between venturi valve and air horn wall. Using a 5/32" Allen wrench, turn WOT adjustment screw until maximum open gap is set to specification. Install new expansion plug in access hole.

OVERHAUL

DISASSEMBLY

Upper Body – 1) Install carburetor on holding stand to prevent damage to throttle plates. Remove fuel inlet fitting, filter, gasket, and spring. Remove "E" clip, and disengage accelerator pump and choke control rods.

2) Remove air cleaner stud. Remove 7 screws holding air horn and note position of screws. Remove upper body, invert it and place on clean work bench. Remove float hinge pin, float assembly and gasket.

3) Remove fuel inlet valve, seat and gasket. Remove accelerator pump link retaining screw and nut. Remove accelerator pump adjustment nut, link, overtravel spring, "E" clip and washer.

4) Remove accelerator pump rod and dust seal. Remove "E" clip from choke hinge pin and slide pin out. Remove cold enrichment rod adjustment nut by turning counterclockwise.

NOTE: Epoxy on nut cavity may cause choke control rod to break. If rod breaks, a new rod and swivel assembly must be installed.

5) Remove cold enrichment rod lever, adjustment swivel, control vacuum regulator and adjustment nut as an assembly. Slide rod out of upper body. Remove 2 Torx head screws while holding venturi valve cover with Cover Holder (T81L-2100-H15).

6) Invert carburetor, holding venturi valve cover in place. Remove valve cover, gasket and bearings as an assembly. Using Pivot Pin Remover/Installer (T77L-9928-A), press tapered plugs out of venturi valve pivot pins.

7) Push venturi pivot pins out and slide venturi valve to rear, freeing it from housing. Remove venturi valve pivot pin bushings. Remove metering rod pins (on outboard side of venturi valve), metering rods, and springs.

NOTE: Identify throttle/choke rods for proper reassembly. Always block venturi valve wide open when working on the jets.

8) Using Jet Plug Remover (T77L-9533-B), remove plugs in upper body housing. Using Jet Wrench (T77L-9533-A), turn main metering jets clockwise, counting number of turns until they bottom in housing. Note number of turns for reassembly reference. Turn jet assembly counterclockwise to remove.

9) Remove "O" rings and identify jets as throttle or choke side, for reassembly reference. Remove accelerator pump plunger and disassemble. Remove venturi valve limiter adjustment screw from throttle side of venturi valve. Remove 1/8" pipe plug in fuel inlet boss for cleaning.

Main Body – 1) Remove venturi valve diaphragm cover screws. Tap cover lightly and remove cover, spring guide, and spring. Carefully loosen diaphragm and slide out of main body. Invert carburetor and catch accelerator pump check ball and weight.

2) Place carburetor on clean surface. Remove 5 throttle body retaining screws and remove throttle body. Using a 1 5/8" socket, remove feedback stepper motor, gasket, pintle valve and pintle spring.

Throttle Body – 1) Remove throttle return control solenoid, dashpot and bracket. Disconnect kickdown return spring. Using a 1/4" drill bit, drill off choke cap retaining screw heads. Carefully remove choke cap and remove remaining portion of screws with small locking pliers.

2) Remove choke thermostatic lever and screw. Slide choke shaft and lever assembly from housing. Remove fast idle cam and "E" clip. Remove fast idle cam adjustment screw and choke diaphragm rod "E" clip that attaches rod to fast idle intermediate lever. Disengage unloader rod (if equipped).

3) Remove fast idle intermediate lever, choke control diaphragm cover screws, cover, and return spring. Remove choke control diaphragm and rod. Remove choke housing bushing (if necessary).

CAUTION: Before pressing out choke housing bushing, file or grind off staked areas.

4) Remove idle speed adjustment screw, throttle shaft retaining nut and spring (if equipped). Remove fast idle adjustment lever, nylon bushing, fast idle lever and fast idle adjustment screw. Remove unloader lever (if equipped). Remove large "E" clip.

5) If throttle plates are to be removed, lightly scribe them to ensure proper reassembly. File off end of throttle plate screws. Remove screws and plates. Discard screws. To remove throttle shaft assembly, drive limiter lever stop pin down until it is flush with shaft.

6) Remove "E" clip next to venturi valve limiter lever. Slide throttle shaft assembly from housing and remove transmission kickdown adjustment screw (if equipped). Remove venturi valve limiter lever and bushing assembly.

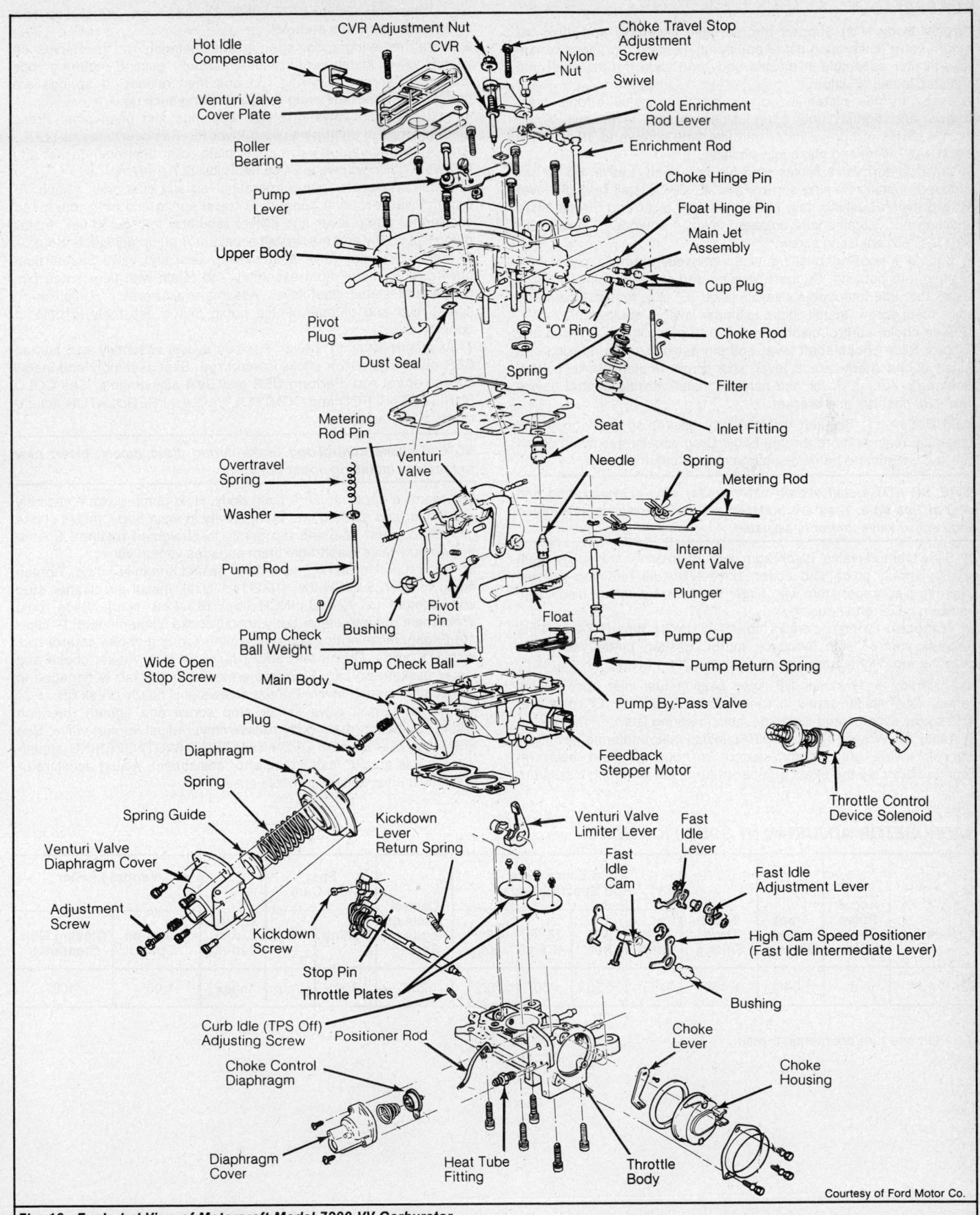

Fig. 13: Exploded View of Motorcraft Model 7200 VV Carburetor

Courtesy of Ford Motor Co.

1989 MOTORCRAFT CARBURETORS
Model 7200 VV 2-Barrel (Cont.)

REASSEMBLY

Throttle Body – 1) Support throttle shaft assembly and drive out venturi valve limiter stop pin (if equipped). Discard pin. Place venturi valve limiter assembly in throttle body and slide throttle shaft into position. Install "E" clip.

2) Place throttle plates in correct position. Install throttle plate screws and tighten until snug. Close throttle lever and center throttle plates in bore. Tighten throttle plate screws to 10-15 INCH lbs. (1.1-1.7 N.m) and stake into position.

3) Drive venturi valve limiter stop pin into shaft. Leave 1/8" of pin exposed. Install retaining screws and "E" clip. Install fast idle lever "E" clip, nylon bushing, fast idle adjustment lever and throttle shaft retaining nut. Install choke unloader lever (if equipped). Install curb idle (TPS off) adjusting screw.

4) If choke housing bushing was removed, carefully press new bushing into housing. Support housing and stake bushing in place. Install fast idle intermediate lever, large "E" clip, fast idle cam and adjustment screw. Install choke unloader lever (if equipped).

5) Slide choke control diaphragm rod into position, engage rod and "E" clip. Slide choke shaft lever and pin assembly into housing and install choke thermostatic lever and screw. Install choke control diaphragm spring, cover and screws. Install throttle control device solenoid, dashpot and bracket.

Main Body – 1) Position throttle body gasket on main body and assemble main body to throttle body. Drop accelerator pump check ball and weight into pump discharge charge channel.

NOTE: DO NOT install venturi valve limiter stop screw, spring and plug at this time. They are installed after carburetor is assembled and venturi valve limiter is adjusted.

2) Slide venturi valve diaphragm into position. Install diaphragm spring, spring guide and cover. Loosely install retaining screws. Depress diaphragm stem with finger to prevent pinching diaphragm between cover and housing.

3) Diagonally tighten screws to 15-22 INCH lbs. (1.7-2.5 N.m). Release stem. Install feedback motor, gasket, pintle valve, and pintle spring. Tighten motor to 8-10 ft. lbs. (11-14 N.m).

Upper Body – 1) Install 1/8" pipe plug in fuel inlet boss. Install venturi valve limiter screw in venturi valve. Lubricate "O" rings with mild soapy solution and install on main metering jets.

2) Using Jet Wrench (T77L-9533-A), install main metering jets. Turn jets clockwise until lightly seated in housing. Turn each jet counterclockwise the exact number of turns noted during disassembly. Using Plug Driver (T77L-9533-C), install jet plugs. Tap tool lightly until it bottoms on housing.

3) Install metering rods, springs and metering rod pivot pins on venturi valve. Install venturi valve, carefully guiding metering rods into jets. Depress metering rod and then release. If springs are correctly installed, metering rods will spring back up.

4) Install venturi valve pivot pin bushings and pivot pins. Press tapered plugs in pivot pins using Pivot Pin Remover/Installer (T77L-9928-A). Install venturi valve cover plate roller bearings, gasket and screws. Tighten screws to 24-35 INCH lbs. (2.7-4.0 N.m).

5) Install accelerator pump operating rod and dust seal. Attach "E" clip and washer. Slide pump over travel spring and onto rod. Insert accelerator pump lever and swivel assembly into pump link. Install pump link screw and nut. Install accelerator pump adjustment nut.

6) Install fuel inlet valve seat gasket, seat and valve. Install float bowl gasket. Install float assembly and retain with float hinge pin. Check and adjust float level. Assemble accelerator pump return spring, cup and plunger. Place pump piston assembly in hole of upper body.

7) Assemble lever to swivel. Position swivel assembly and tighten CER nut 4-5 turns on choke control rod. Seat assembly and install choke control rod. Perform CER and CVR adjustments. See COLD ENRICHMENT ROD and CONTROL VACUUM REGULATOR adjustments in this article.

NOTE: If choke control rod broke during disassembly, insert new rod prior to installing upper body.

8) Assemble upper body to main body. Hold pump piston assembly with finger and guide it into pump cavity in main body. Install choke control rod dust seal and tap gently to straighten retainer. Ensure that venturi valve diaphragm stem engages venturi valve.

9) Install fuel filter spring, new filter, gasket and inlet fitting. Tighten fitting to 90-125 INCH lbs. (10.2-14.1 N.m). Install air cleaner stud and tighten to 72-108 INCH lbs. (8.1-12.2 N.m). Slide cold enrichment rod into upper body. Install choke hinge pin and "E" clip.

10) Engage accelerator pump operating rod and choke control rod. Install "E" clips. Check and adjust fast idle cam. Adjust choke and install gasket and cap. Ensure thermostat spring tab is engaged in slotted choke shaft lever. Tighten screws until heads break off.

11) Install venturi valve limiter stop screw and tighten retention spring (omitted in main body reassembly). Adjust venturi valve. See VENTURI VALVE WIDE OPEN THROTTLE (WOT) OPENING adjustment in this article. Install plug after adjustment. Adjust accelerator pump lash after setting curb idle speed.

CARBURETOR ADJUSTMENT SPECIFICATIONS

Application	Accel. Pump Lever Lash [1]	Float Level Setting	Float Drop Setting	Cold Enrichment Rod Specifications				Control Vacuum Regulator Setting	Fast Idle Cam		Choke Cover Setting	Venturi Limiter	
				0°F Start	0°F Run	75°F Start	75°F Run		Setting	Stop		Maximum Open	Closing Gap Clearance
E2AE-AJA	.010" [1]	1.040"	1.460"	.490"	.350"	.460"	.125"	.250"	.360"	2nd	Index	1.00"	.400"

[1] – Plus one turn counterclockwise.

APPLICATION

CHRYSLER MOTORS & ROCHESTER CARBURETOR NO.

Application	Part No.
5.2L (VIN 4 or S) V8	
Rochester	17085433
Chrysler Motors	4306433

IDENTIFICATION

The Rochester E4ME carburetor numbers are stamped vertically on float bowl, near secondary throttle. *See Fig. 1.* This number must be used for ordering replacement components and performing adjustments. Carburetor identification number must be transferred onto new float bowl if float bowl is replaced.

These carburetors are used with a computerized engine control system. This is indicated by the first letter "E" of identification number. The last letter of identification number indicates type of choke used. Letter "E", indicates an electric choke.

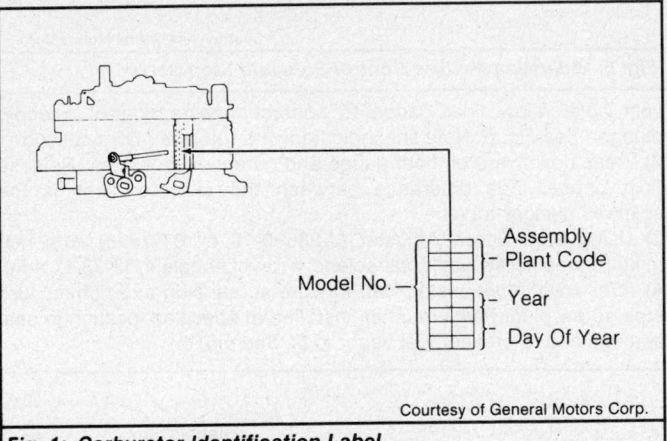

Fig. 1: Carburetor Identification Label

Courtesy of General Motors Corp.

DESCRIPTION

The 2-stage, downdraft design, E4ME carburetor is composed of 3 main components, air horn, float bowl and throttle body. E4ME models utilize a single primary vacuum break assembly.

The E4ME is a feedback type carburetor used in conjunction with the computerized engine control system. Carburetor is equipped with an electrically-actuated Mixture Control (MC) solenoid mounted in the float bowl. Fuel delivery is controlled by the MC solenoid through signals from the computer. Fuel metering is controlled by stepped metering rods and jets.

E4ME models use an Idle Stop Solenoid (ISS). This solenoid is used to increase idle when A/C is operated (if equipped) or extends the plunger during deceleration to improve emissions.

TESTING
FLOAT LEVEL (ON-VEHICLE)

1) Operate engine until choke is fully open. Install Float Gauge (J-34935-1) in vent slot. *See Fig. 2.* Allow gauge to float freely. DO NOT press downward on float gauge or float damage may occur.
2) Observe indicator mark in relation to top of casting. This reading should be within 2/32" of float level specification. See CARBURETOR ADJUSTMENT SPECIFICATIONS table at end of article. Excessive fuel pump pressure will cause a high float level.
3) Remove air horn and adjust float level if not within specification. See FLOAT LEVEL under ADJUSTMENTS in this article.

ELECTRIC CHOKE

NOTE: *Electric choke must be tested only when choke thermostat temperature is approximately 70°F (21°C).*

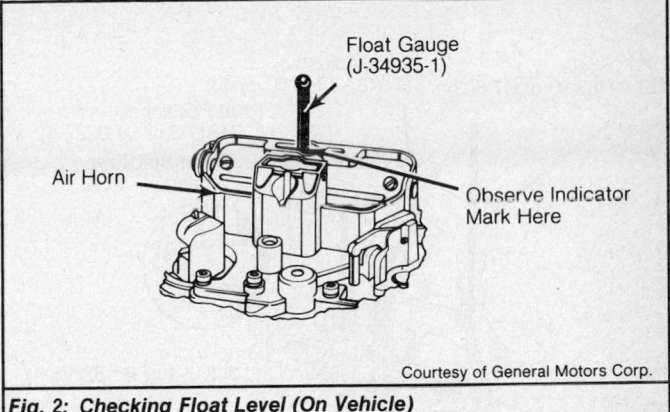

Fig. 2: Checking Float Level (On Vehicle)

Courtesy of General Motors Corp.

1) Choke should be cool, allowing choke valve to fully close when throttle is opened. Start engine and note time required for choke to fully open. Choke should fully open within 5 minutes.
2) If choke opening time was not within specification, start engine and check voltage at choke heater connection. If voltage is between 12-15 volts, inspect ground between choke cover and choke housing.
3) Replace electric choke unit if grounds are correct. If voltage is low or no voltage exists, check wiring and connections. Power for choke unit may be provided through oil pressure switch. Ensure switch is operating properly.

VACUUM BREAK

1) Inspect vacuum break for bleed hole in vacuum tube. Plug bleed hole with tape prior to testing vacuum break. Using vacuum pump, apply 15 in. Hg vacuum to vacuum break and note vacuum reading.
2) Vacuum reading should be held for at least 20 seconds. Apply finger pressure to plunger to determine if plunger has obtained full travel. Replace vacuum break if plunger did not obtain full travel or failed to hold vacuum.

IDLE STOP SOLENOID (ISS)

1) Turn ignition on. DO NOT start engine. Turn A/C unit on. Open throttle, allowing solenoid plunger to extend. Disconnect solenoid wire and note plunger operation.
2) Plunger should retract away from throttle. Install wire. Plunger should extend. If plunger failed to operate, check voltage at solenoid wire. Replace solenoid if voltage exists. Inspect and repair wiring circuit if no voltage exists.

ADJUSTMENTS
FLOAT LEVEL

1) Remove air horn, solenoid plunger, air horn gasket and metering rods. Remove plastic float bowl insert. If solenoid lean mixture screw requires removal, use Mixture Control Tool (J-28696 or BT-7928). Count and record number of turns required to lightly seat mixture screw prior to removal.
2) Install Bracket (J-34817-1 or BT-8227A-1) on float bowl. *See Fig. 3.* Install Float Positioner (J-34817-3 or BT-8227-A) on float bowl with pin contacting outer edge of float lever.
3) Using "T" Scale (J-9789-90 or BT-8037), measure distance from top of casting to top of float, approximately 3/16" from large end of float. Float level must be within 2/32" of float level specification. See CARBURETOR ADJUSTMENT SPECIFICATIONS table at end of article.
4) If float level requires adjustment, use Float Adjuster (J-34817-15 or BT-8233) to bend float lever for correct setting. Recheck float level after each adjustment. Ensure float alignment is straight and float does not contact float bowl.
5) Lightly seat lean mixture screw and readjust to original location (if removed). Reverse removal procedure for remaining components. Tighten air horn in correct sequence. *See Fig. 17.*

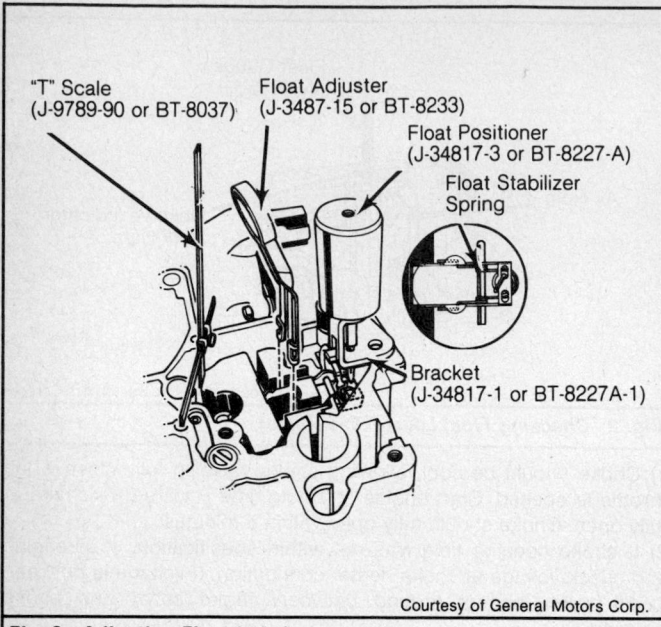

Courtesy of General Motors Corp.

Fig. 3: Adjusting Float Level

MIXTURE CONTROL SOLENOID MIXTURE SCREW

1) Install Mixture Control Solenoid Gauge (J-33815-1 or BT-8253-A) over throttle lever side metering jet guide. Temporarily install solenoid plunger.

2) Install lean mixture screw 6 threads. Install rich limit stop. Hold solenoid plunger downward against solenoid stop. Using Mixture Adjuster (J-28696-10 or BT-7928), slowly turn lean mixture screw in or out until solenoid plunger just contacts solenoid stop and mixture control solenoid gauge. See Fig. 4.

3) Adjustment is correct when solenoid plunger is contacting BOTH the solenoid stop and gauge. Remove solenoid plunger and gauge. Install plug at proper location. See Fig. 6.

MIXTURE CONTROL SOLENOID STOP SCREW

1) With solenoid lean mixture screw properly adjusted and air horn installed, install Float Gauge (J-34935-1 or BT-8420-A) in air horn

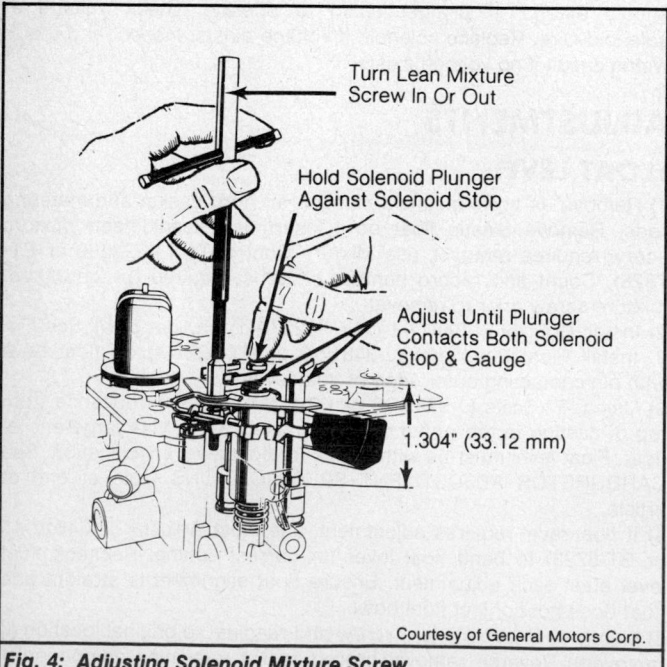

Courtesy of General Motors Corp.

Fig. 4: Adjusting Solenoid Mixture Screw

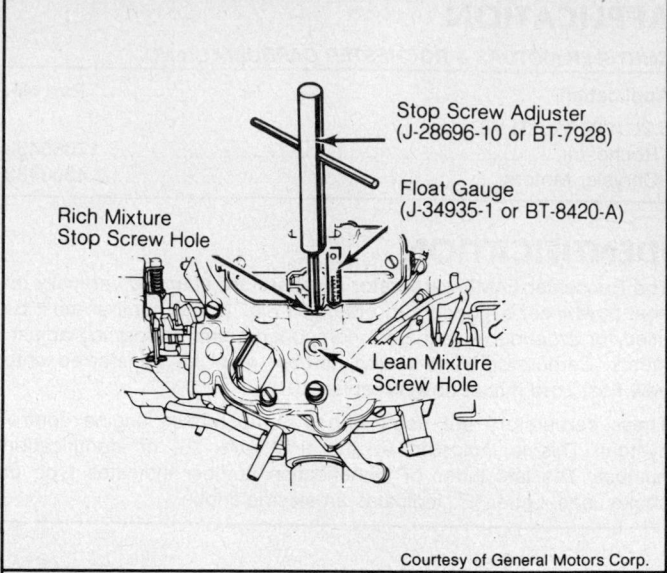

Courtesy of General Motors Corp.

Fig. 5: Adjusting Mixture Control Solenoid Stop Screw

vent hole. Allow float gauge to contact mixture control solenoid plunger. See Fig. 5. Note line indicated with top of air horn casting.

2) Press downward on float gauge and note indicator mark. Release float gauge. This difference between the indicator lines is the solenoid plunger travel.

3) Using Stop Screw Adjuster (J-28696-10 or BT-7928), turn rich mixture stop screw until total solenoid travel equals 4/32" (3.17 mm).

4) After adjustment, install lean mixture screw plug and rich mixture stop screw plug. Plugs must be installed at specified location to seal settings and to prevent fuel vapor loss. See Fig. 6.

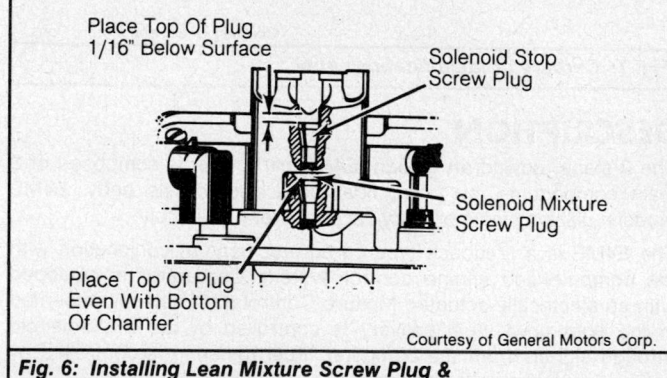

Courtesy of General Motors Corp.

Fig. 6: Installing Lean Mixture Screw Plug & Solenoid Stop Screw Plug

AIR BLEED VALVE

1) Install Air Bleed Valve Gauge (J-33815-2 or BT-8253-B) in throttle side of vent hole of air horn so gauge contacts solenoid plunger. See Fig. 7.

2) Position upper end of air bleed valve gauge over open cavity next to valve. Hold gauge downward so solenoid plunger is against solenoid stop and rotate gauge. Adjust air bleed valve so gauge pivots over and just contacts top of valve. See Fig. 7.

AIR VALVE SPRING

1) Loosen shaft lock screw using Allen wrench. Rotate spring fulcrum pin counterclockwise until throttle valves open. See Fig. 8.

2) Rotate spring fulcrum pin clockwise until throttle valves close. Then rotate spring fulcrum pin proper amount of revolutions. See CARBURETOR ADJUSTMENT SPECIFICATIONS table at end of article.

3) Hold spring fulcrum pin and tighten lock screw. Apply a light coat of grease to spring contact area.

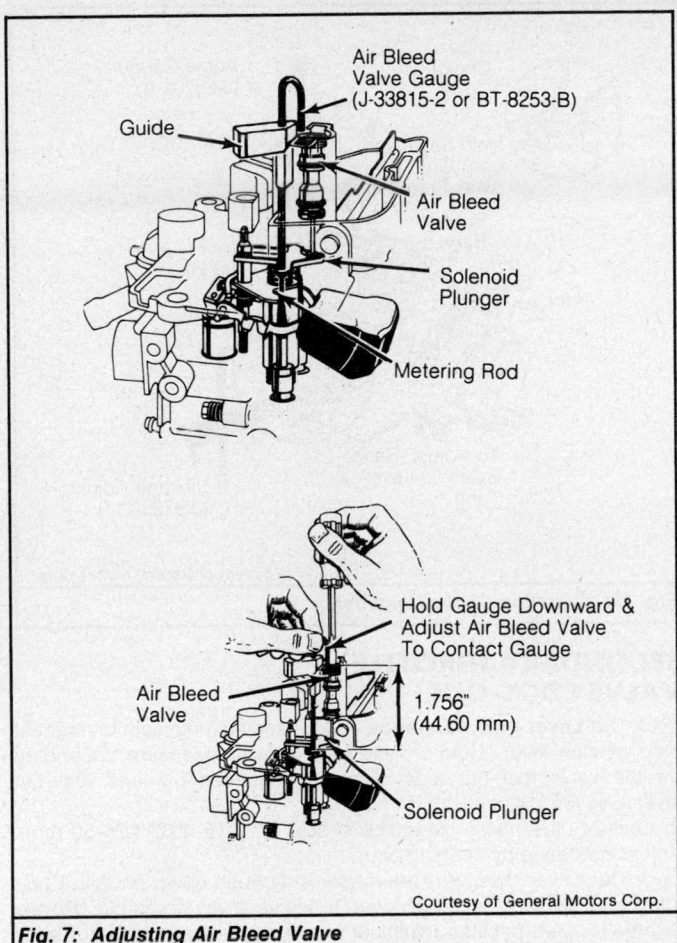

Fig. 7: *Adjusting Air Bleed Valve*

CHOKE COIL LEVER

1) Remove choke cover retaining rivets. Remove choke cover and coil assembly from choke housing. *See Fig. 9.* Position fast idle cam on highest step of fast idle lever.

2) Push upward on choke coil lever to close choke valve. Install a .120" (3.04 mm) drill or pin gauge in choke housing hole. *See Fig. 9.* Lower edge of choke lever should just contact pin gauge. Bend choke rod to adjust.

CHOKE ROD (FAST IDLE CAM)

1) Install rubber band to vacuum break lever of intermediate choke shaft. *See Fig. 10.* Open throttle, allowing choke valve to close. Install Angle Gauge (J-26701-A) on choke valve.

2) Adjust angle gauge to choke rod specification. See CARBURE-TOR ADJUSTMENT SPECIFICATIONS table at end of article. Place fast idle cam on second step of cam lever.

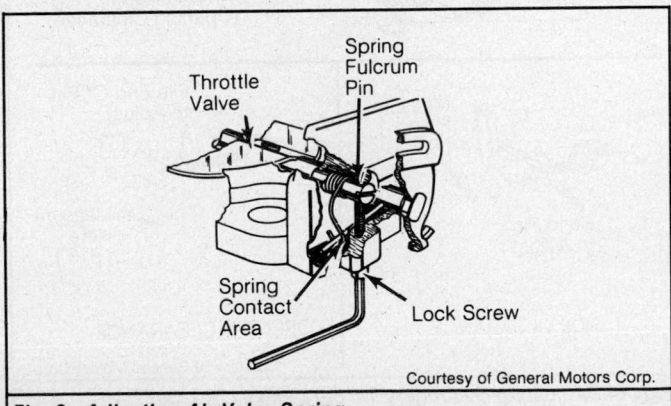

Fig. 8: *Adjusting Air Valve Spring*

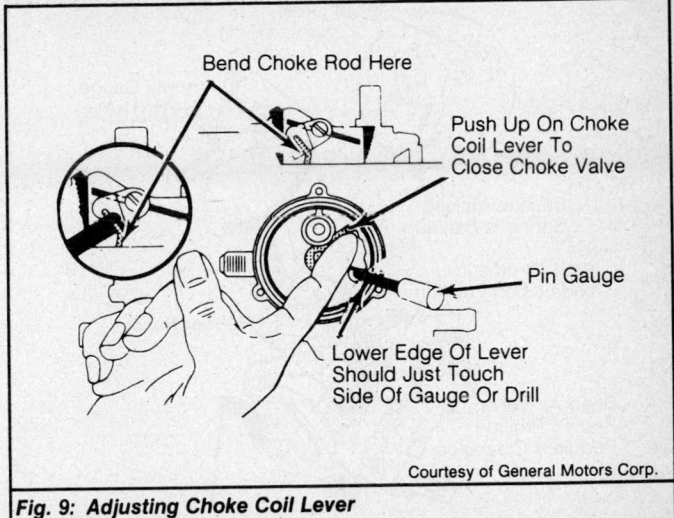

Fig. 9: *Adjusting Choke Coil Lever*

3) If cam lever does not contact cam, adjust fast idle screw. Bend tang on fast idle assembly until angle gauge bubble is centered. *See Fig. 10.*

PRIMARY VACUUM BREAK

NOTE: Choke coil lever and choke rod (fast idle cam) adjustments must be correct before performing this adjustment.

1) Install rubber band to vacuum break lever of intermediate choke shaft. Open throttle, allowing choke valve to close. Install Angle Gauge (J-26701-A) on choke valve. *See Fig. 11.*

2) Adjust angle gauge to specification. See CARBURETOR AD-JUSTMENT SPECIFICATIONS table at end of article. Plug vacuum break bleed holes (if equipped).

3) Using vacuum pump, apply 15 in. Hg vacuum to vacuum break. Ensure bucking spring is seated. *See Fig. 11.* If air valve rod restricts vacuum break plunger from retracting, release vacuum and bend rod to allow full plunger travel.

4) Reapply vacuum and note bubble reading on angle gauge. Adjustment is correct when angle gauge bubble is centered. Adjust screw located on bucking screw to center bubble.

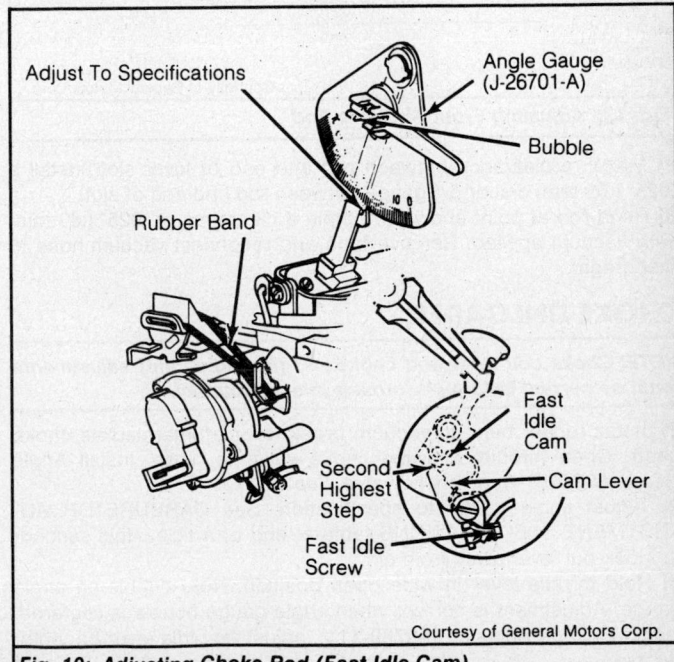

Fig. 10: *Adjusting Choke Rod (Fast Idle Cam)*

1989 ROCHESTER CARBURETORS
E4ME 4-Barrel (Cont.)

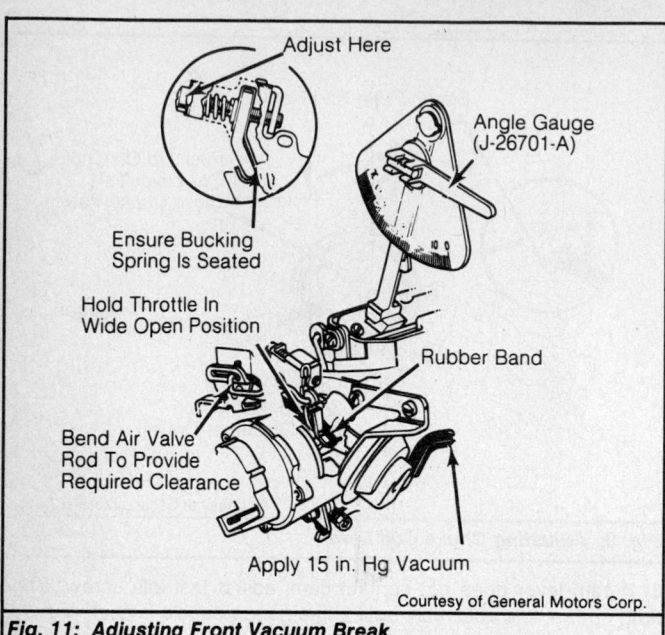

Fig. 11: Adjusting Front Vacuum Break

AIR VALVE ROD – FRONT

NOTE: Choke coil lever and choke rod (fast idle cam) adjustments must be correct before performing this adjustment.

1) Plug vacuum break bleed hole (if equipped). Using vacuum pump, apply 15 in. Hg vacuum to vacuum break. Ensure air valves are fully closed. *See Fig. 12.*

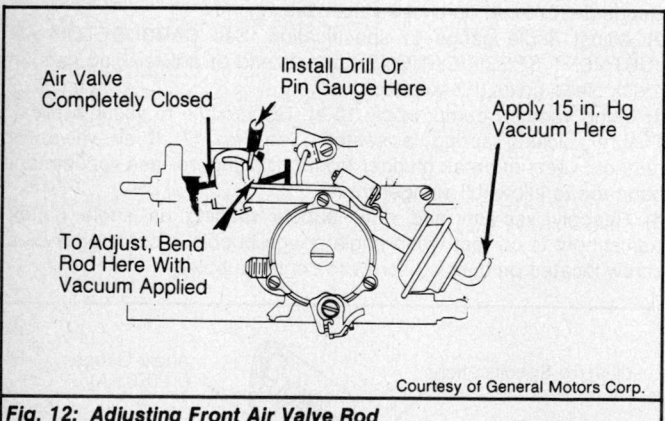

Fig. 12: Adjusting Front Air Valve Rod

2) Measure clearance between rod and end of lever slot. Install a .025" (.63 mm) drill or pin gauge between rod and end of slot.
3) Bend rod at point shown to obtain a clearance of .025" (.63 mm) with vacuum applied. Remove tape and reconnect vacuum hose to diaphragm.

CHOKE UNLOADER

NOTE: Choke coil lever and choke rod (fast idle cam) adjustments must be correct before performing this adjustment.

1) Install rubber band to vacuum break lever of intermediate choke shaft. Open throttle, allowing choke valve to close. Install Angle Gauge (J-26701-A) on choke valve. *See Fig. 13.*
2) Adjust angle gauge to specification. See CARBURETOR ADJUSTMENT SPECIFICATIONS table at end of article. Hold secondary lock-out lever away from pin.
3) Hold throttle lever in wide open position. Note bubble on angle gauge. Adjustment is correct when angle gauge bubble is centered. Using Linkage Adjuster (J-9789-111), adjust fast idle lever to center bubble.

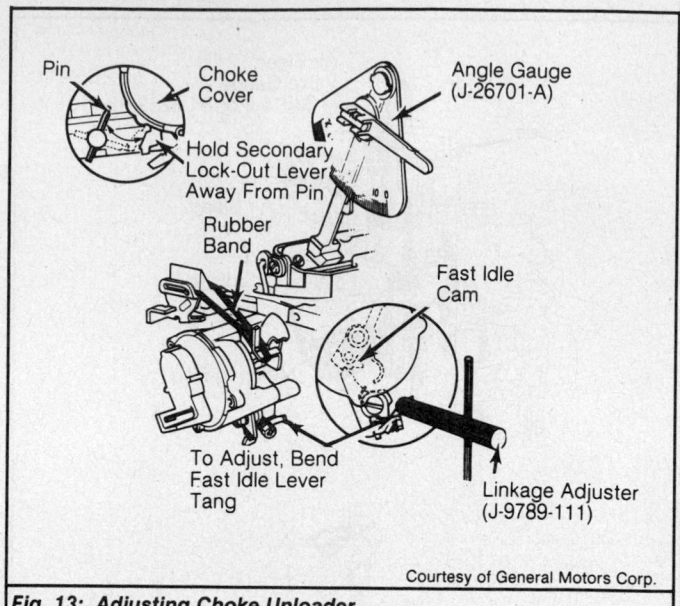

Fig. 13: Adjusting Choke Unloader

SECONDARY THROTTLE VALVE LOCK-OUT

Lock-Out Lever Side Clearance – 1) Place fast idle cam on highest step of cam lever. Hold throttle lever closed. Measure secondary throttle valve lock-out side clearance between pin and lock-out lever. *See Fig. 14.*
2) Lock-out lever side clearance should be .010-.020" (.25-50 mm). Adjust clearance by bending pin.
Lock-Out Lever Opening Clearance – 1) Push down on tail of fast idle cam, allowing lock-out lever to move away from pin. Rotate throttle lever to position minimum clearance between lock-out lever and pin. *See Fig. 14.*
2) Measure specified opening clearance between end of pin and lock-out lever toe. Clearance should be .015" (.38 mm). Adjust clearance by filing end of pin.

OVERHAUL
DISASSEMBLY

Idle Mixture Screw Plug – 1) Idle mixture screw plugs should be removed (if equipped) prior to disassembly of carburetor. Invert

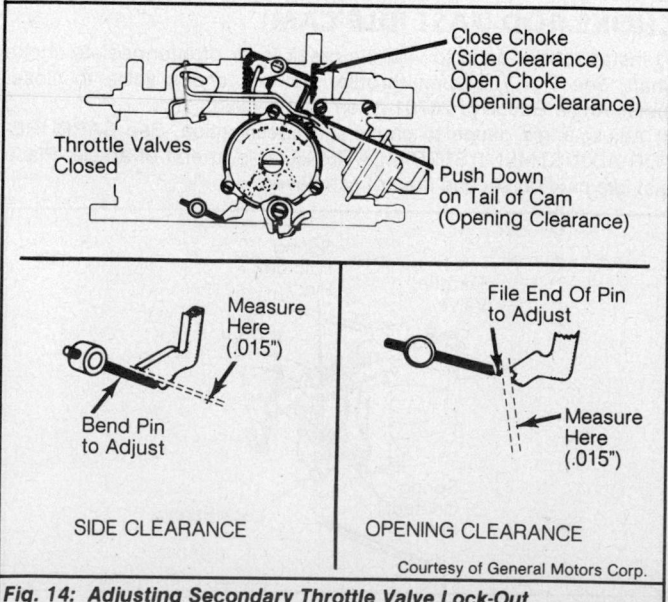

Fig. 14: Adjusting Secondary Throttle Valve Lock-Out

carburetor. Using hacksaw, saw 2 parallel cut areas in throttle body between locator points near one idle mixture plug. See Fig. 15.

2) Distance between cut areas should be near size of punch to be used for plug removal. Cut downward to the plug. Cut area should not exceed more than 1/8" beyond locator points.

3) Place flat punch near end of cut areas. Holding punch at a 45 degree angle, drive punch inward toward throttle body to break casting away. Use a center punch to break plug and expose idle mixture screw. Repeat procedure for remaining plug.

Air Horn – 1) Place carburetor in Holding Fixture (J-9789-118). Remove fuel filter, spring and fuel inlet nut. Remove ISS assembly. Remove primary and secondary vacuum break assemblies and linkage (if equipped).

2) Air bleed valve cover must be removed. Seal bowl vents and air inlets with tape. Using a 7/64" drill bit, drill out head of air bleed valve cover retaining rivet.

3) Remove rivets and air bleed valve cover. Clean metal shavings from top of carburetor. Remove air bleed valve assembly. Remove "O" rings from air bleed valve.

4) Remove secondary metering rod holder retaining screw. Remove metering rod holder and metering rods. Remove choke lever retaining screw. Remove choke lever.

5) Pull upward on choke link. Hold intermediate choke lever outward while twisting choke link from lever. Remove pump link retainer at pump lever. Remove pump link from pump lever. DO NOT remove pump lever from air horn.

6) Remove air horn-to-float bowl retaining screws. Lift air horn straight up from main body. Use care not to damage mixture control solenoid connector and small tubes protruding from air horn. DO NOT attempt to remove small tubes.

7) Using small screwdriver, remove seals from air horn. Remove solenoid adjusting screw plug and adjusting screw (if equipped). See Fig. 16.

Float Bowl – 1) Remove air horn-to-float bowl gasket. Remove mixture control solenoid plunger. Remove accelerator pump assembly. Remove spring and cup from accelerator pump.

2) Remove mixture control solenoid-to-air horn gasket. Remove solenoid connector retaining screws. Using Mixture Control Adjuster (J-28696-10 or BT-7928), remove solenoid mixture adjusting screw and rich limit stop.

3) Remove solenoid plunger. Remove primary metering rods and springs. Remove float bowl insert. Remove mixture control solenoid assembly. DO NOT remove plunger return spring or connector wires from solenoid.

4) Remove solenoid return spring and adjusting screw spring. Remove float, float needle and hinge pin.

5) Using Needle Seat Remover/Installer (J-22769), remove needle seat and gasket. Using Metering Jet Remover (J-28696-4 or BT-7928), remove primary jets.

CAUTION: DO NOT remove secondary jets. Secondary jets are pressed in float bowl. If jets are damaged, float bowl must be replaced.

---

6) Remove discharge plug retainer, discharge ball and pump well baffle. Drill out choke cover retaining rivet heads. Remove choke cover retainers. Remove choke cover, stat assembly and gasket. Remove choke housing-to-float bowl retaining screw and washer.

7) Remove choke housing. Remove choke housing-to-float bowl seal. Remove secondary throttle lock-out lever. Remove intermediate choke lever. Invert float bowl. Remove intermediate choke shaft seal.

8) Remove internal choke stat lever retaining screw. Remove choke stat lever, intermediate choke shaft, lever and link assembly and fast idle cam. Separate fast idle cam from shaft. Remove intermediate choke shaft seal.

Throttle Body – 1) Using Idle Mixture Socket (J-29030-B or BT-7610B), remove idle mixture screws and springs. Note and record number of turns required for idle mixture screw removal for reassembly reference.

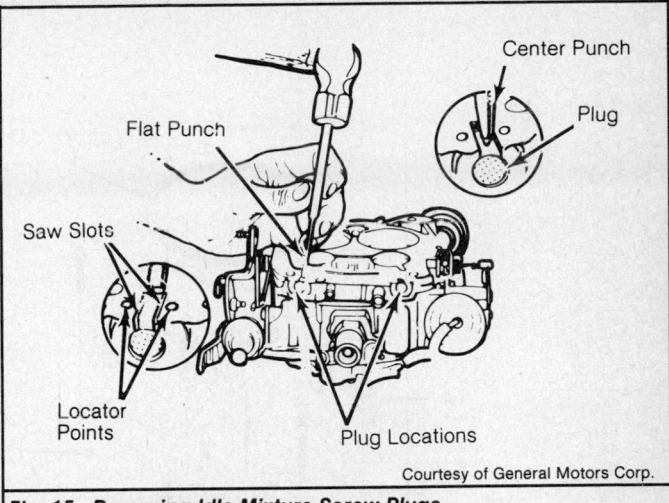

Fig. 15: Removing Idle Mixture Screw Plugs

Courtesy of General Motors Corp.

2) Remove throttle body-to-float bowl retaining screws. Separate throttle body and gasket from float bowl.

CLEANING & INSPECTION

1) Clean parts thoroughly in carburetor cleaner. DO NOT soak solenoids, choke cover and stat assembly, plastic, or rubber parts in cleaner. Rinse all metal parts with HOT water.

2) Blow dry with compressed air. Choke shaft must operate freely in air horn. Inspect idle mixture screws for grooves or nicks. Replace if damaged.

3) Inspect float for damage or fuel absorption. Inspect all solenoids for damaged wiring. Using ohmmeter, check mixture control solenoid resistance. Replace solenoid if resistance is not between 20-26 ohms.

4) Check mixture control solenoid for ground. Place one ohmmeter lead on solenoid housing and remaining lead on one solenoid terminal. Resistance should be infinite. Replace solenoid if grounded.

5) Pump system operation should be checked. Install new pump cup and spring on pump plunger. Install pump discharge ball, plug and pump well baffle in float bowl. Fill float chamber and pump well with clean solvent.

6) Seal 2 pump discharge passages located on top of float bowl surface. Push pump assembly downward in well area. Pump should not reach bottom of travel area. Only movement should be compression of the duration spring.

7) Excessive pump travel indicates improper seating of pump cup, worn pump well or pump discharge plug is leaking. Repair defective components.

8) Refill float chamber and pump well with clean solvent. Slowly move pump downward in pump well until solvent appears at top of pump discharge passages. Remove pump assembly and note solvent level in passages.

9) Solvent level should not decrease. If level decreases, check for missing discharge ball, improper discharge ball seating or defective ball or seat. Repair as necessary.

CAUTION: Float bowl containing a machined pump well may be identified by the letters "MW" stamped on front of float bowl near fuel filter. Ensure replacement float bowl contains proper lettering.

REASSEMBLY

Float Bowl Assembly – 1) Install new float bowl-to-throttle body gasket. Ensure all passages align. Install throttle body and retaining screw.

2) Install carburetor on holding fixture. Install idle mixture screws and springs. Adjust to location recorded during disassembly. Install intermediate choke shaft seal in choke housing with seal lips toward float bowl.

1989 ROCHESTER CARBURETORS
E4ME 4-Barrel (Cont.)

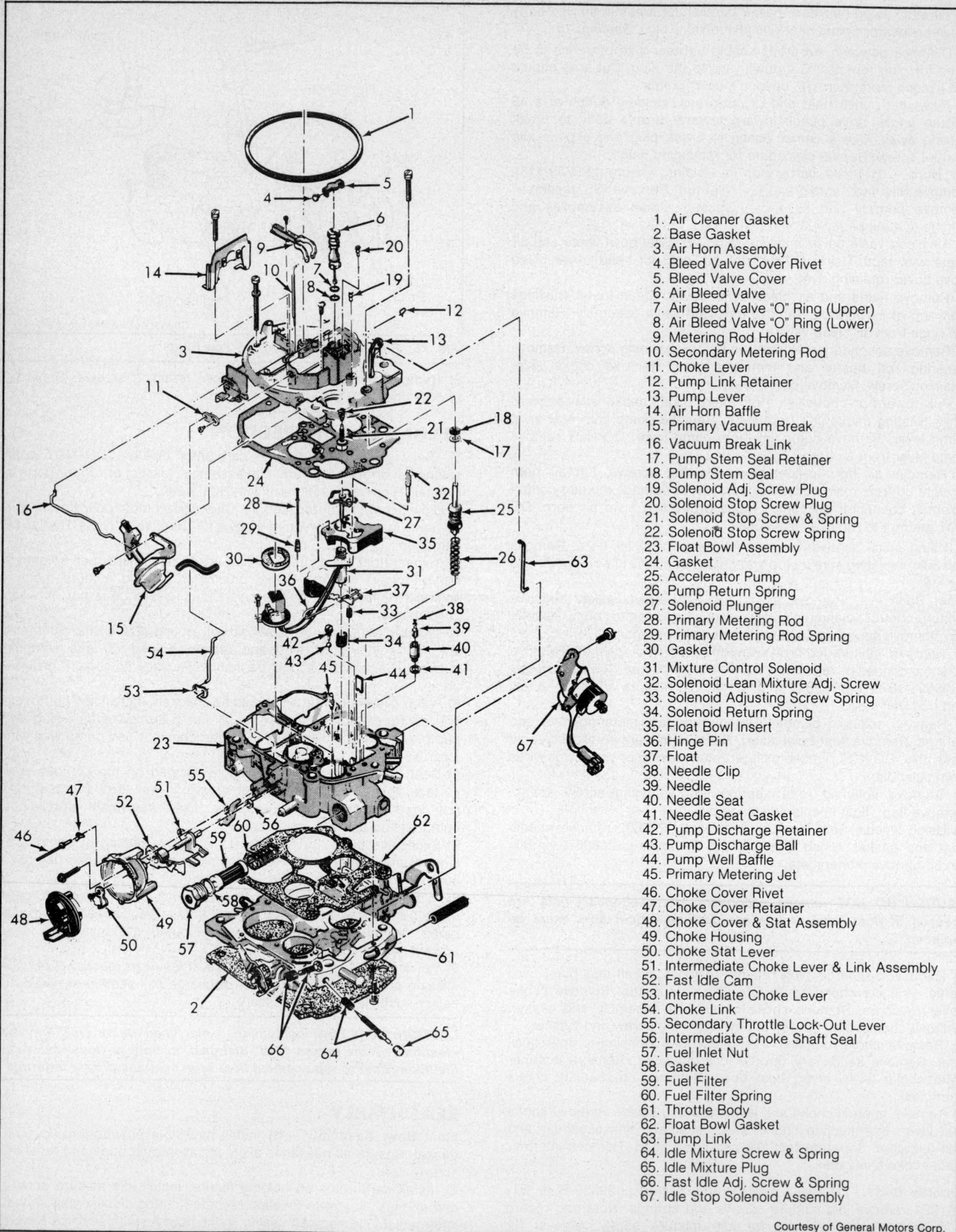

1. Air Cleaner Gasket
2. Base Gasket
3. Air Horn Assembly
4. Bleed Valve Cover Rivet
5. Bleed Valve Cover
6. Air Bleed Valve
7. Air Bleed Valve "O" Ring (Upper)
8. Air Bleed Valve "O" Ring (Lower)
9. Metering Rod Holder
10. Secondary Metering Rod
11. Choke Lever
12. Pump Link Retainer
13. Pump Lever
14. Air Horn Baffle
15. Primary Vacuum Break
16. Vacuum Break Link
17. Pump Stem Seal Retainer
18. Pump Stem Seal
19. Solenoid Adj. Screw Plug
20. Solenoid Stop Screw Plug
21. Solenoid Stop Screw & Spring
22. Solenoid Stop Screw Spring
23. Float Bowl Assembly
24. Gasket
25. Accelerator Pump
26. Pump Return Spring
27. Solenoid Plunger
28. Primary Metering Rod
29. Primary Metering Rod Spring
30. Gasket

31. Mixture Control Solenoid
32. Solenoid Lean Mixture Adj. Screw
33. Solenoid Adjusting Screw Spring
34. Solenoid Return Spring
35. Float Bowl Insert
36. Hinge Pin
37. Float
38. Needle Clip
39. Needle
40. Needle Seat
41. Needle Seat Gasket
42. Pump Discharge Retainer
43. Pump Discharge Ball
44. Pump Well Baffle
45. Primary Metering Jet

46. Choke Cover Rivet
47. Choke Cover Retainer
48. Choke Cover & Stat Assembly
49. Choke Housing
50. Choke Stat Lever
51. Intermediate Choke Lever & Link Assembly
52. Fast Idle Cam
53. Intermediate Choke Lever
54. Choke Link
55. Secondary Throttle Lock-Out Lever
56. Intermediate Choke Shaft Seal
57. Fuel Inlet Nut
58. Gasket
59. Fuel Filter
60. Fuel Filter Spring
61. Throttle Body
62. Float Bowl Gasket
63. Pump Link
64. Idle Mixture Screw & Spring
65. Idle Mixture Plug
66. Fast Idle Adj. Screw & Spring
67. Idle Stop Solenoid Assembly

Fig. 16: *Exploded View of Rochester Model E4ME Carburetor*

3) Install fast idle cam on intermediate choke shaft with stepped areas facing downward. Install cam and choke shaft in housing. Install choke stat lever on intermediate choke shaft. Install retaining screw.

4) Install choke shaft seal in float bowl with seal lips facing outward. Install choke housing seal in float bowl. Install secondary lock-out lever. Using Choke Lever Installer (J-23417), install intermediate choke lever in float bowl cavity.

5) Install choke housing assembly so intermediate choke shaft engages with intermediate choke lever. Ensure fast idle cam is located above vacuum break lever.

6) Install choke housing retaining screws. Check choke linkage for freedom of movement. Adjust choke coil lever adjustment. See CHOKE COIL LEVER under ADJUSTMENTS in this article.

7) Install pump well baffle with slot area toward bottom of float bowl. Install pump discharge ball and spring (if equipped). Install discharge ball plug. Install primary metering jets.

8) Using Needle Seat Installer (J-22769), install needle seat and gasket. Install float needle on float. Ensure float needle does not engage with slot area on float.

9) Install float hinge pin with open end facing pump well. Install float assembly. Adjust float level. See FLOAT LEVEL under ADJUST-MENTS in this article.

10) Install mixture control solenoid return spring and adjusting screw spring. Install mixture control solenoid with solenoid pin aligned with float bowl hole.

11) Install solenoid retaining screw and connector-to-air horn gasket. Adjust solenoid mixture screw. See MIXTURE CONTROL SOLENOID MIXTURE SCREW under ADJUSTMENTS in this article.

12) Install float bowl insert, primary metering rods and springs. Install new cup and spring on accelerator pump. Install accelerator pump and spring. Install float bowl-to-air horn gasket. Install mixture control solenoid plunger.

Air Horn – 1) Install pump stem seal and TPS seal with seal lips facing outward. Install seal retainers. Stake seal retainers in 3 places. Install mixture control solenoid stop screw and spring. Using Stop Screw Adjuster (J-28696-4), lightly seat stop screw then back out 1/4 turn.

2) Hold air horn gasket downward while installing air horn. Ensure accelerator pump aligns with hole of air horn. Ensure air horn tubes align with float bowl and gasket. Install air horn screws. Tighten screws in proper sequence. *See Fig. 17.*

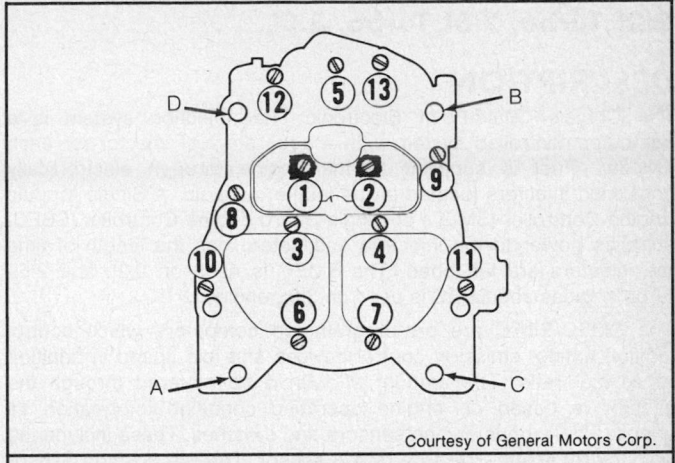

Courtesy of General Motors Corp.

Fig. 17: Air Horn & Throttle Plate Tightening Sequence

3) Install pump link in throttle lever and pump lever. Install pump link retainer. Install choke link in intermediate choke lever while holding fast idle cam upward.

4) Install choke lever on choke link. Engage choke lever with choke shaft. Install retaining screw. Install secondary metering rods and holder. Ends of metering rods must face each other. Install holder retaining screw.

5) Operate air valves to ensure freedom of movement. Coat new "O" rings for air bleed valve with ATF. Install "O" rings on air bleed valve with thick ring in upper groove and thin ring in lower groove.

6) Install air bleed valve. Adjust air bleed valve. See AIR BLEED VALVE under ADJUSTMENTS in this article. Install and adjust vacuum break assemblies.

7) Install ISS. Install spring, fuel filter and fuel inlet nut. Tighten fuel inlet nut to 46 ft. lbs. (62 N.m). Place fast idle cam on highest step.

8) Install choke cover, stat assembly and gasket in choke housing. Ensure coil tang engages with choke stat lever and cover notch aligns with housing projection. Install choke cover retainers and rivets. Perform necessary adjustments. See ADJUSTMENTS in this article.

9) Install carburetor to intake manifold using new base gasket. Tighten bolts A-D in sequence to 12 ft. lbs. (16 N.m). *See Fig. 17.*

CARBURETOR ADJUSTMENT SPECIFICATIONS

| Application | Float Level | Accel. Pump | Idle Air Bleed | Air Valve Spring [1] | Choke Coil Lever | Choke Rod | Vacuum Break | | Air Valve Rod | Auto. Choke | Choke Unloader | Secondary Lock-Out |
							Primary	Secondary				
E4ME 17085433	14/32	TR	....	7/8	.120"	20°	30°	.....	.025"	TR	25°	.015"

TR – Tamper Resistant
[1] – Specification is numbers of turns.

1989 FUEL INJECTION
Chrysler Motors Multi-Point Fuel Injection

2.2L Turbo, 2.5L Turbo, 3.0L

DESCRIPTION

The Chrysler Multi-Point Electronic Fuel Injection system is a computer controlled system with a separate fuel injector for each cylinder. Fuel is supplied to the engine through electronically controlled injectors located in the intake manifold. A Single Module Engine Controller (SMEC) or Single Board Engine Controller (SBEC) supplies power to the injectors and determines the length of time the injectors are left open. The SMEC is used on 2.2L and 2.5L turbo engines and SBEC is used on 3.0L engines.

The SMEC/SBEC are pre-programmed computers which control ignition timing, emission control devices and idle speed in addition to air/fuel ratio. The amount of fuel to be metered through the injector is based on engine operating condition information as supplied by various engine sensors and switches. These include the Manifold Absolute Pressure (MAP) sensor, Throttle Position Sensor (TPS), oxygen sensor, coolant temperature sensor, vehicle distance/speed sensor and fuel charge temperature sensor.

OPERATION

AIR INDUCTION

On turbo models, air is drawn through the air cleaner and forced through the throttle body by the turbocharger. Wastegate is controlled by the SMEC and can increase turbo boost to higher levels for brief periods of time. The amount of air entering the engine is controlled by a cable operated throttle valve in the throttle body.

On all models, the throttle body houses the Throttle Position Sensor (TPS) and Automatic Idle Speed (AIS) motor. The TPS is an electrical resistor which is connected to the throttle valve. The TPS transmits a signal to the SMEC in relation to throttle valve angle.

From this signal, the SMEC/SBEC calculates fuel injector "on" time to provide adequate air/fuel mixture.

The AIS motor controls the flow of air through the throttle body during engine idle. The motor opens and closes an air by-pass on the back of the throttle body to increase or decrease idle speed as engine load varies. The SMEC/SBEC monitors the AIS motor and issues a change command to the injectors to increase or decrease the amount of fuel injected.

FUEL DELIVERY

Fuel is drawn through a filter sock on one end of the fuel pump and is forced out the opposite end. Two check valves are used. One relieves internal fuel pump pressure and regulates maximum fuel pressure output.

The other check valve, located near pump outlet, restricts fuel flow in either direction when pump is not running. Fuel not used by the engine is returned to the tank by a fuel return line.

Power to the fuel pump is supplied through the Automatic Shut-Down (ASD) relay of the SMEC/SBEC. When the SMEC/SBEC receives a signal from the distributor during engine cranking, it grounds ASD motor, closing ASD contacts. When contacts are closed, power is applied to fuel pump.

When distributor signal is lost, the SMEC/SBEC opens the ASD motor, which cuts power supply to fuel pump. This prevents fuel flow should the vehicle be involved in an accident or if engine stalls.

FUEL INJECTORS

The fuel injectors are an electric solenoid powered and controlled by the SMEC. The SMEC determines when and how long the injector should operate. When an electric current is supplied to the injector, the armature and pintle move a short distance against a spring, opening a small orifice. Since fuel is under high pressure a fine spray is developed.

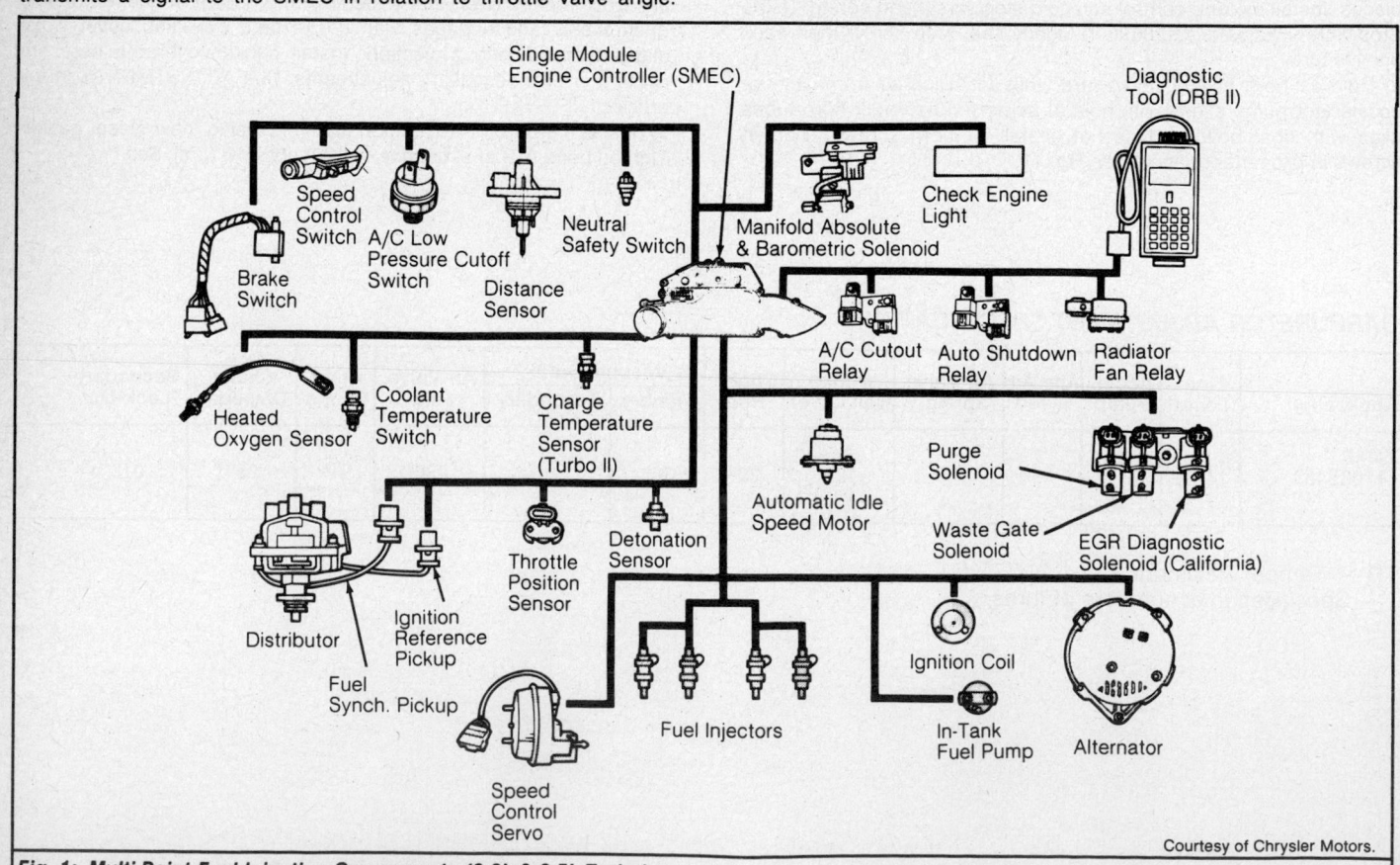

Courtesy of Chrysler Motors.

Fig. 1: Multi-Point Fuel Injection Components (2.2L & 2.5L Turbo)

1989 FUEL INJECTION
Chrysler Motors Multi-Point Fuel Injection (Cont.)

2-23

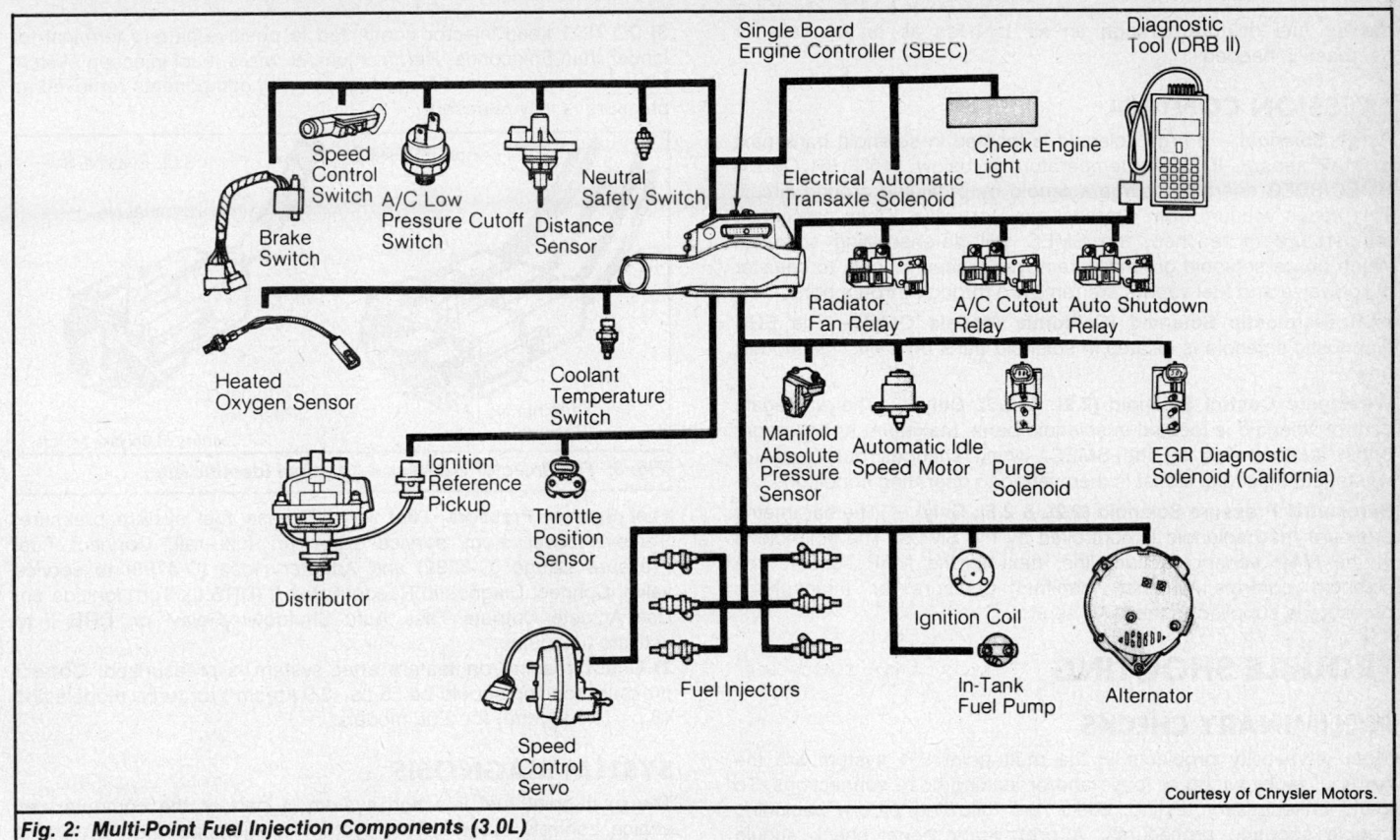

Fig. 2: Multi-Point Fuel Injection Components (3.0L)

Courtesy of Chrysler Motors.

SINGLE MODULE ENGINE CONTROLLER (SMEC) & SINGLE BOARD ENGINE CONTROLLER (SBEC)

The SMEC (2.2L and 2.5L) and SBEC (3.0L) contain circuits necessary to drive ignition coil, fuel injectors and alternator field. They contain a 14-pin connector and a 60-pin connector (60-pin only for SBEC). The SMEC/SBEC are digital computers containing microprocessors. They receive input signals from various switches and sensors.

The SMEC and SBEC then compute the fuel injector pulse width, spark advance, ignition coil dwell, idle speed, purge, cooling fan start and alternator charge rate. The SMEC/SBEC contain voltage converters which converts battery voltage to 9 volts output. The SMEC and SBEC are located on the right inner fender panel.

NOTE: For more information on SMEC and SBEC, see COMPUTER-IZED ENGINE CONTROLS section.

SENSORS & SWITCHES

Manifold Absolute Pressure (MAP) Sensor – The MAP sensor, located in the engine compartment on the right shock tower, monitors manifold vacuum via vacuum line attached to throttle body. The MAP sensor supplies the SMEC/SBEC with an electrical signal which indicates manifold vacuum and barometric pressure. This information helps to determine air/fuel ratio.

Oxygen Sensor – Oxygen sensor is mounted in exhaust manifold or turbo outlet. The oxygen sensor monitors oxygen content of exhaust gases and generates voltage signals proportional to oxygen content.

Voltage signal to the SMEC/SBEC is low when oxygen content of exhaust gases is high, indicating lean air/fuel mixture. If oxygen content decreases (mixture becomes richer), signal voltage will increase.

Charge & Coolant Temperature Sensors – Two temperature sensors are used on this system. The charge temperature sensor, which is mounted in the intake manifold, measures temperature of incoming air/fuel mixture. The coolant temperature sensor, which is mounted in thermostat housing, measures temperature of engine coolant.

Information provided by these 2 sensors allows the SMEC/SBEC to demand slightly richer air/fuel mixtures and higher idle speeds during cold engine operation.

If coolant temperature sensor should fail, the information supplied by the charge temperature sensor is sufficient to determine engine operating temperature and engine warm-up cycles until the coolant temperature sensor can be replaced.

Throttle Position Sensor (TPS) – The TPS is an electric resistor which is activated by throttle shaft movement. It is mounted on the throttle body and senses angle of throttle blade opening.

A voltage signal is produced by the sensor which varies with this angle. This signal is transmitted to the SMEC/SBEC where it is used to adjust air/fuel ratio during acceleration, deceleration, idle, and wide open throttle.

Detonation Sensor (2.2L & 2.5L) – The detonation sensor is mounted on intake manifold. Detonation is converted into an electrical signal which is sent to the SMEC. The SMEC will change spark advance and/or boost as needed.

Engine Switches – Several switches provide operating information to the SMEC/SBEC. These include neutral safety, A/C clutch, brake light and idle switches. When the SMEC/SBEC senses one or more of these switches is on, the AIS motor will receive a signal to increase idle speed.

AUTOMATIC IDLE SPEED MOTOR (AIS)

The automatic idle speed motor is operated by the SMEC/SBEC. Data from throttle position sensor, speed sensor, coolant temperature sensor, and various switch operations, are used by the SMEC/SBEC to adjust engine idle. The AIS adjusts the air portion of

2-24

1989 FUEL INJECTION
Chrysler Motors Multi-Point Fuel Injection (Cont.)

the air fuel mixture through an air by-pass as an increase or decrease is needed.

EMISSION CONTROL

Purge Solenoid – Purge solenoid is located in solenoid bank next to MAP sensor. If engine temperature is below 145°F (61°C), the SMEC/SBEC energizes purge solenoid by providing ground circuit. This keeps vacuum from charcoal canister valve. When prescribed temperature is reached, the SMEC will de-energizing solenoid. When purge solenoid ground is removed, vacuum flows to canister purge valve and fuel vapors are removed through throttle body.

EGR Diagnostic Solenoid (California Models Only) – The EGR diagnostic solenoid is located in solenoid bank on California models only.

Wastegate Control Solenoid (2.2L & 2.5L Only) – The wastegate control solenoid is located in solenoid bank. Maximum turbocharger boost is controlled by the SMEC, which changes duty cycle of wastegate solenoid. Boost is then varied to operating conditions.

Barometric Pressure Solenoid (2.2L & 2.5L Only) – The barometric pressure read solenoid is controlled by the SMEC. The solenoid is in the MAP sensor vacuum line, next to the MAP sensor. The solenoid controls whether manifold pressure or atmospheric pressure is supplied to the MAP sensor.

TROUBLE SHOOTING

PRELIMINARY CHECKS

Most driveability problems in the multi-point EFI system are the result of faulty wiring or loose and/or leaking hose connections. To avoid unnecessary testing, check the following before beginning trouble shooting procedures. A preliminary visual check should include:
- Air ducts at air cleaner, turbocharger and throttle body.
- All electrical connections at components.

Check vacuum lines for tight, leak-free connections in these areas:
- Throttle body.
- Solenoid bank.
- Vapor canister.
- PCV valve to turbocharger vacuum port.
- Backpressure transducer.
- MAP sensor.

Ensure the following electrical connectors are properly attached:
- 14-pin and 60-pin connector at SMEC/SBEC.
- Connectors at ASD relay.
- Connectors at solenoid bank.
- Speed/distance sensor connector (in-line with speedometer cable).
- Charge temperature sensor connector.
- Throttle body connector.
- Fuel injector connectors.
- O_2 sensor connector.
- Coolant temperature sensor connector.
- Distributor connectors.
- Connector at detonation sensor.
- Radiator fan relay connectors.
- Ground eyelet mounting onto intake manifold.

TESTING & DIAGNOSIS

FUEL SYSTEM PRESSURE TESTING

Fuel System Pressure Release – 1) Fuel pressure must be fully released before opening fuel loop or removing any fuel carrying components. To release pressure in tank, open fuel tank cap slowly.
2) To release remaining pressure in system, disconnect 2-pin connector from fuel injector. Using jumper wire, connect injector harness ground terminal No. 1 to ground. Connect injector harness positive terminal No. 2 to positive battery terminal with second jumper wire. *See Fig. 3.*

3) DO NOT keep injector connected to positive battery terminal for longer than 5 seconds. Remove jumper wires. Fuel injection system loop can now be opened and fuel carrying components removed as pressure is fully released.

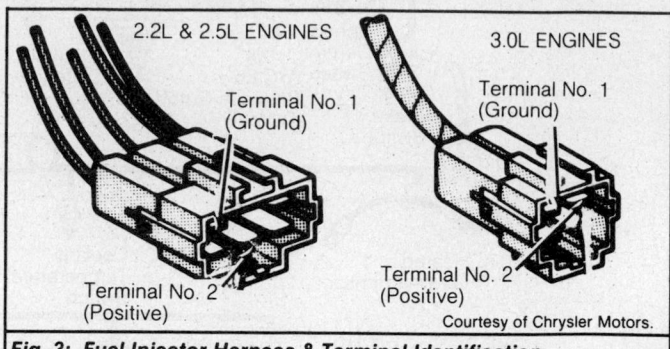

Fig. 3: Fuel Injector Harness & Terminal Identification

Fuel System Pressure Test – 1) Release fuel system pressure. Remove cover from service valve on fuel rail. Connect Fuel Pressure Gauge (C-3292) and Adapter Hose (C-4799) to service valve. Connect Diagnostic Readout Box II (DRB II). Turn ignition on. Use Actuate Outputs Test "Auto Shutdown Relay" on DRB II to activate fuel pump.
2) Check reading on testers after system is pressurized. Correct pressure reading should be 55 psi (3.9 kg/cm²) for turbo models and 48 psi (3.3 kg/cm²) for 3.0L models.

SYSTEM DIAGNOSIS

The multi-point fuel injection system is part of the computerized engine controls system. This system is equipped with "On-Board Diagnosis," which has a self-diagnostic capability that checks several circuits.

If abnormal signals occur often enough to indicate a valid problem, the SMEC/SBEC will store the fault code for later display. If problem is either repaired or disappears by itself, the SMEC/SBEC will remove the fault code after 50-100 engine starts.

When a fault code is set, the "Check Engine Light" comes on. Located on instrument panel, this light informs operator that malfunction in system has occurred and immediate service is required.

The SMEC will attempt to compensate for failure of a component by using input from remaining sensors. If the "Check Engine Light" comes on or certain driveability and engine performance problems exist, the source of these difficulties may be determined by displaying and recording fault codes. Check FAULT CODES to determine questionable circuit.

FAULT CODES

NOTE: For fault codes and code descriptions, see appropriate article in COMPUTERIZED ENGINE CONTROLS section.

REMOVAL & INSTALLATION

PRECAUTIONS

Before removing any fuel system components, system pressure must be relieved. See FUEL SYSTEM PRESSURE RELEASE under FUEL SYSTEM PRESSURE TESTING. It is not necessary to remove throttle body from intake manifold to remove components.

If any components such as hoses or clamps are replaced, ensure they are replaced with components designed for EFI use. Always reassemble throttle body components with new "O" rings and seals.

1989 FUEL INJECTION
Chrysler Motors Multi-Point Fuel Injection (Cont.)

2-25

THROTTLE POSITION SENSOR

Removal & Installation – Disconnect negative battery cable and throttle body wiring connector. Remove 2 screws mounting throttle position sensor to throttle body. Remove throttle position sensor off throttle shaft. To install, remove removal procedure.

THROTTLE BODY

Removal & Installation – 1) Disconnect negative battery cable. Remove screws attaching air cleaner to throttle body. Loosen hose clamp and remove air cleaner adapter. Remove accelerator, speed control and transmission kickdown cables and return spring.
2) Remove throttle cable bracket from throttle body. Disconnect electrical connector. Disconnect vacuum hoses from throttle body. Loosen screws attaching throttle body to intake manifold. Remove throttle body. To install, reverse removal procedure.

AUTOMATIC IDLE SPEED (AIS) MOTOR

Removal & Installation – Remove air cleaner. Disconnect battery negative cable and 4-pin AIS connector. Remove temperature sending unit from throttle body housing. Remove 2 Torx screws that secure AIS. Remove AIS motor. Ensure "O" ring is removed from throttle body. To install, reverse removal procedure. Use new "O" ring. Install 2 mounting screws and tighten to 17 INCH lbs. (2 N.m).

NOTE: Measure exposed pintle before starting installation. If exposed pintle measures more than 1" (25 mm), reconnect battery and retract pintle with Actuate Outputs Test Open/Close. See appropriate article in COMPUTERIZED ENGINE CONTROLS section.

FUEL PUMP UNIT

Removal & Installation – With fuel tank removed from vehicle, use hammer and brass punch to carefully tap lock ring counterclockwise and release pump. Remove fuel pump and "O" ring seal from tank. Discard old seal. To install, reverse removal procedure, making sure seal area is clean. Take care not to overtighten pump.

FUEL INJECTOR RAIL ASSEMBLY

Removal – 1) Release fuel system pressure. Disconnect negative battery cable. Remove air cleaner assembly. Disconnect knock sensor and fuel injector wiring connectors. Loosen supply hose clamp and return hose clamp at fuel pressure regulator and remove hoses.
2) Remove fuel pressure regulator vacuum hose from regulator. Remove fuel pressure regulator-to-fuel rail attaching nuts. Remove fuel pressure regulator from fuel rail. Remove PCV vacuum harness and vacuum vapor harness from intake manifold.
3) Remove fuel rail to valve cover bracket screw. Disconnect knock sensor connector. Remove fuel rail-to-intake manifold attaching screws. Remove fuel rail and injector assembly so injectors come straight out of ports. Use care to not damage "O" rings. Remove fuel rail assembly from vehicle.
4) Cover injector ports with a rag while injectors are serviced. Do not remove fuel injectors until fuel rail assembly has been removed from vehicle.
Installation – 1) Seat injectors in cups (if removed) and install lock rings. Ensure injector holes are clean. Lube injector "O" rings with drop of oil. Install injector assemblies in sockets. Install 2 attaching bolts and ground straps. Tighten bolts to pull fuel rail into place evenly with each injector in its own hole.
2) To complete installation, reverse removal procedure. All wiring, hoses and ground straps must be in original positions. Use ATM tester or start vehicle to check for fuel leaks.

FUEL INJECTORS

Removal – Remove injector wiring connector from injector. Position fuel rail assembly so fuel injectors are accessible. Remove injector lock ring off fuel rail and injector. Pull injector straight out of fuel rail receiver cup.

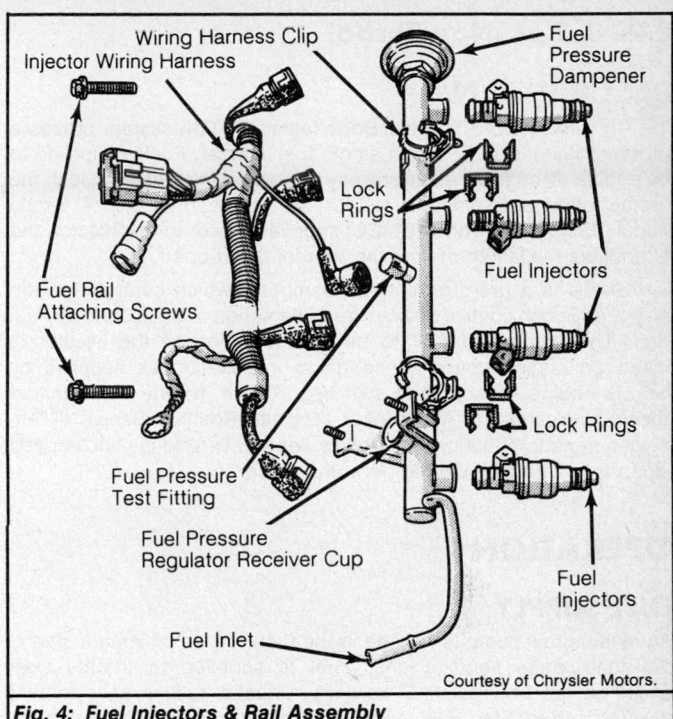

Fig. 4: Fuel Injectors & Rail Assembly

Inspection – Check injector "O" ring for damage. If injector is to be reused, install a protective cap over the injector tip to prevent damage.
Installation – Lubricate injector "O" ring with oil before installation. Install injector top end into fuel rail cup. Use care to not damage "O" ring during installation. Install injector lock ring. To complete installation, reverse removal procedure.

FUEL PRESSURE REGULATOR

Removal & Installation – 1) Perform fuel system pressure release procedure. Disconnect negative battery cable. Remove vacuum hose from fuel pressure regulator. Loosen fuel return hose clamp at fuel pressure regulator and remove hose. Wrap a rag around hose to collect fuel spillage.
2) Remove fuel pressure regulator attaching nuts. Remove fuel pressure regulator from rail. Before installation of regulator, lubricate "O" ring with a drop of oil. To install, reverse removal procedure.

SINGLE MODULE ENGINE CONTROLLER (SMEC) & SINGLE BOARD ENGINE CONTROLLER (SBEC)

Removal & Installation – Remove air cleaner duct from SMEC/SBEC. Remove battery. Remove mounting screws and electrical connectors. To install, reverse removal procedure.

OXYGEN SENSOR

Removal & Installation – Using Sensor Socket (C-4907), remove oxygen sensor from exhaust manifold. Using 18 mm x 1.5 x 6E tap, clean threads in exhaust manifold. New oxygen sensors come with anti-seize on threads. If old sensor is to be reused, coat threads with anti-seize compound. Tighten oxygen sensor to 20 ft. lbs. (27 N.m).

WIRING DIAGRAMS

NOTE: For wiring diagrams, see appropriate article in COMPUTERIZED ENGINE CONTROLS section.

1989 FUEL INJECTION
Chrysler Motors Throttle Body Injection

2.2L & 2.5L (Non-Turbo)

DESCRIPTION

The Chrysler Motors Throttle Body Injection (TBI) system utilizes a throttle-body assembly with a single fuel injector. Fuel is supplied to the engine through an electronically controlled injector located in the throttle body assembly on top of the intake manifold. A Single Module Engine Controller (SMEC) supplies power to the injector and determines the length of time the injector is left open.

The SMEC is a pre-programmed computer which controls ignition timing, emission control devices and idle speed in addition to air/fuel ratio. The amount of fuel to be metered through the injector is based on engine operating condition information as supplied by various engine sensors and switches. These include the Manifold Absolute Pressure (MAP) sensor, Throttle Position Sensor (TPS), oxygen sensor, coolant temperature sensor, vehicle distance/speed sensor and throttle body temperature sensor.

OPERATION

FUEL SUPPLY

An electric fuel pump is located in the fuel tank as an integral part of the fuel gauge sending unit. Fuel is supplied to throttle body assembly at 14.5 psi (1.0 kg/cm²). Unused fuel is sent to tank through return line. Fuel pump voltage is supplied by Automatic Shutdown Relay (ASD).

SINGLE MODULE ENGINE CONTROLLER (SMEC)

The SMEC contains circuits necessary to drive ignition coil, fuel injector and alternator field. It contains a 14-pin connector and a 60-pin connector. *See Fig. 2.* The SMEC is a digital computer containing a microprocessor. It receives input signals from various switches and sensors. It then computes the fuel injector pulse width, spark advance, ignition coil dwell, idle speed, purge, cooling fan start and alternator charge rate. The SMEC is located on the right inner fender panel.

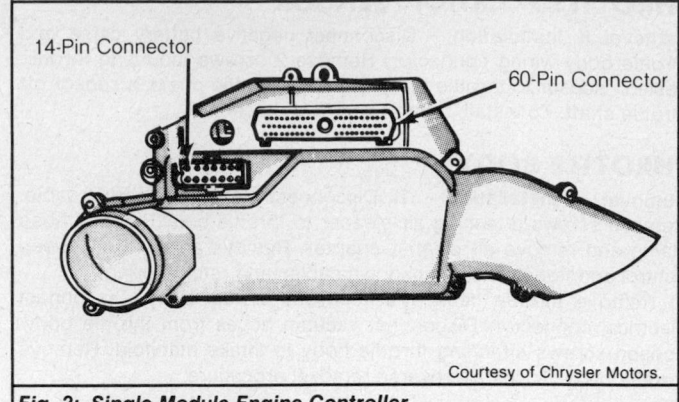

Courtesy of Chrysler Motors.

Fig. 2: Single Module Engine Controller

THROTTLE BODY

The throttle body is mounted on intake manifold. It houses fuel injector, pressure regulator, throttle position sensor, throttle body temperature sensor and automatic idle speed motor. Airflow is controlled by a throttle blade which is operated by conventional throttle linkage.

FUEL INJECTOR

The fuel injector is an electronic solenoid. The SMEC determines when and for how long the injector should be energized. While electrical current is supplied to the injector, a spring loaded check ball is lifted from its seat. Fuel then flows in a cone shaped spray pattern before entering air stream. *See Fig. 3.* Fuel is supplied to injectors at constant 14.5 psi (1.0 kg/cm²).

FUEL PRESSURE REGULATOR

The fuel pressure regulator is located downstream of the fuel injector on the fuel rail. Its function is to regulate fuel pressure at constant 14.5 psi (1.0 kg/cm²).

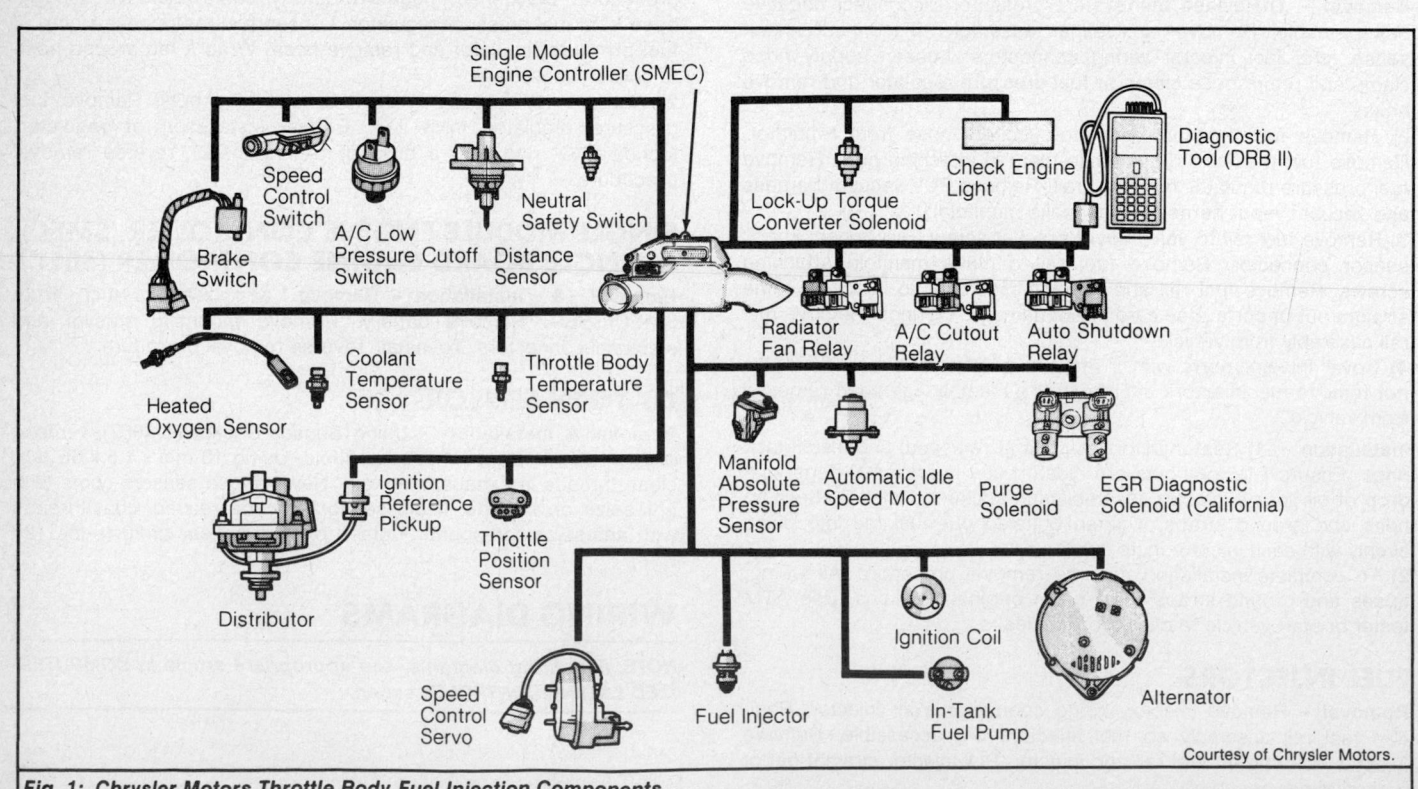

Courtesy of Chrysler Motors.

Fig. 1: Chrysler Motors Throttle Body Fuel Injection Components

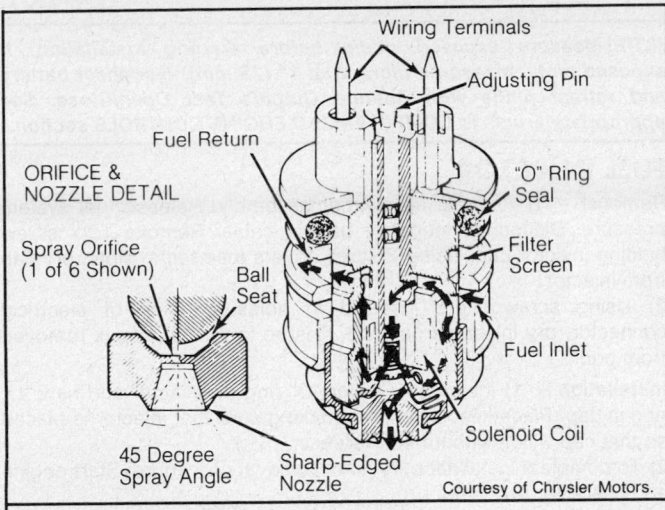

Fig. 3: Cross-Sectional View of Fuel Injector

(Labels in figure: Wiring Terminals, Adjusting Pin, Fuel Return, "O" Ring Seal, Filter Screen, ORIFICE & NOZZLE DETAIL, Spray Orifice (1 of 6 Shown), Ball Seat, Fuel Inlet, 45 Degree Spray Angle, Sharp-Edged Nozzle, Solenoid Coil, Courtesy of Chrysler Motors.)

AUTOMATIC IDLE SPEED MOTOR (AIS)

The AIS motor, mounted on throttle body, is controlled by a signal from SMEC. Data from throttle position sensor, speed sensor, coolant temperature sensor, and various switch operations, are used by SMEC to adjust engine idle to a predetermined speed.

PURGE SOLENOID

The SMEC controls purge solenoid based upon engine temperature. When engine operating temperature reaches 145°F (61°C), fuel vapors will be purged through throttle body.

ENGINE SENSORS & SWITCHES

Manifold Absolute Pressure (MAP) Sensor – The MAP sensor, which is located on right front shock tower, monitors manifold vacuum through a vacuum hose connecting MAP sensor and throttle body. This sensor supplies the SMEC with manifold vacuum and barometric pressure signals. This information is used to determine air/fuel ratio.

Oxygen Sensor – The oxygen sensor is located in the exhaust manifold near the header pipe flange. It monitors oxygen content of exhaust and produces a voltage signal which is proportional to oxygen content. If oxygen content is high (lean air/fuel mixture), a low voltage signal is sent to the SMEC. As oxygen content decreases (richer mixture), signal voltage becomes higher.

Coolant Temperature Sensor – The coolant temperature sensor is mounted in thermostat housing. The coolant sensor voltage signal varies with coolant temperature. The SMEC will command slightly richer air/fuel mixtures and higher idle speeds during cold engine operation. Coolant temperature sensor also functions as control for electric cooling fan.

Throttle Body Temperature Sensor – This sensor is mounted in the throttle body to measure fuel temperature. Fuel temperature input signal controls mixture used in hot start situations.

Throttle Position Sensor (TPS) – The TPS is an electric resistor, mounted on throttle body, and is activated by movement of the throttle shaft. The voltage signal produced by TPS varies with angle of throttle blade opening. This signal is transmitted to the SMEC and is used to adjust air/fuel ratio during various throttle positions in different operating conditions.

Engine Switches – Several switches provide operating information to the SMEC. These include idle, neutral safety, A/C clutch and brake light switches. Whenever one or more of these switches completes its circuit, the SMEC signals AIS to change idle speed to specific RPM.

TROUBLE SHOOTING

PRELIMINARY CHECKS

Most driveability problems in the throttle body fuel injection system result from faulty wiring and/or leaking vacuum hoses and hose connections. To avoid unnecessary component testing, visual check should be performed before beginning trouble shooting procedures. A preliminary visual check should include:
- Air ducts at air cleaner and throttle body.
- All electrical connections at components.

Check vacuum lines for tight leak-free connections in these areas:
- Throttle body (2 front, 2 rear).
- Purge solenoid.
- Charcoal canister.
- PCV valve to intake manifold vacuum port.
- EGR backpressure transducer.
- MAP sensor.

Ensure the following electrical connectors are properly attached:
- 60-pin and 14-pin SMEC connectors.
- MAP sensor connector.
- Purge solenoid connector.
- Speed sensor connector.
- Throttle body temperature sensor connector.
- Radiator fan relay connector.
- AIS motor connector.
- TPS connector.
- A/C cut-out relay.
- Ground eyelet on left cylinder head.
- Fuel injector connector.
- Oxygen sensor connector.
- Coolant temperature sensor connector.
- Distributor connector.

TESTING & DIAGNOSIS

FUEL SYSTEM PRESSURE RELEASE

1) Fuel injection system holds constant pressure of 14.5 psi (1.0 kg/cm²). This pressure must be released before disconnecting any fuel carrying components. To release pressure in tank, open fuel tank cap slowly.

2) To release remaining pressure in system, disconnect 2-pin connector from fuel injector. Using jumper wire, connect injector harness ground terminal No. 1 to ground. Connect injector harness terminal No. 2 to positive battery terminal with second jumper wire. *See Fig. 4.*

3) DO NOT keep injector connected to positive battery terminal for longer than 5 seconds. Remove jumper wires. Fuel injection system can now be opened and fuel carrying components removed as pressure is fully released.

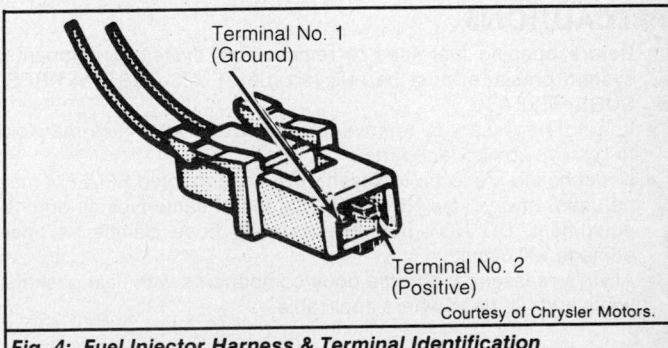

Fig. 4: Fuel Injector Harness & Terminal Identification

(Labels in figure: Terminal No. 1 (Ground), Terminal No. 2 (Positive), Courtesy of Chrysler Motors.)

FUEL SYSTEM PRESSURE TEST

1) Release fuel system pressure. Disconnect 5/16" hose from engine fuel line assembly. Connect Fuel System Pressure Testers (C-3292 and C-4749) between fuel filter outlet hose and throttle

body. Connect Diagnostic Readout Box II (DRB II). Turn ignition on. Use Actuate Outputs Test "Auto Shutdown Relay" on DRB II to activate fuel pump.

2) Check reading on testers after system is pressurized. The correct pressure reading should be 13.5-15.5 psi (.95-1.09 kg/cm²). If system pressure is correct, remove testers. Reconnect fuel hose to throttle body using a new hose clamp of same type as original equipment.

3) If pressure reading is low, move pressure tester so reading is taken between fuel supply line and fuel filter inlet hose. Repeat pressure test. If reading is correct, replace fuel filter.

4) If reading is still low, lightly squeeze fuel return hose. Replace fuel pressure regulator if pressure now increases. If pressure continues to read low, fuel pump is defective or fuel pump intake filter is plugged.

5) If pressure reading is high, disconnect fuel return hose at throttle body. Connect separate hose to throttle body/fuel pressure regulator with open end in clean container. Repeat pressure test. If reading is still high, check for plugged fuel injector. If injector is okay, replace fuel pressure regulator. If reading is correct, check all return lines for restrictions.

SYSTEM DIAGNOSIS

The throttle body fuel injection system is part of the computerized engine controls system. This system is equipped with "On-Board Diagnostics," which has capability to check several circuits.

If abnormal signals occur often enough to indicate a valid problem, the SMEC will store the fault code for later display. If problem is either repaired or disappears by itself, the SMEC will remove the fault code after 50-100 engine starts.

When a fault code is set, the "Check Engine Light" comes on. Located on instrument panel, this light informs operator that malfunction in system has occurred and immediate service is required.

The SMEC will attempt to compensate for failure of a component by using input from remaining sensors. If the "Check Engine Light" comes on or certain driveability and engine performance problems exist, the source of these difficulties may be determined by displaying and recording fault codes. Check FAULT CODES to determine questionable circuit.

FAULT CODES

NOTE: For fault codes and code descriptions, see appropriate article in COMPUTERIZED ENGINE CONTROLS section.

REMOVAL & INSTALLATION

PRECAUTIONS

- Before opening fuel lines to remove fuel system components, system pressure must be relieved. See FUEL SYSTEM PRESSURE RELEASE.
- It is not necessary to remove throttle body from intake manifold to remove component parts.
- If fuel hoses are to be replaced, only hose marked EFI/EFM may be used. Always use NEW hose clamps of same type as original equipment. DO NOT use aviation style hose clamps as hose damage will occur.
- Always reassemble throttle body components with new gaskets, seals and "O" rings where applicable.

AUTOMATIC IDLE SPEED (AIS) MOTOR

Removal & Installation – Remove air cleaner. Disconnect battery negative cable and 4-pin AIS connector. Remove temperature sending unit from throttle body housing. Remove 2 Torx screws that secure AIS. Remove AIS motor. Ensure "O" ring is removed from throttle body. To install, reverse removal procedure. Use new "O" ring. Install 2 mounting screws and tighten to 17 INCH lbs. (2 N.m).

NOTE: Measure exposed pintle before starting installation. If exposed pintle measures more than 1" (25 mm), reconnect battery and retract pintle with Actuate Outputs Test Open/Close. See appropriate article in COMPUTERIZED ENGINE CONTROLS section.

FUEL INJECTOR

Removal – **1)** Remove air cleaner assembly. Release fuel system pressure. Disconnect negative battery cable. Remove Torx screw holding injector cap. Using 2 screwdrivers inserted in slots, pry cap from injector.

2) Using screwdrivers inserted in holes on side of electrical connector, pry injector from pod. Ensure lower "O" ring is removed from pod.

Installation – **1)** Install new lower "O" ring on injector and new "O" ring in cap. Place injector in pod, making sure that injector is placed so that cap will fit without interference.

2) To complete installation, reverse removal procedure. Start engine and check for fuel leaks.

FUEL PUMP UNIT

Removal & Installation – With fuel tank removed from vehicle, use hammer and brass punch to carefully tap lock ring counterclockwise and release pump. Remove fuel pump and "O" ring seal from tank. Discard old seal. To install, reverse removal procedure, making sure seal area is clean. Take care not to overtighten pump.

MANIFOLD ABSOLUTE PRESSURE (MAP) SENSOR

Removal & Installation – Remove vacuum hose and wiring harness from sensor. Remove sensor mounting screws and remove sensor. To install, reverse removal procedure. Ensure vacuum hose and electrical connectors are properly attached.

OXYGEN SENSOR

Removal & Installation – Use Sensor Socket (C-4907), to remove oxygen sensor from exhaust manifold. Clean threads in exhaust manifold, using 18 mm x 1.5 x 6E tap. New oxygen sensors come with anti-seize compound on threads. If old sensor is to be reused, coat threads with anti-seize compound. Tighten oxygen sensor to 20 ft. lbs. (27.2 N.m).

SINGLE MODULE ENGINE CONTROLLER (SMEC)

Removal & Installation – Remove air cleaner duct from SMEC. Remove battery. Remove 2 module mounting screws. Remove wiring connectors from module and remove module. To install, reverse removal procedure.

THROTTLE BODY

Removal – **1)** Remove air cleaner. Release fuel system pressure. Disconnect battery negative cable. Disconnect wiring connectors and vacuum lines from throttle body. Remove throttle, speed control and transmission kickdown cables as necessary.

2) Remove return spring. Loosen fuel intake and return hose clamps. Twist and pull off each hose. Remove throttle body mounting screws. Lift throttle body from engine.

Installation – Install throttle body on intake manifold with new gasket. To complete installation, reverse removal procedure.

THROTTLE POSITION SENSOR (TPS)

Removal & Installation – Disconnect battery negative cable and 3-pin TPS connector. Remove 2 screws holding TPS to throttle body. Lift TPS off throttle shaft. Remove "O" ring. To install, reverse removal procedure. Use new "O" ring.

WIRING DIAGRAMS

NOTE: For wiring diagrams, see appropriate article in COMPUTERIZED ENGINE CONTROLS section.

Premier 3.0L

DESCRIPTION

The 3.0L Eagle Premier uses a multi-point pressure-speed type fuel injection system. The amount of fuel injected into the engine is dependent upon intake manifold pressure and engine speed.

The fuel delivery system includes an in-tank fuel pump, fuel filter, fuel injectors and fuel pressure regulator. The electronic control system consists of an electronic control unit (ECU), input sensors and engine controls which receive output commands.

OPERATION

ELECTRONIC CONTROL UNIT (ECU)

The ECU is located under the instrument panel on the passenger side of the vehicle. Inputs from various engine sensors to ECU are used to determine engine operating conditions and needs.

FUEL INJECTORS

The multi-point fuel injection system has as many fuel injectors as there are cylinders. When voltage is supplied to injector solenoid, armature and plunger move upward against spring. Check ball above injector nozzle moves off seat and opens small orifice at end of injector, resulting in fine spray of fuel.

FUEL PRESSURE REGULATOR

The fuel pressure regulator is located in-line with the fuel return tube. *See Fig. 1.*

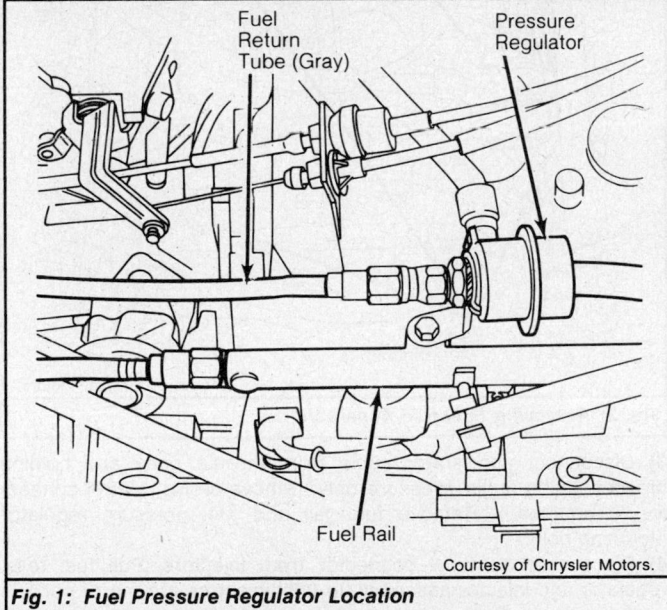

Fig. 1: Fuel Pressure Regulator Location

COOLANT TEMPERATURE SENSOR (CTS)

The coolant temperature sensor is located in the thermostat housing, above water pump. *See Fig. 2.*

OXYGEN SENSOR

The amount of oxygen in exhaust gases varies according to the air/fuel ratio of the intake charge. The oxygen sensor, located in the exhaust pipe, detects this content and transmits a low-votage signal to the ECU.

KNOCK SENSOR

The knock sensor is located above right motor mount and provides input to ECU which retards ignition advance to eliminate knock.

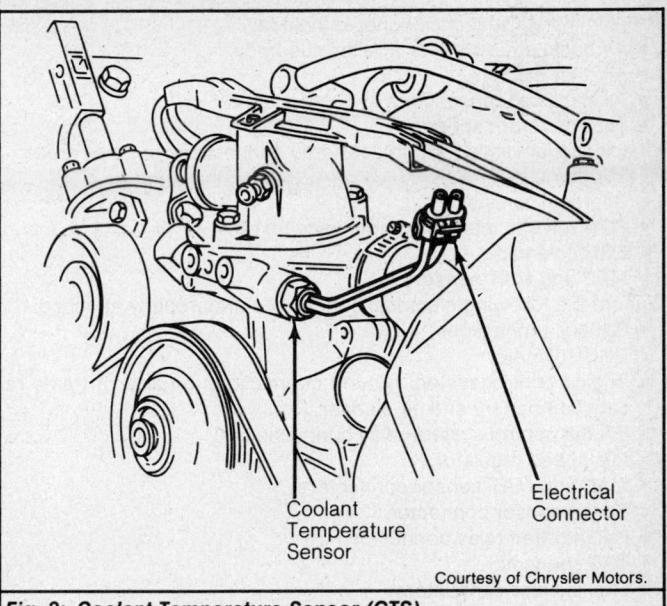

Fig. 2: Coolant Temperature Sensor (CTS)

MANIFOLD ABSOLUTE PRESSURE (MAP) SENSOR

The MAP sensor detects absolute pressure in the intake manifold as well as ambient atmospheric pressure. This information is supplied to the ECU, through voltage signals, as an indication of engine load. The sensor is located on the firewall, next to the brake power booster.

MANIFOLD AIR/FUEL TEMPERATURE (MAT) SENSOR

The MAT sensor provides signal to ECU that changes depending upon temperature of air/fuel mixture in intake manifold. During high temperature conditions, ECU will compensate for changes in density of air.

ENGINE SPEED SENSOR

The engine speed sensor is attached to bellhousing. It senses and counts teeth on flywheel gear ring as they pass during engine operation. Signal from speed sensor provides ECU with engine speed and crankshaft angle.

ADJUSTMENTS

THROTTLE POSITION SENSOR (TPS)

1) The use of Diagnostic Tester (DRB-II) is preferred when adjusting the throttle position sensor. Turn ignition on, engine off. Do not unplug the Throttle Position Sensor (TPS) wire harness connector. Insert voltmeter leads through the back of the wire harness connector.
2) TPS connector is marked "A", "B" and "C". Insert negative lead of voltmeter in terminal "B" and positive lead to terminal "C". Reading should be 5 volts. Insert voltmeter positive lead to terminal "A". Reading should be .4 volt. To adjust, loosen TPS retaining screws and pivot sensor to obtain correct reading.

TROUBLE SHOOTING

PRELIMINARY CHECKS

Most driveability problems in the throttle body fuel injection system result from faulty wiring and/or leaking vacuum hoses and hose connections. To avoid unnecessary component testing, visual check should be performed before beginning trouble shooting procedures.

A preliminary visual check should include:
- Air ducts at air cleaner and throttle body.
- Air filter element.
- All electrical connections at components.
- Throttle return springs.

Check vacuum lines for tight leak-free connections in these areas:
- Throttle body.
- Charcoal canister.
- PCV valve to intake manifold vacuum port.
- EGR solenoid.
- MAP and MAT sensors.

Ensure the following electrical connectors are properly attached:
- Battery connections.
- EGR solenoid.
- Engine control system ground connections on side of frame rail between battery and air cleaner.
- Engine control system relay connections.
- Idle speed regulator.
- MAP and MAT sensor connectors.
- Speed sensor connector.
- Radiator fan relay connector.
- TPS connector.
- Fuel injector connectors.
- Oxygen sensor connector.
- Coolant temperature sensor connector.
- Distributor connector.

TESTING & DIAGNOSIS

NOTE: *For test procedures not covered in this article, see appropriate article in COMPUTERIZED ENGINE CONTROLS section.*

FUEL SYSTEM PRESSURE RELEASE

1) Fuel pressure must be fully released before opening fuel system or removing any fuel carrying components. To release pressure in tank, open fuel tank cap slowly.
2) To release remaining pressure in system, disconnect 4-pin connector from fuel pump/gauge sending unit. This connector is located under vehicle, attached to tab on frame, between fuel tank and fuel filter.
3) Start engine and run until engine dies. Fuel injection system can now be opened and fuel carrying components removed as pressure is fully released. Reconnect connector after work on fuel system has been completed.

FUEL SYSTEM PRESSURE TEST

1) Release fuel system pressure as described in FUEL SYSTEM PRESSURE RELEASE. Remove Black fuel supply tube from fuel rail using Fuel Line Disconnect (6182).
2) Install Fuel Tube Adapter (6175) between Black fuel supply line and fuel rail. Attach 0-60 psi Fuel Pressure Gauge (5069) on port of fuel tube adapter. Start engine and check fuel pressure. Fuel pressure should be 28-30 psi (19.3-20.7 kg/cm²).

SYSTEM DIAGNOSIS

The self-diagnostic capabilities of this system, if properly utilized, can greatly simplify testing. The ECU has been programmed to monitor several different circuits of the engine control system. If a problem is sensed with a monitored circuit, a fault code is stored in the ECU.

The setting of a specific fault code is the result of a particular system failure, NOT the reason for that failure, such as failure of a specific component. The existence of a particular code denotes the probable area of the malfunction, not necessarily the failed component itself.

FAULT CODES

NOTE: *For fault codes and code descriptions, see appropriate article in COMPUTERIZED ENGINE CONTROLS section.*

REMOVAL & INSTALLATION

FUEL RAIL & REGULATOR ASSEMBLY

Removal – 1) Release fuel system pressure as described in FUEL SYSTEM PRESSURE RELEASE in TESTING & DIAGNOSIS section of this article. Disconnect negative battery cable. Disconnect Gray fuel return tube from pressure regulator. Remove Black fuel supply tube from fuel rail using Fuel Line Disconnect (6182).
2) Slide fuel disconnect tube onto nipple and push it forward into quick-connector until handle stops on connector casing. Pull fuel tubes off. *See Fig. 3.* Remove fuel injector wire harness and set aside.

NOTE: **Mark connector locations for reassembly reference.**

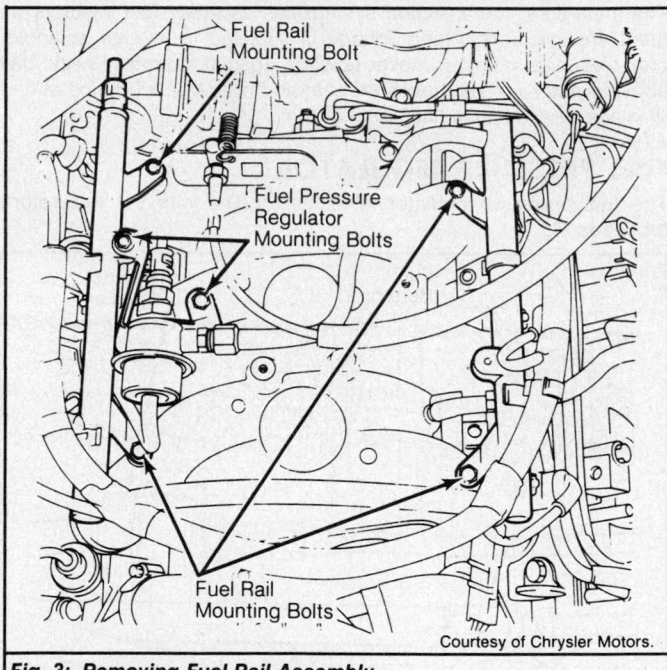

Courtesy of Chrysler Motors.

Fig. 3: Removing Fuel Rail Assembly

3) Disconnect accelerator cable from throttle body and holding bracket. Using finger pressure only, remove cruise control connector (if equipped). Remove fuel rail and fuel pressure regulator mounting bolts.
4) Disconnect electrical connector from injectors. Pull fuel rails, regulator and injector assembly up until injectors are out of ports in intake manifold. Pull assembly out from under transmission cable.

Installation – To install, reverse removal procedure. Check fuel system for leaks.

FUEL INJECTOR

Removal & Installation – Release fuel system pressure as described in FUEL SYSTEM PRESSURE RELEASE in TESTING & DIAGNOSIS section of this article. Remove fuel rail assembly. Remove clip holding fuel injector to fuel rail. *See Fig. 4.* Pull injector from fuel rail. To install, reverse removal procedure

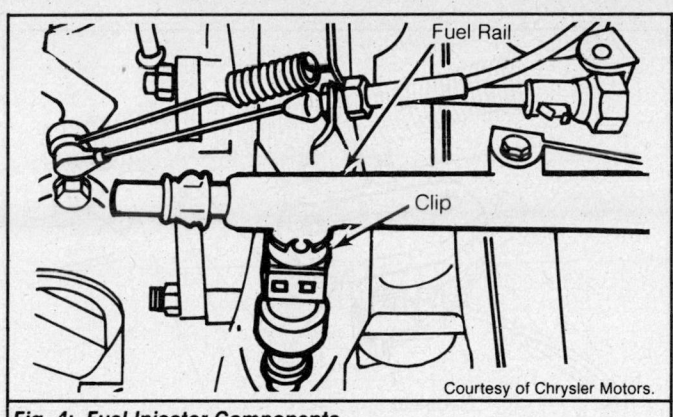

Fig. 4: Fuel Injector Components

THROTTLE BODY

Removal & Installation – 1) Remove air cleaner-to-throttle body mounting screws. Disconnect idle speed actuator inlet hose and move air cleaner to side. Disconnect electrical connector and throttle cable. Using finger pressure, remove cruise control connector.

2) Remove throttle return spring. Remove throttle body nuts at base of throttle body. Remove gasket. To install, reverse removal procedure.

IDLE SPEED REGULATOR

Removal – Remove regulator electrical connector. Remove air inlet hose. Disconnect regulator outlet hose at regulator. Remove regulator clamp bolt and regulator. *See Fig. 5.*

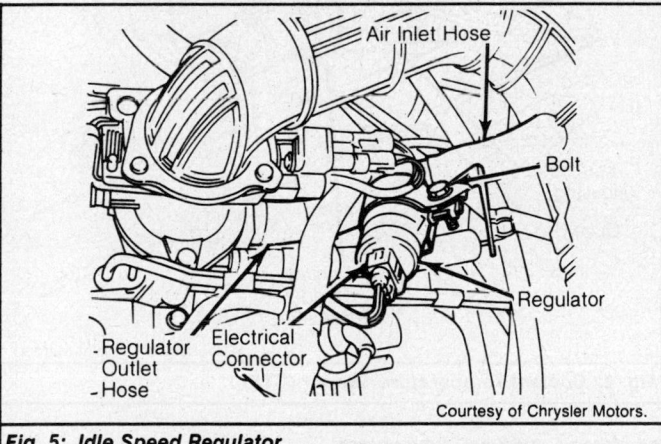

Fig. 5: Idle Speed Regulator

Installation – To install, reverse removal procedure. Ensure regulator is installed with arrow on ports facing throttle body.

MANIFOLD AIR/FUEL TEMPERATURE (MAT) SENSOR

Removal & Installation – Disconnect wire harness connector from MAT sensor. Remove MAT sensor from adaptor. To install, reverse removal procedure.

MANIFOLD ABSOLUTE PRESSURE (MAP) SENSOR

Removal & Installation – Disconnect wire harness connector, vacuum hose and retaining nuts from MAP sensor. Remove sensor from plenum chamber panel. To install MAP sensor, reverse removal procedure.

ELECTRONIC CONTROL UNIT (ECU)

Removal & Installation – Remove retaining screws and bracket that support ECU below glove box. Remove ECU and disconnect wiring harness. To install ECU, reverse removal procedure. *See Fig. 6.*

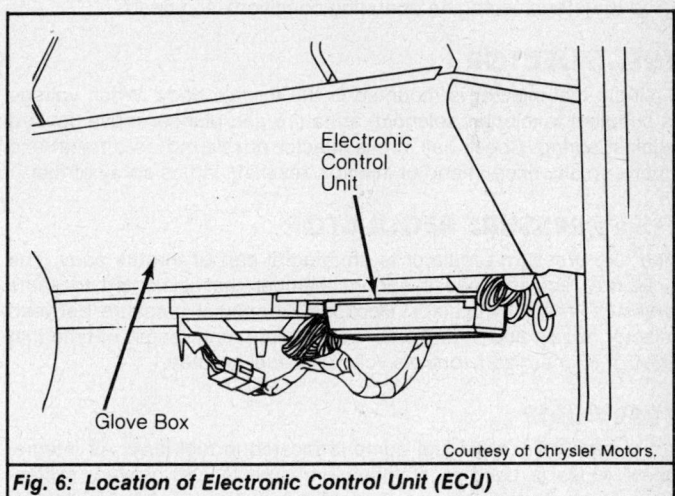

Fig. 6: Location of Electronic Control Unit (ECU)

EGR VALVE

Removal & Installation – Disconnect vacuum and backpressure hoses from EGR valve. Remove EGR valve-to-intake manifold bolts. Remove valve and discard gasket. To install valve, reverse removal procedure. Always use new gasket. Tighten mounting bolts to 20 ft. lbs. (27 N.m).

WIRING DIAGRAMS

NOTE: For wiring diagrams, see appropriate article in COMPUTERIZED ENGINE CONTROLS section.

Premier 2.5L

DESCRIPTION

The 2.5L Eagle Premier Throttle Body Injection (TBI) system injects a metered amount of fuel above throttle blade inside throttle body. The throttle body system has a fuel delivery and electronic control system.

The fuel delivery system includes in-tank fuel pump, fuel filter, fuel injector and fuel pressure regulator. The electronic control system consists of Electronic Control Unit (ECU), input sensors and engine controls which receive output commands.

OPERATION

ELECTRONIC CONTROL UNIT (ECU)

The ECU is located under the instrument panel on the passenger side of the vehicle. Inputs from various engine sensors to ECU are used to determine engine operating conditions and needs.

FUEL INJECTOR

A single fuel injector is mounted in the throttle body. When voltage is supplied to injector solenoid, armature and plunger move upward against spring. Check ball above injector nozzle moves off seat and opens small orifice at end of injector, resulting in fine spray of fuel.

FUEL PRESSURE REGULATOR

The fuel pressure regulator is an integral part of throttle body. The pressure regulator has a spring chamber that is vented to same pressure as tip of injector. Because differential pressure between injector nozzle and spring chamber is same, only length of time that injector is energized controls volume of fuel injected.

FUEL PUMP

An electric roller type fuel pump is located in fuel tank. An integral check valve is used to maintain pressure in fuel delivery system after pump stops running. Fuel pump operation is controlled by ECU.

IDLE SPEED CONTROL (ISC) MOTOR

The ISC motor acts as a movable idle stop to change throttle stop angle. Both engine idle speed and deceleration throttle stop are set by ISC. ECU sends varying voltage outputs to control ISC motor, depending upon engine operating condition.

OXYGEN SENSOR

The oxygen sensor is located in exhaust pipe. ECU receives sensor voltage signal which varies with oxygen content in exhaust gas. Signal is used by ECU as reference for setting air/fuel mixture ratio.

MANIFOLD AIR/FUEL TEMPERATURE (MAT) SENSOR

The MAT sensor provides signal to ECU that changes depending upon temperature of air/fuel mixture in intake manifold. During high temperature conditions, ECU will compensate for changes in density of air.

MANIFOLD ABSOLUTE PRESSURE (MAP) SENSOR

The MAP sensor measures absolute pressure in intake manifold. Both mixture density and ambient barometric pressure are supplied to ECU by MAP sensor. Sensor is mounted in plenum chamber at middle of firewall in engine compartment. Sensor receives manifold pressure information through vacuum line from throttle body. See Fig. 1.

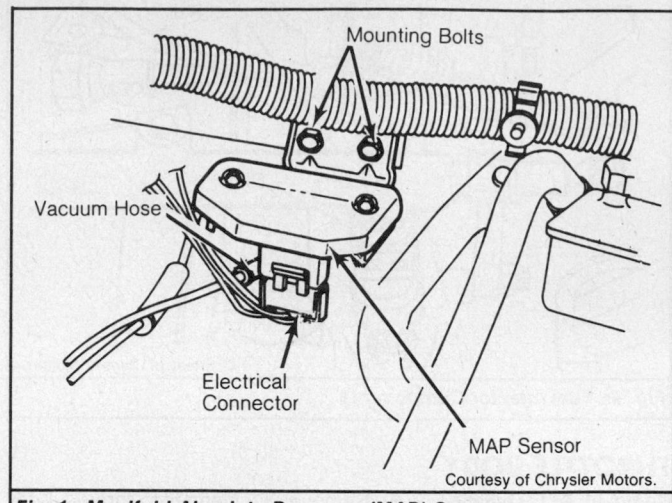

Fig. 1: Manifold Absolute Pressure (MAP) Sensor

COOLANT TEMPERATURE SENSOR (CTS)

The CTS is installed in thermostat housing to provide coolant temperature input signal for ECU. See Fig. 2.

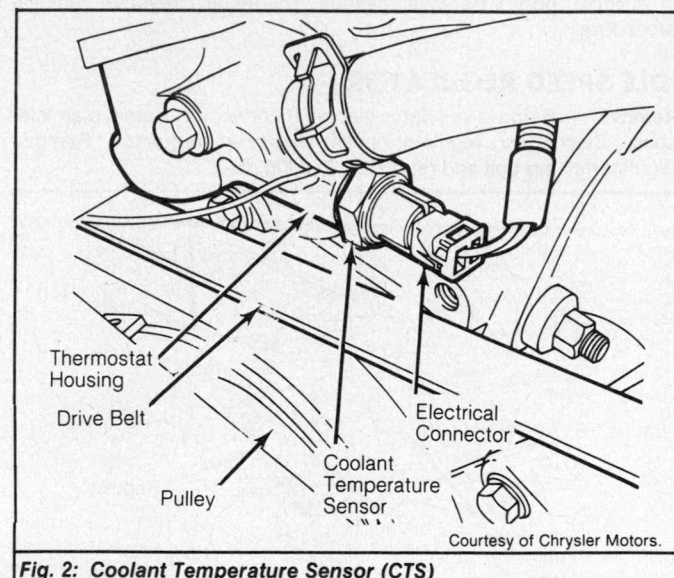

Fig. 2: Coolant Temperature Sensor (CTS)

ENGINE SPEED SENSOR

The engine speed sensor is attached to bellhousing. It senses and counts teeth on flywheel gear ring as they pass during engine operation. Signal from speed sensor provides ECU with engine speed and crankshaft angle. See Fig. 3.

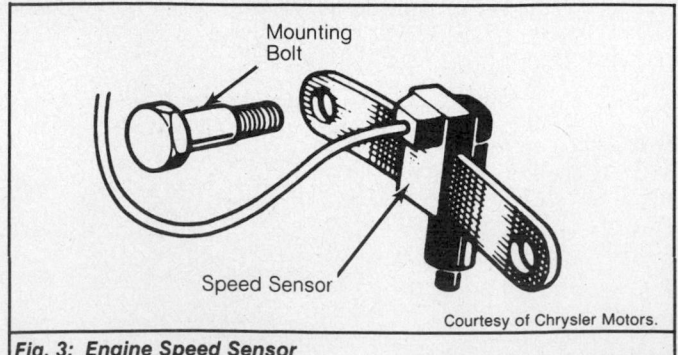

Fig. 3: Engine Speed Sensor

KNOCK SENSOR

The knock sensor is located above right motor mount and provides input to ECU which retards ignition timing to eliminate knock.

ADJUSTMENTS

FUEL PRESSURE REGULATOR

NOTE: See FUEL SYSTEM PRESSURE TEST & FUEL PRESSURE REGULATOR ADJUSTMENT in TESTING & DIAGNOSIS section of this article.

HOT (SLOW) IDLE RPM

1) Start engine and warm to normal operating temperature. Disconnect Idle Speed Control (ISC) motor wire connector.
2) Using ISC Tester (8981-320-828), fully extend ISC motor plunger. Adjust plunger screw until engine is running at 3500 RPM. *See Fig. 4.*
3) Remove ISC tester and connect idle speed motor electrical connector. Idle speed should automatically return to normal within a few seconds.

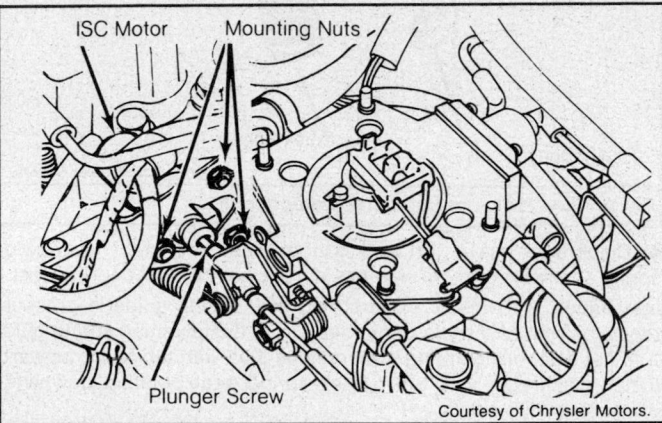

Fig. 4: Idle Speed Control Motor

CURB IDLE SPEED

Application	RPM
2.5L	750

THROTTLE POSITION SENSOR (TPS)

1) The use of Diagnostic Tester (DRB II) is preferred when adjusting thottle position sensor. If digital voltmeter is used, disconnect Idle Speed Control (ISC) motor electrical connector. Connect ISC Tester (7088) and retract ISC plunger until throttle lever contacts the idle stop screw and plunger does not contact the throttle lever.
2) Turn ignition on. On the TPS connector, insert negative lead of voltmeter in terminal "D" and positive lead to terminal "A". Reading should be 5 volts. Insert voltmeter positive lead to terminal "B" and open throttle to wide open position. Reading should be 4.6-4.7 volts. To adjust, loosen TPS retaining screws and pivot sensor to obtain correct reading.

TROUBLE SHOOTING

PRELIMINARY CHECKS

Most driveability problems in the throttle body fuel injection system result from faulty wiring and/or leaking vacuum hoses and hose connections. To avoid unnecessary component testing, visual check should be performed before beginning trouble shooting procedures.

A preliminary visual check should include:
- Air ducts at air cleaner and throttle body.
- Air cleaner pre-heater hose.
- Air filter element.
- All electrical connections at components.
- Throttle return springs.

Check vacuum lines for tight leak-free connections in these areas:
- Throttle body.
- Charcoal canister.
- PCV valve to intake manifold vacuum port.
- EGR solenoid.
- MAP sensor.

Ensure the following electrical connectors are properly attached:
- Battery connections.
- EGR solenoid.
- Engine control system ground connections on side of frame rail between battery and air cleaner.
- Engine control system relays connections.
- Idle Speed Control (ISC) motor.
- MAP sensor connector.
- Speed sensor connector.
- Throttle body temperature sensor connector.
- Radiator fan relay connector.
- TPS connector.
- Fuel injector connector.
- Oxygen sensor connector.
- Coolant temperature sensor connector.
- Distributor connector.

TESTING & DIAGNOSIS

NOTE: For test procedures not covered in this article, see appropriate article in COMPUTERIZED ENGINE CONTROLS section.

FUEL SYSTEM PRESSURE RELEASE

1) Fuel pressure must be fully released before opening fuel system or removing any fuel carrying component. To release pressure in tank, open fuel tank cap slowly.
2) To release remaining pressure in system, disconnect 4-pin connector from fuel pump/gauge sending unit. This connector is located under vehicle, attached to tab on frame, between fuel tank and fuel filter.
3) Start engine and run until engine dies. Fuel injection system can now be opened and fuel carrying components removed as pressure is fully released. Reconnect connector after work on fuel system has been completed.

FUEL SYSTEM PRESSURE TEST & REGULATOR ADJUSTMENT

1) Allow engine to cool before performing pressure test. Release fuel system pressure as described in FUEL SYSTEM PRESSURE RELEASE. Remove air filter cover from throttle body. Slowly remove test port plug from side of pressure regulator, using shop towels to catch any spilled fuel. Test port plug is located near fuel return tube connection.
2) Install Fuel Pressure Test Adapter (6173) into test port. Connect Fuel Pressure Gauge (5069) and start engine. Check fuel pressure with engine at idle. Correct pressure reading should be 14-15 psi (.98-1.09 kg/cm²).
3) If pressure is not within specification, adjust fuel pressure regulator until proper pressure is obtained. Remove plug concealing fuel pressure regulator adjusting screw from nose of fuel pressure regulator using small drift. Tap lightly until plug pops out. With engine at idle speed, adjust screw until fuel pressure reading is 14-15 psi (.98-1.09 kg/cm²).

SYSTEM DIAGNOSIS

The self-diagnostic capabilities of this system, if properly utilized, can greatly simplify testing. The ECU has been programmed to monitor several different circuits of the engine control system. If a problem is sensed with a monitored circuit, a fault code is stored in the ECU.

The setting of a specific fault code is the result of a particular system failure, NOT the reason for that failure, such as failure of a specific component. The existence of a particular code denotes the probable area of the malfunction, not necessarily the failed component itself.

FAULT CODES

NOTE: For fault codes and code descriptions, see appropriate article in COMPUTERIZED ENGINE CONTROLS section.

REMOVAL & INSTALLATION

FUEL INJECTOR

Removal – 1) Release fuel system pressure as described in FUEL SYSTEM PRESSURE RELEASE in TESTING & DIAGNOSIS section of this article. Disconnect negative battery cable. Remove air cleaner and injector wiring connector. Remove injector hold-down plate.

2) Using small pliers, carefully grasp center collar of injector between electrical terminals and carefully remove injector with lifting-twisting motion. Discard both "O" rings. Remove plastic alignment ring from injector. *See Fig. 5.*

Installation – 1) Install new "O" rings. Install alignment ring around injector. Install locating alignment washer to bottom of injector. Tab on top of washer fits into hole in bottom of injector. Tab on bottom side of washer fits into a slot in injector bore.

2) Position injector, alignment ring and spacer ring above throttle body bore. Align tab on bottom of spacer washer with slot in throttle body bore. Install components into bore using pliers. Grasp wedge of injector and push down until injector seats. Ensure injector cannot rotate in bore. Install hold-down plate.

3) Connect injector electrical connector and negative battery cable. Turn ignition switch to "ON" position and check for leaks. Install air cleaner.

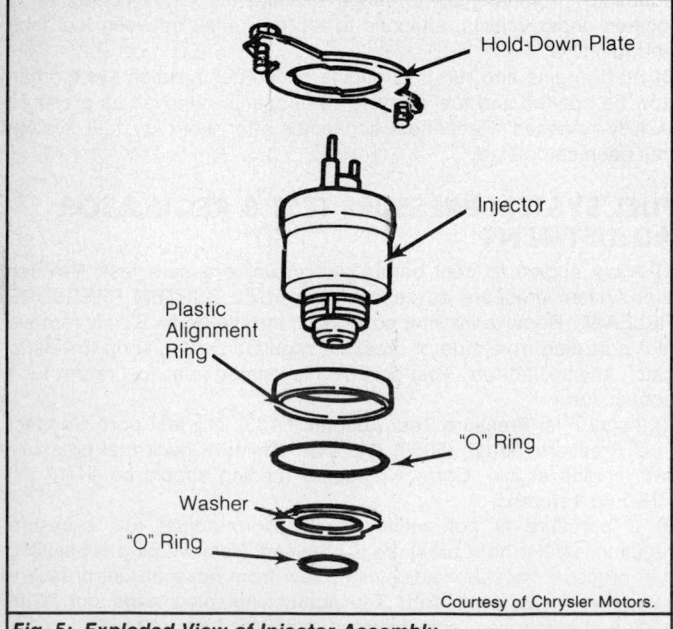

Fig. 5: Exploded View of Injector Assembly

FUEL PRESSURE REGULATOR

Removal – 1) Release fuel system pressure as described in FUEL SYSTEM PRESSURE RELEASE in TESTING & DIAGNOSIS section

of this article. Remove throttle body. Position throttle body on work bench with fuel pressure regulator facing upward. Remove 2 fuel pressure regulator mounting screws opposite of each other.

2) Remove screw heads from 2 screws of same thread size that are 3" long. Use these screws as alignment dowels for removing and installing fuel pressure regulator. Install dowels into bolt holes.

3) Pressure regulator is spring loaded. Hold casing down when removing screws. Remove casing, steel ball, top spring guide, large spring, diaphragm, small spring guide and small spring. *See Fig. 6.*

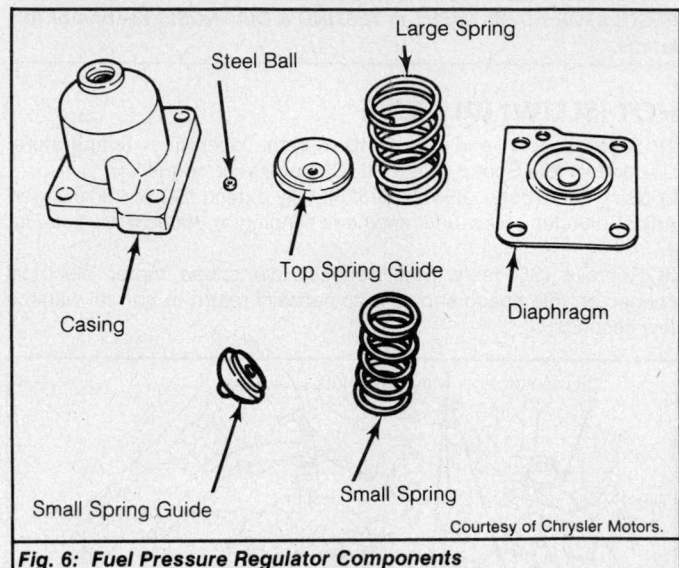

Fig. 6: Fuel Pressure Regulator Components

4) Diaphragm has a top and bottom side. Top side has a wide spring seat while bottom side has a narrower but taller spring seat.

Installation – 1) Install small spring over spring guide in pressure regulator well of throttle body. *See Fig. 7.* Install small spring guide with flat side facing spring and rounded side with tab facing upward. Install diaphragm with narrow/tall spring seat pointing downward over alignment dowels.

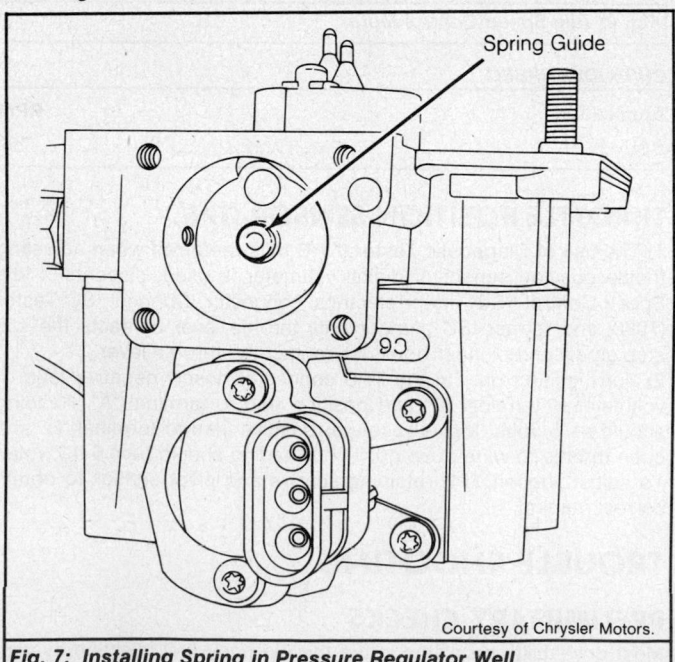

Fig. 7: Installing Spring in Pressure Regulator Well

2) Install large spring into spring seat in diaphragm. Install top spring guide over spring. Install steel ball in center of top spring guide. Install casing over alignment studs. Push down and install screws.

3) Remove alignment dowels and install other 2 screws. Install throttle body.

IDLE SPEED CONTROL (ISC) MOTOR

Removal & Installation – Remove air cleaner. Remove ISC motor mounting nuts. Remove ISC motor from bracket. Disconnect electrical connector. To install ISC motor assembly, reverse removal procedure.

THROTTLE BODY ASSEMBLY

Removal – 1) Release fuel system pressure as described in FUEL SYSTEM PRESSURE RELEASE in TESTING & DIAGNOSIS section of this article. Disconnect negative battery cable. Remove air cleaner. Disconnect throttle cable and cruise control cable (if equipped).

2) Squeeze retainer tabs and disconnect fuel lines by pulling straight out. Note that retainer stays on fuel tube. *See Fig. 8.* Disconnect TPS and ISC motor wire connectors. Remove injector wire connector. Disconnect vacuum connectors from side of throttle body.

3) Remove support brace from cruise control cable bracket (if equipped). Loosen throttle body mounting bolts and remove throttle body. Remove throttle body gasket.

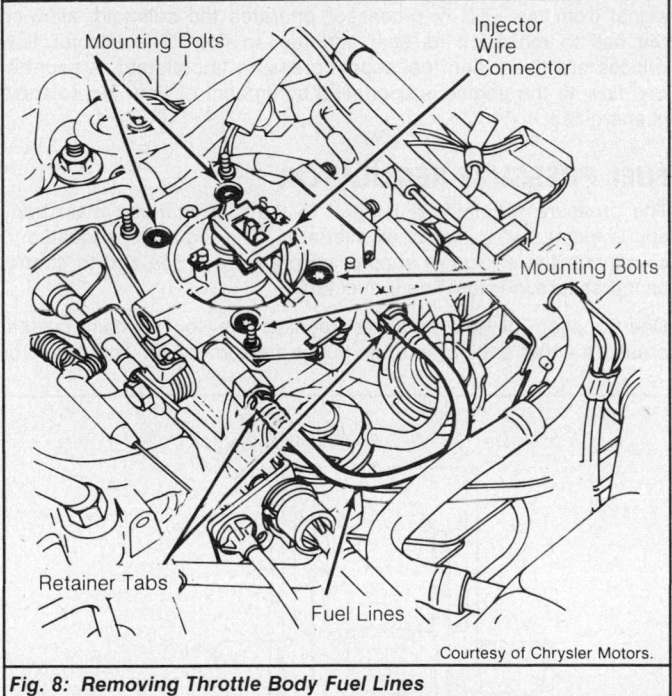

Mounting Bolts

Injector Wire Connector

Mounting Bolts

Retainer Tabs

Fuel Lines

Courtesy of Chrysler Motors.

Fig. 8: Removing Throttle Body Fuel Lines

Installation – Install replacement throttle body assembly on manifold using new gasket. Tighten mounting bolts to 35 INCH lbs. (4

N.m). Reconnect all hoses, wires and cable in order of disassembly. Adjust ISC motor after installation.

MANIFOLD AIR/FUEL TEMPERATURE (MAT) SENSOR

Removal & Installation – Disconnect wire harness connector from MAT sensor. Remove MAT sensor from intake manifold. To install, reverse removal procedure.

MANIFOLD ABSOLUTE PRESSURE (MAP) SENSOR

Removal & Installation – Disconnect wire harness connector, vacuum hose and retaining nuts from MAP sensor. Remove sensor from plenum chamber panel. To install, reverse removal procedure.

ELECTRONIC CONTROL UNIT (ECU)

Removal & Installation – Remove retaining screws and bracket that support ECU below glove box. Remove ECU and disconnect wiring harness. To install, reverse removal procedure. *See Fig. 9.*

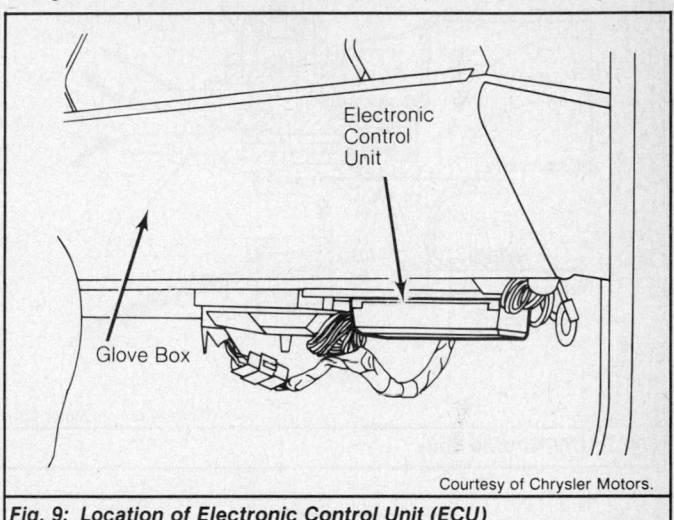

Electronic Control Unit

Glove Box

Courtesy of Chrysler Motors.

Fig. 9: Location of Electronic Control Unit (ECU)

EGR VALVE

Removal & Installation – Disconnect vacuum and backpressure hoses from EGR valve. Remove EGR valve-to-intake manifold bolts. Remove valve and discard gasket. To install valve, reverse removal procedure. Always use new gasket. Tighten mounting bolts to 20 ft. lbs. (27 N.m)

WIRING DIAGRAMS

NOTE: For wiring diagrams, see appropriate article in COMPUTERIZED ENGINE CONTROLS section.

1989 FUEL INJECTION
Ford Motor Co. Central Fuel Injection

Escort 1.9L, Sable, Taurus 2.5L HSC

DESCRIPTION

Central Fuel Injection (CFI) system is single point, pulse time modulated injection system. Fuel is metered into air intake stream according to engine demands by single injector, which is mounted in throttle body on intake manifold.

Fuel is supplied by low pressure electric fuel pump mounted in fuel tank. Fuel is filtered and sent to injector and then to pressure regulator. On 1.9L engines, fuel delivery pressure is maintained at 14.5 psi (1.0 kg/cm²). On 2.5L HSC engines, fuel delivery pressure is maintained at approximately 39 psi (2.7 kg/cm²).

A single injector nozzle is mounted vertically above throttle plate. Fuel pressure regulator is downstream from injector in fuel system. Fuel in excess of that needed for engine demand is returned to fuel tank by fuel return line.

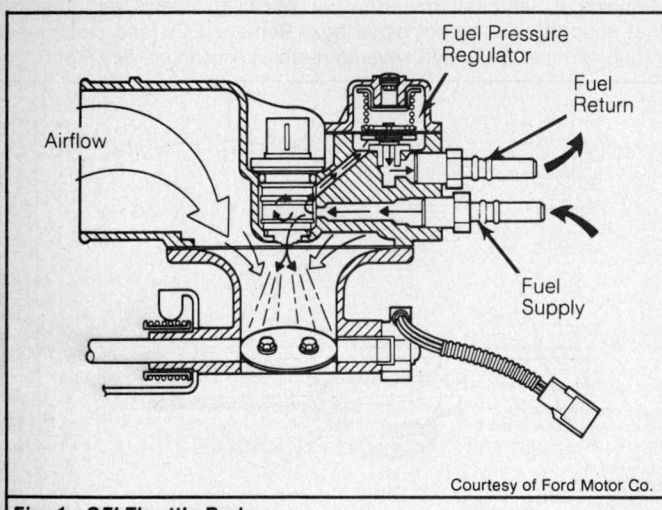

Courtesy of Ford Motor Co.

Fig. 1: CFI Throttle Body

OPERATION

AIR & FUEL CONTROL

Throttle body is comprised of 5 individual components which perform fuel and air metering functions for engine demands. Throttle body assembly mounts to intake manifold and provides for:

- Air Control
- Fuel Injection
- Fuel Pressure Regulation
- Engine Idle Speed Control
- Throttle Position Sensing

AIR CONTROL

Airflow to engine is controlled by single butterfly valve mounted in a die cast aluminum throttle body. Butterfly valve is identical in configuration to throttle plate of carburetor. It is actuated by a similar linkage and pedal cable arrangement.

FUEL INJECTOR NOZZLE

The fuel injector nozzle is mounted vertically above the throttle plate and is an electro-mechanical device which meters and atomizes the fuel delivered to the engine. The injector valve body consists of a solenoid actuated ball and seat assembly. An electrical control signal from the EEC-IV processor operates the solenoid, allowing the ball to move off its seat and fuel to flow. The injector flow orifices are fixed, and fuel supply pressure is constant. Amount of fuel flow to the engine is controlled by amount of time the solenoid is energized.

FUEL PRESSURE REGULATOR

The pressure regulator is integral to the fuel charging main body and is located near rear of air inlet area. The regulator is located to counteract the effects of supply line pressure drops and to control backpressure in return line to fuel tank.

One function of the pressure regulator is to maintain system pressure when engine and fuel pump are turned off. The regulator

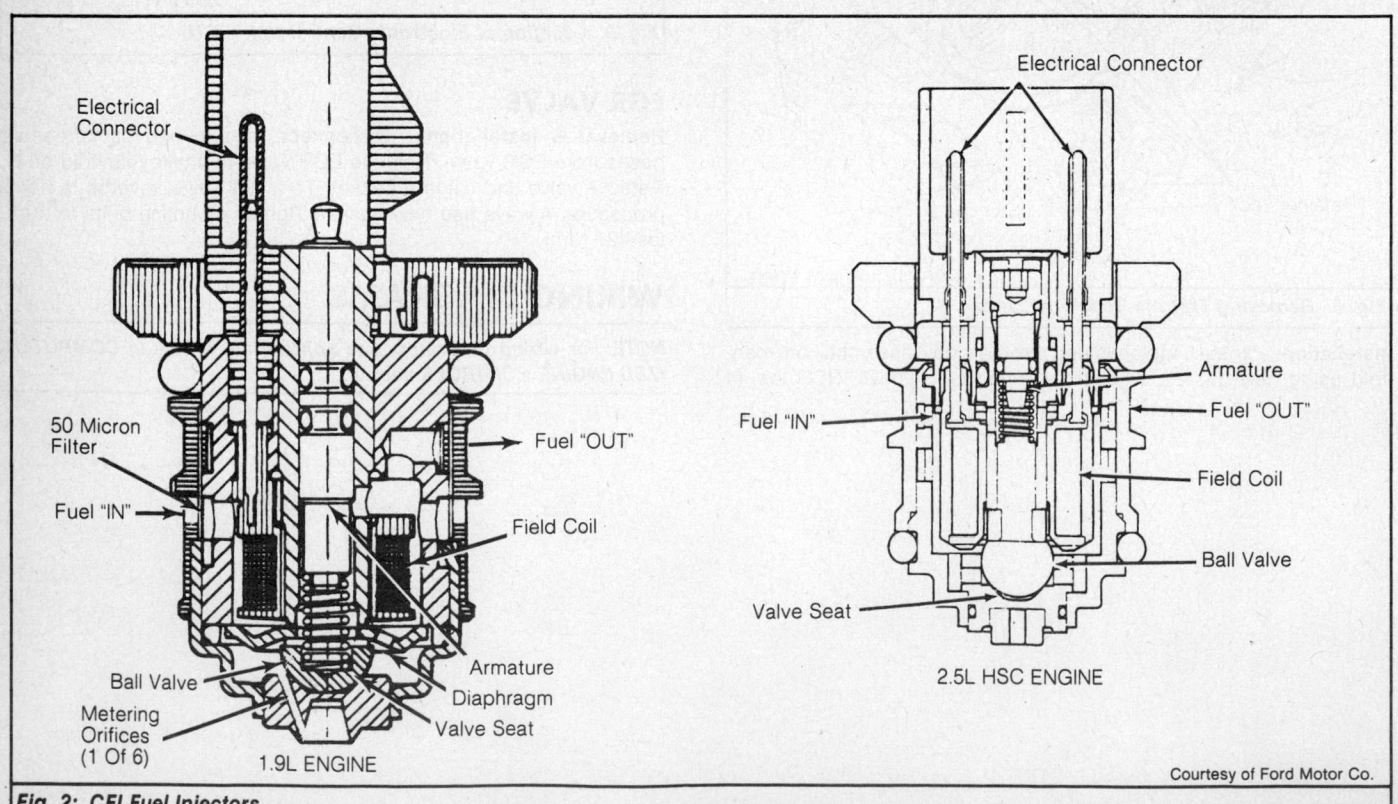

Courtesy of Ford Motor Co.

Fig. 2: CFI Fuel Injectors

1989 FUEL INJECTION
Ford Motor Co. Central Fuel Injection (Cont.)

2-37

functions as a downstream check valve and traps the fuel between itself and fuel pump.

The regulator also maintains fuel pressure when the engine is turned off, controls fuel line vapor formation and allows for rapid restarts and stable idle operation. On 1.9L engines, fuel pressure is maintained at 14.5 psi (1.0 kg/cm²). On 2.5L engines, fuel delivery pressure is maintained at approximately 39 psi (2.7 kg/cm²). On all models, this value may vary from unit to unit. Pressure is adjusted at the factory to compensate for differences in fuel flow among injectors.

IDLE SPEED CONTROL (ISC)
DC MOTOR THROTTLE ACTUATOR

The DC motor actuator controls idle speed by moving the throttle lever. It regulates airflow to maintain desired engine RPM for both warm and cold engine idle speeds.

An Idle Tracking Switch (ITS), integral to the DC motor, is utilized to determine throttle lever contact. It is controlled by the Electronic Control Assembly (ECA). Motor direction is determined by voltage polarity.

THROTTLE POSITION SENSOR (TPS)

A nonadjustable Throttle Position Sensor (TPS) is mounted to the throttle shaft and is used to supply a voltage output signal proportional to the throttle position. The TPS signal is used by the computer to determine engine operating conditions in relation to throttle position.

TROUBLE SHOOTING

PRELIMINARY CHECKS

Check that the following systems and components are in good condition and operating properly before diagnosing problems in fuel injection system:
* Battery condition
* State of tune
* Fuel delivery system
* All wiring and vacuum connections
* Air cleaner and ducting
* Cooling system

SYMPTOMS

Engine Does Not Crank – Check for hydrostatic lock (liquid in cylinder). Repair as needed. Check for starting and charging system problems.

Engine Cranks But Will Not Start – 1) Check fuel tank contents and fuel gauge accuracy. Check for dirt, water or other contamination in fuel.
2) Check ignition system for strong secondary current at spark plugs. If no spark exists or is weak, repair ignition system problem first.
3) Check fuel lines and fittings for leaks. If no leaks are found, check fuel delivery system for proper pressure and volumes. Reset inertia switch if necessary.
4) Check for a defective fuel injector or coolant temperature sensor. Ensure that TPS is not sticking.

Hard Starting (Cold) – 1) Cold enrichment system may not be functioning correctly. Check TPS and DC motor for proper operation and adjustment. Adjust or replace as required.
2) Intake manifold or throttle body gaskets leaking. Replace leaking gaskets as needed.
3) TPS or Coolant Temperature Sensor (CTS) defective.

Rough Idle (Cold) – 1) Cold enrichment cycle not functioning. Check fast idle system for proper operation and adjustment. Adjust or replace as required.
2) Air cleaner duct vacuum motor damaged or stuck open. Replace or service as required. Check for vacuum leaks. Check for leaking injector or injector seals.

Stall, Stumble Or Hesitation (Hot Or Cold) – 1) Cold enrichment system may not be functioning correctly. Check for proper operation and adjustment. Adjust or replace as required.
2) Fuel pump output low. Service or replace as required. Fuel filter clogged. Clean or replace as required after cause is determined.
3) Fuel injector internal filter plugged. Clean or replace injectors as required.
4) Air cleaner vacuum motor damaged. Service or replace as required. Check for bad TPS or coolant temperature sensor.

Hard Starting (Hot) – 1) Cold enrichment system may not be functioning correctly. Check for proper operation and adjustment. Adjust or replace as required. Fuel pressure not within specification. Check fuel pressure regulator.
2) Intake manifold or throttle body gaskets leaking. Replace leaking gaskets as needed. Check for bad TPS or coolant temperature sensor.

Rough Idle (Hot) – Check ignition system. Check for possible intake vacuum leaks.

Stalls On Deceleration/Quick Stop – Throttle position sensor defective. Service as required. Intake manifold or throttle body gaskets leaking. Replace leaking gaskets as necessary.

Lack Of Power – Fuel filter clogged. Fuel injector internal filter plugged. Clean or replace injectors as required. Check fuel delivery and repair as needed.

Reduced Top Speed/Power – 1) Throttle linkage binding. Clean and service as required. Fuel pump delivery volume low. Test fuel delivery system.
2) Fuel filter clogged. Fuel injector internal filter plugged. Clean or replace injectors as required. Repair or replace as needed. Pressure regulator damaged. Repair or replace as needed.

Surge At Cruise – 1) Fuel filter clogged. Fuel pump pressure or delivery volume low. Test fuel delivery system.
2) Fuel contaminated by dirt or water. Drain fuel and clean system as needed. Fuel injector internal filter plugged. Clean or replace injectors as required.

TESTING & DIAGNOSIS

FUEL DELIVERY SYSTEM TEST

NOTE: For additional information regarding testing and repair of system components controlled by the EEC-IV computerized engine control system, see appropriate article in COMPUTERIZED ENGINE CONTROLS section.

INERTIA SWITCH

1) In event of a collision, electrical contacts in inertia switch open and fuel pump automatically shuts off. Fuel pump will shut off even if engine does not stop running. Engine will stop due to lack of fuel.
2) It is not possible to restart engine until inertia switch is manually reset. Inertia switch is located behind access door on right side trim panel in rear cargo space of Sable and Taurus station wagon models. Switch is on left side of trunk in all other models. To reset inertia switch, depress button on switch. *See Fig. 3.*

CAUTION: DO NOT reset inertia switch until fuel system has been inspected for leaks.

CAUTION: Use care when opening fuel lines and testing fuel pressure due to danger of fire in case of fuel spillage. System is under residual pressure which MUST be discharged before opening fuel lines.

Fuel Pump Pressure & Delivery Volume – 1) Disconnect wiring at inertia switch. Inertia switch is located behind trim panel in right rear side of cargo area on Sable and Taurus station wagons and behind trim panel on left side of trunk on all other models. Crank engine for at least 15 seconds to reduce system fuel pressure.

2-38

1989 FUEL INJECTION
Ford Motor Co. Central Fuel Injection (Cont.)

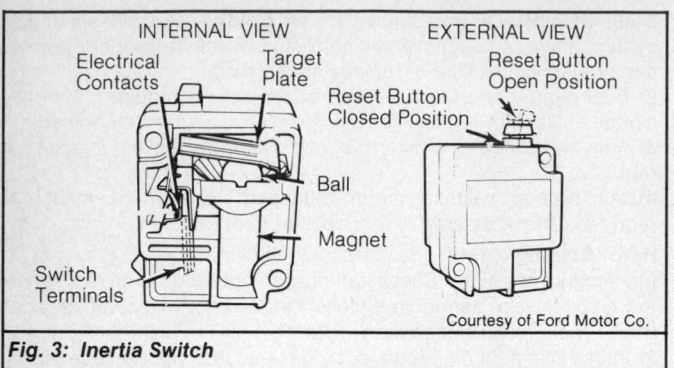

Fig. 3: Inertia Switch

2) Disconnect fuel supply line at throttle body. Install In-Line Adapter (D85L-9974-B) and Fuel Pressure Gauge (T87L-9974-A) on throttle body. Reconnect inertia switch and start engine. Check fuel pressure at idle and when accelerating engine. Pressure should remain stable through entire period of acceleration.

3) If gauge readings are correct, disconnect inertia switch. Crank engine for 15 seconds to reduce fuel pressure. Remove gauge and in-line adapter. Install original fuel line and connect inertia switch. Start engine and check for fuel leaks.

FUEL PRESSURE SPECIFICATIONS: psi (kg/cm²)

Engine	Pressure Engine Running	Pressure KOEO
1.9L	13-17	13-17
	(.91-1.12)	(.91-1.12)
2.5L HSC	39.2	39.2
	(2.7)	(2.7)

INJECTOR RESISTANCE

To measure injector resistance, disconnect injector harness connector. Set ohmmeter on 10-ohm scale. Ensure injector resistance is within specification. See INJECTOR RESISTANCE table.

INJECTOR RESISTANCE

Engine	Ohms (Ω)
All CFI	1.0-2.0

REMOVAL & INSTALLATION

FUEL CHARGING & THROTTLE BODY ASSEMBLY

Removal – 1) Remove air tube clamp at fuel charging assembly air inlet. Remove electrical connector at inertia switch. On Taurus and Sable wagon, inertia switch is located behind access door in right rear cargo area. On others, inertia switch is located in left side of trunk.

2) Release fuel system pressure by cranking engine for 15 seconds. Disconnect throttle cable and transmission throttle lever. Disconnect electrical connector at Idle Speed Control (ISC) motor, Throttle Position Sensor (TPS) and fuel injector.

3) Disconnect fuel inlet and outlet connections. Disconnect PCV vacuum line at fuel charging assembly. Remove retaining nuts and remove fuel charging or throttle body assembly and gasket.

Installation – 1) Clean mounting surface and position new gasket on intake manifold. Position fuel charging or throttle body assembly on intake manifold.

2) On fuel charging assembly, tighten mounting nuts to 15-25 ft. lbs. (20-34 N.m). On throttle body assembly, tighten mounting nuts in proper sequence. See Fig. 4.

3) Connect electrical connectors to ISC, TPS and fuel injector. Connect fuel inlet and outlet connections and PCV vacuum line at fuel charging assembly.

4) Connect throttle cable and transmission throttle lever. Connect electrical connector at inertia switch. Install air tube and clamp at the fuel charging assembly.

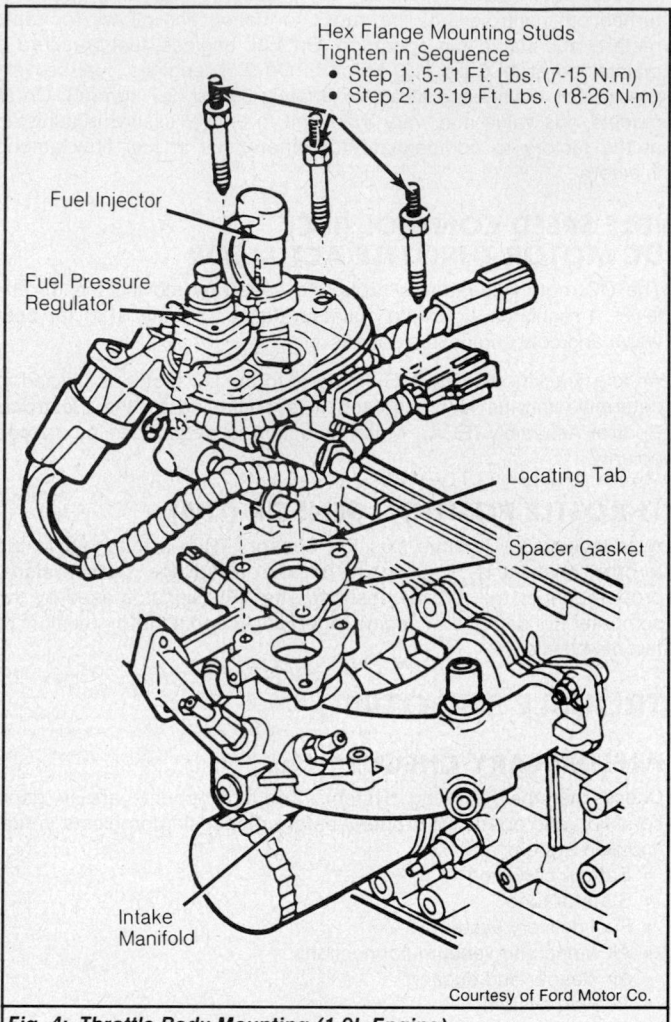

Fig. 4: Throttle Body Mounting (1.9L Engine)

FUEL INJECTOR

Removal & Installation – 1) Release fuel pressure from system. Remove fuel injector retaining screw and retainer. Remove injector and lower "O" ring.

2) To install, lubricate a new lower "O" ring and injector seat area with clean engine oil (DO NOT use transmission oil). Install lower "O" ring on injector. Lubricate upper "O" ring, clean and lubricate throttle body "O" ring seat.

3) Install injector by centering and applying a steady downward pressure with a slight rotational force. Install injector retainer and retaining screw. Tighten retainer screw to 18-22 INCH lbs. (2.0-2.5 N.m).

FUEL PUMP

Removal – Relieve fuel system pressure. Drain fuel tank. Lower fuel tank enough to disconnect fuel tank hoses and electrical connectors. Disconnect fuel tank hoses and electrical connectors. Remove fuel tank. Using Fuel Tank Sender Wrench (D84P-9275-A), remove fuel pump lock ring. Remove fuel pump.

Installation – 1) Clean fuel pump mounting flange, fuel tank mounting surface and seal ring groove. To hold new seal ring in place during installation, apply a light coating of Long Life Lubricant (C1AZ-19590-BA).

2) Install seal ring in fuel ring groove. Carefully install fuel pump and bracket assembly. Ensure locating keys are in keyway and seal ring

1989 FUEL INJECTION
Ford Motor Co. Central Fuel Injection (Cont.)

2-39

remains in groove. Hold pump assembly in place and install locking ring finger tight. Ensure that all locking tabs are under lock ring tabs. Tighten retainer.

OVERHAUL

FUEL CHARGING ASSEMBLY

NOTE: To prevent damage to throttle plates, place assembly on a stand or pad.

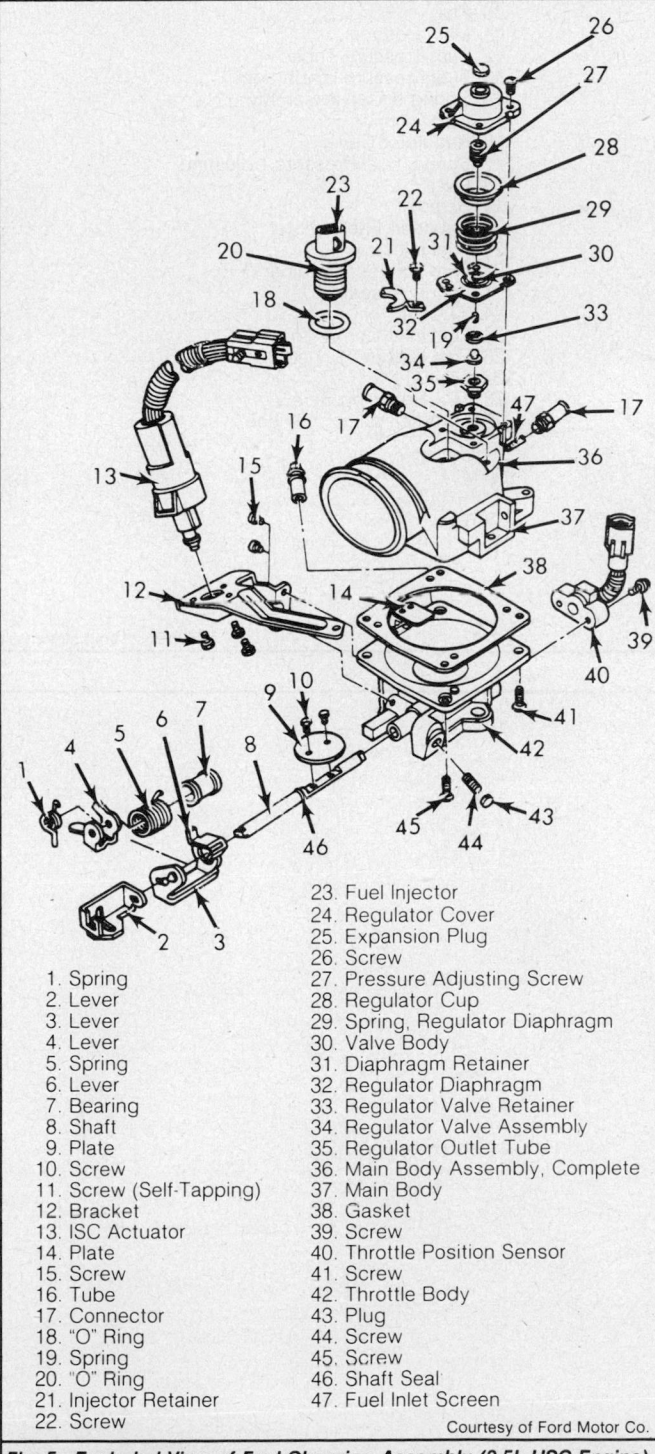

23. Fuel Injector
24. Regulator Cover
25. Expansion Plug
26. Screw
27. Pressure Adjusting Screw
28. Regulator Cup
29. Spring, Regulator Diaphragm
30. Valve Body
31. Diaphragm Retainer
32. Regulator Diaphragm
33. Regulator Valve Retainer
34. Regulator Valve Assembly
35. Regulator Outlet Tube
36. Main Body Assembly, Complete
37. Main Body
38. Gasket
39. Screw
40. Throttle Position Sensor
41. Screw
42. Throttle Body
43. Plug
44. Screw
45. Screw
46. Shaft Seal
47. Fuel Inlet Screen

1. Spring
2. Lever
3. Lever
4. Lever
5. Spring
6. Lever
7. Bearing
8. Shaft
9. Plate
10. Screw
11. Screw (Self-Tapping)
12. Bracket
13. ISC Actuator
14. Plate
15. Screw
16. Tube
17. Connector
18. "O" Ring
19. Spring
20. "O" Ring
21. Injector Retainer
22. Screw

Courtesy of Ford Motor Co.

Fig. 5: Exploded View of Fuel Charging Assembly (2.5L HSC Engine)

Disassembly – 1) Turn fuel charging assembly over and remove 4 retaining screws attaching throttle body to main body. Separate throttle body from main body and set aside.

2) Remove and discard gasket. If scraping is necessary, be careful not to damage gasket surface. Remove fuel pressure regulator and fuel injector. Remove fittings and filter screen from fuel inlet channel. *See Fig. 5 or 6.*

Reassembly – 1) Install fuel injector and fuel pressure regulator. Attach throttle body with new gasket to body. Tighten screws to 38-44 INCH lbs. (4.3-5.0 N.m).

2) Clean and install screen in fuel inlet channel. Clean loose material from fuel fittings and coat with Loctite (290). Install fuel fittings and tighten to 168-190 INCH lbs. (19-23 N.m).

THROTTLE BODY

Disassembly – Remove TPS, ISC motor and bracket assembly from throttle body. If ISC is to be removed from bracket, remove 3 retaining screws.

Reassembly – 1) Attach ISC motor, if removed, to bracket with 3 retaining screws and tighten to 44-50 INCH lbs. (5.0-5.6 N.m). Install ISC motor and bracket assembly and tighten to 38-44 INCH lbs. (4.3-5.0 N.m).

2) Position TPS with connector facing upward toward main body. Rotate counterclockwise only and align screw holes. Tighten screws to 13-16 INCH lbs. (1.5-1.8 N.m).

NOTE: Failure to install the TPS in this manner may result in excessive idle speeds.

3) Position main body to throttle body gasket. Install throttle body to main body with 4 retaining screws. Tighten to 38-44 INCH lbs. (4.3-5.0 N.m).

WIRING DIAGRAMS

See appropriate article in COMPUTERIZED ENGINE CONTROLS section.

2-40

1989 FUEL INJECTION
Ford Motor Co. Central Fuel Injection (Cont.)

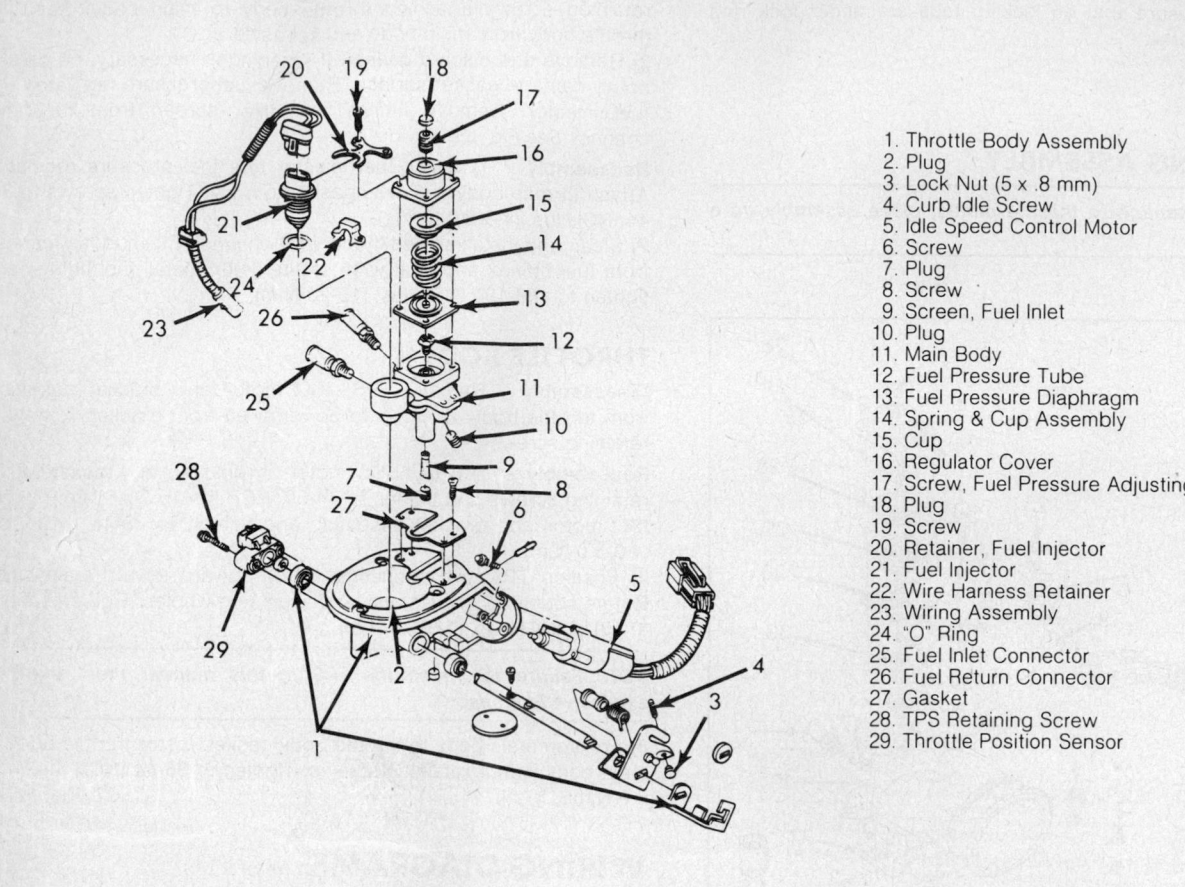

1. Throttle Body Assembly
2. Plug
3. Lock Nut (5 x .8 mm)
4. Curb Idle Screw
5. Idle Speed Control Motor
6. Screw
7. Plug
8. Screw
9. Screen, Fuel Inlet
10. Plug
11. Main Body
12. Fuel Pressure Tube
13. Fuel Pressure Diaphragm
14. Spring & Cup Assembly
15. Cup
16. Regulator Cover
17. Screw, Fuel Pressure Adjusting
18. Plug
19. Screw
20. Retainer, Fuel Injector
21. Fuel Injector
22. Wire Harness Retainer
23. Wiring Assembly
24. "O" Ring
25. Fuel Inlet Connector
26. Fuel Return Connector
27. Gasket
28. TPS Retaining Screw
29. Throttle Position Sensor

Courtesy of Ford Motor Co.

Fig. 6: Exploded View of Throttle Body Assembly (1.9L Engine)

1.9L, 2.2L, 2.2L Turbo, 2.3L, 3.0L, 3.0L SHO, 3.8L, 5.0L

APPLICATION

FUEL INJECTION SYSTEM APPLICATIONS

Vehicle	Engine	Inj. System
Continental	3.8L	SEFI
Cougar, Thunderbird	3.8L [1]	SEFI
Grand Marquis, LTD Crown Victoria, Town Car, Wagon	5.0L	SEFI
Escort	1.9L HO	MPFI
Mark VII	5.0L HO	SEFI
Mustang	2.3L OHC	MPFI
	5.0L MA	SEFI
Probe	2.2L	MPFI
	2.2L Turbo	MPFI
Sable, Taurus	3.0L	MPFI
Taurus	3.0L SHO	SEFI
	3.8L	SEFI
Tempo, Topaz	2.3L HSC	MPFI
	2.3L HSO	MPFI

[1] – Normally aspirated and Supercharged (SC) engines.

FORD MOTOR CO. ENGINE ABBREVIATIONS

Abbreviation	Description
HO	High Output
HSC	High Swirl Combustion
HSO	High Swirl Output
MA	Mass Air (Airflow Meter)
OHC	Overhead Camshaft
SC	Supercharged
SHO	Super High Output

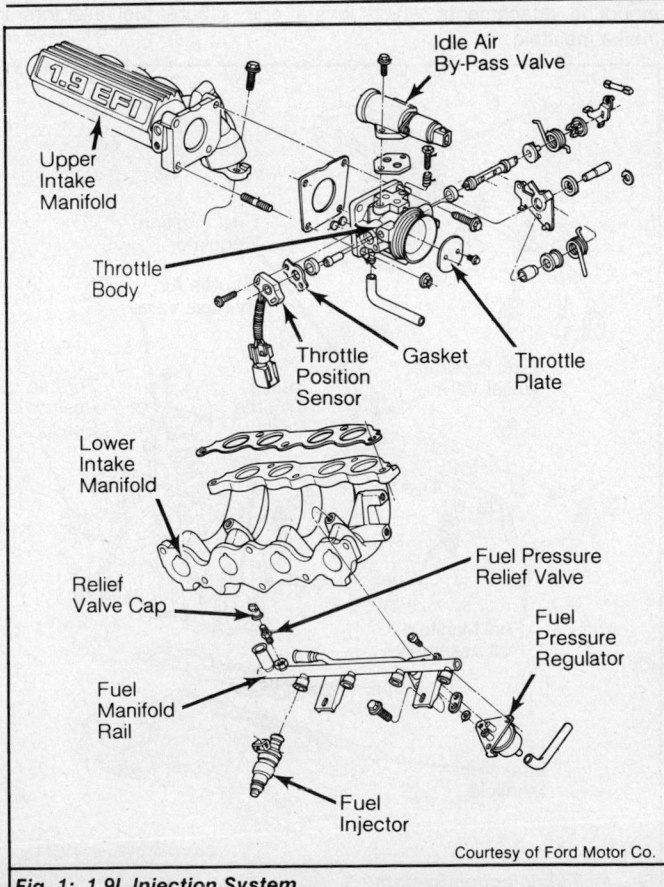

Fig. 1: 1.9L Injection System

Idle Air By-Pass Valve
Upper Intake Manifold
Throttle Body
Throttle Position Sensor
Gasket
Throttle Plate
Lower Intake Manifold
Relief Valve Cap
Fuel Pressure Relief Valve
Fuel Pressure Regulator
Fuel Manifold Rail
Fuel Injector

Courtesy of Ford Motor Co.

Rail "O" Ring Seal
Integral Filter
Electrical Connector
Coil
Armature
Stainless Steel Needle Or Pintle
Washer
Manifold "O" Ring Seal
Pintle Protection Cap
Stainless Steel Body

Courtesy of Ford Motor Co.

Fig. 2: Cutaway View of Fuel Injector

DESCRIPTION

The electronic fuel injection system is a pulse time, Multi-Point Fuel Injection (MPFI) system. On-board Electronic Engine Control (EEC-IV) system has Electronic Control Assembly (ECA) which receives inputs from engine and vehicle sensors to compute required fuel flow rate necessary to maintain prescribed air/fuel ratio throughout entire engine operational range.

Additional airflow metering is provided on 1.9L, 2.2L and 2.2L Turbo engines by a Vane Airflow (VAF) meter. The 5.0L Mass Airflow (MA) engine used in Mustangs uses a Mass Airflow (MA) sensor to measure quantity of air entering the engine.

The ECA controls fuel injectors to meter fuel quantity into intake ports. Injector "on" time is the only controlled variable in fuel delivery system.

OPERATION

FUEL SUPPLY

Fuel is supplied by chassis mounted or in-tank electric fuel pump. Some models use both in-tank low pressure pump and externally mounted high pressure pump. Pump delivers fuel from fuel tank through 20-micron fuel filter to fuel charging manifold assembly.

Fuel charging manifold assembly incorporates electrically actuated fuel injectors directly above each intake port. Injectors spray metered quantity of fuel into intake air. Constant fuel pressure is maintained to injector nozzles by pressure regulator.

Fuel pressure regulator is connected in series with fuel injectors and is positioned downstream from them. Excess fuel supplied by pump, but not consumed by engine, passes through regulator and returns to fuel tank through fuel return line.

On 1.9L, 2.2L Turbo and 2.3L engines, all injectors are energized simultaneously once every crankshaft revolution.

On 2.2L engines, all injectors are energized simultaneously once every crankshaft revolution. When engine speed reaches 4500 RPM, injectors will be energized once every other crankshaft revolution with injectors remaining open longer.

On 3.0L engines, injectors are energized in 3 pairs, in sequence of 1-2, 3-4, 5-6. The injectors are energized once every other crankshaft revolution.

2-42

1989 FUEL INJECTION
Ford Motor Co. Multi-Point Fuel Injection (Cont.)

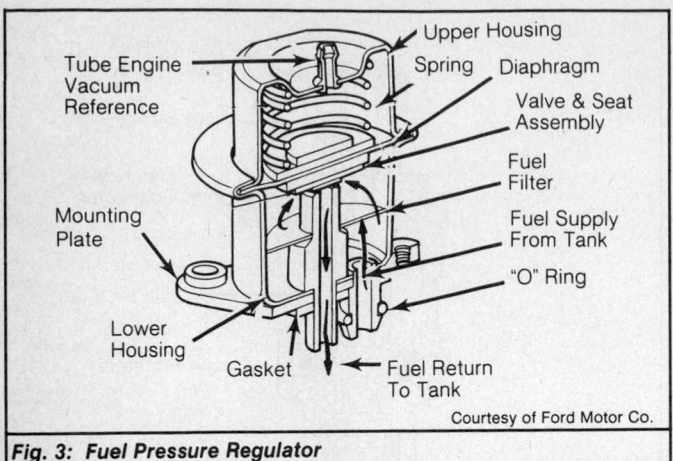

Fig. 3: Fuel Pressure Regulator

Courtesy of Ford Motor Co.

On 3.0L SHO and 5.0L HO engines, injectors are energized once every other crankshaft revolution in sequence with engine firing order.

On 3.8L, 3.8L SC, 5.0L and 5.0L MA engines, all injectors are energized once every crankshaft revolution. Each injector is energized in sequence with ignition firing order.

ECA determines required fuel flow rate necessary to maintain prescribed air/fuel ratio for given engine operation by measuring quantity of air entering engine. Computer determines needed injector pulse width (period of time that injectors are energized) and energizes injector to meter quantity of fuel.

VAF system measures intake air quantity with vane airflow meter and integral air charge temperature sensor. Speed/density control system uses Throttle Position Sensor (TPS), Manifold Absolute Pressure (MAP) sensor and Air Charge Temperature (ACT) sensor to determine intake air quantity.

FUEL INJECTORS

Fuel injector nozzles are solenoid operated valves which meter and atomize fuel delivered to engine. Injectors are mounted in lower intake manifold with their nozzles injecting fuel just upstream of engine intake valves.

Injector bodies consist of solenoid actuated pintle and needle valve assembly. Electrical control signal from ECA unit activates injector solenoid, causing pintle to move inward off its seat, allowing fuel to flow.

Since injector flow orifice is fixed and fuel pressure at injector tip is constant, fuel flow to engine is regulated by how long solenoid is energized. This length of time is known as "pulse width". Atomization spray is obtained by shape of pintle.

FUEL PRESSURE REGULATOR

Fuel pressure regulator is attached to fuel supply manifold assembly downstream of fuel injectors. It regulates fuel pressure supplied to injectors. Regulator is diaphragm operated relief valve in which one side of diaphragm senses fuel pressure and other side is subjected to intake manifold pressure.

Fuel pressure is controlled by spring preload applied to diaphragm. Balancing one side of diaphragm with manifold pressure maintains constant fuel pressure at injectors. Excess fuel is by-passed through regulator and returned to fuel tank.

VANE AIRFLOW METER (VAF) ASSEMBLY

1.9L, 2.2L & 2.2L Turbo – Vane Airflow (VAF) meter assembly contains 2 sensors, airflow vane assembly and Vane Air Temperature (VAT) sensor. VAT measures temperature of incoming air.

VAF measures volume of air entering engine. Airflow moves vane which is mounted on pivot pin. Vane is connected to variable resistor (potentiometer). Output of potentiometer, which is connected to 5-volt reference signal from ECA, varies with volume of air flowing though meter.

Intake air volume and temperature inputs are used by ECA to compute fuel flow necessary for optimum air/fuel ratio.

BAROMETRIC PRESSURE (BP) SENSOR

2.2L & 2.2L Turbo – The BP sensor is mounted on right side of engine compartment firewall. It senses atmospheric pressure and provides information to the ECA.

MASS AIRFLOW (MA) SENSOR

5.0L Mustang – The mass airflow sensor measures airflow to intake system. Sensor output is used by ECA to calculate injector pulse width. This sensor has no moving parts. A heated, glass covered, platinum wire is used to heat air flowing through a fixed orifice to a temperature sensing wire. The temperature of air reaching sensor wire indicates amount of air which has flowed past the heated wire and through MA sensor.

MAP & ACT SENSORS

Manifold Absolute Pressure (MAP) sensor compares manifold vacuum and manifold pressures to obtain manifold absolute pressures. Resulting input signal from sensor provides ECA with engine load and air density information. This sensor is located on firewall in engine compartment or on air cleaner.

Air Charge Temperature (ACT) sensor measures air/fuel mixture temperature. Resulting input signal from sensor provides ECA with density correction factor, which is used to calculate airflow and to proportion cold enrichment fuel flow. This sensor is located in intake manifold runner or side of throttle body.

FUEL SUPPLY MANIFOLD ASSEMBLY

Fuel supply manifold assembly (fuel rail) delivers high pressure fuel from fuel pump supply line to fuel injectors. Fuel rail consists of tubular rail or stamping with injector connectors. Fuel pressure regulator is mounted on flange attached to rail. Rail also has mounting attachments which locate and secure fuel injectors in intake manifold.

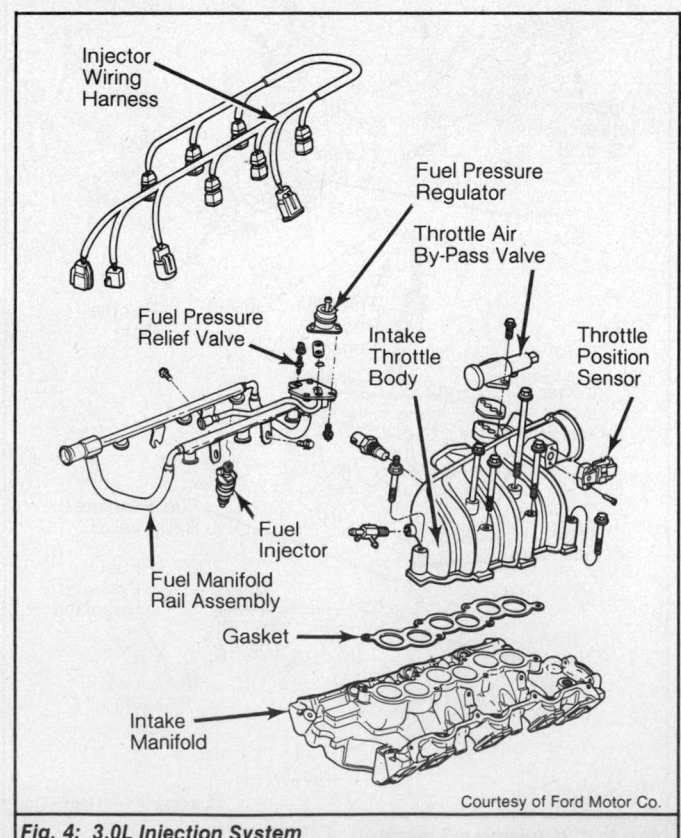

Courtesy of Ford Motor Co.

Fig. 4: 3.0L Injection System

1989 FUEL INJECTION
Ford Motor Co. Multi-Point Fuel Injection (Cont.)

2-43

THROTTLE BODY ASSEMBLY

Throttle body assembly controls airflow to engine through a butterfly valve. Throttle position is controlled by either linkage or cable/cam mechanism. Body is one-piece aluminum casting with single bore and air by-pass channel.

Air by-pass channel carries idle airflow which is regulated by air by-pass valve. Air by-pass valve is controlled by ECA to adjust both cold and warm idle speeds. Air by-pass valve uses solenoid valve to vary volume of idle airflow allowed to enter by-pass channel.

AIR INTAKE SYSTEM

Air intake system on 3.0L engine incorporates throttle body and air intake manifold in one-piece unit. Runner lengths are tuned for optimum engine torque output. Manifold provides mounting flanges for throttle body assembly, fuel supply manifold, accelerator controls, EGR valve and supply tube.

Vacuum ports are provided to support various engine accessories. Mounting sockets for fuel injectors are machined to prevent both air and fuel leakage. Pockets in which injectors are mounted are placed so injectors spray fuel directly in front of each intake valve.

FUEL PUMP CONTROL

When ignition switch is turned to "ON" position, EEC power relay is energized (contacts closed). Power is provided to fuel pump relay and to timer in ECA. Fuel pump receives power through fuel pump relay contacts. If ignition switch is not turned to "START" position, timer in ECA will open ground circuit after approximately one second. ECC senses engine speed and shuts off fuel pump by opening ground circuit to fuel pump relay when engine stops, or when engine speed drops to less than 120 RPM.

Opening ground circuit de-energizes fuel pump relay (contacts opened) and de-energizes fuel pump. This function allows pressurization of fuel system. When ignition switch is turned to "START" position, ECA operates fuel pump relay to provide fuel for starting engine while cranking.

INERTIA SWITCH

CAUTION: Do not reset inertia switch until complete fuel system has been inspected for leaks.

In event of collision, electrical contacts in inertia switch will open. This will automatically shut off fuel pump. Fuel pump will shut off even if engine does not stop running. Engine will stop shortly due to lack of fuel. It will not be possible to restart engine until inertia switch is manually reset. To reset inertia switch, depress button on top of switch.

On most RWD vehicles, inertia switch is located in trunk, on left hinge support or behind trim panel.

On LTD Crown Victoria and Grand Marquis station wagon models, switch is located in left rear side storage compartment.

On 3-door Mustang, it is located near left taillight. On FWD, switch is located behind trim panel in left side of trunk.

On Taurus and Sable station wagon models, switch is located behind access door in right rear cargo area.

TROUBLE SHOOTING

PRELIMINARY CHECKS

Following systems and components must be in good condition and operating properly before beginning diagnosis of fuel injection system:
- Battery condition
- State of tune
- Fuel delivery system
- All wiring and vacuum connections
- Air cleaner and ducting
- Cooling system

NOTE: Some vehicles may not include all components listed in this section.

Engine Does Not Crank – Check starting and charging systems. Repair any problems with these systems before attempting to repair fuel injection system.

Engine Cranks But Does Not Start – **1)** Ensure fuel tank contains adequate amount of fuel. Do not assume that fuel gauge is correct. Check fuel for dirt, water or other contamination.
2) Check ignition system for strong secondary current at spark plugs. If no spark exists or if spark is weak, repair ignition system before continuing with fuel injection diagnosis.
3) Check fuel lines and fittings for leaks. If no leaks are found, check fuel delivery system for proper operation, pressure and volume.
4) Check if inertia switch is tripped and reset if necessary. Check for defective injector, sticking Throttle Position Sensor (TPS), or defective Coolant Temperature Switch (CTS).

NOTE: For problems requiring EEC-IV diagnosis, see FORD MOTOR CO. EEC-IV article in COMPUTERIZED ENGINE CONTROLS section.

Hard to Start - (Cold) – Inoperative ISC motor, EEC-IV diagnosis required. TPS stuck at Wide Open Throttle (WOT), or inoperative injector. Crank engine with TPS disconnected. Check for injector discharge at injector.

Rough Idle (Cold) – Injector leaking or inoperative. Check operation of injector. Injector "O" ring seal leaking. Perform injector/regulator leakage test. Check for possible vacuum leak.

Stall, Stumble, Hesitation (Hot or Cold) – TPS failure. EEC-IV diagnosis required.

Hard Start (Hot) – **1)** Inoperative ISC motor. EEC-IV diagnosis required. TPS stuck at WOT. EEC-IV diagnosis required. Injector leaking or inoperative. Check for fuel discharge while cranking engine.
2) Excessive fuel pressure. Service pressure regulator and fuel return line. Contaminated fuel pressure regulator valve and seat.

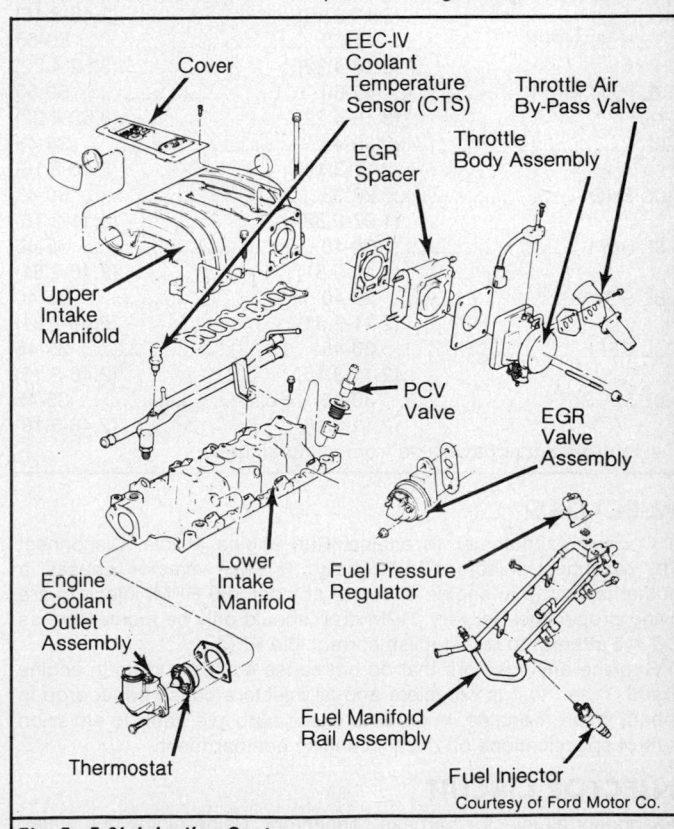

Fig. 5: 5.0L Injection System

Courtesy of Ford Motor Co.

2-44

1989 FUEL INJECTION
Ford Motor Co. Multi-Point Fuel Injection (Cont.)

Service pressure regulator or check fuel pressure bleed down after engine has been turned off. Injector "O" ring seal leaking. Perform injector leakage test.

Rough Idle (Hot) – Injector leaking or inoperative. Check operation of injector. Injector "O" ring leaking. Perform injector leakage test.

Stalls On Deceleration/Quick Stop – ISC inoperative. EEC-IV diagnosis required.

Lack Of Power – Fuel filter may be clogged. Check fuel delivery and repair as needed.

Reduced Top Speed/Power – Plugged injectors. Check injector discharge at injector. Damaged fuel pressure regulator. Service or replace as necessary.

Surges At Cruise – Plugged or leaking injectors. Check injector operation. Check also for restricted fuel filter.

TESTING & DIAGNOSIS

FUEL PUMP

The fuel pump may be activated by grounding the fuel pump lead at the SELF-TEST connector. Use a jumper lead, and ground the "FP" terminal with the ignition on. This activates the fuel pump. *See Fig. 6.* For additional circuit test information, see CIRCUIT TEST C2, of FORD MOTOR CO. EEC-IV article in COMPUTERIZED ENGINE CONTROLS section.

CAUTION: Inspect fuel system for leaks or damage before resetting inertia switch or testing fuel pump.

FUEL PRESSURE SPECIFICATIONS: psi (kg/cm²)

Engine	Pressure Engine Running	Pressure KOEO
1.9L MPFI	30-45 (2.11-3.16)	35-45 (2.46-3.16)
2.2L & 2.2L Turbo	27-40 (1.90-2.81)	[1]
2.3L OHC MPFI	30-45 (2.11-3.16)	35-45 (2.46-3.16)
2.3L HSC MPFI	45-60 (3.16-4.22)	50-60 (3.52-4.22)
2.3L HSO MPFI	45-60 (3.16-4.22)	50-60 (3.52-4.22)
3.0L	30-45 (2.11-3.16)	35-45 (2.46-3.16)
3.0L SHO	28-33 (1.97-2.32)	30-45 (2.11-3.16)
3.8L SEFI	30-40 (2.11-2.81)	35-40 (2.46-2.81)
3.8L SC	30-40 (2.11-2.81)	35-40 (2.46-2.81)
5.0L SEFI	30-45 (2.11-3.16)	35-45 (2.46-3.16)
5.0L MA SEFI	30-45 (2.11-3.16)	35-45 (2.46-3.16)

[1] – Information not available from manufacturer.

INJECTORS

1) Connect tachometer to engine. Run engine at idle. Disconnect and reconnect injectors individually. If each injector causes a momentary drop in engine speed of at least 100 RPM, injectors are giving proper fuel delivery. RPM drop should only be momentary as ISC will attempt to re-establish correct idle RPM.

2) Replace any injectors that do not cause sufficient drop in engine speed. When test is complete and all injectors cause equal drop in speed, shut off engine. In order to check curb idle, refer to emission control specifications on decal in engine compartment.

INJECTOR CIRCUIT

Disconnect all injector harness connectors. Using digital ohmmeter, check resistance across terminals of each injector. See INDIVIDUAL

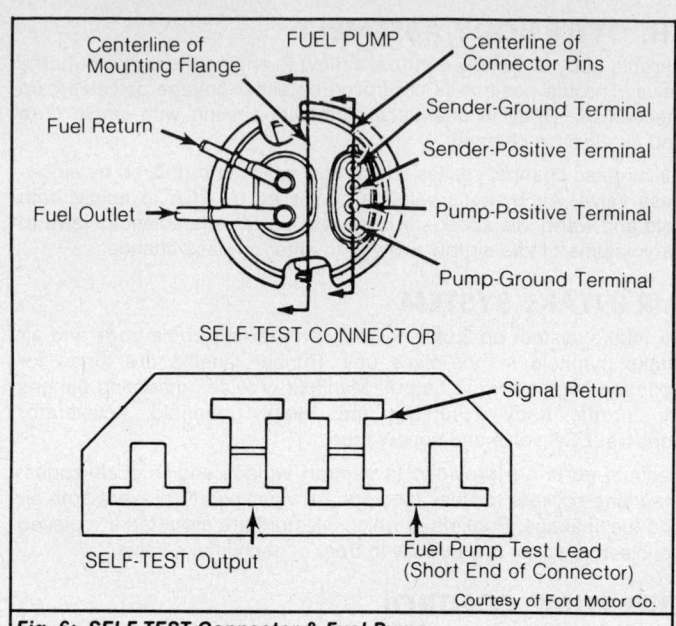

Fig. 6: SELF-TEST Connector & Fuel Pump

Courtesy of Ford Motor Co.

INJECTOR RESISTANCE table. Disconnect injector bank harness connector, check resistance of injector bank. See INJECTOR BANK RESISTANCE table. Repair wiring or replace any injector circuit not within specification.

INDIVIDUAL INJECTOR RESISTANCE

Engine	Ohms (Ω)
1.9L MPFI	2.0-2.7
2.2L	
Non-Turbo	12-16
Turbo	11-15
2.3L OHC	15.0-19.0
2.3L HSC	13.5-16.0
2.3L HSO	13.5-16.0
3.0L	15.0-18.0
3.0L SHO	13.5-16.0
3.8L MPFI	13.5-16.0
5.0L	
Mustang	1.5-19
All Other Models	13.5-19

INJECTOR BANK RESISTANCE

Engine	Ohms
1.9L MPFI	1.2-1.8
2.2L & 2.2L Turbo	[1]
2.3L OHC	7.0-9.5
2.3L HSC	7.0-9.5
2.3L HSO	7.0-9.5
3.0L	5.0-6.5
3.0L SHO	[1]
All 5.0L	[1]

[1] – Information not available from manufacturer.

NOTE: For further component testing and information, see FORD MOTOR CO. EEC-IV article in COMPUTERIZED ENGINE CONTROLS sections.

REMOVAL & INSTALLATION

PREPARATION

Before removing fuel charging assembly or servicing components installed on engine, following steps MUST be performed:

- Turn ignition off.
- Disconnect negative battery lead.
- Remove fuel cap to relieve tank pressure.
- Release system pressure. See FUEL SYSTEM PRESSURE RELEASE.
- Disconnect fuel supply and return lines.
- On 1.9L models, disconnect injector wiring harness by disconnecting ECT sensor in heater supply tube under lower intake manifold. Disconnect air by-pass connector from EEC harness.

FUEL SYSTEM PRESSURE RELEASE

2.2L & 2.2L Turbo – Relieve fuel line pressure by starting engine and disconnecting fuel pump relay. After engine stalls turn ignition off. Reconnect fuel pump relay.

All Other Models – Remove fuel tank cap. Using Fuel Pressure Gauge (T80L-9974-B), release pressure from system at pressure relief valve (schrader valve) on fuel injection manifold rail.

FUEL LINE CONNECTOR

Removal (Spring Lock Coupling) – 1) Using Spring Lock Coupling Remover (D87L-9280-A for 3/8" or D87L-9280-B for 1/2"), remove clip from coupling. Place remover over coupling so intrusion is positioned on cage opening side of coupling. See Fig. 7.

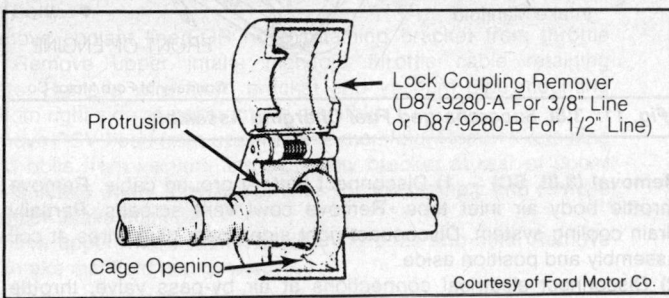

Fig. 7: Disconnecting Fuel Line Spring Lock Coupling

2) Close remover over coupling. Push remover into cage opening to release female fitting from garter spring. Pull male and female halves of coupling apart. Remove tool from disconnected spring lock coupling.

Installation – 1) Ensure garter spring in cage of male fitting is not damaged, replace if necessary. Clean all dirt from both pieces of coupling. Check "O" rings for damage and replace if necessary using proper fuel resistant "O" rings.

2) Lubricate "O" rings and inside of female fitting with clean engine oil. Snap fitting together. Install retaining clip onto coupling. Ensure horseshoe portion of clip is over the coupling. See Fig. 8. Do not install retaining clip over rubber fuel line.

Removal (Hairpin Clip Coupling) – Remove hairpin clip from fitting. Spread each clip leg about 1/8" to disengage body. Push legs into fitting. While pulling lightly on triangular end of clip. Work it clear of tube and fitting. Pull fitting and steel line in axial direction. Use twisting motion while pulling fitting loose.

Installation – Insert clip into any 2 adjacent openings with triangular portion pointing away from fitting opening. Install clip to fully engage the body. Clean end of fitting. Aign fitting and tube axially and push fitting onto tube end. When fitting is engaged, a definite click will be heard.

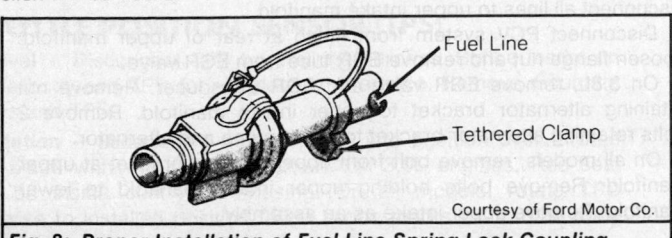

Fig. 8: Proper Installation of Fuel Line Spring Lock Coupling

FUEL CHARGING ASSEMBLY

Removal (1.9L & 2.3L Tempo & Topaz) – 1) Remove air cleaner outlet tube between vane air meter and air throttle body by loosening 2 clamps. Disconnect and remove accelerator and speed control cables from accelerator mounting bracket and throttle lever.

2) Disconnect top manifold vacuum fitting connections by disconnecting both rear vacuum line for dash panel vacuum tree and vacuum line at intake tee. Disconnect hoses from PCV valve at intake manifold.

3) Disconnect vacuum line at EGR valve, fuel pressure regulator and MAP sensor (if equipped). Disconnect EGR tube from upper intake manifold by loosening compression nut while supporting connector. Remove only upper bolt to disconnect upper manifold support bracket.

4) Disconnect wiring at main engine harness and ECT sensor (if equipped). Disconnect fuel lines. Remove manifold mounting nuts. Disconnect lower manifold support bracket by removing top bolt. Remove manifold with wiring harness and gasket.

Installation – 1) Clean and inspect mounting faces of fuel charging manifold assembly and cylinder head. Surface must be clean and flat. Clean and lubricate manifold stud threads. Install new gasket. Install manifold assembly to head and tighten top middle nut finger tight.

2) Install fuel return line in fuel supply manifold. Install 2 manifold mounting nuts finger tight. Install remaining 3 manifold mounting nuts and tighten all nuts. Connect upper and lower manifold support brackets and tighten bolts. Install EGR tube with oil coated compression nut.

3) Connect vacuum lines to throttle body port. Connect large PCV vacuum line to upper manifold. Reconnect all manifold vacuum lines. Connect accelerator and speed control cables. Install air supply tube and tighten clamps.

4) Reconnect wiring harness at ECT sensor and EEC harness. Connect fuel supply hose from fuel filter to fuel rail. Connect fuel return line. Connect battery ground and refill cooling system.

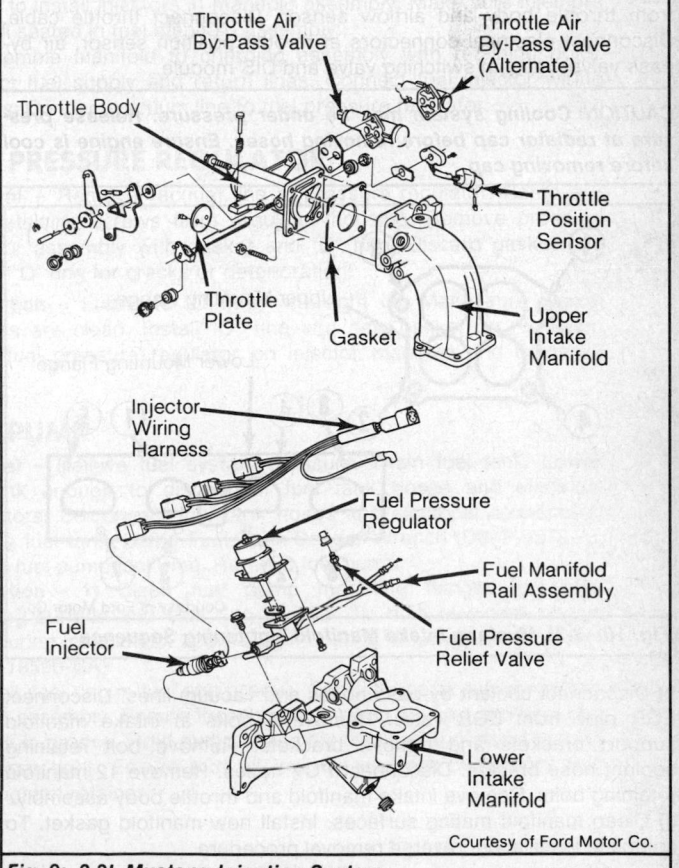

Fig. 9: 2.3L Mustang Injection System

2-48

1989 FUEL INJECTION
Ford Motor Co. Multi-Point Fuel Injection (Cont.)

VANE AIR METER

Removal (1.9L) – 1) Disconnect air cleaner outlet hose from air meter assembly and position hose out of way. Remove air intake tube from air cleaner. Disengage 2 spring clamps. Remove air cleaner front cover and air cleaner filter panel.

2) Remove 4 screws and washers from flange of air cleaner where it attaches to vane air meter assembly. Pull air cleaner base away from vane air meter and remove air cleaner gasket. Remove electrical connector from vane air meter assembly. Remove 3 screws and washers attaching vane air meter to bracket and remove air meter. Note location and size of mounting screws for reassembly reference.

Installation – 1) Clean mounting surfaces. Mount vane air meter on air cleaner tray, making sure gasket is seated and aligned. Secure air meter assembly to air meter bracket with 3 special screw/washer assemblies (2 of No. N605786-S2 and 1 No. N605789-S2 screw). These screws are different sizes and must go in correct opening.

2) Connect vane air meter inlet hose and tighten clamp. Install air cleaner housing/vane meter bracket to fenderwell with 4 retaining screws. Connect all hoses to air cleaner housing. Connect air meter electrical connector. Install air cleaner element and housing cover.

Removal (2.2L & 2.2L Turbo) – Disconnect negative battery cable. Disconnect airflow meter electrical connector. Remove air duct from air filter cover. Remove air filter cover attaching bolts and cover. Remove vane airflow meter attaching nuts from inside air cleaner cover. Remove airflow meter.

Installation – To install, reverse removal procedure.

MASS AIRFLOW SENSOR (MA)

Removal & Installation (5.0L) – The MA sensor is attached to the air inlet duct at the rear of the air filter assembly. Disconnect wiring harness connector. Remove air filter duct and loosen clamps on MA sensor. Remove sensor. To install, reverse removal procedure.

WIRING DIAGRAMS

See appropriate article in COMPUTERIZED ENGINE CONTROLS section.

TIGHTENING SPECIFICATIONS

Application	Ft. Lbs. (N.m)
EGR Tube	
1.9L	18-28 (24-38)
2.3L	
Mustang	18-28 (24-38)
Tempo & Topaz	30-40 (40-54)
Fuel Injector Manifold-to-Fuel Charging Assembly	
5.0L	
HO	[1]
All Others	12-18 (16-24)
3.8L & 3.8L SC	[2]
All Others	15-22 (20-30)
Lower Intake Manifold-to-Head Bolts	
1.9L & 5.0L	23-25 (31-34)
2.3L	
Mustang	14-22 (19-30)
Tempo & Topaz	12-15 (16-20)
3.0L	20-28 (26-38)
3.0L SHO	11-17 (15-23)
3.8L & 3.8L SC	23 (31)
Throttle Body Mounting Bolts	
1.9L	15-22 (20-30)
3.8L & 3.8L SC	24 (33)
All Others	12-15 (16-20)
Upper-to-Lower Intake Manifold Bolts	
5.0L HO	12-18 (16-24)
All Others	15-22 (20-30)
	INCH Lbs. (N.m)
Air By-Pass Valve-to-Throttle Body	71-97 (8-11)
EGR Tube (All Except 2.3L)	71-102 (8-11.5)
Fuel Pressure Relief Valve	48-84 (6-10)
Fuel Pressure Regulator-to-	
Injector Manifold	27-40 (2.9-4.3)
TPS-to-Throttle Body	
2.3L Tempo & Topaz	25-30 (2.8-3.4)
3.8L & 3.8L SC	19 (2.1)
All Others	14-16 (1.6-1.8)
Vane Air Meter Mounting Screws	71-106 (8-12)

[1] – Bolts should be tightened to 71-102 INCH lbs. (8-12 N.m).
[2] – Bolts should be tightened to 87 INCH lbs. (10 N.m).

APPLICATION

CHRYSLER MOTORS

Application	VIN Engine Code
2.2L 4-Cyl. Turbo II	A
2.5L 4-Cyl. Turbo I	J

DESCRIPTION

The turbocharging system is mounted on the manifold side of the engine. It includes a turbine assembly, center housing rotating assembly, compressor assembly, wastegate, and throttle body. The turbine is spun by exhaust gas causing compressor wheel to draw in air.

Maximum manifold pressure (boost) is controlled by the exhaust wastegate. Operation of the wastegate is controlled by a solenoid and the Single Module Engine Controller (SMEC).

OPERATION

COMPRESSOR

Air is drawn into the compressor through an air inlet duct and the throttle body. Forced air from turbocharger enters into the intake manifold. Exhaust gas is directed into the turbocharger turbine housing where it is used to increase speed of the turbine.

TURBINE ASSEMBLY

The turbine is connected to the compressor by a shaft. The exhaust gas passes across the turbine wheel blades. This forces the turbine wheel to rotate. Increased exhaust gas volume and pressure causes an increase in turbine speed. Faster rotation of the turbine increases compressor output.

WASTEGATE & ACTUATOR

The wastegate limits intake manifold pressure to a pre-set maximum. The actuator is a pressure-sensitive diaphragm. Operation of the wastegate is controlled by a solenoid and the SMEC.

As maximum boost pressure is obtained, the actuator causes the wastegate to open. At this point, a portion of the exhaust gas is diverted around the turbine and enters the header pipe directly. The wastegate is mounted to the turbine assembly.

OIL SUPPLY

Turbochargers must have constant flow of clean engine oil for proper operation. Oil is supplied directly into the center housing of turbocharger. Oil feed pipe runs from fitting on the engine block to the turbocharger center housing. Engine oil is returned into the engine block by a tube attached to housing of turbocharger. Change oil, filter and flush turbocharger with clean oil ANYTIME there is oil contamination.

TESTING

WASTEGATE ACTUATOR ASSEMBLY

1) Remove hose from wastegate actuator assembly. Connect cooling system pressure tester to wastegate diaphragm. Slowly apply pressure and note wastegate actuator rod operation.

2) Actuator rod should not move more than .015" (.38 mm) at 4 psi (.28 kg/cm²). If actuator rod does not move at 5 psi (.35 kg/cm²), 4 psi (.28 kg/cm²) for Turbo II, wastegate is faulty. Turbocharger must be replaced if wastegate fails to operate at proper pressure.

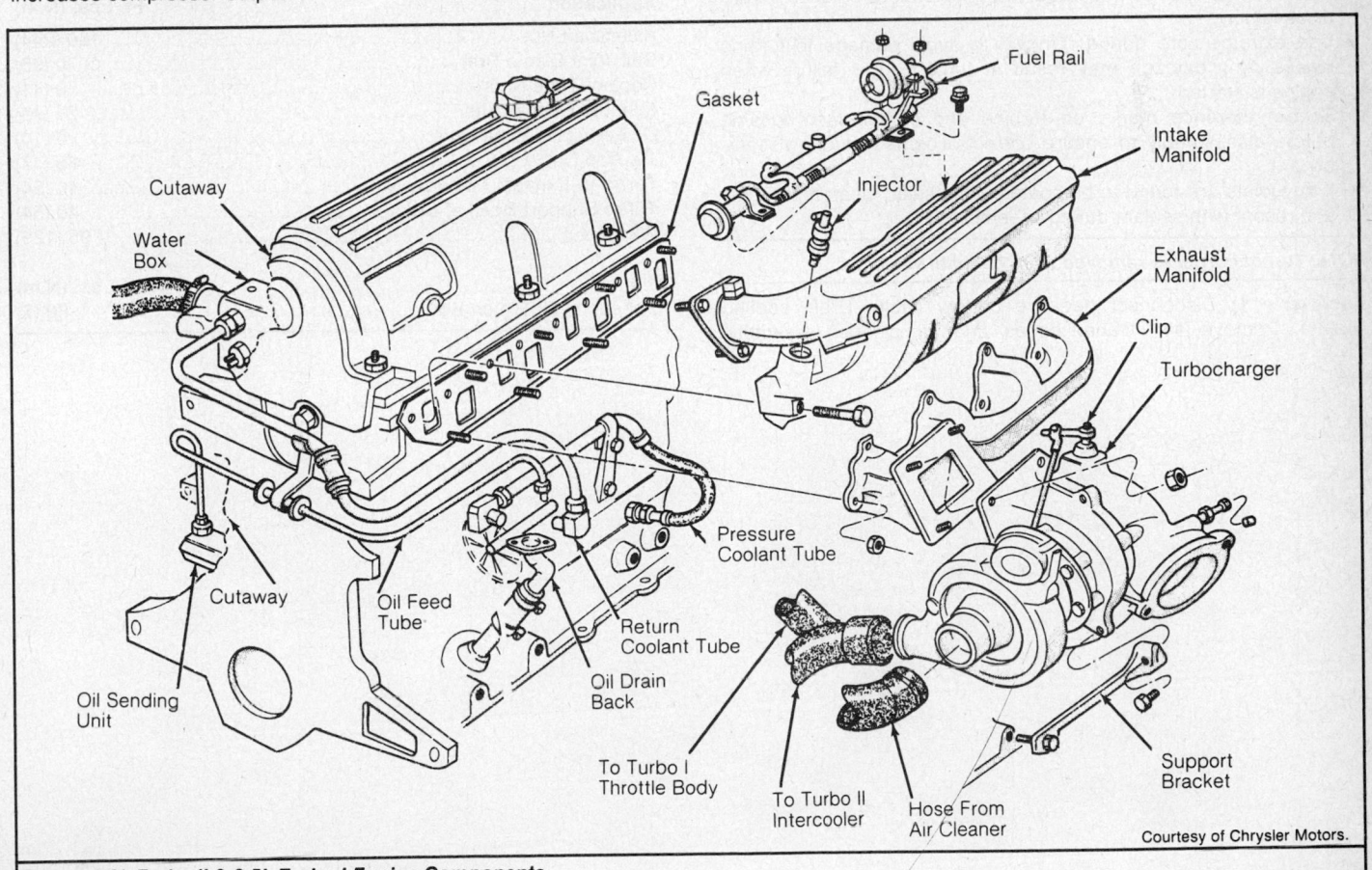

Courtesy of Chrysler Motors.

Fig. 1: 2.2L Turbo II & 2.5L Turbo I Engine Components

INTERNAL INSPECTION

NOTE: Each turbocharger has a unique noise level when operating. If the sound cycles up and down, check for air restrictions in the intake tube and for dirt build-up in the compressor housing or wheel. If a high-pitched noise or whistle occurs, check for inlet air or exhaust gas leak.

TURBOCHARGER

1) Remove exhaust outlet pipe from turbocharger housing. Using a mirror, observe movement of the wastegate while operating the actuator linkage manually.

2) If wastegate fails to open or close, replace turbocharger assembly. Spin the compressor wheel and check for binding. Replace turbocharger if binding exists.

3) Remove the oil drain back from the center housing. Check center housing for sludging in the oil drain area. If necessary, replace the engine oil. If heavily sludged or caked, replace turbocharger assembly.

4) Remove the throttle body and inspect compressor wheel and housing for signs of oil leakage, gouges, nicks, or distortion. If damaged or oil leakage, replace turbocharger assembly.

REMOVAL & INSTALLATION

NOTE: If turbocharger is being replaced, change engine oil and filter.

REMOVAL PRECAUTIONS

Prior to any unit repair on a turbocharging system, several general precautions should be considered.

- Clean area around turbocharger with non-caustic solution before disassembly.
- Use extreme care during removal to avoid damage to turbine blades. Any damage may result in turbocharger failure when engine is started.
- Scribe reference marks on turbine and compressor housing before disassembly to ensure correct alignment during assembly.
- If any joints are found to be coated with sealer, clean thoroughly and recoat with sealant during assembly.

NOTE: Turbocharger is removed from beneath vehicle.

Removal – 1) Disconnect negative battery cable. Drain cooling system. Remove air cleaner hoses and air cleaner assembly.

Remove front engine through bolt and tilt engine towards front of vehicle.

2) Disconnect and remove coolant hose from water box and turbocharger housing. Disconnect oil feed line at turbocharger. Remove wastegate rod retaining clip. Remove 3 (leaving one lower nut) turbocharger-to-exhaust manifold nuts. Disconnect oxygen sensor electrical connector. Disconnect necessary vacuum hoses.

3) Remove right front drive axle spindle nut. Raise and support vehicle. Remove speedometer pinion assembly from transaxle. Tap axle shaft end lightly with brass hammer to free axle shaft from hub splines. Remove lower ball joint clamp bolt. Separate lower ball joint from steering knuckle.

4) Pull out on hub/steering knuckle assembly and separate axle shaft from hub. Grasp both CV joints at outer housings, to prevent separation and pull axle shaft out of transaxle or intermediate shaft. Remove axle shaft from vehicle.

5) Remove turbocharger-to-block support bracket. Disconnect and remove oil drain tube from turbocharger. Remove one remaining turbocharger-to-exhaust manifold nut. Disconnect articulating exhaust pipe joint from turbocharger housing.

6) Remove lower coolant line and fitting at turbocharger. Lift turbocharger off exhaust manifold studs and lower assembly down and out of vehicle.

NOTE: When replacing turbocharger, pour fresh engine oil directly into oil feed line fitting on turbocharger before installing oil feed line.

Installation – To install, reverse removal procedures. Ensure turbocharger tightening specifications are followed. Apply anti-seize compound to exhaust manifold studs. Ensure that turbine wheel turns freely before installing exhaust pipe.

TIGHTENING SPECIFICATIONS

Application	Ft. Lbs. (N.m)
Axle Shaft Nut	180 (244)
Ball Joint Clamp Bolt	70 (95)
Coolant Tube Nuts	30 (41)
Exhaust Flange Nuts	21 (28)
Oil Feed Line Tube Nuts	10 (14)
Tie Rod Nut	35 (47)
Turbo-to-Exhaust Manifold Nuts	40 (54)
Turbo Support Bracket Bolts	40 (54)
Wheel Nut	95 (129)

Application	INCH Lbs. (N.m)
Speedometer Pinion Bolt	60 (7)

2.2L Probe

DESCRIPTION

The turbocharger is a blow-through type system. Fuel is introduced downstream of the compressor. This is an "on-demand" system that boosts engine output at high-load/high-speed conditions.

The turbocharger is equipped with a charge air cooler (intercooler) mounted between the turbocharger and the throttle body. The intercooler cools air flowing out of the turbocharger. This cooling, along with turbo boost, improves combustion efficiency and engine horsepower.

The turbocharger boost control system provides electronic variable boost control. The boost control provides regulation of the exhaust by-pass device or wastegate. If a fault develops in the wastegate, actuator, or solenoid valve, resulting in excessive boost pressures, an overboost warning chime will sound. The warning chime is actuated by the vane airflow meter through the ECA. A knock sensor and knock control unit combine to retard the engine spark advance when engine knocking occurs due to overboost.

The 5 major components of the turbocharger are compressor, turbine, wastegate actuator, wastegate, and a water-cooled center housing.

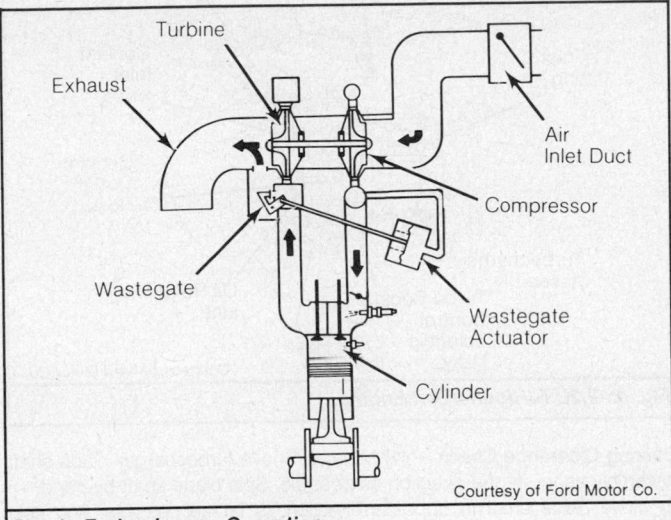

Fig. 1: Turbocharger Operation

Courtesy of Ford Motor Co.

OPERATION

As engine load increases and throttle is opened, more air/fuel mixture flows into the combustion chamber. As this mixture is burned, a greater volume of hot exhaust gas enters exhaust system. The exhaust gas passes through the exhaust intake port on the turbocharger and into the turbine housing, where it provides drive to the turbine wheel.

The turbine wheel is connected by a shaft to the compressor wheel. As compressor speed increases, it compresses incoming air and forces a denser air/fuel mixture into combustion chambers resulting in increased engine power output.

COMPRESSOR

The compressor is a centrifugal, radial outflow type which receives its drive from the turbine by means of a connecting shaft. It compresses incoming air, increasing its density and discharges the air to intake ports.

TURBINE

The turbine is a centripetal, radial in-flow type. Exhaust gases passing through turbine assembly cause turbine wheel to rotate, which in turn causes compressor wheel to rotate. Rotational speed is governed by flow-rate of the exhaust gas. As engine speed increases, turbine speed increases, resulting in increased compressor speed and pressure.

WASTEGATE & WASTEGATE ACTUATOR

The wastegate controls amount of pressure introduced into intake manifold. As pressure approaches a preset limit, wastegate actuator begins to open wastegate, permitting a portion of exhaust gases to by-pass turbine wheel and directly into exhaust pipe. *See Fig. 1.*

CENTER HOUSING

The center housing is a water-cooled assembly which houses bearings, compressor, turbine wheel and oil seals.

OIL SUPPLY

NOTE: ANYTIME there is evidence of ANY oil contamination, the oil and oil filter must be changed and the turbocharger assembly flushed with clean oil.

Whenever the oil is changed, the turbocharger should be primed prior to engine operation. Disconnect coil secondary wire at distributor cap and ground coil wire. Crank engine (30 seconds maximum per cycle) until oil light goes out or oil pressure gauge indicates positive pressure in system. Reconnect coil wire.

NOTE: Immediately shutting down an engine that has been operating at high RPM for an extended period of time can damage the engine and/or turbocharger.

REMOVAL & INSTALLATION

TURBOCHARGER

NOTE: The turbocharger cannot be rebuilt or overhauled. If ANY component malfunctions except wastegate actuator, it will be necessary to replace the entire turbocharger assembly

Prior to removal of turbocharger, the following precautions should be observed:
- Area surrounding turbocharger should be cleaned with a non-caustic cleaner.
- All engine openings should be covered with clean cloth after unit removal to prevent entry of foreign matter.
- Ensure blades are not nicked or otherwise damaged. An imbalance condition could result and lead to severe damage.
- If any internal engine component is replaced, oil and filter should be changed and turbocharger should be flushed with clean oil.
- Prior to installing turbocharger on engine, gently spin blades to ensure freedom of movement.

Removal – 1) Disconnect negative battery cable. Drain cooling system. Disconnect throttle body inlet tube from turbocharger. Remove heat shields from exhaust manifold and turbocharger assembly.

2) Disconnect O_2 sensor electrical connector (if necessary). Disconnect oil feed and return lines from turbocharger. Disconnect coolant inlet and return hose from turbocharger.

3) Remove EGR tube from exhaust manifold. Disconnect turbo boost control solenoid. Remove mounting bolt from turbocharger retaining bracket located under the turbocharger. Remove O_2 sensor (if necessary).

4) Remove converter inlet pipe from turbocharger joint pipe. Remove exhaust manifold and turbocharger as an assembly. Separate exhaust manifold, turbocharger-to-converter inlet pipe, joint pipe and heat shield assembly from turbocharger.

Installation – 1) Fill oil cavity of turbocharger with oil. To install, reverse removal procedure. After installation, disconnect coil wire and crank engine for 20 seconds. Connect coil wire. Start engine and run at idle for 30 seconds.

2) Stop engine, disconnect negative battery cable and depress brake pedal for at least 5 seconds to cancel malfunction code. Reconnect negative battery cable.

CAUTION: Always replace exhaust manifold-to-turbocharger gasket and/or joint pipe gasket if bent or cracked. Use only specified nuts to mount the exhaust manifold and pipe to turbocharger.

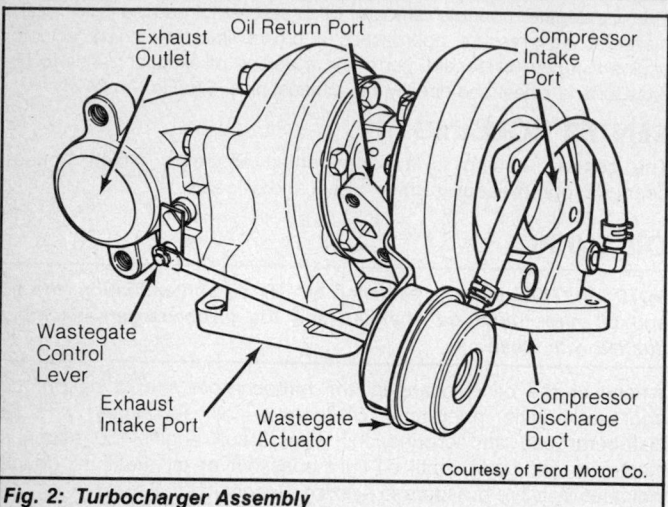

Fig. 2: Turbocharger Assembly

Courtesy of Ford Motor Co.

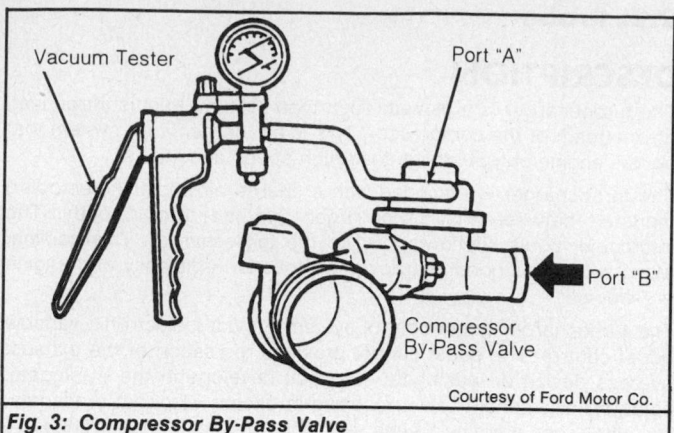

Fig. 3: Compressor By-Pass Valve

Courtesy of Ford Motor Co.

INTERCOOLER

Removal – Remove front facia (if necessary). Remove front bumper assembly (if necessary). Remove intercooler housing mounting nuts. Remove clamps on both inlet and outlet air hoses on intercooler assembly. Remove intercooler.

Installation – To install, reverse removal procedure.

TESTING

Boost Pressure Check – 1) With engine cool, disconnect air hose from the turbo boost control solenoid valve on the turbocharger. Connect vacuum/pressure gauge to control solenoid.

2) Start engine and allow it to warm-up to normal operating temperature. Increase engine speed to 4000 RPM. If gauge reads any positive pressure above zero, perform OVERBOOST WARNING CHIME CHECK. If gauge does not read any positive pressure above zero, preform TURBO BOOST CONTROL SOLENOID VALVE CHECK.

Overboost Warning Chime Check – 1) Start the engine and run at 2000 RPM. Remove the air filter upper housing. Push measuring plate of vane airflow meter to fully open position.

2) Ensure warning buzzer sounds and engine speed drops or engine stalls. If not, see appropriate article in COMPUTERIZED ENGINE CONTROL section of this manual. Turn off engine and replace air filter upper housing.

Compressor By-Pass Valve Function Check – With compressor by-pass valve removed from the vehicle, apply a vacuum of 9.8-15.7 in. Hg to port "A" of the valve. *See Fig. 3.* Blow through port "B" to verify air flows. If air does not flow, replace compressor by-pass valve.

Turbo Boost Control Solenoid Valve Check – 1) Remove small air tube from turbocharger inlet air hose. Disconnect turbo boost control solenoid valve electrical connector. *See Fig. 4.*

2) Blow through small air tube and ensure air will not flow. Apply 12 volts to one terminal of the electrical connector and ground the other terminal.

3) Blow through the air tube and ensure that air flows through the tube. If solenoid valve does not pass test, replace solenoid valve.

Wastegate Function Check – With a cool engine and exhaust manifold heat shields removed, disconnect the wastegate actuator hose at solenoid end. Using Pressure Regulator (T79P-6634-A), apply 8.5 psi (.6 kg/cm²) of air pressure. If wastegate actuator does not move when pressure is applied, replace wastegate actuator assembly.

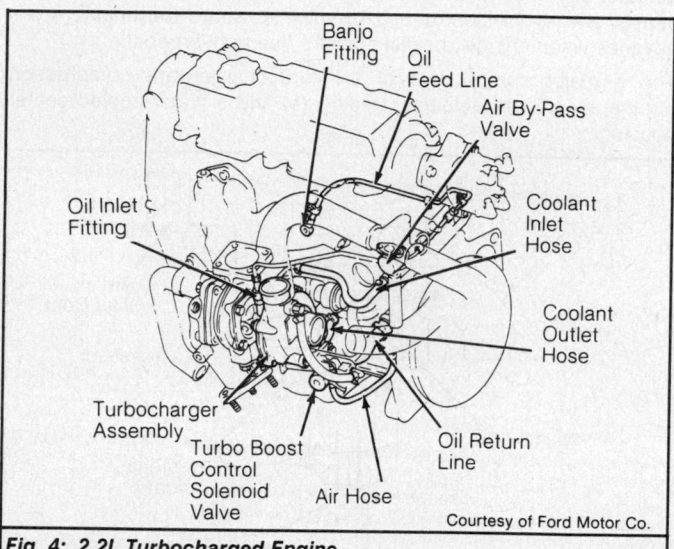

Fig. 4: 2.2L Turbocharged Engine

Courtesy of Ford Motor Co.

Bearing Clearance Check – 1) Manually move turbocharger blade shaft assembly as far in one direction as possible. Spin blade shaft by hand.

2) Move blade shaft in opposite direction as far as possible, and spin blade shaft by hand.

3) If neither turbine blade nor compressor blade contacts any portion of their respective housings, bearings are still good.

4) If either blade contacts with their respective housing, bearings are worn, and turbocharger should be replaced.

Knock Sensor, Knock Sensor Control Unit & ECA – See appropriate article in COMPUTERIZED ENGINE CONTROL section of this manual.

Turbo Seal Leakage Check – Remove compressor outlet hose and front exhaust pipe from the turbocharger. Visually inspect the removed pipes and their connecting passages in turbo housing for presence of oil. If oil is present, replace turbocharger assembly.

TIGHTENING SPECIFICATIONS

Application	Ft. Lbs. (N.m)
Exhaust Manifold-to-Turbocharger Nuts	27-46 (37-62)
Joint Pipe/Heat Shield Assembly-to-Turbocharger Nuts	27-46 (37-62)

3.8L Cougar XR7, Thunderbird Super Coupe

DESCRIPTION

The supercharger is matched to the engine by its displacement and belt ratio and can provide excess airflow at any engine speed. The supercharger contains 2, 3-lobed rotors. The helical shape and specialized porting provides a smooth discharge flow and low level of noise during operation. The rotors are supported by ball bearings in front and needle bearings at the rear. Drive gears are pressed into place, therefore the supercharger is replaced as a unit and is not serviceable.

The supercharger is not a bolt-on option. It is part of an integrated engine system. Many components from a supercharged engine are not interchangeable from a non-supercharged engine. All models are equipped with an air-to-air intercooler which cools the pressurized air from the supercharger. By cooling the pressurized air from the supercharger, air density will be increased, which will improve engine combustion, horsepower and torque.

At low throttle, the engine runs under normal engine vacuum. To prevent supercharger cavitation, reduced performance and increased temperatures, a vacuum controlled by-pass valve is installed at the supercharger outlet. The by-pass valve allows a controlled amount of air back into the supercharger. As throttle opening is increased, the by-pass valve actuator closes the by-pass valve, which directs all air from supercharger to intake manifold. This occurs as soon as throttle opens, resulting in immediate response.

OPERATION

The supercharger is a blow-through type system with port fuel injection. The supercharger is belt driven off the crankshaft. The throttle body controls amount of intake air to the supercharger through the inlet plenum.

Air from supercharger is routed through the intercooler and then to the intake manifold. At partial throttle or when vacuum is present in the intake system, a vacuum controlled by-pass valve reroutes some discharged air from supercharger back through intake plenum to prevent supercharger cavitation.

TROUBLE SHOOTING

See SUPERCHARGER TROUBLE SHOOTING article in this section. See appropriate EEC-IV article in COMPUTERIZED ENGINE CONTROLS section.

REMOVAL & INSTALLATION

AIR BY-PASS VALVE ACTUATOR

Disconnect vacuum hose. Remove supercharger and inlet assembly. Remove actuator-to-supercharger retaining bolt. Remove 2 self-tapping screws. Rotate actuator to allow rod to pass through keyed slot in by-pass lever and remove actuator.

INTAKE ELBOW ASSEMBLY

Removal – Remove cowl vent screens. Disconnect electrical connection at intake air temperature sensor. Disconnect vacuum lines at intake elbow. Remove intercooler outlet tube. Loosen clamps at air by-pass valve inlet hose. Slide hose to free elbow assembly. Remove 3 elbow-to-manifold retaining bolts and remove elbow.

Installation – Clean and inspect gasket surfaces. Install gasket on intake manifold. Install intake elbow and tighten retaining bolts. Slide air by-pass hose into position. Align paint stripe on hose with rib on elbow assembly. To complete installation, reverse removal procedure.

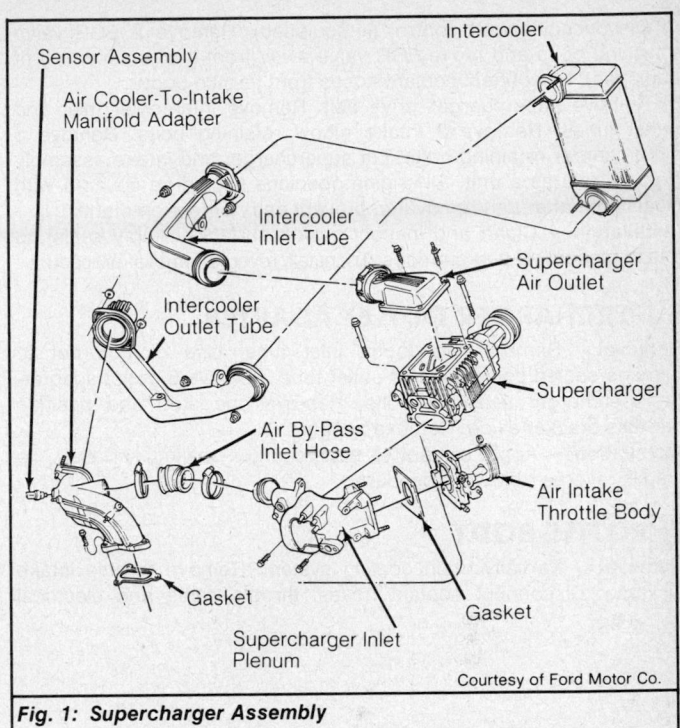

Fig. 1: **Supercharger Assembly**

INTERCOOLER

Removal – Remove retaining nuts connecting upper and lower intercooler tube-to-intercooler. Remove upper (intake) intercooler tube. Remove intercooler retaining bolts. Push down slightly on intercooler to release it from retaining clips.

Installation – Apply teflon tape to intercooler tube sealing connections. To install, reverse removal procedure.

PLENUM ASSEMBLY

Removal – 1) Partially drain coolant. Remove cowl vent screens, elbow assembly and throttle valve intake air tube. Disconnect throttle cable. Disconnect coolant hoses at throttle housing. Remove throttle cable bracket retaining bolts and position bracket aside. Disconnect PCV tube.

2) Disconnect vacuum lines to plenum assembly and EGR transducer. Disconnect electrical connections at throttle position sensor, idle air by-pass valve and EGR transducer. Remove EGR retaining bolts and pull EGR away from plenum (if equipped). Remove EGR transducer bracket mounting screw and remove transducer. Remove plenum assembly retaining bolts.

Installation – Apply sealant to plenum mating joints. To install, reverse remove procedure.

SUPERCHARGER

NOTE: The supercharger cannot be rebuilt or overhauled. If supercharger malfunctions, it will be necessary to replace entire supercharger assembly

Removal – 1) Clean area surrounding supercharger. Disconnect battery ground cable. Remove throttle body air inlet tube. Remove cowl vent screens. Partially drain cooling system. Disconnect right side spark plug wires at coil assembly and position aside.

2) Disconnect electrical connections at air by-pass valve, throttle position sensor and air charge temperature sensors. Disconnect vacuum lines from inlet plenum assembly.

3) Remove EGR transducer from bracket and disconnect vacuum line. Disconnect PCV tube. Disconnect throttle linkage at throttle housing. Remove linkage bracket attaching bolts and position bracket aside.

4) Disconnect speed control (if equipped). Remove 2 EGR valve attaching bolts and move EGR valve away from intake assembly (if equipped). Disconnect coolant hoses from throttle body.

5) Remove supercharger drive belt. Remove intercooler inlet and outlet tubes. Remove 3 intake elbow retaining bolts. Remove 3 supercharger retaining bolts. Lift supercharger and intake assembly from vehicle as a unit. All engine openings should be covered with clean cloth after unit removal to prevent entry of foreign matter.

Installation – Clean and inspect gasket surfaces. Apply sealer to intake plenum mating surfaces. To install, reverse removal procedure.

SUPERCHARGER OUTLET ADAPTER

Removal – Remove intercooler inlet tube. Use caution not to damage sealed connection of outlet tube. Remove 3 outlet adapter-to-supercharger retaining bolts. Remove one stud and position harness bracket aside. Remove adapter.

Installation – Apply sealant to supercharger sealing surfaces. To install, reverse remove procedure.

THROTTLE BODY

Removal – Partially drain cooling system. Remove throttle intake air tube. Disconnect coolant hoses, throttle cable and electrical connectors from throttle body. Remove throttle body retaining nuts and throttle body.

Installation – Clean all gasket surfaces. Replace intake plenum gaskets. To install, reverse remove procedure.

TIGHTENING SPECIFICATIONS

Application	Ft. Lbs. (N.m)
Intake Elbow Bolts	[1]
Intercooler Outlet Tube-to-Bracket Bolt or Stud	52-70 (71-95)
Intercooler Outlet Tube-to-Bracket Nut	30-40 (40-54)
Intercooler Tube Retaining Nuts	14-22 (19-30)
Intercooler-to-Radiator Support Retaining Bolts	14-22 (19-30)
Joint Pipe/Heat Shield Assembly-to-Supercharger Nuts	27-46 (37-62)
Supercharger Adapter Collar Nut	48 (65)
Supercharger Outlet Retaining Bolts	14-22 (19-30)
Supercharger Retaining Bolts	
8 mm	14-22 (19-30)
12 mm	52-70 (71-95)
Throttle Body Retaining Bolts	14-22 (19-30)

[1] – Should be tightened to 72-108 INCH lbs. (8-12 N.m).

1989 FUEL PUMPS
Ford Motor Co. Inertia Switch

DESCRIPTION

Fuel injected models use an electrical interrupt switch in the fuel system. This inertia switch disables the fuel delivery system when the vehicle is struck violently or when vehicle roll-over takes place.

OPERATION

In the event of a collision or vehicle roll-over, electrical contacts within the inertia switch shut off fuel supply to the electric fuel pump. Fuel supply will be interrupted even if the engine is still running. Switch contacts are normally closed, but open upon impact or roll-over. A reset button is located on the switch assembly. If the electrical circuit trips, it is not possible to re-start the vehicle unless the switch is reset by depressing the reset button. Anytime the switch opens, the fuel system should be inspected for damage prior to resetting.

On LTD Crown Victoria and Grand Marquis station wagon models, switch is located in left rear side storage compartment.

On Mustang, it is located near left taillight.

On Taurus and Sable station wagon models, switch is located behind access door in right rear cargo area.

On all other vehicles, inertia switch is located in trunk, on left hinge support or behind trim panel.

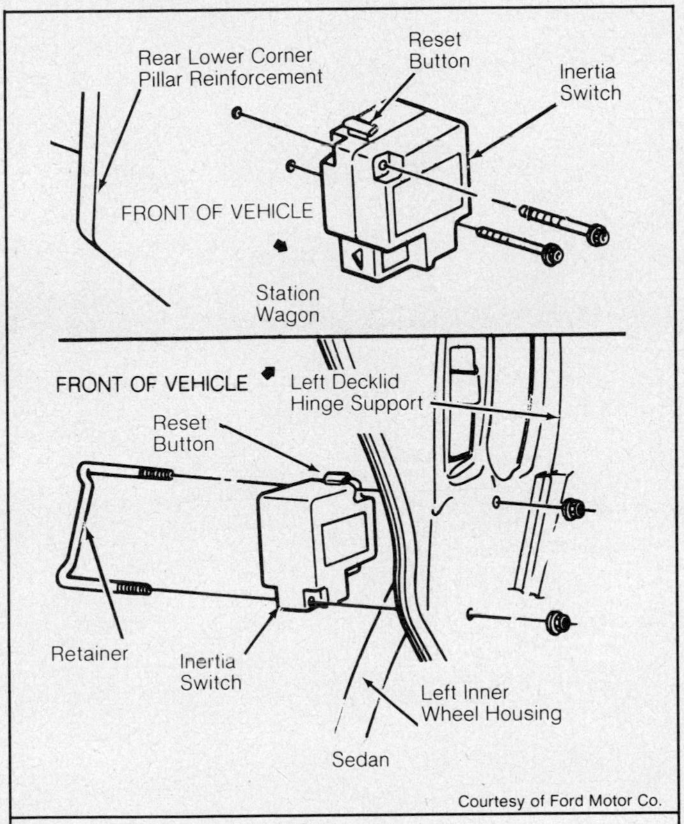

Fig. 1: Inertia Switch (Sable & Taurus)

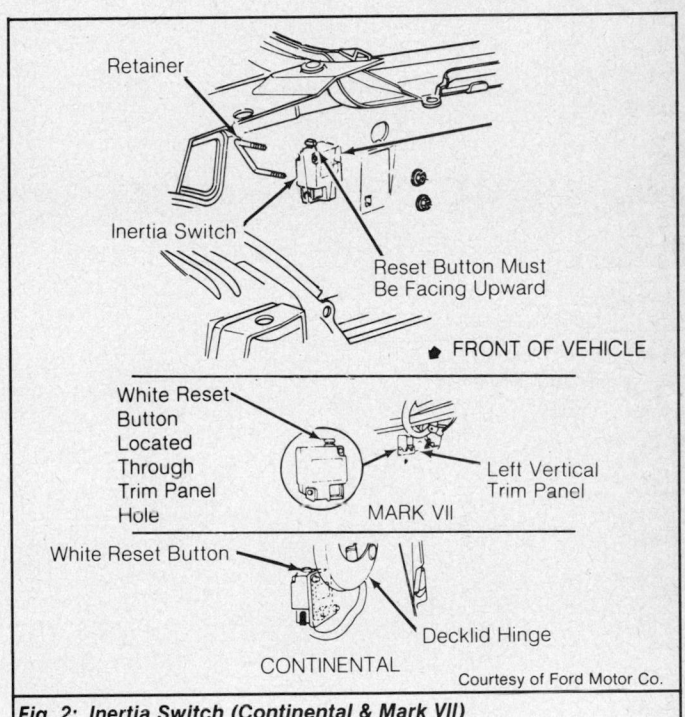

Fig. 2: Inertia Switch (Continental & Mark VII)

Section 3
EXHAUST EMISSION SYSTEMS

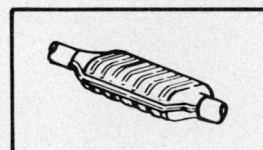

CONTENTS

EMISSION STANDARDS   Page

Chrysler Motors, Eagle &
  Ford Motor Co. 3-2

POSITIVE CRANKCASE VENTILATION SYSTEM

Chrysler Motors, Eagle &
  Ford Motor Co. 3-3

CATALYTIC CONVERTERS   Page

Chrysler Motors, Eagle &
  Ford Motor Co. 3-4

THERMOSTATIC AIR CLEANERS

Chrysler Motors, Eagle &
  Ford Motor Co. 3-5

EXHAUST EMISSION SYSTEMS

Chrysler Motors
  Emission Control Application Table 3-7
  Emission Components 3-8
  Exhaust Gas Recirculation (EGR) 3-10
  Air Injection Systems 3-12
  Electric Assist Choke 3-14
  Fuel Evaporation Control System 3-15
  Vacuum Diagrams 3-16

Eagle
  Emission Control Application Table 3-18
  Emission Components 3-19
  Exhaust Gas Recirculation (EGR) 3-21
  Evaporative Emission Control 3-22
  Vacuum Diagrams 3-23

Ford Motor Co.
  Emission Control Application Table 3-24
  Emission Components 3-25
  Exhaust Gas Recirculation (EGR)
    Except Probe 3-33
    Probe 3-37
  Thermactor Systems 3-40
  Fuel Evaporation Systems – Except Probe 3-43
  Fuel Evaporation Systems – Probe.................... 3-46
  Vacuum Diagrams 3-49

NOTE: **ALSO SEE GENERAL INDEX.**

1989 EXHAUST EMISSION SYSTEMS
Emission Standards & Tune-Ups

MANUFACTURING STANDARDS

Federal and state governments have established air quality standards during the past 20 years. Automobile manufacturers design their vehicles to conform to standards where the vehicle will be sold. These standards cover carbon monoxide (CO), hydrocarbons (HC) and oxides of nitrogen (NOx).

Federal and California standards which must be met by manufacturers are specified in units easily measured in a testing laboratory. Since 1970, these standards have been in "grams per mile". This means no vehicle, whether 2-cylinder or V8, may emit more than a set weight (in grams) of pollutants for each mile it travels. Since large engines burn more fuel than smaller ones, they must be "cleaner" per gallon burned if they are to meet these standards.

When manufacturers certify vehicles, the cars are placed on a dynamometer and the exhaust gases are collected in a bag. After the vehicle runs for a specified time, the gases are analyzed and weighed. Engines and emission systems are designed so the weight of emissions will be less than the specified grams per mile.

Infra-red exhaust analyzers are commonly used in automotive test stations. They use a test probe placed in the exhaust stream, and measure the percentage of CO in the exhaust gas, or parts per million of HC. These are not the same units used by the manufacturer when the car is certified. (NOx emissions can be measured only in a laboratory).

TUNE-UP STANDARDS

When a tune-up is performed, the mechanic must have specifications to use when adjusting the vehicle. The first few years of emission-regulated vehicles were adjusted using carbon monoxide percentage or hydrocarbon parts per million. These are the units measured by an exhaust gas analyzer.

In the past few years, manufacturers have made their vehicles much cleaner (measured in grams per mile). The CO% and HC ppm have become very low, especially when measured AFTER a catalytic converter. It has become hard to accurately measure the effect of turning the idle mixture screws.

One solution to this problem requires the use of artificially-enriched propane adjustments. The added propane boosts the emissions by a known amount, and makes the effect of turning the mixture screws easily measureable. However, CO and HC can only be accurately measured while the propane is being added.

As computer-controlled systems were developed, it became possible for the vehicle to adjust its own mixture throughout the entire engine operating range, not just at idle. These "feedback" systems use oxygen sensors to measure how much unburned oxygen is left in the exhaust. The computer can then determine when the air/fuel mixture is too rich or too lean, and correct it as necessary. Even if a mechanic incorrectly adjusts the mixture, most computers can compensate enough so the vehicle will still run clean. In fact, newer cars burn fuel so completely that changes in the pollutant level after the catalytic converter are hard to measure accurately.

Although many shops have exhaust gas analyzers which measure tailpipe emissions, computer-controlled engines normally do NOT have CO or HC specifications for tuning. These specifications would be neither useful or possible for adjusting new vehicles. This manual provides procedures and specifications given by the manufacturers and does not necessarily list CO or HC specifications.

STATE TEST STANDARDS

Some states have established standards for testing used vehicles to see if they are still running clean. Generally speaking, these standards are given in CO% and HC ppm. They can be checked with an exhaust gas analyzer. Typical standards for newer cars would be less than 2.0% CO (non-catalyst) or 0.5% CO (with catalyst) and less than 200 ppm of HC. If vehicle emissions are below these levels, the vehicle passes inspection. The important thing to remember is that these specifications are NOT to be used for TUNING. They are only for testing to see if the vehicle is functioning properly. If it isn't, it must be tuned using the manufacturer's procedures and specifications, then tested again.

Test standards change each year and vary from state to state, and even by county within each state. It is not possible to provide an accurate and up-to-date list in this manual. Specifications can be obtained from your local county or state government. Remember that these standards are ONLY for test purposes. The manufacturer's adjustment procedures and specifications MUST be used when actually tuning a vehicle.

**Chrysler Motors, Eagle,
Ford Motor Co.**

DESCRIPTION

The Positive Crankcase Ventilation (PCV) system is designed to prevent contaminating hydrocarbons, created in the crankcase, from escaping into the atmosphere.

Crankcase vapors are routed from the crankcase through a vacuum controlled ventilating valve or PCV, into the intake manifold. When vapors reach the intake manifold, they are mixed with air/fuel and burned in the combustion process.

OPERATION

With the engine operating, fresh air enters the PCV system through the air cleaner assembly. Fresh air flows through the crankcase breather and into the rocker arm cover compartment.

Entering fresh air combines with blow-by gases and unburned air/fuel mixture of the crankcase. Combined gases are drawn into the intake manifold, through the PCV valve, by manifold vacuum. Crankcase gases mix with air/fuel mixture and are burned in the combustion chamber. *See Fig. 1.*

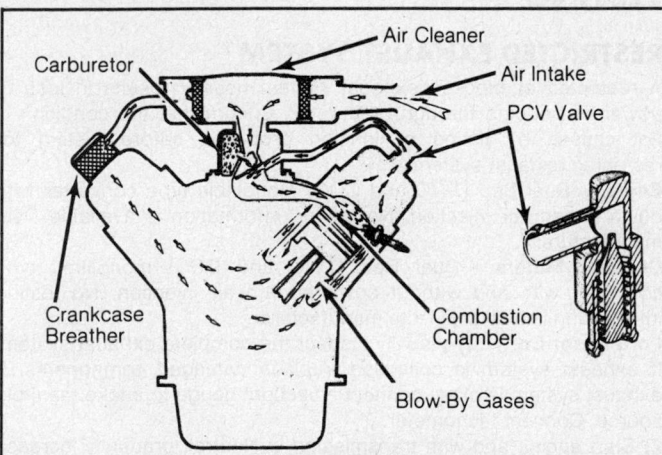

Fig. 1: Typical Positive Crankcase Ventilation System

The PCV valve is held closed by spring pressure when the engine is not running. This prevents hydrocarbon fumes from collecting in the intake manifold, resulting in hard starting.

When the engine is running, manifold vacuum pulls the PCV valve open, allowing crankcase vapors to enter the intake manifold. A baffle in the rocker arm cover prevents engine oil from being drawn into the intake manifold.

If the engine backfires through the intake manifold, the PCV valve closes and prevents any flow of gases through it. This is to prevent the ignition of fumes in the crankcase.

SERVICE PROCEDURES

An engine may idle slow or rough due to a clogged PCV valve or system. Never adjust idle speeds without first checking entire PCV system.

CAUTION: If a PCV system component becomes clogged, all crankcase ventilation will stop and serious engine damage may occur.

ALL MODELS

PCV Valve – Remove and replace PCV valve every 30,000 miles. Do not attempt to clean valve. Replacement intervals may become shorter under severe service.

Filter Element – Filter element should be replaced every 30,000 miles.

FORD MOTOR CO. 1.9L

Testing Dual Orifice Valves – 1) Ford Motor Company's 1.9L engine is equipped with a Dual Orifice PCV system. Periodic inspection is required. Check for proper hose routing and/or blocked, cracked or broken hoses. Clean as required.

2) Place transmission in Park or Neutral set parking brake, block wheels. Turn A/C to "OFF". Bring engine to operating temperature.

3) Remove vacuum control hose at throttle body port. Apply manifold vacuum to port. If there is significant change in engine RPM, go on to step **4)**. If not replace dual orifice assembly.

4) Remove crankcase vent connector from side of air clearner. Hold a stiff piece of paper over open end of vent connector for one minute. If vacuum holds paper in place PCV system is good. If not go on to step **5)**.

5) Remove vacuum hose (small) at crankcase vent connector. Place stiff paper over vacuum hose. If vacuum holds paper, replace crankcase vent connector. If not go to step **6)**.

6) Remove dual orifice valve and check that valve is clear. If not, clear or replace as necessary.

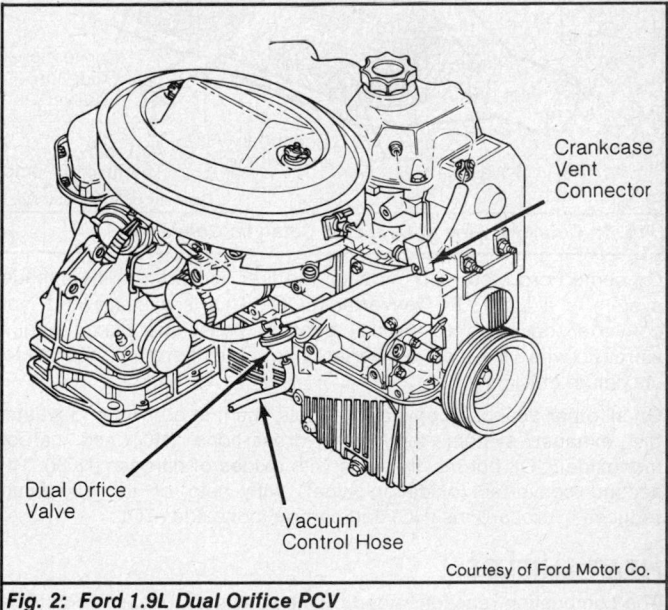

Courtesy of Ford Motor Co.

Fig. 2: Ford 1.9L Dual Orifice PCV

1989 EXHAUST EMISSION SYSTEMS
Catalytic Converters

**Chrysler Motors, Eagle,
Ford Motor Co.**

DESCRIPTION & OPERATION

CATALYTIC CONVERTERS

The Catalytic Converter is an exhaust emission control device. Its function involves the reduction of carbon monoxide (CO), oxides of nitrogen (NOx) and hydrocarbons (HC). The converter, mounted in the exhaust stream works as a gas reactor by speeding up the chemical reaction between the exhaust gas components with the goal of reducing the amount of pollutants in the engine exhaust.

The combustion reaction, aided by the catalyst, causes a temperature increase in the area of the reactor. Heat shields and carefully located components are essential for safe operation. DO NOT remove shields or reroute exhaust system.

NOTE: Use only unleaded fuel on vehicles equipped with a catalytic converter. If leaded fuel is used, coating and destruction of the catalytic surfaces will result, requiring replacement.

On some models, a Three Way Catalyst (TWC) is used in conjunction with a Conventional Oxidation Catalyst (COC) contained in the same canister. Working with this, there often is an air injection pipe that injects air between these 2 beds to help further oxidize the exhaust gases. This is a dual bed converter. *See Fig. 1.*

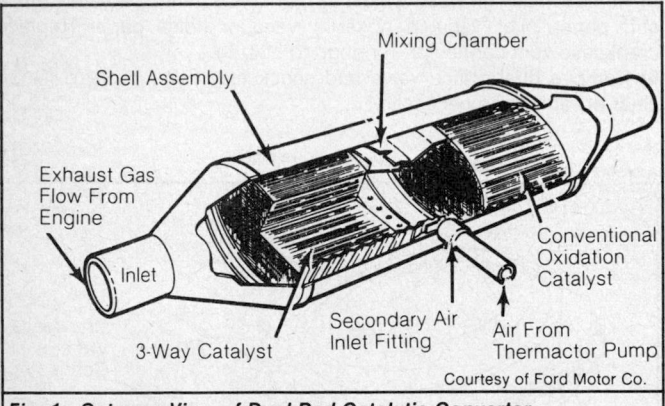

Fig. 1: Cutaway View of Dual Bed Catalytic Converter

On some Ford Motor Co. models, the first converter in the exhaust system is a Light Off Converter (LOC). This is a single bed type converter designed to control exhaust emissions during engine warm-up when the main converter is not at temperature required for maximum efficiency.

On all other dual bed converter models, the first converter (3-way) in the exhaust system reduces hydrocarbons (HC) and carbon monoxide (CO), but mainly deals with oxides of nitrogen (NOx). The second converter (oxidation type), with help of the air pump, reduces hydrocarbons (HC) and carbon monoxide (CO).

HEAT SHIELDS

The combustion reaction, aided by the converter, releases additional heat into the exhaust system. Temperatures in catalytic converters can reach 1600°F (870°C) under normal conditions. Special heat shields are therefore used to protect the underbody and under-vehicle components from extreme heat.

NOTE: Avoid application of rust prevention compounds or under-coating to heat shields or exhaust system floor pan area. These compounds reduce the efficiency of the heat shield resulting in excessive floor pan temperatures and objectionable fumes.

SERVICE PROCEDURES

MAINTENANCE

There is no scheduled maintenance of a catalytic converter, it is designed to last the lifetime of the vehicle. If it does not perform correctly, replace it. Failure of the converter can often be traced to other engine malfunctions. Any engine condition that allows large amounts of unburned fuel into the converter will cause the catalytic converter to fail. These conditions include: checking cylinders by removing or shorting spark plug wires, excessively rich fuel mixture and weak or misadjusted ignition system.

TESTING

RESTRICTED EXHAUST SYSTEM

A restricted or blocked exhaust system usually results in loss of power or popping through carburetor. Ensure that the condition is not caused by timing or ignition problems before testing for restricted exhaust system.

Eagle – Dual Bed (TWC and COC) monolithic type converter with down stream air injection. No testing information is available from manufacturer.

Chrysler Motors – Dual Bed (TWC and COC) monolithic type converter with and without down stream air injection. No testing information is available from manufacturer.

Ford Motor Co. – **1)** Visually inspect the complete exhaust system. If exhaust system is collapsed, replace damaged components. If exhaust system is okay, connect a vacuum gauge to intake manifold source. Connect tachometer.

2) Start engine and with transmission in Neutral, gradually increase engine speed to 2000 RPM. Check manifold vacuum reading on gauge. If manifold vacuum is greater than 16 in. Hg, exhaust system is okay.

3) If manifold vacuum is less than 16 in. Hg, turn engine off and disconnect exhaust from exhaust manifold(s). Repeat step **2)**. If manifold vacuum is less than 16 in. Hg, remove exhaust manifold(s).

4) Check ports for casting flash by dropping a length of chain into each port. DO NOT use a wire or light to check ports, restriction may be small enough to cause excessive backpressure at high RPM.

5) Check for restriction. If restriction is present, remove casting flash. If flash cannot be removed, replace exhaust manifold. If no restriction is present, exhaust system is okay.

6) If manifold vacuum is greater than 16 in. Hg, reconnect exhaust system to manifold(s). Disconnect muffler(s). Repeat step **2)**.

7) If manifold vacuum is less than 16 in. Hg, replace catalytic converter and check to ensure converter debris has not entered muffler. If manifold vacuum is greater than 16 in. Hg, replace muffler.

Chrysler Motors, Eagle, Ford Motor Co.

DESCRIPTION

During cold engine operation most passenger cars preheat the air entering the carburetor or the fuel injection unit. This system maintains incoming air temperature to a point where the carburetor or fuel injection system can be kept lean to reduce hydrocarbon (HC) emissions, and reduce carburetor icing.

Most passenger cars are equipped with dry type air cleaners with a replaceable air filter element. These air inlet systems have various sensors, switches and vacuum motors to control inlet air temperature. There are also various sensors present in the air cleaner for other engine control systems.

OPERATION

Most systems regulate air inlet temperature by using air from a cool air source as well as heated air from heat shroud which is mounted on exhaust manifold. The duct and valve that regulates airflow from these two sources is located inside the air cleaner, on outside of air cleaner or remotely mounted in one of the inlet tubes. Airflow is regulated by vacuum motor operated door. Motor operation is controlled by delay valves, temperature sensors and other vacuum controlled systems, depending upon vehicle application.

The air control door temperature sensor closes when the temperature of air entering the air cleaner is less than the calibration of the temperature sensor. This allows engine vacuum to operate the air control door vacuum motor, and warm manifold air to be routed to the intake. *See Fig. 2.*

When engine vacuum is applied to the vacuum motor, the air control door closes off the intake of outside air. Air is then drawn into the air cleaner from around the exhaust manifold.

As air inside the air cleaner warms, the temperature sensor begins to open, bleeding off vacuum to the vacuum motor. As vacuum to vacuum motor decreases, the air control door begins to open.

As air control door opens, outside air is allowed to enter air cleaner assembly. When air entering air cleaner reaches a predetermined temperature, the air control door opens completely, and closes off the intake of heated air.

VACUUM CONTROL TEMPERATURE SENSOR

The vacuum control temperature sensor controls the operation of the air control door. During initial start-up situations, this valve

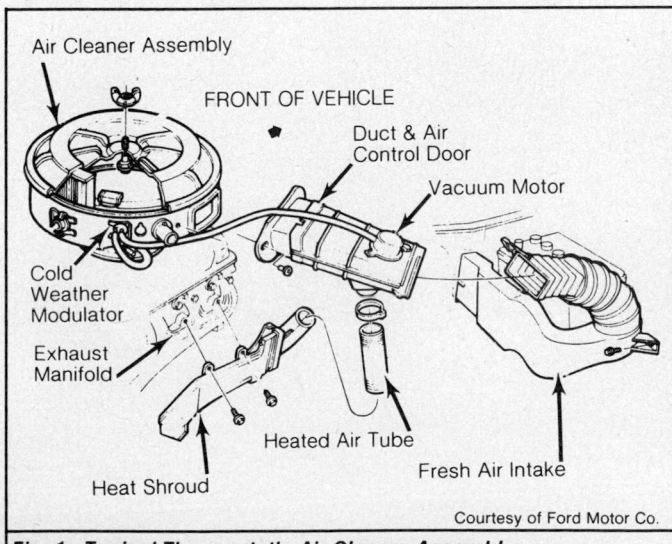

Fig. 1: Typical Thermostatic Air Cleaner Assembly

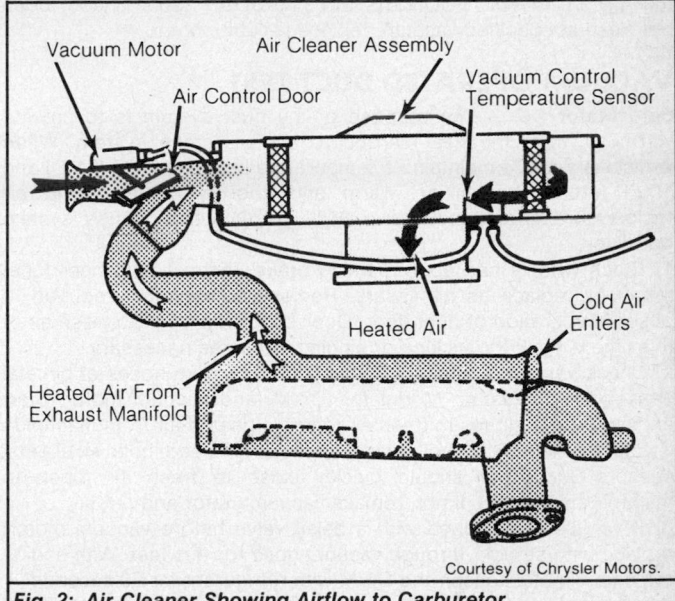

Courtesy of Chrysler Motors.

Fig. 2: Air Cleaner Showing Airflow to Carburetor

directs engine vacuum to the air control vacuum motor. The motor closes the air intake door, allowing the intake of heated manifold air. When the intake air temperature reaches a precalibrated value, this valve opens, allowing the intake of cooler outside air.

TESTING

VACUUM CONTROL TEMPERATURE SENSOR

Chrysler Motors & Eagle – 1) Tape a thermometer close to vacuum control temperature sensor located inside air cleaner. Leave wing nut(s) off top of air cleaner so that top can be quickly removed to read thermometer during test.

2) With engine cold, temperature below vacuum control temperature sensor specifications, check air control door in air cleaner. It should be in fully open position (open to outside air).

3) Start engine. As soon as engine starts, door should move to fully heated air position (closed to outside air). Continue running engine and watch air control door. When door reaches fully open position, quickly remove air cleaner top and read thermometer.

4) Compare thermometer reading with specifications. If reading is not to specification, perform vacuum motor test. If vacuum motor is okay, replace sensor.

VACUUM CONTROL TEMPERATURE SENSOR SPECIFICATIONS

Application	Heated Air Temp. °F (°C)	Fresh Air Temp. °F (°C)
Chrysler Motors		
2.2L & 2.5L	115 (46)	140 (60)
5.2L	50 (10)	100 (38)
Eagle		
2.5L	85 (29)	85 (29)
3.0L	50 (10)	70 (21)

VACUUM MOTOR TEST

Chrysler Motors & Eagle – 1) Remove air cleaner from vehicle. Disconnect vacuum hose from vacuum motor. Apply 20 in. Hg vacuum to motor and pinch off hose. Vacuum should not leak down more than 10 in. Hg in 5 minutes. If vacuum motor does leak down, replace it.

2) Connect a vacuum pump to vacuum motor. Apply specified amount of vacuum to vacuum motor to close heated air door. See the AIR CONTROL DOOR CLOSING VACUUM table. If door does not close at specified vacuum, replace vacuum motor.

VACUUM OPERATED DUCT TEST

Ford Motor Co. – The purpose of the duct system is to provide warm air from the heat shroud to the air intake system. When vehicle is warm it maintains a temperature between 70°F (21°C) and 105°F (40°C) by mixing warm and cool air. Surrounding air temperature should be above 60°F (15°C) when testing system operation.

1) Block wheels and apply parking brake. Inspect heat riser tube, repair or replace as necessary. Remove components required to observe operation of duct door. Door should be open to fresh air at this time. Check for sticking or binding, repair as necessary.

2) Check vacuum source and condition of vacuum hoses at bimetal sensor, Cold Weather Modulator (CWM) and vacuum motor. Start engine. If door closes to fresh air (open to heated air from manifold), go on to step **3)**. If not, place finger over bleed hole in bimetal sensor. Duct door should quickly close to fresh air (open to manifold heated air). If not, replace vacuum motor and retest.

3) If vehicle is equipped with a delay valve before vacuum motor, replace with straight through vacuum hose for this test. With engine off, cool bimetal sensor and CWM with refrigerant for 20 seconds.

CAUTION: Do not cool sensor with refrigerant while engine is running. If drawn into intake system, poisonous phosgene gas will be exhausted into work area. Perform test in well ventilated area.

4) Restart engine. Door should fully close to fresh air (open to manifold heated air). If not, replace sensor. Stop engine, cool CWM and sensor. Restart and run engine briefly (under 15 seconds). Door should close to fresh air (open to manifold heated air). See the AIR CONTROL DOOR CLOSING VACUUM table.

5) Shut off engine and observe door. On vehicles without CWM, the door will slowly open to fresh air (closed to manifold heated air) in 10 to 30 seconds. Vehicles with CWM, the door should not open to fresh air (closed to manifold heated air) for at least 2 minutes. If less replace CWM. Cool CWM and sensor, then retest.

AIR CONTROL DOOR CLOSING VACUUM

Application	Vacuum In. Hg
Chrysler Motors	
2.2L & 2.5L	2-4
5.2L	8.5
Eagle	
2.5L & 3.0L	16
Ford Motor Co.	16

COLD WEATHER MODULATOR

Ford Motor Co. (Only) – Using a vacuum pump with gauge, apply 16 in. Hg of vacuum to motor side of modulator. Determine if modulator holds or leaks within the correct temperature range. See COLD WEATHER MODULATOR SPECIFICATIONS table in this article.

COLD WEATHER MODULATOR SPECIFICATIONS

Modulator Color	Holds Vacuum @ °F (°C)	Leaks Vacuum @ °F (°C)
Black		
Normally Open	20 (-6.7°C)	35 (2)
Blue		
Normally Open	40 (4)	55 (13)
Green		
Normally Open	50 (10)	76 (24)
Yellow		
Normally Closed	65 (18)	50 (10)

1989 CHRYSLER MOTORS

Engine & Fuel System	Emission Control Systems & Devices	Remarks
2.2L (135") 4-Cyl. TBI	**PCV, EVAP, TWC, BP/EGR, SMEC,** [1] EGR-DS, BP/EGR-TRANS, CPS, HAD, HATS, MAP, O$_2$, PR-RV	[1] – Calif. only.
2.2L (135") 4-Cyl. MPFI Turbo II	**PCV, EVAP, TWC, SMEC,** ASOV, BS, CPS, MAP, O$_2$, PR-RV, WSTGT, WSTGT-SOL, VAC-CV, VQRV	[2] – Non-Calif.
2.5L (153") 4-Cyl. TBI	**PCV, EVAP, TWC, BP/EGR, SMEC,** [1] EGR-DS, BP/EGR-TRANS, CPS, HAD, HATS, MAP, O$_2$, PR-RV	[3] – Police only.
2.5L (153") 4-Cyl. MPFI Turbo I	**PCV, EVAP, TWC,** [1] **BP/EGR, SMEC,** [1] EGR-DS, EGR-SOL, BP/EGR-TRANS, BS, CPS, MAP, O$_2$, PR-RV, WSTGT, WSTGT-SOL, VAC-CV, VQRV	
3.0L (181") V6 TBI	**PCV, EVAP, TWC,** [1] **BP/EGR, SBEC,** [1] BP/EGR-TRANS, CPS, [1] EGR-SOL, IAST, MAP, O$_2$, PR-RV, VAC-CV	
5.2L (318") V8 2-Bbl.	**PCV, TAC, AIS, EVAP, TWC, EGR, SPK,** ASRV, ASRV-SOL, CVSCC, [2] EGR-DV, EGR-SOL, ESA, HADV, HATS, O$_2$, VBOV	
5.2L (318") V8 4-Bbl. [3]	**PCV, TAC, AIS, EVAP, TWC, EGR, SPK,** ASRV, ASRV-SOL, BVV, CVSCC, EGR-AMP, EGR-SOL, HATS, O$_2$, TDDV	

AIS – Air Injection System
ASOV – Air Shutoff Valve
ASRV – Air Switching Relief Valve
ASRV-SOL – Air Switching Relief Valve Solenoid
BP/EGR – Backpressure EGR
BP/EGR-TRANS – Backpressure EGR Transducer
BS – Barometer Solenoid
BVV – Bowl Vent Valve
CEC – Computerized Engine Control
CPS – Canister Purge Solenoid
CTS – Charge Temp. Switch/Coolant Temp. Switch
CVSCC – Coolant Vacuum Switch Cold Closed
CVSCO – Coolant Vacuum Switch Cold Open
EGR – Exhaust Gas Recirculation
EGR-AMP – EGR Amplifier
EGR-DS – EGR Diagnostic Solenoid
EGR-DV – EGR Vacuum Delay Valve
EGR-SOL – EGR Solenoid
ESA – Electronic Spark Advance
EVAP – Evaporative Control System

HAD – Heated Air Diaphragm
HADV – Heated Air Delay Valve
HATS – Heated Air Temp. Sensor
IAST – Inlet Air Surge Tank
MAP – Manifold Absolute Pressure Sensor
MPFI – Multi-Point Fuel Injection
O$_2$ – Oxygen Sensor
PCV – Positive Crankcase Ventilation
PR-RV – Pressure Relief-Rollover Valve
SBEC – Single Board Engine Controller
SMEC – Single Module Engine Controller
TAC – Thermostatic Air Cleaner
TBI – Throttle Body Injection
TDDV – Trap Door Delay Valve
TWC – Three-Way Catalyst
VAC-CV – Vacuum Check Valve
VBOV – Vacuum Bleed-Off Valve
VQRV – Vacuum Quick Release Valve
WSTGT – Wastegate
WSTGT-SOL – Wastegate Solenoid

1989 EXHAUST EMISSION SYSTEMS
Chrysler Motors Emission Components

Chrysler Motors vehicles utilize several types of devices to control emissions. These figures show the physical appearance of typical components. Operation and method of actuation is provided for most devices. Refer to specific system within this section for testing purposes.

HEATED AIR VACUUM DIAPHRAGM	When signaled by air temperature sensor, heated air vacuum diaphragm regulates position of heat control door within the air cleaner duct to allow warm or cold air in carburetor or throttle body.
HEATED AIR TEMPERATURE SENSOR	Sensor is located inside air cleaner housing. The sensor, operating at a predetermined temperature range, controls the vacuum diaphragm that operates the heat control door in snorkel assembly.
AIR INJECTION CHECK VALVE (AICV)	Air injection check valve has a one-way diaphragm which prevents hot exhaust gases from backing up into hose and pump. Valve will protect the system in the event of pump belt failure, abnormally high exhaust system pressure, or if air hose ruptures.
AIR SWITCHING/RELIEF VALVE (ASRV)	Air switching/relief valve directs air injection to either the exhaust port or downstream injection port. In addition, valve regulates system pressure by controlling output of the air pump at high engine speeds. When pressure reaches a predetermined point, some of the air pump output is diverted to the atmosphere through the silencer. Air injection is initially directed to exhaust ports. As engine warms up, EGR and O_2 feedback system will begin to operate. When this occurs, air injection must be switched to the downstream injection port for proper system operation.
CANISTER PURGE SOLENOID Canister Purge Solenoid	The purge solenoid is controlled by the Single Module Engine Controller (SMEC) or the Single Board Engine Controller (SBEC). When engine temperature is less than 145°F (61°C), the SMEC/SBEC grounds the purge solenoid, energizing it. This prevents vacuum from reaching the charcoal canister valve. When temperature is greater than 145°F (61°C), the SMEC/SBEC de-energizes the solenoid by turning ground off. Once this occurs, vacuum will flow from canister purge valve and purge fuel vapors through the throttle body.

CHARGE TEMPERATURE SENSOR	The charge temperature sensor is mounted on intake manifold and measures the temperature of the air/fuel mixture. This information is used by the Single Module Engine Controller (SMEC) to modify air/fuel mixture.
COOLANT TEMPERATURE SENSOR	The coolant temperature sensor, located in thermostat housing, provides data on engine operating temperature to the Single Module Engine Controller (SMEC) or the Single Board Engine Controller (SBEC). Sensor is a variable resistor with a range of 104°F to 265°F (-40°C to 129°C). This sensor is also used to control cooling fan.
COOLANT VACUUM SWITCH COLD OPEN (CVSCO)	Switch is mounted on thermostat housing. Switch provides manifold vacuum into air delivery switching system after a cold start until coolant temperature reaches a certain level. After coolant temperature reaches 108-125°F (42-52°C), the switch closes and vacuum is cut off from the switch.
COOLANT VACUUM SWITCH COLD CLOSED (CVSCC)	Vacuum switch is mounted in thermostat housing. When engine coolant temperature reaches 108-125°F (42-52°C), vacuum switch opens. Vacuum is then allowed to operate vapor canister control valve. This allows vapor canister to purge.
HEATED OXYGEN SENSOR	This sensor is electrically heated internally for faster switching when engine is running. Sensor monitors oxygen content in exhaust and converts it to electrical voltage. Sensor acts as a rich-lean switch. Voltage is transmitted to the Single Module Engine Controller (SMEC) or the Single Board Engine Controller (SBEC), which then changes the air/fuel mixture.
MANIFOLD ABSOLUTE PRESSURE (MAP) SENSOR	The sensor transmits information on manifold vacuum conditions and barometric pressure to the Single Module Engine Controller (SMEC) or the Single Board Engine Controller (SBEC). The MAP sensor data on engine load is used with data from other sensors to determine the correct air/fuel mixture.

DESCRIPTION

Exhaust Gas Recirculation (EGR) system is used on all models except 2.2L turbo. The EGR allows a predetermined amount of exhaust gas to recirculate to the intake manifold, diluting the incoming air/fuel mixture. This diluting of the air/fuel mixture reduces peak combustion temperatures. The lower combustion temperature reduces emissions of oxides of nitrogen (NOx).

California models use on-board diagnostics for the EGR system. The diagnostic system uses a solenoid in the vacuum line to the EGR valve.

OPERATION

A backpressure type EGR system is used on 2.2L and 2.5L throttle body fuel injected engines. The backpressure transducer measures the amount of exhaust backpressure and varies the strength of the vacuum signal to the EGR valve. The signal vacuum is bled off into the atmosphere when exhaust backpressure to the EGR drops below a calibrated value.

On 5.2L engines, an electronically controlled EGR system is used. The system consists of Spark Control Computer (SCC), Charge Temperature Sensor (CTS), EGR solenoid and EGR delay system (4-Bbl. models).

On California models, an on-board diagnostic system checks the entire EGR system for failures and is activated and monitored only during selected engine/driving conditions to avoid misdiagnosis. When monitored, the EGR solenoid is energized, disabling the EGR. The O_2 feedback system is monitored to see if a change occurs. The mixture should go lean and the system will try to richen the mixture. The SMEC monitors EGR system performance and registers a fault code if the system has failed or effectiveness has lessened, and turns on the "CHECK ENGINE" light.

VACUUM CONTROL SYSTEM

Except 5.2L 4-Bbl. Engine – As the throttle blade opens, a slotted port in the carburetor base or throttle body is exposed to an increasing percentage of manifold vacuum. This port is connected through an external nipple to an EGR solenoid and/or transducer and then to the EGR valve. The flow rate is dependent on manifold vacuum, throttle position and exhaust gas backpressure.

5.2L 4-Bbl. Engine – The venturi vacuum control system utilizes a vacuum tap at the throat of the carburetor venturi to provide a vacuum control signal. Because of the low signal strength, it is necessary to use a vacuum amplifier to increase vacuum to the level that will operate the EGR valve.

Elimination of EGR at wide open throttle is accomplished by a dump diaphragm which compares venturi and manifold vacuum to determine when wide open throttle is achieved. At wide open throttle, the internal reservoir is dumped, limiting output to the EGR valve to manifold vacuum.

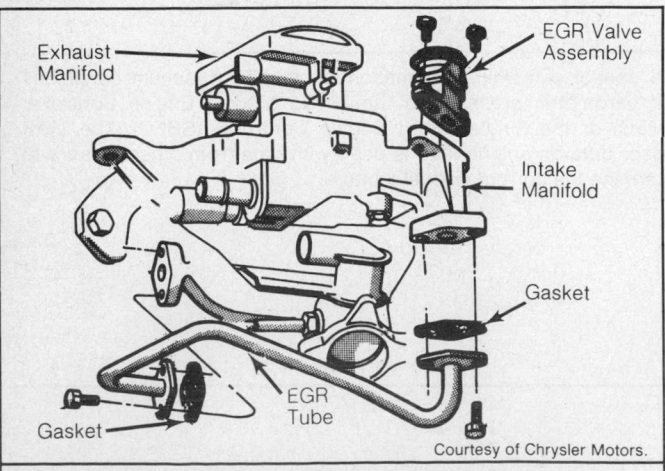

Fig. 1: 2.2L & 2.5L Fuel Injected Engines EGR System

Courtesy of Chrysler Motors.

The valve opening point is set above the manifold vacuum available at wide open throttle, permitting the valve to be closed at wide open throttle. This system is dependent primarily on engine intake airflow, as indicated by the venturi signal, and is also affected by intake vacuum and exhaust pressure.

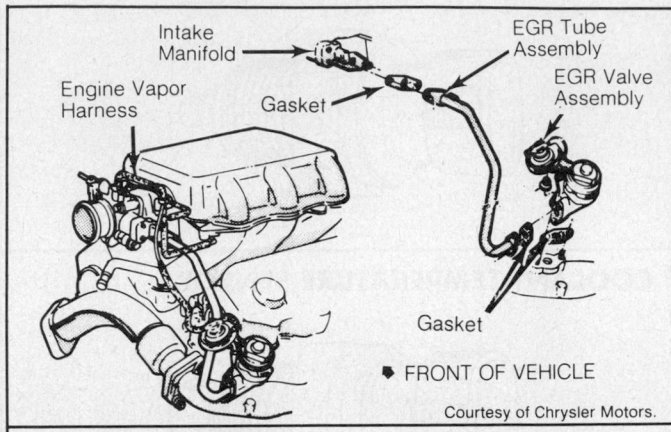

Fig. 2: 3.0L Engine EGR System

Courtesy of Chrysler Motors.

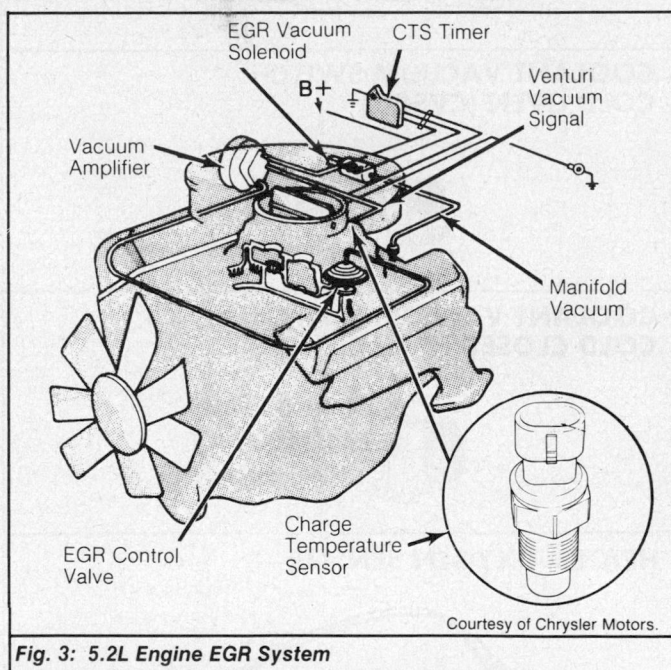

Fig. 3: 5.2L Engine EGR System

Courtesy of Chrysler Motors.

CHARGE TEMPERATURE SENSOR

5.2L 4-Bbl. Engine – The Charge Temperature Sensor (CTS) is installed in the No. 8 intake manifold runner. The sensor signals the computer when to operate the air switching, EGR and spark advance systems.

EGR DELAY SYSTEM

5.2L 4-Bbl. Engine – Some vehicles are equipped with an EGR delay system that is incorporated in the Spark Control Computer (SCC) and controls the EGR solenoid. The solenoid is connected between the carburetor venturi vacuum signal nipple and vacuum amplifier by hoses. The system is designed to prevent EGR operation for about 60 seconds after the ignition is turned on.

TESTING

EGR SYSTEM ON-BOARD DIAGNOSTICS

California Models – On-board diagnostics for EGR system are part of vehicle diagnostic system. If a malfunction is indicated by the

"CHECK ENGINE" light and a fault code for EGR system is stored, see appropriate article in COMPUTERIZED ENGINE CONTROLS section of this manual.

EGR SOLENOID

1) Ensure that all vacuum hoses are routed properly and not leaking. Disconnect electrical plug from solenoid valve (located in front of right front strut tower). Connect either solenoid terminal to ground. Connect other terminal to positive battery terminal.
2) This should activate the solenoid valve and shut off control vacuum to the EGR system. You should hear a "click" from the solenoid as it is connected to battery positive terminal.
3) To test valve operation, start engine and let it idle. Raise engine speed to about 2000 RPM. Watch EGR control valve stem. EGR control valve stem should move. If stem does not move, replace solenoid.

SYSTEM FUNCTIONAL CHECK

NOTE: To ensure proper operation of the EGR system all passages and moving parts must be free from plugging or sticking as a result of deposits. Clean or replace components and hoses as necessary.

Except 5.2L Engines – 1) Warm engine to operating temperature. Attach a tachometer to the engine. Run engine at idle in Neutral an additional 70 seconds. Accelerate the engine abruptly to approximately 2000 RPM, but not over 3000 RPM.
2) During this procedure, check the EGR valve stem for movement. Visible movement of the valve stem should occur. Repeat test to confirm operation. Movement of the stem indicates that the control system is functioning correctly.
3) If EGR valve stem does not move, check for cracked, leaking, disconnected or plugged hoses. Verify correct hose routing. Disconnect hose harness from EGR valve/transducer and connect a vacuum pump to harness.
4) Start engine and raise engine speed to 2000 RPM and hold. Apply 10 in. Hg vacuum to EGR while checking for EGR valve movement. If no movement occurs, replace EGR valve/transducer assembly.
5) If valve opens approximately 1/8", hold vacuum constant and check for valve diaphragm leakage. Valve should remain open for at least 30 seconds. If leakage occurs, replace valve/transducer assembly. If valve is okay, check control system.
6) If EGR valve stem did not move in step 2), but operates normally on external vacuum source, remove throttle body and check port in throttle bore for blockage. Use a solvent to remove deposits and check flow with light air pressure. Normal operation should be restored.
7) If engine will not idle, or if engine stalls or idles very rough or slow, check for leaking EGR valve. With engine running, remove vacuum hose from EGR valve. If removing the vacuum hose does not correct rough idle, remove EGR valve/transducer assembly. Check valve for proper seating. Replace assembly as necessary.
8) Also check EGR-to-intake manifold tube for leak. On 2.2L and 2.5L models, loosen tube and tighten to 25 ft. lbs. (34 N.m). On 3.0L models, remove tube and inspect gasket. Tube end should be uniformly indented on gasket, with no signs of leakage.
9) If there are signs of leakage, replace gaskets and tighten flange nuts to 17 ft. lbs. (23 N.m). If leak persists, replace EGR tube and gaskets.

5.2L Engine – 1) Warm engine to operating temperature, and let idle at least 2 minutes after warm-up in Park or Neutral. Disconnect hose at EGR valve and attach a vacuum gauge to hose.
2) Open throttle quickly several times. A fluctuation of several in. Hg of vacuum should be observed during throttle movement. Disconnect vacuum gauge. Attach a vacuum pump to the EGR valve. With engine running, apply 10 in. Hg vacuum to the valve. The engine speed should drop several hundred RPM, stumble or stall.
3) Disconnect the vacuum pump and reconnect vacuum hose to EGR valve. If system operated as described, system is operating

correctly. If system did not operate as decribed, remove connector from charge temperature sensor (mounted in intake manifold air passage). Using an ohmmeter, check sensor resistance. See CHARGE TEMPERATURE SENSOR RESISTANCE table.

CHARGE TEMPERATURE SENSOR RESISTANCE

Temperature °F (°C)	Ohms
-40 to 20 (-40 to -7)	382,000-22,000
50-100 (10-38)	36,000-3300
140-245 (60-118)	3900-176

4) If resistance is not as specified, replace sensor. If resistance is okay, repair wiring between computer and sensor for an open or short circuit. With engine cold and not running, connect a voltmeter to Gray wire at EGR solenoid. Set parking brake and start engine.
5) With engine temperature less than 70°F (21°C) for 2-Bbl. models and less than 50°F (10°C) for 4-Bbl. models, voltmeter should read zero to one volt. If voltage reading is more than one volt, turn engine off. Disconnect computer 12-pin connector. Connect voltmeter to connector cavity No. 7 and ground. Turn ignition switch to "RUN" position.
6) Voltmeter reading should be within one volt of battery voltage. If voltage reading is okay, replace computer. If there is zero volts, repair open circuit in wiring harness to ignition switch.
7) On 5.2L 4-Bbl. models, remove venturi vacuum hose from carburetor. With engine at idle, apply 1-2 in. Hg vacuum to vacuum hose. Engine speed should drop at least 150 RPM and EGR valve stem should visibly move at least 1/8".
8) If this does not occur, replace vacuum amplifier. If system works properly, check carburetor for plugged vacuum tap. Use carburetor cleaner to clean passage and blow through with compressed air.
9) On 5.2L 2-Bbl. models, remove ported vacuum hose from carburetor. With engine at idle, apply at least 5 in. Hg vacuum to EGR vacuum tap hose. Engine idle speed should drop as EGR valve opens. If idle speed does not drop, check carburetor for plugged vacuum tap. Use carburetor cleaner to clean passage and blow through with compressed air.

NOTE: DO NOT use drill or wire to clean carburetor control passages, as calibration of control orifices may be changed, resulting in unsatisfactory vehicle operation.

10) On 5.2L 4-Bbl. models, if engine will not idle, or if engine stalls or idles very rough or slow, disconnect and plug EGR vacuum hose. Recheck idle. If idle is now okay, replace amplifier. If vacuum hose removal does not correct problem, remove EGR valve. Inspect valve and clean as necessary. Replace EGR valve as necessary.
11) If there is poor Wide Open Throttle (WOT) performance, disconnect and plug EGR hose. Road test vehicle. If performance is restored, replace amplifier.

SERVICING

EGR VALVE

1) Inspect valve for deposits with particular attention to the poppet and seat area. If deposits exceed a thin film, valve should be cleaned. Cleaning is aided by applying a liberal amount of manifold heat control solvent, or equivalent, to the poppet and seat area, allowing deposits to soften.

CAUTION: Extreme care should be taken when using solvent cleaners to prevent spilling of solvent on valve diaphragm.

2) Use an external vacuum source to open poppet and then scrape deposit from this area. If wear of stem or other moving components is noted, valve should be replaced.

NOTE: Do not push valve stem manually. Use an external vacuum source only.

1989 EXHAUST EMISSION SYSTEMS
Chrysler Motors Air Injection Systems

2.2L TBI, 2.5L TBI, 5.2L

DESCRIPTION

The air injection system adds a controlled amount of fresh air to the exhaust gases at the exhaust manifold, or downstream to the catalyst to aid in oxidation of the exhaust gases. This results in reduced levels of carbon monoxide (CO) and hydrocarbon (HC) emissions.

The 2.2L and 2.5L TBI system uses an Air Aspirator System (AAS). This system uses an aspirator valve, hoses and tubing. The 5.2L system consists of a belt driven air pump, a switching/relief valve, relief valve solenoid, hoses, and check valves.

OPERATION

AIR PUMP

5.2L Engines – The air pump is mounted on front of engine and is belt driven. Intake air for the pump is drawn in through a centrifugal filter fan on front of pump. Pump discharge air is directed to air switching/relief valve.

ASPIRATOR VALVE & RESONATOR

2.2L & 2.5L TBI Engines – The air aspirator valve is a reed-type, one-way check valve. This valve is connected to a tube from the exhaust catalyst. A fresh air hose is connected to the valve and to the TBI air filter assembly. When exhaust negative pressure pulses are strong enough to create a vacuum pulse, the reed valve in the aspirator valve is drawn open, allowing fresh air to enter the catalyst.

Positive pulses (pressure) in the exhaust cause the reed valve to remain closed, protecting the connecting hose, resonator and air filter assembly from exhaust gases. The resonator is installed between the aspirator valve and air filter housing to minimize exhaust noise under hood. *See Fig. 1.*

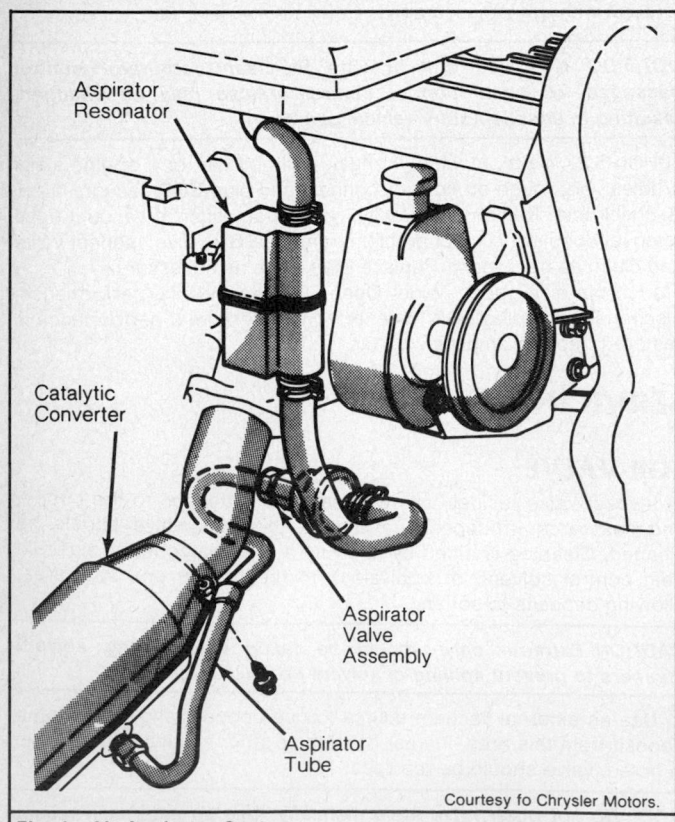

Fig. 1: Air Aspirator System

Courtesy fo Chrysler Motors.

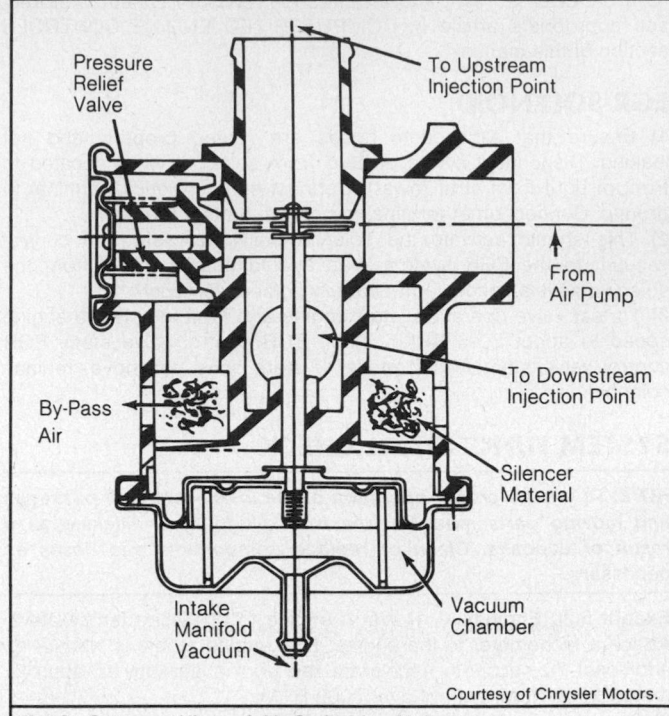

Courtesy of Chrysler Motors.

Fig. 2: Cutaway View of Air Switching Valve

AIR SWITCHING/RELIEF VALVE

5.2L Engines – This valve directs air injection flow to either a location near exhaust ports or to downstream injection point. The valve also serves as a relief valve at high engine speeds.

A vacuum signal from an Air Switching Relief Valve Solenoid (ASRV-SOL), causes switching valve to open. This routes air pump airflow into exhaust ports. When ASRV-SOL shuts off vacuum to the switching valve, a bleed orifice in the vacuum hose allows vacuum signal to go to zero, causing the switching valve to route pump air to downstream injection point. *See Fig. 2.*

CHECK VALVE

5.2L Engines – This valve is located in the injection tube assemblies that lead to exhaust manifold(s) or to the downstream injection point. Valve has a one-way reed valve which prevents hot exhaust gases from backing up into hoses and pump. This valve protects the system in event of air pump belt failure, abnormally high exhaust system pressure or air hose rupture.

SERVICE PROCEDURES

Complete system should be checked at regular intervals. On 5.2L models, engine tune-up should be checked to verify proper engine vacuum whenever air injection system is not operating properly. Belts must be in good condition and set to proper tension.

AIR PUMP

5.2L Engines – 1) Servicing of air pump is limited to replacement of centrifugal fan filter or entire pump. Do not clamp pump in a vise or use a hammer on pump housing.

NOTE: DO NOT lubricate air pump. Wipe all oil off of pump housing. Oil in the pump will cause rapid deterioration and failure of internal pump components.

2) To replace centrifugal filter, insert needle nose pliers between filter fins and break fan from hub. Install new fan, using pulley and bolts to draw fan down evenly. Do not press or hammer on air pump shaft.

1989 EXHAUST EMISSION SYSTEMS
Chrysler Motors Air Injection Systems (Cont.)

3-13

NOTE: Fan might have a slight squeal until sealing lip is worn in. Air injection system is not completely noiseless. Normal noise increases in pitch as engine speed increases.

TESTING

AIR SWITCHING VALVE

5.2L Engines – With engine running, apply vacuum to valve. Air should be injected upstream only. If air escapes from silencer ports or is applied upstream and downstream, valve is faulty and must be replaced.

CHECK VALVE

CAUTION: Exhaust temperatures are hot. Use extreme care when checking for leaks.

5.2L Engines – Remove air supply hose from check valve inlet tube. With engine operating, listen for exhaust leakage at check valve. If exhaust gases escape from valve, valve must be replaced. Also check for leaks at all other connections.

AIR ASPIRATOR VALVE

2.2L & 2.5L TBI Engines – Remove air supply hose from aspirator valve inlet. With engine at idle in neutral, the negative exhaust pulses (vacuum) can be felt at the inlet. If hot exhaust gases are felt escaping from the valve, the valve must be replaced.

1989 EXHAUST EMISSION SYSTEMS
Chrysler Motors Electric Assist Choke

All RWD Models

DESCRIPTION

All RWD passenger cars are equipped with an electric assist choke to help reduce emissions during engine warm-up. A dual-stage control unit assists engine warm-up in summer and winter operation by allowing more current to reach the choke heating element when temperature is more than 80°F (27°C).

OPERATION

NOTE: Information on 5.2L 4-Bbl. models is not available from manufacturer.

On 2-Bbl. models, electrical current is supplied from the oil pressure switch. A minimum of 4 psi (.28 kg/cm²) oil pressure is required to close contacts in the oil pressure switch and provide electrical current to choke control switch. The control then routes power to the choke heating element.

The dual-stage control unit will shorten choke duration when temperatures are more than 80°F (27°C), and it will stabilize choke operation in the winter (summer electric assist is hotter than winter heat level). Engine temperature controls a switch inside the dual-stage control. At temperatures less than 55°F (13°C), electric power is reduced by a resistor. When temperatures are more than 80°F (27°C), the resistor is by-passed and full heat is supplied. This action shortens choke duration.

Engines started in winter conditions will experience 2 levels of choke heat. A low heat level is used during engine warm-up and high heat level is used after engine warm-up.

TESTING

FUNCTIONAL CHECK

1) Check test light by connecting between battery terminals of car battery. Observe intensity of light. Before starting engine, remove ignition harness electrical connector from control switch. See Fig. 1.
2) Connect test light to choke terminal of control switch and ground. Start engine and allow to reach normal operating temperature. Apply 12 volts to ignition harness terminal of control switch. If test light does not light or does not have same intensity as in step 1), control switch is defective and should be replaced.

CHOKE HEATING ELEMENT

1) Disconnect battery voltage (B+) wire from the control switch. Connect an ohmmeter lead to choke housing or choke retainer screw. Touch other lead to a bare portion of choke wire connector at switch (not the battery voltage terminal).
2) Resistance of 4-12 ohms indicates the heating element is electrically functional. Replace choke assembly if ohmmeter readings indicate an open or short circuit.

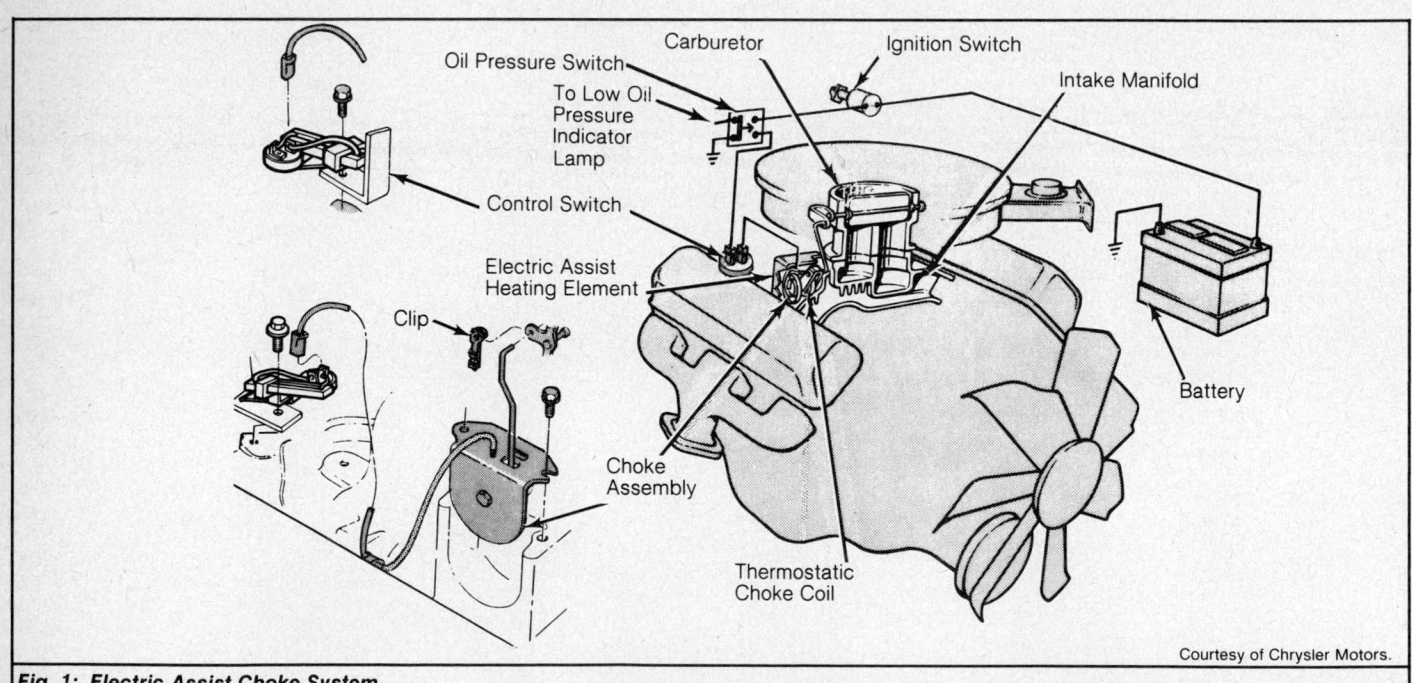

Courtesy of Chrysler Motors.

Fig. 1: Electric Assist Choke System

DESCRIPTION

The purpose of the Fuel Evaporation Control System is to prevent the escape of gasoline vapors from the fuel tank into the atmosphere. When fuel vaporizes in the fuel tank and fuel bowl (carburetor models), the vapors are temporarily held in the charcoal canister until they can be drawn into the intake manifold when the engine is running.

OPERATION

CANISTER PURGE SOLENOID

The purge solenoid is controlled by the Single Module Engine Controller (SMEC), or Single Board Engine Controller (SBEC) on 3.0L models. When engine temperature is less than 145°F (61°C), the SMEC or SBEC grounds the purge solenoid, energizing it. This prevents vacuum from reaching the charcoal canister valve.

When engine temperature reaches 145°F (61°C), the SMEC or SBEC de-energizes the solenoid by turning the ground off. Once this happens, vacuum will flow to canister purge valve and purge the fuel vapors.

CHARCOAL CANISTER

A sealed, maintenance free, charcoal canister is used on all models. Fuel vapors from the fuel tank, throttle body or carburetor are temporarily stored in the canister until they can be drawn into the intake manifold.

PRESSURE-VACUUM FILLER CAP

Fuel tank is sealed with a pressure-vacuum relief filler cap. Relief valves in fuel tank filler cap operate only to prevent excessive pressure or vacuum in fuel tank. Proper replacement cap must be used to replace original cap.

ROLLOVER/VAPOR SEPARATOR

All models are equipped with a rollover/vapor separator valve to prevent fuel leakage if vehicle is accidentally rolled over. This valve is located on top of fuel tank.

MAINTENANCE

Charcoal canister purge control valve can be checked by disconnecting the 3/16" vacuum hose to canister and connecting an auxiliary vacuum source in its place. Delay valve must hold 10 in. Hg. vacuum. If not, replace canister.

Generally, replacement is only required if vehicle is frequently driven in dusty areas or filter is dirty or clogged. All hoses should be inspected periodically and replaced if necessary. Use only fuel resistant hose for replacement of any evaporative hoses.

1989 EXHAUST EMISSION SYSTEMS
Chrysler Motors Vacuum Diagrams

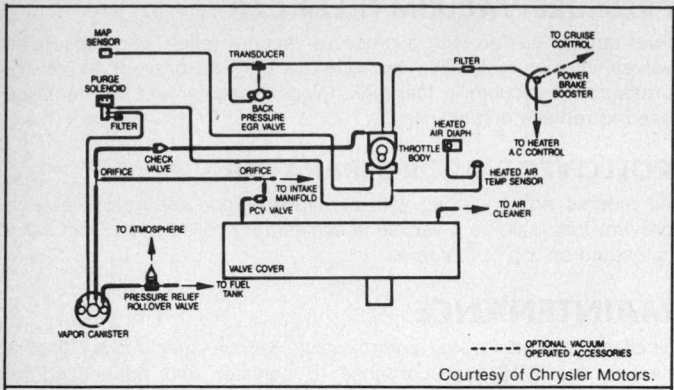

Fig. 1: Vacuum Hose Routing – 2.2L & 2.5L EFI Federal & High Altitude

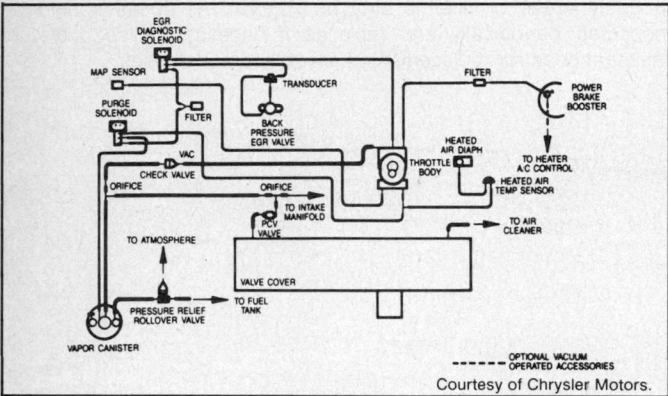

Fig. 2: Vacuum Hose Routing – 2.2L & 2.5L EFI California

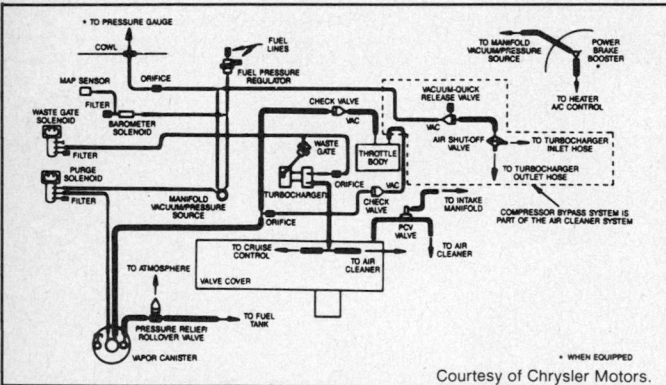

Fig. 3: Vacuum Hose Routing – 2.5L Turbo I Federal

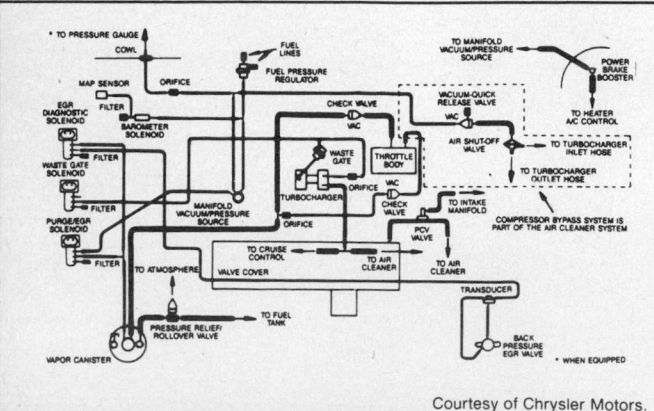

Fig. 4: Vacuum Hose Routing – 2.5L Turbo I California

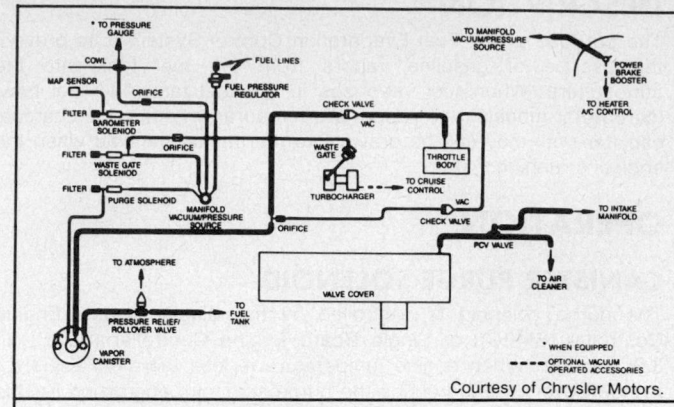

Fig. 5: Vacuum Hose Routing – 2.2L Turbo II 50 State

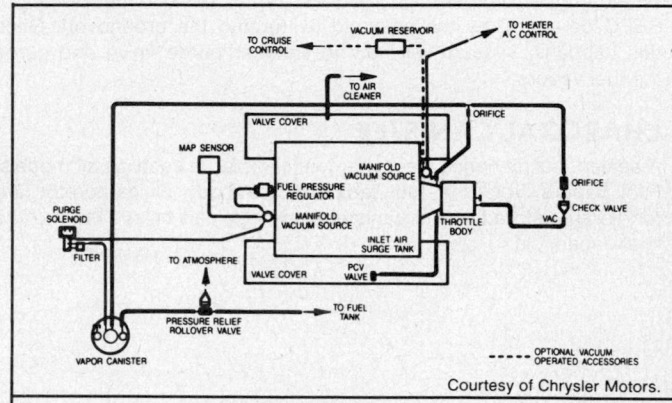

Fig. 6: Vacuum Hose Routing – 3.0L Federal & High Altitude w/Anti-Lock Brakes

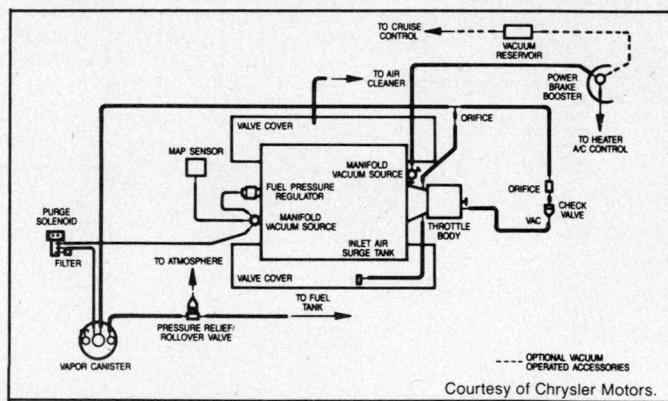

Fig. 7: Vacuum Hose Routing – 3.0L Federal & High Altitude w/o Anti-Lock Brakes

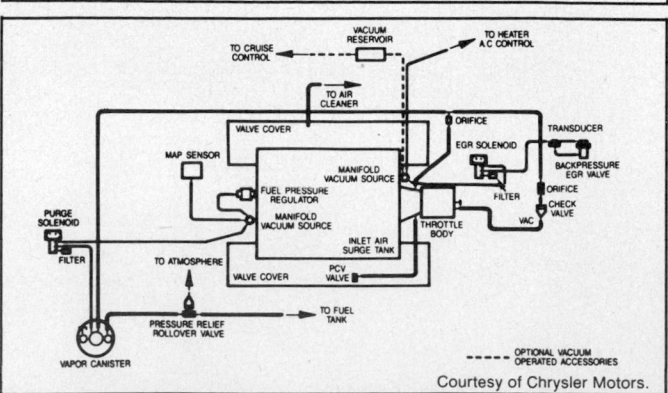

Fig. 8: Vacuum Hose Routing – 3.0L California w/Anti-Lock Brakes

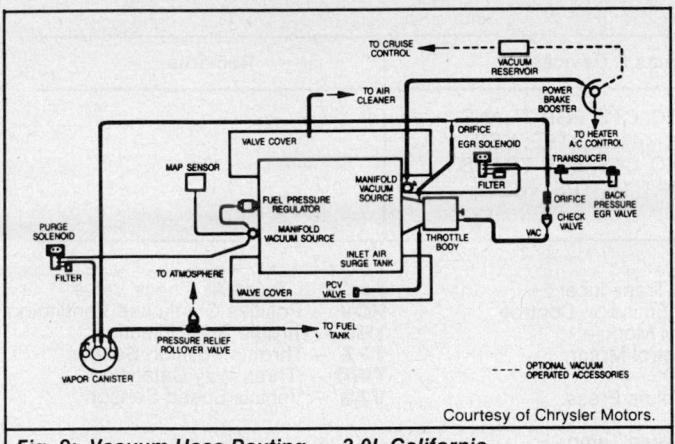

Fig. 9: Vacuum Hose Routing – 3.0L California w/o Anti-Lock Brakes

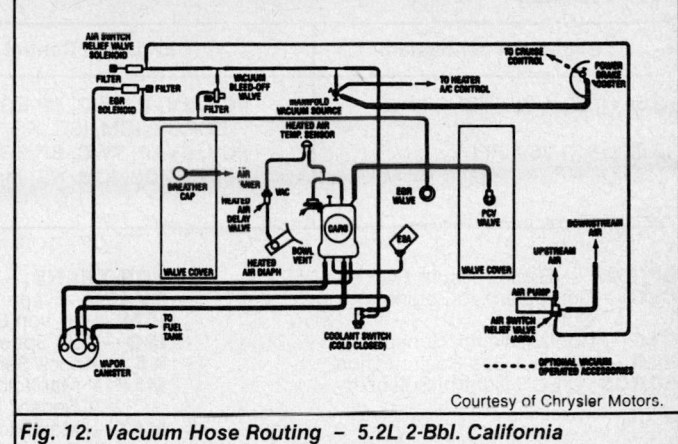

Fig. 12: Vacuum Hose Routing – 5.2L 2-Bbl. California

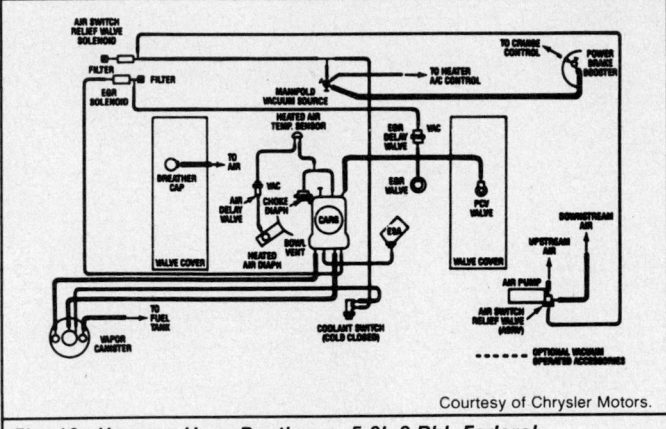

Fig. 10: Vacuum Hose Routing – 5.2L 2-Bbl. Federal & High Altitude w/A999 Transmission

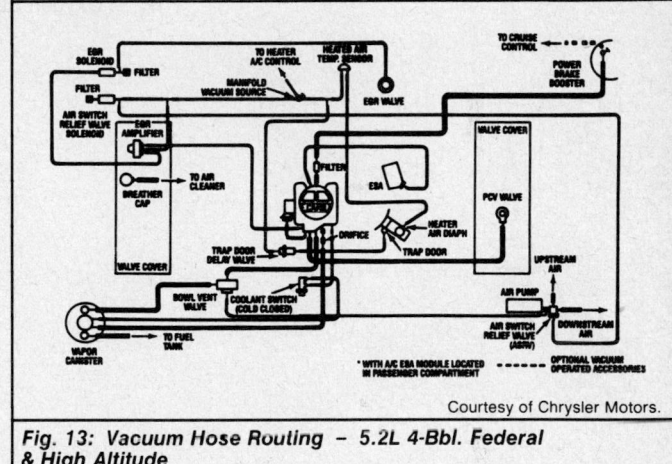

Fig. 13: Vacuum Hose Routing – 5.2L 4-Bbl. Federal & High Altitude

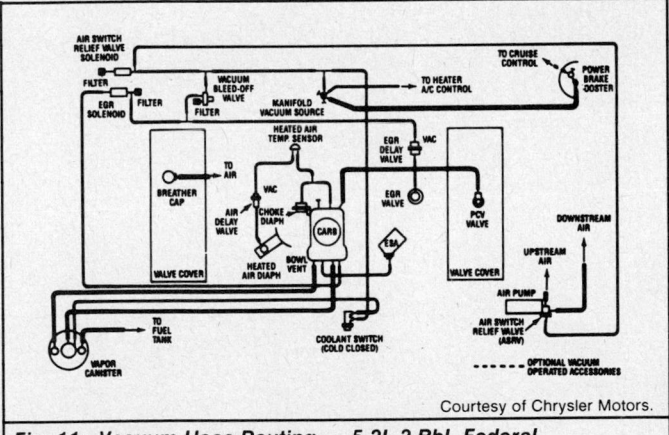

Fig. 11: Vacuum Hose Routing – 5.2L 2-Bbl. Federal & High Altitude w/o A999 Transmission

1989 EXHAUST EMISSION SYSTEMS
Eagle Emission Control Application

1989 EAGLE

Engine & Fuel System	Emission Control Systems & Devices	Remarks
2.5L (135") 4-Cyl. TBI	**PCV, EVAP, TWC, BP/EGR, CEC**, CTS, EGR-TRANS, EGRCS, ICM, ISC, KS, MAP, MAT, O₂, TPS, VSS	
3.0L (181") V6 MPFI	**PCV, EVAP, TWC, BP/EGR, CEC**, CTS, EGR-TRANS, EGRCS, ICM, KS, MAP, MAT, O₂, TPS, VSS	

BP/EGR – Backpressure EGR
CEC – Computerized Engine Control
CTS – Coolant Temp. Sensor
EGR – Exhaust Gas Recirculation
EGRCS – EGR Control Solenoid

EGR-TRANS – EGR Transducer
EVAP – Evaporative Emission Control
ICM – Ignition Control Module
ISC – Idle Speed Control Motor
KS – Knock Sensor
MAP – Manifold Absolute Press. Sensor
MAT – Manifold Absolute Temp. Sensor
MPFI – Multi-Point Fuel Injection
O₂ – Oxygen Sensor

PACV – Pulse Air Check Valve
PCV – Positive Crankcase Ventilation
TBI – Throttle Body Injection
TPS – Throttle Position Sensor
TWC – Three-Way Catalytic
VSS – Vehicle Speed Sensor

Premier

Eagle Premier models utilize several types of devices to control emissions. Although originally intended for a specific purpose, many of the devices are now used in various parts of multiple systems. These figures show the physical appearance of typical components. Operation and method of actuation is provided for most devices. Refer to specific system within this section for testing purposes.

COMPONENT & SYMBOL	OPERATION
EGR BACKPRESSURE TRANSDUCER	A vacuum bleed hole, located inside the transducer, vents EGR vacuum to the atmosphere until sufficient exhaust backpressure is applied, closing the bleed hole. When this happens, vacuum is routed to the EGR and normal EGR operation begins.
EGR SOLENOID	When engine is running, vacuum is applied to the solenoid. If the ECU has energized the solenoid, vacuum will not flow through the solenoid and transducer. If the ECU has not energized the solenoid, vacuum will flow to the transducer.
EGR VALVE	The EGR valve will begin to function, as vacuum is applied through the EGR transducer. As vacuum increases at the EGR valve diaphragm, the EGR pintel will be lifted from its seat, allowing exhaust gases to flow into the intake manifold.
KNOCK SENSOR	Knock sensor is a tuned piezoelectric crystal transducer that is located in the cylinder head (2.5L) or engine block (3.0L). Knock sensor provides ECU with an electrical signal that is created by vibrations that correspond to its center frequency of 5550 Hz. Vibration from engine knock causes the crystal inside the sensor to vibrate and produce the electrical signal. Based on input, ECU can selectively retard ignition timing of any single cylinder or a combination of cylinders to eliminate a knock condition.
MANIFOLD ABSOLUTE PRESSURE (MAP) SENSOR	The Manifold Absolute Pressure (MAP) sensor reacts to absolute pressure in the intake manifold and provides an analog voltage signal for the ECU. Manifold pressure is used to supply mixture density information and ambient barometric pressure information to the ECU. The sensor is remote mounted and a tube from the throttle body provides its input pressure.

COMPONENT & SYMBOL	OPERATION
MANIFOLD AIR TEMPERATURE (MAT) SENSOR	The Manifold Air Temperature (MAT) sensor is located in the intake tract, either in the throttle body adapter at rear of intake manifold (3.0L) or between No. 3 and No. 4 intake manifold runners (2.5L). The sensor projects into air stream and sends an analog voltage reading to ECU to represent changes in manifold air temperature.
OXYGEN SENSOR	The oxygen sensor is located in the exhaust manifold (2.5L) or "Y" pipe (3.0L). It measures the oxygen content in the exhaust gas and provides a variable voltage to the ECU accordingly. The ECU then adjusts the air/fuel mixture based on the voltage received from the oxygen sensor and other inputs. A lean air/fuel mixture causes a greater oxygen content in the exhaust gas and a rich air/fuel mixture causes less oxygen content. The oxygen sensor is heated to decrease initial warm-up time of the sensor.
THROTTLE POSITION SENSOR (TPS)	The Throttle Position Sensor (TPS) is a variable resistor mounted on fuel injection throttle body and is connected to throttle valve shaft. The sensor indicates shaft position by analog voltage to the ECU.

Premier

DESCRIPTION & OPERATION

The Exhaust Gas Recirculation (EGR) system is designed to lower peak combustion temperatures of gases in the combustion chambers due to lower concentrations of oxygen in the intake mixture, and thereby reducing formation of oxides of nitrogen (NOx).

This reduction of peak combustion temperatures is accomplished by introducing metered amounts of exhaust gas into the air/fuel mixture. The EGR system used on the 2.5L and 3.0L engines is controlled by the Electronic Control Unit (ECU). This system consists of a diaphragm actuated EGR valve, EGR valve solenoid, EGR backpressure transducer, connecting vacuum hoses and ECU.

EGR VALVE

The EGR valve is mounted on the side of the intake manifold. It is normally held closed by spring pressure. When enough vacuum is applied through the EGR backpressure transducer, the EGR valve opens allowing exhaust gas recirculation. *See Fig. 1.*

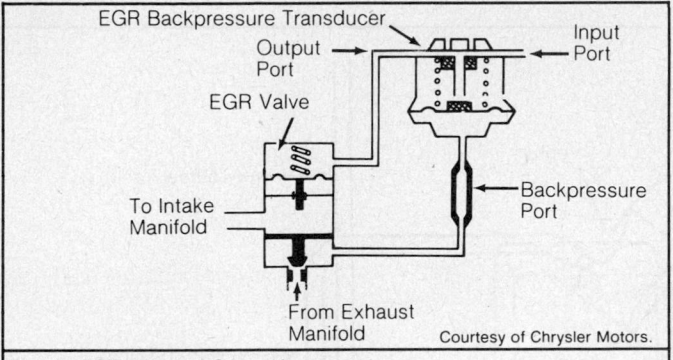

Fig. 1: EGR Internal Operation

EGR BACKPRESSURE TRANSDUCER

A vacuum bleed hole, located inside the transducer, vents EGR vacuum to the atmosphere until sufficient exhaust backpressure is applied, closing the bleed hole. When this happens, vacuum is then routed to the EGR valve and normal EGR operation begins.

EGR SOLENOID

When engine is running, vacuum is applied to the solenoid. If the ECU has energized the solenoid, vacuum will not flow through the solenoid and transducer. If the ECU has not energized the solenoid, vacuum will flow to the transducer.

TESTING

EGR SOLENOID

1) With engine at normal operating temperature, connect vacuum gauge to manifold vacuum. *See Fig. 2 and 3.* Vacuum gauge should read a minimum of 15 in. Hg. If vacuum is low, check hose for damage, kinks and proper connection. If vacuum is okay, proceed to step **2)**.

2) Disconnect vacuum line from transducer side of solenoid (output side) and connect vacuum gauge. If the reading is zero inches of vacuum, go on to step **3)**. If not, check solenoid/ECU operation with Diagnostic Readout Box (DRB-II), repair as necessary.

3) Disconnect electrical connector at solenoid. Vacuum gauge should now show vacuum present. If there is no vacuum, replace solenoid. Proceed to EGR VALVE.

EGR VALVE

1) Disconnect the EGR solenoid electrical connector. By-pass backpressure transducer by connecting EGR solenoid output directly to EGR valve. If EGR valve is good, the engine should idle

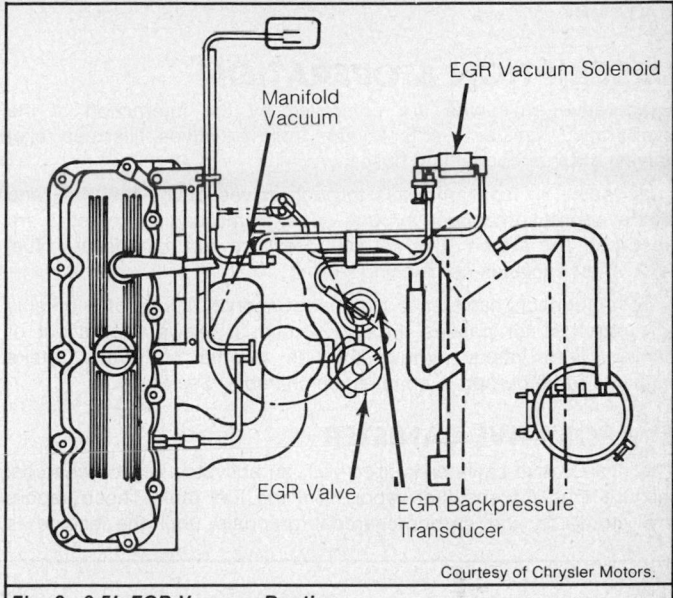

Fig. 2: 2.5L EGR Vacuum Routing

roughly or stall. Proceed to BACKPRESSURE TRANSDUCER. If idle does not change, go to step **2)**.

2) Disconnect vacuum hose from EGR and replace with hand operated vacuum pump. Apply at least 12 in. Hg of vacuum to valve. If engine now idles roughly or dies, check vacuum lines between EGR valve and intake manifold also check the line between transducer and EGR base. If no leaks are found, proceed to BACKPRESSURE TRANSDUCER.

3) If idle did not change in step **2)**, remove EGR valve. Inspect both the EGR valve and exhaust passage in manifold for blockage, repair as necessary. If no blockage is found, replace EGR valve.

BACKPRESSURE TRANSDUCER

Disconnect and plug the output (EGR) side of transducer. Disconnect and remove transducer from vehicle. Apply 1-2 lbs. of regulated air pressure to transducer backpressure port. *See Fig. 1.* Apply at least 12 in. Hg of vacuum to input port. Replace transducer if it will not hold vacuum.

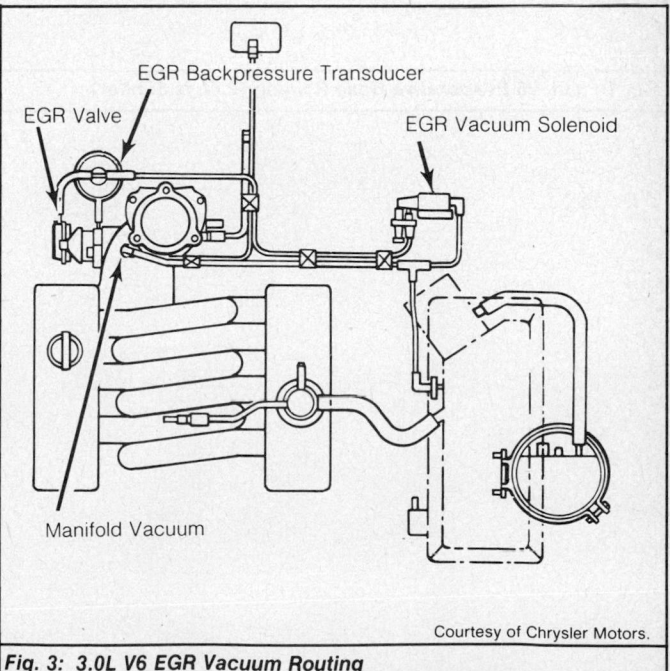

Fig. 3: 3.0L V6 EGR Vacuum Routing

1989 EXHAUST EMISSION SYSTEMS
Eagle Evaporative Emission Control

Premier

DESCRIPTION & OPERATION

Evaporative emissions are controlled by the interaction of the evaporative canister, fuel tank vents, rollover valves, filler cap relief valves and interconnecting hoses.

Fuel vapors in fuel tank pass through valves of the fuel tank and into evaporative canister through hose. In the canister, vapors are absorbed and stored. This controls pressure that may occur in fuel tank when engine is not running.

A hose connects canister to air cleaner snorkel. Inside of snorkel is a venturi. As air passes through venturi, it draws vapors out of canister into intake airflow, through throttle body and intake manifold to be burned in combustion chamber. *See Fig. 1.*

EVAPORATIVE CANISTER

The evaporative canister is filled with an activated carbon/charcoal mixture that absorbs fuel vapor from the fuel tank. These vapors are stored in the carbon/charcoal granuals until the engine is started, initiating canister purge. During canister purge function, vapors are drawn through the purge hose into engine by a venturi located in the air cleaner.

FUEL FILLER PRESSURE CAP

The fuel filler cap is a 2-way relief valve. Normally closed to the atmosphere during engine operation, the relief valve will open at a pressure of 1.5 psi (10 kPa) or a vacuum of 1.8 in. Hg (6 kPa). After relieving pressure or vacuum, valve closes again, preventing venting of vapors to atmosphere.

ROLLOVER VALVE

Fuel tank is equipped with 2 rollover valves. These dual function valves route fuel vapor to the evaporative canister while vehicle is not being operated and prevents fuel flow through tank vent hoses if vehicle should roll over.

The rollover valve consists of a plunger and spring, plunger seat and orfice. In the normal open position, fuel vapor passes through valve to purge canister. During vehicle rollover, the valve is inverted and the plunger seats in orfice, preventing fuel flow through valve.

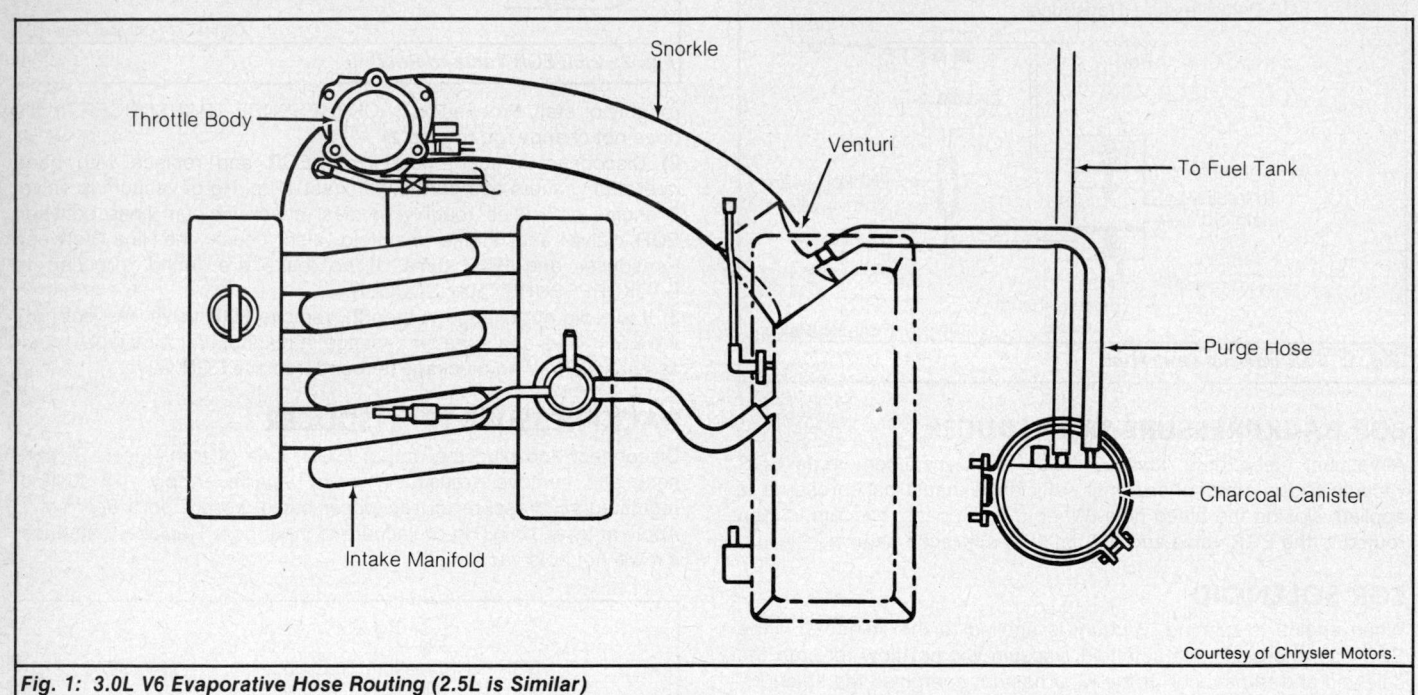

Courtesy of Chrysler Motors.

Fig. 1: 3.0L V6 Evaporative Hose Routing (2.5L is Similar)

Premier

VAPOR & AIR HOSES	▭
VACUUM HOSES	▬

EGR Solenoid

MAP Sensor

Air Temperature Switch

Crankcase Vent Air In

To Fuel Tank

Transducer

EGR Valve

Manifold Vacuum

Vacuum Motor

Evaporative Canister

Crankcase Air Out

Throttle Body

FRONT OF VEHICLE

Air Filter

Metered Orifice

Metered Orifice

Courtesy of Chrysler Motors.

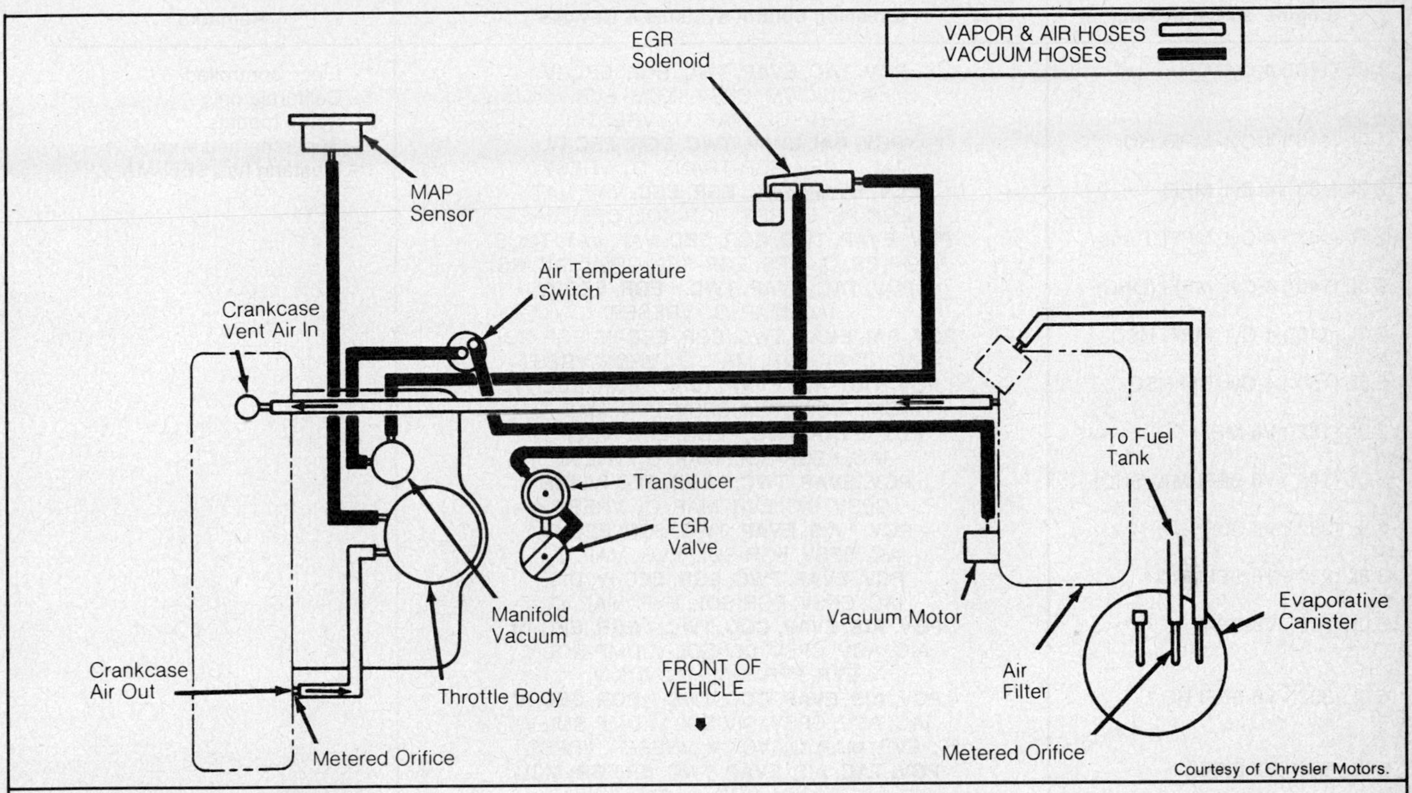

Fig. 1: 2.5L 4-Cyl. Vacuum Diagram

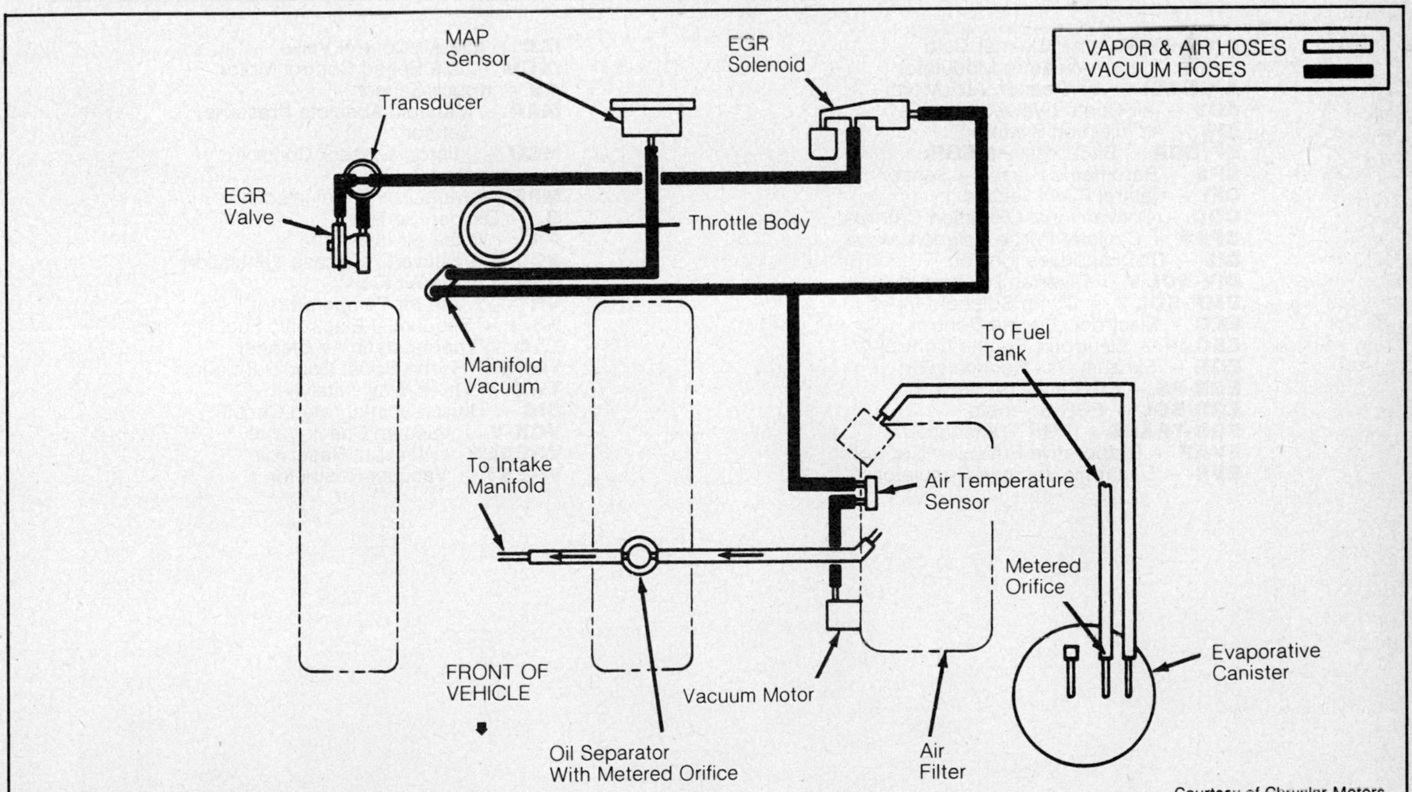

VAPOR & AIR HOSES	▭
VACUUM HOSES	▬

MAP Sensor

EGR Solenoid

Transducer

EGR Valve

Throttle Body

To Fuel Tank

Manifold Vacuum

Air Temperature Sensor

To Intake Manifold

Metered Orifice

Evaporative Canister

FRONT OF VEHICLE

Vacuum Motor

Oil Separator With Metered Orifice

Air Filter

Courtesy of Chrysler Motors.

Fig. 2: 3.0L V6 Vacuum Diagram

1989 EXHAUST EMISSION SYSTEMS
Ford Emission Control Application

1989 FORD MOTOR CO.

Engine & Fuel System	Emission Control Systems & Devices	Remarks
1.9L (116") 4-Cyl. CFI	PCV, TAC, EVAP, TWC, EGR, EEC-IV, A/CL-CWM, CPSV, ISCM, EVR, EGR-SOL, MAP, O$_2$, VREST	[1] – Elect. controlled.
1.9L (116") 4-Cyl. MPFI HO	PCV, PAI, EVAP, TWC, EGR, EEC-IV, IAC, CPSV, EGR-TRANS, O$_2$, VREST	[2] – California only.
2.2L (133") 4-Cyl. MPFI	PCV, EVAP, TWC, EGR, EEC, VAF, VAT, [2] EGR-PS, O$_2$, BPS, EGR-SOL, CPSV, IAC	[3] – Some models.
2.2L (133") 4-Cyl. MPFI Turbo	PCV, EVAP, TWC, EGR, EEC, VAF, VAT, TBCS [2] EGR-PS, O$_2$, BPS, EGR-SOL, CPSV, IAC, KS	[4] – Supercharged engine.
2.3L (140") 4-Cyl. MPFI (OHC)	PCV, TAC, EVAP, TWC, [1] EGR, EEC-IV, IAC, MAP, O$_2$, VRESER	[5] – Mustang has SEFI-MA.
2.3L (140") 4-Cyl. MPFI HSC	PCV, PAI, EVAP, TWC, EGR, EEC-IV, EGR-SOL, IAC, CPSV, EVR, MAP, O$_2$, VRDV, VREST	
2.5L (150") 4-Cyl. CFI HSC	PCV, TAC, AIS, EVAP, TWC, [1] EGR, EEC-IV, ISCM, A/CL-CWM, CPSV, EVR, MAP, O$_2$	
3.0L (182") V6 MPFI	PCV, EVAP, TWC, [2] EGR, EEC-IV, CPSV, IAC, [2] EGR-SOL, MAP, O$_2$, VREST	
3.0L (182") V6 SEFI-MA (SHO)	PCV, EVAP, TWC, [2] EGR, EEC-IV, DIS, CPSV, IAC, EVR, MAP, O$_2$, VREST	
3.8L (232") V6 SEFI	PCV, [3] AIS, EVAP, TWC, EGR, EEC-IV, IAC, CPSV, EGR-SOL, EVR, MAP, O$_2$,	
3.8L (232") V6 SEFI-MA [4]	PCV, EVAP, TWC, EGR, EEC-IV, DIS, IAC, CPSV, EGR-SOL, EVR, MAP, O$_2$	
5.0L (302") V8 SEFI	PCV, AIS, EVAP, COC, TWC, [1] EGR, EEC-IV, AIC, ACV, CPSV, DIV-SOL V, DMP-SOL V, EVR, FPR, MAP, O$_2$, VCK-V,	
5.0L (302") V8 SEFI HO [5]	PCV, AIS, EVAP, COC, TWC, [1] EGR, EEC-IV, IAC, ACV, CPSV, DIV-SOL V, DMP-SOL V, EVR, MAP, O$_2$, VCK-V, VRESER, VREST	
5.8L (351") V8 2-Bbl.	PCV, TAC, AIS, EVAP, TWC, BP/EGR, MCU, ACV, COC, O$_2$, UIC	

A/CL-CWM – Air Cleaner Cold Weather Modulator
A/CL-MR – Air Cleaner Vac. Motor
ACV – Air Control Valve
AIS – Air Injection System
BP/EGR – Backpressure EGR
BPS – Barometric Pressure Sensor
CFI – Central Fuel Injection
COC – Conventional Oxidation Catalytic
CPSV – Canister Purge Solenoid Valve
DIS – Distributorless Ignition
DIV-SOL V – Diverter Solenoid Valve
DMP-SOL V – Dump Solenoid Valve
EEC – Electronic Engine Control
EEC-IV – Electronic Engine Control-IV
EGR – Exhaust Gas Recirculation
EGR-PS – EGR Position Sensor
EGR-SOL – EGR Solenoid
EGR-TRANS – EGR Transducer
EVAP – Evaporative Emission Control
EVR – Electronic Vacuum Regulator

IAC – Idle Air Control Valve
ISCM – Idle Speed Control Motor
KS – Knock Sensor
MAP – Manifold Absolute Pressure Sensor
MCU – Microprocessor Control Unit
MPFI – Multi-Point Fuel Injection
O$_2$ – Oxygen Sensor
PAI – Pulse Air Injection
PCV – Positive Crankcase Ventilation
VAF – Vane Air Flow
VAT – Vane Air Temperature
SEFI – Sequential Electronic Fuel Injection
TAC – Thermostatic Air Cleaner
TBCS – Turbo Boost Control Solenoid
TWC – Three-Way Catalytic
UIC – Universal Integrated Circuit
VCK-V – Vacuum Check Valve
VRESER – Vacuum Reservoir
VREST – Vacuum Restrictor

Ford Motor Co. vehicles utilize several types of devices to control emissions. Although originally intended for a specific purpose, many of the devices are now used in various parts of the system. These figures show the physical appearance of typical components and their identification symbols found on Emission Control Diagrams. Operation and method of actuation is provided for most devices. Refer to specific system within this section for testing procedures.

COMPONENT & SYMBOL	OPERATION
AIR BY-PASS VALVE AIR BPV AIR BPV AIR BPV AIR BPV	Vacuum operated valves may be normally open or closed. Valves direct airflow from thermactor air pump to exhaust system or atmosphere as required. May be mounted on air pump or in-line (remote). Normally closed valves supply air to the exhaust system with medium and high applied vacuum signals during normal modes, short idles and some acceleration. With low or no vacuum applied, the pump air is dumped through the silencer ports of the valve. Normally open valves with a vacuum vent provide a timed air dump during deceleration and also dump when a vacuum pressure difference is maintained between the signal port and the vent port.
AIR CHARGE TEMPERATURE (ACT) SENSOR	The ACT sensor is threaded into the intake manifold or throttle body. It senses air/fuel mixture temperature and provides instant information to EFI system. The ACT sensor is also used as a density corrector for airflow calculation and to proportion the cold enrichment fuel flow.
AIR CHECK VALVE & PULSE AIR VALVE	One-way valve allows thermactor air to enter exhaust system while preventing exhaust gases from passing in the opposite direction. Pulse air valve is not interchangeable with air check valve.
AIR CLEANER COLD WEATHER MODULATOR A/CL CWM	A cold weather modulator is sometimes used in addition to the air cleaner temperature control sensor, to control the inlet air temperature. The cold weather modulator traps vacuum in the system, so air control door will not switch to cold air when vacuum drops during acceleration. The cold weather modulator only works when the outside air is cold.
AIR CLEANER TEMPERATURE SENSOR ○ A/CL BI MET	This bi-metallic sensor is installed in the lower air cleaner tray and is subject to temperature changes within the air cleaner. At a given temperature, the sensor bleeds off vacuum to the air cleaner air control door, permitting the vacuum motor to open the duct door and allow fresh air in while shutting off full heat.
AIR CLEANER VACUUM MOTOR A/CL DV	Regulates position of air control door within air cleaner duct to allow warm or cold air in as signaled by the air cleaner temperature sensor and cold weather modulator.
AIR SILENCER SILN	The air silencer is a combination silencer and filter for air supply pumps that are not equipped with an impeller type centrifugal air filter fan or for pulse air (thermactor II) systems. The air silencer is mounted in a convenient position in the engine compartment and is connected to the air supply pump or pulse air valve inlet by means of a flexible hose.

1989 EXHAUST EMISSION SYSTEMS
Ford Motor Co. Emission Components (Cont.)

COMPONENT & SYMBOL	OPERATION
AIR SUPPLY CONTROL VALVES (ACV)	Operated by vacuum to direct air pump output to exhaust manifold or downstream to catalytic converter, depending on system requirements.
AIR SUPPLY PUMP	Pump is belt driven, positive displacement, vane type that provides air for the air injection system. It is available in 11 cubic inch and 19 cubic inch sizes. Various drive belt pulley ratios permit a wider range of vehicle applications.
BAROMETRIC ABSOLUTE PRESSURE SENSOR	The Barometric Absolute Pressure (BAP) sensor provides information to ECU regarding altitude and engine load. The ECU in response adjusts spark advance, EGR flow and air/fuel ratio.
CANISTER PURGE REGULATOR VALVE (CPRV)	Normally closed solenoid valve controls the flow of fuel vapors from canister to intake manifold. Opened or closed by a signal from the electronic control assembly during various engine operating modes.
CANISTER PURGE VALVE (PURGE CV)	Vacuum operated purge valve controls flow of fuel vapors from carbon canister to engine.
CARBON CANISTER	Fuel vapors from fuel tank and carburetor bowl are stored in a carbon canister until the vehicle is operated, at which time, the vapors will purge from the canister into the engine for consumption. There are 2 canister sizes. In some applications, dual canisters are used on vehicles with large fuel tanks.
CARBURETOR FUEL BOWL SOLENOID VENT VALVE (SV-CBV)	A normally open valve is located in the fuel bowl vent line. The vent valve closes off the fuel bowl vent line when the engine is running and returns to normally open position when ignition is turned off.

1989 EXHAUST EMISSION SYSTEMS
Ford Motor Co. Emission Components (Cont.)

3-27

COMPONENT & SYMBOL	OPERATION
CARBURETOR FUEL BOWL THERMAL VENT VALVE TVV	Inserted in carburetor-to-canister vent line, valve is closed when engine compartment is cold. This prevents fuel tank vapors (generated when fuel tank heats up before engine compartment) from being vented through carburetor fuel bowl.
COMBINATION AIR BY-PASS & AIR CONTROL VALVE ACV	The combination air by-pass and air control valve combines the functions of the by-pass valve and the air control valve into a single unit. There are 2 types of normally closed valves, the non-bleed type and the bleed type, all of which look alike. One distinguishing feature will be that the bleed type will have the percent of bleed molded into the plastic case.
DUAL THERMACTOR AIR CONTROL SOLENOID VALVE SOL V	The dual thermactor air control solenoid valve assembly consists of 2 closed solenoid valves, one controlling the thermactor air by-pass valve and the other controlling the thermactor diverter valve. Both are vented when de-energized, sourced by the intake manifold vacuum reservoir and controlled by the ECU system.
EGR BACKPRESSURE VARIABLE TRANSDUCER	A vacuum bleed hole, located inside the transducer, vents EGR vacuum to the atmosphere until sufficient exhaust backpressure is applied, closing the bleed hole. When this happens, vacuum is then routed to the EGR and normal operation begins.
EGR LOAD CONTROL WOT VALVE LCV	This valve dumps EGR vacuum at or near wide open throttle.
EGR SOLENOID VACUUM VALVE ASSEMBLY SOL V	The dual EGR solenoid valve assembly consists of 2 solenoid valves. One is a vacuum vent valve which supplies vacuum to the EGR when energized. The second valve is a vent valve which vents the EGR valve to the atmosphere when de-energized. Both solenoid valves receive variable duty cycle signals from the ECU according to EGR requirements.

COMPONENT & SYMBOL	OPERATION
EGR VACUUM CONTROL VALVE FILTER O—[FLTR]	The EGR vacuum control valve filter is used to vent various emission control components to the atmosphere.
EGR VACUUM REGULATOR (EVR)	The vacuum regulator is an electromagnetic device which controls vacuum output to EGR valve. The EVR is used in place of EGR Solenoid Vacuum Vent Valve Assembly. Regulator operation is measured as a duty cycle, increased duty is increased vacuum to EGR.
EGR VALVE POSITION (EVP) SENSOR	This sensor is attached to the EGR valve assembly and indicates position of EGR valve to the EEC system. It is located on top of the electronic EGR type valve.
ELECTRONIC CONTROL ASSEMBLY	The Electronic Control Assembly (ECA) is a microprocessor which is the center of the EEC-IV system. The ECA generates output signals to control various relays, solenoids and other actuators. The ECA contains a specific calibration for optimizing emissions, fuel economy and driveability. Based on information received and programmed into its memory, the ECA generates output signals to control various relays, solenoid and other actuators.
ELECTRONIC EGR VALVE	The Electronic EGR (EEGR) valve is required in EEC systems where EGR flow is controlled according to computer demands of EGR valve position sensor. The EGR valve is operated by a vacuum signal from dual EGR solenoid valves or electronic vacuum regulator.
EXHAUST HEAT CONTROL VALVE	Used to divert hot gases from the exhaust manifold to the intake manifold riser pad to heat the incoming air/fuel charge. Two types are used, a bi-metallic spring type and a vacuum actuated type.
EXTERNAL BACKPRESSURE TRANSDUCER EGR VALVE	The valve and transducer assembly, which consists of a modified ported EGR valve and a remote transducer, is used on selected engines. This assembly works the same as the integral backpressure transducer EGR valve and is diagnosed and serviced as an assembly only. Valve functional checks are the same as those for the integral backpressure transducer EGR valve.

1989 EXHAUST EMISSION SYSTEMS
Ford Motor Co. Emission Components (Cont.)

3-29

COMPONENT & SYMBOL	OPERATION
FEEDBACK CARBURETOR ACTUATOR MOTOR	Used on 7200 model carburetors, the actuator motor is threaded into carburetor body. Its actuator shaft moves a fuel metering pintle valve to produce a leaner/richer air/fuel mixture. Actuator shaft moves in response to signals from oxygen sensor and MCU system.
FILTER ASSEMBLY-VACUUM VENT VREST FLTR	The vacuum vent filter is used to filter air being drawn into the vacuum system when a vacuum bleed is required. It is a nylon tee with a restrictor and an open cell foam on one leg.
FUEL-VAPOR SEPARATOR SA-FA	The fuel-vapor separator is use in vacuum systems to prevent fuel contaminating a vacuum operated device.
HEATED EXHAUST GAS OXYGEN (HEGO) SENSOR	The oxygen sensor supplies the ECU with a signal which indicates either a rich or lean condition during engine operation. The sensor is heated to reduce initial warm-up time.
IDLE SPEED CONTROL (AIR BY-PASS) SOLENOID	Solenoid is mounted to the throttle body of fuel injected engines. Solenoid controls engine idle speed by regulating air volume by-passing throttle plates. This solenoid is controlled by the ECU.
IGNITION BAROMETRIC PRESSURE SWITCH	This switch is used to control spark timing and/or other electrical devices depending on barometric pressure. In normal operation, timing is increased above the switching altitude and retarded below the switching altitude. This switch operates in only an ON or OFF mode, below 3000 feet or above 4600 feet.
INTEGRAL BACKPRESSURE VARIABLE TRANSDUCER (VBT) EGR VALVE	The integral backpressure transducer EGR valve combines inputs of exhaust backpressure and EGR port vacuum into one unit. The valve requires both inputs to function. The valve will not function on vacuum alone. This backpressure valve is available in 2 types, poppet and tapered pintle.
INTEGRAL RELAY CONTROL MODULE	The module interfaces with the EEC-IV to control the cooling fan, A/C clutch and fuel pump.

1989 EXHAUST EMISSION SYSTEMS
Ford Motor Co. Emission Components (Cont.)

COMPONENT & SYMBOL	OPERATION
KNOCK SENSOR	Knock sensor is a piezoelectric accelerometer. The sensor reacts to engine ignition knock and provides information to ECU for timing and fuel correction.
MANIFOLD ABSOLUTE PRESSURE (MAP) SENSOR	The ECU uses manifold vacuum input from the MAP sensor to determine engine load. It is also used as a barometric sensor for altitude compensation.
MANIFOLD PRESSURE WARNING INDICATOR SWITCH	This switch is used to trigger a warning light and buzzer when overboost occurs on turbocharged vehicles.
PORTED EGR VALVE	The ported EGR valve is operated by a vacuum signal from the carburetor EGR signal port which actuates the valve diaphragm. As the vacuum increases sufficiently to overcome the power spring, the valve is opened, allowing EGR flow. The amount of flow is dependent on tapered pintle or poppet position, which is a direct result of the vacuum signal.
PRESSURE FEEDBACK ELECTRONIC EGR TRANSDUCER	The Pressure Feedback Electronic (PFE) EGR transducer converts a varying exhaust pressure signal into a proportional analog voltage which is digitized by the ECA. The ECA uses the signal received from PFE transducer to optimize EGR flow.
PRESSURE FEEDBACK ELECTRONIC (PFE) EGR VALVE EGR	This valve consists of a conventional ported EGR valve which has a tube attached to it to sense backpressure. A pressure transducer is used with this valve to send an electrical signal to ECA corresponding to amount of backpressure. The EGR flow is proportional to amount of pressure drop across the sensing tube.
SOLENOID VACUUM VALVE SOL V	The normally close solenoid valve consists of 2 vacuum ports with an atmospheric vent. The valve assembly can be with or without control bleed. When de-energized, outlet port of valve is opened to atmospheric vent and closed to inlet port. When energized, outlet port is opened to inlet port and closed to atmospheric vent. The control bleed is provided to prevent contamination entering solenoid valve from intake manifold. This solenoid valve is used on throttle kicker and EGR shutoff.
TEMPERATURE VACUUM SWITCH (TVS) TVS	The TVS incorporates a bi-metallic disc to open or close vacuum ports and may be used in conjunction with distributor, canister purge or EGR systems.

1989 EXHAUST EMISSION SYSTEMS
Ford Motor Co. Emission Components (Cont.)

COMPONENT & SYMBOL	OPERATION
THERMACTOR IDLE VACUUM (TIV) VALVE VAC / IVV	Prevents excessive underbody temperature of exhaust system by diverting secondary air pump output during extended engine idle. This valve also cuts EGR operation during heavy turbo boost modes.
THROTTLE POSITION SENSOR (TPS) TP	The TPS supplies ECA with a signal proportional to opening angle of throttle body throttle plates.
VACUUM BOWL VENT VALVE & VACUUM/ THERMOSTATIC BOWL VENT VALVE V-CBV	The vacuum bowl vent valve and vacuum/thermostatic bowl vent valve are vacuum and vacuum/temperature actuated on/off valves. Vacuum bowl vent valve and vacuum/thermostatic bowl vent valve are similar in appearance. The valves are used in evaporative emission system to control vapor flow from the carburetor bowl to carbon canister. With either valve, the flow path from the bowl to the canister is closed by manifold vacuum when the engine is running. The thermostatic valve also closes the bowl-to-canister flow path when the temperature of the valve is 90°F (32°C) or less (even without manifold vacuum). When the temperature of the valve is 120°F (49°C) or more, the valve is open (unless closed by manifold vacuum).
VACUUM CHECK VALVE VCK-V	A vacuum check valve blocks airflow in one direction. It allows free airflow in the other direction.
VACUUM CONTROL VALVES (VCV) 2-PORT / VCV 3-PORT / VCV 4-PORT / VCV	Temperature operated vacuum switches have 2 or more ports. They utilize wax pellet or bi-metallic material to either open or close the vacuum ports when normal engine operating temperature is reached. Valves are normally mounted in some part of cooling system so that the base is immersed in coolant. May be normally open or normally closed. One version includes an electrical vacuum switch on its top.
VACUUM DELAY VALVES VDV / VRDV / DV-TW	Inserted in vacuum lines to provide for gradual application or release of vacuum to engine or emission control devices. May be one-way or two-way valves depending on function and part of system affected.
VACUUM REGULATOR (2-PORT) VRV	The 2-port vacuum regulator provides a constant output signal when input signal is greater than a preset level. At a lower input vacuum, output equals input.

1989 EXHAUST EMISSION SYSTEMS
Ford Motor Co. Emission Components (Cont.)

COMPONENT & SYMBOL		OPERATION
	VACUUM REGULATOR (3 & 4-PORT) VRV	The 3-port and 4-port regulators are used to control vacuum advance to the distributor.
	VACUUM RESERVOIR VRESER VRESER	The vacuum reservoir stores vacuum and provides "muscle" vacuum. It prevents rapid fluctuations or sudden drops in a vacuum signal such as seen during acceleration.
	VACUUM RESTRICTOR V REST L REST T REST	This orifice-type flow restrictor is used in several emission calibrations to control the flow rate and/or actuation timing of components and systems.
	VACUUM VENT VALVES VACVV-D	Controls induction of fresh air into system to prevent accumulation of fuel vapors which could cause decay of vacuum diaphragms. May be vent valve only or combined vent and delay valve. Valves should always be mounted so ports point downward.

DESCRIPTION

The Exhaust Gas Recirculation (EGR) system distributes small amounts of exhaust gas into the intake mixture. This lowers combustion temperatures due to lower concentrations of oxygen. Lowering of combustion temperatures reduces amount of NOx emissions. The amount of exhaust gas recycled and timing of EGR valve opening are controlled by engine vacuum, exhaust system backpressure, altitude, temperature, throttle angle and engine speed.

Typical systems consist of an EGR valve, vacuum reservoir, check valve, Ported Vacuum Switch (PVS) and/or a Temperature Vacuum Switch (TVS). The following 5 types of EGR valves are used:

- Backpressure Variable Transducer (BVT)
- External Backpressure Transducer EGR Valve
- Electronic (EEGR)
- Integral Backpressure (IBP) Transducer
- Ported
- Pressure Feedback Electronic (PFE)

OPERATION

EGR VALVES

Backpressure Variable Transducer (BVT) EGR System (1.9L MPFI) – The valve and transducer assembly consists of a modified ported EGR valve and a remote transducer. This assembly works the same as the integral backpressure transducer EGR valve and is diagnosed and serviced as an assembly only. Valve functional checks are the same as those for the integral backpressure transducer EGR valve. *See Fig. 1.*

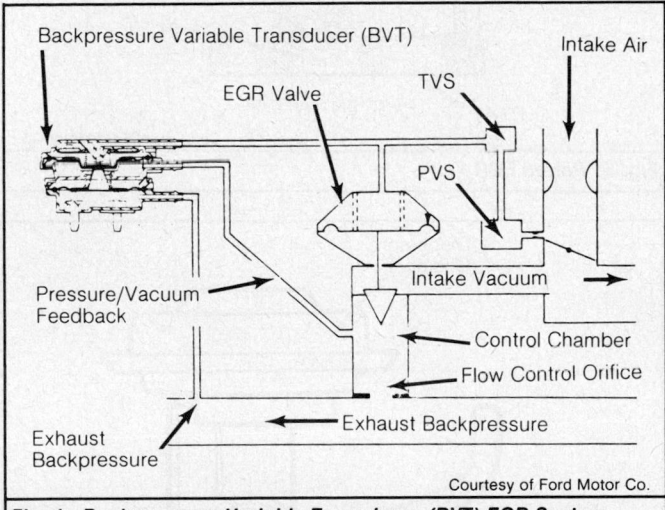

Fig. 1: *Backpressure Variable Transducer (BVT) EGR System*

Electronic (EEGR) EGR Valve – This valve is operated by a vacuum signal from one of the dual EGR solenoid valves or the electronic vacuum regulator. As vacuum overcomes closing spring pressure, the diaphragm is actuated, lifting pintle off its seat and causing exhaust gas to flow. Flow is proportional to pintle position. The EVP sensor on the valve sends an electrical signal relevant to valve position to the Electronic Control Assembly (ECA). *See Fig. 2.*

The electronic EGR valve assembly is not serviceable. The EVP sensor and EGR valve are serviced separately. The EVP sensor mounted on top of the valve sends out electrical signals to the Electronic Control Assembly (ECA) which indicate how far the EGR valve is open.

The ECA then signals the EGR control solenoids to maintain or alter the control vacuum supply to the EGR valve as required. Vacuum is obtained from the intake manifold and is bled off or applied to the EGR diaphragm by the ECA. A cooler is sometimes used to reduce gas temperatures and detonation. This valve operates only during partial throttle mode. It is closed in all other modes.

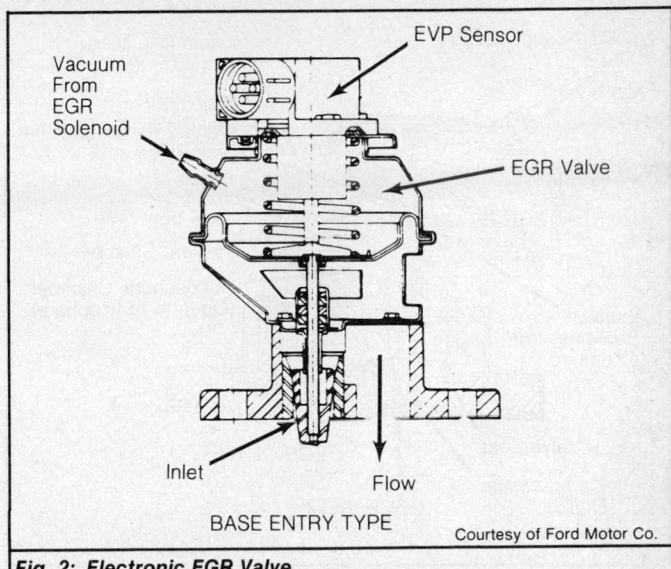

Fig. 2: *Electronic EGR Valve*

External Transducer EGR Valve & Integral Backpressure (IBP) Transducer EGR Valve – These EGR valves combine inputs of exhaust backpressure and EGR port vacuum. Both inputs are required for valve operation.

The integral backpressure transducer EGR valve combines an exhaust gas backpressure transducer within its housing. *See Fig. 3.* On external transducer EGR valve type, the exhaust gas backpressure transducer is mounted to the exterior of EGR valve. *See Fig. 4.* On both types, transducer controls EGR function by venting control vacuum in relation to exhaust backpressure.

In order for valve to operate, sufficient exhaust backpressure is required to close a bleed valve located inside the vacuum diaphragm housing. Until this bleed valve closes, all vacuum routed to the valve has no effect. When bleed valve closes, vacuum is applied to diaphragm. The valve opens allowing exhaust gas to flow. Flow rate is dependent on source vacuum, exhaust pressure, control setting and orifice size.

Poppet valves are rapid opening. Flow rate is limited by size of valve orifice or opening in carburetor spacer plate.

Internal tapered stem valves use a pintle which moves the tapered portion of the valve up or down against its valve seat. Flow rate is determined by the amount of movement off the seat.

Ported EGR Valve – This valve is operated by a vacuum signal from the carburetor EGR port which actuates the EGR valve diaphragm. When vacuum is increased enough to overcome the diaphragm closing spring pressure, the valve opens, allowing EGR flow. Amount of flow is dependent on pintle or poppet position which is a direct result of the strength of the vacuum signal and valve type.

Pressure Feedback Electronic (PFE) EGR Valve – This valve consists of a conventional ported EGR valve which has a tube attached to it to sense backpressure. A pressure transducer is used with this valve to send an electrical signal to ECA, corresponding to amount of backpressure. The EGR flow is proportional to amount of pressure drop across the sensing tube.

EGR SYSTEM COMPONENTS

Backpressure Variable Transducer (BVT) – This remotely mounted regulator modulates the vacuum signal to the EGR valve. It is one of the components in the BVT EGR valve system. It uses 2 backpressure inputs to control vacuum supply to the EGR valve. One input is from the EGR valve control chamber, the other is downstream from the flow control orifice.

EGR Load Control (WOT) Valve – This valve dumps EGR vacuum at or near wide open throttle. This valve senses venturi vacuum at a

3-34

1989 EXHAUST EMISSION SYSTEMS
Ford Motor Co. EGR — Except Probe (Cont.)

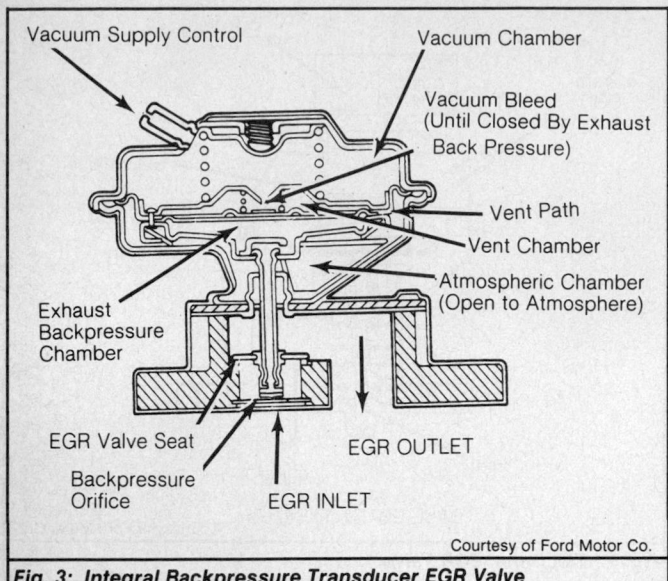

Fig. 3: Integral Backpressure Transducer EGR Valve

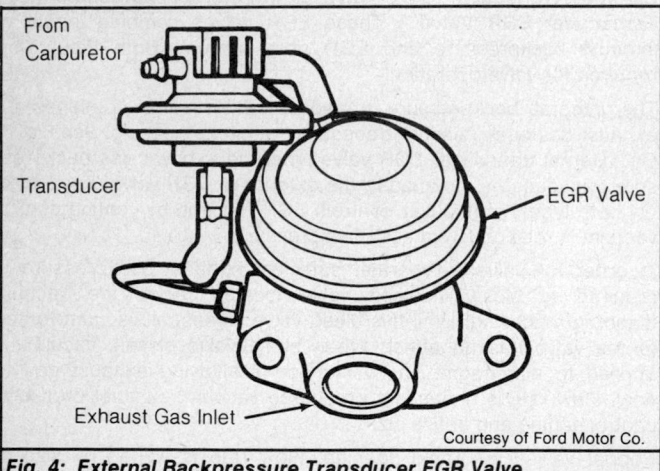

Fig. 4: External Backpressure Transducer EGR Valve

predetermined level and causes the EGR valve to close. When engine load is then reduced from wide open throttle, the EGR load control valve closes and completes the vacuum pathway to the EGR.

EGR Solenoid Vacuum Valve Assembly – This assembly consists of 2 solenoid valves, one to supply vacuum to the EGR valve when energized, the other vents EGR vacuum source to the atmosphere when de-energized. Solenoids are controlled by the ECA. The vacuum supply line has a restrictor in its inlet port to reduce its flow compared to the vent solenoid, which is unrestricted.

EGR Vacuum Control Valve Filter – This component is a small in-line filter that is inserted into the vent lines to protect the various system components which have a vent line open to the atmosphere.

EGR Valve Position Sensor (EVP) – The EVP is attached to the top of the EGR valve. It measures the amount the EGR valve opens and sends a corresponding signal to the ECA. The ECA uses this signal to adjust EGR opening signal. The EVP sensor is removable from the EGR valve and is serviced separately.

EGR Vacuum Regulator – The EGR Vacuum Regulator (EVR) is a solenoid valve which controls vacuum output to EGR valve. The EVR replaces the EGR solenoid vacuum vent valve assembly. When EVR is energized, the vent closes and increases the vacuum level. As EVR duty cycle is increased, an increased vacuum signal goes to the EGR valve.

Pressure Feedback Electronic EGR Transducer – Converts exhaust pressure to a proportional analog electrical signal which is sent to the ECA. The ECA uses this signal to regulate EGR flow and control exhaust emissions.

Temperature Vacuum Switch (TVS) – Temperature vacuum switch is used to delay EGR operation to provide better cold engine driveability. Switch contains a normally open bi-metallic disc which allows free airflow in vacuum line. When closed, it blocks airflow by sealing against an "O" ring.

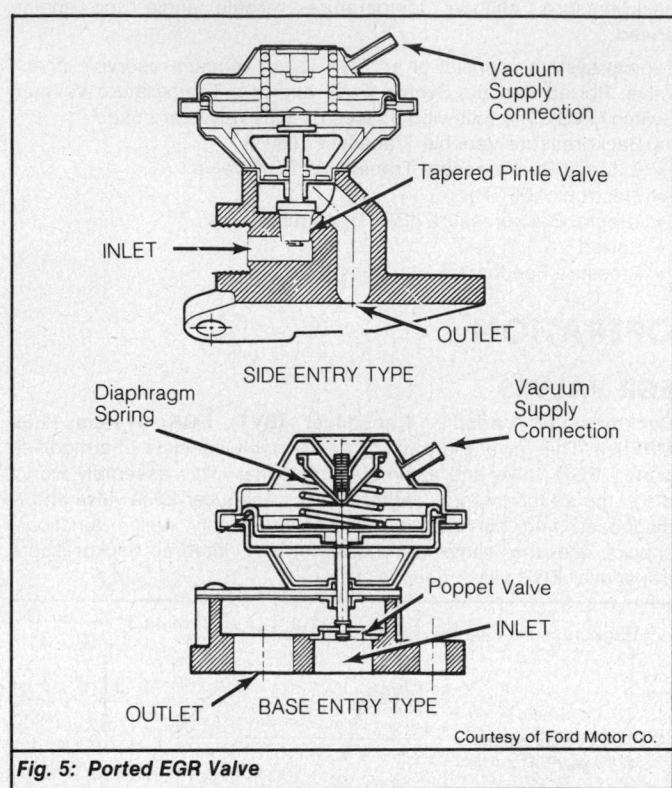

Fig. 5: Ported EGR Valve

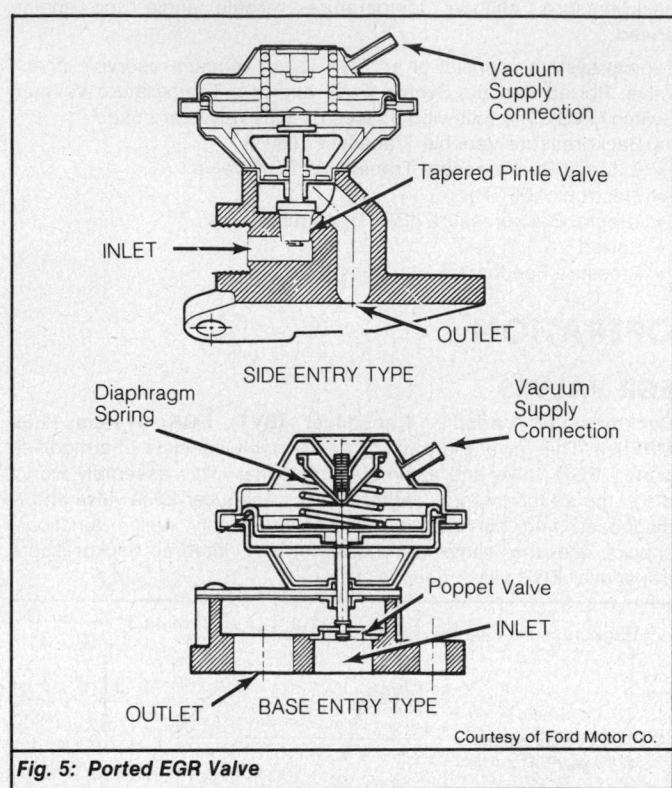

Fig. 6: Pressure Feedback Electronic (PFE) EGR Valve

TROUBLE SHOOTING

ENGINE STALLS ON DECELERATION (HOT OR COLD)

EGR valve stuck open, or not closing fully. BVT malfunction. EGR mounting flange gasket leaking or loose. Vacuum Control Valve (VCV) or TVS malfunction. Blocked or restricted EGR flow ports. WOT valve malfunction. Vacuum leak at EVP sensor. Idle speed too low. Ignition timing retarded.

ROUGH IDLE (HOT OR COLD)

EGR valve receiving vacuum from misrouted hoses. EGR valve not closing fully or stuck open, blown gasket or attachment loose, air bleeds plugged (backpressure valves). TVS or PVS opening too early when engine cold. EFI computer malfunction. Vacuum regulator leaking (BVT system). WOT valve malfunction. Idle set too low.

POOR PART THROTTLE PERFORMANCE (RUNS ROUGH, SURGES, HESITATES)

EGR valve stuck closed. BVT system malfunction. Leaky valve diaphragm or flange gasket. Vacuum restricted to EGR valve or EGR disconnected. TVS and/or PVS not opening, load control (WOT) valve venting or EGR passages blocked. Insufficient backpressure (exhaust leaks) to operate EGR system. EVP sensor "O" ring leaking or sensor loose (EEC). Ignition timing retarded.

SPARK KNOCK OR PING

EGR valve leaking at mounting or internally. Vacuum Control Valve (VCV) or TVS malfunction. Plugged or restricted passage ways or ports. Exhaust leaks provide insufficient backpressure to activate valve. Ignition timing too far advanced.

ENGINE STALLS AT IDLE (COLD)

EGR valve leaking at mounting or internally. PVS or TVS malfunction. Ignition timing retarded. BVT system malfunction. Idle speed too low. Vacuum leak at EVP sensor. WOT valve malfunction.

ENGINE STALLS AT IDLE (HOT)

EGR valve leaking at mounting or internally. PVS or TVS malfunction. Ignition timing retarded. Idle speed too low. Vacuum leak at EVP sensor. WOT valve malfunction. Blocked or restricted passageways

VERY LOW POWER AT FULL THROTTLE

Load control (WOT) valve not venting or EGR valve stuck open. EGR mounting gasket leaking. Vacuum leak at EVP sensor. BVT system malfunction. Ignition timing retarded. Blocked or restricted passageways

POOR FUEL ECONOMY

NOTE: If EGR related, poor fuel economy is usually accompanied by detonation or other symptom of restricted or no EGR flow.

EGR valve leaking at mounting or internally. PVS or TVS malfunction. Ignition timing retarded. BVT system malfunction. Vacuum leak at EVP sensor. WOT valve malfunction. Blocked EGR passages or ports. Insufficient exhaust backpressure to operate EGR valve.

TESTING

EGR VALVES

Backpressure Variable Transducer (BVT) EGR System – 1) Ensure vacuum hoses are correctly routed and in serviceable condition. Start and ensure there is no vacuum to EGR valve at idle (engine at normal operating temperature). Install a tachometer.
2) Disconnect Idle Speed Control (ISC) connector (MPFI and SEFI engines). Disconnect and plug vacuum supply hose from EGR valve nipple. Ensure engine idle speed is within specification.
3) Using a hand pump, slowly apply 5-10 in. Hg vacuum to EGR valve. With vacuum applied, idle speed should drop about 100 RPM (engine may stall). If speed does not drop, replace EGR valve. If speed drops, release vacuum and ensure engine speed returns to normal ±25 RPM.
4) Reconnect ISC connector and EGR supply hose. Disconnect vacuum connection at BVT. *See Fig. 7.* Lightly blow into hose to port "C" until relief valve closes and at the same time apply 5-10 in. Hg of

vacuum to port "E", using a hand vacuum pump. Port "E" should hold vacuum as long as there is pressure to port "C".
5) Apply 5-10 in. Hg vacuum to ports "B" and "C". These ports should hold vacuum. Replace transducer if any ports do not hold vacuum. Reconnect vacuum hoses to BVT ports.

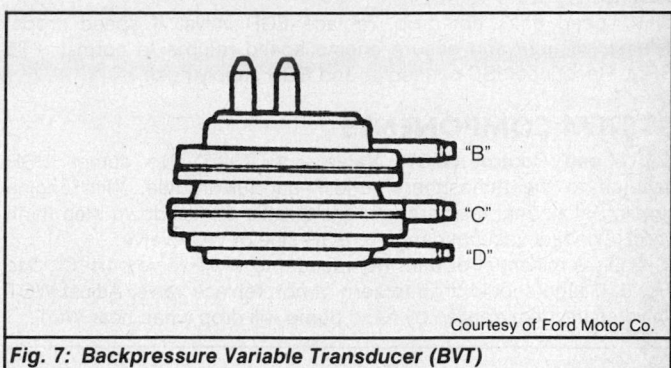

Courtesy of Ford Motor Co.

Fig. 7: Backpressure Variable Transducer (BVT)

Electronic (EEGR) EGR Valve – 1) Ensure vacuum hoses are correctly routed and in serviceable condition. Start engine and ensure there is less than 2.5 in. Hg of vacuum to EGR valve at idle (engine at normal operating temperature). Install a tachometer.

NOTE: The EVR control solenoid has a small constant vent leak. The vacuum signal to the EGR valve should be less than 1.0 in. Hg at idle.

2) Disconnect ISC (Air By-pass Valve) connector (1.9L SEFI engines). Disconnect and plug vacuum supply hose from EGR valve nipple. Ensure engine idle speed is within specification. Using a hand pump, slowly apply 5-10 in. Hg vacuum to EGR valve nipple.
3) Replace EGR valve if engine does not stall, idle speed does not drop 100 RPM (minimum) or idle speed does not return to normal when vacuum is removed.
4) Reconnect ISC. Reconnect EGR valve vacuum supply.

External Backpressure Transducer EGR Valve & Integral Backpressure (IBP) Transducer EGR Valve – 1) Ensure vacuum hoses are correctly routed and in serviceable condition. There should be no vacuum to EGR valve at idle (engine at normal operating temperature). Install a tachometer.
2) Plug the exhaust tailpipe(s) to increase exhaust backpressure for testing purposes. Leave a 1/2" hole to allow exhaust gases to escape. Disconnect and plug vacuum supply hose from EGR valve nipple. Do not disconnect external transducer from the EGR valve (if equipped). Start engine and ensure engine idle speed is within specification.
3) Using a hand pump, slowly apply 5-10 in. Hg vacuum to EGR valve. With vacuum applied, idle speed should drop about 100 RPM (engine may stall). If speed does not drop, replace EGR valve. If speed drops, release vacuum and ensure engine speed returns to normal ±25 RPM.
4) Reconnect EGR supply hose. Remove plugs from exhaust tailpipe.
Ported EGR Valve – 1) Ensure vacuum hoses are correctly routed and in serviceable condition. There should be no vacuum to EGR valve at idle (engine at normal operating temperature). Disconnect ISC connector. Install a tachometer.
2) Disconnect and plug vacuum supply hose from EGR valve nipple. Start engine and ensure engine idle speed is within specification. Using a hand pump, slowly apply 5-10 in. Hg vacuum to EGR valve. With vacuum applied, idle speed should drop about 100 RPM (engine may stall).
3) If speed does not drop, replace EGR valve. If speed drops, release vacuum and ensure engine speed returns to normal ±25 RPM. Reconnect ISC connector and EGR supply hose.
Pressure Feedback Electronic (PFE) EGR Valve – 1) Ensure vacuum hoses are correctly routed and in serviceable condition. There should be no vacuum to EGR valve at idle (engine at normal operating temperature). Disconnect ISC connector. Install a tachometer.

3-36

1989 EXHAUST EMISSION SYSTEMS
Ford Motor Co. EGR — Except Probe (Cont.)

2) Disconnect and plug vacuum supply hose from EGR valve nipple. Start engine and ensure engine idle speed is within specification. Using a hand pump, slowly apply 5-10 in. Hg vacuum to EGR valve. With vacuum applied, idle speed should drop about 100 RPM (engine may stall).

3) If speed does not drop, replace EGR valve. If speed drops, release vacuum and ensure engine speed returns to normal ±25 RPM. Reconnect ISC connector and EGR supply hose.

SYSTEM COMPONENTS

EGR Load Control (WOT) Valve – 1) This valve dumps EGR vacuum to the atmosphere at or near full throttle. With engine running at normal temperature, set throttle on kickdown step (high cam). Connect vacuum gauge to EGR side of WOT valve.

2) Apply a minimum of 6 in. Hg vacuum to WOT valve port "C". *See Fig. 8.* Gauge should drop to zero. If not, replace valve. Adjust WOT valve so vacuum applied by hand pump will drop when near WOT.

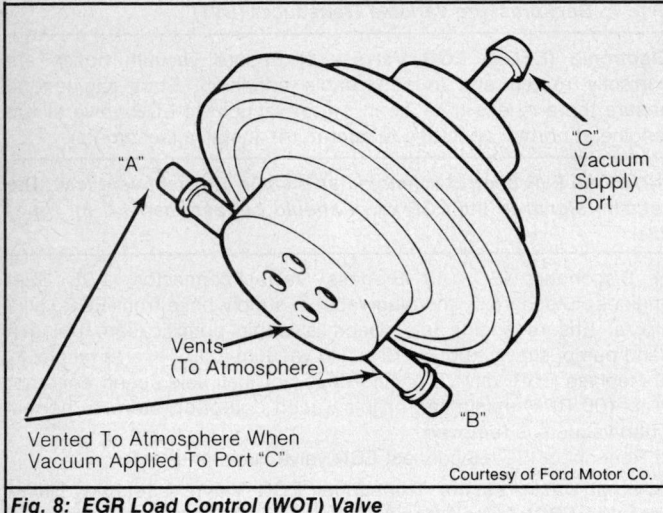

Courtesy of Ford Motor Co.

Fig. 8: EGR Load Control (WOT) Valve

EGR Solenoid Vacuum Valve Assembly – 1) The resistance of each solenoid should be 32-64 ohms. Replace any solenoid which is not in this resistance range. The vent valve should allow flow when the solenoid is de-energized.

2) The control valve should allow flow when the solenoid is energized. The valves may have a very small leakage rate during testing.

EGR Valve Position Sensor (EVP) – For EVP sensor testing procedures, see appropriate article in COMPUTERIZED ENGINE CONTROLS section.

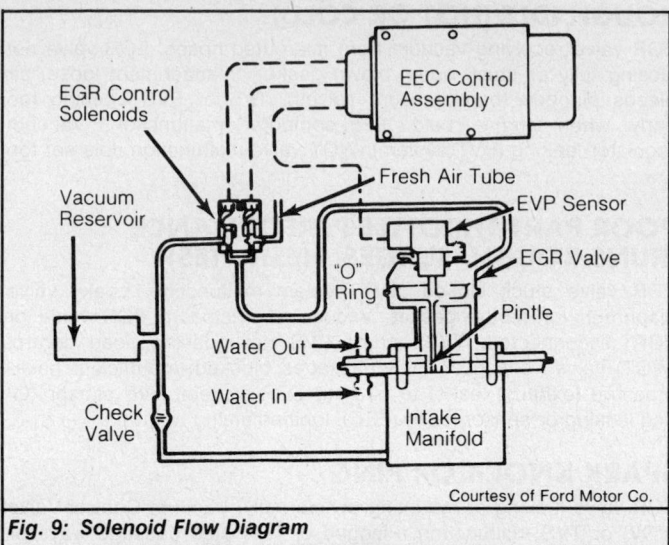

Courtesy of Ford Motor Co.

Fig. 9: Solenoid Flow Diagram

Pressure Feedback Electronic (PFE) EGR Transducer – For PFE EGR transducer testing procedure, see appropriate article in COMPUTERIZED ENGINE CONTROLS section.

Temperature Vacuum Switch (TVS) – Using a vacuum pump, apply 16 in. Hg of vacuum to the motor side of the switch. Ensure vacuum switch meets specifications. See VACUUM SWITCH SPECIFICATIONS table.

VACUUM SWITCH SPECIFICATIONS [1]

Color Switch Closes F° (C°)	Switch Opens F° (C°)
White	
50 (10)	Above 76 (24.4)
Brown	
15 (-9)	Above 30 (-1)
Red	
60 (18)	Below 50 (10)
Purple	
40 (4)	Above 55 (13)

[1] – Must hold a minimum of 5 in. Hg vacuum for 30 seconds.

EGR Solenoid Vacuum Valve Assembly – With the solenoid disconnected, check the resistance between the solenoid terminals. Resistance should be 51-108 ohms. Replace solenoid if not to specification. Ports should allow flow of air when solenoid is energized. Operational signal for solenoid is supplied by the ECA.

DESCRIPTION

The Exhaust Gas Recirculation (EGR) system distributes exhaust gas into the intake mixture. This lowers combustion temperatures due to lower concentrations of oxygen. Lowering of combustion temperatures reduces amount of NOx emissions. The non-turbocharged engine EGR is vacuum controlled and the turbocharged engine uses electrical control. *See Fig. 1.*

OPERATION

On non-turbocharged engines, amount of exhaust gas recirculation is controlled by ported vacuum and exhaust gas pressure. The EGR valve should be closed when any one of the following conditions is met: sudden acceleration, sudden deceleration, closed throttle deceleration, idle, radiator coolant below 63°F (17°C), engine coolant below 158°F (70°C) or engine speed below 1500 RPM.

On turbocharged engines, amount of exhaust gas recirculation is controlled by engine conditions. The EGR valve will be half closed during sudden acceleration. The EGR valve will be fully closed when any one of the following conditions is met: throttle plate is closed, sudden deceleration, radiator coolant below 63°F (17°C) or engine coolant below 104°F (40°C).

EGR SYSTEM COMPONENTS

EGR Backpressure Variable Transducer – The EGR backpressure variable transducer modulates EGR vacuum so amount of gas flow is in proportion to throttle opening. It does this by sensing exhaust backpressure and bleeding off some of the vacuum when backpressure is low. Since exhaust pressure depends on engine load, it is equivalent to throttle opening signal.

The EGR backpressure variable transducer is mounted just above the EGR valve.

EGR Control Solenoid Valve – There are 2 different EGR control solenoids used on turbocharged and non-turbocharged engines.

The turbocharged engine uses a dual type EGR control solenoid. One is a vacuum valve which supplies vacuum to the EGR valve when energized, and the second is a vent valve which vents the EGR valve vacuum to atmosphere when de-energized. Both solenoid valves receive variable duty cycle signals from the ECA according to EGR requirements.

The non-turbocharged engine uses a single EGR control solenoid. The solenoid supplies vacuum to the EGR valve when de-energized and vents vacuum through its air filter when energized. It also receives a signal from the ECA according to EGR requirements. Both turbocharged and non-turbocharged EGR solenoid valves are mounted on the firewall.

EGR Valve – The turbocharged engine uses an electronic EGR valve where EGR flow is controlled according to ECA demands by means of an EGR valve position sensor attached to the valve. The EGR valve is operated by a vacuum signal from EGR control solenoid valve.

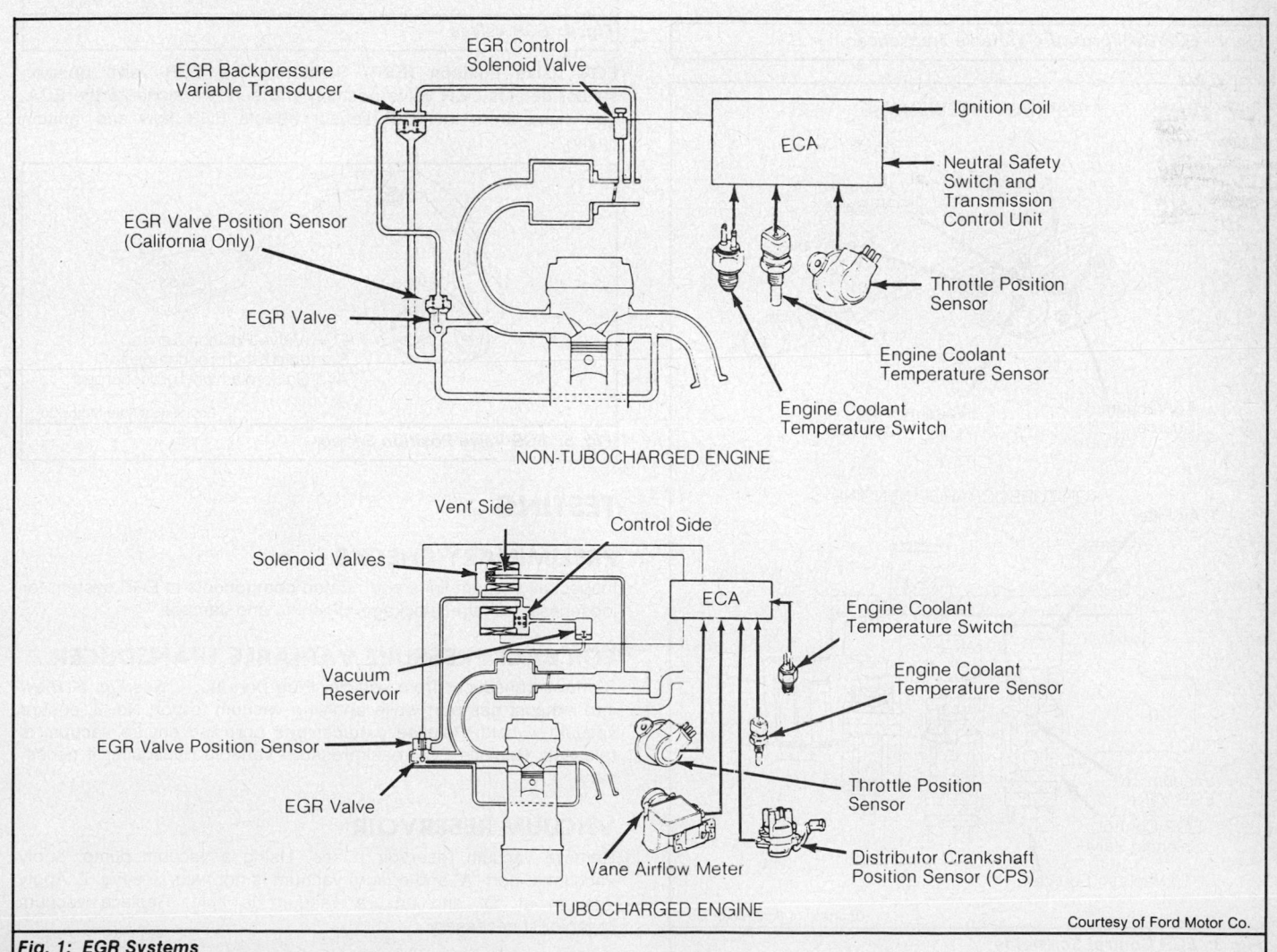

NON-TUBOCHARGED ENGINE

TUBOCHARGED ENGINE

Courtesy of Ford Motor Co.

Fig. 1: *EGR Systems*

3-38

1989 EXHAUST EMISSION SYSTEMS
Ford Motor Co. EGR — Probe (Cont.)

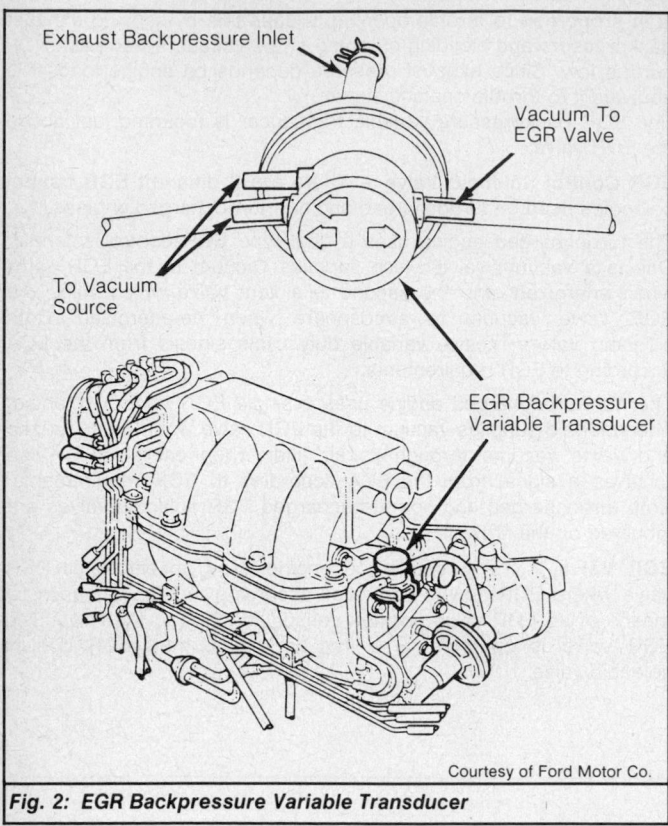

Fig. 2: EGR Backpressure Variable Transducer

The non-turbocharged engine incorporates a modified ported EGR valve and a remote backpressure transducer where the EGR vacuum applied to EGR valve is modulated by sensing exhaust backpressure and bleeding off some vacuum when the backpressure is low. This provides EGR flow proportional to engine load. Vacuum supplied to EGR transducer is controlled by an EGR control solenoid valve.

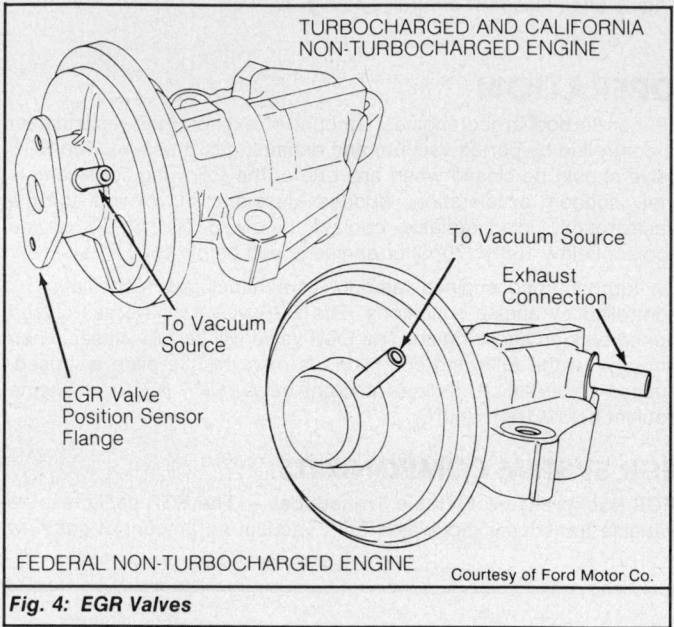

Fig. 4: EGR Valves

EGR Valve Position (EVP) Sensor – The EGR valve position sensor detects EGR valve position and sends a signal to the ECA. The signal from the EVP sensor affects EGR flow and ignition timing.

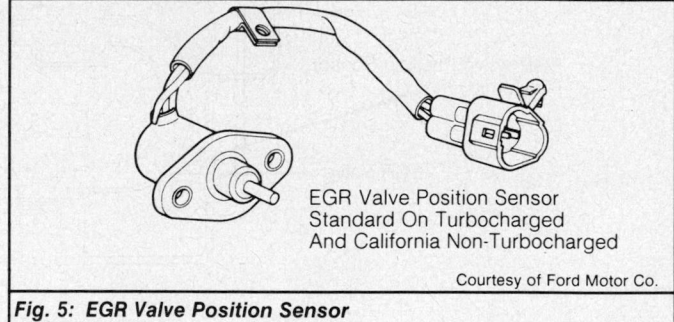

Fig. 5: EGR Valve Position Sensor

Fig. 3: EGR Control Solenoids

TESTING

PRELIMINARY CHECKS
Inspect all vacuum lines and related components in EGR system for looseness, leakage, blockage, pinching and damage.

EGR BACKPRESSURE VARIABLE TRANSDUCER
Remove transducer from vehicle. Plug port No. 1. *See Fig. 6.* Blow into exhaust gas port while applying vacuum to port No. 3, ensure vacuum is held. Release exhaust gas port and ensure vacuum is released. Replace EGR backpressure variable transducer if necessary.

VACUUM RESERVOIR
Remove vacuum reservoir hoses. Using a vacuum pump, apply vacuum at port "A" and ensure vacuum is not held. *See Fig. 7.* Apply vacuum at "B" and ensure vacuum is held. Replace vacuum reservoir if necessary.

1989 EXHAUST EMISSION SYSTEMS
Ford Motor Co. EGR — Probe (Cont.)

3-39

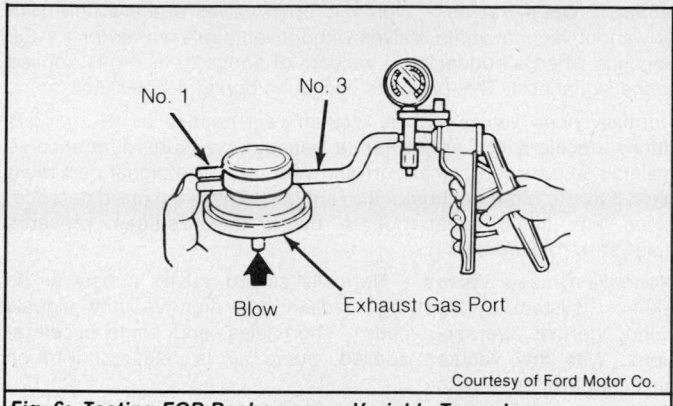

Fig. 6: Testing EGR Backpressure Variable Transducer

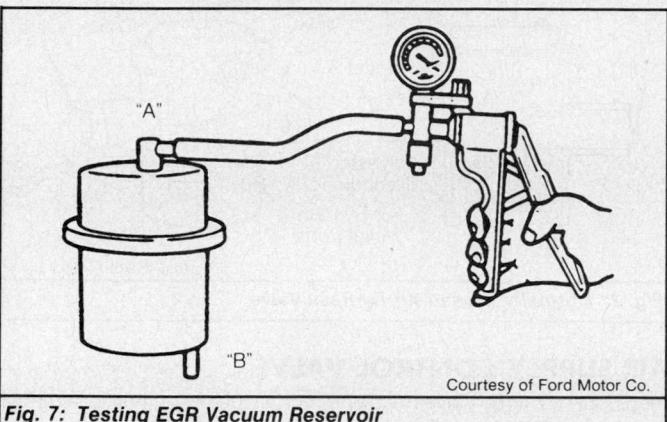

Fig. 7: Testing EGR Vacuum Reservoir

EGR VENT SOLENOID VALVE

Disconnect vacuum hoses and solenoid valve connection. Blow through vent hose "B" and verify that air flows. Apply 12 volts and ground the connector. See Fig. 8. Blow through the vent hose and ensure air does not flow. Replace EGR control solenoid valve if necessary.

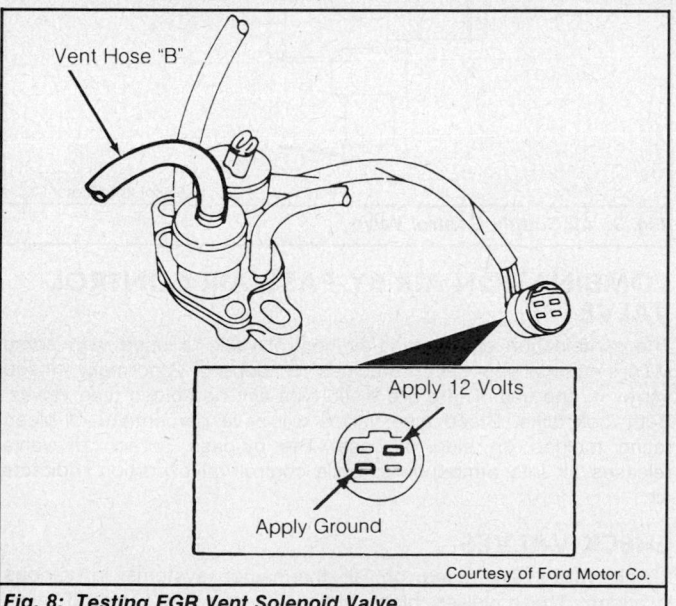

Fig. 8: Testing EGR Vent Solenoid Valve

EGR VALVE

Manually move the valve diaphram and ensure valve moves freely and spring resistance is present. With engine at operating temperature and idling, apply vacuum to the valve. Ensure engine runs roughly at 1.6-2.4 in. Hg of vacuum and stalls at any greater vacuum. Replace EGR valve if necessary.

EGR SHUTOFF SOLENOID

With vacuum hoses and solenoid valve connections disconnected, blow through vacuum hose at port "A" and ensure that air flows from port "B". Apply 12 volts and ground to connections. See Fig. 9. Blow through vacuum hose and verify air flows from the filter. Replace valve if necessary.

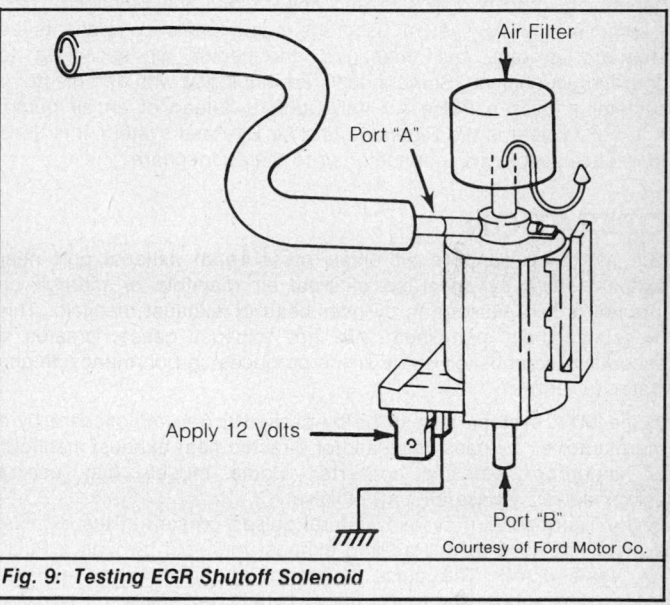

Fig. 9: Testing EGR Shutoff Solenoid

NOTE: For further testing, see PROBE COMPUTERIZED ENGINE CONTROL article.

1989 EXHAUST EMISSION SYSTEMS
Ford Motor Co. Thermactor Systems

All 5.0L Engines, Continental 3.8L, Escort 1.9L HO, Police 5.8L, Taurus 2.5L, Sable 3.8L, Taurus 3.8L, Tempo, Topaz

DESCRIPTION

The Thermactor Exhaust Emission Control system reduces carbon monoxide (CO) and hydrocarbon (HC) content of exhaust gases. It injects fresh air into the exhaust gas stream which continues combustion of unburned gases. A typical system consists of an air supply pump, air by-pass valve, centrifugal filter, check valve(s), air control valve, air manifold and air hoses.

Individual systems may vary in number and type of components, depending upon engine size and application. The Managed Thermactor Air (MTA) system uses the same basic components as standard system, but "manages" thermactor air according to operating conditions. Some models are equipped with Thermactor II system. It uses a Pulse Air Valve (PAV) instead of an air pump. Another system is the Extended Idle Air By-Pass system, it is used to release secondary thermactor air to the atmosphere.

OPERATION

The air pump supplies air under pressure to exhaust port near exhaust valve by either an external air manifold or through an internal drilled passage in cylinder head or exhaust manifold. This pressurized air, combined with hot exhaust gases, creates a secondary combustion stage which produces carbon monoxide and water.

In the MTA system, air can be by-passed to the atmosphere by a thermactor air by-pass valve and/or directed near exhaust manifold, or underbody catalytic converter. Some models may use a combined air by-pass/air control valve.

In the Thermactor II system, natural pulses present in the exhaust system are used to pull air into exhaust manifold through a Pulse Air Valve (PAV). The pulse air valve is connected to exhaust manifold by a tube, and to air cleaner by a hose.

In the Extended Idle Air By-Pass system, a normally closed Idle Tracking Switch (ITS) opens when throttle returns to idle. The ITS signals EEC module to activate by-pass solenoid valve which causes thermactor secondary air to be released into atmosphere.

AIR PUMP

The air pump is a belt-driven, positive displacement, vane type pump. It is available in 11 and 19 cu. in. sizes. Either pump may be driven with different pulley ratios for different applications. Air is received from a remote silencer/filter attached to air inlet nipple of pump or through a centrifugal fan on front of the pump. The by-pass valve performs pressure relief.

AIR BY-PASS VALVES

The 2 types of air by-pass valves are those normally open and those normally closed. These valves may be mounted in-line or directly to air pump.

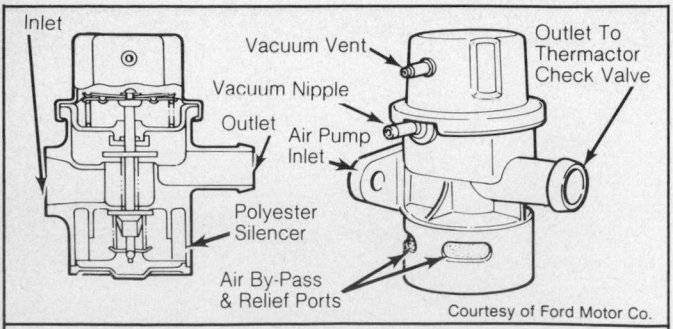

Fig. 1: Normally Open Air By-Pass Valve

Normally Open Valves – Normally open valves are available with or without vacuum vents. Valves without vents release air for 1.1-2.8 seconds when a sudden high vacuum of about 20 in. Hg is applied to the signal port. This prevents backfiring during deceleration.

Normally open valves with a vacuum vent release air at intervals during deceleration, and when a vacuum pressure difference is maintained between signal port and vent port. The signal port must have 3 in. Hg more vacuum than vent port. The pressure difference, along with timed release of air during these stages, prevents catalyst from overheating.

Normally Closed Valves – Normally closed valves supply air to exhaust system by applying medium and high vacuum signals during normal operating modes, short idles, and some accelerations. With low vacuum applied, pump air is released through silencer ports of valve.

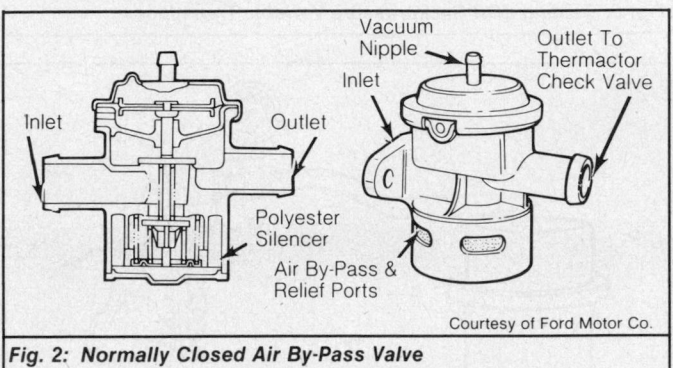

Fig. 2: Normally Closed Air By-Pass Valve

AIR SUPPLY CONTROL VALVE

Air Supply Control Valves (ACV) direct air pump output to exhaust manifold or catalyst, depending upon engine control system.

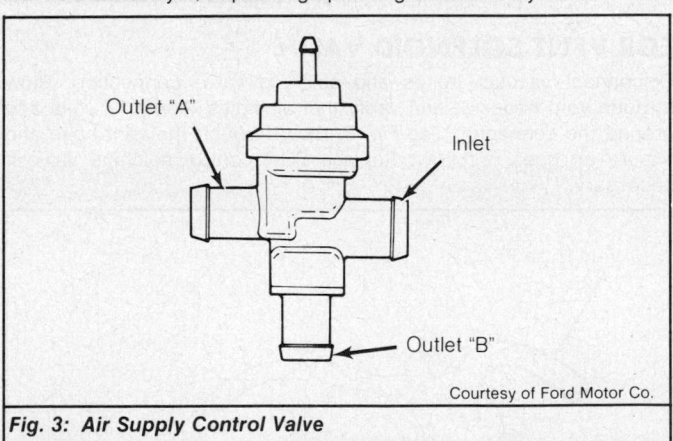

Fig. 3: Air Supply Control Valve

COMBINATION AIR BY-PASS/AIR CONTROL VALVE

The combination air by-pass/air control valve is used with some MTA systems. The valve combines functions of 2 normally closed valves in one unit. There are bleed type and non-bleed type valves. Both look alike. Bleed type valves will have percentage of bleed rating molded on side of case. The by-pass portion of valve releases air into atmosphere, while control valve portion redirects air.

CHECK VALVES

Check valves are used on all thermactor systems in various locations. These valves block airflow in one direction and allow airflow in the other direction.

1989 EXHAUST EMISSION SYSTEMS
Ford Motor Co. Thermactor Systems (Cont.)

3-41

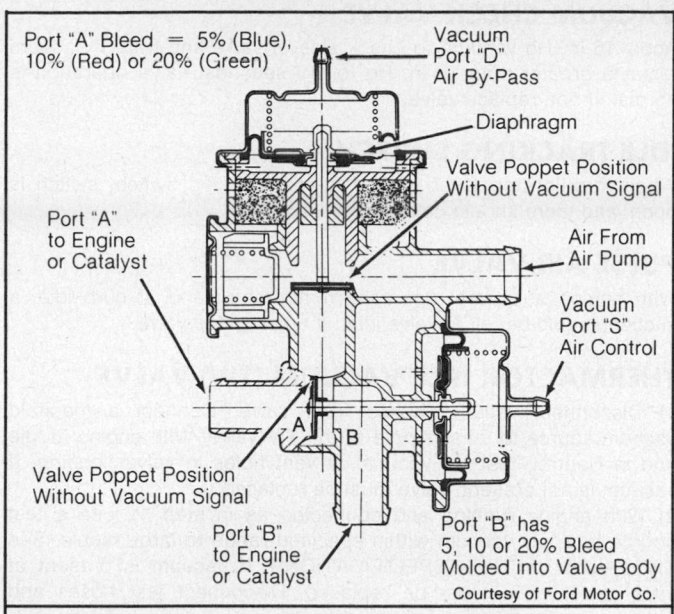

Port "A" Bleed = 5% (Blue), 10% (Red) or 20% (Green)

Vacuum Port "D" Air By-Pass

Diaphragm

Valve Poppet Position Without Vacuum Signal

Port "A" to Engine or Catalyst

Air From Air Pump

Vacuum Port "S" Air Control

Valve Poppet Position Without Vacuum Signal

Port "B" to Engine or Catalyst

Port "B" has 5, 10 or 20% Bleed Molded into Valve Body

Courtesy of Ford Motor Co.

Fig. 4: Combination Air By-Pass/Air Control Valve

IDLE TRACKING SWITCH

5.8L V8 Engine – The Idle Tracking Switch (ITS), located on carburetor, is a mechanically operated electric switch held open by throttle linkage when throttle is closed. It is used on the Extended Idle Air By-Pass system.

When ITS is opened, EEC module is signaled to deactivate the normally closed solenoid. When this happens, vacuum is removed from normally closed by-pass valve and thermactor air is released into atmosphere.

PULSE AIR VALVE

The Pulse Air Valve (PAV) replaces the air pump on some thermactor systems. It permits air to be drawn into exhaust system by vacuum created by exiting exhaust pulse. This allows fresh air to complete oxidation of exhaust gases and blocks backflow of high pressure exhaust pulses.

DUAL THERMACTOR AIR CONTROL SOLENOID VALVE ASSEMBLY

The dual thermactor air control solenoid valve assembly consists of 2 normally closed solenoid valves with vents, one controls thermactor air by-pass valve and the other controls thermactor diverter valve. Both valves pass air when deactivated and do not pass air when activated.

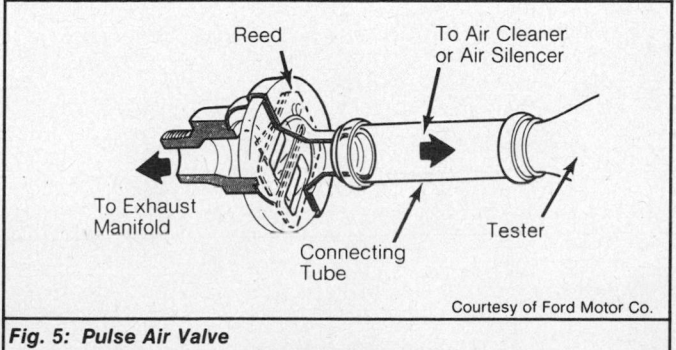

Reed

To Air Cleaner or Air Silencer

To Exhaust Manifold

Connecting Tube

Tester

Courtesy of Ford Motor Co.

Fig. 5: Pulse Air Valve

ANTI-BACKFIRE (GULP) VALVE

The anti-backfire valve, located downstream from the air by-pass valve, diverts a portion of thermactor air to intake manifold during periods of sudden decrease of intake manifold pressure.

AIR SILENCER/FILTER

The air silencer, mounted in engine compartment, is a combination silencer and filter for the Pulse Air (PA) system, or for an air supply pump not equipped with an impeller type centrifugal air filter fan. It is connected to system by means of a flexible hose.

ELECTRONIC CONTROL ASSEMBLY

The Electronic Control Assembly (ECA), is the center of the EEC-IV system. It receives information from sensors, evaluates data and sends signals to various relays, solenoids, and other actuators to control system output.

THERMACTOR IDLE VACUUM (TIV) VALVE

The Thermactor Idle Vacuum (TIV) valve vents the vacuum signal to atmosphere when preset manifold vacuum or pressure is exceeded. During periods of extended idle conditions, this valve is used to divert thermactor airflow to limit exhaust temperature, and to cut EGR in a heavy boost mode for turbocharged applications.

TESTING

AIR PUMP

Check belt tension and adjust to specification. Disconnect air supply hose from control valve. Observe airflow from pump outlet with engine running. Flow should increase as engine speed is increased.

AIR BY-PASS VALVE

Normally Open Valve Without Vacuum Vent – 1) With engine at normal operating temperature, parking brake applied, and transmission in Park or Neutral, disconnect air supply line at valve outlet. Disconnect vacuum line at vacuum nipple.
2) With engine at 1500 RPM, air should be heard and felt at valve outlet. Connect a direct vacuum line from any manifold vacuum source to vacuum nipple on valve. Air at outlet should be momentarily decreased. Air pump supply air should be heard at silencer ports.
3) Reconnect vacuum and thermactor lines. If valve fails any test and air pump functions properly, replace valve.

Normally Open Valve With Vacuum Vent – 1) With engine at normal operating temperature, parking brake applied, and transmission in Park or Neutral, disconnect air supply line at valve outlet. Disconnect all vacuum lines from vacuum nipple and vent.
2) With engine at 1500 RPM, air pump supply should be heard and felt at outlet. Connect a vacuum line from vacuum nipple to one of vacuum fittings on intake manifold. With vacuum vent open to atmosphere and engine speed at 1500 RPM, no air should be felt at outlet since all air is by-passed through silencer ports.
3) Using same direct line to an intake manifold vacuum source, cap vacuum vent. Increase engine speed to 2000 RPM and suddenly release throttle. A momentary interruption of air pump supply should be felt at valve outlet.
4) If valve fails any test and air pump is operating properly, replace valve. Reconnect all vacuum and thermactor lines.

Normally Closed Valve – 1) With engine at normal operating temperature, parking brake applied and transmission in Park or Neutral, disconnect air supply line at valve outlet. Remove vacuum line and ensure that a vacuum signal is present at nipple.
2) Remove any delay valves or restrictors in line. Vacuum must be present at nipple before proceeding. With engine speed at 1500 RPM and vacuum line connected to nipple, air pump supply air should be heard and felt at outlet.
3) With engine at 1500 RPM, disconnect vacuum line. Air at outlet should be significantly decreased or shut off. Air pump supply air should be heard or felt at silencer ports.
4) If valve fails any test and air pump is operating properly, replace valve. Reconnect all vacuum lines.

3-42

1989 EXHAUST EMISSION SYSTEMS
Ford Motor Co. Thermactor Systems (Cont.)

COMBINATION AIR BY-PASS/AIR CONTROL VALVE

Normally Closed Valve With Or Without Bleed – 1) With engine at normal operating temperature, parking brake applied and transmission in Park or Neutral, disconnect hoses from ports "A" and "B". *See Fig. 4.* Disconnect and plug line to port "D". With engine speed at 1500 RPM, air should flow from by-pass vents.

2) Reconnect line to port "D". Disconnect and plug line to port "S". Ensure vacuum is present in line to port "D". With engine speed at 1500 RPM, air should flow from port "B" and no air should flow from port "A".

3) Apply 8-10 in. Hg vacuum to port "S". With engine speed at 1500 RPM, air should flow from port "A". If valve has a vacuum bleed, some lesser amount of air will flow from port "A" or "B" and main discharge will change when vacuum is applied to port "S".

4) If valve fails any test, it must be replaced. Reconnect all vacuum hoses.

AIR SUPPLY CONTROL VALVE

1) Verify that air is being supplied to valve inlet by disconnecting inlet supply hose. Disconnect hoses at valve outlets "A", "B" and at vacuum nipple. With engine speed at 1500 RPM, airflow should be heard and felt at valve outlet "B" and little or no air at valve outlet "A". *See Fig. 3.*

2) Using a direct vacuum line from manifold vacuum source, connect line to vacuum nipple. Airflow should be detected at valve outlet "A" and little or no air at valve outlet "B". If valve fails any test, replace valve. Reconnect all lines.

VACUUM CHECK VALVE

Apply 16 in. Hg vacuum to check side of valve and trap. If vacuum remains greater than 15 in. Hg for 10 seconds, valve operation is normal. If not, replace valve.

IDLE TRACKING SWITCH

When throttle stop lever is against idle tracking switch, switch is open, and there should be no continuity.

PULSE AIR VALVE

With engine at normal operating temperature and at curb idle, a suction should be felt at valve inlet. If not, replace valve.

THERMACTOR IDLE VACUUM (TIV) VALVE

1) Disconnect vacuum hoses from valve. Connect a manifold vacuum source to small nipple of the TIV valve. With engine at idle and in Neutral, test for vacuum at vent holes in valve housing. If vacuum is not present, valve must be replaced.

2) With engine running and connected as in step **1)**, use a test source to apply vacuum within specified range to large nipple. See TIV VALVE VACUUM SPECIFICATIONS. If vacuum is present at vent holes, valve must be replaced. Disconnect test hoses and reconnect original hoses.

TIV VALVE VACUUM SPECIFICATIONS

Application Color/Letters	Vacuum In. Hg
Ash (Gray)	1.5-3.0
Red	3.5-4.5
TUR (Decal Code)	1.5-2.5

Except Probe

DESCRIPTION

The Evaporative Emission Control System (EECS) is designed to prevent fuel vapors (hydrocarbons) from being emitted from the fuel system into atmosphere. The system consists of a sealed fuel tank, pressure/vacuum relief fuel cap, fuel tank vapor valve, vapor tube and hoses, and a carbon canister.

Carbureted Engines – Carbureted engines are equipped with a fuel bowl solenoid vent valve, purge control valve, canister purge regulator valve, vacuum/thermostatic bowl vent valve, thermal vent valve and vacuum bowl vent valve. Carbon canister is purged by drawing vapors into intake manifold.

Fuel Injected Engines – Fuel injected engines are equipped with an in-line purge solenoid or a purge valve. Carbon canister is purged by drawing vapors into air cleaner.

NOTE: *Not all listed components are used on any one system. Component usage depends on calibration of complete vehicle.*

OPERATION

FILL CONTROL/VENT SYSTEM

Fill limiting is accomplished through configuration of fill neck and/or internal vent lines within fill neck and tank. Vent system is designed to permit air space in 10-12 percent of tank when tank is filled to capacity. Air space provides for thermal expansion of fuel as well as being an aid to in-tank vapor vent system.

VAPOR VENT SYSTEM

System provides a vapor space above gasoline surface in fuel tank. This area is sufficient to permit adequate breathing space for tank vapor valve assembly.

All vapor valves are mounted on fuel tank and use a small orifice that allows only vapor and not liquid fuel to pass into line running to canister.

Fuel vapors trapped in sealed fuel tank are vented though vapor valve assembly on top of fuel tank. Vapors are routed through a single vapor line to carbon canister in engine compartment.

Vapors are stored in carbon canister until they are purged into engine while engine is operating.

On vehicles equipped with fuel/vapor return lines, vapor generated in fuel supply line is continuously vented back to fuel tank. Venting prevents engine surging from fuel enrichment and assists in hydrocarbon emission control.

CARBON CANISTER

Fuel vapors from fuel tank and carburetor bowl are stored in carbon-filled canister. There are 2 different canister sizes used: .97 qts. (.93L) and 1.5 qts. (1.4L).

CARBURETOR VENTING

Fuel vapors which might otherwise collect in carburetor bowl and pass directly into atmosphere are vented to carbon canister when engine is stopped. Flow of vapors is controlled by a fuel bowl vent valve or a fuel bowl thermal vent valve.

When engine is started, vapors will be drawn into engine for burning. The time at which vapors are drawn into engine will depend on operating mode of engine, when purging system is most efficient.

PURGE CONTROL VALVE

Purge control valve, located in line with carbon canister, controls flow of fuel vapors from carbon canister to intake manifold. *See Fig. 1.* Air should not flow through PCV purge line port, unless more than 16 in. Hg vacuum is applied to carburetor vacuum port.

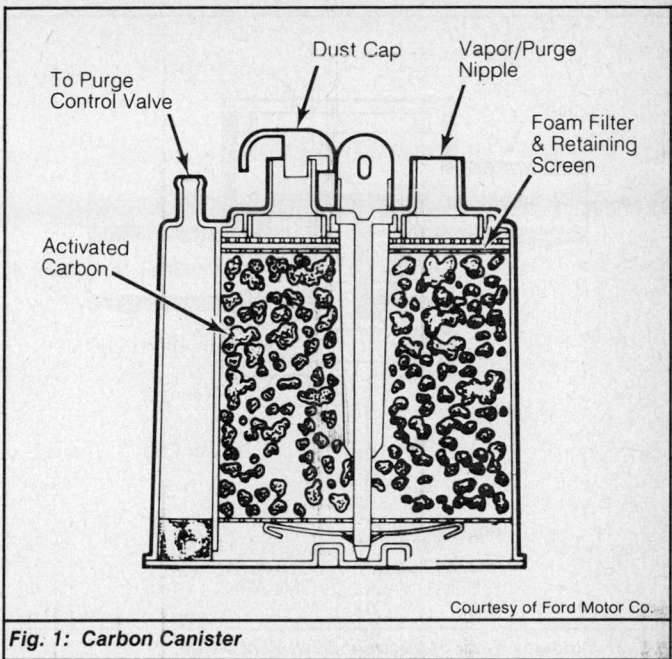

Courtesy of Ford Motor Co.

Fig. 1: Carbon Canister

PURGE CONTROL SOLENOID VALVE

Purge control solenoid valve controls vapor flow from canister to intake manifold. Being normally closed, it is opened by a signal from Electronic Control Assembly (ECA).

FUEL BOWL SOLENOID VENT VALVE

Fuel bowl solenoid vent valve, located in fuel bowl vent line, is normally open. It is used on Motorcraft 7200 carburetors. These carburetors are equipped with a built-in fuel bowl vent valve.

When ignition is turned on, vent valve closes fuel bowl vent line and returns to normal open position when ignition is turned off.

NOTE: *If carburetor displays a lean air/fuel mixture condition, inspect either purge solenoid valve or fuel bowl solenoid valve for proper closing during engine operation.*

NOTE: *On EECS equipped vehicles with 7200 carburetors, a rich air/fuel mixture will result from an open or leaking valve.*

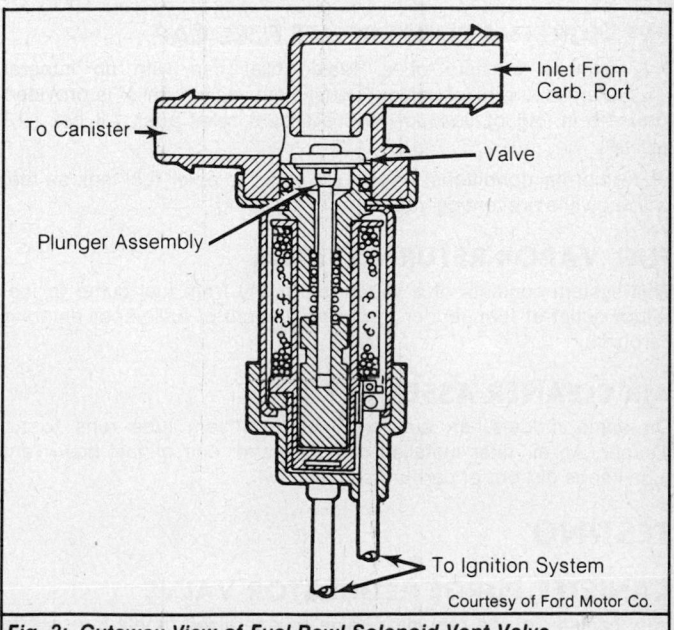

Courtesy of Ford Motor Co.

Fig. 2: Cutaway View of Fuel Bowl Solenoid Vent Valve

3-44

1989 EXHAUST EMISSION SYSTEMS
Ford Motor Co. Fuel Evaporation Systems (Cont.)

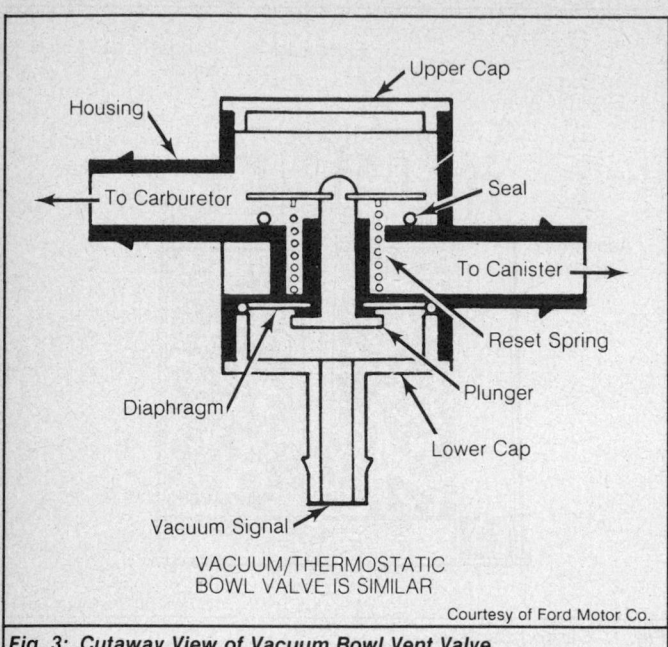

Fig. 3: Cutaway View of Vacuum Bowl Vent Valve

FUEL BOWL THERMAL VENT VALVE

Thermal vent valve, located in carburetor-to-canister vent line, is closed when engine compartment temperature is cold. This prevents fuel tank vapors, generated when fuel tank heats up before engine compartment does, from being vented through carburetor fuel bowl.

VACUUM BOWL VALVE & VACUUM/THERMOSTATIC BOWL VALVE

Vacuum bowl valve and vacuum/thermostatic bowl valve, similar in appearance, are located in carburetor-to-canister vent line, and are vacuum and vacuum/temperature operated "ON/OFF" valves.

Vacuum bowl valve remains open, until manifold vacuum (when engine is operating) causes it to close. Vacuum/thermostatic bowl vent remains closed with temperature less than 90° F (32° C) and open with temperature greater than 120° F (48° C), unless closed by manifold vacuum.

PRESSURE/VACUUM RELIEF FUEL CAP

This system consists of a sealed filler cap with an integral pressure/vacuum relief valve. Fuel system vacuum relief is provided after 1.0 in. Hg of vacuum, and pressure relief after 1.8 psi. (.13 kg/cm²)

Under normal conditions, fill cap allows air to enter fuel tank as fuel is used while preventing vapors from escaping.

FUEL VAPOR RETURN SYSTEM

This system consists of a vapor return line from fuel pump to fuel return outlet of fuel sender, reducing amount of fuel vapor entering carburetor.

AIR CLEANER ASSEMBLY

On some models, an auxiliary fuel bowl vent tube runs to air cleaner. An air filter installed on air cleaner end of fuel bowl vent tube keeps dirt out of carburetor fuel bowl.

TESTING

CANISTER PURGE REGULATOR VALVE

With canister purge regulator valve de-energized, apply 5 in. Hg to vacuum source port. If air passes through valve, it should be

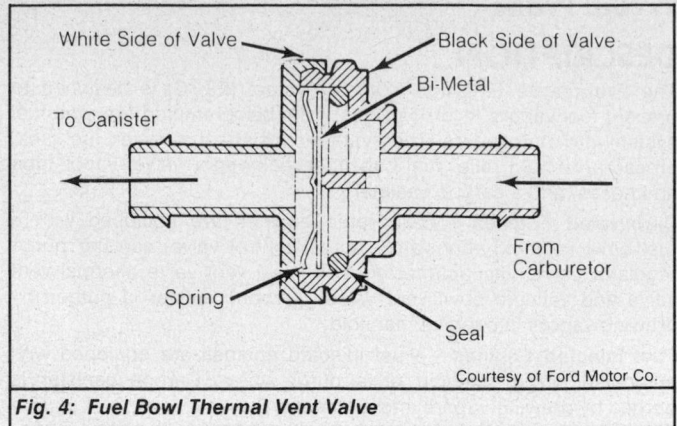

Fig. 4: Fuel Bowl Thermal Vent Valve

replaced. Apply 9-14 volts to valve. The valve should open and pass air. If valve does not open, replace valve.

FUEL BOWL SOLENOID VENT VALVE

Apply 9-14 volts to vent valve. See Fig. 2. The valve should close and not allow air to pass. If valve does not close or leaks at carburetor port when voltage is applied, replace valve.

FUEL BOWL THERMAL VENT VALVE

At 90° F (32° C) and colder, the vent valve should be fully closed. See Fig. 4. At 120° F (48° C) and hotter, the vent valve should be fully open. At temperatures between 90° F (32 C°) and 120° F (48° C), the valve may be either open or closed.

PURGE CONTROL VALVE

NOTE: Do not apply vacuum to port "C", as valve will be permanently damaged.

Apply vacuum to port "A". Air should flow through valve. See Fig. 5. Apply vacuum to port "B", valve should not allow air to flow (except for valves E5VE-AA, E4VE-AA or E77E-AA which should allow a slight flow). Apply and maintain 16 in. Hg of vacuum to port "A", apply vacuum to port "B". Air should pass through valve.

VACUUM BOWL VENT VALVE

Without vacuum applied to vacuum signal nipple, air should flow between carburetor port and canister port. See Fig. 3. With vacuum

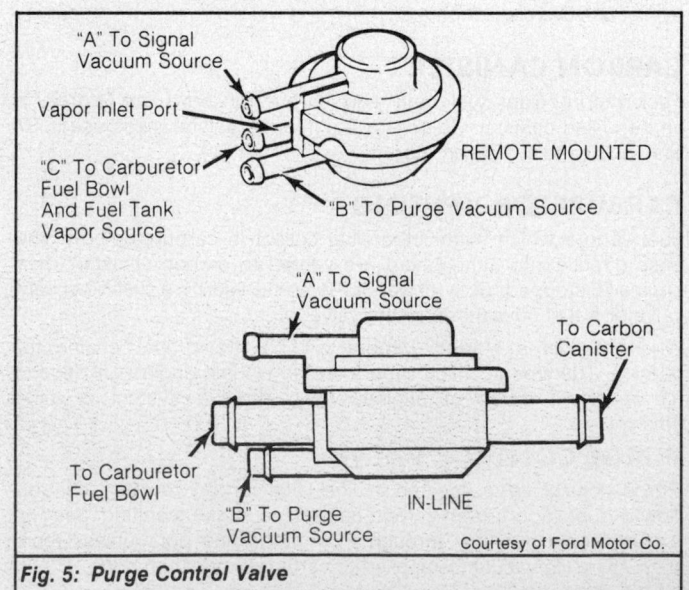

Fig. 5: Purge Control Valve

1989 EXHAUST EMISSION SYSTEMS
Ford Motor Co. Fuel Evaporation Systems (Cont.)

3-45

applied at vacuum signal nipple, air should not flow between carburetor port and canister port.

VACUUM/THERMOSTATIC BOWL VALVE

1) With valve at a temperature of 90° F (32° C) or less, airflow between carburetor port and canister port of valve should be very restrictive or not allowed at all. *See Fig. 3.*

2) With valve at a temperature of 120° F (48° C) and without vacuum applied to vacuum nipple, air should flow between carburetor port and canister port. With vacuum applied at vacuum signal nipple, air should not flow between carburetor port and canister port.

MAINTENANCE

Replace charcoal canister filter every 30,000 miles. All hoses and connections should be checked periodically for cracks, leaks or other damage and replaced as necessary.

1989 EXHAUST EMISSION SYSTEMS
Ford Motor Co. Fuel Evaporation Systems

Probe

DESCRIPTION

The Evaporative Emission Control System (EECS) is designed to prevent fuel vapors (hydrocarbons) from being emitted from the fuel system into atmosphere. For components used in this system, *See Fig. 1.*

OPERATION

The first stage of purge operation occurs when throttle plates are open and a ported vacuum signal is sent to Vacuum Control Valve (VCV). If engine coolant temperature is above 129° F (53° C), ported vacuum signal is sent to No. 1 Purge Control Valve. Manifold vacuum on No. 1 Purge Control Valve draws fuel vapors through an orifice and delivers the vapors to intake manifold.

The second stage of purge operation occurs when engine speed is above 1500 RPM and engine coolant temperature is above 140° F (60° C). The ECA turns on the Canister Purge Control Solenoid and allows vacuum to enter canister purge valve. Manifold vacuum then draws fuel vapors though an additional larger orifice increasing total amount of purge flow.

CANISTER PURGE REGULATOR (CPR) SOLENOID VALVE

The Canister Purge Regulator (CPR) solenoid valve controls vacuum applied to canister purge valve. When the CPR solenoid is energized, vacuum is supplied to the canister purge valve which regulates second stage purge from carbon canister to intake manifold. When de-energized, the vacuum is vented to atmosphere through the valve air filter. The CPR solenoid valve is controlled by a signal from the ECA.

The CPR solenoid valve is mounted on center of firewall next to pressure regulator control solenoid valve. *See Fig. 2.*

CANISTER PURGE VALVE

The canister purge valve regulates evaporative fumes from carbon canister to intake manifold. The valve is controlled by canister purge regulator solenoid valve as determined by the ECA. Valve is located near vacuum tubing assembly behind intake manifold. *See Fig. 3.*

CARBON CANISTER

Fuel vapors from fuel tank are stored in the carbon canister until vehicle is operated. Vapors will purge from canister into engine for consumption. The carbon canister is mounted in rear left corner of engine compartment.

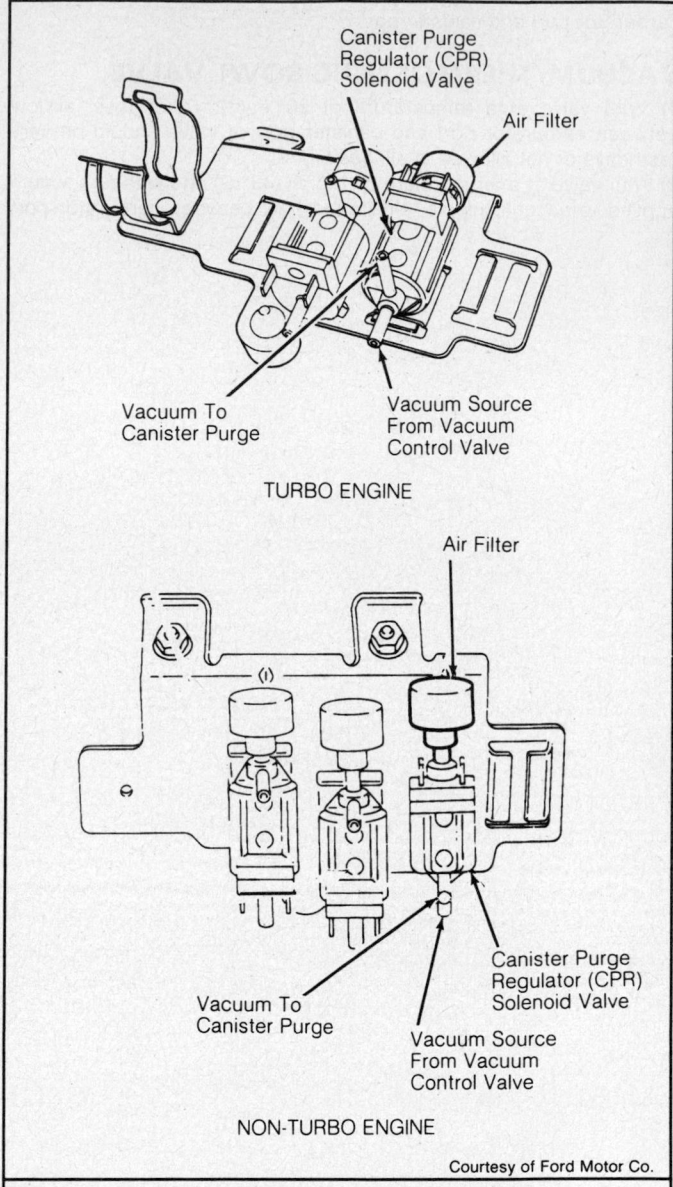

TURBO ENGINE

NON-TURBO ENGINE

Courtesy of Ford Motor Co.

Fig. 2: Canister Purge Regulator (CPR) Solenoid Valve

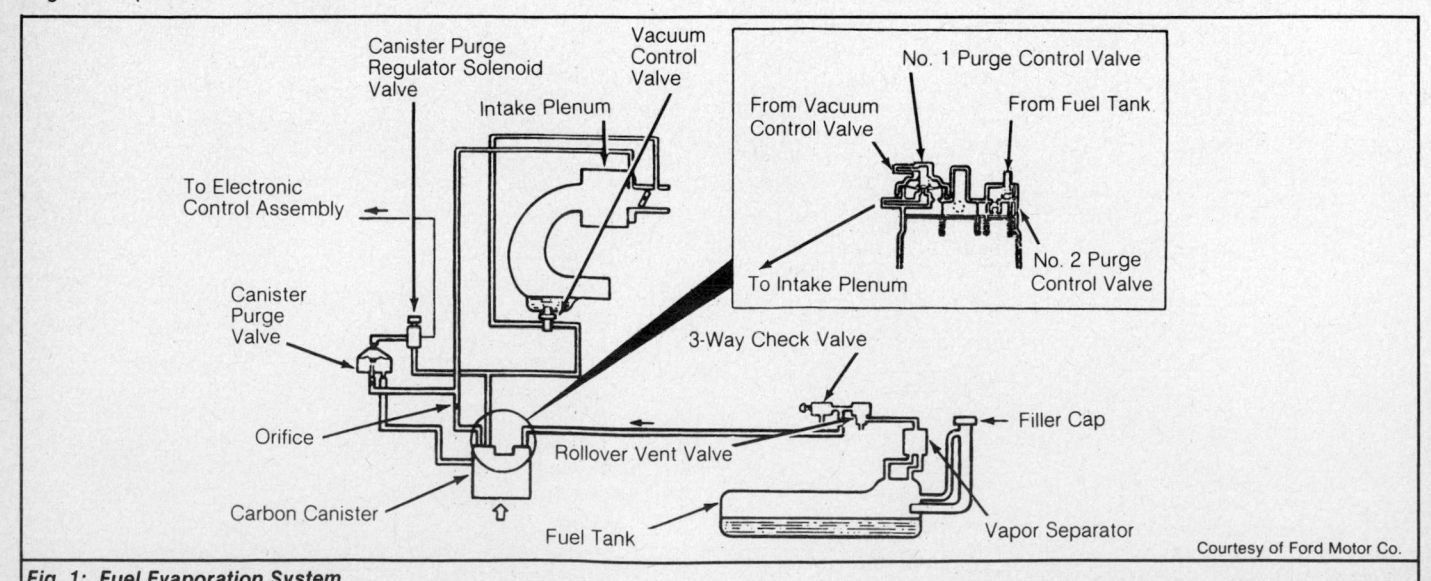

Courtesy of Ford Motor Co.

Fig. 1: Fuel Evaporation System

1989 EXHAUST EMISSION SYSTEMS
Ford Motor Co. Fuel Evaporation Systems (Cont.)

3-47

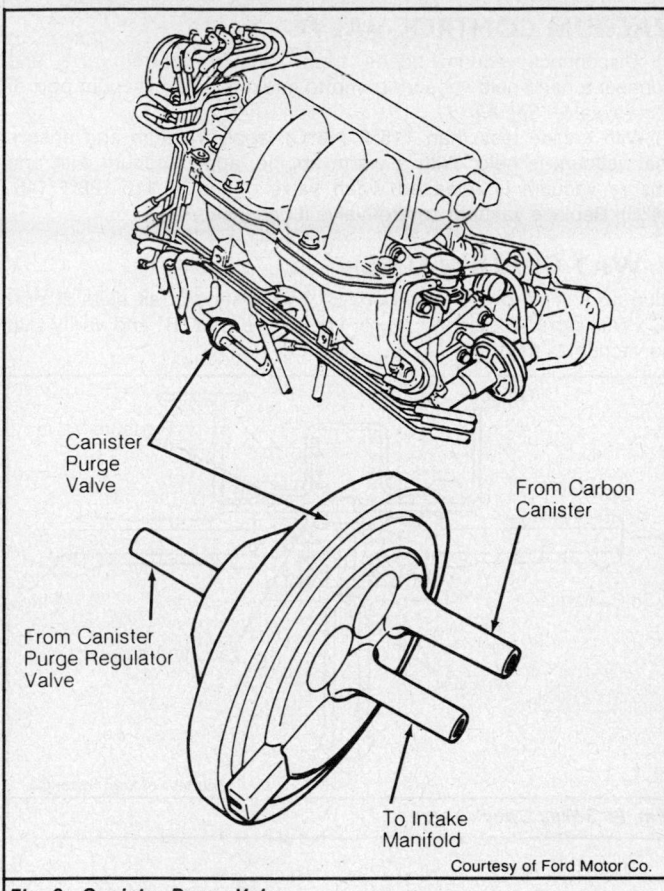

Fig. 3: Canister Purge Valve

Canister Purge Valve
From Carbon Canister
From Canister Purge Regulator Valve
To Intake Manifold
Courtesy of Ford Motor Co.

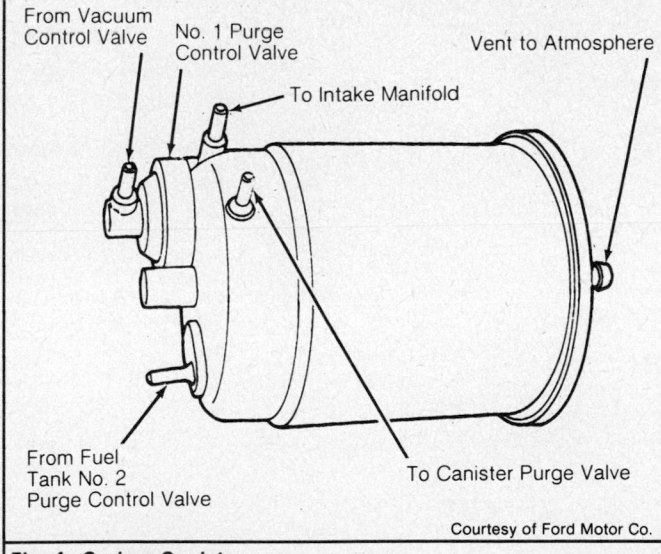

Fig. 4: Carbon Canister

From Vacuum Control Valve
No. 1 Purge Control Valve
To Intake Manifold
Vent to Atmosphere
From Fuel Tank No. 2 Purge Control Valve
To Canister Purge Valve
Courtesy of Ford Motor Co.

TESTING

Check all fuel vapor lines, vacuum lines and components in EVAP system for looseness, leakage, blockage, pinching and damage. Use a hand held vacuum pump to check for blockage in fuel vapor line.

CANISTER PURGE CONTROL SOLENOID VALVE

1) With canister purge control solenoid valve removed from the vehicle. Connect test vacuum hoses. See Fig. 5. Blow air through valve from hose "A". Ensure air exits through the vent.

2) Apply 12 volts to one terminal of solenoid valve and ground the other terminal. Blow air through the valve from hose "A". Ensure air exits at port "B". Replace canister purge control solenoid valve if necessary.

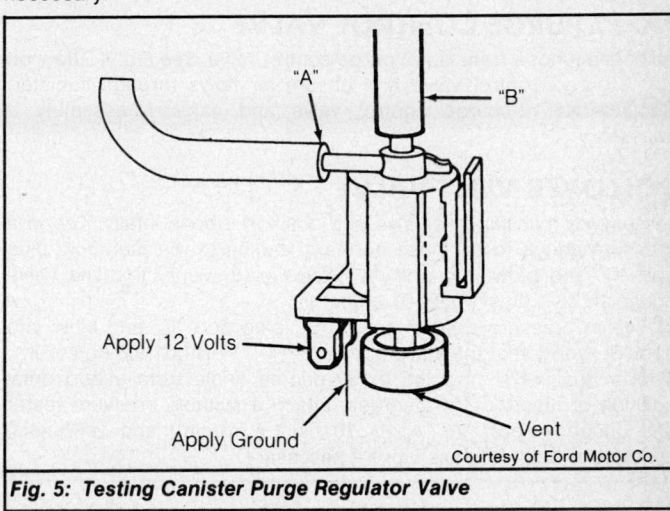

Fig. 5: Testing Canister Purge Regulator Valve

"A"
"B"
Apply 12 Volts
Apply Ground
Vent
Courtesy of Ford Motor Co.

CANISTER PURGE VALVE

Remove valve from vehicle. Apply 2.6-4.2 in Hg. of vacuum to port "C". See Fig. 6. Ensure that vacuum holds at port "C" and that air will flow through ports "A" and "B". Replace canister purge valve if necessary.

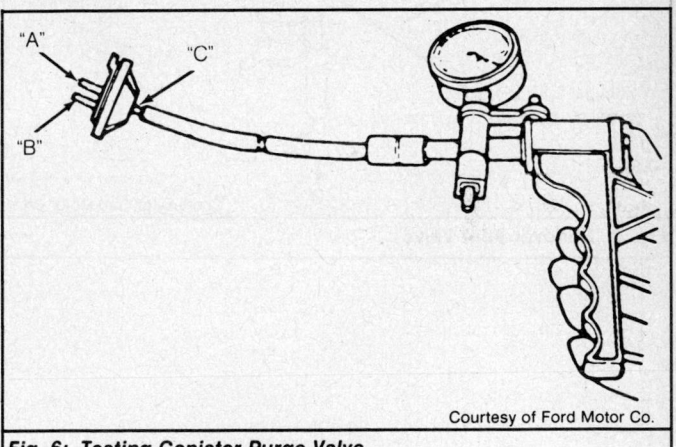

Fig. 6: Testing Canister Purge Valve

"A"
"C"
"B"
Courtesy of Ford Motor Co.

NO. 1 PURGE CONTROL VALVE

1) Connect test vacuum hoses. See Fig. 7. Apply vacuum to No. 1 purge control valve and ensure that air does not flow through the valve while blowing into port "A".

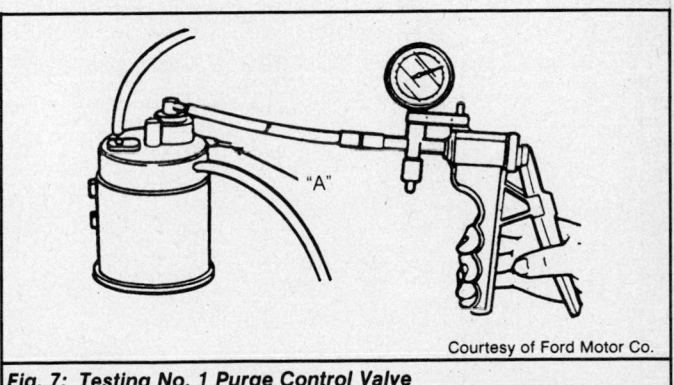

Fig. 7: Testing No. 1 Purge Control Valve

"A"
Courtesy of Ford Motor Co.

3-48

1989 EXHAUST EMISSION SYSTEMS
Ford Motor Co. Fuel Evaporation Systems (Cont.)

2) With 4.3 in Hg. of vacuum applied ensure vacuum is held and air flows through the valve while blowing into port "A". Replace No. 1 purge control valve carbon canister assembly if necessary.

NO. 2 PURGE CONTROL VALVE

Disconnect hose from No. 2 purge control valve. *See Fig. 4.* Blow on No. 2 purge control valve and ensure air flows through canister. Replace No. 2 purge control valve and canister assembly if necessary.

ROLLOVER VENT VALVE

1) Remove rollover vent valve and position it horizontally. Tee in a pressure gauge to the hose normally leading to the fuel tank, plug port "C" and blow into port "A". *See Fig. 8.* Verify that the valve opens at .78-1.0 psi (.055-.07 kg/cm²)

2) Tee in pressure gauge at port "B", plug port "C" and blow into port "B". Verify that the valve opens at .14-.71 psi (.01-.05 kg/cm²).

3) With the valve mounted at 90 degree angle from a horizontal position or inverted 180 degrees, attach a suitable pressure tester and gauge at port "A", apply 10 psi (.7 kg/cm²) and verify that pressure is held. Replace valve if necessary.

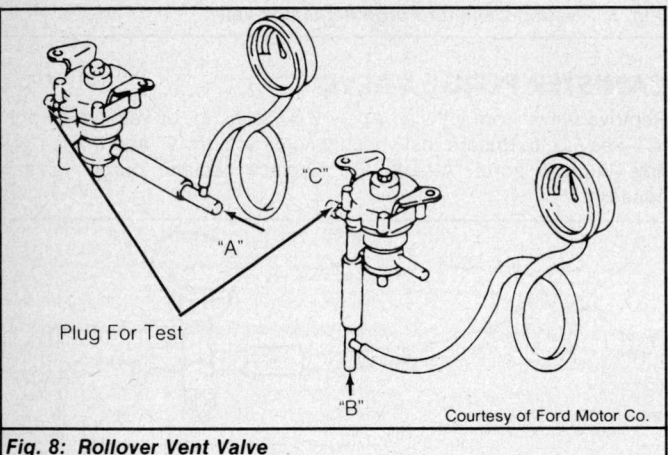

Fig. 8: Rollover Vent Valve

VACUUM CONTROL VALVE

1) Disconnect vacuum hoses from vacuum control valve and connect a hand held vacuum pump to intake plenum vacuum port of control valve. *See Fig. 1.*

2) With engine less than 115°F (46°C), apply vacuum and ensure that vacuum is held. With a warm engine, apply vacuum with and ensure vacuum is released when valve opens at 115-129°F (46-54°C). Replace vacuum control valve if necessary.

3-WAY CHECK VALVE

Plug port "A". Blow air into port "B" and verify that air exits at port "C". With port "A" blocked, apply vacuum to port "B" and verify that no vacuum is held. *See Fig. 9.*

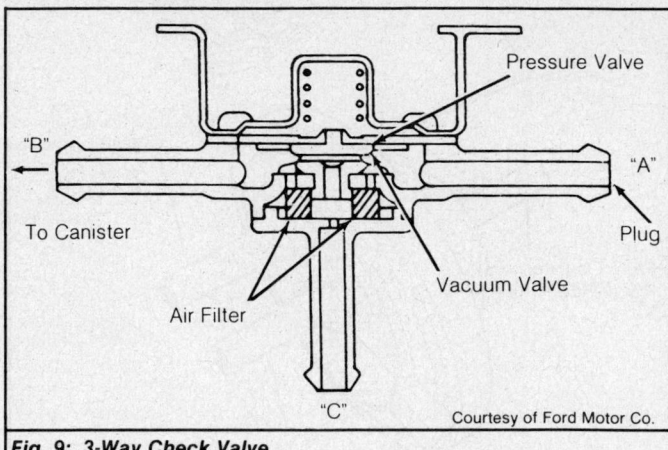

Fig. 9: 3-Way Check Valve

CALIBRATION NUMBER IDENTIFICATION

To identify engine calibration number, locate engine code label on valve cover at front of engine. *See Fig. 1.* Calibration codes usually begin with a number indicating current model year. For example, calibrations for 1989 usually begin with "9". Each vehicle is also equipped with an emission control data decal which applies to that vehicle and engine. *See Fig. 2.* These decals are usually located on underside of hood or other visible engine compartment location.

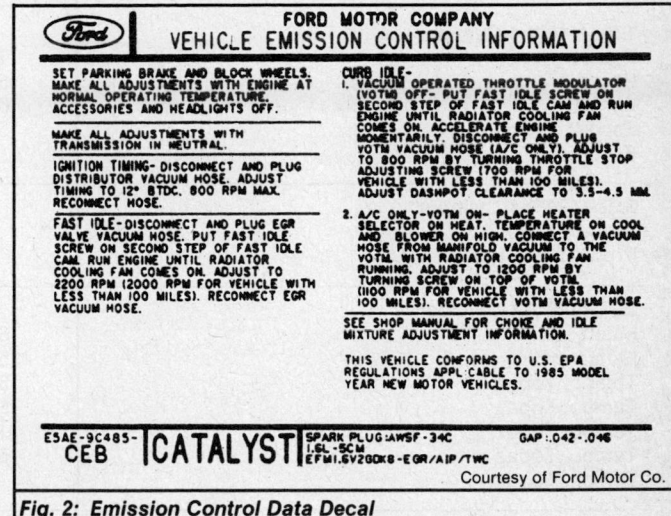

Fig. 2: Emission Control Data Decal

Courtesy of Ford Motor Co.

NOTE: *To locate appropriate vacuum diagram, refer to Fig. No. listed in 1989 FORD MOTOR CO. VACUUM DIAGRAM INDEX in this article.*

Courtesy of Ford Motor Co.

Fig. 1: Engine Calibration Code Label Styles

A/CL BIMET – Air Cleaner Temperature Sensor	**SA-FA** – Fuel Vacuum Separator
A/CL CWM – Air Cleaner Cold Weather Modulator	**SOL** – Distributor Modulator Valve Assembly 3-Port
A/CL DV – Air Cleaner Duct and Vacuum Motor	**SOL V** – Distributor Modulator Valve Assembly 1-Port
ACT – Air Charge Temperature Sensor	**SV-CBV** – Carburetor Fuel Bowl Solenoid Vent Valve
ACV – Air Control Valve	**TAB** – Thermal Air Bleed
AIR BPV – Air By-Pass Valve	**TAD** – Thermactor Diverter
ANTI B/F – Anti-Backfire Valve	**T REST** – Vacuum Restrictor
BVT – EGR Backpressure Modulator	**TSP-VOTM** – Throttle Solenoid Positioner w/Vacuum
CBV – Vacuum Bowl Vent & Vacuum Thermostatic Bowl Vent Valve	Operated Throttle Modulator
	TVS – Temperature Vacuum Switch
COMP VLV – Hot Idle Compensator	**TVV** – Carburetor Fuel Bowl Thermal Vent Valve
CPRV – Canister Purge Valve	**VACVV-D** – Vacuum Vent Valve
DV-TW – Vacuum Delay Valve	**VCS** – Vacuum Control Solenoid
EGRC – EGR Control	**VDV** – Vacuum Delay Valve
EGRV – EGR Vent	**VO ISC** – Vacuum Orifice Idle Speed Control
EVR – Emission Vacuum Regulator	**VOTM** – Vacuum Operated Throttle Modulator
FLTR – EGR Vacuum Control Valve Filter	**VRDV** – Vacuum Delay Valve
FPR – Fuel Pump Relay	**VRESSER** – Vacuum Reservoir
IVV – Thermactor Idle Vacuum Valve	**VREST** – Vacuum Restrictor
SILN – Air Silencer	**VREST FLTR** – Vacuum Vent Filter Assembly
LCV – EGR Load Control (WOT) Valve	**VRV** – EGR Venturi Vacuum Amplifier
MAP – Manifold Absolute Pressure Sensor	**VVA** – EGR Venturi Vacuum Amplifier
PURGE CV – Canister Purge Valve	

1989 EXHAUST EMISSION SYSTEMS
Ford Motor Co. Vacuum Diagrams (Cont.)

1989 FORD MOTOR CO. VACUUM DIAGRAM INDEX

Engine & Model	Application	Transmission	Calibration	Fig. No.
1.9L (116") 4-Cylinder				
Escort	Federal	Manual	8-07A-R11	3
Escort	50-State	Manual	8-07E-R10	4
Escort	50-State	Manual	8-07F-R11	3
Escort	50-State	Auto.	8-08A-R11	3
Escort	Calif.	Manual	9-07S-R00	1
2.2L (134") 4-Cylinder				
Probe (Turbo)	1	1	1	5
Probe (Non-Turbo)	1	1	1	6
2.3L (140") 4-Cylinder				
Mustang	50-State	Manual	8-05A-R10	7
Mustang	50-State	Auto.	8-06A-R10	7
Tempo, Topaz	50-State	Manual	8-25C-R00	8
Tempo, Topaz	50-State	Manual	8-25F-R00	8
Tempo, Topaz	Federal	Auto.	8-26D-R10	8
Tempo, Topaz	50-State	Auto.	8-26E-R00	8
Tempo, Topaz	Calif.	Auto.	8-26T-R10	8
2.5L (153") 4-Cylinder				
Taurus	Federal	Auto.	9-20F-R00	9
Taurus	50-State	Auto.	9-20T-R00	9
3.0L (183") 6-Cylinder				
Sable, Taurus	Federal	Auto. O/D	8-10A-R00	1
Taurus	Federal	Manual	9-09C-R00	1
Taurus	Calif.	Manual	9-09P-R00	1
Sable, Taurus	Calif.	Auto. O/D	9-10S-R10	10
Taurus	Calif.	1	9-10S-R11	10
3.8L (230") 6-Cylinder				
Sable, Taurus	Federal	Auto. O/D	8-16C-R00	12
Thunderbird	Federal	Manual	9-15A-R00	1
Thunderbird	Calif.	Manual	9-15S-R00	1
Cougar, Thunderbird	Federal	Auto.	9-16A-R00	1
Sable, Taurus	Federal	Auto. O/D	9-16C-R10	11
Continental	Federal	Auto. O/D	9-16D-R00	1
Continental	Federal	Auto. O/D	9-16D-R10	11
Cougar, Thunderbird	50-State	Auto. O/D	9-16F-R00	14
Sable, Taurus	Calif.	Auto. O/D	9-16Q-R00	1
Sable, Taurus	Calif.	Auto. O/D	9-16Q-R10	11
Continental	Calif.	Auto. O/D	9-16R-R00	1
Continental	Calif.	Auto. O/D	9-16R-R10	11
Cougar, Thunderbird	Calif.	Auto.	9-16S-R00	1
Cougar, Thunderbird	Calif.	Auto. O/D	9-16T-R10	13

1 – Information not available from manufacturer.

1989 Exhaust Emission Systems
Ford Motor Co. Vacuum Diagrams (Cont.)

3-51

1989 FORD MOTOR CO. VACUUM DIAGRAM INDEX

Engine & Model	Application	Transmission	Calibration	Fig. No.
5.0L (302") V8				
Mustang	Federal	Manual	7-21A-R00	15
Mustang	Calif.	Manual	8-21P-R10	16
Town Car	Federal	Auto. O/D	8-22B-R00	17
Ford, Mercury, Town Car	Federal	Auto. O/D	8-22C-R00	17
Mark VII (exc. LSC)	Federal	Auto. O/D	8-22D-R00	15
Ford, Mercury	Federal	Auto. O/D	8-22E-R00	17
Ford, Mercury	Federal	Auto. O/D	8-22G-R00	17
Ford (Police), Mercury	Federal	Auto. O/D	8-22I-R00	17
Ford, Mercury	Federal	Auto. O/D	8-22J-R00	17
Mark VII (LSC)	50-State	Auto. O/D	8-22L-R00	16
Ford, Mercury, Town Car	Calif.	Auto. O/D	8-22M-R00	17
Mercury	Calif.	Auto. O/D	8-22N-R00	17
Mustang	Calif.	Auto. O/D	8-22P-R12	16
Ford, Mercury, Town Car	Calif.	Auto. O/D	8-22Q-R00	17
Mark VII (exc. LSC)	Calif.	Auto. O/D	8-22R-R00	15
Ford, Mercury	Calif.	Auto. O/D	8-22S-R00	17
Mustang (Convertible)	Federal	Manual	9-21C-R05	15
Mustang	Federal	Auto. O/D	9-22A-R00	16
5.8L (351") V8				
Ford (Police)	50-State	Auto. O/D	7-24P-R10	18

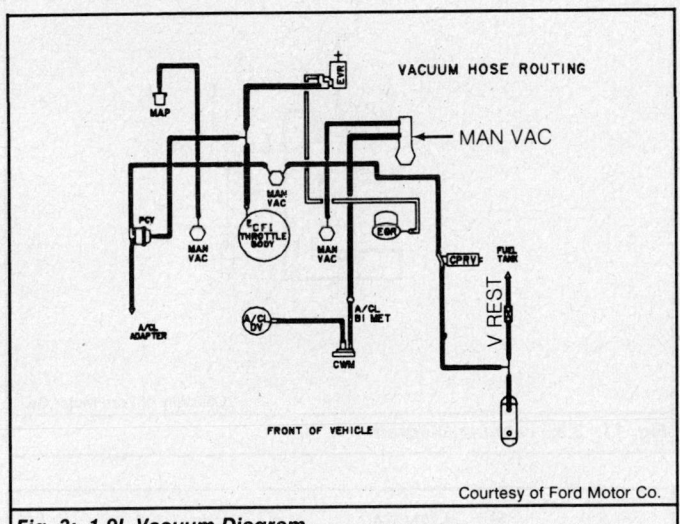

Fig. 3: 1.9L Vacuum Diagram

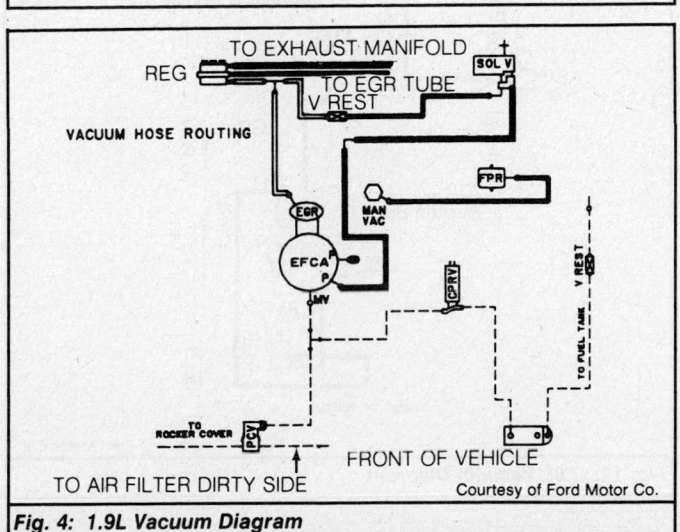

Fig. 4: 1.9L Vacuum Diagram

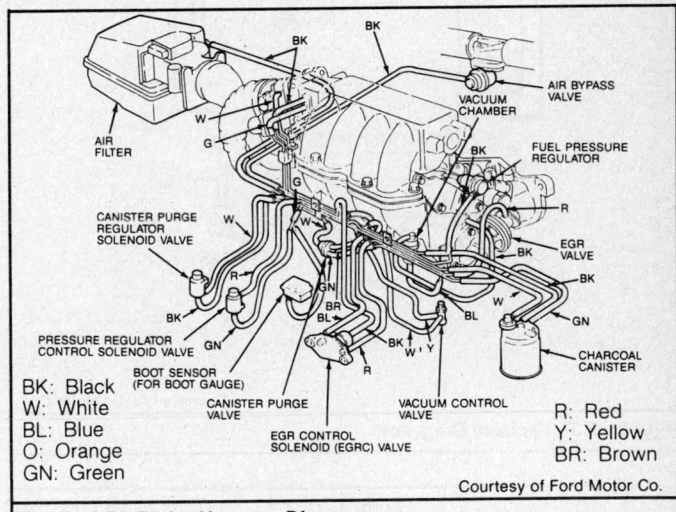

Fig. 5: 2.2L Turbo Vacuum Diagram

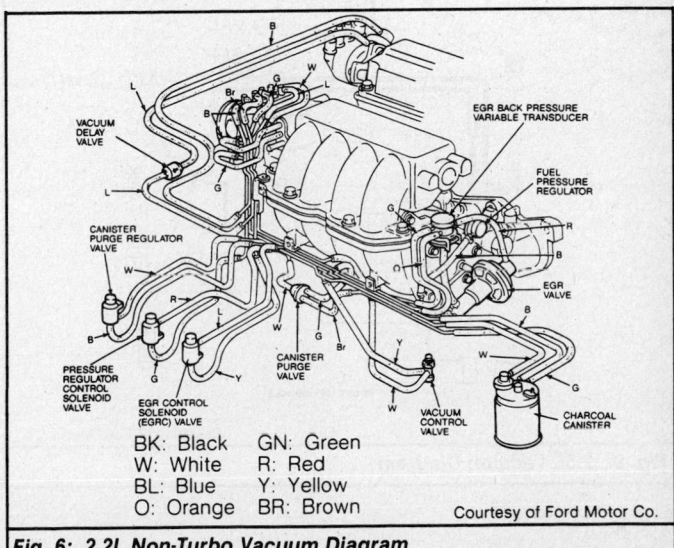

Fig. 6: 2.2L Non-Turbo Vacuum Diagram

1989 EXHAUST EMISSION SYSTEMS
Ford Motor Co. Vacuum Diagrams (Cont.)

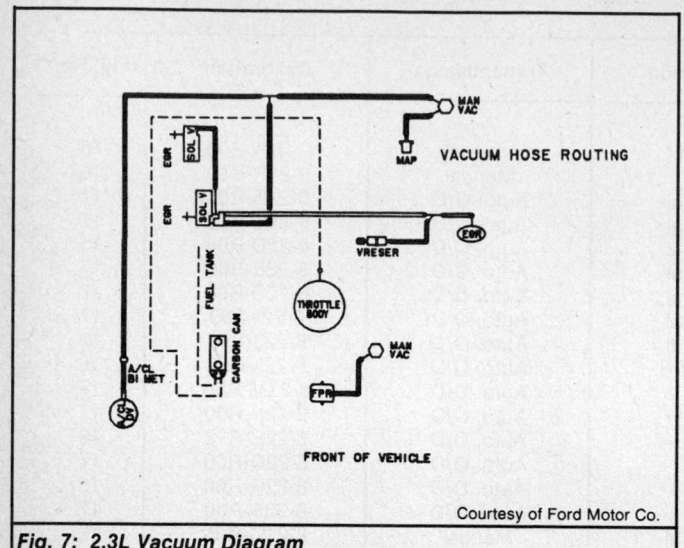

Courtesy of Ford Motor Co.

Fig. 7: 2.3L Vacuum Diagram

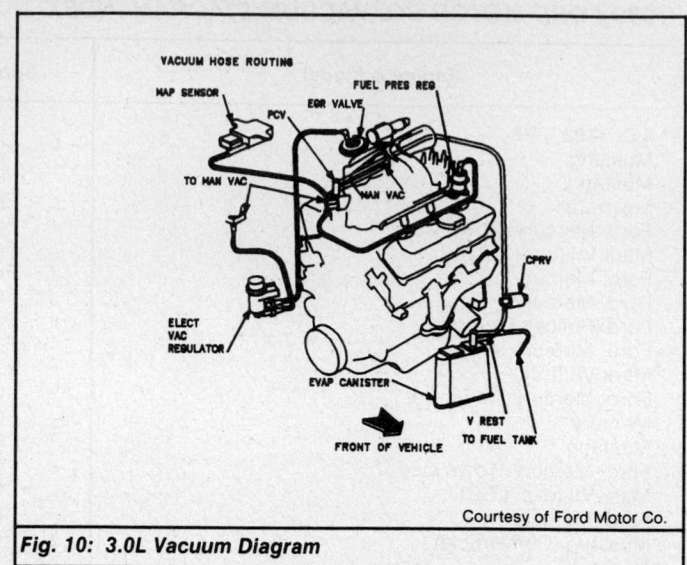

Courtesy of Ford Motor Co.

Fig. 10: 3.0L Vacuum Diagram

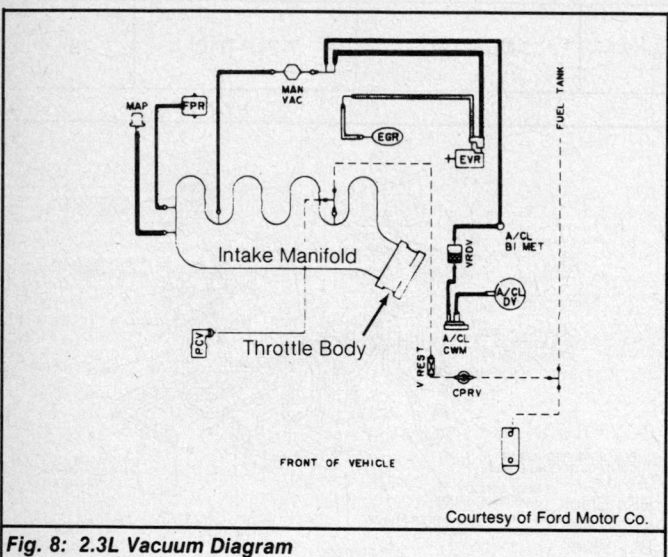

Courtesy of Ford Motor Co.

Fig. 8: 2.3L Vacuum Diagram

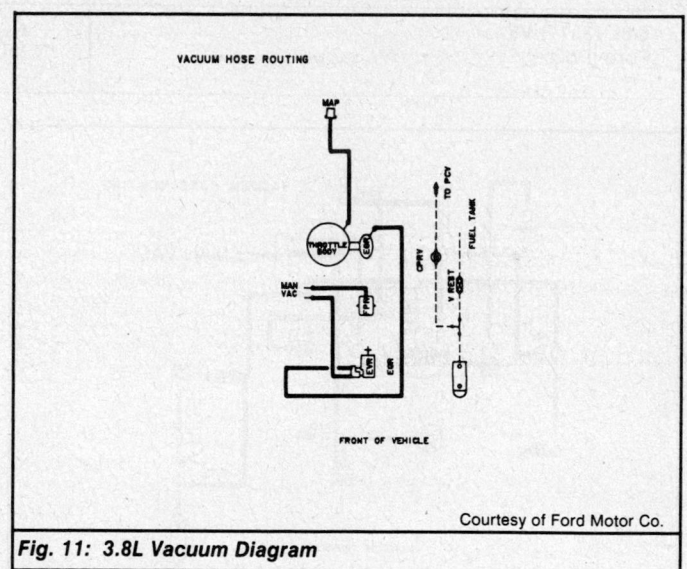

Courtesy of Ford Motor Co.

Fig. 11: 3.8L Vacuum Diagram

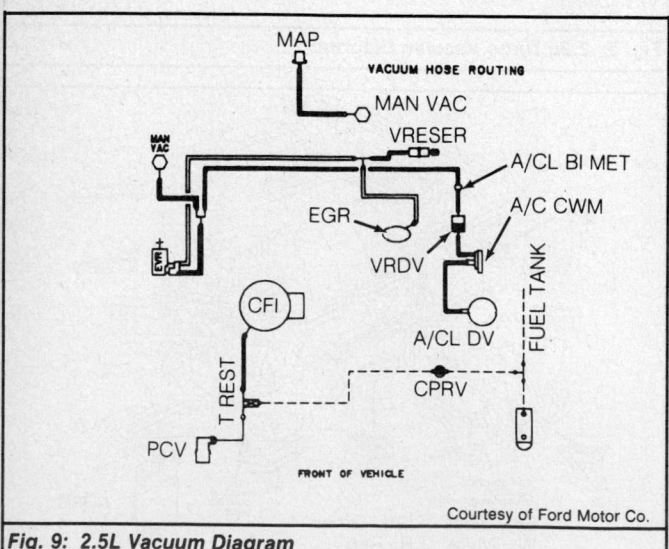

Courtesy of Ford Motor Co.

Fig. 9: 2.5L Vacuum Diagram

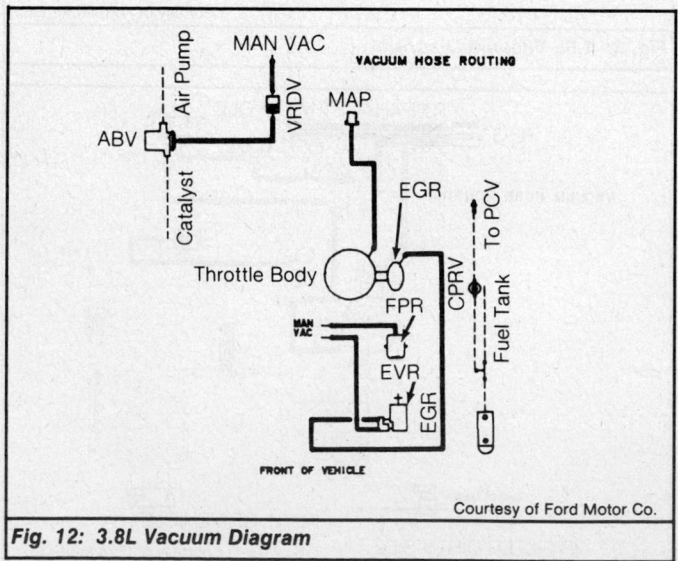

Courtesy of Ford Motor Co.

Fig. 12: 3.8L Vacuum Diagram

1989 EXHAUST EMISSION SYSTEMS
Ford Motor Co. Vacuum Diagrams (Cont.)

3-53

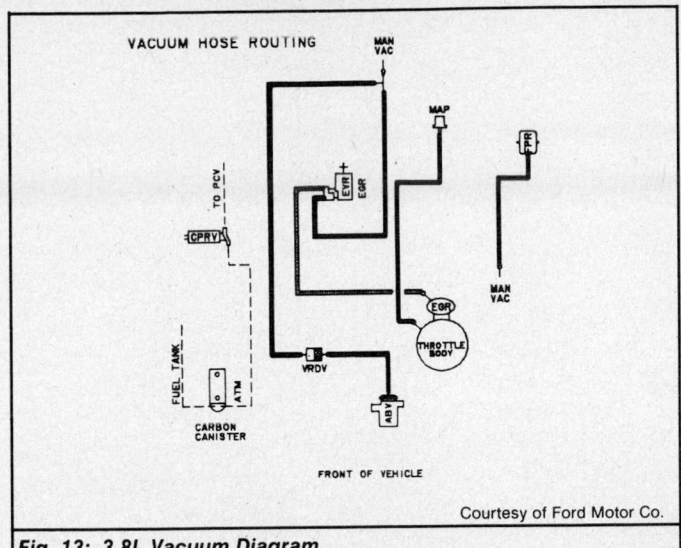

Fig. 13: 3.8L Vacuum Diagram

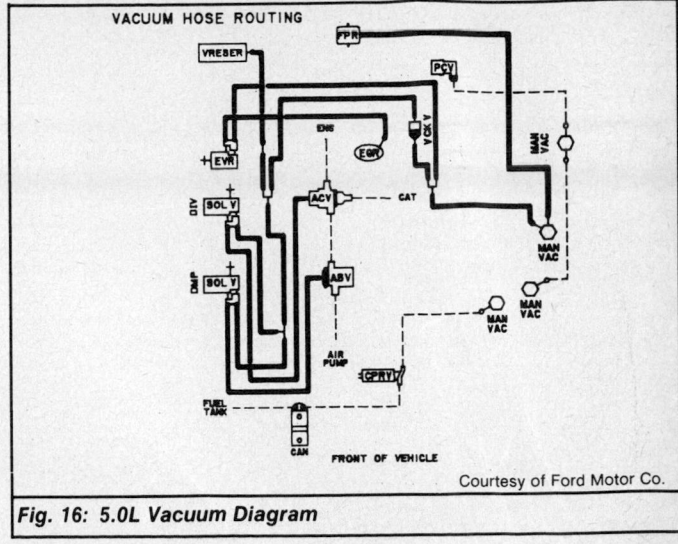

Fig. 16: 5.0L Vacuum Diagram

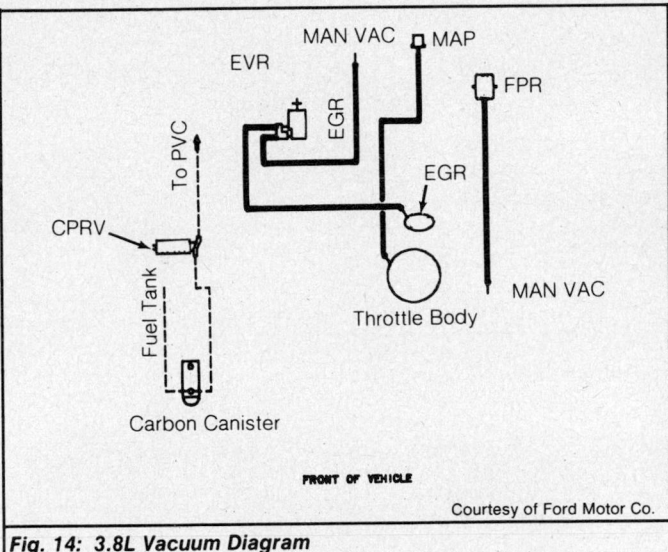

Fig. 14: 3.8L Vacuum Diagram

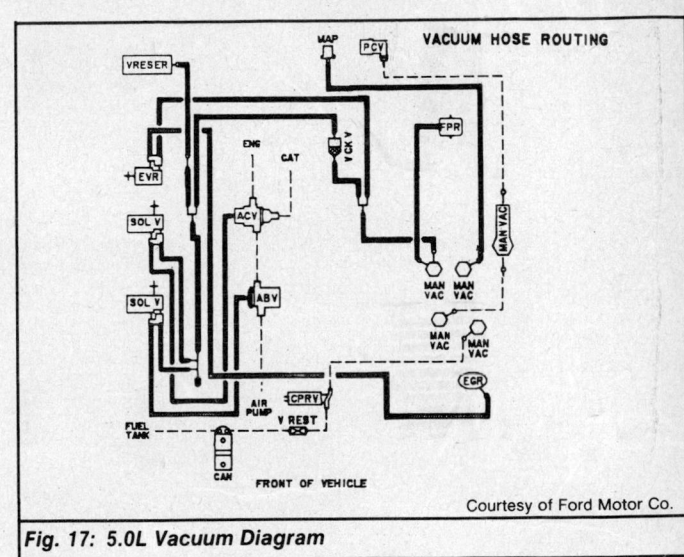

Fig. 17: 5.0L Vacuum Diagram

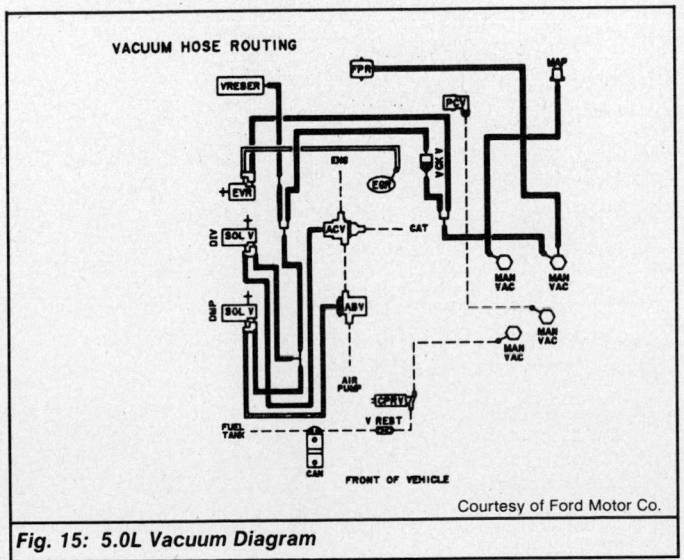

Fig. 15: 5.0L Vacuum Diagram

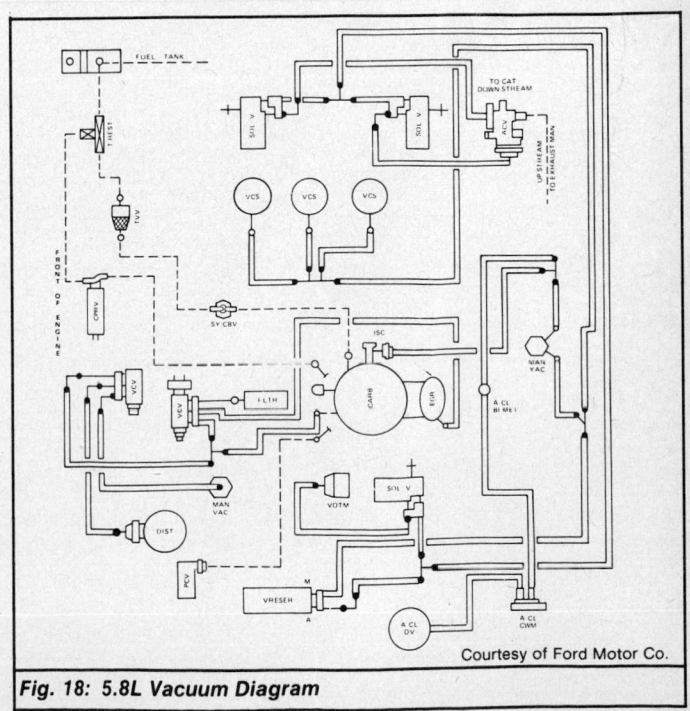

Fig. 18: 5.8L Vacuum Diagram

Section 4

ELECTRICAL

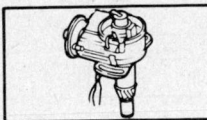

CONTENTS

TROUBLE SHOOTING   Page

Ignition Systems 4-2
Charging Systems 4-26
Starting Systems 4-58

DISTRIBUTORS & IGNITION SYSTEMS

Chrysler Motors
  Electronic Spark Control (ESC) 4-3
  Hall Effect Electronic Ignition 4-7
  Optical Ignition 4-8
Eagle
  Electronic Ignition 4-11

DISTRIBUTORS & IGNITION SYSTEMS (Cont.)   Page

Ford Motor Co.
  Distributorless Ignition System 4-13
  Motorcraft Dura-Spark II Ignition (UIC) 4-17
  Motorcraft TFI-IV Ignition 4-21

ALTERNATORS & REGULATORS

Chrysler Motors
  Bosch 90-Amp 4-27
  Chrysler Motors 90 & 120-Amp
    With External Regulator 4-31
  Nippondenso 75, 90 & 120-Amp
    With Integral Regulator 4-34
  Nippondenso 90 & 120-Amp
    With External Regulator 4-38
  Chrysler Motors Regulator 4-42
Eagle
  Delco-Remy 85, 100 & 105-Amp 4-44
Ford Motor Co.
  Mitsubishi Internal Alternator-Regulator 4-46
  Motorcraft Integral Alternator-Regulator
    w/External Fan 4-49
  Motorcraft Integral Alternator-Regulator
    w/Internal Fan 4-53
  Motorcraft With External Regulator 4-55

STARTER REMOVAL

Chrysler Motors, Eagle & Ford Motor Co. 4-60

STARTERS

Chrysler Motors FWD
  Bosch & Nippondenso 4-61
Chrysler Motors RWD
  Nippondenso 4-64
Eagle
  Bosch & Mitsubishi 4-67
Ford Motor Co.
  Mazda 4-70
  Motorcraft 4-74

NOTE: **ALSO SEE GENERAL INDEX**

1989 IGNITION SYSTEMS
Trouble Shooting

IGNITION SECONDARY QUICK CHECK CHART

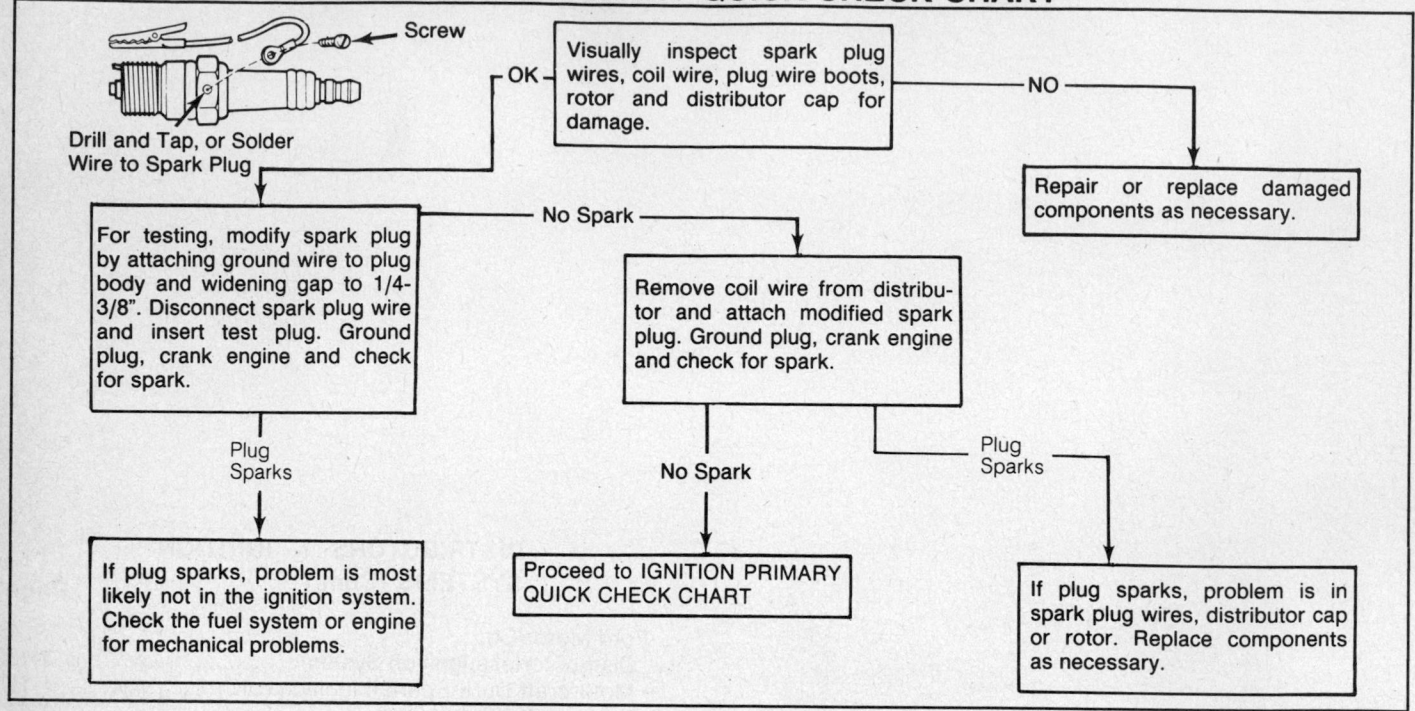

Screw

Drill and Tap, or Solder Wire to Spark Plug

Visually inspect spark plug wires, coil wire, plug wire boots, rotor and distributor cap for damage.

— OK

— NO

Repair or replace damaged components as necessary.

For testing, modify spark plug by attaching ground wire to plug body and widening gap to 1/4-3/8". Disconnect spark plug wire and insert test plug. Ground plug, crank engine and check for spark.

— No Spark —

Remove coil wire from distributor and attach modified spark plug. Ground plug, crank engine and check for spark.

Plug Sparks

No Spark

Plug Sparks

If plug sparks, problem is most likely not in the ignition system. Check the fuel system or engine for mechanical problems.

Proceed to IGNITION PRIMARY QUICK CHECK CHART

If plug sparks, problem is in spark plug wires, distributor cap or rotor. Replace components as necessary.

IGNITION PRIMARY QUICK CHECK CHART

Inspect all ignition primary wiring for broken, frayed, split or cut wires. Also check for loose, corroded or disconnected connectors.

Check battery voltage. Should be at least 11.5 volts.

— OK

— NO—

Repair or replace components as necessary.

NO

OK

Replace or recharge battery.

Check for battery voltage at positive terminal of coil.

OK

NO

Check air gap of pick-up coil in distributor.

OK

Check wires from battery/ignition switch to coil. Also check coil primary and secondary resistance.

OK

Check resistance of ballast resistor (if used) for correct value.

NO

Check pick-up coil resistance for correct value.

NO

Adjust or replace as necessary.

NO

NO

OK

Check control module for good ground connections.

Replace ballast resistor if value is not to speciation.

Replace pick-up coil if not to specification.

OK

If vehicle still fails to run, turn to appropriate article in this manual for complete primary ignition checks with specifications.

RWD Models

DESCRIPTION

The Electronic Spark Control (ESC) system consists of a spark control computer, various engine sensors, a specially-calibrated carburetor, and a single or dual pick-up distributor. The ESC system is designed to burn a lean air/fuel mixture with a minimum of emissions.

OPERATION

SPARK CONTROL COMPUTER

The Spark Control Computer (SCC) is located on the air cleaner assembly. It gives the system the capability of igniting a lean air/fuel mixture according to different modes of engine operation by delivering an infinite amount of variable advance curve. The computer determines optimum ignition advance.

The SCC signals the ignition coil to produce the voltage required for ignition purposes. The voltage produced is based on the demands of air/fuel ratio, air and coolant temperature, load and RPM. The computer consists of one electronic printed circuit board which receives signals from all the sensors and computes the appropriate ignition advance. The computer reaction time is measured in milliseconds.

SYSTEM OPERATION

The 2 functional modes of the Spark Control Computer are "Start" and "Run". The "Start" mode operates while cranking and starting only. The "Run" mode operates after the engine has started and during normal engine operation. The 2 modes never operate at the same time.

During cranking and starting the pick-up coil sends a signal to the computer which is in the "Start" mode. The "Run" mode is by-passed. During this time a fixed ignition advance is used. Advance is determined by distributor position (base timing).

The pick-up coil continues to send a signal to the computer after the engine starts. The computer is now in the "Run" mode and "Start" mode is by-passed. The amount of timing advance in the "Run" mode is controlled by the computer, based upon information received from the engine sensors.

Engine RPM and vacuum are the 2 factors determining ignition advance. When ignition event occurs depends on computer programming. Advance from vacuum will be provided when the carburetor switch is open. The amount of advance is programmed into the computer and is proportional to the amount of vacuum and engine RPM.

Advance from an increase in RPM will be given by the computer when the carburetor switch is open and the computer is programmed to engine RPM. If there is a failure of the "Run" mode of the computer, the "Limp-In" mode will come into service and allow the vehicle to be driven in for repair. Performance and economy will be greatly reduced because of fixed and therefore retarded timing. If the "Start" mode or both pick-up coils fail, the vehicle will not start or run.

SENSORS

The ESC computer analyzes data transmitted from as many as 8 engine sensors in order to determine optimum ignition advance. *See Fig. 1.* These sensors include the distributor pick-up coils, vacuum transducer, coolant temperature sensor, carburetor switch, detonation sensor, oxygen sensor, distance sensor and charge temperature switch (if equipped).

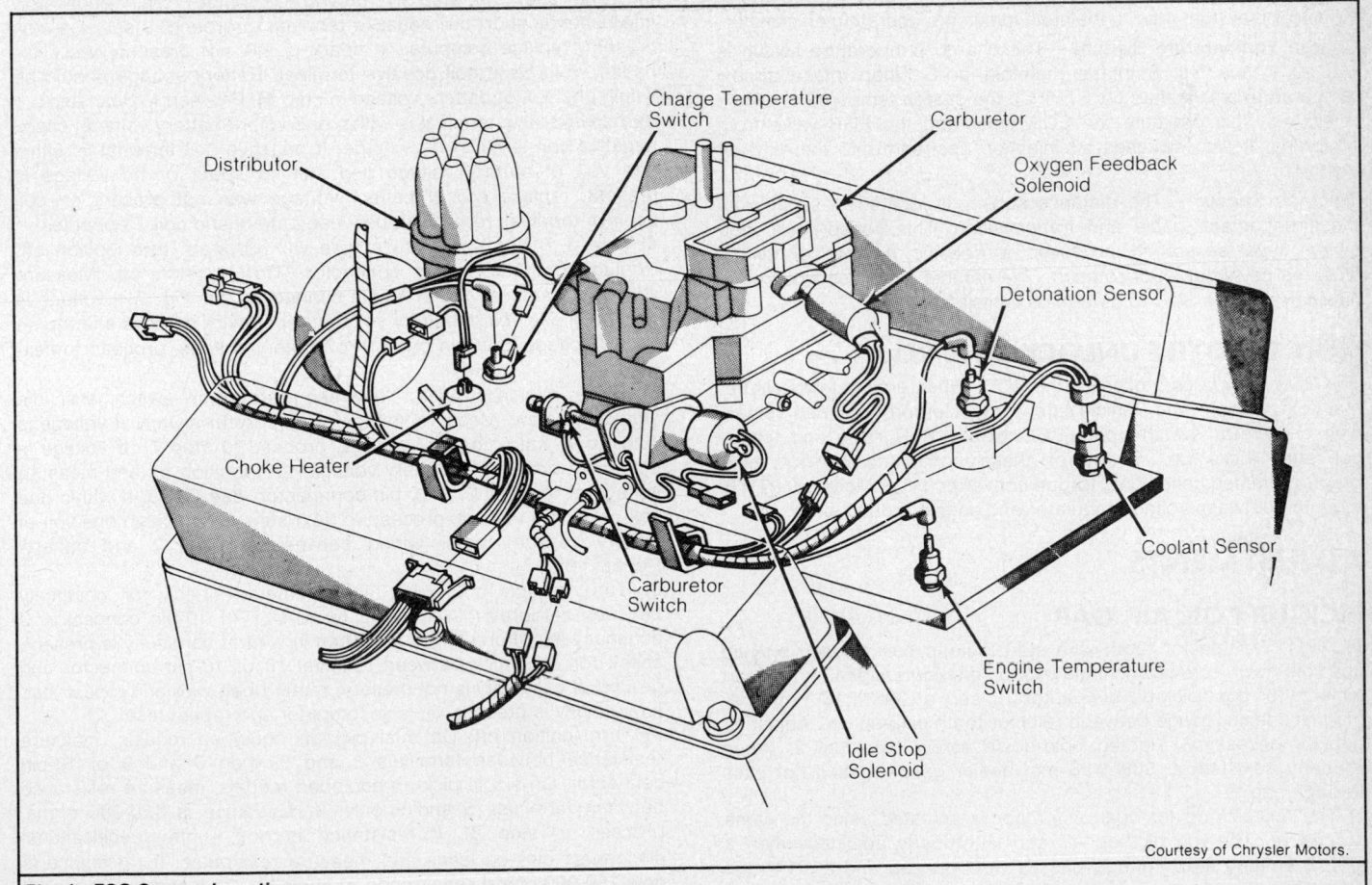

Courtesy of Chrysler Motors.

Fig. 1: *ESC Sensor Locations*

Magnetic Pick-Up Assembly – The pick-up coil assembly is located in the distributor. The start pick-up coil signals the computer correct timing advance under starting conditions. The computer reacts to this sensor during cranking only. After the engine is started, the run pick-up coil takes over. The run pick-up coil supplies base timing advance information to the computer.

The computer modifies spark advance based on information from remaining sensors. The start pick-up coil can be identified by its 2-prong male connector. The run pick-up coil can be identified by its connector having one male terminal and one female terminal.

Coolant Sensor – On 2-Bbl. Federal models the coolant sensor is mounted in the charge temperature area of the intake manifold. It is located in the intake manifold on all other models. The coolant sensor informs the computer of engine temperature. This prevents changing of the air/fuel ratio until the engine reaches normal operating temperature. It also controls the amount of spark advance when engine is cold.

Vacuum Transducer – The vacuum transducer is located on the spark control computer. It signals engine operating vacuum data to the computer. Manifold vacuum is one of the factors used in determining appropriate ignition timing or changes in air/fuel ratio.

Carburetor Switch – The carburetor switch (if equipped) is located on the end of the carburetor idle stop. It signals the computer when engine is at idle. The computer cancels spark advance at idle and controls idle air/fuel ratio.

Detonation Sensor – A detonation sensor is located in the No. 2 intake manifold port. The computer will retard ignition timing a maximum of 20 degrees when detonation is detected by the sensor. Timing is returned to its original advance when detonation is no longer detected.

Oxygen Sensor – The oxygen sensor is located in the exhaust manifold. Its purpose is to inform the computer of the percentage of oxygen in the exhaust gases. Based on this data, the computer adjusts the air/fuel ratio to maintain maximum operating efficiency.

Charge Temperature Switch – The charge temperature switch is located in the No. 8 intake manifold port. When intake airflow temperature is less than 60°F (15°C), the charge temperature switch is closed. This prevents the EGR timer and the EGR valve from operating. It also switches air injection upstream into the exhaust manifold.

Distance Sensor – The distance sensor is located in series with the speedometer cable and transmission. This sensor is a reed switch type sensor. It produces a specific number of switch closures per input shaft rotation. The number of switch closures is calculated by the SCC to determine vehicle speed.

PART THROTTLE UNLOCK (PTU) RELAY

The PTU relay is controlled by the SCC. When engine temperature, manifold vacuum and vehicle speed meet preprogrammed values, with carburetor switch open, SCC closes PTU relay and torque converter locks up. If any of these conditions do not meet preprogrammed conditions, torque converter will not lock up. PTU is mounted between voltage regulator and engine ground strap.

ADJUSTMENTS

PICK-UP COIL AIR GAP

1) Align one reluctor tooth with start pick-up coil. Loosen pick-up coil hold-down screw. On single pick-up distributors and on the start pick-up for dual pick-up distributors, insert a .006" (.15 mm) non-magnetic feeler gauge between reluctor tooth pick-up coil. Adjust air gap as necessary. Tighten hold-down screw. *See Fig. 2.* When properly adjusted, a .008" (.20 mm) feeler gauge should not pass through gap.

2) The run pick-up for dual distributor is adjusted using the same procedure. The run pick-up air gap is properly adjusted when a .012" (.31 mm) feeler gauge passes through gap and a .014" (.36 mm) feeler gauge will not pass through.

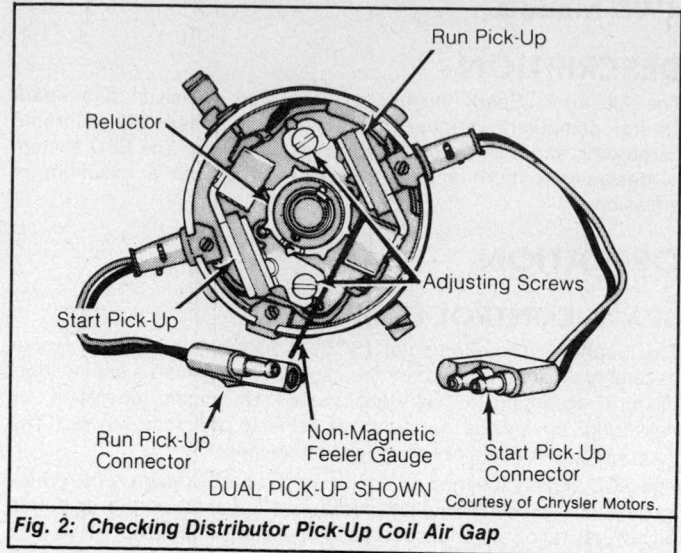

Fig. 2: Checking Distributor Pick-Up Coil Air Gap

TESTING

ESC SYSTEM DIAGNOSIS

1) Measure and record battery voltage. If battery is not at least 12.2 volts, charge or replace battery as necessary prior to any testing. If battery is within specifications, turn ignition on. Hold coil wire near a ground and intermittently short coil negative terminal to ground. If spark is present but engine will not start, proceed to step 4). If no spark is present proceed to next step.

2) If no spark in step 1), unplug computer 10-pin connector. Intermittently short coil negative terminal to ground. If spark is now present, replace computer. If spark is still not present, check for battery voltage at coil positive terminal. Battery voltage should be within one volt of battery voltage in step 1). Proceed to next step.

3) If coil positive terminal is within one volt of battery voltage, check negative coil terminal for voltage. If negative coil terminal is within one volt of battery voltage and still no spark or no voltage is present, replace coil. If battery voltage was not present on coil positive terminal, repair wire between battery and coil. Repeat test.

4) If step 1) has spark but engine will not start, turn ignition off. Unplug computer 10-pin connector. Turn ignition on. Measure voltage at terminal one of 10-pin connector. *See Fig. 3.* If voltage is not within one volt of battery voltage, repair wire harness and repeat test. If voltage is within one volt of battery voltage, proceed to next step.

5) Place a thin insulator between carburetor switch and idle adjusting screw. Measure voltage at carburetor switch. If voltage is within one volt of battery voltage, proceed to step 7). If voltage is not within one volt of battery voltage, turn ignition on and measure voltage at terminal 2 of 10-pin connnector. *See Fig. 3.* If within one volt of battery voltage, proceed to next step. If not within one volt of battery voltage, repair wiring between terminal 2 and battery. Repeat test.

6) Turn ignition off. Using an ohmmeter, check for continuity between carburetor switch and terminal 7 of 10-pin connector. If continuity is not present, repair open in wire. If continuity is present, check for continuity between terminal 10 of 10-pin connector and ground. If continuity is not present, repair open wire and repeat test. If continuity is present, replace computer and repeat test.

7) Turn ignition off. On dual pick-up equipped models, measure resistance between terminals 3 and 9, then 5 and 9 of 10-pin connector. On single pick-up equipped models, measure resistance between terminals 5 and 9 only. If resistance is 150-900 ohms, proceed to step 8). If resistance is not within specifications, disconnect pick-up leads and measure resistance. If resistance is now 150-900 ohms, repair open or short in wiring and repeat test. If resistance is still not within specifications, replace pick-up coil(s), set air gap and repeat test.

8) Attach one ohmmeter lead to ground. Use other lead to check for ground or short at each pick-up coil lead. If short is found, replace pick-up coil(s), set air gap and repeat test. If no short is found, reconnect all connectors and start engine. If engine still does not start, replace computer.

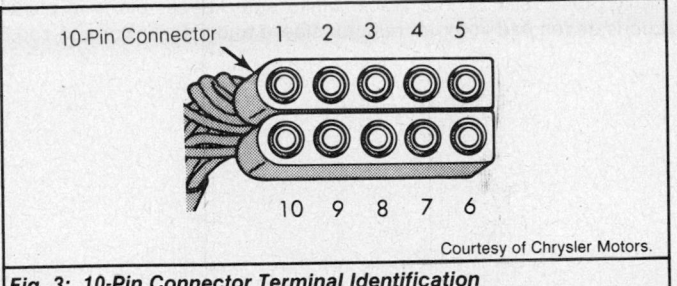

10-Pin Connector

Courtesy of Chrysler Motors.

Fig. 3: 10-Pin Connector Terminal Identification

COMPUTER CONTROLLED SPARK ADVANCE

1) Warm vehicle engine to normal operating temperature. Place a thin piece of insulating material between curb idle adjusting screw and carb switch (ensure no contact is being made).

2) Remove and plug vacuum line at vacuum transducer on SCC computer. Connect auxiliary vacuum supply to vacuum transducer and set vacuum at 16 in. Hg. Increase engine speed to 2000 RPM, wait one minute and compare timing advance against specifications. If correct advance cannot be obtained, replace SCC computer.

CARBURETOR SWITCH

NOTE: Grounding the carburetor switch eliminates all spark advance on most systems.

1) With key off, disconnect 10-way connector from SCC computer. With throttle completely closed, check for continuity between pin No. 7 and ground. If no continuity is present, check wire and carburetor switch for an open or short. Recheck basic timing.

2) With throttle open, check for continuity between pin No. 7 and ground. There should be no continuity.

CHARGE TEMPERATURE SENSOR

With key off, disconnect wire connector from charge temperature sensor. Connect ohmmeter between terminals of charge temperature sensor. Temperature sensor should have approximately 2500 ohms at room temperature (70°F) and more than 6000 ohms at normal operating temperature (200°F).

DETONATION SENSOR

1) Connect an adjustable timing light or magnetic timing light to the engine. Start engine and run it to at least 1200 RPM. Connect an auxiliary vacuum supply to vacuum transducer and apply 16 in. Hg. Tap lightly on intake manifold near detonation sensor with a small metal object.

2) Using a timing light look for a decrease in spark advance. The decrease in timing should directly respond to the strength of the tapping. The maximum decrease in timing is 20 degrees. Shut off engine and disconnect timing light.

ELECTRONIC EGR

NOTE: The engine temperature sensors must be working properly before performing this test.

1) With engine cold and ignition switch in the "OFF" position, connect a voltmeter between Gray wire of EGR solenoid and ground. Start engine. Voltmeter should read less than one volt.

2) It should remain at less than one volt until engine reaches normal operating temperature and electronic EGR has timed out. Solenoid

should then de-energize and voltmeter should read charging system voltage. If not, replace solenoid and repeat this step.

NOTE: Federal 318 CID, 2-barrel engines have no thermal delay below 60°F (15°C). They will follow EGR time delay schedule only.

3) If voltmeter reads charging system voltage before EGR timer has timed out, replace computer or externally mounted EGR timer. If the engine is started hot, the EGR solenoid will only be energized for the length of the time delay schedule, it will then de-energize.

ELECTRONIC THROTTLE CONTROL SYSTEM

NOTE: The spark control system is integral with the electronic throttle system. A solenoid mounted on the carburetor is energized whenever the A/C compressor, Electronic Backlite (EBL) or electronic timers are activated. The electronic timers used in the ignition system operate when the throttle is closed (plus a time delay of 2 seconds) or after an engine start condition.

1) Connect a tachometer to engine. Start engine and run until normal operating temperature is reached. Depress accelerator and let up. A higher than curb idle speed should be seen for the length of the EGR timer.

2) On vehicles equipped with A/C, turn on A/C and EBL. Depress accelerator pedal momentarily. This should cause a higher than normal curb idle speed. Turning the A/C and EBL off, should cause a normal curb idle speed.

3) If speed increases do not occur, disconnect 3-way connector at carburetor. Check the solenoid with an ohmmeter by measuring the resistance from Black wire terminal to ground. If resistance is not between 15-35 ohms, replace the solenoid.

4) Start vehicle and measure the voltage of the Black wire of 3-way connector before the delay times out. The voltmeter should read charging voltage. If not, replace SCC computer.

5) Turning on the A/C or EBL should also produce a charging system voltage on the Black wire of the 3-way connector after the delay has timed out. If not, check the wiring to the instrument panel for an open.

SYSTEM STARTING TEST

1) Turn ignition on. Disconnect coil wire from distributor cap. Hold end of coil wire approximately 1/4" away from a good engine ground. Using a jumper wire, intermittently ground coil negative terminal. Look for a bright Blue spark.

2) If spark is acceptable, intermittently ground negative coil terminal while slowly moving coil wire away from ground. Look for arcing at the coil tower. If arcing occurs, replace coil. If spark is weak or no spark is produced, perform ESC SYSTEM DIAGNOSIS. If spark is acceptable and there is no arcing at coil, check ignition system secondary circuit.

OVERHAUL

DISASSEMBLY

1) Remove distributor cap. Using 2 screwdrivers, pry off rotor from shaft. Remove reluctor by prying up from bottom of reluctor using 2 pry bars or screwdrivers with a maximum width of 7/16". Do not distort or damage reluctor teeth.

2) Remove 2 screws and lock washers attaching plate to housing. Lift out plate and pick-up coils as an assembly. Do not attempt to remove peened distributor cap clamps.

3) If distributor has more than .006" (.15 mm) shaft side play, replace housing shaft and reluctor sleeve by removing shaft retaining pin and sliding retainer off end of shaft.

4) Use a file to clean burrs from around pin hole in shaft and remove lower thrust washer. To remove shaft, push up through top of distributor housing.

4-6

1989 DISTRIBUTORS & IGNITION SYSTEMS
Chrysler Motors Electronic Spark Control (ESC) (Cont.)

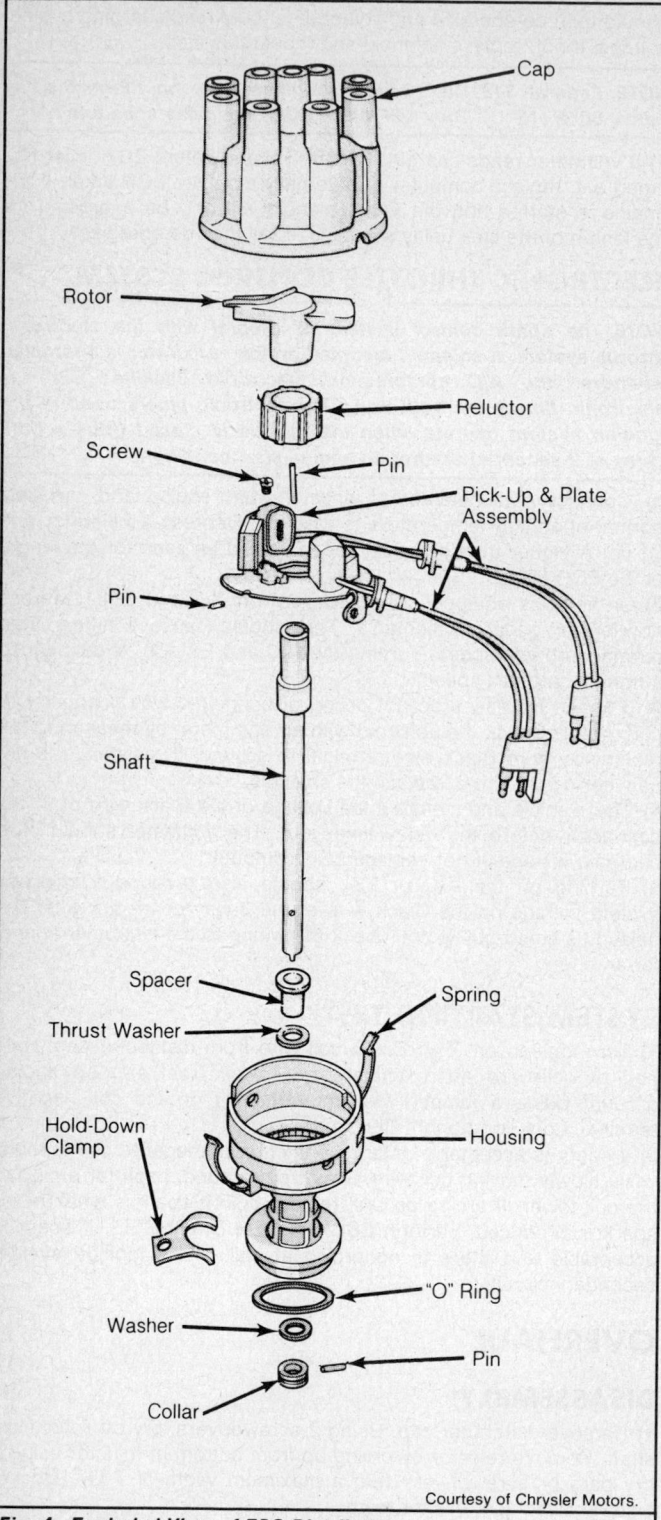

Cap

Rotor

Reluctor

Screw

Pin

Pick-Up & Plate Assembly

Pin

Shaft

Spacer

Thrust Washer

Spring

Hold-Down Clamp

Housing

"O" Ring

Washer

Pin

Collar

Courtesy of Chrysler Motors.

Fig. 4: Exploded View of ESC Distributor

REASSEMBLY

1) Inspect all bearing surfaces and pivot pins for rough, loose or binding surfaces. Lubricate and install upper thrust washer on shaft and slide shaft into distributor housing.

2) Install distributor shaft retainer and pin. Install lower plate, upper plate, and pick-up coils as an assembly.

3) Position reluctor keeper pin into place on reluctor sleeve and firmly press reluctor into place. Make sure keeper pin is in place. Lubricate felt pad in top of reluctor sleeve and install rotor and cap.

2.2, 2.5L Engines

DESCRIPTION & OPERATION

The electronic ignition system features a Hall Effect distributor, engine sensors and a Single Module Engine Controller (SMEC). The SMEC controls entire ignition system. Different engine conditions require changes in timing advance. The SMEC has a built in microprocessor which continually receives input from engine sensors. The SMEC electronically advances or retards ignition timing, providing an infinite number of advance curves.

During cold and warm engine operation, the microprocessor uses some unique advance curves to reduce engine emissions and improve driveability. The amount of advance is determined by coolant temperature, engine RPM, and available manifold vacuum. During the crank/start mode, the SMEC will provide a fixed amount of advanced timing to ensure a quick efficient start.

When no ignition signal is present with ignition in "RUN" position, the auto shutdown (ASD) relay interrupts power to electric fuel pump, fuel injectors, and ignition coil.

SENSORS

Coolant Temperature Sensor (CTS) – The coolant temperature sensor is located near the thermostat housing. It sends the SMEC information regarding engine operating temperatures. The sensor's range is from -40°F to 265°F (-40°C to 129°C). This sensor is also used to operate radiator fan.

Hall Effect Pick-Up – The pick-up assembly supplies engine RPM, ignition timing data, and fuel injection synchronization (turbo engines) to the SMEC to adjust ignition spark as required for engine running condition. The pick-up assembly is located in the distributor.

Manifold Absolute Pressure (MAP) Sensor – The MAP sensor monitors manifold vacuum. It is connected to a throttle body vacuum nipple on 2.2L and 2.5L non-turbo engines, and connected to intake manifold nipple on 2.2L and 2.5L turbo engines. This sensor sends information on vacuum conditions and barometric pressure to the SMEC.

ADJUSTMENTS

Initial timing can be adjusted in conventional manner by changing distributor position. No adjustments can be made to Hall Effect pick-up unit. Dwell and timing advance cannot be adjusted.

TESTING

NOTE: For test procedures not covered in this article, see appropriate article in COMPUTERIZED ENGINE CONTROLS section.

IGNITION SYSTEM SPARK TEST

1) Remove coil secondary wire from distributor center tower. Hold end of wire about 1/4" from a good engine ground. Crank engine and check for spark. If there is spark, slowly move coil secondary wire away from ground while cranking engine. Check for arcing at coil tower. If arcing occurs, replace ignition coil.

2) If spark is weak, inconsistent or there is no spark, proceed to FAILURE TO START TEST. If spark is okay and there is no arcing at coil tower, check distributor cap, rotor, spark plug wires and spark plugs. If components are okay, ignition system is working properly and is not the cause of no start condition. Check fuel system and engine mechanical condition.

FAILURE TO START TEST

CAUTION: Perform IGNITION SYSTEM SPARK TEST first. Failure to do so may result in lost diagnostic time or incorrect test results.

1) Ensure sufficient battery voltage (12.4 volts) is present for cranking and ignition systems. Crank engine for 5 seconds while monitoring voltage at coil positive terminal. If voltage remains near

zero during cranking, see appropriate article in COMPUTERIZED ENGINE CONTROLS section.

2) If reading is close to battery voltage but drops to zero after 1-2 seconds of cranking, see appropriate article in COMPUTERIZED ENGINE CONTROLS section. If voltage remains close to battery voltage for entire 5 seconds, turn ignition off. Remove 14-pin connector from SMEC. Ensure terminals of 14-pin connector are not damaged, causing a poor connection.

3) Disconnect ignition coil positive lead. Connect a jumper wire between coil positive terminal and battery positive terminal. Using a jumper wire with a .33 microfarad capacitor, momentarily ground terminal No. 12 of 14-pin connector. A spark should be seen when ground connection is removed.

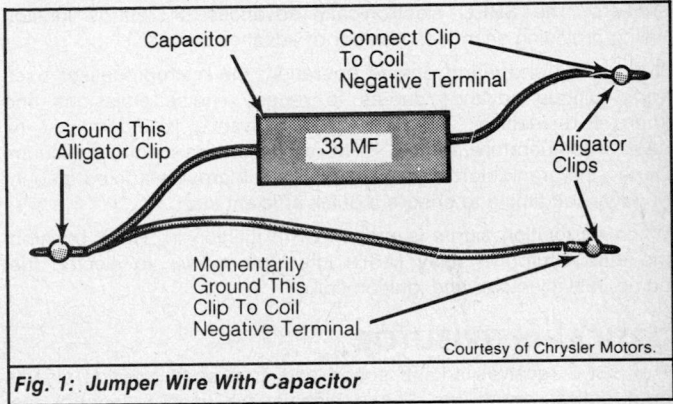

Courtesy of Chrysler Motors.

Fig. 1: Jumper Wire With Capacitor

4) If a spark is generated, replace SMEC. If no spark is seen, use jumper wire with capacitor to ground coil negative terminal directly. *See Fig. 1.* If spark is produced, repair wiring harness for an open circuit. If no spark is produced, replace ignition coil.

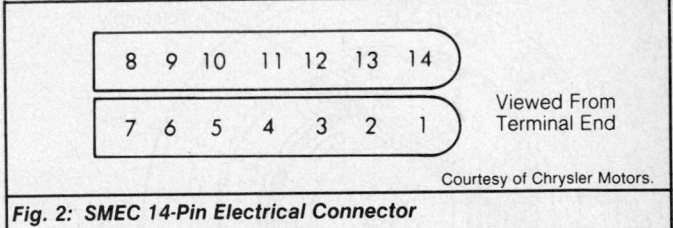

Courtesy of Chrysler Motors.

Fig. 2: SMEC 14-Pin Electrical Connector

POOR PERFORMANCE TESTS

Basic Timing – Ensure initial timing is adjusted to specification. See appropriate article in TUNE-UP section.

Ignition Coil Voltage Supply Test – Ensure IGNITION SYSTEM SPARK TEST has been performed.

Coolant Temperature Sensor (CTS) Test – Turn ignition off. Disconnect coolant sensor. Connect ohmmeter to coolant sensor terminals. With coolant temperature about 70°F (21°C), sensor resistance should be 7000-13,000 ohms. With coolant temperature at 200°F (93°C), sensor resistance should be 700-1000 ohms.

Manifold Absolute Pressure (MAP) Sensor Test – See appropriate article in COMPUTERIZED ENGINE CONTROLS section.

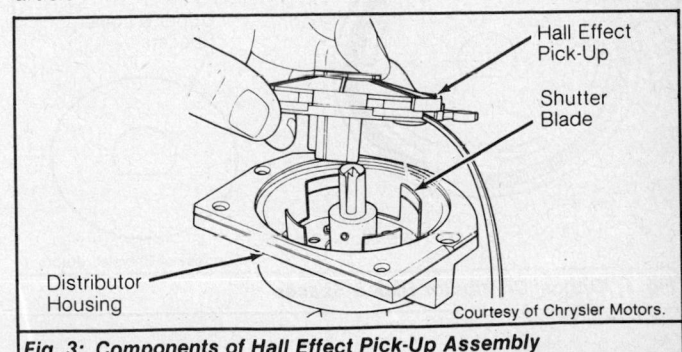

Courtesy of Chrysler Motors.

Fig. 3: Components of Hall Effect Pick-Up Assembly

3.0L Engine

DESCRIPTION

The electronic ignition system features an optical distributor, engine sensors and a Single Board Engine Controller (SBEC).

OPERATION

SINGLE BOARD ENGINE CONTROLLER (SBEC)

The SBEC controls entire ignition system. Different engine conditions require changes in timing advance. The SBEC has a built-in microprocessor which continually receives input from engine sensors. The SBEC electronically advances or retards ignition timing providing an infinite number of advance curves.

During cold and warm engine operation, the microprocessor uses some unique advance curves to reduce engine emissions and improve driveability. The amount of advance is determined by coolant temperature, engine RPM, and available manifold vacuum. During the crank/start mode, the SBEC will provide a fixed amount of advanced timing to ensure a quick efficient start.

When no ignition signal is present with ignition in "RUN" position, the auto shutdown relay (ASD) interrupts power to electric fuel pump, fuel injectors, and ignition coil.

OPTICAL DISTRIBUTOR

The SBEC receives engine speed and crankshaft position signals from optical distributor. These signals are used to control fuel injection, ignition timing and idle speed. The timing member is a thin disk, mounted on the distributor shaft and driven at 1/2 crankshaft speed.

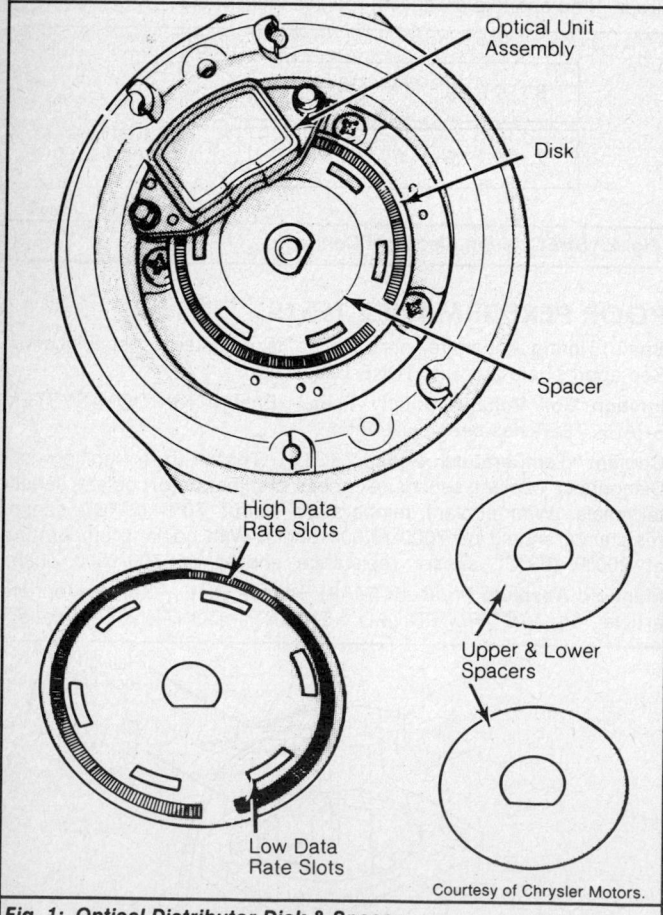

Fig. 1: Optical Distributor Disk & Spacer

Courtesy of Chrysler Motors.

Disk has 2 sets of slots on its surface. The outer, "high data rate" set of slots occurs at intervals of 2 degrees of crankshaft rotation. It is used for ignition timing at engine speeds up to 1200 RPM to increase timing accuracy.

During cranking and idle, engine speed changes with firing pulse of each cylinder. The "high data rate" signal is used to trigger ignition at correct crankshaft position regardless of these speed changes.

The inner, "low data rate" set contains 6 slots, which are correlated to piston TDC for each cylinder. This set is used to trigger fuel injection system and operation at speeds greater than 1200 RPM where speed changes due to individual firing pulses are small. This set of slots is also used for ignition timing. Light Emitting Diodes (LED's) and photo diodes are mounted in facing positions on opposite sides of the disk, in-line with the slots.

Masks over LED's and photo diodes focus light beams onto photo diodes. As each slot passes between diodes, light beam is turned on and off. This creates an alternating voltage in each photo diode which is converted into on-off pulses by an integrated circuit within the distributor.

These pulses are transmitted to SBEC. Distributor also delivers firing pulses from coil to each individual cylinder through a cap and rotor. A cover between rotor and case protects against high voltage damage to electronic circuitry and optical system contamination.

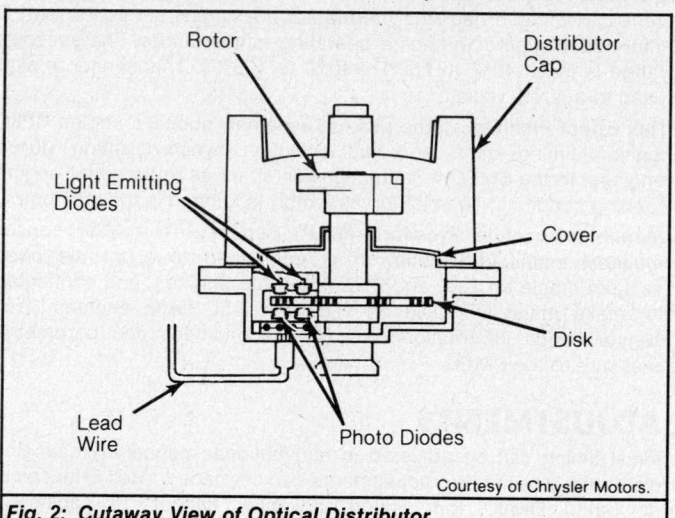

Courtesy of Chrysler Motors.

Fig. 2: Cutaway View of Optical Distributor

SENSORS

Coolant Temperature Sensor (CTS) – The coolant temperature sensor is located near the thermostat housing. It sends the SBEC information regarding engine operating temperatures. The sensors range is from -40°F to 265°F (-40°C to 129°C). This sensor is also used to operate radiator fan.

Manifold Absolute Pressure (MAP) Sensor – MAP sensor monitors manifold vacuum. It is connected to a vacuum nipple on air intake plenum and electrically to SBEC. This sensor sends information on vacuum conditions and barometric pressure to SBEC.

ADJUSTMENTS

No adjustments can be made to optical distributor. Dwell and timing advance cannot be adjusted. Initial fixed timing can be adjusted by changing distributor position.

TESTING

NOTE: For test procedures not covered in this article, see appropriate article in COMPUTERIZED ENGINE CONTROLS section.

IGNITION SYSTEM SPARK TEST

1) Remove coil secondary wire from distributor center tower. Hold end of wire about 1/4" from a good engine ground. Crank engine and check for spark. If there is spark, slowly move coil secondary wire away from ground while cranking engine. Check for arcing at coil tower. If arcing occurs, replace ignition coil.

2) If spark is weak, inconsistent or there is no spark, proceed to FAILURE TO START TEST. If spark is okay and there is no arcing at coil tower, check distributor cap, rotor, spark plug wires and spark plugs. If components are okay, ignition system is working properly and is not the cause of no start condition. Check fuel system and engine mechanical condition.

FAILURE TO START TEST

CAUTION: Perform IGNITION SYSTEM SPARK TEST first. Failure to do so may result in lost diagnostic time or incorrect test results.

1) Determine that sufficient battery voltage is present for cranking and ignition systems (12.4 volts). Crank engine for 5 seconds while monitoring voltage at coil positive terminal. If coil voltage remains near zero during entire period of cranking, see appropriate article in COMPUTERIZED ENGINE CONTROLS section.

2) If voltage is close to battery voltage and drops to zero after 1-2 seconds of cranking, see NO START TEST in appropriate article in COMPUTERIZED ENGINE CONTROLS section.

3) If voltage remains close to battery voltage during the entire 5 seconds, turn ignition off. Remove 60-pin connector from SBEC. Check 60-pin connector for spread or loose terminals. Remove lead from positive terminal of ignition coil. Install a jumper wire between battery positive terminal and positive terminal of coil.

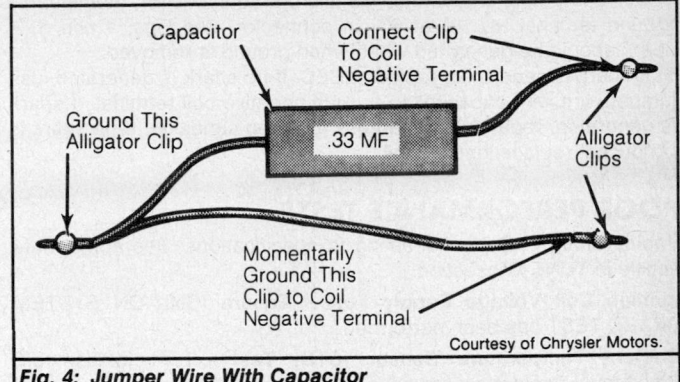

Courtesy of Chrysler Motors.

Fig. 4: Jumper Wire With Capacitor

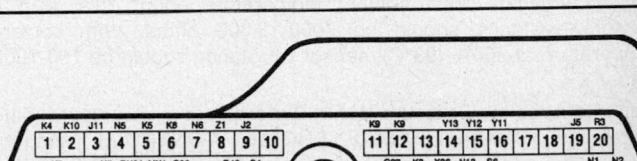

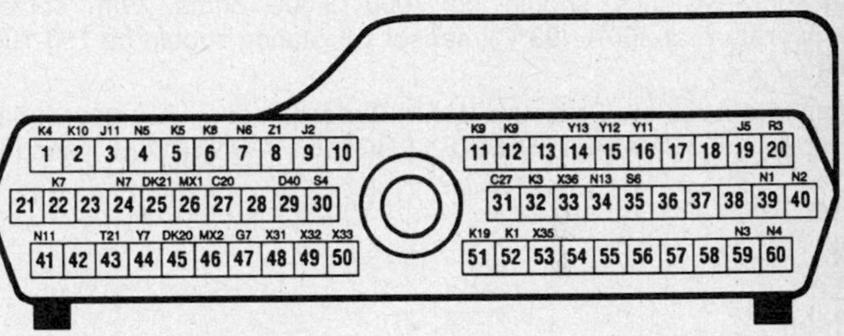

Courtesy of Chrysler Motors.

Fig. 5: Terminal Side View of 60-Pin Electrical Connector

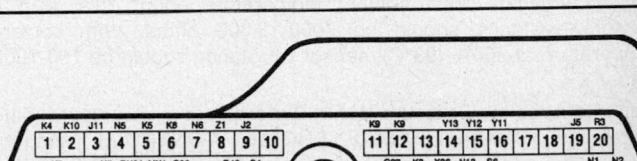

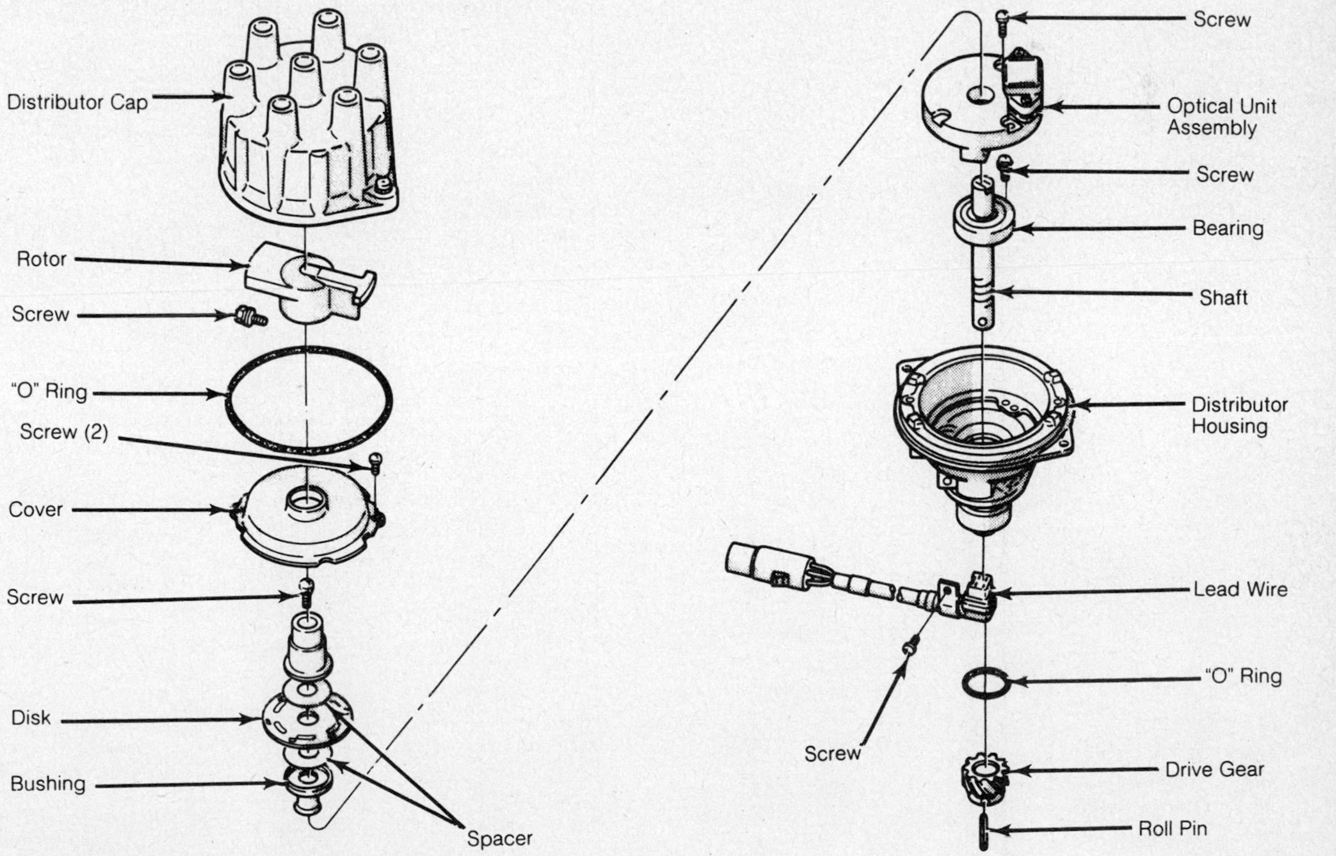

Courtesy of Chrysler Motors.

Fig. 3: Exploded View of 3.0L V6 Optical Distributor

4) Using a jumper wire with a .33 microfarad capacitor, momentarily ground terminal No. 19 of 60-pin connector. *See Figs. 4 and 5*. A spark should be generated when when ground is removed.

5) If spark is generated, replace SBEC. If no spark is generated, use jumper wire with capacitor to ground negative coil terminal. If spark is generated, repair wiring harness for open condition. If no spark is produced, replace ignition coil.

POOR PERFORMANCE TESTS

Basic Timing – Set initial timing to specifications. See appropriate acticle in TUNE-UP section.

Ignition Coil Voltage Supply Test – Ensure IGNITION SYSTEM SPARK TEST has been performed.

Coolant Temperature Sensor (CTS) Test – Turn ignition off. Disconnect coolant sensor connector. Connect ohmmeter to coolant sensor terminals. With coolant temperature about 70°F (21°C), sensor resistance should be 7000-13,000 ohms. With coolant temperature at 200°F (93°C), sensor resistance should be 700-1000 ohms.

Manifold Absolute Pressure (MAP) Sensor Test – See appropriate article in COMPUTERIZED ENGINE CONTROLS section.

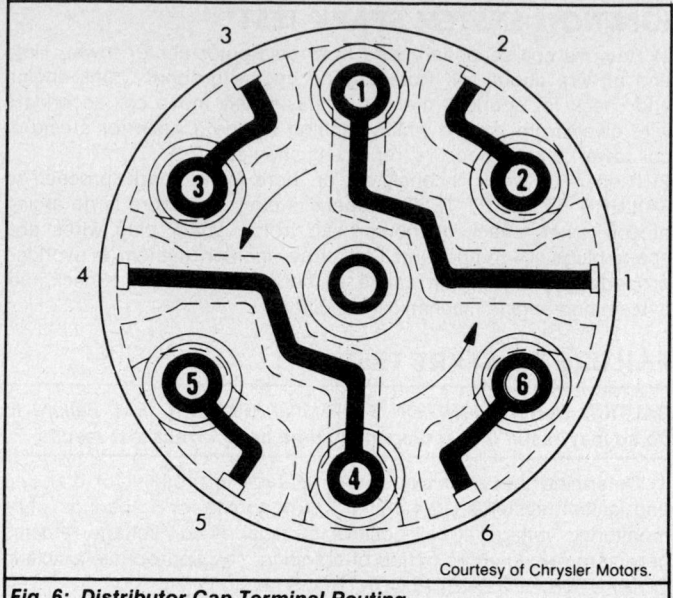

Courtesy of Chrysler Motors.

Fig. 6: Distributor Cap Terminal Routing

Premier

DESCRIPTION

The 2.5L and 3.0L electronic ignition system consists of 4 main components. The Ignition Control Module (ICM), is a solid state unit that generates voltage through the coil to fire the spark plugs. The Electronic Control Unit (ECU), processes information from the sensors to trigger the ICM. Sensors send information on engine conditions to the ECU. The distributor and rotor, determines which cylinder receives ignition voltage.

OPERATION

DISTRIBUTOR

The distributor, cap and rotor function is limited to the distribution of high voltage current produced in the coil, to the appropriate cylinder. Use standard procedures to examine cap and rotor for arcing or burning of terminals and cracks in cap.

ELECTRONIC CONTROL UNIT

The electronic control unit compares information received from the sensors with precalculated values in memory and outputs commands to the ignition control module based on the coordination of sensor input and engine requirements. The 4 input factors used to determine electronic spark advance are: coolant temperature, engine RPM, manifold air temperature and manifold absolute pressure.

IGNITION CONTROL MODULE

Electrical feed to ignition control module, only occurs with ignition in the "START" and "RUN" positions. The ECU sends a 5-volt square wave signal to the ICM. Depending on the signal received from the ECU, the ignition control module will advance or retard the ignition timing according to engine load. When the leading edge of this signal contacts the ICM ignition circuitry, the ICM charges the coil primary windings.

When coil saturation is complete, the ICM opens the primary windings to collapse the magnetic field and induce a high voltage rise in the secondary windings. This voltage is passed through the coil wire, distributor cap and rotor to the spark plugs.

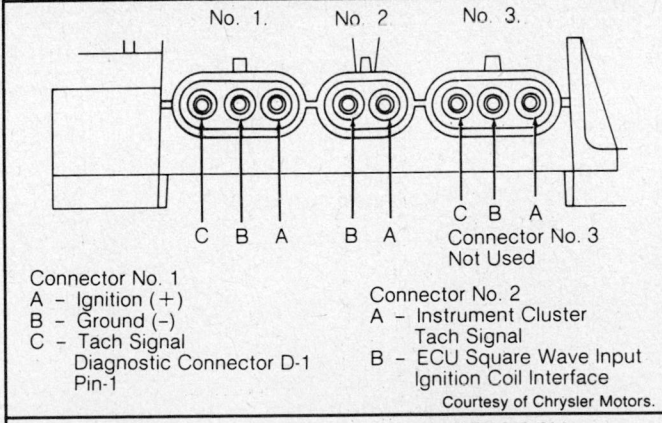

Connector No. 1
A – Ignition (+)
B – Ground (–)
C – Tach Signal
Diagnostic Connector D-1
Pin-1

Connector No. 2
A – Instrument Cluster
Tach Signal
B – ECU Square Wave Input
Ignition Coil Interface

Courtesy of Chrysler Motors.

Fig. 1: Ignition Control Module Connectors (2.5L & 3.0L)

SENSORS

Coolant Temperature Sensor (CTS) – CTS is located in the water jacket behind the throttle body. The resistence of the sensor changes as coolant temperature varies, producing varied input voltages to the ECU.

When a cold engine input is received, the ECU responds by: changing the injector pulse width to richen the air/fuel mixture,

increasing idle speed, advancing ignition timing and energizing the EGR valve solenoid (to prevent EGR valve operation).

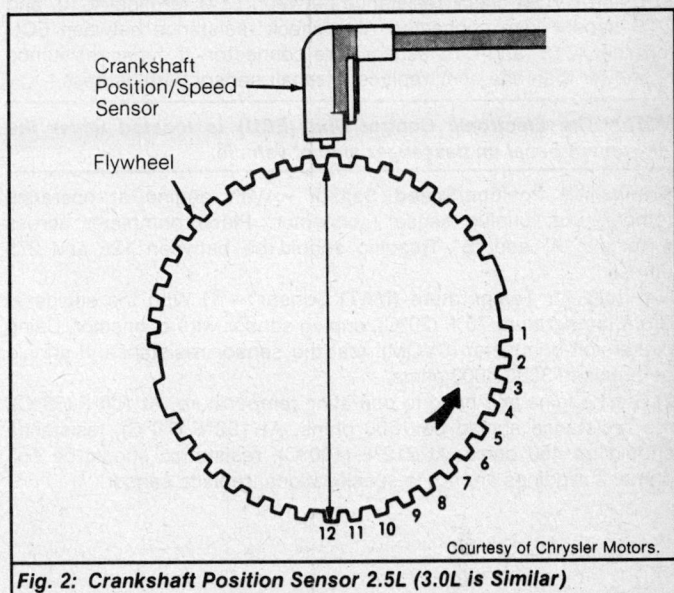

Courtesy of Chrysler Motors.

Fig. 2: Crankshaft Position Sensor 2.5L (3.0L is Similar)

Crankshaft Position/Speed Sensor (CPS) – CPS is attached to the flywheel housing. In this position it able to magnetically detect the large trigger teeth located at 90 degrees before each TDC on the 2.5L (120 degrees apart on 3.0L), as well as the 19 smaller teeth separating each large tooth. *See Fig. 2.*

As the large tooth passes under the sensor, a large voltage spike is created in the sensor that alerts the ECU to begin counting the smaller voltage spikes induced when the smaller teeth pass the sensor. After counting 12 voltage spikes (teeth) the piston is at TDC. With this information, the ECU can advance or retard the ignition timing in relation to flywheel position and sensor inputs.

Knock Sensor – Knock sensor is located on passenger side of engine block by the oil filter on 2.5L (just above oil pan on 3.0L). It is built to respond to the frequency emitted by an engine knock. When the sensor detects this frequency, it signals the ECU which responds by retarding the ignition timing on the appropriate cylinder(s).

Manifold Absolute Pressure (MAP) Sensor – MAP sensor is mounted on dash panel, under the hood. A vacuum hose connects it to the throttle body. As the engine load changes, so does the manifold pressure. This causes the resistance of the MAP sensor to change and vary the voltage to the ECU accordingly. This voltage reading supplies the ECU with information pertaining to ambient barometric pressure while engine is cranking (start-up) and engine load, while running.

Manifold Air Temperature (MAT) Sensor – MAT sensor is installed in the intake manifold with the sensor element projecting into the air/fuel flow. As the manifold air temperature changes, the resistance of the sensor changes causing voltage input to the ECU to change.

TESTING

NOTE: *For test procedures not covered in this article, see appropriate article in COMPUTERIZED ENGINE CONTROLS section.*

SENSORS

Coolant Temperature Sensor (CTS) – **1)** With the engine at room temperature 70°F (20°C), unplug sensor wire connector. Using digital volt-ohmmeter (DVOM), test the sensor resistance. It should be between 3000-4000 ohms.
2) Start engine and bring to operating temperature. At 100°F (38°C) the resistance should be 1600 ohms, at 160°F (70°C) resistance

should be 450 ohms and at 212°F (100°C) resistance should be 185 ohms. If readings are not to specifications, replace sensor.

3) Using DVOM check resistance between ECU terminal "C10" and CTS sensor wire connector. Also check resistance between ECU terminal "D12" and CTS sensor wire connector. If either resistance is greater than one ohm, replace or repair sensor wire harness.

NOTE: The Electronic Control Unit (ECU) is located under the instrument panel on passenger side of vehicle.

Crankshaft Position/Speed Sensor – With engine at operating temperature, unplug sensor connector. Place ohmmeter across terminals "A" and "B". Reading should be between 125 and 275 ohms.

Manifold Air Temperature (MAT) Sensor – 1) With the engine at room temperature 70°F (20°C), unplug sensor wire connector. Using digital volt-ohmmeter (DVOM), test the sensor resistance. It should be between 3000-4000 ohms.

2) Start engine and bring to operating temperature. At 100°F (38°C), the resistance should be 1600 ohms. At 160°F (70°C), resistance should be 450 ohms. At 212°F (100°C), resistance should be 185 ohms. If readings are not to specifications, replace sensor.

3) Using DVOM, check resistance between ECU terminal "C8" and MAT sensor wire connector. Also check resistance between ECU terminal "D3" and MAT sensor wire connector. If either resistance is greater than one ohm, replace or repair sensor wire harness.

Manifold Absolute Pressure (MAP) Sensor – 1) Inspect vacuum hoses at sensor and throttle body, repair if necessary. Turn ignition switch to "ON" position but do not start engine. Using DVOM, check MAP output voltage at terminal "B" (marked on sensor body). Output voltage should be 4-5 volts. If okay, check ECU terminal "C6" for the same voltage. Repair sensor wire harness if necessary.

2) Test sensor terminal "C" for a supply voltage of 4.5 to 5.5 volts. If okay, check sensor wire connector from ECU terminal "C14" for same reading. Repair sensor wire harness if necessary.

3) If voltage is not as specified with engine not running, replace sensor. If okay, start engine and bring to operating temperature. With engine at idle, check output voltage as in step 1). Reading should be between 1.5-2.1 volts. If not, replace sensor.

4) Using ohmmeter, test for proper ground at sensor connector terminal "A" and at ECU terminal "D3". Repair as necessary.

Tempo & Topaz 3.8L SEFI, Taurus 3.0L SHO

DESCRIPTION & OPERATION

The Distributorless Ignition System (DIS) consists of a crankshaft mounted Hall Effect Profile Ignition Pickup (PIP) sensor, a camshaft driven Hall Effect Cylinder Identification (CID) sensor, a 6 tower DIS coil, and a DIS ignition module. The DIS ignition system eliminates the distributor by using multiple coils.

Each coil fires 2 spark plugs at the same time. Spark plugs are paired so as one fires during compression stroke, the other fires during exhaust stroke. Their are 3 coils mounted together in a "coil pack". Each coil pack has 3 tach wires, one for each coil.

The crank sensor is a digital output hall device that sends out a signal called Profile Ignition Pickup (PIP). The PIP is produced by a rotating metallic vane mounted on crankshaft damper assembly. The crankshaft sensor has 3 teeth and generates 3 PIP signals for every one revolution of the crankshaft.

The Cylinder Identification (CID) signal is generated by a single toothed vane cup hall device driven by camshaft that produces one signal every camshaft revolution, or once every 2 crankshaft revolutions. See Fig. 1. The 3.0L SHO CID sensor is mounted at end of the rear camshaft. The 3.8L SC CID sensor is mounted in normal distributor location. See Fig. 2 or 3.

The PIP output is a 50% duty cycle (50% on and 50% off) signal that provides base spark timing information. The CID signal output is also a 50% duty cycle signal and is used so DIS module knows which coil to fire. CID signal is high (10-12 volts) for half of the cam revolution (180 degrees) and low the other half. See Fig. 4.

The EEC-IV processor determines spark angle (SPOUT) using the PIP signal to establish base timing. The SPOUT signal is produced and sent by EEC-IV processor to DIS module and serves 2 purposes. The leading edge of the signal fires the coil and trailing edge of the signal controls dwell timing. This feature is called Computer Controlled Dwell (CCD).

The Ignition Diagnostic Monitor (IDM) is an output from DIS module that provides diagnostic information concerning the ignition system to EEC-IV module for self-test.

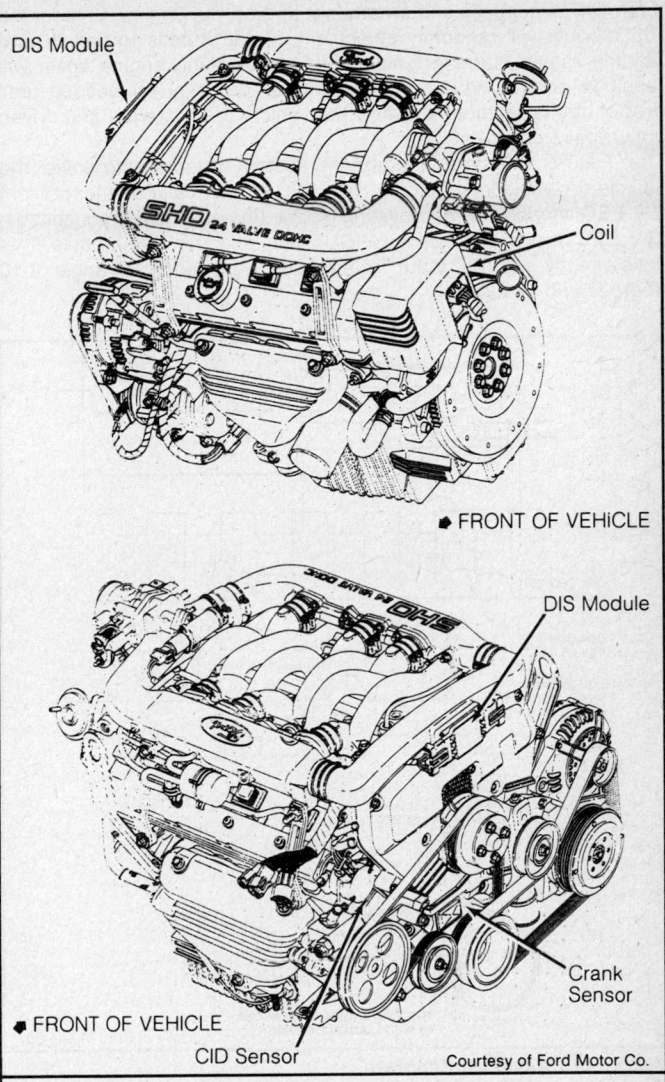

← FRONT OF VEHICLE

Fig. 2: 3.0L SHO Engine DIS Component Locations

Courtesy of Ford Motor Co.

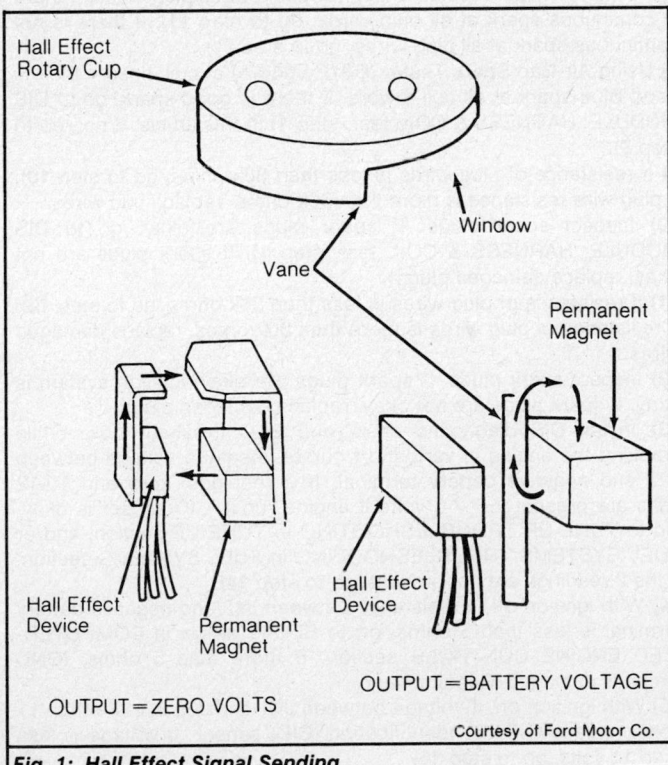

OUTPUT=ZERO VOLTS   OUTPUT=BATTERY VOLTAGE

Courtesy of Ford Motor Co.

Fig. 1: Hall Effect Signal Sending

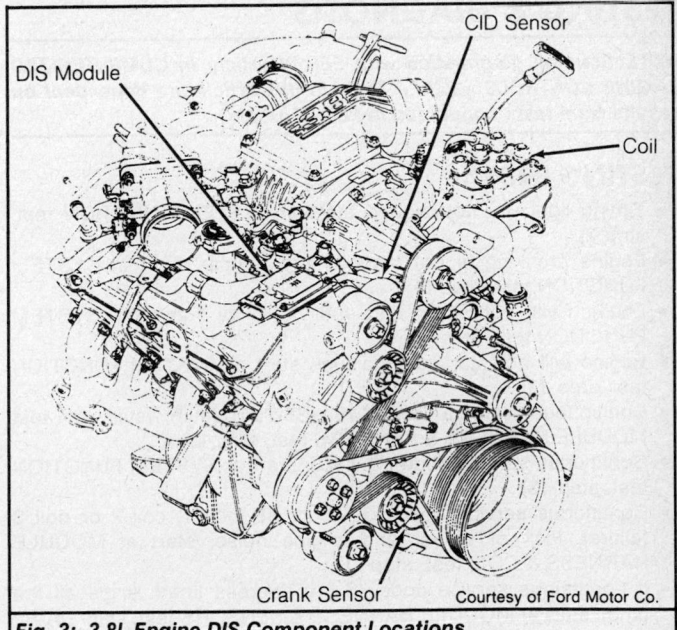

Courtesy of Ford Motor Co.

Fig. 3: 3.8L Engine DIS Component Locations

If the CID circuit fails and an attempt to start the engine is made, the DIS module will randomly select one of the 3 coils to fire. If hard starting results, turning ignition off and cranking engine again will result in another "guess". Several attempts may be needed until proper coil is selected allowing the vehicle to be started and driven until repairs can be made.

The Failure Effects Management system attempts to keep the vehicle driveable in spite of certain EEC system failures that prevent the EEC module from providing spark angle or dwell commands. The EEC processor opens SPOUT line and the DIS module fires coils directly from PIP input. This results in a fixed spark angle of 10 degrees and fixed dwell.

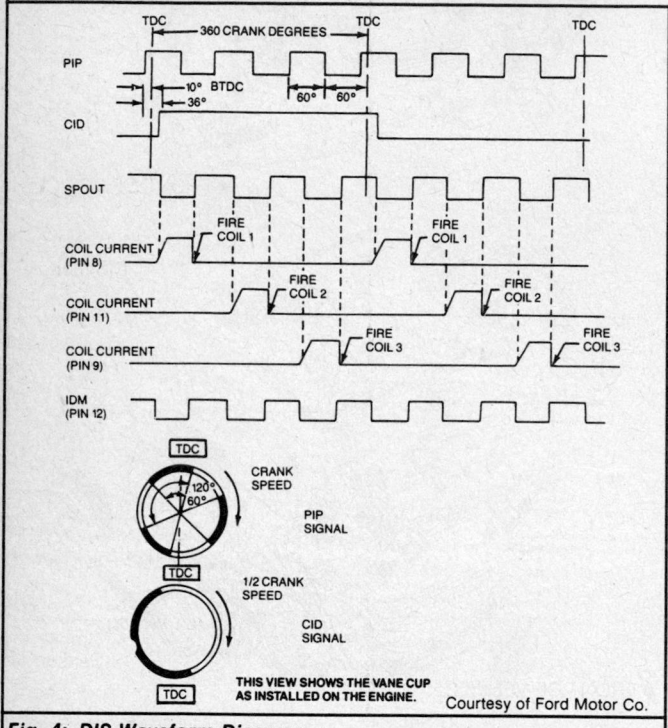

Fig. 4: DIS Waveform Diagram

TESTING & DIAGNOSIS

NOTE: Start all diagnostics with EEC-IV article in COMPUTERIZED ENGINE CONTROLS section. Tests in this article are dependent on results from tests conducted in EEC-IV article.

TESTING INDEX

- Timing light will not trigger, start at SYSTEM FUNCTION test, step 7).
- Engine cranking is not smooth and regular, start at SYSTEM FUNCTION test, step 6).
- Engine will not start and fuel is okay, start at SYSTEM FUNCTION test, step 7).
- Engine will not start and no fuel, start at SYSTEM FUNCTION test, step 13).
- Conitinuous service code 18 (SPOUT fault), start at test MODULE HARNESS & SENSORS test, step 13).
- Continuous service code 19 (CID), start at SYSTEM FUNCTION test, step 13).
- Continuous service code 45, 46 or 48 (coil 1, coil 2 or coil 3 failure), lack of power and engine noise, start at MODULE HARNESS & COIL test, step 1).
- If continuous service code 49 (10 degrees spark angle all the time), start at MODULE HARNESS & SENSORS test, step 15).

PRELIMINARY

Visually inspect engine compartment to ensure all vacuum hoses and spark plug wires are properly connected. Examine all wiring harnesses and connectors for damage. Ensure DIS module mounting screws are tight. Ensure battery is fully charged and accessories are off. When making measurements on a wiring harness, both a visual inspection and a continuity test shoud be preformed.

Inspect connector pins for damage when directed to remove a connector. Spark timing adjustments are not possible. When making voltage checks, a ground reading means any failure within a range of 0-1 volt. Also VBAT readings mean any value that falls within a range of 10-12 volts. When using the spark plug firing indicator, place grooved end as close as possible to plug boot, a very weak flashing may be caused by a fouled plug.

SYSTEM FUNCTION

1) Disconnect SPOUT jumper. See EEC-IV article in COMPUTERIZED ENGINE CONTROL section. If spark angle is 7-13 degrees BTDC, go to step **2)**. If not, go to step **3)**.

2) With SPOUT jumper connected during Self-Test. Is spark angle 27-33 degrees BTDC. If not, replace DIS module. If so, go to step **4)**.

3) Inspect vane cups on back of crankshaft damper. Replace any bent or damaged cups. If vane cups are okay, replace crank sensor.

4) Crank engine. If cranking is smooth and regular (does not backfire or pause), go to step **7)**. If cranking is not smooth and regular, go to step **5)**

5) Using Neon Spark Tester (Champion CT-436), crank engine while watching for continuous spark at all plug wires. If a continuous spark is present at all plug wires, go to step **6)**. If not, go to step **8)**.

6) Install DIS Diagnostic Cable (Hickok HK-100-306) and EEC breakout box. *See Fig. 5*. While cranking engine in very short bursts, measure voltage between J51 and J2. *See Fig. 6*. If 2 readings of zero and 10-12 volts are observed during cranking (5.4-7.4 volts if engine runs), replace DIS module. If the 2 readings are not present, go to DIS MODULE, HARNESS & SENSORS test in this article step **1)**.

7) Using neon spark tester, check for spark at all plug wires. If there is continuous spark at all plug wires, go to step **11)**. If there is not continuous spark at all plug wires, go to step **8)**.

8) Using Air Gap Spark Tester (D81P-6666-A) at coil, ensure their is good Blue spark at all coil towers. If there is good spark, go to DIS MODULE, HARNESS & COIL test, step **1)** in this article. If not, go to step **9)**.

9) If resistance of plug wires is less than 30k ohms, go to step **10)**. If plug wire resistance is more than 30k ohms, replace bad wires.

10) Inspect spark plugs. If spark plugs are okay, go to DIS MODULE, HARNESS & COIL test, step **1)**. If spark plugs are not okay, replace damaged plugs.

11) If resistance of plug wires is less than 30k ohms, go to step **12)**. If resistance of plug wires is more than 30k ohms, replace damaged wires.

12) Inspect spark plugs. If spark plugs are okay, ignition system is okay. If spark plugs are not okay, replace damaged plugs.

13) Install DIS diagnostic cable and EEC breakout box. While cranking the engine in very short bursts, measure voltage between J22 and negative battery terminal. If 2 readings, zero and 10-12 volts are present (5.5-7.5 volts if engine runs), CID sensor is okay. Go to TUNE-UP TROUBLESHOOTING in TUNE-UP section, and/or FUEL SYSTEMS TROUBLESHOOTING in FUEL SYSTEMS section. If the 2 readings are not present, go to step **14)**.

14) With ignition off, if resistance between J42 and negative battery terminal is less than 5 ohms, go to EEC-IV article in COMPUTERIZED ENGINE CONTROLS section. If more than 5 ohms, IGND circuit is damaged. Repair circuit.

15) With ignition on, if voltage between J41 and J55 is more than 11 volts, replace Cylinder Identification (CID) sensor. If voltage is less than 11 volts, go to step **16)**.

16) Remove CID sensor from tee and repeat voltage check between J41 and J55. If 11 volts is present, replace CID sensor. If 11 volts is not present, VBATCS circuit has a fault. Repair harness.

17) Install DIS diagnostic cable and EEC breakout box. While cranking engine in very short bursts, measure voltage between J33 and negative terminal of battery. If 2 readings, zero and 10-12 volts (5.5-7.5 volts if engine runs) are present, PIP sensor is okay, go to TUNE-UP TROUBLESHOOTING in TUNE-UP section and/or FUEL SYSTEMS TROUBLESHOOTING in FUEL SYSTEMS section. If the voltage readings are not present, go to step **18)**.

18) If resistance between J55 and negative terminal of battery is less than 5 ohms, go to step **19)**. If resistance is more than 5 ohms, IGN GND circuit has a fault. Repair IGN GND circuit.

19) With ignition on, if voltage between J56 and J55 is more than 11 volts, replace PIP sensor. If less than 11 volts, go to step **20)**.

20) Remove PIP sensor from crank sensor tee. With ignition on, if voltage between J56 and J55 is more than 11 volts, replace PIP sensor. If 11 volts is not present, VBAT circuit has a fault. Repair harness.

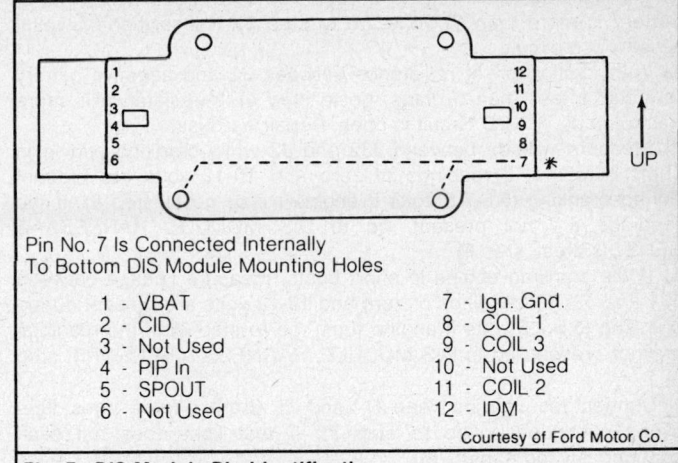

Pin No. 7 Is Connected Internally
To Bottom DIS Module Mounting Holes

1 - VBAT	7 - Ign. Gnd.
2 - CID	8 - COIL 1
3 - Not Used	9 - COIL 3
4 - PIP In	10 - Not Used
5 - SPOUT	11 - COIL 2
6 - Not Used	12 - IDM

Courtesy of Ford Motor Co.

Fig. 7: DIS Module Pin Identification

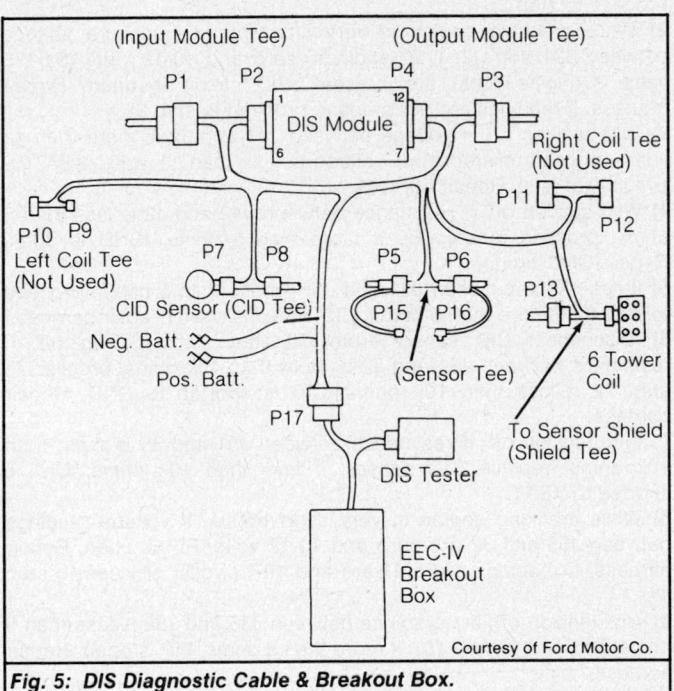

Fig. 5: DIS Diagnostic Cable & Breakout Box.

Courtesy of Ford Motor Co.

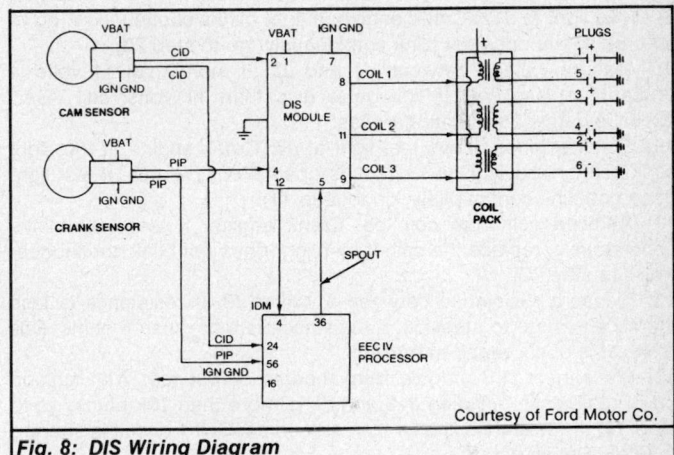

Courtesy of Ford Motor Co.

Fig. 8: DIS Wiring Diagram

DIS MODULE, HARNESS & COIL

1) Install DIS Diagnostic Cable (Hickok HK-100-306) and EEC breakout box. If there is continuous spark at any coil wire while cranking engine, go to step **6)**. If there is not continuous spark at any coil wire, go to step **2)**.

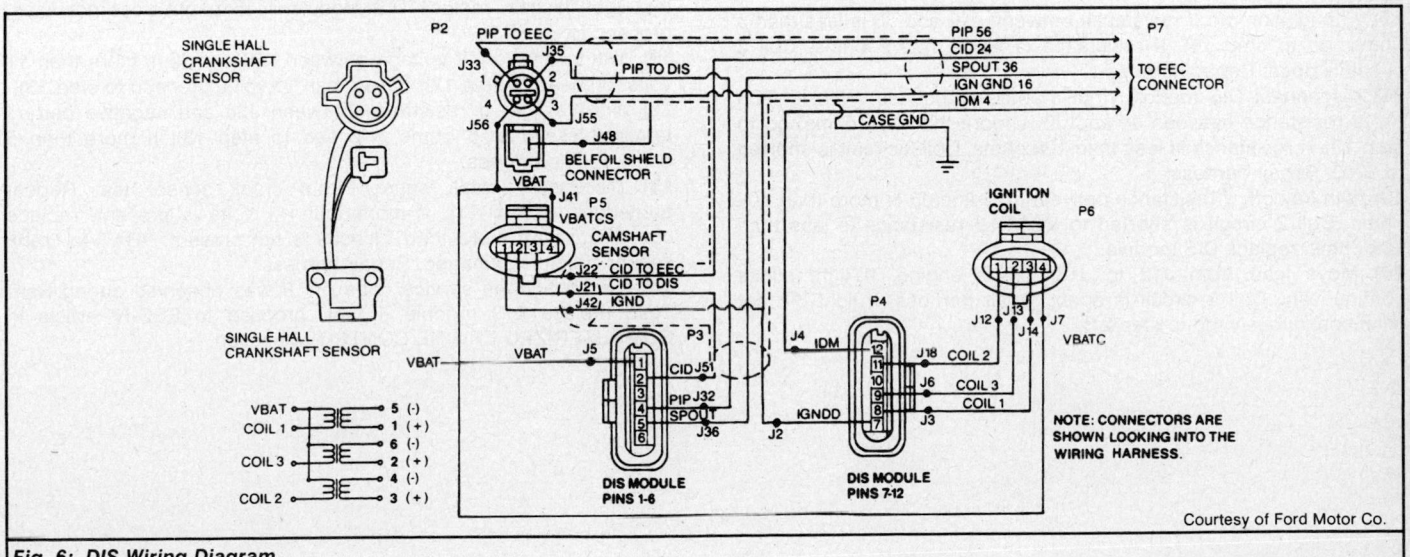

Fig. 6: DIS Wiring Diagram

Courtesy of Ford Motor Co.

2) With ignition on, if voltage between J5 and negative terminal of battery is more than 11 volts, go to step 3). If less than 11 volts, repair open circuit.

3) With ignition off, if resistance between J2 and negative battery terminal is less than 5 ohms, go to step 4). If resistance is more than 5 ohms, IGNDD circuit is open. Repair harness.

4) Measure voltage between J32 and J2 while cranking engine in short bursts. If 2 readings of zero and 10-12 volts are present during cranking (5.5-7.5 volts if engine runs), go to step 5). If the readings are not present, go to DIS MODULE, HARNESS & SENSORS test, step 8).

5) While cranking engine in short busts, measure voltage between J51 and J2. If 2 readings of zero and 10-12 volts are present during cranking (5.5-7.5 volts if engine runs), go to step 6). If the readings are not present, go to DIS MODULE, HARNESS & SENSORS, step 1).

6) Connect test light between J14 and J5. Crank engine. If test light blinks continuously, go to step 7). If test light does not blink continuously, go to step 10).

7) Move test light to J13. Crank engine. If light blinks continuously, go to step 8). If test light does not blink continuously, go to step 15).

8) Move light to J12. Crank engine. If light blinks continuously, go to step 9). If light does not blink continuously, go to step 20).

9) Measure voltage between J7 and J2. If more than 11 volts is present, replace coil. If voltage is less than 11 volts, coil VBAT circuit is damaged. Repair harness.

10) On all engines, move test light to J3. Crank engine. If test light blinks continuously, Coil 1 circuit is open. Repair circuit. If test light does not blink continuously, go to step 11).

11) Remove coil from coil tee. Crank engine. If test light blinks continuously, replace the coil. If test light does not blink continuously, go to step 12).

12) Measure resistance between J14 and J3. If resistance is less than 5 ohms, go to step 13). If resistance is more than 5 ohms, Coil 1 circuit is open, repair harness.

13) Disconnect DIS module from module output tee. With ignition off, if resistance between J18 and J2 is more than 10k ohms, go to step 14). If resistance is less than 10k ohms, Coil 1 circuit is shorted to GND. Repair harness.

14) With ignition off, if resistance between J18 and J5 is more than 10k ohms. Replace DIS module. If less than 10k ohms, Coil 1 circuit is shorted to VBAT.

15) Move lead from J13 to J6. Crank engine. If test light blinks continuously, Coil 3 circuit is open. Repair harness. If test light does not blink continuously, go to step 16).

16) Remove coil from coil tee. Crank engine. If test light blinks continuously, replace coil. If test light does not blink continuously, go to step 17).

17) With ignition off, if resistance between J13 and J6 is less than 5 ohms, go to step 18). If resistance is more than 5 ohms, Coil 3 circuit is open. Repair harness.

18) Disconnect DIS module from module output tee. With ignition off, if resistance between J6 and J2 is more than 10k ohms, go to step 19). If resistance is less than 10k ohms, Coil 2 circuit is shorted to GND. Repair harness.

19) With key off, if resistance between J13 and J5 is more than 10k ohms, Coil 2 circuit is shorted to VBAT. If resistance is less than 10k ohms, replace DIS module.

20) Move lead from J12 to J18. Crank engine. If light blinks continuously, Coil 2 circuit is open, repair harness. If light did not blink continuously, go to step 21).

21) Remove the coil from coil tee. Crank engine. If light blinks continuously, replace coil. If light does not blink continuously, go to step 22).

22) Measure resistance between J3 and J14. If resistance is less than 5 ohms, go to step 23). If resistance is more than 5 ohms, Coil 1 circuit is open. Repair harness.

23) With ignition off, disconnect module from module output tee. If resistance between J3 and J2 is more than 10k ohms, proceed to step 24). If resistance is less than 10k ohms, Coil 1 circuit is shorted to GND. Repair harness

24) With key off, if resistance between J3 and J5 is more than 10k ohms, replace DIS module. If less than 10k ohms, Coil 1 circuit is shorted to VBAT. Repair harness.

DIS MODULE, HARNESS & SENSORS

1) Disconnect module from DIS input tee. While cranking engine in very short bursts. Measure voltage between J51 and J2. If 2 readings, zero and 10-12 volts (5.5-7.5 volts if engine runs) are present, replace DIS module. If the readings are not present, proceed to step 2).

2) While cranking engine in very short bursts, measure voltage between J21 and J2. If 2 readings, zero and 10-12 volts (5.5-7.5 volts if engine runs) are present, CID circuit is open. Repair harness. If readings are not present, proceed to step 3).

3) With ignition on, if voltage between J41 and J2 is more than 11 volts, proceed to step 4). If voltage is less than 11 volts, VBATCS circuit is at fault. Repair harness.

4) With ignition off, if resistance between J42 and J2 is less than 5 ohms, proceed to step 5). If more than 5 ohms, IGND is open. Repair IGND circuit.

5) If resistance between J21 and J51 is less than 5 ohms, proceed to step 6). If more than 5 ohms, CID circuit is open. Repair harness.

6) Disconnect CID sensor from CID tee. With ignition off, if resistance between J51 and J2 is more than 10k ohms, proceed to step 7). If less than 10k ohms, CID is shorted to GND. Repair harness.

7) With ignition off, if resistance between J51 and J5 is more than 10k ohms, replace CID sensor. If less than 10k ohms, CID is shorted to VBAT.

8) While cranking engine in very short bursts, if voltage readings between J35 and J2 are zero and 10-12 volts, PIP is open. Repair harness. If readings are not zero and 10-12 volts, proceed to step 9).

9) With ignition off, if resistance between J35 and J32 is less than 5 ohms, proceed to step 10). If more than 5 ohms, PIP is open. Repair harness.

10) Disconnect DIS module from DIS input tee. Repeat step 8). If test light flashes, replace DIS module. If test light does not flash, proceed to step 11).

11) With ignition on, if voltage between J56 and J2 is more than 11 volts, proceed to step 12). If less than 11 volts, proceed to step 13).

12) With key off, if resistance between J55 and negative battery terminal less than 5 ohms, proceed to step 13). If more than 5 ohms, repair harness.

13) Disconnect crank sensor from crank sensor tee. Repeat procedure in step 11). If more than 11 volts is present, replace crank sensor. If more than 11 volts is not present, VBAT to crank sensor circuit is damaged. Repair harness.

14) If a continuous service code of 18 was observed during Self-Test, replace DIS module. If not, proceed to EEC-IV article in COMPUTERIZED ENGINE CONTROLS section.

5.8L LTD Crown Victoria (Police)

DESCRIPTION

The Dura-Spark II ignition system consists of a breakerless distributor, an ignition module, ignition coil, battery, ignition switch, ignition ballast resistor and necessary wiring. *See Fig. 1.*

Two different ignition modules are used. The standard ignition module uses 2 connectors with a total of 6 wires. The Universal Ignition Module (UIM) has 3 connectors and a total of 8 wires. The UIM type is connected to the Microprocessor Control Unit (MCU) to control spark retard, via knock sensor.

OPERATION

DISTRIBUTOR

The distributor provides a signal to ignition module which controls timing. The rotating reluctor causes fluctuations in a magnetic field produced by stator/pick-up coil assembly magnet. These fluctuations induce a voltage in the stator/pick-up coil which sends a signal to ignition module.

The occurrence of this signal to ignition module, in relation to initial spark timing, is controlled by centrifugal and vacuum advance mechanisms. Centrifugal advance controls spark timing in response to engine RPM. Vacuum advance controls spark timing in response to engine load.

IGNITION MODULE

Two types of ignition modules are used. The standard ignition module uses 2 connectors with a total of 6 wires. The Universal Ignition Module (UIM) has 3 connectors and a total of 8 wires. The UIM type is connected to the MCU to control spark retard, via knock sensor.

Both ignition modules perform the function of turning off current flow through ignition coil in response to a control signal from the stator/pick-up coil assembly. The UIM can respond to another control signal from either an ignition barometric pressure switch or MCU, depending on engine calibration. This allows UIM to provide additional spark timing control under various operating conditions.

IGNITION COIL

Ignition coil is energized whenever ignition switch is on. Coil has a positive "BATT" terminal, a negative "TACH" terminal, and a secondary high voltage terminal. A special connector attaches the ignition module Green wire to "TACH" terminal. An ignition feed wire from ignition switch is attached to "BATT" terminal.

SYSTEM PRECAUTIONS

Battery must be fully charged. Ensure system components have good grounds. Visually inspect for properly routed vacuum hoses. Ensure electrical connectors and wiring harnesses are not damaged, burned, loose or broken. Wiggle wires while making wiring harness and/or connector tests. Keep ignition off while removing/installing ignition components. Accessories should be turned off.

Use care when removing spark plug wires to avoid damage. Under no circumstances are plug wires to be punctured with any type of probe device. Lightly coat entire inner surface of plug wire boots with silicone dielectic compound whenever removed from spark plug, distributor cap or coil.

ADJUSTMENTS

Initial ignition timing and spark plug gap are the only adjustments which can be made to this ignition system. Refer to Vehicle Emission Control (VEC) information decal.

TESTING

SPARK PLUG/COIL WIRE RESISTANCE

1) Remove distributor cap with plug/coil wires attached. Disconnect plug wire from spark plug or coil wire from coil. Connect ohmmeter between plug wire end and corresponding terminal inside cap. DO NOT puncture spark plug wire.
2) If reading is less than 7000 ohms per foot, plug/coil wire is okay. If reading is greater than 7000 ohms per foot, remove plug/coil wire from distributor cap and recheck. If reading is greater than 7000 ohms per foot, replace plug/coil wire.

START CIRCUIT

NOTE: A spark plug with a broken electrode is not sufficient to check for spark and may lead to incorrect results.

1) Attach Spark Tester (D81P-6666-A) between ignition coil wire and engine ground. Crank engine with the ignition switch. If spark is present, proceed to RUN CIRCUIT. If no spark is present, check coil wire resistance as previously described.
2) If coil wire resistance is okay, verify rotation of distributor shaft. Check ignition coil for damage or carbon tracking. If these items are okay, proceed to SUPPLY VOLTAGE CIRCUIT test.

RUN CIRCUIT

1) With the spark tester attached to coil wire, turn the ignition switch from "OFF" to "RUN" to "OFF" position several times. Sparks should occur each time ignition switch is cycled. If no sparks occur,

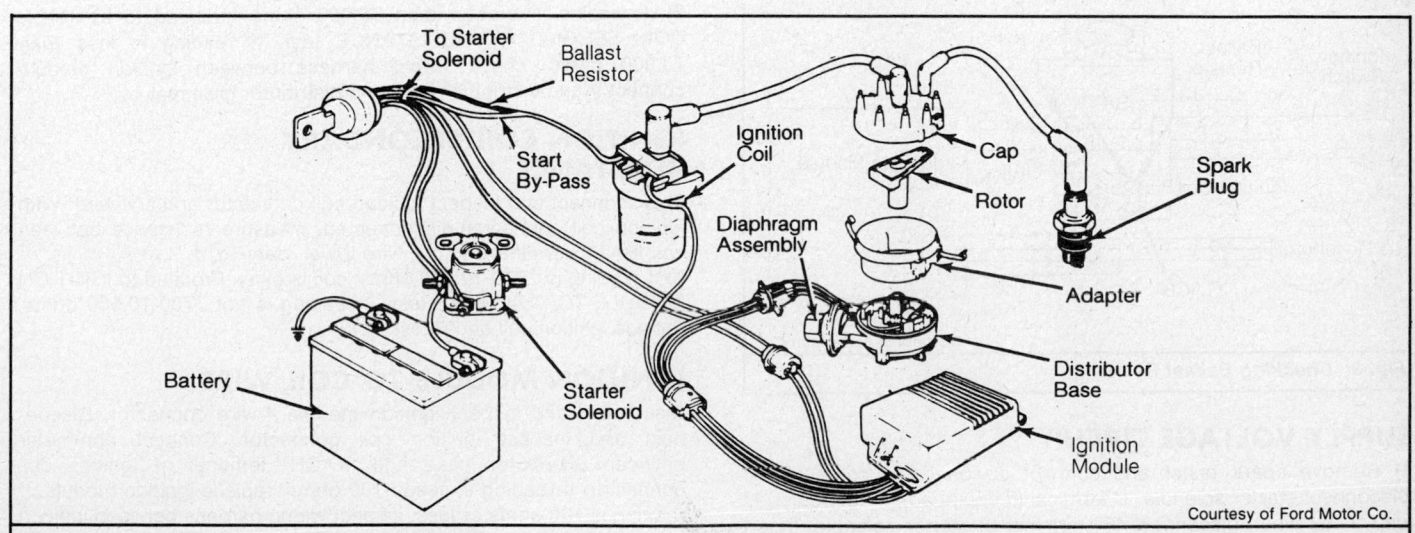

Courtesy of Ford Motor Co.

Fig. 1: Dura-Spark II Ignition System Schematic

proceed to IGNITION MODULE VOLTAGE test.

2) If sparks occurred, check distributor cap, adapter, and rotor for cracks, carbon tracking, or lack of silicone dielectric compound. Ensure roll pin is securing reluctor in distributor. *See Fig. 5.*

3) Ensure Orange and Purple wires are not crossed between distributor and ignition module. If UIM type module is used, proceed to SPARK TIMING ADVANCE test in this article.

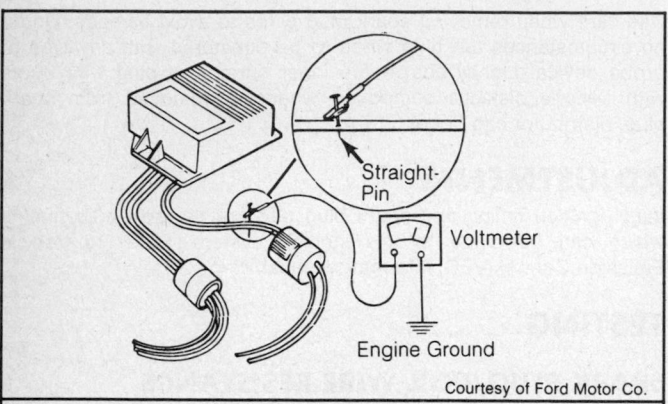

Fig. 2: Checking Ignition Module Voltage

Courtesy of Ford Motor Co.

IGNITION MODULE VOLTAGE

1) With ignition switch off, insert a small straight-pin into Red wire of ignition module. *See Fig. 2.* DO NOT allow straight-pin to contact an electrical ground. Attach voltmeter negative lead to distributor base and measure battery voltage. Turn ignition switch to "RUN" position and measure voltage at straight-pin.

2) If voltage is at least 90% of battery voltage, proceed to BALLAST RESISTOR test. If reading is less than 90% of battery voltage, check wiring harness between ignition module and ignition switch. If wiring harness is okay, check for defective ignition switch. After test, turn ignition off and remove straight-pin.

BALLAST RESISTOR

1) Disconnect and inspect Red and White wire connector at ignition module. Disconnect and inspect ignition coil connector. Attach an ohmmeter between coil connector "BATT" terminal and Red wire on harness side of connector. *See Fig. 3.*

2) If resistance is 0.8-1.6 ohms, problem is either intermittent or not in ignition system. If resistance is less than 0.8 ohms or more than 1.6 ohms, replace ballast resistor. After test, reconnect all connectors.

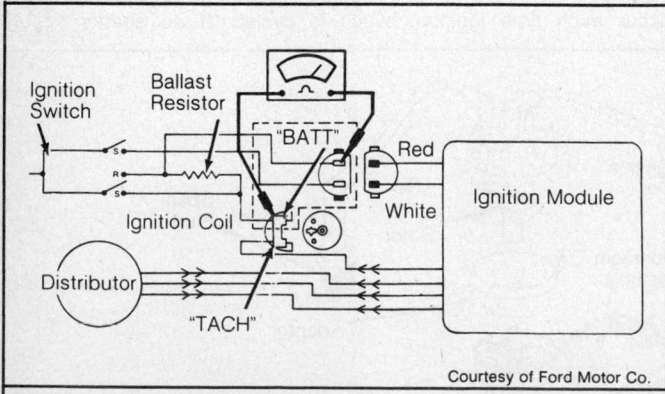

Fig. 3: Checking Ballast Resistor

Courtesy of Ford Motor Co.

SUPPLY VOLTAGE CIRCUIT

1) Remove spark tester and connect disconnected components. Disconnect starter solenoid "I" terminal (if equipped). If not equipped with "S" terminal, disconnect "S" terminal of starter solenoid. Insert

small straight-pins in Red and White wires on ignition module. DO NOT allow straight-pins to contact an electrical ground.

2) Measure battery voltage. Connect voltmeter negative lead to distributor base, and note voltmeter reading in each circuit. See SUPPLY VOLTAGE CIRCUIT TEST table. Wiggle wiring harness while measuring voltage.

SUPPLY VOLTAGE CIRCUIT TEST

Wire/ Terminal	Circuit	Ignition Sw. Test Position
Red	Run	Run
White	Start	Start
"BATT"	Ballast Resistor	Start

3) If voltage readings are at least 90% of battery voltage, proceed to IGNITION COIL SUPPLY VOLTAGE test. If readings are less than 90% of battery voltage, check for faulty wiring harness and/or connectors.

4) Check radio interference capacitor on ignition coil. Check for worn or damaged ignition switch. After testing circuits, turn ignition off. Remove straight-pins and connect disconnected wires.

IGNITION COIL SUPPLY VOLTAGE

1) Connect all disconnected electrical connectors. Connect negative lead of voltmeter to distributor base and positive lead to "BATT" terminal of ignition coil. Turn ignition switch to "RUN" position. Read voltmeter. Turn ignition off.

2) If 6-8 volts is present, proceed to STATOR/PICK-UP COIL ASSEMBLY & WIRING HARNESS test. If reading is not 6-8 volts, proceed to IGNITION COIL PRIMARY RESISTANCE test.

STATOR/PICK-UP COIL ASSEMBLY & WIRING HARNESS

1) Disconnect ignition module 4-wire connector. Inspect connector for dirt, corrosion, or damage. Using an ohmmeter, check resistance between terminals No. 3 and 8 of the distributor harness connector. *See Fig. 4.* Wiggle wiring harness while measuring resistance.

2) If reading is between 400-1300 ohms, proceed to IGNITION MODULE-TO-DISTRIBUTOR WIRING HARNESS check. If resistance is not 400-1300 ohms, proceed to STATOR/PICK-UP COIL check.

IGNITION MODULE-TO-DISTRIBUTOR WIRING HARNESS

1) Disconnect ignition module 4-wire connector. Connect one lead of an ohmmeter to distributor base. Alternately connect other ohmmeter lead to terminals No. 3 and 8 of the connector on the distributor wiring harness side. *See Fig. 4.*

2) If reading is greater than 70,000 ohms, proceed to IGNITION COIL SECONDARY RESISTANCE test. If reading is less than 70,000 ohms, check wiring harness between ignition module connector and distributor including distributor grommet.

IGNITION COIL SECONDARY RESISTANCE

1) Disconnect and inspect ignition coil connector and coil wire. With ignition coil connector disconnected, measure resistance between coil "BATT" terminal and coil wire tower. *See Fig. 4.*

2) If reading is 7700-10,500 ohms, coil is okay. Proceed to IGNITION MODULE-TO-COIL WIRE test. If reading is not 7700-10,500 ohms, replace ignition coil and retest.

IGNITION MODULE-TO-COIL WIRE

Disconnect and inspect ignition module 4-wire connector. Disconnect and inspect ignition coil connector. Connect ohmmeter between distributor base and "TACH" terminal of ignition coil connector. If reading exceeds 100 ohms, replace ignition module. If reading is 100 ohms or less, inspect wiring harness between ignition module and coil.

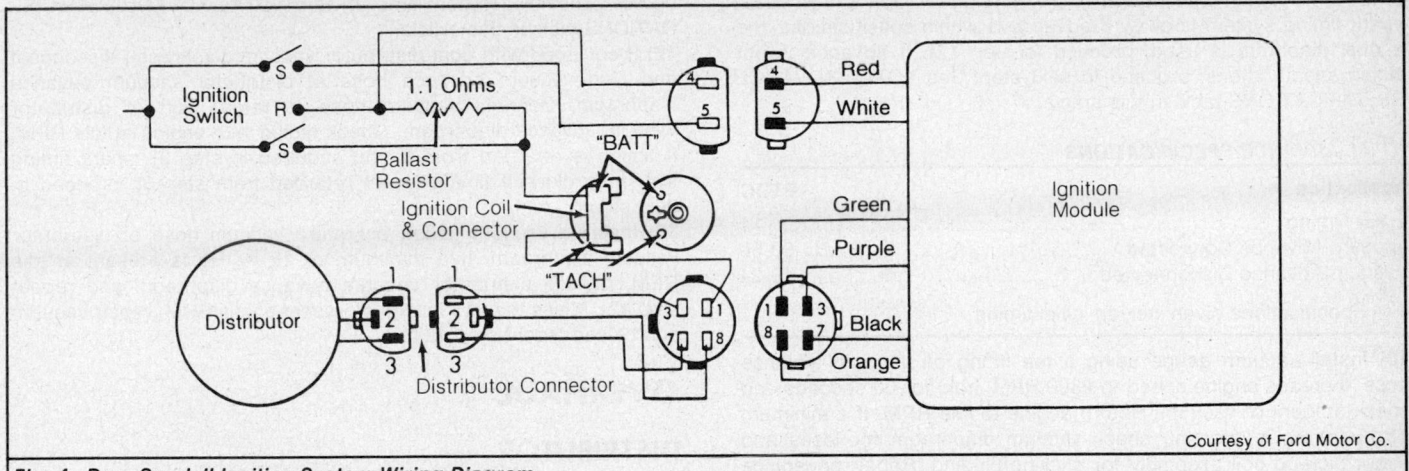

Courtesy of Ford Motor Co.

Fig. 4: Dura-Spark II Ignition System Wiring Diagram

STATOR/PICK-UP COIL

1) Disconnect distributor connector. See Fig. 4. Inspect connector for dirt, corrosion, or damage. Using an ohmmeter, measure stator/pick-up coil resistance across terminals No. 1 and 3 at distributor connector.

2) If reading is 400-1300 ohms, stator/pick-up coil is okay. Inspect wiring harness between distributor and ignition module. If reading is not 400-1300 ohms, replace stator/pick-up coil assembly.

IGNITION COIL PRIMARY RESISTANCE

Disconnect ignition coil connector. Attach ohmmeter leads between "BATT" and "TACH" terminals on ignition coil. If reading is .8-1.6 ohms, ignition coil is okay. Proceed to PRIMARY CIRCUIT CONTINUITY test. If reading is not .8-1.6 ohms, replace coil.

PRIMARY CIRCUIT CONTINUITY

1) Insert a small straight-pin in ignition module Green wire. DO NOT allow straight-pin to contact an electrical ground. Connect voltmeter between distributor base and pin in Green wire.

2) Turn ignition switch to run and measure voltage. If reading exceeds 1.5 volts, proceed to GROUND CIRCUIT CONTINUITY test. If reading is 1.5 volts or less, check wire between ignition module and ignition coil. After test, remove straight-pin.

GROUND CIRCUIT CONTINUITY

1) Insert a small straight-pin in control module Black wire. DO NOT allow straight-pin to contact an electrical ground. Connect negative voltmeter lead to distributor base and positive lead to straight-pin in Black wire. Turn ignition switch to run and measure voltage.

2) If reading exceeds 0.5 volt, proceed to DISTRIBUTOR GROUND CIRCUIT CONTINUITY test. If reading is 0.5 volt or less, replace ignition module. After test, remove straight-pin.

DISTRIBUTOR GROUND CIRCUIT CONTINUITY

1) Disconnect distributor connector. Inspect connector for dirt, corrosion, or damage. Connect ohmmeter between distributor base and terminal No. 2 of distributor side connector. See Fig. 4. Wiggle distributor grommet while measuring resistance.

2) If reading is less than one ohm, circuit is okay. Check wiring harness and connectors between distributor and ignition module. If reading exceeds one ohm, check ground screw in distributor housing. After test, reconnect distributor.

SPARK TIMING ADVANCE

Preliminary Check – 1) Inspect engine compartment to ensure all vacuum hoses and spark plug wires are properly routed and securely attached. Use vehicle's emission label as guide.

2) Examine all wiring harnesses and connectors for damage, overheated wires, and loose or broken terminals. Ensure that battery is fully charged and all accessories are off.

Timing Test – 1) Disconnect and plug distributor vacuum hose(s). Connect timing light and tachometer to engine. If UIM equipped, disconnect UIM connector (Yellow and Black wire). Install jumper wire between UIM connector terminals (Yellow and Black wire).

2) With engine at normal operating temperature, ensure engine RPM is at or below vehicle emission control information decal specifications. Adjust if necessary.

NOTE: Some vehicles may be equipped with a Positive-Buy Timing from factory. Vehicles with Positive-Buy Timing will have a label on distributor diaphragm and a Torx distributor hold-down bolt.

3) Check and record initial timing. If equipped with Positive-Buy Timing, initial timing may vary by plus or minus 4 degrees. If not equipped with Positive-Buy Timing, initial timing may vary by plus or minus 2 degrees. If not within specifications, reset timing.

4) If UIM equipped, remove jumper wire and reconnect UIM connector. Check and record initial timing at specified RPM. Compare reading with recorded initial timing from step 3). If timing is not the same, refer to FORD MOTOR CO. V8 MCU CONTROL SYSTEM article in COMPUTERIZED ENGINE CONTROLS section. If timing is the same, disconnect Yellow and Black wire connector at UIM. If engine stalls, spark retard is operating properly. Proceed to step 7). If engine does not stall, proceed to next step.

5) Check and compare initial timing at specified RPM with step 4). If timing is retarded from recorded timing in step 4), retard operation is okay. Proceed to step 7). If timing is not retarded, proceed to next step.

6) If timing was not retarded in step 5), substitute a new ignition module. Connect Red and White wire connector. Connect 4 wire connector. Install jumper wire on Yellow and Black wire connector terminals of UIM. Check initial timing at specified RPM. If timing is the same as in step 3), repeat step 4). If ignition module substitution appears to correct problem, reconnect original module and repeat this step. If timing is not the same as in step 3), substitute another ignition module and repeat this step.

7) Disconnect distributor vacuum advance. Increase engine speed to 2500 RPM. Check and record spark timing. Return engine to idle RPM. If timing advance is within specifications, proceed to next step. If timing advance is not within specifications, replace distributor and repeat this step. See TOTAL ADVANCE SPECIFICATIONS table in this article.

8) Recheck initial timing at specified timing RPM. If initial timing is the same as in step 4), proceed to next step. If timing is not the same as in step 4), replace distributor and repeat step 7).

9) Connect distributor vacuum advance without spark delay valve (if equipped). Increase engine speed to 2500 RPM and hold for 60 seconds. Check spark timing. Return engine speed to idle RPM. If

advance is within specifications and a single diaphram is used, spark timing system is okay. If advance is within specifications and a dual diaphram is used, proceed to step **12)**. If advance is not within specifications, proceed to next step. See TOTAL ADVANCE SPECIFICATIONS table in this article.

TOTAL ADVANCE SPECIFICATIONS

Application	BTDC
Initial Timing	14
Vacuum Advance Connected [1]	50-60
Vacuum Advance Disconnected [1]	19-24

[1] – Specifications given include initial timing.

10) Install vacuum gauge using a tee fitting on vacuum advance hose. Increase engine speed to 2500 RPM, hold for 60 seconds and check amount of vacuum. Return engine to idle RPM. If a minimum of 15 in. Hg is present, check vacuum diaphragm for leaks and stator/pick-up coil assembly for sticking/binding. Repair or replace as necessary and repeat step **9)**. If less than 15 in. Hg is present, check for vacuum lock-out components. If equipped with vacuum lock-out components, proceed to next step. If not equipped with vacuum lock-out components, repair vacuum source to vacuum advance.

11) Disconnect original distributor vacuum advance hose and plug. Install a separate vacuum hose from an intake manifold vacuum source to distributor advance. Increase engine speed to 2500 RPM. Check timing. Return engine to idle RPM. If timing is within specifications, repair original vacuum source and repeat step **9)**. If timing is not within specifications, check and repair or replace leaking distributor vacuum advance or sticking/binding stator/pick-

up coil assembly. Repeat step **9)**. See TOTAL ADVANCE SPECIFICATIONS table in this article.

12) If equipped with dual distributor vacuum diaphragm, disconnect and plug vacuum advance hose at distributor vacuum advance diaphragm. Connect vacuum hose to retard port of distributor vacuum advance diaphragm. Check timing with engine at idle RPM. If timing is retarded from timing acquired in step **3)**, spark timing system is okay. If timing is not retarded from step **3)**, proceed to next step.

13) Install a vacuum gauge on retard vacuum hose of distributor vacuum diaphragm. If a minimum of 15 in. Hg is present at idle RPM, replace distributor vacuum advance diaphragm and repeat step **12)**. If less than 15 in. Hg is present at idle RPM, repair vacuum source and repeat step **12)**.

OVERHAUL

DISTRIBUTOR

Disassembly & Reassembly – 1) Remove distributor cap, rotor, and adapter. Disconnect distributor wiring harness. Using 2 screwdrivers, carefully pry reluctor from sleeve and plate assembly. See *Fig. 5*. Remove roll pin. DO NOT pinch stator wires when removing reluctor.

2) Remove retaining clip from base plate. Remove base ground screw and separate rubber grommet from base. Remove "E" clip holding vacuum advance diaphragm rod to pick-up coil assembly.

3) Lift vacuum advance rod off post. See *Fig. 5*. Move diaphragm rod out against housing. Remove pick-up coil assembly. To reassemble, reverse disassembly procedure. Install new roll pin when installing reluctor.

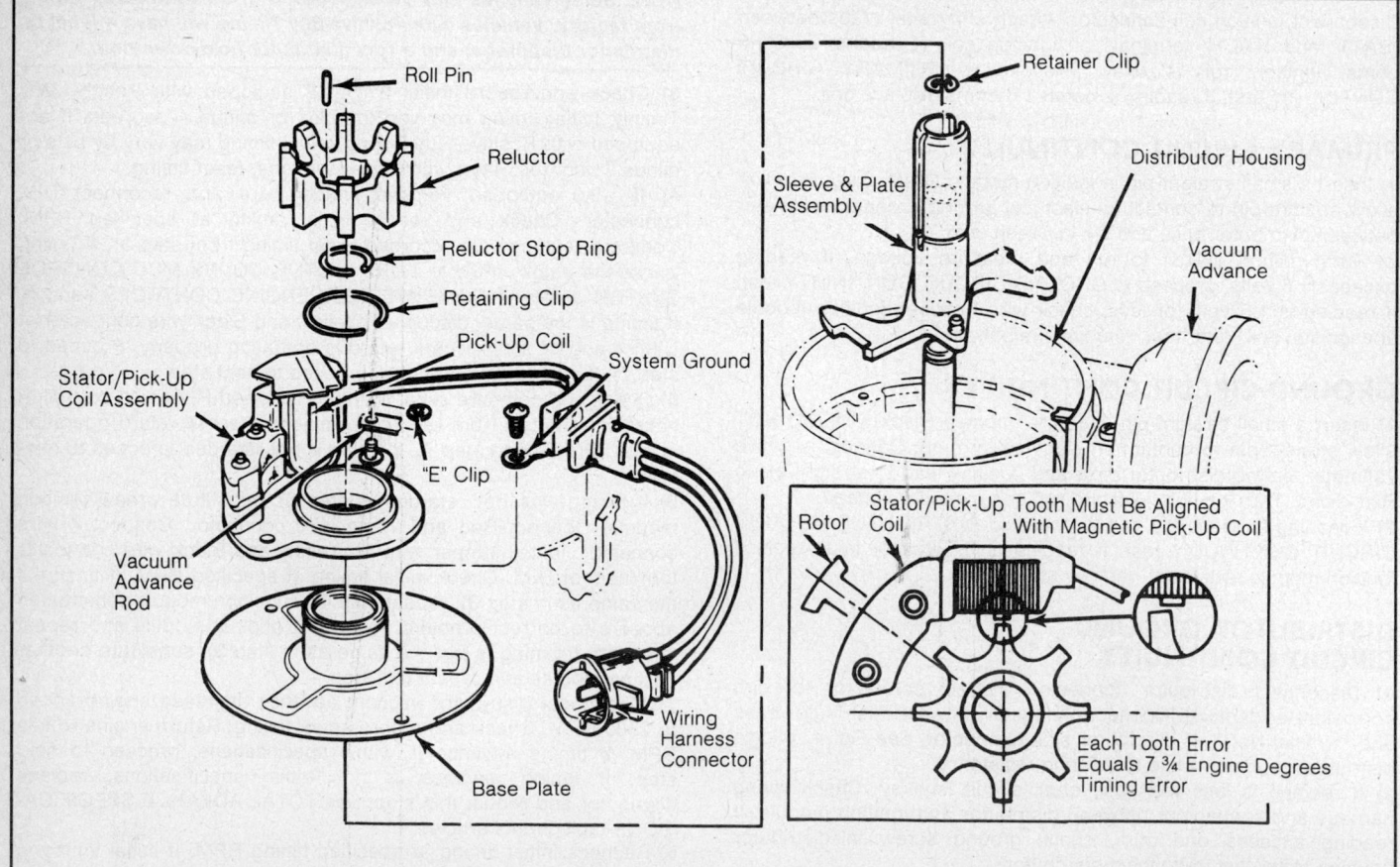

Courtesy of Ford Motor Co.

Fig. 5: Exploded View of Dura-Spark II Distributor

Except 5.8L MCU (Police)

DESCRIPTION

All EEC-IV controlled engines use the TFI-IV ignition system. The TFI-IV distributor is a gear driven, die cast unit. A Hall Effect stator assembly is used to trigger the ignition coil. This distributor does not use conventional centrifugal/vacuum advance mechanisms. *See Fig. 1 or 2.* On models with 3.8L engines, a "closed bowl" distributor is used. The TFI ignition module is mounted on the cowl behind the engine (Continental, Sable and Taurus) or the radiator crossmember (Cougar and Thunderbird). On all others, the TFI ignition module is integrally mounted on base of distributor.

The TFI ignition module used on manual transaxle equipped vehicles features a push start mode. This feature allows vehicle to be push started if necessary. An "E" core ignition coil is used.

OPERATION

The TFI-IV distributor uses a Hall Effect switch mechanism to switch primary voltage and send a Profile Ignition Pickup (PIP) to the Electronic Control Assembly (ECA) and TFI module on 3.8L engines. On all models, the ECA uses PIP input signal to produce an output signal called SPOUT that is sent to the TFI ignition module to be used to trigger discharge of coil secondary voltage.

Secondary voltage is distributed through a conventional cap, rotor and spark plug wires.

TESTING

CAUTION: DO NOT short any terminal directly to ground.

PRELIMINARY STEPS

1) Visually inspect engine compartment to ensure that all vacuum hoses and spark plug wires are properly routed and securely connected. Examine all wiring harnesses and connectors for insulation damage, burnt or overheated wires, and loose or broken terminals.

2) Ensure that battery is fully charged and that all accessories are off. Check that TFI ignition module is securely fastened to distributor base. Obtain Spark Tester (D81P-6666-A). See Fig. 3. A spark plug with a broken side electrode is NOT recommended as it may lead to incorrect results.

3) When inspecting wiring harness, both a visual inspection and a continuity check should be performed. When checking continuity perform a "WIGGLE" test to assist in finding intermittent faults.

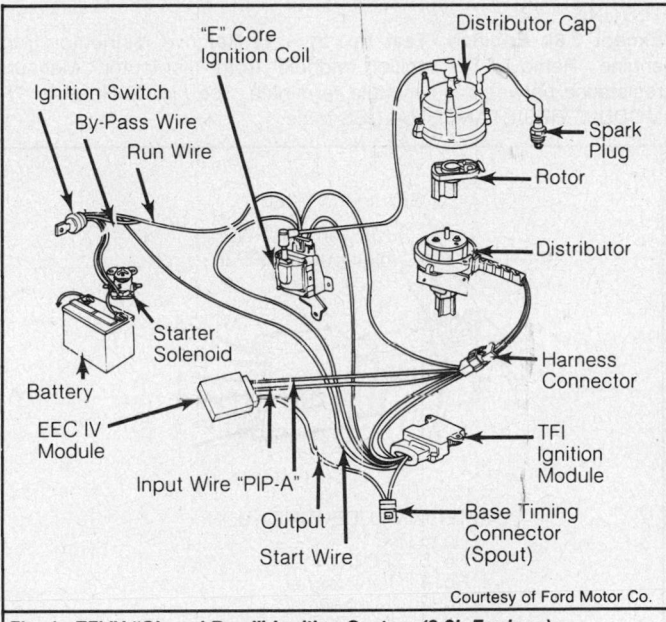

Fig. 1: TFI-IV "Closed Bowl" Ignition System (3.8L Engines)

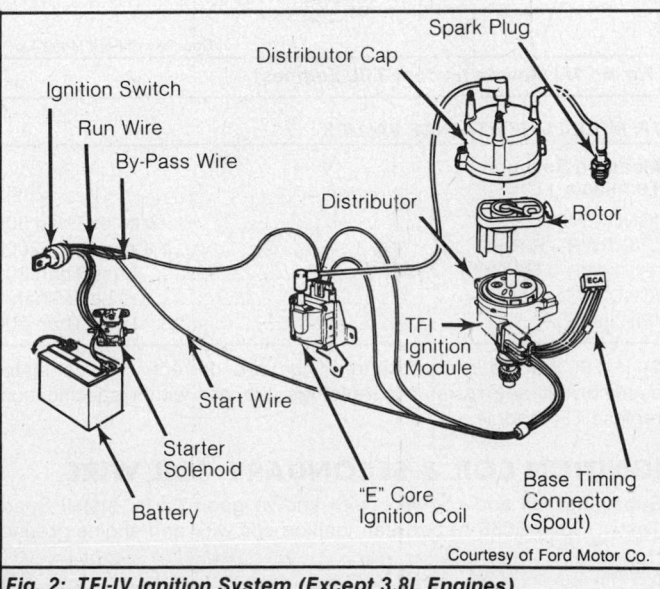

Fig. 2: TFI-IV Ignition System (Except 3.8L Engines)

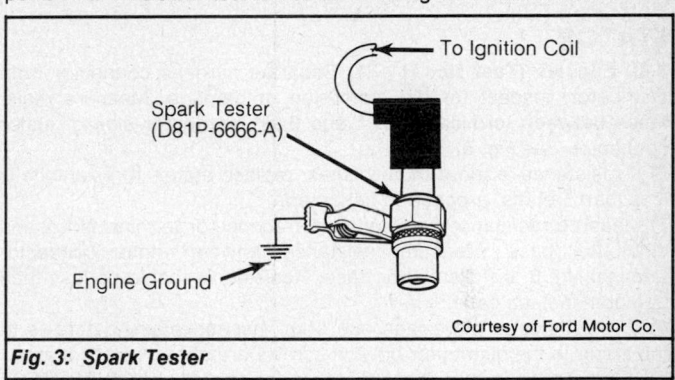

Fig. 3: Spark Tester

Crank Mode – 1) Connect Spark Tester (D81P-6666-A) between ignition coil wire and engine ground. Crank engine while checking for spark at tester. If spark occurs, inspect distributor cap and rotor for damage or carbon tracking.

2) If no spark occurs, remove distributor cap and crank engine to ensure distributor shaft rotates. If distributor shaft does not rotate while cranking engine, repair as necessary. If distributor rotates go to STATOR test.

Run Mode – 1) Place transmission in Park or Neutral and set parking brake. Disconnect wire at "S" terminal of starter relay and attach remote starter switch.

2) Connect Spark Tester (D81P-6666-A) between ignition coil wire and engine ground. Turn ignition switch to "RUN" position. Using remote starter switch, crank engine while watching for spark at tester. If spark is present, ignition system is okay. If spark was not present, go to next test.

TFI CONNECTOR VOLTAGE CHECK

1) Disconnect wiring harness connector from TFI module. Inspect connector for dirt, corrosion, or damage. Repair if necessary. Disconnect wire at "S" terminal of starter solenoid.

2) Attach negative voltmeter lead to distributor base. Measure voltage at battery. With negative lead of voltmeter still connected to distributor base, check voltages at TFI ignition module wiring harness terminals. See WIRING HARNESS TEST table. See Fig. 4.

3) If all readings are at least 90% of battery voltage, replace TFI module. If any reading is less than 90% of battery voltage, inspect wiring harness and connectors. Also check for a worn or damaged ignition switch. Repair or replace as necessary.

WIRING HARNESS TEST

Connector Terminal No.	Wire (Circuit)	Ignition Switch Test Position
3	Run	"RUN" or "START"
4	Start	"START"

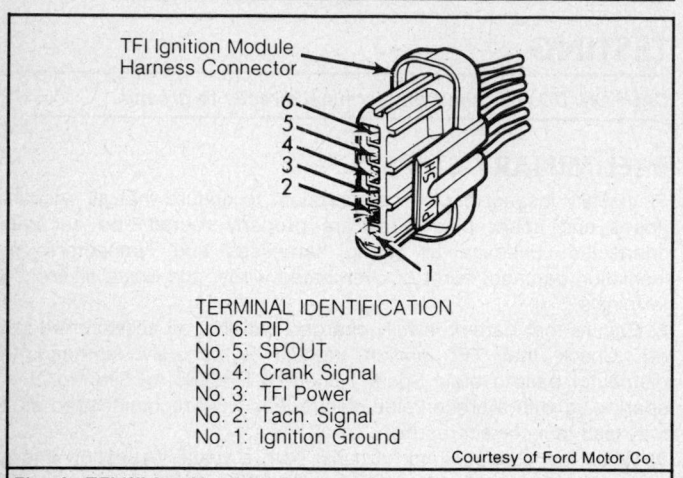

TERMINAL IDENTIFICATION
No. 6: PIP
No. 5: SPOUT
No. 4: Crank Signal
No. 3: TFI Power
No. 2: Tach. Signal
No. 1: Ignition Ground

Courtesy of Ford Motor Co.

Fig. 4: TFI Wiring Harness Connector

STATOR

3.8L Engines (Test No. 1) – 1) Separate harness connector from distributor. Inspect for dirt, corrosion or damage. Measure resistance between terminals No. 1 and 5 on distributor side of stator connector. See Fig. 5.

2) If resistance is more than 5 ohms, replace stator. If resistance is less than 5 ohms, proceed to next step.

3) Measure resistance between stator connector terminal No. 2 and distributor base. Measure resistance between stator connector terminal No. 6 and distributor base. Resistance should be less than one ohm in each case.

4) If resistance is more than one ohm, inspect retaining screws to the stator in the distributor bowl. If screws are okay, replace stator.

5) If resistance is less than one ohm, go to 3.8L ENGINES (TEST NO. 2) under STATOR TESTING.

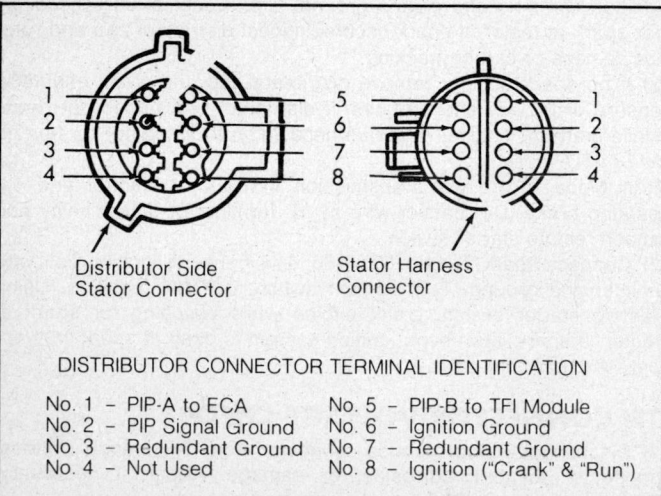

DISTRIBUTOR CONNECTOR TERMINAL IDENTIFICATION

No. 1 – PIP-A to ECA	No. 5 – PIP-B to TFI Module
No. 2 – PIP Signal Ground	No. 6 – Ignition Ground
No. 3 – Redundant Ground	No. 7 – Redundant Ground
No. 4 – Not Used	No. 8 – Ignition ("Crank" & "Run")

Courtesy of Ford Motor Co.

Fig. 5: Stator Connector (3.8L Engine)

3.8L Engines (Test No. 2) – 1) Place transmission in Park or Neutral and set parking brake. Disconnect harness connector from TFI module. Using DVOM, attach negative lead to distributor base and positive lead to TFI harness connector terminal No. 6. Disconnect wire at "S" terminal of starter relay and attach remote starter switch.

2) Crank engine using remote starter switch while watching DVOM. If DVOM varies between 3-6 volts, stator is okay. Remove remote starter switch. Reconnect wire to starter relay and connector to TFI module.

3) If DVOM did not vary between 3-6 volts during testing in step **2)**, replace stator. Remove remote starter switch. Reconnect wire to starter relay and connector to TFI module.

Except 3.8L Engines (Test No. 1) – 1) Place transmission in Park or Neutral and set parking brake. Disconnect harness connector from TFI module. Using DVOM, attach negative lead to distributor base and positive lead to TFI harness connector terminal No. 6. Disconnect wire at "S" terminal of starter relay and attach remote starter switch.

2) Crank engine using remote starter switch while watching DVOM. If DVOM varies between 3-6 volts, stator is okay. Remove DVOM and remote starter switch. Reconnect wire to starter relay and connector to TFI module.

3) If voltmeter did not vary between 3-6 volts during testing in step **2)**, remove distributor cap and ensure rotor rotates when engine is cranked. If rotor rotation is okay, remove DVOM and remote starter switch. Reconnect wire to starter relay and connector to TFI module and go to EXCEPT 3.8L ENGINES (TEST NO. 2) under STATOR TESTING.

Except 3.8L Engines (Test No. 2) – 1) Remove distributor from engine. Remove TFI ignition module from distributor. Measure resistance between TFI module terminals. See Fig. 6. Refer to TFI MODULE RESISTANCE VALUES table.

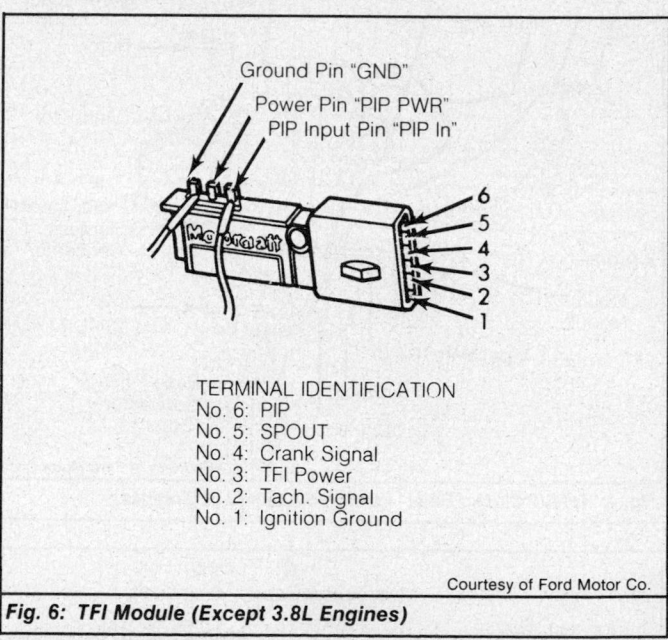

TERMINAL IDENTIFICATION
No. 6: PIP
No. 5: SPOUT
No. 4: Crank Signal
No. 3: TFI Power
No. 2: Tach. Signal
No. 1: Ignition Ground

Courtesy of Ford Motor Co.

Fig. 6: TFI Module (Except 3.8L Engines)

TFI MODULE RESISTANCE VALUES

Measure Between Terminals	Ohms
"GND"-"PIP In"	Greater Than 500
"PIP PWR"-"PIP In"	Less Than 2000
"PIP PWR"-"TFI PWR"	Less Than 200
"GND"-"IGN GND"	Less Than 2
"PIP In"-"PIP"	Less Than 200

2) If TFI module resistance readings are correct, replace stator assembly. If any resistance readings are not within specification, replace TFI module.

IGNITION COIL & SECONDARY COIL WIRE

Substitute coil and coil wire with known good parts. Install Spark Tester (D81P-6666-A) between ignition coil wire and engine ground.

Crank engine. Turn ignition off. If spark is present, determine if coil and/or secondary wire was cause of no spark, replace part(s) as necessary.

WIRING

3.8L Engines (Test No. 1) – 1) Disconnect in-line connector near TFI module. Install Spark Tester (D81P-6666-A) between ignition coil wire and engine ground. Crank engine. Turn ignition off.

2) If spark was present, check PIP-A and ignition ground wires for continuity. Service as necessary. If wires are okay, see EEC-IV article in COMPUTERIZED ENGINE CONTROL section. If spark was not present, go to next test.

3.8L Engines (Test No. 2) – 1) Disconnect wiring harness from stator and TFI module. Measure resistance between terminal No. 5 of the stator harness connector and terminal No. 6 of the TFI harness connector. *See Figs. 4 and 5.*

2) If resistance is less than 5 ohms, go to IGNITION COIL SUPPLY VOLTAGE TEST in this article. If resistance is more than 5 ohms. Inspect and service wiring between the distributor and TFI module (PIP-B circuit).

All Others – Disconnect in-line connector near TFI module. Install Spark Tester (D81P-6666-A) between ignition coil wire and engine ground. Crank engine. Turn ignition off. If spark was present, check PIP and ignition ground wires for continuity. Service wiring as necessary. If wires are okay, see EEC-IV article in COMPUTERIZED ENGINE CONTROL section. If spark was not present, go to IGNITION COIL SUPPLY VOLTAGE test.

IGNITION COIL SUPPLY VOLTAGE

1) Attach negative voltmeter lead to distributor base. Measure voltage at battery. Place ignition switch in "RUN" position. Measure voltage at coil positive terminal. Turn ignition off. If reading was 90% of battery voltage, go to TFI SUPPLY VOLTAGE test.

2) If reading is less than 90% of battery voltage, inspect wiring harness between ignition coil and ignition switch for an open and also check for a worn or damaged ignition switch. When testing is complete, reconnect ignition module harness connector. Repair or replace parts as necessary.

TFI SUPPLY VOLTAGE

3.8L Engines – 1) Disconnect wire at "S" terminal of starter relay. Attach negative voltmeter lead to distributor base. Measure battery voltage.

2) Following TFI SUPPLY VOLTAGE CHECK table, measure connector terminal voltage using straight pin inserted into connector terminal and turning ignition switch to position shown in table.

3) Turn ignition switch to "OFF" position. Remove straight pin. Reconnect wire to "S" terminal of starter relay. If voltage measured in each case was greater than 90% of battery voltage, go to STATOR SUPPLY VOLTAGE test. If voltage measured in each case was less than 90% of battery voltage, check for faults in wiring harness, connectors or damaged ignition switch.

All Others – 1) Disconnect wiring harness from TFI module and inspect connector terminals for damage. Disconnect wire at "S" terminal of starter relay. Attach negative voltmeter lead to distributor base. Measure battery voltage.

2) Following TFI SUPPLY VOLTAGE CHECK table, measure connector terminal voltage using straight pin inserted into connector terminal and turning ignition switch to position shown in table. *See Fig. 4.*

3) Turn ignition switch to "OFF" position. Remove straight pin. Reconnect wire to "S" terminal of starter relay. If voltage measured in each case was greater than 90% of battery voltage, check for faults in wiring between the coil and TFI module terminal No. 2 or any additional wiring or components connected to that circuit.

4) If voltage measured in each case was less than 90% of battery voltage, check for faults in wiring harness, connectors or damaged ignition switch.

TFI SUPPLY VOLTAGE CHECK

Connector Terminal No.	Wire (Circuit)	Ignition Switch Test Position
3.0L California		
3	Run	"RUN" or "START"
All Others		
3	Run	"RUN" or "START"
4	Start	"START"

STATOR SUPPLY VOLTAGE

3.8L Engine – 1) Attach negative voltmeter lead to distributor base. Measure voltage at battery. Place ignition switch in "RUN" position. Measure voltage at terminal No. 8 of harness side of stator connector. Turn ignition off.

2) If reading was 90% of battery voltage, go to TFI WIRING HARNESS test. If reading was less than 90% of battery voltage, check wiring between stator and ignition switch or damaged ignition switch.

TFI WIRING HARNESS

3.8L Engines – 1) With wiring harness connected to stator, measure resistance between distributor base and terminal No. 1 of the TFI ignition module harness connector. *See Fig. 4.*

2) If resistance is less than one ohm, inspect for faults in wiring between coil and TFI module terminal No. 2, or any additional wiring or components connected to that circuit. Repair wiring as necessary.

3) If resistance is more than one ohm, inspect wiring between harness connector at TFI module and harness connector at distributor ground circuit.

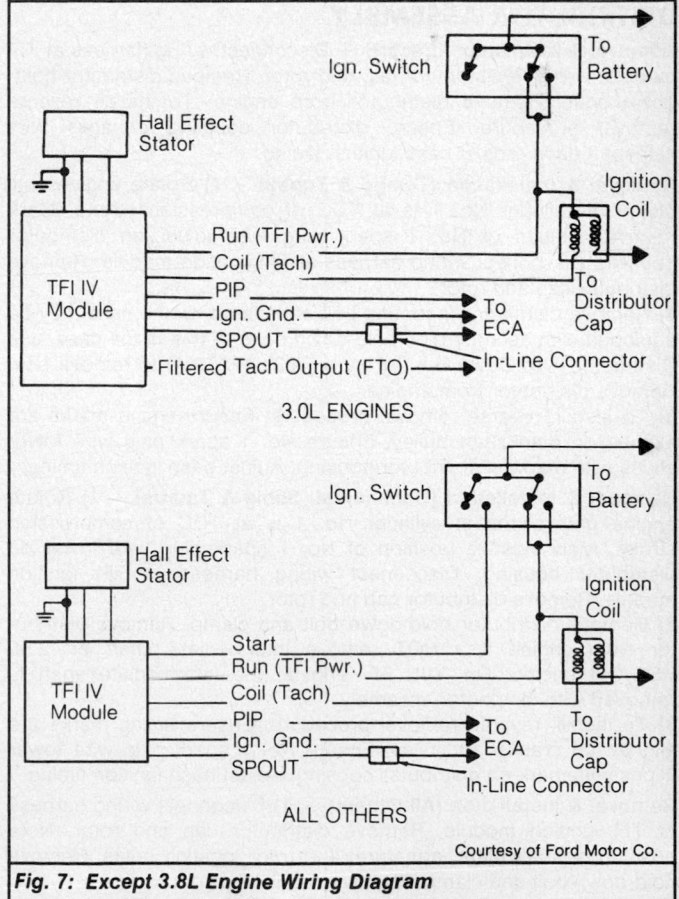

Courtesy of Ford Motor Co.

Fig. 7: Except 3.8L Engine Wiring Diagram

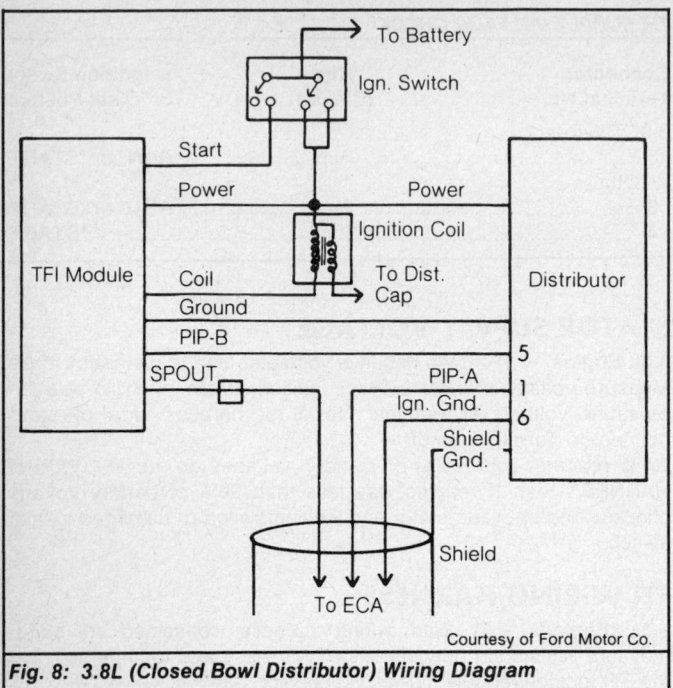

Fig. 8: 3.8L (Closed Bowl Distributor) Wiring Diagram

Courtesy of Ford Motor Co.

NOTE: For further testing, see EEC-IV article in COMPUTERIZED ENGINE CONTROLS section.

REMOVAL & INSTALLATION

DISTRIBUTOR ASSEMBLY

Removal & Installation (Escort) – Disconnect wiring harness at TFI module. Remove distributor cap and rotor. Remove distributor hold-down bolts. Remove distributor from engine. To install, reverse removal procedure. Ensure distributor coupling engages with camshaft drive. Adjust base ignition timing.

Removal & Installation (Tempo & Topaz) – **1)** Rotate engine until piston in cylinder No. 1 is at TDC of compression stroke. Mark relative position of No. 1 spark plug wire tower on distributor housing. Disconnect wiring harness at TFI ignition module. Remove distributor cap and rotor.

2) Remove distributor mounting bolt and clamp. Some units may be equipped with security-type hold-down bolts. If this is the case, use Distributor Hold-Down Bolt Wrench (T82L-12270-A) to remove bolt. Remove distributor from engine.

3) To install, reverse removal procedure. Ensure timing marks are aligned on crankshaft pulley. Ensure No. 1 spark plug wire tower aligns with mark on distributor housing. Adjust base ignition timing.

Removal & Installation (Continental, Sable & Taurus) – **1)** Rotate engine until piston in cylinder No. 1 is at TDC of compression stroke. Mark relative position of No. 1 spark plug wire tower on distributor housing. Disconnect wiring harness at TFI ignition module. Remove distributor cap and rotor.

2) Remove distributor hold-down bolt and clamp. Remove distributor from engine. DO NOT remove intermediate shaft on 2.5L HSC/CFI engine. On 3.0L EFI engine, the intermediate shaft is removed with distributor assembly.

3) To install, reverse removal procedure. Ensure timing marks are aligned on crankshaft pulley. Ensure No. 1 spark plug wire tower aligns with mark on distributor housing. Adjust base ignition timing.

Removal & Installation (All Others) – **1)** Disconnect wiring harness at TFI ignition module. Remove distributor cap and rotor. Note position of shaft plate, armature, and rotor locating holes. Remove hold-down bolt and clamp. Remove distributor from engine.

2) To install, reverse removal procedure. Ensure that position of shaft plate, armature, and rotor locating holes are in the same

position as during removal. Ensure TFI ignition module is properly oriented on engine.

TFI IGNITION MODULE

Removal (3.8L Engines) – **1)** Using a Phillips screwdriver, remove leaf screen attaching screws from top of cowl. Separate engine compartment/cowl seal from leaf screen and cowl dash extension panel near TFI ignition module.

2) Lift screen to allow access to TFI ignition module. Press up on harness connector latch from under TFI module shroud to disconnect harness connector from module. Remove 2 module retaining nuts and washers. Remove TFI ignition module and heat-sink as an assembly.

Installation – **1)** To install, insert module and heat-sink, with heat-sink facing down, into cowl dash extension to allow nuts to be installed. Install washers.

2) Install and tighten nuts to 44-70 INCH lbs. (5-8 N.m). Connect harness connector to module. Install leaf screen. Position seal on leaf screen and cowl dash extension.

Removal & Installation (All Others) – **1)** Remove distributor from engine. With distributor on workbench, remove 2 module mounting screws. Slide right side of module down toward distributor mounting flange, and then back up. Move left side of module down toward distributor mounting flange and then back up.

2) Alternate sliding right and left sides of module until module terminals are disengaged from connector in distributor. Any attempt to pull module from mounting surface prior to moving it toward distributor flange WILL BREAK module electrical connector pins.

3) To install, reverse removal procedure. Apply a 1/32" thick ribbon of Silicone Dielectric Compound (D7AZ-19A331-A) to TFI ignition module base plate. Adjust base ignition timing.

STATOR

Removal (Escort) – **1)** Remove distributor. Using a small screwdriver, remove drive coupling spring. Using compressed air, blow dirt and oil away from end of distributor. Mark orientation of drive coupling to shaft.

2) Align drive pin with slot in base. Support distributor and drive pin out with a 3/32" drift and small hammer. See Fig. 9. Remove drive coupling and set aside for reassembly.

3) Ensure shaft is free of nicks or burrs. If burrs are present, polish shaft with emery paper to remove minor burrs. Wipe shaft clean after polishing. Pull up on shaft plate to remove shaft from distributor.

4) Remove screws and TFI ignition module. See TFI IGNITION MODULE REMOVAL & INSTALLATION (ALL OTHERS). Wipe grease from base and module to keep surfaces free of dirt. Remove octane rod retaining screw and octane rod assembly.

5) Remove screws retaining stator connector in distributor bowl. Save screws for installation. Gently pull up on stator to remove from bowl.

6) Inspect base bushing, oil seal, spring retainer, "O" ring, and distributor housing for wear, cracks, or other damage. If necessary, replace spring retainer or "O" ring. If distributor housing, bushing, or oil seal are damaged, replace entire distributor assembly.

Installation – **1)** Place stator over bushing and press down on seat. Place stator connector in position. Tab should fit in notch of base and fastening eyelets should align with screw holes. Position wires away from moving parts.

2) Install and tighten stator screws. With seal on octane rod, insert rod in holes. Install octane rod through distributor base hole. Place end of rod onto same post as original stator. Install and tighten octane rod screw.

3) Wipe back of TFI ignition module and distributor mounting plate clean. Apply Silicone Dielectric Compound (D7AZ-19A331-A) to back of module and spread evenly.

4) Turn distributor base upside-down so that stator connector is in full view. Insert TFI ignition module, making sure that module pins are inserted into stator connector.

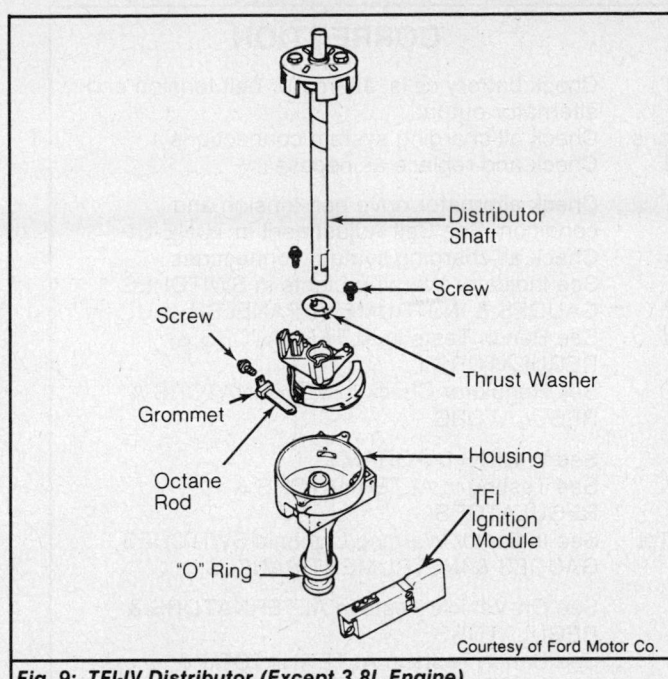

Fig. 9: TFI-IV Distributor (Except 3.8L Engine)

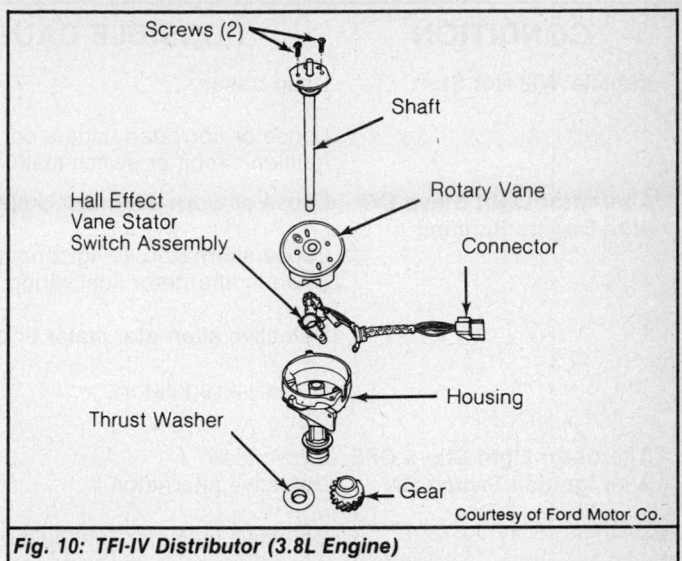

Fig. 10: TFI-IV Distributor (3.8L Engine)

5) Fully seat module into connector and against base. Install and tighten TFI module screws. Lubricate distributor shaft, just below armature, with light oil. DO NOT overlubricate.

6) Insert shaft assembly through base bushing. Place drive coupling over shaft and line up mark made during removal. Start pin into drive coupling and shaft.

7) Support distributor and drive pin into shaft until end of pin is flush with step in drive coupling. Check drive coupling for freedom of movement. Ensure that pin does not extend beyond step in coupling in either direction.

8) Remove distributor from support. Check distributor for freedom of rotation. Install drive coupling spring in groove of drive coupling. Install distributor. Check base timing.

Removal (All Others) – 1) Remove distributor from engine. On all except Continental, remove screws and TFI ignition module from distributor. See TFI IGNITION MODULE REMOVAL & INSTALLATION (ALL OTHERS). Wipe grease from base and module to keep surfaces free of dirt.

2) On all models, hold gear and loosen armature screws, DO NOT hold armature. Remove screws and armature. Using a felt tip pen, mark armature and gear for installation reference. Remove and discard roll pin in gear.

3) Place distributor in Axle Bearing Remover (T75L-1165-B). Press off gear using arbor press and Pinion Bearing Cone Remover (D79L-4621-A). Using emery cloth, remove burrs from distributor shaft. Remove shaft from distributor assembly.

4) Remove thrust washer from distributor and save for installation. See Fig. 10. Remove screw and octane rod assembly. Save octane rod and screw for installation. Remove stator assembly screws and stator. Save screws for installation.

5) Inspect base bushing, "O" ring, and distributor housing for wear, cracks, or other damage. If necessary, replace "O" ring. If distributor housing or bushings are worn, replace entire distributor assembly.

Installation – 1) Place stator assembly over bushing and press down to seat. Place stator connector in position. Tab should fit in notch of base and fastening eyelets should align with screw holes. Position wires away from moving parts. Install and tighten stator screws.

2) Install octane rod through distributor base hole. Place end of rod onto same post as original stator. Install and tighten octane rod screw. Install thrust washer on top of bushing (if equipped). Lubricate distributor shaft, just below armature, with light oil. DO NOT overlubricate.

3) Install shaft through base bushing. Place a 1/2" deep well socket over shaft, invert assembly and place in arbor press. If distributor uses a screw-down rotor, invert assembly and place in arbor press. Place distributor drive gear on shaft. Align marks made during removal.

4) Place a 5/8" deep well socket over shaft and gear. Press gear until holes align with holes in shaft. If holes do not line up, press gear off and try once more. DO NOT try to align holes using a drift or roll pin.

5) Insert new roll pin through gear and shaft. If armature was removed, install armature. Tighten armature screws. Check distributor for freedom of rotation. If armature contacts stator, replace distributor.

6) Wipe back of TFI ignition module and distributor mounting plate clean. Apply Silicone Dielectric Compound (D7AZ-19A331-A) to back of module and spread evenly.

7) Turn distributor base upside-down so that stator connector is in full view. Insert TFI module. Ensure that module pins are inserted into stator connector.

8) Fully seat TFI ignition module into connector and against base. Install and tighten TFI module screws. See Fig. 10. Install distributor. Check base timing.

TIGHTENING SPECIFICATIONS

Application	Ft. Lbs. (N.m)
Distributor Hold-Down Bolts	
Except 1.9L Engine	17-25 (23-34)

	INCH Lbs. (N.m)
Armature Screws	25-35 (3-4)
Distributor Hold-Down Bolts	
1.9L Engine	48-60 (5-7)
Octane Rod Screw	25-35 (3-4)
Stator Assembly Screws	25-35 (3-4)
TFI Ignition Module Screws	25-35 (3-4)

1989 CHARGING SYSTEMS
Trouble Shooting

CONDITION	POSSIBLE CAUSE	CORRECTION
Vehicle Will Not Start	Dead battery	Check battery cells, alternator belt tension and alternator output
	Loose or corroded battery connections	Check all charging system connections
	Ignition circuit or switch malfunction	Check and replace as necessary
Alternator Light Stays ON With Engine Running	Loose or worn alternator drive belt	Check alternator drive belt tension and condition. See Belt Adjustment in TUNE-UP
	Loose alternator wiring connections	Check all charging system connections
	Short in alternator light wiring	See Indicator Warning Lights in SWITCHES, GAUGES & INSTRUMENT PANELS
	Defective alternator stator or diodes	See Bench Tests in ALTERNATORS & REGULATORS
	Defective regulator	See Regulator Check in ALTERNATORS & REGULATORS
Alternator Light Stays OFF With Ignition Switch ON	Blown fuse	See WIRING DIAGRAMS
	Defective alternator	See Testing in ALTERNATORS & REGULATORS
	Defective indicator light bulb or socket	See Indicator Warning Lights in SWITCHES, GAUGES & INSTRUMENT PANELS
Alternator Light Stays ON With Ignition Switch OFF	Short in alternator wiring	See On-Vehicle Tests in ALTERNATORS & REGULATORS
	Defective rectifier bridge	See Bench Tests in ALTERNATORS & REGULATORS
Lights or Fuses Burn Out Frequently	Defective alternator wiring	See On-Vehicle Tests in ALTERNATORS & REGULATORS
	Defective regulator	See Regulator Check in ALTERNATORS & REGULATORS
	Defective battery	Check and replace as necessary
Ammeter Gauge Shows Discharge	Loose or worn drive belt	Check alternator drive belt tension and condition. See Belt Adjustment in TUNE-UP
	Defective wiring	Check all wires and wire connections
	Defective alternator or regulator	See Bench Tests and On-Vehicle Tests in ALTERNATORS & REGULATORS
	Defective ammeter, or improper ammeter wiring connections	See Testing in SWITCHES, GAUGES & INSTRUMENT PANELS
Noisy Alternator	Loose drive pulley	Tighten drive pulley attaching nut
	Loose mounting bolts	Tighten all alternator mounting bolts
	Worn or dirty bearings	See Bearing Replacement in ALTERNATORS & REGULATORS
	Defective diodes or stator	See Bench Tests in ALTERNATORS & REGULATORS
Battery Does Not Stay Charged	Loose or worn drive belt	Check alternator drive belt tension and condition. See Belt Adjustment in TUNE-UP
	Loose or corroded battery connections	Check all charging system connections
	Loose alternator connections	Check all charging system connections
	Defective alternator or battery	See On-Vehicle Tests and Bench Tests in ALTERNATORS & REGULATORS
	Defective alternator stator or diodes	See Bench Tests in ALTERNATORS & REGULATORS
	Add-on electrical accessories exceeding alternator capacity	Install larger capacity alternator
Battery Overcharged - Uses Too Much Water	Defective battery	Check alternator output and repair as necessary
	Defective alternator	See On-Vehicle Tests and Bench Tests in ALTERNATORS & REGULATORS
	Excessive alternator voltage	Check alternator output and repair as necessary

Chrysler Motors

DESCRIPTION

A 90-amp (90RS) alternator is used on some FWD 2.5L SPFI and 2.5L Turbo I MPFI engines. The charging system consists of a Single Module Engine Controller (SMEC), check engine light and battery. The alternator consists of a rotor, stator, rectifiers, front and rear covers and drive pulley. *See Fig. 4.* The electronic voltage regulator is contained within the SMEC and is not serviceable.

OPERATION

Alternator diodes convert AC current to DC current. The engine controller monitors critical input and output of the charging system, making sure it is working properly.

The engine controller will store in memory any failures within the monitored circuits. Engine controller will translate a failure in the form of fault codes when on-board diagnostics are entered.

The self-diagnostic capabilities of this system, if properly utilized, can greatly simplify testing. The engine controller has been programmed to monitor several different circuits of the engine control system.

If a problem is sensed with a monitored circuit, a fault code is stored in the engine controller's memory. The check engine light will illuminate and engine controller will enter limp-in mode.

In this mode, engine controller attempts to compensate for the failure of a particular component by substituting information from other sources. This will allow vehicle to be operated until proper repairs can be made.

TESTING & DIAGNOSIS

SYSTEM DIAGNOSIS

If a charging system malfunction is suspected, perform ON-VEHICLE TESTS in this article. Repair as necessary. If no problem is found using ON-VEHICLE TESTS, refer to ENTERING ON-BOARD DIAGNOSTICS in this article.

ON-VEHICLE TESTS

Alternator Output Wire Resistance Test – Alternator output wire resistance test will show amount of voltage drop across alternator output wire between alternator "BAT" terminal and positive battery post.

1) Charge battery as necessary. Turn ignition switch to "OFF" position. Disconnect negative battery cable. Disconnect alternator output wire from alternator "BAT" terminal.

2) Using a 0-150 ampere scale DC ammeter, connect positive ammeter lead to alternator "BAT" terminal and negative lead to disconnected alternator output wire. *See Fig. 1.*

3) Using a voltmeter (0-18 volts minimum), connect positive voltmeter lead to disconnected alternator output wire and negative lead to positive battery cable.

CAUTION: Alternator has 2 field terminals. See Fig. 2. One field terminal has Dark Green wire and other field terminal has Dark Blue wire. DO NOT connect jumper wire to alternator field terminal Dark Blue wire.

---

4) Remove air hose between SMEC and air cleaner. Connect one end of jumper wire to ground and other end to alternator field terminal Dark Green wire on rear side of alternator.

5) Connect engine tachometer and reconnect negative battery cable. Connect Variable Carbon Pile Rheostat (C-3950) between battery terminals. Be sure carbon pile is in "OPEN" or "OFF" position before connecting leads.

6) Start engine and reduce engine speed to idle. Adjust engine speed and carbon pile to maintain 20 amps flowing in circuit. Observe voltmeter reading. Voltage drop should not be more than .5 volt.

7) If higher voltage drop is indicated, inspect, clean and tighten all connections between alternator "BAT" terminal and positive battery post. Voltage drop test may be performed at each connection to locate connection with excessive resistance. If resistance tested satisfactorily, reduce engine speed, turn off carbon pile and ignition switch.

8) Disconnect negative battery cable. Remove test ammeter, voltmeter, carbon pile and tachometer. Remove jumper wire between alternator Dark Green field wire and ground.

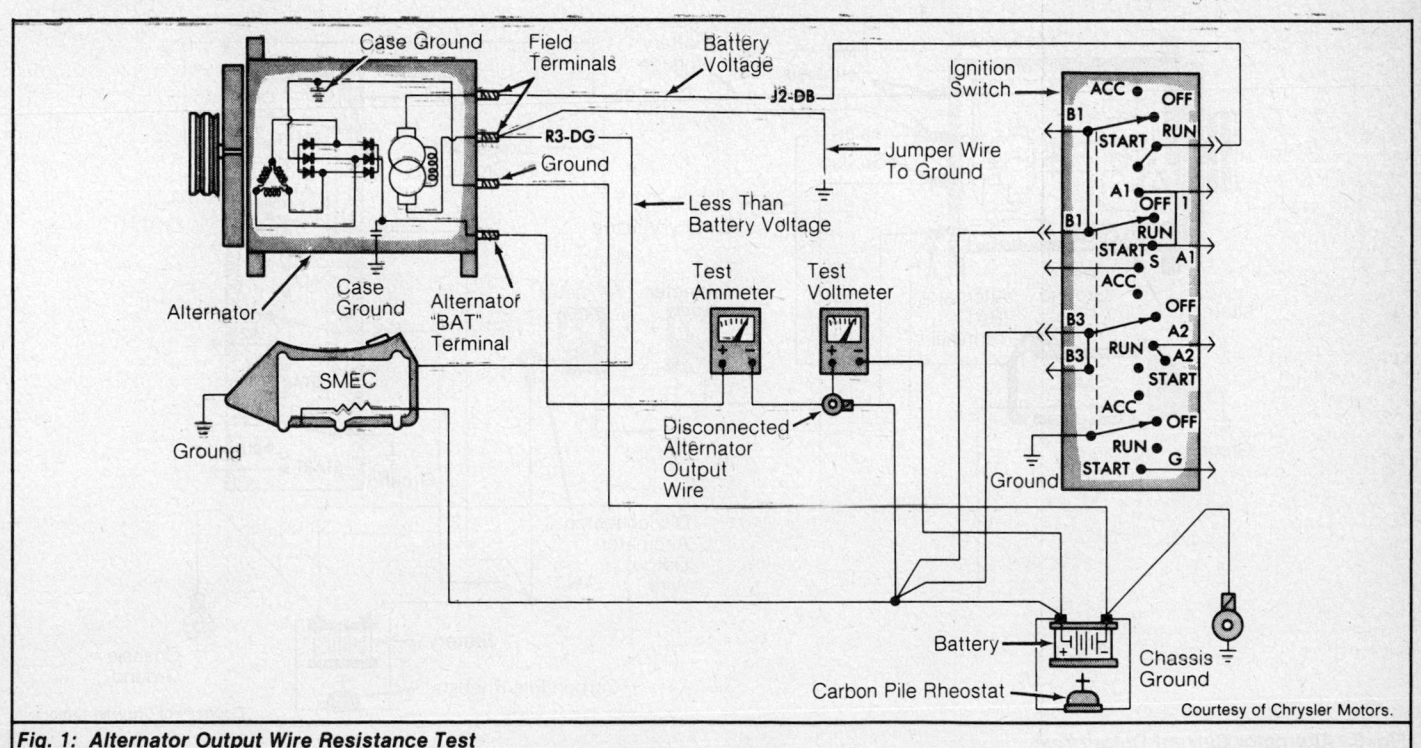

Fig. 1: Alternator Output Wire Resistance Test

9) Connect alternator output wire to alternator "BAT" terminal. Reconnect negative battery cable and hose between SMEC and air cleaner.

Current Output Test – The current output test determines whether or not alternator is capable of delivering its rated current output.

1) Charge battery as necessary. Disconnect negative battery cable. Disconnect alternator output wire at alternator "BAT" terminal. *See Fig. 2.* Using a 0-150 ampere scale DC ammeter, connect positive ammeter lead to alternator "BAT" terminal and negative lead to disconnected alternator output wire. *See Fig. 3.*

2) Using a voltmeter (0-18 volts range minimum), connect positive voltmeter lead to disconnected alternator "BAT" terminal and negative lead to good ground.

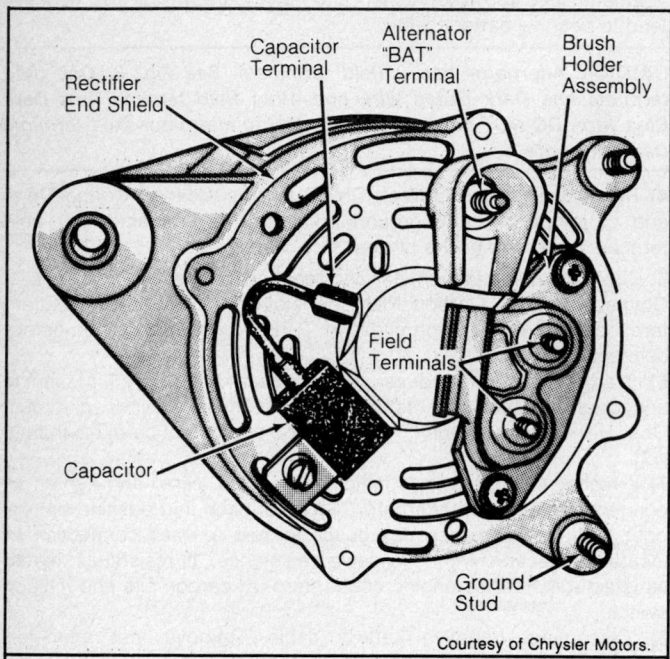

Fig. 2: Alternator Terminal Identification

Courtesy of Chrysler Motors.

3) Connect engine tachometer and reconnect negative battery cable. Connect Variable Carbon Pile Rheostat (C-3950) between battery terminals. Be sure carbon pile is in "OPEN" or "OFF" position before connecting leads.

CAUTION: Alternator has 2 field terminals. See Fig. 2. One field terminal has Dark Green wire and other field terminal has Dark Blue wire. DO NOT connect jumper wire to alternator field terminal Dark Blue wire.

4) Remove air hose between SMEC and air cleaner. Connect one end of jumper wire to ground and other end to alternator field terminal Dark Green wire on back of alternator.

5) Start engine and reduce engine speed to idle. Adjust carbon pile and engine speed in increments until engine speed is 1250 RPM and voltmeter reads 15 volts. DO NOT allow voltage to read more than 16 volts.

6) If voltmeter reads less than specified and alternator output wire resistance is not excessive, alternator should be removed from vehicle and bench tested. See BENCH TESTS in this article. After current output test is completed reduce engine speed, turn off carbon pile and ignition switch.

7) Disconnect negative battery cable. Remove test ammeter, voltmeter, tachometer and carbon pile. Remove jumper wire between alternator field terminal Dark Green wire and ground.

8) Reconnect alternator output wire to alternator "BAT" terminal. Reconnect negative battery cable and hose between SMEC and air cleaner.

ENTERING ON-BOARD DIAGNOSTICS

Diagnostic Readout Box – The DRB-II (C-4805) is a diagnostic tool that is plugged into the vehicle diagnostic connector. The DRB-II is used to put the system into diagnostic test mode, circuit actuation test mode, switch test mode, sensor test mode and engine running test mode. These 5 test modes are required to properly diagnose the system. The following is a description of each test mode:

Diagnostic Test Mode – This mode is used to see if there are any fault codes stored in engine controller's memory.

Circuit Actuation Test Mode (ATM) – This mode is used to turn a specific circuit on and off to check it.

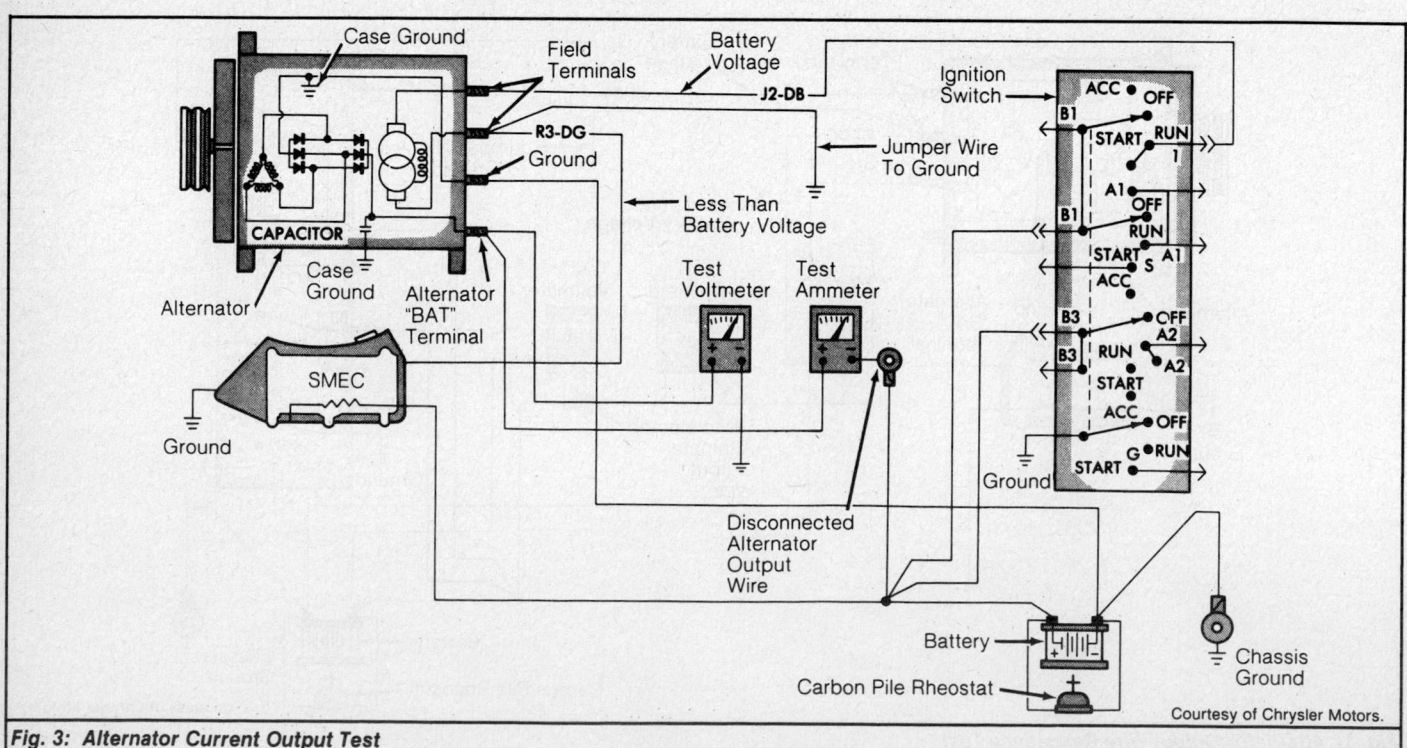

Courtesy of Chrysler Motors.

Fig. 3: Alternator Current Output Test

Switch Test Mode – This mode is used to determined if specific inputs are being received by the engine controller.

Sensor Test Mode – This mode is used to see the output signals of certain sensors as received by the engine controller when engine is not running.

Engine Running Test Mode – This mode is used to see sensor ouput signals as received by the engine controller while the engine is running. Also, this test mode will be used to establish some specific engine running conditions required for diagnosis.

NOTE: Charging system is controlled by SMEC. For proper diagnosis of system, DRB-II (C-4805) is necessary for complete testing of charging system. For more information on testing charging system, refer to appropriate article in COMPUTERIZED ENGINE CONTROLS section.

Check Engine Light Diagnostic Mode – 1) Start engine (if possible). Move transmission shift lever through all positions, engine in Park. Turn A/C switch on, then off (if equipped).

2) Turn engine off. Without starting engine again, turn ignition on, off, on, off and on. Check engine light will come on for 2 seconds as a bulb check, followed by fault codes. Record 2-digit fault codes as displayed by flashing check engine light.

3) For example, code 23 is displayed as flash, flash, 4 second pause, flash, flash, flash. After a slightly longer pause, any other codes stored are displayed in numerical order.

4) Once check engine light begins to flash fault codes, it cannot be stopped. If you loose count, it will be necessary to start over. Code 55 indicates end of fault code display. Refer to appropriate article in COMPUTERIZED ENGINE CONTROLS section.

NOTE: Check engine light cannot be used to perform actuation test mode, sensor test modes, or engine running test.

DRB-II Diagnostic Mode – 1) Attach DRB-II Tester (C-4805) to self-test connector. Connector is located in engine compartment near left shock tower.

2) Start engine (if possible). Move transmission shift lever through all positions, ending in Park. Turn A/C switch on, then off (if equipped).

3) Turn engine off. Without starting engine again, turn ignition on, off, on, off and on within 5 seconds. Enter vehicle model year and engine size. Read fault data on DRB-II. Refer to appropriate article in COMPUTERIZED ENGINE CONTROLS section.

Check Engine Light Switch Test Mode – After all codes are displayed, switch function can be verified. The light will turn on or off when a switch is turned on or off. Once the check engine light begins to display fault codes, it cannot be stopped. If you loose count it will be necessary to start all over again.

Limp-In Mode – If SMEC senses incorrect data or no data from battery voltage, coolant temperature sensor, Manifold Absolute Pressure (MAP) sensor or Throttle Position Sensor (TPS), engine controller will put system in limp-in mode and illuminate check engine light.

The following is a description of each charging system limp-in mode:

Battery Voltage Sense – If this signal drops below 4 volts after engine has been running for one minute fault code 16 is recorded in memory and check engine light is turned on. At this time SMEC will operate charging system at a fixed rate.

Battery Voltage Too High – If SMEC senses battery voltage is more than one volt above the desired control voltage, fault 45 is recorded in memory and check engine light is turned on.

If these 2 sensor signals return to within specification while engine is running, check engine light will turn off and charging system will return to normal operation. Fault codes will remain in memory, but

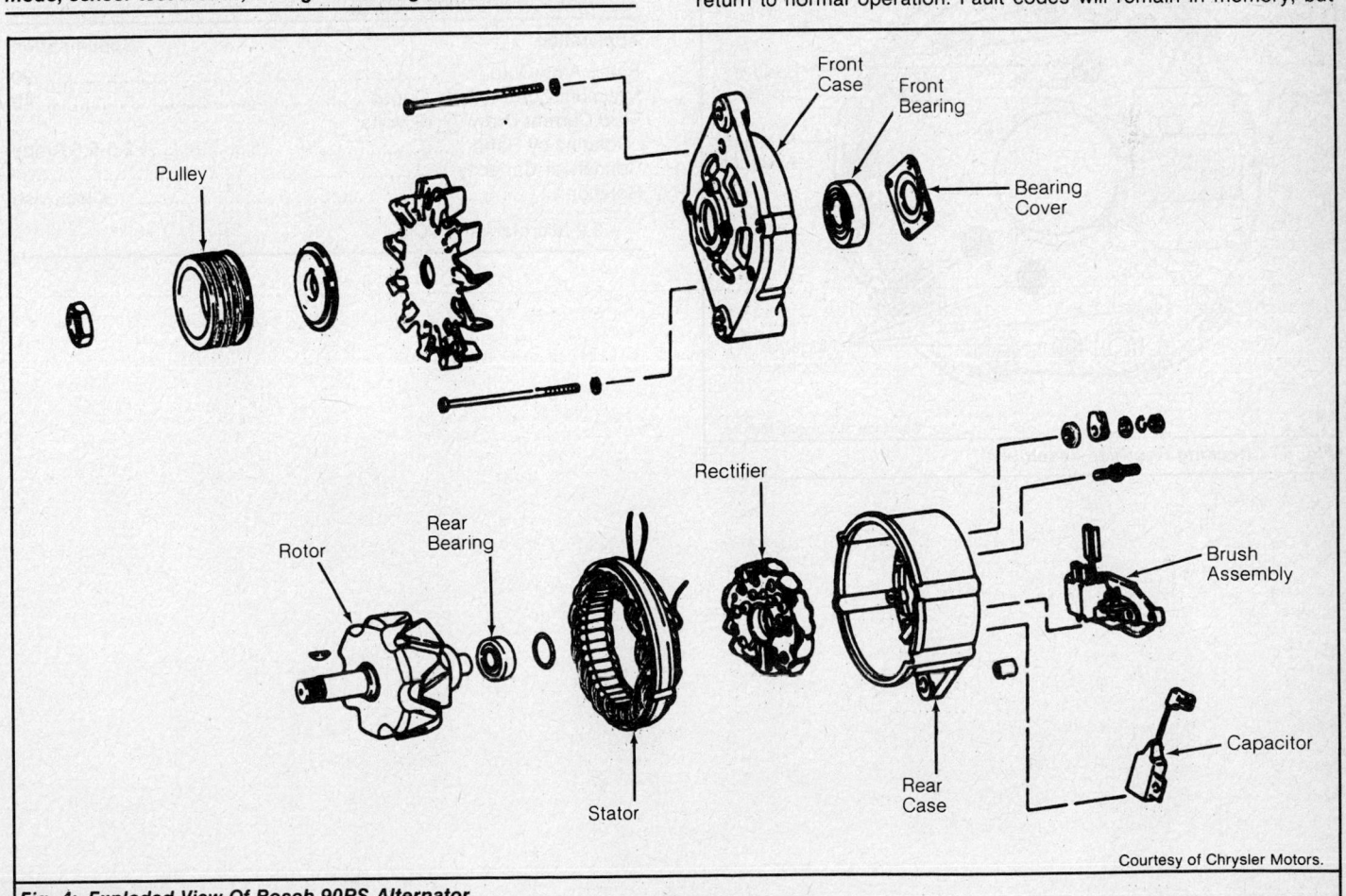

Courtesy of Chrysler Motors.

Fig. 4: Exploded View Of Bosch 90RS Alternator

will be cleared after 50-100 engine starts if the fault does not happen again.

BENCH TESTS

Rotor Assembly Test – 1) Check field slip rings for excessive wear or roughness. If slip ring has only minor damage, clean with fine emery cloth. If slip rings are too badly damaged, rotor must be replaced.

2) Using an ohmmeter, test for continuity from one slip ring to other. Test should show closed circuit. Using an ohmmeter, test for continuity from both field coil slip rings to rotor shaft or core.

3) Test should show open circuit. If failure is detected in either test, replace rotor assembly.

Stator Assembly Test – 1) Check stator for worn or broken leads, distorted frame, or burned windings. Clean small area of stator frame for making good electrical contact. Using an ohmmeter, test for continuity from stator leads to frame. Test should show an open circuit.

2) Test for continuity from one stator lead to other leads. Test should show closed circuit. If failure is detected in either test, replace stator assembly.

Rectifier Test – 1) Check rectifier assembly for poor solder joints, cracks, or signs of overheating. Using an ohmmeter, test for continuity from positive diode pin to positive heat sink. *See Fig. 5.*

2) Reverse ohmmeter test probes and repeat test. Test should show continuity in one direction only. Test for continuity from negative diode pin to negative heat sink.

3) Reverse ohmmeter test probes and repeat test. Test should show continuity in one direction only. If failure is detected in either test, replace rectifier assembly.

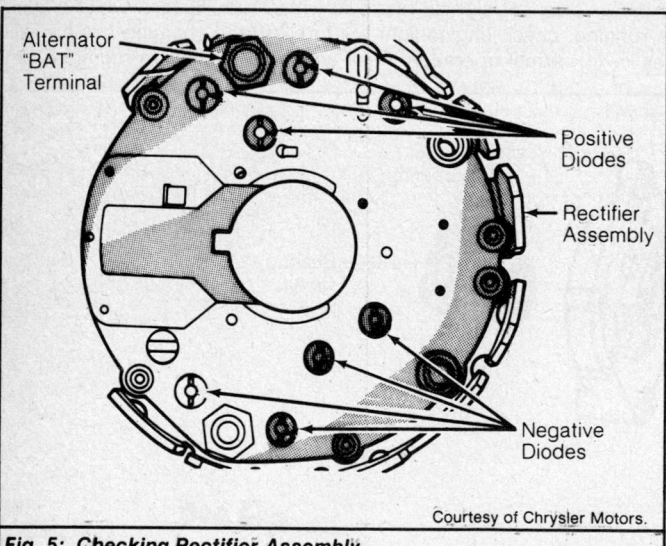

Fig. 5: Checking Rectifier Assembly

Courtesy of Chrysler Motors.

Brush Holder Test – 1) When testing brushes and brush springs, make sure that brushes move smoothly in brush holder. Sticking brushes require replacement of brush holder assembly.

2) Using an ohmmeter, touch one test lead to inner brush, and other test lead to field terminal. If there is no continuity, replace brush assembly. Using an ohmmeter, touch one test lead to outer brush and other test lead to field terminal. If there is no continuity, replace brush assembly. *See Fig. 6.*

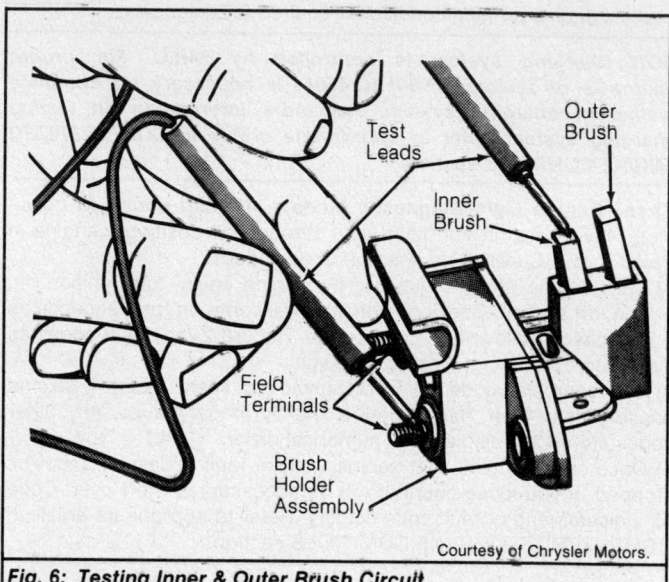

Courtesy of Chrysler Motors.

Fig. 6: Testing Inner & Outer Brush Circuit

ALTERNATOR SPECIFICATIONS

Application	Specification
Rated Amp Output	90
Minimum Current Amp Ouput	40
Field Current Draw @ 12 Volts	
Rotating by Hand	2.5-5.0 Amps
Condenser Capacity	1
Rotation	Clockwise

[1] – 2.2 Microfarad ± 20%.

Chrysler Motors: Diplomat, Fifth Avenue, Grand Fury

DESCRIPTION

The 90RS alternator is standard equipment on most rear wheel drive models. A 120RS alternator is used when equipped with police or taxi package. Alternators use an external electronic voltage regulator to control the amount of current that passes through the alternator.

ON-VEHICLE TEST

NOTE: Before performing following test, check battery to verify full charge. False readings could result if test is performed with weak or defective battery.

OUTPUT WIRE RESISTANCE

1) With ignition off, disconnect negative battery cable. Remove output wire from alternator "B+" terminal. See Fig. 2. Using 0-100 amp ammeter, connect positive test lead to alternator "B+" terminal and negative test lead to disconnected alternator output wire.

2) Using voltmeter, connect positive test lead to disconnected alternator output wire and negative lead to positive battery cable at battery post. Disconnect voltage regulator connector. Connect jumper wire from Green wire in connector to ground. See Fig. 1.

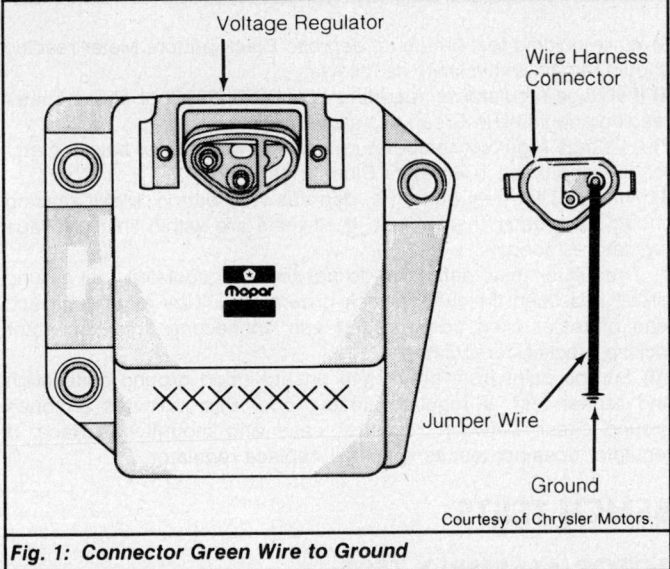

Fig. 1: Connector Green Wire to Ground

CAUTION: Do not connect blue wire of regulator wiring connector to ground. Do not spread connector terminals with jumper wire.

3) Connect tachometer to engine. Reconnect negative battery cable. Be sure carbon pile is in "OPEN" or "OFF" position before connecting leads. Connect Variable Carbon Pile Rheostat (C-3950) in series between battery terminals.

4) Start engine. Immediately reduce to idle speed. Adjust engine speed and carbon pile to maintain 20 amps. Voltmeter reading should not exceed voltage drop of .5 volt.

5) If higher voltage drop is indicated, inspect, clean and tighten all alternator output wire circuit connections. Voltage drop test can be performed at each connection to locate excessive resistance.

6) If resistance tested satisfactorily, turn off carbon pile and ignition. Disconnect negative battery cable. Remove ammeter, voltmeter, variable carbon pile rheostat and tachometer. Remove jumper wire connected between voltage regulator connection and ground.

7) Reinstall voltage regulator connector and alternator output wire to alternator "B+" terminal. Reinstall negative battery cable.

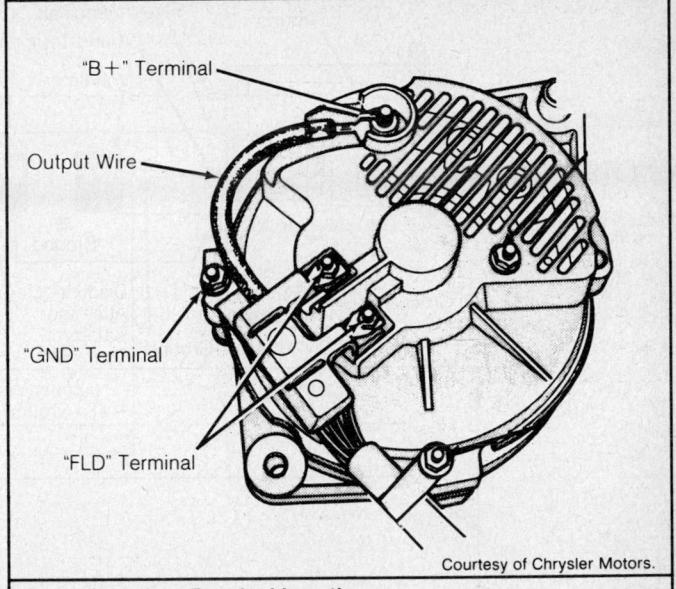

Fig. 2: Alternator Terminal Locations

CURRENT OUTPUT TEST

1) Ensure battery is fully charged. Verify ignition is off and disconnect negative battery cable. Disconnect alternator output wire from alternator "B+" terminal. See Fig. 2. Using 0-100 amp ammeter, connect positive test lead to alternator "B+" terminal and negative test lead to disconnected alternator output wire. See Fig. 3.

2) Using voltmeter, connect positive test lead to alternator "B+" terminal and negative lead to ground. Disconnect voltage regulator connector. Connect a jumper wire from Green wire to ground. See Fig. 1.

CAUTION: Do not connect Blue wire of regulator wiring connector to ground. Do not spread connector terminals with jumper wire.

3) Attach negative battery cable and connect tachometer to engine. Be sure carbon pile is in "OPEN" or "OFF" position before connecting leads. Install Variable Carbon Pile Rheostat (C-3950) in series between battery terminals.

4) Start engine. Immediately reduce engine to idle speed. Adjust carbon pile and engine speed in increments until 1250 RPM is reached and voltmeter reads 15 volts. Do not allow voltage to exceed 16 volts.

5) Ammeter reading should be within specifications. See ALTERNATOR SPECIFICATIONS TABLE at end of this article. If reading is less than specified and alternator output wire resistance is not excessive, alternator should be removed and bench tested. See BENCH TESTS in this article.

6) After test is complete, reduce engine speed. Turn off carbon pile and ignition. Disconnect negative battery cable. Remove ammeter, voltmeter, variable carbon pile rheostat and tachometer.

7) Remove jumper wire connected between voltage regulator connection and ground. Reinstall voltage regulator connector and alternator output wire to alternator "B+" terminal. Reinstall negative battery cable.

TESTING VOLTAGE REGULATOR WITHOUT REGULATOR TESTER (C-4133)

1) Ensure battery is fully charged. Turn ignition off. Connect positive voltmeter lead to positive battery cable. Connect negative voltmeter lead to good chassis ground. Connect tachometer to engine.

2) With all lights and accessories off, Start engine and adjust to 1250 RPM. Check voltmeter readings. If voltage readings are as specified, regulator is working properly. See VOLTAGE CHART.

4-32

1989 ALTERNATORS & REGULATORS
Chrysler Motors 90 & 120-Amp Alternators (Cont.)

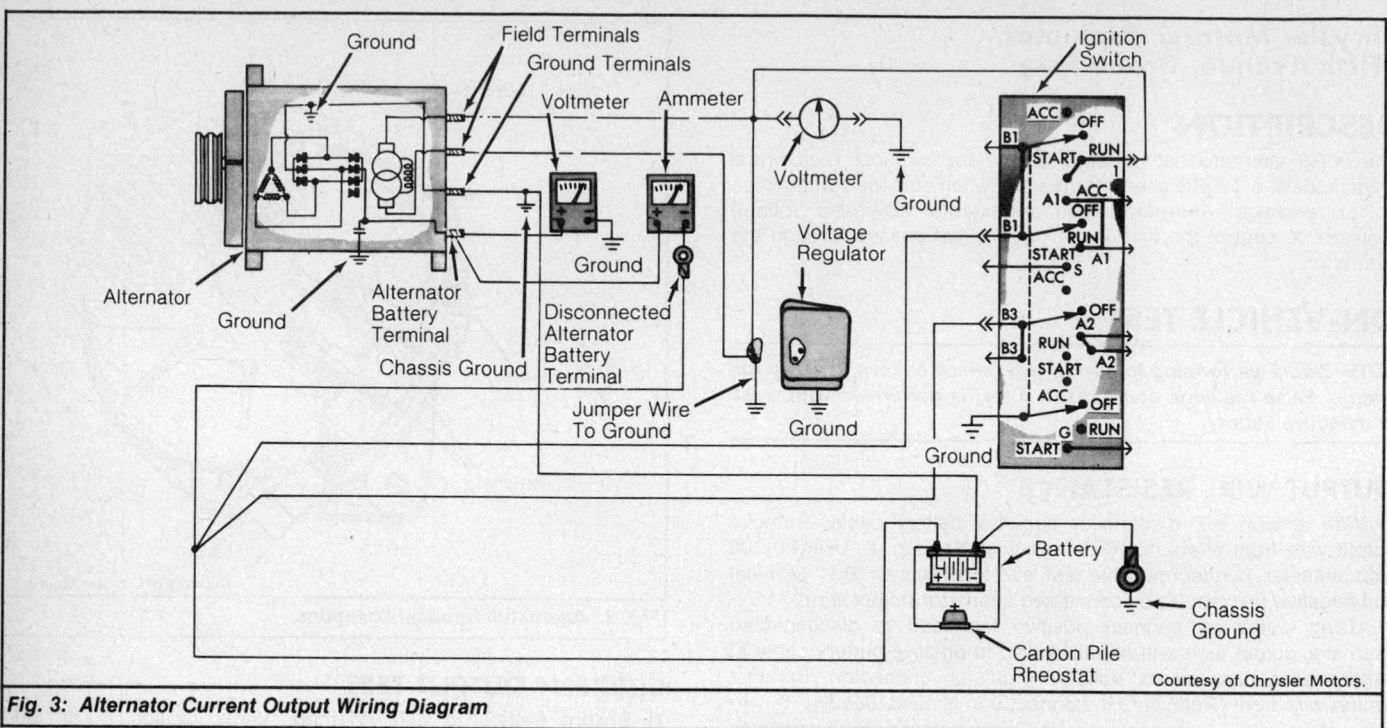

Fig. 3: Alternator Current Output Wiring Diagram

Courtesy of Chrysler Motors.

VOLTAGE CHART

Temperature	Voltage
-20°F (-30°C)	14.9-15.8
80°F (27°C)	13.9-14.4
140°F (60°C)	13.0-13.7
Above 140°F (60°C)	Less Than 13.6

3) If voltage is greater than or less than specifications, check for good voltage regulator ground. Voltage regulator ground is obtained through regulator case, mounting screws and sheet metal of vehicle.

4) Check ground circuit for an open circuit. If an open circuit is found, clean all connections in voltage regulator ground circuit and retest.

5) Turn ignition off. Disconnect voltage regulator connector. Ensure terminals of connector are not spread open, causing an open or intermittent connection.

NOTE: DO NOT start engine or distort terminals with voltmeter test leads.

6) Turn ignition on. Check for battery voltage at voltage regulator connector Blue and Green terminals. Both Blue and Green terminals should read battery voltage. Turn ignition off. If battery voltage is not present, check Blue and Green wires for an open circuit.

7) If all tests are satisfactory, replace regulator and repeat test. Remove voltmeter and tachometer.

TESTING VOLTAGE REGULATOR WITH REGULATOR TESTER (C-4133)

1) Disconnect voltage regulator connector. Plug in power cord of Voltage Regulator Tester (C-4133). Connect ground wire from tester to good body ground near regulator.

2) Plug voltage regulator tester connector into regulator on vehicle. Place tester knob to regulator test position. Press test button on tester. Voltage reading should be within limits as follows:

3) If voltage regulator temperature is at 80°F (27°C) or above, meter reading should be in Green or Yellow range.

4) If voltage regulator temperature is at 80°F (27°C) or below, meter reading should be in Green or Blue range.

5) While holding test button in, depress Black button. Meter reading should remain within limits as follows:

6) If voltage regulator temperature is at 80°F (27°C) or above, meter reading should be in Green or Yellow range.

7) If voltage regulator temperature is at 80°F (27°C) or below, meter reading should be in Green or Blue range.

8) While holding test button in, depress Red button. Meter reading should be greater than .7 volt. If all tests are within limits, voltage regulator is good.

9) If regulator tests defective, do not replace regulator until ground circuit has been checked. Check ground circuit by moving ground lead of tester from body ground and connecting it to connector locking bracket of regulator.

10) Scrape paint from bracket to ensure good ground connection and repeat test. If regulator tests good, this indicates an open ground circuit between regulator case and mounting surface. If regulator does not test as specified, replace regulator.

BENCH TESTS

ROTOR ASSEMBLY TEST

1) Remove rotor from alternator. Check field slip rings for excessive wear or roughness. If slip ring has only minor damage, clean with fine emery cloth. If slip rings are badly damaged, rotor must be replaced.

2) Using ohmmeter, connect each probe to a rotor slip ring. Ohmmeter needle should show continuity. If no meter movement, replace rotor.

3) Connect one ohmmeter probe to slip ring and other probe to rotor shaft. Ohmmeter reading should be infinity. Reading other than infinity indicates rotor is shorted to shaft and must be replaced.

STATOR ASSEMBLY TEST

1) Remove stator from alternator. Connect one ohmmeter probe to one stator lead and other probe to stator laminated core. Ohmmeter reading should be infinity.

2) If meter needle moves, stator winding is shorted to core and must be replaced. Repeat test for each stator lead. Do not touch probes or stator leads, as an incorrect reading will result.

1989 ALTERNATORS & REGULATORS
Chrysler Motors 90 & 120-Amp Alternators (Cont.)

4-33

3) Connect one ohmmeter probe to stator lead and other probe to another stator lead. If no meter movement occurs, stator coil is open and must be replaced. Repeat tests with other stator leads.

RECTIFIER TEST

1) Separate positive diode leads from negative diode leads. Using a volt/ohmmeter, test for continuity from positive heat sink to each positive diode leads.

2) Reverse ohmmeter test leads and repeat test. Test should show continuity in one direction only.

3) Test for continuity from negative heat sink to each negative diode leads. Reverse ohmmeter test leads and repeat test. Test should show continuity in one direction only. If meter readings are not as specified, replace rectifier assembly.

BRUSH HOLDER TEST

1) When testing brushes and brush springs make sure that brushes move smoothly in brush holder. Sticking brushes require replacement of brush holder assembly.

2) Using an ohmmeter, touch one test lead to inner brush and other test lead to field terminal. One field terminal should be open and other terminal should be closed. If meter readings are not as specified, replace brush holder assembly.

3) Using an ohmmeter, touch one test lead to outer brush and other test lead to field terminal. One field terminal should be open and other terminal should be closed. If meter readings are not as specified, replace brush holder assembly.

ALTERNATOR SPECIFICATION TABLE

Application	Specification
Rated Amp Output for 90 Amp Alt.	90 Amp
Rated Amp Output for 120 Amp Alt.	120 Amp
Minimum Output for 90 Amp Alt. [1]	87 Amp
Minimum Output for 120 Amp Alt. [1]	98 Amp
Field Current Draw [2]	2.5-5.0 Amp
Capacitor Capacity	[3]
Rotation	Clockwise

[1] – Minimum full field 1250 RPM.
[2] – At 12 volts while rotating by hand.
[3] – .5 Microfarad ± 20%.

1989 ALTERNATORS & REGULATORS
Nippondenso 75, 90 & 120-Amp Alternators

Chrysler Motors

DESCRIPTION

A 75-amp (75HS) alternator is used on some FWD models equipped with 2.5L SPFI, 2.5L Turbo I MPFI and 3.0L MPFI engines. A 90-amp (90HS) and 120-amp (120HS) may also be used on some FWD models equipped with 3.0L MPFI engines. Charging system consists of a Single Module Engine Controller (SMEC) on 2.5L engines or Single Board Engine Controller (SBEC) on 3.0L engines and check engine light and battery on all models.

The alternator consists of a rotor, stator, rectifiers, front and rear covers and drive pulley. The electronic voltage regulator is contained within the engine controller and is not serviceable as a separate component.

OPERATION

Alternator diodes convert AC current to DC current. The engine controller monitors critical input and output of the charging system, making sure it is working properly.

The engine controller will store in memory any failures within the monitored circuits. Engine controller will translate a failure in the form of fault codes when on-board diagnostics are entered.

The self-diagnostic capabilities of this system, if properly utilized, can greatly simplify testing. The engine controller has been programmed to monitor several different circuits of the engine control system.

If a problem is sensed with a monitored circuit, a fault code is stored in the engine controller's memory. The check engine light will illuminate and engine controller will enter limp-in mode.

In this mode, engine controller attempts to compensate for the failure of a particular component by substituting information from other sources. This will allow vehicle to be operated until proper repairs can be made.

TESTING & DIAGNOSIS

SYSTEM DIAGNOSIS

If a charging system malfunction is suspected, perform ON-VEHICLE TESTS in this article. Repair as necessary. If no problem is found using ON-VEHICLE TESTS, refer to ENTERING ON-BOARD DIAGNOSTICS in this article.

ON-VEHICLE TESTS

Alternator Output Wire Resistance Test – Alternator output wire resistance test will show amount of voltage drop across alternator output wire between alternator "BAT" terminal and positive battery post.
1) Charge battery as necessary. Turn ignition switch to "OFF" position. Disconnect negative battery cable. Disconnect alternator output wire from alternator "BAT" terminal.
2) Using a 0-150 ampere scale DC ammeter, connect positive ammeter lead to alternator "BAT" terminal and negative lead to disconnected alternator output wire. *See Fig. 1.*
3) Using a voltmeter (0-18 volts minimum), connect positive voltmeter lead to disconnected alternator output wire and negative lead to positive battery cable.

CAUTION: Alternator has 2 field terminals. See Fig. 2. One field terminal has Dark Green wire and other field terminal has Dark Blue wire. DO NOT connect jumper wire to alternator field terminal Dark Blue wire.

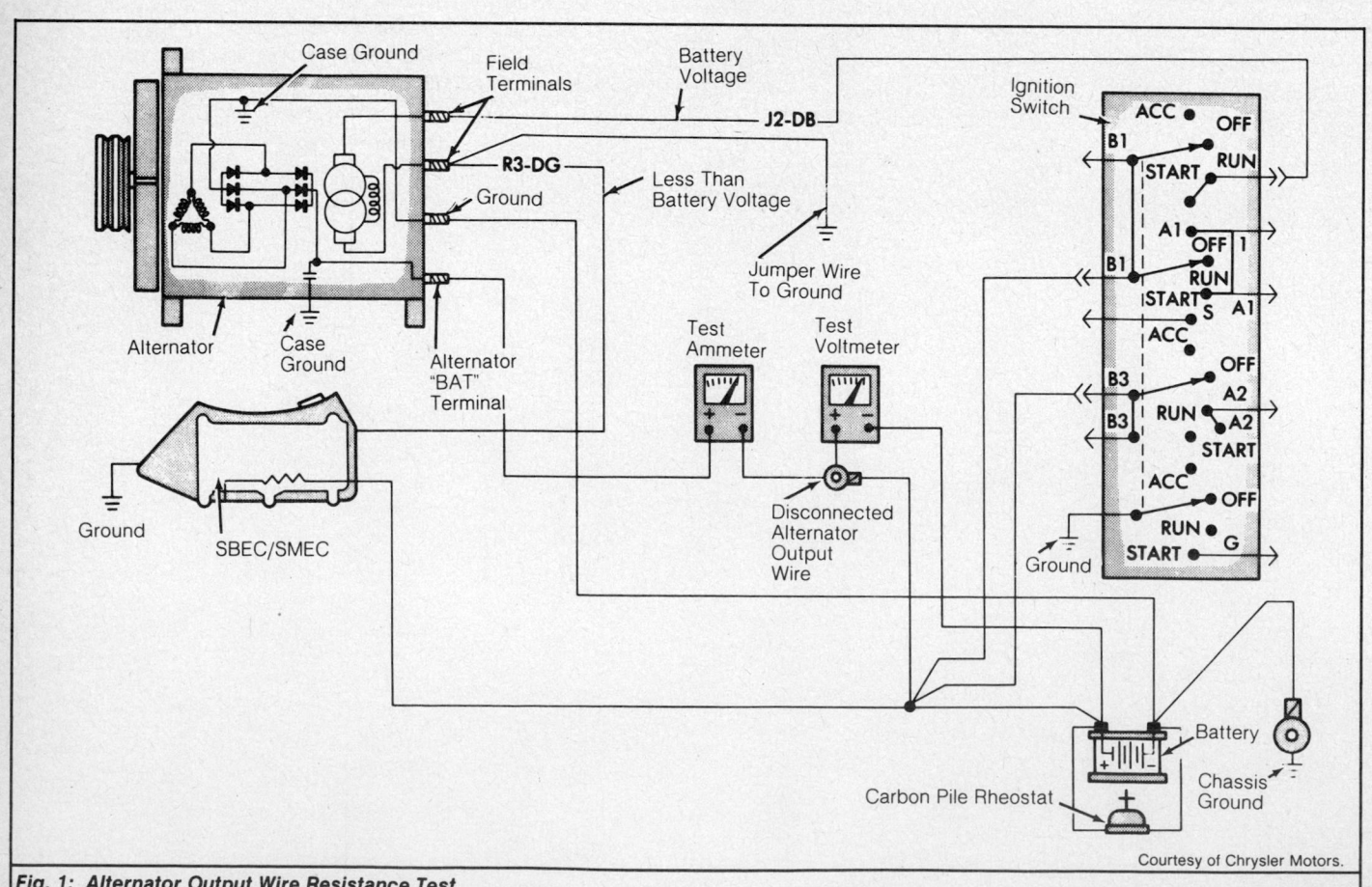

Fig. 1: Alternator Output Wire Resistance Test

Courtesy of Chrysler Motors.

1989 ALTERNATORS & REGULATORS
Nippondenso 75, 90 & 120-Amp Alternators (Cont.)

4-35

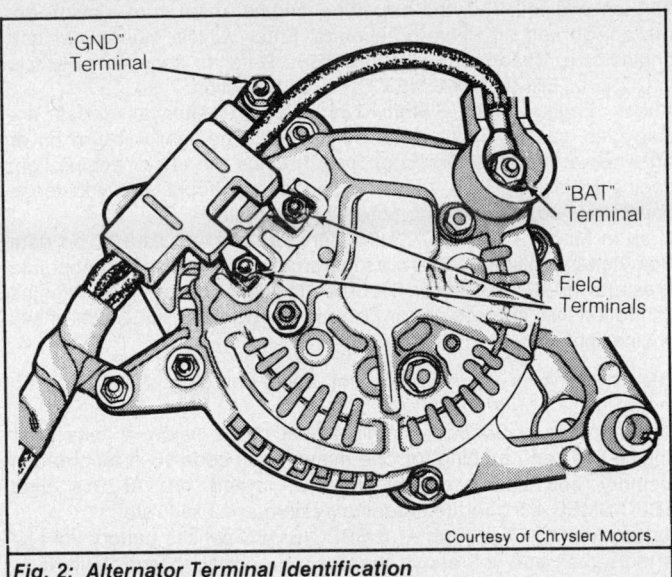

Fig. 2: Alternator Terminal Identification

Courtesy of Chrysler Motors.

Observe voltmeter reading. Voltage drop should not be more than .5 volt.

7) If higher voltage drop is indicated, inspect, clean and tighten all connections between alternator "BAT" terminal and positive battery post. Voltage drop test may be performed at each connection to locate connection with excessive resistance. If resistance tested satisfactorily, reduce engine speed, turn off carbon pile and ignition switch.

8) Disconnect negative battery cable. Remove test ammeter, voltmeter, carbon pile and tachometer. Remove jumper wire between alternator Dark Green field wire and ground.

9) Connect alternator output wire to alternator "BAT" terminal. Reconnect negative battery cable and hose between SBEC/SMEC and air cleaner.

Current Output Test – The current output test determines whether or not alternator is capable of delivering its rated current output.

1) Charge battery as necessary. Disconnect negative battery cable. Disconnect alternator output wire at alternator "BAT" terminal. *See Fig. 2.* Using a 0-150 ampere scale DC ammeter, connect positive ammeter lead to alternator "BAT" terminal and negative lead to disconnected alternator output wire. *See Fig. 3.*

2) Using a voltmeter (0-18 volts range minimum), connect positive voltmeter lead to disconnected alternator "BAT" terminal and negative lead to good ground.

3) Connect engine tachometer and reconnect negative battery cable. Connect Variable Carbon Pile Rheostat (C-3950) between battery terminals. Be sure carbon pile is in "OFF" position before connecting leads.

CAUTION: *Alternator has 2 field terminals. See Fig. 2. One field terminal has Dark Green wire and other field terminal has Dark Blue wire. DO NOT connect jumper wire to alternator field terminal Dark Blue wire.*

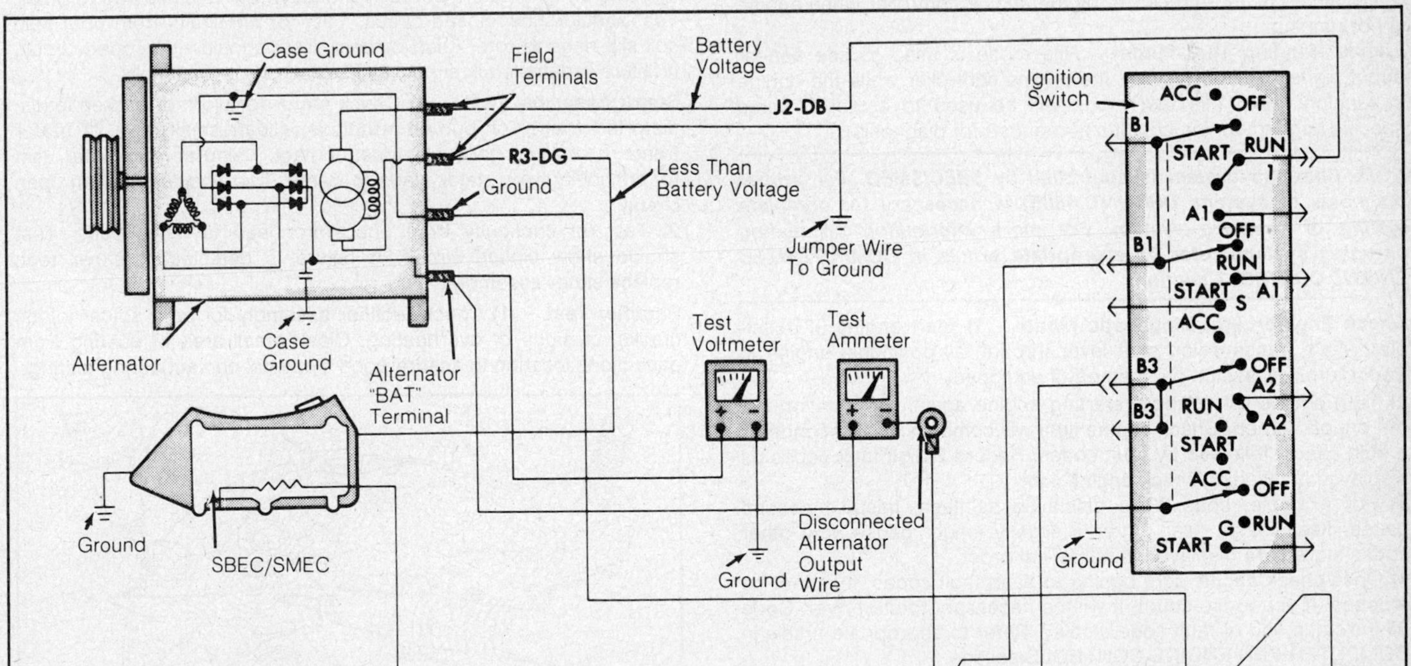

4) Remove air hose between SBEC/SMEC and air cleaner. Connect one end of jumper wire to ground and other end to alternator field terminal Dark Green wire on rear side of alternator.

5) Connect engine tachometer and reconnect negative battery cable. Connect Variable Carbon Pile Rheostat (C-3950) between battery terminals. Be sure carbon pile is in "OFF" position before connecting leads.

6) Start engine and reduce engine speed to idle. Adjust engine speed and carbon pile to maintain 20 amps flowing in circuit.

Fig. 3: Alternator Current Output Test

Courtesy of Chrysler Motors.

4-36

1989 ALTERNATORS & REGULATORS
Nippondenso 75, 90 & 120-Amp Alternators (Cont.)

4) Remove air hose between SBEC/SMEC and air cleaner. Connect one end of jumper wire to ground and other end to alternator field terminal Dark Green wire on back of alternator.

5) Start engine and reduce engine speed to idle. Adjust carbon pile and engine speed in increments until engine speed is 1250 RPM and voltmeter reads 15 volts. DO NOT allow voltage to read more than 16 volts.

6) Ammeter should read within specification. See ALTERNATOR SPECIFICATIONS table at end of this article. If alternator amperage reads less than specified and alternator output wire resistance is not excessive, alternator should be removed and bench tested. See BENCH TESTS in this article. After current output test is completed, reduce engine speed, turn off carbon pile and ignition switch.

7) Disconnect negative battery cable. Remove test ammeter, voltmeter, tachometer and carbon pile. Remove jumper wire between alternator field terminal Dark Green wire and ground.

8) Reconnect alternator output wire to alternator "BAT" terminal. Reconnect negative battery cable and hose between SBEC/SMEC and air cleaner.

ENTERING ON-BOARD DIAGNOSTICS

Diagnostic Readout Box – The DRB-II (C-4805) is a diagnostic tool that is plugged into the vehicle diagnostic connector. The DRB-II is used to put the system into diagnostic test mode, circuit actuation test mode, switch test mode, sensor test mode and engine running test mode. These 5 test modes are required to properly diagnose the system. The following is a description of each test mode:

Diagnostic Test Mode – This mode is used to see if there are any fault codes stored in engine controller's memory.

Circuit Actuation Test Mode (ATM) – This mode is used to turn a specific circuit on and off to check it.

Switch Test Mode – This mode is used to determined if specific inputs are being received by the engine controller.

Sensor Test Mode – This mode is used to see the output signals of certain sensors as received by the engine controller when engine is not running.

Engine Running Test Mode – This mode is used to see sensor ouput signals as received by the engine controller while the engine is running. Also, this test mode will be used to establish some specific engine running conditions required for diagnosis.

NOTE: Charging system is controlled by SBEC/SMEC. For proper diagnosis of system, DRB-II (C-4805) is necessary for complete testing of charging system. For more information on testing charging system, refer to appropriate article in COMPUTERIZED ENGINE CONTROLS section.

Check Engine Light Diagnostic Mode – 1) Start engine (if possible). Move transmission shift lever through all positions, engine in Park. Turn A/C switch on, then off (if equipped).

2) Turn engine off. Without starting engine again, turn ignition on, off, on, off and on. Check engine light will come on for 2 seconds as a bulb check, followed by fault codes. Record 2-digit fault codes as displayed by flashing check engine light.

3) For example, code 23 is displayed as flash, flash, 4 second pause, flash, flash, flash. After a slightly longer pause, any other codes stored are displayed in numerical order.

4) Once check engine light begins to flash fault codes, it cannot be stopped. If you loose count, it will be necessary to start over. Code 55 indicates end of fault code display. Refer to appropriate article in COMPUTERIZED ENGINE CONTROLS section.

NOTE: Check engine light cannot be used to perform actuation test mode, sensor test modes, or engine running test.

DRB-II Diagnostic Mode – 1) Attach DRB-II Tester (C-4805) to self-test connector. Connector is located in engine compartment near left shock tower.

2) Start engine (if possible). Move transmission shift lever through all positions, ending in Park. Turn A/C switch on, then off (if equipped).

3) Turn engine off. Without starting engine again, turn ignition on, off, on, off and on within 5 seconds. Enter vehicle model year and engine size. Read fault data on DRB-II. Refer to appropriate article in COMPUTERIZED ENGINE CONTROLS section.

Check Engine Light Switch Test Mode – After all codes are displayed, switch function can be verified. The light will turn on or off when a switch is turned on or off. Once the check engine light begins to display fault codes, it cannot be stopped. If you loose count it will be necessary to start all over again.

Limp-In Mode – If SBEC/SMEC senses incorrect data or no data from battery voltage, coolant temperature sensor, Manifold Absolute Pressure (MAP) sensor or Throttle Position Sensor (TPS), engine controller will put system in limp-in mode and illuminate check engine light.

The following is a description of each charging system limp-in mode:

Battery Voltage Sense – If this signal drops below 4 volts after engine has been running for one minute fault code 16 is recorded in memory and check engine light is turned on. At this time SBEC/SMEC will operate charging system at a fixed rate.

Battery Voltage Too High – If SBEC/SMEC senses battery voltage is more than one volt above the desired control voltage, fault 45 is recorded in memory and check engine light is turned on.

If these 2 sensor signals return to within specification while engine is running, check engine light will turn off and charging system will return to normal operation. Fault codes will remain in memory, but will be cleared after 50-100 engine starts if the fault does not happen again.

BENCH TESTS

Rotor Assembly Test – 1) Check field slip rings for excessive wear or roughness. If slip rings have only minor damage, clean with fine emery cloth. If slip rings are badly damaged, rotor must be replaced.

2) Using an ohmmeter, test for continuity from one slip ring to other. Test should show closed circuit. Test for continuity from both field coil slip rings to rotor shaft or core. Test should show open circuit. If failure is detected in either test, replace rotor assembly.

Stator Assembly Test – 1) Check stator for worn or broken leads, distorted frame, or burned windings. Clean small area of stator frame for making good electrical contact. Using an ohmmeter, test for continuity from stator leads to frame. Test should show an open circuit.

2) Test for continuity from one stator lead to other leads. Test should show closed circuit. If failure is detected in either test, replace stator assembly.

Rectifier Test – 1) Check rectifier assembly for poor solder joints, cracks, or signs of overheating. Clean small area of coating from each diode location to assure good electrical contact during testing.

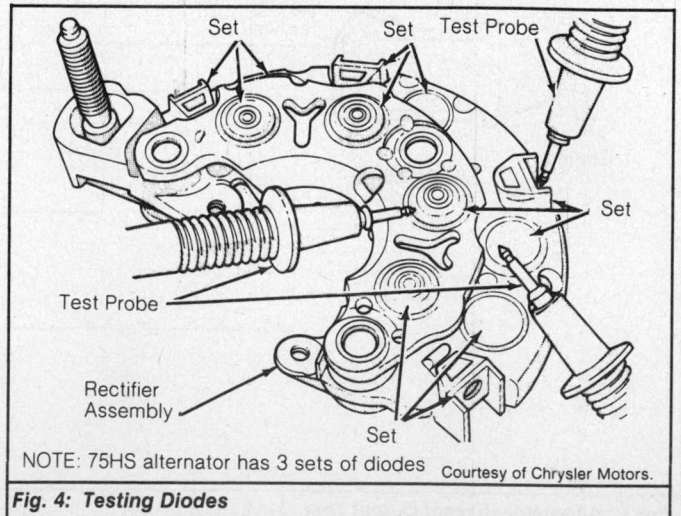

NOTE: 75HS alternator has 3 sets of diodes   Courtesy of Chrysler Motors.

Fig. 4: Testing Diodes

1989 ALTERNATORS & REGULATORS
Nippondenso 75, 90 & 120-Amp Alternators (Cont.)

4-37

2) Using an ohmmeter, connect positive test probe to negative diode and negative probe to stator terminal. Ohmmeter should read 7-11 ohms resistance. Move positive test probe to positive diode, no continuity should be detected. *See Fig. 4.* Perform same test procedure on each stator terminal to diode set.

NOTE: *75HS alternator has 3 sets of diodes. 90HS and 120HS alternators have 4 sets of diodes.*

3) Connect negative ohmmeter probe to positive diode and positive probe to stator terminal. Ohmmeter should read 7-11 ohms resistance. Move negative test probe to negative diode, no continuity should be detected. Perform same test procedure on each stator terminal to diode set. If rectifier does not test as specified, replace rectifier assembly.

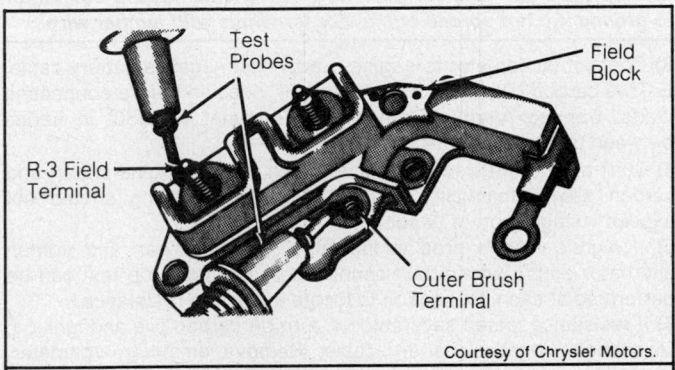

Fig. 5: Field Block R-3 Terminal Test

Brush Holder Test – When testing brushes and brush springs, make sure that brushes move smoothly in brush holder. Sticking brushes require replacement of brush holder assembly. Using an ohmmeter, touch one test lead to inner brush and other test lead to field terminal. One should show open and other should be closed. Repeat procedure on outer brush. If brush holder does not test as specified, replace brush holder.

Field Block Tests – 1) Using an ohmmeter, test for continuity from outer brush terminal to R-3 field terminal, circuit should test closed. *See Fig. 5.*

2) Test for continuity from inner brush terminal to J-2 field terminal, circuit should test closed. *See Fig. 6.*

3) Test for continuity from J-2 field terminal to R-3 terminal, circuit should test open. *See Fig. 7.*

4) Turn field block over and test for continuity across radio suppression capacitor terminals, circuit should test open. *See Fig. 8.* If field block does not test as specified, replace field block.

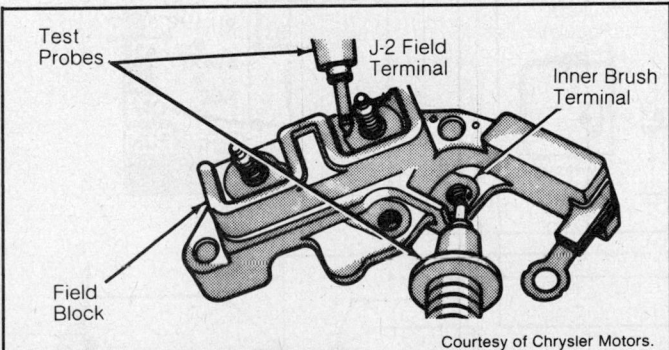

Fig. 6: Field Block J-2 Terminal Test

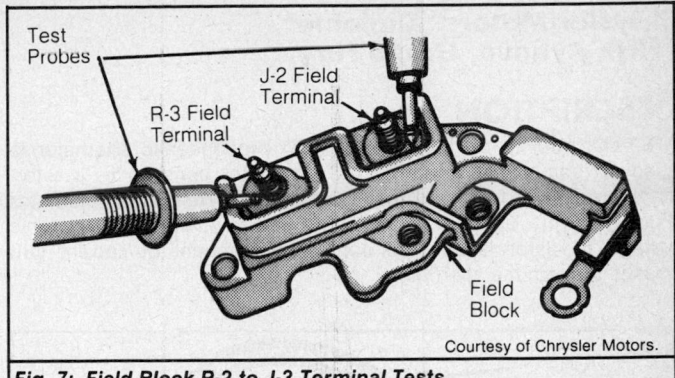

Fig. 7: Field Block R-2 to J-3 Terminal Tests

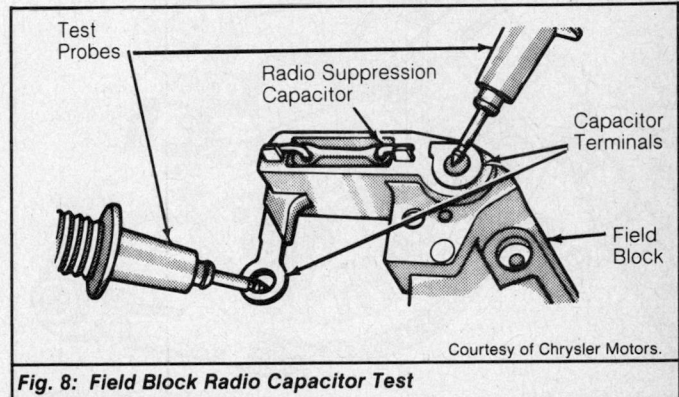

Fig. 8: Field Block Radio Capacitor Test

ALTERNATOR SPECIFICATIONS

Application	Specification
Rated Amp Output	
75 Amp (75HS)	75
90 Amp (90HS)	90
120 Amp ((120HS)	120
Minimum Current Amp Ouput	
75 Amp [1]	68
90 Amp [1]	87
120 Amp [1]	98
Field Current Draw	
75 Amp @ 12 Volts	
Rotating By Hand	2.5-5.0 Amps
90 Amp @ 12 Volts	
Rotating By Hand	2.5-5.0 Amps
120 Amp @ 12 Volts	
Rotating By Hand	2.5-5.0 Amps
Condenser Capacity	
75 Amp	[2]
90 Amp	[2]
120 Amp	[2]
Rotation	
75 Amp	Clockwise
90 Amp	Clockwise
120 Amp	Clockwise

[1] – Full Fielded @ 1250 RPM.
[2] – 0.5 Microfarad ± 20%.

1989 ALTERNATORS & REGULATORS
Nippondenso 90 & 120-Amp Alternators

Chrysler Motors: Diplomat, Fifth Avenue, Grand Fury

DESCRIPTION

A 90-amp (90HS) or 120-amp (120HS) Nippondenso alternator is used on some RWD models. The alternator consists of a rotor, stator, rectifiers, front and rear covers and drive pulley. Alternator diodes convert AC current to DC. The use of an external electronic voltage regulator is used to control the amount of current that passes through the alternator.

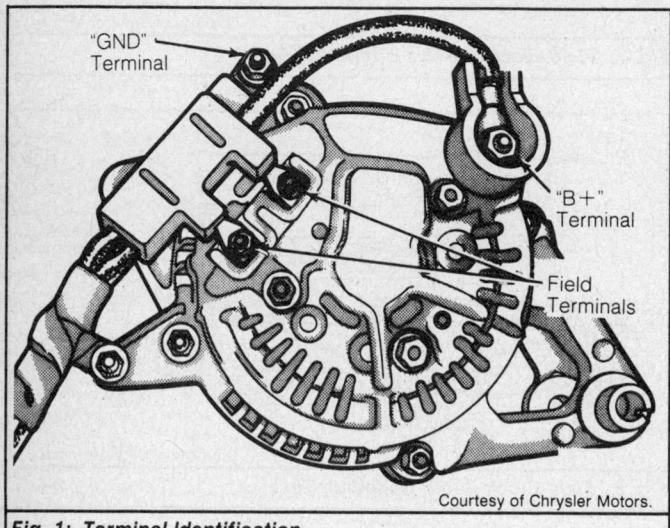

Fig. 1: Terminal Identification

Courtesy of Chrysler Motors.

ON-VEHICLE TEST

OUTPUT WIRE RESISTANCE

1) Ensure battery is fully charged. With ignition off, disconnect negative battery cable. Remove output wire from alternator "B+" terminal. *See Fig. 1.* Using a 0-100 amp ammeter, connect positive ammeter lead to alternator "B+" terminal and negative lead to disconnected alternator output wire. *See Fig. 2.*

2) Using a voltmeter, connect positive lead to disconnected alternator output wire and negative lead to positive battery post. Disconnect voltage regulator harness connector. Connect jumper wire from voltage regulator harness connector Green wire terminal to ground. *See Fig. 3.*

CAUTION: Do not connect Blue wire of regulator wiring connector to ground. Do not spread connector terminals with jumper wire.

3) Connect tachometer to engine. Reconnect negative battery cable. Ensure carbon pile is in "OPEN" or "OFF" position before connecting leads. Connect Varible Carbon Pile Rheostat (C-3950) in series between battery terminals.

4) Start engine and reduce to idle speed. Adjust engine speed and carbon pile to maintain 20 amps. Voltmeter reading should not exceed voltage drop of .5 volt.

5) If higher voltage drop is indicated, inspect, clean and tighten alternator output wire circuit connections. Voltage drop test can be performed at each connection to locate excessive resistance.

6) If resistance tested satisfactorily, turn off carbon pile and ignition. Disconnect negative battery cable. Remove ammeter, voltmeter, variable carbon pile rheostat and tachometer. Remove jumper wire connected between voltage regulator harness connector and ground.

7) Reconnect voltage regulator harness connector and alternator output wire to alternator "B+" terminal. Reconnect negative battery cable.

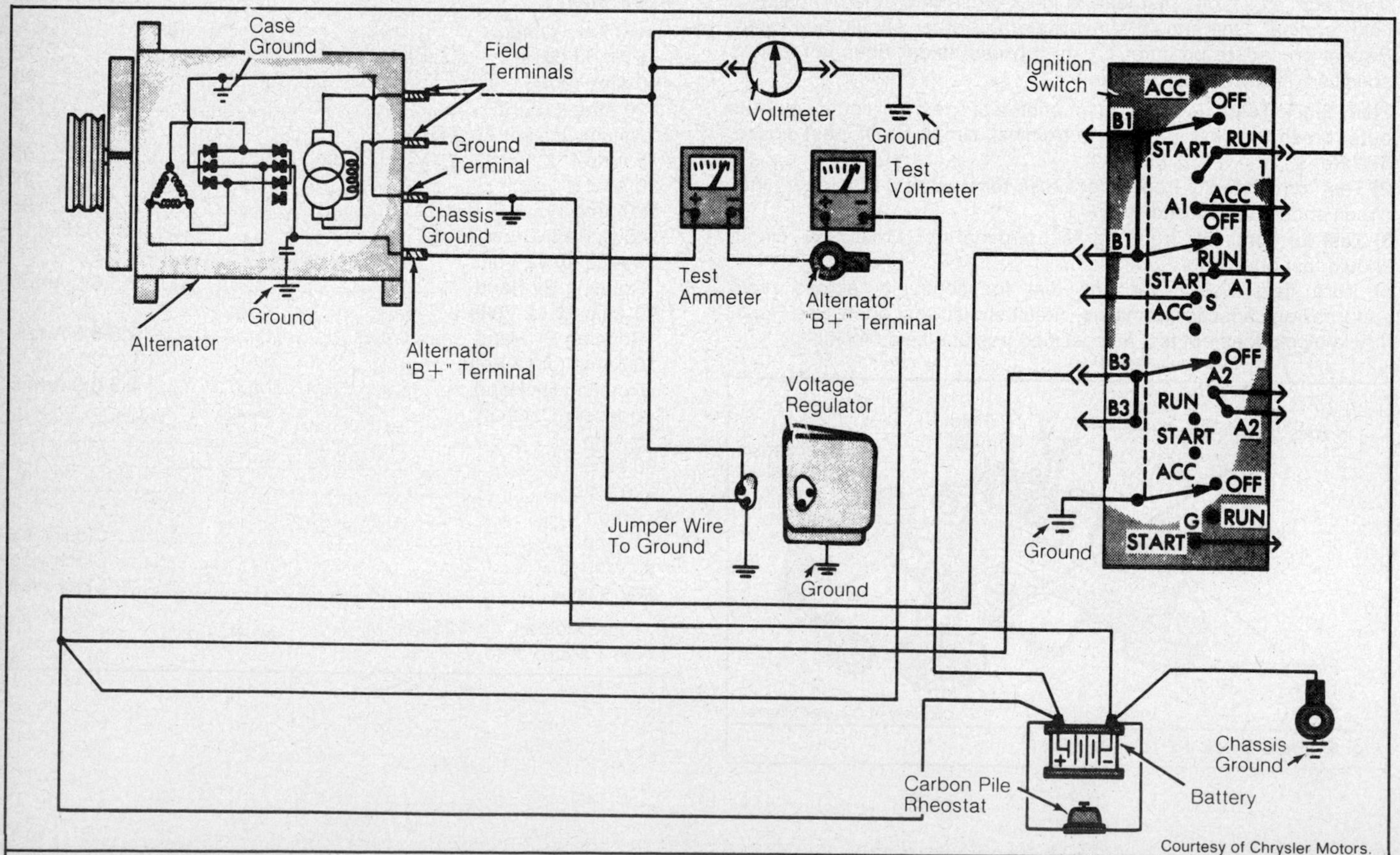

Fig. 2: Output Wire Resistance Test

Courtesy of Chrysler Motors.

CURRENT OUTPUT TEST

1) Ensure battery is fully charged. With engine off, disconnect negative battery cable at battery post. Disconnect alternator output wire from alternator "B+" terminal. *See Fig. 1*. Using a 0-100 amp ammeter, connect positive ammeter lead to alternator "B+" terminal and negative lead to disconnected alternator output wire. *See Fig. 4*.

2) Using a voltmeter, connect positive test lead to alternator "B+" terminal and negative lead to ground. Disconnect voltage regulator harness connector. Connect jumper wire from voltage regulator harness connector Green wire terminal to ground. *See Fig. 3*.

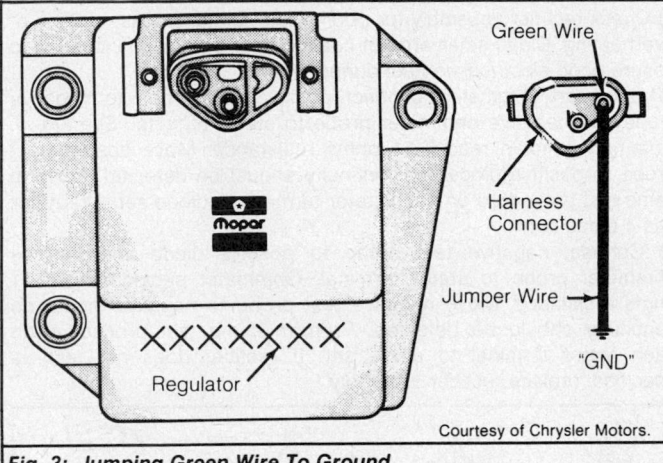

Fig. 3: *Jumping Green Wire To Ground*

CAUTION: Do not connect Blue wire of regulator wiring connector to ground. Do not spread connector terminals with jumper wire.

3) Reconnect negative battery cable and connect tachometer to engine. Ensure carbon pile is in "OPEN" or "OFF" position before connecting leads. Install Variable Carbon Pile Rheostat (C-3950) in series between battery terminals.

4) Start engine and reduce to idle speed. Adjust carbon pile and engine speed in increments until 1250 RPM is reached and voltmeter reads 15 volts. Do not allow voltage to exceed 16 volts.

5) Ammeter reading should be within specifications. See ALTERNATOR SPECIFICATIONS table at end of this article. If reading is less than specified and alternator output wire resistance is not excessive, alternator should be removed and bench tested. See BENCH TESTS in this article.

6) After test is complete, reduce engine speed. Turn off carbon pile and ignition. Disconnect negative battery cable. Remove ammeter, voltmeter, variable carbon pile rheostat and tachometer.

7) Remove jumper wire connected between voltage regulator harness connector and ground. Reconnect voltage regulator harness connector and alternator output wire to alternator "B+" terminal. Reconnect negative battery cable.

TESTING VOLTAGE REGULATOR WITHOUT REGULATOR TESTER (C-4133)

1) Ensure battery is fully charged. Turn ignition off. Connect positive voltmeter lead to positive battery cable. Connect negative voltmeter lead to chassis ground. Connect tachometer to engine.

2) Turn lights and accessories off. Start engine and adjust to 1250 RPM. Observe voltmeter reading. If voltage reading is as specified, regulator is working properly. See VOLTAGE CHART.

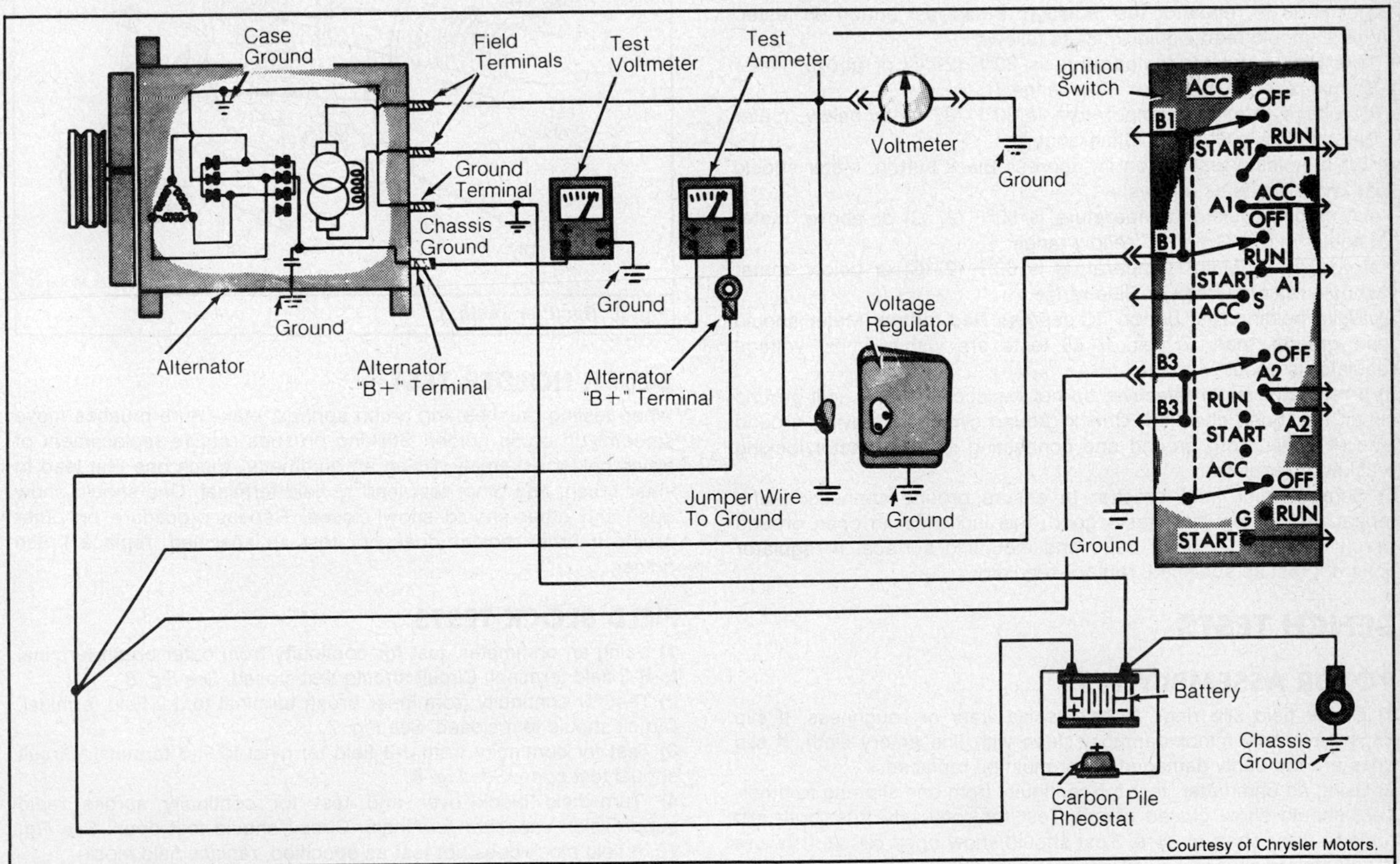

Fig. 4: *Current Output Test*

VOLTAGE CHART

Temperature	Voltage
-20°F (-30°C)	14.9-15.8
80°F (27°C)	13.9-14.4
140°F (60°C)	13.0-13.7
Above 140°F (60°C)	Less Than 13.6

3) If voltage is greater than or less than specifications, check for good voltage regulator ground. Voltage regulator ground is obtained through regulator case, mounting screws and sheet metal of vehicle.

4) Check ground circuit for an open. If an open circuit is found, clean all connections in voltage regulator ground circuit and retest.

5) Turn ignition off. Disconnect voltage regulator connector. Ensure terminals of connector are not spread open, causing an open or intermittent connection.

NOTE: DO NOT start engine or distort terminals with voltmeter test leads.

6) Turn ignition on. Check for battery voltage at voltage regulator harness connector Blue and Green terminals. Both Blue and Green terminals should read battery voltage. Turn ignition off. If battery voltage is not present, check Blue and Green wires for an open.

7) If all tests are satisfactory, replace regulator and repeat test. Remove voltmeter and tachometer.

TESTING VOLTAGE REGULATOR WITH REGULATOR TESTER (C-4133)

1) Disconnect voltage regulator connector. Plug in power cord of Voltage Regulator Tester (C-4133). Connect ground wire from tester to ground near regulator.

2) Plug voltage regulator tester connector into regulator. Place tester knob to regulator test position. Press test button on tester. Voltage should read within limits as follows:
- If voltage regulator temperature is 80°F (27°C) or above, meter should read in Green or Yellow range.
- If voltage regulator temperature is 80°F (27°C) or below, meter should read in Green or Blue range.

3) While holding test button in, depress Black button. Meter should read within limits as follows:
- If voltage regulator temperature is 80°F (27°C) or above, meter should read in Green or Yellow range.
- If voltage regulator temperature is 80°F (27°C) or below, meter should read in Green or Blue range.

4) While holding test button in, depress Red button. Meter should read greater than .7 volt. If all tests are within limits, voltage regulator is good.

5) If regulator tests defective, do not replace regulator until ground circuit has been checked. Check ground circuit by moving ground lead of tester from ground and connecting it to connector locking bracket of regulator.

6) Scrape paint from bracket to ensure ground connection and repeat test. If regulator tests good, this indicates an open ground circuit between regulator case and mounting surface. If regulator does not test as specified, replace regulator.

BENCH TESTS

ROTOR ASSEMBLY TEST

1) Check field slip rings for excessive wear or roughness. If slip rings have only minor damage, clean with fine emery cloth. If slip rings are too badly damaged, rotor must be replaced.

2) Using an ohmmeter, test for continuity from one slip ring to other. Test should show closed circuit. Test for continuity from both slip rings to rotor shaft or core. Test should show open circuit. If failure is detected in either test, replace rotor assembly.

STATOR ASSEMBLY TEST

1) Check stator for worn or broken leads, distorted frame or burned windings. Clean small area of stator frame to ensure good electrical contact. Using an ohmmeter, test for continuity from stator leads to frame. Test should show an open circuit.

2) Test for continuity from one stator lead to other leads. Test should show closed circuit. If failure is detected in either test, replace stator assembly.

RECTIFIER TEST

1) Check rectifier assembly for poor solder joints, cracks or signs of overheating. Clean small area of coating from each diode location to assure good electrical contact during testing.

2) Using an ohmmeter, connect positive test probe to negative diode and negative ohmmeter probe to stator terminal. *See Fig. 5.* Ohmmeter should read 7-11 ohms resistance. Move positive test probe to positive diode, no continuity should be detected. Perform same test procedure on each stator terminal to diode set. Alternator has 4 diode sets.

3) Connect negative test probe to positive diode and positive ohmmeter probe to stator terminal. Ohmmeter should read 7-11 ohms resistance. Move negative test probe to negative diode, no continuity should be detected. Perform same test procedure on each stator terminal to diode set. If rectifier does not test as specified, replace rectifier assembly.

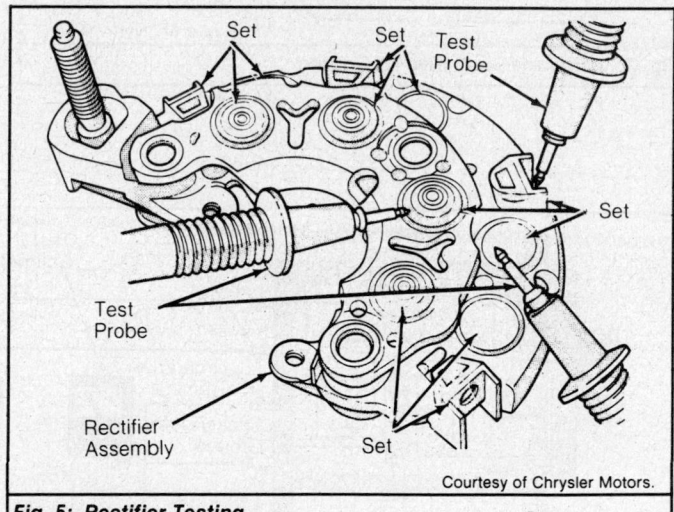

Courtesy of Chrysler Motors.

Fig. 5: Rectifier Testing

BRUSH HOLDER TEST

When testing brushes and brush springs, make sure brushes move smoothly in brush holder. Sticking brushes require replacement of brush holder assembly. Using an ohmmeter, touch one test lead to inner brush, and other test lead to field terminal. One should show open and other should show closed. Repeat procedure on outer brush. If brush holder does not test as specified, replace brush holder.

FIELD BLOCK TESTS

1) Using an ohmmeter, test for continuity from outer brush terminal to R-3 field terminal. Circuit should test closed. *See Fig. 6.*

2) Test for continuity from inner brush terminal to J-2 field terminal. Circuit should test closed. *See Fig. 7.*

3) Test for continuity from J-2 field terminal to R-3 terminal. Circuit should test open. *See Fig. 8.*

4) Turn field block over and test for continuity across radio suppression capacitor terminals. Circuit should test open. *See Fig. 10.* If field block does not test as specified, replace field block.

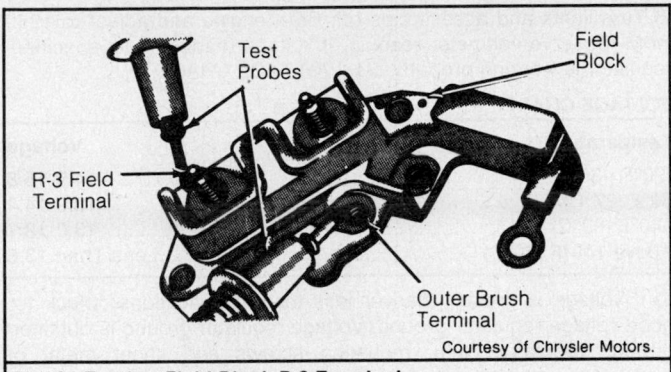

Fig. 6: Testing Field Block R-3 Terminal

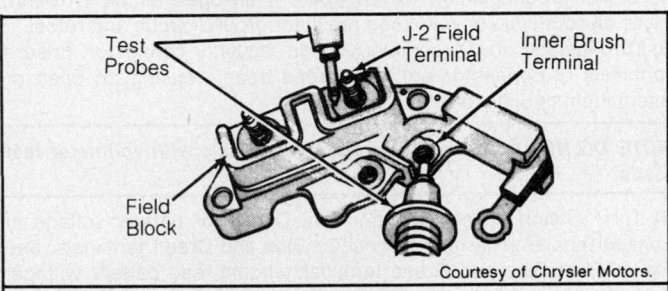

Fig. 7: Testing Field Block J-2 Terminal

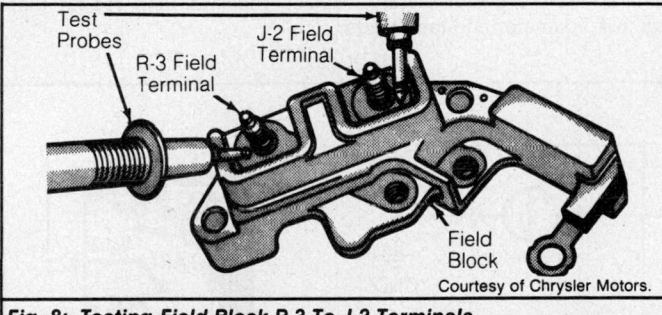

Fig. 8: Testing Field Block R-3 To J-2 Terminals

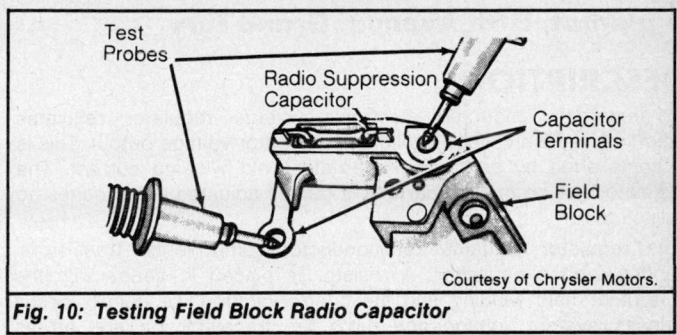

Fig. 10: Testing Field Block Radio Capacitor

90-AMP (90HS) ALTERNATOR SPECIFICATIONS

Application	Specification
Rated Amp Output	90
Minimum Current Amp Ouput [1]	87
Field Current Draw @ 12 Volts	
Rotating By Hand	2.5-5.0 Amps
Condenser Capacity	[2]
Rotation	Clockwise

[1] – Full Fielded @ 1250 RPM.
[2] – 0.5 Microfarad ± 20%.

120-AMP (120HS) ALTERNATOR SPECIFICATIONS

Application	Specification
Rated Amp Output	120
Minimum Current Amp Ouput [1]	98
Field Current Draw @ 12 Volts	
Rotating By Hand	2.5-5.0 Amps
Condenser Capacity	[2]
Rotation	Clockwise

[1] – Full Fielded @ 1250 RPM.
[2] – 0.5 Microfarad ± 20%.

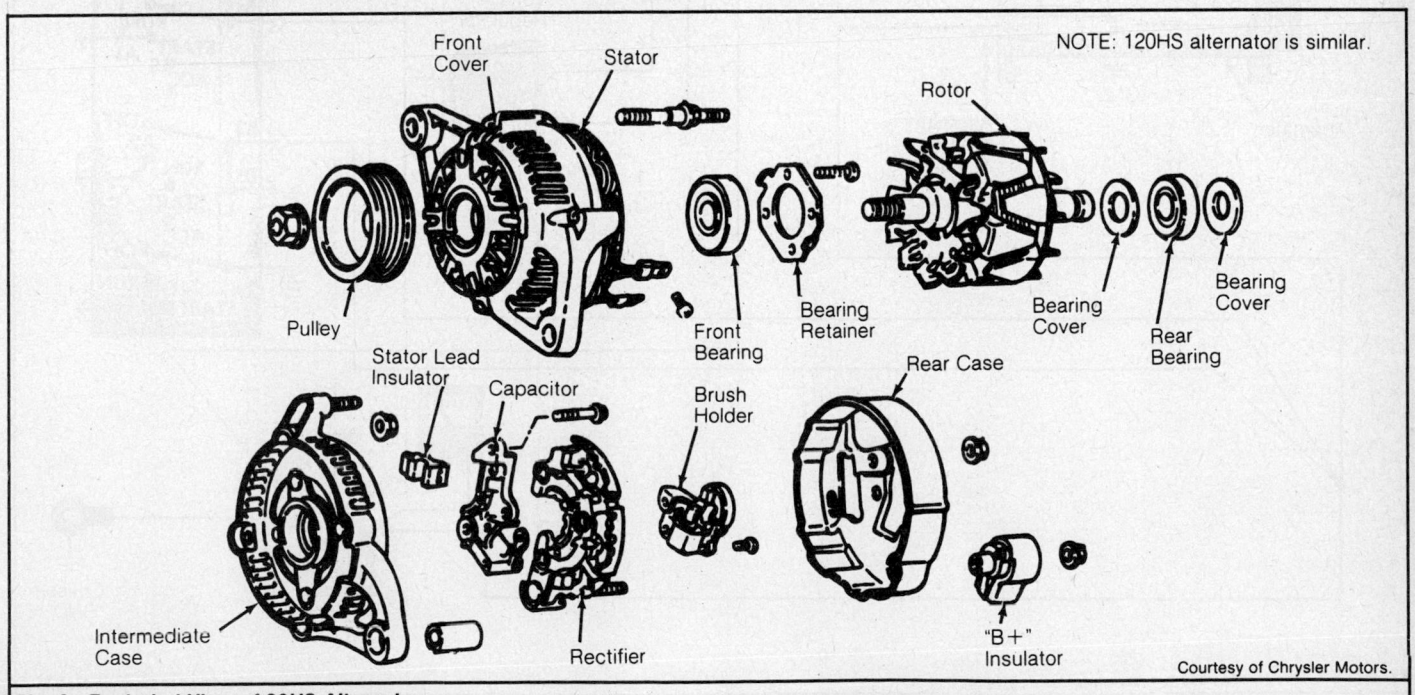

NOTE: 120HS alternator is similar.

Fig. 9: Exploded View of 90HS Alternator

1989 ALTERNATORS & REGULATORS
Chrysler Motors Regulator

Diplomat, Fifth Avenue, Grand Fury

DESCRIPTION

An externally mounted electronic voltage regulator regulates electrical system voltage by limiting alternator voltage output. This is accomplished by controlling alternator field winding current. The regulator has no moving parts. It is factory adjusted and requires no adjustment.

The regulator contains semiconductor components, transistors, diodes, and a capacitor. A resistor is placed in series with the alternator field winding and the control circuit. The control circuit senses system voltage and turns the transistor on and off as required. The transistor cycles many times per second when the engine is running.

During conditions of low engine speed and high electrical loads, the alternator field is required to be continuously in the "ON" state. Under these conditions, the transistor is not cycling rapidly and field voltage is increased in order to meet system demand. The electronic voltage regulator control circuit can also vary regulated system voltage up or down as temperature changes.

TESTING VOLTAGE REGULATOR WITHOUT REGULATOR TESTER (C4133)

NOTE: Ensure battery is fully charged and in good condition before performing the following regulator tests.

1) Turn ignition to the "OFF" position. Connect positive voltmeter lead to positive battery cable. Connect negative voltmeter lead to chassis ground. Connect tachometer to engine. *See Fig. 1.*

2) Turn lights and accessories off. Start engine and adjust to 1250 RPM. Observe voltmeter reading. If voltage reading is as specified, regulator is working properly. See VOLTAGE CHART.

VOLTAGE CHART

Temperature	Voltage
-20°F (-30°C)	14.9-15.8
80°F (27°C)	13.9-14.4
140°F (60°C)	13.0-13.7
Above 140°F (60°C)	Less Than 13.6

3) If voltage is greater than or less than specifications, check for good voltage regulator ground. Voltage regulator ground is obtained through regulator case, mounting screws and sheet metal of vehicle.

4) Check ground circuit for an open. If an open circuit is found, clean all connections in voltage regulator ground circuit and retest.

5) Turn ignition off. Disconnect voltage regulator connector. Ensure terminals of connector are not spread open, causing an open or intermittent connection.

NOTE: DO NOT start engine or distort terminals with voltmeter test leads.

6) Turn ignition in the "ON" position. Check for battery voltage at voltage regulator harness connector Blue and Green terminals. *See Fig. 2.* Both Blue and Green terminals should read battery voltage. Turn ignition off. If battery voltage is not present, check Blue and Green wires for an open.

7) If all tests are satisfactory, replace regulator and repeat test. Remove voltmeter and tachometer.

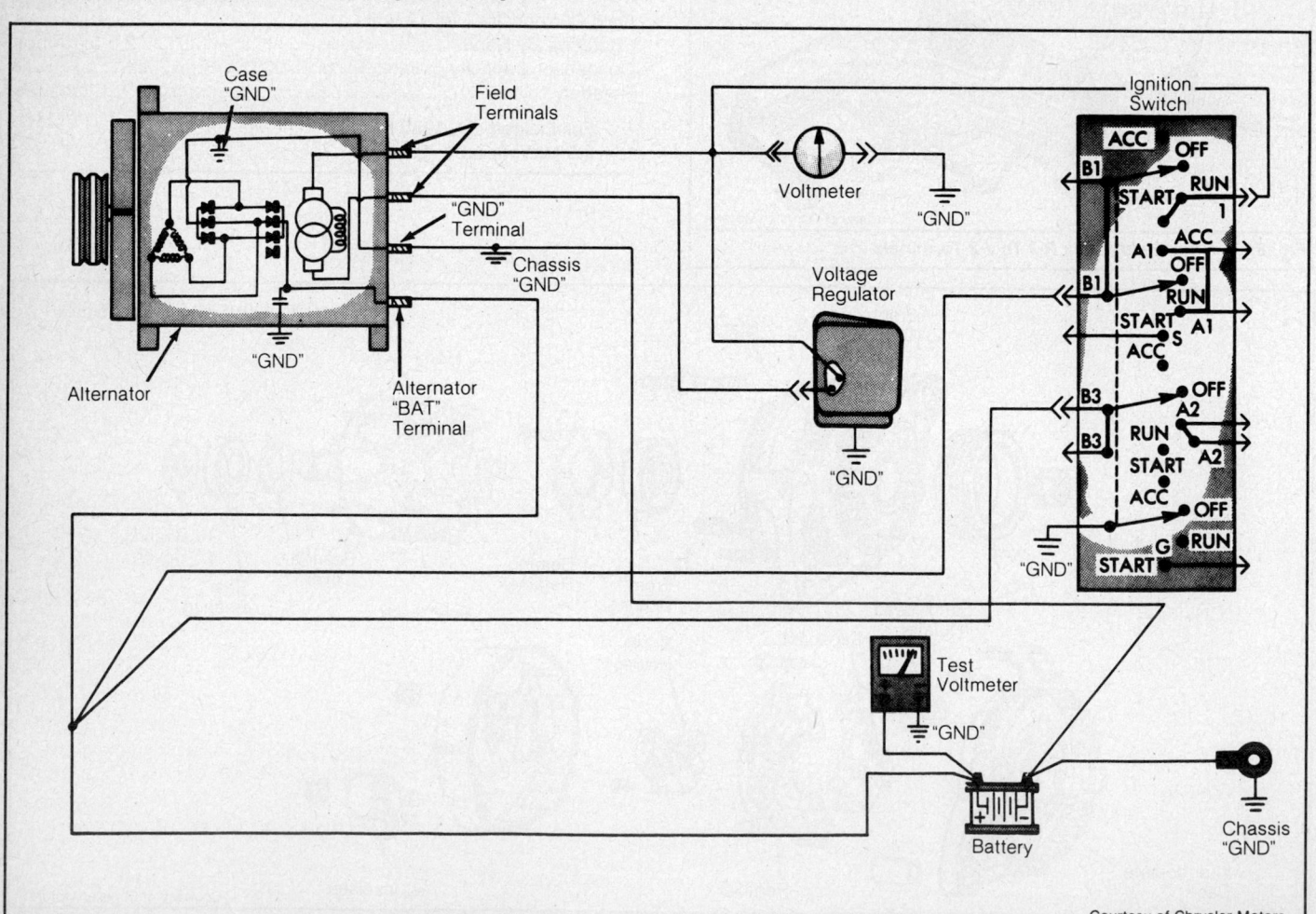

Courtesy of Chrysler Motors.

Fig. 1: Testing Voltage Regulator Without Tester (C-4133)

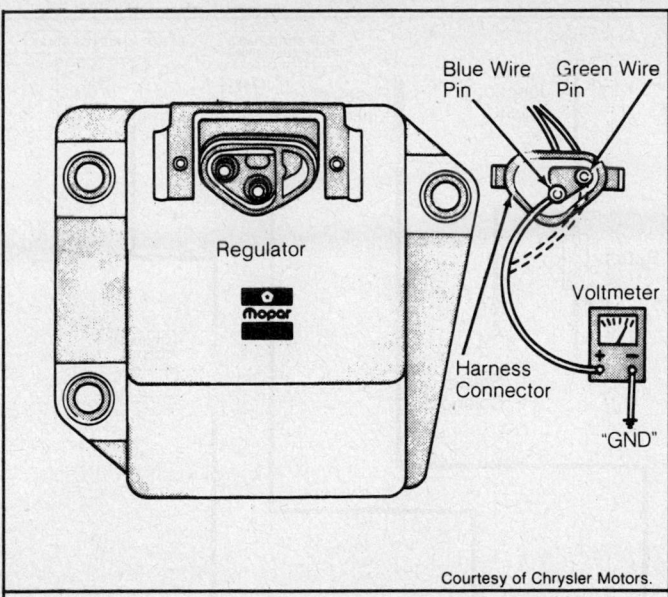

Blue Wire Pin

Green Wire Pin

Regulator

Voltmeter

Harness Connector

"GND"

Courtesy of Chrysler Motors.

Fig. 2: Testing Regulator Harness Connector Wires For Battery Voltage

TESTING VOLTAGE REGULATOR WITH REGULATOR TESTER (C-4133)

1) Disconnect voltage regulator connector. Plug in power cord of Voltage Regulator Tester (C-4133). Connect ground wire from tester to ground near regulator.

2) Plug voltage regulator tester connector into regulator. Place tester knob to regulator test position. Press test button on tester. Voltage should read within limits as follows:

- If voltage regulator temperature is 80°F (27°C) or above, meter should read in Green or Yellow range.
- If voltage regulator temperature is 80°F (27°C) or below, meter should read in Green or Blue range.

3) While holding test button in, depress Black button. Meter should read within limits as follows:

- If voltage regulator temperature is 80°F (27°C) or above, meter should read in Green or Yellow range.
- If voltage regulator temperature is 80°F (27°C) or below, meter should read in Green or Blue range.

4) While holding test button in, depress Red button. Meter should read greater than .7 volt. If all tests are within limits, voltage regulator is good.

5) If regulator tests defective, do not replace regulator until ground circuit has been checked. Check ground circuit by moving ground lead of tester from ground and connecting it to connector locking bracket of regulator.

6) Scrape paint from bracket to ensure ground connection and repeat test. If regulator tests good, this indicates an open ground circuit between regulator case and mounting surface. If regulator does not test as specified, replace regulator.

1989 ALTERNATORS & REGULATORS
Delco-Remy 85, 100 & 105-Amp Alternators

Eagle

DESCRIPTION

Eagle Premier is equipped with a Delco-Remy CS130 alternator (85, 100 or 105-amp). Alternator does not use a diode trio. If charging system voltage is too high or too low when engine is running, regulator will cause charge indicator light to turn on. Regulator is enclosed in a solid mold, mounted inside alternator. Alternator is not serviceable. If alternator is defective, a new unit must be installed.

NOTE: Manufacturer does not recommend disassembling and servicing CS alternators. If alternator is defective, a new unit must be installed.

ADJUSTMENTS

No adjustment or maintenance is required on alternator assembly. Regulator voltage is preset and no adjustment is provided.

TROUBLE SHOOTING

BATTERY CABLES & DRIVE BELT

1) Inspect condition of battery cables and terminals. Clean, tighten or replace as necessary.
2) Ensure battery is fully charged and tested okay. Charge and/or replace battery as necessary.
3) Inspect drive belt condition and tension. Adjust belt tension or replace as necessary.

ALTERNATOR CONNECTIONS

1) Inspect alternator output "B+" terminal connection. Clean and tighten as necessary.
2) Disconnect alternator harness plug from alternator. Install a jumper wire between alternator harness plug "L" terminal to ground. *See Fig. 1.* Battery indicator light should glow.
3) If battery indicator light does not glow, Check fuse number 15 (10-amp) in fusebox. Fuse box is located on right side of kick panel.
4) If fuse is good, check for bad battery indicator light bulb. If bulb is okay, repair open to fuse number 15. Remove jumper wire.
5) Using a voltmeter, connect positive voltmeter lead to alternator harness plug terminal "F" and negative lead to ground. *See Fig. 1.* With ignition switch in the "ON" position, voltmeter should read battery voltage. If voltmeter does not read battery voltage, repair open from "F" terminal wire to ignition switch.
6) Connect positive voltmeter lead to alternator harness plug "B+" terminal and negative lead to ground. Voltmeter should read battery voltage. If voltmeter does not read battery voltage, repair open in "B+" terminal wire.
7) Ensure clean engine-to-chassis ground connections. Repair as necessary.

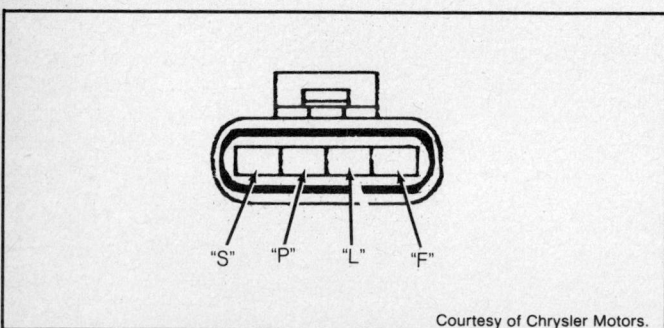

Fig. 1: Alternator Harness Plug Terminal Identification

Courtesy of Chrysler Motors.

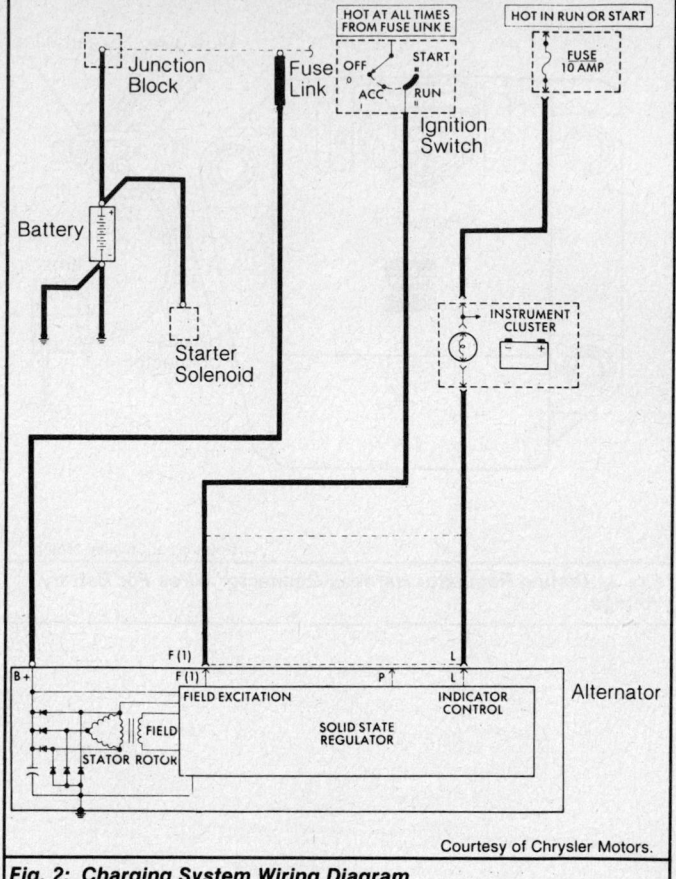

Courtesy of Chrysler Motors.

Fig. 2: Charging System Wiring Diagram

ON-VEHICLE TESTS

CURRENT OUTPUT TEST

NOTE: Battery must be fully charged and in good condition before proceeding with current output test.

1) Using an ammeter, connect ammeter in series with positive battery cable. Using a voltmeter, connect positive voltmeter lead to positive battery post and negative lead to negative battery post. Connect carbon pile rheostat to battery. Ensure carbon pile rheostat is in the "OFF" position before connecting to battery.
2) Start engine and allow 15 minutes for warm-up. Ensure a charging rate of 13 volts before testing output. Adjust engine RPM according to specification. See ALTERNATOR SPECIFICATIONS table at end of this article.
3) Turn carbon pile to match alternator output. Battery voltage should not drop below 13 volts. If alternator output is not according to specification, replace alternator.

CURRENT LEAKAGE TEST

CAUTION: Ensure all accessories are off and doors are not opened when ammeter is connected. Failure to do so could result in ammeter damage.

Current leakage refers to power being drained from battery with ignition switch off. Battery drain should not exceed 20mA (.020 amps). Typical draw is .10mA. At least 20mA are needed to supply electronic control unit, digital clock and electronically tuned radio memory.

1989 ALTERNATORS & REGULATORS
Delco-Remy 85, 100 & 105-Amp Alternators (Cont.)

4-45

1) Check to ensure no accessories are on. Excessive battery drain can be caused by items left on, such as reading lights, dome light and trunk light.

2) Excessive battery drain can also be caused by bad alternator diodes, shorted stator windings, shorted regulator and intermittent short in wiring.

3) Using an ammeter capable of sustaining over 10 amps, connect ammeter in series between positive battery cable and positive battery post. If current leakage is less than 10 amps, connect an ammeter set at 10-amp range in series between positive battery cable and positive battery post.

4) If voltage draw is less than 1 amp, connect an ammeter set at 100mA range in series between positive battery cable and positive battery post.

5) Main power branches can be isolated by removing one lead at a time from 100-amp main fuse. Further isolation can be located by removing circuit breakers and fuses.

6) Ammeter reading will drop once current leakage is found. Repair as necessary.

BENCH TESTS

NOTE: Bench testing is not available from manufacturer.

ALTERNATOR SPECIFICATION TABLE

Application	Current Output
CS130	
@ 800 RPM [1]	
85-Amp	48 Amps
100-Amp	51 Amps
105-Amp	60 Amps
@ 1200 RPM [2]	
85-Amp	61 Amps
100-Amp	65 Amps
105-Amp	74 Amps
@ 2000 RPM [3]	
85-Amp	70 Amps
100-Amp	78 Amps
105-Amp	84 Amps

[1] – Alternator RPM 2250.
[2] – Alternator RPM 3350.
[3] – Alternator RPM 5600.

TIGHTENING SPECIFICATIONS

Application	Ft. Lbs. (N.m)
Lower Mount Bolt	20 (27)
Upper Mount Bolt	30 (40)

1989 ALTERNATORS & REGULATORS
Mitsubishi Internal Alternator-Regulator

Ford Motor Co.: Probe

DESCRIPTION

Alternator has an internal fan and Integrated Circuit (IC) electronic voltage regulator. Internal IC electronic voltage regulator is part of the rotor, brush and brush holder. *See Fig. 4.* Voltage regulator automatically reduces regulated voltage when ambient temperature increases, so battery charging voltage is maintained at the proper level. Charging system voltage is maintained at an operating range of 14.1-14.7 volts. Alternating current is rectified to direct current by 6 diodes. A check engine warning light is used to indicate charging system malfunction.

ON-VEHICLE TESTS

BATTERY VOLTAGE TEST

Connect voltmeter negative lead to negative battery post and positive lead to positive battery post. Record battery voltage for comparison with other test results.

NOTE: Low state of battery charge may be caused by low current output from alternator. This can occur on vehicles operated under frequent stop and start conditions in high temperatures coupled with high electrical loads. New pulley and belt kit are available from manufacturer to correct this condition.

AMPERAGE OUTPUT TEST

1) Connect ammeter in series with positive battery cable. Connect voltmeter negative lead to negative battery post and positive lead to positive battery post.
2) Turn on as many electrical accessories as possible. Start engine and accelerate to 2500-3000 RPM. If alternator amperage output is within 10 percent of rated output, alternator is functioning properly. If amperage output is less than 90 percent of rated output, proceed to VOLTAGE OUTPUT TEST.

CHARGING SYSTEM VOLTAGE OUTPUT TEST

NOTE: Battery must be fully charged for following test and alternator wiring plug must remain connected.

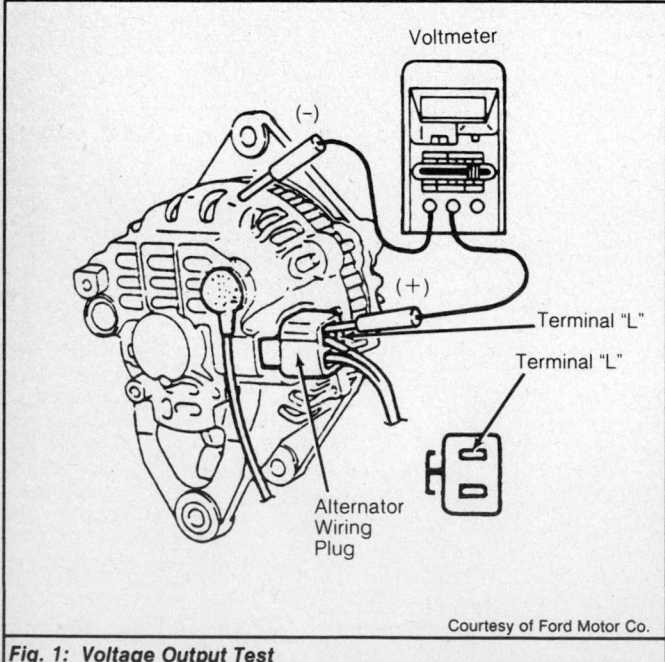

Fig. 1: Voltage Output Test

1) Turn off all electrical accessories. Connect ammeter in series to positive battery cable. Start engine and accelerate to 2500 RPM.
2) If ammeter reading is less than 5 amps, proceed to ROTOR FIELD COIL TEST. If ammeter reading is more than 5 amps, voltage loss in charging circuit is indicated. Check battery, alternator and engine ground cable connections.
3) Connect voltmeter positive lead to terminal "L" on alternator and negative voltmeter lead to alternator rear housing. *See Fig. 1.*
4) If reading at terminal "L" is less than 14.4 volts at 68°F (20°C), proceed to REGULATOR POWER SOURCE TEST. If reading at terminal "L" is between 14.4-15.0 volts at 68°F (20°C), problem in stator or rectifier is indicated. See appropriate test under BENCH TESTS in this article.

REGULATOR POWER SOURCE TEST

NOTE: Alternator wiring plug must be disconnected for the following test.

1) Disconnect alternator wiring plug. Turn ignition switch to "ON" position (engine not running). Connect voltmeter positive lead to alternator wiring plug terminal "S". *See Fig. 2.* Connect negative voltmeter lead to alternator rear housing.
2) If reading is same as battery voltage, proceed to ROTOR FIELD COIL TEST. If reading is less than battery voltage, problem is indicated between terminal "S" wire and battery.

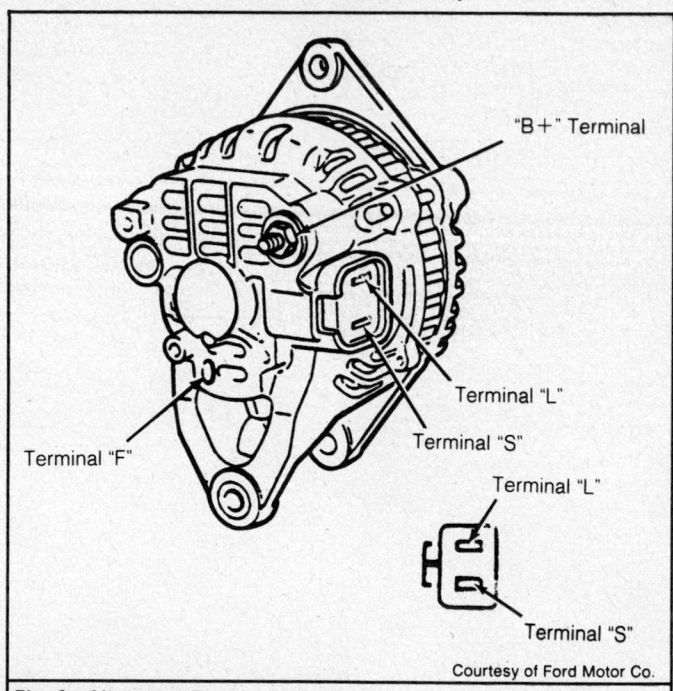

Fig. 2: Alternator Terminal Locations

ROTOR FIELD COIL TEST

NOTE: Terminal "F" is internal and can be accessed through hole in rear housing of alternator. Be sure ohmmeter probe does not touch alternator housing while performing the following test.

1) Disconnect negative battery cable at battery. Disconnect alternator output wire at "B+" terminal. Disconnect alternator wiring plug. Set ohmmeter in "x1" range. Connect one probe to alternator terminal "L" and other probe to terminal "F". *See Fig. 2.*
2) If ohmmeter reading is between 3 and 6 ohms, good alternator field is indicated. Proceed to "L" TERMINAL VOLTAGE TEST. If reading is less than 3 ohms or more than 6 ohms, problem is indicated in field rotor, slip rings or brushes. Remove alternator for further testing. See appropriate tests under BENCH TESTS in this article.

"L" TERMINAL VOLTAGE TEST

1) If previously disconnected, connect alternator output wire to "B+" terminal at rear alternator housing and negative battery terminal to battery. Disconnect alternator wiring plug if not previously disconnected.

2) With ignition switch in "ON" position (engine not running), connect voltmeter positive lead to alternator wiring plug "L" terminal and negative voltmeter lead to alternator rear housing. See Fig. 2.

3) If reading is 1-3 volts, problem is indicated in stator or rectifier. Remove alternator for further testing. See appropriate test under BENCH TESTS in this article.

4) If reading is more than 3 volts, problem is indicated in IC regulator. Remove alternator for further testing. See appropriate test under BENCH TESTS in this article.

ALTERNATOR VOLTAGE OUTPUT TEST

NOTE: Battery must be fully charged and battery voltage test should be performed before beginning the following test. See BATTERY VOLTAGE TEST under ON-VEHICLE TESTS in this article.

1) Connect alternator wiring plug if previously disconnected. Turn all electrical accessories off. Connect ammeter to positive battery cable.

2) Start engine and accelerate to 2500 RPM. Record ammeter reading. If ammeter reading is less than 5 amps, proceed to step 5). If more than 5 amps, see VOLTAGE OUTPUT TEST in this article.

NOTE: Alternator wiring plug must be connected for following test.

3) Connect voltmeter positive lead to alternator terminal "L". See Fig. 3. Connect negative voltmeter lead to alternator rear housing. Accelerate engine to 2500 RPM. If voltage reading is more than 15.0 volts at 68°F (20°C), proceed to REGULATOR POWER SOURCE TEST. If voltage is between 14.4-15.0 volts, alternator is operating properly.

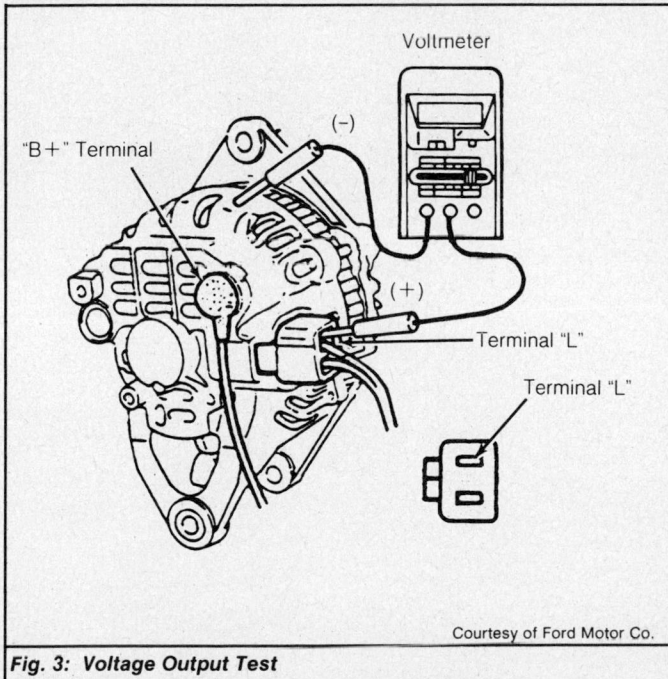

Fig. 3: Voltage Output Test

REGULATOR POWER SOURCE TEST

1) Disconnect alternator wiring plug. Turn ignition switch to "ON" position (engine not running). Connect positive voltmeter lead to terminal "S" of alternator wiring plug. See Fig. 2. Connect voltmeter negative lead to alternator rear housing. Record voltage reading.

2) If voltage at terminal "S" is same as battery voltage, proceed to ROTOR FIELD COIL TEST. If voltage at terminal "S" is less than battery voltage, problem is indicated in wiring between ignition switch and terminal "S". Reconnect alternator wiring plug.

ROTOR FIELD COIL CHECK

NOTE: Terminal "F" is internal and can be accessed through hole in rear housing of alternator. Be sure ohmmeter probe does not touch alternator housing while performing this test.

1) Disconnect negative battery cable, alternator wiring plug and "B+" wire at alternator output terminal.

2) Set ohmmeter in "x1" range. Connect one ohmmeter probe to alternator terminal "L" and other probe to alternator terminal "F". See Fig. 2.

3) If ohmmeter reading is between 3-6 ohms, problem in IC regulator is indicated. If reading is less than 3 ohms or more than 6 ohms, problem is indicated in rotor field coil, slip rings or brushes. Remove alternator for further testing. See appropriate test under BENCH TESTS in this article.

BENCH TESTS

RECTIFIER TESTING

1) Set ohmmeter to "x1" range. Check for continuity between positive diode lead and heat sink on positive diode side. There should be continuity from diode lead to heat sink, and no continuity in opposite direction. Repeat test for each diode. If meter readings are not as specified, replace rectifier assembly.

2) Repeat test for negative diodes. Check for continuity between negative diode lead and heat sink at negative diode side. There should be continuity from diode lead to heat sink, and no continuity in opposite direction. Repeat test for each diode. If meter readings are not as specified, replace rectifier assembly.

STATOR COIL GROUNDED TEST

1) Inspect stator laminations closely for signs of overheating. A burnt spot usually indicates shorted stator winding. Remove stator from alternator. Set ohmmeter on "x1000" scale. Connect one ohmmeter probe to one stator lead and other probe to stator laminated core. Ohmmeter reading should be infinity.

2) If meter needle moves, stator winding is shorted to core and must be replaced. Repeat test for each stator lead. Do not touch probes or stator leads, an incorrect reading will result.

STATOR COIL OPEN TEST

Remove stator from alternator. Set ohmmeter on "x1" scale. Connect one ohmmeter probe to stator lead and other probe to another stator lead. If no meter movement occurs, stator coil is open and must be replaced. Repeat test with other stator leads. Do not touch probes or stator leads, or an incorrect reading will result.

ROTOR OPEN OR SHORT CIRCUIT TEST

1) Remove rotor from alternator. Set ohmmeter on "x1" scale. Connect each probe to one rotor slip ring. Reading should be 2.0-2.6 ohms. Higher reading indicates damaged slip ring solder connection or broken wire.

2) Lower reading indicates shorted wire or slip ring. Replace rotor if damaged. Connect one ohmmeter probe to slip ring and other probe to rotor core.

3) Ohmmeter reading should be infinity. Reading other than infinity indicates rotor is shorted to shaft and must be replaced. Damaged slip ring terminals or solder touching rotor shaft will cause shorted condition.

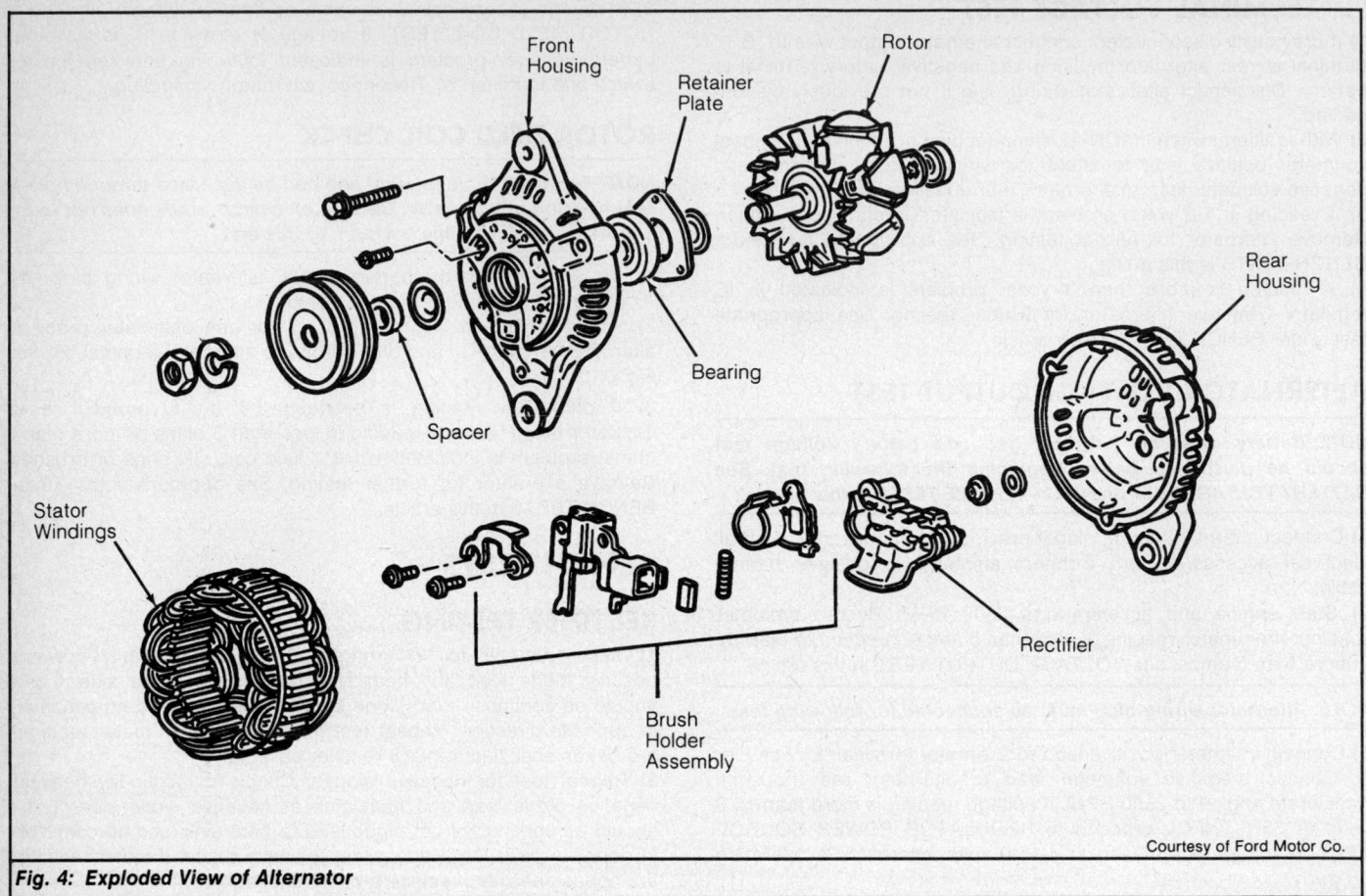

Fig. 4: Exploded View of Alternator

Courtesy of Ford Motor Co.

NOTE: Only specifications listed are available from manufacturer.

ALTERNATOR SPECIFICATIONS

Application	In. (mm)
Brush Length	
New	.65 (16.5)
Wear Limit	.30 (8)

Ford Motor Co.

DESCRIPTION

The Motorcraft Integral Alternator-Regulator (IAR) system with external fan, has an electronic voltage regulator mounted on the rear side of the alternator. Current is supplied from alternator/regulator system to rotating field of alternator through 2 brushes contacting 2 slip rings. Alternating current is rectified to direct current by 6 diodes. See Figs. 1 and 8.

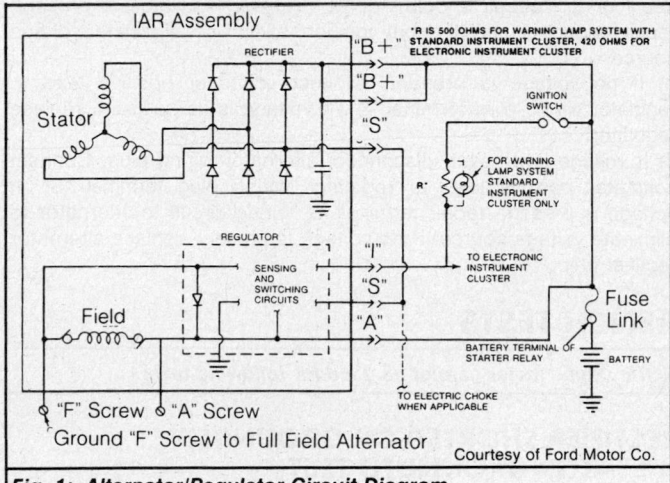

Fig. 1: Alternator/Regulator Circuit Diagram

ON-VEHICLE TESTS

BATTERY VOLTAGE TEST

Connect voltmeter negative lead to negative battery post and positive lead to positive battery post. Record battery voltage for comparison with other test results.

NO-LOAD TEST

1) Attach tachometer to engine. Start engine and operate at 1500 RPM with no electrical load (foot off brake and doors closed).
2) Voltmeter reading should be taken when needle stops moving. This may require a few minutes. Voltmeter reading should increase 2.5 volts more than battery voltage.
3) If voltage increases properly, proceed to LOAD TEST. If voltage increases more than 2.5 volts, proceed to HIGH VOLTAGE TEST. If there is no voltage increase, proceed to LOW VOLTAGE TEST.

LOAD TEST

1) Attach tachometer to engine. Start engine and turn on heater or A/C blower motor to high position. Turn headlights on high beam. Increase engine speed to 2000 RPM.
2) Voltmeter should indicate a minimum of .5 volt increase more than battery voltage. If system conforms to that reading, alternator operation is normal. If voltage reading is less than .5 volt more than battery voltage, proceed to LOW VOLTAGE TEST.

HIGH VOLTAGE TEST

1) If voltmeter reading indicates high voltage (greater than 2.5 volts more than battery voltage), turn ignition switch to "ON" position (engine not running). Connect voltmeter negative lead to rear of alternator housing.
2) Connect voltmeter positive lead to alternator output terminal of starter solenoid and record voltage. Connect voltmeter positive lead to terminal "A" screw of regulator. See Fig. 2. Compare voltage difference recorded at alternator output terminal of starter.
3) If voltage difference between 2 locations is more than .5 volt, service circuit "A" wiring to eliminate high resistance condition. Repeat NO-LOAD TEST.

4) If high voltage condition is still present, check ground connection from firewall to engine and engine to battery. Also, check for loose regulator grounding screws. See Fig. 2.
5) If high voltage condition still exists, connect voltmeter negative lead to rear of alternator housing. With ignition switch in "OFF" position, connect voltmeter positive lead to terminal "A" screw of regulator and record reading. Connect voltmeter positive lead to terminal "F" screw of regulator. See Fig. 2.
6) Check if different voltage is present at terminals "A" and "F" screw of regulator. Different voltage readings indicates a defective regulator, grounded brush leads or grounded rotor coil. Repair entire alternator/regulator assembly.
7) If same voltage is present at both terminals (battery voltage) and circuits tested in previous steps are okay, replace voltage regulator.

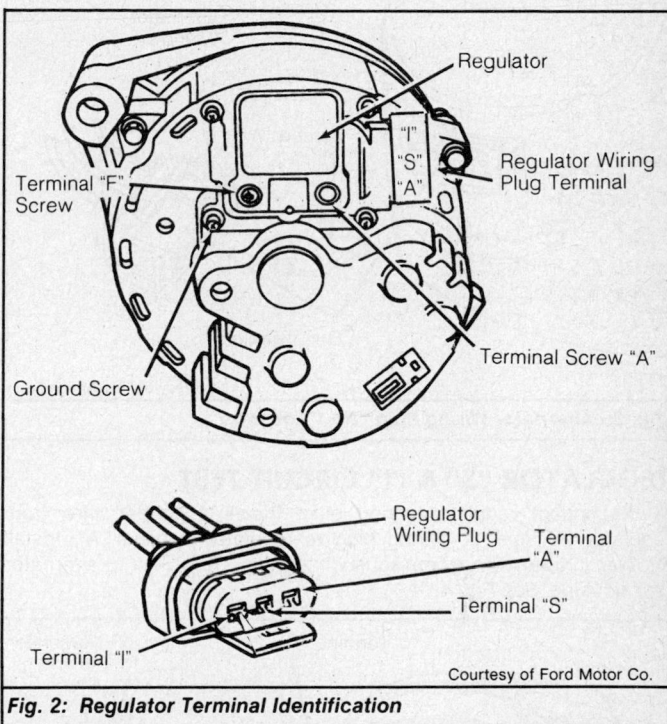

Fig. 2: Regulator Terminal Identification

LOW VOLTAGE TEST

1) If voltmeter does not indicate more than .5 volt more than battery voltage, disconnect regulator wiring plug and connect an ohmmeter between terminals "A" and "F" screw of regulator. See Fig. 2.
2) Ohmmeter should indicate more than 2.4 ohms. If less than 2.4 ohms, check alternator for shorted rotor or field circuit and replace regulator. See FIELD OPEN OR SHORT CIRCUIT TEST and ROTOR OPEN OR SHORT CIRCUIT TEST in this article. Repeat LOAD TEST.

NOTE: Damage to regulator may result if regulator is replaced before checking alternator for shorted rotor and field circuit.

3) If ohmmeter reading is greater than 2.4 ohms, reconnect regulator wiring plug and connect voltmeter negative lead to rear alternator housing. Connect voltmeter positive lead to terminal "A" screw of regulator. Meter should read battery voltage. If voltage is not present, service "A" circuit wiring. Repeat LOAD TEST.
4) With ignition off, connect voltmeter positive lead to terminal "F" screw of regulator. If battery voltage is present, proceed to step 5). If battery voltage is not present, repair circuit "F". Repeat LOAD TEST.
5) Turn ignition switch to "ON" position (engine not running). Voltmeter should indicate 1.5 volts or less. If more than 1.5 volts are present, perform REGULATOR "S" & "I" CIRCUIT TEST in this article and repair if necessary. Repeat LOAD TEST.

4-50

1989 ALTERNATORS & REGULATORS
Integral Alternator-Regulator w/External Fan (Cont.)

6) If 1.5 volts or less is indicated, disconnect alternator wiring plug and connect 12-gauge jumper wire between alternator "B+" terminal and "B+" alternator wiring plug. *See Fig. 3.* Connect voltmeter positive lead to "B+" terminal or alternator plug. Repeat LOAD TEST. If results are now satisfactory (.5 volt more than battery voltage), repair wiring harness from alternator to starter relay.

7) If voltmeter still indicates less than .5 volt more than battery voltage, connect jumper wire from rear alternator housing to "F" terminal screw of regulator. *See Fig. 2.* Repeat LOAD TEST. If voltmeter indicates more than .5 volt more than battery voltage, replace regulator. If less than .5 volt more than battery voltage, service alternator.

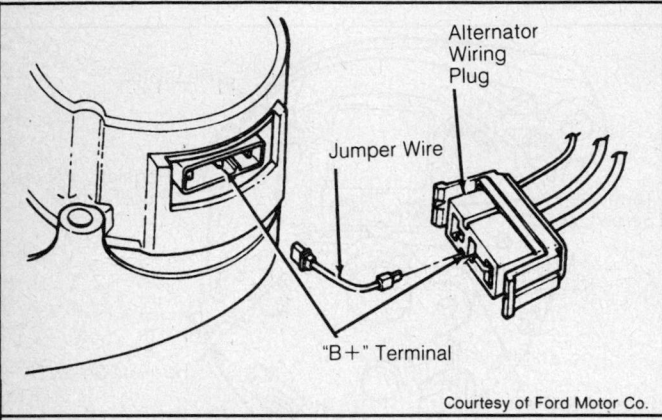

Fig. 3: Alternator Wiring Plug "B+" Location

REGULATOR "S" & "I" CIRCUIT TEST

1) Disconnect regulator wiring plug. Install a jumper wire from regulator terminal "A" wiring plug to regulator terminal "A". Install another jumper wire from regulator terminal "F" screw to alternator rear housing. *See Fig. 4.*

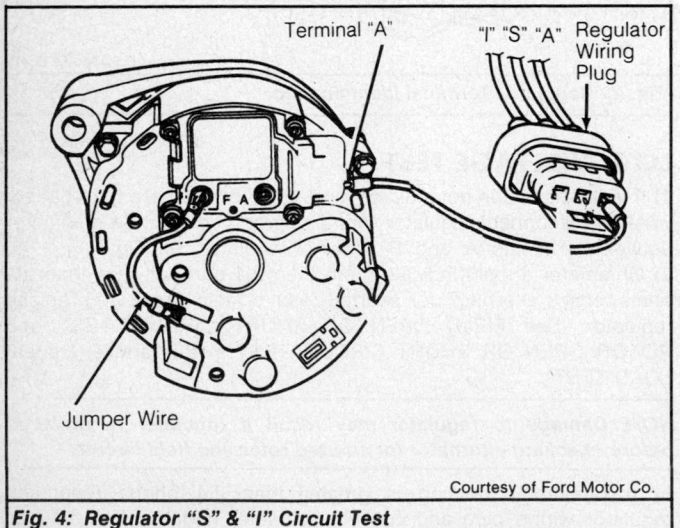

Fig. 4: Regulator "S" & "I" Circuit Test

2) With engine idling, connect voltmeter negative lead to battery ground terminal. Connect voltmeter positive lead to regulator wiring plug terminal "S" and then to terminal "I". Voltage at "S" terminal should be about 1/2 of terminal "I".

3) If voltage is okay, remove jumper wire. Connect regulator wiring plug. Repeat LOAD TEST. If no voltage is present, remove jumper wire and repair faulty wiring circuit or alternator.

4) Connect voltmeter positive lead to positive battery terminal. Connect regulator wiring plug. Repeat LOAD TEST.

FIELD CIRCUIT DRAIN TEST

NOTE: Connect voltmeter negative lead to alternator rear housing for following voltage readings.

1) Turn ignition switch to "OFF" position. Connect voltmeter positive lead to regulator terminal "F" screw. *See Fig. 2.* Battery voltage should be present.

2) If less than battery voltage is present, disconnect regulator wiring plug and connect voltmeter positive lead to wiring plug terminal "I". *See Fig. 2.* Voltage should not be present. If voltage is present, repair wiring circuit "I" from ignition switch to eliminate voltage source.

3) If no voltage is present, connect voltmeter positive lead to regulator wiring plug terminal "S". If voltage is not present, replace regulator.

4) If voltage is present, disconnect alternator wiring plug. Connect voltmeter positive lead to regulator wiring plug terminal "S". If voltage is present, repair terminal "S" wiring circuit to alternator to eliminate voltage source. If no voltage is present, replace alternator rectifier unit.

BENCH TESTS

NOTE: Digital meter cannot be used for following tests.

RECTIFIER SHORTED OR GROUNDED & STATOR GROUNDED TEST

1) Using an ohmmeter set in "x1" range, connect one probe to alternator rectifier "B+" terminal and other probe to "STA" terminal. *See Fig. 5.* Reverse terminal probes and repeat test.

2) Ohmmeter should read about 6.5 ohms resistance in one direction and infinity when probes are reversed. Same reading in both directions indicates bad positive diode or shorted radio suppression capacitor.

3) Perform same test using "STA" terminal and rear alternator housing. Same reading in both directions indicates bad negative diode, grounded stator winding, grounded stator terminal or shorted radio suppression capacitor.

4) If in preceding tests, no needle movement is indicated in one direction, or high resistance (considerably more than 6.5 ohms) is indicated in other direction, open circuit exists in rectifier assembly.

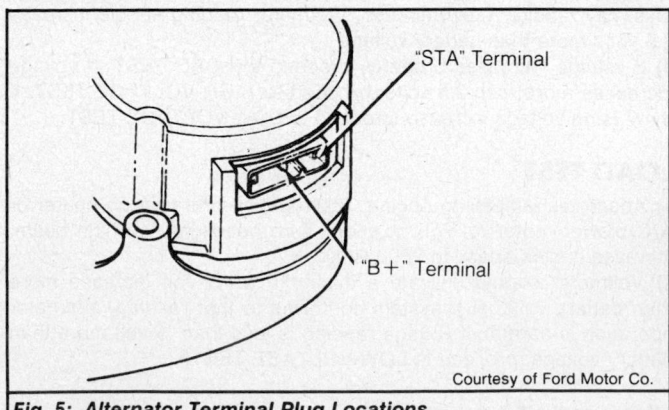

Fig. 5: Alternator Terminal Plug Locations

FIELD OPEN OR SHORT CIRCUIT TEST

1) Set ohmmeter in "x1" range. Touch regulator terminal "A" with one probe. Touch terminal "F" of regulator with other probe and spin alternator pulley. *See Fig. 6.* Reverse ohmmeter connections and repeat test.

2) In one test, ohmmeter should read between 2.2-100 ohms resistance and may fluctuate while pulley is spinning. In reverse connection, ohmmeter should fluctuate between 2.2-9 ohms.

3) An infinite reading in one test and about 9 ohms resistance in reverse test indicates open brush lead, worn or stuck brushes, bad rotor assembly or loose mounting screws at regulator brush holder.

4) Resistance reading of less than 2.2 ohms in both tests indicates shorted rotor or bad regulator. Reading considerably greater than 9 ohms in both tests indicates a defective regulator or loose terminal "F" screw.

5) Connect ohmmeter probe to alternator rear housing. Connect other probe to terminal "F" screw. *See Fig. 2.* Reverse probes and repeat test. Ohmmeter should read infinite in one direction and approximately 9 ohms in other direction. Reading less than infinite in both directions indicates grounded brush lead or bad regulator. Reading greater than 9 ohms resistance in both directions indicates bad regulator or damaged terminal connection.

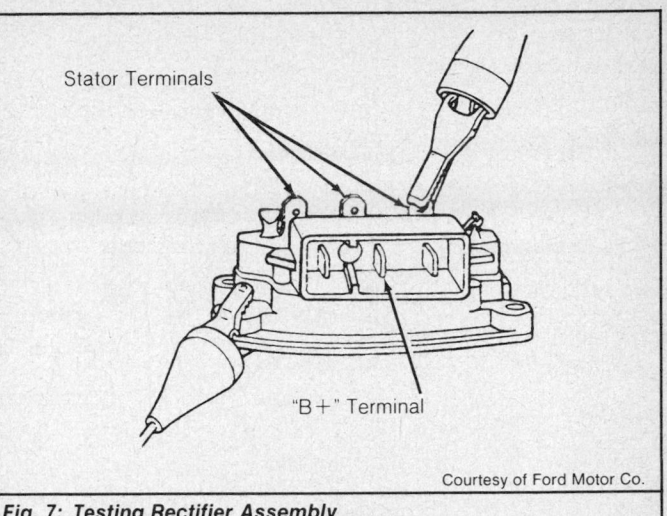

Fig. 7: Testing Rectifier Assembly

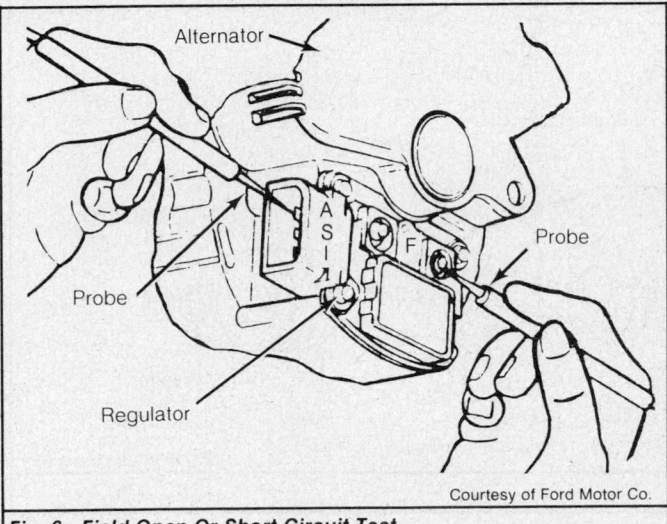

Fig. 6: Field Open Or Short Circuit Test

RECTIFIER ASSEMBLY TEST

1) Remove rectifier assembly from alternator. Set ohmmeter to "x1" range. To test positive set of diodes, connect one ohmmeter probe to "B+" terminal and contact each of 3 stator lead terminals with other probe.

2) Reverse probes and repeat test. All diodes should show readings of about 7 ohms resistance in one direction and infinite readings with probes reversed.

3) Repeat test for negative set of diodes by connecting one probe to rectifier assembly base plate and contact each of 3 stator lead terminals with other probe. *See Fig. 7.* If meter readings are not as specified in step **2)**, replace rectifier assembly.

RADIO SUPPRESSION CAPACITOR TEST

NOTE: This is an open or shorted circuit test and does not measure capacitance value.

1) Set ohmmeter to "x1000" range. Connect one ohmmeter probe to "B+" terminal and other probe to rectifier base plate assembly. Reverse probes while observing indicator needle.

2) One position should give an infinite reading, indicating reverse current direction through diodes. Other position should read about 1000 ohms resistance, indicating forward direction of current. Same reading in both directions indicates inoperative rectifier assembly.

3) To check capacitor, connect probes to rectifier assembly "B+" terminal and base plate. If needle jumps momentarily and then returns to previous position, capacitor is okay. If needle does not jump, replace rectifier assembly. Radio suppression capacitor must be replaced as a complete unit.

STATOR COIL GROUNDED TEST

1) This test is to determine if stator coil is operating properly. Remove stator from alternator. Set ohmmeter in "x1000" range.

2) Connect one ohmmeter probe to one stator lead and other probe to stator laminated core. Ohmmeter reading should be infinity.

3) If meter needle moves, stator winding is shorted to core and stator must be replaced. Repeat test for each stator lead.

NOTE: Do not touch hands to metal probes or to stator lead, or incorrect reading will result.

STATOR COIL OPEN TEST

Disconnect stator from rectifier assembly. Place ohmmeter in "x1" range. Connect one ohmmeter probe to one stator lead and touch other probe to another stator lead. If no meter movement occurs, an open exists and stator should be replaced. Repeat test for each stator lead.

NOTE: A single open phase cannot be detected on alternators with a "delta" connected stator.

ROTOR OPEN OR SHORT CIRCUIT TEST

1) Remove rotor from alternator. Set ohmmeter to "x1" range. Contact each probe to one rotor slip ring. Meter should read 2.0-3.9 ohms resistance. Higher readings indicates damaged slip ring solder connection or broken wire.

2) Lower readings indicates shorted wire or slip ring. Replace rotor if damaged. Contact ohmmeter probe to one slip ring and other probe to rotor shaft. Ohmmeter reading should be infinity. Readings other than infinity indicate rotor is shorted to shaft. Replace rotor if shorted.

ALTERNATOR SPECIFICATIONS

Application	In. (mm)
Brush Length	
New	.48 (12.2)
Wear Limit	.25 (6.4)
Slip Rings	
Minimum Diameter	1.2 (31)
Maximum Runout	.0005 (.013)

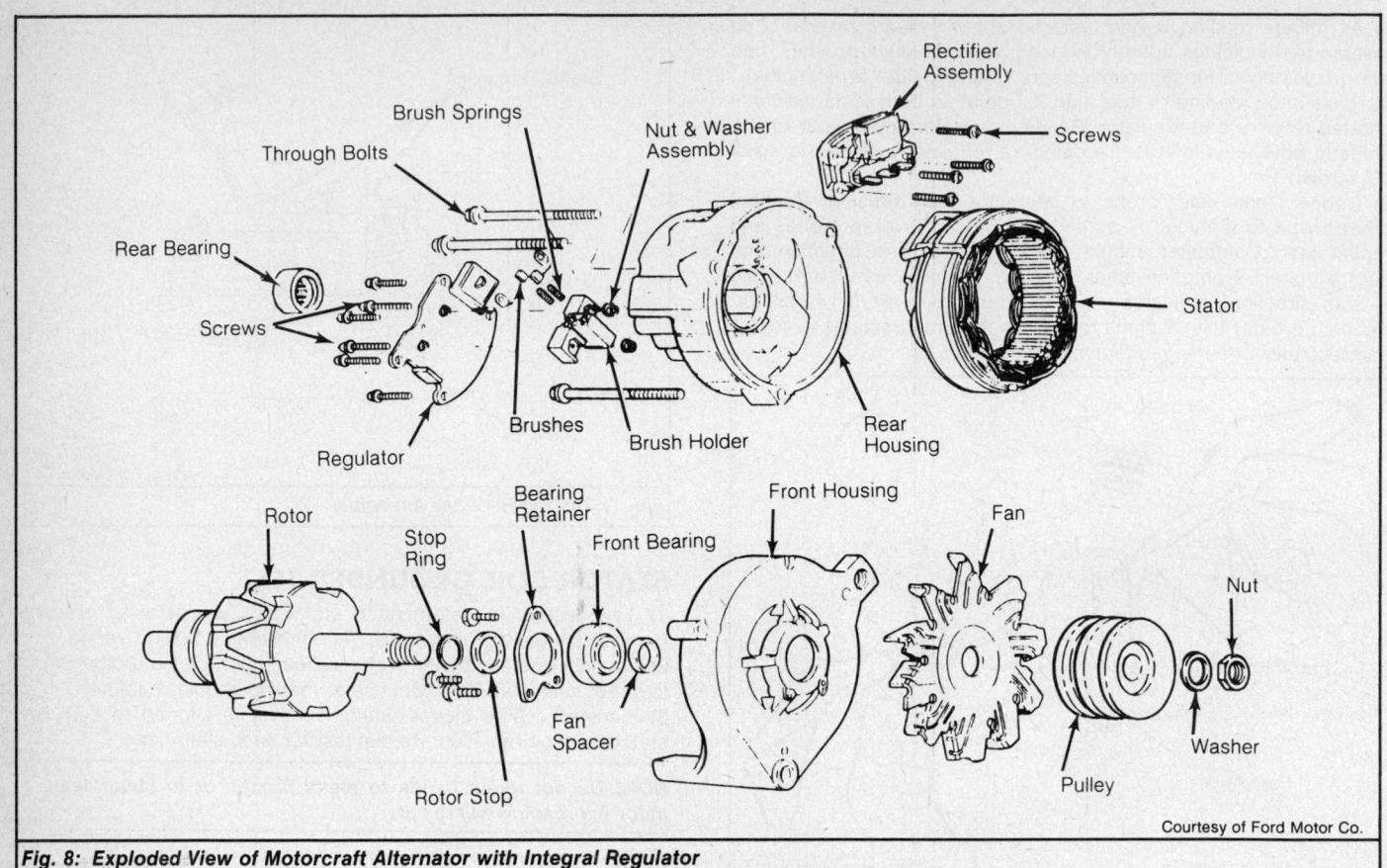

Fig. 8: Exploded View of Motorcraft Alternator with Integral Regulator

Courtesy of Ford Motor Co.

TIGHTENING SPECIFICATIONS

Application	Ft. Lbs. (N.m)
Pulley Nut	60-100 (81-136)

	INCH Lbs. (N.m)
Regulator Grounding Screws	15-25 (2-3)
Bearing Retainer Screws	25-42 (3-5)
Brush Holder Screw	20-30 (2-3)
Rectifier Screws	25-35 (3-4)
Regulator Mount Screws	25-35 (3-4)
Through Bolt	35-60 (4-7)

Ford Motor Co.

DESCRIPTION

The Motorcraft Integral Alternator-Regulator (IAR) system with internal fan, has an electronic voltage regulator mounted on the rear side of the alternator. Current is supplied from alternator/regulator system to rotating field of alternator through 2 brushes contacting 2 slip rings. Alternating current is rectified to direct current by 6 diodes. *See Fig. 2.*

ON-VEHICLE TESTS

BATTERY VOLTAGE TEST

Connect voltmeter negative lead to negative battery post and positive lead to positive battery post. Record battery voltage for comparison with other test results.

NO-LOAD TEST

1) Attach tachometer to engine. Start engine and operate at 1500 RPM with no electrical load (foot off brake and doors closed).
2) Voltmeter reading should be taken when needle stops moving. This may require a few minutes. Voltmeter reading should increase 2.0 volts greater than battery voltage.
3) If voltage increases properly, proceed to LOAD TEST. If voltage increases greater than 2.0 volts, proceed to HIGH VOLTAGE TEST. If there is no voltage increase, proceed to REGULATOR "A" & "I" CIRCUIT TEST.

LOAD TEST

1) Attach tachometer to engine. Start engine and turn heater or A/C blower motor to high position. Turn headlights on high beam. Increase engine speed to 2000 RPM.
2) Voltmeter should indicate a minimum of .5 volt increase greater than battery voltage. If system conforms to that reading, alternator operation is normal. If voltage reading is .5 volt less than battery voltage, proceed to REGULATOR "A" & "I" CIRCUIT TEST.

HIGH VOLTAGE TEST

1) If voltmeter reading indicates high voltage (2.0 volts greater than battery voltage), disconnect regulator wiring plug and connect jumper wire to terminals "A" and "I" of regulator plug. *See Fig. 1.*
2) Turn ignition switch to "ON" position (engine not running). Connect voltmeter negative lead to alternator rear housing. Connect voltmeter positive lead to alternator output connection at starter solenoid and then to regulator terminal "A" of wiring plug.
3) If voltage difference is greater than .5 volt, service "A" circuit wiring to eliminate high resistance. If voltage is same as battery voltage at both locations, replace regulator.

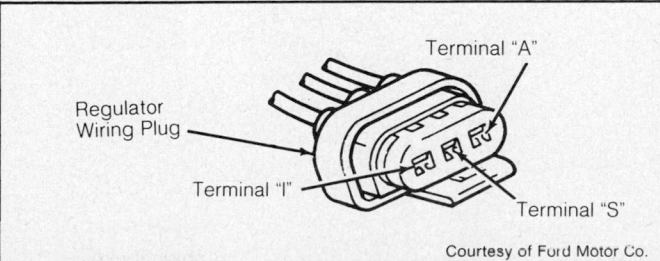
Courtesy of Ford Motor Co.
Fig. 1: Regulator Wiring Plug Terminal Locations

REGULATOR "A" & "I" CIRCUIT TEST

1) Turn ignition switch to "ON" position (engine not running). Ensure charge indicator (alternator or battery) light is on. Disconnect regulator wiring plug . Connect jumper wire to regulator wiring plug terminal "I" to battery negative terminal. *See Fig. 1.*

2) Turn ignition switch to "ON" position (engine not running). Ensure charge indicator light comes on. If indicator light does not come on, check for burned bulb and replace if necessary. If bulb checks good, repair open "I" circuit wiring. Repeat REGULATOR "A" & "I" CIRCUIT TEST.
3) If indicator light is on, remove jumper wire. Connect voltmeter negative lead to battery negative terminal. Connect voltmeter positive lead to regulator wiring plug terminal "A". Battery voltage should be indicated. If battery voltage is not indicated, service "A" circuit wiring.
4) If battery voltage is indicated, clean and tighten ground connections to engine and alternator.
5) Turn ignition switch to "ON" position (engine not running). If indicator light still does not light, repair complete alternator/regulator assembly.

BENCH TESTS

NOTE: Digital meter cannot be used for following tests.

RECTIFIER ASSEMBLY TEST

1) Set ohmmeter in "x1" range. Connect one ohmmeter probe to positive diode lead and other probe to heat sink at positive side. Reverse ohmmeter probes. There should be about 7 ohms resistance in one direction from diode lead to heat sink and infinite reading with probes reversed. If meter readings are not as specified, replace positive rectifier assembly.
2) Set ohmmeter in "x1" range. Connect one ohmmeter probe to negative diode lead and other probe to heat sink at negative side. Reverse ohmmeter probes. There should be about 7 ohms resistance in one direction from heat sink to negative diode. If meter readings are not as specified, replace negative rectifier assembly.

RADIO SUPPRESSION CAPACITOR TEST

NOTE: This is an open or shorted circuit test and does not measure capacitance value.

1) Set ohmmeter to "x1000" range. Connect one ohmmeter probe to "B+" terminal and other probe to rectifier base plate assembly. Reverse probes while observing indicator needle.
2) One position should give an infinite reading, indicating reverse current direction through diodes. Other position should read about 1000 ohms resistance, indicating forward direction of current. Same reading in both directions indicates inoperative rectifier assembly.
3) To check capacitor, connect probes to rectifier assembly "B+" terminal and base plate. If needle jumps momentarily and then returns to previous position, capacitor is okay. If needle does not jump, replace rectifier assembly. Radio suppression capacitor must be replaced as a complete unit.

STATOR COIL GROUNDED TEST

1) This test is to determine if stator coil is operating properly. Remove stator from alternator. Set ohmmeter in "x1000" range.
2) Connect one ohmmeter probe to one stator lead and other probe to stator laminated core. Ohmmeter reading should be infinity.
3) If meter needle moves, stator winding is shorted to core and stator must be replaced. Repeat test for each stator lead.

NOTE: Do not touch hands to metal probes or to stator leads or incorrect reading will result.

STATOR COIL OPEN TEST

Disconnect stator from rectifier assembly. Place ohmmeter in "x1" range. Connect one ohmmeter probe to one stator lead and touch other probe to another stator lead. If no meter movement occurs, an open exists and stator should be replaced. Repeat test for each stator lead.

4-54

1989 ALTERNATORS & REGULATORS
Integral Alternator-Regulator w/Internal Fan (Cont.)

ROTOR OPEN OR SHORT CIRCUIT TEST

1) Remove rotor from alternator. Set ohmmeter to "x1" range. Contact each probe to one rotor slip ring. Meter should read 2.0-3.9 ohms. Higher readings indicates damaged slip ring solder connection or broken wire.

2) Lower readings indicates shorted wire or slip ring. Replace rotor if damaged. Contact ohmmeter probe to one slip ring and other probe to rotor shaft. Ohmmeter reading should be infinity. Readings other than infinity indicate rotor is shorted to shaft. Replace rotor if shorted.

NOTE: Only specifications listed are available from manufacturer.

ALTERNATOR SPECIFICATIONS

Application	In. (mm)
Brush Length Wear Limit	.30 (8)

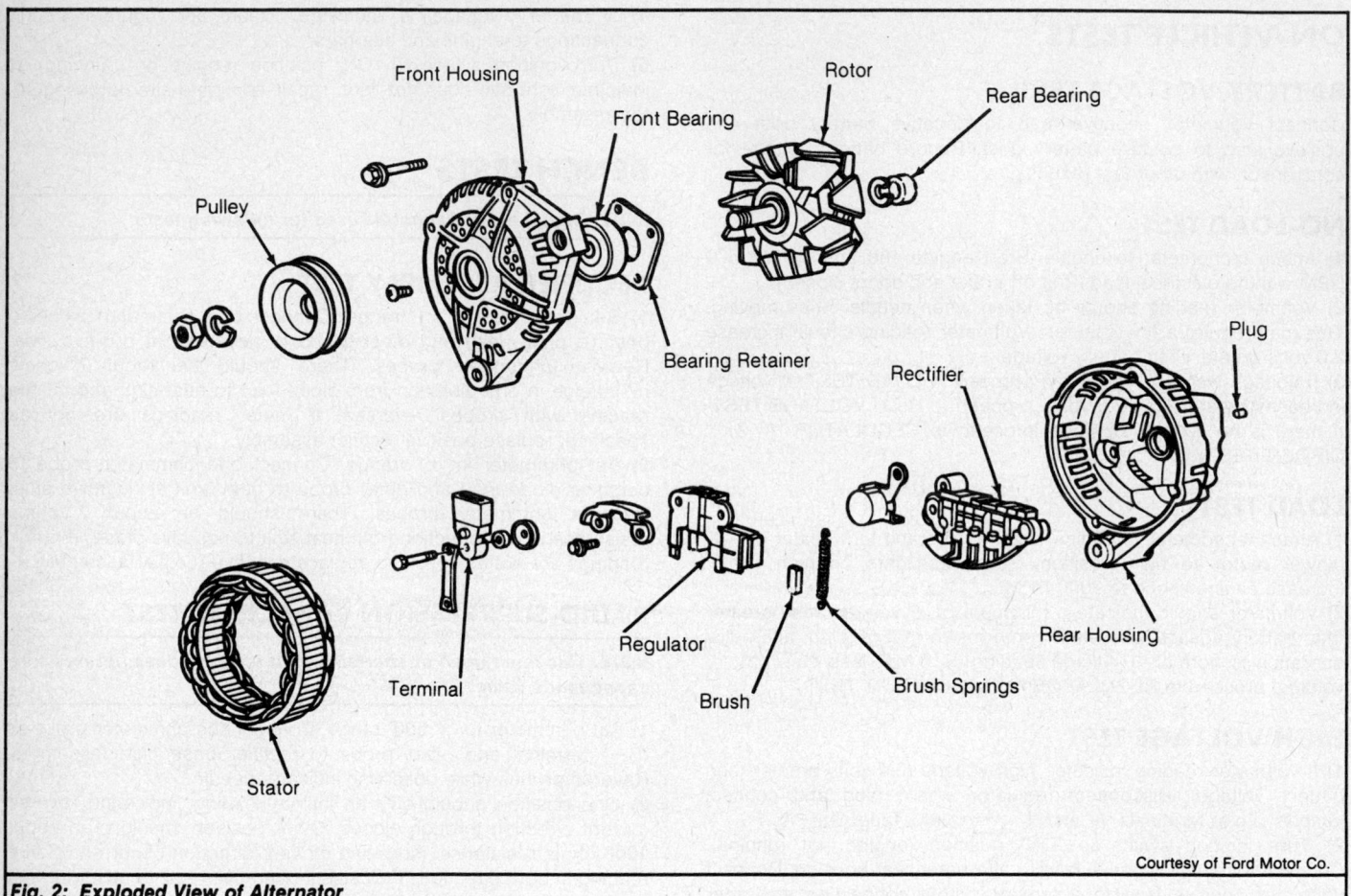

Fig. 2: Exploded View of Alternator

Courtesy of Ford Motor Co.

Ford Motor Co.

DESCRIPTION

Current is supplied from the alternator/regulator system to rotating field of alternator through 2 brushes and 2 slip rings. Power is produced in the form of alternating current and is rectified to direct current by 6 diodes. See Fig. 1. If equipped, the heated windshield and heated windshield control module are components of the charging system. See Fig. 4.

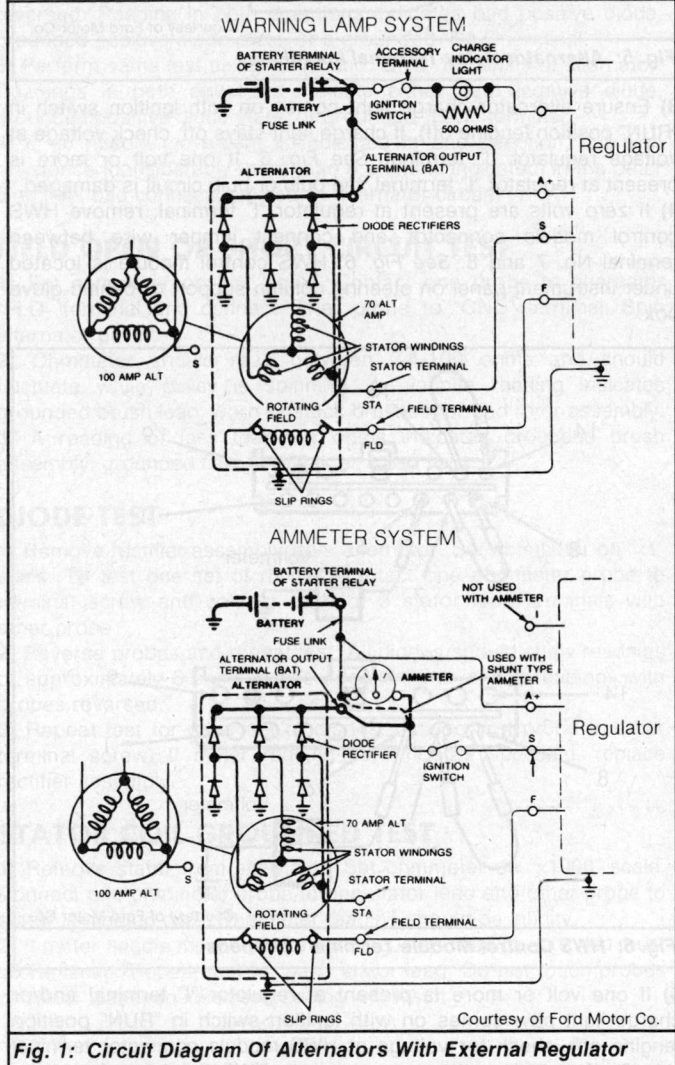

Fig. 1: Circuit Diagram Of Alternators With External Regulator

ON-VEHICLE TESTS

BATTERY VOLTAGE TEST

Connect negative lead of voltmeter to negative battery post and positive lead to positive battery post. Record battery base voltage for comparison with other test results.

NO-LOAD TEST

1) Attach tachometer to engine. Start engine and operate at 1500 RPM with no electrical load (foot off brake and doors closed).
2) Record voltmeter reading when needle stops moving. Voltmeter reading should increase 1-2 volts more than battery voltage.
3) If voltage increases properly, proceed to LOAD TEST. If voltage increases more than 2.5 volts, proceed to OVERVOLTAGE TEST. If there is no voltage increase, proceed to UNDERVOLTAGE TEST.

LOAD TEST

1) Attach tachometer to engine. Start engine and turn on A/C-heater blower motor to high position. Turn headlights on high beam. Increase engine speed to 2000 RPM.
2) If voltmeter indicates a minimum of .5 volt increase over battery voltage, alternator operation is normal. If voltage increase is less than .5 volt, proceed to UNDERVOLTAGE TEST.

OVERVOLTAGE TEST

1) If voltmeter reading indicates overvoltage (more than 2.5 volts greater than battery voltage), connect jumper wire between regulator base and alternator frame. Repeat NO LOAD TEST.
2) If overvoltage condition disappears, check ground connections at regulator, alternator, from firewall to engine and from engine to battery.
3) If overvoltage condition is still present, disconnect regulator wiring plug and repeat NO LOAD TEST. If condition is corrected, replace regulator.
4) If overvoltage condition is still present with regulator disconnected, a short is indicated in wiring harness between alternator and regulator ("A" and "F" circuits). Repair short circuit and reconnect voltage regulator plug.

UNDERVOLTAGE TEST

1) If voltmeter does not indicate .5 volt more than battery voltage, disconnect wiring plug from regulator and connect an ohmmeter from "F" terminal of plug to battery ground.
2) Ohmmeter should indicate more than 2.4 ohms. If less than 2.4 ohms, repair grounded field circuit and repeat LOAD TEST.
3) If field circuit is satisfactory (more than 2.4 ohms resistance), disconnect regulator wiring plug at regulator and connect jumper wire between "A" and "F" terminals on regulator wiring plug. See Fig. 3. Repeat LOAD TEST.
4) If voltmeter now indicates .5 volt greater than battery voltage, regulator or wiring harness is defective. Service regulator or wiring as necessary. Perform REGULATOR "S" & "I" CIRCUIT TEST.
5) If undervoltage problem is still present, remove jumper wire at regulator plug and leave plug disconnected from regulator. Disconnect wire from "FLD" terminal on alternator. See Fig. 2.
6) Connect a jumper wire to "FLD" and "BAT" terminals on alternator. Repeat LOAD TEST. If results are okay (.5 volt more than battery voltage), repair wiring harness from alternator to regulator.
7) If voltmeter still indicates undervoltage, move positive lead of voltmeter to "BAT" terminal. If battery voltage now exists, repair or replace alternator. If reading is zero volts, repair "BAT" wire to starter relay.

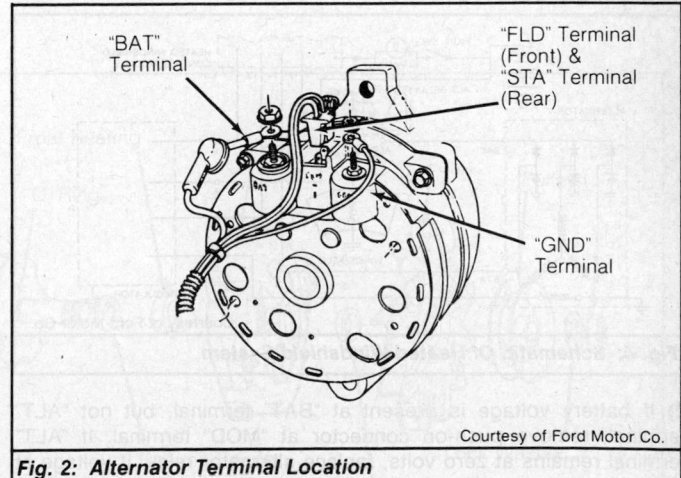

Fig. 2: Alternator Terminal Location

Courtesy of Ford Motor Co.

1989 STARTING SYSTEMS
Trouble Shooting

CONDITION	POSSIBLE CAUSE	CORRECTION
Starter Fails to Operate	Dead battery or bad connections between starter and battery	Check battery charge and all wires and connections to starter
	Ignition switch faulty or misadjusted	Adjust or replace ignition switch
	Open circuit between starter switch and ignition terminal on starter relay	Check and repair wires and connections as necessary
	Starter relay or starter defective	See ON-VEHICLE or BENCH TESTS in STARTERS
	Open solenoid pull-in wire	See ON-VEHICLE or BENCH TESTS in STARTERS
Starter Does Not Operate and Headlights Dim	Weak battery or dead battery cell	Charge or replace battery as necessary
	Loose or corroded battery connections	Ensure battery connection are clean and tight
	Internal short in starter windings	See ON-VEHICLE or BENCH TESTS in STARTERS
	Grounded starter fields	See ON-VEHICLE or BENCH TESTS in STARTERS
	Armature rubbing on pole shoes	Check for worn armature bushings or bent aramture shaft
Starter Turns but Engine Does Not Rotate	Starter drive slipping	Replace starter drive
	Pinion shaft rusted or dry	Lubricate pinion shaft
	Starter not engaging flywheel	Check starter alignment
	Converter drive plate hub broken	Replace converter drive plate
	Broken teeth on engine flywheel	Replace flywheel and check for starter pinion gear damage
Starter Will Not Crank Engine	Faulty starter drive	Replace starter drive
	Broken clutch housing	Replace or repair clutch housing
	Broken flywheel teeth	Replace flywheel and check for starter pinion gear damage
	Armature shaft sheared or reduction gear teeth stripped	Repair or replace starter
	Weak battery	Charge or replace battery as necessary
	Faulty solenoid	See ON-VEHICLE or BENCH TESTS in STARTERS
	Poor grounds	Check all ground connections for tight and clean connections
	Ignition switch faulty or misadjusted	Replace ignition switch as necessary
Starter Cranks Engine Slowly	Battery weak or defective	Charge or replace battery as necessary
	Engine overheated	Check engine cooling system
	Ignition timing too far advanced	Reset ignition timing
	Engine oil too heavy	Check that proper viscosity oil is used
	Poor battery-to-starter connections	Check that all connections between battery and starter are clean and tight
	Current draw too low or too high	See Bench Tests in STARTERS
	Bent armature, loose pole shoe screws or worn bearings	Repair or replace starter
	Burned solenoid contacts	Replace solenoid
	Faulty starter	Replace starter
Starter Engages Engine Only Momentarily	Engine timing too far advanced	See Ignition Timing In TUNE-UP
	Overrunning clutch not operating	Replace overrunning clutch. See appropriate article in STARTERS
	Broken starter clutch housing	See appropriate article in STARTERS
	Broken teeth on engine flywheel	Replace flywheel and check starter pinion gear for damage
	Weak drive assembly thrust spring	See appropriate article in STARTERS
	Weak hold-in coil	See Bench Tests in STARTERS

CONDITION	POSSIBLE CAUSE	CORRECTION
Starter Drive Will Not Engage Starter Relay Does Not Close	Defective pull-in coil	Replace starter solenoid
	Dead battery	Charge or replace battery as necessary
	Faulty wiring	Check all wiring and connections leading to relay
	Neutral safety switch faulty	Replace neutral safety switch
	Starter relay faulty	Replace starter relay or starter solenoid
Starter Drive Will Not Disengage	Starter motor loose on mountings	Tighten starter attaching bolts
	Worn drive end bushing	Repair or replace starter bushings
	Damaged engine flywheel teeth	Replace flywheel and check starter pinion gear for damage
	Drive yolk return spring broken or missing	Replace return spring
	Faulty ignition switch	Replace ignition switch
	Solenoid contact switch plunger stuck	Replace starter solenoid
	Faulty starter relay	Replace starter relay
	Insufficient clearance between winding leads to solenoid terminal and main contact in solenoid	Replace starter solenoid
	Starter clutch not disengaging	Replace starter clutch
	Faulty wiring	Check all wiring leading to solenoid
	Broken connections inside switch cover	Repair connections or replace solenoid
	Open hold-in wire	Replace solenoid
Low Current Draw	Worn brushes or weak brush springs	Replace brushes or brush springs as necessary
High Pitched Whine During Cranking Before Engine Fires but Engine Fires and Cranks Normally	Distance too great between starter pinion and flywheel	Align starter or check that correct starter and flywheel are being used
High Pitched Whine After Engine Fires With Key Released. Engine Fires and Cranks Normally	Distance too small between starter pinion and flywheel. Flywheel runout contributes to the intermittent nature	Align starter or check that correct starter and flywheel are being used

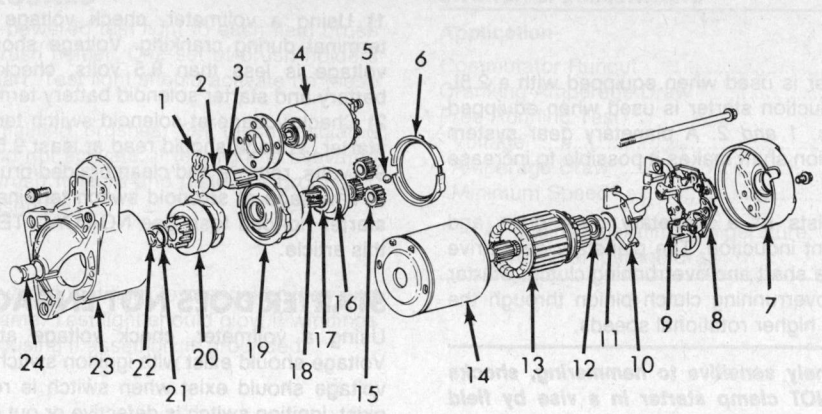

1. Clutch Fork	9. Brush Spring Set	17. Washer
2. Washer	10. Brushes	18. Drive Shaft
3. Rubber Retainer	11. Wave Washer	19. Gear Housing
4. Solenoid	12. Bearing	20. Clutch Gear Assembly
5. Shaft Ball	13. Armature	21. Stop Ring
6. Packing Ring	14. Frame	22. Snap Ring
7. End Cover	15. Planetary Gear Set	23. End Housing
8. Brush Holder Assembly	16. "Z" Washer	24. Bushing

Courtesy of Chrysler Motors.

Fig. 2: Exploded View Of Mitsubishi Starter

STARTER MOTOR TESTS

1) Check pinion gear for freedom of movement by turning it on shaft. Check armature for freedom of movement by prying on pinion gear to engage it with shaft.

2) If gear and armature do not rotate freely, starter should be disassembled. If pinion gear and armature rotate freely, proceed to NO-LOAD TEST in this article.

3) No rotation and high current flow indicate one or more of the following:

- Connecting terminal or armature windings shorted to ground.
- Seized bearings.

4) No rotation and no current flow conditions indicate one or more of the following:

- Open armature windings (inspect commutator for burned commutator bars after disassembly).
- Broken brush springs, worn brushes, protruding insulation between commutator bars, or other causes that could prevent good contact between brushes and commutator.

NO-LOAD TEST

1) Install starter in soft-jawed vise with mounting flange. Install voltmeter between solenoid terminal and starter frame.

2) Connect a switch, ammeter and fully charged battery in series with starter motor. See Fig. 3. Ensure switch is in the "OPEN" position prior to connecting battery.

3) Close switch and note armature RPM, voltage and amperage. Reading should be within specification. See STARTER SPECIFICA-TIONS table at end of article.

CAUTION: Overheating, caused by excessive starter operation, will damage starter. DO NOT operate starter for more than 30 seconds at a time without allowing starter to cool for at least 2 minutes.

4) Disconnect electrical connections with switch in "OPEN" position only. Repair or replace starter if not within specification.

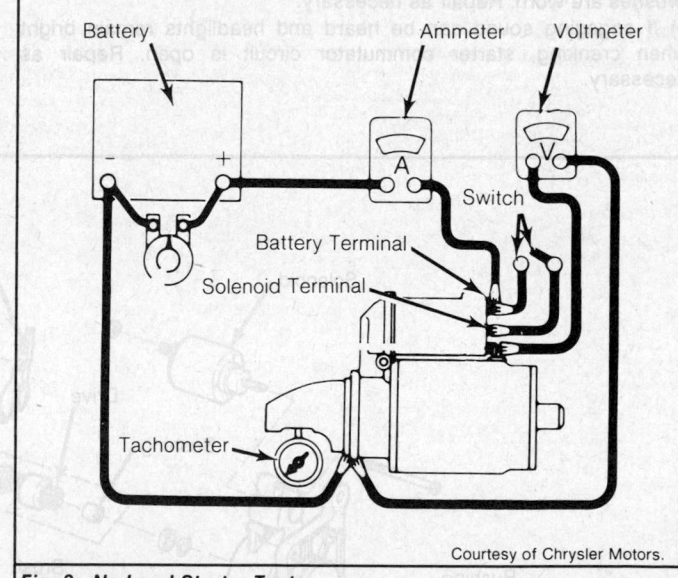

Courtesy of Chrysler Motors.

Fig. 3: No-Load Starter Test

STARTER MOTOR

Inspection – 1) Inspect field housing and permanent magnets for damage. Magnets are permanently attached to field housing. DO NOT remove magnets from field housing. They are permanently attached. If field housing or magnets are damaged, replace them as an assembly.

2) Inspect condition of bushing in armature end of drive shaft. Replace planetary gear assembly and pinion shaft if worn or damaged. Inspect armature shaft bushing and bearing. Replace either part if worn.

3) If bushing or bearing has worn to point where armature-to-frame contact has occured, replace starter.

4) Inspect brushes and brush holder. Replace brushes if damaged or worn below minimum length. See STARTER SPECIFICATIONS table at end of this article. Replace brush holder if cracked, bent or distorted.

ARMATURE TESTING

Ground Test – Place armature in growler. Touch one lead of self-powered test light to armature core and remaining lead to each commutator bar. If test light is activated, armature is grounded. Replace armature.

Short Test – Place armature in growler. Hold thin steel blade parallel and just above armature while armature is rotating in growler. Replace armature if blade vibrates.

Balance Test – 1) Place armature in growler. Place growler selector switch in "GROWLER" position. Position meter test leads across adjacent commutator bars.

2) Adjust voltage control until pointer indicates highest voltage on scale. Test all commutator bars. Voltage should exist at all commutator bars. If no voltage exists, commutator bar is shorted. Replace armature if shorted.

Runout Test – Place armature in a pair of "V" blocks. Using dial indicator, check commutator and armature core runout. If runout exceeds specification, replace armature. See STARTER SPECIFICATIONS table.

STARTER SPECIFICATIONS

Application	Specifications
Bosch Starter	
Cold Cranking Amps	130 Amps
Cold Cranking Voltage	9.6 Volts
Minimum Brush Length	.35" (9 mm)
No-Load Test	75 Amps @ 2900 RPM
Runout	
Commutator	.0004" (.01 mm)
Armature	.003" (.08 mm)
Mitsubishi Starter	
Cold Cranking Amps	130 Amps
Cold Cranking Voltage	9.6 Volts
Minimum Brush Length	.31" (8 mm)
No-Load Test	80 Amps @ 2500 RPM
Runout	
Commutator	.001" (.03 mm)
Armature	.003" (.08 mm)

TIGHTENING SPECIFICATIONS

Application	Ft. Lbs. (N.m)
Mounting Bolts	20 (21)

	INCH Lbs.
Solenoid "B+" Nut	9 (80)
Solenoid Wire-to-Starter	9 (80)

Ford Motor Co.: Probe

DESCRIPTION

Starting system consists of a starter motor, solenoid, battery, ignition switch, neutral safety switch (A/T) or clutch engage switch (M/T) and necessary cables and wires. *See Fig. 1.*

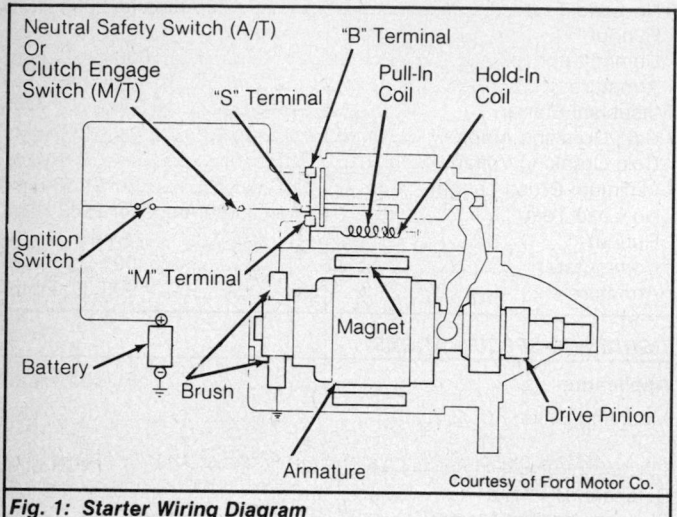

Fig. 1: Starter Wiring Diagram

TROUBLE SHOOTING

ENGINE CRANKS SLOWLY

Undercharged battery. Loose or corroded cable connections. Bad starter.

ENGINE WILL NOT CRANK

Undercharged battery. Bad ignition switch. Bad clutch engage switch (M/T) or neutral safety switch (A/T). Loose or corroded cable connections. Bad starter.

STARTER SPINS BUT ENGINE WILL NOT CRANK

Bad starter. Bad flywheel ring gear and/or starter drive pinion.

PRELIMINARY TESTS

Ensure battery is fully charged and load tested okay. If starter will not crank engine with fully charged battery, proceed with the following test.

1) Using a digital voltmeter, connect positive voltmeter lead to starter solenoid terminal "S" and negative lead to starter housing.
2) Turn ignition switch to "START" position and observe voltmeter reading. If voltage at terminal "S" is more than 8 volts, starter or circuit malfunction is indicated. See STARTER FEED CIRCUIT TEST and STARTER GROUND CIRCUIT TEST under TESTING & DIAGNOSIS in this article.
3) If voltage is not present at starter solenoid terminal "S", malfunction in circuit to terminal "S" is indicated. Proceed to TESTING & DIAGNOSIS.

TESTING & DIAGNOSIS

ON-VEHICLE TESTS

Ignition Switch – 1) Check main circuit breaker in interior fuse box. Fuse box is located just above left kick panel. If circuit breaker is open, check and repair circuit as necessary.
2) After problem in circuit is corrected, reset circuit breaker by pushing Red reset button.

3) Remove lower panel and defroster duct to gain access to steering column wiring. Disconnect 4 ignition switch snap connectors located to left of steering column.
4) Using an ohmmeter, check continuity of switch terminals. *See Fig. 2.* Turn ignition switch to "ACC" position. Connect one ohmmeter probe to terminal "B" and other probe to "ACC" terminal. Ohmmeter should show continuity.
5) Turn ignition switch to "ON" position. Connect one ohmmeter probe to terminal "B" and other probe to "ACC" terminal. Ohmmeter should show continuity. Move one ohmmeter probe to "IGN-1" terminal and then to "IGN-2" terminal. Ohmmeter should show continuity at both terminals.
6) Turn ignition switch to "START" position. Connect one ohmmeter probe to terminal "B" and other probe to "IGN-1" terminal and then to "ST" terminal. Ohmmeter should show continuity at both terminals. If ohmmeter does not read as indicated in any of the ignition switch positions, replace ignition switch.

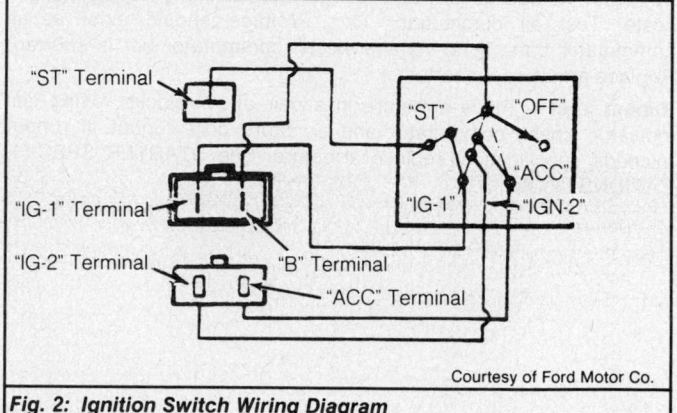

Fig. 2: Ignition Switch Wiring Diagram

Clutch Engage Switch (M/T) – 1) Clutch engage switch is located next to clutch pedal. Unplug 2 terminal switch connector.
2) Using a digital ohmmeter, check resistance between both connector terminals. Ohmmeter should show continuity when switch rod is depressed and no continuity when released.
3) Replace clutch engage switch if ohmmeter does not read as indicated.
Neutral Safety Switch (A/T) – 1) Unplug 3 terminal neutral safety switch connector located under battery tray.
2) Place shift lever in Park or Neutral. Using an ohmmeter, connect ohmmeter probes between terminals "A" and "B". *See Fig. 3.* Ohmmeter should show continuity between both terminals. If ohmmeter does not read as indicated, replace neutral safety switch.

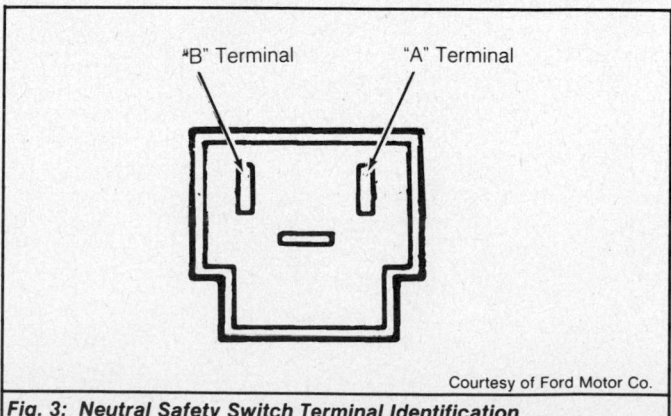

Fig. 3: Neutral Safety Switch Terminal Identification

Starter Feed Circuit Test – 1) Disconnect coil wire from distributor cap. Connect remote starter switch between starter solenoid terminal "S" and positive battery post.

NOTE: Make all voltmeter connections at component terminal rather than cable or wire end.

2) Using a digital voltmeter set at low voltage scale, connect positive voltmeter lead to positive battery post and negative lead to solenoid terminal "M". *See Fig. 4.*

3) Engage remote starter switch. Voltmeter should read .5 volt or less. If voltage at terminal "M" is greater than .5 volt, move negative voltmeter lead to solenoid terminal "B" and repeat test.

4) If voltage at terminal "B" reads less than .5 volt, problem is either in solenoid connections or contacts.

5) Clean solenoid terminals "B", "S" and "M". Repeat steps **1)** through **5)**. If voltmeter still reads higher than .5 volt at terminal "M" and lower than .5 volt at terminal "B", problem is in solenoid contacts. Remove starter for repair.

6) If voltmeter reads more than .5 volt at terminal "B", clean cables and connections at solenoid. If voltmeter still reads more than .5 volt, problem is either bad positive battery connection or cable. Repair as necessary.

7) To locate excessive voltage drop, move voltmeter negative lead toward battery and check each connection point. When high voltmeter reading disappears, last connection point checked is the problem.

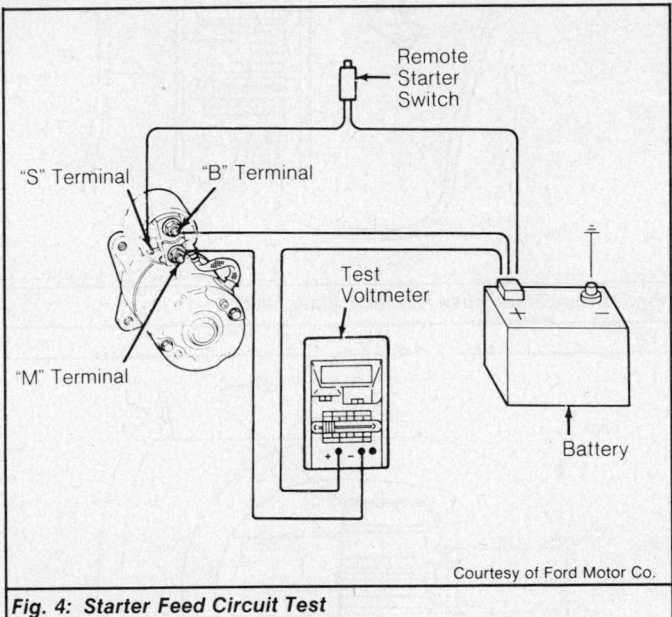

Courtesy of Ford Motor Co.

Fig. 4: Starter Feed Circuit Test

Starter Ground Circuit Test – 1) Slow starter cranking condition can be caused by resistance in ground or return portion of cranking circuit. Check voltage drop in ground circuit as follows:

NOTE: Make all voltmeter connections at component terminal rather than cable or wire end.

2) Disconnect coil wire from distributor cap. Connect remote starter switch between starter solenoid terminal "S" and positive battery terminal.

3) Using a digital voltmeter set at lowest voltage scale, connect positive voltmeter lead to starter housing and negative lead to negative battery post.

4) Engage remote starter switch and observe voltmeter reading. Voltmeter should read .2 volt or less. If voltage drop is more than .2 volt, clean negative cable connections at battery and chassis. Also, clean engine ground cable connections at front cover and engine mount bracket.

5) If voltage drop is still excessive, repair or replace negative battery cable and/or engine ground cable as necessary. Repeat starter circuit test after repair to ensure problem has been corrected.

6) If battery and cables test okay and starter motor still cranks slowly, or not at all, remove starter for repair.

BENCH TESTS

ARMATURE

1) Using a digital ohmmeter, determine if armature is grounded by checking for continuity between commutator and core. If ohmmeter shows continuity, replace armature.

2) Determine if armature is insulated by checking for continuity between commutator and shaft. If ohmmeter shows continuity, replace armature.

3) Place armature on "V"-blocks. Using a dial indicator, check commutator runout. If runout is more than .002" (.05 mm), use a lathe to repair commutator. If diameter of commutator is 1.13" (28.8 mm) or less, replace armature.

4) Check commutator to ensure it is free of burnt spots and scoring. If commutator surface is dirty, wipe with cloth. Remove burnt spots with fine emery cloth. If commutator is excessively scored, use lathe to refinish commutator face.

NOTE: Do not use emery cloth on commutator face

5) If depth of groove between commutator segments is .008" (.02 mm) or less, undercut insulating meterial using appropriate tool with sharp point. Undercut until groove depth of .020-.031" (.5-.8 mm) is reached.

6) If armature laminations show signs of having contacted field coil pole-pieces, check that pole-pieces are tight in field frame housing. Check armature for excessive runout (bent shaft). If armature shaft is bent, replace armature.

SOLENOID

1) Check solenoid for wiring damage between terminals "S" and "M". *See Fig. 5.* Using a digital ohmmeter, check for continuity between terminals "S" and "M". Replace solenoid if there is no continuity.

2) Check for internal wire damage between terminal "S" and solenoid body. Connect one ohmmeter probe to solenoid body and other probe to terminal "S". Replace solenoid if there is no continuity.

3) Check for ground between terminals "M" and "B". Connect ohmmeter probes between terminals "M" and "B". Replace solenoid if there is continuity.

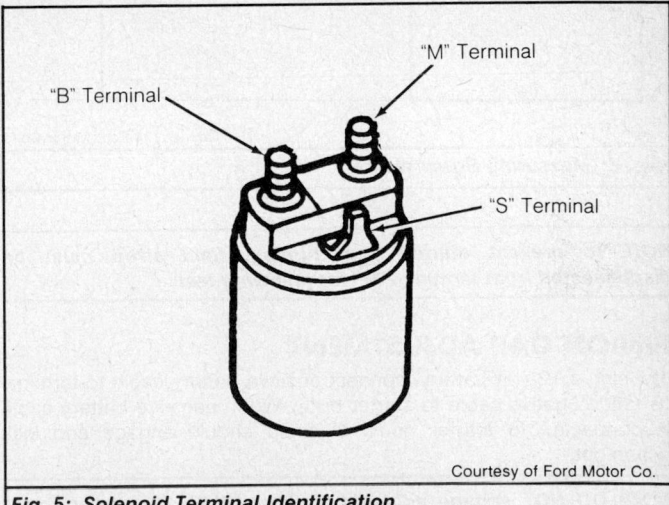

Courtesy of Ford Motor Co.

Fig. 5: Solenoid Terminal Identification

ARMATURE SHAFT BEARING

Check bearing for abnormal noise, looseness or binding. If any of these problems exists, replace bearing.

DRIVE PINION

1) Inspect wear pattern on pinion drive gear and flywheel. Inspect entire circumference of flywheel for damage when pinion drive gear teeth are damaged. Replace pinion gear and/or flywheel as necessary.

2) Turn pinion shaft by hand and hold overrunning clutch. Replace overrunning clutch if pinion turns in both directions or does not turn.

NOTE: _Overrunning clutch is packed with grease and sealed. DO NOT wash in solvent._

FIELD HOUSING

Check field housing for damage. Replace as necessary.

INTERNAL & PLANETARY GEARS

Check internal and planetary gears for wear or damage. Replace as necessary.

BRUSHES & BRUSH HOLDER

1) Check brushes for wear by measuring amount of useable brush remaining. Replace brushes if near wear limit line. _See Fig. 6._

2) Using a digital ohmmeter, check for continuity between insulated brush holders and brush plate. Replace brush holder if there is continuity. _See Fig. 7._

3) Check that brushes slide smoothly inside brush holder. Clean brush channels as necessary.

4) Using a spring balance, measure force of brush spring. Spring force is measured at moment brush spring separates from brush. Replace brush spring if force is below 1.5 lbs. (6.7 N).

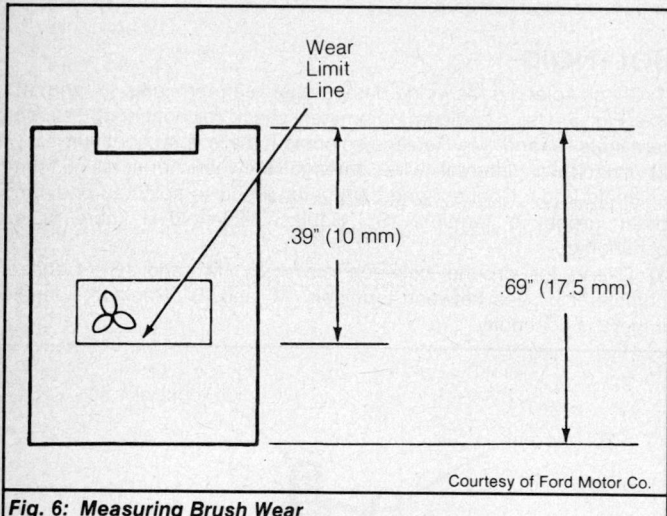

Courtesy of Ford Motor Co.

Fig. 6: Measuring Brush Wear

NOTE: _To prevent starter from turning, field strap must be disconnected from terminal "M" for following test._

PINION GAP ADJUSTMENT

1) Using a 12-volt battery, connect positive battery cable to terminal "S" and negative cable to starter body. When negative battery cable is connected to starter body, solenoid should engage and kick pinion out.

NOTE: _DO NOT engage solenoid for more than 20 seconds at a time. If test must be repeated, wait 3 minutes between attempts._

2) With pinion extended, measure gap between pinion and collar. Gap should be .02-.08" (.5-2 mm). _See Fig. 8._

3) If gap is not within specified range, add or substract shims between solenoid and drive end housing until pinion gap is within specification. Reconnect solenoid terminal "M".

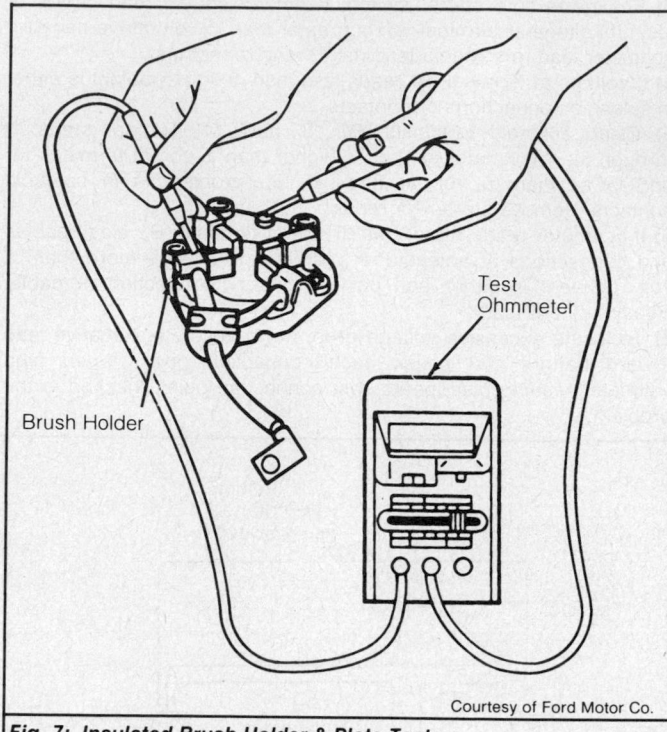

Courtesy of Ford Motor Co.

Fig. 7: Insulated Brush Holder & Plate Test

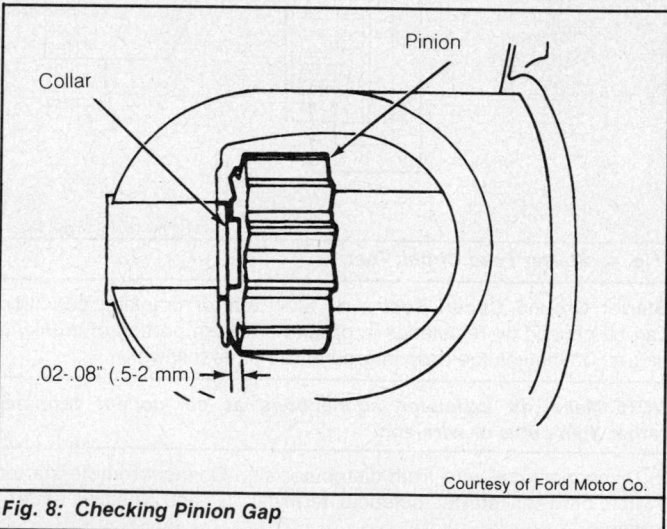

Courtesy of Ford Motor Co.

Fig. 8: Checking Pinion Gap

STARTER NO-LOAD TEST

1) Connect battery, voltmeter, ammeter and remote starter switch to starter. _See Fig. 10._

2) Engage remote starter switch, starter should turn smoothly. Voltmeter should read 11 volts and ammeter should read no more than 90 amps.

3) If voltage is lower or amperage is higher than specification, disassemble starter and determine cause.

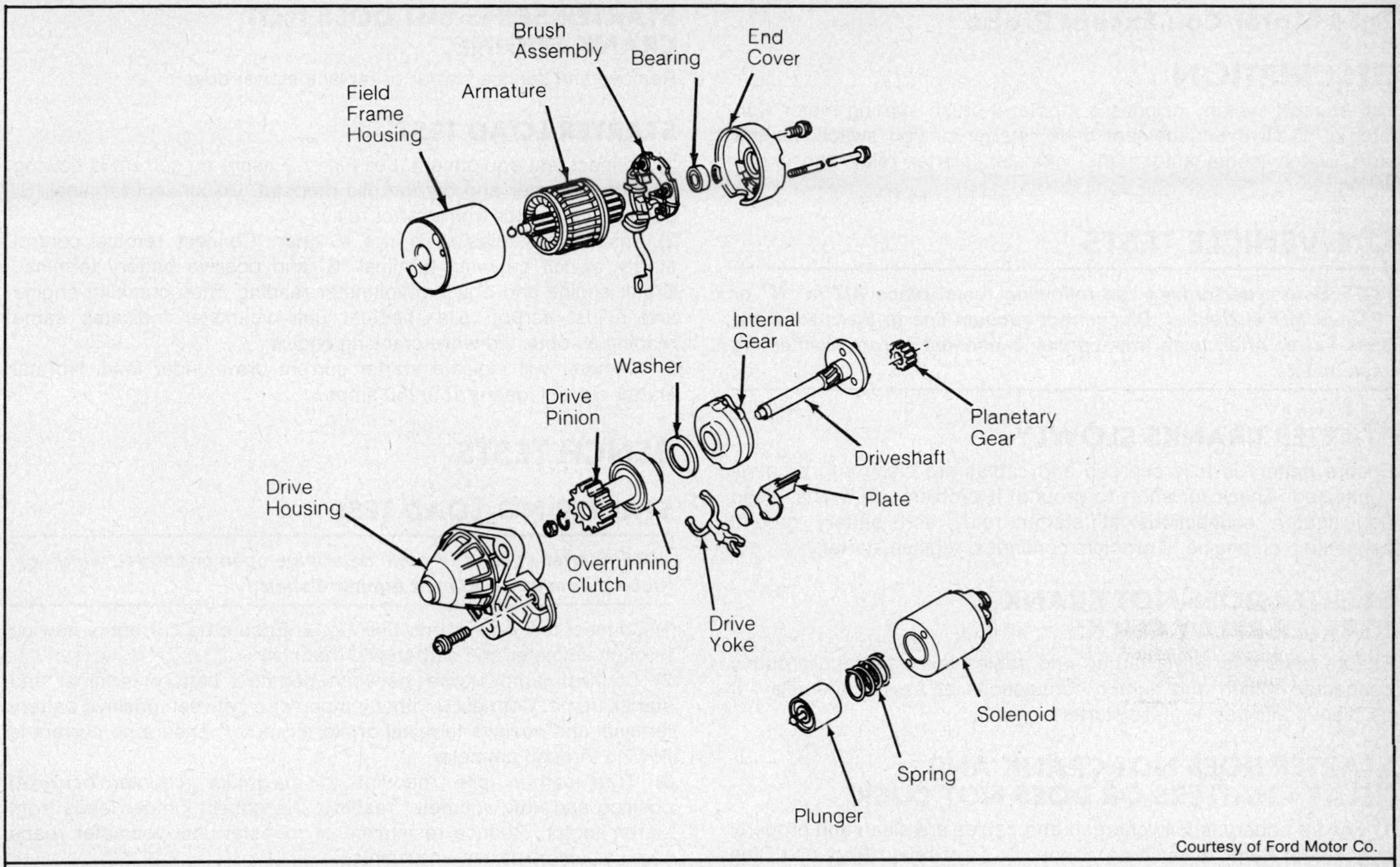

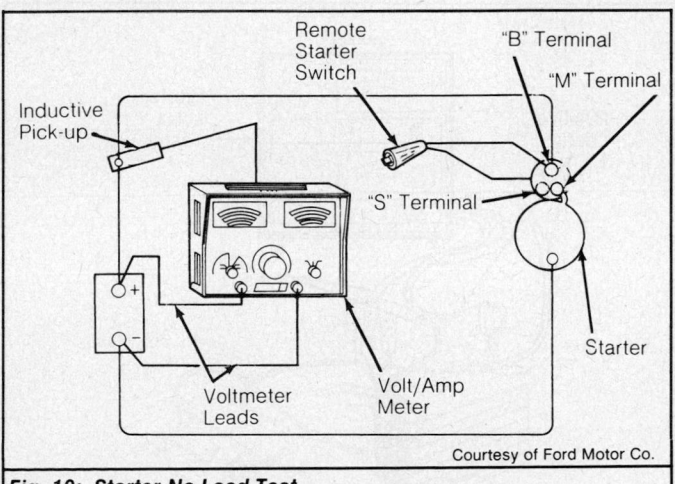

Fig. 9: Exploded View Of Starter Assembly

Courtesy of Ford Motor Co.

Fig. 10: Starter No-Load Test

Courtesy of Ford Motor Co.

STARTER SPECIFICATIONS

Application	Specifications
Commutator	
Runout	.002" (.05 mm)
Outer Diameter	.13" (28.8 mm)
Groove Depth	.020-.031" (.5-.8 mm)
Pinion Gap	.02-.08" (.5-2 mm)
Brush Spring Force [1]	1.5 lbs. (6.7 N)

[1] - Replace spring if below specification.

TIGHTENING SPECIFICATIONS

Application	Ft. Lbs. (N.m)
Starter Motor	
Mounting Bolts	23-34 (31-46)

	INCH Lbs. (N.m)
Solenoid	
"B" & "M" Terminal Nuts	90-110 (10-11)

1989 STARTERS
Motorcraft

Ford Motor Co.: Except Probe

DESCRIPTION

The starting system includes a 4-pole, 4-brush starting motor with integral positive engagement drive, starter-ignition switch, neutral start switch (some auto. trans. models), starter relay and circuit wiring.

ON-VEHICLE TESTS

NOTE: Before performing the following tests, place A/T in "N" or "P" and M/T in Neutral. Disconnect vacuum line to thermactor by-pass valve. After tests, run engine 3 minutes before connecting vacuum line.

STARTER CRANKS SLOWLY

Ensure battery is fully charged and cables are clean and properly connected. Check for short to ground. If problem still exists, clean and tighten connections at starter relay and battery ground connection on engine. If problem continues, replace starter.

STARTER DOES NOT CRANK, STARTER RELAY CLICKS

Ensure battery is fully charged and cables are clean and properly connected. Clean and tighten connections at starter and relay. If problem continues, replace starter.

STARTER DOES NOT CRANK AND RELAY CHATTERS OR DOES NOT CLICK

1) Ensure battery is fully charged and cables are clean and properly connected. Remove push-on connector from relay (Red with Blue stripe wire).
2) Ensure connection is clean and secure, and relay bracket is grounded. If connections are okay, check operation of relay with jumper wire.
3) Ensure ignition switch is off. Using a jumper wire, connect one end of jumper wire to now exposed terminal on starter relay and other end to battery positive post.
4) If this corrects problem, check ignition switch, neutral switch and wiring in starting circuit for open or loose connections. If jumper wire across relay does not correct problem, replace relay.

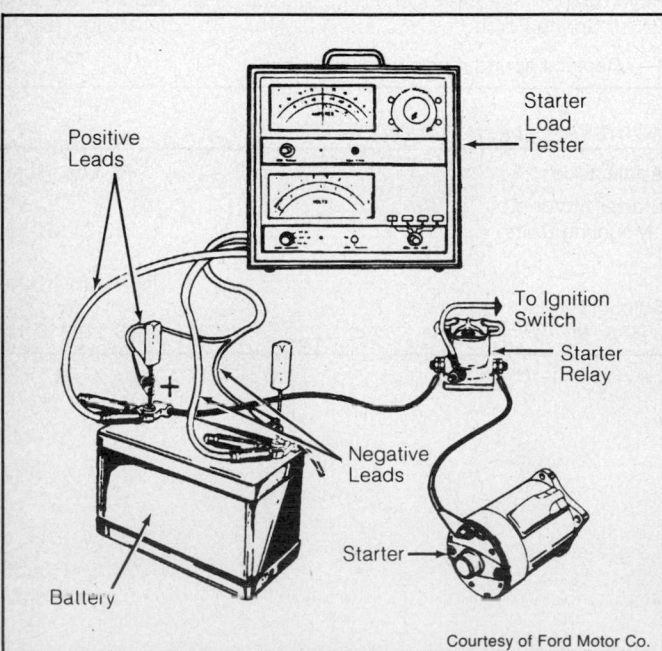

Fig. 1: Starter Load Test Connections

STARTER SPINS BUT DOES NOT CRANK ENGINE

Remove and service starter or replace starter drive.

STARTER LOAD TEST

1) Connect test equiptment. See Fig. 1. Ensure no current is flowing through ammeter and carbon pile rheostat. Disconnect terminal "S" push-on connector from starter relay.
2) Ensure transmission is not in gear. Connect remote control starter switch between terminal "S" and positive battery terminal. Crank engine and observe voltmeter reading. Stop cranking engine and adjust carbon pile rheostat until voltmeter indicates same reading as obtained while cranking engine.
3) Ammeter will indicate starter current draw under load. Normal starter current load is 150-250 amps.

BENCH TESTS

STARTER NO-LOAD TEST

NOTE: Starter no-load test will determine open or shorted windings, rubbing armature and bent armature shaft.

1) Connect test equipment. See Fig. 2. Ensure no current is flowing through ammeter and carbon pile rheostat.
2) Connect jumper wire between negative battery terminal and starter frame. Connect another jumper wire between positive battery terminal and positive terminal of starter motor. Ensure no current is flowing through ammeter.
3) Turn carbon pile rheostat to maximum (counterclockwise) position and note voltmeter reading. Disconnect jumper leads from starter motor. Reduce resistance of rheostat until voltmeter reads same as when starter was running.
4) Ammeter will indicate starter draw under no load. Normal starter draw under no load is 80 amps.

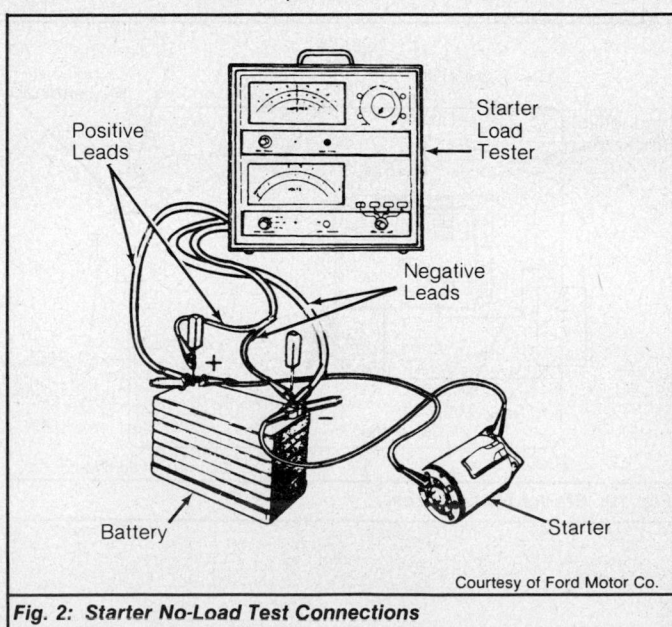

Fig. 2: Starter No-Load Test Connections

ARMATURE OPEN CIRCUIT TEST

An open armature circuit can be detected by inspecting commutator for evidence of burning. If burning is present, replace armature assembly. Check for damage to other related components.

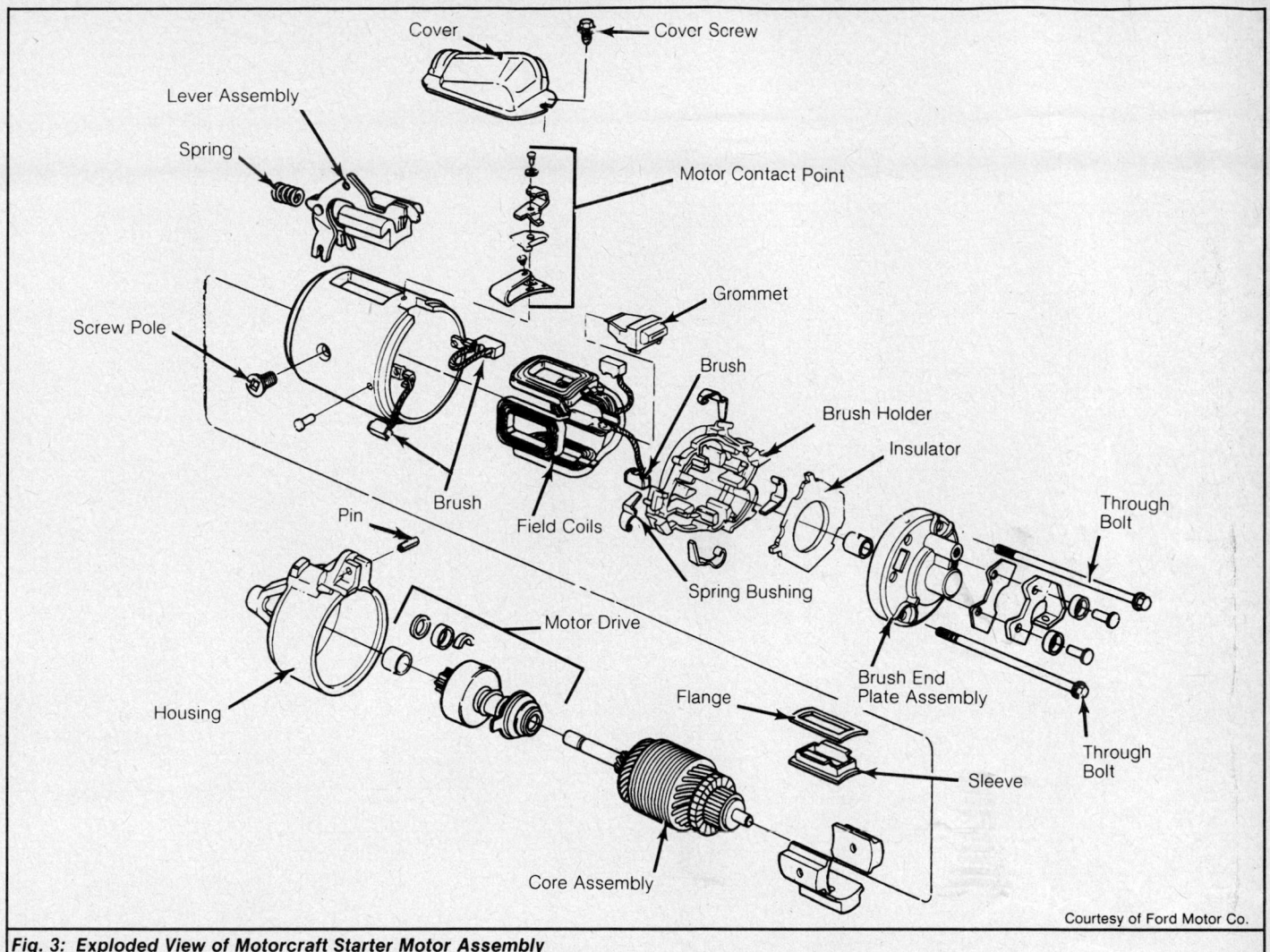

Fig. 3: Exploded View of Motorcraft Starter Motor Assembly

Courtesy of Ford Motor Co.

ARMATURE & FIELD GROUNDED CIRCUIT TEST

NOTE: This test will determine if field winding insulation has failed, permitting a conductor to contact frame or armature core.

1) Using a voltmeter, connect negative voltmeter lead to negative battery terminal and positive lead to commutator. Connect jumper wire between positive battery terminal and armature core. If any voltage is indicated, windings are grounded and armature should be replaced.
2) Connect jumper wire between negative battery terminal and starter frame. Connect negative voltmeter lead to positive battery terminal and positive lead to field coil eyelet terminal. If any voltage is indicated, field windings are grounded and should be replaced.

STARTER SPECIFICATIONS

Application	Specification
Brush Length	
Original	.45" (11.4 mm)
Service Limit	.25" (6.4 mm)
Brush Spring Tension	80 oz. (2.3 kg)
Load Test Current Draw	150-250 Amps
No-Load Test Current Draw	80 Amps

TIGHTENING SPECIFICATIONS

Application	Ft. Lbs. (N.m)
Starter-to-Engine Bolts	15-20

	INCH Lbs. (N.m)
Brush End Plate	
Through Bolts	55-80 (6-9 N.m)

Section 5

WIRING DIAGRAMS

CONTENTS

**WIRING DIAGRAM
EXPLANATION & SYMBOLOGY**   **Page**

All Models 5-2

CHRYSLER

Fifth Avenue 5-26
LeBaron Coupe & Convertible 5-55
LeBaron Sedan 5-47
New Yorker 5-31

DODGE

Aries 5-14
Daytona 5-19
Diplomat 5-26
Dynasty 5-31
Lancer 5-47
Omni 5-43
Shadow 5-63
Spirit 5-4

EAGLE

Premier 5-69

FORD

Escort 5-106
LTD Crown Victoria & Wagon 5-114
Mustang 5-134
Probe 5-141
Taurus 5-153
Tempo 5-166
Thunderbird 5-92

LINCOLN

Continental 5-80
Mark VII 5-124
Town Car 5-174

MERCURY

Cougar 5-92
Grand Marquis & Wagon 5-114
Sable 5-153
Topaz 5-166

PLYMOUTH

Acclaim 5-4
Gran Fury 5-26
Horizon 5-43
Reliant 5-14
Sundance 5-63

NOTE: **ALSO SEE GENERAL INDEX**

1989 WIRING DIAGRAMS
Explanation & Symbology

INTRODUCTION

Mitchell obtains wiring diagrams and technical service bulletins, containing wirng diagram changes, from the domestic and import manufacturers. These are checked for accuracy and are all redrawn into a consistent format for easy use.

All diagrams are arranged with the front of the vehicle at the left side of the first page and the rear of the vehicle at the right side of the last page. Accessories are shown near the end of the diagram. Components are shown in their approximate location on the vehicle. Due to the constantly increasing number of components on vehicles today, it is impossible to show exact locations.

In the past, when cars were simpler, diagrams were simpler. All components were connected by wires, and diagrams seldom exceeded 4 pages in length. Today some wiring diagrams require more than 16 pages. It would be impractical to expect a service technician to trace a wire from page 1 across every page to page 16.

Removing some of the wiring maze reduces eyestrain and time wasted searching across several pages. Today, Mitchell diagrams now follow a much improved format, which permits space for internal details of relays and switches.

Any wires that don't connect directly to their components are identified on the diagram to indicate where they go. There is a legend on the first page of each diagram, detailing component location. It refers you to sub-systems, using grid NUMBERS at the top and bottom of the page and grid LETTERS on each side. This grid system works in a manner similar to that of a road map.

HOW TO USE MITCHELL'S WIRING DIAGRAMS

1) On the first page of the diagram, you will find a listing of major electrical components or systems. Locate the specific component or system you wish to trace. A grid number and letter will follow the component's name.

2) Use the grid NUMBERS (arranged horizontally across the top and bottom of each page) to find the page of the wiring diagram that contains the component you're seeking. When you reach this page, use the grid LETTER/NUMBER combination to find the component's location.

3) Locate the circuit you need to service. The internals are shown for switches and relays to assist you in understanding how the circuit operates.

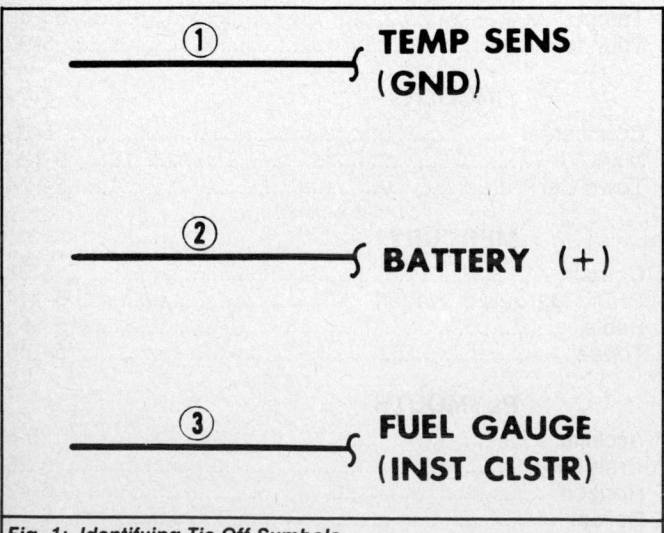

Fig. 1: Identifying Tie-Off Symbols

4) If the wires are not drawn all the way to another component (across several pages), a reference will tell you their final destination.

5) Again, use the legend on the first page of the wiring diagram to determine the grid number and letter of the referenced component. You can then turn directly to it without tracing wires across several pages.

6) The symbols shown in *Fig. 1* are called tie-offs. The first tie-off indicates that the circuit goes to the temperature sensor, and is also a ground circuit. The second tie-off indicates that the circuit goes to the battery positive terminal. The third tie-off leads to a particular component and the location is also given.

7) The lines shown in *Fig. 2* are called options. Which path or option to take depends on what engine or systems the vehicle has.

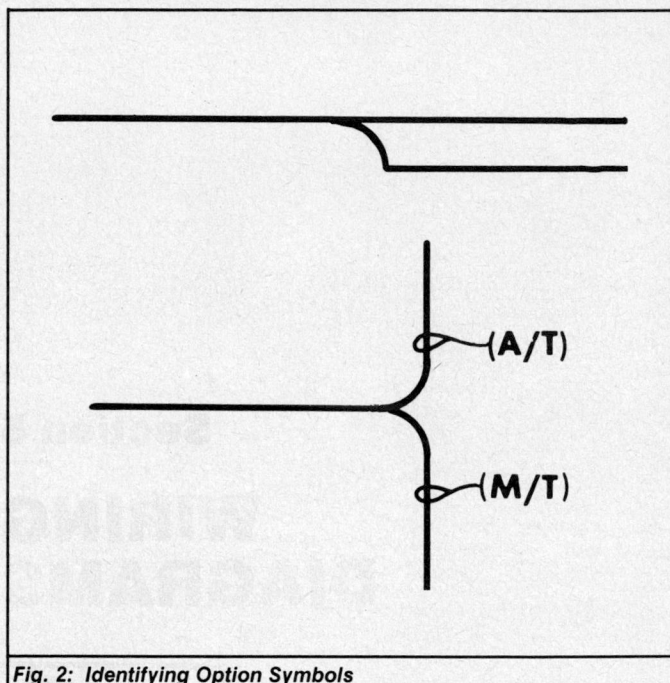

Fig. 2: Identifying Option Symbols

COLOR ABBREVIATIONS

Color	Normal	Optional
BLACK	BLK	BK
BLUE	BLU	BU
BROWN	BRN	BN
CLEAR	CLR	CR
DARK BLUE	DK BLU	DK BU
DARK GREEN	DK GRN	DK GN
GREEN	GRN	GN
GRAY	GRY	GY
LIGHT BLUE	LT BLU	LT BU
LIGHT GREEN	LT GRN	LT GN
ORANGE	ORG	OG
PINK	PNK	PK
PURPLE	PPL	PL
RED	RED	RD
TAN	TAN	TN
VIOLET	VIO	VI
WHITE	WHT	WT
YELLOW	YEL	YL

IDENTIFYING WIRING DIAGRAM SYMBOLS

NOTE: Standard wiring symbols are used on Mitchell diagrams. The list below will help clarify any symbols that are not easily understood at a glance. Most components are labeled "Motor", "Switch" or "Relay" in addition to being drawn with the Standard Symbol.

 CIRCUIT BREAKER

 COIL (Internal)

 CONNECTOR

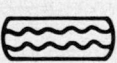 DIODE (In-Line)

DIODE (Internal)

DIODE (Light Emitting)

DEFOGGER GRID

FUSE

 FUSIBLE LINK

 GROUND

 GLOW PLUG, RESISTOR (In-line), MIRROR HEATER

 INJECTOR, PHOTOCELL

 INTERNAL FUSE, THERMAL LIMITER

 LAMP (Dual Element)

 LAMP (Single Element)

 MOTOR

 RESISTOR (Internal)

 SENSOR, THERMISTOR

 SOLENOID

 SOLID STATE DEVICE, TRANSISTOR

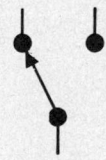 SWITCH (Internal)

 TWO PIN SWITCH

 VARIABLE RESISTOR OR POTENTIOMETER

IDENTIFYING WIRING DIAGRAM ABBREVIATIONS

NOTE: Abbreviations used on Mitchell diagrams are normally self-explanatory. To assist you, however, we have included a 5-page list of abbreviations elsewhere in this manual.

1989 CHRYSLER MOTORS
Acclaim & Spirit

COMPONENT LOCATOR:

A/C CLUTCH RELAY .... C 26-27
A/C SYSTEM .... B-C 24-27
ALT .... E 3
ASHTRAY LIGHT .... B 19
AUTO SHUTDOWN RLY (2.5L) .... B 7
AUTO SHUTDOWN RLY (TURBO) ..... B 11
AUTO SHUTDOWN RLY (3.0L) .... B 15
BACK-UP LT RLY (3.0L) .... B 20
BATTERY .... A 2
BEAM SELECT SW .... E 22
BRAKE WARN LT SW .... A 17
CIG LTR LT .... C 19
COURTESY LIGHTS .... D-E 32-35
CRUISE CTRL SYSTEM .... A-B 26-27
DEFOG SWITCH .... B-C 32
DIR FLASHER .... A 16
DIR SWITCH .... D-E 20
DOOR AJAR SWITCHES .... C 30
DOOR LOCKS .... B-C 34-35
ECM (2.5L) .... A-E 4
ECM (2.5L TURBO) .... A-E 8
ECM (3.0L) .... A-E 12
ELECT TRANS CTRL (ETC) MOD ..... A 20-23
ENG COMPT LT & SW .... B 1
ETC DIAG CONN .... D 28
FOG LT RLY .... C 23
FUEL TANK UNIT .... A 31
FUS LINKS .... D 2
FUSE BLOCK .... C-E 17-18
HAZARD FLASHER .... A 16
HAZARD FLASHER SW .... E 21
HEADLT SW .... D-E 3
HEATER SYSTEM .... A 24
HORN RELAY .... A 16
IGN SW .... A 18-19
INST CLSTR .... A-C 28-30
LT OUTAGE MODULES .... D-E 29-31
NEUTRAL SAFETY SW (3.0L) .... B 2
NEUTRAL SAFETY/BACK-UP
  LIGHT SWITCH (2.5L) .... B 2
POWER MIRRORS .... C 32-34
POWER SEAT SW .... B 32
POWER WINDOWS .... A 32-35
RAD FAN RELAY .... C 26-27
RELAY MODULE .... A 16-17
SAFETY SHUTDOWN RLY .... C 21
SEAT BELT WARN MOD .... E 28
STARTER RLY .... A 3
STOP LT SW .... B 26
TIME DELAY RELAY .... D 34
TRIP COMPUTER .... D 28
VISUAL MESSAGE CENTER .... C 28-31
WIPER SYSTEM .... D-E 24-27

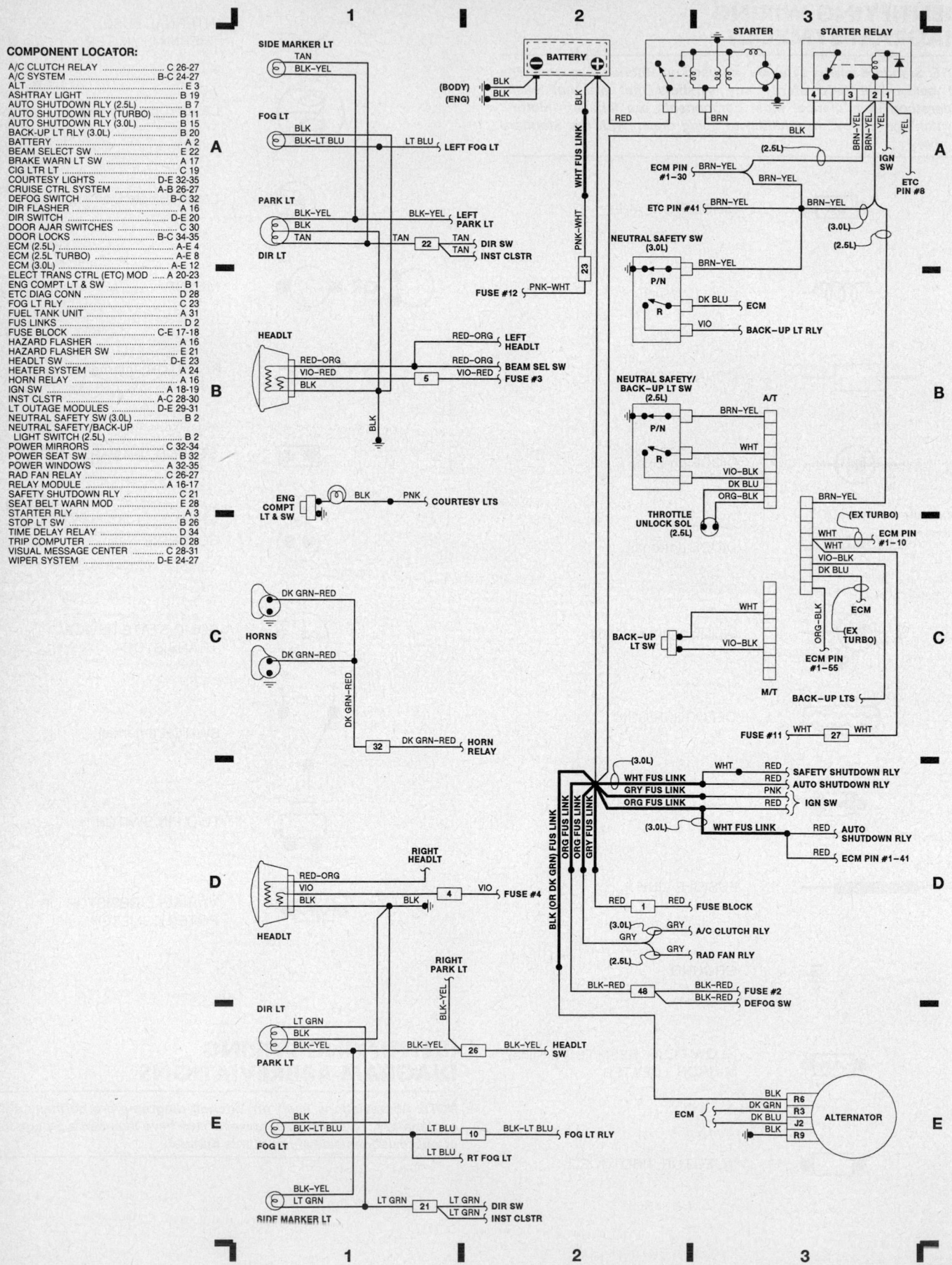

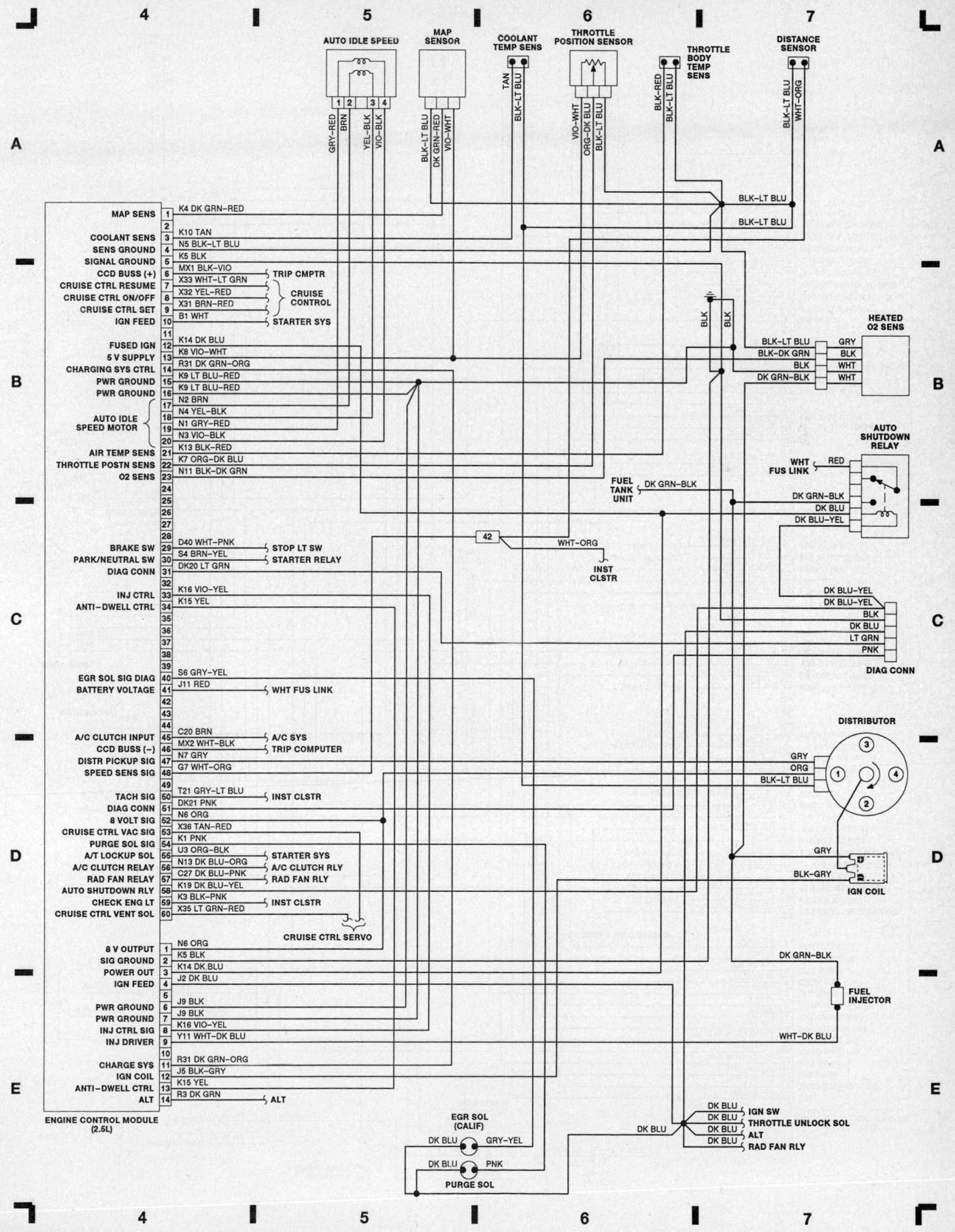

1989 CHRYSLER MOTORS
Acclaim & Spirit (Cont.)

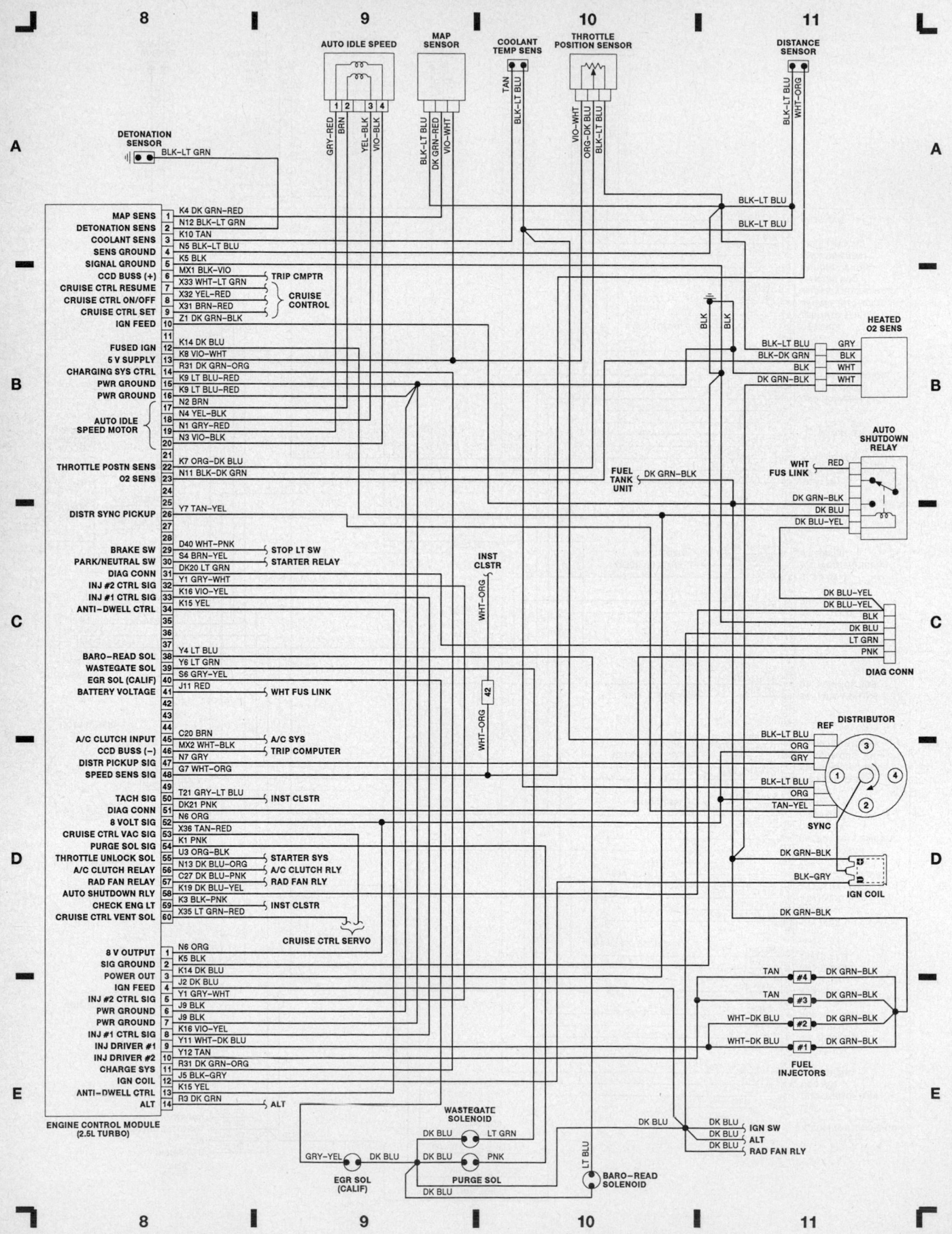

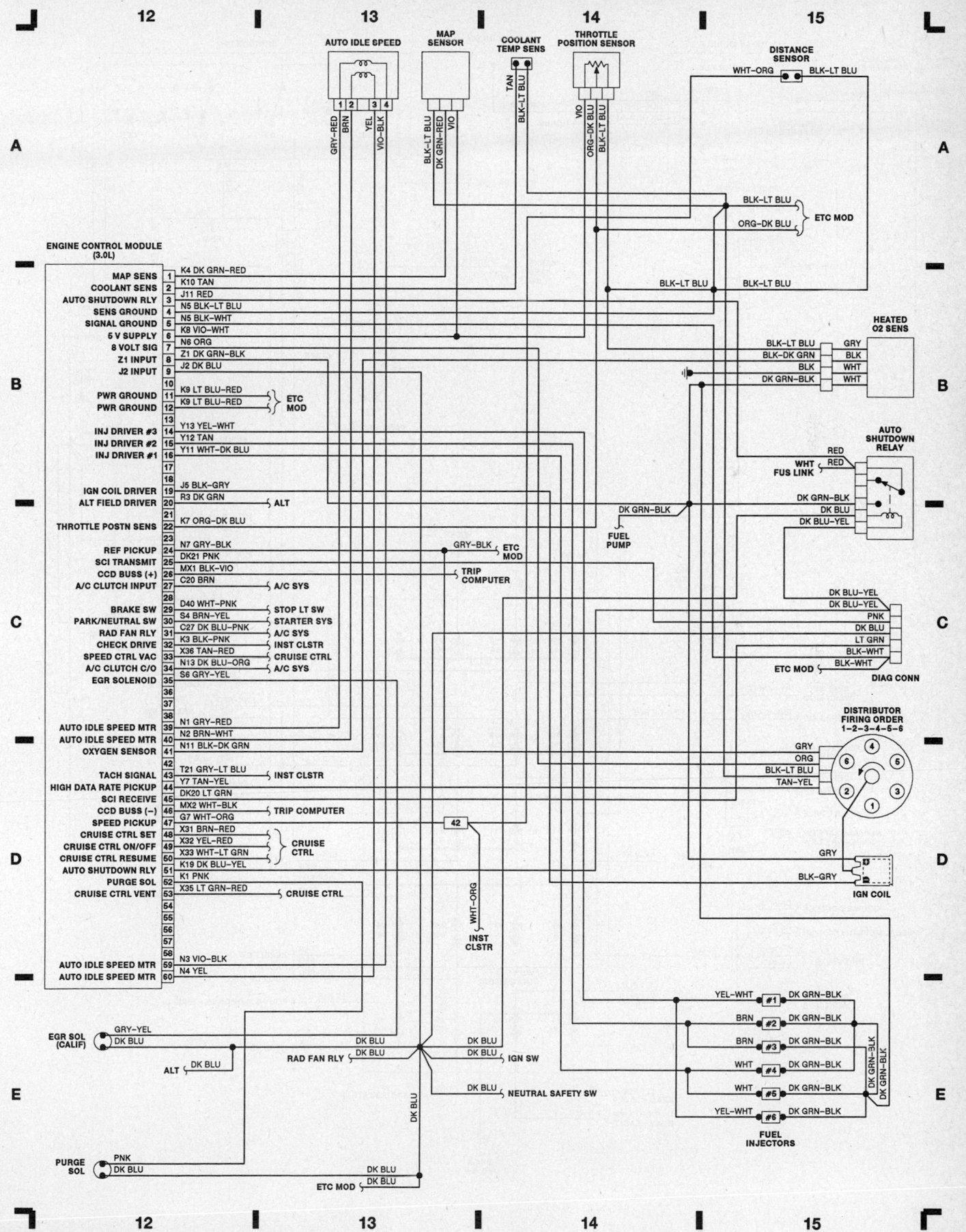

1989 CHRYSLER MOTORS
Acclaim & Spirit (Cont.)

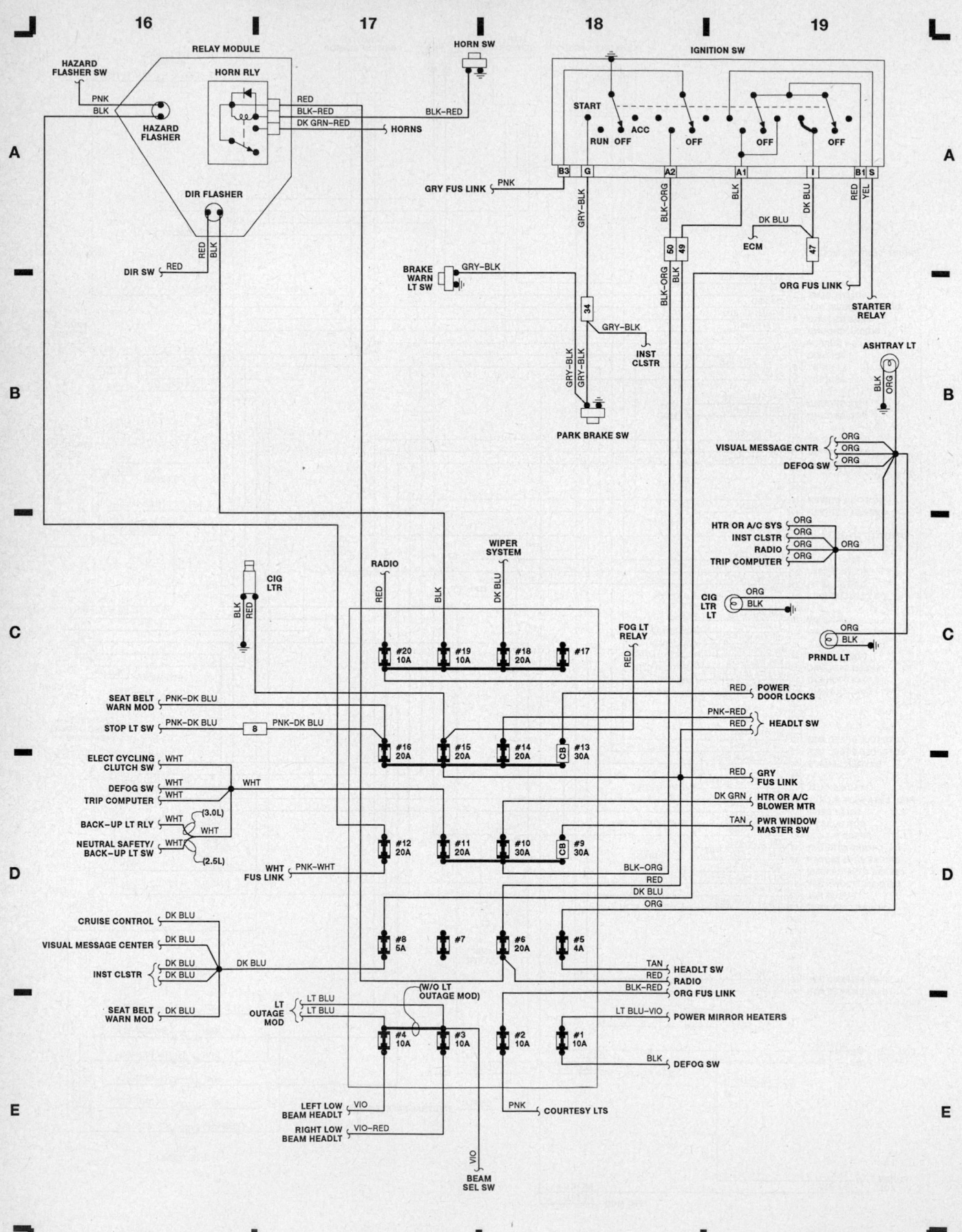

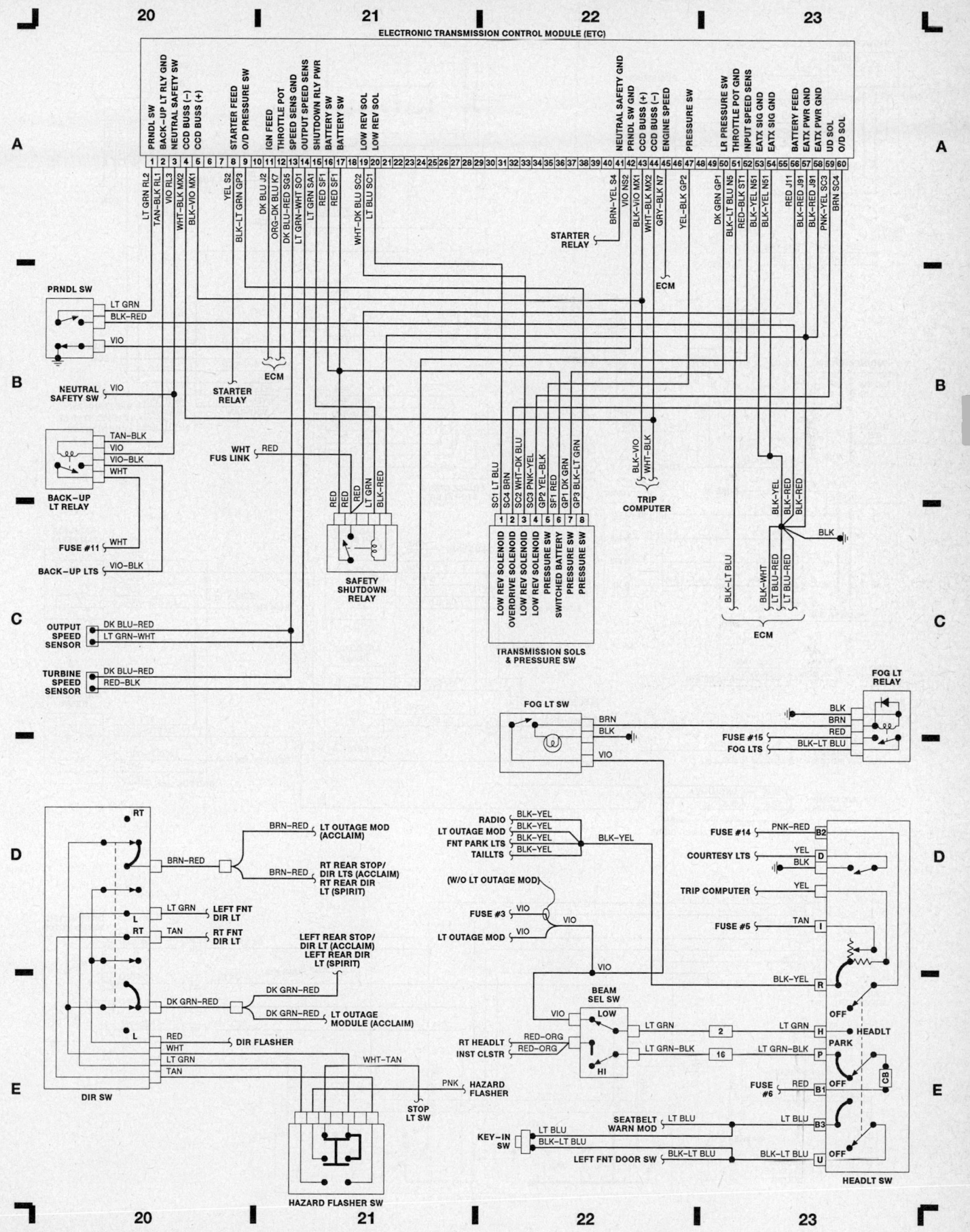

1989 CHRYSLER MOTORS
Acclaim & Spirit (Cont.)

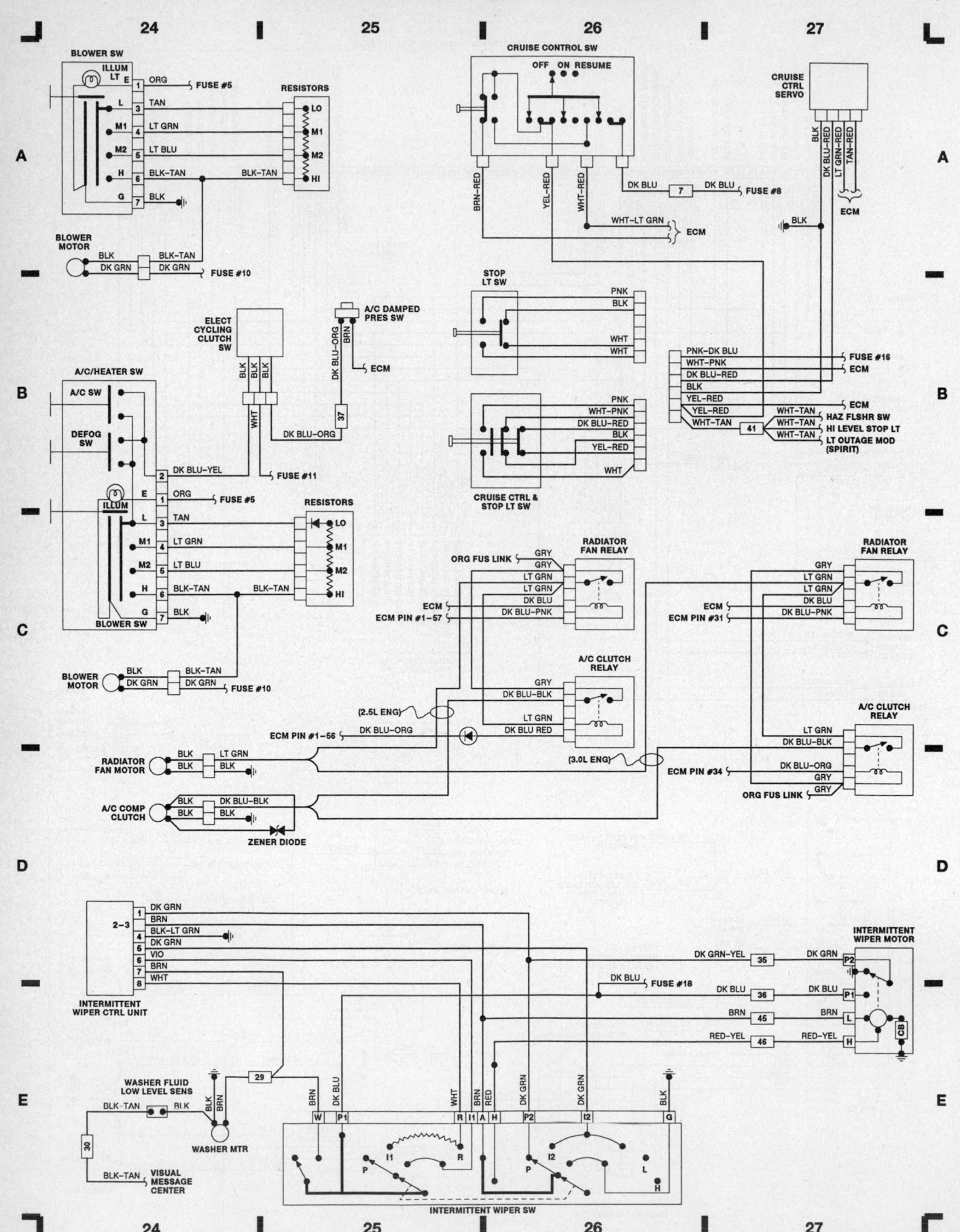

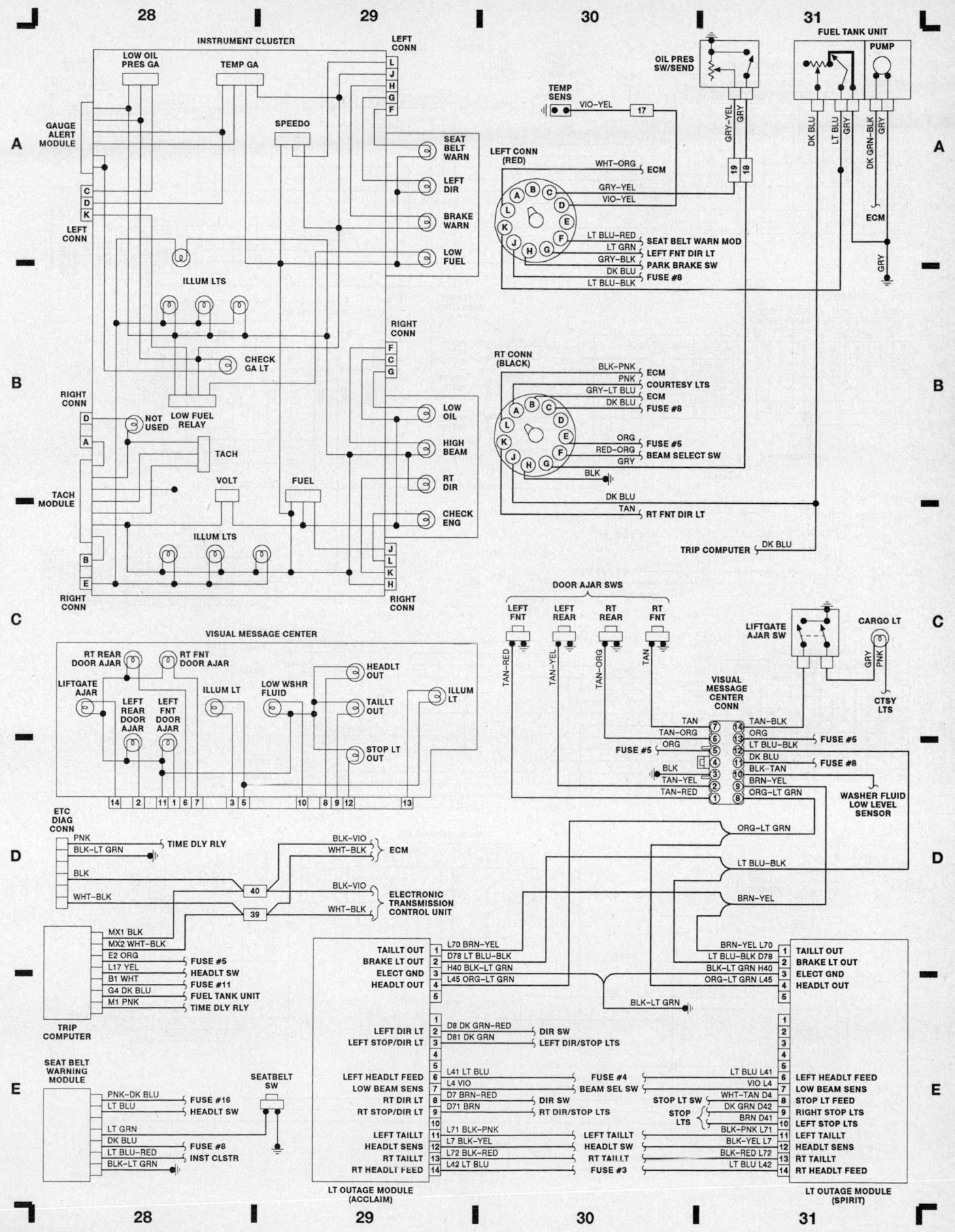

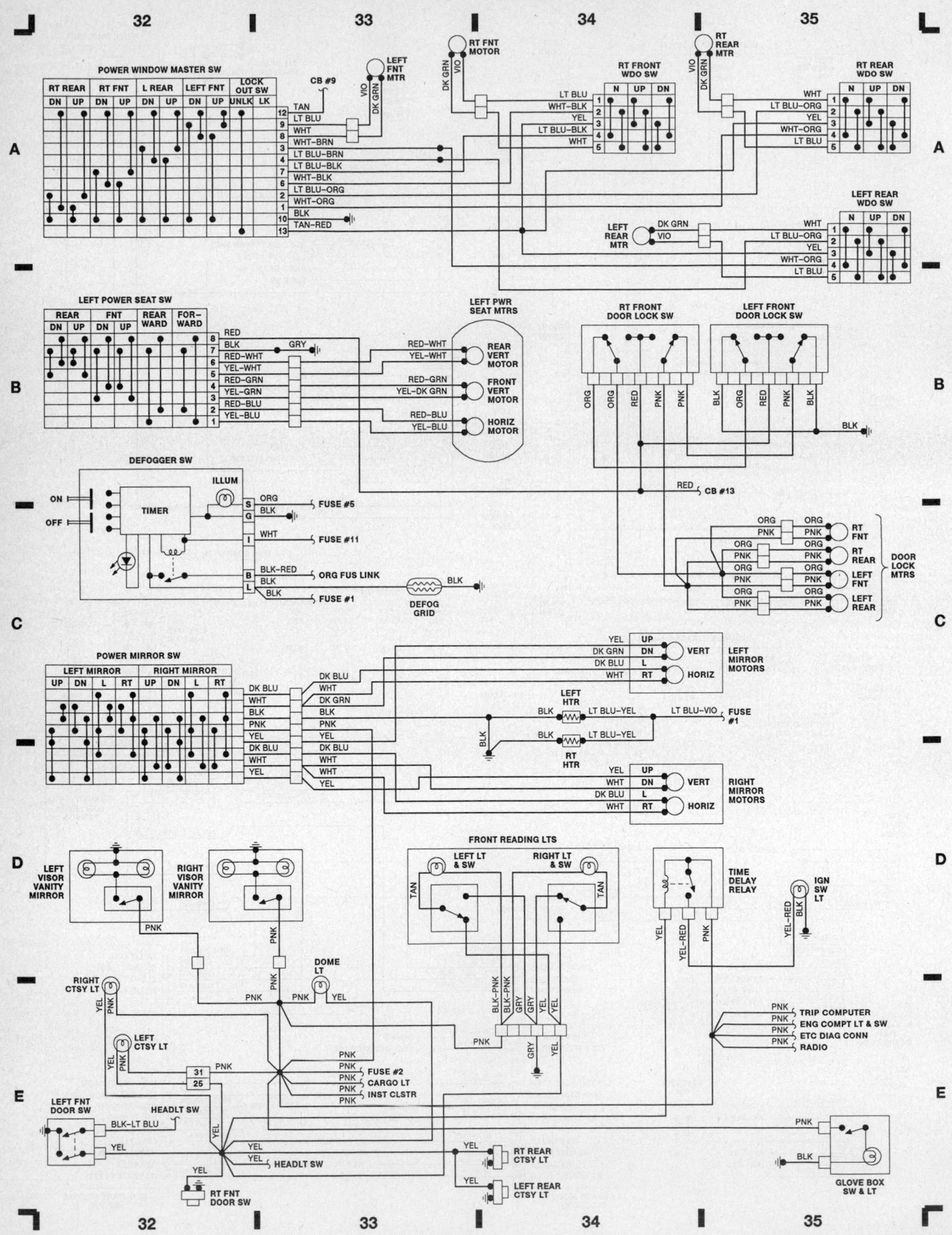

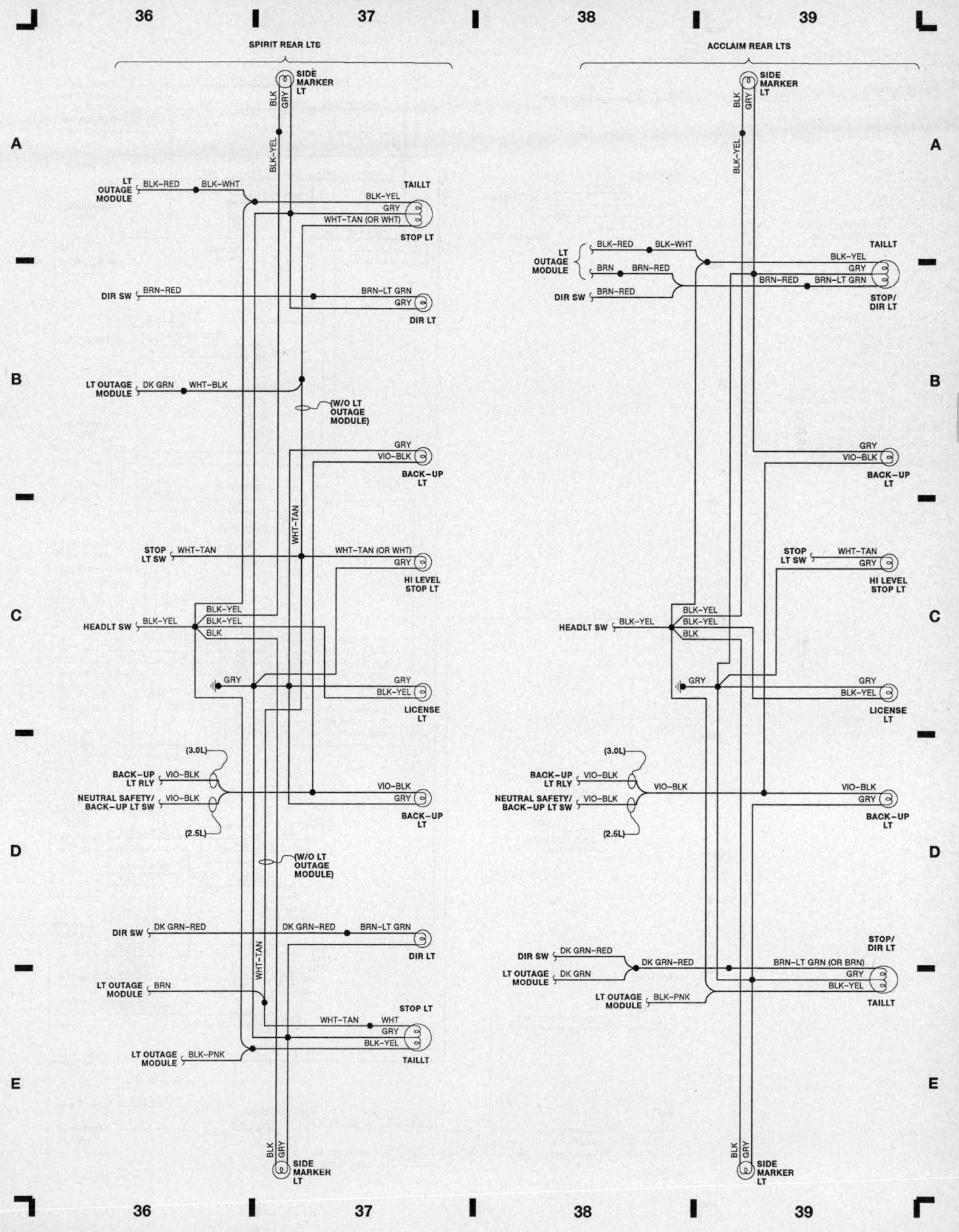

1989 CHRYSLER MOTORS
Aries & Reliant

COMPONENT LOCATOR:

A/C CLUTCH RLY .... D 3
A/C SW .... A 16
ALTERNATOR .... B 3
AUTO SHUTDOWN RLY .... B 7
BACK-UP LT SW .... C 3
BATTERY .... A 2
BEAM SEL SW .... A 11
BUZZER .... E 12
CIG LTR .... E 8
CRUISE CTRL SERVO .... E 4
CRUISE CTRL SW .... B 15
DEFOG SW .... B 16
DISTANCE SENS .... C 2-3
DIR SW .... A 8
DOME/MAP LTS .... C-B 17
DOOR LOCKS .... D-E 16
DOOR SWS .... C-D 11
ENGINE CTRL MODULE (ECM) .. A-E 4
FUEL PUMP/SENS .... B 19
FUS LINKS .... A 2
FUSE BLOCK .... D-E 9-10
GLOVE BOX LT .... E 8
HAZARD SW .... C 8
HEADLIGHT SW .... B 11
HEATER SW .... C 16
HORN RLY/SW .... E 3
IGNITION SW .... A 9-10
INSTRUMENT CLUSTER .... A-B 12-13
LIFTGATE AJAR LT SW .... C 19
NEUTRAL SAFETY/BACK-UP LT SW . C 3
OIL PRES SENS .... D 13
PARK BRAKE SW .... D 13
RADIATOR FAN RLY .... D 3
SEAT BELT SW .... E 12
STARTER RELAY .... B 3
STOP LT SW (W/ CRUISE CTRL) ... A 15
STOP LT SW (W/O CRUISE CTRL) .. C 8
TEMP SENS .... C 13
THROTTLE UNLOCK SOL .... C 3
TIME DELAY RELAY .... D-E 9
TRUNK/CARGO LT & SWS .... C 18-19
WIPER/WASHER SYS (FNT) .... D-E 13-15
WIPER/WASHER SYS (REAR) .. D-E 12
WIPER/WASHER SYS (2 SPEED) . C 13-15

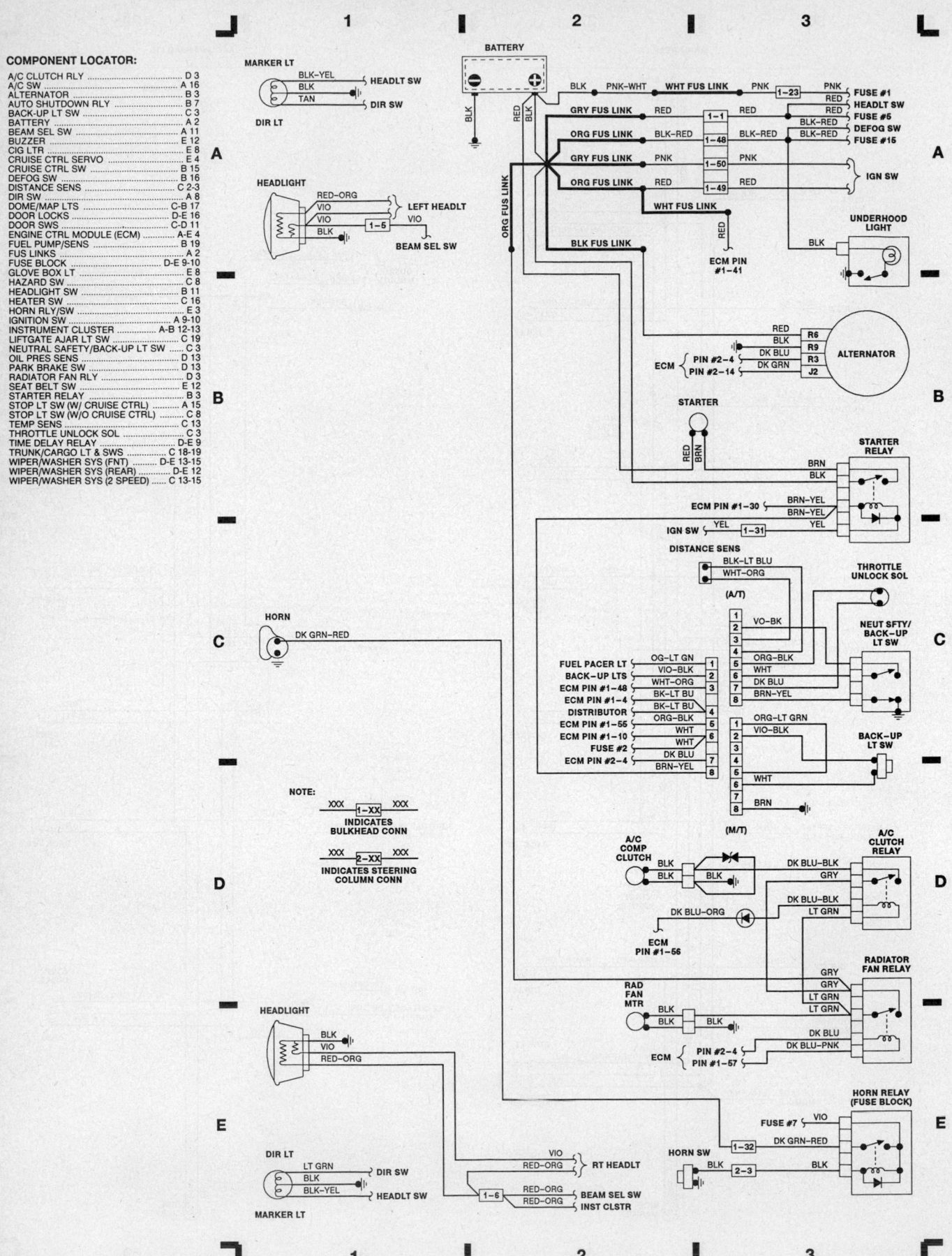

1989 CHRYSLER MOTORS
Aries & Reliant (Cont.)

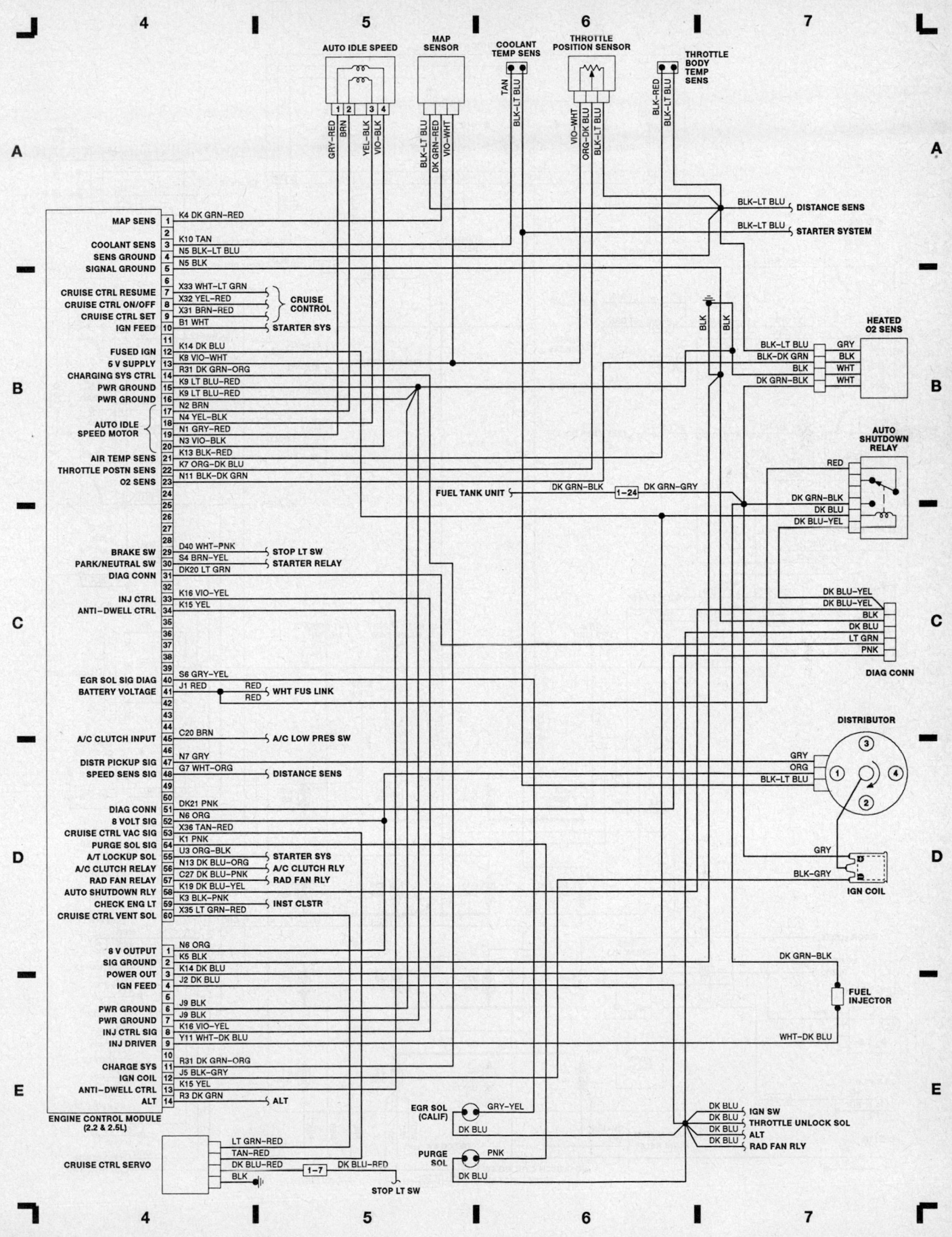

1989 CHRYSLER MOTORS
Aries & Reliant (Cont.)

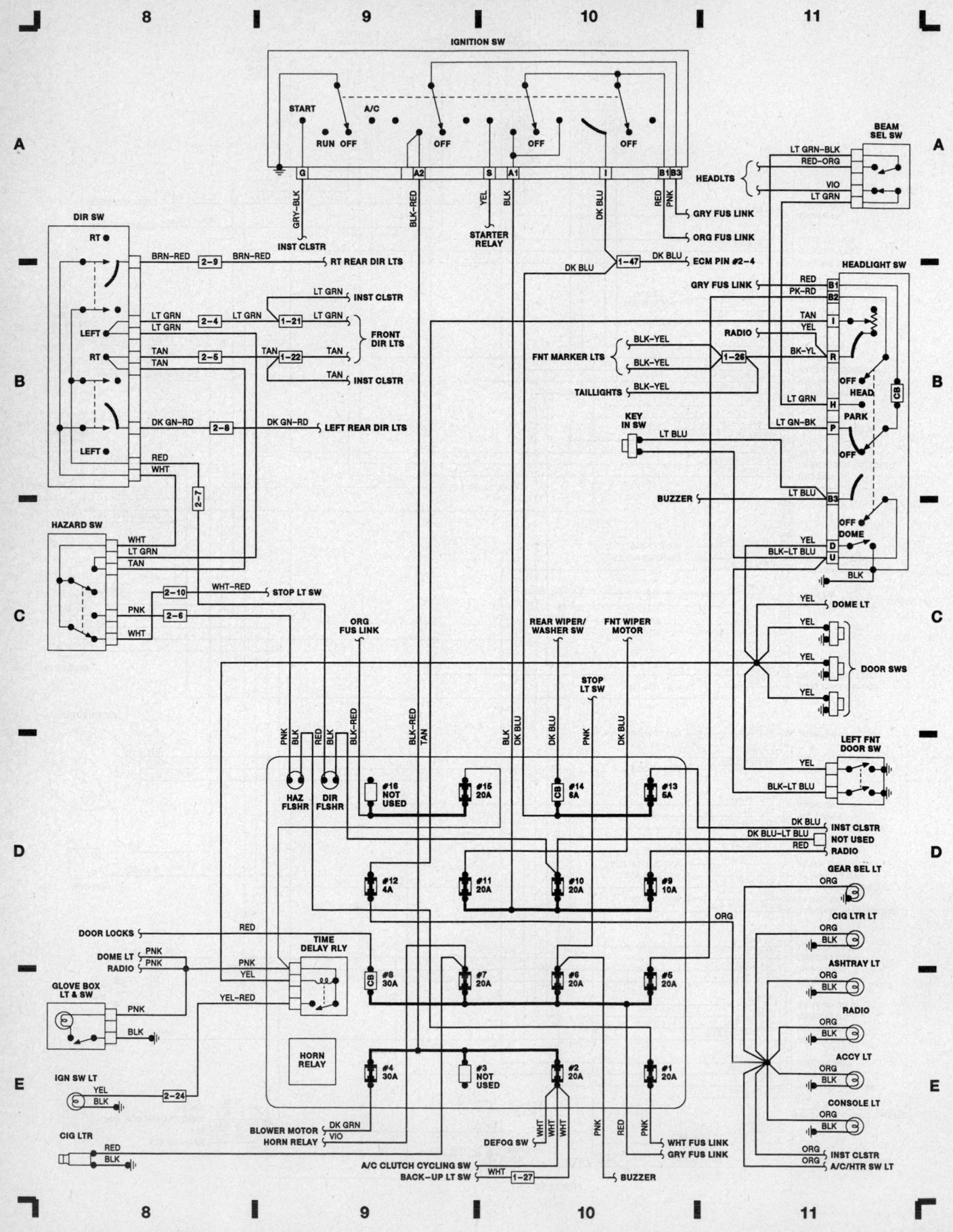

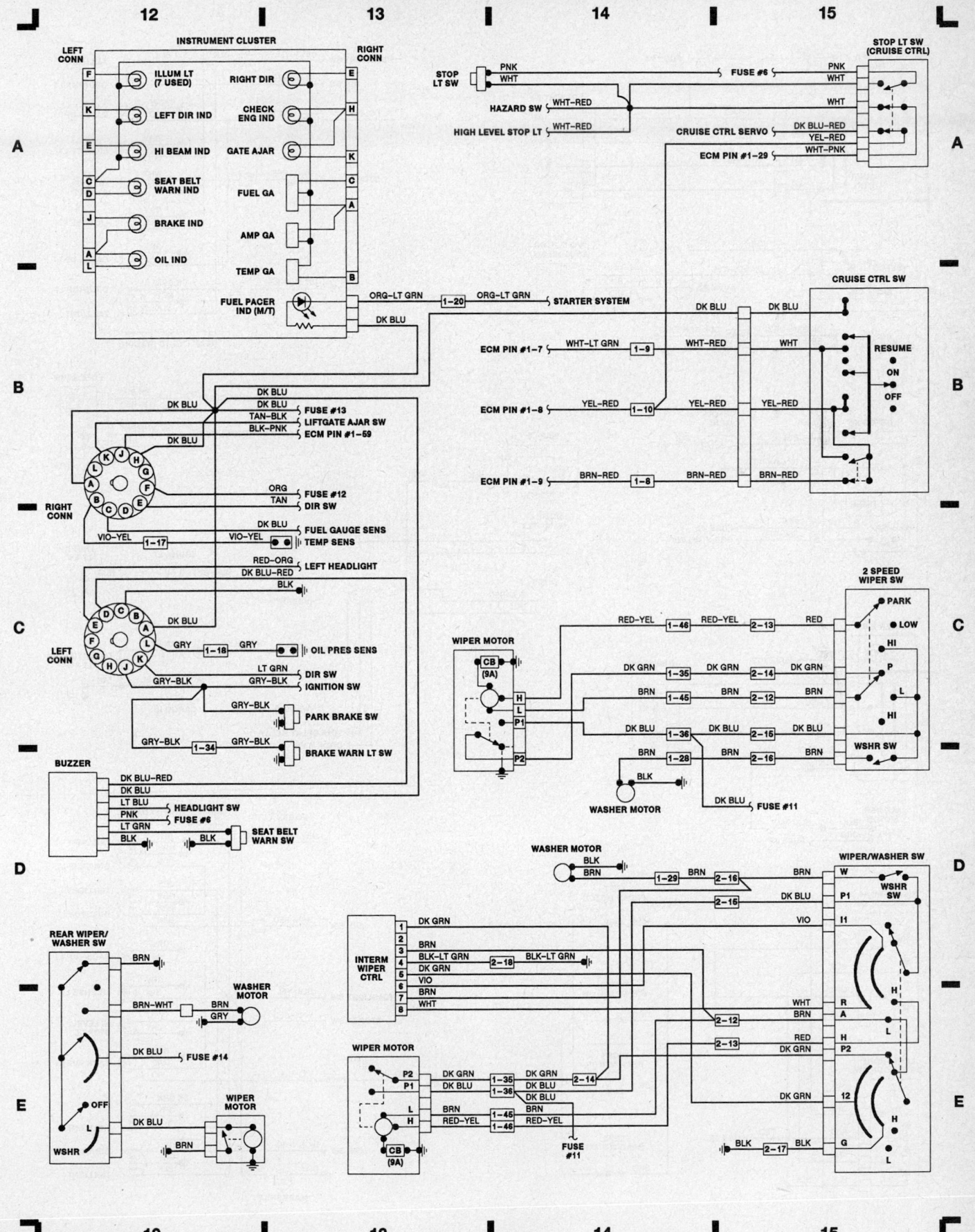

1989 CHRYSLER MOTORS
Aries & Reliant (Cont.)

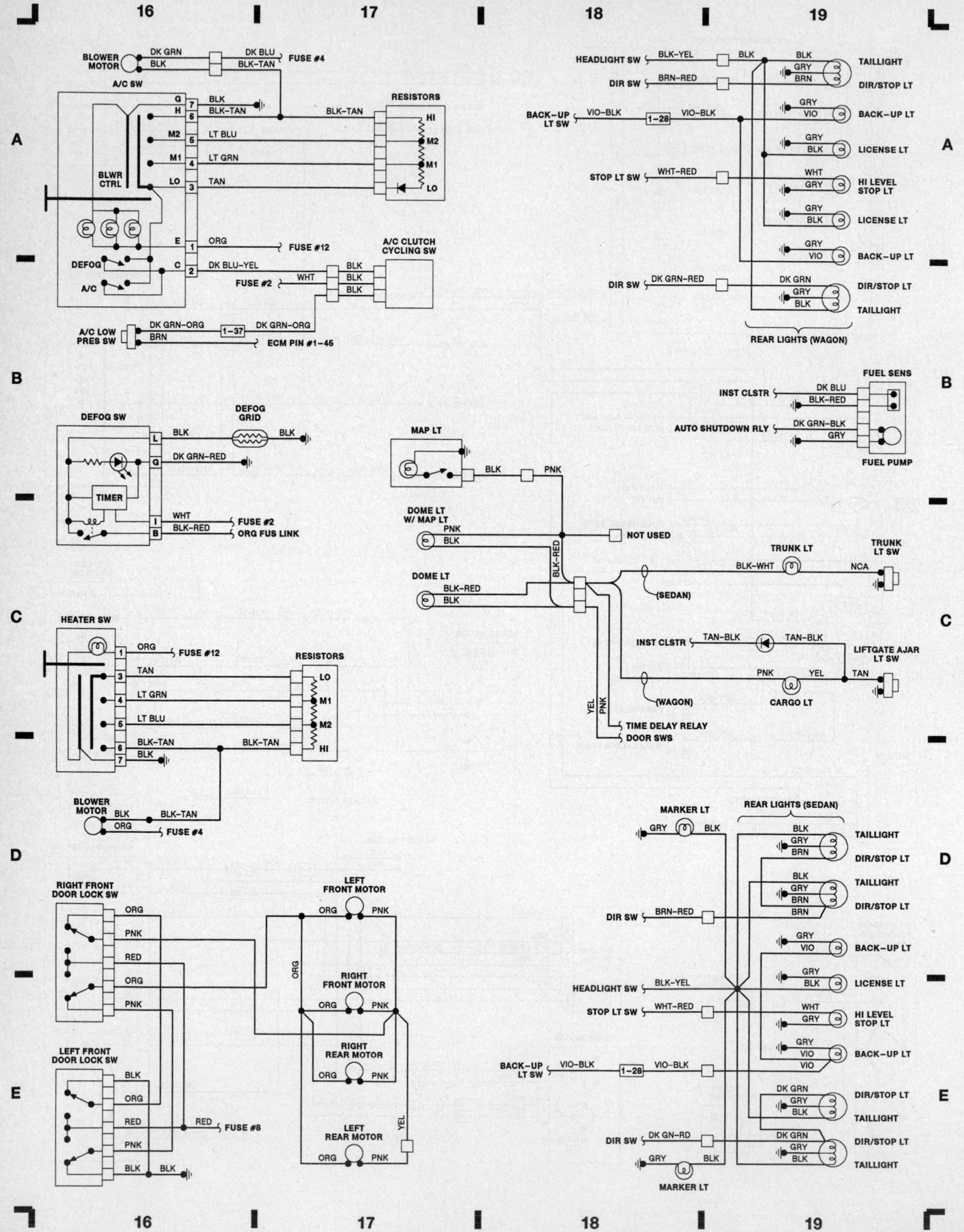

COMPONENT LOCATOR:

A/C CLUTCH RELAY	D 3
A/C LOW PRES SW	B 19
A/C SWITCH	A 19
AIR BAG SYSTEM	D-E 22-23
ALTERNATOR	B 3
AMBIENT AIR TEMP SENS	C 22
AUTO SHUTDOWN RLY	B 7
AUTO SHUTDOWN RLY (TURBO)	B-C 11
BACK-UP LT SW	C-D 3
BATTERY	A 1
BEAM SEL SW	A 15
BLOWER MOTOR	A 19, C 19
BRAKE WARN SW	A 12
CHIME MODULE	E 16-18
CONCEALED HEADLIGHT CTRL	E 19
CRUISE CTRL SERVO	E 4, E 8
CRUISE CTRL SW	A-B 16
DEFOG SW	C 19
DIR SW	B 12
DISTANCE SENS	C 2
DISTRIBUTOR	C-D 7
DISTRIBUTOR (TURBO)	C-D 11
DOME/INTERIOR LTS	D 24
DOOR AJAR SWS	A 21
DOOR LT SWS	D-E 24-26
ENGINE CONTROL MOD (ECM)	A-E 4-7
ENGINE CONTROL MOD (TURBO)	A-E 8-11
FOG LT SW & RELAY (NO INFO AVAILABLE)	B 2
FUEL TANK UNIT	E 21-22
FUS LINKS	A 2
FUSE BLOCK	D-E 13-14
GLOVE BOX LT & SW	E 24
HAZARD SW	C 12
HEADLIGHT SW	B-C 15
HEATER SW	B 19
HORN SYSTEM	E 3
IGNITION SW	A 13-14
ILLUMINATED ENTRY RLY	D 19
INSTRUMENT CLUSTER (ANALOG)	A-B 22-23
INSTRUMENT CLUSTER (ELECT)	D-E 20
KEY IN SW	C 15
MIRROR HEATERS	B 25-26
NEUTRAL SAFETY SW	C 3
OIL PRES SENS & SW	C 20
OVERHEAD CONSOLE	C 23
PARK BRAKE SW	A 12
POWER DOOR LOCKS	A 24-25
POWER MIRRORS	B 25-26
POWER SEAT	B-C 24
POWER WINDOW SW	A 26
RADIATOR FAN RELAY	D-E 3
SEAT/SHOULDER BELT SWS	E 17-18
STARTER RELAY	B 3
STARTER SYSTEM	B-D 2-3
STOP LT SW	B 16
STOP LT SW (CRUISE CTRL)	A 16
TEMP SW	C 22
THROTTLE UNLOCK SOL	C 3
TRIP NAVIGATOR	D 23
UNDERHOOD LT & SW	A 3
VISUAL MESSAGE CENTER	A 22-23
WIPER/WASHER SYSTEMS	C-E 16-17

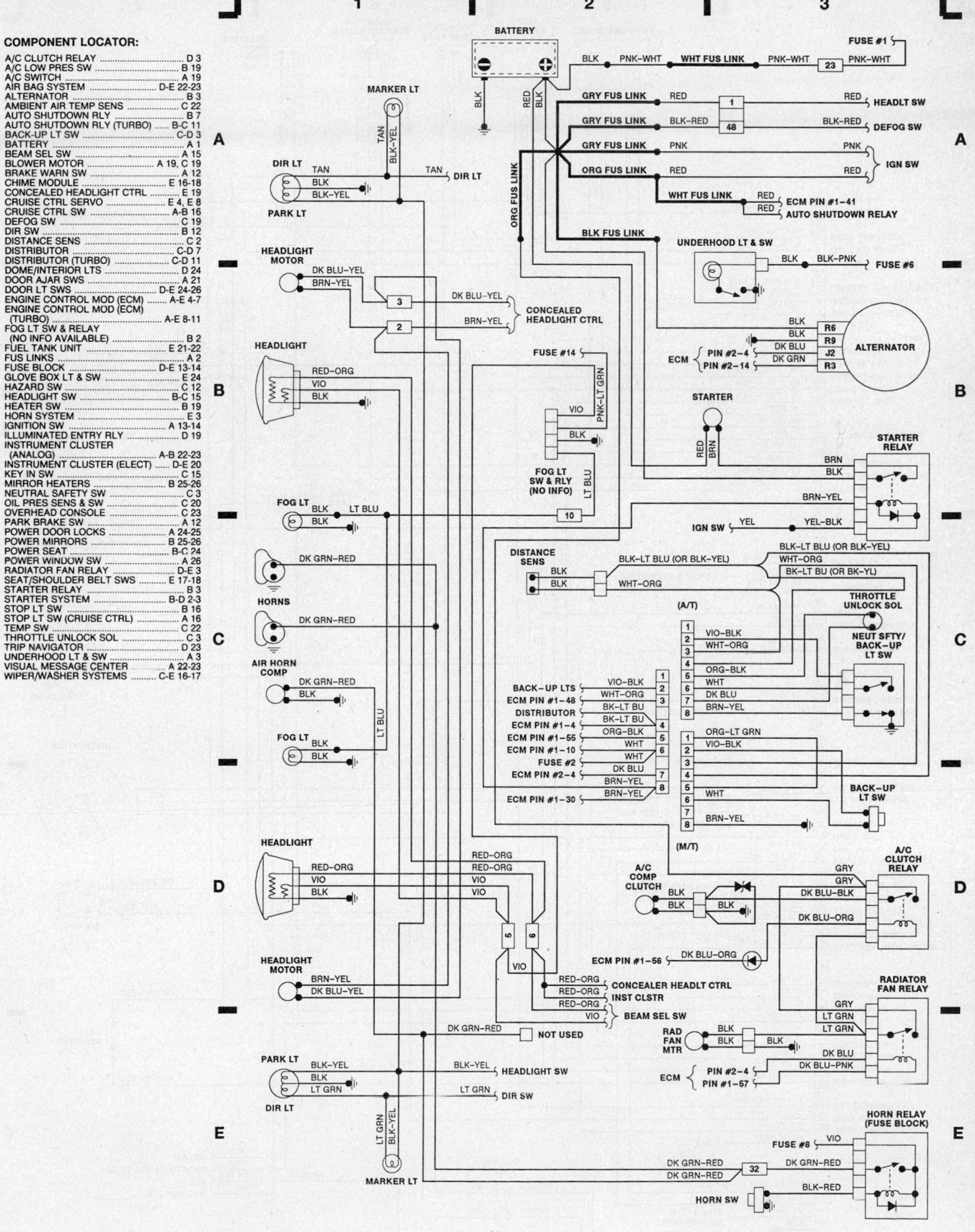

1989 CHRYSLER MOTORS
Daytona (Cont.)

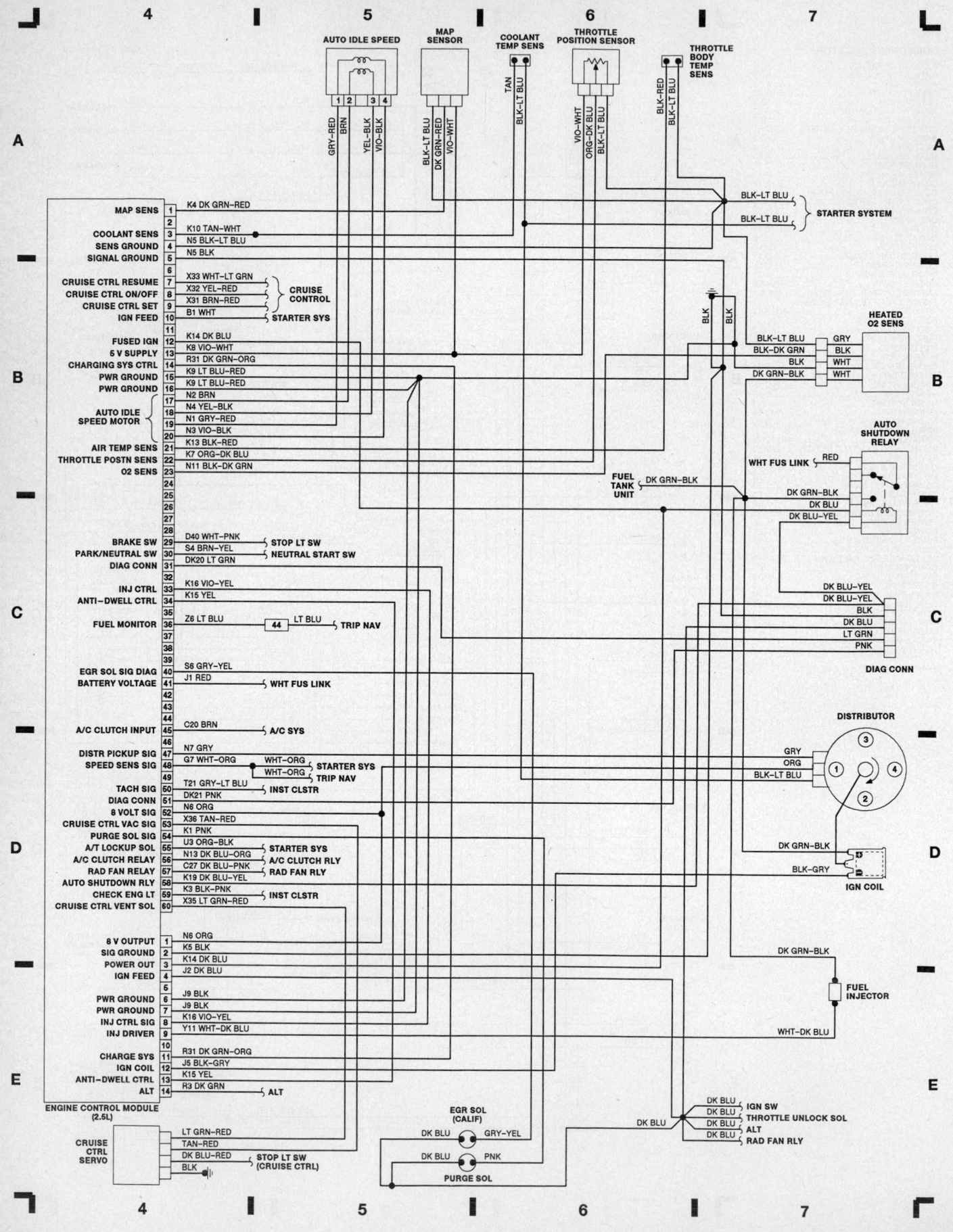

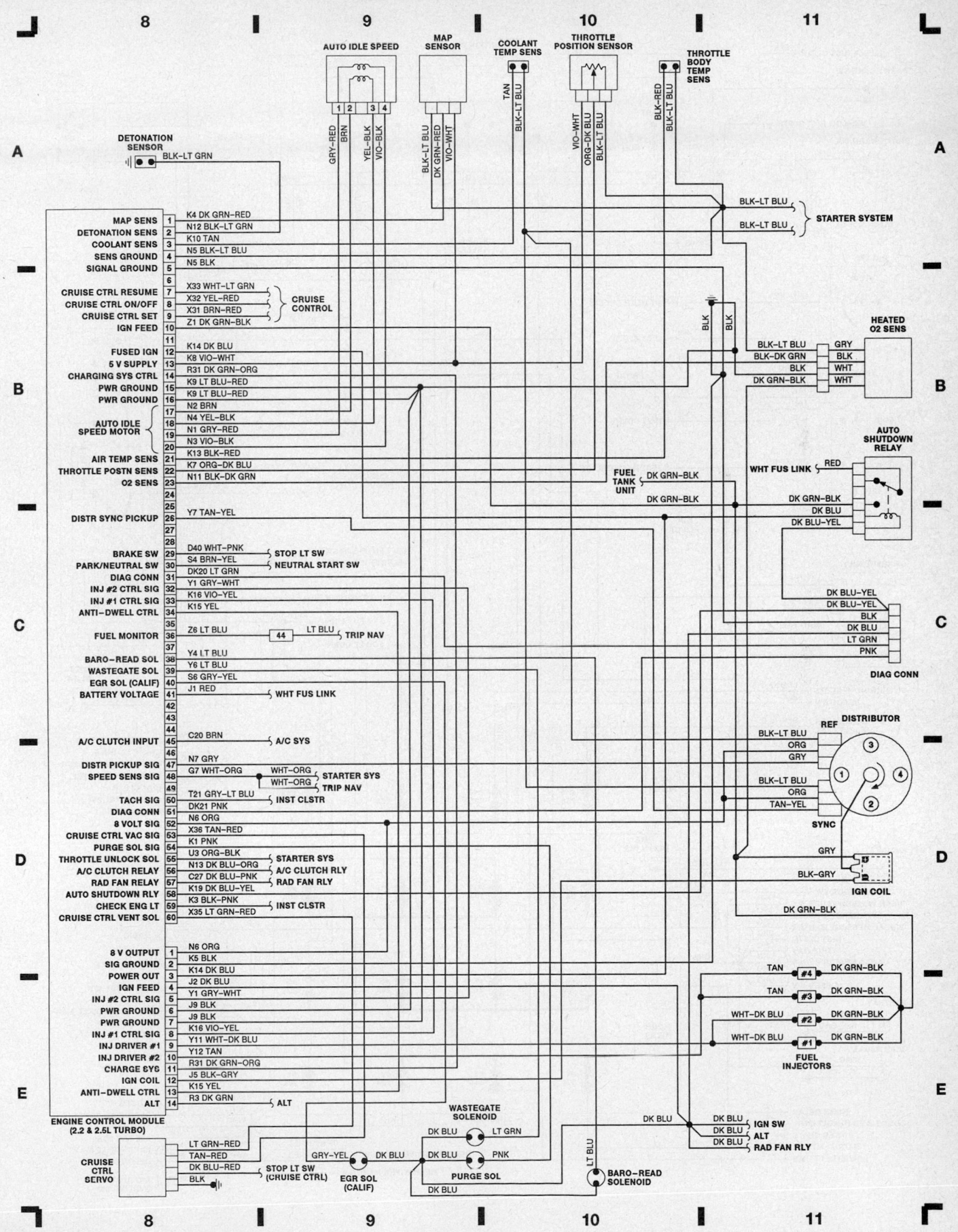

1989 CHRYSLER MOTORS
Daytona (Cont.)

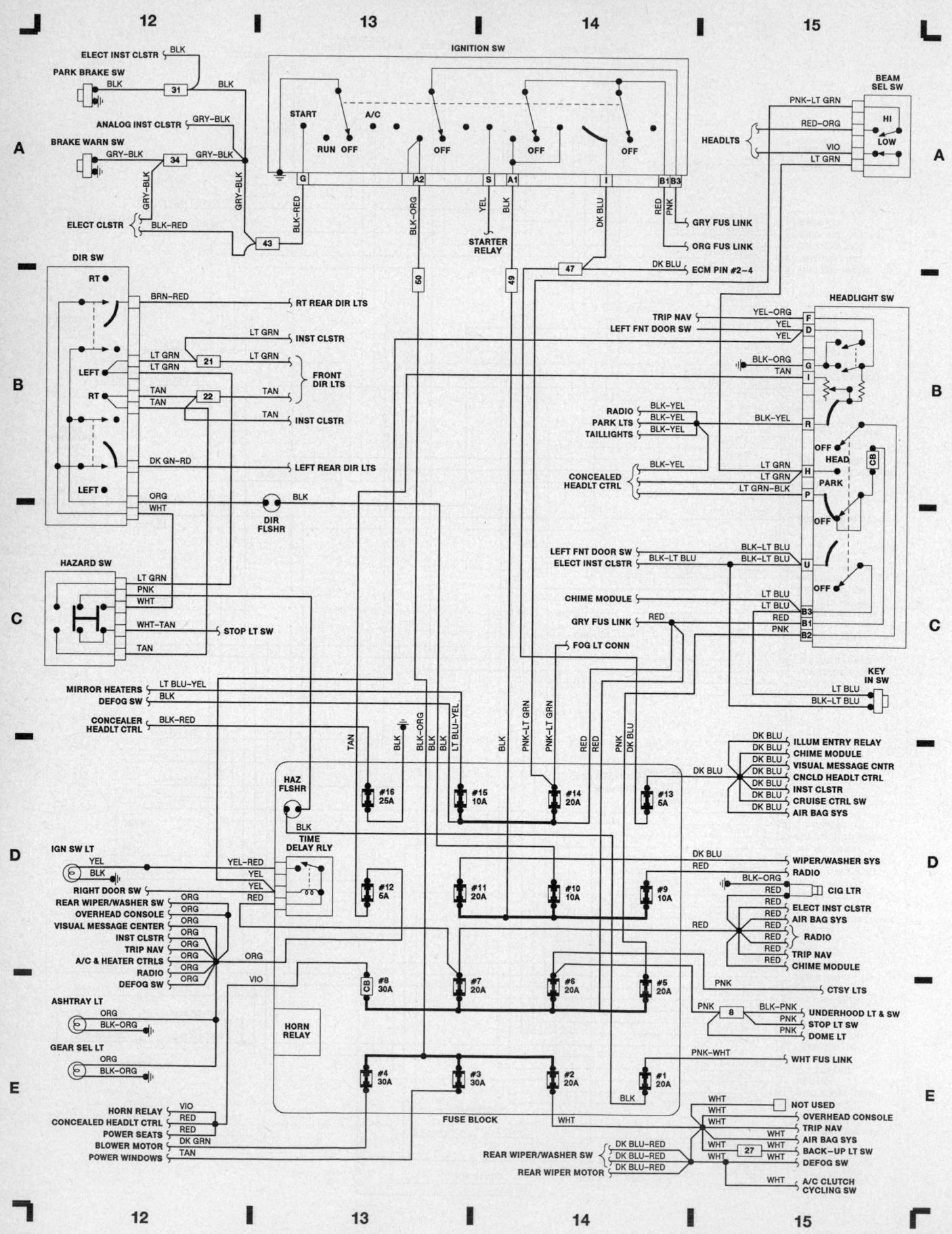

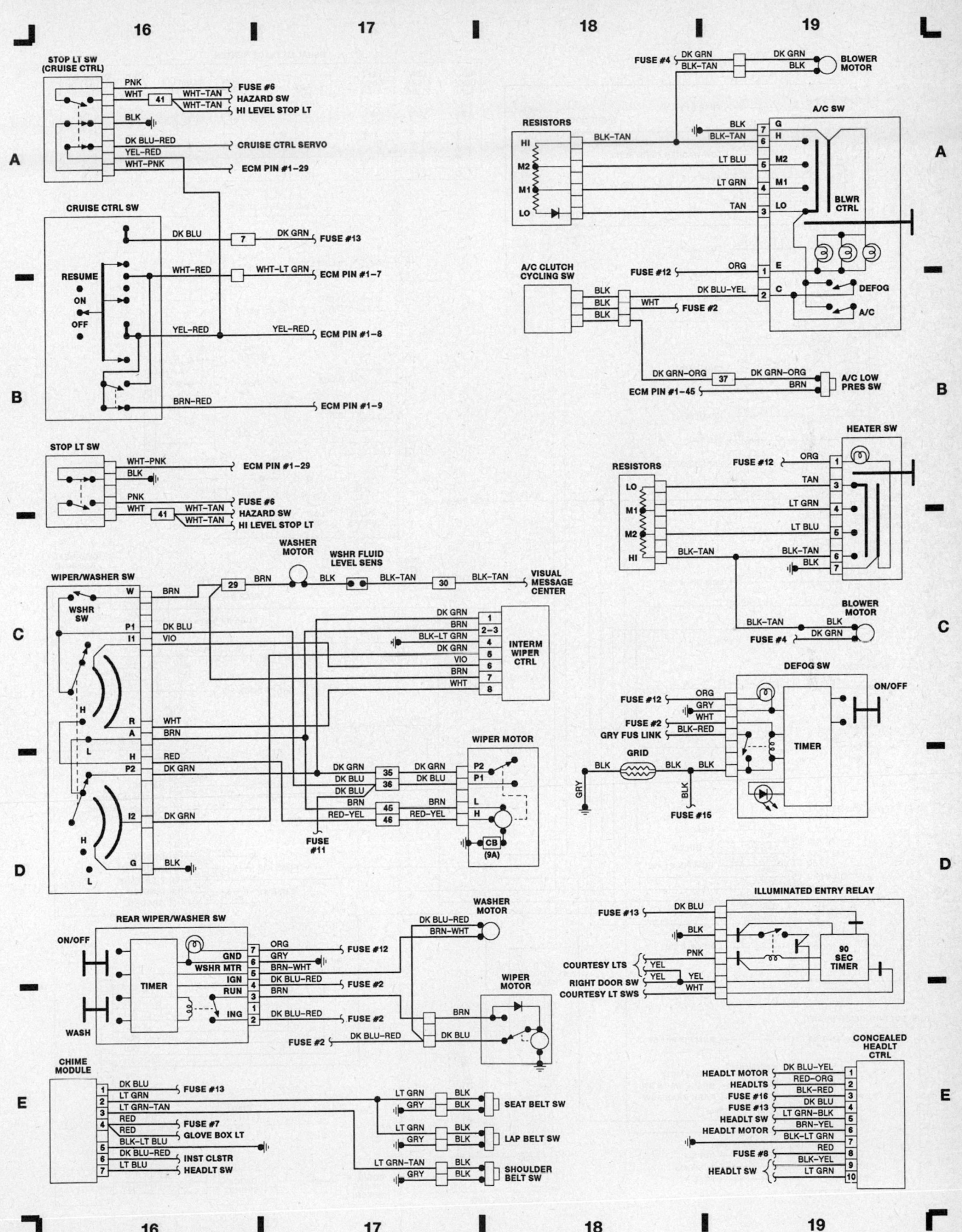

1989 CHRYSLER MOTORS
Daytona (Cont.)

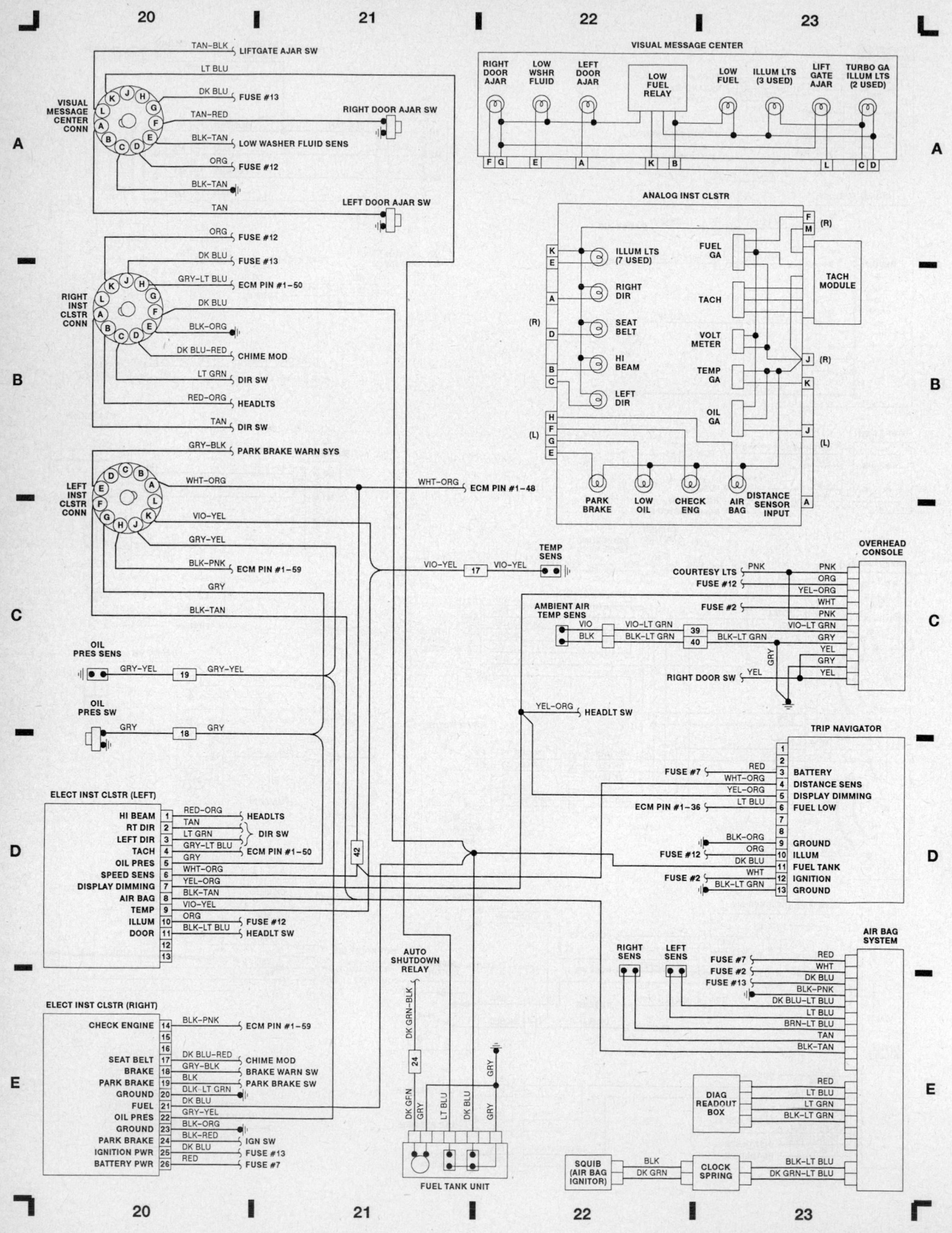

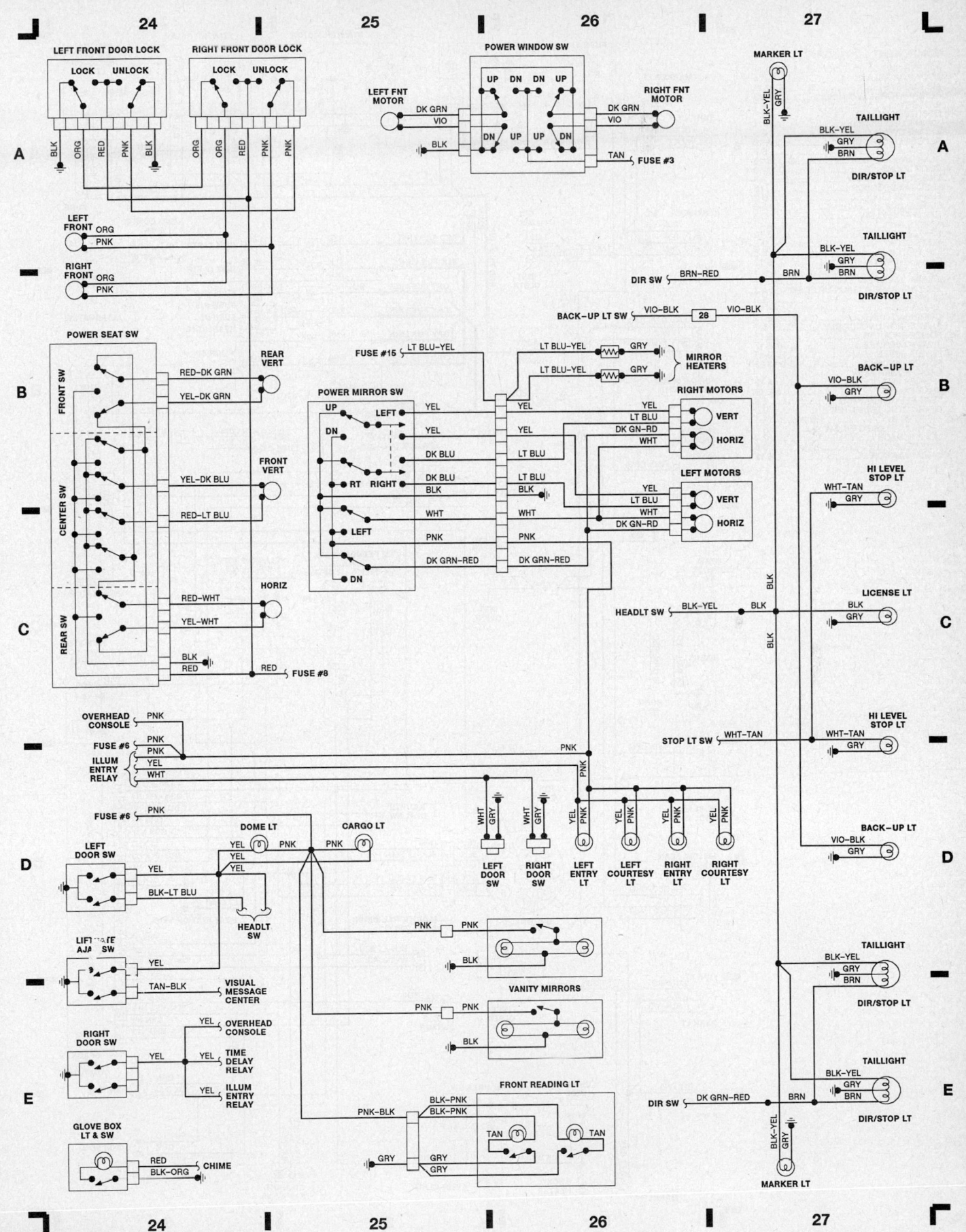

1989 CHRYSLER MOTORS
Diplomat, Fifth Avenue & Gran Fury

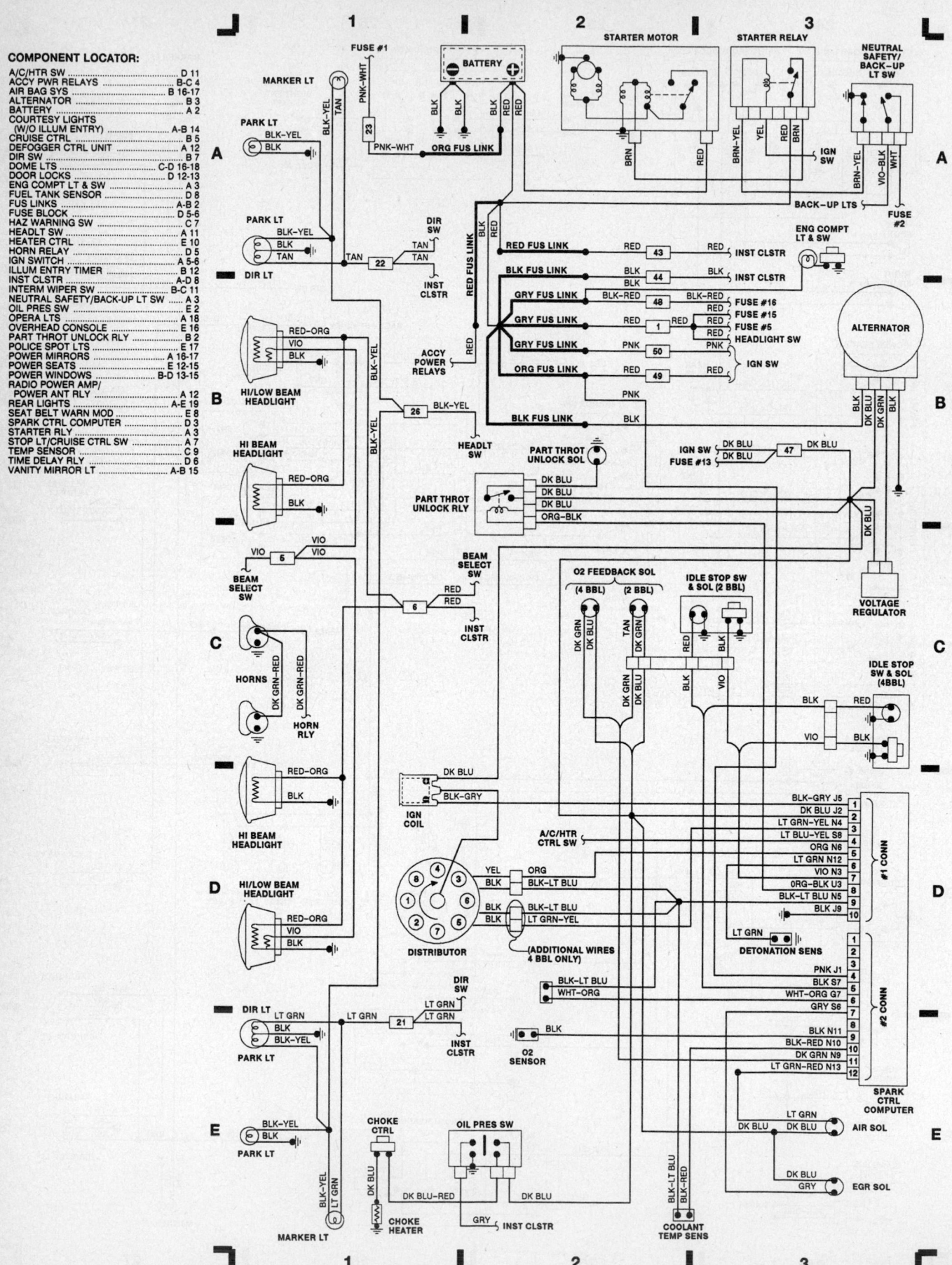

COMPONENT LOCATOR:

A/C/HTR SW .... D 11
ACCY PWR RELAYS .... B-C 4
AIR BAG SYS .... B 16-17
ALTERNATOR .... B 3
BATTERY .... A 2
COURTESY LIGHTS
  (W/O ILLUM ENTRY) .... A-B 14
CRUISE CTRL .... B 5
DEFOGGER CTRL UNIT .... A 12
DIR SW .... B 7
DOME LTS .... C-D 16-18
DOOR LOCKS .... D 12-13
ENG COMPT LT & SW .... A 3
FUEL TANK SENSOR .... D 8
FUS LINKS .... A-B 2
FUSE BLOCK .... D 5-6
HAZ WARNING SW .... C 7
HEADLT SW .... A 11
HEATER CTRL .... E 10
HORN RELAY .... D 5
IGN SWITCH .... A 5-6
ILLUM ENTRY TIMER .... B 12
INST CLSTR .... A-D 8
INTERM WIPER SW .... B-C 11
NEUTRAL SAFETY/BACK-UP LT SW .. A 3
OIL PRES SW .... E 2
OPERA LTS .... A 18
OVERHEAD CONSOLE .... E 16
PART THROT UNLOCK RLY .... B 2
POLICE SPOT LTS .... E 17
POWER MIRRORS .... A 16-17
POWER SEATS .... E 12-15
POWER WINDOWS .... B-D 13-15
RADIO POWER AMP/
  POWER ANT RLY .... A 12
REAR LIGHTS .... A-E 19
SEAT BELT WARN MOD .... E 8
SPARK CTRL COMPUTER .... D 3
STARTER RLY .... A 3
STOP LT/CRUISE CTRL SW .... A 7
TEMP SENSOR .... C 9
TIME DELAY RLY .... D 6
VANITY MIRROR LT .... A-B 15

1989 CHRYSLER MOTORS
Diplomat, Fifth Avenue & Gran Fury (Cont.)

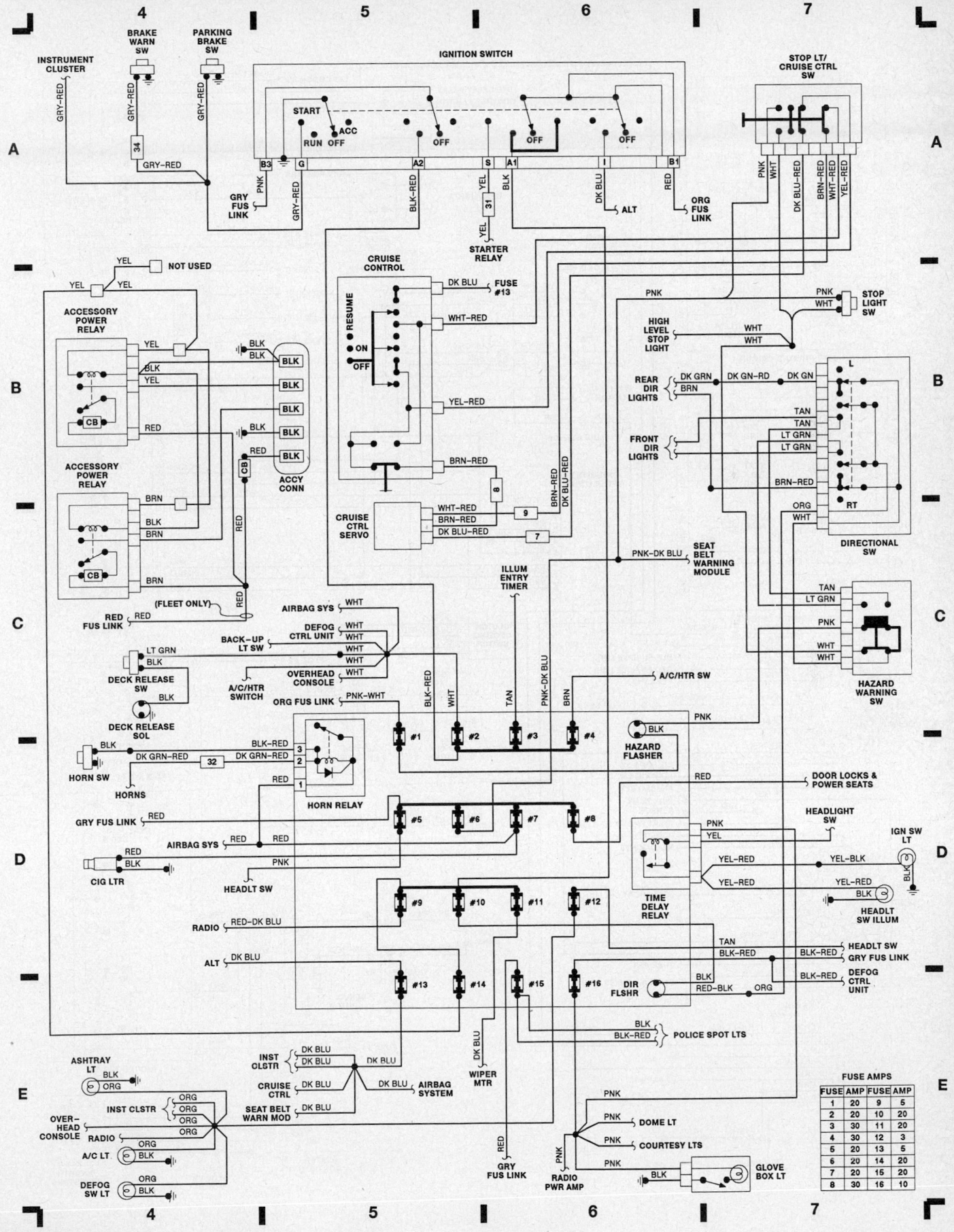

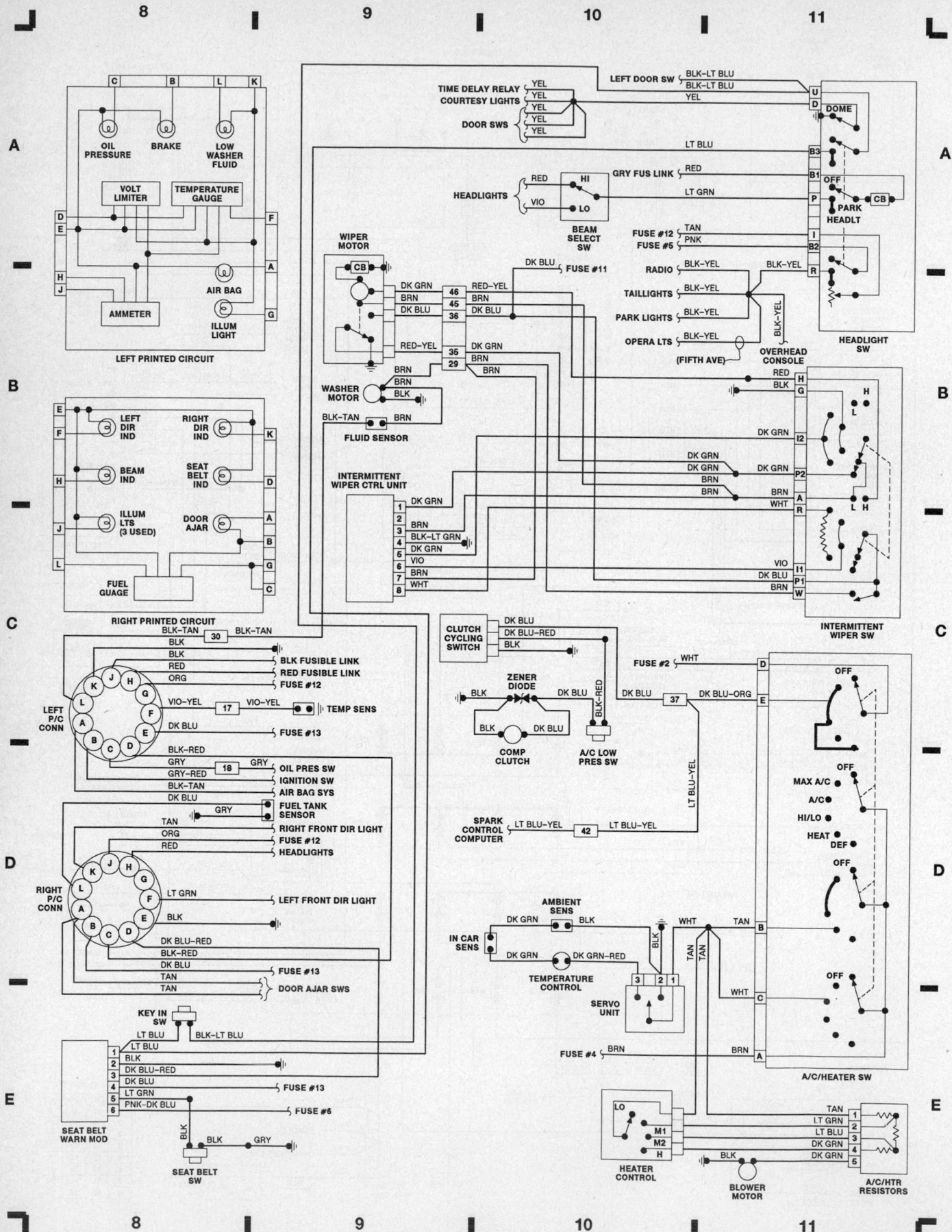

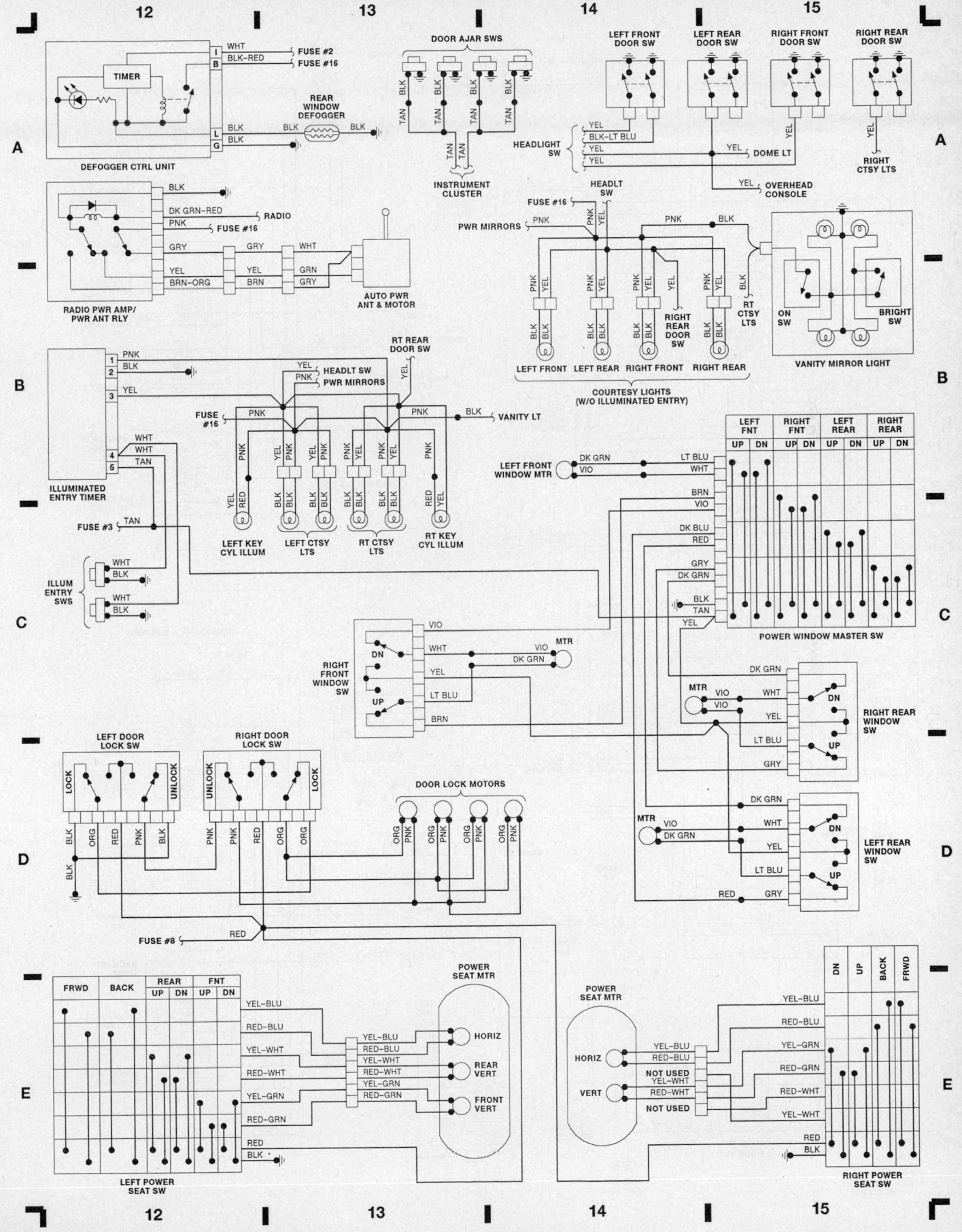

1989 CHRYSLER MOTORS
Diplomat, Fifth Avenue & Gran Fury (Cont.)

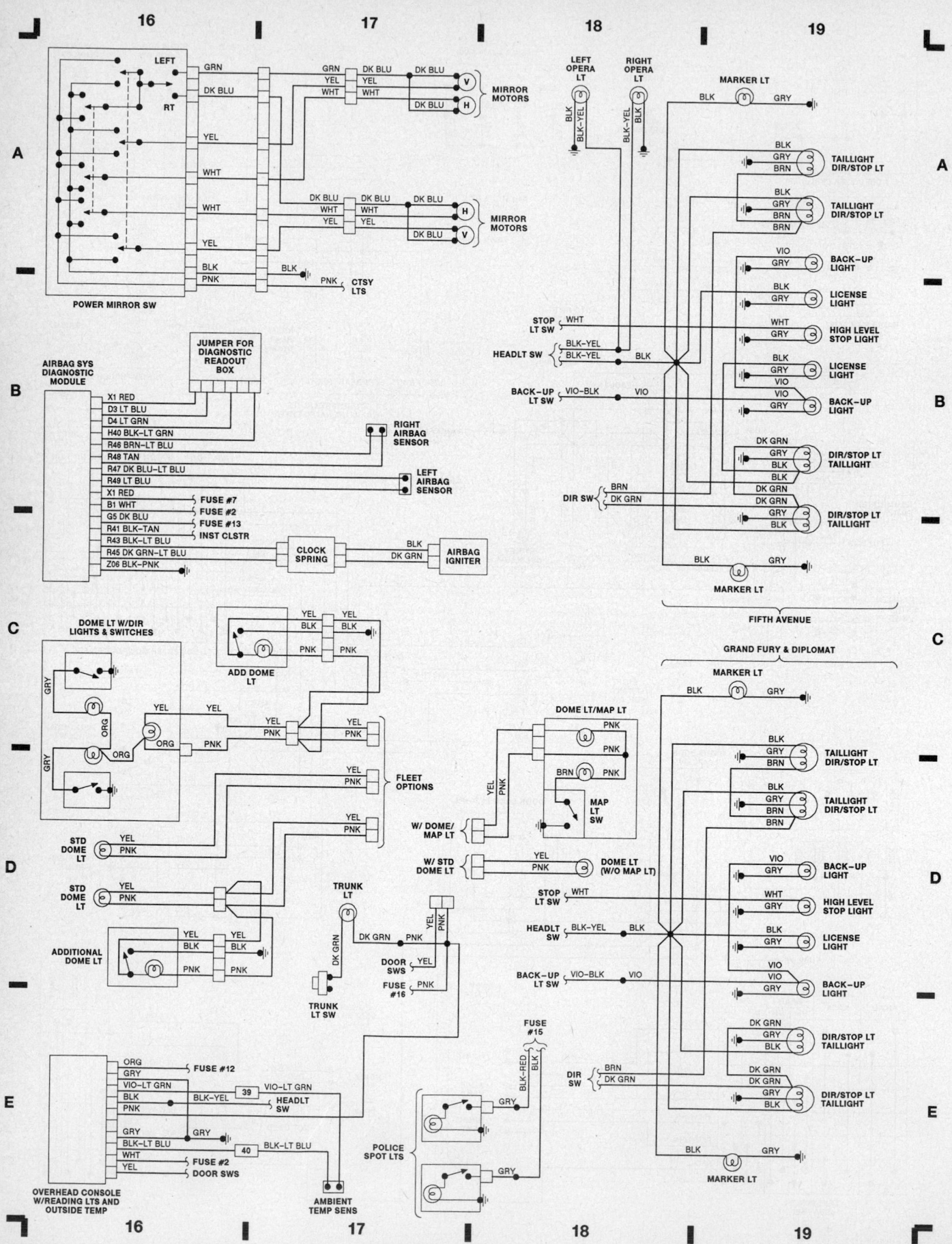

1989 CHRYSLER MOTORS
Dynasty & New Yorker

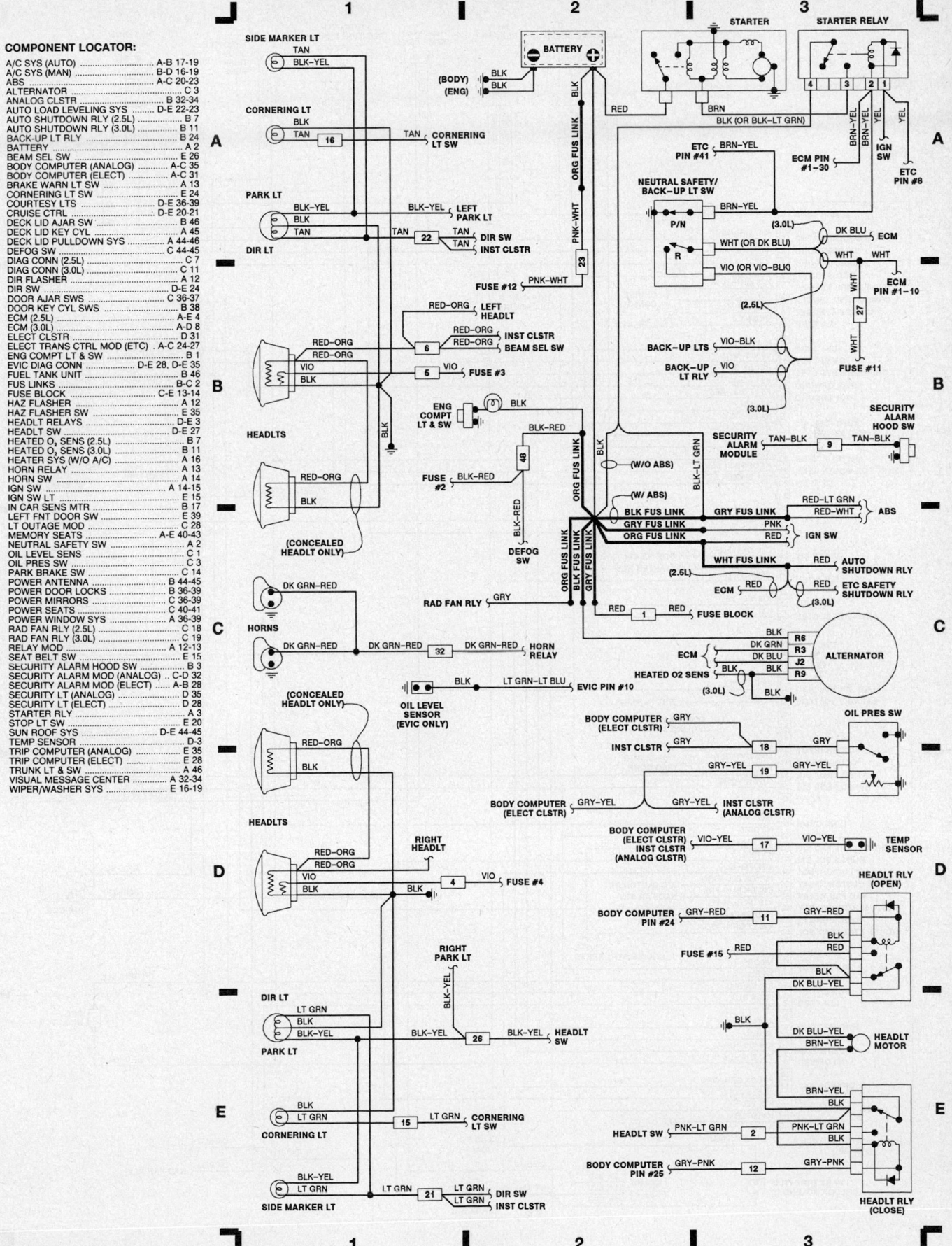

COMPONENT LOCATOR:

A/C SYS (AUTO) .... A-B 17-19
A/C SYS (MAN) .... B-D 16-19
ABS .... A-C 20-23
ALTERNATOR .... C 3
ANALOG CLSTR .... B 32-34
AUTO LOAD LEVELING SYS .... D-E 22-23
AUTO SHUTDOWN RLY (2.5L) .... B 7
AUTO SHUTDOWN RLY (3.0L) .... B 11
BACK-UP LT RLY .... B 24
BATTERY .... A 2
BEAM SEL SW .... E 26
BODY COMPUTER (ANALOG) .... A-C 35
BODY COMPUTER (ELECT) .... A-C 31
BRAKE WARN LT SW .... A 13
CORNERING LT SW .... E 24
COURTESY LTS .... D-E 36-39
CRUISE CTRL .... D-E 20-21
DECK LID AJAR SW .... B 46
DECK LID KEY CYL .... A 45
DECK LID PULLDOWN SYS .... A 44-46
DEFOG SW .... C 44-45
DIAG CONN (2.5L) .... C 7
DIAG CONN (3.0L) .... C 11
DIR FLASHER .... A 12
DIR SW .... D-E 24
DOOR AJAR SWS .... C 36-37
DOOR KEY CYL SWS .... B 38
ECM (2.5L) .... A-E 4
ECM (3.0L) .... A-D 8
ELECT CLSTR .... D 31
ELECT TRANS CTRL MOD (ETC) .... A-C 24-27
ENG COMPT LT & SW .... B 1
EVIC DIAG CONN .... D-E 28, D-E 35
FUEL TANK UNIT .... B 46
FUS LINKS .... B-C 2
FUSE BLOCK .... C-E 13-14
HAZ FLASHER .... A 12
HAZ FLASHER SW .... E 35
HEADLT RELAYS .... D-E 3
HEADLT SW .... D-E 27
HEATED O₂ SENS (2.5L) .... B 7
HEATED O₂ SENS (3.0L) .... B 11
HEATER SYS (W/O A/C) .... A 16
HORN RELAY .... A 13
HORN SW .... A 14
IGN SW .... A 14-15
IGN SW LT .... E 15
IN CAR SENS MTR .... B 17
LEFT FNT DOOR SW .... E 39
LT OUTAGE MOD .... C 28
MEMORY SEATS .... A-E 40-43
NEUTRAL SAFETY SW .... A 2
OIL LEVEL SENS .... C 1
OIL PRES SW .... C 3
PARK BRAKE SW .... C 14
POWER ANTENNA .... B 44-45
POWER DOOR LOCKS .... B 36-39
POWER MIRRORS .... C 36-39
POWER SEATS .... C 40-41
POWER WINDOW SYS .... A 36-39
RAD FAN RLY (2.5L) .... C 18
RAD FAN RLY (3.0L) .... C 19
RELAY MOD .... A 12-13
SEAT BELT SW .... E 15
SECURITY ALARM HOOD SW .... B 3
SECURITY ALARM MOD (ANALOG) .... C-D 32
SECURITY ALARM MOD (ELECT) .... A-B 28
SECURITY LT (ANALOG) .... D 35
SECURITY LT (ELECT) .... D 28
STARTER RLY .... A 3
STOP LT SW .... E 20
SUN ROOF SYS .... D-E 44-45
TEMP SENSOR D-3
TRIP COMPUTER (ANALOG) .... E 35
TRIP COMPUTER (ELECT) .... E 28
TRUNK LT & SW .... A 46
VISUAL MESSAGE CENTER .... A 32-34
WIPER/WASHER SYS .... E 16-19

1989 CHRYSLER MOTORS
Dynasty & New Yorker (Cont.)

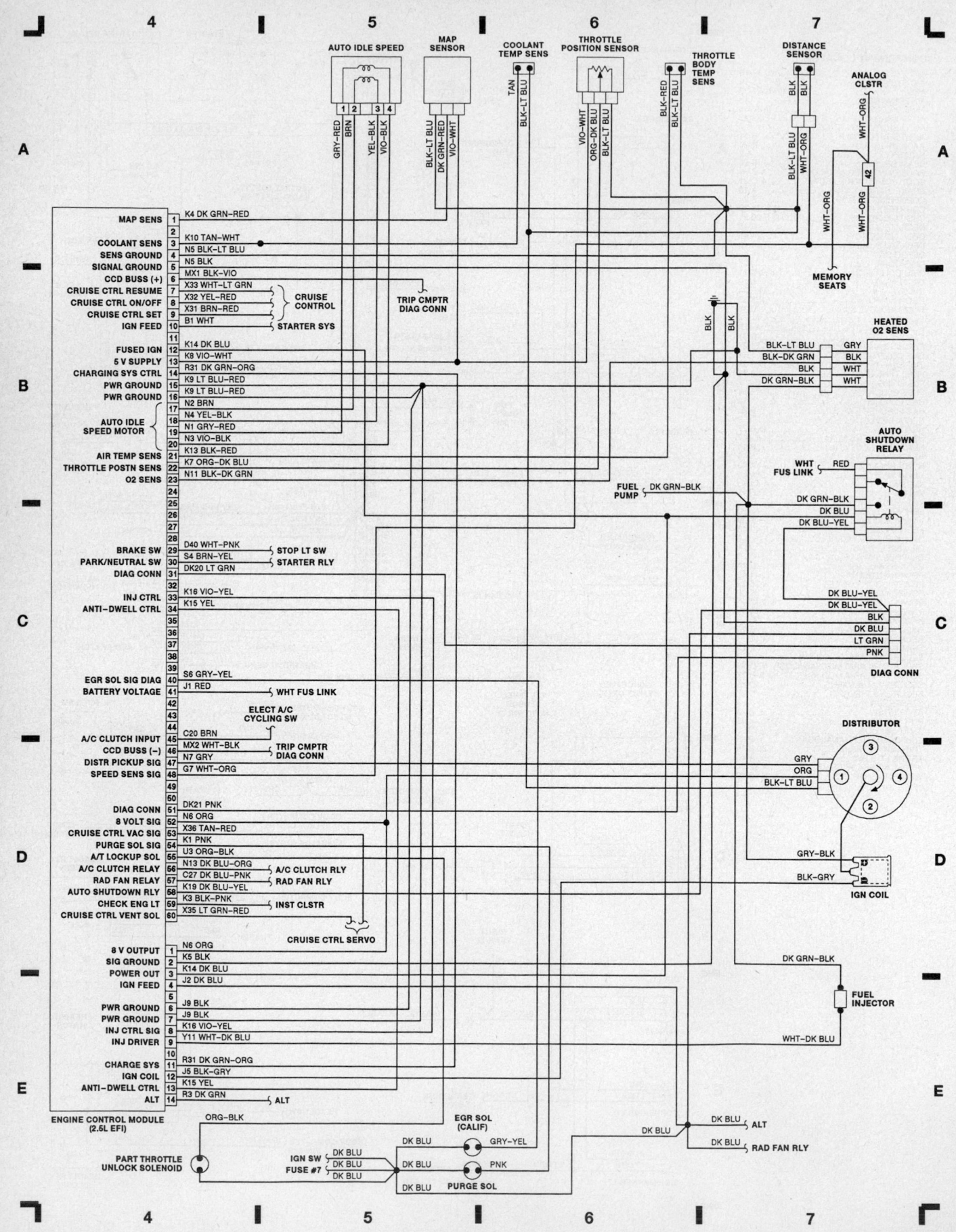

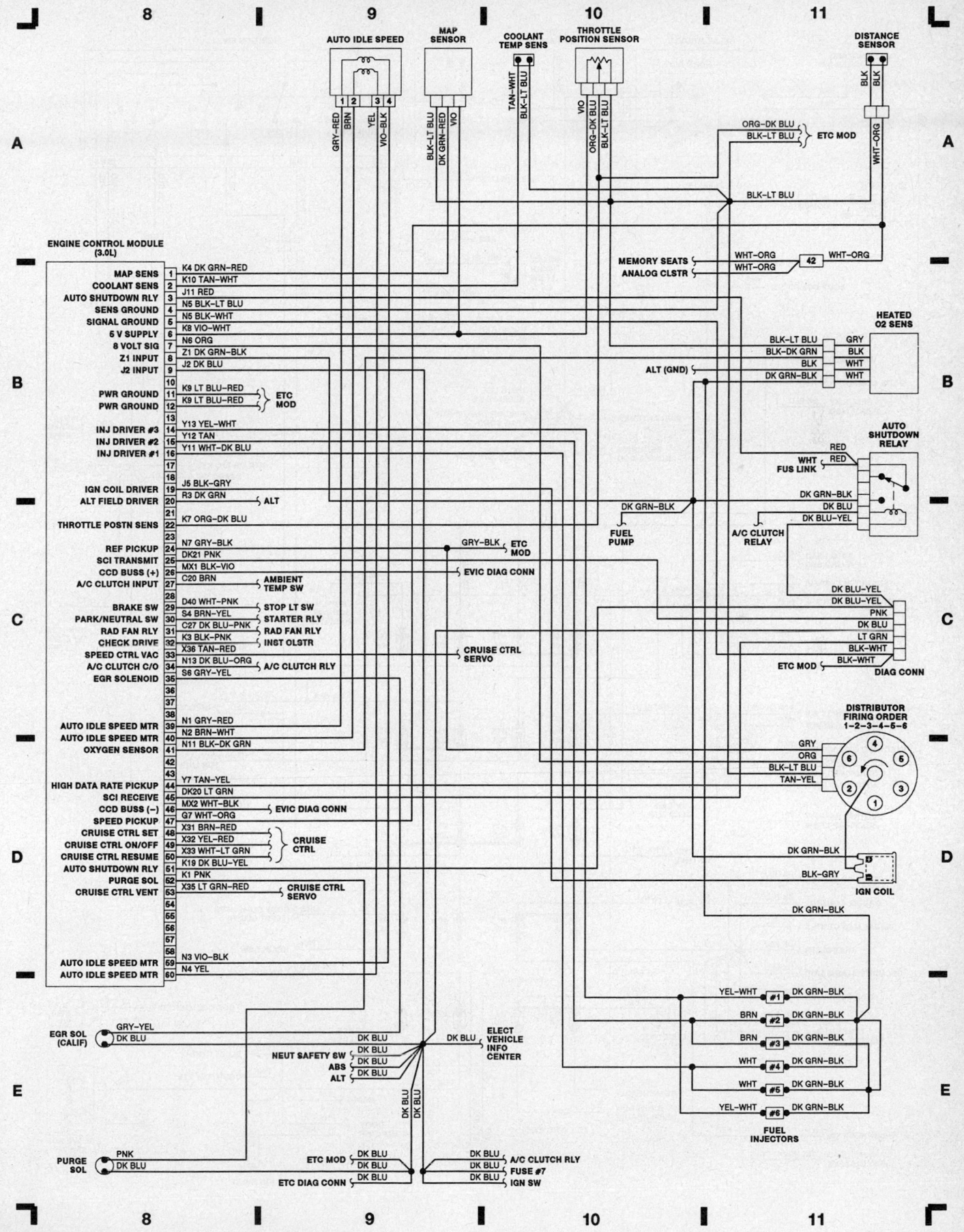

1989 CHRYSLER MOTORS
Dynasty & New Yorker (Cont.)

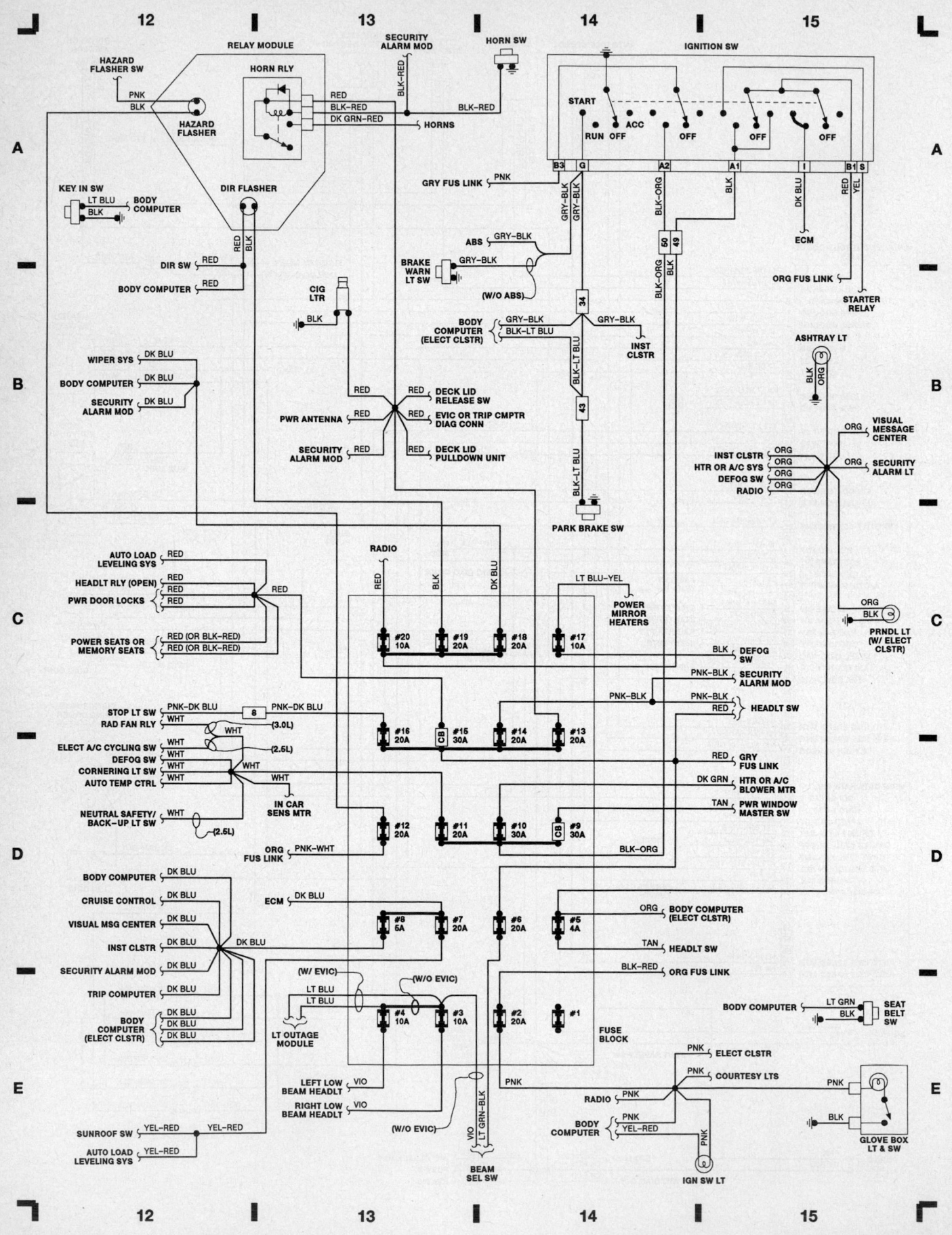

1989 CHRYSLER MOTORS
Dynasty & New Yorker (Cont.)

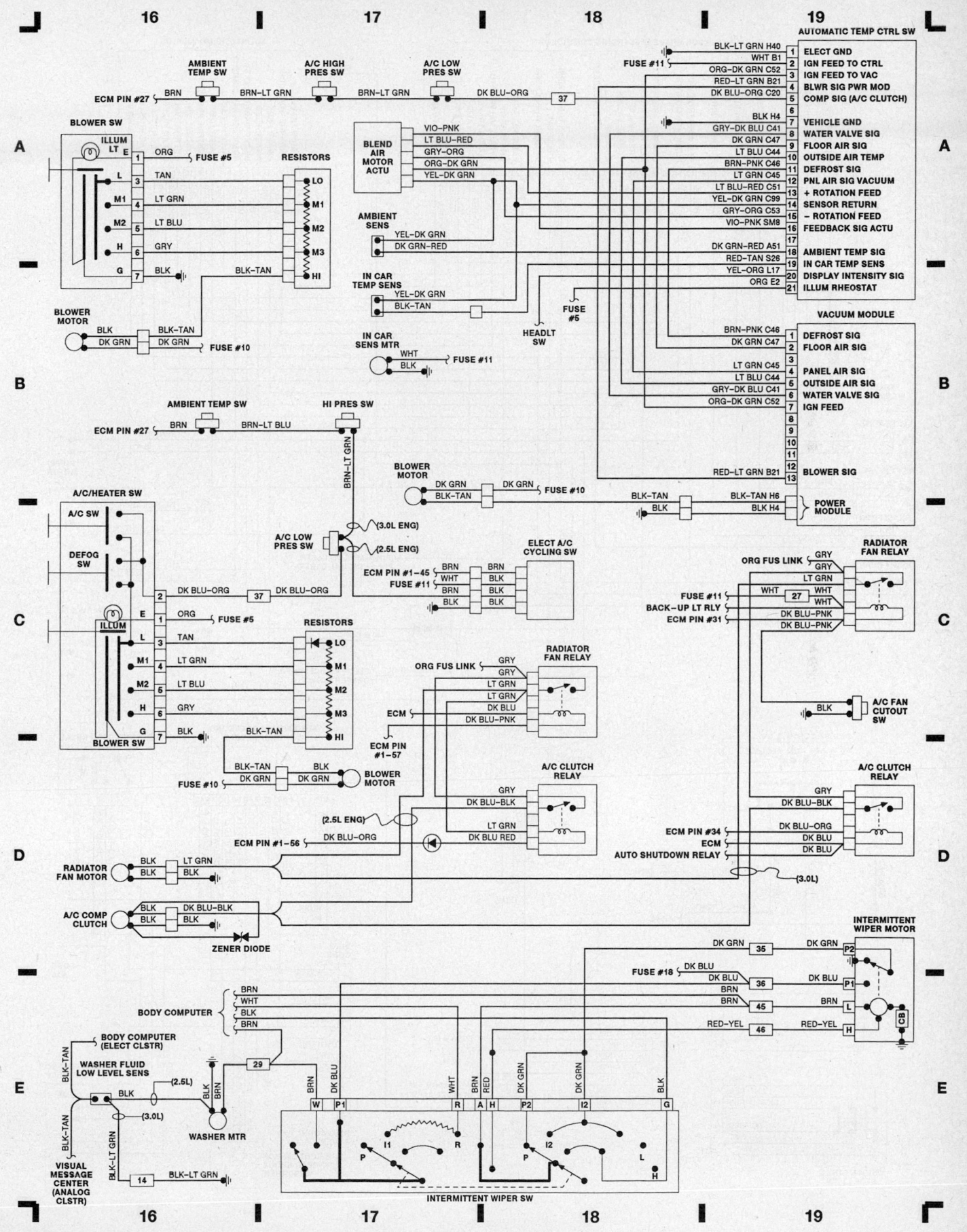

1989 CHRYSLER MOTORS
Dynasty & New Yorker (Cont.)

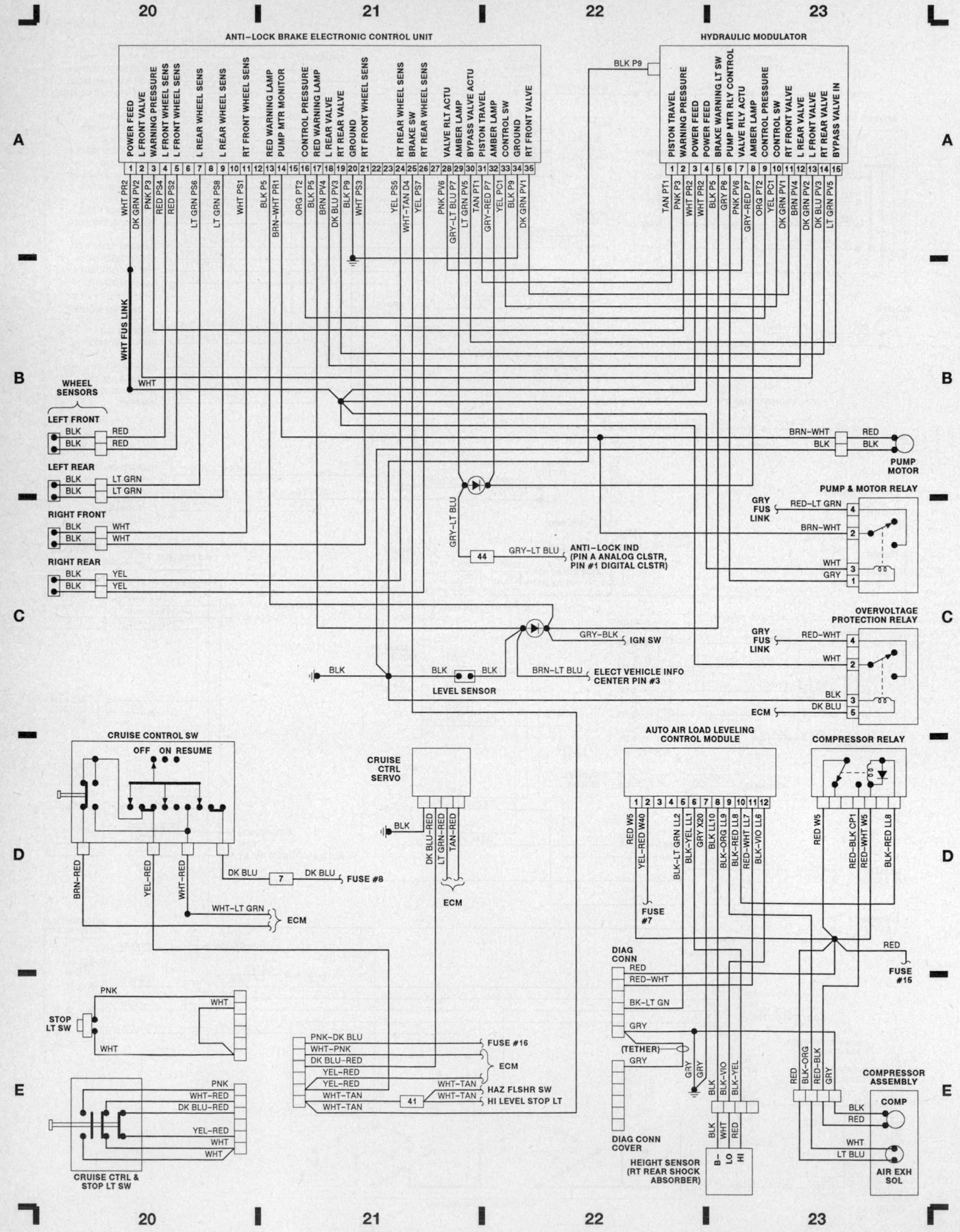

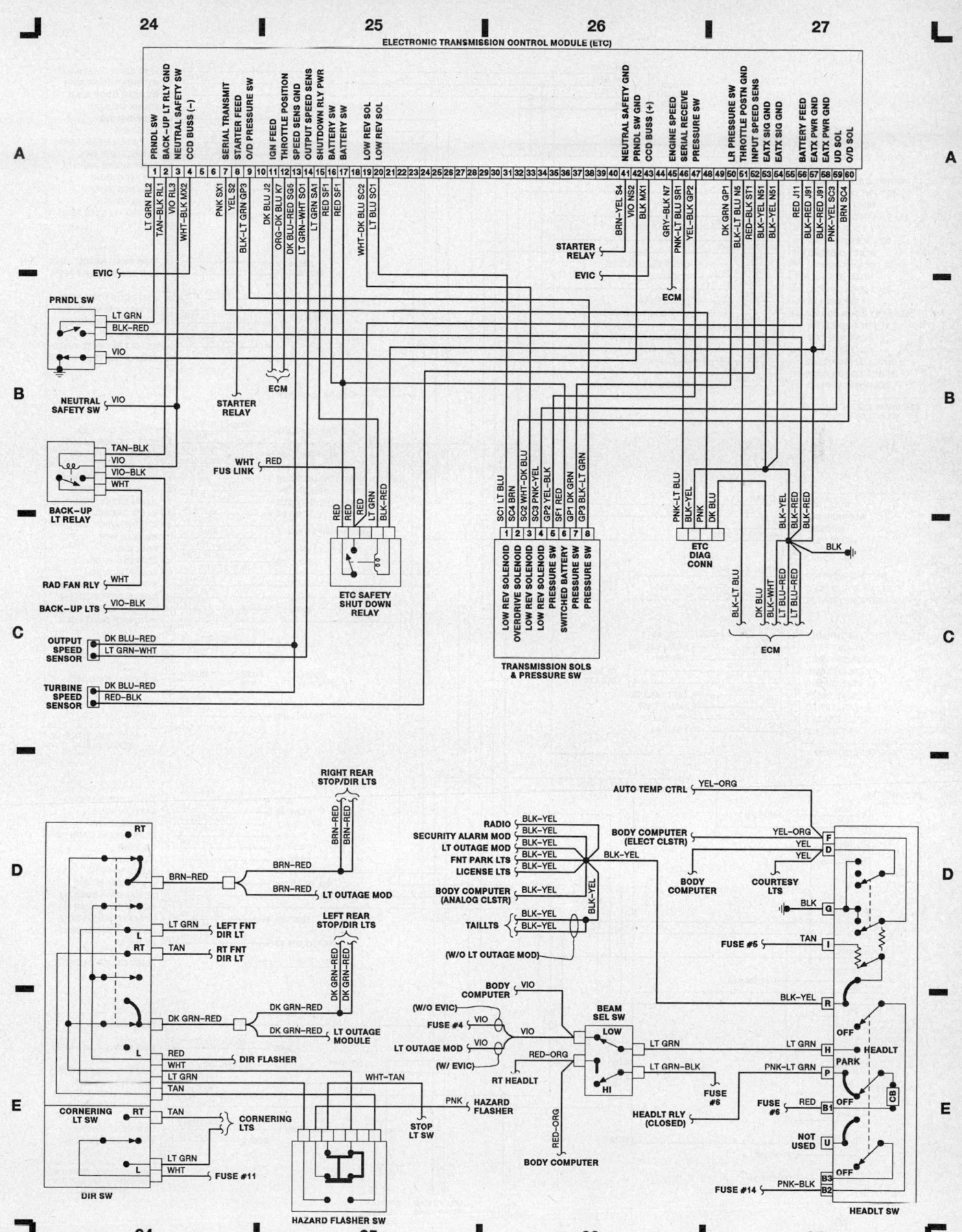

1989 CHRYSLER MOTORS
Dynasty & New Yorker (Cont.)

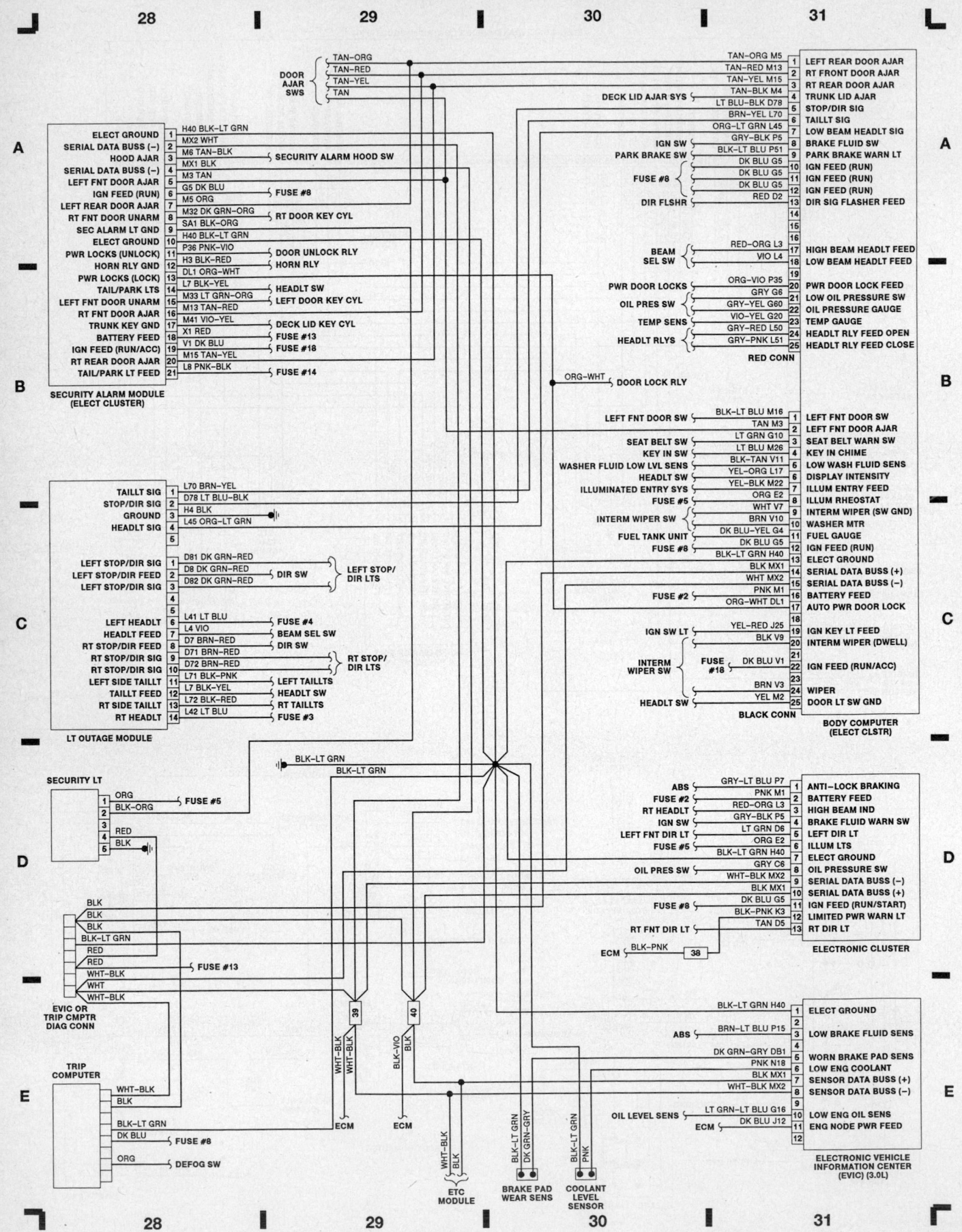

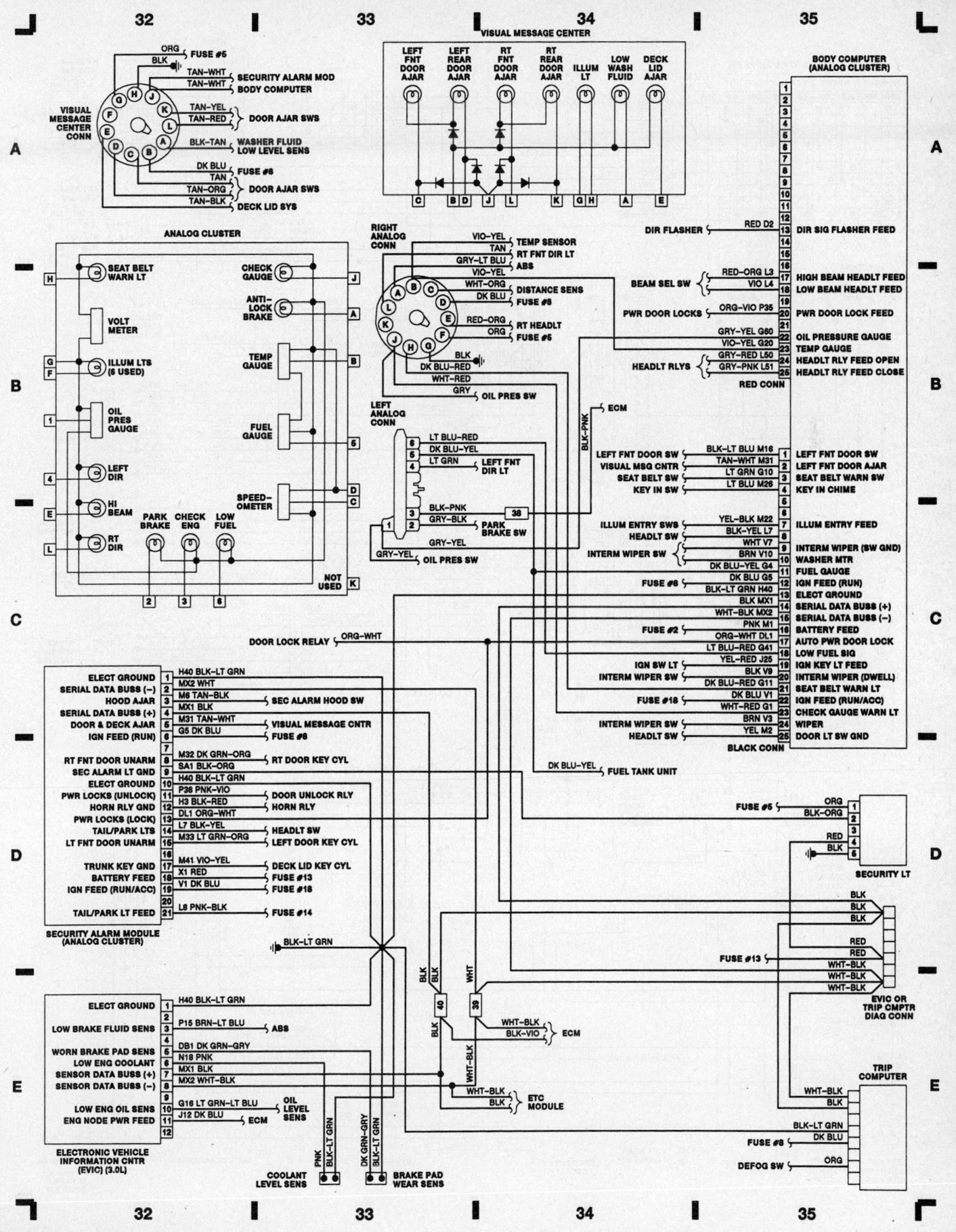

1989 CHRYSLER MOTORS
Dynasty & New Yorker (Cont.)

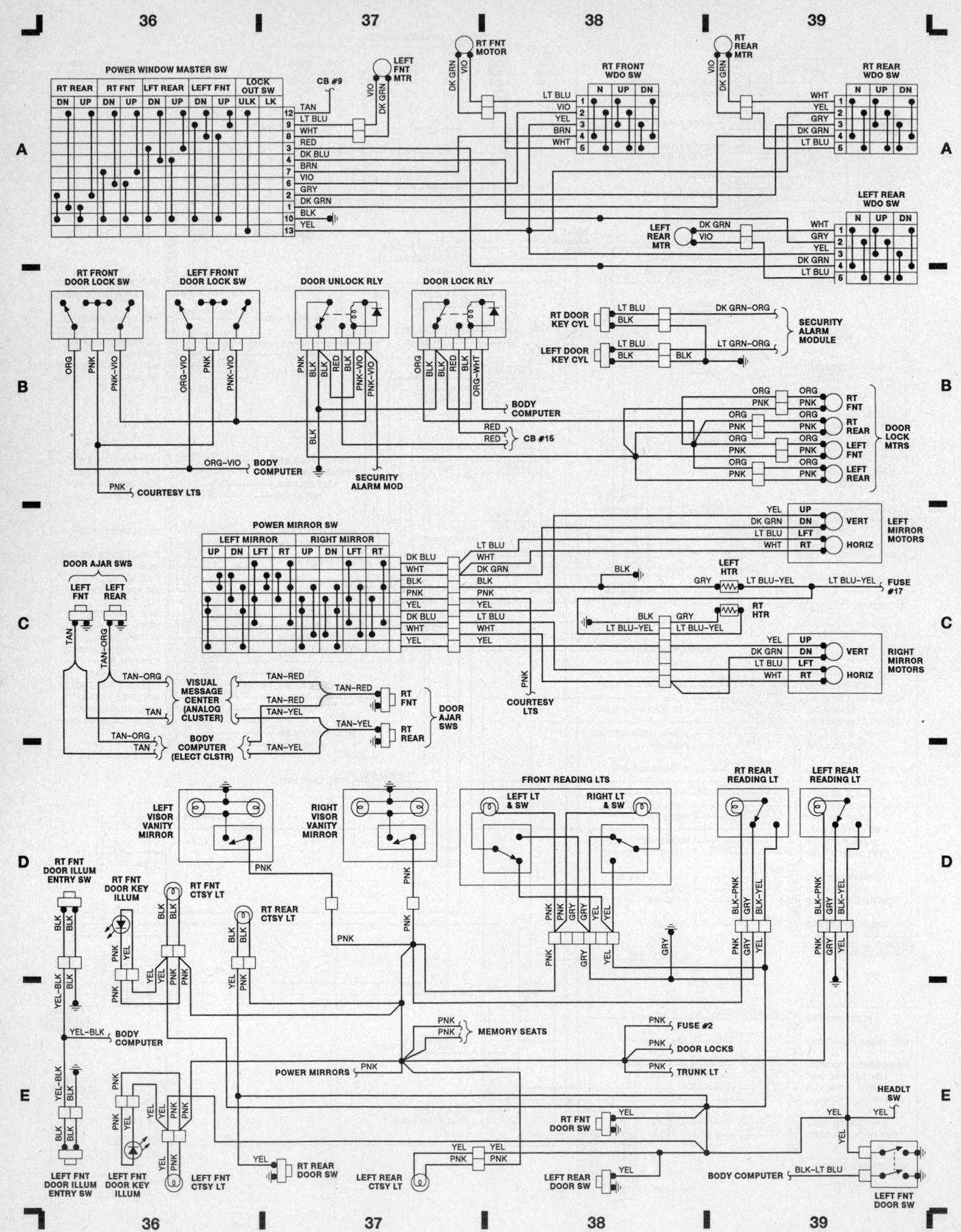

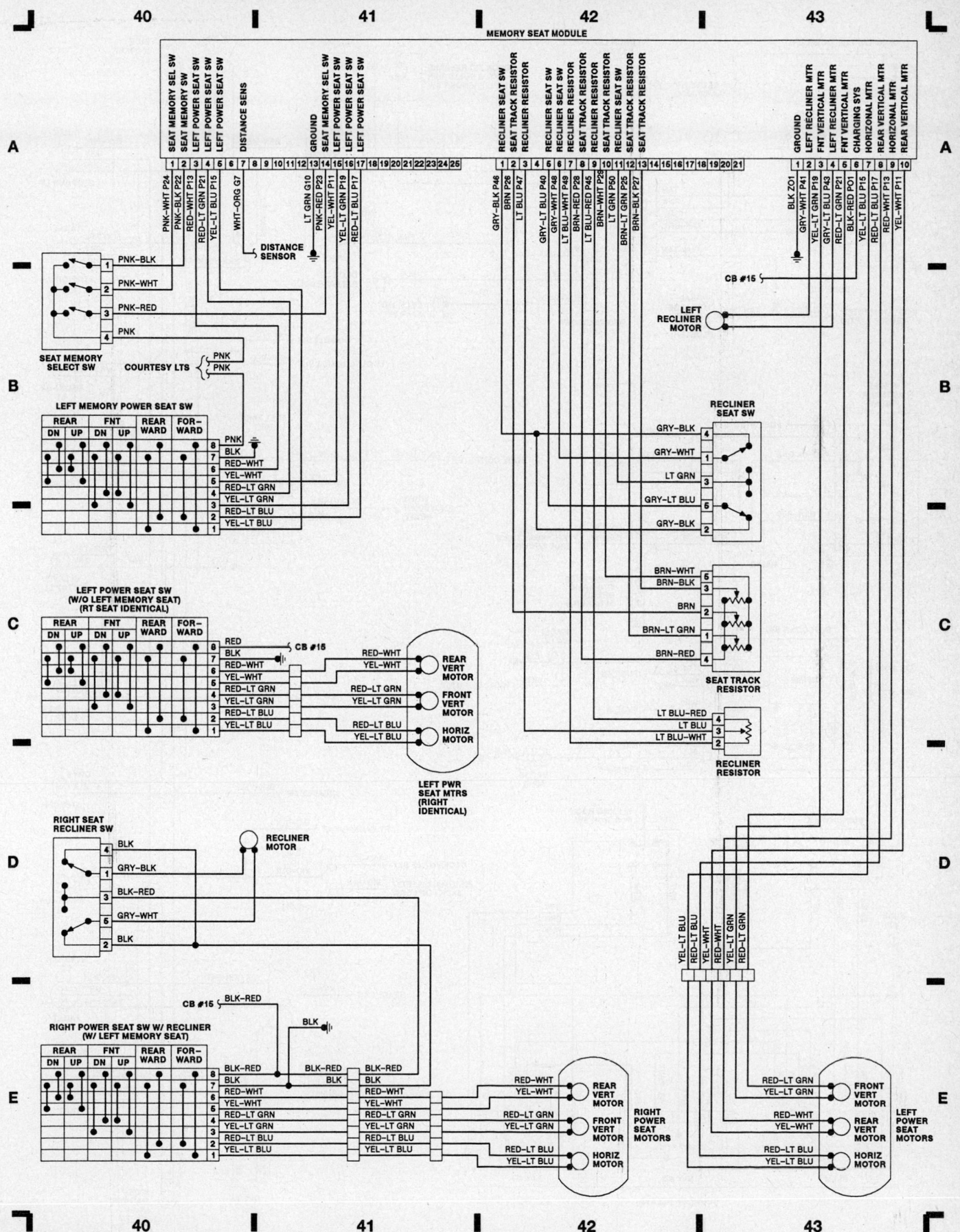

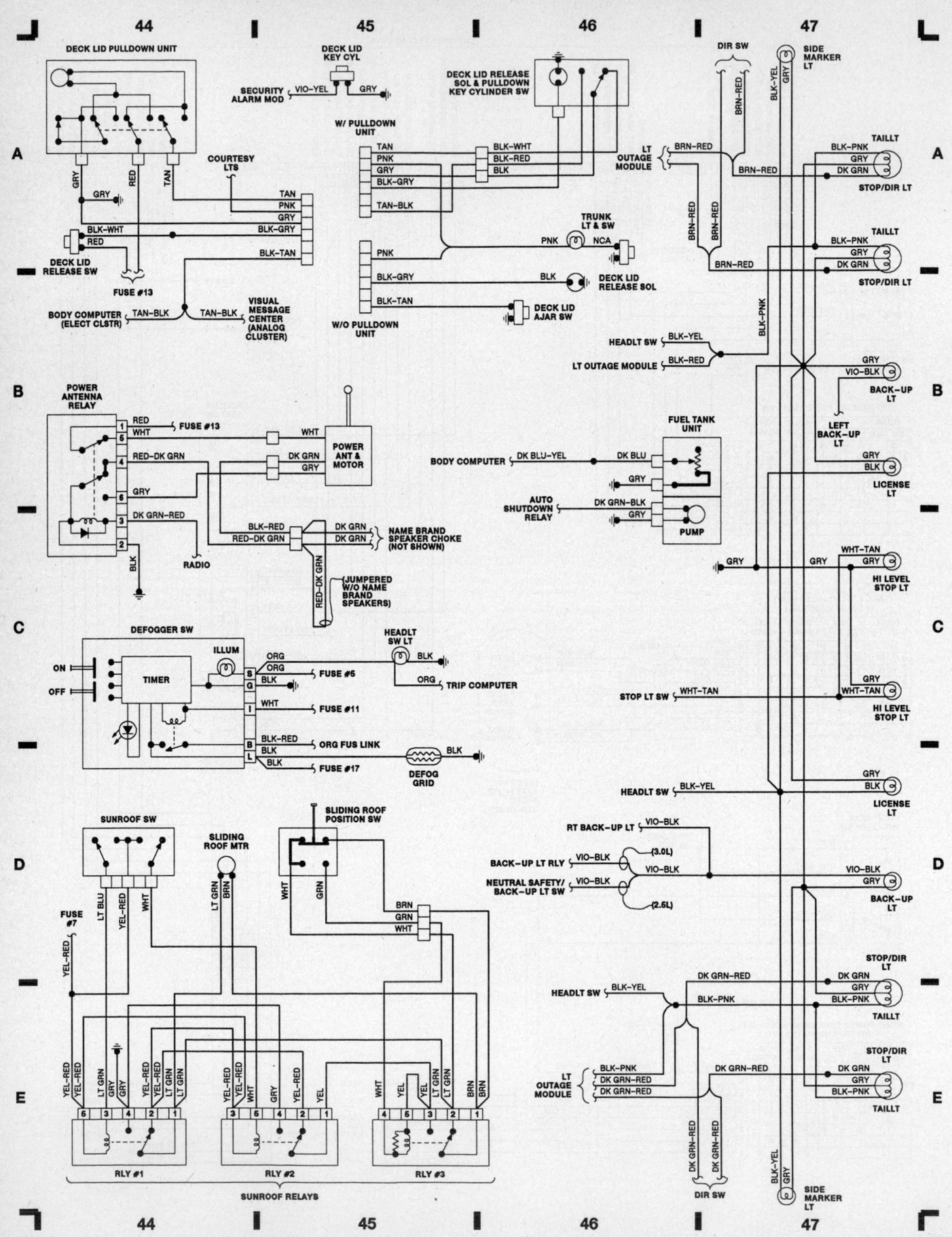

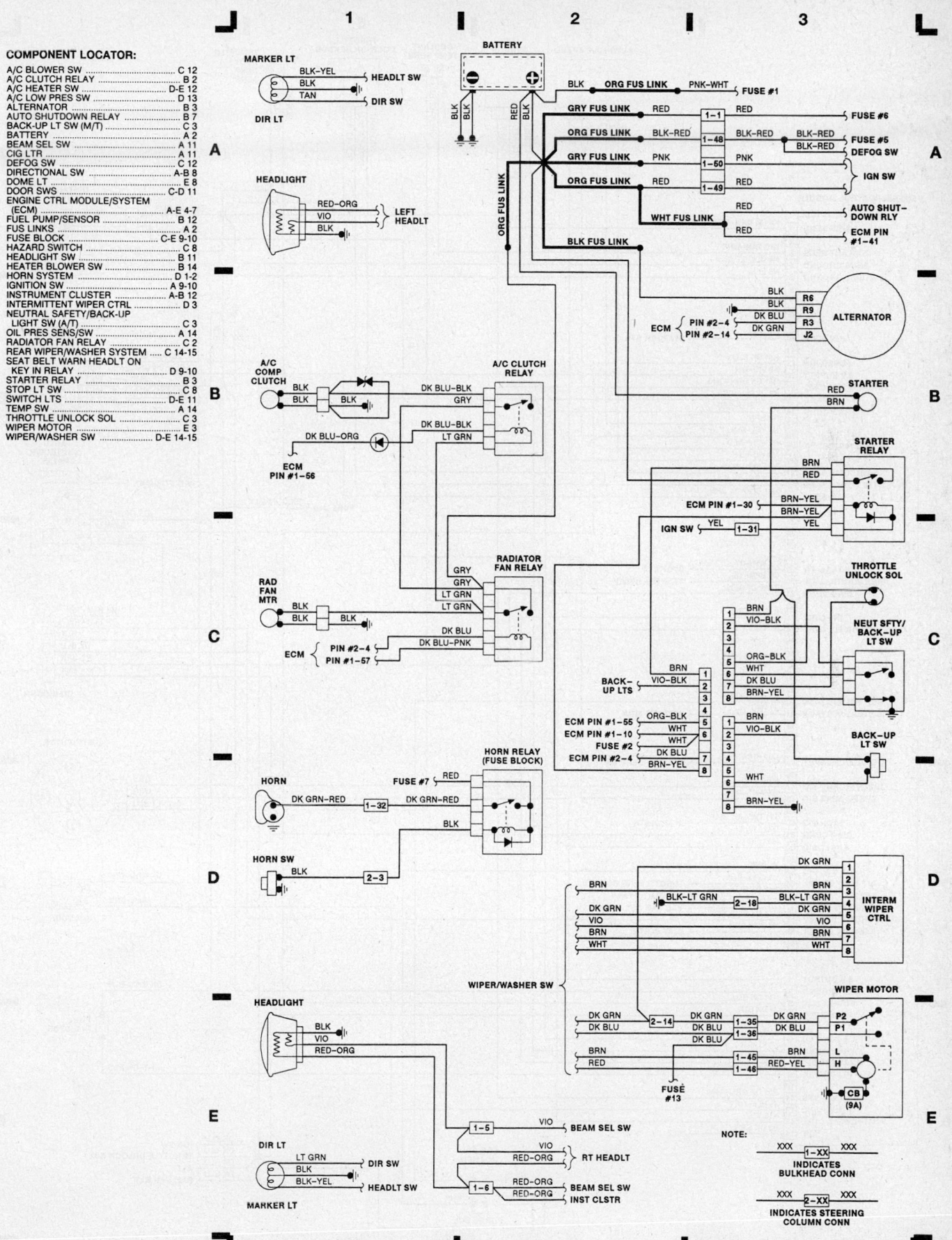

COMPONENT LOCATOR:

A/C BLOWER SW	C 12
A/C CLUTCH RELAY	B 2
A/C HEATER SW	D-E 12
A/C LOW PRES SW	D 13
ALTERNATOR	B 3
AUTO SHUTDOWN RELAY	B 7
BACK-UP LT SW (M/T)	C 3
BATTERY	A 2
BEAM SEL SW	A 11
CIG LTR	A 11
DEFOG SW	C 12
DIRECTIONAL SW	A-B 8
DOME LT	E 8
DOOR SWS	C-D 11
ENGINE CTRL MODULE/SYSTEM (ECM)	A-E 4-7
FUEL PUMP/SENSOR	B 12
FUS LINKS	A 2
FUSE BLOCK	C-E 9-10
HAZARD SWITCH	C 8
HEADLIGHT SW	B 11
HEATER BLOWER SW	B 14
HORN SYSTEM	D 1-2
IGNITION SW	A 9-10
INSTRUMENT CLUSTER	A-B 12
INTERMITTENT WIPER CTRL	D 3
NEUTRAL SAFETY/BACK-UP LIGHT SW (A/T)	C 3
OIL PRES SENS/SW	A 14
RADIATOR FAN RELAY	C 2
REAR WIPER/WASHER SYSTEM	C 14-15
SEAT BELT WARN HEADLT ON KEY IN RELAY	D 9-10
STARTER RELAY	B 3
STOP LT SW	C 8
SWITCH LTS	D-E 11
TEMP SW	A 14
THROTTLE UNLOCK SOL	C 3
WIPER MOTOR	E 3
WIPER/WASHER SW	D-E 14-15

1989 CHRYSLER MOTORS
Horizon & Omni (Cont.)

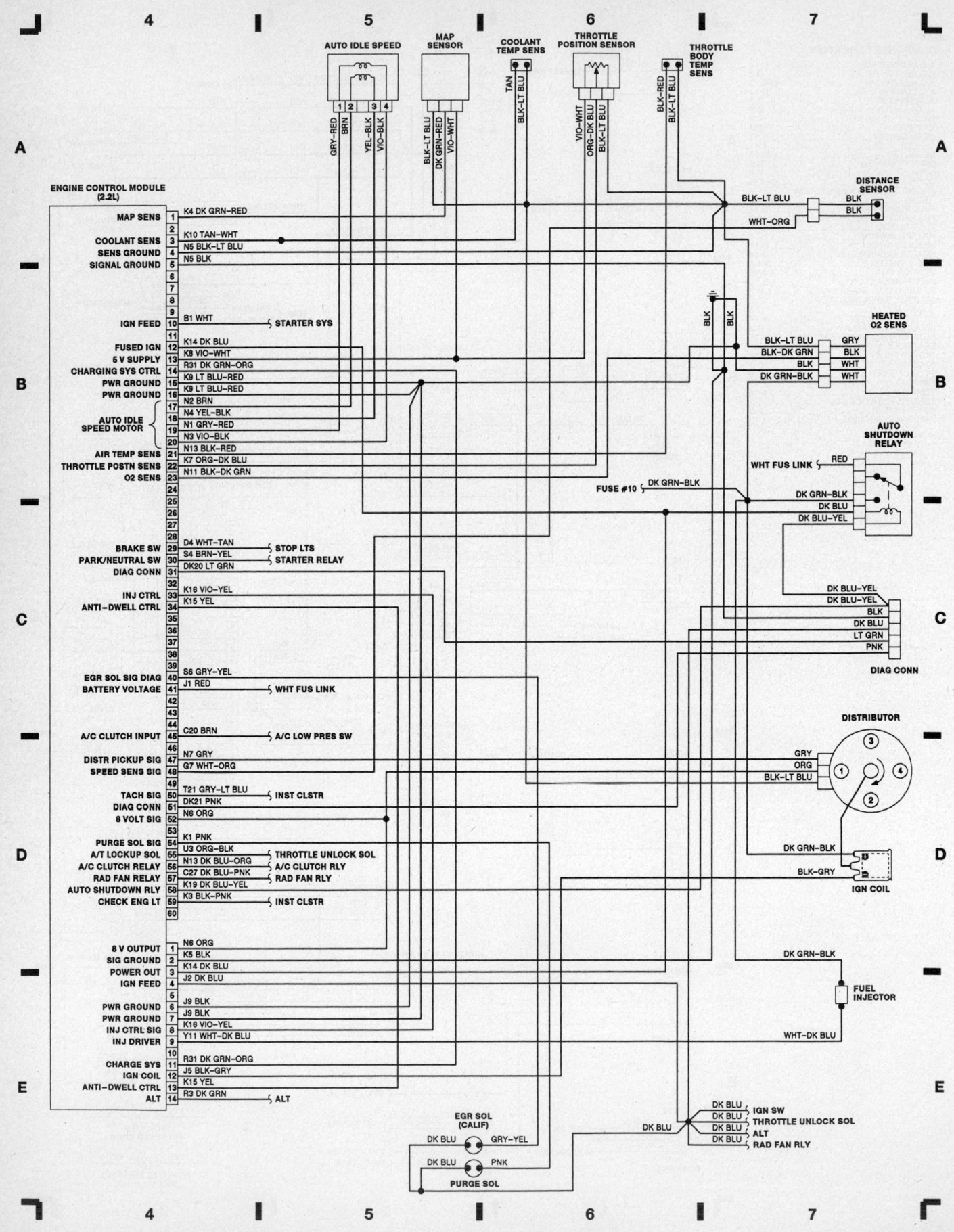

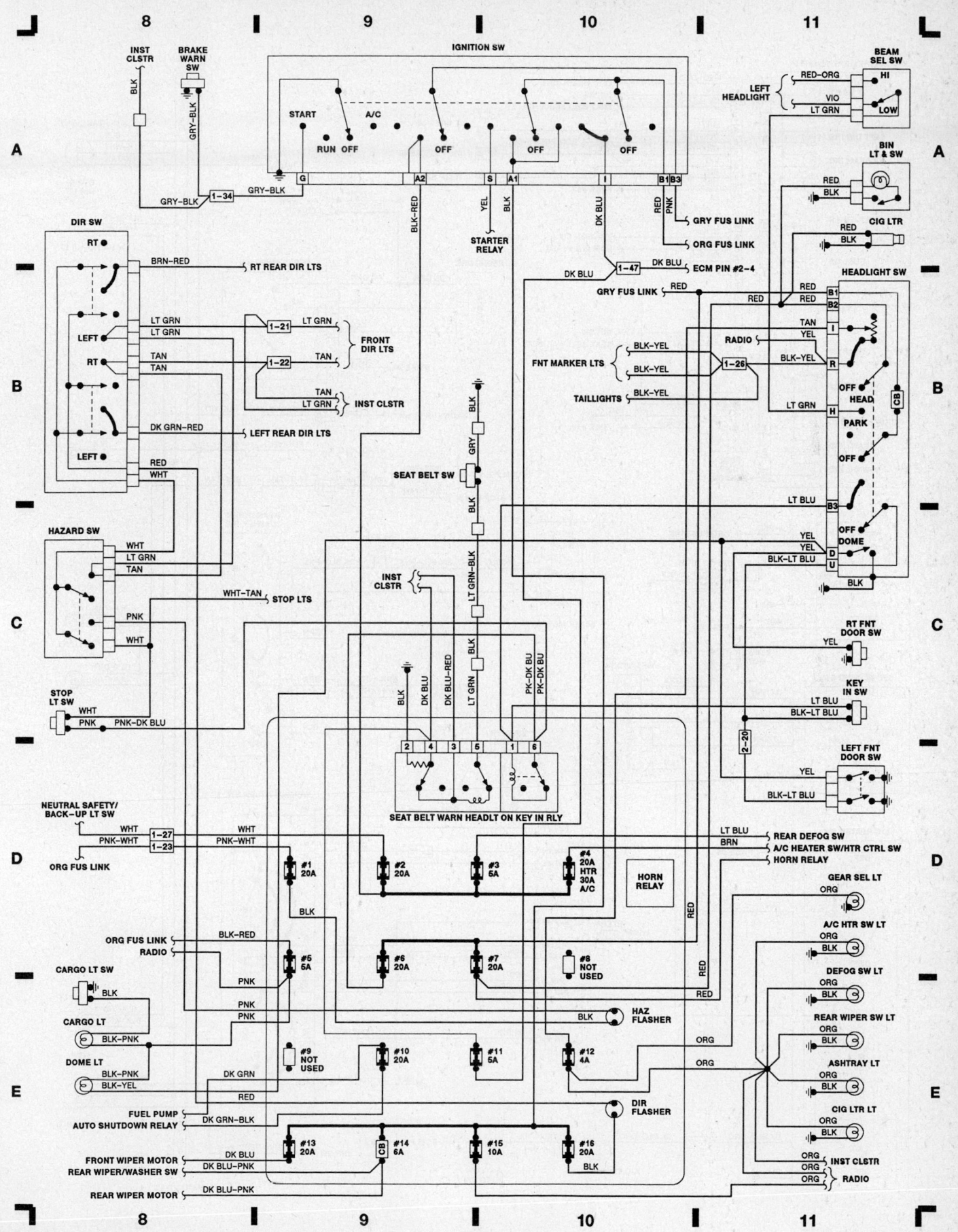

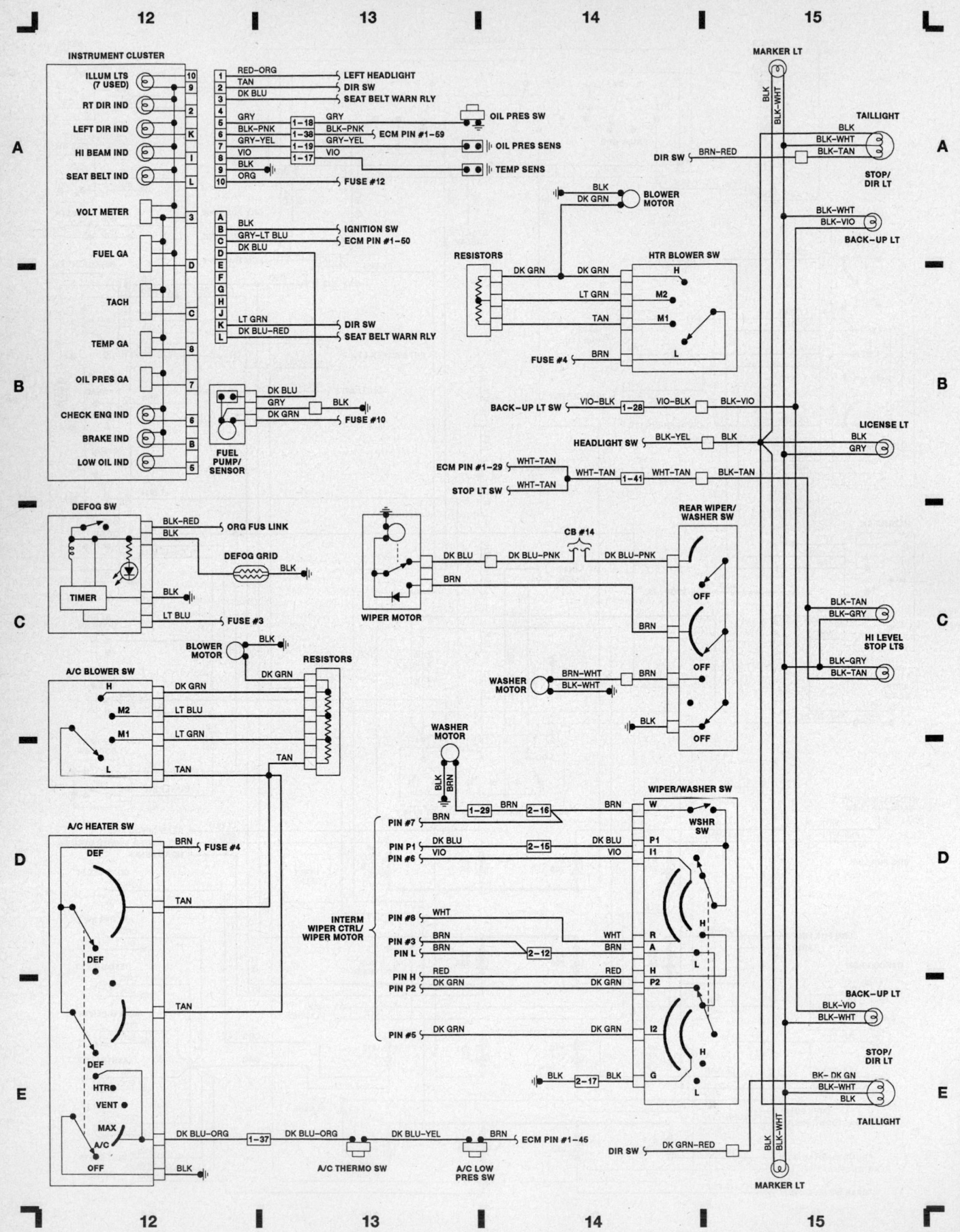

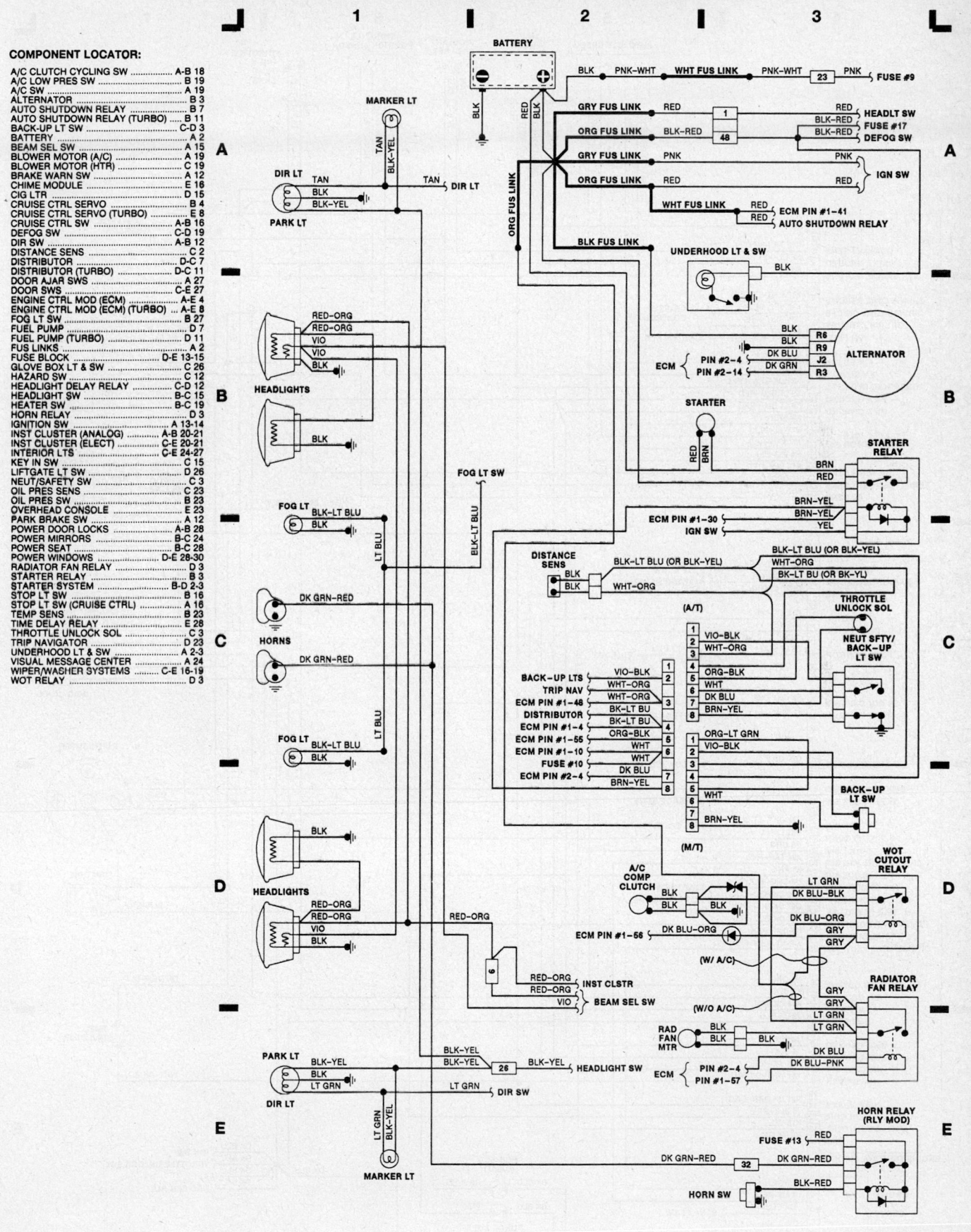

COMPONENT LOCATOR:

A/C CLUTCH CYCLING SW .... A-B 18
A/C LOW PRES SW .... B 19
A/C SW .... A 19
ALTERNATOR .... B 3
AUTO SHUTDOWN RELAY .... B 7
AUTO SHUTDOWN RELAY (TURBO) ... B 11
BACK-UP LT SW .... C-D 3
BATTERY .... A 2
BEAM SEL SW .... A 15
BLOWER MOTOR (A/C) .... A 19
BLOWER MOTOR (HTR) .... C 19
BRAKE WARN SW .... A 12
CHIME MODULE .... E 16
CIG LTR .... D 15
CRUISE CTRL SERVO .... B 4
CRUISE CTRL SERVO (TURBO) ...... E 8
CRUISE CTRL SW .... A-B 16
DEFOG SW .... C-D 19
DIR SW .... A-B 12
DISTANCE SENS .... C 2
DISTRIBUTOR .... D-C 7
DISTRIBUTOR (TURBO) .... D-C 11
DOOR AJAR SWS .... A 27
DOOR SWS .... C-E 27
ENGINE CTRL MOD (ECM) .... A-E 4
ENGINE CTRL MOD (ECM) (TURBO) ... A-E 8
FOG LT SW .... B 27
FUEL PUMP .... D 7
FUEL PUMP (TURBO) .... D 11
FUS LINKS .... A 2
FUSE BLOCK .... D-E 13-15
GLOVE BOX LT & SW .... C 26
HAZARD SW .... C 12
HEADLIGHT DELAY RELAY .... C-D 12
HEADLIGHT SW .... B-C 15
HEATER SW .... B-C 19
HORN RELAY .... D 3
IGNITION SW .... A 13-14
INST CLUSTER (ANALOG) .... A-B 20-21
INST CLUSTER (ELECT) .... C-E 20-21
INTERIOR LTS .... C-E 24-27
KEY IN SW .... C 15
LIFTGATE LT SW .... D 26
NEUT/SAFETY SW .... C 3
OIL PRES SENS .... C 23
OIL PRES SW .... B 23
OVERHEAD CONSOLE .... E 23
PARK BRAKE SW .... A 12
POWER DOOR LOCKS .... A-B 28
POWER MIRRORS .... B-C 24
POWER SEAT .... B-C 28
POWER WINDOWS .... D-E 28-30
RADIATOR FAN RELAY .... D 3
STARTER RELAY .... B 3
STARTER SYSTEM .... B-D 2-3
STOP LT SW .... B 16
STOP LT SW (CRUISE CTRL) .... A 16
TEMP SENS .... B 23
TIME DELAY RELAY .... E 28
THROTTLE UNLOCK SOL .... C 3
TRIP NAVIGATOR .... D 23
UNDERHOOD LT & SW .... A 2-3
VISUAL MESSAGE CENTER .... A 24
WIPER/WASHER SYSTEMS .... C-E 16-19
WOT RELAY .... D 3

1989 CHRYSLER MOTORS
Lancer & LeBaron Sedan (Cont.)

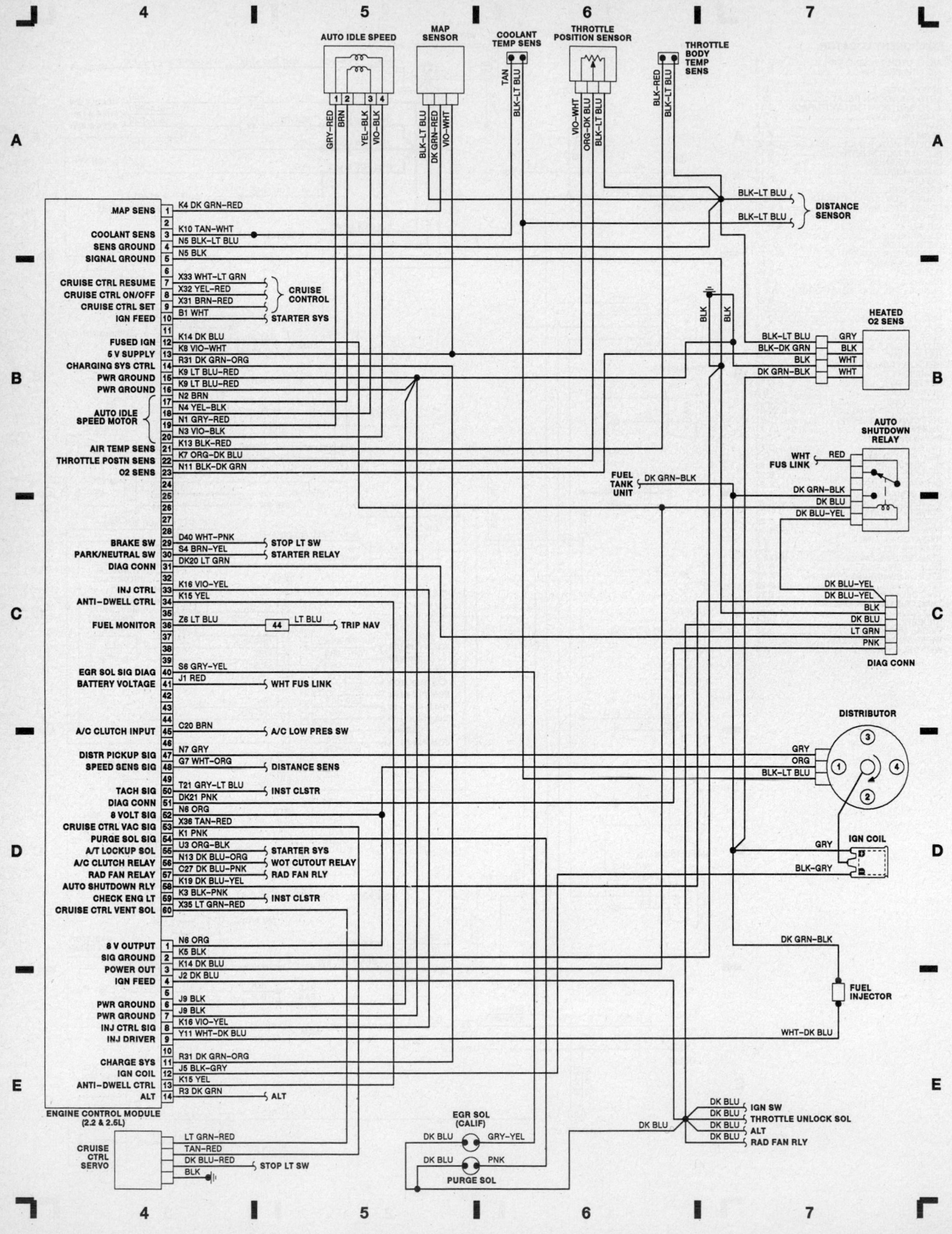

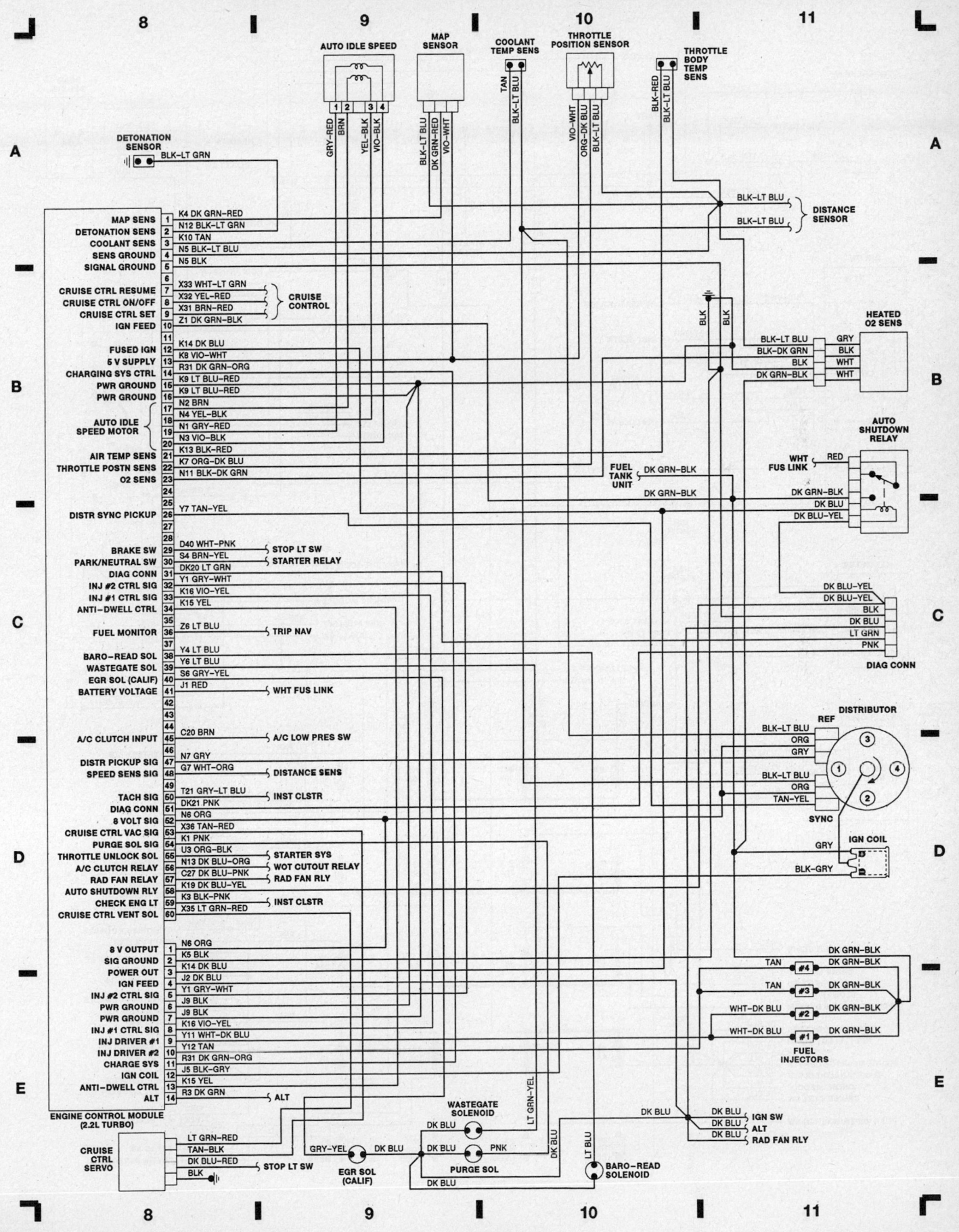

1989 CHRYSLER MOTORS
Lancer & LeBaron Sedan (Cont.)

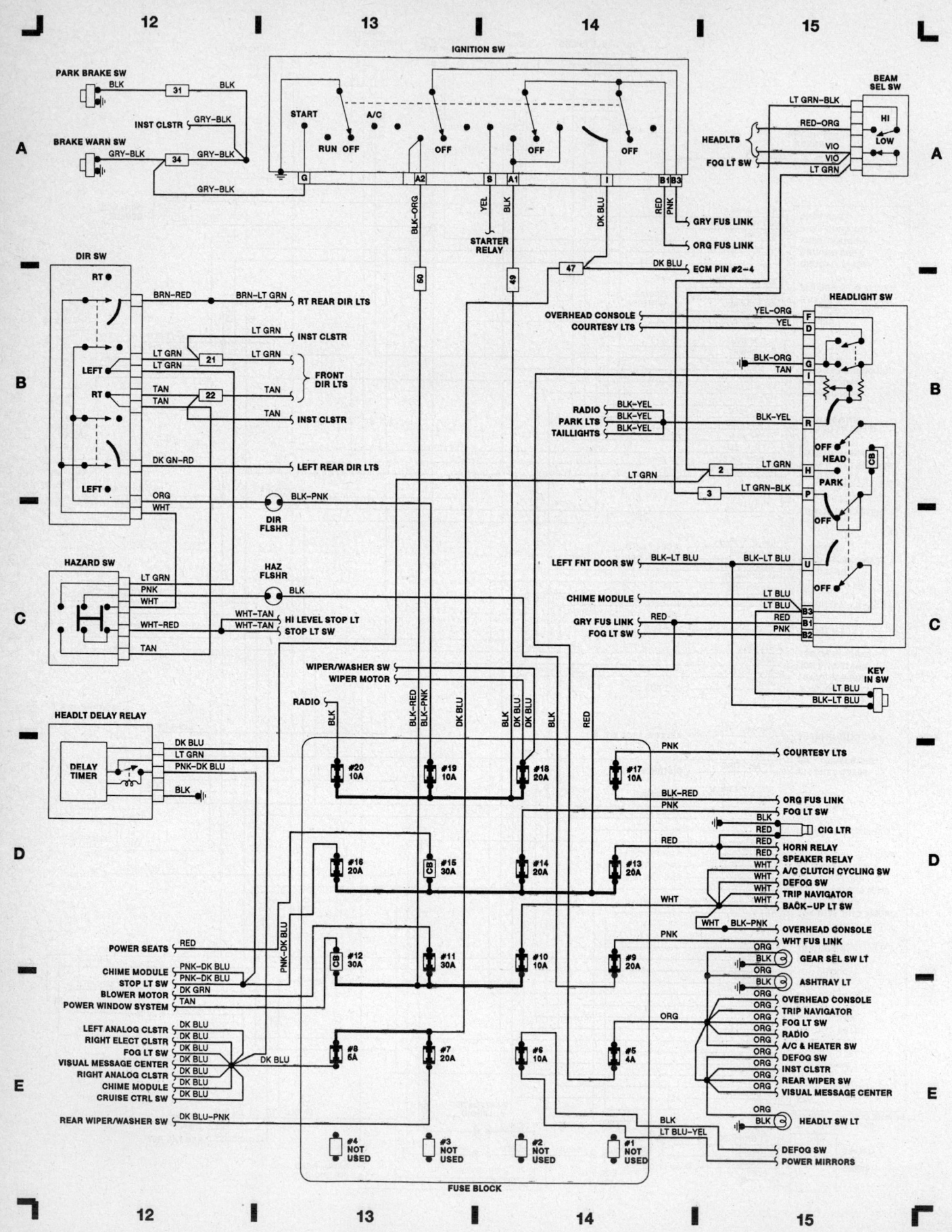

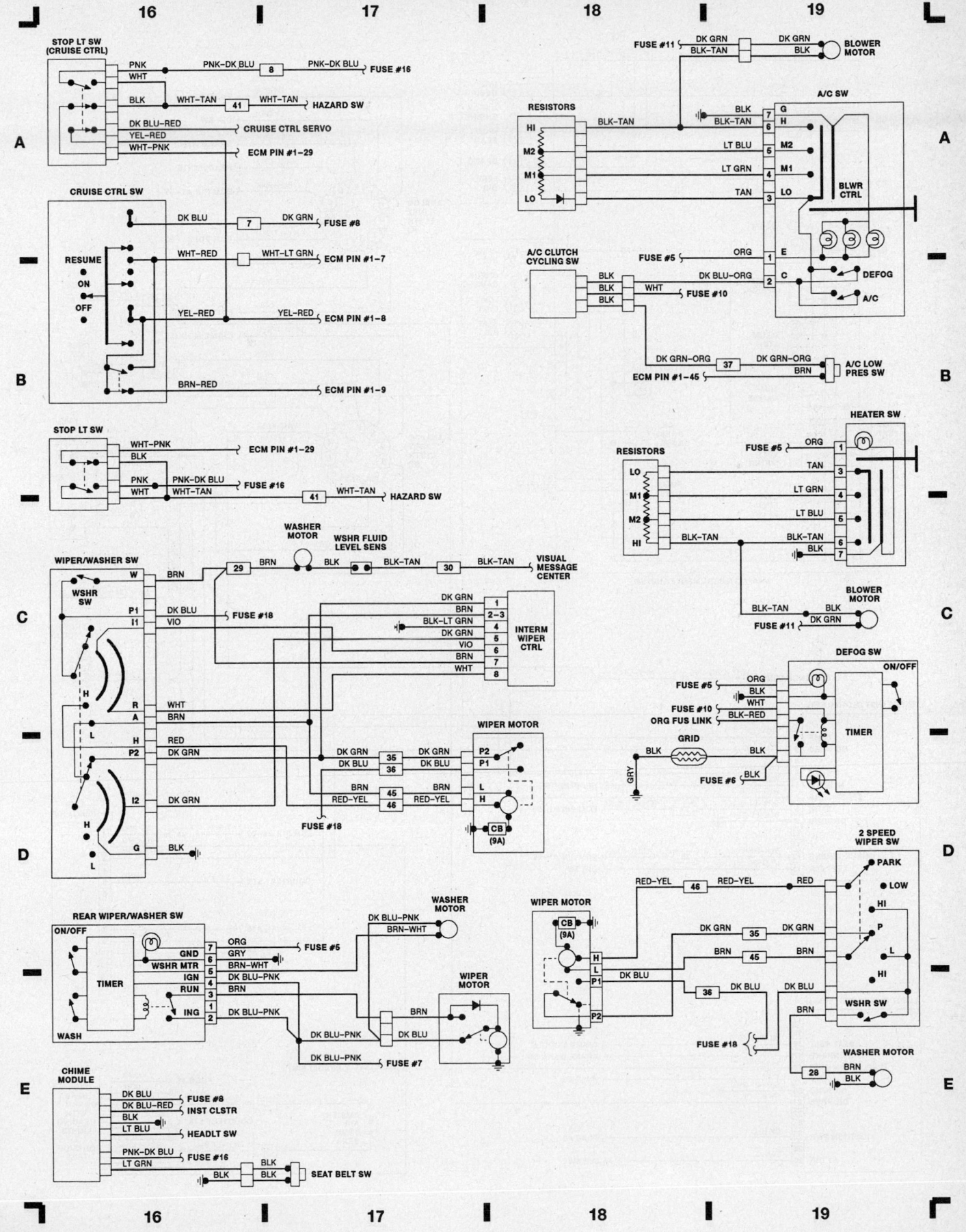

1989 CHRYSLER MOTORS
Lancer & LeBaron Sedan (Cont.)

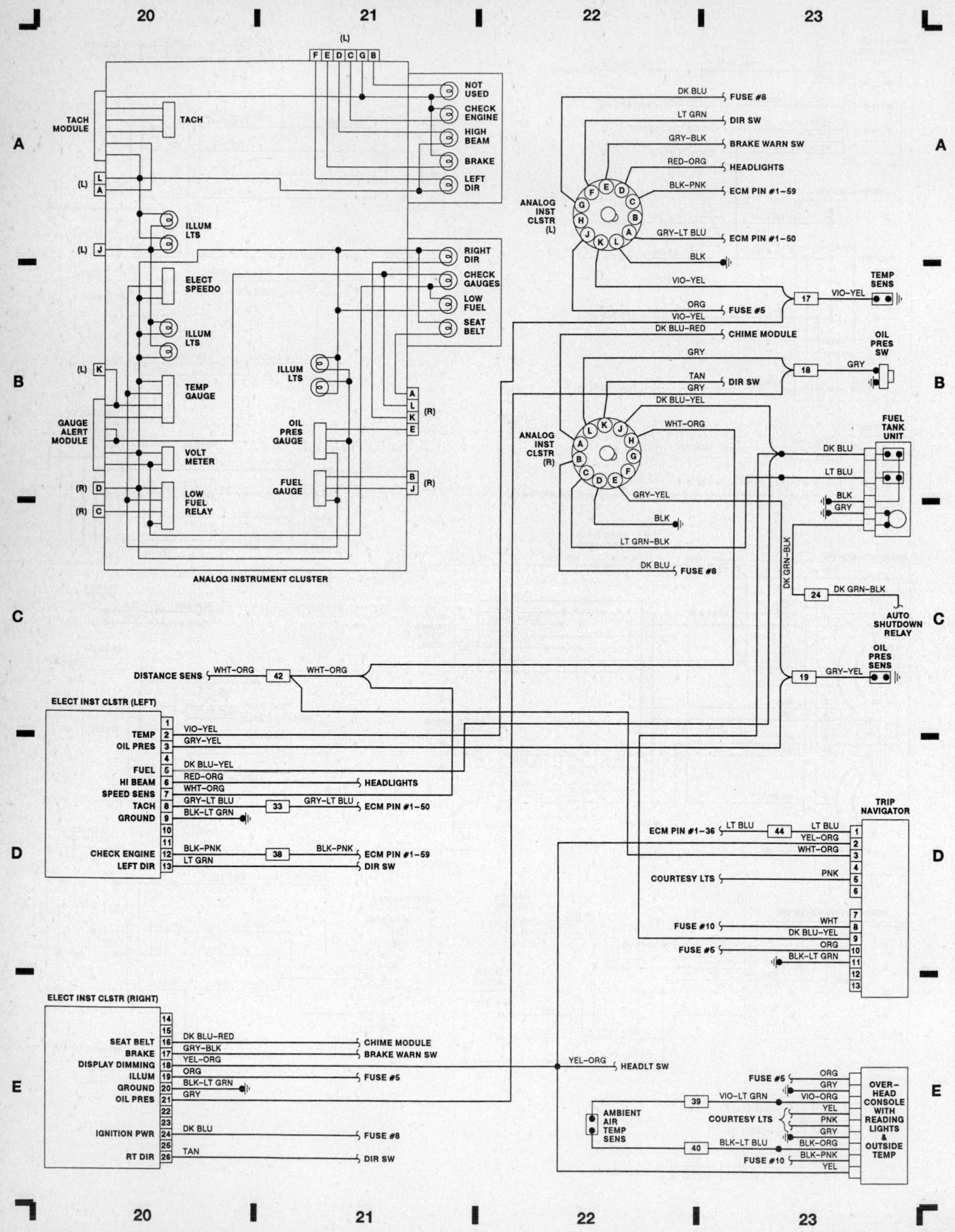

1989 CHRYSLER MOTORS
Lancer & LeBaron Sedan (Cont.)

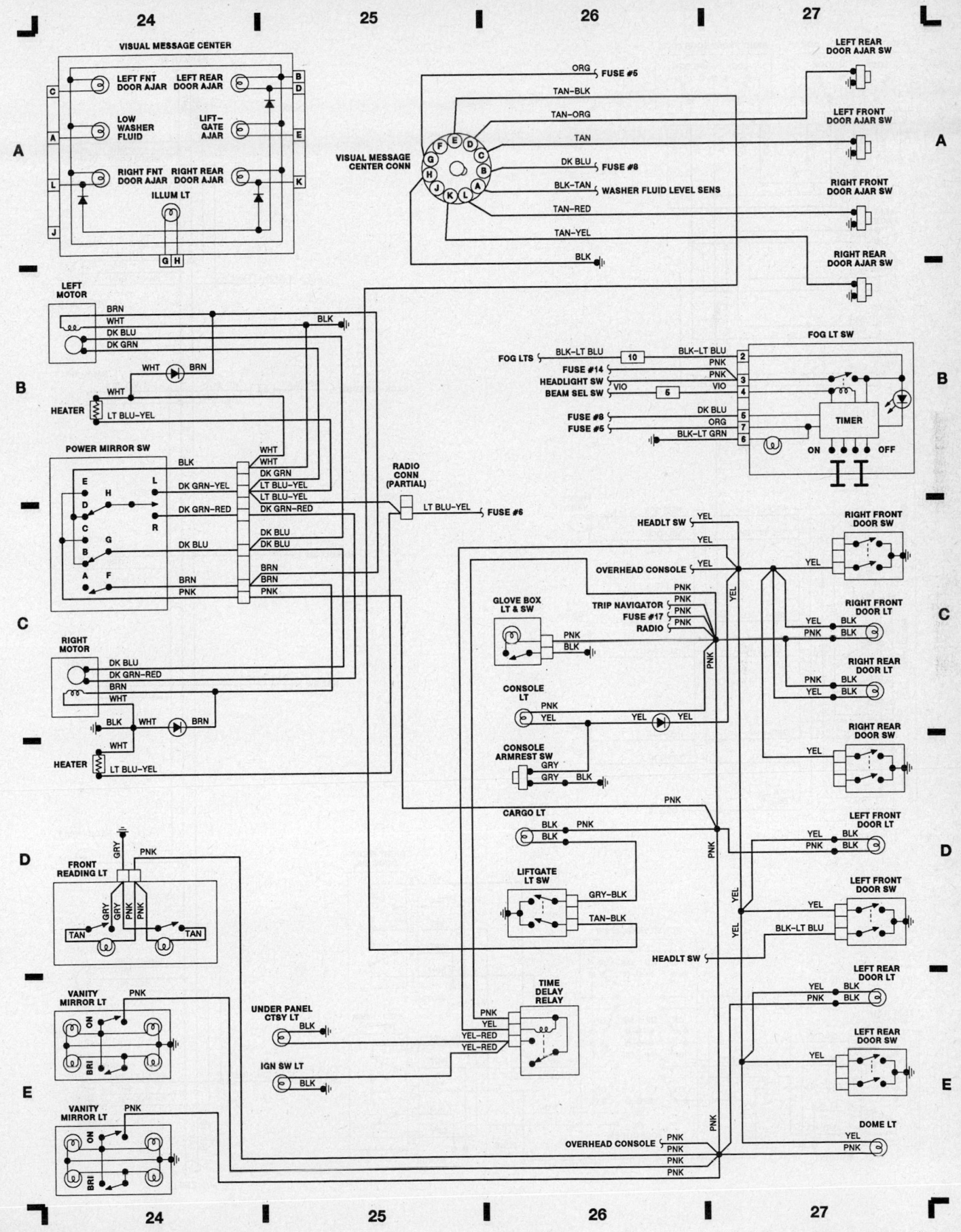

1989 CHRYSLER MOTORS
Lancer & LeBaron Sedan (Cont.)

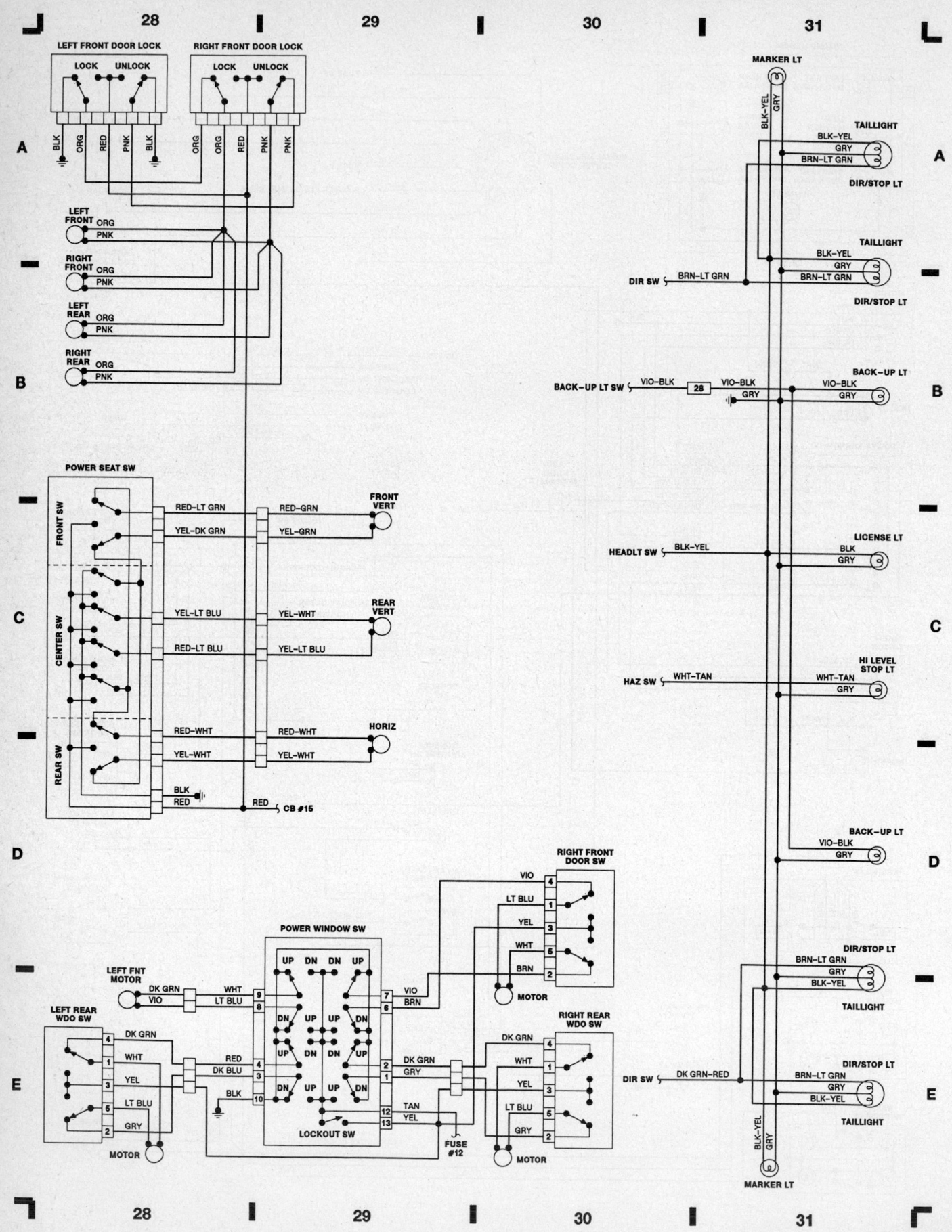

1989 CHRYSLER MOTORS
LeBaron Coupe & Convertible

COMPONENT LOCATOR:

A/C BLOWER MOTOR .... B 26
A/C CLUTCH CYCLING SW .... A-B 18
A/C LOW PRES SW .... B 19
A/C RELAY .... D 3
A/C SW .... A 19
AIR BAG SYSTEM .... B 27
ALTERNATOR .... B 3
AUTOMATIC TEMP CTRL SYS ...... C-E 25-27
AUTO SHUTDOWN RLY .... B 7
AUTO SHUTDOWN RLY (TURBO) .... B 11
BACK-UP LT SWS .... C-D 3
BATTERY .... A 2
BEAM SEL SW .... A 15
BLOWER MOTOR .... A 19, C 19
BRAKE FLUID LEVEL SENS .... D 21
BRAKE PAD WEAR SENS .... D-E 21-22
BRAKE WARN SW .... C 23
CHIME MODULE .... E 16
CIG LTR .... D 15
CONCEALED HEADLIGHT CTRL .... E 19
COOLANT LEVEL SENS .... C-D 22
COURTESY LIGHTS .... C-E 30
CRUISE CTRL SERVO .... E 4
CRUISE CTRL SERVO (TURBO) .... C 11
CRUISE CTRL SW .... A 16
DEFOG SYSTEM (CONV) .... A-B 26-27
DEFOG SYSTEM (COUPE) .... C 19
DIAG CONN .... C 7
DIAG CONN (TURBO) .... C 11
DIRECTIONAL SW .... A-B 12
DIR FLASHER .... C 12-13
DISTANCE SENS .... C 2
DOOR AJAR SWS .... B 24
DOOR SWS .... C-E 30
ELECT CTRL MOD (ECM) .... A-E 4-9
ELECT CTRL MOD (ECM) (TURBO) .. A-E 8-9
ELECT MONITOR .... D-E 20
FUEL TANK UNIT .... C-D 23
FUS LINKS .... A 2
FUSE BLOCK .... D-E 13-14
GLOVE BOX LT & SW .... E 17
HAZARD FLASHER .... D 13
HAZARD SW .... C 12
HEADLT OUTAGE TOROID .... E 22
HEADLIGHT SW .... B-C 15
HEATER SYSTEM .... B-C 18-19
HORN SYSTEM .... E 3
IGNITION SW .... A 13-14
ILLUMINATED ENTRY RLY .... D 19
INST CLSTR (ANALOG) .... D-E 22-23
INST CLUSTER (ELECT) .... A-B 20
KEY IN SW .... C 15
LIFTGATE AJAR SW .... A 24
NEUTRAL/SAFETY SW .... C 3
OIL PRES SW .... A 22, B 22
OVERHEAD CONSOLE .... D 24
PARK BRAKE SW .... C 23
POWER ANTENNA RELAY .... A 28
POWER DOOR LOCKS .... A 29-30
POWER MIRRORS .... B-C 28-29
POWER MODULE .... B 25
POWER SEAT .... A 29-30
POWER TOP SW .... D 16-17
POWER WINDOWS .... D-E 28-29
RADIATOR FAN RELAY .... D 3
STARTER SYSTEM .... B-C 2-3
STOP LIGHT OUTAGE TOROID .... B 30
STOP LT SW .... B 16
STOP LT SW (CRUISE CTRL) .... A 16
SWITCH LIGHT MODULE .... A 27
TEMP SENS .... A 22, C 22
TIME DELAY RELAY .... D 13
TRAN PRES SW .... C-D 22
TRIP NAVIGATOR .... E 24
TRUNK LIGHT .... A 25
VISUAL MESSAGE CNTR .... A-B 25-26
VOICE ALERT .... C 20
WIPER/WASHER SYSTEM .... C-D 16-18

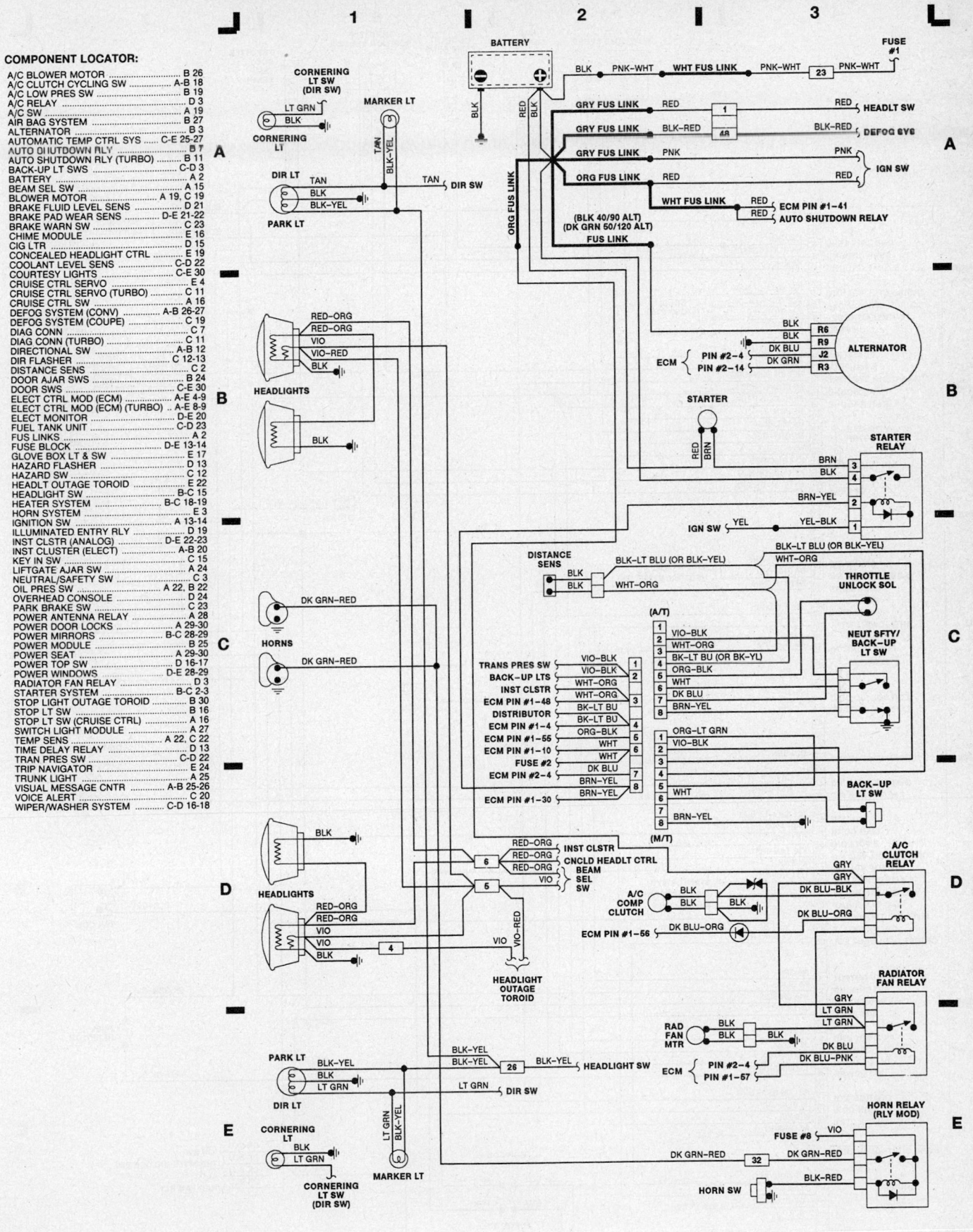

1989 CHRYSLER MOTORS
LeBaron Coupe & Convertible (Cont.)

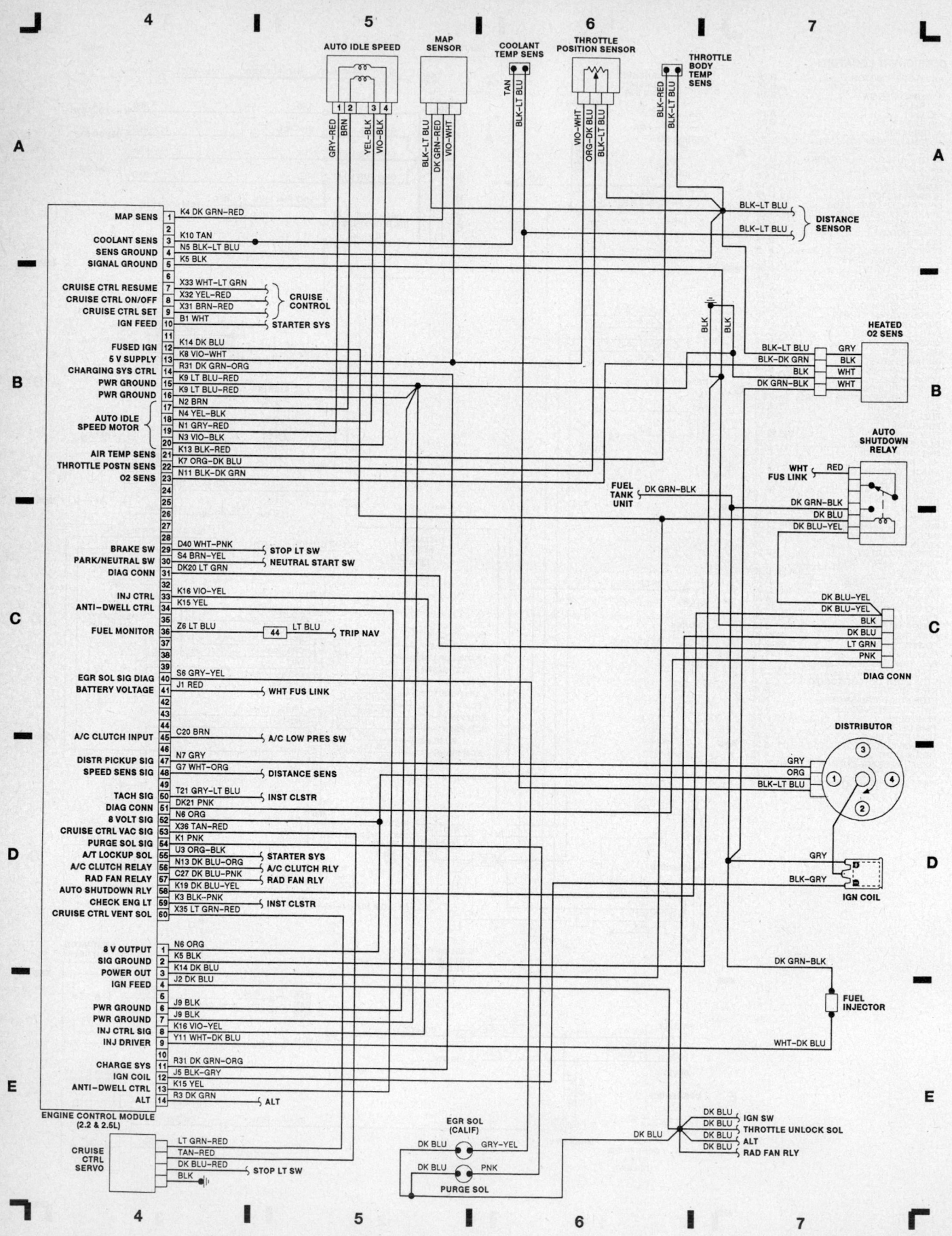

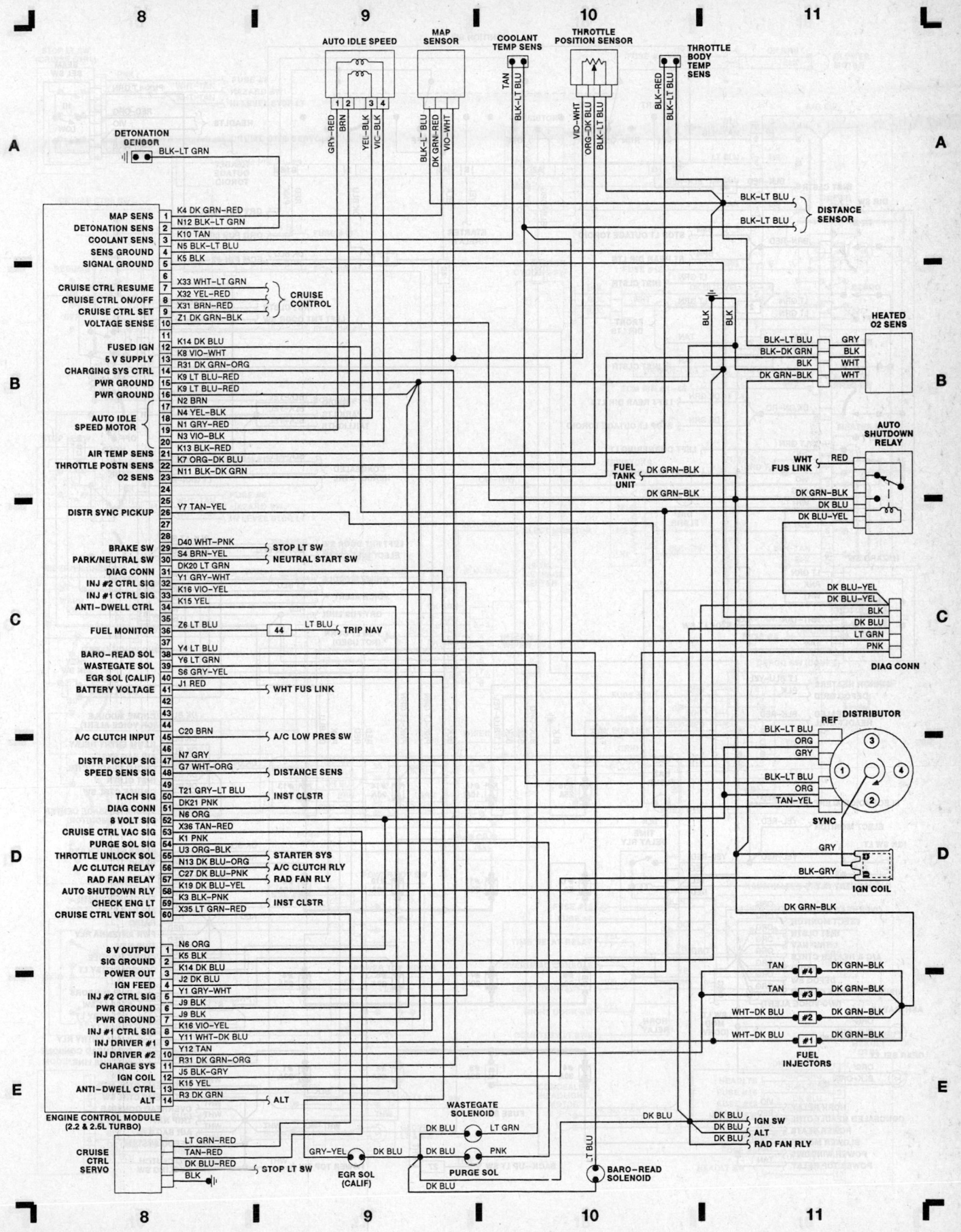

1989 CHRYSLER MOTORS
Shadow & Sundance (Cont.)

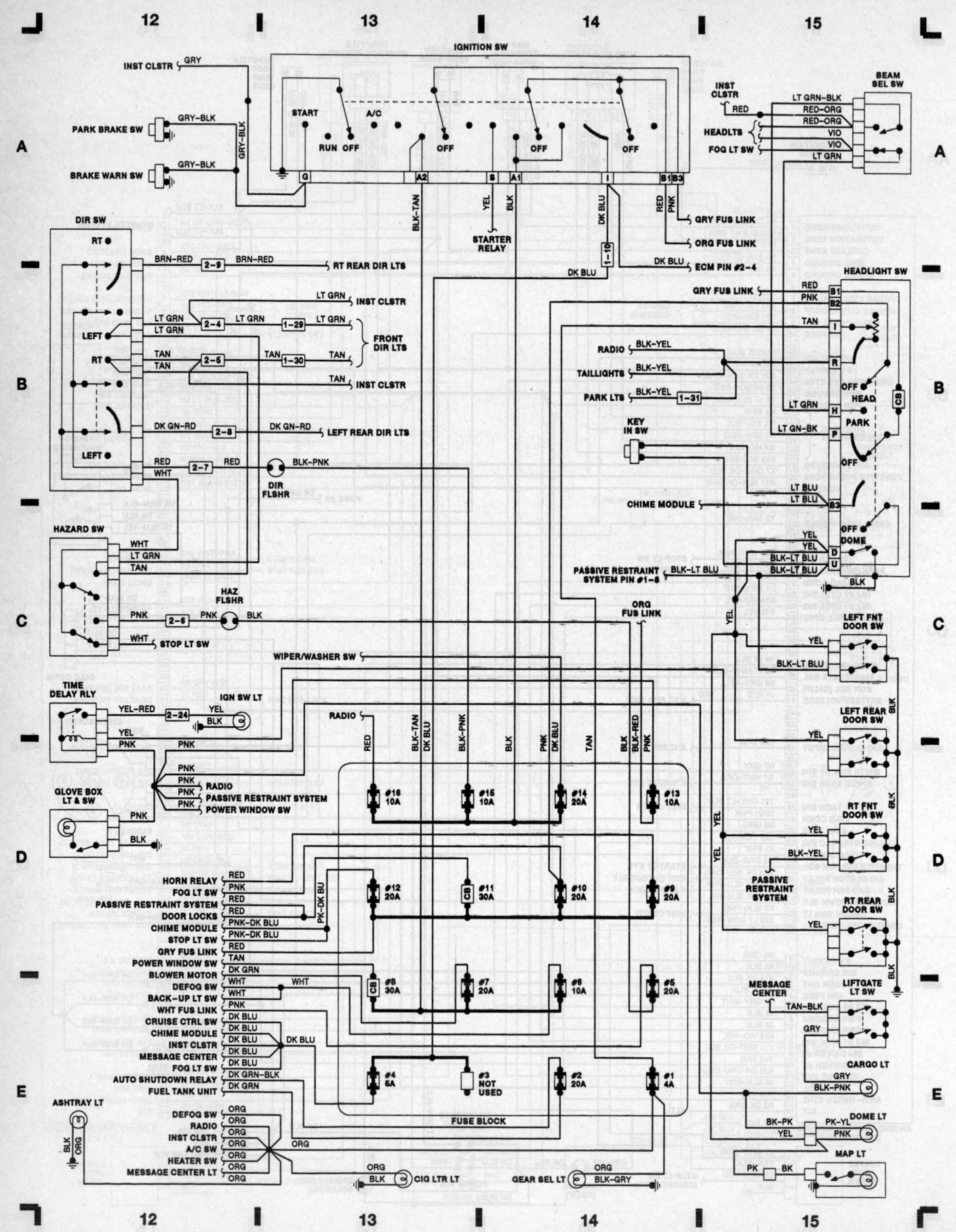

1989 CHRYSLER MOTORS
Shadow & Sundance (Cont.)

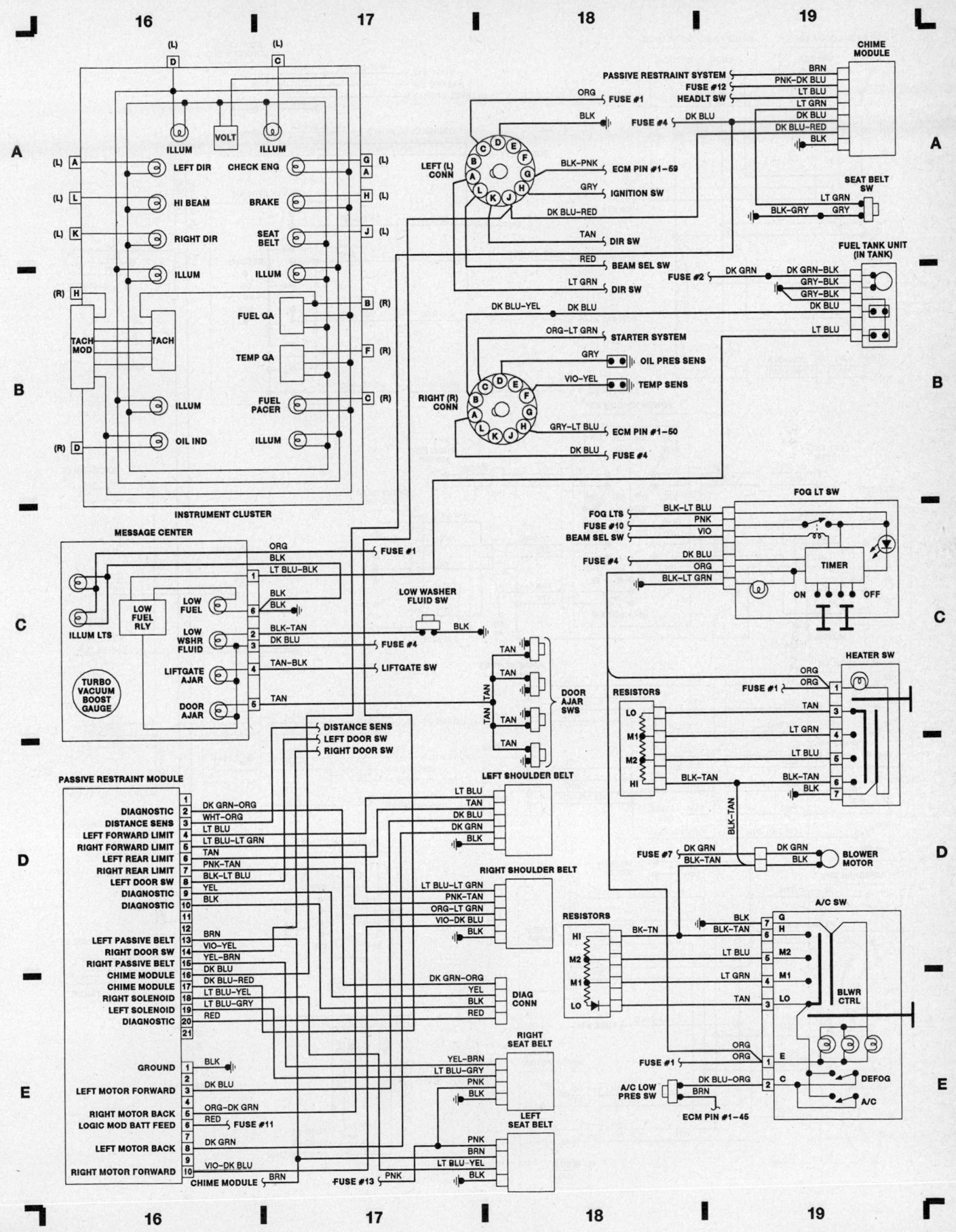

1989 CHRYSLER MOTORS
Shadow & Sundance (Cont.)

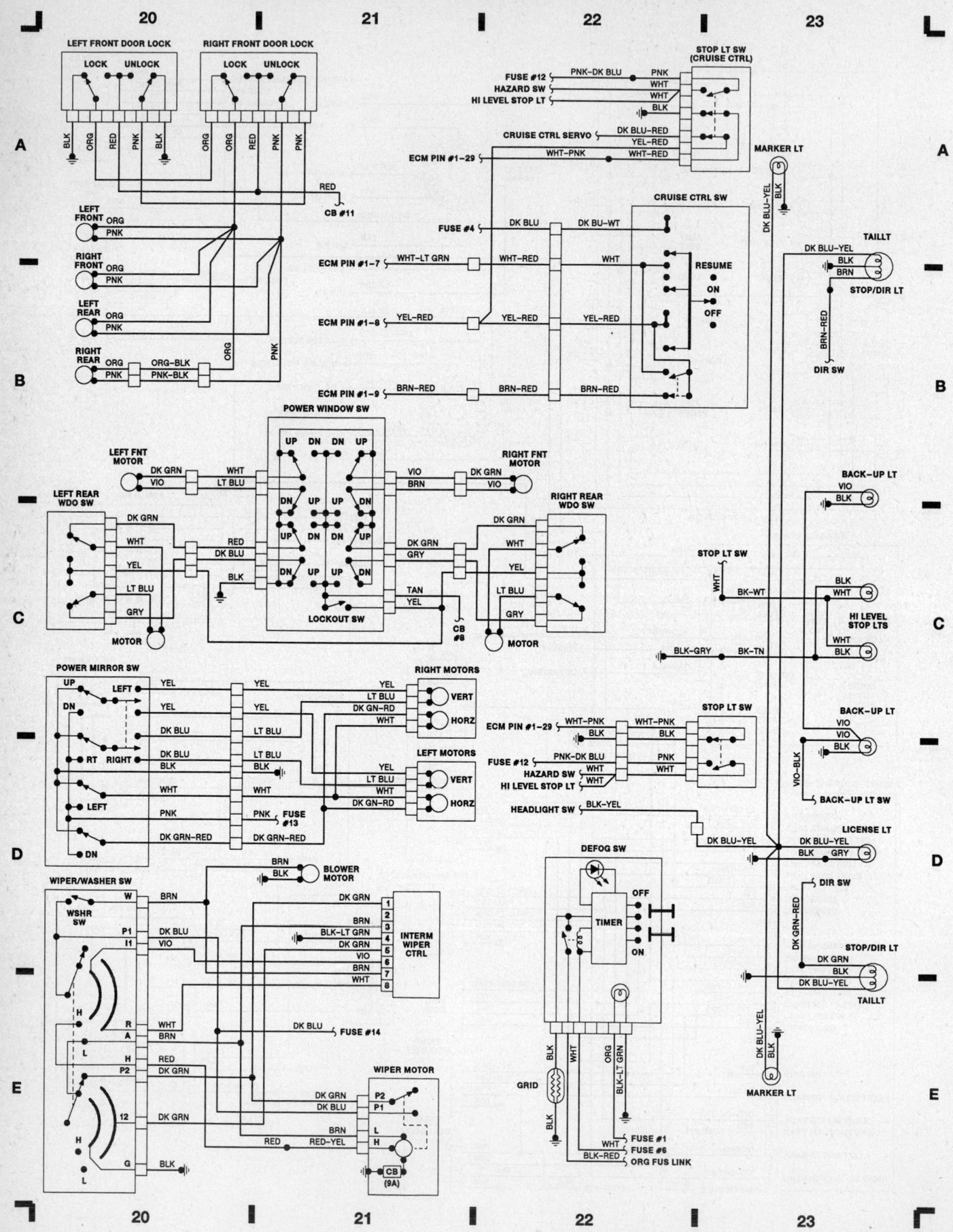

1989 EAGLE
Premier

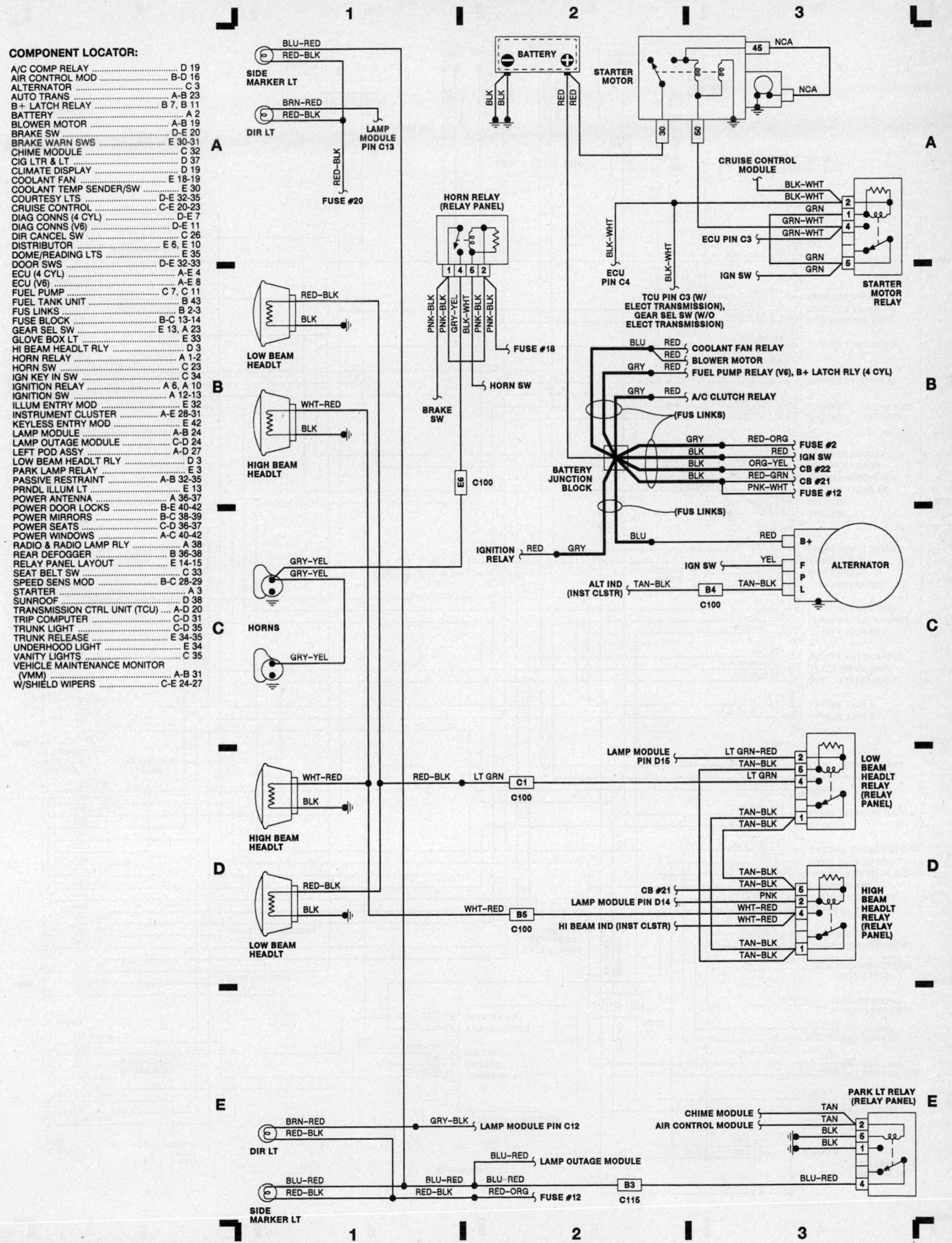

COMPONENT LOCATOR:

A/C COMP RELAY	D 19
AIR CONTROL MOD	B-D 16
ALTERNATOR	C 3
AUTO TRANS	A-B 23
B+ LATCH RELAY	B 7, B 11
BATTERY	A 2
BLOWER MOTOR	A-B 19
BRAKE SW	D-E 20
BRAKE WARN SWS	E 30-31
CHIME MODULE	C 32
CIG LTR & LT	D 37
CLIMATE DISPLAY	D 19
COOLANT FAN	E 18-19
COOLANT TEMP SENDER/SW	E 30
COURTESY LTS	D-E 32-35
CRUISE CONTROL	C-E 20-23
DIAG CONNS (4 CYL)	D-E 7
DIAG CONNS (V6)	D-E 11
DIR CANCEL SW	C 26
DISTRIBUTOR	E 6, E 10
DOME/READING LTS	E 35
DOOR SWS	D-E 32-33
ECU (4 CYL)	A-E 4
ECU (V6)	A-E 8
FUEL PUMP	C 7, C 11
FUEL TANK UNIT	B 43
FUS LINKS	B 2-3
FUSE BLOCK	B-C 13-14
GEAR SEL SW	E 13, A 23
GLOVE BOX LT	E 33
HI BEAM HEADLT RLY	D 3
HORN RELAY	A 1-2
HORN SW	C 23
IGN KEY IN SW	C 34
IGNITION RELAY	A 6, A 10
IGNITION SW	A 12-13
ILLUM ENTRY MOD	E 32
INSTRUMENT CLUSTER	A-E 28-31
KEYLESS ENTRY MOD	E 42
LAMP MODULE	A-B 24
LAMP OUTAGE MODULE	C-D 24
LEFT POD ASSY	A-D 27
LOW BEAM HEADLT RLY	D 3
PARK LAMP RELAY	E 3
PASSIVE RESTRAINT	A-B 32-35
PRNDL ILLUM LT	E 13
POWER ANTENNA	A 36-37
POWER DOOR LOCKS	B-E 40-42
POWER MIRRORS	B-C 38-39
POWER SEATS	C-D 36-37
POWER WINDOWS	A-C 40-42
RADIO & RADIO LAMP RLY	A 38
REAR DEFOGGER	B 36-38
RELAY PANEL LAYOUT	E 14-15
SEAT BELT SW	C 33
SPEED SENS MOD	B-C 28-29
STARTER	A 3
SUNROOF	D 38
TRANSMISSION CTRL UNIT (TCU)	A-D 20
TRIP COMPUTER	C-D 31
TRUNK LIGHT	C-D 35
TRUNK RELEASE	E 34-35
UNDERHOOD LIGHT	E 34
VANITY LIGHTS	C 35
VEHICLE MAINTENANCE MONITOR (VMM)	A-B 31
W/SHIELD WIPERS	C-E 24-27

1989 EAGLE
Premier (Cont.)

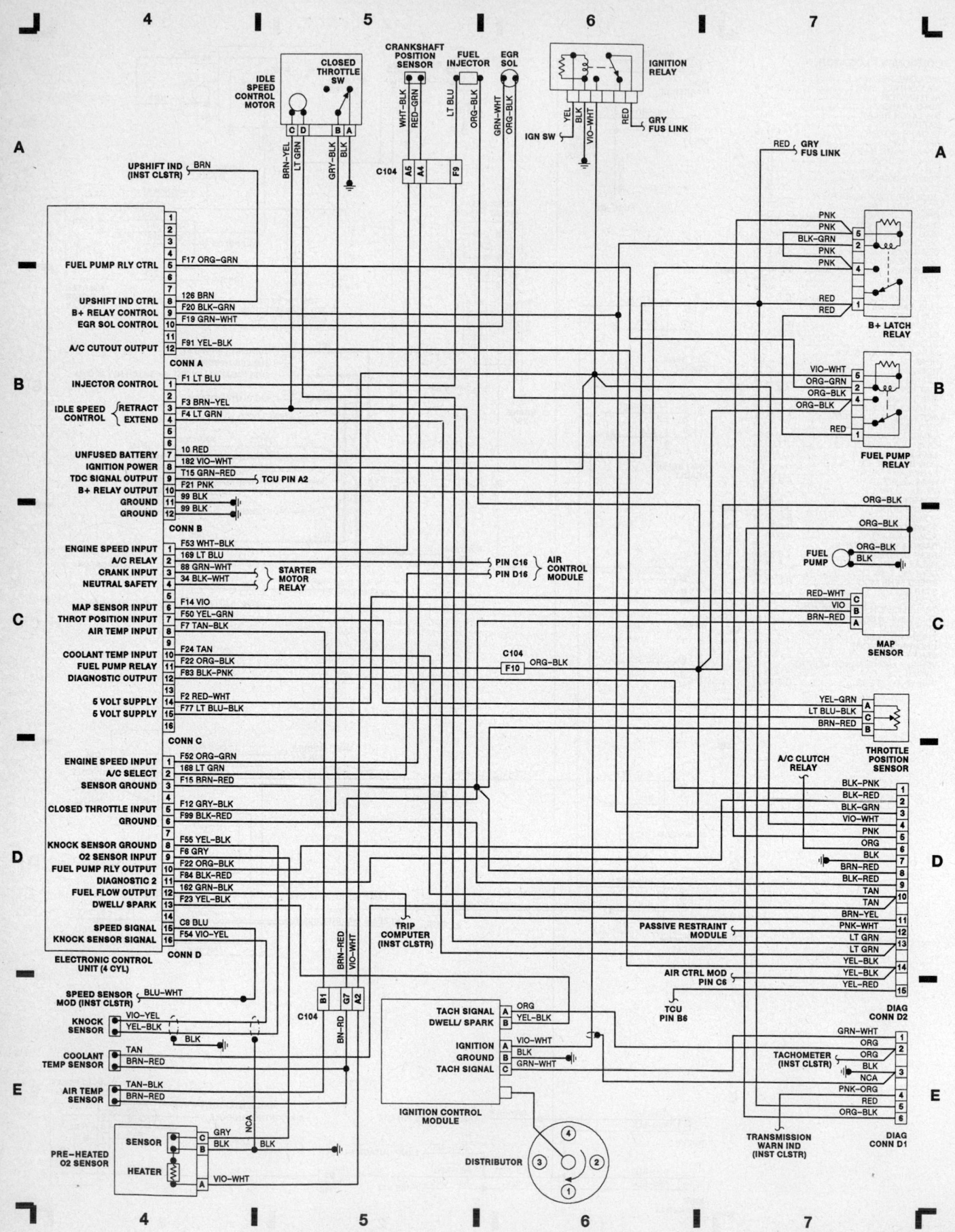

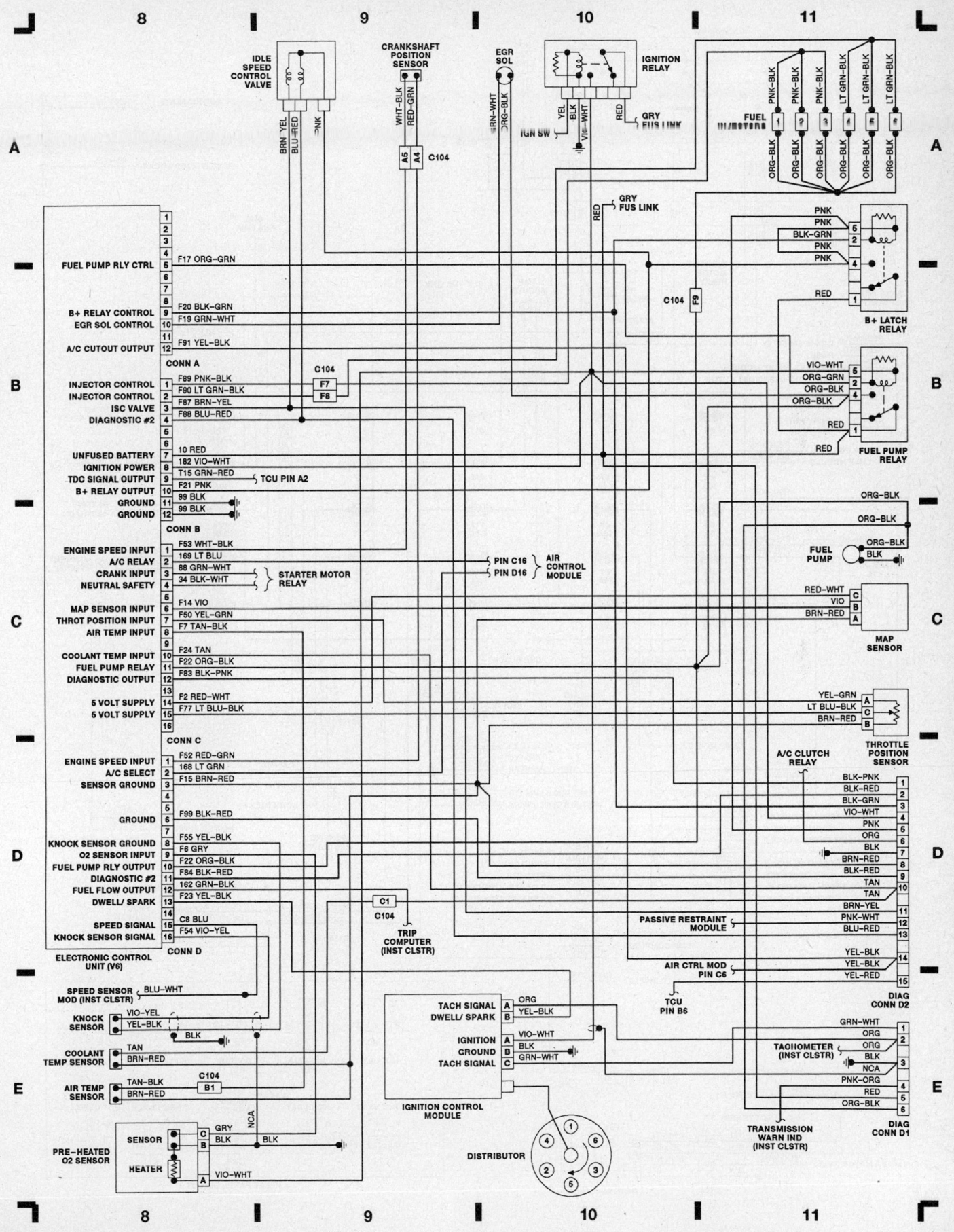

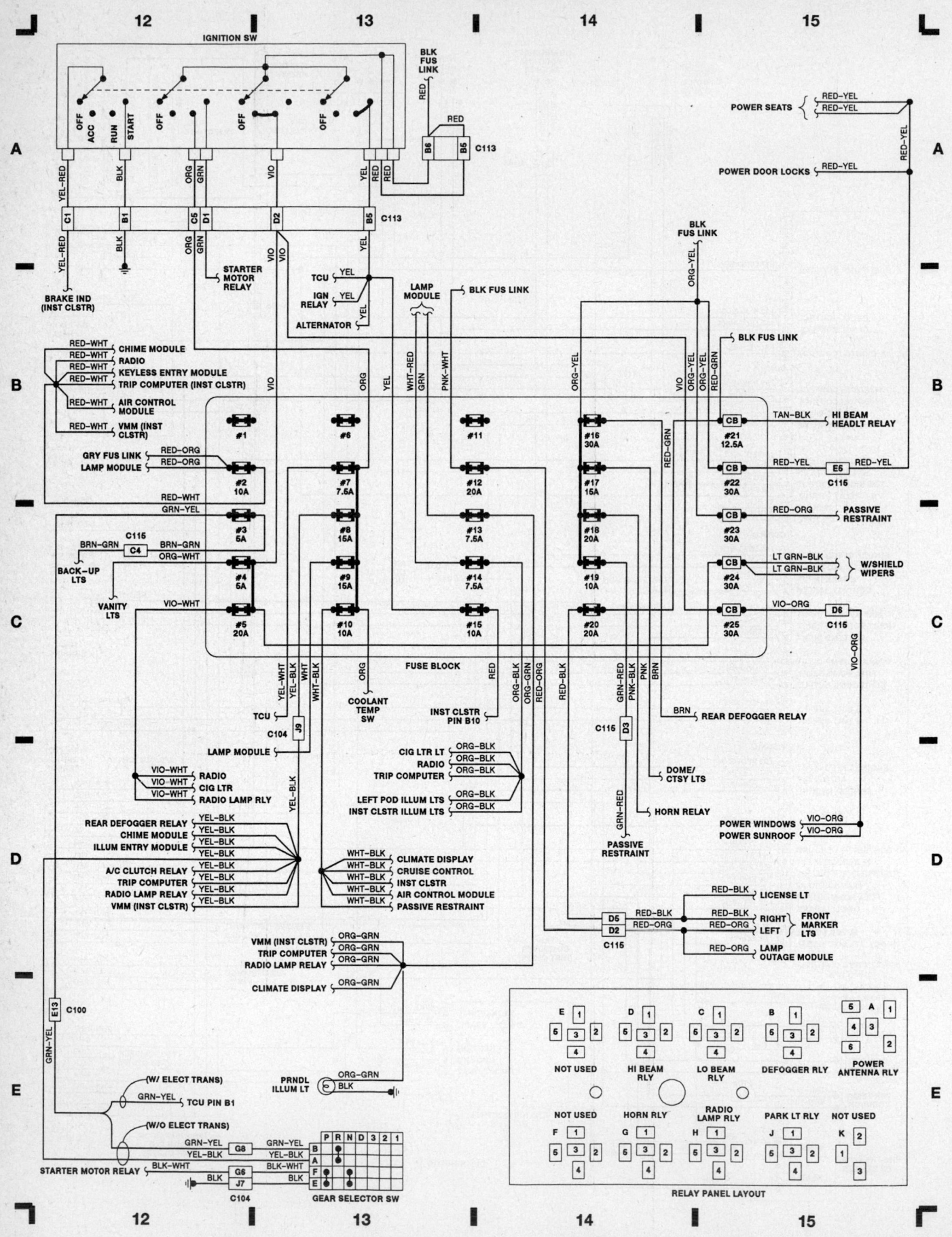

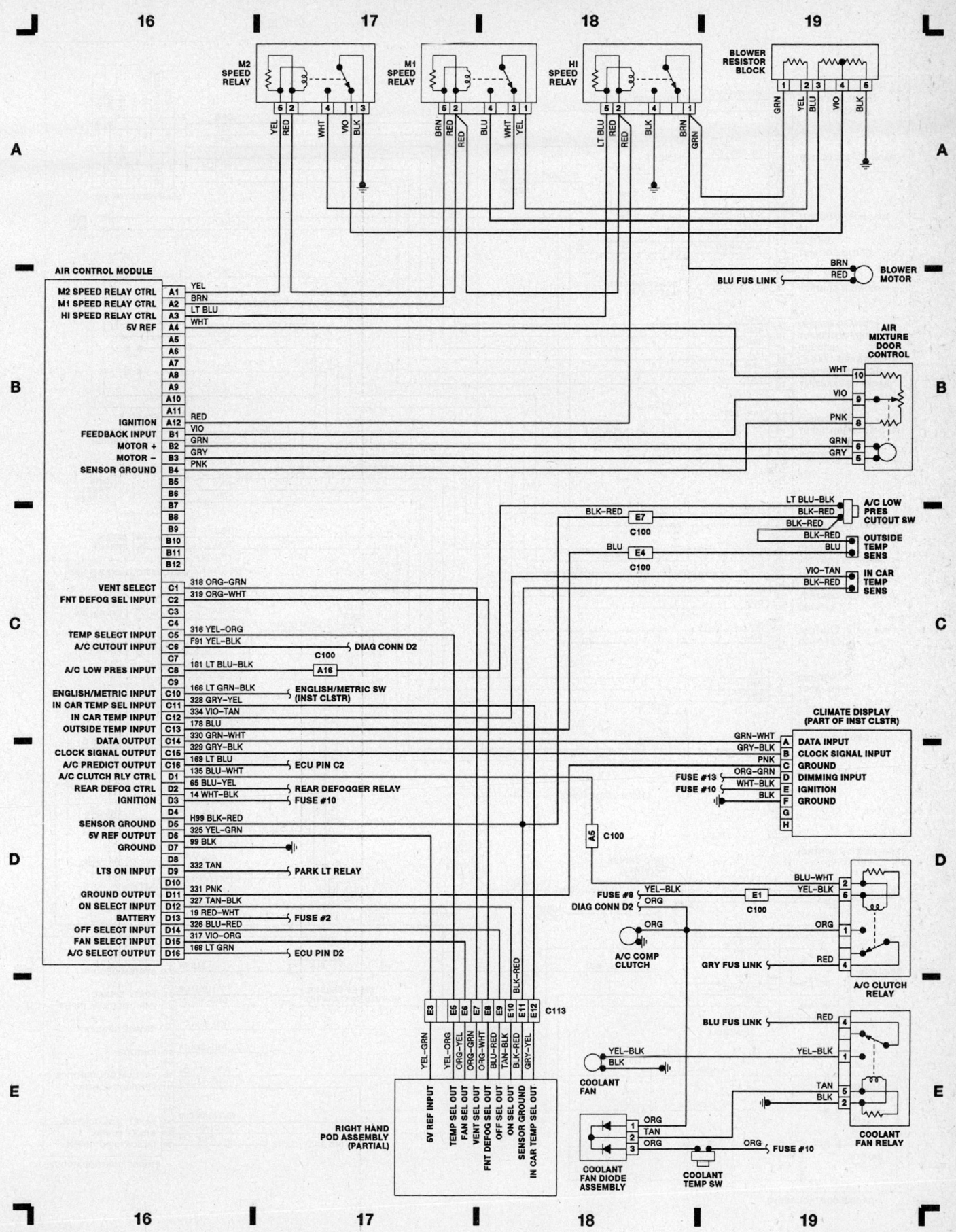

1989 EAGLE
Premier (Cont.)

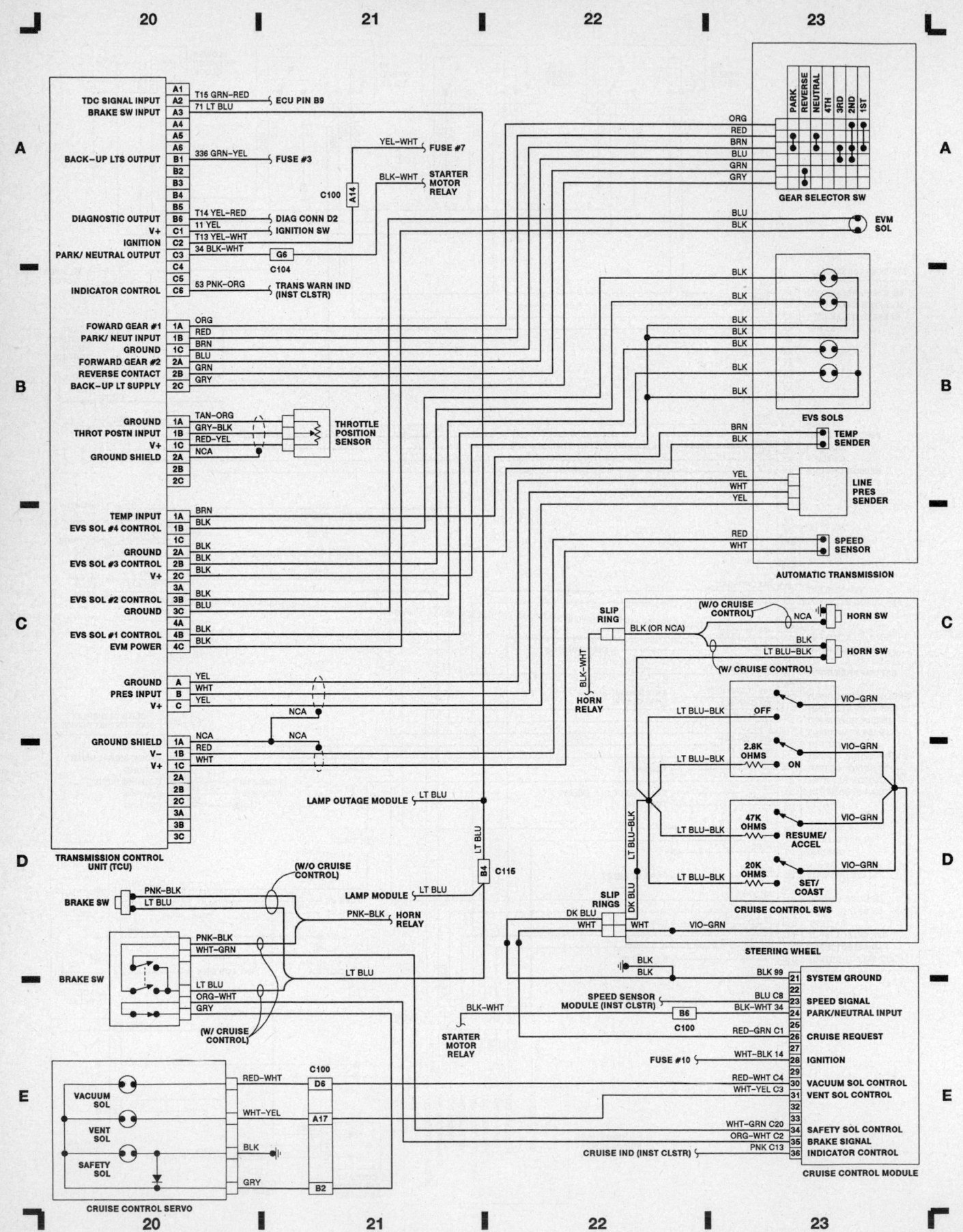

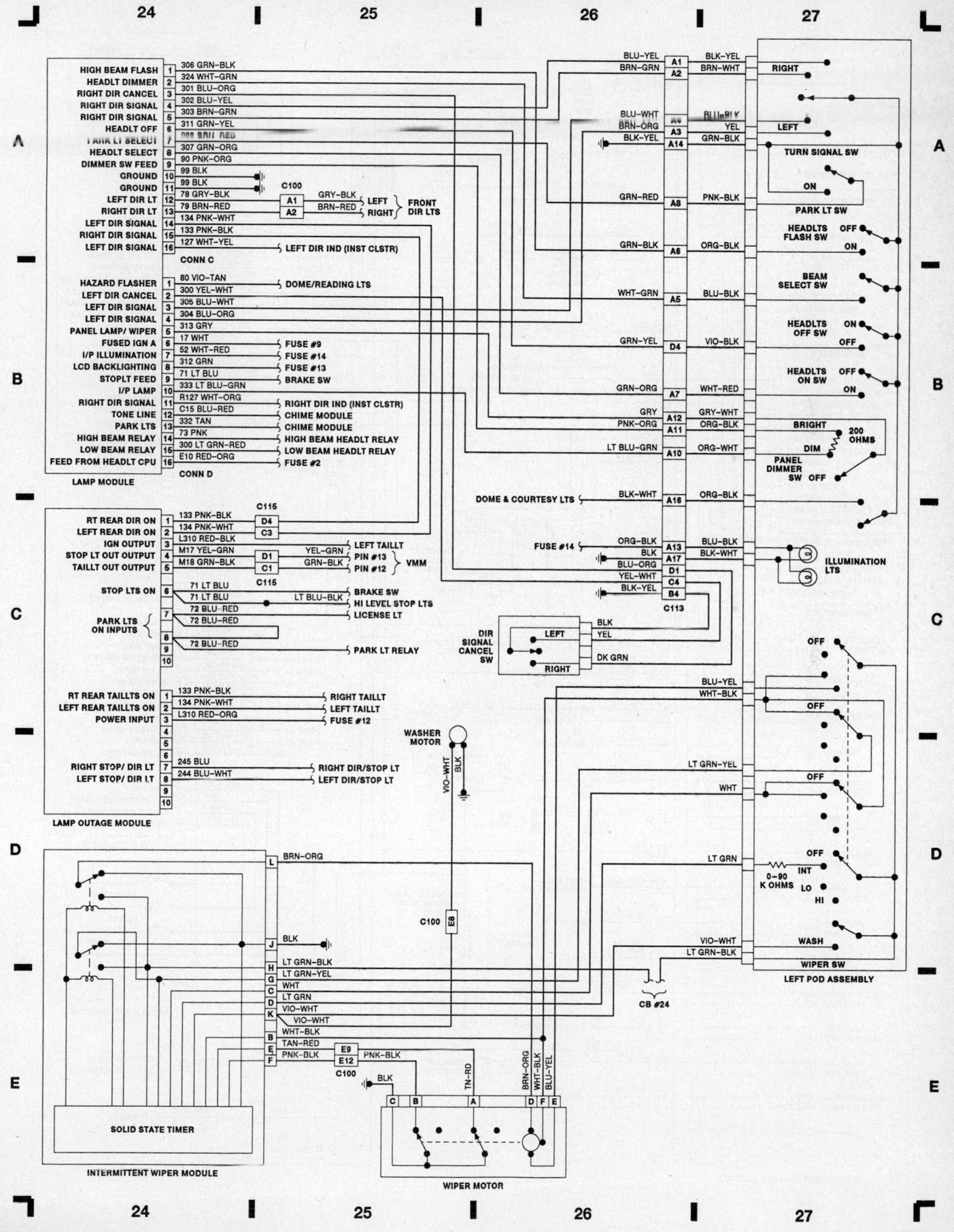

1989 EAGLE
Premier (Cont.)

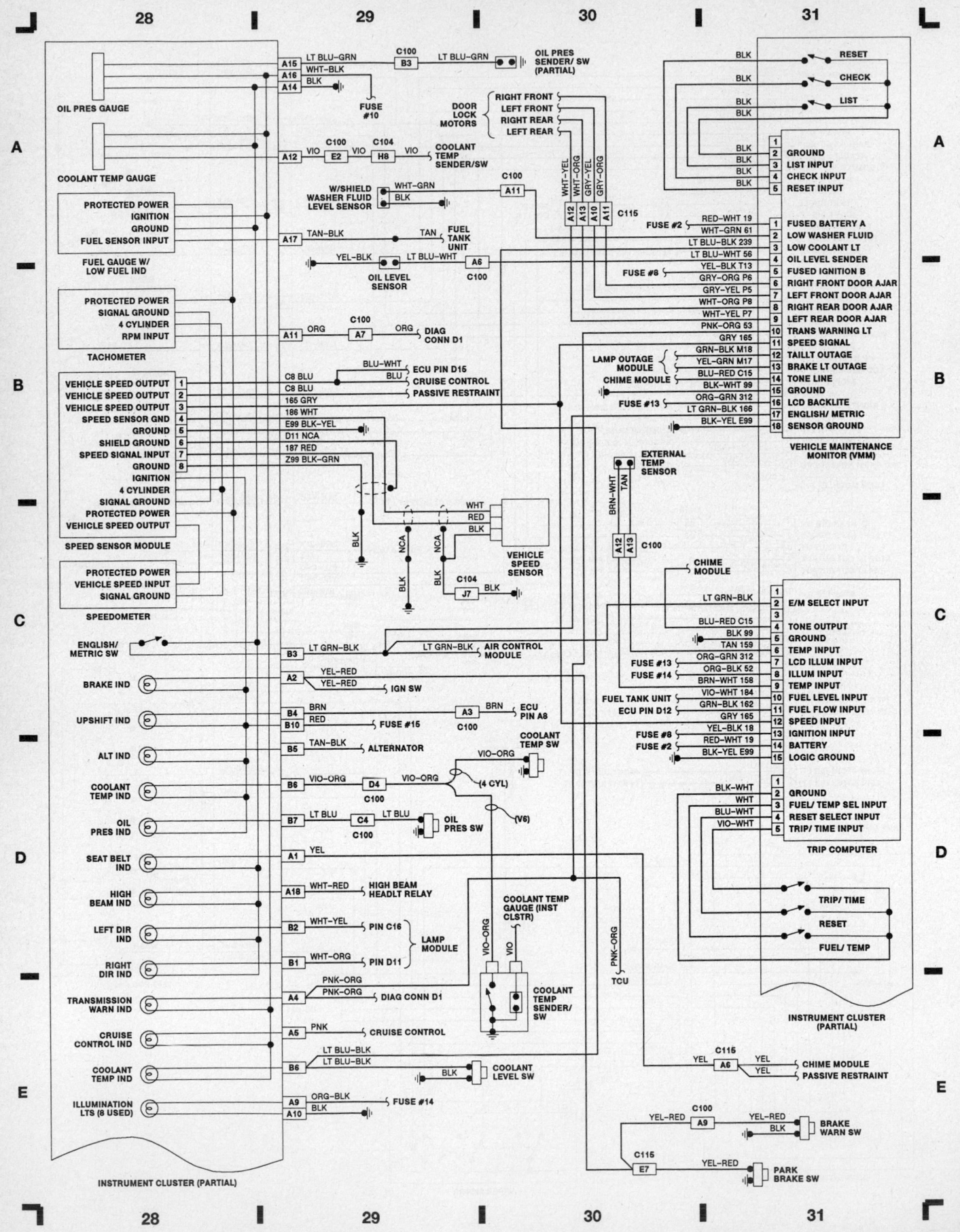

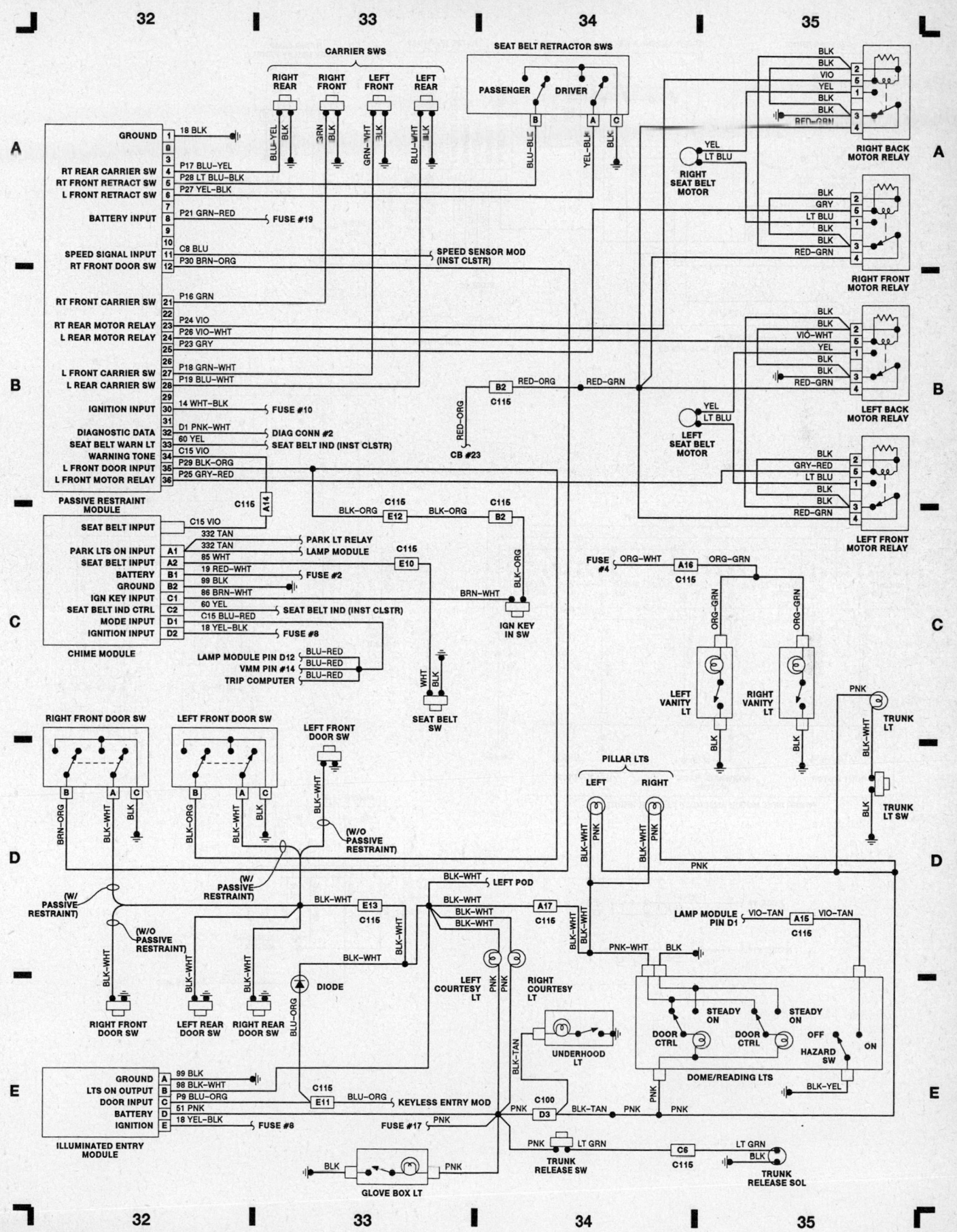

1989 EAGLE
Premier (Cont.)

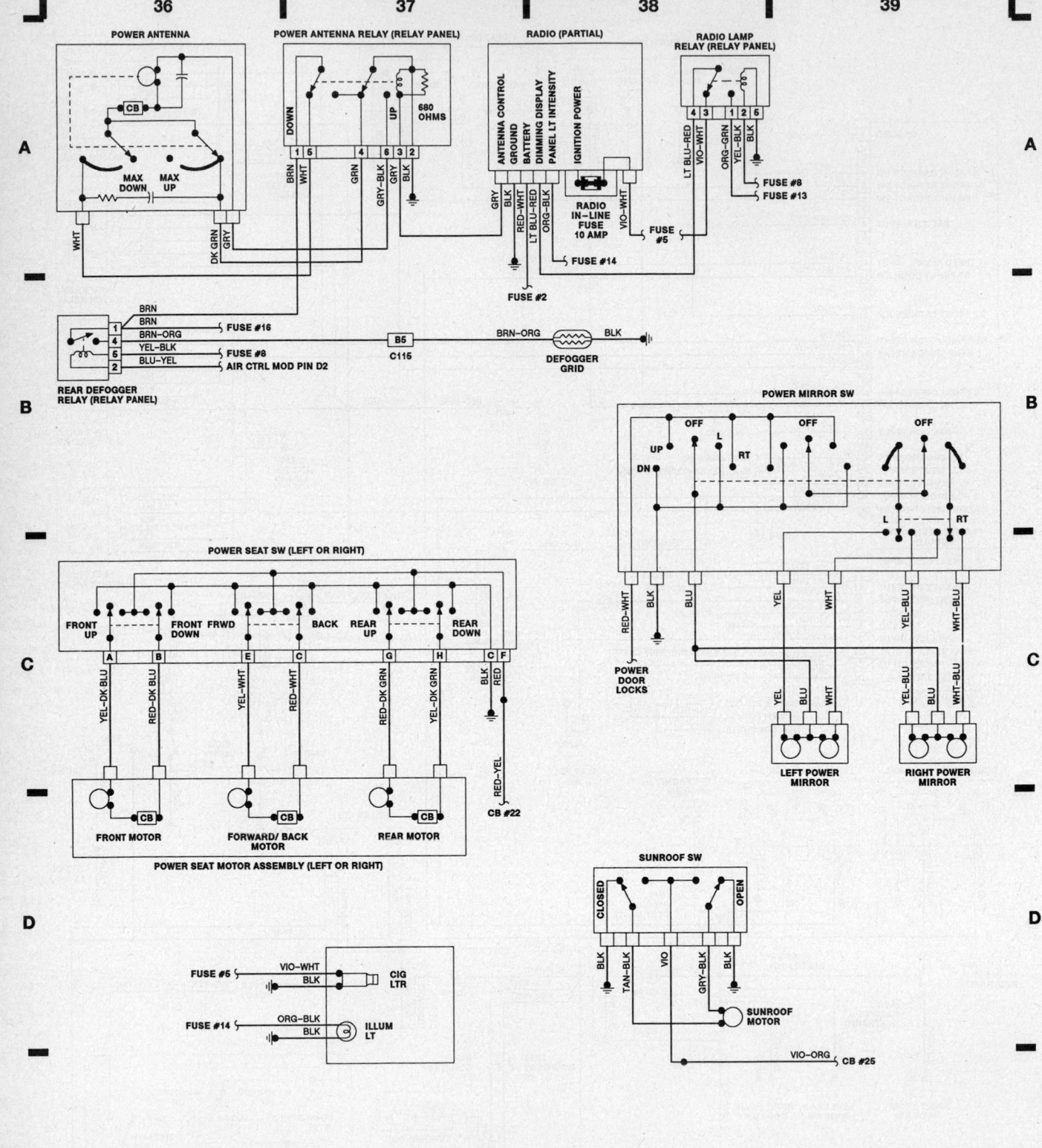

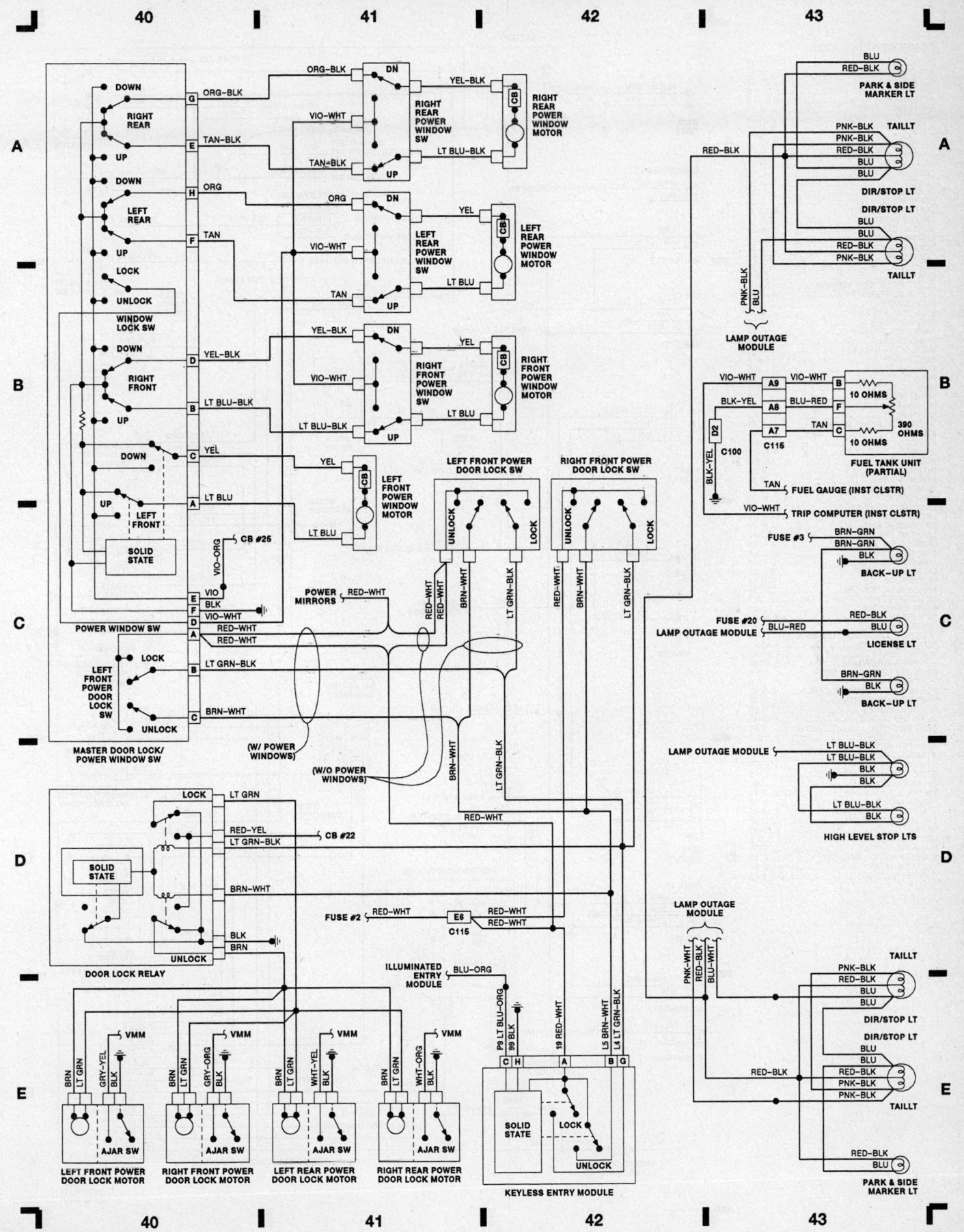

1989 Ford Motor Co.
Continental

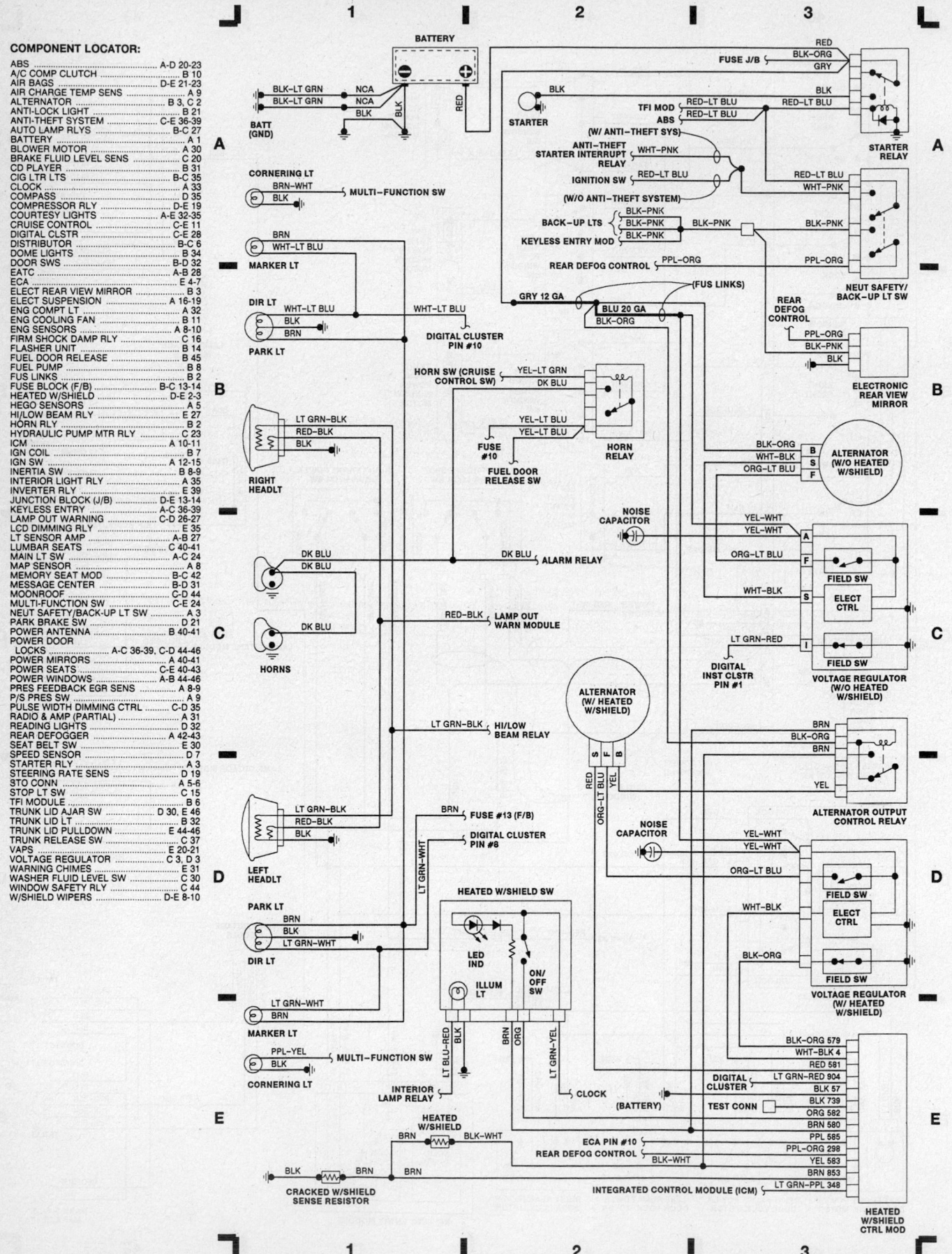

COMPONENT LOCATOR:

ABS .... A-D 20-23
A/C COMP CLUTCH .... B 10
AIR BAGS .... D-E 21-23
AIR CHARGE TEMP SENS .... A 9
ALTERNATOR .... B 3, C 2
ANTI-LOCK LIGHT .... B 21
ANTI-THEFT SYSTEM .... C-E 36-39
AUTO LAMP RLYS .... B-C 27
BATTERY .... A 1
BLOWER MOTOR .... A 30
BRAKE FLUID LEVEL SENS .... C 20
CD PLAYER .... B 31
CIG LTR LTS .... B-C 35
CLOCK .... A 33
COMPASS .... D 35
COMPRESSOR RLY .... D-E 19
COURTESY LIGHTS .... A-E 32-35
CRUISE CONTROL .... C-E 11
DIGITAL CLSTR .... C-E 28
DISTRIBUTOR .... B-C 6
DOME LIGHTS .... B 34
DOOR SWS .... B-D 32
EATC .... A-B 28
ECA .... E 4-7
ELECT REAR VIEW MIRROR .... B 3
ELECT SUSPENSION .... A 16-19
ENG COMPT LT .... A 32
ENG COOLING FAN .... B 11
ENG SENSORS .... A 8-10
FIRM SHOCK DAMP RLY .... C 16
FLASHER UNIT .... B 14
FUEL DOOR RELEASE .... B 45
FUEL PUMP .... B 8
FUS LINKS .... B 2
FUSE BLOCK (F/B) .... B-C 13-14
HEATED W/SHIELD .... D-E 2-3
HEGO SENSORS .... A 5
HI/LOW BEAM RLY .... E 27
HORN RLY .... B 2
HYDRAULIC PUMP MTR RLY .... C 23
ICM .... A 10-11
IGN COIL .... B 7
IGN SW .... A 12-15
INERTIA SW .... B 8-9
INTERIOR LIGHT RLY .... A 35
INVERTER RLY .... E 39
JUNCTION BLOCK (J/B) .... D-E 13-14
KEYLESS ENTRY .... A-C 36-39
LAMP OUT WARNING .... C-D 26-27
LCD DIMMING RLY .... E 35
LT SENSOR AMP .... A-B 27
LUMBAR SEATS .... C 40-41
MAIN LT SW .... A-C 24
MAP SENSOR .... A 8
MEMORY SEAT MOD .... B-C 42
MESSAGE CENTER .... B-D 31
MOONROOF .... C-D 44
MULTI-FUNCTION SW .... C-E 24
NEUT SAFETY/BACK-UP LT SW .... A 3
PARK BRAKE SW .... D 21
POWER ANTENNA .... B 40-41
POWER DOOR
  LOCKS .... A-C 36-39, C-D 44-46
POWER MIRRORS .... A 40-41
POWER SEATS .... C-E 40-43
POWER WINDOWS .... A-B 44-46
PRES FEEDBACK EGR SENS .... A 8-9
P/S PRES SW .... A 9
PULSE WIDTH DIMMING CTRL .... C-D 35
RADIO & AMP (PARTIAL) .... A 31
READING LIGHTS .... D 32
REAR DEFOGGER .... A 42-43
SEAT BELT SW .... E 30
SPEED SENSOR .... D 7
STARTER RLY .... A 3
STEERING RATE SENS .... D 19
3TO CONN .... A 5-6
STOP LT SW .... C 15
TFI MODULE .... B 6
TRUNK LID AJAR SW .... D 30, E 46
TRUNK LID LT .... B 32
TRUNK LID PULLDOWN .... E 44-46
TRUNK RELEASE SW .... C 37
VAPS .... E 20-21
VOLTAGE REGULATOR .... C 3, D 3
WARNING CHIMES .... E 31
WASHER FLUID LEVEL SW .... C 30
WINDOW SAFETY RLY .... C 44
W/SHIELD WIPERS .... D-E 8-10

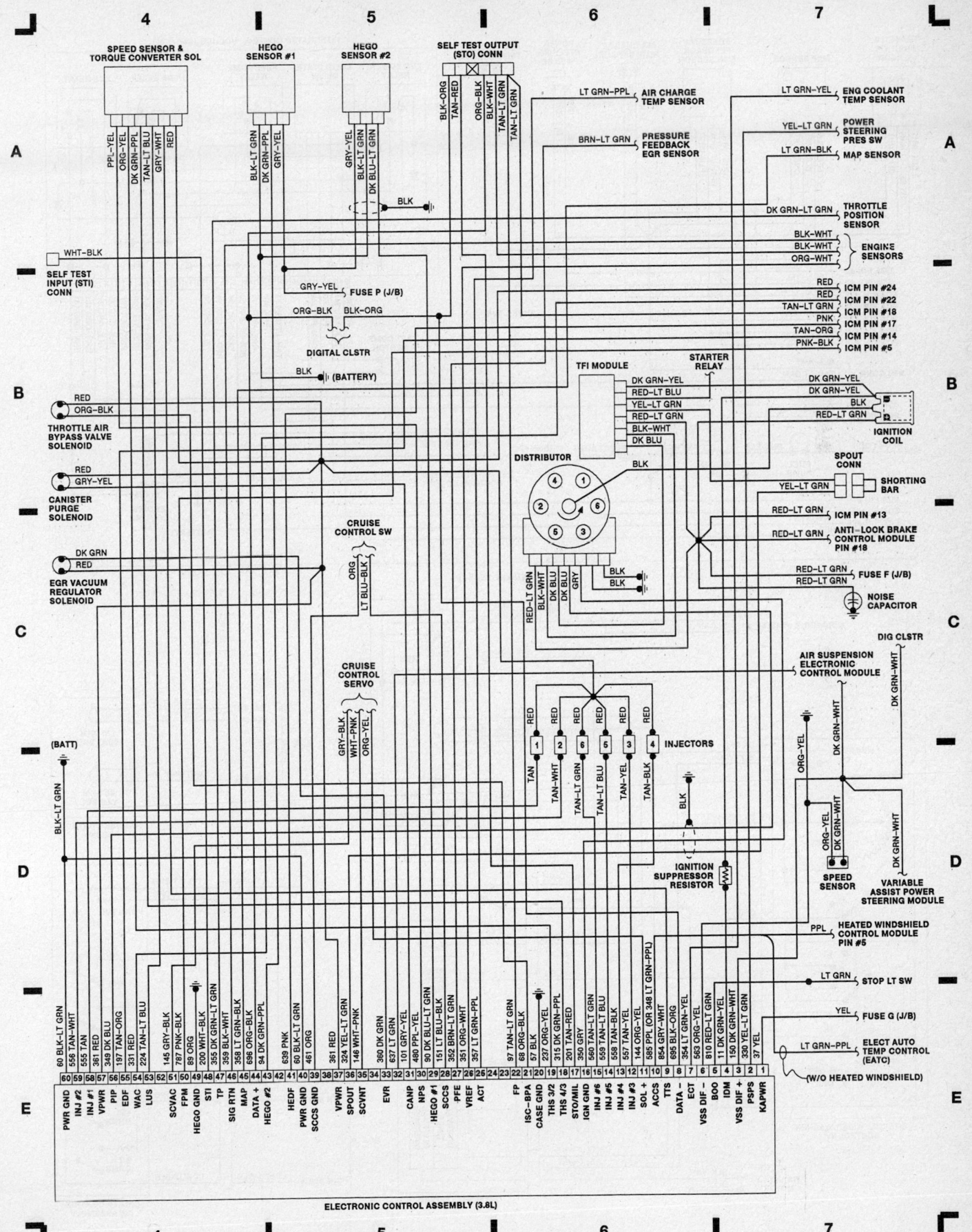

ELECTRONIC CONTROL ASSEMBLY (3.8L)

1989 Ford Motor Co.
Continental (Cont.)

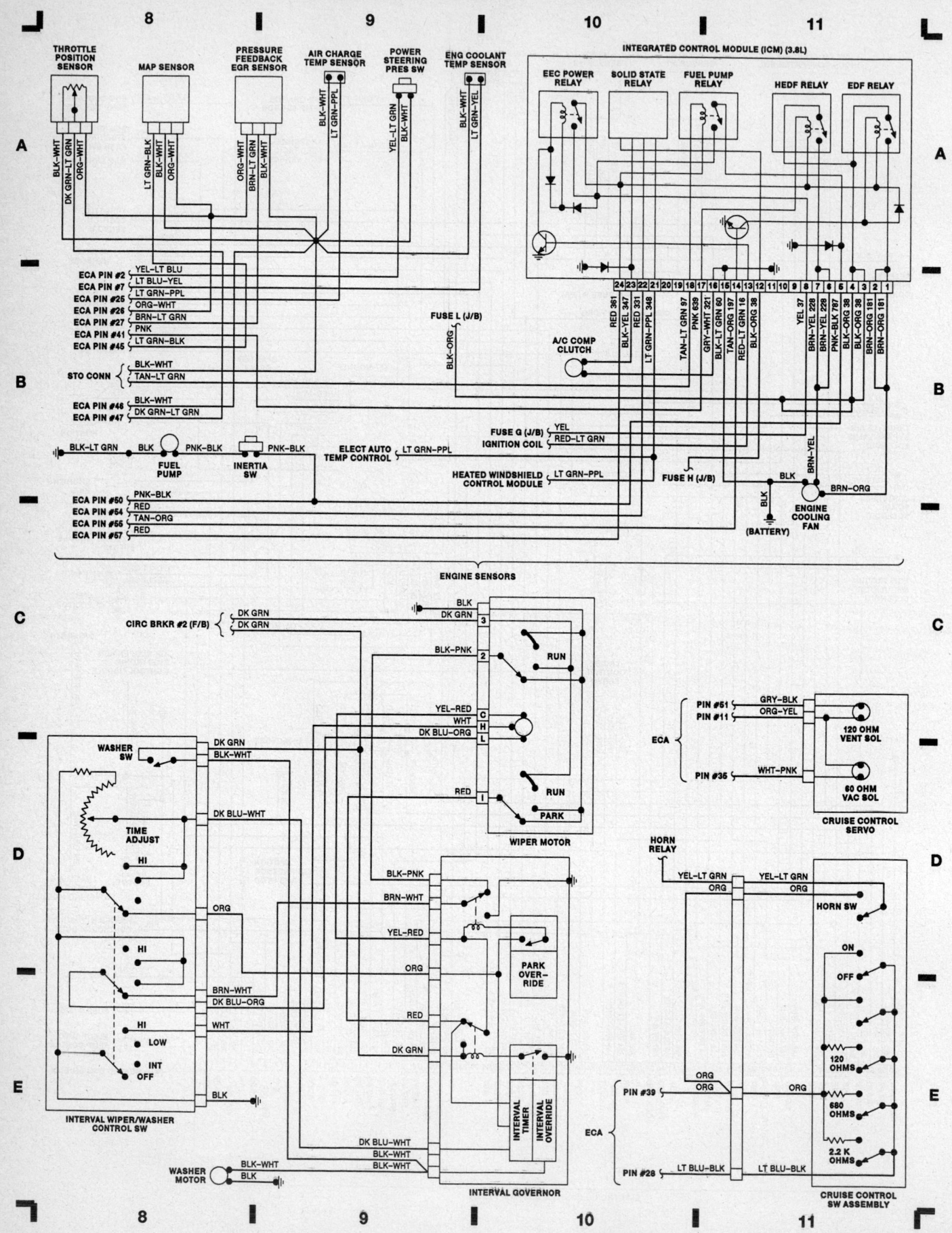

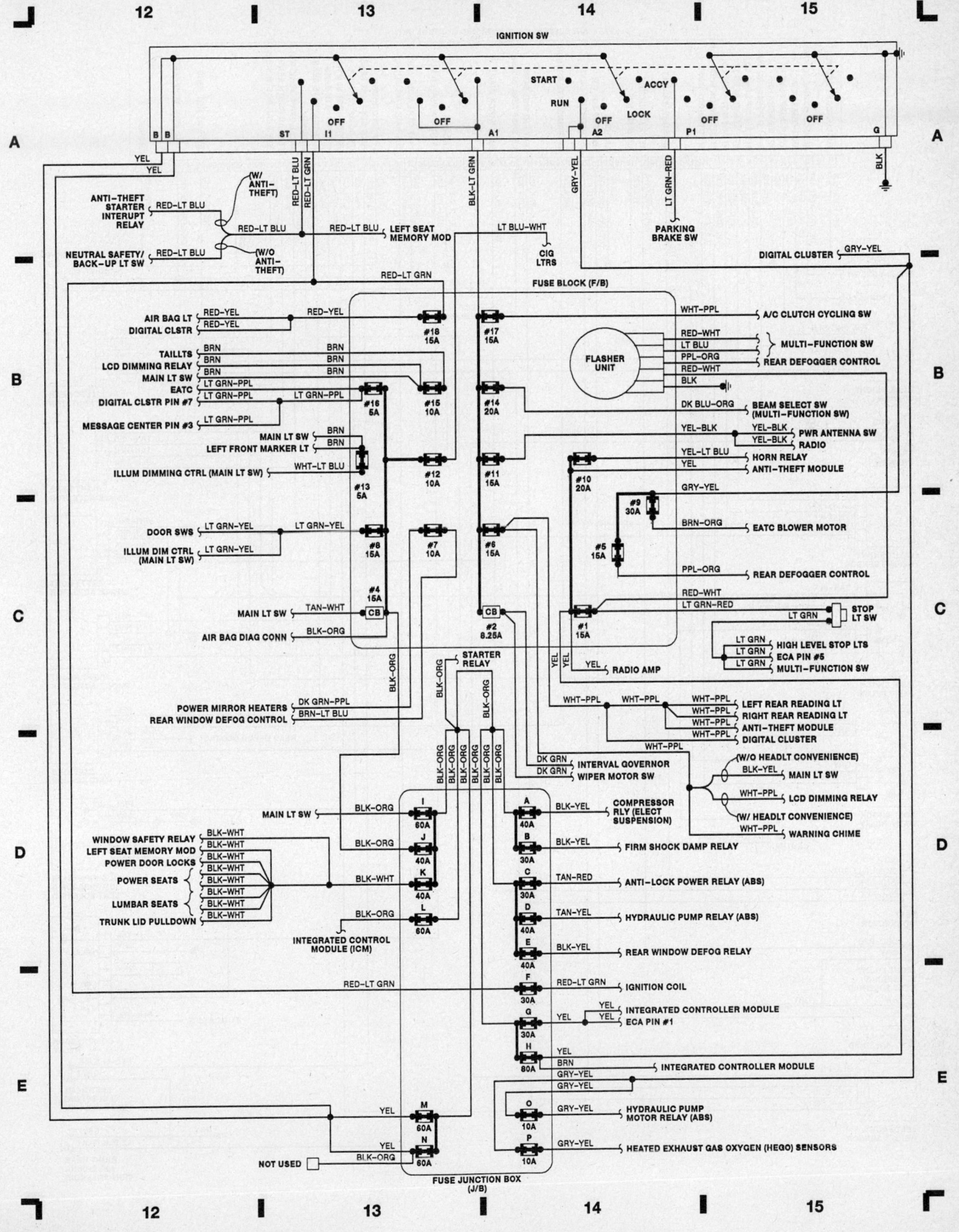

1989 FORD MOTOR CO.
Continental (Cont.)

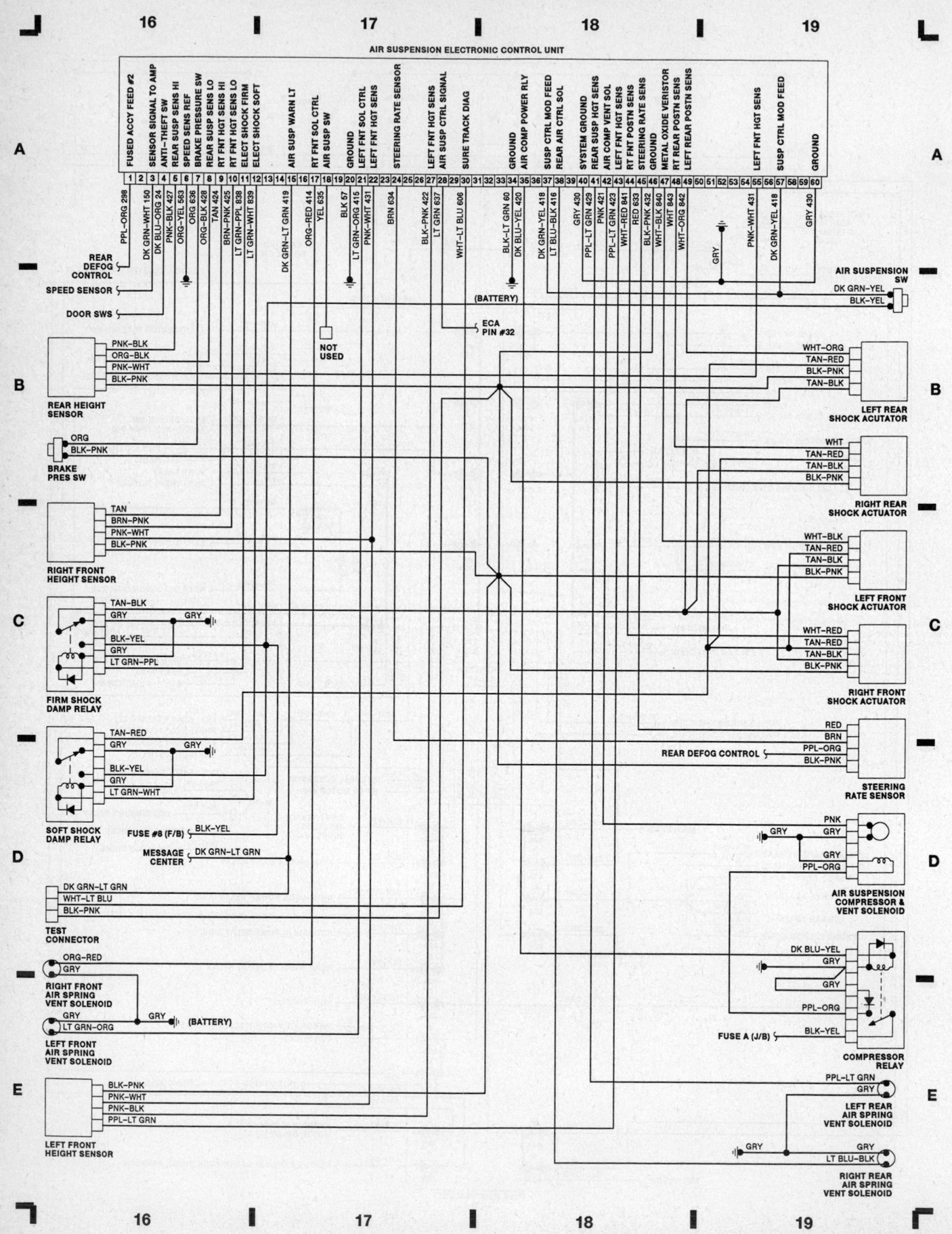

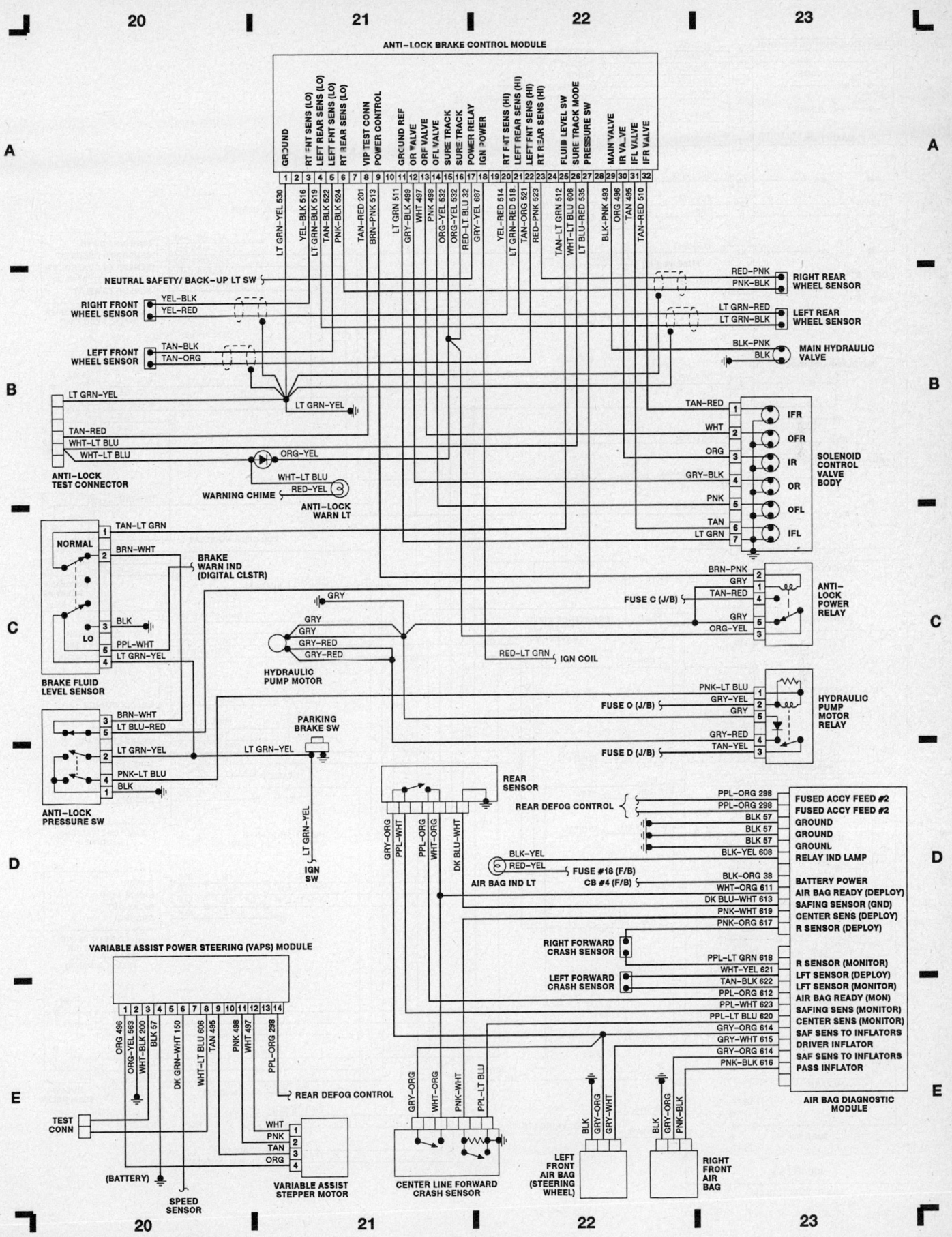

1989 FORD MOTOR CO.
Continental (Cont.)

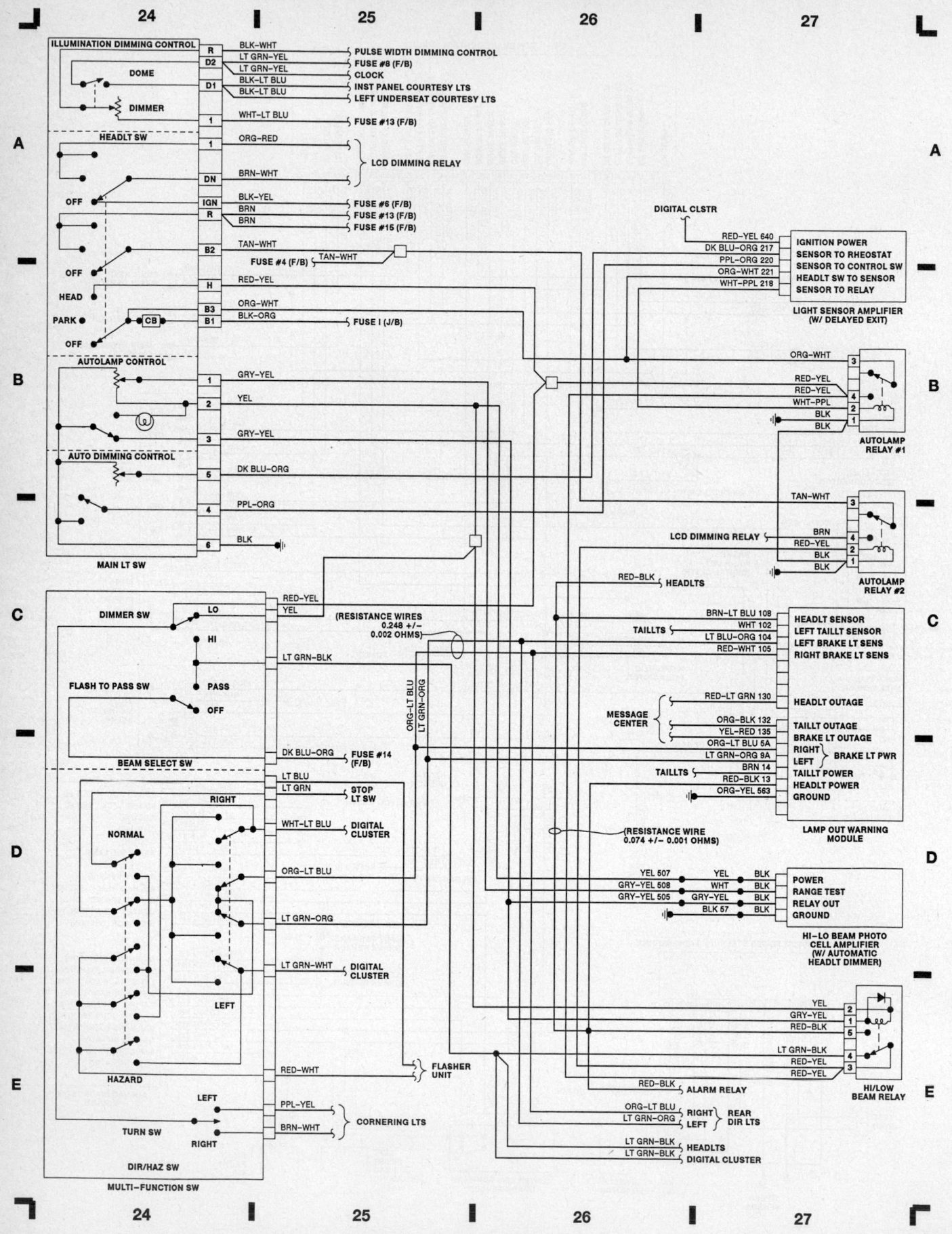

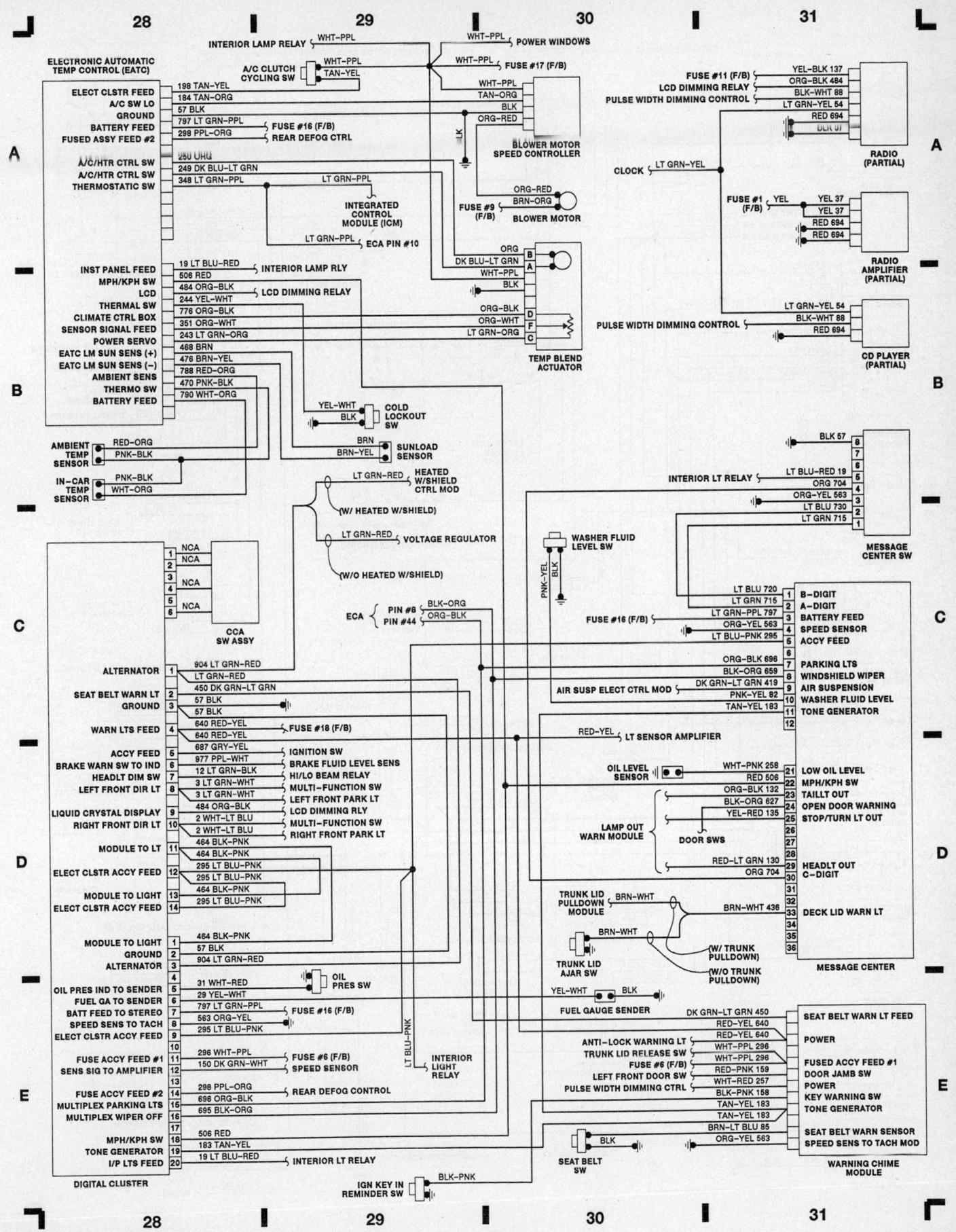

1989 FORD MOTOR CO.
Continental (Cont.)

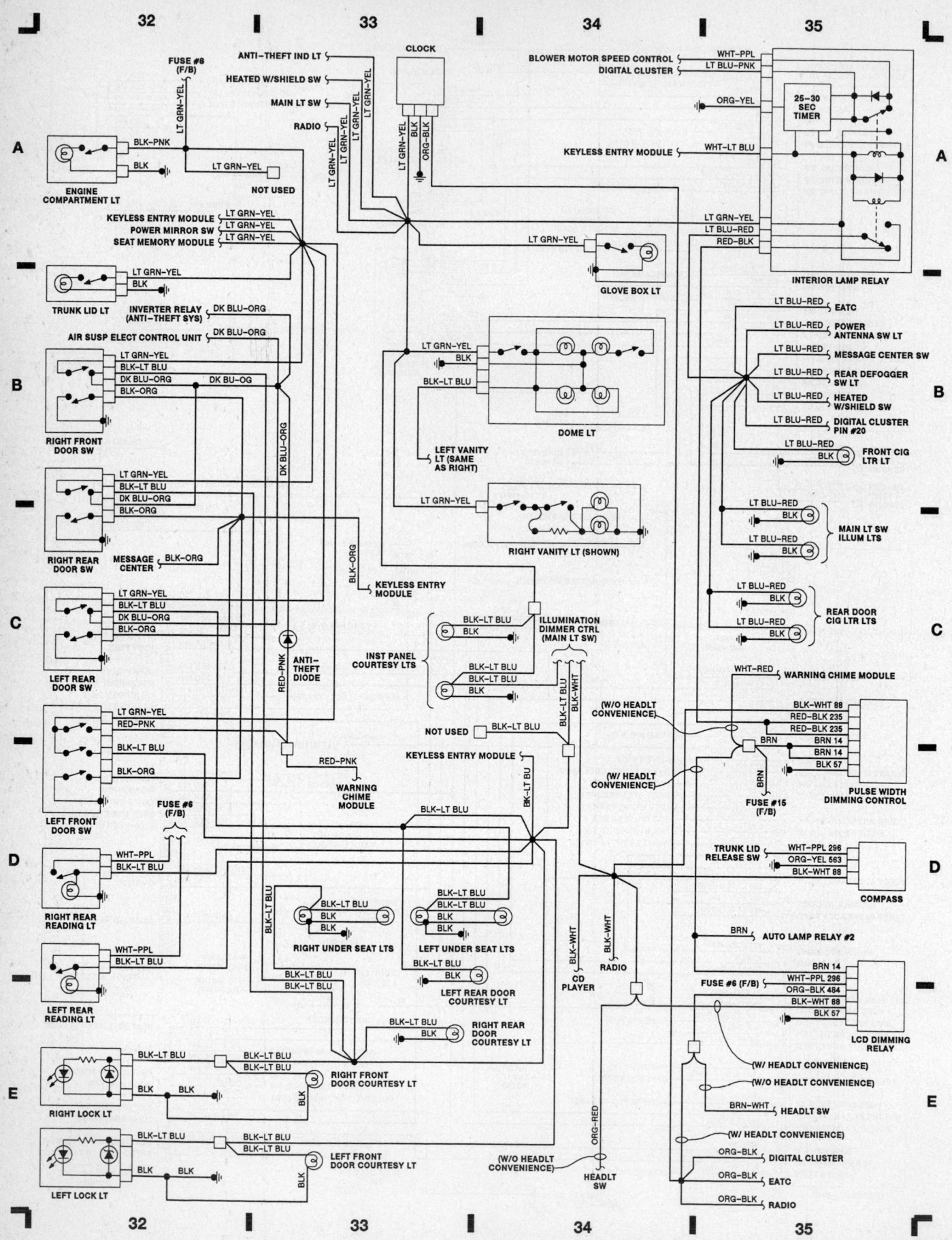

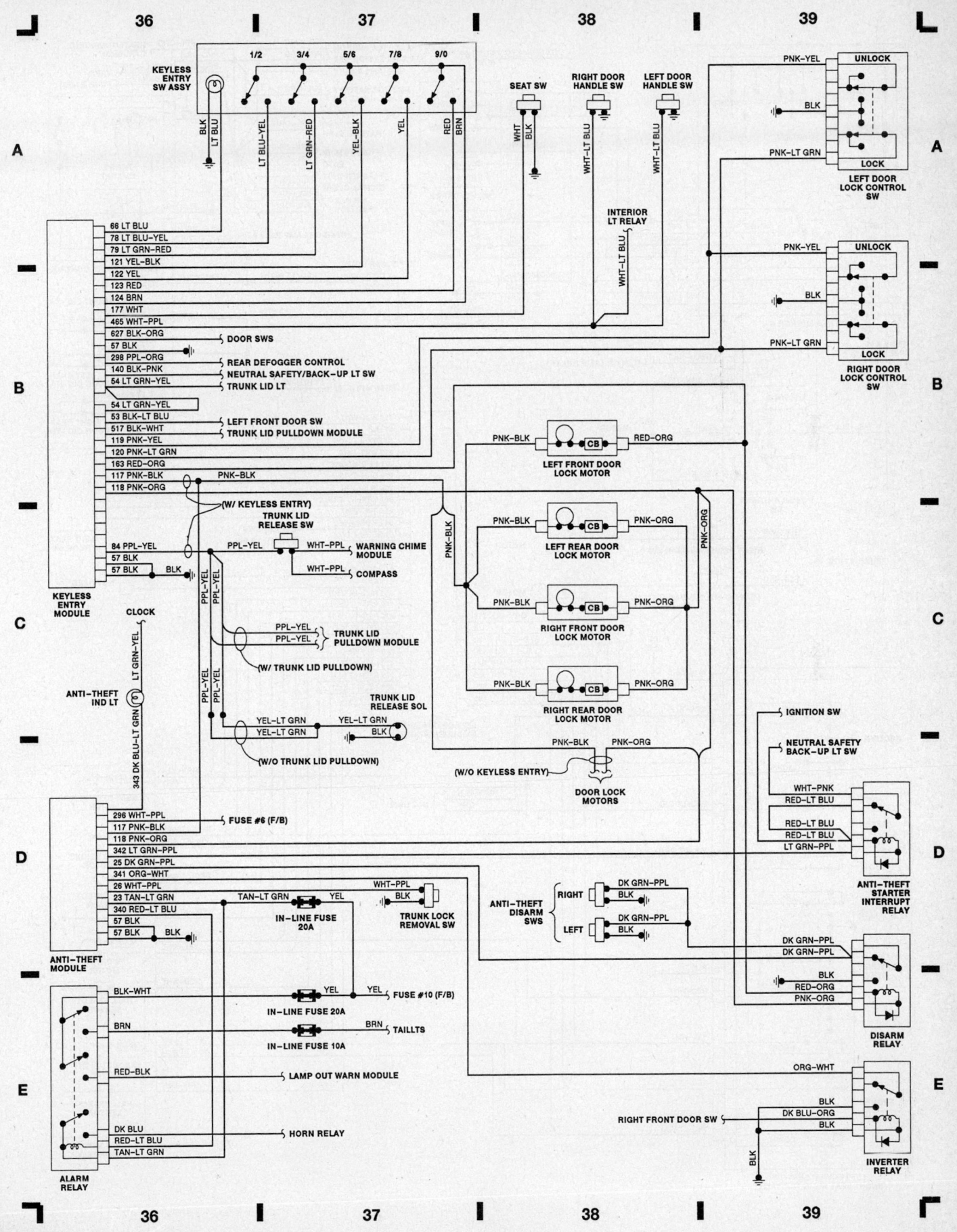

1989 Ford Motor CO.
Continental (Cont.)

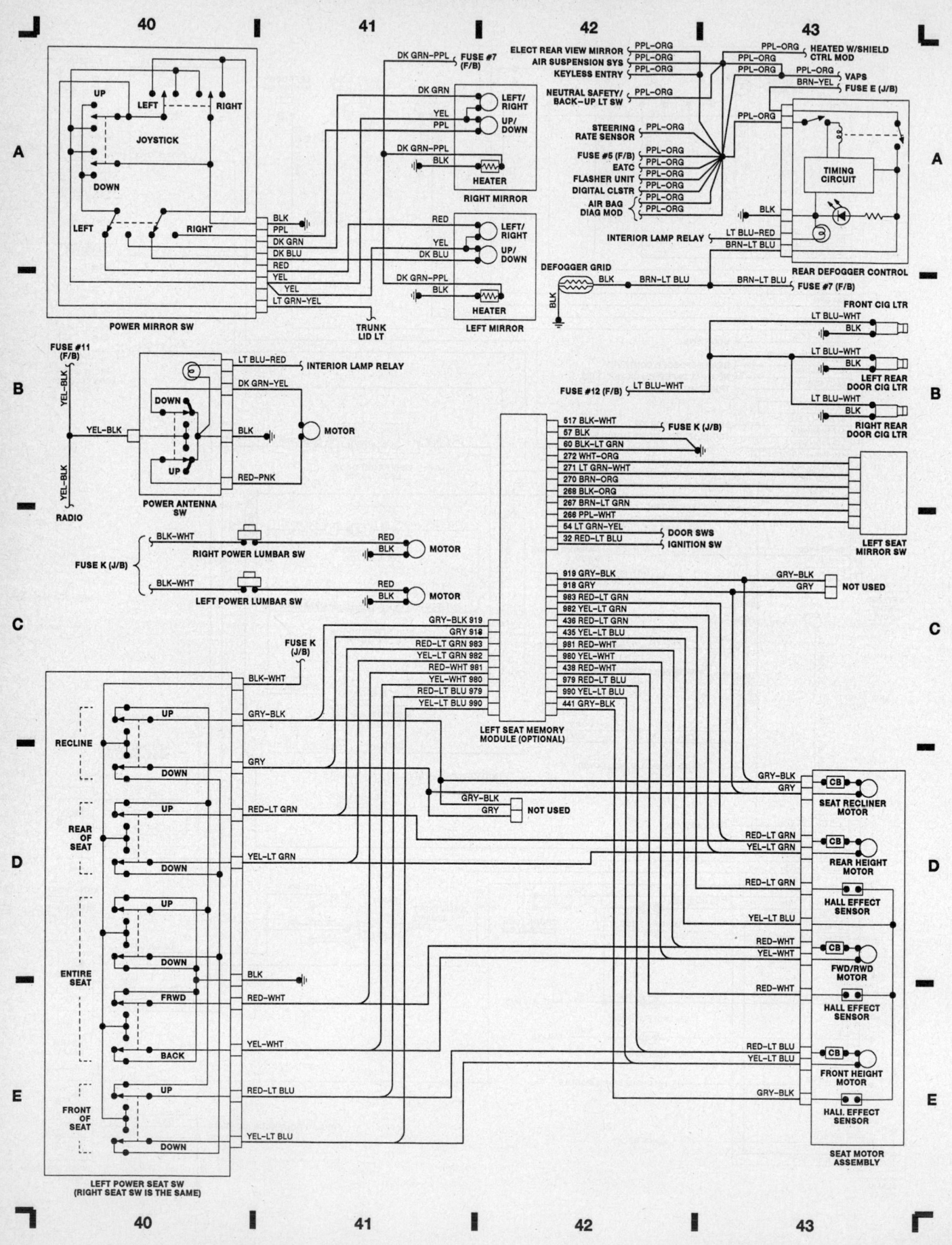

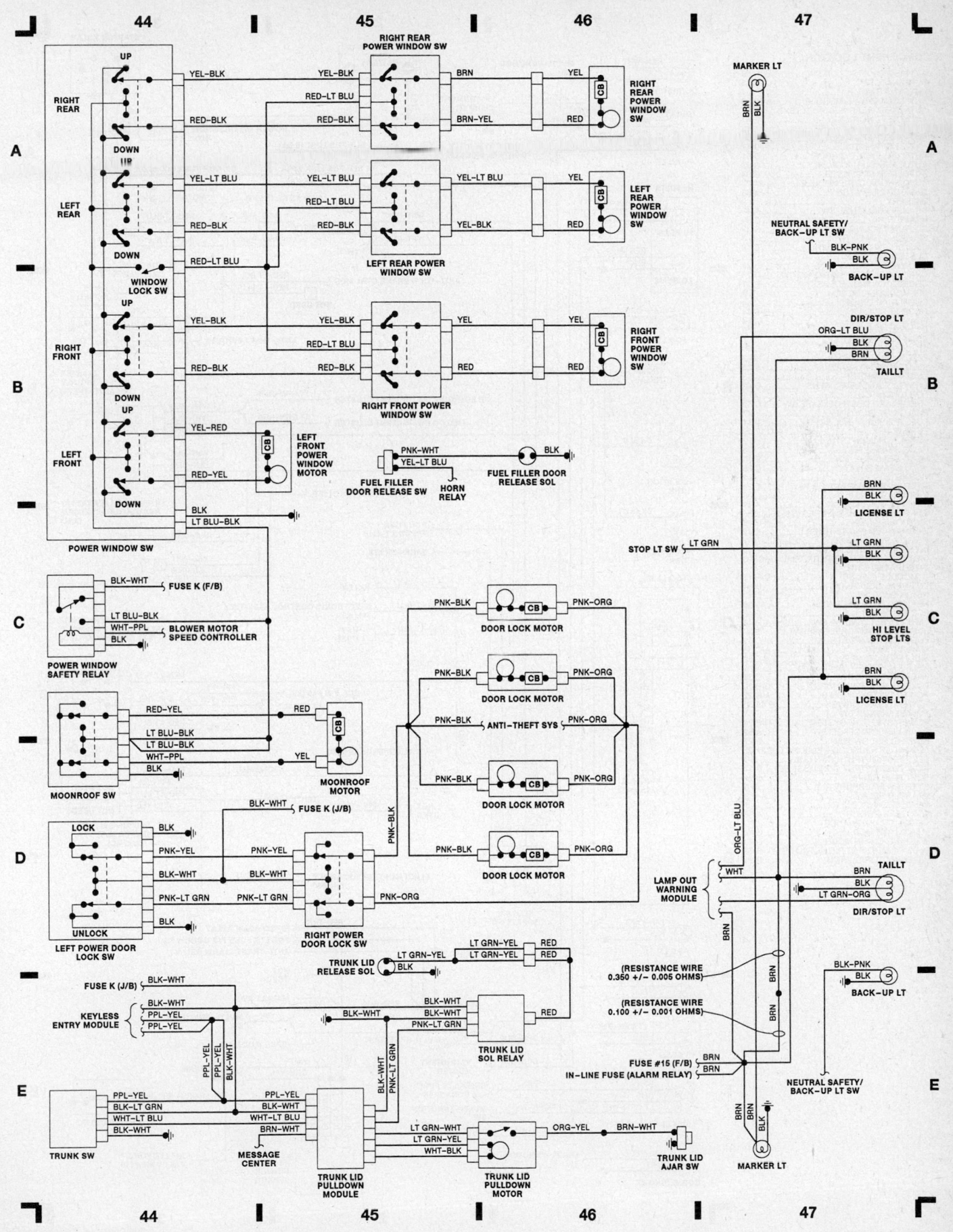

1989 Ford Motor Co.
Cougar & Thunderbird

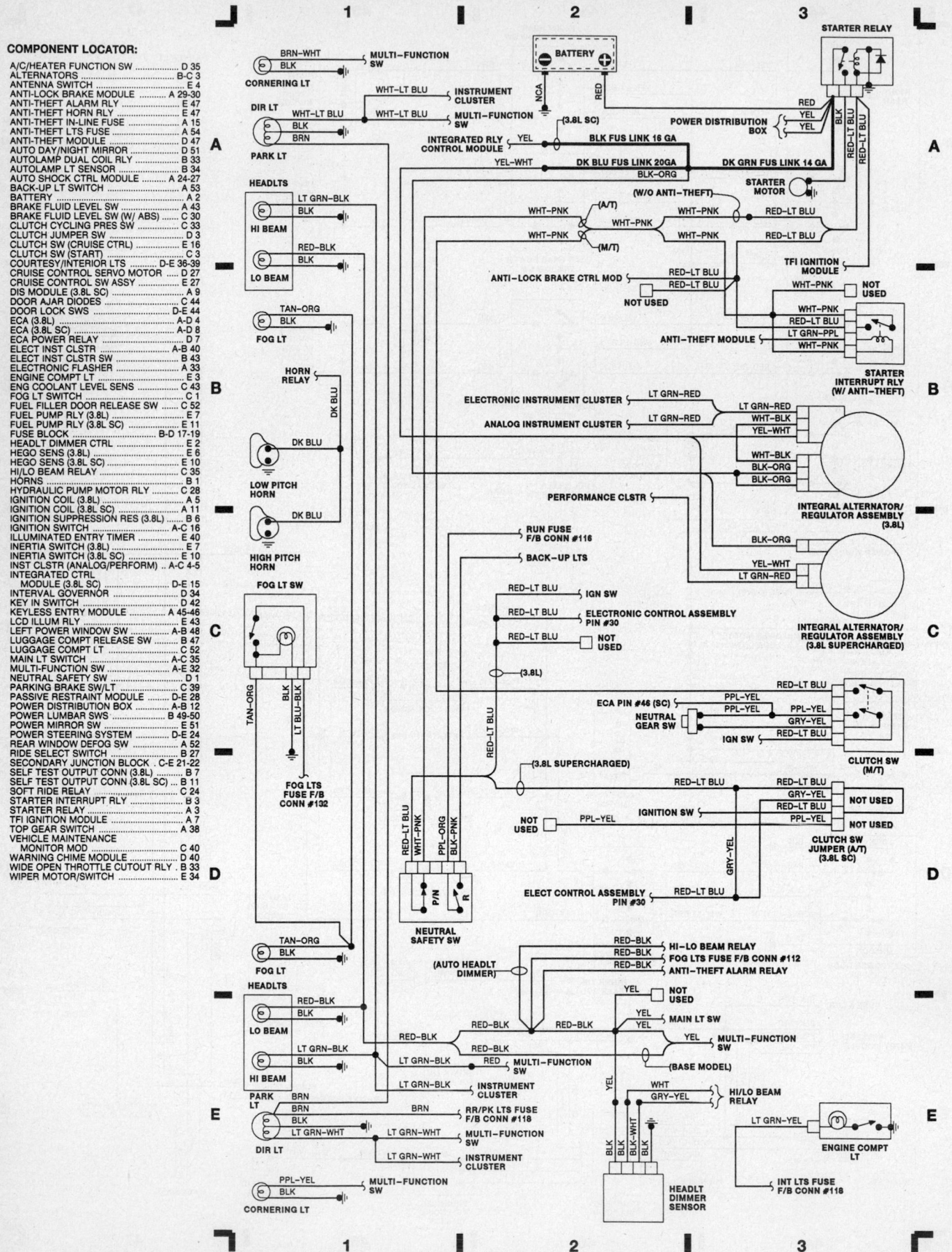

COMPONENT LOCATOR:

A/C/HEATER FUNCTION SW .... D 35
ALTERNATORS .... B-C 3
ANTENNA SWITCH .... E 4
ANTI-LOCK BRAKE MODULE .... A 29-30
ANTI-THEFT ALARM RLY .... E 47
ANTI-THEFT HORN RLY .... E 47
ANTI-THEFT IN-LINE FUSE .... A 15
ANTI-THEFT LTS FUSE .... A 54
ANTI-THEFT MODULE .... D 47
AUTO DAY/NIGHT MIRROR .... D 51
AUTOLAMP DUAL COIL RLY .... B 33
AUTOLAMP LT SENSOR .... B 34
AUTO SHOCK CTRL MODULE .... A 24-27
BACK-UP LT SWITCH .... A 53
BATTERY .... A 2
BRAKE FLUID LEVEL SW .... A 43
BRAKE FLUID LEVEL SW (W/ ABS) ... C 30
CLUTCH CYCLING PRES SW .... C 33
CLUTCH JUMPER SW .... D 3
CLUTCH SW (CRUISE CTRL) .... E 16
CLUTCH SW (START) .... C 3
COURTESY/INTERIOR LTS .... D-E 36-39
CRUISE CONTROL SERVO MOTOR ... D 27
CRUISE CONTROL SW ASSY .... E 27
DIS MODULE (3.8L SC) .... A 9
DOOR AJAR DIODES .... C 44
DOOR LOCK SWS .... D-E 44
ECA (3.8L) .... A-D 4
ECA (3.8L SC) .... A-D 8
ECA POWER RELAY .... D 7
ELECT INST CLSTR .... A-B 40
ELECT INST CLSTR SW .... B 43
ELECTRONIC FLASHER .... A 33
ENGINE COMPT LT .... E 3
ENG COOLANT LEVEL SENS .... C 43
FOG LT SWITCH .... C 1
FUEL FILLER DOOR RELEASE SW ... C 52
FUEL PUMP RLY (3.8L) .... E 7
FUEL PUMP RLY (3.8L SC) .... E 11
FUSE BLOCK .... B-D 17-19
HEADLT DIMMER CTRL .... E 2
HEGO SENS (3.8L) .... E 6
HEGO SENS (3.8L SC) .... E 10
HI/LO BEAM RELAY .... C 35
HORNS .... B 1
HYDRAULIC PUMP MOTOR RLY .... C 28
IGNITION COIL (3.8L) .... A 7
IGNITION COIL (3.8L SC) .... A 11
IGNITION SUPPRESSION RES (3.8L) ... B 6
IGNITION SWITCH .... A-C 16
ILLUMINATED ENTRY TIMER .... E 40
INERTIA SWITCH (3.8L) .... E 7
INERTIA SWITCH (3.8L SC) .... E 10
INST CLSTR (ANALOG/PERFORM) ... A-C 4-5
INTEGRATED CTRL
MODULE (3.8L SC) .... D-E 15
INTERVAL GOVERNOR .... D 34
KEY IN SWITCH .... D 42
KEYLESS ENTRY MODULE .... A 45-46
LCD ILLUM RLY .... E 43
LEFT POWER WINDOW SW .... A-B 48
LUGGAGE COMPT RELEASE SW ... B 47
LUGGAGE COMPT LT .... C 52
MAIN LT SWITCH .... A-C 35
MULTI-FUNCTION SW .... A-E 32
NEUTRAL SAFETY SW .... D 1
PARKING BRAKE SW/LT .... C 39
PASSIVE RESTRAINT MODULE ..... D-E 28
POWER DISTRIBUTION BOX .... A-B 12
POWER LUMBAR SWS .... B 49-50
POWER MIRROR SW .... E 51
POWER STEERING SYSTEM .... D-E 24
REAR WINDOW DEFOG SW .... A 52
RIDE SELECT SWITCH .... B 33
SECONDARY JUNCTION BLOCK ... C-E 21-22
SELF TEST OUTPUT CONN (3.8L) ... B 7
SELF TEST OUTPUT CONN (3.8L SC) ... B 11
SOFT RIDE RELAY .... C 24
STARTER INTERRUPT RLY .... B 3
STARTER RELAY .... A 3
TFI IGNITION MODULE .... A 7
TOP GEAR SWITCH .... A 38
VEHICLE MAINTENANCE
MONITOR MOD .... C 40
WARNING CHIME MODULE .... D 40
WIDE OPEN THROTTLE CUTOUT RLY ... B 33
WIPER MOTOR/SWITCH .... E 34

1989 Ford Motor Co.
Cougar & Thunderbird (Cont.)

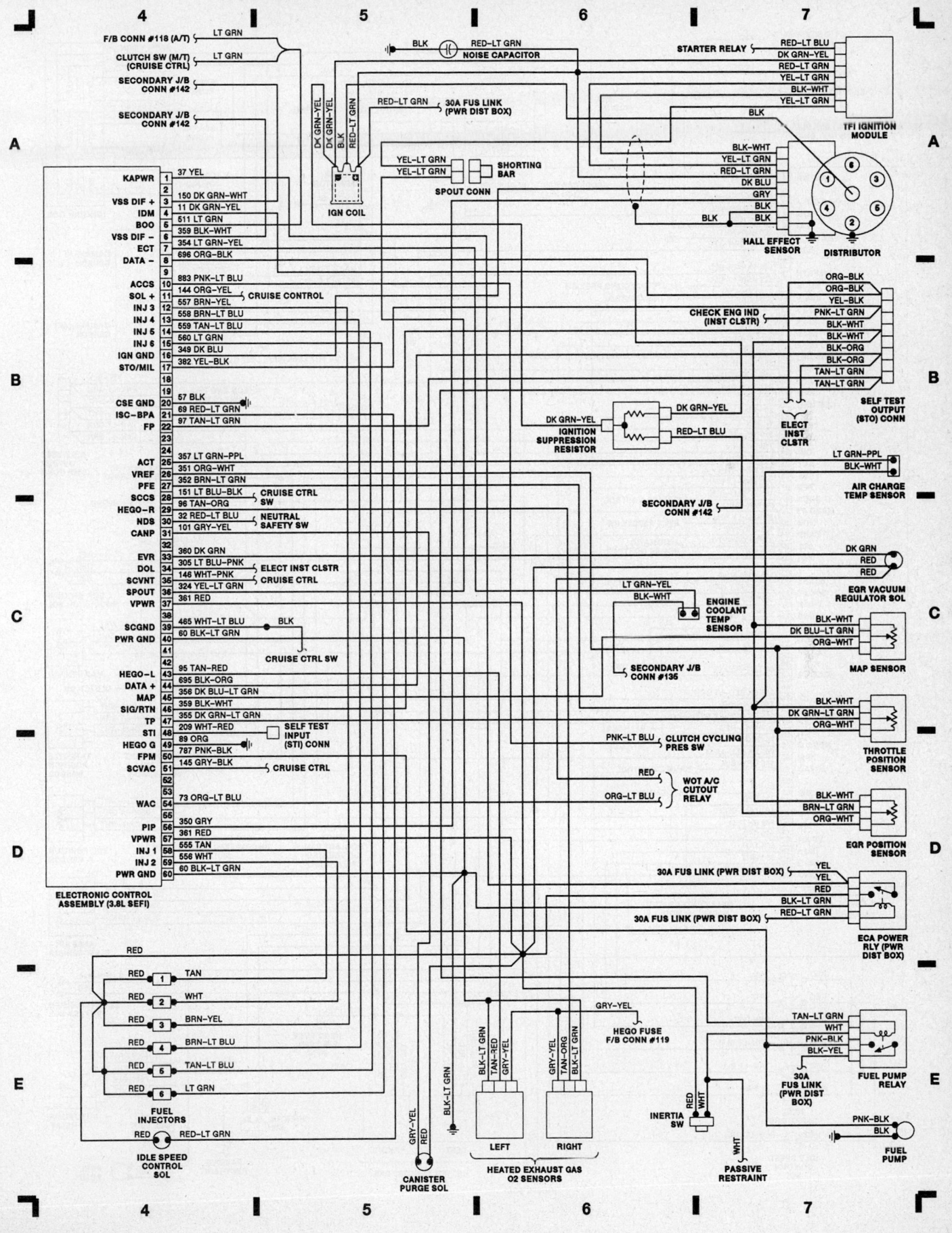

1989 FORD MOTOR CO.
Cougar & Thunderbird (Cont.)

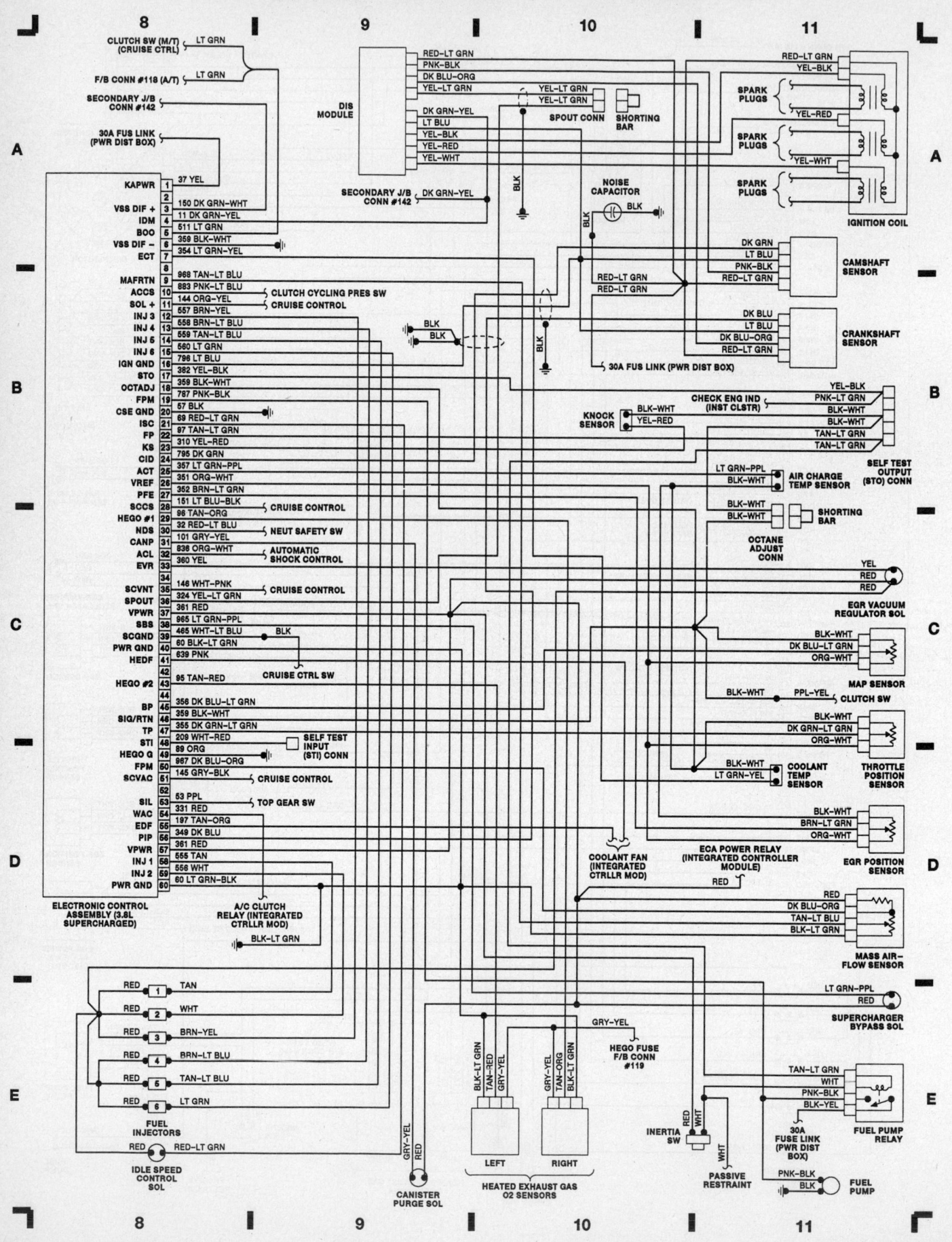

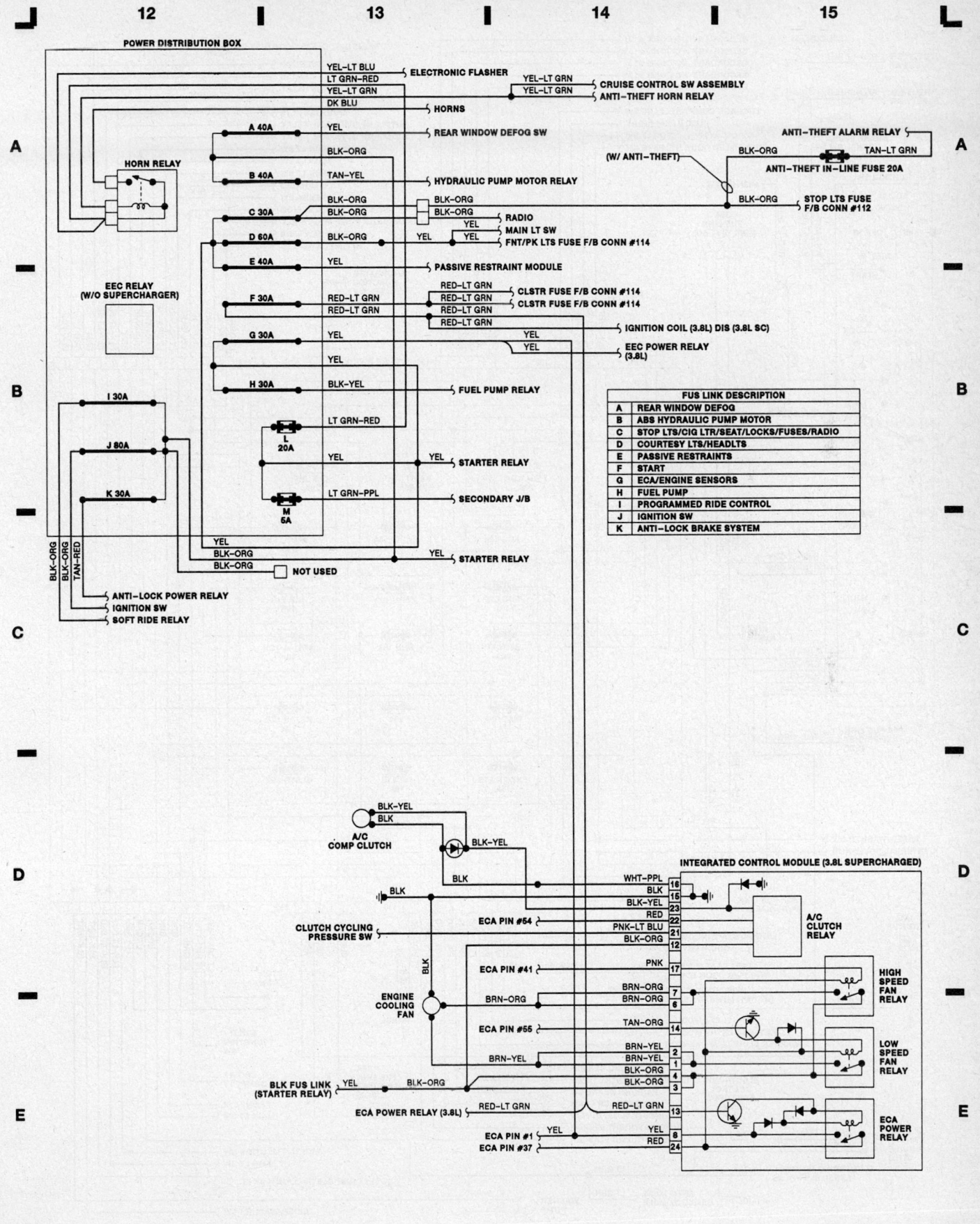

FUS LINK DESCRIPTION	
A	REAR WINDOW DEFOG
B	ABS HYDRAULIC PUMP MOTOR
C	STOP LTS/CIG LTR/SEAT/LOCKS/FUSES/RADIO
D	COURTESY LTS/HEADLTS
E	PASSIVE RESTRAINTS
F	START
G	ECA/ENGINE SENSORS
H	FUEL PUMP
I	PROGRAMMED RIDE CONTROL
J	IGNITION SW
K	ANTI-LOCK BRAKE SYSTEM

1989 Ford Motor Co.
Cougar & Thunderbird (Cont.)

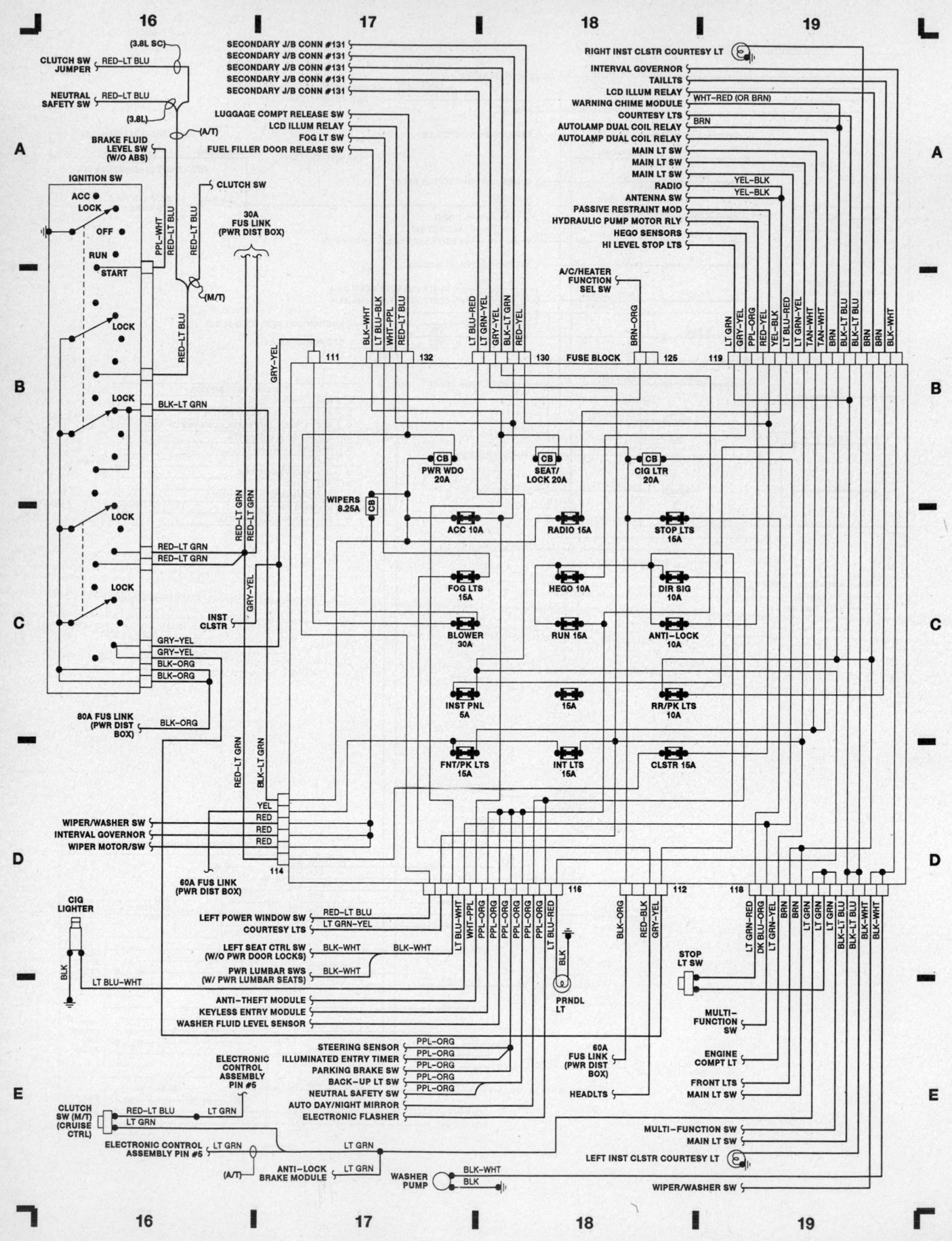

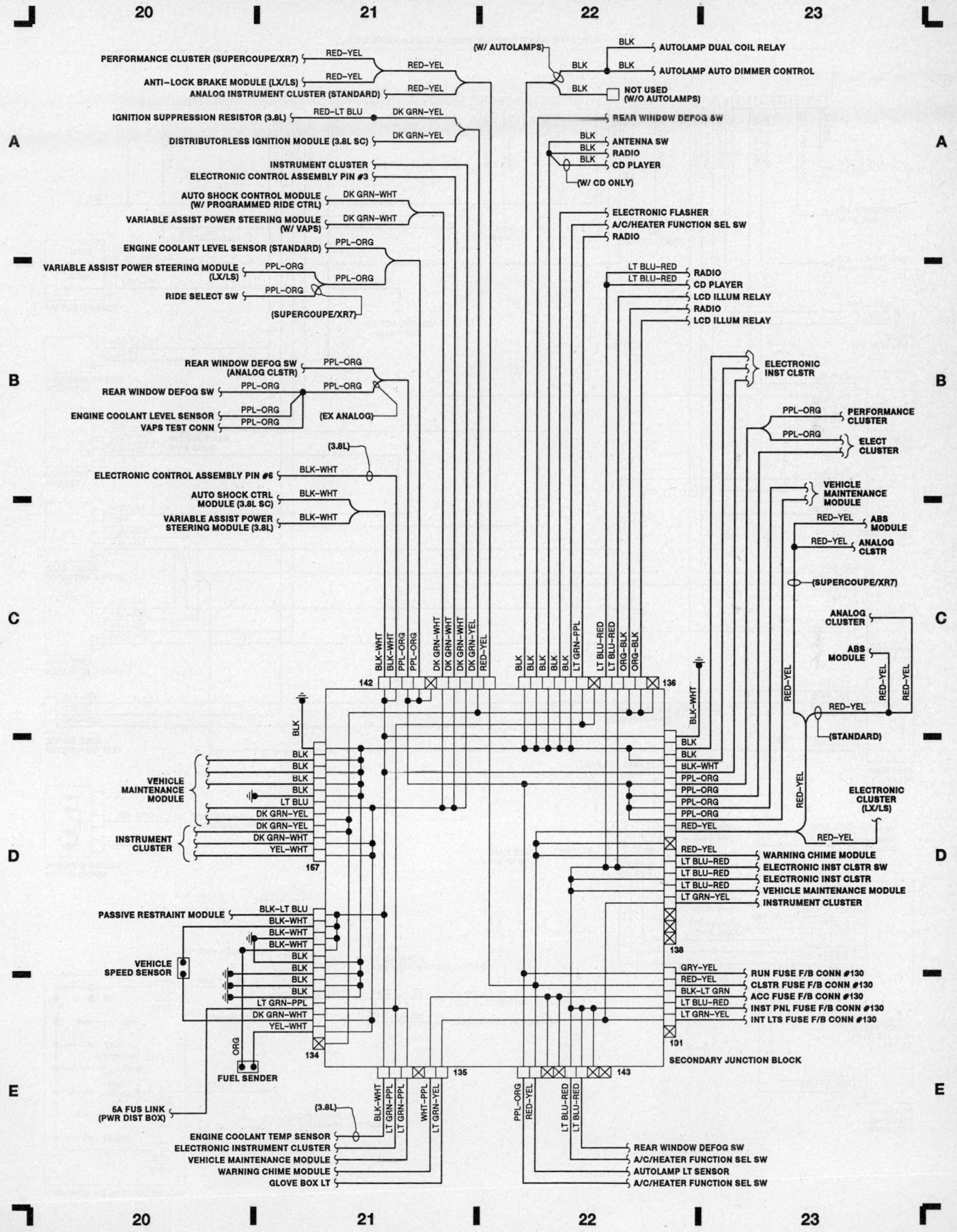

1989 Ford MOTOR CO.
Cougar & Thunderbird (Cont.)

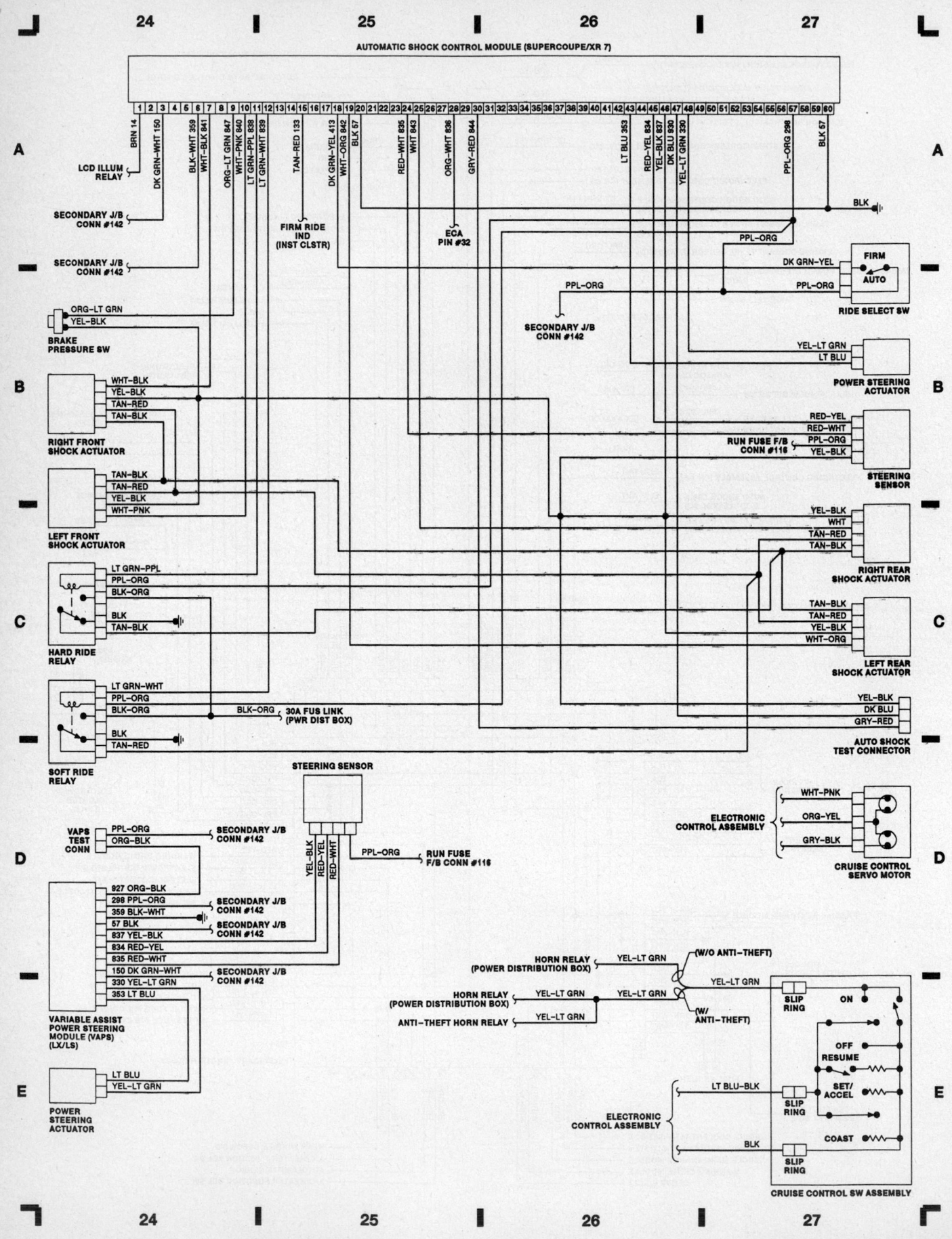

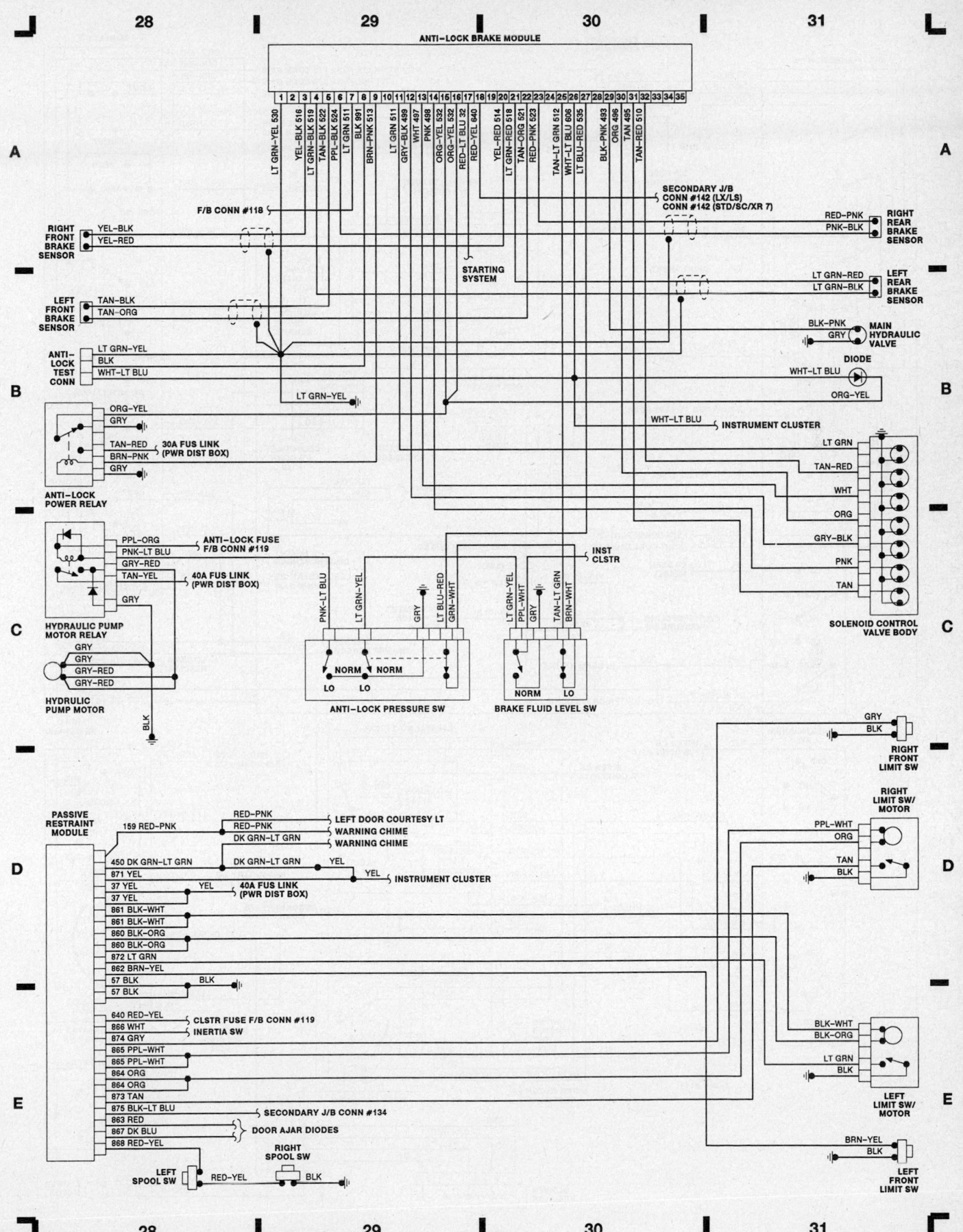

1989 Ford Motor Co.
Cougar & Thunderbird (Cont.)

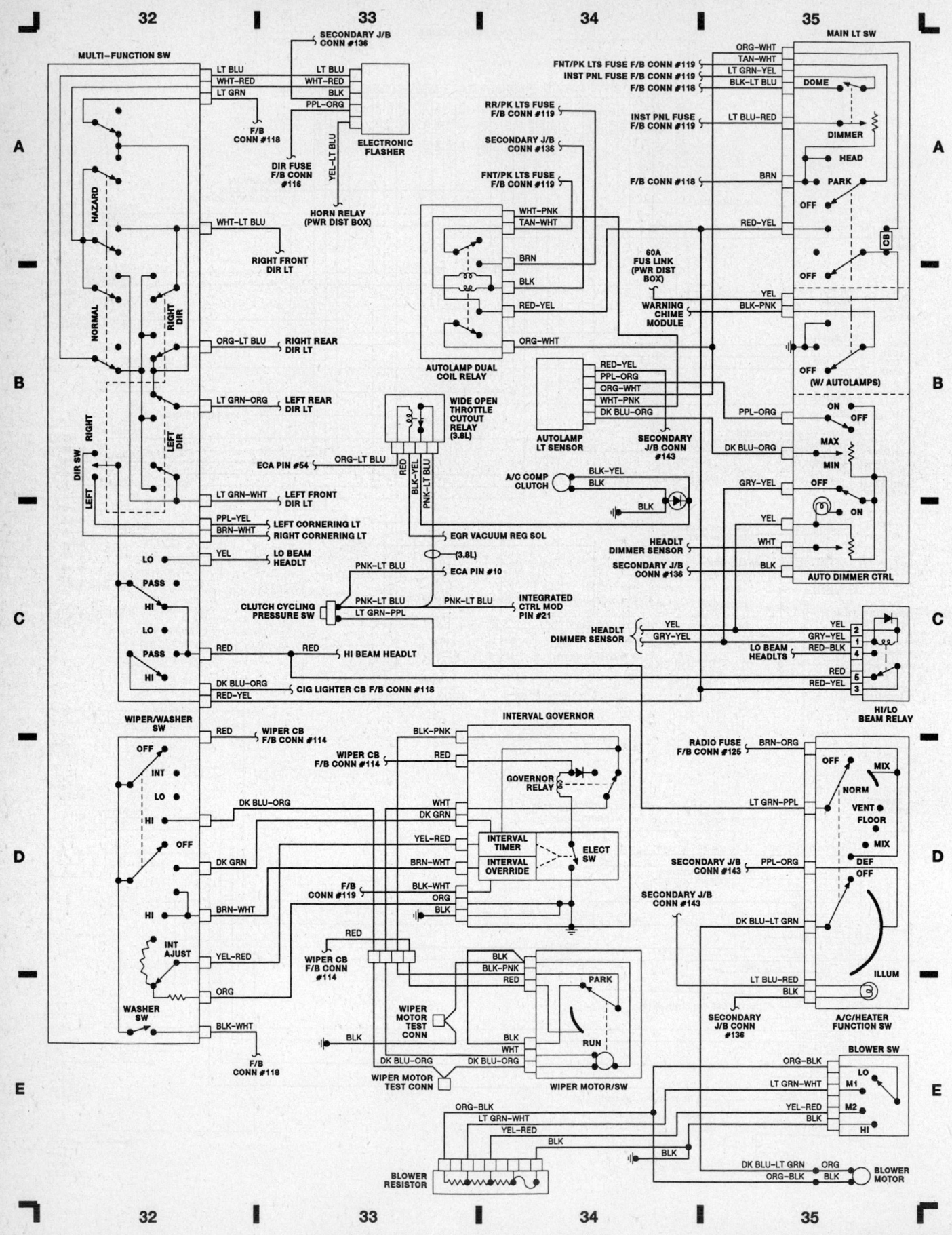

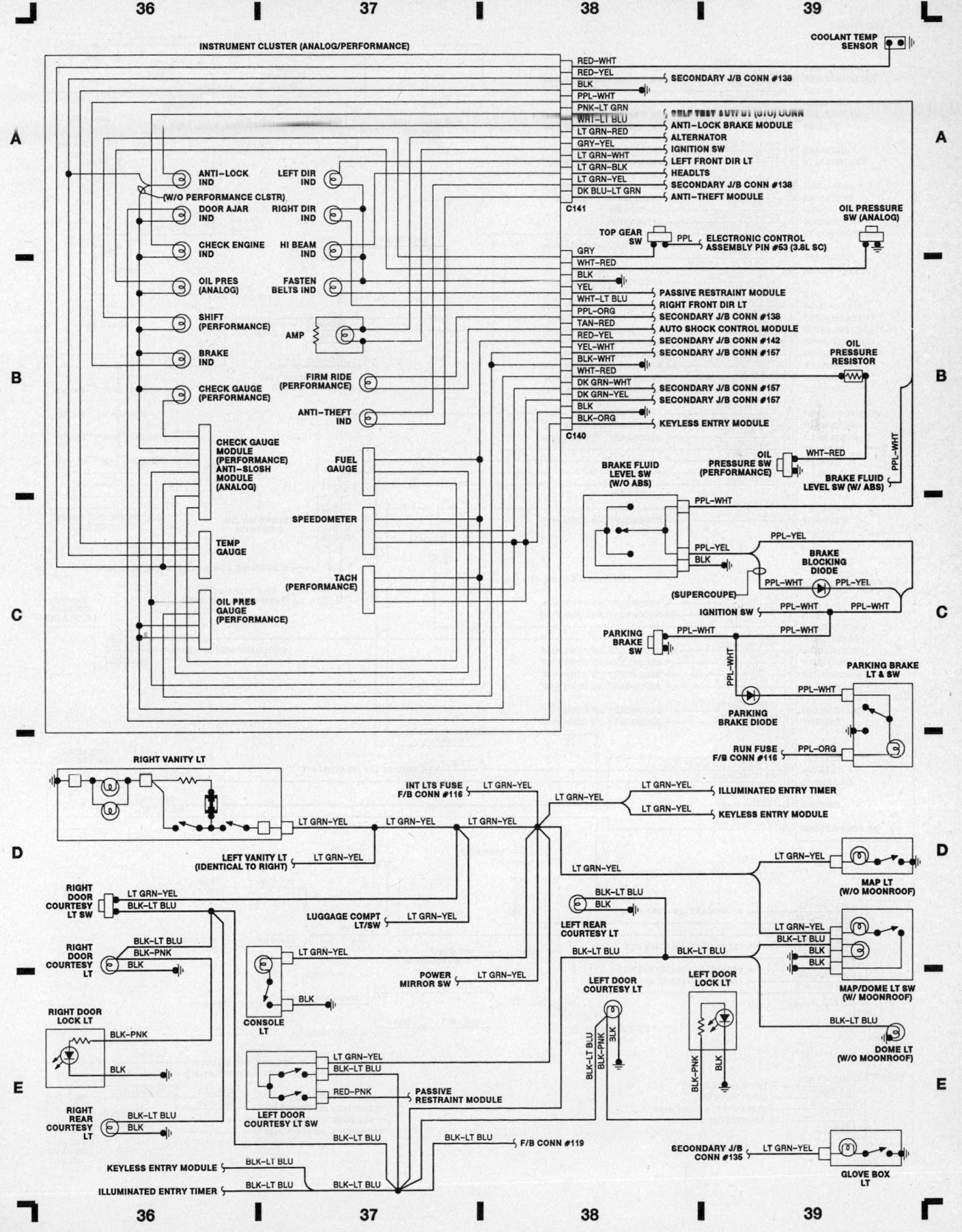

1989 Ford Motor Co.
Cougar & Thunderbird (Cont.)

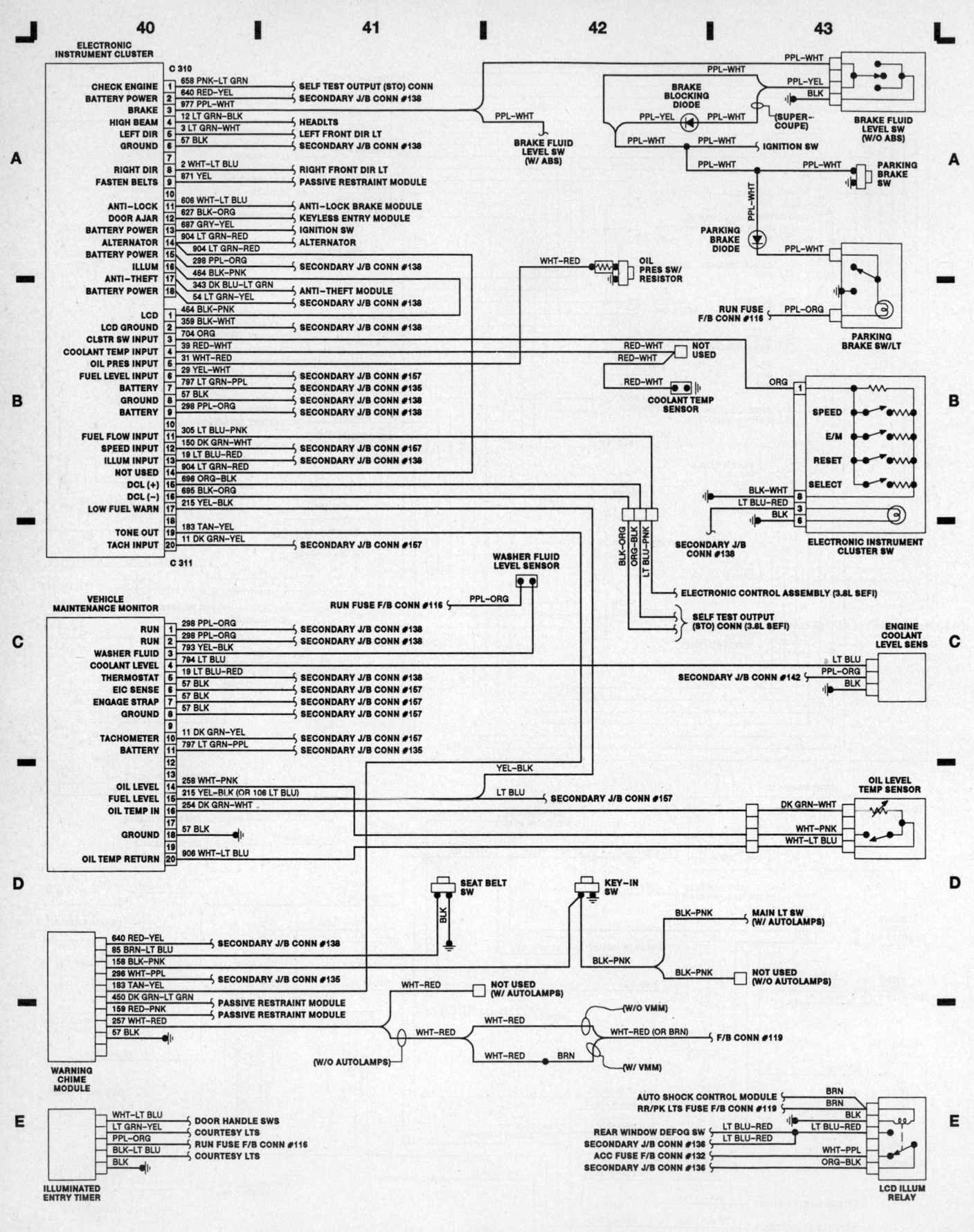

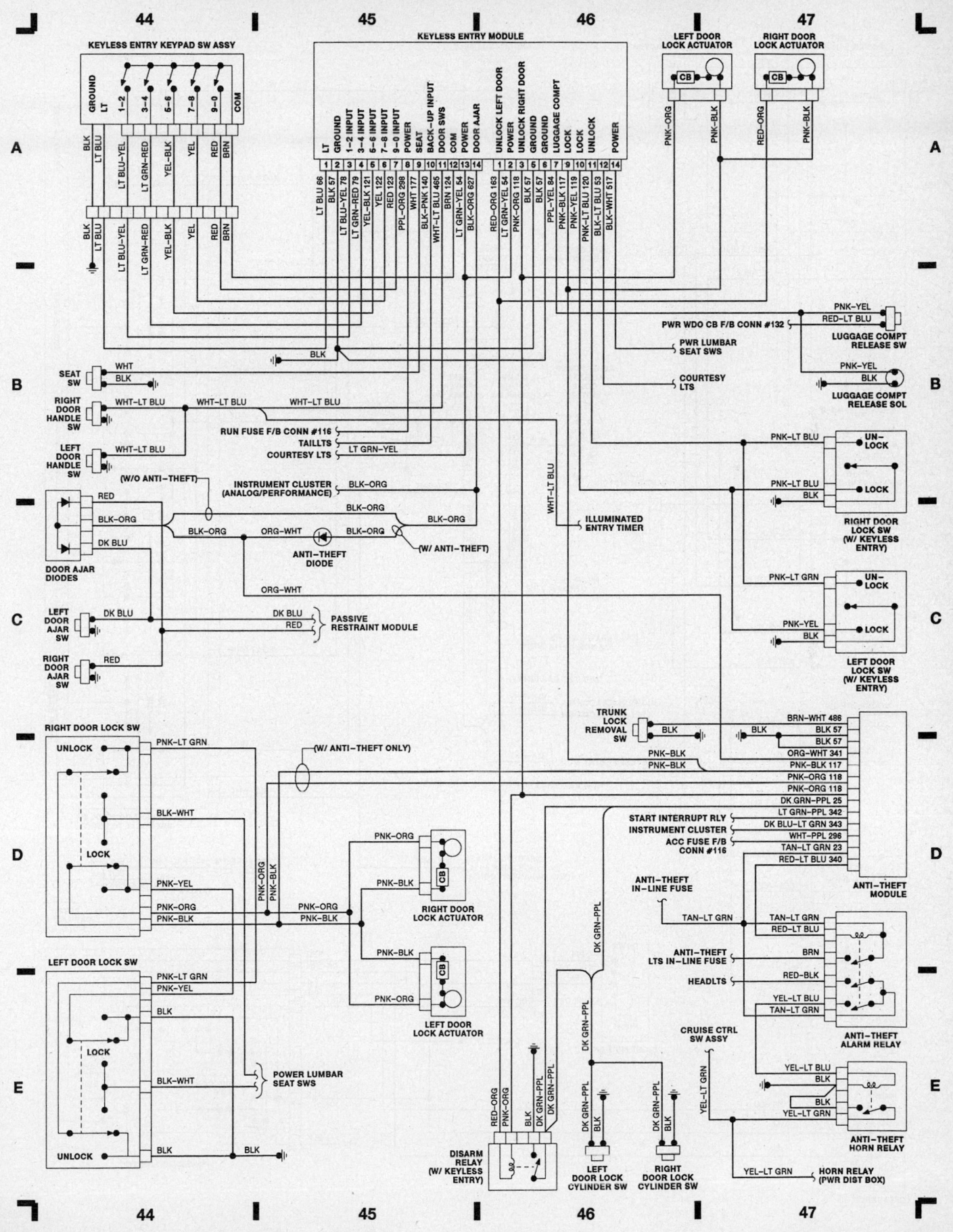

1989 Ford Motor Co.
Cougar & Thunderbird (Cont.)

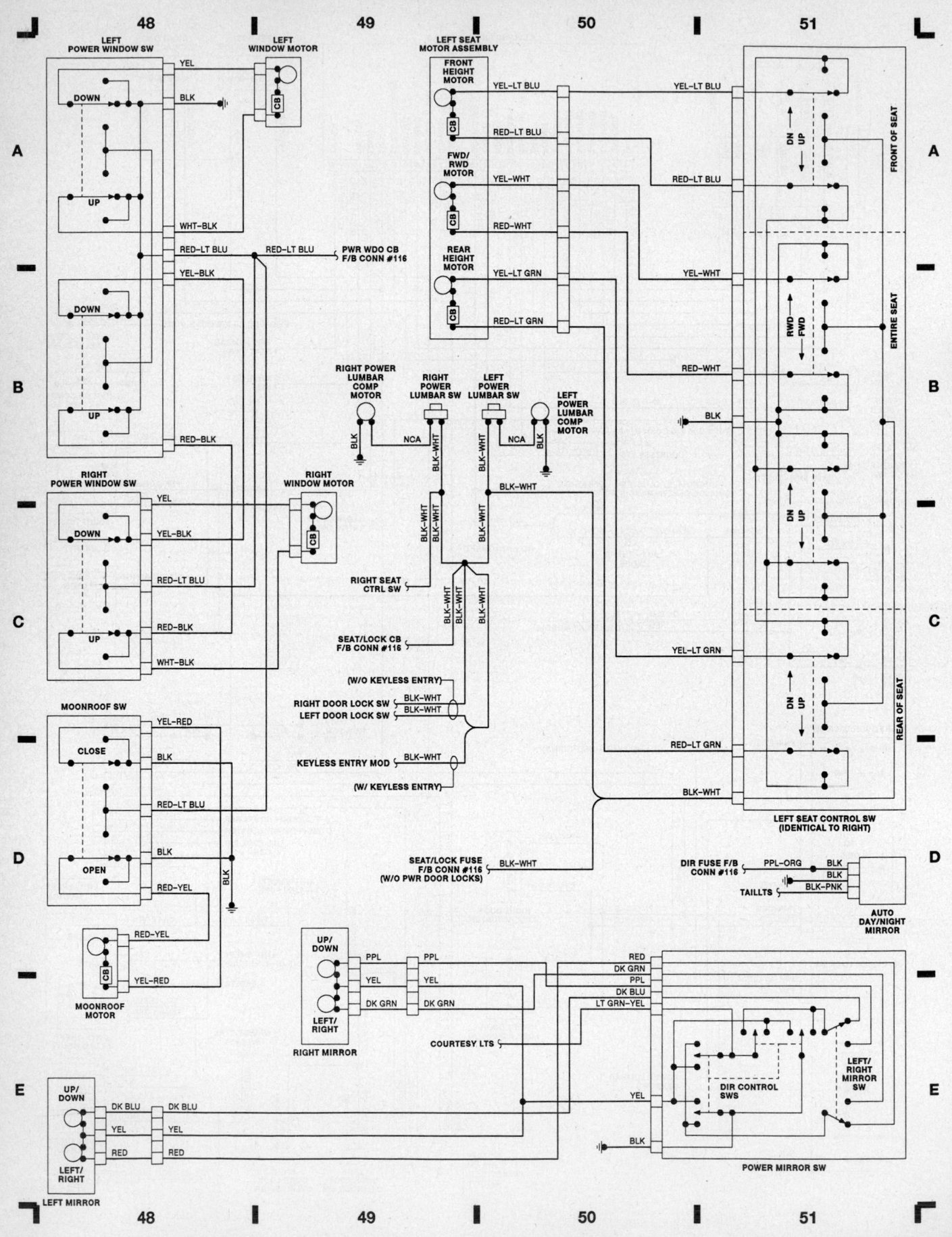

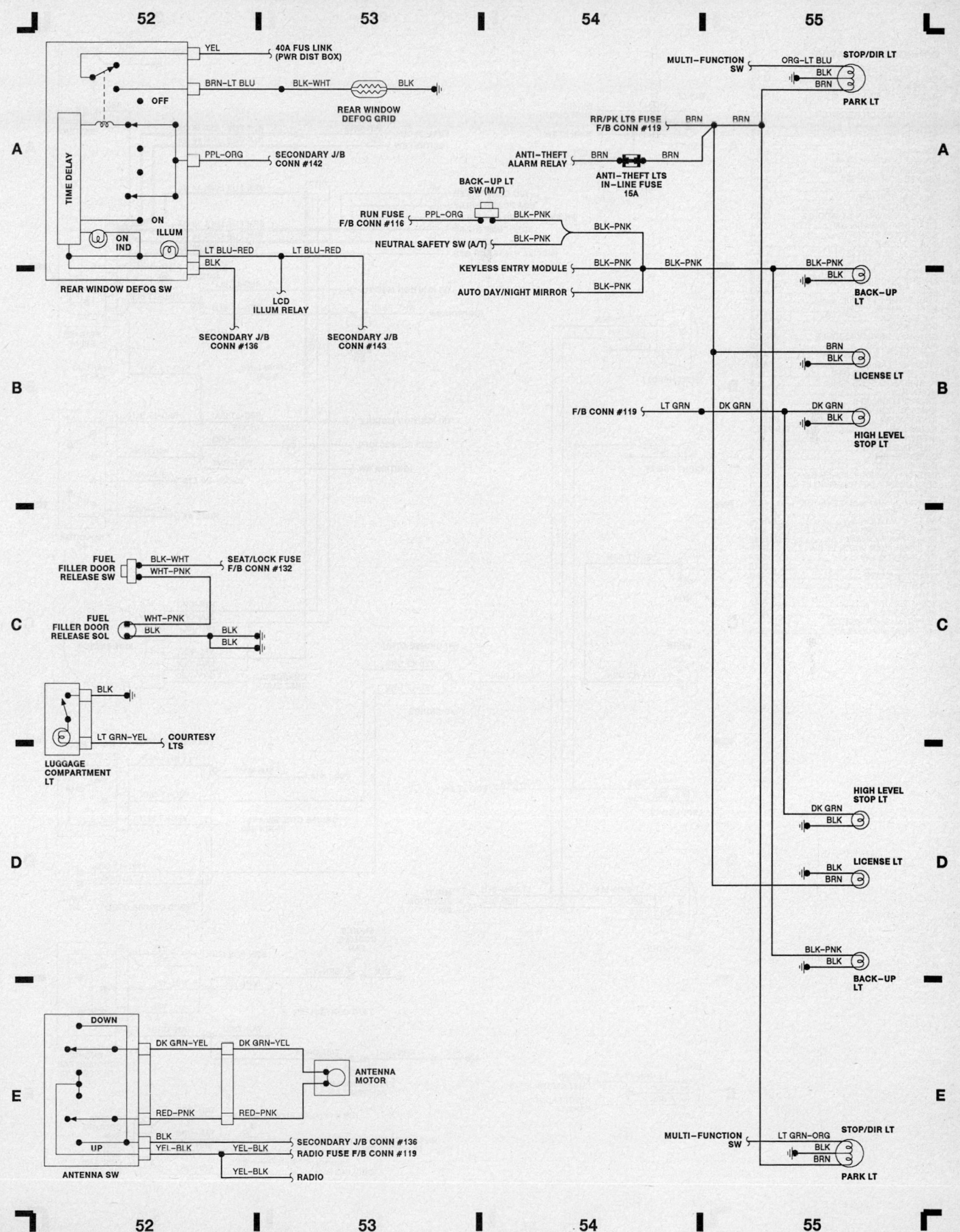

1989 Ford Motor Co.
Escort

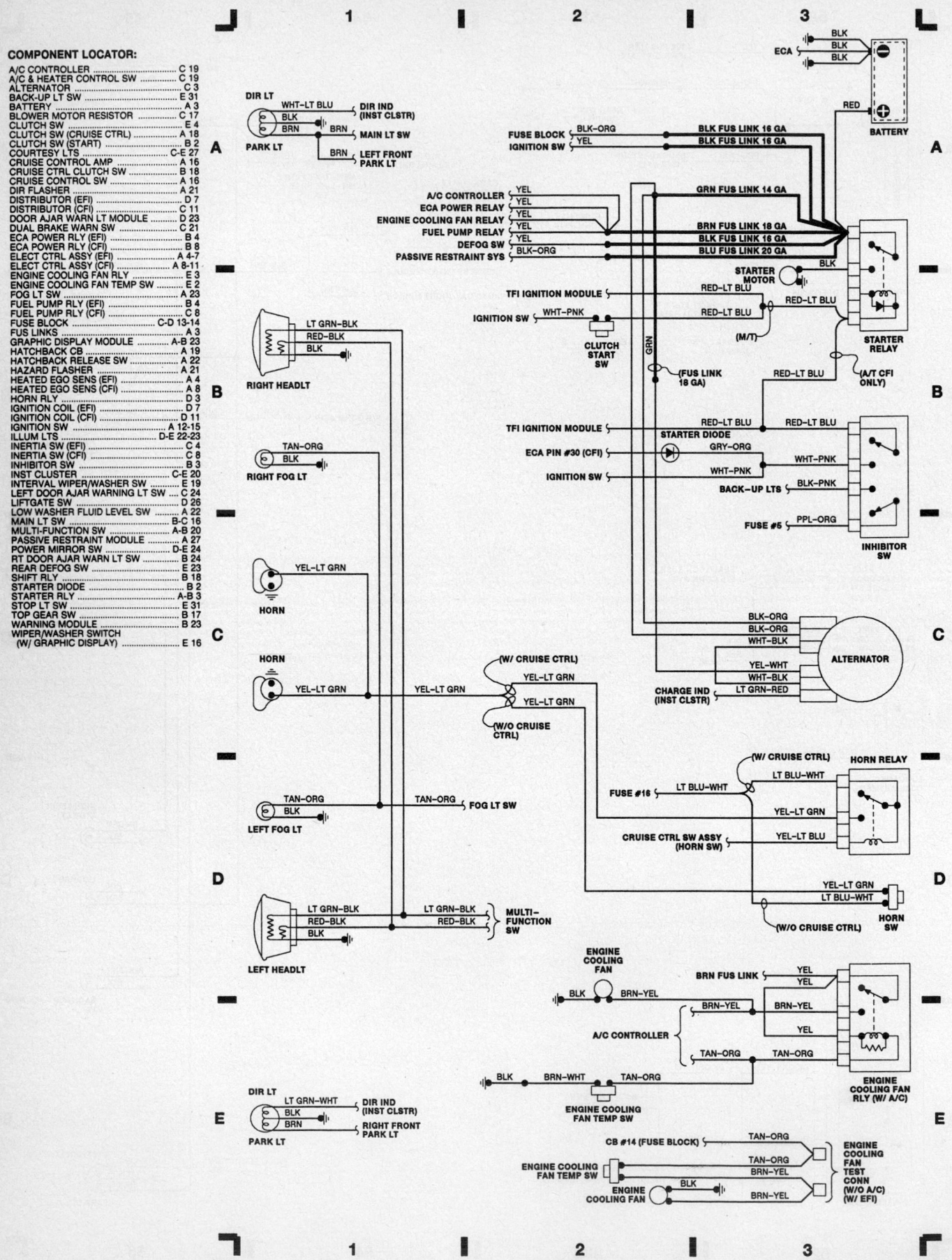

COMPONENT LOCATOR:

A/C CONTROLLER .... C 19
A/C & HEATER CONTROL SW .... C 19
ALTERNATOR .... C 3
BACK-UP LT SW .... E 31
BATTERY .... A 3
BLOWER MOTOR RESISTOR .... C 17
CLUTCH SW .... E 4
CLUTCH SW (CRUISE CTRL) .... A 18
CLUTCH SW (START) .... B 2
COURTESY LTS .... C-E 27
CRUISE CONTROL AMP .... A 16
CRUISE CTRL CLUTCH SW .... B 18
CRUISE CONTROL SW .... A 16
DIR FLASHER .... A 21
DISTRIBUTOR (EFI) .... D 7
DISTRIBUTOR (CFI) .... C 11
DOOR AJAR WARN LT MODULE .... D 23
DUAL BRAKE WARN SW .... C 21
ECA POWER RLY (EFI) .... B 4
ECA POWER RLY (CFI) .... B 8
ELECT CTRL ASSY (EFI) .... A 4-7
ELECT CTRL ASSY (CFI) .... A 8-11
ENGINE COOLING FAN RLY .... E 3
ENGINE COOLING FAN TEMP SW ...... E 2
FOG LT SW .... A 23
FUEL PUMP RLY (EFI) .... B 4
FUEL PUMP RLY (CFI) .... C 8
FUSE BLOCK .... C-D 13-14
FUS LINKS .... A 3
GRAPHIC DISPLAY MODULE .... A-B 23
HATCHBACK CB .... A 19
HATCHBACK RELEASE SW .... A 22
HAZARD FLASHER .... A 21
HEATED EGO SENS (EFI) .... A 4
HEATED EGO SENS (CFI) .... A 8
HORN RLY .... D 3
IGNITION COIL (EFI) .... D 7
IGNITION COIL (CFI) .... D 11
IGNITION SW .... A 12-15
ILLUM LTS .... D-E 22-23
INERTIA SW (EFI) .... C 4
INERTIA SW (CFI) .... C 8
INHIBITOR SW .... B 3
INST CLUSTER .... C-E 20
INTERVAL WIPER/WASHER SW .... E 19
LEFT DOOR AJAR WARNING LT SW ... C 24
LIFTGATE SW .... D 26
LOW WASHER FLUID LEVEL SW .... A 22
MAIN LT SW .... B-C 16
MULTI-FUNCTION SW .... A-B 20
PASSIVE RESTRAINT MODULE .... A 27
POWER MIRROR SW .... D-E 24
RT DOOR AJAR WARN LT SW .... B 24
REAR DEFOG SW .... E 23
SHIFT RLY .... B 18
STARTER DIODE .... B 2
STARTER RLY .... A-B 3
STOP LT SW .... E 31
TOP GEAR SW .... B 17
WARNING MODULE .... B 23
WIPER/WASHER SWITCH
(W/ GRAPHIC DISPLAY) .... E 16

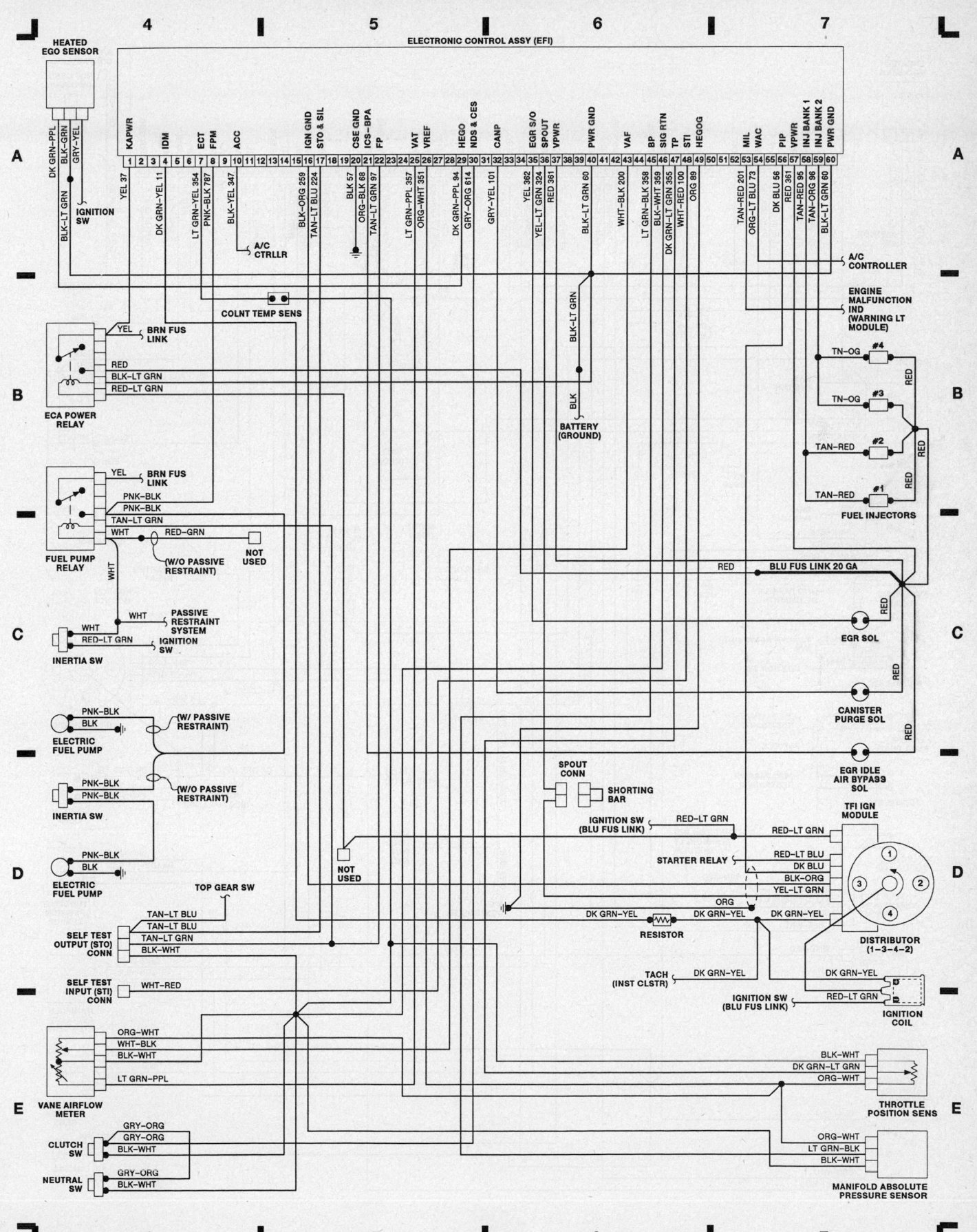

1989 Ford Motor Co.
Escort (Cont.)

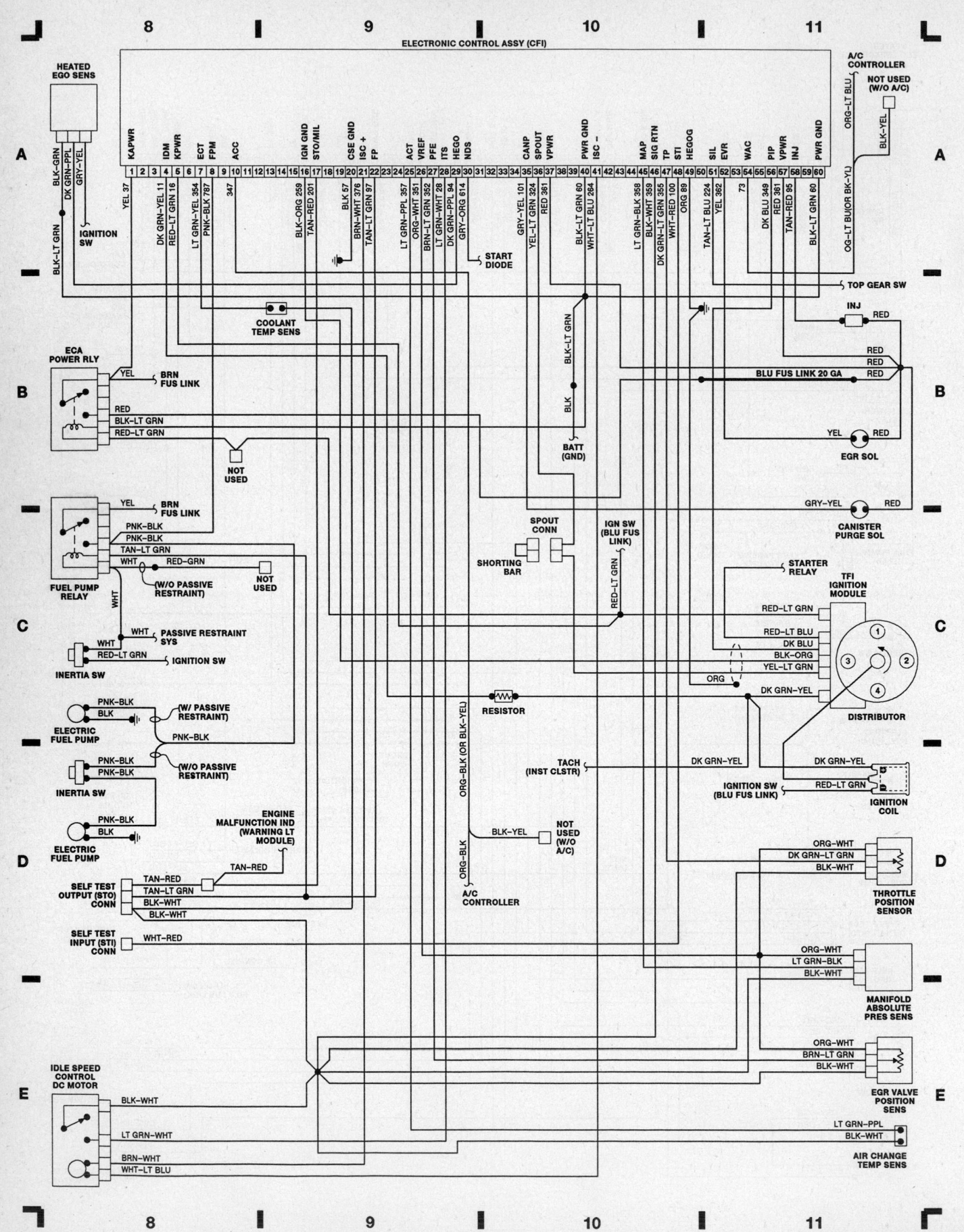

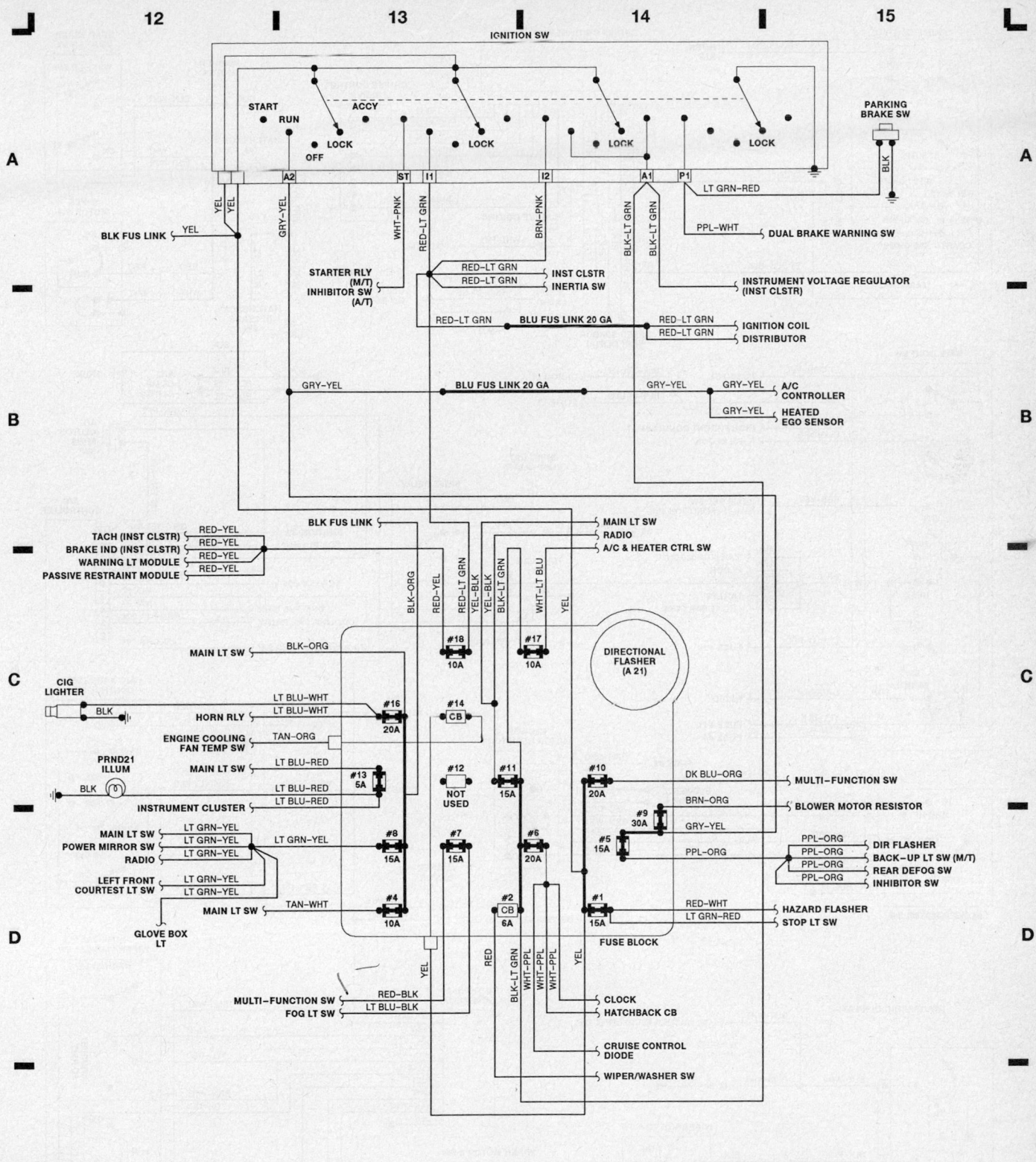

1989 Ford Motor Co.
Escort (Cont.)

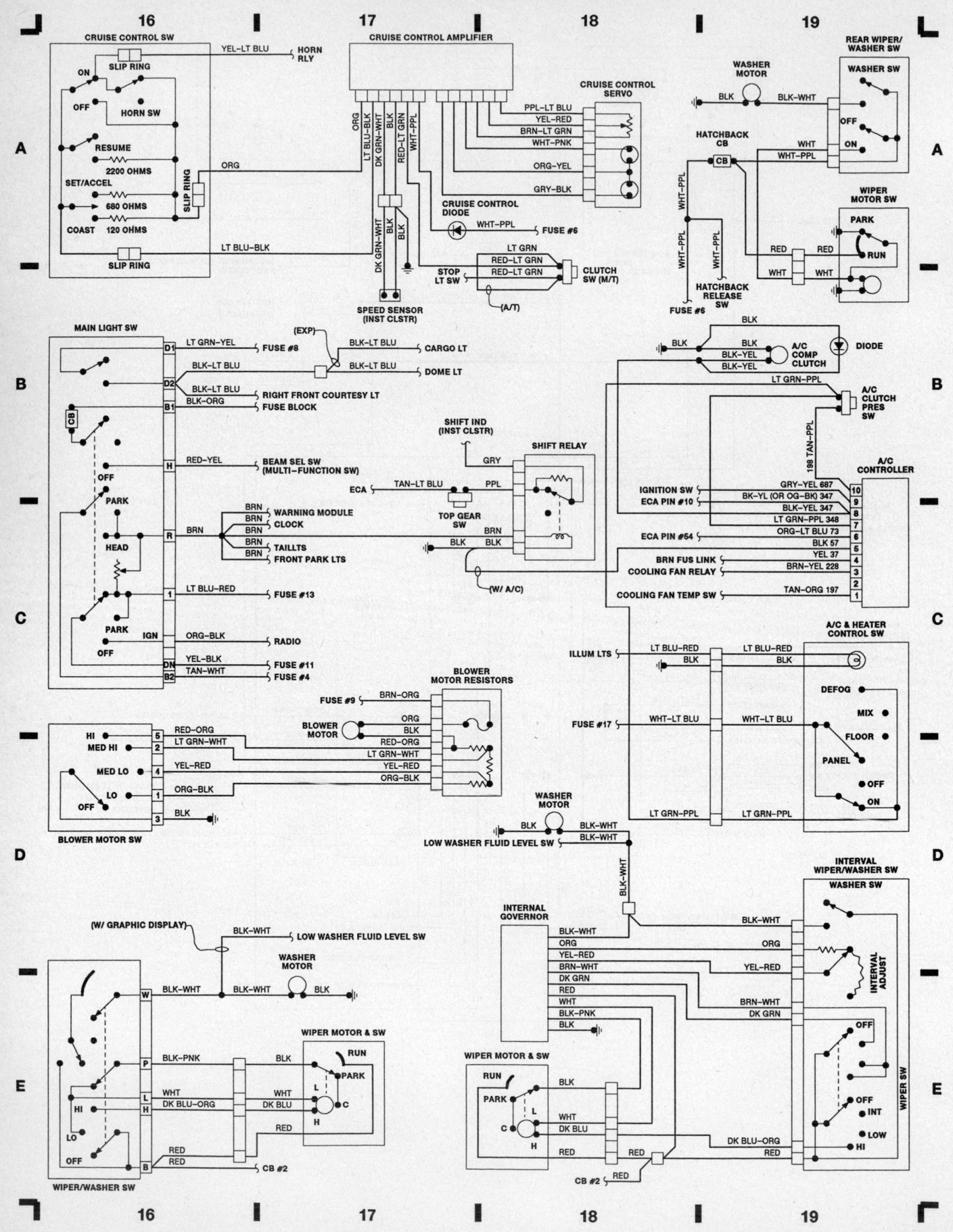

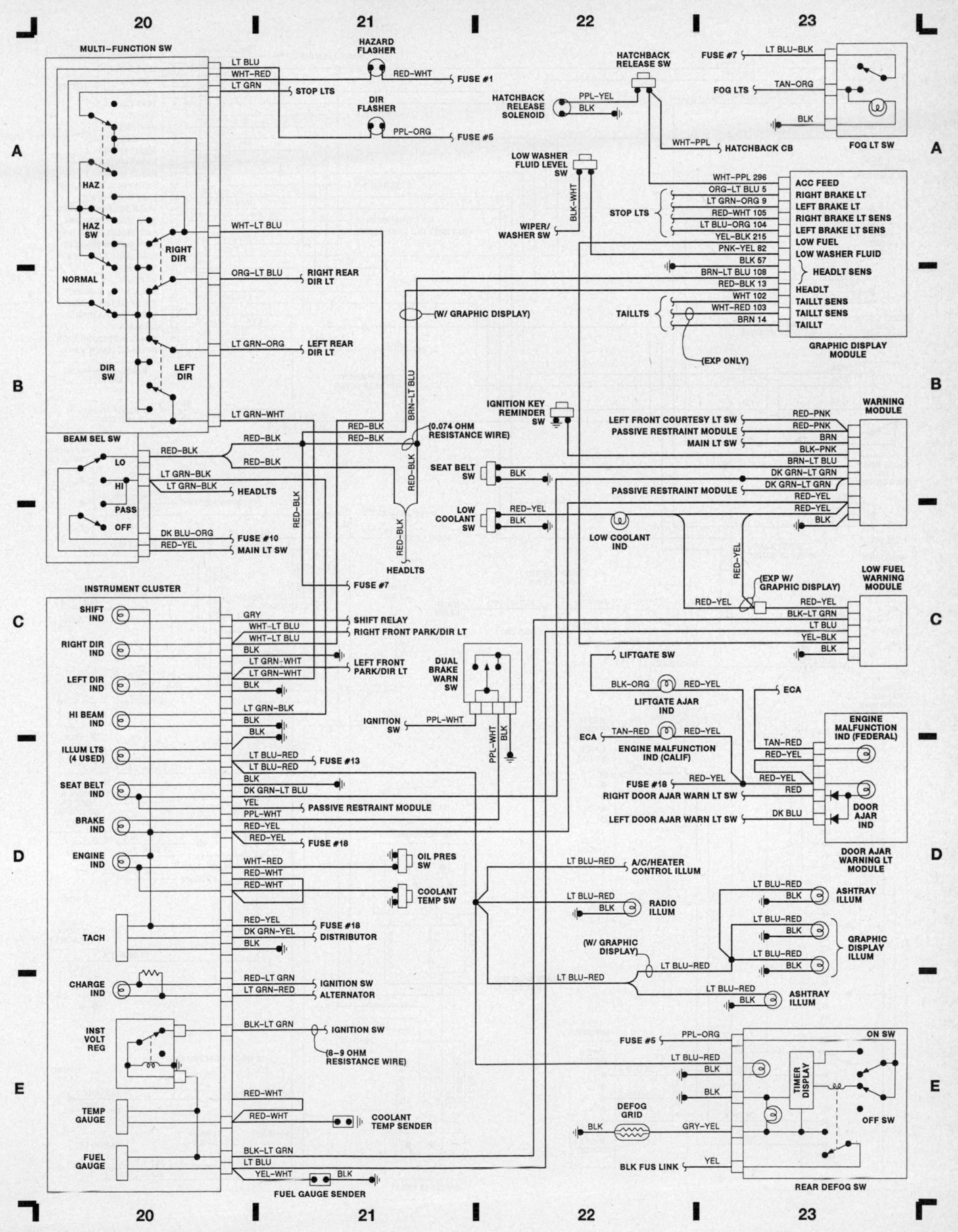

1989 Ford Motor Co.
Escort (Cont.)

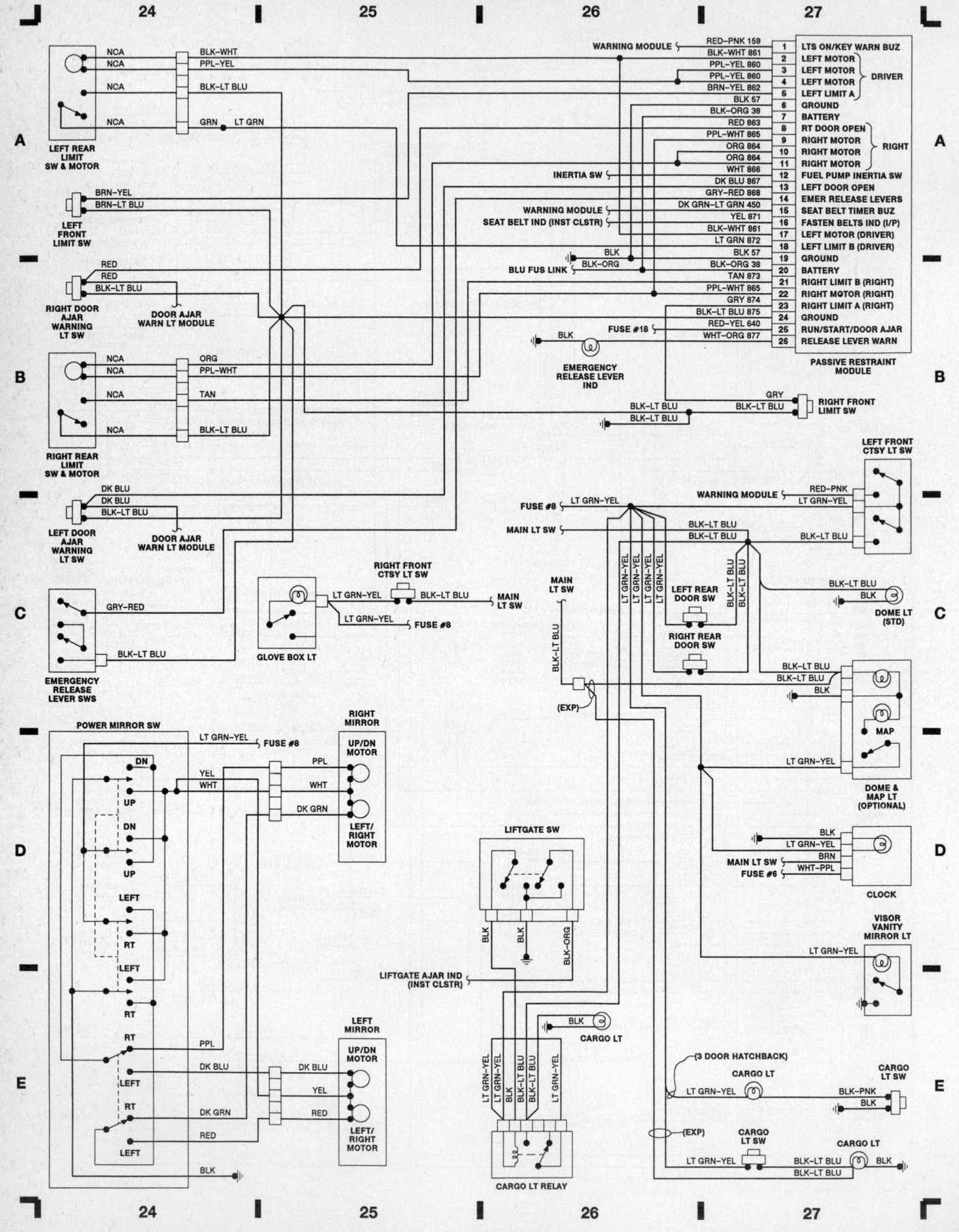

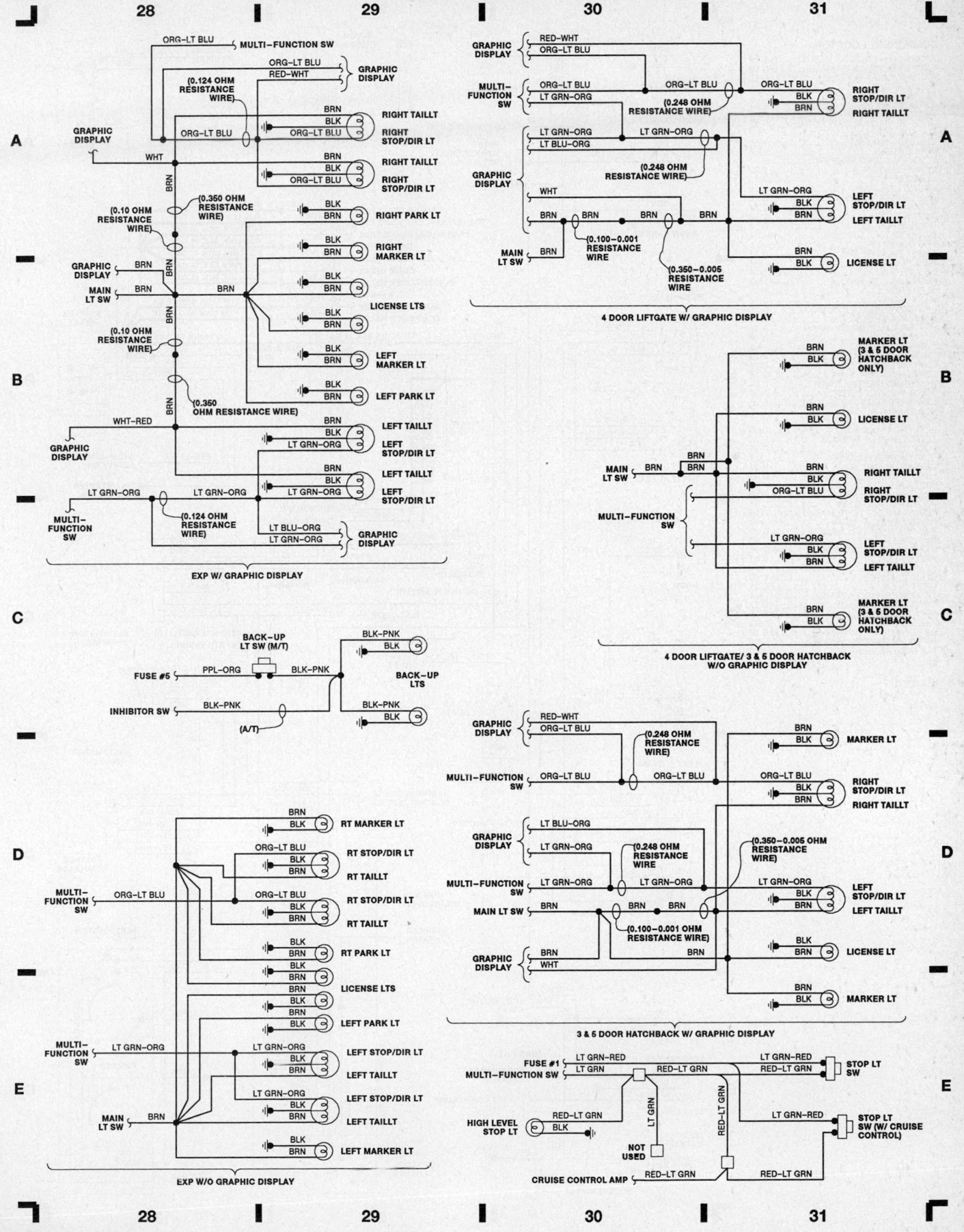

1989 Ford Motor Co.
LTD Crown Victoria, Grand Marquis & Wagons

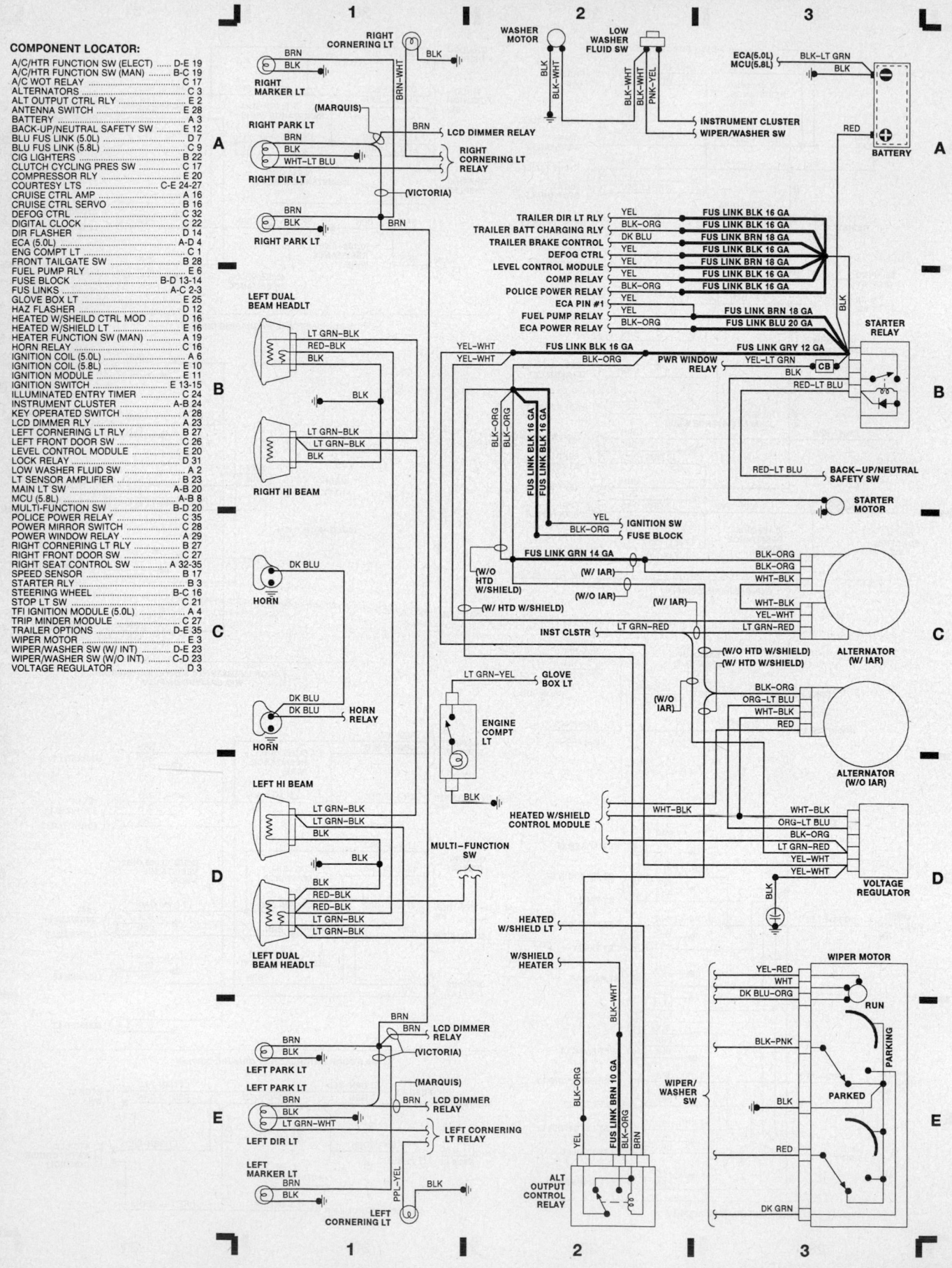

COMPONENT LOCATOR:

A/C/HTR FUNCTION SW (ELECT) ...... D-E 19
A/C/HTR FUNCTION SW (MAN) .... B-C 19
A/C WOT RELAY .... C 17
ALTERNATORS .... C 3
ALT OUTPUT CTRL RLY .... E 2
ANTENNA SWITCH .... E 28
BATTERY .... A 3
BACK-UP/NEUTRAL SAFETY SW .... E 12
BLU FUS LINK (5.0L) .... D 7
BLU FUS LINK (5.8L) .... C 9
CIG LIGHTERS .... B 22
CLUTCH CYCLING PRES SW .... C 17
COMPRESSOR RLY .... E 20
COURTESY LTS .... C-E 24-27
CRUISE CTRL AMP .... A 16
CRUISE CTRL SERVO .... B 16
DEFOG CTRL .... C 32
DIGITAL CLOCK .... C 22
DIR FLASHER .... D 14
ECA (5.0L) .... A-D 4
ENG COMPT LT .... C 1
FRONT TAILGATE SW .... B 28
FUEL PUMP RLY .... E 6
FUSE BLOCK .... B-D 13-14
FUS LINKS .... A-C 2-3
GLOVE BOX LT .... E 25
HAZ FLASHER .... D 12
HEATED W/SHEILD CTRL MOD .... D 16
HEATED W/SHIELD LT .... E 16
HEATER FUNCTION SW (MAN) .... A 19
HORN RELAY .... C 16
IGNITION COIL (5.0L) .... A 6
IGNITION COIL (5.8L) .... E 10
IGNITION MODULE .... E 11
IGNITION SWITCH .... E 13-15
ILLUMINATED ENTRY TIMER .... C 24
INSTRUMENT CLUSTER .... A-B 24
KEY OPERATED SWITCH .... A 28
LCD DIMMER RLY .... A 23
LEFT CORNERING LT RLY .... B 27
LEFT FRONT DOOR SW .... C 26
LEVEL CONTROL MODULE .... E 20
LOCK RELAY .... D 31
LOW WASHER FLUID SW .... A 2
LT SENSOR AMPLIFIER .... B 23
MAIN LT SW .... A-B 20
MCU (5.8L) .... A-B 8
MULTI-FUNCTION SW .... B-D 20
POLICE POWER RELAY .... C 35
POWER MIRROR SWITCH .... C 28
POWER WINDOW RELAY .... A 29
RIGHT CORNERING LT RLY .... B 27
RIGHT FRONT DOOR SW .... C 27
RIGHT SEAT CONTROL SW .... A 32-35
SPEED SENSOR .... B 17
STARTER RLY .... B 3
STEERING WHEEL .... B-C 16
STOP LT SW .... C 21
TFI IGNITION MODULE (5.0L) .... A 4
TRIP MINDER MODULE .... C 27
TRAILER OPTIONS .... D-E 35
WIPER MOTOR .... E 3
WIPER/WASHER SW (W/ INT) .... D-E 23
WIPER/WASHER SW (W/O INT) ...... C-D 23
VOLTAGE REGULATOR .... D 3

1989 Ford Motor Co.
LTD Crown Victoria, Grand Marquis & Wagons (Cont.)

5-115

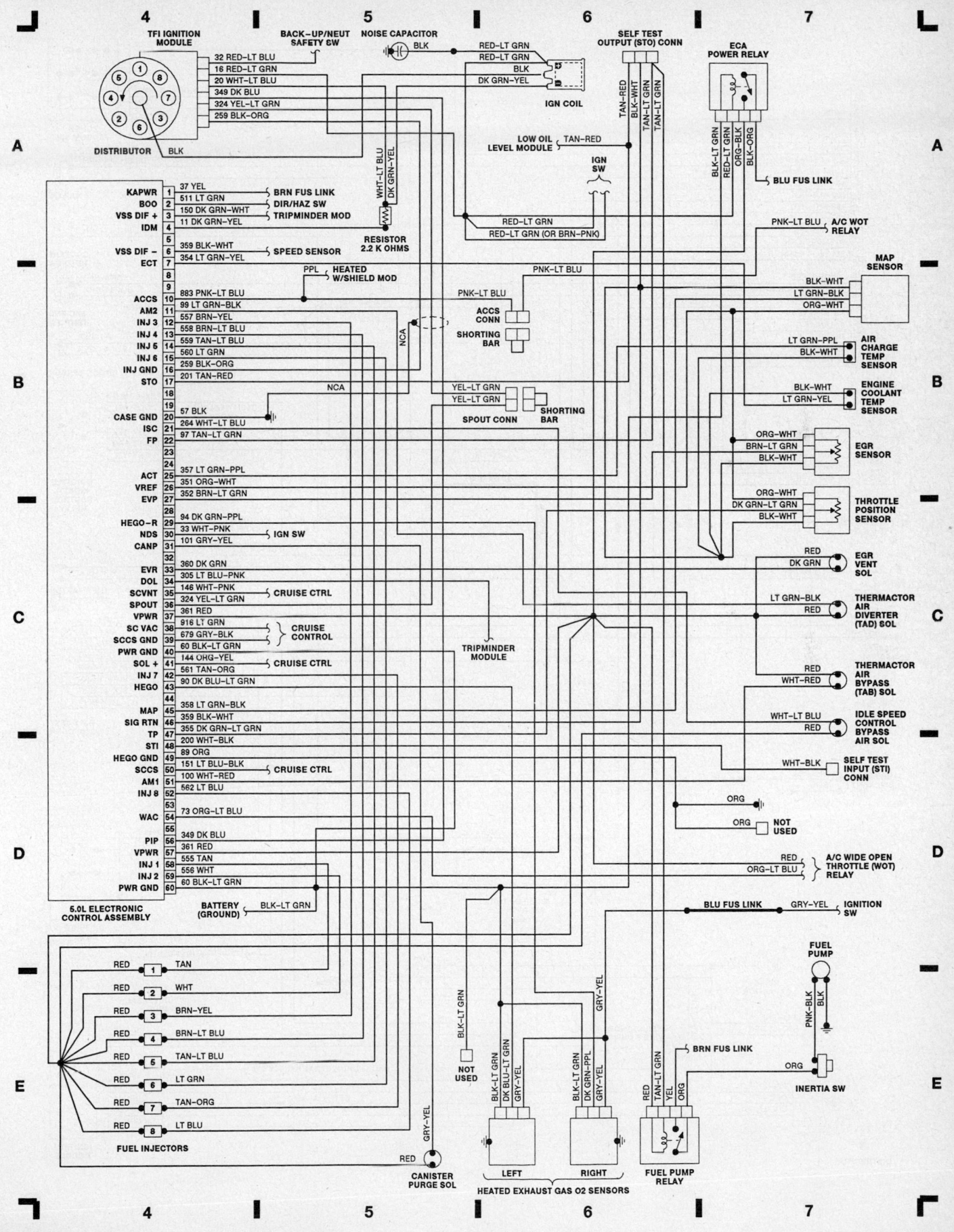

5-116

1989 Ford Motor Co.
LTD Crown Victoria, Grand Marquis & Wagons (Cont.)

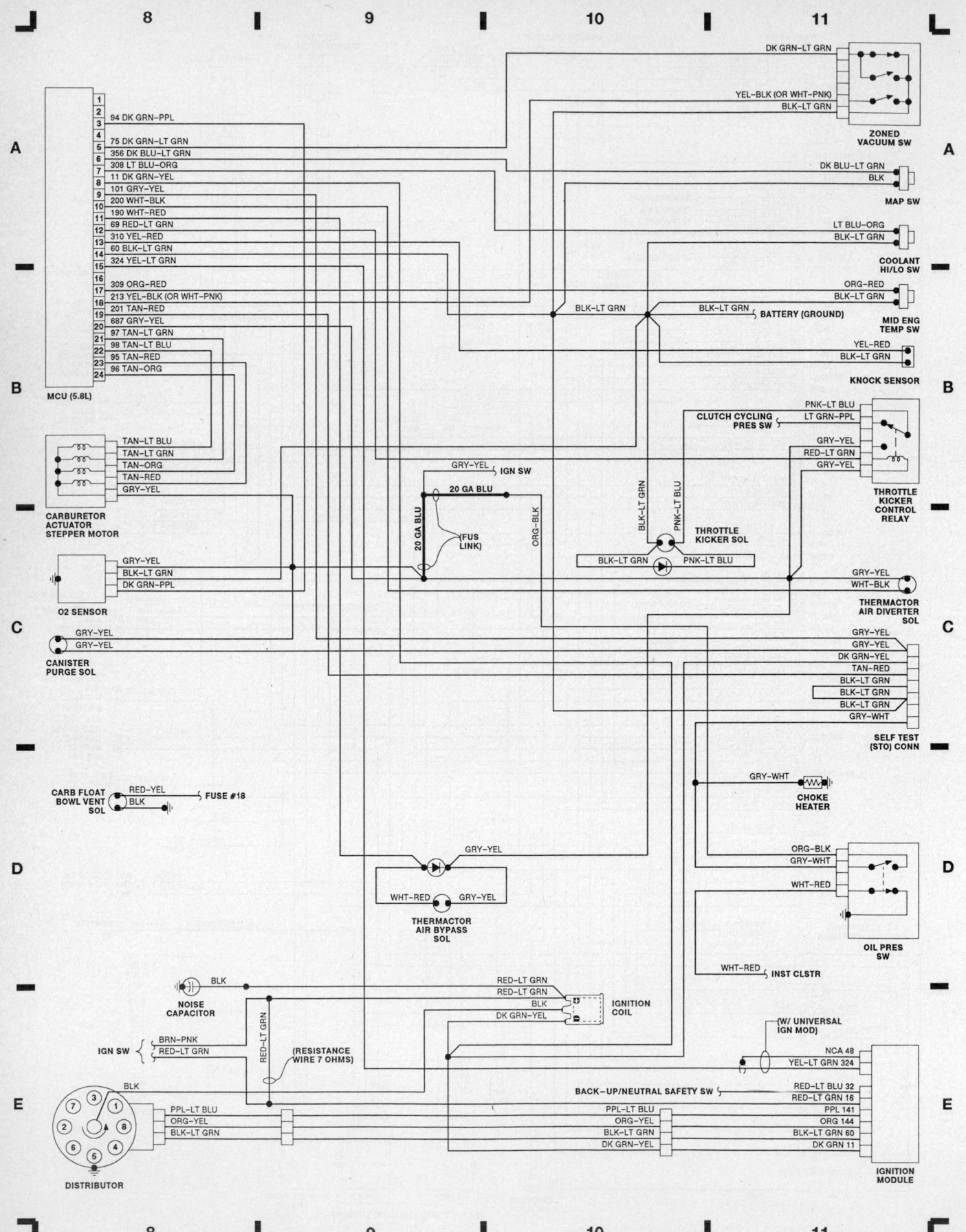

1989 Ford Motor Co.
LTD Crown Victoria, Grand Marquis & Wagons (Cont.)

5-117

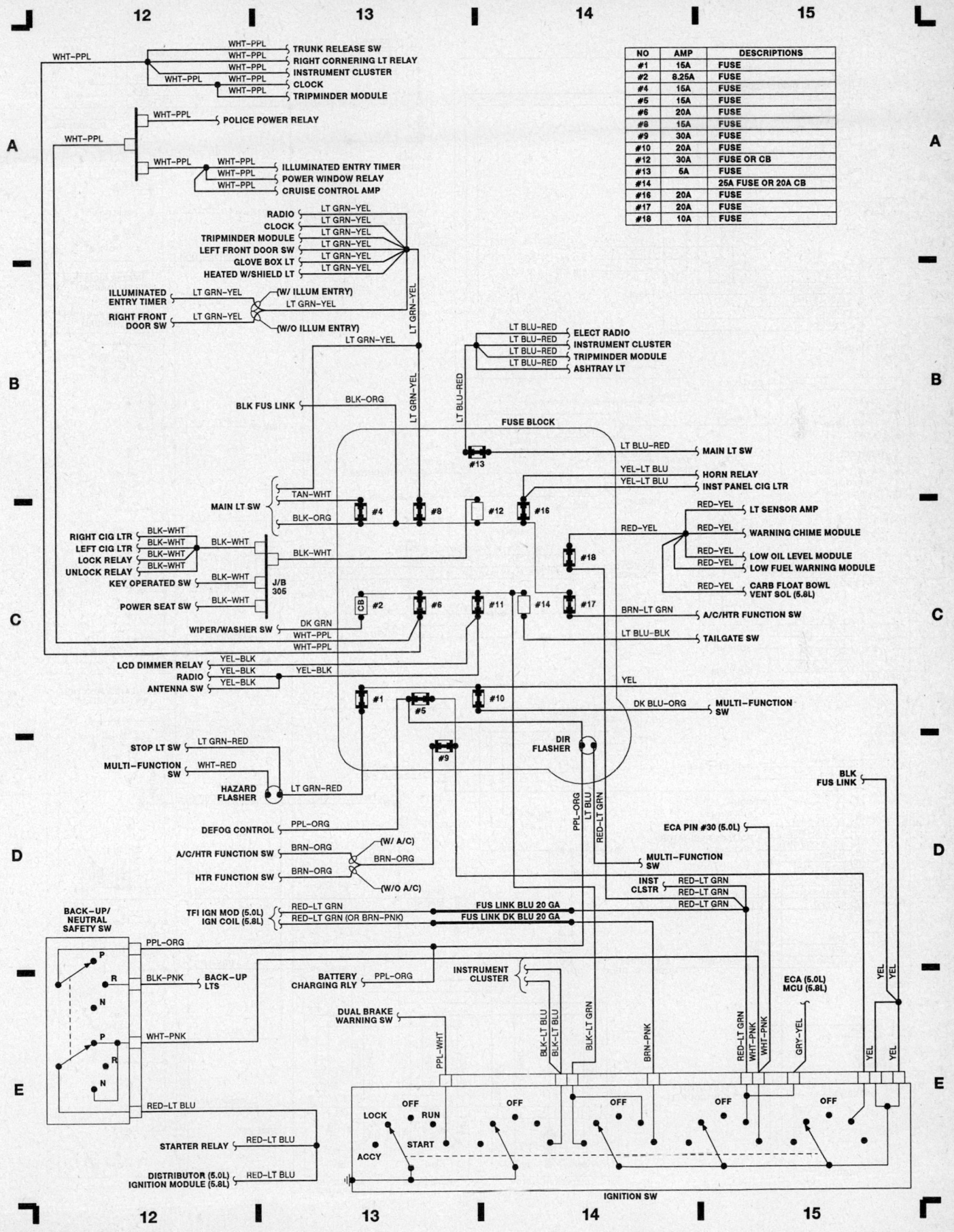

NO	AMP	DESCRIPTIONS
#1	15A	FUSE
#2	8.25A	FUSE
#4	15A	FUSE
#5	15A	FUSE
#6	20A	FUSE
#8	15A	FUSE
#9	30A	FUSE
#10	20A	FUSE
#12	30A	FUSE OR CB
#13	5A	FUSE
#14		25A FUSE OR 20A CB
#16	20A	FUSE
#17	20A	FUSE
#18	10A	FUSE

1989 FORD MOTOR CO.
LTD Crown Victoria, Grand Marquis & Wagons (Cont.)

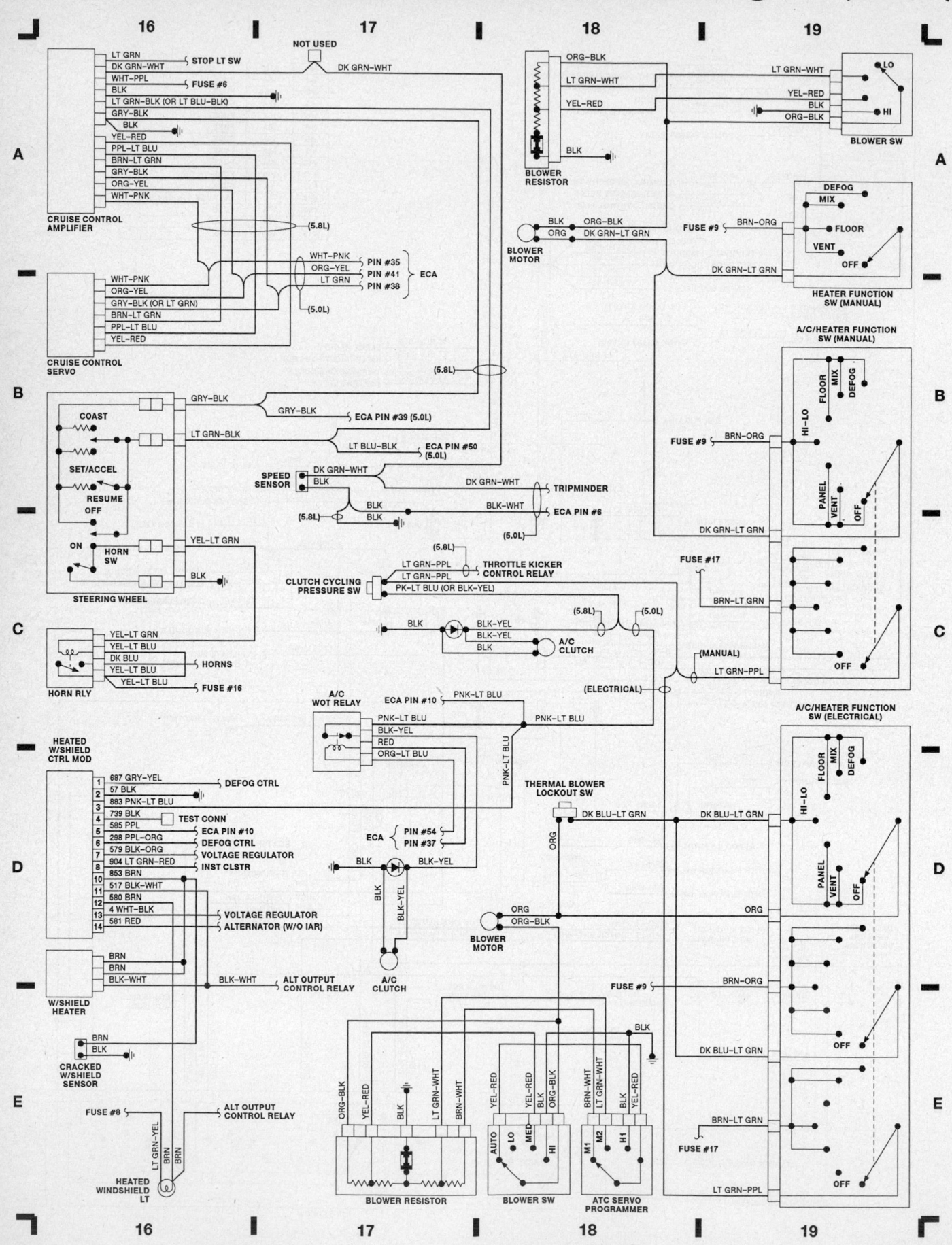

1989 Ford Motor Co.
LTD Crown Victoria, Grand Marquis & Wagons (Cont.)

5-119

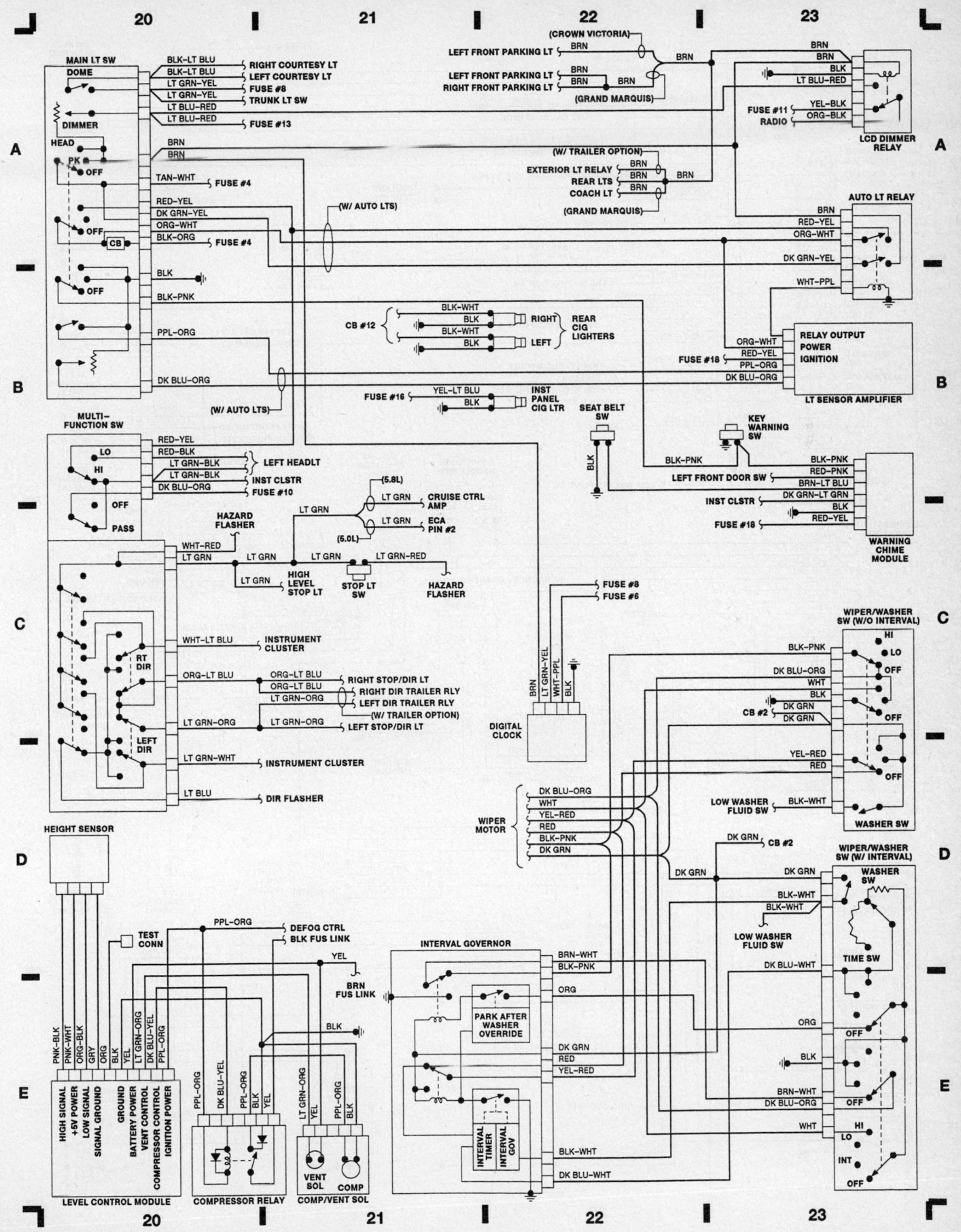

1989 Ford Motor CO.
LTD Crown Victoria, Grand Marquis & Wagons (Cont.)

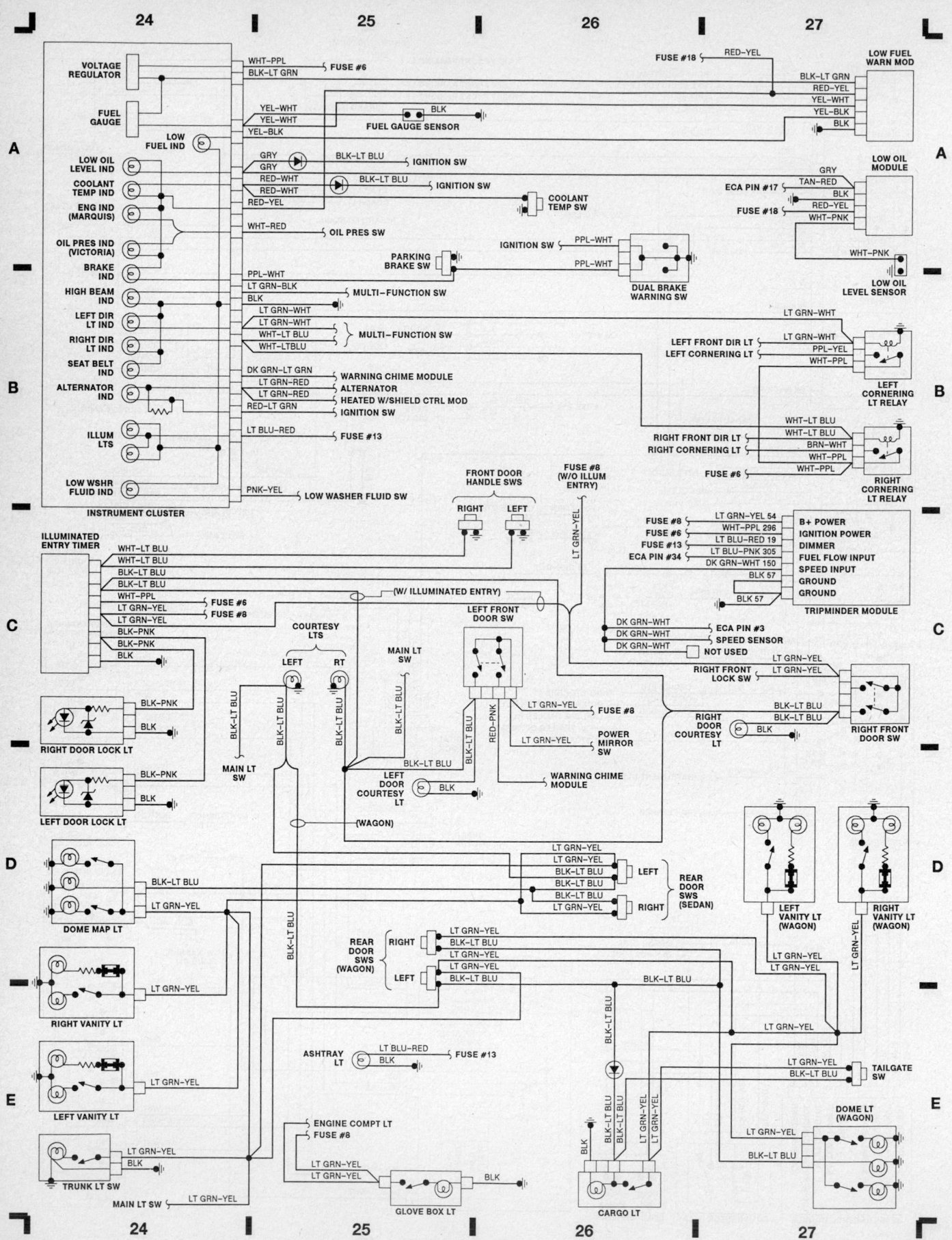

1989 Ford Motor Co.
LTD Crown Victoria, Grand Marquis & Wagons (Cont.)

5-121

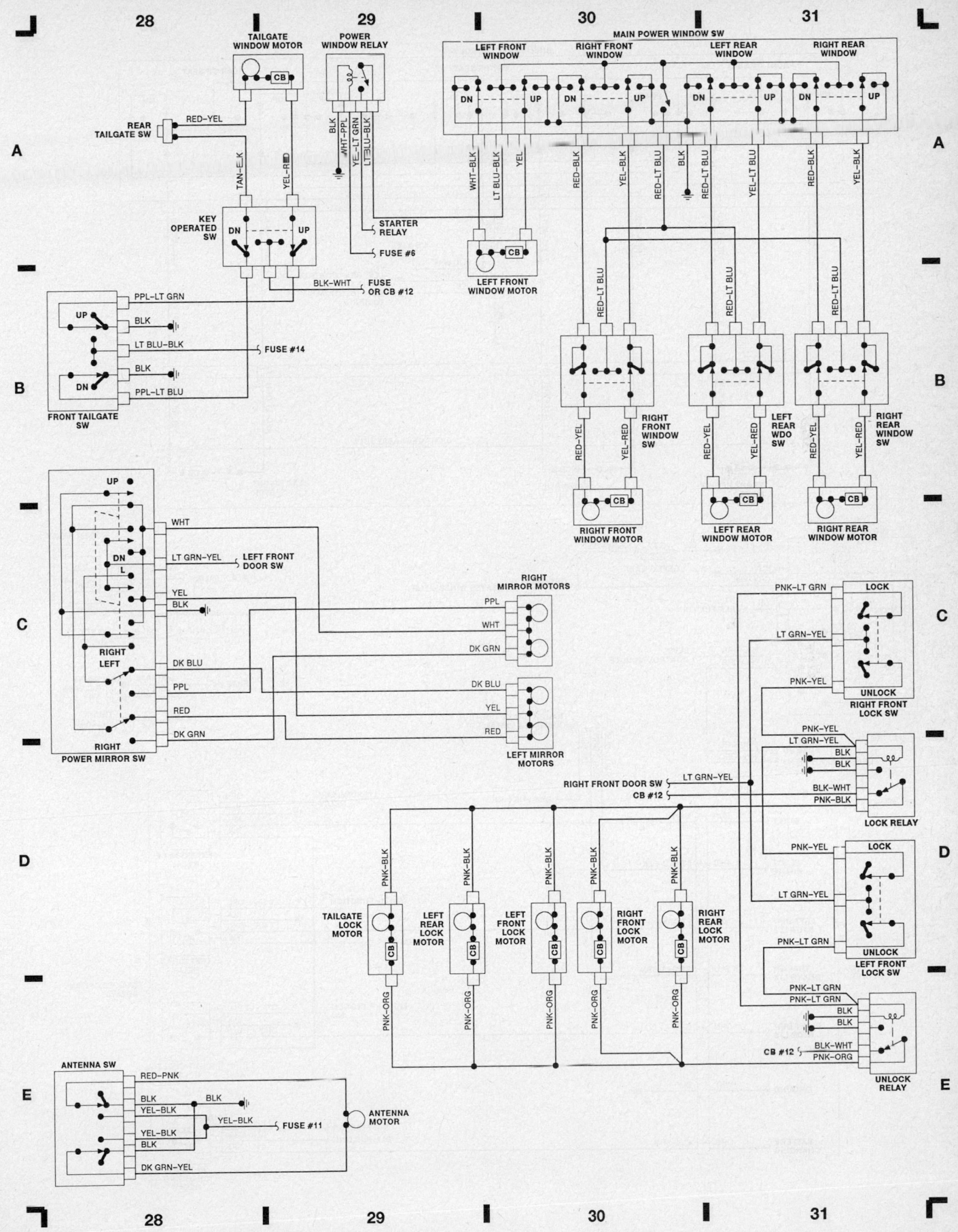

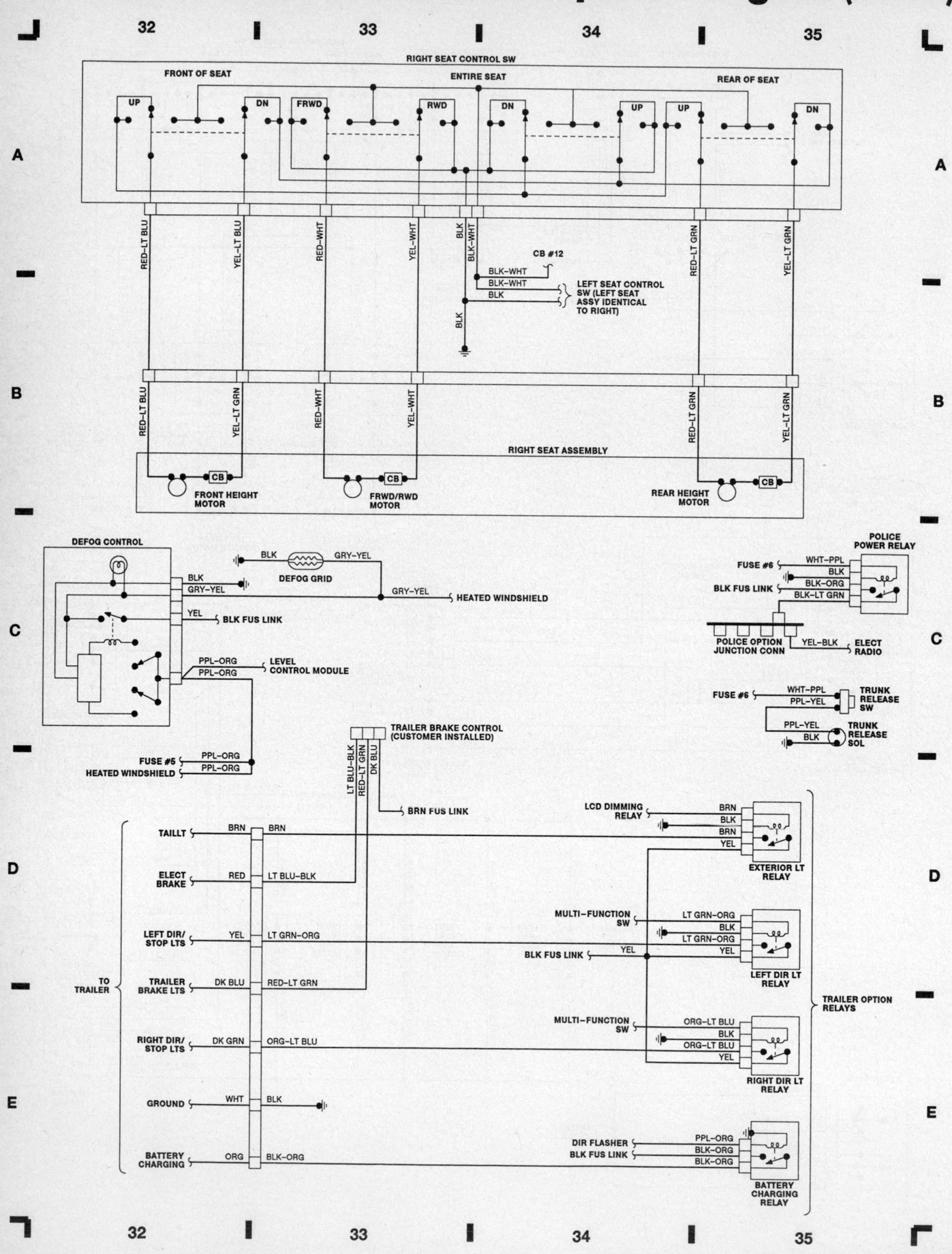

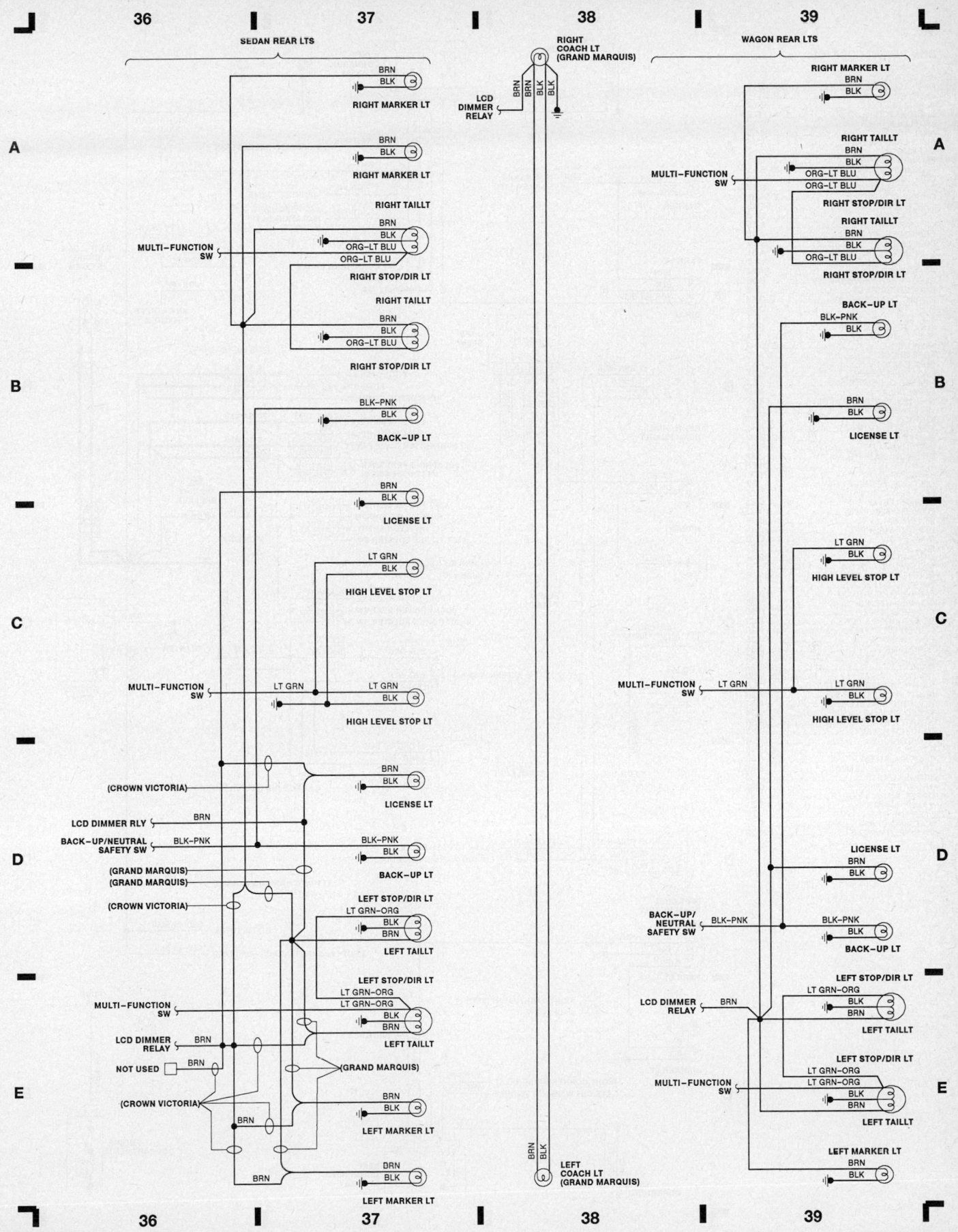

1989 Ford Motor Co.
Mark VII

COMPONENT LOCATOR:

A/C SYSTEM .... C-E 20-22
A/C WOT CUTOUT RLY .... D-E 20
ABS .... C-E 12-15
AIR SUSPENSION .... A-B 12-15
ALARM RELAY .... B 38
ALTERNATOR .... C 2
ANTI-LOCK PRES SW .... C 12
ANTI-THEFT .... A-B 36-38
AUTO LAMP RELAY .... A 19
BATTERY .... A 3
BLOWER MOTOR .... E 21
BRAKE FLUID LEVEL SW .... C 13, B 11
CIG LTRS .... C 38
COMPRESSOR RELAY .... B 14
CRUISE CONTROL .... E 34-35
DEFOG GRID .... E 19
DIR FLASHER .... C 10
DIR/HAZ SWITCH .... E 16
DISARM RELAY .... A 38
DISTRIBUTOR .... E 7
DOME/MAP LTS .... A 31
ECA .... A 4-7
ECA POWER RELAY .... B-C 4
ELECT REAR VIEW MIRROR .... B 38
ENGINE COMPT LT .... E 3
FLASH TO PASS RELAY .... C-D 19
FOG LTS SW .... D 19
FOG LTS .... C 1
FUEL DOOR RELEASE .... E 38
FUEL PUMP RELAY .... B 4
FUS LINKS .... B-C 2-3
FUSE BLOCK .... C-D 9-10
GLOVE BOX LT .... A 31
HAZARD FLASHER .... E 17
HEATED O₂ SENSORS .... E 4
HORN RELAY .... B 2
HYDRAULIC PUMP MTR RLY .... E 12
HI-LOW BEAM RELAY .... C 19
IGNITION COIL .... C 7
IGNITION SWITCH .... A 8-11
INST CLSTR .... A-E 24-27
INST ILLUM LTS .... B-C 34
INTERIOR LAMP RELAY .... C 32
INVERTER RELAY .... A 38
KEYLESS ENTRY .... D-E 28-31
LEFT CORNERING LT RLY .... E 2
LEFT FRONT DOOR SW .... A 28
LOW OIL LEVEL RLY .... C 23
LOWER WARN MOD .... D 23
LT SENSOR AMP .... B 19
LTS OUT WARNING .... A 32-34
MAIN LT SW .... A-C 16
MESSAGE CENTER .... E 27
MOONROOF .... E 32
MULTI-FUNCTION SW .... E 16
NEUT SAFETY/BACK-UP LT SW ..... C 8
OVERHEAD MODULE .... A 23
PARK BRAKE SWITCH .... A-B 11
POWER ANTENNA .... D 38
POWER BOLSTER .... D 38
POWER DOOR LOCKS .... D-E 29
POWER MIRRORS .... E 36
POWER SEATS .... B-C 36
POWER WINDOWS .... D 35
REAR DEFOGGER .... E 19
RADIO .... B-C 27
READING LT SWS .... B 28, B 30
RIGHT CORNERING LT RLY .... A 2
RIGHT FRONT DOOR SW .... A 30
ROOF IND MODULE .... A 23
SPEED SENSOR .... C 34
STARTER INTERRUPT RLY .... B 36
STARTER RELAY .... C 3
STO CONN .... D 4
STOP LT SW .... E 17-18
TRUNK AJAR SW .... E 38
TRUNK LID PULLDOWN .... E 32
TTRUNK LIGHT .... A 30
TRUNK RELEASE .... D 33
UPPER WARN MODULE .... B 23
VANITY LIGHTS .... B-C 31
VOLTAGE REGULATOR .... D 2
WARNING CHIME .... D 32
W/ SHIELD WIPERS .... A-B 20-22

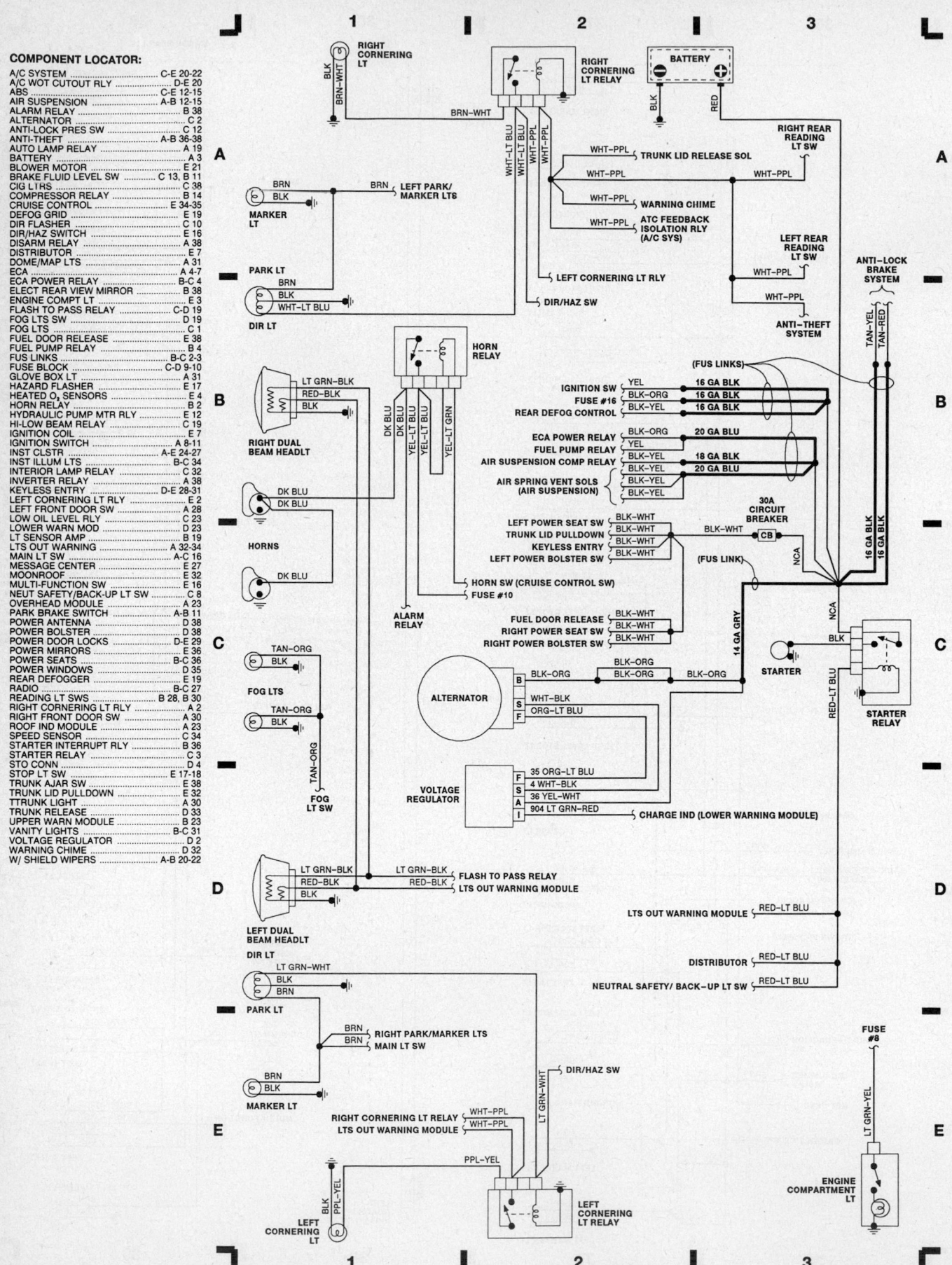

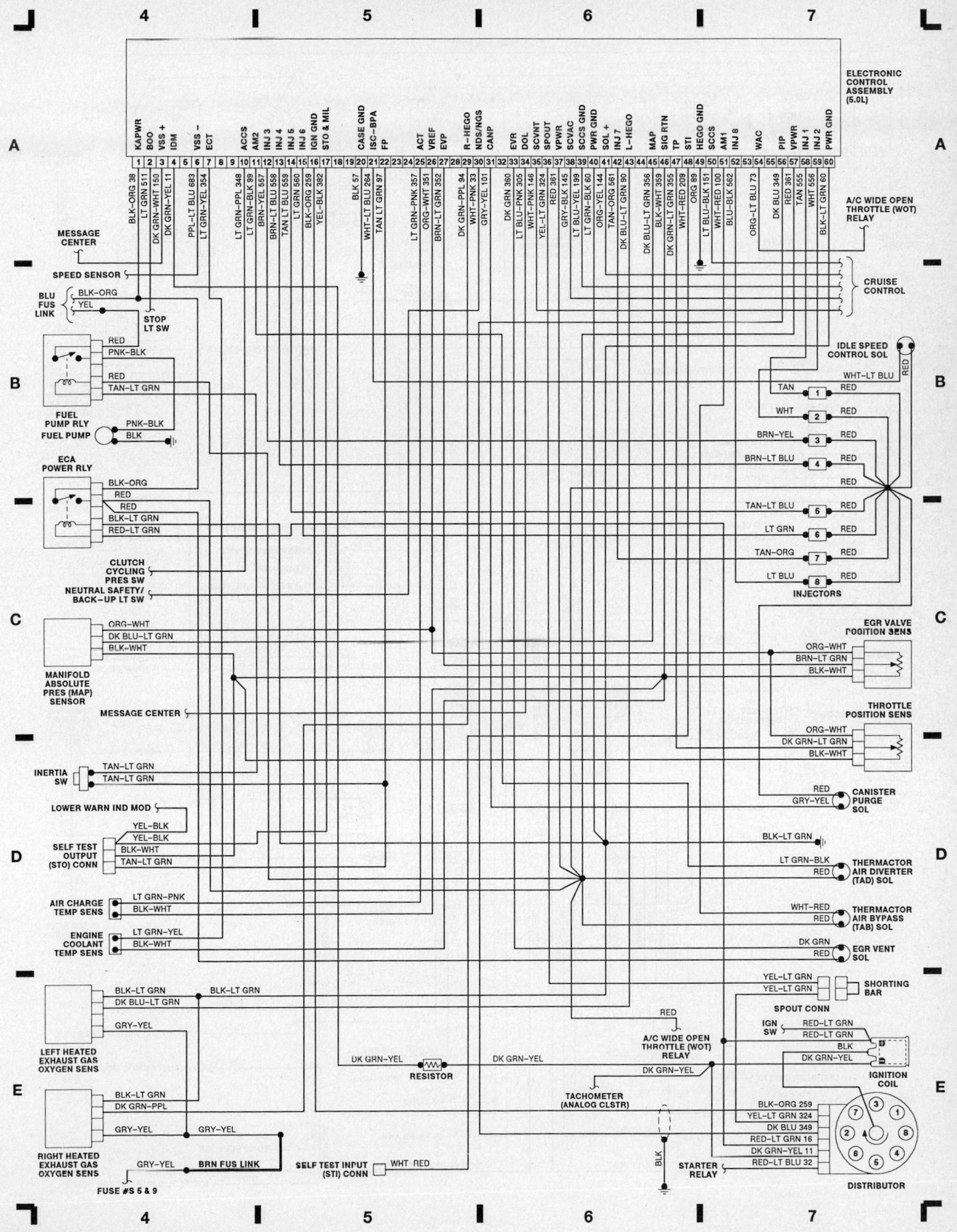

1989 Ford Motor Co.
Mark VII (Cont.)

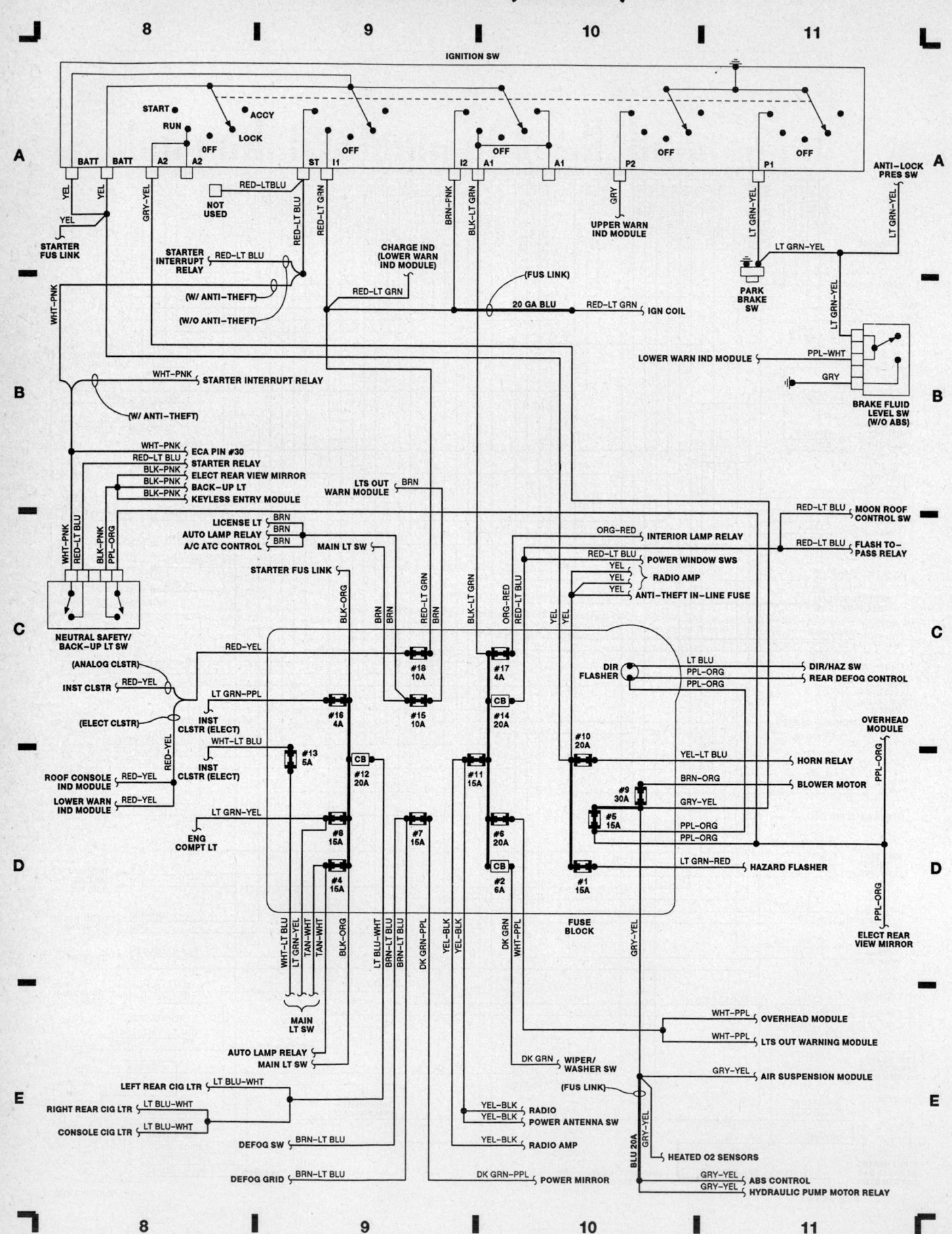

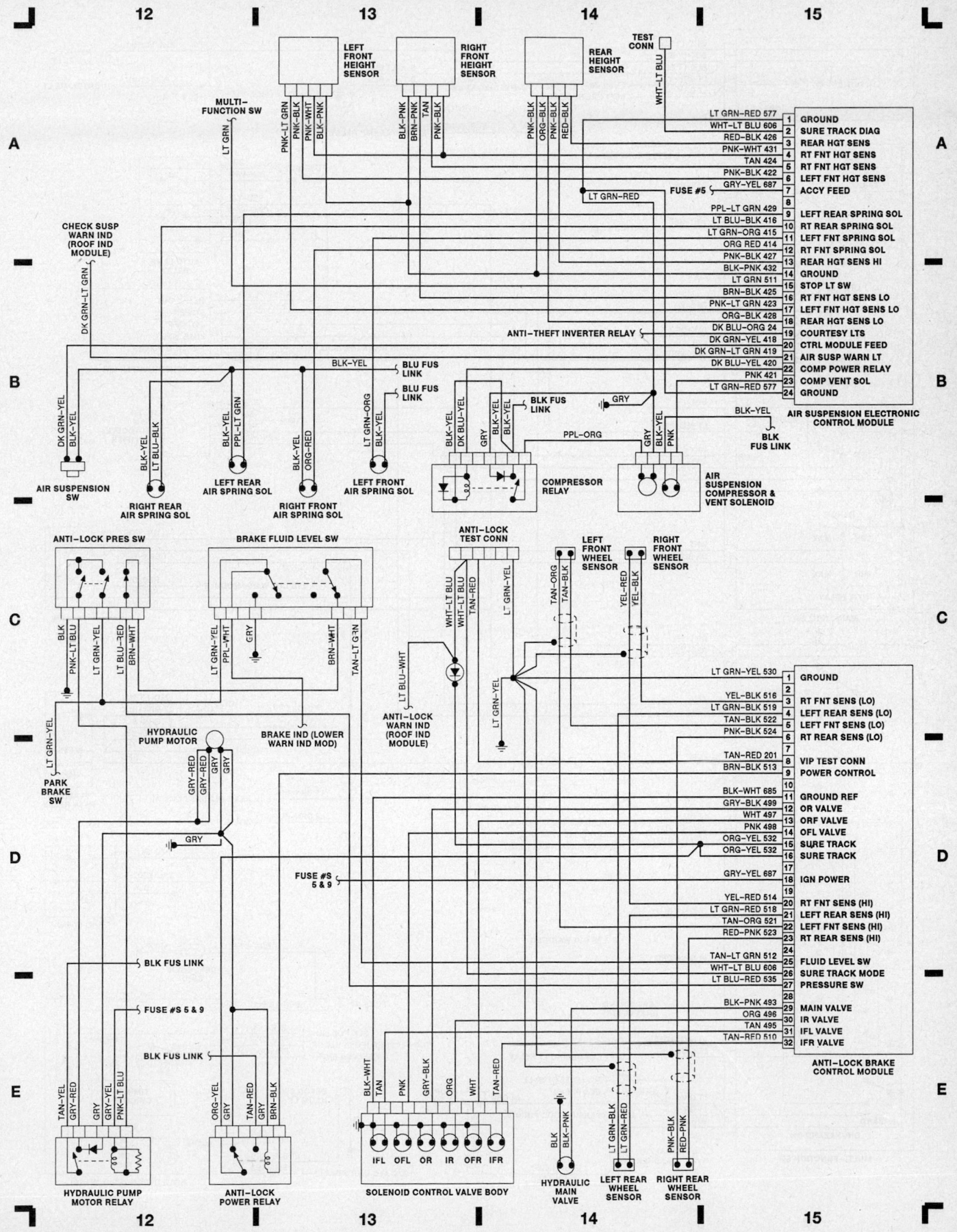

1989 Ford MOTOR CO.
Mark VII (Cont.)

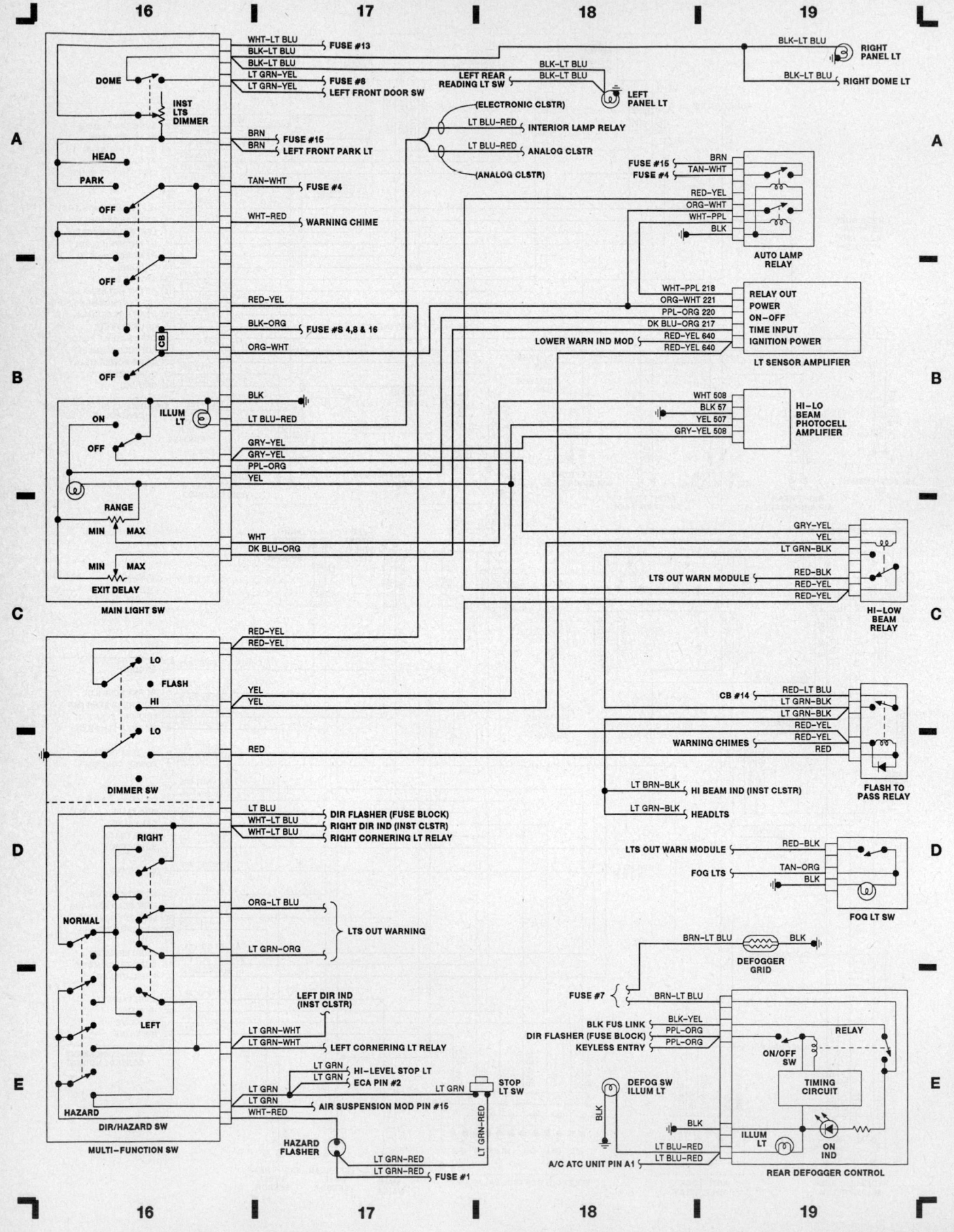

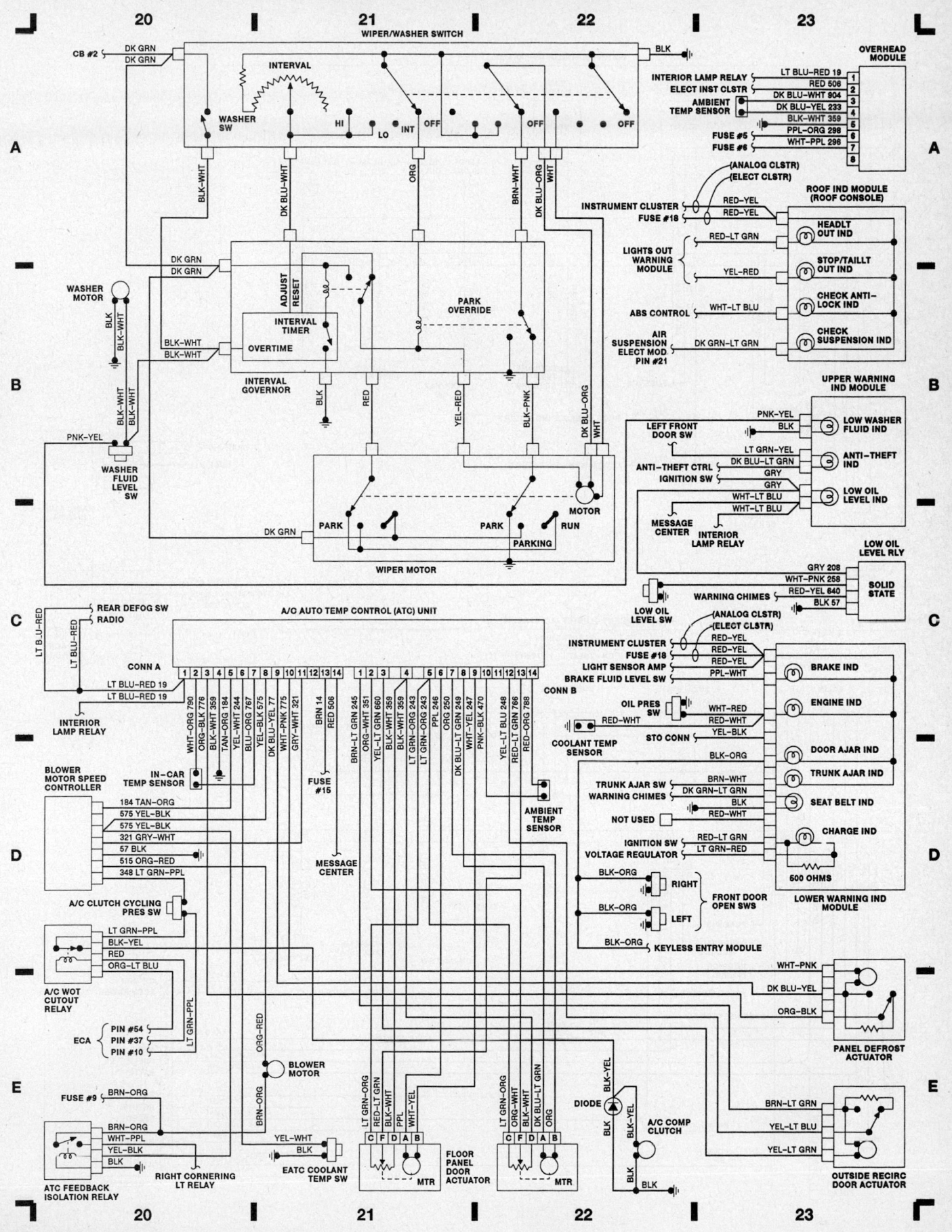

1989 Ford Motor Co.
Mark VII (Cont.)

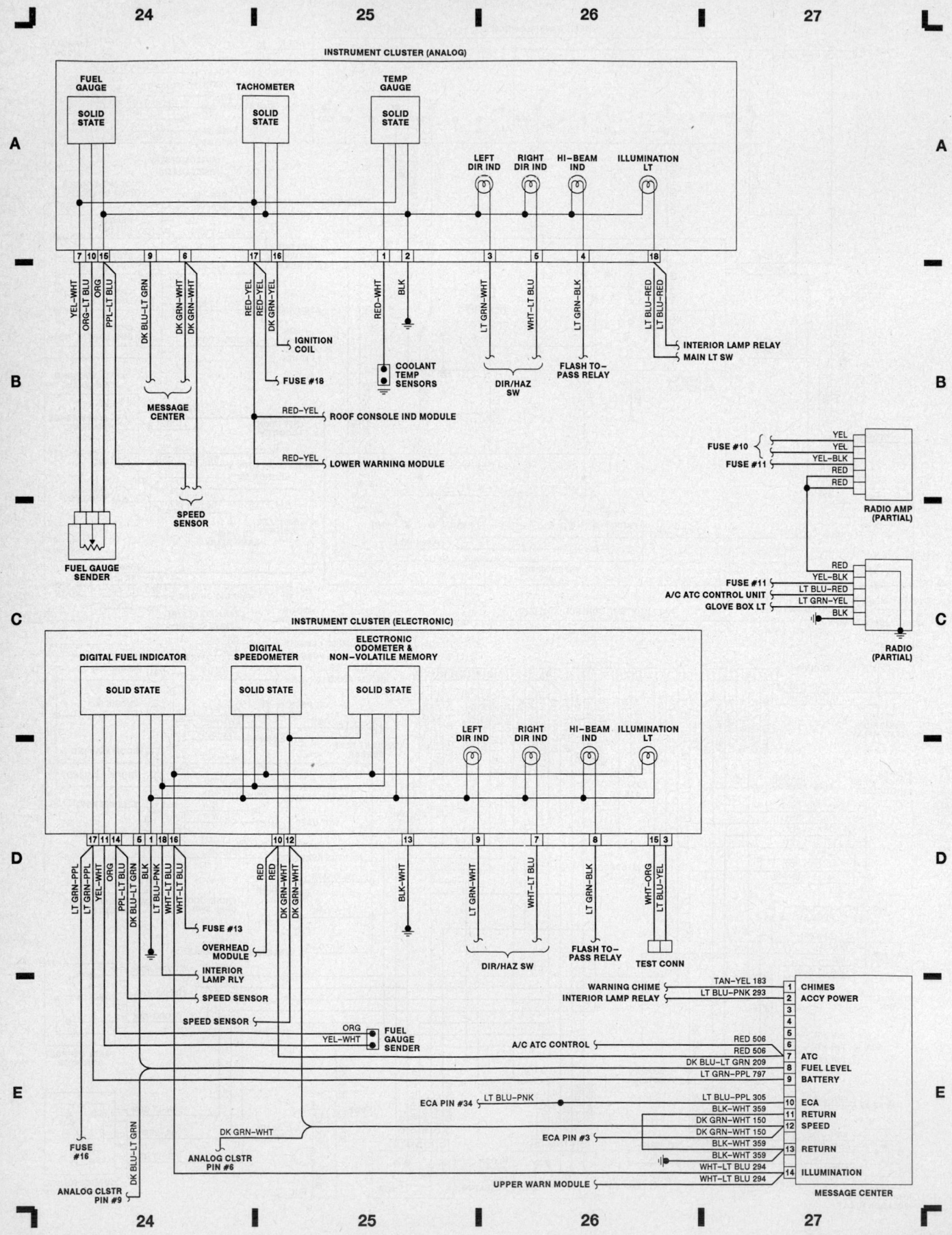

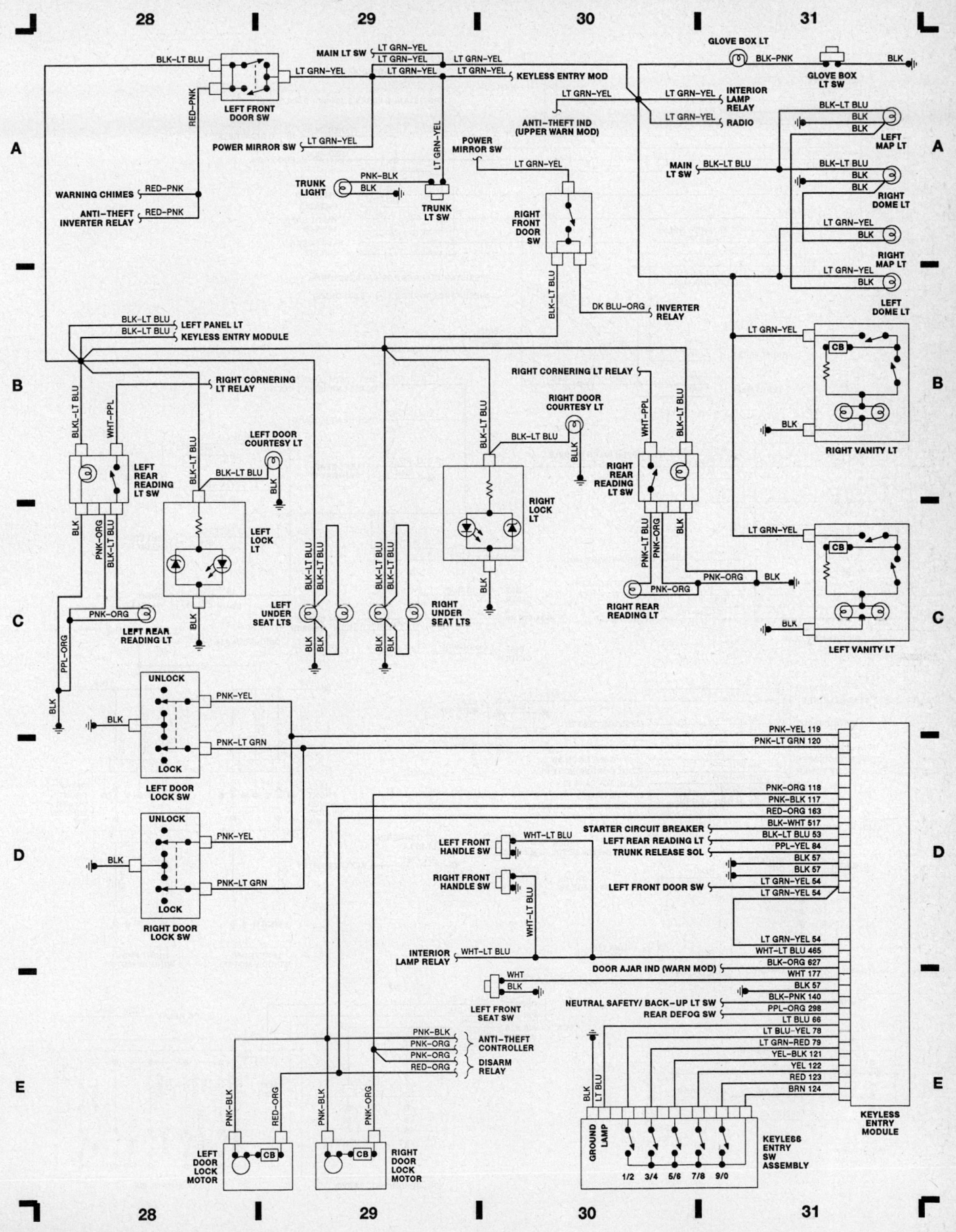

1989 Ford Motor Co.
Mark VII (Cont.)

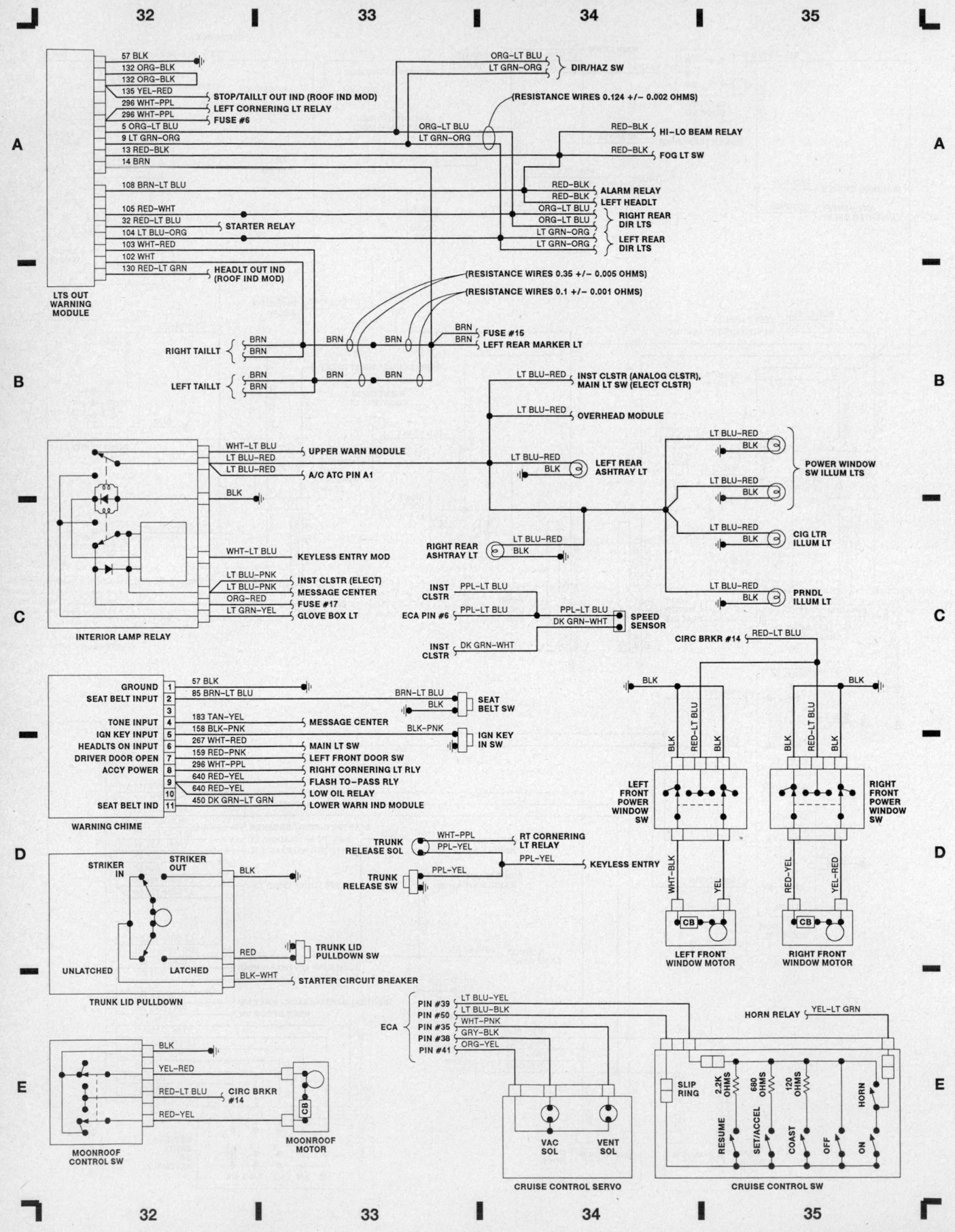

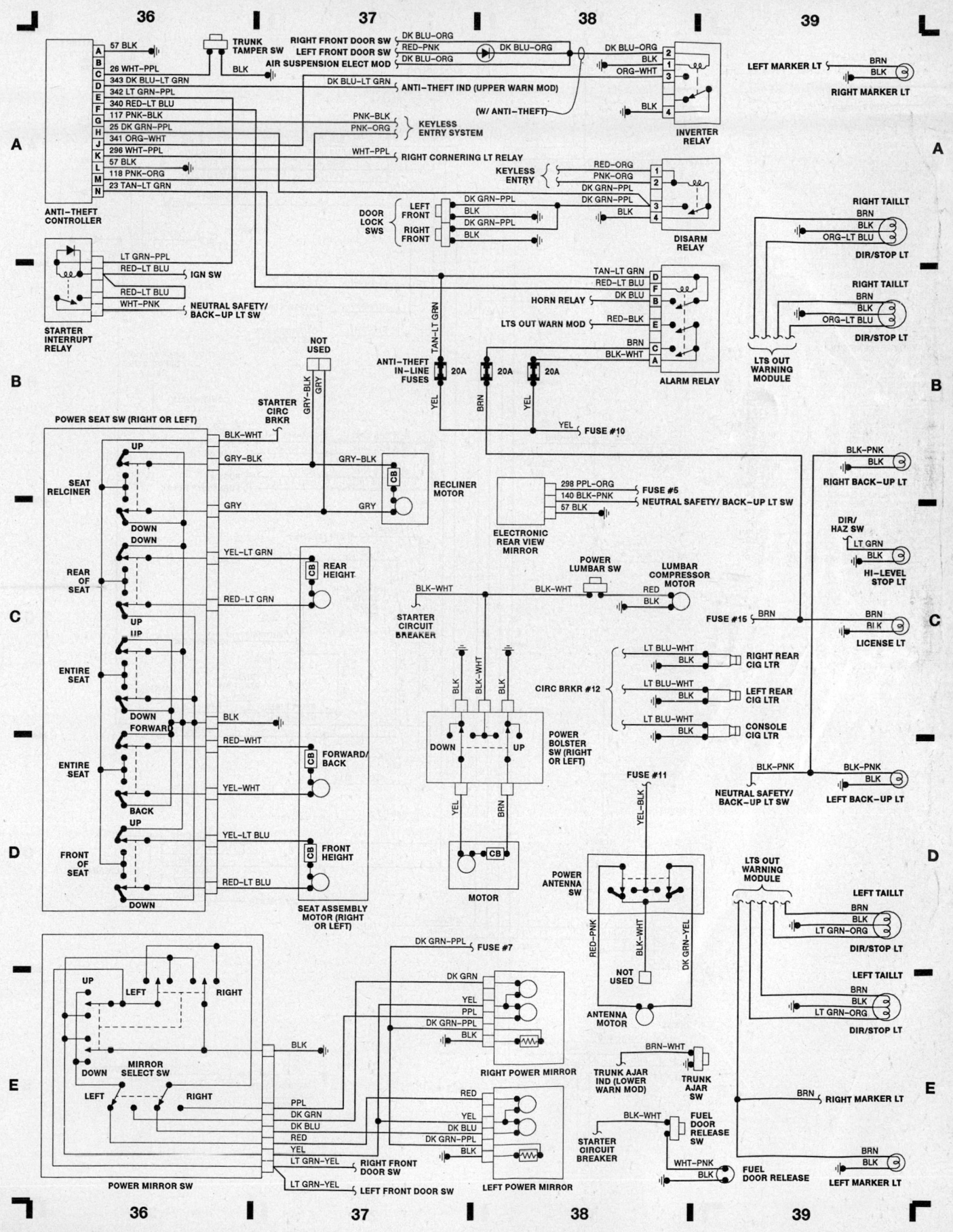

1989 Ford Motor Co.
Mustang

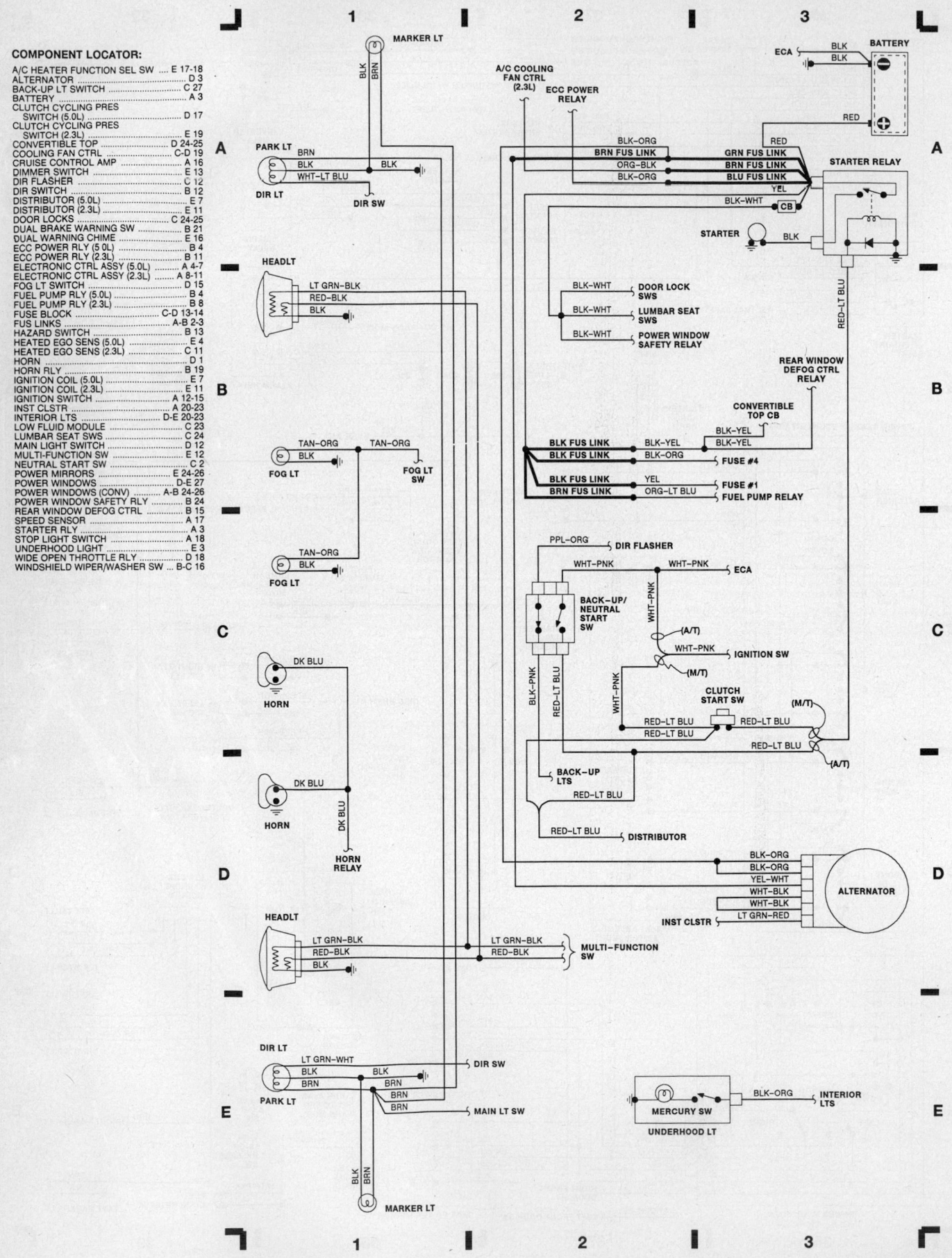

COMPONENT LOCATOR:

A/C HEATER FUNCTION SEL SW .... E 17-18
ALTERNATOR .... D 3
BACK-UP LT SWITCH .... C 27
BATTERY .... A 3
CLUTCH CYCLING PRES
  SWITCH (5.0L) .... D 17
CLUTCH CYCLING PRES
  SWITCH (2.3L) .... E 19
CONVERTIBLE TOP .... D 24-25
COOLING FAN CTRL .... C-D 19
CRUISE CONTROL AMP .... A 16
DIMMER SWITCH .... E 13
DIR FLASHER .... C 12
DIR SWITCH .... B 12
DISTRIBUTOR (5.0L) .... E 7
DISTRIBUTOR (2.3L) .... E 11
DOOR LOCKS .... C 24-25
DUAL BRAKE WARNING SW .... B 21
DUAL WARNING CHIME .... E 16
ECC POWER RLY (5.0L) .... B 4
ECC POWER RLY (2.3L) .... B 11
ELECTRONIC CTRL ASSY (5.0L) ... A 4-7
ELECTRONIC CTRL ASSY (2.3L) ... A 8-11
FOG LT SWITCH .... D 15
FUEL PUMP RLY (5.0L) .... B 4
FUEL PUMP RLY (2.3L) .... B 8
FUSE BLOCK .... C-D 13-14
FUS LINKS .... A-B 2-3
HAZARD SWITCH .... B 13
HEATED EGO SENS (5.0L) .... E 4
HEATED EGO SENS (2.3L) .... C 11
HORN .... D 1
HORN RLY .... B 19
IGNITION COIL (5.0L) .... E 7
IGNITION COIL (2.3L) .... E 11
IGNITION SWITCH .... A 12-15
INST CLSTR .... A 20-23
INTERIOR LTS .... D-E 20-23
LOW FLUID MODULE .... C 23
LUMBAR SEAT SWS .... S 24
MAIN LIGHT SWITCH .... D 12
MULTI-FUNCTION SW .... E 12
NEUTRAL START SW .... C 2
POWER MIRRORS .... E 24-26
POWER WINDOWS .... D-E 27
POWER WINDOWS (CONV) .... A-B 24-26
POWER WINDOW SAFETY RLY ... B 24
REAR WINDOW DEFOG CTRL ...... B 17
SPEED SENSOR .... A 3
STARTER RLY .... A 3
STOP LIGHT SWITCH .... A 18
UNDERHOOD LIGHT .... E 3
WIDE OPEN THROTTLE RLY .... D 18
WINDSHIELD WIPER/WASHER SW ... B-C 16

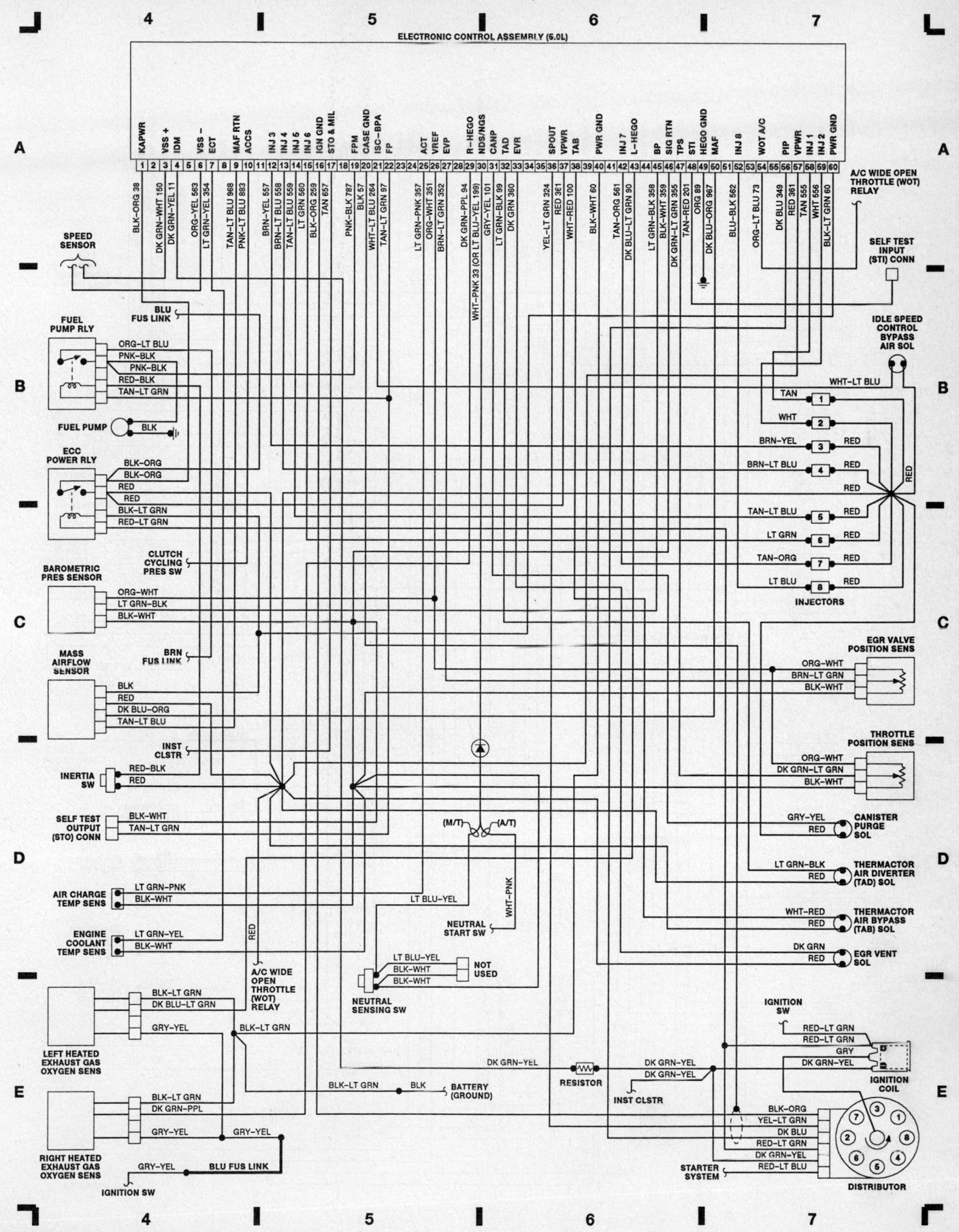

1989 FORD MOTOR CO.
Mustang (Cont.)

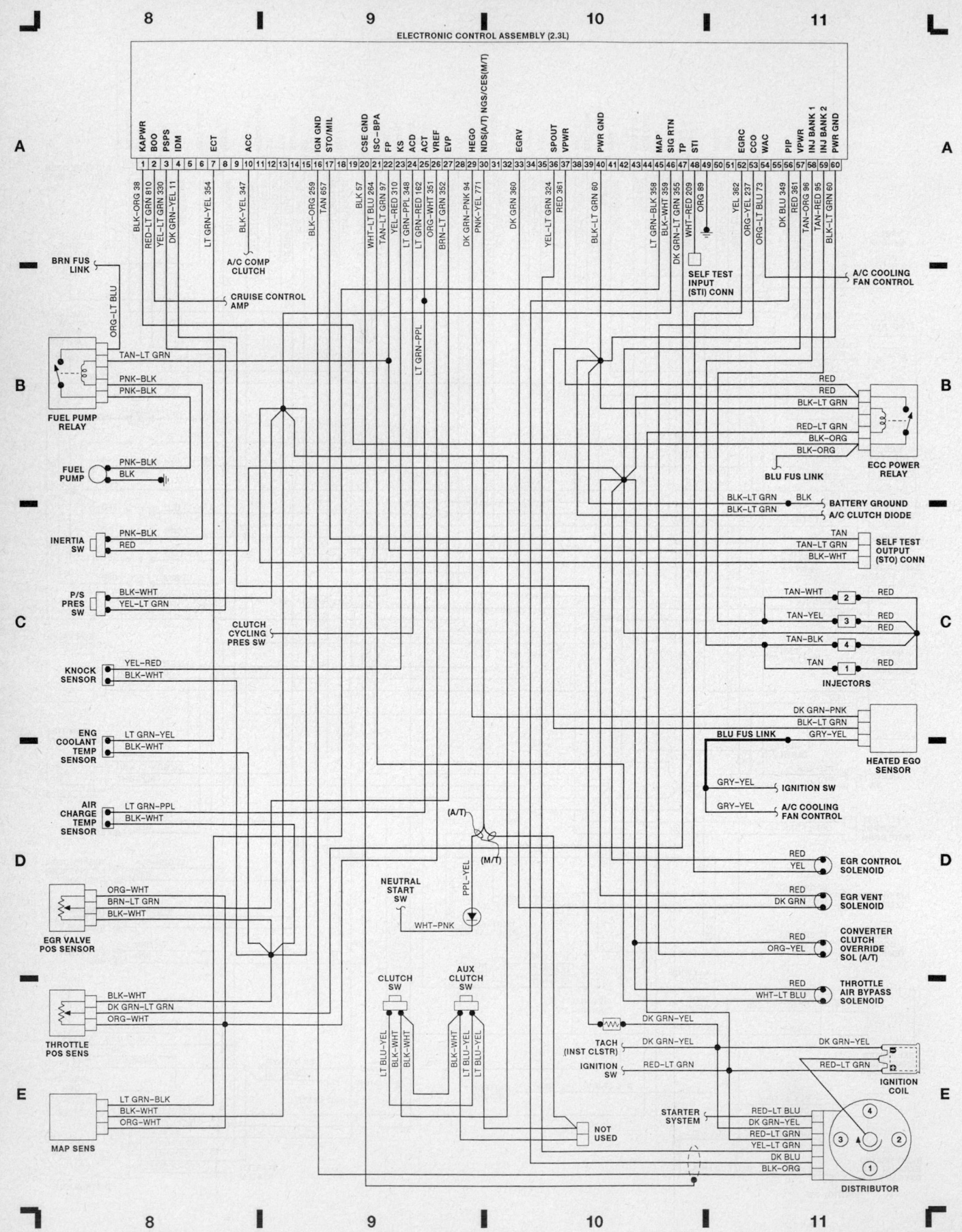

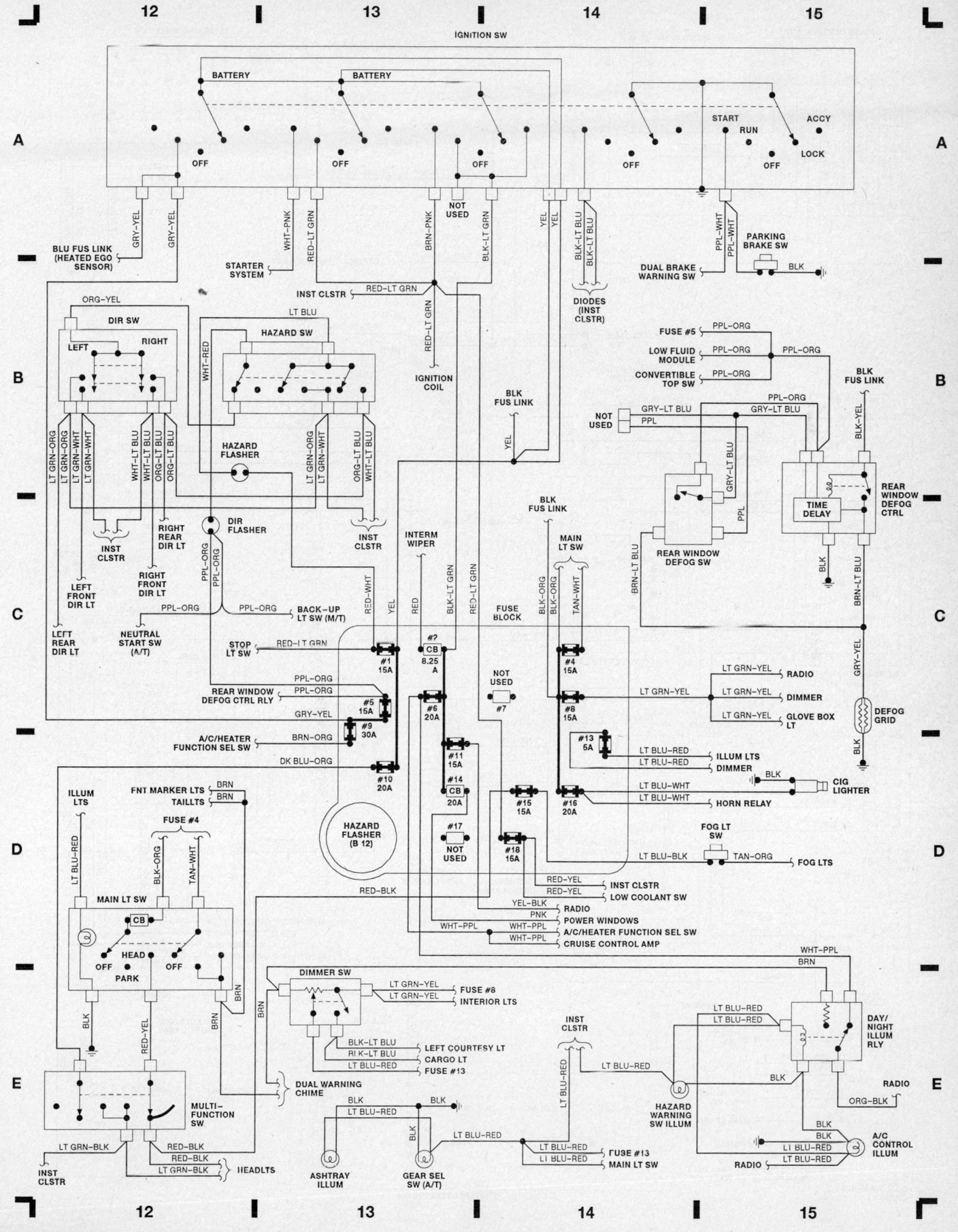

1989 Ford Motor Co.
Mustang (Cont.)

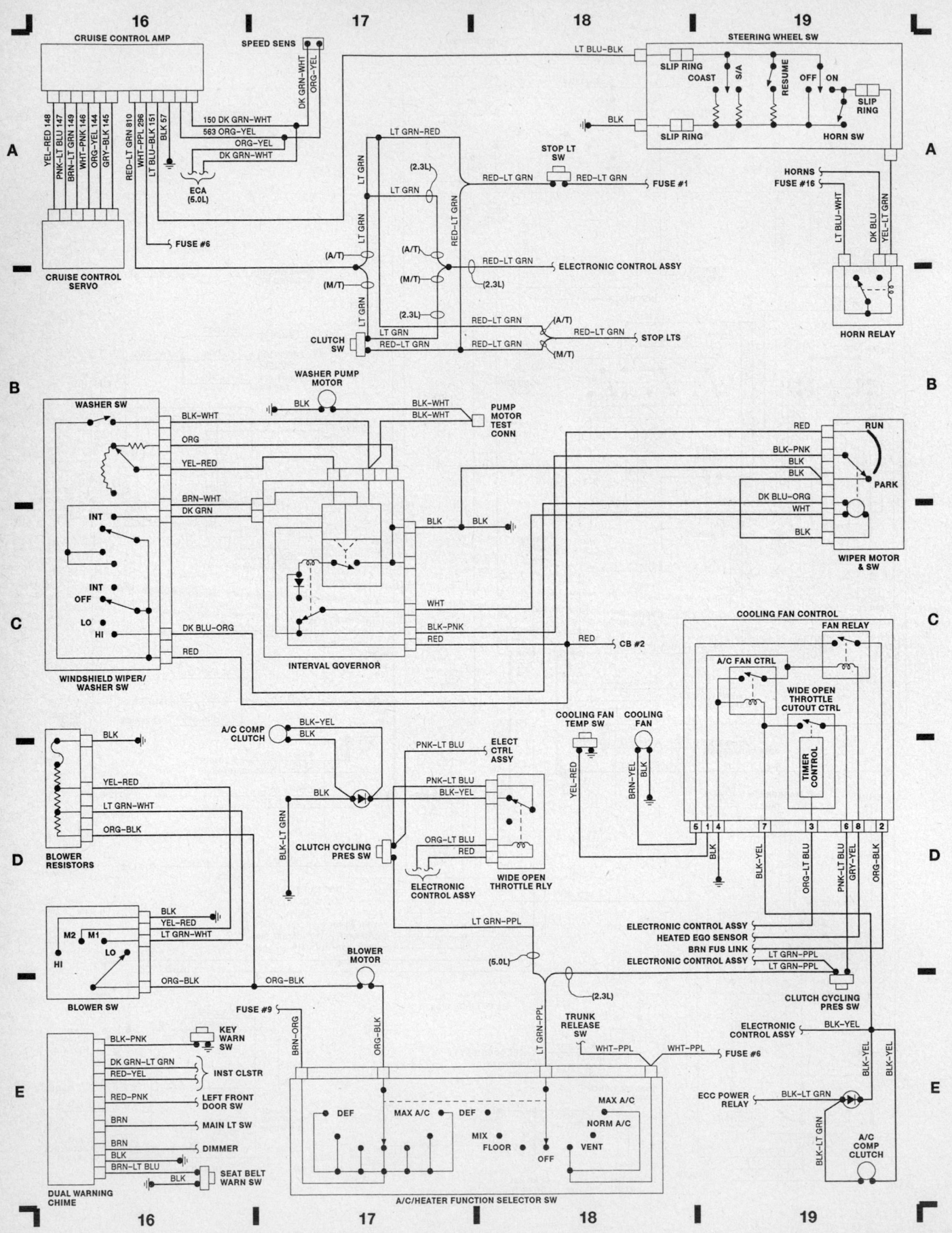

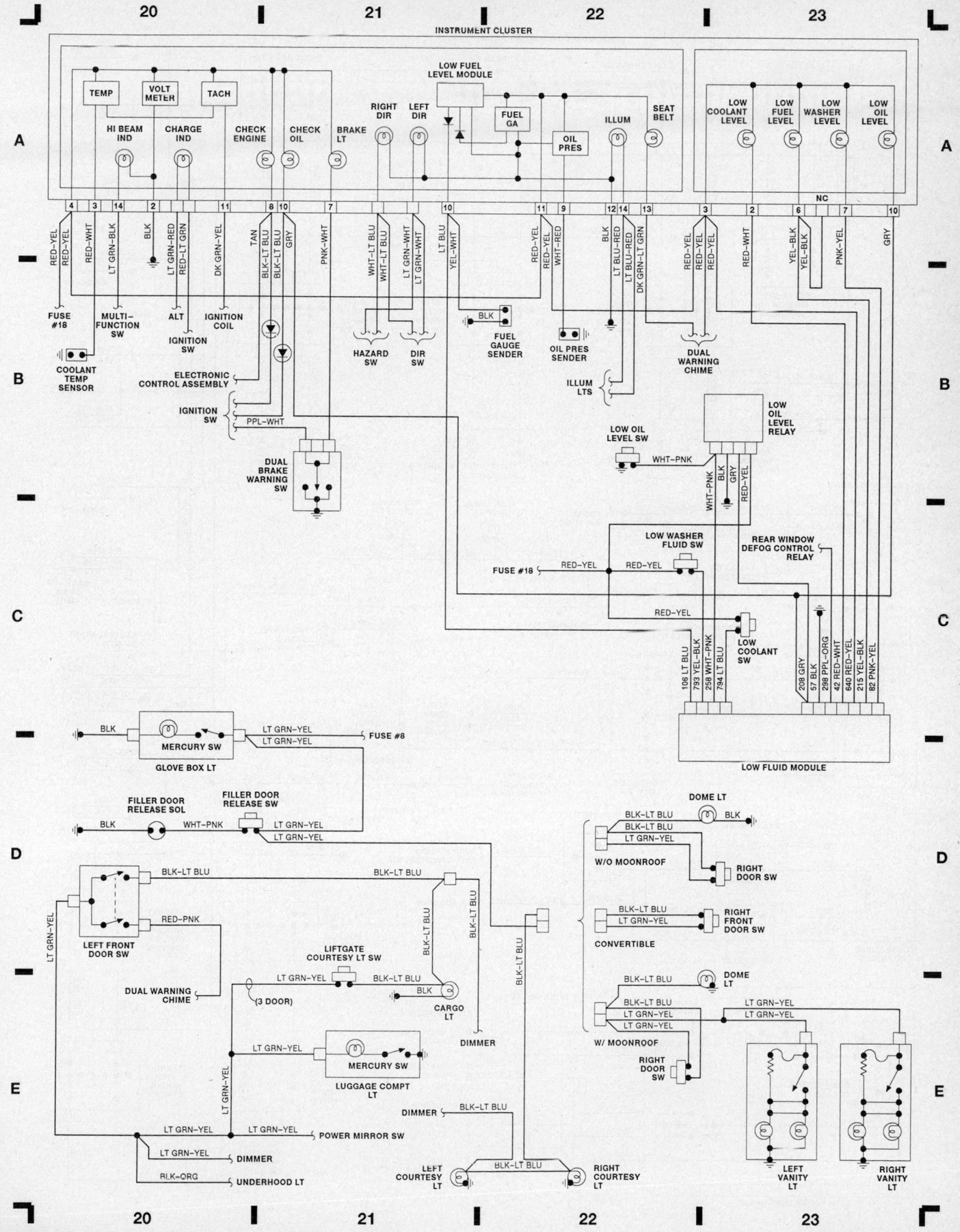

1989 Ford Motor Co.
Mustang (Cont.)

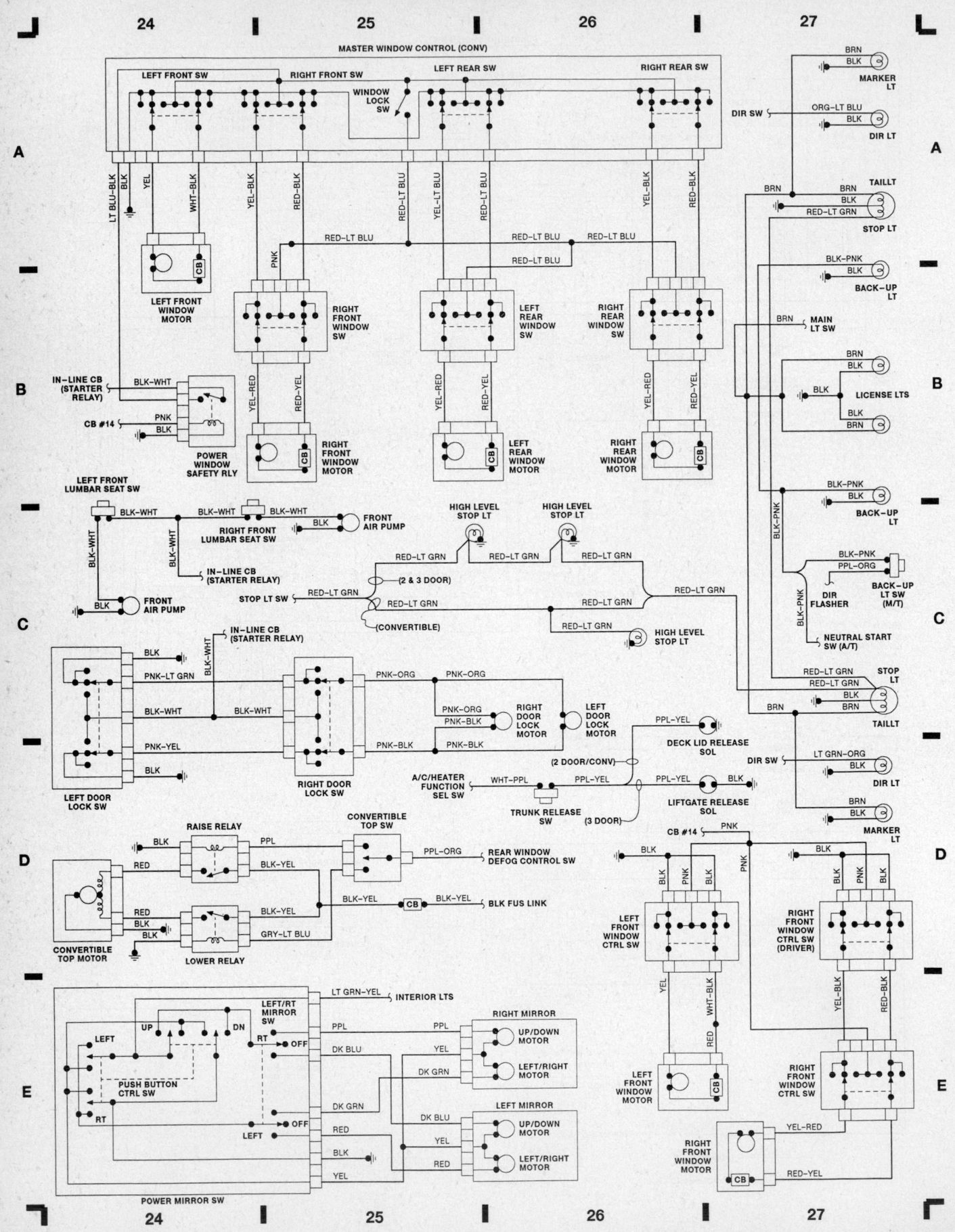

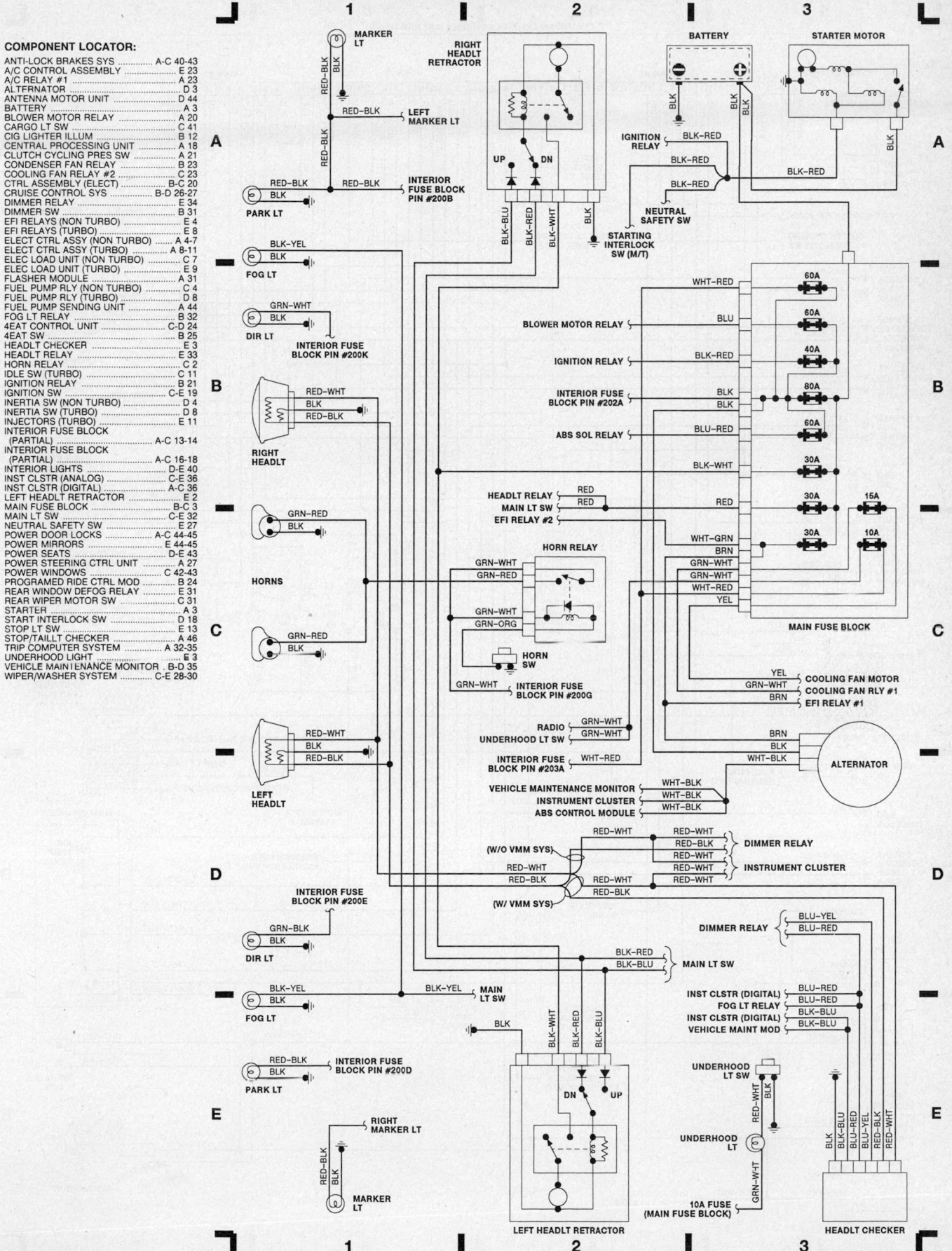

COMPONENT LOCATOR:

ANTI-LOCK BRAKES SYS .... A-C 40-43
A/C CONTROL ASSEMBLY .... E 23
A/C RELAY #1 .... A 23
ALTERNATOR .... D 3
ANTENNA MOTOR UNIT .... D 44
BATTERY .... A 3
BLOWER MOTOR RELAY .... A 20
CARGO LT SW .... C 41
CIG LIGHTER ILLUM .... B 12
CENTRAL PROCESSING UNIT .... A 18
CLUTCH CYCLING PRES SW .... A 21
CONDENSER FAN RELAY .... B 23
COOLING FAN RELAY #2 .... C 23
CTRL ASSEMBLY (ELECT) .... B-C 20
CRUISE CONTROL SYS .... B-D 26-27
DIMMER RELAY .... E 34
DIMMER SW .... B 31
EFI RELAYS (NON TURBO) .... E 4
EFI RELAYS (TURBO) .... E 8
ELECT CTRL ASSY (NON TURBO) .... A 4-7
ELECT CTRL ASSY (TURBO) .... A 8-11
ELEC LOAD UNIT (NON TURBO) .... C 7
ELEC LOAD UNIT (TURBO) .... E 9
FLASHER MODULE .... A 31
FUEL PUMP RLY (NON TURBO) .... C 4
FUEL PUMP RLY (TURBO) .... D 8
FUEL PUMP SENDING UNIT .... A 44
FOG LT RELAY .... B 32
4EAT CONTROL UNIT .... C-D 24
4EAT SW .... B 25
HEADLT CHECKER .... E 3
HEADLT RELAY .... E 33
HORN RELAY .... C 2
IDLE SW (TURBO) .... C 11
IGNITION RELAY .... B 21
IGNITION SW .... C-E 19
INERTIA SW (NON TURBO) .... D 4
INERTIA SW (TURBO) .... D 8
INJECTORS (TURBO) .... E 11
INTERIOR FUSE BLOCK
  (PARTIAL) .... A-C 13-14
INTERIOR FUSE BLOCK
  (PARTIAL) .... A-C 16-18
INTERIOR LIGHTS .... D-E 40
INST CLSTR (ANALOG) .... C-E 36
INST CLSTR (DIGITAL) .... A-C 36
LEFT HEADLT RETRACTOR .... E 2
MAIN FUSE BLOCK .... B-C 3
MAIN LT SW .... C-E 32
NEUTRAL SAFETY SW .... E 27
POWER DOOR LOCKS .... A-C 44-45
POWER MIRRORS .... E 44-45
POWER SEATS .... D-E 43
POWER STEERING CTRL UNIT .... A 27
POWER WINDOWS .... C 42-43
PROGRAMED RIDE CTRL MOD .... B 24
REAR WINDOW DEFOG RELAY .... E 31
REAR WIPER MOTOR SW .... C 31
STARTER .... A 3
START INTERLOCK SW .... D 18
STOP LT SW .... E 13
STOP/TAILLT CHECKER .... A 46
TRIP COMPUTER SYSTEM .... A 32-35
UNDERHOOD LIGHT .... E 3
VEHICLE MAINTENANCE MONITOR . B-D 35
WIPER/WASHER SYSTEM .... C-E 28-30

1989 FORD MOTOR CO.
Probe (Cont.)

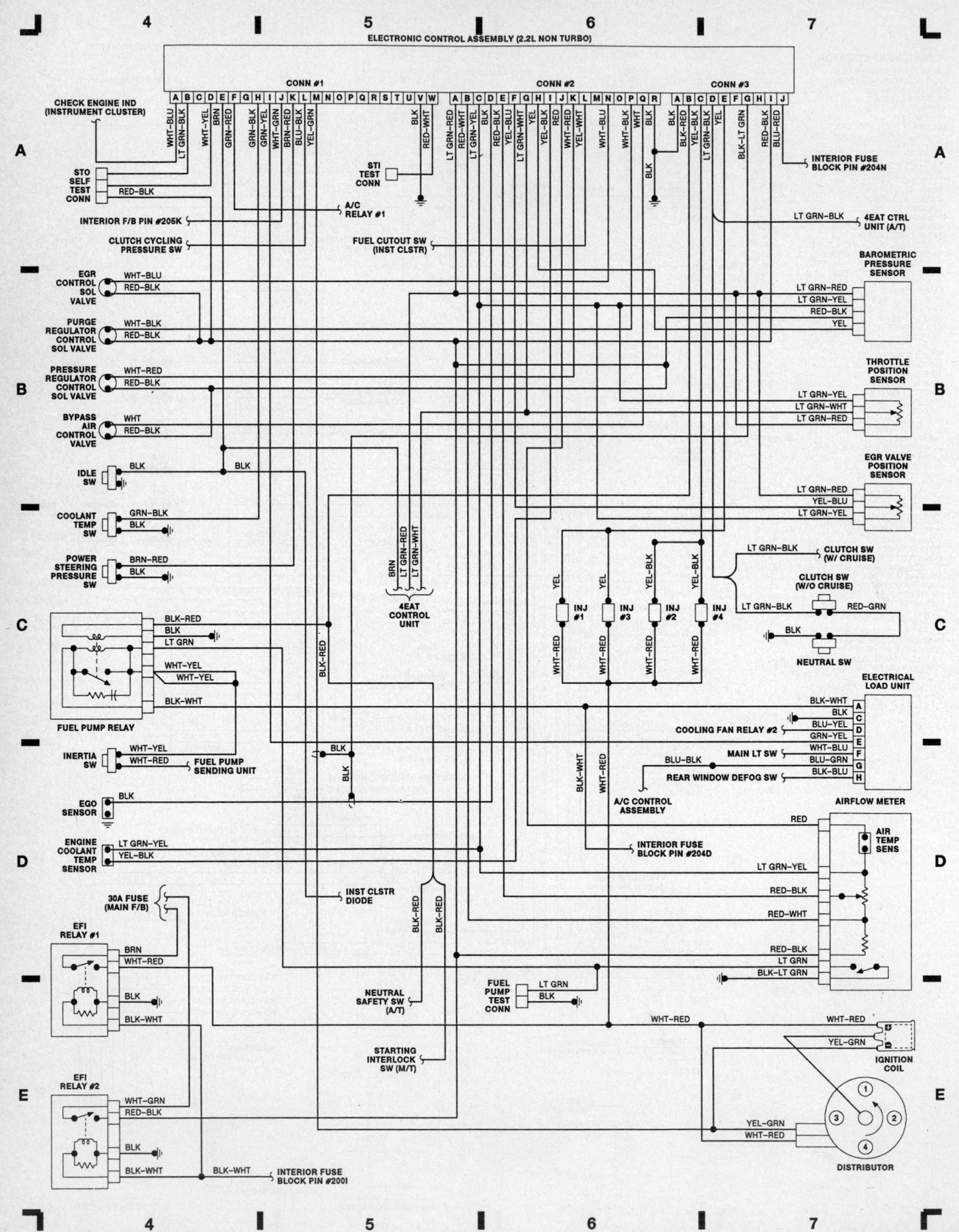

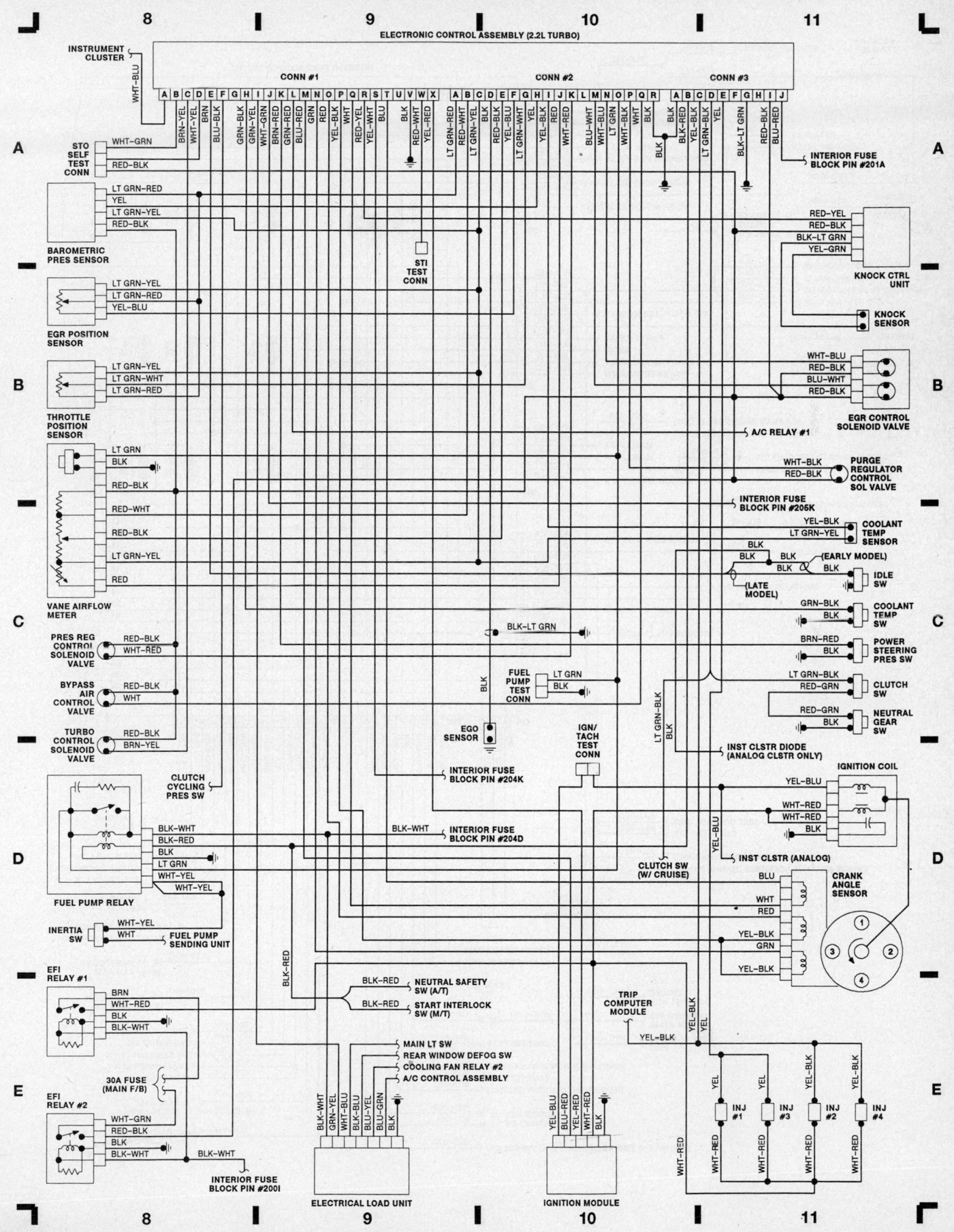

1989 Ford Motor Co.
Probe (Cont.)

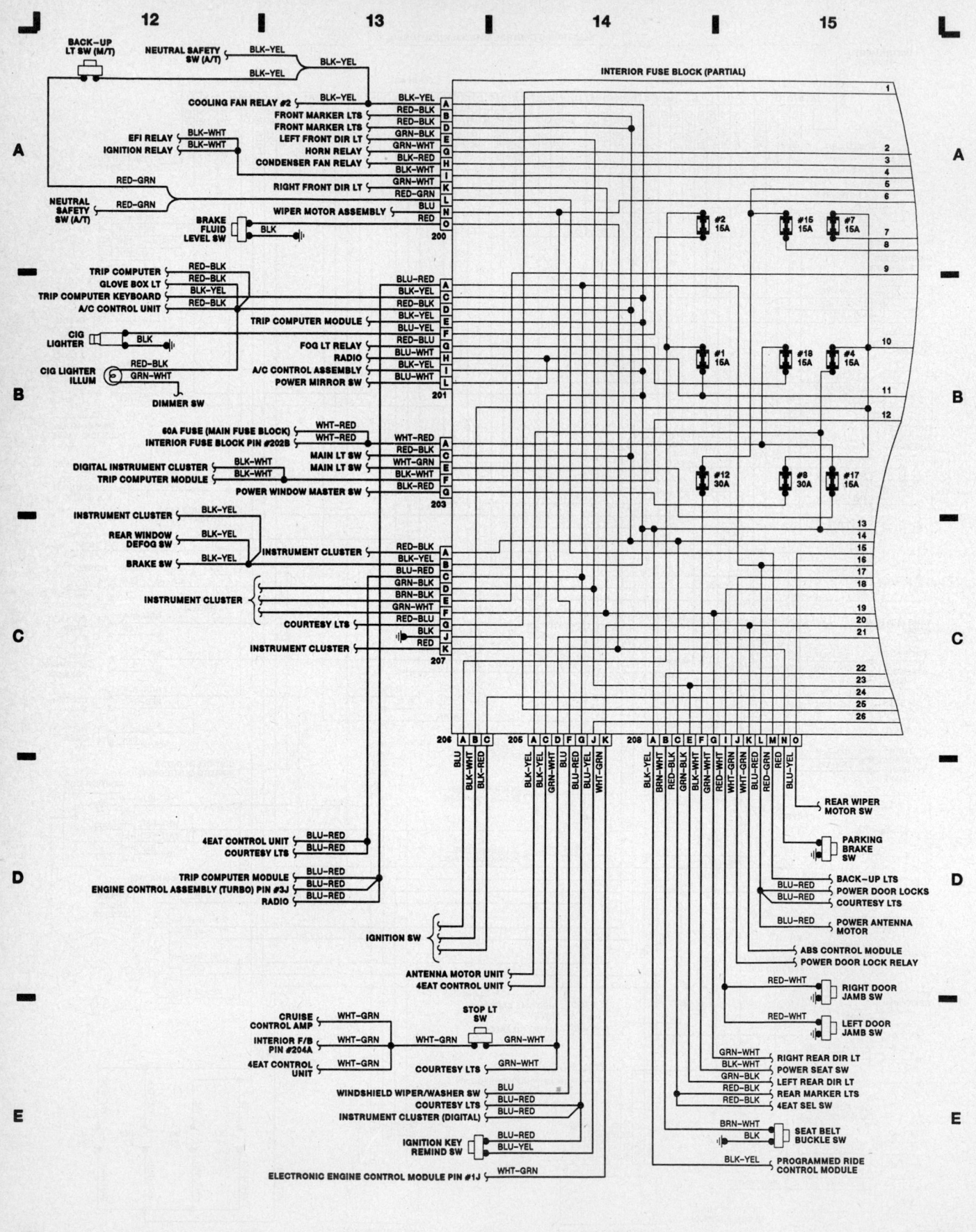

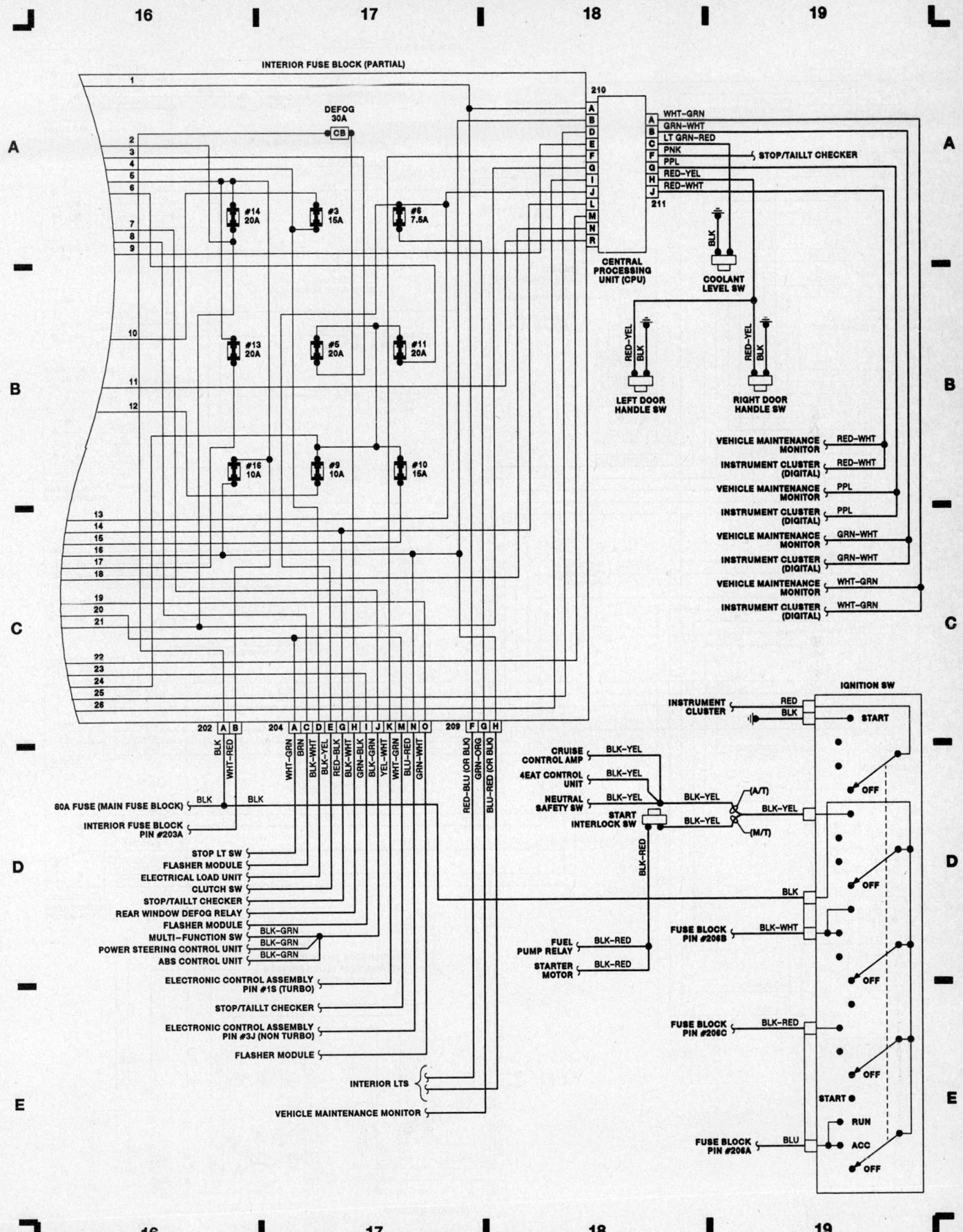

1989 Ford Motor Co.
Probe (Cont.)

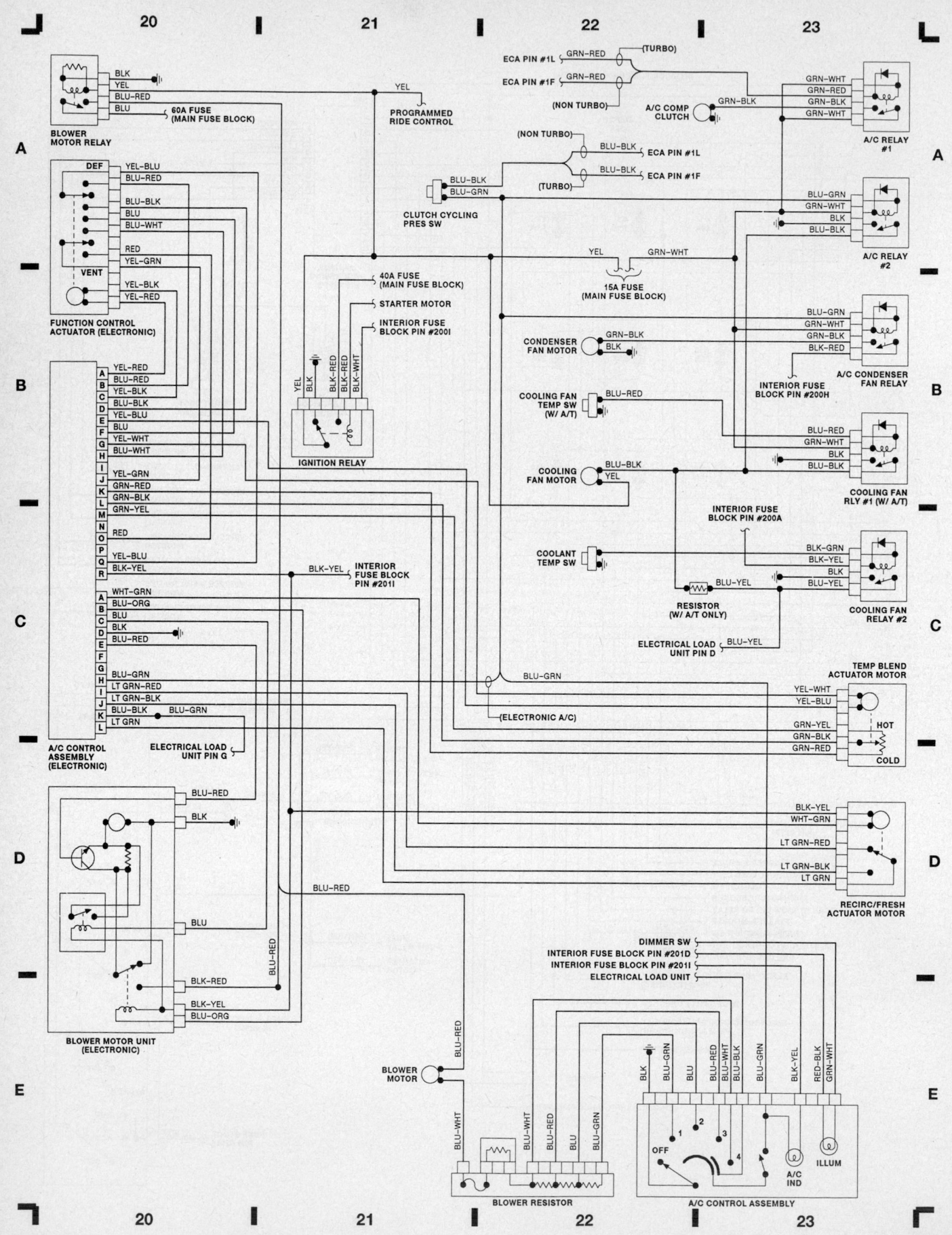

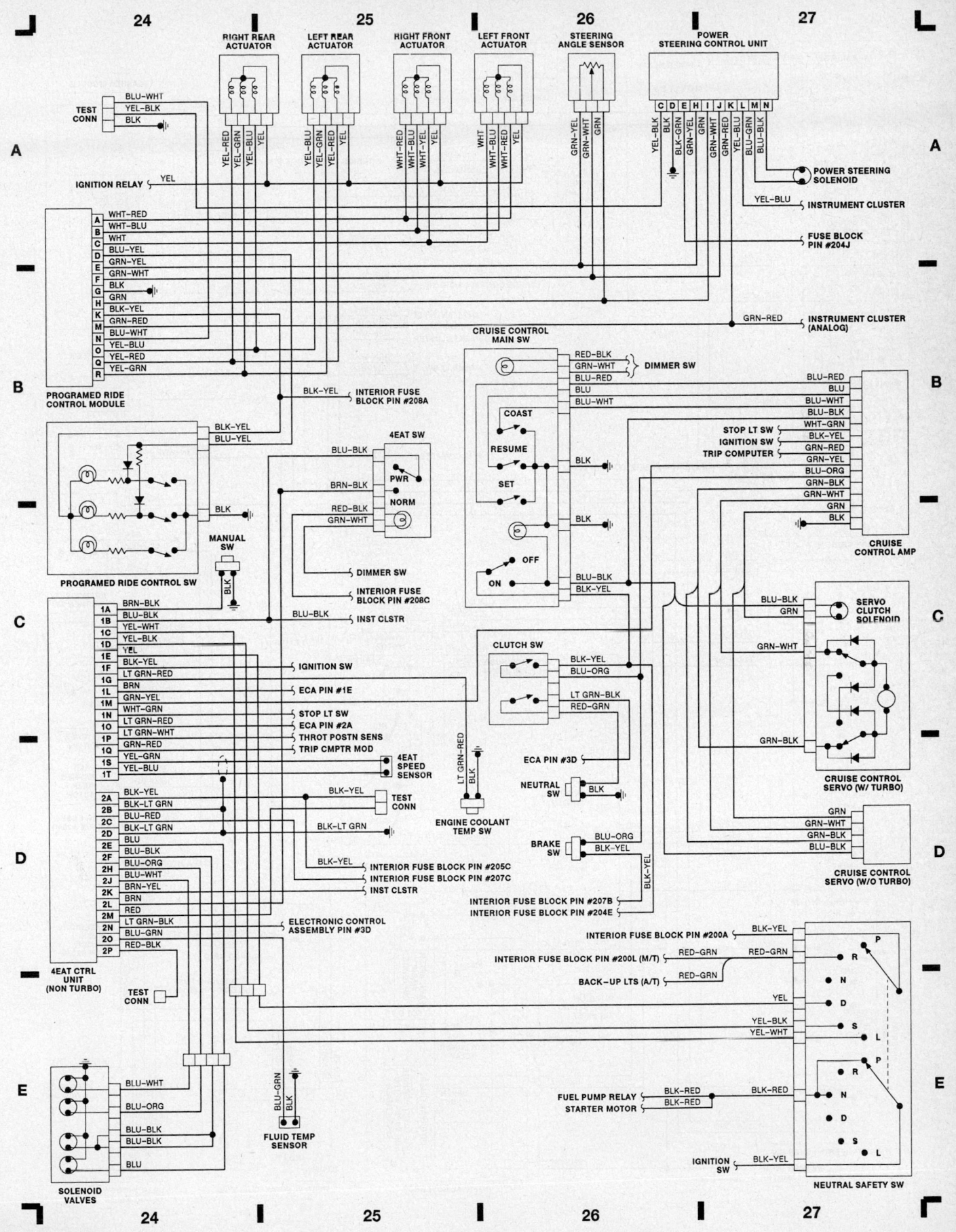

1989 Ford Motor Co.
Probe (Cont.)

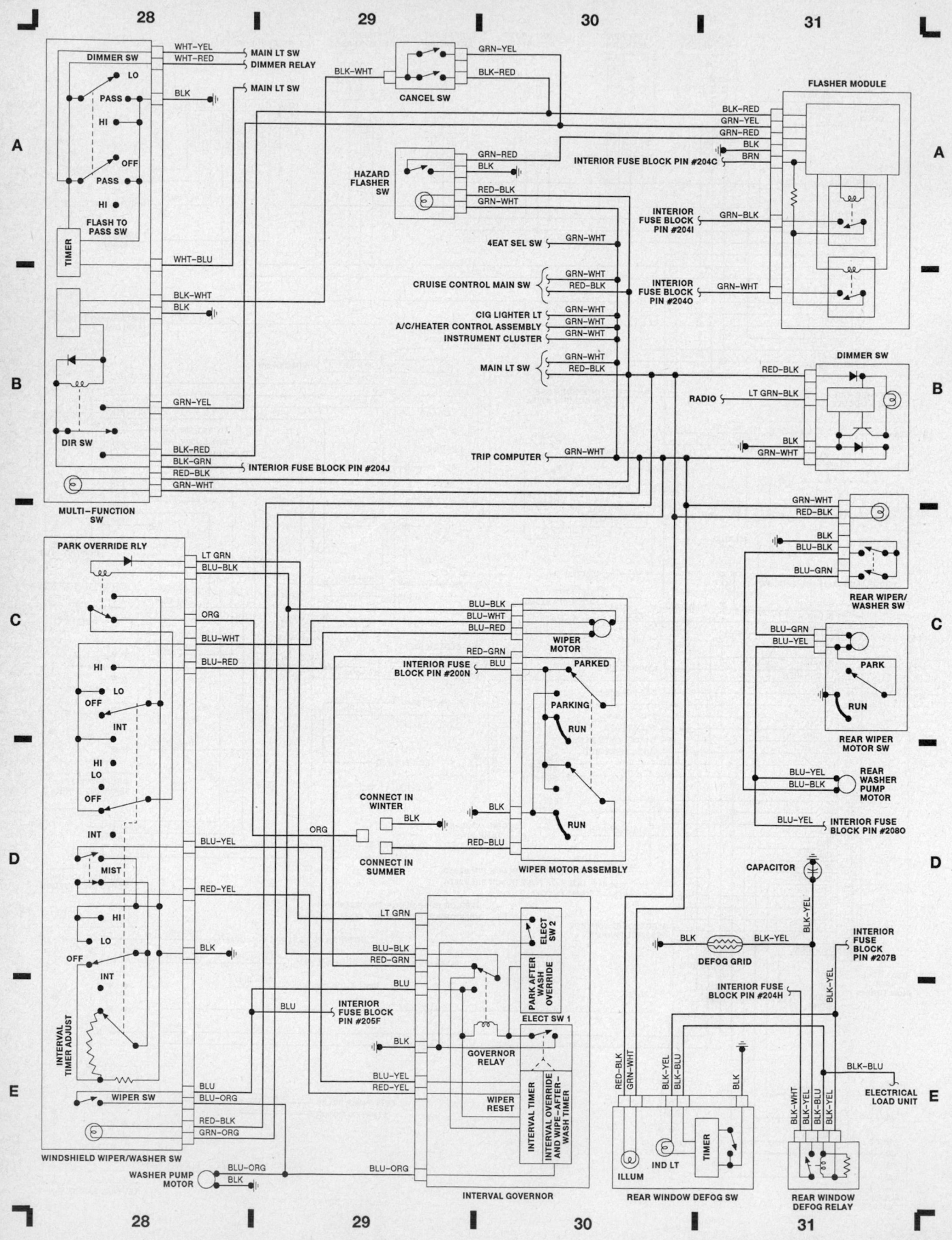

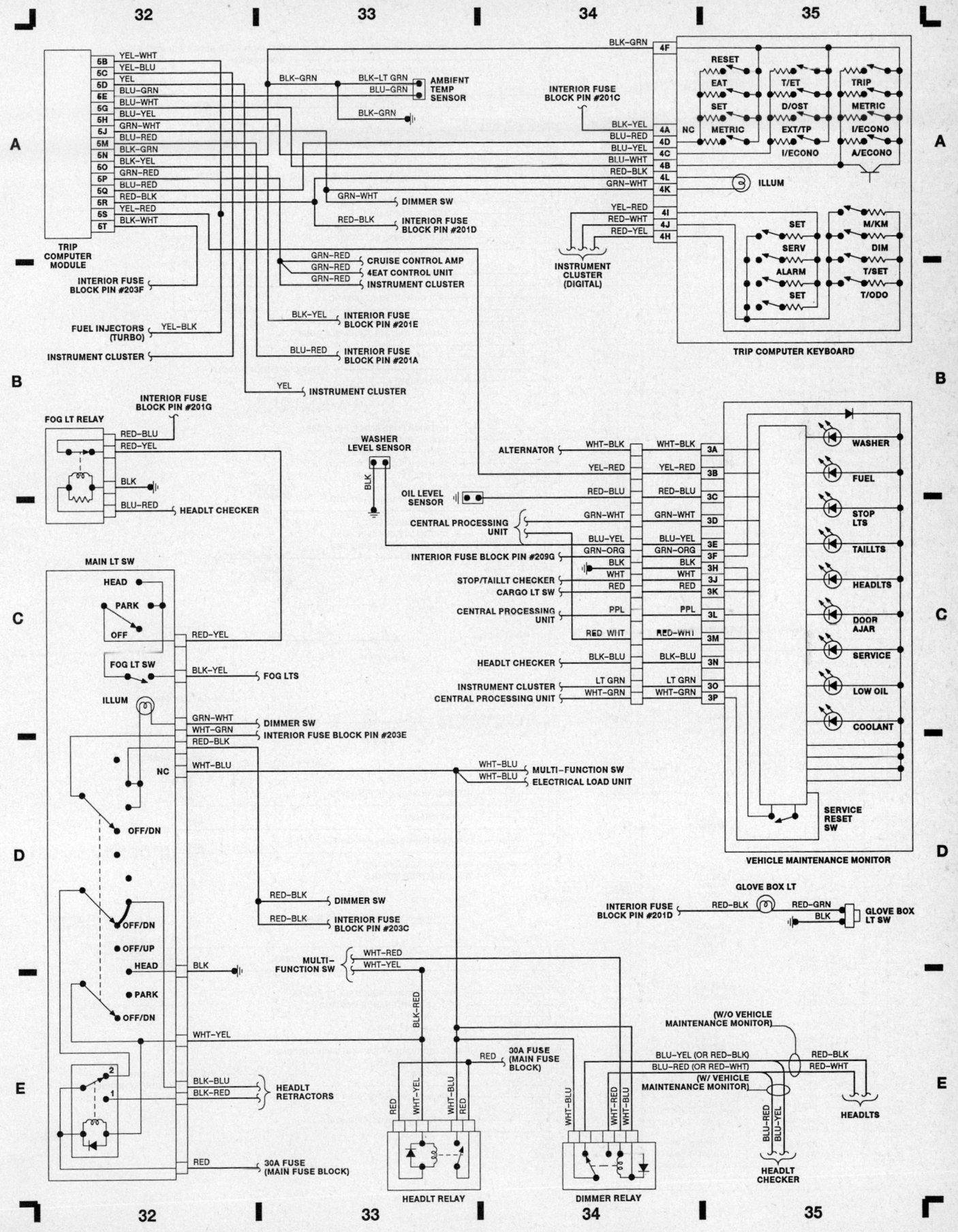

1989 Ford Motor Co.
Probe (Cont.)

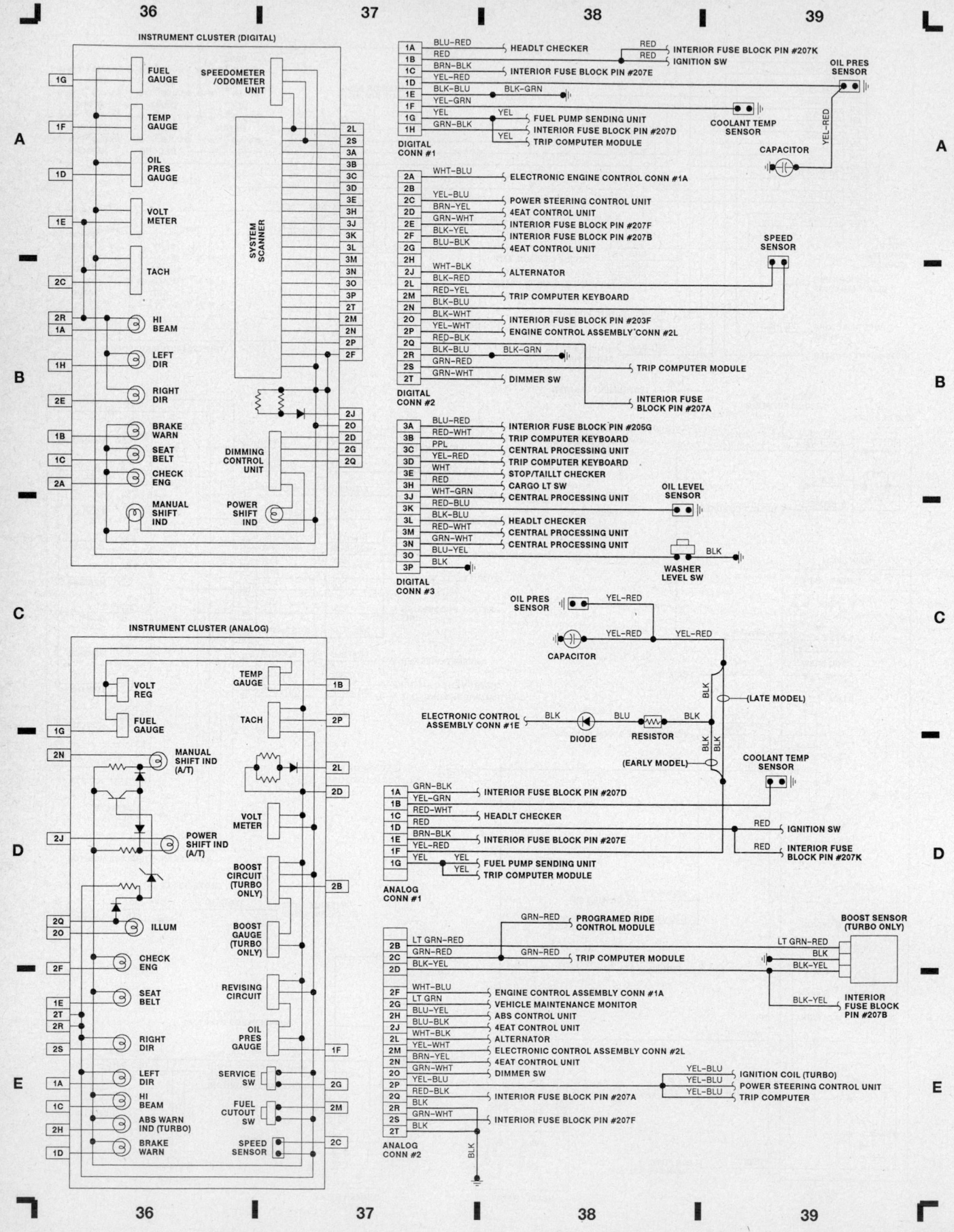

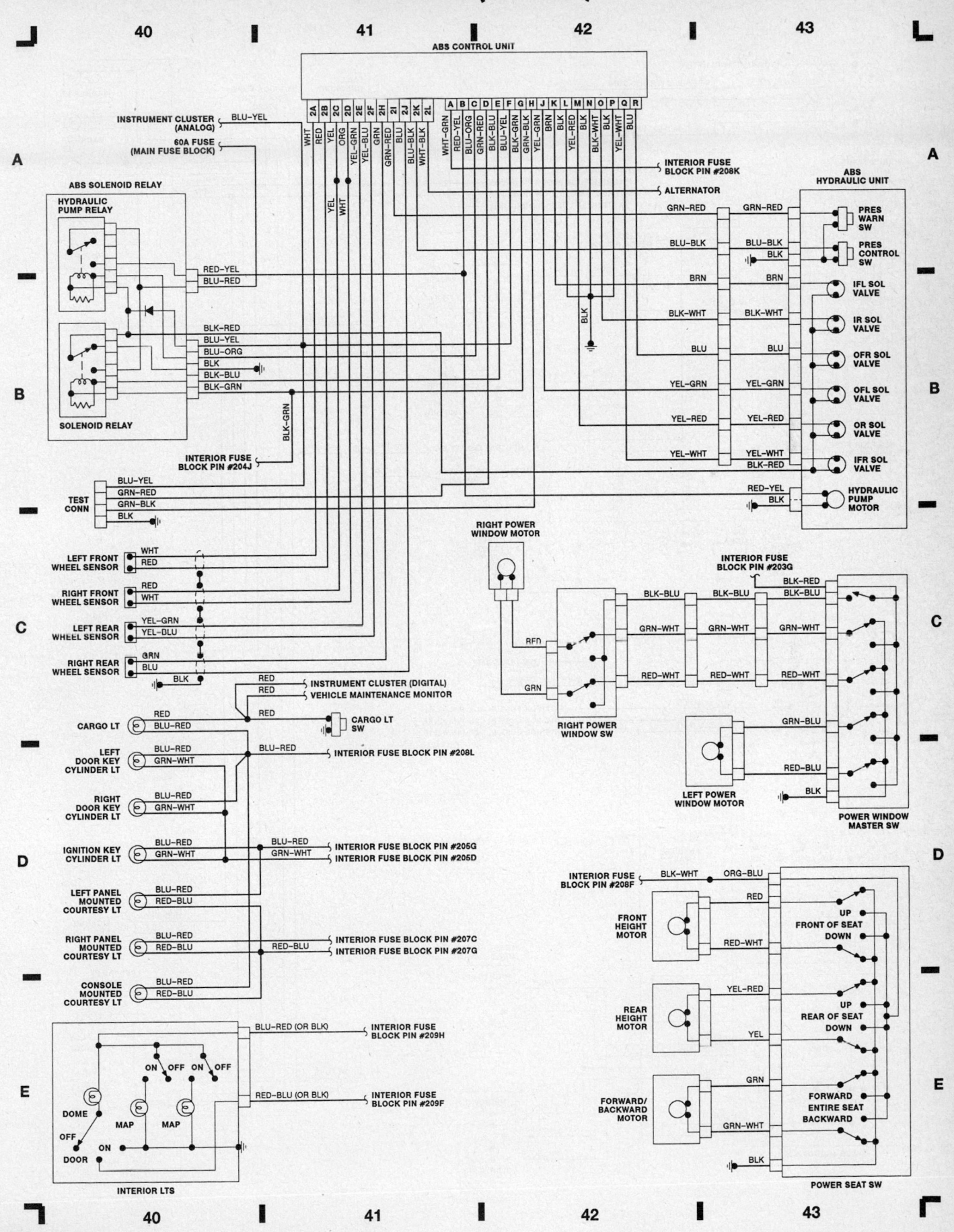

1989 Ford Motor Co.
Probe (Cont.)

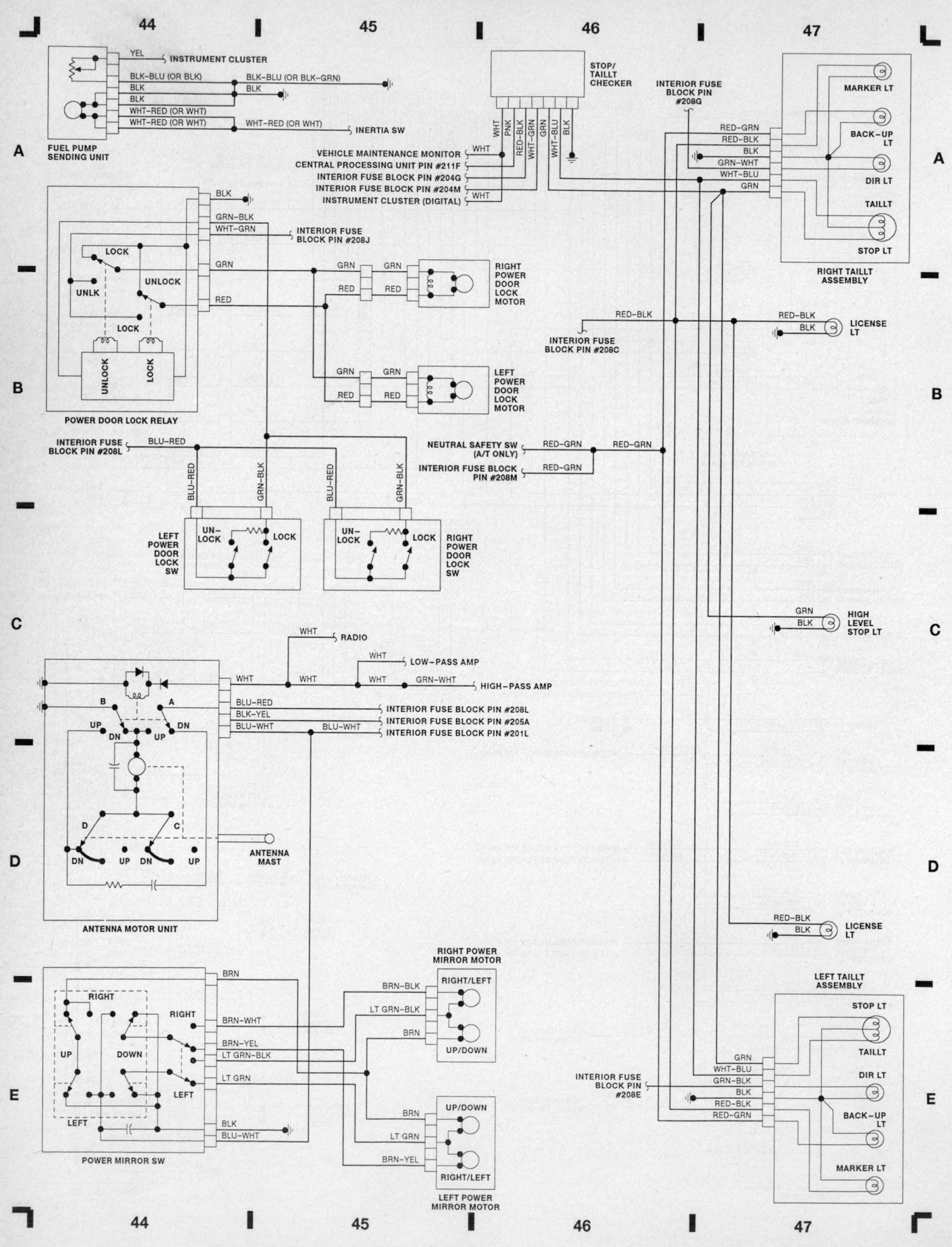

1989 Ford Motor Co.
Sable & Taurus

Component Locator:

A/C CLUTCH CYCLING SW .... C 29, D 29
A/C/HEATER FUNCTION SW .... B-D 28
ALTERNATOR .... B D 3
ALT OUTPUT CONTROL RELAY .... C-D 3
AUTO A/C (EATC) MODULE .... A-B 28
AUTO LAMP DUAL RELAY .... E 39
AUTO LAMP TIME CONTROL SW ... E 31
BACK-UP LIGHT SW .... C 49
BATTERY .... A 1-2
BLOWER MOTOR .... A 31, C 30
CHECK ENGINE IND .... C 6, C 10, E 15, E 21
CIG LIGHTER ASSEMBLY .... C-D 39
CORNERING LTS (TAURUS) .... A 1, E 1
CRUISE CONTROL SERVO .... E 24
CRUISE CONTROL SW .... E 34
DIAGNOSTIC WARNING MODULE .... B-C 32
DIGITAL CLOCK .... D 36
DISTRIBUTOR .... C 7, C 11, C 21
DISTRIBUTORLESS IGNITION SYSTEM
  (DIS) MODULE .... C-D 12-13
DOOR AJAR SWS .... A-B 48
DOOR COURTESY LTS .... B 36
DOOR LOCK SWS .... A 44, A 47
DOOR SWS .... A 36-37
ELECT CLUSTER SW ASSEMBLY .. A-B 40
ELECT CONTROL ASSEMBLY
  (ECA) 2.5L .... B-E 4
ELECT CONTROL ASSEMBLY
  (ECA) 3.0L EFI .... B-E 8
ELECT CONTROL ASSEMBLY
  (ECA) 3.0L SHO .... A 12-15
ELECT CONTROL ASSEMBLY
  (ECA) 3.8L .... A 20-23
ELECT FLASHER .... C 34-35
ENGINE COMPT LT .... E 2
FOG LTS .... B-D 1
FOG LIGHT SW .... A 32
FUEL INJECTORS .... E 6, E 10, E 13, C 21
FUSE BLOCK .... C-D 25-26
FUS LINK (BATTERY) .... A 2
FUS LINK (ALTERNATOR) .... B-C 2
FUS LINK (ALT OUTPUT
  CONTROL RELAY) .... C 3
FUS LINK (IGNITION SW) .... B 26
FUS LINK (STARTER RELAY) .... A 2-3
GLOVE COMPT SW & LT .... A 28
HEATED EXHAUST GAS OXYGEN (HEGO)
  SENSOR #1 .... D 6, D 10, E 14, E 22
HEATED EXHAUST GAS OXYGEN
  (HEGO) SENSOR #2 ...... E 14, E 22
HEATED WINDSHIELD .... D 31
HEATED WINDSHIELD CONTROL
  MODULE .... C 31
HEATED WINDSHIELD SW .... B-C 31
HORNS .... C 1
HORN RELAY .... E 35
IGNITION COIL .... B 7, B 11, D-E 12, D 20
IGNITION SW .... A-C 24
ILLUMINATION DIMMING RELAY ... C 39
ILLUMINATED ENTRY TIMER ...... B-C 37
INST CLSTR (ANALOG) .... A-D 43
INST CLSTR (ELECT) .... A-E 41-42
INTEGRATED CONTROL MODULE
  (ICM) 2.5L .... A-B 7
INTEGRATED CONTROL MODULE
  (ICM) 3.0L EFI .... A-B 11
INTEGRATED CONTROL MODULE
  (ICM) 3.0L SHO .... A 18-19
INTEGRATED CONTROL MODULE
  (ICM) 3.8L .... E 16-17
INTERVAL GOVERNOR .... D 32-33
KEYLESS ENTRY MODULE .... B-C 47
LCD DIMMING RELAY .... D-E 38
LIFTGATE AJAR SW .... A 48
LIFTGATE RELEASE RELAY .... E 49
LIFTGATE RELEASE SW .... E 49-50
LIGHT SENSOR/AMPLIFIER .... D-E 31
MAIN LIGHT SWITCH .... D-E 36
MOON ROOF CONTROL SW .... C 48
NEUTRAL SAFETY/BACK-UP
  LIGHT SWITCH .... A-B 27
POWER ANTENNA SW .... D 48
POWER MIRROR SW .... E 46-47
POWER SEAT CONTROL SW ...... D 44-46
POWER WINDOW SAFETY RELAY . A-B 44
RADIO .... C-D 36
REAR COURTESY LTS .... A-B 38
REAR WINDOW DEFOGGER
  CONTROL .... C-D 34
SELF TEST INPUT
  (STI) CONN .... E 6, E 10, E 15, E 23
SELF TEST OUTPUT
  (STO) CONN .... C 6, C 11, E 14-15, E 21-22
SPEED SENSOR .... B 4, A 8, A 20
SPOUT CONN .... B 6, B 10, B 12, C 20
STARTER RELAY .... A 2
STOP LIGHT SWITCH .... C 53
TFI MODULE .... C 7, C 11, C-D 21
TOP GEAR SW (M/T) .... E 5
UPSHIFT DIMMER RELAY (M/T) ... E 25-26
VOLTAGE REGULATOR .... C 1, D 2
WARNING CHIME MODULE .... E 28, E 20
WASHER FLUID LEVEL SW .... E 2
WIPER MOTOR (FRONT) .... E 3
WIPER/WASHER SW (FRONT) ... E 32-33
WIPER/WASHER SW (REAR) ..... E 48

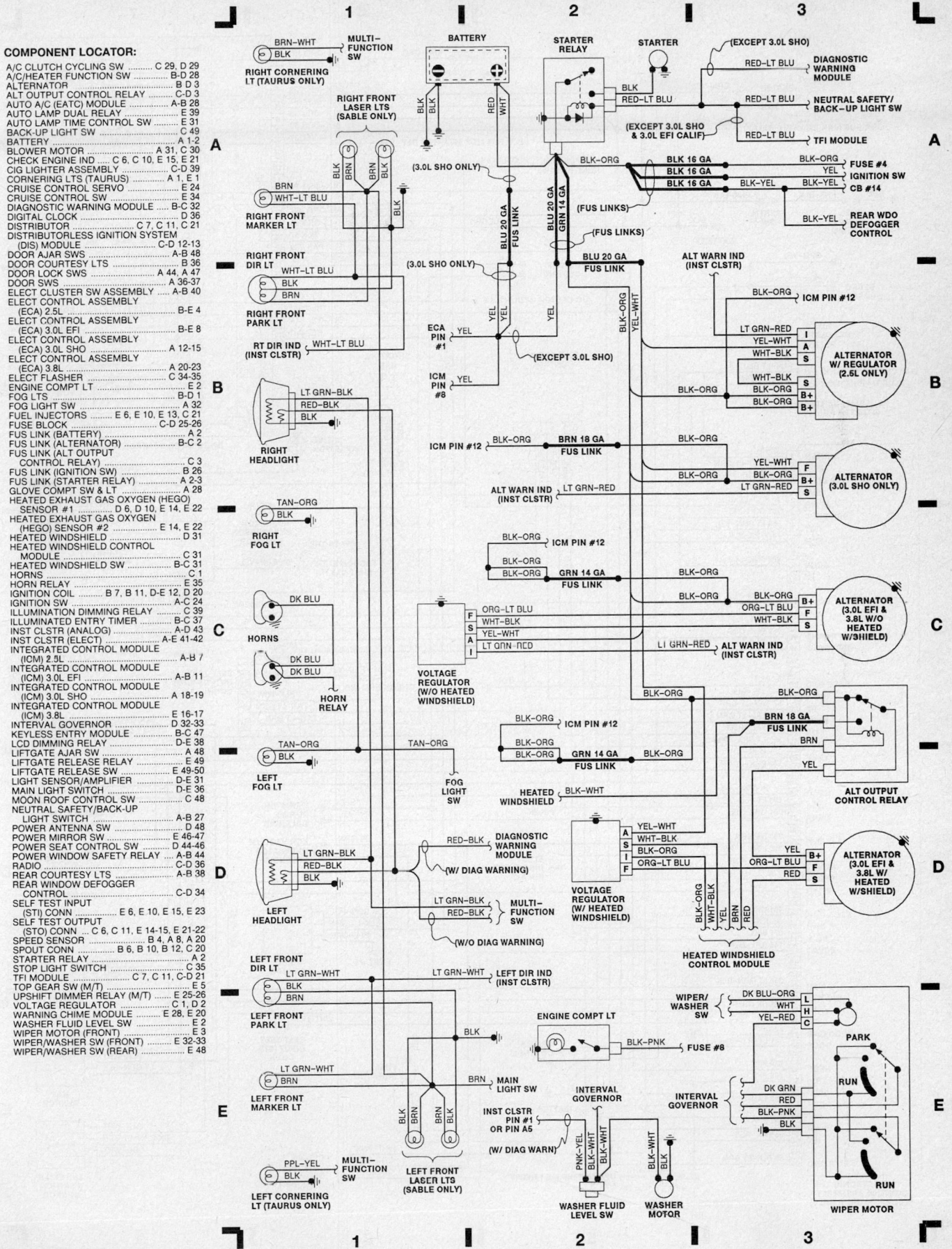

1989 FORD MOTOR CO.
Sable & Taurus (Cont.)

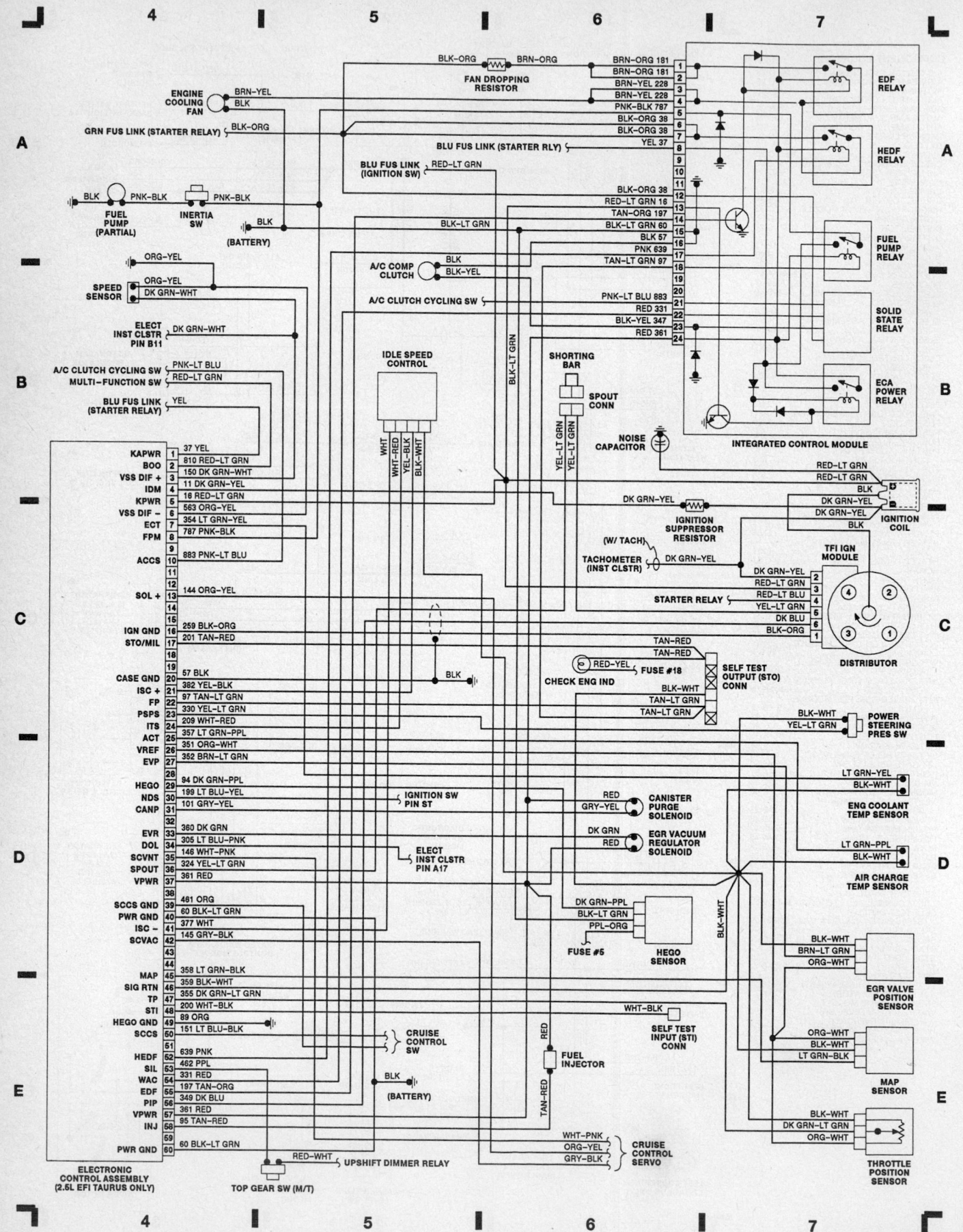

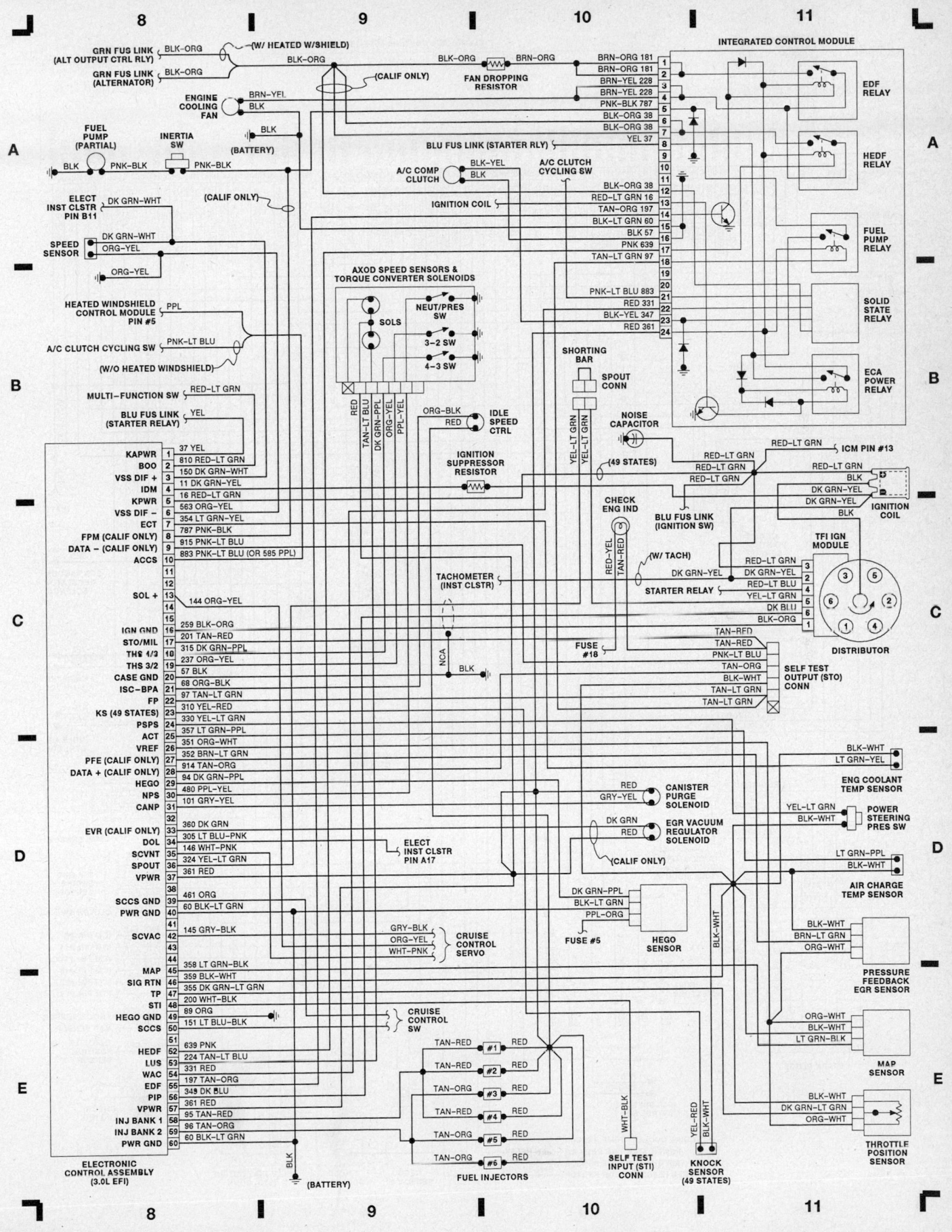

1989 FORD MOTOR CO.
Sable & Taurus (Cont.)

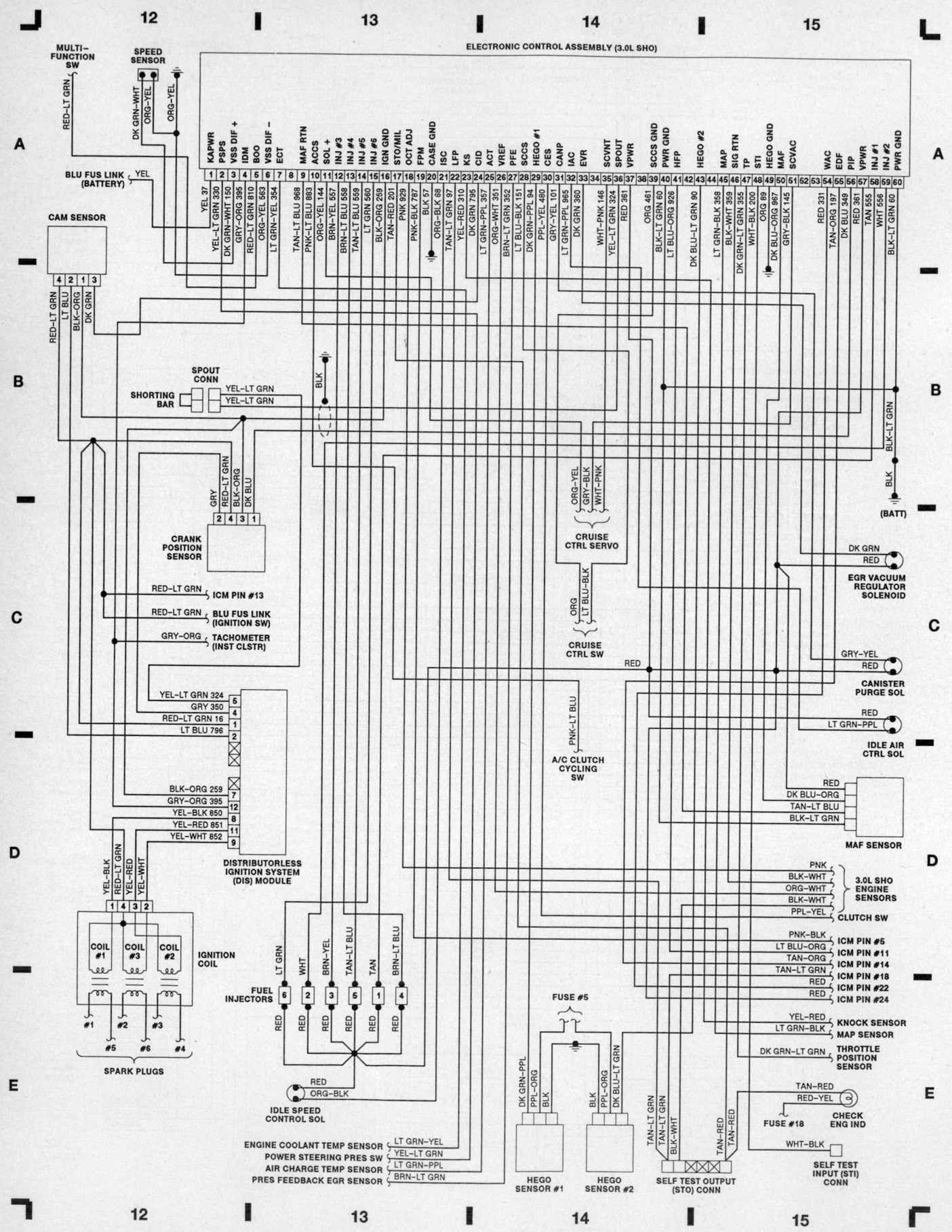

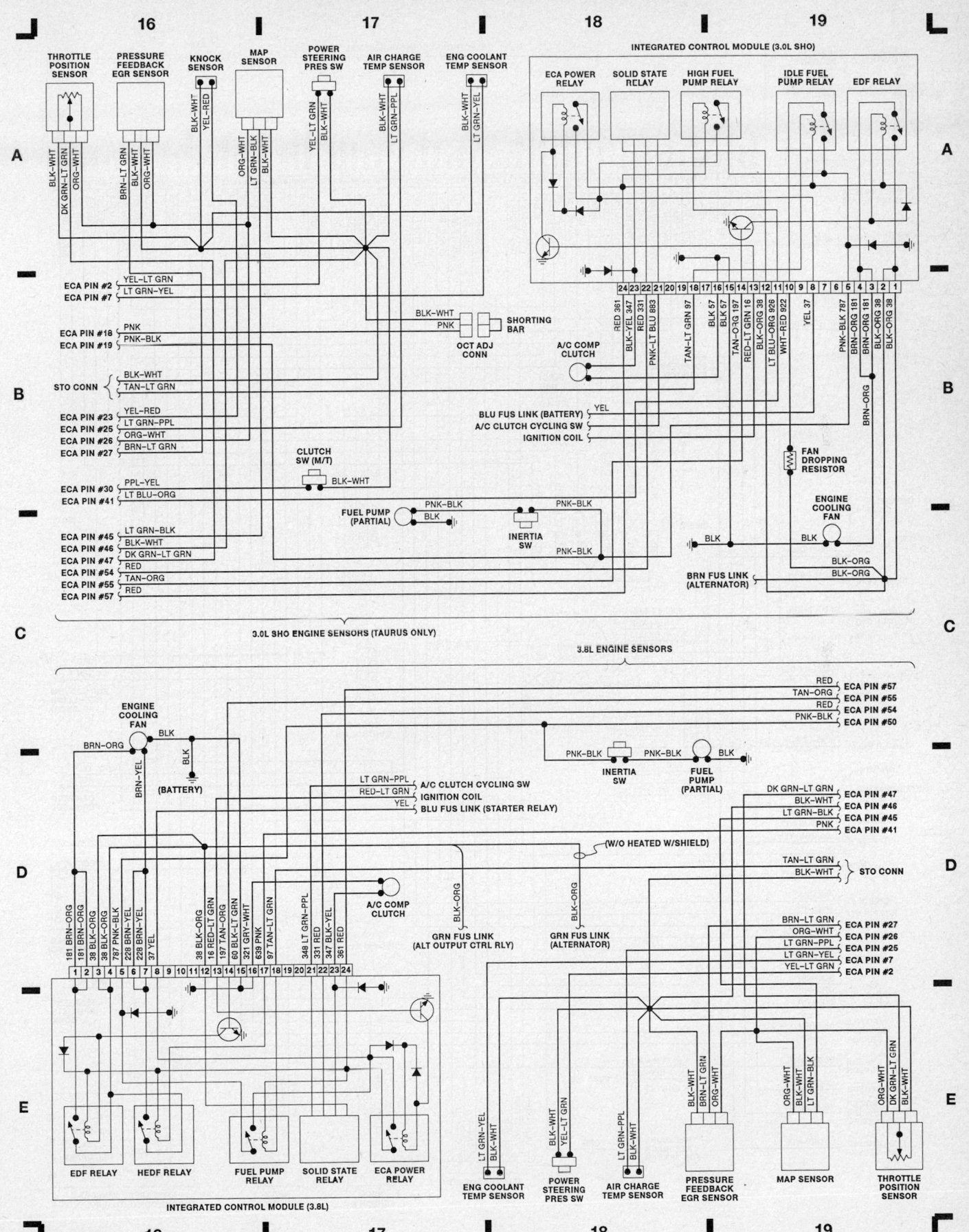

1989 Ford Motor Co.
Sable & Taurus (Cont.)

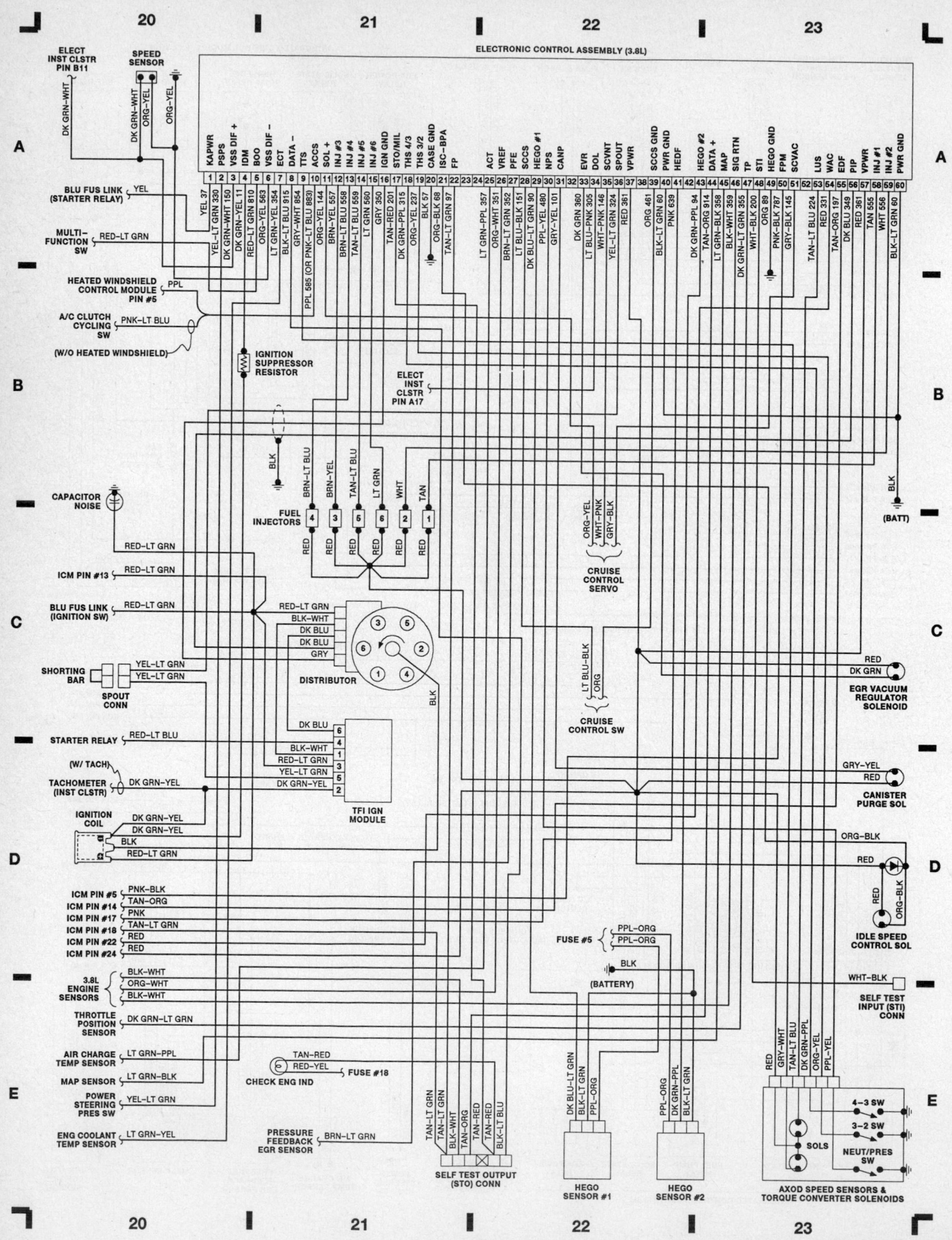

ELECTRONIC CONTROL ASSEMBLY (3.8L)

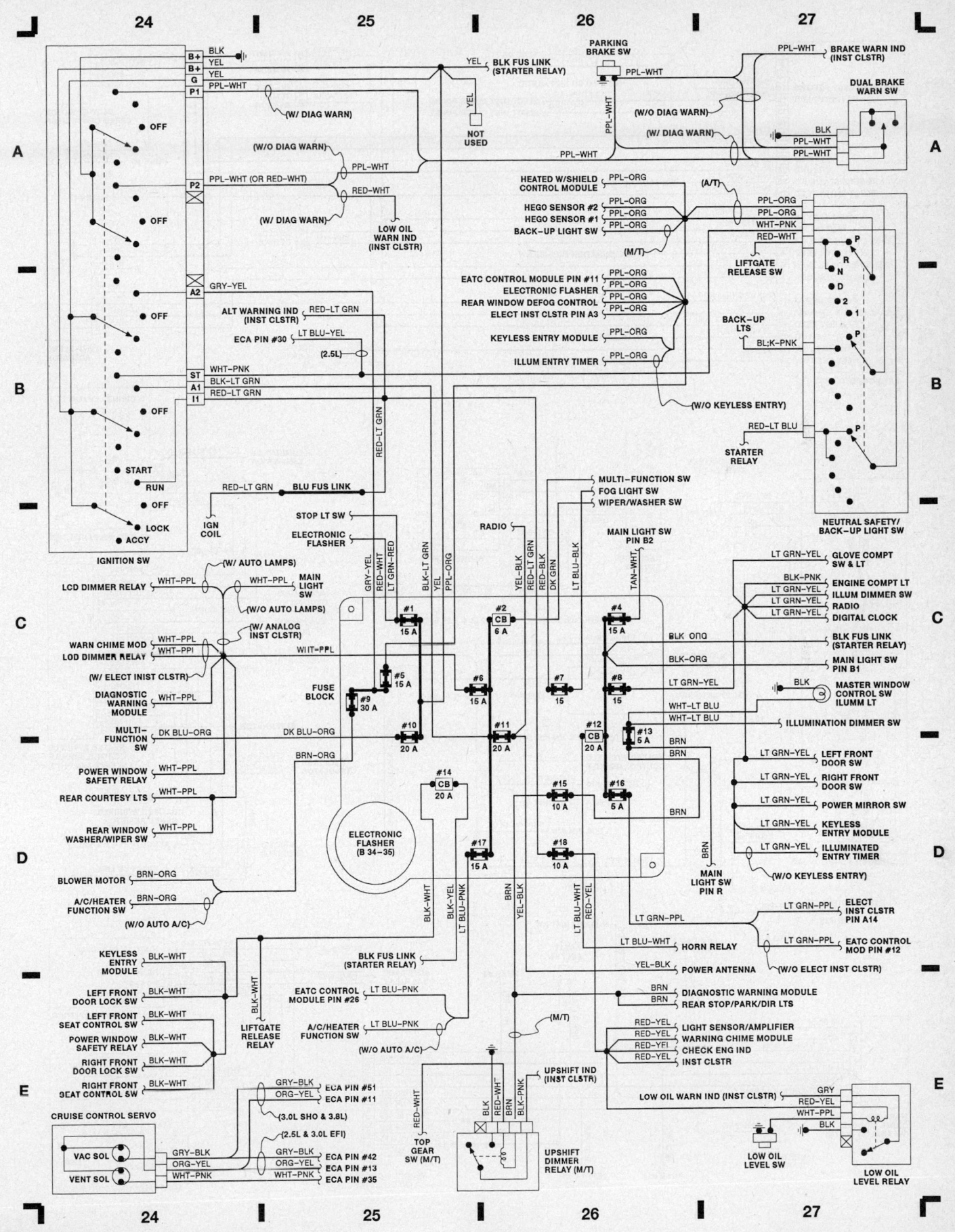

1989 Ford Motor CO.
Sable & Taurus (Cont.)

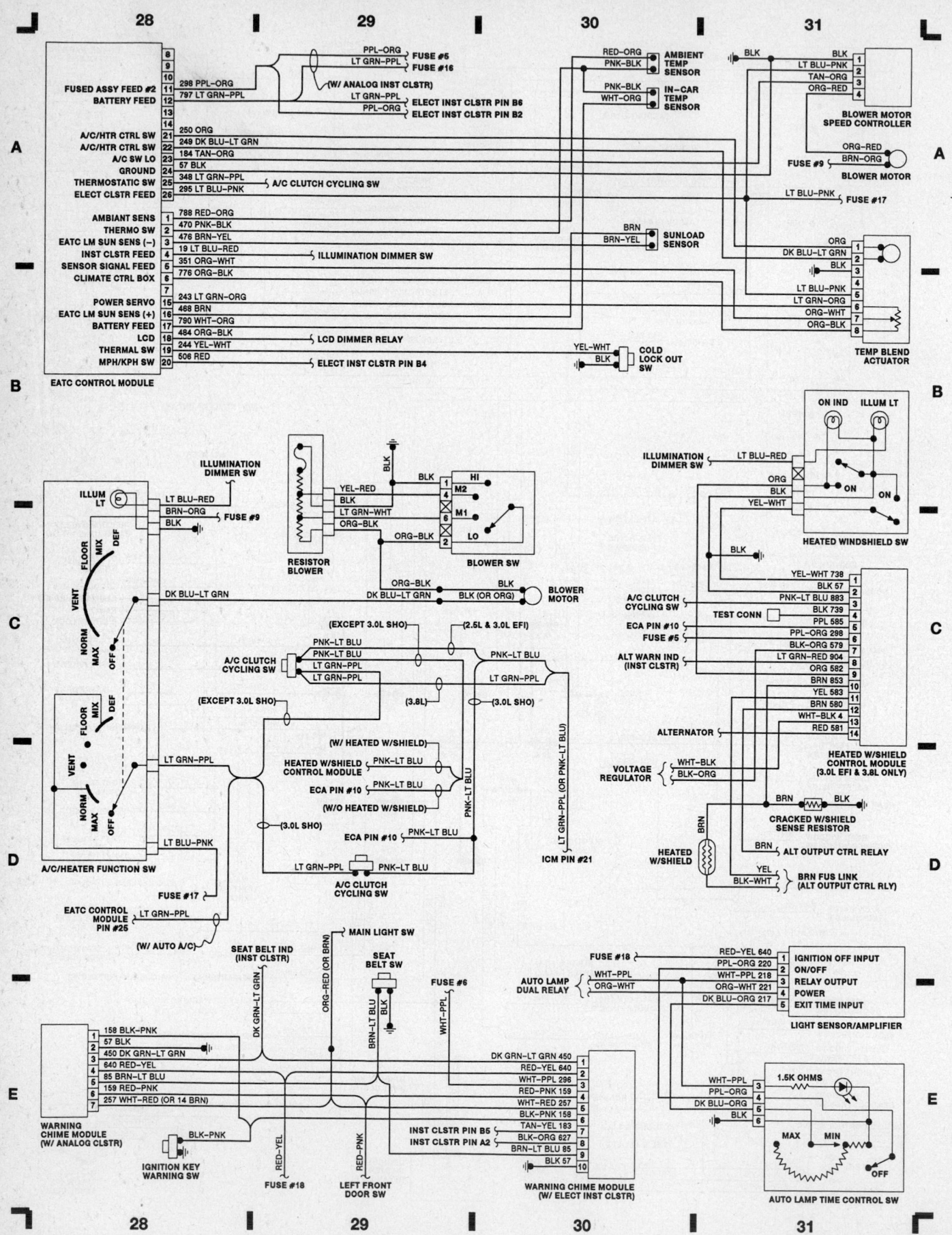

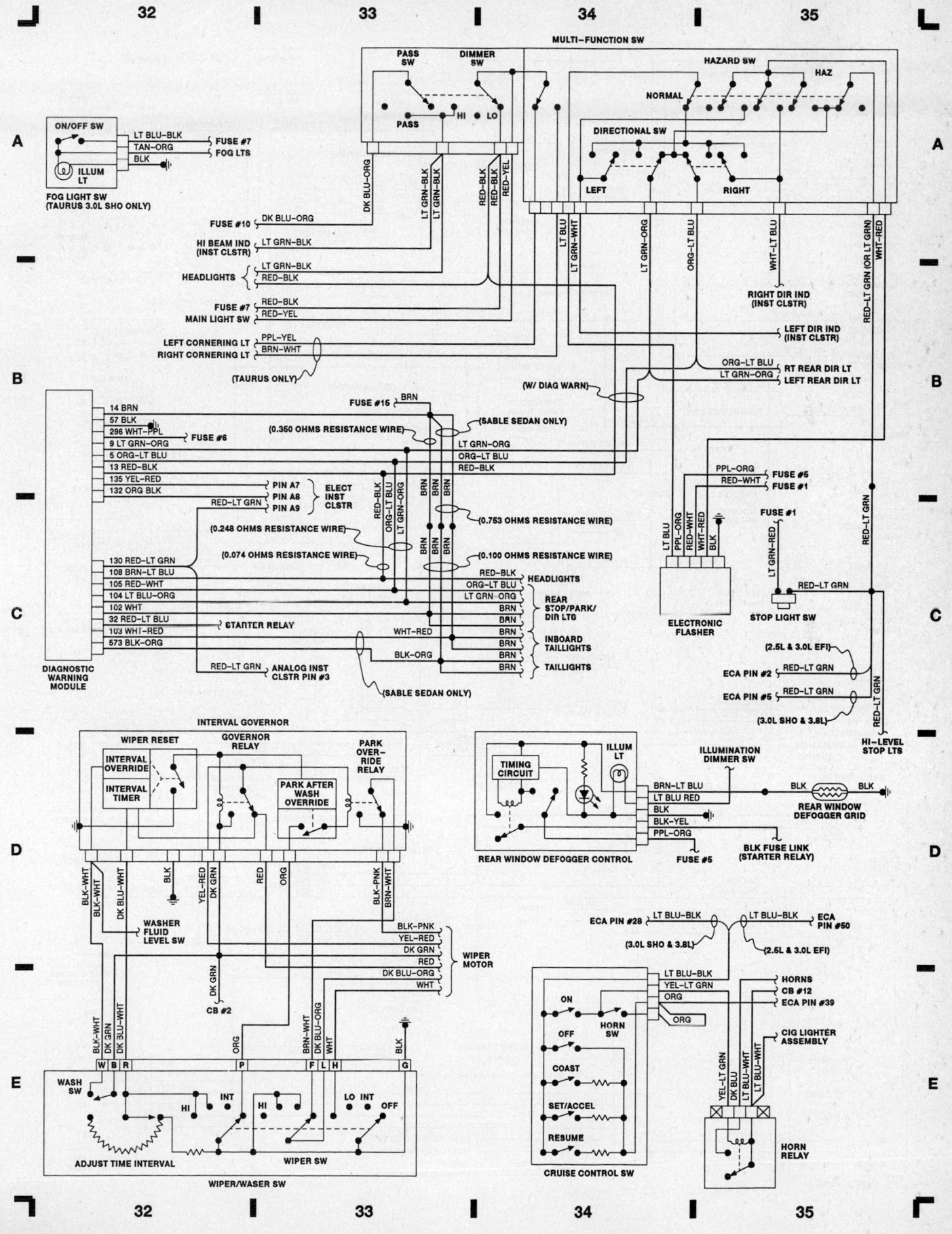

1989 FORD MOTOR CO.
Sable & Taurus (Cont.)

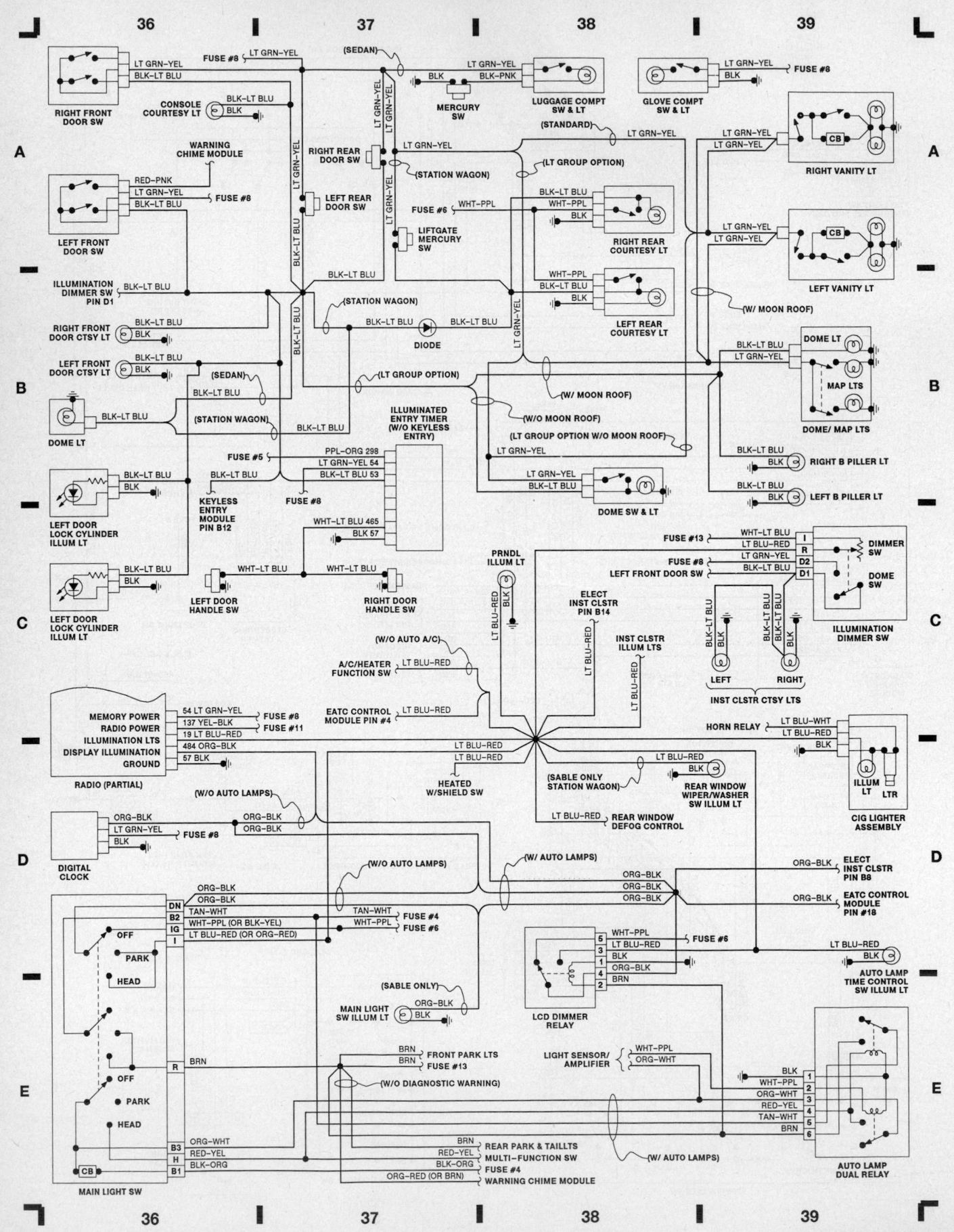

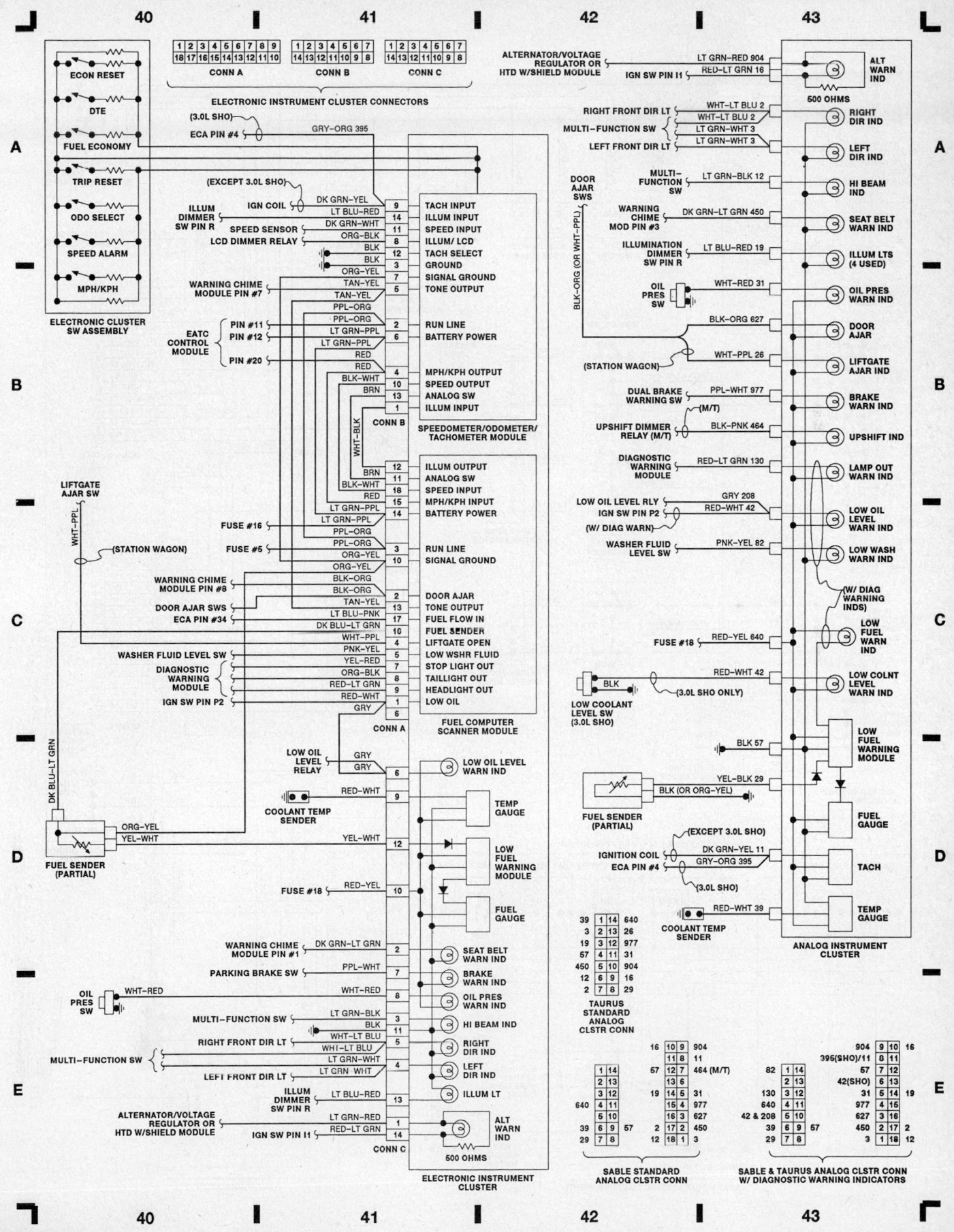

1989 Ford Motor Co.
Sable & Taurus (Cont.)

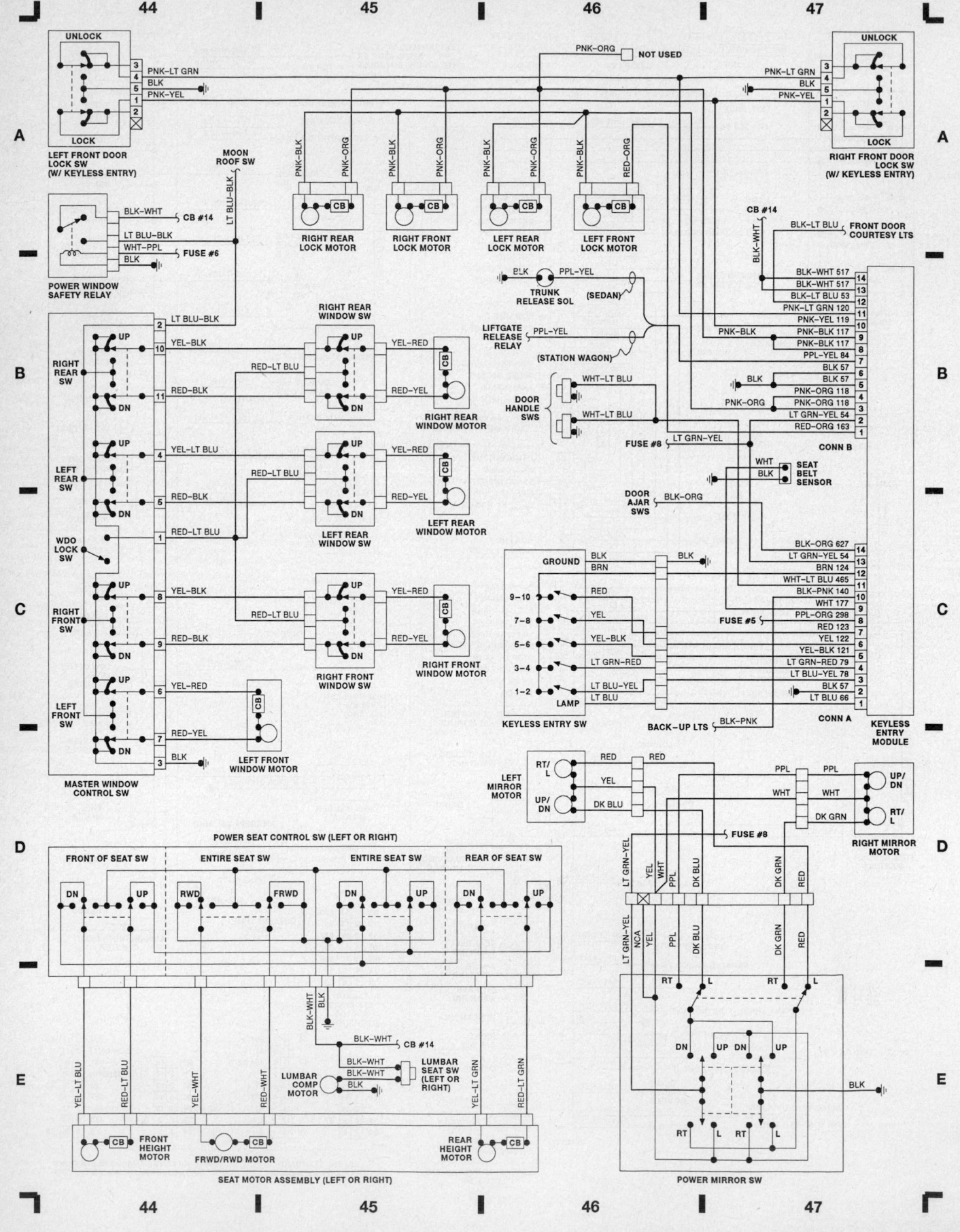

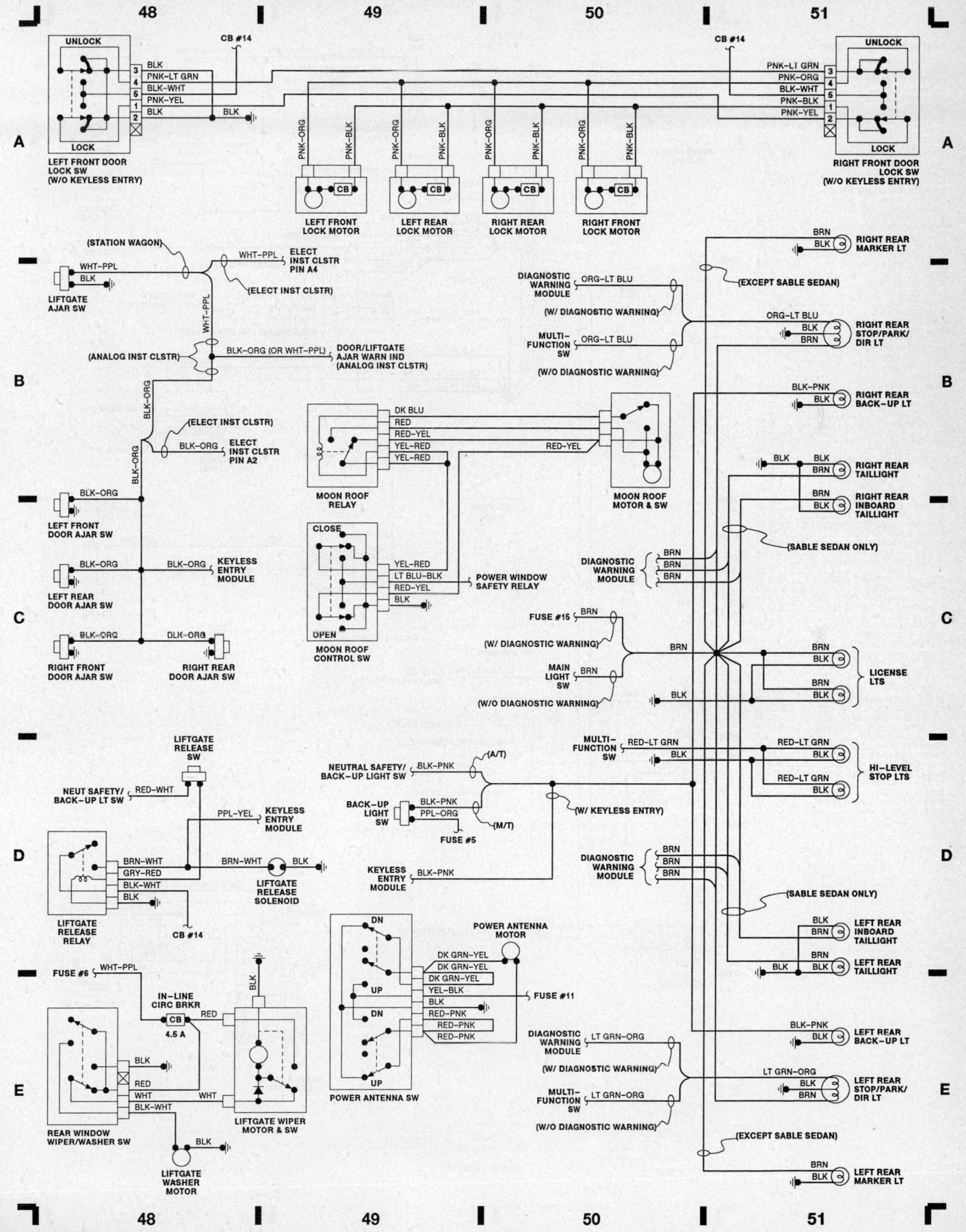

1989 Ford Motor Co.
Tempo & Topaz

COMPONENT LOCATOR:

A/C COOLING FAN CONTROLLER .... D-E 15
A/C/HEATER CONTROL .... E 13
AIR BAG DIAGNOSTIC MODULE ...... B-C 15
ALTERNATOR .... B 3
BACK-UP LIGHT SW .... C 29
BATTERY .... A 1-2
BLOWER SWITCH .... D 12
CLUTCH CYCLING PRESSURE SW ...... D 14
CLUTCH INTERRUPT SW .... C 3
CLUTCH SW (M/T) .... A 6
COOLING FAN TEMP SW .... A 2, E 14
COOLING FAN RELAY .... A 3
CRUISE CONTROL AMPLIFIER .... A 7
CRUISE CONTROL SW .... B-C 16
DIRECTIONAL FLASHER .... B 18
DISTRIBUTOR .... C 7
DOOR LOCK CONTROL
   RELAY (2 DOOR) .... A 28
DRIVERS SEAT CONTROL SW .... D 24-27
DUAL BRAKE WARNING SW .... C-D 21-22
ECA RELAY .... B 5-6
ELECTRONIC CONTROL ASSEMBLY . B-E 4
ENGINE COMPARTMENT LT .... E 1-2
FUEL FILLER DOOR RELEASE SW .... E 28
FUEL PUMP RELAY .... B 5
FUEL SENDER .... C 29
FUSE BLOCK .... A-B 9-10
FUSIBLE LINKS ... A-B 1-2, D-E 9, E 10-11
4WD RELAYS .... A 4
4WD SWITCH .... A 5
GLOVE BOX LT & SW .... D-E 20
HAZARD FLASHER .... B 19
HEGO SENSOR .... D 6
HORN RELAY .... B 17-18
HORNS .... C-D 1
HORN SWITCH .... B 8
IGNITION COIL .... B-C 7
IGNITION DIODE (A/T) .... D 10
IGNITION SWITCH .... E 8-10
ILLUM ENTRY TIMER .... D 23
INERTIA SWITCH .... B 4, A 13
INSTRUMENT CLUSTER ...... A-C 20, A-B 23
LEFT COURTESY LT .... D 20
LEFT DOOR LOCK SW (2 DOOR) ...... A 30
LEFT FRONT DOOR SW .... D 22
LEFT FRONT DOOR LOCK
   SWITCH (4 DOOR) .... A 24
LEFT REAR DOOR SW .... E 21
LUMBAR SEAT SW .... E 24
MAIN LIGHT SWITCH .... A-B 16
MASTER WINDOW CONTROL SW ... B-D 24
MULTI-FUNCTION SW .... A 17-19
NEUTRAL SAFETY SW .... C-D 11
PARKING BRAKE SW .... E 8
PASSIVE RESTRAINT DIODE
   ASSEMBLY .... B 12
PASSIVE RESTRAINT MODULE .... A-B 12
POWER MIRROR SW .... C-D 26-27
POWER WINDOW SAFETY SW ...... A-B 24
REAR WINDOW DEFOG RELAY .... B-C 28
RIGHT DOOR LOCK
   SWITCH (2 DOOR) .... A 30
RIGHT FRONT DOOR
   LOCK SW (4 DOOR) .... A 27
RIGHT REAR DOOR SW .... E 21
SELF TEST INPUT
   (STI) CONN .... E 5
SELF TEST OUTPUT
   (STO) CONN .... C 6
SHIFT IND DIMMER RELAY .... C-D 20
STARTER RELAY .... B-C 1-2
STOP LIGHT SWITCH .... C 10
STEERING WHEEL HORN SW ...... B-C 16
TOP GEAR SWITCH .... E 5
TRUNK LIGHT .... D 29
TRUNK RELEASE SWITCH .... D 28
WARNING CHIME MODULE .... A-B 15
WASHER FLUID LEVEL SW .... E 2
WASHER MOTOR .... E 3
WIPER MOTOR .... D-E 3
WIPER INTERVAL GOVERNOR ..... C-D 16-17
WIPER/WASHER SW .... D-E 16, C-D 19

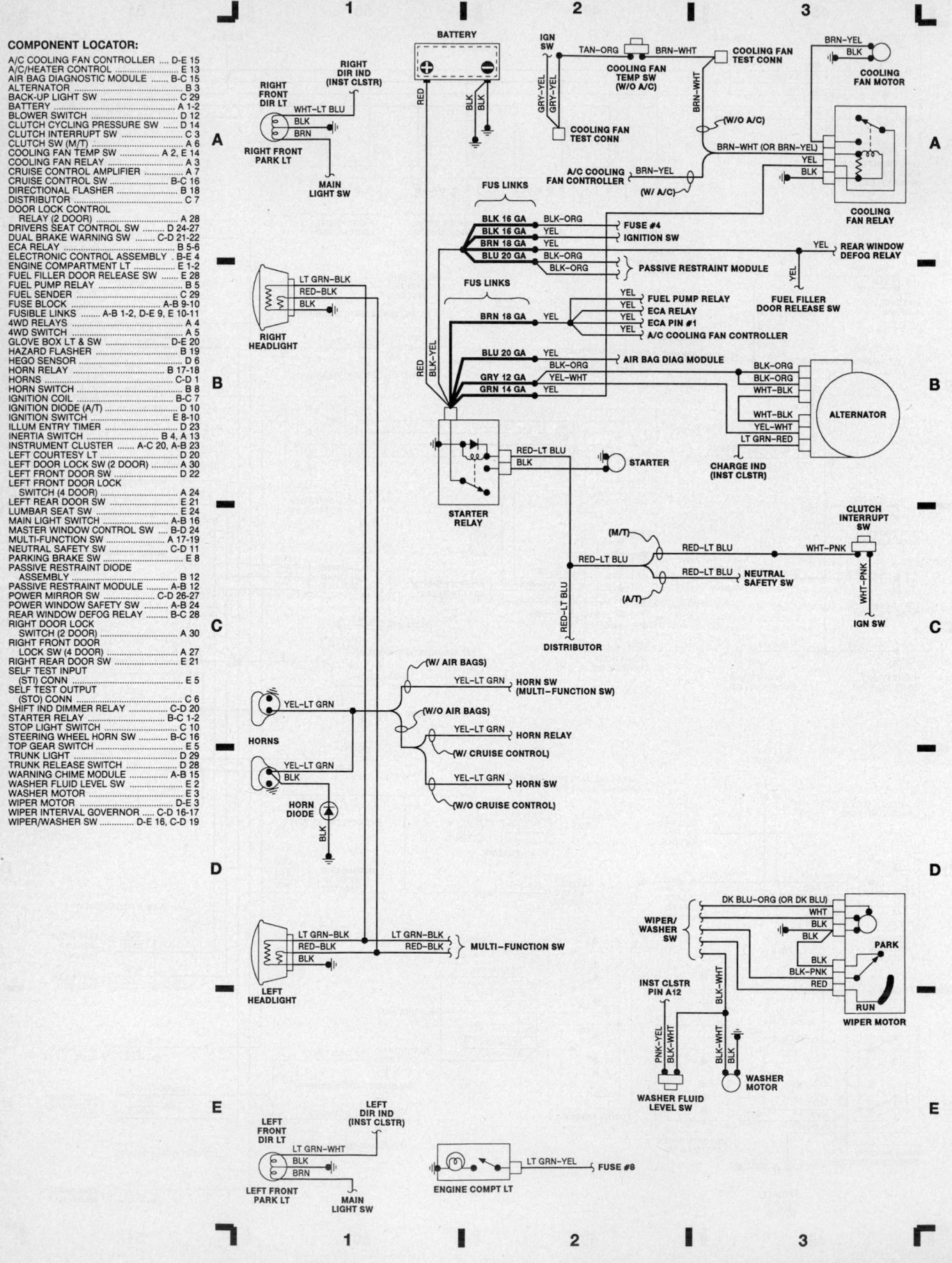

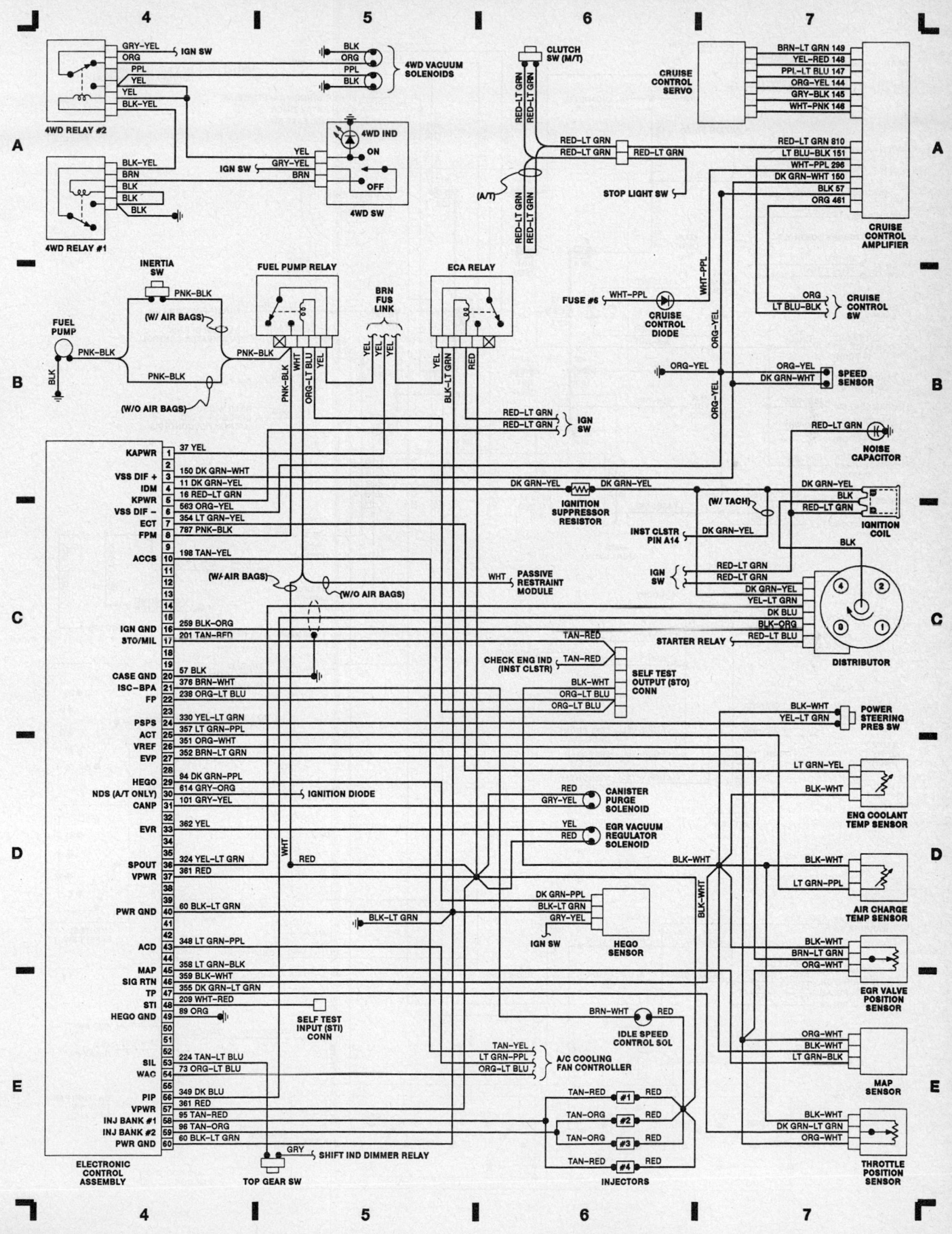

1989 Ford Motor Co.
Tempo & Topaz (Cont.)

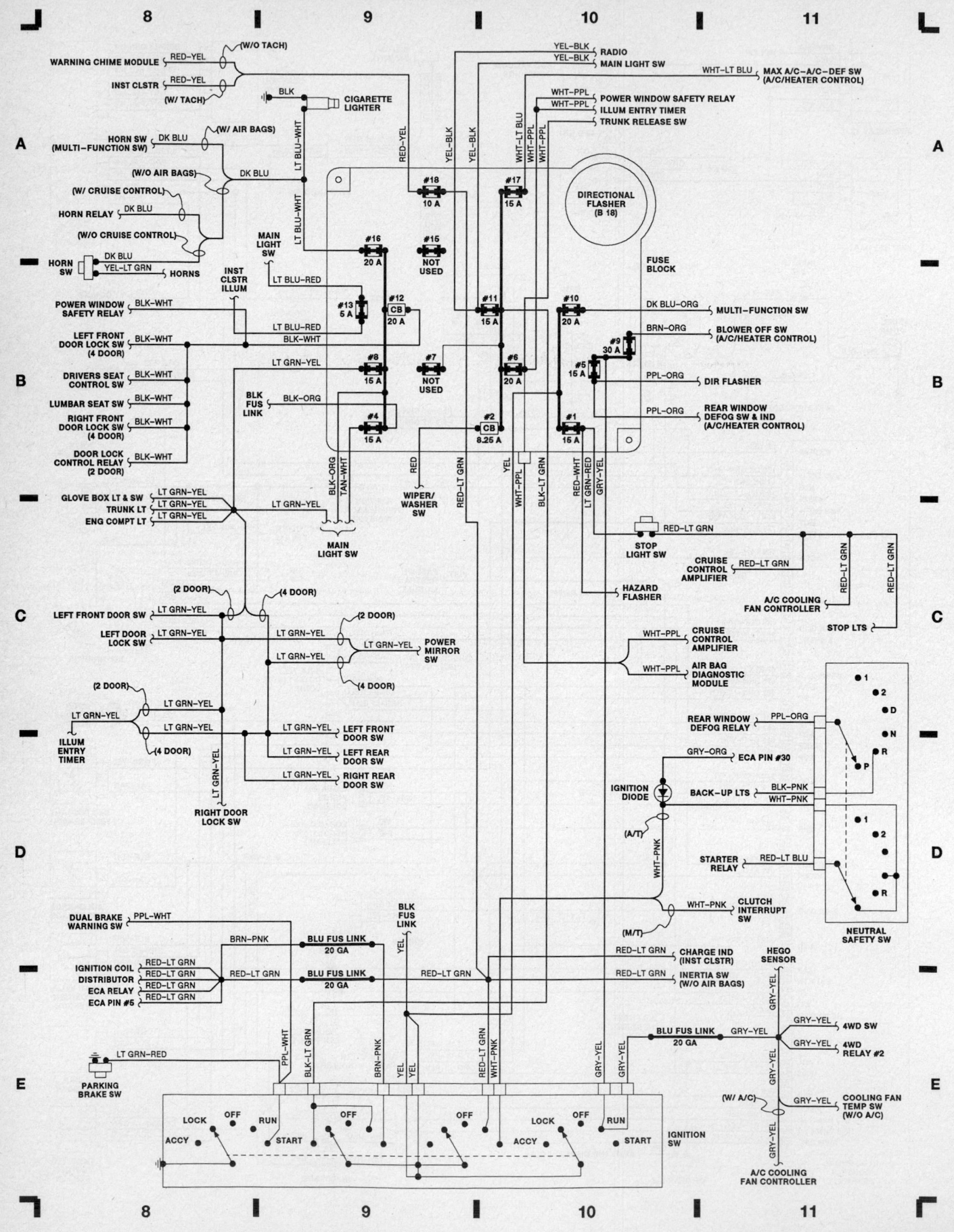

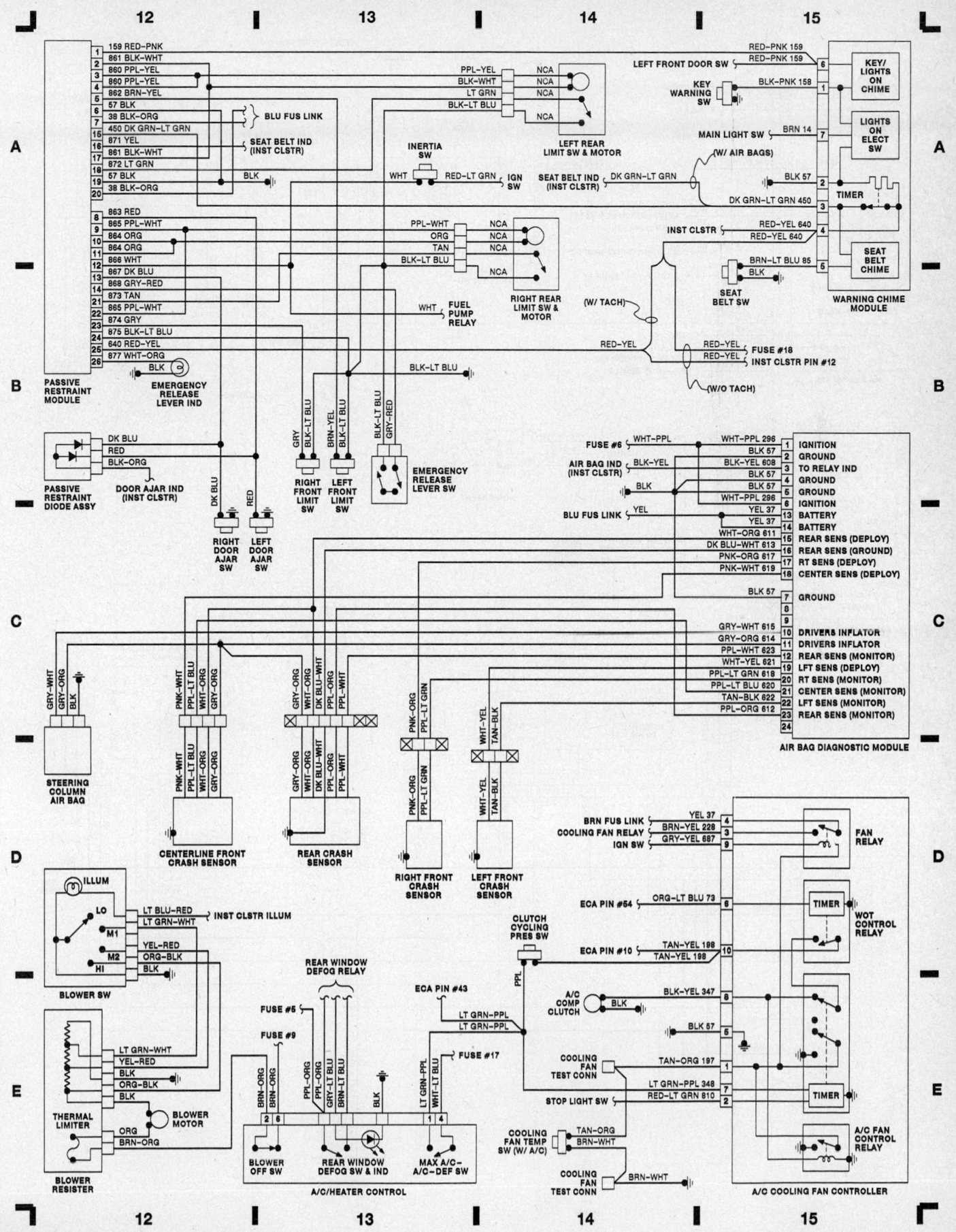

1989 Ford Motor Co.
Tempo & Topaz (Cont.)

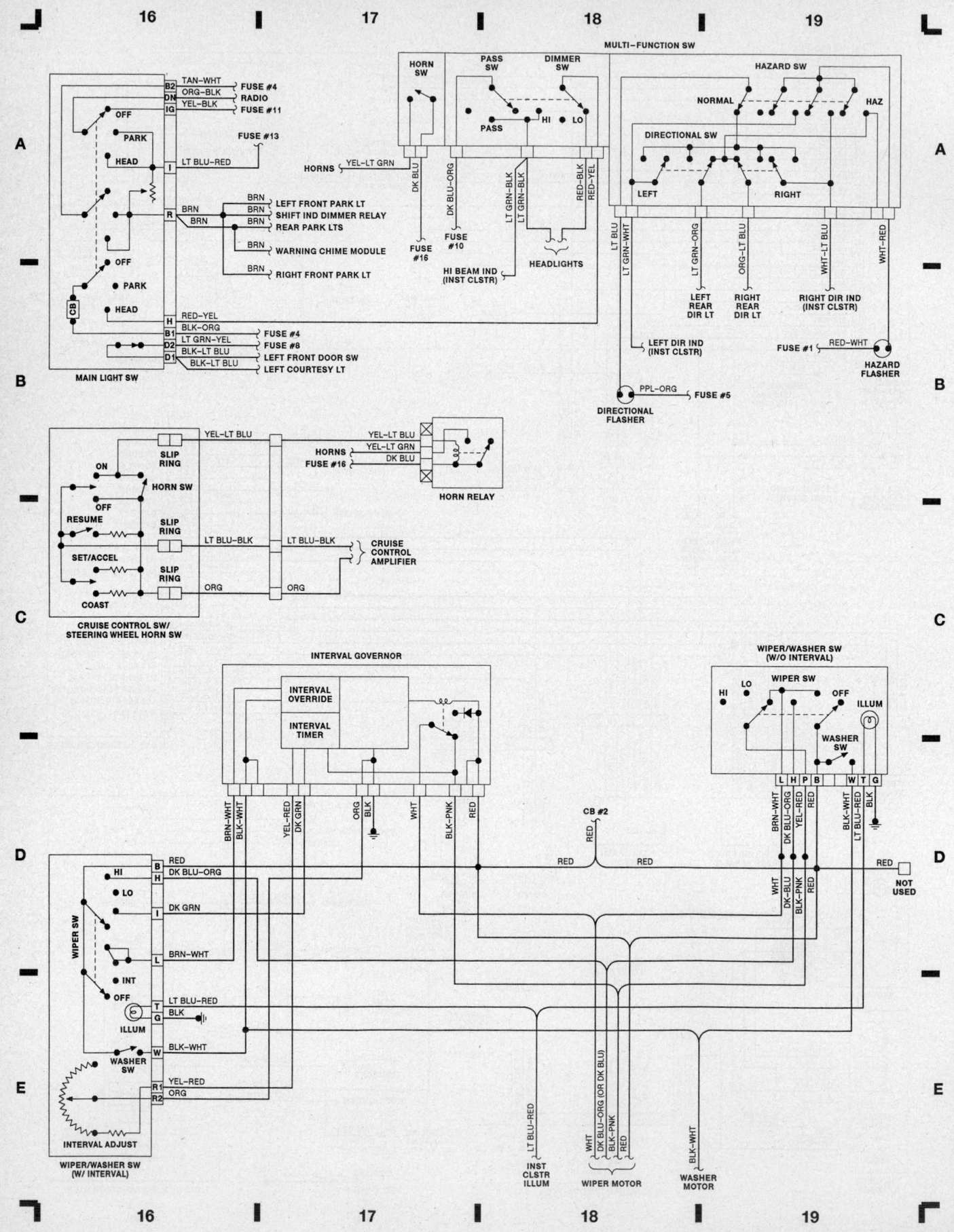

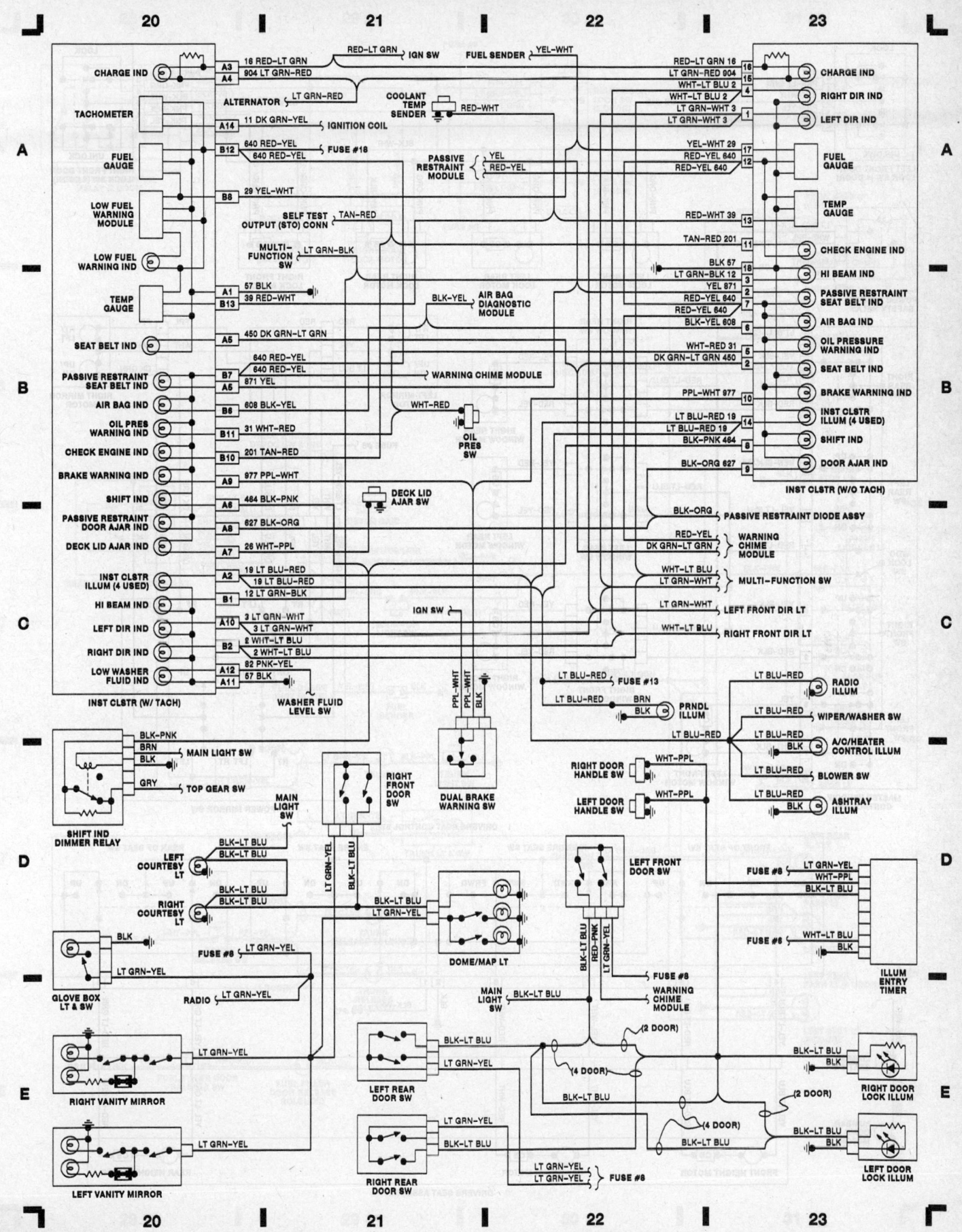

1989 Ford Motor Co.
Town Car

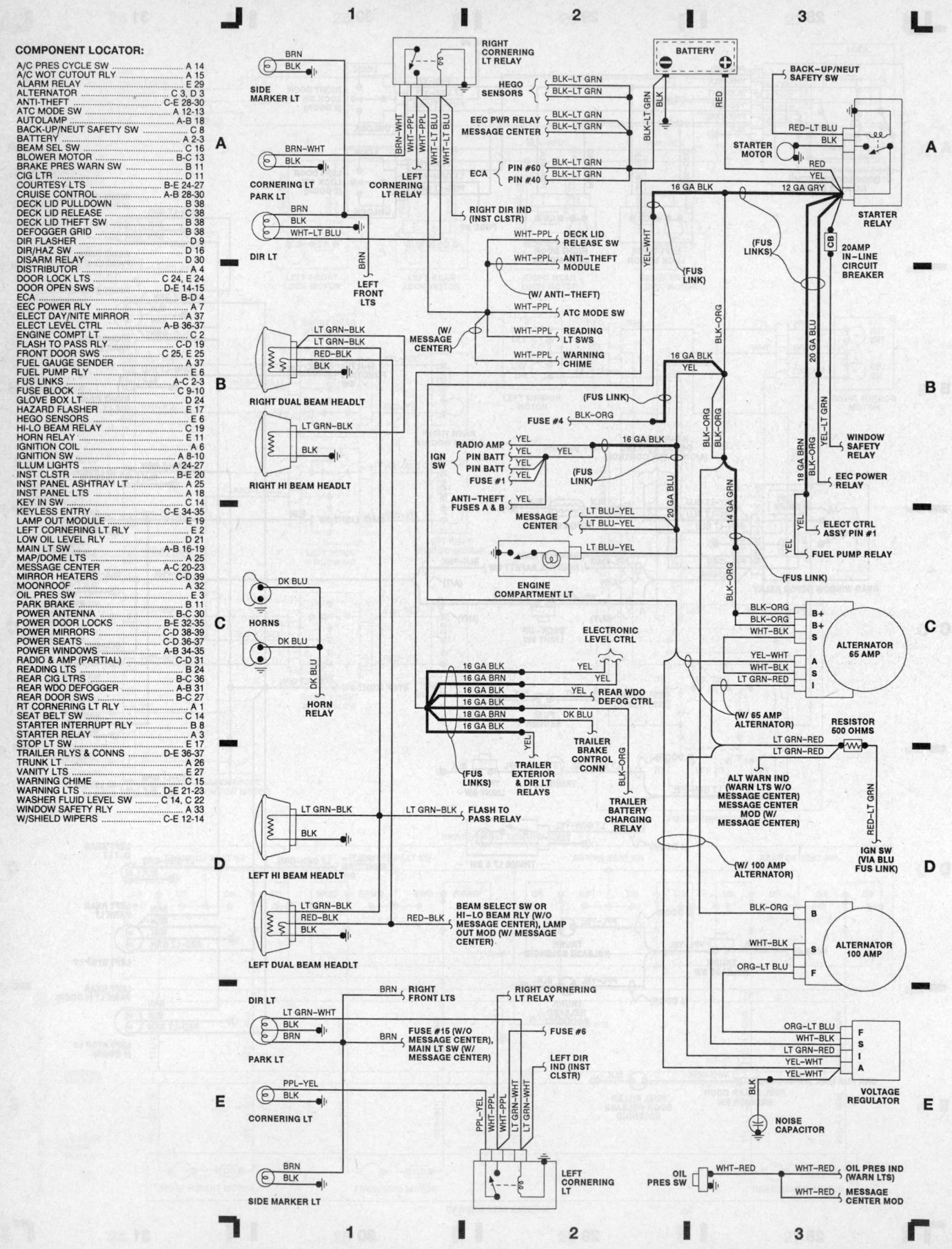

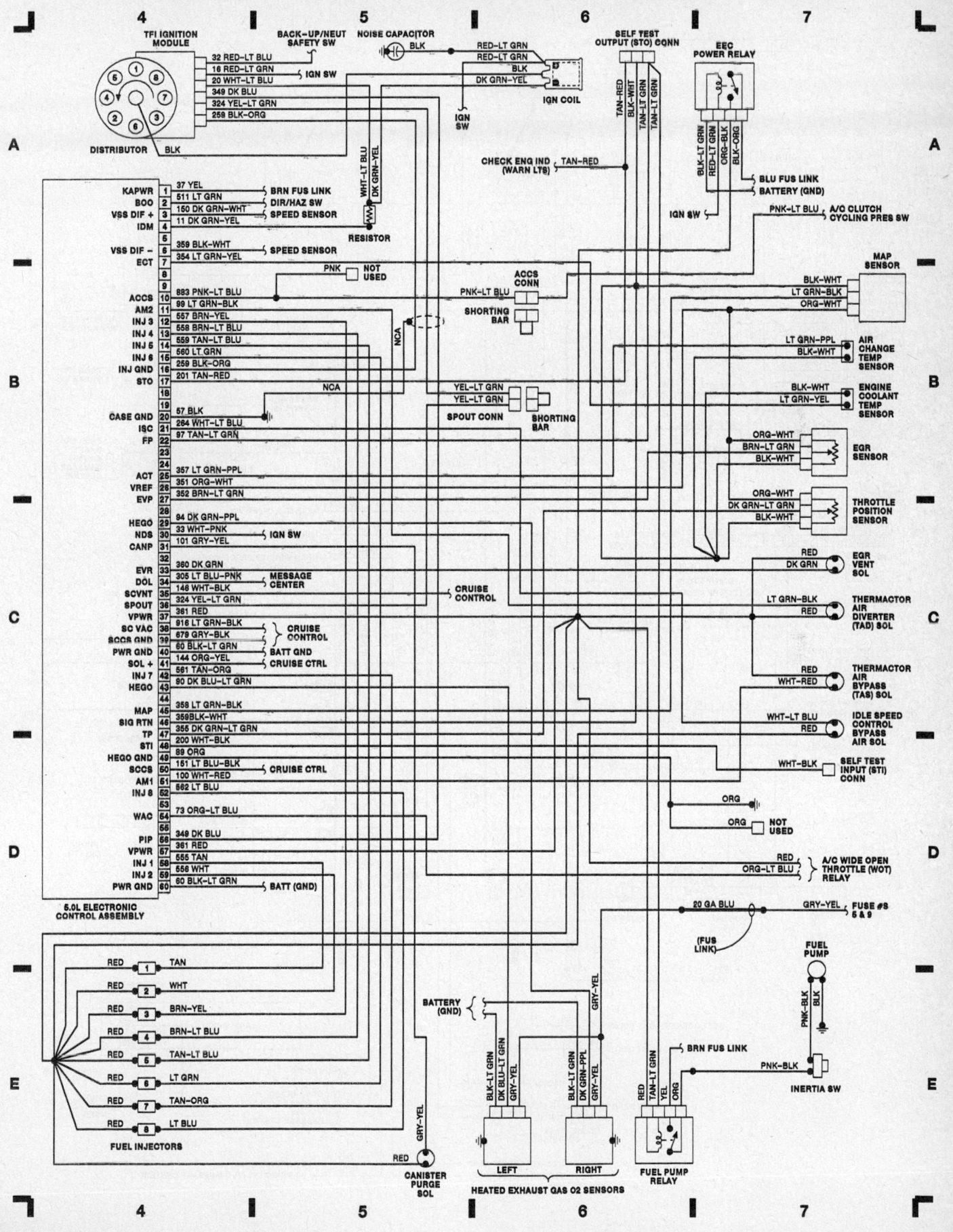

1989 FORD MOTOR CO.
Town Car (Cont.)

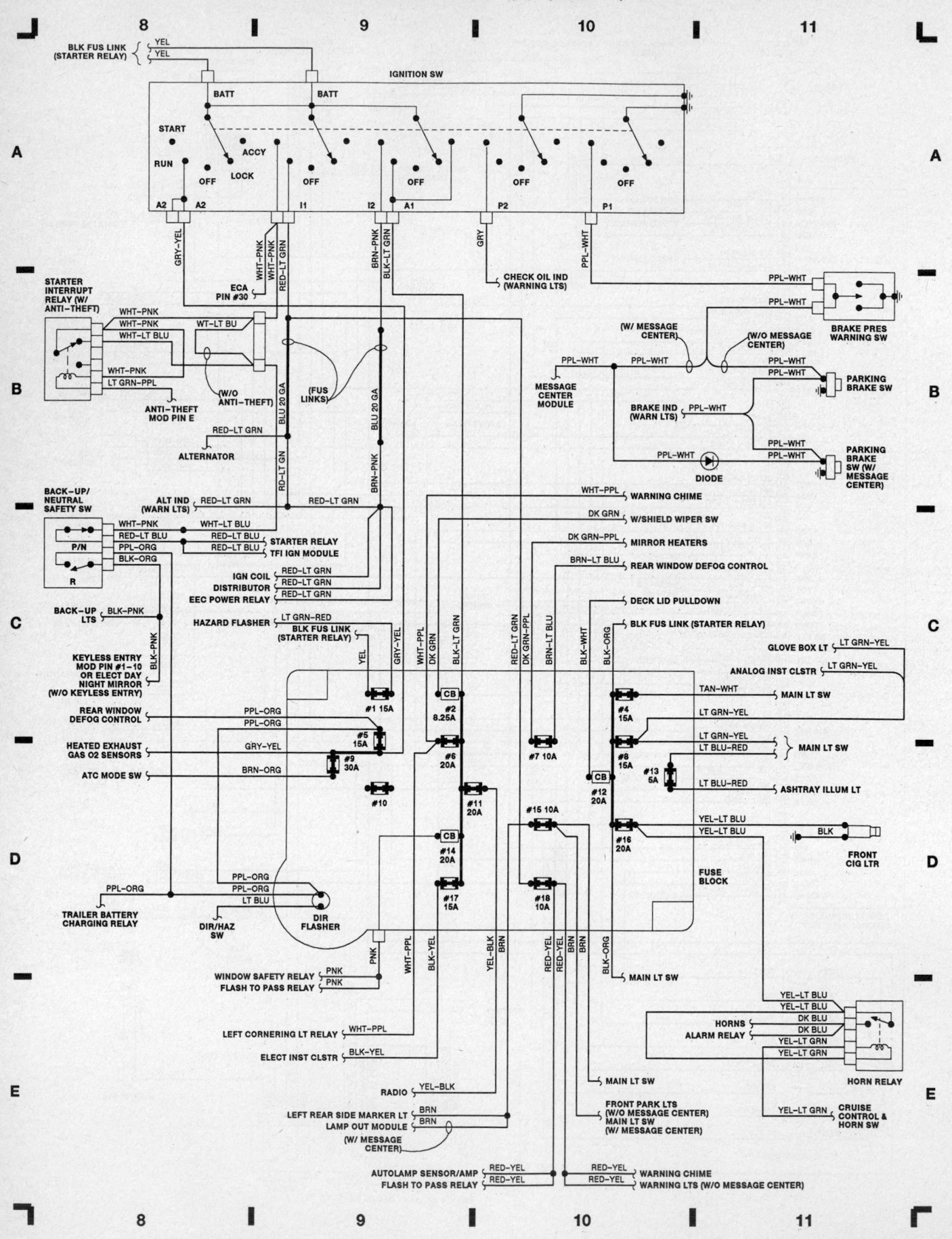

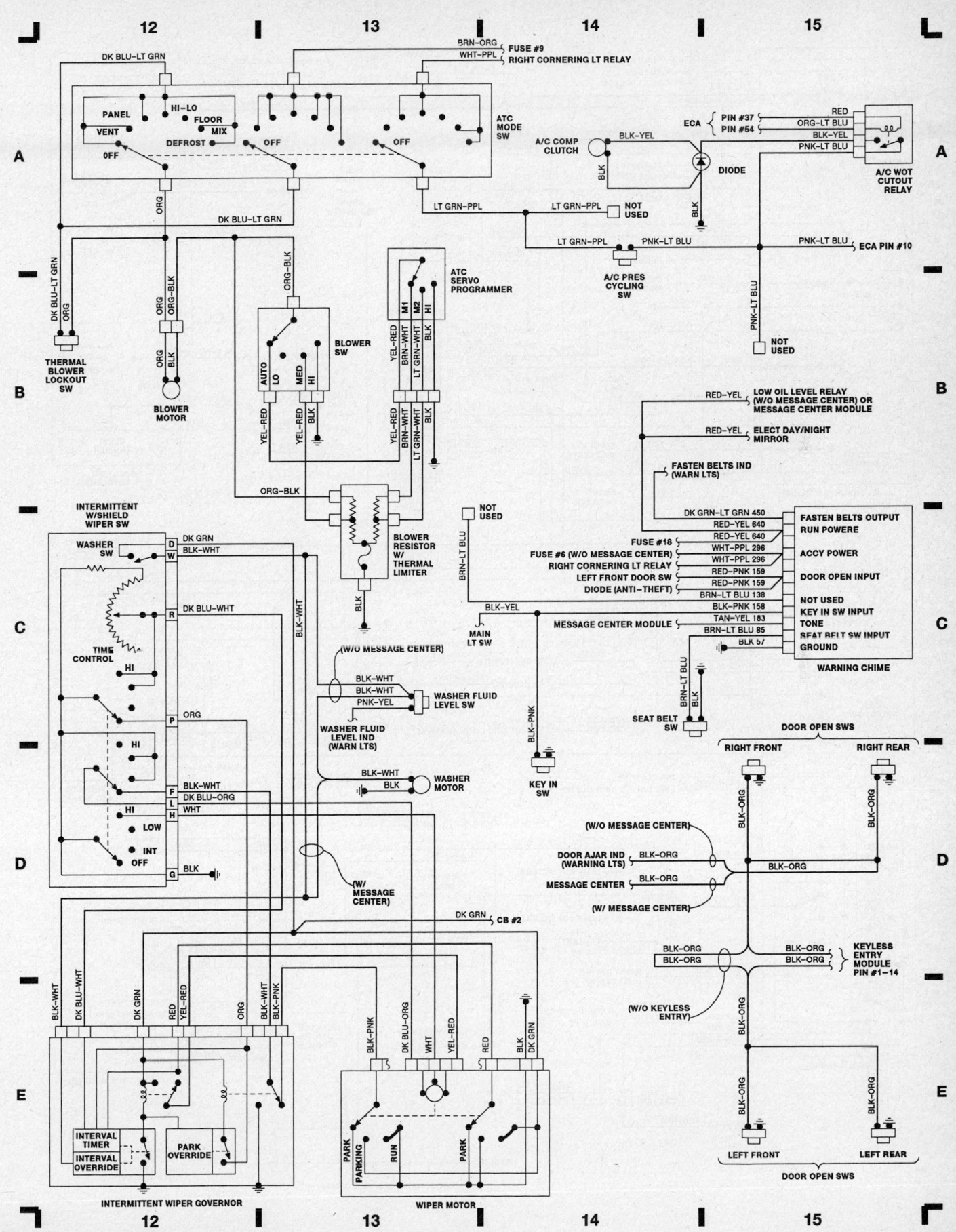

1989 Ford Motor Co.
Town Car (Cont.)

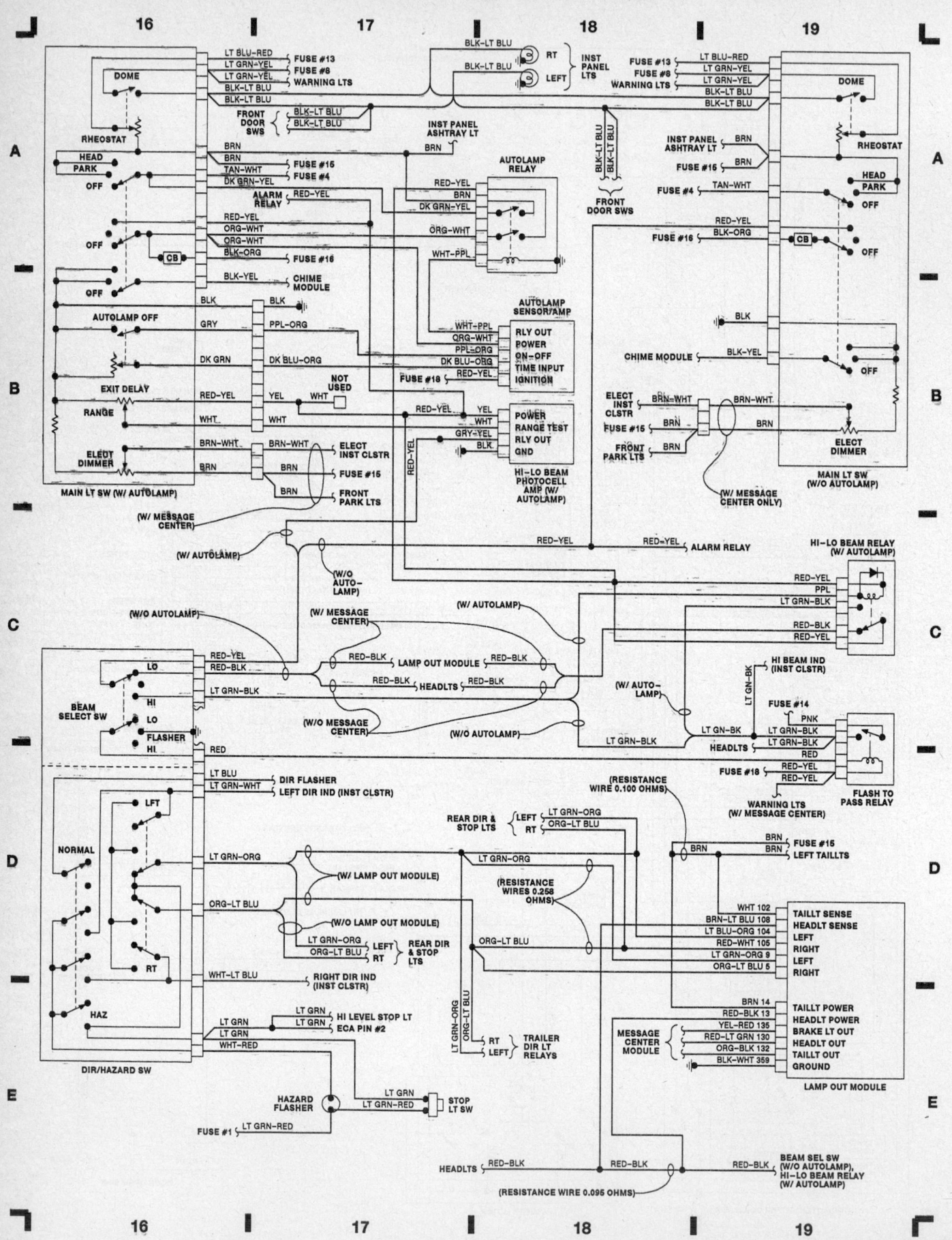

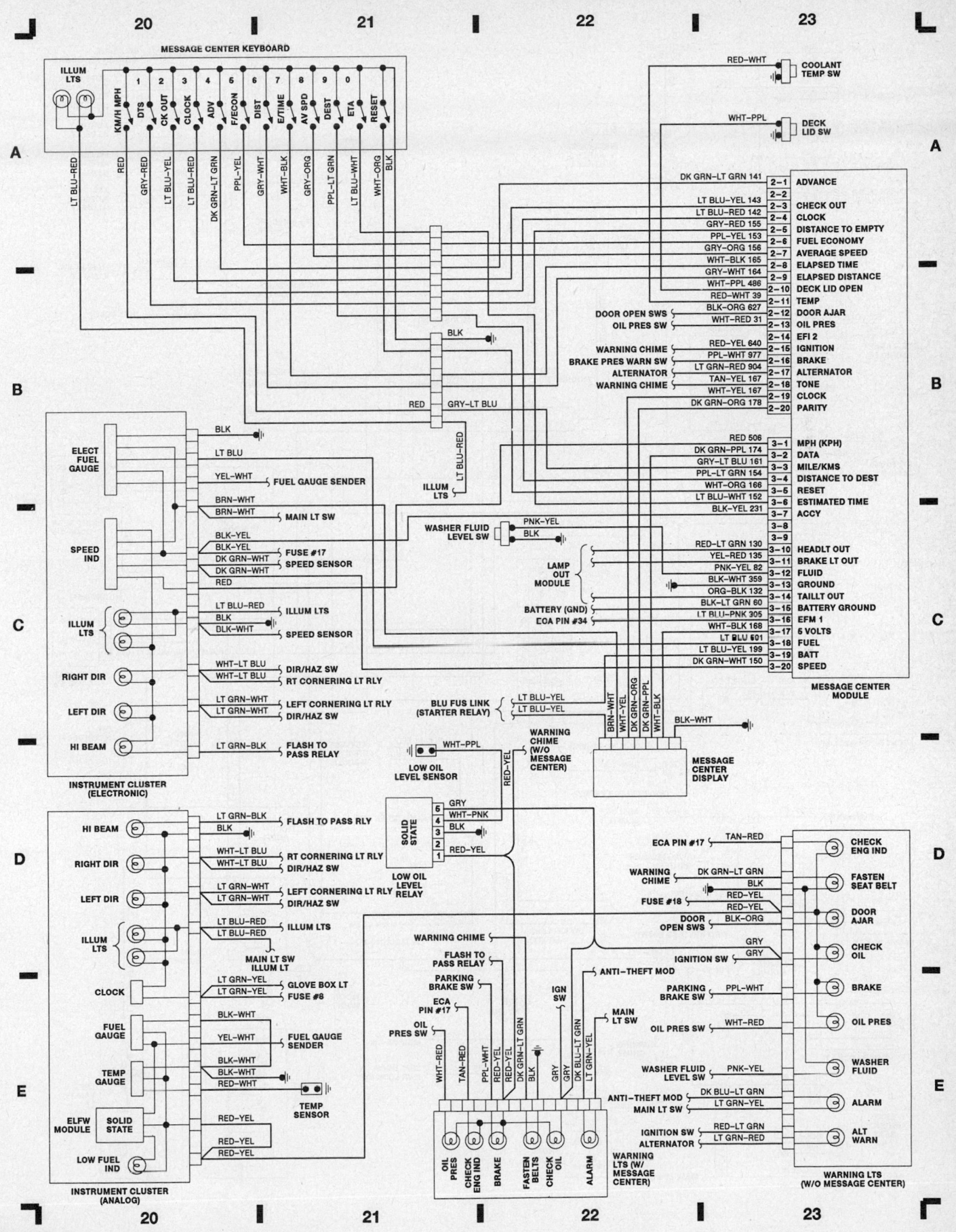

1989 Ford Motor Co.
Town Car (Cont.)

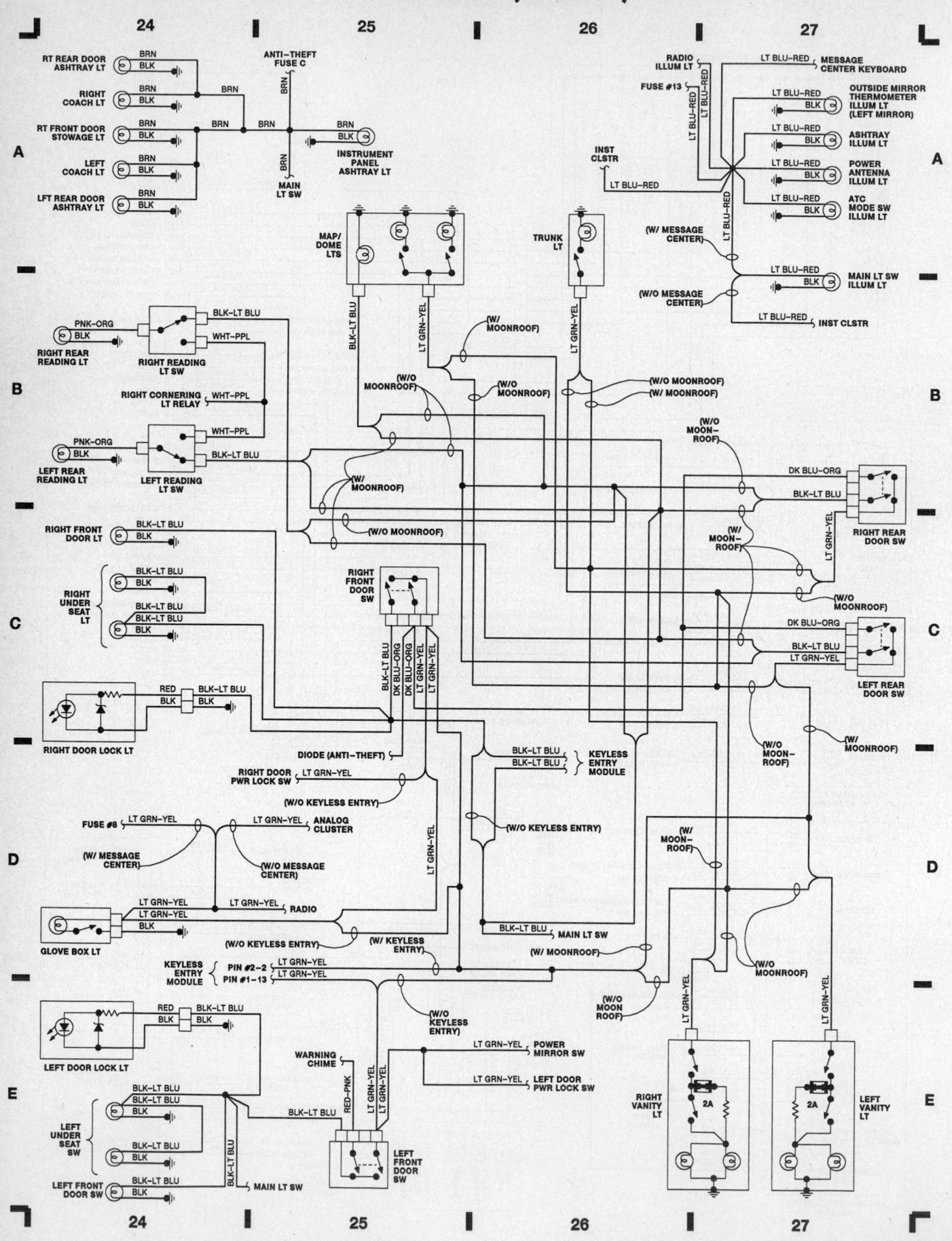

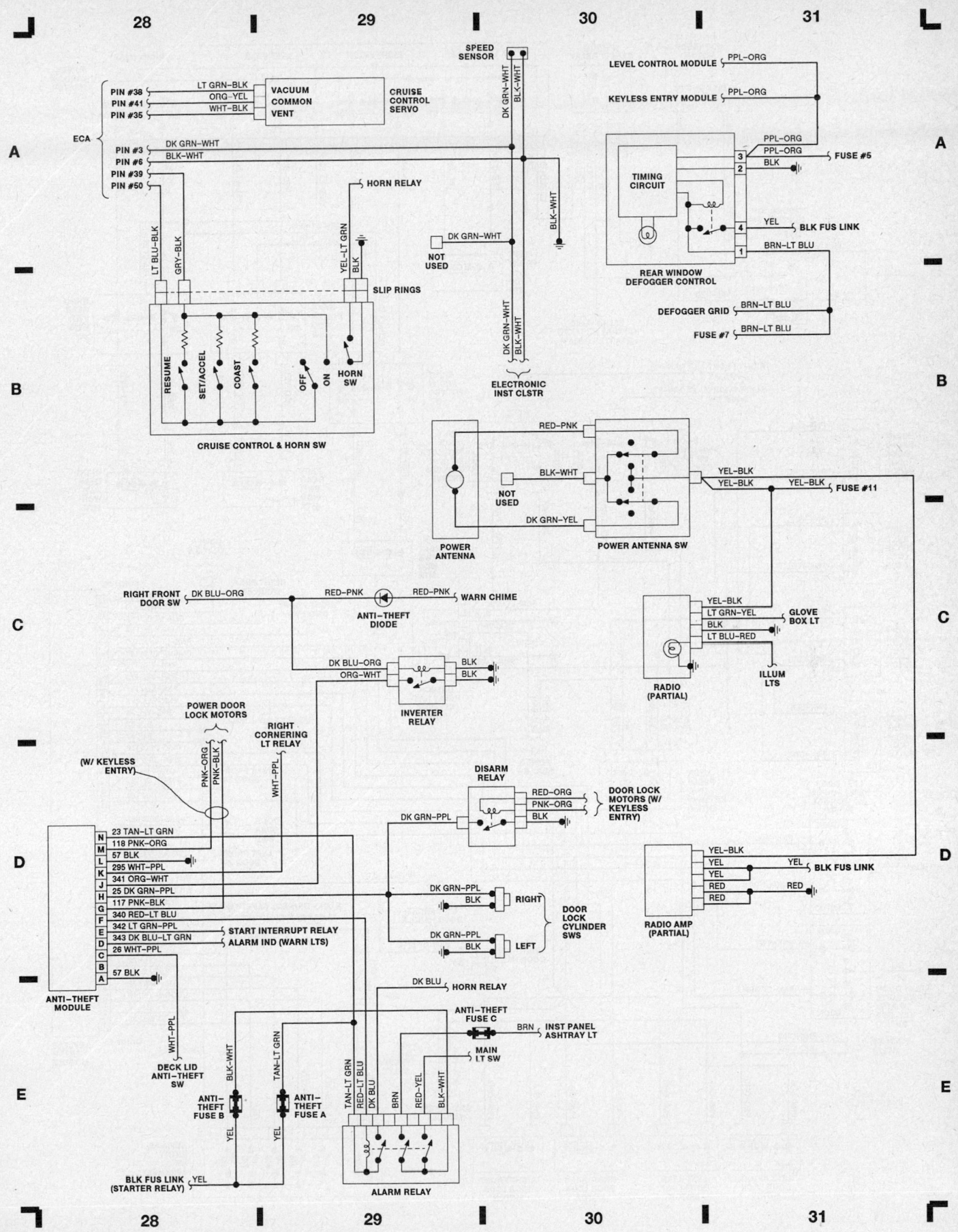

1989 Ford Motor Co.
Town Car (Cont.)

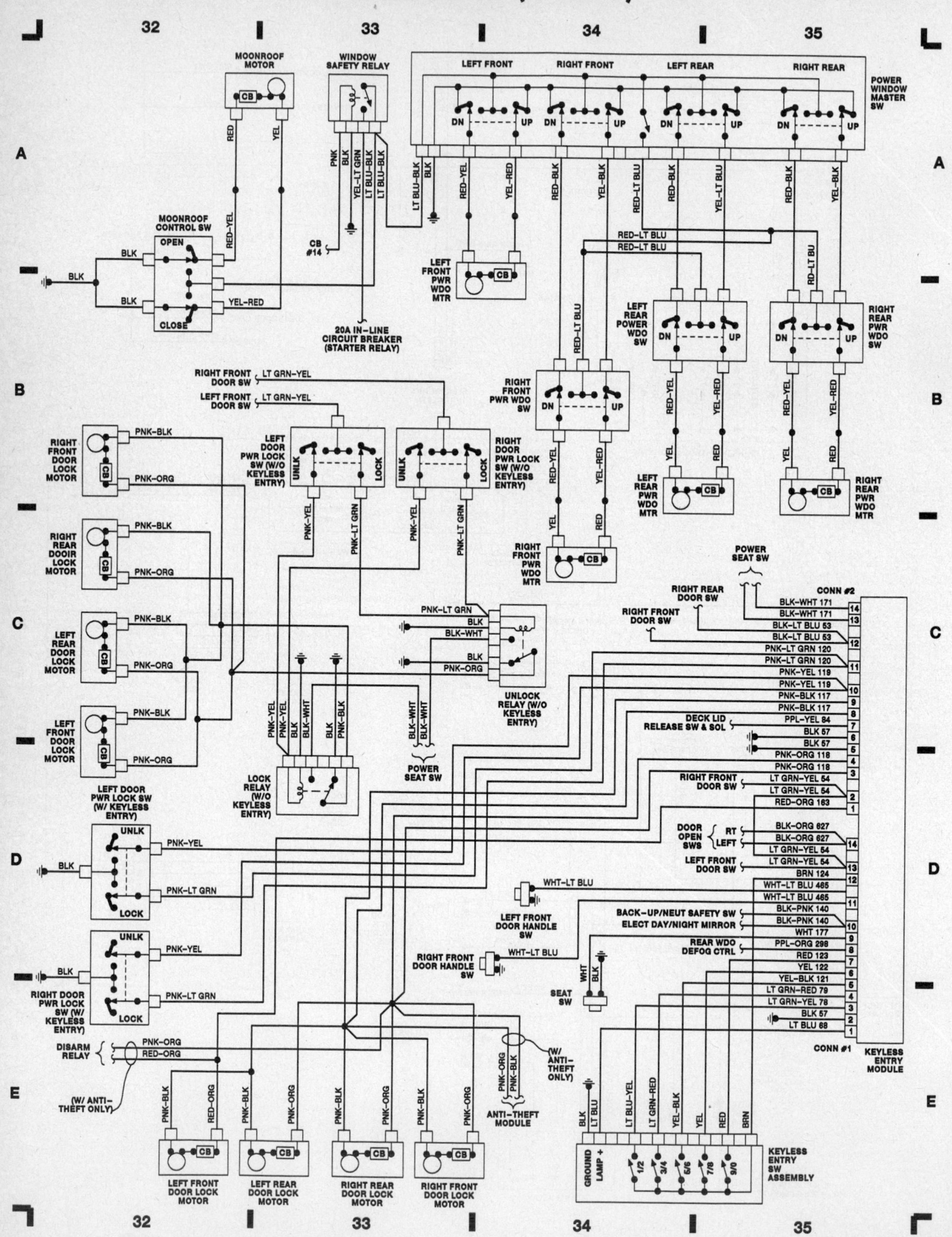

1989 Ford Motor Co.
Town Car (Cont.)

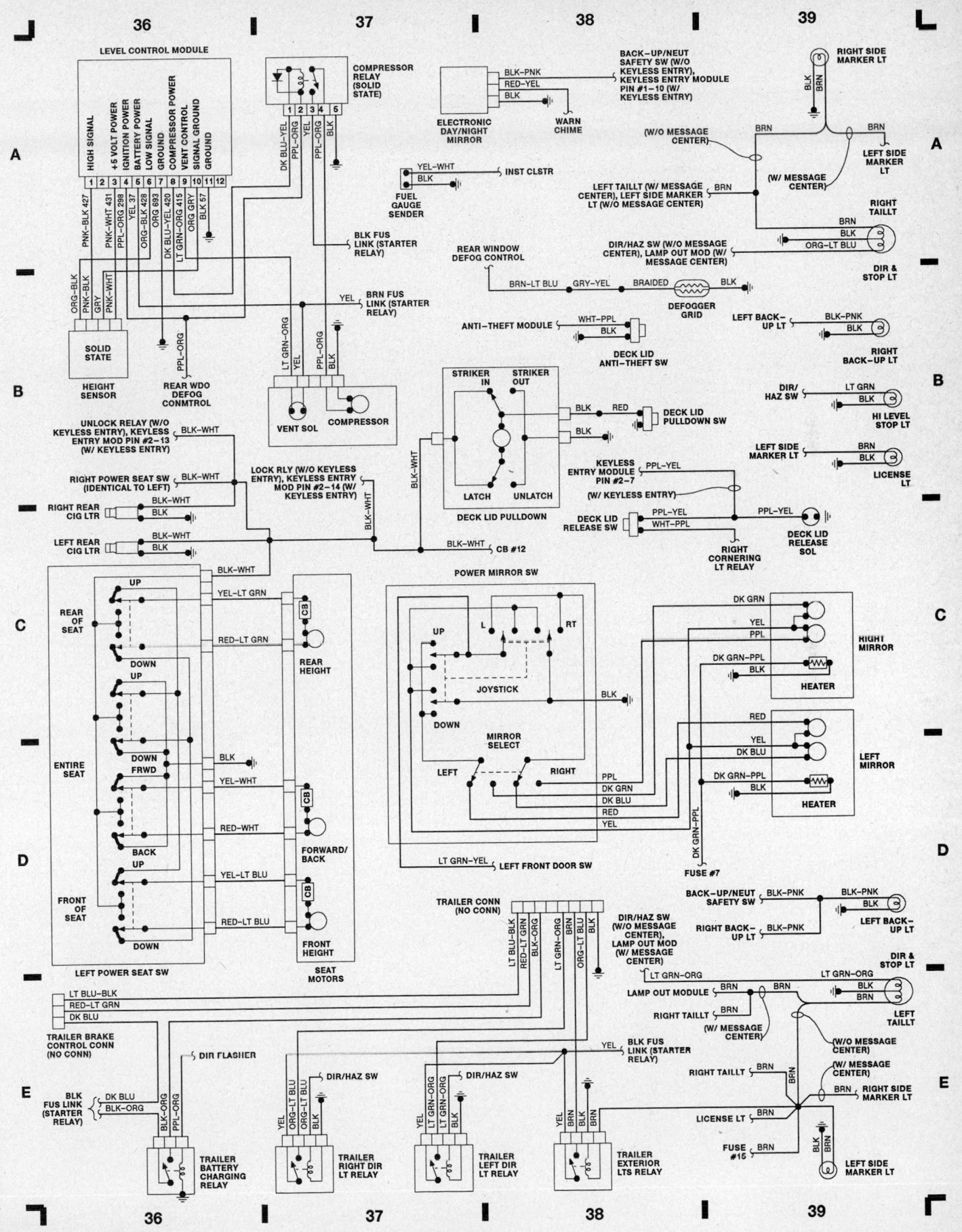

Section 6

ACCESSORIES & EQUIPMENT

CONTENTS

AIR BAG RESTRAINT SYSTEMS   Page
Chrysler Motors 6-2

ANTI-THEFT SYSTEM
Chrysler Motors 6-15
Ford Motor Co. 6-17

CRUISE CONTROL SYSTEMS
Chrysler Motors 6-20
Eagle 6-24
Ford Motor Co.
  EEC-IV Controlled 6-26
  Except EEC-IV Controlled 6-33

DEFOGGERS
Chrysler Motors Rear Window Defogger 6-36
Ford Motor Co. Rear Window Defogger 6-37

DOOR & TAILGATE LOCKS
Chrysler Motors Door & Trunk Release 6-39
Eagle Power Door Locks 6-40
Eagle Trunk Release 6-41
Ford Motor Co.
  Keyless Entry System 6-42
  Liftgate, Tailgate & Trunk Release 6-47
  Side Doors 6-48

HEADLIGHT DOORS – AUTOMATIC
Chrysler Motors 6-51

HEADLIGHT DIMMER – AUTOMATIC
Ford Motor Co. 6-53

HEADLIGHTS – AUTOMATIC
Ford Motor Co. Autolamp 6-56

HEATED WINDSHIELD   Page
Ford Motor Co. 6-58

POWER ANTENNAS
Chrysler Motors 6-63
Ford Motor Co. 6-64

POWER CONVERTIBLE TOPS
Chrysler Motors 6-66
Ford Motor Co. 6-68

POWER MIRRORS
Chrysler Motors Side Mirrors 6-71
Eagle 6-74
Ford Motor Co. Rear View & Side Mirrors 6-75

POWER SEATS
Chrysler Motors
  Acclaim & Spirit 6-78
  Except Acclaim & Spirit 6-80
  Memory Seat & Recliner 6-83
Eagle 6-87
Ford Motor Co.
  Probe 6-89
  Except Probe 6-91

POWER WINDOWS
Chrysler Motors
  Acclaim & Spirit Side Windows 6-95
  FWD Side Windows 6-97
  RWD Side Windows 6-100
Eagle 6-101
Ford Motor Co.
  Side Windows 6-103
  Tailgate Window 6-106

SUN & MOON ROOFS – ELECTRIC
Chrysler Motors 6-107
Ford Motor Co. 6-109

SWITCHES & INSTRUMENT PANELS
Chrysler Motors
  Standard 6-112
  Electronic Instrument Cluster 6-122
Eagle 6-127
Ford Motor Co.
  Standard Except Probe 6-132
  Probe Standard 6-137
  Electronic Instrument Cluster
    Cougar & Thunderbird 6-145
    Mark VII 6-154
    Probe 6-160
    Sable & Taurus 6-168
    Town Car 6-179

WIPER/WASHER SYSTEMS
Chrysler Motors
  Dynasty & New Yorker 6-189
  Except Dynasty & New Yorker 6-191
  Liftgate 6-194
Ford Motor Co.
  Probe – Front & Rear 6-195
  Except Probe 6-198
  Liftgate 6-204

NOTE: ALSO SEE GENERAL INDEX.

1989 AIR BAG RESTRAINT SYSTEMS
Chrysler Motors (Cont.)

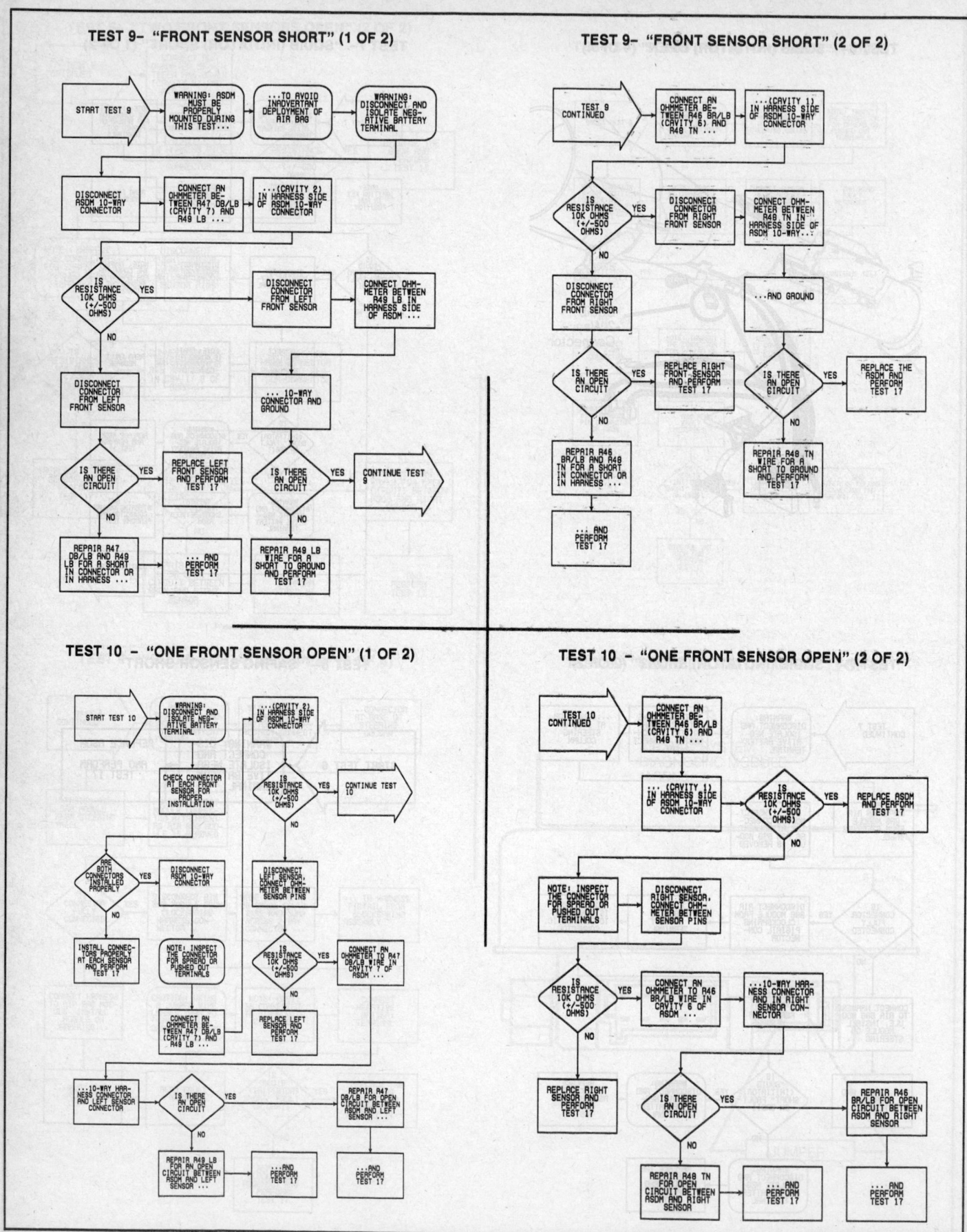

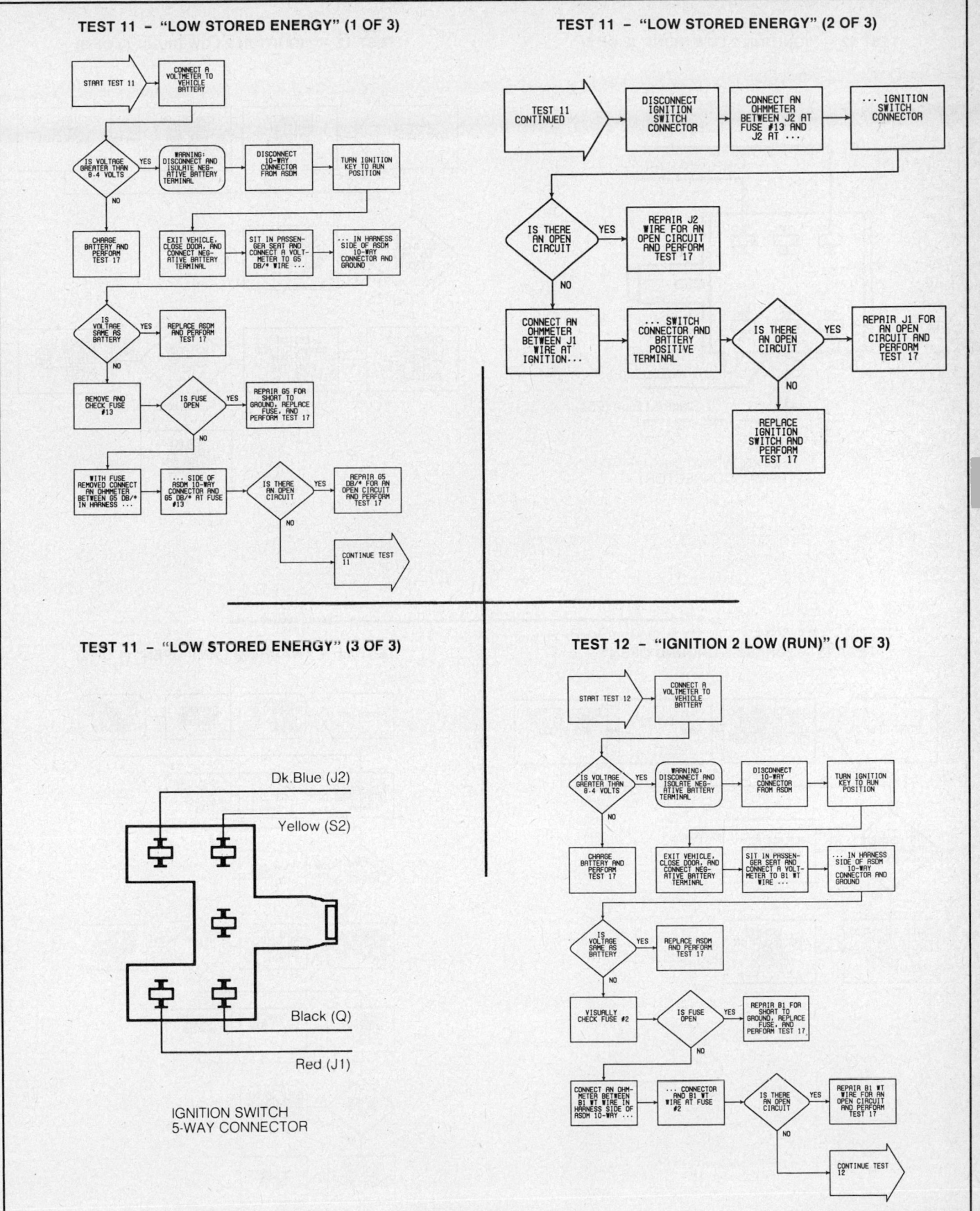

TEST 11 – "LOW STORED ENERGY" (1 OF 3)

TEST 11 – "LOW STORED ENERGY" (2 OF 3)

TEST 11 – "LOW STORED ENERGY" (3 OF 3)

IGNITION SWITCH
5-WAY CONNECTOR

Dk.Blue (J2)

Yellow (S2)

Black (Q)

Red (J1)

TEST 12 – "IGNITION 2 LOW (RUN)" (1 OF 3)

TEST 12 – "IGNITION 2 LOW (RUN)" (2 OF 3)

Pink (J10)

Black/Red (Q20)

B3 B1

A2

A2

B3 G

Gray/Black (P5)

Black/Lt.Blue (P51)

IGNITION SWITCH
6-WAY CONNECTOR

TEST 12 – "IGNITION 2 LOW (RUN)" (3 OF 3)

TEST 12 CONTINUED → DISCONNECT IGNITION SWITCH CONNECTOR → CONNECT AN OHMMETER BETWEEN Q20 AT FUSE #2 AND Q20 AT ... → ... IGNITION SWITCH CONNECTOR

IS THERE AN OPEN CIRCUIT — YES → REPAIR Q20 WIRE FOR AN OPEN CIRCUIT AND PERFORM TEST 17

NO ↓

CONNECT AN OHMMETER BETWEEN J10 WIRE AT IGNITION... → SWITCH CONNECTOR AND BATTERY POSITIVE TERMINAL → IS THERE AN OPEN CIRCUIT — YES → REPAIR J10 FOR AN OPEN CIRCUIT AND PERFORM TEST 17

NO ↓

REPLACE IGNITION SWITCH AND PERFORM TEST 17

TEST 13 – "CHASSIS GROUND OPEN"

START TEST 13 → CONNECT ONE END OF A JUMPER WIRE TO GROUND AND TOUCH OTHER ... → ...END TO ASDM → CHECK FOR FAULT CODES IN AIR BAG SYSTEM

IS "CHASSIS GROUND OPEN" ON DRB II — YES → REPLACE ASDM AND PERFORM TEST 17

NO ↓

CHECK ASDM FOR PROPER INSTAL-LATION AND USE OF PROPER SCREWS ... → ...(SCREWS ARE YELLOW IN COLOR) PERFORM TEST 17

TEST 14 – "WARNING LAMP OPEN" (1 OF 2)

PERFORM TEST 14 → WARNING! DISCONNECT AND ISOLATE NEGA-TIVE BATTERY TERMINAL → DISCONNECT ASDM 10-WAY CONNECTOR → NOTE: INSPECT THE CONNECTOR FOR SPREAD OR PUSHED OUT TERMINALS

WITH IGNITION IN RUN POSITION CONNECT NEG-ATIVE BATTERY TERMINAL → CONNECT ONE END OF A JUMPER WIRE TO R41 BK/TN IN HARNESS... → ...SIDE OF ASDM 10-WAY CON-NECTOR AND TOUCH OTHER END TO GROUND

DOES LAMP LIGHT WHEN CIRCUIT GROUNDED — YES → REPLACE ASDM AND PERFORM TEST 17

NO ↓

WARNING! DISCONNECT AND ISOLATE NEG-ATIVE BATTERY TERMINAL → REMOVE INSTRU-MENT CLUSTER AS REQUIRED TO PERMIT ACCESS TO WARNING LAMP → IS LAMP OPEN — YES → REPLACE AIR BAG SYSTEM WARNING LAMP AND PERFORM TEST 17

NO ↓

CONNECT AN OHMMETER BETWEEN R41 BK/TN IN CLUSTER... → ...CONNECTOR AND R41 BK/TN WIRE IN ASDM ... → 10-WAY HARNESS CONNECTOR

IS THERE AN OPEN CIRCUIT — YES → REPAIR THE R41 BK/TN WIRE FOR AN OPEN CIRCUIT AND PERFORM TEST 17

NO ↓

REPLACE THE INSTRUMENT CLUSTER PRINTED CIRCUIT ... → ...AND PERFORM TEST 17

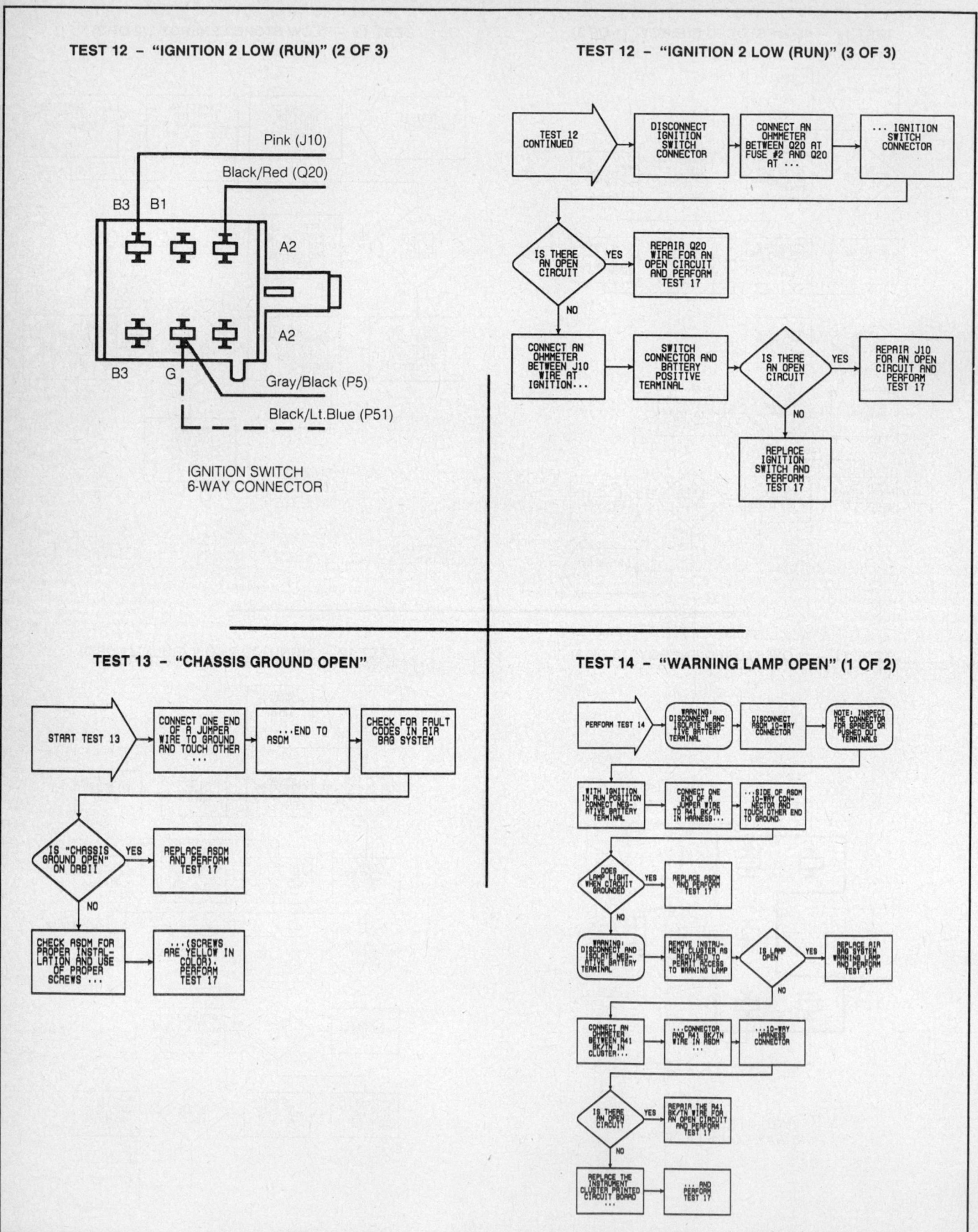

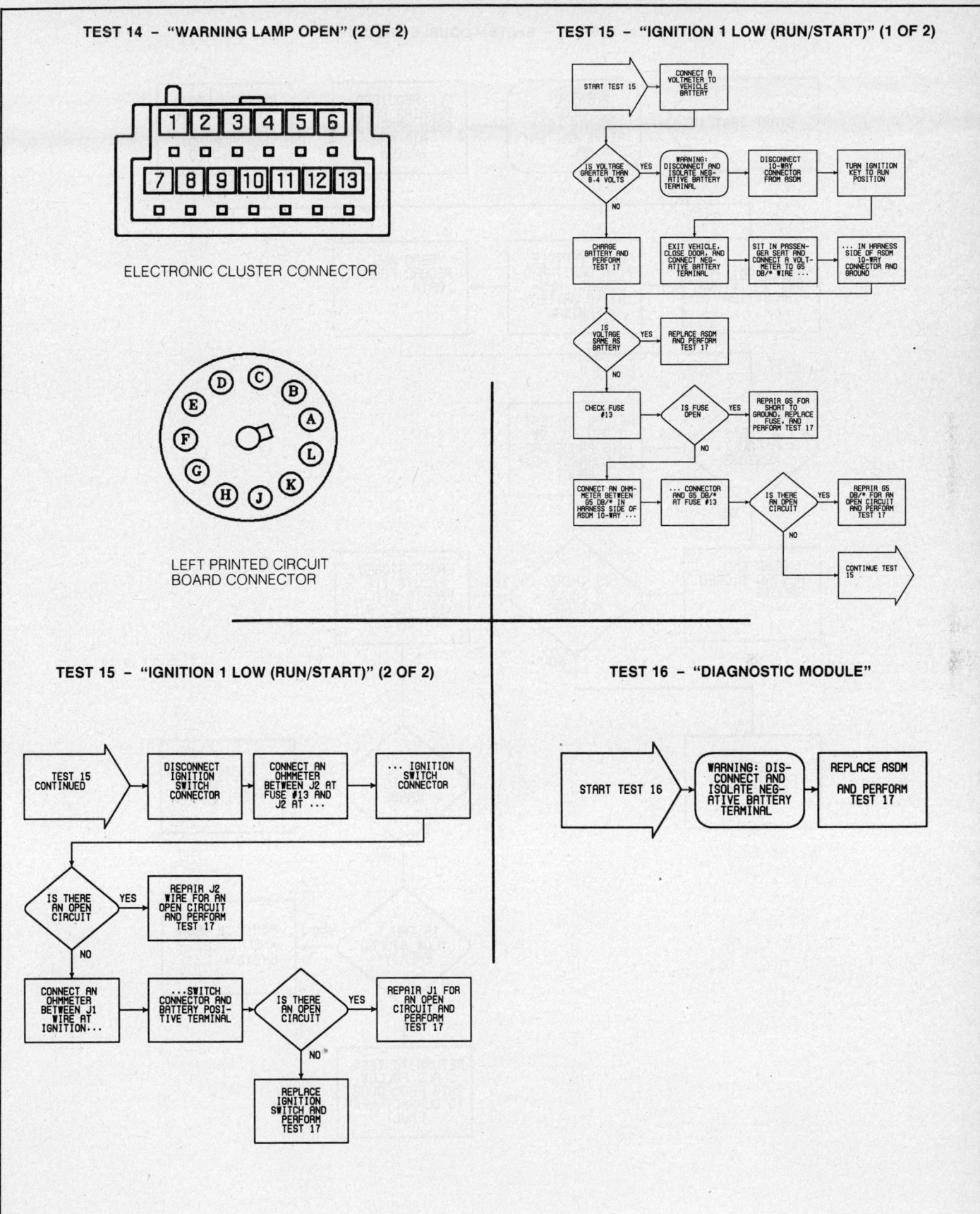

TEST 14 – "WARNING LAMP OPEN" (2 OF 2)

ELECTRONIC CLUSTER CONNECTOR

LEFT PRINTED CIRCUIT BOARD CONNECTOR

TEST 15 – "IGNITION 1 LOW (RUN/START)" (1 OF 2)

TEST 15 – "IGNITION 1 LOW (RUN/START)" (2 OF 2)

TEST 16 – "DIAGNOSTIC MODULE"

1989 AIR BAG RESTRAINT SYSTEMS
Chrysler Motors (Cont.)

TEST 17 – SYSTEM DOUBLE CHECK?

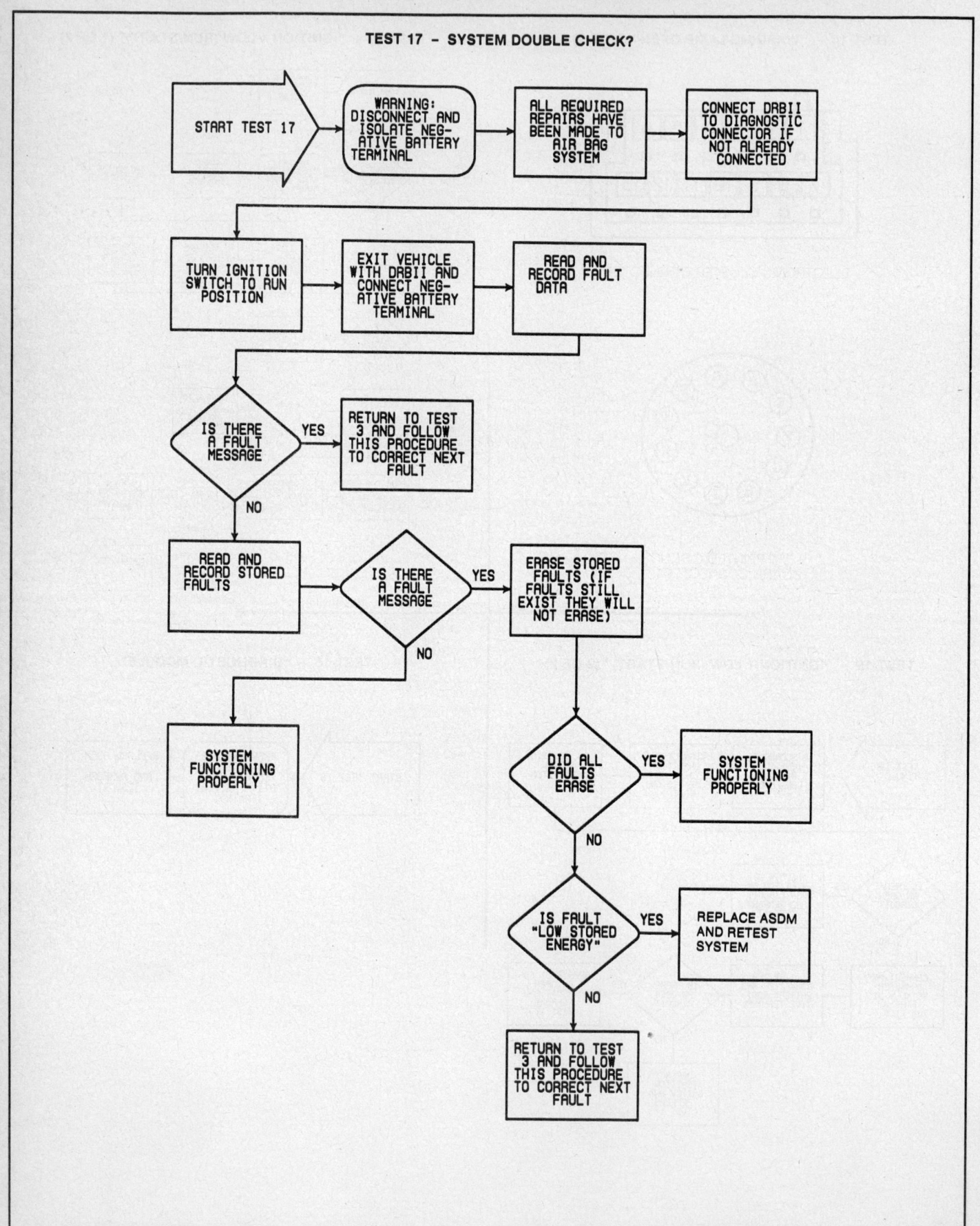

Dynasty, New Yorker

DESCRIPTION

The Chrysler Vehicle Theft Security System (VTSS) consists of an anti-theft control module, Single Board Engine Controller (SBEC) indicator light and the necessary circuitry to integrate the parking lights, tail lights, horn, hood switch, door switch and all lock switches into the system. The system is activated by securing the vehicle with the power door lock switch when exiting.

The VTSS is a 2-part theft deterrent system. Primarily, the horn, parking and tail light are used to deter forced entry. Additionally, an engine-start disable system operates when a method other than the proper ignition key is used to start engine. System checks and diagnostics are used for evaluation of the theft deterrent system.

OPERATION

Anti-theft system is "armed" when ignition key is removed and doors are locked using the power door lock switch. To verify system activation, the "SECURITY ALARM" light on the instrument panel will flash for 15 seconds. If the "SECURITY ALARM" light remains on, hood, deck lid or doors are not properly closed.

If forced entry is attempted, alarm warning system will trip, causing fuel system to be disabled, horn to sound and exterior lights to flash for 18 minutes (horn will sound for 3 minutes). System is "disarmed" by unlocking either front door with key or by turning ignition on.

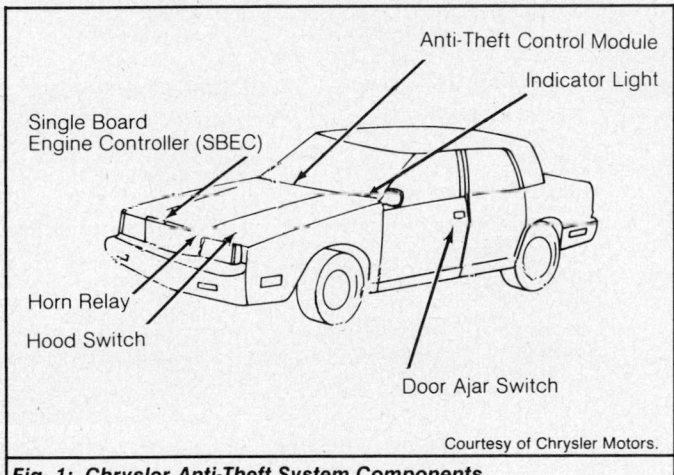

Single Board
Engine Controller (SBEC)

Anti-Theft Control Module

Indicator Light

Horn Relay

Hood Switch

Door Ajar Switch

Courtesy of Chrysler Motors.

Fig. 1: Chrysler Anti-Theft System Components

TROUBLE SHOOTING

1) Trouble shooting is designed to verify correct system operation or to isolate defective components. This is accomplished by entering the self-diagnostic mode and testing each system independently.

2) Cycle the ignition from "LOCK" to "ACCESSORY" position 3 times. With ignition in the "ACCESSORY" position, park and tail lights will flash and horn will sound twice to verify trunk key cylinder is in correct position. Turn key off to deactivate the verification process. System will remain in self-diagnostic mode.

3) While in self-diagnostic mode, a system performance check can be done to eliminate unnecessary diagnostic procedure. Complete the following procedure to isolate system in which the malfunction exists.

- Close all doors. Open, then close each door individually. The horn should sound once when the door ajar switch opens and once when the switch closes.
- Open, then close the hood. The horn should sound once when the hood opens and once when the hood closes.
- Lock, then unlock the doors using the power door lock switch. The horn should sound once at each position.
- Insert key into each door lock cylinder. Rotate to the lock and unlock position. The horn should sound once at each position.

- Insert key into ignition. Cycle the ignition from the "OFF" to the "RUN" position. The horn should sound once after each cycle to indicate correct system operation and then exit anti-theft control module from self-diagnostic mode.

4) All procedures require a one second pause between switch rotation or false signal(s) will result. If horn does not pulse correctly, failure of switch, anti-theft control module or circuitry of system tested is indicated.

TESTING

1) Cycle the ignition from "LOCK" to "ACCESSORY" position 3 times. Leave ignition in the "ACCESSORY" position. If park and tail lights do not flash, proceed to step **6)**. If horn does not sound 2 times, proceed to step **5)**.

2) If park and tail lights flash and horn sounds 2 times, vehicle is in self-diagnostic mode. Check indicator "SET" light. If light is not flashing, check for defective bulb or circuitry. If light is flashing, turn ignition to the "OFF" position.

3) Check switches using system diagnosis. See Chrysler Motors Body Control Computer in COMPUTERIZED ENGINE CONTROLS section. If switches test bad, repair as necessary and retest system. If switches test good, turn ignition on and wait 5 seconds. If indicator "SET" light remains off, turn ignition off. "Arm" system by closing and locking door using the power door lock switch. Test is complete if system operates correctly.

4) If indicator "SET" light remained on in step **3)**, problem is in wiring harness between anti-theft control module and SBEC. See appropriate chassis wiring diagram in WIRING DIAGRAMS section. If system will not "arm" suspect that SBEC module has recently been replaced. Crank engine 20 times and re-test system.

5) If horn did not sound 2 times in step **1)**, check fuse and replace if blown. If fuse is not blown, check decklid switch for continuity and replace if switch is open. If switch is okay, check wiring between switch and anti-theft control module. *See Fig. 3.* If wiring is okay, replace anti-theft control module.

6) If park and tail lights did not flash in step **1)**, check fuse and replace if blown. If fuse is not blown, check anti-theft control module connector from wiring harness side for battery voltage at Pins No. 6, 14, 18 and 19. If wiring is okay, replace anti-theft control module.

CONNECTOR PIN CHART

Pin No.	Wire Color	Function	Voltage
1	Black/Green	Ground	Zero
2	White	Data Bus (-)	2.5
3	Tan/Black	Hood Ajar	[1] 8.5
4	Black	Data Bus (+)	2.5
5 [7]	Tan	LF Door Ajar	[1] 5
5 [8]	White/Tan	All Doors	[1] 5
6	Blue	Ign. Feed	[2] 12
7 [7]	Orange	LR Door Ajar	[1] 5
8	Green/Orange	RF Door Lock	[3] 12
9	Black/Orange	Ind. Set Light	[4] 12
10	Black/Green	Ground	[1] Zero
11	Pink/Purple	Power Door Lock	[6] 12
12	Black/Red	Horn Relay (-)	[4] 12
13	Orange/White	Power Door Lock	[6] 12
14	Black/Yellow	Tail/Park Lights	12 (on)
15	Green/Orange	LF Door Key	[3] 12
16 [7]	Tan/Red	RF Door Ajar	[1] 5
17	Purple/Yellow	Trunk Lock (-)	[5] 12
18	Red	Battery Feed	12
19	Blue	Ignition Feed	[2] 12
20 [7]	Tan/Yellow	RR Door Ajar	[1] 5
21	Pink/Black	Tail/Park	12

[1] - Zero volts when open.
[2] - With key on.
[3] - Zero volts when unlocked.
[4] - Zero volts when on.
[5] - Zero volts with key removed.
[6] - In the unlocked position.
[7] - Electronic cluster only.
[8] - Mechanical cluster only.

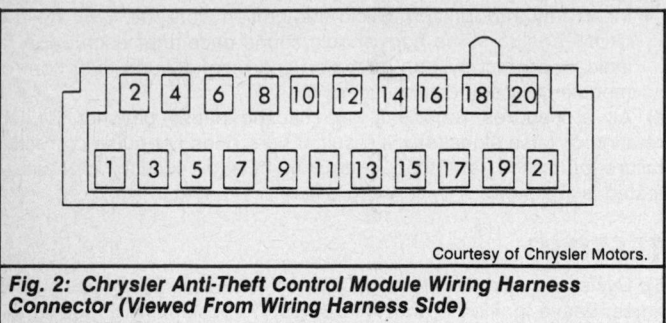

Fig. 2: Chrysler Anti-Theft Control Module Wiring Harness Connector (Viewed From Wiring Harness Side)

Courtesy of Chrysler Motors.

REMOVAL & INSTALLATION

THEFT CONTROL MODULE

NOTE: *If theft control is being removed, but not replaced, module must be disconnected while engine is running or anti-theft system will be "armed" and engine will not start.*

Removal & Installation – 1) Remove upper right instrument panel silencer and glove box assembly. Remove mounting bracket-to-instrument panel attaching screws. Disconnect anti-theft control module wiring harness connector and remove attaching screws. *See Fig. 3.*

2) To install, reverse removal procedure. If engine will not start, anti-theft system has disabled fuel injection system. Cycle ignition switch on and off. Remove ignition key and exit vehicle. With driver's door closed, lock and unlock door with key. Open door and start engine.

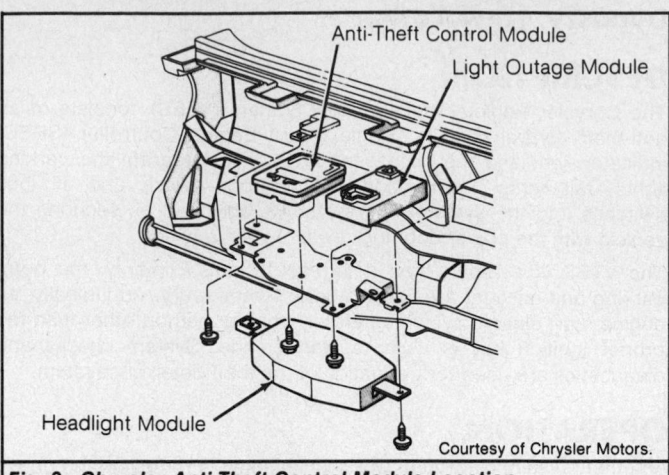

Fig. 3: Chrysler Anti-Theft Control Module Location

Courtesy of Chrysler Motors.

WIRING DIAGRAMS

For wiring diagrams, refer to appropriate chassis wiring diagram in WIRING DIAGRAMS section.

Continental, Cougar, Mark VII, Thunderbird, Town Car

DESCRIPTION

The anti-theft system consists of an electronic control module, protective switches, alarm relay, starter interrupt relay, anti-theft warning light, door key unlock switches (driver and passenger), courtesy light inverter relay, luggage compartment lock cylinder tamper switch, and on vehicles equipped with keyless entry, a disarm relay.

The protective switches are located in door and trunk locks. On Town Car models, control module and alarm relay are located in instrument panel above glove box. The starter interrupt and courtesy light inverter relay are located under right side of instrument panel. On all other models, control module, alarm relay, and courtesy light inverter relay are in the luggage compartment, under package tray. The starter interrupt relay is located under the center of the instrument panel. *See Figs. 1 through 3.*

OPERATION

The system is "armed" when the ignition switch is turned to the "OFF" position, the door is opened, the door lock switch is activated or the last 2 buttons of the keyless entry keyboard are pressed simultaneously and the door is closed. The system acknowledges an armed state by activating the anti-theft light on the instrument panel. The system is activated when a passenger compartment door is opened without a key, or when the trunk lock cylinder is removed. The alarm warning system will trip, causing the horn to sound intermittently and the low beam headlights, taillights and parking lights to flash.

The starter interrupt relay will cause the starter to cease functioning. The system is "disarmed" by unlocking either front door with a key or inputting the keyless entry code. System also disarms automatically within 2-4 minutes after alarm has been activated and returns automatically to armed state.

TROUBLE SHOOTING

ARMING SEQUENCE VERIFICATION

1) Start vehicle, turn ignition switch to "OFF" position. Close all doors. If warning light is off, go to next step. If warning light blinks, go to step **4)**. If warning light is on steady, go to step **9)**.
2) Open a vehicle door. If warning light does not blink, go to step **5)**. If light does blink, activate electric door lock switch or press buttons 7 and 9 of keyless entry (if equipped). If warning light glows continuously, go to next step. If not, go to step **7)**.
3) Close vehicle door. Check that warning light turns off after 32 seconds. If it does, arming sequence is verified. If not, replace control module.
4) Using a voltmeter, check voltage of circuit No. 341 (Orange/White wire) at terminal "J" of control module. *See Fig. 4.* If voltage is greater than 9 volts, replace module and retest system. If voltage is less than 2 volts, courtesy light door switch contacts may be shorted to battery voltage, inverter relay contacts may be shorted to ground or relay may be damaged.
5) Check that courtesy lights are on. If they are, go to step **6)**. If not, check door courtesy light switch, circuit No. 24 (Dark Blue/Orange wire) or circuit No. 159 (Red/Pink wire). Retest system.
6) Measure voltage at terminal "J" of control module. If less than 2 volts, replace module and retest system. If 2 volts or more, check that courtesy light inverter relay turns on and relay contacts close when doors close. Service as required and retest system.
7) Check if doors lock. If they do, go to step **8)**. If not, refer to ELECTRIC DOOR LOCK article or KEYLESS ENTRY SYSTEMS article in this section. Service as required and retest system.
8) Check that voltage at terminal "M" (circuit No. 118 - Pink/Orange wire) is less than 2 volts and a momentary battery voltage signal is applied to terminal "G" (circuit No. 117 - Pink/Black wire) when

door lock switch is activated. If okay, replace control module. If not, repair circuits.
9) Disconnect harness connector from control module. If warning light is still on, service circuit No. 343 (Dark Blue/Light Green wire) and retest system. If light goes off, replace control module and retest system.

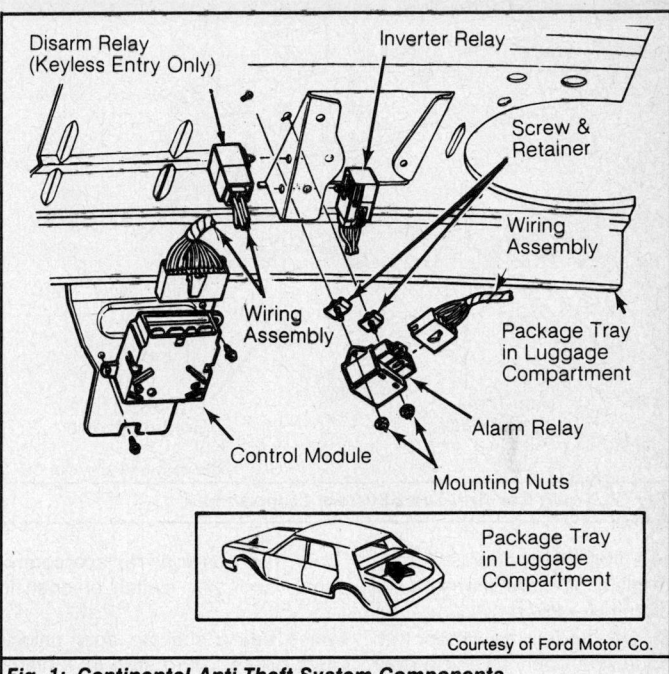

Fig. 1: Continental Anti-Theft System Components

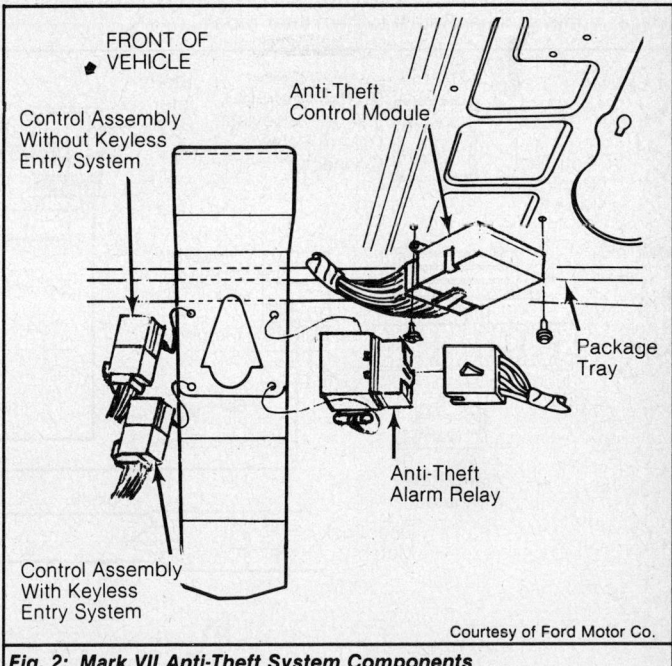

Fig. 2: Mark VII Anti-Theft System Components

DISARMING MODES VERIFICATION

1) Unlock and open a vehicle door. If light blinks, refer to ARMING SEQUENCE VERIFICATION in this article. If alarm sounds, and door key input is okay, go to step **3)**. If not, try other door key, keyless entry code or disconnect battery to stop alarm and go to next step.
2) Using voltmeter, check voltage at terminal "H" (circuit No. 25 - Dark Green/Purple wire) of control module. *See Fig. 4.* If less than

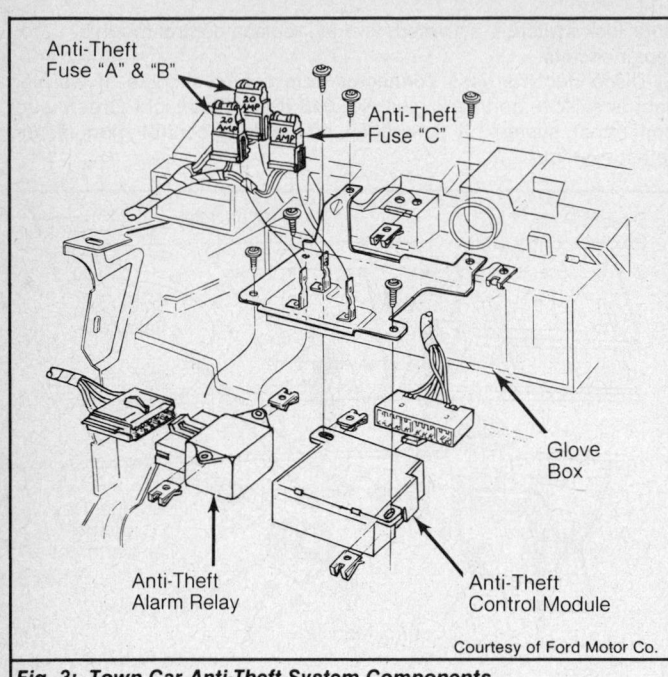

Fig. 3: Town Car Anti-Theft System Components

Courtesy of Ford Motor Co.

one volt when door switch is in unlocked position, replace control module. If more than one volt, repair door key switch or open in circuit No. 25.

3) On models equipped with keyless entry, activate door unlock code and open a vehicle door. If light blinks, go to step **4)**. If alarm sounds, use door key to stop alarm. Repair alarm disarm relay, open in circuit No. 25 or refer to TESTING in KEYLESS ENTRY article in this section. Retest system after repair.

4) On all models, open vehicle door and activate electric lock switch. If light glows steadily, disarm modes are verified. If light blinks, go to step **5)**.

5) Check that a momentary battery voltage signal is applied to terminal "M" (circuit No. 118 - Pink/ Orange wire) when unlock switch is activated. If it does, replace control module. If not, repair and/or replace circuit No. 118 and retest system.

6) Turn ignition key to "ACC" or "RUN" and open vehicle door. If alarm light blinks, disarm modes are verified. If alarm sounds, use door key to stop alarm and go to next step.

7) Check voltage of terminal "K" (circuit No. 296 - White/Purple wire) of control module. If greater than 9 volts with ignition key in "RUN" or "ACC" position, replace control module. If less than 9 volts, repair ignition switch or circuit No. 296 for open circuit. Retest system.

ALARM ACTIVATION VERIFICATION

1) With window down, unlock and open a door from inside vehicle. If alarm turns on and off, go to next step. If alarm does not turn off, go to step **6)**. If alarm turns on continuously, replace control module and retest system.

2) If horns turn off and on, go to step **3)**. If not, repair alarm relay contact and/or circuit No. 1 (Dark Blue wire) and retest system. *See Fig. 4.*

3) If tail and parking lights turn off and on, go to step **4)**. If not, repair alarm relay contact and/or circuit No. 14 (Brown wire) and retest system.

4) If low beam headlights turn off and on, system is okay. If not, repair alarm relay contact and/or circuit No. 13 (Red/Black wire) and retest system. Attempt to start vehicle. If vehicle starts, proceed to step **5)**. If it does not start, system is okay.

5) Measure voltage at terminal "E" (circuit No. 342 - Light Green-/Purple wire) of control module. If less than 2 volts, repair starter interrupt relay or open in circuit No. 33 (White/Pink wire). If greater than 2 volts, replace control module and retest system.

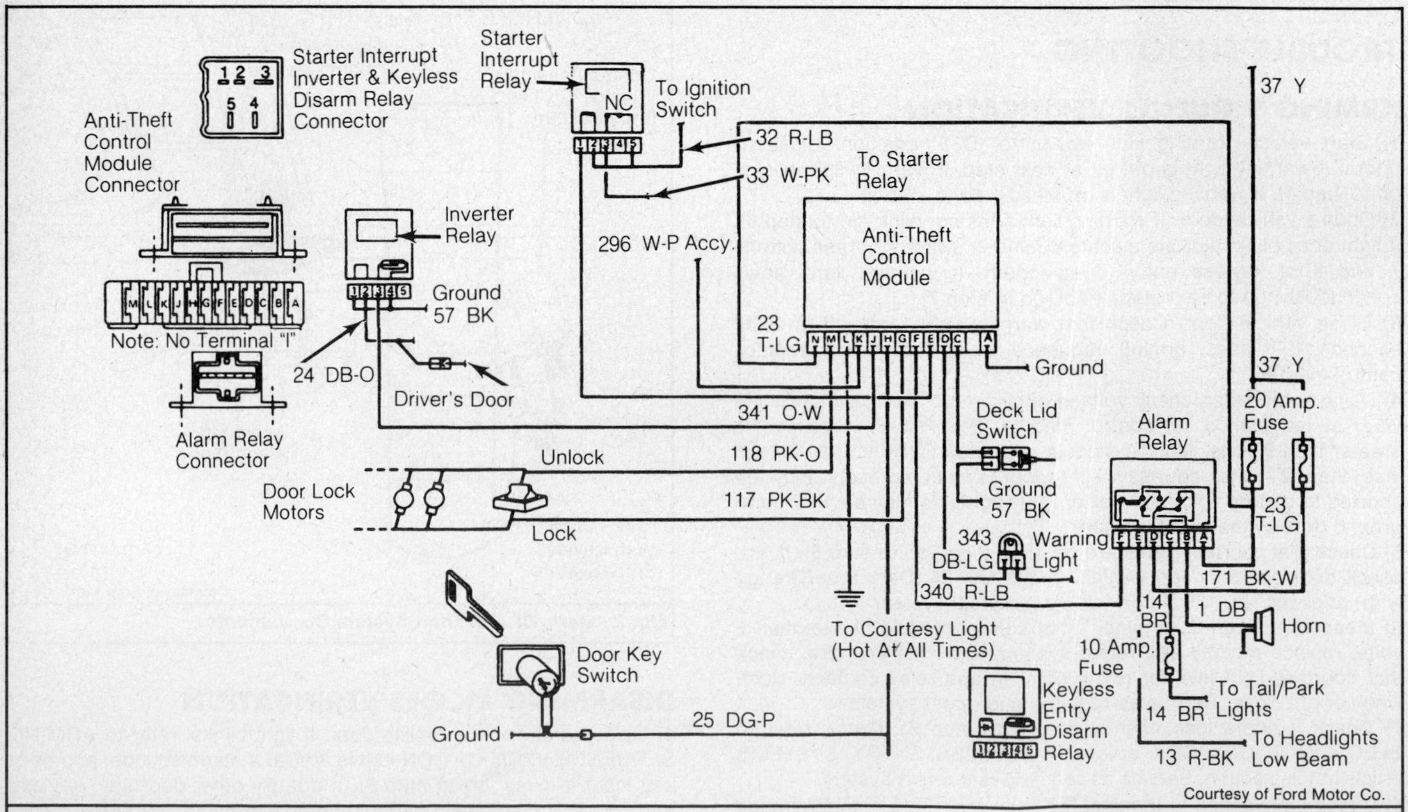

Fig. 4: Mark VII Anti-Theft System Wiring Schematic

Courtesy of Ford Motor Co.

6) Measure voltage at terminal "F" (circuit No. 340 - Red/Light Blue wire). If voltage switches between 12 volts and less than 2 volts, repair alarm relay and retest system. If voltage reads steady battery voltage, replace control module. If voltage reads below 2 volts, repair open in circuit No. 23 (Tan/Light Green wire) and retest system.

7) Arm alarm system, open trunk and remove lock cylinder. If alarm activates, system is okay. If alarm does not activate, measure voltage at terminal "C" (circuit No. 486 - Brown/White wire). If less than 2 volts, replace control module and retest system. If greater than 2 volts, repair circuit No. 486 and/or trunk lock cylinder switch and retest system.

ALARM DEACTIVATION VERIFICATION

1) With window down, arm alarm system. Unlock and open a door from inside vehicle. Insert key and turn to "unlock" position. If alarm activates and turns off, go to step 3). If alarm is continuous, go to next step.

2) With key in "unlock" position, measure voltage of terminal "H" of control module. See Fig. 4. If less than one volt, replace control module. If greater than one volt, repair door key switch or open in circuit No. 25 (Dark Green/Purple wire). Retest system.

3) If equipped with keyless entry system, arm and activate alarm as in step 1). Activate keyless entry door unlock code. If alarm turns off, system is okay. Go to step 5). If alarm is continuous, go to next step.

4) Press unlock code. Check that battery voltage is applied momentarily to circuit No. 163 (Red/ Orange wire). This turns keyless entry alarm disarm relay on, which provides a ground to circuit No. 25 (Dark Green/Purple wire). If not, repair relay or circuits No. 25, 118 or 163 as required. Retest system.

5) With window down, arm alarm system. Unlock and open door from inside vehicle. Wait 4 minutes. If alarm activates and shuts off, system is okay. If alarm continues, replace control module and retest system.

VEHICLE WILL NOT START

1) Insert door key and turn to unlock position. Using a jumper, short terminals No. 3 and 5 of starter interrupt relay. See Fig. 4. Start vehicle. If vehicle starts, go to next step. If vehicle will not start, system is okay.

2) Check voltage at terminal "1 C" of starter interrupt relay or terminal "E" (circuit No. 342 - Light Green/Purple wire) of control module. If greater than 2 volts, replace relay and retest system. If less than 2 volts, replace control module.

ALARM LIGHT ALWAYS ON

Ensure alarm system is disarmed. If light is still on, insert door key and turn to "unlock" position. If light turns off, replace control module and retest system. If light remains on, repair short in circuit No. 343 (Dark Blue/Light Green wire) and retest system. See Fig. 4.

ALARM LIGHT DOES NOT WORK

1) Turn ignition switch to "OFF" position. Using a jumper, short terminal "D" (circuit No. 343 - Dark Blue/Light Green wire) of control module to ground. See Fig. 4. If light turns on, go to step 2). If light remains off, repair warning light or open in circuit No. 343 and retest system.

2) Measure voltage of terminal "N" (circuit No. 23 - Tan/Light Green wire). If greater than 9 volts, go to step 3). If less than 9 volts, replace fuse and/or repair circuits No. 23 and 37 (Yellow). Retest system.

3) Measure voltage of terminal "K" (circuit No. 296 - White/Purple wire). If less than 9 volts, go to step 4). If greater than 9 volts, repair short in circuit No. 296 and retest system.

4) Open a vehicle door. Activate electric door lock switch. If light glows, system is okay. If not, replace control module and retest system.

HORN, HEADLIGHTS AND/OR TAILLIGHTS ALWAYS ON

Remove control module connector. If horn and lights remain on, replace alarm relay and retest system. If they turn off, replace control module and retest system.

TESTING

DOOR LOCK SWITCH

Ensure that key is removed from door lock. Measure switch resistance. If not more than 25,000 ohms, replace switch. Rotate key 45 degrees from center of travel. Measure switch resistance. If not less than 200 ohms, replace switch.

DECK LID LOCK TAMPER SWITCH

Measure installed switch resistance. If not more than 25,000 ohms, replace switch.

REMOVAL & INSTALLATION

CONTROL MODULE

Removal & Installation – 1) Disconnect battery ground cable. Open luggage compartment deck lid. Remove 2 screws on each side of defroster nozzle opening. Remove 6 screws from underside of instrument panel pad brow. Remove one screw from each end of pad.

2) Disconnect electrical connector from control module. Remove 2 screws attaching control module and remove module. To install, reverse removal procedure and test system for proper operation. See Figs. 1 through 3.

ALARM RELAY

Removal & Installation – Disconnect battery ground cable. Open luggage compartment deck lid. Disconnect wiring connector from alarm relay. Remove 2 nuts attaching alarm relay to package tray. Remove alarm relay. To install, reverse removal procedure and test system for proper operation. See Figs. 1 through 3.

DISARM RELAY

Removal & Installation – Disconnect battery ground cable. Open luggage compartment deck lid. Disconnect electrical connector from disarm relay. Remove disarm relay by pulling away from brace. To install, reverse removal procedure and test system for proper operation. See Figs. 1 through 3.

INVERTER RELAY

Removal & Installation – Disconnect battery ground cable. Open luggage compartment deck lid. Disconnect electrical connector to inverter relay. Remove inverter relay by pulling away from package tray brace. To install, reverse removal procedure and test system for proper operation. See Figs. 1 through 3.

STARTER INTERRUPT RELAY

Removal & Installation – Disconnect battery ground cable. Disconnect electrical connector from starter interrupt relay (located under instrument panel to right-hand side of steering column). Remove starter interrupt relay by pulling away from brace. To install, reverse removal procedure and test system for proper operation.

WIRING DIAGRAMS

For wiring diagrams, refer to appropriate chassis wiring diagram in WIRING DIAGRAMS section.

1989 CRUISE CONTROL SYSTEMS
Ford Motor Co. — EEC-IV Controlled

Continental, Cougar, Grand Marquis (5.0L), LTD Crown Victoria (5.0L), Mark VII, Sable, Taurus, Thunderbird, Town Car, Wagon

DESCRIPTION

The cruise control system consists of operator controls, a servo (throttle actuator) assembly, a speed sensor, a clutch switch, a stoplight switch, a vacuum dump valve, an amplifier assembly, a horn relay, wiring harnesses and vacuum hoses.

Control switches are located in steering wheel. The servo assembly is mounted in engine compartment, and is connected to throttle linkage with an actuator cable. The brake and clutch switches are located on brake pedal support bracket below dashboard. The speed control sensor is located on transaxle or transmission. Models with electronic dashboard use a special connection to speedometer in place of a speed sensor.

On the Integrated Vehicle Speed Control (IVSC), the speed control amplifier assembly function is integrated into the EEC-IV Electronic Control Assembly (ECA).

OPERATION

The cruise control is only operational at speeds above 30 MPH. The system is activated when cruise control switch is set to "ON" position and "SET/ACCEL" or "SET" button is depressed and released. The vehicle speed will be maintained until a new speed is set, the brake or clutch pedal is depressed, or until system is turned off. When the system has been deactivated by depressing brake or clutch pedal, the driver can re-establish the set speed by pressing and releasing "RESUME" button.

When brake pedal is depressed, an electrical signal from stoplight is sent to the amplifier, turning off system. In addition (when brake pedal is depressed), the vacuum dump valve mechanically releases vacuum from servo, thus releasing the throttle independently of the amplifier control.

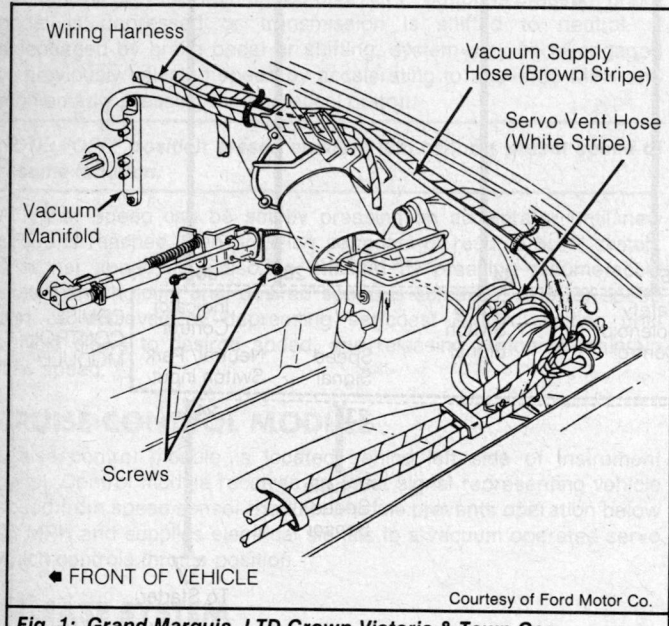

Fig. 1: Grand Marquis, LTD Crown Victoria & Town Car Automatic Cruise Control Components

Courtesy of Ford Motor Co.

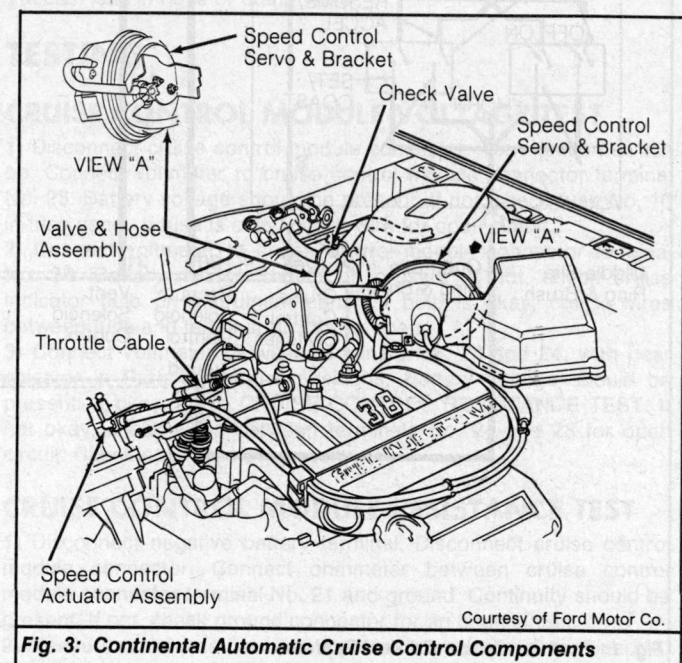

Fig. 3: Continental Automatic Cruise Control Components

Courtesy of Ford Motor Co.

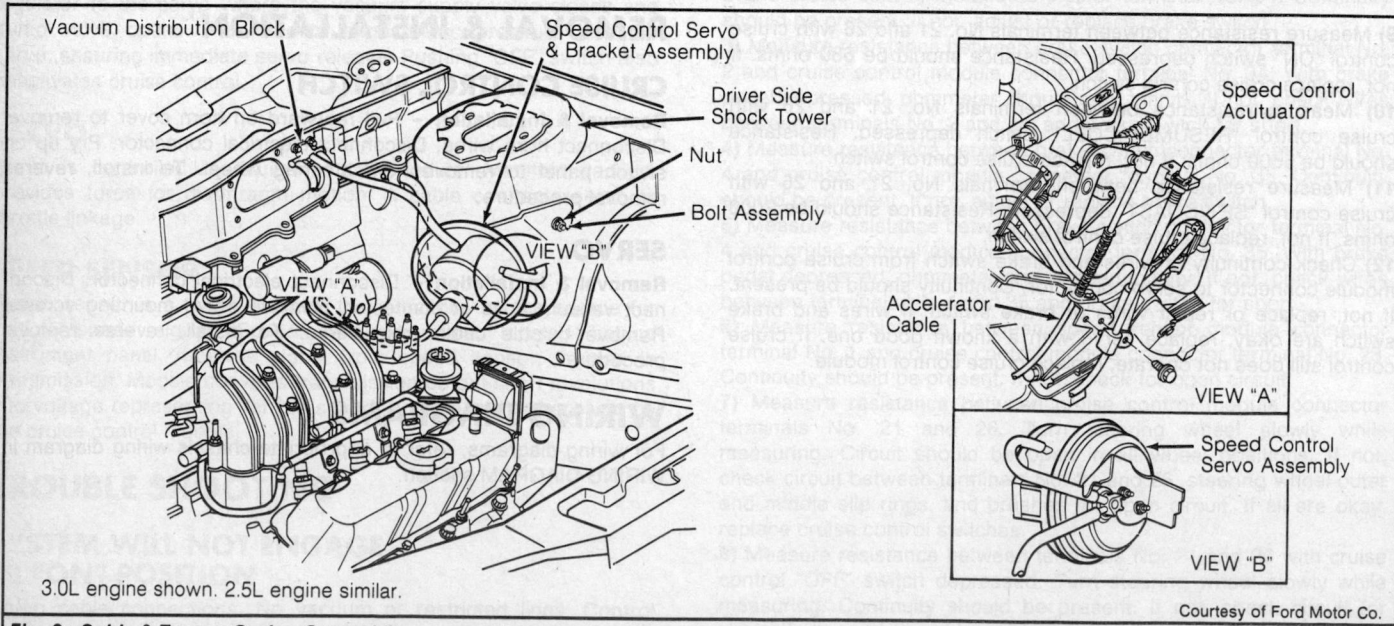

Fig. 2: Sable & Taurus Cruise Control Component Location

Courtesy of Ford Motor Co.

1989 CRUISE CONTROL SYSTEMS
Ford Motor Co. — EEC-IV Controlled (Cont.)

6-27

Ford

CRUISE CONTROL QUIC
KEY ON, ENGINE OFF (K

Service Code

11 ....
23 ....
47 ....
48 ....
49 ....
53 ....
63 ....
67 ....
74 ....
75 ....
81 ....
82 ....

¹ – Refer to ELECTRO
COMPUTERIZED E
manual for diagnosi
QUICK TEST.

CRUISE CONTROL QUICK
KEY ON, ENGINE RUNNIN

Service Code

11 ....
27 ....
28 ....
36 ....
37 ....

Circuit Tests Instructions
any circuit tests unless in
assumes that a fault has
to enter a specific servic
direction from the QUICK
cause replacement of non
2) DO NOT replace any p
they should be replaced.
3) When more than one
service with first code rece
4) DO NOT measure volta
test lights to it, unless othe
5) Isolate both ends of a
checking for shorts or con

• REFER TO THE FOLLOW
  NECESSARY DURING C

  Vacuu
  Distrib

Fig. 6: Cruise Control Circu

ADJUSTMENTS

LINKAGE

Remove speed control actuator cable retaining clip. Push actuator cable through adjuster until slight tension is felt. Insert cable retaining clip and snap into place.

VACUUM DUMP VALVE

1) Dump valve should be adjusted so that there is no vacuum leakage when brake pedal is not depressed, and there is vacuum leakage when pedal is depressed. Check with vacuum pump.
2) If adjustment is required, hold brake pedal in depressed position and push valve into valve collar as far as it will go. Place a .050-.100" (1.27-2.54 mm) shim between White valve button and pad (adapter on some models) on brake pedal.
3) Pull brake pedal fully rearward and remove shim. Valve button should now be slightly above or just touching in pad (adapter) on brake pedal.

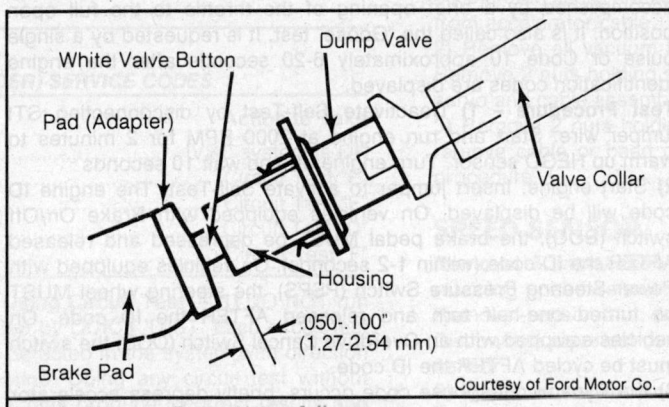

Fig. 4: Vacuum Dump Valve Adjustment

CLUTCH SWITCH

Prop clutch pedal in full-up position (pawl fully released from sector). Loosen switch mounting screw. Slide switch forward toward clutch pedal until switch plunger cap is approximately .030" (.76 mm) from contacting switch housing. Tighten attaching screw to complete adjustment.

TROUBLE SHOOTING

Check all electrical and vacuum connections. Press brake pedal and check brake lights work. If not, repair brake light circuit. Check clutch switch on manual transmission vehicles. Check servo and throttle linkage for free operation. If components appear to be in good condition, proceed to TESTING procedures.

TESTING

QUICK TEST

Description – The QUICK TEST diagnostic procedure is a functional test of the EEC-IV system. It consists of the following basic test steps and must be carefully followed in sequence, otherwise misdiagnosis, or replacement of non-faulty components may result.
  • VISUAL CHECK & VEHICLE PREPARATION
  • EQUIPMENT HOOK-UP
  • KEY ON ENGINE OFF (KOEO) SELF-TEST
  • KEY ON ENGINE RUNNING (KOER) SELF-TEST
  • CONTINUOUS MONITOR MODE (WIGGLE TEST)
  • DIAGNOSIS BY SYMPTOM

After all tests, servicing, or repairs have been completed, repeat QUICK TEST to ensure all EEC-IV systems work properly.

The KOEO and KOER SELF-TESTS are intended to detect faults present at time of testing, not intermittent faults. Intermittent faults are detected by CONTINUOUS SELF-TESTS, which is entered after the KOER SELF-TEST, and stored in the ECA memory.

NOTE: Correct test results for system are dependent on the correct operation of several related non-EEC components and systems. All non-EEC problems should be corrected before attempting to diagnose the EEC system.

VISUAL CHECK & VEHICLE PREPARATION

Before hooking up any equipment to diagnose the EEC system, make the following visual checks and perform the preparation procedures:
  • Verify condition of air cleaner and air ducting.
  • Check all vacuum hoses for leaks, restrictions, and proper routing.
  • Check the EEC-IV system wiring harness electrical connections for corrosion, bent or broken pins, loose wires or terminals, and proper routing.
  • Check the ECA, sensors and actuators for physical damage.
  • Check engine coolant level.
  • Perform all necessary safety precautions to prevent personal injury or vehicle damage.
  • Set parking brake and place shift lever in "P" for automatic transmissions, and Neutral for manual transmissions. DO NOT move shift lever during test unless specifically directed to do so.
  • Turn off all lights and accessories. Ensure vehicle doors are closed when making voltage or resistance readings.
  • Start engine and idle until upper radiator hose is hot and pressurized, and throttle is off fast idle. Check for leaks around exhaust manifold, exhaust gas oxygen sensor, and vacuum hose connections.
  • Turn ignition off. Service items as required, then go to EQUIPMENT HOOK-UP.

SELF-TEST CONNECTOR LOCATIONS

Application	Location
Continental & Mark VII	Right rear of engine compartment
Cougar & Thunderbird	In front of left shock tower
Grand Marquis, LTD Crown Victoria, Town Car & Wagon	Left inner fender above wheelwell
Taurus & Sable	
2.5L CFI (Taurus Only)	Right rear of engine
3.0L & 3.8L	Right rear of engine compartment below MAP sensor

EQUIPMENT HOOK-UP

Analog Volt/Ohmmeter (VOM) – **1)** Turn ignition switch to "OFF" position. Set VOM at 0-15V DC range and connect positive lead of VOM to positive battery terminal.
2) Connect negative VOM lead to pin No. 4 (STO) on Self-Test connector. *See Fig. 5.* Connect timing light, and go to KOEO SELF-TEST. KOEO SELF-TEST is activated by connecting jumper wire from Self-Test Input (STI) pigtail to pin No. 2 (Signal Return) on Self-Test connector with the ignition on.

STAR Tester – Turn ignition switch to "OFF" position. Connect color coded adapter cable leads to diagnostic tester. Connect adapter cable's 2 service connectors to vehicle Self-Test and STI connectors. Connect timing light. Go to KOEO SELF-TEST.

"CHECK ENGINE" Light (MIL) & "MESSAGE CENTER" (Lincoln Continental) – With ignition on, connect a jumper wire between STI and pin No. 2 of Self-Test connector. No additional special equipment hookup is required.

6-28

6-30

1989 CRUISE CONTROL SYSTEMS
Ford Motor Co. — EEC-IV Controlled (Cont.)

Ford

STAR HOOKUP (WITH
ADAPTER CABLE ASS…

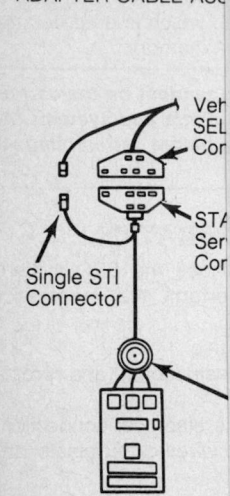

Veh…
SEL…
Con…

STA…
Ser…
Con…

Single STI
Connector

Fig. 5: Self-Test Connec…

KEY ON ENGINE

Test Procedure – 1) Tu…
all procedures of PREP…
been followed. Engine sh…
2) Turn ignition on. If us…
(MIL) light, connect a jur…
to pin No. 2 (Signal Retur…
the KOEO Self-Test. If St…
in down position at th…
Continental models may …
3) The ECA will run th…
various solenoids and s…
cycle the codes will appe…

NOTE: DO NOT depress …
Ensure ignition switch is …
connector to pin No. 2 of …

4) The first set of code…
codes. They will be repe…
signal and then the CON…
will also be repeated twic…
5) A KOEO code 11 indic…
code 11 must be pre…
CONTINUOUS MEMORY…
the order they appear. S…
each repair, repeat KOEO…
6) If no KOEO codes are …
Code 10 (separator pulse…
to verify that other servic…
KOEO CONTINUOUS ME…
All other Continuous Mer…
testing.

KOEO CONTINUOUS MEM

Application

All Engines ....
5.0L MA, 3.0L SHO, 3.8L …

3.0L SHO, 3.8L SC ....

ENGAGEMENT SWITCH

NOTE: See STEERING COLUMN SWITCHES article in STEERING section for engagement switch REMOVAL & INSTALLATION procedure.

WIRING DIAGRAMS

For wiring diagrams, refer to appropriate chassis wiring diagram in WIRING DIAGRAM section.

CIRCUIT TEST A
CRUISE CONTROL SWITCHES

Enter this test only when Codes 47, 48 or 49 are received in KEY ON, ENGINE OFF SELF-TEST. To prevent replacement of good components, ensure horn relay and/or fuses (non-IVSC areas) are not at fault. This circuit test is intended to diagnose only speed control switches, brush assembly, slip ring assembly, wiring harness and ECA.

1) Service Code 47 appears. If "OFF", "COAST", "ACCEL" and "RESUME" buttons are pressed during IVSC KEY ON, ENGINE OFF, go to step 2). If not, perform IVSC KEY ON, ENGINE OFF SELF-TEST.

2) If switch does not function, turn key off. Wait 10 seconds. Disconnect ECA 60-pin connector. Inspect for damage. Service as necessary. Install Breakout Box (34J593), leaving ECA disconnected. Measure resistance between test pin No. 50 and test pin No. 39 per diagram.

3) If resistances are within range, replace ECA. If not, replace switches. If resistance values fluctuate within ranges while steering wheel is rotated, or goes above ranges, clean brushes and slip rings and lubricate slip rings. If not, switches are okay.

RESISTANCE RANGES

Range (Ohms)	Button	Ohm Resistance
200	"OFF"	0-4
200	"COAST"	114-126
2000	"ACCEL"	646-714
5000	"RESUME"	2090-2310

4) Service Code 48 appears. If "OFF", "COAST", "ACCEL" and "RESUME" buttons are pressed during IVSC KEY ON, ENGINE OFF QUICK TEST, go to next step. If not, perform IVSC KEY ON, ENGINE OFF QUICK TEST.

5) If switch is stuck with key off, wait 10 seconds. Disconnect ECA 60-pin connector. Inspect for damage. Service as necessary. Install breakout box, leaving ECA disconnected. DVOM range should be on 5000-ohm scale. If resistance reading is 0-2310 ohms, replace switches. If not, replace ECA.

6) Service Code 49 has appeared. If "OFF", "COAST", "ACCEL" and "RESUME" buttons are pressed during IVSC KEY ON, ENGINE OFF QUICK TEST, go to step 7). If not, perform IVSC KEY ON, ENGINE OFF QUICK TEST.

7) Turn key off and wait 10 seconds. Disconnect ECA 60-pin connector. Inspect for damage. Service as necessary. Install breakout box, leaving ECA disconnected. Disconnect speed control switch plug in steering column shroud. Set DVOM on 200-ohm scale.

8) Measure resistance between test pin No. 39 of 60-pin connector and ground terminal of disconnected speed control switch plug. If resistance reading is greater than 5 ohms, service open circuit between EEC-IV connector pin No. 39 and switch plug ground terminal. If not, replace ECA.

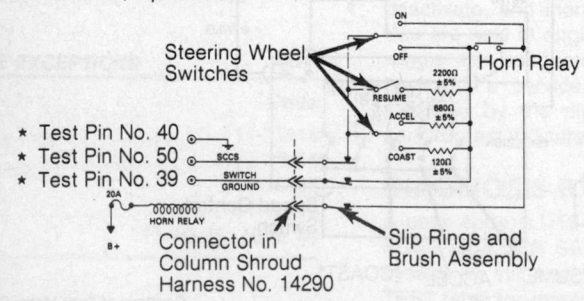

Steering Wheel Switches

ON
OFF
2200Ω ±5%
Horn Relay
RESUME
680Ω ±5%
ACCEL
COAST
1200Ω ±5%

★ Test Pin No. 40
★ Test Pin No. 50
★ Test Pin No. 39
SCCS
SWITCH GROUND

20A
HORN RELAY
B+
Connector in Column Shroud Harness No. 14290
Slip Rings and Brush Assembly

★ TEST PINS LOCATED ON BREAKOUT BOX.

CIRCUIT TEST B
BRAKE ON/OFF (BOO)

Enter this circuit test only when service Codes 74 or 75 are received in KEY ON, ENGINE OFF SELF-TEST. To prevent replacement of good components, ensure brake light, brake switch and/or fuses (non-IVSC areas) are not at fault. This circuit test is intended to diagnose BOO circuit and ECA.

1) Service Code 74 has appeared. If brake is pressed during KEY ON, ENGINE OFF SELF-TEST, go to next step. If not, perform KEY ON, ENGINE OFF SELF-TEST and press brake once during test.

2) Turn key off and wait 10 seconds. Disconnect ECA 60-pin connector. Inspect for damage. Service as necessary. Install breakout box, leaving ECA disconnected. Set DVOM on 20-volt scale. Measure voltage between test pin No. 2 and test pin No. 40 at breakout box while depressing and releasing brake. If voltage cycles, replace ECA and retest. If not, go to next step.

3) Turn key off. Install breakout box. Disconnect ECA. Set DVOM on 200-ohm scale. Disconnect BOO circuit from 14290 harness (12-pin connector). Measure resistance between test pin No. 2 at breakout box and ground. If resistance reading is greater than 5 ohms, service stoplight circuit. If not, service BOO circuit short to ground.

4) Turn key off and wait 10 seconds. Disconnect ECA 60-pin connector. Inspect for damage. Service as necessary. Install breakout box, leaving ECA disconnected. Set DVOM on 20-volt scale. Measure voltage between test pin No. 2 and test pin No. 40 at breakout box while depressing and releasing brake. If voltage cycles, replace ECA and perform QUICK TEST. If not, go to next step.

5) Turn key off. Install breakout box. Disconnect ECA. Set DVOM on 20-volt scale. Disconnect BOO circuit from 14290 harness (12-pin connector). Measure voltage between test pin No. 2 at breakout box and engine block ground. If voltage reading is greater than 10.5 volts, service BOO circuit short to power. If not, BOO circuit is okay. Service stoplight circuit.

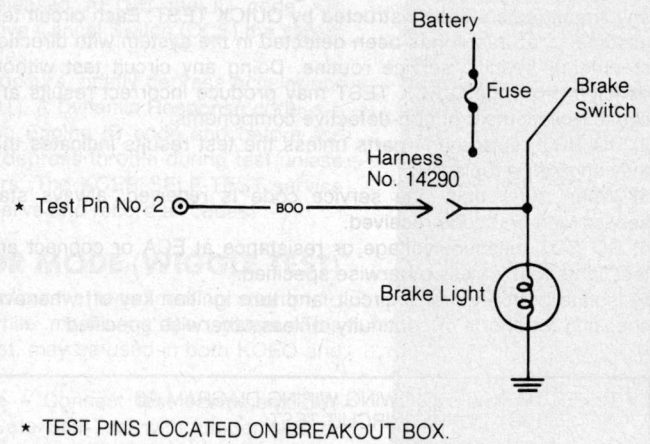

Battery
Fuse
Brake Switch
Harness No. 14290
★ Test Pin No. 2 — BOO —
Brake Light

★ TEST PINS LOCATED ON BREAKOUT BOX.

CIRCUIT TEST C
SERVO SOLENOIDS

Enter circuit test only when service Codes 81 or 82 are received in KEY ON, ENGINE OFF SELF-TEST. This circuit test is intended to diagnose only servo vent solenoid, servo vacuum solenoid, circuits SOL+, SCVNT, SCVAC, and ECA.

1) Turn key off. Disconnect ECA 60-pin connector. Inspect for damage. Service as necessary. Install breakout box, leaving ECA disconnected. Set DVOMon 200-ohm scale. Measure resistance between test pin No. 13 and test pin No. 35. If resistance is 100-150 ohms, replace ECA and repeat QUICK TEST. If resistance is less than 100 ohms, replace servo and repeat QUICK TEST. If resistance is greater than 150 ohms, go to step 2).

2) Disconnect harness connector from servo. Set DVOM on 200-ohm scale. Measure resistance between test pin No. 13 and SOL+ circuit at harness connector. If resistance is greater than 5 ohms, service open circuit and repeat QUICK TEST. If resistance is less than 5 ohms, go to step 3).

1989 CRUISE CONTROL SYSTEMS
Ford Motor Co. — EEC-IV Controlled (Cont.)

6-31

3) Disconnect harness connector from servo. Set DVOM on 200-ohm scale. Measure resistance between test pin No. 35 and SCVNT circuit at harness connector. If resistance is greater than 5 ohms, service open circuit and repeat QUICK TEST. If resistance is less than 5 ohms, go to step **4)**.

4) Disconnect harness connector from servo. Set DVOM on 200-ohm scale. Measure resistance between SOL+ and SCVNT circuit pins on servo connector. If resistance is greater than 150 ohms, replace servo and repeat QUICK TEST.

5) Turn key off. Disconnect ECA 60-pin connector. Inspect for damage. Service as necessary. Install breakout box, leaving ECA disconnected. Set DVOM on 200-ohm scale. Measure resistance between test pin No. 13 and test pin No. 42. If resistance is 40-75 ohms, replace ECA and repeat QUICK TEST. If resistance is less than 40 ohms, replace servo and repeat QUICK TEST. If resistance is greater than 75 ohms, go to step **6)**.

6) Disconnect harness connector from servo. Set DVOM on 200-ohm scale. Measure resistance between test pin No. 13 and SOL+ circuit at harness connector. If resistance is greater than 5 ohms, service open circuit and repeat QUICK TEST. If resistance is less than 5 ohms, go to next step.

7) Disconnect harness connector from servo. Set DVOM on 200-ohm scale. Measure resistance between test pin No. 42 and SCVAC circuit at harness connector. If resistance is greater than 5 ohms, service open circuit and repeat QUICK TEST. If resistance is less than 5 ohms, replace servo and repeat QUICK TEST.

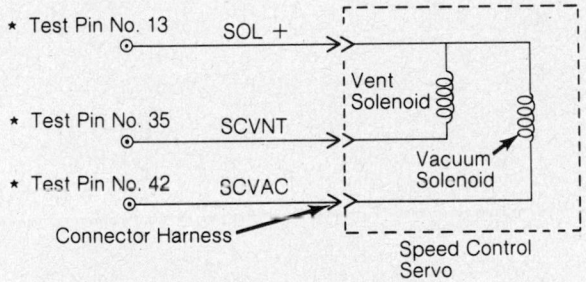

★ Test Pin No. 13 — SOL +
★ Test Pin No. 35 — SCVNT
★ Test Pin No. 42 — SCVAC
Connector Harness
Vent Solenoid
Vacuum Solenoid
Speed Control Servo

★ TEST PINS LOCATED ON BREAKOUT BOX.

CIRCUIT TEST D

SPEED DOES NOT INCREASE DURING DYNAMIC TEST

Enter this test only when Code 36 is received in KOER SELF-TEST. This circuit test is intended to diagnose actuator cable adjustment, vacuum hose connections, dump valve adjustment and ECA.

1) Service Code 36 appears. Repeat KEY ON, ENGINE RUNNING SELF-TEST. Ensure speed control "ON" button is pressed before pressing "STAR" push button. If Code 36 is still present, go to next step. If not, increased-vehicle-speed test passed. Service any other service codes that appear as necessary.

2) If actuator cable is attached to throttle body accelerator linkage, go to next step. If not, connect servo cable to throttle body accelerator linkage. Repeat QUICK TEST.

3) If servo vacuum supply hose is connected to servo and vacuum manifold, go to next step. If not, connect hoses and repeat QUICK TEST. If dump valve hose is connected to servo and to dump valve, go to next step. If not, connect hoses and repeat QUICK TEST.

4) If dump valve is adjusted properly so that valve is closed when brake pedal is not depressed, replace ECA. If not, adjust dump valve and repeat QUICK TEST.

CIRCUIT TEST E

SYSTEM DOES NOT HOLD SPEED DURING DYNAMIC TEST

Enter this circuit test only when service Codes 27 and/or 28 are in KEY ON, ENGINE RUNNING SELF-TEST. This circuit test is intended to diagnose speed control servo and vacuum hose connections (servo-to-manifold and servo-to-dump valve).

1) Service Code 27 appears. Repeat KEY ON, ENGINE RUNNING SELF-TEST. Ensure speed control "ON" button is pressed before pressing "STAR" push button. If Code 27 is still present, go to next step. If Code 27 is not present, servo leak down test passed. Service any other service code that may appear.

2) If servo vacuum supply hose is not tightly connected to servo and vacuum manifold, and is not free of cuts or cracks, service vacuum hoses. Repeat QUICK TEST. If okay, replace servo and repeat QUICK TEST. If dump valve hose is not tightly connected to servo and dump valve, and is not free of cuts or cracks, service vacuum hoses. Repeat QUICK TEST. If okay, replace servo and repeat QUICK TEST.

3) Service Code 28 appears. Repeat KEY ON, ENGINE RUNNING SELF-TEST. Ensure speed control "ON" button is pressed before pressing "STAR" push button. If Code 28 is still present, replace servo and repeat QUICK TEST. If not, servo leaks-up-test passed. Service any other service codes that appear as necessary.

CIRCUIT TEST F

SPEED DOES NOT DECREASE DURING DYNAMIC TEST

Enter this circuit test only when service Code 37 is received in KEY ON, ENGINE RUNNING SELF-TEST. This circuit test is intended to diagnose actuator cable adjustment, throttle shaft and linkage, throttle position sensor and ECA.

1) Service Code 37 appears. Repeat KEY ON, ENGINE RUNNING SELF-TEST. Ensure speed control "ON" button is pressed before pressing "STAR" push button. If Code 37 is still present, go to next step. If not, decrease vehicle speed test passed. Service any other service codes that appear as necessary.

2) If throttle shaft or throttle linkage is binding, service to eliminate binding and repeat QUICK TEST. If not, go to step **3)**.

3) If acutator cable binds, replace actuator cable. If not, go to step **4)**.

4) If throttle position sensor is binding, replace throttle position sensor and repeat QUICK TEST. If not, replace ECA and repeat QUICK TEST.

CIRCUIT TEST G

SPEED SENSOR

Enter this circuit test only when directed by KEY ON, ENGINE RUNNING SELF-TEST. This circuit test is intended to diagnose speed sensor resistance, short in sensor input circuit, and open in sensor input circuit.

1) Turn key off, and wait 10 seconds. Disconnect ECA 60-pin connector. Inspect for damage. Service as necessary. Install breakout box, leaving ECA disconnected. Set DVOM to 2000-ohm scale. Measure resistance between test pin No. 3 and test pin No. 6. If DVOM reads less than 180 ohms or greater than 420 ohms, go to step **2)**. If DVOM reading is 180-240 ohms, replace ECA and repeat QUICK TEST.

2) Turn key off. Remove connector from vehicle speed sensor. Set DVOM on 2000-ohm scale. Measure resistance between 2 connector pins on speed sensor. If DVOM reads less than 180 ohms or greater than 240 ohms, replace speed sensor and repeat QUICK TEST. If DVOM reading is 180-240 ohms, repair open in wire harness between sensor and EEC-IV pins No. 3 and No. 6. Repeat QUICK TEST.

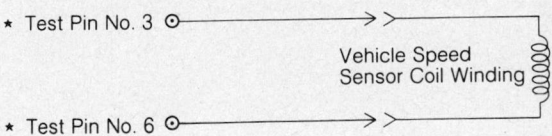

★ Test Pin No. 3
★ Test Pin No. 6
Vehicle Speed Sensor Coil Winding

★ TEST PINS LOCATED ON BREAKOUT BOX.

6-32

1989 CRUISE CONTROL SYSTEMS
Ford Motor Co. — EEC-IV Controlled (Cont.)

CIRCUIT TEST Q

Enter this circuit test only when directed from KEY ON, ENGINE RUNNING or KEY ON, ENGINE OFF SELF-TEST. This circuit test is intended to diagnose only ECA and harness circuits (signal return, STO, STI, and ground).

1) Turn key off and wait 10 seconds. Disconnect ECA 60-pin connector and inspect for damage. Service as necessary. Install breakout box, leaving ECA disconnected. Set DVOM to 200-ohm scale. Measure resistance between SELF-TEST input at SELF-TEST single pin connector and test pin No. 48 at breakout box. If less than 5 ohms, go to next step. If greater than 5 ohms, correct open in circuit.

2) Install breakout box. Set DVOM to 200-ohm scale. Measure resistance between SELF-TEST output at SELF-TEST connector and test pin No. 17 at breakout box. If less than 5 ohms, go to step **3)**. If greater than 5 ohms, correct open in circuit.

3) Install breakout box. Turn key off. Measure resistance between EGO ground on engine and test pin No. 49 at breakout box. If less than 5 ohms, go to step **4)**. If greater than 5 ohms, check and service EGO sensor ground wire or open circuit.

4) Install breakout box. Set DVOM on 200,000-ohm scale. Measure resistance between SELF-TEST output at SELF-TEST connector and engine block ground. If resistance is greater than 10,000 ohms, replace ECA and repeat QUICK TEST. If not, service shorts to ground and repeat QUICK TEST.

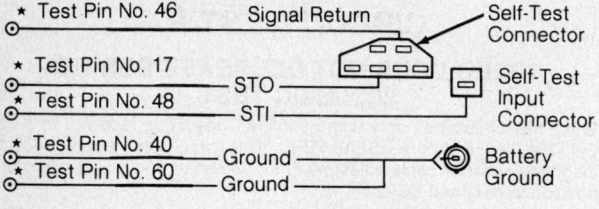

* Test Pin No. 46 — Signal Return — Self-Test Connector
* Test Pin No. 17 — STO
* Test Pin No. 48 — STI — Self-Test Input Connector
* Test Pin No. 40 — Ground
* Test Pin No. 60 — Ground — Battery Ground

★ Test pins on breakout box. All harness connectors viewed into mating surface.

Escort, Grand Marquis (5.8L), LTD Crown Victoria (5.8L), Mustang, Probe, Tempo, Topaz

DESCRIPTION

The cruise control system consists of operator controls, a servo (throttle actuator) assembly, a speed sensor, a clutch switch, a stoplight switch, a vacuum dump valve, an amplifier assembly, a horn relay, wiring harnesses and vacuum hoses.

On Probe, control switches are located on dashboard. On other models, control switches are located in steering wheel. The servo assembly is mounted in engine compartment, and is connected to throttle linkage with an actuator cable. The brake and clutch switches are located on brake pedal support bracket below dashboard. The speed control sensor is located on transaxle or transmission. Models with electronic dashboard use a special connection to speedometer in place of a speed sensor. Amplifier assembly is located below steering column on instrument panel reinforcement.

OPERATION

The cruise control is only operational at speeds above 30 MPH. The system is activated when cruise control switch is set to "ON" position and "SET/ACCEL" or "SET" button is depressed and released. The vehicle speed will be maintained until a new speed is set, the brake or clutch pedal is depressed, or until system is turned off. When the system has been deactivated by depressing brake or clutch pedal, the driver can re-establish the set speed by pressing and releasing "RESUME" button.

When brake pedal is depressed, an electrical signal from stoplight is sent to the amplifier, turning off system. In addition (when brake pedal is depressed), the vacuum dump valve mechanically releases vacuum from servo, thus releasing the throttle independently of the amplifier control.

ADJUSTMENTS

LINKAGE

Actuator Cable Type (Probe) – 1) On turbo models equipped with electric actuator, remove plastic cover. On all models, loosen lock nut and adjusting nuts.
2) Pull on cable housing without moving actuator rod. Position outer adjusting nut until there is .039-.118" (1-3 mm) clearance between outer adjusting nut and bracket. Tighten inside lock nut. On turbo models, replace electric actuator plastic cover.
Actuator Cable Type (Other Models) – Remove speed control actuator cable retaining clip. Push actuator cable through adjuster until slight tension is felt. Insert cable retaining clip and snap into place.
Bead Type Chain (Escort, Tempo & Topaz) – Remove locking pin. Pull bead chain through adjuster. Insert locking pin in best hole of adjuster for tight bead chain without opening throttle plate.

VACUUM DUMP VALVE

1) Dump valve should be adjusted so that there is no vacuum leakage when brake pedal is not depressed, and there is vacuum leakage when pedal is depressed. Check with vacuum pump.
2) If adjustment is required, hold brake pedal in depressed position and push valve into valve collar as far as it will go. Place a .050-

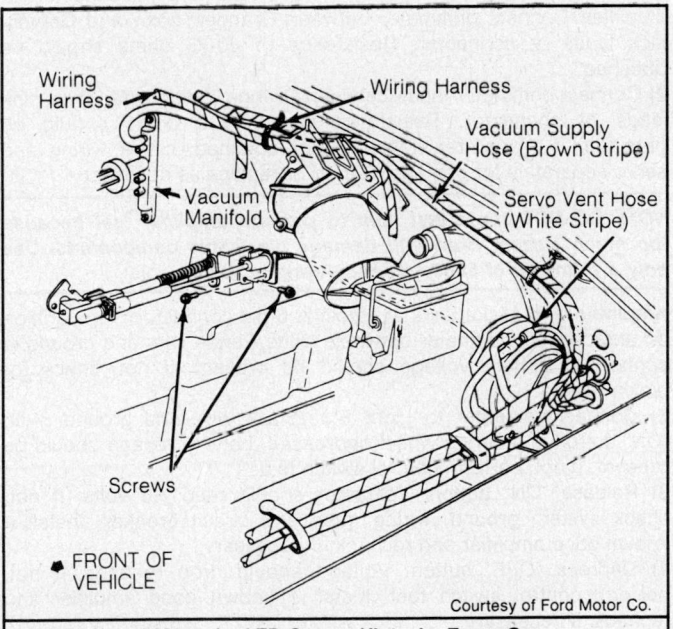

Fig. 1: Grand Marquis, LTD Crown Victoria, Town Car Automatic Cruise Control Components

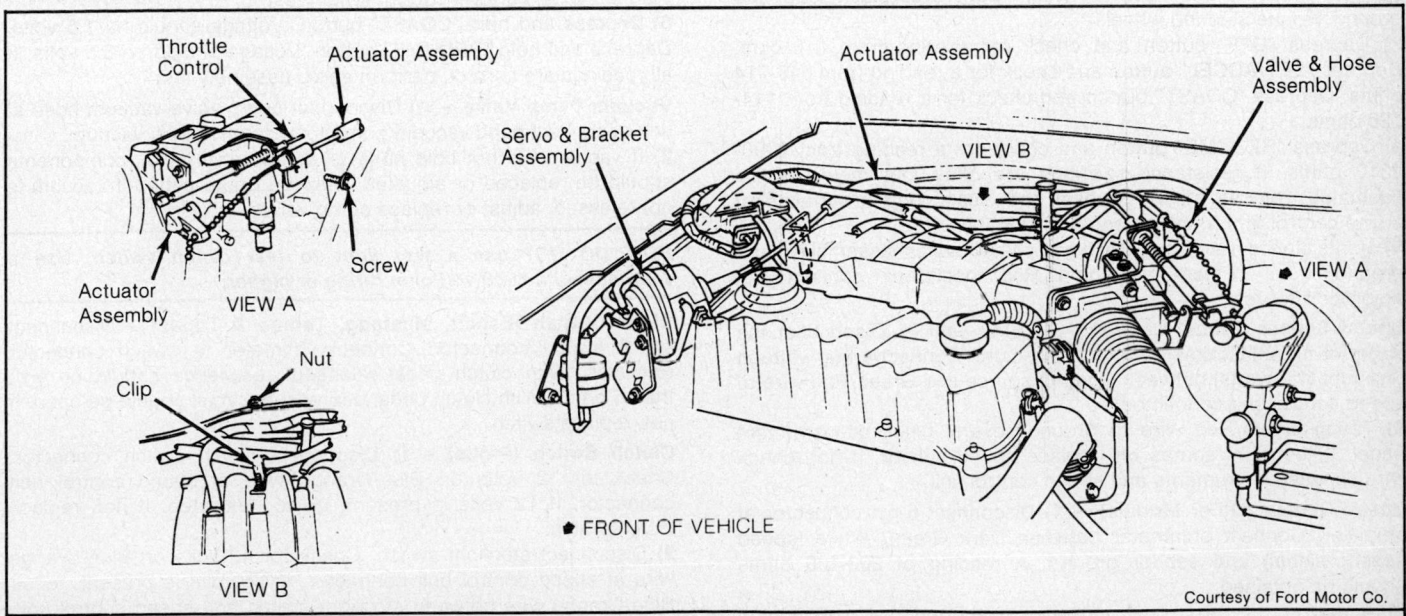

Fig. 2: Tempo & Topaz Cruise Control Component Location

6-34

1989 CRUISE CONTROL SYSTEMS
Ford Motor Co. – Except EEC-IV Controlled (Cont.)

.100" (1.27-2.54 mm) shim between White valve button and pad (adapter on some models) on brake pedal.

3) Pull brake pedal fully rearward and remove shim. Valve button should now be slightly above or just touching in pad (adapter) on brake pedal.

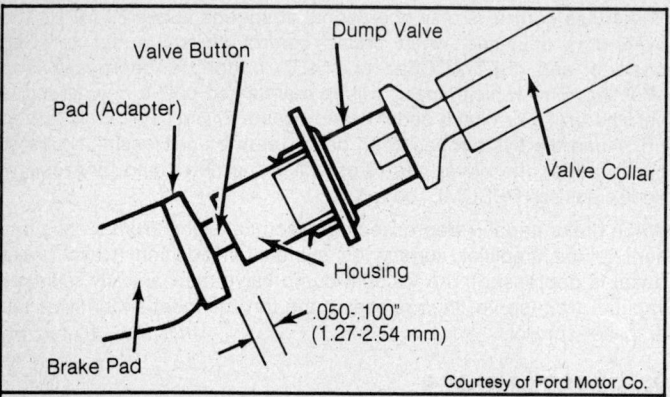

Fig. 3: Vacuum Dump Valve Adjustment

CLUTCH SWITCH

Prop clutch pedal in full-up position (pawl fully released from sector). Loosen switch mounting screw. Slide switch forward toward clutch pedal until switch plunger cap is approximately .030" (.76 mm) from contacting switch housing. Tighten attaching screw to complete adjustment.

TROUBLE SHOOTING

Check all electrical and vacuum connections. Press brake pedal and check brake lights work. If not, repair brake light circuit. Check clutch switch on manual transmission vehicles. Check servo and throttle linkage for free operation. If components appear to be in good condition, proceed to TESTING procedures.

TESTING

Control Switches – 1) Check main feed fuse and stoplight fuse. If fuse is okay, turn ignition off and disconnect 6-pin connector at amplifier assembly. Connect voltmeter between Light Blue/Black lead and ground.
2) Turn ignition on. Depress "ON" button and check for battery voltage. Connect ohmmeter between Light Blue/Black lead and ground. Rotate steering wheel.
3) Depress "OFF" button and check for reading from 0-1 ohm. Depress "SET/ACCEL" button and check for a reading from 646-714 ohms. Depress "COAST" button and check for a reading from 114-126 ohms.
4) Depress "RESUME" button and check for a reading from 2090-2310 ohms. If resistance readings are okay, but meter needle fluctuates, remove steering wheel and clean contact surfaces of cruise control ground brush and turn signal brush.
5) If resistance readings are high, check switch assemblies and ground circuit in steering column. Reconnect 6-pin connector at amplifier after test.

Speed Sensor (Probe Models) – 1) Stop vehicle. Disconnect the larger of the 2 instrument panel connectors. Connect a low wattage test light (1.4 watts) between 12 volts source and Green/Red wire of speed control unit connector.
2) Touch Green/Red wire to ground several times at instrument panel. If test light comes on, replace speed sensor. If not, check wire between instruments and speed control unit.

Speed Sensor (Other Models) – 1) Disconnect 6-pin connector at amplifier. Connect ohmmeter between Dark Green/ White (speed sensor signal) and sensor ground. A reading of 200-300 ohms should be obtained.
2) A reading of zero ohms indicates a shorted coil, and a high reading indicates an open coil in sensor or open wire in harness.

Repeat test at sensor. Replace sensor if resistance is not within 200-300 ohms. Repair wire harness if sensor resistance is okay.
3) If ohmmeter reads 200-300 ohms and speedometer operates properly within needle waver, sensor is probably good. Substitute a known good sensor if necessary to check operation.

Servo Assembly (Escort, Tempo & Topaz) – 1) Separate 8-pin connector at amplifier. Connect an ohmmeter between Orange/Yellow and Gray/Black wires at servo connector. Resistance should be 40-70 ohms.
2) Connect ohmmeter between Orange/Yellow and White/Pink wires. Resistance reading should be 110-140 ohms.
3) Connect Purple/Lt. Brown between Brown/Lt. Green leads. A resistance of 40,000-60,000 ohms chould be obtained. Connect ohmmeter between Yellow/Red and Brown/Lt. Green leads. A resistance of 20,000-30,000 ohms should be obtained.
4) If proper resistance is not obtained, check wiring and servo separately for damage. Replace or repair as necessary.

Servo Assembly (Mustang) – 1) Separate 8-pin connector at amplifier. Connect ohmmeter between Orange/Yellow and Gray/Black leads at connector. Resistance of 40-75 ohms should be obtained.
2) Connect ohmmeter leads between Orange/Yellow and White/pink leads of connector. Resistance of 100-150 ohms should be obtained. If proper resistance is not obtained, check wiring and servo separately for damage. Repair or replace as necessary.

NOTE: DO NOT use a test light to perform amplifier test because too much current draw will damage electronic components. Use only a voltmeter of 5000 volt/ohm rating or higher.

Amplifier – 1) Make tests at amplifier 6-pin connector. Turn ignition on and connect voltmeter between White/Purple wire and ground in connector. Battery voltage should be present. If not, check for blown fuse.
2) Connect voltmeter to Light Blue/Black wire and ground. With "ON" button in steering wheel depressed, battery voltage should be present. If not, perform control switch test.
3) Release "ON" button. Voltmeter should read 7.8 volts. If not, check system ground, wiring, fuse and circuit breaker. Install a known good amplifier and recheck, if necessary.
4) Depress "OFF" button. Voltage should drop to zero. If not, perform control switch test. Install a known good amplifier and recheck, if necessary.
5) Depresss and hold "SET-ACCEL" button. Voltmeter should read 4.5 volts. Rotate steering wheel several times. If voltage varies more than 0.5 volts, perform control switch test.
6) Depress and hold "COAST" button. Voltage should be 1.5 volts. Depress and hold "RESUME" button. Voltage should be 6.5 volts. If all readings are correct, perform servo assembly test.

Vacuum Dump Valve – 1) Disconnect dump valve vacuum hose at servo, connect hand vacuum pump to hose and apply vacuum.
2) If vacuum will not hold hose or dump valve leaks, components should be replaced or adjusted. Step on brake pedal. If vacuum is not released, adjust or replace dump valve.

NOTE: DO NOT use a test light to test clutch switch. Use a voltmeter with 5000 volt/ohm rating or higher.

Clutch Switch (Escort, Mustang, Tempo & Topaz) – Disconnect clutch switch connector. Connect voltmeter to switch connector terminals. With clutch pedal released, resistance should be less than 5 ohms. With clutch pedal depressed, circuit should be open. If not, replace switch.

Clutch Switch (Probe) – 1) Disconnect clutch switch connector. Check for 12 volts on Blue/Orange wire at speed control unit connector. If 12 volts is present, go to next step. If not, replace clutch switch.
2) Disconnect stoplight switch. Check for 12 volts on Blue/Orange wire at speed control unit connector. If 12 volts is present, repair Blue/Orange wire between stoplight switch and speed control unit. If not, replace stoplight switch.

1989 CRUISE CONTROL SYSTEMS
Ford Motor Co. — Except EEC-IV Controlled (Cont.)

6-35

REMOVAL & INSTALLATION

SERVO ASSEMBLY

Removal & Installation – 1) Remove air cleaner. Remove retaining clip screw and disconnect actuator cable or bead chain from accelerator cable bracket. Disconnect actuator cable with adjuster from accelerator cable.

2) Remove all vacuum hoses and electrical connector from servo. Remove 2 nuts holding servo to mounting bracket. Carefully remove servo and cable assembly.

3) Remove 2 nuts holding cable cover to servo. Pull off cover and remove cable or bead chain assembly. To install, reverse removal procedure.

AMPLIFIER

Removal & Installation – Remove screws securing amplifier to mounting bracket. Disconnect electrical connections to amplifier and remove amplifier. To install, reverse removal procedure.

SPEED SENSOR

Removal & Installation (All Models Except Escort, Tempo & Topaz) – 1) Raise vehicle on hoist. Remove bolt retaining speed sensor mounting clip to transmission or transaxle. Remove sensor and driven gear from transmission or transaxle. Disconnect electrical connector and speedometer cable from speed sensor.

2) Disconnect speedometer cable by pulling it out of speed sensor. Do not attempt to remove spring retainer clip with speedometer cable in sensor. Remove driven gear retainer. Remove driven gear from sensor. To install, reverse removal procedure.

Removal & Installation (Escort, Tempo & Topaz) – 1) The speed sensor is located on transaxle (Tempo/Topaz), or in engine compartment (Escort). Raise vehicle on hoist and loosen retaining nut holding sensor in transmission. Remove sensor from transmission.

2) Disconnect electrical connector from sensor. Disconnect speedometer cable by pulling it out of speed sensor. DO NOT attempt to remove spring retainer clip with speedometer cable in sensor. To install, reverse removal procedure.

ENGAGEMENT SWITCH

NOTE: See STEERING COLUMN SWITCHES article in STEERING section for engagement switch REMOVAL & INSTALLATION procedure.

WIRING DIAGRAMS

For wiring diagrams, refer to appropriate chassis wiring diagram in WIRING DIAGRAM section.

1989 DEFOGGERS
Ford Motor Co. Rear Window Defogger (Cont.)

REMOVAL & INSTALLATION

CONTROL SWITCH

Removal & Installation (Continental) – Remove right hand instrument panel molding. Remove cluster opening finish panel. Depress switch mounting fingers on either side and pull out switch. Disconnect electrical connector. To install, reverse removal procedure.

Removal & Installation (LTD Crown Victoria, Grand Marquis, Tempo, Topaz & Town Car) – Remove knob from control lever. Remove applique. Remove screws retaining climate control head to instrument panel. Remove control head. Remove control assembly from climate control head assembly. Disconnect electrical connector. To install, reverse removal procedure.

Removal & Installation (Cougar & Thunderbird) – Remove instrument panel trim. Remove electrical connector from control assembly. Push on connector base of control assembly to push control assembly out of trim panel. To install, reverse removal procedure.

Removal & Installation (Escort & Mark VII) – Remove instrument cluster trim panel applique. Remove control assembly retaining screw. Pull control assembly out from instrument panel. Disconnect electrical connector. Remove control assembly. To install, reverse removal procedure.

Removal & Installation (Mustang) – Disengage 2 locking tabs on right side of control by pushing tabs in with a small screwdriver and pulling on right side of control. Using screwdriver, pry left side of control out of instrument panel. Pull control completely out of opening and disconnect 2 connectors. To install, reverse removal procedures.

Removal & Installation (Probe) – 1) Disconnect negative battery terminal. Remove cluster module from vehicle. Remove pushbutton from switch housing by gently prying it off with a screwdriver.
2) Remove mounting screws from defroster switch housing from behind cluster module. Turn rotary headlight switch to "ON" position, to provide clearance for defroster switch removal.
3) Remove defroster switch from behind of cluster module. Disconnect electrical connector. To install, reverse removal procedure.

Removal & Installation (Sable & Taurus) – On Sable models, remove instrument cluster finish panel. On Taurus models, remove lower left finish panel. On all models, disconnect electrical connector. Depress spring locking tabs on control switch and push out of finish panel. To install, reverse removal procedure.

RELAY TIMER

Removal & Installation (Continental & Mustang) – Remove relay control assembly from under instrument panel, on left side, by rotating the assembly 90 degrees. Fit assembly through access hole. Disconnect electrical connector. To install, reverse removal procedure.

WIRING DIAGRAMS

For wiring diagrams, refer to appropriate chassis wiring diagram in WIRING DIAGRAMS section.

Chrysler Motors Door & Trunk Release

DESCRIPTION

The power door lock system includes 2 control switches, a door lock motor for each door and wiring harness. Power is supplied through a 30-amp circuit breaker in fuse panel. The control switches are located on front arm rests of door panels. The trunk release system includes a release button, 6-amp circuit breaker, and latch with an internal solenoid.

OPERATION

All doors are locked by moving either front door locking knobs or switches. Doors can be locked and unlocked manually by using lock knobs. When locked, only left front door can be unlocked by pulling inside door handle. Trunk solenoid is energized only when push button is depressed.

TESTING

NOTE: Battery must be fully charged before testing.

CIRCUIT BREAKER

Pull out circuit breaker so that terminals still contact terminals in fuse block. Using voltmeter, ground negative lead. Place positive lead on each terminal of circuit breaker. Ensure 12 volts exist at both terminals. If voltmeter reads 12 volts at only one terminal, replace circuit breaker. If neither terminal shows 12 volts, check for an open or shorted circuit to circuit breaker.

DOOR LOCK SWITCH VOLTAGE

Remove driver's side door lock switch. Carefully separate multiple terminal block on wiring harness from switch body. Connect test light to Black wire (ground) and touch Red wire terminal with test light point. If test light comes on, wiring circuit between battery and switch is okay. It test light does not light, check 30-amp main fuse (circuit breaker) or for a broken wire.

DOOR LOCK SWITCHES

Remove switch from mounting location. Using an ohmmeter check continuity between switch terminals. See DOOR LOCK SWITCH CONTINUITY table. *See Fig 1.*

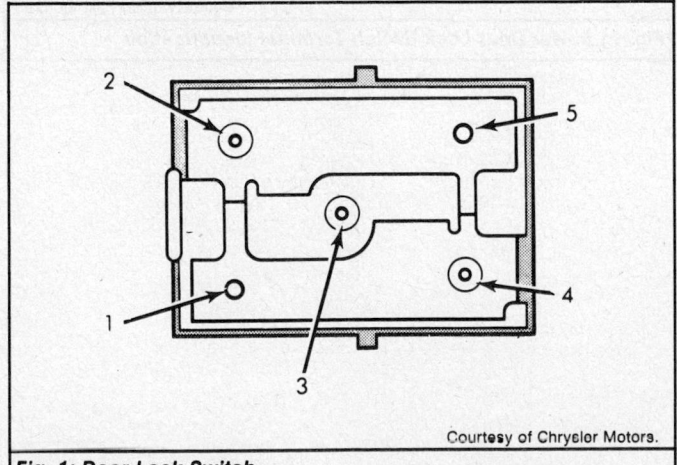

Courtesy of Chrysler Motors.

Fig. 1: Door Lock Switch

DOOR LOCK SWITCH CONTINUITY

Switch Position	Continuity Between Pins
OFF	1 & 4, 2 & 5
LOCK	3 & 4, 2 & 5
UNLOCK	1 & 4, 2 & 3

DOOR LOCK MOTOR

System Check – Ensure battery is fully charged. To determine which motor is faulty, check each door for electrical lock and unlock. Work switch with each motor disconnected. If none of motors work, problem may be a shorted motor. Disconnecting defective motor will allow others to work.

Individual Check – 1) Disconnect connector near motor. Connect 12-volt power source to Orange wire terminal of motor connector and ground Pink wire terminal. Door should lock.
2) Connect 12-volt power source to Pink wire and ground Orange wire. Door should unlock. If motor does not function properly, inspect harness for broken wiring. If wiring is okay, replace door lock motor.

POWER TRUNK PULL-DOWN SYSTEM

Dynasty & New Yorker – 1) Open trunk. With latch switch released, continuity should exist between Black/Red wire terminal and Black wire terminal of latch pull-down connector. With latch switch depressed, continuity should exist between Black wire terminal and Black/White wire terminal. If pull-down latch does not test properly, replace latch.

2) Remove pull-down motor connector. Connect a 12-volt positive source to Pink wire terminal of motor and ground Gray wire terminal. Pull-down bar should retract. Ground Tan wire terminal with positive source still connected to Pink wire terminal. Pull-down bar should raise to open position. If pull-down limit switch is depressed at this time, motor should stop. If these results are not obtained, replace pull-down motor assembly.

HATCHBACK/TRUNK RELEASE

1) Turn ignition switch to "ON" or "ACC" position, trunk should unlock when release button is pressed. If trunk does not unlock, open trunk manually and separate connector at solenoid. Connect voltmeter between solenoid connector and ground.

2) With button pressed, at least 10 volts must be present. If less than 10 volts are indicated, check power feed and wiring. If voltage is present, check solenoid ground connection.

3) With solenoid removed, check plunger spring and plunger for free movement of at least 5/8" (16 mm). Reinstall solenoid. Adjust trunk latch and striker so trunk closes with a moderate slam. If trunk does not lock, replace latch assembly.

REMOVAL & INSTALLATION

ELECTRIC DOOR LOCK MOTORS

Removal & Installation – Remove door release and window regulator handles. Remove trim panel and plastic water shields. Disconnect locking motor from wiring harness. Disconnect motor link at latch. Remove rivets and remove motor from door. Reverse removal procedure to install.

WIRING DIAGRAMS

For wiring diagrams, refer to appropriate chassis wiring diagram in WIRING DIAGRAMS section.

1989 DOOR & TAILGATE LOCKS
Eagle Power Door Locks

Premier

DESCRIPTION

The master door lock switch receives constant voltage from fuse No. 2. Circuit breaker No. 22 applies battery voltage at all times to the door lock relay. Closing a door lock or master door lock switch applies battery voltage to door lock relay terminal No. 1. This energizes the lock coil, causing voltage to travel from terminal No. 5, through normally open lock contacts, to door lock relay terminal No. 4. Door lock relay terminal No. 2 is ground.

TESTING

NO POWER TO SYSTEM

Check fuse No. 2. If fuse is bad, replace. Check battery side of fuse. If battery voltage is not present, repair open circuit to battery. Check and replace circuit breaker No. 22 as necessary. Check terminal No. 5 of door lock relay connector. If battery voltage is not present, repair open circuit to fuse block.

DOOR LOCK RELAY

NOTE: Door lock relay is located behind passenger side kick panel.

1) Remove door lock relay. Using an ohmmeter, check continuity between door lock relay connector terminal No. 2 and ground. If no continuity is present, repair open circuit to ground.
2) Position door lock switch in "LOCK" position. Using a voltmeter, check voltage between door lock relay connector terminal No. 1 and ground. If battery voltage is not present, repair open to fuse block.
3) Position door lock switch in "UNLOCK" position. Using a voltmeter, check voltage between door lock relay connector terminal No. 3 and ground. If battery voltage is not present, repair open to fuse block.
4) Position door lock switch in "LOCK" position. Using a jumper wire, jump door lock relay connector terminal No. 1 to terminal No. 4, and jump terminal No. 6 to terminal No. 2. If doors lock, replace relay. If not, go to next step.
5) Position door lock switch in "UNLOCK" position. Using a jumper wire, jump door lock relay connector terminal No. 3 to terminal No. 6, and jump terminal No. 4 to terminal No. 2. If doors unlock, replace relay. If not, reinstall relay and go to DOOR LOCK MOTOR INOPERATIVE test.

DOOR LOCK MOTOR INOPERATIVE

Position any door lock switch in "LOCK" position. Install a voltmeter in place of motor. If battery voltage is present, replace motor. If voltage is not present, repair open in motor circuit.

DOOR LOCKS INOPERATIVE FROM ONE SWITCH

1) Using a voltmeter, check power output terminal of inoperative switch. *See Fig. 1.* If battery voltage is present, switch is okay. If not, repair open in circuit from fuse panel.
2) Position door lock switch in "UNLOCK" position. Using a voltmeter, check power output terminal of switch. *See Fig. 1.* If battery voltage is present, repair open to door lock relay. If not, replace switch.
3) Position door lock switch in "LOCK" position. Using a voltmeter, check power terminal of switch. If battery voltage is present, repair open to door lock relay. If not, replace switch.

WIRING DIAGRAMS

For wiring diagrams, see appropriate chassis wiring diagram in WIRING DIAGRAM section.

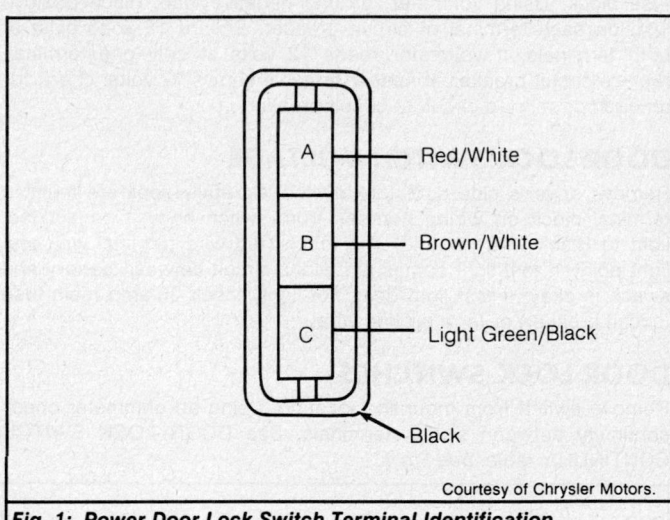

Courtesy of Chrysler Motors.

Fig. 1: Power Door Lock Switch Terminal Identification

Premier

DESCRIPTION

Electric trunk release system consists of a glove box mounted power trunk switch, a trunk latch solenoid and necessary wiring. Battery voltage is supplied from fuse No. 17.

TESTING

TRUNK LID DOES NOT RELEASE (SWITCH DEPRESSED)

1) Using a voltmeter, ensure battery voltage is present between power trunk switch terminal "A" and ground. If battery voltage is not present, repair open circuit to fuse No. 17.

2) Ensure battery voltage is present between power trunk switch terminal "B" and ground. If battery voltage is not present, replace power trunk switch.

3) Ensure battery voltage is present between luggage compartment release solenoid terminal "B" and ground. If battery voltage is not present, repair open circuit to power trunk switch.

4) Using an ohmmeter, check continuity between luggage compartment release solenoid terminal "A" and ground. If continuity is present, replace luggage compartment release solenoid. If no continuity is present, repair open circuit to ground.

REMOVAL & INSTALLATION

POWER TRUNK SWITCH

Removal & Installation – Open glove box and remove glove box liner screws. Remove glove box liner. Lift tab on back of switch and unplug connector. *See Fig. 1.* Remove power trunk switch by pushing on it from inside glove box. To install, reverse removal procedure.

ACTUATOR

Removal & Installation – Open trunk. Remove actuator mounting screws. Remove actuator rod from linkage rod. *See Fig. 2.* Unplug electrical connector and remove actuator. To install, reverse removal procedure.

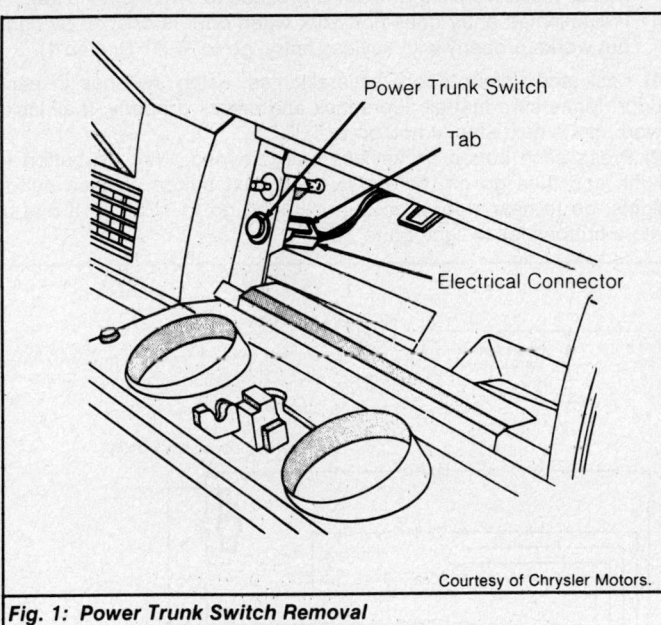

Courtesy of Chrysler Motors.

Fig. 1: Power Trunk Switch Removal

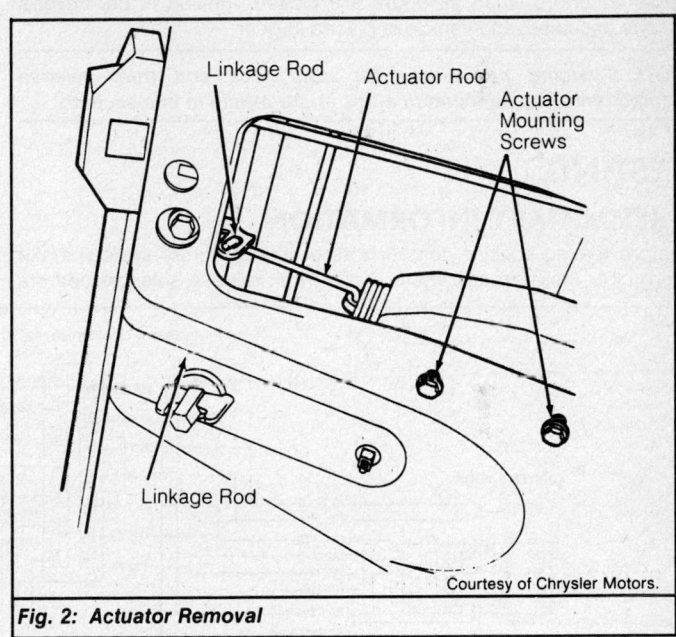

Courtesy of Chrysler Motors.

Fig. 2: Actuator Removal

WIRING DIAGRAMS

For wiring diagrams, see appropriate chassis wiring diagram in WIRING DIAGRAM section.

1989 DOOR & TAILGATE LOCKS
Ford Motor Co. Keyless Entry System

Continental, Cougar, Mark VII, Sable, Taurus, Thunderbird, Town Car

DESCRIPTION

The system components include a driver's seat switch, a keypad, wiring harnesses, and a keyless entry module. On Town Car, module is located behind right side kick panel. On all other models, module is located below rear package shelf in luggage compartment. The system also includes the power door locks and power trunk release.

OPERATION

The keyless entry system enables vehicle to be locked and unlocked without use of a key. The system's operation is controlled by a 5-button keypad on driver's door and keyless entry module.

Pressing correct combination will unlock driver's door and turn on courtesy lights. Pressing additional buttons will open remaining doors, lock all doors or open trunk lid. The system automatically locks all doors when all doors are closed, ignition is on, driver's seat is occupied, and vehicle is placed in gear.

NOTE: Servicing procedures for door lock and trunk release components can be found in appropriate article in this section.

TESTING

PRELIMINARY INFORMATION

Before testing specific components of keyless entry system, make sure door lock actuator motors and trunk release solenoid operate correctly when activated by manual switches. Check for binding linkages and poor wire connections. Lubricate or repair as necessary.

The keyless entry module cannot be serviced and must be replaced as an assembly. Perform QUICK TEST to determine which component needs to be serviced and perform tests as directed. Do not make any other repairs until tests are completed. After repairs, perform QUICK TEST to ensure system works properly.

QUICK TEST

Ensure battery is fully charged. Disconnect and reconnect battery to reset system. If none of the complaints that follow are the problem, go directly to step 1). If any of the complaints that follow seem to be the problem, go to appropriate test.

- If door locks bind when manually operated, proceed to TEST E, step **1)**.
- If system does not operate in freezing temperature, proceed to TEST E, step **19)**.
- If door locks work only when engine is running, proceed to TEST E, step **20)**.
- If door locks work intermittently, proceed to TEST E, step **18)**.
- If illuminated entry does not work when door is opened by hand but works properly with keyless entry, go to TEST D, step **1)**.

1) Lock and unlock doors several times, using switches in each door. Make sure that all doors lock and unlock properly. If all locks work, go to next step. If not, go to TEST E.

2) Press each button on keyless entry keypad. Wait for button to light, and then go off, before pushing next button. If each button lights, go to next step. If no buttons light, go to TEST B. If one or more buttons fail to light, go to TEST C.

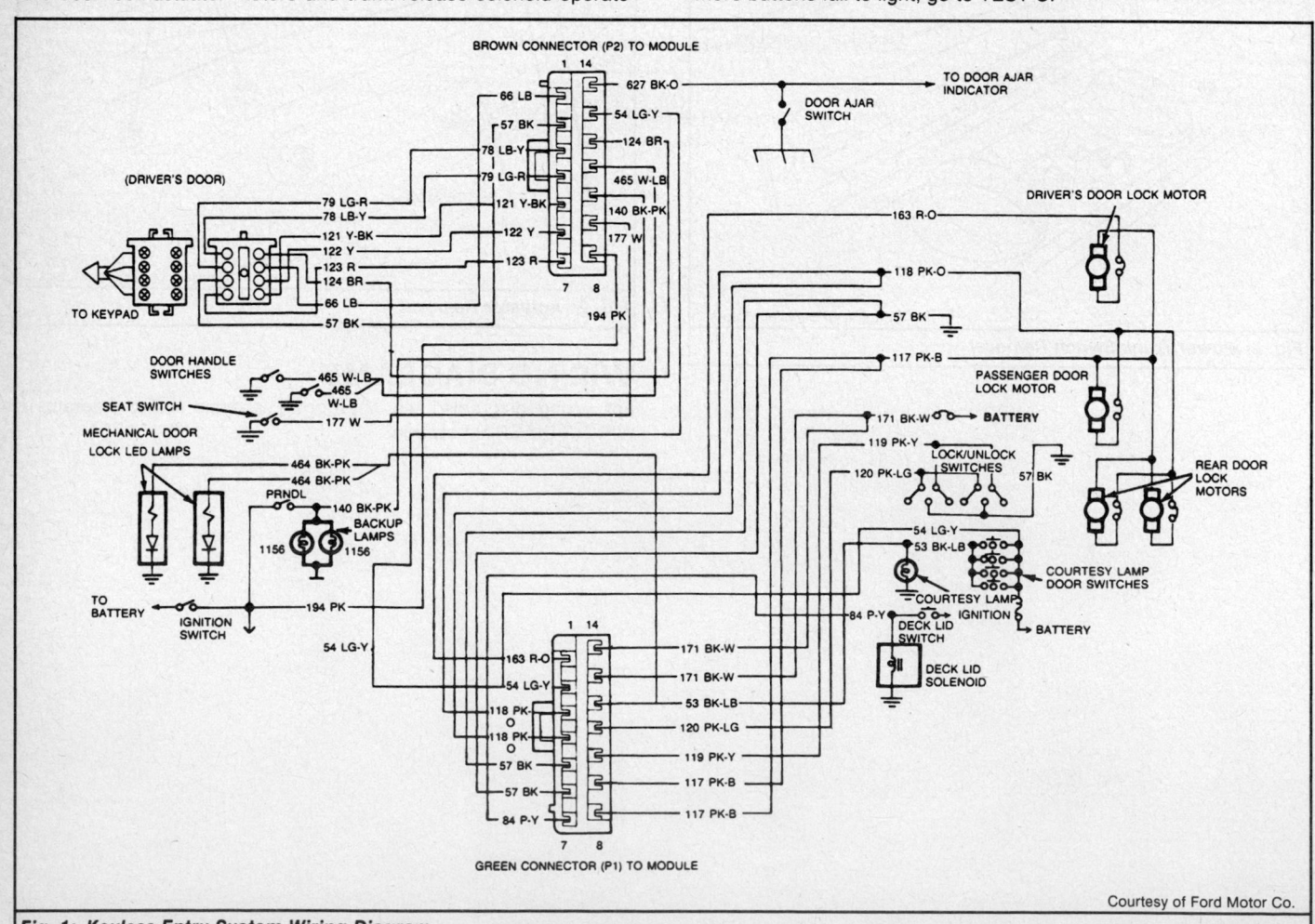

Fig. 1: Keyless Entry System Wiring Diagram

Courtesy of Ford Motor Co.

1989 DOOR & TAILGATE LOCKS
Ford Motor Co. Keyless Entry System (Cont.)

6-43

3) With ignition off and key out of ignition lock, close all doors and trunk. Make sure all doors are unlocked. Simultaneously press "7/8" and "9/0" buttons on keypad. If all doors lock, go to next step. If some doors fail to lock, replace keyless entry module and repeat QUICK TEST. If all doors fail to lock, go to TEST C.

4) Unlock driver's door using permanent code. Code is printed on keyless entry module. If driver's door unlocks, go to next step. If driver's door fails to unlock, go to TEST C.

5) Wait until light on keypad goes out. Re-enter permanent code and press "3/4" button within 5 seconds to unlock all other door(s). If other door(s) unlock, go to next step. If other door(s) fail to unlock, go to TEST C.

6) Wait until light on keypad goes out. Re-enter permanent code and press "5/6" button within 5 seconds to unlock trunk. If trunk unlocks, go to next step. If trunk does not unlock, go to TEST F. If trunk is always unlocked, go to TEST F, step **5)**.

7) Sit in driver's seat. Ensure transmission is in "PARK" position and that interior lights are off. Close all doors, leaving them unlocked. Turn ignition on. Move transmission selector lever to "R" position, and then to "D" position. If all doors lock, go to next step. If some doors fail to lock, go to TEST A.

8) Stay in driver's seat. Place transmission in "D" position, and turn ignition on. Open and then close driver's door. If door locks when closed, go to next step. If not, go to TEST A.

9) Stay in driver's seat. Place transmission in "D" position, and turn ignition on. Open driver's door, and then depress interior light switch with left foot. If door locks, go to TEST A, step **15)**. If door does not lock, go to next step.

10) Place transmission in "PARK" position. Turn ignition off and remove key. Get out of vehicle and close door. Press any button on keypad. If interior lights and keyhole lights for both doors come on, go to next step. If not, go to TEST D.

11) Wait until interior lights go out. Press any keypad button to turn interior lights back on again. Within 5 seconds, press "7/8" and "9/0" buttons simultaneously to turn off lights. If lights go out, go to next step. If not, go to TEST D.

12) With ignition off, transmission in "PARK" and driver's door closed, lift outside handle to open door. Within 25 seconds, get into vehicle and turn ignition on. If lights come on when handle is lifted and then go off when ignition is turned on, go to next step. If lights come on, but do not go out, replace keyless entry module and repeat QUICK TEST. If lights do not come on, go to TEST D.

13) Enter permanent code on keypad. Press "1/2" button to alert system to accept alternate code. Press the following buttons in sequence and within 5 seconds of each other: "9/0", "7/8", "5/6", "3/4", and "1/2". If keypad lights go out, go to next step. If lights stay on, replace keyless entry module and repeat QUICK TEST.

14) Close and lock doors. Press the following buttons in sequence: "9/0", "7/8", "5/6", "3/4", and "1/2". If driver's door unlocks, go to next step. If door stays locked, repeat steps **12)** and **13)**. If system still malfunctions, replace keyless entry module and repeat QUICK TEST.

15) When all keypad lights are off, enter permanent code. Depress "1/2" button within 5 seconds after entering code and wait until keypad lights go out. Close and lock driver's door. Press the following buttons in sequence: "9/0", "7/8", "5/6", "3/4", and "1/2". If doors remain locked, keyless entry system is okay. If some doors unlock, replace keyless entry module and repeat QUICK TEST.

TEST A, AUTOMATIC LOCKING SYSTEM

This test checks driver's seat switch, courtesy light and switches, back-up light switch, keyless entry module, door ajar switch, and related circuits.

1) Using ohmmeter, check continuity between pin No. 2 of Brown connector and ground. If continuity exists, go to next step. If not, repair Black wire in Brown connector. See KEYLESS ENTRY MODULE CONNECTOR TERMINAL IDENTIFICATION.

TEST A (Cont.)

2) Turn ignition off. Disconnect Brown connector. With driver's seat unoccupied, check continuity between pins No. 2 and 9 of connector. If no continuity exists, go to step **4)**. If continuity exists, go to next step.

3) Disconnect driver's seat switch. Check for short between pin No. 9 of Brown connector and ground. If short is found, repair White wire and repeat QUICK TEST. If no short is found, replace seat switch and repeat QUICK TEST.

4) Have an assistant sit in driver's seat. Check continuity between pins No. 2 and 9 in Brown connector. If continuity exists, go to step **6)**. If not, go to next step.

5) With driver's seat occupied, check continuity between pin No. 9 of Brown connector and driver's seat switch connector White wire. If continuity exists, replace seat switch and repeat QUICK TEST. If no continuity exists, repair White wire and repeat QUICK TEST.

6) Using voltmeter, check voltage between pins No. 2 and 13 of Brown connector. If reading is 10 volts or more, go to next step. If reading is less than 10 volts, check for open or shorts in circuits No. 54B and 54C. See KEYLESS ENTRY SYSTEM WIRING DIAGRAM. Repeat QUICK TEST.

7) Check that dome/courtesy lights come on when each courtesy light switch is operated. If lights come on, go to next step. If not, repair switch or wiring and repeat QUICK TEST.

8) Disconnect Green connector. With all doors closed, check voltage between pin No. 12 of Green connector and ground. If reading is zero volts, go to next step. If reading is more than zero volts, replace door switch or repair Black/Light Blue wire. Wire is shorted to battery voltage. Repeat QUICK TEST.

9) Close all doors. Open any door and check voltage at pin No. 12 of Green connector. Repeat procedure for every other door. If all readings are 10 volts or more, go to next step. If not, replace door switch(es) or repair Black/Light Blue wire. Repeat QUICK TEST.

10) Turn ignition off. Check voltage between pin No. 8 of Brown connector and ground. If reading is zero volts, go to next step. If reading is more than zero volts, repair or replace ignition switch. Repeat QUICK TEST.

11) Turn ignition on. Check voltage between pin No. 8 of Brown connector and ground. If reading is 10 volts or more, go to step **13)**. If reading is less than 10 volts, go to next step.

12) Turn ignition off. Check for short between pin No. 8 of Brown connector and ground. Also check for continuity between pin No. 8 and ignition switch circuit No. 194B (Town Car) or 298 (all other models). If wiring is okay, go to next step. If not, replace ignition switch or repair circuit No. 194B or 298. Repeat QUICK TEST.

13) Turn ignition on. With transmission in "R" position, check voltage between pin No. 10 of Brown connector and ground. Shift transmission into all other positions. If reading is 10 volts in "R" and zero volts in any other position, replace keyless entry module. If reading is less than 10 volts in "R" or more than zero volts in all other positions, go to next step.

14) Test operation of back-up light switch by placing transmission in "R" position. Make sure back-up lights come on. If switch is okay, check for open or short in Black/Pink wire. If switch is defective, replace switch and repeat QUICK TEST.

15) Using an ohmmeter, check resistance between pin No. 14 of Brown connector and ground. Lift outside door handle to open door latch, observe ohmmeter, and then close latch with a screwdriver. If reading is greater than 10,000 ohms with latch closed and less than 10 ohms with latch open, replace keyless entry module and repeat QUICK TEST.

1989 DOOR & TAILGATE LOCKS
Ford Motor Co. Side Doors

Continental, Cougar, Grand Marquis, LTD Crown Victoria, Mark VII, Mustang, Sable, Taurus, Tempo, Thunderbird, Topaz, Town Car

DESCRIPTION

The power door lock system is controlled by rocker switches or push buttons. The driver's and passenger's door lock switches/buttons are on the door armrests. On Cougar, LTD Crown Victoria (4-door), Grand Marquis (4-door), Tempo, Thunderbird, Topaz, and Town Car models, door lock/unlock relays control the power distribution. On all other models, power is supplied directly to the switches and door lock motors.

OPERATION

On models with door lock/unlock relays, both wires of each lock motor are normally grounded through the relays. When the door lock switch/button is pressed to "LOCK", the lock relay operates. Current flows through the relay to the motors and grounds through the normally closed contacts of the unlock relay. To unlock, the door lock switch/button is pressed to "UNLOCK" and the unlock relay operates. Current flows through all the motors in the opposite direction and grounds through the lock relay.

On models without door lock/unlock relays, the door lock motors are normally grounded through both control switches. When a control switch is pressed to the "LOCK" position, current is applied through that switch to the motors and grounded through the normally closed contacts of the other switch. Power and ground are reversed when the control switch is pressed to the "UNLOCK" position.

TROUBLE SHOOTING

ONE DOOR LOCK DOES NOT OPERATE

Check for binding and interference around latch and all linkage. Lubricate latch and manually cycle latch 10 times. Check for voltage at motor connector, operating switch in both positions. See MOTOR in TESTING section of this article. Replace motor if necessary.

ALL DOOR LOCKS DO NOT OPERATE

Check for blown fuse and replace if necessary. Check wiring and connections between circuit breaker and door lock switches for open or short. Check relay and bracket attaching screws for poor ground. Check left control switch for open ground circuit. See DOOR LOCK SWITCH in TESTING section of this article.

DOOR LOCKS OPERATE ONE WAY ONLY

Check for corroded wiring and loose connections between relays and door lock switches. Check relay for malfunction. See RELAY in TESTING section of this article. Check ground circuit from left control switch.

DOOR LOCKS OPERATE INTERMITTENTLY

Check for loose connectors and tighten if necessary. Check relay and bracket attaching screws for poor ground. Check left control switch for poor ground. See DOOR LOCK SWITCH in TESTING section of this article.

DOOR LOCKS OPERATE FROM ONE SWITCH ONLY

Check wiring and connections between fuse and inoperative switch for open or shorted circuit. Test control switch for malfunction. See DOOR LOCK SWITCH in TESTING of this article.

DOOR LOCKS OPERATE WITH ENGINE RUNNING ONLY

Ensure battery is fully charged. Check for corroded wiring and loose connections. Check for interference around latch and all linkage. Lubricate latch and manually cycle latch 10 times.

DOOR LOCKS DO NOT OPERATE IN BELOW FREEZING WEATHER

Bring vehicle into heated garage to allow lock system to thaw. Verify that all locks now work. Check for interference around night latch and all linkage. Lubricate latch and manually cycle latch 10 times. It may be necessary to remove door trim panel to lubricate entire latch and linkage system.

TESTING

MOTOR

Apply 12 volts directly to motor terminals. The motor should finish its travel in one second or less. Reverse test leads and retest. Using an ammeter, check current draw. Current draw should not exceed 6 amps.

DOOR LOCK SWITCH

NOTE: Use a self-powered test light to perform switch continuity tests.

Continental & Town Car (Master Switch) – 1) Remove switch from vehicle. With switch in normal (Neutral) position, continuity should not exist between terminals No. 12, 13, and 14. See Fig. 1.
2) With switch in "LOCK" position, continuity should exist between terminals No. 12 and 13. With switch in "UNLOCK" position, continuity should exist between terminals No. 12 and 14. If continuity is incorrect, replace switch.

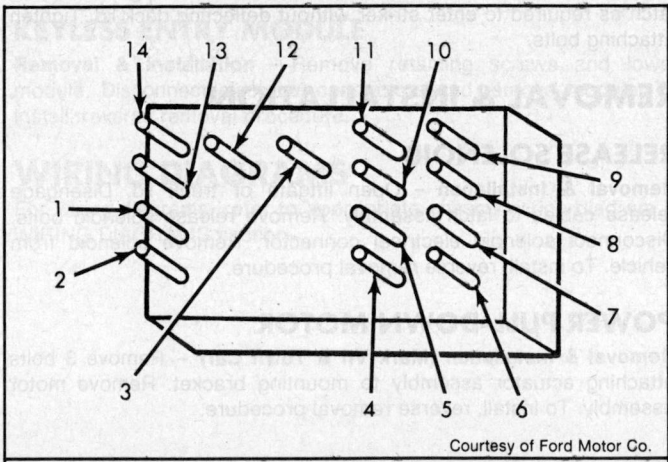

Courtesy of Ford Motor Co.

Fig. 1: Continental & Town Car (Master Switch) Door Lock Switch Terminal Identification

Town Car (Passenger Door Only), LTD Crown Victoria, Grand Marquis & Mark VII – 1) With switch in normal (Neutral) position, there should be continuity between terminals No. 1 and 3, terminals No. 2 and 5, and between terminals No. 4 and 6. See Fig. 2.
2) With toggle switch pushed downward, there should be continuity between terminals No. 2, 4 and 5. Continuity should also exist between terminals No. 1 and 3. Terminal No. 6 should not have continuity with any other terminal.
3) With toggle switch pushed upward, there should be continuity between terminals No. 2, 3 and 5. Continuity should also exist between terminals No. 4 and 6. Terminal No. 1 should not have continuity with any other terminal.

1989 DOOR & TAILGATE LOCKS
Ford Motor Co. Side Doors (Cont.)

6-49

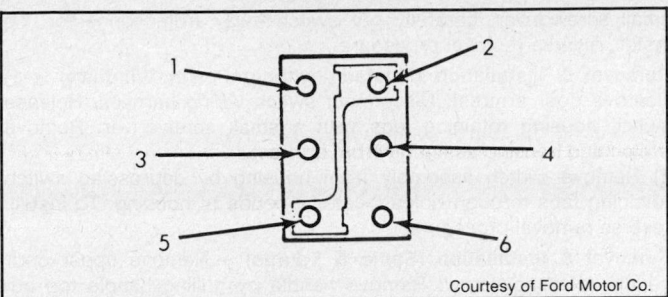

Fig. 2: LTD Crown Victoria, Grand Marquis, Mark VII & Town Car Door Lock Switch Terminal Identification

Cougar & Thunderbird – 1) With switch in normal (Neutral) position, there should be no continuity between terminals. With switch in "LOCK" position, there should be continuity between terminals No. 2 and 3. Terminal No. 1 should not have continuity with any other terminal.

2) With switch in "UNLOCK" position, there should be continuity between terminals No. 1 and 2. *See Fig. 3.* Terminal No. 3 should not have continuity with any other terminal. If continuity is incorrect, replace switch.

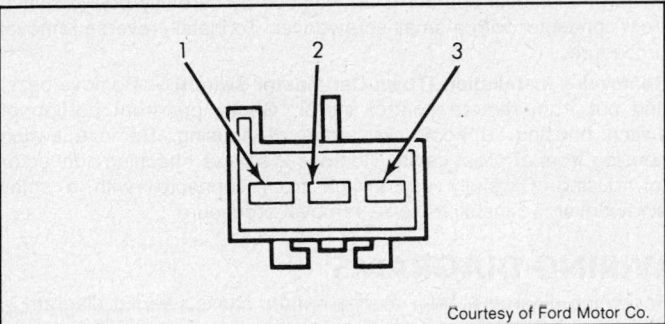

Fig. 3: Cougar & Thunderbird Door Lock Switch Terminal Identification

Continental, Mustang, Sable & Taurus – 1) Position switch so that raised portion of switch knob (marked "L") is to right, with 5 terminals toward you. With switch in normal (Neutral) position, there should be continuity between terminals No. 1 and 2, and between terminals No. 3 and 4. Terminal No. 5 should not have continuity with any other terminal.

2) When "L" portion of switch is pushed, there should be continuity between terminals No. 1 and 5, and between terminals No. 3 and 4.

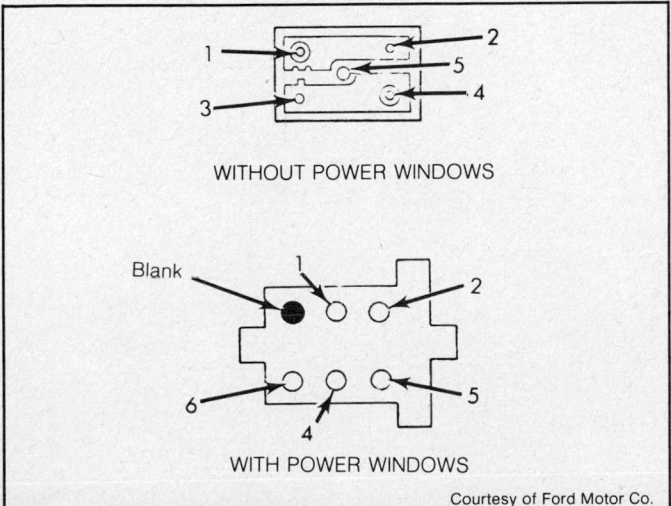

WITHOUT POWER WINDOWS

WITH POWER WINDOWS

Fig. 4: Continental, Mustang, Sable & Taurus Door Lock Switch Terminal Identification

See Fig. 4. Terminal No. 2 should not have continuity with any other terminal.

3) When "U" portion of switch is pushed, there should be continuity between terminals No. 1 and 2, and between terminals No. 4 and 5. Terminal No. 3 should not have continuity with any other terminal. If continuity is incorrect, replace switch.

Tempo & Topaz (2-Door) – Check for continuity between terminals with switch in normal (Neutral) position. If there is continuity, replace switch. With switch held in "LOCK" position, there should be continuity between terminals No. 1 and 2. *See Fig. 5.* With switch held in "UNLOCK" position, there should be continuity between terminals No. 2 and 3. If switch fails test, replace switch.

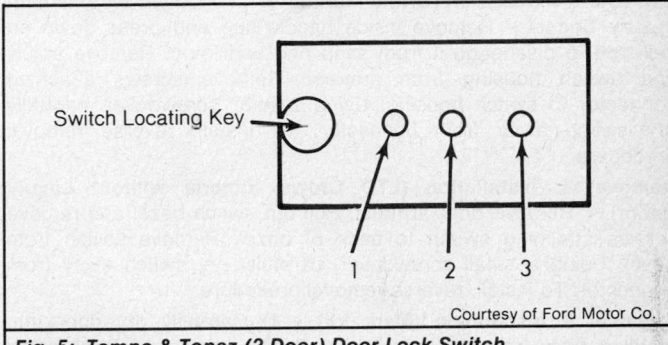

Fig. 5: Tempo & Topaz (2-Door) Door Lock Switch Terminal Identification

RELAY

Cougar, Tempo, Thunderbird & Topaz – 1) Find door lock relays. On Cougar and Thunderbird, relays are located under passenger's seat. On Tempo and Topaz, relays are located in luggage compartment, under center of package tray.

2) Using a voltmeter, verify that terminal No. 4 on relays has 12 volts. *See Fig. 6.* Terminals No. 1 and 5 should be grounded. If not, check ground connection.

3) Disconnect relays. Ground terminal No. 1 on relays. Apply voltage to terminals No. 2 and 4 on each relay. Connect a test light between terminal No. 3 and ground. If test light does not light, replace relay(s).

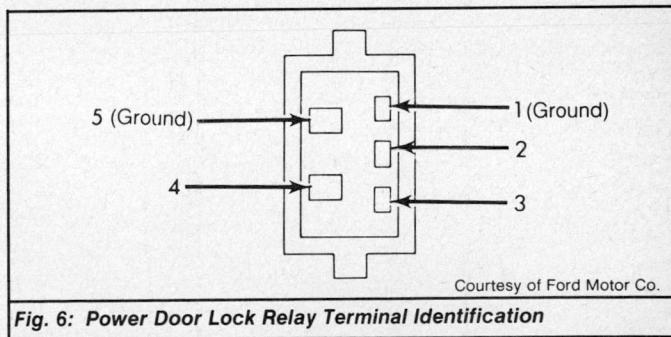

Fig. 6: Power Door Lock Relay Terminal Identification

REMOVAL & INSTALLATION

DOOR LOCK ACTUATOR MOTOR

Removal & Installation – Remove door trim panel and water shield. Disconnect actuator motor link from door latch. Remove screws or drill out rivets attaching actuator motor to door. Disconnect wiring connector. Remove motor. To install, reverse removal procedure.

DOOR LOCK SWITCH

Removal & Installation (Continental) – On right front door, remove screw from under ashtray lid. Using a small screwdriver, carefully pry end of housing upward until housing can be removed from

6-50

1989 DOOR & TAILGATE LOCKS
Ford Motor Co. Side Doors (Cont.)

armrest. Remove screws retaining connector to housing. Using a small screwdriver, carefully pry switch away from connector. To install, reverse removal procedure.

Removal & Installation (Cougar & Thunderbird with Luxury Decor) – Remove armrest plate assembly. Disconnect wiring connector. Remove nuts attaching switch to armrest plate assembly. To install, reverse removal procedure.

Removal & Installation (Cougar & Thunderbird without Luxury Decor) – Remove armrest pad. Pull wiring connector up through access hole in armrest base and disconnect. Remove door trim panel. Carefully pry up on wiring retainers at armrest base. Remove nuts holding switch to base. To install, reverse removal procedure.

Removal & Installation (Grand Marquis & LTD Crown Victoria with Luxury Decor) – Remove inside handle cup and press down on lock rod to disengage it from snap ring and knob. Remove screw and switch housing from armrest. Remove screws attaching connector to switch housing. Using a small screwdriver, carefully pry switch away from connector. To install, reverse removal procedure.

Removal & Installation (LTD Crown Victoria without Luxury Decor) – Remove door armrest. Pull out switch bezel and remove screws attaching switch to back of bezel. Remove switch from bezel. Using a small screwdriver, carefully pry switch away from connector. To install, reverse removal procedure.

Removal & Installation (Mark VII) – 1) Carefully pry door trim molding away from door trim panel. Remove door trim finish panel retaining screws and panel. Remove screws retaining power seat switch to finish panel. Disengage power door lock wiring retainer from power seat switch.

2) Move power seat switch to expose power door lock switch connector. Remove 2 screws holding power door lock connector to finish panel. Remove connector. Using a small screwdriver, carefully pry switch away from connector. To install, reverse removal procedure.

Removal & Installation (Mustang with Power Windows) – Remove switch housing attaching screw and rotate housing up and out of armrest. Remove connector attaching screws from switch. Using a

small screwdriver, carefully pry switch away from connector. To install, reverse removal procedure.

Removal & Installation (Mustang without Power Windows) – 1) Remove door armrest. Disconnect switch wiring harness. Release switch housing retaining legs with a small screwdriver. Remove switch and housing assembly from armrest.

2) Remove switch assembly from housing by depressing switch retaining tabs through holes located at ends of housing. To install, reverse removal procedure.

Removal & Installation (Sable & Taurus) – Remove upper door handle retaining screw. Remove handle by pulling handle top out and up. Remove 2 switch mounting plate retaining screws. Using a screwdriver, carefully pry switch plate from door panel. Rotate switch plate and remove electrical connector. Remove switch. To install, reverse removal procedure.

Removal & Installation (Tempo & Topaz) – 1) On 2 door models, insert small screwdriver in slot at bottom of switch-to-bezel assembly. Carefully pry assembly from trim panel. Spread 2 connector latch tabs and disconnect electrical connector. Remove switch. To install, reverse removal procedure.

2) On 4 door models, remove switch housing attaching screw and rotate housing up and out of armrest. Remove 2 connector attaching screws from bottom of switch housing. Switch is held in place by electrical contact pins. Remove by carefully prying switch from connector with a small screwdriver. To install, reverse removal procedure.

Removal & Installation (Town Car Master Switch) – Remove bezel and nut from remote control mirror. Gently pry front portion of switch housing. Unhook rear edge of housing. Remove switch housing from armrest cavity. Remove 2 screws attaching connector to housing. Carefully pry switch from connector with a small screwdriver. To install, reverse removal procedure.

WIRING DIAGRAMS
For wiring diagrams, refer to appropriate chassis wiring diagram in WIRING DIAGRAMS section.

Daytona, LeBaron GTS, New Yorker

DESCRIPTION

Daytona models use 2 headlight door drive motors with internal ground switches to prevent headlights from illuminating until headlight doors are fully open. The headlight ground switch is part of headlight door drive motor assembly and cannot be serviced separately.

LeBaron GTS and New Yorker models use a single motor, centrally located behind radiator grille, linked to headlight doors by a torsion bar. The headlight door drive motors are equipped with a manual override hand wheel to open or close headlight doors if a failure should occur or servicing is required. Access to hand wheel can be gained through a flap covered hole in the sight shield behind bumper fascia, under the hood. Several turns of the hand wheel may be required to visually notice movement in headlight door assemblies.

OPERATION

The headlight system is controlled by a Concealed Headlight Control Module (CHCM). The CHCM is located in instrument panel under the top cover. The CHCM receives input information from the ignition switch, headlight switch and headlight dimmer switch.

The CHCM controls the time delay headlight system (if equipped). By turning off ignition switch and then turning off headlight switch, the CHCM will allow headlights to remain on for 75 seconds before they automatically turn off and close the headlight doors.

The CHCM also controls headlight doors when the passing lights are used. With headlights turned off, actuating headlight dimmer switch will signal the CHCM to open headlight doors. The operator then has 2 seconds to flash the bright lights before the CHCM closes the headlight doors. Holding headlight dimmer switch in the engaged position will signal the CHCM to keep headlight doors open until dimmer switch is released. Actuating headlight dimmer switch with parking lights on will signal the CHCM to open headlight doors and keep them open until headlights are turned off.

ADJUSTMENTS

Adjustment procedures are not available from manufacturer.

TROUBLE SHOOTING

BOTH HEADLIGHT DOORS INOPERATIVE

Turn on headlights and place ignition switch in "RUN" position. If headlight doors do not operate check following possible causes:

- Burned out fuse, circuit breaker or fusible link caused by a short to body ground.
- Wire connector or pin inside connector disengaged at any connector or component in system.
- Defective electronic component.
- Defective electronic module.
- Subfreezing weather conditions, mechanical failure, corroded or misaligned assemblies.

ONE HEADLIGHT DOOR INOPERATIVE

Turn on headlights and place ignition switch in "RUN" position. If only one headlight door opens check following possible causes:

Daytona

- Wire connector or pin in connector disengaged at any junction or component forward of engine comparatment dash panel.
- Corroded wire terminals.
- Headlight door crank link arm disconnected or broken.
- Defective motor.
- Subfreezing weather conditions, mechanical failure, corroded or misaligned assemblies.

LeBaron GTS & New Yorker

- Headlight door pivot or crank seized.
- Headlight torsion bar sleeve or clip excessively worn or broken.
- Headlight door crank screw missing or broken.
- Headlight torsion bar broken of disengaged.

HEADLIGHT DOOR OPERATES ERRATICALLY

Check following possible causes:

- Headlight door pivot or crank seized.
- Corroded or misaligned assemblies.
- Stripped motor reduction gears.
- Defective motor.
- Defective electronic module.

HEADLIGHT DOOR FITS POORLY

Check following possible causes:

Daytona

- Headlight door bumper fascia mounting bracket or adjustable stops misaligned.

LeBaron GTS & New Yorker

- Headlight door pivot bracket or door/crank lateral adjustment collar misaligned.
- Pivot bushings worn or missing.
- Up or down stop bumper missing.
- Defective motor.

REMOVAL & INSTALLATION

HEADLIGHT DOOR

Removal & Installation (Daytona) – 1) Remove manual override hand wheel cover and open headlight door. Remove headlight trim bezel. Remove "E" ring from motor crank and separate link arm from crank.

2) Remove 2 pivot screws from headlight door assembly. Carefully rotate headlight assembly upward and out of bumper fascia. To install, reverse removal procedure.

Removal & Installation (LeBaron GTS) – 1) Remove radiator grille from grille bezel. Remove retaining clip from torsion bar coupling sleeve.

2) Slide coupling sleeve from door crank and loosen door adjustment collar set screw. Remove door crank attaching screw located in access hole below adjustment collar when headlight door is open. Remove door crank from pivot bushing. Remove pivot screw from outside pivot bracket.

3) Position outside end of headlight door under bumper fascia support and lift inside end of door to clear bumper fascia opening. Remove headlight door from vehicle. *See Fig. 1.* To install, reverse removal procedure.

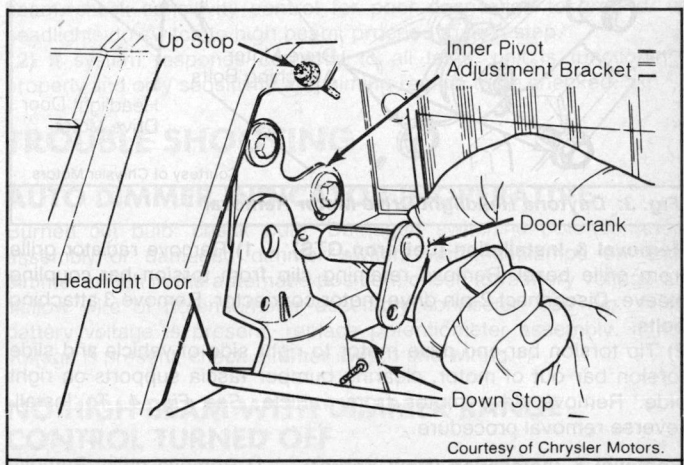

Up Stop

Inner Pivot Adjustment Bracket

Headlight Door

Door Crank

Down Stop

Courtesy of Chrysler Motors.

Fig. 1: LeBaron GTS Headlight Door Crank Removal

1989 POWER ANTENNAS
Ford Motor Co.

Continental, Cougar, LTD Crown Victoria, Grand Marquis, Mark VII, Thunderbird, Sable, Taurus, Town Car

DESCRIPTION & OPERATION

The power antenna is activated by an instrument panel mounted switch which controls antenna height as selectd by operator. The power antenna system consists of the antenna assembly with mast, motor and switch.

TROUBLE SHOOTING

ANTENNA DOES NOT RAISE OR LOWER

1) Check for battery voltage at antenna motor connector. With switch actuated to "UP" position, Red/Pink wire should have battery voltage. With switch actuated to "DOWN" position, Dark Green/Yellow wire should have battery voltage.
2) If voltage is not present on one or both of the connectors, check fuse and antenna switch wiring. If voltage is present at both connectors, replace antenna motor assembly.

FADING OR WEAK RECEPTION

Check antenna connections. If connections are properly mated but reception is still poor, replace antenna cable.

TESTING

ANTENNA TEST

1) Using an ohmmeter, connect one lead to tip of antenna cable and other lead to tip of antenna and check for continuity. Connect one lead to tip of antenna cable and other lead to ground behind sheath of antenna cable. There should be no continuity.
2) If any ohmmeter reading is unsatisfactory, replace antenna mast and cable assembly. If results are satisfactory, antenna mast and cable assembly are okay.

REMOVAL & INSTALLATION

ANTENNA MOTOR

Removal & Installation (Continental & Mark VII) – 1) Lower antenna. Disconnect battery cable. Remove cap on antenna base. Remove nut securing antenna to base. Remove 2 screws attaching base to right quarter panel. Remove base and gasket assembly. Disconnect electrical connector and antenna cable.
2) From inside trunk, remove bolt retaining tube and bracket motor assembly to trunk. Remove antenna by pulling down through quarter panel. To install, reverse removal procedure.

Removal & Installation (Cougar & Thunderbird) – 1) Lower antenna and remove right cowl trim panel. Drop glove box by detaching holding straps from instrument panel. Remove antenna cable clip holding antenna lead and motor wiring to A/C-heater assembly. Disconnect wiring from radio.
2) Disconnect antenna motor wiring at rear of antenna switch. Remove rear attaching screws of right front wheel splash shield for access to lower antenna attaching bolt. Remove bolt from bottom of motor.
3) Remove trim nut from top of motor tube. Remove antenna through fender/splash shield access. To install, reverse removal procedure.

Removal & Installation (LTD Crown Victoria & Grand Marquis) – 1) Lower antenna. Disconnect antenna lead from power antenna near right plastic fender apron. Disconnect antenna motor wires from antenna overlay wire assembly connector.
2) Remove antenna nut and chrome trim stanchion. Partially loosen right fender from vehicle to gain access to antenna. Remove power antenna support bracket bolt and remove antenna. To install, reverse removal procedure.

Removal & Installation (Sable & Taurus) – 1) Lower antenna. Push inward on sides of glove box door. Place door in hinged downward position. Disconnect antenna from radio. Disconnect antenna cable from retaining clips on A/C-heater assembly.
2) Remove right front fender liner. Disconnect antenna cable and electrical connector from antenna base. Pull cable through hole in door hinge pillar and remove antenna cable assembly from wheelwell.
3) Remove antenna nut and stanchion on right front fender. Remove antenna base attaching screw and remove antenna. To install, reverse removal procedure.

Removal & Installation (Town Car) – 1) Lower antenna and remove luggage compartment left trim panel. Disconnect lead-in cable from antenna. Disconnect antenna motor wires at electrical connectors. *See Fig. 1.* Remove trim nut from antenna. Remove bolt from antenna mounting bracket located at bottom of motor.
2) Remove antenna assembly from vehicle. To install, reverse removal procedure. Ensure that underside of quarter panel is clean to ensure a good ground.

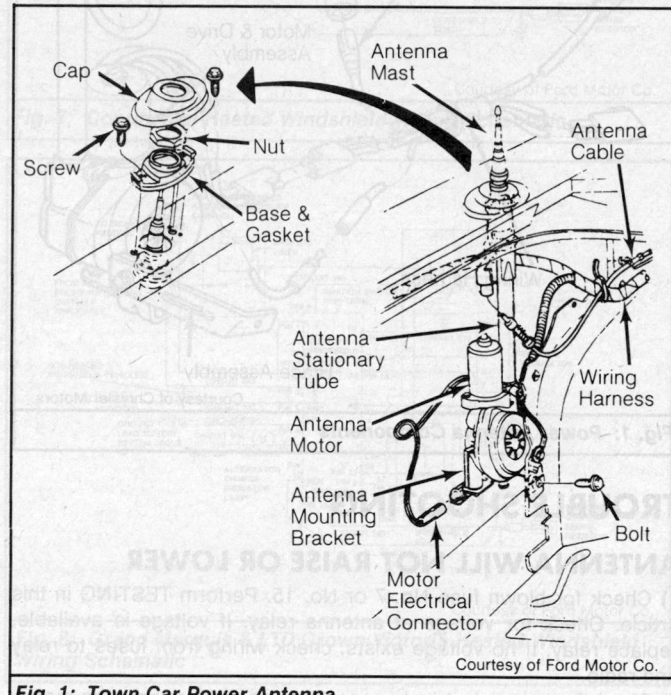

Fig. 1: Town Car Power Antenna

ANTENNA MAST

NOTE: If antenna mast is bent or broken, it may be replaced without replacing motor and tube assembly.

Removal – 1) Remove trim nut and stanchion. Slide 9/16" (14 mm) socket over mast. Loosen retaining nut inside tube and slide it partway up mast. Raise antenna to run plastic drive wire, at bottom of mast, out of motor.
2) Pull wire and mast all the way out of tube by hand. Note direction teeth are facing on plastic drive wire. Saw off damaged portion of antenna mast. Remove burrs from mast and slide nut and contact tube off stationary tube.

Installation – 1) To install replacement mast, ensure teeth on plastic drive wire face same direction as noted during removal of broken mast. Teeth should face toward antenna motor. Push end of plastic drive wire down into tube. Push it around curve at bottom of tube until end enters drive mechanism.
2) Run motor in down mode while pushing on plastic drive wire. Continue until about 12" (305 mm) of wire has been drawn into tube. Stop motor and insert bottom of antenna mast into tube. Lower mast. Slide contact tube and nut down antenna mast. Tighten nut. Raise and lower antenna several times to ensure proper operation.

ANTENNA SWITCH

Removal & Installation (Cougar & Thunderbird) – Remove screws at bottom of power antenna switch finish cover and remove cover. Remove 2 screws from switch assembly and remove switch. Disconnect wiring connector. To install, reverse removal procedure.

Removal & Installation (LTD Crown Victoria & Grand Marquis) – Remove steering column cover. Remove applique retaining power antenna switch in instrument panel. Remove antenna switch mounting screws from front of instrument panel. Disconnect electrical connector and remove switch. To install, reverse removal procedure.

Removal & Installation (Continental, Mark VII, Sable, Taurus & Town Car) – Remove trim applique and antenna switch from instrument panel. Remove antenna switch mounting screws. Remove antenna switch from trim applique. Disconnect wiring connector. To install, reverse removal procedure.

WIRING DIAGRAMS

For wiring diagrams, refer to appropriate chassis wiring diagram in WIRING DIAGRAMS section.

Premier

DESCRIPTION

Electric remote control mirrors are controlled by a dual-control switch mounted on driver's door. The left/right switch directs current to desired mirror. The horizontal/vertical switch directs current to electric motor in mirror assembly, controlling up/down and left/right adjustment. There is a built-in overrun feature which prevents damage to control motor in the event that mirror is moved by hand.

TESTING

NOTE: Refer to Fig. 1 for all testing.

MIRRORS DO NOT OPERATE (POWER DOOR LOCKS OKAY)

1) Using a voltmeter, measure voltage between power mirror switch connector terminal "A" to ground. If battery voltage is present, circuit is okay. If not, repair open circuit from fuse No. 19.

2) Using an ohmmeter, measure resistance between power mirror switch connector terminal "G" to ground. If resistance is not present, perform POWER MIRROR SWITCH test. If resistance is present, repair open to ground.

POWER MIRROR MOTOR

Ground terminal "C" of left and right mirror switch connector. Using a jumper wire, jump terminal "A" of power mirror switch connector to terminal "B", then to terminal "A" of left and right mirror switch connector. Motors should move and stop at end of mirror travel. Reverse power and ground leads and motors should move in opposite direction.

POWER MIRROR SWITCH

Using an ohmmeter, check resistance between power mirror switch terminals with switch in appropriate position. See appropriate POWER MIRROR SWITCH TEST table.

LEFT POWER MIRROR SWITCH TEST

Switch Position	Terminals	Resistance
Down	A & B	No
	F & G	No
	All Others	Yes
Up	A & F	No
	B & G	No
	All Others	Yes
Off	All	Yes
Left	A & D	No
	F & G	No
	All Others	Yes
Right	A & F	No
	D & G	No
	All Others	Yes

RIGHT POWER MIRROR SWITCH TEST

Switch Position	Terminals	Resistance
Down	A & C	No
	F & G	No
	All Others	Yes
Up	A & F	No
	G & C	No
	All Others	Yes
Off	All	Yes
Left	A & D	No
	F & G	No
	All Others	Yes
Right	A & F	No
	E & G	No
	All Others	Yes

WIRING DIAGRAMS

For wiring diagrams, see appropriate chassis wiring diagram in WIRING DIAGRAM section.

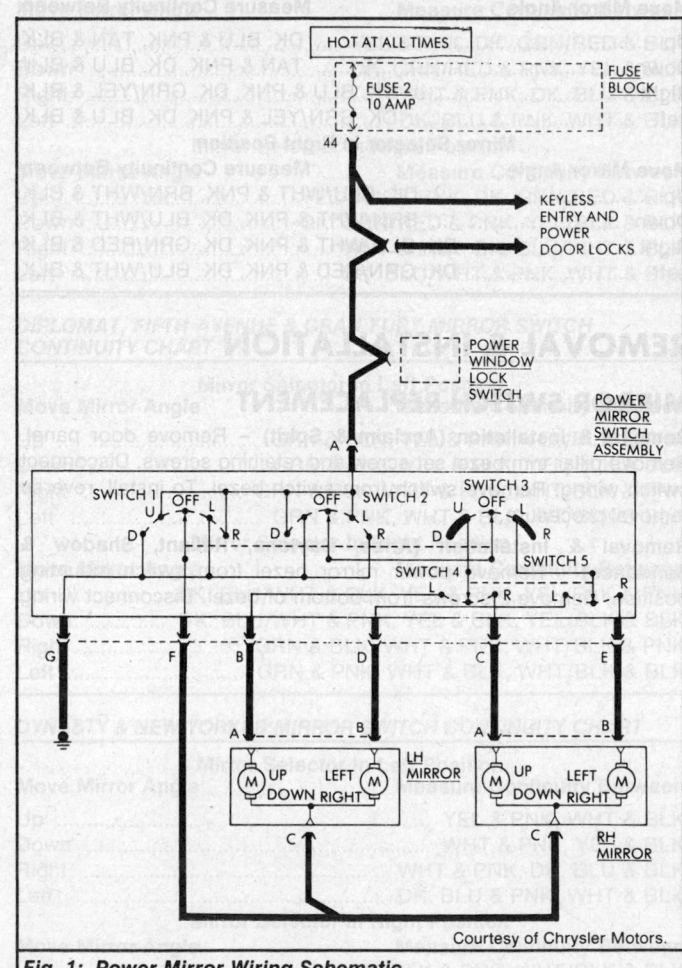

Fig. 1: Power Mirror Wiring Schematic

DESCRIPTION

The electric side view mirror assemblies consist of mirror head with integral servo motor and dash mounted mirror control switch. Side view mirrors on Continental and Mark VII incorporate an electronic heating element for mirror glass defrosting.

Continental, Grand Marquis, LTD Crown Victoria, Mark VII and Town Car are equipped with optional electronic rear view mirror which automatically "flips" to reduce glare during night driving. This mirror is controlled by 2 light sensitive photocells. Outside light level is measured by a sensor on backside of mirror housing. A second sensor, located inside the mirror, detects approaching rear light. Mirror locks in normal position whenever transmission gear selector is placed in "REVERSE".

OPERATION

Side view mirror is moved up, down, left or right by depressing control switch push button with arrow indicating desired direction. A selector switch controls which mirror is to be adjusted.

TROUBLE SHOOTING

ELECTRONIC REAR VIEW MIRROR

NOTE: If back-up light switch is defective or back-up lights are on, mirror will not automatically "flip" to reduce glare.

Rear View Mirror Does Not Operate – 1) Check connectors for good contact. Check for blown fuse. If fuse is okay, pull electrical feed connector from rear of mirror.

2) Turn ignition switch to "RUN" position. Place transmission gear selector in "PARK" position and mirror switch in "AUTO" position. Check for battery voltage between Red/Yellow and Black wire at feed harness.

3) If no voltage is present at feed harness, check for voltage from Red/Yellow wire to a known good ground to determine which circuit is open. Service as required.

4) With voltage present, securely plug mirror feed connector into back of mirror and check for proper operation. If mirror does not operate correctly, remove mirror and check mirror on bench using outside power source. If mirror fails to function properly, it must be replaced.

SIDE MIRRORS

Side Mirrors Do Not Operate (Except Probe) – 1) Check 15-amp courtesy light fuse in fuse panel. If fuse is okay, remove switch assembly. Check for power to switch by connecting test light across Light Green/Yellow wire (circuits No. 54) and Black wire (circuit No. 57). *See Fig. 3.*

2) If no power is present, connect Light Green/Yellow wire (circuit No. 54) to ground and check for open in Light Green/Yellow wire and Black wire (circuit 57). If open, trace circuit and correct problem. If power is present, connect jumper wire across connector terminals and check continuity.

3) If mirrors can be operated while by-passing switch, replace switch.

One Mirror Does Not Operate (Except Probe) – Remove door trim panel. Verify wiring harness is connected to motor. Using test lamp, check for circuit continuity in harness connector by operating switch. *See Fig. 3.* If there is no continuity, trace circuit to connector in floor console panel and check circuit for loose wires and connectors. If continuity is correct, replace motor assembly.

Probe – 1) Check radio fuse. If fuse is okay go to step **2)**. If fuse is blown, replace fuse. If fuse blows again, check for short to ground in Black/White wire at remote control mirror switch.

2) With key in "ON" position, check for 12 volts (11-13 volts permissible) on Black/White wire at remote control mirror switch connector. If voltage is not present repair Black/White wire between fuse panel and remote control mirror switch. If voltage is present, go to step **3)**.

3) Turn ignition switch to "OFF" position. Check for continuity between ground and Black wire at remote control mirror switch. If continuity is present, replace remote control mirror switch. If no continuity is present repair Black wire between remote control mirror switch and ground.

4) If one or more remote control mirror switch position is not working, remove remote control mirror switch from console. Check for voltage at connector while moving switch. If all switch positions test okay, go to step **5)**. If all switch positions do not test okay, replace remote control mirror switch. *See Fig. 1.*

When switch is in resting position, 0 volts should be on all wires.

Switch Position		LG	BR/Y	BR	BR/BK	LG/BK
Left Mirror	Up	0V	X	12V	X	X
	Down	12V	X	0V	X	X
	Left	12V	0V	X	X	X
	Right	0V	12V	X	X	X
Right Mirror	Up	X	X	12V	X	0V
	Down	X	X	0V	X	12V
	Left	X	X	X	0V	12V
	Right	X	X	X	12V	0V

12V = (11V – 13V)
0V = (0V – 1V)
X = Does not apply

VOLTMETER

REMOTE CONTROL MIRROR SWITCH C305

BL/W LG/BK BR/BK

BR BK LG BR/Y

Courtesy of Ford Motor Co.

Fig. 1: Probe Remote Control Mirror Switch Test

When switch is in resting position, 0 volts should be on all wires.

Switch Position		BR/BK	BR	BR/W
Left Mirror	Up	0V	12V	X
	Down	12V	0V	X
	Left	0V	X	12V
	Right	12V	X	0V

12V = (11V — 13V)
0V = (0V — 1V)
X = Does not apply

Switch Position		BR/BK	BR	BR/W
Right Mirror	Up	0V	12V	X
	Down	12V	0V	X
	Left	12V	X	0V
	Right	0V	X	12V

VOLTMETER

REMOTE CONTROL MIRROR MOTOR C500 OR C600

BR/BK BR

BR/W

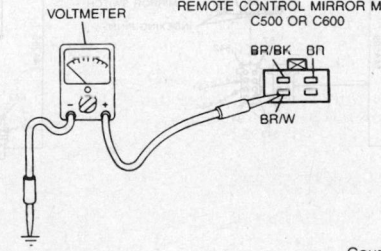

Courtesy of Ford Motor Co.

Fig. 2: Probe Remote Control Mirror Motor Test

SPORT SEAT CONTROL SWITCHES

Daytona & LeBaron – Remove each switch from its mounting position. Move switch to specified location and use an ohmmeter to check continuity between pins indicated in AIR CONTROL SWITCH CONTINUITY and SEAT WING SWITCH CONTINUITY tables. If continuity is not proper, replace switch.

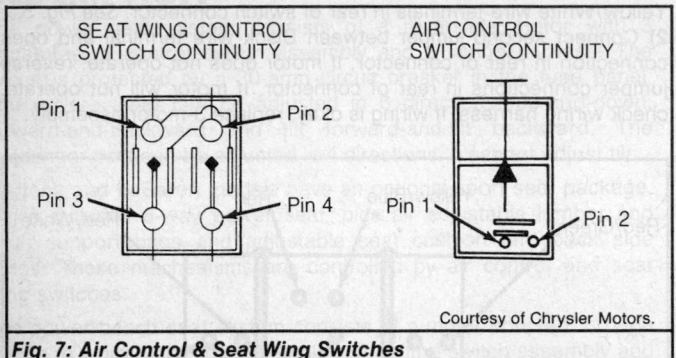

Fig. 7: Air Control & Seat Wing Switches

AIR CONTROL SWITCH CONTINUITY

Mode	Continuity Between Pins 1 & 2
Off	No
Deflate	No
Inflate	Yes

SEAT WING SWITCH CONTINUITY

Mode	Continuity Between Pins
Out	1-4, 2-3
Off	None
In	1-3, 2-4

REMOVAL & INSTALLATION

SEAT ASSEMBLY (FWD MODELS)

Removal – Remove adjuster attaching bolts and nuts from floor pan. Move adjuster as needed for access. Disconnect negative battery cable. Disconnect wiring harness power lead at carpet. Remove assembly from vehicle.

Installation – Position seat assembly in vehicle. Connect wiring harness. Install and tighten mounting bolts and nuts. Connect negative battery cable.

SEAT ASSEMBLY (RWD MODELS)

NOTE: Passenger side 4-way seat adjuster (if equipped) must be positioned fully forward before removal.

Removal – Disconnect negative battery cable. From underneath vehicle, remove mounting nuts holding seat assembly to floor pan. Tilt seat and disconnect wiring harness. Remove assembly from vehicle.

Installation – Position seat assembly in vehicle. Connect wiring harness. From underneath vehicle, install and tighten mounting nuts. Connect negative battery cable and check seat operation.

ADJUSTER

Removal & Installation – Remove seat assembly. Lay seat on its back. Remove bolts attaching adjuster to seat assembly. Disconnect

wiring at switch. Remove any tie straps holding cable housing to seat. To install, reverse removal procedure.

MOTOR

Removal – Remove seat assembly. Lay seat on its back. Remove motor mounting screws. Carefully disconnect housings and cables from motor. Remove motor.

Installation – Position motor onto support of seat assembly. Synchronize left side and right side adjuster positions. Connect housings and cables to motor. Install and tighten motor mounting screws and bolt securing motor to adjuster. Install seat assembly.

CABLE & HOUSING (BUCKET SEAT)

Removal – Remove motor assembly from seat. Disconnect cable from motor. Remove clamp from cable housing. Slide cable and housing out of connector. Check cable for kinks and wear.

Installation – Insert cable and housing into connector. Synchronize right and left side adjusters. Install motor assembly and seat assembly in vehicle.

CABLE & HOUSING (POWER BENCH SEAT)

Removal – Remove seat assembly. See SEAT ASSEMBLY under REMOVAL & INSTALLATION in this article. Disconnect motor. Remove Corbin clamp from cable housing. Slide cable and housing out of bracket for seat adjuster. Remove 2 screws from bracket. Remove cables from motor.

Installation – Insert cable and housing into bracket. Install Corbin clamp. Synchronize left and right adjuster positions. With bracket in position, insert cables in motor. Install 2 bracket screws. Install motor assembly.

TRANSMISSION

Transmissions are not removable and no maintenance is required. If transmission fails, replace entire seat adjuster assembly.

WIRING DIAGRAMS

For wiring diagrams, refer to appropriate chassis wiring diagram in WIRING DIAGRAMS section.

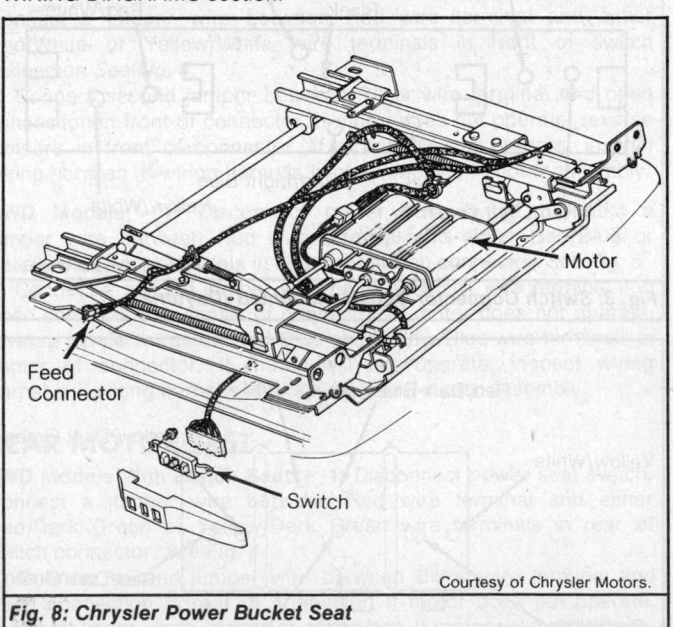

Fig. 8: Chrysler Power Bucket Seat

Dynasty, New Yorker

DESCRIPTION

The Dynasty and New Yorker have an optional power memory seat and recliner package, along with 6-position power seat. The power recliner uses a motor and cable to allow driver to control angle of seat back. The system has a memory seat control module, 2 memory switches, an adjuster assembly switch, a power recliner motor, a recliner drive hinge and 3 seat motors.

OPERATION

The memory seat allows driver to set and retain 2 seat and 2 recline positions. The system uses sensors (potentiometers) to determine seat position. The driver can recall a seat position from memory, as long as vehicle is not moving and seat belt is unbuckled. Self-tests are built-in to check component function.

SYSTEM SOFT LIMITS

This system activates when seat motor or recliner motor reaches its mechanical travel limit. The control module shuts off drive to that motor, sensing a stall condition, and records a soft limit for travel. The control module will not allow motor to drive past that point. To override soft limits, activate switch twice in proper direction.

SETTING SYSTEM SOFT LIMITS

Whenever control module or motor assembly are replaced, new system soft limits must be set. To do this, perform memory seat self-test. See MEMORY SEAT SELF-TEST under TESTING in this article. After completing test, control module will have set and stored its soft limits.

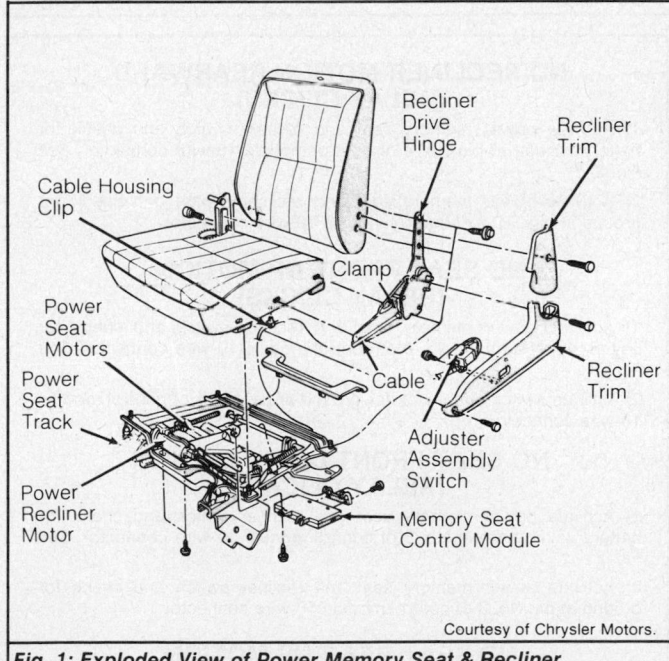

Courtesy of Chrysler Motors.

Fig. 1: Exploded View of Power Memory Seat & Recliner

REMOVAL & INSTALLATION

SEAT ASSEMBLY

Removal & Installation – Remove track adjuster bolts and nuts from floor pan. Disconnect negative battery cable. Disconnect wiring harness power lead at carpet. Remove seat. To install, reverse removal procedure.

POWER RECLINER MOTOR & CABLE

Removal – 1) Remove seat. See SEAT ASSEMBLY under REMOVAL & INSTALLATION in this article. Remove recliner trim for access to recliner and recliner cable. *See Fig. 1.* Remove cable housing clip from cushion frame. Remove cable housing clamp from recliner transmission. Remove cable.

2) Place seat upside down on clean surface. Remove 4 track-to-cushion frame bolts. Remove 2 motor attachment screws from track cross strap. Disconnect recliner motor connectors. Remove recliner motor and cable.

Installation – 1) Install recliner motor and cable. Ensure cable is equipped with cable housing clip and clamp. Connect wiring. Install recliner motor-to-seat track front cross strap.

2) Align seat track with cushion frame. Route cable housing toward recliner through gap between cushion frame and track side strap. Install seat track to cushion frame.

3) Install cable. Ensure cable's square drive end connects with square hole in transmission worm gear. Install cable housing into transmission housing. Install cable housing-to-transmission housing clamp. Clamp prongs point toward floor. Install cable housing clip in cushion frame. Install seat outboard side shields. Install seat.

POWER RECLINER DRIVE HINGE

Removal – 1) Remove recliner trim. Remove 4 recliner-to-seat frame screws. Seat trim may cover screws on some models. Disconnect cable housing clamp at transmission.

2) Carefully, disconnect cable from transmission. DO NOT pull cable from motor. If cable pulls from motor, see POWER RECLINER MOTOR & CABLE under REMOVAL & INSTALLATION in this article.

Installation – 1) Install cable, ensuring square-drive cable end seats in recliner drive hinge worm gear. Seat cable housing into transmission housing.

2) Install cable housing-to-transmission clamp. Clamp prongs point toward floor. Install 4 recliner-to-seat frame screws. Install seat outboard side shields. Set system soft limits.

MEMORY CONTROL MODULE

Removal & Installation – Remove seat. See SEAT ASSEMBLY under REMOVAL & INSTALLATION in this article. Place seat upside down on clean surface. Remove memory control module-to-seat track screws. Disconnect control module wiring. Remove memory control module. To install, reverse removal procedure. Set system soft limits. See SYSTEM SOFT LIMITS under OPERATION in this article.

RECLINER SWITCH

Removal & Installation – Remove recliner trim. Disconnect recliner switch wiring. Remove recliner switch screws from side shields. Remove recliner switch. To install, reverse removal procedure.

TESTING

Ensure battery is fully charged and all electrical connections are proper before any testing.

MEMORY SEAT SELF-TEST

Press memory switches "1" and "2" and hold for between 5-10 seconds to enter switch self-test mode.

- Three seconds after releasing switches, control module should move seat to a mid-travel position.
- Within 10 seconds, move seat switch to activate a seat motor. Check for seat movement in all switch positions: seat track forward, rearward, front upward and front downward.
- With 10 seconds of last seat movement, press memory switches "1" and "2" for at least 5 seconds and release. Seat should move to a full downward and rearward position. Module should move seat until it comes to a stall in 8 positions: forward, rearward,

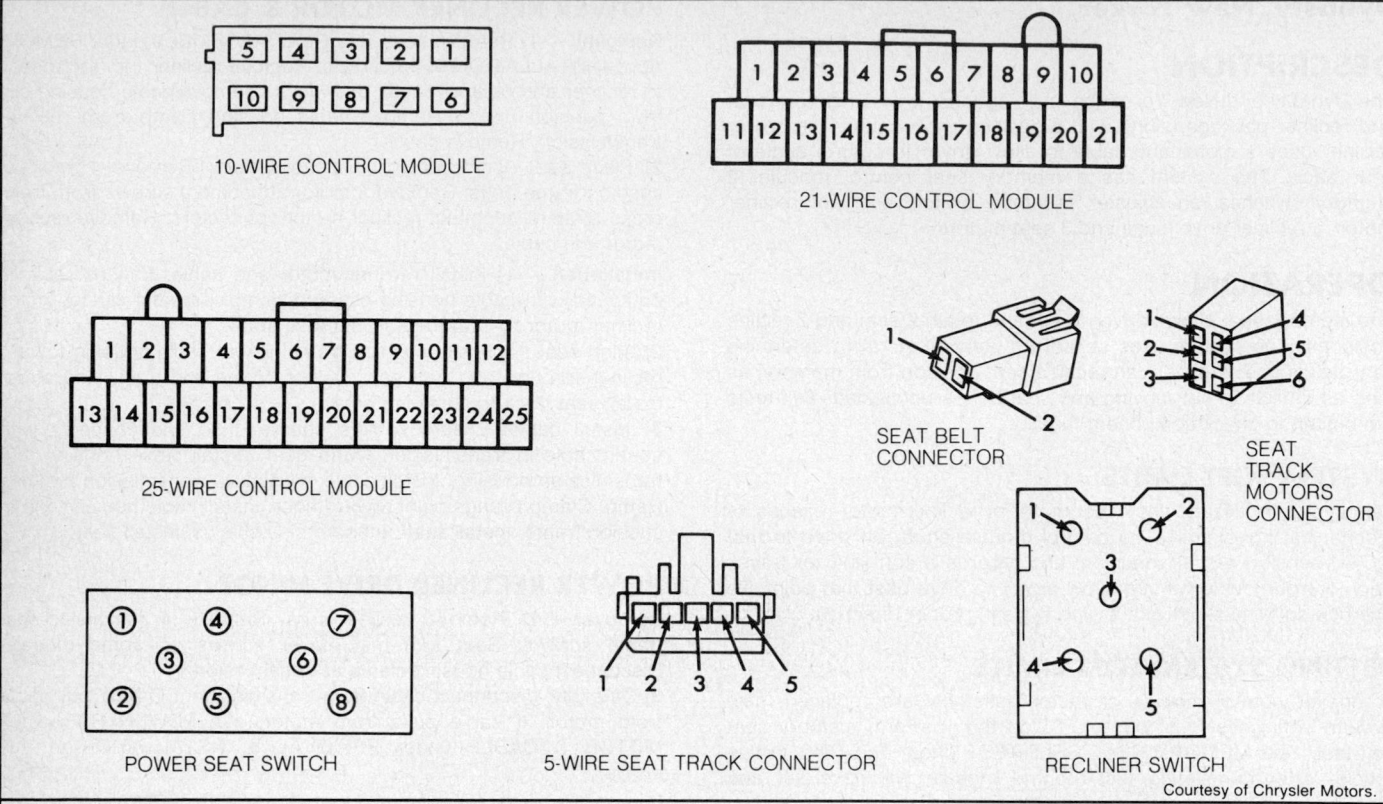

10-WIRE CONTROL MODULE

21-WIRE CONTROL MODULE

25-WIRE CONTROL MODULE

SEAT BELT CONNECTOR

SEAT TRACK MOTORS CONNECTOR

POWER SEAT SWITCH

5-WIRE SEAT TRACK CONNECTOR

RECLINER SWITCH

Courtesy of Chrysler Motors.

Fig. 2: Power Memory Seat & Recliner Connectors

front up, front down, rear up, rear down, recliner forward and recliner downward.

- If a problem exists, control module will not move seat for that function.
- After all motors have run to stall, the system will pause for 3 seconds, then return to mid-travel position. Control module will move seat through its positions for a 2 second run.
- If a problem is found, control module will go into a loop and move only problem part of system.
- To exit loop, press "SET," "1" or "2" buttons to repair fault. When seat stops, system will return to normal operating mode.
- If a problem is found, see TROUBLE SHOOTING in this article.

WIRING DIAGRAMS

For wiring diagrams, refer to appropriate chassis wiring diagram in WIRING DIAGRAMS section.

TROUBLE SHOOTING

NO SYSTEM OPERATION

1) Check circuit breaker for voltage at both terminals. Activate power memory seat and recliner switch and check for continuity between ground side of 2-wire connector under driver's seat and pin No. 1 of control module 10-wire connector. *See Figs. 1 & 2.*

2) Activate switch and check continuity between 2-wire connector under driver's seat and pin No. 6 of control module 10-wire connector.

NO RECLINER MOTION FORWARD (RELAY CLICKS)

1) Activate power memory seat and recliner switch and check for battery voltage at pin No. 2 of control module 10-wire connector. *See Fig. 2.*

2) Activate power memory seat and recliner switch and check for ground at pin No. 4 of control module 10-way connector.

NO RECLINER MOTION REARWARD (RELAY CLICKS)

1) Activate power memory seat and recliner switch and check for battery voltage at pin No. 4 of control module 10-wire connector. *See Fig. 2.*

2) Activate power memory seat and recliner switch and check for ground at pin No. 2 of control module 10-wire connector.

NO SEAT FRONT UP MOTION (RELAY CLICKS)

1) Activate power memory seat and recliner switch and check for battery voltage at pin No. 3 of control module 10-wire connector. *See Fig. 2.*

2) Activate switch and check for ground at pin No. 5 of control module 10-wire connector.

NO SEAT FRONT DOWN MOTION (RELAY CLICKS)

1) Activate power memory seat and recliner switch and check for battery voltage at pin No. 5 of control module 10-wire connector. *See Fig. 2.*

2) Activate power memory seat and recliner switch and check for ground at pin No. 3 of control module 10-wire connector.

NO SEAT REAR UP MOTION (RELAY CLICKS)

1) Activate power memory seat and recliner switch and check for battery voltage at pin No. 10 of control module 10-wire connector. *See Fig. 2.*

2) Activate switch and check for ground at pin No. 9 of control module 10-wire connector.

NO SEAT REAR DOWN MOTION
(RELAY CLICKS)

1) Activate power memory seat and recliner switch and check for battery voltage at pin No. 9 of control module 10-wire connector. *See Fig. 2.*

2) Activate switch and check for ground at pin No. 10 of control module 10-wire connector.

NO SEAT FORWARD MOTION
(RELAY CLICKS)

1) Activate power memory seat and recliner switch and check for battery voltage at pin No. 7 of control module 10-wire connector. *See Fig. 2.*

2) Activate power memory seat and recliner switch and check for ground at pin No. 8 of control module 10-wire connector.

NO SEAT REARWARD MOTION
(RELAY CLICKS)

1) Activate power memory seat and recliner switch and check for battery voltage at pin No. 8 of control module 10-wire connector. *See Fig. 2.*

2) Activate switch and check for ground at pin No. 7 of control module 10-wire connector.

NO RECLINER MOTION

1) Check for battery voltage at pin No. 11 of control module 21-wire connector. *See Fig. 2.*

2) Check for ground at pin No. 3 of recliner switch wiring harness.

NO MANUAL RECLINER MOTION
(MOVES IN RECALL MODE ONLY)

1) Check wiring harness in seat for short.

2) Check for ground at pin No. 3 of recliner switch. Check for defective wiring harness. If either condition exists, replace control module. *See Fig. 2.*

NO MANUAL RECLINER MOTION FORWARD
(MOVES IN RECALL MODE ONLY)

1) Activate power memory seat and recliner switch and check for battery voltage at pin No. 5 of control module 21-wire connector. *See Fig. 2.*

2) Activate switch and check for battery voltage at pin No. 2 of recliner switch wiring harness.

3) Check harness in seat for shorts.

NO RECLINER MOVEMENT REARWARD
(MOVES IN RECALL MODE ONLY)

1) Activate power memory seat and recliner switch and check for battery voltage at pin No. 6 of control module 21-wire connector. *See Fig. 2.*

2) Activate switch and check for battery voltage at pin No. 4 of recliner switch harness.

3) Check wiring harness for shorts.

NO RECLINER MOVEMENT IN RECALL
(RECLINER MOVES MANUALLY
WITHOUT STALL DETECTION)

1) Check for 5 volts at pin No. 9 of control module 21-wire connector. *See Fig. 2.*

2) Check for 5 volts at pin No. 2 of recliner position sensor connector.

3) Check harness in seat for short.

4) Check for ground at pin No. 7 of control module 21-wire connector.

5) Check for battery voltage at pin No. 4 of recliner position sensor connector. This is position sensing circuit ground side. If battery voltage exists here, repair wiring and replace control module.

6) Check for continuity between pin No. 3 of control module 21-wire connector and pin No. 3 of recliner position sensor connector.

7) While switch is activated, circuit voltage is between 1-5 volts. Testing should be done in ground circuit.

NO MOVEMENT IN RECALL
(SEAT MOVES MANUALLY
WITHOUT STALL DETECTION)

1) Check for 5 volts at pin No. 9 of control module 21-wire connector. *See Fig. 2.* This is a 5-volt feed from control module for recliner position sensor.

2) Check harness in seat for short.

NO FORWARD, REARWARD, FRONT VERTICAL
OR REAR VERTICAL SEAT TRACK MOTION
(IN RECALL MODE)

1) Check for 5 -volts at pin No. 10 of control module 21-wire connector and pin no. 5 of seat track position 5-way sensor connector. *See Fig. 2.* (This is 5-volt feed from control module for all seat position sensors.)

2) Check harness in seat for short.

3) Check for continuity between pin No. 8 of control module 21-wire harness and pin No. 4 of of seat track position sensor 5-wire connector.

4) This is ground side of position sensor circuit. If battery voltage exists here, repair wiring and replace control module.

NO SEAT TRACK/RECLINER MOTION
IN RECALL MODE (WILL MOVE
MANUALLY WITHOUT STALL DETENTION)

1) Check for 5 volts at pin No. 10 of control module 21-wire connector and pin No. 5 of seat track 5-wire connector. *See Fig. 2.*

2) Check harness in seat for short.

NO FRONT VERTICAL MOTION
(IN RECALL MODE)

1) Check for continuity between pin No. 2 of control module 21-wire connector and pin No. 2 of seat track position sensor 5-way connector. *See Fig. 2.*

2) Check wiring harness for shorted wires in seat. With power memory seat and recliner switch activated, circuit voltage should be between 1-5 volts. (Testing should be done in ground circuit.)

NO FORWARD/REARWARD MOTION
(IN RECALL MODE)

1) Check for continuity between pin No. 12 of control module 21-wire connection and pin No. 1 of seat track 5-wire position sensor connector. *See Fig. 2.*

2) Check wiring harness in seat for shorts. With switch activated, circuit voltage should be between 1-5 volts. Testing should be done in ground circuit.

NO REAR UPWARD/DOWNWARD MOTION
(IN RECALL MODE)

1) Check for continuity between pin No. 13 of control module 21-wire connection and pin No. 3 of seat track 5-wire position sensor connector. *See Fig. 2.*

2) Check wiring harness in seat for shorts. With switch activated, circuit voltage should be between 1-5 volts. Testing should be done in ground circuit.

NO FORWARD SEAT MOTION
(MOVES FORWARD IN RECALL MODE ONLY)

1) Activate switch and check for battery voltage at pin No. 5 of control module 25-wire connector and at from pin No. 8 of seat switch 8-wire connector in driver's door. *See Fig. 2.*

2) Check for broken or shorted wire between switch and control module.

NO REARWARD SEAT MOTION
(MOVES REARWARD IN RECALL MODE ONLY)

1) Activate switch and check for battery voltage at pin No. 17 of control module 25-wire connector coming from pin No. 7 of seat switch 8-wire connector in driver's door. *See Fig. 2.*

2) Check for broken or shorted wire between switch and control module.

NO FRONT DOWNWARD SEAT MOTION
(MOVES DOWNWARD IN RECALL MODE ONLY)

1) Activate switch and check for battery voltage at pin No. 4 of control module 25-wire connector coming and at pin No. 8 of seat switch 8-wire connector in driver's door. *See Fig. 2.*

2) Check for broken or shorted wire between switch and control module.

NO FRONT UPWARD/DOWNWARD MOTION
(MOVES UPWARD IN RECALL MODE ONLY)

1) Activate switch and check for battery voltage at pin No. 16 of control module 25-wire connector coming from pin No. 5 of seat switch 8-wire connector in driver's door. *See Fig. 2.*

2) Check for broken or shorted wire between switch and control module.

NO REAR DOWNWARD MOTION
(MOVES DOWNWARD IN RECALL MODE ONLY)

1) Activate switch and check for battery voltage at pin No. 3 of control module 25-wire connector coming from pin No. 1 of seat switch 8-wire connector in driver's door. *See Fig. 2.*

2) Check for broken or shorted wire between switch and control module.

NO REAR UPWARD MOTION
(MOVES UPWARD IN RECALL MODE ONLY)

1) Activate switch and check for battery voltage at pin No. 15 of control module 25-wire connector coming from pin No. 4 of seat switch 8-wire connector in driver's door. *See Fig. 2.*

2) Check for broken or shorted wire between switch and control module.

NO MEMORY RECALL/SET IN "1" SET
(CANNOT ENTER SELF-TEST)

1) Activate power memory seat and recliner switch and check for battery voltage at pin No. 14 of control module 25-wire connector coming from pin No. 2 of memory switch 4-wire connector in driver's door. *See Fig. 2.*

2) Check for broken or shorted wire between switch and control module. Check battery feed to switch.

NO MEMORY RECALL/SET IN "2" SET
(CANNOT ENTER SELF-TEST)

1) Activate switch and check for battery voltage at pin No. 1 of control module 25-wire connector coming from pin No. 2 of memory switch 4-wire connector in driver's door. *See Fig. 2.*

2) Check for broken or shorted wire between switch and control module. Check battery feed to switch.

NO "SET" IN EITHER MEMORY POSITION
(ONLY PREVIOUS MEMORY RECALLED)

1) Activate "SET" switch and check for battery voltage at pin No. 2 of control module 25-wire connector coming from pin No. 4 of memory switch 4-wire connector in driver's door. *See Fig. 2.*

2) Check for broken or shorted wire between switch and control module. Check battery feed to switch.

MEMORY RECALL/SET CAN BE SET
WITH VEHICLE MOVING/BELT UNBUCKLED

1) Check distance sensor. If distance sensor is faulty, other vehicle systems will be affected.

2) Check for continuity between pin No. 7 of control module 25-wire connector and pin No. 13 of 25-wire connector mounted at right side of instrument panel.

3) Check for broken or shorted wire between control module and instrument panel connector. *See Fig. 2.*

NO MEMORY POSITIONS RECALLED
(SELF-TEST SYSTEM WILL NOT WORK)

1) Check for continuity between pin No. 13 of control module 25-wire connector and pin No. 1 of 2-wire seat belt switch. *See Fig. 2.*

2) Check for broken or shorted wire between control module and seat belt switch.

Premier

DESCRIPTION & OPERATION

Power seats can be adjusted in 6 directions by a 3-armature reversible motor, drive cables and transmission assemblies. Electrical circuit is protected by a 30-amp circuit breaker located on the fuse panel.

TESTING

NOTE: Refer to Fig. 1 for all testing.

POWER SEAT MOTORS DO NOT OPERATE

1) Check circuit breaker No. 22 and replace as necessary. Using a voltmeter, check voltage between left and right seat switch connector terminal "F" and ground. Battery voltage should be present. If not, repair open circuit to fuse block.

2) Using an ohmmeter, measure resistance between left and right seat switch connector terminal "C" and ground. If no continuity is present, repair open to fuse ground circuit. If continuity is present, go to SWITCH TEST.

SEAT SWITCH TEST

Using an ohmmeter, check continuity between terminals shown in SEAT SWITCH CONTINUITY table.

SEAT SWITCH CONTINUITY

Switch Position	Continuity Between
Driver Seat	
Front Rocker Up	A & D, B & F
Front Rocker Down	B & D, A & F
Center Joystick Up .... A & D, D & G, B & F, F & H
Center Joystick Down .... B & D, D & H, A & F, F & G
Center Joystick Forward	C & D, E & F
Center Joystick Back	D & E, C & F
Rear Rocker Up	D & G, F & H
Rear Rocker Down	D & H, F & G
Switch Open .... [1] D & F
Passenger Seat	
Front Rocker Up	D & G, F & H
Front Rocker Down	D & H, F & G
Center Joystick Up .... A & D, D & G, B & F, H & F
Center Joystick Down .... B & D, D & H, A & F, F & G
Center Joystick Forward	D & E, C & F
Center Joystick Back	D & C, E & F
Rear Rocker Up	A & D, B & F
Rear Rocker Down	B & D, A & F
Switch Open .... [1] D & F

[1] – No continuity.

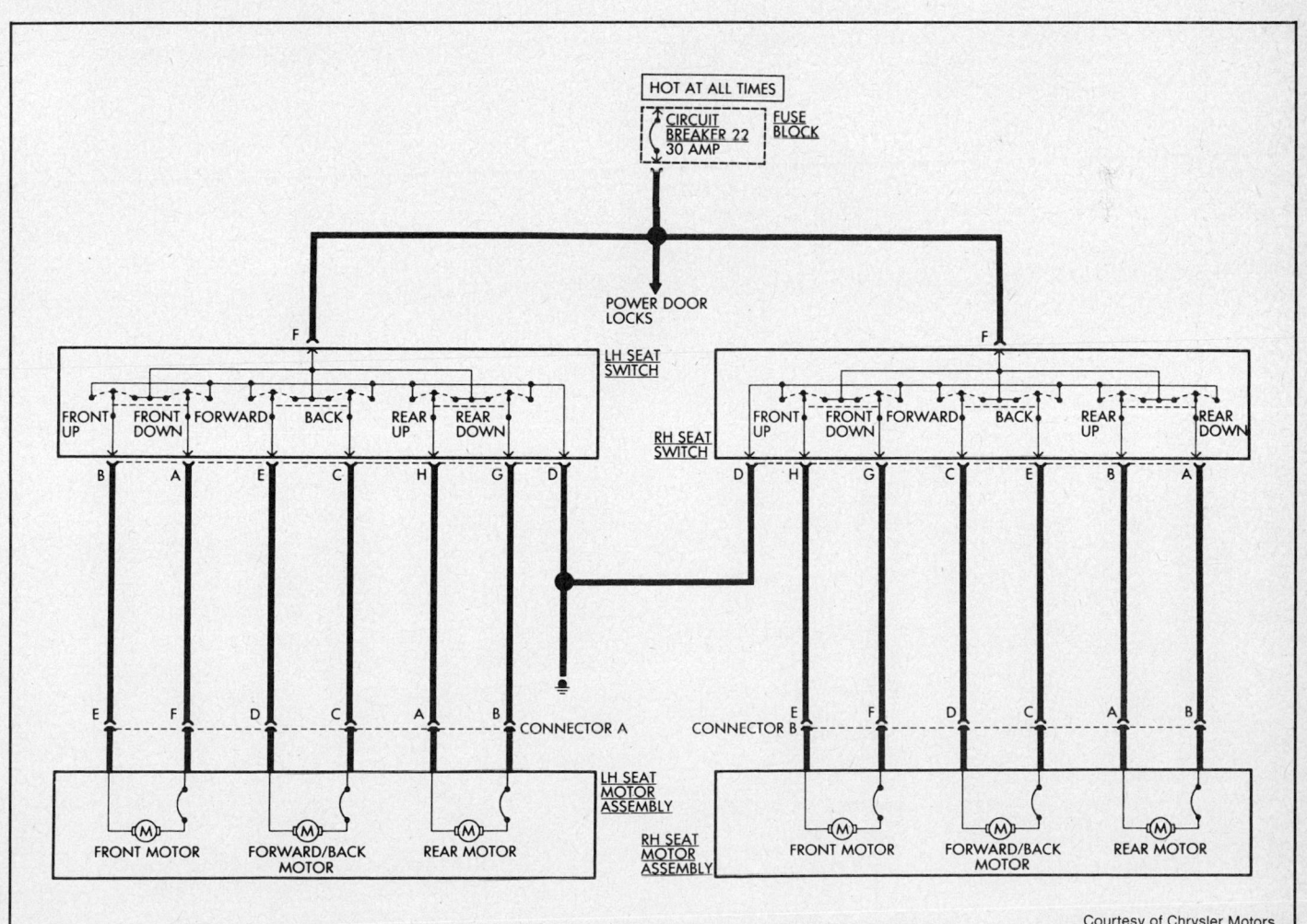

Fig. 1: Power Seat Wiring Schematic

Courtesy of Chrysler Motors.

1989 POWER SEATS
Eagle (Cont.)

SEAT MOTOR TEST

1) Disconnect seat motor harness connector. With switch in "REAR UP" position, use a voltmeter and check voltage between harness connector terminal "A" and ground. If battery voltage is present, go to next step. If battery voltage is not present, repair open circuit to seat switch.

2) Using a voltmeter, check voltage between harness connector terminal "B" and ground with seat switch in "REAR DOWN" position. If battery voltage is present, go to next step. If battery voltage is not present, repair open circuit to seat switch.

3) Using a voltmeter, check voltage between harness connector terminal "C" and ground with seat switch in "BACK" position. If battery voltage is present, go to next step. If battery voltage is not present, repair open circuit to seat switch.

4) Using a voltmeter, check voltage between harness connector terminal "D" and ground with seat switch in "FORWARD" position. If battery voltage is present, go to next step. If battery voltage is not present, repair open circuit to seat switch.

5) Using a voltmeter, check voltage between harness connector terminal "E" and ground with seat switch in "FRONT UP" position. If battery voltage is present, go to next step. If battery voltage is not present, repair open circuit to seat switch.

6) Using a voltmeter, check voltage between harness connector terminal "F" and ground with seat switch in "FRONT DOWN" position. If battery voltage is present, replace seat motor assembly. If battery voltage is not present, repair open circuit to seat switch.

1989 POWER SEATS
Ford Motor Co. Probe

DESCRIPTION & OPERATION

The 6-way power seat system uses a screw-type drive for seat adjustments. Three reversible armature motors are controlled by a switch mounted on the lower side of the driver's seat.

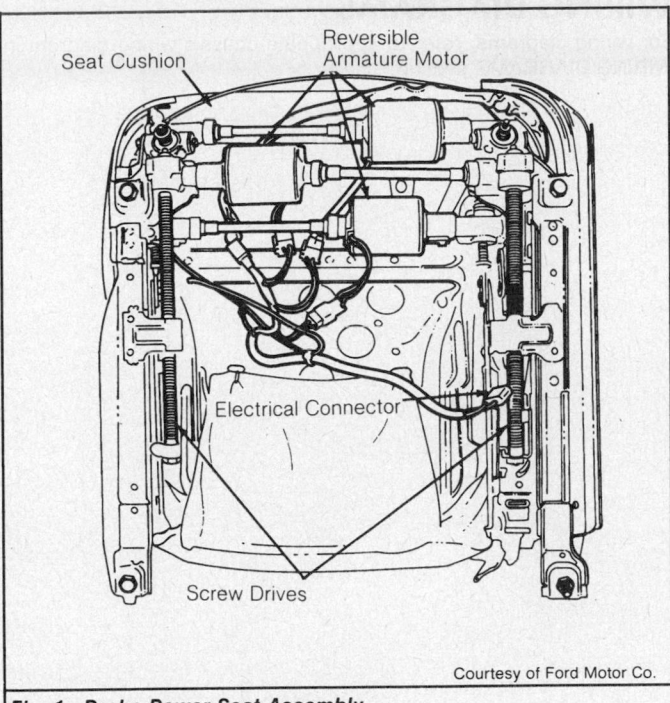

Courtesy of Ford Motor Co.

Fig. 1: Probe Power Seat Assembly

TROUBLE SHOOTING

SEAT DOES NOT OPERATE

No voltage at Orange/Blue wire of power seat switch (Check 30 amp fuse, No. 12). Defective power seat switch. Poor continuity through Black wire from power seat switch to power seat ground. Power seat ground is under trim panel near high-mount brake light.

POWER SEAT DOES NOT OPERATE IN ONE DIRECTION ONLY

Track mechanism binding or defective. No continuity through wires to affected motor. Defective motor. Malfunctioning power seat switch.

TESTING & DIAGNOSIS

POWER SUPPLY TEST

1) Check for 12 volts at Black/White wire of power seat switch connector. *See Fig. 2.*
2) If no voltage is present, check fuse No. 12. If fuse is okay, check continuity of Black/White wire between fuse panel and power seat switch.
3) If voltage is present, check Blue wire between power seat connector and power seat switch.

POWER SEAT SWITCH TEST

Check for correct voltages when power seat switch is placed in each seat position. *See Fig. 2.* If all voltages are correct, replace power seat switch.

MOTOR & HARNESS TEST

1) Disconnect power seat motor connectors. Disconnect power seat motor from linkage.
2) Using chart in *Fig. 2* as a guide, check for correct voltages at power seat motor connectors. *See Fig. 3.* If voltages are not correct, check harness between motor and power seat switch.
3) Apply 12 volts to motors for 2 seconds. *See Fig. 3.* Reverse power supply leads for 2 seconds. Motors should operate properly in both directions.

SWITCH POSITION		WIRE COLOR					
		R	R/W	Y/R	Y	GN	GN/W
FRONT	UP	12V	0 V	0 V	0 V	0 V	0 V
FRONT	DOWN	0 V	12V	0 V	0 V	0 V	0 V
REAR	UP	0 V	0 V	12V	0 V	0 V	0 V
REAR	DOWN	0 V	0 V	0 V	12V	0 V	0 V
SEAT	FORWARD	0 V	0 V	0 V	0 V	12V	0 V
SEAT	BACKWARD	0 V	0 V	0 V	0 V	0 V	12V

* When switch is in resting position, there should be 0 (zero) volts on all wires.

12 volts (11-13 volts–
0 volts (0-3 volts)

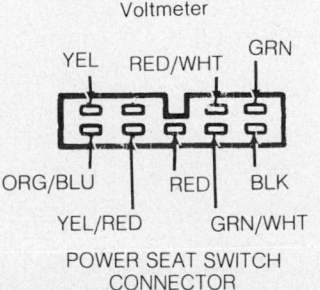

POWER SEAT SWITCH
CONNECTOR

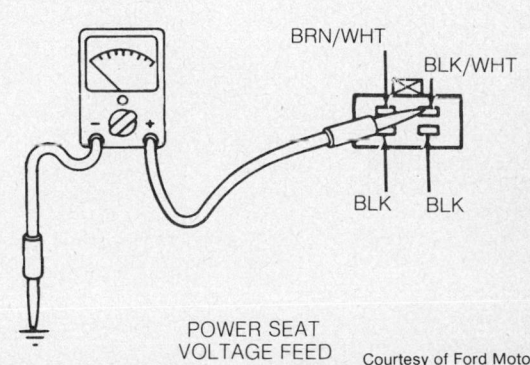

POWER SEAT
VOLTAGE FEED

Courtesy of Ford Motor Co.

Fig. 2: Testing Power Seat Switch

1989 POWER SEATS
Ford Motor Co. Probe (Cont.)

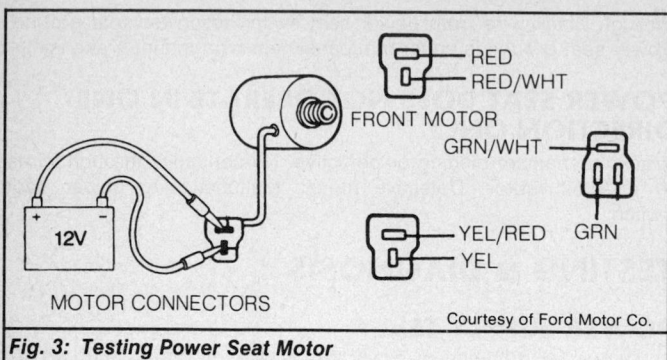

RED
RED/WHT
FRONT MOTOR
GRN/WHT
YEL/RED
YEL
GRN
12V
MOTOR CONNECTORS

Courtesy of Ford Motor Co.

Fig. 3: Testing Power Seat Motor

NOTE: *Manufacturer does not give removal and installation procedure for power seat motor.*

WIRING DIAGRAMS

For wiring diagrams, refer to appropriate chassis wiring diagram in WIRING DIAGRAMS section.

Continental, Cougar, Grand Marquis, LTD Crown Victoria, Mark VII, Sable, Taurus, Tempo, Thunderbird, Topaz, Town Car

DESCRIPTION

The 6-way power seats provides horizontal, vertical and vertical tilt adjustments. On Tempo and Topaz models, only the driver's seat is powered. Continental, Cougar, Mark VII and Thunderbird models have an optional power recliner which provides tilt adjustment of the seat back only.

NOTE: This article only includes information on the 6-way power seats, not power recliner or articulating sport options.

The horizontal and vertical drive units are serviced separately. The motor is serviced as an assembly. The flexible shafts can be replaced individually.

OPERATION

6-WAY POWER SEAT

NOTE: The Grand Marquis, LTD Crown Victoria and Town Car may be equipped with either the rack and pinion or the screw drive seat system.

Rack & Pinion Type (Cougar, Mark VII, Tempo, Thunderbird & Topaz) – The rack and pinion drive system consists of a reversible 3 armature motor, switch and housing, vertical drive gears and horizontal rack and pinion drives.

The pinion housing and motor is attached to the movable section of the track and is responsible for horizontal movement. Vertical movement is controlled by a worm and sector gear arrangement. Drive units are located at the front and rear of the seat. The tilt function is controlled by actuating either the front or rear worm and sector gear.

Screw Drive Type (Continental, Sable & Taurus) – The screw-type drive system consists of a reversible armature motor, vertical and horizontal screw drives, a control switch and housing assembly.

Horizontal movement is controlled by a transmission, lead screw and motor which are attached to the movable section of the track. Vertical drive units are located on the left side of the movable track. The motor assembly is serviced only as an assembly. The flexible shafts can be replaced individually.

PROGRAMMABLE SEAT

The Continental models offer a programmable seat memory which provides the storing and recalling of 3 driver's seat positions. The switch includes 3 buttons marked "SET", "1" and "2". A third position is activated by pressing buttons "1" and "2" at the same time. Pressing the "SET" button lights the LED in the button and start a second timer to show operator that the memory is not open for a seat position input.

If "1" or "2" or both buttons are not pressed within 5 seconds, the light will go out and the memory will be closed for further operator input. The originally stored seat position will be retained. System is operational only when transmission is in "PARK" or "NEUTRAL" position with engine either running or off.

The programmable seat functions are controlled by an electronic module located under the driver's seat. The module is capable of some self-diagnostics. A self-test button and Light Emitting Diode (LED) are located on the top of the module. *See Fig. 1.* The seat controls are wired through the module. If the module is not functioning, the memory or manual controls will not work. There are sensors on the seat track which determine movement. If the sensors are not connected, the seat memory or manual controls will not operate.

TESTING

CIRCUIT PROTECTION

Electrical protection is by a 20-amp circuit breaker. See CIRCUIT BREAKER LOCATIONS table.

CIRCUIT BREAKER LOCATIONS

Model	Location
Mark VII	Left hand fenderwell, near starter relay.
All Other Models	In fuse panel.

GROUNDING PRECAUTIONS

The programmable seat module ground should be short as possible. Module ground wire should not be spliced to any other circuit in the harness. The module and motor power feed wires should never be spliced together.

PROGRAMMABLE SEAT CONTROL SWITCH TEST

1) With "1" button pressed, continuity should be present between terminals No. 1 and No. 2. With "2" button pressed, continuity should be present between terminals No. 1 and No. 3. With "SET" button pressed, continuity should be present between terminals No. 1 and No. 4.

2) To test LED in "SET" switch, ground terminal No. 5 and connect terminal No. 6 to battery positive. LED should glow. *See Fig. 1.* See PROGRAMMABLE SEAT SWITCH CONNECTOR FUNCTION table.

PROGRAMMABLE SEAT SWITCH CONNECTOR FUNCTION

Pin No.	Wire Color	Function
1	PPL/WHT	LED Drive
2	BRN/LT. GRN	LED Return
3	BLK/ORN	Set Button
4	BRN/ORN	Pos. 2 Button
5	LT. GRN/WHT	Pos. 1 Button
6	WHT/ORG	Common

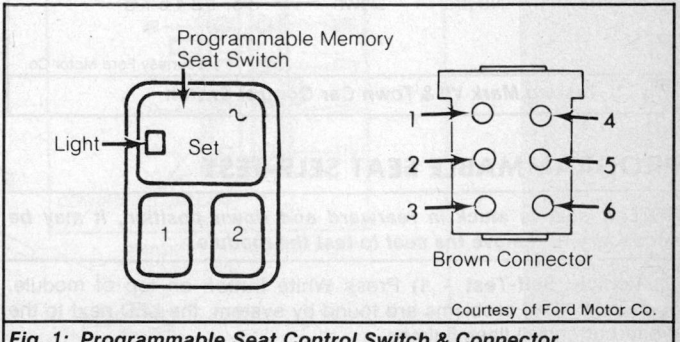

Fig. 1: Programmable Seat Control Switch & Connector

Courtesy of Ford Motor Co.

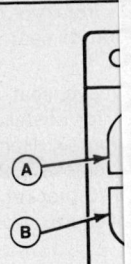

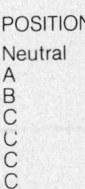

POSITION

Neutral
A
B
C
C
C
D
E

Fig. 4: Testing C... Switch

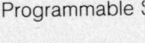

Programmable S...

To Se...

Fig. 6: Programm...

1989 POWER SEATS
Ford Motor Co. Except Probe (Cont.)

POWER SEA

NOTE: For testing
5.

| Note: | Termir |
| | Termir |

To Test Switch
While Still
Attached to Cor

**4-WAY
KNOB**

Neutral
Forward
Rearward
Up
Down
Neutral
Neutral
Neutral
Neutral

To Test Switch
While Not
Attached to Co

**4-WAY
KNOB**

Neutral
Forward
Rearward
Up
Down
Neutral
Neutral
Neutral
Neutral

Fig. 2: Testing

PROGRAM

NOTE: If seat is
necessary to re

On-Vehicle Sel
See Fig. 6. If nc
White button wi

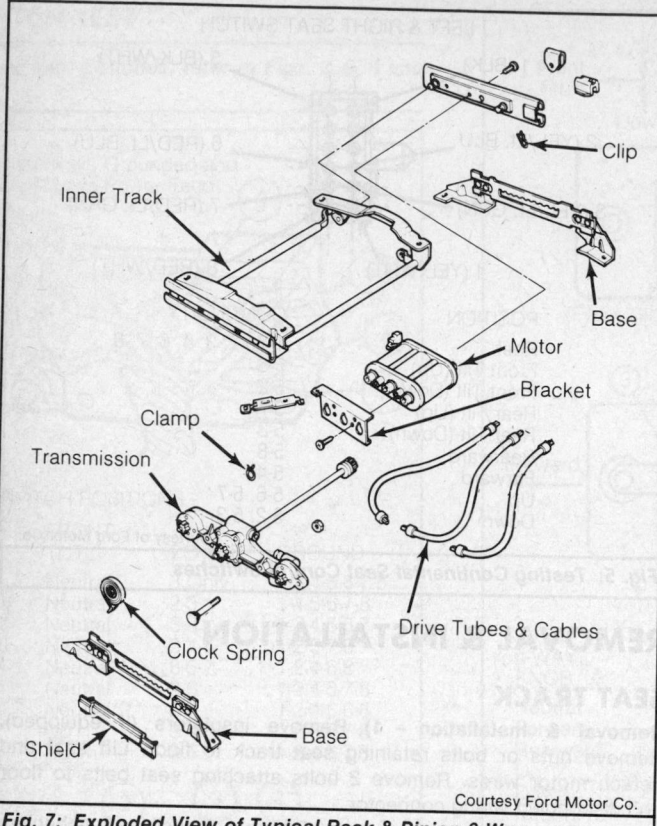

Courtesy Ford Motor Co.

**Fig. 7: Exploded View of Typical Rack & Pinion 6-Way
Power Seat Assembly**

2) Remove cable retaining brackets and drive cables from motor. To install, reverse removal procedures. Check operation of seat in all directions.

Removal & Installation (Screw-Type Drive) – Remove seat from vehicle. Remove track from seat. Mark cables for installation purposes. Remove nut from stabilizer rod. See Fig. 8. Remove motor bracket mounting screw. Lift motor and remove cables. Remove motor from stabilizer rod. Remove 2 motor-to-bracket lock nuts. Remove motor. To install, reverse removal procedure.

WIRING DIAGRAMS

For wiring diagrams, refer to appropriate chassis wiring diagram in WIRING DIAGRAMS section.

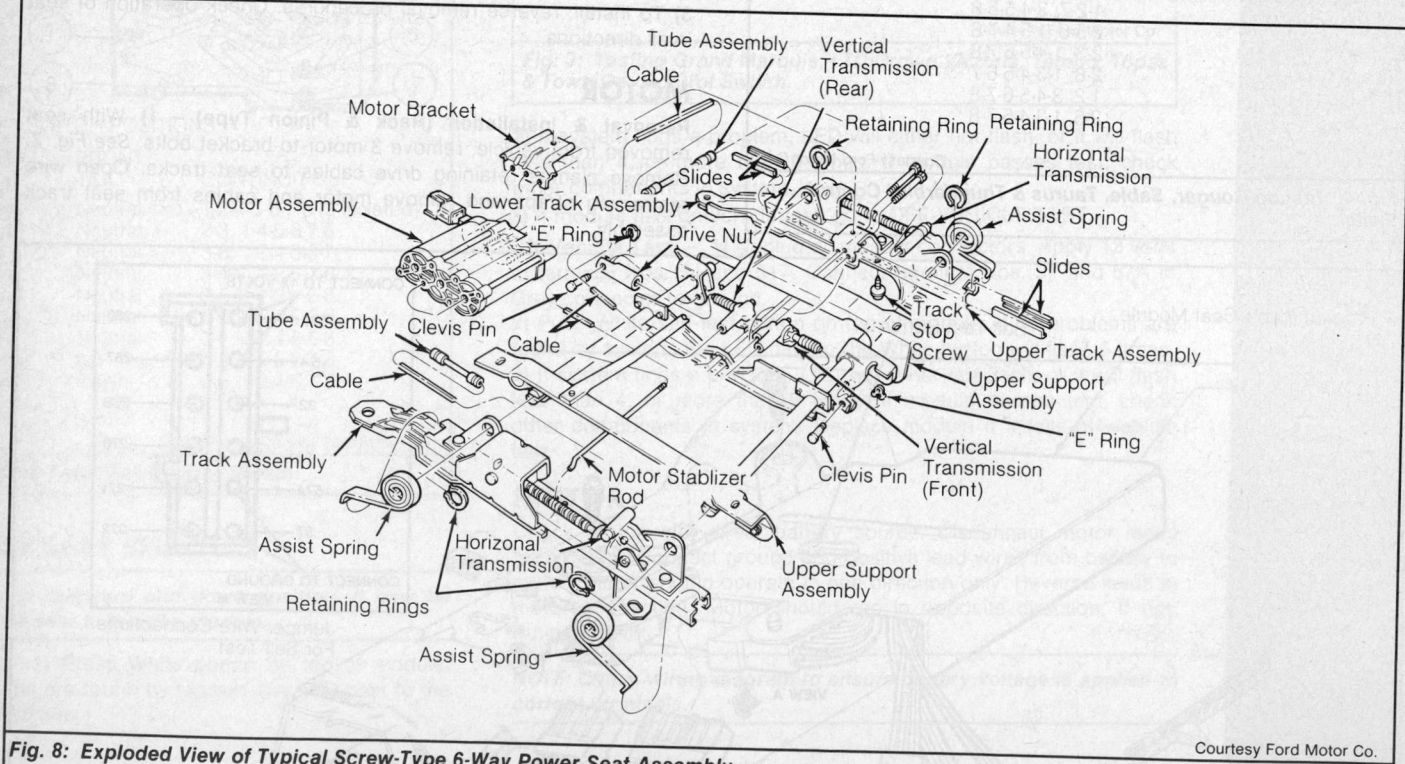

Fig. 8: Exploded View of Typical Screw-Type 6-Way Power Seat Assembly

Courtesy Ford Motor Co.

Acclaim, Spirit
DESCRIPTION

Front and rear door windows are lifted and lowered by a permanent magnet drive motor. The system consists of a master switch on driver's side, 3 door switches, 4 window lift motors and regulators and interconnecting wiring. Each motor is grounded through master switch on driver's door by a Black wire attached to left cowl panel.

TESTING

WIRING VOLTAGE TEST

This test determines whether voltage is continuous through body harness to power window switch. Remove switch. Separate multiple terminal block on wiring harness from switch. With ignition on, connect test light between Black wire terminal and Tan wire terminal. If test light glows, circuit is okay. If test light does not glow, check 30-amp circuit breaker or wiring from circuit breaker to door.

WINDOW LIFT MOTOR TEST

Remove door trim panel for access to motor. See SWITCH & DOOR TRIM PANEL under REMOVAL & INSTALLATION in this article. Connect positive and negative leads from a test battery to window lift motor terminals. *See Fig. 1.* The motor should operate in one direction. Reverse current through same terminals and motor should operate in opposite direction. If window does not move, remove motor and inspect gear and pinion. See WINDOW MOTOR under REMOVAL & INSTALLATION in this article.

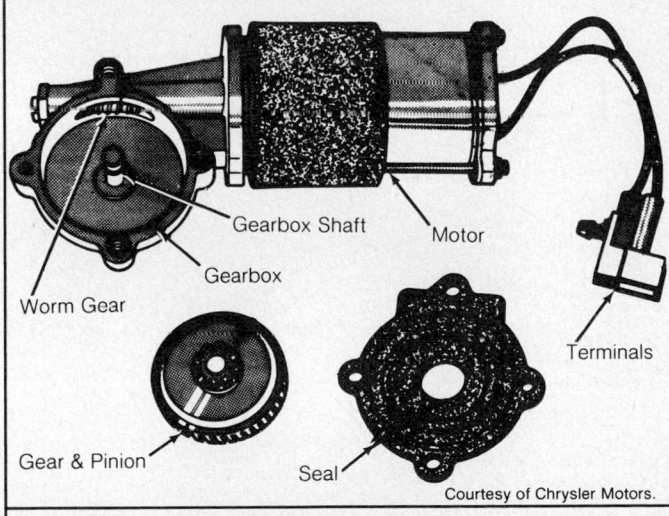

Fig. 1: Window Lift Motor Components

WINDOW CHANNEL TEST

The window must slide freely in glass channels or tubes and tracks for power window motors to operate properly. Disconnect window from regulator and move window up and down by hand to determine if it slides freely.

With window in up or down stop position, move glass slightly from side to side, front to rear and up and down. If glass moves in any direction, it is loose in tracks. Repair as required.

WINDOW LIFT SWITCH TEST

Remove switch. See SWITCH & DOOR TRIM PANEL under REMOVAL & INSTALLATION in this article. Use ohmmeter and refer to MASTER WINDOW SWITCH CONTINUITY CHART, RIGHT FRONT DOOR SWITCH CONTINUITY CHART and REAR DOORS SWITCH CONTINUITY CHART to check window switches. For pin location, *See Fig. 2.* Replace switch in question if it fails any continuity test.

MASTER WINDOW SWITCH CONTINUITY CHART

Switch Position	Check Continuity Between
OFF	Pins 2 & 4; Pins 2 & 5
	Pins 2 & 6; Pins 2 & 7
	Pins 2 & 8; Pins 2 & 9
	Pins 2 & 10; Pins 2 & 11
DRIVER'S UP	Pins 3 & 5; Pins 2 & 7
RIGHT FRONT UP	Pins 3 & 4; Pins 2 & 6
LEFT REAR UP	Pins 3 & 9; Pins 2 & 11
RIGHT REAR UP	Pins 3 & 8; Pins 2 & 10
DRIVER'S DOWN	Pins 3 & 7; Pins 2 & 5
RIGHT FRONT DOWN	Pins 3 & 6; Pins 2 & 4
LEFT REAR DOWN	Pins 3 & 11; Pins 2 & 9
RIGHT REAR DOWN	Pins 2 & 8; Pins 3 & 10
WINDOW LOCK	Pins 1 & 3 & 8

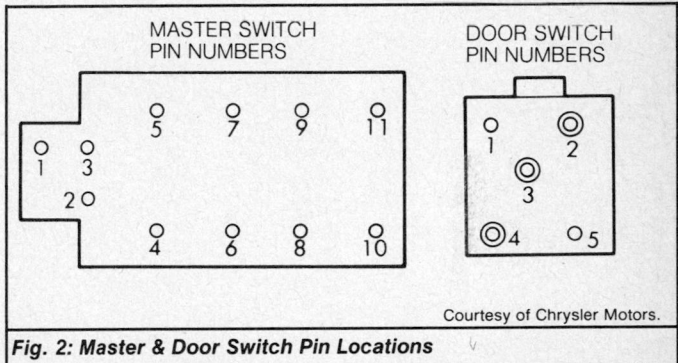

Fig. 2: Master & Door Switch Pin Locations

RIGHT FRONT DOOR SWITCH CONTINUITY CHART

Switch Position	Check Continuity Between
OFF	Pins 1 & 4; Pins 2 & 5
UP	Pins 2 & 3; Pins 1 & 4
DOWN	Pins 3 & 4; Pins 2 & 5

REAR DOORS SWITCH CONTINUITY CHART

Switch Position	Check Continuity Between
OFF	Pins 1 & 4; Pins 2 & 5
UP	Pins 3 & 4; Pins 2 & 5
DOWN	Pins 2 & 3; Pins 1 & 4

REMOVAL & INSTALLATION

SWITCH & DOOR TRIM PANEL

Removal & Installation – Move window down. Disconnect negative battery cable. Lift forward edge and unsnap power window switch plate. Disconnect wiring. Remove inside door handle cover. Remove 3 screws and inside handle bezel. Disconnect wiring at quick disconnect. Remove screw from top of armrest through inside handle opening. Disengage 8 clips fastening trim panel to door. Remove trim panel. To install, reverse removal procedure.

WINDOW MOTOR

Removal – 1) Raise window to up position. Block window. Window must stay in this position when motor is separated from spring load regulator. Disconnect motor electrical connector.

2) Remove 3 motor-to-regulator mounting screws. Remove motor tie down bracket-to-inner panel screw. Reach through opening in inner door panel and behind regulator to remove motor retaining screws. Remove motor from regulator.

Installation – 1) Tap threads in new motor screw holes before installation. Install motor on regulator. Ensure motor gearbox engages with regulator sector teeth. *See Fig. 3.* Position motor so center post gearbox fits into pilot hole. Rotate or rock motor to align 3 motor gearbox screws.

2) Install 3 gearbox screws and one tiedown bracket screw. Tighten to 50-60 INCH lbs. (5-7 N.m). To complete installation, reverse removal procedure.

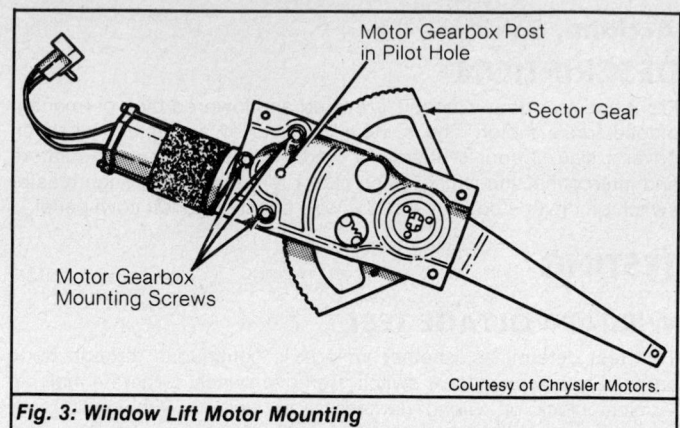

Courtesy of Chrysler Motors.

Fig. 3: Window Lift Motor Mounting

Aries, Daytona, Dynasty, Lancer, LeBaron, LeBaron GTS, New Yorker, Reliant, Shadow, Sundance

DESCRIPTION

Power windows are operated by a permanent magnet type electric motor, mounted in each door. A master control switch provides ground to each motor. A circuit breaker is used to protect circuit.

Electric motor operation is changed by reversing electric current flow. The motor rotates worm gear in gearbox mounted to electric motor. Worm gear rotates pinion gear, which meshes with window regulator.

Three different types of electric window regulators are used: conventional, flexible drive and cable drive. On conventional regulator, operation of pinion gear rotates sector gear attached to window. On flexible drive window regulators, pinion gear meshes with a flexible track attached to window. A cable-driven power quarter window is used on LeBaron convertible.

TESTING

SWITCH VOLTAGE TEST

Performing switch voltage test determines if voltage is available at wiring harness. Remove control switch from trim panel. Carefully separate terminal block from switch body. Using test light, connect test light lead to Black or Gray wire terminal. Turn ignition on and touch other test light lead to Tan wire terminal. If test light glows, wiring harness and circuit breaker are okay. If test light does NOT glow, inspect wiring harness and circuit breaker. Perform WINDOW CONTROL SWITCH TEST to determine if window switch is defective.

MOTOR LIFT TEST

Remove appropriate door panel. Check motor by connecting positive lead of a 12 volt test battery to either motor terminal.

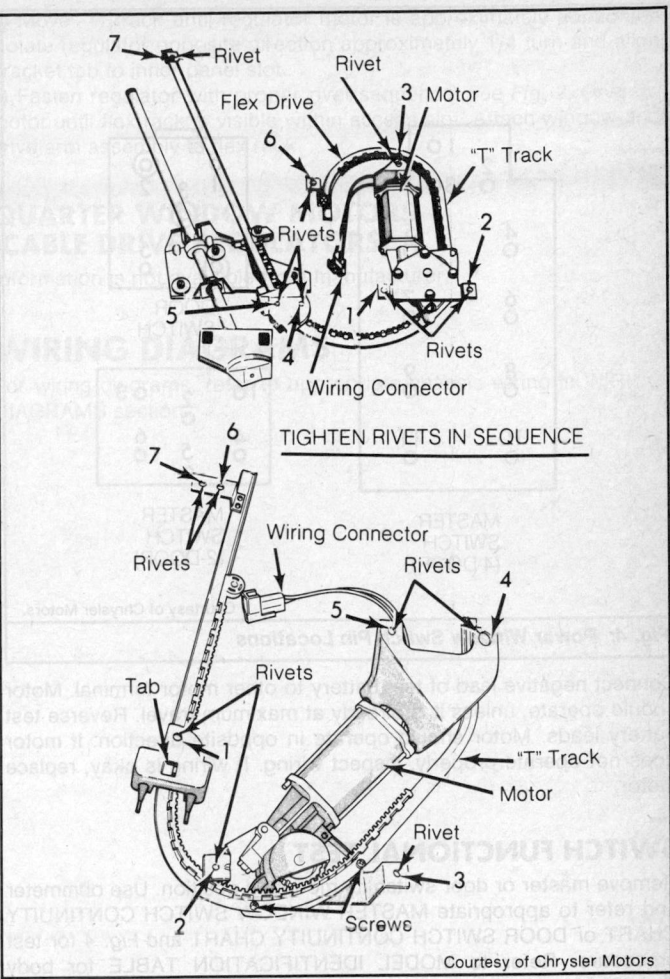

TIGHTEN RIVETS IN SEQUENCE

Courtesy of Chrysler Motors.

Fig. 2: Flexible Drive Window Regulator

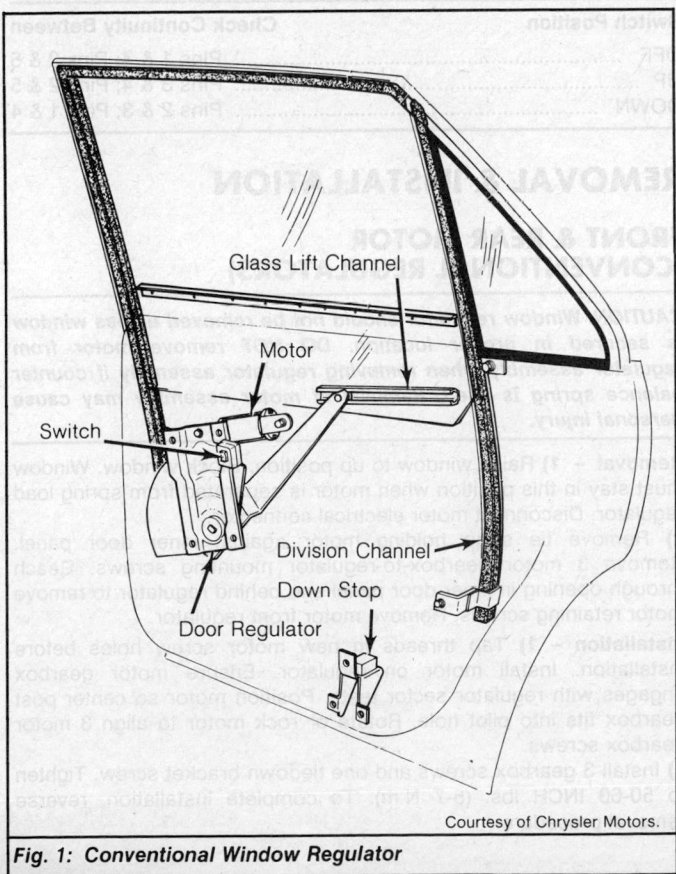

Courtesy of Chrysler Motors.

Fig. 1: Conventional Window Regulator

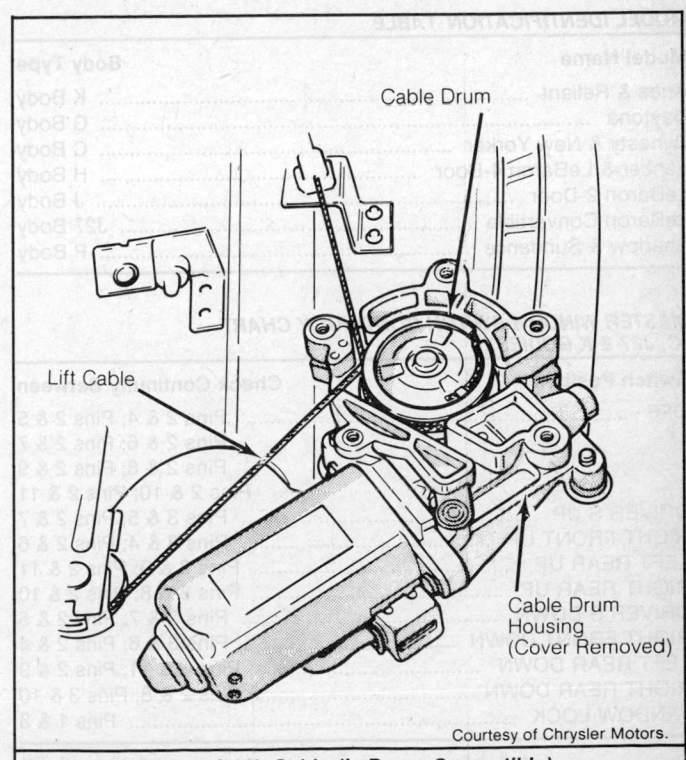

Courtesy of Chrysler Motors.

Fig. 3: Cable Drum & Lift Cable (LeBaron Convertible)

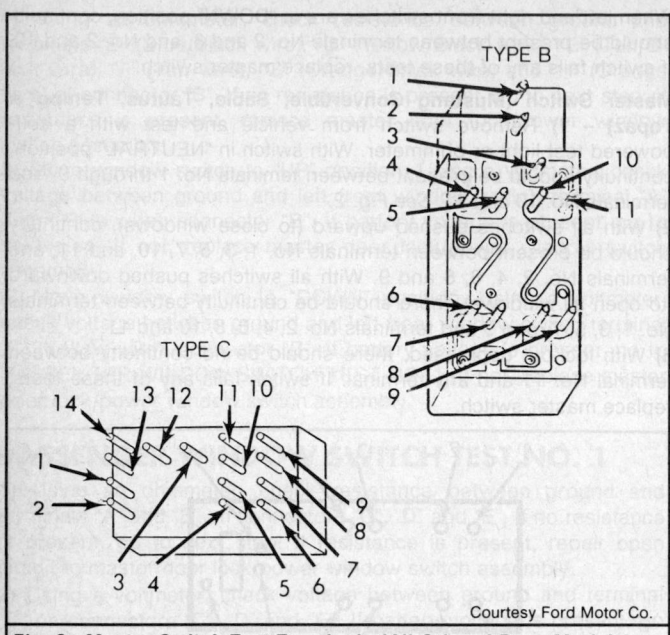

Fig. 3: Master Switch Test Terminals (All Other 4-Door Models)

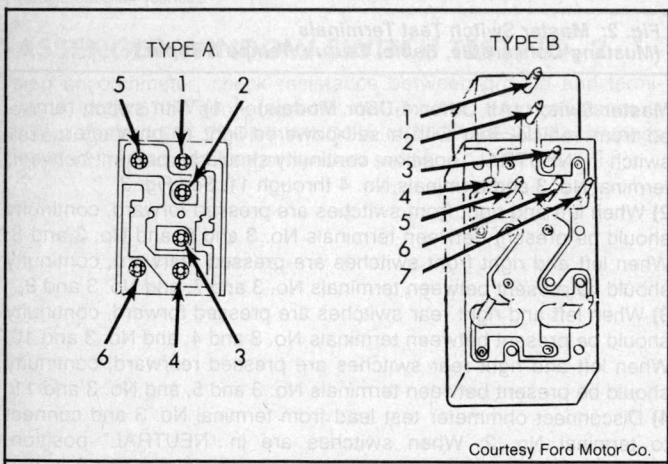

Fig. 4: Master Switch Test Terminals (2-Door Models, Type A & B)

Master Switch (2-Door Models, Type B) – 1) With switch removed from vehicle, test with a self-powered test light or ohmmeter. Connect one test lead on terminal No. 3. With switch in "NEUTRAL" position, terminals No. 4 through 7 should have continuity to terminal No. 3. *See Fig. 4.*

2) Push switches forward. Terminals No. 5 and 7 of the switch should lose continuity to terminal No. 3. Push switch rearward. Terminals No. 4 and 6 should lose continuity to terminal No. 3. Remove test lead from terminal No. 3 and connect to terminal No. 2. Push switch forward.

3) Terminals No. 5 and 7 should have continuity to terminal No. 2. Push switch rearward. Terminals No. 4 and 6 should have continuity to terminal No. 2. If switch fails any of these tests, replace switch.

Single Window Switch (Sable, Taurus, Tempo & Topaz) – 1) With switch removed from vehicle, test with a self-powered test light or ohmmeter. With switch in "NEUTRAL" position, check for continuity between terminals No. 1 and 2, and No. 3 and 4. Terminal No. 5 should be disconnected from all other terminals. *See Fig. 5.*

2) With switch pushed upward (to close windows), continuity should be present between terminals No. 1 and 5, and No. 3 and 4. Terminal No. 2 should be disconnected from all other terminals.

3) With switch pushed in downward position (to open windows), continuity should be present between terminals No. 1 and 2, and No. 4 and 5. Terminal No. 3 should be disconnected from all other terminals. If switch fails any of these tests, replace switch.

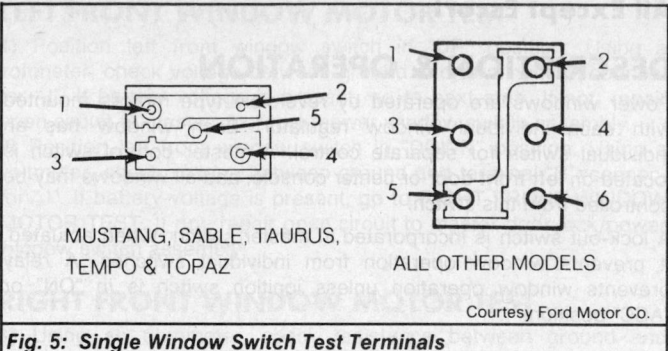

MUSTANG, SABLE, TAURUS, TEMPO & TOPAZ   ALL OTHER MODELS

Courtesy Ford Motor Co.

Fig. 5: Single Window Switch Test Terminals

Single Window Switch (All Other Models) – 1) Remove switch from vehicle. Test with a self-powered test light or ohmmeter. With switch in "NEUTRAL" position, continuity should be present between terminals No. 1 and 3, No. 2 and 5, and No. 4 and 6. *See Fig. 5.*

2) With the switch pushed downward, continuity should be present between terminals No. 2, 4 and 5, and No. 1 and 3. Terminal No. 6 should be disconnected from any other terminal.

3) With switch pushed upward, continuity should be present between terminals No. 2, 3 and 5, and No. 4 and 6. Terminal No. 1 should be disconnected from any other terminal. If switch does not test as stated, replace switch.

REMOVAL & INSTALLATION

ELECTRIC MOTOR

Removal & Installation – 1) Raise window to full up position (if possible) and support. Disconnect battery ground cable. Remove inner door trim panel and protective cover.

2) Locate and mark area of door panel covering motor mounting screws. Some models may have dimples over mounting screw locations. Disconnect motor wiring connector. Ensure that no wires are routed directly under mounting screw areas.

3) On Sable and Taurus models, remove 2 forward regulator mounting plate rivets. Remove 3 electric motor mounting screws. Push regulator mounting plate outward to remove motor.

4) On all other models, using a 3/4" hole saw with a 1/4" pilot, drill inner door panel to expose motor mounting screws. Remove drilled shavings from door.

5) Lock regulator arm in fixed position to prevent counterbalance spring from unwinding. Remove motor mounting screws and remove motor. To install, reverse removal procedure.

POWER WINDOW RELAY

Removal & Installation (Grand Marquis, LTD Crown Victoria, Mark VII & Town Car) – Disconnect battery ground. Locate relay in right lower pillar, behind right side kick panel. Disconnect relay connector and remove retaining screw. Remove relay. To install, reverse removal procedure.

Removal & Installation (All Other Models) – Disconnect battery ground. Remove screw attaching relay to left reinforcement to brake pedal support. Disconnect wires from relay and remove. To install, reverse removal procedure.

POWER WINDOW SWITCH

Removal & Installation (Continental) – On left door remove end screw securing housing assembly. On right door remove screw from under ash tray lid. Carefully pry end of housing up until housing can be removed. Remove 2 screws attaching connector to housing. Pry switch from connector. To install, reverse removal procedure.

Removal & Installation (Grand Marquis & LTD Crown Victoria) – Remove screw from front of bezel and lift bezel and switch away from arm rest. Remove bezel and nut from mirror remote control. Remove 2 nuts from bezel studs and separate switch from bezel. Pull switch from connector. To install, reverse removal procedure.

Removal & Installation (Mark VII & Town Car) – 1) Remove bezel and nut from mirror remote control. Remove ashtray and screw from rear end of bezel on right door. Remove 2 screws from rear half of bezel on rear doors.

2) Lift bezel and switch from armrest. Remove connector retaining screws and separate the switch from bezel. Pry switch from connector to remove. To install, reverse removal procedure.

Removal & Installation (Sable & Taurus) – 1) Remove door pull handle retaining screw and pull handle out of door. Remove 2 switch plate retaining screws. Using a flat-bladed tool, carefully pry switch plate away from door panel. Remove switch housing attaching screw and rotate switch housing up and out of armrest.

2) Remove 2 connector attaching screws from switch housing. Switch is held in place by electrical contact pins. Carefully pry switch from connector. To install, reverse removal procedure.

Removal & Installation (All Other Models) – Remove the switch bezel retaining screw from bottom of bezel. Pivot lower edge of bezel out and up to remove bezel. Pry switch from connector to remove. To install, reverse removal procedure.

WIRING DIAGRAMS

For wiring diagrams, refer to appropriate chassis wiring diagram in WIRING DIAGRAMS section.

1989 POWER WINDOWS
Ford Motor Co. Tailgate Window

LTD Crown Victoria, Grand Marquis

DESCRIPTION & OPERATION

The electric tailgate window is operated by a reversible motor and regulator assembly mounted inside the tailgate. An instrument panel control switch and key-actuated tailgate lock switch operate the power window. A limit switch prevents operation when tailgate is open.

ADJUSTMENTS

NOTE: Separate adjustment procedures are included for each adjustment. This permits for partial glass adjustment. If a complete glass adjustment is required, complete all adjustments in the order presented. All window mechanism adjustments must be performed with trim panel removed.

GLASS POSITION FULL-UP

Inspection – Tailgate glass should be properly positioned within the glass opening to ensure a good glass seal with the weatherstrip. The top edge of the glass should also be parallel to top of glass opening when glass is closed.

Adjustment – loosen each upper stop bracket attaching nut and check the glass fit. If glass fit is not as specified, loosen equalizer bracket nuts. Move glass until top edge of glass is parallel to glass opening. Tighten equalizer bracket attaching nuts. After glass has been positioned in opening, move upper stop brackets down firmly against stops and tighten attaching nuts.

GLASS POSITION SIDE-TO-SIDE

Inspection – The tailgate glass should be positioned from side-to-side to form a good seal overlap with the side weatherstrips.

Adjustment – Loosen 2 lower left side guide-to-bracket attaching screws. Move glass from side-to-side as necessary to obtain a good glass overlap with weatherstrip on each side of glass. Tighten guide attaching screws after glass has been moved to desired position.

GLASS TILT IN & OUT

Inspection – The top edge of the tailgate glass should form a good seal against weatherstrip.

Adjustment – Loosen guide-to-bracket and lower run attaching screws. Move the run in or out as necessary to move the glass top edge against the weatherstrip and obtain a good seal. Tighten attaching screws after good seal is obtained.

TESTING

WINDOW MOTOR

If window does not operate, check fuses. If okay, check for correct limit switch adjustment. Ensure ground connection at dashboard switch is properly grounded. If window operates from one switch but not the other, check continuity of both switches in both "UP" and "DOWN" positions.

REMOVAL & INSTALLATION

TAILGATE GLASS

Removal – 1) Remove tailgate trim panel and watershield. Remove tailgate inner panel lower access cover. Lower tailgate to "DOWN" position. Raise glass until glass brackets are accessible.
2) Remove center pin from glass-to-glass bracket rivets with a drift punch. Drill heads from rivets with 1/4" drill and remove rivets. Disconnect wires from rear window defroster terminals, if so equipped. Slide glass from tailgate.

Installation – Position glass into tailgate and glass brackets. Ensure spacers are placed between glass and glass bracket. Install nuts and bolts or blind rivets to attach glass bracket to glass. Torque must not exceed 36-60 INCH lbs. (4-7 N.m). To adjust glass, see ADJUSTMENTS in the article.

MOTOR WITH REGULATOR

Removal – 1) Remove tailgate glass. Remove glass brackets from regulator arm rollers and equalizer bracket. Disconnect motor wires at connector.
2) Remove 4 regulator attaching rivets. Remove regulator. Driil a 5/16" hole though regulator sector gear and plate. Install a 1/4" bolt and nut through hole to prevent sector gear from moving. Remove motor assembly from regulator.

Installation – Position regulator and install with rivets or bolts. Connect wiring. Replace glass and secure with rivets. Check motor operation.

MOTOR WITHOUT REGULATOR

Removal – Remove tailgate inner panel and watershield. Disconnect wires. Remove motor-to-regulator screws. Remove motor and drive.

Installation – Position motor and drive but do not tighten bolts. Connect wiring. Cycle motor and check alignment. Tighten bolts to 50-85 INCH lbs. (5.6-9.6 N.m). Replace trim panel.

GLASS RUN

Removal – 1) Remove tailgate trim panel and watershield. Remove glass from tailgate. Remove outside belt moulding and weatherstrip from tailgate. Remove upper and lower run attaching screws.
2) Remove glass bracket and run from tailgate. Remove glass bracket and guides from run. To remove guides, remove 2 screws attaching each guide to glass bracket.

Installation – Install guides on glass bracket. Notice the lower right hand guide is different from the other guides. Install weatherstrip and outside belt moulding. Install tailgate glass. Install tailgate trim panel and watershield.

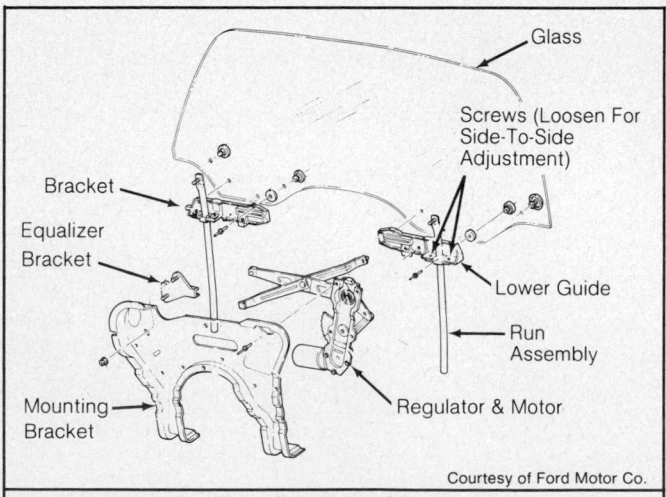

Courtesy of Ford Motor Co.

Fig. 1: Identificaton Of Tailgate Power Window Components

WIRING DIAGRAMS

For wiring diagrams, refer to appropriate chassis wiring diagram in WIRING DIAGRAMS section.

**Diplomat, Dynasty, Fifth Avenue,
Gran Fury, Lancer, LeBaron GTS,
New Yorker**

DESCRIPTION & OPERATION

The sun roof is operated by a switch on the headliner. The motor is located near the switch and actuates the sun roof panels by means of the drive cables. The system is protected by a 20-amp fuse.

If necessary, the sun roof can be closed manually by using a crank handle provided in the glove box. First, remove the plug in the headliner. Using the handle, remove the screw and washers. Insert the handle into the winding gear and turn until the roof closes.

ADJUSTMENTS

SLIDING GLASS PANEL (VERTICAL ALIGNMENT)

Standard Adjustment – 1) To adjust front sliding glass panel, open panel half way and loosen front guide bolts using a 7 mm open end wrench. Adjust panel then tighten guide bolts.

2) Adjust rear of sliding glass panel by placing panel in vent position. Loosen rear cam attaching bolts, adjust panel and then tighten cam bolts.

Optional Adjustment – To adjust panel in the closed position, first unscrew and slide bezel rearward to access adjusting bolts. Loosen adjusting bolts to adjust panel. Tighten bolts, then reverse removal procedure to complete adjustment.

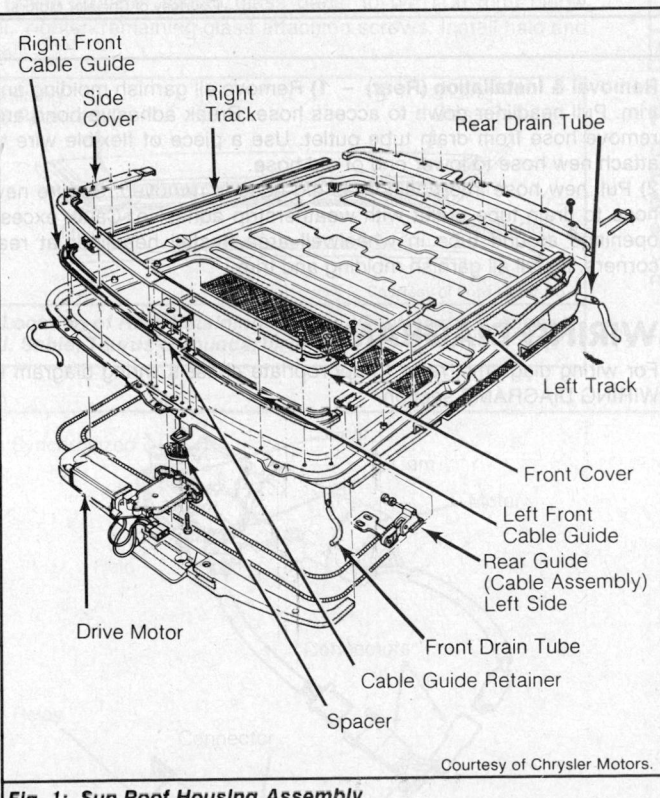

Fig. 1: Sun Roof Housing Assembly

Courtesy of Chrysler Motors.

Right Front
Cable Guide

Side
Cover

Right
Track

Rear Drain Tube

Left Track

Front Cover

Left Front
Cable Guide

Rear Guide
(Cable Assembly)
Left Side

Drive Motor

Front Drain Tube

Cable Guide Retainer

Spacer

MAINTENANCE

DRAIN TUBES

Check drain holes at all four corners of roof panel. These holes (and drain tubes) should always be open and free of any foreign materials. If drains are plugged, clean with compressed air or

flexible wire. If drains can not be cleaned, replace drain tubes. See DRAIN TUBES in REMOVAL & INSTALLATION section of this article.

LUBRICATION

Periodically clean off any dirt that may have accumulated on guide rail covers and check for proper lubrication of cables.

During cable replacement, lubricate cables with Lubriplate, or its equivalent.

REMOVAL & INSTALLATION

DRIVE MOTOR

Removal & Installation – Drop headliner at rear of housing. Disconnect 2-wire connector from drive motor assembly. Remove 2 hex head screws attaching drive motor to mounting bracket. To install, reverse removal procedure.

NOTE: Use care not to stretch or distort headliner when removing drive motor.

DRIVE GEAR

Removal & Installation – Drop headliner at rear of housing. Remove 2 screws from lower retainer cover. Remove "C" clip attaching drive gear to motor shaft. To install, reverse removal procedure.

GLASS PANEL

Removal – Open sliding glass panel halfway. Pull sunshade fully rearward. Remove 5 screws attaching bezel to glass panel. Slide bezel rearward into housing. Close sun roof and remove front guide shoulder bolts. Remove 4 screws from rear guide assembly. Remove glass panel upward through roof opening.

Installation – To install, reverse removal procedure. Check for proper sun roof operation.

CABLE ASSEMBLY

Removal & Installation – 1) Drop headliner at rear of housing. Remove cable guide lower retainer cover. Disengage cable from drive gear and slide glass panel to forward position. Remove sliding glass panel. Remove bezel by pulling forward and rotating.

2) Remove sunshade by applying light hand pressure upward to disengage from track. Remove 2 screws retaining each panel actuator. Remove 3 screws retaining each track. Lift front track up and disengage from housing. Remove cable assembly from track at rear of housing. To install, reverse removal procedure.

MAGNETIC SENSOR

Removal & Installation – Open sun roof. Remove welt cord and drop headliner on left side of opening. Disconnect sensor from harness. Loosen left-hand track by removing 3 attaching screws. Deflect the track upward enough to remove sensor from bottom side of track. To install, reverse removal procedure.

ELECTRONIC MODULE ASSEMBLY

Removal & Installation – Remove headliner at rear of housing. Separate connector at module assembly and remove module. To install, reverse removal procedure.

WIND DEFLECTOR

Removal & Installation – 1) Open sliding glass panel. Remove screws attaching wind deflector arm to blade. Remove welt cord from around sun roof opening. Carefully peel away headlining from front end sides of sun roof opening.

2) Remove 4 bolts attaching brackets to housing. It may be necessary to loosen front 3 housing bolts. Deflect housing

IDENTIFICATION

VEHICLE BODY INDENTIFICATION

Body Type	Model Name
FWD	
A Body	Acclaim & Spirit
C Body	Dynasty & New Yorker
G Body	Daytona
H Body	Lancer & LeBaron GTS
J Body	LeBaron
K Body	Aries & Reliant
L Body	Horizon & Omni
P Body	Shadow & Sundance
RWD	
M Body	Chrysler Fifth Avenue
M Body	Dodge Diplomat
M Body	Plymouth Grand Fury

DESCRIPTION & OPERATION

STANDARD INSTRUMENT CLUSTER

FWD Models – The standard instrument cluster and "Rallye" type cluster (used on L body) incorporates magnetic type gauges. The types of gauges included on standard instrument clusters are: oil pressure gauge, coolant temperature gauge, charging system voltage gauge and fuel level gauge. When the ignition switch is in the "OFF" position, gauges WILL show a reading; however, readings are only accurate when ignition switch is in the "ON" position.

RWD Models – The standard instrument cluster used on RWD vehicles include gauges for fuel, coolant temperature and charging system amperage. These gauges use small Red lamps which signal when a warning condition exists such as: low fuel, low oil pressure, low washer fluid, seat belt reminder, brake system, door ajar, air bag, overheated engine coolant, or alternator system not working properly. The fuel and temperature gauges operate on an effective 5 volts supplied by the voltage limiter.

TACHOMETER

A, G, H, J, L & P Bodies – The tachometer used on standard instrument clusters incorporates an electronic drive module that drives the magnetic type tachometer gauge.

MESSAGE CENTER

A, C, G, H, J & P Bodies – The message center is a car graphic warning lamp module that will display warnings for low fuel, low windshield washer fluid, door ajar and trunk ajar situations. Some models also display headlamp out, tail lamp out and brake lamp out warning lights. Lamps are operated by a lamp outage module. On G and J bodies equipped with turbocharged engines, an optional turbo gauge is available on the message center that displays engine vacuum and turbo boost pressures.

NAVIGATOR

G, H & J Bodies – The electronic navigator provides the driver with information supplementary to standard vehicle instrumentation. The display is operational only when the ignition switch is in the "ON" position or if "TIME" button is depressed. Information that can be displayed is: current time, day of week, date, distance to empty, current fuel efficiency, trip distance, trip average speed, trip fuel efficiency, distance to destination, trip elapsed time, trip fuel consumed, estimated time until arrival, and estimated time and date of arrival. The navigator system evaluates input signals from digital sensors to determine distance traveled and fuel consumed, as well as requiring an analog input from the fuel gauge. An alpha-numeric vacuum fluorescent display with 2 rows of 10 characters each is used to display the value and units of measure requested. Battery power must be supplied continuously to maintain trip information and current time.

TRAVELER

A & C Bodies – The traveler is a 5 function computer that uses vacuum flourescent displays to display trip miles (ODO), average miles per gallon or miles per gallon (ECO), trip elapsed time (ET), and estimated distance to empty (DTE). Traveler computer is located in the instrument cluster with the message center on A bodies, and is located above the headlight switch on C bodies.

WARNING LAMPS & INDICATOR LIGHTS

A Body – The A body instrument clusters have warning lamps and indicator lights for 8 different systems. These systems include: left and right turn signals, low fuel level, low oil pressure, high beam indicator, seat belt reminder, brake system, check engine and check gauges.

C Body – The C body instrument clusters have warning lamps for 5 systems. Systems included are: brakes, seat belt, low fuel, anti-lock (for optional anti-lock brake system), and check engine (power loss). The standard cluster also includes a "CHECK GAUGE" indicator which will illuminate in a warning situation. This will notify driver to check for a problem in coolant temperature, oil pressure, or electrical system.

K Body – The K body instrument clusters have warning lamps for 4 systems. Systems included are: brakes, seat belt warning, check engine system, and low oil pressure. Some vehicles are equipped with an indicator lamp module which operate other systems such as: door ajar, low fuel, low washer fluid and deck lid (liftgate) ajar warning lamps.

L Body – The L body instrument cluster has warning lamps for low oil pressure, brake system and seat belt.

P Body – The P body instrument cluster has warning lamps for 4 systems. Systems included are: low oil pressure, brakes, seat belt warning and check engine system. The low oil pressure gauge uses a 2 function combination oil unit that turns oil light off (when normal oil pressure is present), and provides a resistance to oil gauge that varies with oil pressure.

GAUGE ALERT SYSTEM (RWD MODELS)

The ammeter, fuel and temperature gauges have a small Light Emitting Diode (LED) mounted in each gauge dial. These LEDs will illuminate if the gauge is monitoring a condition that is not normal. The electronic sensor circuit is mounted on the gauge housing. The printed circuit board is permanently attached and cannot be serviced separately. If replacement becomes necessary, gauge and printed circuit board must be replaced as an assembly.

Ammeter Gauge LED – The ammeter LED works independent of the ammeter gauge. When voltage drops to about 11.2 volts, the LED will illuminate and alert the driver of problems in the charging system. The LED will remain illuminated until these conditions are corrected.

Fuel Gauge LED – The fuel gauge LED works in conjunction with the fuel gauge. When the indicator moves to about 1/8 of a tank of fuel remaining, the LED will illuminate and alert the driver of a low fuel condition.

Temperature Gauge LED – The temperature gauge LED works in conjunction with the temperature gauge. When the gauge reaches 240-260°F (116-127°C), the engine temperature LED will illuminate and alert the driver of an overheating condition. The LED will remain on until the engine temperature returns to normal.

DIAGNOSIS

NOTE: All of the following procedures must be performed with the ignition switch in the "ON" position with the engine off.

BRAKE SYSTEM WARNING LIGHT

Brake Light "ON" With Parking Brake Released – Check for leaking fluid in brake system, grounded wiring, shorted parking brake or brake warning switch, or faulty brake system proportioning valve unit.

Brake Light "OFF" With Parking Brake Applied – Check for burned out bulb, disconnected or faulty bulb socket, broken wire or wire disconnected at parking brake switch.

Brake Light "ON" When Service Brake Is Applied – Check for leaking fluid in brake system, grounded wiring or shorted brake warning switch, or faulty brake system proportioning valve unit.

Brake Light Fails To Turn "ON" When Testing Service Brakes – Check for an open circuit in wiring leading to service brake switch. Check for loose bulkhead connector, faulty service brake switch, or faulty service brake system proportioning valve unit.

FUEL GAUGE SYSTEM

Fuel Gauge Does Not Read Full – Make sure fuel tank is full. Check for faulty wiring or components. Use tester or known good fuel gauge sending unit. Check all wiring including ground. If wiring is okay, check for faulty fuel gauge sending unit, faulty voltage limiter (if used), faulty fuel gauge or faulty printed circuit board.

Fuel Gauge Inoperative or Erratic – Check for faulty wiring or components. Use tester or known good fuel gauge sending unit. Check all wiring including ground clip. If wiring is okay, check for faulty fuel gauge sending unit, faulty voltage limiter (if used), faulty fuel gauge or faulty printed circuit board.

Fuel Gauge Inaccurate – 1) Make sure tank is not deformed. Check mounting flange of fuel tank sending unit. Check tank for sending unit interference. Check for faulty wiring or components. Use tester or known good fuel gauge sending unit.
2) Check all wiring including ground clip. If wiring is okay, check for faulty fuel gauge sending unit, faulty voltage limiter (if used), faulty fuel gauge or faulty printed circuit board.

Fuel Gauge Does Not Read Empty – 1) Make sure fuel tank is empty and not deformed. Check mounting flange of fuel tank sending unit. Check tank for sending unit interference. Check for faulty wiring or components. Use tester or known good fuel gauge sending unit.
2) Check all wiring including ground clip. If wiring is okay, check for faulty fuel gauge sending unit, faulty voltage limiter (if used), faulty fuel gauge or faulty printed circuit board.

NAVIGATOR

See CHRYSLER ELECTRONIC INSTRUMENT CLUSTER article in this section for navigator diagnosis.

SPEEDOMETER

Speedometer Inoperative – Check for disconnected cable, damaged cable assembly or broken core, defective speedometer, or damaged speedometer drive pinion gear.

Speedometer Needle Fluctuates – Check for cable not properly routed, cable not properly connected, bent core tip or kinked core, or a defective speedometer.

Speedometer Inaccurate – Check for cable not properly connected, speedometer not properly calibrated, incorrect speedometer drive pinion gear, or damaged drive pinion gear.

Speedometer Noisy Or Ticking – Check for damaged or improperly routed cable assembly, cable not properly connected, defective upper core plastic tip, bent core tip, or kinked core.

Speedometer Noisy Or Squealing – Check for a defective speedometer.

NOTE: In extremely cold weather, a slight squeal on initial running of vehicle is normal and does not indicate a malfunction.

DIAGNOSIS & TESTING

CAUTION: Disconnect negative battery cable BEFORE servicing instrument panel. When power is required for test purposes, reconnect battery cable for test purposes ONLY. Disconnect negative battery cable after completion of test and before continuing service procedures.

AMMETER (RWD MODELS)

RWD Models – Turn headlights on. DO NOT start engine. Ammeter needle should move toward "D" (discharge position). If ammeter shows discharge, ammeter is okay. If needle does not move, check for faulty wiring or for loose terminal connections. If terminals are secure, ammeter is defective. If meter moves toward "C" or charge position, connections are reversed.

AMMETER GAUGE ALERT SYSTEM (RWD MODELS)

NOTE: The ammeter gauge alert system used on RWD models is a shunt type ammeter gauge. A small portion of main vehicle current is tapped off of main power source to supply the ammeter. Main vehicle current is in a separate lead located in the engine compartment wiring.

1) Ensure that LED on ammeter gauge is not illuminated. Check that charging system is working properly and battery is fully charged. Turn ignition on. DO NOT start engine.
2) Create a heavy electrical load by turning on headlights, windshield wipers and stoplights. LED should light up within one minute. If not, gauge alert system is malfunctioning. Replace ammeter.
3) If LED illuminates, start engine and maintain engine speed at 2000 RPM. LED should go out. If not, gauge alert system is malfunctioning. Replace ammeter.

BRAKE SYSTEM WARNING LIGHT

1) The brake system warning light should only illuminate when the parking brake is applied with the ignition switch in the "ON" position, or if one of the 2 service brake systems fail when brake pedal is applied.
2) Turn ignition switch to the "ON" position. DO NOT start engine. Apply parking brake. If brake warning light fails to go on, check for a burned out bulb, a disconnected socket, or a broken or disconnected wire at brake switch.
3) Release parking brake. Warning light should go out. If light stays on, check brake system for leaks, grounded wires, shorted parking brake warning switch, or faulty brake warning switch in service brake warning system.
4) To test service brake warning system, raise and support vehicle on a hoist and open a brake wheel cylinder bleed screw while an assistant depresses the brake pedal and observes the warning light. Brake warning light should illuminate.
5) If brake warning light fails to illuminate, check for burned out bulb, disconnected socket, or check for broken or disconnected wire at the brake warning light switch. Brake warning light switch is on the brake line "T" fitting mounted on the frame rail in engine compartment.
6) If bulb is not burned out and wire continuity is okay, replace brake warning switch in the brake line "T" fitting.

CAUTION: If wheel cylinder bleeder has been opened, ensure that brake system has been bled properly and that master cylinder brake fluid level is correct.

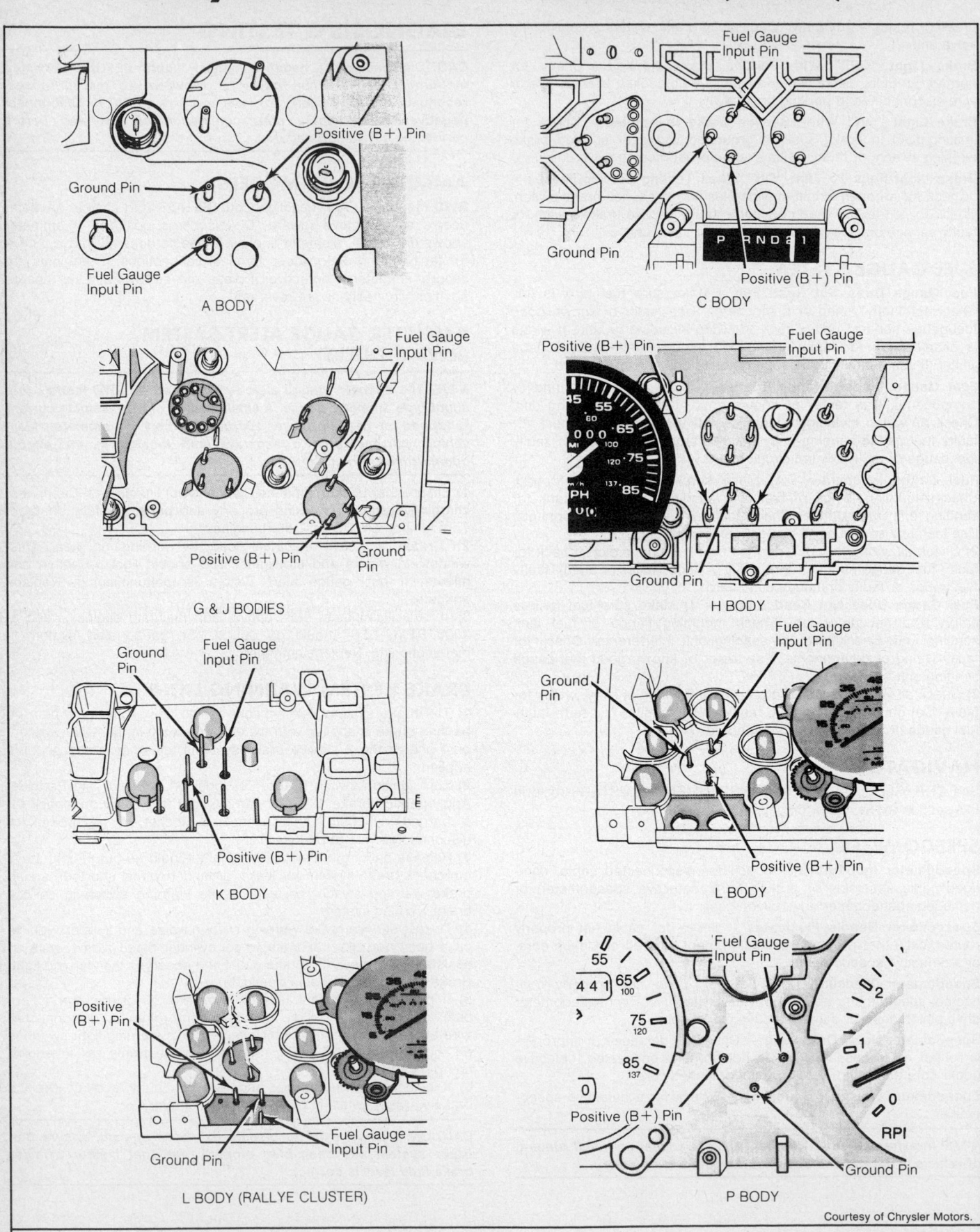

Fig. 1: Fuel Gauge Circuit Test (FWD Models)

Courtesy of Chrysler Motors.

FUEL GAUGE ALERT SYSTEM (RWD MODELS)

1) Disconnect wire from fuel tank sending unit. Connect wire to one lead of Gauge Tester (C-3826A) and remaining tester lead to ground. Turn ignition switch to the "ON" position.

2) If gauge alert function is okay, LED will illuminate when selector tester is in the "E" position. LED will not illuminate when tester is in the "1/2" or "FULL" position. If LED does not work as indicated, replace gauge.

FUEL GAUGE CIRCUIT TEST

FWD Models – 1) Remove fuel gauge assembly or combination fuel/temperature, or fuel/tachometer gauge assembly. Check for continuity in wire between fuel tank sending unit and gauge (fuel gauge input pin).

2) With ignition switch in the "ON" position, battery voltage should exist across the positive (B+) pin and ground pin. If test results of either test is incorrect, replace wire or fuel gauge. *See Fig. 1.*

RWD Models (With Gauge Tester) – 1) Disconnect fuel sending unit connector at fuel tank sending unit. Connect one lead of Gauge Tester (C-3826A) to harness side connector terminal for Dark Blue (DB) wire and the other lead of tester to terminal for Gray (GY) wire.

2) Turn ignition switch to the "ON" position. Turn tester knob to the "L" position and observe gauge. Gauge should read "EMPTY". Turn tester knob to the "1/2" position. Gauge should read plus or minus 2 pointer widths within the "1/2" mark on gauge. Turn knob on tester to the "F" position. Gauge should read "FULL" plus 2 pointer widths, plus or minus one pointer width.

3) If gauge responds to tests, but does not operate with sending unit connected, replace sending unit. If gauge does not respond properly to tests, check for loose connections, broken wires, open printed circuit or a faulty gauge.

RWD Models (Without Gauge Tester) – 1) Disconnect sending unit connector just forward of fuel tank. Connect a known good sending unit to harness side of sending unit connector.

2) Retain float arm of sending unit to its empty (stop) position and turn ignition switch to the "ON" position. Gauge should read "EMPTY" or below. Move sending unit float arm to its full (stop) position. Gauge should read "FULL" or above. Allow at least 2 minutes on each test for an accurate gauge reading.

3) If gauge responds to above tests but does not operate with sending unit connected, replace sending unit. If gauge does not respond properly to tests, check for loose connections, broken wires, open printed circuit or a faulty gauge.

LOW OIL PRESSURE WARNING LIGHT (P BODY)

1) Turn ignition switch to the "ON" position. DO NOT start engine. Oil pressure warning light should illuminate. If light fails to illuminate, check for a broken or disconnected wire at oil pressure combination unit located at front of engine.

2) If wire at connector is okay, disconnect connector from switch and ground connector to engine using a jumper wire. With ignition switch in the "ON" position, oil light should illuminate. If light fails to illuminate, check for a burned out bulb or disconnected socket in cluster.

COMBINATION OIL SENDING UNIT (P BODY)

1) With engine off, disconnect combination oil sending unit locking connector. *See Fig. 2.* Measure resistance between sending unit terminal and metal housing of sending unit. There should be 0 (zero) ohms.

2) Start engine. There should be between 30-55 ohms, depending on engine speed, oil temperature, and oil viscosity. If reading is not within specifications, replace sending unit.

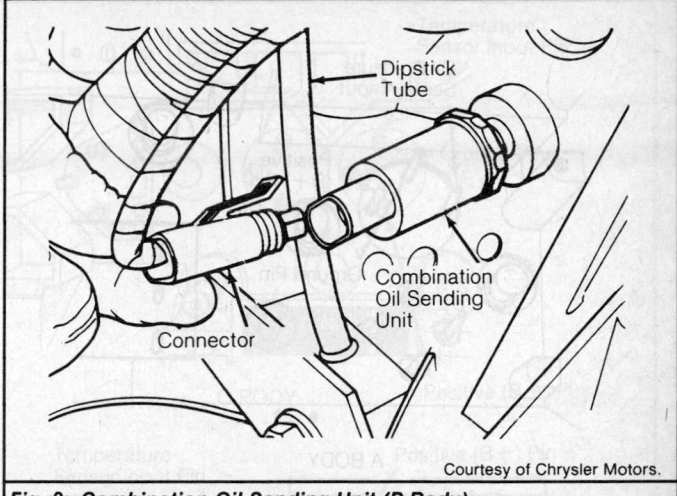

Fig. 2: Combination Oil Sending Unit (P Body)

Courtesy of Chrysler Motors.

OIL PRESSURE GAUGE CIRCUIT TEST

A, C, G, H, J & L Bodies – Remove oil pressure gauge or combination oil pressure/temperature, oil pressure/temperature-/voltmeter gauge assembly from cluster. Check for continuity in the wire between oil pressure sensor and oil pressure sensor input pin. With ignition switch in the "ON" position, check for battery voltage at positive (B+) pin and ground pin. If voltage reading is incorrect, replace oil pressure gauge. *See Fig. 3.*

SENDING UNITS (FUEL TANK, TEMPERATURE & OIL PRESSURE)

NOTE: When a problem occurs with any gauge requiring a sensor or sending unit to operate it, before disassembling cluster to test gauge(s), check for loose connections or faulty wiring before replacing gauge or sending unit.

1) Disconnect connector lead from sending unit or sensor being tested. Turn ignition switch to the "ON" position and ground connector lead.

2) A grounded input should cause gauge to read at or above its maximum reading. If gauge does not respond as indicated, problem is in gauge or in wiring.

TEMPERATURE GAUGE ALERT SYSTEM (RWD MODELS)

1) Disconnect wire from temperature gauge sending unit. Connect sending unit wire to one lead of Gauge Tester (C-3826A) and remaining tester lead to ground. Turn ignition on.

2) If gauge alert function is okay, LED will illuminate when selector tester is in the "F" position. It will not illuminate when in "1/2" position. If LED does not work as indicated, replace temperature gauge.

TEMPERATURE GAUGE (RWD MODELS)

RWD Models – 1) Disconnect wire from temperature sending unit. Connect one lead of Gauge Tester (C-3826A) to sending unit wire and remaining tester lead to ground. Place pointer of tester to "E" position and turn ignition on.

2) Gauge should show "C" (COLD), plus or minus 1/8". Place tester pointer to the "1/2" position. Gauge should advance to within operating range, left of half way mark on dial. Place tester pointer to the "F" position. Gauge should advance to the "H" (HOT) position on dial.

3) If gauge responds to tests performed with tester, but does not operate with sending unit connected to gauge, check sending unit and replace if necessary. If gauge does not respond properly to

VOLTMETER CIRCUIT TEST (FWD MODELS)

Remove voltmeter assembly. With ignition switch in the "ON" position, check for battery voltage across positive (B+) pin and ground pin. *See Fig. 5*. Voltmeter readings should indicate regulated alternator output or battery voltage, whichever is greater.

ENGINE OIL PRESSURE WARNING SYSTEM (RWD MODELS)

1) Turn ignition on. DO NOT start engine. If oil light does not come on, check for a burned out bulb, damaged bulb socket, open wiring or defective switch. If light comes on, start engine and let it idle. If light goes out, warning light is okay.

2) If light stays on after starting engine, immediately turn engine off and check for grounded wiring. If wiring is okay, check for low oil level. If necessary, test engine oil pressure. If engine oil pressure is low, service engine as required. If pressure is okay, replace defective switch.

NAVIGATOR

See CHRYSLER MOTORS ELECTRONIC INSTRUMENT CLUSTER article in this section for navigator diagnosis or testing.

REMOVAL & INSTALLATION

CAUTION: Disconnect negative battery cable BEFORE servicing instrument panel. When power is required for test purposes, reconnect battery cable. Disconnect battery cable before removing or installing instrument panel components.

BEZEL

Removal & Installation (C Body) – 1) Move gear selector lever to the "L" position. Remove all Torx head screws from bezel. Pry bezel loose from fasteners on lower portion of bezel. Lift bezel over steering wheel.

2) To install, position bezel to instrument panel. Secure bezel to panel with Torx head screws and snap lower edges of bezel into place.

Removal & Installation (G & J Bodies) – Remove 5 screws from top of cluster bezel. Pull bezel rearward to disengage 3 clips on bottom of bezel and remove bezel. To install, position bezel over cluster and snap bezel clips into clip attaching points.

Removal & Installation (H Body) – Move gear selector lever to the "L" position. Remove 11 Torx head screws from bezel and lift cluster bezel over steering wheel. To install, position bezel to instrument panel and secure with Torx head screws.

Removal & Installation (K Body) – Move gear selector lever to the "1" position. Remove 6 screws from cluster bezel. Remove cluster bezel by snapping bezel off of 5 retaining clips. To install, snap bezel into place and secure with screws.

Removal & Installation (L Body) – 1) Remove cluster bezel lower attaching screws. Allow bezel to drop slightly so that locating pins on top of bezel are free from cluster mask.

2) Remove bezel rearward away from cluster assembly. To install, position bezel to cluster ensuring that locating pins are inserted properly into cluster mask. Secure with attaching screws.

Removal & Installation (P Body) – Remove 4 screws holding bezel to instrument panel. Remove bezel over steering wheel. To install, reverse removal procedure.

Removal & Installation (RWD Models) – Remove 4 mounting screws located along upper edge of bezel. Position gear selector lever to the "1" position. Remove bezel by pulling rearward and unsnapping 4 lower fasteners. To install, position bezel into place on cluster. Install upper mounting screws and tighten securely. Snap in 4 lower fasteners.

HEADLIGHT SWITCH

Removal & Installation (A, K & P Bodies) – 1) Remove cluster bezel. Remove 3 screws securing headlight switch mounting plate to base panel. Pull headlight switch and plate rearward. Disconnect wiring connectors from switch.

2) Remove knob and stem by depressing button on switch. Snap out escutcheon. Remove nut attaching switch to mounting plate and remove switch from plate.

3) To install, place switch on mounting plate and tighten nut. Snap in escutcheon. Install knob and stem by depressing button on switch. Position headlight switch and connect wiring connectors.

4) Install screws securing headlight switch mounting plate to base panel. Install cluster bezel.

Removal & Installation (C & H Bodies) – 1) Remove headlight and accessory switch module from instrument panel. Press button on underside of headlight switch and pull knob and shaft to remove.

2) Remove switch assembly and escutcheon from switch module by removing 4 attaching screws. Remove headlight switch mounting plate from switch by removing retaining nut. To install, reverse removal procedure.

Removal & Installation (G & J Bodies) – 1) Remove cluster bezel. Remove 3 screws securing headlight switch mounting plate to base panel. Pull headlight switch and plate rearward. Disconnect wiring connectors from switch.

2) Remove knob and stem by depressing button on switch. Snap out escutcheon and remove nut attaching switch to mounting plate. Remove switch from mounting plate.

Removal & Installation (L Body) – 1) Reach under instrument panel and disengage headlight switch knob and shaft by depressing button on switch lower surface.

2) Remove switch knob and shaft. Remove 4 bezel attaching screws and remove left bezel. Remove headlight switch mounting screws. Remove switch from panel and disconnect wiring harness connector. Separate switch and bracket by removing bracket retainer.

Removal & Installation (RWD Models) – 1) Remove cluster bezel. Remove 2 screws mounting switch module and pull assembly out and let hang loose in order to gain access to headlight switch.

2) While depressing headlight switch stem release button (located on bottom of switch), pull knob and stem from switch bezel. Insert a Phillips head screwdriver through stem opening in switch bezel and remove headlight switch mounting nut.

3) Disconnect wiring harness connector from switch. Remove headlight switch.

4) To install, position switch to module, install mounting nut and tighten securely. Connect wiring harness and install mounting screws and tighten securely. Install cluster bezel.

INSTRUMENT CLUSTER

Removal & Installation (A Body) – 1) Remove cluster bezel. On column shift vehicles disconnect gear shift indicator wire. Remove 4 screws attaching cluster housing to base panel.

2) Pull cluster assembly rearward, then reach behind cluster and disconnect wiring harness. Remove cluster assembly.

Removal & Installation (C Body) – 1) Remove cluster assembly. Remove lower steering column cover and disconnect gear indicator pointer cable. Remove cluster assembly.

2) To install, position cluster assembly while routing gear selector indicator needle cable through base panel. Place gear selector lever in the "N" position. Pull cable so needle is between the "R" and "N" positions and let cable snap back.

3) Install cable to shift housing and move gear selector lever to the "P" position. Install cluster mask and lens assembly. Install lower steering column cover and cluster bezel.

Removal & Installation (G & J Bodies) – 1) Remove cluster bezel. Remove 4 screws attaching cluster housing to base panel. Pull cluster assembly rearward, then reach under and disconnect wiring harness. Remove cluster assembly.

2) To install, connect wiring harness, position cluster assembly and secure to base panel with screws. Install cluster bezel.

Removal & Installation (H Body) – Remove cluster bezel and lower steering column cover. Remove mask and lens assembly. Remove cluster assembly. To install cluster assembly, reverse removal procedure.

Removal & Installation (K Body) – 1) Remove cluster bezel. Remove rearward screws from instrument panel upper pad assembly. Lift rearward edge of instrument panel upper pad.

2) With pad raised, remove 2 screws from top of cluster. Remove 2 screws from bottom of cluster to panel. Lift rearward edge of upper pad and pull cluster rearward. Disconnect wiring and speedometer cable. Remove cluster assembly.

3) To install, connect wiring and speedometer cable to cluster. Raise upper pad and position cluster in instrument panel opening. Secure cluster to panel with screws. Install upper pad screws and install cluster bezel.

Removal & Installation (L Body) – 1) Remove cluster bezel. Remove 4 screws attaching cluster to base panel. Pull cluster rearward and disconnect speedometer cable and wiring connectors. Remove cluster assembly.

2) To install, connect speedometer cable and wiring. Position cluster assembly into panel opening and secure with screws. Install bezel.

Removal & Installation (P Body) – Remove instrument cluster bezel. Remove 4 instrument cluster retaining screws and move cluster rearward and toward center of vehicle to remove. To install, reverse removal procedure.

Removal & Installation (RWD Models) – 1) Remove cluster bezel. Remove 3 screws attaching cluster and printed circuit board assembly to carrier. Pull assembly away from carrier and disconnect electrical leads. Remove assembly from instrument panel.

2) To install, position cluster and printed circuit board assembly into instrument panel and connect electrical leads. Secure cluster assembly with screws. Install cluster bezel.

MESSAGE CENTER

Removal & Installation (A, C, G, H, J & P Bodies) – 1) Remove cluster bezel. Remove message center mounting screws. Pull unit rearward and disconnect wiring. To install, reverse removal procedure.

2) Remove center bezel assembly. Remove message center or turbo gauge/message center mounting screws. Pull module rearward, disconnect wiring and vacuum connectors and remove from vehicle. To install, reverse removal procedure.

NAVIGATOR

Removal & Installation (G & J Bodies) – Remove cluster bezel. Remove 4 screws and disconnect wiring to navigator. Remove navigator assembly. To install, connect wiring connector and position navigator to instrument panel and secure with screws. Install cluster bezel.

Removal & Installation (H Body) – Remove 2 Torx head screws and pull navigator straight out. Disconnect wiring harness connectors from navigator and remove navigator assembly. To install, align clips and push navigator straight into console opening. Secure navigator with mounting screws.

PRINTED CIRCUIT BOARD

Removal & Installation (A Body) – 1) Remove cluster assembly. Remove tachometer drive module, low fuel relay and gauge alert module. Remove all cluster bulbs.

2) Remove mounting screws securing printed circuit board to cluster housing and remove printed circuit board. To install, reverse removal procedure.

Removal & Installation (C & K Bodies) – Remove cluster assembly. Twist out all cluster bulbs. Remove screws securing printed circuit board to cluster housing. To install, reverse removal procedure.

Removal & Installation (G, J, L & P Bodies) – 1) Remove cluster assembly. Remove tachometer drive module and twist out all cluster bulbs. Remove mounting screws securing printed circuit board to cluster housing.

2) To install, carefully align printed circuit board to cluster housing and reverse removal procedure.

Removal & Installation (H Body) – Remove cluster assembly. Remove tachometer drive module. Remove gauge alert module. Twist out all cluster bulbs. Remove mounting screws securing printed circuit board to cluster housing and remove printed circuit board. To install, reverse removal procedure.

Removal & Installation (RWD Models) – 1) Remove cluster bezel. Remove instrument cluster assembly from carrier. Remove printed circuit board from cluster housing by prying apart at alternator and temperature gauges. Voltage limiter can be accessed at this time if necessary.

2) To install, position and push voltage limiter into printed circuit board (if removed). Position and push printed circuit board on cluster housing assembly. Install gauge cluster assembly to carrier. Install cluster bezel.

WIRING DIAGRAMS

For wiring diagrams, refer to appropriate chassis wiring diagram in WIRING DIAGRAMS section.

diagnostic function, press "SET" button and then another function button.

Fuel Level Diagnostic Function – 1) If "RANGE" function is not correct, check navigator using fuel level diagnostic function. Press "SPD" button and within 5 seconds, simultaneously press "US/MET" and "RESET" buttons, then press "SET" button.

2) Enter 124 into navigator. Display should read 30 or less for full tank and above 229 for empty tank. For example, a tank with 5 gallons should show reading of approximately 185. Replace navigator if fuel level function is okay.

3) If fuel level function indicates a failure, check instrument cluster fuel gauge operation. If fuel gauge works properly, test fuel tank sending unit. To deactivate diagnostic function, press "SET" button and then another function button.

REMOVAL & INSTALLATION

INSTRUMENT CLUSTER

Removal & Installation (Daytona & LeBaron) – 1) Remove cluster bezel retaining screws. Move bezel reward to disengage bezel retaining clips and remove cluster bezel. *See Fig. 4.* Remove instrument cluster retaining bolts.

2) Move instrument cluster outward and disconnect electrical connection. Remove instrument cluster. To install, reverse removal procedure.

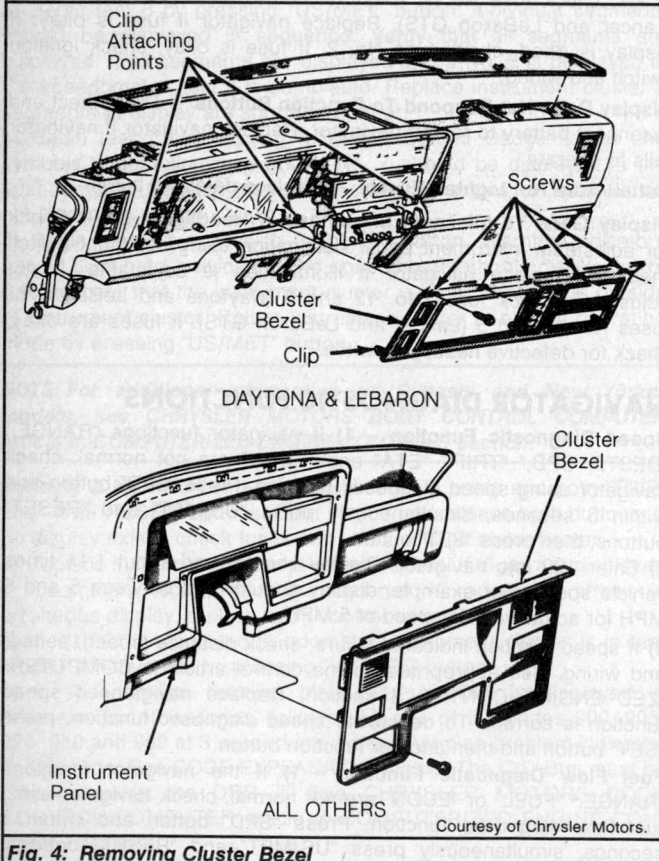

DAYTONA & LEBARON

ALL OTHERS

Courtesy of Chrysler Motors.

Fig. 4: Removing Cluster Bezel

Removal & Installation (Dynasty & New Yorker) – 1) Place gear selector lever in the lowest position. Remove screws from cluster bezel and remove cluster bezel. *See Fig. 4.*

2) Remove lower steering column cover. Disconnect shift indicator cable at steering column shift housing. Remove instrument cluster

retaining screws. Disconnect electrical connection and remove instrument cluster.

3) To install, reverse removal procedure. With shift indicator cable installed through instrument cluster, position gear selector lever in Neutral. Pull shift indicator cable so pointer is between Reverse and Neutral. Release cable and allow to snap back. Install shift cable in shift housing. Install remaining components.

Removal & Installation (Lancer & LeBaron GTS) – 1) Place gear selector lever in the lowest position. Remove screws from cluster bezel and remove cluster bezel. *See Fig. 4.*

2) Remove lower steering column cover. Remove knob from "TRIP RESET" button. Remove mask and lens from instrument cluster. Remove instrument cluster retaining screws. Disconnect electrical connection and remove instrument cluster. To install, reverse removal procedure.

NAVIGATOR

Removal & Installation – 1) On Daytona & LeBaron models, remove cluster bezel retaining screws. Move bezel reward to disengage bezel retaining clips and remove bezel. *See Fig. 4.*

2) On Lancer & LeBaron GTS models, place gear selector lever in the lowest position. Remove screws from cluster bezel and remove cluster bezel. *See Fig. 4.*

3) On all models, remove navigator retaining screws. Disconnect wiring connector and remove navigator. To install, reverse removal procedure.

ADJUSTMENTS

ODOMETER ADJUSTMENT

Daytona & LeBaron – Information not available by manufacturer.

Dynasty & New Yorker – Mileage information is stored in the body control computer. If instrument panel is changed, the original odometer reading will be obtained.

Lancer & LeBaron GTS – 1) If instrument cluster is replaced, vehicle's actual mileage can be programmed into new instrument cluster.

NOTE: Mileage can only be adjusted on instrument clusters with less than 10 accumulated miles.

2) Simultaneously press and hold "TRIP RESET" and "US/MET" buttons. Turn ignition on and release both buttons. Odometer will illuminate, displaying all zeroes with the first digit flashing.

3) Press and release "US/MET" button to change value of first (flashing) digit. Press "TRIP RESET" button to start second digit flashing. Press and release "US/MET" button to change value of second digit.

4) Adjust remaining odometer digits by pressing "TRIP RESET" button to start digit flashing, then pressing "US/MET" button to change digit value.

5) Once all odometer digits are adjusted to vehicle mileage, simultaneously press "TRIP" and "TRIP RESET" buttons. This locks in the adjusted odometer reading and returns instrument cluster to normal operation.

NOTE: An asterisk appears in the odometer display if mileage is adjusted. Adjustment can be made 3 times if incorrect mileage is entered, as long as less than 10 actual miles have been registered on the instrument cluster.

WIRING DIAGRAMS

For wiring diagrams, refer to appropriate chassis wiring diagram in WIRING DIAGRAMS section.

Premier

DESCRIPTION & OPERATION

Gauges – The instrument panel incorporates 3 magnetic type gauges: temperature, fuel and oil gauges. Current flows through the coils of each gauge creating 2 opposing magnetic fields. The sending unit used for each gauge is a variable resistor. The resistor varies magnetic field for each gauge which in turn controls needle position.

circuit. The vehicle speed sensor generates an AC voltage signal. This signal is buffered by the speed module and is sent to the speedometer circuit board in the instrument cluster. The solid state circuit drives the pointer of the speedometer.

Tachometer – With the ignition in the "RUN" or "START" positions, voltage is applied to the solid state tachometer. With the engine running, the tachometer receives an engine speed signal from the negative side of the ignition coil and displays engine speed or RPM.

Warning Indicators – The warning indicators receive battery voltage when the ignition switch is in the "ACC" or "RUN" positions. All warning indicators require a ground signal to turn each indicator light on.

TRIP COMPUTER

The trip computer monitors the following circuits: vehicle speed, fuel level, fuel flow, and outside temperature. Fuel and vehicle speed inputs are used to calculate fuel economy and average speed.

The trip computer has 8 primary functions and uses 3 function control buttons to select each function. The "ENGLISH/METRIC" display select button (located on far left side of instrument panel) is used to select either English or Metric measurements.

When the "TRIP/TIME" button is pressed, the functions on the left side of computer will display: time, stopwatch, distance, and average speed. When the "FUEL/TEMP" button is pressed, the functions on the right side of the computer will display: temperature, range, average economy, and instantaneous economy. The indicator light will move from function to function as you press each button.

When the ignition switch is on, the computer will display the current time. The "RESET" button is used to enter or exit the time setting mode. If battery is disconnected, the trip computer will flash "12:00 AM" until the time has been set.

VEHICLE MAINTENANCE MONITOR (VMM)

The Vehicle Maintenance Monitor (VMM) displays messages of conditions monitored by various input signals. The VMM is capable of self-diagnostics and will also display service reminder messages. Conditions monitored are: oil level, coolant level, windshield washer fluid level, vehicle speed and door ajar inputs. When the ignition switch is turned on, all segments of the VMM will be illuminated briefly. After this "bulb check", the display will indicate any monitored system message(s) in the order of highest priority. The system messages, their abbreviations, and order of priority are listed as follows:

Door Ajar "DOOR" – This message will display when the appropriate door(s) is (are) illuminated on the vehicle outline. Close door(s) to reset.

Brake Lamp Out "LAMP" – This message is activated when the brakes are applied and a bulb is burned out. To reset, replace bulb.

Tail Lamp Out "LAMP" – This message is activated when the tail lamps are on and a bulb is burned out. To reset, replace bulb.

Coolant Fluid Low "COOLANT" – This message is displayed when coolant level is low. To reset, add engine coolant as required.

Oil Low "OIL" – Oil level is monitored 12 minutes after the ignition switch is turned to the "OFF" position. After 3 consecutive detections of low oil, the message will be displayed. After adding oil, the display may be reset by pressing the "RESET" button while the oil level message is displayed and holding the button until a beep is heard. The display will automatically reset after the VMM sees 3

correct oil level readings. It is important to remember that the vehicle must be at normal operating temperture and turned off for 12 minutes to check oil level readings. This must happen 3 times consecutively to reset the display.

Washer Fluid Low "WASHER" – This message is displayed when windshield washer fluid is low. To reset, add windshield washer fluid as required.

Service Transmission "TRANS" – This message indicates a fault in the automatic transmission on 4-cylinder vehicles.

Perform Service "SERVICE" – This message is activated at 7500 mile intervals to indicate that regular service and maintenance is due. To reset, perform required service, then press the "RESET" button until a beep is heard.

Oil Level Fault "SENSOR" – This message will be reset when oil level is corrected.

Coolant Level Fault "SENSOR" – This message will be reset when coolant level is corrected.

Washer Level Fualt "SENSOR" – This message will be reset when washer level is corrected.

"MILES (KMS) TO SERVICE" – This message indicates the distance (or interval) to next scheduled service. When a fault condition is present, the monitor also sends a signal to the chime module.

All Systems Okay "MONITOR" – If all systems monitored are found to be normal, the VMM will display "MONITOR".

The VMM uses the vehicle speed input to calculate the distance traveled. It automatically notifies the driver (after a pre-programmed number of miles has elapsed) to perform a particular service on the vehicle.

When the lamps are on, the vehicle maintenance monitor display intensity is adjustable by using the panel dimmer switch. The monitor receives a signal from the "ENGLISH/METRIC" switch to display either English or Metric measurements.

The VMM also has the capability of self-diagnostics. It checks the monitor, the sensors and their circuits without the use of any special tools.

TESTING

MORE THAN ONE INDICATOR OR GAUGE DOES NOT OPERATE

Ignition Switch In "RUN" Position – Inspect fuses No. 10 and 15 and replace if needed. Check for battery voltage at battery side of fuse and repair open from ignition switch if needed. Check for battery voltage at terminals No. 16 and 10 of connector A and repair open from fuse if needed. Inspect instrument cluster printed circuit for cracks or poor contacts and replace printed circuit if necessary. See Fig. 7.

Ignition Switch "OFF" & Battery Disconnected – Check continuity between instrument cluster terminal No. 14 of connector A and ground. There should be zero (0) ohms. If not, repair open to ground.

COOLANT TEMP. GAUGE DOES NOT OPERATE (OTHERS GAUGES OKAY)

Ignition Switch In "RUN" Position – 1) Disconnect coolant temperature sender connector. Needle should move to the full "COLD" position. If it does, go to next step. If it does not, check wire to cluster and printed circuit for a short to ground. If okay, replace coolant temperature gauge.

2) Momentarily touch terminal No. 2 (Brown/Red wire) of coolant temperature sender connector to ground. Needle should move to the full "HOT" position. If it does, replace temperature sender. If it does not, check for an open between sender and instrument cluster.

3) Inspect instrument cluster printed circuit for cracks or a poor connection. If okay, replace coolant temperature gauge. If not okay, replace printed circuit.

FUEL GAUGE DOES NOT OPERATE (OTHER GAUGES OKAY)

Ignition Switch In "RUN" Position – 1) Disconnect fuel tank unit connector. Needle should move to the far "EMPTY" position. If it does, go to next step. If it does not, check wire to cluster and printed circuit for a short to ground. If okay, replace fuel gauge.

2) Momentarily touch terminal C of fuel tank connector to ground. Needle should move to the "FULL" position. If it does, replace fuel gauge sender. If it does not, check for open between fuel gauge sender and instrument cluster.

3) Inspect instrument cluster printed circuit for cracks or a poor connection. If okay, replace fuel gauge. If not okay, replace printed circuit.

TACHOMETER DOES NOT OPERATE (OTHER GAUGES OKAY)

Engine Running – 1) Connect an AC voltmeter to terminal A of ignition control module connector. Refer to IGNITION CONTROL MODULE VOLTAGE (AC) table to compare engine RPM and corresponding voltage readings. If voltage readings are not within specifications, replace ignition coil.

2) Connect an AC voltmeter to terminal No. 11 of instrument cluster connector B. Refer to IGNITION CONTROL MODULE VOLTAGE (AC) table to compare engine RPM and voltage readings. If voltage readings are not within specifications, repair open between ignition coil and instrument cluster.

3) Inspect instrument cluster printed circuit for cracks or a poor connection. If okay, replace tachometer. If not okay, replace printed circuit.

IGNITION CONTROL MODULE VOLTAGE (AC)

Engine RPM	AC Volts
1000	6.8
1500	8.1
2000	9.4
2500	10.7
3000	12.0
3500	13.3

OIL PRESSURE GAUGE DOES NOT OPERATE (OTHER GAUGES OKAY)

Ignition Switch In "RUN" Position – 1) Disconnect oil pressure sender/switch connector. Needle should move to the low or "L" position of gauge. If not, check wires to cluster and printed circuit for an open. If okay, replace oil pressure gauge.

2) Momentarily touch terminal of oil pressure sender/switch connector to ground. Needle should move to the maximum or "H" position of gauge. If it does, replace oil pressure sender/switch. If it does not, check wire to cluster and printed circuit for an open. If okay, replace oil pressure gauge.

SPEEDOMETER DOES NOT OPERATE

1) Operate cruise control. If cruise control does not operate correctly, go to next step. If cruise control operates correctly, check wires between speedometer and speed module. If wires are okay, replace speedometer assembly.

2) If cruise control does not operate correctly, check vehicle speed sensor. If speed sensor is okay, check speed sensor wire to cluster. If speed sensor wire is okay, go to next step. If speed sensor wire is not okay, repair or replace faulty wires.

3) If speed sensor wire is okay, check the power and ground wires to speed module and repair or replace if needed. If wires are okay, replace speed module.

BRAKE INDICATOR LIGHT STAYS ON

Ignition Switch In "RUN" Position – 1) Ground the park brake switch connector. Indicator light should turn on. If not, repair open from instrument cluster. If light turns on, replace park brake switch.

2) Ground terminal B of brake warning switch connector. Indicator light should turn on. If not, repair open from instrument cluster. If light turns on, go to next step.

3) Jumper terminal B to terminal A of brake warning switch connector. Indicator light should go on. If not, repair open from ground. If light turns on, replace brake warning switch.

HIGH TEMP., OIL LEVEL OR COOLANT LEVEL INDICATOR LIGHT STAYS ON

Ignition Switch In "RUN" Position – Disconnect switch connector of circuit being tested. Indicator light should turn off. If not, repair short to ground between switch and instrument cluster. If indicator light turns off, replace switch.

HIGH TEMP., OIL LEVEL OR COOLANT LEVEL INDICATOR LIGHT DOES NOT COME ON

Ignition Switch In "RUN" Position – 1) Ground switch connector of circuit being tested. Indicator light should turn on. If not, go to next step. If indicator light turns on, replace switch. Before replacing coolant level switch, check continuity from terminal B of coolant level switch connector to ground. Continuity must exist before replacing switch. If not, repair wiring.

2) Check indicator light bulb and replace if necessary. Check continuity between cluster and switch. If continuity does not exist, repair open from instrument cluster. If continuity does exist, replace instrument cluster printed circuit.

TRIP COMPUTER SELF-DIAGNOSTICS

The trip computer self-diagnostics consists of 5 tests. When the self-diagnostics cycle starts, the trip computer starts with Test 1. The sequence of tests from that point on is determined by which switch is depressed.

• Depressing the "TRIP/TIME" switch initiates Test 2 when the "ENGLISH/METRIC" switch is in the "ENGLISH" position.
• Depressing the "TRIP/TIME" switch initiates Test 3 when the "ENGLISH/METRIC" switch is in the "METRIC" position.
• Depressing the "FUEL/TEMP" switch initiates Test 4 when the "ENGLISH/METRIC" switch is in the "ENGLISH" position.
• Depressing the "FUEL/TEMP" switch initiates Test 5 when the "ENGLISH/METRIC" switch is in the "METRIC" position.
• Switching the ignition switch to the "OFF" position exits the self-diagnostics WITHOUT resetting any fault conditions.
• Depressing the "RESET" switch returns the trip computer to displaying the current time and WILL reset any existing fault conditions.

To Enter Self-Diagnostics – To enter the trip computer self-diagnostic mode, turn ignition switch to the "RUN" position while depressing the "TRIP/TIME" and "RESET" switches simultaneously.

Test 1 – The trip computer will display size of the vehicles fuel tank (in gallons) and will also display one of two different software revision levels (version 2 or version 3) for approximately one second.

With version 2 software, every segment in the display is illuminated and then extinguished. This segment testing will continue until the "TRIP/TIME" switch or the "FUEL/TEMP" switch is depressed, or if self-diagnostics mode is exited.

With version 3 software, the software revision level and fuel tank size code will continue to display until the "TRIP/TIME" switch or the "FUEL/TEMP" switch is depressed, or if self-diagnostics mode is exited.

Test 2 – The trip computer will display the condition of the temperature telltale lights or if a failure of the ambient air temperature sensor input is detected. The letters "CO" will display if there is an open detected in the circuit. The letters "CS" wll display if there is a short detected in the circuit. If there is no failure detected, the instantaneous temperature will be displayed.

Test 3 – The trip computer will display the condition of the average speed telltale lights and the frequency of the speed sensor. This frequency begins at zero (0) and increases as the vehicle speed increases.

Test 4 – The trip computer will display the condition of the range telltale lights or if a failure of the fuel level sensor input is detected. The letters "CO" will display if there is an open detected in the circuit. The letters "CS" will display if there is a short detected in the circuit. If there are no failures detected, the fuel level will be displayed in liters.

Test 5 – The trip computer will display the condition of the instant economy telltale lights or if a failure of the fuel flow input is detected. The letters "CO" will display if a failure of the fuel flow input occurs. If a failure is not detected, the frequency of the fuel flow sensor will be displayed. This frequency will vary as the vehicle speed is increased.

TRIP COMPUTER DOES NOT DISPLAY OR INCORRECT INFORMATION DISPLAYED

Ignition Switch In "RUN" Position – 1) Inspect fuse Nos. 8 and 19 (without passive restraint) of fuse No. 2 (with passive restraint). Replace fuse(s) if necessary.

2) Check for battery voltage at terminals No. 13 and 14 of trip computer connector. If battery voltage does not exist, repair open to fuse block. If battery voltage does exist, replace trip computer when testing for a no display or a no lamps on fault. If voltage does exist when testing for an incorrect information fault, perform the TRIP COMPUTER SELF-DIAGNOSTICS test.

INSTRUMENT PANEL DOES NOT ILLUMINATE

See NO INSTRUMENT PANEL ILLUMNIATION in this article.

TRIP COMPUTER DOES NOT CHANGE MODE

Disconnect Connector B On Trip Computer – 1) Check continuity between terminals No. 2 and 3 of connector B while depressing the "FUEL/TEMP" switch. There should be zero (0) ohms. If not, replace mode select switch.

2) Check continuity between terminals No. 2 and 4 of connector B while depressing the "RESET" switch. There should be zero (0) ohms. If not, replace mode select switch.

3) Check continuity between terminals No. 2 and 5 of connector B while depressing the "TRIP/TIME" select switch. There should be zero (0) ohms. If not, replace mode select switch.

NO INSTRUMENT PANEL ILLUMINATION

Headlight Switch In "PARK" Or "ON" Positions – 1) Check for battery voltage at terminal R of left hand module connector. If voltage is not present, check fuse No. 9 or check for an open to ignition switch or from battery.

2) Check for battery voltage at terminal P of left hand module connector with panel dimmer switch in the "DIM" position. If voltage is not present, replace left hand module.

3) Check for battery voltage at terminal S of left hand module connector with panel dimmer switch in the "BRIGHT" position. If voltage is not present, replace left hand module.

4) Check for battery voltage at terminal D10 of lamp module connector with panel dimmer switch in the "DIM" position. If voltage is not present, replace left hand module.

5) Check for battery voltage at terminal C9 of lamp module connector with panel dimmer switch in the "BRIGHT" position. If voltage is not present, repair open to left hand module.

6) Check for battery voltage at terminals D7 and D8 of lamp module connector. If battery voltage is not present, replace lamp module.

7) Check for battery voltage at terminals No. 22 and 23 at fuse block. If voltage is not available, repair open to lamp module.

8) Check for battery voltage at each components supply wires. If battery voltage is not available, repair open to fuse Nos. 13 and 14.

9) Check ground wire continuity for each component being tested. There should be zero (0) ohms. If not, repair open to ground.

NO ILLUMINATION IN ONE COMPONENT

Headlight Switch In "ON" Position & Panel Dimmer Switch In "BRIGHT" Position – Check for battery voltage to component or bulb being tested. If battery voltage is not present, repair open to respective splice. Check for continuity to ground on ground wire of component being tested. There should be zero (0) ohms, If not, repair open to ground.

VMM SELF-DIAGNOSTICS

To activate the diagnostics mode, simultaneously press and hold the "CHECK" and "LIST" switches, then turn the ignition switch to the "RUN" position. With these switches pressed, turn the ignition switch to the "ON" position. The diagnostic program will start and loop continously. To exit the diagnostic mode, simultaneously press the "CHECK" and "LIST" switches.

There are 2 modes for the diagnostic program: automatic mode and manual mode. In the automatic mode, the program will automatically perform all the tests in sequence. The sequence of tests will repeat until the diagnostic routine is exited. In the manual mode, each test will be performed individually and will only progress to the next test when the "CHECK" switch is pressed. Modes can be changed by pressing the "ENGLISH/METRIC" switch. If the instrument cluster is in the English mode, the program is in the automatic mode. If the instrument cluster is in the Metric mode, the program is in the manual mode.

VMM DOES NOT CHANGE MODE

Connector B disconnected – 1) Check continuity between terminals No. 2 and 4 of B connector while depressing the "CHECK" switch. there should be zero (0) ohms. If not, replace mode select switch.

2) Check continuity between terminals No. 2 and 3 of B connector while depressing the "LIST" switch. There should be zero (0) ohms. If not, replace mode select switch.

3) Check continuity between terminals No. 2 and 5 of B connector while depressing the "RESET" switch. There should be zero (0) ohms. If not, replace mode select switch.

VMM DOES NOT DISPLAY OR INCORRECT INFORMATION DISPLAYED

Ignition Switch In "RUN" Position (Engine Running) – 1) Inspect fuse Nos. 8 and 19 (without passive restraint) and fuse No. 2 (with passive restraint). Replace fuse(s) if necessary.

2) Check for battery voltage at terminals No. 1 and 5 of connector A. If battery voltage does not exist, repair open to fuse block.

Ignition Switch In "OFF" Position – 1) Check continuity at terminals No. 15 and 18 of connector A. There should be zero (0) ohms. If not, repair open to ground. If ohms reading is correct, replace VMM when testing for a no display fault, or perform a self-diagnostic test if testing for an incorrect information fault.

2) With all doors closed, check continuity (one at a time) between each terminals No. 6, 7, 8 and 9 of connector A and ground. There should be an infinite ohms reading. If not, check circuit for a short to ground.

REMOVAL & INSTALLATION

CHIME MODULE

Removal & Installation – Disconnect negative battery cable. Reach up under the drivers side of the instrument panel, between steering column and kick panel near floor, and unplug chime module. *See Fig. 1.* To install chime module, reverse removal procedures.

CLUSTER ASSEMBLY

Removal & Installation – 1) Disconnect negative battery cable. Remove screws and instrument panel lower cover (if equipped). Loosen screw holding shift indicator anchor bracket in place. *See Fig. 2.*

2) Remove shift indicator cable anchor by sliding to keyhole position. Remove wire from rear of gearshift lever pulley. Remove instrument cluster bezel screws and remove bezel.

3) Remove cluster retaining screws. *See Fig. 3.* Move gearshift lever to the "1" position. Tilt cluster forward and disconnect electrical connectors. Remove cluster assembly. *See Fig. 4.*

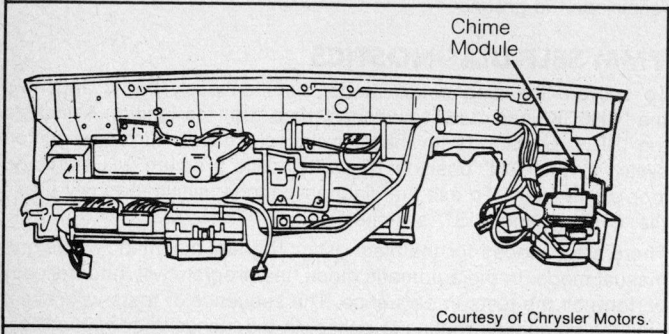

Fig. 1: Location of Chime Module

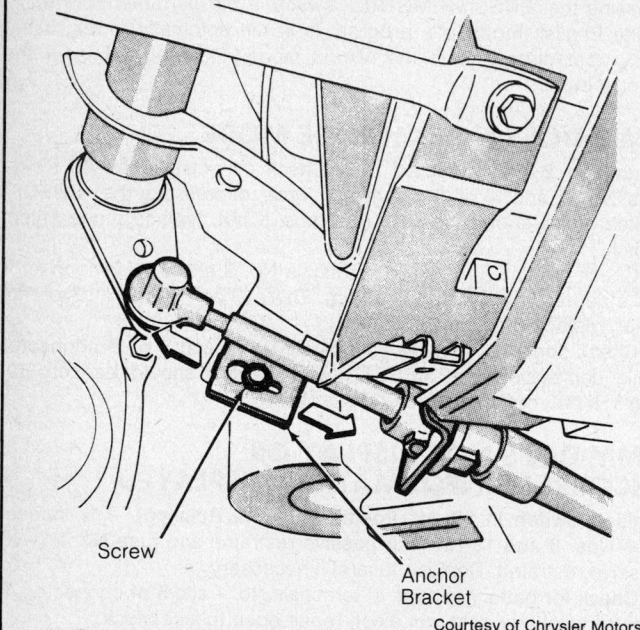

Fig. 2: Removing Shift Indicator Bracket

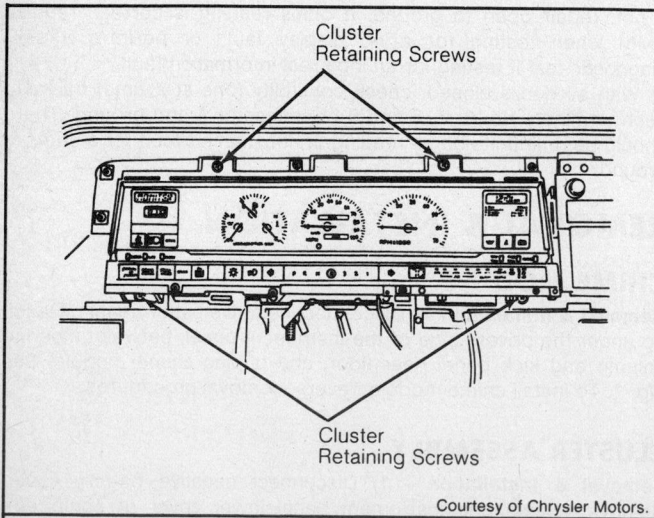

Fig. 3: Removing Cluster Assembly Retaining Screws

4) To install cluster assembly, guide shift indicator wire into instrument panel and down to shift linkage. Connect electrical connectors. Install cluster assembly and secure with screws.

5) Loop shift wire over pulley. Install shift cable anchor onto screw. Move gearshift lever to the "N" position and check position of shift indicator. If pointer is not aligned with the "N" on the display, slide anchor until indicator is positioned correctly, then tighten screw. Check for proper positioning of indicator in all positions.

6) Install bezel and secure with screws. Install instrument panel lower trim cover (if equipped).

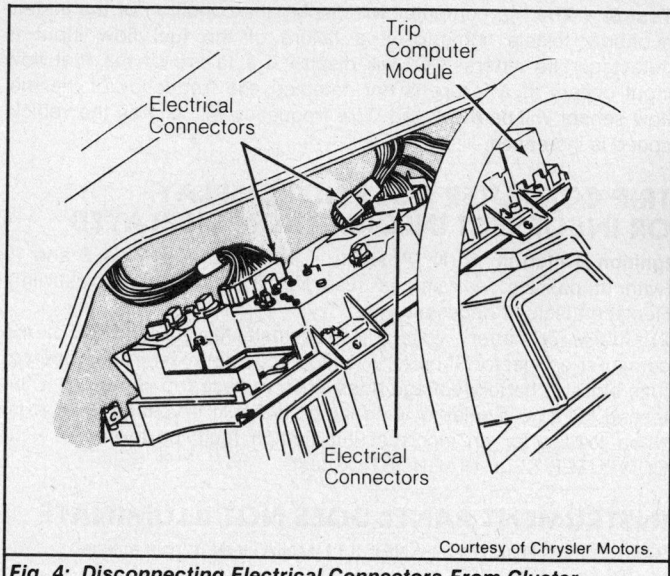

Fig. 4: Disconnecting Electrical Connectors From Cluster

SPEEDOMETER

CAUTION: Wear clean gloves when handling the cluster assembly. Finger prints and finger nails will mar the surface.

Removal – 1) Remove cluster assembly. Remove control switch panel. Remove lens screws and lens. Remove screws retaining Black mask and remove mask.

2) Remove all screws and nuts retaining cluster and dial assemblies. Remove cluster and dial assemblies from cluster. *See Fig. 5.*

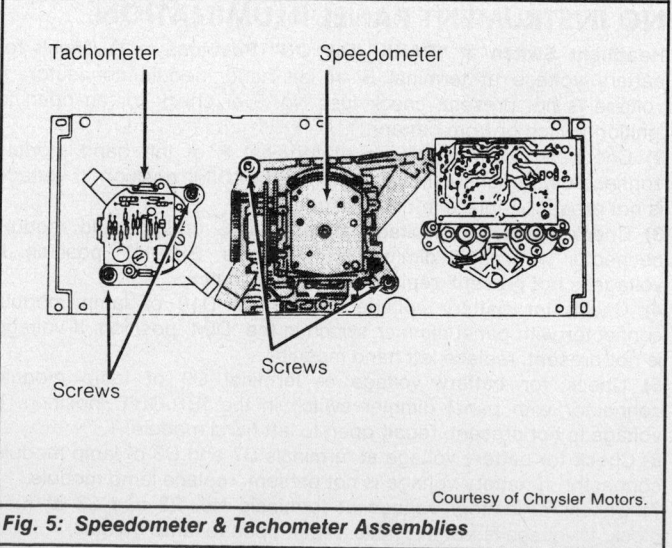

Fig. 5: Speedometer & Tachometer Assemblies

3) When removing speedometer assembly, grasp the pointer hub and slowly rotate pointer assembly clockwise and counterclockwise until pointer contacts trip reset shaft, while gently pulling upward on hub away from dial surface. Repeat this procedure approximately 5 to 15 times until pointer assembly lifts off movement shaft. Remove screws and separate speedometer from face plate.

Installation – 1) Position speedometer and secure with screws. Grasp pointer by hub and gently place bushing onto movement shaft. Pointer tip should be indicating approximately 90 MPH (140 KPH).

2) Rotate pointer assembly counterclockwise while gently pushing down on hub toward the dial surface (a slight resistance should be felt). Clearance between hub underside and dial surface should be .020-.060" (.50-1.52 mm) before pointer tip is in line with the zero horizontal graduation.

3) Stop when the pointer tip comes in line with the zero horizontal graduation. If pointer tip does NOT align with the horizontal graduation, perform either of the 2 following steps:

4) If pointer is too high, continue rotating assembly counterclockwise until alignment is achieved. Repeat procedure if necessary.

5) If pointer is too low, rotate pointer assembly clockwise until rotational resistance is felt (this does not refer to contact with trip reset shaft). Continue rotating in direction of resistance to compensate for initial misalignment. Release hub allowing pointer assembly to rotate back to its reset position. Repeat procedure if necessary.

6) To install cluster assembly, reverse removal procedure.

TACHOMETER

CAUTION: Wear clean gloves when handling the cluster assembly. Finger prints and finger nails will mar the surface.

Removal – 1) Remove cluster assembly. Remove control switch panel. Remove lens screws and lens. Remove screws retaining Black mask and remove mask.

2) Remove all screws and nuts retaining cluster and dial assemblies. Remove cluster and dial assemblies.

3) Grasp pointer hub and slowly rotate pointer assembly counterclockwise while gently pulling upward on the hub away from dial surface (approximately 5 to 15 turns are required).

4) Remove screws attaching tachometer to face plate and remove tachometer assembly from face plate.

Installation – 1) Position tachometer and secure with screws. Grasp the pointer by the hub and gently place the bushing onto movement shaft. The pointer tip shold be indicating approximately 6000 RPM.

2) Rotate pointer assembly counterclockwise while gently pushing down on hub toward dial surface (a slight resistance should be felt). Clearance between the hub underside and dial surface shoud be .020-.060" (.50-1.52 mm) before pointer tip is in line with zero horizontal graduation.

3) If pointer in NOT properly aligned to the horizontal graduation, perform either of the 2 following steps:

4) If pointer is too high, continue rotating assembly counterclockwise until alignment is achieved. Repeat procedure if necessary.

5) If pointer is too low, rotate pointer assembly clockwise until rotational resistance is felt (this does not refer to contact with trip reset shaft). Continue rotating in direction of resistance to compensate for initial alignment. Release hub allowing pointer assembly to rotate back to its reset position. Repeat procedure if necessary.

6) To install cluster assembly, reverse removal procedure.

TRIP COMPUTER

Removal & Installation – Remove cluster assembly. Remove screws attaching computer module to instrument cluster. Disconnect electrical connector. Remove computer module. *See Fig. 4.*

VEHICLE MAINTENANCE MONITOR (VMM)

Removal & Installation – Remove cluster assembly. Remove screws attaching VMM module to instrument cluster and disconnect electrical connector. Remove computer module. *See Fig. 6.* To install, reverse removal procedure.

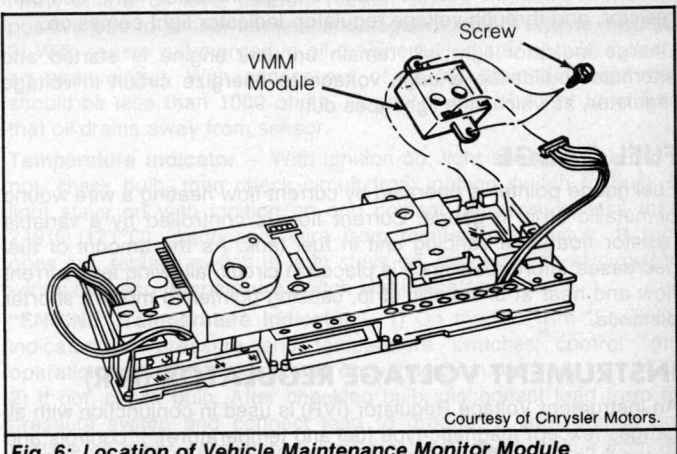

Courtesy of Chrysler Motors.

Fig. 6: Location of Vehicle Maintenance Monitor Module

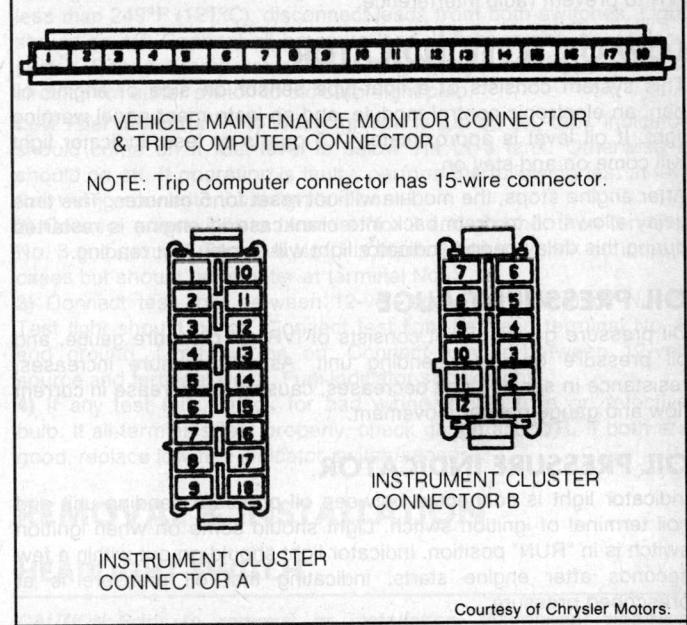

VEHICLE MAINTENANCE MONITOR CONNECTOR & TRIP COMPUTER CONNECTOR

NOTE: Trip Computer connector has 15-wire connector.

INSTRUMENT CLUSTER CONNECTOR A

INSTRUMENT CLUSTER CONNECTOR B

Courtesy of Chrysler Motors.

Fig. 7: Electrical Connector Identification

WIRING DIAGRAMS

For wiring diagrams, refer to appropriate chassis wiring diagram in WIRING DIAGRAMS section.

6-138

1989 SWITCHES & INSTRUMENT PANELS
Ford Motor Co. Probe — Standard (Cont.)

TURN SIGNAL SWITCH

Removal & Installation – 1) Disconnect negative battery cable. Remove steering wheel. Remove instrument cluster. See INSTRUMENT CLUSTER under REMOVAL & INSTALLATION in this article.
2) Remove attaching screw from turn signal arm and remove arm. Remove 2 attaching screws from turn signal switch. Remove turn signal switch from back of instrument cluster. To install, reverse removal procedure.

HAZARD SWITCH

Removal & Installation – 1) Disconnect negative battery cable. Remove steering wheel. Remove instrument cluster. See INSTRUMENT CLUSTER under REMOVAL & INSTALLATION in this article.
2) Remove attaching screws from hazard switch. Remove switch from back of instrument cluster. To install, reverse removal procedure.

PANEL DIMMER SWITCH

Removal & Installation – 1) Disconnect negative battery cable. Remove instrument cluster. See INSTRUMENT CLUSTER under REMOVAL & INSTALLATION in this article.
2) Gently press in on lock tab on both side of dimmer switch. Remove dimmer switch through front of instrument cluster. To install, reverse removal procedure.

HEADLIGHT SWITCH

Removal & Installation – Remove turn signal switch assembly. See TURN SIGNAL SWITCH under REMOVAL & INSTALLATION in this article. Remove rotary switch knob from headlight switch stem by gently pulling knob away from switch. Remove attaching screws from rotary switch housing. Remove headlight switch. To install, reverse removal procedure.

FRONT & REAR WIPER/WASHER SWITCH

Removal & Installation – 1) Remove instrument cluster. See INSTRUMENT CLUSTER under REMOVAL & INSTALLATION in this article. Remove front washer/interval switch rate control knob and front wiper/washer switch knob by gently pulling knob away from switch.
2) Remove attaching screws from front wiper/washer switch. Remove front wiper/washer switch. To remove rear wiper/washer switch, remove switch retaining screws. Remove switch button by releasing tangs. Remove switch through front of instrument cluster. To install, reverse removal procedure.

NOTE: The following diagnostic charts, circuits and illustrations are supplied courtesy of Ford Motor Co.

TESTING & DIAGNOSIS

FUEL GAUGE INOPERATIVE

1) Turn ignition switch on (engine not running). Check fuel gauge and warning lights for proper operation. If warning lights are inoperative and fuel gauge reads empty, go to INSTRUMENT CLUSTER FUSE CHECK NO. 1.
2) If warning lights are operative and fuel gauge reads empty, go to FUEL GAUGE CHECK. If fuel gauge always reads full, go to FUEL GAUGE SHORT CHECK NO. 1. If fuel gauge is not accurate, go to FUEL GAUGE TESTING.

INSTRUMENT CLUSTER FUSE CHECK NO. 1

Check 15-amp instrument cluster fuse in interior fuse panel. Fuse panel is located just above left kick panel. If fuse is okay, go to WARNING LIGHT SYSTEM CHECK. If fuse is blown, replace fuse. If fuse blows again, check for shorts to ground in Black/Yellow wire between gauges and fuse panel. Repair as necessary.

FUEL GAUGE CHECK

1) Ground Yellow wire at instrument cluster 8-pin connector. See INSTRUMENT CLUSTER 8-PIN TERMINAL IDENTIFICATION illustration. Instrument cluster 8-pin connector is located on right side of dash, near steering column.
2) Observe fuel gauge reading. If fuel gauge reads full, go to FUEL GAUGE CONTINUITY CHECK NO. 1. If fuel gauge is inoperative, replace fuel gauge.

Instrument Cluster 8-pin Terminal Identification

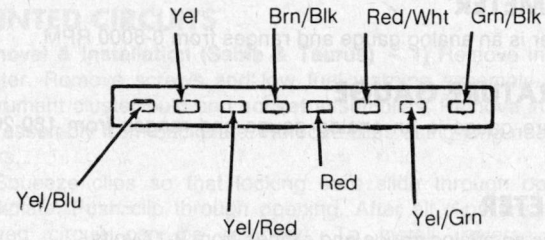

FUEL GAUGE CONTINUITY CHECK NO. 1

1) Ground Yellow wire at fuel tank sending unit 6-pin connector. See FUEL TANK SENDING UNIT 6-PIN TERMINAL IDENTIFICATION illustration. Fuel tank sending unit 6-pin connector is located on front of fuel tank.
2) Observe fuel gauge reading. If fuel gauge reads full, go to FUEL GAUGE CONTINUITY CHECK NO. 2. If fuel gauge does not read full, repair Yellow wire between gauges and fuel tank sending unit.

Fuel Tank Sending Unit 6-Pin Terminal Identification

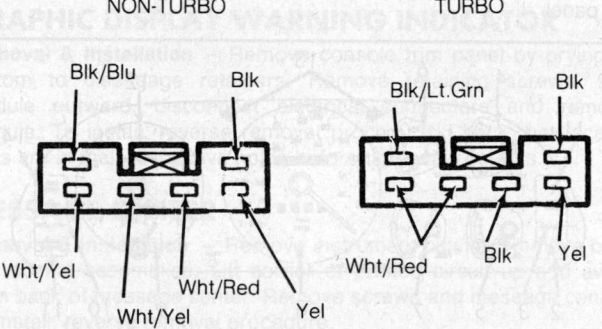

FUEL GAUGE CONTINUITY CHECK NO. 2

1) On non-turbo models, ground Black/Blue wire at fuel tank sending unit 6-pin connector. On turbo models equipped with Vehicle Maintenance Monitor (VMM), ground Black/Light Green wire. See FUEL TANK SENDING UNIT 6-PIN TERMINAL IDENTIFICATION illustration. Fuel tank sending unit 6-pin connector is located on front of fuel tank.
2) Observe fuel gauge reading. If fuel gauge reads correctly, repair Black wire between fuel tank sending unit and ground. If fuel gauge does not read correctly, replace fuel tank sending unit.

1989 SWITCHES & INSTRUMENT PANELS
Ford Motor Co. Probe – Standard (Cont.)

6-139

FUEL GAUGE SHORT CHECK NO. 1

1) Disconnect instrument cluster 8-pin connector. Instrument cluster 8-pin connector is located on right side of dash, near steering column.

2) Observe fuel gauge reading. If fuel gauge reads full, replace fuel gauge. If fuel gauge does not read full, go to FUEL GAUGE SHORT CHECK NO. 2.

FUEL GAUGE SHORT CHECK NO. 2

1) Reconnect instrument cluster 8-pin connector if previously disconnected. Disconnect fuel tank sending unit 6-pin connector. Fuel tank sending unit 6-pin connector is located on front of fuel tank.

2) Observe fuel gauge reading. If fuel gauge reads full, repair Yellow wire between gauges and fuel tank sending unit. If fuel gauge does not read full, replace fuel tank sending unit.

FUEL GAUGE TESTING

1) Disconnect fuel tank sending unit 6-pin connector. Fuel tank sending unit 6-pin connector is located on front of fuel tank. Using Gauge System Tester (Rotunda 021-00055), connect one lead to Yellow terminal wire of fuel tank sending unit 6-pin connector and other lead to ground. See TESTING FUEL GAUGE illustration.

2) Set tester to resistance values shown in illustration. Turn ignition on and check to see that needle indicator displays correct values. Continue inspection for 2 minutes on each setting, to correctly judge accuracy of gauge.

3) Allowable error is twice the width of fuel gauge needle. If fuel gauge readings are correct, go to FUEL GAUGE SENDING UNIT CHECK. If fuel gauge readings are not correct, replace fuel gauge.

Testing Fuel Gauge

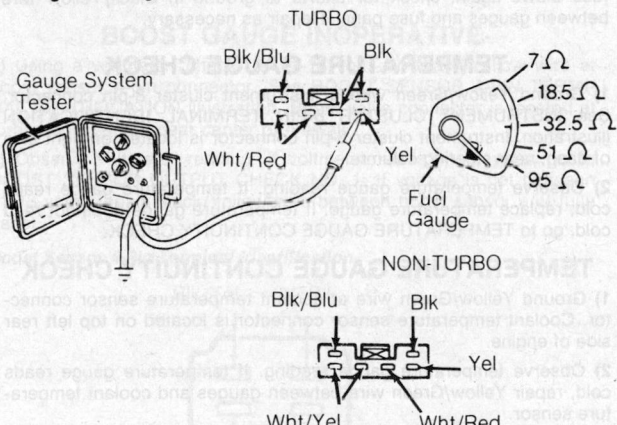

FUEL GAUGE SENDING UNIT CHECK

1) Remove fuel tank sending unit. To remove sending unit, remove service hole cover. Disconnect main fuel hose. Remove fuel tank sending unit.

2) Connect ohmmeter to fuel tank sending unit connector "A" and "B" terminals. Compare resistance values. See CHECKING FUEL GAUGE SENDING UNIT illustration.

Checking Fuel Gauge Sending Unit

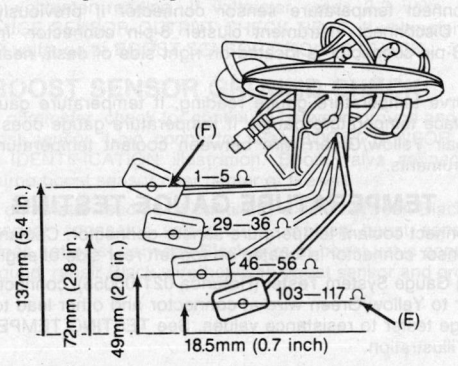

FUEL GAUGE SENDING UNIT CHECK (CONT.)

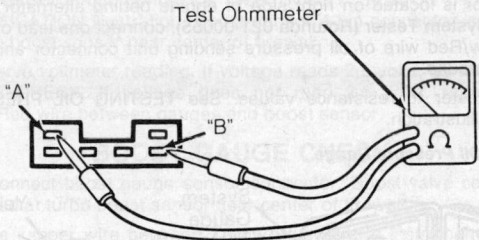

3) If resistance values are same as listed, check for loose or dirty connections at fuel tank sending unit connector. If resistance values are not same as listed, replace fuel tank sending unit.

OIL PRESSURE GAUGE INOPERATIVE

1) Turn ignition on (engine not running). Check oil pressure gauge and warning lights for proper operation.

2) If warning lights are not working and oil pressure gauge reads low, go to INSTRUMENT CLUSTER FUSE CHECK NO. 2.

3) If oil pressure switch reads low, go to OIL PRESSURE GAUGE CHECK.

4) If oil pressure gauge reads high, go to OIL PRESSURE GAUGE SHORT CHECK NO. 1.

5) If oil pressure gauge is not accurate, go to OIL PRESSURE GAUGE TESTING.

INSTRUMENT CLUSTER FUSE CHECK NO. 2

Check 15-amp instrument cluster fuse in interior fuse panel. Fuse panel is located just above left kick panel. If fuse is okay, go to WARNING LIGHT SYSTEM CHECK. If fuse is blown, replace fuse. If fuse blows again, check for shorts to ground in Black/Yellow wire between gauges and fuse panel. Repair as necessary.

OIL PRESSURE GAUGE CHECK

1) Ground Yellow/Red wire at instrument cluster 8-pin connector. See INSTRUMENT CLUSTER 8-PIN TERMINAL IDENTIFICATION illustration. Instrument cluster 8-pin connector is located on right side of dash, near steering column.

2) Observe oil pressure gauge reading. If oil pressure gauge reads high, go to OIL PRESSURE GAUGE CONTINUITY CHECK NO. 1.

3) If oil pressure gauge does not read high, replace oil pressure gauge.

OIL PRESSURE GAUGE CONTINUITY CHECK NO. 1

1) Ground Yellow/Red wire at oil pressure sending unit connector. Oil pressure switch connector is located on right side of engine behind alternator.

2) If oil pressure gauge reads high, replace oil pressure sending unit. If oil pressure gauge does not read high, repair Yellow/Red wire between gauges and oil pressure sending unit.

OIL PRESSURE GAUGE SHORT CHECK NO. 1

1) Disconnect instrument cluster 8-pin connector. Instrument cluster 8-pin connector is located on right side of dash, near steering column.

2) Observe oil pressure gauge reading. If oil pressure gauge reads high, replace oil pressure gauge.

3) If oil pressure gauge does not read high, go to OIL PRESSURE GAUGE SHORT CHECK NO. 2.

OIL PRESSURE GAUGE SHORT CHECK NO. 2

1) Reconnect instrument cluster 8-pin connector if previously disconnected. Disconnect oil pressure gauge sending unit connector. Oil pressure switch connector is located on right side of engine behind alternator.

2) Observe oil pressure gauge reading. If oil pressure gauge reads high, repair Yellow/Red wire between gauges and oil pressure sending unit. If oil pressure gauge does not read high, replace oil pressure sending unit.

REMOVAL & INSTALLATION

INSTRUMENT CLUSTER

NOTE: Electronics within instrument cluster are not serviceable.

Removal – 1) Disconnect negative battery cable. Remove headlight switch knob. Carefully pull away instrument cluster finish panel while detaching spring clips surrounding finish panel.

2) Unplug connector on rear of switch assembly. Disconnect auto lamp module connector (if equipped). Place clean soft cloth over steering column shroud to prevent scratching cluster finish.

3) Remove 4 cluster retaining screws. Pull bottom of cluster towards steering wheel. Reaching behind cluster, unplug 2 connectors. Swing bottom of cluster out to clear top of cluster from pad and remove.

Installation – Insert top of instrument cluster under pad leaving bottom out. Plug in 2 connectors. Seat instrument cluster and install 4 retaining screws. Reconnect negative battery cable and check instrument cluster operation. Install cluster finish panel. To complete installation, reverse removal procedure.

ILLUMINATION BULBS

Removal & Installation – 1) Remove instrument cluster. See INSTRUMENT CLUSTER under REMOVAL & INSTALLATION in this article. Allow illumination bulbs to cool before replacing. Find light bar on right side (rear view) of cluster assembly.

2) Unplug 3-pin connector secured by locking tab. Carefully depress tab on top of light bar cover. Slowly pull light bar out from end of cluster. To install, reverse removal procedure.

AUTOLAMP SWITCH

Removal & Installation – Remove autolamp switch assembly from instrument cluster finish panel (snaps out). Disconnect wiring connector and remove switch. *See Fig. 2.* To install, reverse removal procedure.

HEADLIGHT SWITCH

Removal & Installation – 1) Disconnect negative battery cable. Remove 2 cluster finish panel retaining screws. Remove headlight switch knob (pulls off). Remove cluster finish panel (snaps off) and disconnect electrical connector to headlight dimmer sensor assembly.

2) Using opening in instrument panel, depress shaft release button on switch and remove shaft. Remove headlight switch retaining nut and pull switch through opening. Disconnect headlight switch wiring connector. *See Fig. 2.* To install, reverse removal procedure.

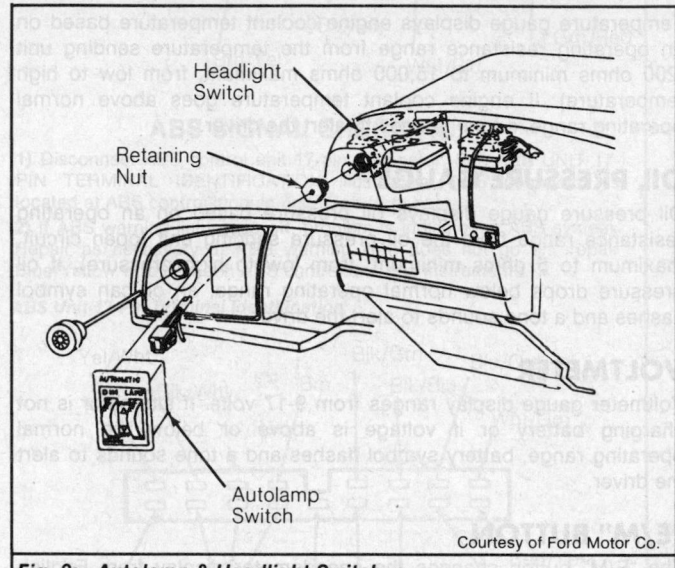

Courtesy of Ford Motor Co.

Fig. 2: Autolamp & Headlight Switches

1989 SWITCHES & INSTRUMENT PANELS
Cougar & Thunderbird Electronic Instrument Cluster (Cont.)

6-147

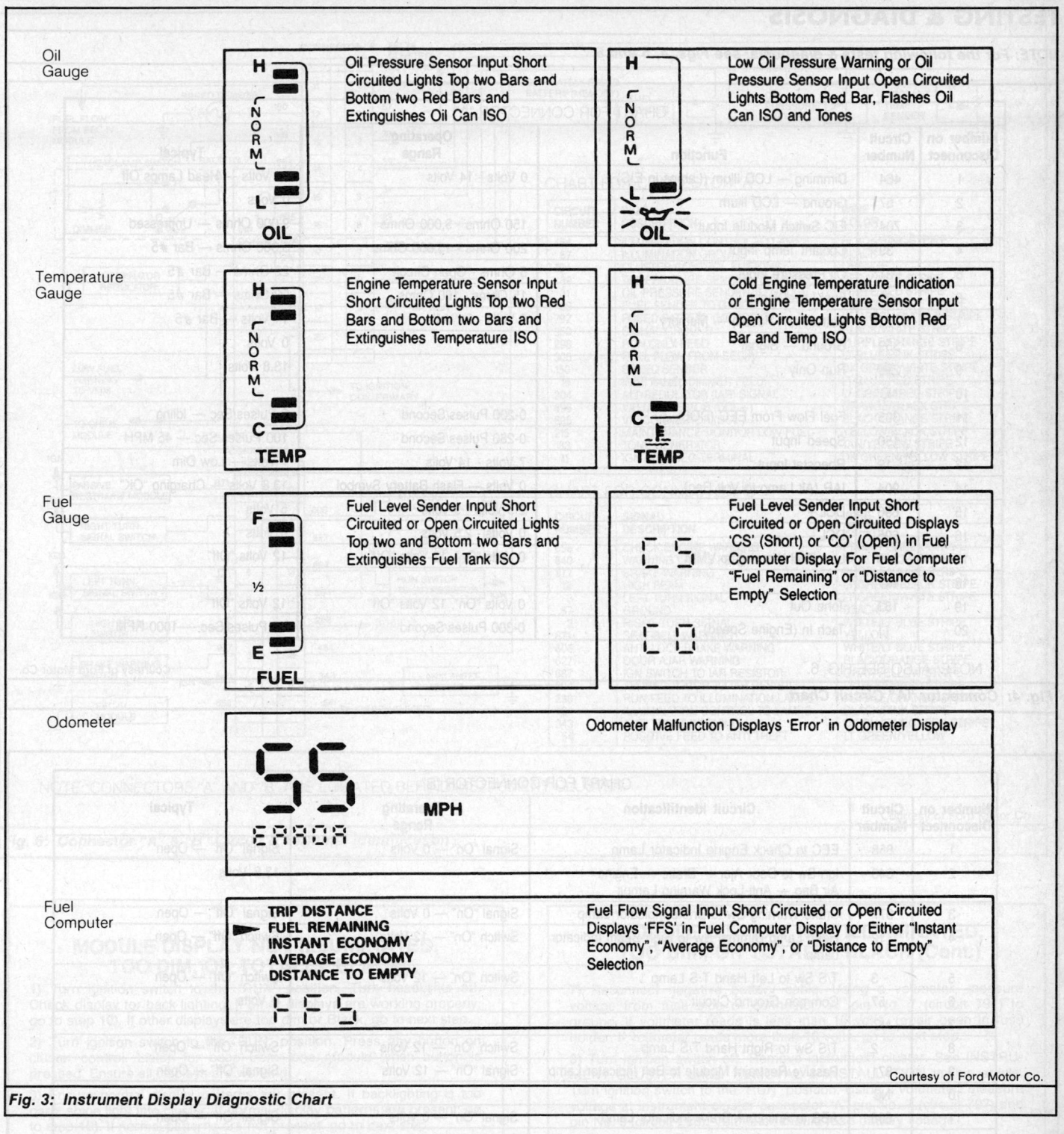

Oil Gauge	Oil Pressure Sensor Input Short Circuited Lights Top two Bars and Bottom two Red Bars and Extinguishes Oil Can ISO	Low Oil Pressure Warning or Oil Pressure Sensor Input Open Circuited Lights Bottom Red Bar, Flashes Oil Can ISO and Tones
Temperature Gauge	Engine Temperature Sensor Input Short Circuited Lights Top two Red Bars and Bottom two Bars and Extinguishes Temperature ISO	Cold Engine Temperature Indication or Engine Temperature Sensor Input Open Circuited Lights Bottom Red Bar and Temp ISO
Fuel Gauge	Fuel Level Sender Input Short Circuited or Open Circuited Lights Top two and Bottom two Bars and Extinguishes Fuel Tank ISO	Fuel Level Sender Input Short Circuited or Open Circuited Displays 'CS' (Short) or 'CO' (Open) in Fuel Computer Display For Fuel Computer "Fuel Remaining" or "Distance to Empty" Selection
Odometer		Odometer Malfunction Displays 'Error' in Odometer Display
Fuel Computer	TRIP DISTANCE / FUEL REMAINING / INSTANT ECONOMY / AVERAGE ECONOMY / DISTANCE TO EMPTY	Fuel Flow Signal Input Short Circuited or Open Circuited Displays 'FFS' in Fuel Computer Display for Either "Instant Economy", "Average Economy", or "Distance to Empty" Selection

Courtesy of Ford Motor Co.

Fig. 3: Instrument Display Diagnostic Chart

DESCRIPTION

The Mark VII Electronic Instrument Cluster (EIC) is divided into 3 sections: the Electronic Instrument Module (EIM), the Non-Volatile Memory Module (NVMM) and Conventional Feature Section (CFS).

ELECTRONIC INSTRUMENT MODULE (EIM)

The EIM consists of digital fuel gauge, digital speedometer, and an electronic odometer. All displays share common electronic circuitry (i.e. power supply, dimming control, and computer) within the EIM.

When ignition switch is in "RUN" or "ACC" positions or the door handle is pulled, the EIM is illuminated at maximum display brightness and is operational.

NON-VOLATILE MEMORY MODULE (NVMM)

The NVMM provides permanent memory for odometer, fuel gauge, and diagnostic counts.

CONVENTIONAL FEATURE SECTION (CFS)

This section consists of turn signal indicators and a high beam indicator.

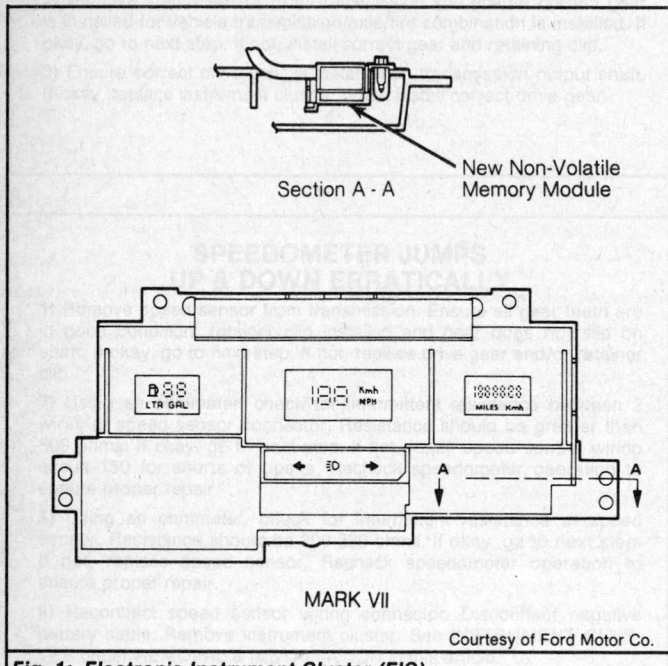

Fig. 1: Electronic Instrument Cluster (EIC)

Courtesy of Ford Motor Co.

Section A - A — New Non-Volatile Memory Module

MARK VII

OPERATION

SPEEDOMETER

The electronic digital speedometer is located in the center display section of EIM. It can display vehicle speeds from zero to a maximum of 85 MPH or 137 km/h.

Speed information is provided by a transmission mounted variable reluctance speed sensor. This sensor also provides speed information directly to message center and cruise control module.

The speedometer will initiate a 2-second self-test sequence which will allow verification of speedometer display segment illumination when cluster is first turned on. If speedometer system is in good condition, the following display will be shown. See Fig. 2.

ODOMETER

The odometer is located in the right display section of EIM. Accumulated distance traveled will be shown on a 6 1/2 digit, seven-segment display with decimal point. The odometer is capable of displaying from 00000.0 to 199999.9.

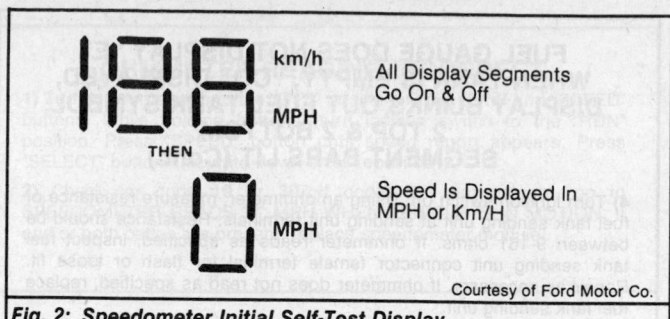

Fig. 2: Speedometer Initial Self-Test Display

Courtesy of Ford Motor Co.

All Display Segments Go On & Off

Speed Is Displayed In MPH or Km/H

Distance information is provided by the same transmission-mounted sensor used to provide information to the speedometer. The odometer accumulated mileage is stored in the NVMM at every 10 mile interval. Mileage is also stored when the ignition is turned off.

FUEL DISPLAY

The digital fuel display is located in left section of EIM. Fuel level is displayed on two, 7-segment digits. Also displayed is an International Standards Organization (ISO) fuel pump symbol and the appropriate display unit (gallons or liters). For fuel levels greater than 20 gallons (75.7 liters) an "F" will be displayed (indicating full) and for fuel levels less than 1 gallon (3.78 liters) an "E" will be displayed (indicating empty).

When cluster is first turned on, a 2 second self-test sequence will be initiated. This allows driver to verify illumination of all display segments. If fuel display is operating correctly, all displays will come on and then go off.

Low Fuel Displays – A continuous flashing ISO fuel pump symbol provides a low fuel warning. Symbol will begin to flash when fuel display indicates 2 gallons (7.5 liters). At zero usable fuel, the "E" begins to flash along with fuel pump symbol.

Service Alerts – If an open circuit in fuel display circuit exists, a "CO" will be displayed. If a short circuit in fuel display circuit exists, a "CS" will be displayed. These displays will be shown until condition is corrected.

REMOVAL & INSTALLATION

NOTE: Removal and installation procedures for components not listed here will be found in FORD MOTOR CO. SWITCHES & INSTRUMENT PANELS article in this section.

INSTRUMENT CLUSTER

1) Disconnect negative battery cable. Remove 4 screws retaining instrument cluster finish panel. Rotate top of panel toward steering wheel. Disconnect electrical and air sensor connectors from right side of panel. Remove panel. See Fig. 3.
2) Remove 6 screws retaining instrument panel top pad and rotate pad toward steering gear. Remove pad. Remove 4 screws and carefully pull out instrument cluster. See Fig. 3. Disconnect wiring harness from cluster. To install, reverse removal procedure.

ELECTRONIC INSTRUMENT MODULE (EIM)

1) Remove instrument cluster. Remove screws retaining NVMM cable connector at back of EIM. Remove cable from under 2 retaining tabs.
2) Remove EIM flex connector from 4 mounting tabs on backplate. Remove EIM by sliding it rearward. To install, reverse removal procedure.

NON-VOLATILE MEMORY MODULE (NVMM)

1) Remove instrument cluster. Remove screw retaining NVMM cable connector to back of EIM. Remove cable from under 2 retaining tabs. Remove connector.

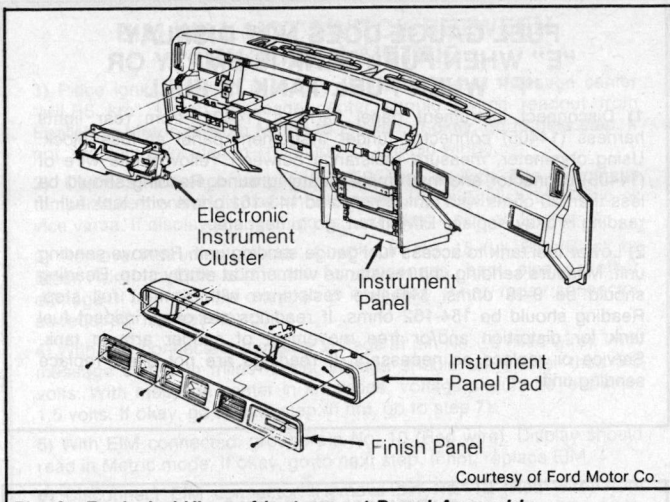

Electronic Instrument Cluster

Instrument Panel

Instrument Panel Pad

Finish Panel

Courtesy of Ford Motor Co.

Fig. 3: Exploded View of Instrument Panel Assembly

2) Remove extra cable stored in lower backplate. Remove module retaining screws. Remove module by lifting mounting tab upward to disengage. To install, reverse removal procedure.

WIRING DIAGRAMS

For wiring diagrams, refer to appropriate chassis wiring diagram in WIRING DIAGRAMS section.

TESTING & DIAGNOSIS (INSTRUMENT CLUSTER)

NOTE: In the following diagnostic testing, circuits and illustrations are supplied courtesy of Ford Motor Co. For connector and harness identification, see Figs. 4, 5, 6, and 7.

DISPLAY TOTALLY BLANK

1) Place ignition switch in "ACC" position. Check illumination of other EIM displays. If other displays are lit, replace EIM. If other displays are not lit, go to next step.

2) Check illumination of message center. If message center is lit, go to step 6). If not, check message center and instrument cluster 4-amp fuses (Nos. 16 and 17). If fuses are okay, go to step 5). If fuses are blown, go to next step.

3) Before replacing fuse(s), turn ignition off. Disconnect negative battery cable. Connect ohmmeter between Light Green/Purple wire at fuse block and ground. Check for short circuit. If short exists, repair circuit wiring. If not shorted, check Orange/Red wire from fuse box to instrument illumination module 8-wire connector for short circuit using same procedure.

4) Place ignition switch in "ACC" position. Measure voltage at Light Blue/Pink wire of interior lamp relay. If reading is at least 10 volts, go to next step. If reading is less than 10 volts, repair:

- Light Blue/Pink wire from interior lamp relay to EIM pin No. 18 and message center.
- Light Green/Purple wire from fuse block to EIM pin No. 17 and message center.

5) Place ignition switch in "ACC" position. Measure voltage at Light Blue/Pink wire at EIM connector. If voltage is at least 10 volts, go to next step. If voltage is incorrect, replace interior lamp relay.

6) Check EIM connector terminals for cleanliness. Ensure connector is securely attached. If connector is okay, go to next step. If connector is not okay, clean terminals and properly secure connector to EIM.

7) Disconnect EIM harness connector. Measure voltage between Light Blue/Pink wire (pin No. 18) and Black/White wire (pin No. 13). If reading is greater than 10 volts, go to next step. If reading is less than

DISPLAY TOTALLY BLANK (Cont.)

10 volts, repair Light Blue/Pink wire and/or Black/White wire (ground), behind instrument panel, right side of steering column.

8) Disconnect EIM harness connector. Measure voltage between Light Green/Purple wire (pin No. 17) and Black/White wire (pin No. 13). If reading is greater than 10 volts, go to next step. If reading is less than 10 volts, repair Light Green/Purple wire and/or Black/White wire (ground).

9) Remove EIM. Check instrument cluster ground terminal for good metal-to-metal contact. Ground terminal is located on shake brace, below instrument cluster. Service as required. If connection is okay, replace EIM.

Cluster Ground Connectors

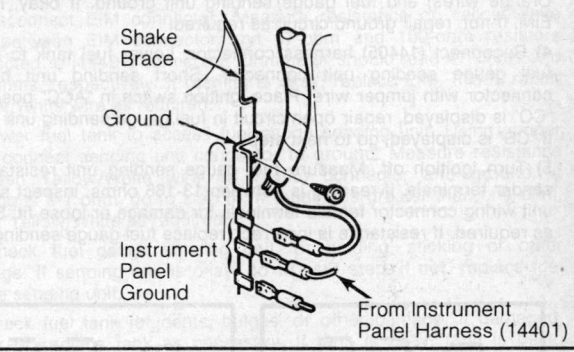

Shake Brace

Ground

Instrument Panel Ground

From Instrument Panel Harness (14401)

DISPLAY BRIGHTNESS DOES NOT CHANGE WITH DIMMING CONTROL

1) Place ignition switch in "ACC" position. With headlights on, check dimming of other displays while rotating dimmer switch. If other displays dim, replace EIM. If no displays dim, go to next step.

2) With headlights on, check dimming of message center while rotating dimmer switch. If message center dims, go to step 6). If not, check instrument panel fuse (No. 13). If fuse is okay, go to step 4). If not, go to next step.

3) Before replacing fuse, turn ignition off. Using ohmmeter, check for short to ground in White/Light Blue wire (at fuse panel). If shorted, repair White/Light Blue wire. If not, replace fuse.

4) Measure input voltage at instrument panel fuse (No. 13). If reading is greater than 10 volts, go to next step. If reading is less than 10 volts, repair White/Light Blue wire at headlight switch as required.

5) Check parking light/taillight fuse (No. 4). If fuse is okay, go to step 6). If not, check for short to ground in Light Blue/Red wire. If shorted, repair Light Blue/Red wire. If not, replace fuse.

6) Remove EIC/EIM from instrument panel. Disconnect harness connector. Measure rheostat voltage between Light Blue/Red wire (pin No. 2) and ground. Reading should be less than 3 volts with headlights off and greater than 5 volts with headlights on. Go to next step.

7) Turn ignition off. Measure voltage changes between Brown/White wire (pin No. 16) and ground. With dimmer switch in full counterclockwise position, reading should be battery voltage. With dimmer switch in full clockwise position, reading should be 1/2 battery voltage. If readings are correct, replace EIM. If not, repair White/Light Blue wire.

Dimmer Control Circuit

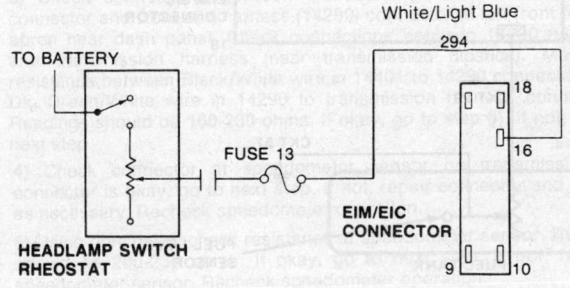

White/Light Blue

294

TO BATTERY

FUSE 13

HEADLAMP SWITCH RHEOSTAT

EIM/EIC CONNECTOR

18

16

9

10

FUEL GAUGE CONTINUITY CHECK NO. 2

1) On non-turbo models, ground Black/Blue wire at fuel tank sending unit 6-pin connector. On turbo models equipped with Vehicle Maintenance Monitor (VMM), ground Black/Light Green wire. See FUEL TANK SENDING UNIT 6-PIN TERMINAL IDENTIFICATION illustration. Fuel tank sending unit 6-pin connector is located on front of fuel tank.

2) Observe fuel gauge reading. If fuel gauge reads correctly, repair Black wire between fuel tank sending unit and ground. If fuel gauge does not read correctly, replace fuel tank sending unit.

FUEL GAUGE SHORT CHECK NO. 1

1) Disconnect instrument cluster 8-pin connector. Instrument cluster 8-pin connector is located on right side of dash, near steering column.

2) Observe fuel gauge reading. If fuel gauge reads full, replace fuel gauge. If fuel gauge does not read full, go to FUEL GAUGE SHORT CHECK NO. 2.

FUEL GAUGE SHORT CHECK NO. 2

1) Reconnect instrument cluster 8-pin connector if previously disconnected. Disconnect fuel tank sending unit 6-pin connector. Fuel tank sending unit 6-pin connector is located on front of fuel tank.

2) Observe fuel gauge reading. If fuel gauge reads full, repair Yellow wire between gauges and fuel tank sending unit. If fuel gauge does not read full, replace fuel tank sending unit.

FUEL GAUGE TESTING

1) Disconnect fuel tank sending unit 6-pin connector. Fuel tank sending unit 6-pin connector is located on front of fuel tank. Using Gauge System Tester (Rotunda 021-00055), connect one lead to Yellow terminal wire of fuel tank sending unit 6-pin connector and other lead to ground. See TESTING FUEL GAUGE illustration.

2) Set tester to resistance values. See FUEL GAUGE RESISTANCE VALUES SPECIFICATIONS table. Turn ignition on and check to see that needle indicator displays correct values. Continue inspection for 2 minutes on each setting, to correctly judge accuracy of gauge.

3) Allowable error is twice the width of fuel gauge needle. If fuel gauge readings are correct, go to FUEL GAUGE SENDING UNIT CHECK. If fuel gauge readings are not correct, replace fuel gauge.

Testing Fuel Gauge

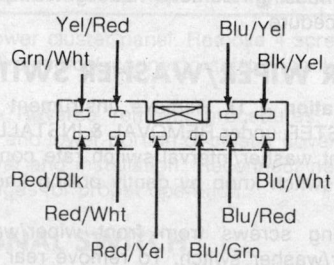

FUEL GAUGE RESISTANCE VALUES SPECIFICATIONS TABLE

Segment	Resistance
1-10	Less Than 8
1-9	8-14
1-8	14-20
1-7	20-25
1-6	25-30
1-5	30-37
1-4	37-46
1-3	46-63
1-2	63-86
1	86-98

FUEL GAUGE SENDING UNIT CHECK

1) Remove fuel tank sending unit. To remove sending unit, remove service hole cover. Disconnect main fuel hose. Remove fuel tank sending unit.

2) Connect ohmmeter to fuel tank sending unit connector "A" and "B" terminals. Compare resistance values. See CHECKING FUEL GAUGE SENDING UNIT illustration.

Checking Fuel Gauge Sending Unit

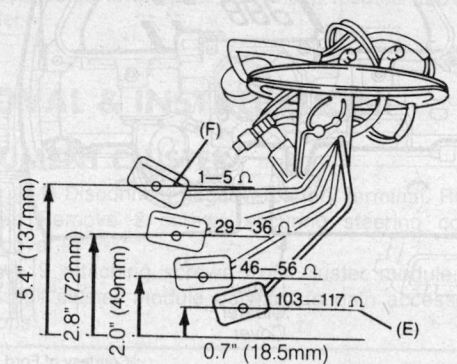

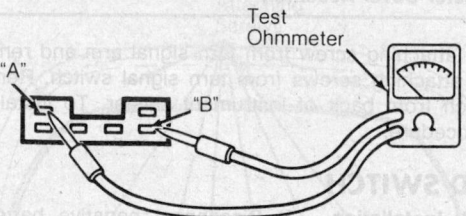

3) If resistance values are same as listed, check for loose or dirty connections at fuel tank sending unit connector. If resistance values are not same as listed, replace fuel tank sending unit.

KEYBOARD INOPERATIVE

1) Operate all electronic instrument keyboard keys. If keyboard is not working, go to KEYBOARD FUNCTION CHECK NO. 1.

2) If one or more of electronic keyboard keys are not working, go to KEYBOARD FUNCTION CHECK NO.1.

3) If "ALARM", "SET UP", "SET DOWN" or "DIM OFF" are not working, go to KEYBOARD FUNCTION CHECK NO. 2.

4) If "M/KM", "T/ODO", "T/SET" or "SERV OFF" are not working, go to KEYBOARD FUNCTION CHECK NO. 4.

KEYBOARD FUNCTION CHECK NO. 1

1) Ground Red/White wire at instrument keyboard 10-pin connector. Instrument keyboard 10-pin connector is located behind trip computer keyboard. See ELECTRONIC INSTRUMENT KEYBOARD TERMINAL IDENTIFICATION illustration.

Electronic Instrument Keyboard Terminal Identification

2) If keyboard works, repair Red/White wire between keyboard and electronic instrument cluster.

3) If keyboard still does not work, replace keyboard.

KEYBOARD FUNCTION CHECK NO. 2

1) Using Gauge System Tester (Rotunda 021-00055), connect one lead of tester to Yellow/RED wire at instrument keyboard 10-pin connector and other lead to ground.

2) Instrument keyboard 10-pin connector is located behind trip computer keyboard. See ELECTRONIC INSTRUMENT KEYBOARD TERMINAL IDENTIFICATION illustration.

3) Slowly adjust resistance from 0-1000 ohms and back to 0 again. Check to see if "ALARM", "SET UP", "SET DOWN" or "DIM OFF" functions are working. If no functions are working, go to KEYBOARD FUNCTION CHECK NO. 3.

4) If all functions are working, replace keyboard. If only some functions are working, replace gauges.

KEYBOARD FUNCTION CHECK NO. 3

1) Using Gauge System Tester (Rotunda 021-00055), connect one lead of tester to Yellow/Red wire at instrument cluster 14-pin connector and other lead to ground.

2) Instrument cluster 14-pin connector is located behind instrument cluster, near steering column. See INSTRUMENT CLUSTER 14-PIN TERMINAL IDENTIFICATION illustration.

Instrument Cluster 14-Pin Terminal Identification

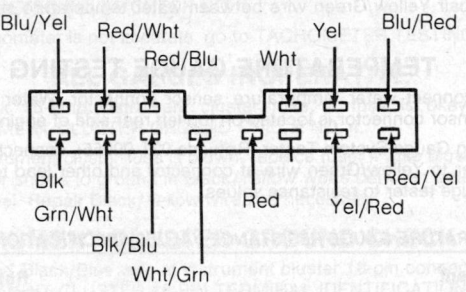

3) Slowly adjust resistance from 0-1000 ohms and back to 0. Check to see that "ALARM", "SET UP", "SET DOWN" and "DIM OFF" functions are working.

4) If some or no functions are working, replace gauges. If all functions are working, repair Yellow/Red wire between gauges and keyboard.

KEYBOARD FUNCTION CHECK NO. 4

1) Using Gauge System Tester (Rotunda 021-00055), connect one lead of tester to Red/Yellow wire at instrument keyboard 10-pin connector.

2) Instrument keyboard 10-pin connector is located behind trip computer keyboard. See ELECTRONIC INSTRUMENT KEYBOARD TERMINAL IDENTIFICATION illustration.

3) Slowly adjust resistance from 0-1000 ohms and back to 0. Check to see that "M/KM", "T/ODO", "T/SET" and "SERV OFF" functions are working.

4) If no functions are working, go to KEYBOARD FUNCTION CHECK NO. 5. If all functions are working, replace keyboard. If some functions are working, replace gauges.

KEYBOARD FUNCTION CHECK NO. 5

1) Using Gauge System Tester (Rotunda 021-00055), connect one lead of tester to Red/Yellow wire at instrument cluster 14-pin connector.

2) Instrument cluster 14-pin connector is located behind instrument cluster, near steering column. See INSTRUMENT CLUSTER 14-PIN TERMINAL IDENTIFICATION illustration.

3) Slowly adjust resistance from 0-1000 ohms and back to 0. Check to see that "M/KM", "T/ODO", "T/SET" and "SERV OFF" functions are working.

4) If some or no functions are working, replace gauges. If all functions are working, repair Red/Yellow wire between gauges and keyboard.

NOTE: Oil pressure gauge testing is not available from manufacture.

SPEEDOMETER OPERATION CHECK

Operate vehicle at various speeds and check the operation of speedometer. If speedometer is not working, go to INSTRUMENT CLUSTER FUSE CHECK. If speedometer is inaccurate, go to SPEEDOMETER CALIBRATION CHECK.

INSTRUMENT CLUSTER FUSE CHECK

1) Check 15-amp instrument cluster fuse in interior fuse block. Fuse panel is located just above left kick panel. If fuse is okay, go to SPEEDOMETER SUPPLY CHECK.

2) If fuse is blown, replace fuse. If fuse blows again, check for shorts to ground in Black/Yellow wire at instrument cluster 18-pin connector. Repair Black/Yellow wire as needed.

3) Instrument cluster 18-pin connector is located behind instrument cluster. See INSTRUMENT CLUSTER 18-PIN TERMINAL IDENTIFICATION illustration.

Instrument Cluster 18-Pin Terminal Identification

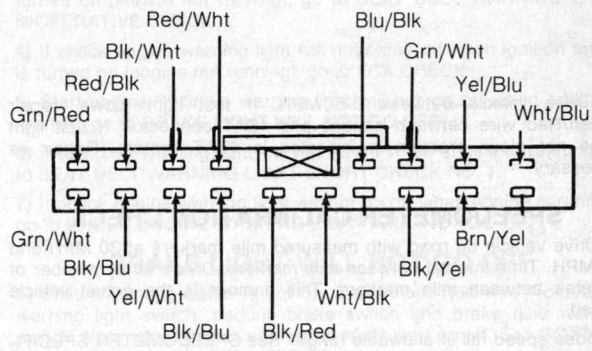

SPEEDOMETER SUPPLY CHECK

1) Check for 11-13 volts on Black/Yellow wire at instrument cluster 18-pin connector. Instrument cluster 18-pin connector is located behind instrument cluster. See INSTRUMENT CLUSTER 18-PIN TERMINAL IDENTIFICATION illustration.

2) If voltmeter reads 11-13 volts at Black/Yellow wire, go to SPEEDOMETER SIGNAL CHECK NO. 1. If voltmeter does not read 11-13 volts at Black/Yellow wire, repair Black/Yellow wire between gauges and fuse panel.

SPEEDOMETER SIGNAL CHECK NO. 1

1) Place test light between a 12-volt source and Green/Red wire at instrument cluster 18-pin connector. Instrument cluster 18-pin connector is located behind instrument cluster. See INSTRUMENT CLUSTER 18-PIN TERMINAL IDENTIFICATION illustration.

2) Drive vehicle between 0-5 MPH. If test light glows, replace speedometer. If test light does not glow and vehicle has an automatic transmission, go to SPEEDOMETER SIGNAL CHECK NO. 2.

SPEEDOMETER SIGNAL CHECK NO. 2

1) Place test light between a 12-volt source and Green/Red wire at Electronically Controlled Automatic Transmission (4EAT) connector.

2) The 4EAT connector is located at 4EAT control unit, forward of left side of instrument panel. See 4EAT TERMINAL IDENTIFICATION illustration.

6-176

1989 SWITCHES & INSTRUMENT PANELS
Sable & Taurus Electronic Instrument Cluster (Cont.)

ODOMETER READING INCORRECT, INCREASES OR DECREASES A LARGE AMOUNT

1) Enter self-test mode (hold in "TRIP RESET" button and turn ignition switch from "OFF" to "RUN" position). Observe zeroes on digital display and then release "TRIP RESET" button.

2) Test one, as indicated by "01" in the ones and tenths digit of odometer, should pass by displaying a "P" on the speedometer ones digit and sounding a constant pass tone. If okay, go to next step. If not, replace speedometer module.

3) Advance from test one to odometer memory test by pressing "TRIP RESET" button until "07" is displayed in odometer. Test passes if "P" is displayed in speedometer ones digit and a pass tone is heard. If okay, go to next step. If not, replace speedometer module.

4) Check speedometer for correct operation. If okay, go to SPEEDOMETER CONSTANTLY READS TOO HIGH OR TOO LOW and SPEED INDICATOR JUMPS UP AND DOWN ERRATICALLY tests.

MILEAGE CONSTANTLY READS TOO HIGH OR TOO LOW

1) Check speedometer for correct operation. If okay, go to next step. If not, go to SPEEDOMETER CONSTANTLY READS TOO HIGH OR TOO LOW test.

2) Check display for proper operation. If okay, go to next step. If not, go to DISPLAY SCRAMBLED, SEGMENTS HALF LIT, SEGMENTS MISSING, INCORRECT DISPLAY, DISPLAY STUCK WITH ALL SEGMENTS ON test.

3) Check odometer memory by advancing from test one of self-test to odometer memory test by pressing "TRIP RESET" button until "07" is displayed in odometer. Test passes if "P" is displayed in speedometer ones digit and a pass tone is heard. If okay, system is okay. If not, go to ODOMETER READING INCORRECT, INCREASES OR DECREASES A LARGE AMOUNT test.

TRIP ODOMETER MALFUNCTIONING, REGULAR ODOMETER DISPLAYED

1) Place ignition switch in "RUN" position. After initial display test and seat belt reminder chime have finished, press "ODO SEL" button and listen for beep. If beep is heard, replace speedometer module. If not, go to next step.

2) Remove trim panel to expose cluster. Verify connector from switch to electronic instrument cluster is secure and properly aligned. If okay, go to next step. If not, repair connector as required and recheck.

3) Remove switch module assembly and go to SWITCH TEST (MODULE DOES NOT RESPOND TO BUTTONS) test. If okay, replace speedometer module. If not, replace switch assembly.

TRIP ODOMETER WILL NOT RESET

1) Place ignition switch in "RUN" position. After initial display test and seat belt reminder chime have finished, press "TRIP" button. Press "TRIP RESET" button and listen for beep. If beep is heard, replace speedometer module. If not, go to next step.

2) Remove trim panel to expose cluster. Verify connector from switch to electronic instrument cluster is secure and properly aligned. If okay, go to next step. If not, repair connector as required and recheck.

3) Remove switch module assembly and go to SWITCH TEST (MODULE DOES NOT RESPOND TO BUTTONS) test. If okay, replace speedometer module. If not, replace switch assembly.

SPEED ALARM CANNOT BE SET, DOES NOT RESPOND TO SPEED ALARM BUTTON

1) With vehicle moving at less than 20 MPH (32 km/h), speed alarm will not set and button will not beep. If correct, system is okay. If not, go to next step.

2) With vehicle moving at least 20 MPH (32 km/h), press "SPEED ALARM" button and listen for beep. If beep is heard, replace speedometer module. If not, go to next step.

3) Remove trim panel to expose cluster. Verify connector from switch to electronic instrument cluster is secure and properly aligned. If okay, go to next step. If not, repair connector as required and recheck.

4) Remove switch module assembly and go to SWITCH TEST (MODULE DOES NOT RESPOND TO BUTTONS) test. If okay, replace speedometer module. If not, replace switch assembly.

"SERVICE" LIGHT DOES NOT GO OUT WHEN RESET

1) Verify 3 beeps are heard when service reminder is reset (simultaneously push both "ODO SEL" and "TRIP RESET" buttons). If beeps are heard, replace speedometer module. If not, go to next step.

2) Press "ODO SEL" button. Display should change between regular and trip odometers. If okay, go to next step. If not, go to SWITCH TEST (MODULE DOES NOT RESPOND TO BUTTONS) test.

3) Call up odometer with "ODO SEL" button. Press "TRIP RESET" button. Trip odometer should zero. If okay, replace speedometer module. If not, go to SWITCH TEST (MODULE DOES NOT RESPOND TO BUTTONS) test.

NO BEEPS WHEN SERVICE REMINDER IS RESET

1) Press instrument cluster buttons and listen for beep. If okay, go to next step. If not, go to SWITCH TEST (MODULE DOES NOT RESPOND TO BUTTONS) test.

2) Press "ODO SEL" button. Display should change between regular and trip odometers. If okay, go to next step. If not, go to SWITCH TEST (MODULE DOES NOT RESPOND TO BUTTONS) test.

3) Call up trip odometer with "ODO SEL" button. Press "TRIP RESET" button. Trip odometer should zero. If okay, replace speedometer module. If not, go to SWITCH TEST (MODULE DOES NOT RESPOND TO BUTTONS) test.

FUEL COMPUTER/SYSTEM SCANNER MODULE DISPLAY BLANK (BUT BACK LIGHTED)

1) Place ignition switch in "RUN" position. If display is back lighted but blank, verify seedometer/tachometer module is functioning. If okay, go to next step. If not, got to step 3).

2) Remove instrument cluster. See INSTRUMENT CLUSTER under REMOVAL & INSTALLATION in this article. Place ignition switch in "RUN" position. Check voltage on pin "3A" and pin "14A" is equal to battery voltage (10 volts minimum). If okay, go to next step. If not, repair open in circuit.

3) Check continuity between pin "10A" and battery ground cable. If okay, replace fuel computer module. If not, repair open in fuel module ground circuit (from cluster to ground).

4) Place ignition switch in "RUN" position. Check fuel computer module/system scanner fuse. If okay, go back to step 2). If not, go to next step.

5) Before replacing fuse, turn ignition off. Disconnect negative battery cable. Connect ohmmeter from circuit side of fuse to ground. If no short is found, replace fuse. If shorted, repair short in circuit.

FUEL COMPUTER DISPLAY NOT ILLUMINATED, TOO DIM, OR TOTALLY BLACK

1) Place ignition switch in "RUN" position. Check for back lighting of speedometer/tachometer display. If other module is okay, go to next step. If not, go to step 3).

2) Disconnect negative battery cable. Check for continuity between pin "1C" and pin "12A". See INSTRUMENT CLUSTER PIN CONNECTOR IDENTIFICATION illustration. If okay, replace burned out bulb(s). If not, repair wiring as necessary.

3) Remove instrument cluster. See INSTRUMENT CLUSTER under REMOVAL & INSTALLATION in this article. Measure resistance between pin "3C" and pin "11B". Reading should be less than one ohm. If correct, go to next step. If not, repair illumination ground.

4) Place ignition switch in "RUN" position. Check display for back lighting. Turn headlights on. Move dimmer control to maximum brightness. Check for display back lighting.

5) If display does not light in "RUN" position or with headlights on, go to next step. If display is illuminated in "RUN" position but not with headlights on, go to step 7). If display is too dim, go to step 8).

6) Connect negative battery cable. Measure voltage on pin "8C" (LCD illumination line). If voltage is more than 10 volts, replace cluster. If voltage is less than 10 volts, repair illumination circuits, fuses, or headlight switch.

7) Turn headlight switch on. Move dimmer to maximum brightness. Measure voltage on pin "8C". If voltage is greater than 10 volts, replace cluster. If voltage is less than 10 volts, repair illumination circuits, fuses, or headlight switch.

8) Place ignition switch in "RUN" position. Check for burned out bulbs. If bulbs are on, go to next step. If not, replace burned out bulb(s).

9) Check for correct bulb type. Replace bulbs if not of correct type. If bulbs are of correct type, go back to steps 6) and 7).

INSTANTANEOUS FUEL ECONOMY ALWAYS READS "0" MILES/GALLON OR "99" LITERS/100 KM

1) Verify speedometer is operating properly. If okay, go to next step. If not, go to SPEEDOMETER READS "0" MPH WHEN VEHICLE IS IN MOTION test.

2) Remove instrument cluster. See INSTRUMENT CLUSTER under REMOVAL & INSTALLATION in this article. Check continuity between pin "10C" of speedometer and pin "18A" of fuel computer. See INSTRUMENT CLUSTER PIN CONNECTOR IDENTIFICATION illustration. If okay, replace fuel computer module. If not, repair wiring in circuit as necessary.

INSTANTANEOUS FUEL ECONOMY ALWAYS READS "99" LITERS/100 KM OR "0" MILES/GALLON

1) Verify continuity and absence of shorts in fuel flow circuit. If okay, go to next step. If not, repair wiring in circuit as necessary.

2) Verify proper operation of electronic engine control fuel flow function. See appropriate article in COMPUTERIZED ENGINE CONTROLS section. If okay, replace fuel computer module. If not, repair or replace fuel flow sensor system as required.

DTE ALWAYS READS "0" MILES

1) Remove instrument cluster. See INSTRUMENT CLUSTER under REMOVAL & INSTALLATION in this article. Check continuity of pin "16A" to fuel sending unit. If okay, go to next step. If not, repair open in circuit wiring as necessary.

2) Measure fuel sending unit resistance between pin "16A" and pin "10A" (ground). With tank full, reading should be less than 5 ohms resistance. With tank empty, reading should be more than 140 ohms resistance. If okay, replace fuel computer module. If not, repair circuit wiring or replace fuel sending unit.

FUEL COMPUTER DISPLAY SCRAMBLED, SEGMENTS HALF LIT, SEGMENTS MISSING, INCORRECT DISPLAY, DISPLAY STUCK WITH ALL SEGMENTS ON

1) Place ignition switch in "RUN" position. Observe fuel computer display. Go to next step if all segments come on, go off and then return to normal. If not, replace fuel computer module.

2) Hold "FUEL ECON" button in and turn ignition switch from "OFF" to "RUN" position. Observe zeroes on upper digital display and then release "FUEL ECON" button. If "F" is displayed, replace fuel computer module.

3) If display does not go into self-test mode (no zeroes displayed), "FUEL ECON" button was not held down properly, or button is damaged. Go to SWITCH TEST (MODULE DOES NOT RESPOND TO BUTTONS) test. If display has "P" on it, go to next step.

4) Enter self-test mode as in step 2). Advance to display test portion (test 12) of self-test by pressing "FUEL ECON" button until display No. 1 appears. See FUEL COMPUTER/SYSTEM SCANNER MODULE SELF-TEST DISPLAYS.

5) Inspect display for problems as test is advanced through each step by pressing "FUEL ECON" button. Ensure displays match illustrations. If okay, system is working properly. If not, replace fuel computer module.

FUEL COMPUTER MODULE WILL NOT SWITCH BETWEEN ENGLISH & METRIC

1) Verify English/Metric function is operating properly in speedometer/tachometer module. If okay, go to next step. If not, go to SPEEDOMETER & ODOMETER WILL NOT SWITCH BETWEEN ENGLISH & METRIC test.

2) Remove instrument cluster. See INSTRUMENT CLUSTER under REMOVAL & INSTALLATION in this article. Check continuity between pin "15A" and pin "4C". If okay, replace fuel computer module. If not, repair wiring in circuit as required.

FUEL GAUGE INOPERATIVE, POINTER DOES NOT MOVE

1) Verify fuel gauge is inoperative. If pointer does not move, go to next step. If pointer moves, go to FUEL GAUGE INACCURATE test.

2) Check power to cluster by turning ignition on. Observe all other gauges and warning lights for proper operation. If necessary, use voltmeter to check voltage at "B+" terminal of cluster connector.

3) If other gauges and warning lights operate properly (voltage is present at cluster), go to FUEL GAUGE INACCURATE test. If other gauges and warning lights do not operate properly (no voltage at cluster), repair wiring in power circuit.

FUEL GAUGE INACCURATE

1) Connect Instrument Gauge System Tester (Rotunda 021-00055) in fuel gauge sending unit circuit. Disconnect connector under instrument panel and connect tester to cluster side of connector. Set tester to "LOW" (22 ohms). If gauge reads "E" (empty), go to next step. If pointer does not move, replace gauge.

2) Set tester to "HIGH" (145 ohms). If gauge reads "F" (full), go to next step. If pointer does not move, replace gauge.

3) Check fuel gauge sending unit circuit wiring for shorts or opens with ohmmeter. If circuit is okay, replace sending unit. If not, repair circuit wiring as necessary.

TEMP/OIL GAUGE INOPERATIVE, POINTER DOES NOT MOVE

1) Verify temp/oil gauge is inoperative. If pointer does not move, go to next step. If pointer moves, go to TEMP/OIL GAUGE INACCURATE test.

2) Check power to cluster by turning ignition on. Observe all other gauges and warning lights for proper operation. If necessary, use voltmeter to check voltage at "B+" terminal of cluster connector.

3) If other gauges and warning lights operate properly (voltage is present at cluster), go to TEMP/OIL GAUGE INACCURATE test. If other gauges and warning lights do not operate properly (no voltage at cluster), repair wiring in power circuit.

TEMP/OIL GAUGE INACCURATE

1) Connect Instrument Gauge System Tester (Rotunda 021-00055) in fuel gauge sending unit circuit. Disconnect connector at sending unit and connect tester to cluster side of connector. Set tester to "LOW" (73 ohms). If gauge reads "C" or "L", go to next step. If pointer does not move, go to step **3)**.

2) Set tester to "HIGH" (10 ohms). If gauge reads "H", replace sending unit. If pointer does not read "H", go to next step.

3) Check temp/oil sending unit circuit wiring for shorts or opens with ohmmeter. If circuit is okay, replace gauge. If not, repair circuit wiring as necessary.

DESCRIPTION

The Electronic instrument cluster system consists of a bar-type fuel gauge, digital speedometer, message center display module (if equipped), message center keyboard, message center control module, tone generator, sensors and related wiring.

OPERATION

The instrument cluster and message center are illuminated and operational only when ignition switch is in "RUN" or "ACC" positions. The instrument panel and message center display illumination is at maximum brightness for daytime driving. Turning on headlights or parking lights automatically dims panel and message center for night time driving. While headlights or parking lights are on, the degree of display brightness can be manually adjusted by turning headlight switch knob.

FUEL GAUGE

The system consists of an electronic fuel gauge module with vacuum fluorescent bar graph display and modified fuel gauge sending unit. The display is divided into 4 groups of 8 segments each. Fuel level is indicated by those segments (bars) which are brightly illuminated. The word "EMPTY" appears when all segments are off.

The fuel gauge has a built-in diagnostic feature to detect an open circuit in fuel gauge sending unit wiring. Under an open condition, no bars are lit and the "E", "1/2" and "F" symbols flash continuously.

DIGITAL SPEEDOMETER

The digital speedometer displays vehicle speed in numerals. The odometer and transmission selector, although enclosed in cluster, are mechanical in design and not an integral part of the electronic cluster. Maximum readings of speedometer are 85 MPH and 137 km/h.

The mechanical cable from the transmission to the cluster is of conventional design. The difference occurs at the head of the speedometer assembly where the magnetic drive formerly used has been replaced by a slotted wheel with 16 slots. As this wheel rotates, an optical sensor counts each slot passing by and creates an electrical pulse for each slot.

These electrical pulses are sent to car speedometer electronics. Here they are counted and totaled every .45 seconds. The number of pulses generated in this time period are proportional to the speed of the vehicle. The speedometer indication is updated each .45 seconds in the MPH mode. In the Km/h mode a different time period is used.

Whenever ignition switch is turned from "OFF" position to either "RUN" or "ACC" positions, speedometer will display "188" for 2 seconds, turn off for 2 seconds and then display "0 MPH" (if vehicle is not moving). The "188" display ensures all light segments are functional.

MESSAGE CENTER

The message center keyboard allows direct access to the message center. Keyboard is functional only with ignition switch in "RUN" or "ACC" positions.

The message center displays a digital clock with AM/PM, month, date, and day of week indications. It also calculates estimated time of arrival, average vehicle speed, average/instantaneous fuel economy, distance to empty, distance remaining to destination, and elapsed time/distance since last reset.

The message center also displays a variety of warnings. These warnings include oil pressure below prescribed value, engine temperature above prescribed value, inadequate brake system pressure, headlight, tail light, brake light and charging system failure, door and trunk ajar.

TESTING & DIAGNOSIS

NOTE: The following diagnostic charts, circuits and illustrations are supplied courtesy of Ford Motor Co.

FUEL GAUGE DISPLAY TOTALLY BLANK

1) Place ignition switch in "ACC" position. Check for illumination of other displays in instrument cluster. If other displays are illuminated, go to next step. If not, repair circuit as required.

2) Measure voltage between ground and ignition terminals of fuel gauge. If voltage is at least 10 volts, replace gauge. If voltage is less than 10 volts, check for open in circuit between ground terminal and vehicle ground. Repair as required.

Fuel Gauge Circuit

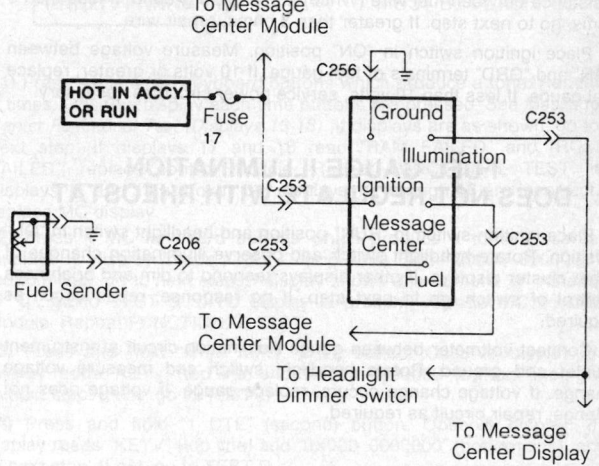

FUEL GAUGE "E", "1/2" & "F" SYMBOLS FLASH

1) Unplug connector at fuel gauge sending unit and short wiring connector terminals with jumper wire. Place ignition switch in "ACC" position and check gauge symbols. If "E", "1/2" or "F" symbols continue flashing, go to next step. If symbols do not continue flashing, go to step 3).

2) Check Black wire at fuel gauge sending unit for proper ground. If ground connection is okay, go to step 4). If ground connection is not okay, repair ground circuit.

3) Remove fuel gauge sending unit. Using ohmmeter, check unit for open circuit. If reading is greater than 300 ohms, replace sending unit. If reading is less than 300 ohms, inspect female connector for damage or loose fit. Correct if necessary.

4) Reconnect fuel gauge sending unit and short fuel gauge stud (with Yellow/White wire) to ground stud at back of fuel gauge. Place ignition switch in "ACC" position and check symbols for continued flashing. If symbols still flash, replace fuel gauge. If symbols do not flash, repair open circuit between fuel gauge and sending unit.

FUEL GAUGE INACCURATE, ERRATIC OR ALWAYS INDICATES EMPTY

1) Turn all accessories off. Place ignition switch in "RUN" position. Note number of bars brightly displayed on fuel gauge. Turn ignition off. Turn fan to "HIGH" position and push in cigarette lighter. Place ignition switch in "RUN" position. If fewer bars are brightly displayed, repair fuel gauge ground circuit. If same number of bars are displayed, go to next step.

2) Check for loose, corroded or damaged connection at sender and sending unit ground (in trunk). Check resistance of Black wire. If less than one ohm, go to next step. If greater than one ohm, repair wiring.

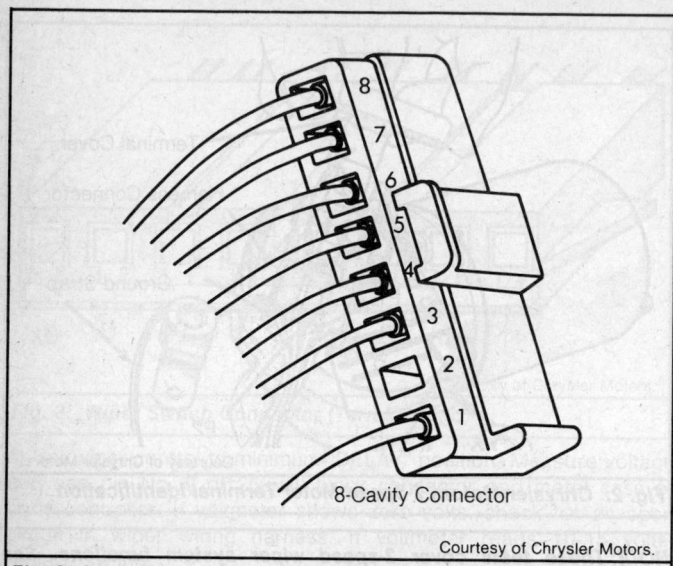

8-Cavity Connector

Courtesy of Chrysler Motors.

Fig. 3: Intermittent Wiper Module Connector Terminal Locations

to "OFF" position. With motor harness disconnected, connect voltmeter or test light to ground strap and "P_1" terminal of wiring connector.

2) If voltage is NOT present, check for open in wiring harness or switch. If voltage is present, connect ohmmeter or continuity tester between terminals "L" and "P_2." If continuity exists, replace motor. If continuity does NOT exist, repair open in switch or harness.

INTERMITTENT FUNCTION TESTS

NOTE: These tests cover intermittent wiper system function. See TWO-SPEED FUNCTION TESTS for normal wiper system test procedures.

Wipers Do Not Delay In "DELAY" Position – **1)** Place wiper switch in "LOW" position and disconnect 8-way connector at intermittent wiper module. For location, see INTERMITTENT WIPER MODULE under REMOVAL & INSTALLATION in this article. Check contacts for dirt and damage. Place wiper switch in "LOW" position. Connect test light between cavity Nos. 1 and 3 of wiper module connector. *See Fig. 3.* The light should flash once every cycle.

2) If light flashes periodically, replace wiper module. If light does not flash periodically, check with test light between terminals "P_1" and "P_2" at motor. If periodic flashing is at motor, check wiring to intermittent wiper module.

Wipers Do Not Operate With Switch In "DELAY" Position – **1)** Place wiper switch in "MAXIMUM DELAY" position and remove connector from intermittent wiper module. Connect voltmeter negative lead to cavity No. 4 and voltmeter positive lead to cavity No. 6. *See Fig. 3.*

2) If no voltage is present check switch and wiring. If more than 10 volts are present, place switch in "LOW" position. Connect voltmeter negative lead to cavity No. 4 and voltmeter positive lead to cavity No. 3. If there are more than 10 volts, replace intermittent wiper module. If more than 10 volts are not present, check wiring.

Wipers Operate Only Once In Intermittent Mode – **1)** Place switch in "MAXIMUM DELAY" position and connect voltmeter negative lead to cavity No. 4 and voltmeter positive lead to cavity No. 8. If voltmeter reads zero volts, check switch and wiring. If more than 10 volts are present, replace intermittent wiper module.

More Than 30 Seconds Delay or Inadequate Variation in Delay – Variations in delay should be as follows:
- Minimum Delay – 1/2-2 seconds
- Maximum Delay – 10-30 seconds

If there is excessive delay or no variations in delay, see INTERMITTENT WIPE SWITCH TEST under TESTING in this article.

Wipers Do Not Run Continually When Wash Control Is Operated During Delay Mode – Disconnect intermittent wiper module connector. Connect a voltmeter between cavity No. 4 and No. 7. Depress wash switch. If voltage reads zero, check switch and wiring. If voltage is 10-15 volts, replace intermittent wiper module.

Wipers Start Erractically During Delay Mode – Ensure grounds at instrument panel, wiper motor, wiper switch and intermittent wiper module are clean and tight. If condition is not corrected, replace intermittent wiper module.

INTERMITTENT WIPE SWITCH TEST

Disconnect intermittent wiper switch connector. With a continuity tester or ohmmeter, test for continuity between terminals in switch shown in INTERMITTENT WIPER SWITCH CONTINUITY chart. For terminal identification, *See Fig. 4.* For test purposes, going clockwise:
- First is "OFF" position
- Counterclockwise rotation is "DELAY" position
- Next detent is "LOW" position
- Full counterclockwise is "HIGH" position

INTERMITTENT WIPER SWITCH CONTINUITY

Switch Position	[1] Continuity
Off	L & P_2
Delay	P_1 & I_1
	R & I_1
	I_2 & G
Low	P_1 & L
High	P_1 & H

[1] – Resistance at maximum delay: 270,000-330,000 ohms. Resistance at minimum delay: zero (with ohmmeter set on high ohm scale).

REMOVAL & INSTALLATION

MOTOR & LINKAGE

Removal (Horizon & Omni) – **1)** Remove wiper arms. Remove tie down nuts and washers from pivots. Open hood. Remove plastic motor cover and washer hose attaching clip. Disconnect wiring harness. Remove 3 mounting bolts. Disengage pivots from cowl top mounting positions.

2) Remove wiper motor, bracket, cranks, pivots and drive link assembly from cowl plenum chamber. Ensure pivot marked "L" is

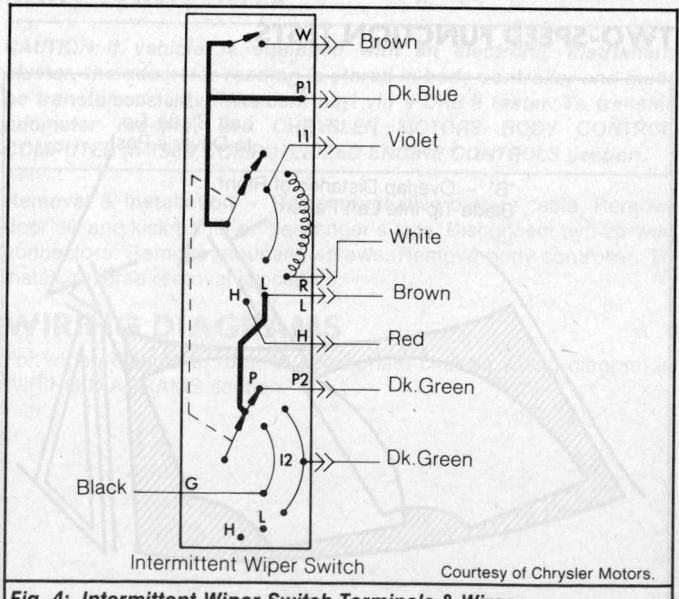

Intermittent Wiper Switch

Courtesy of Chrysler Motors.

Fig. 4: Intermittent Wiper Switch Terminals & Wires

positioned to driver's side of vehicle. On bench, remove drive crank from motor. To install, reverse removal procedure.

Removal (Aries, Daytona, LeBaron & Reliant) – 1) Ensure wiper arms are in "PARK" position. Open hood. Remove wiper arms. Disconnect hoses from "T" fitting. Remove cowl top plastic cover. Remove pivot screws. Remove wiper motor cover and disconnect wiring harness. Remove 3 motor mounting nuts.

2) Push pivots down into cowl chamber. Pull motor out until it clears mounting studs. Move motor as far to driver's side as possible. Pull right pivot and link out through opening. Shift motor inward. Remove motor, left link and pivot. Clamp motor crank in vise and remove nut from motor shaft.

NOTE: Do not rotate motor shaft from "PARK" position.

Installation (Aries, Daytona, LeBaron & Reliant) – 1) Assemble linkage to motor. Ensure crank fits over "D" slot on motor shaft. Install mounting nut and tighten to 95 INCH lbs. (11 N.m).
2) Place left pivot and link into plenum chamber and slide left as far as possible. Motor should clear studs and crank should be behind sheet metal. Push right pivot and link through opening. Move assembly right and position on studs. Install motor mounting nuts and pivot screws. Tighten to 55 INCH lbs. (6 N.m). To complete installation, reverse removal procedure.

Removal & Installation (Acclaim, Lancer, LeBaron GTS, Shadow, Spirit & Sundance) – Open hood and remove wiper arms. Remove cowl top plastic cover. Remove attaching screws or mounting nuts from pivots. Disconnect wiper motor wiring harness. Remove 3 motor mounting bracket-to-body bolts. Remove wiper motor bracket and linkage assembly from cowl. To install, reverse removal procedure.

Removal & Installation (Diplomat, Fifth Avenue & Gran Fury) – Disconnect negative battery. Remove cowl screen. Hold drive crank with wrench while removing crank nut. Remove drive crank and wiring harness. Remove mounting bolts and motor. Remove linkage assembly. To install, reverse removal procedure. Tighten pivot nuts to 95 INCH lbs. (11 N.m).

WIPER SWITCH

Removal & Installation (Acclaim & Spirit) – Information not available from manufacturer.

Removal (Horizon & Omni) – 1) Disconnect connector for wiper and turn signal switch. Remove lower column cover. Remove horn button. Remove wiper switch access cover. Turn ignition off. Turn steering wheel so access hole in hub is at 3 o'clock position.
2) Using a flat screwdriver, loosen turn signal lever screw. Disengage dimmer push rod from wiper switch. Disconnect wiring and remove switch.

Installation (Horizon & Omni) – To install, reverse removal procedure. Ensure dimmer push rod is properly positioned in wiper switch.

Removal & Installation (All Models Except Horizon & Omni) – 1) Remove steering wheel. On vehicles with standard steering column, proceed to **2)**. On tilt column models, remove lock plate cover, lock plate, lower instrument panel bezel and shift indicator. Remove 2 bolts holding column to lower panel reinforcement. Remove 4 mounting bracket attaching bolts and remove mounting bracket.
2) On all columns, remove wiring through steering column. Remove turn signal switch. Remove lock housing cover attaching screws. Remove lock housing cover. Pull wiper switch up from column while guiding wires through column opening. To install, reverse removal procedure.

INTERMITTENT WIPER MODULE

NOTE: All intermittent wiper modules have 8-way harness connectors and mount by slipping into mounting bracket.

Removal & Installation (Acclaim & Spirit) – The intermittent wiper module is attached to a bracket, right of steering column. Remove lower steering column cover. Slide module from bracket. Disconnect wiring. To install, reverse removal procedure.

Removal & Installation (Aries, Daytona, LeBaron & Reliant) – The intermittent wiper module is attached to a bracket below fuse box. Disconnect wiring. Slide module from bracket. To install, reverse removal procedure.

Removal & Installation (Lancer & LeBaron 4-Door) – The intermittent wiper module is attached to bottom of steering column. Disconnect wiring. Remove module from bracket. To install, reverse removal procedure.

Removal & Installation (Horizon & Omni) – The intermittent wiper module is attached to a bracket on brake pedal support bracket. Disconnect wiring. Remove module from bracket. To install, reverse removal procedure.

Removal & Installation (Shadow & Sundance) – The intermittent wiper module is attached to a bracket to right of steering column, behind steering column cover. Disconnect wiring. Slide module from bracket. To install, reverse removal procedure.

WIRING DIAGRAMS

For wiring diagrams, refer to appropriate chassis wiring diagram in WIRING DIAGRAMS section.

1989 WIPER/WASHER SYSTEMS
Chrysler Motors Liftgate

Daytona, Horizon, Lancer, LeBaron GTS, Omni

DESCRIPTION & OPERATION

The rear window/liftgate wiper system includes a circuit breaker, wiring harness, control switch, washer motor and single speed wiper motor. Wiper motor automatically parks wiper blade at lower edge of rear window when control switch is turned to "OFF" position.

TESTING

WIPER MOTOR

Horizon & Omni – 1) Remove plastic motor cover. Disconnect electrical connector from motor. With ignition on, check for voltage at Blue wire.

2) Turn liftgate wiper switch to "ON" position. Check for voltage at Blue and Brown wires. If 12 volts are present in both steps, circuit breaker, switch and wiring are okay. If 12 volts are NOT present in either step, check circuit breaker, switch and wiring.

3) With ignition on and liftgate wiper switch in "OFF" position, check for voltage between Blue and Brown wires. If battery voltage is NOT present, check ground wire to switch. If battery voltage is present in steps **1)** and **2)**, apply battery voltage to terminal on liftgate wiper motor switch plate (open terminal). See Fig. 1.

4) If motor does not operate, replace motor. If motor operates and drive shaft rotates, replace switch plate. If motor operates, but drive shaft does NOT rotate, inspect motor drive mechanism and replace parts as needed.

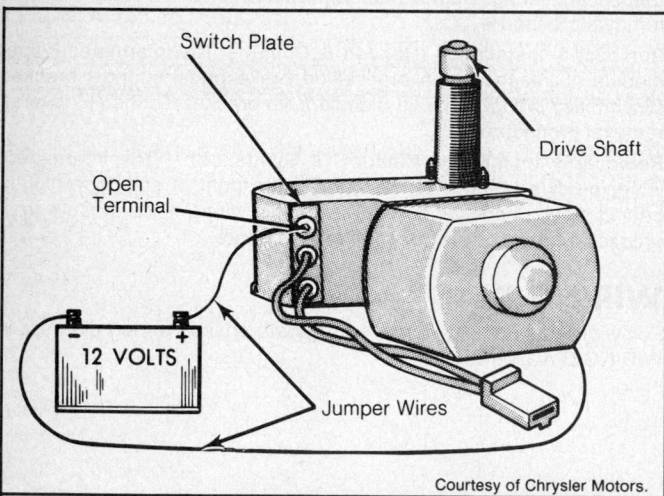

Fig. 1: *Testing Liftgate Wiper Motor (Horizon & Omni)*

Daytona – 1) Remove liftgate lower cover. Disconnect electrical connector from motor. With ignition on and liftgate wiper switch in "OFF" position, check for battery voltage at Blue wire.

2) Turn ignition switch and liftgate wiper switch to "ON" position. Check for battery voltage at Blue and Brown wires. If battery voltage is present in both step, check circuit breaker, switch and wiring. If battery voltage is NOT present in either step, check circuit breaker, switch and wiring.

3) With ignition switch in "ON" position and wiper switch in "OFF" position, check for battery voltage between Blue and Brown wires. If battery voltage is NOT present, check ground wire to liftgate switch. If voltage is present, replace motor.

Lancer & LeBaron GTS – Information not available from manufacturer.

REMOVAL & INSTALLATION

WASHER RESERVOIR & PUMP

Removal & Installation (Daytona, Lancer & LeBaron GTS) – 1) Open liftgate and remove right rear quarter panel. If necessary, remove rear speaker. Remove 2 reservoir mounting screws. Disconnect wiring harness and filler tube.

2) Disconnect washer hose and block pump outlet. Remove reservoir and pump assembly. Empty reservoir and loosen pump filter and nut. Disconnect inner and outer portions of pump and remove. To install, reverse removal procedure.

Removal Installation (Horizon & Omni) – 1) Open liftgate. Remove plastic cap and 2 mounting retainer screws from reservoir filler. Disconnect wiring harness from washer pump. Remove 2 side panel reservoir mounting screws.

2) Disconnect washer hose from reservoir. Remove reservoir and pump assembly through side panel access hole. Empty reservoir and loosen pump filter and nut. Disconnect inner and outer portions of pump and remove. To install, reverse removal procedure.

WIPER MOTOR & LINKAGE

Removal & Installation (Daytona) – Remove wiper arm assembly. Open liftgate. Remove trim panel. Disconnect motor wiring harness. Remove grommet from liftgate glass. Remove 2 screws fastening bracket to liftgate. Remove motor from liftgate. See Fig. 2. To install, place new grommet in liftgate glass. Reverse removal procedure.

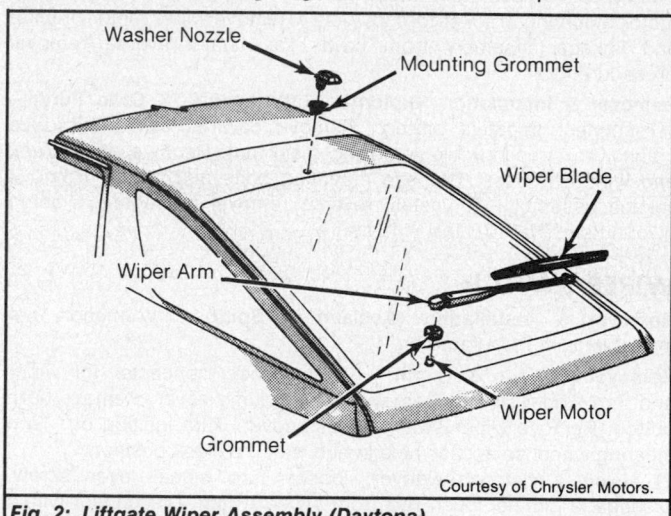

Fig. 2: *Liftgate Wiper Assembly (Daytona)*

Removal & Installation (Horizon & Omni) – Open liftgate. Remove plastic motor cover. Remove wiper arm from shaft. Remove pivot shaft nut, ring and seal. Disconnect motor wiring harness. Remove motor attaching screws and remove motor. To install, reverse removal procedure. Install sealing washer approximately 1/2" (12 mm) down motor output shaft.

Removal (Lancer & LeBaron GTS) – Remove wiper arm and blade assembly. Open liftgate and remove trim panel. Disconnect motor wiring harness. Remove 4 motor-to-liftgate bracket attaching screws. Remove motor.

Installation (Lancer & LeBaron GTS) – Position motor so pivot shaft and hose nipple pass through grommet and shaft cover. Ensure shaft cover and grommet are seated to liftgate and motor. To complete installation, reverse removal procedure.

WIRING DIAGRAMS

For wiring diagrams, refer to appropriate chassis wiring diagram in WIRING DIAGRAMS section.

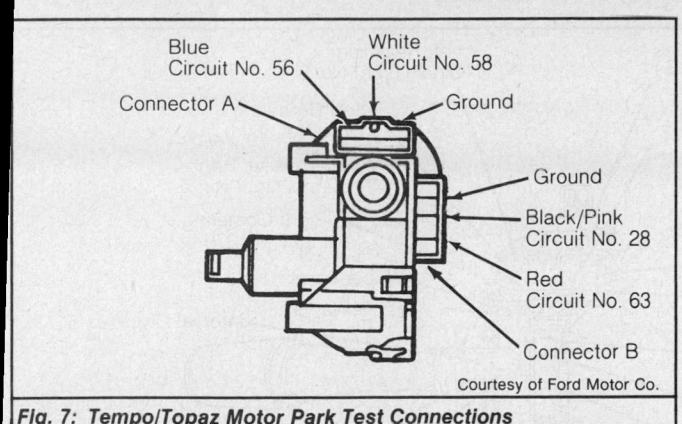

Blue Circuit No. 56 — White Circuit No. 58

Connector A — Ground

Ground

Black/Pink Circuit No. 28

Red Circuit No. 63

Connector B

Courtesy of Ford Motor Co.

Fig. 7: Tempo/Topaz Motor Park Test Connections

WIPER SWITCH CONTINUITY

Unplug multi-function switch connector under steering column. Test circuits with self-powered test light or ohmmeter. An ohmmeter is required for intermittent wiper test. If switch does not show required continuity, or poor continuity is found in any position, replace switch. To perform wiper switch continuity test use appropriate WIPER SWITCH CONTINUITY TEST table. See Figs. 8 and 9.

COUGAR & THUNDERBIRD WIPER SWITCH CONTINUITY TEST

Switch Position	Terminal No. (Wire Color)	Continuity
Washer Switch		
ON	63 To 941 (RED To BLK/WHT)	Yes
OFF	63 To 941 (RED To BLK/WHT)	No
Wiper Switch		
LO & HI	63 To 993 (RED To BRN/WHT)	Yes
All Others	63 To 993 (RED To BRN/WHT)	No
INT.	63 To 65 (RED To Dk GRN)	Yes
All Others	63 To 65 (RED/ To Dk GRN)	No
HI	56 To 63 (Dk BLU/ORG To RED)	Yes
All Others	56 To 63 (Dk BLU/ORG To RED)	Yes
Intermittent		
INT. & OFF	67 To 589 (YEL/RED To ORG)	[1]
LOW & HI	57 To 590 (YEL/RED To ORG)	Yes

[1] – Rotate control clockwise. Resistance reading should smoothly increase from minimum 420 ohms to 13,000 ohms maximum.

ESCORT WIPER SWITCH CONTINUITY TEST

Application	Switch Position	Terminal Continuity
Standard	OFF	P, L
	LOW	B, L
	HIGH	B, H
	WASH	B, W
With Interval	OFF	None
	LOW	B, L
	HIGH	B, H, L
	INTERVAL	[1] B, L
	Wash	B, W

[1] – Minimum variable resistance between R1 & R2 is 420-880 ohms with a maximum of 7000-13,000 ohms.

GRAND MARQUIS, LTD CROWN VICTORIA, MARK VII & TOWN CAR WIPER SWITCH CONTINUITY TEST

Switch Position	Terminal Continuity
OFF	F-L, P-G
LOW	R, L, G
HIGH	R, H, G
WASH	B+, W
Intermittent	[1] L, G

[1] – Minimum variable resistance between G, R is 420-880 ohms with a maximum of 7000-13,000 ohms.

MUSTANG WIPER SWITCH CONTINUITY TEST

Wiper Switch Position	Terminal Number	Continuity
OFF	B+ to W	No
ON	B+ to W	Yes
ON or OFF, Wash OFF	B+ to H,L,I,W	No
LO, Wash OFF	B+ to L	Yes
	[1] B+ to H,I,W	No
HI, Wash OFF	B+ to L,H	YES
	[1] B+ to W,I	No
Interval at MAX, Wash OFF [2]	B+ to I	Yes
	B+ to H,L,W	No

[1] – R1-R2 resistance should be more than 420 ohms but less than 880 ohms. This is interval circuit set at minimum time setting.

[2] – R1-R2 resistance greater than 7000 ohms, but less than 13,000 ohms.

SABLE & TAURUS WIPER SWITCH CONTINUITY TEST

Switch Position	Terminal No. (Wire Color)	Continuity
Washer Switch		
ON	65 To 941 (Dk GRN To BLK/WHT)	Yes
OFF	65 To 941 (Dk GRN To BLK/WHT)	No
Wiper Switch		
OFF	56 To 993 (BRN/WHT To Dk BLU/ORG)	Yes
	57 To 589 (BLK To ORG)	Yes
All Others	56 To 993 (BRN/WHT To Dk BLU/ORG)	No
	57 To 589 (BLK To ORG)	No
LO & INT.	56 To 57 (Dk BLU/ORG To BLK)	Yes
All Others	56 To 57 (Dk BLU/ORG To BLK)	No
HI	57 To 58 (BLK To WHT)	Yes
All Others	57 To 58 (BLK To WHT)	Yes
Intermittent		
INT. & OFF	57 To 590 (BLK To Dk BLU/WHT)	[1]
LO & HI	57 To 590 (BLK To Dk BLU/WHT)	Yes

[1] – Rotate control clockwise. Resistance reading should smoothly increase from minimum 420 ohms to 13,000 ohms maximum.

DESCRIPTION & OPERATION

Front windshield wiper motor is located in engine compartment and is directly connected to wiper linkage. Wiper motor is a 2-speed, permanent magnet with 3 brushes. When control selector is in "LOW" position, low speed brush and common brush are used and motor operates at low speed.

When control selector is in "HIGH" position, high speed brush and common brush are used. Current by-passes a portion of armature winding, causing motor to operate faster.

When control selector is in "INT" position, wipers make single wipes which are separated by an adjustable pause through an interval governor attached to relay panel under driver's side of dash. See Fig. 2. The mist function provides a single wipe cycle. When wipe cycle is completed, wiper arm is returned to park position.

The rear (liftgate) wiper system is a single speed wiper motor with an on or off control selector. Single speed motor is mounted inside liftgate.

operate through 3 or 4 cycles. Install wiper arm and blade assembly with tip of wiper blade .79-1.18" (20.1-30.0 mm) from bottom of windshield or rear window. Install and tighten retaining cap.

TESTING

FRONT WIPER

NOTE: For connector terminal identification in the following tests, see Fig. 1.

Wipers Inoperative – Check wiper fuse and replace if necessary. If fuse blows again, check for short to ground in BLU wires at wiper/washer switch, interval governor and front wiper motor. Repair BLU wire as necessary. If fuse is okay, proceed to INTERMITTENT SUPPLY CHECK.

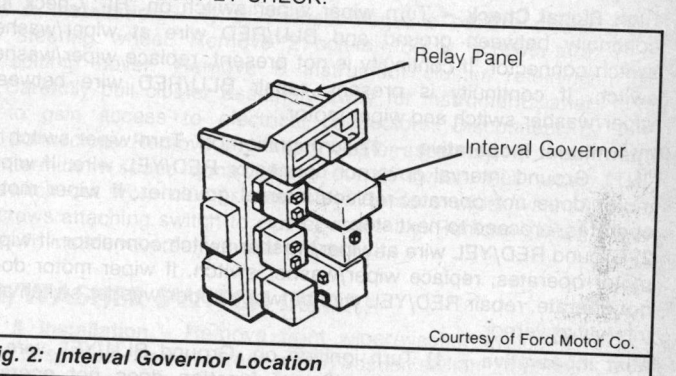

Relay Panel

Interval Governor

Courtesy of Ford Motor Co.

Fig. 2: Interval Governor Location

Intermittent Supply Check – Check for 11-13 volts on BLU wire at interval governor connector. If specified voltage is not present, repair BLU wire between fuse panel and interval governor. If specified voltage is present, proceed to WIPER MOTOR INTERMITTENT SUPPLY CHECK.

Wiper Motor Intermittent Supply Check – Check for 11-13 volts on BLU/BLK wire at interval governor connector. If specified voltage is not present, proceed to INTERVAL GOVERNOR GROUND. If specified voltage is present, proceed to WIPER MOTOR SUPPLY CHECK.

Interval Governor Ground – Check for continuity between ground and BLK wire of interval governor connector. If continuity is not present, repair BLK wire between interval governor and ground. If continuity is present, proceed to SIGNAL GROUND CHECK.

Signal Ground Check – 1) Check for continuity between ground and LT GRN wire of interval governor connector. If continuity is not present, replace interval governor. If continuity is present, proceed to next step.

2) Disconnect wiper/washer switch connector. Check for continuity between ground and LT GRN wire of interval governor connector. If continuity is not present, replace wiper/washer switch. If continuity is present, repair LT GRN wire between wiper/washer switch and interval governor connector.

Wiper Motor Supply Check – Check for 11-13 volts on BLU/BLK wire at wiper motor connector. If specified voltage is not present, repair BLU/BLK wire between interval governor and wiper motor. If specified voltage is present, replace wiper motor.

Low Speed Inoperative – Turn ignition off. Disconnect both large and small wiper motor connectors. Using a 12-volt source at small connector, attach positive side to BLU/BLK wire and negative side to BLU/WHT wire. If wiper motor does not operate, replace wiper motor. If wiper motor does operate, proceed to LOW SIGNAL CHECK.

Low Signal Check – 1) Turn wiper switch on "LO". Check for continuity between ground and BLU/WHT wire of wiper/washer switch connector. If no continuity is present, replace wiper/washer switch. If continuity is present, proceed to next step.

2) Check for continuity between ground and BLU/WHT wire at small wiper motor connector. If continuity is not present, repair BLU/WHT

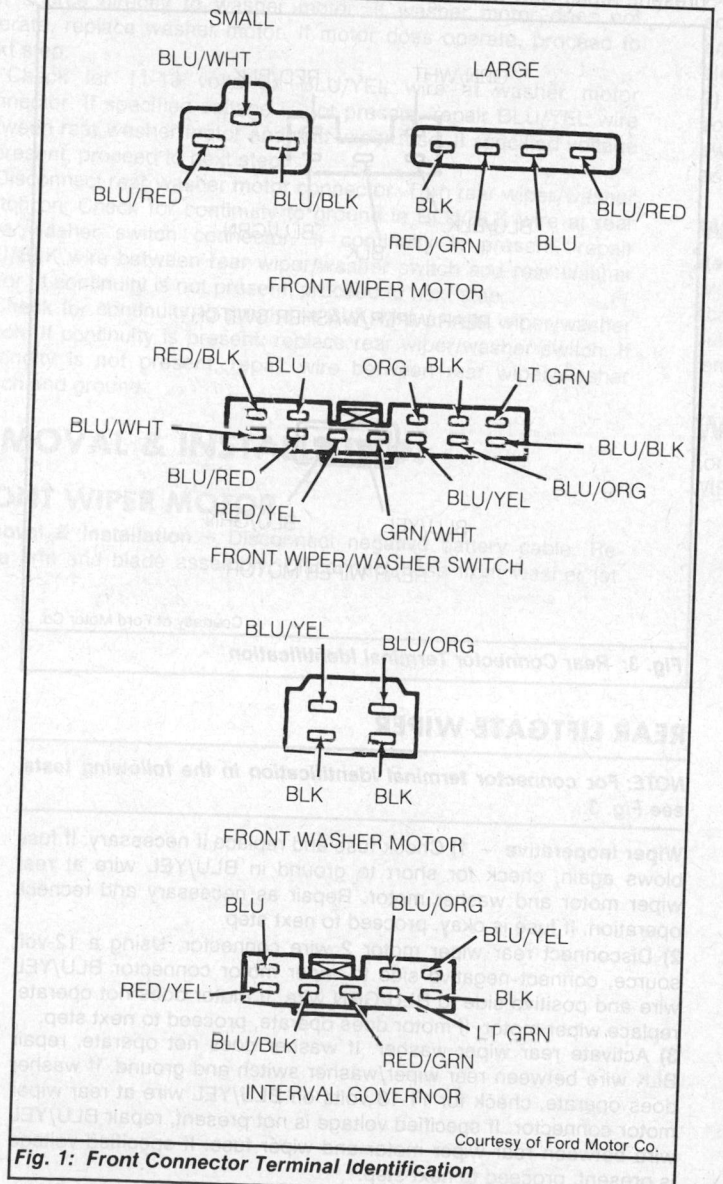

Rotunda Starting & Charging Tester

Red

Common Brush Terminal

Low Speed

High Speed

Connector A (Motor Switch)

Fig. 1: Testing Wiper Marquis, LTD Crown V

Rotunda Starting & Charging Tester

Ground (G1

Park Return Circuit No. 28

Ground (G2

Fig. 2: Testing Wiper M (Cougar & Thunderbird

SMALL

BLU/WHT

LARGE

BLU/RED BLU/BLK BLK BLU/RED

RED/GRN BLU

FRONT WIPER MOTOR

RED/BLK BLU ORG BLK LT GRN

BLU/WHT BLU/BLK

BLU/RED BLU/YEL BLU/ORG

RED/YEL GRN/WHT

FRONT WIPER/WASHER SWITCH

BLU/YEL BLU/ORG

BLK BLK

FRONT WASHER MOTOR

BLU BLU/ORG

BLU/YEL

RED/YEL BLK

BLU/BLK LT GRN

RED/GRN

INTERVAL GOVERNOR

Courtesy of Ford Motor Co.

Fig. 1: Front Connector Terminal Identification

ADJUSTMENTS

Front & Rear (Liftgate) – Unscrew retaining cap and remove wiper arm and blade assembly. Turn wipers on and allow motor to

DESCRIPTION

Two wiper systems are...
(wipers come to rest b...
high/low speed wipe...
permanent magnet mot...

Wiper motor location...
extension, inboard of r...
gear cover. Park mech...
supplied to motor throu...

OPERATION

INTERVAL SYST...

Low and high speed w...
of the control switch. ...
result is single wipes s...

Interval operation is c...
switch variable resist...
available and contro...
positioned at end of ...
pause control activate...
until after a pause of u...

Washer switch is inte...
pulling lever towards ...
system differ from s...
windshield washer ca...
operating position, inc...

TROUBLE SHO...

WIPERS DO N...

Check for open circ...
defective wiper switch...
components as neces...

MOTOR STOPS ...
TURNED OFF ...
(DOES NOT CO...

Continental, Grand M...
Taurus & Town Ca...
DIAGNOSIS & TESTI...
Escort, Mustang, Te...
in DIAGNOSIS & TES...

WIPERS GO IN...
MOTOR CONTI...

Replace wiper motor....

WIPERS CONT...
"OFF" OR "INT...

Continental, Cougar...
Thunderbird...
CONTINUITY test in...
test.

2) If wiper switch i...
switch to washer pur...
switch "OFF", replac...
3) If washer switch...
Leave interval goveri...
4) On all models Cou...
circuit 63 terminal ...
harness. On Courga...
park feed circuit and ...
5) All models, if...
no continuity is pres...

Mustang – 1) Disconnect battery negative cable. Disconnect linkage and electrical plug from wiper motor. Connect Green ammeter lead from Rotunda Starting and Charging Tester (07800005) to battery positive post.
2) Attach jumper wire from ground terminal on connector A to body ground. Connect positive (Red) lead from tester to low-speed terminal on connector A. See Fig. 5. Read current draw.
3) Remove positive (Red) tester lead from low-speed terminal and connect positive lead to high-speed terminal at connector A. See Fig. 5. Current draw should not exceed 3 amperes in either test.

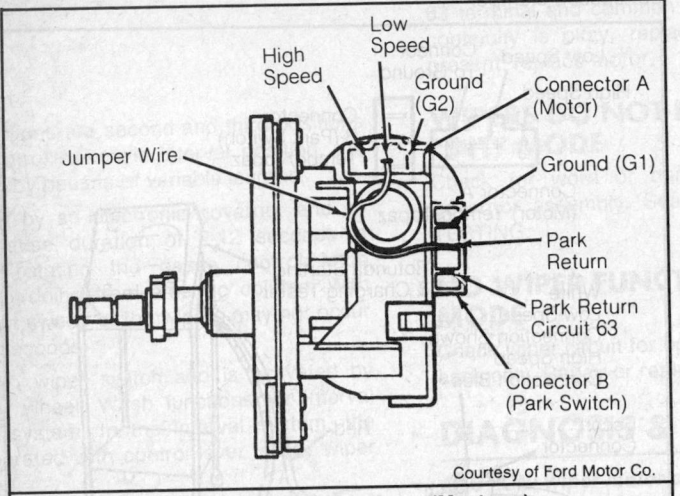

Fig. 5: Testing Wiper Motor Current Draw (Mustang)

MOTOR CONTINUITY TEST

All Except Escort, Mark VII, Mustang, Tempo & Topaz – 1) Remove motor park switch connector (connector B). Turn ignition switch "ON".
2) On Continental, Grand Marquis, LTD Crown Victoria, Sable, Taurus & Town Car, check for voltage on circuit 65 (Dark Green wire). See Fig. 1. On Cougar and Thunderbird, check for voltage on park feed circuit (Red wire). See Fig. 2. On all models, if battery voltage is not present, repair circuit. if voltage is present, go to next step.
2) Check motor ground wiring at switch connector. If continuity exists to ground, go to next step. If no continuity, service circuit as required.
3) Unplug wiper motor connectors. With an ohmmeter, ensure there is less than one ohm resistance between circuit terminal No. 28 and low-speed terminal in wiring harness. If continuity is not present, repair wire as required. If continuity is okay, leave connectors unplugged and go to next step.
4) Check for continuity to ground at circuit terminal No. 28 on wiper motor. If open, replace wiper motor. If ground is present, leave connectors unplugged and go to next step.
5) Measuring between wiring harnesses, ensure there is less than one ohm resistance between circuit terminal No. 63 and connector A common brush terminal (circuit terminal No. 63 and G2 ground on Courgar and Thunderbird. If continuity is not present, repair circuit as required. If lack of continuity is traced to interval governor, check wiper switch for continuity. See WIPER SWITCH CONTINUITY TEST.
6) Replace wiper switch if continuity is not present. If continuity is present in switch and lack of continuity has been traced to interval governor, replace governor.
7) On all except Cougar and Thunderbird, if continuity between circuits 63 and common brush terminal is okay, leave connectors unplugged. Check for continuity between circuits No. 63 and No. 65 on wiper motor. If open, replace motor.

Mark VII – 1) Turn ignition switch "ON". Remove motor park switch connector. See Fig. 4. Check for battery voltage on circuit No. 65. If

no voltage is present, repair wire as necessary. If voltage is present, go to next step.
2) Ensure motor housing is grounded through cup screw and housing ground strap. If ground is okay, go to next step.
3) Unplug wiper motor. Check continuity between circuits No. 28 and No. 56, in the wiring harness. If no continuity, trace and repair circuit. If continuity is okay, leave motor unplugged and go to next step.
4) Check for ground between circuit No. 28 on motor and body ground. If open, replace wiper motor. If ground is okay, leave motor disconnected and go to next step.
5) Ensure there is less than one ohm resistance between circuits No. 61 and No. 62, in the wiring harness. If continuity is okay, go to step 7). If no continuity is present, trace and repair wiring.
6) If open circuit is traced to interval governor, check wiper switch for continuity between Orange and Black wire terminals on wiper switch. Replace switch if defective. If wiper switch and wiring is okay, replace interval governor.
7) If continuity between circuits No. 61 and No. 62 in step 5) is okay, leave motor disconnected. Check for continuity between circuit terminals No. 61 and No. 65 on WIPER MOTOR. Replace wiper motor if there is an open circuit.

MOTOR PARK TEST

Escort & Mustang – 1) Turn ignition switch "ON". Turn on wipers. Stop wiper system with ignition switch so wipers are not in depressed park mode. On Mustang, Connect terminal 63 (Red wire) to positive battery terminal. Connect both ground terminals (G1 and G2) to body ground. See Fig. 5.
2) On Escort, jumper Red wire terminal to battery positive terminal. Jumper Black wire terminal to White wire terminal. See Fig. 6.
3) The wipers should run not more than one full cycle and park. If motor will not park or will not run to park position, replace motor. If motor parks, check windshield wiper manual control switch and wiring for continuity.
4) If switch and wiring test okay, replace interval governor if wiper will not stop in "OFF" or "INT" position of switch. See INTERVAL GOVERNOR LOCATION table.

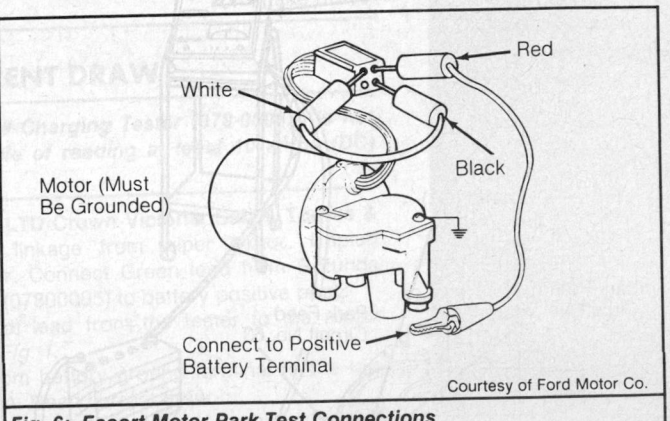

Fig. 6: Escort Motor Park Test Connections

Tempo & Topaz – 1) Turn ignition switch to "RUN" position. Place wiper switch in "OFF" position. Check for voltage at circuits 58 (White wire), 28 (Black/Pink wire) and 63 (Red wire) at motor connectors. See Fig. 7.
2) If voltage is present on all 3 circuits and wiper blades are not in "PARK" position, ground connector "A" and connector "B" ground terminals to body. If motor parks, service motor ground. If motor does not move to "PARK" position, replace motor.
3) If voltage check shows only voltage at circuit 63 (Red wire), replace wiper motor. If voltage check shows voltage at circuits 63 (Red wire) and 28 (Black/Pink wire) only, replace wiper switch. If voltage is still not present at circuit 58 (White wire), trace circuits 28 (Black and 58 (White wire) back to wiper switch to determine source of problem.

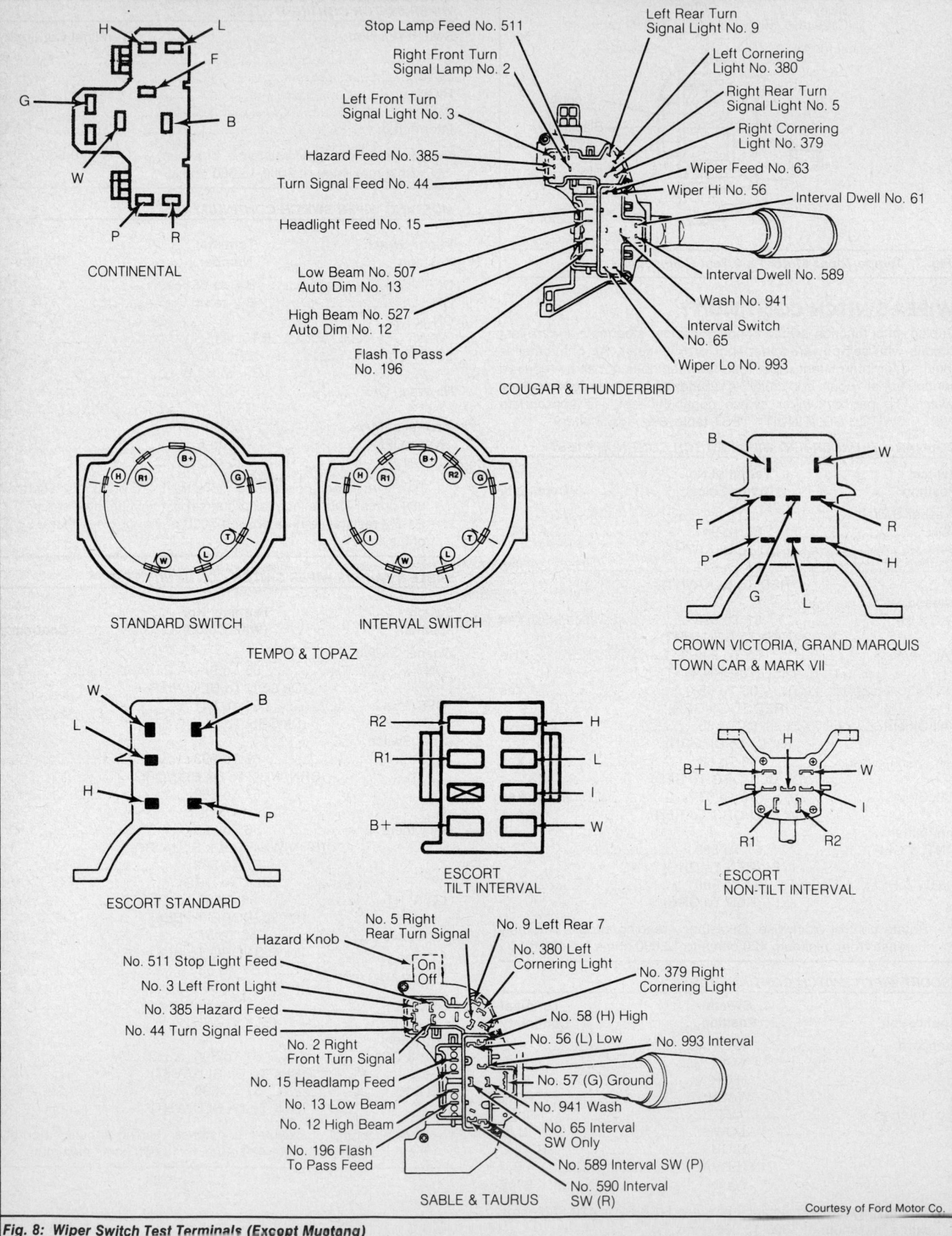

Fig. 8: Wiper Switch Test Terminals (Except Mustang)

TEMPO/TOPAZ WIPER SWITCH CONTINUITY TEST

Application	Switch Position	Terminal Continuity
Standard	OFF	R1, L
	LOW	B+, L
	HIGH	B+, H
	WASH	B+, W
With Interval	OFF	None
	INTERVAL	[1]B+, I
	LOW	B+, L
	HIGH	B+, H, L
	Wash	B+, W

[1] – Minimum variable resistance between R1-R2 is 420-880 ohms with a maximum of 7000-13,000 ohms.

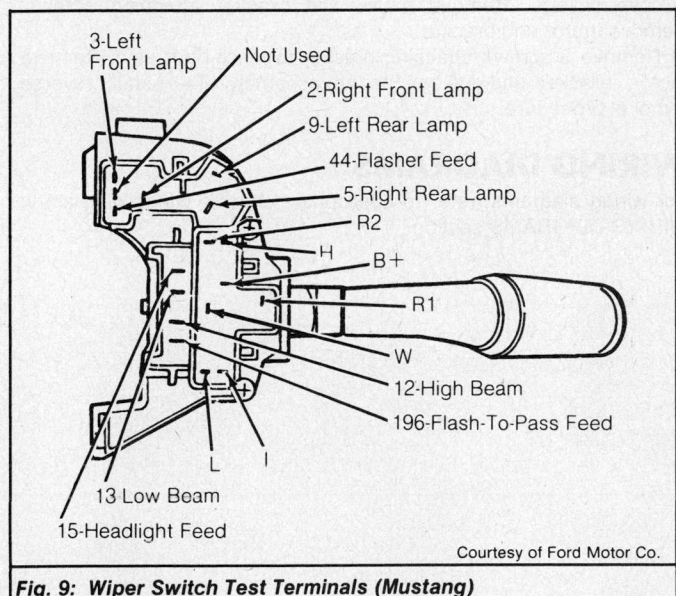

3-Left Front Lamp — Not Used
2-Right Front Lamp
9-Left Rear Lamp
44-Flasher Feed
5-Right Rear Lamp
R2
H — B+
R1
W
12-High Beam
196-Flash-To-Pass Feed
L — I
13 Low Beam
15-Headlight Feed

Courtesy of Ford Motor Co.

Fig. 9: Wiper Switch Test Terminals (Mustang)

WINDSHIELD WASHERS

Washers Do Not Operate – 1) Check fluid level in reservoir. Fill if necessary. Activate washer switch. If motor is inoperative go to step **2)**. If motor operates but will not squirt fluid, visually inspect washer nozzles for blockage and hose for kinks. Disconnect hose at reservoir and check for blockage at washer pump outlet.

2) Using a voltmeter or test lamp, check for voltage at washer pump by activating washer switch. If voltage is present go to next step. If voltage is not present go to step **4)**.

3) With an ohmmeter, check ground at washer pump. If ground is not present, service ground. If ground is good, replace pump.

4) Using a voltmeter or test lamp, check for power at wiper switch by operating wipers. If wipers operate, go to step **6)**. If wipers do not operate, go to next step.

5) Using a voltmeter or test lamp, check for power out of washer switch or wash circuit. If no voltage is present go to step **8)**. If voltage is present, go to step **7)**.

6) Activate heater blower. If blower does not operate, service open circuit in power feed wiring. If blower operates, go to next step.

7) Check wiper/wash circuit breaker. If circuit breaker is blown, replace circuit breaker. If circuit breaker is okay, go to next step.

8) Check for power to switch. If no power is available, check for electrical system fault before replacing wipe/wash switch. If power is available, service wipe/wash wiring and connectors.

REMOVAL & INSTALLATION

NOTE: To remove wiper arm and blade assembly, raise blade end of wiper arm. Move slide latch away from pivot shaft. Wiper arm can be removed without the use of tools.

WIPER MOTOR

Removal & Installation (Cougar, Mark VII & Thunderbird) – 1) Turn wipers on. When blades are straight up, turn ignition off. Disconnect battery. Remove arm and blade assemblies. Remove left side cowl screen.

2) Disconnect linkage drive arm from motor crank pin after removing clip. Disconnect electrical connector. Remove motor attaching screws and motor. To install, ensure motor is in park position and reverse removal procedure.

Removal & Installation (All Others) – 1) Disconnect battery ground cable. Disconnect 2 push-on wire connectors from motor. Remove hood seal. Remove right side arm assembly. Remove windshield wiper linkage cover by removing 2 attaching screws and hose clip.

2) Remove linkage retaining clip from operating arm on motor by lifting locking tab up and pulling clip away from pin. Remove 3 bolts retaining motor to dash panel extension. Remove motor. To install, ensure motor is in "PARK" position and reverse removal procedure.

WIPER SWITCH & INTERMITTENT GOVERNOR

Removal – Disconnect battery. Remove split steering column cover retaining screw. Separate the 2 halves and disconnect multiple connector at rear of wiper switch. Disconnect multiple connector at main wiring loom. Remove governor retaining screws and remove interval governor. To install, reverse removal procedure.

WIRING DIAGRAMS

For wiring diagrams, refer to appropriate chassis wiring diagram in WIRING DIAGRAMS section.

1989 WIPER/WASHER SYSTEMS
Ford Motor Co. Liftgate

Escort, Sable, Taurus

DESCRIPTION

The optional window wiper/washer assembly consists of a motor mounted inside the liftgate and a single-speed switch located on the instrument panel. Wiper motor is protected by an in-line circuit breaker.

OPERATION

Turning the wiper switch controls operation of the wiper motor. Pressing the switch operates the washer, but does not turn on the wiper. When the control switch is turned off, the park circuit returns the wiper blade to a side or bottom position.

TESTING

Rear Wiper Inoperative – 1) Turn ignition and rear wiper on. If motor operates but wiper does not, check linkage. If linkage is okay replace motor. If motor does not operate, check circuit breaker.

2) If circuit breaker is okay, turn ignition and wiper off. On Escort non-wagon models, remove liftgate inner trim panel. On Escort wagon models, remove license plate housing and disconnect license plate light connector. On all models, disconnect wiper motor connector.

3) Attach a good ground to Black wire or directly to wiper motor housing. Apply battery voltage to White wire on motor connector. If wiper motor operates check wire between switch and wiper motor.

If wire is okay, replace switch. If wiper motor does not operate, replace motor.

4) Apply battery voltage to Red wire. Wiper should operate and then stop in park position. If not, replace motor. If wiper stops at park, check wire between switch and motor. If wire is okay, replace switch.

REMOVAL & INSTALLATION

WIPER MOTOR

Removal & Installation – 1) Remove wiper arm and blade. Remove pivot shaft attaching nut and spacers. Remove liftgate inner trim panel (if equipped). On wagon models, disconnect license light wiring and remove housing.

2) Disconnect electrical connector to wiper motor. Pry off arm and remove linkage. Remove motor and bracket attaching screws. Remove motor and bracket.

3) Remove 3 screws attaching bracket to inner door skin. Remove motor, bracket and linkage as an assembly. To install, reverse removal procedure.

WIRING DIAGRAMS

For wiring diagrams, refer to appropriate chassis wiring diagram in WIRING DIAGRAMS section.

Section 7

ENGINES & ENGINE COOLING

CONTENTS

TROUBLE SHOOTING

	Page
Cooling Systems	7-128
Gasoline Engines	7-2

ENGINE OVERHAUL PROCEDURES

All Engines	7-5

CHRYSLER MOTORS ENGINES

2.2L & 2.5L 4-Cylinder	7-17
3.0L V6	7-27
5.2L V8	7-34

EAGLE ENGINES

2.5L 4-Cylinder	7-42
3.0L V6	7-49

FORD MOTOR CO. ENGINES

	Page
1.9L 4-Cylinder	7-60
2.2L 4-Cylinder	7-68
2.3L HSC & HSO 4-Cylinder	7-75
2.5L HSC 4-Cylinder	7-75
2.3L OHC 4-Cylinder	7-82
3.0L V6	7-89
3.0L SHO V6	7-96
3.8L & 3.8L Supercharger (SC) V6	7-103
5.0L, 5.0L HO & 5.8L V8	7-111

ENGINE REMOVAL & INSTALLATION

Chrysler Motors	7-118
Eagle	7-120
Ford Motor Co.	7-122

OIL PAN REMOVAL

Chrysler Motors	7-126
Eagle	7-126
Ford Motor Co.	7-126

COOLING SYSTEM TROUBLE SHOOTING

All Models	7-128

GENERAL COOLING SYSTEM SERVICING

All Models	7-129

ENGINE COOLANT SPECIFICATIONS

All Models	7-130

ENGINE COOLING FANS

Flex-Blade Fans	7-131
Electric Cooling Fans	
Chrysler Motors	7-132
Eagle Premier	7-134
Ford Motor Co.	7-135

SERPENTINE DRIVE BELTS

Chrysler Motors, Eagle & Ford Motor Co.	7-153

NOTE: ALSO SEE GENERAL INDEX

CYLINDER HEAD REPLACEMENT

REMOVAL

Remove intake and exhaust manifolds and valve cover. Cylinder head and camshaft carrier bolts (if equipped), should be removed only when engine is cold. On many aluminum cylinder heads, removal while hot will cause cylinder head warpage. Mark rocker arm or overhead cam components for location.

Remove rocker arm components or overhead cam components. Components must be installed in original location. Individual design rocker arms may utilize shafts, ball-type pedestal mounts or no rocker arms. For all design types, wire components together and identify according to corresponding valve. Remove cylinder head bolts. Note length and location. Some applications require cylinder head bolts be removed in proper sequence to prevent cylinder head damage. See Fig. 1. Remove cylinder head.

INSTALLATION

Ensure all surfaces and head bolts are clean. Check that head bolt holes of cylinder block are clean and dry to prevent block damage when bolts are tightened. Clean threads with tap to ensure accurate bolt torque.

Install head gasket on cylinder block. Some manufacturer's may recommend sealant be applied to head gasket prior to installation. Note that all holes are aligned. Some gasket applications may be marked so certain area faces upward. Install cylinder head using care not to damage head gasket. Ensure cylinder head is fully seated on cylinder block.

Some applications require head bolts be coated with sealant prior to installation. This is done if head bolts are exposed to water passages. Some applications require head bolts be coated with light coat of engine oil.

Install head bolts. Head bolts should be tightened in proper steps and sequence to specification. See Fig. 1. Install remaining components. Tighten all bolts to specification. Adjust valves if required. See VALVE ADJUSTMENT in this article.

NOTE: Some manufacturers require that head bolts be retightened after specified amount of operation. This must be done to prevent head gasket failure.

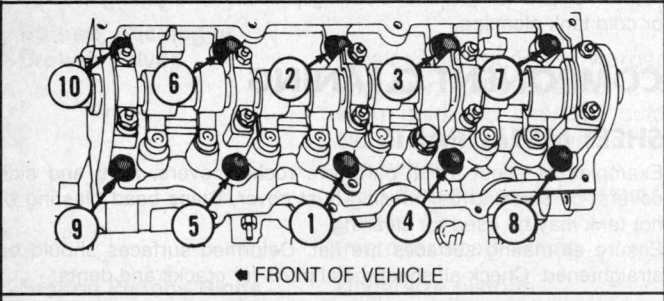

Fig. 1: Typical Cylinder Head Tightening or Loosening Sequence

VALVE ADJUSTMENT

Engine specifications will indicate valve train clearance and temperature at which adjustment is to be made on most models. In most cases, adjustment will be made with a cold engine. In some cases, both a cold and a hot clearance will be given for maintenance convenience.

On some models, adjustment is not required. Rocker arms are tightened to specification and valve lash is automatically set. On some models with push rod actuated valve train, adjustment is made at push rod end of rocker arm while other models do not require adjustment.

Clearance will be checked between tip of rocker arm and tip of valve stem in proper sequence using a feeler gauge. Adjustment is made

by rotating adjusting screw until proper clearance is obtained. Lock nut is then tightened. Engine will be rotated to obtain all valve adjustments to manufacturer's specifications.

Some models require hydraulic lifter to be bled down and clearance measured. Different length push rods can be used to obtain proper clearance. Clearance will be checked between tip of rocker arm and tip of valve stem in proper sequence using a feeler gauge.

Overhead cam engines designed without rocker arms actuate valves directly on a cam follower. A hardened, removable disc is installed between the cam lobe and lifter. Clearance will be checked between cam heel and adjusting disc in proper sequence using a feeler gauge. Engine will be rotated to obtain all valve adjustments.

On overhead cam engines designed with rocker arms, adjustment is made at valve end of rocker arm. Ensure that the valve to be adjusted is riding on the heel of the cam on all engines. Clearance will be checked between tip of rocker arm and tip of valve stem in proper sequence using a feeler gauge. Adjustment is made by rotating adjusting screw until proper clearance is obtained. Lock nut is then tightened. Engine will be rotated to obtain all valve adjustments to manufacturer's specifications.

CYLINDER HEAD OVERHAUL

CYLINDER HEAD DISASSEMBLY

Mark valves for location. Using valve spring compressor, compress valve springs. Remove valve locks. Carefully release spring compressor. Remove retainer or rotator, valve spring, spring seat and valve. See Fig. 2.

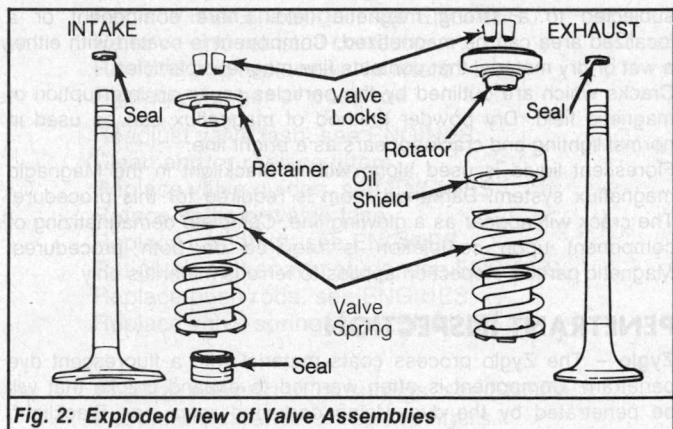

Fig. 2: Exploded View of Valve Assemblies

CYLINDER HEAD CLEANING & INSPECTION

Clean cylinder head and valve components using approved cleaning methods. Inspect cylinder head for cracks, damage or warped gasket surface. Place straightedge across gasket surface. Determine clearance at center of straightedge. Measure across both diagonals, longitudinal centerline and across the head at several points. See Fig. 3.

On cast cylinder heads, if warpage exceeds .003" (.08 mm) in a 6" span, or .006" (.15 mm) over total length, cylinder head must be resurfaced. On most aluminum cylinder heads, if warpage exceeds .002" (.05 mm) in any area, cylinder head must be resurfaced. Warpage specification may vary with manufacturer.

Cylinder head thickness should be measured to determine amount of material which can be removed before replacement is required. Cylinder head thickness must not be less than manufacturer's specifications.

If cylinder head required resurfacing, it may not align properly with intake manifold. On "V" type engines, misalignment is corrected by machining intake manifold surface that contacts cylinder head. Cylinder head may be machined on surface that contacts intake manifold. Using oil stone, remove burrs or scratches from all sealing surfaces.

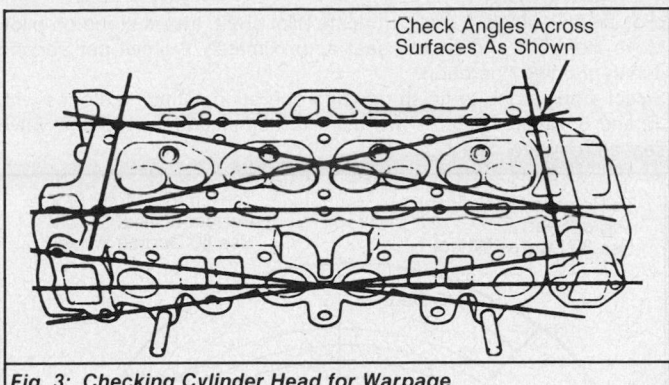

Fig. 3: *Checking Cylinder Head for Warpage*

VALVE SPRINGS

Inspect valve springs for corroded or pitted valve spring surfaces which may lead to breakage. Polished spring ends caused by a rotating spring, indicates that spring surge has occurred. Replace springs showing evidence of these conditions.

Inspect valve springs for squareness using a 90 degree straight-edge. *See Fig. 4.* Replace valve spring if out-of-square exceeds manufacturer's specification.

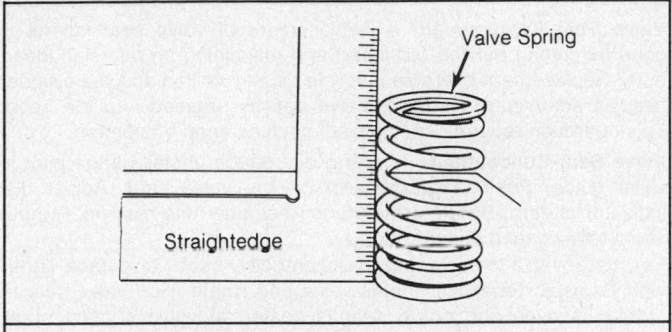

Fig. 4: *Checking Valve Spring Squareness*

Using vernier caliper, measure free length of all valve springs. Replace springs if not within specification. Using valve spring tester, test valve spring pressure at installed and compressed heights. *See Fig. 5.*

Usually compressed height is installed height minus valve lift. Replace valve spring if not within specification. It is recommended to replace all valve springs when overhauling cylinder head.

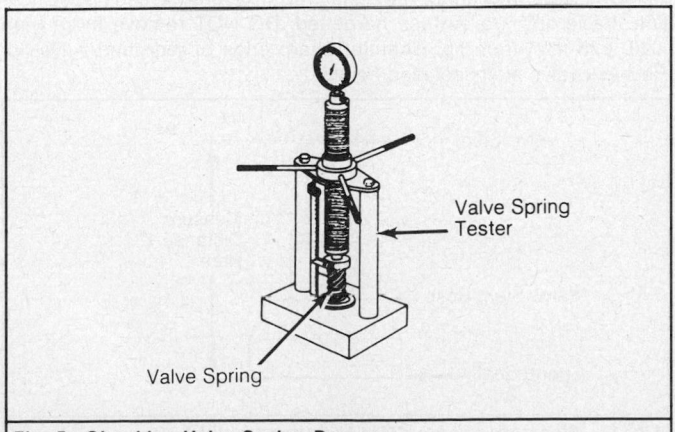

Fig. 5: *Checking Valve Spring Pressure*

VALVE GUIDE

Measuring Valve Guide Clearance – Check valve stem-to-guide clearance. Ensure valve stem diameter is within specifications.

Install valve in valve guide. Install dial indicator assembly on cylinder head with tip resting against valve stem just above valve guide. *See Fig. 6.*

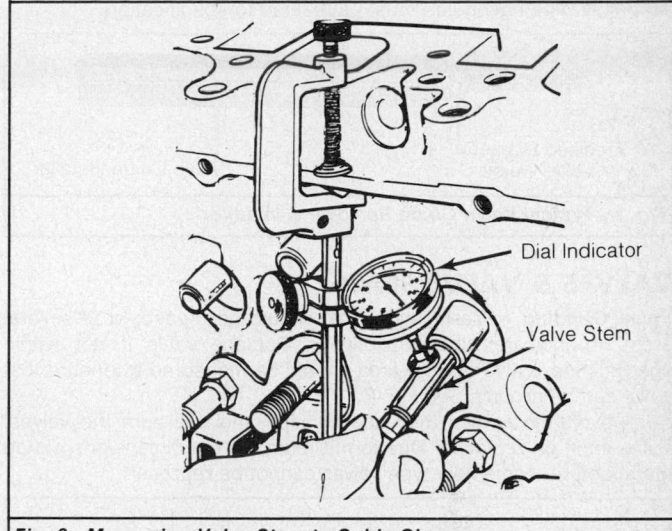

Fig. 6: *Measuring Valve Stem-to-Guide Clearance*

Lower valve approximately 1/16" below valve seat. Push valve stem against valve guide as far as possible. Adjust dial indicator to zero. Push valve stem in opposite direction and note reading. Clearance must be within specification.

If valve guide clearance exceeds specification, valves with oversize stems may be used or valve guide must be replaced. On some applications, a false guide is installed, then reamed to proper specification. Valve guide reamer set is used to ream valve guide to obtain proper clearance for new valve.

Reaming Valve Guide – Select proper reamer for valve stem. Reamer must be of proper length to provide clean cut through entire length of valve guide. Install reamer in valve guide and rotate to cut valve guide. *See Fig. 7.*

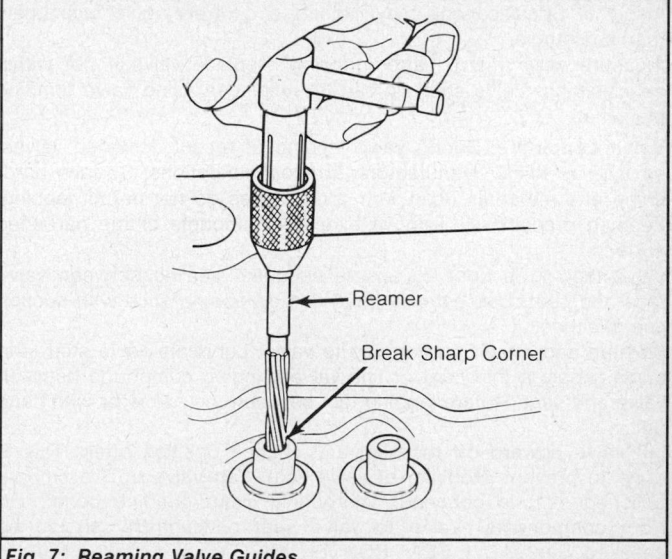

Fig. 7: *Reaming Valve Guides*

Replacing Valve Guide – Replace valve guide if clearance exceeds specification. Valve guides are either pressed, hammered or shrunk in place, depending upon cylinder head design and type of metal used.

Remove valve guide from cylinder head by pressing or tapping on a stepped drift. *See Fig. 8.* Once valve guide is installed, distance from cylinder head to top of valve guide must be checked. This distance must be within specification.

Aluminum heads are often heated before installing valve guide. Guide is sometimes chilled in dry ice before installation. Combination of a heated head and chilled guide insures a tight guide fit upon assembly. The new guide must be reamed to specification.

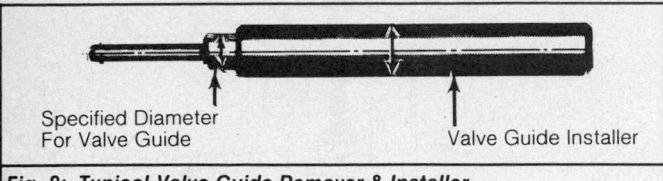

Fig. 8: Typical Valve Guide Remover & Installer

VALVES & VALVE SEATS

Valve Grinding – Valve stem O.D. should be measured in several areas to indicate amount of wear. Replace valve if not within specification. Valve margin area should be measured to ensure that valve can be ground. *See Fig. 9.*

If valve margin is less than specification, this will burn the valves. Valve must be replaced. Due to minimum margin dimensions during manufacture, some new type valves cannot be reground.

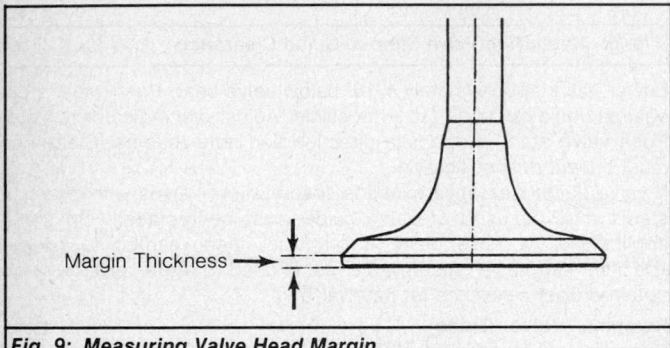

Fig. 9: Measuring Valve Head Margin

Resurface valve to proper angle specification using valve grinding machine. Follow manufacturer's instructions for valve grinding machine. Specifications may indicate a different valve face angle than seat angle.

Measure valve margin after grinding. Replace valve if not within specification. Valve stem tip can be refinished using valve grinding machine.

Valve Lapping – During valve lapping of recent designed valves, be sure to follow manufacturer's recommendations. Surface hardening and materials used with some valves do not permit lapping. Lapping process will remove excessive amounts of the hardened surface.

Valve lapping is done to ensure adequate sealing between valve face and seat. Use either a hand drill or lapping stick with suction cup attached.

Moisten and attach suction cup to valve. Lubricate valve stem and guide. Apply a thin coat of fine valve grinding compound between valve and seat. Rotate lapping tool between the palms or with hand drill.

Lift valve upward off the seat and change position often. This is done to prevent grooving of valve seat. Lap valve until a smooth polished seat is obtained. Thoroughly clean grinding compound from components. Valve to valve seat concentricity should be checked. See VALVE SEAT CONCENTRICITY.

CAUTION: Valve guides must be in good condition and free of carbon deposits prior to valve seat grinding. Some engines contain an induction hardened valve seat. Excessive material removal will damage valve seats.

Valve Seat Grinding – Select coarse stone of correct size and angle for seat to be ground. Ensure stone is true and has a smooth surface. Select correct size pilot for valve guide dimension. Install

pilot in valve guide. Lightly lubricate pilot shaft. Install stone on pilot. Move stone off and on the seat approximately 2 times per second during grinding operation.

Select a fine stone to finish grinding operation. Grinding stones with 30 and 60 degree angles are used to center and narrow the valve seat as required. *See Fig. 10.*

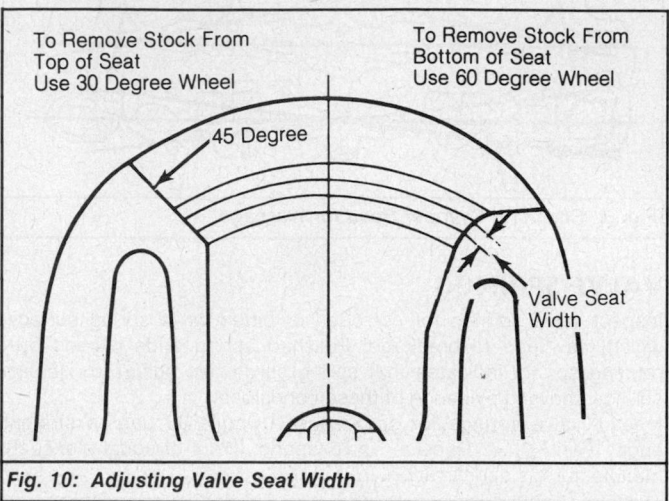

Fig. 10: Adjusting Valve Seat Width

Valve Seat Replacement – Replacement of valve seat inserts is done by cutting out the old insert and machining an oversize insert bore. Replacement oversize insert is usually chilled and the cylinder head is sometimes warmed. Valve seat is pressed into the head. This operation requires specialized machine shop equipment.

Valve Seat Concentricity – Using dial gauge, install gauge pilot in valve guide. Position gauge arm on the valve seat. Adjust dial indicator to zero. Rotate arm 360 degrees and note reading. Runout should not exceed specification.

To check valve-to-valve seat concentricity, coat valve face lightly with Prussian Blue dye. Install valve and rotate it on valve seat. If pattern is even and entire seat is coated at valve contact point, valve is concentric with the seat.

CYLINDER HEAD REASSEMBLY

Valve Stem Installed Height – Valve stem installed height must be checked when new valves are installed or when valves or valve seats have been ground. Install valve in valve guide. Measure distance from tip of valve stem to spring seat. *See Fig. 11.* Distance must be within specifications.

Remove valve and grind valve stem tip if height exceeds specification. Valve tips are surface hardened. DO NOT remove more than .010" (.25 mm) from tip. Chamfer sharp edge of reground valve tip. Recheck valve stem installed height.

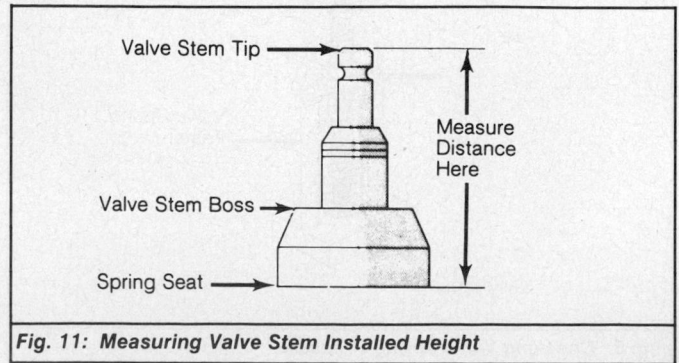

Fig. 11: Measuring Valve Stem Installed Height

VALVE STEM OIL SEALS

Valve stem oil seals must be installed on valve stem. *See Fig. 2.* Seals are needed due to pressure differential at the ends of valve guides. Atmospheric pressure above intake guide, combined with manifold vacuum below guide, causes oil to be drawn into the cylinder.

Exhaust guides also have pressure differential created by exhaust gas flowing past the guide, creating a low pressure area. This low pressure area draws oil into the exhaust system.

Replacement (On Vehicle) – Mark rocker arm or overhead cam components for location. Remove rocker arm components or overhead cam components. Components must be installed in original location. Remove spark plugs. Valve stem oil seals may be replaced by holding valves against seats using air pressure.

Air pressure must be installed in cylinder using an adapter for spark plug hole. An adapter can be constructed by welding air hose connection to spark plug body with porcelain removed.

Rotate engine until piston is at top of stroke. Install adapter in spark plug hole. Apply a minimum of 140 psi (9.8 kg/cm²) line pressure to adapter. Air pressure should hold valve closed. If air pressure does not hold valve closed, check for damaged or bent valve. Cylinder head must be removed for service.

Using valve spring compressor, compress valve springs. Remove valve locks. Carefully release spring compressor. Remove retainer or rotator and valve spring. Remove valve stem oil seal.

If oversized valves have been installed, oversized oil seals must be used. Coat valve stem with engine oil. Install protective sleeve over end of valve stem. Install new oil seal over valve stem and seat on valve guide. Remove protective sleeve. Install spring seat, valve spring and retainer or rotator. Compress spring and install valve locks. Remove spring compressor. Ensure valve locks are fully seated.

Install rocker arms or overhead cam components. Tighten all bolts to specification. Adjust valves if required. Remove adapter. Install spark plugs, valve cover and gasket.

VALVE SPRING INSTALLED HEIGHT

Valve spring installed height should be checked during reassembly. Measure height from lower edge of valve spring to the upper edge. DO NOT include valve spring seat or retainer. Distance must be within specifications. If valves and/or seats have been ground, a valve spring shim may be required to correct spring height. See Fig. 12.

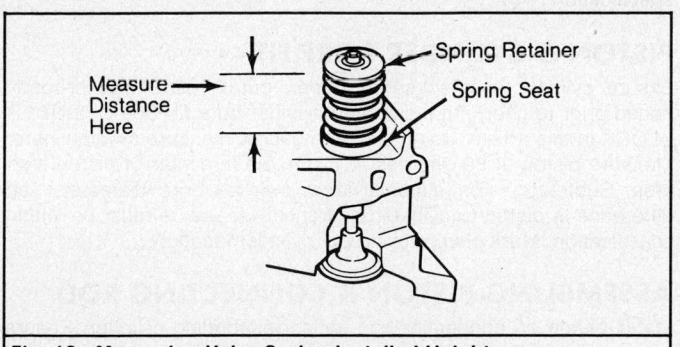

Fig. 12: Measuring Valve Spring Installed Height

ROCKER ARMS & ASSEMBLIES

Rocker Studs – Rocker studs are either threaded or pressed in place. Threaded studs are removed by locking 2 nuts on the stud. Unscrew the stud by turning the jam nut. Coat new stud threads with Loctite and install. Tighten to specification.

Pressed in stud can be removed using a stud puller. Ream stud bore to proper specification and press in a new oversize stud. Pressed in studs are often replaced by cutting threads in the stud bore to accept a threaded stud.

Rocker Arms & Shafts – Mark rocker arms for location. Remove rocker arm retaining bolts. Remove rocker arms. Inspect rocker arms, shafts, bushings and pivot balls (if equipped) for excessive wear. Inspect rocker arms for wear in valve stem contact area. Measure rocker arm bushing I.D. Replace bushings if excessively worn.

The rocker arm valve stem contact point can be reground, using special fixture for valve grinding machine. Remove minimum amount of material as possible. Ensure all oil passages are clear. Install rocker arms in original locations. Ensure rocker arm is properly seated in push rod. Tighten bolts to specification. Adjust valves if required. See VALVE ADJUSTMENT in this article.

PUSH RODS

Remove rocker arms. Mark push rods for location. Remove push rods. Push rods can be steel or aluminum, solid or hollow. Hollow push rods must be internally cleaned to ensure oil passage to rocker arms is cleaned. Check push rods for damage, such as loose ends on steel tipped aluminum types.

Check push rod for straightness. Roll push rod on a flat surface. Using feeler gauge, check clearance at center. Replace push rod if bent. The push rod can also be supported at each end and rotated. A dial indicator is used to detect bends in the push rod.

Lubricate ends of push rod and install push rod in original location. Ensure push rod is properly seated in lifter. Install rocker arm. Tighten bolts to specification. Adjust valves if required. See VALVE ADJUSTMENT in this article.

LIFTERS

Hydraulic Lifters – Before replacing a hydraulic lifter for noisy operation, ensure noise is not caused by worn rocker arms or valve tips. Hydraulic lifter assemblies must be installed in original locations. Remove rocker arm assembly and push rod. Mark components for location. Some applications require intake manifold, or lifter cover removal. Remove lifter retainer plate (if used). To remove lifters, use a hydraulic lifter remover or magnet. Different type lifters are used. See Fig. 13.

On sticking lifters, disassemble and clean lifter. DO NOT mix lifter components or positions. Parts are select-fitted and are not interchangeable. Inspect all components for wear. Note amount of wear in lifter body-to-camshaft contact area. Surface must have smooth and convex contact face. If wear is apparent, carefully inspect cam lobe.

Inspect push rod contact area and lifter body for scoring or signs of wear. If body is scored, inspect lifter bore for damage and lack of lubrication. On roller type lifters, inspect roller for flaking, pitting, loss of needle bearings and roughness during rotation.

Measure lifter body O.D. in several areas. Measure lifter bore I.D. of cylinder block. Some models offer oversized lifters. Replace lifter if damaged.

If lifter check valve is not operating, obstructions may be preventing it from closing or valve spring may be broken. Clean or replace components as necessary.

Check plunger operation. Plunger should drop to bottom of the body by its own weight when assembled dry. If plunger is not free, soak lifter in solvent to dissolve deposits.

Lifter leak-down test can be performed on lifter. Lifter must be filled with special test oil. New lifters contain special test oil. Using lifter leak-down tester, perform leak-down test following manufacturer's instructions. If leak-down time is not within specifications, replace lifter assembly.

Lifters should be soaked in clean engine oil several hours prior to installation. Coat lifter base, roller (if equipped) and lifter body with ample amount of molykote or camshaft lubricant. See Fig. 13. Install lifter in original location. Install remaining components. Valve lash adjustment is not required on most hydraulic lifters. Preload of hydraulic lifter is automatic. Some models may require adjustment.

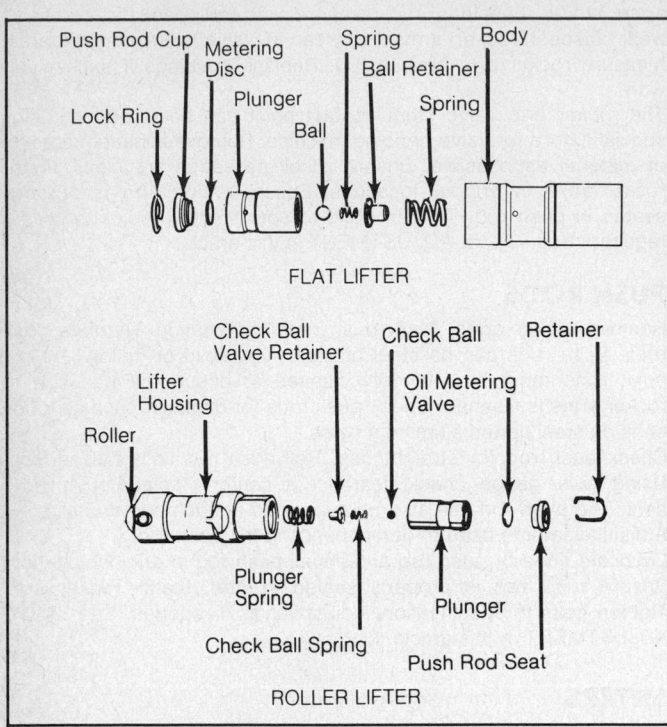

FLAT LIFTER

ROLLER LIFTER

Fig. 13: Typical Hydraulic Valve Lifter Assemblies

Mechanical Lifters – Lifter assemblies must be installed in original locations. Remove rocker arm assembly and push rod. Mark components for location. Some applications require intake manifold or lifter cover removal. Remove lifter retainer plate (if used). To remove lifters, use lifter remover or magnet.

Inspect push rod contact area and lifter body for scoring or signs of wear. If body is scored, inspect lifter bore for damage and lack of lubrication. Note amount of wear in lifter body-to-camshaft contact area. Surface must have smooth and convex contact face. If wear is apparent, carefully inspect cam lobe.

Coat lifter base, roller (if equipped) and lifter body with ample amount of molykote or camshaft lubricant. Install lifter in original location. Install remaining components. Tighten bolts to specification. Adjust valves. See VALVE ADJUSTMENT in this article.

PISTONS, CONNECTING RODS & BEARINGS

RIDGE REMOVAL

Ridge in cylinder wall must be removed prior to piston removal. Failure to remove ridge prior to removing pistons will cause piston damage in piston ring lands or grooves.

With piston at bottom dead center, place rag in bore to trap metal chips. Install ridge reamer in cylinder bore. Adjust ridge reamer using manufacturer's instructions. Remove ridge using ridge reamer. DO NOT remove an excessive amount of material. Ensure ridge is completely removed.

PISTON & CONNECTING ROD REMOVAL

Note top of piston. Some pistons may contain a notch, arrow or be marked "FRONT". Piston must be installed in proper direction to prevent damage with valve operation.

Check that connecting rod and cap are numbered for cylinder location and which side of cylinder block the number faces. Proper cap and connecting rod must be installed together. Connecting rod cap must be installed on connecting rod in proper direction to ensure bearing lock procedure. Mark connecting rod and cap if necessary. Pistons must be installed in original location.

Remove cap retaining nuts or bolts. Remove bearing cap. Install stud protectors on connecting rod bolts. This protects cylinder walls from scoring during removal. Ensure proper removal of ridge. Push piston and connecting rod from cylinder. Connecting rod boss can be tapped with a wooden dowel or hammer handle to aid in removal.

PISTON & CONNECTING ROD

Disassembly – Using ring expander, remove piston rings. Remove piston pin retaining rings (if equipped). On pressed type piston pins, special fixtures and procedures according to manufacturer must be used to remove piston pins. Follow manufacturer's recommendations to avoid piston distortion or breakage.

Cleaning – Remove all carbon and varnish from piston. Pistons and connecting rods may be cleaned in cold type chemical tank. Using ring groove cleaner, clean all deposits from ring grooves. Ensure all deposits are cleaned from ring grooves to prevent ring breakage or sticking. DO NOT attempt to clean pistons using wire brush.

Inspection – Inspect pistons for nicks, scoring, cracks or damage in ring areas. Connecting rod should be checked for cracks using Magnaflux procedure. Piston diameter must be measured in manufacturer's specified area.

Using telescopic gauge and micrometer, measure piston pin bore of piston in 2 areas, 90 degrees apart. This is done to check diameter and out-of-round.

Install proper bearing cap on connecting rod. Ensure bearing cap is installed in proper location. Tighten bolts or nuts to specification. Using inside micrometer, measure inside diameter in 2 areas, 90 degrees apart.

Connecting rod I.D. and out-of-round must be within specification. Measure piston pin bore I.D. and piston pin O.D. All components must be within specification. Subtract piston pin diameter from piston pin bore in piston and connecting rod to determine proper fit. Connecting rod length must be measured from center of crankshaft journal inside diameter to center of piston pin bushing using proper caliper. Connecting rods must be the same length. Connecting rods should be checked on an alignment fixture for bent or twisted condition. Replace all components which are damaged or not within specification.

PISTON & CYLINDER BORE FIT

Ensure cylinder is checked for taper, out-of-round and properly honed prior to checking piston and cylinder bore fit. See CYLINDER BLOCK in this article. Using dial bore gauge, measure cylinder bore. Measure piston at 90 degrees to piston pin in center of piston skirt area. Subtract piston diameter from cylinder bore diameter. The difference is piston-to-cylinder clearance. Clearance must be within specification. Mark piston for proper cylinder location.

ASSEMBLING PISTON & CONNECTING ROD

Install piston on connecting rod for corresponding cylinder. Ensure reference marking on top of piston corresponds with connecting rod and cap number. See Fig. 14.

Lubricate piston pin and install in connecting rod. Ensure piston pin retainers are fully seated (if equipped). On pressed type piston pins, follow manufacturer's recommended procedure to avoid distortion or breakage.

CHECKING PISTON RING CLEARANCES

Piston rings must be checked for side clearance and end gap. To check end gap, install piston ring in cylinder which it is to be installed. Using an inverted piston, push ring to bottom of cylinder in smallest cylinder diameter.

Using feeler gauge, check ring end gap. See Fig. 15. Piston ring end gap must be within specification. Ring breakage will occur with insufficient ring end gap.

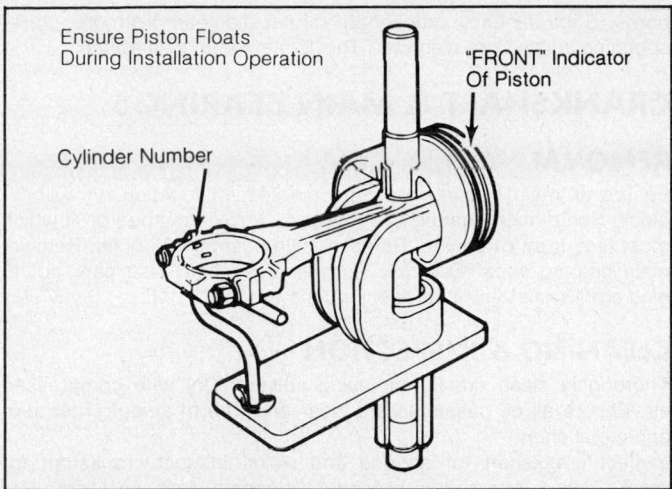

Fig. 14: Typical Piston Pin Installation

Some manufacturers permit correcting insufficient ring end gap by using a fine file while other manufacturers recommend using another ring set. Mark rings for proper cylinder installation after checking end gap.

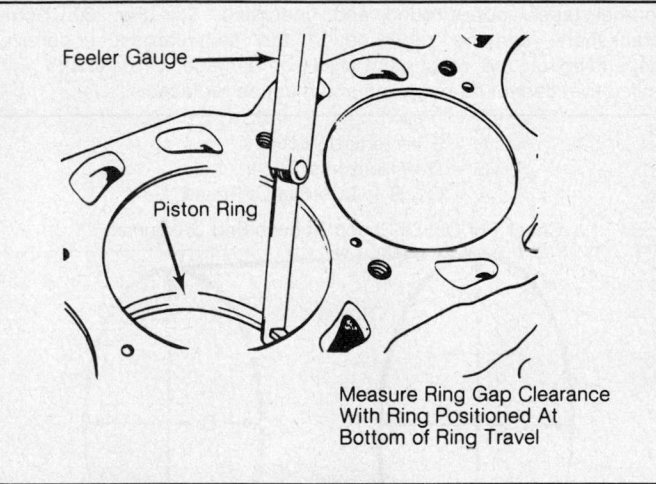

Fig. 15: Checking Piston Ring End Gap

For checking side clearance, install rings on piston. Using feeler gauge, measure clearance between piston ring and piston ring land. Check side clearance in several areas around piston. Side clearance must be within specification.

If side clearance is excessive, piston ring grooves can be machined to accept oversized piston rings (if available). Normal practice is to replace piston.

PISTON & CONNECTING ROD INSTALLATION

Cylinders must be honed prior to piston installation. See CYLINDER HONING under CYLINDER BLOCK in this article.

Install upper connecting rod bearings. Lubricate upper bearings with engine oil. Install lower bearings in rod caps. Ensure bearing tabs are properly seated. Position piston ring gaps according to manufacturer's recommendations. See Fig. 16. Lubricate pistons, rings and cylinder walls.

Install ring compressor. Use care not to rotate piston rings. Compress rings with ring compressor. Install plastic tubing protectors over connecting rod bolts. Install piston and connecting rod assembly. Ensure piston notch, arrow or "FRONT" mark is toward front of engine. See Fig. 17.

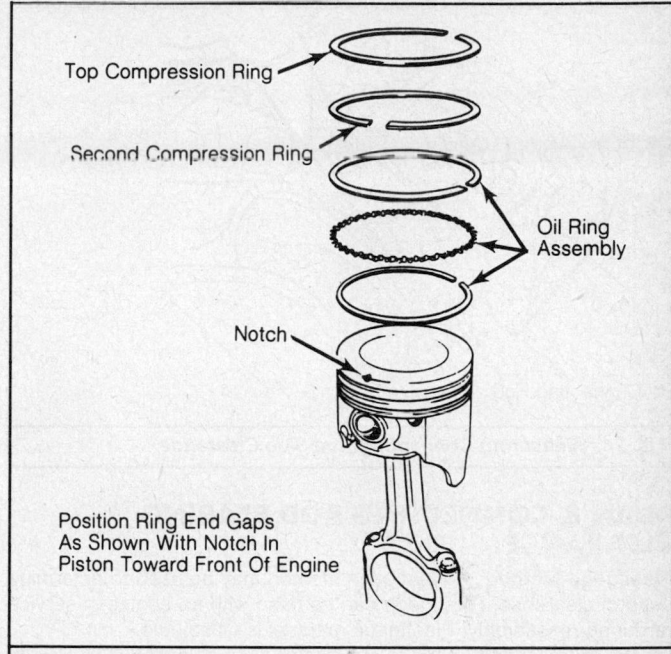

Fig. 16: Typical Piston Ring End Gap Positioning

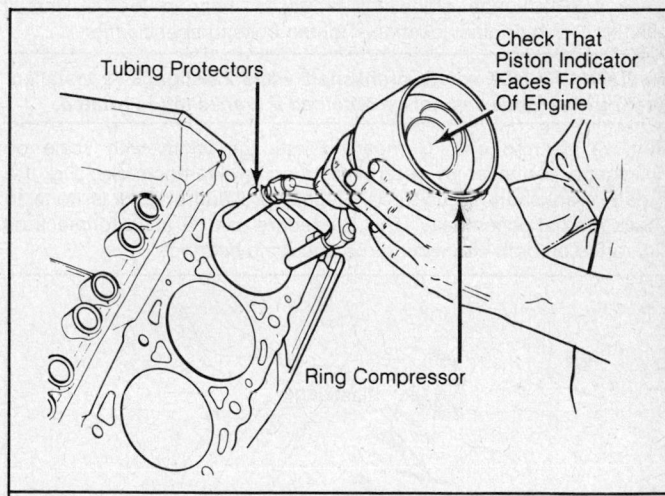

Fig. 17: Installing Piston & Connecting Rod Assembly

Carefully tap piston into cylinder until rod bearing is seated on crankshaft journal. Remove protectors. Install rod cap and bearing. Lightly tighten connecting rod bolts. Repeat procedure for remaining cylinders. Check bearing clearance. See MAIN & CONNECTING ROD BEARING CLEARANCE in this article.

Once clearance is checked, lubricate journals and bearings. Install bearing caps. Ensure marks are aligned on connecting rod and cap. Tighten rod nuts or bolts to specification. Ensure rod moves freely on crankshaft. Check connecting rod side clearance. See CONNECTING ROD SIDE CLEARANCE in this article.

CONNECTING ROD SIDE CLEARANCE

Position connecting rod toward one side of crankshaft as far as possible. Using feeler gauge, measure clearance between side of connecting rod and crankshaft. See Fig. 18. Clearance must be within specifications.

Check for improper bearing installation, wrong bearing cap or insufficient bearing clearance if side clearance is insufficient. Connecting rod may require machining to obtain proper clearance. Excessive clearance usually indicates excessive wear at crankshaft. Crankshaft must be repaired or replaced.

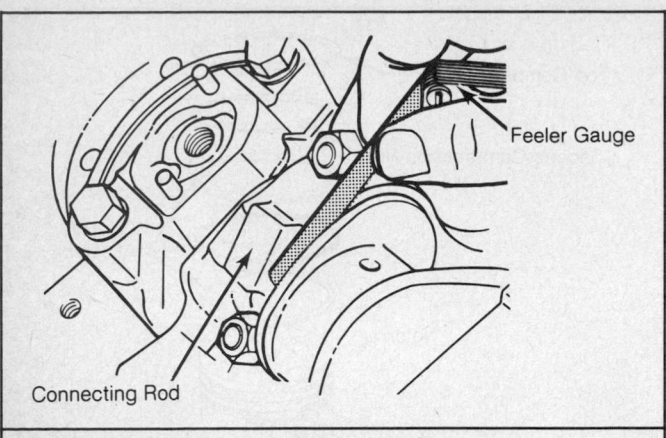

Fig. 18: Measuring Connecting Rod Side Clearance

MAIN & CONNECTING ROD BEARING CLEARANCE

Plastigage Method – Plastigage method may be used to determine bearing clearance. Plastigage can be used with an engine in service or during reassembly. Plastigage material is oil soluble.

Ensure journals and bearings are free of oil or solvent. Oil or solvent will dissolve material and false reading will be obtained. Install small piece of Plastigage along full length of bearing journal. Install bearing cap in original location. Tighten bolts to specification.

CAUTION: DO NOT rotate crankshaft while Plastigage is installed. Bearing clearance will not be obtained if crankshaft is rotated.

Remove bearing cap. Compare Plastigage width with scale on Plastigage container to determine bearing clearance. *See Fig. 19.* Rotate crankshaft 90 degrees. Repeat procedure. This is done to check journal eccentricity. This procedure can be used to check oil clearance on both connecting rod and main bearings.

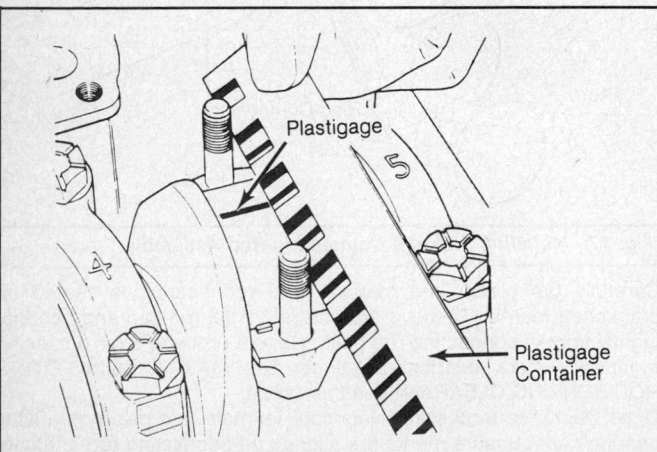

Fig. 19: Measuring Bearing Clearance

Micrometer & Telescopic Gauge Method – A micrometer is used to determine journal diameter, taper and out-of-round dimensions of the crankshaft. See CLEANING & INSPECTION under CRANKSHAFT & MAIN BEARINGS in this article.

With crankshaft removed, install bearings and caps in original location on cylinder block. Tighten bolts to specification. On connecting rods, install bearings and caps on connecting rods. Install proper connecting rod cap on corresponding rod. Ensure bearing cap is installed in original location. Tighten bolts to specification.

Using a telescopic gauge and micrometer or inside micrometer measure inside diameter of connecting rod and main bearings

bores. Subtract each crankshaft journal diameter from the corresponding inside bore diameter. This is the bearing clearance.

CRANKSHAFT & MAIN BEARINGS

REMOVAL

Ensure all main bearing caps are marked for location on cylinder block. Some main bearing caps have an arrow stamped on it which must face front of engine. Remove main bearing cap bolts. Remove main bearing caps. Carefully remove crankshaft. Use care not to bind crankshaft in cylinder block during removal.

CLEANING & INSPECTION

Thoroughly clean crankshaft using solvent. Dry with compressed air. Ensure all oil passages are clear and free of sludge, rust, dirt, and metal chips.

Inspect crankshaft for scoring and nicks. Inspect crankshaft for cracks using Magnaflux procedure. Inspect rear seal area for grooving or damage. Inspect bolt hole threads for damage. If pilot bearing or bushing is used, check pilot bearing or bushing fit in crankshaft. Inspect crankshaft gear for damaged or cracked teeth. Replace gear if damaged. Check that oil passage plugs are tight (if equipped).

Using micrometer, measure all journals in 4 areas to determine journal taper, out-of-round and undersize. *See Fig. 20.* Some crankshafts can be reground to the next largest undersize, depending on the amount of wear or damage. Crankshafts with rolled fillet cannot be reground and must be replaced.

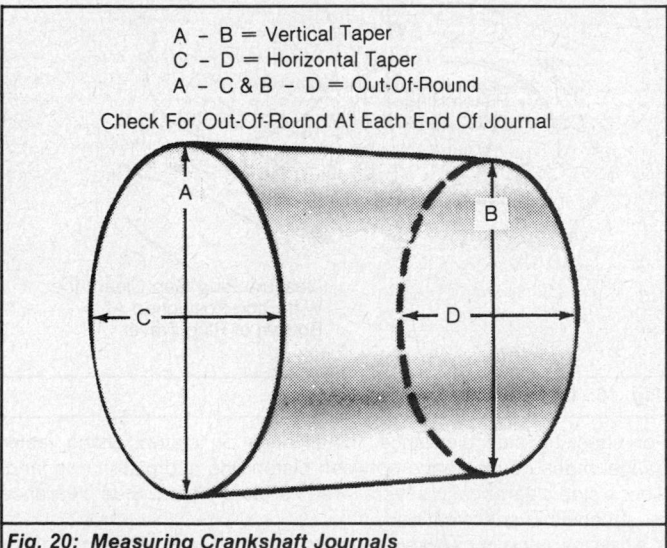

A – B = Vertical Taper
C – D = Horizontal Taper
A – C & B – D = Out-Of-Round

Check For Out-Of-Round At Each End Of Journal

Fig. 20: Measuring Crankshaft Journals

Crankshaft journal runout should be checked. Install crankshaft in "V" blocks or bench center. Position dial indicator with tip resting on the main bearing journal area. *See Fig. 21.* Rotate crankshaft and

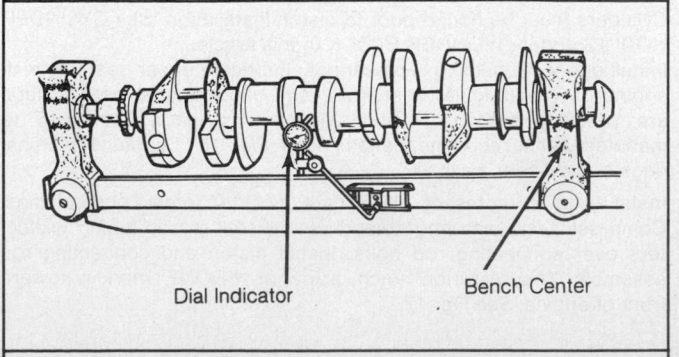

Fig. 21: Measuring Crankshaft Main Bearing Journal Runout

note reading. Journal runout must not exceed specification. Repeat procedure on all main bearing journals. Crankshaft must be replaced if runout exceeds specification.

INSTALLATION

Install upper main bearing in cylinder block. Ensure lock tab is properly located in cylinder block. Install bearings in main bearing caps. Ensure all oil passages are aligned. Install rear seal (if removed).

Ensure crankshaft journals are clean. Lubricate upper main bearings with clean engine oil. Carefully install crankshaft. Check each main bearing clearance using Plastigage method. See MAIN & CONNECTING ROD BEARING CLEARANCE in this article.

Once clearance is checked, lubricate lower main bearing and journals. Install main bearing caps in original location. Install rear seal in rear main bearing cap (if removed). Some rear main bearing caps require sealant to be applied in corners to prevent oil leakage.

Install and tighten all bolts except thrust bearing cap to specification. Tighten thrust bearing cap bolts finger tight only. Thrust bearing must be aligned. On most applications, crankshaft must be moved rearward then forward. Procedure may vary with manufacturer. Thrust bearing cap is then tightened to specification. Ensure crankshaft rotates freely. Crankshaft end play should be checked. See CRANKSHAFT END PLAY in this article.

CRANKSHAFT END PLAY

Dial Indicator Method – Crankshaft end play can be checked using dial indicator. Mount dial indicator on rear of cylinder block. Position dial indicator tip against rear of crankshaft. Ensure tip is resting against flat surface.

Pry crankshaft rearward. Adjust dial indicator to zero. Pry crankshaft forward and note reading. Crankshaft end play must be within specification. If end play is not within specification, check for faulty thrust bearing installation or worn crankshaft. Some applications offer oversized thrust bearings.

Feeler Gauge Method – Crankshaft end play can be checked using feeler gauge. Pry crankshaft rearward. Pry crankshaft forward. Using feeler gauge, measure clearance between crankshaft and thrust bearing surface. *See Fig. 22.*

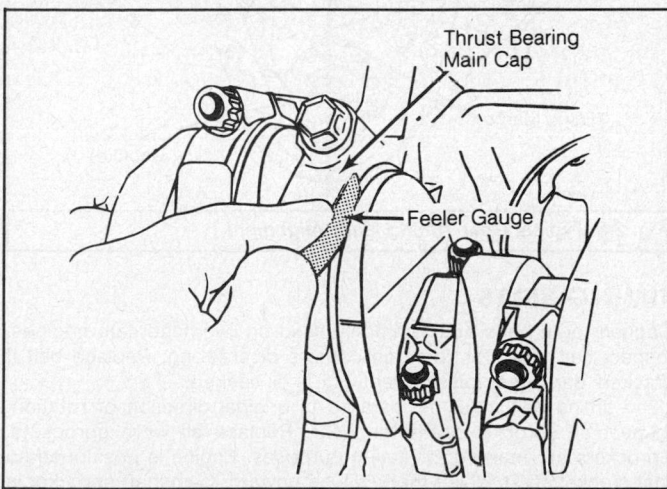

Fig. 22: Checking Crankshaft End Play

Crankshaft end play must be within specification. If end play is not within specification, check for faulty thrust bearing installation or worn crankshaft. Some applications offer oversized thrust bearings.

CYLINDER BLOCK

Block Cleaning – Only cast cylinder blocks should be hot tank cleaned. Aluminum cylinder blocks should be cleaned using cold tank method. Cylinder block is cleaned in order to remove carbon deposits, gasket residue and water jacket scale. Remove oil gallery plugs, freeze plugs and cam bearings prior to block cleaning.

Block Inspection – Visually inspect the block. Check suspected areas for cracks using the Dye Penetrant inspection method. Block may be checked for cracks using the magnaflux method.

Cracks are most commonly found at the bottom of cylinders, main bearing saddles, near expansion plugs and between cylinders and water jackets. Inspect lifter bores for damage. Inspect all head bolt holes for damaged threads. Threads should be cleaned using tap to ensure proper head bolt torque. Consult machine shop concerning possible welding and machining (if required).

Cylinder Bore Inspection – Inspect bore for scoring or roughness. Cylinder bore is dimensionally checked for out-of-round and taper using dial bore gauge. For determining out-of-round, measure cylinder parallel and perpendicular to the block centerline. Difference in the 2 readings is the bore out-of-round. Cylinder bore must be checked at top, middle and bottom of piston travel area.

Bore taper is obtained by measuring bore at the top and bottom. If wear has exceeded allowable limits, block must be honed or bored to next available oversize piston dimension.

Cylinder Honing – Cylinder must be properly honed to allow new piston rings to properly seat. Cross-hatching at correct angle and depth is critical to lubrication of cylinder walls and pistons.

A flexible drive hone and power drill are commonly used. Drive hone must be lubricated during operation. Mix equal parts of kerosene and SAE 20W engine oil for lubrication.

Apply lubrication to cylinder wall. Operate cylinder hone from top to bottom of cylinder using even strokes to produce 45 degree cross-hatch pattern on the cylinder wall. DO NOT allow cylinder hone to extend below cylinder during operation.

Recheck bore dimension after final honing. Wash cylinder wall with hot soapy water to remove abrasive particles. Blow dry with compressed air. Coat cleaned cylinder walls with lubricating oil.

Deck Warpage – Check deck for damage or warped gasket surface. Place a straightedge across gasket surface of the deck. Using feeler gauge, measure clearance at center of straightedge. Measure across width and length of cylinder block at several points. If warpage exceeds specifications, deck must be resurfaced. If warpage exceeds manufacturer's maximum tolerance for material removal, replace block.

Deck Height – Distance from crankshaft centerline to block deck is called the deck height. Measure and record front and rear main journals of crankshaft. To compute this distance, install crankshaft and retain with center main bearing and cap only. Measure distance from crankshaft journal to block deck, parallel to cylinder centerline. Add one half of main bearing journal diameter to distance from crankshaft journal to block deck. This dimension should be checked at front and rear of cylinder block. Both readings should be the same.

If difference exceeds specifications, cylinder block must be repaired or replaced. Deck height and warpage should be corrected at the same time.

Main Bearing Bore & Alignment – For checking main bearing bore, remove all bearings from cylinder block and main bearing caps. Install main bearing caps in original location. Tighten bolts to specification. Using inside micrometer, measure main bearing bore in 2 areas 90 degrees apart. Determine bore size and out-of-round. If diameter is not within specification, block must be align-bored.

For checking alignment, place a straightedge along centerline of main bearing saddles. Check for clearance between straightedge and main bearing saddles. Block must be align-bored if clearance is present.

Expansion Plug Removal – Drill hole in center of expansion plug. Remove with screwdriver or punch. Use care not to damage sealing surface.

Expansion Plug Installation – Ensure sealing surface is free of burrs. Coat expansion plug with sealer. Using wooden dowel or pipe of slightly smaller diameter, install expansion plug. Ensure expansion plug is evenly located.

Oil Gallery Plug Removal – Remove threaded oil gallery plugs using appropriate wrench. Soft, press-in plugs are removed by drilling into plug and installing a sheet metal screw. Remove plug with slide hammer or pliers.

Oil Gallery Plug Installation – Ensure threads or sealing surface is clean. Coat threaded oil gallery plugs with sealer and install. Replacement soft press-in plugs are driven in place with a hammer and drift.

CAMSHAFT

CLEANING & INSPECTION

Clean camshaft with solvent. Ensure all oil passages are clear. Inspect cam lobes and bearing journals for pitting, flaking or scoring. Using micrometer, measure bearing journal O.D.

Support camshaft at each end with "V" blocks. Position dial indicator with tip resting on center bearing journal. Rotate camshaft and note reading. If reading exceeds specification, replace camshaft.

Check cam lobe lift by measuring base circle of camshaft using micrometer. Measure again at 90 degrees to tip of cam lobe. Cam lift can be determined by subtracting base circle diameter from tip of cam lobe measurement.

Different lift dimensions are given for intake and exhaust cam lobes. Reading must be within specifications. Replace camshaft if cam lobes or bearing journals are not within specifications.

Inspect camshaft gear for chipped, eroded or damaged teeth. Replace gear if damaged. On camshafts using thrust plate, measure distance between thrust plate and camshaft shoulder. Replace thrust plate if not within specification.

CAMSHAFT BEARINGS

Removal & Installation – Remove camshaft rear plug. Camshaft bearing remover is assembled with shoulder resting against bearing to be removed according to manufacturer's instructions. Tighten puller nut until bearing is removed. Remove remaining bearings, leaving front and rear bearings until last. These bearings act as guide for camshaft bearing remover.

To install new bearings, puller is rearranged to pull bearings toward the center of block. Ensure all lubrication passages of bearing are aligned with cylinder block. Coat new camshaft rear plug with sealant. Install camshaft rear plug. Ensure plug is even in cylinder block.

CAMSHAFT INSTALLATION

Lubricate bearing surfaces and cam lobes with ample amount of Molykote or camshaft lubricant. Carefully install camshaft. Use care not to damage bearing journals during installation. Install thrust plate retaining bolts (if equipped). Tighten bolts to specification. On overhead camshafts, install bearing caps in original location. Tighten bolts to specification. Check end play.

CAMSHAFT END PLAY

Using dial indicator, check end play. Position dial indicator on front of engine block. Position indicator tip against camshaft. Push camshaft toward rear of engine and adjust indicator to zero.

Move camshaft forward and note reading. Camshaft end play must be within specification. End play may be adjusted by relocating gear, shimming thrust plate or replacing thrust plate depending on manufacturer.

TIMING CHAINS & BELTS

TIMING CHAINS

Timing chains will stretch during operation. Limits are placed upon amount of stretch before replacement is required. Timing chain stretch will alter ignition timing and valve timing.

To check timing chain stretch, rotate crankshaft to eliminate slack from one side of timing chain. Mark reference point on cylinder block. Rotate crankshaft in opposite direction to eliminate slack from remaining side of timing chain. Force other side of chain outward and measure distance between reference point and timing chain. See Fig. 23. Replace timing chain and gears if not within specification.

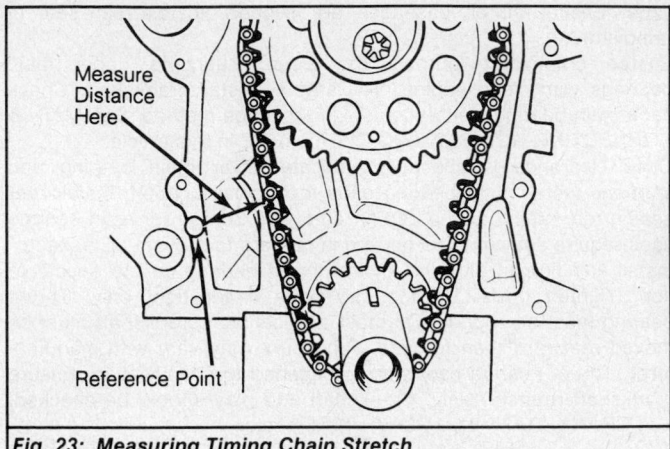

Fig. 23: Measuring Timing Chain Stretch

Timing chains must be installed so that timing marks on camshaft gear and crankshaft gear are aligned according to manufacturer. See Fig. 24.

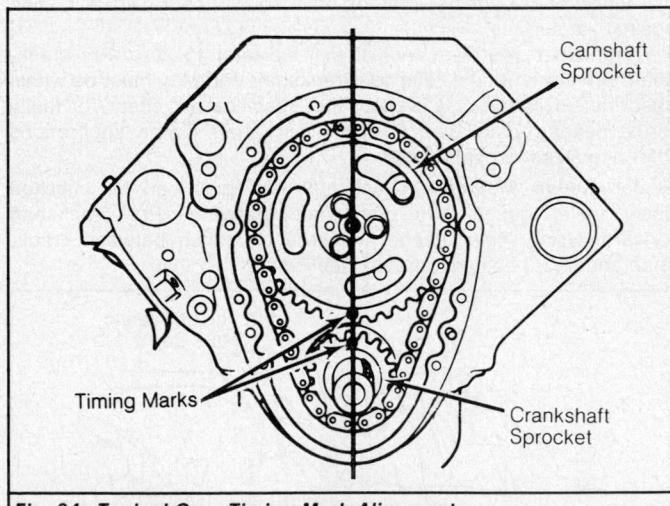

Fig. 24: Typical Gear Timing Mark Alignment

TIMING BELTS

Cogged tooth belts are commonly used on overhead cam engines. Inspect belt teeth for rounded corners or cracking. Replace belt if cracked, damaged, missing teeth, or is oil soaked.

Used timing belt must be installed in original direction of rotation. Inspect all sprocket teeth for wear. Replace all worn sprockets. Sprockets are marked for timing purposes. Engine is positioned so that crankshaft sprocket mark will be upward. Camshaft sprocket is aligned with reference mark on cylinder head and timing belt is installed. See Fig. 25.

TENSION ADJUSTMENT

If guide rails are used with spring loaded tensioners, ensure at least half of original rail thickness remains. Spring loaded tensioner should be inspected for damage.

Ensure all timing marks are aligned. Adjust belt tension using manufacturer's recommendations. Belt tension may require checking using tension gauge. See Fig. 26.

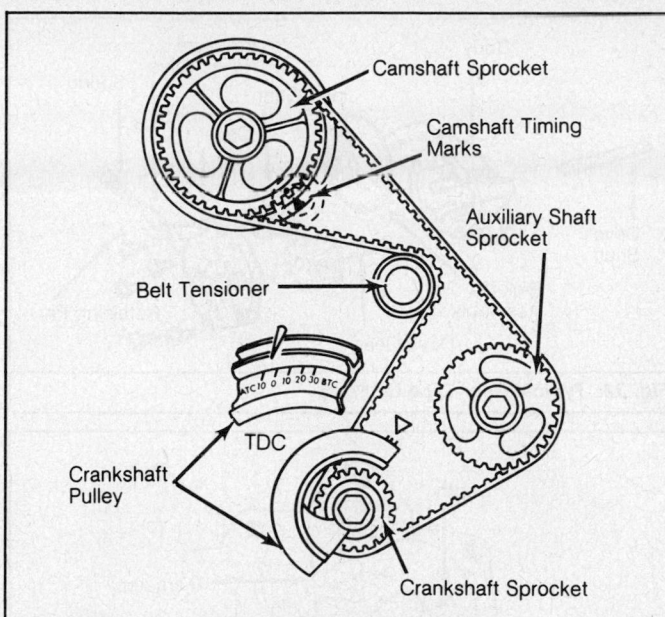

Fig. 25: *Typical Camshaft Belt Sprocket Alignment*

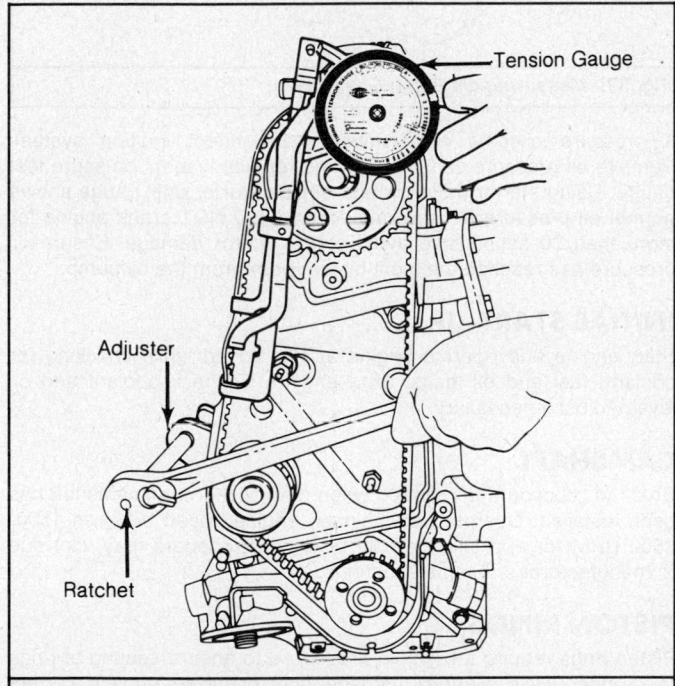

Fig. 26: *Typical Timing Belt Tension Adjustment*

TIMING GEARS

TIMING GEAR BACKLASH & RUNOUT

On engines where camshaft gear operates directly on crankshaft gear, gear backlash and runout must be checked. To check backlash, install dial indicator with tip resting on tooth of camshaft gear. Rotate camshaft gear as far as possible. Adjust indicator to zero. Rotate camshaft gear in opposite direction as far as possible and note reading.

To determine timing gear runout, mount dial indicator with tip resting on face edge of camshaft gear. Adjust indicator to zero. Rotate camshaft gear 360 degrees and note reading. If backlash or runout exceed specifications, replace camshaft and/or crankshaft gear.

REAR MAIN OIL SEAL INSTALLATION

One-Piece Type Seal – For one-piece type oil seal installation, coat block contact surface of seal with sealer if seal is not factory coated. Ensure seal surface is free of burrs. Lubricate seal lip with engine oil and press seal into place using proper oil seal installer. *See Fig. 27.*

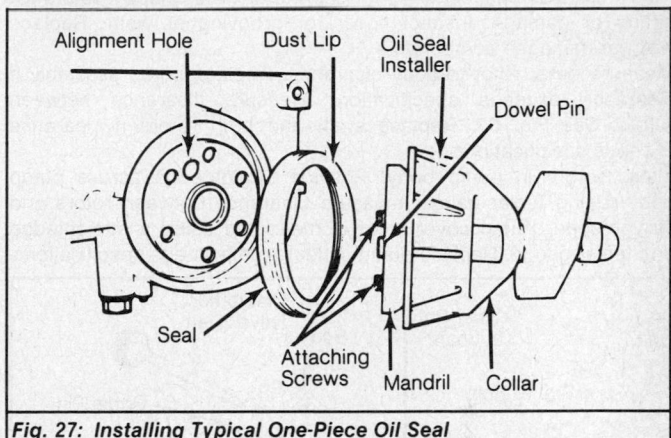

Fig. 27: *Installing Typical One-Piece Oil Seal*

Rope Type Seal – For rope type rear main oil seal installation, press seal lightly into seat area. Using seal installer, fully seat seal in bearing cap or cylinder block.

Trim seal ends even with block parting surface. Some applications require sealer to be applied on main bearing cap prior to installation. *See Fig. 28.*

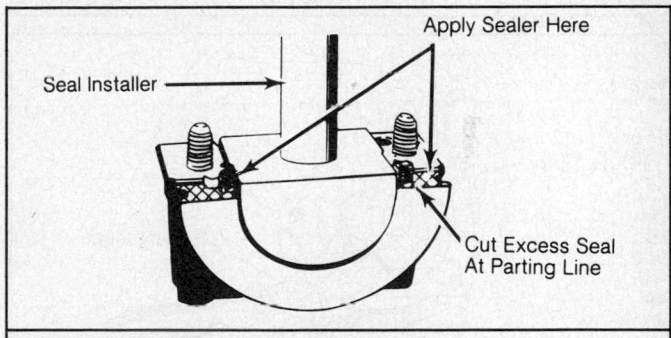

Fig. 28: *Typical Rope Seal Installation*

Split-Rubber Type Seal – Follow manufacturer's procedures when installing split-rubber type rear main oil seals. Installation procedures vary with engine type. See appropriate ENGINE article in this section. *See Fig. 29.*

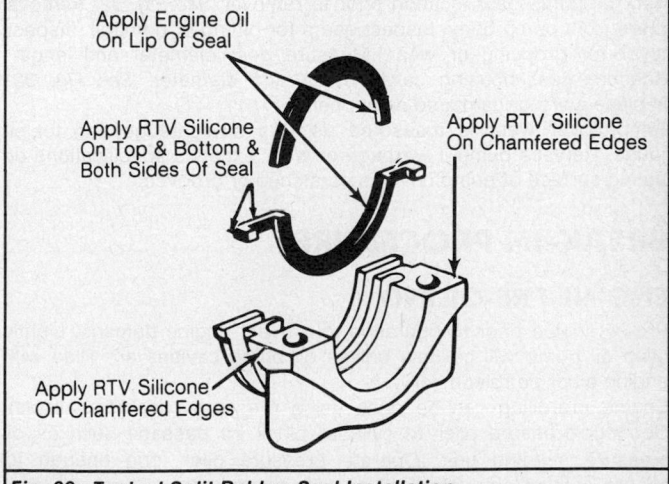

Fig. 29: *Typical Split-Rubber Seal Installation*

1989 ENGINE OVERHAUL PROCEDURES
All Engines (Cont.)

OIL PUMP

ROTOR TYPE

Mark oil pump rotor locations prior to removal. *See Fig. 30.* Remove outer rotor and measure thickness and diameter. Measure inner rotor thickness. Inspect shaft for scoring or wear. Inspect rotors for pitting or damage. Inspect cover for grooving or wear. Replace worn or damaged components.

Measure outer rotor-to-body clearance. Replace pump assembly if clearance exceeds specification. Measure clearance between rotors. *See Fig. 31.* Replace shaft and both rotors if clearance exceeds specifications.

Install rotors in pump body. Position straightedge across pump body. Using feeler gauge, measure clearance between rotors and straightedge. Pump cover wear is measured using a straightedge and feeler gauge. Replace pump if clearance exceeds specification.

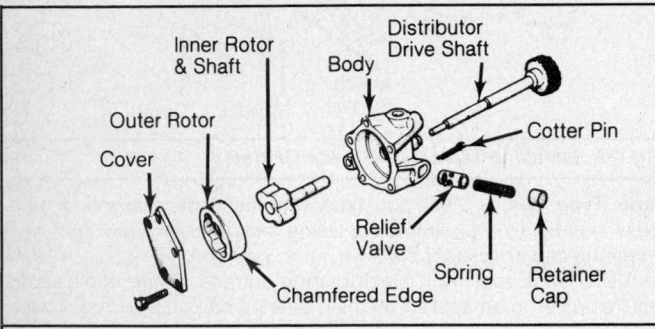

Fig. 30: Typical Rotor Type Oil Pump

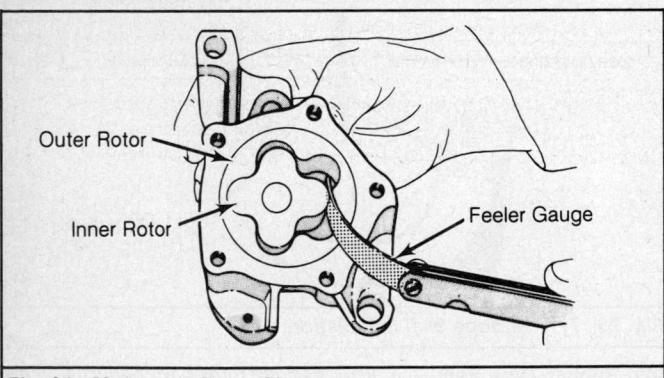

Fig. 31: Measuring Rotor Clearance

GEAR TYPE

Mark oil pump gear location prior to removal. *See Fig. 32.* Remove gears from pump body. Inspect gears for pitting or damage. Inspect cover for grooving or wear. Measure gear diameter and length. Measure gear housing cavity depth and diameter. *See Fig. 33.* Replace worn or damaged components.

Pump cover wear is measured using a straightedge and feeler gauge. Replace pump if warpage or wear exceeds specifications or mating surface of pump cover is scratched or grooved.

BREAK-IN PROCEDURE

ENGINE PRE-OILING

Pre-oil engine prior to operation to prevent engine damage. Lightly oiled oil pump will cavitate unless oil pump cavities are filled with engine oil or petroleum jelly.

Engine pre-oiling can be done using pressure oiler (if available). Connect pressure oiler to cylinder block oil passage such as oil pressure sending unit. Operate pressure oiler long enough to ensure correct amount of oil has filled crankcase. Check oil level while pre-oiling.

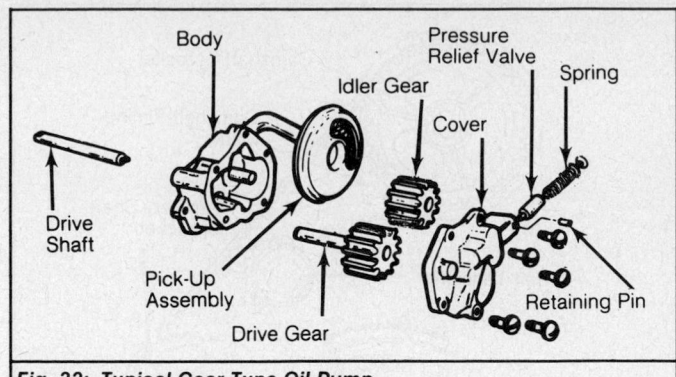

Fig. 32: Typical Gear Type Oil Pump

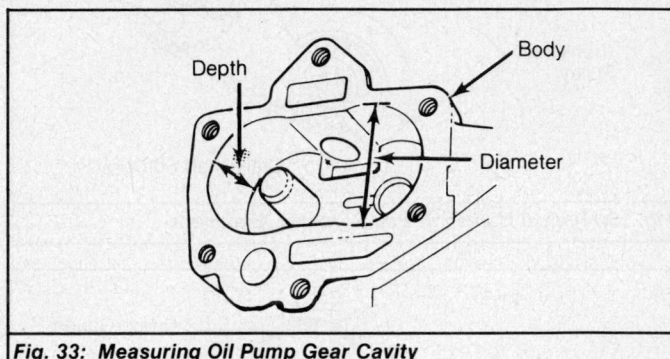

Fig. 33: Measuring Oil Pump Gear Cavity

If pressure oiler is not available, disconnect ignition system. Remove oil pressure sending unit and replace with oil pressure test gauge. Using starter motor, rotate engine starter until gauge shows normal oil pressure for several seconds. DO NOT crank engine for more than 30 seconds to avoid starter motor damage. Ensure oil pressure has reached the most distant point from the oil pump.

INITIAL START-UP

Start engine and operate engine at low speed while checking for coolant, fuel and oil leaks. Stop engine. Recheck coolant and oil level. Adjust if necessary.

CAMSHAFT

Break-in procedure is required when new or reground camshaft has been installed. Operate and maintain engine speed between 1500-2500 RPM for approximately 30 minutes. Procedure may vary due to manufacturer's recommendations.

PISTON RINGS

Piston rings require a break-in procedure to ensure seating of rings to cylinder walls. Serious damage may occur to rings if correct procedures are not followed.

Extremely high piston ring temperatures are obtained during break-in process. If rings are exposed to excessively high RPM or high cylinder pressures, ring damage can occur. Follow piston ring manufacturer's recommended break-in procedure.

FINAL ADJUSTMENTS

Check or adjust ignition timing and dwell (if applicable). Adjust valves (if necessary). Adjust idle speed and mixture. Retighten cylinder heads (if required). If cylinder head or block is aluminum, retighten bolts when engine is cold. Follow the engine manufacturer's recommended break-in procedure and maintenance schedule for new engines.

NOTE: Some manufacturer's require that head bolts be retightened after specified amount of operation. This must be done to prevent head gasket failure.

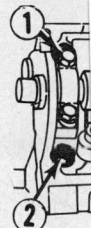

Fig. 5: Cylinder He...

CAUTION: Use prop...
Diameter of head...
indentified by the "...
bolt WILL thread in...
cylinder block bolt h...

NOTE: The 2.2L Turb...
gasket which it NOT...
I engines in prior ye...

Installation – 1) Ins...
block. Install bolts a...
bolts to specificatio...
Tighten bolts in prop...
2) When tightening...
turn, torque should...
torque does not exce...

TIMING BELT

Removal – 1) Disco...
belts. Remove alter...
compressor from mo...
nect refrigerant lines...
2) Raise and suppo...
Remove water pump...
lower timing belt cov...
engine.
3) Remove right engin...
timing belt tensioner...

Installation – 1) Rem...
Align timing marks or...
See Fig. 6. Rotate...
sprocket align with...
sprocket small hole m...
line. See Fig. 6.

2) Install timing be...
horizontally on large...
lock nut (if necessary...
axis of horizontal posi...
3) Rotate crankshaft...
Tighten tensioner reta...

NOTE: For engine repair procedures not covered in this article, see ENGINE OVERHAUL PROCEDURES article at beginning of this section.

ENGINE IDENTIFICATION

Engine may be identified using Vehicle Identification Number (VIN) stamped on metal tab located near lower left corner of windshield. The 8th character identifies the engine model.

Engine serial number must be used when ordering replacement components. On 2.2L engines, serial number is stamped on rear of cylinder block, directly below cylinder head. On 2.5L engines, serial number is located on right front of cylinder block, next to exhaust manifold stud.

ENGINE IDENTIFICATION CODES

Engine	Code
2.2L Turbo II	A
2.2L TBI	D
2.5L Turbo I	J
2.5L TBI	K

ADJUSTMENTS

VALVE ARRANGEMENT

E-I-E-I-E-I-E-I (Front-to-rear).

HYDRAULIC VALVE LASH ADJUSTERS

1) No adjustment of lash adjusters is required. If disassembled for cleaning purposes, reassemble using new retainer caps.
2) Adjusters must be at least partially full of oil prior to installation. Little or no plunger travel should exist when adjuster is depressed.

NOTE: Always service hydraulic valve lash adjusters as complete assemblies. Internal components of valve lash adjusters are not interchangeable.

DRY LASH

1) Dry lash is amount of clearance between installed camshaft base circle and rocker arm pad. Valve lash adjuster must be completely collapsed and free of oil when checking clearance.
2) Remove retainer cap from valve lash adjuster. Disassemble and drain oil. Install adjuster when completely collapsed. Using feeler gauge, measure clearance between camshaft base circle and rocker arm pad.
3) Clearance should be .024-.060" (.62-1.52 mm). If not within specifications, check for wear on related parts and replace as required. Fill adjusters with engine oil. Reassemble using new retainer cap. Allow 10 minutes for adjusters to bleed down before rotating camshaft.

REMOVAL & INSTALLATION

NOTE: For reassembly reference, label all electrical connectors, vacuum hoses and fuel lines before removal. Also place mating marks on engine hood and other major assemblies before removal.

ENGINE

NOTE: See ENGINE REMOVAL & INSTALLATION article at end of ENGINE section.

INTAKE & EXHAUST MANIFOLDS

NOTE: Exhaust and intake manifolds use a one-piece mounting gasket. Both manifolds must be removed to perform service to either manifold.

Removal (Non-Turbo) – 1) Disconnect battery. Drain cooling system. Disconnect water crossover. Disconnect air cleaner hoses and remove air cleaner.
2) Disconnect throttle cable and kickdown cable (if equipped). Disconnect and mark electrical connections from throttle body.

CAUTION: Fuel system is under pressure. Pressure must be released prior to disconnecting any fuel system component.

3) To release fuel pressure, loosen gas cap at tank. Remove wiring harness connector from injector. Ground one injector terminal. Connect a 12-volt jumper wire to remaining injector terminal. DO NOT apply voltage for longer than 10 seconds.
4) Disconnect and mark vacuum hoses to throttle body. Disconnect fuel lines from throttle body. Disconnect exhaust pipe from exhaust manifold. Remove intake and exhaust manifold bolts. Remove manifolds.

Removal (Turbo) – 1) Disconnect battery. Drain cooling system. Disconnect intercooler hoses, air intake and outlet hoses from turbo. Disconnect air inlet hose at throttle body. Disconnect air intake hoses from air cleaner assembly. Remove air cleaner.
2) Disconnect throttle cable and kickdown cable (if equipped). Disconnect and mark electrical connections at throttle body. Disconnect PCV hose and brake booster vacuum hose.
3) Disconnect and mark vacuum hoses to throttle body. On Turbo II models, disconnect charge air temperature sensor located on intake manifold.

CAUTION: Fuel system is under pressure. Pressure must be released prior to disconnecting any fuel system component.

4) To release fuel pressure, loosen gas cap at tank. Remove wiring harness connector from injector. Ground one injector terminal. Connect a 12-volt jumper wire to remaining injector terminal. DO NOT apply voltage for longer than 10 seconds.
5) Remove throttle body-to-intake manifold nuts. Separate throttle body from intake manifold. Disconnect knock sensor and all fuel injector wiring connectors.
6) Remove fuel hose from fuel injector rail. Remove fuel return hose at fuel pressure regulator. See Fig. 1.

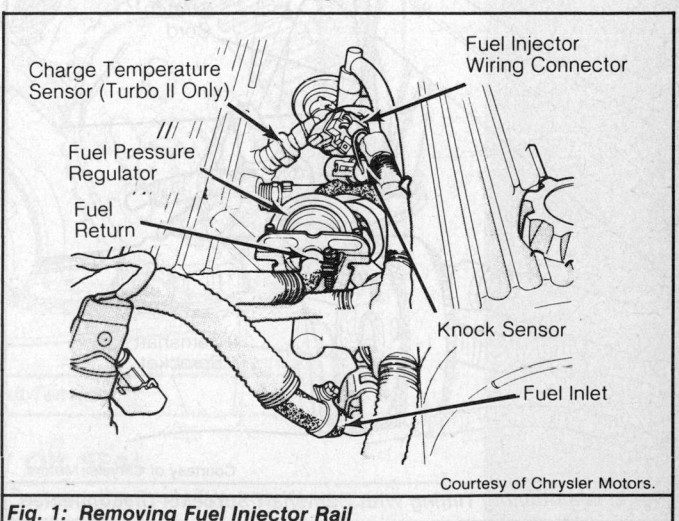

Fig. 1: Removing Fuel Injector Rail

Courtesy of Chrysler Motors.

7) Disconnect vacuum hose from fuel pressure regulator. Remove fuel pressure regulator-to-fuel injector rail nuts. Separate fuel pressure regulator from fuel rail.

1989 CHRYSLER MOTORS ENGINES
2.2L & 2.5L 4-Cylinder (Cont.)

8) Remove fuel inj
fuel injector rail r
injectors from intak
9) Remove front er
Disconnect exhaus
wheel. Remove righ
AXLES section.
10) Remove O₂ s
cylinder block brac
wastegate rod-to-g
11) Remove oil re
Disconnect coolant
and exhaust manifo

Installation – 1) M
(.15 mm) per 12" (30
be coated with Seal
NOT use sealant.
gasket.
2) On all models,
manifold. Tighten b
and working outwar
3) On turbo models
all line fittings with
"O" rings with clean
4) Ensure fuel ra
tightening. Reverse
nents. Tighten bolts
5) Fill cooling syste
Allow air to bleed
reaches thermostat

CYLINDER HE

NOTE: When remov
separation of cam
maintain camshaft,
service procedures
sprocket while ass
tension. See Fig. 2.

Fig. 2: Maintaining

Removal – 1) Re
timing belt. Remove
remove A/C compr
side.

FRONT CRANKSHAFT SPROCKET OIL SEAL

Removal – Remove front covers and timing belt. Remove crankshaft sprocket retaining bolt. Using Crankshaft Sprocket Puller/Installer (C-4685) with puller insert, remove crankshaft sprocket. *See Fig. 8*. Using Crankshaft Sprocket Seal Remover (C-6341), remove front crankshaft sprocket oil seal. *See Fig. 9*.

Installation – Using Crankshaft Seal Installer (C-6342), install new seal in far enough so it is even with seal retainer surface. *See Fig. 10*. Install crankshaft sprocket using Crankshaft Sprocket Puller/Installer (C-4685) and Thrust Bearing. *See Fig. 8*. Install timing belt and ensure proper alignment on all belt sprockets.

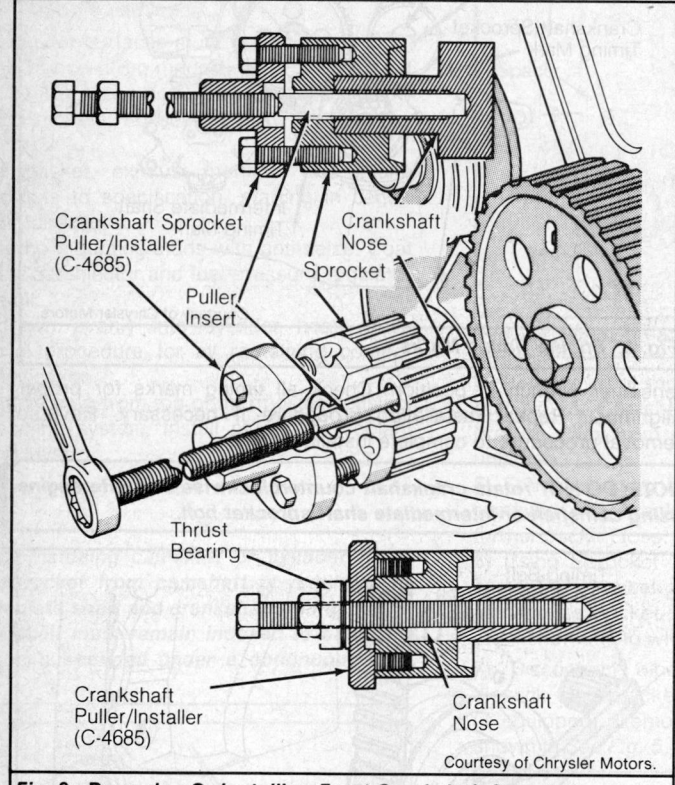

Courtesy of Chrysler Motors.

Fig. 8: Removing Or Installing Front Crankshaft Sprocket

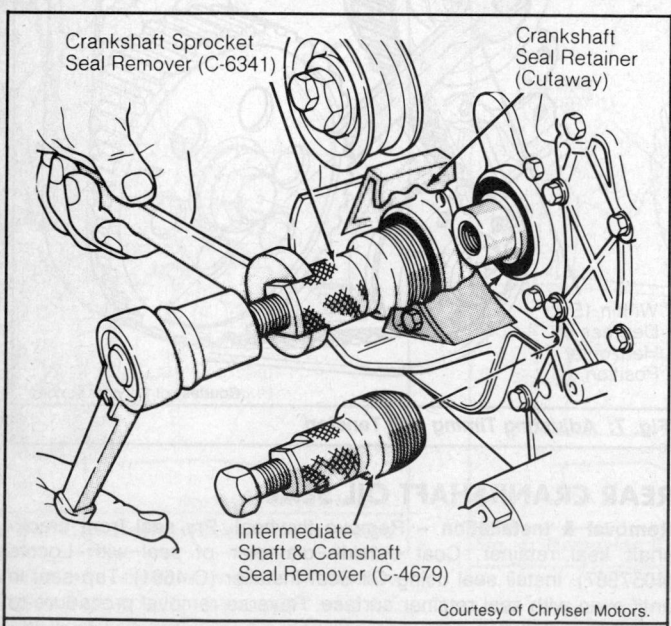

Courtesy of Chrysler Motors.

Fig. 9: Front Crankshaft Sprocket Oil Seal Remover

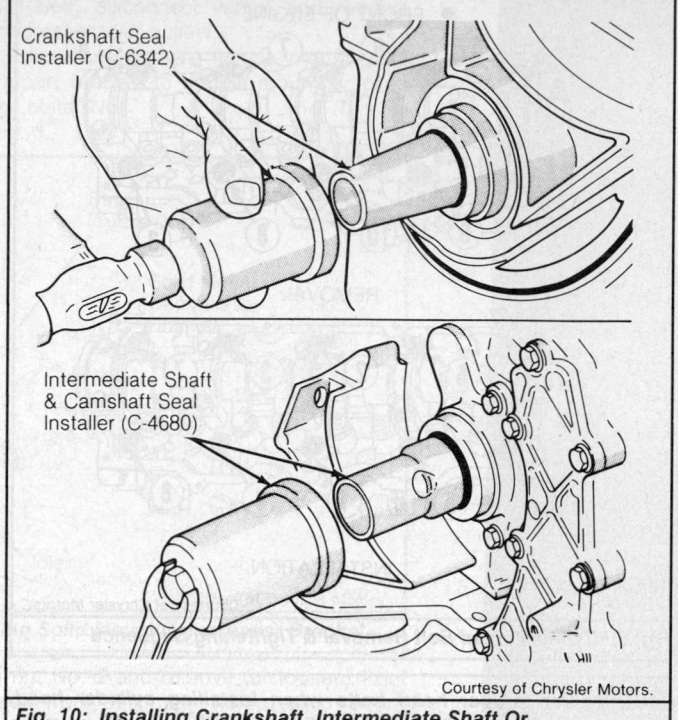

Courtesy of Chrysler Motors.

Fig. 10: Installing Crankshaft, Intermediate Shaft Or Camshaft Seals

BALANCE SHAFTS (2.5L ONLY)

Removal & Installation (Gears & Shafts) – 1) Remove oil pan, oil pick-up, timing belt covers, timing belt, crankshaft belt sprocket and front crankshaft oil seal retainer. Remove balance shaft chain cover, chain guide and chain tensioner.

2) Remove balance shaft chain sprocket retaining bolts and crankshaft chain sprocket torx bolts. Remove chain and sprocket assembly. Remove front gear cover retaining stud. Remove cover and balance shaft gears. Remove carrier rear cover and remove balance shafts from carrier.

3) To install balance shafts and gears, reverse removal procedure using ALIGNING BALANCE SHAFTS procedure in this article to ensure correct timing of balance shafts and crankshaft.

Removal & Installation (Carrier Assembly & Shafts) – 1) The following components will remain intact during carrier removal. Gear cover, gears, balance shafts and rear cover.

2) Remove chain cover. Remove lower chain sprocket bolt. Loosen tensioner pivot and adjusting bolts. Move chain driven balance shaft inboard by using driven chain sprocket. Sprocket should remain hanging in lower chain loop. Remove carrier-to-crankcase attaching bolts and remove carrier assembly.

3) To install balance shafts and carrier assembly, reverse removal procedure using ALIGNING BALANCE SHAFTS procedure to ensure correct timing of balance shafts, chain and crankshaft.

Aligning Balance Shafts – 1) With balance shafts installed in carrier, position carrier (if removed) on crankcase and install 6 balance carrier bolts. Tighten bolts to specifications.

2) Turn both balance shafts until shaft keyways are facing upward (parallel to vertical centerline of engine). Install short hub drive gear on (sprocket) driven shaft, and long hub gear on (gear) driven shaft. After installation, ensure that balance shaft keyways remain facing upward when timing gear alignment marks are together. *See Fig. 11*.

3) Install gear cover and tighten double ended stud to 105 INCH lbs. (12 N.m). Install crankshaft chain (upper) sprocket with timing mark on sprocket aligned with upper nickel plated link of chain. Tighten socket head torx bolts to specification.

1989 CHRYSLER MOTORS ENGINES
2.2L & 2.5L 4-Cylinder (Cont.)

7-21

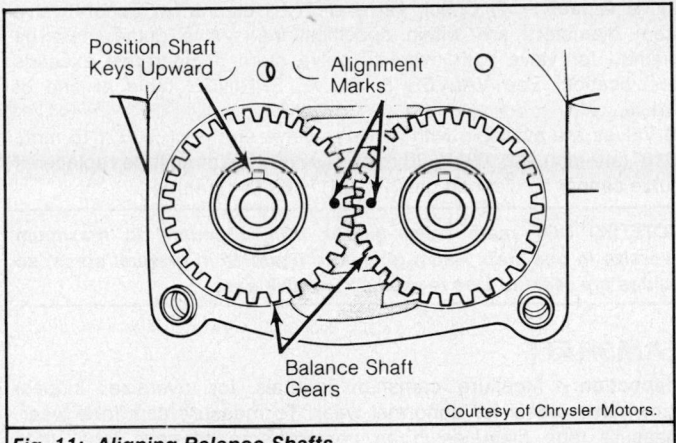

Fig. 11: Aligning Balance Shafts

4) Rotate crankshaft until number one cylinder is at Top Dead Center (TDC). Timing marks on crankshaft chain sprocket, along with upper nickel plated link, should align with parting line on left side of number one main bearing cap. *See Fig. 12.*

5) Place balance shaft chain (lower) sprocket into timing chain so that timing mark (Yellow dot) of sprocket aligns with lower nickel plated link on chain. *See Fig. 12.*

NOTE: Upper and lower nickel plated chain links are exactly 8 links apart from each other. Each link should align with timing marks of upper and lower chain sprockets respectively.

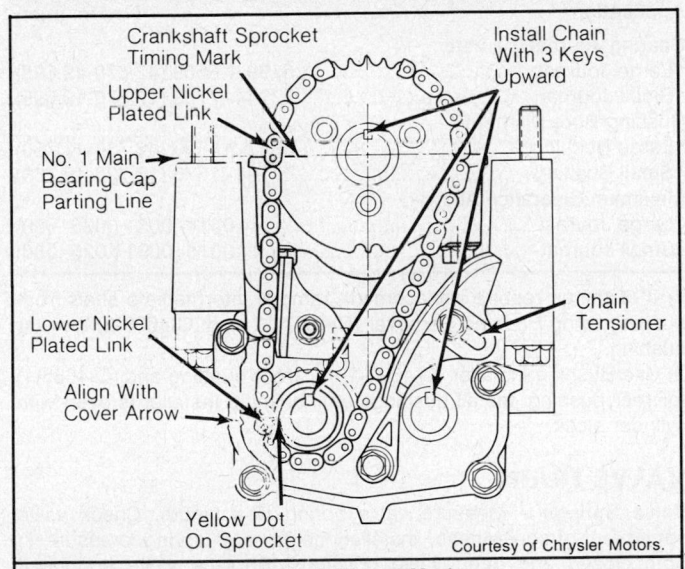

Fig. 12: Aligning Balance Shaft Timing Marks

6) With balance shaft properly aligned, slide balance shaft chain sprocket onto nose of left balance shaft. Balance shaft may have to be pushed in slightly to allow for clearance. Reverse removal procedure to complete installation.

NOTE: Balance shaft timing is set correctly when timing mark (Yellow dot) on balance shaft chain (lower) sprocket and lower nickel plated chain link are aligned with arrow on chain cover. See Fig. 12.

CAMSHAFT

Removal – 1) Remove front covers and timing belt. Remove valve cover and oil baffle (if equipped). Using Sprocket Holder (C-4687) with Adapter (C-4687-1), hold camshaft sprocket and remove sprocket bolt. *See Fig. 4.* Remove camshaft sprocket.

2) Using Seal Remover (C-4679), remove camshaft seal. *See Fig. 9.* Mark rocker arms for location. On each rocker arm, rotate camshaft until base circle contacts rocker arm.

3) Using Spring Compressor (C-4682), compress valve spring. Remove rocker arm and mark for location. Ensure camshaft bearing caps are marked for location.

4) Loosen camshaft bearing cap nuts several turns. Using soft-faced mallet, tap rear of camshaft to loosen bearing caps. Remove camshaft bearing cap bolts so camshaft does not bind in cylinder head, damage to camshaft and/or bearing thrust surfaces may result. Remove camshaft and oil seals.

Inspection – 1) Inspect camshaft and cylinder head for damage. Measure bearing journals. Replace camshaft if not within specification. See CAMSHAFT table at end of article.

2) Measure camshaft lobe on outer edges and in rocker contact surface areas. Replace camshaft if difference between both readings exceeds .010" (.25 mm). Ensure proper sized camshaft is used when replacing.

NOTE: If an oversized camshaft is used, cylinder head must have oversized camshaft bores also. Oversized camshafts are identified by Green painted barrel with letters "O/JS" stamped on air pump end of camshaft. An oversized cylinder head is identified by Green painted bearing caps with letters "O/JS" stamped to rear of oil gallery plug on air pump end of cylinder head.

Installation – 1) Install camshaft on cylinder head. Arrows on bearing caps Nos. 1 through 4 should point toward timing belt. Apply anaerobic sealer to Nos. 1 and 5 bearing caps at cap-to-cylinder head surfaces.

2) Install No. 1 bearing cap at timing belt end and No. 5 bearing cap at rear of cylinder head. Ensure arrows on bearing caps Nos. 1 through 4 point toward timing belt. Install bearing cap bolts and tighten bolts alternately (working from middle outward) to specification.

3) After installation of camshaft, check camshaft end play using a dial indicator. If end play exceeds specification, camshaft and/or cylinder head should be replaced.

4) Coat camshaft oil seal lips with oil. Using Intermediate Shaft & Camshaft Seal Installer (C-4680), install camshaft oil seal flush with camshaft bearing cap. *See Fig. 10.* Install rocker arms to their original positions.

CAUTION: Ensure valve spring retainer locks are fully seated after installing rocker arms.

5) If replacing camshaft sprocket, ensure proper sprocket is used. Camshaft sprockets on 2.2L engines use a 4 hole pattern in sprocket hub, while camshaft sprockets on 2.5L engines use a 6 hole pattern.

6) Install timing belt and covers. Reverse removal procedure to complete installation of remaining components. Tighten all bolts to specification.

INTERMEDIATE SHAFT

CAUTION: Distributor MUST be removed before attempting to remove intermediate shaft.

Removal – Remove front covers and timing belt. Hold intermediate sprocket using Sprocket Holder (C-4687) with Adapter (C-4687-1). *See Fig. 4.* Remove intermediate shaft sprocket bolt and remove sprocket. Remove intermediate shaft front retainer bolts, retainer and remove intermediate shaft.

Installation – Replace intermediate shaft seal at this time. Apply a 1/16" bead of anaerobic gasket material to form gasket on intermediate shaft front retainer. Install retainer and tighten bolts to specification. Lubricate distributor drive gear before installing. Install timing belt and front covers.

7-22

1989 CHRYSLER MOTORS ENGINES
2.2L & 2.5L 4-Cylinder (Cont.)

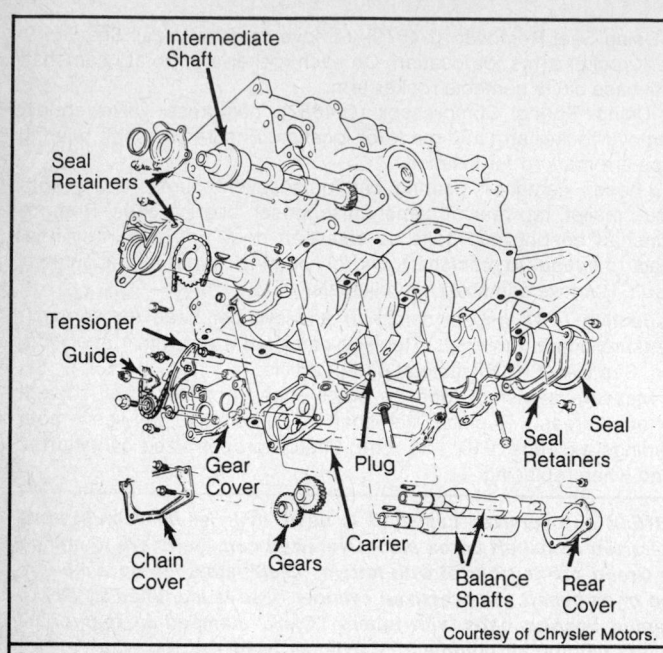

Fig. 13: Exploded View of 2.5L Engine

WATER PUMP

Removal – 1) Drain cooling system. Remove upper and lower radiator hoses. Remove air conditioning compressor from mounting bracket. DO NOT disconnect lines. Remove alternator. Remove water pump by-pass hose. Remove water pump retaining bolts. Remove water pump from cylinder block.
2) Remove water pump pulley. Remove water pump-to-housing bolts. Separate water pump from housing. Remove "O" ring from housing groove.

Installation – 1) Apply 1/8" bead of RTV sealant to housing. Install water pump on housing. Tighten retaining bolts to specification. Install new "O" ring from housing groove.
2) Install water pump pulley. Reverse removal procedures for remaining components. Tighten bolts to specification. Fill cooling system. Remove plug from top of thermostat housing. Allow air to bleed from cooling system. Install plug once coolant reaches thermostat housing level.

NOTE: For information on cooling system capacities and see ENGINE COOLANT SPECIFICATIONS article in this section.

OIL PAN

See appropriate OIL PAN REMOVAL article in this section.

OVERHAUL

CYLINDER HEAD

Inspection – 1) Inspect cylinder head for cracks and warpage. Cylinder head must be resurfaced or replaced if warpage exceeds specification. If cylinder head replacement is required, ensure proper cylinder head is used.
2) Inspect camshaft journals for scoring and journal caps for oversize markings. When servicing cylinder head or camshaft, it is necessary to ensure that oversized camshafts are used only with oversized heads and vice-versa.
3) After grinding valves or valve seats, install valve into cylinder and measure distance from spring seat of cylinder head to tip of valve. Distance should be 1.960-2.009" (49.78-51.03 mm). Grind valve tip if necessary.

Valve Guides – 1) Check valve stem oil clearance. Ensure valve stem diameters are within specifications. Valve guide must be reamed for valve with oversize valve stem if clearance exceeds specification. See VALVES & VALVE SPRINGS table at end of article.
2) Valves are available with oversize valve stems of .006" (.15 mm), .016" (.40 mm) and .031" (.80 mm). Cylinder head must be replaced if guide cannot be cleaned using a .031" (.80 mm) reamer.

NOTE: DO NOT ream valve guides from standard to maximum oversize in one step. Ream guides to oversize in gradual steps, so guides are reamed true in relation to valve seat.

CAMSHAFT

Inspection – Measure camshaft journals for oversize. Inspect camshaft journals for abnormal wear. To measure cam lobe wear, measure lobe diameter in an unworn area of each lobe, then measure lobe diameter in worn area of cam lobe. Subtract the difference between readings. Camshaft bearing journal wear or lobe wear should not exceed .010" (.25 mm).

INTERMEDIATE SHAFT

Inspection – 1) Inspect bearing journals and bushings for damage. Measure bearing journal diameters. Measure intermediate shaft bushing bore diameters. Determine maximum oil clearance. Replace shaft and/or bushings if not within specification. See INTERMEDIATE SHAFT SPECIFICATIONS table.

INTERMEDIATE SHAFT SPECIFICATIONS

Application	In. (mm)
Bearing Journal Diameter	
Large Journal	1.6799-1.6809 (42.670-42.695)
Small Journal	.7744-.7753 (19.670-19.695)
Bushing Bore Diameter	
Large Bushing	1.6823-1.6830 (42.730-42.750)
Small Bushing	.7764-.7776 (19.720-19.750)
Maximum Clearance Allowed	
Large Journal	.0014-.0031 (.035-.080)
Small Journal	.0010-.0031 (.025-.080)

2) If bushings require replacement, remove intermediate shaft front bushing using Bushing Remover (C-4697-2), and (C-4686-2) for rear bushing.
3) Use Bushing Installer (C-4697-1) for front bushing and (C-4686-1) for rear bushing. Install bushings until bushing installer is even with cylinder block.

VALVE TRAIN

Valve Springs – Measure valve spring free length. Check valve spring out-of-squareness, installed height and spring pressure in both closed and open valve positions. Replace valve springs if necessary.

Valves & Valve Seats – 1) If valve face and/or valve seats have been ground, valve tip-to-valve spring seat dimension must be measured. Grind valve tip (if necessary) to give a 1.960-2.009" (49.78-51.03 mm) installed height when measured from spring seat.
2) Valve tip diameter should be no less than .275" (6.99 mm) after grinding. If necessary, tip chamfer should be reground to prevent seal damage when valve is installed.

CAUTION: If more than .020" (.50 mm) has been ground from valve tip, measure clearance between installed rocker arm and valve spring retainer. If clearance is less than .050" (1.27 mm), bottom of rocker arm must be ground for proper clearance.

---

3) Measure stem diameter of each valve. Replace valve if not within specification. Measure valve minimum margin after grinding each valve. Replace valve if less than specification.

1989 CHRYSLER MOTORS ENGINES
2.2L & 2.5L 4-Cylinder (Cont.)

7-23

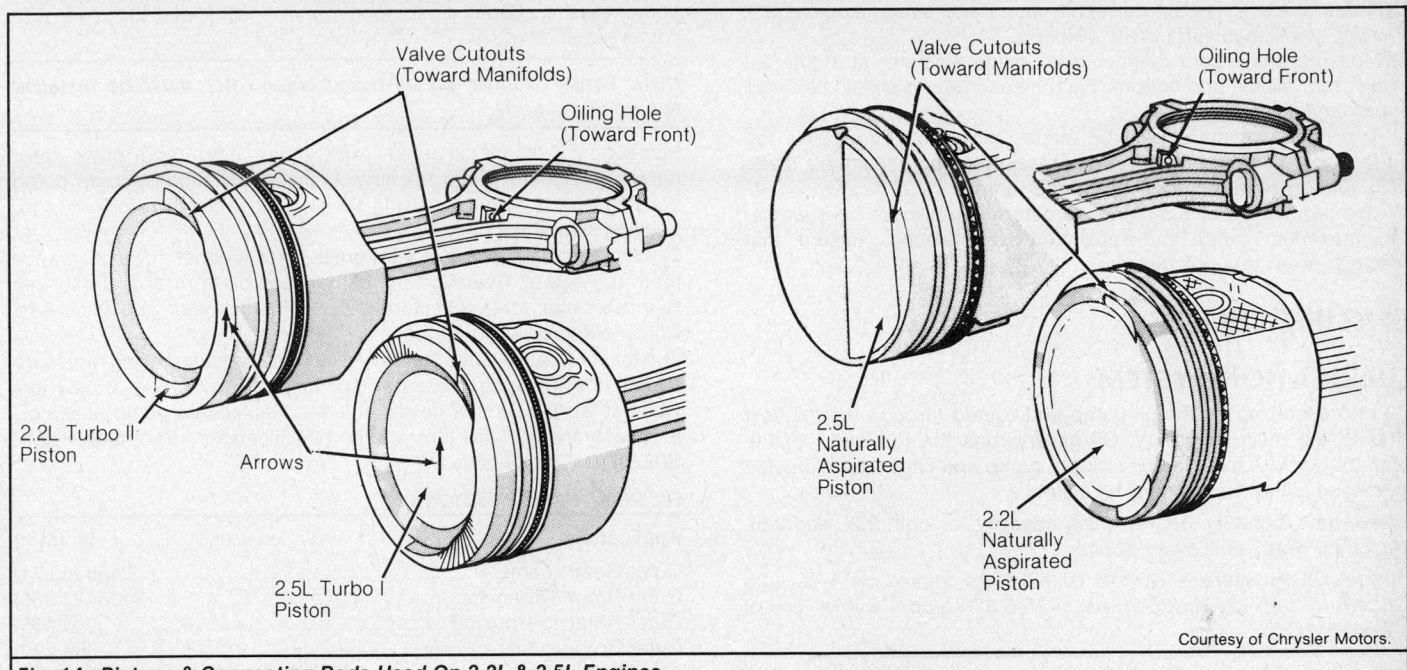

Fig. 14: Pistons & Connecting Rods Used On 2.2L & 2.5L Engines

Valve Stem Oil Seals – Ensure that oversize valve stem seals are used when oversize valves are installed.

Hydraulic Valve Lash Adjusters – 1) No adjustment of lash adjusters is required. If adjuster is disassembled for cleaning purposes, reassemble using new caps.

2) Adjusters must be at least partially full of oil prior to installation. Little or no plunger travel should exist when adjuster is depressed.

NOTE: Always service hydraulic valve lash adjusters as complete assemblies. Internal components of valve lash adjusters are not interchangeable.

CYLINDER BLOCK

Pistons & Connecting Rods – 1) Before removing pistons, mark each piston top with matching cylinder number and mark connecting rod to match rod cap. Valve clearance cutout(s) on piston heads should face manifold side of engine.

2) Pistons on turbocharged engines will have an arrow facing toward front of engine. Oiling hole on connecting rod must face toward front (timing belt end) of engine. *See Fig. 14.*

PISTON SIZING LOCATIONS

Engine Size	Location Area To Measure In. (mm) [1]	Piston-to-Cyl. Clearance In. (mm)
2.2L TBI	1.14 (28.9)	.0005-.0015 (.013-.038)
2.2L Turbo II	2.38 (60.4)	.0005-.0015 (.013-.038)
2.5L TBI	1.87 (47.4)	.0010-.0020 (.025-.050)
2.5L Turbo I	1.48 (37.5)	.0060-.0018 (.152-.045)

[1] – Measure diameter of piston skirt at this location. Measured from top of piston.

Piston Rings – 1) Ensure ring end gap and side clearances are within specifications. Ensure No. 1 and 2 piston rings (marked "TOP") are installed in the proper direction.

2) Position ring gaps in proper location. Oil ring rail gaps are installed 180 degrees apart from each other. *See Fig. 15.*

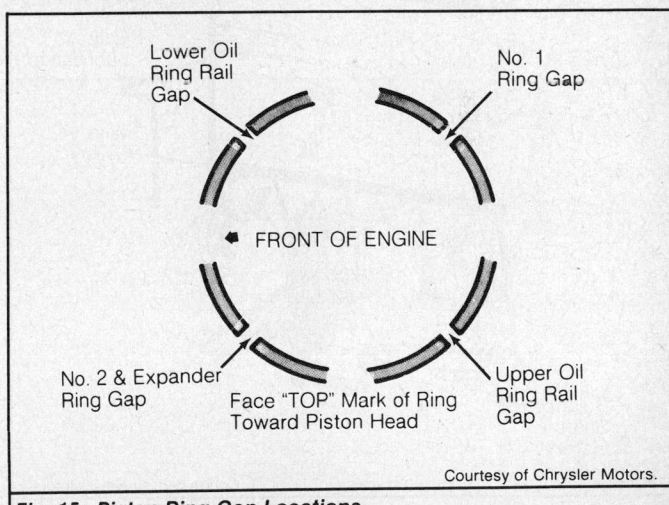

Fig. 15: Piston Ring Gap Locations

NOTE: A correct piston-to-bore clearance must be established when fitting pistons to cylinder block. Chrysler Motors 4-cylinder engines use pistons designed specifically for each engine configuration. Piston clearance and sizing locations vary with with respect to engine configuration. When measuring pistons, use the PISTON SIZING LOCATIONS table to determine the appropriate sizing location (area in which to measure piston skirt) and recommended piston-to-cylinder bore clearance.

7-24

1989 CHRYSLER MOTORS ENGINES
2.2L & 2.5L 4-Cylinder (Cont.)

Cylinder Block – 1) Using a feeler gauge and straightedge, check cylinder block head surface for warpage.

2) Measure and record cylinder bore inside diameter at 3 different levels, top, middle and bottom. Each measurement should be taken in perpendicular directions.

3) Top measurement should be made .375" (9.52 mm) below top surface of cylinder bore. Bottom measurement should be made .375" (9.52 mm) from bottom of cylinder bore.

4) Use recorded measurements to determine cylinder bore diameter, maximum taper and maximum out-of-round. Ensure that readings are within specifications.

ENGINE OILING

LUBRICATION SYSTEM

Oil is pressurized by the oil pump and routed through the full flow filter to the main oil gallery. Oil gallery runs the full length of the cylinder block. A modified oil pick-up, pump and check valve provide increased oil flow to the main oil gallery.

Crankshaft Capacity – Crankcase capacity for both 2.2L and 2.5L engines is 4 qts. (3.8L) with oil filter.

Normal Oil Pressure – Normal oil pressure should be 4 psi (.28 kg/cm²) at curb idle, or 25-90 psi (1.75-6.32 kg/cm²) with engine at 3000 RPM.

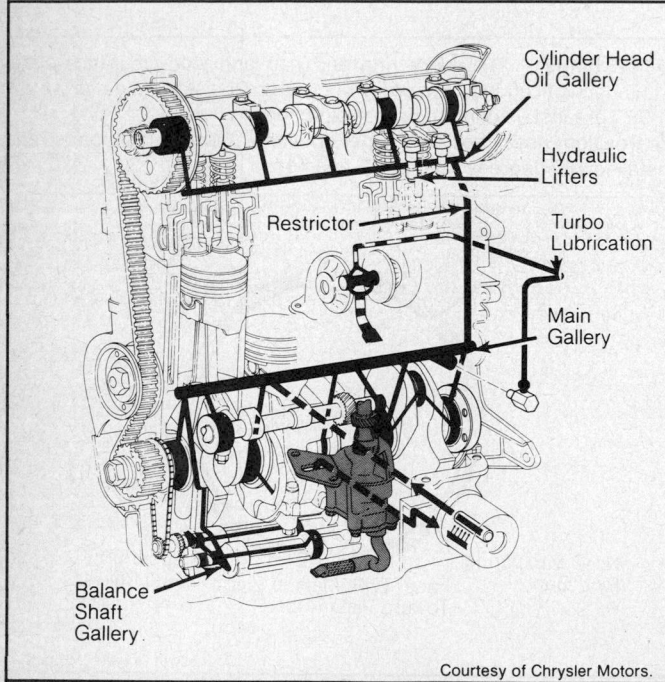

Fig. 16: Engine Oiling System (2.5L Turbo I)

OIL PUMP

Removal – Remove oil pan. Remove oil pick-up tube-to-oil pump bolt. Remove pick-up tube and "O" ring. Remove oil pump-to-cylinder block bolts. Remove oil pump.

Disassembly – Remove oil pump cover-to-pump housing bolts. Remove pump cover. Remove inner and outer rotors. *See Fig. 17.* Remove oil pressure relief valve pin, cup, spring and valve from oil

pump housing. Clean all components in solvent and blow dry with compressed air.

NOTE: Large chamfer on oil pump outer rotor must be installed toward pump body.

Inspection – 1) Install inner rotor (drive gear) and outer rotor (driven gear) into pump housing. Place straightedge across pump housing and both gears. Using feeler gauge, check rotor gears-to-housing clearance.

2) With rotors installed, check outer rotor-to-inner rotor clearance (between gears). Check clearance between outer rotor and housing. Remove outer rotor. Measure outer rotor diameter and thickness. Check pump cover for flatness.

3) Measure relief valve spring free length. Using spring pressure tester, check spring pressure. Spring pressure should be 20 lbs. when compressed to a height of 1.34". Replace oil pump assembly if measurements are not within specifications. See OIL PUMP SPECIFICATIONS table.

OIL PUMP SPECIFICATIONS

Application	In. (mm)
Outer Rotor Diameter	2.469 (62.71)
Outer Rotor Thickness	.9435 (23.965)
Outer Rotor-to-Housing	.014 (.35)
Outer Rotor-to-Inner Rotor	.008 (.20)
Pump Cover Flatness	.003 (.07)
Rotor Gears-to-Housing [1]	.001-.0035 (.02-.088)
Valve Spring Free Length	1.95 (49.5)

[1] – Measured by using straightedge across housing.

Reassembly – Install and lubricate outer rotor in pump housing with large chamfered edge toward pump housing. Lubricate inner rotor shaft and drive gear. Install inner rotor and drive gear. Install pump cover. Tighten bolts to specification. Install pressure relief valve in pump housing. Ensure relief valve slides freely in its bore. Install spring, cup and pin.

Installation – 1) Apply Loctite Sealer (515) to oil pump housing-to-cylinder block surface. Align slot in oil pump drive gear. Install oil pump. Rotate pump back and forth to ensure proper seating while tightening retaining bolts.

2) Tighten to specification. Install new "O" ring on pick-up tube. Reverse removal procedures to complete installation. Tighten bolts to specification.

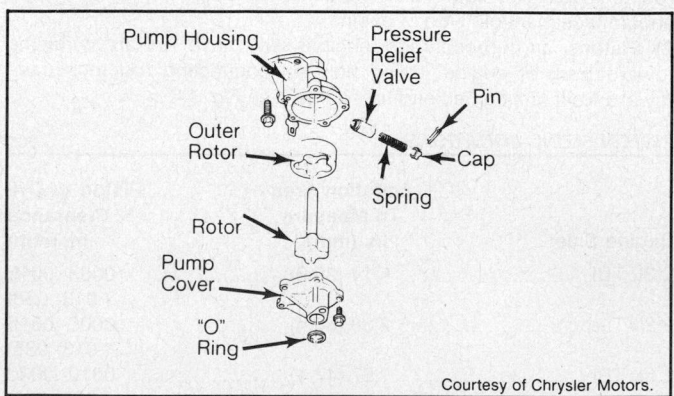

Courtesy of Chrysler Motors.

Fig. 17: Exploded View of Oil Pump Assembly

1989 CHRYSLER MOTORS ENGINES
2.2L & 2.5L 4-Cylinder (Cont.)

7-25

TIGHTENING SPECIFICATIONS

Application	Ft. Lbs. (N.m)
Air Pump Mounting Bolt	21 (29)
Balance Shaft Carrier-to-Cylinder Block Bolt	40 (54)
Balance Shaft Chain Sprocket Bolt	21 (29)
Balance Shaft Chain Sprocket-to-Crankshaft Bolt	11 (15)
Camshaft Bearing Cap Bolt	18 (24)
Camshaft Sprocket Bolt	65 (88)
Coolant Tube-to-Thermostat Housing	30 (41)
Connecting Rod Cap Nut	[1] 40 (54)
Crankshaft Belt Sprocket Bolt	50 (68)
Crankshaft Pulley Bolt	20 (27)
Cylinder Head Bolt	
Step 1	45 (61)
Step 2	65 (88)
Step 3	[1] 65 (88)
Exhaust Manifold Nut	17 (23)
Flywheel Bolt	70 (95)
Fuel Rail Bolt	21 (29)
Intake Manifold Bolt	17 (23)
Intermediate Shaft Sprocket Bolt	65 (88)
Main Bearing Cap Bolt	[1] 30 (41)
Oil Pick-Up Tube-to-Pump Bolt	21 (29)
Oil Pump-to-Block Bolt	17 (23)
Socket Head Torx Bolts	10 (13)
Timing Belt Tensioner Bolt	45 (61)
Turbo Oil Feed Line	10 (14)

TIGHTENING SPECIFICATIONS (Cont.)

Application	Ft. Lbs. (N.m)
Turbo Support Bracket Bolt	
Lower	40 (54)
Upper	20 (27)
Turbo-to-Exhaust Manifold Nut	40 (54)
Water Pump Housing Mounting Bolt	
Lower	40 (54)
Upper	21 (29)

Application	INCH Lbs. (N.m)
Balance Shaft Chain Adjustment Bolt	105 (12)
Balance Shaft Chain Guide Nut	105 (12)
Balance Shaft Chain Tensioner Bolt	105 (12)
Balance Shaft Cover Bolt	105 (12)
Fuel Pressure Regulator Nut	65 (7.3)
Front Seal Retainer Bolt	105 (12)
Intermediate Shaft Retainer Bolt	105 (12)
Oil Pump Cover Bolt	105 (12)
Crankshaft Rear Seal Retainer Bolt	105 (12)
Timing Belt Cover Bolt	40 (4.5)
Valve Cover Bolt	105 (12)
Water Pump Pulley Bolt	105 (12)
Water Pump-to-Housing Bolt	105 (12)

[1] – Tighten an additional 1/4 turn.

ENGINE SPECIFICATIONS

GENERAL SPECIFICATIONS

Year	Displacement		Fuel System	HP@RPM	Torque Ft. Lbs.@RPM	Compr. Ratio	Bore		Stroke	
	Cu. In.	Liters					In.	mm	In.	mm
1989										
2.2L Base	135	2.2	TBI	93@4800	122@3200	9.5:1	3.44	87.5	3.62	92.0
2.2L Turbo II	135	2.2	MPFI	174@5200	200@2400	8.0:1	3.44	87.5	3.62	92.0
2.5L Base	153	2.5	TBI	100@4400	135@2800	8.9:1	3.44	87.5	4.09	103.8
2.5L Turbo I	153	2.5	MPFI	155@4800	180@2000	7.8:1	3.44	87.5	4.09	103.8

PISTONS, PINS & RINGS

Engine	Pistons		Pins			Rings		
	Clearance In. (mm)	Diameter In. (mm)	Diameter In. (mm)	Piston Fit In. (mm)	Rod Fit In. (mm)	Ring No.	End Gap In. (mm)	Side Clearance In. (mm)
Non-Turbo								
2.2L	.0005-.0015 (.013-.038)	3.443-3.445 (87.45-87.50)	.....		.....	No. 1	.010-.020 (.25-.51)	.0015-.0031 (.038-.079)
2.5L	.0010-.0020 (.025-.050)	3.442-3.445 (87.43-87.50)	.....		.....	No. 2	.011-.021 (.28-.53)	.0015-.0037 (.038-.094)
						No. 3	.015-.055 (.38-1.40)	
Turbo								
2.2L	.0005-.0015 (.013-.038)	3.443-3.445 (87.45-87.50)		[1]	.....	No. 1	.010-.020 (.25-.51)	.0016-.0030 (.041-.076)
2.5L	.0006-.0018 (.015-.046)	3.443-3.444 (87.45-87.48)		[1]	.....	No. 2	.009-.019 (.29-.48)	.040-.090 (1.02-2.29)
						No. 3	.015-.055 (.38-1.40)	

[1] – On Turbocharged engines only, piston pin end play should be 0-.035" (0.0-.89 mm).

1989 CHRYSLER MOTORS ENGINES
2.2L & 2.5L 4-Cylinder (Cont.)

ENGINE SPECIFICATIONS (Cont.)

CONNECTING RODS

Engine	Side Play In. (mm)	Max. Bend & Twist In. (mm)	Pin Bore Dia. In. (mm)	Large Bore Dia. In. (mm)	Center-to-Center In. (mm)
2.2L & 2.5L	.005-.013 (.13-.33)	.003 (.08)	.....	.....	.....

CRANKSHAFT, MAIN & CONNECTING ROD BEARINGS

Engine	Crankshaft				Main Bearings		Connecting Rod Bearings	
	End Play In. (mm)	Runout In. (mm)	Journal Taper In. (mm)	Journal Out-of-Round In. (mm)	Journal Diameter In. (mm)	Oil Clearance In. (mm)	Journal Diameter In. (mm)	Oil Clearance In. (mm)
2.2L & 2.5L	.002-.007 (.05-.18)	.....	.0004 (.010)	.005 (.13)	2.362-2.363 (59.99-60.02)	.0004-.0028 (.010-.071)	1.968-1.969 (49.99-50.01)	.0008-.0034 (.020-.086)

CYLINDER HEAD

Engine	Max. Cylinder Head Warp In. (mm)	Valve Seats				Valve Guides		
		Seat Angle	Maximum Runout In. (mm)	Seat Width In. (mm)	Seat Bore Diameter In. (mm)	Valve Stem Oil Clearance In. (mm)	Valve Guide I.D. In. (mm)	Valve Guide Bore I.D. In. (mm)
2.2L & 2.5L	.004 (.10)	45°	.002 (.05)	.....	.....	.....	.....	.....
Intake				.069-.089 (1.75-2.26)	1.593 (40.46)	.0009-.0026 (.023-.066)		
Exhaust				.059-.078 (1.50-1.98)	1.371 (34.82)	.0030-.0047 (.076-.119)		

VALVES & VALVE SPRINGS

Engine	Valves					Valves Springs			Pressure Lbs. @ In. (Kg @ mm)	
	Head Dia. In. (mm)	Stem Dia. In. (mm)	Face Angle	Min. Margin In. (mm)	Max. Refinish In. (mm)	Free Length In. (mm)	Out-of-Square In. (mm)	Installed Height In. (mm)	Valve Closed	Valve Open
2.2L & 2.5L										
Intake	1.60 (40.6)	.3124 (7.935)	45°	.031 (.79)	.....	2.39 (60.71)	.079 (2.01)	1.62-1.68 (41.2-42.7)	108@1.65 (49.0@42.0)	195@1.22 (88.5@31.0)
Exhaust	1.39 (35.3)	.3103 (7.882)	45°	.047 (1.19)	.....	2.39 (60.71)	.079 (2.01)	1.62-1.68 (41.2-42.7)	108@1.65 (49.0@42.0)	195@1.22 (88.5@31.0)

CYLINDER BLOCK

Engine	Max. Block Warp In. (mm)	Cylinder Bore		
		Standard Diameter In. (mm)	Maximum Taper In. (mm)	Maximum Out-of-Rnd In. (mm)
2.2L & 2.5L	.004 (.10)	3.440-3.450 (87.38-87.63)	.005 (.13)	.002 (.05)

NOTE: *For engine repair procedures not covered in this article, see ENGINE OVERHAUL PROCEDURES article at beginning of this section.*

ENGINE IDENTIFICATION

The engine can be identified by the 8th character of the Vehicle Identification Number (VIN). The VIN is located on a metal tag on upper left corner of dashboard and is visible through windshield. The engine can also be identified by the Engine Identification Number (EIN). The EIN is located on left side of engine block between the core plug and rear face of block.

ENGINE IDENTIFICATION CODE

Engine	Code
3.0L (181")	3

ADJUSTMENTS

VALVE ARRANGEMENT

Right Bank – I-E-I-E-I-E (Front-to-rear).
Left Bank – E-I-E-I-E-I (Front-to-rear).

NOTE: *There are no applicable adjustments for this engine.*

REMOVAL & INSTALLATION

NOTE: *For reassembly reference, label all electrical connectors, vacuum hoses and fuel lines before removal. Also place mating marks on engine hood and other major assemblies before removal.*

ENGINE

NOTE: *See ENGINE REMOVAL & INSTALLATION article at end of ENGINE section.*

INTAKE MANIFOLDS

CAUTION: *Fuel system is under pressure. Fuel pressure must be released before disconnecting fuel lines.*

Removal – 1) Loosen gas cap to release fuel tank pressure. Remove wiring harness connector from any injector. Ground one injector terminal. Connect jumper wire to other terminal and touch battery positive terminal with jumper. DO NOT appply voltage to injector for longer than 10 seconds. Remove jumper wires.
2) Disconnect negative and positive battery cables. Drain cooling system. Remove air cleaner-to-throttle body hose. Disconnect accelerator cable and transaxle kickdown linkage. Disconnect Automatic Idle Speed (AIS) motor and Throttle Position Sensor (TPS) wiring harness connectors from throttle body. Remove vacuum hoses from throttle body.
3) Remove air cleaner-to-throttle body hose. Remove EGR tube flange from intake plenum. Disconnect wiring connectors from charge temperature sensor and coolant temperature sensor. Remove vacuum hoses from air intake plenum. Remove fuel hoses from fuel rail.
4) Remove 8 bolts and nuts retaining intake plenum to intake manifold. Remove air intake plenum. Cover intake manifold ports when servicing. Remove vacuum hoses from fuel rail and fuel pressure regulator. Disconnect fuel injector wiring harness from engine wiring harness.
5) Remove fuel pressure regulator from fuel rail. Remove fuel rail attaching bolts. Remove fuel rail assembly from intake manifold. Disconnect radiator and heater hoses from manifold. Remove 8 mounting nuts and washers. Remove intake manifold. *See Fig. 1.*

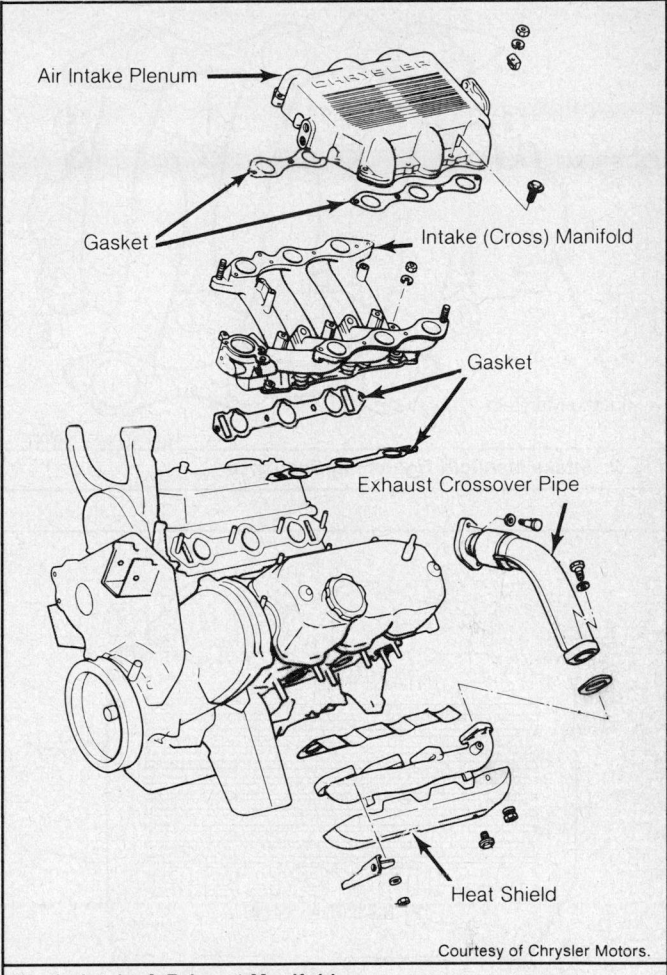

Courtesy of Chrysler Motors.

Fig. 1: Intake & Exhaust Manifolds

Inspection – Clean all gasket mating surfaces. Check for damage or cracks on all mounting surfaces. Check for clogged coolant and fuel passages in manifold. Check mounting surfaces for warpage.

INTAKE MANIFOLD WARPAGE

Application	In. (mm)
Intake Plenum Mounting Surface	
Standard	.004 (.15)
Maximum	.008 (.30)
Cylinder Head Mounting Surface	
Standard	.003 (.10)
Maximum	.005 (.20)

Installation – 1) Position intake manifold gasket on cylinder head. Install intake manifold. Install 8 washers and nuts. Tighten nuts to specification in several steps.
2) Ensure injector holes are clean. Lubricate injector "O" rings. Install injector until firmly seated in port. Install fuel rail and tighten mounting bolts. Install fuel pressure regulator and hose assembly on fuel rail. Install manifold attaching bolts and tighten to specification. *See Fig. 2.*
3) Install fuel supply and return tube, and vacuum crossover tube hold-down bolts. Tighten fuel pressure regulator hose clamps. Connect injector wiring harness. Connect vacuum hoses to fuel pressure regulator and fuel rail assembly. Install intake manifold gasket with beaded sealant side up on lower manifold.
4) Position intake plenum on lower manifold. Tighten mounting bolts and nuts to specification. *See Fig. 3.* Connect fuel line to fuel rail. Connect vacuum harness to intake plenum. Reconnect charge temperature sensor and coolant temperature sensor. Connect EGR tube flange to intake plenum.

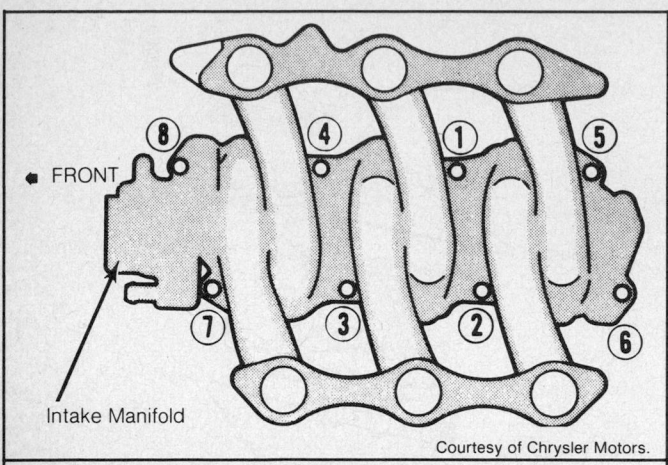

Fig. 2: Intake Manifold Tightening Sequence

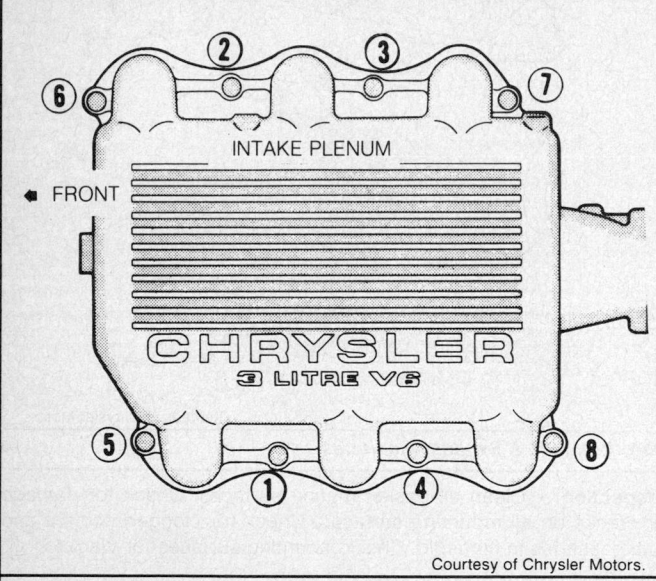

Fig. 3: Intake Plenum Tightening Sequence

5) Tighten flange bolts to specification. Connect brake booster and PCV hoses to intake plenum. Connect AIS motor and TPS electrical connectors. Connect vacuum vapor harness to throttle body. Install throttle cable and transaxle kickdown linkage.

6) Install air inlet hose assembly. Install upper radiator hose and heater hose to intake manifold. Fill and bleed cooling system. Connect battery cable.

EXHAUST MANIFOLDS

Removal & Installation – 1) Raise vehicle and disconnect exhaust pipe from rear exhaust manifold flange. Disconnect EGR tube from rear manifold. Disconnect O_2 sensor wiring. Remove crossover pipe mounting bolts. Remove nuts attaching rear manifold to cylinder head.

2) Lower vehicle. Remove screws attaching heat shield to front manifold. Remove bolts attaching crossover pipe to front manifold. Remove nuts attaching front manifold to cylinder head. Remove front exhaust manifold. Check manifolds for cracks and damage. Check mounting surfaces for warpage.

3) To install, reverse removal procedure. Install gasket with numbers 1-3-5 embossed on top, on rear exhaust manifold. Install gasket with numbers 2-4-6 embossed on top, on front exhaust manifold. Tighten mounting bolts and nuts to specification.

CYLINDER HEAD

Removal – 1) Disconnect negative battery cable. Drain cooling system. Remove air cleaner assembly. Loosen accessory drive belts. Remove A/C compressor mounting bolts and set compressor aside. Remove A/C compressor mounting bracket and drive belt tensioner. Remove power steering/alternator belt tensioner. Remove power steering pump and set aside.

2) Raise vehicle and remove right inner fender shield. Remove crankshaft pulleys and vibration damper. Lower vehicle and support engine. Separate engine mount from engine bracket. Raise engine slightly. Remove engine mount bracket. Label and disconnect all wiring, hoses, lines and linkages from throttle body, distributor, manifolds and cylinder head.

3) Remove timing belt cover, noting length of bolts for reinstallation reference. Align timing marks on front and rear camshaft sprockets and timing mark on crankshaft sprocket. *See Fig. 6.* Mark timing belt direction of rotation for reinstallation reference.

4) Loosen timing belt tensioner. Remove timing belt. Using Camshaft Sprocket Holder (MB990775), hold camshaft sprocket and loosen camshaft sprocket retaining bolt. Remove retaining bolt and sprocket.

5) Remove spark plug wires. Remove valve covers. Check auto lash adjuster free play. Insert a small wire through air bleed hole in rocker arm and VERY LIGHTLY push the auto adjuster check ball down. While holding the check ball down, check rocker arm for free play. If there is no play, replace adjuster.

6) Install Auto Lash Adjuster Retainers (MD998443). *See Fig. 4.* Remove distributor adapter. Loosen, but DO NOT remove camshaft bearing cap bolts. Remove rocker arms, shafts and bearing shafts as an assembly. Remove camshafts. Remove cylinder head bolts in sequence and remove cylinder head. *See Fig. 5.*

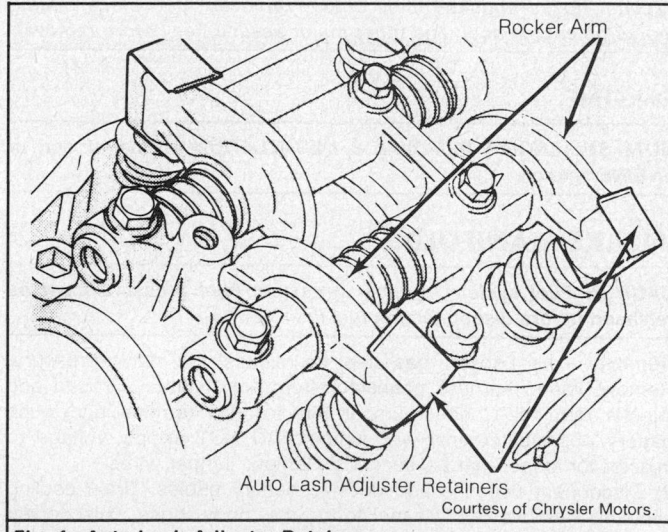

Fig. 4: Auto Lash Adjuster Retainers

Cleaning & Inspection – Clean gasket surfaces on block and cylinder head. Check cylinder head for cracks, damage or warpage. Resurface head if warped beyond .002" (.05 mm). DO NOT grind more than .008" (.2 mm) from surface of head or head surface on block. Replace head if not within specification.

Installation – 1) To install, reverse removal procedure. Install new gasket over cylinder head dowels on block. Tighten cylinder head bolts in sequence using 2-3 steps. *See Fig. 5.* Lubricate and install camshaft.

2) Install rocker shaft assemblies, applying sealant to bearing cap mating surfaces at both ends of head. Ensure arrows on rocker shaft assemblies are pointing in same direction as arrows on cylinder heads.

3) Install new camshaft seals using Seal Installer (MD998713). Install end seal plug using Installer (MD998306). To complete installation, reverse removal procedure. To install timing belt, see

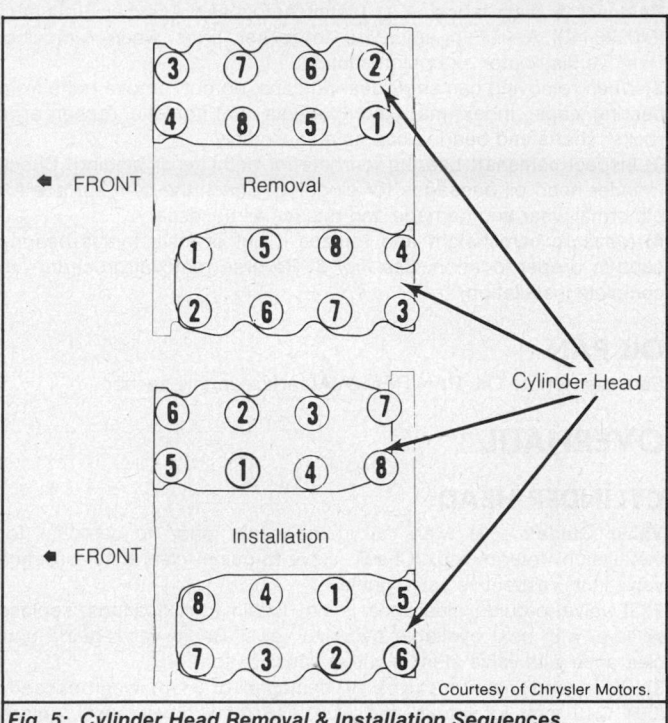

Fig. 5: Cylinder Head Removal & Installation Sequences

INSTALLATION under FRONT COVER & TIMING BELT. Tighten all bolts to specification. See ENGINE TIGHTENING SPECIFICATIONS chart.

FRONT COVER & TIMING BELT

Removal – 1) Support engine and transmission with floor jack. Remove front engine mount bracket. Remove upper (front outer) timing belt cover. Align timing marks on front and rear camshaft sprockets and timing mark on crankshaft sprocket. See Fig. 6.

2) Remove crankshaft pulleys and vibration damper. Loosen timing belt tensioner bolt and remove timing belt.

Inspection – Inspect timing belt for cracks, debris damage, missing teeth or loose cords.

Installation – 1) Ensure all timing marks are aligned. Install timing belt on crankshaft sprocket first and while keeping belt tight on tension side, install belt on the front (radiator side) camshaft sprocket.

2) Install belt on water pump pulley and on the rear camshaft sprocket and finally on timing belt tensioner. Loosen tensioner bolt and allow spring to tension belt.

3) Turn crankshaft 2 full turns clockwise. Turn smoothly and in clockwise direction only. Recheck timing marks on sprockets and then tighten timing belt tensioner to 23 ft. lbs. (31 N.m). To complete installation, reverse removal procedure.

NOTE: Turn crankshaft smoothly and ONLY in a clockwise direction.

REAR CRANKSHAFT OIL SEAL

NOTE: Rear main bearing oil seal is a one-piece unit mounted on the oil seal housing. Housing and seal can be accessed when engine or transmission is removed.

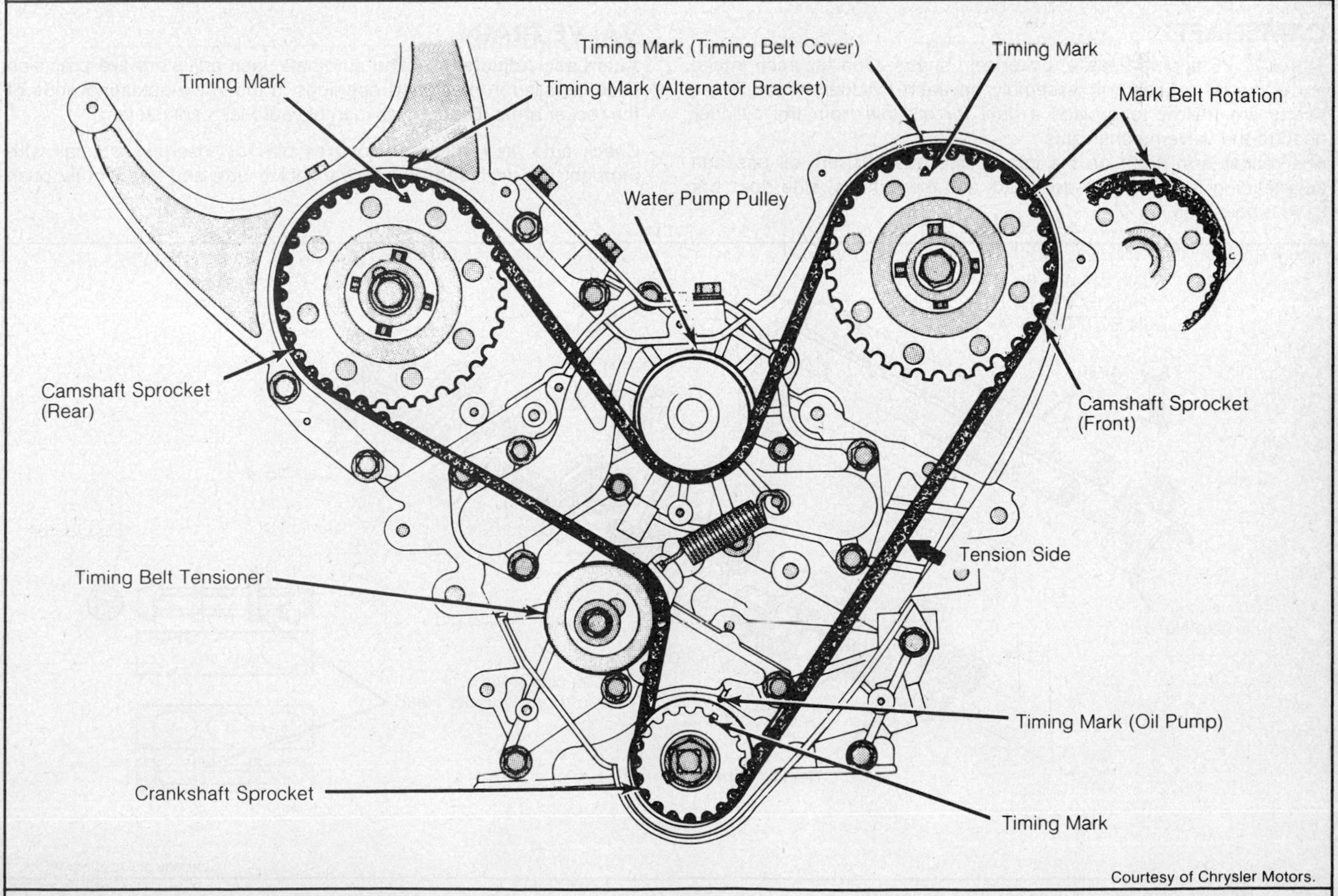

Timing Mark

Timing Mark (Timing Belt Cover)

Timing Mark

Timing Mark (Alternator Bracket)

Mark Belt Rotation

Water Pump Pulley

Camshaft Sprocket (Rear)

Camshaft Sprocket (Front)

Tension Side

Timing Belt Tensioner

Timing Mark (Oil Pump)

Crankshaft Sprocket

Timing Mark

Courtesy of Chrysler Motors.

Fig. 6: Timing Mark & Sprocket Locations

1989 CHRYSLER MOTORS ENGINES
3.0L V6 (Cont.)

Removal & Installation – 1) To remove rear main oil seal housing, remove 5 retaining bolts from housing. Carefully pry oil seal from housing using care not to damage seal bore. Throughly clean all mating surfaces.

2) Install rear crankshaft oil seal in housing using Seal Driver (MD998718). Apply RTV gasket to oil seal housing to block surface. Apply light coating of engine oil to entire circumference of oil seal lip. Install seal assembly on cylinder block and tighten bolts to 104 INCH lbs. (12 N.m).

WATER PUMP

NOTE: Water pump is driven by the timing belt. Refer to TIMING BELT removal and installation procedure in this article for removal of timing belt.

Removal – 1) With timing belt removed, drain cooling system and remove upper radiator hose. Remove air conditioning compressor (without discharging system) and alternator from engine brackets and secure both units to one side.

2) Disconnect lower radiator hose, by-pass/heater hose and screws holding water pump to engine. Remove water pump.

NOTE: Pump housing and body assemblies are serviced separately. Replace all "O" rings and rubber gaskets. Clean all mating surfaces before assembling halves together. Tighten housing bolts to 106 INCH lbs. (30 N.m).

Installation – 1) Install water pump on engine using new gasket. Tighten top 3 bolts to 22 ft. lbs. (30 N.m), and lower bolt to 50 ft. lbs. (68 N.m).

2) Install by-pass/heater hose and lower radiator hose. Attach alternator and air conditioning compressor to brackets. Connect upper radiator hose and install drive belt. Refill cooling system and check for leaks.

CAMSHAFT

The 3.0L V6 engine uses 4 rocker arm shafts. One for each intake and exhaust rocker arm assembly on each cylinder head. These shafts are hollow to provide a duct for oil flow from the cylinder head to the valve mechanisms.

The rocker arm shaft on the intake side has a 3 mm oil passage hole leading from the cylinder head, and the exhaust side does not have a hole. *See Fig. 7.*

Removal & Installation – 1) Install Auto Lash Adjuster Retainers (M0998443) to retain adjusters to rocker arms when removing. Remove distributor extension section.

2) When removing camshaft bearing caps, do not remove bolts from bearing caps. Index mark components and remove rocker arm, rocker shafts and bearing cap as an assembly.

3) Inspect camshaft bearing journals for damage or binding. Check cylinder head oil passages for clogging. Check the cam surface for abnormal wear and damage and replace as necessary.

4) Measure cam height and replace if out of limit. Install bearing caps to proper location. *See Fig. 8.* Reverse removal procedure to complete installation.

OIL PAN

See appropriate OIL PAN REMOVAL article in this section.

OVERHAUL

CYLINDER HEAD

Valve Guides – 1) Mark all components prior to removal for installation referencing. Check valve-to-guide clearance of each valve in its respective valve guide.

2) If valve-to-guide clearance is not within specifications, replace valve(s) with next available oversize valve. Ream valve guide until clearance with valve stem is within specification.

3) Clean and inspect valves. If damaged or stem wear exceeds .004" (.10 mm) for intake and .006" (.15 mm) for exhaust, replace valve. Do not reuse valve stem seals.

Valve Stem Oil Seals – Do not reuse valve stem seals. Coat valve stems with oil and insert in cylinder heads. Press new shields or seals squarely over valve guide, using valve stem as a positioning aid. Do not force seal against top of guide.

VALVE TRAIN

Auto Lash Adjusters – The automatic lash adjusters are precision units installed in machined openings in the valve actuating ends of the rocker arms. Do not disassemble auto lash adjusters.

Check auto lash adjusters for free play by inserting a small wire throught the air bleed hole in the rocker arm and very lightly push

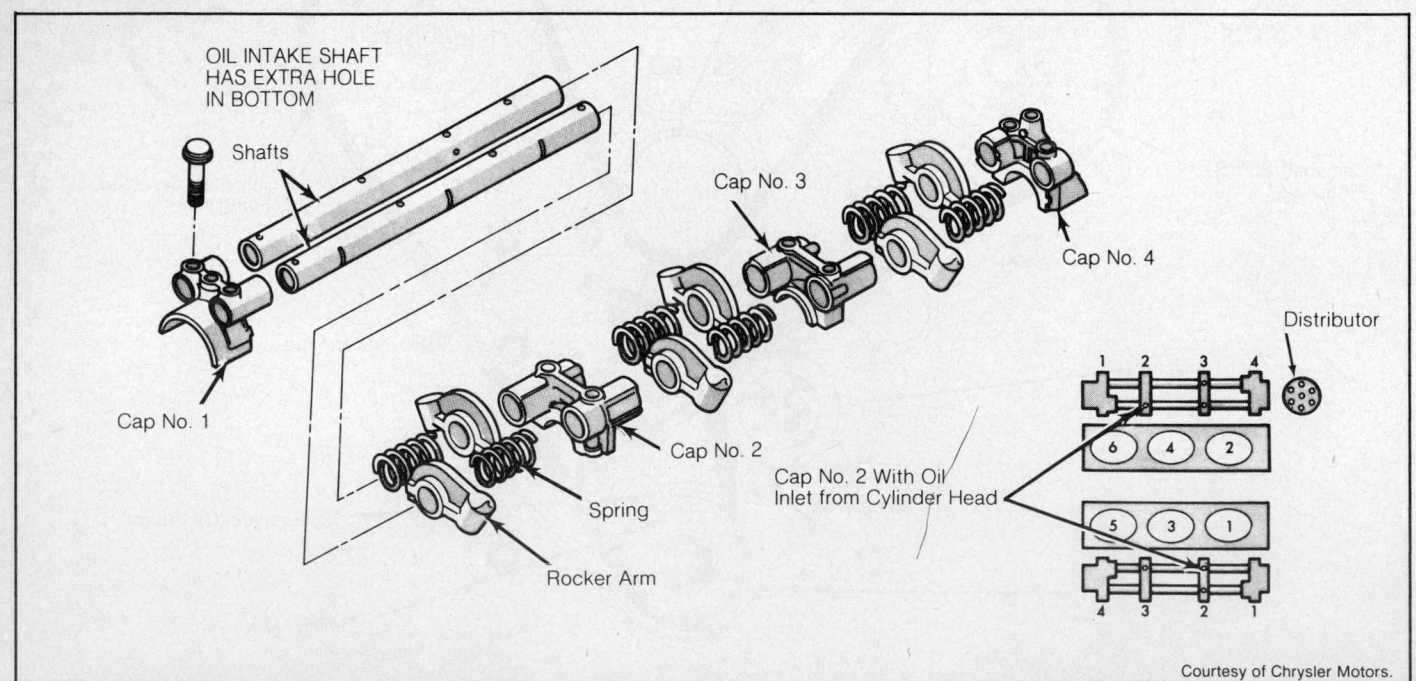

Fig. 7: Rocker Arm Shaft & Rocker Arm Assembly

Courtesy of Chrysler Motors.

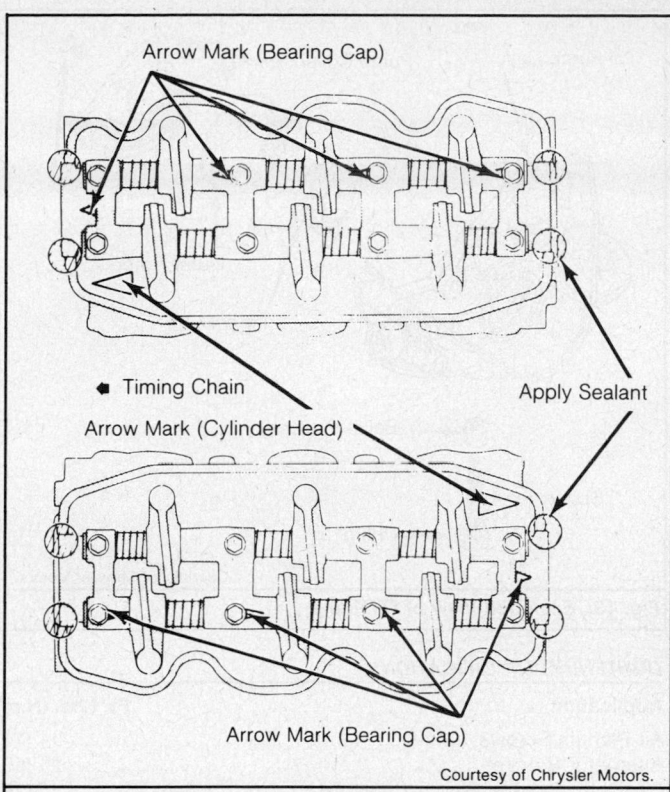

Fig. 8: Camshaft Bearing Cap Position

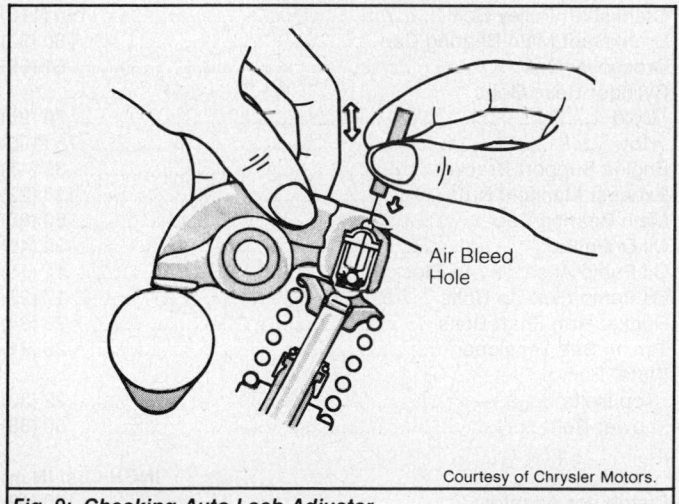

Fig. 9: Checking Auto Lash Adjuster

auto adjuster check ball down. See Fig. 9. Move rocker up and down to check free play. If there is no play, replace the adjuster.

Valve Springs – Inspect valve springs for installed height, tension free length and maximum out-of-square. See ENGINE SPECIFICATIONS tables at end of this article.

CYLINDER BLOCK

Fitting Pistons – 1) Pistons should be measured approximately .08" (2 mm) above the bottom of the piston skirt across the thrust face.

2) Measure cylinder bore at three different levels in perpendicular directions. Top measurement should be made .38" (10 mm) below the top surface of cylinder bore. Bottom measurement should be made .38" (10 mm) from the bottom of cylinder bore. See Fig. 10.

3) Oversize pistons are available in .25 mm increments; .25 mm, .50 mm and 1.0 mm.

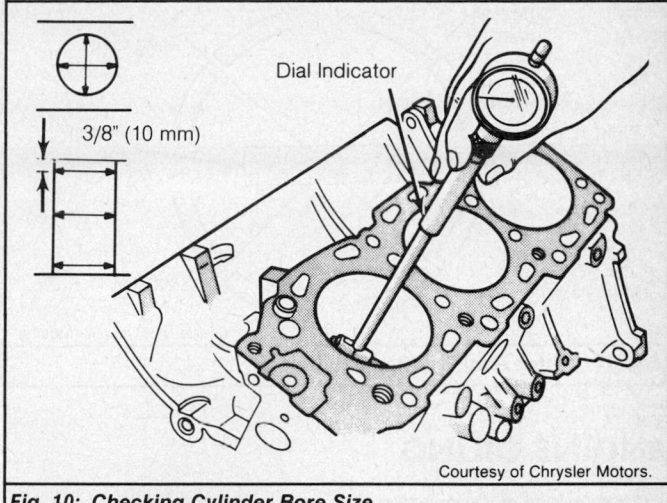

Fig. 10: Checking Cylinder Bore Size

Crankshaft Main Bearings – 1) Use Plastigage method to check main bearing clearance. Measure clearance by installing main bearing cap and tightening bolts to specified torque. Remove bearing caps and measure Plastigage on scale.

2) All upper bearing shells in the crankcase have oil grooves. All lower bearing shells installed in the monoblock main bearing cap are plain. Crankshaft end play is controlled by thrust washers on number 3 main bearing journal.

3) Install upper main bearing shells. Ensure that they are aligned with oil holes and bearing tabs are seated in block tabs.

Piston & Rod Assembly – 1) Ensure pistons and rods are installed in cylinder from which they were removed. For cylinders No. 1, 3, and 5, install pistons with the "R" mark (top of piston), toward the front (timing belt side) of engine block. For cylinders No. 2, 4, and 6, install piston with the "L" mark toward the front of engine block. See Fig. 11.

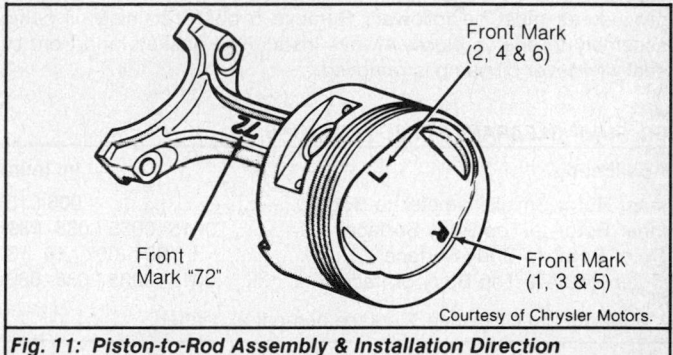

Fig. 11: Piston-to-Rod Assembly & Installation Direction

2) Before installing piston and rod assemblies into cylinder block, follow ring arrangements and installation procedure. See Fig. 12.

Crankshaft Thrust Washer Main Bearing – Engine uses different types of thrust washer bearings. One type uses positioning tabs, while the other type is plain. One SET of tab type thrust washer bearings are installed in the block and one SET of plain type thrust washer bearings are installed in the No. 3 main bearing cap. Install main bearing caps with arrows facing the front (timing belt end) of block.

Connecting Rod Bearings – Ensure rod caps are marked for proper identification before removing. Remove rod cap and use Plastigage method to check for proper bearing clearance. If clearance is not within specifications, replace with correct under-sized bearing. Install rod cap with bearing insert and tighten nuts to specification. Check connecting rod side-to-side clearances.

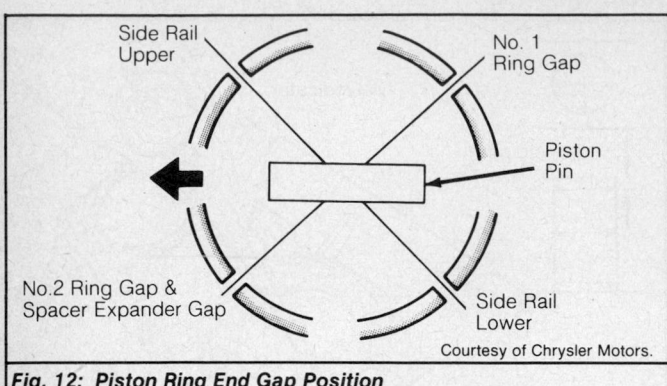

Fig. 12: Piston Ring End Gap Position

Courtesy of Chrysler Motors.

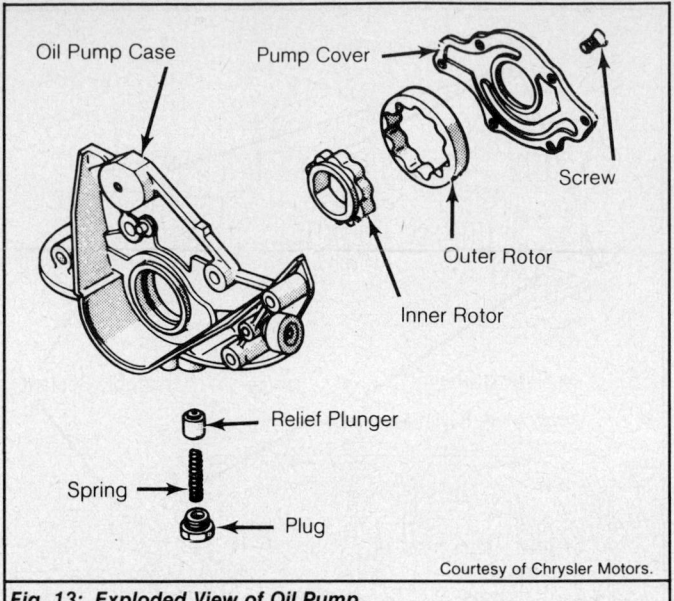

Courtesy of Chrysler Motors.

Fig. 13: Exploded View of Oil Pump

ENGINE OILING

LUBRICATION SYSTEM

The engine lubrication system is a full flow filtration, pressure feed type. The oil pump is mounted on the front cover. The pump inner rotor is installed on and rotates with the crankshaft. The engine oil pan contains a baffle plate to control oil level fluctuation during engine operation.

Crankcase Capacity – Crankcase capacity is 4.5 qts. (4.3L) including oil filter.

Normal Oil Pressure – Normal oil pressure on a fully warmed up engine is 100 psi @ 3000 RPM (45.36 kg @ 3000 RPM).

OIL PUMP

Removal & Installation – 1) Oil pump is mounted on timing belt end of block with inner pump rotor indexed and driven by crankshaft nose. Oil pump housing also retains crankshaft front oil seal and provides front oil pan closure.

2) To remove oil pump, timing belt removal and installation procedures must be followed. Remove 5 bolts retaining oil pump assembly to engine block. Always install new gaskets and front oil seal whenever oil pump is removed.

OIL PUMP CLEARANCE SPECIFICATIONS

Application	In. (mm)
Inner Rotor Small Diameter-to-Body	[1] .006 (.15)
Inner Rotor-to-Top Body Surface	.0015-.0035 (.038-.089)
Outer Rotor-to-Body Surface	.004-.007 (.10-.18)
Outer Rotor-to-Top Body Surface	.0015-.0035 (.038-.089)

[1] – Maximum clearance. Replace pump if exceeded.

TIGHTENING SPECIFICATIONS

Application	Ft. Lbs. (N.m)
Air Plenum Screws	11 (15)
Alternator Bracket	21 (29)
Camshaft Bearing Cap	15 (20)
Camshaft Sprocket Bolt	70 (95)
Connecting Rod Cap Nut	38 (52)
Crankshaft Pulley Bolt	150 (110)
Crankshaft Main Bearing Cap	60 (80)
Crossover Bolt	51 (69)
Cylinder Head Bolts	
Cold	70 (95)
Hot	75 (100)
Engine Support Bracket	35 (45)
Exhaust Manifold Nuts	16 (22)
Main Bearing Cap	60 (80)
Oil Drain Plug	30 (40)
Oil Pump Assembly-to-Block	11 (15)
Oil Pump Pick-Up Bolts	17 (23)
Rocker Arm Shaft Bolts	25 (34)
Timing Belt Tensioner	23 (31)
Water Pump	
Top Bolts	22 (30)
Lower Bolt	50 (68)

Application	INCH Lbs. (N.m)
Distributor Adaptor	120 (13)
Oil Pan Bolts	50 (6)
Oil Pump Cover	120 (13)
Rear Oil Seal Retainer	104 (12)
Rocker Cover	88 (10)
Thermostat Housing	113 (12)

ENGINE SPECIFICATIONS

GENERAL SPECIFICATIONS

Year	Displacement		Fuel System	HP@RPM	Torque Ft. Lbs.@RPM	Compr. Ratio	Bore		Stroke	
	Cu. In.	Liters					In.	mm	In.	mm
1989	181	3.0	MPFI	140@4800	170@2800	8.8:1	3.586	91.08	2.99	76.0

ENGINE SPECIFICATIONS (Cont.)

PISTONS, PINS & RINGS

Engine	Pistons		Pins			Rings		
	Clearance In. (mm)	Diameter In. (mm)	Diameter In. (mm)	Piston Fit In. (mm)	Rod Fit In. (mm)	Ring No.	End Gap In. (mm)	Side Clearance In. (mm)
3.0L	.0008-.0015 (.020-.038)	3.585-3.586 (91.05-91.08)	.....	.....	.....	1	.012-.018 (.304-.457)	.0020-.0035 (.050-.088)
						2	.010-.016 (.254-.406)	.0008-.0015 (.020-.038)

CRANKSHAFT, MAIN & CONNECTING ROD BEARINGS

Engine	Crankshaft				Main Bearings		Connecting Rod Bearings	
	End Play In. (mm)	Runout In. (mm)	Journal Taper In. (mm)	Journal Out-of-Round In. (mm)	Journal Diameter In. (mm)	Oil Clearance In. (mm)	Journal Diameter In. (mm)	Oil Clearance In. (mm)
3.0L	.002-.010 (.050-.254)	.....	.0002 (.005)	.001 (.025)	2.361-2.362 (59.96-59.99)	.0006-.0020 (.015-.050)	1.968-1.969 (49.98-50.01)	.0006-.0020 (.015-.050)

CONNECTING RODS

Engine	Side Play In. (mm)	Max. Bend & Twist In. (mm)	Pin Bore Dia. In. (mm)	Large Bore Dia. In. (mm)	Center-to-Center In. (mm)
3.0L	.004-.010 (.101-.254)	.0019 (.048)	.....	2.0866-2.0868 (52.999-53.005)	5.547-5.551 (140.89-140.99)

VALVES & VALVE SPRINGS

Engine	Valves					Valves Springs			Pressure Lbs. @ In. (Kg @ mm)	
	Head Dia. In. (mm)	Stem Dia. In. (mm)	Face Angle	Min. Margin In. (mm)	Max. Refinish In. (mm)	Free Length In. (mm)	Out-of-Square In. (mm)	Installed Height In. (mm)	Valve Closed	Valve Open
3.0L Intake	1.69 (42.9)	.313-.314 (7.95-7.97)	45°	.028 (.71)	.....	1.99 (50.5)	[1]	.....	.....	73@1.59 (33@40.4)
Exhaust	1.37 (34.9)	.312-.313 (7.92-7.95)	45°	.059 (1.50)	.....	1.99 (50.5)	[1]	.....	.....	73@1.59 (33@40.4)

[1] – Service limit is 4 degrees maximum out-of-square.

CYLINDER HEAD

Engine	Max. Cylinder Head Warp In. (mm)	Valve Seats				Valve Guides		
		Seat Angle	Maximum Runout In. (mm)	Seat Width In. (mm)	Seat Bore Diameter In. (mm)	Valve Stem Oil Clearance In. (mm)	Valve Guide I.D. In. (mm)	Valve Guide Bore I.D. In. (mm)
3.0L	.002 (.050)	44°	.....	.....	.....	[1] .004 (.10)	.314-.315 (7.98-8.00)	.5140-5143 (13.056-13.063)

[1] – For intake valve guide clearance. Exhaust valve guide clearance is .006" (.15 mm).

CYLINDER BLOCK

Engine	Max. Block Warp In. (mm)	Cylinder Bore		
		Standard Diameter In. (mm)	Maximum Taper In. (mm)	Maximum Out-of-Rnd In. (mm)
3.0L	.002 (.05)	3.59 (91.2)	.0008 (.020)	.0008 (.020)

1989 CHRYSLER MOTORS ENGINES
5.2L V8

ENGINE IDENTIFICATION

The 8th character of the Vehicle Identification Number (VIN) identifies engine cubic inch displacement and carburetor type. The VIN plate is attached to the upper left side of instrument panel and is visible through the windshield.

The Engine Identification Number (EIN) is on a pad located on the right side of block, to the rear of engine mount. The Engine Serial Number (ESN) is located on the left front corner of block, below the cylinder head, and must be referenced to when ordering engine replacement parts.

ENGINE IDENTIFICATION CODES

Engine	Code
5.2L (318")	
2-Bbl. Standard	P
4-Bbl.	
Standard	4
Heavy Duty	S

Special Engine Marks – Information identifying undersize crankshaft journals, oversize cylinder bores, tappets and valve stems is stamped in various locations on engine (depending on engine). Information and location is decoded as follows:

R or M – Numbers 1, 2, 3, or 4 following R or M indicates .001" undersize rod or main bearing journals and which (number) journal is undersized. Stamp is on No. 8 crankshaft counterweight.

RX or MX – Indicates all rod or main bearing journals are .010" undersize. Stamped on the No. 8 crankshaft counterweight.

A – Indicates .020" oversize cylinder bore. Stamped after engine identification number.

♦ – Indicates .008" oversize tappets. Stamped on top pad at front of engine and on a flat surface at outside of each tappet bore.

X – Indicates .005" oversize valve stems. Stamped on milled pad adjacent to two .375" tapped holes on each end of cylinder head.

ADJUSTMENTS

VALVE ARRANGEMENT

E-I-I-E-E-I-I-E (Both banks, front-to-rear).

VALVE CLEARANCE ADJUSTMENT

No valve adjustments are necessary on this engine.

REMOVAL & INSTALLATION

NOTE: For reassembly reference, label all electrical connectors, vacuum hoses and fuel lines before removal. Also place mating marks on engine hood and other major assemblies before removal.

ENGINE

NOTE: See ENGINE REMOVAL & INSTALLATION article at end of ENGINE section.

INTAKE MANIFOLD

Removal – **1)** Disconnect battery ground and drain cooling system. Remove air cleaner, alternator, and fuel line to carburetor. Disconnect upper radiator hose, by-pass hose and heater hoses.

2) Disconnect accelerator linkage. Label and disconnect all electrical wiring to intake manifold. Remove distributor cap, wires and vacuum hose. Remove evaporative control system and closed ventilation system. Remove valve covers. Remove intake manifold bolts. Remove intake manifold, coil and carburetor as an assembly.

Inspection – Clean all gasket mating surfaces. Check intake manifold-to-cylinder head mounting surfaces for warpage. Gasket surfaces must not be warped more than .006" (.15 mm) per foot of manifold length. Check crossover passages for carbon deposits and clean as necessary.

Installation – **1)** Clean all gasket mating surfaces. Coat bottom of intake manifold side gaskets lightly with sealer and install on cylinder heads. Apply a thin even coat of quick drying cement to front and rear manifold gaskets and block surfaces.

CAUTION: On engines with 4-Bbl. carburetors, do not use any sealer on side intake manifold gaskets.

2) Install front and rear manifold gaskets on block, making sure that hole in gaskets engage dowels in block and end holes lock into tangs of head gaskets. Apply a bead of RTV sealer to each of 4 manifold-to-cylinder head gasket corners.

3) Lower intake manifold carefully into position and install bolts. Tighten bolts in proper sequence shown in *Fig. 1* using 3 steps to obtain specification.

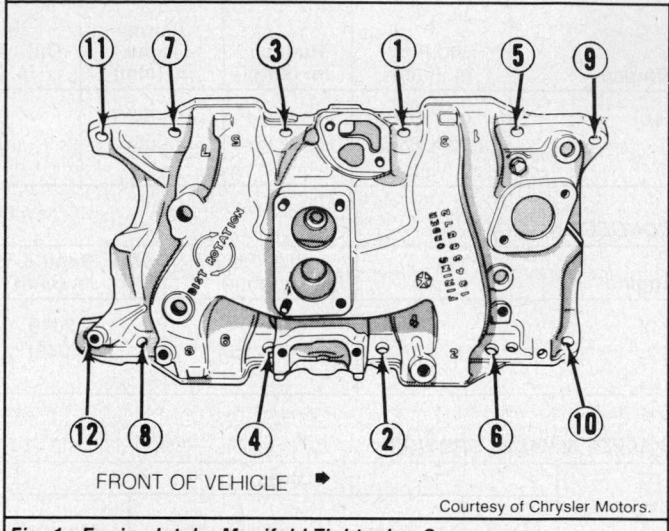

FRONT OF VEHICLE ➡

Courtesy of Chrysler Motors.

Fig. 1: Engine Intake Manifold Tightening Sequence

EXHAUST MANIFOLDS

Removal – Disconnect exhaust pipes from manifolds. Remove exhaust manifold bolts and nuts. If studs are removed with nuts, replace studs and install in head with sealer. Thoroughly clean gasket material from manifold and head mating surfaces.

Inspection – Check exhaust manifold-to-cylinder head mounting surface for warpage. Gasket surfaces must not be warped more than .006" (.15 mm) per foot of manifold length. Check manifold mating surfaces for pitting or cracks and replace if necessary.

NOTE: Coolant leak may develop if thread sealer is not used on threads of exhaust manifold studs.

Installation – Install new gasket over studs of cylinder head. Install exhaust manifolds. Install conical washers on outboard arms of manifolds. Coat threads on bolts and studs with anti-seize compound and install. Tighten bolts and nuts to specification starting from the center, working outward. Install exhaust pipes and tighten to specification.

CYLINDER HEAD

Removal – Remove intake and exhaust manifolds. Remove rocker shaft assemblies. Remove push rods and mark each one to ensure installation in original locations. Remove cylinder head bolts, cylinder heads and gaskets.

Installation – **1)** With all gasket surfaces and bolt holes clean, place head gaskets on block and install heads. After cleaning threads on head bolts, coat threads with sealer. Install head bolts and tighten in sequence as shown in *See Fig. 2*. Use 2 steps to obtain proper torque specification.

2) When rocker arm assemblies are being installed, notch on rocker shaft end must face center of engine and point to rear on right bank and to front on left bank. Long stamped steel retainers go in No. 2 and No. 4 positions. *See Fig. 3.*

3) When tightening support bracket bolts, tighten bolts slowly and evenly to allow lifters time to bleed down to operating length, then tighten to specifications.

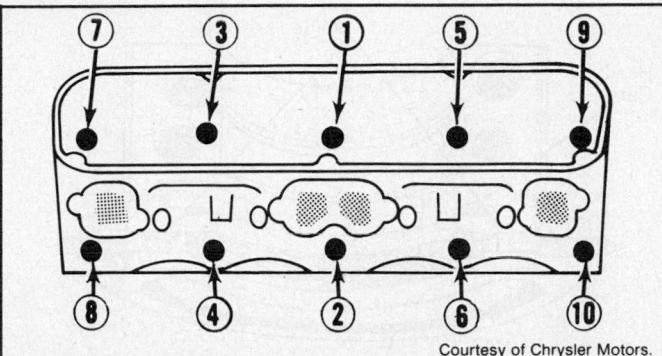

Fig. 2: Cylinder Head Tightening Sequence

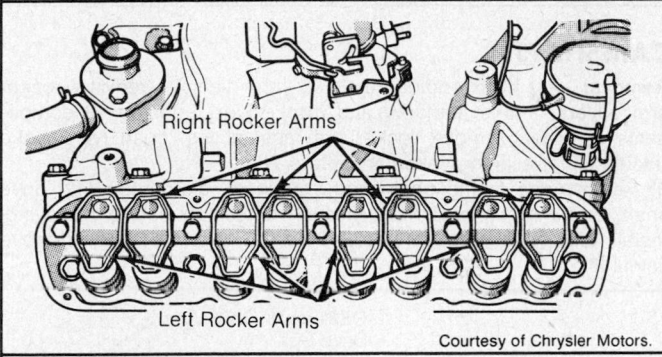

Fig. 3: Location of Rocker Arms

FRONT COVER & OIL SEAL

Removal – 1) Disconnect negative battery cable. Loosen and remove belts from crankshaft pulley. Remove radiator shroud retainer screws and set shroud back over engine. Remove fan and shroud from engine.

2) Remove crankshaft pulley from vibration damper. Remove vibration damper bolt and washer from end of crankshaft. Install a vibration damper puller and remove vibration damper from crankshaft.

3) If just removing front seal, pry seal out, being careful not to damage crankshaft seal surface or seal bore of cover. If removing cover, drain cooling system and remove water pump and power steering pump.

4) Remove fuel lines and fuel pump. Loosen lower oil pan-to-cover bolts and remove front bolts on each side of cover. Remove chain case cover and gasket using extreme caution to avoid damaging oil pan gasket.

Installation – 1) If installing front cover go to step **4)**. If only replacing seal, install new seal by installing threaded shaft part of Seal Installer (C-4251) into threads of crankshaft. Place seal into opening with seal spring towards inside of engine.

2) Place Installer Adapter (C-4251-3) with thrust bearing and nut on Seal Installer shaft. Tighten nut until tool is flush with timing chain cover. *See Fig. 4.* Seal surfaces on vibration damper must be free of varnish, dirt or nicks.

3) If necessary, use 400 grit paper to polish vibration damper. Lubricate seal and damper surfaces. Install vibration damper using Installer (C-3688). Install retainer bolt and washer and torque to specification.

NOTE: Timing cover oil seal may be installed in timing cover before installing on engine.

4) Ensure that mating surfaces of chain case cover and cylinder block are clean, dry and free from burrs. Install chain cover with new gasket to engine block. Apply 1/8" diameter bead of silicone sealer to oil pan gasket. Do not tighten chain case cover bolts at this time.

5) Lubricate lip of front seal with lubriplate and align vibration damper hub slot to crankshaft drive. Damper will act as a pilot for crankshaft seal. Place Installer (C-3688) in position and press vibration damper on crankshaft. Remove tool.

6) Install all cover bolts finger tight. Tighten front chain case cover bolts to specification first, then tighten lower oil pan bolts. Install vibration damper retainer bolt and washer and tighten to specification.

7) Install pulley to damper and tighten to specification. Install fuel pump, fuel lines and water pump housing assemblies using new gaskets. Install power steering pump, fan, belts and hoses. Reconnect battery and fill cooling system.

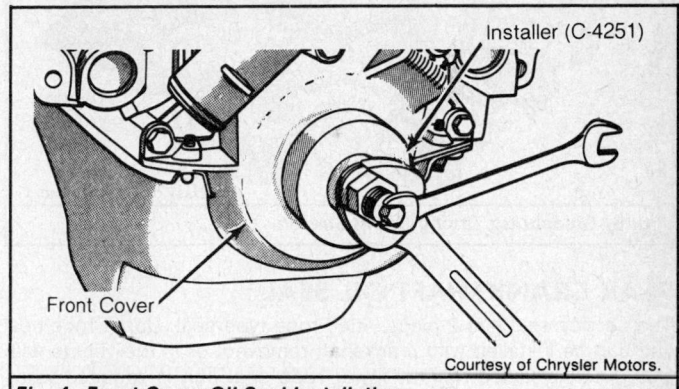

Fig. 4: Front Cover Oil Seal Installation

TIMING CHAIN

Removal – With front cover removed, align timing chain sprockets as shown in *See Fig. 5.* Remove camshaft sprocket attaching bolt, with washer and fuel pump eccentric. Remove timing chain with crankshaft and camshaft sprockets.

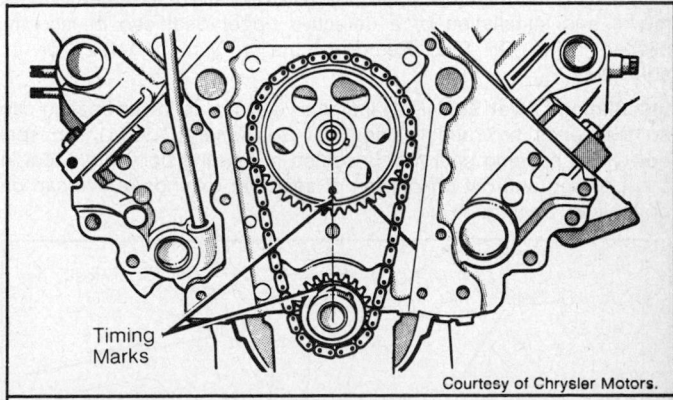

Fig. 5: Timing Chain Sprocket Alignment

Installation – 1) Place camshaft and crankshaft sprockets on bench with timing marks on imaginary centerline through bore of both sprockets. Place timing chain around both sprockets.

2) If necessary, turn crankshaft and camshaft to line up with keyway location in crankshaft sprocket and camshaft sprocket. Slide both sprockets evenly over their respective shafts, with new chain installed on sprockets.

3) Use a straightedge to measure alignment of timing marks. Install fuel pump eccentric, washer and camshaft sprocket bolt and tighten.

Chain Stretch Test – 1) Place a torque wrench and socket over camshaft sprocket bolt and apply 30 ft. lbs. (41 N.m) torque in direction of rotation with cylinder heads installed, or 15 ft. lbs. (20 N.m) with heads removed.

2) Block crankshaft to prevent rotation. Place scale next to chain link and apply 30 ft. lbs. (41 N.m) torque in reverse direction of rotation with heads installed, or 15 ft. lbs. (20 N.m) with heads removed. If there is more than 1/8" (3 mm) movement from original mark, replace chain. *See Fig. 6.*

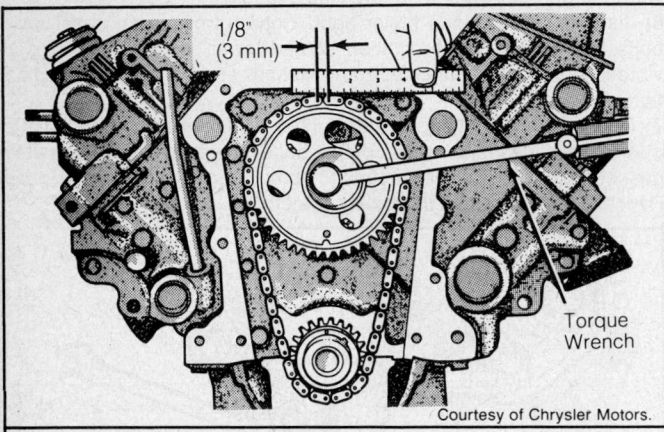

Fig. 6: Measuring Timing Chain Stretch

REAR CRANKSHAFT OIL SEAL

The service seal is a 2 piece, fitted rope type seal. Upper rope seal half can be installed with crankshaft removed, or in the vehicle with crankshaft installed. A new lower rope seal half is required when installing upper seal.

Installation Upper Seal (Crankshaft Removed) – 1) Install new rear bearing oil seal in cylinder block so that both ends protrude. Using Seal Positioner (C-3511) tap seal down into position until tool is seated in bearing bore.

2) Hold tool in this position and cut off portion of seal that extends below the block on both sides as shown in *Fig. 7*. Install crankshaft.

Removal & Installation Upper Seal (Crankshaft Installed) – Removal and installation of a defective upper seal can be accomplished using Oil Seal Remover/Installer Tool (KD-492), or its equivalent.

Installation Lower Seal – 1) Install a new seal in lower bearing cap so that ends protrude. Using Seal Positioner (C-3511), tap seal down into position until tool is seated in bearing bore. Hold tool in this position and cut off portion of seal that extends above cap on both sides. *See Fig. 7.*

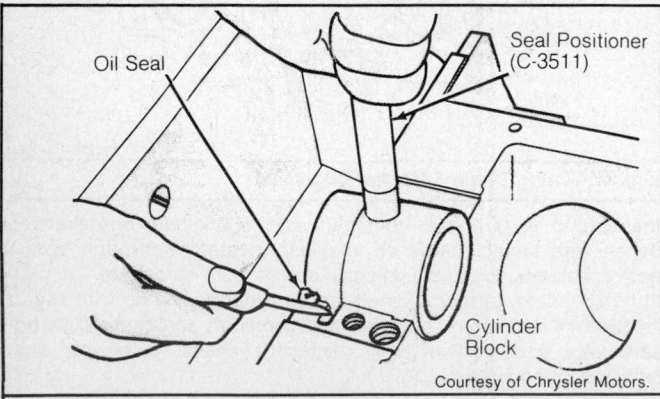

Fig. 7: Trimming Upper or Lower Oil Seal

2) Install cap seals into slots in bearing cap as shown in *Fig. 8*. If this is not done oil leakage will occur. Lightly oil seals with engine oil and assemble bearing cap to cylinder block. Install cleaned and oiled cap bolts and torque to specification.

3) If replacing seal in vehicle, reinstall oil pump and add sealer at bearing cap to block joint to provide sealing to oil pan end. Install clean oil pan with new gaskets and tighten bolts to specification.

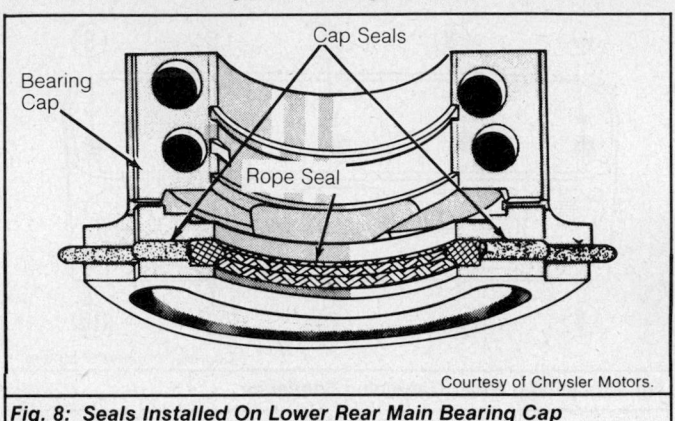

Fig. 8: Seals Installed On Lower Rear Main Bearing Cap

CAMSHAFT

Removal – 1) With engine removed from vehicle, remove rocker arm covers, intake manifold and front cover. Keeping all components in order, remove rocker arm assemblies, push rods, yoke retainer, lifter aligning yokes and lifters.

2) Remove the timing chain and sprockets, distributor with drive shaft, and thrust plate. Note location of oil tab before removing. Install long bolt into threaded hole of camshaft and remove camshaft.

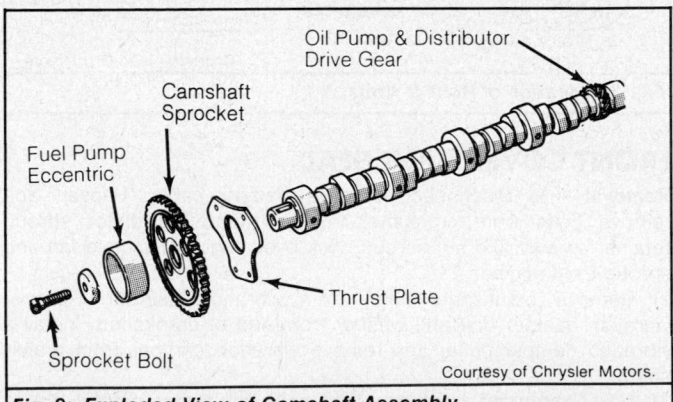

Fig. 9: Exploded View of Camshaft Assembly

Installation – Lubricate camshaft lobes and bearing journals. Insert camshaft to within 2" (50.8 mm) of its fully installed position in cylinder block. Install Camshaft Holder (C-3509) in distributor drive hole and hold in position using distributor retainer plate bolt. Install camshaft to proper depth. To complete installation, reverse removal procedure.

NOTE: Camshaft Holder (C-3509) will prevent camshaft from being pushed in too far and knocking out camshaft core plug. Leave tool installed until both sprockets and chain are secured.

WATER PUMP

Removal – 1) Drain cooling system. If equipped with air conditioning, remove shroud from radiator and position out of the way. Remove radiator and shroud.

2) Loosen alternator adjusting strap bolt and pivot bolt. Loosen power steering and air pumps (if equipped). Remove all drive belts. On engines without air conditioning, remove alternator bracket attaching bolts from water pump. Swing alternator out of the way and tighten pivot bolt.

3) On engines with air conditioning, remove alternator, adjusting bracket, and power steering pump attaching bolts. Set assembly to one side. Remove fan blade, spacer (or fluid unit), bolts and pulley as an assembly.

4) Disconnect heater and by-pass hoses. Remove air conditioning compressor pulley and field coil assembly. Remove water pump-to-compressor front mount bracket bolts and bracket. Remove pump retaining bolts and water pump assembly. Discard gasket and clean mating surfaces.

Installation – 1) Install water pump using a new gasket. Tighten pump bolts to 30 ft. lbs. (41 N.m). Install and position heater hoses, then tighten clamps. On engines without air conditioning, install alternator front braket and tighten to 30 ft. lbs. (41 N.m).

2) On engines with air conditioning, install compressor front bracket. Tighten compressor bracket bolts to 50 ft. lbs. (68 N.m) and water pump retainer bolts to 30 ft. lbs. (41 N.m). Install alternator, adjusting bracket and power steering pump. Tighten all bolts to 30 ft. lbs. (41 N.m). Install compressor clutch assembly.

3) Install fan, spacer (or fluid unit), pulley and bolts as an assembly. Install all belts and adjust belt tensions. Connect heater hose and install radiator. Refill cooling system.

OIL PAN

NOTE: See appropriate OIL PAN REMOVAL article in this section.

OVERHAUL

CYLINDER HEAD

Valve Guide Servicing – 1) Remove valve springs, retainers, locks and stem seals. Remove valves and keep in order for reinstallation in original location. Remove carbon and varnish accumulation from inside of valve guides.

2) Clean and inspect valves. If damaged or stem wear exceeds .002" (5 mm), replace valve. Install Sleeve (C-3973) over valve stem and install valve and sleeve together into guide bore.

3) Attach dial indicator to cylinder head and set it at right angle to valve stem being measured. *See Fig. 10.* Total side play should not exceed .017" (.431 mm).

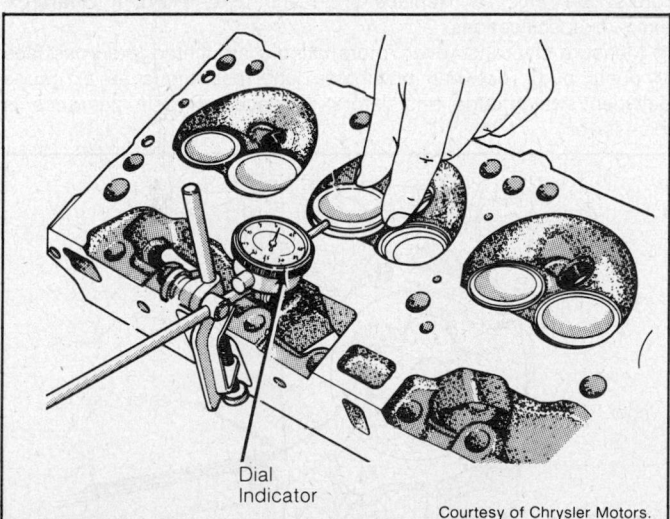

Fig. 10: *Measuring Valve Stem-to-Guide Clearance*

4) If reading is excessive or stems are scuffed or scored, ream guides for installation of valves with oversize stems. Replacement valves with oversized stems are available in .005" (.127 mm), .015" (.381 mm) and .030" (.762 mm) sizes.

NOTE: Do not attempt to ream guides from standard diameter to .030" (.076 mm) oversize in one step. Gradually increase reamer size to obtain the required diameter.

Valve Stem Oil Seals – Install new cup shields on all exhaust valves stems and seals over intake valve guides. Coat valve stems lightly with oil and insert in cylinder heads. Intake valve stem seals should be pushed firmly and squarely over valve guide using the valve stem as a guide. DO NOT force seal against top of guide. When installing valve retainer locks, compress the spring only enough to install locks.

Valve Spring Installed Height – 1) Valve springs must be square within .078" (1.98 mm). Installed height of springs is measured from bottom surface of spring seat in cylinder head, to bottom surface of spring retainer. If spacers are installed, measure from top of spacer surface.

2) If installed spring height is greater than maximum allowable, install spacers in increments of .063" (1.60 mm) into head counterbore to bring spring height back to normal. If spacers are installed, measure from top of spacer.

VALVE SPRING INSTALLED HEIGHT

Application	In. (mm)
Spring Height [1]	1.625-1.688 (41.27-42.86)

[1] – Measured from spring seat, to retainer.

VALVE TRAIN

Rocker Arm Shaft Assembly – Rocker arms are stamped steel type and identified as right or left. Design difference between rocker arms is in the outward position of the push rod cavity and valve contact pad. *See Fig. 11.*

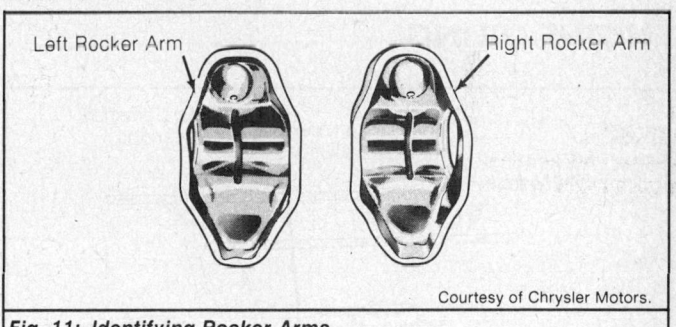

Fig. 11: *Identifying Rocker Arms*

VALVES

Removal – With cylinder head removed, compress valve springs using a valve spring compressor. Remove valve retaining locks, retainers, valve springs, valves and cup seals.

Installation – To install, reverse removal procedure. Compress spring only enough to install valve retaining locks. If valves or seats are reground, check valve stem height with Valve Gauge (C-396B) as shown in *See Fig. 12.* If valve is too long, grind off tip until length is within limits marked on gauge. Check valve spring installed height.

CYLINDER BLOCK ASSEMBLY

Piston & Rod Assembly – Notch on top of piston must face toward front of engine and larger chamfer of connecting rod bore must be positioned toward crankshaft journal fillet.

Fitting Pistons – When measuring, each piston should be measured 90 degrees to piston pin axis at top of skirt. Measure cylinder bore halfway down at 90 degrees to crankshaft center line. Pistons and cylinder bores should be measured at normal room temperature, 70°F (21°C).

1989 CHRYSLER MOTORS ENGINES
5.2L V8 (Cont.)

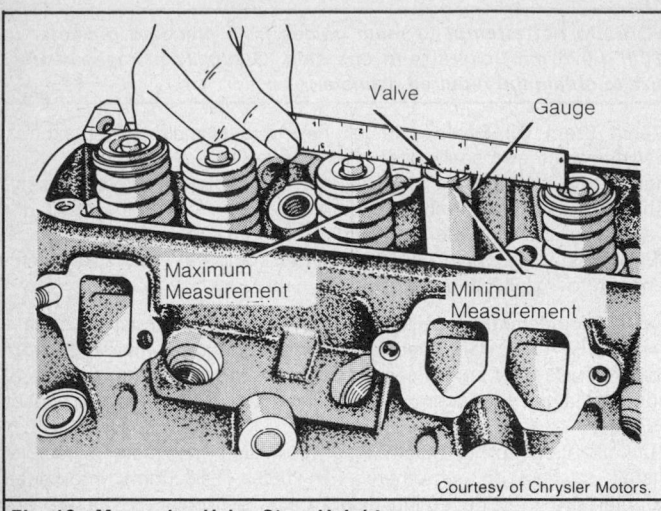

Fig. 12: Measuring Valve Stem Height

Crankshaft Main & Rod Bearings – Use Plastigage method to check main bearing and rod bearing clearances. Measure clearance by loosening each bearing cap, one at a time, while all others remain tight. If clearance is not within specifications, replace bearing insert. New bearing inserts are available in standard and .001", .002", .003", .010" and .012" undersize.

NOTE: When assembled to pistons correctly, rods are not interchangeable from one bank to another. Fit all rod and piston assemblies to one bank until completed, before continuing to next bank.

ENGINE OILING

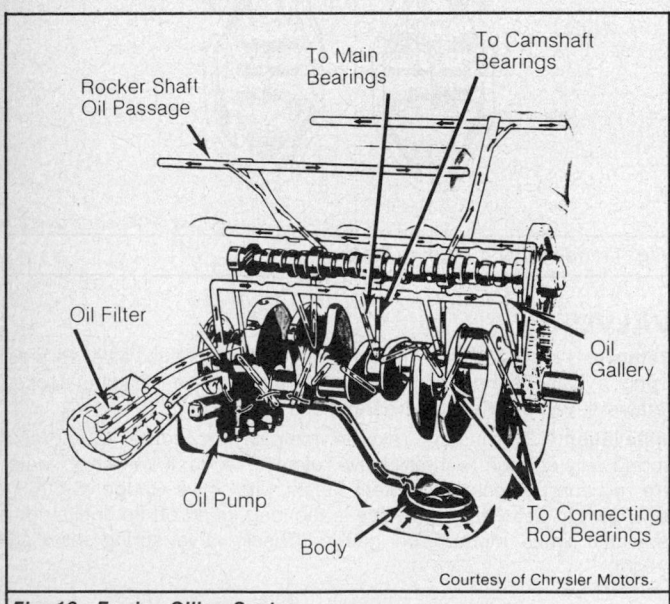

Fig. 13: Engine Oiling System

LUBRICATION SYSTEM

Oil Pump – Engine oiling system is a full pressure type. Oil pressure is supplied by a rotor type oil pump that is driven by the distributor driveshaft. Oil pump is bolted to bottom of rear main bearing cap and is internally regulated.

Crankcase Capacity – Engine crankcase capacity is 4 qts. (3.8L). Add 1 qt. (.9L) with filter change.

Oil Pressure (Hot) – Normal oil pressure is 30-80 psi (2.1-5.6 kg/cm²) @ 3000 RPM.

OIL PUMP

Removal & Disassembly – **1)** With oil pan removed, remove pump retaining bolts and pump from main bearing cap. Remove cotter pin from pump housing. Drill a .125" (3.17 mm) hole into the relief valve retainer cap.

2) Insert a sheet metal screw into the cap. While holding pump, clamp the screw into a vise. Using a shoft hammer, tap on pump body until retainer cap is pulled from body. Remove relief valve and spring from pump body.

3) Remove pump cover retaining bolts and cover. Remove inner rotor, shaft, and outer rotor. Wash all parts in solvent and inspect for wear or damage.

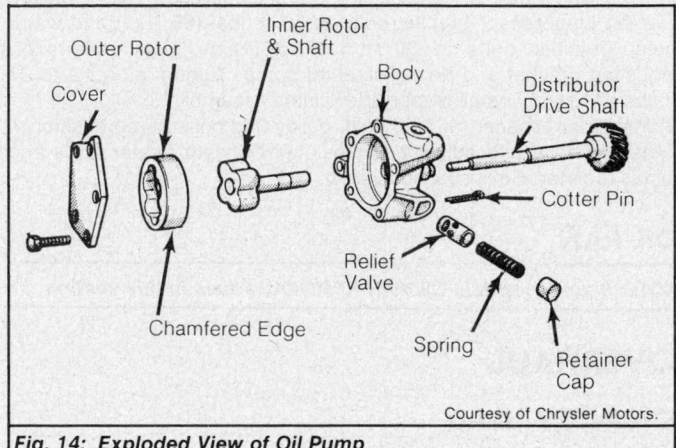

Fig. 14: Exploded View of Oil Pump

Inspection – **1)** Measure pump cover wear using a straightedge and feeler gauge. Replace pump if wear exceeds specifications or if mating surfaces are scratched or grooved.

2) Measure outer rotor thickness and diameter. Replace rotor if either is less than specifications. Measure inner rotor thickness and replace rotor and shaft assembly if less than specifications.

3) Measure outer rotor-to-body clearance and replace pump assembly if clearance is excessive. Measure clearance between rotors. See Fig. 15. Replace shaft and both rotors if clearance exceeds specifications.

4) Measure clearance over rotors using a straightedge across face of pump body, between bolt holes, and inserting a feeler gauge between straightedge and rotors. Replace pump if clearance is excessive.

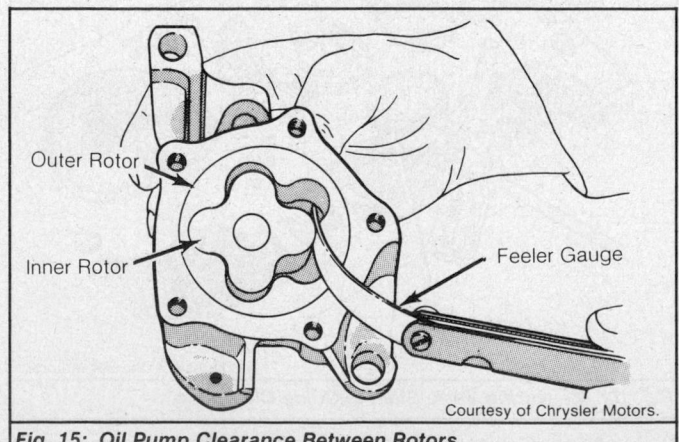

Fig. 15: Oil Pump Clearance Between Rotors

Reassembly & Installation – **1)** Reverse removal procedure to complete reassembly. Prime the pump by filling rotor cavity with oil while rotating pump shaft. Place pump on engine, install retaining bolts and tighten to specification.

2) Pressure relief valve spring has free length of 2.031-2.047" (51.59-51.99 mm). Spring should test 16.2-17.2 lbs. (7.3-7.8 kg) when compressed to 1.344" (32.13 mm).

OIL PUMP SPECIFICATIONS

Application	In. (mm)
Clearance Between Rotors	¹ .010 (.25)
Clearance Over Inner Rotor	¹ .004 (.10)
Clearance Over Outer Rotor	¹ .004 (.10)
Inner Rotor Thickness	² .825 (20.95)
Oil Pump Cover	¹ .0015 (.003)
Outer Rotor Diameter	² 2.469 (62.71)
Outer Rotor-To-Body Clearance	¹ .014 (35)

¹ – Maximum.
² – Minimum.

TIGHTENING SPECIFICATIONS

Application	Ft. Lbs. (N.m)
Camshaft Sprocket Bolt	50 (68)
Camshaft Thrust Plate Bolts	18 (24)
Connecting Rod Cap Nut	45 (61)
Crankshaft Bolts	100 (136)
Cylinder Head Bolts	
Step 1	50 (68)
Step 2	105 (143)
Exhaust Manifold	
Bolts	20 (27)
Nut	15 (20)
Flex Plate-to-Converter Bolts	23 (31)
Flex Plate-to-Crankshaft Bolts	55 (75)
Front (Timing Chain) Cover Bolts	35 (47)
Intake Manifold Bolts	
Step 1	25 (34)
Step 2	40 (54)
Step 3	45 (61)
Main Bearing Cap Bolts	85 (115)
Oil Pan Bolts	17 (23)
Oil Pump Attaching Bolts	30 (41)
Rocker Shaft Bracket Bolt	17 (23)
Vibration Damper Nut	100 (136)
Water Pump Bolts	30 (41)

	INCH Lbs. (N.m)
Oil Pump Cover Bolts	95 (11)
Rocker Arm Cover Bolts	95 (11)

ENGINE SPECIFICATIONS

GENERAL SPECIFICATIONS

Year	Displacement		Fuel System	HP@RPM	Torque Ft. Lbs. @RPM	Compr. Ratio	Bore		Stroke	
	Cu. In.	Liters					In.	mm	In.	mm
1989										
Std.	318	5.2	2-Bbl	140@3600	265@2000	9.0:1	3.91	99.3	3.31	8.4
H.P.	318	5.2	4-Bbl	175@4000	250@3200	8.4:1	3.91	99.3	3.31	8.4

CRANKSHAFT, MAIN & CONNECTING ROD BEARINGS

Engine	Crankshaft				Main Bearings		Connecting Rod Bearings	
	End Play In. (mm)	Runout In. (mm)	Journal Taper In. (mm)	Journal Out-of-Round In. (mm)	Journal Diameter In. (mm)	Oil Clearance In. (mm)	Journal Diameter In. (mm)	Oil Clearance In. (mm)
5.2L	.002-.009 (.05-.22)	.....	.001 (.025)	.001 (.025)	2.499-2.500 (63.47-63.50)	.005-.002 (.127-.055)	2.124-2.125 (53.94-53.97)	.0005-.0025 (.012-.063)

CONNECTING RODS

Engine	Side Play In. (mm)	Max. Bend & Twist In. (mm)	Pin Bore Dia. In. (mm)	Large Bore Dia. In. (mm)	Center-to-Center In. (mm)
5.2L	.006-.014 (.15-25.4)	.....	.9819-.9834 (24.940-24.978)	.....	.....

1989 CHRYSLER MOTORS ENGINES
5.2L V8 (Cont.)

ENGINE SPECIFICATIONS (Cont.)

PISTONS, PINS & RINGS

| Engine | Pistons | | Pins | | | Rings | | |
	Clearance In. (mm)	Diameter In. (mm)	Diameter In. (mm)	Piston Fit In. (mm)	Rod Fit In. (mm)	Ring No.	End Gap In. (mm)	Side Clearance In. (mm)
5.2L	.0005-.0015 (.012-.038)	....	.9841-.9843 (24.996-25.001)	.00025-.0075 (.0063-.0190)	Press Fit	1 & 2	.010-.020 .254-.508	.0015-.0030 (.038-.076)
						3	.015-.055 (.381-1.40)	.0002-.0050 (.005-.127)

VALVES & VALVE SPRINGS

| Engine | Valves | | | | | Valves Springs | | | | |
	Head Dia. In. (mm)	Stem Dia. In. (mm)	Face Angle	Min. Margin In. (mm)	Max. Refinish In. (mm)	Free Length In. (mm)	Out-of-Square In. (mm)	Installed Height In. (mm)	Pressure Lbs. @ In. (Kg @ mm) Valve Closed	Valve Open
5.2L Std. Intake	1.78 (45.2)	.372-.373 (9.44-9.47)	45°	.031 (.79)	.....	2.00 (50.8)	.063 (1.6)	1.63-1.69 (41.3-42.9)	78-88@1.69 (35-40@42.8)	170-184@1.31 (77-83@33.4)
Exhaust	1.50 (38.1)	.371-.372 (9.42-9.44)	45°	.047 (1.19)	.....	2.00 (50.8)	.063 (1.6)	1.63-1.69 (41.3-42.9)	78-88@1.69 (35-40@42.8)	170-184@1.31 (77-83@33.4)
5.2L H.P. Intake	1.88 (47.8)	.372-.373 (9.43-9.46)	45°	.031 (.79)	.....	2.10 (53.3)	.080 (2.03)	1.63-1.69 (41.3-42.9)	108-118@1.66 (49-54@42.1)	186-200@1.25 (84-91@31.8)
Exhaust	1.60 (40.6)	.371-.372 (9.41-9.43)	45°	.047 (1.19)	.....	2.10 (53.3)	.080 (2.03)	1.63-1.69 (41.3-42.9)	108-118@1.66 (49-54@42.1)	186-200@1.25 (84-91@31.8)

CYLINDER HEAD

| Engine | Max. Cylinder Head Warp In. (mm) | Valve Seats | | | | Valve Guides | | |
		Seat Angle	Maximum Runout In. (mm)	Seat Width In. (mm)	Seat Bore Diameter In. (mm)	Valve Stem Oil Clearance In. (mm)	Valve Guide I.D. In. (mm)	Valve Guide Bore I.D. In. (mm)
5.2L Intake	[1] .00075 (.019)	45°	.002 (.05)	.065-.085 (1.65-2.15)	.....	[2] .001-.003 (.03-.08)	.....	.374-.375 (9.49-9.52)
Exhaust		45°	.002 (.05)	.080-.100 (2.03-2.54)	.....	[2] .002-.004 (.05-.10)	.....	.374-.375 (9.49-9.52)

[1] – Not to exceed this amount per inch of measured area.
[2] – On H.P. engine, valve stem oil clearance is .0025-.0045" (.063-.114 mm).

CAMSHAFT

Engine	Journal Diameter In. (mm)	Oil Clearance In. (mm)	Bearing Bore In. (mm)	Runout In. (mm)	End Play In. (mm)	Lobe Lift In. (mm)	Lobe Height In. (mm)
5.2L No. 1	1.998-1.999 (50.74-50.77)	.001-.003 (.025-.076)	2.000-2.001 (50.80-50.82)	.....	.002-.010 (.050-.254)	.....	.....
No. 2	1.982-1.983 (50.34-50.36)	.001-.003 (.025-.076)	1.984-1.985 (50.39-50.41)				
No. 3	1.967-1.968 (49.96-49.98)	.001-.003 (.025-.076)	1.969-1.970 (50.01-50.03)				
No. 4	1.951-1.952 (49.55-49.58)	.001-.003 (.025-.076)	1.953-1.954 (49.60-49.63)				
No. 5	1.561-1.562 (39.36-39.66)	.001-.003 (.025-.076)	1.563-1.564 (39.68-39.71)				

ENGINE SPECIFICATIONS (Cont.)

VALVE LIFTERS

Engine	Diameter In. (mm)	Bore Diameter In. (mm)	Oil Clearance In. (mm)
5.2L	.9035-.9040 (22.948-22.961)	.9048-.9059 (22.981-23.009)	.0008-.0024 (.020-.060)

CYLINDER BLOCK

Engine	Max. Block Warp In. (mm)	Cylinder Bore		
		Standard Diameter In. (mm)	Maximum Taper In. (mm)	Maximum Out-of-Rnd In. (mm)
5.2L	.....	3.910-3.912 (99.31-99.36)	.010 (.254)	.005 (.127)

1989 EAGLE ENGINES
2.5L 4-Cylinder

Premier

NOTE: For engine repair procedures not covered in this article, see ENGINE OVERHAUL PROCEDURES article at beginning of this section.

ENGINE IDENTIFICATION

Engine may be identified by Vehicle Identification Number (VIN) attached to instrument panel on driver's side and visible through windshield. The VIN contains 17 characters. The 8th character identifies the engine and the 10th character identifies the model year.

ENGINE IDENTIFICATION CODE

Engine	Code
2.5L (150") TBI	H

SPECIAL ENGINE MARKS

Some engines may be manufactured with oversize or undersize components as follows: Cylinder bores, camshaft bearing bores, main bearing journals and connecting rod journals. These are identified by a letter code stamped on the side of block, below No. 4 cylinder spark plug. *See Fig. 1.* Use this code to obtain proper parts. See OVERSIZE/UNDERSIZE CODES table in this article.

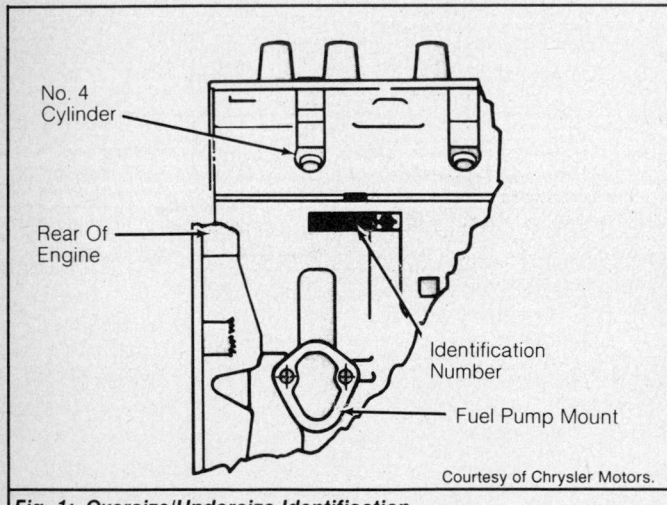

Courtesy of Chrysler Motors.

Fig. 1: Oversize/Undersize Identification

OVERSIZE/UNDERSIZE CODES

Code	Component
P	1 or More Connecting Rod
M	All Main Bearing Journals
PM	All Main Bearing Journals & 1 or More Connecting Rod
B	All Cylinder Bores
C	All Camshaft Bearing Bores

ADJUSTMENTS

VALVE ARRANGEMENT

E-I-I-E-E-I-I-E (Front-to-rear).

VALVE CLEARANCE ADJUSTMENT

There are no adjustments necessary for the 2.5L engine.

REMOVAL & INSTALLATION

NOTE: For reassembly reference, label all electrical connectors, vacuum hoses and fuel lines prior to removal. Match mark engine hood and all other major components prior to removal.

ENGINE

NOTE: See ENGINE REMOVAL & INSTALLATION article at end of ENGINE section.

FUEL PRESSURE RELEASE

Fuel pressure must be released prior to disconnecting any fuel lines or hoses. Remove fuel filler cap. Disconnect fuel pump/sender connector. Connector is located between fuel filter and fuel tank, next to the vapor hose "Y". Start engine and run until engine stalls.

INTAKE/EXHAUST MANIFOLD ASSEMBLY

1) Release fuel pressure as previously described. Disconnect negative battery cable and drain cooling system. Remove air inlet hose from throttle body and air cleaner assembly. Loosen accessory belts. Remove power steering belt. Remove power steering pump and brackets and set aside.

2) Wrap shop raps around fuel lines prior to disconnecting. Disconnect Black fuel supply tube and Gray fuel return tube from throttle body by squeezing retaining tabs and pulling. Disconnect throttle cable from throttle body. Using your fingers only, remove cruise control connector at throttle body.

3) Mark and disconnect necessary electrical connectors. Pull wiring harness away from manifold. Mark and disconnect vacuum hoses as necessary. Loosen EGR tube nut at intake manifold and bolts securing EGR tube to exhaust manifold. Remove heater hoses from front and rear of intake manifold.

4) Separate inlet pipe from exhaust manifold. Starting from center and working evenly outward, remove intake/exhaust manifold bolts. Remove intake/exhaust manifold as an assembly. Remove gaskets. Separate intake and exhaust manifold by removing EGR tube. *See Fig. 2.*

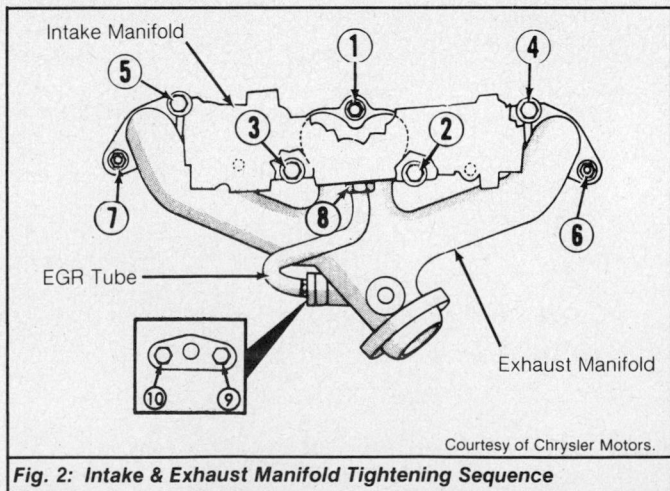

Courtesy of Chrysler Motors.

Fig. 2: Intake & Exhaust Manifold Tightening Sequence

Installation – Clean all gasket mating surfaces. Replace gaskets and exhaust manifold alignment spacers. Install intake manifold gasket on cylinder head. Install intake/exhaust manifold assembly. Install bolts and tighten finger tight. Install new EGR gasket and attach EGR tube to exhaust manifold. Tighten intake/exhaust manifold bolts in sequence to specifications. *See Fig. 2.* To complete installation, reverse removal procedure.

VALVE COVER & ROCKER ARMS

NOTE: Lifters may be removed without removing cylinder head.

Removal & Installation – 1) Remove heater hose holders from valve cover. Mark and disconnect vacuum hose from valve cover. Remove valve cover bolts, valve cover and gasket. Remove bolts retaining bridge, pivot and rocker arms. Keeping components together, remove rocker arms and push rods.

2) Lubricate components with oil conditioner during installation. To install, reverse removal procedure. Tighten rocker arm bolts evenly, one turn at a time.

CYLINDER HEAD

NOTE: Cylinder head should only be removed when engine is cold.

Removal – 1) Disconnect negative battery cable and drain cooling system. Remove accessory belts. With hoses attached, remove accessories and brackets. Remove coolant hoses thermostat housing.

2) Mark and disconnect necessary electrical connectors and vacuum hoses. Remove valve cover, rocker arms and push rods as previously described. Remove intake/exhaust manifolds as previously described.

3) If cylinder head bolts have NEVER been removed, apply paint to top of bolts to ensure bolts are discarded next time. If bolts have paint on top or you are not sure of previous removal, discard head bolts. Remove cylinder head bolts, and keep in order to ensure bolt location.

4) Remove cylinder head assembly. If prying is necessary, use a screwdriver at boss in front of engine. Use care not to damage gasket mating surfaces. Remove and discard cylinder head gasket.

Inspection – Clean all gasket mating surfaces. Remove all carbon deposits from cylinder head combustion chambers. Check cylinder head gasket surfaces for warpage. If not within specifications, machine or replace cylinder head. See ENGINE SPECIFICATIONS tables at end of this article.

NOTE: Cylinder head gasket is a composition type. DO NOT use gasket sealer. Gasket must be installed dry.

Installation – 1) Install dowels in bolt hole Nos. 8 and 10. *See Fig. 3.* Place head gasket on cylinder block with numbers facing up. Install cylinder head on block. Coat threads of head bolt No. 7 with Loctite PST sealant. Install head bolts, except Nos. 8 and 10.

2) Remove dowels and install Nos. 8 and 10 cylinder head bolt. Tighten bolts in sequence to specifications. See TIGHTENING SPECIFICATIONS table in this article. *See Fig. 3.* To complete installation, reverse removal procedure.

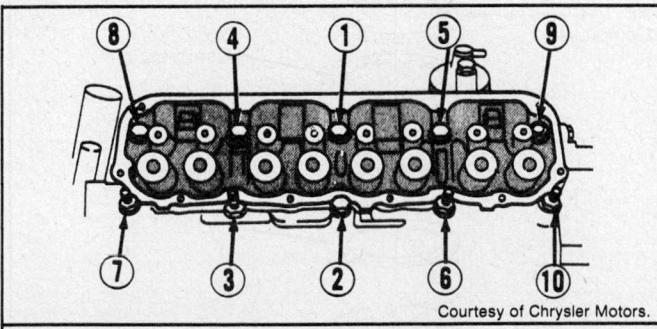

Fig. 3: Cylinder Head Tightening Sequence

CAUTION: Rotate crankshaft in direction of normal operation only.

CRANKSHAFT FRONT SEAL

Removal & Installation – Disconnect negative battery cable. Remove accessory belts. Remove cooling fan and shroud. Remove vibration damper bolt and washer. Using a universal puller, remove vibration damper. Remove seal with a front cover seal remover. Apply sealer to outer diameter of seal and engine oil to crankshaft. Install seal with Front Timing Cover Alignment and Seal Installer (6139). To complete installation, reverse removal procedure.

FRONT TIMING COVER

Removal – 1) Disconnect negative battery cable. Remove accessory belts. Remove cooling fan and shroud. Remove vibration damper bolt and washer. Using a universal puller, remove vibration damper. Remove water pump pulley. Remove accessories and brackets as necessary.

2) Remove oil pan-to-front timing cover bolts. Remove front timing cover-to-cylinder block bolts. Remove front timing cover and gaskets. Remove crankshaft oil seal.

Installation – 1) Cut protuding portion of oil pan gasket flush with block face. Apply sealing compound to both sides of timing cover gasket and position gasket on cylinder block. Cut new gasket to fit removed portion of oil pan gasket and cement in position.

2) Apply a liberal amount of sealer to oil pan front seal tabs and position oil pan seal on front timing cover. Apply engine oil to seal lip on oil pan. Replace crankshaft front oil seal and lubricate seal lip. Position front timing cover to cylinder block.

3) Install Front Timing Cover Alignment and Seal Installer (6139). Install front timing cover bolts and tighten to specifications. Remove alignment tool and use it to install a new crankshaft seal. To complete installation, reverse removal procedure.

CAUTION: Rotate crankshaft in direction of normal operation only.

TIMING CHAIN & GEARS

NOTE: To remove timing chain tensioner, oil pan must be removed.

Removal – Remove front timing cover as previously described. Rotate crankshaft and align timing marks on camshaft and crankshaft gears. *See Fig. 4.* Note position of oil slinger and remove. Turn timing chain tensioner lever in unlock (down) position and push in on tensioner block. Hold block in and turn tensioner lever to lock (up) position. Remove camshaft gear bolt and washer. Remove camshaft gear, chain and crankshaft gear as an assembly.

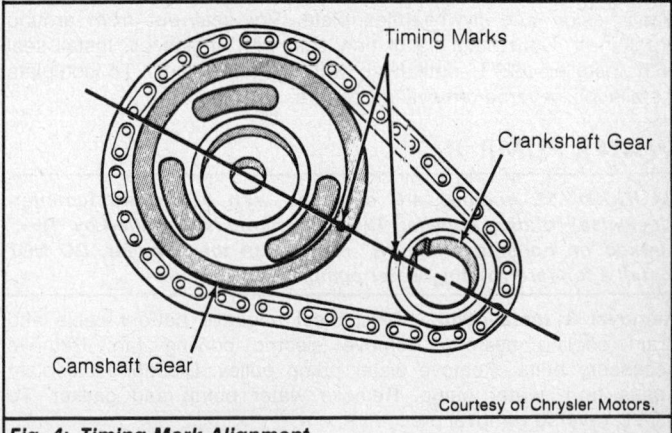

Fig. 4: Timing Mark Alignment

Installation – 1) Ensure tensioner block is retracted. Align timing marks on camshaft and crankshaft gears. *See Fig. 4.* Install chain and gears as an assembly. Install camshaft gear bolt and washer.

2) Rotate crankshaft and position camshaft gear timing mark at 1 o'clock. The crankshaft gear key way should be at 3 o'clock position. *See Fig. 5.* Count number of chain pins as shown. There must be 20 pins.

3) With timing chain properly installed, release timing chain tensioner. Tensioner must be in unlock position for proper operation. To complete installation, reverse removal procedure.

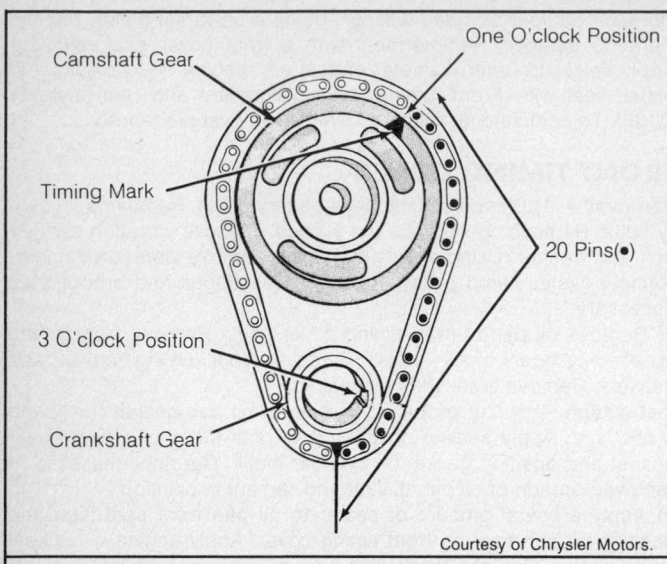

Fig. 5: Verifying Timing Chain & Gear installation

CAMSHAFT

Removal & Installation – 1) Disconnect negative battery cable and drain cooling system. Remove radiator and A/C condenser (if equipped). Position timing mark at TDC of compression stroke. Match mark distributor housing-to-rotor and to-cylinder block. Remove distributor and spark plug wires.

2) Remove valve cover, rocker arms, push rods, lifters and timing chain and gears as previously described. Pull camshaft out front of engine. Lubricate camshaft with Mopar oil supplement. To install, reverse removal procedure.

Inspection – Check camshaft lobes and journals for wear. Check distributor drive gear. Check camshaft bearing clearance. If camshaft bearings need replacing, engine must be removed from vehicle.

REAR MAIN BEARING OIL SEAL

Removal & Installation – Rear main seal is a one-piece. Remove transmission and flywheel/flex plate. Pry seal out from around crankshaft. Coat outer lip of new seal with engine oil. Install seal with Installer (6271) until flush with cylinder block. To complete installation, reverse removal procedure.

WATER PUMP

CAUTION: 2.5L engines are equipped with a reverse (counter-clockwise) rotating impeller. The water pump is identified by "REV" marked on housing or an "R" marked on the impeller. DO NOT install a forward rotating water pump.

Removal & Installation – Disconnect negative battery cable and drain cooling system. Remove electric cooling fan. Remove accessory belts. Remove water pump pulley. Disconnect coolant hoses from water pump. Remove water pump and gasket. To install, reverse removal procedure.

OIL PAN

NOTE: See appropriate OIL PAN REMOVAL article in this section.

OIL PUMP

Removal & Installation – Remove oil pan. See appropriate OIL PAN REMOVAL article in this section. Remove oil pump attaching bolts. Remove oil pump. Oil pump is replaced as complete assembly only. See OIL PUMP under OVERHAUL for inspection. If oil pump

inlet tube and strainer assembly is moved within oil pump body, a replacement tube and strainer must be installed to assure an airtight seal. To install, reverse removal procedure.

OVERHAUL

NOTE: Keep components together to ensure installation to original location and position.

CYLINDER HEAD

Valve Springs & Seals – These components may be replaced with cylinder head installed on engine, using compressed air method. Intake and exhaust valve seals are not interchangeable.

Valve Guides – Valve guides are an integral part of cylinder head and are not replaceable. If guide-to-valve clearance is excessive, ream guide to fit available oversize valve. Oversize valve seals must be used with valves having .015" (.38 mm) oversize stems. If proper clearance cannot be achieved with oversize valve, cylinder head must be replaced.

Valve Seat – Valve seat replacement information is not available from manufacturer. Service valve seats after valve guide service.

Valves – After valve service, check valve margin. Replace valve if worn beyond specifications. Valve stems may be resurfaced and rechamfered when worn. Do not remove more than .01" (.3 mm) from valve stem.

CYLINDER BLOCK ASSEMBLY

Inspection – Check block for cylinder head gasket surface warpage. Check cylinder bores for wear, taper, out-of-round and piston fit. Machine or replace as necessary. See ENGINE SPECIFICATIONS table at end of this article. DO NOT use rigid-type hones to remove glaze on cylinder wall.

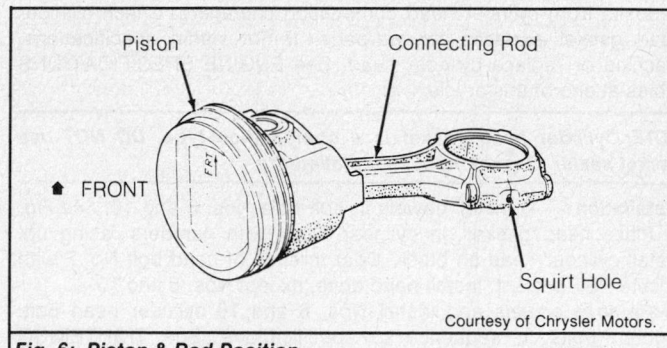

Fig. 6: Piston & Rod Position

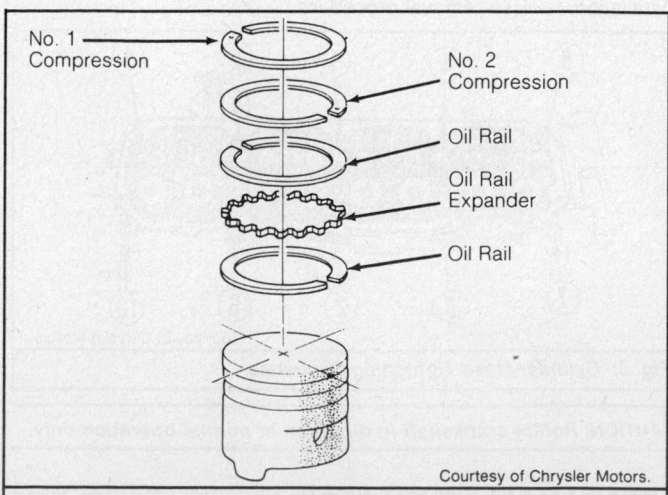

Fig. 7: Piston Ring End Gap Position

Crankshaft	Corresponding Connecting Rod Bearing Insert Color Code	
Color Code and Diameter inches (Journal Size)	Upper Insert Size	Lower Insert Size
Yellow — 53.2257-53.2079 mm 2.0955-2.0948 inch Standard	Yellow — Standard	Yellow — Standard
Orange — 53.2079-53.1901 mm 2.0948-2.0941 inch Undersize (0.0178 mm or 0.0007 inch)	Yellow — Standard	Black — Undersize 0.025 mm 0.001 inch
Black — 53.1901-53.1723 mm 2.0941-2.0933 inch Undersize (0.0356 mm or 0.0014 inch)	Black — Undersize 0.025 mm 0.001 inch	Black — Undersize 0.025 mm 0.001 inch
Red — 53.9717-53.9539 mm 2.0855-2.0848 inch Undersize (0.254 mm or 0.010 inch)	Red — Undersize 0.254 mm 0.001 inch	Red — Undersize 0.254 mm 0.001 inch

Courtesy of Chrysler Motors.

Fig. 8: Rod Bearing Identification & Selection

Piston & Rod Assembly – Ensure pistons and rods are marked with cylinder number prior to removal. Ensure arrow on piston top faces front of engine. *See Fig. 6.* Match mark piston-to-rod prior to disassembly. Piston pin must be pressed out of piston and rod. See ENGINE SPECIFICATIONS tables at end of this article.

Piston Rings – Check end gap and side clearance of rings. Replace piston and/or rings as necessary. See ENGINE SPECIFICATIONS tables at end of this article. Properly position ring end gaps on piston. *See Fig. 7.* Piston rings are marked with a dot facing upward when installed on piston. One dot is No. 1 compression ring and 2 dots is No. 2 compression ring.

Fitting Pistons – Check piston-to-bore clearance. Machine or replace with oversize pistons as necessary. See ENGINE SPECIFICATIONS tables at end of this article.

Connecting Rod Bearing – Each rod bearing insert is select fit from factory using different sizes of bearing inserts. A color code is on the edge of bearing insert. Crankshaft rod journal is color coded on the adjacent counterweight toward rear of crankshaft. Use color code chart to obtain a proper fitting bearing. *See Fig. 8.*

Crankshaft & Main Bearings – 1) Main bearing caps are marked with journal number. An arrow is used to indicate engine front to ensure caps are installed properly. Crankshaft end play is controlled by No. 2 main bearing journal by means of a thrust bearing.
2) Main bearing journal size is identified by a color coded paint on adjacent counterweight toward rear of crankshaft with the exception of rear main bearing. Rear main bearing color code is on crankshaft rear flange. Main bearing insert is color coded on its edge.
3) Use the MAIN BEARING FITTING CHART to determine and select necessary replacement bearings. *See Fig. 9.* If paint codes are not present or visible crankshaft journals must be measured.

Thrust Bearing – 1) Install all main bearing caps. Tighten cap Nos. 1, 3, 4 and 5 to 40 ft. lbs. (54 N.m). Tighten again to 70 ft. lbs. (95 N.m). Final tighten to 80 ft. lbs. (109 N.m).

2) Push crankshaft forward and rearward. Load crankshaft either front or rear and tighten cap No. 2 using same 3 steps to tighen cap Nos. 1, 3, 4, and 5. Check end play and replace thrust bearing as necessary.

ENGINE OILING

ENGINE LUBRICATING SYSTEM

Crankcase Capacity – Crankcase capacity is 4 qts. (3.8L) without filter change and 5 qts. (4.7L) with filter change.
Normal Oil Pressure – At idle speed, engine oil pressure should be 25-35 psi (1.8-2.5 kg/cm). At 1600 RPM or more, oil pressure should be 37-75 psi (2.6-5.3 kg/cm).

OIL PUMP

Inspection – 1) Remove oil pump cover bolts and remove cover. Measure end clearance and gear-to-body clearance. If not within specifications, replace oil pump assembly. See OIL PUMP SPECIFICATIONS table in this article.
2) If inlet tube and strainer assembly was moved in oil pump body, install a replacement inlet tube and strainer assembly. Apply a light film of Permatex No. 2 sealant around tube end. Drive tube into body with Installer (7624). Ensure tube is positioned properly for mounting. Fill gear cavity with petroleum jelly for self-priming. Apply a thin bead of Loctite (515) to housing cover surface.

OIL PUMP SPECIFICATIONS

Application	In. (mm)
Gear-to-Body	.002-.004 (.05-.10)
Gear End Clearance	
Using Plastigage	.002-.006 (.05-.15)
Using Feeler Gauge	.004-.008 (.10-.20)

1989 EAGLE ENGINES
2.5L 4-Cylinder (Cont.)

NO. 1 JOURNAL

Crankshaft No. 1 Main Bearing Journal Color Codes and Diameter In Inches (mm)	Cylinder Block No. 1 Main Bearing Bore Color Code and Size In Inches (mm)	Bearing Insert Color Code	
		Upper Insert Size	Lower Insert Size
Yellow — 2.5001 to 2.4996 (Standard) (63.5025 to 63.4898 mm)	Yellow — 2.6910 to 2.6915 (68.3514 to 68.3641 mm)	Yellow — Standard	Yellow — Standard
	Black — 2.6915 to 2.6920 (68.3641 to 68.3768 mm)	Yellow — Standard	Black — 0.001-Inch Undersize (0.025 mm)
Orange — 2.4996 to 2.4991 (0.0005 Undersize) (63.4898 to 63.4771 mm)	Yellow — 2.6910 to 2.6915 (68.3514 to 68.3641 mm)	Yellow — Standard	Black — 0.001-Inch Undersize — (0.001 mm)
	Black — 2.6915 to 2.6920 (68.3461 to 68.3768 mm)	Black — 0.001-Inch Undersize (0.025 mm)	Black — 0.001-Inch Undersize (0.025 mm)
Black — 2.4991 to 2.4986 (0.001 Undersize) (63.4771 to 63.4644 mm)	Yellow — 2.6910 to 2.6915 (68.3514 to 68.3641 mm)	Black — 0.001-Inch Undersize — (0.025mm)	Black — 0.001-Inch Undersize — (0.025 mm)
	Black — 2.6915 to 2.6920 (68.3461 to 68.3768 mm)	Black — 0.001-Inch Undersize (0.025 mm)	Green — 0.002-Inch Undersize (0.051 mm)
Green — 2.4986 to 2.4981 (0.0015 Undersize) (63.4644 to 63.4517 mm)	Yellow — 2.6910 to 2.6915 (68.3514 to 68.3641 mm)	Black — 0.001-Inch Undersize — (0.025 mm)	Green — 0.002-Inch Undersize (0.051 mm)
Red — 2.4901 to 2.4896 (0.010 Undersize) (63.2485 to 63.2358 mm)	Yellow — 2.6910 to 2.6915 (68.3514 to 68.3641 mm)	Red — 0.010-Inch Undersize (0.254 mm)	Red — 0.010-Inch Undersize — (0.254 mm)

NOTE: With Green and Red Coded Crankshaft Journals, Use Yellow Coded Cylinder Block Bores Only.

NOS. 2-5 JOURNALS

Crankshaft Main Bearing Journal 2-3-4-5 Color Code and Diameter In Inches (Journal Size)	Bearing Insert Color Code	
	Upper Insert Size	Lower Insert Size
Yellow — 2.5001 to 2.4996 (Standard) (63.5025 to 63.4898 mm)	Yellow — Standard	Yellow — Standard
Orange — 2.4996 to 2.4991 (0.0005 Undersize) (63.4898 to 63.4771 mm)	Yellow — Standard	Black — 0.001-Inch Undersize (0.025 mm)
Black — 2.4991 to 2.4986 (0.001 Undersize) (63.4771 to 63.4644 mm)	Black — 0.001-Inch Undersize (0.025 mm)	Black — 0.001-Inch Undersize (0.025 mm)
Green — 2.4986 to 2.4981 (0.0015 Undersize) (63.4644 to 63.4517 mm)	Black — 0.001-Inch Undersize (0.025 mm)	Green — 0.002-Inch Undersize (0.051 mm)
Red — 2.4901 to 2.4896 (0.010 Undersize) (63.2485 to 63.2358 mm)	Red — 0.010 Inch Undersize (0.054 mm)	Red — 0.010-Inch Undersize (0.254 mm)

Courtesy of Chrysler Motors.

Fig. 9: Main Bearing Fitting Chart

TIGHTENING SPECIFICATIONS

Application	Ft. Lbs. (N.m)
Camshaft Gear Bolt	80 (109)
Connecting Rod Nut	33 (45)
Crankshaft Pulley	20 (27)
Cylinder Head Bolt [1]	
1st Step	
Tighten All To	22 (30)
2nd Step	
Tighten All To	45 (61)
3rd Step	
Recheck All To	45 (61)
4th Step	
Nos. 1-6 & 8-10	110 (149)
No. 7	100 (136)
5th Step	Recheck 4th step
Intake/Exhaust Manifold [2]	
Nos. 1, 6, 7 & 8	30 (41)
Nos. 2-5	32 (43)
Nos. 9 & 10	14 (19)

TIGHTENING SPECIFICATIONS (Cont.)

Application	Ft. Lbs. (N.m)
Main Bearing Cap Bolt	80 (109)
Oil Pan Bolt	
1/4 x 20 Bolt	7 (10)
5/16 x 18 Bolt	11 (15)
Oil Pump	
Long Bolt	17 (23)
Short Bolt	10 (14)
Rocker Arm Bolt	19 (26)
Vibration Damper-to-Crankshaft	80 (109)
Water Pump Bolt	13 (18)
Water Pump Pulley Bolt	20 (27)

	INCH Lbs. (N.m)
Front Timing Cover-to-Block	62 (7)
Valve Cover Bolt	70 (8)

[1] – Tighten in sequence. *See Fig. 3.*
[2] – Tighten in sequence. *See Fig. 2.*

1989 EAGLE ENGINES
2.5L 4-Cylinder (Cont.)

ENGINE SPECIFICATIONS

GENERAL SPECIFICATIONS

| Year | Displacement | | Fuel System | HP@RPM | Torque Ft. Lbs.@RPM | Compr. Ratio | Bore | | Stroke | |
	Cu. In.	Liters					In.	mm	In.	mm
1989	150	2.5	TBI	1	1	9.2:1	3.88	98.6	3.19	81.0

1 – Information not available from manufacturer.

PISTONS, PINS & RINGS

| Engine | Pistons | | Pins | | | Rings | | |
	Clearance In. (mm)	Diameter In. (mm)	Diameter In. (mm)	Piston Fit In. (mm)	Rod Fit In. (mm)	Ring No.	End Gap In. (mm)	Side Clearance In. (mm)
2.5L	.0013-.0021 (.033-.053)	1	.9306 (23.637)	.0005 (.013)	Press Fit	No. 1 & 2 No. 3 (Oil)	.01-.02 (.3-.5) .015-.055 (.38-1.40)	.001-.003 (.03-.08) .001-.008 (.03-.20)

1 – Information not available from manufacturer.

CRANKSHAFT, MAIN & CONNECTING ROD BEARINGS

| Engine | Crankshaft | | | | Main Bearings | | Connecting Rod Bearings | |
	End Play In. (mm)	Runout In. (mm)	Journal Taper In. (mm)	Journal Out-of-Round In. (mm)	Journal Diameter In. (mm)	Oil Clearance In. (mm)	Journal Diameter In. (mm)	Oil Clearance In. (mm)
2.5L	.0015-.0065 (.038-.165)	.....	.0005 (.013)	.0005 (.013)	2.4994-2.5001 (63.485-63.503)	.002 (.05)	2.0934-2.0955 (53.172-53.226)	.0015-.0020 (.038-.051)

CONNECTING RODS

Engine	Side Play In. (mm)	Max. Bend & Twist In. (mm)	Pin Bore Dia. In. (mm)	Large Bore Dia. In. (mm)	Center-to-Center In. (mm)
2.5L	.010-.019 (.25-.48)	.001 (.03)	.9288-.9298 (23.591-23.617)	2.2080-2.2085 (56.083-56.096)	6.123-6.127 (155.52-155.625)

CYLINDER HEAD

| Engine | Max. Cylinder Head Warp In. (mm) | Valve Seats | | | | Valve Guides | | |
		Seat Angle	Maximum Runout In. (mm)	Seat Width In. (mm)	Seat Bore Diameter In. (mm)	Valve Stem Oil Clearance In. (mm)	Valve Guide I.D. In. (mm)	Valve Guide Bore I.D. In. (mm)
2.5L	1 .001 (.03)	44.3°	.0025 (.046)	.04-.06 (1.0-1.5)	.....	.001-.003 (.03-.08)	.313 (7.95)	.....

1 – Specification given is within a 1" (25 mm) area. Within a 6" (152 mm) area, no more than .002" (.05 mm).

1989 EAGLE ENGINES
2.5L 4-Cylinder (Cont.)

ENGINE SPECIFICATIONS (Cont.)

CAMSHAFT

Engine	Journal Diameter In. (mm)	Oil Clearance In. (mm)	Bearing Bore In. (mm)	Runout In. (mm)	End Play In. (mm)	Lobe Lift In. (mm)	Lobe Height In. (mm)
2.5L	[1] 2.029 (51.54)	.001-.003 (.03-.08)	.....	.001 (.03)	Zero Zero	[2] .24 (6.1)	.....

[1] – Journal No. 1 listed. All others as follow:
Journal No. 2 is 2.019" (51.28 mm).
Journal No. 3 is 2.009" (51.03 mm).
Journal No. 4 is 1.999" (50.78 mm).
[2] – Intake listed. Exhaust is .25" (6.4 mm).

VALVES & VALVE SPRINGS

Engine	Valves					Valves Springs				
	Head Dia. In. (mm)	Stem Dia. In. (mm)	Face Angle	Min. Margin In. (mm)	Max. Refinish In. (mm)	Free Length In. (mm)	Out-of-Square In. (mm)	Installed Height In. (mm)	Pressure Lbs. @ In. (Kg @ mm)	
									Valve Closed	Valve Open
2.5L										
Intake	1.908 (48.46)	.311-.313 (7.90-7.93)	45°	.0312 (.792)	.01 (.3)	1.967 (49.96)	.....	1.64 (41.66)	80-90@1.64 (36-41@41.66)	200@1.126 (91@30.89)
Exhaust	1.498 (38.05)	.311-.313 (7.90-7.93)	45°	.0312 (.792)	.01 (.3)	1.967 (49.96)	.....	1.64 (41.66)	80-90@1.64 (36-41@41.66)	200@1.126 (91@30.89)

VALVE LIFTERS

Engine	Diameter In. (mm)	Bore Diameter In. (mm)	Oil Clearance In. (mm)
2.5L	.904 (22.96)	.....	.0010-.0025 (.030-.064)

CYLINDER BLOCK

Engine	Max. Block Warp In. (mm)	Cylinder Bore		
		Standard Diameter In. (mm)	Maximum Taper In. (mm)	Maximum Out-of-Rnd In. (mm)
2.5L	[1] .001 (.03)	3.8751-3.8775 (98.428-98.489)	.001 (.03)	.001 (.03)

[1] – Specification is within a 1" (25 mm) area. For within a 6" (152 mm) area, no more than .002" (.05 mm).

1989 EAGLE ENGINES
3.0L V6

Premier

NOTE: For engine repair procedures not covered in this article, see the ENGINE OVERHAUL PROCEDURES article at the beginning of this section.

ENGINE IDENTIFICATION

Engine may be identified by the Vehicle Identification Number (VIN) located on top of instrument panel near lower left corner of windshield. The 8th character of VIN identifies the engine and 10th character "K" indicates 1989 model.

Partial VIN number is stamped on rear corner of cylinder block. Engine identification tag is located on right side of cylinder block below exhaust manifold. *See Fig. 1.*

ENGINE IDENTIFICATION CODE

Engine	Code
3.0 MPFI	U

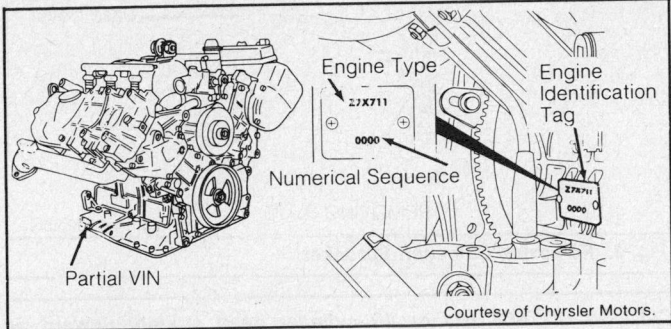

Fig. 1: Cylinder Block Identification

ADJUSTMENTS

VALVE ARRANGEMENT

Intake Manifold Side – Intake valves.

Exhaust Manifold Side – Exhaust valves.

VALVE CLEARANCE ADJUSTMENT

No valve adjustment is required, as hydraulic valve lifters are used.

REMOVAL & INSTALLATION

NOTE: For reassembly reference, label all electrical connectors, vacuum hoses and fuel lines before removal. Also place mating marks on engine hood and other major assemblies before removal.

ENGINE

NOTE: See ENGINE REMOVAL & INSTALLATION article at end of ENGINE SECTION.

INTAKE MANIFOLD

CAUTION: Fuel system is under pressure. Fuel pressure must be released prior to disconnecting or servicing fuel system components.

Removal – **1)** Fuel pressure must be released. Remove fuel tank filler cap. Disconnect fuel pump/sender connector. Connector is located between fuel filter and fuel tank, next to the vapor hose "Y". Start engine and operate until it stalls. Reinstall fuel tank cap.
2) Disconnect negative battery cable. Reinstall fuel pump/sender connector. Remove air intake duct and control cables from throttle body. Disconnect necessary vacuum hoses and electrical connections.

CAUTION: DO NOT use excessive pressure while removing cruise control cable connector (if equipped). If connector is broken, cable must be replaced.

3) Disconnect EGR tube and EGR valve transducer vacuum hose. Place shop towel around fuel lines as some residual line pressure may exist.
4) Disconnect fuel supply and return lines. To disconnect lines, install Fuel Line Tool (6182) into fuel line connector until handle contacts the connector and disconnect fuel line. Remove intake manifold bolts, manifold and "O" rings from cylinder head.

Installation – To install, reverse removal procedure using new "O" rings. Ensure all control cables are properly adjusted.

EXHAUST MANIFOLD

Removal – **1)** Disconnect negative battery cable. Disconnect EGR tube from manifold. Raise and support vehicle. Disconnect catalytic converter from "Y" pipe and pull backward from hanger.
2) Disconnect oxygen sensor. Remove "Y" pipe bracket-to-transaxle bracket bolts. Disconnect "Y" pipe from exhaust manifolds.
3) For right manifold applications, remove dipstick tube. Remove exhaust manifold nuts, manifold and gasket. Note direction of gasket installation.
4) For left manifold applications, remove hot air tube. Disconnect electrical connections at starter and ground cable. Remove lower manifold nuts and remove starter. Remove remaining exhaust manifold nuts, manifold and gasket. Note direction of gasket installation.

Installation – **1)** To install, reverse removal procedure. Ensure gaskets are installed with ring area toward cylinder head and tab area toward oil pan. *See Fig. 2.*
2) Apply Loctite to stop area on dipstick prior to installation. DO NOT tighten "Y" pipe bracket-to-transaxle bracket through bolts until all other bolts have been tightened.

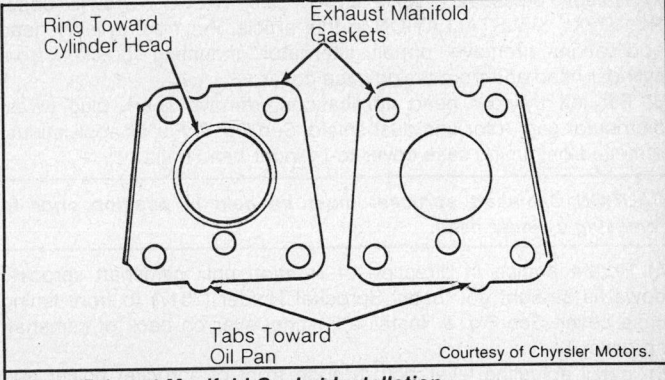

Fig. 2: Exhaust Manifold Gasket Installation

CAMSHAFT

Removal – **1)** With cylinder head removed, remove camshaft cover and gasket from rear of cylinder head if not previously removed. Loosen camshaft thrust plate bolt.
2) Rotate thrust plate upward and tighten bolt. Remove camshaft from cylinder head. Mark camshaft location for reassembly reference.

CAUTION: Right and left camshafts are not interchangeable. Left camshaft has both lobes for each cylinder on the same side and the right camshaft has both lobes on opposite sides. Mark camshaft location for reassembly reference.

Inspection – Inspect camshaft for wear or damage. Replace components as necessary. No other information available from manufacturer.

Installation – 1) To install, reverse removal procedure using new rear cover gasket. Coat camshaft with Super Oil Conditioner (J-8993431) prior to installation.

2) Check camshaft end play. Replace components if end play is not correct. See ENGINE SPECIFICATIONS tables at end of article. Apply Loctite to rear cover bolts prior to installation.

VALVE COVERS

Removal – 1) Disconnect negative battery cable. For right valve cover applications, remove accessory drive belt. Remove A/C compressor with hoses attached and lay aside. Remove spark plug wires and wire holder. Remove valve cover bolts, valve cover and gasket.

2) For left valve cover applications, remove air intake from throttle body. Remove brake booster hose from throttle body. Disconnect vacuum hoses from valve cover. Remove air cleaner assembly.

3) Remove power steering reservoir bolts. Move coolant recovery bottle in air cleaner location. Disconnect control cables at throttle body. Remove idle speed regulator bracket at rear of valve cover. Remove spark plug wire holder, valve cover bolts, valve cover and gasket.

Installation – To install, reverse removal procedure using new gaskets. Apply Sealant (J-8993317) on top of timing case cover and cylinder head joining areas prior to valve cover installation. To install remaining components, reverse removal procedure.

CYLINDER HEAD

CAUTION: Cylinder head must be removed with engine cold to prevent warpage to cylinder head. Exhaust manifold must be installed AFTER cylinder head is installed to prevent damage to cylinder head gaskets.

Removal – 1) Remove intake manifold. See INTAKE MANIFOLD under REMOVAL & INSTALLATION in this article. Drain cooling system. Remove exhaust manifold. See EXHAUST MANIFOLD under REMOVAL & INSTALLATION in this article.

2) Remove necessary valve cover. See VALVE COVERS under REMOVAL & INSTALLATION in this article. For right cylinder head applications, remove upper alternator mounting bracket from cylinder head and front timing case cover.

3) For left cylinder head applications, remove spark plug wires, distributor cap, rotor and dust shield. *See Fig. 8.* For all applications, remove front timing case cover-to-cylinder head bolts.

CAUTION: Camshaft sprocket must be held in position prior to removing cylinder head.

4) Rotate engine in direction of rotation until camshaft sprocket dowel is straight up. Install Sprocket Holder (7317) to front timing case cover. *See Fig. 3.* Install adjusting lever on back of camshaft sprocket.

5) Install adjusting lever bolt through front of sprocket holder and into adjusting lever. Push adjusting lever upward as far as possible and tighten adjusting lever bolt.

6) For right cylinder head applications, remove plug from front timing case cover for access to camshaft thrust bolt. *See Fig. 3.* Remove cylinder head bolts and rocker arm shaft assembly.

7) Reinstall one cylinder head bolt in center of cylinder head. Tighten bolt approximatey 2 turns. Remove camshaft cover and gasket from rear of cylinder head.

8) Loosen camshaft thrust plate bolt. Rotate thrust plate upward and tighten bolt. Camshaft can now move backward as camshaft sprocket bolt is removed. Loosen camshaft sprocket bolt. Move camshaft backward until bolt is free of camshaft and camshaft is away from camshaft sprocket.

9) Install drift punches in front and rear cylinder head bolt holes on exhaust manifold side. Tap on drift punches to push dowels downward below head gasket.

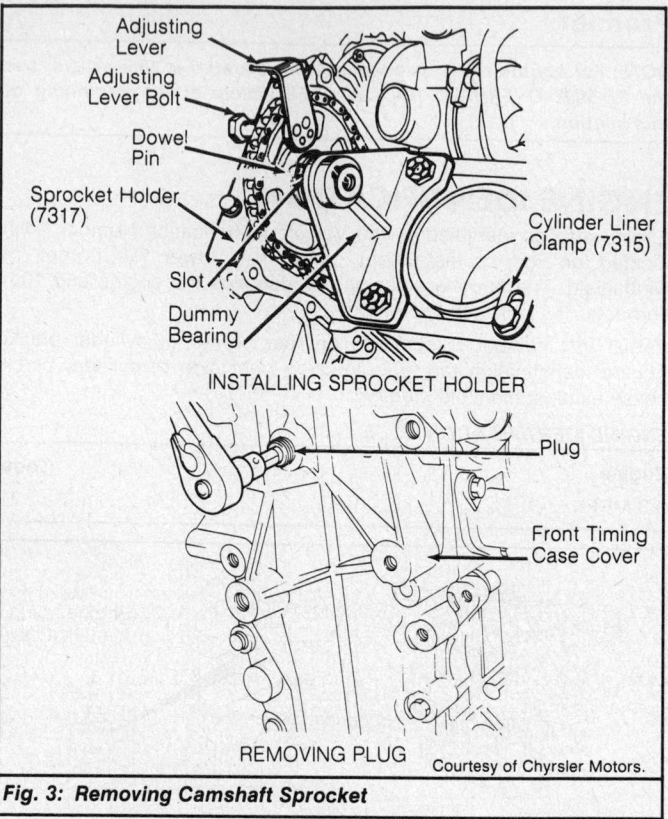

Fig. 3: Removing Camshaft Sprocket

CAUTION: DO NOT pry or lift cylinder head straight upward or cylinder liners may come out of cylinder block.

10) Place wooden block on rear of intake manifold area and tap with hammer. Place wooden block on front of exhaust manifold area and tap with hammer. Repeat procedure until cylinder head is free.

11) Remove remaining cylinder head bolt, cylinder head and gasket. Install Cylinder Liner Clamps (7315) on cylinder block to retain cylinder liners. Using Dowel Remover (7314), remove cylinder head dowels from cylinder block.

CAUTION: DO NOT rotate engine with sprocket holder installed.

12) Ensure all surfaces are clean. Cylinder liner protrusion should be checked. See CYLINDER LINER under CYLINDER BLOCK ASSEMBLY in this article.

13) If crankshaft needs to be rotated with cylinder head removed, install Cylinder Liner Clamps (7315) on cylinder liners. Install dummy bearing on rear of camshaft sprocket. *See Fig. 3.* Align slot of dummy bearing with camshaft sprocket dowel pin. *See Fig. 3.*

14) If gap area exists between bottom of dummy bearing and cylinder block, use washers to shim for tight fit. Install bolts to secure dummy bearing to cylinder block. Before engine can be rotated, the sprocket holder must be removed from the front timing case cover.

CAUTION: Cylinder Liner Clamps (7315) must be installed before rotating engine. Once dummy bearing is installed, remove sprocket holder from front timing case cover prior to rotating engine.

Inspection – Inspect cylinder head warpage and height. See CYLINDER HEAD under OVERHAUL in this article.

Installation – 1) Remove cylinder liner clamps. Install sprocket holder and remove dummy bearing (if installed). Cut front timing case cover gaskets even with cylinder head gasket surface. Install sections from replacement gasket and secure to front timing case cover with weatherstrip adhesive.

1989 EAGLE ENGINES
3.0L V6 (Cont.)

2) Install 3 mm punch into cylinder block holes located below cylinder head dowels. Install dowels until they contact the punch. Install cylinder head gasket. Ensure proper cylinder head gasket is used. Different style gaskets are used for left and right applications.

CAUTION: Proper cylinder head gasket must be installed. Different style gaskets are used for left and right applications.

3) Place small bead of sealant where cylinder head gasket contacts the front timing case cover gasket. Install cylinder head. Install front timing case cover-to-cylinder head bolts finger tight.

4) Install camshaft in camshaft sprocket. Ensure dowel pin is aligned with slot area. Install sprocket retaining bolt finger tight. Remove sprocket holder assembly. Tighten camshaft sprocket bolt to specification.

5) Reposition camshaft thrust plate and tighten bolt to specification. Remove punches installed for dowel pin installation. Install rocker arm shaft assembly. Ensure rocker arm shaft pins are aligned with cylinder head. Apply light coat of engine oil to cylinder head bolts and install.

6) Tighten cylinder head bolts in sequence to 44 ft. lbs. (60 N.m). *See Fig. 4.* Loosen all bolts in sequence. Tighten No. 1 bolt to 15 ft. lbs. (20 N.m).

7) Place Graduated Disc Tool (7321) on No. 1 bolt. Tighten graduated disc clockwise until stem contacts cylinder head or components to prevent disc from turning. *See Fig. 4.* Tighten bolt to 106 degrees ± 2 degrees. Repeat procedure on remaining bolts in sequence.

8) To install remaining components, reverse removal procedure. Ensure plug in front timing case cover is coated with thread sealant prior to installation.

9) Apply sealant at front timing case cover-to-cylinder head joint areas prior to installing valve cover. Install camshaft rear cover using new gasket. Apply Loctite to rear cover bolts prior to installation.

10) Fill cooling system. To bleed air from cooling system, place hose on bleed valve located on thermostat housing. Place hose in container and open bleed valve while filling cooling system.

11) Close bleed valve once steady stream exists. Fill cooling system to proper level. Operate engine for 15 minutes at 2000 RPM. Allow engine to cool for at least 6 hours and tighten head bolts in sequence an additional 45 degrees. Ensure each bolt is torqued to 52 ft. lbs. (71 N.m).

CAUTION: Cylinder head bolts must be tightened an additional 45 degrees in sequence once engine has operated at 2000 RPM for 15 minutes and then allowed to cool for at least 6 hours. Ensure each bolt is torqued to 52 ft. lbs. (71 N.m).

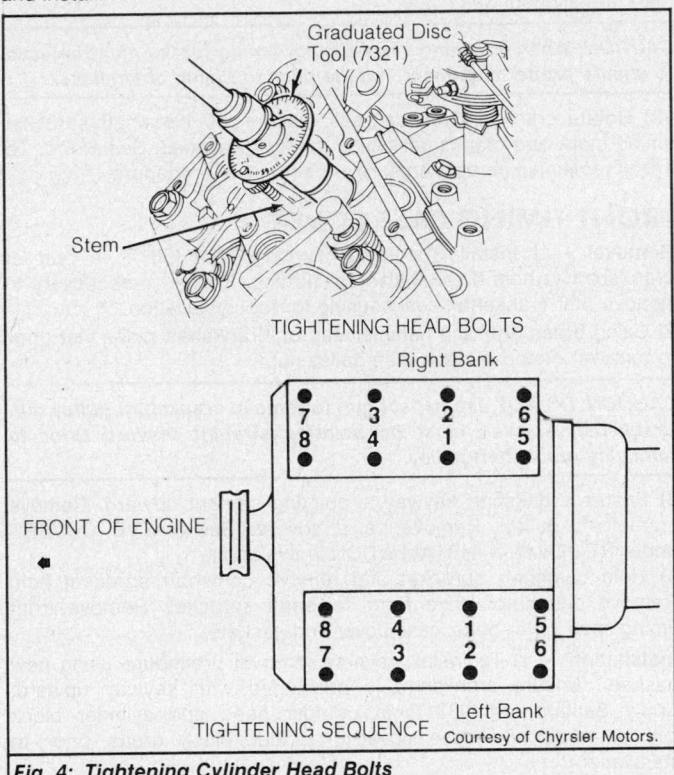

TIGHTENING HEAD BOLTS

Right Bank

| 7 | 3 | 2 | 6 |
| 8 | 4 | 1 | 5 |

FRONT OF ENGINE

| 8 | 4 | 1 | 5 |
| 7 | 3 | 2 | 6 |

TIGHTENING SEQUENCE — Left Bank

Courtesy of Chyrsler Motors.

Fig. 4: Tightening Cylinder Head Bolts

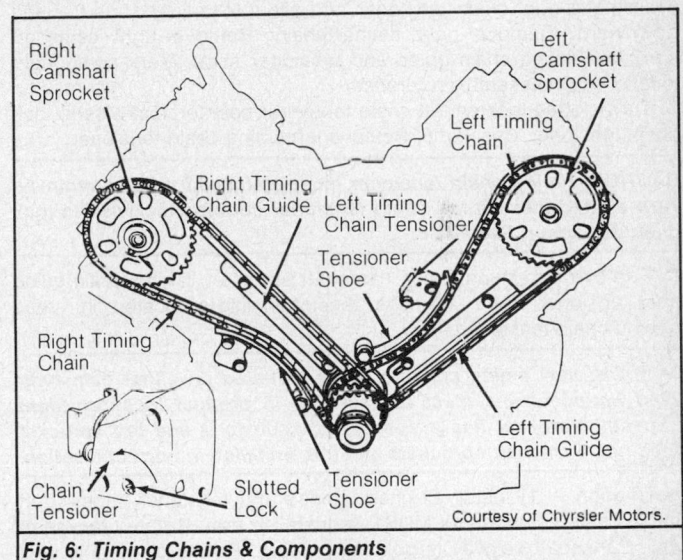

Courtesy of Chyrsler Motors.

Fig. 6: Timing Chains & Components

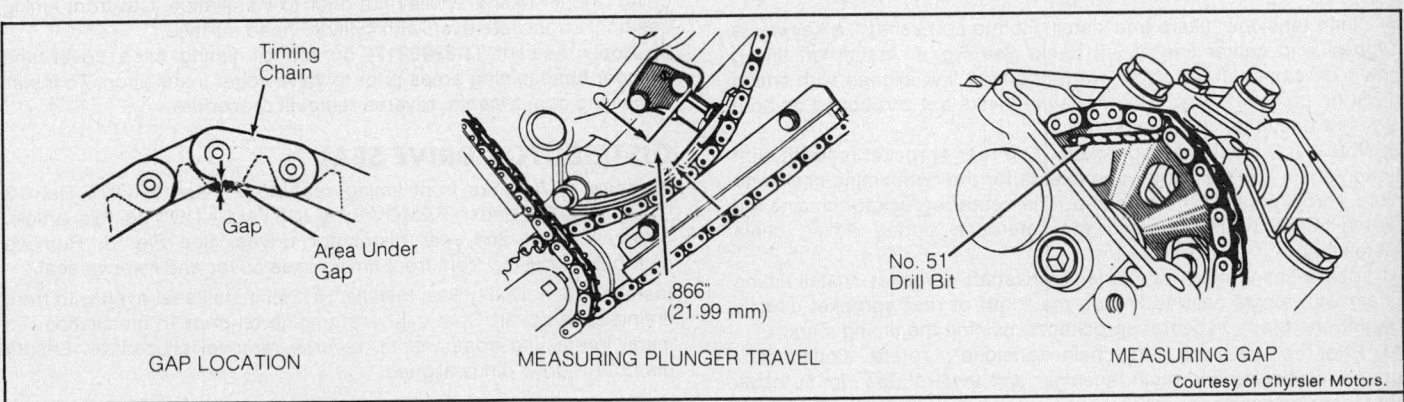

GAP LOCATION — MEASURING PLUNGER TRAVEL — MEASURING GAP

.866" (21.99 mm)

No. 51 Drill Bit

Courtesy of Chyrsler Motors.

Fig. 5: Measuring Timing Chain Wear

1989 EAGLE ENGINES
3.0L V6 (Cont.)

TIMING CHAINS & SPROCKETS

CAUTION: Camshaft sprockets, timing chains and components must be marked for location. Components are different and must be installed in original location.

Removal – 1) Remove front timing case cover. See FRONT TIMING CASE COVER under REMOVAL & INSTALLATION in this article.

2) Timing chain and sprocket wear can be determined prior to removal. Remove valve covers. See VALVE COVERS under REMOVAL & INSTALLATION in this article. Pull upward on timing chain and note gap clearance between bottom of timing chain and bottom of area between sprocket teeth. See Fig. 5.

3) Maximum gap clearance should not exceed .067" (1.70 mm) with tensioner plunger travel of .866" (21.99 mm). To measure gap clearance, use a No. 51 drill bit. See Fig. 5. If solid end of drill bit fits into the gap, the timing chains, tensioners, guides, sprockets and tensioner shoes must be replaced.

4) To remove timing chains and sprockets, rotate crankshaft until crankshaft keyway is pointing upward. Remove oil pump sprocket bolts, oil pump sprocket and oil pump drive chain. See Fig. 14.

5) Remove right camshaft sprocket bolt. Turn slotted lock on right chain tensioner counterclockwise to lock chain tensioner. See Fig. 6.

CAUTION: Timing chain tensioner must be locked prior to removal. Turn slotted lock on right chain tensioner counterclockwise to lock chain tensioner. See Fig. 6.

6) Remove right chain tensioner and allow tensioner shoe to hang downward. Remove right timing chain. Remove right camshaft sprocket, timing chain guide and tensioner shoe. Mark component location for reassembly reference.

7) Turn slotted lock on left chain tensioner counterclockwise to lock chain tensioner. See Fig. 6. Remove left timing chain tensioner.

CAUTION: Timing chain tensioner must be locked prior to removal. Turn slotted lock on left chain tensioner counterclockwise to lock chain tensioner. See Fig. 6.

8) Remove left timing chain, camshaft sprocket, timing chain guide and tensioner shoe. Remove tensioner filters located in areas behind chain tensioners.

CAUTION: New timing chains can be installed on either camshaft. Used timing chains must be installed in original location. Right camshaft sprocket has a spacer attached to it and left sprocket does not. Camshaft sprockets must be installed in correct location.

Installation – 1) Install all chain guides and tensioner shoes. Left timing chain components MUST be installed first. Rotate crankshaft until crankshaft keyway is pointing upward. Rotate camshafts until slot is correctly positioned. See Fig. 7.

2) Clean tensioner filters and install. Rotate crankshaft so keyway is aligned with center line of left bank. See Fig. 7. Install left timing chain on camshaft sprocket with unpainted link aligned with timing mark on camshaft gear. Ensure painted links are positioned on both sides of unpainted link. See Fig. 7.

3) Note the 3 crankshaft sprockets. The rear sprocket is for the left timing chain and the center sprocket is for the right timing chain and front sprocket is for the oil pump. The center sprocket contains the timing mark which is used for reference during timing chain installation.

4) Locate timing mark on center crankshaft sprocket. Install timing chain with single painted link on the tooth of rear sprocket directly behind the tooth on center sprocket containing the timing mark.

5) Prior to installing left chain tensioner, rotate slotted lock counterclockwise and push tensioner arm inward. See Fig. 6. Install tensioner so tensioner arm is positioned in tensioner shoe. Tighten tensioner retaining bolts to specification.

6) For right timing chain installation, rotate crankshaft 150 degrees until timing mark on crankshaft center sprocket is aligned with lower oil pump mounting bolt. See Fig. 7.

7) Install right timing chain on camshaft sprocket with unpainted link aligned with timing mark on camshaft gear. Ensure painted links are positioned on both sides of unpainted link. See Fig. 7.

8) Locate timing mark on center crankshaft sprocket. Install timing chain with single painted link (on bottom of timing chain) on center sprocket in alignment with timing mark. See Fig. 7.

9) Prior to installing right chain tensioner, rotate slotted lock counterclockwise and push tensioner arm inward. See Fig. 6. Install tensioner so tensioner arm is positioned in tensioner shoe. Tighten tensioner retaining bolts to specification.

10) Install right camshaft sprocket bolt. Push both tensioner shoes in to release tensioner from locked position. Allow tensioners to expand against timing chain. Ensure tensioners are in released position.

11) Valve timing should be checked. Rotate crankshaft 180 degrees. Ensure right camshaft sprocket timing mark and crankshaft timing mark are aligned. See Fig. 7.

CAUTION: When checking valve timing, timing marks must be used to ensure proper alignment, not the painted timing chain links.

12) Rotate crankshaft 90 degrees. Ensure left camshaft sprocket timing mark and crankshaft timing mark are aligned. See Fig. 7. To install remaining components, reverse removal procedure.

FRONT TIMING CASE COVER

Removal – 1) Install Crankshaft Turning Tool (6072) in rear of crankshaft to hold crankshaft from turning. It may be necessary to remove rear crankshaft seal housing for tool installation.

2) Using brass drift and hammer, tap on crankshaft pulley nut prior to removal. Remove crankshaft pulley nut.

CAUTION: DO NOT use impact gun to remove crankshaft pulley nut. Crankshaft keyway must be pointing straight upward prior to removing crankshaft pulley.

3) Ensure crankshaft keyway is pointing straight upward. Remove crankshaft pulley. Remove valve covers. See VALVE COVERS under REMOVAL & INSTALLATION in this article.

4) Hold camshaft sprocket and remove camshaft sprocket bolt. Remove distributor drive from camshaft sprocket. Remove front timing case cover bolts, case cover and gaskets.

Installation – 1) To install, reverse removal procedure using new gaskets. Ensure crankshaft is positioned with keyway upward. Apply Sealant (J-8993317) at cylinder head and cylinder block joining areas and case cover-to-cylinder block areas prior to installation.

2) Apply Loctite to 4 bottom mounting bolts of front timing case cover and crankshaft pulley nut prior to installation. Cut front timing case cover gaskets even with cylinder head surface.

3) Apply Sealant (J-8993317) on top of timing case cover and cylinder head joining areas prior to valve cover installation. To install remaining components, reverse removal procedure.

DISTRIBUTOR DRIVE SEAL

Removal – Remove front timing case cover. See FRONT TIMING CASE COVER under REMOVAL & INSTALLATION in this article. Separate front and rear distributor drives. See Fig. 8. Remove distributor housing from front timing case cover and remove seal.

Installation – Using Seal Installer (6126), install seal even with front timing case cover. Coat seal with engine oil prior to installation. To install remaining components, reverse removal procedure. Ensure distributor drive pin is aligned.

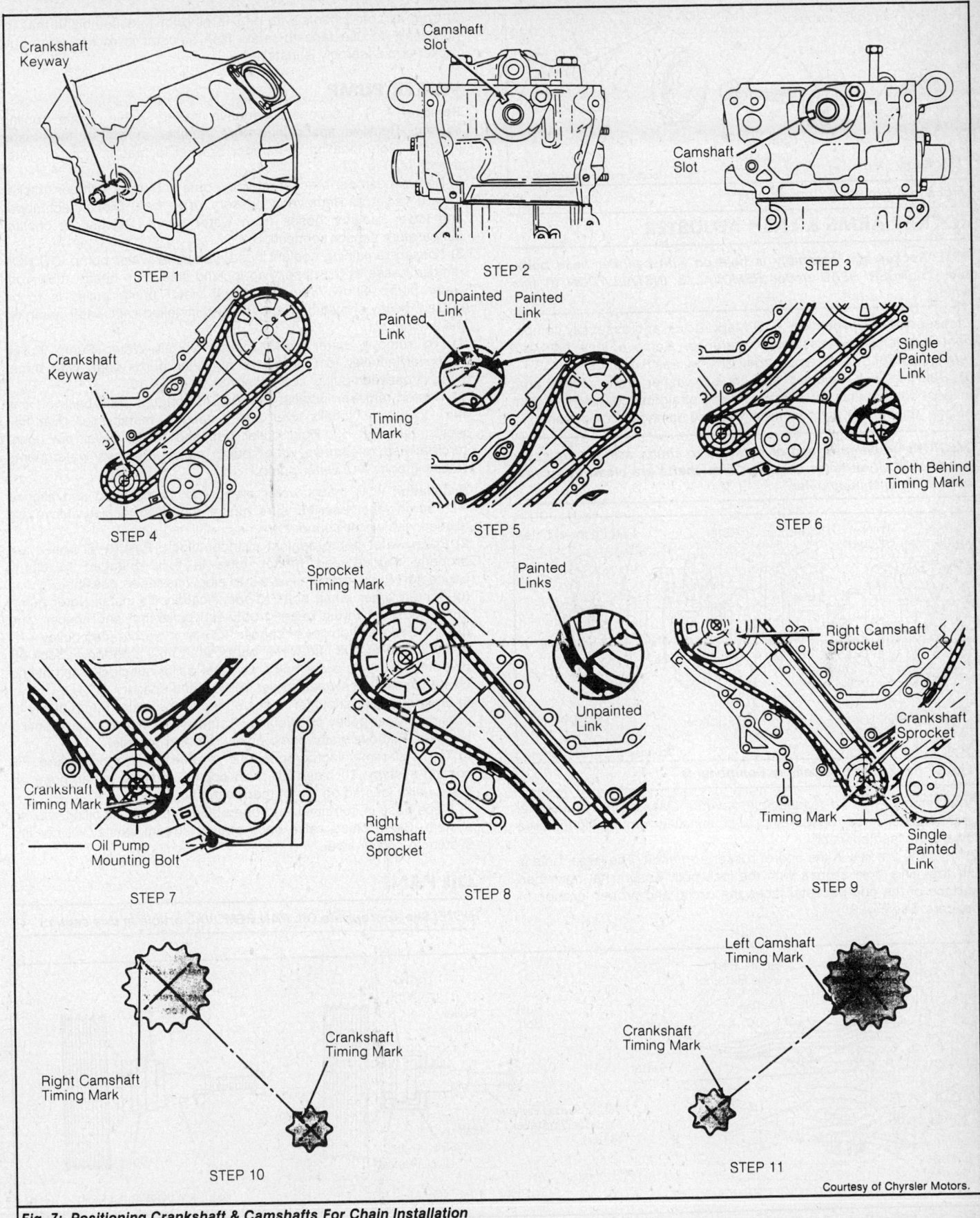

Fig. 7: Positioning Crankshaft & Camshafts For Chain Installation

Courtesy of Chyrsler Motors.

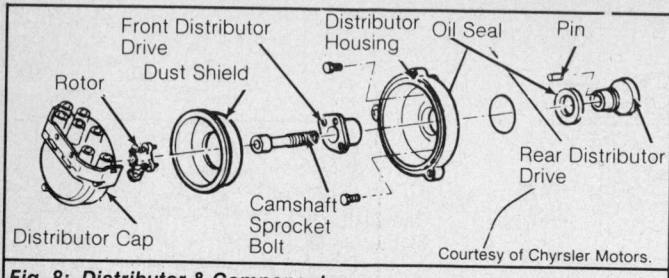

Fig. 8: Distributor & Components

ROCKER ARMS & LASH ADJUSTER

NOTE: Rocker arm assembly is held on with cylinder head bolts. See CYLINDER HEAD under REMOVAL & INSTALLATION in this article.

Disassembly & Inspection – 1) Mark rocker arm assembly component location for reassembly reference. Remove lock bolt and remove rocker arm assembly components. *See Fig. 9.*
2) Remove lash adjuster and thrust washer from rocker arm. Inspect components for damage. Using straightedge, check bottom of lash adjuster for a crown area. Replace damaged components.

CAUTION: Oil plugs in end of rocker arm shafts are not replaceable. Ensure all oil holes of rocker arm shafts are clean to provide lubrication to lash adjuster.

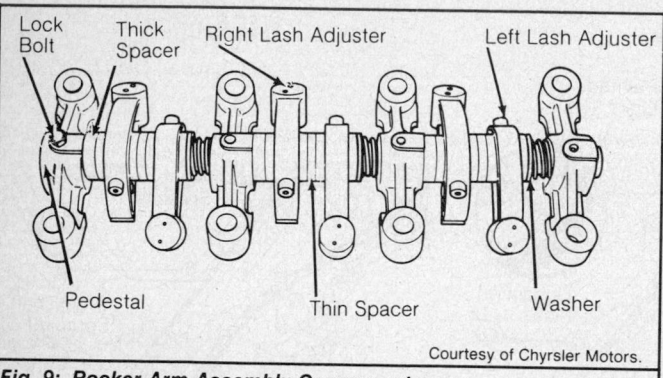

Fig. 9: Rocker Arm Assembly Components

Reassembly – 1) To reassemble, reverse disassembly procedure. Lash adjuster thrust washer should be installed with the slotted area toward the lash adjuster.
2) Note the 2 holes in the end of rocker arm shaft. The larger hole is the top. This hole aligns with the lock bolt. Ensure flat machined surface of the end pedestal faces the circlip and proper location of spacers. *See Fig. 9.*

3) Coat all components with engine oil prior to assembly. It may be necessary to use tape to retain lash adjuster in rocker arms until rocker arm assembly is installed.

WATER PUMP

Removal – 1) Disconnect negative battery cable. Drain cooling system. Remove spark plug wire retainer at top of thermostat housing. Note location of damper bracket located in front of water pump. *See Fig. 10.*
2) Remove damper bracket retaining nuts and move damper bracket toward radiator. Remove accessory drive belt. Disconnect upper and lower radiator hoses from water pump. Disconnect coolant temperature sensor connection.
3) Loosen remaining coolant hose clamps at water pump. DO NOT remove hoses at this time. Tap locking sleeve on heater tube from water pump elbow. *See Fig. 10.* If water pump pulley is to be reused, pulley should be removed and installed with water pump on the engine.
4) To remove water pump pulley, install Water Pump Pulley Remover/Installer (6160) in end of water pump shaft with thrust bearing between pulley and puller nut. *See Fig. 10.*
5) Tighten remover/installer bolt until it bottoms, then back off one turn. Install half shells over pulley flanges. Install shell over half shells. *See Fig. 10.* Hold puller bolt and rotate puller nut counterclockwise to remove water pump pulley. Remove water pump retaining bolts and water pump.

Installation – 1) Install water pump with pump tilted and aligned with all coolant hoses. Ensure heater tube and locking sleeve are aligned with elbow connector.
2) Place water pump against cylinder block. Ensure all hoses are properly aligned and heater tube is fully engaged in elbow connector. Push locking sleeve into elbow as far as possible.
3) Tighten water pump bolts to specification. To install water pump pulley, position thrust bearing between puller nut and spacer. *See Fig. 10.* Ensure shoulder of spacer fits inside water pump pulley.
4) Rotate puller bolt into water pump shaft until it bottoms. Back off bolt one turn. Hold puller bolt and rotate puller nut clockwise until no clearance exists between thrust bearing and spacer.
5) Ensure spacer shoulder is positioned inside water pump pulley to provide proper pulley positioning. Rotate puller nut clockwise until it bottoms. Remove water pump pulley remover/installer.
6) To install remaining components, reverse removal procedure. Fill cooling system. To bleed air from cooling system, install hose on bleed valve located on top of thermostat housing.
7) Place hose in container and open bleed valve while filling cooling system. Close bleed valve once steady stream exists. Fill cooling system to proper level.

OIL PAN

NOTE: See appropriate OIL PAN REMOVAL article in this section.

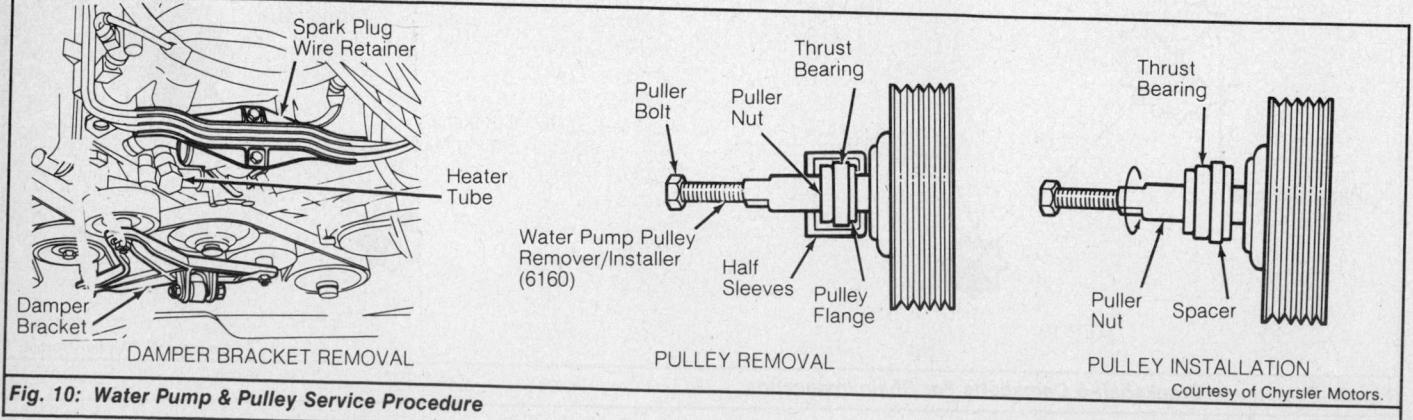

Fig. 10: Water Pump & Pulley Service Procedure

OVERHAUL

CYLINDER HEAD

Inspection – Inspect cylinder head for warpage at deck surface and manifold surfaces. Cylinder head cannot be resurfaced. Replace cylinder head if warpage exceeds specification. See ENGINE SPECIFICATIONS tables at end of article. Cylinder head height should be 4.363" (110.82 mm).

CAUTION: Cylinder head cannot be resurfaced. Replace cylinder head if warpage exceeds specification.

Valve Seats – No service procedure is given by manufacturer. Valve seats must be ground if valve guides are replaced.

Valve Guides – 1) Valve guides can be replaced if valve stem oil clearance is not within specification. See ENGINE SPECIFICATIONS tables at end of article. Stock valve guides do not contain grooves while replacement valve guides contain 2 grooves for identification purposes.

2) To change valve guide, press valve guide from cylinder head. Replacement valve guide MUST NOT be the same diameter as that removed.

CAUTION: Replacement valve guide must not be the same diameter as that removed. The replacement valve guide must be installed with a .0039" (.099 mm) interference fit. Replacement valve guide O.D. is .526" (13.36 mm). Intake valve guide length is 1.772" (45.01 mm) and exhaust valve guide length is 1.929" (48.99 mm).

3) Machine cylinder head to obtain a .0039" (.099 mm) interference fit between valve guide and cylinder head at 16.5 degrees. The replacement valve guide O.D. is .526" (13.36 mm).

4) Valve guide should be installed so the distance from bottom of valve guides to top of valve seat is 1.181" (29.99 mm) on intake valves or 1.024" (26.01 mm) on exhaust valves.

5) After installation, ream valve guides to .315" (8.00 mm) prior to grinding the valves. Valve seats must be ground if valve guides are replaced.

Seat Correction Angles – Information not available from manufacturer.

VALVE TRAIN

Valve Stem Oil Seals – Using Valve Stem Oil Seal Installer (6187) for intake valves or (6200) for exhaust valves, install oil seals until installer bottoms.

CYLINDER BLOCK ASSEMBLY

Piston & Ring Installation – 1) Top compression ring and the oil scraper ring can be installed in either direction. Second compression ring must be installed with identification mark toward top of piston. Rings must be properly spaced. *See Fig. 11.*

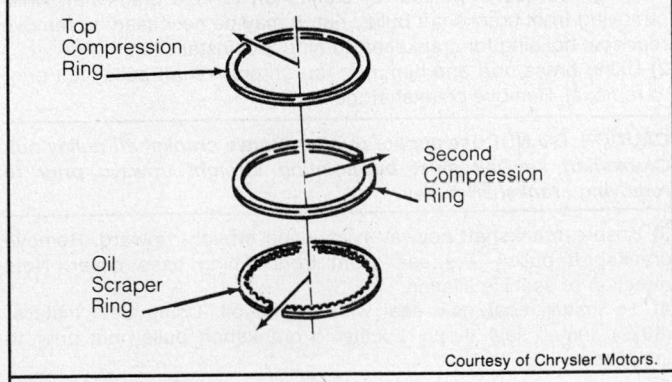

Courtesy of Chrysler Motors.

Fig. 11: Piston Ring Positioning

CAUTION: Piston assembly MUST NOT be installed from top of cylinder liner. Piston must be installed from bottom of cylinder liner using ring compressor.

2) Using ring compressor, install piston from bottom of cylinder liner. Piston must not be installed from top of cylinder liner, as no chamfer exists on top of cylinder liner.

CAUTION: Piston must not be removed from top of cylinder liner. Piston must be removed from bottom of cylinder liner once cylinder liner is removed from cylinder block. Mark piston position on connecting rod if piston is to be removed from connecting rod.

Piston & Rod Assembly – 1) To remove piston pin, use 1500 watt heating plate to heat connecting rod piston pin area until piston pin can be removed. Remove piston pin and piston from connecting rod. Note direction of ARROW on top of piston in relation to shoulder on connecting rod. *See Fig. 12.*

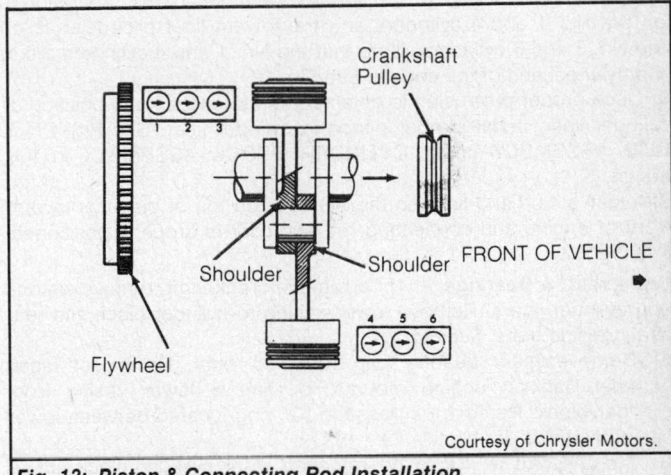

Courtesy of Chrysler Motors.

Fig. 12: Piston & Connecting Rod Installation

2) To install, use 1500 watt heating plate to heat connecting rod piston pin area. Place small piece of solder on connecting rod pin area.

3) Heat connecting rod until solder melts. With piston pin installed in piston, install piston and connecting rod on anvil from Piston Pin Remover/Installation Kit (7305).

4) Ensure ARROW on top of piston and shoulder of connecting are properly positioned according to piston location. *See Fig. 12.* Using piston pin remover/installation kit components, install piston pin while solder is melted. Ensure piston pin and connecting rod are centered in piston.

CAUTION: The ARROW on top of piston and shoulder of connecting rod should be properly positioned according to piston location. See Fig. 12. Piston must not be removed from top of cylinder liner. Piston must be removed from bottom of cylinder liner once cylinder liner is removed from cylinder block.

Cylinder Liner – 1) With oil pan and cylinder head removed, place cylinder number reference mark on connecting rod and cap. Remove oil pump inlet tube and baffle. It may be necessary to remove lower casing for access to connecting rod nuts. See CRANKSHAFT & BEARINGS under CYLINDER BLOCK ASSEMBLY in this article.

2) Remove connecting rod nuts and connecting rod cap. Place reference mark on cylinder liner location and cylinder block. Remove cylinder liner clamp. Remove cylinder liner and piston assembly.

3) To install original cylinder liners, install cylinder liner and piston assembly using the same thickness cylinder liner seal as that removed. The cylinder liner seals are color coded. Ensure reference marks are aligned on cylinder block and cylinder liner.

4) To install new cylinder liners, install new cylinder liner and seal in cylinder block. Using dial indicator, measure cylinder liner protrusion on both sides of cylinder liner at 90 degree angle from adjacent cylinder liner.

5) Cylinder liner protrusion should be within .0051-.0078" (.129-.198 mm). Check variance between adjacent cylinder liners. Variance should not exceed .0016" (.041 mm) between cylinders.

6) Cylinder liner protrusion can be modified by using different thickness cylinder liner seals. See CYLINDER LINER SEAL SPECIFICATIONS table.

CYLINDER LINER SEAL SPECIFICATIONS

Seal Color	Thickness In. (mm)
Blue	.006 (.15)
Red	.004 (.10)
Silver	.005 (.12)

7) Adjust cylinder liner protrusion so the highest liner protrusion is on the No. 1 and 4 cylinders and the lowest liner protrusion is on the No. 3 and 6 cylinders. Note that the No. 1 and 4 cylinders are at the flywheel end of the engine. See Fig. 12.

8) Once proper protrusion is obtained, mark location and position of cylinder liner. Install proper piston in cylinder liner. See PISTON & ROD ASSEMBLY under CYLINDER BLOCK ASSEMBLY in this article.

9) Install piston and liner so the ARROW on top of piston is toward front of engine and connecting rod shoulder is properly positioned. See Fig. 12.

Crankshaft & Bearings – 1) To remove crankshaft, remove pistons and cylinder liners. Remove lower casing-to-cylinder block and rear seal housing bolts. See Fig. 13.

2) Remove main bearing cap retaining nuts. Using soft-faced hammer, tap on engine mounts to remove lower casing from cylinder block. Remove oil passage "O" ring located between lower casing and cylinder block.

3) If crankshaft is not to be removed from cylinder block, install Clamps (6071) over front and rear main bearing studs. Install retaining nuts to hold clamps. If crankshaft is to be removed, remove timing chains. See TIMING CHAINS & SPROCKETS under REMOVAL & INSTALLATION in this article. Remove rear crankshaft seal housing. Remove clamps, main bearing caps, bearings and crankshaft.

CAUTION: Note direction of main bearing cap installation. Caps are installed with tabs toward the front of engine.

4) To install, coat thrust washer surfaces with Super Oil Conditioner (J-8993431) prior to installation. Install thrust washers with grooves facing away from main bearing cap. Ensure upper thrust washer tab is aligned with notch of cylinder block.

5) Install crankshaft, main bearings and main bearing caps. Main bearing caps must be installed in original location with the TABS toward front of engine.

6) Install Clamps (6071) over front and rear main bearing studs. Install retaining nuts and tighten to 20 ft. lbs. (27 N.m). Check crankshaft end play. Install different thickness thrust washers if end play is not within specification. See ENGINE SPECIFICATIONS tables at end of article.

7) Install rear seal housing and gasket with bolts finger tight. Install new "O" ring in oil passage located between lower casing and cylinder block. Apply Sealant (J-8993317) at lower casing-to cylinder block sealing surface.

CAUTION: Lower casing must only be installed using Alignment Plate (6140) to provide correct alignment.

8) Install lower casing. Install washers and all retaining nuts and bolts finger tight ONLY. Position lower casing forward and install Alignment Plate (6140) with machined bosses toward rear of engine.

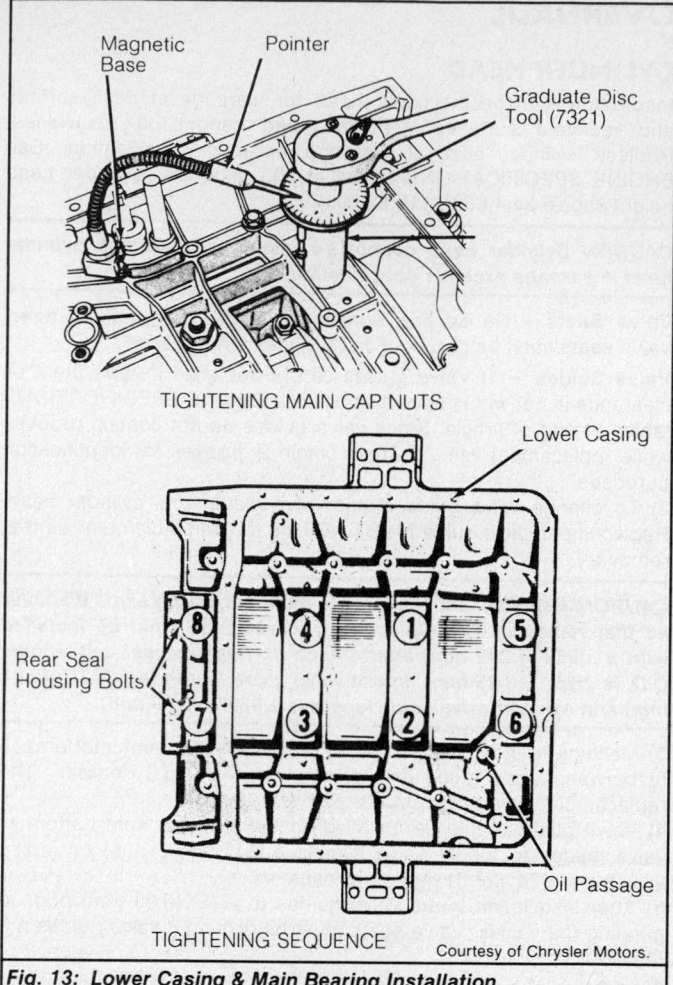

TIGHTENING MAIN CAP NUTS

TIGHTENING SEQUENCE

Courtesy of Chrysler Motors.

Fig. 13: Lower Casing & Main Bearing Installation

9) Slightly tighten rear seal housing bolts. Move lower casing against alignment plate and tighten main bearing cap nuts in sequence to 20 ft. lbs. (27 N.m). See Fig. 13.

10) Place Graduated Disc Tool (7321) on No. 1 bolt. Tighten graduated disc clockwise until stem contacts solid component to prevent disc from turning. See Fig. 13. Install magnetic base and position pointer at 75 degree mark.

11) Tighten nuts in sequence until zero on dial aligns with the pointer. Remove alignment plate. Tighten lower casing-to-rear seal housing bolts, then remaining rear seal housing bolts. Tighten lower casing-to-cylinder block bolts. Install remaining components.

Front Crankshaft Seal – 1) To remove front seal, install Crankshaft Turning Tool (6072) on rear of crankshaft to hold crankshaft while removing front crankshaft pulley nut. It may be necessary to remove rear seal housing for crankshaft turning tool installation.

2) Using brass drift and hammer, tap on crankshaft pulley nut prior to removal. Remove crankshaft pulley nut.

CAUTION: DO NOT use impact gun to remove crankshaft pulley nut. Crankshaft keyway must be pointing straight upward prior to removing crankshaft pulley.

3) Ensure crankshaft keyway is pointing straight upward. Remove crankshaft pulley. Pry seal from front timing case cover. Note direction of seal installation.

4) To install, coat new seal with engine oil. Using Seal Installer (6077), install seal. Apply Loctite to crankshaft pulley nut prior to installation.

Rear Crankshaft Seal – 1) To remove seal, remove flywheel. Remove lower casing-to-rear seal housing bolts. Remove seal housing bolts, seal housing and gasket. Pry seal from housing.

1989 EAGLE ENGINES
3.0L V6 (Cont.)

2) To install, install seal housing using new gasket with all bolts loosely installed. Tighten seal housing-to-cylinder block bolts to specification, then tighten lower casing-to-seal housing bolts.

3) Coat seal surfaces with engine oil. Install seal on Seal Installer (7224). Drive seal into seal housing until seal installer bottoms. Remove seal installer and install remaining components.

ENGINE OILING

LUBRICATION SYSTEM

The crankshaft driven oil pump provides pressurized lubrication to the main oil gallery. *See Fig. 14.*

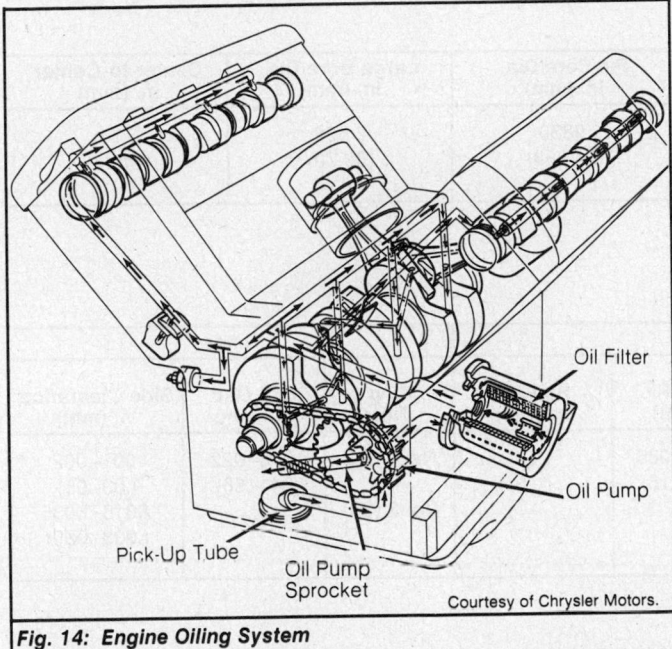

Oil Filter

Oil Pump

Pick-Up Tube

Oil Pump Sprocket

Courtesy of Chrysler Motors.

Fig. 14: Engine Oiling System

Crankcase Capacity – Engine oil capacity is approximately 6 qts. (5.7L) with filter change. Recheck oil level after changing filter.

Normal Oil Pressure – Normal oil pressure is 14.7 psi (1.0 kg/cm²) at idle and 60 psi (4.2 kg/cm²) at 4000 RPM with engine at normal operating temperature.

OIL PUMP

Removal & Disassembly – 1) Remove front timing case cover. See FRONT TIMING CASE COVER under REMOVAL & INSTALLATION in this article. Rotate crankshaft so keyway is facing upward. Remove oil pump sprocket bolts, sprocket and chain.

2) Remove oil pump cover bolts and pump cover. Remove cotter pin, retainer, spring and pressure relief valve.

Reassembly & Installation – 1) Inspect components for damage. Replace pump assembly if components are damaged. To reassem-

ble, reverse disassembly procedure. Coat components with engine oil. Pressure relief valve must be installed with open end toward spring.

2) To install, reverse removal procedure. Apply Loctite to oil pump sprocket bolts prior to installation. To prime the oil pump, remove oil filter and pour oil through hole located below oil filter threaded adapter. Install remaining components.

TIGHTENING SPECIFICATIONS

Application	Ft. Lbs. (N.m)
Camshaft Sprocket Bolt	59 (80)
Connecting Rod Nut	35 (47)
Crankshaft Pulley Nut [1]	133 (180)
Cylinder Head Bolt [2]	
Step 1	44 (60)
Step 2	Loosen Completely
Step 3	15 (20)
Step 4	106 Degrees ± 2 Degrees
Step 5	[3]
Exhaust Manifold Nut	13 (18)
Intake Manifold Bolt	11 (15)
Lower Casing-to-Cylinder Block Bolt	13 (18)
Main Bearing Cap Nut [4]	
Step 1	20 (27)
Step 2	Additional 75 Degrees
Water Pump Bolt	20 (27)

	INCH Lbs. (N.m)
Camshaft Rear Cover Plate Bolt [1]	53 (6)
Camshaft Thrust Plate Bolt	108 (12)
Oil Pan Bolt	108 (12)
Oil Pump Cover Bolt	108 (12)
Oil Pump Inlet Tube Bolt	108 (12)
Oil Pump Sprocket Bolt [1]	53 (6)
Rear Seal Housing-to-Cylinder Block Bolt	132 (15)
Rear Seal Housing-to-Lower Casing Bolt	108 (12)
Rocker Arm Shaft Lock Bolt	53 (6)
Front Timing Case Cover Bolt [5]	108 (12)
Timing Chain Guide Bolt	53 (6)
Timing Chain Tensioner Bolt	53 (6)
Timing Chain Tensioner Shoe Bolt	108 (12)
Valve Cover Bolt	108 (12)

[1] – Apply thread sealant to threads.

[2] – Tighten in sequence. See Fig. 4.

[3] – Operate engine at 1800-2000 RPM for 15 minutes, allow to cool for 6 hours, then tighten head bolts an additional 45 degrees in sequence. See Fig. 4. Ensure each bolt is torqued to at least 52 ft. lbs. (71 N.m).

[4] – Alignment Plate (6140) and lower casing must be installed. See text for procedure. Tighten nuts in sequence. See Fig. 13.

[5] – Apply thread sealant to threads on bottom 4 bolts.

ENGINE SPECIFICATIONS

GENERAL SPECIFICATIONS

Year	Displacement		Fuel System	HP@RPM	Torque Ft. Lbs.@RPM	Compr. Ratio	Bore		Stroke	
	Cu. In.	Liters					In.	mm	In.	mm
1989	182	3.0L	MPFI	[1]	171@3750	9.3:1	3.66	93.0	2.87	72.9

[1] – Information not available from manufacturer.

1989 EAGLE ENGINES
3.0L V6 (Cont.)

ENGINE SPECIFICATIONS (Cont.)

CRANKSHAFT, MAIN & CONNECTING ROD BEARINGS

| | Crankshaft | | | | Main Bearings | | Connecting Rod Bearings | |
Engine	End Play In. (mm)	Runout In. (mm)	Journal Taper In. (mm)	Journal Out-of-Round In. (mm)	Journal Diameter In. (mm)	Oil Clearance In. (mm)	Journal Diameter In. (mm)	Oil Clearance In. (mm)
3.0L	.003-.011 (.08-.28)	.....	.....	.....	2.7576-2.7583 (70.043-70.061)	.0015-.0035 (.038-.089)	2.3611-2.3618 (59.972-59.990)	.....

CONNECTING RODS

Engine	Side Play In. (mm)	Max. Bend & Twist In. (mm)	Pin Bore Dia. In. (mm)	Large Bore Dia. In. (mm)	Center-to-Center In. (mm)
3.0L	.008-.015 (.20-.38)	[1] .003 (.08)	.9830 (24.968)	2.508 (63.70)	5.75 (146.1)

[1] – Bend is listed. Twist is .002" (.05 mm).

PISTONS, PINS & RINGS

| | Pistons | | Pins | | | Rings | | |
Engine	Clearance In. (mm)	Diameter In. (mm)	Diameter In. (mm)	Piston Fit In. (mm)	Rod Fit In. (mm)	Ring No.	End Gap In. (mm)	Side Clearance In. (mm)
3.0L	.....	.....	.9839-.9843 (24.991-25.001)	.0015-.0085 (.038-.216)	.....	No. 1 & 2	.016-.022 (.41-.56)	.001-.002 (.03-.05)
						No. 3 (Oil)	.....	.0015-.0035 (.038-.089)

VALVES & VALVE SPRINGS

| | Valves | | | | | Valves Springs | | | Pressure Lbs. @ In. (Kg @ mm) | |
Engine	Head Dia. In. (mm)	Stem Dia. In. (mm)	Face Angle	Min. Margin In. (mm)	Max. Refinish In. (mm)	Free Length In. (mm)	Out-of-Square In. (mm)	Installed Height In. (mm)	Valve Closed	Valve Open
3.0L Intake	1.783 (45.29)	.315 (8.00)	45°	.059 (1.50)	.....	1.909 (48.49)	.....	1.575 (40.01)	76@1.575 (35@40.01)	155@1.220 (70@31.00)
Exhaust	1.516 (38.51)	.315 (8.00)	45°	.067 (1.70)	.....	1.909 (48.49)	.....	1.575 (40.01)	76@1.575 (35@40.01)	155@1.220 (70@31.00)

CYLINDER HEAD

| | Max. Cylinder Head Warp In. (mm) | Valve Seats | | | | Valve Guides | | |
Engine		Seat Angle	Maximum Runout In. (mm)	Seat Width In. (mm)	Seat Bore Diameter In. (mm)	Valve Stem Oil Clearance In. (mm)	Valve Guide I.D. In. (mm)	Valve Guide Bore I.D. In. (mm)
3.0L [1]	[2] .002 (.05)	45°	.....	.....	.....	.....	.315 (8.00)	.....

[1] – Cylinder head height is 4.363" (110.82 mm).

[2] – Maximum warpage is listed. Surface is not resurfaceable.

1989 EAGLE ENGINES
3.0L V6 (Cont.)

ENGINE SPECIFICATIONS (Cont.)

CAMSHAFT

Engine	Journal Diameter In. (mm)	Oil Clearance In. (mm)	Bearing Bore In. (mm)	Runout In. (mm)	End Play In. (mm)	Lobe Lift In. (mm)	Lobe Height In. (mm)
3.0L	.....	.....	.....	.....	.0030-.0055 (.076-.140)	.....	.....

CYLINDER BLOCK

Engine	Max. Block Warp In. (mm)	Cylinder Bore		
		Standard Diameter In. (mm)	Maximum Taper In. (mm)	Maximum Out-of-Rnd In. (mm)
3.0L	.....	¹ 3.6614-3.6618 (93.000-93.010)	²	

¹ – Inside diameter of liner with 1 notch on liner top is listed. Liner with 2 notches on top is 3.6618-3.6622" (93.010-93.020 mm). Liner with 3 notches on top is 3.6622-3.6626" (93.020-93.030 mm).

² – Liner protrusion is .0051-.0078" (.130-.198 mm).

1989 FORD MOTOR CO. ENGINES
1.9L 4-Cylinder (Cont.)

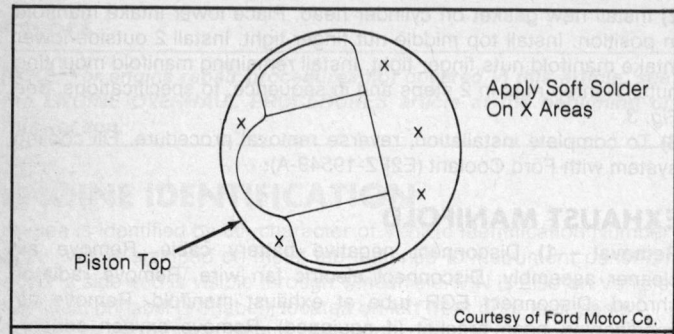

Fig. 4: Checking Piston Squish Height

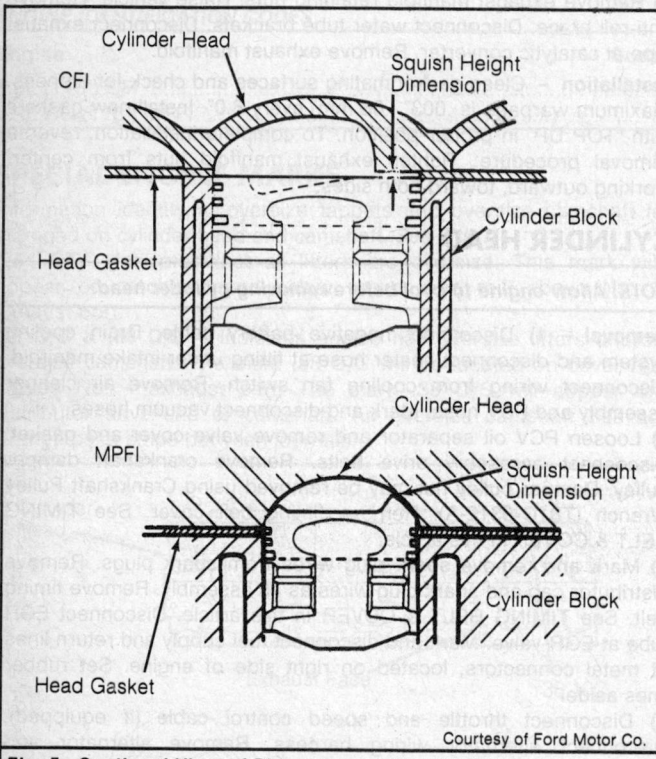

Fig. 5: Sectional View of Piston Squish Height

4) Rotate crankshaft and move piston through its TDC position. Remove cylinder head. Measure thickness of compressed solder to determine squish height at TDC. See SQUISH HEIGHT SPECIFICATIONS table.

SQUISH HEIGHT SPECIFICATIONS

Model	In. (mm)
CFI	.046-.060 (1.17-1.52)
MPFI	.039-.070 (.99-1.78)

5) If no parts other than head gasket are replaced, piston squish height should be within specifications. If parts other than head gasket are replaced and piston squish height is out of specifications, replace parts again. Recheck piston squish height. Clean and tap all cylinder head bolt threads in engine block.

CAUTION: DO NOT install cylinder head without performing piston squish height. See INSPECTION under CYLINDER HEAD in this article. DO NOT reuse cylinder head bolts.

Installation – 1) Ensure gasket mating surfaces are clean. Ensure camshaft timing mark is aligned with cylinder head mark (keyway at 9:00 o'clock position). No. 1 piston must be at TDC of compression stroke.

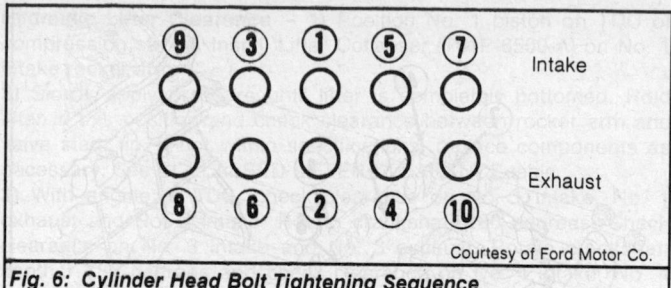

Fig. 6: Cylinder Head Bolt Tightening Sequence

2) Position cylinder head gasket on engine block. Replace cylinder head bolts. Apply light coat of engine oil to new cylinder head bolts. Install NEW cylinder head bolts.

3) Tighten all cylinder head bolts in sequence to 44 ft. lbs. (60 N.m). *See Fig. 6.* Loosen all cylinder head bolts 2 turns. Retighten cylinder head bolts in sequence to 44 ft. lbs. (60 N.m). Again in sequence, tighten cylinder head bolts 90 degrees. To complete tightening, tighten cylinder head bolts in sequence a final 90 degrees.

4) To complete installation, reverse removal procedure. Fill cooling system with Ford Coolant (E2FZ-19549-A).

TIMING BELT & COVER

CAUTION: DO NOT rotate camshaft with timing belt removed and piston at TDC. Rotate crankshaft to 90 degrees BTDC before turning camshaft.

Removal – 1) Disconnect negative battery cable. Remove accessory belts. Position No. 1 piston on TDC and align crankshaft damper mark with TDC mark on cover. Remove timing belt cover. Check camshaft sprocket timing mark to ensure alignment with mark on cylinder head.

2) If mark on camshaft sprocket and cylinder head do not align, rotate crankshaft until they are aligned. Position timing cover and ensure crankshaft damper mark align with TDC mark on cover. Remove timing cover if reinstalled. Remove crankshaft damper bolt using Crankshaft Pulley Wrench (T81P-6312-A). Remove crankshaft damper.

3) Ensure timing marks are in alignment. Loosen both belt tensioner attaching bolts. Pry tensioner away from belt and tighten one tensioner bolt. Remove timing belt from camshaft sprocket and water pump. Remove belt from crankshaft sprocket.

Installation – 1) Ensure timing marks are all aligned. Position timing belt on crankshaft sprocket. Install timing belt over remaining sprockets in a counterclockwise direction. Keep belt tight on crankshaft sprocket-to-camshaft sprocket side during installation. Loosen tensioner bolt and allow tensioner to snap against timing belt.

2) Tighten one tensioner bolt. Install crankshaft damper. Using Damper Holding Wrench (YA-826), hold damper stationary and tighten damper bolt to specification. Ensure camshaft timing marks are aligned. Position timing belt cover and check crankshaft timing mark alignment. Remove cover if aligned and proceed to next step. Repeat procedures if not aligned.

CAUTION: To prevent engine damage, DO NOT crank engine if camshaft and crankshaft timing marks are not in proper alignment.

3) Seat timing belt by rotating crankshaft several revolutions. DO NOT turn crankshaft counterclockwise. Check that camshaft timing marks are still aligned.

4) Position timing belt cover on engine and check crankshaft timing mark alignment. Damper mark must align with TDC pointer on cover. If timing marks are not in alignment, remove timing belt and repeat procedure. If timing mark alignment is correct, remove timing belt cover.

NOTE: Do not set belt tension when engine is hot.

5) Loosen timing belt tensioner bolt. Tensioner will apply correct load on belt. Tighten both tensioner bolts. To complete installation, reverse removal procedure.

CAMSHAFT OIL SEAL (FRONT)

Removal & Installation – Remove timing belt. See TIMING BELT & COVER in this article. Remove camshaft sprocket. Pry camshaft seal out, using care not to damage surfaces. Lubricate new camshaft seal lip with SAE 30 motor oil. Use Camshaft Seal Replacer (T81P-6292-A) and install seal. To complete installation, reverse removal procedure.

CAMSHAFT BEARINGS

See INSPECTION under CAMSHAFT in this article.

CAMSHAFT

Removal – 1) Disconnect negative battery cable. Remove air cleaner assembly, PCV hose and accessory drive belts. Set No. 1 piston to TDC of compression stroke.
2) Remove crankshaft damper retaining bolt and washer using Crankshaft Pulley Wrench (T81P-6312-A). Remove damper. Remove valve cover and gasket.
3) Remove timing belt cover. See TIMING BELT & COVER in this article. Check camshaft and cylinder head for oversized markings. See SPECIAL ENGINE MARKS under ENGINE IDENTIFICATION in this article.

NOTE: Mark all components prior to removal for installation reference.

---

4) Remove rocker arm bolts. Remove fulcrums, rocker arms, lifter retainer guides and lifter guides. *See Fig. 7.* Leave lifters in at this time.
5) Mark spark plug wires and disconnect wires from spark plugs. Remove spark plugs. If necessary, check the camshaft lobe lift. *See Fig. 8.*

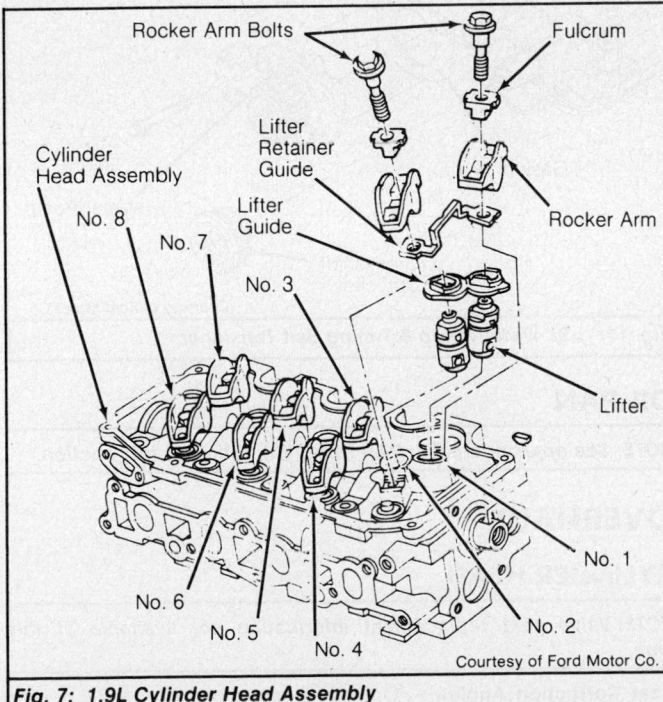

Fig. 7: 1.9L Cylinder Head Assembly

CAUTION: DO NOT rotate crankshaft with timing belt removed.

6) Remove lifters. Noting location of ignition rotor and distributor, remove distributor assembly. Loosen tension bolts and remove timing belt from camshaft sprocket.

7) Remove camshaft sprocket, Woodruff key and camshaft thrust plate. Remove ignition coil and bracket. Carefully remove camshaft through rear of cylinder head (transaxle side). Check camshaft seal and replace if necessary.

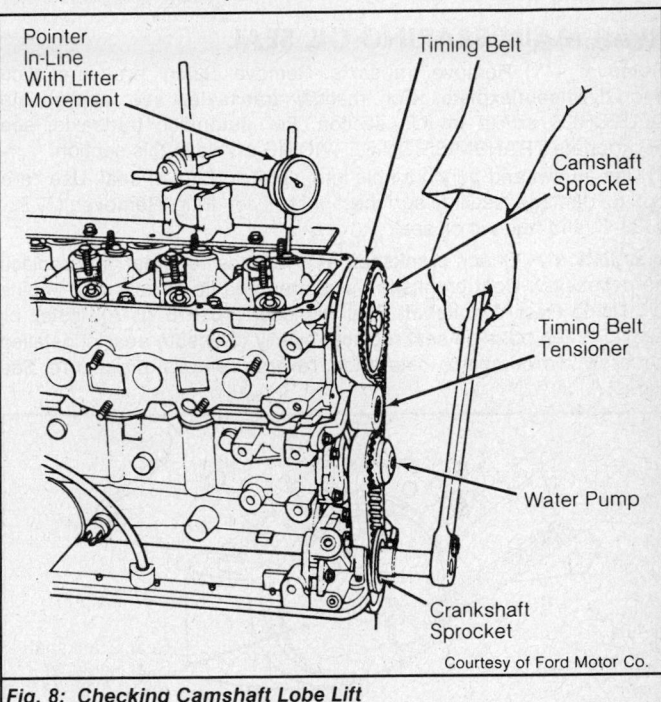

Fig. 8: Checking Camshaft Lobe Lift

Inspection – 1) Check camshaft and lifter for wear or damage. See ENGINE SPECIFICATIONS tables at end of article. Replace camshaft and lifters as necessary.
2) Check camshaft bores in cylinder head for size, taper, roundness, alignment and finish. Camshaft journals and bores in cylinder head may be machined .015" (.38 mm), to accommodate undersize bearings. Camshaft replacement is suggested.

CAUTION: When installing rocker arms, always bleed down lifters BEFORE rotating crankshaft or serious damage may result. Ensure oil gallery plug is installed in distributor end of camshaft.

Installation – 1) Thoroughly clean all bearing surfaces. Coat camshaft journals, lobes and thrust plate groove with heavy SF engine oil. Install camshaft seal (if removed), with Camshaft Seal Replacer (T81P-6292-A). Lubricate camshaft seal lip with SAE 30 engine oil.
2) Install camshaft through rear of cylinder head (transaxle side). Install camshaft thrust plate and tighten bolts. Install Woodruff key.
3) Align camshaft sprocket and Woodruff key. Install camshaft sprocket. Apply Teflon sealer to bolt. Install washer and bolt. Tighten to specification.
4) Check camshaft end play. Replace thrust plate as neccessary. Rotate camshaft until Woodruff key is in 12 o'clock position (aligned with timing mark on cylinder head).

NOTE: Ensure lifters and rocker arms are installed in original position.

---

5) Lubricate valve lifter bore with heavy SF engine oil. Install lifter, with hole in plunger facing upward. Install lifter guides over lifter flats, with notch on guide toward exhaust side. *See Fig. 7.*
6) Lubricate top of lifter and valve tip with heavy SF engine oil. Position lifter retainer guides into slots in lifter guides, on both intake and exhaust sides. Ensure notch on lifter retainer guide is with exhaust lifter. *See Fig. 7.*

NOTE: To prevent damage, DO NOT rotate camshaft until lifters are bled down.

7) Lubricate and install rocker arms. Install timing belt. See TIMING BELT & COVER in this article. To complete installation, reverse removal procedure. Fill cooling system with specified coolant only and bleed system.

REAR MAIN BEARING OIL SEAL

Removal – 1) Remove transaxle. Remove clutch, preasure plate and flywheel/flexplate. For manual transaxle, see appropriate CLUTCHES article in this section. For automatic transaxle, see appropriate TRANSMISSION SERVICING article in this section.

2) Use an awl and punch a hole into metal surface of seal. Use care not to damage sealing surfaces. Install Jet Plug Remover (T77L-9533-B) and remove oil seal.

Installation – Check crankshaft seal surface for wear and replace as necessary. Coat crankshaft seal area and lip of seal with engine oil. Using Rear Crankshaft Seal Replacer (T81P-6701-A), install oil seal. Tighten bolts on seal replacer evenly to ensure seal is installed squarely. To complete installation, reverse removal procedure. *See Fig. 9.*

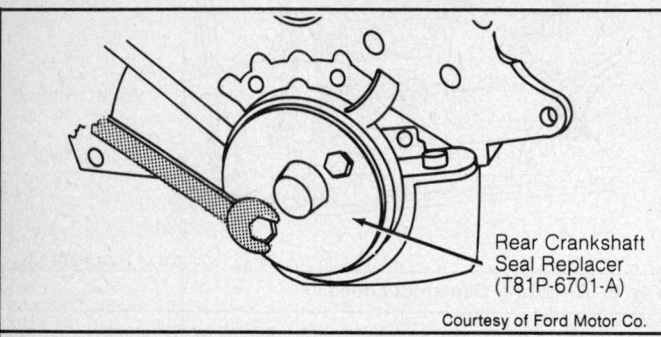

Rear Crankshaft Seal Replacer (T81P-6701-A)

Courtesy of Ford Motor Co.

Fig. 9: Installing Crankshaft Rear Main Oil Seal

FRONT CRANKSHAFT OIL SEAL

Removal & Installation – Remove timing belt, crankshaft damper and crankshaft sprocket. See TIMING BELT & COVER in this article. Pry out oil seal using care not damage sealing surfaces. Install oil seal with Seal Installer (T81P-6700-A). To complete installation, reverse removal.

WATER PUMP

Removal – 1) Disconnect negative battery cable. Drain cooling system. Remove drive belts. Remove timing belt. See TIMING BELT & COVER in this article.

2) Remove the rearward front timing cover stud. Remove the heater return tube hose connection at water pump inlet tube. *See Fig. 10.*

3) Remove alternator bracket, if necessary. Remove water pump inlet tube retainers. Remove water pump bolts. Remove water pump and gasket.

NOTE: Use only Ford Cooling System Fluid (E2FZ-19549-A) at a 50/50 ratio.

Installation – 1) Clean all gasket mating surfaces. Hold water pump inlet tube gasket with mounting flange bolts. Apply pipe sealant with Teflon to water pump mounting bolts.

2) Intstall water pump and new gasket on engine. Evenly tighten bolts to specifications. Ensure water pump impeller rotates freely. To complete installation, reverse removal procedure.

NOTE: For information on cooling system capacity, see ENGINE COOLANT SPECIFICATIONS article.

OIL PUMP

See OIL PUMP under ENGINE OILING in this article.

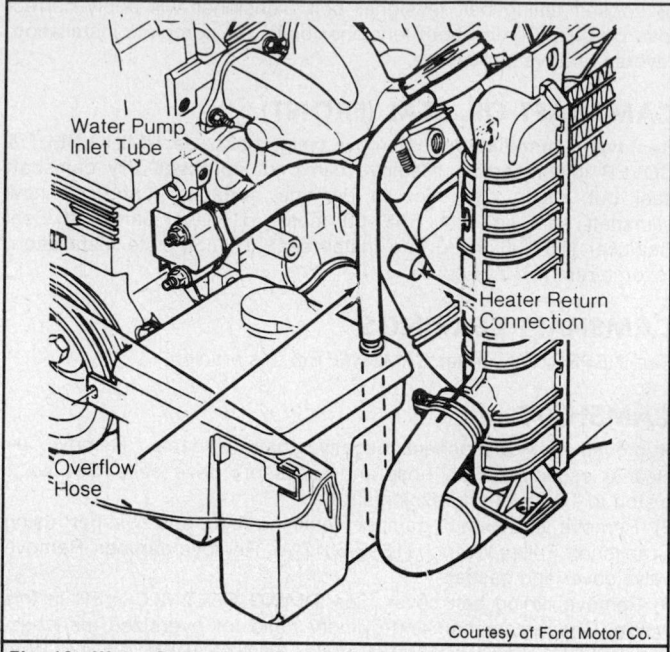

Water Pump Inlet Tube

Heater Return Connection

Overflow Hose

Courtesy of Ford Motor Co.

Fig. 10: Water Pump Inlet Tube-to-Water Pump

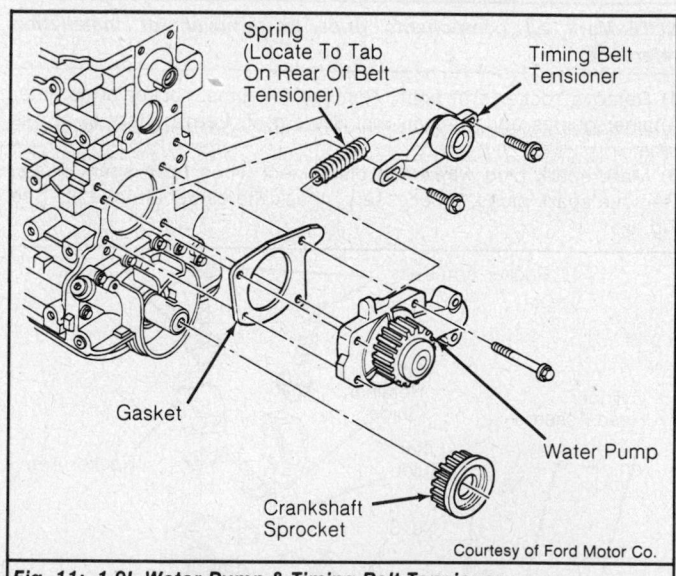

Spring (Locate To Tab On Rear Of Belt Tensioner)

Timing Belt Tensioner

Gasket

Water Pump

Crankshaft Sprocket

Courtesy of Ford Motor Co.

Fig. 11: 1.9L Water Pump & Timing Belt Tensioner

OIL PAN

NOTE: See appropriate OIL PAN REMOVAL article in this section.

OVERHAUL

CYLINDER HEAD

NOTE: Valve seat replacement information not available at this time.

Seat Correction Angles – On intake seats, use only a 77 degree angle grinding stone to remove stock from bottom of seat. On exhaust seats, use only a 70 degree angle grinding stone to remove stock from bottom of seat. Use an 18 degree grinding stone to remove stock from top of all seats. DO NOT lap valves.

Valves & Valve Guides – Mark all components prior to removal for installation reference. Check valve-to-guide clearance. *See Fig. 12.* If not within specifications, replace valve(s) with next available oversize valve. Ream valve guide until clearance is within specification. See ENGINE SPECIFICATIONS tables at end of article.

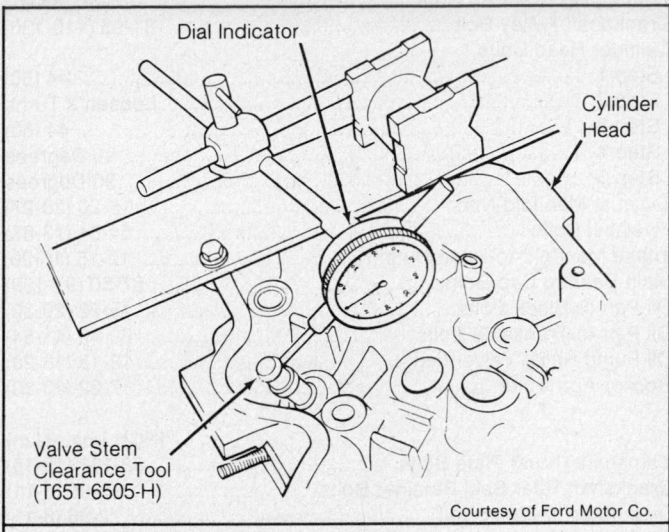

Fig. 12: Checking Valve-To-Guide Clearance

CYLINDER BLOCK ASSEMBLY

Piston & Rod Assembly – Ensure pistons and rods are installed in original locations. Ensure arrow on top of piston faces front of engine and oil squirt hole in rod faces intake manifold side of engine. *See Fig. 13.* Install rings on piston with ring ends 90 degrees apart. *See Fig. 14.*

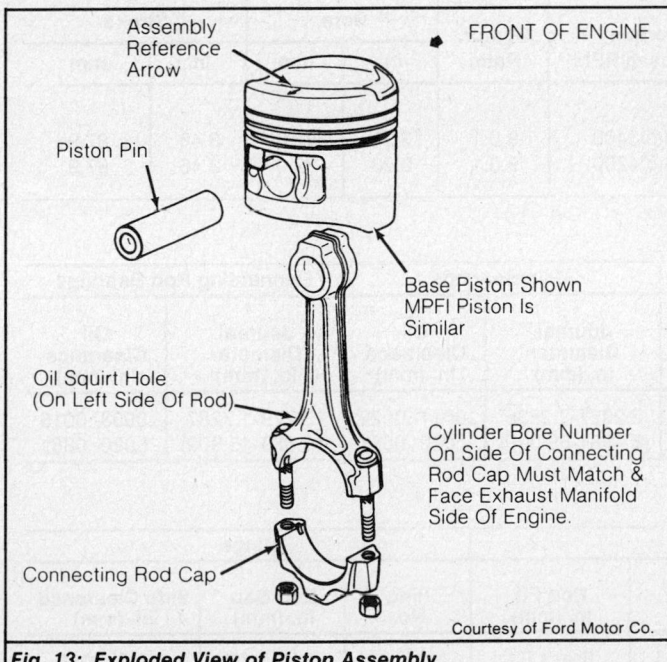

Fig. 13: Exploded View of Piston Assembly

Fitting Pistons – Standard size pistons are color coded Red, Blue or Yellow on the piston dome. If piston-to-bore clearance is in lower one-third of specified clearance, use a Red piston. If clearance is in middle of specified clearance, use Blue piston. The Yellow piston is .004" (.10 mm) oversize. Use proper piston to acquire specified clearance.

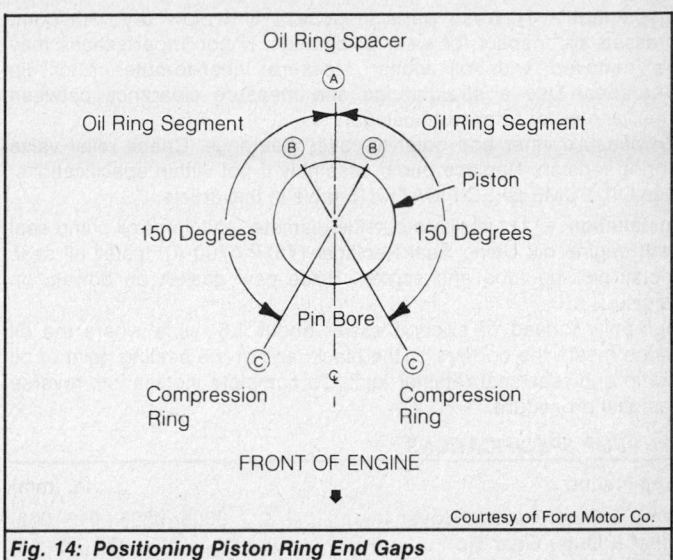

Fig. 14: Positioning Piston Ring End Gaps

Crankshaft & Bearings – 1) If oil clearance is not within specifications with standard bearings, use .002" (.050 mm) undersize and recheck clearance. Always replace rod or main bearings in pairs.

NOTE: Main bearing caps are numbered from No. 1 to No. 5. Arrow on cap points toward from of engine.

2) Before checking crankshaft end play, tighten main bearing caps to specification. Thrust bearing is center main bearing in block.

Flywheel – Maximum flywheel cluch face runout limit is .007" (.18 mm) T.I.R. Replace flywheel if more than .045" (1.14 mm) needs to be machined from original surface.

Cylinder Block – 1) Using a straightedge and feeler gauge, ensure cylinder block head gasket surface is flat within .003" (.08 mm) over entire surface. Check cylinder bore for wear, taper, out-of-round and piston fit. See ENGINE SPEIFICATIONS tables at end of this article.

2) Use ONLY equal parts of kerosene and SAE 20 motor oil for honing cylinder bores. Install and tighten main bearing caps to specifications before cylinder refinishing. Use ONLY a spring-loaded type cylinder hone. After honing, allow cylinders to cool. Clean bore with detergent and water solution. Tap cylinder head bolt threads in cylinder block.

ENGINE OILING

LUBRICATION SYSTEM

Engine oiling is a full pressure system. Oil pump is bolted to front of cylinder block with pump drive gear positioned directly over crankshaft. Oil pump is driven directly by crankshaft.

Crankcase Capacity – Crankcase capacity is 4 qts. (3.8L) with filter change, 3.5 qts. (3.3L) without filter change.

Normal Oil Pressure – Oil pressure is 35-65 psi (2.40-4.50 kg/cm²) at 2000 RPM, with engine at normal operating temperature.

OIL PUMP

Removal – Disconnect negative battery cable. Remove timing belt, crankshaft damper and sprocket. Disconnect starter cable and remove starter. Drain engine oil and remove oil pan. See appropriate OIL PAN REMOVAL article in this section. Remove oil pump retaining bolts. Pull oil pump assembly and gasket from engine. Remove oil pump seal.

Disassembly & Reassembly – If oil pump is found to be defective, complete unit must be replaced.

1989 FORD MOTOR CO. ENGINES
1.9L 4-Cylinder (Cont.)

Inspection – 1) Wash parts in solvent and blow dry with compressed air. Inspect for wear or damage. Minor imperfections may be removed with oil stone. Measure inner-to-outer rotor tip clearance. Use a straightedge and measure clearance between inner and outer rotor-to-housing.

2) Measure inner and outer-to-cover clearance. Check relief valve spring tension. Replace pump assembly if not within specifications. See OIL PUMP SPECIFICATIONS table in this article.

Installation – 1) Lubricate outside diameter and lip of oil pump seal with engine oil. Using Seal Replacer (T81P-6700-A), install oil seal. Install pick-up tube and screen. Place new gasket on dowels on engine.

2) Apply a bead of silicone sealer about 1.8" wide where the oil pump meets the corners of the block, and at the sealing point of oil pump and rear seal retainer joint. To complete installation, reverse removal procedure.

OIL PUMP SPECIFICATIONS

Application	In. (mm)
Inner & Outer Gear-to-Cover	.0005-.0035 (.013-.009)
Inner & Outer Gear Tip	.002-.007 (.05-.18)
Outer Gear-to-Housing	.0029-.0063 (.074-.160)
Relief Valve-to-Bore [1]	.0008-.0031 (.020-.079)

[1] – Relief valve spring tension is 9.3-10.3 lbs. @ 1.11 in. (4.2-4.6 kg @ 28.2 mm).

TIGHTENING SPECIFICATIONS

Application	Ft. Lbs. (N.m)
Belt Tensioner Bolts	17-20 (23-27)
Camshaft Sprocket-to-Camshaft Bolts	71-84 (95-115)
Connecting Rod Cap Nuts	26-30 (35-41)
Crankshaft Pulley Bolt	81-96 (110-130)
Cylinder Head Bolts [1]	
Step 1	44 (60)
Step 2	Loosen 2 Turns
Step 3	44 (60)
Step 4	90 Degrees
Step 5	90 Degrees
Exhaust Manifold Nuts	15-20 (20-27)
Flywheel Bolts	54-64 (73-87)
Intake Manifold-to-Head Nuts [2]	12-15 (16-20)
Main Bearing Cap Bolts	67-80 (91-109)
Oil Pan-to-Block Bolts	15-22 (20-30)
Oil Pan-to-Transaxle Bolts	30-40 (41-54)
Oil Pump Relief Valve Plug	12-15 (16-20)
Rocker Arm Bolts	17-22 (23-30)

Application	INCH Lbs. (N.m)
Camshaft Thrust Plate Bolts	88-132 (10-15)
Crankshaft Rear Seal Retainer Bolts	72-96 (8-11)
Distributor-to-Block Bolt	72-96 (8-11)
Oil Pump	
Cover Bolts	72-108 (8-12)
Pick-Up Tube Bolts	88-124 (10-14)
Pump-to-Block Bolts	72-96 (8-11)
Valve Cover-to-Head Bolts	72-96 (8-11)

[1] – Tighten bolts in sequence. See Fig. 6.
[2] – See Fig. 2 for tightening sequence.

ENGINE SPECIFICATIONS

GENERAL SPECIFICATIONS

Year	Displacement Cu. In.	Displacement Liters	Fuel System	HP@RPM	Torque Ft. Lbs.@RPM	Compr. Ratio	Bore In.	Bore mm	Stroke In.	Stroke mm
1989										
CFI	116	1.9	Central F.I.	90@4600	106@3400	9.0:1	3.23	82.0	3.46	87.9
EFI HO	116	1.9	Multi-Port F.I.	110@5200	115@4200	9.0:1	3.23	82.0	3.46	87.9

CRANKSHAFT, MAIN & CONNECTING ROD BEARINGS

Engine	Crankshaft End Play In. (mm)	Crankshaft Runout In. (mm)	Crankshaft Journal Taper In. (mm)	Crankshaft Journal Out-of-Round In. (mm)	Main Bearings Journal Diameter In. (mm)	Main Bearings Oil Clearance In. (mm)	Connecting Rod Bearings Journal Diameter In. (mm)	Connecting Rod Bearings Oil Clearance In. (mm)
1.9L	.004-.008 (.10-.20)	.002 (.05)	.0003 (.008)	.0003 (.008)	2.2827-2.2835 (57.981-58.000)	.0011-.0022 (.028-.056)	1.7279-1.7287 (43.889-43.909)	.0008-.0015 (.020-.038)

PISTONS, PINS & RINGS

Engine	Pistons Clearance In. (mm)	Pistons Diameter In. (mm)	Pins Diameter In. (mm)	Pins Piston Fit In. (mm)	Pins Rod Fit In. (mm)	Ring No.	Rings End Gap In. (mm)	Rings Side Clearance In. (mm)
1.9L	.0016-.0024 (.040-.060)	[1] 3.224-3.225 (81.89-81.92)	.8119-.8124 (20.622-20.634)	.0003-.0005 (.007-.013)	Press Fit	1	.010-.020 (.25-.50)	.0015-.0032 (.038-.081)
						2	.010-.020 (.25-.50)	.0015-.0035 (.038-.089)
						3 (Oil)	.016-.055 (.04-1.40)	Snug Fit

[1] – Diameter for Red coded standard piston. For other standard pistons see following:
Blue: 3.225-3.226" (81.92-81.94 mm).
Yellow (.004" Oversize): 3.226-3.227" (81.94-81.97 mm).

ENGINE SPECIFICATIONS (Cont.)

CYLINDER BLOCK

Engine	Max. Block Warp In. (mm)	Cylinder Bore		
		Standard Diameter In. (mm)	Maximum Taper In. (mm)	Maximum Out-of-Rnd In. (mm)
1.9L [1]	.003 (.08)	3.23 (82.0)	.010 (.25)	.005 (.13)

[1] – Main bearing bore diameter is 2.4523-2.4528" (62.288-62.301 mm).

VALVE LIFTERS

Engine	Diameter In. (mm)	Bore Diameter In. (mm)	Oil Clearance In. (mm)
1.9L	.8740-.8745 (22.199-22.212)	.8754-.8766 (22.235-22.353)	.0009-.0026 (.023-.066)

CAMSHAFT

Engine	Journal Diameter In. (mm)	Oil Clearance In. (mm)	Bearing Bore In. (mm)	Runout In. (mm)	End Play In. (mm)	Lobe Lift In. (mm)	Lobe Height In. (mm)
1.9L	[1] 1.8007-1.8017 (45.738-45.763)	.0013-.0033 (.034-.084)	1.8030-1.8040 (45.796-45.822)	[2] .005 (.13)	.0018-.0060 (.046-.152)	.240 (6.09)	.....

[1] – Out of round limit is .003" (.08 mm).
[2] – Measured at center bearing.

VALVES & VALVE SPRINGS

Engine	Valves					Valves Springs			Pressure Lbs. @ In. (Kg @ mm)	
	Head Dia. In. (mm)	Stem Dia. In. (mm)	Face Angle	Min. Margin In. (mm)	Max. Refinish In. (mm)	Free Length In. (mm)	Out-of-Square In. (mm)	Installed Height In. (mm)	Valve Closed	Valve Open
1.9L Intake	1.66 (42.1)	.3159-.3167 (8.03-8.043)	45°	.031 (.79)	.010 (.25)	[1] 1.86 (47.2)	.060 (1.52)	[2] 1.44-1.48 (36.6-37.6)	[3] 95@1.46 (42@37.1)	200@1.09 (89@27.7)
Exhaust	1.50 (38.1)	.3149-.3156 (7.996-8.017)	45°	.031 (.79)	.010 (.25)	[1] 1.86 (47.2)	.060 (1.52)	[2] 1.44-1.48 (36.6-37.6)	[3] 95@1.46 (42@37.1)	200@1.09 (89@27.7)

[1] – For engine with Central Fuel Injection. On High Output engines with multi-port fuel injection, free length is 1.90" (48.3 mm).
[2] – For high output engine with multi-port fuel injection. Specifications not available for base engine with Central Fuel Injection.
[3] – For engine with Central Fuel Injection. On High Output engine with multi-port fuel injection, spring pressure is as follows:
Valve Closed: 95 Lbs. @ 1.46" (42 kg @ 37.1 mm).
Valve Open: 216 Lbs. @ 1.02" (96 kg @ 25.8 mm).

CONNECTING RODS

Engine	Side Play In. (mm)	Max. Bend & Twist In. (mm)	Pin Bore Dia. In. (mm)	Large Bore Dia. In. (mm)	Center-to-Center In. (mm)
1.9L	[1] .004-.011 (.10-.28)	.002 (.05)	.8106-.8114 (20.589-20.610)	1.8460-1.8468 (46.888-46.909)	5.193-5.196 (131.90-131.98)

[1] – Service limit is .014" (.36 mm).

CYLINDER HEAD

Engine	Max. Cylinder Head Warp In. (mm)	Valve Seats				Valve Guides		
		Seat Angle	Maximum Runout In. (mm)	Seat Width In. (mm)	Seat Bore Diameter In. (mm)	Valve Stem Oil Clearance In. (mm)	Valve Guide I.D. In. (mm)	Valve Guide Bore I.D. In. (mm)
1.9L [1] Intake	[2] .006 (.15)	[3] 45°	.003 (.08)	.069-.091 (1.75-2.31)	[4] 1.572-1.573 (39.93-39.95)	.0008-.0027 (.020-.069)	.3174-.3187 (8.062-8.095)	.5310-.5324 (13.487-13.523)
Exhaust		45°	.003 (.08)	.069-.091 (1.75-2.31)	1.375-1.573 (34.93-39.95)	.0018-.0037 (.046-.095)	.3174-.3187 (8.062-8.095)	.5310-.5324 (13.487-13.523)

[1] – Distributor shaft bearing bore diameter is 1.852-1.854" (47.04-47.09 mm).
[2] – .003" (.08 mm) per 6" (152.4) maximum.
[3] – Seat correction angles for top angle is 18 degrees on intake and exhaust. Bottom correction is 77 degrees on intake and 70 degrees on exhaust.
[4] – For engines with Central Fuel Injection. On MPFI engines, valve seat bore diameters are as follows:
Intake: 1.723-1.724" (43.76-43.79 mm).
Exhaust: 1.506-1.507" (38.25-38.28 mm).

1989 FORD MOTOR CO. ENGINES
2.2L 4-Cylinder

Probe

NOTE: For engine repair procedures not covered in this article, see the ENGINE OVERHAUL PROCEDURES article at the beginning of this section.

ENGINE IDENTIFICATION

Engine may be identified by the Vehicle Identification Number (VIN) located on top of instrument panel near lower left corner of windshield. The VIN number is also stamped on Vehicle Certification lable (VC lable), mounted on the left front door pillar. The 8th character of VIN identifies the engine and 10th character "K" indicates 1989 model.

ENGINE IDENTIFICATION CODES

Engine	Code
2.2L Non-Turbo	C
2.2L Turbo	L

ADJUSTMENTS

VALVE ARRANGEMENT

Firewall Side – Intake valves.
Exhaust Manifold Side – Exhaust valves.

VALVE CLEARANCE ADJUSTMENT

No valve adjustment is required, as hydraulic valve lifters are used.

REMOVAL & INSTALLATION

NOTE: For reassembly reference, label all electrical connectors, vacuum hoses and fuel lines before removal. Also place mating marks on engine hood and other major assemblies before removal.

ENGINE

NOTE: See ENGINE REMOVAL & INSTALLATION article at end of ENGINE SECTION.

INTAKE MANIFOLD

CAUTION: Fuel system is under pressure. Fuel pressure must be released prior to disconnecting or servicing fuel system components.

Removal – 1) Fuel pressure must be released. Disconnect fuel pump relay. See Fig. 1. Start engine and operate until it stalls. Disconnect negative battery cable. Reconnect fuel pump relay.

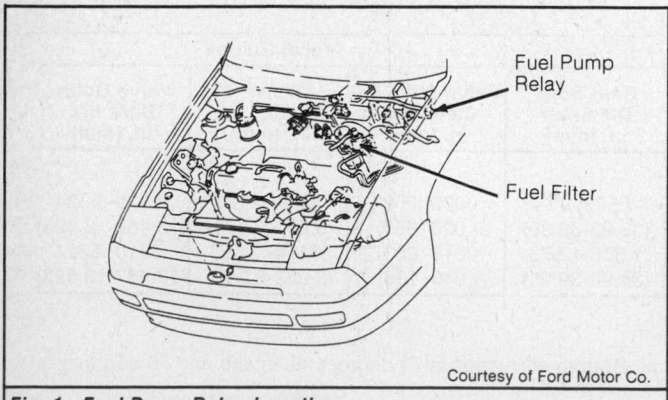

Fuel Pump Relay

Fuel Filter

Courtesy of Ford Motor Co.

Fig. 1: Fuel Pump Relay Location

2) Drain cooling system. Disconnect necessary coolant hoses and vacuum lines. Disconnect throttle body control cables and air intake duct. Remove all hose, wiring and control cable brackets.

3) Remove PCV hose from upper intake manifold. Remove upper intake manifold and gasket. See Fig. 2. Disconnect fuel lines from fuel rail. Disconnect fuel injector electrical connections and coolant temperature switch (if equipped).

4) Disconnect all fuel line brackets from intake manifold. Remove fuel rail bolts, spacers and fuel rail with fuel injectors. Disconnect EGR pipe. Remove lower intake manifold bolts, manifold and gasket.

Installation – To install, reverse removal procedure using new gaskets and "O" rings. Coat "O" rings with engine oil prior to installation. Ensure proper adjustment of all control cables.

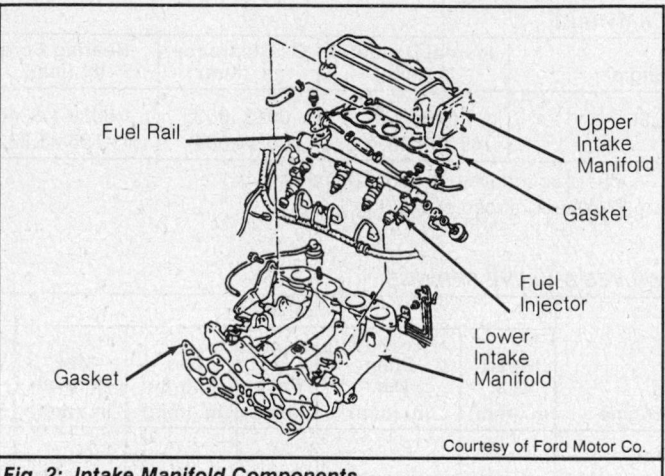

Fuel Rail

Upper Intake Manifold

Gasket

Fuel Injector

Lower Intake Manifold

Gasket

Courtesy of Ford Motor Co.

Fig. 2: Intake Manifold Components

EXHAUST MANIFOLD

Removal (Turbo) – 1) Disconnect negative battery cable and oxygen sensor connector. Drain cooling system. Disconnect hoses from air inlet and compressor housing of turbo.

2) Remove manifold heat shields. Disconnect oil feed and return lines, and coolant lines from turbo. Remove EGR tube from exhaust

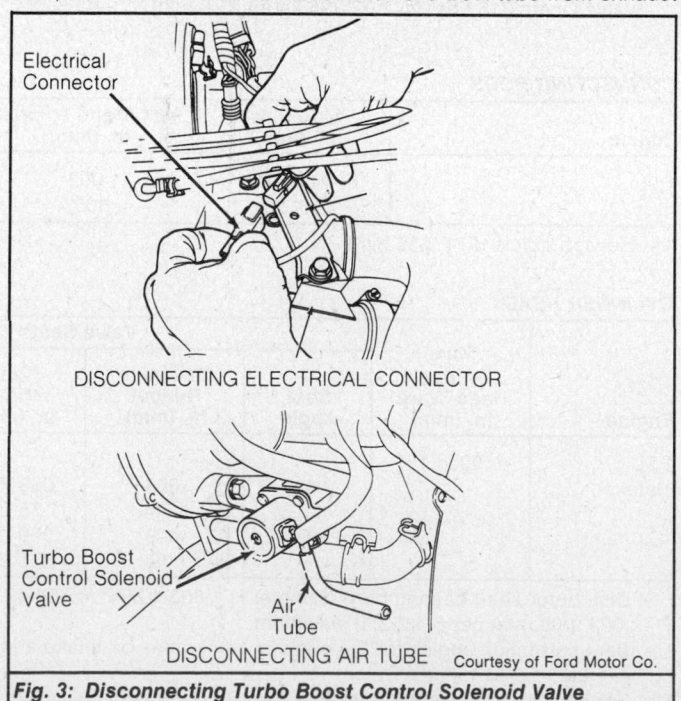

Electrical Connector

DISCONNECTING ELECTRICAL CONNECTOR

Turbo Boost Control Solenoid Valve

Air Tube

DISCONNECTING AIR TUBE Courtesy of Ford Motor Co.

Fig. 3: Disconnecting Turbo Boost Control Solenoid Valve

manifold. Disconnect electrical connections and air tube from turbo boost control solenoid valve. *See Fig. 3.*

3) Remove mounting bracket from lower side of turbo. Discharge A/C system and remove line from A/C compressor (if necessary). Disconnect oxygen sensor. Disconnect catalytic converter pipe from turbo joint pipe.

4) Remove exhaust pipe from joint pipe attached to turbo housing. Remove exhaust manifold bolts, exhaust manifold with turbo and gaskets. Remove turbo from exhaust manifold.

Installation – 1) To install, reverse removal procedure using new gaskets. Install gasket with raised area against exhaust manifold. Ensure special type nuts are installed to retain turbo on exhaust manifold.

2) Pour .85 ozs. (.02L) of engine oil in oil feed passage of turbo prior to installing oil feed line.

CAUTION: If turbo was removed from exhaust manifold, ensure special type nuts are used for turbo installation. Pour .85 ozs. (.02L) of engine oil in oil feed passage of turbo prior to installing oil feed line.

---

3) Once all components are installed and cooling system is filled, disconnect coil wire at ignition coil. Crank engine for approximately 20 seconds. Reconnect coil wire.

4) Start engine and allow to idle for 30 seconds. Stop engine and disconnect negative battery cable. Depress brake pedal for at least 5 seconds to cancel trouble code. Reconnect negative battery cable.

Removal (Non-Turbo) – Disconnect oxygen sensor connector. Disconnect exhaust pipe from manifold. Remove outer heat shield. Remove exhaust manifold bolts, manifold, inner shield and gaskets.

Installation – To install, reverse removal procedure using new gaskets. Install gasket with raised area against exhaust manifold.

CAMSHAFT

Removal – 1) Remove timing belt, camshaft sprocket and front housing. See TIMING BELT & SPROCKETS under REMOVAL & INSTALLATION in this article. Remove rear housing. *See Fig. 4.* Using dial indicator, check camshaft end play.

2) Replace camshaft or cylinder head if end play is not within specification. See ENGINE SPECIFICATIONS tables at end of article. Remove rocker arms and lash adjusters. See ROCKER ARMS & LASH ADJUSTERS under REMOVAL & INSTALLATION in this article. Mark camshaft bearing cap location for reassembly reference. Remove camshaft bearing caps and camshaft.

CAUTION: Camshaft bearing cap location must be marked prior to removing bearing caps. Bearing caps are installed so that the arrow on the caps points toward front of the engine.

Inspection – Inspect camshaft journal diameter, lobe lift, oil clearance and runout. See ENGINE SPECIFICATIONS tables at end of article. Replace components if not within specification.

Installation – 1) To install, reverse removal procedure. Coat camshaft and camshaft bearing caps with engine oil prior to installation. Install camshaft with dowel pin facing straight up.

2) Apply silicone sealant in front and rear camshaft bearing cap areas prior to installation. *See Fig. 7.* Install camshaft bearing caps with ARROW pointing toward front of engine.

CAUTION: Camshaft bearing caps must be installed in original location with ARROW toward front of the engine. The No. 3 bearing cap contains an oil passage from the cylinder head and must be installed in correct location. Silicone sealant must be applied in front and rear camshaft bearing cap areas prior to installation. See Fig. 7.

---

3) To install remaining components, reverse removal procedure. Ensure components are installed in original location. Ensure all timing marks are aligned.

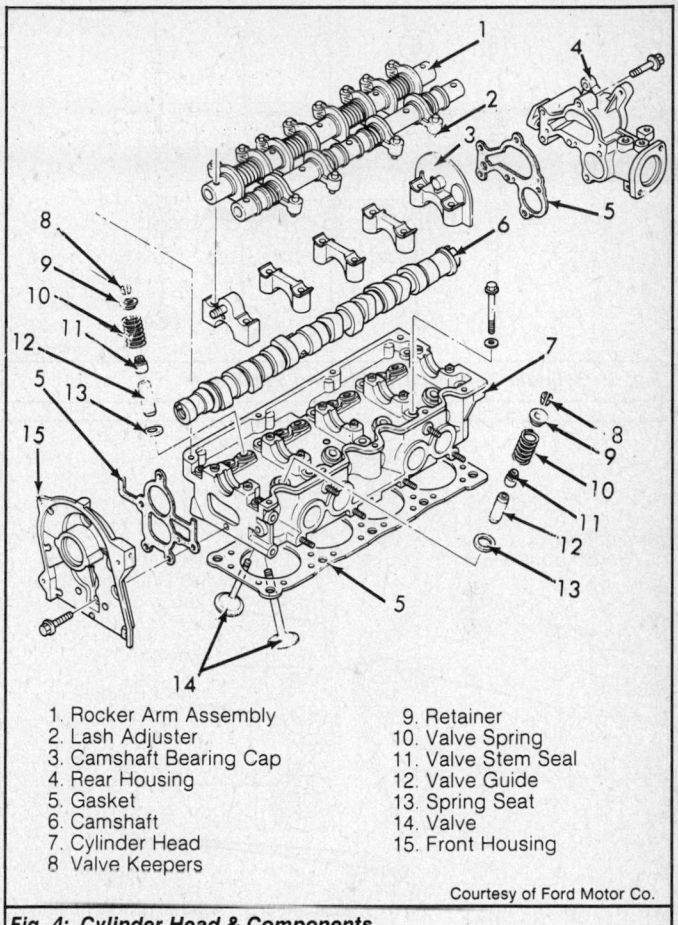

1. Rocker Arm Assembly	9. Retainer
2. Lash Adjuster	10. Valve Spring
3. Camshaft Bearing Cap	11. Valve Stem Seal
4. Rear Housing	12. Valve Guide
5. Gasket	13. Spring Seat
6. Camshaft	14. Valve
7. Cylinder Head	15. Front Housing
8. Valve Keepers	

Courtesy of Ford Motor Co.

Fig. 4: Cylinder Head & Components

CYLINDER HEAD

Removal – 1) Remove intake manifold. See INTAKE MANIFOLD under REMOVAL & INSTALLATION in this article. Remove exhaust manifold. See EXHAUST MANIFOLD under REMOVAL & INSTALLATION in this article.

2) Remove timing belt. See TIMING BELT & SPROCKETS under REMOVAL & INSTALLATION in this article. Remove valve cover. Place reference mark on distributor and remove distributor.

3) Remove engine lifting hooks and engine ground strap. Remove necessary coolant hoses. Disconnect electrical connections at thermostat housing. Remove cylinder head bolts, cylinder head and gasket.

Inspection – Inspect cylinder head warpage. See CYLINDER HEAD under OVERHAUL in this article. Inspect block deck surface warpage. See CYLINDER BLOCK ASSEMBLY under OVERHAUL in this article.

CAUTION: Ensure proper type cylinder head gasket is used. Different type gasket is used for non-turbo and turbo models.

Installation – 1) To install, reverse removal procedure. Ensure cylinder head bolt threads and cylinder block are clean. Ensure proper type cylinder head gasket is used. Different type gasket is used for non-turbo and turbo models.

2) Apply light coat of oil to head bolts threads and seating surface prior to installation. Tighten cylinder head bolts to specification in 2 steps using proper sequence. *See Fig. 5.* To install remaining components, reverse removal procedure. Ensure all timing marks are aligned.

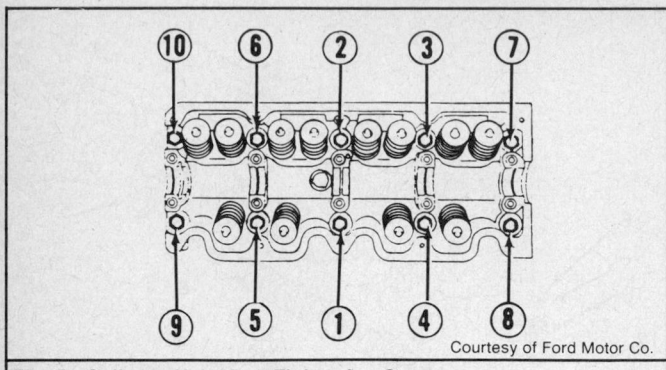

Fig. 5: Cylinder Head Bolt Tightening Sequence

Courtesy of Ford Motor Co.

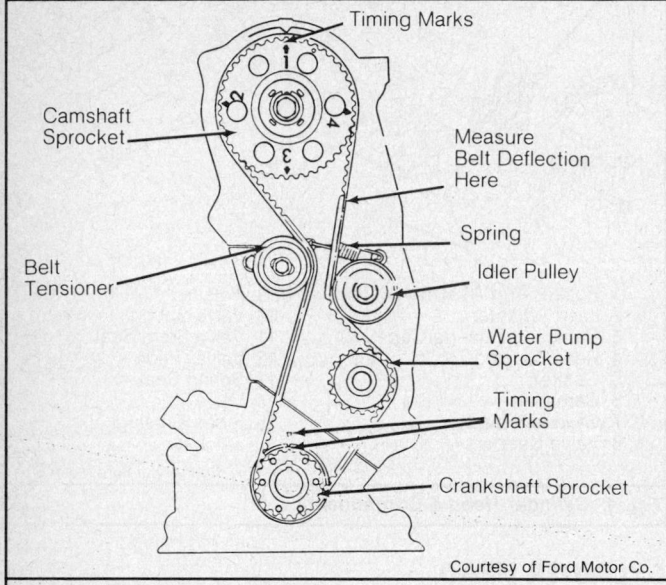

Fig. 6: Timing Belt & Components

Courtesy of Ford Motor Co.

TIMING BELT & SPROCKETS

Checking Timing – 1) Disconnect negative battery cable. Remove right inner fender panel. Remove accessory drive belt. Remove upper timing belt cover.

2) Rotate engine in direction of rotation and position No. 1 cylinder on TDC of compression stroke. Ensure crankshaft pulley notch aligns with mark on lower timing belt cover.

3) Ensure the No. 1 on camshaft sprocket is aligned with mark on cylinder head. See Fig. 6. If No. 1 is not aligned, rotate engine one revolution and recheck alignment. If No. 1 is not aligned, timing belt must be removed, sprockets properly positioned, and reinstalled.

CAUTION: Timing belt must be marked for direction of rotation if belt is to be reinstalled.

Removal – 1) Remove timing belt cover. See TIMING BELT COVER under REMOVAL & INSTALLATION in this article. Rotate crankshaft so the No. 1 on camshaft sprocket is aligned with mark on cylinder head and crankshaft sprocket timing mark is aligned with mark on oil pump housing. See Fig. 6.

2) Mark timing belt direction of rotation if belt is to be reused. Remove spring from belt tensioner. Remove belt tensioner retaining bolt and belt tensioner. Remove timing belt.

3) If camshaft sprocket requires removal, hold camshaft sprocket and remove sprocket retaining bolt. Remove camshaft sprocket. If crankshaft sprocket requires removal, remove sprocket retaining bolt and remove crankshaft sprocket.

Installation – 1) To install crankshaft and camshaft sprockets, reverse removal procedure. Ensure No. 1 mark on camshaft sprocket aligns with camshaft dowel pin. Tighten sprocket retaining bolts to specification.

2) Rotate crankshaft so the No. 1 on camshaft sprocket is aligned with mark on cylinder head and crankshaft sprocket timing mark is aligned with mark on oil pump housing. See Fig. 6.

3) Install timing belt in original direction of rotation. Install belt tensioner and spring. Temporarily position belt tensioner with spring fully extended and tighten retaining bolt.

4) Ensure no looseness exists on timing belt at water pump sprocket and idler pulley locations.

5) Loosen belt tensioner bolt and allow tension to be applied to timing belt. Rotate engine 2 full revolutions in direction of rotation. Ensure all timing marks are aligned. Tighten belt tensioner bolt.

6) Measure belt deflection half way between idler pulley and camshaft sprocket. See Fig. 6. Belt deflection should be .30-.33" (7.6-8.4 mm) with 22 lbs. (9 kg) pressure. If deflection is incorrect, repeat step **5)** or replace belt tensioner. To install remaining components, reverse removal procedure.

TIMING BELT COVER

Removal – 1) Remove accessory drive belts. Remove right inner fender panel. Remove crankshaft pulley and sprocket baffle plate. Sprocket baffle plate is located behind crankshaft pulley. Note direction of sprocket baffle plate installation.

2) Support engine and remove retaining nuts and dowels from right engine mount. Remove engine mount. Remove bolts from upper and lower timing belt covers. Remove timing belt covers and gaskets.

Installation – To install, reverse removal procedure using new gaskets. Ensure sprocket baffle plate is installed with curved outer lip toward the crankshaft pulley.

FRONT HOUSING & CAMSHAFT SEAL

Removal & Installation – 1) Remove valve cover. Remove timing belt and camshaft sprocket. See TIMING BELT & SPROCKETS under REMOVAL & INSTALLATION in this article. Remove front housing bolts, front housing and gasket. Remove seal from housing. Note direction of seal installation.

2) To install, lubricate front housing and seal with engine oil. Using press and Seal Installer (T88C-6701-AH), install seal in front housing. Install front housing and new gasket. Install remaining components. Apply silicone sealant to designated areas prior to installing valve cover. See Fig. 7.

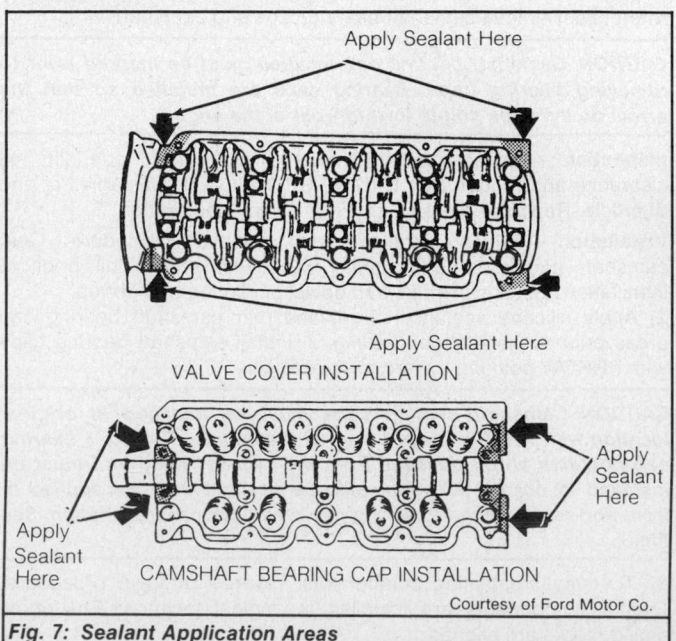

Fig. 7: Sealant Application Areas

Courtesy of Ford Motor Co.

FRONT CRANKSHAFT SEAL

Seal is contained in oil pump housing. No information is available from manufacturer for on vehicle service.

REAR CRANKSHAFT SEAL

Removal – Remove transaxle. On M/T models, remove clutch and pressure plate. On all models, remove flywheel or flexplate. Remove seal housing and gasket. *See Fig. 8.* Remove seal from housing. Note direction of seal installation.

Installation – Coat seal and housing with engine oil. Using press and Seal Installer (T88C-6701-BH), install seal in housing. Seal must be installed with hollow side toward the crankshaft. Install seal housing with new gasket. Trim gasket even with cylinder block. Install remaining components.

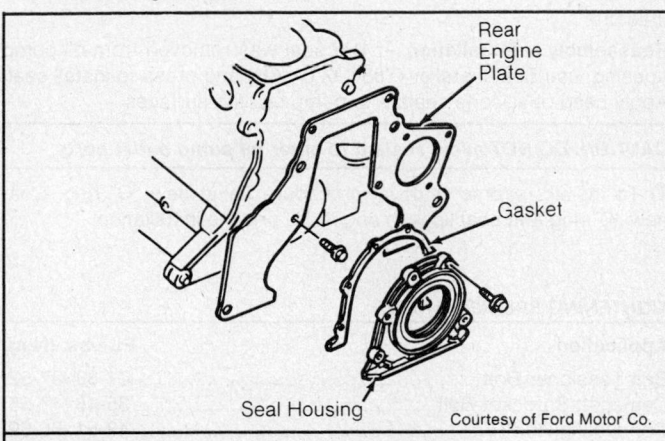

Fig. 8: Rear Crankshaft Seal & Components

Courtesy of Ford Motor Co.

ROCKER ARMS & LASH ADJUSTERS

Removal – Remove valve cover. Mark component location prior to removal. Remove rocker arm assembly bolts evenly, starting at the ends and working inward. Remove rocker arm assembly.

CAUTION: Rocker arm location must be noted. Intake side shaft contains twice as many oil holes as the exhaust side. Different type stepped ends are used on the rear of the shafts. See Fig. 9.

Disassembly & Inspection – 1) Mark rocker arm assembly component location for reassembly reference. Disassemble rocker arm assemblies. DO NOT remove lash adjuster unless necessary.
2) Inspect components for damage. Measure rocker arm I.D. and rocker arm shaft O.D. Determine oil clearance. Maximum oil clearance is .004" (.10 mm). Replace necessary components. Inspect lash adjusters for damage. Remove only if damaged.
Reassembly & Installation – 1) Coat components with engine oil. Install lash adjuster (if removed) using new "O" ring. Install components in original location. Intake side shaft contains twice as many oil holes as the exhaust side. Different type stepped ends are used on the rear of the shafts. *See Fig. 9.*

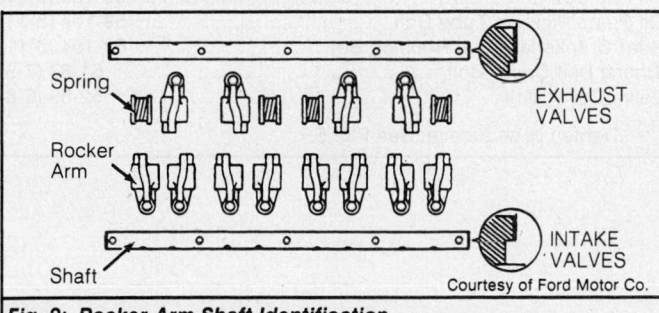

Fig. 9: Rocker Arm Shaft Identification

Courtesy of Ford Motor Co.

2) Ensure all camshaft bearing caps are installed with arrow pointing toward front of engine. If camshaft bearing caps were removed, ensure silicone sealant is applied in proper areas. *See Fig. 7.* To install, reverse removal procedure. Tighten rocker arm bolts evenly to specification starting from the center and working outward.

WATER PUMP

Removal & Installation – Drain cooling system. Remove timing belt. See TIMING BELT & SPROCKETS under REMOVAL & INSTALLATION in this article. Remove water pump bolts, water pump and "O" ring. To install, reverse removal procedure using new "O" ring. Fill cooling system.

OIL PAN

NOTE: See appropriate OIL PAN REMOVAL article in this section.

OVERHAUL

CYLINDER HEAD

Inspection – Inspect cylinder head for warpage at deck surface and manifold surfaces. Resurface cylinder head if warpage exceeds specification. See ENGINE SPECIFICATIONS tables at end of article.
Valve Seats – No replacement procedure is given from manufacturer.
Valve Guides – 1) Valve guide can be replaced if valve stem oil clearance is not within specification. See ENGINE SPECIFICATIONS tables at end of article.
2) To remove valve guide, heat cylinder head in water to approximately 190°F (90°C). Using Valve Guide Remover/Installer (T87C-6510-A) and hammer, drive valve guide toward the camshaft side of the cylinder head.
3) To install, use valve guide remover/installer and install valve guide until valve guide protrusion is .752-.772" (19.10-19.61 mm) above cylinder head. *See Fig. 10.*

NOTE: Exhaust valve guides are installed for both intake and exhaust valves when valve guides are replaced.

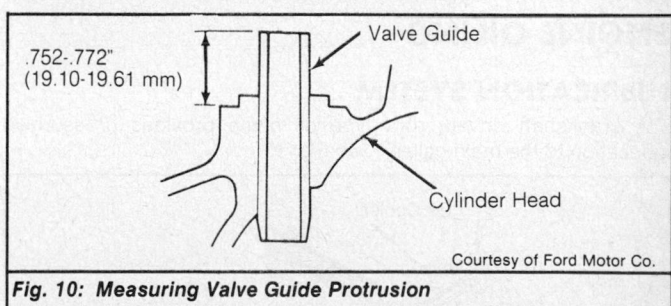

Fig. 10: Measuring Valve Guide Protrusion

Courtesy of Ford Motor Co.

Seat Correction Angles – Information not available from manufacturer.

VALVE TRAIN

Valve Stem Oil Seals – Use Valve Stem Oil Seal Installer (T87C-6510-B) for seal installation.

CYLINDER BLOCK ASSEMBLY

Piston Ring Installation – Piston rings must be installed with identification mark toward top of piston and rings properly spaced. *See Fig. 11.* Oil ring expander should be installed so ends of ring are positioned over solid area of piston, not over piston oil drain hole.

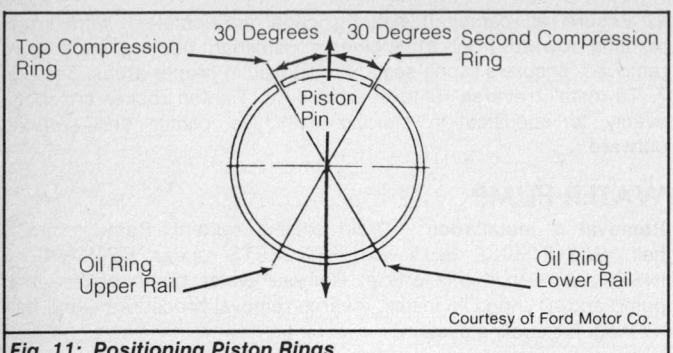

Fig. 11: Positioning Piston Rings

Piston & Rod Assembly – Piston should be installed on connecting rod with "F" mark opposite the connecting rod oil hole. *See Fig. 12.* Piston and connecting rod must be installed with "F" mark on top of the piston toward the front of engine.

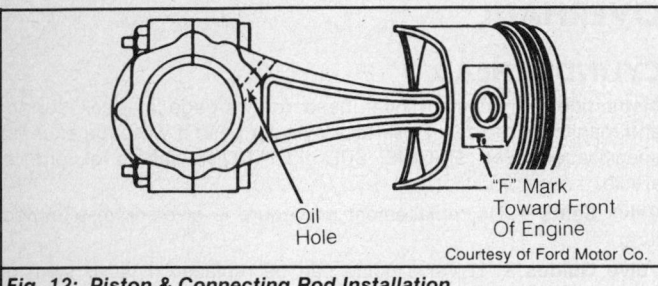

Fig. 12: Piston & Connecting Rod Installation

Fitting Pistons – Piston diameter should be measured .709" (18.01 mm) below oil ring groove and 90 degrees to piston pin.

Crankshaft & Bearings – Thrust bearing alignment procedures are not available from manufacturer. Main bearing caps must be installed with arrow pointing toward front of engine.

Cylinder Block – Using feeler gauge and straightedge, inspect deck surface for warpage. Warpage should not exceed specification. See ENGINE SPECIFICATIONS tables at end of article. Replace cylinder block if more than .008" (.20 mm) material is removed from deck surface.

ENGINE OILING

LUBRICATION SYSTEM

The crankshaft driven, rotor-type oil pump provides pressurized lubrication to the main gallery. *See Fig. 13.*

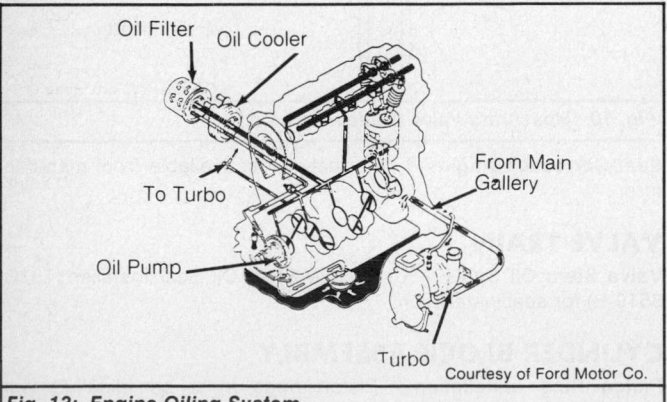

Fig. 13: Engine Oiling System

Normal Oil Pressure – Normal oil pressure is 57 psi (4.0 kg/cm²) at 3000 RPM with engine at normal operating temperature.

Crankcase Capacity – Engine oil capacity is approximately 4.5 qts. (4.3L) without filter change or 4.9 qts. (4.6L) with filter change. Recheck oil level after changing filter.

OIL PUMP

Removal – 1) Remove timing belt and crankshaft sprocket. See TIMING BELT & SPROCKETS under REMOVAL & INSTALLATION in this article. Remove oil pan. See appropriate OIL PAN REMOVAL article in this section.

2) Remove oil pump pick-up tube. Remove oil pump bolts, oil pump, gasket and "O" ring.

Disassembly & Inspection – Information not available from manufacturer.

Reassembly & Installation – 1) If seal was removed from oil pump housing, use Seal Installer (T88C-6701-AH) and press to install seal. Apply bead of silicone sealant to pump sealing surfaces.

CAUTION: DO NOT allow sealant to enter oil pump outlet ports.

2) To install, reverse removal procedure using new "O" ring. Coat new "O" ring and seal lip with engine oil prior to installation.

TIGHTENING SPECIFICATIONS

Application	Ft. Lbs. (N.m)
Belt Tensioner Bolt	27-38 (37-52)
Camshaft Sprocket Bolt	35-48 (47-65)
Connecting Rod Nut	48-51 (65-69)
Crankshaft Sprocket Bolt	108-116 (1465-157)
Cylinder Head Bolt	[1] 59-64 (80-87)
Exhaust Manifold Bolt	16-21 (22-29)
Exhaust Manifold Heat Shield Bolt	14-22 (19-30)
Flywheel or Flexplate Bolt	71-76 (96-103)
Front Housing Bolt	14-19 (19-26)
Fuel Rail Bolt	14-19 (19-26)
Intake Manifold Bolt	
Lower Manifold	14-22 (19-30)
Upper Manifold	14-22 (19-30)
Main Bearing Cap Bolt	61-65 (83-88)
Oil Pump Bolt	
8 mm	14-19 (19-26)
10 mm	27-38 (37-52)
Rear Engine Plate Bolt	14-22 (19-30)
Rear Housing Bolt	14-19 (19-26)
Rocker Arm Shaft Assembly Bolt	13-20 (18-27)
Thermostat Housing Nut	14-22 (19-30)
Turbo Retaining Nut	20-29 (27-39)
Water Pump Bolt	14-19 (19-26)

	INCH Lbs. (N.m)
Crankshaft Pulley Bolt	109-152 (12-17)
Oil Pan Bolt	69-104 (8-11)
Oil Pump Pick-Up Tube Bolt	69-104 (8-11)
Rear Crankshaft Seal Housing Bolt	69-104 (8-11)
Timing Belt Cover Bolt	61-87 (7-9)
Valve Cover Bolt	52-69 (6-8)

[1] – Tighten in sequence. See Fig. 5.

ENGINE SPECIFICATIONS

GENERAL SPECIFICATIONS

| Year | Displacement | | Fuel System | HP@RPM | Torque Ft. Lbs.@RPM | Compr. Ratio | Bore | | Stroke | |
	Cu. In.	Liters					In.	mm	In.	mm
1989										
Non-Turbo	134	2.2	MPFI	110@4700	130@3000	8:5:1	3.39	86.1	3.70	93.9
Turbo	134	2.2	MPFI	145@4300	190@3500	7:8:1	3.39	86.1	3.70	93.9

PISTONS, PINS & RINGS

| Engine | Pistons | | Pins | | | Rings | | |
	Clearance In. (mm)	Diameter In. (mm)	Diameter In. (mm)	Piston Fit In. (mm)	Rod Fit In. (mm)	Ring No.	End Gap In. (mm)	Side Clearance In. (mm)
2.2L	.0014-.0030 (.036-.076)	3.3836-3.3844 (85.943-85.963)	.8651-.8654 (21.973-21.981)	.0003-.0009 (.008-.023)	.0005-.0015 (.013-.038)	No. 1	.008-.014 (.20-.35)	.001-.003 (.02-.07)
						No. 2	.006-.012 (.15-.30)	.001-.003 (.02-.07)
						No. 3 (Oil)	[1]	.....

[1] – End gap is .006-.014" (.15-.35 mm) on turbo models or .012-.035" (.30-.89 mm) on non-turbo models.

CRANKSHAFT, MAIN & CONNECTING ROD BEARINGS

| Engine | Crankshaft | | | | Main Bearings | | Connecting Rod Bearings | |
	End Play In. (mm)	Runout In. (mm)	Journal Taper In. (mm)	Journal Out-of-Round In. (mm)	Journal Diameter In. (mm)	Oil Clearance In. (mm)	Journal Diameter In. (mm)	Oil Clearance In. (mm)
2.2L	.0031-.0071 (.078-.180)	.0012 (.030)	.....	.002 (.05)	2.3597-2.3604 (59.936-59.954)	[1]	2.0055-2.0061 (50.940-50.955)	.0011-.0026 (.027-.066)

[1] – Oil clearance is .0010-.0017" (.025-.043 mm) on all journals except No. 3. Oil clearance on No. 3 journal is .0012-.0019" (.030-.048 mm).

CONNECTING RODS

Engine	Side Play In. (mm)	Max. Bend & Twist In. (mm)	Pin Bore Dia. In. (mm)	Large Bore Dia. In. (mm)	Center-to-Center In. (mm)
2.2L	[1] .004-.010 (.10-.25)	.0016 Per 3.94 (.041 Per 100.1)	.8640-.8645 (21.945-21.958)	.....	.....

[1] – Service limit is .012" (.30 mm).

CYLINDER HEAD

| Engine | Max. Cylinder Head Warp In. (mm) | Valve Seats | | | | Valve Guides | | |
		Seat Angle	Maximum Runout In. (mm)	Seat Width In. (mm)	Seat Bore Diameter In. (mm)	Valve Stem Oil Clearance In. (mm)	Valve Guide I.D. In. (mm)	Valve Guide Bore I.D. In. (mm)
2.2L	.006 (.15)	45°	.....	.047-.063 (1.19-1.60)	.....	.008 (.02)	.2760-.2768 (7.010-7.030)	.....

1989 FORD MOTOR CO. ENGINES
2.2L 4-Cylinder (Cont.)

ENGINE SPECIFICATIONS (Cont.)

CAMSHAFT

Engine	Journal Diameter In. (mm)	Oil Clearance In. (mm)	Bearing Bore In. (mm)	Runout In. (mm)	End Play In. (mm)	Lobe Lift In. (mm)	Lobe Height In. (mm)
2.2L							
No. 1 & 5	1.2575-1.2585 (31.940-31.965)	.0014-.0033 (.035-.083)	.....	.0012 (.030)	.003-.008 (.08-.20)	.....	1
No. 2, 3 & 4	1.2563-1.2573 (31.910-31.935)	.0026-.0045 (.066-.114)	.....	.0012 (.030)	.003-.008 (.08-.20)	.....	1

1 – Lobe height is 1.626-1.630" (41.30-41.40 mm) on intake valves with wear limit of 1.620" (41.15 mm). Lobe height is 1.646-1.650" (41.81-41.91 mm) on exhaust valves with wear limit of 1.640" (41.66 mm).

VALVES & VALVE SPRINGS

	Valves					Valves Springs				
Engine	Head Dia. In. (mm)	Stem Dia. In. (mm)	Face Angle	Min. Margin In. (mm)	Max. Refinish In. (mm)	Free Length In. (mm)	Out-of-Square In. (mm)	Installed Height In. (mm)	Pressure Lbs. @ In. (Kg @ mm) Valve Closed	Valve Open
2.2L										
Intake	.....	.2744-.2750 (6.969-6.985)	45°	.....	.....	1 1.949 (49.50)	.067 (1.70)	.....	.....	.....
Exhaust	.....	.2742-.2748 (6.965-6.979)	45°	.....	.....	1 1.984 (50.39)	.067 (1.70)	.....	.....	.....

1 – Minimum free length is 1.902" (48.31 mm) for intake valves or 1.937" (49.19 mm) for exhaust valves.

CYLINDER BLOCK

Engine	Max. Block Warp In. (mm)	Cylinder Bore Standard Diameter In. (mm)	Maximum Taper In. (mm)	Maximum Out-of-Rnd In. (mm)
2.2L	1 .006 (.15)	3.3858-3.3866 (85.999-86.019)	.0007 (.018)	.0007 (.018)

1 – Replace cylinder block if more than .008" (.20 mm) material is removed.

Taurus, Tempo, Topaz

NOTE: For engine repair procedures not covered in this article, see ENGINE OVERHAUL PROCEDURES article at beginning of this section.

ENGINE IDENTIFICATION

Engine may be identified by the Vehicle Identification Number (VIN) at top of instrument panel near windshield on left side of vehicle and visible from outside. VIN number is also stamped on Safety Certification Decal on left front door lock face panel and on Engine Identification Label on valve cover.

The VIN number contains 17 characters. The 8th character identifies the engine and the 10th character identifies the model year. To determine if the engine is High Swirl Combustion (HSC) or High Swirl Output (HSO), use the emission calibration number label located on the drivers door or pillar.

ENGINE IDENTIFICATION CODES

Engine	¹ Code
2.3L (140") HSC MPFI	X
2.3L (140") HSO MPFI	S
2.5L (153") HSC CFI	D

¹ – Eight character of VIN.

ADJUSTMENTS

VALVE ARRANGEMENT

I-E-I-E-E-I-E-I (Front-to-rear).

HYDRAULIC LIFTER ASSEMBLY

Hydraulic Lifter Clearance – 1) Place No. 1 piston on TDC of compression stroke. Install Lifter Collapser (T81P-6500-A) on No. 1 intake rocker arm.

2) Slowly apply pressure until lifter is completely bottomed. Check clearance between rocker arm and valve stem tip. If not within specifications, replace components as necessary. See COLLAPSED LIFTER CLEARANCE table.

3) With engine at TDC, check clearance on No. 1 intake, No. 1 exhaust, No. 2 intake and No. 3 exhaust. Rotate crankshaft 180 degrees and check clearance on No. 2 exhaust, No. 3 intake, No. 4 intake and No. 4 exhaust.

COLLAPSED LIFTER CLEARANCE

Application	In. (mm)
2.3L & 2.5L	.072-.174 (1.83-4.42)

REMOVAL & INSTALLATION

NOTE: For reassembly reference, label all electrical connectors, vacuum hoses and fuel lines before removal. Also place mating marks on engine hood and other major assemblies before removal.

ENGINE

NOTE: See ENGINE REMOVAL & INSTALLATION article at end of ENGINE section.

INTAKE & EXHAUST MANIFOLDS

Removal – 1) Disconnect negative battery cable. Drain cooling system. Remove air cleaner assembly. Remove heat stove tube at heat shield. Disconnect throttle cable. Mark and remove vacuum lines and electrical connectors.

2) Remove 3 nuts attaching exhaust manifold to inlet pipe. Remove exhaust manifold heat shield assembly. Disconnect oxygen sensor. Disconnect throttle linkage. Remove thermactor check valve hose at tube. Remove EGR valve and bracket. Disconnect coolant inlet tube at intake manifold.

3) Relieve the fuel pressure at pressure relief valve. See Fig. 1. Disconnect fuel lines using Spring Lock Coupling (D87-9280-A for 3/8"; D87L-9280-B for 1/2"). Remove heater hose at fitting located under intake manifold. Remove intake and exhaust manifold bolts. Remove intake and exhaust manifolds. See Fig. 1.

Inspection – Clean and check gasket mating surface. Intake and exhaust manifold warpage should not exceed .005" (.12 mm) overall. Cylinder head mating surface should not exceed .007" (.18 mm) warpage overall.

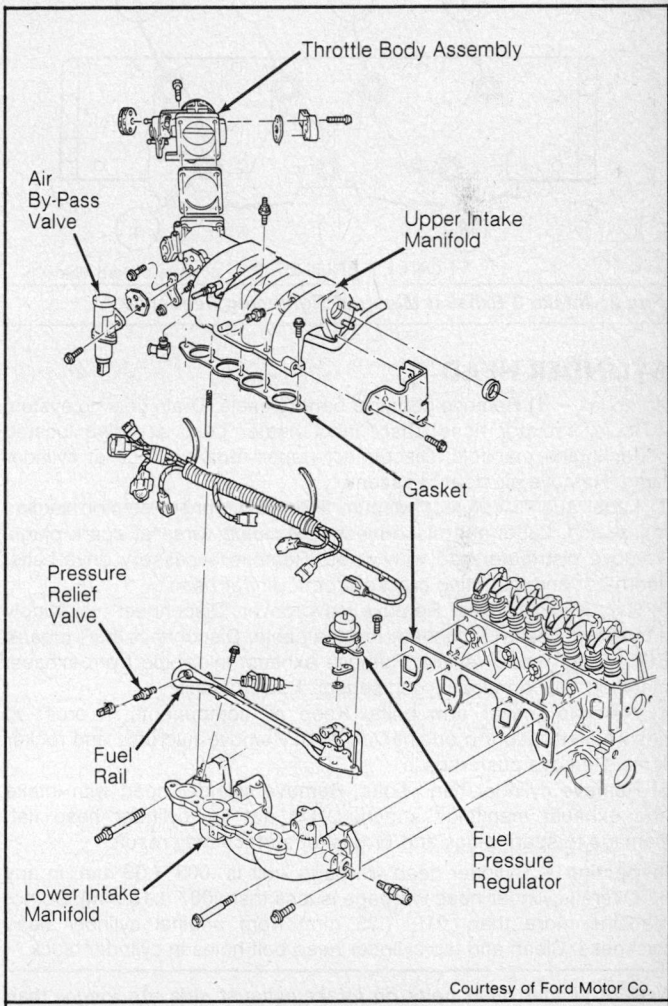

Courtesy of Ford Motor Co.

Fig. 1: 2.3L HSC Intake Manifold Assembly

Installation – 1) Position exhaust manifold on cylinder head with Exhaust Manifold Alignment Studs (T84P-6065-B) in holes No. 2 and 3. See Fig. 2. Install attaching bolts in remaining holes. Remove guide studs and install bolts. Tighten exhaust manifold bolts in 2 steps and sequence. See Fig. 2.

2) Coat new intake manifold gasket with sealer. Position intake manifold and gasket on cylinder head. Tighten bolts to specifications and in sequence. See Fig. 2. To complete installation, reverse removal procedure.

1989 FORD MOTOR CO. ENGINES
2.3L HSC/HSO & 2.5L HSC 4-Cylinder (Cont.)

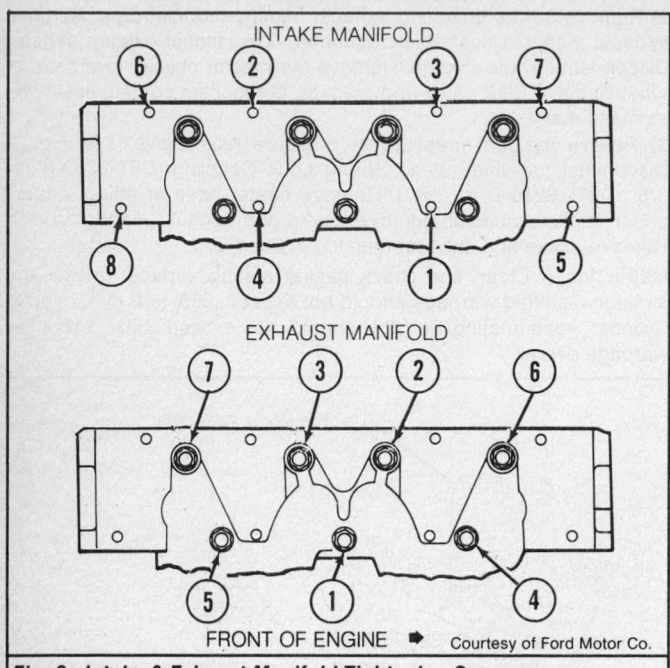

Fig. 2: Intake & Exhaust Manifold Tightening Sequence

CYLINDER HEAD

Removal – 1) Remove negative battery cable. Drain cooling system at lower radiator hose. Disconnect heater hose at fitting located under intake manifold. Disconnect upper radiator hose at cylinder head. Remove air cleaner assembly.

2) Label and disconnect vacuum lines. Disconnect electric cooling fan switch. Label and disconnect spark plug wires at spark plugs. Remove distributor cap with wires. Remove accessory drive belts, alternator and mounting bracket from cylinder head.

3) Remove PCV hose. Remove valve cover. Disconnect fuel supply and return lines. Disconnect throttle cable. Disconnect EGR tube at EGR valve. Raise vehicle. Remove exhaust inlet pipe from exhaust manifold. Disconnect oxygen sensor. Lower vehicle.

4) Remove rocker arm bolts. Keep all components in order to ensure installation to original location. Remove fulcrums and rocker arms. Remove push rods.

5) Remove cylinder head bolts. Remove cylinder head with intake and exhaust manifolds attached. Do not lay cylinder head flat. Damage to spark plugs and/or gasket surface may result.

Inspection – Cylinder head warpage limit is .003" (.08 mm) in any 6". Overall cylinder head warpage is less than .007" (.18 mm). Do not machine more than .010" (.25 mm) from original cylinder head thickness. Clean and tap cylinder head bolt holes in cylinder block.

NOTE: Cylinder head bolts on intake/exhaust side are longer than spark plug side of cylinder head.

Installation – 1) Use 2 old cylinder head bolts and cut the head off, to use as guide pins. Slot top of old bolts for screwdriver access. Install fabricated guide pins in bolt hole Nos. 7 and 10. *See Fig. 3.* Install head gasket. Ensure marked side of gasket is in proper position.

2) Install cylinder head. Install cylinder head bolts until snug. Remove 2 guide pins and install 2 cylinder head bolts. Tighten cylinder head bolts in 2 steps and sequence. *See Fig. 3.*

3) Align crankshaft sprocket timing mark with camshaft sprocket timing mark (TDC on compression stroke). Install push rods, rocker arms and fulcrums on No. 1 intake and exhaust, No. 2 intake and No. 3 exhaust. *See Fig. 4.*

4) Tighten rocker arm bolts to specifications. Completely collapse lifter by applying pressure on push rod before rotating engine.

5) Rotate crankshaft 180 degrees. Install push rods, rocker arms and fulcrums on No. 2 exhaust, No. 3 intake and No. 4 intake and exhaust. Tighten rocker arm bolts to specifications. Completely collapse lifters and rotate crankshaft 180 degrees.

6) To complete installation, reverse removal procedure. Tighten all bolts and nuts to specifications. Change oil and filter. Fill fluid levels. Start engine and check for leakage.

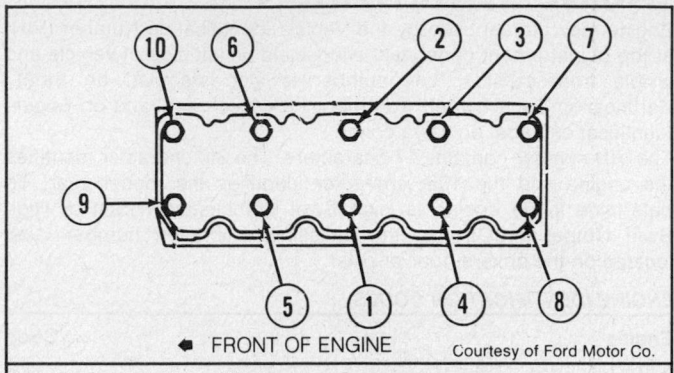

Fig. 3: Cylinder Head Tightening Sequence

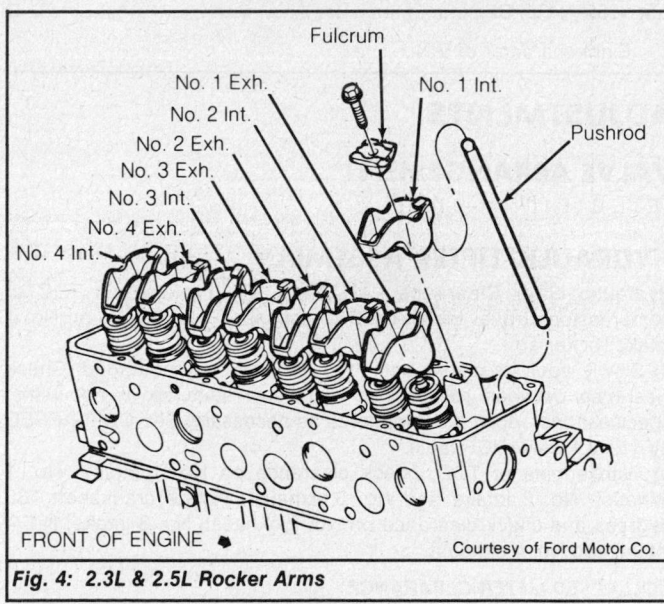

Fig. 4: 2.3L & 2.5L Rocker Arms

FRONT COVER & TIMING CHAIN

Removal – 1) On Tempo and Topaz models, engine must be removed from vehicle. See ENGINE REMOVAL & INSTALLATION article at end of ENGINE section. Remove oil dipstick.

2) Remove accessory drive belts. Remove crankshaft damper bolt and washer. Remove crankshaft damper with Remover (T77F-4220-B). Remove front cover oil seal using Seal Remover (T74P-6700-A). Remove bolts from front cover and necessary oil pan bolts.

3) Pry top of front cover away from cylinder block. Remove front cover and gasket. Check timing chain and components. See INSPECTION. Align camshaft sprocket and crankshaft sprocket timing marks.

4) Remove camshaft sprocket retaining bolt and washer. Slide camshaft sprocket, crankshaft sprocket and timing chain assembly forward. Remove as an assembly.

Inspection – 1) Clean gasket mating surfaces. Check timing chain tensioner blade and timing chain vibration damper for wear. Check timing chain deflection by rotating crankshaft counterclockwise to take up slack on left side of chain. Mark a reference point on cylinder block and measure from this point to chain.

2) Move crankshaft in opposite direction to take up slack on right side of chain. Force left side of chain out with fingers. Measure

1989 FORD MOTOR CO. ENGINES
2.3L HSC/HSO & 2.5L HSC 4-Cylinder (Cont.)

7-77

distance between reference point and chain. The difference between the 2 measurements is the deflection. If not within specifications, replace necessary components. See TIMING CHAIN SPECIFICATIONS table in this article.

TIMING CHAIN SPECIFICATIONS

Application	In. (mm)
Timing Chain Deflection (Max.)	.500 (12.70)
Tensioner Wear (Max.)	.06 (1.5)

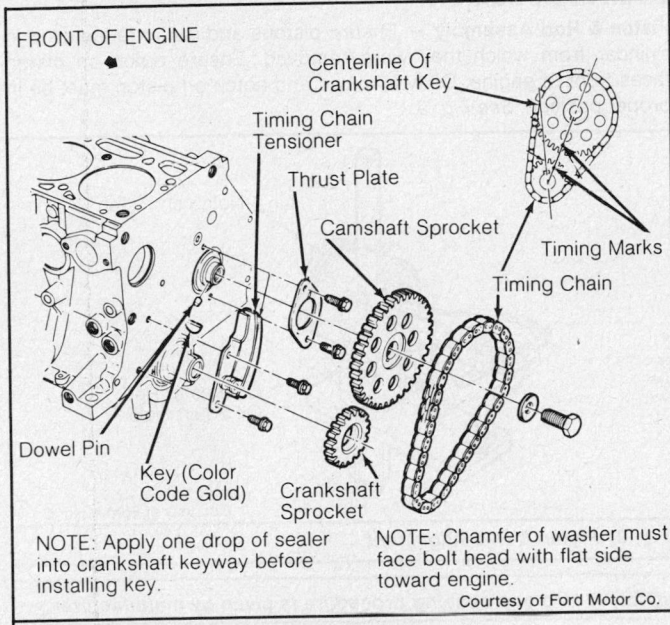

FRONT OF ENGINE

NOTE: Apply one drop of sealer into crankshaft keyway before installing key.

NOTE: Chamfer of washer must face bolt head with flat side toward engine.

Courtesy of Ford Motor Co.

Fig. 5: Exploded View of Timing Chain

Installation – 1) Apply drop of sealer in crankshaft keyway or to crankshaft key. Install key in crank. Align camshaft sprocket and crankshaft sprocket timing marks. Slide timing chain and sprockets into position. On cranskshaft sprocket with chamfers around keyway, fill keyway chamfer cavity with Threadlock and Sealer (E0AZ-19554-Z), flush with front face of sprocket.
2) Install camshaft bolt and washer. Ensure flat side of washer faces camshaft sprocket.

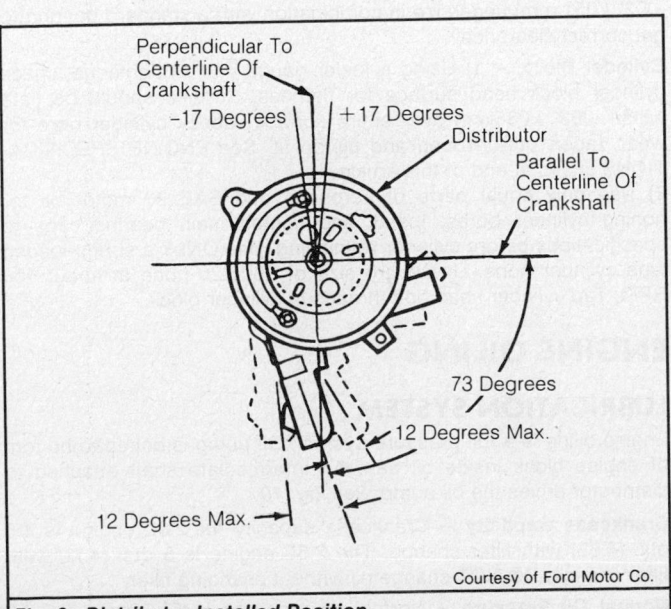

Courtesy of Ford Motor Co.

Fig. 6: Distributor Installed Position

3) Oil timing chain, sprockets and tensioner after installation. Position gasket on cover. DO NOT install front cover oil seal until cover is installed on block.
4) Install Front Cover Aligner (T84P-6019-C) on crankshaft. Install front cover and gasket. Install front cover bolts and tighten to specifications. Remove aligner.
5) Coat hub of crankshaft with multipurpose grease. Using Pinion Seal Installer (T83T-4676-A), install new front cover seal. To complete installation, reverse removal procedure.

DISTRIBUTOR

Removal & Installation – With engine at TDC of compression stroke, use *Fig. 6* as reference for installing the distributor.

REAR CRANKSHAFT OIL SEAL

Removal – Remove transaxle. On manual transaxle models, remove clutch disc, pressure plate and flywheel. See appropriate article in CLUTCHES section. On automatic transaxle models, remove flexplate. See appropriate article in TRANSMISSION SERVICING section. Using an awl, punch a hole into metal surface of seal. Pry out seal.

Installation – Check crankshaft seal surface for wear and replace as necessary. Coat crankshaft seal area and lip of oil seal with engine oil. Using Rear Crankshaft Seal Replacer (T81P-6701-A), install oil seal. Tighten bolts on seal replacer evenly, to ensure seal is installed squarely. To complete installation, reverse removal procedure.

FRONT CRANKSHAFT OIL SEAL

Removal & Installation – Remove accessory belts. Remove bolt and washer from crankshaft damper. Remove crankshaft damper with Differential Side Bearing Puller (T77F-4220-B1). Pry out front oil seal. Coat new seal with Long-Life Lubricant (C1AZ-19859-B). Use Pinion Oil Seal Installer (T83T-4676-A) and install new oil seal. To complete installation, reverse removal procedure.

WATER PUMP

Removal & Installation – Disconnect negative battery cable and drain cooling system. Remove accessory belts. Remove water pump inlet tube. Remove water pump retaining bolts. Remove water pump and gasket. Clean gasket mating surfaces. Position new gasket and water pump on engine block. To complete installation, reverse removal procedure.

NOTE: For information on cooling system capacity, see ENGINE COOLANT SPECIFICATIONS article.

CAMSHAFT

Engine must be removed from vehicle to remove camshaft. No on-vehicle procedures are given by manufacturer.

OIL PAN

See appropriate OIL PAN REMOVAL article in this section.

OVERHAUL

CYLINDER HEAD

Valve Seats – 1) On 2.3L models, use only a 77 degree angle grinding stone to remove stock from bottom of intake seat. On exhaust seats, use only a 70 degree angle grinding stone to remove stock from bottom of seat. Use an 18 degree grinding stone to remove stock from top of all seats.
2) On 2.5L models, use only a 60 degree angle grinding stone to remove stock from bottom of all seats. Use a 30 degree angle grinding stone to remove stock from top of all seats.

1989 FORD MOTOR CO. ENGINES
2.3L HSC/HSO & 2.5L HSC 4-Cylinder (Cont.)

Valves & Valve Guides – **1)** Mark all components prior to removal for installation reference. Check valve-to-guide clearance of each valve in its respective valve guide. See Fig. 7.

2) If valve-to-guide clearance is not within specifications, replace valve(s) with next available oversize valve. Ream valve guide until clearance with valve stem is within specification. See ENGINE SPECIFICATIONS tables at end of article.

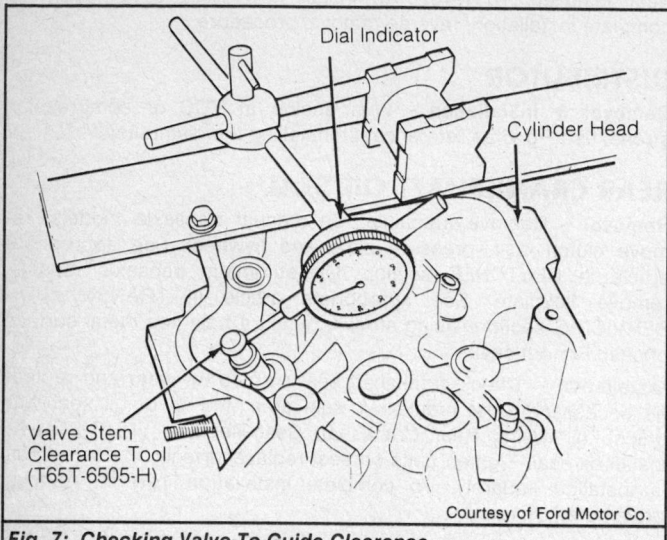

Fig. 7: Checking Valve-To-Guide Clearance

VALVE TRAIN

Valve Springs – Inspect valve springs for installed height, tension, free length and maximum out-of-square. See ENGINE SPECIFICATIONS tables at end of this article.

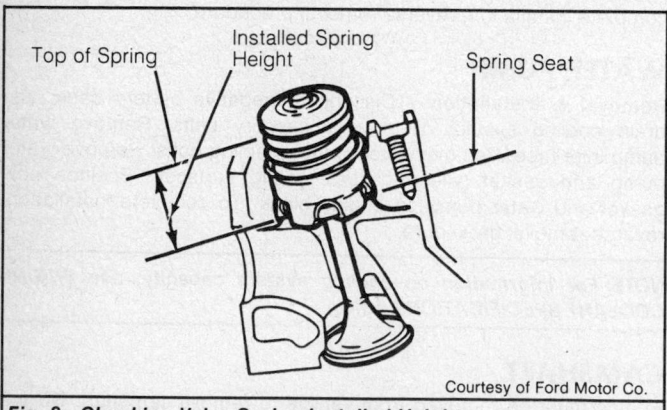

Fig. 8: Checking Valve Spring Installed Height

CAMSHAFT

NOTE: Camshaft bearings are prefinished to size. No reaming is required for standard or .015" undersize journal diameters.

Removal – **1)** Remove engine and transaxle. Drain engine oil. Remove accessory belts, pulley, cylinder head, and distributor assembly.

2) Using a magnet, remove lifters. Keep in order of removal to ensure lifters are installed to original location. Remove front cover timing chain and sprockets. Check camshaft end play.

3) Remove camshaft thrust plate. Pull camshaft out front of engine, using care not to damage journals or bearings.

Inspection – Clean all components and gasket mating surfaces. Check lobe lift and camshaft-to-bearing clearance.

Bearing Replacement – Use Camshaft Bearing Replacer (T65L-6250-A) to replace bearings. Ensure oil holes in bearings and cylinder block are aligned and new rear bearing bore plug is installed.

Installation – Coat camshaft lobes and journals with SAE 50 engine oil. Slide camshaft in through front of block. Install thrust plate. Ensure camshaft turns freely. To complete installation, reverse removal procedure.

CYLINDER BLOCK

Piston & Rod Assembly – Ensure pistons and rods are installed in cylinder from which they were removed. Ensure notch on piston faces front of engine. Oil hole in rod and notch on piston must be in proper position. See Fig. 9.

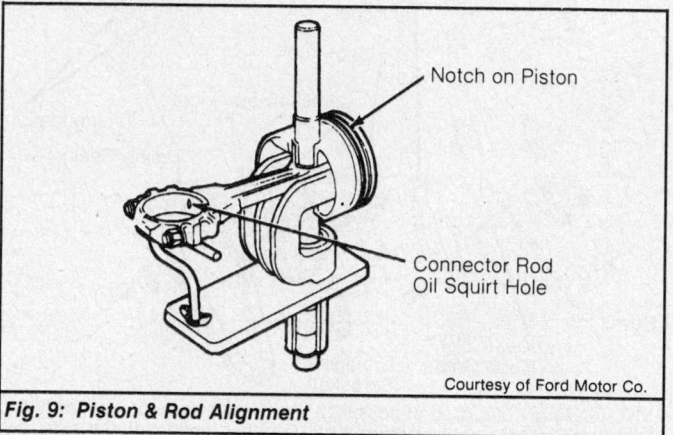

Fig. 9: Piston & Rod Alignment

NOTE: No ring gap spacing procedure is given by manufacturer.

Fitting Pistons – **1)** Check piston-to-bore clearance. Standard size pistons are color coded Red, Blue or Yellow on the piston dome. See ENGINE SPECIFICATIONS table at end of article.

2) If bore diameter is in lower one-third of specifications, use a Red coded piston. If bore diameter is in middle one-third of specifications, use a Blue coded piston.

3) If bore diameter is in upper one-third of specifications, use Yellow coded piston. The Yellow coded piston is .004" (.10 mm) oversize.

Crankshaft Main & Rod Bearings – If oil clearance cannot be obtained with standard bearings, try one-half of a .001" (.025 mm) or .002" (.051 mm) undersize in combination with a standard bearing to get correct clearance.

Cylinder Block – **1)** Using a feeler gauge and straightedge, check cylinder block head surface for flatness. Surface should be flate within .003" (.08 mm) over entire surface. Check cylinder bore for wear, taper, out-of-round and piston fit. See ENGINE SPECIFICATIONS tables at end of this article.

2) Use only equal parts of kerosene and SAE 20 motor oil for honing cylinder bores. Install and tighten main bearing caps to specifications before cylinder refinishing. Use ONLY a spring-loaded type cylinder hone. Use a grit size of 180-220 hone at about 500 RPM. Tap cylinder head bolt threads in cylinder block.

ENGINE OILING

LUBRICATION SYSTEM

Engine oiling is a full pressure system. Oil pump is bolted to bottom of engine block inside oil pan. An intermediate shaft attached to distributor drives the oil pump. See Fig. 10.

Crankcase Capacity – Crankcase capacity for 2.3L engine is 4.5 qts. (4.3L) with filter change. The 2.5L engine is 5 qts. (4.7L) with filter change. DO NOT change oil without changing filter.

Normal Oil Pressure – Normal oil pressure is 55-70 psi (3.9-4.9 kg/cm²) at 2000 RPM (engine hot).

1989 FORD MOTOR CO. ENGINES
2.3L HSC/HSO & 2.5L HSC 4-Cylinder (Cont.)

7-79

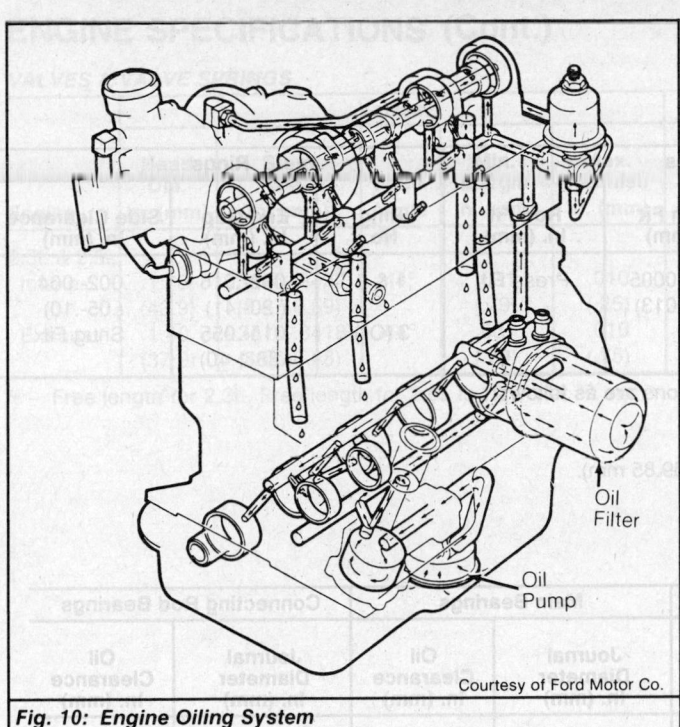

Fig. 10: Engine Oiling System

Courtesy of Ford Motor Co.

OIL PUMP

Removal & Installation – Remove oil pan. Remove oil pump and pick-up tube attaching bolts. Remove oil pump assembly. Remove pick-up tube from oil pump. To install, reverse removal procedure. Install new gaskets. Fill oil pump inlet port with engine oil. Rotate oil pump shaft until oil flows from outlet.

Inspection – Remove cover. Clean all components in solvent and dry with compressed air. Check inside of housing, outer race and rotor for wear and damage. Replace pump assembly if necessary. Measure inner rotor tip clearance. Measure rotor end play. Check relief valve spring and replace pump assembly as necessary. See OIL PUMP SPECIFICATIONS table.

OIL PUMP SPECIFICATIONS

Application	Specification
Driveshaft-to-Housing Clearance	.0014-.0026" (.036-.066 mm)
Outer Race-to-Housing Clearance	.001-.012" (.03-.31 mm)
Relief Valve Spring Tension	
2.3L	14.2-16.2 Lbs. @ 1.2" (6.4-7.3 kg @ 30.4 mm)
2.5L	15.2-17.2 Lbs. @ 1.2" (6.9-7.8 kg @ 30.4 mm)
Relief Valve-to-Bore Clearance	.0015-.0029" (.038-.074 mm)
Inner Rotor Tip Clearance	.004" (.10 mm)

TIGHTENING SPECIFICATIONS

Application	Ft. Lbs. (N.m)
Camshaft Sprocket Bolt	41-56 (55-75)
Connecting Rod Cap Nut	21-26 (28-35)
Crankshaft Damper Bolt	140-170 (190-230)
Cylinder Head Bolt	
Step 1	51-59 (69-80)
Step 2	70-76 (95-103)
Distributor Hold-Down Bolt	17-25 (23-34)
Exhaust Manifold Bolt	
Step 1	5-7 (7-10)
Step 2	20-30 (27-41)
Flywheel Mount Bolt	54-64 (73-87)
Intake Manifold Bolt	[1] 15-23 (20-31)
Intake Manifold Support Bracket Bolt	30-40 (41-54)
Main Bearing Cap Bolt	52-66 (71-90)
Oil Pan Bolts [2]	
Engine Block Bolts	15-22 (20-30)
Transaxle Bolts	30-39 (41-53)
Oil Pump Mount Bolt	30-39 (41-53)
Rocker Arm Bolt	
Step 1	5-8 (7-11)
Step 2	20-27 (27-38)
Water Pump Mount Bolt	15-23 (20-30)

	INCH Lbs. (N.m)
Camshaft Tensioner Bolt	72-108 (8-12)
Camshaft Thrust Plate Bolt	72-108 (8-12)
Crankshaft Seal Retainer Bolt	72-108 (8-12)
Timing Cover Bolts	72-108 (8-12)

[1] – Tighten intake manifold to specification in 2 steps. Tightening torque applies to intake manifold-to-cylinder head and upper-to-lower intake manifold bolts.

[2] – If oil pan is installed with engine out of vehicle, a transaxle case or other fixture must be bolted to engine to align pan with rear face of block.

ENGINE SPECIFICATIONS

GENERAL SPECIFICATIONS

Year	Displacement		Fuel System	HP@RPM	Torque Ft. Lbs.@RPM	Compr. Ratio	Bore		Stroke	
	Cu. In.	Liters					In.	mm	In.	mm
1989										
HSC	140.	2.3	MPFI	98@4400	124@2200	9.0:1	3.68	93.5	3.30	84.0
HSO	140	2.3	MPFI	100@4400	126@3200	9.0:1	3.68	93.5	3.30	84.0
HSC	153	2.5	CFI	90@4400	130@2600	9.0:1	3.68	93.5	3.58	91.0

CONNECTING RODS

Engine	Side Play In. (mm)	Max. Bend & Twist In. (mm)	Pin Bore Dia. In. (mm)	Large Bore Dia. In. (mm)	Center-to-Center In. (mm)
2.3L & 2.5L	.0035-.0105 (.088-.266)	[1] .0029 (.074)	.9096-.9112 (23.104-23.144)	2.2388-2.2396 (56.866-56.886)	5.4555-5.4585 (138.569-138.646)

[1] – Specification is for twist. Bend limit is .0015" (.038 mm).

7-86

1989 FORD MOTOR CO. ENGINES
2.3L OHC 4-Cylinder (Cont.)

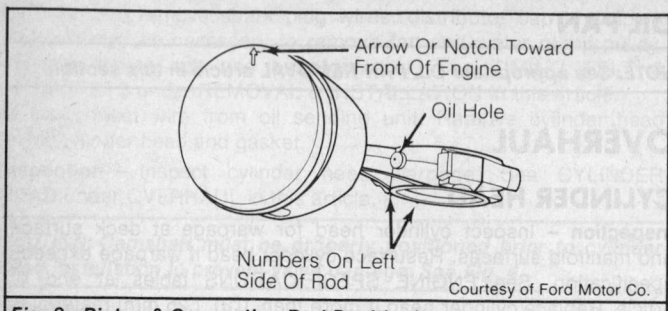

Fig. 9: Piston & Connecting Rod Positioning

3) If bore diameter is in lower one-third of specification, use Red piston. If bore diameter is in middle one-third of specification, use Blue piston. If bore diameter is in upper one-third of specification, use oversize piston. See PISTON SIZE CODE CHART table in this article. Ensure clearance is within specification. See ENGINE SPECIFICATIONS tables at end of article.

PISTON SIZE CODE CHART

Code	Size In. (mm)
Red	3.7764-3.7770 (95.920-95.936)
Blue	3.7776-3.7782 (95.951-95.966)
.003 OS	N/A

Cylinder Block – If cylinder block requires that cylinders be bored, ensure all main bearing caps are installed and tightened to specification prior to boring.

ENGINE OILING

LUBRICATION SYSTEM

The distributor driven, rotor-type oil pump provides pressurized lubrication to the main gallery. *See Fig. 10.*

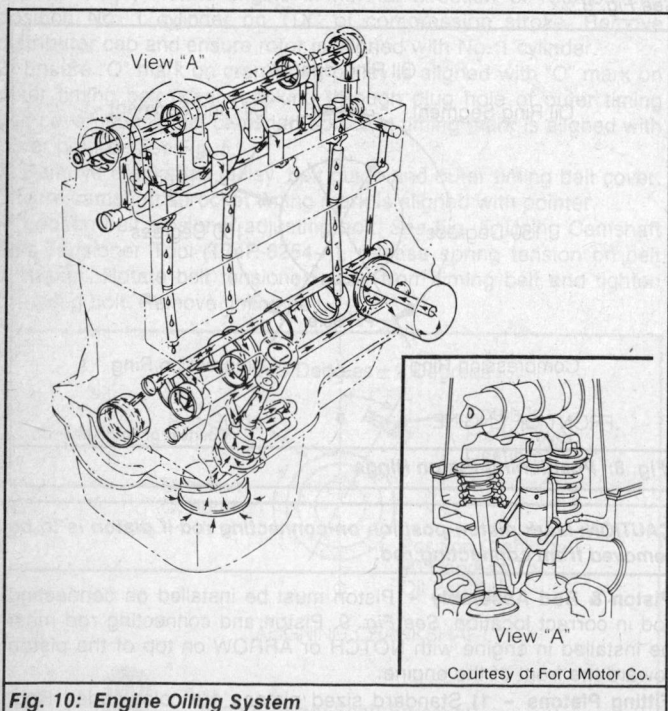

Fig. 10: Engine Oiling System

Crankcase Capacity – Engine oil capacity is approximately 5 qts. (4.7L) with filter change. Recheck oil level after changing filter.

Normal Oil Pressure – Normal oil pressure is 40-60 psi (2.8-4.2 kg/cm²) at 2000 RPM with engine at normal operating temperature.

OIL PUMP

Removal – Remove oil pan. See appropriate OIL PAN REMOVAL article in this section. Remove pick-up tube-to-block mounting bolt. Remove oil pump retaining bolts, oil pump and shaft.

Disassembly & Inspection – 1) Remove pick-up tube from pump. Remove pump cover. Mark rotor location and remove rotors. Inspect components for damage. Measure rotor tip clearance, outer rotor-to-housing clearance and rotor end clearance.
2) Check clearance between pressure relief valve and bore, and spring tension. Replace pump assembly if not within specification. See OIL PUMP SPECIFICATIONS table.

OIL PUMP SPECIFICATIONS

Application	In. (mm)
Maximum Rotor End Clearance	.004 (.10)
Maximum Rotor Tip Clearance	.010 (.25)
Outer Rotor-To-Housing	.001-.013 (.02-.33)
Relief Valve-To-Bore [1]	.0015-.0030 (.038-.076)

[1] – Relief valve spring tension is 15.2-17.2 lbs. @ 1.20" (6.5 kg @ 30.4 mm).

Reassembly & Installation – To reassemble, reverse disassembly procedure. Ensure rotors are installed in original location. To install, reverse removal procedure using new gaskets. Oil pump must be free to rotate after installation. Prime oil pump prior to starting engine.

TIGHTENING SPECIFICATIONS

Application	Ft. Lbs. (N.m)
Auxiliary Shaft Sprocket Bolt	28-40 (38-54)
Belt Tensioner	
Adjusting Bolt	14-21 (19-29)
Pivot Bolt	28-40 (38-54)
Camshaft Sprocket Bolt [1]	50-71 (68-96)
Connecting Rod Nut	
Step 1	25-30 (34-41)
Step 2	30-36 (41-49)
Crankshaft Pulley Bolt	103-133 (140-180)
Cylinder Head Bolt [2]	
Step 1	50-60 (68-81)
Step 2	80-90 (109-122)
Exhaust Manifold Bolt [3]	
Step 1	15-17 (20-23)
Step 2	20-30 (27-41)
Flywheel Bolt	54-64 (73-87)
Fuel Rail Bolt	14-21 (19-29)
Intake Manifold-to-Head Bolt/Nut [4]	20-29 (27-39)
Main Bearing Cap Bolt	
Step 1	50-60 (68-81)
Step 2	75-85 (102-115)
Oil Pan Bolt	10-14 (14-19)
Oil Pump Pick-Up Tube-to-Pump Bolt	14-21 (19-29)
Oil Pump-to-Block Bolt	14-21 (19-29)
Throttle Body Bolt	14-21 (19-29)
Upper-to-Lower Intake Manifold Bolt [4]	15-22 (20-30)

Application	INCH Lbs. (N.m)
Auxiliary Shaft Cover Bolt	72-108 (8-12)
Auxiliary Shaft Retainer Plate Bolt	72-108 (8-12)
Camshaft Retainer Thrust Plate Bolt	72-108 (8-12)
Front Cover Bolt	72-108 (8-12)
Oil Pump Cover Bolt	90-130 (10-15)
Valve Cover Bolt	60-96 (6-11)

[1] – Install NEW bolt. DO NOT reuse bolt.
[2] – Tighten to specification in sequence. See Fig. 4.
[3] – Tighten to specification in sequence. See Fig. 3.
[4] – Tighten to specification in sequence. See Fig. 2.

1989 FORD MOTOR CO. ENGINES
2.3L OHC 4-Cylinder (Cont.)

7-87

ENGINE SPECIFICATIONS

GENERAL SPECIFICATIONS

Year	Displacement		Fuel System	HP@RPM	Torque Ft. Lbs.@RPM	Compr. Ratio	Bore		Stroke	
	Cu. In.	Liters					In.	mm	In.	mm
1989	140	2.3	EFI	88@4000	132@2600	9:5:1	3.78	96.0	3.126	79.40

PISTONS, PINS & RINGS

Engine	Pistons		Pins			Rings		
	Clearance In. (mm)	Diameter In. (mm)	Diameter In. (mm)	Piston Fit In. (mm)	Rod Fit In. (mm)	Ring No.	End Gap In. (mm)	Side Clearance In. (mm)
2.3L	.0030-.0038 (.076-.097)	[1]	[2] .9118-.9124 (23.159-23.175)	.0003-.0005 (.008-.013)	Press Fit	No. 1	.010-.020 (.25-.50)	.002-.004 (.05-.10)
						No. 2	.010-.020 (.25-.50)	.002-.004 (.05-.10)
						No. 3 (Oil)	.010-.049 (.25-1.24)	.....

[1] – On Red color coded pistons, diameter is 3.7764-3.7770" (95.920-95.936 mm). Blue color coded pistons is 3.7776-3.7782" (95.951-95.966 mm). Oversized pistons are available in .003" (.08 mm).

[2] – Standard diameter listed. Available in .001" (.02 mm) and .002" (.05 mm) oversizes.

CRANKSHAFT, MAIN & CONNECTING ROD BEARINGS

Engine	Crankshaft				Main Bearings		Connecting Rod Bearings	
	End Play In. (mm)	Runout In. (mm)	Journal Taper In. (mm)	Journal Out-of-Round In. (mm)	Journal Diameter In. (mm)	Oil Clearance In. (mm)	Journal Diameter In. (mm)	Oil Clearance In. (mm)
2.3L	[1] .004-.008 (.10-.20)	.005 (.13)	.0006 (.015)	.0006 (.015)	2.3982-2.3990 (60.914-60.935)	.0008-.0026 (.020-.066)	2.0465-2.0472 (51.981-51.998)	.0008-.0026 (.020-.066)

[1] – Service limit is .012" (.30 mm).

CONNECTING RODS

Engine	Side Play In. (mm)	Max. Bend & Twist In. (mm)	Pin Bore Dia. In. (mm)	Large Bore Dia. In. (mm)	Center-to-Center In. (mm)
2.3L	[1] .0035-.0105 (.089-.267)	[2]	.9012-.9096 (22.890-23.104)	2.1720-2.1728 (55.169-55.189)	5.2031-5.2063 (132.158-132.240)

[1] – Service limit is .014" (.36 mm).

[2] – Maximum bend is .012" (.30 mm) and twist is .024" (.61 mm).

ENGINE SPECIFICATIONS (Cont.)

CRANKSHAFT, MAIN & CONNECTING ROD BEARINGS

| Engine | Crankshaft | | | | Main Bearings | | Connecting Rod Bearings | |
	End Play In. (mm)	Runout In. (mm)	Journal Taper In. (mm)	Journal Out-of-Round In. (mm)	Journal Diameter In. (mm)	Oil Clearance In. (mm)	Journal Diameter In. (mm)	Oil Clearance In. (mm)
3.0L	.004-.008 (.10-.20)	.....	[1] .0003 (.008)	.0003 (.008)	2.5190-2.5198 (63.983-64.003)	.0010-.0014 (.025-.036)	2.1253-2.1261 (53.983-54.003)	.0010-.0014 (.025-.036)

[1] - Specifications listed is per 1" (25.4 mm).

CONNECTING RODS

Engine	Side Play In. (mm)	Max. Bend & Twist In. (mm)	Pin Bore Dia. In. (mm)	Large Bore Dia. In. (mm)	Center-to-Center In. (mm)
3.0L	.006-.014 (.15-.36)	[1] .0015 (.038)	.9096-.9112 (23.104-23.145)	2.250 (57.15)	5.53 (140.5)

[1] - Specifications listed is bend and per 1" (25.4 mm). Twist is .002" (.05 mm) per 1" (25.4 mm).

PISTONS, PINS & RINGS

| Engine | Pistons | | Pins | | | Rings | | |
	Clearance In. (mm)	Diameter In. (mm)	Diameter In. (mm)	Piston Fit In. (mm)	Rod Fit In. (mm)	Ring No.	End Gap In. (mm)	Side Clearance In. (mm)
3.0L	.0014-.0022 (.036-.056)	[1]	.912 (23.17)	.0002-.0005 (.005-.013)	Press Fit	No. 1	.01-.02 (.25-.51)	.0012-.0031 (.031-.079)
						Oil Ring	.010-.049 (.25-1.25)	.0006 Max. (.015 Max.)

[1] - Pistons are color coded. See FITTING PISTONS under OVERHAUL in this article.

VALVES & VALVE SPRINGS

| Engine | Valves | | | | | Valves Springs | | | | |
| | Head Dia. In. (mm) | Stem Dia. In. (mm) | Face Angle | Min. Margin In. (mm) | Max. Refinish In. (mm) | Free Length In. (mm) | Out-of-Square In. (mm) | Installed Height In. (mm) | Pressure Lbs. @ In. (Kg @ mm) | |
									Valve Closed	Valve Open
3.0L Intake	1.57 (39.9)	.3126-.3134 (7.940-7.960)	44°	.0313 (.794)	.....	1.84 (46.7)	.06 (1.5)	1.58 (40.1)	65 @ 1.58 (30 @ 40.1)	180 @ 1.16 (82 @ 29.5)
Exhaust	1.30 (33.0)	.3121-.3129 (7.927-7.948)	44°	.0313 (.794)	.....	1.84 (46.7)	.06 (1.5)	1.58 (40.1)	65 @ 1.58 (30 @ 40.1)	180 @ 1.16 (82 @ 29.5)

CYLINDER HEAD

| Engine | Max. Cylinder Head Warp In. (mm) | Valve Seats | | | | Valve Guides | | |
		Seat Angle	Maximum Runout In. (mm)	Seat Width In. (mm)	Seat Bore Diameter In. (mm)	Valve Stem Oil Clearance In. (mm)	Valve Guide I.D. In. (mm)	Valve Guide Bore I.D. In. (mm)
3.0L	.007 (.18)	45°	.001 (.03)	[1] .06-.08 (1.5-2.0)	.....	[2] .0010-.0028 (.025-.071)	.3145 (7.988)	.....

[1] - Intake listed. Exhaust is .08-.10" (2.0-2.5 mm).
[2] - Intake listed. Exhaust is .0015-.0033" (.038-.084 mm).

ENGINE SPECIFICATIONS (Cont.)

CAMSHAFT

Engine	Journal Diameter In. (mm)	Oil Clearance In. (mm)	Bearing Bore In. (mm)	Runout In. (mm)	End Play In. (mm)	Lobe Lift In. (mm)	Lobe Height In. (mm)
3.0L	2.0074-2.0084 (50.988-51.013)	.001-.003 (.03-.08)	¹ 2.1536 (54.701)	....	.001-.005 (.03-.13)	.26 (6.60)	....

¹ – Bore Nos. 1 & 4 listed. Bore Nos. 2 & 3 are 2.1334-2.1344" (54.188-54.214 mm).

VALVE LIFTERS

Engine	Diameter In. (mm)	Bore Diameter In. (mm)	Oil Clearance In. (mm)
3.0L	.874 (22.20)	.8752-.8767 (22.230-22.268)	.0007-.0027 (.018-.069)

CYLINDER BLOCK

Engine	Max. Block Warp In. (mm)	Cylinder Bore		
		Standard Diameter In. (mm)	Maximum Taper In. (mm)	Maximum Out-of-Rnd In. (mm)
3.0L	¹ .003 (.08)	3.50 (88.9)	.002 (.05)	.002 (.05)

¹ – Specification listed is within a 6" (152 mm) area.

1989 FORD MOTOR CO. ENGINES
3.0L SHO V6

Taurus

NOTE: For engine repair procedures not covered in this article, see ENGINE OVERHAUL PROCEDURES article at beginning of this section.

DESCRIPTION

The 3.0L SHO engine is a high performance V6 with DOHC, 24 valves and Sequential Electronic Fuel Injection (SEFI). The 3.0L SHO is manufactured by Yamaha. Left and right bank intake camshafts are timing belt driven. Exhaust camshafts are timing chain driven through intake camshafts at rear of engine.

A Distributorless Ignition System (DIS) with a 3 pack coil assembly is used. DIS logic module is mounted on front intake section. *See Fig. 3.* Spark plugs are centrally located in combustion chambers. Air intake system utilizes a secondary and primary intake port. Secondary port is opened and closed by a vacuum operated intake air control valve.

ENGINE IDENTIFICATION

Engine may be identified from Vehicle Identification Number (VIN). VIN is stamped on a plate, on top of instrument panel and visible through windshield. VIN contains 17 characters. The 8th character identifies engine.

An engine code calibration number label is located in engine compartment, in front of radiator. This label contains engine calibration number, engine build date, engine plant code and an engine code.

An emission calibration number label is located on upper radiator sight shield. This label identifies engine calibration number, engine code number and revision level.

All label numbers are necessary for determining correct and unique parts to specific enignes. DO NOT remove labels at any time. Record these numbers for future reference.

ENGINE IDENTIFICATION CODE

Engine	Code
3.0L (182") SEFI	Y

ADJUSTMENTS

VALVE ARRANGEMENT

Intake Valves – Inboard (both banks).
Exhaust Valves – Outboard (both banks).

VALVE CLEARANCE ADJUSTMENT

1) Disconnect negative battery cable. Remove intake manifold assembly. See INTAKE MANIFOLD under REMOVAL & INSTALLATION in this article. Remove valve covers. See VALVE COVERS under REMOVAL & INSTALLATION in this article.
2) Rotate crankshaft, in direction of normal operation only, until camshaft lobe is as shown. *See Fig. 1.* Using a feeler gauge, check clearance between camshaft and lifter shim. If not within specifications, replace shim. See VALVE CLEARANCE table in this article.

VALVE CLEARANCE

Application	In. (mm)
Intake	.006-.010 (.15-.25)
Exhaust	.010-.014 (.25-.35)

3) To replace shim, insert lifter compressor under camshaft, next to lobe and rotate down to depress lifter. *See Fig. 1.* Insert lifter holder and remove lifter compressor. Using a pick, lift and remove shim.

4) Determine size of removed shim by either the number on bottom side of shim or measuring with micrometer. Install appropriate shim with numbers facing downward. Repeat procedure for each valve.

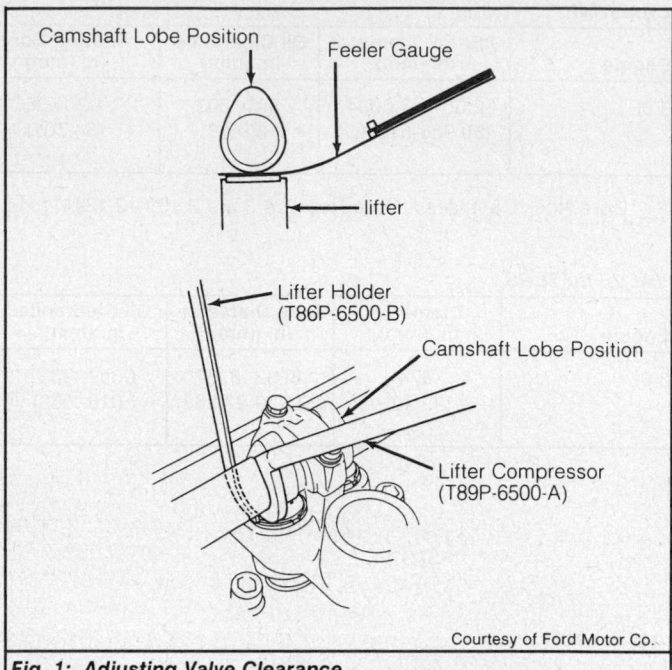

Courtesy of Ford Motor Co.

Fig. 1: Adjusting Valve Clearance

REMOVAL & INSTALLATION

NOTE: For reassembly reference, label all electrical connectors, vacuum hoses and fuel lines prior to removal. Match mark engine hood and all other major components prior to removal.

ENGINE

NOTE: See ENGINE REMOVAL & INSTALLATION article at end of ENGINE section.

FUEL PRESSURE RELEASE

Release fuel pressure prior to disconnecting any fuel lines. Remove fuel filler cap. Attach a fuel pressure gauge to pressure relief valve on right side fuel rail. *See Fig. 2.* Release fuel pressure through fuel gauge into a container.

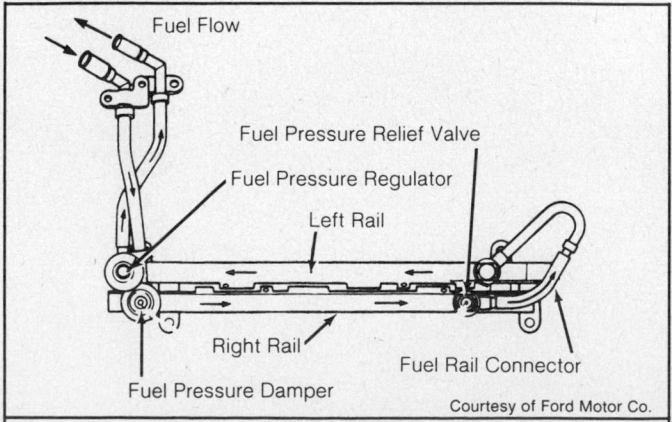

Courtesy of Ford Motor Co.

Fig. 2: Fuel Rail Component Identification

1989 FORD MOTOR CO. ENGINES
3.0L SHO V6 (Cont.)

INTAKE MANIFOLD

Removal – **1)** Disconnect negative battery cable and partially drain cooling system. Mark and disconnect electrical connectors and vacuum hoses from intake manifold. Remove air intake duct. Disonnect coolant lines and cable from throttle body.

2) Note location and remove bolts and one stud retaining brackets to intake manifold. *See Fig. 3.* Bolts and studs MUST be installed to original location and position.

3) Mark brackets and remove lower bracket bolts with brackets. Remove 12 bolts retaining intake manifold to cylinder heads. Remove intake manifold and gaskets.

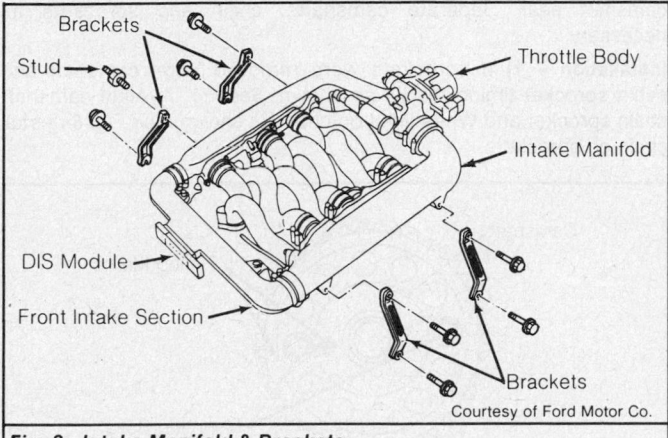

Fig. 3: Intake Manifold & Brackets

Courtesy of Ford Motor Co.

Installation – Lightly oil all attaching bolts/stud threads. Clean all gasket mating surfaces. Position intake manifold gasket on cylinder heads. Install intake manifold. Install 12 retaining bolts finger tight. Tighten bolts to specifications. To complete installation, reverse removal procedure.

EXHAUST MANIFOLD

NOTE: To remove right side exhaust manifold, cylinder head must be removed. See CYLINDER HEAD under REMOVAL & INSTALLATION in this article.

Removal & Installation (Left Side) – Remove oil dip stick tube support bracket. Remove power steering pump pressure and return hoses. Remove inlet pipe from exhaust manifold. Remove heat shield attaching bolts. Remove exhaust manifold bolts and manifold. Lightly oil bolt threads prior to installation. To complete installation, reverse removal procedure.

VALVE COVERS

Removal – **1)** Disconnect negative battery cable. Release fuel pressure as previously described. Mark and disconnect all necessary electrical connectors and vacuum hoses. Remove intake manifold as previously described. Mark and disconnect spark plug wires from spark plugs.

2) For left valve cover, remove oil fill cap and ignition coil pack cover. For right valve cover, disconnect fuel lines. On both sides, remove valve cover bolts and remove valve cover(s).

Installation – Lightly oil bolt/stud threads prior to installation. Using solvent, clean valve cover gasket mating surfaces. Install new valve cover gasket and spark plug hold gaskets on valve cover. To complete installation, reverse removal procedure.

CYLINDER HEADS

Removal – **1)** Disconnect negative battery cable and drain cooling system. Remove air intake duct. Remove intake manifold as previously described. Remove accessory drive belts, left idler and bracket. Remove right front wheel and inner fender splash shield. Remove upper timing belt cover. Remove crankshaft damper with a universal damper puller.

2) Disconnect crankshaft sensor wiring assembly located at lower timing belt cover. Remove lower timing belt cover. Align timing marks as shown. *See Fig. 4.* Release timing belt tension by loosening tensioner nut. Rotate tensioner away from timing belt with a hex head wrench and tighten nut to hold tensioner.

3) Remove center timing belt cover. Match mark timing belt with camshaft sprockets and direction of rotation to ensure reassembly to original location and position. Remove valve covers as previously described. Remove intake camshaft sprockets.

4) Remove upper and center rear timing belt covers. On left cylinder head, remove exhaust manifold. On right cylinder head, exhaust manifold is removed with cylinder head. Remove cylinder head bolts evenly. Remove cylinder head and gasket.

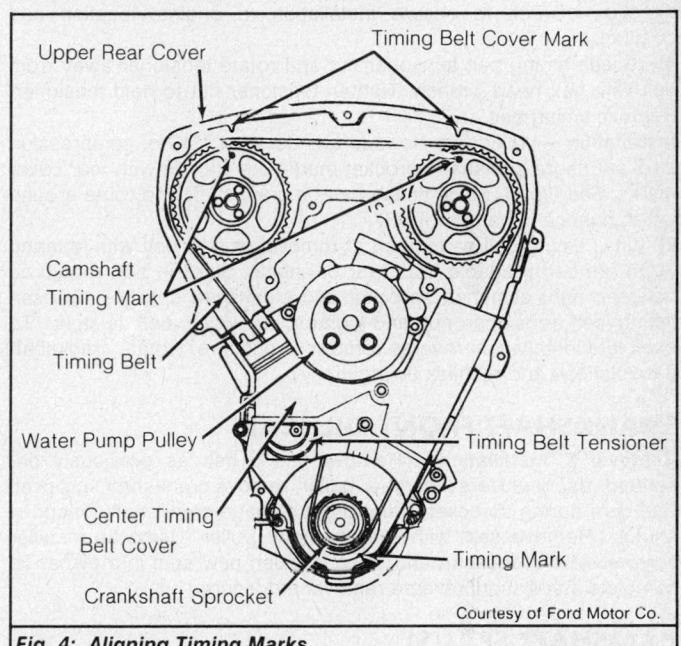

Fig. 4: Aligning Timing Marks

Courtesy of Ford Motor Co.

Installation – Clean gasket mating surfaces. Replace dowels if damaged. Properly position gasket on block. Install cylinder head. Lightly oil bolt/stud threads and install finger tight. Tighten head bolts in sequence to specifications. *See Fig. 5.* To complete installation, reverse removal procedure.

SAME SEQUENCE FOR BOTH BANKS

Courtesy of Ford Motor Co.

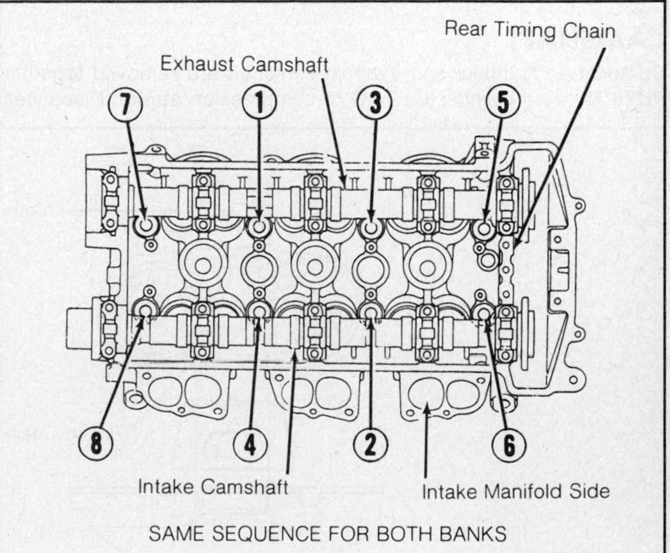

Fig. 5: Cylinder Head Tightening Sequence

1989 FORD MOTOR CO. ENGINES
3.0L SHO V6 (Cont.)

TIMING BELT COVER, BELT & WATER PUMP

Removal – 1) Disconnect negative battery cable. Position No. one piston on TDC of compression stroke. Disconnect DIS module and remove front intake section. *See Fig. 3.* Remove accessory belts. Remove engine roll damper support. Remove upper timing belt cover.

2) Remove right front wheel and splash shield. Remove crankshaft damper with universal damper puller. Remove accessory belt tensioner. Remove center timing belt cover. Remove lower timing belt cover. Remove 6 water pump bolts, water pump and gasket (if replacing).

3) Check camshaft sprocket timing mark alignment. *See Fig. 4.* If reusing timing belt, match mark belt with camshaft sprockets and direction of belt to ensure installation to original location and position.

4) Loosen timing belt tensioner nut and rotate tensioner away from belt with hex head wrench. Tighten tensioner nut to hold tensioner. Remove timing belt.

Installation – 1) Ensure No. one cylinder is at TDC of compression stroke. Ensure camshaft sprocket marks are aligned with rear cover marks. *See Fig. 4.* Place timing belt on crankshaft and route around left to right camshaft sprocket.

2) Install timing belt as marked at removal or new belt with lettering "KOA" on belt readable from rear of engine. Slack in belt should be between right camshaft sprocket and crankshaft sprocket. Loosen timing belt tensioner nut and tighten nut when belt is tight. To complete installation, reverse removal procedure. Rotate crankshaft 2 revolutions and recheck timing marks.

CRANKSHAFT FRONT OIL SEAL

Removal & Installation – Remove timing belt as previously described. Using universal damper puller, remove crankshaft sprocket. Use care during sprocket removal not damage crankshaft sensor or shutter. Remove seal with slide hammer puller. Using an installer screwed into crankshaft end threads, push new seal into place. To complete installation, reverse removal procedure.

CAMSHAFT SEAL(S)

Removal & Installation – Remove timing belt as previously described. Note location of dowel pins and remove camshaft sprockets. Remove seal with a seal puller. Apply silicone sealer to seal outer diameter and seal seating surface. Install camshaft seal with Camshaft Seal Expander and Replacer (T89P-6256-A & B). To complete installation, reverse removal procedure.

CAMSHAFT

Removal – 1) Intake and exhaust camshaft are removed together. Place No. one cylinder on TDC of compression stroke. Disconnect negative battery cable. Remove intake manifold, valve cover and timing belt as previously described.

2) Note location of dowel pins and remove camshaft sprocket(s). Mark bearing caps with engine front and sequence number for installation reference. Evenly and in 2 or 3 steps, loosen camshaft bearing caps in reverse sequence of tightening. *See Fig. 9.*

NOTE: Chain tensioners are not interchangeable from left to right.

3) Remove camshaft bearing caps. Remove camshaft chain tensioner mounting bolts at rear of engine. Remove intake and exhaust camshaft with chain and tensioner as an assembly. Discard camshaft seal. Separate camshafts, chain and sprockets as necessary.

Installation – 1) If sprockets were removed, align camshaft and cahin sprocket timing marks as shown. *See Fig. 7.* Align camshaft chain sprocket and White links on chain as shown. *See Fig. 8.* Install chain on sprockets.

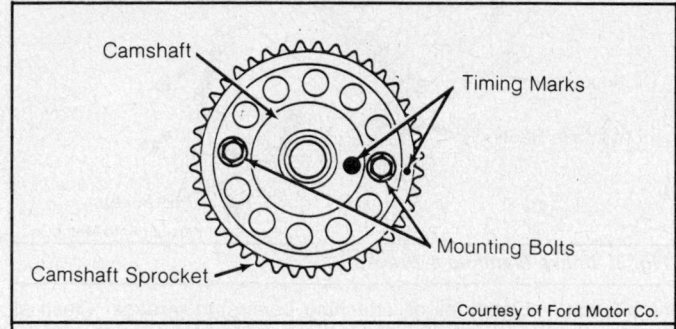

Fig. 7: Aligning Camshaft & Rear Chain Sprocket

Courtesy of Ford Motor Co.

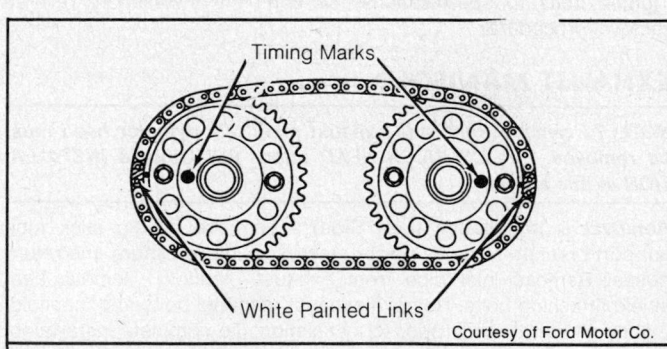

Fig. 8: Aligning Camshaft Chain Sprockets & Chain

Courtesy of Ford Motor Co.

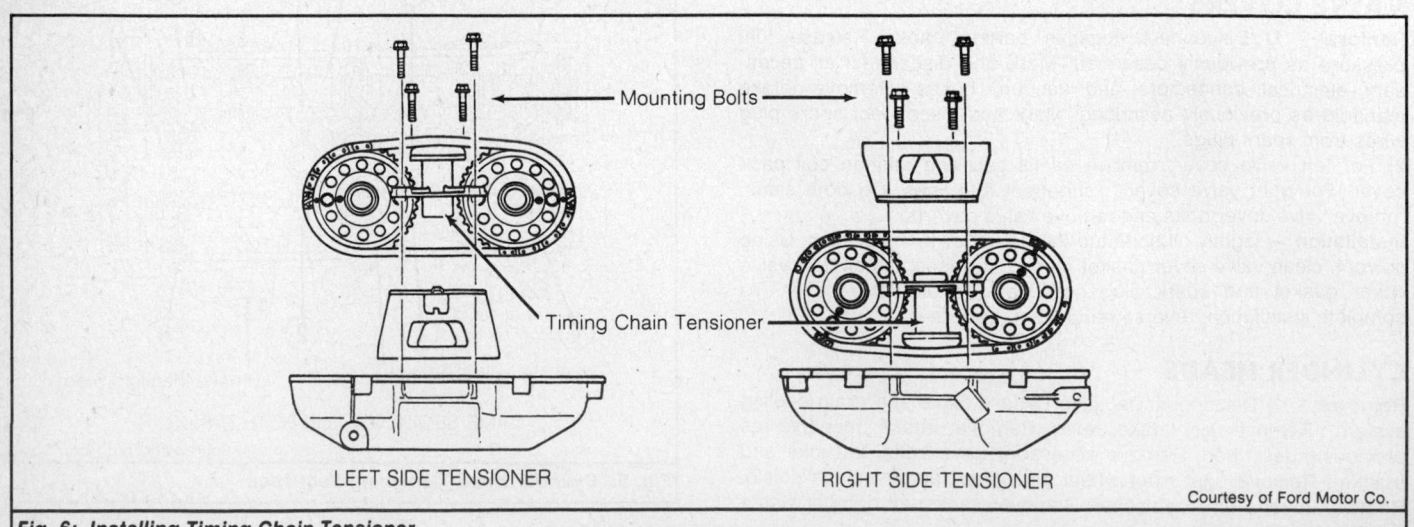

LEFT SIDE TENSIONER

RIGHT SIDE TENSIONER

Courtesy of Ford Motor Co.

Fig. 6: Installing Timing Chain Tensioner

2) Rotate camshafts approximately 60 degrees counterclockwise. Position tensioner between chain sprockets and position camshaft assembly in cylinder head. *See Fig. 6.* Apply a light coat of engine oil to camshaft bearing journals. Install bearing cap Nos. 2-5 and loosely install bolts. Ensure bearing caps are installed to original location and position.

3) Apply Silicone Sealer (D6AZ-19579C) to outer diameter of new camshaft seal and seal mating surface on cylinder head. Install camshaft seal with Camshaft Seal Expander and Replacer (T89P-6256-A & B). Apply a .10" (2.5 mm) bead of silicone sealer to No. 1 bearing cap. DO NOT apply sealer to journal surface.

4) Install bearing cap and bolts loosely. Tighten bearing caps in sequence in 2 or 3 steps. On left bank camshafts, apply pressure to chain tensioner to avoid damage during tightening. *See Fig. 9.* Install tensioner attaching bolts and tighten to specifications.

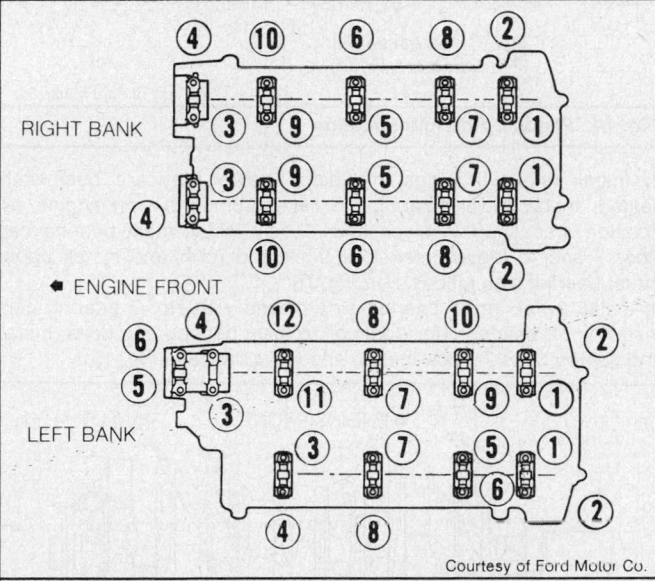

Fig. 9: Camshaft Bearing Cap Tightening Sequence

5) Rotate camshaft 60 degrees clockwise and check timing mark alignment. *See Fig. 10.* Rotate camshafts until timing marks align with valve cover mating surface. Set Camshaft Positioner (T89P-6256-C) over camshaft. *See Fig. 11.* Flats on camshafts must align with flats on positioner.

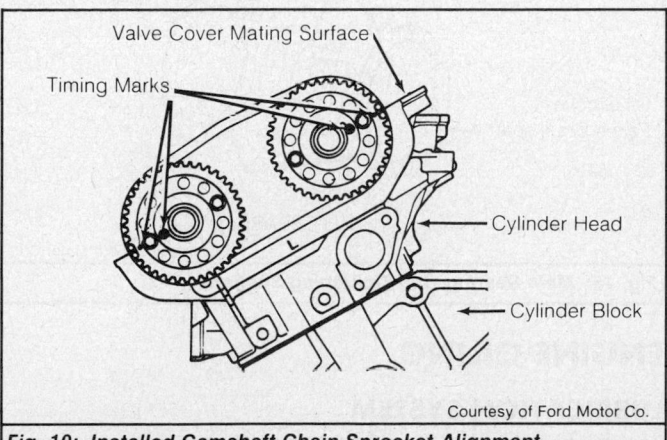

Fig. 10: Installed Camshaft Chain Sprocket Alignment

6) If positioner does not fit and/or timing marks do not align as in step **5)**, repeat complete installation procedure. To complete installation, reverse removal procedure.

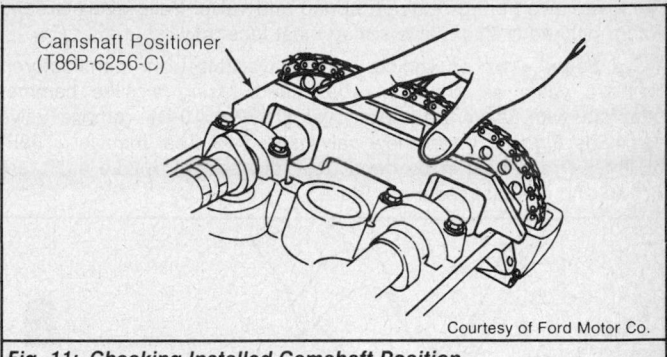

Fig. 11: Checking Installed Camshaft Position

WATER PUMP

See TIMING BELT COVER, BELT & WATER PUMP under REMOVAL & INSTALLATION in this article.

NOTE: For information on cooling system capacity, see ENGINE COOLANT SPECIFICATIONS article.

OIL PAN

NOTE: See appropriate OIL PAN REMOVAL article in this section.

OIL PUMP

Removal & Installation – Remove oil pan. See appropriate OIL PAN REMOVAL article in this section. Remove timing belt as previously described. Remove crankshaft sprocket. Remove oil pump pick-up tube. Remove oil pump-to-cylinder block retaining bolts. Remove oil pump assembly from front of engine. To install, reverse removal procedure. See INSPECTION under OIL PUMP at end of this article.

OVERHAUL

NOTE: Keep components together and marked to ensure installation to original location and position.

CYLINDER HEAD

Valves – **1)** Remove cylinder head with camshafts installed. Place cylinder head assembly in a holding fixture. Using a dial indicator, check camshaft end play prior to camshaft removal. If end play is greater than specifications, replace camshaft and/or cylinder head.

2) Remove camshafts from cylinder head. See CAMSHAFT under REMOVAL & INSTALLATION in this article. Remove shim and lifter. Using Valve Spring Compressor/Stand (T89P-6565-A) and Pivot Bar (T87C-6565-A), remove valve keepers with a magnet. *See Fig. 12.*

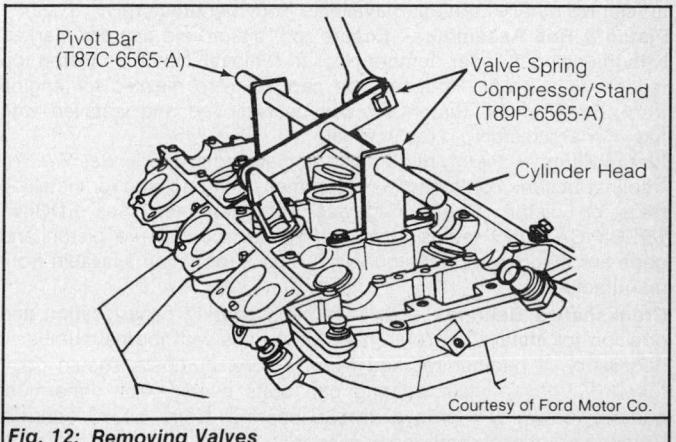

Fig. 12: Removing Valves

Remove valve spring retainer, spring and valve. Yellow painted end (wider pitched end) of valve spring must face upward.

Valve Seals – No on vehicle service available from manufacturer. Remove valve as previously described. Using a slide hammer attached with Valve Seal Remover (T89P-6510-D), remove valve seal. *See Fig. 13.* Install new valve seal with Seal Installer (T89P-6510-C). Press seal in by hand until fully seated. Intake seals are Brown and exhaust seals are Black.

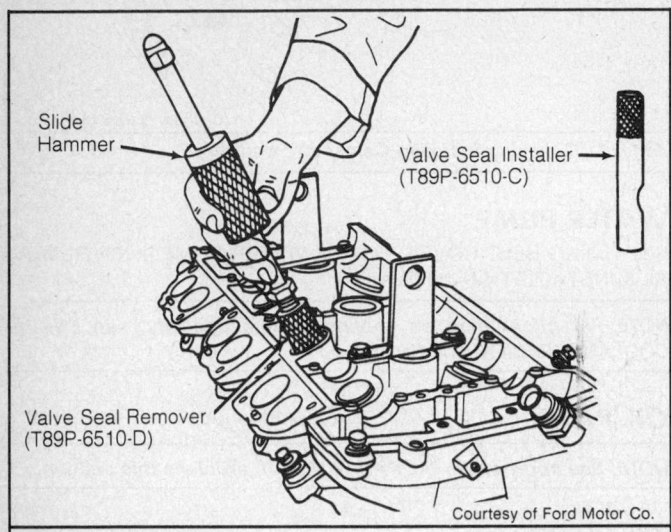

Fig. 13: *Replacing Valve Seals*

Valve Guides – Valve guides must be serviced prior to valve or seat service. Valve guide may be replaced or reamed to fit oversize valves. If replacing guide, guide is driven out through bottom of cylinder head. New guide is installed through top of cylinder head until fully seated.

Valve & Valve Seat – Machine valve to specifications as necessary. Do not remove more than .01" (.3 mm) from valve stem. Valve seat replacement information not available from manufacturer. Use a 75 degree stone for narrowing bottom of seat. Use a 30 degree stone for narrowing top of seat.

Camshaft Bearings – Information not available from manufacturer.

Cylinder head – Cylinder head surfaces can not be machined. If warpage exceeds specifications, replace cylinder head. See ENGINE SPECIFICATIONS tables at end of this article.

CYLINDER BLOCK ASSEMBLY

NOTE: Keep components together and marked to ensure installation to original location and position.

Cylinder Block – Check cylinder bore for wear, taper, out-of-round and piston fit. See ENGINE SPECIFICATIONS tables at end of this article. No other information available from manufacturer.

Piston & Rod Assembly – Ensure rod, piston and cap are marked with matching cylinder number prior to removal. Notch on piston top faces engine front. Rod and rod cap are also marked for engine front. *See Fig. 14.* Piston pin can be removed and installed with hammer and piston pin replacer kit.

Piston Rings – Piston rings must be installed properly. *See Fig. 14.* Use instructions contained in replacement ring package for installing rings on piston. Check ring gap and clearance. See ENGINE SPECIFICATIONS tables at end of this article. Ensure piston end gaps are staggered on piston. No further information available from manufacturer.

Crankshaft & Bearings – **1)** Note main bearing caps location and position for installation reference. Mark caps with journal number if necessary. If number marked from factory, numbers should point forward. Loosen main bearing cap bolts evenly, from innermost bearing outward. Remove thrust bearing from No. 3 journal. Remove crankshaft and upper bearings.

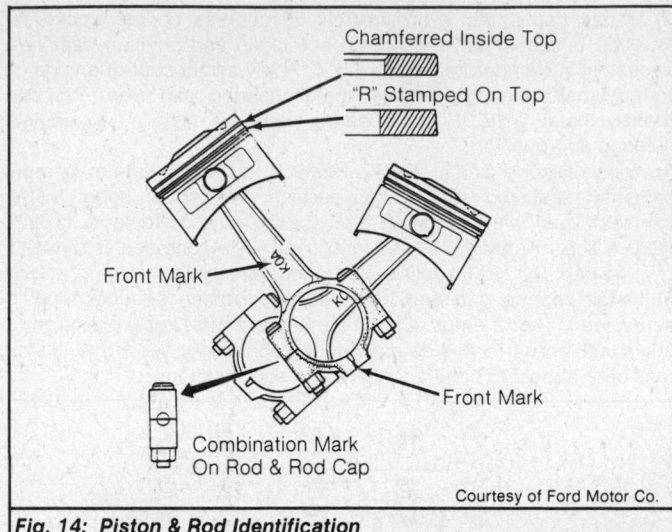

Fig. 14: *Piston & Rod Identification*

2) Install upper bearings in block. Ensure they are completely seated. Install lower bearings in caps. Lubricate with engine oil. Position crankshaft in block and loosely install main bearing cap Nos. 1 and 4. Move crankshaft back and forth and install upper thrust bearing side pieces. *See Fig. 15.*

3) Install lower thrust bearing side pieces with No. 3 bearing cap. Install No. 2 bearing cap. Apply oil to main bearing cap bolts. Install and tighten bolts in sequence to specifications. *See Fig. 15.*

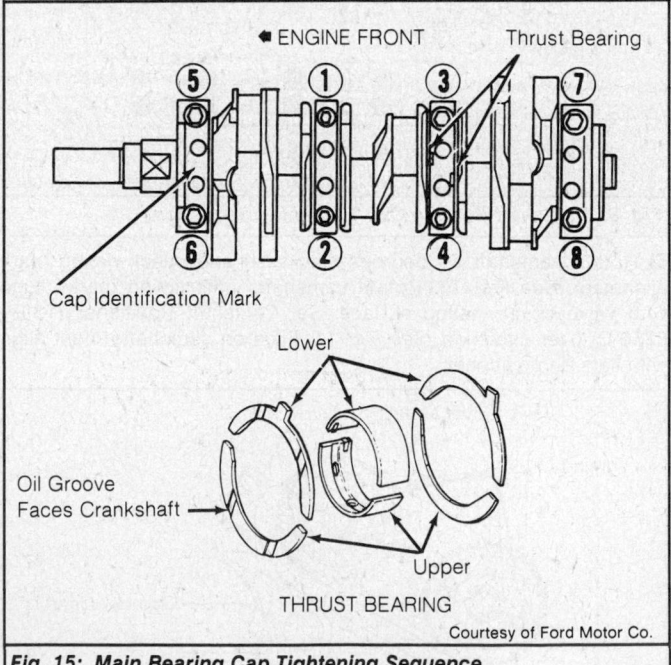

Fig. 15: *Main Bearing Cap Tightening Sequence*

ENGINE OILING

LUBRICATION SYSTEM

Engine lubrication is of force-feed type in which oil is supplied under pressure to crankshaft and rod bearings, lifters and camshaft bearings. Oil pump is mounted to front of engine, behind crankshaft timing belt sprocket.

Crankcase Capacity – Crankcase capacity is 5 qts. (4.7L) with filter changed.

Minimum Oil Pressure – Minimum oil pressure with engine at normal operating temperature is 12.8 psi (.84 kg/cm²) at idle.

OIL PUMP

Inspection – If any component is not within specifications, complete oil pump assembly must be replaced. See OIL PUMP SPECIFICATIONS table in this article. Check inner rotor tip-to-outer rotor tip with rotors removed from housing. Check rotor end play with gears installed in housing.

OIL PUMP SPECIFICATIONS

Application	In. (mm)
Inner Rotor Shaft-to-Housing	.0012-.0037 (.031-.094)
Inner Rotor Tip-to-	
Outer Rotor Tip	.0024-.0071 (.061-.180)
Outer Rotor-to-Housing	.0039-.0069 (.099-.175)
Rotor End Play	.0012-.0035 (.031-.089)
Relief Valve-to-Bore	.0020-.0035 (.051-.089)

TIGHTENING SPECIFICATIONS

Application	Ft. Lbs. (N.m)
Camshaft Bearing Caps [1]	[1] 12-16 (16-22)
Camshaft Chain Sprockets-to-	
Camshafts (Rear)	10-13 (14-18)
Chain Tensioner	11-14 (14-19)
Camshaft Timing Belt Sprockets (Front)	15-18 (20-24)
Connecting Rod Caps	
1st Step	22-26 (30-35)
2nd Step	33-36 (45-49)
Crankshaft Damper-to-Crankshaft	113-126 (153-171)
Cylinder Head Bolts [2]	
1st Step	37-50 (50-68)
2nd Step	62-68 (84-92)
EGR Tube-to-EGR Valve	19-25 (26-34)
Exhaust Manifold	26-38 (35-52)
Exhaust Manifold Heat Shield	11-17 (15-23)
Flywheel-to-Crankshaft [3]	
1st Step	37-50 (50-68)
2nd Step	62-68 (84-92)

TIGHTENING SPECIFICATIONS Cont.)

Application	Ft. Lbs. (N.m)
Front Intake Section-to-Intake Manifold	11-17 (15-23)
Fuel Rail Assembly	11-17 (15-23)
Intake Manifold & Brackets	11-17 (15-23)
Knock Sensor	22-28 (30-38)
Main Bearing Caps [4]	
1st Step	36-51 (49-67)
2nd Step	58-64 (79-87)
Oil Level Sensor	16-24 (22-33)
Oil Pan [5]	11-17 (15-23)
Oil Pressure Switch	12-17 (16-23)
Oil Pump-to-Block	11-17 (15-23)
Pressure Plate-to-Flywheel	12-24 (16-33)
Spark Plugs	17-19 (23-26)
Transaxle-to-Engine	25-35 (34-47)

	INCH Lbs. (N.m)
Oil Pump Pick-Up Tube	70-96 (8-11)
Outer Timing Belt Covers	60-90 (7-10)
Rear Oil Seal Retainer-to-Block	55-82 (6-9)
Rear Timing Belt Cover	70 (8)
Thermostat Housing	60-96 (7-11)
Throttle Body-to-Intake	18-26 (2-3)
Valve Cover	96-132 (11-15)
Water Pump-to-Front Cover	60-72 (7-8)

[1] – Tighten in sequence and in 2 steps evenly. *See Fig. 9.*
[2] – Tighten in sequence. *See Fig. 5.*
[3] – Tighten in a crisscross pattern.
[4] – Tighten in sequence. *See Fig. 15.*
[5] – Oil pan must be tightened in sequence. See appropriate OIL PAN REMOVAL article in this section.

ENGINE SPECIFICATIONS

GENERAL SPECIFICATIONS

Year	Displacement		Fuel System	HP@RPM	Torque Ft. Lbs.@RPM	Compr. Ratio	Bore		Stroke	
	Cu. In.	Liters					In.	mm	In.	mm
1989	182	3.0	SEFI	220@6200	200@4800	.....	3.5	88.9	3.2	80.0

CRANKSHAFT, MAIN & CONNECTING ROD BEARINGS

Engine	Crankshaft				Main Bearings		Connecting Rod Bearings	
	End Play In. (mm)	Runout In. (mm)	Journal Taper In. (mm)	Journal Out-of-Round In. (mm)	Journal Diameter In. (mm)	Oil Clearance In. (mm)	Journal Diameter In. (mm)	Oil Clearance In. (mm)
3.0L	.0008-.0087 (.020-.221)	....	.0008 (.020)	.0008 (.020)	2.5187-2.5197 (63.975-64.000)	.0031 (.079)	2.0463-2.0472 (51.976-51.999)	.0031 (.079)

CONNECTING RODS

Engine	Side Play In. (mm)	Max. Bend & Twist In. (mm)	Pin Bore Dia. In. (mm)	Large Bore Dia. In. (mm)	Center-to-Center In. (mm)
3.0L	.0138 (.351)	....	.827 (21.01)	2.165 (54.99)	5.77-5.78 (146.6-146.8)

1989 FORD MOTOR CO. ENGINES
3.0L SHO V6 (Cont.)

ENGINE SPECIFICATIONS (Cont.)

PISTONS, PINS & RINGS

| Engine | Pistons | | Pins | | | Rings | | |
	Clearance In. (mm)	Diameter In. (mm)	Diameter In. (mm)	Piston Fit In. (mm)	Rod Fit In. (mm)	Ring No.	End Gap In. (mm)	Side Clearance In. (mm)
3.0L	.0012-.0020 (.031-.051)	3.502-3.504 (88.95-89.002)	.8269 (21.003)	Press Fit	.0002-.00043 (.005-.011)	1	.012-.018 (.31-.46)	.0008-.0024 (.020-.061)
						2	.012-.018 (.31-.46)	.0006-.0022 (.015-.056)
						Oil	.008-.020 (.20-.51)	.0024-.0059 (.061-.150)

VALVES & VALVE SPRINGS

| Engine | Valves | | | | | Valves Springs | | | Pressure Lbs. @ In. (Kg @ mm) | |
	Head Dia. In. (mm)	Stem Dia. In. (mm)	Face Angle	Min. Margin In. (mm)	Max. Refinish In. (mm)	Free Length In. (mm)	Out-of-Square In. (mm)	Installed Height In. (mm)	Valve Closed	Valve Open
3.0L										
Intake	1.38 (35.1)	.235 (5.97)	45.5°	.02 (.5)	.....	1.76 (44.7)	.....	.....	42@1.52 (19@38.6)	121@1.19 (55@30.2)
Exhaust	1.18 (30.0)	.235 (5.97)	45.5	.02 (.5)	.....	1.76 (44.7)	.....	.....	42@1.52 (19@38.6)	121@1.19 (55@30.2)

CAMSHAFT

Engine	Journal Diameter In. (mm)	Oil Clearance In. (mm)	Bearing Bore In. (mm)	Runout In. (mm)	End Play In. (mm)	Lobe Lift In. (mm)	Lobe Height In. (mm)
3.0L	1.2189-1.2195 (30.960-30.975)	.001-.003 (.03-.08)	1.221 (31.01)	.....	.012 (.31)	[1] .335 (8.51)	[2] 1.646 (41.81)

[1] – Intake listed. Exhaust is .315" (8.00 mm).
[2] – Intake listed. Exhaust is 1.626" (41.30 mm).

CYLINDER HEAD

| Engine | Max. Cylinder Head Warp In. (mm) | Valve Seats | | | | Valve Guides | | |
		Seat Angle	Maximum Runout In. (mm)	Seat Width In. (mm)	Seat Bore Diameter In. (mm)	Valve Stem Oil Clearance In. (mm)	Valve Guide I.D. In. (mm)	Valve Guide Bore I.D. In. (mm)
3.0L	.008 (.20)	45°	.....	.039-.055 (.99-1.40)	.....	[1] .001-.002 (.03-.05)	.236-.237 (5.99-6.02)	

[1] – Intake listed. Exhaust is .001-.003" (.03-.08 mm).

CYLINDER BLOCK

| Engine | Max. Block Warp In. (mm) | Cylinder Bore | | |
		Standard Diameter In. (mm)	Maximum Taper In. (mm)	Maximum Out-of-Rnd In. (mm)
3.0L	.002 (.05)	3.5039-3.5051 (88.100-89.030)	.0008 (.020)	.0004 (.010)

VALVE LIFTERS

Engine	Diameter In. (mm)	Bore Diameter In. (mm)	Oil Clearance In. (mm)
3.0L	1.2587-1.2596 (31.971-31.994)	.....	.003 (.08)

1989 FORD MOTOR CO. ENGINES
3.8L & 3.8L Supercharger (SC) V6

Continental, Cougar, Sable, Taurus, Thunderbird

NOTE: For engine repair procedures not covered in this article, see ENGINE OVERHAUL PROCEDURES article at beginning of this section.

ENGINE IDENTIFICATION

The engine may be identified by the Vehicle Identification Number (VIN) stamped on a metal tab attached to the instrument panel and visible through windshield on driver's side. The VIN number is also stamped on both Safety Certification Decals, mounted on the driver's front door lock panel and on Engine Identification Label, mounted on the valve cover. The VIN number contains 17 characters. The 8th character identifies the engine and the 10th character establishes the model year.

All label numbers are necessary for determining correct and unique parts to specific engines. DO NOT remove labels at any time. Record these numbers for future reference.

ENGINE IDENTIFICATION CODES

Engine	Code
Continental, Sable & Taurus	
3.8L (232") V6	4
Cougar & Thunderbird [1]	
3.8L (232") V6	3
3.8L SC (232") V6	[2] R

[1] – The Cougar and Thunderbird 3.8L engine does not use a balance shaft. All other models with the 3.8L engine use a balance shaft.

[2] – Some early models may have a C code.

ADJUSTMENTS

VALVE ARRANGEMENT

Right Side – I-E-I-E-I-E.
Left Side – E-I-E-I-E-I.

NOTE: "Right" and "Left" refer to right and left side of the engine NOT the vehicle.

VALVE CLEARANCE ADJUSTMENT

1) Valve and/or valve seat refacing will diminish clearance and cause improper valve operation. Push rods are available in shorter and longer sizes to compensate for dimensional changes.

2) Attach auxiliary starter to relay and battery. With ignition off, position No. 1 piston on TDC of compression stroke. Completely collapse No. 1 intake valve lifter and hold lifter collapsed. Measure clearance between rocker arm and valve stem with feeler gauge.

3) Using VALVE ADJUSTMENT SEQUENCE table in this article, position crankshaft and check appropriate valves. If clearances are not within specifications, replace push rods as necessary. See COLLAPSED LIFTER CLEARANCE table in this article.

4) If push rod(s) is replaced, ensure corresponding cylinder piston is below TDC. It will be necessary to remove rocker arm to replace push rod. DO NOT operate engine after installing push rod until lifter has leaked down to normal operating position.

VALVE ADJUSTMENT SEQUENCE

Crankshaft Position [1]	Intake Valve	Exhaust Valve
No. 1 Cyl. at TDC	Nos. 1, 3, 6	Nos. 1, 2, 4
Rotate 360°	Nos. 2, 4, 5	Nos. 3, 5, 6

[1] – Begin with No. 1 cylinder at TDC of compression stroke and rotate crankshaft degrees given for each set of valves to be checked.

COLLAPSED LIFTER CLEARANCE

Application	In. (mm)
3.8L & 3.8L SC	.089-.189 (2.26-4.80)

REMOVAL & INSTALLATION

NOTE: For reassembly reference, label all electrical connectors, vacuum hoses and fuel lines prior to removal. Match mark engine hood and all other major components prior to removal.

ENGINE

NOTE: See ENGINE REMOVAL & INSTALLATION article at end of ENGINE section.

FUEL PRESSURE RELEASE

On fuel injected models, fuel pressure must be released prior to disconnecting any fuel lines or hoses. Remove fuel filler cap. Attach a fuel pressure gauge to pressure relief valve on fuel rail. *See Fig. 1.* Release fuel pressure through fuel gauge into a container.

CAUTION: The 3.8L engines have aluminum cylinder heads and requires Ford Cooling System Fluid (E2FZ-19549-AA) at 50/50 mixture.

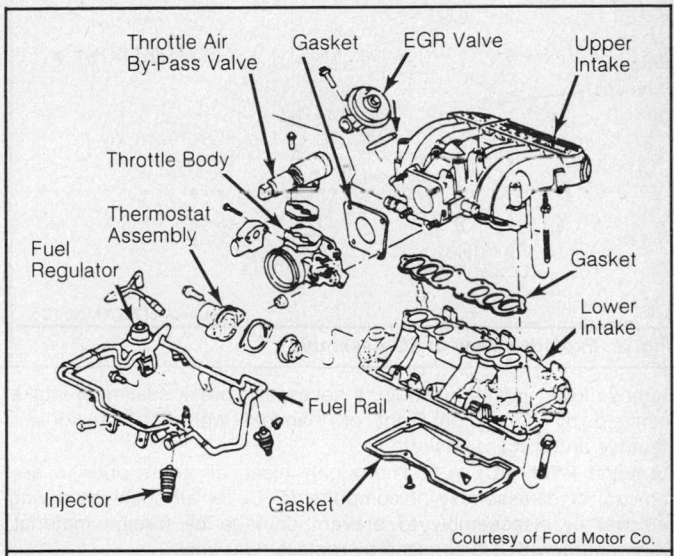

Fig. 1: Exploded View of Intake Manifold (Without SC)

Courtesy of Ford Motor Co.

INTAKE MANIFOLDS

NOTE: Some models will vary in removal and installation of some components, due to location and accessories.

Removal (Without SC) – 1) Disconnect negative battery cable and drain cooling system. Release fuel pressure as previously described. Remove air cleaner assembly and heat tube. Disconnect and set aside throttle body linkage.

2) Disconnect thermactor air supply hose at check valve. Disconnect fuel line as necessary. Remove necessary coolant hoses. Remove heater tube with fuel lines attached.

3) Mark and disconnect necessary vacuum hoses and electrical connectors. Remove necessary accessories and/or brackets. Remove EGR valve assembly. Remove spark plug wires from left front of intake manifold and set aside. Mark and remove upper intake bolts. Remove upper intake manifold. *See Fig. 1.*

4) Remove fuel rail and injectors as an assembly. Remove heater coolant outlet hose. Mark and remove lower intake manifold bolts.

1989 Ford Motor Co. Engines
3.8L & 3.8L Supercharger (SC) V6 (Cont.)

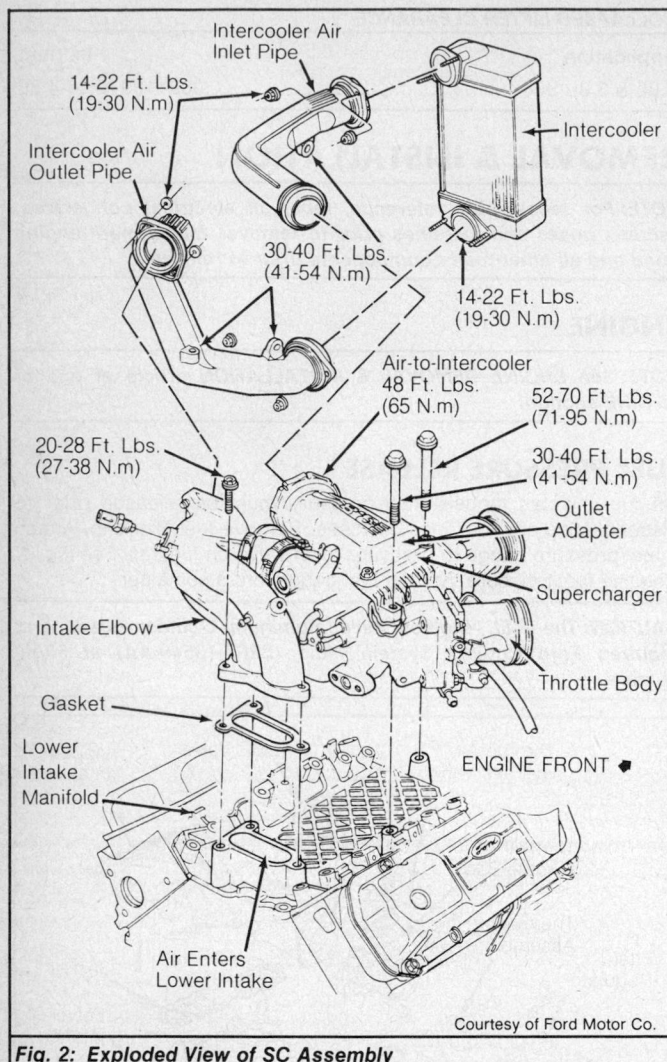

Fig. 2: Exploded View of SC Assembly

Courtesy of Ford Motor Co.

Remove lower intake manifold. If necessary, break sealing of intake manifold by prying on front of manifold with flat screwdriver. Remove and discard gaskets.

Removal (With SC) – 1) Thoroughly clean all areas prior to any removal or disassembly of components. Cover all openings during removal or disassembly to prevent damage by foreign material. Supercharger (SC) is serviced by replacement only.

2) Disconnect negative battery cable and drain cooling system. Remove air inlet duct. Remove cowl vent screens. Disconnect right side plug wires at coil assembly and position out of way. Mark and disconnect necessary electrical connectors and vacuum hoses.

3) Remove EGR transducer from bracket. Disconnect PCV tube. Disconnect linkage at throttle body. Remove EGR valve. Disconnect coolant hoses from throttle body. Remove SC drive belt. Remove intercooler air inlet and outlet pipes. Mark and evenly remove SC mounting bolts. *See Fig. 2.*

4) Lift complete SC assembly off lower intake manifold. Remove and discard gasket. Evenly remove lower intake manifold bolts. Remove lower intake manifold and discard gaskets.

Installation – 1) Clean all gasket surfaces thoroughly. Apply a small amount of Gasket and Trim Adhesive (19B508-AA) to cylinder head gasket surface to hold intake gaskets in place. Install side gaskets. Apply 1/8" bead of Silicone Sealer (D6AZ-19562-B) to each mating corner. Install front and rear intake manifold end seals.

2) Carefully install lower intake manifold. Lightly oil bolt and stud threads. Install bolts/studs finger tight as marked at removal. Tighten in sequence to specifications. *See Fig. 3.* On models without SC, to complete installation, reverse removal procedure. Ensure components are installed to original location and position.

3) On SC models, install SC assembly. Install bolts as marked during removal. Tighten bolts to specifications as shown. *See Fig. 2.* Install Teflon tape to mating surfaces of intercooler inlet and outlet pipes. Keep tape close to inner diameter and overlap ends 1/4".

4) Install the outlet pipe. Loosely install the retaining nut at the alternator/power steering pump bracket and pipe flange nuts. Apply Anti-Seize Compound (ESE-M12A-4A) to threads on air inlet pipe. Position air inlet pipe in place. Loosely install retaining nuts and adapter collar.

5) Tighten bolts to specification in following order: Outlet pipe-to-intake elbow. Outlet pipe-to-bracket nut. Outlet pipe-to-bracket bolt. Inlet pipe-to-outlet adapter spanner. Inlet pipe-to-bracket nut. Outlet pipe-to-intercooler. Inlet pipe-to-intercooler. *See Fig. 2.*

6) Install SC drive belt. To complete SC model installation, reverse removal procedure.

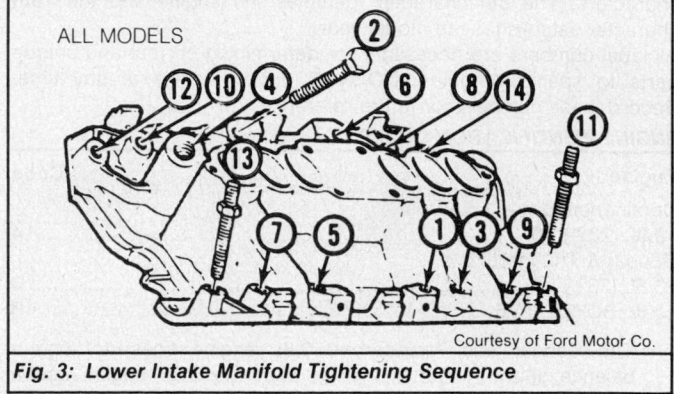

Fig. 3: Lower Intake Manifold Tightening Sequence

Courtesy of Ford Motor Co.

EXHAUST MANIFOLDS

Removal – 1) On left side (with SC), intercooler outlet pipe and inlet pipe must be removed. Proceed to step **2)**.

2) On left side (without SC), remove oil dipstick tube support bracket. Mark and disconnect plug wires from spark plugs. Separate inlet pipe from exhaust manifold. Remove exhaust manifold bolts and manifold.

3) On right side (all models), remove air cleaner assembly and heat tube. Disconnect downstream thermactor hose from check valve. Mark and remove coil wire and plug wires from spark plugs. Remove spark plugs. Remove outer heat shield from exhaust manifold. Disconnect EGR tube. Remove transaxle dipstick tube and thermactor downstream tube. Separate inlet pipe from exhaust manifold. Remove exhaust manifold bolts and manifold.

Installation – Lightly oil all bolt and stud threads prior to installation. A slight warpage, causing misalignment, may be corrected by elongating bolt holes as necessary. DO NOT elongate lower rear bolt hole on No. 2 cylinder for right side or lower front bolt hole on No. 5 cylinder for left side. To complete installation, reverse removal procedure.

VALVE COVERS

Removal & Installation – On SC models, intercooler inlet and outlet pipes must be removed for right side valve covers. On models without SC, upper intake mainfold must be removed. Lightly oil bolt/stud threads prior to installation. To complete installation, reverse removal procedure.

CYLINDER HEAD

NOTE: Some models may differ in removal and installation of some components due to location and accessories.

Removal – 1) Disconnect negative battery cable and drain cooling system. Remove air cleaner assembly and heat tube. Remove accessories with hoses attached and set aside as necessary. Remove accessory drive belt idler, thermactor pump assembly, hoses and PCV valve.

1989 FORD MOTOR CO. ENGINES
3.8L & 3.8L Supercharger (SC) V6 (Cont.)

7-105

2) Remove upper and lower intake manifold, valve covers and exhaust manifolds as previously described. Loosen rocker arm bolts and pivot rocker arms off push rods. Mark and remove pushrods. Remove cylinder head bolts, noting location of different size bolts for installation. Discard cylinder head bolts. Remove cylinder head(s) and gaskets.

Inspection A cleaning solvent for intake manifold gasket surfaces is required. Check dowels in cylinder block and replace if necessary. Check for cracks and warpage. Replace head if cracked. DO NOT machine more than .010" (.25 mm) from original cylinder head surface. Clean and tap cylinder head bolt holes in cylinder block. See ENGINE SPECIFICATIONS tables at end of this article.

NOTE: Always use NEW cylinder head bolts. The 3.8L engine has aluminum cylinder heads and requires Ford Cooling System Fluid (E2FZ-19549-A) at 50/50 mixture.

Installation – 1) Place head gasket on cylinder block. Install cylinder head. Apply a thin coat of Teflon Pipe Sealant (D8AZ-19554-A) to threads of NEW short cylinder head bolts. DO NOT apply sealant to long cylinder head bolts.

2) Install cylinder head. Tighten cylinder head bolts to in sequence to specifications. See TIGHTENING SPECIFICATIONS table at end of this article. *See Fig. 4.* Dip each push rod in Oil Conditioner (D9AZ-19579-C) and install push rods in original position. Prior to installing rocker arm on push rod, rotate crankshaft until push rod is in full down position. Position rocker arm on push rod and tighten bolt to 43 INCH lbs. (5 N.m) maximum.

3) Repeat procedure for remaining push rods and rocker arms. Final tightening of rocker arms may be done with camshaft in any position. To complete installation, reverse removal procedure. Tighten all bolts/nuts to specifications. Change oil and filter. Fill cooling system with specified coolant. Check for leakage.

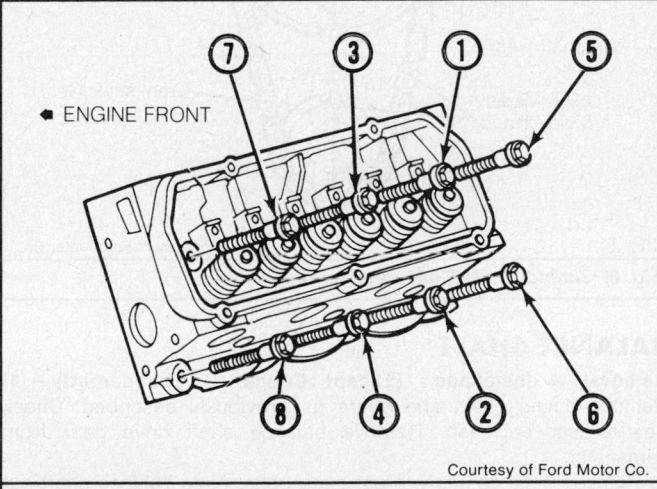

Fig. 4: Cylinder Head Tightening Sequence

WATER PUMP

CAUTION: The 3.8L engine has aluminum cylinder heads and requires Ford Cooling System Fluid (E2FZ-19549-A) at 50/50 mixture.

Removal & Installation (Cougar & Thunderbird) – 1) Disconnect negative battery cable and drain cooling system. Remove air cleaner and heater tube assembly. Remove fan clutch assembly and shroud. Remove accessory belts and water pump pulley. Remove accessories with hoses attached and set aside (as equipped). Disconnect by-pass and heater hose from water pump.

2) Remove water pump attaching bolts. Remove water pump assembly. *See Fig. 5.* Clean gasket mating surfaces and replace gasket using Gasket and Trim Adhesive (D7AZ-19B508-AA). Lightly oil bolt/stud threads prior to installation. To complete installation, reverse removal procedure. Tighten all bolts/nuts to specifications.

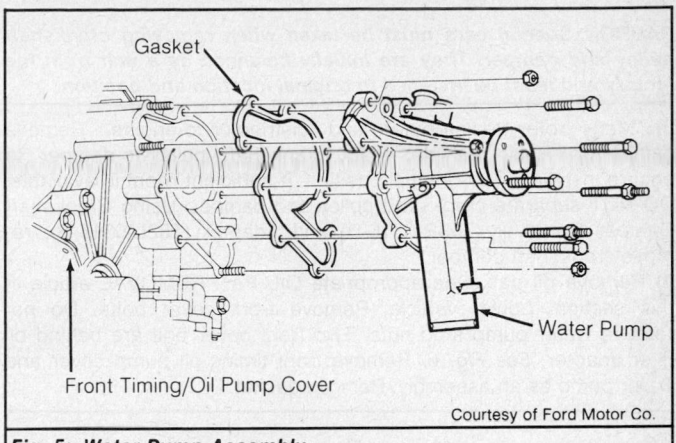

Fig. 5: Water Pump Assembly

Removal & Installation (Except Cougar & Thunderbird) – 1) Disconnect negative battery cable and drain cooling system. Remove lower nut on both right-hand engine mounts. Raise engine. Remove accessory belts and water pump pulley. Remove power steering with hoses attached and set aside (if equipped).

2) Remove A/C compressor front bracket and leave compressor attached (if equipped). Disconnect by-pass and heater hose from water pump. Remove water pump attaching bolts. Remove water pump and gasket. *See Fig. 5.*

3) Clean gasket mating surfaces and replace gasket using Gasket and Trim Adhesive (D7AZ-19B508-AA). Lightly oil bolt/stud threads prior to installation. To complete installation, reverse removal procedure. Tighten all bolts/nuts to specifications.

NOTE: For information on cooling system capacity, see ENGINE COOLANT SPECIFICATIONS article.

FRONT CRANKSHAFT SEAL

CAUTION: Special care must be taken when removing crankshaft pulley and damper. They are initially balanced as a unit from the factory and must be installed to original location and position.

Removal & Installation – 1) Front crankshaft seal may be replaced without removing front timing/oil pump cover. On FWD models, it may be necessary to raise engine to gain access. On RWD models, remove fan, clutch and shroud. Loosen accessory belts and remove belts from crankshaft pulley.

2) Remove bolt retaining damper on crankshaft. Using Crankshaft Damper Remover (T58P-6316-D) and Adapter (T82L-6316-B), remove crankshaft damper. Using screwdriver, pry seal out. Lubricate seal and sealing surfaces with engine oil. Using Seal Installer (T82L-6316-A and T70P-6B070-A), install seal. To complete installation, reverse removal procedure.

FRONT TIMING/OIL PUMP COVER

NOTE: On FWD models, it may be necessary to raise engine to gain access for removal and installation. See WATER PUMP under REMOVAL & INSTALLATION in this article.

Removal – 1) Disconnect negative battery cable and drain cooling system. Drain engine oil. Remove oil filter. Remove air cleaner assembly with heat tube. Remove accessory belts and water pump pulley. Remove fan shroud, fan and clutch assembly. Remove power steering pump/bracket assembly with hoses attached (if equipped). Remove A/C compressor front bracket (if equipped).

2) Disconnect by-pass hose, heater hose, upper and lower radiator hose. Mark and remove spark plug wires from spark plugs. Disconnect coil wire. Remove distributor cap and wire assembly. Position No. 1 cylinder on TDC of compression stroke. Ignition rotor should be at No. 1 cylinder.

7-106

1989 Ford MOTOR CO. ENGINES
3.8L & 3.8L Supercharger (SC) V6 (Cont.)

CAUTION: Special care must be taken when removing crankshaft pulley and damper. They are initially balanced as a unit from the factory and must be installed to original location and position.

3) Mark rotor-to-distributor and distributor-to-engine. Remove distributor. Raise vehicle. Mark crankshaft pulley-to-damper to ensure installation to original position. If sufficient room is available, DO NOT separate crankshaft pulley and damper. Using Crankshaft Damper Remover (T58P-6316-D) and Adapter (T82L-6316-B), remove crankshaft damper.

4) Remove oil pan. See appropriate OIL PAN REMOVAL article in this section. Lower vehicle. Remove front cover bolts. Do not remove water pump stud nuts. Two front cover bolt are behind oil filter adapter. *See Fig. 6.* Remove front timing/oil pump cover and water pump as an assembly. Remove gasket.

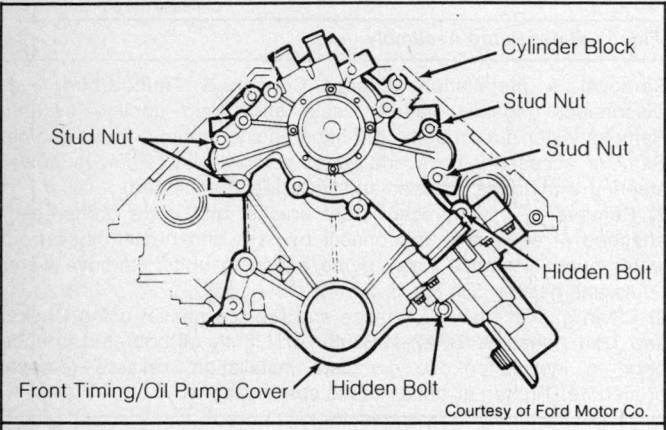

Fig. 6: Front Timing/Oil Pump Cover Assembly

Installation – Lightly oil bolt/stud threads prior to installation. Using Gasket and Trim Adhesive (D7AZ-19BO8-A) to hold cover gasket in place, install gasket on block. Apply engine oil to crankshaft seal lip. Install front timing/oil pump cover and water pump as an assembly. Install cover bolts and tighten evenly to specifications. To complete installation, reverse removal procedure.

TIMING CHAIN & GEARS

NOTE: On Cougar and Thunderbird models, balance shaft is not used in 1989. A spacer has replaced the balance shaft drive gear behind the camshaft gear.

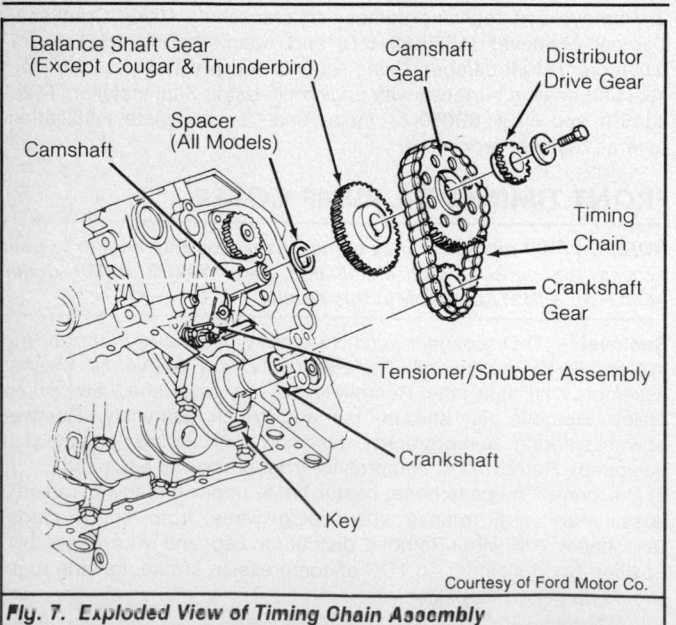

Fig. 7. Exploded View of Timing Chain Assembly

Removal – 1) Remove front timing/oil pump cover as previously described. Ensure timing marks on gears are aligned. Remove camshaft bolt and washer. Remove distributor drive gear. Remove camshaft gear, crankshaft gear and timing chain. *See Fig. 7.* If crankshaft gear is difficult to remove, carefully pry off with a pair of screwdrivers evenly positioned on gear.

2) On FWD models, remove timing chain tensioner/snubber by first pulling back on ratcheting mechanism and installing a pin through hole in bracket. *See Fig. 7.*

Installation – 1) Lightly oil all bolt/stud threads prior to installation. Ensure crankshaft key is at 12 o'clock. On FWD models, install tensioner/snubber with ratcheting mechanism in retracted position and pin in bracket hole facing outward.

2) Install crankshaft gear, camshaft gear and timing chain as an assembly. Ensure timing marks are aligned. *See Fig. 8.* If not aligned, rotate camshaft or crankshaft as necessary. Ensure camshaft is at No. 1 cylinder TDC of compression stroke and not 180 degrees off.

3) Thoroughly coat timing chain and gears with Oil Conditioner (ESE-M2C39-F). To complete installation, reverse removal procedure.

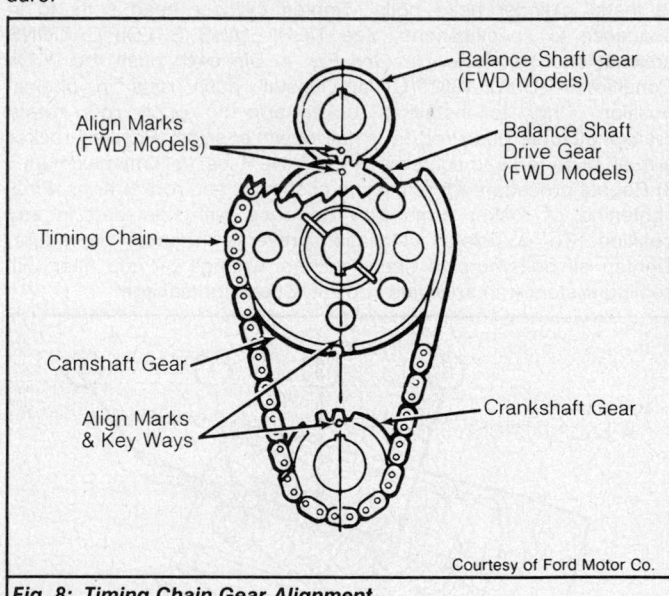

Fig. 8: Timing Chain Gear Alignment

BALANCE SHAFT

Removal & Installation (Except Cougar & Thunderbird) – 1) Remove timing chain and gears as previously described. Check gear-to-gear backlash. Remove balance shaft drive gear from camshaft.

2) Remove balance shaft thrust plate bolts. Slide balance shaft out front of engine. To install, reverse removal procedure. Ensure gear marks are properly aligned. *See Fig. 8.* Coat gears with Lubricant (ESE-M2C39-F).

CAMSHAFT

NOTE: On FWD models, engine must be removed from vehicle to remove camshaft. See ENGINE REMOVAL & INSTALLATION article at end of ENGINE section. Proceed to step 2).

Removal – 1) On RWD models, disconnect negative battery and drain cooling system. Remove radiator, A/C condenser (if equipped) and grille.

2) On all models, remove intake manifolds, valve covers and timing chain and gears as previously described. Remove lifter guide plate retainer and guide plates. Keeping lifters in order, remove lifters. Check camshaft end play. Remove camshaft key, spacer and thrust plate. Pull camshaft out front of engine. Use care not to damage camshaft bearings.

1989 FORD MOTOR CO. ENGINES
3.8L & 3.8L Supercharger (SC) V6 (Cont.)

Inspection – Clean all components and gasket mating surfaces. Check clearance of camshaft-to-bearings. Check lift of each lobe in consecutive order and record each reading. See ENGINE SPECIFICATIONS tables at end of this article. Replace as necessary.

Installation – Lubricate camshaft lobes and bearing surfaces with Oil Conditioner (D9AZ-19579-C). Install camshaft using care not to damage bearings and journal surfaces. To complete installation, reverse removal procedure. Ensure components are installed to original position.

REAR MAIN BEARING OIL SEAL

Removal & Installation – Rear main bearing oil seal is a one piece seal. Remove transmission/transaxle. Remove flex plate/flywheel. Punch hole in metal portion of seal with an awl. Remove seal with a slide hammer. Lubricate seal and mating surfaces with Lubricant (ESE-M2C39-F). Install seal with Rear Main Seal Installer (T82L-6701-A). Rear face of seal must be within .005" (.13 mm) of rear face of cylinder block.

OIL PAN

NOTE: See appropriate OIL PAN REMOVAL aritcle in this section.

OIL PUMP

Removal & Installation – Oil pump is part of the front timing cover. See FRONT TIMING/OIL PUMP COVER under REMOVAL & INSTALLATION in this article.

OVERHAUL

NOTE: Keep components together and marked to ensure installation to original location and position.

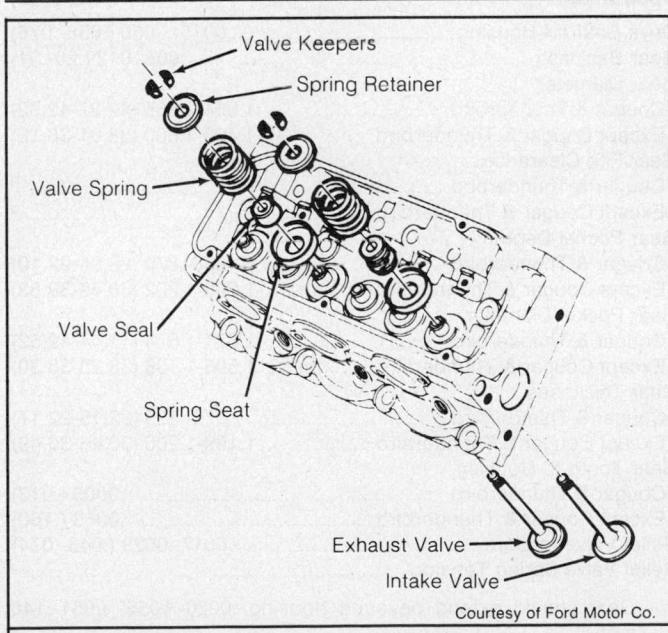

Fig. 9: Exploded View of Cylinder Head Assembly

CYLINDER HEAD

NOTE: No on-vehicle service of valve springs or valve seals available from manufacturer. Lubricate all valves, valve stems and valve guides with heavy oil during installation. Use Multi-Purpose Grease (D0AZ-19584-AA) on valve tips.

Valve Guide – Valve guides may be reamed for available oversize valves. If oversized valves are used, oversized valve seals must also be used. Valve guides may also be bore out and replaced with a service guide if oversized valves and seals are not available. Ream guides until proper clearance of valve stem is achieved.

Valve Seat – Valve seat replacement information is not available from manufacturer. Follow tool manufacturer instructions for servicing valve seats. If seats are serviced, valves must be serviced or replaced.

Valves – Check valves and machine or replace as necessary. See ENGINE SPECIFICATIONS tables at end of this article. Do not remove more than .01" (.3 mm) from end of valve stem. Interference angle of valve and seat must not be lapped out.

CYLINDER BLOCK ASSEMBLY

Inspection – 1) Check cylinder block head gasket surface for warpage. Check cylinder bore for wear, taper, out-of-round and piston fit. See ENGINE SPECIFICATIONS tables at end of this article.

2) Install all main bearing caps and tighten to specifications prior to cylinder bore machining. Use only equal parts of kerosene and SAE 20 motor oil for honing cylinder bores. Use a spring pressure-type cylinder hone. After honing, allow cylinders to cool. Thoroughly clean bore with detergent and water solution.

Camshaft & Balance Shaft Bearings – Engine must be removed from vehicle. Replace camshaft bearing with a bearing replacer kit. Bearings are not interchangeable from one bore to another. Ensure oil holes in bearing and bore are properly aligned. Use sealing compound on rear bearing core plug when installing.

Piston & Rod Assembly – 1) Ensure pistons and rods are measured and installed in cylinder from which it was removed. Ensure notch or dome on piston top and button on connecting rod faces front of engine. See Fig. 10. Check piston fit before assembling piston on rod.

2) Check piston pin fit. If piston pin is to be replaced, replace piston and pin as an assembly. See ENGINE SPECIFICATIONS tables at end of this article.

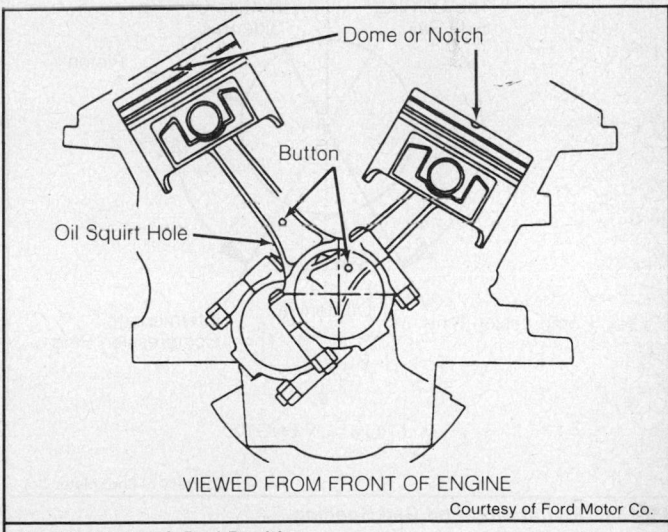

VIEWED FROM FRONT OF ENGINE

Courtesy of Ford Motor Co.

Fig. 10: Piston & Rod Position

Fitting Pistons – 1) Check piston-to-bore clearance. See ENGINE SPECIFICATIONS tables at end of this article. Standard size pistons are color coded Red, Blue or Yellow on the piston dome. See PISTON SIZE CODES table in this article.

2) If bore diameter is in lower one-third of standard specifications, use a Red coded piston. If bore diameter is in middle one-third of standard specifications, use a Blue coded piston. If bore diameter is in upper one-third of standard specifications, use Yellow coded piston. The Yellow coded piston is .004" (.10 mm) oversize. See PISTON SELECTION table in this article.

3) Check piston top-to-deck clearance. Clearance must be .27" (6.9 mm) below deck to .25" (6.4 mm) above deck. Measure with piston at TDC and parallel to crankshaft on true centerline of piston. No further information available from manufacturer.

7-108

1989 FORD MOTOR CO. ENGINES
3.8L & 3.8L Supercharger (SC) V6 (Cont.)

4) When installing piston and rod assembly, install in the following order: Cylinder No. 1 and No. 5, cylinder No. 2 and No. 6, cylinder No. 3 and No. 4. Tighten connecting rod nuts to correct torque. See TIGHTENING SPECIFICATIONS table at end of this article.

PISTON SIZE CODES

Code	In. (mm)
Red	3.8095-3.8101 (96.761-96.777)
Blue	3.8107-3.8113 (96.792-96.807)
Yellow	3.8119-3.8125 (96.822-96.836)

PISTON SELECTION

Bore Diameter In. (mm)	Piston Required Code
3.8110-3.8122 (96.799-96.830)	Red
3.8122-3.8134 (96.830-96.860)	Blue
3.8134-3.8146 (96.860-96.891)	Yellow

Fitting Rings – 1) Measure ring end gap. If ring end gap is less than specifications, remove necessary amount from end of ring. If ring gap is greater than specifications, use a different set of rings. Ensure rings are installed in cylinder bore in which they were measured.

2) Check piston ring side clearance. If lower lands of piston have high steps, replace piston. Replace piston and rings if side clearance is not within specifications. Properly set ring ends on piston before installing pistons into cylinder. *See Fig. 11.* See ENGINE SPECIFICATIONS tables at end of this article.

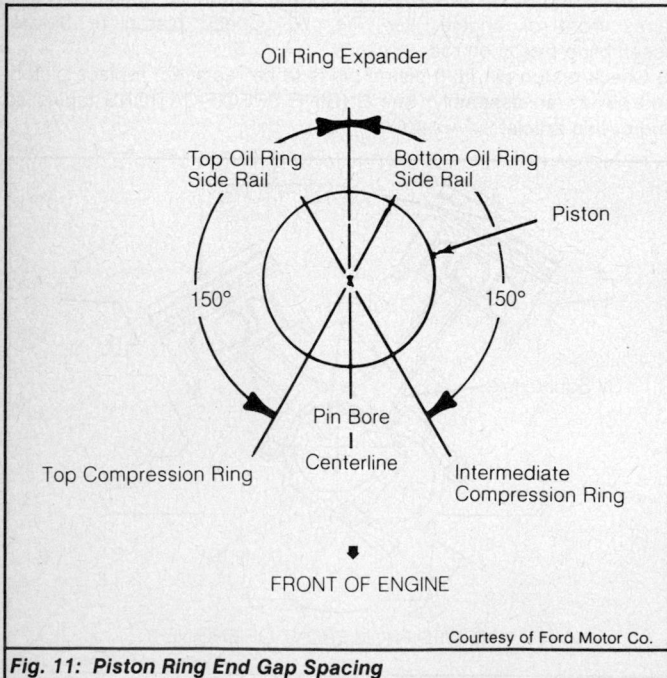

Fig. 11: Piston Ring End Gap Spacing

CAUTION: The No. 4 main bearings (upper and lower) are unique to supercharged (SC) engines and journal is .01" (.3 mm) undersized as designed. DO NOT regrind journal to .01" (.3 mm) undersize.

Crankshaft & Bearings – 1) Prior to measuring and installing main bearing, loosen lower intake manifold attachments. Use Plastigage method and check clearance. Check crankshaft for nicks, scratches, scores and wear. Machine or replace crankshaft as necessary. See ENGINE SPECIFICATIONS tables at end of this article.

2) Journal refinishing is limited to .01" (.5 mm) undersize. Check crankshaft end play. See THRUST BEARING ALIGNMENT in this article. Replace thrust bearing as necessary.

3) If rear main bearing was removed, remove all traces of sealant from cap and block. Apply a 1/8" bead of silicone sealer to main bearing cap-to-cylinder block parting ling. Lubricate journal and bearings. Install main bearing cap.

Thrust Bearing – Lubricate journal and bearings. Install main bearing cap. Tighten bolts finger tight. Pry crankshaft forward against thrust surface on upper bearing insert. While holding bearing cap to the rear. While holding crankshaft forward, tighten main bearing cap.

ENGINE OILING

LUBRICATION SYSTEM

The lubrication is a force-feed type. The oil is supplied under full pressure to crankshaft, connecting rods, camshaft bearing and valve lifters. A controlled volume of oil is supplied to rocker arms and push rods. All other moving parts are lubricated by splash or gravity flow.

Crankcase Capacity – Crankcase capacity is 4 qts. (3.8L) without filter. On Cougar and Thunderbird models, 5 qts. (4.7L) with filter change. On all other models, 4.5 qts. (4.3L) with filter change. DO NOT change oil without filter.

Normal Oil Pressure (Hot) – Normal oil pressure is 40-60 psi (2.8-4.2 kg/cm²) at 2500 RPM.

OIL PUMP

Inspection – Check oil pump gear end play, side clearance, gear thickness, gear pocket depth, gear diameter and front gear pocket diameter. If not within specifications, replace components as necessary. See OIL PUMP SPECIFICATIONS table in this article.

OIL PUMP SPECIFICATIONS

Application	In. (mm)
Drive Shaft-to-Housing	.0015-.0030 (.038-.076)
Gear Backlash	.008-.012 (.20-.31)
Gear Diameter	
Cougar & Thunderbird	1.664-1.666 (42.27-42.32)
Except Cougar & Thunderbird	1.498-1.500 (38.01-38.10)
Gear End Clearance	
Cougar & Thunderbird	[1]
Except Cougar & Thunderbird	[2]
Gear Pocket Depth	
Cougar & Thunderbird	.868-.870 (22.05-22.10)
Except Cougar & Thunderbird	1.200-1.202 (30.49-30.53)
Gear Pocket Diameter	
Cougar & Thunderbird	1.671-1.674 (42.44-42.52)
Except Cougar & Thunderbird	1.505-1.508 (38.23-38.30)
Gear Thickness	
Cougar & Thunderbird	.872-.873 (22.15-22.17)
Except Cougar & Thunderbird	1.199-1.200 (30.46-30.49)
Gear Tooth-to-Housing	
Cougar & Thunderbird	.0005 (.013)
Except Cougar & Thunderbird	.0063 (.160)
Relief Valve-to-Bore	.0017-.0029 (.043-.074)
Relief Valve Spring Tension	[3]

[1] – Gear should extend beyound housing .0020-.0055" (.051-.140 mm).

[2] – Gear should be recessed in .0004-.0034" (.010-.085 mm).

[3] – Spring tension should be 15.2-17.1 lbs. @ 1.20" (6.9-7.8 kg @ 30.5 mm).

7-109

1989 FORD MOTOR CO. ENGINES
3.8L & 3.8L Supercharger (SC) V6 (Cont.)

TIGHTENING SPECIFICATIONS

Application	Ft. Lbs. (N.m)
Camshaft Sprocket Bolt	
Except Continental	15-22 (20-30)
Continental	30-36 (41-49)
Cylinder Head Bolts [1]	
1st Step	37 (50)
2nd Step	45 (61)
3rd Step	52 (70)
4th Step	59 (80)
5th Step	Back off 2-3 turns
6th Step	Repeat steps 1-4
Connecting Rod Nut	
1st Step	31-36 (42-49)
2nd Step	Back off 2-3 turns
3rd Step	31-36 (42-49)
Damper-to-Crankshaft Bolt	93-121 (126-165)
Continental	104-132 (141-180)
Exhaust Manifold	15-22 (20-30)
Flywheel-to-Crankshaft Bolts	54-64 (73-87)
Front Timing/Oil Pump	
Cover-to-Cylinder Block	15-22 (20-30)
Intake Manifold Bolts [2]	
Without SC	
1st Step	7 (10)
2nd Step	15 (20)
3rd Step	24 (32)
With SC	
1st Step	7.5 (10.2)
2nd Step	11 (15)

TIGHTENING SPECIFICATIONS (Cont.)

Application	Ft. Lbs. (N.m)
Intercooler Pipes	[3]
Main Bearing Cap	
Bolts	65-74 (88-100)
No. 2 Cap Stud	67-81 (91-110)
Sable & Taurus	65-81 (88-110)
Pulley-to-Damper Bolt [4]	20-28 (27-38)
Rocker Arm Bolt	
Except Continental	
1st Step	5-11 (7-15)
2nd Step	18-26 (25-35)
Continental	
1st Step	4 (5)
2nd Step	18-26 (25-35)
Supercharger-to-Intake Manifold Bolts	[3]
Valve Lifter Guide Retainer	6-10 (8-14)
Water Pump Bolt	15-22 (20-30)

Application	INCH Lbs. (N.m)
Fuel Rail Mount Bolt	71-104 (8-11.7)
Oil Pan-to-Cylinder Block Bolt	80-106 (9-12)
Spark Plug	60-132 (7-15)
Valve Cover Bolt	71-101 (8-11)
Water Pump Pulley Bolt	71-101 (8-11)

[1] – Tighten in sequence. *See Fig. 4.*
[2] – Tighten in sequence. *See Fig. 3.*
[3] – Tighten SC components as shown. *See Fig. 2.*
[4] – Damper and pulley are balanced as a unit at the factory and must be installed to original position.

ENGINE SPECIFICATIONS

GENERAL SPECIFICATIONS

Year	Displacement		Fuel System	HP@RPM	Torque Ft. Lbs.@RPM	Compr. Ratio	Bore		Stroke	
	Cu. In.	Liters					In.	mm	In.	mm
1989	232	3.8	EFI	[1] 140@3800	[2] 215@2200	[3] 9.0:1	3.81	96.8	3.39	86.1

[1] – Models without SC listed. Models with SC is 210 @ 4000.
[2] – Models without SC listed. Models with SC is 315 @ 2600.
[3] – Models without SC listed. Models with SC is 8.2:1.

CRANKSHAFT, MAIN & CONNECTING ROD BEARINGS

Engine	Crankshaft				Main Bearings		Connecting Rod Bearings	
	End Play In. (mm)	Runout In. (mm)	Journal Taper In. (mm)	Journal Out-of-Round In. (mm)	Journal Diameter In. (mm)	Oil Clearance In. (mm)	Journal Diameter In. (mm)	Oil Clearance In. (mm)
3.8L	.004-.008 (.10-.20)	....	[1] .0003 (.008)	.0003 (.008)	[2] 2.5190-2.5198 (63.983-64.003)	[3] .0010-.0014 (.025-.036)	2.3103-2.3111 (58.682-58.702)	.0010-.0014 (.025-.036)

[1] – Specifications listed is per 1" (25.4 mm).
[2] – Models without SC listed. Models with SC is as follows:
  Journal Nos. 1-3 are 2.5186-2.5194" (63.972-63.993 mm).
  Journal No. 4 is 2.5092-2.5100" (63.734-63.754 mm).

[3] – Models without SC listed. Models with SC is as follows:
  Journal Nos. 1-3 are .0009-.0026" (.023-.066 mm).
  Journal No. 4 is .0014-.0032" (.036-.081 mm).

CONNECTING RODS

Engine	Side Play In. (mm)	Max. Bend & Twist In. (mm)	Pin Bore Dia. In. (mm)	Large Bore Dia. In. (mm)	Center-to-Center In. (mm)
3.8L	.0047-.0114 (.119-.290)	[1] .0016 (.041)	.9096-.9112 (23.104-23.145)	2.4266-2.4274 (61.636-61.656)	5.914 (150.22)

[1] – Specifications listed is bend and per 1" (25.4 mm). Twist is .003" (.08 mm) per 1" (25.4 mm).

1989 FORD MOTOR CO. ENGINES
3.8L & 3.8L Supercharger (SC) V6 (Cont.)

ENGINE SPECIFICATIONS (Cont.)

PISTONS, PINS & RINGS

Engine	Pistons		Pins			Rings		
	Clearance In. (mm)	Diameter In. (mm)	Diameter In. (mm)	Piston Fit In. (mm)	Rod Fit In. (mm)	Ring No.	End Gap In. (mm)	Side Clearance In. (mm)
3.8L	[1] .0014-.0032 (.036-.081)	[2]	.912 (23.17)	.0002-.0005 (.005-.013)	Press Fit	No. 1	.011-.021 (.28-.55)	.0016-.0034 (.041-.086)
						No. 2	.009-.020 (.23-.51)	.0016-.0034 (.041-.086)
						Oil Ring	.015-.058 (.38-1.47)	.0006 Max. (.015 Max.)

[1] – Models without SC listed. Models with SC is .0040-.0045" (.102-.114 mm).
[2] – Pistons are color coded. See FITTING PISTONS under OVERHAUL in this article.

VALVES & VALVE SPRINGS

Engine	Valves					Valves Springs				
	Head Dia. In. (mm)	Stem Dia. In. (mm)	Face Angle	Min. Margin In. (mm)	Max. Refinish In. (mm)	Free Length In. (mm)	Out-of-Square In. (mm)	Installed Height In. (mm)	Pressure Lbs. @ In. (Kg @ mm)	
									Valve Closed	Valve Open
3.8L										
Intake	1.78 (45.2)	.3415-.3423 (8.67-8.69)	45.8°	.0313 (.794)	.....	2.02 (51.3)	.06 (1.5)	1.65 (41.9)	85 @ 1.65 (39 @ 41.9)	220 @ 1.18 (100 @ 30.0)
Exhaust	1.46 (37.1)	.3410-.3418 (8.661-8.682)	45.8°	.0313 (.794)	.....	2.02 (51.3)	.06 (1.5)	1.65 (41.9)	85 @ 1.65 (39 @ 41.9)	220 @ 1.18 (100 @ 30.0)

CYLINDER HEAD

Engine	Max. Cylinder Head Warp In. (mm)	Valve Seats				Valve Guides		
		Seat Angle	Maximum Runout In. (mm)	Seat Width In. (mm)	Seat Bore Diameter In. (mm)	Valve Stem Oil Clearance In. (mm)	Valve Guide I.D. In. (mm)	Valve Guide Bore I.D. In. (mm)
3.8L	.007 (.18)	44.5°	.003 (.08)	.06-.08 (1.5-2.0)	[2] 1.8532 (47.071)	[1] .0010-.0028 (.025-.071)	.3433-.3443 (8.720-8.745)	....

[1] – Intake listed. Exhaust is .0015-.0033" (.038-.084 mm).
[2] – Intake minimum specifications listed. Maximum is 1.8542" (47.097 mm). Exhaust maximum is 1.5645" (39.738 mm).

CAMSHAFT

Engine	Journal Diameter In. (mm)	Oil Clearance In. (mm)	Bearing Bore In. (mm)	Runout In. (mm)	End Play In. (mm)	Lobe Lift In. (mm)	Lobe Height In. (mm)
3.8L	2.0505-2.0515 (52.083-52.108)	.001-.003 (.03-.08)	[1] 2.191 (55.65)	.01 (.3)	[2]	[3] .245 (6.22)	....

[1] – No. 1 & 4 bore listed. No. 2 & 3 bore is 2.177" (55.30 mm).
[2] – No end play. Camshaft is restrained by spring.
[3] – Intake is listed. Exhaust is .259" (6.58 mm).

CYLINDER BLOCK

Engine	Max. Block Warp In. (mm)	Cylinder Bore		
		Standard Diameter In. (mm)	Maximum Taper In. (mm)	Maximum Out-of-Rnd In. (mm)
3.8L	[1] .003 (.08)	3.81 (96.8)	.002 (.05)	.002 (.05)

[1] – Specification listed is within a 6" (152 mm) area.

VALVE LIFTERS

Engine	Diameter In. (mm)	Bore Diameter In. (mm)	Oil Clearance In. (mm)
3.8L	.874 (22.20)	....	.0007-.0027 (.018-.069)

Grand Marquis, LTD Crown Victoria Mark VII, Mustang, Town Car

NOTE: For engine repair procedures not covered in this article, see ENGINE OVERHAUL PROCEDURES article at beginning of this section.

ENGINE IDENTIFICATION

Engine may be identified from Vehicle Identification Number (VIN). VIN is stamped on a plate, on top of instrument panel and visible through windshield. VIN contains 17 characters. The 8th character identifies engine.

An engine code information label is located on front of engine. This label contains engine calibration number, engine build date, engine plant code and engine code.

An emission calibration number label is located on driver's door or door post pillar. This label identifies engine calibration number, engine code number and revision level.

All label numbers are necessary for determining correct and unique parts to specific enignes. DO NOT remove labels at any time. Record these numbers for future reference.

ENGINE IDENTIFICATION CODES

Engine	Code
5.0L HO (302") SEFI	E
5.0L (302") SEFI	F
5.8L (351") 2-Bbl.	G

ADJUSTMENTS

VALVE ARRANGEMENT

Right Side – I-E-I-E-I-E-I-E (front-to-rear).
Left Side – E-I-E-I-E-I-E-I (front-to-rear).

VALVE CLEARANCE ADJUSTMENT

1) Valve and/or valve seat refacing will diminish clearance and cause improper valve operation. Push rods are available in shorter and longer sizes to compensate for dimensional changes.

VALVE ADJUSTMENT SEQUENCE

Crankshaft Position [1]	Intake Valve	Exhaust Valve
5.0L		
No. 1 Cyl. at TDC	Nos. 1, 7, 8	Nos. 1, 5, 4
Rotate 360°	Nos. 4, 5	Nos. 2, 6
Rotate 90°	Nos. 2, 3, 6	Nos. 7, 3, 8
5.0L HO & 5.8L		
No. 1 Cyl. at TDC	Nos. 1, 4, 8	Nos. 1, 3, 7
Rotate 360°	Nos. 3, 7	Nos. 2, 6
Rotate 90°	Nos. 2, 5, 6	Nos. 4, 5, 8

[1] – Begin with No. 1 cylinder at TDC of compression stroke and rotate crankshaft degrees given for each set of valves to be checked.

COLLAPSED LIFTER CLEARANCE

Application	In. (mm)
Allowable	
5.0L	.071-.171 (1.80-4.34)
5.0L HO & 5.8L	.098-.198 (2.49-5.03)
Desired	
5.0L & 5.8L	.096-.146 (2.44-3.71)
5.0L HO	.123-.146 (3.12-3.71)

2) Disconnect terminals I and S at starter relay. Attach auxiliary starter to relay and battery. With ignition off, position No. 1 piston on TDC of compression stroke. Completely collapse No. 1 intake valve lifter and hold lifter collapsed. Measure clearance between rocker arm and valve stem with feeler gauge.

3) Using VALVE ADJUSTMENT SEQUENCE table in this article, position crankshaft and check appropriate valves. If clearances are not within specifications, replace push rods as necessary. See COLLAPSED LIFTER CLEARANCE table in this article.

REMOVAL & INSTALLATION

NOTE: For reassembly reference, label all electrical connectors, vacuum hoses and fuel lines prior to removal. Match mark engine hood and all other major components prior to removal.

ENGINE

NOTE: See ENGINE REMOVAL & INSTALLATION article at end of ENGINE section.

FUEL PRESSURE RELEASE

On fuel injected models, fuel pressure must be released prior to disconnecting any fuel lines or hoses. Remove fuel filler cap. Attach a fuel pressure gauge to pressure relief valve on left front corner of engine. Release fuel pressure through fuel gauge into a container.

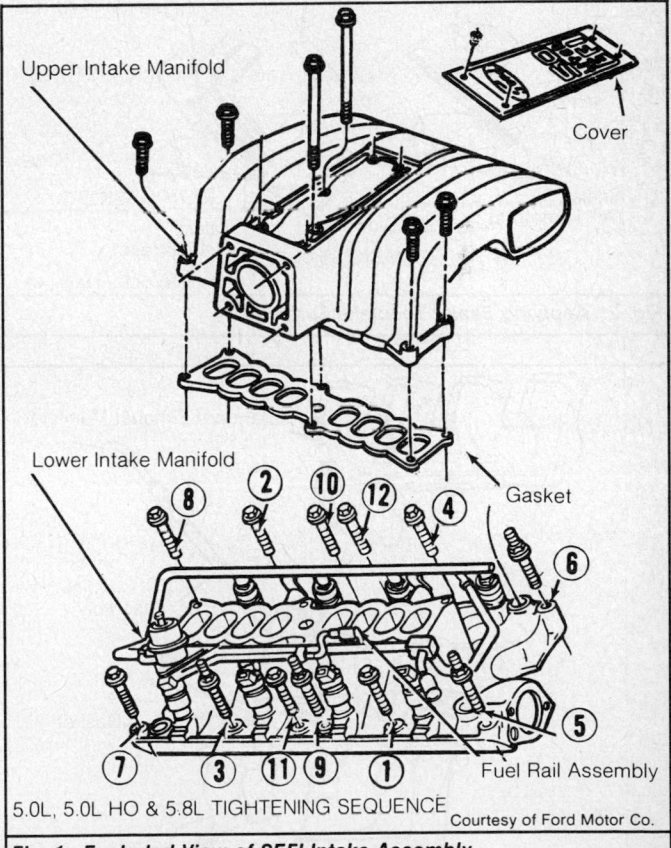

5.0L, 5.0L HO & 5.8L TIGHTENING SEQUENCE
Courtesy of Ford Motor Co.

Fig. 1: Exploded View of SEFI Intake Assembly

INTAKE MANIFOLD

Removal (5.0L & 5.0L HO) – 1) Disconnect negative battery cable and drain cooling system. Release fuel pressure as previously described. Mark and disconnect necessary linkage and cables (as equipped). Mark and disconnect vacuum hoses at intake manifold. Remove distributor cap and spark plug wires as an assembly. Mark and remove distributor. Remove coolant hoses as necessary.

1989 FORD MOTOR CO. ENGINES
5.0L, 5.0L HO & 5.8L V8 (Cont.)

2) Mark and disconnect electrical connectors as necessary. Disconnect fuel injector wiring harness. Remove upper intake manifold cover plate. Remove 6 upper intake manifold bolts. Remove upper intake manifold. *See Fig. 1.*

3) Remove accessory brackets attached to lower intake manifold. Remove heater tube assembly from lower intake manifold. Remove lower intake manifold bolts evenly. Remove lower intake manifold. Remove gaskets and seals.

Removal (5.8L) – 1) Disconnect negative battery cable and drain cooling system. Remove air cleaner assembly. Disconnect linkage at carburetor. Mark and disconnect electrical connectors and vacuum lines as necessary. Mark and disconnect spark plug wires and remove distributor cap assembly.

2) Disconnect fuel line at carburetor. Mark position of distributor and remove distributor assembly. Remove necessary coolant hoses. Remove by-pass hose at thermostat housing. Remove intake manifold and carburetor assembly.

Installation – 1) Clean all gasket surfaces. Apply a .125" (3.18 mm) bead of Silicone Rubber Sealer (D6AZ-19562-A) without gaskets installed as shown. *See Fig. 2.* Install front and rear seals. Install intake manifold gaskets. Ensure holes in gasket and cylinder block are properly aligned.

2) Apply a .063" (1.60 mm) bead of the silicone sealer with gaskets installed as shown. *See Fig. 2.* Install intake manifold (or lower intake) and bolts. Tighten bolts in sequence to specifications. To complete installation, reverse removal procedure.

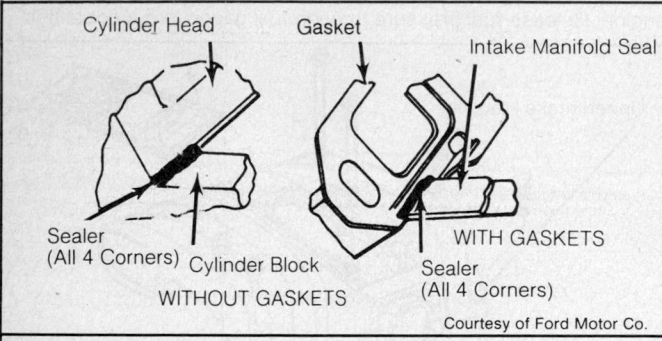

Fig. 2: Applying Sealer To Intake Surfaces

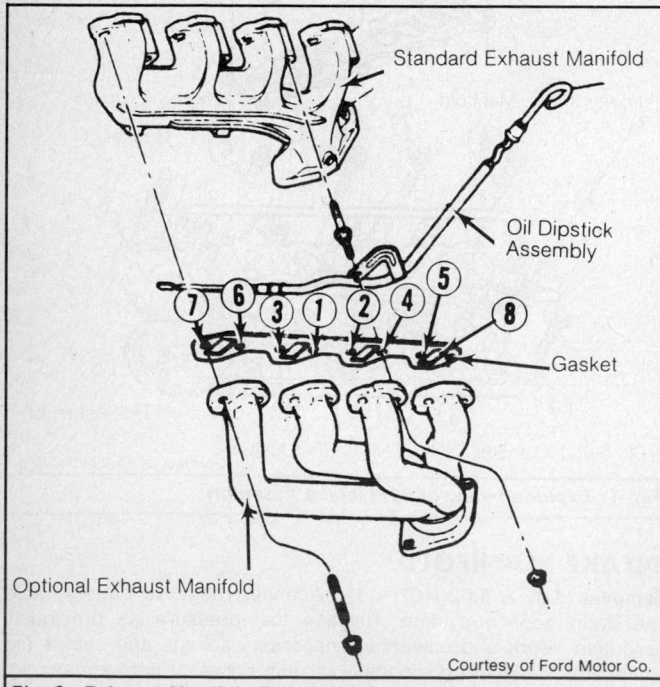

Fig. 3: Exhaust Manifold Tightening Sequence

EXHAUST MANIFOLD

Removal & Installation – Exhaust manifolds can be removed with engine in vehicle. Oil dipstick and tube must be removed for left manifold removal. Spark plug wires and spark plugs should be removed to avoid damage. To install, reverse removal procedure. Tighten exhaust manifold in sequence. *See Fig. 3.*

VALVE COVERS

Removal & Installation – Remove PCV valve and pipes as necessary. Remove thermactor by-pass valve and hoses as necessary. Mark and remove spark plug wires from spark plugs and valve cover. Remove upper intake manifold as necessary (if equipped). Remove valve cover bolts, valve cover and gasket (if equipped). To install, reverse removal procedure.

CYLINDER HEAD

NOTE: Allow sufficient cool down time prior to performing service.

Removal & Installation – 1) Disconnect negative battery cable. Remove exhaust manifold(s), intake manifold(s) and valve cover(s) as previously described. Remove necessary accessories and/or brackets attached to cylinder head(s). Loosen rocker arms and rotate them off of push rods. Keeping push rods in order, remove push rods.

2) Remove cylinder head bolts. Remove cylinder head and gasket. Clean gasket surfaces. Check for surface warpage. Surface must not be machined more than .01" (.3 mm) from original. Properly position new head gasket over dowels. Install cylinder head and bolts. Tighten cylinder head bolts in sequence to specifications. *See Fig. 4.* To complete installation, reverse removal procedure.

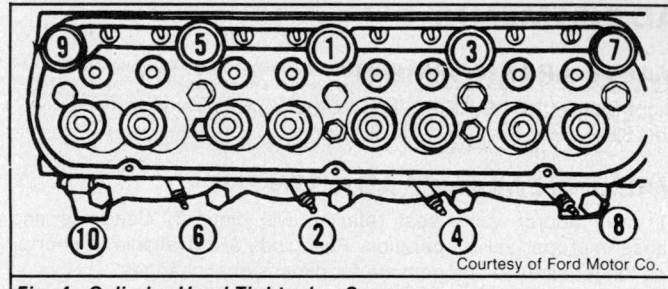

Fig. 4: Cylinder Head Tightening Sequence

WATER PUMP

Removal – 1) Disconnect negative battery cable and drain cooling system. Remove fan shroud attaching bolts and position shroud over cooling fan. Remove fan, clutch and shroud. Remove accessory belts. Remove necessary accessories and/or brackets attached to water pump. Remove necessary coolant hoses.

2) Remove water pump bolts, water pump and gasket. *See Fig. 5.*

Installation – Coat both sides of new gasket with Perfect Seal Sealing Compound (B5A-19554-A) and install gasket on front cover. Install water pump and tighten bolts finger tight. Evenly and alternately, tighten bolts to specifications. To complete installation, reverse removal procedure.

NOTE: For information on cooling system capacity, see ENGINE COOLANT SPECIFICATIONS article.

FRONT TIMING COVER & SEAL

NOTE: It is not necessary to remove timing cover to replace seal.

Removal – 1) Perform step 1) in REMOVAL under WATER PUMP. Drain engine oil. Remove crankshaft pulley. Remove crankshaft damper with a puller. Remove seal if not removing front timing cover. Remove bolts retaining oil pan-to- front timing cover. Using a

1989 Ford Motor Co. Engines
5.0L, 5.0L HO & 5.8L V8 (Cont.)

7-113

thin blade, cut oil pan gasket flush with cylinder block prior to separating front timing cover.

2) Remove front timing cover retaining bolts. Remove front cover and water pump as an assembly. *See Fig. 5.* Remove and discard gaskets. If front cover removal is restricted by oil pan, oil pan-to-cylinder block may be loosened to allow ample clearance. Oil pan gasket may then have to be replaced.

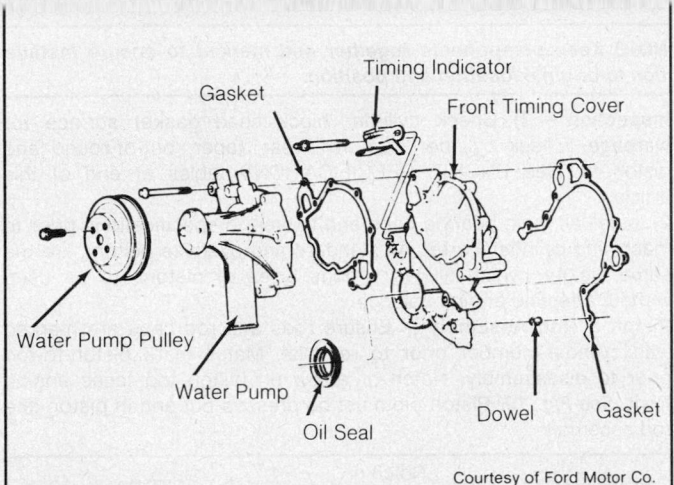

Fig. 5: Exploded View of Front Timing Cover Assembly

NOTE: Gasket and Trim Adhesive (D7AZ-19B508-AA) is recommended to retain gaskets during installation.

Installation – 1) Coat oil pan gasket surface with sealer. Cut and position required sections of new gasket. Apply silicone sealer to mating corner. Position front timing cover to cylinder block. Ensure gaskets are in proper position. Install Front Cover Aligner (T61P-6019-B) through oil seal. *See Fig. 6.*

2) Coat front timing cover bolts with oil resistant sealer and install bolts. While pushing on aligner, tighten oil pan-to-cover bolts. Tighten front timing cover bolts to specifications and remove aligner. To complete installation, reverse removal procedure.

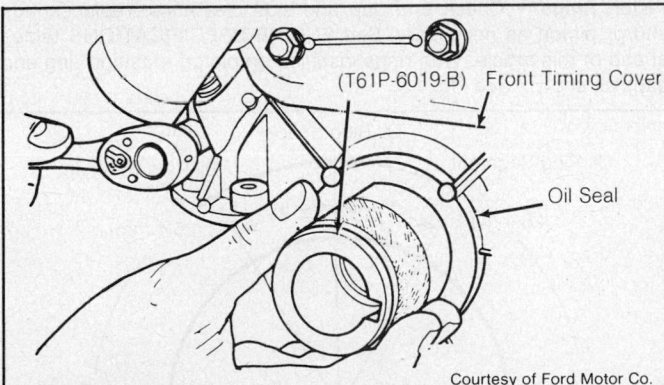

Fig. 6: Installing Front Timing Cover

TIMING CHAIN & GEARS

Removal – 1) Rotate crankshaft and position No. 1 cylinder at TDC on compression stroke. Remove front timing cover as previously described. Check timing chain deflection. See ENGINE OVERHAUL PROCEDURES article at beginning of this section.

2) Check timing gear mark alignment. *See Fig. 7.* Remove fuel pump eccentric from camshaft (if equipped). Slide camshaft gear, crankshaft gear and chain off as an assembly.

Installation – Place timing chain around camshaft and crankshaft gear. Align timing marks and slide assembly into position. *See Fig. 7.* Install fuel pump eccentric on camshaft. Lubricate timing chain

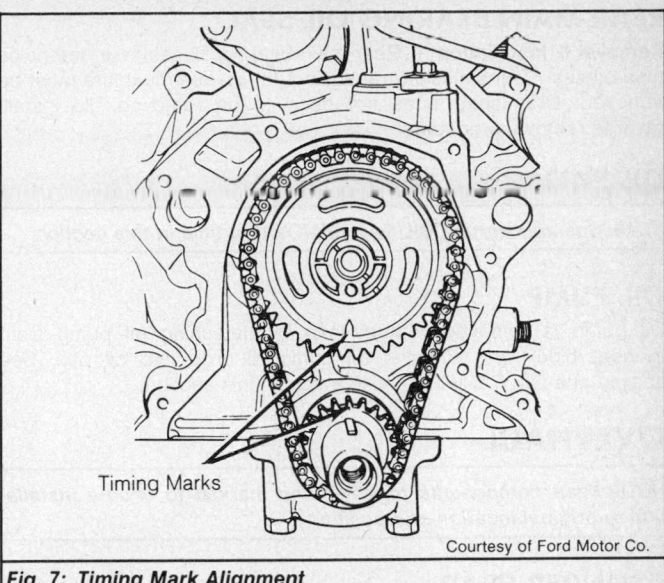

Fig. 7: Timing Mark Alignment

and gears with engine oil. To complete installation, reverse removal procedure.

CAMSHAFT

NOTE: Engine must be removed to install camshaft bearings.

Removal – Disconnect negative battery cable and drain cooling system. Remove radiator, A/C condenser and necessary grille components. Remove intake manifold(s), valve covers and timing gears as previously described. Remove lifter guide retainer, guide plate and lifters. Remove camshaft thrust plate. *See Fig. 8.* Carefully slide camshaft out of cylinder block.

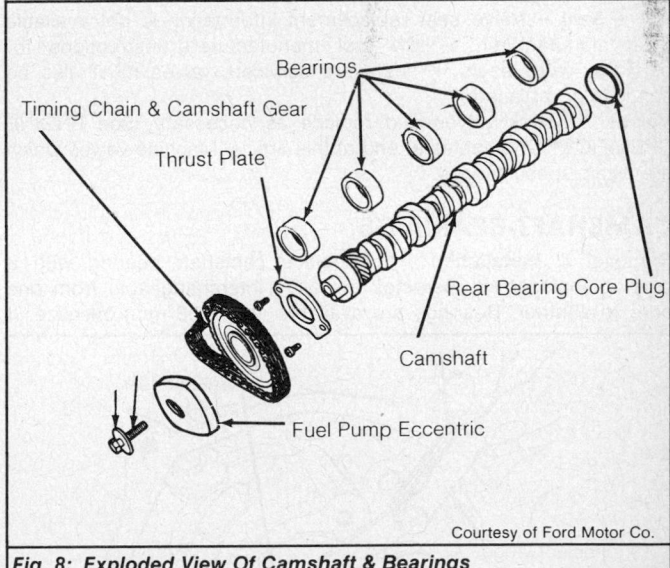

Fig. 8: Exploded View Of Camshaft & Bearings

Inspection – Check camshaft for scratched, pits and loose fit in bearings. Check for out-of-round journals. Check for runout at center journal. If not within specifications, replace camshaft and bearings as necessary.

Installation – Lubricate camshaft journals with heavy engine oil. Apply Multi-Purpose Grease (DOAZ-19584-AA) to camshaft lobes. Carefully slide camshaft into cylinder block. Install camshaft thrust plate with groove towards cylinder block. Check camshaft end play and replace thrust plate if necessary. Lubricate components during installation. To complete installation, reverse removal procedure.

1989 FORD MOTOR CO. ENGINES
5.0L, 5.0L HO & 5.8L V8 (Cont.)

REAR MAIN BEARING OIL SEAL

Removal & Installation – Rear main bearing oil seal is a one-peice type oil seal. Transmission/transaxle and flywheel/flexplate must be removed. Crankshaft does not need to be removed. To install, reverse removal procedure.

OIL PAN

NOTE: See appropriate OIL PAN REMOVAL article in this section.

OIL PUMP

Oil pump is removed with oil pan by detaching oil pump from cylinder block and allowing oil pump to drop into oil pan. See appropriate OIL PAN REMOVAL article in this section.

OVERHAUL

NOTE: Keep components together and marked to ensure installation to original location and position.

CYLINDER HEAD

NOTE: All valves, valve stems and valve guides are to be lubricated with heavy oil. Lubricate valve tips with with Multi-Purpose Grease (DOAZ-19584-AA).

Valve Seal, Springs & Rotators – These components may be replaced with cylinder head installed using the compressed air method.

Valve Guides – Check and service valve guides prior to valve and seat service. Oversize valves are available. Guide is reamed to fit oversize valve. If oversize valves and guides are used, oversize valve seals must also be installed. If oversize components are not available, bore out original guide and replace with service guides. Ream guide to proper clearance for standard valve.

Valve Seat – Valve seat replacement information is not available from manufacturer. Follow tool manufacturers instructions for servicing valve seats. If seats are serviced, valves must also be serviced or replaced.

Valves – Check valves and replace as necessary. See ENGINE SPECIFICATIONS tables at end of this article. Machine valves which are within specifications.

CAMSHAFT BEARINGS

Removal & Installation – 1) Replace camshaft bearing with a bearing replacer kit. Bearings are NOT interchangeable from one bore to another. Bearings are available .015" (.38 mm) oversize. If

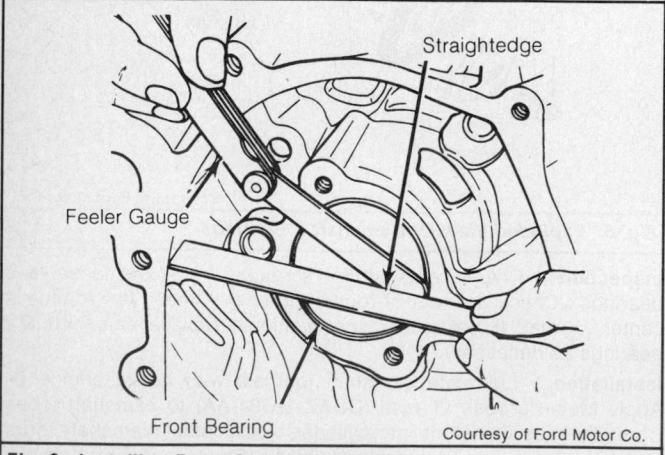

Fig. 9: Installing Front Camshaft Bearing

camshaft can not be machined to accommodate oversize bearings, camshaft and/or bearings must be replaced.
2) Ensure oil holes in bearings and in bores are aligned. Front camshaft bearing must be installed .005-.020" (.13-.51 mm) below front face of cylinder block. *See Fig. 9.* Use sealing compound on rear bearing core plug when installing plug.

CYLINDER BLOCK ASSEMBLY

NOTE: Keep components together and marked to ensure installation to original location and position.

Inspection – 1) Check cylinder block head gasket surface for warpage. Check cylinder bore for wear, taper, out-of-round and piston fit. See ENGINE SPECIFICATIONS tables at end of this article.
2) Install all main bearing caps and tighten to specifications prior to machining cylinder bores. All standard and oversize pistons are the same weight, which allows various sizes of pistons to be used without affecting engine balance.

Piston & Rod Assembly – Ensure rods and rod caps are marked with cylinder number prior to removal. Match mark piston-to-rod prior to disassembly. Notch or arrow on piston top faces engine front. *See Fig. 10.* Piston pin must be pressed out and in piston and rod assembly.

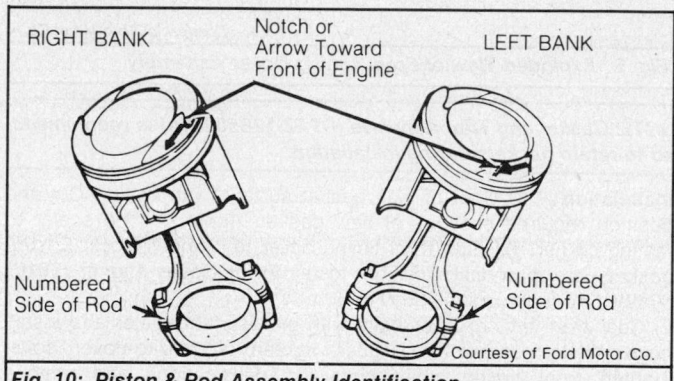

Fig. 10: Piston & Rod Assembly Identification

Piston Rings – Check end gap and side clearance. replace rings and/or piston as necessary. See ENGINE SPECIFICATIONS tables at end of this article. With rings installed on piston, position ring end gaps as shown. *See Fig. 11.*

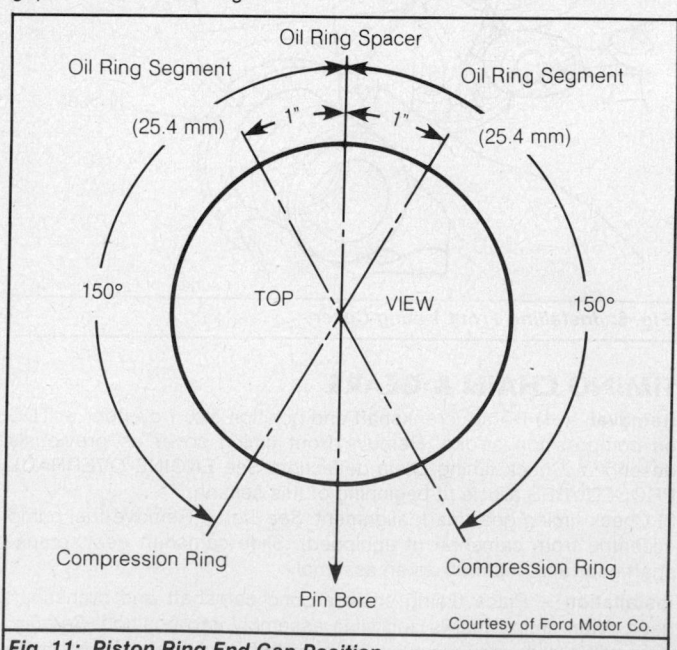

Fig. 11: Piston Ring End Gap Position

ENGINE SPECIFICATIONS (Cont.)

VALVES & VALVE SPRINGS

		Valves				
Engine	Head Dia. In. (mm)	Stem Dia. In. (mm)	Face Angle	Min. Margin In. (mm)	Max. Refinish In. (mm)	Free Lengt In. (mm)
5.0L & HO						
Intake	1.78 (45.2)	.342 (8.69)	44°	.0313 (.795)	.....	2.03 (51.6)
Exhaust	1.46 (37.1)	.3415 (8.674)	44°	.0313 (.795)	.....	[1] 1.88 [1] (47.8
5.8L						
Intake	1.78 (45.2)	.342 (8.69)	44°	.0313 (.795)	.....	2.03 (51.6)
Exhaust	1.46 (37.1)	.3415 (8.674)	44°	.0313 (.795)	.....	1.87 (47.5)

[1] – Non HO model listed. On HO models, free length is 1.79" (45.5 mm).
[2] – Information not available from manufacturer.

CYLINDER HEAD

		Valve Seats		
Engine	Max. Cylinder Head Warp In. (mm)	Seat Angle	Maximum Runout In. (mm)	Seat Width In. (mm)
5.0L, 5.0L HO & 5.8L	[1] .003 (.08)	45°	.002 (.05)	.06-.08 (1.5-2.0)

[1] – Specification is within 6". Overall warpage is .006" (.15 mm).
[2] – Intake listed. Exhaust is .0015-.0032" (.038-.081 mm).

CAMSHAFT

Engine	Journal Diameter In. (mm)	Oil Clearance In. (mm)	Bearing Bore In. (mm)	
5.0L, 5.0L HO 5.8L	[1] 2.0805-2.0815 (52.845-52.870)	.006 (.15)	[2] 2.0825-2.0835 (52.896-52.921)	

[1] – No. 1 journal listed. All others as follows:
No. 2 journal is 2.0655-2.0665 (52.464-52.489 mm).
No. 3 journal is 2.0505-2.0515 (52.070-52.108 mm).
No. 4 journal is 2.0355-2.0365 (51.702-51.727 mm).
No. 5 journal is 2.0205-2.0215 (51.321-51.346 mm).
[2] – No. 1 bearing listed. All others as follows:
No. 2 bearing is 2.0675-2.0685 (52.515-52.540 mm).
No. 3 bearing is 2.0525-2.0535 (52.134-52.159 mm).
No. 4 bearing is 2.0375-2.0385 (51.753-51.778 mm).
No. 5 bearing is 2.0225-2.0235 (51.372-51.397 mm).

VALVE LIFTERS

Engine	Diameter In. (mm)	Bore Diameter In. (mm)	Oil Clearance In. (mm)
5.0L, 5.0L HO & 5.8L	.8740-.8745 (22.200-22.212)	.....	.0007-.0027 (.018-.069)

Fitting Pistons – 1) Check piston-to-bore clearance. Machine or replace as necessary. All standard and oversize pistons are the same weight, which allows various sizes of pistons to be used without affecting engine balance.

2) Standard pistons are color coded Red, Blue and Yellow on piston dome. If piston-to-bore clearance is in lower one-third of specifications, use Red piston. If clearance is in middle of specifications, use Blue piston. Yellow piston is .004" (.10 mm) oversize. Use proper piston to obtain clearance specifications.

Crankshaft & Bearings – If replacing rear main bearing engine must be removed. All other bearings may be replaced in vehicle. Upper and lower main bearings are not interchangeable. Check crankshaft journal and bearing fit. Replace or machine as necessary. See ENGINE SPECIFICATIONS tables at end of this article.

Crankshaft Thrust Bearing – 1) Check crankshaft end play and replace thrust bearing (No. 3 journal) as necessary. To install thrust bearing, lubricate journal and thrust bearing with engine oil. Install thrust bearing, main bearing cap and tighten bolts finger tight.

2) Pry crankshaft forward against thrust surface of upper half of bearing. While holding crankshaft froward, pry thrust bearing cap rearward. This will align thrust surfaces of both halves of bearing. Continue holding crankshaft forward and tighten thrust bearing cap to specifications.

ENGINE OILING

LUBRICATION SYSTEM

Crankcase Capacity – Crankcase capacity on all models is 4 qts. (3.8L) without filter and 5 qts. (4.7L) with filter.
Normal Oil Pressure (Hot) – Oil pressure at 2000 RPM should be 40-60 psi (2.8-4.2 kg/cm²).

OIL PUMP

Inspection - If oil pump is not within specifications, oil pump must be replaced as an assembly. See OIL PUMP SPECIFICATIONS table in this article. Measure inner-to-outer rotor tip clearance with gears removed from housing and feeler gauge inserted 1/2".

OIL PUMP SPECIFICATIONS

Application	In. (mm)
Assembled End Clearance	.004 (.10)
Inner-to-Outer Rotor Tip	.01 (.3)
Outer Race-to-Housing	.001-.013 (.03-.33)
Relief Valve-to-Bore [1]	.0015-.0030 (.038-.076)

[1] – Relief valve spring tension is as follows:
On 5.0L and 5.0L HO models, 10.6-12.2 lbs. @ 1.704" (4.8-5.5 kg @ 43.3 mm).
On 5.8L models, 18.2-20.2 lbs. @ 2.49" (8.3-9.2 kg @ 63.3 mm).

TIGHTENING SPECIFICATIONS

Application	Ft. Lbs. (N.m)
Camshaft Gear Bolt	40-45 (54-61)
Camshaft Thrust Plate Bolt	9-12 (12-16)
Connecting Rod Nut	19-24 (26-32)
Cylinder Head Bolt	
5.0L & 5.0L HO [1]	
1st Step	55-65 (76-88)
2nd Step	65-72 (88-98)
5.8L [1]	
1st Step	85 (115)
2nd Step	95 (129)
3rd Step	105-112 (142-152)
Damper-to-Crankshaft Bolt	70-90 (95-122)
Distributor Hold Down Bolt	18-26 (24-35)
Exhaust Manifold [2]	18-24 (24-32)
Fan-to-Water Pump Bolt	
5.0L & 5.0L HO	15-22 (20-30)
5.8L	12-18 (16-24)
Flywheel Bolt	75-85 (102-115)
Front Timing Cover	12-18 (16-24)
Fuel Pump Bolt (5.8L)	19-27 (26-37)
Intake Manifold	
5.8L [3]	
1st Step	15-20 (20-27)
2nd Step	23-25 (31-34)
Lower Intake Manifold-to-Cylinder Head	
5.0L & 5.0L HO [3]	
1st Step	15-20 (20-27)
2nd Step	23-25 (31-34)
Main Bearing Cap Bolt	
5.0L & 5.0L V8	60-70 (81-95)
5.8L	60-70 (81-95)
Oil Pump Mount Bolt	22-32 (30-43)
Oil Pan-to-Block Bolt	
5.8L	9-11 (12-15)
Pick-Up Tube-to-Oil Pump	
5.0L & 5.0L HO	12-18 (16-24)
5.8L	10-15 (14-20)
Pick-Up Tube-to-Bearing Cap Nut	22-32 (30-43)
Pulley-to-Damper Bolt	35-50 (47-68)
Rocker Arm Bolt	18-25 (24-34)
Spark Plug	
5.8L	10-15 (14-20)
Upper Intake-to-Lower Intake Manifold	
5.0L & 5.0L HO [4]	12-18 (16-24)
Water Pump Mount Bolt	12-18 (16-24)

Application	INCH Lbs. (N.m)
Oil Pan-to-Block Bolt	
5.0L & 5.0L HO	72-108 (8-12)
Spark Plug	
5.0L & 5.0L HO	60-120 (7-14)
Valve Cover Bolt	
5.0L & 5.0L HO	72-108 (8-12)
5.8L	36-60 (4-7)

[1] – Tighten in sequence. See Fig. 4.
[2] – Tighten in sequence. See Fig. 3.
[3] – Tighten in sequence and repeat 2nd step after engine has reached normal operating temperature. See Fig. 1.
[4] – Tighten evenly.

1989 FORD MOTO
5.0L, 5.0L HO & 5

ENGINE SPECIFICATIONS

GENERAL SPECIFICATIONS

| Year | Displacement | | Fuel System | HP@RPM | Ft. L |
	Cu. In.	Liters			
1989					
5.0L & HO	302	5.0L	SEFI	¹ 150@3200	² 27
5.8L	351	5.8L	2-Bbl.	180@3600	28

¹ – Non HO is listed. On 5.0L HO models, 225 @ 4200.
² – Non HO is listed. On 5.0L HO models, 300 @ 3200.
³ – Non HO is listed. On 5.0L HO models, 9.0:1.

CRANKSHAFT, MAIN & CONNECTING ROD BEARINGS

| Engine | Crankshaft | | | |
	End Play In. (mm)	Runout In. (mm)	Journal Taper In. (mm)	Journal Out-of-Round In. (mm)
5.0L & HO	.004-.008 (.10-.20)	.005 (.13)	.0004 (.010)	.0006 (.015)
5.8L	.004-.008 (.10-.20)	.005 (.13)	.0004 (.010)	.0006 (.015)

CONNECTING RODS

Engine	Side Play In. (mm)	Max. Bend & Twist In. (mm)
5.0L & HO	.01-.02 (.3-.5)	¹ .012 (.31)
5.8L	.01-.02 (.3-.5)	¹ .012 (.31)

¹ – Bend is listed. Twist is .024" (.61 mm).

PISTONS, PINS & RINGS

| Engine | Pistons | | | Pins |
	Clearance In. (mm)	Diameter In. (mm)	Diameter In. (mm)	Piston F In. (mm
5.0L & HO	¹ .0014-.0022 (.036-.056)	²	.912 (23.17)	.0003 (.008)
5.8L	.0018-.0026 (.046-.066)	²	.912 (23.17)	.0003-.00 (.008-.01

¹ – 5.0L listed. On 5.0L HO models, .003-.004" (.08-.10 mm).
² – See FITTING PISTONS under CYLINDER BLOCK ASSEMBLY in this art

---

tion and remove hood. Release fuel system pressure at fuel rail service valve.

2) Disconnect fuel lines using appropriate spring lock coupling tool. Place correct size spring lock coupling tool against coupling. Push tool into cage opening to release garter spring. Pull coupling apart and remove tool. See Fig. 1.

3) Discharge A/C system. Disconnect alternator wiring, cooling fan electrical connector, transaxle cooling lines and pressure switch wiring. Disconnect heater hoses at engine. Disconnect power steering hoses and hose brackets.

4) Disconnect A/C compressor clutch wiring. Disconnect A/C discharge and suction lines at compressor. Disconnect power steering pump tube bracket, ECC wire harness and vacuum lines. Disconnect ground wires at engine and throttle cable at throttle valve.

5) Remove engine oil dipstick. Remove upper radiator sight shield and integrated controller relay. Remove air cleaner assembly. Remove cooling fan shroud. Disconnect upper radiator hose at engine. Remove coolant recovery reservoir. Remove air suspension compressor and position out of way (if equipped).

6) Remove transaxle support retaining bolts and remove support. Remove A/C compressor mounting bolts and remove A/C compressor. Raise vehicle on hoist. Drain engine oil and remove oil filter. Disconnect oxygen sensor wiring. Release tension on drive belts and remove crankshaft pulley assembly.

7) Remove drive belt tensioner assembly. Remove starter. Remove catalytic converter housing cover. Remove catalytic converter and inlet pipe assemble. Remove nuts from left and right engine mounts. Match mark flex plate and torque converter and remove attaching nuts.

8) Remove oil level indicator sensor. Disconnect lower radiator hose at engine. Loosen but do not remove engine-to-transaxle bolts. Partially lower vehicle. Remove left and right front wheels. Remove drive belts. Remove water pump pulley bolts and remove pulley.

9) Remove radiator. Remove distributor cap and position out of way. Remove distributor rotor. Remove exhaust manifold lock bolts. Remove thermactor attaching bolts and remove thermactor. Disconnect oil pressure sender wire.

10) Install engine lifting equipment on engine lifting eyes. Remove engine-to-transaxle bolts. Position jack under transaxle. Lift transaxle slightly as engine is lifted. Pull engine free of transaxle and remove engine.

Installation – To install, reverse removal procedure. Check fluid levels. Start engine and check for leaks.

Removal (Cougar & Thunderbird) – 1) Mark hinges for reinstallation and remove hood. Drain crankcase and cooling system. Disconnect battery and alternator ground cables from engine. Remove windshield wiper module and left side cowl screen.

2) Remove air cleaner tube and air cleaner assembly. On supercharged models, remove upper intercooler tube at supercharger and cooler assemblies. Remove bolt retaining cooler tube to power steering bracket. Remove cooler tube.

3) Remove radiator upper shield. Release drive belt tension and remove belts. Disconnect cooling fan electrical connector. Remove radiator shroud and cooling fan assembly.

4) Remove upper radiator hose. Disconnect automatic transmission cooler lines. Disconnect heater hoses. Disconnect lower radiator hose at water pump. Remove radiator retaining bolts and remove radiator. On supercharged models, remove 2 push pins retaining intercooler before removing radiator.

5) On non-supercharged models, disconnect power steering pressure hose. Remove power steering bracket assembly and place power steering pump to one side.

6) Discharge A/C system. Disconnect compressor clutch electrical connector. Disconnect and plug A/C lines at compressor. Remove A/C compressor mount bolts. Remove A/C compressor.

7) Remove cooling system reservoir. Remove engine wire harness shield. Remove accelerator cable and bracket and place to one side. Release fuel system pressure at fuel rail service valve.

8) Disconnect fuel lines using appropriate spring lock coupling tool. Place correct size spring lock coupling tool against coupling. Push tool into cage opening to release garter spring. Pull coupling apart and remove tool. See Fig. 1.

9) Disconnect engine control module wiring and all engine electrical harnesses. Label and disconnect all vacuum hoses. On non-supercharged models, disconnect ground wire assembly and coil wire.

10) On supercharged models, disconnect DIS module wiring. Remove coil pack retaining bolts and position coil pack to one side. Remove lower intercooler tube-to-supercharger bolts.

11) Remove intercooler tube-to-power steering bracket bolts. Remove alternator wiring and bracket bolts. Remove alternator. Remove power steering bracket bolts and place power steering pump to one side.

12) On all models, disconnect cannister purge hoses. Disconnect one end of throttle control valve cable. Raise vehicle on hoist and drain engine oil. Remove oil filter.

13) On supercharged models, remove 2 nuts attaching lower intercooler tube to intercooler. Remove intercooler.

14) On all models, remove exhaust pipe-to-manifold nuts. Remove left side exhaust shield. Disconnect oxygen sensor electrical connector. Remove inspection cover. Mark flex plate-to-torque converter for reassembly. Remove flex plate bolts.

15) Remove engine-to-transmission bolts. Remove engine mount through bolts. On supercharged models, remove left side mount retaining strap. On all models, remove crankshaft pulley assembly. Remove starter mount bolts. Remove starter.

16) Remove ground cable and starter harness retainers. Disconnect oil level indicator electrical connector. Disconnect oil pressure sender wiring.

17) Partially lower vehicle. Place floor jack under transmission. Install engine lifting equipment. Carefully pull engine forward to clear transmission. Lift engine up and out of vehicle.

Installation – To install, reverse removal procedure. Ensure all fluid levels are correct. Recharge A/C system. Start and run engine to check for leaks.

V8

5.0L & 5.8L

Removal (All Models) – 1) Mark hinges for reinstallation and remove hood. Drain crankcase and cooling system. Disconnect battery and alternator ground cables from engine. Remove air cleaner and intake duct assembly. On 5.8L models, disconnect fuel lines at carburetor.

2) On 5.0L models, release fuel pressure at fuel rail service valve. Disconnect fuel lines using appropriate spring lock coupling tool. Place correct size spring lock coupling tool against coupling. Push tool into cage opening to release garter spring. Pull coupling apart and remove tool. See Fig. 1.

3) On all models, disconnect upper and lower radiator hoses. Disconnect transmission oil cooler lines from radiator. Remove bolts attaching fan shroud to radiator. Remove radiator.

4) Remove fan, spacer, belt, pulley and shroud. Remove alternator bolts and position alternator aside. Disconnect oil pressure sending unit wire from sending unit.

5) Disconnect accelerator cable. Disconnect speed control cable (if equipped). Disconnect throttle valve vacuum line from intake manifold (if equipped). Disconnect transmission filler tube bracket from engine block. On vehicles equipped with A/C, remove A/C compressor leaving lines attached, and set aside.

6) Disconnect power steering pump bracket from cylinder head. Remove drive belt. Position pump aside. Disconnect brake vacuum line from intake manifold.

7) Disconnect heater hoses from water pump and intake manifold. Disconnect coolant temperature sending unit wire from sending unit. Remove flywheel/converter housing-to-engine upper bolts.

8) Disconnect primary wiring connector from ignition coil. Remove wire harness and position aside. Disconnect ground strap from block.

(middle columns — partially obscured)

4-CYLIN

2.2L (135"

1) Disconnect
reinstallation. R
and heater hos
lines from rad
assembly.
2) Remove air
sor and power
aside (if equip
hoses connect
vacuum lines ar
3) Remove gas
harness from a
negative termin
NOT leave injec
jumper wires. R
4) Remove alte
On manual tra
transaxle hous
exhaust pipe a
aside. Support t
5) On automa
inspection cove
converter-to-fle
housing to preve
6) Install engine
Remove ground
Remove bolts at
7) Mark front er
engine mount l
manual transax
insulator throug
remove from veh
8) To install, rev
install. DO NOT
and bolts have
damper weight r
9) If drive axl
gine/transaxle a
mount verticle
crossmember fa
obtain correct c
LENGTH SPECI
10) Tighten mou
axle shaft length
Fill cooling syste
above thermos
reaches plug ope

Fig. 1: Measurin

4-C

1.9L

NOTE:
recor
trans
distan
transa
rail.
Prope
alignm
mm).

Remo
hood.
airflov
inertia
fuel p
2) On
lock c
agains
spring
3) On
Remo
Remo
positi
remov
4) Dis
transa
from
6)
hoses
Remo
5) On
clip. C
tube.
openi
6) Dis
cable
therm
brack
7) Ra
return
brace
restric
8) On
Disco
cover
9) Re
timing
autom
Remo
10) O
Remo
Attach
throug
11) C
insula
transa
housir
conve

Install
axle s
front
Re
check

2.2L

NOTE:

Remo
locati
transa
from

9) Raise front of vehicle. Disconnect starter cable from starter. Remove starter. Disconnect exhaust pipes from exhaust manifolds. Disconnect engine support insulators.

10) Disconnect transmission cooler lines from retainer and remove converter housing inspection cover. Disconnect converter from flex plate. Secure converter assembly in housing. Remove remaining converter housing-to-engine bolts.

11) Lower vehicle and support transmission. Attach engine hoist and carefully separate engine from transmission. Remove engine.

Installation – To install, reverse removal procedure. Check fluid levels. Start engine and check for leaks.

FORD MOTOR CO. TIGHTENING SPECIFICATIONS

Application	Ft. Lbs. (N.m)
4-Cylinder	
1.9L	
Left Side Front	
Bracket-to-Crossmember Bolts	30-42 (41-57)
Motor Mount Bracket-to-Transaxle Bolts	25-35 (34-48)
Motor Mount Through Bolts	55-75 (75-102)
Left Side Rear	
Motor Mount-to-Transaxle Bolts	55-75 (75-102)
Motor Mount Through Bolts	25-35 (34-48)
Right Side	
Motor Mount-to-Bracket Bolts	65-70 (88-95)
Motor Mount-to-Engine Bolts	35-40 (48-54)
Motor Mount Through Bolts	65-70 (88-95)
2.2L	1
2.3L OHC	
Converter-to-Flex Plate Bolts	27-49 (37-66)
Crossmember-to-Frame Bolts	50-70 (68-95)
Motor Mount Bracket-to-Engine Bolts	33-45 (45-61)
Motor Mount Bracket-to-Frame Bolts	70-90 (95-122)
Rear Mount-to-Crossmember Bolts	25-35 (34-48)
Rear Mount-to-Transmission Bolts	50-70 (68-95)
2.3L HSC & HSO	
CV Hub Nut	180-200 (244-271)
Intermediate Bracket-to-Engine Bracket Bolts	75-100 (102-135)
Insulator Bracket-to-Body Bracket Bolts	75-100 (102-135)
Roll Restrictor-to-Transaxle Bolts	25-45 (34-61)
Shift Stabilizer-to-Transaxle Bolts	23-35 (31-47)
Shifter-to-Input Shaft Bolts	7-10 (10-14)

FORD MOTOR CO. TIGHTENING SPECIFICATIONS (Cont.)

Application	Ft. Lbs. (N.m)
2.5L [2]	
Left Front Insulator-to-Bracket Nut	75-100 (102-135)
Left Front Insulator-to-Transaxle Bolts	25-37 (34-50)
Left Rear Insulator-to-Body Bolts	75-100 (102-135)
Left Rear Insulator-to-Transaxle Bolts	35-50 (48-68)
Right Insulator Nuts	75-100 (100-135)
Right Intermediate Bracket Bolt	55-75 (75-102)
V6	
3.0L [2]	
A/C Bracket Bolt	40-55 (54-75)
Engine Mount Bolt	40-55 (54-75)
Left Engine Damper	
Bolt	21-30 (28-41)
Nut	21-30 (28-41)
Left Insulator/Support Nut & Bolt	70-96 (95-130)
Right Engine Damper	
Bolt	40-55 (54-75)
Nut	21-30 (28-41)
Rt. Front/Rt. Rear	
Insulator-to-Frame Bolt	55-75 (75-102)
3.8L [2]	
Crossmember-to-Frame Bolts	35-50 (48-68)
Fan/Clutch Assembly Bolts	12-18 (16-24)
Motor Mount-to-Engine Bolts	35-50 (48-68)
Motor Mount-to-Frame Bolts	70-100 (95-135)
Rear Mount-to-Trans. Bolts	50-70 (68-95)
V8	
5.0L [2]	
Crossmember-to-Frame Bolts	35-50 (48-68)
Motor Mount Through Bolts	35-50 (48-68)
Motor Mount-to-Crossmember Bolts	57-65 (77-88)
Motor Mount-to-Engine Bolts	35-60 (48-81)
Rear Mount-to-Trans. Bolts	50-70 (68-95)
5.8L [2]	
Insulator Bracket Bolt	35-60 (48-81)
Motor Mount Bolts	26-38 (35-52)
Motor Mount Stud	35-60 (48-81)
Motor Mount Through Bolt	40-46 (54-62)
Rear Engine Mount Bolts	50-70 (68-95)
Rear Engine Mount Nuts	35-50 (48-68)

[1] – Probe tightening specifications not available from manufacturer.

[2] – Always replace self-locking fasteners.

1989 OIL PAN REMOVAL
Chrysler Motors

4-CYLINDER

2.2L & 2.5L

Disconnect negative battery cable and remove engine oil dipstick. Drain crankcase, remove oil pan bolts and oil pan.

V6

3.0L

Drain crankcase, remove oil pan bolts and oil pan. When installing oil pan, tighten bolts in a crisscross pattern working from the center outward.

V8

5.2L

Disconnect negative battery cable and remove engine oil dipstick. Raise and support vehicle. Drain crankcase. Remove steering and idler arm ball joints from steering linkage center link. Remove center link. Remove exhaust crossover pipe, starter and starter mounting stud. Remove flywheel access cover, oil pan bolts and oil pan.

CHRYSLER MOTORS TIGHTENING SPECIFICATIONS

Application	INCH Lbs. (N.m)
4-Cylinder	
2.2L	204 (23)
2.5L	
M6 Bolts	108(12)
M8 Bolts	204 (23)
V6	
3.0L	53 (6)
V8	
5.2L	204 (23)

Eagle

Premier

4-CYLINDER

2.5L

Disconnect negative battery cable. Raise and support vehicle. Drain engine oil. Disconnect exhaust pipe at exhaust manifold. Disconnect hanger at catalytic converter and lower exhaust pipe. Remove starter and wire out of way. Remove oil pan bolts. Remove oil pan.

V6

3.0L

NOTE: To remove oil pan, it is necessary to remove front anti-sway bar and engine cradle.

1) With vehicle weight on front wheels, remove anti-sway bar retainers. Place nut on one sway bar retainer bolt lower control arm and tighten to retain ball joint positions.

2) Raise vehicle on side arm type hoist. Drain engine oil. Loosen engine mount stud and nut assemblies to obtain clearance for engine cradle removal. Remove front tires. Remove lower ball joint retaining bolts and separate lower control arms from steering knuckles.

3) Remove bolts retaining rear of transaxle to crossmember. Lower vehicle. Install Engine Support Bar (MS 1900) and raise engine as far as possible. Place dolly under engine cradle. Remove cradle mounting bolts. Raise vehicle off engine cradle. Remove oil pan.

EAGLE TIGHTENING SPECIFICATIONS

Application	Ft. Lbs. (N.m)
4-Cylinder	1
V6	
Engine Cradle Mounting Bolts	92 (125)
Oil Pan	1
Steering Knuckle-to-Ball Joint	77 (105)
Transaxle-to-Crossmember Nuts	20 (27)

1 - Tighten to 108 INCH lbs. (12 N.m).

Ford Motor Co.

4-CYLINDER

1.9L

Escort – 1) Disconnect negative battery cable. Raise and support vehicle. Drain crankcase. Disconnect lower radiator hose. Remove sway bar (if equipped). Disconnect cable at starter. Remove starter.
2) Disconnect interfering exhaust pipe. Remove oil pan retaining bolts and oil pan. Remove oil pan gasket.

2.2L

Probe – 1) Disconnect negative battery cable. Raise and support vehicle. Remove right splash shield at front fender wheel opening. Drain engine oil. Remove engine-to-flywheel housing support bracket.
2) Remove front section of exhaust pipe. Remove exhaust pipe support bracket. Remove flywheel housing dust cover bolts and remove cover. Remove oil pan bolts. Remove oil pan.

2.3L OHC

Mustang – 1) Disconnect negative battery cable and remove fan shroud. If equipped with electric fan, disconnect power lead and remove fan and shroud assembly. Drain cooling system and disconnect upper and lower hoses at radiator.
2) Raise and support vehicle. Drain crankcase. Remove right and left engine support through bolts. Using a jack, raise engine as far as possible and place support blocks between the mounts and crossmember pedestals. Remove jack.
3) Remove shake brace, sway bar retaining bolts and lower sway bar. Remove steering gear retaining bolts and lower gear. Disconnect starter wiring, remove starter. Remove oil pan bolts, lower pan to crossmember and remove pan.

NOTE: No. 4 piston must be at TDC for oil pan to clear crankshaft.

2.3L HSC & HSO

Tempo & Topaz – 1) Disconnect negative battery cable. Raise and support vehicle. Drain crankcase. Remove lower radiator hose to drain coolant. On manual transaxle models, remove roll resistor. On all models, remove starter wiring and starter.
2) Disconnect exhaust pipe bracket from oil pan. Remove heater return hose at lower radiator and water pump inlet tube locations. Remove tube support tabs and position air conditioning line aside. Remove oil pan bolts and oil pan.

2.5L HSC

Taurus – 1) Disconnect negative battery cable. Raise and support vehicle. Drain crankcase. Drain coolant by removing lower radiator hose. Remove roll restrictor (MTX only). Disconnect starter cable.

2) Remove starter. Disconnect exhaust pipe from oil pan. Remove engine coolant tube located at lower radiator hose, at water pump and at tabs on oil pan. Position air conditioner line off to side. Remove oil pan.

V6

3.0L & 3.0L SHO

Sable & Taurus – 1) Disconnect negative battery cable and remove oil level dipstick. Raise and support vehicle. Remove electrical connector and retainer clip at low oil level sensor (if equipped).

2) Drain oil from crankcase. Remove starter motor. Disconnect EGO sensor. Remove exhaust pipe assembly and lower engine/flywheel dust cover from converter housing. Remove oil pan attaching bolts and oil pan.

3.8L

Continental, Sable & Taurus – Disconnect negative battery cable. Raise and support vehicle. Drain crankcase. Remove oil filter. Remove catalytic converter assembly. Remove starter motor. Remove converter housing cover. Remove bolts retaining oil pan assembly. Remove oil pan assembly.

Cougar & Thunderbird – 1) Disconnect battery ground cable. Remove air intake duct assembly. Remove 2 bolts attaching sight shield and place sight shield aside. Remove hood weather seal. Remove wiper arms. Remove left side cowl vent screen. Remove wiper module.

2) Install engine lifting eyes. Install Engine Support Fixture (D87L-6000-A). Raise vehicle on hoist. Remove engine mount through bolts. On supercharged models, remove left side engine mount retaining strap.

3) Partially lower vehicle. Raise engine at support fixture. Raise vehicle. Remove starter. Drain engine oil and remove oil filter. Remove lower engine wire loom, ground strap and transmission cooler lines.

4) Remove oil pan-to-bellhousing bolts. Remove crankshaft position sensor shield bolts (if equipped). Remove remaining oil pan bolts. Remove steering shaft pinch bolts and separate steering shaft.

5) Position transmission jack under front of subframe. Remove 6 rearward bolts on front of subframe. Loosen 2 front subframe bolts. Remove lower strut-to-control arm bolts and nuts. Lower subframe. Remove oil pan.

V8

5.0L & 5.8L

Mark VII & Mustang – 1) Disconnect negative battery cable. Remove fan shroud bolts and position shroud over fan. Remove oil level indicator from left-hand side of cylinder block. Remove air cleaner tube.

2) Raise and support vehicle. Drain engine oil. Remove starter motor wires and starter. Remove catalytic converter and muffler inlet pipes. Remove engine mount-to-No. 2 crossmember bolts.

3) Remove No. 3 crossmember and support assemblies. Remove steering gear attaching bolts and position steering gear forward out of work area. Raise and support engine for clearance of oil pan removal.

4) Remove oil pan attaching bolts and lower oil pan. Remove oil pump and pick-up tube assembly to drop into oil pan. Remove oil pan.

Grand Marquis, LTD Crown Victoria, Town Car & Wagon – 1) Remove air cleaner, disconnect accelerator and kickdown rods at carburetor (police model), or throttle valve on all others, and remove accelerator mounting bracket. Remove fan shroud bolts and position shroud over fan. Disconnect wiring from harness and remove wiper motor.

2) Disconnect windshield washer hose and remove wiper motor mounting cover. Remove dipstick and dipstick tube retaining bolt at exhaust manifold. Remove thermactor air dump tube retaining clamp and thermactor crossover tube at rear of engine.

3) Raise vehicle and drain crankcase. Remove filler tube and drain crankcase. Disconnect starter wiring, remove starter. Relieve fuel pressure and disconnect fuel line. Disconnect inlet pipes from exhaust manifold.

4) Remove exhaust gas oxygen sensor from exhaust manifold and thermactor secondary air tube-to-converter housing clamps. Disconnect exhaust pipes to catalytic converter outlet. Remove catalytic converter secondary air tube and inlet pipes to exhaust manifold.

5) Remove rear engine mount through bolts and shift crossover bolts at transmission. Disconnect transmission kickdown rod. Remove flywheel access cover. Remove brake line retainer from front crossmember. Using a jack, raise engine as far as possible.

6) Place support blocks between engine mounts and chassis brackets. Remove jack. Disconnect low oil sensor from oil pan. Remove oil pan bolts and lower pan. Remove oil pump pick-up tube assembly and place in oil pan. Remove oil pan.

FORD MOTOR CO. TIGHTENING SPECIFICATIONS

Application	INCH Lbs. (N.m)
4-Cylinder	
1.9L	71-97 (8-11)
2.2L	[1]
2.3L	
6 mm Bolts	62-97 (7-11)
8 mm Bolts	97-115 (11-13)
2.3L HSC & HSO	71-106 (8-12)
2.5L HSC	[2]
V6	
3.0L	71-106 (8-12)
3.0L SHO	[3]
3.8L	
Oil Pan Bolts	80-106 (9-12)
Subframe Bolts (Supercharged)	[4]
V8	
5.0L & 5.8L	106-133 (12-15)

[1] – Information not supplied by manufacturer.
[2] – Tighten to 15-23 ft. lbs. (20-30 N.m).
[3] – Tighten to 11-17 ft. lbs. (15-23 N.m.)
[4] – Tighten to 70-95 ft. lbs. (95-130 N.m).

1989 ENGINE COOLING SYSTEMS
Cooling System Trouble Shooting

CONDITION	POSSIBLE CAUSE	CORRECTION
Engine Overheats With or Without Coolant Loss	Low coolant level	Add coolant, see ENGINE COOLING
	Thermostat stuck closed	Replace thermostat, see ENGINE COOLING
	Faulty fan clutch	Replace fan clutch, see ENGINE COOLING
	Faulty electric fan motor	Replace motor
	Faulty thermal relay switches	Check switches and connections
	Water distribution tube clogged	Flush system, see ENGINE COOLING
	Radiator air flow passages blocked	Clean or replace radiator
	Plugged or restricted radiator	Flush or replace radiator
	Incorrect coolant concentration	Refill with proper amount of coolant
	Incorrect ignition timing	Reset ignition timing
	Faulty ignition advance	Check and/or replace
	Exhaust system restricted	Correct restriction
	Broken or slipping fan belt	Replace fan belt
	Water pump shaft broken	Replace water pump, see ENGINES
	Leaking freeze plug(s)	Replace freeze plug(s)
	Faulty radiator pressure cap	Replace pressure cap, see ENGINE COOLING
Engine Overheats With Internal Coolant Leakage	Warped or cracked intake manifold	Replace intake manifold, see ENGINES
	Blown cylinder head gasket	Replace head gasket, see ENGINES
	Warped/cracked cylinder head/block	Resurface or replace head or block
Engine Fails to Reach Normal Temperature	Thermostat stuck in open position	Replace thermostat, see ENGINE COOLING
	Temperature gauge or light defective	Inspect gauge, light or sending unit
	Faulty temperature sending unit	Replace sending unit
	Faulty thermal relay switches	Replace switches
	Incorrect thermostat	Replace thermostat, see ENGINE COOLING
	Radiator capacity too large	Check radiator application
Poor Coolant Flow	Plugged or restricted radiator	Flush or replace radiator
	Restricted cylinder head or block	Flush entire cooling system
	Collapsed lower radiator hose	Replace lower hose
	Faulty water pump	Replace water pump, see ENGINES
Coolant Loss	Radiator cap not holding pressure	Pressure test radiator cap
	Radiator, reservoir or heater core leaks	Repair radiator, reservoir or heater
	Water pump seal or gasket leaking	Replace seal or gasket, see ENGINES
	Cylinder head gasket leaking	Replace head gasket, see ENGINES
	Incorrect cylinder head bolt torque	Retighten bolts, see ENGINES
	Air in system	Bleed cooling system, see ENGINE COOLING
	Faulty water control valve	Replace control valve
Recovery System Inoperative	Low coolant level	Add coolant as required
	Leak in system	Inspect system, see ENGINE COOLING
	Radiator cap loose or defective	Inspect and/or replace as required
	Overflow tube clogged or leaking	Remove tube restriction
	Recovery bottle vent restricted	Remove vent restriction
No Coolant Flow Through Heater Core	Plugged return pipe in water pump	Inspect or replace water pump, see ENGINES
	Heater hose collapsed or plugged	Remove restriction and/or replace hose
	Plugged heater core and/or thermostat	Remove blockage in core or housing
	Plugged cylinder head heater flow hole	Flush system, see ENGINE COOLING
	Faulty water valve	Replace water valve
Cooling System Noise	Water pump bearing worn	Replace water pump, see ENGINES
	Fan contacting shroud	Reposition fan and/or shroud
	Loose water pump impeller	Replace water pump, see ENGINES
	Dry fan belt	Replace fan belt
	Rough surface on drive pulley	Smooth surface or replace pulley
	Improper alignment of fan belts	Reposition and/or replace belts

**Chrysler Motors, Eagle Premier,
Ford Motor Co.**

DESCRIPTION

The engine cooling system consists of a radiator, radiator cap, water pump, thermostat, cooling fan, heater core, engine coolant passages and connecting hoses. A coolant recovery reservoir is used on most vehicles to maintain radiator level during expansion and contraction of coolant.

Engine cooling fans range from belt driven flex or clutch type, to electronically controlled electric cooling fans. Electric cooling fans operate only when conditions require fan operation. When trouble shooting electric cooling fans, refer to appropriate ELECTRIC COOLING FANS article in this section.

MAINTENANCE

CAUTION: DO NOT remove radiator cap while engine is running. Sudden release of pressure can cause boiling and hot steam release. Use extreme caution when removing radiator cap on warm engines.

PRESSURE TESTING

Remove radiator cap. Inspect radiator and radiator cap sealing surfaces. Many radiators use plastic filler neck. The sealing surface of this plastic may distort if vehicle has overheated.

Install pressure tester on radiator cap. Increase pressure slowly and observe pressure tester gauge. Replace radiator cap if pressure is not released as specified on radiator cap. See Fig. 1.

Install pressure tester and pressurize cooling system to radiator cap specification. Inspect all hose connections, water pump, radiator and engine for any signs of leakage. Correct any leaks. See Fig. 2

Release pressure, but leave pressure tester connected. Start and run engine for a few minutes while observing pressure tester. If pressure build up rapidly, a compression leak to cooling system is indicated. Check for possible defective head gasket, improper head bolt torque and cracked cylinder head.

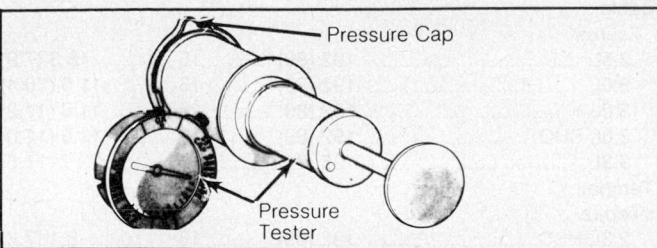

Fig. 1: Testing Radiator Cap

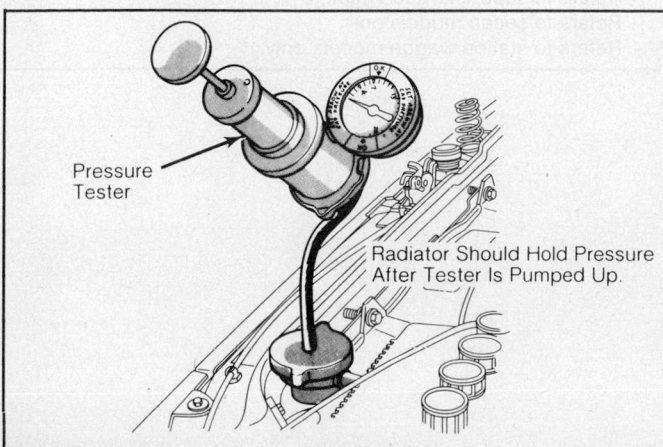

Fig. 2: Pressure Testing Cooling System

Commercially available testers can be used to identify cylinder compression leaks into cooling system by detecting gasoline fumes (Hydrocarbons) at radiator fill neck.

DRAINING

Remove radiator cap. Ensure heater coolant valve (if equipped) is open. Open drain cocks or remove plugs in radiator and engine block. Inspect drained coolant for signs of excessive rust or oily film. Oil contamination of coolant is an indication of defective engine gaskets, leaking automatic transmission (transaxle) cooling lines or engine oil cooler (if equipped). Clean radiator cooling fins as necessary to ensure proper air flow.

FLUSHING

NOTE: Many vehicles use an aluminum/plastic radiator and aluminum and different alloy materials in engine block, heads and gaskets. Ensure material used for cleaning and flushing is compatible with these materials.

Back flushing is an effective way of removing scale and rust from cooling systems. Radiator and heater core should be isolated when flushing engine to avoid plugging cores with scale and rust. Remove thermostat before flushing engine. If power flush equipment is used, refer to equipment manufacturer's operation instructions to avoid cooling system or equipment damage. Replace thermostat after flushing is complete.

REFILLING

Fill radiator with a 50 percent mixture of water and anti-freeze. Install radiator cap to first notch to keep spillage to a minumum. Start and run engine until upper radiator hose warm indicating thermostat is open. Remove radiator cap carefully and add coolant mixture until system is full. Install radiator cap. Fill coolant recovery reservoir to "FULL COLD" mark. See Fig. 3. Run engine until engine temperature stabilizes. Check cooling system for leaks.

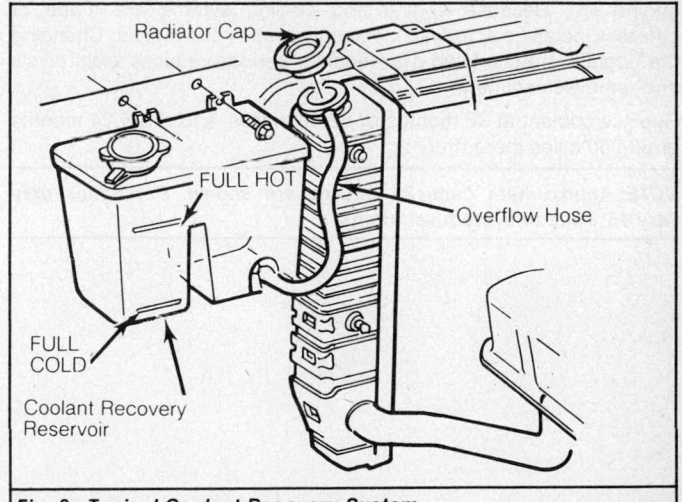

Fig. 3: Typical Coolant Recovery System

THERMOSTAT

If vehicle is slow to warm to operating temperature, or overheating is occurring with radiator top hose cooler than lower radiator hose, replace thermostat and check cooling system for leaks.

COOLANT MIXTURE

Using an anti-freeze tester with temperature compensating feature, test anti-freeze for correct mixture. On vehicles using aluminum engine and/or cooling system parts, refer to owners manual for specific information on coolant type and mixture required.

1989 ENGINE COOLING SYSTEMS
Engine Coolant Specifications

Chrysler Motors, Eagle Premier, Ford Motor Co.

DESCRIPTION

THERMOSTAT

Most thermostats are thermal wax pellet type. As coolant temperatures rise the wax begins to expand. This expansion over comes spring tension allowing the thermostat to open. Some thermostats also incorporate an additional bleed hole to allow a small amount of circulation to help eliminate air locks.

PRESSURE CAP

Modern cooling systems use a closed system type cap. This system allows for coolant expansion during engine operation. As coolant expands and builds pressure, some coolant is permitted to bleed past the cap into the overflow tank. When the engine cools and coolant contracts, the cap allows the coolant in the over flow tank to siphon back into the system.

The pressure cap also increases pressure in the cooling system. The increased pressure raises the boiling point, one pound of pressure raises the boiling point approximately 10° F (12.2° C).

COOLANT MIXTURE

Engine coolant must be mixed with water to a specific percent. A 100% coolant mixture could cause system over heating or premature system failure. Coolants are designed to function best when mixed with water. The percentage of coolant to water can vary depending on climate condition, but a 50/50 mixture is a standard percentage. Engine coolant should also include an aluminum protection additive. This will help protect against metal deterioration.

MAINTENANCE

Periodic maintenance is necessary for extended cooling system and engine life. Because engine and cooling sytems are made of different metals, electrolysis begins to destroy the metals. Changing the coolant at scheduled maintenance periods reduces electrolysis and removes sediment.

Replace coolant at 36 months or 52,500 miles, and every 24 months or 30,000 miles thereafter.

NOTE: Approximate capacity figures are shown. Capacities may vary 15% due to system variations.

COOLING SYSTEM SPECIFICATIONS

Application	Therm. F° (C°)	Pres. Cap psi	Coolant Cap. Qts. (L)
CHRYSLER MOTORS			
Lebaron, New Yorker			
2.5L	195 (91)	16	8.0 (7.6)
3.0L	195 (91)	16	9.5 (9.0)
Reliant, Sundance			
2.2L	195 (91)	16	8.5 (8.1)
2.2L Turbo	195 (91)	16	8.5 (8.1)
All Other FWD	195 (91)	16	9.0 (8.5)
All RWD	195 (91)	16	16.0 (15.1)
EAGLE			
Premier			
2.5L	195 (91)	18	9.6 (9.1)
3.0L	195 (91)	18	9.6 (9.1)
FORD MOTOR CO.			
Continental			
3.8L	197 (91)	16	12.1 (11.5)
Cougar, Thunderbird			
3.8L	195 (91)	16	11.8 (11.2)
3.8L [1]	195 (91)	16	25.5 (24.1)
Escort			
1.9L	192 (89)	16	7.9 (7.5)
1.9L H.O.	192 (89)	16	7.9 (7.5)
LTD Crown Victoria, Grand Marquis, Town Car, Wagon			
5.0L	195 (91)	16	14.4 (13.6)
Mark VII			
5.0L	195 (91)	16	14.1 (13.3)
Mustang			
2.3L	192 (89)	16	9.2 (8.7)
5.0L H.O.	195 (91)	16	14.1 (13.3)
Probe			
2.2L	195 (91)	16	7.9 (7.5)
Sable, Taurus			
2.5L	192 (89)	16	8.3 (7.9)
3.0L [2]	192 (89)	16	11.0 (10.4)
3.0L [3]	192 (89)	16	11.8 (11.2)
3.0L SHO	192 (89)	16	11.6 (11.0)
3.8L	195 (91)	16	12.1 (11.5)
Tempo, Topaz			
2.3L HSC	192 (89)	16	8.1 (7.6)
2.3L HSO	192 (89)	16	8.1 (7.6)

[1] – Refers to supercharged engines.
[2] – Refers to sedan models only.
[3] – Refers to station wagon models only.

Chrysler Motors, Ford Motor Co.

DESCRIPTION

The flex-blade fan assembly is designed to allow blades to flex as engine RPM increases. Blade pitch decreases as RPM increases, thereby saving power and decreasing noise level. Keep fan belt adjusted to proper tension as necessary. *See Fig. 1.*

Many air conditioned models use a thermostatically controlled fluid fan and torque control clutch. Thermal control drive is a silicone-filled coupling connecting fan to a fan pulley, and is operated by an internal control valve. The control valve is operated by a temperature sensitive bi-metallic coil (or strip) and controls flow of silicone through the clutch. *See Fig. 2.*

During periods of operation when radiator discharge air temperature is low, fan clutch speeds are slowed, decreasing fan speed and increasing engine warm-up. High radiator discharge air temperature causes bi-metallic coil or strip to allow a greater flow of silicone to enter clutch. This increases drag between driven member and driving member resulting in a higher fan speed and increased cooling.

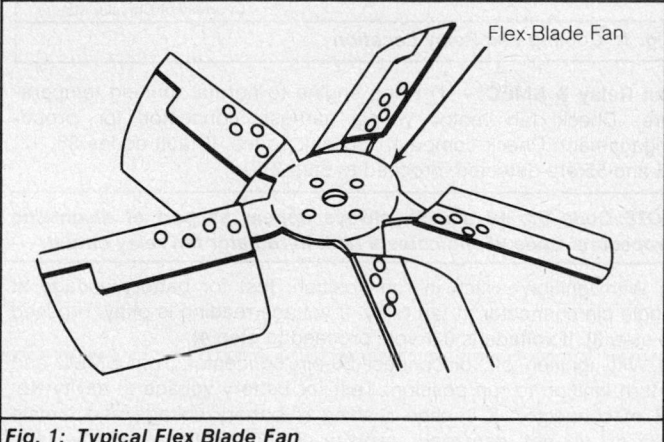

Fig. 1: Typical Flex Blade Fan

TESTING

Thermostatically Controlled Fan Assembly – **1)** In cases of engine overheating or insufficient air conditioning, start with a cool engine to ensure complete fan clutch disengagement. Cover radiator grille to induce high engine temperature.

2) Start engine and operate at 2000 RPM. On all models except Chrysler Motors, turn on air conditioning (if equipped). When radiator discharge air temperature gets hot, a fan roar will be noticed when fan clutch engages.

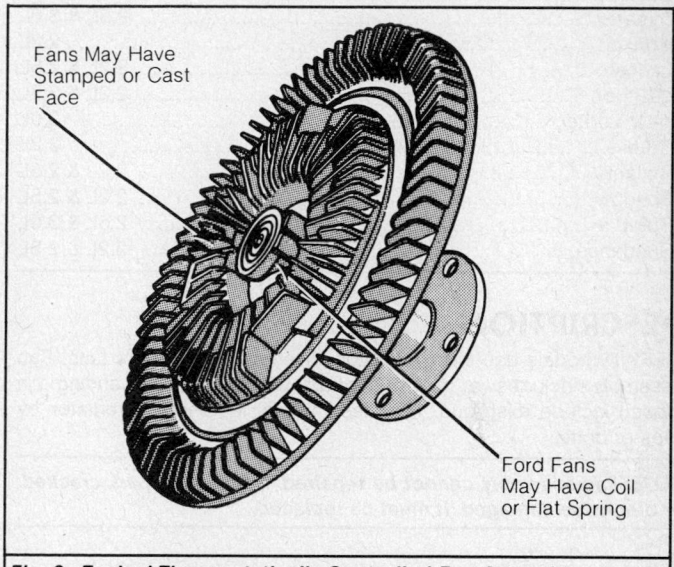

Fans May Have Stamped or Cast Face

Ford Fans May Have Coil or Flat Spring

Fig. 2: Typical Thermostatically Controlled Fan Assembly

NOTE: It takes approximately 5-10 minutes for temperature to become hot enough to allow engagement of fan clutch. While operating engine under this condition, observe temperature light or gauge to prevent overheating. If car overheats, remove cover from radiator grille.

3) When clutch engages, remove radiator grille cover and turn A/C off to assist in engine cooling. After several minutes fan clutch should disengage. This can be determined by a reduction in fan speed and roar. If fan clutch fails to function as described, it should be replaced.

1989 ENGINE COOLING SYSTEMS
Chrysler Motors Electric Cooling Fans

1989 ELECTRIC COOLING FAN APPLICATIONS

Application	Engine
Passenger Cars	
Acclaim	2.5L & 3.0L
Aries	2.2L & 2.5L
Daytona	2.5L
Dynasty	2.5L & 3.0L
Horizon	2.2L
Lancer	2.2L & 2.5L
LeBaron	2.2L & 2.5L
New Yorker	3.0L
Omni	2.2L
Reliant	2.2L & 2.5L
Shadow	2.2L & 2.5L
Spirit	2.5L & 3.0L
Sundance	2.2L & 2.5L

DESCRIPTION

All FWD models use electric motor driven cooling system fans. Fan assembly includes a motor support which may (depending on model) include a shroud. Fan assembly is fastened to radiator by clips or bolts.

NOTE: Fan assembly cannot be repaired. If fan is warped, cracked, or otherwise damaged, it must be replaced.

OPERATION

Fan control is accomplished two ways. The fan always runs when A/C compressor clutch is engaged. In addition, fan is turned on by temperature of coolant which is sensed by coolant temperature sensor which sends a message to the Single Module Engine Controller (SMEC). The SMEC turns on fan through a fan relay. *See Figs. 1 and 2.*

Switching through the SMEC provides for fan control. Fan should not run during cranking until engine starts. Fan should always run when A/C clutch is engaged.

On non-A/C equipped vehicles or with A/C off, fan should run at vehicle speeds above 40 MPH only if coolant temperature reaches 230°F (110°C), and will turn off when temperature drops to 220°F (104°C).

At speeds below 40 MPH, fan switches on at 210°F (99°C) and off at 200°F (93°C). With vehicle stopped and engine at idle, fan will run only under following conditions: below 60°F (16°C) ambient temperature, and from 100°F (38°C) to 195°F (97°C) coolant temperature. Fan will only run for 3 minutes at idle speed.

NOTE: At idle with A/C off, temperature gauge will rise slowly to about 5/8 gauge travel, fan will come on and gauge will quickly drop to about 1/2 gauge travel. This is normal.

TROUBLE SHOOTING

Electric Fan Motor – To check electric fan motor, disconnect fan motor wire connector. Observing correct polarity, connect a 12-volt battery source and ground to fan motor connector. Positive side of connector is male and negative side is female. If fan runs normally, motor is functioning properly. If not, replace motor.

NOTE: If motor is noticeably overheated, system voltage may be too high. Check charging system.

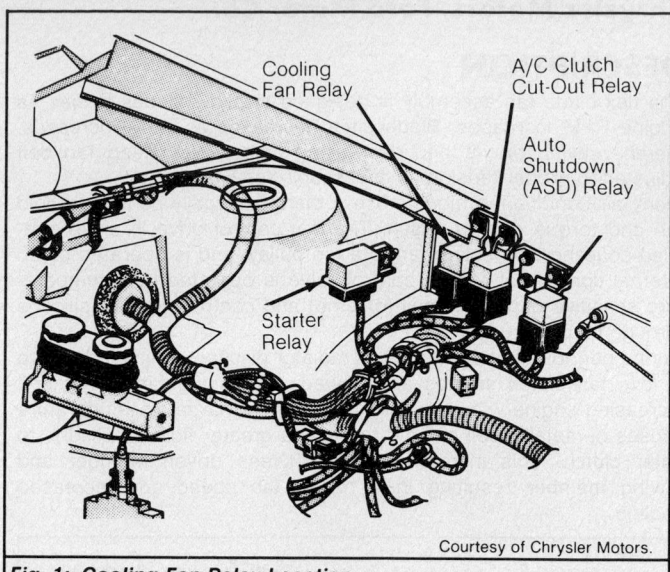

Courtesy of Chrysler Motors.

Fig. 1: Cooling Fan Relay Location

Fan Relay & SMEC – 1) Bring engine to normal running temperature. Check fan motor wiring harness connector for proper engagement. Check computer for fault codes. If fault codes 88, 12, 35 and 55 are detected, proceed to step 2).

NOTE: Code 88, 12 and 55 always appear as part of diagnostic procedure. Code 35 indicates a fault in radiator fan relay circuit.

2) With ignition switch in run position, test for battery voltage at single pin connector at fan relay. If voltage reading is okay, proceed to step 3). If voltage is 0-1 volt, proceed to step 4)

3) With ignition off, disconnect 60-pin connector from SMEC and return ignition to run position. Test for battery voltage at cavity No. 57 of connector. If voltage reading is battery voltage and female terminal is not damaged, replace SMEC. With a zero voltage reading, repair open or short in wiring circuit.

4) With ignition off, disconnect 60-pin connector from SMEC and return ignition to run position. Test for battery voltage at single pin connector of fan relay. If voltage reading is battery voltage, replace the SMEC. If voltage reading is 0-1 volt, proceed to step 5).

5) With ignition in run position, test for battery voltage at Blue wire in 3-way connector of fan relay. If voltage is battery voltage, replace fan relay. If voltage reading is zero, repair open or short in wiring circuit. Turn ignition off, connect 60-pin connector to SMEC and test system.

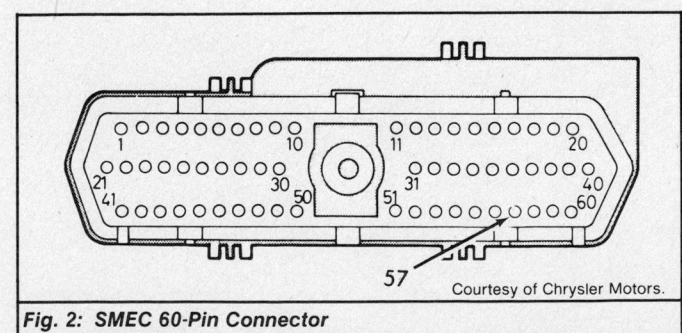

Courtesy of Chrysler Motors.

Fig. 2: SMEC 60-Pin Connector

1989 ENGINE COOLING SYSTEMS
Chrysler Motors Electric Cooling Fans (Cont.)

7-133

WIRING DIAGRAMS

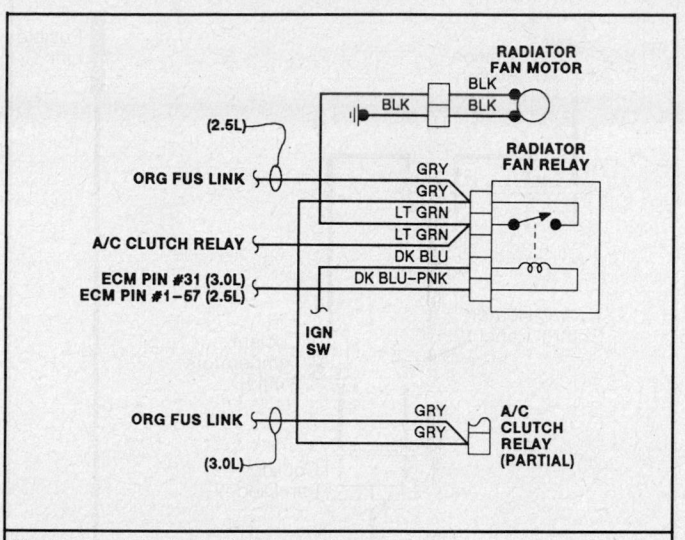

Fig. 3: Acclaim & Spirit Wiring Diagram

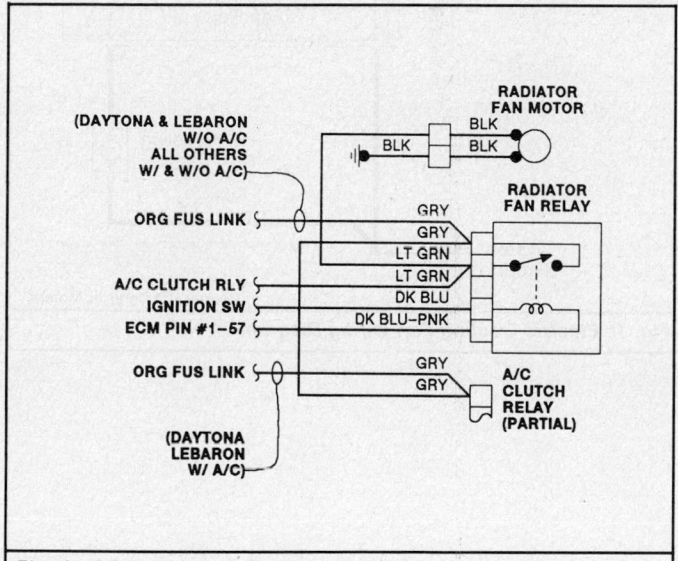

Fig. 4: Aries, Daytona, Dynasty (2.5L), Horizon, LeBaron, Omni & Reliant Wiring Diagram

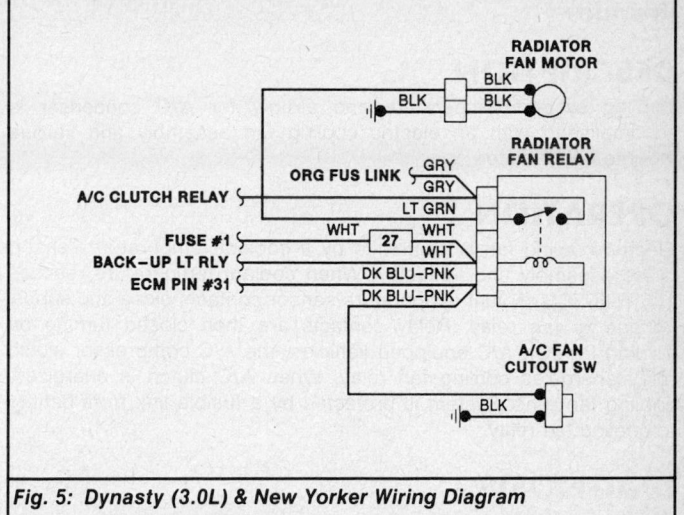

Fig. 5: Dynasty (3.0L) & New Yorker Wiring Diagram

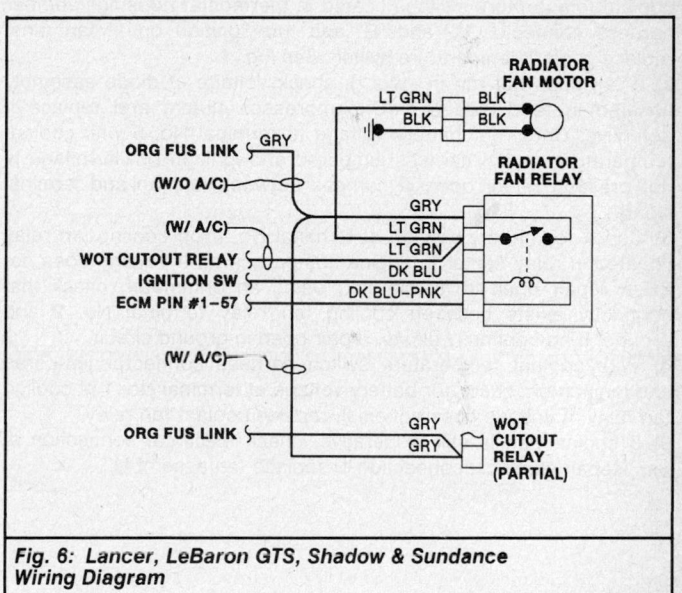

Fig. 6: Lancer, LeBaron GTS, Shadow & Sundance Wiring Diagram

1989 ENGINE COOLING SYSTEMS
Eagle Electric Cooling Fans

Premier

DESCRIPTION

Cooling system temperature and airflow for A/C condenser is accomplished with an electric cooling fan assembly and shroud mounted on radiator.

OPERATION

Electric cooling fan is controlled by a coolant temperature sensor, diode assembly and fan relay. When coolant temperature reaches 188°F (87°C), coolant temperature sensor contacts close and supply voltage to fan relay. Relay contacts are then closed turning on cooling fan. On A/C equipped vehicles, the A/C compressor clutch relay energizes cooling fan relay. When A/C clutch is energized, cooling fan runs. System is protected by a fusible link from battery to cooling fan relay.

DIAGNOSIS

1) If cooling fan is inoperative, disconnect electrical connector at coolant temperature switch (located in thermostat housing). Jumper harness connector "A" and "B" and turn ignition on. If fan runs, replace coolant temperature switch. *See Fig. 1.*

2) If fan does not run in step **1)**, check voltage at diode assembly (located in feed wire to A/C compressor clutch) and replace if defective. Check for battery voltage at terminal No. 5 with coolant temperature switch harness jumpered and ignition on. If voltage is not present, repair open in harness between ignition and terminal No. 5.

3) Check for battery voltage at terminal No. 4 on cooling fan relay (located in relay center in engine compartment). If voltage does not exist, repair open in fusible link. Using an ohmmeter, check that continuity exists between cooling fan relay terminal No. 2 and ground. If no continuity exists, repair open in ground circuit.

4) With coolant temperature switch harness connector jumpered and ignition on, check for battery voltage at terminal No. 1 at cooling fan relay. If voltage does not exist, replace coolant fan relay.

5) If coolant fan is still inoperative, check electrical connection at fan. Repair electrical connection or replace fan assembly.

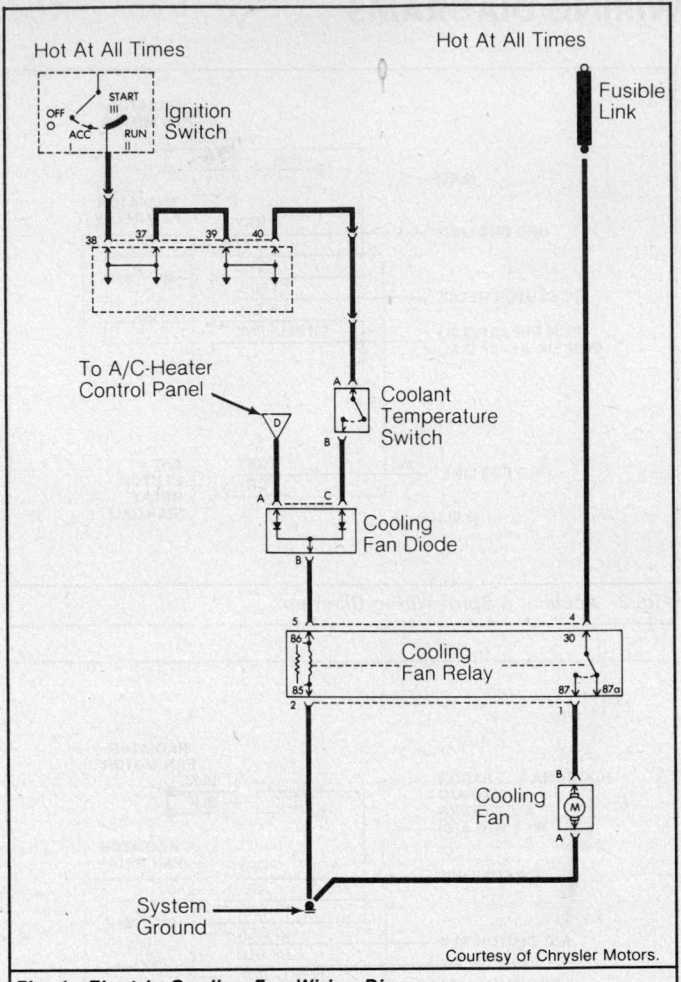

Courtesy of Chrysler Motors.

Fig. 1: Electric Cooling Fan Wiring Diagram

Ford Motor Co. Electric Cooling Fans (Cont.)

at Blue/Black wire is less than 10 volts, repair Blue/Black wire from cooling fan relay to cooling fan motor.

TEST 17, A/C Pressure Switch Ground Check – Turn ignition on. Turn A/C and blower off. Disconnect A/C pressure switch connector. Using a jumper wire, jumper Blue/Green wire in connector to ground. If cooling fan runs, go to TEST 18. If cooling fan does not run, go to TEST 19.

TEST 18, A/C Pressure Switch Operation Check – With engine at idle, A/C and blower on, measure voltage at A/C pressure switch terminals while observing A/C compressor clutch cycling. A/C pressure switch is functioning properly if:

- When A/C compressor clutch is off, Blue/Green wire has 0-4 volts and Blue/Black wire has 10-14 volts.
- When A/C compressor clutch is on, Blue/Green wire has 0-4 volts and Blue/Black wire has 0-4 volts.

If switch is functioning properly, go to TEST 22. If switch is not functioning properly, replace A/C pressure switch.

TEST 19, A/C Relay Operation Check – Remove A/C relay (located in engine compartment in main fuse block). Using jumper wires, supply battery voltage to terminal "A" and ground terminal "B" of relay. Using an ohmmeter, check resistance between terminals "C" and "D". If resistance is less than 5 ohms with voltage applied, and more than 10,000 ohms with voltage disconnected, go to TEST 20. If resistance is not correct, replace A/C relay.

TEST 20, A/C Condenser Fan Relay Ground Check – Turn ignition off. Remove A/C relay. Using an ohmmeter, check resistance between relay connector Black wire and ground. If resistance is less than 5 ohms, go to TEST 21. If resistance is more than 5 ohms, repair ground circuit.

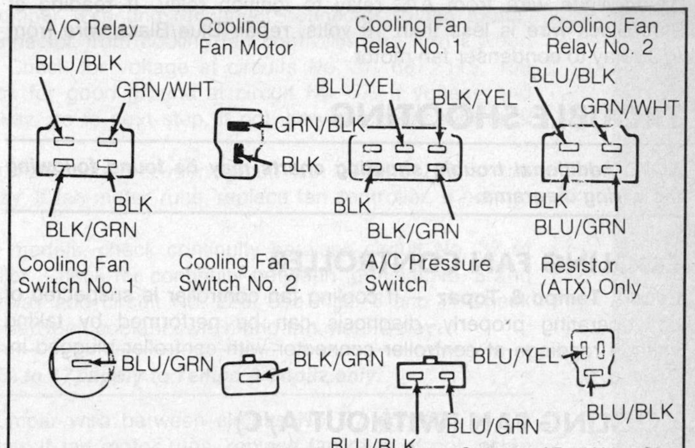

Courtesy of Ford Motor Co.

Fig. 3: Probe Electric Fan Connectors

TEMPO & TOPAZ 2.3L

TEST 1: Ignition switch in "OFF" position.

Connector Pin Number	Voltmeter should read
1	0-volts
2	(not used)
3	0-volts
4	Battery voltage
5	0-volts
6	0-volts
7	0-volts
8	0-volts
9	0-volts
10	0-volts

TEST 2: Ignition switch in "RUN" position, engine running with A/C and defrost off.

Connector Pin Number	Voltmeter should read
1	Battery voltage with coolant temperature switch open.
2	(not used)
3	0-volts with coolant temperature switch open — Battery voltage with coolant temperature switch closed.
4	Battery voltage
5	0-volts — continuity with ground
6	6-volts
7	0-volts
8	0-volts
9	Battery voltage
10	0-volts

TEST 3: Ignition switch in "RUN" position, engine running with A/C and defrost on.

Connector Pin Number	Voltmeter should read
1 (c)	0-volts with clutch cycling pressure switch closed/or coolant temperature switch closed.
2	(not used)
3 (c)	Battery voltage with coolant temperature switch closed and/or clutch cycling pressure switch closed (a) — 0-volts otherwise.
4	Battery voltage
5	0-volts
6	6-volts during normal operation — 0-volts during wide-open throttle operation (b).
7	Battery voltage
8 (a)	Battery voltage when A/C clutch cycling pressure switch is closed and throttle is normal (c) — 0-volts with cycling switch open or throttle closed.
9	Battery voltage
10	Battery voltage when A/C clutch cycling pressure switch and high pressure cut-out switch closed — 0-volts if switch is open.

(a) When Pin 6 is grounded, Pin 8 will have 0 volts.

(b) High pressure cutout switch (if used) must also be closed.

(c) On fan controllers with prefix E53Z or later the fan motor will stay energized when the WOT switch is open. The fan motor will stay energized if the A/C cycling pressure switch opens for less than 2-3 minutes.

NOTE: Indicated voltages in the 50 states and Canada procedures can vary, depending on the type of meter used.

ESCORT 1.9L ENGINE WITH A/C

TEST 1: Ignition switch in "OFF" position.

Connector Pin Number	Voltmeter should read
1	12-volts with coolant temperature switch open.
2	(not used)
3	0 voltage (with coolant temperature switch open)
4	Battery voltage
5	0-volts
6	0-volts
7	0-volts
8	0-volts
9	0-volts
10	0-volts

TEST 2: Ignition switch in "RUN" position, engine running with A/C and defrost off.

Connector Pin Number	Voltmeter should read
1	Battery voltage with coolant temperature switch open — Less than 1-volt with coolant temperature switch closed.
2	(not used)
3	0-volts with coolant temperature switch open — Battery voltage with coolant temperature switch closed.
4	Battery voltage
5	0-volts
6	6-volts
7	0-volts
8	0-volts
9	Battery voltage
10	0-volts

TEST 3: Ignition switch in "RUN" position, engine running with A/C and defrost on.

Connector Pin Number	Voltmeter should read
1	Less than 1.0-volt with coolant temperature switch closed.
2	(not used)
3	Battery voltage with temperature switch and/or clutch cycling pressure cut-out switch closed — 0-volts if both switches are open.①
4	Battery voltage
5	0-volts
6	Wide-open throttle: 0 volts Not wide-open throttle: 6-volts
7	Battery voltage
8	Battery voltage with clutch cycling, switch closed or not wide-open throttle 0-volts if A/C cycling switch open or wide-open throttle.
9	Battery voltage
10	Battery voltage with clutch cycling pressure switch closed.

①On fan controllers with prefix E5EZ or later, the fan motor will stay energized when the WOT switch is open. The fan motor will stay energized if the A/C cycling pressure switch opens for less than 2-3 minutes.

Courtesy of Ford Motor Co.

Fig. 2: Escort (1.9L), Tempo & Topaz (2.3L) Cooling Fan Controller Pin Voltage Specifications

Ford Motor Co. Electric Cooling Fans

1989 ELECTRIC COOLING FAN APPLICATIONS

Application	Engine
Ford Motor Co.	
Continental	3.8L
Cougar & Thunderbird	3.8L
Escort	1.9L
Mustang	2.3L
Probe	2.2L
Sable	2.5L, 3.0L & 3.8L
Taurus	2.5L, 3.0L, 3.0L SHO & 3.8L
Tempo	2.3L
Topaz	2.3L

NOTE: This article contains the Integrated Relay Controller Module (IRCM) tests. This test is part of Ford's Electronic Engine Control (EEC) IV system. Only the procedure required to test the (cooling fan) integrated controller is included. Other diagnostic codes may appear while performing integrated controller electrical diagnosis. For complete information on Ford's EEC IV system, see COMPUTERIZED ENGINE CONTROL section in this manual.

DESCRIPTION

FORD MOTOR CO.

Continental, Cougar, Sable, Taurus & Thunderbird – The electric cooling fan system consists of a 2-speed fan on all 2.5L (automatic transaxle), 3.0L, 3.0L SHO and 3.8L engines or a 1-speed fan on 2.5L engines with manual transaxle, and an electric motor attached to a fan shroud located behind the radiator. On 2.5L and 3.0L engines with automatic transaxle, low speed cooling fan motor operation is achieved by using a dropping resistor in series with the motor. All others use a 2-speed fan motor. The electro-drive cooling fan operates only when the ignition switch is in the "RUN" position.

Escort, Tempo & Topaz – The electric cooling fan system consists of a fan and electric motor attached to a fan shroud located behind the radiator. The system utilizes a coolant temperature switch mounted in the thermostat housing. Vehicles equipped with air conditioning have a cooling fan controller and cooling fan relay. On vehicles with a standard heater, the engine cooling fan is powered through the cooling fan relay.

Mustang – The system is designed to have engine cooling fan operation, whenever the A/C compressor is operating or whenever the engine coolant temperature reaches 221°F (105°C) with the ignition switch in the "ON" position. A cooling fan controller is used to energize cooling fan. The cooling fan controller is located under instrument panel, between steering column and left side cowl panel.

Probe – The system is designed to energize the electric cooling fan through use of coolant temperature sensors and relays. The electric cooling fan is mounted behind radiator. Air conditioning equipped vehicles have a second electric cooling fan to draw air through A/C condenser.

OPERATION

FORD MOTOR CO.

CAUTION: Disconnect the cooling fan prior to performing any underhood service. The fan could cycle if the ignition switch is left in the "ON" position even though the engine is not running.

Continental, Cougar, Sable, Taurus & Thunderbird – The cooling fan is controlled by the Integrated Relay Controller Module (IRCM) and EEC-IV module, which will energize the cooling fan under the following conditions:

- Engine temperature is higher than normal. Low-speed fan comes on at 215°F (102°C), and goes off at 210°F (99°C).
- A/C is on and vehicle speed is below 43 MPH.
- Cooling fan is turned on high speed if engine temperature is higher than desirable and fan has been operating at a low speed. Fan comes on at 230°F (110°C), and goes off at 224°F (107°C). During idle, cooling fan is turned on high fan speed at 236°F (113°C).
- Cooling fan will turn off (providing engine coolant temperature is not too high) if driver demand is Wide Open Throttle (WOT) or A/C is not operating.

When A/C low side pressure is low, the clutch cycling pressure switch cuts off power to the ECA, which then interrupts the compressor and engine cooling fan operation, providing the engine coolant temperature does not call for fan operation.

Several different controllers are available depending on application. Proper operation of the system cannot be obtained unless the correct controller is used.

Escort, Tempo & Topaz – The electric cooling fan operates only when ignition switch is in the "RUN" position on Tempo and Topaz vehicles. The cooling fan will operate whenever cooling fan temperature switch is closed on Escort.

If vehicle is equipped with A/C, the cooling fan is controlled by a cooling fan controller and fan relay. The cooling fan motor is energized when the A/C cycling pressure switch closes with the select lever in "A/C" or "DEFROST" position. The A/C clutch coil will be energized once voltage is available at the fan motor. The A/C clutch will cycle with A/C clutch cycling pressure switch.

The cooling fan motor will stay energized as A/C clutch cycles if cycling pressure switch opening intervals are less than 2-3 minutes in duration. If coolant temperature switch closes in A/C mode at 210°F (99°C) on Escort, fan motor will run continuously until coolant temperature drops below 193°F (89°C).

Two different fan controllers are used. Proper operation of the cooling system cannot be obtained unless proper fan controller is used. Each controller is identified with a color code and part number.

The cooling fan operates when engine coolant temperature goes above 210°F (99°C) or when A/C is operated. When A/C low side pressure is low, the clutch cycling pressure switch signals A/C fan controller to cut off power to A/C clutch field coil, fan motor and throttle solenoid kicker.

The cooling fan controller on Escort is located under instrument panel, forward of evaporator mounting bracket. On Tempo and Topaz, controller is mounted on right cowl panel under instrument panel. The controller can be serviced through glove compartment opening.

Mustang – The cooling fan controller consists of 2 relays mounted on a printed circuit board. One relay powers the fan motor, the other relay powers A/C compressor clutch coil.

When engine coolant temperature reaches 221°F (105°C), the cooling fan temperature switch (located in heater hose tube) will close, completing ground circuit to fan relay coil in cooling fan controller. When the relay is energized, contacts close to complete circuit for engine cooling fan motor operation. The fan will continue to operate until engine coolant temperature drops to approximately 201°F (94°C).

During A/C operation, A/C clutch cycling pressure switch controls evaporator temperature by controlling compressor operation. The pressure switch will cause the fan relay to operate first (within 2-4 seconds of start-up), then A/C relay will operate if voltage is available at fan motor terminal. The A/C compressor will cycle together with the A/C pressure switch. The cooling fan motor will remain on for A/C pressure switch open intervals less than 2 minutes.

The fan motor will de-energize if A/C pressure remains open for more than 2 minutes or if ignition switch is turned to the "OFF" position. Under wide open throttle conditions, the A/C compressor will de-energize, but cooling fan motor will continue operating. Turning A/C or defrost demand switch to "OFF" position will not disengage cooling fan motor for 2-3 minutes unless ignition switch is turned to "OFF" position.

7-136

1989 ENGINE COOLING SYSTEMS
Ford Motor Co. Electric Cooling Fans (Cont.)

Probe – The cooling fan can run when ignition switch is in the "RUN" position. Models with automatic transaxle have 2 coolant sensors and 2 relays to energize low or high fan speed. Models with manual transaxle have one coolant sensor and one relay for high speed fan operation only. *See Fig. 1.*

The cooling fan is turned on low speed when coolant temperature reaches 177°F (97°C) or higher. Cooling fan is turned on high speed when coolant temperature reaches 226°F (108°C). Manual transaxle models use one relay and only the high speed value for operation. The auxiliary condenser fan used on A/C equipped models runs continuously while A/C compressor clutch is engaged.

CAUTION: The cooling fan will run if the ignition is on and electrical wire is disconnected from coolant sensor. Ensure ignition is off before disconnecting wiring.

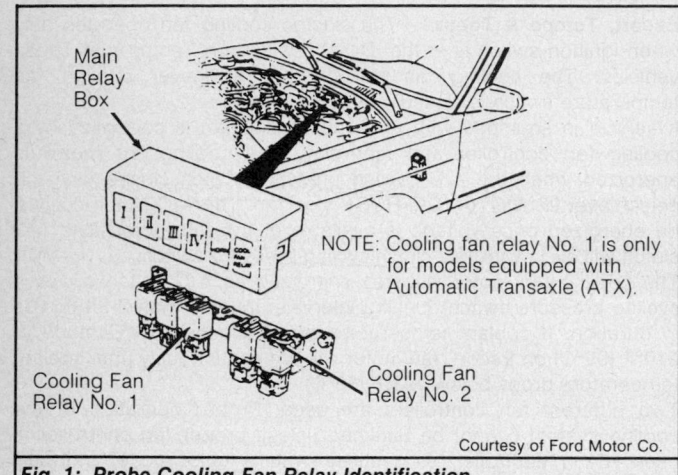

NOTE: Cooling fan relay No. 1 is only for models equipped with Automatic Transaxle (ATX).

Fig. 1: Probe Cooling Fan Relay Identification

Courtesy of Ford Motor Co.

TESTING

PROBE

Probe – The electric cooling fan and condenser fan (on A/C equipped models) use coolant switches and relays to control fan(s) operation. To diagnosis Probe electric fan(s), use the following testing sequence. *See Fig. 3.*

TEST 1, System Check – Visually inspect all relays, switches, circuits and fuses for damage, opens, shorts or bad connections. Repair as required.
- If cooling fan does not run, go to TEST 2.
- If cooling fan is always on, go to TEST 6.
- If cooling fan has no high speed operation, go to TEST 12.
- If cooling fan does not operate with A/C on, go to TEST 17.

TEST 2, Cooling Fan Motor Operational Check – With ignition on and engine off, jumper cooling fan motor connector Blue/Black wire to ground. If cooling fan runs, go to TEST 5. If cooling fan fails to run, go to TEST 3.

TEST 3, Cooling Fan Voltage Supply Check – With ignition on and engine off, measure voltage at cooling fan connector. Using a voltmeter, measure voltage between Yellow wire and ground. If voltage is more than 10 volts, go to TEST 4. If voltage is less than 10 volts, repair Yellow wire circuit from ignition relay to cooling fan motor.

TEST 4, Cooling Fan Motor Ground Check – Disconnect electrical connector at cooling fan motor. Using a jumper wire, jumper Blue/Black wire terminal to ground. Apply battery voltage to Blue/Red wire terminal. If cooling fan motor runs, check connector for corrosion, bad crimps and loose connectors. If cooling fan motor does not run, check cooling fan motor harness for open or short. Check that cooling fan blades are free of obstructions. If okay, replace cooling fan motor.

TEST 5, Cooling Fan Switch No. 1 – With key on and engine off, disconnect cooling fan switch No. 1 (Black/Green wire). If cooling fan runs, go to TEST 6. If cooling fan does not run, go to TEST 7.

TEST 6, Cooling Fan Switch No. 1 Operation Check – Disconnect cooling fan switch No. 1. Using an ohmmeter, check resistance between switch No. 1 terminal and ground. Resistance should be less than 5 ohms with cold engine. Resistance should be more than 10,000 ohms with engine coolant temperature greater than 177°F (97°C). If resistance checks are NOT okay, replace cooling fan switch No. 1. If resistance values are okay, go to TEST 17 for manual transaxle equipped vehicles. For automatic transaxle equipped vehicles, go to TEST 12.

TEST 7, Cooling Fan Relay Function Check – Remove cooling fan relay No. 1. Using jumper wires, supply battery voltage to "A" terminal and ground terminal "B" of relay No. 1. Using an ohmmeter, check resistance between terminals "C" and "D". If resistance is more than 10,000 ohms with voltage applied, and less than 5 ohms with voltage disconnected, go to TEST 8. If resistance is not correct, replace relay No. 1.

TEST 8, Cooling Fan Relay Ground Check – Ignition off. Remove cooling fan relay No. 1. Using an ohmmeter, check resistance between relay connector Black wire and ground. If resistance is less than 5 ohms, go to TEST 9. If resistance is more than 5 ohms, repair ground circuit.

TEST 9, Cooling Fan Relay Power Check – Turn key on. Remove cooling fan relay No. 1. Using a voltmeter, check voltage between Black/Yellow and Blue/Yellow terminals. If both readings are more than 10 volts, repair Black/Green wire from relay to cooling fan switch. If reading at Black/Yellow is less than 10 volts, repair Black/Yellow wire from fuse panel to relay. If reading at Blue/Yellow wire is less than 10 volts, go to TEST 10.

TEST 10, Power Check At Resistor – Turn ignition on. Remove cooling fan relay No. 1. Using a voltmeter, check voltage between resistor Blue/Yellow wire terminal and ground. If voltage is more than 10 volts, repair Blue/Yellow wire from resistor to relay. If voltage is less than 10 volts, go to TEST 11.

TEST 11, Power Check To Resistor – Turn ignition on. Remove cooling fan relay No. 1. Using a voltmeter, Check voltage between resistor Blue/Black wire terminal and ground. If reading is more than 10 volts, replace resistor. If reading is less than 10 volts, repair Blue/Black wire from motor to resistor.

TEST 12, Cooling Fan Switch No. 2 Ground Check – Turn ignition on. Disconnect cooling fan switch No. 2 (Black/Green wire). Jump Black/Green wire to ground. If cooling fan runs, go to TEST 13. If cooling fan does not run, go to TEST 14.

TEST 13, Cooling Fan Switch No. 2 Operation Check – Turn ignition off. Disconnect cooling fan switch No. 2 (Black/Green wire). Using an ohmmeter, check resistance between Black/Green wire and ground. Resistance should be more than 10,000 ohms with cold engine. Resistance should be less than 5 ohms with engine coolant temperature greater than 226°F (108°C). If resistance checks are NOT okay, replace cooling fan switch No. 2. If resistance values are okay, go to TEST 17.

TEST 14, Cooling Fan Relay Operation Check – Remove cooling fan relay No. 2. Using jumper wires, supply battery voltage to terminal "A" and ground terminal "B" of relay No. 2. Using an ohmmeter, check resistance between terminals "C" and "D". If resistance is less than 5 ohms with voltage applied, and more than 10,000 ohms with voltage disconnected, go to TEST 15. If resistance is not correct, replace relay No. 2.

TEST 15, Cooling Fan Relay Ground Check – Turn ignition off. Remove cooling fan relay No. 2. Using an ohmmeter, check resistance between relay connector Black wire and ground. If resistance is less than 5 ohms, go to TEST 16. If resistance is more than 5 ohms, repair ground circuit.

TEST 16, Cooling Fan Relay Power Check – Turn key on. Remove cooling fan relay No. 2. Using a voltmeter, check voltage between Blue/Black and Green/White terminals. If both readings are more than 10 volts, repair Black/Green wire from relay to cooling fan switch. If reading at Green/White wire is less than 10 volts, repair Green/White wire from cooling fan relay to ignition relay. If reading

7-138   7-140

1989 ENGINE COOLING SYSTEMS
Ford Motor Co. Electric Cooling Fans (Cont.)

Fig. 7: Tempo & Topaz (With A/C) Wiring Schematic

Courtesy of Ford Motor Co.

Fig. 8: Mustang (2.3L) Wiring Schematic

Courtesy of Ford Motor Co.

1989 ENGINE COOLING SYSTEMS
Ford Motor Co. Electric Cooling Fans (Cont.)

7-141

COOLING FAN INOPERATIVE

Mustang – 1) Disconnect fan motor lead and install a jumper wire between negative lead and ground. Install jumper lead between positive lead and battery voltage. If fan motor does not run, replace fan motor. If fan motor runs, reconnect fan motor lead and go to next step

2) Disconnect coolant temperature switch connector and install a jumper wire between connector and ground on circuit No. 45. Turn ignition switch on. If fan motor runs, check coolant temperature switch ground circuit No. 45. See Fig. 8. If okay, replace coolant temperature switch. If fan motor does not run, go to next step.

3) With ignition off, remove jumper wire. Check continuity of circuit No. 45 from cooling fan controller (terminal No. 1) to coolant temperature switch. If no continuity is present, fix open in circuit No. 45. If continuity is present, install jumper wire between coolant temperature switch and ground and go to next step.

4) Install a jumper wire between circuit No. 687 of cooling fan controller connector (terminal No. 8) and battery voltage. If motor runs, check ignition feed circuit No. 687 for an open. See Fig. 8. If motor does not run, remove jumper wire and go to next step.

5) Disconnect cooling fan controller connector. Jumper circuit No. 228 (terminal No. 5) to battery voltage. If motor runs, remove jumper wire and go to next step. If not, check for open in circuit No. 228.

6) Install a jumper wire between circuits No. 68 (terminal No. 2) and No. 228 (terminal No. 5) at the cooling fan controller connector. If motor does not run, check circuit No. 68 for an open. If fan motor does run, replace cooling fan controller and remove jumper from coolant temperature switch.

COOLING FAN WORKS,
BUT DOES NOT OPERATE IN A/C MODE

Mustang – 1) Turn A/C switch to "ON" position. Wait for 5 seconds. If fan motor does not operate, go to next step. If fan motor goes off and on repeatedly, go to step **7)**.

2) Check 20 amp fuse in fuse panel. If fuse is blown, replace it. If not, disconnect A/C clutch cycle pressure switch connector and install a jumper wire between terminals of connector. If fan motor runs, go to next step. If not, go to step **6)**.

3) Check A/C system for loss of refrigerant charge. If refrigerant level is low, add refrigerant. If refrigerant pressure is above 50 psi (3.5 cm/kg²), go to next step.

4) Check for continuity between terminals of A/C clutch cycling pressure switch with connector removed. If continuity is present, go to next step. If not, replace A/C clutch cycling pressure switch.

5) Check for voltage of circuit No. 348 at A/C clutch cycling pressure switch connector. See Fig. 8. If voltage is present, go to step **7)**. If no voltage is present, go to next step.

6) Check for voltage at circuits No. 296 and 348 at function selector switch in instrument panel. If voltage is present on circuit No. 296, but not on circuit No. 348, A/C control assembly is defective. If no voltage is present at circuit No. 296, check for short on circuits No. 296 and 297 to the ignition switch.

7) Check for voltage on circuit No. 883 (pin No. 6) of cooling fan controller. See Fig. 8. If voltage is present, go to next step. If voltage is not present, repair open in circuit No. 883 to the controller.

8) With fan controller connected, ground circuit No. 57 (pin No. 4) of the controller. If fan runs, repair ground circuit No. 57. If not, replace fan controller.

INTEGRATED RELAY CONTROLLER

Continental, Cougar, Sable, Taurus & Thunderbird – The Integrated Relay Controller Module (IRCM) interfaces with the EEC-IV system to provide control of the cooling fan, A/C clutch, and fuel pump. The module incorporates the ECC power relay which supplies current to the EEC-IV system. See Figs. 9-18.

The location of the IRCM for all models is on the radiator support bracket. The operating voltage of the IRCM is between 7-17 volts.

For diagnostic information concerning A/C components controlled the IRCM and/or for the IRCM itself, see the following A/C INTEGRATED RELAY CONTROLLER trouble shooting charts.

NOTE: Trouble shooting charts and flow-charts supplied Courtesy of Ford Motor Co., may be found following the wiring diagrams.

WIRING DIAGRAMS

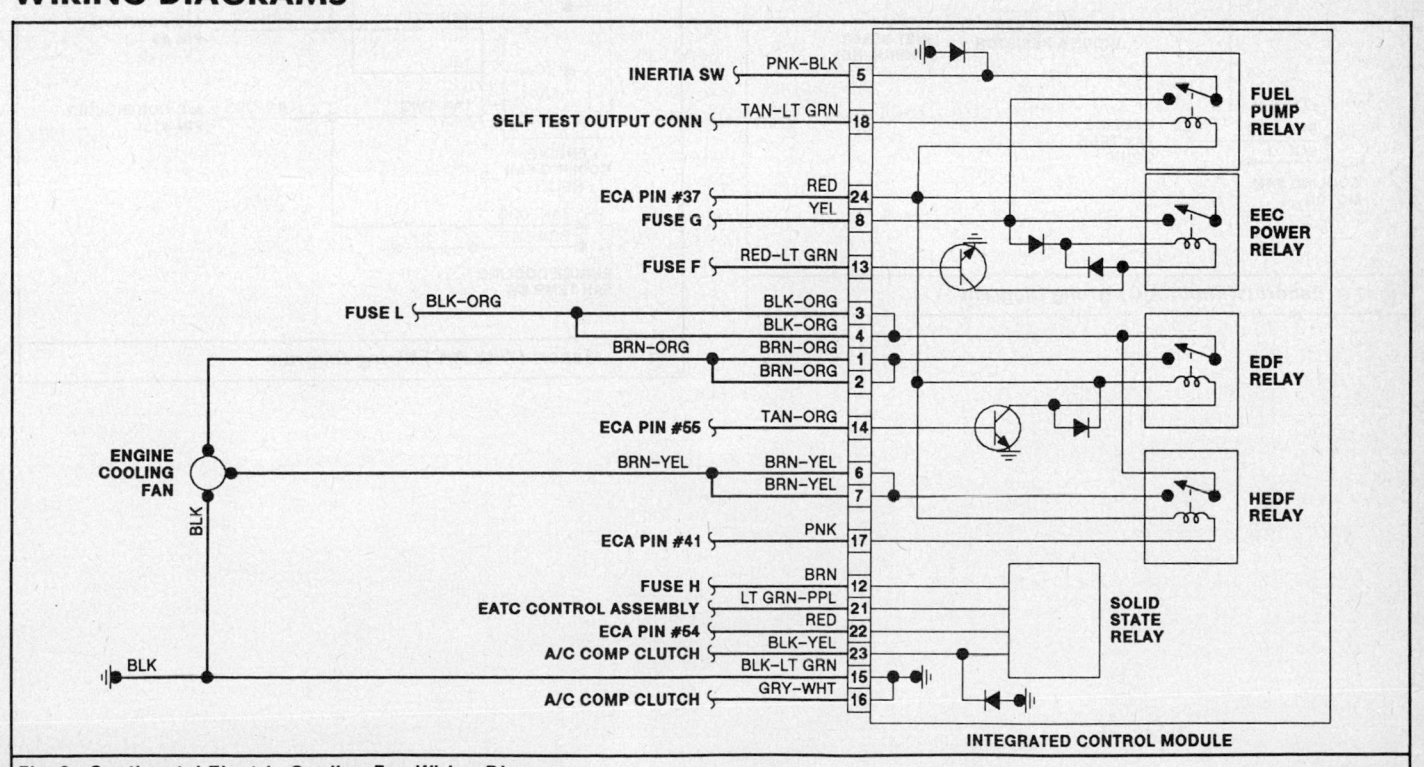

Fig. 9: Continental Electric Cooling Fan Wiring Diagram

1989 ENGINE COOLING SYSTEMS
Ford Motor Co. Electric Cooling Fans (Cont.)

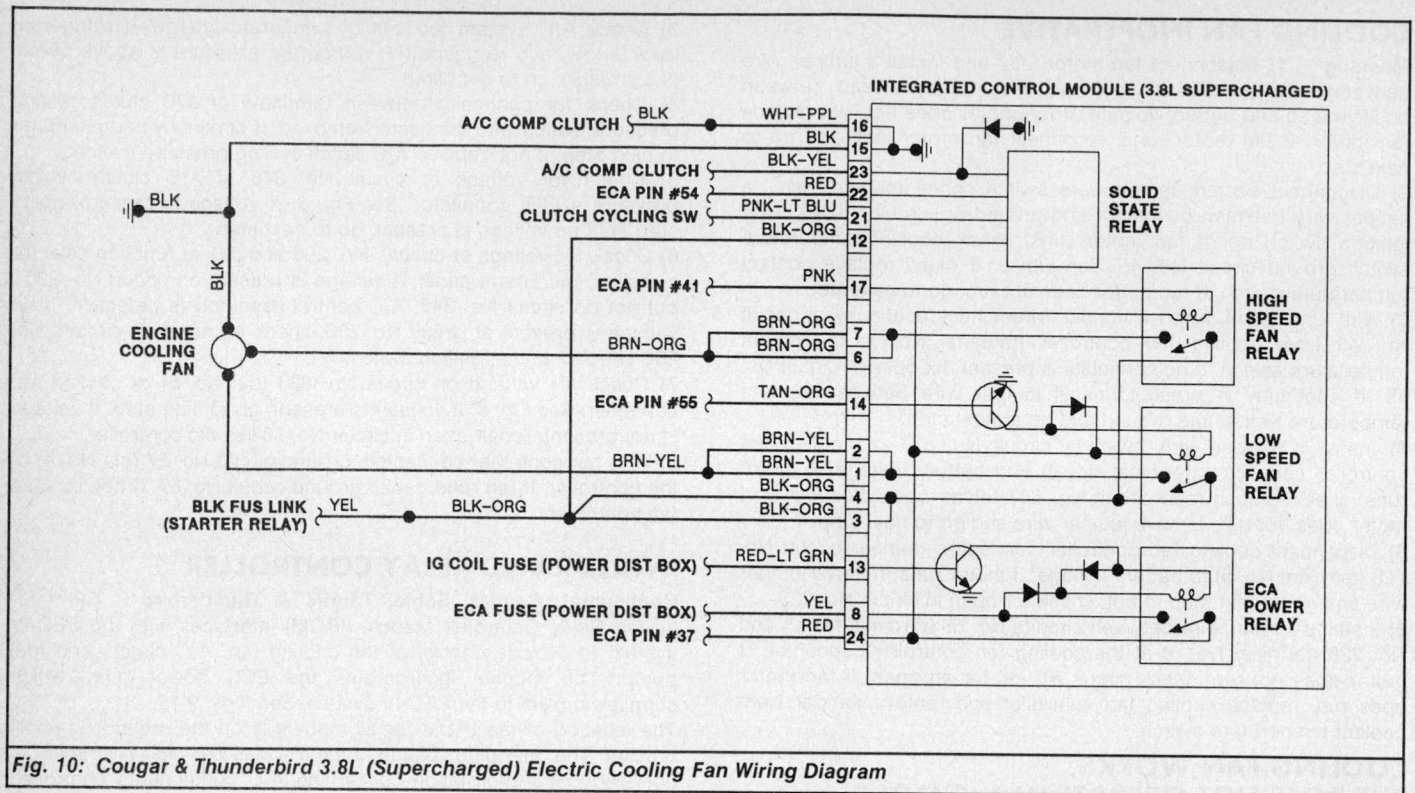

Fig. 10: Cougar & Thunderbird 3.8L (Supercharged) Electric Cooling Fan Wiring Diagram

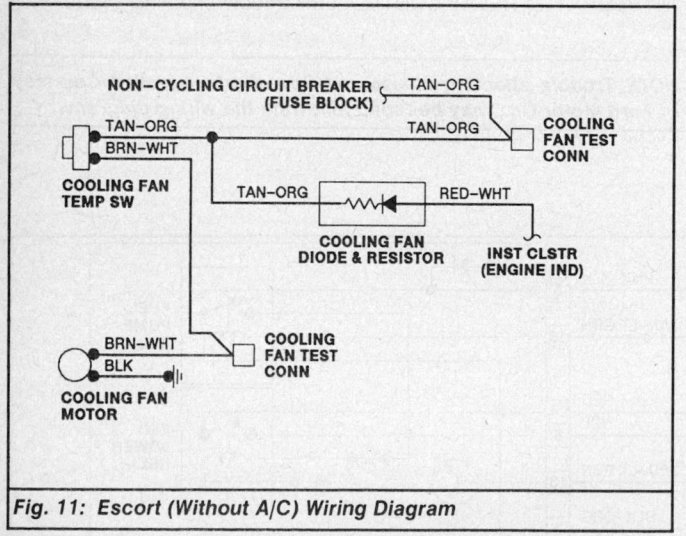

Fig. 11: Escort (Without A/C) Wiring Diagram

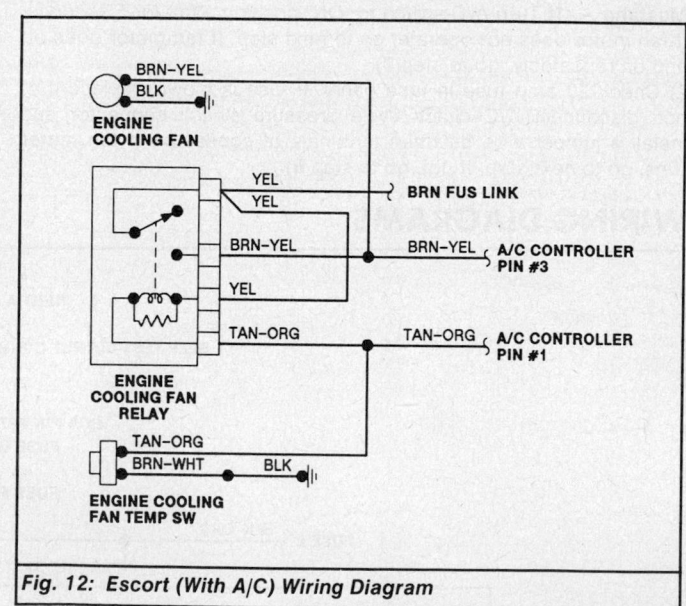

Fig. 12: Escort (With A/C) Wiring Diagram

1989 ENGINE COOLING SYSTEMS
Ford Motor Co. Electric Cooling Fans (Cont.)

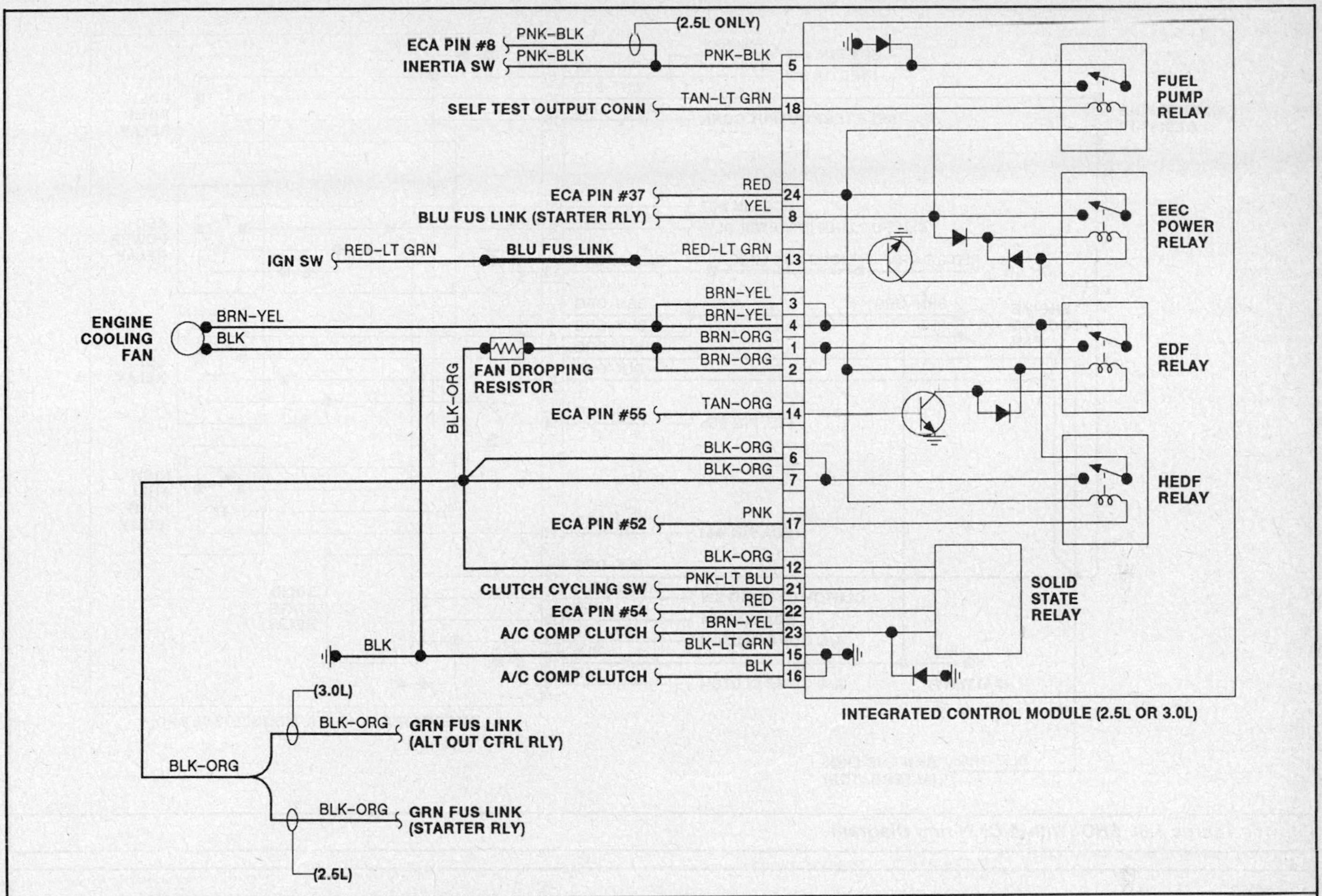

7-143

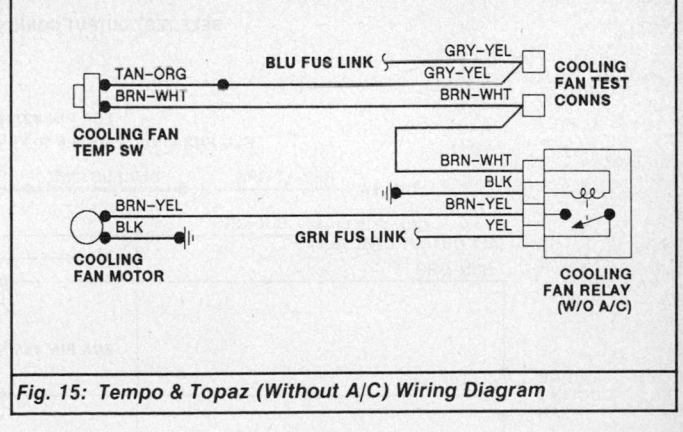

Fig. 13: Sable & Taurus 2.5L & 3.0L (With A/C) Wiring Diagram

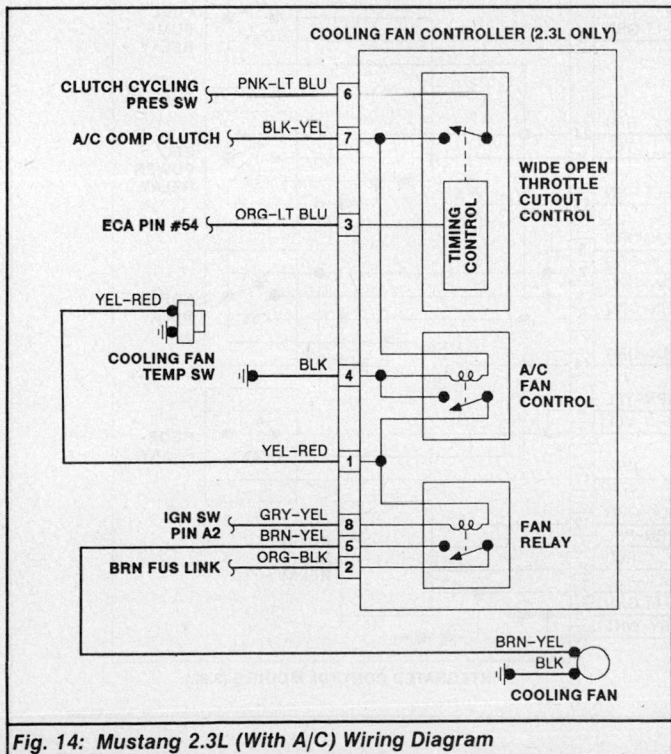

Fig. 14: Mustang 2.3L (With A/C) Wiring Diagram

Fig. 15: Tempo & Topaz (Without A/C) Wiring Diagram

1989 ENGINE COOLING SYSTEMS
Ford Motor Co. Electric Cooling Fans (Cont.)

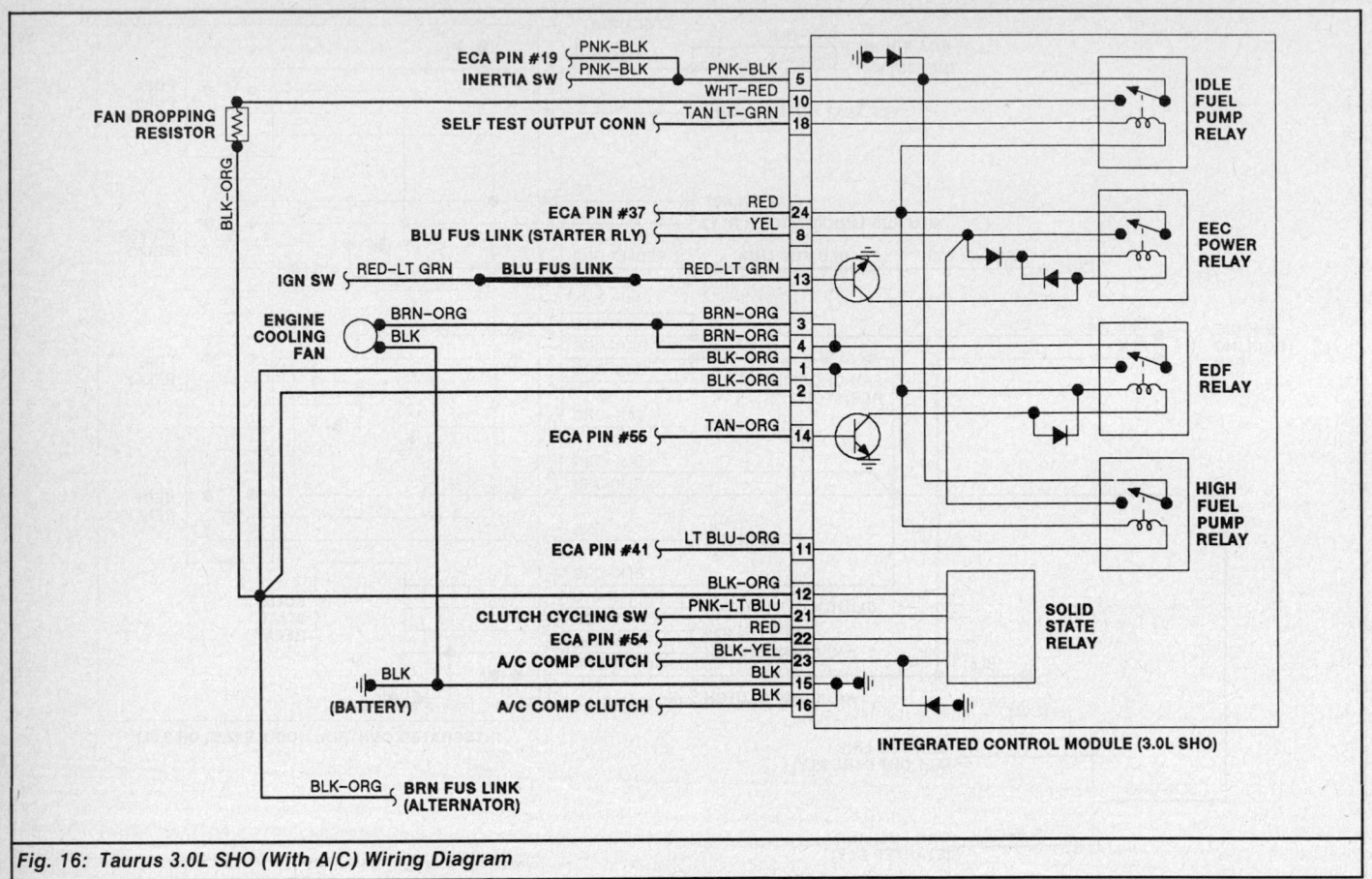

Fig. 16: Taurus 3.0L SHO (With A/C) Wiring Diagram

Fig. 17: Sable & Taurus 3.8L (With A/C) Wiring Diagram

1989 ENGINE COOLING SYSTEMS
Ford Motor Co. Electric Cooling Fans (Cont.)

7-145

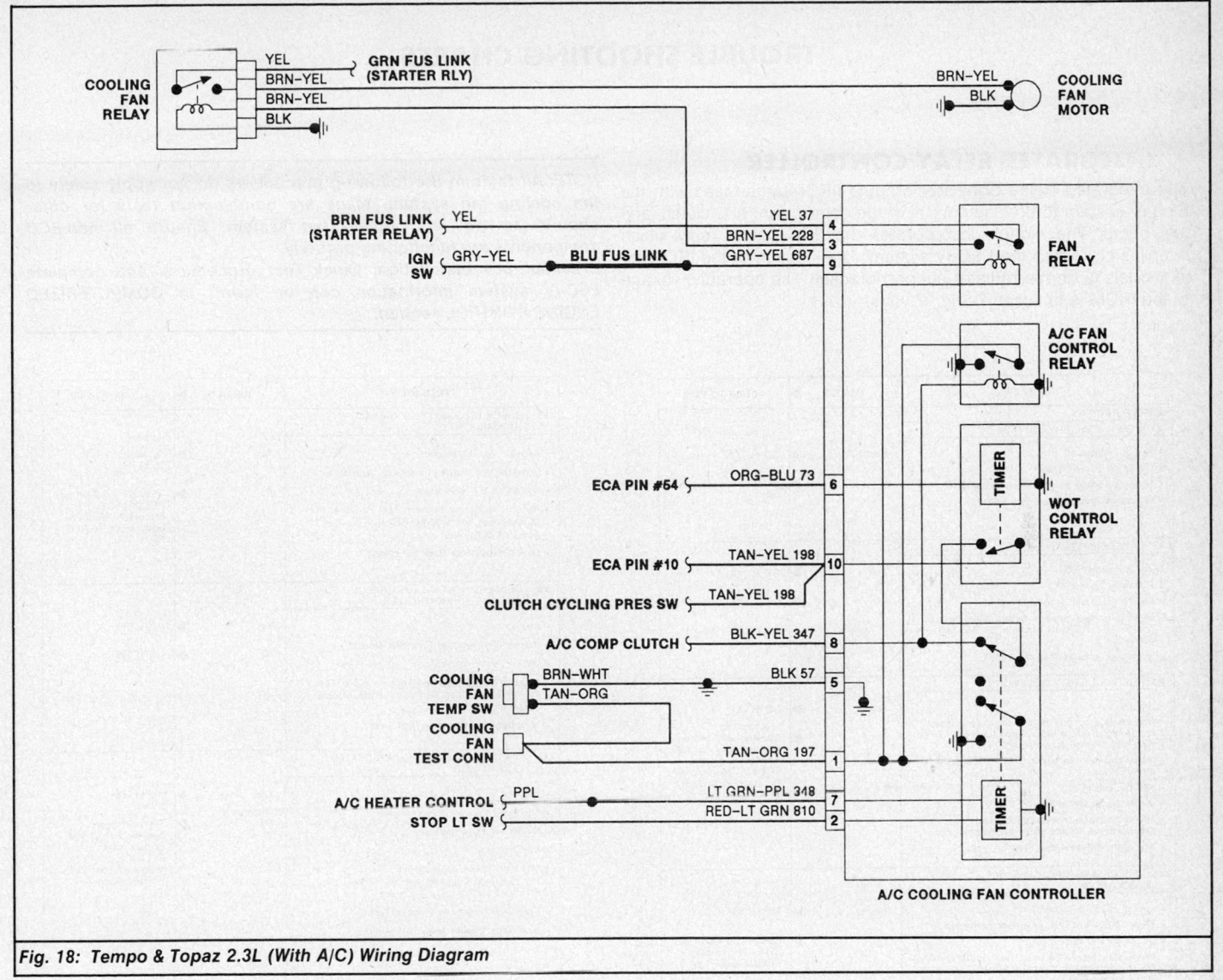

Fig. 18: *Tempo & Topaz 2.3L (With A/C) Wiring Diagram*

7-146

1989 ENGINE COOLING SYSTEMS
Ford Motor Co. Electric Cooling Fans (Cont.)

TROUBLE SHOOTING CHARTS

INTEGRATED RELAY CONTROLLER

The Integrated Relay Controller Module (IRCM) interfaces with the EEC-IV system to provide control of the cooling fan, A/C clutch, and fuel pump. The module incorporates the ECC power relay which supplies current to the EEC-IV system. The location of the IRCM for all models is on the radiator support bracket. The operating voltage of the IRCM is between 7 and 17 volts.

NOTE: All tests in the following procedures do not apply solely to the cooling fan system. Many are combination tests for other circuits as well as cooling fan system. Ensure all non-ECC components are functioning properly.
Breakout box installation, Quick Test procedures and complete EEC-IV system information can be found in COMPUTERIZED ENGINE CONTROL section.

TEST STEP	RESULT ▶	ACTION TO TAKE
VEHICLE BATTERY		
X1 CHECK BATTERY VOLTAGE		
• Key on, engine off. • DVOM on 20 volt scale. • Measure voltage across battery terminals. • **Is voltage greater than 10.5 volts?**	Yes ▶ No ▶	GO to X2 . SERVICE discharged battery.
X2 CHECK BATTERY GROUND		
• Key on, engine off. • Processor connected. • DVOM on 20 volt range. • Measure voltage between battery negative post and SIGNAL RETURN circuit in the Self-Test connector. • **Is voltage greater than 0.5 volts?**	Yes ▶ No ▶	GO to X3 . GO to X6 .
X3 GROUND FAULT ISOLATION		
• Key off. • Disconnect processor 60 pin connector. Inspect for damaged or pushed out pins, corrosion, loose wires etc. Service as necessary. • Install breakout box and connect processor to breakout box. • Key on, engine off. • DVOM on 20 volt scale. • Measure voltage between battery negative post and Test Pins 40 and 60 at the breakout box. • **Are both voltages less than 0.5 volts?**	Yes ▶ No ▶	GO to X4 . Circuit(s) with greater than 0.5 volts has high resistance or open. SERVICE open ground circuit. RERUN Quick Test.
X4 PROCESSOR GROUND FAULT ISOLATION		
• Key off, wait 10 seconds. • Breakout box installed, processor connected. • DVOM on 200 ohm scale. • Measure resistance between Test Pin 46 and Test Pin 40 and between Test Pin 46 and Test Pin 60 at the breakout box. • **Are both resistances less than 5 ohms?**	Yes ▶ No ▶	GO to X5 . REMOVE breakout box. REPLACE processor. RERUN Quick Test.

TEST STEP	RESULT ▶	ACTION TO TAKE
X5 CHECK CONTINUITY OF SIGNAL RETURN CIRCUIT		
• Key off, wait 10 seconds. • Breakout box installed, processor connected. • DVOM on 200 ohm scale. • Measure resistance between Test Pin 46 at the breakout box and SIGNAL RETURN circuit at Self-Test connector. • **Is resistance less than 5.0 ohms?**	Yes ▶ No ▶	System OK. RUN Quick Test. REMOVE breakout box. RECONNECT processor. SERVICE open circuit. RERUN Quick Test.
X6 MEASURE VOLTAGE AND GROUND TO INTEGRATED CONTROLLER		
• Key off. • Disconnect Integrated Controller Module. • DVOM on 20 volt scale. • Measure voltage between Test Pin 8 and Test Pin 15 at the Integrated Controller vehicle harness connector. • **Is voltage greater than 10.5 volts?**	Yes ▶ No ▶	GO to X7 . GO to X9 .
X7 CHECK KEY POWER TO INTEGRATED CONTROLLER		
• Key off. • Integrated Controller disconnected. • DVOM on 20 volt scale. • Key on. • Measure voltage between Pin 13 and Pin 15 at the Integrated Controller vehicle harness connector. • Refer to schematic in Pinpoint Test X. • **Is voltage greater than 10.5 volts?**	Yes ▶ No ▶	GO to X8 . SERVICE open between Pin 13 and ignition switch. RECONNECT Integrated Controller. RERUN Quick Test.

ABBREVIATIONS

A/C: Air Conditioning
ACCS: A/C Cycling Switch
DVOM: Digital Volt/Ohm Meter (see VOM)
ECT: Engine Coolant Temperature sensor
EDF: Electric Drive Fan relay assembly
EEC: Electronic Engine Control
FP: Fuel Pump
FPM: Fuel Pump Monitor

GND or GRND: Ground
HEDF: High Speed Electro Drive Fan relay or circuit
KOEO: Key On Engine Off
KOER: Key On Engine Running
VOM: Analog Volt/Ohm Meter (see DVOM)
VPWR: Vehicle Power supply voltage (regulated 10-14 volts)
WAC: WOT A/C Cut-off switch or circuit
WOT: Wide Open Throttle

Courtesy of Ford Motor Co.

1989 ENGINE COOLING SYSTEMS
Ford Motor Co. Electric Cooling Fans (Cont.)

7-147

TROUBLE SHOOTING CHARTS (Cont.)

TEST STEP	RESULT	ACTION TO TAKE
X8 MEASURE CONTINUITY OF VPWR • Key off. • Integrated Controller disconnected. • Disconnect processor 60 pin connector. Inspect for damaged or pushed out pins, corrosion, loose wires, etc. Service as necessary. • Install breakout box, leave processor disconnected. • DVOM on 200 ohm scale. • Measure resistance between Test Pin 37 and 57 at the breakout box and Test Pin 24 at the Integrated Controller harness. • **Is resistance greater than 5.0 ohms?**	Yes ▶ No ▶	REMOVE breakout box. RECONNECT processor. SERVICE open in VPWR circuit. RECONNECT Integrated Controller. RERUN Quick Test. REMOVE breakout box. RECONNECT processor. REPLACE Integrated Controller. RERUN Quick Test.
X9 MEASURE CONTINUITY OF POWER GROUND TO INTEGRATED CONTROLLER • Key off. • Integrated Controller disconnected. • DVOM on 200 ohm scale. • Measure resistance between battery negative post and at Test Pin 15 at the Integrated Controller connector. • **Is resistance greater than 5.0 ohms?**	Yes ▶ No ▶	RECONNECT Integrated Controller. SERVICE open in battery ground to Pin 15 (Integrated Controller harness connector). RERUN Quick Test. RECONNECT Integrated Controller. SERVICE open in battery positive to Pin 8 (Integrated Controller harness connector). RERUN Quick Test.

TEST STEP	RESULT	ACTION TO TAKE
X12 CHECK POWER-TO-PUMP CIRCUIT CONTINUITY • Key off. • DVOM on 200 ohm scale. • Disconnect Integrated Controller. • Fuel pump(s) disconnected. • Measure resistance between Pin 5 at the integrated controller vehicle harness connector and POWER-TO-PUMP(S) circuit at the fuel pump vehicle harness connector. • **Is resistance less than 5.0 ohms?**	Yes ▶ No ▶	REPLACE Integrated Controller. RECONNECT all components. RERUN Quick Test. SERVICE open in POWER-TO-PUMP(S) circuit. RECONNECT Integrated Controller. RERUN QuicK Test.
X14 CHECK POWER-TO-PUMP(S) FOR SHORTS TO POWER • Key off. • Disconnect Integrated Controller. • Disconnect fuel pumps. • DVOM on 200,000 ohm scale. • Measure resistance between Pin 5 and Pin 24 at the Integrated Controller vehicle harness connector. • Measure resistance between Pin 5 at the Integrated Controller vehicle harness connector and battery positive post. • **Is either resistance less than 10,000 ohms?**	Yes ▶ No ▶	SERVICE short circuit. RECONNECT all components. ATTEMPT to start vehicle. If vehicle runs, RERUN Quick Test. If vehicle will not run, REPLACE Integrated Controller. RERUN Quick Test. RECONNECT fuel pump. REPLACE Integrated Controller. RERUN Quick Test.

TEST STEP	RESULT	ACTION TO TAKE
X10 CODE 72: **INTERMITTENT OPEN IN VPWR CIRCUIT** **NOTE: Code 72 indicates that while key power was present, VPWR had an interrupt, or interference from electrical noises caused the processor to reset, resulting in possible stalls, high idle rpm, lack of power on acceleration or other drive symptoms.** Possible Causes: — Intermittent open in VPWR circuit from integrated controller to processor. — EEC power relay intermittent malfunction. — Intermittent open in VBAT circuit to integrated controller. — Intermittent open in KEY POWER circuit to integrated controller. — EEC harness too close to the distributor spark plug wires and other vehicle harnesses. • Using Continuous Monitor Mode (Engine Running) per Quick Test Appendix. Observe VOM or STAR LED for indication of a fault while performing the following: • Shake, bend and twist harness from integrated controller to the processor, to the ignition switch and to battery positive. • **Is a fault indicated or does Code 72 reappear in continuous memory if Quick Test is rerun?**	Yes ▶ No ▶	CHECK for proper routing of EEC harness. SERVICE as necessary. If OK SERVICE intermittent VPWR circuit. RERUN Quick Test. INSPECT component and harness connectors of integrated controller and processor, for loose or damaged pins, corrosion, etc. SERVICE as necessary. If OK, ROAD TEST vehicle through a variety of drive modes. If symptom exists, REPLACE integrated controller, otherwise testing complete. RERUN Quick Test.
X11 CHECK POWER-TO-PUMP(S) CIRCUIT • Key on, engine off. • Locate and disconnect fuel pump(s). • DVOM on 20 volt scale. • Measure voltage between CHASSIS GROUND and POWER-TO-PUMP(S) circuit at fuel pump during crank mode. • **Is voltage greater than 8.0 volts during crank?**	Yes ▶ No ▶	CHECK electric fuel pump operation. GO to X12

TEST STEP	RESULT	ACTION TO TAKE
SERVICE CODE: 87/83 **X15 CHECK CONTINUITY OF FUEL PUMP CIRCUIT** Service Code 87 or 83 indicates that the voltage output for the high or low fuel pump circuit did not change when activated during Key On Engine Off Self-Test. Possible causes are: — Open or grounded fuel pump circuit — Open or grounded processor driver — Disconnected or open solenoid • Key off. • Disconnect processor 60 pin connector. Inspect for damaged or pushed out pins, corrosion, loose wires, etc. Service as necessary. • Install breakout box, leave processor disconnected. • Disconnect Integrated Controller. • DVOM on 200 ohm scale. For Service Code 87: • Measure resistance between Test Pin 22 at the breakout box and Pin 18 at the Integrated Controller vehicle harness connector. • **Is resistance less than 5.0 ohms?** For Service Code 83: • Measure resistance between Test Pin 41 at the breakout box and Pin 11 at the Integrated Controller vehicle harness connector. • **Is resistance less than 5.0 ohms?**	Yes ▶ No ▶	GO to X16 SERVICE open in fuel pump circuit. REMOVE breakout box. RECONNECT processor and controller. RERUN Quick Test.

1989 ENGINE COOLING SYSTEMS
Ford Motor Co. Electric Cooling Fans (Cont.)

TROUBLE SHOOTING CHARTS (Cont.)

TEST STEP	RESULT ▶	ACTION TO TAKE
X16 CHECK APPROPRIATE FUEL PUMP CIRCUIT FOR SHORTS TO POWER AND GROUND • Key off. • Breakout box installed, processor disconnected. • Integrated Controller disconnected. • DVOM on 200,000 ohm scale. For Service Code 87: • Measure resistance between Test Pin 22 and Test Pins 37, 57 and battery positive post and between Test Pin 22 and Test Pins 40, 60 and battery negative. For Service Code 83: • Measure resistance between Test Pin 41 and Test Pins 37, 57 and battery positive post and between Test Pin 41 and Test Pin 40, 60 and battery negative. • **Are all resistances greater than 10,000 ohms?**	Yes ▶ No ▶	GO to X17. REMOVE breakout box. SERVICE the appropriate fuel pump circuit shorts to power or ground. RECONNECT all components. RERUN Quick Test. If code 87 or 83 is still present, GO to X17.
X17 CHECK RESISTANCE OF FUEL PUMP RELAY COIL • Key off. • Breakout box installed, processor disconnected. • Integrated Controller disconnected. • DVOM on 200 ohm scale. • Measure resistance of Integrated Controller from Pin 18 to 24 or from Pin 11 to 24 as appropriate. • **Is resistance between 65 and 100 ohms?**	Yes ▶ No ▶	REMOVE breakout box. REPLACE processor. RECONNECT Integrated Controller. RERUN Quick Test. REMOVE breakout box. RECONNECT processor. REPLACE Integrated Controller. RERUN Quick Test.
X20 NO FAN (HIGH OR LOW) • Key off. • Disconnect Integrated Controller. • DVOM on 20 volt scale. • Measure voltage between battery negative post and Pins 1, 2, 6 and 7, (except 3.8L GO to pins 3 and 4) respectively at the Integrated Controller vehicle harness connector. • **Is voltage greater than 10.5 volts?**	Yes ▶ No ▶	GO to X21. RECONNECT Integrated Controller. SERVICE open in battery power circuit. RE-EVALUATE symptom.

TEST STEP	RESULT ▶	ACTION TO TAKE
X24 VERIFY COOLING FAN GROUND • Key off. • Cooling fan disconnected. • Integrated Controller disconnected. • Jumper Pin 3 to Pin 6 at Integrated Controller vehicle harness connector. • DVOM on 20 volt scale. • Measure voltage between voltage positive at cooling fan harness connector and negative battery post. • **Is voltage greater than 8.0 volts?**	Yes ▶ No ▶	SERVICE Open in ground circuit to fan. RECONNECT Integrated Controller and cooling fan. RE-EVALUATE symptom. SERVICE open in power-to-fan circuit from 3 and 4 of Integrated Controller harness connector to cooling fan connector. RECONNECT cooling fan and controller, RE-EVALUATE symptom.
X25 JUMPER HIGH ELECTRIC-DRIVE SIGNAL (HEDF) TO GROUND • Key off. • Inspect processor 60 pin connector for damaged or pushed out pins, corrosion, loose wires, etc. Service as necessary • Install breakout box, leave processor disconnected. • Integrated Controller connected. • Key on. • Jumper Test Pin 52 to Test Pin 40 at breakout box. • **Does fan speed change from low to high?**	Yes ▶ No ▶	GO to X26. REMOVE breakout box. REPLACE Integrated Controller. RECONNECT processor. RE-EVALUATE symptom.

TEST STEP	RESULT ▶	ACTION TO TAKE
X21 CHECK FAN MOTOR • Key off. • Integrated Controller disconnected. • Jumper Pin 3 to Pin 6 at Integrated Controller harness. • **Does fan run?**	Yes ▶ No ▶	GO to X22. GO to X23.
X22 CHECK FAN RUNNING MODE (LOW) • Key off. • Disconnect processor. • Reconnect Integrated Controller. • Key on. • **Does fan run at low speed?**	Yes ▶ No ▶	GO to X25. REPLACE Integrated Controller. RECONNECT processor and controller. RE-EVALUATE symptom.
X23 MEASURE BATTERY VOLTAGE SUPPLY AT FAN — BYPASSING INTEGRATED CONTROLLER • Key Off. • Disconnect cooling fan. • Integrated Controller disconnected. • Jumper Pin 3 to Pin 6 at Integrated Controller vehicle harness connector. • DVOM on 20 volt scale. • Measure voltage at cooling fan vehicle harness connector. • **Is voltage greater than 8.0 volts?**	Yes ▶ No ▶	RECONNECT Integrated Controller. REPLACE fan motor. RE-EVALUATE symptom. GO to X24.

TEST STEP	RESULT ▶	ACTION TO TAKE
X26 CHECK ECT SENSOR • Key off, wait 10 seconds. • Breakout box installed. • Connect processor to breakout box. • Check engine coolant level. • Warm engine to operating temperature before taking ECT resistance measurement. • Key off, wait 10 seconds. • Disconnect harness from ECT sensor. • DVOM on 200,000 ohm scale. • Measure resistance of the ECT sensor. • **Is the resistance between 1500 ohms and 2000 ohms?**	Yes ▶ No ▶	For 3.8L SEFI SC, GO to X27. All others, REMOVE breakout box. REPLACE processor. RECONNECT harness to ECT sensor. RECONNECT Integrated Controllers. RE-EVALUATE symptom. REMOVE breakout box. REPLACE ECT sensor. RECONNECT all components. RE-EVALUATE symptom.
X27 CHECK A/C PRESSURE SWITCH HARNESS CONTINUITY • Key off. • Breakout box installed, processor connected. • Disconnect A/C pressure switch. • DVOM on 200,000 ohm scale. • Measure resistance between Test Pin 2 at the breakout box and A/C pressure switch vehicle harness connector, also between Test Pin 46 at the breakout box and SIGNAL RETURN at the switch vehicle harness connector. • **Are both resistances less than 5 ohms?**	Yes ▶ No ▶	GO to X28. REMOVE breakout box. SERVICE open circuit. RECONNECT all components. RERUN Quick Test.
X28 VERIFY HEDF OPERATION • Key off. • A/C pressure switch disconnected. • Jumper A/C pressure circuit to SIGNAL RETURN at the switch vehicle harness connector. • Key on. • **Is HEDF on?**	Yes ▶ No ▶	REPLACE A/C PRESSURE switch. REMOVE breakout box. REPLACE processor. RERUN Quick Test.

Courtesy of Ford Motor Co.

1989 ENGINE COOLING SYSTEMS
Ford Motor Co. Electric Cooling Fans (Cont.)

7-149

TROUBLE SHOOTING CHARTS (Cont.)

TEST STEP	RESULT ▶	ACTION TO TAKE
X30 SERVICE CODE 83: CHECK RESISTANCE OF HEDF CONTROLLER CIRCUIT • Service Code 83 indicates a High Electro Drive Fan (HEDF)/circuit failure. • Key off. • Disconnect Integrated Controller. • DVOM on 200 ohm scale. • Measure resistance between Pin 17 and Pin 24 at the Integrated Controller. • **Is the resistance reading between 50 ohms and 100 ohms?**	Yes ▶ No ▶	GO to X31 . REPLACE controller. RERUN Quick Test.
X31 CHECK HEDF PROCESSOR SIGNAL TO INTEGRATED CONTROLLER FOR OPEN • Key off. • Disconnect processor 60 pin connector. Inspect for damaged or pushed out pins, corrosion, loose wires, etc. Service as necessary. • Install breakout box, leave processor disconnected. • Integrated Controller disconnected. • DVOM On 200 ohms scale. • Measure resistance between Test Pin 52 at breakout box and Pin 17 of Integrated Controller vehicle harness connector. • **Is resistance less than 5 ohms?**	Yes ▶ No ▶	GO to X32 REMOVE breakout box. SERVICE open in HEDF circuit. RECONNECT all components. RERUN Quick Test.
X32 CHECK FOR SHORTS TO GROUND IN THE HEDF CIRCUIT • Key off. • Breakout box installed, processor disconnected. • Integrated Controller disconnected. • DVOM on 200,000 ohm scale. • Measure resistance between Test Pin 52 and Test Pin 40. • **Is resistance greater than 10,000 ohms?**	Yes ▶ No ▶	GO to X33 REMOVE breakout box. RECONNECT processor and Integrated Controller. SERVICE short to ground in HEDF circuit. RERUN Quick Test.

TEST STEP	RESULT ▶	ACTION TO TAKE
X37 CHECK EDF FOR SHORT TO GROUND • Key on. • Breakout box installed, processor disconnected. • Connect Integrated Controller. • Jumper Test Pin 55 to Test Pin 40 or 60. • **Does fan continue to run?**	Yes ▶ No ▶	REMOVE breakout box. RECONNECT processor. REPLACE controller. RE-EVALUATE symptom. REMOVE breakout box. RECONNECT controller. REPLACE processor. RE-EVALUATE symptom.
X38 CHECK A/C PRESSURE SWITCH INPUT • Key off. • Disconnect vehicle harness at the A/C pressure switch. • Key on. • **Does fan still run?**	Yes ▶ No ▶	RECONNECT the vehicle harness connector to the A/C pressure switch. GO to X39 REPLACE the A/C pressure switch. RE-EVALUATE symptom.
X39 CHECK A/C PRESSURE SWITCH FOR SHORT TO GROUND • Key on. • Disconnect processor 60 pin connector. Inspect for damaged or pushed out pins, corrosion, loose wires. Service as necessary. • Install breakout box, leave processor disconnected. • Disconnect Integrated Controller. • DVOM on 200,000 ohm scale. • Measure resistance between Test Pin 2 and Test Pins 40, 46 and 60. • **Is resistance less than 10,000 ohms?**	Yes ▶ No ▶	SERVICE short circuit. REMOVE breakout box. RECONNECT the processor and the integrated controller. RE-EVALUATE the symptom. GO to X35 .

TEST STEP	RESULT ▶	ACTION TO TAKE
X33 CHECK FOR SHORTS TO POWER IN THE HEDF CIRCUIT • Key off. • Breakout box installed, processor disconnected. • Integrated Controller disconnected. • DVOM on 200,000 ohms scale. • Measure resistance between Test Pin 52 and Test Pin 37. • **Is resistance greater than 10,000 ohms?**	Yes ▶ No ▶	REMOVE breakout box. REPLACE Processor. RECONNECT all components. RERUN Quick Test. REMOVE breakout box. SERVICE short to power. RECONNECT all components. RERUN Quick Test. If code 83 is still present, REPLACE processor. RERUN Quick Test.
X35 LOW SPEED FAN ALWAYS "ON" • Key off. • Disconnect processor 60 pin connector. Inspect for damaged or pushed out pins, corrosion, loose wires. Service as necessary. • Install breakout box, leave processor disconnected. • Disconnect the Integrated Controller. • DVOM on 200 ohm scale. • Measure the resistance between Test Pin 55 and controller vehicle harness Pin 14. • **Is resistance less than 5 ohms?**	Yes ▶ No ▶	GO to X36 . REMOVE breakout box. SERVICE open in EDF circuit. RECONNECT all components. RE-EVALUATE symptom.
X36 CHECK EDF CIRCUIT FOR SHORTS TO POWER • Key off. • Breakout box installed, processor disconnected. • Processor and Integrated Controller disconnected. • DVOM on 200,000 ohm scale. • Measure resistance between Test Pin 55 and Test Pin 37 and between Test Pin 55 and battery positive post. • **Is resistance less than 10,000 ohms?**	Yes ▶ No ▶	SERVICE short to power in EDF circuit. GO to X37 . GO to X37 .

TEST STEP	RESULT ▶	ACTION TO TAKE
X40 CHECK FAN VOLTAGE • Key off. • Disconnect Integrated Controller. • DVOM on 20 volt scale. • Measure voltage between battery negative post and Pin 1 and Pin 2, (except 3.8L GO to pins 3 and 4) respectively at the Integrated Controller vehicle harness connector. • **Is voltage greater than 10.5 volts?**	Yes ▶ No ▶	GO to X41 . RECONNECT controller. SERVICE open in battery power circuit. RE-EVALUATE symptom.
X41 CHECK FAN MOTOR • Key off. • Integrated Controller disconnected. • Jumper Pin 1 to Pin 3 at Integrated Controller harness. • **Does fan run?**	Yes ▶ No ▶	GO to X42 . GO to X43 .
X42 CHECK FAN RUNNING MODE • Key off. • Disconnect processor. • Connect Integrated Controller. • Key on. • **Does fan run?**	Yes ▶ No ▶	GO to X46 . GO to X44 .
X43 MEASURE BATTERY VOLTAGE SUPPLY AT FAN — BYPASSING INTEGRATED CONTROLLER • Key off. • Disconnect cooling fan. • Integrated Controller disconnected. • Jumper Pin 1 to Pin 3 at Integrated Controller vehicle harness connector. • DVOM on 20 volt scale. • Measure voltage at cooling fan vehicle harness connector. • **Is voltage greater than 8.0 volts?**	Yes ▶ No ▶	RECONNECT all components. CHANGE fan. RE-EVALUATE symptom. GO to X45 .

7-150

1989 ENGINE COOLING SYSTEMS
Ford Motor Co. Electric Cooling Fans (Cont.)

TROUBLE SHOOTING CHARTS (Cont.)

TEST STEP	RESULT ▶	ACTION TO TAKE
X44 CHECK EDF CIRCUIT FOR SHORT TO GROUND • Key off. • Processor and controller disconnected. • DVOM on 200,000 ohm scale. • Measure resistance from Pin 14 to Pin 15 at Integrated Controller vehicle harness connector. • **Is resistance greater than 10,000 ohms?**	Yes No	REPLACE Integrated Controller. RECONNECT processor and controller. RE-EVALUATE symptom. SERVICE short to ground in EDF circuit. RECONNECT processor and Integrated Controller. RE-EVALUATE symptom.
X45 VERIFY COOLING FAN GROUND • Key off. • Cooling fan disconnected. • Integrated Controller disconnected. • Jumper Pin 1 to Pin 3 at Integrated Controller vehicle harness connector. • DVOM on 20 volt scale. • Measure voltage between voltage positive at cooling fan harness connector and negative battery post. • **Is voltage greater than 8.0 volts?**	Yes No	SERVICE open in ground circuit to fan. RECONNECT Integrated Controller, RE-EVALUATE symptom. SERVICE open in power-to-fan circuit from 3 and 4 of Integrated Controller harness connector to cooling fan connector. RECONNECT controller. RE-EVALUATE symptom.
X46 CHECK ECT SENSOR • Reconnect processor. • Check engine coolant level. • Warm engine to operating temperature before taking ECT resistance measurement. • Key off, wait 10 seconds. • Harness disconnected from ECT sensor. • DVOM on 200,000 ohm scale. • Measure resistance of the ECT sensor. • **Is the resistance reading between 1500 ohms and 2000 ohms?**	Yes No	REPLACE processor. RECONNECT harness to ECT sensor. RECONNECT Integrated Controller. RE-EVALUATE symptom. REPLACE ECT sensor. RECONNECT all components. RE-EVALUATE symptom.

TEST STEP	RESULT ▶	ACTION TO TAKE
X53 CHECK WAC OUTPUT FOR PROPER ELECTRICAL OPERATION • Key on, engine off. • A/C demand switch to A/C on position. • Breakout box installed, processor connected. • DVOM on 20 volt scale. • Connect DVOM positive test lead to Test Pin 37 and negative test lead to Test Pin 54. • While observing DVOM, depress and release the throttle several times. • **Does voltage output change?**	Yes No	GO to X54. GO to X57.
X54 CHECK FOR VOLTAGE AT A/C CLUTCH SWITCH • Key on, engine off. • A/C demand switch to A/C on position. • DVOM on 20 volt scale. • Breakout box installed, processor connected. • Integrated Controller connected. • Measure voltage between Test Pin 10 and Test Pin 40 at breakout box. • **Is voltage greater than 10.5 volts?**	Yes No	GO to X55. GO to X56.
X55 CHECK CONTINUITY OF ACCS TO INTEGRATED CONTROLLER • Key off, wait 10 seconds. • Breakout box installed. • Processor disconnected. • Integrated Controller disconnected. • DVOM on 200 ohm scale. • Measure resistance between Test Pin 10 at breakout box and Pin 21 at controller harness connector. • **Is resistance less than 5 ohms?**	Yes No	REMOVE breakout box. RECONNECT processor. REPLACE Integrated Controller. RE-EVALUATE symptom. REMOVE breakout box. RECONNECT all components. SERVICE open in ACCS circuit. RE-EVALUATE symptom.

TEST STEP	RESULT ▶	ACTION TO TAKE
X50 CHECK FOR VOLTAGE AT A/C CLUTCH • Key on, engine off. • A/C demand switch to A/C ON position. • Start engine. • DVOM on 20 volt scale. • Check voltage at A/C clutch harness connector. • **Is voltage greater than 10.5 volts?**	Yes No	CHECK A/C harness for short to voltage or defective A/C compressor clutch. GO to X51.
X51 CHECK FOR CONTINUITY FROM INTEGRATED CONTROLLER TO A/C CLUTCH • Key off. • Disconnect Integrated Controller. • DVOM on 200 ohm scale. • Measure resistance between Pin 23 of the controller harness and power side of the A/C clutch harness connector and between Pin 16 of the controller harness and ground side of the A/C clutch harness connector. • **Are both resistances less than 5 ohms?**	Yes No	GO to X52. SERVICE open in power to A/C clutch or ground to A/C clutch. RE-EVALUATE symptom.
X52 ENTER OUTPUT STATE CHECK (REFER TO QUICK TEST APPENDIX) **NOTE: Do not use STAR tester for this Step, use VOM/DVOM.** • Key off, wait 10 seconds. • Disconnect processor 60 pin connector. Inspect for damaged or pushed out pins, corrosion, loose wires, etc. Service as necessary. • Install breakout box and connect processor to breakout box. • DVOM on 20 volt scale. • Connect DVOM negative test lead to STO and positive test lead to battery positive. • Jumper STI to SIGNAL RETURN. • Perform Key On Engine Off Self-Test until the completion of the Continuous Test Codes. • DVOM will indicate zero volts. • Depress and release the throttle. • **Did DVOM reading change to a high voltage reading?**	Yes No	REMAIN in Output State Check. GO to X53. DEPRESS throttle to WOT and RELEASE. If STO voltage does not go high, GO to Pinpoint Test Step QC1. LEAVE equipment hooked up.

TEST STEP	RESULT ▶	ACTION TO TAKE
X56 CHECK CONTINUITY OF ACCS CIRCUIT • Key off, wait 10 seconds. • Breakout box installed, processor connected. • A/C demand switch to A/C ON position. • Integrated Controller connected. • DVOM on 200 ohm scale. • Measure resistance between Test Pin 10 and A/C demand switch. • **Is resistance less than 5 ohms?**	No Yes	SERVICE open in circuit. RERUN Quick Test. REMOVE breakout box. RECONNECT all components. EEC-IV system OK. CHECK wiring harness for damage or poor connections.
X57 CHECK CONTINUITY IN WAC TO INTEGRATED CONTROLLER CIRCUIT • Key off, wait 10 seconds. • Breakout box installed. • Disconnect processor. • Disconnect Integrated Controller. • DVOM on 200 ohm scale. • Measure resistance between Test Pin 54 and Pin 22 at Integrated Controller harness. • **Is resistance less than 50 ohms?**	No Yes	REMOVE breakout box. RECONNECT all components. SERVICE open in WAC circuit. RE-EVALUATE symptom. GO to X58.
X58 CHECK WAC CIRCUIT FOR SHORTS TO GROUND • Key off, wait 10 seconds. • Breakout box installed, processor disconnected. • Integrated Controller disconnected. • DVOM on 200,000 ohm scale. • Measure resistance between Test Pin 54 and Test Pin 40 and between Test Pin 54 and Test Pin 46 and between Test Pin 54 and battery negative post. • **Are all resistances greater than 10,000 ohms?**	Yes No	GO to X59. REMOVE breakout box. RECONNECT all components. SERVICE shorts to ground in WAC circuit. RE-EVALUATE symptom.

NOTE: See COMPUTERIZED ENGINE CONTROL section for Test Step QC1.

1989 ENGINE COOLING SYSTEMS
Ford Motor Co. Electric Cooling Fans (Cont.)

7-151

TROUBLE SHOOTING CHARTS (Cont.)

TEST STEP	RESULT ▶	ACTION TO TAKE
X59 CHECK WAC CIRCUIT FOR SHORTS TO POWER • Key off, wait 10 seconds. • Breakout box installed, processor disconnected. • Integrated Controller disconnected. • DVOM on 200,000 ohm scale. • Measure resistance between Test Pin 54 and Test Pin 37 and between Test Pin 54 and battery positive. • **Are both resistances greater than 10,000 ohms?**	Yes ▶ No ▶	GO to **X60** REMOVE breakout box. RECONNECT all components. SERVICE short to power in WAC circuit. GO to **X60**
X60 CHECK FOR VOLTAGE AT A/C CLUTCH • Key off, wait 10 seconds. • Breakout box installed, processor disconnected. • Connect Integrated Controller. • A/C clutch disconnected. • A/C demand switch to A/C ON position. • Key on, engine off. • Measure voltage at A/C clutch harness connection. • **Is voltage greater than 10.5 volts?**	Yes ▶ No ▶	REMOVE breakout box. RECONNECT all components. REPLACE processor. RE-EVALUATE symptom. REMOVE breakout box. RECONNECT all components. REPLACE Integrated Controller. RE-EVALUATE symptom.
X80 SERVICE CODE 88: CHECK EDF PROCESSOR SIGNAL TO INTEGRATED CONTROLLER FOR SHORTS TO GROUND **NOTE: If fan is always on with Code 88, GO to X82** • Key off. • Disconnect processor 60 pin connector. Inspect for damaged or pushed out pins, corrosion, and loose wires, etc. Service as necessary. • Install breakout box, leave processor disconnected. • Disconnect Integrated controller. • DVOM on 200,000 ohm scale. • Measure resistance between Test Pin 55 and Test Pin 40. • **Is resistance less than 10,000 ohms?**	Yes ▶ No ▶	SERVICE short to ground in EDF circuit. RECONNECT all components. RERUN Quick Test. GO to **X81**

TEST STEP	RESULT ▶	ACTION TO TAKE
X84 CHECK EDF SHORT TO GROUND • Key off. • Breakout box installed, processor disconnected. • Integrated controller connected. • Key on, engine off. • Jumper test Pin 55 to Test Pin 40 or 60. • **Does fan continue to run?**	Yes ▶ No ▶	REMOVE breakout box. REPLACE Integrated Controller. RECONNECT all components. RERUN Quick Test. REMOVE breakout box. REPLACE processor. RECONNECT all components. RERUN Quick Test.
X90 SERVICE CODE 95: CHECK INERTIA SWITCH Key On Engine Off Service Code 95 indicates that one of the following has occurred. — Open circuit in/or between the fuel pump and FPM circuit (see schematic) — Poor fuel pump ground — FUEL PUMP circuit short to power — Fuel pump relay contacts always closed • Key off, wait 10 seconds. • Locate and disconnect fuel pump inertia switch. • DVOM on 200 ohm scale. • Measure resistance of the fuel pump inertia switch. • **Is resistance less than 5.0 ohms?**	Yes ▶ No ▶	RECONNECT inertia switch. GO to **X91** REPLACE or RESET inertia switch. RERUN Quick Test.
X91 VERIFY THAT FUEL PUMP IS OFF • Key off. • Listen for motor noise from fuel pump. • **Is fuel pump off?**	Yes ▶ No ▶	GO to **X93** GO to **X92**

TEST STEP	RESULT ▶	ACTION TO TAKE
X81 CHECK FAN RUNNING MODE • Key off. • Breakout box installed, processor disconnected. • Connect integrated controller. • Key on, engine off. For 2.5L MTX ───▶ Does fan run? For 2.5L, 3.0L and 3.8L AXOD ───▶ Does fan run at low speed?	Yes ▶ No ▶	REMOVE breakout box. REPLACE processor. RECONNECT all components. RERUN Quick Test. REMOVE breakout box. REPLACE Integrated Controller. RECONNECT all components. RERUN Quick Test.
X82 FAN ALWAYS ON WITH CODE 88: CHECK EDF PROCESSOR SIGNAL TO INTEGRATED CONTROLLER FOR OPEN CIRCUIT • Key off. • Disconnect processor 60 pin connector. Inspect for damaged or pushed out pins, corrosion, and loose wires, etc. Service as necessary. • Install breakout box, leave processor disconnected. • Disconnect Integrated Controller. • DVOM on 200 ohm scale. • Measure resistance between Test Pin 55 and Integrated Controller harness Pin 14. • **Is resistance less than 5 ohms?**	Yes ▶ No ▶	GO to **X83** REMOVE breakout box. SERVICE open in EDF circuit. RECONNECT all components. RERUN Quick Test.
X83 CHECK EDF CIRCUIT FOR SHORTS TO POWER • Key off. • Breakout box installed, processor disconnected. • Integrated controller disconnected. • DVOM on 200,000 ohm scale. • Measure resistance between Test Pin 55 and Test Pin 37, and between Test Pin 55 and battery positive. • **Is resistance less than 10,000 ohms?**	Yes ▶ No ▶	SERVICE short to power in EDF circuit, then GO to **X84**. GO to **X84**

TEST STEP	RESULT ▶	ACTION TO TAKE
X92 CHECK FOR FUEL PUMP RELAY ALWAYS CLOSED • Key off. • Locate and disconnect integrated controller. • **Does fuel pump shut off when controller is disconnected?**	Yes ▶ No ▶	REPLACE Integrated Controller. RERUN Quick Test SERVICE short to power in POWER-TO-PUMP/FPM circuit. RECONNECT integrated controller. RERUN Quick Test.
X93 CHECK CONTINUITY OF FPM CIRCUIT • Key off. • Disconnect processor 60 pin connector. Inspect for damaged or pushed out pins, corrosion, loose wires, etc. Service as necessary. • Install breakout box, leave processor disconnected. • Disconnect integrated controller. • DVOM on 200 ohm scale. • Measure resistance between FPM circuit at the breakout box and integrated controller harness connector pin 5. • **Is resistance less than 5.0 ohms?**	Yes ▶ No ▶	GO to **X94** REMOVE breakout box. RECONNECT processor and integrated controller. SERVICE open circuit. RERUN Quick Test.
X94 CHECK FOR CONTINUITY BETWEEN FPM CIRCUIT AND GROUND • Key off. • Breakout box installed, processor disconnected. • Integrated controller disconnected. • DVOM on 200 ohm scale. • Measure resistance between FPM circuit at the breakout box and battery negative post. • **Is resistance less than 5.0 ohms?**	Yes ▶ No ▶	REMOVE breakout box. RECONNECT integrated controller. REPLACE processor. RERUN Quick Test. REMOVE breakout box. RECONNECT processor and integrated controller. CHECK electric Fuel Pump circuit for open or poor ground.

Courtesy of Ford Motor Co.

1989 CLUTCHES
Clutch Trouble Shooting

CONDITION	POSSIBLE CAUSE	CORRECTION
Chattering or Grabbing	Incorrect clutch adjustment	Adjust clutch
	Oil, grease or glaze on facings	Disassemble and clean or replace
	Loose "U" joint flange	See DRIVE AXLES
	Worn input shaft spline	Replace input shaft
	Binding pressure plate	Replace pressure plate
	Binding release lever	See CLUTCHES
	Binding clutch disc hub	Replace clutch disc
	Unequal pressure plate contact	Replace worn/misaligned components
	Loose/bent clutch disc	Replace clutch disc
	Incorrect transmission alignment	Realign transmission
	Worn pressure plate, disc or flywheel	Replace damaged components
	Broken or weak pressure springs	Replace pressure plate
	Sticking clutch pedal	Lubricate clutch pedal & linkage
	Incorrect clutch disc facing	Replace clutch disc
	Engine loose in chassis	Tighten all mounting bolts
Failure To Release	Oil or grease on clutch facings	Clean or replace clutch disc
	Incorrect release lever or pedal adjustment	See CLUTCHES
	Dust or dirt on clutch disc	Clean or replace
	Worn or broken clutch facings	Replace clutch disc
	Bent clutch disc or pressure plate	Replace damaged components
	Clutch disc hub binding on input shaft	Clean or replace clutch disc and/or input shaft
	Binding pilot bearing	Replace pilot bearing
	Sticking release bearing sleeve	Replace release bearing and/or sleeve
	Binding clutch cable	See CLUTCHES
	Defective clutch master cylinder	Replace master cylinder
	Defective clutch slave cylinder	Replace slave cylinder
	Air in hydraulic system	Bleed hydraulic system
Rattling	Weak or broken release lever spring	Replace spring and check alignment
	Damaged pressure plate	Replace pressure plate
	Broken clutch return spring	Replace return spring
	Worn splines on clutch disc or input shaft	Replace clutch disc and/or input shaft
	Worn clutch release bearing	Replace release bearing
	Dry or worn pilot bearing	Lubricate or replace pilot bearing
	Unequal release lever contact	Align or replace release lever
	Incorrect pedal free play	Adjust free play
	Warped or damaged clutch disc	Replace damaged components
Slipping	Pressure springs worn or broken	Replace pressure plate
	Oily, greasy or worn clutch facings,	Clean or replace clutch disc
	Incorrect clutch alignment	Realign clutch assembly
	Warped clutch disc or pressure plate	Replace damaged components
	Binding release levers or clutch pedal	Lubricate and/or replace release components
Squeaking	Worn or damaged release bearing	Replace release bearing
	Dry or worn pilot or release bearing	Lubricate or replace bearing assembly
	Pilot bearing turning in crankshaft	Replace pilot bearing and/or crankshaft
	Worn input shaft bearing	Replace bearing and seal
	Incorrect transmission alignment	Realign transmission
	Dry release fork between pivot	Lubricate release fork and pivot
Heavy and/or Stiff Pedal	Sticking release bearing sleeve	Replace release bearing and/or sleeve
	Dry or binding clutch pedal hub	Lubricate and align components
	Floor mat interference with pedal	Lay mat flat in proper area
	Dry or binding ball/fork pivots	Lubricate and align components
	Faulty clutch cable	Replace clutch cable
Noisy Clutch Pedal	Faulty interlock switch	Replace interlock switch
	Self-adjuster ratchet noise	Lubricate or replace self-adjuster
	Speed control interlock switch	Lubricate or replace interlock switch

CONDITION	POSSIBLE CAUSE	CORRECTION
Clutch Pedal Sticks Down	Binding clutch cable	See CLUTCHES
	Springs weak in pressure plate	Replace pressure plate
	Binding in clutch linkage	Lubricate and free linkage
Noisy	Dry release bearing	Lubricate or replace release bearing
	Dry or worn pilot bearing	Lubricate or replace bearing
	Worn input shaft bearing	Replace bearing
Transmission Click	Weak springs in pressure plate	Replace pressure plate
	Release fork loose on ball stud	Replace release fork and/or ball stud
	Oil on clutch disc damper	Replace clutch disc
	Broken spring in slave cylinder	Replace slave cylinder

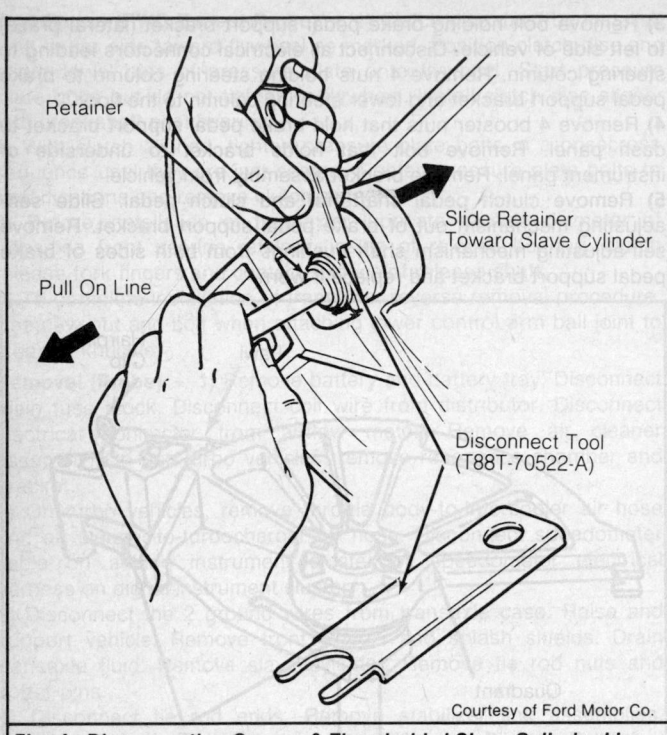

Fig. 4: Disconnecting Cougar & Thunderbird Slave Cylinder Line

Courtesy of Ford Motor Co.

MASTER CYLINDER

Removal & Installation (Thunderbird) – 1) Disconnect hydraulic lines from master cylinder. Remove 2 push pins retaining master cylinder reservoir to left front shock tower. Disconnect clutch pedal from pushrod.

2) Rotate master cylinder 45 degrees counterclockwise. Carefully pull master cylinder through firewall. To install, reverse removal procedure.

Removal & Installation (Probe) – Disconnect clutch master cylinder hydraulic line. Remove clutch master cylinder mounting bolts. Remove master cylinder. To install, reverse removal procedure.

CLUTCH PILOT BEARING

Removal – Remove transmission or transaxle, pressure plate and clutch disc. Pull pilot bearing from crankshaft using proper puller.

Installation – 1) Ensure that crankshaft pilot bore is clean and free from nicks or burrs. Lightly coat pilot bearing bore of crankshaft with Lubricant (C1AZ-19590-B).

2) On 2.3L, install pilot bearing (with seal end toward transmission) using Clutch Aligner (T71P-7137-H) and Pilot Bearing Installer (T71P-7137-C). Carefully tap pilot bearing squarely into bore until flush with flywheel. See Fig. 5.

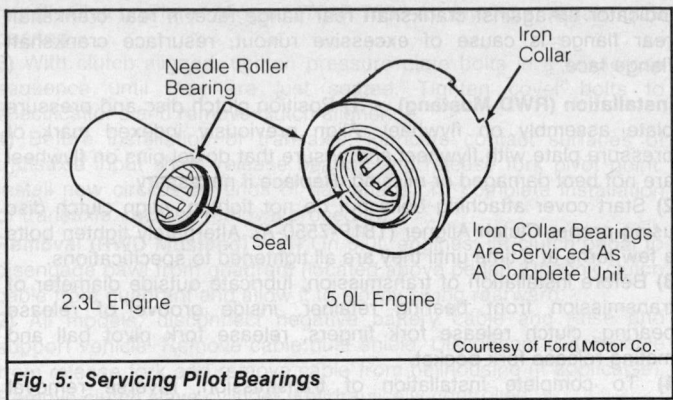

Fig. 5: Servicing Pilot Bearings

Courtesy of Ford Motor Co.

3) On 5.0L, install pilot bearing using Pilot Bearing Installer (T81P-7120-B). Carefully tap pilot bearing squarely into bore until flush with flywheel. Check that needle bearings are not damaged or repositioned in collar.

4) On Probe, install pilot bearing using proper driver so surface of pilot bearing facing transaxle is .150-.165" (3.8-4.2 mm) below surface of crankshaft flange.

NOTE: Care must be taken when installing transmission, so that input shaft does not damage bearing.

TIGHTENING SPECIFICATIONS

Application	Ft. Lbs. (N.m)
FWD Except Probe	
Bellhousing-to-Engine Bolts	28-38 (38-52)
Bracket-to-Clutch Pedal Bolts	25-30 (34-40)
Flywheel-to-Crankshaft Bolts	59-69 (80-94)
Pedal-to-Support Bracket Nuts	15-25 (20-34)
Pressure Plate-to-Flywheel Bolts	12-24 (16-33)
Release Fork Bolt	30-40 (40-55)
Probe	
Crossmember Bolts	27-40 (37-55)
Crossmember Nuts	55-69 (75-94)
Extension Bar-to-Transaxle	23-34 (31-46)
Flywheel-to-Crankshaft Bolts	71-75 (96-102)
Gusset Plate-to-Transaxle Bolts	27-38 (37-52)
Pressure Plate-to-Flywheel Bolts	13-20 (18-27)
RWD (Mustang)	
2.3L	
Bellhousing-to-Engine Bolts	28-38 (38-52)
Flywheel-to-Crankshaft Bolts	56-64 (76-87)
Pressure Plate-to-Flywheel Bolts	12-24 (16-33)
5.0L	
Bellhousing-to-Engine Bolts	38-55 (52-75)
Clutch Pedal Attaching Nuts	17-26 (23-36)
Flywheel-to-Crankshaft Bolts	75-85 (102-116)
Pressure Plate-to-Flywheel Bolts	12-24 (16-33)
Steering Column Attaching Nut	20-37 (27-50)
Support Bracket-to-Dash Panel Bolt	13-25 (18-34)

Section 9

DRIVE AXLES

CONTENTS

TROUBLE SHOOTING   **Page**

Drive Axle Trouble Shooting
RWD Vehicles 9-2
FWD Vehicles 9-3
Drive Axle Gear Tooth Patterns
All Models 9-4

DRIVE AXLES

Chrysler Motors RWD
7 1/4" & 8 1/4" Ring Gear 9-5
Ford Motor Co.
All-Wheel Drive Rear Axle 9-9
RWD 7 1/2" & 8 3/4" Ring Gear 9-13

POSITIVE TRACTION DIFFERENTIALS

Cone Brake Type
Chrysler Motors RWD 9-17
Clutch Pack Type
Ford Motor Co. RWD 9-18

PROPELLER SHAFT ALIGNMENT

Chrysler Motors
RWD Models 9-20
Ford Motor Co.
RWD Models 9-21

UNIVERSAL JOINTS

All Models 9-24

FWD AXLE SHAFTS

Chrysler Motors 9-25
Eagle 9-31
Ford Motor Co. 9-32

NOTE: ALSO SEE GENERAL INDEX

1989 DRIVE AXLES
Trouble Shooting RWD Vehicles

CONDITION	POSSIBLE CAUSE	CORRECTION
General Knocking or Clunking	Excessive differential side gear clearance	See OVERHAUL in DRIVE AXLES
	Worn axle pinion shaft or shaft bore	See OVERHAUL in DRIVE AXLES
	Excessive end play of axle shafts-to-axle pinion shaft	See OVERHAUL in DRIVE AXLES
	Damaged gear teeth	See OVERHAUL in DRIVE AXLES
	Improper axle shaft spline fit	See OVERHAUL in DRIVE AXLES
	Excessive total axle backlash	See OVERHAUL in DRIVE AXLES
	Incorrect driveline angle	See PROPELLER SHAFT ALIGNMENT
Clunking During Initial Engagement	Excessive differential side gear clearance	See OVERHAUL in DRIVE AXLES
	Excessive ring and pinion backlash	See OVERHAUL in DRIVE AXLES
	Worn or loose pinion shaft	See OVERHAUL in DRIVE AXLES
Gear Howl or Whine	Excessive pinion bearing wear	See OVERHAUL in DRIVE AXLES
	Incorrect pinion depth	See OVERHAUL in DRIVE AXLES
	Incorrect ring gear backlash	See OVERHAUL in DRIVE AXLES
	Excessive ring gear runout	See OVERHAUL in DRIVE AXLES
	Incorrect bearing preload	See OVERHAUL in DRIVE AXLES
Clicking or Chatter on Turns	Wrong lubricant in differential	Drain and fill with proper lubricant
	Clutch plates worn	See LUBRICATION in POSITIVE TRACTION DIFFERENTIALS
	Differential side gears or pinion worn	See OVERHAUL in DRIVE AXLES
Grunt Noise on Stops	Lack of lubricant in propeller shaft slip yoke	See UNIVERSAL JOINTS
Groan in Forward or Reverse	Wrong lubricant in differential	Drain and fill with proper lubricant
Knock in Driveline at Low Speed	Worn or damaged universal joints	See UNIVERSAL JOINTS
	Side gear hub bore in differential oversize	See OVERHAUL in DRIVE AXLES
Snap or Click in Driveline	Loose upper or lower control arm bushing bolts	See REAR SUSPENSION
	Loose companion flange	See OVERHAUL in DRIVE AXLES
Scraping Noise	Slinger, companion flange or yoke rubbing axle carrier	See OVERHAUL in DRIVE AXLES
Car Will Not Move	Broken axle shaft	See OVERHAUL in DRIVE AXLES
	Broken pinion stem	See OVERHAUL in DRIVE AXLES
	Axle lock-up	See OVERHAUL in DRIVE AXLES
	Broken gear teeth	See OVERHAUL in DRIVE AXLES
Axle Backlash	Excessive ring and pinion clearance	See OVERHAUL in DRIVE AXLES
	Loose fitting differential pinion shaft	See OVERHAUL in DRIVE AXLES
	Excessive side gear-to-case clearance	See OVERHAUL in DRIVE AXLES
Leakage at Differential or Propeller Shaft	Rough outside surface on splined yoke	See OVERHAUL in DRIVE AXLES
	Worn drive pinion seal	See OVERHAUL in DRIVE AXLES
	Worn cover gasket, or axle shaft seal	See OVERHAUL in DRIVE AXLES

CONDITION	POSSIBLE CAUSE	CORRECTION
Roughness, Shudder or Vibration Upon Heavy Acceleration	Double cardan joint ball seats or ball set spring worn or broken	See UNIVERSAL JOINTS
	Incorrect propeller shaft angle	See PROPELLER SHAFT ALIGNMENT
	Worn or damaged universal joints	See UNIVERSAL JOINTS
Roughness, Vibration or Body Boom Experienced at Any Speed	Rough rear wheel bearings	See OVERHAUL in DRIVE AXLES
	Unbalanced or damaged propeller shaft	Check and/or balance propeller shaft
	Unbalanced or damaged tires	Check and/or balance tires
	Worn or damaged universal joints	See UNIVERSAL JOINTS
	Damaged propeller shaft, or undercoating on propeller shaft	Check propeller shaft, repair as necessary
	Tight universal joints	Lubricate or replace as necessary
	Burrs or gouges on companion flange	Resurface or replace flange
	Propeller shaft or companion shaft runout too great	Repair or replace as necessary
	Excessive looseness at slip yoke spline	See OVERHAUL in DRIVE AXLES

Trouble Shooting FWD Vehicles

CONDITION	POSSIBLE CAUSE	CORRECTION
Grease Leaks	Joint boot torn, split or cracked	See DISASSEMBLY in FWD AXLES SHAFTS
Clicking Noise on Cornering	Damaged or worn outboard joint	See DISASSEMBLY in FWD AXLES SHAFTS
Clunk Noise on Acceleration	Damaged or worn inboard joints	See DISASSEMBLY in FWD AXLES SHAFTS
	Transaxle gears or bearings	
Vibration or Shudder on Acceleration	Sticking, damaged or worn joints	See DISASSEMBLY in FWD AXLES SHAFTS
	Excessive alignment or spring height	
Squealing or Humming	Insufficient or ImproperJoint Lubrication	See DISASSEMBLY in FWD AXLES SHAFTS
	Defective wheel bearing	See HUB & BEARING ASSEMBLY in FWD AXLES SHAFTS

REMOVAL & INSTALLATION

REAR DIFFERENTIAL ASSEMBLY

NOTE: Remove rear axle assembly and place on work bench to perform all repairs.

Removal – 1) Raise and support vehicle. Position a jack under axle assembly. Remove exhaust system from catalytic converter back. Mark drive shaft-to-yoke flanges for reassembly. Remove rear "U" joint bolts retaining drive shaft. Lower drive shaft. Remove torque tube support bracket mounting bolts. Remove damper and position drive shaft out of way.

2) Remove left and center axle support mounting bolts. Lower differential assembly enough to remove bolts retaining inner axle shafts. Remove both axle shafts from differential and support with wire. Lower and remove differential.

CAUTION: Apply Loctite 242 (Ford specification E0AZ-14554-A) to all removed "U" joint bolts before being reused.

Installation – Position differential under vehicle and raise enough to connect axle shafts. Attach axle shafts. To complete installation, reverse removal procedure. Tighten all bolts/nuts to specifications. Fill differential with specified lubricant.

AXLE SHAFTS

Removal & Installation – Remove rear suspension control arm bolt. Index inner and outer axle shaft-to-yoke. Remove "U" joint bolts. Slide axle shafts together and remove axle shaft. To install, reverse removal procedure. Ensure larger diameter shaft is installed inboard. Tighten bolts/nuts to specification.

OVERHAUL

AXLE SHAFTS

Disassembly – 1) Remove axle shaft to be repaired and place on work bench. See AXLE SHAFTS under REMOVAL & INSTALLATION in this article. Cut and remove boot clamps. Mark axle shaft at splined joint before separating. Carefully separate axle shaft.
2) Remove and discard "U" joint snap rings. Using "U" Joint Remover (T74P-4635-C), remove bearings from yoke.

Reassembly – 1) Fill boot with approximately 10 grams of Multi-purpose Long-Life Lubricant (C1AZ-19590-B). Coat splines with same lubricant. Install new original equipment clamps and boot on shaft with external splines. Carefully install axle shafts. Ensure splines are properly aligned. Do not force shafts together.
2) Remove excess grease and air pressure from boot and slip yoke. Install clamps on boot and retain with Clamp Pliers (T63P-9171-A). To complete installation, reverse disassembly procedure.

REAR DIFFERENTIAL ASSEMBLY

Disassembly – 1) Remove differential. See REAR DIFFERENTIAL ASSEMBLY under REMOVAL & INSTALLATION in this article. Place differential assembly on work bench. Remove protective shield (boot) from torque tube and differential. Remove 4 Allen head bolts retaining torque tube to differential and remove torque tube.
2) Remove 2 mounting bolts retaining support bracket to torque tube. Pull input shaft from torque tube and place shaft in a vise with protected jaws. Remove adapter sleeve snap ring. Position shaft vertically in vise. Remove adapter sleeve.
3) Use a 2 jaw-type puller and remove splined coupling from shaft. Remove splined coupling "O" ring. Remove sleeve spring snap ring. Remove sleeve spring, flatwasher and adapter sleeve retaining ring. *See Fig. 1.*
4) Place yoke side of input shaft in vise. Remove snap ring retaining bearing to shaft. Use a press and remove bearing and bracket from shaft. Replace bracket if it is bent or damaged. Remove seal from torque tube with a 3 jaw-type puller and discard seal.
5) Remove differential housing cover bolts. Remove cover and drain lubricant. Remove both side gear snap rings and remove both inner

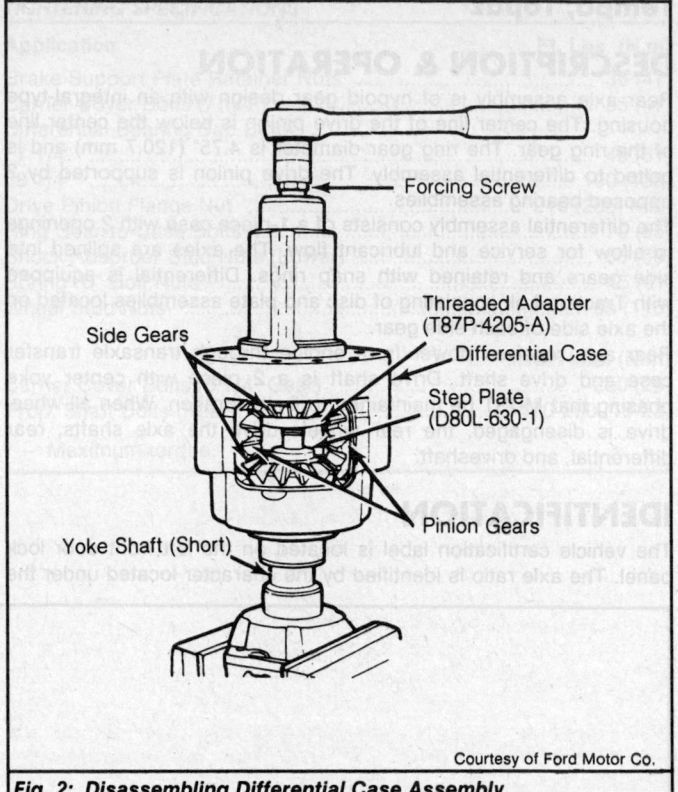

Courtesy of Ford Motor Co.

Fig. 2: Disassembling Differential Case Assembly

yoke shafts. Use a 3 jaw-type puller and slide hammer to remove RH yoke shaft bearing and seal from right yoke bore in differential housing. Remove left side yoke shaft seal.
6) Remove 4 bolts from bearing retaining cap on left side of differential. Remove bearing retaining cap and discard "O" ring. Remove differential case assembly from differential housing. Use a 2 jaw-type puller and remove side bearings. Tag bearings and shims for reassembly.
7) Remove ring gear retaining bolts. Alternately tap sides of ring gear free from case. Place differential case on short yolk shaft and mount yolk end in vise. Remove roll pin retaining pinion gear shaft to case. Remove pinion gear shaft from roll pin side of case.
8) Remove differential case from short yolk shaft and place on bench with short yolk shaft side down. Place Step Plate (D80L-630-1) in center of lower side gear. Install forcing screw through long yoke shaft bore. Place Threaded Adapter (T87P-4205-A) between step plate and upper side gear. *See Fig. 2.* Thread forcing screw into adapter.
9) Remount differential case on short yoke shaft in vise. Tighten forcing screw until pinion gears become loose. Use feeler gauge and push pinion gear thrust washers from differential case. Do not mix thrust washers and pinion gears. Rotate differential case until pinion gears can be removed. Remove pinion gears.
10) Remove differential case from short yoke shaft. Remove tooling. Remove one side gear at a time using care not to drop clutch pack. DO NOT mix components.
11) Remove and discard drive pinion adapter "O" ring at drive pinion. Remove staked portion on pinion nut and remove nut. Tap drive pinion with soft hammer and remove drive pinion. Retain preload spacer and shim(s) for reassembly. Remove outer drive pinion bearing. Press inner bearing from drive pinion and retain any shim(s).
12) Remove inner and outer drive pinion bearing races and side bearing races with 3 jaw-type puller and slide hammer. Remove left and center support bushing from axle housing (if replacing), with a "C" clamp and appropriate adapter.

Inspection – 1) Thoroughly clean components with clean solvent (except clutch pack). Inspect all bearings and races for pitting, scoring and damage. Inspect ring gear and drive pinion for tooth

1989 DRIVE AXLES
Ford Motor Co. All-Wheel Drive Rear Axle (Cont.)

9-11

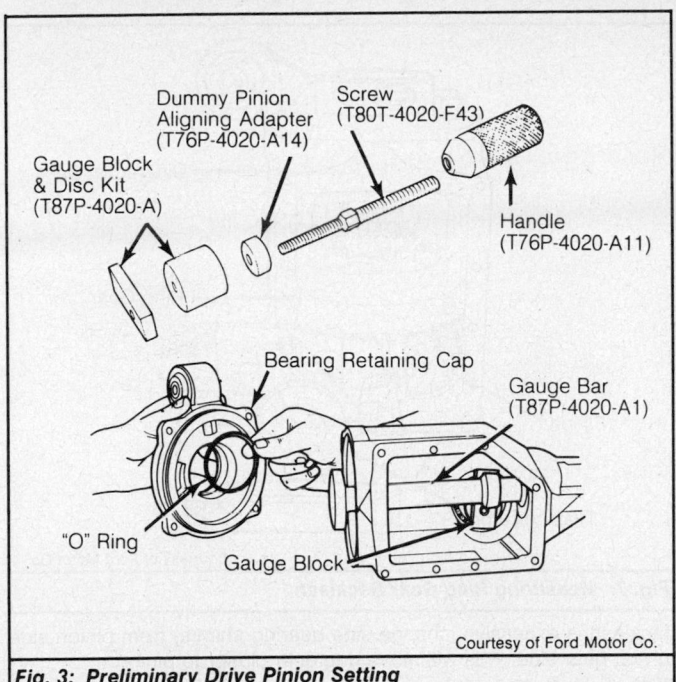

Fig. 3: Preliminary Drive Pinion Setting

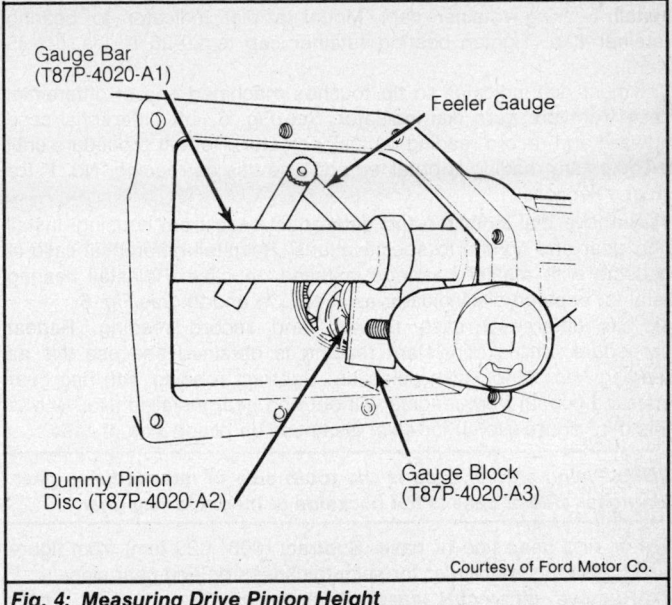

Fig. 4: Measuring Drive Pinion Height

contact pattern, cracks or damage. Replace ring and drive pinion as a set only.

2) Check differential case for cracks and damage. Ensure pinion gear thrust washer surface of case is not damaged. Inspect pinion gears, side gears and pinion gear shaft for wear or damage. Inspect clutch pack for wear or burnt surfaces.

3) Inspect axle housing for cracks and damage. Check for metal or contamination in bottom of axle housing. Inspect axle shaft for wear and damage. Check boots for cracks or splits. Replace defective components as necessary.

Reassembly – 1) Lubricate clutch pack with Friction Modifier Additive (C8AZ-19B546-A). Reassemble left side gear and clutch pack. With short shaft side of differential case facing up, install left side gear assembly with retainers aligned with differential case.

2) Hold left hand side gear in place and turn differential case over. Reassemble and install right side gear as stated in step **1)**. Ensure retainers are aligned with differential case. Install tooling used during disassembly. *See Fig. 2.* Place differential case on short yoke shaft and tighten forcing-screw slightly.

3) Place differential pinion gears and thrust washers in position in opening of case. Ensure gears are 180 degrees apart so they correctly align with pinion shaft bore. Ensure pinion gears are in proper mesh with side gears. Rotate differential case until pinion gears are aligned with shaft bore.

4) With differential pinion gears installed, tighten forcing screw until side gears become loose. Lubricate and install pinion gear thrust washers. Ensure washers line up with holes and remove tooling. Install pinion gear shaft and roll pin. DO NOT install ring gear at this time. Set differential case aside.

Drive Pinion Height – 1) Place differential housing on bench. Install both drive pinion bearing races in case. From Gauge Block and Disc Kit (T87P-4020-A), install Gauge Disc (T87P-4020-A2), Handle (T76P-4020-A11), Screw (T80T-4020-F43), and Dummy Pinion Aligning Adapter (T76P-4020-A14) into drive pinion bearing bore. *See Fig. 3.*

2) Install Gauge Block (T87P-4020-A3) from kit, into long yoke shaft bearing bore. Install "O" ring from kit into bearing retaining cap bore and install cap on differential housing. Tighten retaining cap. Use feeler gauges to determine the clearance between gauge block and gauge bar shoulder. This is the base reading.

3) Examine drive pinion for etched marking (+) or (-) followed by a single digit number. This number represents thousandths of an inch (+3 = .003" or -5 = .005). HOWEVER, in using this number to

modify the base reading, REVERSE the indicated sign to subtract a positive number from the base reading or add a negative number.

An example: If your base reading is .008 and the drive pinion is etched -5, convert -5 to +.005 and add this to your base reading for an adjusted reading of .013. This adjusted reading is the shim thickness required between drive pinion and inner pinion bearing. This is the preliminary drive pinion height setting.

4) Mount shim and bearing on drive pinion shaft and press into place. Install preload spacer, preload shims and "O" ring on shaft. Install assembly into differential housing. Install drive pinion outer bearing. Install and tighten pinion nut, but do not stake at this time.

Pinion Rotation Torque – Use an INCH lb. torque wrench and measure pinion rotation torque. Rotation torque should be 15-35 INCH lbs. (1.7-4 N.m) with NEW bearings. If not within specifications, add or remove preload shims. When differential case assembly is installed (with NEW bearings) in differential housing the rotational torque specification increases to 19-42 INCH lbs. (2.2-4.8 N.m). If not within specifications, add or remove preload shims.

Assembled Pinion Drive Check – From Gauge Block and Disc Kit (T87P-4020-A), install Gauge Bar (T87P-4020-A1), in differential housing and Dummy Pinion Gauge Disc (T87P-4020-A2) between gauge bar and button on drive pinion. *See Fig. 4.* Using feeler gauges, determine clearance. The clearance should be .018" to .022". Use thicker or thinner shim installed in preliminary drive pinion height setting to obtain this clearance. With rotation torque at specifications, stake pinion nut.

Side Bearing End Play – 1) Install Master Bearings (T87P-4222-A) on differential case. *See Fig. 5.* Place differential housing in a vise with bearing retainer cap upward. Install differential case in housing.

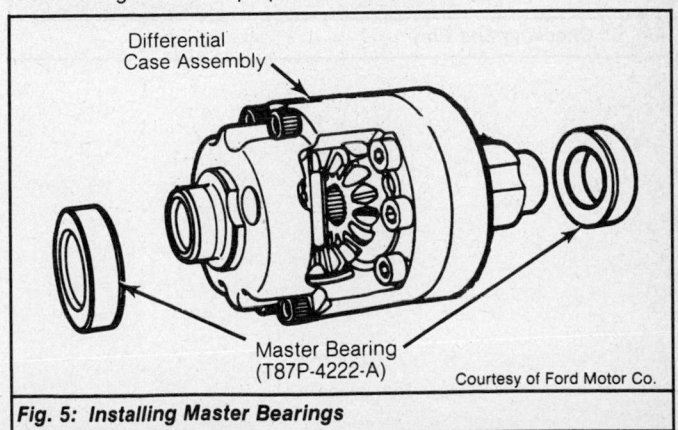

Fig. 5: Installing Master Bearings

9-12

1989 DRIVE AXLES
Ford Motor Co. All-Wheel Drive Rear Axle (Cont.)

Install bearing retainer cap. Mount a dial indicator to bearing retainer cap. Tighten bearing retainer cap to 20-26 ft. lbs. (27-35 N.m).

2) Adjust dial indicator so tip touches machined end of differential case trunnion. Zero dial indicator. *See Fig. 6.* Lift differential case upward and record reading on dial indicator. Repeat procedure until a consistant reading is obtained and use this as reading "No. 1" for shim selection.

3) Remove dial indicator and differential case from housing. Install ring gear and tighten to specifications. Reinstall differential case in housing with master bearings installed on case. Reinstall bearing retainer cap and dial indicator as in step 1) and 2). *See Fig. 6.*

4) Lift differential case upward and record reading. Repeat procedure until a consistant reading is obtained and use this as reading "No. 2" for shim selection. Subtract reading with ring gear installed (No. 2) from reading without ring gear installed (No. 1). Use this third figure (No. 3) for shim thickness on pinion side of case.

NOTE: *Pinion side of case is the tooth side of mounted ring gear. Ring gear side of case is the backside of mounted ring gear.*

5) For ring gear side of case. Subtract .008" (.20 mm) from figure No. 3. Use this remainder for shim thickness on ring gear side.

6) Remove differential case. Remove master bearings. Install selected shim(s) to proper side and install side bearings with an appropriate size driver. Install side bearing race in bearing retainer cap with appropriate size driver. Thoroughly lubricate bearings and races.

Ring Gear Backlash – 1) Install differential case assembly in housing. Install and tighten bearing retainer cap. Mount a dial indicator and measure ring gear backlash at 3 equally spaced points. *See Fig. 7.* Backlash should be .004-.006" (.10-.15 mm). If

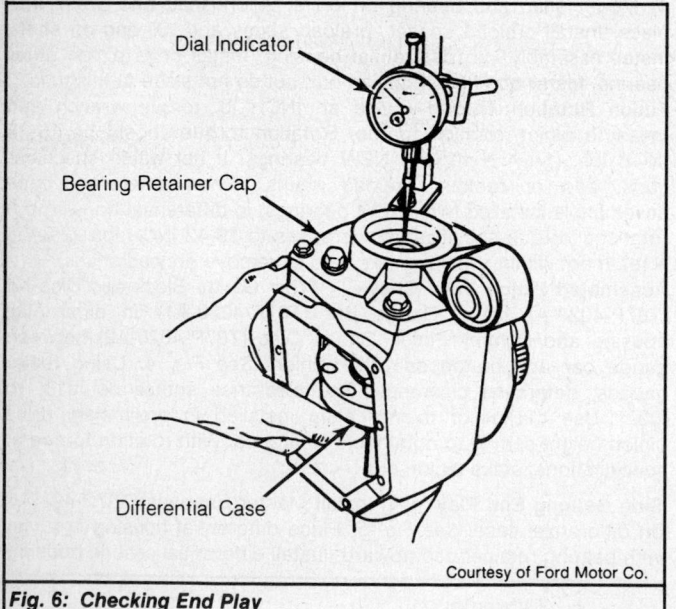

Fig. 6: *Checking End Play*

Dial Indicator
Bearing Retainer Cap
Differential Case
Courtesy of Ford Motor Co.

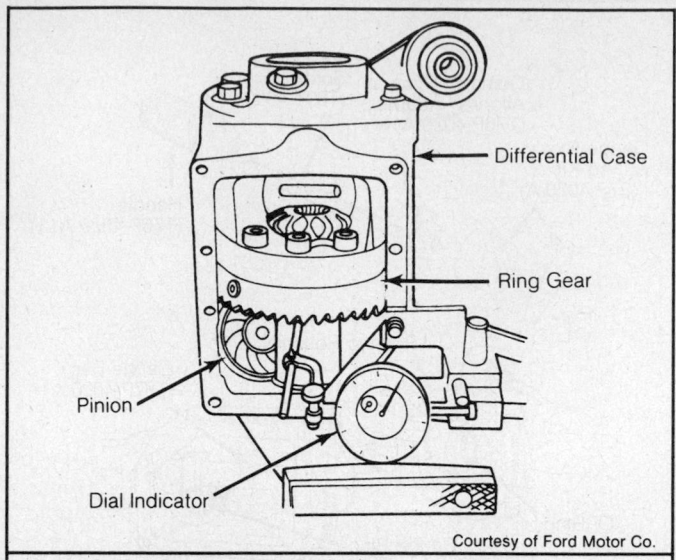

Differential Case
Ring Gear
Pinion
Dial Indicator
Courtesy of Ford Motor Co.

Fig. 7: *Measuring Ring Gear Backlash*

backlash is excessive, change side bearing shim(s) from pinion side to ring gear side. This will move ring gear closer to pinion.

2) If backlash is less than specifications, change shim(s) from ring gear side to pinion side. This will move ring gear away from pinion. With backlash within specifications, check total pinion rotating torque. Pinion rotating torque with case assembly installed should be 19-42 INCH lbs. (2.2-4.8 N.m).

Final Assembly – With backlash and pinion rotating torque within specification, complete reassembly by reversing disassembly procedure. Install axle shaft bearings in differential housing with name on bearing facing axle shaft (outboard side). Ensure to align all matching marks made at disassembly. Tighten all bolts/nuts to specifications. Fill differential assembly with specified lubricant.

TIGHTENING SPECIFICATION

Application	Ft. Lbs. (N.m)
Bearing Retainer Cap Bolt	20-26 (27-35)
Differential Cover Bolt	7-12 (9-16)
Differential Housing Support Bolt	70-80 (95-108)
Drive Shaft-to-Torque Tube Bolt	15-17 (21-23)
Pinion Nut	180-210 (244-285)
Ring Gear Mounting Bolt	29-37 (39-50)
Torque Tube-to-Housing Bolt	40-50 (54-68)
Torque Tube-to- Mounting Bracket Bolt	45-50 (61-68)
Torque Tube Mounting Bracket-to- Crossmember Bolt	45-50 (61-68)
Torque Tube Support Bearing Bolt	23-30 (31-41)
"U" Joint Retaining Bolt	15-17 (21-23)

Ford

(T79P-4020-A)
PINION DEPTH
2) Install new
cups must be
gauge will not f
3) Install neces
Press inner be
against shims.
pinion in axle
pinion bearing.
4) Check that a
Seal Installer (
cocked during
lips with multi-p
5) Check pinic
companion flan
marks on comp
companion flar
lubricant. Install
6) Using Compa
flange and gra
TIONS table a
flange or install
bearing preload
ASSEMBLY SP

**NOTE: If desire
must be install
obtained.**

7) Lubricate all
thrust washers
washers exactly
and mesh with s
8) Install ring g
threads and tigh
at end of articl
proper sized s
differential case
9) Once proper
backlash and
installed. See D
BACKLASH und
10) Install differ
Install bearing
TIGHTENING S
11) Check ring
GEAR TOOTH
tooth contact p
gauge is used a
backlash may
pattern.
12) Once all ad
cover, brake d
reference mark
lubricant.

ADJUSTM

PINION DE

1) Assemble P
adapter, gauge
mm) for 8 3/4"
bearing over alig
2) Install front
handle onto scr
4. Make sure pi
tightened.

RWD Models

DESCRIPTION

The rear axle is a hypoid design, ring and pinion gear encased in an integral cast iron housing. Differential case and pinion assembly are mounted in axle housing using tapered bearings assemblies. A one piece differential case contains a conventional 2-pinion differential assembly. Semi-floating axle shafts are retained by "C" locks at splined end of axle shafts.

AXLE RATIO & IDENTIFICATION

A metal tag stamped with axle model, date of manufacture, gear ratio, ring gear diameter and assembly plant is mounted under housing cover-to-carrier cap screw. See Fig. 1. Using axle model code, gear ratio may be determined. See AXLE RATIO IDENTIFICATION table.
Ford Motor Co. Vehicle Certification Label attached to left front door lock panel or pillar post also contains axle identification code. From this label, axle identification code can be found in the column marked "AX". Using axle identification code, axle ratio may be determined.

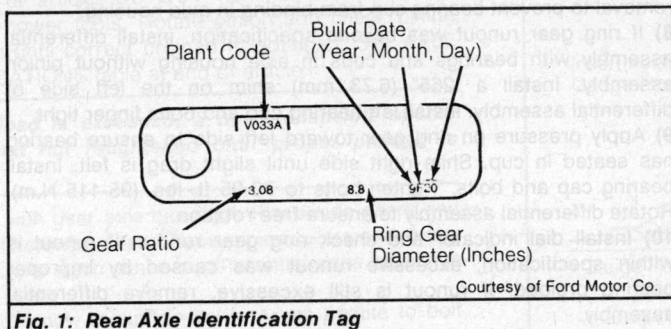

Fig. 1: Rear Axle Identification Tag
Courtesy of Ford Motor Co.

AXLE RATIO IDENTIFICATION

Ratio	Code
7 1/2" Axle	
3.08:1	462-B & 479-B
3.45:1	281-D
3.73:1	266-D
8 3/4" Axle	
2.73:1	030-B, 012-B
3.08:1	014-B, 014-C, 404-F & 033-B
3.27:1	016-B, 016-C, 424-F & 038-B

REMOVAL & INSTALLATION

AXLE SHAFTS & BEARINGS

Removal – 1) Raise and support vehicle. Remove wheels and brake drums. Remove housing cover and drain lubricant. Remove differential pinion shaft lock bolt and pinion shaft.
2) Remove wheel speed sensor to prevent damage during axle shaft removal (if equipped). Push axle toward center and remove "C" locks. Remove axles. Use care not to damage axle seal. Using a slide hammer and puller, remove bearing and seal as a unit.
Installation – 1) Lubricate bearing with rear axle lubricant. Install wheel bearing and seal into axle housing using proper sized driver. Check that seal was not damaged during installation. Lubricate seal lips with multi-purpose lubricant. If seal becomes cocked during installation, remove and replace with a new one.
2) On 8 3/4" ring gears, install "O" ring on splined end of axle shaft. Install axle shaft in axle housing, using care not to damage oil seal. Install "C" locks on axle shafts. Pull shafts outboard to seat locks in counterbore of differential side gears.

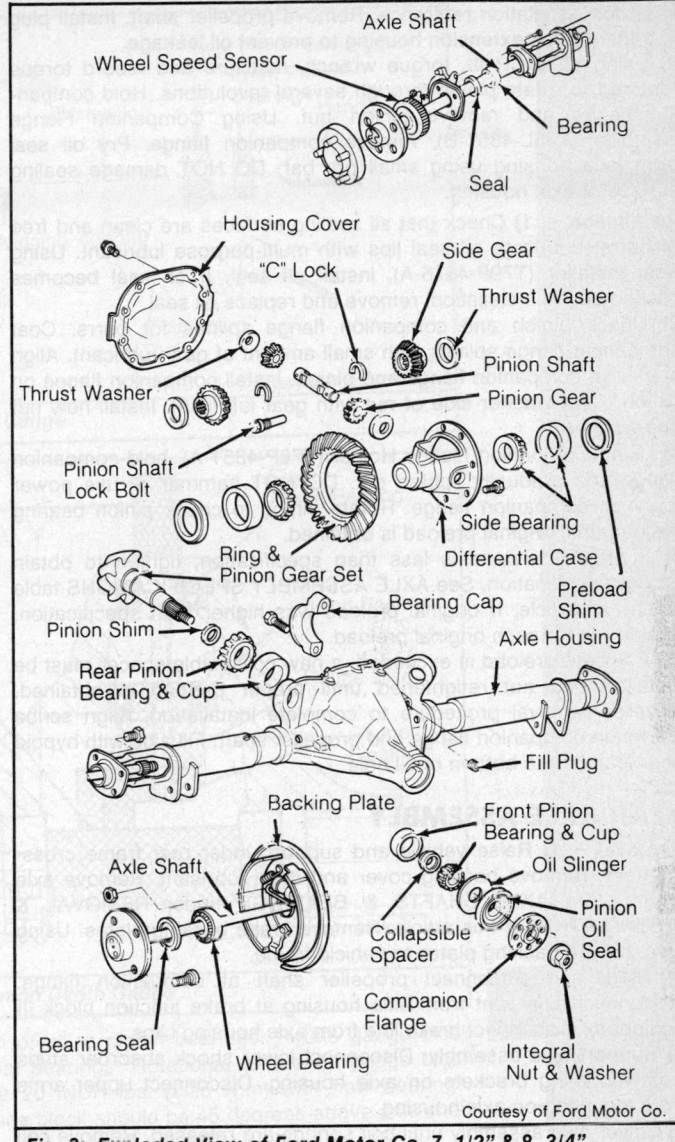

Fig. 2: Exploded View of Ford Motor Co. 7 1/2" & 8 3/4" Integral Housing Axle Assembly
Courtesy of Ford Motor Co.

3) Install pinion shaft and lock bolt and tighten to specification. See TIGHTENING SPECIFICATIONS table at end of article. Check that housing cover sealing surfaces are clean and free of burrs. Apply 1/8-3/16" bead of Silicone Sealer (D6AZ-19562-B) to face of axle housing cover.
4) Install housing cover, identification tag and retaining bolts. Tighten retaining bolts in crisscross pattern. Install wheel speed sensor (if equipped). Refill axle with hypoid gear lubricant.

NOTE: Cover assembly must be installed within 15 minutes of application of sealant.

5) Install and tighten fill plug. On Mark VII and Mustang, remove vent on axle housing tube. Pour 4-8 ozs. (.12-.23L) of hypoid gear lubricant through vent hole. Install vent and tighten.

PINION FLANGE & OIL SEAL

CAUTION: Pinion flange and oil seal replacement affects bearing preload. Preload must be carefully reset during reassembly.

Removal – 1) Raise vehicle. Remove wheels and brake drums. Scribe alignment marks on companion flange, yoke and propeller

9-14   9-16

Ford   # 1989 Drive Axles
Ford Motor Co. – 7 1/2" & 8 3/4" Ring Gear (Cont.)

6) If bearing preload is exceeded before torque specification is reached, replace collapsible spacer. See AXLE ASSEMBLY SPECIFICATIONS table at end of article for proper specification. Install new pinion nut and repeat procedure. DO NOT loosen pinion nut to reduce pinion bearing preload.

DIFFERENTIAL BEARING PRELOAD & RING GEAR BACKLASH

1) With pinion depth set and pinion installed, place differential case and gear assembly, with bearings and cups, into axle housing. Install a .265" (6.3 mm) shim on left side (ring gear side) of differential. Install left bearing cap finger tight.

2) Select largest shim that will fit with a slight drag and install on right side (pinion gear side) of differential. Install right bearing cap and tighten all cap bolts to specification. Rotate gear assembly to ensure free operation.

3) Check ring and pinion backlash. If backlash is within specifications, go to step **7**. If backlash is not within specifications, go to step **5**. If zero backlash was recorded, go to step **4**.

4) If zero backlash was recorded, add .020" (.51 mm) to shim size on right side and subtract .020" (.51 mm) from shim size on left side. Check ring and pinion backlash.

5) If backlash is not within specifications, increase shim thickness on one side and decrease shim thickness on opposite side by same amount. See BACKLASH-TO-SHIM THICKNESS CONVERSION chart for approximate shim change. See Fig. 5.

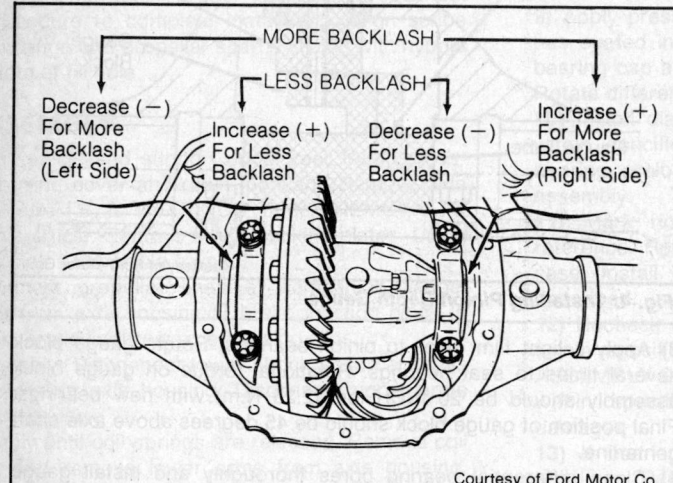

Fig. 5: Backlash Adjustment

Courtesy of Ford Motor Co.

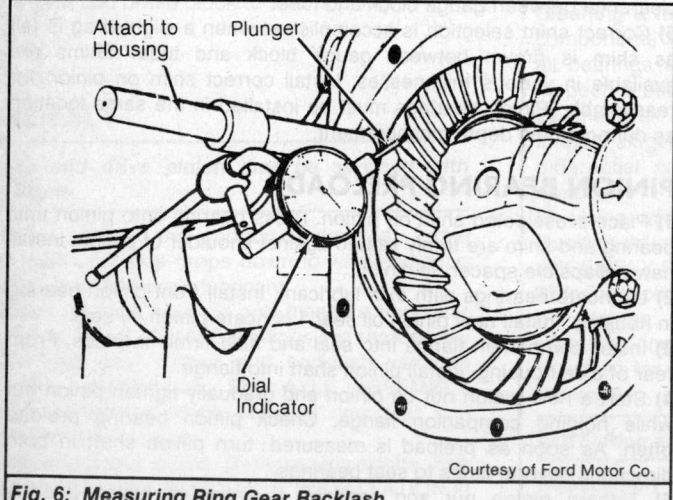

Fig. 6: Measuring Ring Gear Backlash

Courtesy of Ford Motor Co.

6) Install shim and bearing caps. Tighten bearing cap bolts. Rotate gear assembly several times. Recheck backlash. If backlash is within specification, go to step **7**. If not, repeat step **5**.

7) Increase both left and right shim sizes .006" (.15 mm) and reinstall for correct bearing preload. Make sure shims are fully seated and gear assembly turns freely. Using marking compound, check gear tooth contact pattern.

BACKLASH-TO-SHIM THICKNESS CONVERSION

Required Change In Backlash In. (mm)	Required Change In Shim Thickness In. (mm)
.001" (.025 mm)	.002" (.05 mm)
.002" (.051 mm)	.002" (.05 mm)
.003" (.076 mm)	.004" (.10 mm)
.004" (.10 mm)	.006" (.15 mm)
.005" (.13 mm)	.006" (.15 mm)
.006" (.15 mm)	.008" (.20 mm)
.007" (.18 mm)	.010" (.25 mm)
.008" (.20 mm)	.010" (.25 mm)
.009" (.23 mm)	.012" (.30 mm)
.010" (.25 mm)	.014" (.35 mm)
.011" (.28 mm)	.014" (.35 mm)
.012" (.30 mm)	.016" (.41 mm)
.013" (.33 mm)	.018" (.46 mm)
.014" (.36 mm)	.018" (.46 mm)
.015" (.38 mm)	.020" (.51 mm)

AXLE ASSEMBLY SPECIFICATIONS

Application	Specifications
Capacity	
7 1/2" Ring Gear	3.5 pts. (1.7L)
8 3/4" Ring Gear	4.0 pts. (1.9L)
Differential Case Runout	.003 (.08)
Ring Gear Backface Runout	.004" (.10 mm) MAX.
Differential Side Gear	
Thrust Washer Thickness	.030-.032" (.76-.81 mm)
Pinion Gear Thrust Washer	
Thickness	.030-.032" (.76-.81 mm)
Nominal Pinion Shim Thickness	.030" (.76 mm)
Ring Gear Backlash	.008-.015" (.20-.38 mm)
Maximum Backlash Variation	
Between Teeth	.004" (.10 mm)
Pinion Bearing Preload (With Oil Seal)	
Original Bearings	8-14 INCH lbs. (.9-1.6 N.m)
New Bearings	16-29 INCH lbs. (1.8-3.3 N.m)

TIGHTENING SPECIFICATIONS

Application	Ft. Lbs. (N.m)
Axle Vent	11-19 (15-26)
Bearing Cap Bolts	70-85 (95-115)
Brake Backing Plate Bolts	20-40 (27-54)
Oil Filler Plug	15-30 (20-41)
Pinion Shaft Lock Bolt	15-30 (20-41)
Propeller Shaft-to-Companion	
Flange Bolts	70-95 (95-130)
Ring Gear Attaching Bolts [1]	70-85 (95-115)
Rear Cover Bolts	
Plastic Cover	15-20 (20-27)
Metal Cover	25-35 (34-47)
Pinion Nut	
7 1/2" Ring Gear	170 (230) MIN.
8 3/4" Ring Gear	140 (190) MIN.

[1] – Using Loctite.

1989 POSITIVE TRACTION DIFFERENTIALS
Chrysler Motors Cone Brake Type

RWD Models

DESCRIPTION

Positive traction type differential directs major driving force to the wheel with greatest amount of traction. This is accomplished by 2 spring-loaded thrust plates pressing against the differential side gears which are seated into tapered brake cones.

The brake cones fit into a tapered recess in each end of differential cases where outward pressure of thrust plate assembly forces brake cones against recesses, providing resistance to normal differential action. Thrust plate spring load is calibrated to permit some slippage under variable torque conditions. Chrysler Motors uses the Sure-Grip unit which is not serviceable.

IDENTIFICATION

The differential can be identified as a positive traction unit by raising vehicle and rotating one rear wheel with transmission in Neutral. Both rear wheels should rotate in same direction if vehicle is equipped with a positive traction differential. Positive traction unit may also be identified by removing oil fill plug and noting type of differential case used. See Fig. 1.

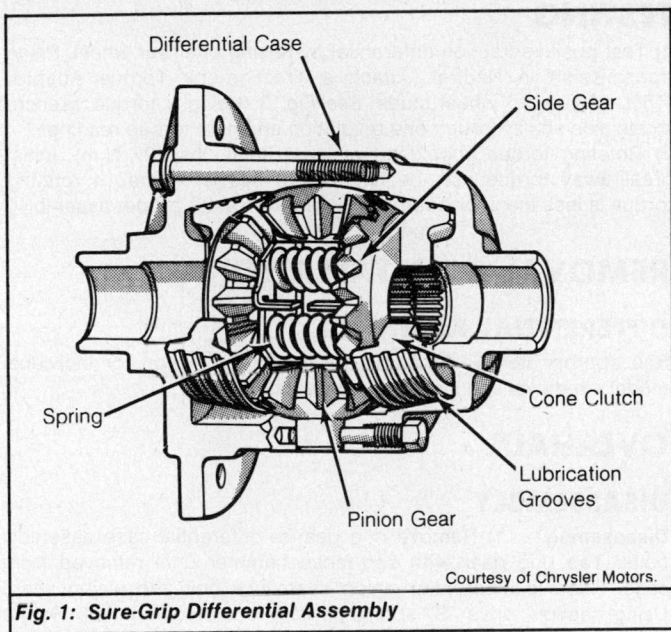

Courtesy of Chrysler Motors.

Fig. 1: Sure-Grip Differential Assembly

REMOVAL & INSTALLATION

DIFFERENTIAL ASSEMBLY

See appropriate DRIVE AXLE article in this section for individual model's removal and installation procedures.

LUBRICATION

Fill axle with Mopar Hypoid Gear Lubricant (4318058) and 4 ounces (.12L) of Mopar Hypoid Gear Oil Additive (4318060). See LUBRICATION CAPACITY table for approximate refill capacity.

LUBRICATION CAPACITY

Application	Pts. (L)
8 1/4" Ring Gear	4.4 (2.1)

TESTING

1) Differential can be tested externally by raising both rear wheels from ground. Place transmission in Park on automatic transmissions, or Low gear on manual transmissions.
2) Attempt to turn one wheel by hand. Wheel assembly must be very difficult to turn. If wheel can be turned easily, differential assembly should be replaced as a complete unit.

OVERHAUL

NOTE: Chrysler Motors Sure-Grip differential units are serviced as a complete assembly only.

INSPECTION

Inspect all gears for damaged teeth. Verify brake cone seats are smooth and free of excessive scoring or damage. If the brake cone or differential case is damaged, replace brake cones and differential case as a unit.

NOTE: To prevent misalignment of splines DO NOT rotate axle after differential and first axle shaft have been installed in axle housing.

AXLE ASSEMBLY SPECIFICATIONS

Application	In. (mm)
Differential Case Runout	.003 (.08)
Ring Gear Backface	.005 (.13)
Ring & Pinion Gear Backlash [1]	.005-.008 (.13-.20)

[1] – At point of minimum backlash.

1989 POSITIVE TRACTION DIFFERENTIALS
Ford Motor Co. Clutch Pack Type

RWD Models

DESCRIPTION

Positive traction type differentials direct major driving force to wheel with greatest amount of traction. This is accomplished by a spring-loaded multiple disc clutch pack behind each side gear. Each clutch pack uses friction surfaced clutch discs splined to the side gear and steel clutch plates held by the differential case.

In operation, preload spring pressure is accompanied by side gear thrust load to compress clutch packs, providing resistance to normal differential action. Preload spring pressure is calibrated to allow some slippage of clutch packs under variable torque conditions such as turning corners.

CAUTION: Use of other than equal size tires on rear axle for extended mileage can result in a reduction of posi-traction effectiveness.

IDENTIFICATION

Differential can be identified as a positive traction unit by raising vehicle and turning one rear wheel. Place transmission in Neutral. Rotate wheels. If both wheels rotate in same direction, differential is a positive traction differential.

All models have an identification tag attached to housing cover bolt. *See Fig. 1.* Axle ratio, ring gear diameter and differential type are contained in axle code. When an "L" appears in the axle code, positive traction differential is indicated. Using axle model code, gear ratio may be determined. See AXLE RATIO IDENTIFICATION table.

LUBRICATION

Fill axle with Ford Hypoid Gear Lubricant (ESP-M2C154-A) and 4 ozs. (.12L) of Ford Friction Modifier (C8AZ-19B546-A). See LUBRICATION CAPACITIES table for approximate capacity.

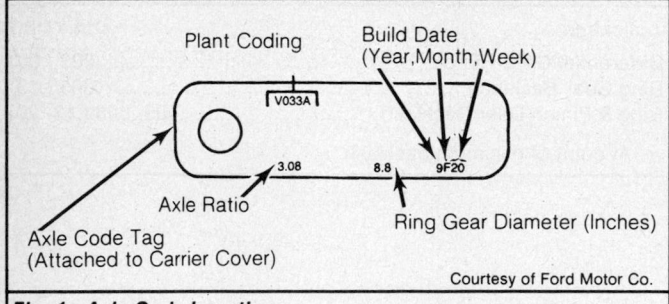

Fig. 1: Axle Code Location

AXLE RATIO IDENTIFICATION

Axle Ratio	Axle Code
Ford Motor Co.	
7 1/2" Ring Gear	
3.08:1	462 B & 479 B
3.45:1	281 D
3.73:1	266 D
8 3/4" Ring Gear	
2.73:1	013 B, 031 B & 201 A
3.08:1	015 B, 015 C, 034 B, 203 F, & 423 F
3.27:1	017 B, 017 C, 039 A, 407 F, & 205 F
3.55:1	037 B & 037 C

LUBRICATION CAPACITIES

Application	Pts. (L)
Ford Motor Co. [1]	
7 1/2" Ring Gear	3.75 (1.7)
8 3/4" Ring Gear	3.75 (1.7)

[1] – Does not include additive.

TESTING

1) Test positive traction differential by raising one rear wheel. Place transmission in Neutral. Attach a Traction-Lok Torque Adapter (T59L-4204-A) to wheel studs. *See Fig. 3.* Using a torque wrench, rotate axle shaft through one revolution and note torque reading.
2) Rotating torque should be at least 20 ft. lbs. (27 N.m). Initial break-away torque may be higher, but this is normal. If rotating torque is less than specified, check differential for proper assembly.

REMOVAL & INSTALLATION

DIFFERENTIAL ASSEMBLY

See appropriate DRIVE AXLE article in this section for individual model's removal and installation procedures.

OVERHAUL

DISASSEMBLY

Disassembly – 1) Remove ring gear-to-differential case assembly bolts. Tap ring gear with soft-faced hammer until removed from case. Remove differential pinion shaft lock bolt and pinion shaft. Using caution, drive "S" spring partially out of differential. Rotate differential 180 degrees.

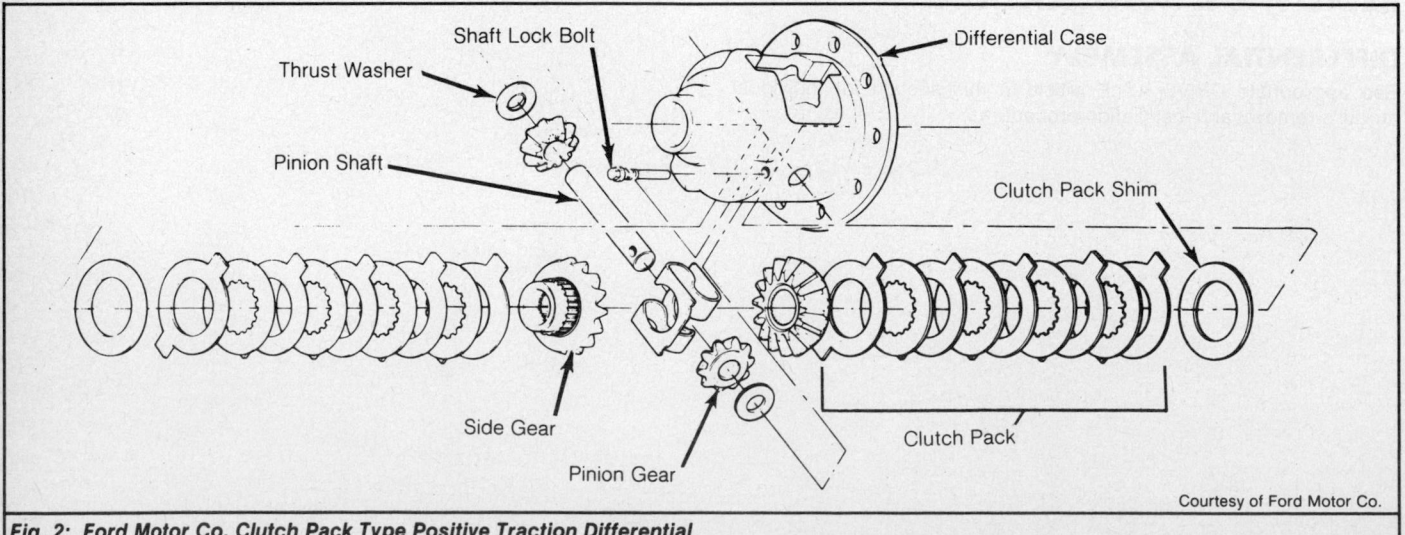

Fig. 2: Ford Motor Co. Clutch Pack Type Positive Traction Differential

1989 POSITIVE TRACTION DIFFERENTIALS
Ford Motor Co. Clutch Pack Type (Cont.)

9-19

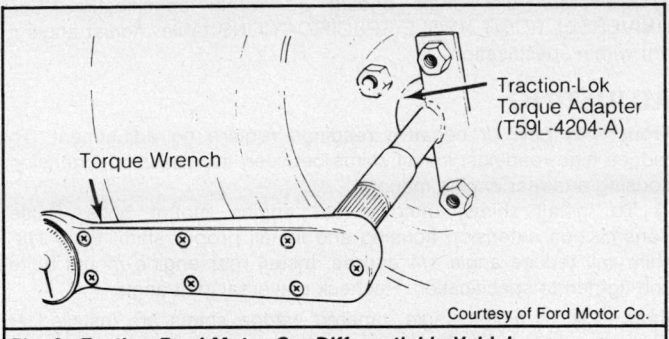

Fig. 3: Testing Ford Motor Co. Differential In Vehicle

2) Grip "S" spring with pliers and remove from differential. Rotate pinion gears with Differential Gear Rotator (T84P-4205-A) to remove gears and washers. Remove side gears, clutch plates and shims from both cavities and label them for reassembly reference.

CLEANING & INSPECTION

Wipe friction plates with clean rag. Check clutch packs for wear or damage. Inspect pinion shaft, pinion gears, and side gears for excessive wear, cracks or scoring. Replace worn or damaged components as necessary.

CLUTCH PACK PRELOAD

1) Lubricate clutch pack with Ford Friction Modifier (C8AZ-19B546-A). Assemble clutch pack on side gear without shims. Install Differential Clutch Gauge (T84P-4946-A) on side gear clutch pack. *See Fig. 5.*

2) Checking with a feeler gauge, select thickest blade that will fit between gauge and clutch pack. This will be required shim thickness. Repeat procedure for remaining side gear.

REASSEMBLY

1) Lubricate all parts for reassembly. Secure differential case in a soft-jawed vise. Install clutch packs and side gears in their original cavities. Position pinion gears and thrust washers on side gears. Install pinion gears and thrust washers and rotate into position. Use a soft-faced hammer to drive "S" spring into case.

2) Install pinion shaft and lock bolt. DO NOT tighten at this time. Mount Traction-Lok Torque Holder (T59L-4204-A) in vise. Position case over holder. Using traction-lok torque holder and torque wrench, measure torque required to rotate one side gear while other side gear is held stationary. *See Fig. 4.*

3) Initial break-away torque for original clutch pack should be more than 20 ft. lbs. (27 N.m). For new clutch packs, break-away torque should be 80-200 ft. lbs. (108-271 N.m). If less than specified, check

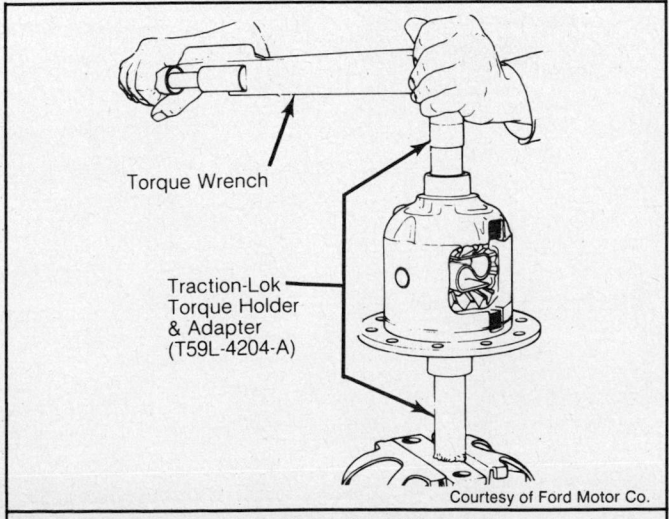

Fig. 4: Bench Testing Ford Motor Co. Differential

differential for proper assembly. Tighten pinion shaft lock bolt. Install ring gear using new bolts.

NOTE: *See appropriate DRIVE AXLE article in this section for additional rear axle specifications.*

REAR AXLE SPECIFICATIONS

Application	INCHES (mm)
Backlash Variation Between Teeth	.004 (.102)
Differential Case Runout	.076 (1.93)
Pinion Gear Thrust Washer	.030-.032 (.762-.813)
Pinion Locating Shim	.030 (.762)
Ring Gear Backface Runout	.004 (.102)
Ring Gear/Pinion Teeth Backlash	.008-.015 (.203-.381)
Side Gear Thrust Washer	.030-.032 (.762-.813)

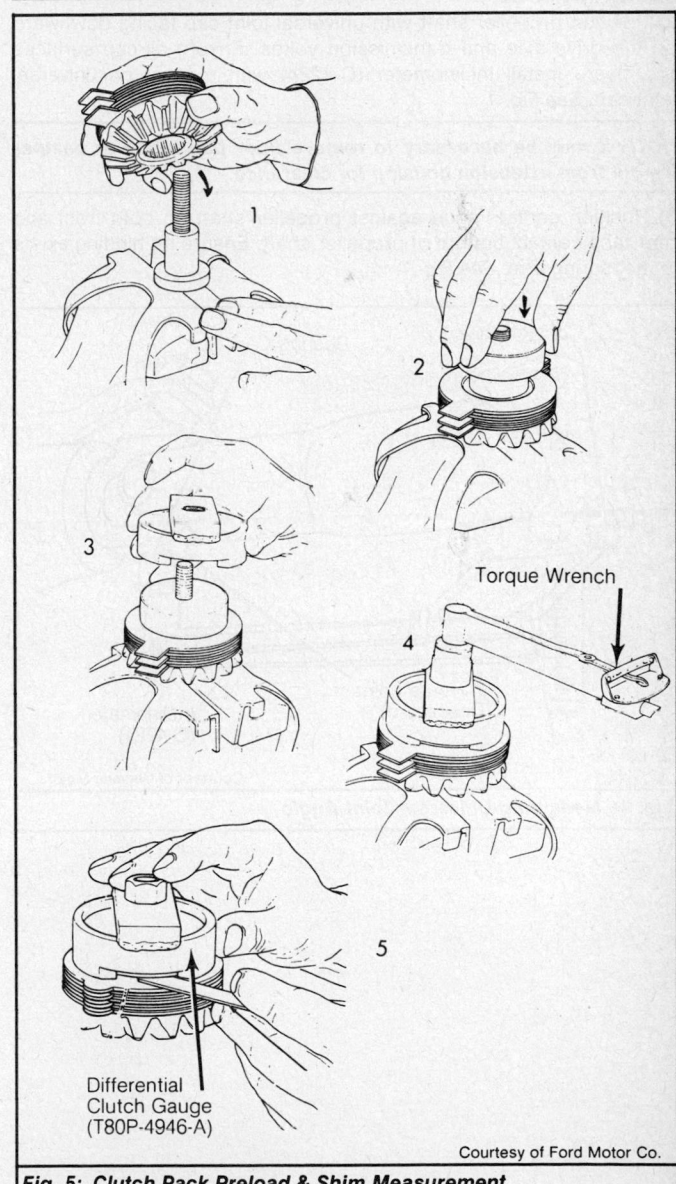

Fig. 5: Clutch Pack Preload & Shim Measurement

TIGHTENING SPECIFICATIONS

Application	Ft. Lbs. (N.m)
Pinion Shaft Lock Bolt	20 (27)
Propeller Shaft-to-Companion Flange Bolts	70-95 (95-130)
Ring Gear Bolts	
7 1/2	80-95 (108-129)
8 1/2"	70-90 (95-122)

1989 PROPELLER SHAFT ALIGNMENT
Chrysler Motors

RWD Models

DESCRIPTION

Universal joint angle must be correct for smooth operation. Axle identification is used for determining proper universal joint angle. Axle identification can be obtained by measuring the O.D. of the inner end of the axle tube housing. The 7 1/4" axle measures 2.50" (63.5 mm) while the 8 1/4" measures 3.00" (76.2 mm).

CHECKING & ADJUSTING

CHECKING

1) Support vehicle under front and rear suspension. DO NOT use frame contact hoist. Car should be level, fuel tank full, and free of excess trunk weight.
2) Position propeller shaft with universal joint cap facing downward on the drive axle and transmission yokes. Ensure all cap surfaces are clean. Install Inclinometer (C-4224) with magnet on universal joint cap. See Fig. 1.

NOTE: It may be necessary to remove floor pan brace or damper weight from extension housing for clearance.

---

3) Position contact shoe against propeller shaft so both front and rear tabs contact bottom of propeller shaft. Ensure no binding exists in measuring arm. See Fig. 1.

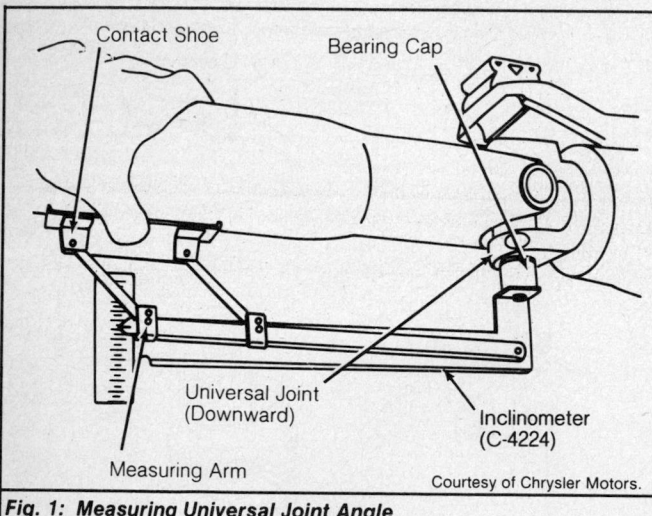

Fig. 1: Measuring Universal Joint Angle
Courtesy of Chrysler Motors.

4) Universal joint angle should be within specification. See UNIVERSAL JOINT ANGLE SPECIFICATIONS table. Adjust angle if not within specification.

ADJUSTING

Front – 1) Low or negative readings require no adjustment. To reduce high readings, install shims between transmission extension housing and rear engine mount.
2) To install shims, remove rear engine mount bolts. Raise transmission extension housing and install proper shim. Each 1/8" shim will reduce angle 1/4 degree. Install rear engine mount bolts and tighten to specification. Recheck universal joint angle.
Rear – 1) To adjust angle, tapered wedge shims are installed at rear axle spring seats. Shims are available in values of 1-4 degrees.
2) For shim installation, loosen leaf spring "U" bolt nuts. Install shim between spring and spring seat. Installing shim with thick end toward rear of vehicle increases angle while installing thick end toward front of vehicle decreases angle. Retighten leaf spring "U" bolt nuts and recheck angle.

CAUTION: DO NOT use shim pack exceeding 1/4" thickness at center of shim pack. If excessive shimming is necessary, check rear springs for damage.

UNIVERSAL JOINT ANGLE SPECIFICATIONS

Application	Front Angle (Degrees)	Rear Angle (Degrees)
7 1/4" Axle	0 ± 1/2	+2 1/4 ± 1/2
8 1/4" Axle	0 ± 1/2	+3 ± 1/2

TIGHTENING SPECIFICATIONS

Application	Ft. Lbs. (N.m)
Leaf Spring "U" Bolt Nut	
7 1/4" Axle	40 (54)
8 1/4" Axle	45 (61)
Rear Engine Mount Bolt	50 (68)

UNIVERSAL JOINT ANGLE &

Application	Univ (From (Degr
Cougar & T-Bird	
Grand Marquis &	
LTD Crown Victoria	
Sedan	
Wagon	
Mark VII	
Front	
Rear	
Mustang	
6 3/4" Axle	
7 1/2" Axle	
Town Car	

¹ - Angles may be ±1/2 deg

RWD Models

NOTE: Information not available from manufacturer for Cougar and Thunderbird or Grand Marquis, LTD Crown Victoria, Town Car and Wagon models with air suspension.

DESCRIPTION

Propeller shaft universal joint angle is controlled by rear axle upper control arms on both coil spring and air suspension models. *See Fig. 1.* Whenever upper control arms are removed, universal joint angle must be checked and adjusted if necessary.

If propeller shaft universal joint angle requires adjustment, upper control arms with adjustable cams may need to be installed (if available).

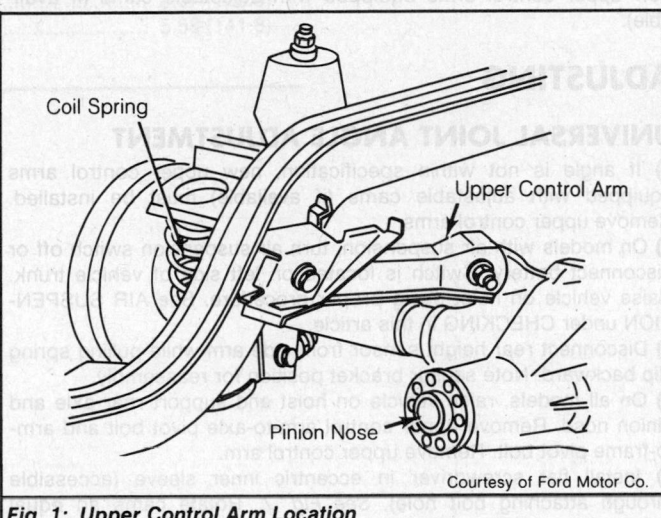

Fig. 1: Upper Control Arm Location

CHECKING

NOTE: Vehicle curb or ride height must be correct prior to checking universal joint angle.

COIL SPRING SUSPENSION

Vehicle Ride Height – 1) Measure vehicle ride height from top of axle housing tube to axle bumper bracket on frame rail for Mark VII and Mustang models. On all other models, measure from top of axle housing to the outer edge of the frame rail. *See Fig. 2.*

2) Adjust ride height if not within specification. See UNIVERSAL JOINT ANGLE & RIDE HEIGHT SPECIFICATIONS table at end of article.

NOTE: Information not available from manufacturer for Grand Marquis, LTD Crown Victoria, Town Car and Wagon models with air suspension.

AIR SUSPENSION

Mark VII – Before checking universal joint angle on models with air suspension, vehicle trim must be performed in addition to front and rear vehicle curb height or ride height.

CAUTION: Electrical power supply for air suspension system must be shut off prior to hoisting, jacking or towing vehicle. Turn off air suspension switch located on left side of vehicle trunk or disconnect battery.

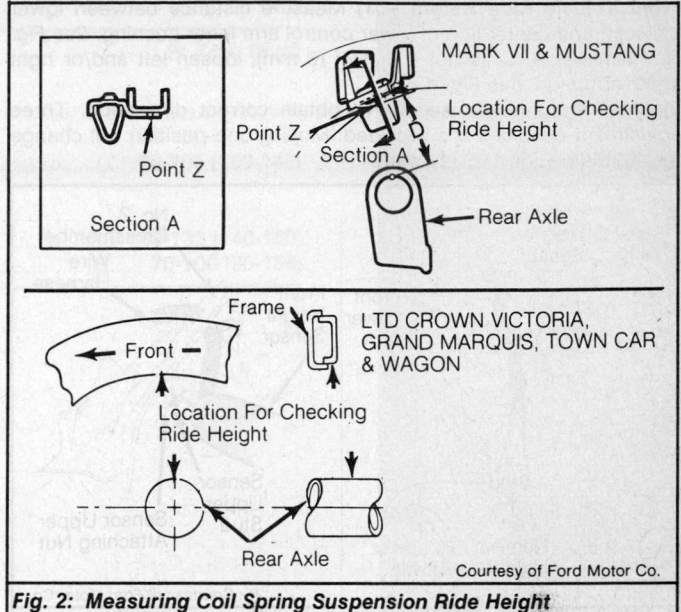

Fig. 2: Measuring Coil Spring Suspension Ride Height

CAUTION: The following hoist restrictions must be observed: use only a "body hoist" and lift vehicle using standard procedures. Place jack stands at each corner as a safety precaution. If "body hoist" is not available, use standard hydraulic floor jack. Raise front of vehicle at No. 2 crossmember. Place jack stands at front corners of body. For rear, use same procedures using the rear jacking location.

Vehicle Trim Setting Procedure – 1) If vehicle temperature differs more than 20°F (11°C) from shop area, allow enough time for temperature of vehicle to adjust.

2) Position vehicle on alignment rack and turn ignition off. Level alignment rack as necessary. Turn ignition on. DO NOT START.

3) After one minute, push trunk release, turn ignition off, and exit vehicle. Allow vehicle 20 seconds to settle to trim height with doors closed, then turn air suspension switch off. Switch is located on left side of vehicle trunk.

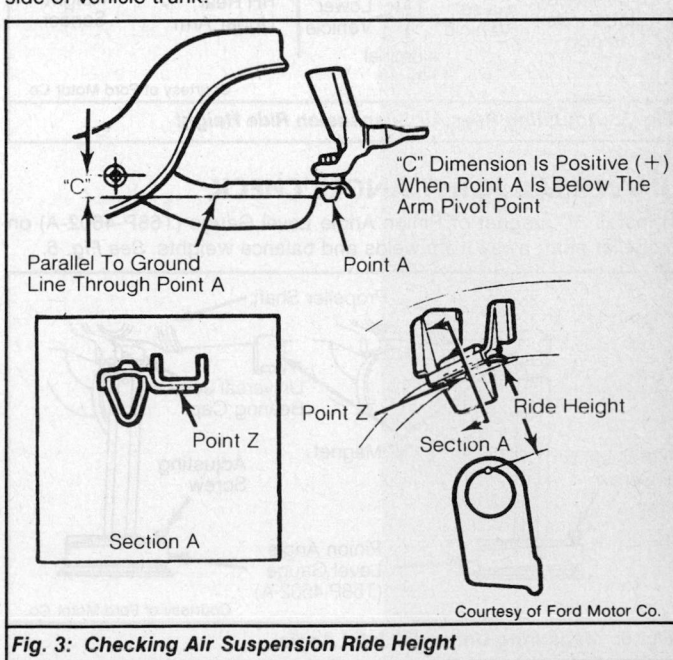

Fig. 3: Checking Air Suspension Ride Height

1989 UNIVERSAL JOINTS
Chrysler Motors, Eagle & Ford Motor Co.

Front Vehicle Ride Height –
ball joint and center line of low
3. If dimension "C" is not a +
lower arm stud. *See Fig. 4.*
2) Move front height sensor
adjustment positions are provi
the "C" dimension 1/2" (12 mm)

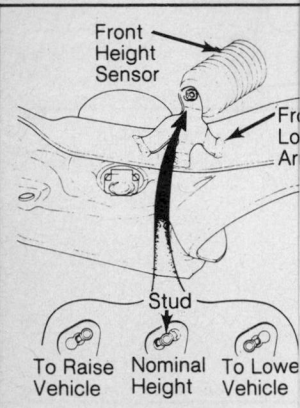

Front
Height
Sensor

Fro
Lo
Ar

Stud

To Raise Nominal To Lowe
Vehicle Height Vehicle

Fig. 4: Adjusting Front Air Su

Rear Suspension Ride Height
axle housing tube to axle bum
Ride height should be within s
ANGLE & RIDE HEIGHT SPEC
2) If adjustment is required, lo
and move up or down. *See Fi*
will change dimension ride heig

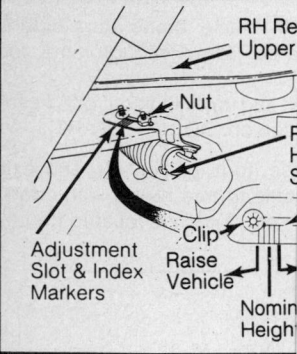

RH Re
Upper

Nut

F
H
S

Adjustment
Slot & Index Raise Clip
Markers Vehicle

Nomin
Height

Fig. 5: Adjusting Rear Air Sus

UNIVERSAL JOINT A

1) Install "V" magnet of Pinion
propeller shaft away from weld

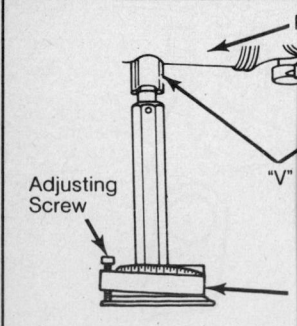

Adjusting
Screw

"V"

Fig. 6: Measuring Universal J

All Models
REMOVAL & INSTALLATION

PROPELLER SHAFT

Removal – Raise and support vehicle with front end slightly lower to prevent loss of transmission fluid. Place reference mark on propeller shaft and differential yoke for reassembly reference. Remove trunnion bearing straps or flange bolts. Slide propeller shaft with slip yoke from transmission output shaft.

NOTE: DO NOT use pry bar or heavy tool to hold propeller shaft while removing strap bolts or flange bolts, as damage to bearing seals may result. DO NOT allow one end of shaft to hang free or bend at a sharp angle.

Installation – 1) Clean sliding yoke splines and outside diameter. Inspect machined surface for nicks, scratches or foreign material. Apply lubricant to splines and outside yoke surface.
2) Install yoke onto transmission output shaft and align shaft with companion flange. Install exposed bearing cups into companion flange with straps and bolts (single joint), or connect propeller shaft flange to companion flange with bolts (constant velocity joint).

OVERHAUL

CROSS & ROLLER TYPE JOINT

NOTE: Some vehicles use an injected nylon ring in place of snap rings or "C" locks. Replacement universal joints use "C" lock rings. Remains of sheared nylon rings must be completely removed in order for new lock rings to seat properly.

Disassembly – Remove bearing cup locks or snap rings. Press out bearing cups using arbor press or vise and supporting tools. Remove trunnion (cross) assembly from yoke. *See Fig. 1.* DO NOT remove seal retainers from cross.

Reassembly – Hold cross between ears of propeller shaft flange. Partially install 2 bearing cups. Align cross with cups. Using arbor press or vise, press cups into yoke until locks or snap rings can be installed. Install locks or snap rings.

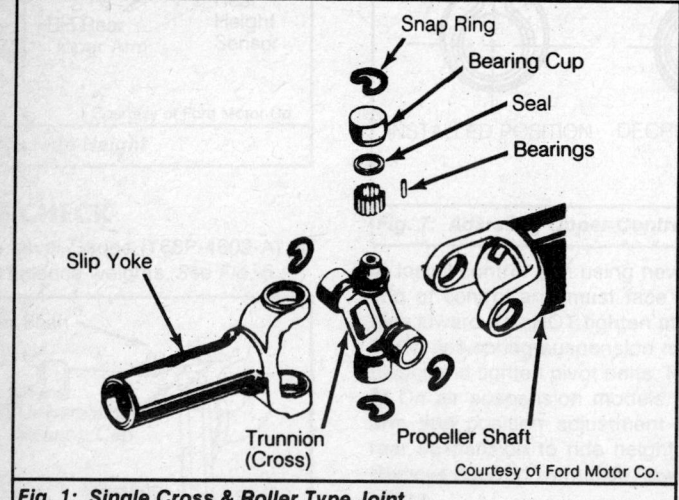

Snap Ring

Bearing Cup

Seal

Bearings

Slip Yoke

Trunnion
(Cross) Propeller Shaft

Courtesy of Ford Motor Co.

Fig. 1: Single Cross & Roller Type Joint

CONSTANT VELOCITY TYPE JOINT

CAUTION: Care must be taken when moving shaft horizontally. Shaft must be supported at both ends or center ball could be damaged. Shaft may be carried in vertical position without resulting damage.

Disassembly – Scribe alignment marks on all yokes for reassembly reference. Press bearing cups from center yoke and continue disassembly as for single cross and roller joint. *See Fig. 2.*

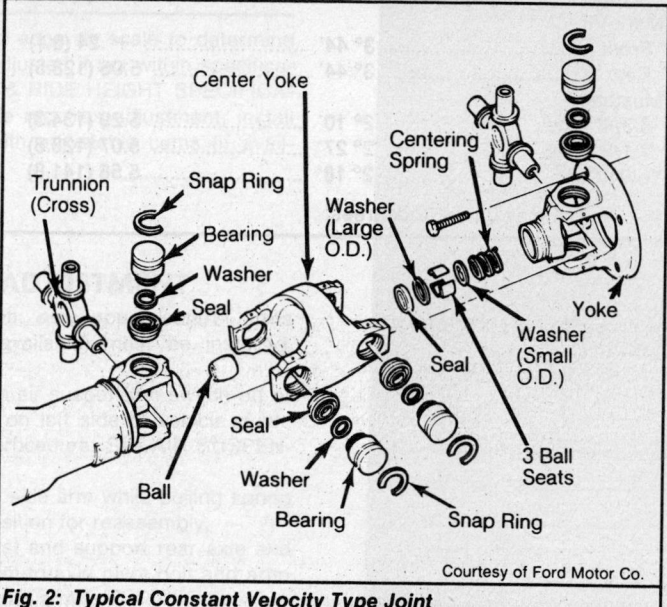

Center Yoke

Trunnion
(Cross) Snap Ring

Bearing

Washer

Seal

Centering
Spring

Washer
(Large
O.D.)

Yoke

Seal

Washer
(Small
O.D.)

Seal

Washer

Ball

Bearing

Snap Ring

3 Ball
Seats

Courtesy of Ford Motor Co.

Fig. 2: Typical Constant Velocity Type Joint

Centering Ball Replacement – 1) Using ball remover, place inner part of tool under ball. Place outer cylinder of tool over ball, thread nut on tool and draw off ball. Place replacement ball on stud. Using tool, drive ball onto stud until ball seats firmly against shoulder at base of stud.
2) Lubricate all components and install in ball seat cavity in following order: spring, washer (smallest OD), ball seats (with largest opening outward to receive ball), washer (largest OD), and seal.
3) Lubricate seal lip and press seal even with seal installer. Fill cavity with grease. Install flange yoke to centering ball. Ensure alignment marks are aligned. Install cross and bearing cups.

Reassembly – Pack all bearing cups with grease. To reassemble, reverse disassembly procedure, ensuring crosses and yokes are in original location. Check for free movement of joint. If binding exists, use brass hammer and seat bearings with sharp rap on yoke. DO NOT hammer on bearing cups or damage may occur.

DESCRIPTION & IDENTIFICATION

Turbocharged models use axle shafts of equal length. All others use unequal length axle shafts. The equal length system uses an intermediate shaft on the right side. Unequal length system has a long axle shaft on right side and short axle shaft on left side. Except for a rubber washer seal attached to right inner CV joint on the equal length type, axle shafts can be serviced the same.

Several different axle shafts are used and are identified by configuration and manufacturer. The types are either A.C.I., G.K.N., SSG or Citroen. The different types are not interchangeable and must not be intermixed. *See Fig. 1.*

LUBRICATION

CV joints require special lubrication. CV joints are enclosed with a boot to contain lubricant and prevent contamination. Periodic lubrication of CV joints is not required but boots should be inspected at regular intervals. The lubricant requirements and quantities are different for inner and outer types of CV joints being serviced. Use only specified lubricant.

If necessary to refill transaxle with fluid, use SAE, SF or SF/CC rated 5W-30 engine oil for manual transaxles. For automatic transaxles, use Mopar ATF Plus (7176). If Mopar ATF is not available, Dexron II may be used.

SERVICE (IN-VEHICLE)

HUB BEARINGS

NOTE: Hub and axle shaft are splined together through knuckle hub bearing and retained by hub nut. New bearings MUST be installed whenever hub is removed.

Removal – 1) Remove dust cap, cotter pin, nut lock and spring washer. With vehicle on ground, apply brakes and loosen wheel nuts and hub nut. Raise and support vehicle. Remove wheel. Remove hub nut and washer. Tap end of axle shaft lightly (if necessary), with brass hammer to free axle shaft from hub splines.
2) Disconnect brake hose retainer from strut damper. Remove lower ball joint clamp bolt. Remove brake caliper and support caliper to vehicle frame. Remove brake rotor. Separate lower ball joint from steering knuckle. Pull steering knuckle out and away from axle shaft.
3) Install Bracket (C-4811-17) to steering knuckle. Install Thrust Button (C-4811-6) inside hub bore. *See Fig. 3.* Install Puller (C-4811-14) and remove hub. *See Fig. 4.* Use a universal puller and remove outer bearing race from hub. Remove bearing retainer from steering knuckle.
4) Pry out bearing seal from machined recess in steering knuckle and thoroughly clean recess. Install Puller Kit (C-4811) and remove bearing from steering knuckle. *See Fig. 5.*

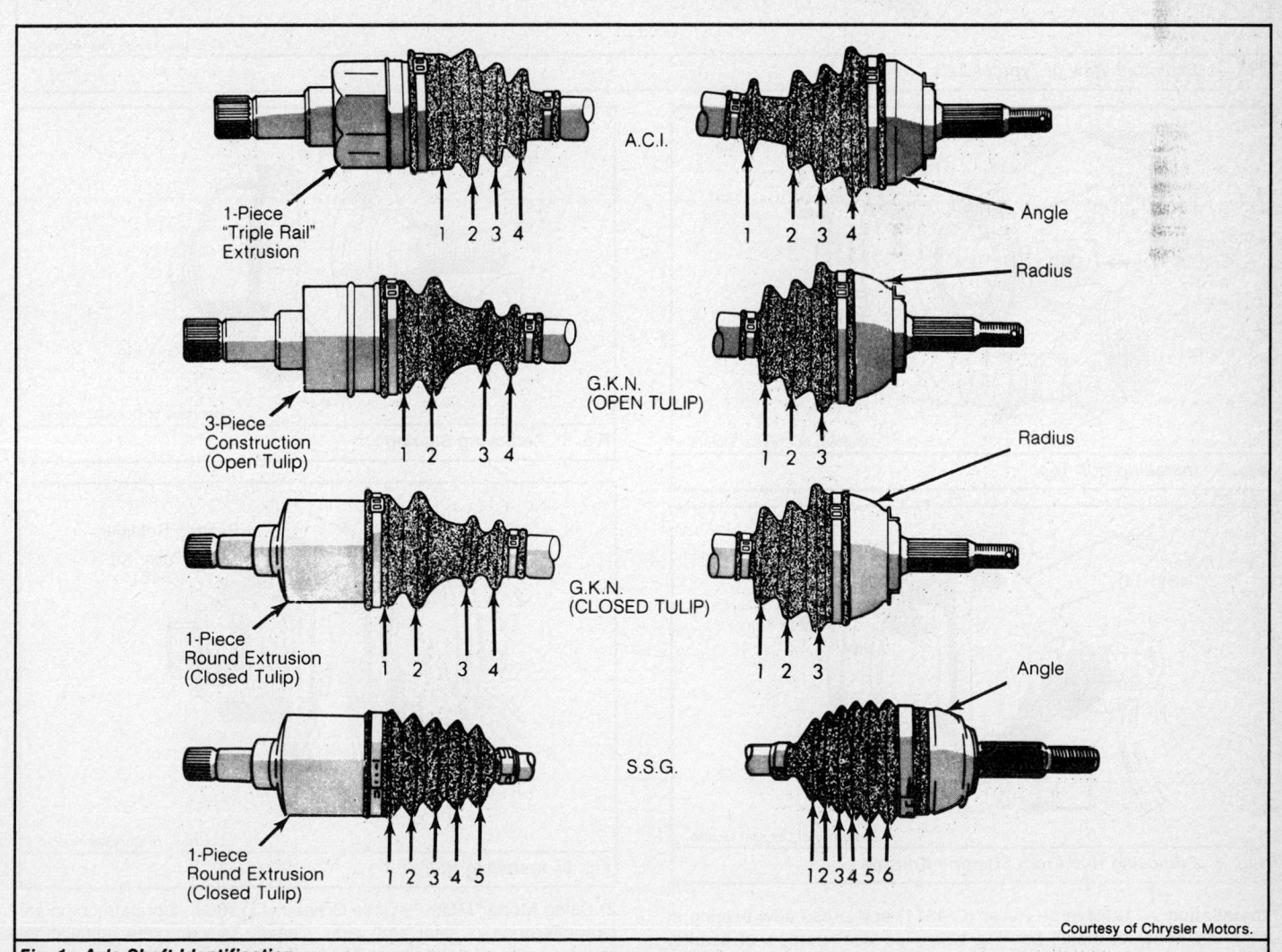

Courtesy of Chrysler Motors.

Fig. 1: Axle Shaft Identification

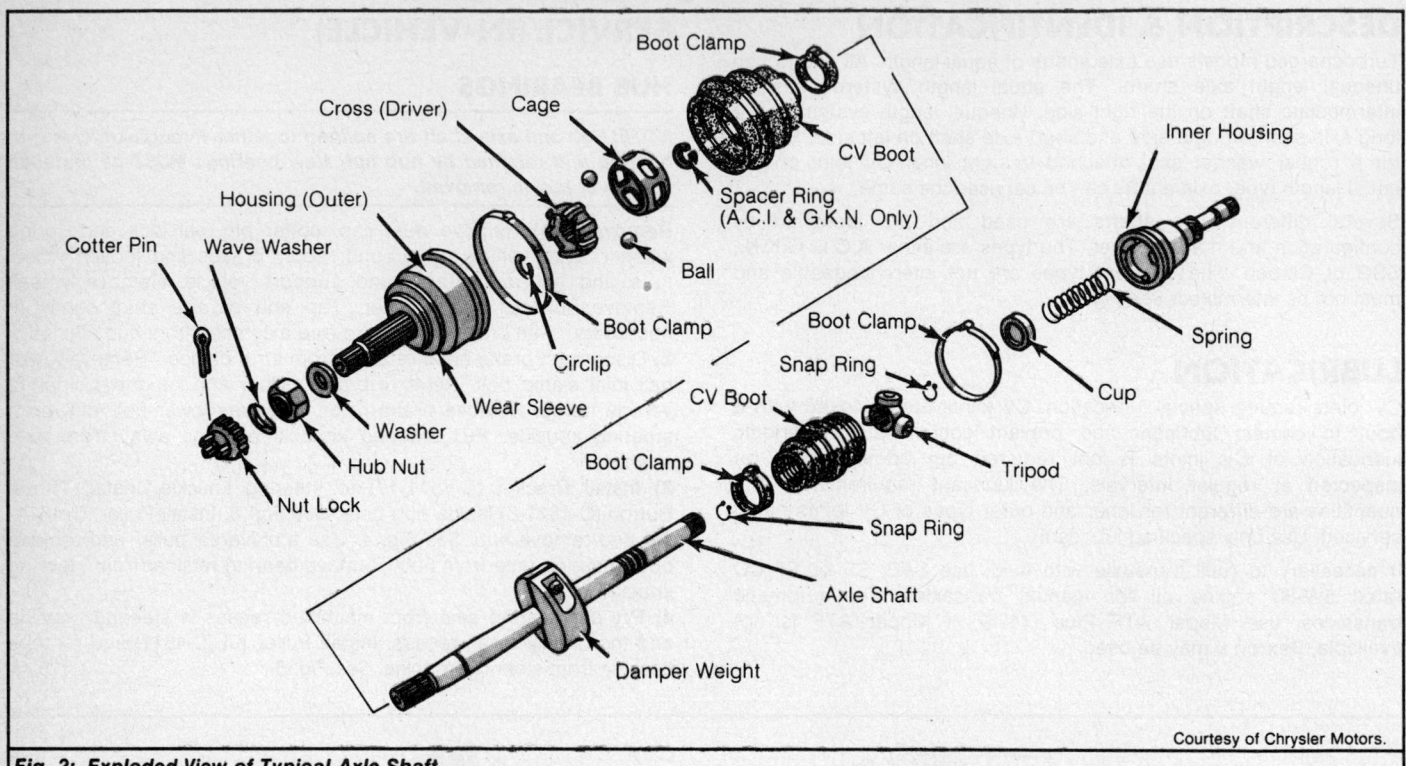

Fig. 2: *Exploded View of Typical Axle Shaft*

Courtesy of Chrysler Motors.

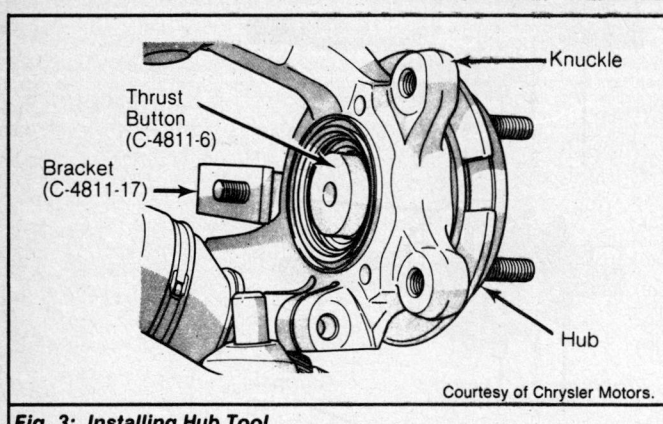

Fig. 3: **Installing Hub Tool**

Courtesy of Chrysler Motors.

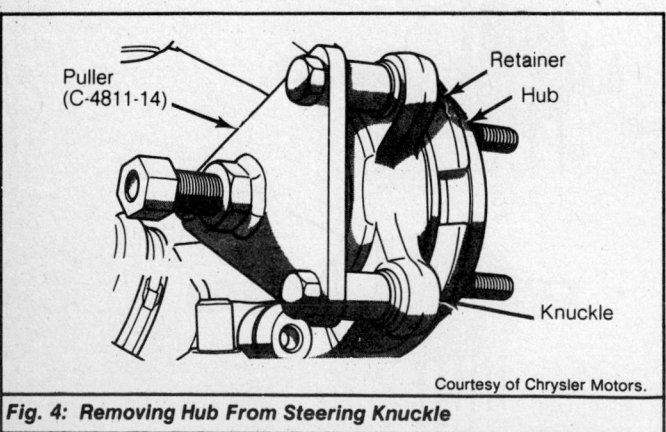

Fig. 4: **Removing Hub From Steering Knuckle**

Courtesy of Chrysler Motors.

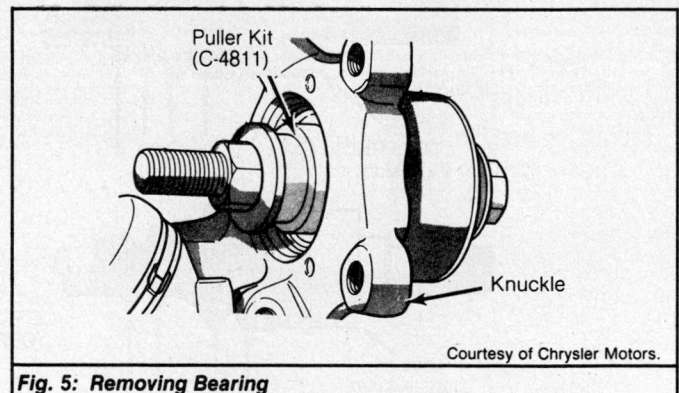

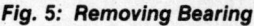

Fig. 5: **Removing Bearing**

Courtesy of Chrysler Motors.

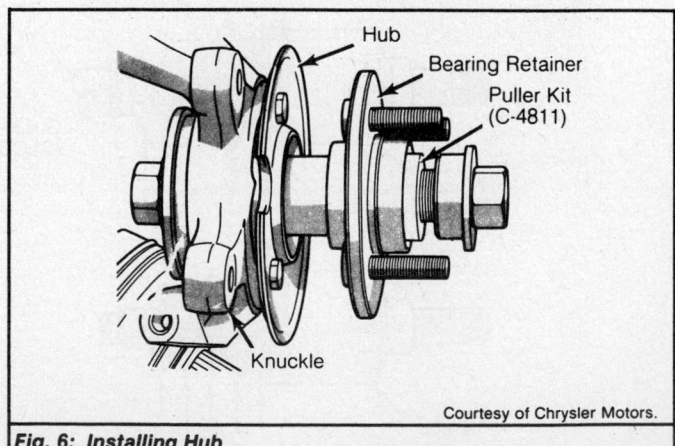

Fig. 6: **Installing Hub**

Courtesy of Chrysler Motors.

Installation – 1) Reverse Puller (C-4811) and press new bearing in steering knuckle. Install bearing with Red seal portion fo bearing facing bearing retainer. Install new seal and bearing retainer. Tighten retainer bolts to specifications. Press hub into steering knuckle with Puller Kit (C-4811). *See Fig. 6.*

2) Using Mopar Multi-Purpose Grease (4318063), lubricate complete circumference of seal and wear sleeve. To complete installation, reverse removal procedure. Tighten all bolts/nuts to specifications. See TIGHTENING SPECIFICATIONS table.

AXLE SHAFTS

Removal – 1) Remove spindle nut. Raise and support vehicle. If removing right axle shaft, remove speedometer pinion assembly from transaxle. Tap axle shaft end lightly with brass hammer to free axle shaft from hub splines. Remove lower ball joint clamp bolt. Separate lower ball joint from steering knuckle.

NOTE: Speedometer drive pinion must be removed before removing right axle shaft.

2) Pull out on hub/steering knuckle assembly and separate axle shaft from hub. Grasp both CV joints at outer housings, to prevent separation and pull axle shaft out of transaxle or intermediate shaft. Remove axle shaft from vehicle.

Installation – Grasp both CV joints at outer housings and insert inner CV joint in transaxle or intermediate shaft. Ensure A.C.I. tripod type CV joint is engaged in housing and boot is not twisted. To complete installation, reverse removal procedure. Tighten all bolts/nuts to specifications. Lubricate seal and wear sleeve with Mopar grease.

OVERHAUL

NOTE: All left axle shafts on FWD models have damper weights. See AXLE SHAFT DAMPER WEIGHTS in this article.

INNER CV JOINT

Disassembly – 1) Remove axle shaft assembly. See AXLE SHAFTS in this article. Identify type of axle shaft being serviced. *See Fig. 1.* Remove boot clamps and slide boot away from joint.
2) On A.C.I. type joints, tripod retaining tabs are an integral part of staked boot retaining collar. On G.K.N. type joints, the tripod retaining tabs are an integral part of the housing cover. Lightly compress CV joint retention spring while bending tabs with pliers. *See Fig. 7.*

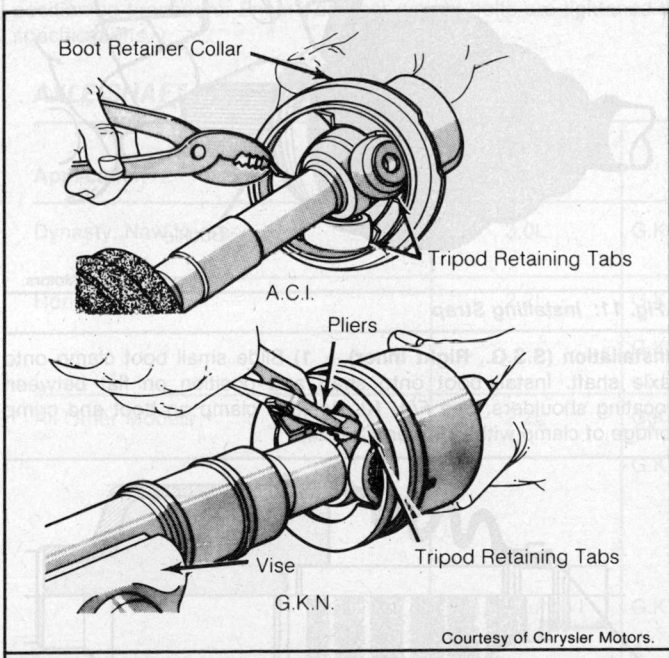

Fig. 7: Separating A.C.I. & G.K.N. Joints

3) S.S.G. type joints utilize a wire ring tripod retainer which expands into a groove. Use a flat tip screwdriver and pry wire out of groove. Slide tripod from housing. Replace wire ring tripod retainer if deformed.
4) With tripod joint removed from housing, tape tripod rollers to hold into place. Remove snap ring from end of axle shaft. Remove tripod from axle shaft.

Inspection – 1) Remove as much grease as possible from tripod assembly. Inspect CV joint housing ball race and tripod components for excessive wear. Inspect spring, spring cup and spherical end of connecting shaft for damage or excessive wear.
2) Clean and check CV joint boot for cracks, tears and/or scuffed areas on interior surfaces. Replace components as necessary.

Reassembly – 1) On Turbo models install rubber washer seal over right inner stub shaft and seat in groove. Lubricate boot and slide boot on axle shaft (if removed). On A.C.I. and G.K.N. type, install tripod with chamfered end toward long length of axle shaft and install retaining ring. *See Fig. 8.* On S.S.G. type, install inner retaining ring, tripod and outer retaining ring.

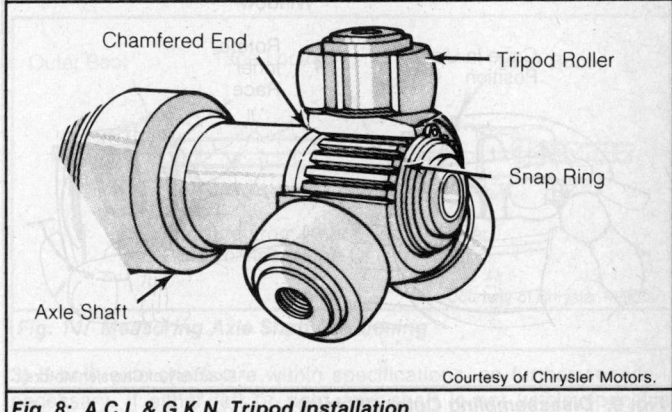

Fig. 8: A.C.I. & G.K.N. Tripod Installation

2) On all types, install tripod snap ring. On A.C.I. type, distribute one packet of grease into boot and remaining one packet into housing. On G.K.N. type, distribute 2 packets of grease into boot and remaining packet into housing. On S.S.G. type, distribute 1/2 packet of grease into housing and remaining amount into boot.

NOTE: On retaining tab type joints, DO NOT bend retaining tabs to original position. Instead, reattach boot to hold housing onto axle shaft. Tripod must be re-engaged in housing when axle shaft is installed in vehicle.

3) Position spring in housing and install spring cup. Place a small amount of grease on concave surface of spring cup. To complete reassembly, reverse disassembly procedure. Ensure spring in housing is centered in housing.

OUTER CV JOINT

Disassembly – 1) Remove axle shaft from vehicle. See AXLE SHAFTS in this article. Remove boot clamps. On A.C.I. and G.K.N. type, support axle shaft in vise with protected jaws. Tap top of CV joint housing to dislodge joint from internal circlip. On S.S.G. type, loosen damper weight bolts and slide it and boot towards inner joint. Expand circlip and slide joint off axle shaft. Reinstall damper weights.
2) On A.C.I. and G.K.N. type, do not remove heavy spacer ring from axle shaft unless replacing shaft. If replacing boot only, do not disassemble further. If CV joint is defective, replace complete unit. If lubricating CV joint proceed to next step.
3) Wipe surplus grease and mark position of inner cross, cage and housing. Clamp splined end of shaft in vise with protected jaws (joint vertical). Press down on one side of inner race to tilt cage and remove ball. *See Fig. 9.* If joint is tight, a hammer and brass drift may be used to tilt cage. DO NOT hit cage. Repeat procedure for remaining balls.
4) Tilt cage and inner race assembly vertically and position 2 opposing cage windows in area between ball grooves. Remove cage and inner race assembly. Turn inner cross 90 degrees to cage and align one of the race spherical lands with cage window. Raise land into cage window and remove inner race. *See Fig. 9.*

Inspection – 1) Check grease for contamination. Wash all parts in solvent and dry with compressed air. Inspect housing ball races for

1989 FWD AXLE SHAFTS
Chrysler Motors (Cont.)

AXLE SHAFT LENGTH SPECIFICATIONS

Application	Engine	Shaft Type	Side of Vehicle	Transaxle	Length In. (mm)
Acclaim, Spirit	2.5L, 3.0L	S.S.G.	Right	All	18.0-18.5 (457-469)
			Left	All	7.7-7.9 (196-200)
		G.K.N. (82-98)	Right	All	18.9-19.2 (481-489)
			Left	All	8.5-8.8 (216-224)
	2.5L Turbo I	S.S.G.	Right	Auto	18.0-18.5 (457-469)
			Left	Auto	7.2-7.9 (184-200)
		S.S.G.	Right	Manual	7.4-7.7 (187-196)
			Left	Manual	7.4-7.7 (187-196)
		G.K.N. (82-98)	Right	Auto	18.9-19.2 (481-489)
			Left	Auto	8.5-8.8 (216-224)
		G.K.N. (82-98)	Right	Manual	8.5-8.8 (216-224)
			Left	Manual	8.5-8.8 (216-224)
Dynasty, New Yorker	2.5L [1] 3.0L	G.K.N. (82-98)	Right	All	18.9-19.2 (481-489)
			Left	All	8.5-8.8 (216-224)
Horizon, Omni	2.2L	A.C.I	Right	Auto	18.5-19.0 (469-478)
			Left	NA	
		G.K.N. (69-92)	Right	Auto	19.6-19.8 (498-504)
			Left	Auto	8.2-8.7 (208-221)
		G.K.N. (69-92)	Right	Manual	19.6-19.8 (498-504)
			Left	Manual	9.4-10.0 (240-253)
All Other Models	2.2L	G.K.N. (82-98)	Right	All	18.9-19.2 (481-489)
			Left	All	8.5-8.8 (216-224)
		A.C.I.	Right	All	18.8-19.1 (477-485)
			Left	All	7.8-8.3 (197-212)
		S.S.G.	Right	All	18.0-18.5 (457-469)
			Left	All	7.2-7.9 (184-200)
	2.2L Turbo II	G.K.N. (82-98)	Right	Manual	8.5-8.8 (216-224)
			Left	Manual	8.5-8.8 (216-224)
	2.5L	G.K.N.(82-98)	Right	All	18.9-19.2 (481-489)
			Left	All	8.5-8.8 (216-224)
		S.S.G.	Right	All	18.0-18.5 (457-469)
			Left	All	7.7-7.9 (196-200)
	2.5L Turbo I	G.K.N.(82-98)	Right	All	18.9-19.2 (481-489)
			Left	All	8.5-8.8 (216-224)
		S.S.G.	Right	Auto	18.0-18.5 (457-469)
			Left	Auto	7.2-7.9 (184-200)
		S.S.G.	Right	Manual	7.4-7.7 (187-196)
			Left	Manual	7.4-7.7 (187-196)

[1] – Information not available from manufacturer.

TIGHTENING SPECIFICATIONS

Application	Ft. Lbs. (N.m)
Ball Joint Clamp Bolt	70 (95)
Brake Caliper Bolt	160 (217)
Brake Hose Retainer Bolt	10 (14)
Damper Weight Bolt	
S.S.G.	21 (28)
G.K.N.	23 (31)
Hub Bearing Retainer Bolt	20 (27)
Inner CV Joint Flange	36 (49)
Intermediate Shaft	
Bracket-to-Bearing Bolt	21 (28)
Bracket-to-Engine Bolt	40 (54)
Spindle Nut	180 (244)
Tie Rod Nut	35 (47)
Wheel Nut	95 (129)

	INCH Lbs. (N.m)
Damper Weight Bolt	
A.C.I.	96 (11)
Speedometer Gear Bolt	60 (7)

Premier

DESCRIPTION

Axle shafts transfer power from transaxle to the front driving wheels. The axle shafts are splined to the wheel hub and secured by a spindle nut. The axle shafts are splined into the transaxle and retained by a roll pin.

LUBRICATION

The transaxle and differential are integral. The transaxle must use ONLY Mercon automatic transmission fluid. The differential uses synthetic 75W-140 hypoid gear lubricant.

NOTE: Vehicle must be raised on a drive on or side mounted swing arm hoist and in special areas of vehicle. See ENGINE REMOVAL & INSTALLATION at end of ENGINE section.

SERVICE (IN-VEHICLE)

HUB & WHEEL BEARINGS

Removal – 1) Raise and support vehicle. Remove front wheel. Remove caliper and support out of way. Hold hub secure and remove spindle nut. Push axle shaft out of hub. If necessary, use a hub puller to push axle shaft out.

NOTE: DO NOT strike end of axle shaft with hammer as axle threads may be damaged.

2) Leave brake rotor attached. Install a hub puller with slide hammer on hub. Remove hub. See Fig. 1. Using a a press and bearing puller, remove bearing race from back side of hub. Remove brake rotor. Remove bolts retaining bearing assembly to steering knuckle. Remove bearing assembly.

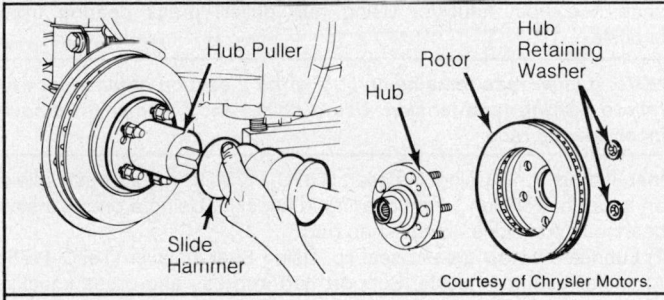

Fig. 1: Removing Front Hub

Installation – 1) Pack bearing with the grease supplied with replacement kit. If not replacing, pack old bearing with EP bearing lubricant. Install one bearing race on back side of bearing assembly. Press remaining bearing race on wheel hub.
2) Install bearing and race assembly on steering knuckle. Install and tighten bearing assembly bolts to specifications. Install brake rotor. Use a brass hammer and tap hub into position. Install drive axle. To complete installation, reverse removal procedure. Tighten bolts/nuts to specifications.

AXLE SHAFTS

Removal – 1) Remove front hub, rotor and bearing. See HUB & WHEEL BEARINGS in this article. Remove axle shaft roll pin, attaching axle shaft to transaxle. See Fig. 2. Remove nut from lower ball joint and leave bolt installed. Loosen 2 upper steering knuckle nuts until they are at end of bolts. The bolts are splined at the head end.
2) Tap nuts with brass hammer to loosen bolts. Remove nuts and bolts. Place a drain pan under transaxle end of axle shaft. Wrap shop rags around CV joint boots to protect boots. Tilt upper steering knuckle away from strut. Remove axle shaft from hub. Slide axle shaft out of transaxle and remove from vehicle.

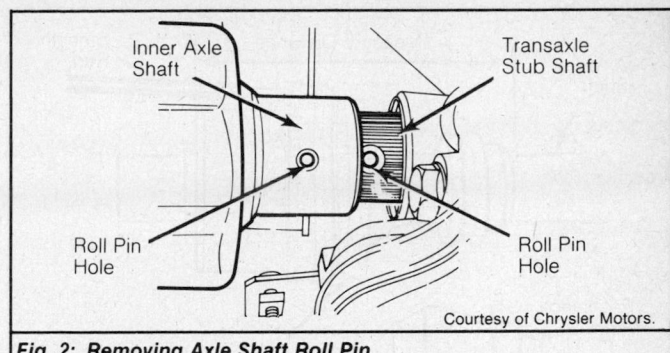

Fig. 2: Removing Axle Shaft Roll Pin

Installation – Tape shop rags around CV joint boots to protect boots during installation. Align axle shaft roll pin hole with output shaft hole and slide axle shaft on output shaft. See Fig. 2. Install a new roll pin. To complete installation, reverse removal procedure. Tighten bolts/nuts to specifications. Check and fill fluid levels.

OVERHAUL

AXLE SHAFTS

NOTE: Inner CV joint can be disassembled and repaired. The outer CV joint must be replaced as an assembly. Both boots can be serviced.

Disassembly (Outer CV Joint) – Remove axle shaft from vehicle. See AXLE SHAFTS in this article. Cut and remove boot clamps using care not to damage boot. Slide boot rearward enough to gain access to plastic retaining ring. Use snap ring pliers and spread the plastic retaining ring. Tap outer CV joint with plastic mallet and remove from axle shaft. Remove boot if replacing. See Fig. 3.

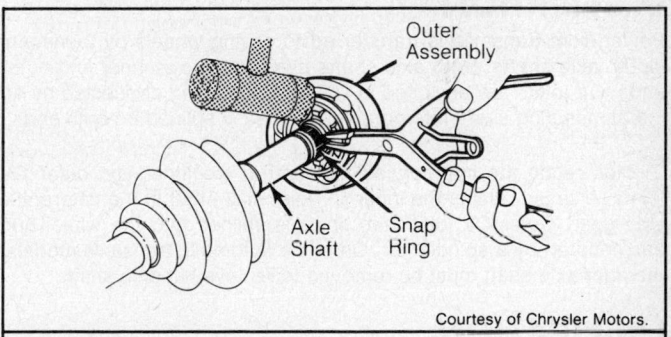

Fig. 3: Removing Outer CV Joint

Reassembly – Replace plastic retaining ring. Ensure tapered end goes into CV joint and segmented end toward axle shaft. Slide CV joint boot onto axle shaft (if removed). Thoroughly lubricate CV joint with grease supplied in kit. Tap CV joint onto axle shaft until retaining ring clicks. To complete installation, reverse removal procedure. Ensure boot is properly positioned before clamping.

Disassembly (Inner CV Joint) – Remove axle shaft. See AXLE SHAFTS in this article. Cut and remove boot clamps using care not to damage boot. Slide boot off CV joint yoke. Slide yoke straight off tripod joint. Remove tripod joint plastic retaining ring with snap ring pliers. Tap tripod joint off axle shaft with plastic mallet. Remove boot if replacing.

Reassembly – 1) Install a new plastic retaining ring in tripod joint with tapered end towards axle shaft and segmented end towards tripod joint. Install boot (if removed). Tap tripod joint onto axle shaft until fully seated in groove on axle shaft. Thoroughly lubricate yoke and tripod joint with grease supplied in kit.
2) Slide yoke onto tripod joint. Position boot on yoke and axle shaft. Bleed air from boot using a smooth rod between boot and yoke. Lift up on boot and allow trapped air to escape. See Fig. 4. Extend and

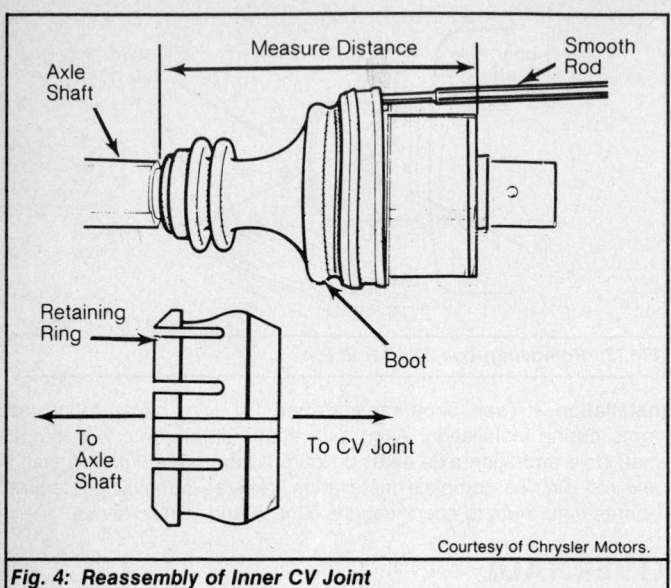

Fig. 4: Reassembly of Inner CV Joint

Courtesy of Chrysler Motors.

retract CV joint until distance is 6.10-6.18" (155-157 mm). To complete installation, reverse removal procedure. Ensure boot is properly seated before installing clamps.

TIGHTENING SPECIFICATIONS

Application	Ft. Lbs. (N.m)
Axle Spindle Nut	181 (245)
Brake Caliper Mounting Bolts	70 (95)
Lower Ball Joint Bolt/Nut	60 (82)
Steering Knuckle-to-Strut	123 (167)
Wheel Lug Nuts	63 (85)

Ford Motor Co.

Continental, Escort, Probe, Sable, Taurus, Tempo, Topaz

DESCRIPTION

Power from transaxle is transferred to driving wheels by 2 unequal length axle shafts. Both axle shafts use CV joints at inner and outer ends. CV joints are enclosed in CV joint boots and connected by an interconnecting shaft. Interconnecting shaft is splined on both ends.

Circlips retain the interconnecting shaft in the inner and outer CV joints. A circlip retains the inner CV joint stub shaft in the differential side gear. Outer CV joint stub shaft is splined into the wheel hub and secured by a spindle nut. On some automatic transaxle models, the right axle shaft must be removed to remove left axle shaft.

LUBRICATION

Front hub bearings are a cartridge design and require no scheduled maintenance. Inner and outer joints utilize 2 different grease specifications. The inner CV joint requires High Temperature Grease (E43Z-19590-A). The outer CV joint requires CV Joint Grease (E2FZ-19590-A). Transaxle lubricant must be filled with Mercon (ESP-M2C185-A).

SERVICE (IN-VEHICLE)

HUB BEARINGS

NOTE: Bearings are preset and cannot be adjusted. If bearing is disassembled, complete bearing unit must be replaced.

Removal (Probe) – 1) Remove front wheels. Carefully raise staked portion of axle nut. Apply brakes and remove axle nut and discard nut. Remove stabilizer bar-to-control arm nut, spacer and bolt.
2) Remove tie rod end cotter pin and nut. Using Tie Rod Separator (T85M-3395-A), disconnect tie rod end. Remove disc brake caliper and wire up out of way. Remove disc brake rotor (if necessary).
3) Remove lower control arm ball joint clamp bolt. Pry downward on lower control arm to separate control arm from knuckle. Remove knuckle-to-strut attaching bolts. Slide knuckle assembly off axle shaft and remove from vehicle.
4) Using a large screwdriver, pry grease seal from hub. Using Hub Puller (T87C-1104-A), press hub from knuckle. Remove bearing snap ring from knuckle. Using hub puller, press bearing from knuckle.

NOTE: If inner race remains on hub, grind a section of inner race to relieve bearing race tension. Use a chisel and hammer to remove inner bearing race.

Installation – 1) Using Installer (T87C-1175-B), install dust shield on knuckle. Position wheel bearing in knuckle. Using a press, install bearing into knuckle. Install snap ring.
2) Lubricate a new grease seal lip. Using Seal Installer (T87C-1175-A), install seal in knuckle. Support hub in press and press knuckle and hub together. Install new axle nut. Tighten all bolts and nuts to specifications. See TIGHTENING SPECIFICATIONS table. Stake new axle nut with blunt nose chisel. To complete installation, reverse removal procedure.

Removal (All Other Models) – 1) Loosen wheel lug nuts. Remove hub nut retainer by turning nut counterclockwise and breaking locking tab. Do not use screwdriver or chisel to remove locking tabs. Continue turning nut until nut retainer is removed. Remove washer. Raise and support vehicle on safety stands. Remove tire/wheel assembly.

NOTE: DO NOT reuse nut retainer.

2) Remove brake caliper by loosening locating pins and rotating caliper off rotor from lower end and lifting upward. Do not remove caliper pins from caliper assembly. Support caliper out of way with wire.
3) Pull rotor from hub. If rotor is restricted, apply rust penetrator to rotor and hub mating surfaces. Install 3-jaw type puller and remove rotor by pulling on outside diameter and pushing on center of hub. If excessive removal force is used, check rotor for lateral runout.

4) Disconnect lower control arm and tie rod from steering knuckle (leave strut attached). Loosen 2 nuts at top of strut mount in engine comparment. Install Hub Remover/Installer (T81P-1104-C) assembly and push CV joint out of hub assembly. See Fig. 1.

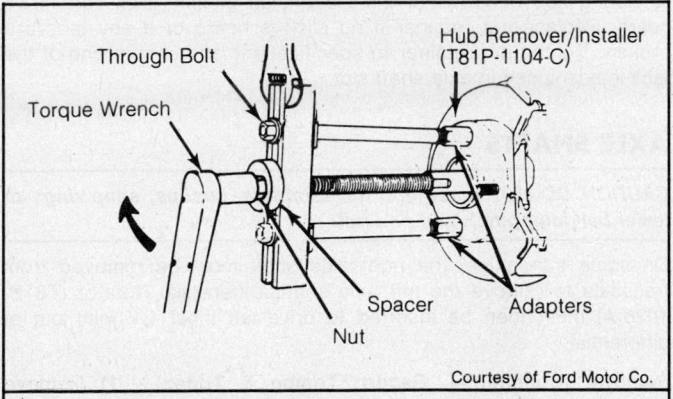

Fig. 1: Separating CV Joint & Knuckle Assembly

5) Hold knuckle assembly with wire and remove strut bolt-to-knuckle. Slide knuckle assembly off stut. Remove wire and place knuckle assembly on bench. Install 2-jaw type puller and remove hub from knuckle. Ensure a shaft protector is used, clears bearing I.D. and is centered. See Fig. 2.

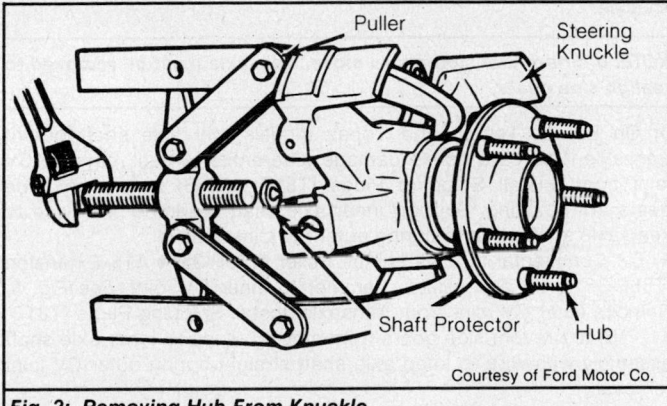

Fig. 2: Removing Hub From Knuckle

6) Using a screwdriver, remove and discard snap ring, which retains bearing in knuckle. Using Bearing Remover/Installer Kit (T83P-1104-AH), place appropriate spacer on inboard side of knuckle, with step side of spacer up. Place spacer and knuckle on press plate. Install bearing remover on inner bearing race. Press bearing out of knuckle and discard. See Fig. 3.

7) Remove axle shaft. See REMOVAL & INSTALLATION under AXLE SHAFTS in this article. Place axle shaft in vise with protected jaws. Remove dust seal by uniformly tapping outer edge with hammer and screwdriver. Discard dust seal.

Installation – 1) With axle shaft in vise, install dust seal on axle shaft with seal flange facing outward. See Fig. 4. Install axle shaft. See REMOVAL & INSTALLATION under AXLE SHAFT in this article.

2) Remove all foreign material from knuckle bearing bore and hub bearing journal. If hub bearing journal is scored or damaged, replace hub assembly. Using bearing remover/installer kit, place knuckle (inboard of knuckle facing up), on appropriate spacer (with step side down). See Fig. 5.

NOTE: Bearing installers must be positioned as indicated to prevent bearing damage during installation.

---

3) Install appropriate bearing installer on bearing outer race face, with undercut side of installer facing bearing. See Fig. 5. Press

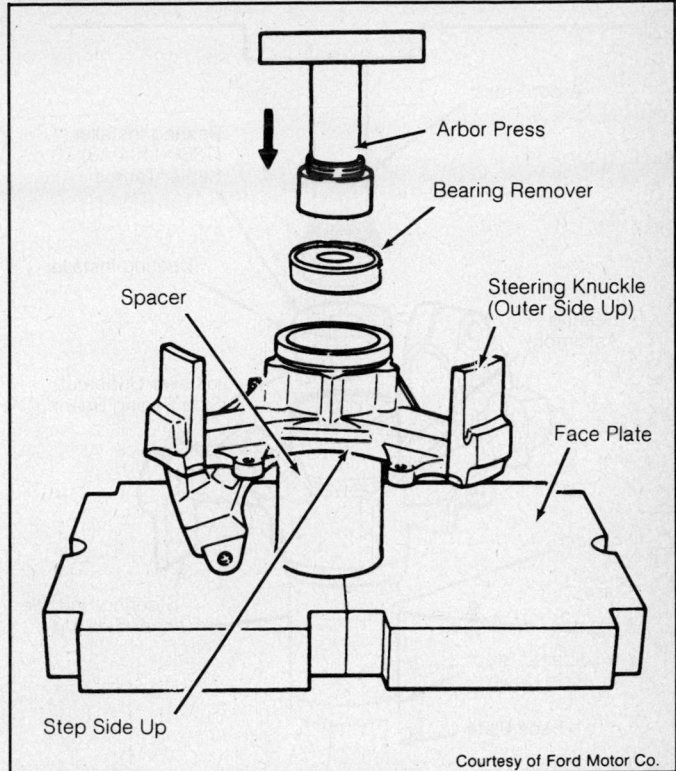

Fig. 3: Removing Hub Bearing From Knuckle

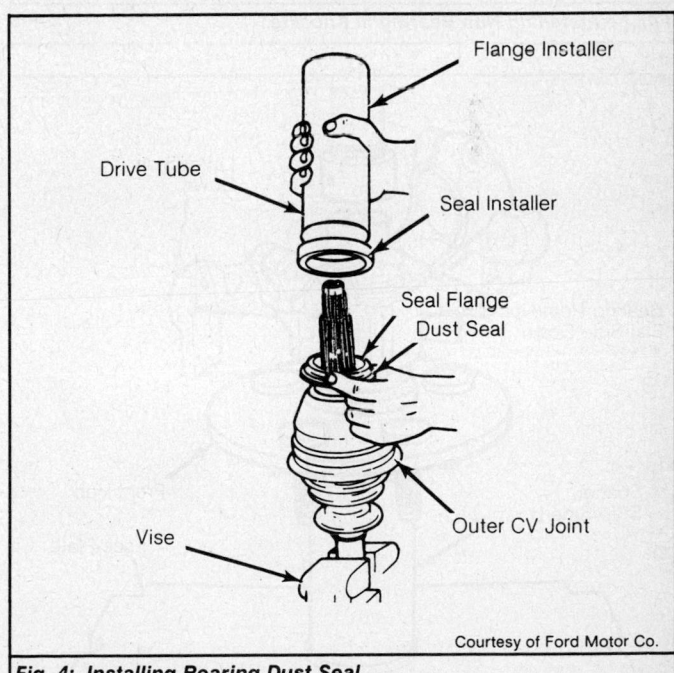

Fig. 4: Installing Bearing Dust Seal

bearing in knuckle until it seats completely against knuckle bore shoulder. Install a new snap ring in knuckle groove. Ensure snap ring is seated properly.

4) Position spacer on face plate with step side down. Position hub on spacer. Position knuckle assembly on hub with outboard side of knuckle down. Position appropriate bearing remover on bearing with flat side down and centered. See Fig. 6.

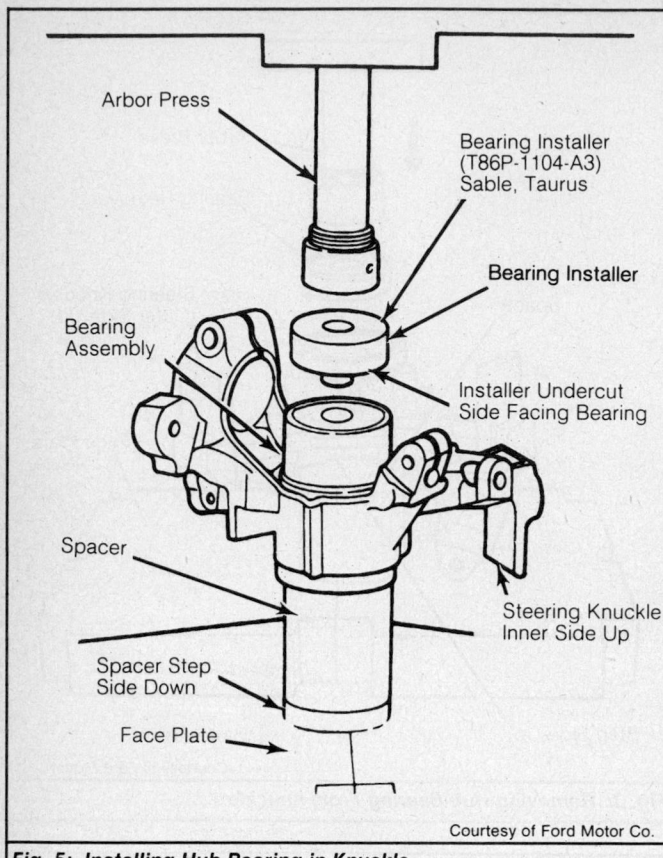

Fig. 5: Installing Hub Bearing in Knuckle

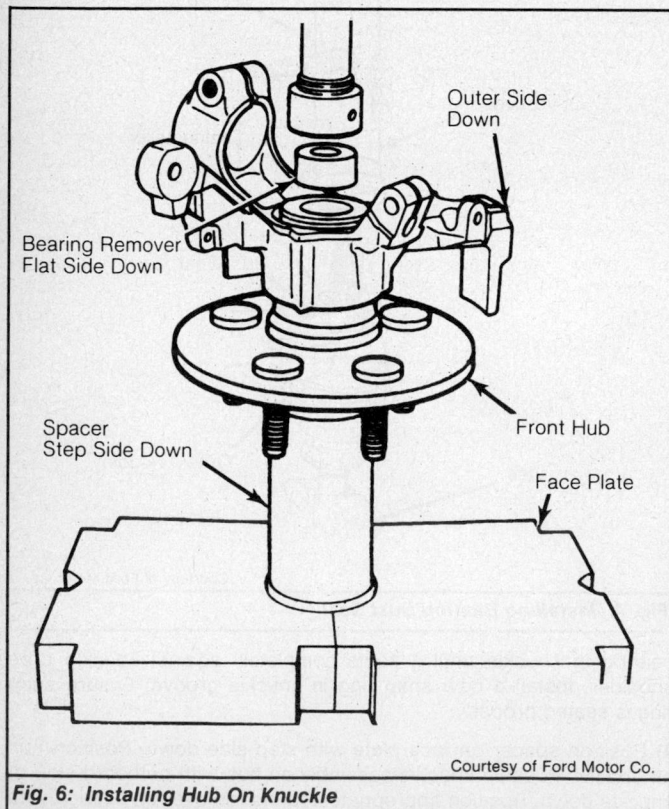

Fig. 6: Installing Hub On Knuckle

NOTE: Do not use power tools to tighten hub nut retainer. Do not move vehicle without tightening hub nut retainer.

5) Press remover until bearing is fully seated on hub. Ensure hub rotates freely on knuckle. To complete installation, reverse removal procedure. Lubricate CV joint splines with SAE 30W oil prior to installing in hub.

6) During hub nut retainer installation, an audible click should be heard. Replace nut retainer if no click is heard or if any tabs are broken. Tighten nut retainer to specifications and ensure one of the tabs is positioned in axle shaft slot.

AXLE SHAFTS

CAUTION: DO NOT reuse hub nut retainers, circlips, snap rings or lower ball joint pinch bolt and nut.

On some transaxles, the right axle shaft must be removed from transaxle to remove the left axle shaft. Differential Rotator (T81P-4026-A) must then be inserted to drive left inner CV joint out of differential.

Removal (Continental, Escort, Tempo & Topaz) – 1) Remove wheel/tire assembly and hub nut retainer. See step 1) in REMOVAL under HUB BEARINGS in this article. Remove bolt attaching brake hose to strut. Remove and discard bolt and nut retaining lower ball joint to steering knuckle. On Continental models, remove anti-lock brake sensor, height sensor link and stabilizer bar link.

2) On all models, move brake rotor shield out of way and pry down on control arm assembly to separate ball joint from steering knuckle.

NOTE: If differential side gears move, transaxle must be removed to realign side gears.

3) On Escort, Tempo and Topaz models, pry axle shaft out of transaxle. Use care not to damage differential oil seal, case or CV joint boot. Install Shipping Plugs (T81P-1177-B) to prevent side gears from moving. Support inner axle shaft assembly with wire to keep axle shaft straight during outer CV joint removal.

4) On Continental models, install Puller (T86P-3514-A1), Extension (T86P-3514-A2) and a slide hammer to inner CV joint. *See Fig. 8.* Remove inner CV joint from transaxle. Install Shipping Plugs (T81P-1177-B) to prevent side gears from moving. Support inner axle shaft assembly with wire to keep axle shaft straight during outer CV joint removal.

NOTE: DO NOT use hammer or similar tool to drive axle shaft from hub.

5) On all models, install Hub Remover/Installer (T81P-1104-C) assembly and push CV joint out of hub assembly. *See Fig. 1.* Remove axle shaft from vehicle.

Installation – Replace inner CV joint circlip. To install axle shaft, reverse removal procedure. Ensure circlip if fully seated in transaxle. During hub nut retainer installation, an audible click should be heard. Replace nut retainer if no click is heard or if any tabs are broken. Tighten nut retainer to specifications and ensure one of the tabs is positioned in axle shaft slot.

Removal (Probe) – 1) Remove front wheels. Carefully raise staked portion of axle nut. Apply brakes and loosen but do not remove axle nut. Remove stabilizer bar-to-control arm nut, spacer and bolt.

2) Remove lower control arm ball joint clamp bolt. Pry downward on lower control arm to separate control arm from knuckle. Remove knuckle-to-strut attaching bolts. Slide knuckle assembly off axle shaft and remove from vehicle.

NOTE: If removing right drive axle, remove dynamic damper from engine block.

3) On manual transaxle models, pull outward on steering knuckle with enough force to disengage axle circlip at transaxle end. DO NOT pull axle all the way out of transaxle or seal may be damaged.

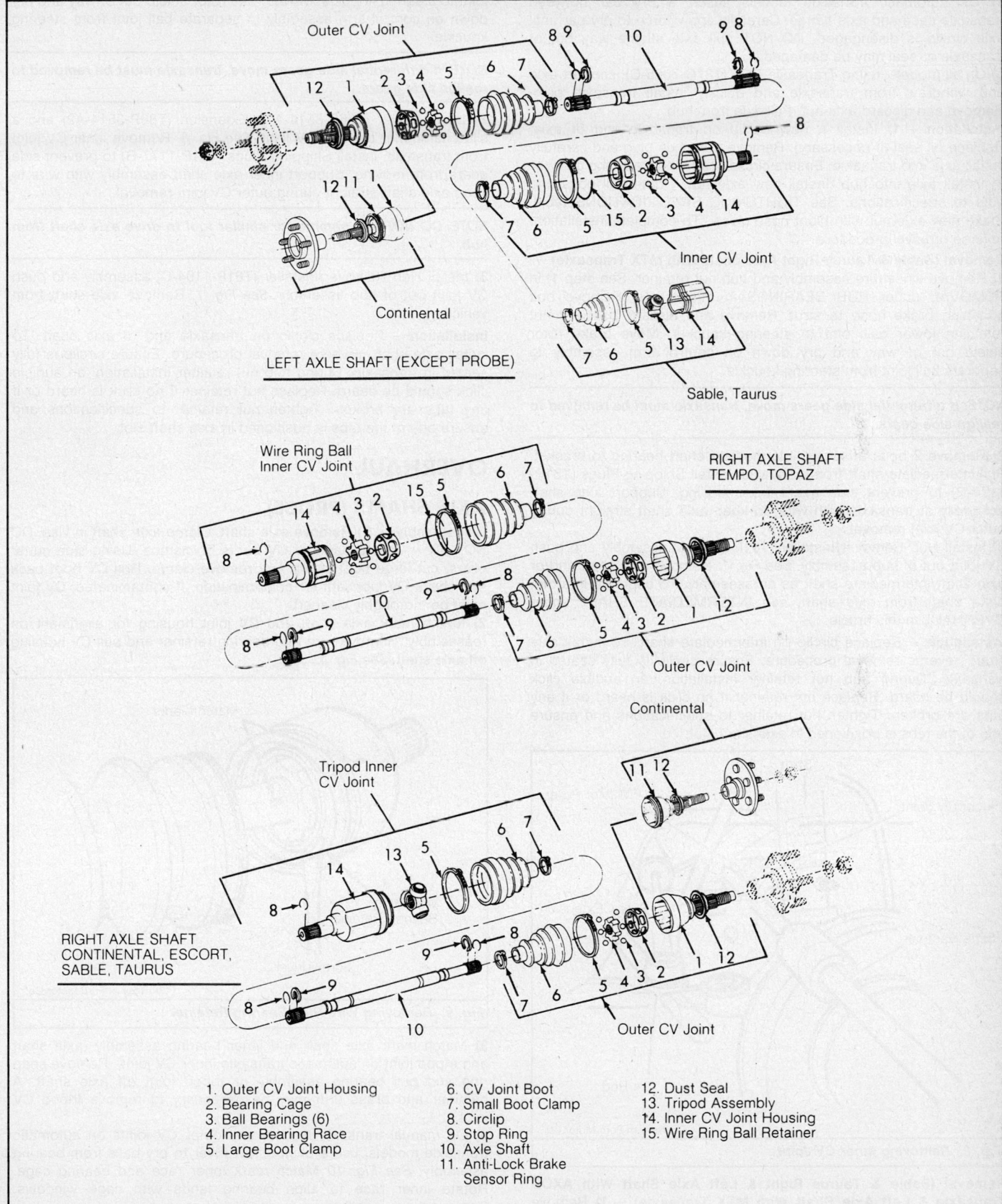

1. Outer CV Joint Housing
2. Bearing Cage
3. Ball Bearings (6)
4. Inner Bearing Race
5. Large Boot Clamp
6. CV Joint Boot
7. Small Boot Clamp
8. Circlip
9. Stop Ring
10. Axle Shaft
11. Anti-Lock Brake Sensor Ring
12. Dust Seal
13. Tripod Assembly
14. Inner CV Joint Housing
15. Wire Ring Ball Retainer

Courtesy of Ford Motor Co.

Fig. 7: Exploded View of Axle Shaft & CV Joint Assemblies

4) On automatic transaxle models, insert a pry bar between transaxle case and axle flange. Carefully apply force to pry bar until axle circlip is disengaged. DO NOT pull axle all the way out of transaxle or seal may be damaged.

5) On all models, using Transaxle Plug (T87C-7025-C), support axle and withdraw from transaxle and quickly install transaxle plug. Remove and discard axle nut. Pull axle from hub.

Installation – 1) Install a new circlip on transaxle end of axle. Replace oil seal (if necessary). Remove transaxle plug and carefully install axle into transaxle. Ensure circlip snaps into retaining groove.

2) Install axle into hub. Install new axle nut. Tighten all bolts and nuts to specifications. See TIGHTENING SPECIFICATIONS table. Stake new axle nut with blunt nose chisel. To complete installation, reverse removal procedure.

Removal (Sable & Taurus Right Axle Shaft With MTX Transaxle) –
1) Remove wheel/tire assembly and hub nut retainer. See step 1) in REMOVAL under HUB BEARINGS in this article. Remove bolt attaching brake hose to strut. Remove and discard bolt and nut retaining lower ball joint to steering knuckle. Move brake rotor shield out of way and pry down on control arm assembly to separate ball joint from steering knuckle.

NOTE: If differential side gears move, transaxle must be removed to realign side gears.

2) Remove 2 bolts attaching intermediate shaft bearing to bracket. Pull intermediate shaft from transaxle. Install Shipping Plugs (T81P-1177-B) to prevent side gears from moving. Support axle shaft assembly at transaxle with wire, to keep axle shaft straight during outer CV joint removal.

3) Install Hub Remover/Installer (T81P-1104-C) assembly and push CV joint out of hub assembly. *See Fig. 1.* Remove axle shaft and/or axle shaft/intermediate shaft as an assembly. To separate intermediate shaft from axle shaft, see INTERMEDIATE SHAFT under OVERHAUL in this article.

Installation – Replace circlip on intermediate shaft. To install axle shaft, reverse removal procedure. Ensure circlip is fully seated in transaxle. During hub nut retainer installation, an audible click should be heard. Replace nut retainer if no click is heard or if any tabs are broken. Tighten nut retainer to specifications and ensure one of the tabs is positioned in axle shaft slot.

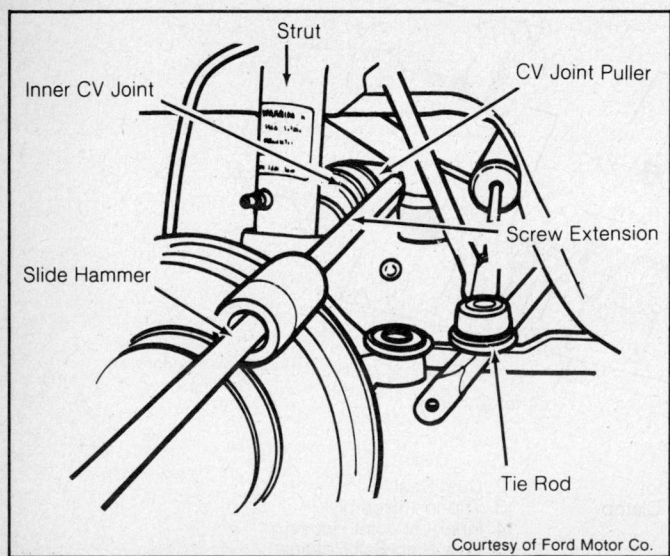

Fig. 8: Removing Inner CV Joint

Removal (Sable & Taurus Right & Left Axle Shaft With AXOD Transaxle & Left Axle Shaft With MTX Transaxle) – 1) Remove wheel/tire assembly and hub nut retainer. See step 1) in REMOVAL under HUB BEARINGS in this article. Remove bolt attaching brake hose to strut. Remove and discard bolt and nut retaining lower ball

joint to steering knuckle. Move brake rotor shield out of way and pry down on control arm assembly to separate ball joint from steering knuckle.

NOTE: If differential side gears move, transaxle must be removed to realign side gears.

2) Install Puller (T86P-3514-A1), Extension (T86P-3514-A2) and a slide hammer to inner CV joint. *See Fig. 8.* Remove inner CV joint from transaxle. Install Shipping Plugs (T81P-1177-B) to prevent side gears from moving. Support inner axle shaft assembly with wire to keep axle shaft straight during outer CV joint removal.

NOTE: DO NOT use hammer or similar tool to drive axle shaft from hub.

3) Install Hub Remover/Installer (T81P-1104-C) assembly and push CV joint out of hub assembly. *See Fig. 1.* Remove axle shaft from vehicle.

Installation – Replace circlip on transaxle end of axle shaft. To install axle shaft, reverse removal procedure. Ensure circlip is fully seated in transaxle. During hub nut retainer installation, an audible click should be heard. Replace nut retainer if no click is heard or if any tabs are broken. Tighten nut retainer to specifications and ensure one of the tabs is positioned in axle shaft slot.

OVERHAUL

AXLE SHAFTS (PROBE)

Disassembly – 1) Remove axle shaft. Clamp axle shaft in vise. DO NOT allow vise to damage CV boots or clamps. Using side cutter pliers, cut large boot clamp and remove clamp. Roll CV boot back and check CV lubricant for contamination. If contaminated, CV joint must be thoroughly cleaned.

2) Match mark axle shaft and CV joint housing for alignment on reassembly. Remove wire ring bearing retainer and pull CV housing off axle shaft. *See Fig. 9.*

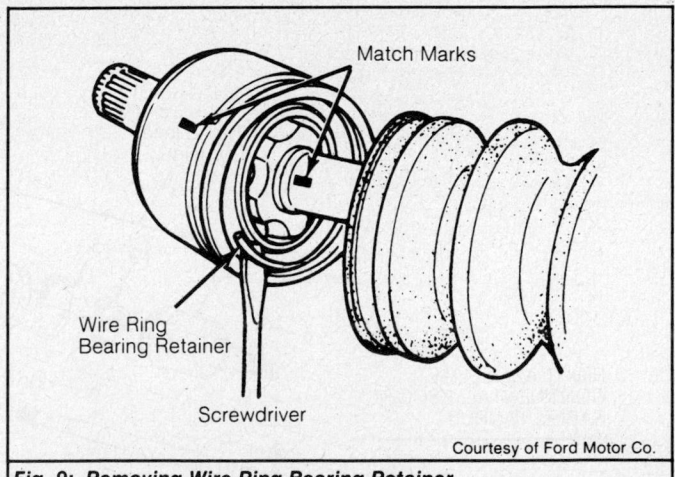

Fig. 9: Removing Wire Ring Bearing Retainer

3) Match mark axle shaft and inner bearing assembly (axle shaft and tripod joint on automatic transaxle inner CV joint). Remove snap ring and pull bearing assembly or tripod joint off axle shaft. A hammer and brass drift may be necessary to remove tripod CV joint.

4) On manual transaxle models and outer CV joints on automatic transaxle models, use a blunt screwdriver to pry balls from bearing assembly. *See Fig. 10* Match mark inner race and bearing cage. Rotate inner race to align bearing lands with cage windows. Remove inner race through larger end of cage.

5) On all models, thoroughly clean all parts. Inspect all bearing surfaces and bearings. CV joints must not have parts interchanged. A damaged CV joint will require a complete CV joint replacement.

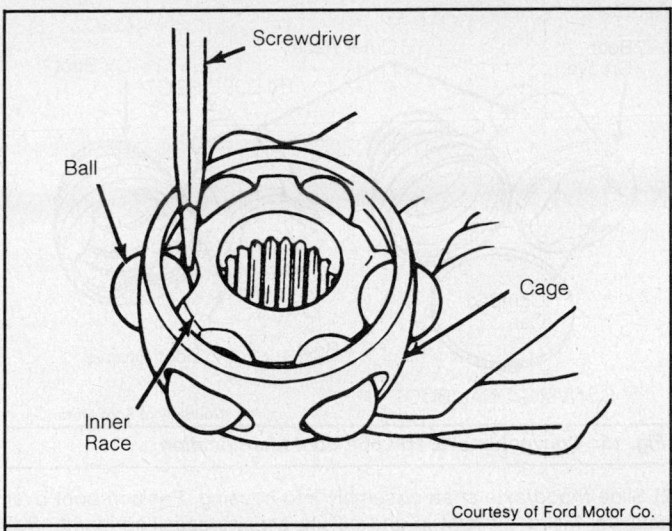

Fig. 10: Removing Balls From Bearing Assembly

Reassembly – **1)** CV joint must be lubricated with CV Joint Grease (E43Z-19590-A) when reassembled. If CV boot is being replaced, tape axle shaft splines to avoid damaging small end of boot when installing over axle.

2) Ensure match marks are aligned during reassembly. Lubricate CV bearing assembly with approximately 2 ounces of specified grease. Put remainder of grease in boot.

3) Lubricate tripod joint with 3.5 ounces of specified grease when reassembling. On all models, ensure CV boot is seated in grooves. Install CV boot clamp on small end and crimp.

4) Insert a blunt screwdriver under large end of CV boot to release trapped air. Install large CV boot clamp and crimp. On tripod CV joint, work CV joint in and out to it's full travel. Position CV joint on axle shaft to achieve 3.5" (90 mm) between CV boot clamps. Crimp boot clamp. *See Fig. 11.*

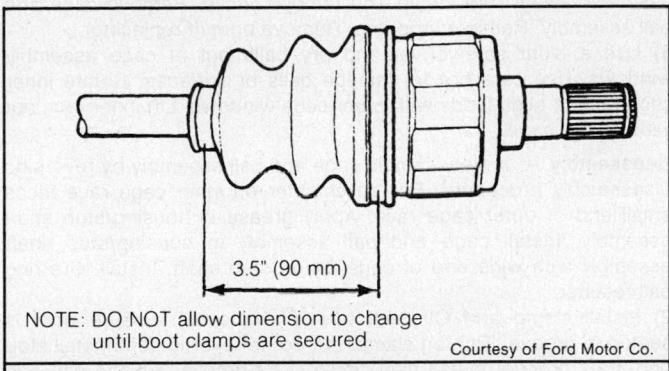

Fig. 11: CV Boot Assembled Length Measurement

AXLE SHAFTS (EXCEPT PROBE)

NOTE: Intermediate shafts are not the same. Note position, location and length to ensure correct installation.

Disassembly & Reassembly (Intermediate Shaft) – **1)** Remove axle shaft and intermediate shaft assembly. See appropriate AXLE SHAFTS in this article. Place intermediate shaft horizontally in a vise. Install Puller (T86P-3514-A1) and slide hammer. Separate axle shaft from intermediate shaft. Place intermediate shaft vertically in vise. Use a flat tip screwdriver and pry seal off.

2) Place intermediate shaft in a press and remove bearing. Place new bearing on intermediate shaft and press into position with a 1 3/16" deep well socket. Position new seal and press into position with same socket. Coat intermediate shaft splines, seal lip and seal cavity with CV Joint Grease (E2FZ-1950-A). Replace circlip and install axle shaft.

Disassembly (Outer CV Joint & Boot) – **1)** Remove axle shaft from vehicle. See AXLE SHAFTS under SERVICE (IN-VEHICLE). Clamp axle shaft horizontally in vise with protected jaws. Cut large boot clamp and pull boot back over axle shaft. Reposition axle shaft in vise. *See Fig. 12.* Use hammer and brass drift to tap inner bearing race sharply and dislodge internal circlip. Use care not to drop CV joint.

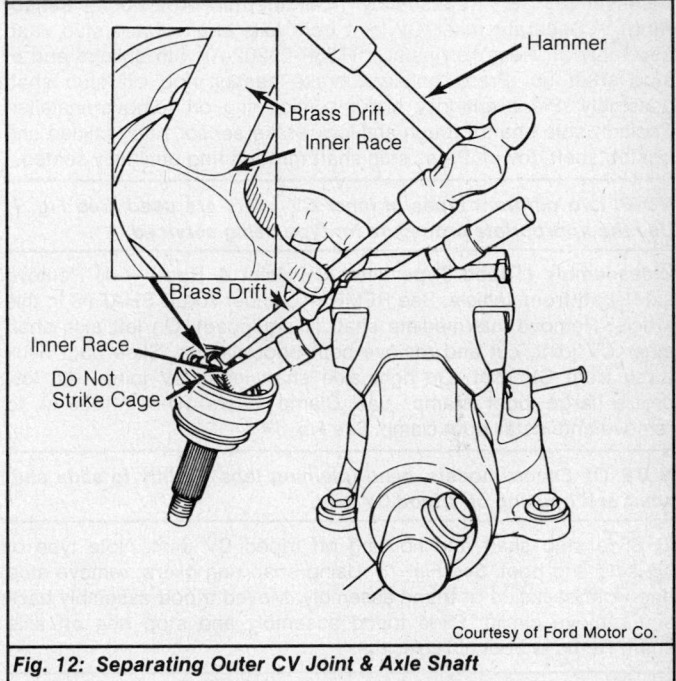

Fig. 12: Separating Outer CV Joint & Axle Shaft

2) Using a small screwdriver, remove and discard circlip and stop ring at end of axle shaft. Remove boot (if replacing). Place CV joint stub shaft in vise with bearing facing up. Press down on inner race enough to tilt cage and remove ball. *See Fig. 13.* Use a hammer and wooden drift and tap on inner race to tilt cage (if necessary).

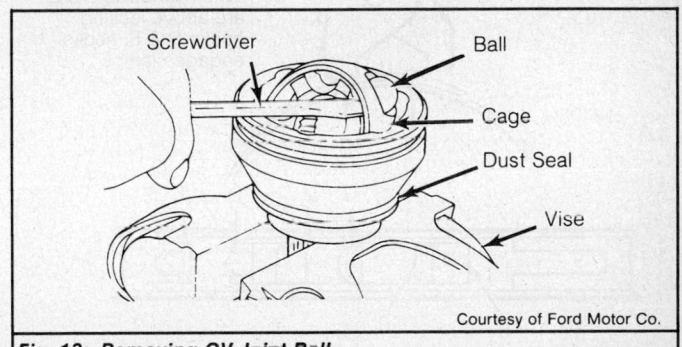

Fig. 13: Removing CV Joint Ball

3) Use a screwdriver without sharp edges (if necessary) to remove balls. Repeat procedure for remaining balls. Pivot cage and inner race assembly until it is straight up and down in outer race. Align cage windows with outer race lands while pivoting cage and lift cage assembly from outer race.

4) With cage assembly removed, pivot inner race until it is straight up and down in cage. Align one inner race land with one cage window and position race through window. Rotate inner race up and out of cage.

NOTE: Components are factory matched and can not be interchanged, mixed or substituted.

Reassembly – **1)** If components are cracked, broken, pitted or worn, replace complete assembly. Apply a light coat of CV Joint Grease (E2FZ-19590-A) on inner and outer races. To reassemble cage and balls, reverse disassembly procedure. Install boot on axle shaft (if removed) and seat in groove. Tighten clamp securely, but do not over tighten.

2) Install stop ring and ensure ring is properly seated. Install new circlip. Pack CV joint and boot with specified CV joint grease. Fill CV joint first and place remaining amount in boot. Total amount of grease required is 3.52 ozs. (100 g). To complete reassembly, reverse disassembly procedure.

Disassembly & Reassembly (Continental Anti-Lock Sensor Ring) – Separate outer CV joint from axle shaft. Place stub shaft assembly on Remover/Installer (T88P-20202-A) with splined end of stub shaft up. Press anti-lock brake sensor ring off stub shaft assembly. Place anti-lock brake sensor ring on remover/installer. Position stub shaft through anti-lock brake sensor ring (splined end of stub shaft down). Press stub shaft through ring until fully seated.

NOTE: *Two different types of inner CV joints are used. See Fig. 7. Use the appropriate procedure for type being serviced.*

Disassembly (Tripod Type Inner CV Joint & Boot) – 1) Remove axle shaft from vehicle. See REMOVAL under AXLE SHAFTS in this article. Remove intermediate shaft (if equipped). On left axle shaft inner CV joint, cut and remove both boot clamps. Slide boot back away from CV joint. On right axle shaft inner CV joint, with low profile large boot clamp, use Clamp Pliers (D-82P-1090-A) to remove and install boot clamp. See Fig. 14.

NOTE: *On Escort models, bend retaining tabs slightly to slide stub shaft and housing off tripod CV joint.*

2) Slide stub shaft and housing off tripod CV joint. Note type of housing and boot. See Fig. 15. Using snap ring pliers, remove stop ring from backside of tripod assembly. Moved tripod assembly back and remove circlip. Slide tripod assembly and stop ring off axle shaft. Remove boot (if replacing).

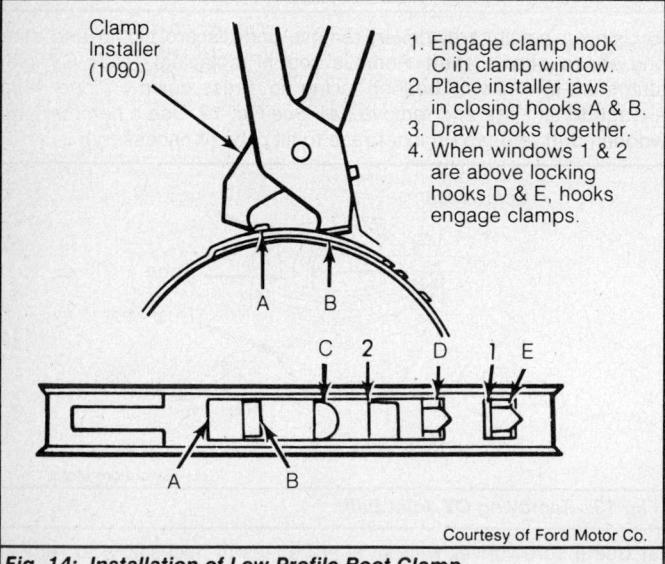

Clamp Installer (1090)

1. Engage clamp hook C in clamp window.
2. Place installer jaws in closing hooks A & B.
3. Draw hooks together.
4. When windows 1 & 2 are above locking hooks D & E, hooks engage clamps.

Courtesy of Ford Motor Co.

Fig. 14: Installation of Low Profile Boot Clamp

NOTE: *On Escort models, fill tri-lobe type boot with 2.1 ozs. (60 g) of specified grease.*

Reassembly – 1) Install small clamp and boot (if removed). Ensure boot is seated in groove on axle shaft and tighten clamp securely, but do not over tighten. Install stop ring on axle shaft, beyond its groove. This will allow new circlip to be installed. Slide tripod assembly on axle shaft with chamfered side toward stop ring.

NOTE: *On Escort models, bend retaining tabs back to original position after reassembly of CV joint into housing.*

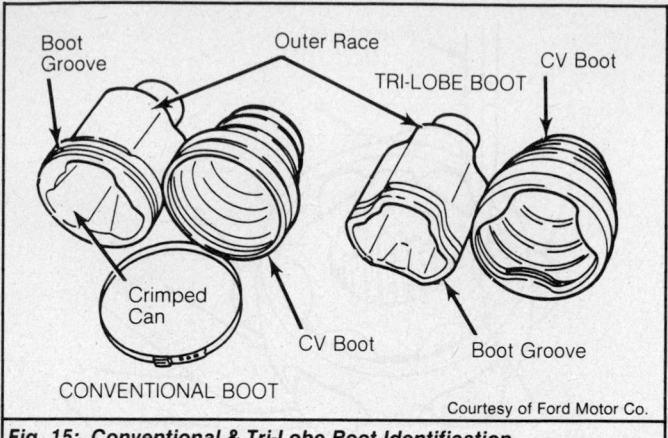

Fig. 15: Conventional & Tri-Lobe Boot Identification

Boot Groove — Outer Race — CV Boot — TRI-LOBE BOOT — Crimped Can — CV Boot — Boot Groove — CONVENTIONAL BOOT

Courtesy of Ford Motor Co.

2) Slide tripod/axle shaft assembly into housing. Position boot over housing. Move CV joint in and out, to acquire specified length. *See Fig. 16.* Ensure boot is properly seated in groove. Wipe excess grease from external surfaces. Remove trapped air by lifting boot off housing with a dull screwdriver.

3) With axle shaft at specified length, air removed and boot properly seated, install boot clamp. Tighten clamp, but do not overtighten. To install low profile type clamps, *see Fig. 14.* To complete reassembly, reverse disassembly procedure. Install a new circlip.

Disassembly (Wire Ring Ball Type CV Joint) – 1) Remove axle shaft from vehicle. See REMOVAL under AXLE SHAFTS in this article. Remove intermediate shaft (if equipped). Note inner CV joint stub shaft length. The lengths are different depending on model being serviced. *See Fig. 17.*

2) Cut large boot clamp and remove clamp. Move boot away from CV joint. Remove wire ring ball retainer. Separate housing from CV joint and axle shaft. Pull cage and ball assembly away from stop ring and slide stop ring down axle shaft. Slide cage and ball assembly away from circlip and remove circlip. Remove cage and ball assembly. Remove stop ring. Remove boot (if replacing).

3) Use a blunt screwdriver and pry balls out of cage assembly windows. Use care not to damage balls or surfaces. Rotate inner cage race to align lands with outer cage windows. Lift inner race out wide end of cage.

Reassembly – 1) Reassemble cage and ball assembly by reversing disassembly procedure. Ensure chamfer on inner cage race faces small end of outer cage race. Apply grease in housing/stub shaft assembly. Install cage and ball assembly in housing/stub shaft assembly with wide end of cage facing stub shaft. Install wire ring ball retainer.

2) Install clamp and CV joint boot (if removed). Ensure boot is seated in groove. Tighten clamp, but do not overtighten. Install stop ring in its groove. Install new circlip in its groove. Fill CV joint and housing with 3.2 ozs. (90 g) of specified grease. Spread 1.4 ozs. (40 g) of specified grease evenly inside boot.

3) Position housing/stub shaft assembly on axle shaft/CV joint assembly. Ensure splines are properly aligned and tap stub shaft end with plastic hammer until CV joint is fully seated. Remove excess grease from external surfaces. Position boot over housing and seat in groove.

4) Move CV joint in and out, to acquire specified length. See Fig. 16. Ensure boot is properly seated in groove. Wipe excess grease from external surfaces. Remove trapped air by lifting boot off housing with a dull screwdriver.

5) With axle shaft at specified length, air removed and boot properly seated, install boot clamp. Tighten clamp, but do not over tighten. On low profile type clamps, *See Fig. 14.* To complete reassembly, reverse disassembly procedure. Install a new circlip.

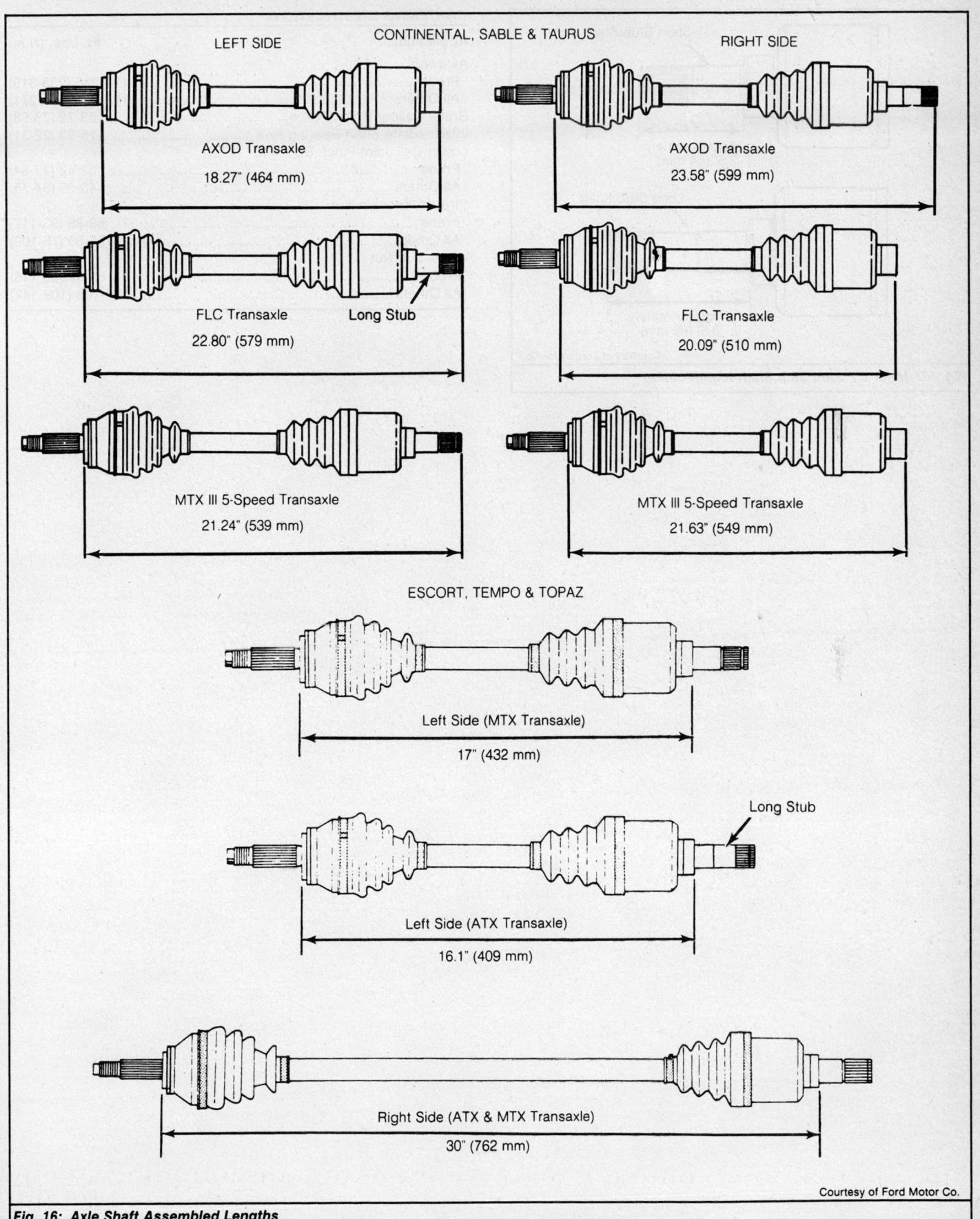

CONTINENTAL, SABLE & TAURUS

LEFT SIDE

AXOD Transaxle
18.27" (464 mm)

FLC Transaxle
22.80" (579 mm)
Long Stub

MTX III 5-Speed Transaxle
21.24" (539 mm)

RIGHT SIDE

AXOD Transaxle
23.58" (599 mm)

FLC Transaxle
20.09" (510 mm)

MTX III 5-Speed Transaxle
21.63" (549 mm)

ESCORT, TEMPO & TOPAZ

Left Side (MTX Transaxle)
17" (432 mm)

Long Stub

Left Side (ATX Transaxle)
16.1" (409 mm)

Right Side (ATX & MTX Transaxle)
30" (762 mm)

Courtesy of Ford Motor Co.

Fig. 16: Axle Shaft Assembled Lengths

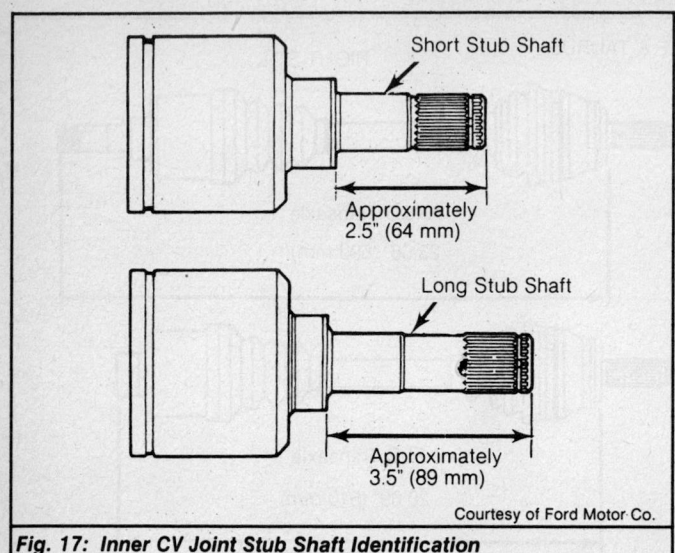

Fig. 17: Inner CV Joint Stub Shaft Identification

TIGHTENING SPECIFICATIONS

Application	Ft. Lbs. (N.m)
Axle Nut	
Probe	174-235 (235-319)
All Others	180-200 (244-271)
Brake Caliper Bolts (Probe)	58-72 (79-98)
Intermediate Shaft Bearing Bolt	16-23 (22-31)
Lower Ball Joint Pinch Bolt	
Probe	32-40 (43-54)
All Others	40-55 (54-75)
Strut-to-Knuckle Nut	
Probe	69-86 (93-117)
All Others	55-80 (75-109)
Wheel Lug Nut	
Probe	65-87 (88-118)
All Others	80-105 (109-142)

Section 10
BRAKES

CONTENTS

BRAKE TROUBLE SHOOTING
                                                        Page
All Models 10-2

HYDRAULIC BRAKE BLEEDING
All Models 10-3

POWER BRAKE UNITS
Chrysler Motors, Eagle
 & Ford Motor Co. Single Diaphragm 10-4

MASTER CYLINDERS   Page
Bendix/Delco-Moraine
 Chrysler Motors, Eagle & Ford Motor Co. 10-6

ANTI-LOCK BRAKE SYSTEMS
SAFETEY PRECAUTIONS
All Models 10-8

ANTI-LOCK BRAKE SYSTEMS
Chrysler Motors
 Dynasty & New Yorker 10-9
Ford Motor Co.
 Continental, Cougar, Mark VII & Thunderbird 10-20
 Probe 10-39

DISC BRAKE SYSTEMS
Chrysler Motors Single Piston
 Front 10-43
 Rear 10-46
Eagle & Ford Motor Co. – Front 10-48
Ford Motor Co. – Rear 10-50

DRUM BRAKE SYSTEMS
Bendix Single Anchor Automatic Adjuster
 Chrysler Motors, Eagle & Ford Motor Co.
 (Except Continental & Mark VII) 10-54

NOTE: ALSO SEE GENERAL INDEX.

1989 BRAKES
Brake Trouble Shooting

CONDITION	POSSIBLE CAUSE	CORRECTION
Brakes Pull Left or Right	Incorrect tire pressure	Inflate tires to proper pressure
	Front end out of alignment	See WHEEL ALIGNMENT
	Mismatched tires	Check tires sizes
	Restricted brake lines or hoses	Check hose routing
	Loose or malfunctioning caliper	See DISC BRAKE SYSTEMS
	Bent shoe or oily linings	See DRUM BRAKE SYSTEMS
	Malfunctioning rear brakes	See DRUM or DISC BRAKE SYSTEMS
	Loose suspension parts	See SUSPENSION
Noises Without Brakes Applied	Front linings worn out	Replace linings
	Bent or broken hardware	See DISC OR DRUM BRAKE SYSTEMS
	Bent shoe or lining	See DRUM BRAKE SYSTEMS
Noises With Brakes Applied	Linings or pads glazed	Replace pads or linings
	Insulator on outboard shoe damaged	See DISC BRAKE SYSTEMS
	Incorrect pads or linings	Replace pads or linings
Brake Rough, Chatters or Pulsates	Uneven pad wear caused by caliper	See DISC BRAKE SYSTEMS
	Excessive lateral runout	Check rotor runout
	Parallelism not to specifications	Reface or replace rotor
	Wheel bearings not adjusted	See SUSPENSION
	Rear drums out-of-round	Reface or replace drums
	Disc pad reversed, steel against rotor	Remove and reinstall pad
Excessive Pedal Effort	Malfunctioning power unit	See POWER BRAKE UNITS
	Partial system failure	Check fluid and pipes
	Caliper piston stuck or sluggish	See DISC BRAKE SYSTEMS
	Master cylinder piston stuck	See MASTER CYLINDERS
	Plugged air filter element	Replace air filter
	Incorrect pads or linings	Replace pads or linings
Excessive Pedal Travel	Partial brake system failure	Inspect complete braking system
	Air trapped in system	See BLEEDING
	Rear brakes not adjusted	See ADJUSTMENTS in DRUM BRAKE SYSTEMS
	Worn drums	Replace drums
	Plugged master cylinder cap	See MASTER CYLINDER
	Improper brake fluid	Replace brake fluid
Pedal Travel Decreasing	Compensating port plugged	See MASTER CYLINDERS
	Swollen cup in master cylinder	See MASTER CYLINDERS
	Master cylinder piston not returning	See MASTER CYLINDERS
	Weak shoe retracting springs	See DRUM BRAKE SYSTEMS
	Wheel cylinder piston sticking	See DRUM BRAKE SYSTEMS
Dragging Brakes	Master cylinder pistons not returning	See MASTER CYLINDERS
	Restricted brake lines or hoses	Check line routing
	Incorrect parking brake adjustment	See DISC OR DRUM BRAKE SYSTEMS
	Parking brake cables frozen	See DISC OR DRUM BRAKE SYSTEMS
	Incorrect installation of disc pad	Remove and replace correctly
	Power booster output rod too long	See POWER BRAKE UNITS
	Brake pedal not returning freely	See DISC or DRUM BRAKE SYSTEMS
Brakes Grab or Uneven Braking Action	Malfunction of combination valve	See HYDRAULIC SYSTEM CONTROL VALVES
	Malfunction of power brake unit	See POWER BRAKE UNITS
	Binding brake pedal	See DISC or DRUM BRAKE SYSTEMS
	Contaminated linings	Replace pads or linings

Chrysler Motors, Eagle, Ford Motor Co.

DESCRIPTION

Hydraulic system bleeding is necessary any time air has been introduced into system. Bleed brakes at all 4 wheels if master cylinder lines have been disconnected or master cylinder has run dry. Bleeding can be accomplished by using pressure bleeding equipment or by manually pumping brake pedal and using a clear bleeder hose.

SERVICING

METERING VALVE

1) On disc brake equipped vehicles, the metering section of the combination valve must be held open before pressure bleeding.
2) Hold metering valve open while pressure bleeding front brakes. Loosen front mounting bolt and install pressure bleeding tool on combination valve, valve stem should be fully depressed. See Fig. 1.

NOTE: Never reintroduce brake fluid that has been drained from hydraulic brake system or that has been allowed to stand in an open container for an extended period of time. Also, do not use fluid that contains a petroleum base. Petroleum based fluids will cause swelling and distortion of rubber parts in hydraulic system.

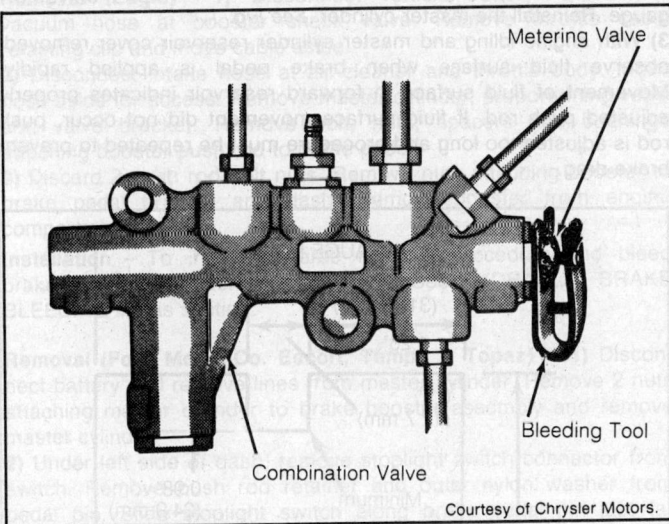

Metering Valve

Bleeding Tool

Combination Valve

Courtesy of Chrysler Motors.

Fig. 1: Combination Valve (Manual Override)

BENCH BLEEDING MASTER CYLINDER

NOTE: Bleed tubes must have a residual pressure check valve installed to keep tubes from siphoning brake fluid.

1) Clamp master cylinder in vise at mounting flange. Install and tighten threaded end of bleed tubes in outlet ports of master cylinder with opposite end of bleeder tube in reservoirs. Fill reservoirs with clean brake fluid so bleed tube ends are submerged in brake fluid.

2) Slowly compress and release piston assemblies until bubbles cease to appear in brake fluid. Remove tubes and plug master cylinder outlets to keep fluid from draining.

MANUAL BLEEDING

NOTE: On Eagle Premier, rear wheels must be at normal ride height. Air can be trapped in wheel cylinder if rear wheels are at full jounce position. Position vehicle on drive-on type hoist or raise rear wheels to normal ride height before bleeding.

1) If vehicle is equipped with power brakes, exhaust vacuum reserve from power unit by depressing brake pedal several times. Fill master cylinder with clean brake fluid. Install bleeder hose to wheel assembly being serviced. Submerge other end of hose in clean glass jar partially filled with clean brake fluid.
2) Depress brake pedal slowly through its full travel and hold. Open bleed screw 3/4-1 turn. Close bleed screw. Release brake pedal. Repeat procedure until brake fluid shows no signs of air bubbles.

PRESSURE BLEEDING

NOTE: On Eagle Premier, rear wheels must be at normal ride height. Air can be trapped in wheel cylinder if rear wheels are at full jounce position. Position vehicle on drive-on type hoist or raise rear wheels to normal ride height before bleeding.

1) To prevent dirt from falling into reservoir, clean master cylinder and cover/diaphram assembly. With pressure tank at least 1/3 full, connect to master cylinder using adapters.
2) Install bleeder hose to wheel assembly being serviced. Submerge other end of hose in clean glass jar partially filled with clean brake fluid. Charge bleeder to specification. See BLEEDING PRESSURES table at end of this article.
3) Open release valve on pressure bleeder. Open bleed screw 3/4-1 turn. Close bleed screw when brake fluid is clear and free of bubbles. Bleed remaining wheel assemblies in sequence and in same manner. Remove pressure bleeding tool.

BLEEDING SEQUENCE

NOTE: When bleeding anti-lock brake systems, refer to BLEEDING BRAKE SYSTEM under ANTI-LOCK BRAKE SYSTEMS in this section. Also, on Eagle Premier, rear wheels must be at normal ride height. Air can be trapped in wheel cylinder if rear wheels are at full jounce position. Position vehicle on drive-on type hoist or raise rear wheels to normal ride height before bleeding.

If vehicle is equipped with power brakes, exhaust vacuum reserve from power unit by depressing brake pedal several times. Bleed master cylinder before bleeding wheel assemblies. Generally, system is bled starting with wheel assembly furthest from master cylinder and working to wheel assembly closest to master cylinder.

BLEEDING PRESSURES

Application	psi (kg/cm²)
Chrysler Motors	35 (2.46)
Eagle Premier	15-20 (1.05-1.40)
Ford Motor Co.	10-30 (.70-2.10)

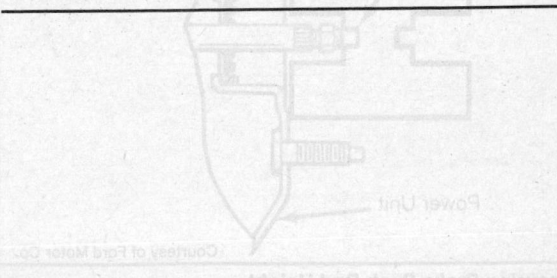

2) Plug all open lines. Disconnect transmission shift cable from transmission and lay aside. Remove all bolts and nuts retaining pump/motor assembly. Remove pump/motor assembly. To install, reverse removal procedure.

PRESSURE & RETURN HOSES

Removal & Installation – Remove pump/motor assembly. Remove pressure and return hoses. To install, reverse removal procedure. Install rubber "O" rings on return hoses. Install steel "O" rings on pressure hoses.

SENSOR BLOCK

Removal – **1)** Depressurize brake system. Unplug all electrical connectors from hydraulic assembly. From under instrument panel, remove clip retaining brake pedal and discard. Remove insulator sound panel from driver's side. Remove nuts retaining hydraulic assembly.

2) From engine compartment, pull hydraulic assembly outward enough to gain access to sensor block. DO NOT disconnect brake lines from hydraulic assembly. Remove sensor block cover.

3) Unplug 12-pin connector from sensor block. Remove 3 bolts retaining sensor block. Carefully remove sensor block. DO NOT damage "O" ring at pressure port.

Installation – To install, reverse removal procedure. Tighten sensor block retaining bolts to 11 ft. lbs. (15 N.m).

HYDRAULIC ASSEMBLY

Removal & Installation – **1)** Disconnect negative battery cable. Turn ignition off. Depress brake pedal 25 times or more to depressurize brake system. Remove air intake ducts. Unplug all electrical connectors from hydraulic assembly.

2) Remove fluid from reservoir. Disconnect pressure and return hoses from hydraulic assembly. Plug all openings. Disconnect all brake lines from hydraulic assembly.

3) From under instrument panel, remove clip and brake pedal pin. Discard clip. Remove driver's side insulator panel. Remove hydraulic assembly. To install, reverse removal procedure. Install new clip. Bleed brake system. See BRAKE BLEEDING in this article.

OVER VOLTAGE & PUMP/MOTOR RELAYS

Removal & Installation – Remove radiator overflow bottle. Remove relay bracket retaining screw. Remove relay. See Fig. 3. To install, reverse removal procedure.

WHEEL SENSORS

NOTE: DO NOT use pliers to remove wheel sensor.

Removal (Front) – Raise front of vehicle and support. Remove wheel. Remove clip retaining sensor wire to fender sheild and strut. Remove sensor head screw. Carefully remove sensor.

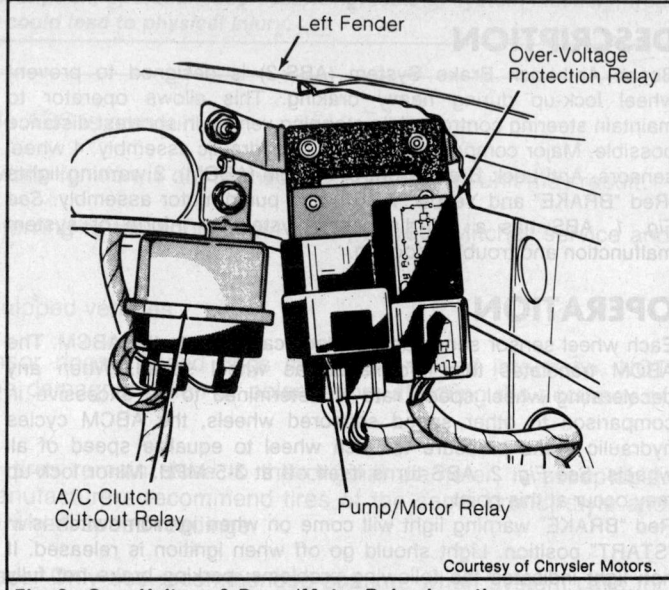

Fig. 3: Over Voltage & Pump/Motor Relay Locations

Removal (Rear) – Raise and support rear of vehicle. Remove sensor grommet from underbody. Pull sensor lead through hole. Remove all wheel sensor lead clips. Remove sensor head screw. Remove wheel sensor.

Installation – To install, reverse removal procedure.

BLEEDING BRAKE SYSTEM

1) Brake system can be bled using manual method or using hydraulic unit to pressurize system. To manually bleed brake system, depressurize brake system before opening any bleeder screw.

2) With ignition off, pump brake pedal 25 times using full pedal strokes. When a definite increase in pedal effort is felt, pump pedal 2 more times. DO NOT turn ignition on any time system is being manually bled.

3) To bleed system using hydraulic unit, depressurize brake system. Ensure reservoir is full. Open bleeder screw. Turn ignition on. Allow pump/motor assembly to run until brake fluid from bleeder screw contains no air.

4) Close bleeder screw. Turn ignition off. Depressurize brake system. Fill reservoir with brake fluid. Perform same procedure as previously described for each wheel.

NOTE: The following charts and diagrams are courtesy of Chrysler Motors.

TROUBLE SHOOTING CHARTS

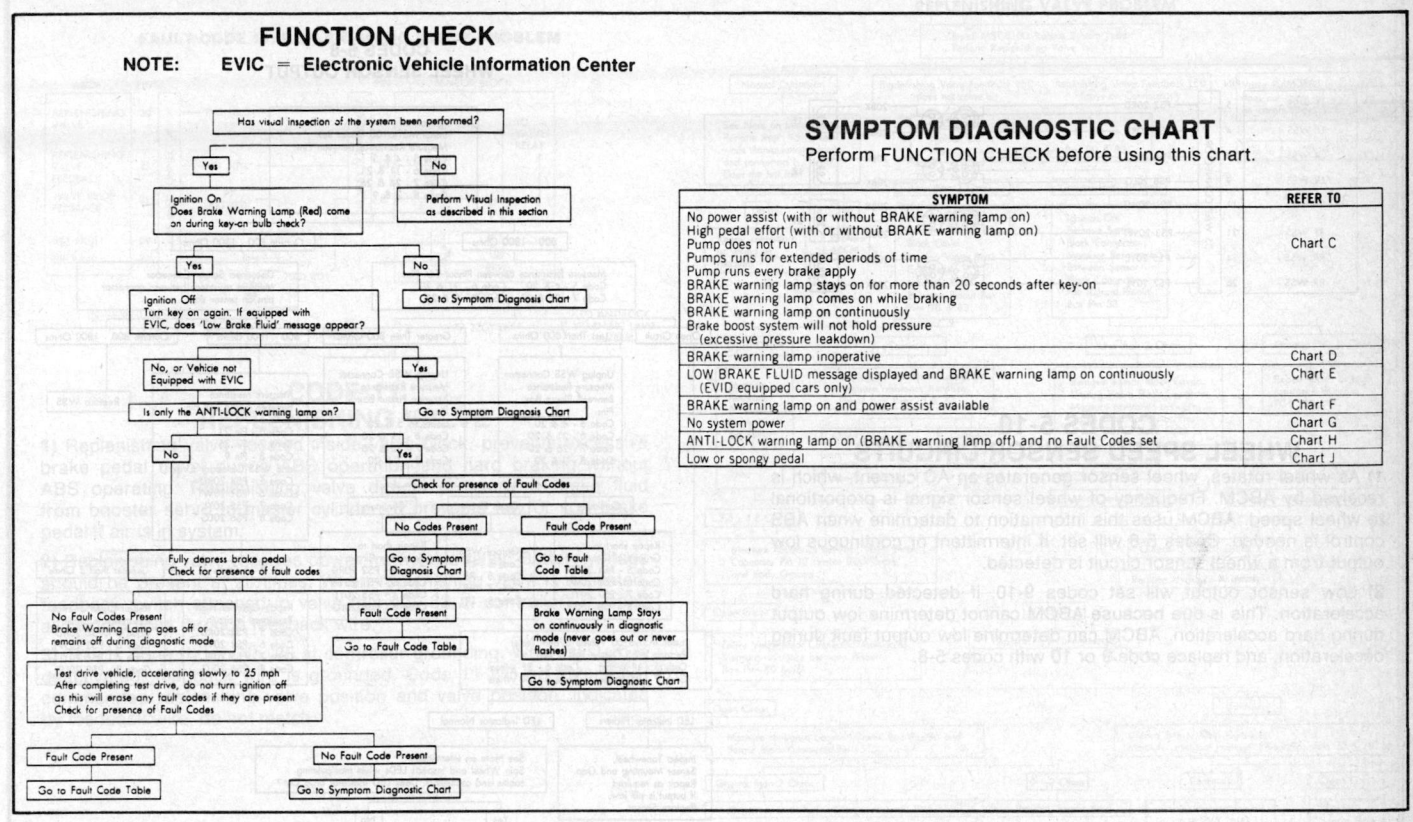

FUNCTION CHECK

NOTE: EVIC = Electronic Vehicle Information Center

SYMPTOM DIAGNOSTIC CHART

Perform FUNCTION CHECK before using this chart.

SYMPTOM	REFER TO
No power assist (with or without BRAKE warning lamp on) High pedal effort (with or without BRAKE warning lamp on) Pump does not run Pumps runs for extended periods of time Pump runs every brake apply BRAKE warning lamp stays on for more than 20 seconds after key-on BRAKE warning lamp comes on while braking BRAKE warning lamp on continuously Brake boost system will not hold pressure (excessive pressure leakdown)	Chart C
BRAKE warning lamp inoperative	Chart D
LOW BRAKE FLUID message displayed and BRAKE warning lamp on continuously (EVID equipped cars only)	Chart E
BRAKE warning lamp on and power assist available	Chart F
No system power	Chart G
ANTI-LOCK warning lamp on (BRAKE warning lamp off) and no Fault Codes set	Chart H
Low or spongy pedal	Chart J

Function Check flowchart:

- Has visual inspection of the system been performed?
  - Yes → Ignition On. Does Brake Warning Lamp (Red) come on during key-on bulb check?
    - Yes → Ignition Off. Turn key on again. If equipped with EVIC, does 'Low Brake Fluid' message appear?
      - No, or Vehicle not Equipped with EVIC → Is only the ANTI-LOCK warning lamp on?
        - No → Fully depress brake pedal. Check for presence of fault codes
          - No Fault Codes Present. Brake Warning Lamp goes off or remains off during diagnostic mode → Test drive vehicle, accelerating slowly to 25 mph. After completing test drive, do not turn ignition off as this will erase any fault codes if they are present. Check for presence of Fault Codes
            - Fault Code Present → Go to Fault Code Table
            - No Fault Code Present → Go to Symptom Diagnostic Chart
        - Yes → Check for presence of Fault Codes
          - No Codes Present → Go to Symptom Diagnosis Chart
          - Fault Code Present → Go to Fault Code Table
            - Fault Code Present → Go to Fault Code Table
            - Brake Warning Lamp Stays on continuously in diagnostic mode (never goes out or never flashes) → Go to Symptom Diagnostic Chart
      - Yes → Go to Symptom Diagnosis Chart
    - No → Go to Symptom Diagnosis Chart
  - No → Perform Visual Inspection as described in this section

---

CODE 1 – LF VALVE
CODE 2 – RF VALVE
CODE 3 – RR VALVE
CODE 4 – LR VALVE

FAULT CODES 1-4: WHEEL CIRCUIT VALVE PROBLEM

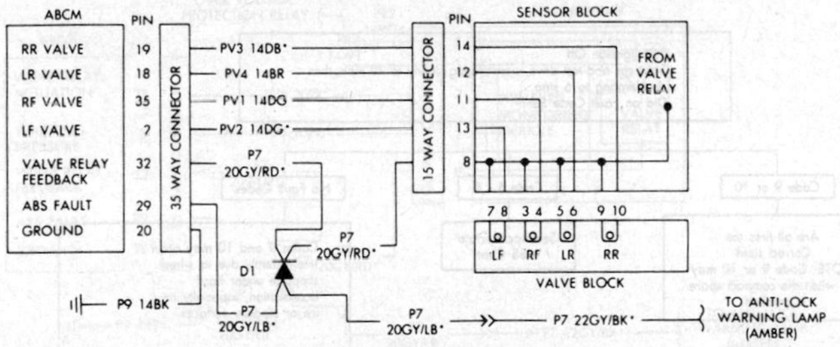

ABCM	PIN
RR VALVE	19
LR VALVE	18
RF VALVE	35
LF VALVE	7
VALVE RELAY FEEDBACK	32
ABS FAULT	29
GROUND	20

35 WAY CONNECTOR
PV3 14DB*
PV4 14BR
PV1 14DG
PV2 14DG*
P7 20GY/RD*
P7 20GY/RD*
P9 14BK
D1
P7 20GY/LB*
P7 20GY/LB*
P7 22GY/BK*

SENSOR BLOCK
15 WAY CONNECTOR
PIN 14 12 11 13 8
FROM VALVE RELAY
7 8 3 4 5 6 9 10
LF RF LR RR
VALVE BLOCK
TO ANTI-LOCK WARNING LAMP (AMBER)

CODES 1-4
WHEEL CIRCUIT VALVE

Valve block, attached to bottom of booster/master cylinder, controls hydraulic fluid pressure to each wheel by amount of electrical ground allowed in the circuit. This is controlled by ABCM. Power to each circuit is received through valve relay, inside sensor block. The ABCM powers the valve relay when ignition is turned on.

Fault Codes 1-4 flowchart:

Ignition off. Install MST-6100 Pinout Box. Measure resistance between
Code 1 - Pins 2 & 32   Code 3 - Pins 19 & 32
Code 2 - Pins 35 & 32   Code 4 - Pins 18 & 32

- 0.8 - 2.5 Ohms → Unplug Sensor Block Connector. Measure Resistance Between Pinout Box Pins: Code 1 - 2 & 20, Code 2 - 35 & 20, Code 3 - 19 & 20, Code 4 - 18 & 20
  - Open Circuit → Connect Sensor Block Conn. Measure Resistance Between Pinout Box Pins: Code 1 - Pins 2 & 32, Code 2 - Pins 35 & 32, Code 3 - Pins 19 & 35, Code 4 - Pins 18 & 32
    - Less than 0.8 Ohms → Replace Hydraulic Assembly
    - Greater than 0.8 Ohms → Install MST-6100 Vehicle System Tester. Perform Wheel Valve Test 5 for: Code 1 - LF Valve, Code 2 - RF Valve, Code 3 - RR Valve, Code 4 - LR Valve
  - Continuity → Repair Short to Ground in Circuit: Code 1 - PV2 14DG*, Code 2 - PV1 14DG, Code 3 - PV3 14DB*, Code 4 - PV4 14BR. NOTE: A short to ground on a valve may cause permanent damage to the Sensor Block. Replace Sensor Block if Problem persists.
- Greater than 2.5 Ohms → Unplug Sensor Block Connector. Measure resistance between Sensor Block Pins: Code 1 - 8 & 13, Code 2 - 8 & 11, Code 3 - 8 & 14, Code 4 - 8 & 12
  - Greater Than 2.5 Ohms → Remove Sensor Block Covers. Unplug Valve Block Connector. Measure Resistance Between Valve Block side of Pins: Code 1 - 7 & 8, Code 2 - 3 & 4, Code 3 - 9 & 10, Code 4 - 5 & 6
    - Greater than 2.5 Ohms → Replace Hydraulic Assembly
    - 0.8 - 2.5 Ohms → Replace Sensor Block
  - 0.8 - 2.5 Ohms → Repair Open or High Resistance in circuit: Code 1 - PV2 14DG*, Code 2 - PV1 14DG, Code 3 - PV3 14DB*, Code 4 - PV4 14BR

Wheel Valve Test results:
- Neither Pressure Hold or Reduce Modes Operate → Unplug Sensor Block Connector. Remove Sensor Block Cover. Unplug Valve Block Connector from Sensor Block. Measure Resistance Between Sensor Block Pins: Code 1 - 8 & 13, Code 2 - 8 & 11, Code 3 - 8 & 14, Code 4 - 8 & 12
  - No Continuity → Replace Hydraulic Assembly
  - Continuity → Replace Sensor Block
- One Mode Operates and the other does not → Replace Hydraulic Assembly
- Both Modes Operate → See NOTE ON INTERMITTENTS. With Ignition On, Manipulate Connectors and Wiring by Hand. Does a Code Set?
  - Yes → Repair Suspect Harness or Connector
  - No → Replace ABCM
- Valve Relay LED does not go out during test → Go to Code 12 Chart

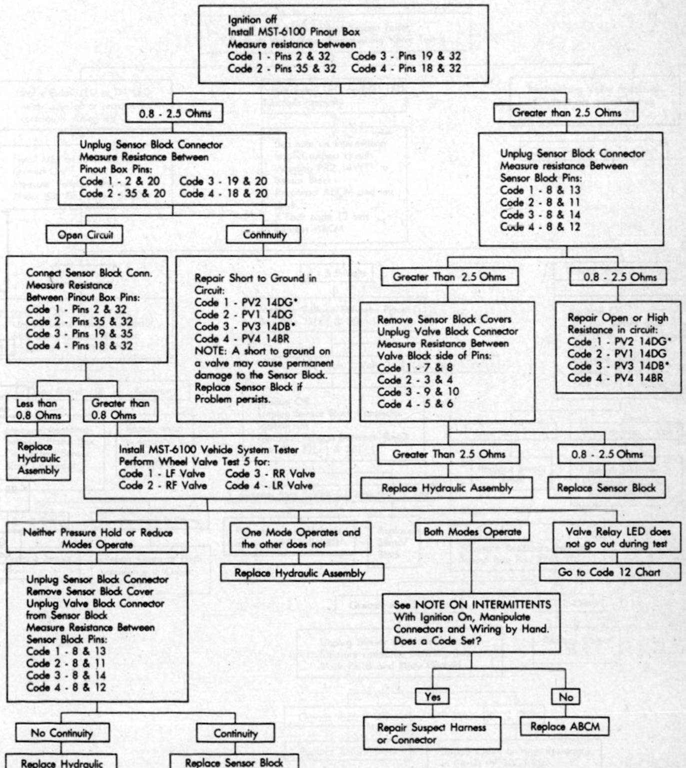

1989 Anti-Lock Brake Systems
Ford Motor Co. Except Probe (Cont.)

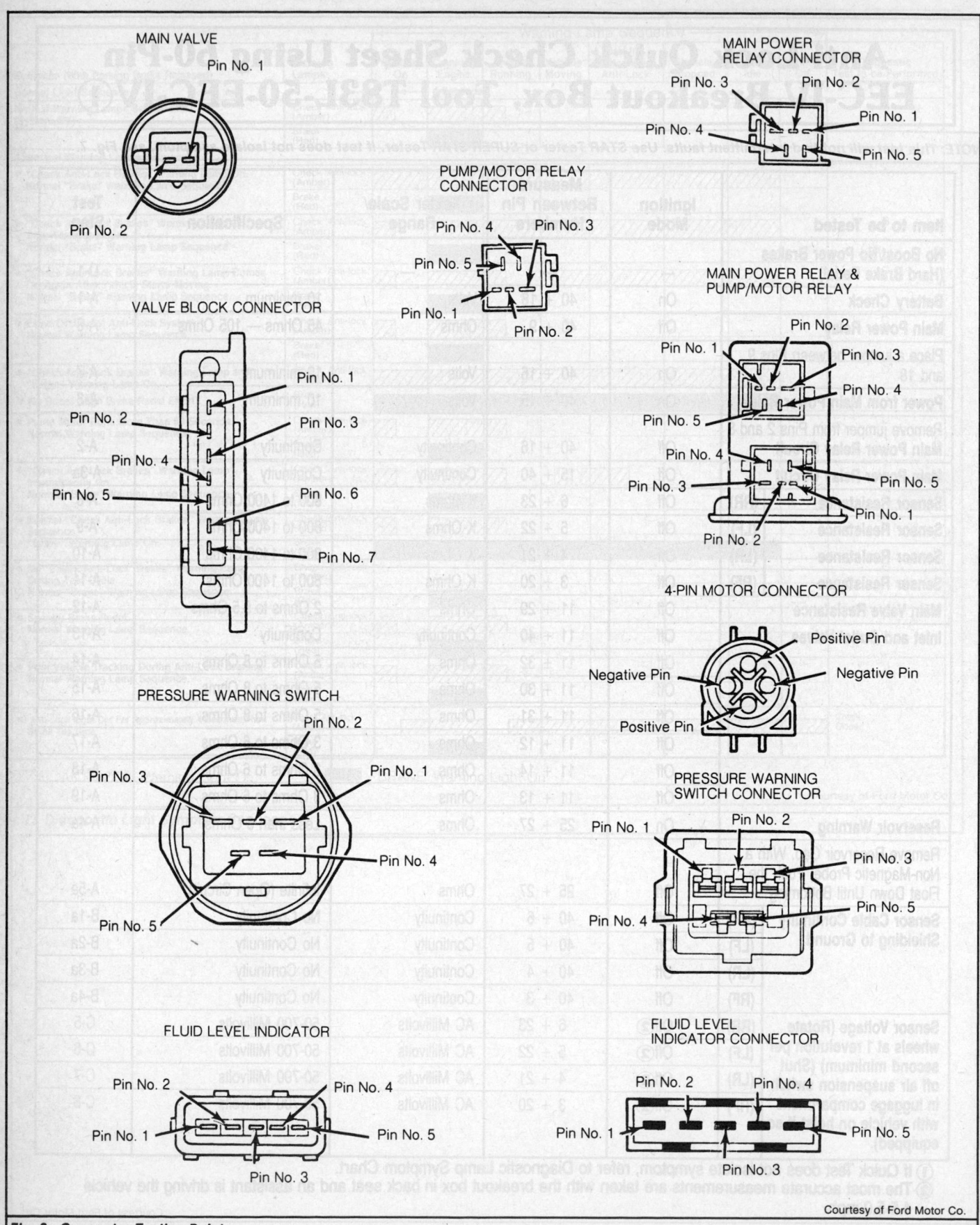

Fig. 9: Connector Testing Points

Courtesy of Ford Motor Co.

1989 ANTI-LOCK BRAKE SYSTEMS
Ford Motor Co. Except Probe (Cont.)

10-27

TROUBLE CODE INDEX

Codes [1]	Procced To Test
11 (EBCM)	AA1
12 (EBCM)	AA2
21 (Main Valve)	BB1
22 (LF Inlet Valve)	CC1
23 (LF Outlet Valve)	CC2
24 (RF Inlet Valve)	CC3
25 (RF Outlet Valve)	CC4
26 (Rear Inlet Valve)	CC5
27 (Rear Outlet Valve)	CC6
31 (LF Wheel Sensor)	DD1
32 (RF Wheel Sensor)	DD6
33 (RR Wheel Sensor)	DD11
34 (LR Wheel Sensor)	DD16
35 (LF Wheel Sensor)	DD1
36 (RF Wheel Sensor)	DD6
37 (RR Wheel Sensor)	DD11
38 (LR Wheel Sensor)	DD16
41 (LF Wheel Sensor)	DD1
42 (RF Wheel Sensor)	DD6
43 (RR Wheel Sensor)	DD11
44 (LR Wheel Sensor)	DD16
45 (LF & One Other Wheel Sensor)	DD21
46 (RF & One Other Wheel Sensor)	DD24
47 (Missing Rear Wheel Sensor)	DD25
48 (Missing 3 or 4 Wheel Sensor)	DD26
51 (LF Outlet Valve)	EE1
52 (RF Outlet Valve)	EE3
53 (Rear Outlet Valve)	EE5
54 (Rear Outlet Valve)	EE7
55 (LF Wheel Sensor)	DD1
56 (RF Wheel Sensor)	DD6
57 (RR Wheel Sensor)	DD11
58 (LR Wheel Sensor)	DD16
61 (Fluid Level Sensor & Pressure Warning Switch)	FF1
71 (LF Wheel Sensor)	EE1
72 (RF Wheel Sensor)	EE3
73 (RR Wheel Sensor)	EE5
74 (LR Wheel Sensor)	EE7
75 (LF Wheel Sensor)	DD1
76 (RF Wheel Sensor)	DD6
77 (RR Wheel Sensor)	DD11
78 (LR Wheel Sensor)	DD16
88 (EBCM)	AA1
99 (EBCM)	AA1

[1] – Any code in twenties must be repaired before other codes can be retrieved.

ON-BOARD SELF-TEST

1) Turn ignition off. Connect STAR Tester to self-test connector, located in luggage compartment. DO NOT operate vehicle or turn steering wheel. Press button on tester. ":00" should appear on tester. Turn ignition on. Check for trouble codes.

2) If no trouble code appears and warning lights are off, vehicle is okay. If trouble codes are indicated, but warning light(s) are on, see ANTI-LOCK QUICK TEST CHECK. If trouble code appears, record code. Release tester button, then depress button again. Wait 45 seconds for second code to appear.

3) If first code starts with 2, service solenoid valve assembly, then repeat test. Continue this procedure to obtain all trouble codes. Service each trouble code. When no new trouble codes appear, turn ignition off. Remove STAR Tester.

4) Turn ignition on. Check warning lights function. Test drive vehicle above 25 MPH. If all warning lights are off, vehicle is okay. If either warning light is on, perform ON-BOARD SELF-TEST again. If power brake does not work, go to step D-1 in TEST D.

NOTE: The following charts A through J are for use with Break-Out Box on all models with ABS. See Fig. 9 for Pin No. locations and testing points.

CIRCUIT TEST A

"ANTI-LOCK" LIGHT ON WITH "BRAKE" LIGHT OFF

1) 32-Pin Plug Testing. Turn ignition off. Unplug 32-pin plug from EBCM. Connect Break-Out Box (T83L-50-EEC-IV) and Adapter (T87P-50-ALA) to 32-pin harness. Set multimeter to DC volts setting. Turn ignition on with engine off. Measure voltage between break-out box pins No. 40 and No. 18. If more than 10 volts present, go to step 2. If less than 10 volts present, go to step 1a.

1a) EBCM Ground Wire. Check battery and fusible link to anti-lock warning light. Remove positive battery cable. Check continuity between break-out box pin No. 40 and ground. If continuity is present, go to step 1b. If no continuity is present, repair or replace circuit No. 530A.

1b) Ignition-to-EBCM Wire. Check continuity between break-out box pin No. 18 and ignition switch wire, circuit No. 687 (Continental), No. 687B (Mark VII) and 640N (Cougar and Thunderbird). If continuity is okay, reconnect positive battery cable. Check power at ignition switch pin with switch "ON". If okay, connect EBCM and recheck symptom. If no continuity, repair or replace circuit No. 687A, 687B or No. 640N.

2) Main Power Relay Secondary Circuit (Normal). Turn ignition off. Check continuity between break-out box pins No. 40 and No. 16. If continuity is present, go to step 3. If no continuity present, go to step 2a.

2a) Main Power Relay Secondary Circuit (Normal). Disconnect main relay from socket. Check for continuity between main power relay socket pins No. 3 and No. 5. If continuity present, go to step 2b. If no continuity present, replace main power relay.

2b) Main Power Relay Secondary Circuit Wiring Harness. Disconnect positive battery cable. Check continuity between main power relay socket pin No. 3 and break-out box pin No. 16. If continuity present, go to step 2c. If no continuity present, repair or replace circuit No. 532A, No. 532B, and 532D (Cougar and Thunderbird) or No. 532, No. 532B, and 532C (all others).

2c) Main Power Relay Secondary Circuit Wiring Harness. Check for continuity between main power relay socket pin No. 5 and body ground. If continuity present, reconnect main power relay, EBCM and battery cable. Recheck symptom. If no continuity present, repair or replace circuit No. 430A or (Cougar and Thunderbird) 430J.

3) Main Power Relay Secondary Circuit – Normal. Check continuity between break-out box pins No. 40 and No. 15. If continuity present, go to step 4. If no continuity present, go to step 3a.

3a) Main Power Relay Secondary Circuit Wiring Harness. Remove main power relay. Check for continuity between main power relay socket pin No. 3 and break-out box pin No. 15. If continuity present, connect main power relay and EBCM. Recheck symptom. If no continuity present, repair or replace circuit No. 532A, 532C or No. 532D (Cougar and Thunderbird) or No. 532, 532B or 532C (all others).

4) Fluid Level Sensor & Pressure Warning Switch Circuit. Turn ignition on with engine off. Measure resistance between break-out box pins No. 25 and No. 27. If resistance is less than 5 ohms, go to step 5. If resistance greater than 5 ohms, go to step 4a.

4a) Fluid Level Sensor Anti-Lock Warning Circuit. Disconnect 5-pin plug on fluid level sensor. Ensure fluid level is at maximum level, marked on reservoir. Measure resistance between sensor pins No. 1 and 2. If less than 2 ohms, go to step 4b. If greater than 2 ohms, replace fluid level sensor.

4b) Pressure Warning Switch Anti-Lock Warning Circuit. Ensure system is pressurized. Unplug 5-pin connector at pressure warning switch. Check continuity between pressure warning switch pins No. 3 and No. 5. If continuity present, go to step 4c. If no continuity present, replace pressure warning switch and pump/motor relay.

4c) EBCM-to-Fluid Level Sensor Circuit. Check for continuity between break-out box pin No. 25 and fluid level sensor connector pin No. 1. If continuity is present, go to step 4d. If no continuity present, repair or replace circuit No. 512, (512A Cougar and Thunderbird).

4d) Fluid Level Sensor-to-Pressure Warning Switch Circuit. Check for continuity between pin No. 2 of 5-pin fluid level sensor connector and pressure warning switch connector pin No. 3. If continuity present, go to step 4e. If no continuity present, repair or replace circuit No. 549 (549A Cougar and Thunderbird).

1989 ANTI-LOCK BRAKE SYSTEMS
Ford Motor Co. Probe (Cont.)

Terminal		Connection or measured item	Check item	Tester connection	Condition	Voltage or resistance
R-27 11-pins	2A (W), 2B (R)	Left front	Voltage (AC)	2A (W) — 2B (R)	Turn wheel 1 revolution per second	More than 0.25V (AC)
			Resistance		—	800—1,200Ω
	2C (Y), 2D (O)	Right front	Voltage (AC)	2C (Y) — 2D (O)	Turn wheel 1 revolution per second	More than 0.25V (AC)
	Wheel-speed sensor		Resistance		—	800—1,200Ω
	2E (Y/G), 2F (Y/L)	Left rear	Voltage (AC)	2E (Y/G) — 2F (Y/L)	Turn wheel 1 revolution per second	More than 0.25V (AC)
			Resistance		—	800—1,200Ω
	2H (G), 2J (L)	Right rear	Voltage (AC)	2H (G) — 2J (L)	Turn wheel 1 revolution per second	More than 0.25V (AC)
			Resistance		—	800—1,200Ω
	2I (G/R)	Low-pressure switch	Continuity	2I (G/R) — Ground	—	Continuity
	2K (L/B)	High-pressure switch	Continuity	2K (L/B) — Ground	—	Continuity
	2L (W/B)	Alternator output	Voltage	2L (W/B) — Ground	Run engine	Approx. 14V
R-27 17-pins	1A (W/G)	Stoplight switch	Voltage	1A (W/G) — Ground	Depress brake pedal	12V
	1B (R/Y)	Motor	Continuity	1B (R/Y) — Ground	—	Continuity
	1C (L/O)	Motor relay	Resistance	1C (L/O)(⊕ test-lead)-1K (BR)	—	Approx. 60—70Ω
	1D (G/R)	Check connector	Continuity	1D (G/R) — (G/R, R-30)	—	Continuity
	1E (B/L)	Fail-safe relay	Resistance	1E (B/L) — 1G (B/G)	—	Approx. 70—80Ω
	1F (L/Y)	Warning lamp	Continuity	1F (L/Y) — Ground	—	Continuity
	1G (B/G)	Battery	Voltage	1G (B/G) — Ground	Turn ignition SW. ON	12V
	1H (G/B)	Check connector	Continuity	1H (G/B) — (G/B, R-30)	—	Continuity
	1J (Y/G)	Solenoid valve		1J(Y/G) — 1K (BR)		
	1K (BR)					
	1M (Y/R)	Solenoid valve	Resistance	1M (Y/R) — 1O (B/W)	—	Approx. 5.5—7.0Ω
	1O (B/W)					
	1Q (Y/W)	Solenoid valve		1Q (Y/W) — 1R (L)		
	1R (L)					
	1L (B)			1L (B) — Ground		
	1N (B)			1N (B) — Ground		
	1P (B)	Ground circuit	Continuity	1P (B) — Ground	—	Continuity
4-pins	(B)			(B, R-30) — Ground		

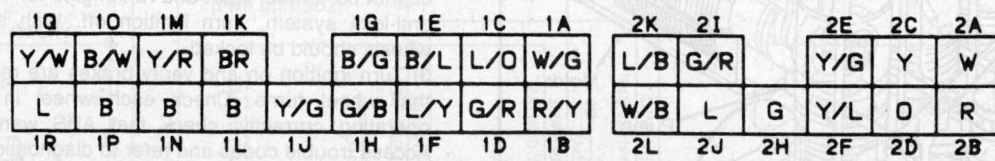

Fig. 3: ABS Control Unit Circuit Test

Courtesy of Ford Motor Co.

WIRE COLOR CONVERSION

Abbreviation	Wire Color
B	Black
G	Green
L	Blue
O	Orange
R	Red
W	White
Y	Yellow
BR	Brown

ABS RELAY BOX

NOTE: The main relay for ABS operation is located in main relay/fuse box in engine compartment.

1) The ABS relay box (under dash above brake pedal) contains a solenoid (fail-safe) relay and an ABS solenoid relay. Locate electrical connectors at relay box.

2) Using an ohmmeter, check that continuity exists between Black/Red and Black wire with ignition off. Turn ignition on. Check that continuity exists between Black/Green and Black/Blue wires. If readings are not as indicated, replace relay box.

1989 ANTI-LOCK BRAKE SYSTEMS
Ford Motor Co. Probe (Cont.)

10-41

3) Turn ignition off. Using an ohmmeter, check that NO continuity exists between Red/Yellow and Blue/Red wires. Turn ignition on. Check that continuity does exists between Red/Yellow and Blue/Red wires. If readings are not as indicated, replace relay box.

TROUBLE SHOOTING

NOTE: For Probe trouble shooting, access trouble codes and use ABS control unit circuit tests to isolate defect.

VISUAL INSPECTION

Check brake fluid level. Ensure parking brake is released. Check all fuses. Check all electrical connectors for corrosion or improper mating.

ACCESSING ABS TROUBLE CODES

Ensure ignition is off. Remove driver's seat to access ABS check connector. Using a jumper wire, jumper Green/Black to Black wire connectors on check connector. Using an analog voltmeter, connect positive voltmeter lead to Green/Red wire connector at check connector and connect negative lead to a known good ground. See Fig. 4.

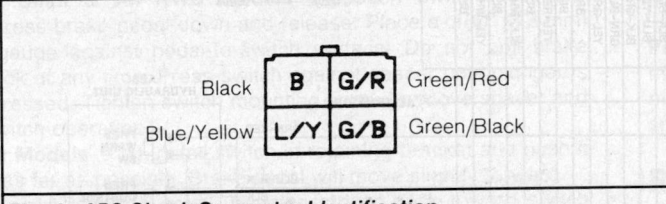

Black	B	G/R	Green/Red
Blue/Yellow	L/Y	G/B	Green/Black

Fig. 4: ABS Check Connector Identification

The voltmeter needle will sweep from 0-12 volts, indicating a trouble code which corresponds to number of needle sweeps. A .5 second pause will occur between needle sweeps of a trouble code, and a 10 second delay will occur between each trouble code. Therefore, a trouble code of 3 will have 3 needle sweeps of on for .5 seconds and off for .5 seconds.

ABS TROUBLE CODES

Code	Fault
1	RF Wheel Speed Sensor
2	LF Wheel Speed Sensor
3	Rear Wheel Speed Sensor
4	RF Sensor Rotor
5	LF Sensor Rotor
6	RR Sensor Rotor
7	LR Sensor Rotor
8	Hydraulic Unit
9-14	Relay Box/Hydraulic Unit
15	Control Unit/Hydraulic Unit
16-18	Control Unit/Harness

CLEARING ABS TROUBLE CODES

NOTE: Disconnecting the battery cable will not clear ABS codes.

Using a jumper wire, jumper Green/Black to Green/Red wire connectors on check connector. See Fig. 4. Turn on ignition. Check that ABS warning light is on. Wait 1-2 seconds and turn off ignition. Disconnect jumper wire. Start and run engine and wait for ABS light to go off. If light does not go off, repeat procedure.

REMOVAL & INSTALLATION

CAUTION: ABS system contains high pressure. System pressure must be discharged before servicing any component, disconnecting any fluid lines or opening fluid reservoir. With ignition off, pump brake pedal a minimum of 20 times using full pedal strokes. When a definite increase in pedal effort is felt, pump brake pedal several more times. Wear eye protection when opening any hydraulic system. For additional information, see ANTI-LOCK BRAKE SYSTEMS SAFETY PRECAUTIONS in this article.

ABS CONTROL UNIT

Removal & Installation – Ensure ignition is off. Remove driver's seat. Disconnect control unit electrical connectors. Remove control unit attaching bolts. Remove control unit. To install, reverse removal procedure.

HYDRAULIC UNIT

CAUTION: Hydraulic unit actuator contains high pressure gas. DO NOT attempt to disassemble or subject actuator to hard shocks or high heat. When actuator is scrapped, high pressure gas must be released. Loosen screw on bottom of accumulator one turn ONLY. This will allow gas to escape.

Removal – 1) Relieve fuel pressure. See appropriate article in FUEL SYSTEMS section. Remove fuel filter bracket bolts and remove fuel filter. Remove air filter assembly and ignition coil (if necessary). Remove wiring harness from bottom of fuel filter and coil bracket. Remove fuel filter and coil mounting bracket.

2) Disconnect electrical connectors at accumulator. Remove 2 banjo bolts and 4 copper washers from brake lines at accumulator. Discard washers. Remove 2 banjo bolts and 4 copper washers at master cylinder. Discard washers. Remove master cylinder-to-accumulator brake lines. Disconnect electrical connector at master cylinder. Remove master cylinder.

3) Remove routing clips from brake lines. Disconnect 4 brake lines at actuator. Remove 3 actuator mounting nuts. Carefully lift actuator from mounting bracket. Inspect actuator mount bushings for damage. Replace if necessary.

Installation – 1) Install actuator in mounting bracket. Tighten mounting bolts to 14-19 ft. lbs. (19-25 N.m). Connect actuator electrical connectors. Connect 4 brake lines at actuator. Using a 6" extension and 10 mm crowfoot wrench, tighten brake lines to 9-16 ft. lbs. (13-22 N.m).

2) Position 2 brake line-to-actuator and install banjo bolts using new copper washers. Tighten banjo bolts to 14-23 ft. lbs. (19-29 N.m). To complete installation, reverse removal procedure. Bleed brake system manually or with pressure bleeder.

WHEEL SPEED SENSORS

Removal & Installation – 1) Raise and support vehicle. Remove appropriate wheel. Remove necessary routing brackets. On rear sensors, open rear hatch and remove necessary interior panels to access electrical connector.

2) On all sensors, disconnect sensor wire connector. Remove 2 mounting bolts and remove sensor. To install, reverse removal procedure. Adjust sensor clearance. See ADJUSTMENTS in this article. Tighten sensor mounting bolts to specification. See TIGHTENING SPECIFICATIONS table.

SENSOR ROTOR

Removal & Installation (Front) – 1) Remove appropriate axle shaft. See FWD AXLE SHAFTS & CV JOINTS in DRIVE AXLE section. Using a soft faced drift and hammer, tap sensor rotor from outboard CV joint housing.

2) Position new sensor rotor on CV housing with chamfered edge toward axle shaft. Carefully tap new sensor rotor on housing. To complete installation, reverse removal procedure. Tighten all bolts

Daytona, Dynasty, LeBaron, New Yorker

DESCRIPTION

The single piston, floating caliper rear disc brake assembly consists of a hub assembly, caliper, disc pads, adapter, rotor, and a mechanically operated parking brake.

Dynasty and New Yorker models use a caliper with a 1.42" (36 mm) piston. Inside the piston assembly is an automatic brake adjuster and self-adjusting parking brake mechanism. The caliper assembly rides on rubber bushings with metal sleeves on 2 bolts which mount assembly to an adapter.

Daytona and LeBaron models use a caliper with a 1.30" (33 mm) piston for 14" brakes and a 1.42" (36 mm) piston for 15" brakes. The parking brake mechanism consists of a small duo-servo brake in caliper mounting adapter. The center of the rotor serves as parking brake drum. The caliper assembly rides on rubber bushings, with TEFLON sleeves on 2 guide pins that attach to the mounting adapter.

ADJUSTMENTS

PARKING BRAKE

1) Raise and support vehicle. Release parking brake and loosen parking brake cable adjusting nut until cables are slack. Tightening adjusting nut until slight drag is felt while rotating rear wheels.

2) Loosen adjusting nut until rear wheels turn freely. Loosen nut an additional 2 full turns. Apply and release parking brake several times to ensure proper operation.

SERVICING

BLEEDING SYSTEM

CAUTION: Vehicles equipped with ABS brake systems MUST follow brake bleeding procedure. See BOSCH ANTI-LOCK BRAKE SYSTEM (ABS) CHRYSLER MOTORS in this section.

See HYDRAULIC BRAKE BLEEDING article in this section for vehicles without ABS brake systems.

DISC PAD INSPECTION

Inspect condition of disc pads anytime wheels are removed. When a disc pad assembly is worn to a thickness of approximately 9/32" (7.14 mm), it should be replaced.

DISC PAD REPLACEMENT

See CALIPER & PADS under REMOVAL & INSTALLATION in this article.

BRAKE ROTOR

Lateral Runout – 1) To check lateral runout, install and tighten lug nuts to hold rotor on hub, tighten wheel bearings until all end play is eliminated. Attach dial indicator to suspension so that dial pointer contacts rotor face approximately one inch from outer edge.

2) Rotate rotor and record measurement. If runout exceeds specifications, check hub lateral runout. *See Fig. 1.*

3) Before removing rotor, chalk mark rotor and one wheel stud on high side of runout. Remove rotor and check hub runout. Runout should not exceed .003" (.08 mm).

4) If runout exceeds specifications, hub must be replaced. If hub runout does not exceed specifications, install rotor on hub 180 degrees from original position. Recheck lateral runout.

5) If runout exceeds specification, refinish or replace rotor as required. Readjust wheel bearings.

Parallelism – To check parallelism, measure thickness of rotor at 12 points around rotor. Make all measurements one inch from edge of rotor. If rotor exceeds specifications, refinish or replace rotor.

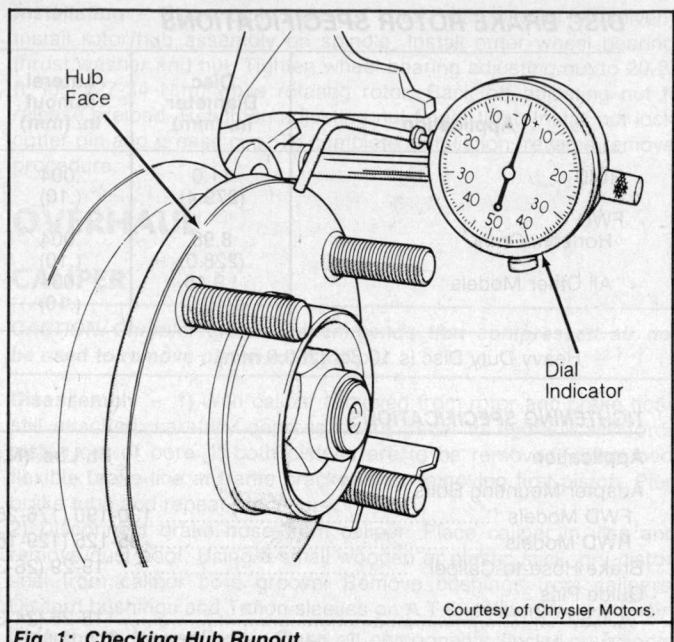

Fig. 1: Checking Hub Runout

REMOVAL & INSTALLATION

CALIPER & PADS

Removal (Dynasty & New Yorker) – 1) Raise and support vehicle. Remove wheel and tire assembly. Drive out disc pad retainer pin and remove 2 caliper mounting bolts. *See Fig. 2.*

2) Lift caliper up and away from disc. Suspend caliper on wire hook to prevent damage to brake hose. Remove disc pads.

NOTE: Rear calipers are not serviceable. If fluid leaks are detected around caliper piston, calipers must be replaced as an assembly.

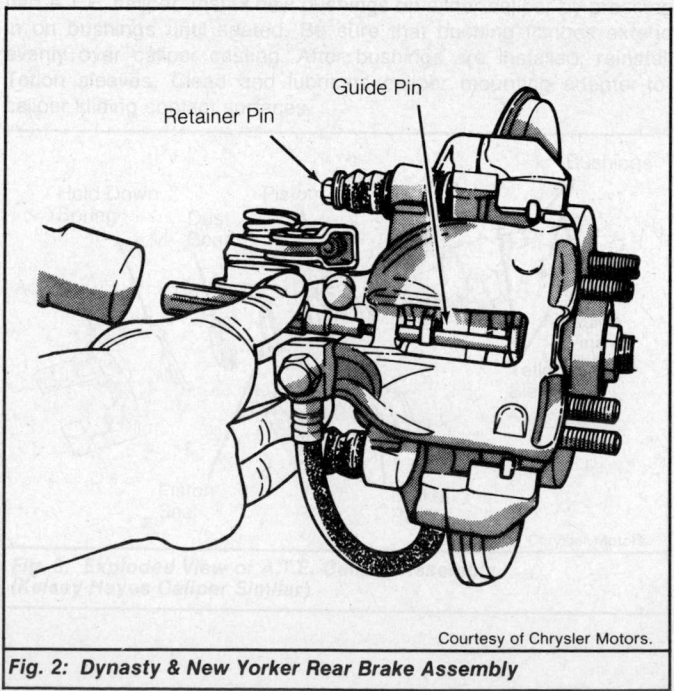

Fig. 2: Dynasty & New Yorker Rear Brake Assembly

Installation – 1) Remove a small amount of brake fluid from master. Slowly push piston back into caliper bores until bottomed. Clean and lubricate caliper sliding contact areas. Install new disc pads.

1989 DISC BRAKE SYSTEMS
Chrysler Motors Single Piston — Rear (Cont.)

10-47

2) Carefully, place caliper over disc and pads. Lower end must be installed first. Install anti-rattle clip through top opening in caliper.

3) Drive disc pad retainer pin through caliper and disc pads. Push down caliper assembly and torque upper and lower caliper mounting bolts. Install wheels and tires. Pump brakes and ensure pedal is firm. Road test and check for leaks.

Removal (Daytona & LeBaron) – Raise and support vehicle. Remove wheel and tire assembly. Remove caliper mounting bolts. Lift caliper up and away from disc. Suspend caliper on wire hook to prevent damage to brake hose. Remove disc pads. If brake fluid is present under or around caliper piston boot, caliper should be overhauled.

Installation – 1) Compress piston to bottom of bore. Install inboard disc pad into caliper piston. Install outboard pad on adapter.

2) Carefully lower caliper over disc and outboard pad. Install guide pins and torque to specification. Pump brakes to ensure pedal is firm. Road test and check for leaks.

OVERHAUL

CALIPER

Dynasty, New Yorker – Rear calipers are not serviceable. If fluid leaks are detected around caliper piston, calipers must be replaced as an assembly.

Disassembly (Daytona & LeBaron) – 1) With caliper removed from rotor and brake hose still attached, carefully depress brake pedal to hydraulically force piston out of bore. If both pistons are to be removed, disconnect flexible brake line at frame bracket after removing first piston. Plug brake tube and repeat procedure.

2) Disconnect brake hose from caliper. Place caliper in vise and remove dust boot. Using a small wooden or plastic stick, pry piston seal from caliper bore groove. Remove bushings from calipers. Discard bushings and Teflon sleeves.

Cleaning & Inspection – Clean all components (including bleeder screw) using alcohol or solvent. Blow out all passages and bores with compressed air. Inspect piston and bore for scoring or pitting. Clean light scoring or corrosion with crocus cloth. Bores with deep scoring may be honed, providing diameter of bore is not increased more than .001" (.025 mm). If specification is exceeded, replace caliper.

Reassembly – 1) Dip new piston seal in clean brake fluid and gently work seal into groove until seated. Coat new piston boot with clean brake fluid, leaving a generous amount inside boot.

2) Position dust boot over piston. Install piston, pushing it past seal, until it bottoms in bore. Position boot in counterbore. Using a hammer and dust boot installer, drive boot into counterbore.

3) Install new bushings on caliper by pressing in on bushings until seated. Be sure that bushing flanges extend evenly over caliper casting. Clean and lubricate caliper-to-mounting bracket contact areas. Install caliper and fill and bleed system. Check brake operation.

DUST BOOT

Removal & Installation – 1) Clean caliper with alcohol or solvent. Using a screwdriver, remove dust boot. Dip new dust boot in clean brake fluid.

2) On Dynasty and New Yorker calipers, position boot over piston and use Dust Boot Installer (C-4383-7) to seat boot into caliper.

3) On Daytona and LeBaron calipers, position boot over piston and install retainer to hold boot to caliper.

BUSHING & SLEEVE

Removal & Installation – Remove old sleeve and bushing from caliper. Clean caliper with alcohol or solvent. Compress new bushings with fingers and work into proper position. Insert new sleeves. Ensure bushing is seated in sleeve grooves.

TIGHTENING SPECIFICATIONS

Application	Ft. Lbs. (N.m)
Brake Hose to Caliper	19-29 (26-40)
Guide Pin Bolts	18 (25)
Wheel Studs	95 (129)

DISC BRAKE ROTOR SPECIFICATIONS

Application	Disc Diameter In. (mm)	Lateral Runout In. (mm)	Parallelism In. (mm)	Original Thickness In. (mm)	Min. Refinish Thickness In. (mm)	Discard Thickness In. (mm)
Dynasty, New Yorker	10.4 (264)	.005 (.13)	.0005 (.013)	.354 (8.99)	.324 (8.23)	[1] .294 (7.46)
Daytona						
Solid	10.57 (268.5)	.005 (.13)	.0005 (.013)	.472 (11.99)	.442 (11.23)	[1] .412 (10.46)
Vented	10.57 (268.5)	.005 (.13)	.0005 (.013)	.866 (21.99)	.836 (21.23)	[1] .806 (20.47)
LeBaron						
Solid	11.3 (287)	.005 (.13)	.0005 (.013)	.472 (11.99)	.442 (11.23)	[1] .412 (10.46)
Vented	11.3 (287)	.005 (.13)	.0005 (.013)	.866 (21.99)	.836 (21.23)	[1] .806 (20.47)

[1] – If specification varies from specification stamped on rotor, specification on rotor should be used.

1989 DISC BRAKE SYSTEMS
Eagle & Ford Motor Co. — Front

Eagle: Premier
Ford Motor Co.: Continental, Cougar, Country Squire, Escort, Grand Marquis, LTD Crown Victoria, Mark VII, Mustang, Probe, Sable, Taurus, Tempo, Thunderbird, Topaz, Town Car

DESCRIPTION

Front disc brakes use a slider-type caliper with a composite rotor. The caliper uses a single piston with a piston seal and dust boot. Caliper is mounted to steering knuckle with 2 locating pins. Rubber insulators isolate the pins from direct contact with caliper.
Caliper assemblies and outer brake pads are NOT interchangeable from left to right side. Inner brake pads are NOT interchangeable from left to right side on Country Squire, Grand Marquis, LTD Crown Victoria, Mark VII, Mustang and Town Car. Inner brake pads may be interchanged from left to right side on all other models.

ADJUSTMENTS

For available adjustments of brakes, see appropriate POWER BRAKE UNITS article in this section.

FRONT WHEEL BEARINGS

FWD Models – The front wheel bearing is a one-piece roller bearing, pressed into the steering knuckle. The hub assembly is pressed into the wheel bearing during assembly. There are no adjustments or servicing required.

RWD Models (Cougar & Thunderbird) – Front wheel bearings are part of hub unit and require no maintenance or adjustment. If replacement is necessary the hub/bearing assembly must be replaced as complete unit. See WHEEL BEARINGS under REMOVAL & INSTALLATION in SUSPENSION section.

RWD Models (Except Cougar & Thunderbird) – **1)** Turn off air suspension switch (if equipped). Raise vehicle, remove wheel cover and grease cap. Remove cotter pin and nut lock. Loosen adjusting nut 3 turns. Rock wheel, hub and rotor assembly in and out several times to push brake pads away from rotor.
2) Tighten adjusting nut to 17-25 ft. lbs. (23-34 N.m) while rotating wheel assembly. Loosen adjusting nut 1/2 turn, then retighten to specifications. See WHEEL BEARING SPECIFICATIONS table in this article.
3) Reinstall nut lock on adjusting nut and insert new cotter pin. Install grease cap and wheel cover. Lower vehicle. Before driving vehicle, pump brake pedal to restore normal brake pedal travel.

WHEEL BEARING SPECIFICATIONS

Application	INCH lbs. (N.m)
Country Squire, Grand Marquis, LTD	
Crown Victoria, Town Car	10-28 (1.1-3.2)
Mark VII, Mustang	10-12 (1.1-1.7)

SERVICING

BLEEDING SYSTEM

See HYDRAULIC BRAKE BLEEDING article in this section.

DISC PAD INSPECTION

Inspect disc pads whenever wheel is removed. If pad thickness is less than specifications, replace complete set of pads. See DISC PAD MINIMUM THICKNESS table in this article. Specification given is remaining thickness of pad material.

DISC PAD MINIMUM THICKNESS

Application	In. (mm)
Eagle	.236 (5.99)
Ford Motor Co.	.125 (3.18)

DISC ROTOR

Lateral Runout – Mount rotor on brake lath and attach a dial indicator. Place indicator pointer on center of braking surface. Rotate rotor and note indicator reading. If not within specifications, machine or replace rotor as necessary. See DISC BRAKE ROTOR SPECIFICATIONS table at end of this article.

Parallelism – Parallelism is the rotor thickness variation. Measure rotor thickness at 6 to 8 areas. If not within specifications, machine or replace rotor as necessary. See DISC BRAKE ROTOR SPECIFICATIONS table at end of this article.

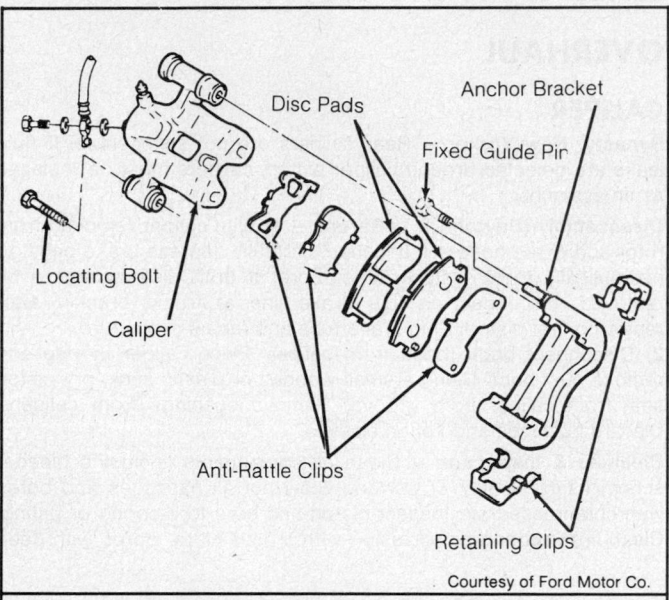

Fig. 1: Exploded View of Caliper & Disc Pads (Probe)

Courtesy of Ford Motor Co.

REMOVAL & INSTALLATION

BRAKE CALIPER & DISC PADS

Removal & Installation – **1)** Remove front wheels. Disconnect and plug brake hose from caliper. Mark caliper with right or left for installation reference.
2) On Probe models, remove caliper attaching bolts. Pivot the caliper up, off brake pads and slide caliper off fixed guide pin. See Fig. 1. Mark anti-rattle clips to ensure installation to original position. Remove brake pads.
3) On all models (except Probe), remove caliper locating pins. Remove caliper and disc pads from rotor.
4) On all models, apply high temperature grease to guide pins and insulators. To complete installation, reverse removal procedure. Refill and bleed system.

BRAKE ROTOR

Removal & Installation – **1)** On FWD models, hub is not removed with rotor. Remove factory retaining clips (if equipped). Remove rotor-to-hub set screw (if equipped).
2) On RWD models, remove dust cap, cotter pin, lock nut, spindle nut, washer and outer bearing. Remove rotor and hub assembly.
3) On all models, reverse removal procedure to install. Adjust wheel bearing as necessary. See FRONT WHEEL BEARINGS under ADJUSTMENT in this article.

1989 DISC BRAKE SYSTEMS
Eagle & Ford Motor Co. – Front (Cont.)

10-49

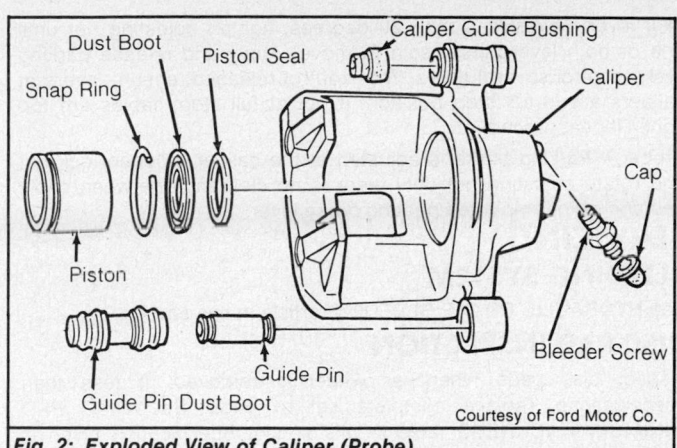

Fig. 2: Exploded View of Caliper (Probe)

Dust Boot — Piston Seal — Snap Ring — Piston — Caliper Guide Bushing — Caliper — Cap — Bleeder Screw — Guide Pin — Guide Pin Dust Boot

Courtesy of Ford Motor Co.

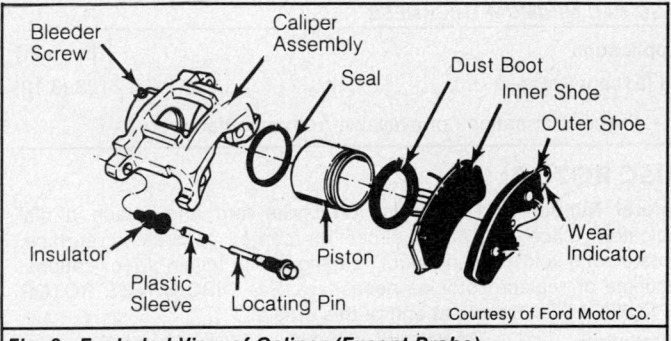

Fig. 3: Exploded View of Caliper (Except Probe)

Bleeder Screw — Caliper Assembly — Seal — Dust Boot — Inner Shoe — Outer Shoe — Wear Indicator — Piston — Locating Pin — Plastic Sleeve — Insulator

Courtesy of Ford Motor Co.

OVERHAUL

BRAKE CALIPER

Disassembly (Probe) – Remove caliper as previously described. Remove caliper guide bushing and dust boot. Remove snap ring. See Fig. 2. Place a piece of wood in caliper and apply air to brake hose bore to remove piston. Remove piston dust boot. Using care not to scratch caliper bore, remove piston bore seal.

Reassembly – Apply a film of clean brake fluid to seal, bore and piston. Install seal in caliper bore. Ensure seal is not twisted. Install dust boot in piston bore. Position piston and using a rocking motion, install piston. Install snap ring. To complete installation, reverse removal procedure.

Disassembly (Except Probe) – Remove caliper as previously described. Place a piece of wood in caliper and apply air to brake hose bore to remove piston. Remove dust boot. See Fig. 3. Using care not to scratch caliper bore, remove piston bore seal.

Reassembly – Apply a film of clean brake fluid to seal, bore and piston. Install seal and dust boot in caliper bore. Spread dust boot over piston and install piston squarely into caliper bore. To complete installation, reverse removal procedure.

TIGHTENING SPECIFICATIONS

Application	Ft. Lbs. (N.m)
Eagle Premier	
Caliper Brake Hose	25 (34)
Caliper Bracket Mounting Bolt	70 (95)
Caliper Mounting Pin	15-22 (20-30)
Wheel Stud Nuts	75 (102)
Ford Motor. Co.	
Anchor Bracket Mounting Bolt	
Probe	58-72 (78-98)
Brake Hose-to-Caliper	
Continental, Cougar, Escort, Sable, Taurus	
Tempo, Thunderbird & Topaz	30-45 (41-60)
LTD Crown Victoria, Grand Marquis	
Mustang & Town Car	20-30 (28-63)
Mark VII	17-25 (23-34)
Probe	16-22 (22-30)
Caliper Locating Pins	
Continental, Cougar, Escort, Sable, Taurus	
Tempo, Thunderbird & Topaz	18-25 (25-34)
LTD Crown Victoria, Grand Marquis	
Mustang & Town Car	40-60 (54-81)
Mark VII	45-65 (61-88)
Probe	23-30 (31-41)
Wheel Stud Nuts	93 (126)
Probe	65-87 (80-118)
All (Except Probe)	85-105 (115-142)

DISC BRAKE ROTOR SPECIFICATIONS

Application	Disc Diameter In. (mm)	Lateral Runout In. (mm)	Parallelism In. (mm)	Original Thickness In. (mm)	Min. Refinish Thickness In. (mm)	Discard Thickness In. (mm)
Eagle Premier	10.43 (265.0)	.003 (.08)	.....	.866 (22.00)	.807 (20.50)	.....
Ford Motor Co.						
Continental	10.16 (258.1)	.002 (.05)	.0004 (.010)	1.02 (26.0)	.....	.974 (24.74)
Cougar & Thunderbird	10.87 (276.10)	.003 (.08)	.0005 (.013)	1.024 (26.01)	[1]	.935 (23.75)
Escort, Tempo & Topaz	9.25 (235.0)	.003 (.08)	.0005 (.013)	.945 (24.0)	[1]	.882 (22.4)
Grand Marquis, LTD Crown Victoria & Town Car	11.08 (281.43)	.003 (.08)	.0005 (.013)	1.03 (26.2)	[1]	.972 (24.69)
Mark VII	10.91 (277.1)	.003 (.08)	.0005 (.013)	1.03 (26.2)	[1]	.972 (24.69)
Mustang						
2.3L	10.08 (256.0)	.003 (.08)	[2] .0005 [2] (.013)	.870 (22.10)	[1]	.810 (20.57)
5.0L	10.91 (277.1)	.003 (.08)	.0005 (.013)	1.03 (26.2)	[1]	.972 (24.69)
Probe	[3] [3]	.004 (.10)	.001 (.03)	[3] [3]	[3] [3]	.97 (24.6)
Sable & Taurus	10.16 (258.0)	.003 (.08)	.0005 (.013)	1.024 (26.01)	[1]	.974 (24.74)

[1] – Minimum refinish is marked on each rotor.
[2] – If equipped with aluminum wheels, .0003" (.008 mm).
[3] – Information not available from manufacturer.

Continental, Mark VII, Probe, Thunderbird

DESCRIPTION

With the exception of the parking brake, rear caliper assembly is similar to the pin slider front brake caliper. The parking brake lever, on back of caliper, is cable operated. Parking brake is self-adjusting.

NOTE: Brake Piston Remover (T75P-2588-A or B) is required for servicing rear disc calipers.

Caliper assembly consists of a pin slider caliper housing with a single piston, inner and outer disc pads, anti-rattle clip and anchor plate. Caliper slides on 2 greased locating pins that act as attaching bolts between caliper and anchor plate. Rubber insulators isolate pins from direct contact with caliper.

NOTE: On Mark VII models, it is possible to overadjust rear brakes. A partial brake system failure with only rear brakes operational, can be encountered. Check and adjust piston position and perform caliper adjustment.

ADJUSTMENTS
PISTON POSITION

Mark VII – 1) Remove rear wheel. Pull caliper assembly outward until inner disc pad is firmly seated against rotor. Measure clearance between outer disc pad and caliper. Clearance must be .0313-.0938" (.795-2.383 mm). If not within specifications, remove caliper.
2) Using piston remover, adjust piston to obtain required gap. Rotating remover shaft counterclockwise will narrow gap and clockwise will widen gap. A clearance greater than .0938" (2.383 mm) may allow adjuster to be pulled out of piston when brake is applied. Piston/adjuster assembly will then need to be replaced.

CALIPER

Mark VII – 1) Start engine and let idle. Pump brakes lightly about 40 times. Allow at least one second between pedal applications. Check parking brake for excess travel and very light effort. If either condition exists, repeat pumping brakes.
2) If either condition still exists, check parking brake cable for proper tension. Parking brake lever at caliper must return to full stop position when released. See PARKING BRAKE under ADJUST-MENTS in this article.

PARKING BRAKE

Continental – 1) Apply and release parking brake a couple times and ensure parking brake is fully released. Tighten adjusting nut against cable adjuster bracket until there is less than .063" (1.59 mm) of movement at either lever on caliper.
2) Apply and release parking brake several times. Recheck movement at levers on calipers. Readjust as necessary.

Thunderbird – 1) Apply and release parking brake fully several times. Place transmission in Neutral. Adjustment is made at equalizer, located between left and right rear wheels. Rotate locking lever away from threaded rod. Tensioner spring will take up cable slack and preload cables.
2) DO NOT pull down on locking lever as it will pull cables down and cause cables to have low tension. Lock tensioner by releasing locking lever. Ensure locking lever is secure by rotating toward threaded rod.
3) Examine tensioner for remaining cable take up capability. If none is present, check all cables, parking brake control and brackets for possible damage or deflection. Replace damaged components and repeat procedure as necessary.

Mark VII – 1) Back off adjusting nut, located near equalizer, until cables are loose. Operate parking brake lever at calipers. If lever moves more than 20 degrees using hand pressure of 50 psi (3.5 kg/cm²), perform piston position and caliper adjustment as previously described.

2) If lever moves less than 20 degrees, tighten adjusting nut until one or both levers just begin to move. Apply and release parking brake control several times. With control released, ensure levers at calipers are in full stop position. If not at full stop, cables are too tight. Repeat procedure.

Probe – Parking brake is adjusted at the caliper. Loosen lock nut and rotate adjusting nut until there is no clearance between cable end and caliper mounted parking brake lever.

SERVICING
BLEEDING SYSTEM

See HYDRAULIC BRAKE BLEEDING article in this section.

DISC PAD INSPECTION

Inspect disc pads whenever wheel is removed. If less than specifications, replace complete set of pads. See DISC PAD MINIMUM THICKNESS table in this article. Specification given is remaining thickness of pad material.

DISC PAD MINIMUM THICKNESS

Application	In. (mm)
All (Except Probe) [1]	.123 (3.12)

[1] – Probe information not available from manufacturer.

DISC ROTOR

Lateral Runout – Mount rotor on brake lath and attach a dial indicator. Place indicator pointer on center of braking surface. Rotate rotor and note indicator reading. If not within specifications, machine or replace rotor as necessary. See DISC BRAKE ROTOR SPECIFICATIONS table at end of this article.

Parallelism – Parallelism is the rotor thickness variation. Measure rotor thickness at 6 to 8 areas. If not within specifications, machine or replace rotor as necessary. See DISC BRAKE ROTOR SPECIFI-CATIONS table at end of this article.

REMOVAL & INSTALLATION
BRAKE CALIPER & DISC PADS

Removal (Continental & Thunderbird) – 1) Remove front wheels. Disconnect and plug brake hose from caliper. On Continental

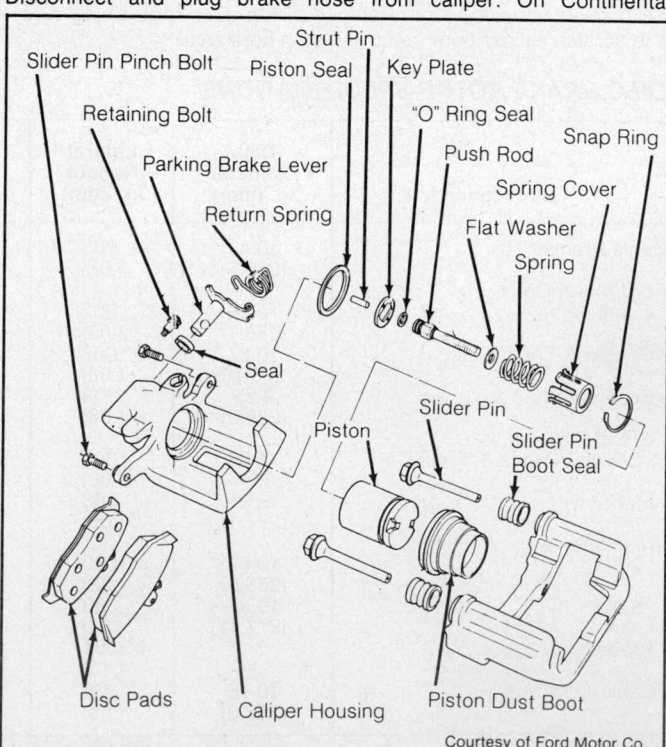

Courtesy of Ford Motor Co.

Fig. 1: Expoded View of Caliper (Continental & Thunderbird)

models, remove retaining clip from parking brake at caliper and disengage cable.

2) On Thunderbird models, release parking brake cable tension at adjustment locking lever. See PARKING BRAKE (THUNDERBIRD) under ADJUSTMENT in this article.

3) Hold slider pin and remove pinch bolt. *See Fig. 1.* Lift caliper assembly away from anchor plate. Remove slider pins and boots from anchor plate.

Installation 1) When installing new pad, caliper piston must be properly retracted. Using piston remover, rotate piston clockwise until piston is fully seated in caliper. Align one of the piston slots with tab on disc pad.

2) Install inner and outer disc pads in anchor plate. Rotate caliper assembly over rotor into position. Ensure disc pads are properly positioned. Clean pinch bolt threads and apply threadlock and sealer. To complete installation, reverse removal procedure. Bleed and adjust as necessary.

Removal (Mark VII) – 1) Remove wheel. Disconnect parking brake cable from caliper. Remove brake hose from caliper. Remove caliper locating pins. Lift caliper away from anchor plate by pushing upward toward anchor plate and rotating lower end out of anchor plate.

2) If insufficient clearance between caliper and disc pads prevent removal of caliper, loosen parking brake end retainer a maximum of 1/2 turn. This will allow piston to be forced back into bore.

3) To loosen end retainer, remove parking brake lever. Match mark end retainer and caliper to ensure no more than 1/2 turn. Force piston back into bore and remove caliper. If more than 1/2 turn is made, caliper must be overhauled.

4) Remove outer disc pad from anchor plate. Remove 2 rotor retainer nuts and remove rotor from axle. Remove inner disc pad.

Installation – 1) If end retainer has been loosened 1/2 turn, install caliper on anchor plate without installing disc pads. Tighten end retainer to 75-96 ft. lbs. (102-130 N.m). Install parking brake lever with arm down and rearward. Tighten retainer bolt to 16-22 ft. lbs (22-30 N.m).

2) If new disc pads are being installed, leave caliper attached to anchor plate as in step **1)**. Using piston remover, screw piston into bore until there is no further inward movement of piston and remover handle is rotated until there is firm seating force. Remove caliper and piston remover.

3) Lubricate anchor plate sliding surface with high temperature grease. Install inner disc pad and anti-rattle clip. Install rotor. Install outer disc pad. Place upper tab of caliper on anchor plate and rotate caliper into position.

4) Perform piston position adjustment. See PISTON POSITION under ADJUSTMENT in this article. Lubricate locating pins and inside insulators with Dielectric Compound (D7AZ-19A331-A). Add one drop of Threadlock and Sealer (EOAC-16554-A) to locating pin threads. To complete installation, reverse removal procedure. Bleed and adjust brakes as necessary.

Removal (Probe) – Remove wheel. Loosen parking brake cable adjusting nut and disengage cable from lever on caliper. Remove brake hose from caliper. Remove caliper retaining bolt and pivot caliper up, off disc pads and remove caliper. Note location of anti-rattle clips, retaining clips and "V" springs for installation reference.

Installation – 1) Install disc pads with anti-rattle clips, retaining clips and "V" springs in proper position, as marked at removal. Using piston remover, rotate piston clockwise until piston is fully seated in caliper. Align groves in piston with opening in caliper. *See Fig. 2.*

2) Lubricate guide pin bushings with high temperature grease. Install caliper on guide pin and pivot caliper onto anchor bracket. To complete installation, reverse removal procedure.

ROTOR

Removal & Installation – 1) Remove caliper and anchor plate or bracket as an assembly. Support out of way with wire.

2) On Probe models, unstake wheel bearing nut and remove nut and washer.

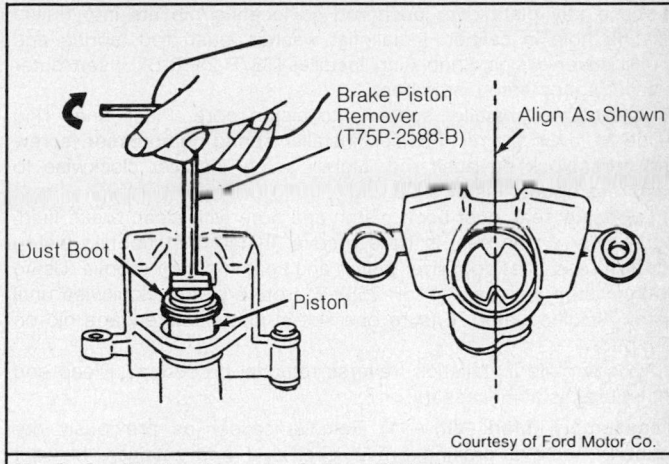

Fig. 2: Positioning Piston in Caliper (Probe)

3) On all other models, remove rotor retaining nuts or bolts.

4) On all models, remove rotor. Remove ABS signal ring (if equipped). To install, reverse removal procedure.

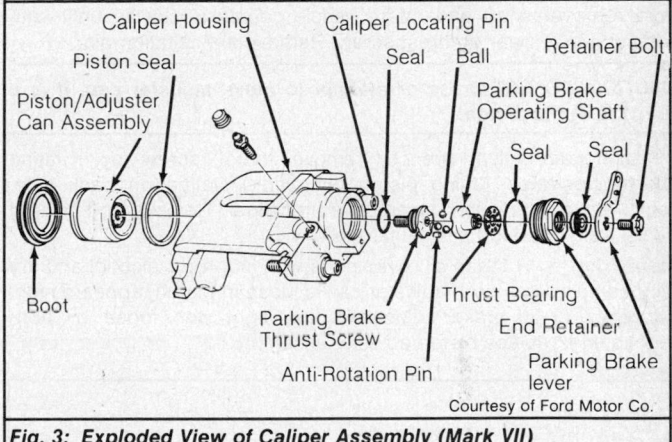

Fig. 3: Exploded View of Caliper Assembly (Mark VII)

OVERHAUL

CAUTION: Components are not interchangeable from side to side.

Disassembly (Continental & Thunderbird) – 1) Remove caliper as previously described. Mount caliper in vise with protected jaws. Using piston remover, rotate piston counterclockwise and remove piston from bore. Remove dust boot and seal from bore.

2) Remove snap ring. Use care, due to snap ring and spring cover under spring load. Remove spring cover, spring, flat washer, key plate and pull out push rod and strut pin from bore. Discard "O" ring from push rod. *See Fig. 1.*

3) Remove parking brake lever return spring. Remove lever retaining bolt and pull lever out of housing. Remove and discard seal.

Inspection – Clean all metal parts with isopropyl alcohol and dry with clean, dry compressed air. Replace components if worn, pitted or scored.

Reassembly – 1) Apply light coat of Silicone Dielectric Compound (D7AZ-19A331-A) to parking brake lever shaft and bore and seal. Press parking brake lever seal into bore and install lever. Install retaining bolt and tighten to 60-84 INCH lbs. (7-10 N.m). Install return spring.

2) Position strut pin in bore and in recess of parking brake lever shaft. Install new "O" ring on push rod and insert push rod into push rod bore of caliper. Ensure strut pin is positioned correctly between shaft recess at end of push rod.

3) Place key plate over push rod so locating nib fits into drilled locating hole in caliper. Install flat washer, push rod, spring and spring cover. Using Snap Ring Installer (T87P-2588-B), insert outer installer spacer into piston bore.

4) Insert inner installer spacer into piston bore. Place snap ring inside of inner spacer. Position installer spring compressor, screw and crossblock on push rod. Lightly screw installer clockwise to compress spring. Install snap ring.

5) Lubricate seal, dust boot, piston and bore with clean brake fluid. Install new piston seal in bore groove. Install dust boot in piston bore. Spread dust boot over piston and seat in piston groove. Using Brake Piston Remover (T75P-2588-B), rotate piston clockwise until piston is fully seated. Ensure one slot in piston will engage nib on disc pad.

6) To complete installation, reverse removal procedure. Bleed and adjust brakes as necessary.

Disassembly (Mark VII) – 1) Remove caliper as previously described. Remove praking brake lever and end retainer. Lift out operating shaft, thrust bearing and balls. *See Fig. 3.* Using magnet or tweezers, remove anti-rotation pin.

2) If anti-rotation pin will not come out, use piston remover and move piston out of caliper until it protrudes 1" from bore. Push piston back into bore with remover. With remover still in position, hold remover shaft and rotate handle counterclockwise until anti-rotation pin is clear of thrust screw. Remove anti-rotation pin.

CAUTION: DO NOT press or attempt to move adjuster can. It is a press fit in the piston.

---

3) Using an Allen wrench, remove thrust screw by rotating counterclockwise. Using piston remover, installed on back side, remove piston/adjuster assembly from caliper. Remove and discard seals, dust boot and pin insulators.

Inspection – 1) Clean all metal parts with isopropyl alcohol and dry with compressed air. If adjuster can is loose in piston, appears high, damaged or if brake adjustment too tight, too loose or non-functioning, replace piston/adjuster assembly.

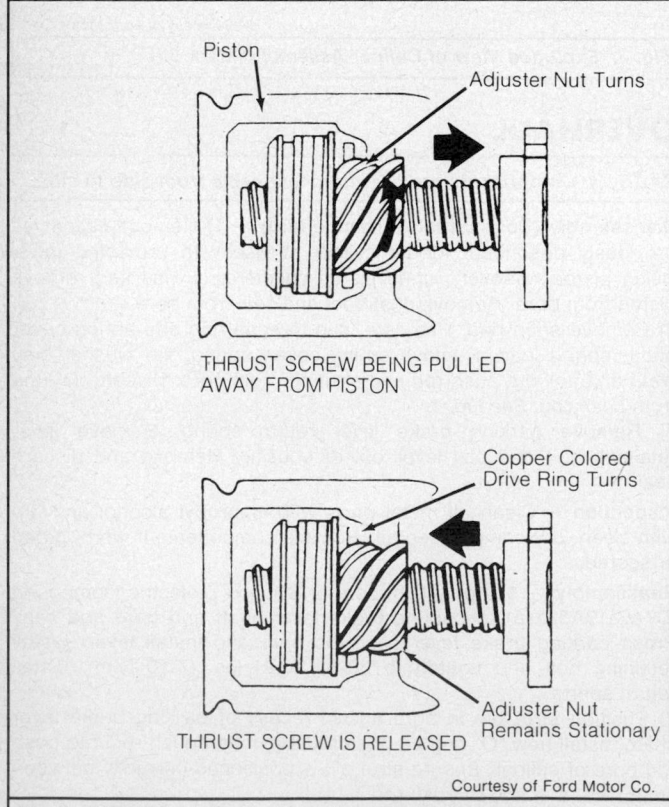

THRUST SCREW BEING PULLED AWAY FROM PISTON

THRUST SCREW IS RELEASED

Courtesy of Ford Motor Co.

Fig. 4: Checking Adjuster Operation (Mark VII)

2) Check adjuster operation. Install thrust screw into adjuster. Pull the 2 pieces apart by hand approximately 1/4" and then release. *See Fig. 4.* If action is not as shown, replace piston assembly.

Reassembly – 1) Use clean brake fluid on components during installation, except on parking brake components. Install seal and ensure it is not twisted and is seated in groove. Install new dust boot by seating the flange squarely in outer groove of caliper bore.

2) Install piston/adjuster assembly in cylinder bore. Spread dust boot over piston and seat in piston groove. Mount caliper in vise. Fill piston/adjuster with clean brake fluid, to bottom edge of thrust screw bore.

3) Install new thrust screw seal in groove on thrust screw. Using Allen wrench, install thrust screw until top surface of thrust screw is flush with bottom of the threaded bore. Use care not to damage seal. Index thrust screw, so notches on thrust screw and caliper housing are aligned. Install anti-rotation pin.

4) Apply a liberal amount of Silicone Dielectric Grease (D7AZ-19A331-A), to all components in parking brake mechanism. Install the 3 balls, operating shaft and thrust bearing. While holding operating shaft firmly seated against internal mechanism to prevent mislocation of balls, install end retainer with new seal.

5) Tighten end retainer. Install parking brake lever with arm down and rearward. Tighten retaining bolt. Using piston remover, bottom piston in bore. To complete installation, reverse removal procedure. Bleed and adjust system as necessary.

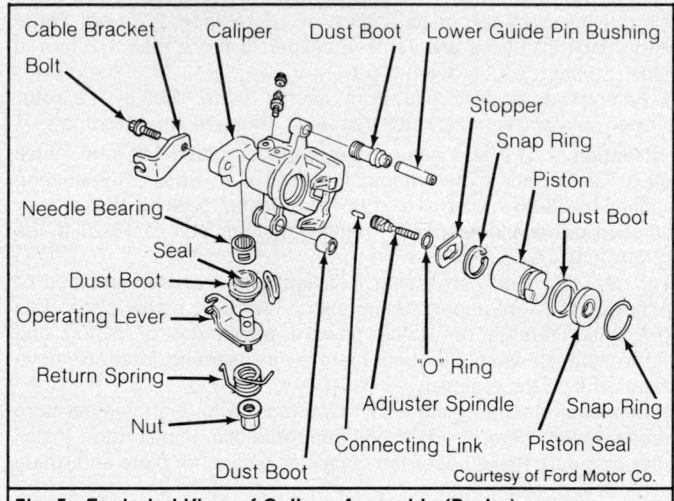

Cable Bracket · Caliper · Dust Boot · Lower Guide Pin Bushing · Bolt · Stopper · Snap Ring · Piston · Dust Boot · Needle Bearing · Seal · Dust Boot · Operating Lever · Return Spring · "O" Ring · Adjuster Spindle · Snap Ring · Piston Seal · Connecting Link · Nut · Dust Boot

Courtesy of Ford Motor Co.

Fig. 5: Exploded View of Caliper Assembly (Probe)

Disassembly (Probe) – 1) Remove caliper as previously described. Open bleeder screw and drain fluid out through brake hose fitting. Remove caliper guide bushing and dust boots. Pry retaining spring off dust boot and discard dust boot.

2) Using Brake Piston Remover (T75P-2588-B), rotate piston counterclockwise and remove piston from adjuster spindle. Carefully remove piston seal. Remove snap ring. *See Fig. 5.* Remove stopper, adjusting spindle and connecting link. Remove and discard "O" ring from adjusting spindle.

3) Remove parking brake return spring. Remove nut and lock washer. Match mark operating lever-to-shaft. Remove operating lever from shaft. Remove seal and dust boot, shaft and needle bearing from caliper.

Reassembly – 1) Lubricate needle bearing with orange grease (supplied with kit). Align slot in bearing with piston bore in caliper and install bearing. Install seal and dust boot. Install shaft and operating lever. Ensure match marks are aligned. Install lock washer and nut.

2) Install connecting link. Ensure connecting link passes through slot in needle bearing and enters shaft. Install new "O" ring on adjusting spindle. Position stopper on adjusting spindle with pins on stopper aligned with holes in caliper bore.

3) Install adjusting spindle and stopper. Install snap ring. Ensure operating lever and adjusting spindle move freely. Install return spring. Install piston seal in caliper bore. Position piston and piston remover.

4) Rotate piston clockwise and install piston onto adjusting spindle. Install piston fully and align grooves in piston with opening in caliper. *See Fig. 2.* To complete installation, reverse removal procedure. Bleed and adjust as necessary.

TIGHTENING SPECIFICATIONS

Application	Ft. Lbs. (N.m)
Continental	
Anchor Plate Retaining Bolt	80-100 (109-136)
Brake Hose-to-Caliper	30-45 (41-61)
Slider Pin Pinch Bolt	23-26 (31-35)
Wheel Stud Nuts	80-105 (109-142)
Mark VII	
Anchor Plate Retaining Bolt	80-110 (109-149)
Brake Hose-to-Caliper	20-30 (27-41)
Caliper Locating Pin	29-37 (39-50)

TIGHTENING SPECIFICATIONS (Cont.)

Application	Ft. Lbs. (N.m)
Mark VII (Cont.)	
End Retainer	75-96 (102-130)
Parking Brake Lever Retaining Bolt	16-22 (22-30)
Wheel Stud Nuts	80-105 (109-142)
Probe	
Anchor Bracket Bolt	33-49 (45-66)
Brake Hose-to-Caliper	16-20 (22-27)
Caliper Retaining Bolt	12-17 (16-23)
Parking Brake Cable Lock Nut	14-21 (19-29)
Wheel Stud Nuts	65-87 (80-118)
Thunderbird	
Anchor Plate Retaining Bolt	80-100 (109-136)
Brake Hose-to-Caliper	18-24 (24-32)
Slider Pin Pinch Bolt	18-24 (24-32)
Wheel Stud Nuts	80-105 (109-142)

DISC BRAKE ROTOR SPECIFICATIONS

Application	Disc Diameter In. (mm)	Lateral Runout In. (mm)	Parallelism In. (mm)	Original Thickness In. (mm)	Min. Refinish Thickness In. (mm)	Discard Thickness In. (mm)
Ford Motor Co.						
Continental	10.16 (258.1)	.002 (.05)	.0005 (.013)	1.02 (25.9)	[1]	.974 (24.74)
Mark VII	11.31 (287.3)	.004 (.10)	.0005 (.013)	.945 (24.00)	[1]	.895 (22.73)
Probe	[2]	.004 (.10)	.001 (.03)	[2]	[1]	.345 (8.76)
Thunderbird	10.16 (258.1)	.003 (.08)	.0005 (.013)	.945 (24.00)	[1]	.895 (22.73)

[1] – Rotor is stamped with minimum refinish thickness.

[2] – Information not available from manufacturer.

1989 DRUM BRAKE SYSTEMS
Bendix Single Anchor Automatic Adjuster

**Chrysler Motors, Eagle, Ford Motor Co.
(Except Continental & Mark VII)**

DESCRIPTION

Units consists of a backing plate, 2 brake shoes, return springs, hold-down spring assemblies, self-adjusting components, and a wheel cylinder. Duo Servo Automatic adjuster consists of a cable (with spring hook and anchor fitting), cable guide, adjusting lever, lever pivot and adjusting screw (star).

AUTOMATIC ADJUSTER

Chrysler Motors – Adjuster screw thread is opposite that of other models; therefore, adjuster moves upward when brakes are applied. A cage and spring on adjuster cable absorbs secondary shoe movement, except when shoe wear results in enough movement to cause adjuster to rotate. This feature reduces possibility of over-adjustment.

Eagle Premier – This non-servo design brake uses an incremental adjuster that adjusts during braking whenever a wear gap appears sufficient to actuate the adjuster wheel. Brake adjustment occurs during forward and rearward braking.

Ford Motor Co. – On duo-servo design brakes, the adjuster uses movement of rear (secondary) shoe during reverse brake application to turn brake adjusting screw. Screw is rotated a small amount to maintain proper lining-to-drum clearance.

Non-servo design brakes use an incremental adjuster that adjusts during braking whenever a wear gap appears sufficient to actuate the adjuster wheel. Brake adjustment occurs during forward and rearward braking.

ADJUSTMENTS

BRAKE SHOE ADJUSTMENT

This adjustment is made only after brake lining replacement or if brake applications are insufficient to actuate automatic adjuster.

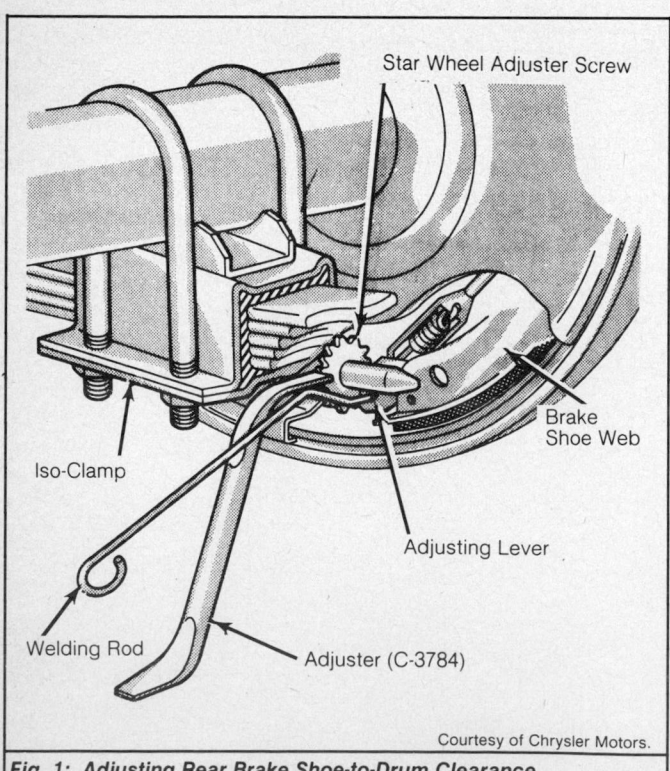

Chrysler Motors – 1) Adjust parking brake after service brake adjustment. Remove adjusting hole covers. Insert Adjuster (C-3784), or thin-bladed screwdriver into star wheel and rotate until road wheel turns with slight drag (locked on Acclaim, Horizon, Omni and Spirit).
2) On all models except Acclaim, Horizon, Omni and Spirit, back off star wheel while using welding rod to push adjusting lever (if equipped) away from star wheel until wheels rotate freely with no drag. *See Fig. 1.*
3) On Acclaim, Horizon, Omni and Spirit, back off adjuster 10 clicks. On all models, adjustments must be equal on both wheels.

NOTE: On RWD models with Iso-Clamp rear suspension, bend welding rod to match angle of adjusting tool plus a 3/4 reverse bend at contact end. See Fig. 1.

Eagle Premier – With drum installed, rotate star adjuster through access hole on backing plate to lock drum. Using a thin screwdriver and brake spoon, push adjuster lever away from star wheel and back of star wheel one complete revolution.
Ford Motor Co. – 1) Remove tire and wheel assembly and brake drum assembly.
2) On all models except Escort, Tempo and Topaz with 7" brakes, use a measuring tool to determine drum diameter and proper shoe diameter. Hold automatic adjusting lever out of engagement while rotating adjusting screw. Adjust brake shoes to fit gauge. Rotate gauge around shoe to ensure proper fit. Install drum assembly.
3) On Escort, Tempo and Topaz with 7" brakes, pivot adjuster quadrant until it meshes with knurled pin and is in 3rd or 4th notch of outboard end of quadrant.
4) On FWD, install drum assembly, outer bearing, keyed washer and hub nut. While rotating hub assembly, tighten wheel bearing nut to 17-25 ft. lbs. (23-34 N.m). Back wheel bearing nut off one half turn. Tighten wheel bearing nut to 26 INCH lbs. (3 N.m).
4) On all models, complete adjustment by applying brakes several times while backing vehicle, with forward movement after each application. Use a minimum 50 lbs. (22 kg) pressure on non-power brakes and 25 lbs. (11 kg) on power brakes.

PARKING BRAKE ADJUSTMENT

Chrysler Motors – 1) Ensure service brakes are properly adjusted. Back off parking brake cable and allow slack in cable. Clean and lubricate cable threads. Using Adjuster (C-3784) and a thin screwdriver inserted in brake adjusting hole to disengage adjusting lever, rotate star wheel to obtain light contact between brake shoe and drum.
2) Back off star wheel until no drag is felt. Adjust parking brake cable adjuster nut until a slight drag is felt while rotating rear wheels. Loosen adjusting nut until wheels just turn freely, then back off nut 2 full turns. Apply and release parking brake several times to make sure rear wheels do not drag.

Eagle Premier – Parking brake is adjusted by removing slack from cable. Cable adjustment location is under vehicle at front cable-to-rear cables junction.

Ford Motor Co. (RWD) – Release parking brake fully. Place transmission in "N" and raise vehicle on axle type hoist. Tighten adjusting nut against cable equalizer or cable adjusting rod until rear brakes drag. Loosen adjusting nut until brakes turn freely, without drag. If equipped, tighten lock nut to 84-120 INCH lbs. (10-14 N.m). Lower vehicle and check brake operation.

Ford Motor Co. (Escort, Sable, Taurus, Tempo & Topaz) – 1) With engine running, pump brakes 3 times before adjusting parking brake. Place transmission in "N" and raise vehicle enough to rotate wheels. Place parking brake lever in 12th notch position.
2) Tighten parking brake lever cable adjusting nut until 1" (25 mm) of threaded rod is exposed beyond nut. Return parking brake handle to "OFF" position and rotate rear wheels. A slight drag is desirable. If no drag is present or lever travels too far, repeat above procedure.

Fig. 1: Adjusting Rear Brake Shoe-to-Drum Clearance

Courtesy of Chrysler Motors.

1989 DRUM BRAKE SYSTEMS
Bendix Single Anchor Automatic Adjuster (Cont.)

10-55

Ford Motor Co. (Probe) – To adjust parking brake, tighten parking brake adjusting nut on left side of parking brake lever, this shortens equalizer cable. Tighten adjusting nut until it takes seven to ten notches of lever movement to fully set parking brake.

VACUUM PARKING BRAKE RELEASE

Ford Motor Co. – **1)** Visually check operation of brake linkage as pedal is depressed and when manual release lever is activated.

CAUTION: Air pressure should never be applied to vacuum system as diaphragm in vacuum motor may be damaged.

2) Ensure a minimum of 10 in. Hg is available at all points where vacuum is applied. Start engine and let idle. Place transmission in "D" and observe that lever moves upward and parking brake releases. If it does not release, check for proper vacuum in system and replace components as necessary.

CLEANING & INSPECTION

NOTE: When servicing brake parts, do not create dust by grinding or sanding linings or using compressed air. Use water dampened shop towel to remove dirt and dust from brake parts during disassembly.

CLEANING

Clean all parts except linings and drums with brake cleaning solvent. To remove brake fluid contamination, clean all parts except brake linings with denatured alcohol. Contaminated brake linings must be replaced.

INSPECTION

1) Pull back wheel cylinder dust boots and check for evidence of leakage. If evidence of leakage is noted, cylinder should be disassembled, inspected and overhauled.
2) Polish brake support plate ledges with fine emery cloth and inspect for grooves that could restrict shoe movement. If grooves exist after polishing, support plate must be replaced.
3) Inspect lining wear pattern. If wear across width of lining is uneven, drums should be checked for distortion, shoes for correct positioning, and support plate for distortion.
4) Inspect all springs for evidence of overheating and fractures. Self-adjusting cables should be inspected for kinks, fraying, or elongation of eyelet. Inspect adjuster screws for freedom of rotation, and adjuster lever for wear and distortion. Replace all defective brake parts.

OVERHAUL

SHOE & LINING REPLACEMENT

Chrysler Motors (RWD) – **1)** Remove brake drums, releasing brake adjustment if necessary. Remove return springs, adjuster cable, overload spring, cable guide and anchor plate. Disengage adjusting lever from spring and remove by working it out from under spring. Remove spring from pivot. Remove shoe-to-shoe spring.
2) Disengage shoes from push rods (if equipped) and remove adjusting wheel assembly. Remove parking brake strut and anti-rattle spring. Remove brake shoe retainers, springs and nails. Disconnect parking brake cable and remove lever. Remove brake shoes.
3) Lubricate all brake shoe contact points and pivot end of parking brake lever. Insert brake lever into hole of secondary shoe from inner side of shoe web. Connect brake lever to cable. Slide secondary shoe against backing plate and anchor pin, while engaging shoe web with push rod (if equipped).
4) Slide parking brake strut behind hub and into lever slot. Install anti-rattle spring on strut.

5) On 10" left brake, spring tab must point up and rearward on outside of shoe web and, point down and forward on inside of shoe web on 10" right brake.
6) On all models, slide primary shoe into position, engaging shoe with push rod (if equipped) and strut. Install anchor plate and adjuster cable. Install primary shoe return spring.
7) While holding cable guide in position on secondary shoe, install return spring through guide and into web. Place other end over anchor pin. Squeeze spring ends around anchor pin with pliers until parallel.

NOTE: Cable guide must remain flat and secondary spring must overlap primary spring.

8) Install adjusting assembly between shoes with star wheel next to secondary shoe. Install shoe-to-shoe spring. Coil must be forward and opposite adjuster lever on 11" brakes.

NOTE: Left star wheel is cadmium plated and stamped "L" on stud end; right star is Black and stamped "R" on stud end. Assemblies must be installed as indicated.

9) Install adjusting lever and spring over pivot pin. Lock lever in position by sliding it lightly rearward. Install shoe retaining nails, retainers and springs.
10) Thread adjuster cable over guide and hook end of overload spring in lever. Install drums. Adjust and bleed brakes. Check for proper brake operation before moving vehicle.

NOTE: Cable eye must be tight against anchor and in a straight line with guide.

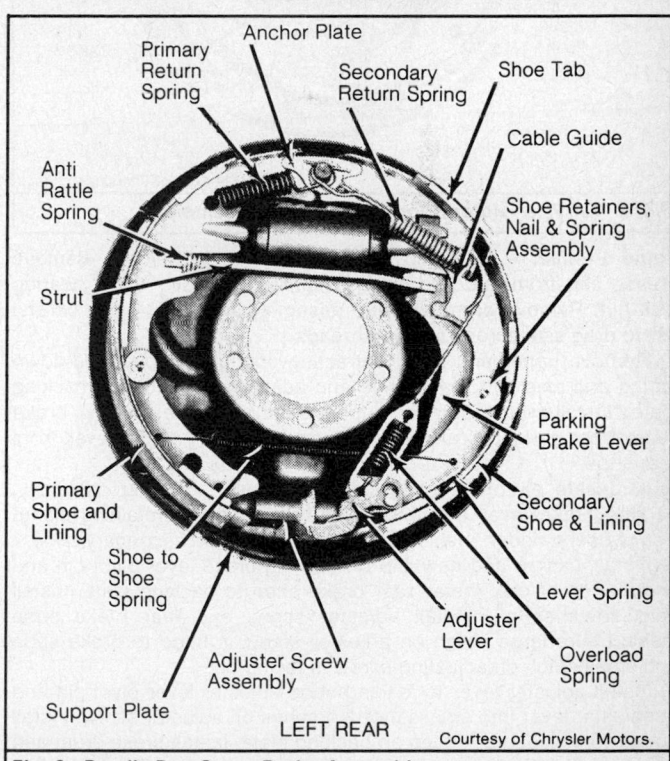

Fig. 2: Bendix Duo-Servo Brake Assembly

Chrysler Motors (FWD) – **1)** Release brake adjustment. Remove grease cap, cotter pin, lock nut and washer. Remove brake drum and bearings. Remove parking brake cable, shoe anchor springs and hold-down springs. Spread shoes and remove adjuster assembly.
2) Remove brake shoes by raising parking brake lever. Pull shoe away from support to remove spring tension and disengaging spring from support. Remove springs from brake shoes.

10-56

1989 DRUM BRAKE SYSTEMS
Bendix Single Anchor Automatic Adjuster (Cont.)

3) Install primary shoe return spring. Install primary shoe while engaging return spring end in support and shoe end under anchor plate. Install secondary shoe and spring in same manner. Spread shoes and install adjuster assembly with 2 stepped forks facing toward outboard side of shoes. Longer fork will be pointing to rear.

4) Install hold-down pins, springs and anchor springs. Compress parking brake cable housing spring to expose cable. Slide cable into parking brake lever. Position washer between parking brake cable housing spring and parking brake lever.

5) Install drum, bearing, washer, nut. While rotating hub and drum assembly, tighten wheel bearing nut to 27-34 ft. lbs. (37-46 N.m). Loosen wheel bearing nut to relieve all preload from bearing. Finger tighten wheel bearing nut. End play should be .001-.003" (.026-.076 mm).

6) Install cotter pin and grease cap. Bleed brakes and check for proper brake operation before moving vehicle.

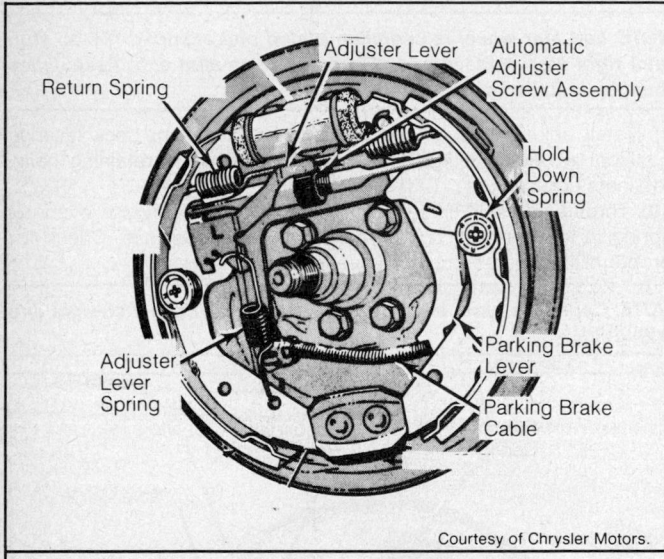

Fig. 3: Chrysler Motors Non-Servo Brake Assembly

Courtesy of Chrysler Motors.

Eagle Premier – 1) Remove wheel and tire assembly. Remove grease cap from hub and drum assembly. Remove wheel bearing lock nut. Remove drum and hub assembly as a unit, being careful not to drag seal across spindle threads.

2) Remove upper and lower retracting spring. Remove hold-down spring and pins. Lift brake shoe and adjuster assembly off backing plate. Install wheel cylinder cup retainer. Remove parking brake cable from parking brake lever. Remove parking brake lever from rear shoe.

3) Lubricate all brake shoe contact points, adjusting assembly, parking brake lever and lever pivot pin. Remove retaining clamp from wheel cylinder. Install parking brake lever on secondary shoe.

4) Install washer and new clip on parking brake lever pivot pin and crimp ends of clip. Install rear brake shoe to backing plate. Install hold down spring. Install adjuster screw and rear brake shoe making sure large notch on adjuster screw is fitted to brake shoe and small notch on adjusting screw is facing out.

5) Install adjuster lever to leading shoe adjuster lever pivot pin and fit adjuster lever into smallest of 2 notches on adjuster screw. Install upper spring. Center shoes on backing plate. Install brake drum and hub assembly. Install new wheel bearing lock nut and lightly tighten. Adjust brakes. Tighten new wheel bearing lock nut to 123 ft. lbs. (167 N.m).

Ford Motor Co. (RWD) – 1) Remove drum, releasing brake adjustment if necessary. Install clamp over wheel cylinder pistons. Remove shoe-to-anchor springs and unhook cable eye from anchor pin. Remove anchor pin plate.

2) Remove hold-down springs, shoes, adjusting screw, pivot nut, socket and automatic adjuster. Remove parking brake link spring and retainer. Disconnect parking brake cable from lever. After removing secondary shoe, disassemble parking brake lever from shoe by removing retaining clip and spring washer.

3) Assemble parking brake lever to secondary shoe and secure with spring washer and retaining clip. Lubricate brake shoe contact points. Position shoes on backing plate and install hold-down springs.

4) Install parking brake link, spring and retainer. Back off parking brake adjustment and connect cable to brake lever. Install anchor pin plate. Place cable eye over anchor pin with crimped side toward drum.

5) Install primary shoe anchor spring. Install cable guide on secondary shoe web with flanged hole fitted into hole in shoe web. Thread cable around anchor guide groove; NOT between guide and shoe web. Install secondary anchor spring. All parts should be flat on anchor pin.

6) Lubricate threads of adjusting screw and turn screw into pivot nut to limit of threads. Back off 1/2 turn and place socket on screw end. Install assembly between shoe ends with adjusting screw toothed wheel nearest secondary shoe.

7) Install cable hook in adjusting lever. Position hooked end of adjuster spring completely into large hole of primary shoe web. Connect loop end of spring to adjuster lever hole. Pull adjuster lever, cable and adjuster spring down and rearward, engaging pivot hook in large hole of secondary shoe web.

8) Ensure shoes are seated and centered on backing plate and that automatic adjuster is operating. Install drums and adjust and bleed brakes. Check for proper brake operation before moving vehicle.

Ford Motor Co. (Escort, Sable, Taurus, Tempo & Topaz) – 1) On FWD models, remove grease cap from hub. Remove cotter pin, nut lock and adjusting nut. Remove flat washer and outer bearing.

2) On all models, remove wheel, drum and hub assembly as a unit, being careful not to drag seal across spindle threads (if equipped). Remove hold-down spring and pins. Lift brake shoe and adjuster assembly off backing plate. Remove parking brake cable from parking brake lever.

3) On 7" brakes remove lower retracting spring, then remove lower primary shoe retracting spring by rotating shoe over adjusting quadrant and disconnecting spring.

NOTE: If drum will not come off, insert a screwdriver through adjustment hole and apply side pressure to adjuster assembly pivot to release brake adjustment. On 8", 8.85" and 9.84" brakes it will be necessary to remove brake line-to-axle retention bracket to gain access to adjuster hole.

4) On 7" brakes, remove secondary shoe-to-parking brake strut retracting spring by pivoting strut downward until it disengages from secondary shoe.

5) On 8", 8.85" and 9.84" brakes, remove retracting springs from lower brake shoe attachment and upper shoe-to-adjuster lever.

6) On 7" brakes, disassemble adjuster by pulling quadrant away from knurled pin and rotating. Remove spring and slide quadrant out of slot.

7) On all models, remove parking brake lever horseshoe retaining clip and spring washer. Lift lever off pin on brake shoe. Apply a light coating of high temperature grease to contact points of brake shoes and backing plate and adjusting screw threads.

8) On 7" brakes, install adjuster quadrant until it meshes with knurled pin in 3rd or 4th notch of outboard end of quadrant.

9) On 8", 8.85" and 9.84" brakes, install stainless steel washer over socket end of adjusting screw and install socket. Turn adjustng screw into adjusting pivot nut to limit of threads and back off 1/2 turn.

10) On all models, assemble parking brake lever to secondary shoe. Install spring washer and new horseshoe clip. Crimp clip until lever is securely fastened.

11) On 8", 8.85" and 9.84" brakes, install parking brake cable to parking brake lever.

1989 DRUM BRAKE SYSTEMS
Bendix Single Anchor Automatic Adjuster (Cont.)

10-57

12) On 7" brakes, install secondary shoe to parking brake strut retracting spring by attaching to slots in each part and pivoting strut to tension spring. Ensure spring end with hook parallel to centerline of coils is installed in hole in shoe web. Installed spring should be flat against shoe and parallel to strut.

13) On all models, attach lower shoe retracting spring to brake shoes.

14) On 7" brakes, install primary shoe to adjuster strut retracting spring.

15) On all models, expand shoe assembly and install over anchor plate and wheel cylinder.

16) On 7" brakes, install parking brake cable to parking brake lever. On all models, install hold-down pins and spring assembly.

17) On 8", 8.85" and 9.84" brakes, install adjuster screw between primary shoe slot and slot in secondary shoe and parking brake lever with socket end of screw assembly in secondary shoe. Ensure letter on socket faces up. Assemble adjusting lever in groove located in parking brake lever pin.

18) On 8", 8.85" and 9.84" brakes, attach upper retracting spring to leading shoe slot. Stretch other end of spring into notch on adjuster lever. Adjuster lever should contact star wheel after installing spring.

19) On all models, install drum assembly.

20) On FWD models, install outer bearing, keyed washer and hub nut. While rotating hub assembly, tighten wheel bearing nut to 17-25 ft. lbs. (23-34 N.m). Back wheel bearing nut off one half turn. Tighten wheel bearing nut to 26 INCH lbs. (3 N.m).

21) On all models, install tire and wheel assembly.

Ford Motor Co. (Probe) – 1) Remove grease cap from hub. Remove cotter pin and hub retaining nut. Remove flat washer and outer bearing. Remove wheel, drum and hub assembly as a unit, being careful not to drag seal across spindle threads.

2) Remove brake shoe return springs and anti-rattle spring. Remove brake shoe hold-down springs. Using a screwdriver, push in and twist hold-down spring to disengage it from hold-down pin.

3) Remove rear brake shoe from the parking brake strut. Remove front brake shoe. Remove wheel cylinder (if necessary).

NOTE: Unless broken or worn, leave parking brake strut adjuster mechanism and adjuster spring in place.

4) Clean backing plate with an approved vacuum cleaner. Remove parking brake strut adjuster mechanism, and adjuster spring (if necessary). Use proper grease to lubricate shoe contact pads, adjuster mechanism toothed quadrant and anchor plate section where the shoes ride.

5) Install and tighten wheel cylinder (if removed). Position rear brake shoe into parking brake strut and install rear hold-down pin and spring. Install brake shoe return springs.

6) Insert a screwdriver between knurled quadrant and parking brake strut. Twist screwdriver until quadrant just touches backing plate. *See Fig 6.* To complete reassembly, reverse remainder of disassembly procedure. Bleed brakes (if necessary).

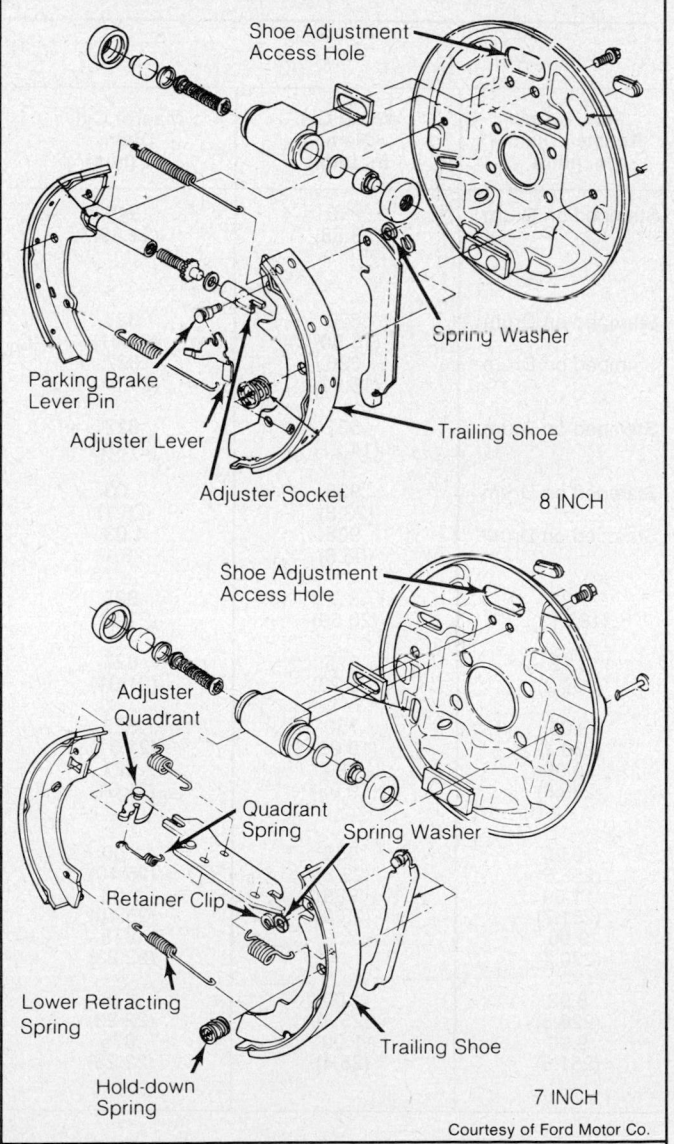

Fig. 4: Ford Motor Co. (Except Probe) Non-Servo Brake Assembly

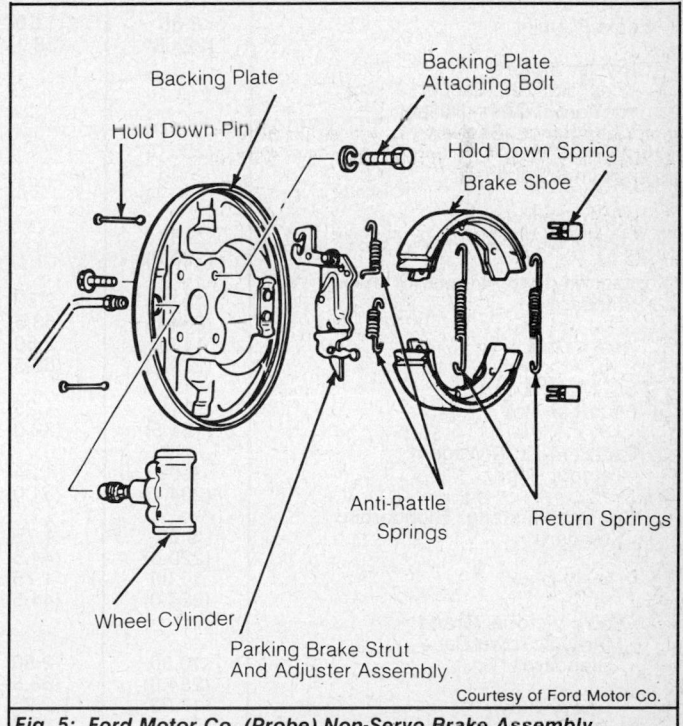

Fig. 5: Ford Motor Co. (Probe) Non-Servo Brake Assembly

10-58

1989 DRUM BRAKE SYSTEMS
Bendix Single Anchor Automatic Adjuster (Cont.)

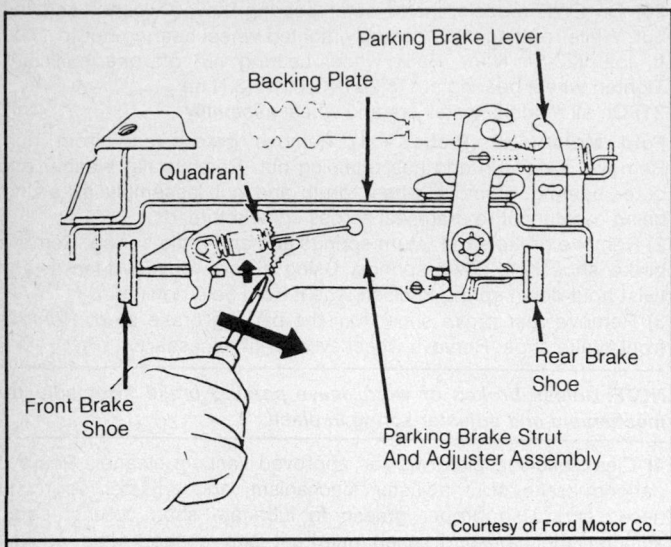

Parking Brake Lever

Backing Plate

Quadrant

Front Brake Shoe

Parking Brake Strut And Adjuster Assembly

Rear Brake Shoe

Courtesy of Ford Motor Co.

Fig. 6: Ford Motor Co. (Probe) Meshing Knurled Quadrant

BLEEDING SYSTEM

See HYDRAULIC BRAKE BLEEDING in this section.

TIGHTENING SPECIFICATIONS

Application	Ft. Lbs. (N.m)
Lug Nuts	
Eagle Premier	65 (85)
Chrysler Motors	
Diplomat, Fifth Avenue,	
Gran Fury	85 (115)
All Others	95 (129)
Ford Motor Co.	
Probe	88-115 (119-156)
All Others	85-105 (115-142)
Rear Wheel Bearing Nuts	
Probe [1]	73-131 (99-178)
Eagle Premier [2]	123 (167)
All Others [3]	

[1] – Always use new nut. Stake nut after tightening.

[2] – Always use new nut.

[3] – Rotate drum and lightly tighten nut to seat bearing. Back off nut and tighten to 17-25 ft. lbs. (23-34 N.m).

DRUM BRAKE SPECIFICATIONS

Application	Drum Diam. In. (mm)	Drum Width In. (mm)	Max. Drum Refinish Diam. In. (mm)	Wheel Cyl. Diam. In. (mm)	Master Cyl. Diam. In. (mm)
Eagle Premier	8.85 (224.8)	1.50 (38.1)	Stamped on Drum	.940 (23.88)	.940 (23.88)
Chrysler Motors					
Aries, Horizon, Lancer, LeBaron, Omni, Reliant, Sundance, Shadow	7.87 (200.0)	.....	Stamped on Drum	.626 (15.90)	.827 (21.01)
Acclaim & Spirit	8.66 (220.0)	.....	Stamped on Drum	.626 (15.90)	.827 (21.01)
Aries, Daytona, LeBaron, New Yorker, Reliant	8.66 (220.0)	.....	Stamped on Drum	.562 (14.27)	.827 (21.01)
Diplomat, Fifth Avenue, Gran Fury Standard	10.00 (254.0)	2.50 (63.5)	Stamped on Drum	.938 (23.8)	1.03 (26.1)
Heavy Duty [1]	11.00 (279.4)	2.50 (63.5)	Stamped on Drum	.938 (23.8)	1.03 (26.1)
Ford Motor Co. Escort (2-Dr.)	7.15 (181.5)	1.26 (32.0)	7.21 (183.13)	.811 (20.59)	.827 (21.01)
Escort (4-Dr. & Wagon), Tempo, Topaz	8.06 (204.7)	1.34 (34.0)	8.12 (206.2)	.875 (22.23)	.827 (21.01)
Cougar, Mustang, Thunderbird Standard	9.00 (229.0)	1.75 (44.5)	9.06 (230.1)	.750 (19.05)	.827 (21.01)
Heavy Duty [1]	10.00 (254.0)	1.75 (44.5)	10.06 (255.5)	.750 (19.05)	.827 (21.01)
Crown Victoria, Grand Marquis, Town Car Standard	10.00 (254.0)	2.50 (63.5)	10.06 (255.5)	.938 (23.8)	1.00 (25.40)
Heavy Duty [1]	11.03 (280.2)	2.25 (57.2)	11.09 (281.7)	.938 (23.8)	1.00 (25.40)
Probe	9.00 (229.0)	.....	9.06 (230.1)	.....	.875 (22.23)
Sable, Taurus Sedan	8.85 (225.0)	1.49 (38.0)	8.92 (226.5)	1.00 (25.4)	.875 (22.23)
Wagon	9.84 (250.0)	1.77 (45.0)	9.90 (251.5)	1.00 (25.4)	.875 (22.23)

[1] – Heavy Duty Models are Station Wagons, Police, Taxi and Trailer Tow.

Section 11

WHEEL ALIGNMENT

CONTENTS

TROUBLE SHOOTING   Page

All Models 11-2

ALIGNMENT PROCEDURES

All Models 11-3
Wheel Lug Nut Tightening
  Specifications 11-4

RIDING HEIGHT SPECIFICATIONS

All Models 11-5

ALIGNMENT SPECIFICATIONS

Chrysler Motors 11-6
Eagle 11-6
Ford Motor Co. 11-6

ADJUSTMENT PROCEDURES

All Models 11-8

JACKING & HOISTING

Chrysler Motors 11-10
Eagle 11-11
Ford Motor Co. 11-11

NOTE: ALSO SEE GENERAL INDEX

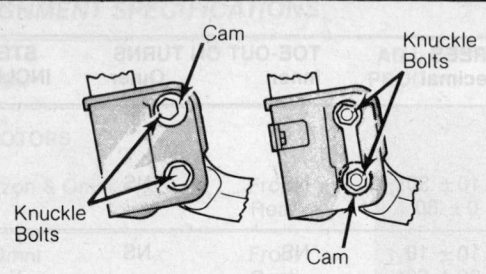

1 – Camber (Front)
Loosen cam and knuckle bolts. Rotate cam bolt to move top of wheel in or out to proper specifications. Tighten bolts to 45 ft. (65 N.m) plus 1/4 turn on "L" body, and 75 ft. lbs. (102 N.m) plus 1/4 turn on all others.

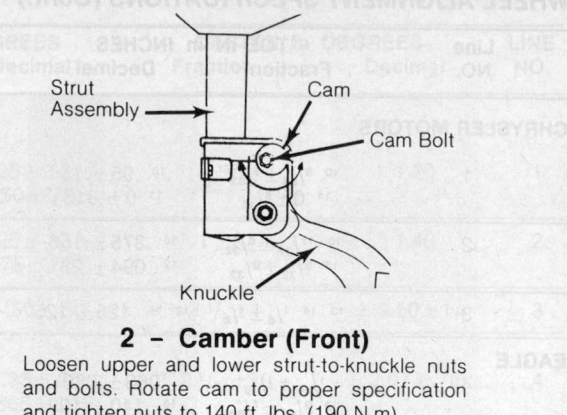

2 – Camber (Front)
Loosen upper and lower strut-to-knuckle nuts and bolts. Rotate cam to proper specification and tighten nuts to 140 ft. lbs. (190 N.m).

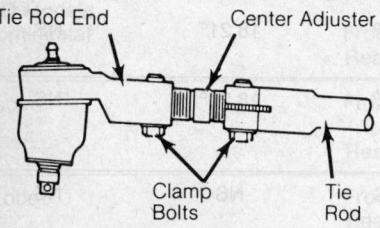

3 – Toe-In (Front)
Loosen tie rod clamp bolts. Adjust to specification by turning adjuster sleeves or center adjuster to proper specifications. On sleeve type adjusters, threaded end of bolts must face toward front of vehicle. Tighten clamp bolts to 41 ft. lbs. (55 N.m).

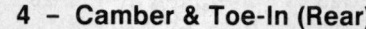

4 – Camber & Toe-In (Rear)
1) Check and record camber and toe angles. Remove both rear tires and brake drum assemblies. Loosen (do not remove) 4 bolts that mount spindle just enough to allow for installation of shims.
2) Arrange shims until proper specifications are met. Tighten spindle mounting bolts to 45 ft. lbs. (61 N.m).

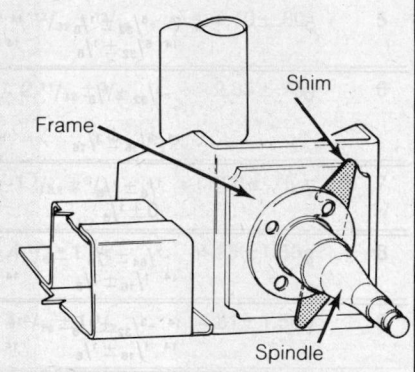

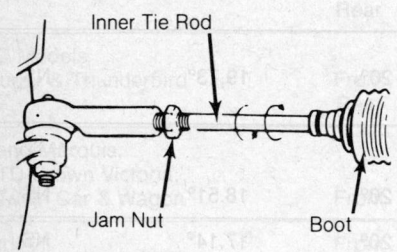

5 – Toe-In (Front & Rear)
Loosen jam nut on inner tie rod. Adjust toe to specification by turning inner tie rod. Do not twist boots (if equipped). Tighten nuts to 45 ft. lbs. (61 N.m).

6 – Camber & Caster (Front)
1) Determine initial camber and caster readings to confirm variance to specifications before loosening pivot bar bolts. Loosen nuts slightly while holding pivot bar (caster/camber).
2) Position claw of Camber/Caster Wrench (C-4576) on pivot bar and pin of tool into holes provided in tower or bracket. Move both ends of upper control arm in or out (in exact equal amounts) to adjust camber. Moving one end of the bar will change caster (and camber).
3) To preserve camber while adjusting caster, move each end of the upper control arm pivot bar (in exact equal amounts) in opposite directions. Tighten pivot bar bolts to 150 ft. lbs. (203 N.m).

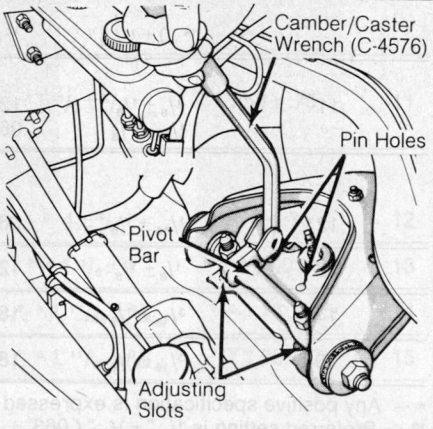

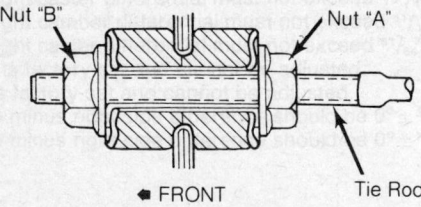

7 – Toe-In (Rear)
Loosen tie rod nut "B" and slide tie rod toward rear of vehicle to increase amount of negative toe. Loosen tie rod nut "A" and slide tie rod toward front of vehicle to increase amount of positive toe. Tighten rod nut "A" to 6-12 ft. lbs. (8-16 N.m), and tighten tie rod nut "B" to 35-50 ft. lbs. (47-68 N.m).

8 – Camber & Caster (Front)

1) Center punch 4 spot welds on alignment plates on upper strut tower. Loosen 3 strut attaching nuts. Using Rotobroach or equivalent, remove 4 spot welds.

2) Remove strut nuts and alignment plate. Clean burrs from tower and alignment plate. Install alignment plate and loosely install nuts. Make alignment adjustments for caster and camber. Tighten strut mount nuts to 20-30 ft. lbs. (27-41 N.m).

3) Drill three 1/8" inch holes through alignment plate and strut tower. Install three 1/8" x 1/4" inch grip range pop rivets.

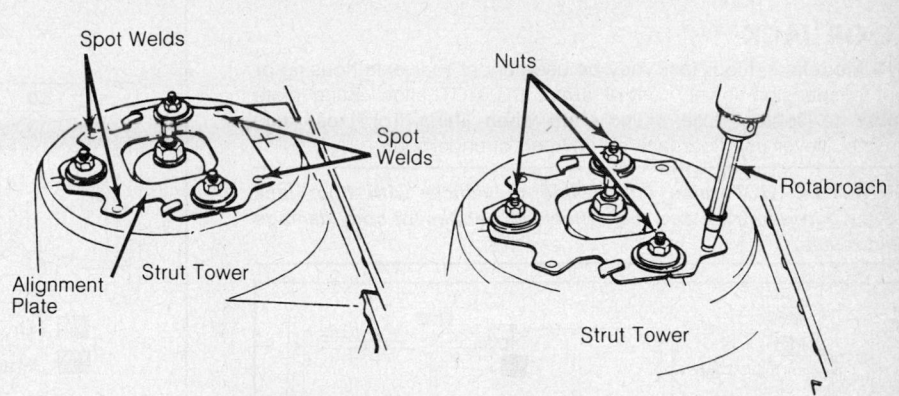

9 – Toe-In (Rear)

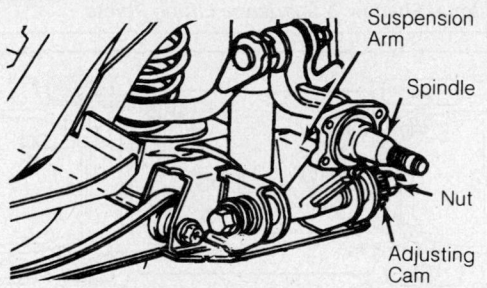

Loosen nut and bolt attaching spindle to lower suspension arm. Turn adjusting cam to obtain required alignment setting. While holding adjusting cam in position, tighten attaching nut to 60-86 ft. lbs. (81-115 N.m).

10 – Toe-In (Rear)

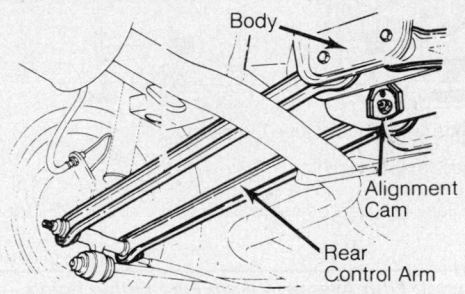

Adjust each wheel by loosening bolt attaching rear control arm to body and rotate alignment cam until the required alignment setting is obtained. Tighten control arm attaching bolt to 40-55 ft. lbs. (54-75 N.m).

11 – Camber (Front)

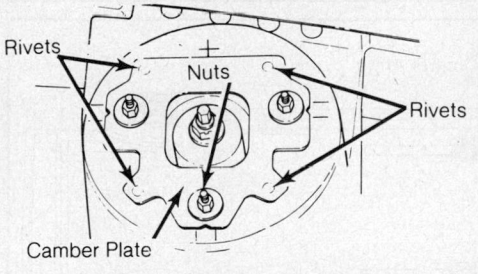

Remove pop rivets on camber plate. Loosen 3 nuts holding strut mount to body apron. Move top of shock strut to obtain required camber angle. Tighten mounting nuts to 50-75 ft. lbs. (68-102 N.m).

12 – Camber & Caster (Front)

1) Check and record camber and caster readings. Insert 2 Caster/Camber Adjusters (T79P-3000-A) into frame holes and tighten nuts finger tight against inner shaft of upper arm. Tighten each nut one additional "hex flat" turn.

2) Loosen upper control arm inner shaft-to-frame attaching bolts to unload pressure. Firmly tap bolts to loosen lower assemblies and adjust camber and caster to specifications. Tighten upper arm inner shaft-to-frame bolts to 100-140 ft. lbs. (136-190 N.m).

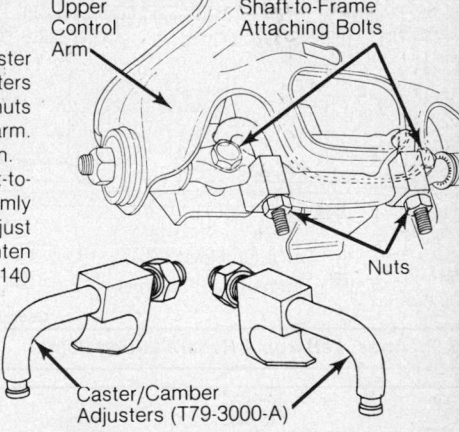

1989 JACKING & HOISTING
Chrysler Motors

LIFTING VEHICLE WITH JACK

FLOOR JACK

RWD Models – Floor jack may be used under rear axle housing or front suspension lower control arms. DO NOT allow lifting plate fingers to contact axle cover plate when lifting from rear axle housing. Never use floor jack on any part of underbody.

CAUTION: DO NOT raise entire side of vehicle with floor jack midway between front and rear wheels or permanent body damage could result.

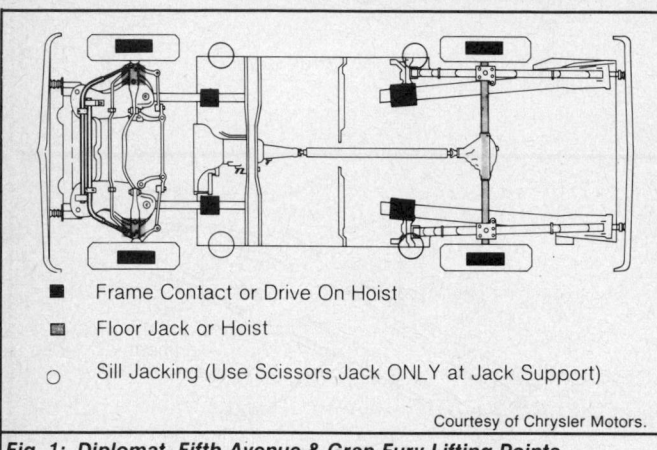

■ Frame Contact or Drive On Hoist

▨ Floor Jack or Hoist

○ Sill Jacking (Use Scissors Jack ONLY at Jack Support)

Courtesy of Chrysler Motors.

Fig. 1: Diplomat, Fifth Avenue & Gran Fury Lifting Points

FWD Models – Floor jack may be used to raise vehicle at locations shown in illustrations. *See Figs. 2-7.* A front floor jack point is located at center of front crossmember (inboard) and at center of rear axle.

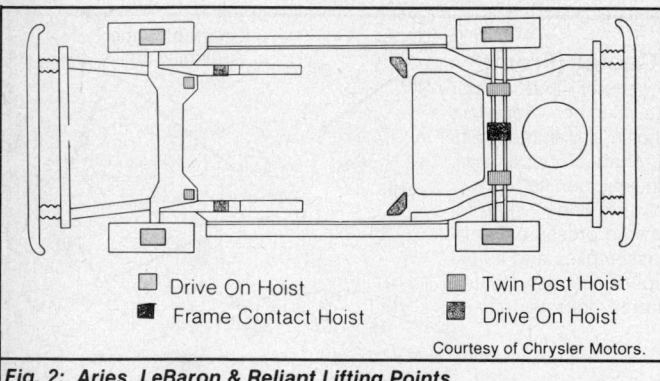

▢ Drive On Hoist   ▨ Twin Post Hoist

▨ Frame Contact Hoist   ▨ Drive On Hoist

Courtesy of Chrysler Motors.

Fig. 2: Aries, LeBaron & Reliant Lifting Points

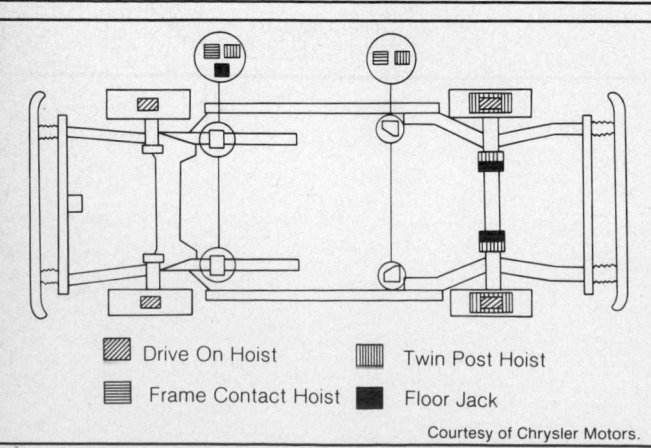

▨ Drive On Hoist   ▥ Twin Post Hoist

▨ Frame Contact Hoist   ■ Floor Jack

Courtesy of Chrysler Motors.

Fig. 3: Caravelle & New Yorker Turbo Lifting Points

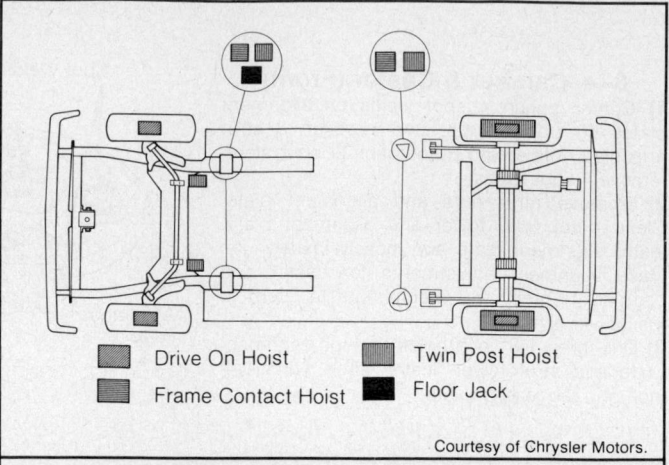

▨ Drive On Hoist   ▥ Twin Post Hoist

▨ Frame Contact Hoist   ■ Floor Jack

Courtesy of Chrysler Motors.

Fig. 4: Daytona, Shadow & Sundance Lifting Points

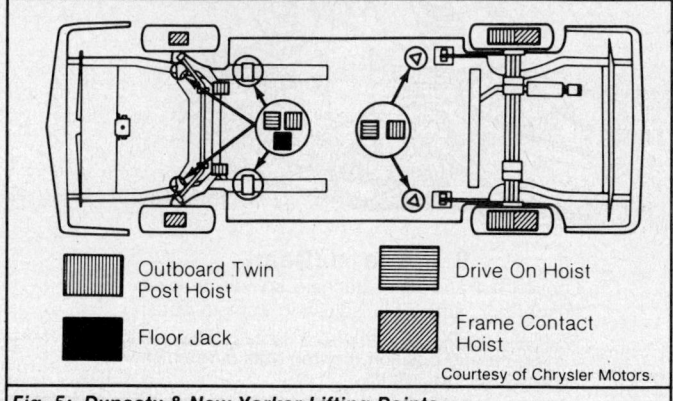

▥ Outboard Twin Post Hoist   ▨ Drive On Hoist

■ Floor Jack   ▨ Frame Contact Hoist

Courtesy of Chrysler Motors.

Fig. 5: Dynasty & New Yorker Lifting Points

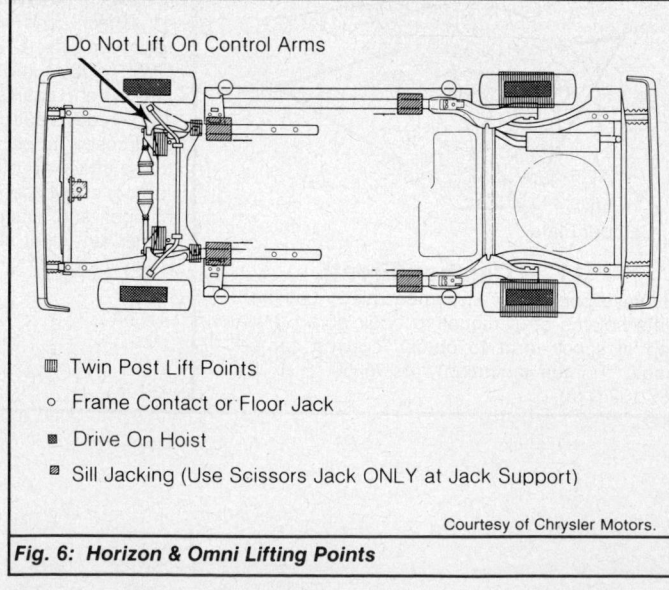

Do Not Lift On Control Arms

▨ Twin Post Lift Points

○ Frame Contact or Floor Jack

▨ Drive On Hoist

▨ Sill Jacking (Use Scissors Jack ONLY at Jack Support)

Courtesy of Chrysler Motors.

Fig. 6: Horizon & Omni Lifting Points

EMERGENCY JACKING

Scissor jack receptacles are located at body sills. DO NOT use floor jack at scissors jack locations. Ensure scissors jack flange is in contact with body sill and jack is engaged in body sill receptacle. Ensure scissor jack engages with locator pin on body sills. Always block opposite wheels and jack on level surface.

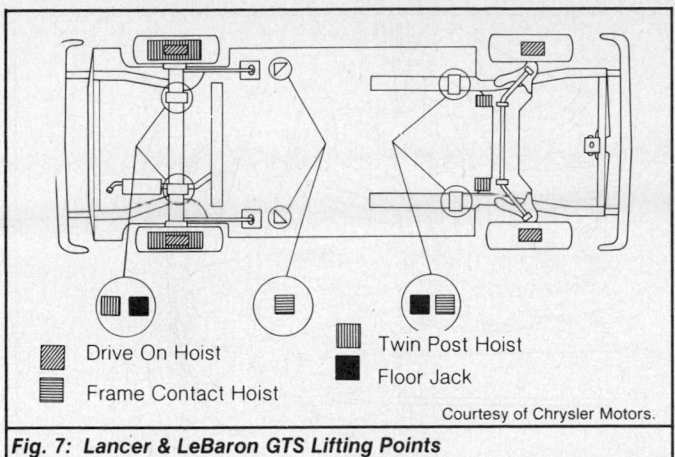

Drive On Hoist

Frame Contact Hoist

Twin Post Hoist

Floor Jack

Courtesy of Chrysler Motors.

Fig. 7: Lancer & LeBaron GTS Lifting Points

LIFTING VEHICLE WITH HOIST

CAUTION: If removing rear axle, fuel tank, spare tire or lift gate on FWD vehicles and single post hoist is used, anchor vehicle to hoist. Place jack stands under vehicle or add weight on rear end of vehicle to prevent tipping when center of gravity changes.

FRAME CONTACT HOIST

Frame contact hoist must be equipped with proper adapters to support vehicle in correct locations. On rear wheel drive models, use adaptor plates to make firm contact with lower control arms and rear axle housing.

AXLE CONTACT HOIST

RWD Models – Hoist should contact lower control arms and rear axle housing.

FWD Models – Axle contact hoist may be used on points shown in illustrations. Do not pick up vehicle at front lower control arms or rear trailing arm suspension.

Eagle

LIFTING VEHICLE WITH JACK

FLOOR JACK

DO NOT raise vehicle with floor jack positioned under axle housing, body side sills or front suspension arms. Use sub-frame rail lift points only. *See Fig. 1.*

BUMPER JACK

1) Bumper jack should be used only on models that are supplied as original equipment and only to change flat tire. If bumper jack is used to raise vehicle for any other reason, subframe rails must be supported by jack stands in event of bumper jack failure.
2) Verify that ground supporting jack is firm and level. If vehicle is not supplied with a bumper type jack, do not lift vehicle by bumper. Failure to use correct equipment could result in vehicle tipping off support. Always block wheels on axle opposite axle being lifted.

LIFTING VEHICLE WITH HOIST

AXLE CONTACT HOIST

CAUTION: The use of axle contact hoist is not recommended.

FRAME CONTACT HOIST

Vehicle can be raised on swivelling arm or a ramp-type drive hoist. If swivelling arm hoist is used, lifting pads should be positioned evenly on subframe rails. Hoist must be equipped with proper adapters so vehicle will be supported at points marked. *See Fig. 8.*

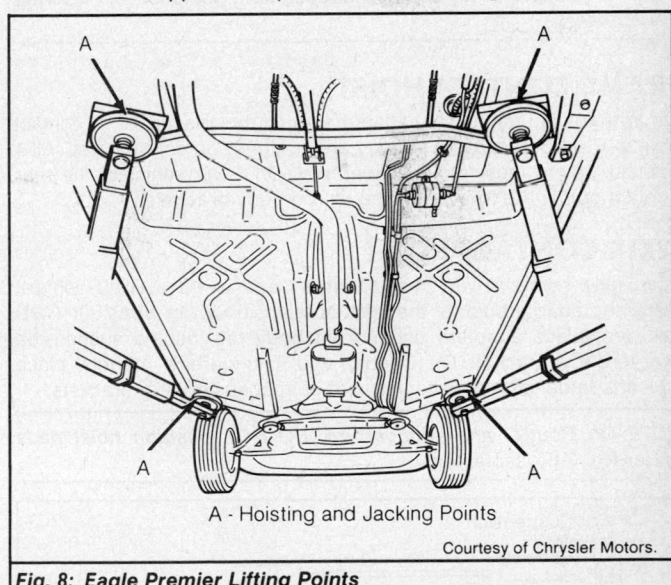

A - Hoisting and Jacking Points

Courtesy of Chrysler Motors.

Fig. 8: Eagle Premier Lifting Points

Ford Motor Co.

LIFTING VEHICLE WITH JACK

FLOOR JACK

FWD Models – Front of vehicle may be raised with floor jack by placing jack under front body rail, behind suspension arm-to-body bracket. Rear of vehicle may be raised by placing jack forward of tie rod bracket or under either rear lower control arm.

Cougar, Mustang & Thunderbird – **1)** The front of the vehicle may be lifted by positioning a jack under the center of No. 2 crossmember. The front end or either side of the rear end may be lifted by positioning floor a jack under the rocker flange at contact points used for jack supplied with vehicle.
2) To lift both sides of rear at once, position floor jack under differential housing. Make sure that jack does not make contact with differential housing cover.

3) Position jack stands under rear axle housing between suspension arm brackets and differential housing. DO NOT place jack stands under suspension arm brackets.

NOTE: On vehicles with air suspension, disconnect electrical power by removing negative battery cable or shutting off air suspension power switch located in trunk. Switch is located in trunk on left front side of inner panel.

Grand Marquis, LTD Crown Victoria, Mark VII & Town Car – 1) Either front side of vehicle may be raised by jack contact at lower arm strut connection, on front crossmember or on side rail to which stabilizer is connected.
2) Front of vehicle may be raised by positioning jack under center of front crossmember. Care must be taken not to contact steering linkage or to compress stabilizer link insulators.
3) For rear of vehicle, position jack under rear axle housing between suspension arm brackets and differential housing. Do not place jack under suspension arm brackets.

BUMPER JACK

A bumper type jack may be used on Grand Marquis, LTD Crown Victoria, Mark VII and Town Car models only. DO NOT raise other vehicles by the bumper at any time.

LIFTING VEHICLE WITH HOIST

CAUTION: Follow hoist manufacturer's instructions. DO NOT allow hoist or adapters to contact suspension, exhaust or steering components.

FRAME CONTACT HOIST

On frame contact hoists, adapters must be placed at 4 contact points. Position adapters so they are centered on contact area. All 4 contact points must contact adapters. On FWD vehicles, the rear contact points are forward of the tie rod body brackets.

AXLE CONTACT HOIST

If an axle contact (twin post) hoist is used to lift a RWD vehicle, place the adapters under the front suspension lower arms. On FWD vehicles, place adapters under front body rail, behind suspension arm-to-body bracket. On Cougar and Thunderbird models, place fork lifts under axle housing inboard of suspension arm brackets.

NOTE: On Cougar and Thunderbird, DO NOT position hoist pads under No. 3 crossmember.

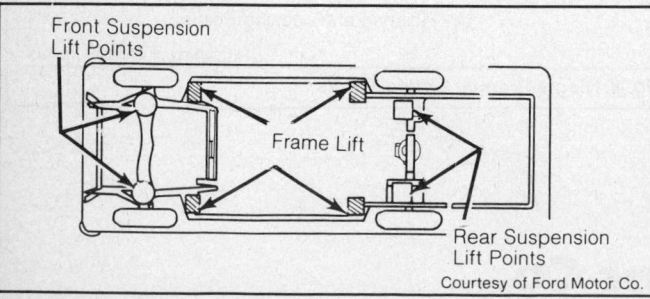

Fig. 9: *Grand Marquis, LTD Crown Victoria & Town Car Lifting Points*

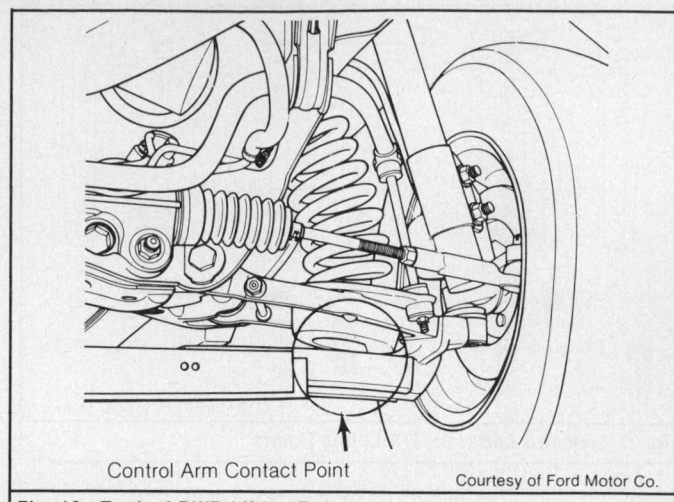

Control Arm Contact Point
Courtesy of Ford Motor Co.

Fig. 10: *Typical RWD Lifting Points*

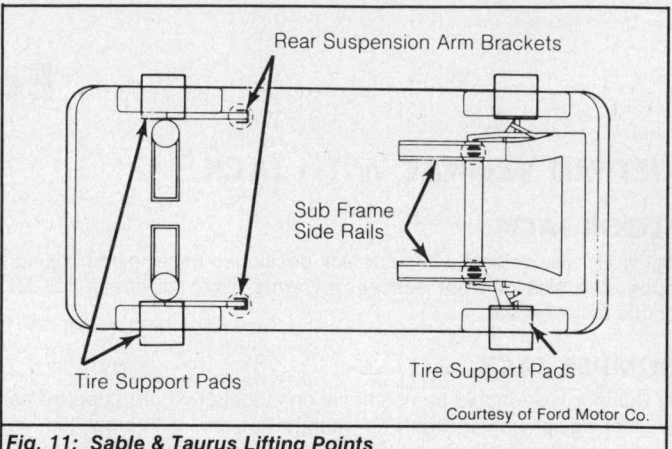

Rear Suspension Arm Brackets
Sub Frame Side Rails
Tire Support Pads
Tire Support Pads
Courtesy of Ford Motor Co.

Fig. 11: *Sable & Taurus Lifting Points*

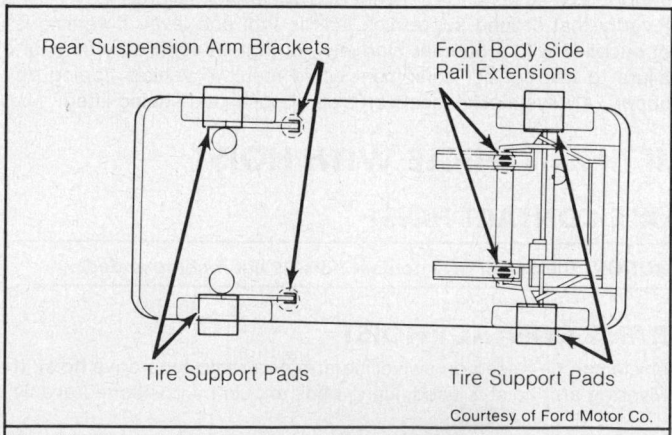

Rear Suspension Arm Brackets
Front Body Side Rail Extensions
Tire Support Pads
Tire Support Pads
Courtesy of Ford Motor Co.

Fig. 12: *Escort, Tempo & Topaz Lifting Points*

Section 12

SUSPENSION

CONTENTS

TROUBLE SHOOTING   Page
All Models 12-2

FRONT SUSPENSION

Chrysler Motors
  FWD Models 12-3
  RWD Models 12-8
Eagle 12-12
Ford Motor Co.
  FWD Models
  Escort, Tempo & Topaz 12-15
  Probe 12-18
  Sable & Taurus 12-21

FRONT SUSPENSION (Cont.)   Page

Ford Motor Co. (Cont.)
  RWD Models
  Continental 12-60
  Cougar & Thunderbird 12-25
  LTD Crown Victoria, Grand Marquis,
  Town Car & Wagon (Enclosed Spring) 12-27
  Mustang 12-30

REAR SUSPENSION

Chrysler Motors FWD
  Except Horizon & Omni 12-33
  Horizon & Omni 12-36
Eagle 12-37
Ford Motor Co.
  FWD Models
  Escort 12-41
  Probe 12-44
  Sable & Taurus 12-46
  Tempo & Topaz 12-49
  RWD Models
  Except Cougar, Mark VII & Thunderbird 12-51
  Continental 12-60
  Cougar & Thunderbird 12-55
  Mark VII 12-92

ELECTRONIC SUSPENSION

Chrysler Motors Rear Level Control
  Dynasty & New Yorker 12-57
Ford Motor Co.
  Air Suspension
  Continental 12-60
  Mark VII 12-92
  Automatic Ride Control
  Cougar XR-7 & Thunderbird Super Coupe 12-109
  Programmed Ride Control
  Probe 12-118
  Rear Level Control
  LTD Crown Victoria, Grand Marquis,
  Town Car & Wagon 12-127

NOTE: **ALSO SEE GENERAL INDEX**

1989 SUSPENSION
Trouble Shooting

CONDITION	POSSIBLE CAUSE	CORRECTION
Abnormal Tire Wear	Unbalanced tires	Check tire balance & rotation
	Incorrect tire inflation	Inflate tires to correct pressure
	Defective suspension components	See SUSPENSION
	Incorrect front end alignment	See WHEEL ALIGNMENT
	Faulty shock absorbers	Replace shock absorbers
Broken Springs	Loose "U" bolts	See SUSPENSION
	Excessive load in vehicle	Remove load or increase suspension support
Car Leans or Sways on Corners	Loose stabilizer bar	See SUSPENSION
	Faulty shocks or mountings	Replace shocks or mountings
	Broken or sagging springs	See SUSPENSION
Car Pulls to One Side	Mismatched or uneven tires	Check tire condition
	Incorrect tire inflation	Inflate tires to correct pressure
	Radial tire belt separation	Replace tire
	Broken or sagging springs	See SUSPENSION
	Loose or worn strut bushings	See SUSPENSION
	Incorrect wheel alignment	See WHEEL ALIGNMENT
	Improper rear axle alignment	Check rear axle alignment
	Power steering gear unbalanced	See STEERING
	Front or rear brake drag	See BRAKES
"Dog" Tracking	Broken rear spring	Replace leaf spring
	Bent rear axle housing	Check rear axle housing
	Incorrect rear wheel alignment	See WHEEL ALIGNMENT
	Frame misalignment	Check frame for damage
Front End Noise	Loose or worn wheel bearings	See Wheel Bearing Adjustment in SUSPENSION
	Incorrect spring installation	See SUSPENSION
	Worn shocks or shock mountings	Replace shocks or mountings.
	Worn struts or strut mountings	Replace struts or strut mountings
	Loose or worn control arm	See SUSPENSION
	Loose steering gear-to-frame bolts	See STEERING
	Worn control arm bushings	See SUSPENSION
	Ball joints not lubricated	Lubricate ball joints & see Ball Joint Checking in SUSPENSION
Front Wheel Shimmy or Vibration	Tires or wheels out of balance	Check tire balance
	Loose steering gear-to-frame bolts	See STEERING
	Propeller shaft unbalanced	Check propeller shaft balance
	Loose or worn wheel bearings	See Wheel Bearing Adjustment in SUSPENSION
	Loose or worn idler arm	See SUSPENSION
	Loose or worn tie rod ends	See SUSPENSION
	Worn upper ball joints	See Ball Joint Checking in SUSPENSION
	Worn strut bushings	Replace strut bushings
Scuffed Tires	Incorrect wheel alignment	See WHEEL ALIGNMENT
	Suspension arm bent or twisted	See appropriate SUSPENSION article
Shock Absorbers Leaking	Worn seals or reservoir tube crimped	Replace shock absorber
Shock Absorber Noise	Loose shock mountings	Check & tighten mountings
	Worn bushings	Replace bushings
	Undercoating on shocks	Remove undercoating
Springs Bottom or Sag	Broken or sagging springs	See SUSPENSION
	Excessive load in vehicle	Remove load or increase suspension support
Spring Noises	Loose "U" Bolts	See SUSPENSION
	Loose or worn bushings	See SUSPENSION
	Worn or missing interliners	See SUSPENSION

1989 FRONT SUSPENSION
Chrysler Motors FWD Models

Acclaim, Aries, Daytona, Dynasty, Horizon, New Yorker, Lancer, LeBaron, LeBaron GTS, Omni, Reliant, Shadow, Spirit, Sundance

DESCRIPTION

The front suspension is a MacPherson type with vertical shock absorbing struts. The top of each strut assembly bolts to upper fender through rubber isolated mounts and the bottom attaches to top of steering knuckle with 2 bolts. One bolt is formed to retain an eccentric cam (for camber adjustment). The caster is fixed and has no adjustment. The lower control arms are interconnected through a rubber isolated stabilizer bar. See Fig. 1 or 5.

ADJUSTMENTS

CAMBER & TOE-IN

See appropriate article in WHEEL ALIGNMENT section.

RIDING HEIGHT

See RIDING HEIGHT SPECIFICATIONS article in WHEEL ALIGNMENT section.

FRONT WHEEL BEARINGS

No lubrication or adjustment is necessary for permanently sealed front bearings. Replace hub nut and washer when removed, as they are not reuseable. Install a new bearing any time hub is removed from knuckle.

BALL JOINT CHECKING

NOTE: Ball joints operate with no free play. Ball joint housing is pressed into control arm with ball joint stud retained in steering knuckle with a clamp bolt.

1) With vehicle on ground and wheels in straight ahead position, grasp grease fitting and attempt to move fitting. No mechanical assistance or added force is needed to check joint. If ball joint is worn, fitting will move easily. If movement is noted, joint should be replaced.
2) Ball joints and control arm pivot bushings that are welded to control arms must be serviced by replacement of complete control arm assembly.

CAUTION: DO NOT raise vehicle by hoisting or jacking against the lower control arms.

REMOVAL & INSTALLATION

STABILIZER BAR

Removal – 1) Raise and support vehicle. Remove stabilizer bar end bushing-to-control arm nuts, bolts and retainers. Detach stabilizer bar-to-crossmember nuts and bolts, and remove holding clamps. See Fig.5.
2) Remove stabilizer bar from vehicle. Inspect for broken or distorted clamps and/or retainers. Replace components as needed. Inspect bushings for wear, deterioration or damage.
3) If inner (crossmember) bushing replacement is required, remove by opening split in bushing. Remove outer (control arm) bushing by cutting or hammering bushing from bar.
4) If outer bushing needs replacement, force the bushing on so that approximately 1/2" of stabilizer bar protrudes.

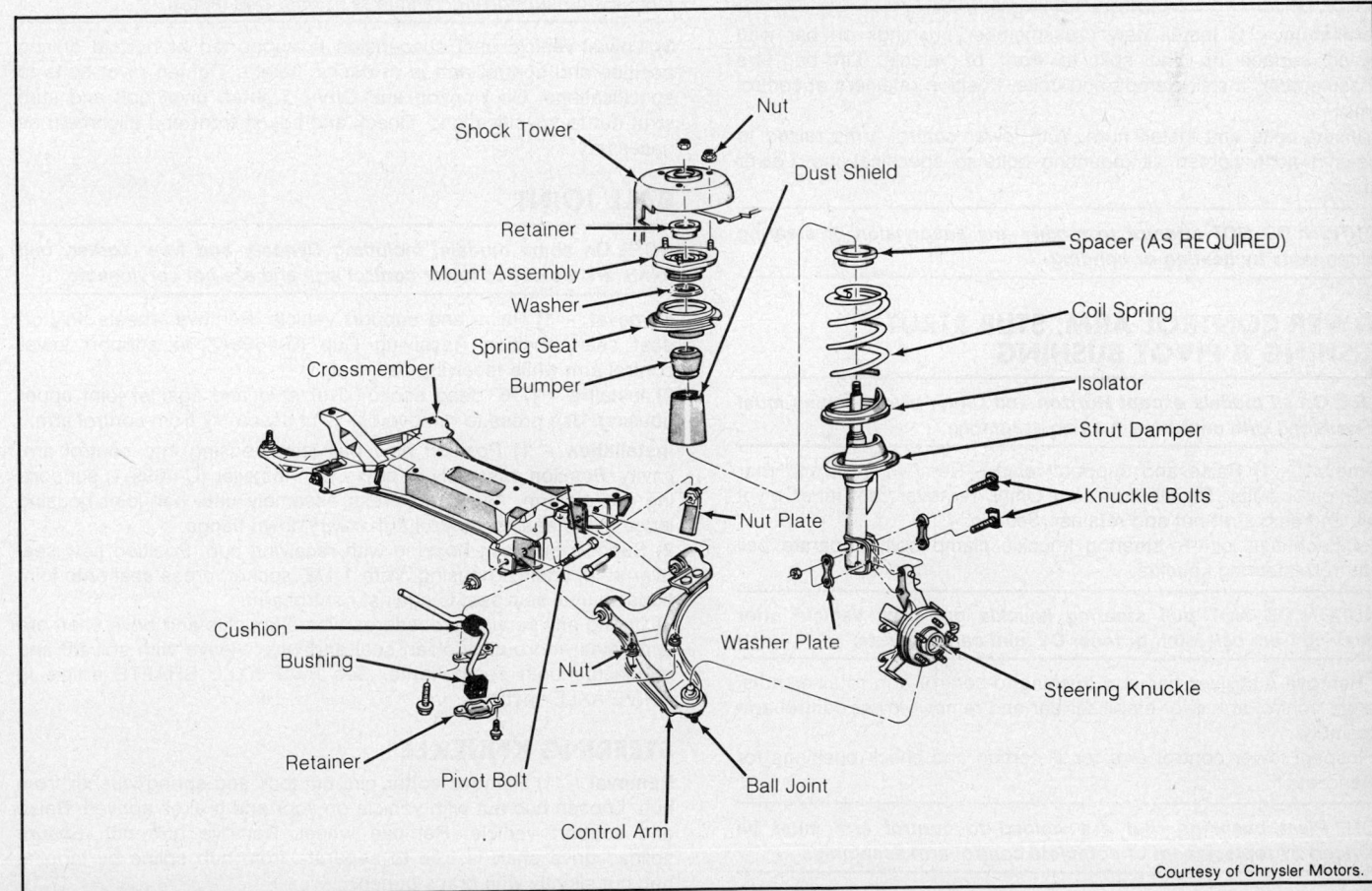

Courtesy of Chrysler Motors.

Fig. 1: Exploded View Of FWD Strut Damper Assembly (Except Dynasty, Horizon, New Yorker & Omni)

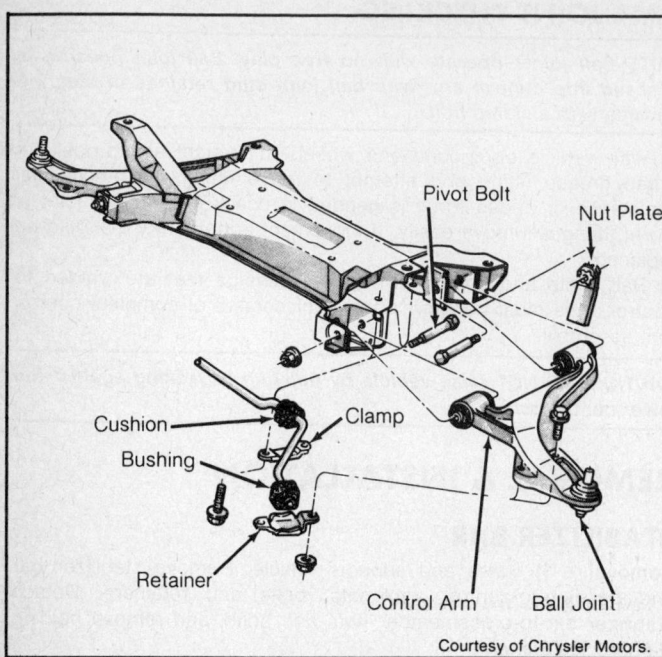

Fig. 2: Sectional View Of Lower Control Arm (Dynasty & New Yorker)

NOTE: On Dynasty and New Yorker, control arm bushings should be oriented as indicated on retainer. On all others, control arm bushing retainers are symmetrical and bend slightly upon installation.

Installation – 1) Install new crossmember bushings on bar with curved surface up and split to front of vehicle. Lift bar into crossmember. Install clamps and bolts. Position retainers at control arms.
2) Insert bolts and install nuts. With lower control arms raised to design height, tighten all mounting bolts to specifications. Lower vehicle.

CAUTION: DO NOT attempt to modify any suspension or steering components by heating or bending.

LOWER CONTROL ARM, STUB STRUT BUSHING & PIVOT BUSHING

NOTE: On all models except Horizon and Omni, pivot bushing must be replaced with control arm as an assembly.

Removal – 1) Raise and support vehicle. Remove front and rear inner pivot bolts. On Horizon and Omni, remove front inner pivot bolt, and stub strut nut and retainer. *See Fig. 4.*
2) Detach ball joint-to-steering knuckle clamp bolt. Separate ball joint from steering knuckle.

CAUTION: DO NOT pull steering knuckle out from vehicle after releasing from ball joint, or inner CV joint can separate.

3) Remove stabilizer bar end bushing-to-control arm retainer nuts. Rotate control arm over stabilizer bar and remove lower control arm assembly.
4) Inspect lower control arm for distortion and check bushings for deterioration.

NOTE: Pivot bushings that are welded to control arm must be serviced by replacement of complete control arm assembly.

Pivot Bushing Replacement (Horizon & Omni) – 1) Inspect control arm pivot bushing for distortion, wear, deterioration, or damage. If replacement of pivot bushing is necessary, position Control Arm Support (C-4700) between lower control arm flanges and around bushing to prevent control arm distortion.
2) Install a 1/2" x 2 1/2" bolt into bushing. With Receiving Cup (C-4699-2) on press base, position control arm inner flange against cup wall to support flange while receiving bushing. Remove bushing by pressing on bolt head.
3) To install pivot bushing, position Control Arm Support (C-4700) between control arm flanges. Install bushing inner sleeve and insulator into cavity of Receiver (C-4699-2).
4) Position assembly onto press base and align control arm to receive bushing. Position Installer (C-4699-1) to support control arm outer flange while receiving bushing. Press bushing into control arm until bushing flange seats against control arm.

Stub Strut Bushing Replacement (Horizon & Omni) – 1) If stub strut bushing needs replacement, slide sleeve out of bushing and pry bushing from crossmember. To install stub strut bushing, position new bushing in crossmember.
2) Fabricate a bushing installer from a 1/2" x 7 1/2" bolt, 2 washers and a piece of 1.2" bar stock (2" x 4 1/2"). Press bushing into position.

Installation – 1) Position control arm over stabilizer bar. Install retainer on stub strut. Install rear stub strut and front pivot bolt into crossmember. Install front pivot bolt and assemble nut finger tight. Install stub strut retainer and assemble nut finger tight.
2) Install ball joint stud into steering knuckle. Install clamp bolt and tighten to specifications. See TIGHTENING SPECIFICATIONS table. Position stabilizer bar end bushing retainer onto control arm. Install retainer bolts and tighten all to specifications.

CAUTION: The control arm pivot bolts must be tightened with suspension supporting vehicle at normal ride height.

3) Lower vehicle until suspension is supported at normal driving position and control arm is at design height. Tighten pivot bolts to specifications. On Horizon and Omni, Tighten pivot bolt and stub strut nut to specifications. Check and adjust front end alignment as necessary.

BALL JOINT

NOTE: On some models, including Dynasty and New Yorker, ball joints are welded to lower control arm and are not serviceable.

Removal – 1) Raise and support vehicle. Remove wheels. Pry off dust seal. Position Receiving Cup (C-4699-2) to support lower control arm while receiving ball joint.
2) Install a 1 1/16" deep socket over stud and against joint upper housing. Use press to remove ball joint assembly from control arm.

Installation – 1) Position new ball joint housing into control arm cavity. Position assembly in press with Installer (C-4699-1) supporting control arm. Align and press assembly until ball joint housing ledge stops against control arm cavity down flange.
2) Support ball joint housing with receiving cup. Position new seal over stud, against housing. With 1 1/2" socket, press seal onto joint housing until seal seat is against control arm.
3) During any service procedures where knuckle and drive shaft are separated, thoroughly clean seal and wear sleeve with solvent and relubricate both components. See FWD AXLE SHAFTS article in DRIVE AXLE section.

STEERING KNUCKLE

Removal – 1) Remove cotter pin, nut lock and spring washer from hub. Loosen hub nut with vehicle on floor and brakes applied. Raise and support vehicle. Remove wheel. Remove hub nut. Ensure splined drive shaft is free to separate from hub spline by tapping hub out slightly with brass punch.

NOTE: *The hub and drive shaft are splined together through the steering knuckle/bearing assembly and retained by the hub nut.*

2) Remove tie rod end from steering knuckle with Remover (C-3894-A). Remove brake hose retaining clamp from strut damper. Remove ball joint stud clamp bolt and caliper mounting bolts. Remove caliper and hang with wire. Remove brake rotor.

3) Separate ball joint stud from knuckle assembly. Pull knuckle assembly out and away from drive shaft.

Installation – 1) Slide drive shaft through hub splines. Install hub with steering knuckle/bearing assembly onto lower control arm ball joint stud. *See Fig. 3.* Install ball joint-to-knuckle clamp bolt and tighten to specifications.

2) Install tie rod end onto knuckle steering arm and tighten nut. Install new cotter pin. Install brake rotor. Install brake caliper assembly. Install caliper mounting bolts and tighten.

3) Attach brake hose retainer to strut damper and tighten. Install washer and tighten hub nut (with brakes applied). Install spring washer, nut lock and new cotter pin. Install wheel. Tighten all nuts and bolts to specifications. SEE TIGHTENING SPECIFICATIONS table. Check and adjust front end alignment as necessary.

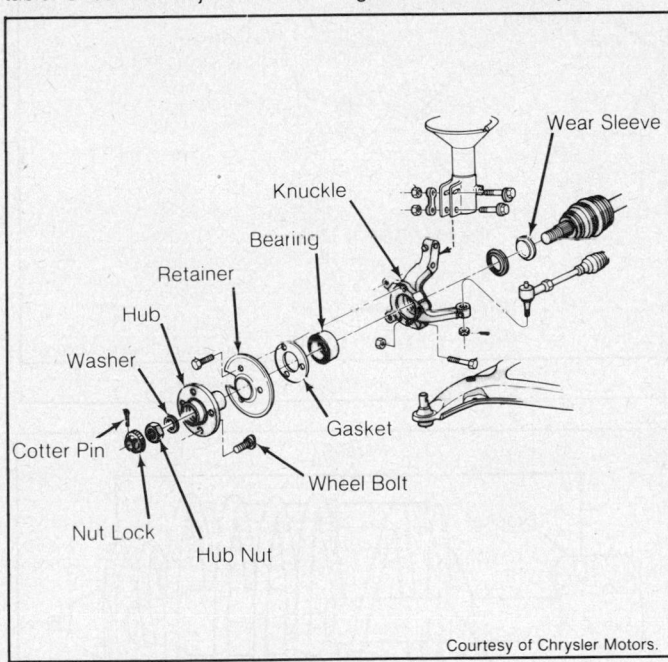

Fig. 3: Sectional View Of Knuckle Assembly

WHEEL BEARINGS, SEAL & HUB ASSEMBLY

NOTE: *The Hub Unit III Front Hub bearing (bolted on hub) is used on certain vehicles. This unit is serviced as a complete assembly, and is attached to the steering knuckle by 4 mounting screws that are removed from rear of knuckle.*

Removal (Pressed On Hub) – 1) Remove steering knuckle as previously described. Separate hub from bearing assembly with Hub/Bearing Remover/Installer Kit (C-4811).

2) Back out one of the bearing retainer screws and install Bracket (C-4811-17) between screw head and retainer. Install Thrust Button (C-4811-6) inside hub bore. Install Puller (C-4811-14) and remove hub. *See Fig. 4.* If inner race remains on hub, use gear puller to remove it.

3) Remove tool (C-4811) and attaching screws from knuckle. Remove 3 screws and bearing retainer. Carefully pry seal from machined recess in knuckle and discard seal. Clean recess. Press bearing out of knuckle.

NOTE: *Inspect hub surfaces for damage before installing new bearing. If damaged replace hub.*

Installation – 1) Press new bearing into steering knuckle. Red seal on bearing faces outboard toward bearing retainer.

2) Install new seal and bearing retainer. Tighten retainer screws to specifications. Press hub into the steering knuckle using Puller Kit (C-4811).

3) Position new seal in recess and drive into place with Installer (C-4698) and hammer. Lubricate full circumference of seal and wear sleeve with multipurpose grease.

4) If necessary, install wear sleeve in constant velocity joint housing using Installer (C-4698). Lubricate full circumference of seal and wear sleeve with grease. Install knuckle onto suspension.

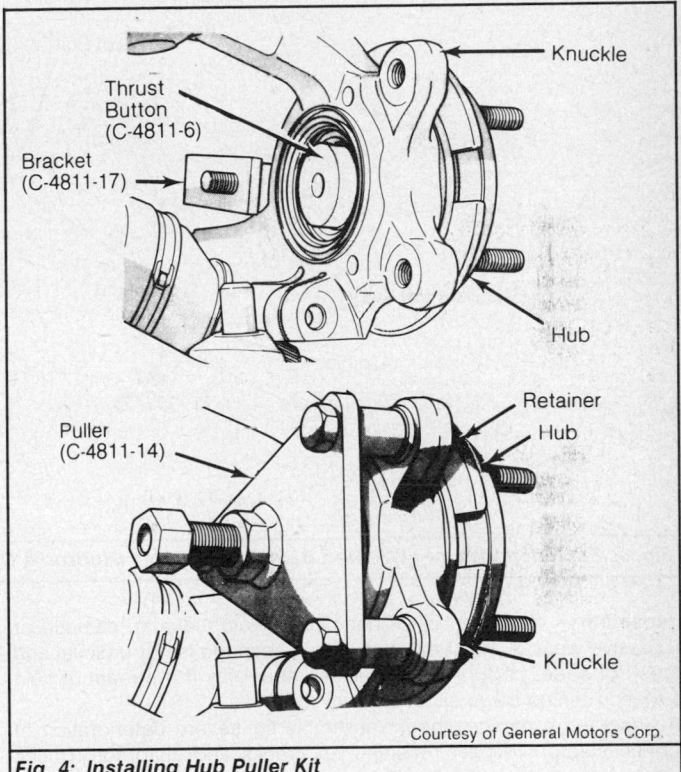

Fig. 4: Installing Hub Puller Kit

STRUT DAMPER ASSEMBLY

NOTE: *Where reassembly procedure includes use of original strut and knuckle, mark outline of strut on knuckle, on Lancer, LeBaron, Shadow and Sundance. On all others, mark cam adjusting bolt position for reassembly and alignment reference.*

Removal – 1) Raise and support vehicle. Remove wheel. Remove cam adjusting bolt, knuckle bolt, washer plate and brake hose-to-damper bracket retaining screw.

2) Remove strut damper-to-fender shield mounting nut washer assemblies. Remove strut damper and coil spring assembly from vehicle.

Disassembly – 1) Compress coil spring with Spring Compressor (C-4838). On Horizon and Omni, ensure 4 coils on spring are compressed. On all others, compress 5 coils. Hold strut rod and remove strut rod nut. Remove retainers and bushings. Remove coil spring.

CAUTION: *Do not grasp or damage strut rod seal surface, or possible seal leakage can result.*

2) Coil springs are rated separately for each side of vehicle depending on optional equipment and type of service. Mark coil spring to ensure it is installed on same side of vehicle.

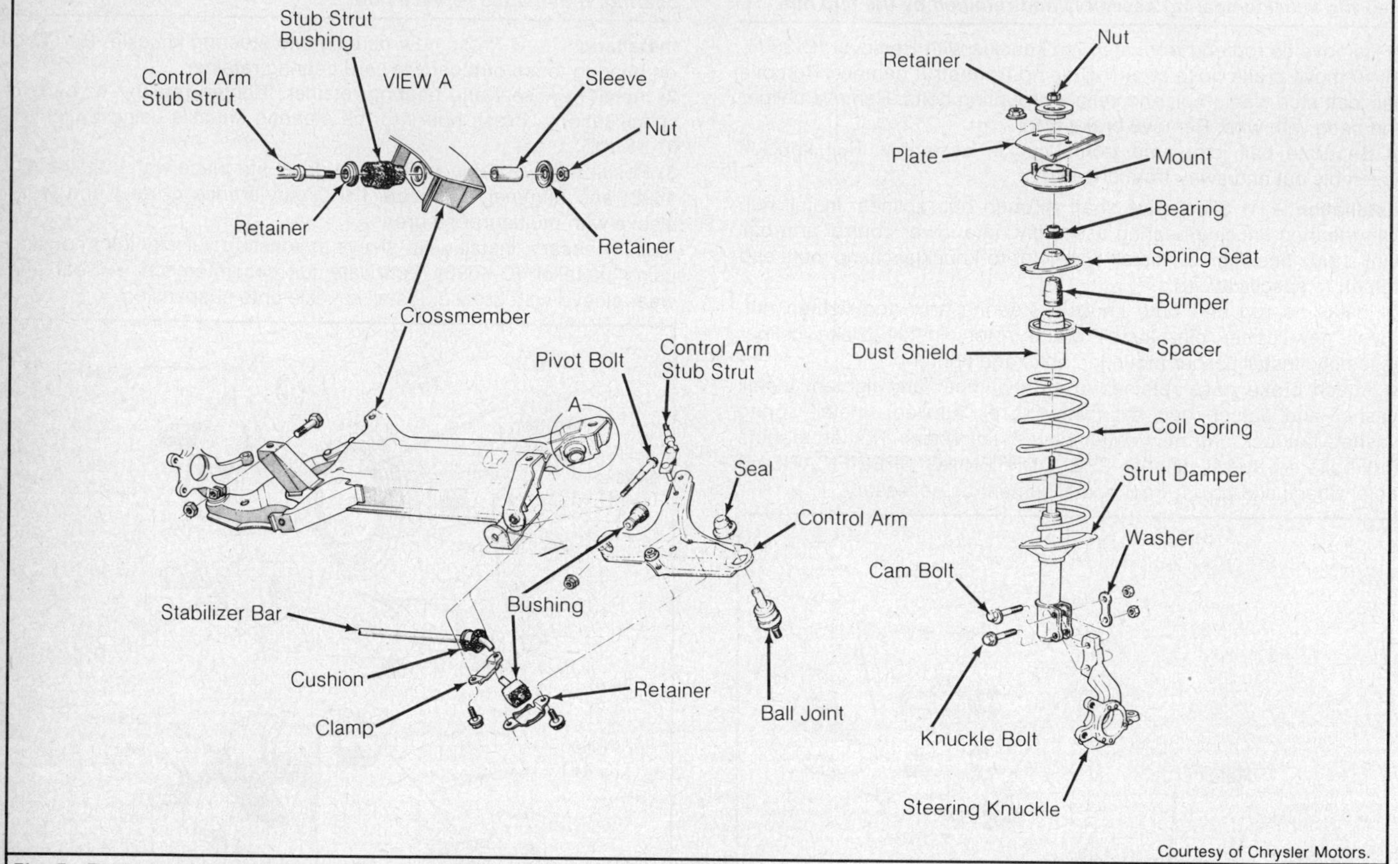

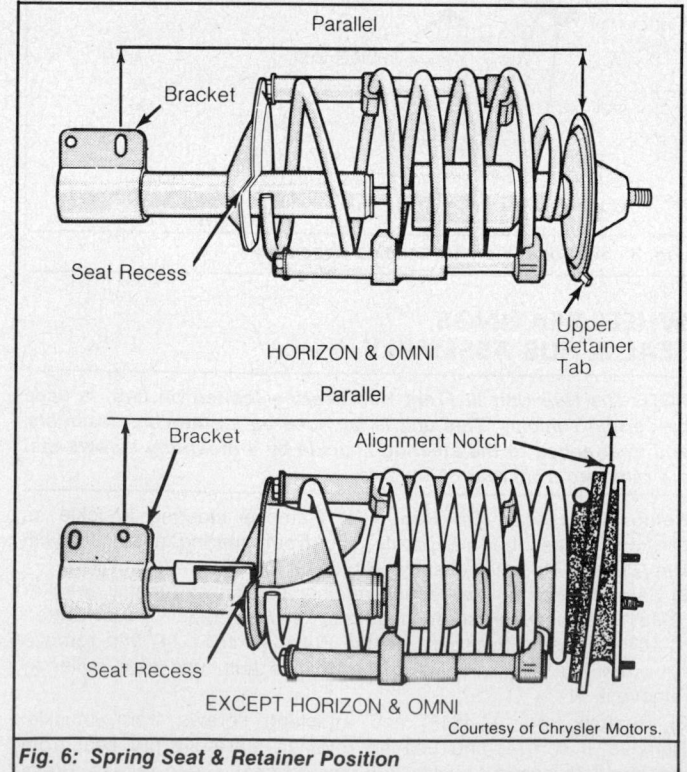

Fig. 5: Exploded View of FWD Strut Damper Assembly (Horizon & Omni)

Courtesy of Chrysler Motors.

Inspection – 1) Inspect strut damper for fluid leakage, damage or excessive wear. A slight amount of fluid seepage is not unusual and does not affect performance. Replace strut only if a stream of fluid is found running down sides of strut.

2) Check strut damper mount assembly for severe deterioration of rubber isolator. Inspect retainers for cracks and distortion. Check bearings for binding. Ensure damper has no flat spots over its entire stroke. Replace all worn parts as necessary.

Reassembly – 1) Install dust shield, isolator (if equipped), jounce bumper, spacer (as required) and spring seat onto top of spring. Install mount assembly, rebound retainer and rod nut.

NOTE: Be certain there is no vertical play between strut cartridge and strut housing before continuing reassembly.

2) Position upper spring retainer alignment tab parallel to damper lower attaching brackets. *See Fig. 7.* Using Strut Rod Nut Assembler (L-4558) tighten rod nut, before releasing the spring compressor. Remove spring compressor.

Installation – 1) Install strut damper and coil spring assembly into fender reinforcement. Install retaining nut and washer assemblies and tighten.

2) Position knuckle neck into strut clamp. Position washer plate (if equipped) cam and knuckle bolts. Attach brake hose retainer-to-damper clamp and tighten screw.

3) Index cam bolt to original mark (or clamp outline to knuckle neck). Place a 4" (or larger) "C" clamp onto strut and knuckle, and tighten just enough to eliminate any looseness between knuckle and strut.

4) Check alignment of index marks and tighten bolts to specification. Remove "C" clamp. Install wheel and lower vehicle.

Parallel

Bracket

Seat Recess

HORIZON & OMNI

Upper Retainer Tab

Parallel

Bracket

Alignment Notch

Seat Recess

EXCEPT HORIZON & OMNI

Courtesy of Chrysler Motors.

Fig. 6: Spring Seat & Retainer Position

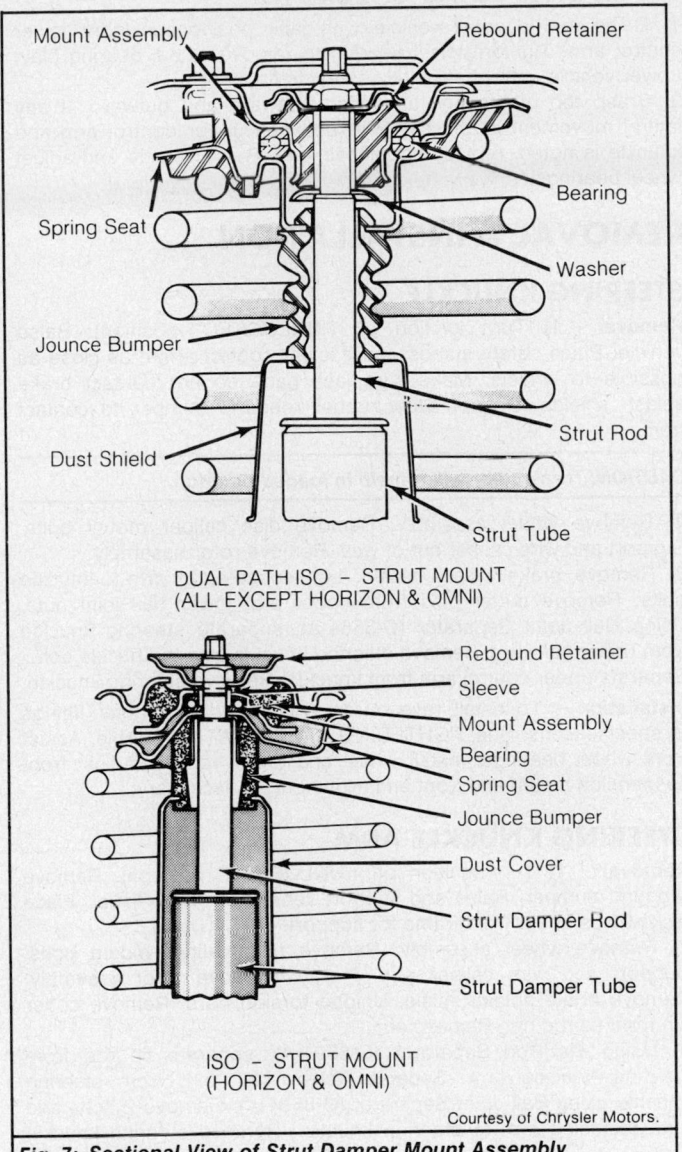

Mount Assembly

Rebound Retainer

Bearing

Washer

Spring Seat

Jounce Bumper

Strut Rod

Dust Shield

Strut Tube

DUAL PATH ISO – STRUT MOUNT
(ALL EXCEPT HORIZON & OMNI)

Rebound Retainer

Sleeve

Mount Assembly

Bearing

Spring Seat

Jounce Bumper

Dust Cover

Strut Damper Rod

Strut Damper Tube

ISO – STRUT MOUNT
(HORIZON & OMNI)

Courtesy of Chrysler Motors.

Fig. 7: Sectional View of Strut Damper Mount Assembly

TIGHTENING SPECIFICATIONS

Application	Ft. Lbs. (N.m)
Ball Joint Stud Clamp Bolt	70 (95)
Bearing Retainer-to-Knuckle Screw	20 (27)
Brake Hose Retainer Screw	10 (13)
Caliper Adapter Mounting Bolt	160 (217)
Control Arm Pivot Bolt/Nut	
Horizon & Omni	95 (129)
All Others	125 (169)
Hub Nut	180 (245)
Stabilizer Bar Clamp/Retainer	
Horizon & Omni	25 (34)
All Other Models	40 (55)
Strut Damper Rod Nut	55 (75)
Strut Damper-to-Steering Knuckle	
Horizon & Omni	[1] 45 (61)
All Other Models	[1] 75 (102)
Strut Damper Upper Retainer Nut	20 (27)
Stub Strut Nut	70 (95)
Tie Rod End Nut	35 (47)
Wheel Lug Nut	95 (129)

[1] – Tighten 1/4 turn beyond specified torque.

1989 FRONT SUSPENSION
Chrysler Motors RWD Models

Diplomat, Fifth Avenue, Gran Fury

DESCRIPTION

All models use an independent torsion bar type suspension. Transverse torsion bars are mounted between outboard ends of lower control arms and forward portion of the suspension crossmember. Each torsion bar is anchored in the front crossmember opposite affected wheel. The sway bar is mounted between both control arms and is bolted to the crossmember, adding a stabilizing effect to the front suspension system.

Height is controlled by the torsion bar anchor adjusting bolts, located on the front crossmember. The right torsion bar is adjusted by the left side and the left torsion bar is adjusted by the right side. Front height specifications must be correct to ensure proper wheel alignment, tire wear, satisfactory ride, and appearance. *See Fig. 1.*

ADJUSTMENTS

CASTER & CAMBER

See appropriate article in WHEEL ALIGNMENT section.

RIDING HEIGHT

See RIDING HEIGHT SPECIFICATIONS article in WHEEL ALIGNMENT section.

FRONT WHEEL BEARINGS

NOTE: Under normal service, front wheel bearings should be inspected, lubricated and adjusted whenever front brakes are serviced or at least every 30,000 miles. For severe service use, check bearings at least every 9000 miles. Lubricate wheel bearings using only high temperature wheel bearing grease.

1) Raise vehicle. Remove tire and wheel. Remove caliper from rotor. Remove rotor assembly. Carefully remove seal and inner bearing from hub.
2) Clean hub and bearings with solvent, mineral spirits or kerosene. Check bearing races for pitting, scoring or other damage. If races need replacement, drive bearing race out of hub with soft steel drift.

NOTE: Replace inner and/or outer bearings and races as matched sets.

3) Check bearings for wear and damage. If bearings are okay, pack bearings with grease. Place inner bearing assembly into inner race.
4) Using seal installer, position seal with lip facing inward, flush with end of hub. Clean spindle and apply light coat of grease. Install brake rotor assembly to spindle. Install outer bearing, thrust washer and adjusting nut.
5) While rotating brake rotor and hub assembly, tighten adjusting nut to 20-25 ft. lbs. (27-34 N.m). Stop rotation and back off adjusting nut 1/4 turn (90 degrees) to release preload. Finger tighten adjusting nut while rotating wheel. Position nut lock over adjusting nut. Install new cotter pin and dust cover. Install wheel.

LOWER BALL JOINT CHECKING

1) Raise and support vehicle. Place jack stands under both lower control arms, as far outboard as possible. Ensure the stands DO NOT contact splash shield and upper control arms DO NOT contact the rebound bumpers.
2) With weight on control arms, place dial indicator and clamp assembly on lower control arm. Position plunger tip against steering knuckle arm and zero dial indicator.
3) Measure axial travel of control arm by raising and lowering wheel with pry bar under center of tire. If control arm axial travel is more than .030" (.76 mm), replace ball joint.

UPPER BALL JOINT CHECKING

1) Raise and support vehicle with jack positioned under lower control arm. Tighten wheel bearing to remove wheel bearing play. Lower vehicle until wheel lightly contacts floor.
2) Grasp top of tire and apply force inward and outward. If any lateral movement at the ball joint between upper control arm and knuckle is noted, replace upper ball joint. Raise vehicle and adjust wheel bearings.

REMOVAL & INSTALLATION

STEERING KNUCKLE

Removal – 1) Turn ignition off ("UNLOCKED" position). Raise vehicle. Place safety stands under lower control arms, as close as possible to wheels. Make sure jack pads do not contact brake splash shields. Do not allow rubber rebound bumper to contact frame.

CAUTION: Torsion bar will remain in loaded position.

2) Remove wheel assembly. Remove disc caliper mount bolts. Support and wire caliper out of way. Remove rotor assembly.
3) Remove brake splash shield. Loosen steering arm-to-knuckle bolts. Remove cotter pins from upper and lower ball joint nuts. Using Ball Joint Separator (C-3564-A), separate steering knuckle from upper ball joint. Remove steering knuckle arm-to-knuckle bolts. Separate upper control arm from knuckle. Remove steering knuckle.

Installation – To install, reverse removal procedure. Tighten fittings to specifications. See TIGHTENING SPECIFICATIONS table. Adjust front wheel bearings. Install wheel and lower vehicle. Adjust front suspension height and front end alignment as necessary.

STEERING KNUCKLE ARM

Removal – 1) Turn ignition off ("UNLOCKED" position). Remove rebound bumper. Raise and support vehicle on frame hoist. Place jack stands under front frame for support.
2) Remove wheel assembly. Remove disc caliper mount bolts. Support and wire caliper out of way. Remove rotor assembly. Remove brake splash shield. Unload torsion bars. Remove cotter pin from tie rod nut. Remove nut.
3) Using Tie Rod Separator (C-3894-A), separate tie rod from steering knuckle arm. Separate lower ball joint from steering knuckle using Ball Joint Separator (C-3564-A). Remove 2 bolts and nuts attaching arm to steering knuckle. Remove steering knuckle arm.

Installation – To install, reverse removal procedure. Tighten fittings to specifications. See TIGHTENING SPECIFICATIONS table. Adjust front wheel bearings. Install wheel and lower vehicle. Adjust front suspension height and front end alignment as necessary.

LOWER BALL JOINT

Removal – 1) Turn ignition off ("UNLOCKED" position). Raise and support vehicle on frame hoist. Place jack stands under front frame for support. Remove front tire and wheel. Remove brake caliper and wire out of way. Remove hub and rotor. Remove brake splash shield. Disconnect shock absorber from lower control arm. Loosen torsion bar.
2) Remove cotter pin and nuts from upper and lower ball joints. Using Ball Joint Separator (C-3564-A), separate lower ball joint from steering knuckle. Use Adapter (C-4212) to press lower ball joint out of control arm.

Installation – 1) Using ball joint remover/installer, press new ball joint into lower control arm. Place new seal over ball joint. Using Seal Adapter (C-4039), press seal retainer down on joint housing until locked in position.
2) Insert ball joint stud into knuckle arm opening. Install stud retaining nut and tighten to specifications. Install new cotter pin and lubricate ball joint.

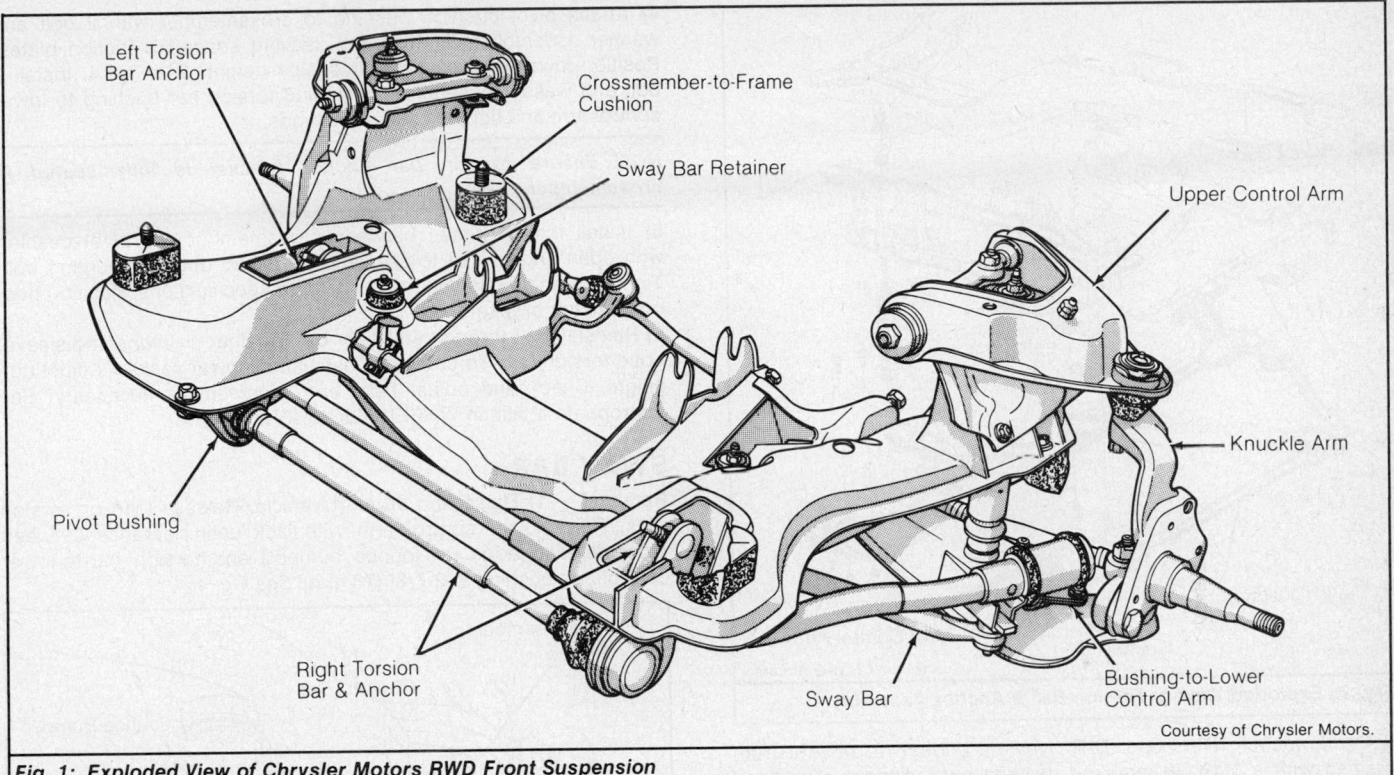

Fig. 1: Exploded View of Chrysler Motors RWD Front Suspension

Labels: Left Torsion Bar Anchor, Crossmember-to-Frame Cushion, Sway Bar Retainer, Upper Control Arm, Knuckle Arm, Pivot Bushing, Right Torsion Bar & Anchor, Sway Bar, Bushing-to-Lower Control Arm

Courtesy of Chrysler Motors.

3) Place load on torsion bar. Reassemble suspension and brake components. Lower vehicle. Adjust torsion bars for proper vehicle height. Check and adjust front end alignment as necessary.

UPPER BALL JOINT

Removal – 1) Raise vehicle. Place jack stand under lower control arm, as close to wheel as possible. Ensure stand does not contact brake splash shield. Rubber rebound bumper must not contact frame.

CAUTION: Torsion bar will remain in loaded position.

2) Remove wheel. Remove cotter pin and nut from upper ball joint. Install Ball Joint Separator (C-3564-A) on lower ball joint stud, allowing tool to rest on knuckle arm.

CAUTION: DO NOT attempt to force stud out of knuckle using separator only.

3) Tighten tool securely to apply pressure to upper stud. Strike knuckle sharply with hammer to loosen stud. Disengage upper ball joint from knuckle.
4) Support knuckle and brake assembly to prevent damage to brake hose or lower ball joint. Using Socket (C-3560), remove upper ball joint.

Installation – 1) Thread ball joint squarely into control arm as far as possible by hand. Ensure ball joint threads engage those of control arm correctly. Seals should always be replaced once they have been removed.
2) Thread ball joint into control arm until it bottoms on housing. Ensure ball joint is tightened to specifications. Using Seal Adapter (C-4039), press new seal over ball joint stud. Ensure seal is seated on ball joint housing.
3) Position upper ball joint stud into steering knuckle. Install nut and tighten to specifications. Install and tighten lower ball joint stud nut into steering knuckle. Install cotter pins. Lubricate ball joint(s). Install brake components and wheel. Check and adjust front end alignment as necessary.

TORSION BAR, BUSHINGS & ANCHOR ASSEMBLY

Removal – 1) Raise front of vehicle. Support vehicle so front suspension is in full rebound position. Release load on both torsion bars. Remove anchor adjusting bolt on torsion bar to be removed. Using a jack, raise lower control arm until clearance between crossmember ledge (at jounce bumper) and torsion bar end bushing is 2 7/8" (73 mm). See Fig. 4.
2) Support lower control arm at this design height (equal to 3 passenger position with vehicle on ground). This is necessary to align stabilizer bar and lower control arm attaching points for disassembly and reassembly.
3) Disconnect sway bar from control arm. Remove 2 bolts attaching torsion bar end bushing to lower control arm. Remove 2 bolts attaching torsion bar pivot bushing to crossmember. See Fig. 2. Remove torsion bar and anchor assembly from the crossmember.

NOTE: Replacement torsion bars include the permanent pivot cushion bushing and replaceable torsion bar-to-lower control arm bushing. Check component condition to determine parts needing replacement.

Inspection – 1) Check torsion bar pivot cushion bushing seals for cuts, tears or severe deterioration that may allow moisture under cushion. If corrosion is evident, replace torsion bar assembly.
2) Inspect torsion bar-to-lower control arm bushings for wear or damage and replace as necessary. Separate torsion bar from anchor. Remove all foreign matter from hex openings in anchors and from hex ends of torsion bar.
3) Inspect torsion bar adjusting bolt and swivel. Replace components if there is any sign of corrosion or other damage. Lubricate bolt and swivel.

Torsion Bar & Arm Bushing Replacement – 1) With torsion bar assembly removed from vehicle, clamp torsion bar-to-lower control arm bushing in soft-jawed vise with rivet head up (hex end of bar down).

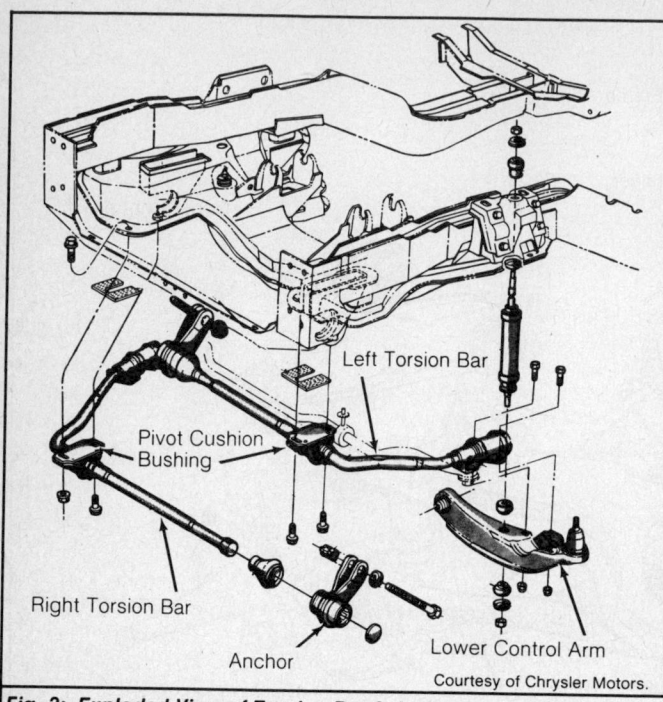

Fig. 2: Exploded View of Torsion Bar & Anchor Assembly

Courtesy of Chrysler Motors.

2) Center punch rivet head. Drill rivet out enough to drive it from bushing with a 5/16" (8 mm) rod. If necessary, remove rivet head flange before driving rivet out. Use care not to enlarge 7/16" (11 mm) diameter hole in torsion bar bushing clamp.

3) Remove bushing from bar and discard. If necessary, clean any roughness under bushing with sandpaper to ease reassembly. Install new bushing by hand. Install new bushing retaining bolt and tighten to specifications.

Installation – 1) Carefully slide torsion bar-to-anchor boot (balloon seal) over end of torsion bar with cupped end toward hex. Coat hex end of torsion bar with lubricant.

2) Install torsion bar hex end into anchor bracket. With torsion bar in a horizontal position, ensure ears of anchor bracket are positioned nearly straight up. See Fig. 3. Position swivel into anchor bracket ears.

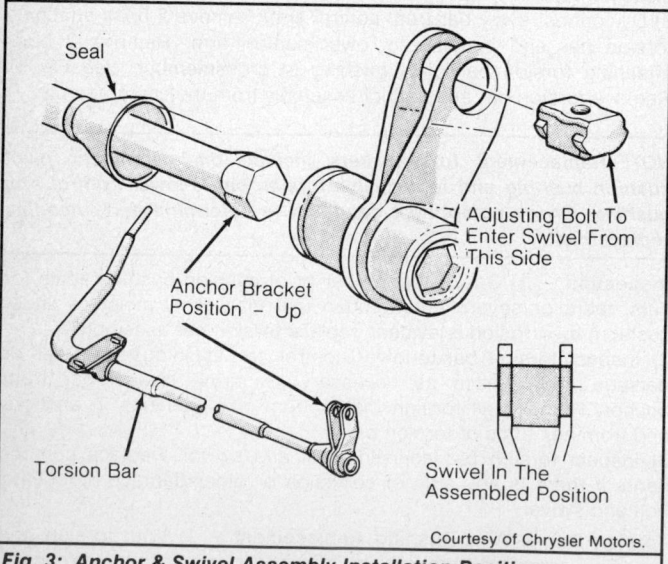

Fig. 3: Anchor & Swivel Assembly Installation Positions

Courtesy of Chrysler Motors.

3) Place bushing end of bar into position on top of lower control arm. Install anchor bracket assembly into crossmember anchor retainer. Install anchor adjusting bearing and bolt.

4) Attach pivot cushion bushing to crossmember with 2 bolt and washer assemblies (finger tight), leaving space for friction plates. Position lower control arms at design height. See Fig. 4. Install 2 bolt and washer assemblies attaching torsion bar bushing to lower control arm and tighten to specifications.

NOTE: Ensure torsion bar anchor bracket is fully seated in crossmember.

5) Install friction plates between crossmember and pivot cushion with open end of slot to rear and bottomed out on mounting bolt. Tighten cushion bushing mount bolts to specifications. Position boot over anchor bracket.

6) Reinstall bolt through stabilizer bar, retainer cushions and sleeve. Load torsion bar. To complete installation, lower vehicle. Adjust ride height. Check and adjust front end alignment as necessary. See appropriate article in WHEEL ALIGNMENT section.

SWAY BAR

Removal – 1) Raise and support vehicle. Release load on torsion bars. Raise lower control arm with jack until clearance between crossmember ledge (at jounce bumper) and torsion bar-to-lower control arm bushing is 2 7/8" (73 mm). See Fig. 4.

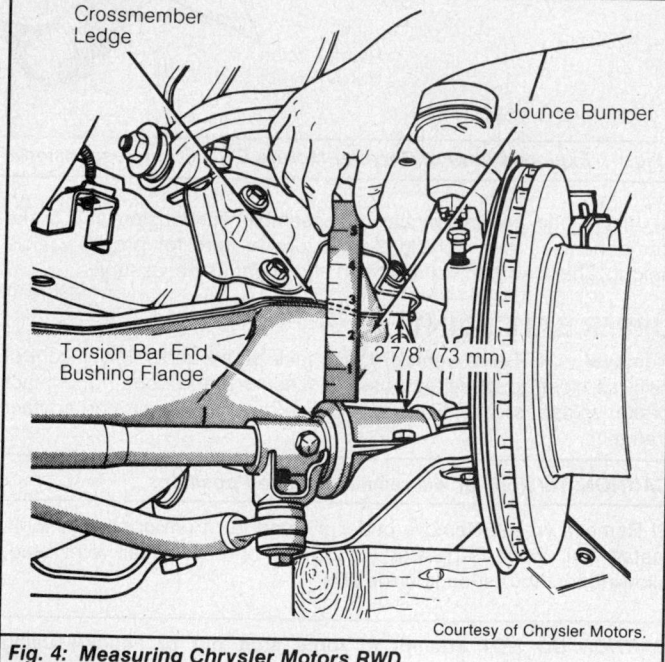

Fig. 4: Measuring Chrysler Motors RWD Front Suspension Design Height

Courtesy of Chrysler Motors.

2) Support control arm in this position during entire removal and installation process. Remove sway bar-to-torsion bar mount bolts, retainer, cushions and sleeves.

3) Remove retainer assembly strap bolts and retainer straps. Remove stabilizer bar. Inspect sway bar rubber bushings and cushions for excessive wear or deterioration and replace parts as necessary.

Installation – 1) Install bolts through sway bar retainer. Install cushions and sleeve. Attach torsion bar-to-lower control arm bushing. Tighten bolt to specifications.

2) Tighten sway bar retainer and strap bolts to specifications. Load torsion bars. Lower vehicle and adjust vehicle height. Check and adjust front end alignment as necessary.

UPPER CONTROL ARM & PIVOT BUSHINGS

Removal – 1) Place ignition switch in "UNLOCKED" and "OFF" position. Raise and support vehicle. Place jack pads under lower control arms near wheel without touching splash shield. Remove wheel and tire assembly. Remove brake caliper if necessary for clearance.

2) Remove cotter pin and nut from upper ball joint. Using Ball Joint Separator (C-3564-A), separate upper ball joint from steering knuckle. Support assembly to prevent damage to brake hose or lower ball joint. From under hood, remove engine splash shield to expose upper control arm pivot shaft.

3) Scribe a line on support bracket, along inboard edge of pivot shaft, for reassembly reference. Remove pivot shaft nut and bolts from upper control arm. Lift control arm away from support bracket and remove from vehicle.

Pivot Bushing Replacement – 1) Place upper control arm in vise. Remove pivot shaft nuts and bushing retainers. Bolt Pivot Bushing Support (C-4253-1) to pivot shaft. Place Pivot Bushing Puller (C-4253-2) over end of pivot shaft and reinstall nut.

2) Snug puller bolts against arm. Turn bolts equally until bushing is free of arm. Remove tool and discard bushing. Repeat procedure for remaining bushing. Remove pivot shaft.

3) Place pivot shaft in control arm and attach Support Bracket Spacer (C-4253-8). Slip new bushings over each end of pivot shaft and pilot into holes in control arm. Install bushing cups over both bushings. Press bushings together until fully seated in control arm.

NOTE: If possible, use press to install pivot bushings together and ensure each bushing flange is bottomed on control arm extrusion.

4) Install retainers and nuts on pivot shaft. Snug nuts against retainers. Pivot shaft bushing retainer nuts are to be tightened to specification AFTER suspension is set to design height.

Installation – Place upper control arm, with ball joint and pivot shaft, on bracket. Install and snug attaching bolts against arm. Set inboard edge of pivot shaft on scribed line of mounting bracket. Tighten bolts to specifications. To complete installation, reverse removal procedure.

LOWER CONTROL ARM & PIVOT BUSHING

Removal – 1) Raise vehicle on hoist and remove wheel. Disconnect lower ball joint as previously described. Remove shock absorber. Release load on both torsion bars.

NOTE: Release tension on both torsion bars even if only one control arm is being removed due to stabilizer bar reaction from opposite torsion bar.

2) Raise lower control arm until clearance between crossmember ledge (at jounce bumper) and torsion bar-to-lower control arm bushing is 2 7/8" (73 mm). *See Fig. 4.* Support control arm at design height. Remove 2 bolts attaching torsion bar end bushing to lower control arm. Remove bushing pivot bolt and control arm.

Pivot Bushing Replacement – 1) Place lower control arm in vise. Install Pivot Bushing Remover/Installer (C-4383) by placing support fixture between flanges of control arm and around bushing.

NOTE: Ensure proper fixture position to prevent control arm distortion during bushing removal.

2) Position cup over flanged bushing end with bolt through cup and bushing. Install pilot, thrust washer, plain washer and nut on through bolt. Press bushing out of lower control arm by holding bolt on cup end and turning nut on pilot end.

3) Discard old pivot bushing. Position flange end of new bushing into cup squarely and press bushing into control arm until bushing flange seats on arm.

Installation – 1) Position lower control arm into crossmember flange. Install pivot bolt and flanged nut finger tight. Reinstall lower ball joint into steering knuckle as previously described.

2) Position control arm supported at design height. *See Fig. 4.* Install 2 bolts attaching torsion bar end bushing to lower control arm and tighten to specifications. Tighten lower control arm pivot bolt to specifications.

3) Install shock absorber stud through lower control arm. Install bushing retainer and nut. Tighten nut to specifications. Install brake rotor assembly and caliper. Reload torsion bar pressure. Install wheel. Lower vehicle and adjust suspension height and front end alignment as necessary.

TIGHTENING SPECIFICATIONS

Application	Ft. Lbs. (N.m)
Ball Joint-to-Lower Control Arm Nut	100 (136)
Ball Joint-to-Upper Control Arm Nut	100 (136)
Disc Brake Caliper Adapter Bolt	110 (150)
Disc Brake Caliper Bolts	15 (20)
Idler Arm Bolt/Nut	70 (95)
Lower Control Arm Pivot Nut	75 (102)
Pitman Arm Nut	175 (238)
Rebound Bumper Bolt	17 (23)
Shock Absorber	
Lower Mount Nut	35 (47)
Upper Mount Nut	25 (34)
Splash Shield Bolts	18 (24)
Sway Bar	
Strap Nut	30 (41)
Cushion Bolt	50 (68)
Steering Knuckle	
Lower Bolt/Nut	160 (217)
Tie Rod End Nut	40 (54)
Torsion Bar Bushing	
Retaining Nut	50 (68)
Torsion Bar	
Pivot Cushion Retainer Nut/Bolt	85 (115)
Torsion Bar-to-Lower Control Arm	
Bushing Nut/Bolt	70 (95)
Upper Control Arm	
Pivot Bushing Nut	110 (150)
Pivot Shaft Bolts	150 (203)

	INCH Lbs. (N.m)
Sway Bar	
Link Retainer Nut	97 (11)

1989 FRONT SUSPENSION
Eagle

Premier

DESCRIPTION

The MacPherson strut front suspension consists of coil springs, control arms with ball joints, wheel hubs and bearings, cast steering knuckles and a stablizer bar.

Tie rods connect to steering arms through strut assembly. The hub and bearing assembly mount to knuckle and hold a replaceable wheel bearing.

ADJUSTMENTS

CASTER & CAMBER

See appropriate article in WHEEL ALIGNMENT section.

RIDING HEIGHT

See RIDING HEIGHT SPECIFICATIONS article in WHEEL ALIGNMENT section.

FRONT WHEEL BEARINGS

NOTE: The hub can be replaced without removing bearing from steering knuckle.

Removal – 1) Raise and support vehicle. Remove wheel, brake caliper and pads. DO NOT disconnect flexible brake line. Using Hub Locking Bar (Rou. 604.01), hold hub and remove drive shaft nut.
2) Install Hub Puller (T. Av. 1050) on hub. Tighten bolt and push drive shaft from hub. Install slide hammer in hub puller and remove hub and rotor. Rotor can be easily separated from hub by removing 2 safety nuts.
3) Using hydraulic press and bearing puller, remove hub bearing race. To remove bearing located on steering knuckle, remove bearing assembly Torx retaining bolts. *See Fig. 1.*

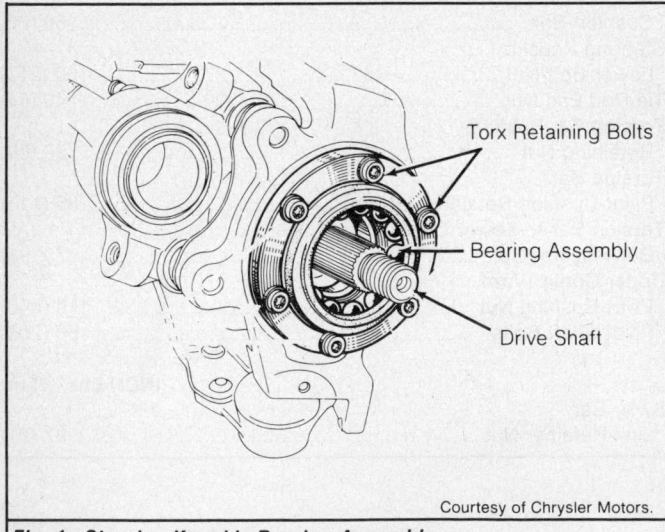

Torx Retaining Bolts
Bearing Assembly
Drive Shaft

Courtesy of Chrysler Motors.

Fig. 1: Steering Knuckle Bearing Assembly

Installation – 1) Discard removable plastic covers from outer edges and bore of new bearing assembly. Remove bearing races from new bearing. Pack bearing with grease supplied with bearing.
2) Press outer bearing race on hub. Install inner race in bearing. Install bearing assembly on steering knuckle. Tighten bolts. See TIGHTENING SPECIFICATIONS table in this article.
3) Lubricate hub bearing race with EP type grease. Install hub on drive shaft and bearing assembly. Using soft-faced hammer, tap hub until 3-4 threads are visible on drive shaft.
4) Install drive shaft nut. Using hub locking bar, hold hub and tighten drive shaft nut to specification. To complete installation, reverse removal procedure.

REMOVAL & INSTALLATION

LOWER BALL JOINT

Removal – 1) Raise and support vehicle. Remove wheel. Place shop towel around drive shaft boot to prevent damage. Loosen stabilizer bar-to-frame retaining bolts. DO NOT remove bolts.
2) Remove stabilizer bar-to-control arm bracket retaining nuts. Remove bracket assembly. Install nuts back on bolts after bracket removal. The stabilizer bar mounting bracket bolts secure lower ball joint to control arm.
3) Move stabilizer bar from control arm. Remove ball joint-to-steering knuckle retaining bolt. Lower stabilizer bar. Loosen lower control arm retaining bolts. DO NOT remove bolts.
4) After lowering control arm, remove plastic washer from ball joint. Remove ball joint retaining bolts. Tap upward on ball joint and remove from control arm.

Installation – 1) To install, reverse removal procedure and note following. Install ball joints and retaining bolts in control arm. DO NOT tighten bolts yet. Install plastic washer on ball joint. Tighten bolts to specification. See TIGHTENING SPECIFICATIONS table in this article.
2) Tighten ball joint and stabilizer bar retaining bolts with vehicle at normal operating height.

STEERING KNUCKLE

NOTE: Hub and bearing are removed as an assembly during steering knuckle service.

Removal – 1) Raise and support vehicle. Remove wheel. Place shop towel around drive shaft boot to prevent damage. Remove brake caliper and pads. DO NOT disconnect flexible brake line.
2) Using Hub Locking Bar (Rou.604.01), hold hub and remove drive shaft nut. Install Hub Puller (T. Av. 1050). Tighten bolt and push drive shaft from hub.
3) Remove rotor-to-hub safety nuts. Remove rotor from hub. Remove bearing assembly-to-steering knuckle Torx retaining bolts through hub access hole.
4) Install rotor and hub puller on hub. Install slide hammer in hub puller. Remove hub and bearing assembly together.
5) Loosen but DO NOT remove stabilizer bar inner bracket retaining bolts at engine cradle. Remove stabilizer bar outer bracket and retaining nuts at control arm. Stabilizer bar outer bracket retaining nuts also hold ball joint to control arm.
6) Remove ball joint-to-steering knuckle bolt. Disconnect ball joint from steering knuckle.
7) Loosen steering knuckle-to-strut retaining bolts. Position nuts at end of bolts. Using soft-faced hammer, tap nut to loosen bolt splines. Remove nuts and retaining bolts. Remove steering knuckle.

CAUTION: Strut-to-steering knuckle bolts are splined. Only nuts should turn. The following procedure must be followed to prevent damage to bolts and splines.

Installation – To install, reverse removal procedure. Ensure ball joint-to-steering knuckle retaining bolt is seated on ball joint stud groove. Align splined strut bolts prior to installation. Tighten all retainers. See TIGHTENING SPECIFICATIONS table in this article.

STRUT DAMPER ASSEMBLY

Removal – 1) Raise and support vehicle. Allow suspension to hang freely. Remove wheel. Remove tie rod-to-strut retaining nut using Joint Extractor (9T.Av. 476). Separate tie rod end from strut.
2) Remove upper strut-to-body retaining bolts. DO NOT remove center nut of strut assembly.

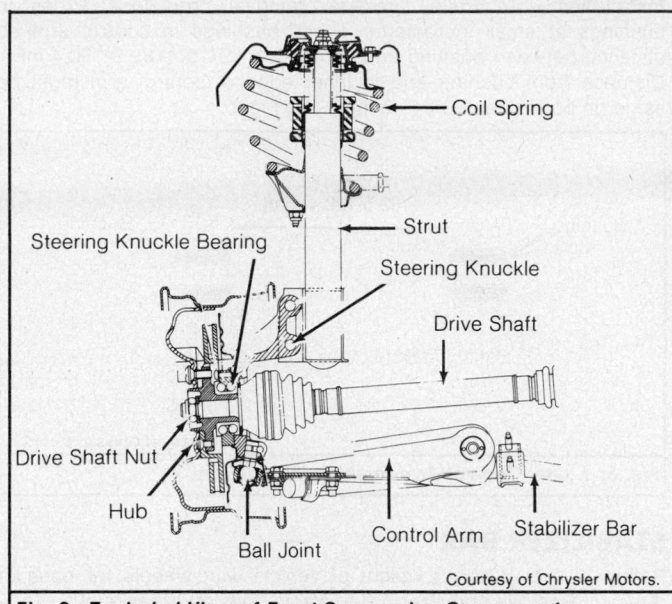

Fig. 2: Exploded View of Front Suspension Components

Courtesy of Chrysler Motors.

CAUTION: DO NOT remove center nut of strut assembly. Coil spring is under excessive pressure. Removal WITHOUT spring compressed may cause personal injury.

---

3) Ensure suspension hangs freely. Loosen steering knuckle-to-strut retaining bolts. Position nuts at end of bolt. Using soft-faced hammer, tap on nut to loosen bolt splines. Remove nuts and retaining bolts.

4) Place shop towel around drive shaft boot to prevent damage. Move control arm downward and remove strut assembly.

Disassembly – **1)** Install lower plate from Spring Compressor (Sus. 1052.99) in a vise. The proper lower adapter plate is stamped with "R-21" on flat side.

2) Install proper lower adapter plate with shoulder downward into lower plate. *See Fig. 3.* Install small adapter plates around lower area of strut assembly. Install strut assembly in lower plate. Ensure strut is properly seated.

3) Upper adapter plate will require modification to fit properly. Drill out proper holes to 7/16" (11.1 mm). *See Fig. 4.* Install upper adapter plate on strut. Align proper holes.

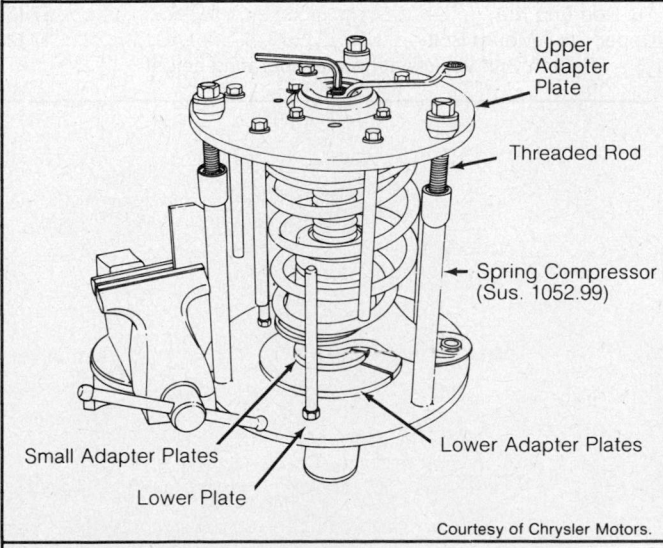

Fig. 3: Compressing Strut Assembly Coil

Courtesy of Chrysler Motors.

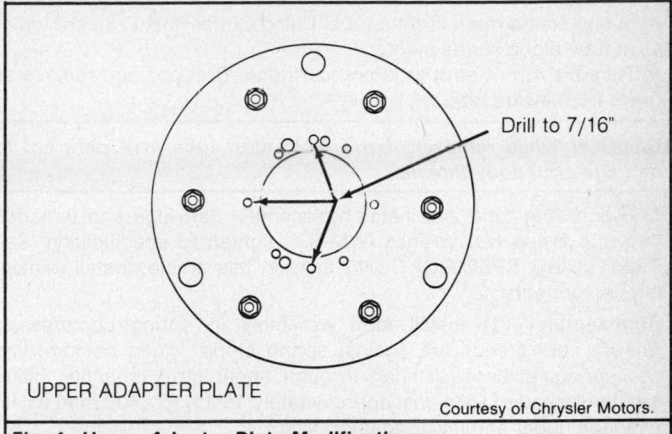

UPPER ADAPTER PLATE

Courtesy of Chrysler Motors.

Fig. 4: Upper Adapter Plate Modification

4) Install strut-to-upper plate retaining bolts. Install threaded rods into lower holes. Lubricate all threaded rods with oil. Slowly tighten threaded rods evenly to compress coil spring approximately 13/32" (10.3 mm).

5) Hold strut shaft and remove center nut from strut shaft. Evenly loosen threaded rods to release spring tension. Remove adapter plate and strut components. *See Fig. 5.*

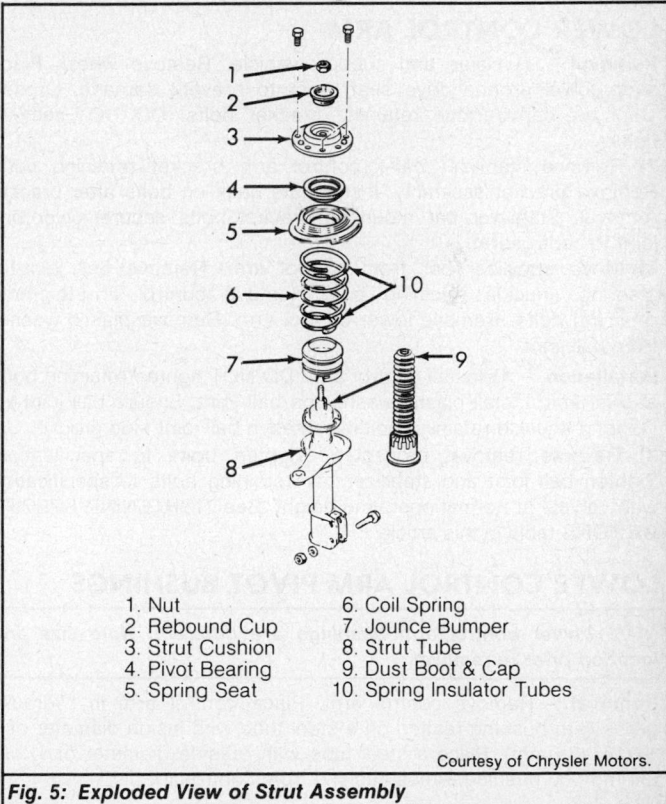

1. Nut	6. Coil Spring
2. Rebound Cup	7. Jounce Bumper
3. Strut Cushion	8. Strut Tube
4. Pivot Bearing	9. Dust Boot & Cap
5. Spring Seat	10. Spring Insulator Tubes

Courtesy of Chrysler Motors.

Fig. 5: Exploded View of Strut Assembly

NOTE: The strut internal piston rod assembly and fluid can be replaced using a service cartridge.

Strut Cartridge Replacement – **1)** Place strut assembly in Strut Clamping Vise (YA-457). DO NOT place in regular vise or damage will result to strut tube. Twist jounce bumper to align tab with opening.

2) Remove jounce bumper and dust boot. Using chisel, remove cap from top of strut. Remove plastic cover. Use care not to damage threads under plastic cover.

3) Measure downward from top of strut tube 7/16-31/64" (11-12 mm) and scribe mark around tube. Using Cutter (MS 776), cut top of strut tube along scribe mark.

4) Remove top of strut tube and cartridge. Drain oil and remove all burrs from inside tube.

> **CAUTION: While removing burrs from strut tube, use care not to damage strut body threads.**

5) Clean strut tube and install replacement cartridge and threaded cap nut. Using Nut Wrench (WM-S3), tighten to specification. See TIGHTENING SPECIFICATIONS table in this article. Install remaining components.

Reassembly – 1) Install strut assembly in spring compressor. Ensure spring ends are against spring stops. When compressing coil spring, guide strut shaft through upper strut mounting plate. Tighten threaded rods until approximately 15 11/16" (400 mm) exists between upper and lower adapter plates.

2) Tighten threaded rods until nut can be installed on strut shaft. Install rebound cup and new retaining nut. Tighten nut to specification. Remove spring compressor.

Installation – Install strut. Install upper retaining bolts. DO NOT tighten until strut is installed in steering knuckle. To complete installation, reverse removal procedure. Tighten bolts to specificaton. Check toe-in setting found in appropriate article in WHEEL ALIGNMENT article.

LOWER CONTROL ARM

Removal – 1) Raise and support vehicle. Remove wheel. Place shop towel around drive shaft boot to prevent damage. Loosen stabilizer bar-to-frame retaining bracket bolts. DO NOT remove bolts.

2) Remove stabilizer bar-to-control arm bracket retaining nuts. Remove bracket assembly. Install nuts back on bolts after bracket removal. Stabilizer bar mounting bracket bolts secure lower ball joint to control arm.

3) Move stabilizer bar from control arm. Remove ball joint-to-steering knuckle retaining bolt. Remove control arm-to-cradle retaining bolts. Remove lower control arm. Remove plastic washer from ball joint.

Installation – 1) Install control arm. DO NOT tighten retaining bolts at this time. Install plastic washer on ball joint. Ensure ball joint-to-steering knuckle retaining bolt is seated in ball joint stud groove.

2) Reverse removal procedure. Tighten bolts to specification. Tighten ball joint and stabilizer bar retaining bolts to specification with vehicle at normal operating height. See TIGHTENING SPECIFICATIONS table in this article.

LOWER CONTROL ARM PIVOT BUSHINGS

> **NOTE: Lower control arm bushings are different. Note size and location prior to removal.**

Removal – Remove control arm. Place control arm in hydraulic press with bushing resting on a steel tube with inside diameter of 1 11/16" (36 mm). Place a steel tube with outside diameter of 1 3/8" (34 mm) on bushing. Press bushing from control arm.

Installation – To install, reverse removal procedure. Press in bushings at small increments. Press bushings in control arm so distance between bushing ends are 7 1/4-7 9/16" (189.5-190.4 mm). Distance from bushing end to inner edge of control arm must be same on both sides 13/64" (5 mm). See Fig. 6.

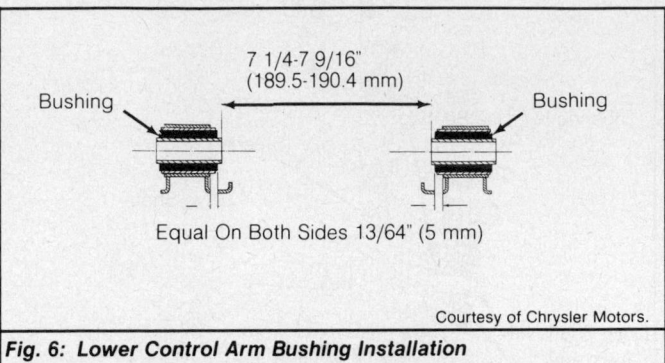

Courtesy of Chrysler Motors.

Fig. 6: Lower Control Arm Bushing Installation

STABILIZER BAR

Removal – 1) Support weight of vehicle with wheels for ease of removal. Remove stabilizer bar-to-frame bolts and brackets.

2) Remove bar-to-control arm bracket retaining nuts and bracket assembly.

3) Reinstall nuts on bolts after outer bracket removal. The stabilizer bar outer bracket bolts secure lower ball joint to control arm.

4) Remove stabilizer bar. Inspect stabilizer bushings and replace as necessary.

Installation – To install, reverse removal procedure. Tighten ball joint and stabilizer bar retaining bolts to specification with vehicle at normal operating height.

TIGHTENING SPECIFICATIONS

Application	Ft. Lbs. (N.m)
Ball Joint-To-Knuckle Bolt	77 (104)
Bearing-To-Steering Knuckle Bolt	11 (15)
Control Arm Mount Bolt	[1] 103 (140)
Drive Axle Nut	181 (245)
Stabilizer Bar & Ball Joint Bolt	[1] 60 (81)
Stabilizer Bar-To-Frame Bolt	21 (28)
Strut Cap Nut	73 (99)
Strut Shaft Nut	52 (71)
Strut-To-Knuckle Nut	123 (167)
Tie Rod End Nut	27 (37)
Upper Strut Mount Bolt	17 (23)

[1] – Tighten with vehicle at normal operating height.

DESCRIPTION

The Escort, Tempo and Topaz front suspension is MacPherson strut type, using gas pressurized struts and cast steering knuckles. The strut assembly includes a rubber isolated top mount with a bearing pivot. The strut assembly is bolted to strut tower and steering knuckle.

A pinch joint is designed into steering knuckle to retain the ball joint stud. A forged control arm is attached to underbody and steering knuckle. A stabilizer bar is connected to both control arms and is secured to crossmember at bracket assemblies. Tie rod ends connect to steering knuckle.

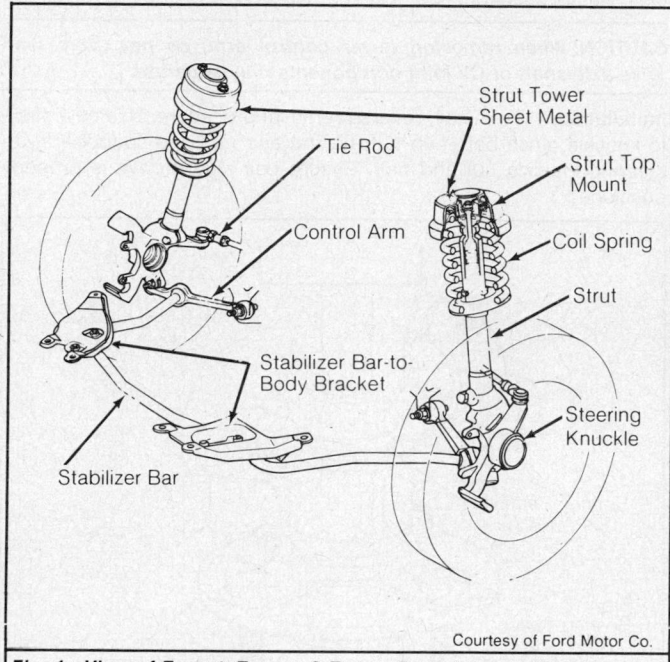

Courtesy of Ford Motor Co.

Fig. 1: View of Escort, Tempo & Topaz Front Suspension

ADJUSTMENTS

CASTER & CAMBER

See appropriate article in WHEEL ALIGNMENT section.

RIDING HEIGHT

See RIDING HEIGHT SPECIFICATIONS article in WHEEL ALIGNMENT section.

FRONT WHEEL BEARINGS

Two opposed and tapered roller bearings and a grease retainer ride in the hub. The bearings are pressed into steering knuckle from inboard side. A snap ring is installed for extra retention. They require no periodic maintenance or adjustment. If bearing is disassembled for any reason, it must be replaced as a unit.

BALL JOINT CHECKING

Raise vehicle so wheels hang freely. Grasp tire by top and bottom edges and move wheel assembly in and out. Any movement between lower end of knuckle and control arm indicates ball joint wear and requires replacement of lower control arm assembly. Check for loose nuts or bolts.

CAUTION: When hoisting FWD vehicles, ensure hoist adapters are positioned properly. See appropriate JACKING & HOISTING article in WHEEL ALIGNMENT section.

REMOVAL & INSTALLATION

CONTROL ARM

Removal – **1)** Raise vehicle. Remove nut and large dished washer from stabilizer bar end. Remove control arm inner pivot nut and bolt.
2) Remove ball joint pinch bolt. A drift punch may be needed to remove pinch bolt. Spread steering knuckle pinch joint with a screwdriver and separate ball joint from knuckle. Remove stabilizer bar spacer from control arm bushing.
3) Remove control arm inner pivot nut and bolt. Pull control arm from underbody and away from stabilizer bar.
Installation – **1)** Connect control arm/ball joint assembly to steering knuckle. Ensure ball joint stud groove is properly positioned. Insert new pinch bolt. Tighten to specification. See TIGHTENING SPECIFICATIONS table at end of article.
2) Insert stabilizer bar spacer into control arm bushing. Clean stabilizer bar threads. Position control arm onto stabilizer bar and inner underbody mounting. Install new nut and bolt. Tighten to specification.

CONTROL ARM PIVOT BUSHING

NOTE: The control arm pivot bushing can be replaced on the vehicle without removing arm from steering knuckle.

Removal & Installation – **1)** Raise vehicle. Remove stabilizer bar-to-control arm nut and large dished washer. Remove control arm pivot bolt and nut. Pull control arm from underbody and away from stabilizer bar.
2) Cut away retaining lip of bushing. Use Control Arm Pivot Bushing Remover and Replacer (T81P-5493-B) and "C" Clamp (T74P-3044-A1) to replace bushing. To install, reverse removal procedure. Tighten to specification.

STABILIZER BAR & "U" BRACKET BUSHINGS

NOTE: When installing bushings on stabilizer bar and in control arms, use only vegetable oil for lubrication. Any mineral or petroleum based oil or brake fluid will deteriorate rubber bushings.

Removal – **1)** Raise vehicle. Remove stabilizer bar-to-control arm nuts and large dished washers from each control arm.
2) Remove stabilizer bar "U" bracket and bolts. Remove stabilizer bar assembly.
Installation – **1)** Slide and position new bushings on stabilizer bar. Clean threads on bar. Install spacers into control arm from front so

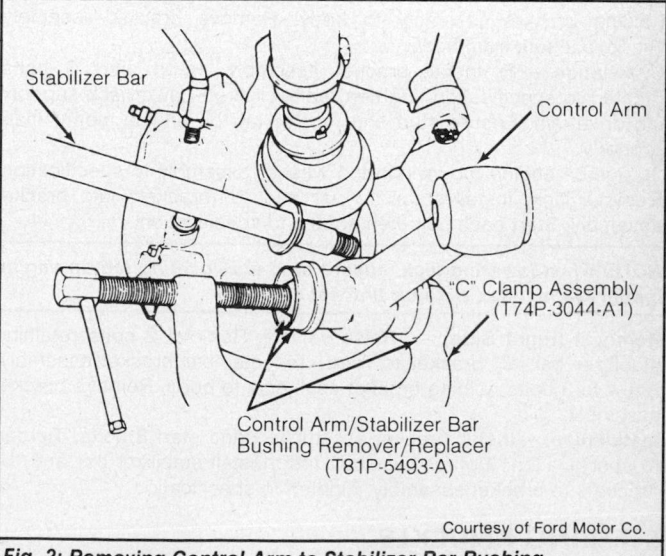

Courtesy of Ford Motor Co.

Fig. 2: Removing Control Arm-to-Stabilizer Bar Bushing

12-16

1989 FRONT SUSPENSION
Ford Motor Co. Escort, Tempo & Topaz (Cont.)

washer end of spacer seats against stabilizer bar machined shoulder. Push mounting brackets over bushings.

2) Insert stabilizer bar end into lower control arm. Using new bolts, attach bar and bushing "U" brackets. Install new nuts and original dished washers with dish pointing away from bushings. Tighten to specification.

STABILIZER BAR-TO-CONTROL ARM BUSHINGS

Removal – 1) Raise vehicle. Remove stabilizer bar-to-control arm nut and dished washer. Remove control arm inner pivot bolt. Pull control arm from underbody and away from stabilizer bar. Remove bushing spacer.

2) Use Control Arm Pivot Bushing Remover and Replacer (T81P-5493-A) and "C" Clamp (T74P-3044-A1) to replace bushing. *See Fig. 2.* Saturate new bushing in vegetable oil before installing. To install, reverse procedure. Tighten to specification.

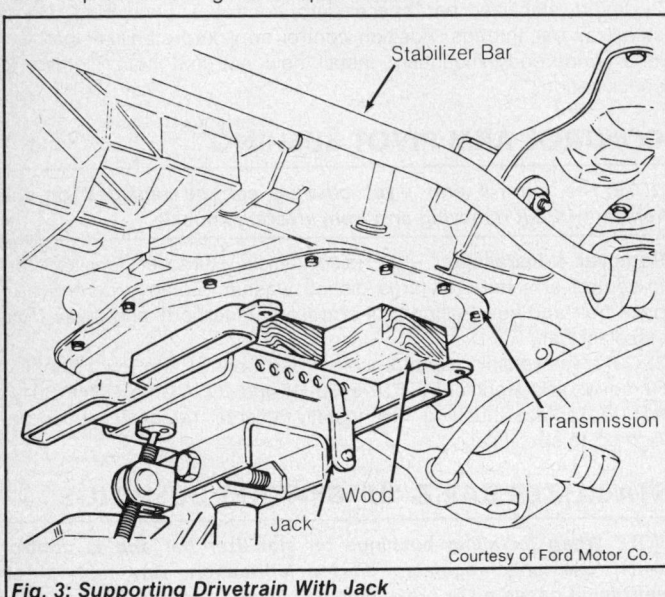

Fig. 3: Supporting Drivetrain With Jack

STABILIZER BAR-TO-CROSSMEMBER BRACKETS

Removal (Left Side) – 1) Raise vehicle. Remove 2 bolts retaining stabilizer bar "U" bracket to front crossmember bracket assembly. With a wood block as a cushion, place a jack under transmission pan to support weight of drivetrain. *See Fig. 3.*

2) Remove engine mount-to-bracket assembly. Remove 3 bolts holding bracket assembly to body. Remove bracket assembly. Remove 3 nuts from body.

Installation – 1) Install bracket assembly. Hand start 3 bolts. Tighten to specification. Tighten rear bolt first. Lower jack supporting drivetrain. Ensure stud and locator tab on engine mount mate properly.

2) Tighten engine mount nut and washer assembly to specification. Remove jack. Install stabilizer bar and "U" brackets into bracket assembly. Start each bolt then tighten to specification.

NOTE: When lowering jack, ensure stud and locating tab on engine mount are in index slots on bracket assembly.

Removal (Right Side) – Raise vehicle. Remove 2 bolts retaining stabilizer bar "U" bracket to front crossmember bracket assembly. Remove 3 bolts holding bracket assembly to body. Remove bracket assembly.

Installation – Install bracket assembly. Hand start 3 bolts. Tighten to specification. Tighten rear bolt first. Install stabilizer bar and "U" brackets to bracket assembly. Tighten to specification.

STEERING KNUCKLE

Removal – 1) Raise vehicle. Remove wheel. Remove cotter pin and slotted nut from tie rod end stud. Using Tie Rod Remover (3290-C)

and Adapter (T81P-3504-W), separate tie rod end from steering knuckle.

2) Remove brake caliper. Loosen (do not remove) top strut mount-to-strut tower nuts.

3) Remove drive axle shaft from hub. See HUB & WHEEL BEARINGS in REMOVAL & INSTALLATION in this article. Remove lower control arm-to-steering knuckle pinch bolt and nut, using a drift punch if necessary. DO NOT use a hammer to separate ball joint from steering knuckle.

4) Using screwdriver, slightly spread knuckle-to-lower arm pinch joint and remove lower arm from knuckle. Remove strut-to-steering knuckle pinch bolt. Using screwdriver, pry knuckle-to-strut pinch joint. Remove steering knuckle and hub assembly.

CAUTION: When removing lower control arm, do not overextend drive axle shaft or CV joint components may separate.

Installation – To install, reverse removal procedure. Use new strut-to-knuckle pinch bolt, hub nut, tie rod end nut, and control arm-to-steering knuckle nut and bolt. Ensure ball stud groove is properly positioned.

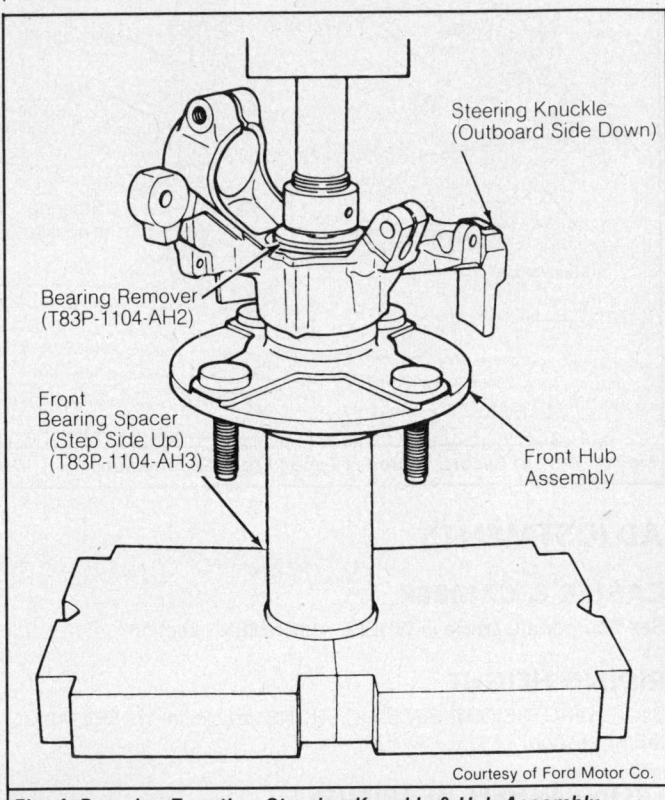

Fig. 4: Pressing Together Steering Knuckle & Hub Assembly

HUB & WHEEL BEARINGS

Removal – 1) Loosen wheel nuts. Remove hub retainer nut and washer. Raise vehicle. Remove front wheel.

2) Loosen brake caliper locating pins and rotate caliper off rotor. Do not remove caliper pins from caliper assembly. Remove caliper from rotor and support.

3) Remove rotor from hub. If excessive force was needed for removal, check rotor for excessive lateral runout before installation and replace as necessary.

4) Disconnect lower control arm and tie rod from steering knuckle. Leave strut attached. Loosen top strut mount-to-apron nuts. Install Hub Remover/Installer (T81P-1104-A & C) and Adapters (T83P-1104 BH) and remove hub.

5) Remove hub, bearing and knuckle assembly by pushing CV joint outer shaft until free. Support drive axle aside with wire. Remove strut bolt and slide hub and knuckle assembly off strut.

1989 FRONT SUSPENSION
Ford Motor Co. Escort, Tempo & Topaz (Cont.)

12-17

6) Remove support wire and place front hub and knuckle assembly on bench. Use Front Hub Puller (D80L-1002-L) and Shaft Protector (D80L-625-1) to remove hub.

Disassembly – Remove bearing snap ring from knuckle. Use press with Front Bearing Spacer (T83P-1104-AH3) step side up on press plate and steering knuckle outboard facing up. Install Front Bearing Remover (T83P-1104-AH2) on bearing inner race and press out bearing.

Reassembly – **1)** Clean knuckle bearing bore and hub bearing journal. If hub bearing journal is scored or damaged, replace hub. Do not attempt to service hub. If bearing is disassembled for any reason, it must be replaced.

2) Place Front Bearing Spacer (T83P-1104-AH3), step side down, on press plate and position knuckle with outboard side down on spacer. Position new bearing inside inboard side of knuckle. Install Front Bearing Installer (T83P-1104-AH1) with undercut side facing bearing on bearing outer race face. Press bearing into knuckle. Ensure bearing seats completely against knuckle bore shoulder. Install snap ring.

3) Place Front Bearing Spacer (T83P-1104-AH3) on arbor press plate and position hub on tool with lugs facing downward. Position knuckle assembly with outboard side down on hub barrel. Place Front Wheel Bearing Remover (T83P-1104-AH2) on inner race of bearing and press until bearing is seated onto hub. Ensure hub rotates freely in knuckle after installation.

NOTE: While tightening hub retainer nut, an audible click will be heard to indicate proper ratchet function. If hub nut is damaged or more than one locking tab is broken, replace hub retainer nut.

Installation – **1)** Connect hub/steering knuckle assembly on vehicle with wire and attach strut loosely to knuckle. Lubricate axle shaft and insert into hub. Ensure splines engage.

2) Install Front Hub Remover/Installer (T81P-1104-C), Adapter (T81P-1104-A) and Wheel Bolt Adapter (T83P-1104-BH) to hub and stub shaft. Tighten to specification. Ensure hub is fully seated. Install washer and hub retaining nut finger tight.

3) Complete installation of front suspension components. Install brake rotor and brake caliper. Install wheel and tighten wheel nuts finger tight. Lower vehicle and block wheels. Manually thread hub nut retainer assembly on axle shaft. Tighten to specification using 1 3/16" (30 mm) socket.

COIL SPRING & STRUT ASSEMBLY

Removal – **1)** Raise vehicle. Loosen, but DO NOT remove, 2 top mount-to-strut tower nuts. Remove wheel. Remove brake flex line-to-strut bolt. Remove strut-to-knuckle pinch bolt. Spread knuckle-to-strut pinch joint. Separate strut from steering knuckle with pry bar.

2) Remove 2 top mount-to-strut tower nuts. Remove strut assembly.

Reassembly – **1)** Install spring compressor in bench mount. Use Spring Compressor (086-00029). Place Deep Socket with External Hex Drive (D81P-18045-A1) or 18 mm socket on strut shaft nut. Insert an 8 mm hex deep socket with 1/4" drive wrench.

2) Remove top shaft mounting nut while holding 1/4" drive socket with suitable extension. Loosen spring compressor and remove top mount bracket assembly, bearing, insulator and spring. To assemble, reverse disassembly procedure.

Installation – To install, reverse removal procedure.

TIGHTENING SPECIFICATIONS

Application	Ft. Lbs. (N.m)
Ball Joint Pinch Bolt	38-45 (52-61)
Control Arm Pivot Bolt	48-55 (65-75)
Control Arm-to-Steering Knuckle Bolts	38-45 (52-61)
Left-Hand Engine Mount-to-Bracket Bolts	55-65 (75-88)
Stabilizer Bar-to-Bracket Bolts	
Escort	85-100 (115-135)
Tempo & Topaz	59-68 (80-92)
Stabilizer Bar Bracket-to-Body Bolts	48-55 (65-75)
Stabilizer Bar-to-Control Arm Nut	98-115 (132-156)
Stabilizer "U" Bracket Clamps-to-Bracket	
Escort	85-100 (115-135)
Tempo & Topaz	59-68 (80-92)
Strut Shaft-to-Top Mount Nut	35-50 (48-68)
Strut Top Mount-to-Strut Tower Nuts	25-30 (37-41)
Strut-to-Steering Knuckle Bolts	55-81 (75-110)
Tie Rod-to-Steering Knuckle Nuts	28-32 (38-43)
Wheel Lug Nuts	85-105 (115-142)

1989 FRONT SUSPENSION
Ford Motor Co. Probe

DESCRIPTION

The MacPherson strut front suspension consists of single wishbone control arms with ball joints, cast steering knuckles and a stabilizer bar.

The lower ball joints are pressed into wide stance control arms, which are supported by rubber bushings at chassis subframe. The front hub and wheel bearings mount inside the steering knuckle.

A Programmed Ride Control (PRC) system is optional. The PRC actuator bolts to the strut mounting block, which houses a rubber mounted strut bearing. The upper end of the coil spring rides in a heavy rubber seat. If the vehicle is not equipped with PRC, the struts are conventional and cannot be interchanged with PRC struts. For more information on PRC, see ELECTRONIC SUSPENSIONS in this section.

ADJUSTMENTS

CASTER & CAMBER

See appropriate article in WHEEL ALIGNMENT section.

RIDING HEIGHT

See RIDING HEIGHT ADJUSTMENTS in WHEEL ALIGNMENT section.

FRONT WHEEL BEARINGS

The front wheel bearings are a one-piece roller bearings pressed into the steering knuckle. The hub assembly is pressed into the wheel bearing during assembly. There are no adjustments or servicing required.

BALL JOINT CHECKING

Raise vehicle so wheels hang freely. Grasp tire by top and bottom edges and move wheel assembly in and out. Any movement between lower end of knuckle and control arm indicates ball joint wear and requires replacement of lower control arm assembly. Check for loose nuts or bolts before replacing control arm.

The ball joint is NOT serviceable and must be replaced with lower control arm assembly. Only the ball joint dust boot is replaceable.

CAUTION: When hoisting FWD vehicles, ensure hoist adapters are positioned properly. See appropriate JACKING & HOISTING article in WHEEL ALIGNMENT section.

REMOVAL & INSTALLATION

LOWER CONTROL ARM & BALL JOINT

Removal & Installation – The ball joint cannot be replaced separately. It can only be replaced with the lower control arm as an assembly.

1) Raise vehicle and remove wheel. Remove brake caliper and support aside. Remove stabilizer bar link assembly mounting bolts from lower control arm. Remove mounting bolt from stabilizer bar bushing. Remove ball joint clamp bolt from steering knuckle.

2) Remove harmonic damper from chassis subframe. Harmonic damper is on driver's side of automatic transmission equipped vehicles only. Remove 2 control arm mounting bolts. Remove lower control arm. To install, reverse removal procedure. See TIGHTENING SPECIFICATIONS in this article.

LOWER CONTROL ARM BUSHINGS

Removal & Installation – 1) Remove lower control arm. See REMOVAL under LOWER CONTROL ARM & BALL JOINT. Place control arm in a vise. Cut away projecting rubber on bushing.

2) Press out bushing using "C" Clamp (T74P-3044-A1), Clamp Tip (T74P-6306-A) and Receiving Cup (T86P-5493-A3). *See Fig. 1.* Use "C" clamp and clamp tip to install bushing. To install, reverse removal procedure.

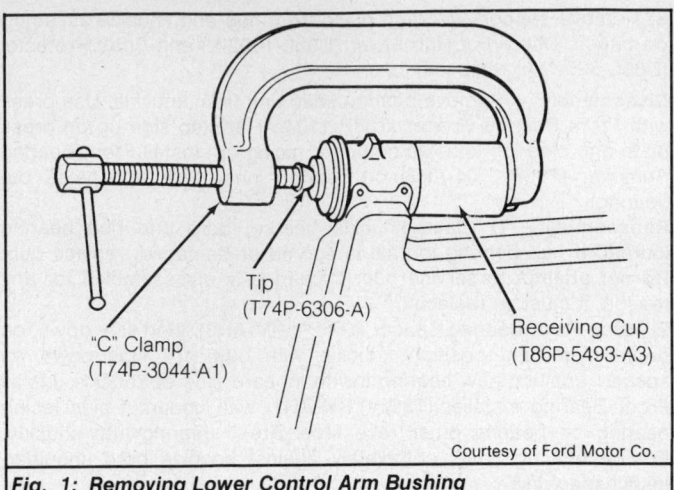

"C" Clamp (T74P-3044-A1)
Tip (T74P-6306-A)
Receiving Cup (T86P-5493-A3)
Courtesy of Ford Motor Co.

Fig. 1: Removing Lower Control Arm Bushing

STABILIZER BAR & LINK ASSEMBLY

Removal – Raise vehicle and remove wheel. Remove stabilizer link mounting bolts from lower control arm. Remove bolts from stabilizer bar bushing brackets. Remove stabilizer bar. *See Fig. 2.*

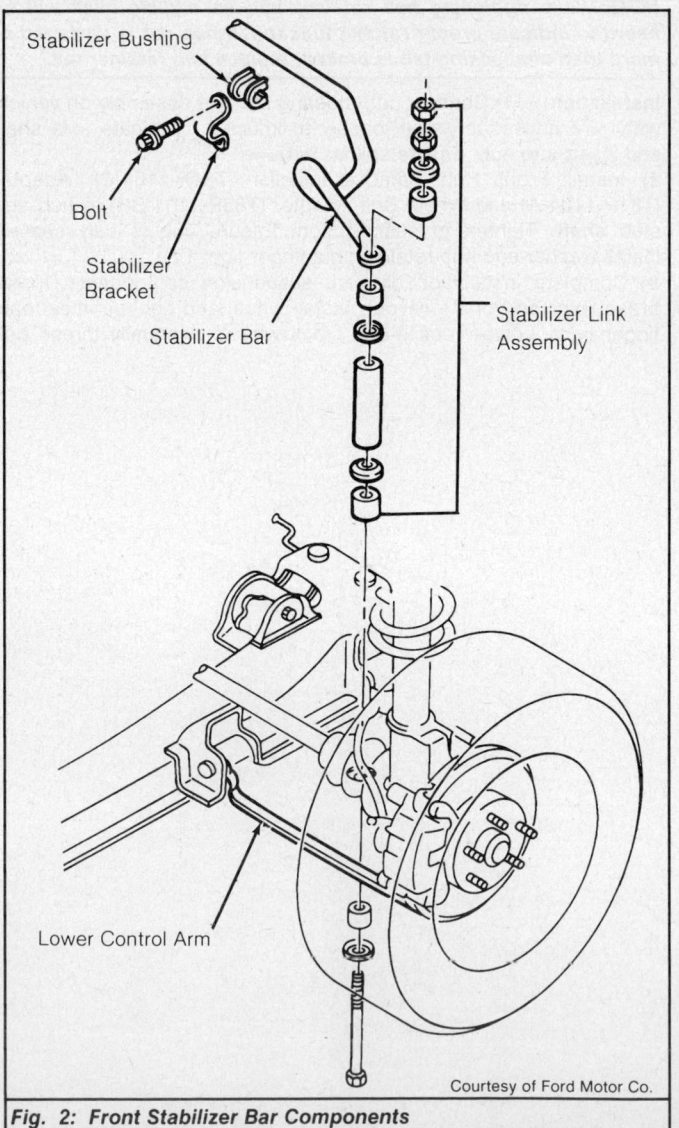

Stabilizer Bushing
Bolt
Stabilizer Bracket
Stabilizer Bar
Stabilizer Link Assembly
Lower Control Arm
Courtesy of Ford Motor Co.

Fig. 2: Front Stabilizer Bar Components

Installation – Install stabilizer link assembly mounting bolts with threads facing upward through lower control arm. Hand tighten only. Install stabilizer bar bushings and torque to specifications. Tighten link assembly nut until .79 " (20 mm) of thread remains above nut. *See Fig. 3.* Install wheel and lower vehicle.

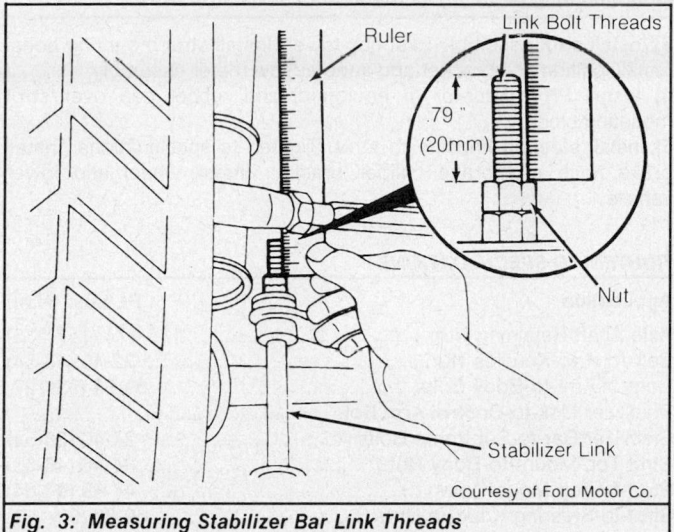

Fig. 3: Measuring Stabilizer Bar Link Threads

STEERING KNUCKLE

Removal – **1)** Raise vehicle and remove wheel. Carefully raise staked portion of axle shaft nut with a hammer and chisel.

2) Remove axle shaft nut and discard. Remove stabilizer bar to control arm attaching bolt, nut washers and bushings. Remove cotter pin and tie rod end attaching nut.

3) Separate tie rod end and steering knuckle using Separator (T85M-3395-A). If tie rod and knuckle do not separate easily, sharply strike steering knuckle with a soft-faced hammer to shock the taper.

4) Remove brake caliper and caliper anchor bracket. Remove rotor by loosening hold-down bolt.

5) Remove ball joint clamp bolt and nut at lower control arm. Pry open control arm to separate ball joint from steering knuckle.

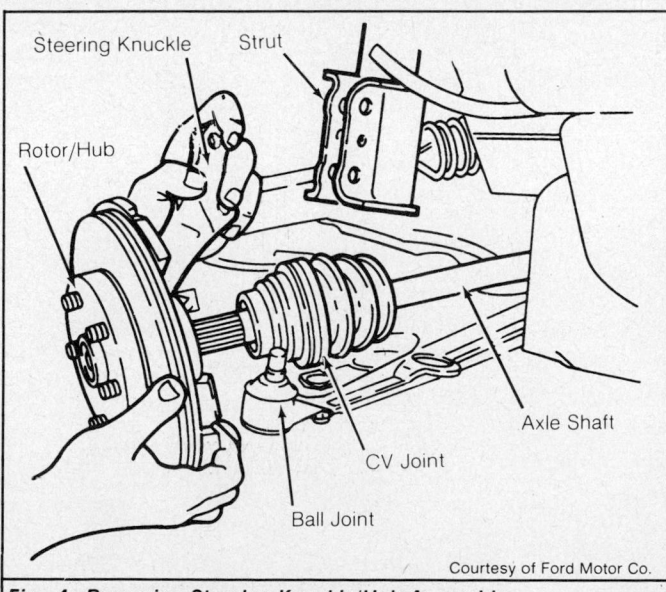

Fig. 4: Removing Steering Knuckle/Hub Assembly

6) Remove steering knuckle-to-strut attaching bolts. Remove steering knuckle, being careful not to damage grease seals. *See Fig. 4.* If wheel hub binds on axle shaft, it can be loosened by lightly tapping threaded end with a plastic faced hammer.

Installation – **1)** Position front hub/steering knuckle assembly over axle shaft and into strut bracket. Install steering knuckle attaching bolts and nuts. Tighten to specifications.

2) Position ball joint through steering knuckle and install clamp bolt and nut. Install brake rotor, caliper anchor bracket and caliper.

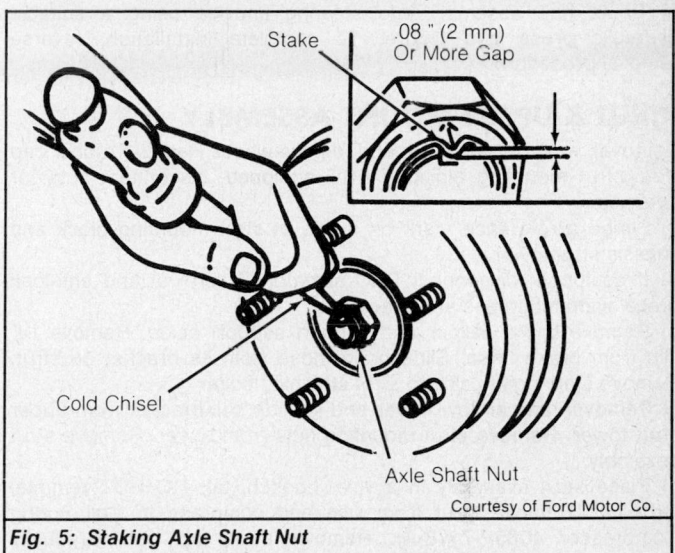

Fig. 5: Staking Axle Shaft Nut

3) Install NEW axle shaft nut and tighten to specifications. Stake axle shaft nut using a rounded-edge cold chisel. *See Fig. 5.*

4) Connect tie rod to steering knuckle. Install stabilizer bar and stabilizer link assembly. Tight to specifications. Install wheel and lower vehicle.

WHEEL HUB & BEARINGS

Removal & Installation – **1)** Remove steering knuckle/wheel hub assembly. See REMOVAL under STEERING KNUCKLE in this article. Remove and discard grease seal.

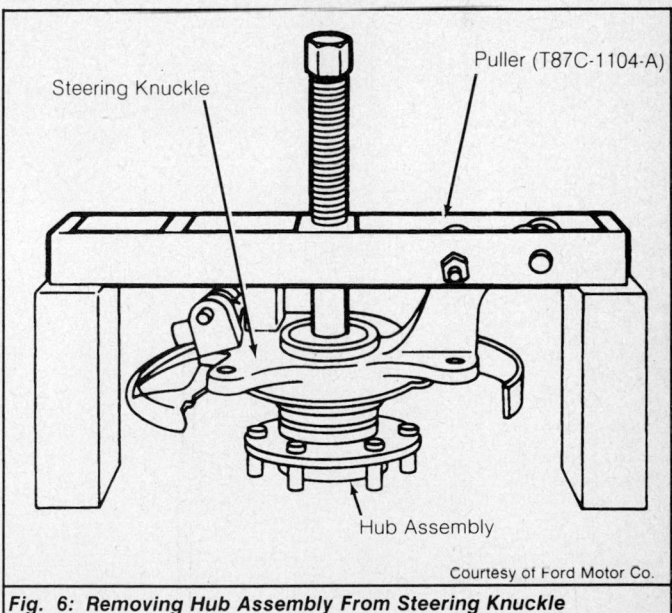

Fig. 6: Removing Hub Assembly From Steering Knuckle

2) Remove hub assembly from steering knuckle using Puller (T87C-1104-A). *See Fig. 6.* If inner bearing race stays on hub, grind a section of race to .197 inch (.5 mm) of the hub. Use a chisel at indent to remove race.

3) Remove snap ring from steering knuckle. Remove wheel bearing using Puller (T87C-1104-A). Leave dust shield on steering knuckle unless damaged.

Installation – 1) Inspect hub and knuckle for cracks, wear or scoring. Install dust shield on knuckle.

2) Position wheel bearing in steering knuckle. Press wheel bearing into knuckle. Install snap ring in knuckle. Install grease seal using Installing Tool (T87C-1175-A).

3) Press hub assembly into steering knuckle using a suitable hydraulic press and fixture. To complete installation, reverse removal procedure.

STRUT & UPPER MOUNT ASSEMBLY

Removal – 1) Raise vehicle and remove wheel. Remove rubber cap from strut mounting block. If PRC equipped, disconnect actuator connector.

2) Scribe a reference mark on inside of strut mounting block and chassis strut tower.

3) If equipped, disconnect PRC actuator (2 screws) and anti-lock brake system harness and bracket.

4) Remove brake caliper and support support aside. Remove "U" clip from brake hose. Slide brake hose from its bracket on strut. Remove steering knuckle to strut attaching bolts.

5) Remove vane airflow meter and ignition coil bracket from upper strut tower. Remove strut mounting nuts from tower. Remove strut assembly.

6) Place strut assembly in a vise. Loosen, but DO NOT remove, strut nut. Remove strut from vise and compress in Coil Spring Compressor (D85P-7178-A). Remove strut top nut. Gradually release compressor. Be careful not to damage threads on strut as it expands.

7) Remove actuator bracket (if equipped), strut mounting block, upper rubber seat, dust boot, bump stopper, and coil spring from strut. Inspect and replace parts as necessary.

Installation – 1) Install coil spring, bump stopper, dust boot and upper rubber seat on new strut. Install strut mounting block. Install PRC bracket (if equipped) ensuring notch on mounting block is 180 degrees from knuckle mounting bracket on strut.

2) Compress coil spring using Compressor (D85P-7178-A). Install strut nut and torque to specifications. Gradually release spring compressor. Remove strut assembly.

NOTE: When installing strut assembly, ensure alignment mark on strut mounting block faces mark on chassis strut tower.

---

3) Install strut assembly in shock tower. Install strut mounting bolts. Install ignition coil bracket and vane airflow meter assembly.

4) Install PRC actuator (if equipped) and rubber cap over strut mounting block.

5) Install steering knuckle to strut. Tighten to specifications. Install brake hose and brake caliper bracket. Install wheel and lower vehicle.

TIGHTENING SPECIFICATIONS

Application	Ft. Lbs. (N.m)
Axle Shaft Retaining Nut	116-174 (157-235)
Ball Joint-to-Knuckle Nut	32-40 (43-54)
Control Arm-to-Body Bolts	69-93 (93-127)
Stabilizer Link-to-Control Arm Bolt	[1]
Stabilizer Bar-to-Subframe Bolts	27-40 (36-54)
Strut Top Mount-to-Body Nuts	34-46 (46-63)
Strut-to-Top Mount Nuts	47-69 (64-84)
Strut-to-Steering Knuckle Nuts	69-86 (93-117)
Tie Rod-to-Steering Knuckle Nuts	22-33 (29-44)
Wheel Nuts	65-87 (88-118)

[1] – Tighten Stabilizer Link bolt until .79 " (20 mm) of thread remain above nut.

DESCRIPTION

The FWD front suspension is a MacPherson strut gas pressurized design. The strut assembly includes a rubber isolated top mount, seat and bearing assembly and coil spring insulator. The strut assembly mounts to the body side apron on the top. The lower strut assembly fits into a pinch joint designed into the steering knuckle. A link assembly runs between the strut and stabilizer bar end. A forged lower control arm attaches to the subframe and steering knuckle at the lower ball joint. A tension strut connects to the lower arm and subframe. *See Fig. 1.*

ADJUSTMENTS

CASTER & CAMBER

See appropriate article in WHEEL ALIGNMENT section.

RIDING HEIGHT

See RIDING HEIGHT SPECIFICATIONS article in WHEEL ALIGNMENT section.

FRONT WHEEL BEARINGS

There are 2 opposed and tapered roller bearings and a grease retainer installed in hub. The bearings are pressed into steering knuckle from inboard side. A snap ring is installed for extra retention. They require no maintenance or adjustment. If bearing is disassembled for any reason, it must be replaced as a unit.

BALL JOINT CHECKING

Raise vehicle so wheels hang freely. Grasp tire by top and bottom edges and move wheel assembly in and out. Any movement between lower end of knuckle and control arm indicates ball joint wear and requires replacement of lower control arm assembly.

CAUTION: *When hoisting FWD vehicles, ensure hoist adapters are positioned properly. See appropriate JACKING & HOISTING article in WHEEL ALIGNMENT section.*

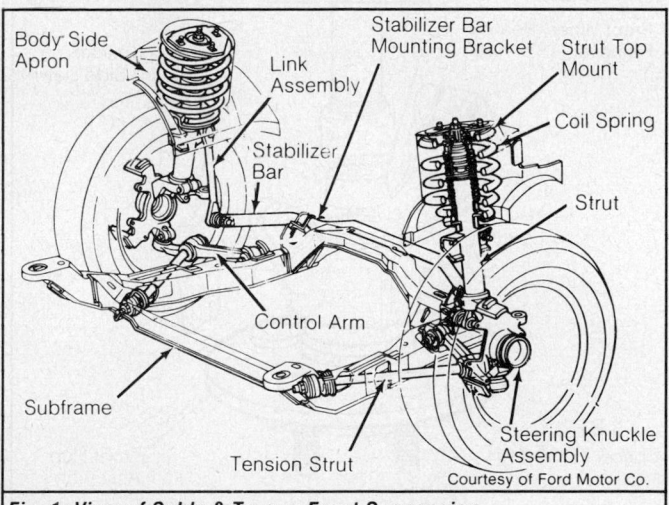

Fig. 1: View of Sable & Taurus Front Suspension

REMOVAL & INSTALLATION

CONTROL ARM

Removal – 1) Raise vehicle. Remove wheel. Remove nut and large dished washer from tension strut. Remove ball joint pinch bolt. A drift punch may be needed to remove pinch bolt. Spread steering knuckle pinch joint with a screwdriver and separate control arm from knuckle.

2) Remove control arm inner pivot nut and bolt. Remove control arm assembly from tension strut.
Installation – 1) Insert tension strut into control arm bushing. Position control arm into subframe bracket. Install nut and bolt and tighten to specification. See TIGHTENING SPECIFICATIONS at end of article. Put ball joint into steering knuckle. Ensure ball joint stud groove is properly positioned. Insert new pinch bolt. Tighten to specification.
2) Clean tension strut threads. Install nut and dished washer with dished side away from control arm bushing. Tighten to specification.

CONTROL ARM INNER PIVOT BUSHING

Removal & Installation – Remove control arm. See CONTROL ARM under REMOVAL & INSTALLATION in this article. Use Bushing Removers (T86P-5493-A2 and T86P-5493-A3) and "C" Clamp (T74P-3044-A1) to remove old bushing from control arm. Use Bushing Installer (T86P-5493-A4) and "C" Clamp (T74P-3044-A1) to install new bushing in control arm.

CONTROL ARM-TO-TENSION STRUT BUSHING

Removal & Installation – Remove lower control arm. See CONTROL ARM under REMOVAL & INSTALLATION in this article. Use Bushing Remover (T86P-5493-A5) and "C" Clamp (T74P-3044-A1) to remove old bushing from control arm. Use Bushing Installer (T86P-5493-A1 and T86P-5493-2) and "C" Clamp (T74P-3044-A1) to install new bushing in control arm. Saturate new bushing with vegetable oil before installing.

TENSION STRUT-TO-SUBFRAME BUSHINGS

Removal & Installation – Remove lower control arm. See CONTROL ARM under REMOVAL & INSTALLATION in this article. Remove nut, washer and bushing from front of tension strut. Pull strut rearward to remove it from subframe. Remove tension strut insulator. Install new bushing on tension strut end and insert into subframe. Install new front bushing. Clean tension strut threads. Tighten to specification.

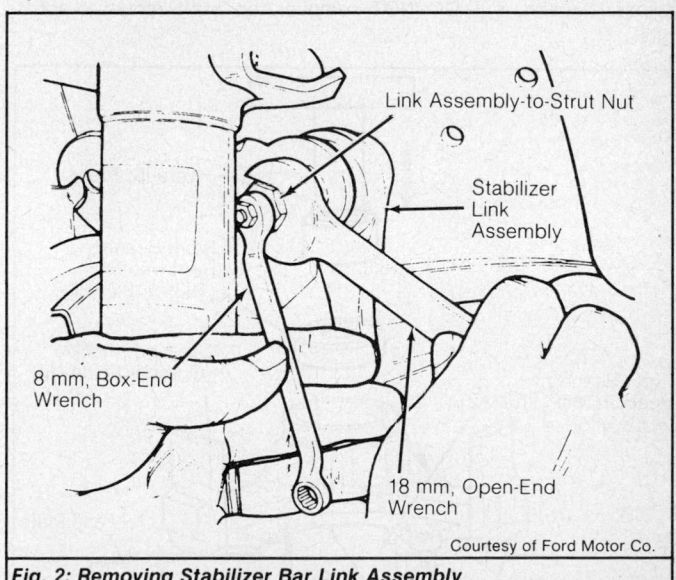

Fig. 2: Removing Stabilizer Bar Link Assembly

STABILIZER BAR & LINK ASSEMBLY

Removal – 1) Raise vehicle. Remove nuts attaching link assembly to stabilizer bar and strut with 8 mm, box-end wrench and 18 mm open-end wrench. *See Fig. 2.*
2) Remove nuts retaining steering gear to subframe. Move gear off subframe. Support subframe with jack stands. Remove 2 rear subframe mounting bolts. Lower rear of subframe for access to stabilizer bar mounting brackets. Remove stabilizer bar "U" bracket bolts and replace bushings.

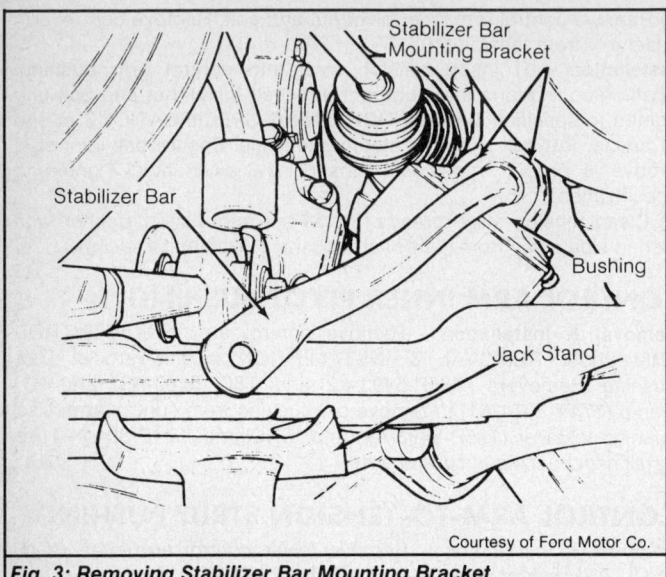

Fig. 3: Removing Stabilizer Bar Mounting Bracket

Installation – 1) Clean stabilizer bar where bushings mount. Lubricate inside of new bushing with vegetable oil. Install on bar. Install "U" brackets and tighten to specification.

2) Raise subframe. Install steering gear and tighten nuts to specification. Install link assembly to stabilizer bar and strut. Tighten to specifications.

STEERING KNUCKLE

Removal – 1) Raise vehicle. Remove wheel. Remove cotter pin and slotted nut from tie rod end stud. Using Tie Rod Remover (TOOL-3290-C) and Adapter (T81P-3504-W), separate tie rod end from steering knuckle.

2) Remove stabilizer link assembly from strut. Remove brake caliper. Loosen, but DO NOT remove, top strut mount-to-apron nuts.

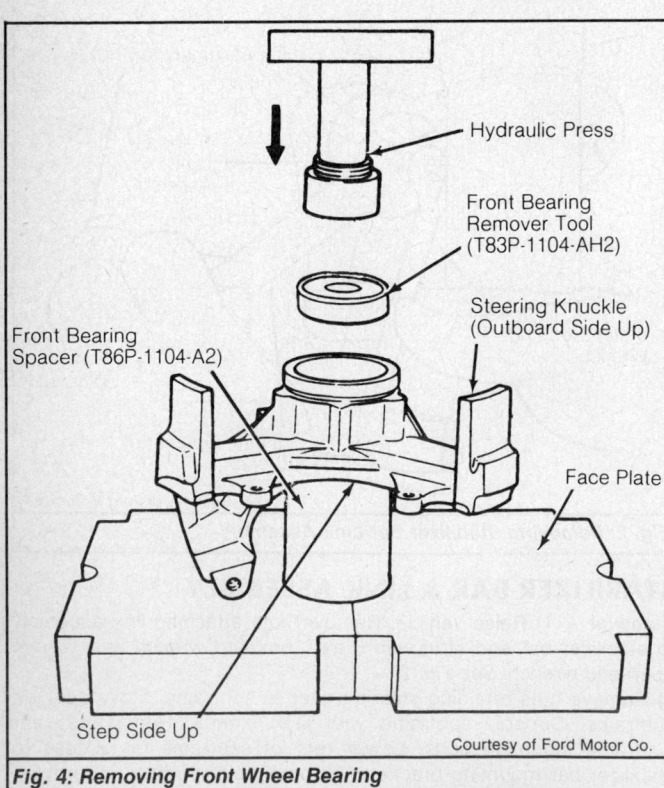

Fig. 4: Removing Front Wheel Bearing

3) Remove drive axle shaft from hub. See HUB & WHEEL BEARINGS under REMOVAL & INSTALLATION in this article. Remove ball joint-to-steering knuckle pinch bolt and nut, using a drift punch if necessary. DO NOT use a hammer to separate ball joint from steering knuckle.

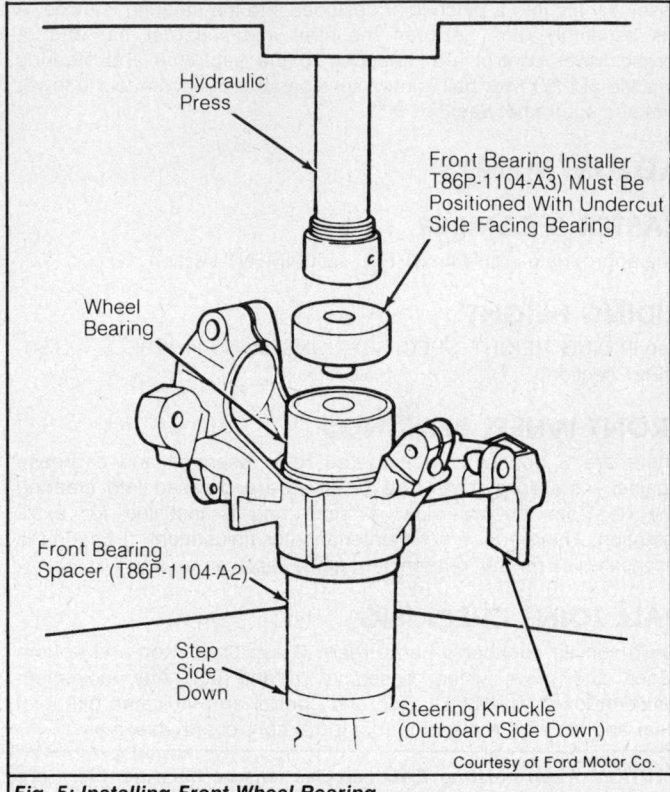

Fig. 5: Installing Front Wheel Bearing

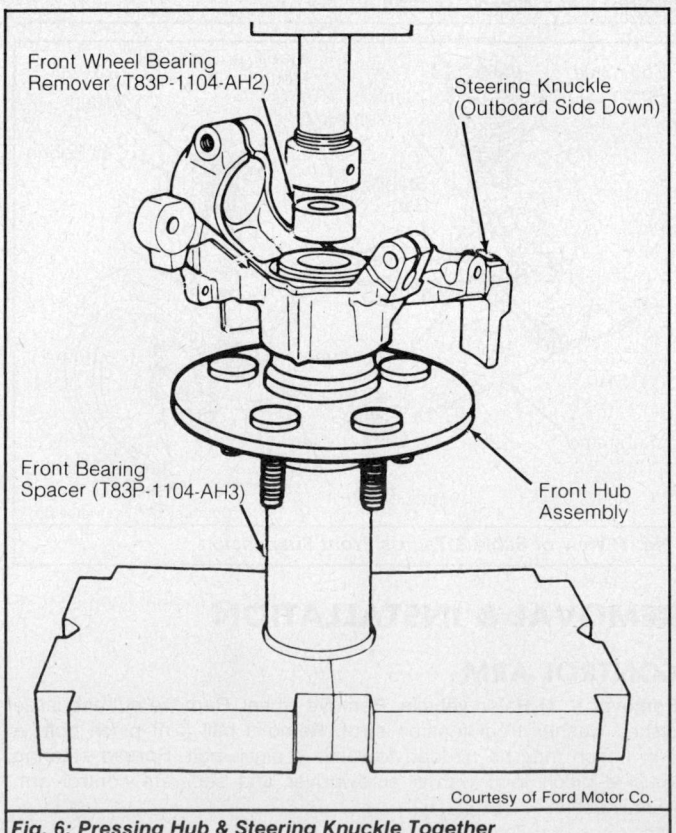

Fig. 6: Pressing Hub & Steering Knuckle Together

4) Using screwdriver, slightly spread knuckle-to-lower arm pinch joint and remove ball joint from knuckle. Remove strut-to-steering knuckle pinch bolt. Using screwdriver, pry knuckle-to-strut pinch joint. Remove steering knuckle and hub assembly.

CAUTION: When removing lower control arm, do not overextend drive axle shaft or CV joint components may separate.

Installation – To install, reverse removal procedure. Use new strut-to-knuckle pinch bolt, hub nut, tie rod end nut, and control arm-to-steering knuckle nut and bolt. Ensure ball stud groove is properly positioned.

HUB & WHEEL BEARINGS

Removal – 1) Loosen wheel nuts. Remove hub retainer nut and washer. Discard nut. Raise vehicle. Remove front wheel.
2) Remove brake caliper by loosening caliper locating pins and rotating caliper off rotor, starting from lower end of caliper and lifting upward. Do not remove caliper pins from caliper assembly. Support caliper with wire out of way.
3) Remove rotor by pulling it off hub bolts. If rotor is difficult to remove, strike rotor sharply between studs with a rubber or plastic hammer.

CAUTION: If excessive force is needed to remove rotor, check for excessive lateral runout before installation and replace as necessary.

4) Remove rotor splash shield. Disconnect control arm and tie rod from steering knuckle. Leave strut attached. Loosen 2 top strut mount-to-apron nuts. Install Hub Remover/Installer (T81P-1104-A and T81P-1104-C) and Adapters (T83P-1104-BH and T86P-1104-A1) and remove hub, bearing and knuckle assembly by pushing CV joint outer shaft until free.
5) Support drive axle aside with wire. Remove strut bolt and slide hub and knuckle assembly off strut. Remove support wire and place front hub and knuckle assembly on bench. Use Front Hub Puller (D80L-1002-L) and Shaft Protector (D80I-625-1) to remove hub.
Disassembly – Remove bearing snap ring from knuckle. Use press with Front Bearing Spacer (T86P-1104-A2) step side up on press plate. Put steering knuckle outboard side up on spacer. Install Front Bearing Remover (T83P-1104-AH2) on bearing inner race and press out bearing. Discard bearing. *See Fig. 4.*
Reassembly – 1) Clean knuckle bearing bore and hub bearing journal. If hub bearing journal is scored or damaged, replace hub. Do not attempt to service hub. If bearing is disassembled for any reason, it must be replaced.
2) Place Front Bearing Spacer (T86P-1104-A2), step side down, on press plate and position knuckle, outboard side down, on spacer. Position new bearing inside inboard side of knuckle. Install Front Bearing Installer (T86P-1104-A3) with undercut side facing bearing on bearing outer surface face. Press bearing into knuckle. *See Fig. 5.* Ensure bearing seats completely against knuckle bore shoulder. Install snap ring.
3) Place Front Bearing Spacer on arbor press plate and position hub on spacer with lugs facing down. Position knuckle assembly with outboard side down on hub barrel. Place Front Wheel Bearing Remover (T83P-1104-AH2) on inner race of bearing and press until bearing is seated onto hub. Ensure hub rotates freely in knuckle after installation. *See Fig. 6.*

NOTE: While tightening hub retainer nut, an audible click will be heard to indicate proper ratchet function. If hub nut is damaged or more than one locking tab is broken, replace hub retainer nut.

Installation – Connect hub/steering knuckle assembly on vehicle with wire and attach strut loosely to knuckle. Lubricate axle shaft and insert into hub. Ensure splines engage. Install Front Hub Remover/Installer (T81P-1104-C), Adapter (T81P-1104-A) and Wheel Bolt Adapter (T83P-1104-BH) to hub and stub shaft. Tighten to 120 ft. lbs. (162 N.m) to ensure hub is fully seated. Install washer and

hub retaining nut finger tight. Complete installation of front suspension components. Install brake rotor and brake caliper. Install wheel and tighten wheel nuts finger tight. Lower vehicle and block wheels. Manually thread hub nut retainer assembly on axle shaft. Using 1 3/16" (30 mm) socket, tighten to specification.

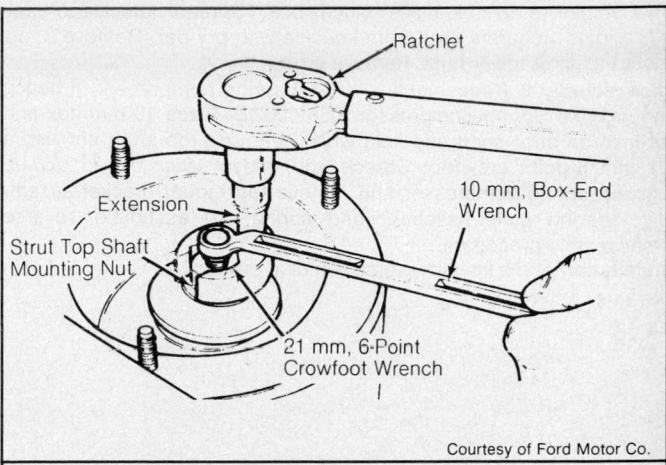

Courtesy of Ford Motor Co.

Fig. 7: Removing Strut Top Shaft Mounting Nut

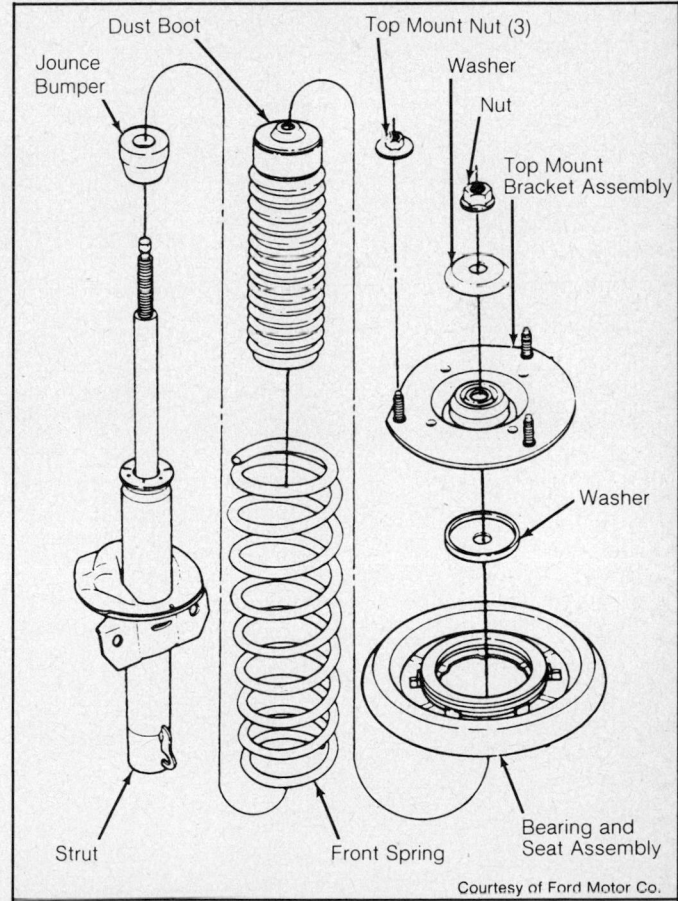

Courtesy of Ford Motor Co.

Fig. 8: Exploded View of Front Strut

COIL SPRING & STRUT ASSEMBLY

Removal – 1) Raise vehicle by control arms. Remove axle shaft nut. See HUB & WHEEL BEARINGS under REMOVAL & INSTALLATION in this article.
2) Loosen, but DO NOT remove, 3 top mount-to-strut tower nuts. Remove wheel. Remove brake caliper and rotor. Remove tie rod

end nut and cotter pin. Disconnect tie rod end from strut. Disconnect stabilizer link from strut.

3) Remove ball joint-to-knuckle pinch joint bolt. Spread knuckle pinch joint with a screwdriver and disconnect control arm at ball joint.

4) Remove strut-to-knuckle pinch bolt. Spread knuckle-to-strut pinch joint. Separate strut from knuckle with pry bar. Remove 3 top mount-to-strut tower nuts. Remove strut.

Disassembly & Reassembly – Install spring compressor in bench mount. Use Spring Compressor (086-00029). Place 10 mm box-end wrench on strut shaft and hold while removing top shaft nut with a 21 mm 6-point crowfoot wrench and ratchet. *See Figs. 7 and 8.* Loosen spring compressor and remove top mount bracket assembly, bearing plate assembly and spring. To assemble, reverse disassembly procedure.

Installation – To install, reverse removal procedure.

TIGHTENING SPECIFICATIONS

Application	Ft. Lbs. (N.m)
Axle (Hub) Retaining Nut	180-200 (245-270)
Ball Joint Pinch Bolt	40-55 (54-75)
Control Arm Pivot Bolt	70-95 (95-129)
Link Assembly-to-Stabilizer Bar Nut	35-48 (48-65)
Link Assembly-to-Strut Nut	55-75 (75-101)
Stabilizer Bar-to-Control Arm Nut	98-115 (132-156)
Stabilizer "U" Bracket-to-Subframe Bolt	21-32 (28-43)
Strut Shaft-to-Top Mount Nut	35-50 (48-68)
Strut Top Mount-to-Strut Tower Nut	22-32 (30-43)
Strut-to-Steering Knuckle Bolt	70-95 (95-129)
Tension Strut-to-Control Arm Nut	70-95 (95-129)
Tension Strut-to-Subframe Nut	21-32 (28-43)
Tie Rod-to-Steering Knuckle Nut	23-25 (31-47)
Wheel Lug Nuts	85-105 (115-142)

DESCRIPTION

Suspension is a long, hot forged spindle with upper and lower control arms, isolated tension strut, stabilizer bar and variable rate coil spring. Suspension geometry features high caster angle and negative camber.

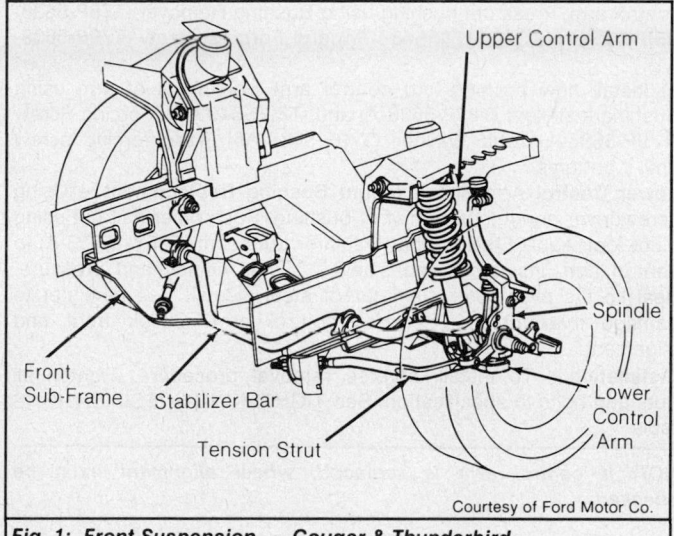

Front Sub-Frame

Upper Control Arm

Spindle

Lower Control Arm

Stabilizer Bar

Tension Strut

Courtesy of Ford Motor Co.

Fig. 1: Front Suspension – Cougar & Thunderbird

ADJUSTMENTS

CASTER & CAMBER

See appropriate article in WHEEL ALIGNMENT section.

RIDING HEIGHT

See RIDING HEIGHT SPECIFICATIONS article in WHEEL ALIGNMENT section.

FRONT WHEEL BEARINGS

Front wheel bearings are part of hub unit and require no maintenance or adjustment. If replacement is necessary the hub/bearing assembly must be replaced as complete unit. See WHEEL BEARINGS under REMOVAL & INSTALLATION in this article.

LOWER BALL JOINT CHECKING

Inspection – 1) Raise vehicle. Place jack stands under lower suspension arms. Attach dial indicator to measure lateral (sideways) movement between spindle and arm.
2) Grasp tire at top and bottom and slowly move in and out. If dial indicator reading exceeds .015" (.40 mm) replace ball joint.

REMOVAL & INSTALLATION

LOWER BALL JOINT

Removal – 1) Raise vehicle. Remove lower control arm. See LOWER CONTROL ARM.
2) Remove and discard joint boot seal. Ball joint can now be pressed out, or C-Frame Ball Joint Remover (T74P-4635-C) may be used.
Installation – To install, reverse removal procedure. Tighten all nuts and bolts to specification. See TIGHTENING SPECIFICATIONS table.

UPPER BALL JOINT

Upper ball joints are part of the upper control arm assembly and are replaced as a unit.

STABILIZER BAR, BUSHINGS & LINK INSULATORS

Removal – 1) Remove air inlet tube. Remove stabilizer bar retaining bracket bolts and brackets. Remove serpentine drive belt.
2) Raise vehicle on hoist. Remove front tire and wheel assemblies. Remove crankshaft vibration damper. Remove cotter pins and castellated nuts at rod ends. Separate tie rod ends from spindles.
3) Remove transmission oil cooler line bracket. Remove nuts from stabilizer link. Separate link studs from spindle and stabilizer bar using Joint Separator (D88L-3006-A).
4) Remove stabilizer bar from vehicles right side. Remove stabilizer bar bushings from stabilizer bar.
Installation – To install, reverse removal procedure. Tighten all nuts and bolts to specification. See TIGHTENING SPECIFICATIONS table.

TENSION STRUT

Removal – 1) Raise vehicle. Remove tire and wheel assembly. Hold tension strut with wrench ON FLATS ONLY while turning nut. Remove front attaching nut and insulator.
2) Mark or note threads visable at tension strut rear frame attaching nut. Back nut off. Remove strut-to-lower control arm nut. Remove lower shock bolt and nut. Remove brake hose bracket bolt.
3) Remove ABS sensor bolt and position sensor out of the way. Pry lower control arm rearward. Remove tension strut.
Reassembly – 1) Deburr insulator sleeves before reassembly. If new sleeves are used, inner sleeve must be shorter than outer sleeve. Up to .025" (6 mm) may be cut from inner sleeve.
2) If replacing tension strut, install nut all the way on threads. Install so nylon insert is facing forward (front of vehicle). *See Fig. 2 .* Install outer sleeve and rear washer. Word "REAR" should be facing out. Install in frame.

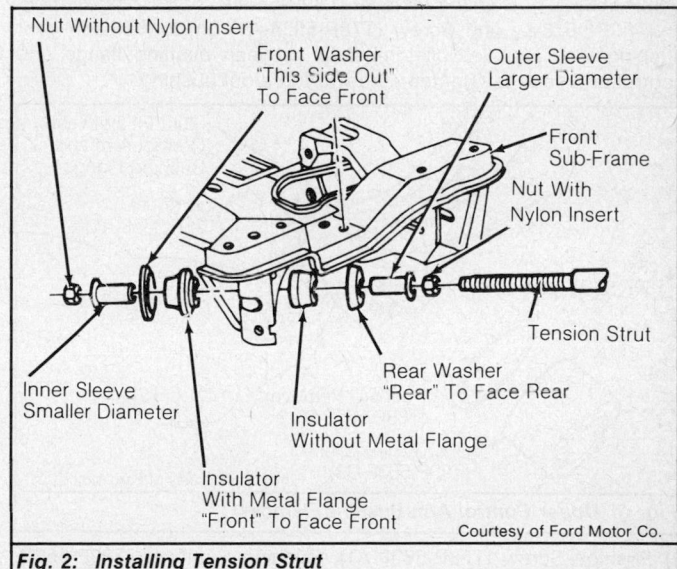

Nut Without Nylon Insert

Front Washer "This Side Out" To Face Front

Outer Sleeve Larger Diameter

Front Sub-Frame

Nut With Nylon Insert

Tension Strut

Rear Washer "Rear" To Face Rear

Insulator Without Metal Flange

Inner Sleeve Smaller Diameter

Insulator With Metal Flange "Front" To Face Front

Courtesy of Ford Motor Co.

Fig. 2: Installing Tension Strut

3) Install front insulator with metal flange toward frame. Install washer, inner sleeve. Loosely install front nut. Install front washer and insulator on rear of tension strut, with cup facing away from insulator.
4) Install tension strut in lower control arm. Install rear insulator with small end toward control arm. Install washer and cup with cup facing rear of vehicle. Return rear torsion strut-to-frame nut to original position.
Installation – To install, reverse removal procedure. Tighten all nuts and bolts to specification. See TIGHTENING SPECIFICATIONS table. Check wheel alignment. See appropriate article in WHEEL ALIGNMENT section.

COIL SPRING

Removal – 1) Remove plastic cover at upper shock mount. Remove automatic ride actuator, if so equipped. Remove 3 upper shock retaining nuts and collar plate from mounting studs in engine compartment.

2) Raise vehicle on hoist. Remove tire and wheel assembly. Remove lower shock mounting bolt and nut. Remove nut at stablizer link upper mounting stud. Separate link studs from spindle and stablizer bar using Joint Separator (D88L-3006-A).

3) Support lower control arm assembly with transmission jack. Raise control arm with jack until stabilizer link can be separated from spindle. Position link out of way. Remove spindle to upper control arm attaching nut and bolt, and discard. Lower jack to separate spindle from upper control arm. Support spindle with wire or other means. Remove jack from lower control arm and remove shock assembly.

Disassembly – Position shock assembly in Rotunda Spring Compressor (086-00029). Mark position of upper mount to coil spring before disassembly. Assembly WILL NOT install in vehicle if upper mount is not properly positioned. Compress spring, remove upper mount. Release spring compressor, remove spring.

Installation – To install, reverse removal procedure. Tighten all nuts and bolts to specification. See TIGHTENING SPECIFICATIONS table.

UPPER CONTROL ARM & BUSHINGS

Removal – 1) Raise vehicle on hoist. Remove tire and wheel assembly. Remove and discard upper spindle to ball joint bolt and nut. Slightly spread spindle at slot. Remove ball joint.

2) Break off flags on upper control arm pivot bolt heads. Using a six-point tool, remove upper control arm bolts. Remove control arm.

Upper Control Arm Bushing Replacement – 1) Assemble Collet (T89P-5638-C1), Bushing Installer (T89P-5638-C3), Bushing Remover (T89P-5638-D) and Screw (T78P-5638-A1) on control arm over bushing. *See Fig. 3.* Collet must fit between bushing flange and control arm surface. Tighten screw to force out bushing.

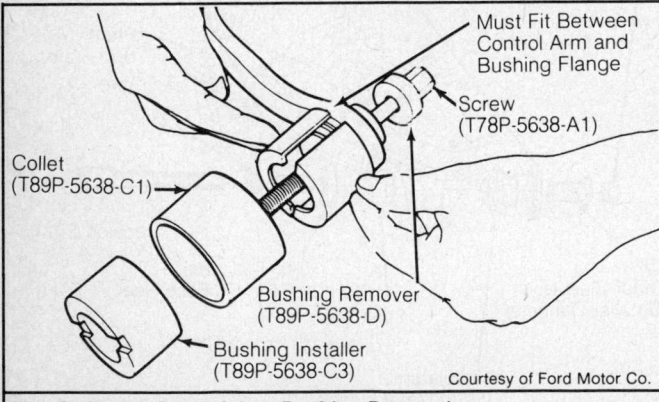

Collet (T89P-5638-C1)

Must Fit Between Control Arm and Bushing Flange

Screw (T78P-5638-A1)

Bushing Remover (T89P-5638-D)

Bushing Installer (T89P-5638-C3)

Courtesy of Ford Motor Co.

Fig. 3: Upper Control Arm Bushing Removal

2) Position Screw (T78P-5638-A1), Bushing Remover (T89P-5638-D), Bushing Installer (T89P-5638-D) on outer side of control arm. Position Bushing Installer (T89P-5638-C3) on inside of control arm with grooves on installer lining up with control arm ridge. Tighten screw until bushing installers bottom out against each other. Reinstall control arm.

Installation – To install, reverse removal procedure. Tighten all nuts and bolts to specification. See TIGHTENING SPECIFICATIONS table.

LOWER CONTROL ARM & BUSHINGS

Removal – 1) Raise vehicle. Remove tire and wheel assembly. Loosen ball joint nut 3 or 4 turns. Rap spindle to separate ball joint. Leave nut in place. Support spindle to prevent excess sagging of upper control arm.

2) Mark position of camber adjustment cam. Remove nut attaching tension strut to control arm. Hold tension strut with wrench ON FLATS ONLY while turning nut. Remove lower shock bolt and nut. Remove pivot (camber) bolt and nut. Remove lower ball joint nut and remove control arm.

Lower Control Arm Bushings Replacement – 1) Remove lower control arm. Press out bushing using Bushing Remover (T78P-5638-A5), Receiving Cup (T78P5638-A4) and Forcing Screw (T79P-5638-A1).

2) Install new bushing into control arm from front of arm using Bushing Installers (T89P-5638-A) and (T89P-5493-B), Forcing Screw (T79P-5638-A1) and Washer (T79P-5638-A6). Turn forcing screw until it bottoms.

Lower Control Arm Shock Mount Bushing Replacement – Using screwdriver pry out either half of bushing. Push other half out using blunt tool. Apply Ford Rubber Insulator Lubricant (E25Y-19553-A) to control arm, insulators and sleeves. Install using hand pressure. Seal lip fits over outer diameter of steel sleeve. Use care not to damage insulator lip. Reinstall control arm. Check front end alignment.

Installation – To install, reverse removal procedure. Tighten all nuts and bolts to specification. See TIGHTENING SPECIFICATIONS table.

NOTE: If control arm is replaced, wheel alignment must be checked.

WHEEL BEARINGS

Removal – 1) Raise vehicle. Remove wheel and tire assembly. Remove grease cap and discard. Remove 2 Torx bolts from brake caliper. Remove caliper assembly and suspend by wire. DO NOT suspend by brake hose.

2) Remove factory clips. Remove rotor. Remove front axle nut and discard. Remove hub and bearing. If necessary, use Hub Puller (T81P-1104-C).

Installation – 1) Install hub and bearing. Install new front axle hub nut and tighten to 183 ft. lbs. (250 N.m).

NOTE: When hub nut is loosened or removed, always replace with new nut. Do not back off hub nut after tightening. Do not use impact tools to tighten.

2) Install rotor and push on nuts. Install grease cap. Install brake caliper. Be sure spring clip is seated properly. Install Torx bolts. Tighten to 25 ft. lbs. (34 N.m). Install wheel and tire.

TIGHTENING SPECIFICATIONS

Application	Ft. Lbs. (N.m)
Axle Hub Nut	183 (250)
Brake Caliper Bolts	25 (34)
Lower Control Arm-to-Ball Joint Nut	80-120 (110-160)
Lower Control Arm-to-Frame Bolt	92-125 (125-170)
Lower Control Arm-to-Shock Nut	103-144 (140-195)
Lower Control Arm-to-Tension Strut Nut	90-120 (120-160)
Shock-to-Upper Mount Nut	37-45 (50-61)
Stabilizer Bar Link-to-Spindle Nut	40-55 (55-75)
Stabilizer Bar Link-to-Stabilzer Bar Nut	40-55 (55-75)
Tension Strut-to-Frame Nut	90-120 (120-160)
Tie Rod End-to-Spindle Nut	[1] 39-54 (53-73)
Upper Control Arm-to-Body Nut	55-90 (75-120)
Upper Control Arm-to-Ball Joint Nut	50-65 (70-90)
Upper Shock Mount-to-Body Nut	16-23 (22-31)

[1] – Tighten to minimum torque, then continue to tighten to nearest cotter pin slot.

LTD Crown Victoria, Grand Marquis, Town Car, Wagon

DESCRIPTION

Front suspension system is of the coil spring type. The coil springs are located between lower control arms and upper frame or front-end sheet metal. Upper or lower ball joints and lower control arm pivot bushings must be replaced with control arm as an assembly. Upper pivot bushings may be replaced individually. Side roll is controlled by stabilizer bar. Stabilizer bar ends are connected to lower control arms. Bar is mounted in rubber bushings held to frame side rails by clamps.

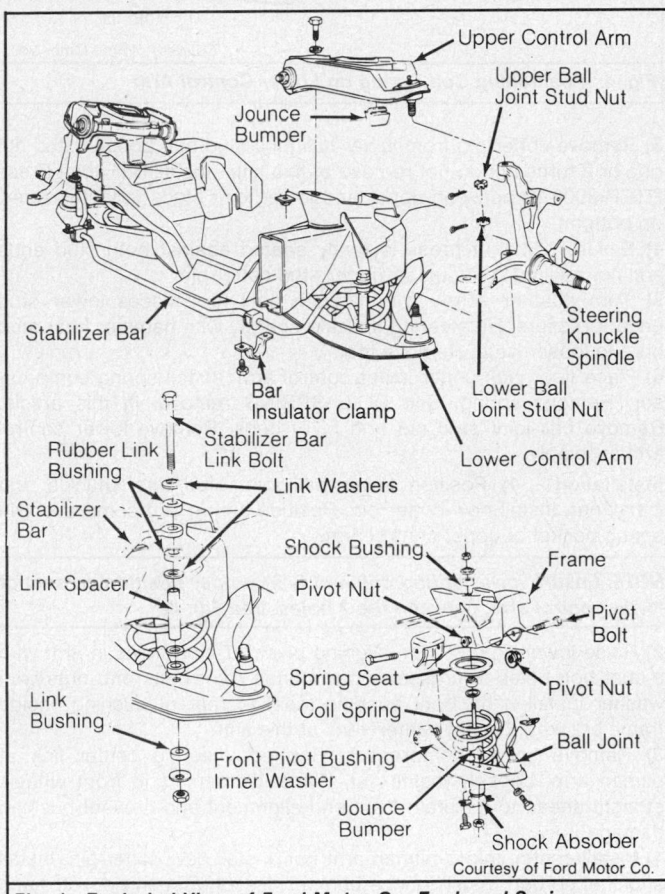

Fig. 1: Exploded View of Ford Motor Co. Enclosed Spring

ADJUSTMENTS

CAMBER, CASTER & TOE-IN

See appropriate article in WHEEL ALIGNMENT section.

RIDING HEIGHT

See RIDING HEIGHT SPECIFICATIONS article in WHEEL ALIGNMENT section.

FRONT WHEEL BEARINGS

1) Raise vehicle. Remove grease cap from hub. Remove cotter pin and nut lock. Loosen adjusting nut 3 turns. Rock wheel assembly in and out to push brake pad away from rotor.
2) While rotating wheel, tighten adjusting nut to 17-25 ft. lbs. (23-34 N.m). Loosen nut 1/2 turn, then tighten to 10-28 INCH lbs. (1.1-3.2 N.m). Place nut lock on nut.
3) Position nut retainer over adjusting nut and align cotter pin hole. Install new cotter pin. Check for free wheel rotation. Install grease

cap. Lower vehicle. Pump brake pedal before driving to restore normal pedal travel.

BALL JOINT CHECKING

Lower Ball Joint – 1) With wheel bearings adjusted, support vehicle in normal driving position (ball joints loaded). Wipe grease fittings and checking surfaces clean.
2) Checking surface should project outside ball joint cover. If surface is inside cover, replace lower control arm assembly. *See Fig. 2.*

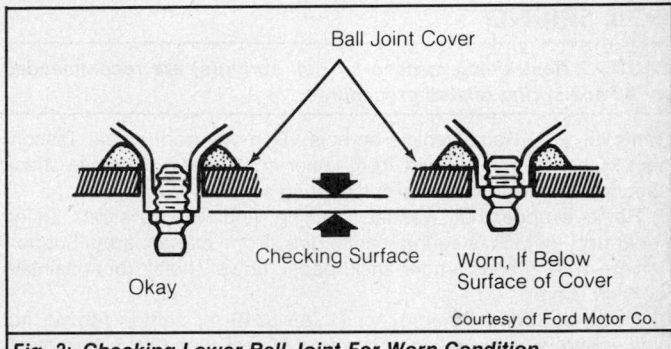

Fig. 2: Checking Lower Ball Joint For Worn Condition

Upper Ball Joint – 1) Ensure wheel bearings are adjusted and lower ball joints properly checked. Raise vehicle. Place floor jacks beneath lower control arms. Hold lower edge of tire and move wheel in and out.
2) While moving wheel, check for play between steering knuckle upper end and upper control arm. Movement indicates ball joint wear. Install new upper control arm assembly.

REMOVAL & INSTALLATION

UPPER & LOWER BALL JOINTS

Replace upper or lower ball joint with control arm as an assembly only. Do not install ball joint or other components in used control arm. See CONTROL ARM procedures in this article.

CAUTION: Gas-charged shock absorbers will extend unassisted during removal. Do not apply heat or flame to shock tube.

SHOCK ABSORBER

Removal – Remove nut, washer and bushing from shock absorber shaft upper end. Raise vehicle on hoist. Support with safety stands. Remove 2 self-tapping screws attaching shock to lower control arm. Remove shock.

Installation – 1) Place washer and new rubber bushing on shock top stud. Position unit inside spring. Install 2 self-tapping screws and tighten to specifications.
2) Remove safety stands. Lower vehicle. Place new bushing and washer on top stud. Install and tighten nut to specifications.

NOTE: If threads in lower control arm become stripped or damaged, install new 5/16" x 18 lock nuts on lower shock mount screws.

STABILIZER BAR, LINK BUSHINGS & INSULATORS

Removal – 1) Raise vehicle. Place jack stands under lower control arms. Remove nut, washer and insulator from each stabilizer bar link bolt. Remove remaining bolts, washers, insulators and spacers. Note locations for reassembly reference.
2) Detach stabilizer bar insulator clamp bolts. Remove clamps and bar assembly. Inspect rubber link bushings and bar insulators for wear, damage and/or deterioration.

3) If replacement is needed, install new stabilizer bar link bushing kit. If insulators need replacement, cut worn insulators from bar.

Installation – 1) Assemble new cup washer and bushing on bolt. Insert bolt through stabilizer bar end (from top). Install new bushings, washers and spacer on link bolt. Install bolt through lower control arm. Install new bushing and cup washer. Install nut.

2) Coat inside of new rubber insulators with rubber lubricant. Slide insulators on stabilizer bar. Using new bolts, clamp bar to frame brackets. Remove jack stands. Lower vehicle.

COIL SPRING

CAUTION: Restraining devices for coil spring(s) are recommended for all coil spring related procedures.

Removal – 1) Raise vehicle on hoist. Remove front wheel. Disconnect stabilizer bar link bolt from lower control arm. Remove shock absorber-to-lower control arm mounting screws.

2) Remove upper nut, washer, bushing, and remove shock. Using separator, detach steering center link from pitman arm. Support vehicle with stands under jack pads. Lower hoist (but maintain working room).

3) Using a Spring Compressor (D78P-5310-A), tighten forcing nut until spring is compressed and is free in seat. *See Fig. 3.* Remove 2 lower control arm pivot bolts, nuts and washer. Detach lower arm from crossmember. Remove spring.

4) If installing new spring, note position of upper and lower spring ends to be sure correct installation is made. Loosen forcing nut to relieve spring tension. Remove compressor (if necessary).

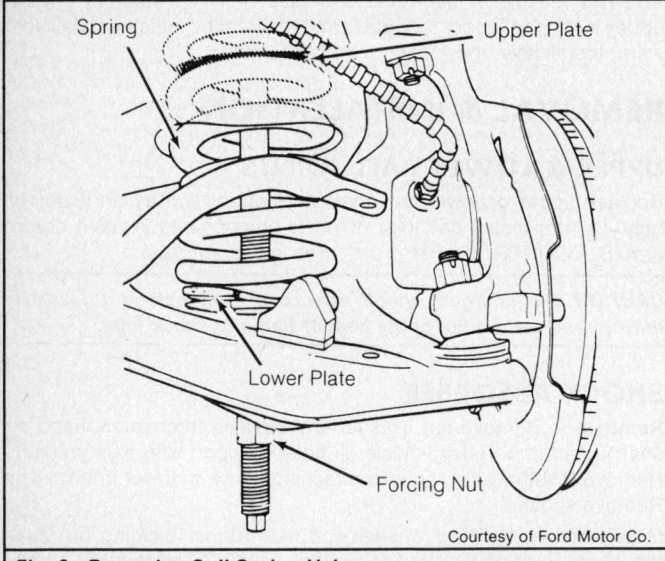

Fig. 3: Removing Coil Spring Using Spring Compressor (D78P-5310-A)

Installation – To install coil spring, reverse removal procedure. Before compressing spring, ensure coil spring end is positioned properly. *See Fig. 4.* When installing lower front pivot bolt, ensure washer is placed on inside of front pivot bushing, next to rear of bushing, inside frame bracket.

NOTE: End of spring must cover hole "B" but not cover hole "A".

LOWER CONTROL ARM ASSEMBLY

Removal – 1) Raise vehicle. Place jack stands under both sides of frame, just behind lower control arms. Remove front wheel. Remove brake caliper, rotor and dust shield.

2) Remove jounce bumper and shock. Detach stabilizer bar link from lower arm. Using separator, pull steering center link off pitman arm.

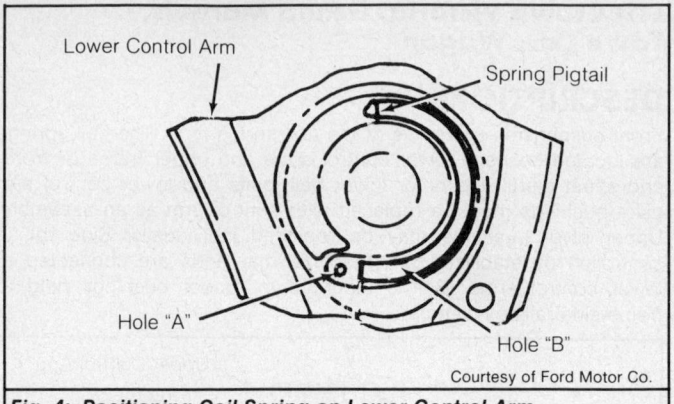

Fig. 4: Positioning Coil Spring on Lower Control Arm

3) Remove cotter pin from lower ball joint stud nut. Loosen stud nut one or 2 turns but do not remove at this time. Install Ball Joint Press (T57P-3006-B) between upper and lower joint studs (adapter screw on bottom).

4) Ensure ball joint press is firmly seated against both stud ends and not against stud nuts or upper stud cotter pin.

5) Turn adapter screw with wrench until tool places lower stud under pressure. Hit steering knuckle sharply with hammer near stud bore to loosen stud. Remove tool.

6) Place floor jack under lower control arm. Install spring compressor. Remove spring. See COIL SPRING removal in this article. Remove ball joint stud nut and pivot bolts. Remove lower control arm assembly.

Installation – 1) Position lower ball joint stud into knuckle and install nut. Install new cotter pin. Position spring and compressor in spring pocket of upper control arm.

NOTE: Ensure lower spring coil end is in proper position on seat of lower control arm, between the 2 holes. See Fig. 4.

2) Raise lower control arm, aligning pivot bushing holes in arm with mount bolt holes in crossmember. Install pivot bolts and nuts with washer installed on front bushing (next to rear of bushing, inside frame bracket). Do not tighten nuts at this time.

3) Remove spring compressor. Connect steering center link at pitman arm. Loosely install nut. Place idler arm and front wheels straight ahead to maintain front end alignment and prevent bushing damage.

4) Install center link-to-pitman arm nut. Install new cotter pin. Install shock absorber. Install jounce bumper. Install dust shield, rotor and caliper. Position stabilizer link to lower control arm and install bolt, link assembly and nut.

5) Using jack, raise control arm to normal riding height. Tighten the lower control arm-to-crossmember pivot bolts to specifications. Install wheel. Check and adjust front end alignment as necessary.

NOTE: Only upper control arm pivot bushings may be replaced individually. Replace lower pivot bushings by replacing complete control arm assembly.

UPPER CONTROL ARM ASSEMBLY

Removal – 1) Raise front of vehicle. Position jack stands under both sides of frame, just behind lower control arms. Remove wheel. Remove upper ball joint stud cotter pin. Loosen stud nut one or 2 turns. Do not remove nut from stud at this time.

2) Install Ball Joint Press (T57P-3006-B) between upper and lower ball joint studs (adapter screw on top). Press must be firmly seated against both stud ends and not against stud nuts or lower stud cotter pin.

3) Turn adapter screw with wrench until upper stud is under pressure. Using hammer, hit steering knuckle sharply near upper stud bore to loosen stud. Remove tool.

4) Place jack under lower control arm to support lower arm and spring assembly. Remove upper control arm pivot bolts and ball joint stud nut. Remove upper arm assembly. If upper control arm is replaced, transfer jounce bumper from old arm.

Upper Control Arm Bushing Replacement – 1) With upper control arm removed, detach nuts and washers from ends of inner shaft. Use "C" Clamp (T74P-3044-A1) and Pivot Bushing Remover Adapters (T79P-3044-A2 and T75P-3044-A1) to remove bushings. Repeat procedure for other side.

NOTE: Front pivot bushing has larger diameter than rear.

2) Position shaft and new bushings in upper control arm. Ensure inner washer is installed on shaft (rear bushing only). Using "C" clamp and adapters, press bushings into upper control arm. Position inner shaft so serrated side contacts frame. *See Fig. 5.*

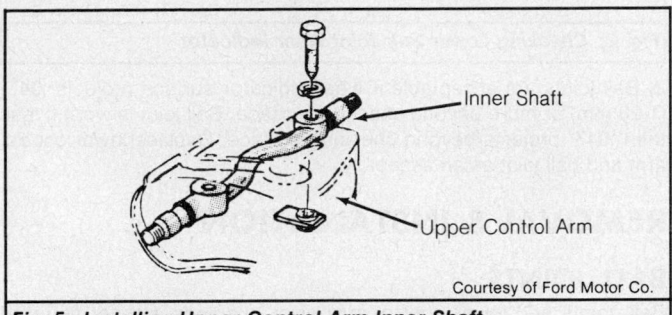

Inner Shaft

Upper Control Arm

Courtesy of Ford Motor Co.

Fig. 5: Installing Upper Control Arm Inner Shaft

3) Install 2 outer washers, with new nuts, on each end of inner shaft. Tighten nuts to specifications.

Installation – Position upper control arm assembly to frame bracket. Install 2 attaching bolts and washers. Connect upper ball joint stud to knuckle. Install nut. Install new cotter pin and front wheel. Remove stands. Lower vehicle. Check and adjust front end alignment as necessary.

STEERING KNUCKLE

Removal – 1) Raise vehicle. Place safety stands under both sides of frame, just behind lower arm. Remove wheel. Remove brake caliper, rotor and dust shield. Detach tie rod end from knuckle arm.

2) Remove cotter pins from both ball joint stud nuts. Loosen nuts one or 2 turns (do not remove nuts at this time). Position ball joint remover between upper and lower joint studs. Seat tool firmly on joint studs, not on stud nuts.

CAUTION: Restraining devices for coil spring(s), are recommended for all coil spring related procedures.

3) Turn tool with wrench until studs are under pressure. Using hammer, hit knuckle near stud bore to break joint stud loose. Position jack under lower arm, at lower ball joint area. Remove upper and lower ball joint stud nuts. Lower jack carefully. Remove knuckle.

Installation – To install, reverse removal procedure. Check and adjust front end alignment as necessary.

WHEEL BEARINGS

NOTE: Under normal service, front wheel bearings should be inspected, lubricated and adjusted whenever front brakes are serviced or at least every 30,000 miles. Lubricate wheel bearings using high temperature wheel bearing grease.

Removal – 1) Raise and support vehicle. Remove front wheel. Remove caliper from knuckle and wire out of way. Remove grease cap from hub. Remove cotter pin, nut retainer, adjusting nut and flat washer from spindle.

2) Remove outer bearing assembly. Pull hub and rotor off spindle. Remove seal. Remove inner bearing from hub.

3) Clean hub and bearings in solvent. Blow dry with compressed air. Do not spin bearings. Inspect bearings and races for scratches, pits, excessive wear or other damage. Replace worn bearings and races in matched sets.

4) If bearing race removal is necessary, pull races from rotor hub using bearing race remover and race puller.

Installation – 1) Install inner or outer bearing race (if removed). Pack bearings with grease. Place inner bearing assembly into inner race. Apply grease to seal lips. Install new seal.

2) Install hub and rotor assembly on knuckle spindle. Install outer bearing assembly, flat washer and nut. Adjust bearing preload. See FRONT WHEEL BEARINGS under ADJUSTMENTS in this article. Install brake caliper. Install wheel and lower vehicle.

TIGHTENING SPECIFICATIONS

Application	Ft. Lbs. (N.m)
Ball Joint-to-Steering Knuckle	
Upper Stud Nut	60-90 (82-122)
Lower Stud Nut	80-120 (109-163)
Brake Dust Shield Bolt	10-15 (13-20)
Caliper Bolts	40-60 (54-82)
Center Link-to-Pitman Arm Nut [1]	43-47 (58-64)
Jounce Bumper Nut	30-35 (40-48)
Lower Control Arm-to-Crossmember	
Pivot Bolt	100-140 (136-190)
Stabilizer Bar-to-Lower Control Arm	
Link Bolt/Nut	9-15 (12-20)
Stabilizer Bar-to-Frame Bracket	
Insulator Clamp Bolt	14-26 (19-35)
Shock Absorber	
Mount Screw [2]	12-18 (16-24)
Upper Mount Nut	22-30 (30-40)
Tie Rod Clamp Bolts	20-22 (27-30)
Upper Control Arm-to-Crossmember	
Pivot Bolt/Nut	100-140 (136-190)
Upper Control Arm	
Inner Shaft Mount Bolt	100-140 (136-190)
Wheel Lug Nut	85-105 (115-142)

[1] – Tighten to lower limit of specification; then, tighten nut to nearest cotter pin slot and insert cotter pin.

[2] – The shock lower mount screws are self-tapping type. If threads in control arm are stripped, use 5/16" x 18 lock nuts on mount screws.

DESCRIPTION

Front suspension is a modified MacPherson strut design. The design uses a strut damper with coil spring located between lower control arm and a spring pocket in crossmember. All models use gas-pressurized hydraulic shock struts. A front stabilizer is also used. See Fig. 1.

The shock struts are non-serviceable and must be replaced as an assembly. The ball joints and lower control arm pivot bushings are not serviced separately and also must be replaced as an assembly.

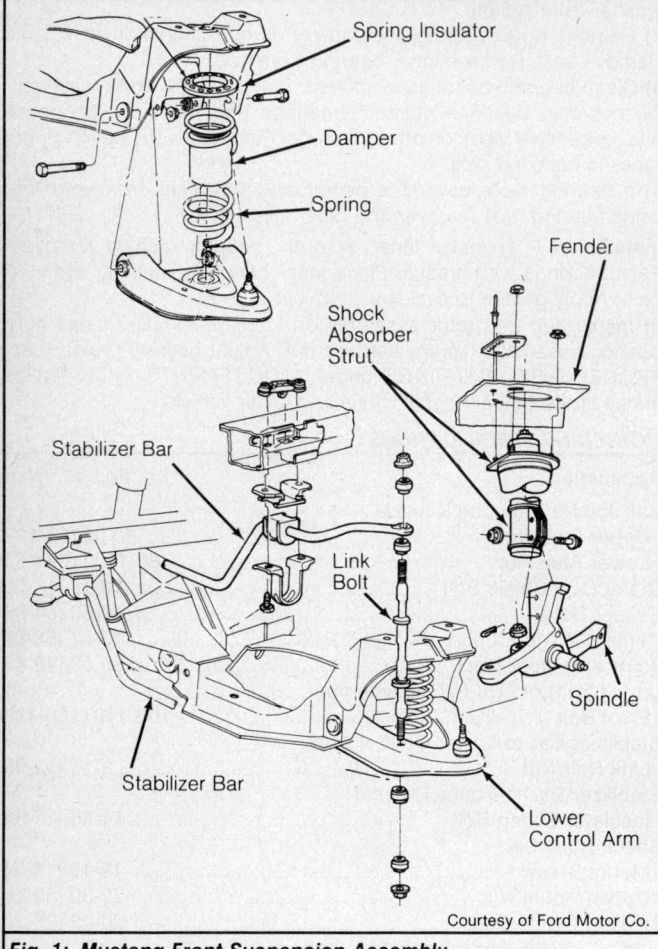

Fig. 1: Mustang Front Suspension Assembly

ADJUSTMENTS

CASTER & CAMBER

See appropriate article in WHEEL ALIGNMENT section.

RIDING HEIGHT

See RIDING HEIGHT SPECIFICATIONS article in WHEEL ALIGNMENT section.

FRONT WHEEL BEARINGS

1) Raise vehicle, remove wheel cover and grease cap. Remove cotter pin and nut lock. Loosen adjusting nut 3 turns. Rock wheel, hub and rotor assembly in and out several times to push brake pads away from rotor.

2) Tighten adjusting nut to 17-25 ft. lbs. (23-34 N.m) while rotating wheel assembly. Loosen adjusting nut 1/2 turn, then retighten to 10-12 INCH lbs. (1.1-1.7 N.m).

3) Reinstall nut lock on adjusting nut and insert new cotter pin. Install grease cap and wheel cover. Lower vehicle. Before driving vehicle, pump brake pedal to restore normal brake pedal travel.

LOWER BALL JOINT CHECKING

1) Support vehicle in normal driving position with both ball joints loaded. On all models, clean dirt and grease from ball joint checking surface. See Fig. 2. Ensure checking surface projects beyond ball joint cover surface or ball joint must be replaced.

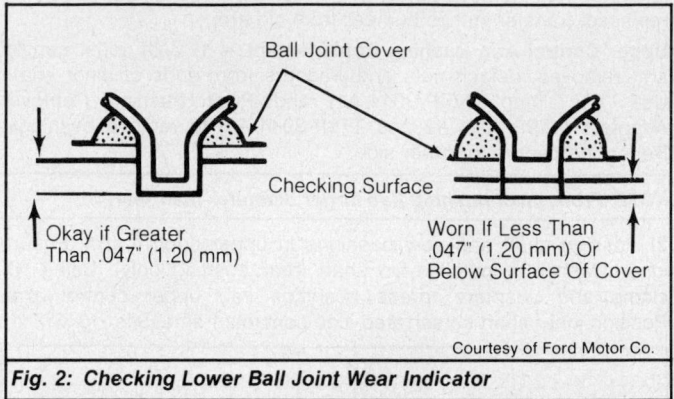

Fig. 2: Checking Lower Ball Joint Wear Indicator

2) Ball joints are acceptable if wear indicator surface projects .047" (1.20 mm) or more beyond checking surface. Ball joint is worn if less than .047" projects beyond checking surface. Replace lower control arm and ball joint as an assembly.

REMOVAL & INSTALLATION

BALL JOINTS

Ball Joints and lower control arm pivot bushings are not serviced separately and must be replaced with lower control arm as an assembly. See LOWER CONTROL ARM.

STABILIZER BAR, BUSHINGS & LINK INSULATORS

Removal – 1) Raise and support vehicle on frame hoist. To disconnect stabilizer bar from stabilizer links, remove nut, washer, and rubber insulator from link bolt. If necessary, remove remaining insulators, washers and spacers.

2) Remove bolts attaching insulator bushing clamp to stabilizer. Remove bar assembly. Detach adapter brackets from clamps. See Fig. 1.

3) Inspect stabilizer bar rubber link insulator and insulator bushings. Replace all worn or damaged components. If replacement is needed cut worn insulator bushings from stabilizer bar with sharp knife.

Installation – 1) Lubricate rubber parts of stabilizer bar with rubber lubricant. Slide new insulator bushings onto stabilizer bar. Reinstall adapter brackets on clamps. See Fig. 1.

2) Using new nut and bolt, secure each end of stabilizer bar to link insulators on lower control arm. Ensure link insulator components are installed in proper order. See Fig. 1.

3) Using new bolts, mount attaching clamps, stabilizer bar and adapter brackets onto frame side rails. Lower vehicle.

COIL SPRING

Removal – 1) Raise vehicle on hoist so control arms hang free. Remove tire and wheel assembly. Remove brake caliper and wire out of way. Remove tie rod end from steering knuckle arm. Disconnect stabilizer bar link from control arm.

2) If necessary, remove steering gear bolts. Position gear so control arm pivot bolt may be removed. Using Spring Compressor (T82P-5310-A), place tool upper plate into position in spring pocket cavity on crossmember.

NOTE: When intalling spring compressor components, ensure hooks on tool upper plate are facing center of vehicle.

3) Install compression rod into lower arm spring pocket hole, through coil spring and into upper plate. Install lower plate, lower ball nut, thrust washer, bearing and forcing nut onto compression rod. Tighten forcing nut on tool until drag on nut is felt.

4) Remove control arm-to-crossmember pivot bolts and nuts. The compression tool forcing nut may have to be tightened or loosened for easier bolt removal. Loosen compression rod forcing nut until spring tension is relieved. Remove forcing nut. Remove compression rod, coil spring and spring insulator.

Installation – 1) Position spring insulator on top of spring. Position spring into lower control arm spring pocket. Ensure spring end is positioned between 2 holes in lower arm spring pocket. See Fig. 3.

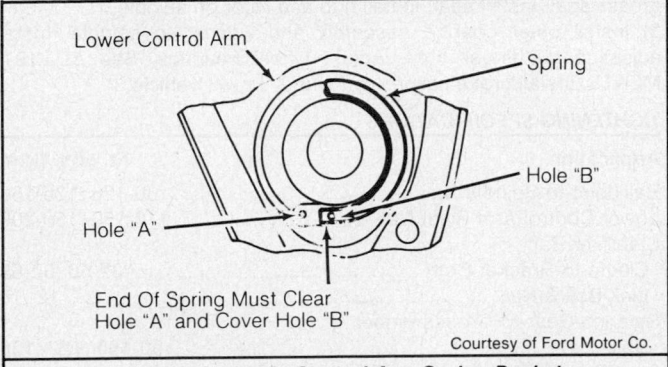

Fig. 3: Positioning Spring In Control Arm Spring Pocket

2) Position spring into upper spring seat in crossmember. Insert compressor rod through control arm and spring, then hook it to upper plate. Ensure upper plate is installed with hooks facing center of vehicle.

3) Install retaining spring compressor components. Tighten forcing nut. Position lower control arm into crossmember. Install new control arm pivot bolt and nuts finger tight. DO NOT tighten bolts and nuts at this time. Remove spring compressor.

4) Using a jack, raise control arm to normal riding height. Tighten control arm pivot bolts to specifications. Remove jack. Install tie rod end into steering knuckle. Install new cotter pin. Install brake caliper and wheel. Lower vehicle.

LOWER CONTROL ARM

Removal – 1) Raise vehicle on hoist so that control arms hang free. Remove wheel. Remove brake caliper and wire out of way. Remove brake rotor and dust shield. Disconnect tie rod assembly from steering knuckle.

2) Remove steering gear bolts (if necessary). Position gear so control arm pivot bolt may be removed. Disconnect stabilizer bar link from lower control arm.

3) Remove cotter pin from ball joint stud nut. Loosen ball joint nut 1 or 2 turns. Do not remove nut at this time. Tap steering knuckle boss sharply to relieve stud pressure. Install Spring Compressor (T82P-5310-A).

4) Tighten forcing nut on spring compressor until drag is felt on nut. Remove ball joint nut. Raise entire strut and steering knuckle assembly. Wire it out of way to obtain working room. Remove control arm-to-crossmember pivot bushing nuts and bolts.

5) The compression tool forcing nut may have to be tightened or loosened for easier bolt removal. Loosen compression rod forcing nut until spring tension is relieved. Remove forcing nut, lower control arm and coil spring.

NOTE: Manufacturer recommends replacing all nuts and bolts, once removed.

Installation – 1) To install, reverse removal procedure. Ensure spring lower end is positioned between 2 holes in lower arm spring pocket. See Fig. 3.

2) Raise lower control arm to normal position before tightening attaching nuts. Tighten ball joint stud nut to specifications. After installation, check front end alignment and adjust if necessary.

STEERING KNUCKLE

Removal – 1) Raise vehicle. Support with safety stands under both sides (at jacking pads, just behind lower control arms). Remove wheel. Remove brake caliper, rotor and dust shield. Remove stabilizer link from lower control arm.

2) Remove tie rod end from steering knuckle. Remove cotter pin from ball joint stud nut. Loosen nut 1 or 2 turns. Do not remove at this time. Tap steering knuckle sharply with hammer to relieve ball joint stud pressure.

CAUTION: Restraining devices for coil springs are recommended during all coil spring related removal procedures.

3) Place a jack under lower control arm. Compress spring and remove stud nut. Remove bolts attaching steering knuckle to shock strut. Compress shock strut until sufficient clearance is obtained. Remove steering knuckle.

Installation – 1) Place steering knuckle on ball joint stud and install stud nut. Do not tighten at this time. Lower shock strut until attaching holes are in line with steering knuckle holes. Install 2 bolts and nuts.

2) Tighten ball joint stud nut and install cotter pin. Do not back off nut to install cotter pin, tighten to align holes. Tighten shock-to-knuckle attaching nuts to specifications.

3) Lower and remove jack. Install remaining components in reverse order of removal. Check front end alignment and adjust as necessary.

NOTE: Do not use impact wrench when replacing gas-pressurized front damper assembly. All strut damper and upper mount assemblies use metric fasteners.

STRUT DAMPER & UPPER MOUNT ASSEMBLY

Removal – 1) Place ignition switch in "UNLOCKED" position. Raise vehicle by lower control arms until wheels are just off ground. From inside engine compartment, remove three 12 mm upper mount attaching bolts. DO NOT drive vehicle with these nuts removed. Do not remove pop rivet holding camber plate in position.

2) Raise vehicle. Place safety stands under frame jacking pads, rearward of wheels. Remove wheel. Remove brake caliper, wire out of way. Remove 2 lower nuts holding strut to steering knuckle, leaving bolts in place.

NOTE: Hold struts firmly during removal of last steering knuckle-to-strut bolt. Gas pressure will cause strut to fully extend when second bolt is removed.

3) Remove strut-to-knuckle mount bolts and push bracket free of knuckle. Lift strut up to compress rod and remove from steering knuckle. Pull down to remove strut from vehicle. Remove upper mount components and jounce bumper from strut if necessary. Inspect and replace components as needed.

4) Upper mounts consist of several parts, assembled on the strut rod and body mounting bracket. See Fig. 4.

NOTE: It is not necessary to replace shock struts in pairs. A damaged or worn strut may be replaced individually.

Installation – 1) If removed, install upper mount and jounce bumper on strut. Position 3 upper mount studs into body mounting pad and camber plate. Start 3 new nuts, engaging as many threads as possible. Extend strut (if necessary) and position in steering knuckle. Install new lower mounting bolts and hand start nuts.

2) Remove suspension load from lower control arms. Tighten lower mount nuts. Raise control arms and tighten 3 strut-to-upper mount nuts (in engine compartment) to specifications.

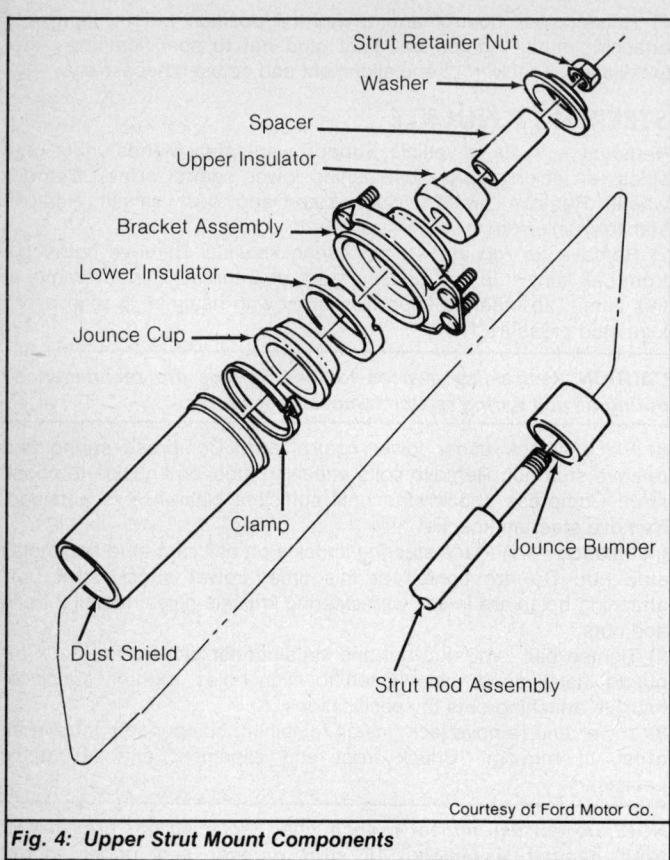

Strut Retainer Nut
Washer
Spacer
Upper Insulator
Bracket Assembly
Lower Insulator
Jounce Cup
Clamp
Jounce Bumper
Dust Shield
Strut Rod Assembly

Courtesy of Ford Motor Co.

Fig. 4: Upper Strut Mount Components

3) Install wheel. Remove safety stands and lower vehicle. Check and adjust front end alignment as needed.

WHEEL BEARINGS

Removal – 1) Raise and support vehicle. Remove wheel. Remove brake caliper and support with wire. Remove grease cap.

2) Remove cotter pin, nut lock, adjusting nut and washer from spindle. Remove outer bearing. Remove hub and rotor from spindle.

3) Remove and discard grease seal. Remove inner bearing from hub. Clean inner and outer bearings in solvent. Use compressed air to dry. DO NOT allow bearings to spin while drying.

4) Inspect bearings for damage or wear. If necessary, replace bearing and race as a set.

Installation – 1) Install new outer bearing race in hub using bearing race installer or drift punch. Install new inner bearing race using Bearing Race Installer (T73T-1202-B).

2) Thoroughly pack bearings with grease. Place inner bearing assembly in inner race. Apply a light film of grease to lips of new grease seal. Install seal. Install hub and rotor on spindle.

3) Install outer bearing assembly and washer to spindle. Install adjusting nut finger tight. Adjust wheel bearings. See ADJUST-MENTS. Install brake caliper and wheel. Lower vehicle.

TIGHTENING SPECIFICATIONS

Application	Ft. Lbs. (N.m)
Ball Joint-to-Spindle Nut	100-120 (136-163)
Lower Control Arm Pivot Nut	110-150 (150-203)
Stabilizer Bar	
Clamp-to-Bracket Bolt	37-50 (50-68)
Link Bolt & Nut	12 (16)
Steering Gear-to-Crossmember	
Bolt	90-100 (122–136)
Strut Damper	
Strut-to-Upper Mount Nut	60-75 (81-102)
Strut-to-Knuckle Mount Nut	140-200 (122-136)
Upper Mount-to Body Nut	50-75 (68-102)
Tie Rod-to-Spindle Nut	35-47 (48-64)
Wheel Bearing Adjusting Nut	¹ 17-25 (23-34)
Wheel Lug Nut	80-105 (109-142)

¹ – Specification is for bearing seating only. Adjust to 10-12 INCH lbs. (1.1-1.7 N.m) after seating.

Acclaim, Aries, Daytona, Dynasty, Lancer, LeBaron, LeBaron GTS, New Yorker, Reliant, Shadow, Spirit, Sundance

DESCRIPTION

Rear suspension is a trailing arm, solid type design. An integral tubular stabilizer bar is positioned inside the axle and is attached to the spindle mounting plates at either end of the axle channel. The trailing arms and coil spring seats are welded directly to the axle. The axle assembly is located fore and aft by blade-type trailing arms, attached to body mounted pivots. A track bar provides lateral stability. Coil springs and vertically-mounted shock absorbers complete the suspension assembly. *See Fig. 1.*

ADJUSTMENTS

CAMBER & TOE-IN

See appropriate article in WHEEL ALIGNMENT section.

RIDING HEIGHT

See RIDING HEIGHT SPECIFICATIONS article in WHEEL ALIGNMENT section.

REAR WHEEL BEARINGS

NOTE: Under normal service, rear wheel bearings should be inspected, lubricated, and adjusted whenever rear brakes are serviced, or at least every 30,000 miles. Lubricate wheel bearings using high temperature wheel bearing grease.

Tighten adjusting nut to 240-300 INCH lbs. (27-33 N.m) while rotating wheel. Stop rotation and back off adjusting nut 1/4 turn. Finger tighten adjusting nut while again rotating wheel. Position lock nut with slots in line with cotter pin hole. Install cotter pin.

REMOVAL & INSTALLATION

SHOCK ABSORBERS

Removal & Installation – Raise vehicle and support axle. Remove wheel and tire assembly. Disconnect air lines (if equipped). Remove upper and lower shock absorber mounting bolts and remove shock absorbers. To install shock absorber, reverse removal procedure. Tighten all nuts and bolts to specifications.

COIL SPRINGS

Removal & Installation – 1) Raise vehicle and support axle assembly. Remove both lower shock absorber mounting bolts. Remove link from track bar-to-load leveling sensor (if equipped). Lower the axle assembly until the spring and upper spring isolator can be removed.

2) Remove 2 screws holding isolator cup to side rail and remove entire assembly. To install coil spring, reverse removal procedure. Tighten shock absorber nuts with weight of vehicle on spring.

NOTE: Do not stretch brake hoses when lowering axle assembly.

TRACK BAR, BRACE & BRACKET

Removal & Installation – 1) Raise vehicle. Raise rear axle to curb height with jack stands. Disconnect load leveling system sensor link from track bar (if equipped). Remove track bar-to-axle pivot bolt and track bar-to-frame pivot bolt.

2) Remove track bar. Remove diagonal brace-to-underbody stud nut and brace. Remove 2 track bar support bracket-to-frame rail bolts and remove bracket.

3) To install track bar and brace, reverse removal procedure. Tighten all bolts to specifications.

PIVOT BUSHING

Removal – 1) Raise vehicle. Remove wheel and tire assembly. Remove brake hose mounting bracket bolt. Disconnect parking brake cable guide at the connector and from the front hanger bracket.

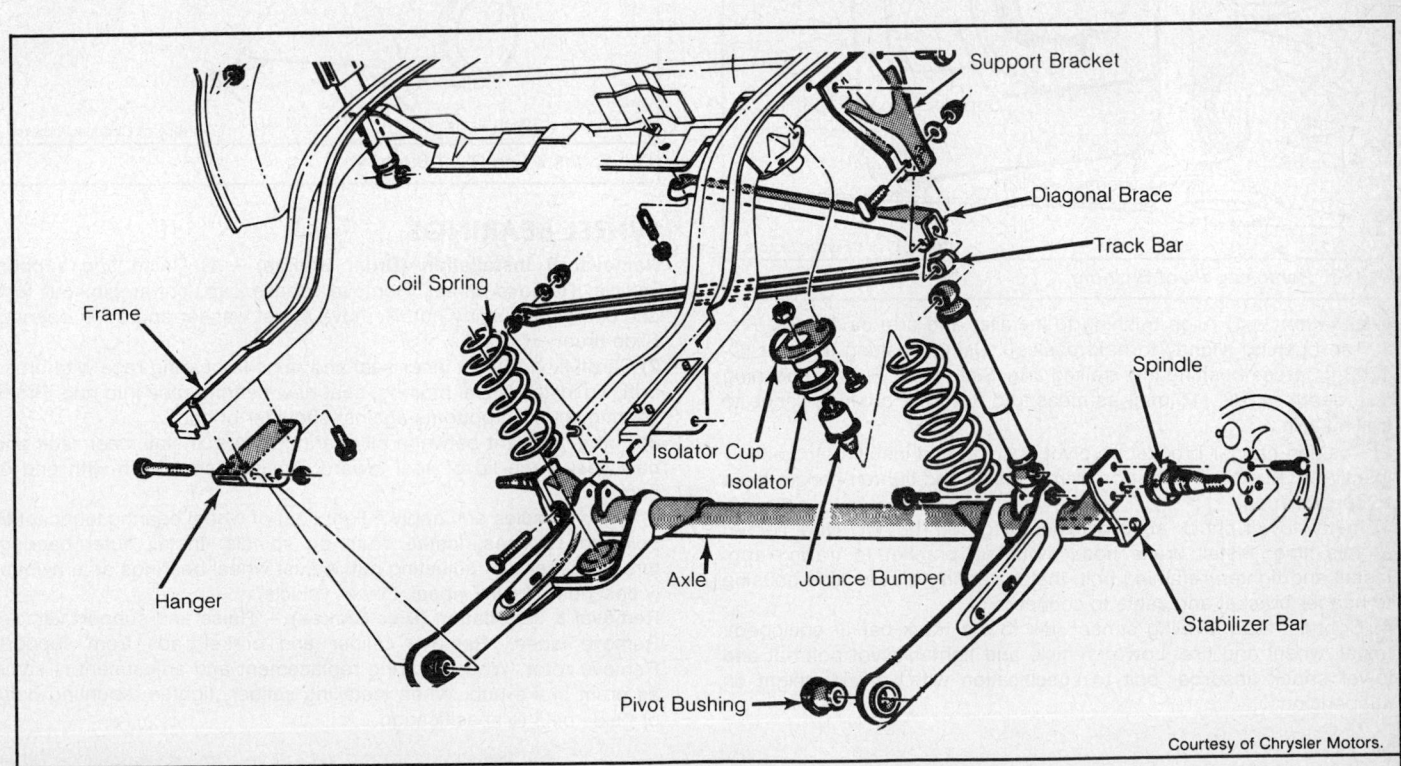

Courtesy of Chrysler Motors.

Fig. 1: Exploded View Of Rear Suspension Assembly

12-34

1989 REAR SUSPENSION
Chrysler Motors FWD — Exc. Horizon & Omni (Cont.)

2) Disconnect load leveling system sensor link from the track bar (if equipped). Support rear axle assembly and remove lower shock absorber mounting bolts. Remove hanger bracket-to-frame side rail bolts. *See Fig. 2.*

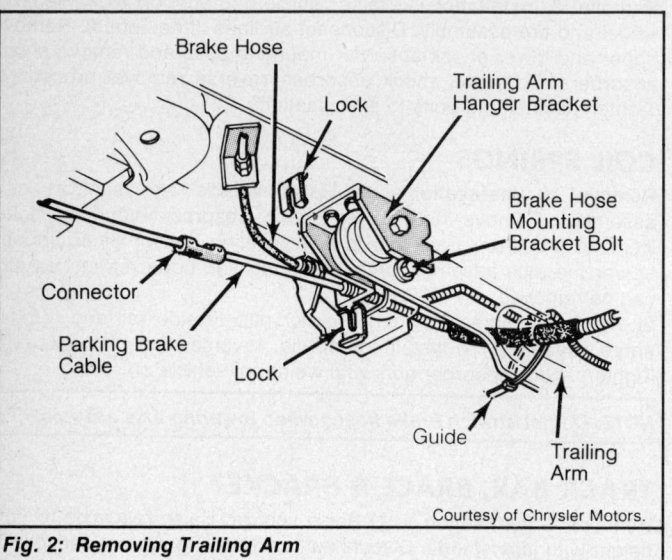

Fig. 2: Removing Trailing Arm

3) Lower axle assembly far enough to remove pivot bolt and hanger bracket. Position Bushing Remover (C-4702-7) over Support Cup (C-4366-1) and Press (C-4212).

4) Position assembly with support cup supporting trailing arm. Turn screw on press into remover and press bushing out. *See Fig. 3.*

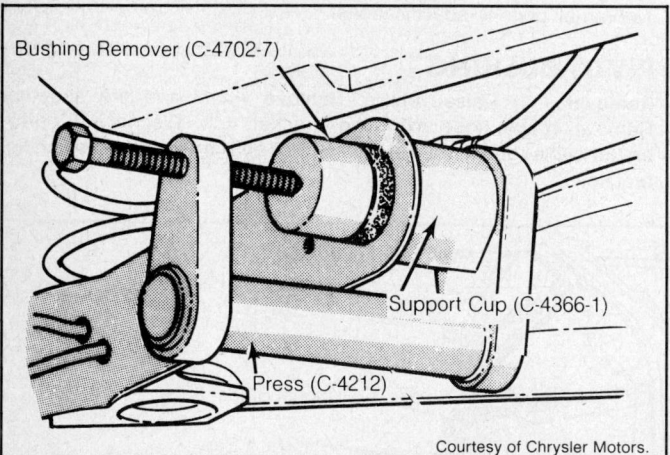

Fig. 3: Removing Pivot Bushing

Installation — 1) Align bushing to installer and arm cavity. *See Fig. 4.* Tap bushing slightly to hold position. Using Bushing Installer (C-4702-2), press bushing into trailing arm. *See Fig. 5.* Press in bushing to a depth of 5/8" (16 mm) as measured from the bushing flange to trailing arm.

2) Position hanger bracket on pivot bushing and install bolt. Loosely install nut. Position hanger on frame. Install and tighten hanger bolts to specification.

3) Install lower shock absorber mounting bolt, but DO NOT tighten at this time. Install brake hose mounting bracket to trailing arm. Install and tighten retaining bolt. Install parking brake cable housing to hanger bracket and cable to connector.

4) Connect load leveling sensor link to the track bar (if equipped). Install wheel and tire. Lower vehicle and tighten pivot bolt nut and lower shock absorber bolt to specification with vehicle weight on suspension.

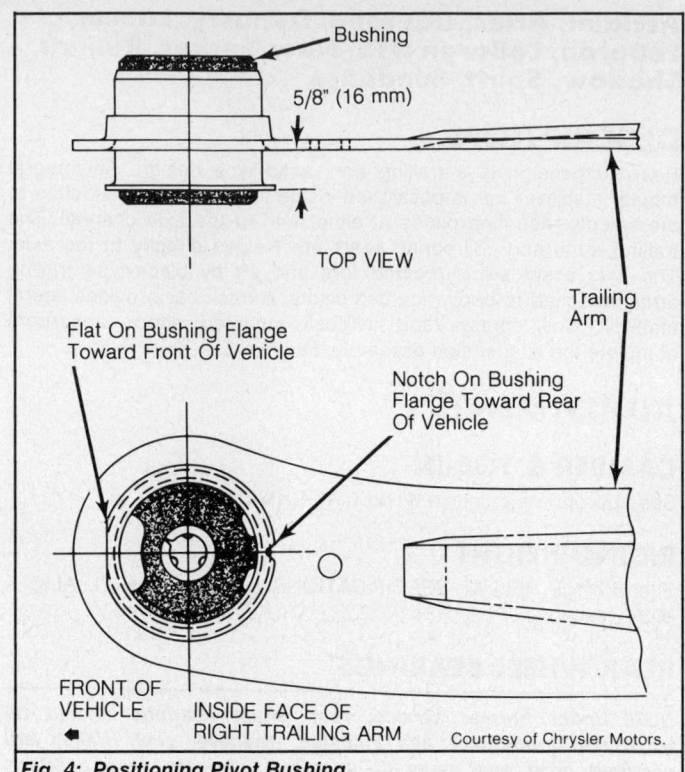

Fig. 4: Positioning Pivot Bushing

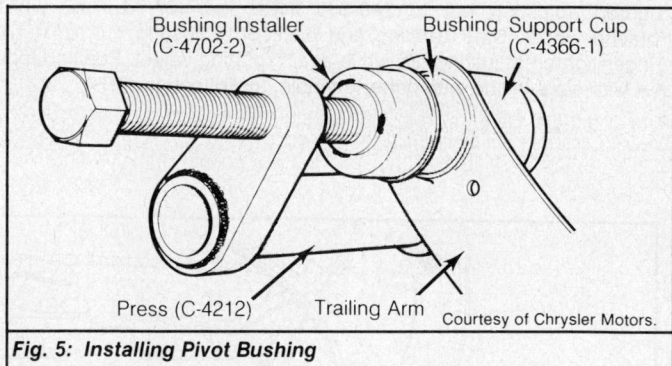

Fig. 5: Installing Pivot Bushing

WHEEL BEARINGS

Removal & Installation (Drum Brakes) — 1) Raise and support vehicle. Remove wheel. Remove grease cap, cotter pin, nut lock and bearing adjusting nut. Remove thrust washer and outer bearing. Slide drum off spindle.

2) Carefully drive out inner seal and remove bearing race with brass drift. To install wheel bearing, seat new bearing race into hub. Press bearing in until it bottoms against shoulder of hub.

3) Force lubricant between all bearing rollers. Install inner race and new seal. Face lip of seal inward. Position seal flush with end of hub.

4) Clean spindles and apply a light coat of wheel bearing lubricant to polished surfaces. Install drum on spindle. Install outer bearing, thrust washer and adjusting nut. Adjust wheel bearings as previously described. Install wheel. Lower vehicle.

Removal & Installation (Disc Brakes) — Raise and support vehicle. Remove wheel. Remove caliper and brake pads from support. Remove rotor. Wheel bearing replacement and adjustment is same as drum brake hub. When installing caliper, tighten mounting bolts or guide pins to specification.

1989 REAR SUSPENSION
Chrysler Motors FWD — Exc. Horizon & Omni (Cont.)

12-35

REAR AXLE ASSEMBLY

Removal & Installation – 1) Raise vehicle and support axle with jack stands. Remove wheels. Separate parking brake cable at connector and detach. Separate brake tube assembly from brake hose at trailing arm support bracket and remove retaining clip.

2) Disconnect height sensor link from track bar, if equipped with automatic load leveling system. Remove lower shock absorber bolts and track bar-to-axle bolts.

3) Support track bar end with wire. Lower axle until spring and isolator assembly can be removed. Support pivot bushing end of trailing arms and axle beam with jack stands.

4) Remove pivot bushing hanger bracket-to-frame bolts. Lower and remove axle assembly from vehicle. If required, remove brake drum assembly, spindle and brake support.

5) To install rear axle, reverse removal procedure. Tighten lower shock absorber bolts and track bar bolts with vehicle weight on the suspension. Bleed brake system.

TIGHTENING SPECIFICATIONS

Application	Ft. Lbs. (N.m)
Drum & Disc Brake Support	
Plate-to-Rear Axle Bolt	45-60 (61-81)
Rear Disc Brake	
Adapter Mount Bolts	176-258 (130-190)
Shock Absorber	
Lower Bolt	45 (61)
Upper Nut	45 (61)
Track Bar	
Diagonal Brace-to-Stud Nut	55 (75)
Support Bracket-to-Frame Bolts	40 (54)
Track Bar-to-Axle Pivot Bolt	70 (95)
Track Bar-to-Frame Pivot Bolt	55 (75)
Track Bar Brace-to-Stud Nut	55 (75)
Trailing Arm	
Hanger Bracket Bolts	40 (54)
Pivot Bolt Nut	45 (61)
Wheel Stud Nuts	95 (129)

	INCH Lbs. (N.m)
Brake Hose Mounting Bracket	95 (11)
Caliper Mount Bolts	155-230 (17-25)
Isolator Cup	70 (8)

DESCRIPTION

Rear suspension is a semi-independent trailing arm type. Some models are equipped with an integral anti-sway bar. Spindles are attached to 2 trailing arms that extend rearward from mounting points on body.

Each arm is isolated from the body by rubber pivot bushings. A crossmember is welded between trailing arms, providing anti-sway stabilization for the rear suspension. Coil springs surrounding shock absorbers are used to dampen road variations. *See Fig. 1.*

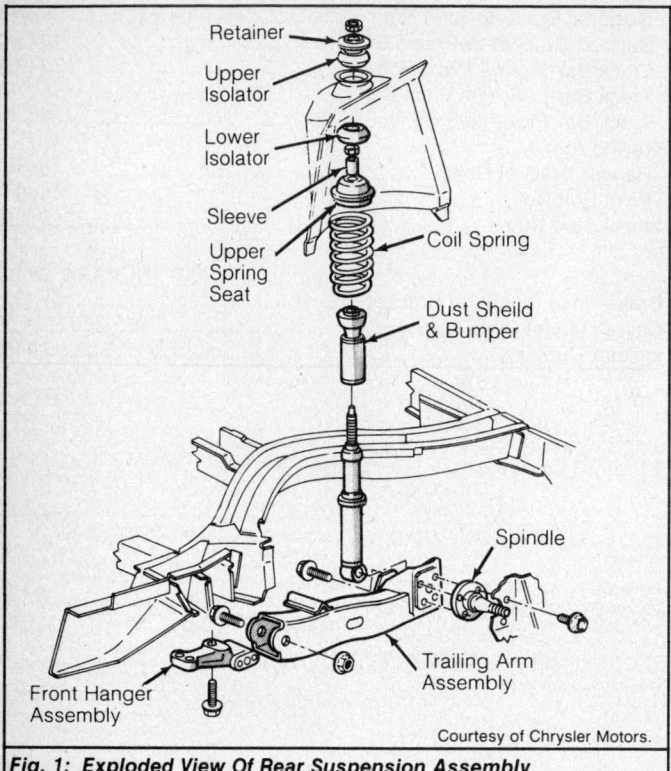

Fig. 1: Exploded View Of Rear Suspension Assembly

Retainer
Upper Isolator
Lower Isolator
Sleeve
Upper Spring Seat
Coil Spring
Dust Sheild & Bumper
Spindle
Trailing Arm Assembly
Front Hanger Assembly
Courtesy of Chrysler Motors.

ADJUSTMENTS

CAMBER & TOE-IN

See appropriate article in the WHEEL ALIGNMENT section.

RIDING HEIGHT

See RIDING HEIGHT SPECIFICATIONS article in WHEEL ALIGNMENT section.

REAR WHEEL BEARINGS

1) Tighten spindle adjusting nut to 240-300 INCH lbs. (27-34 N.m), while rotating wheel. Back off adjusting nut 1/4 turn to release bearing preload. Finger tighten adjusting nut.
2) Position lock nut, aligning one pair of slots in line with cotter pin hole. Install new cotter pin. Adjustment should provide .001-.003" (.03-.08 mm) end play. Clean and install grease cap.

REMOVAL & INSTALLATION

SHOCK ABSORBERS & COIL SPRINGS

Removal – Remove upper shock absorber mounting nut cap, located inside vehicle over rear wheelwell. On 2-door models, remove lower rear trim quarter panel. On all models, remove mounting nut, retainer and isolator. Raise and support vehicle. Remove bottom shock absorber mount bolt. Remove spring and shock absorber from trailing arm bracket.

Disassembly & Reassembly – 1) Compress coil spring using Spring Compressor (C-4838). Tighten spring compressor evenly until pressure is relieved from upper spring seat. Hold flat end of shock rod. Loosen retaining nut. Remove lower isolator, shock rod sleeve and upper spring seat. Remove shock absorber.

CAUTION: If coil spring is not compressed enough, serious injury could occur when retaining nut is loosened.

2) Remove jounce bumper and dust shield from shock rod. Remove lower spring seat. *See Fig. 1.* To reassemble shock assembly, reverse disassembly procedure. Make sure leveled surface on both spring seats are in position against ends of coil spring.

Installation – To install shock assembly, reverse removal procedure. When installing assembly in vehicle, leave lower shock absorber bolt loose. Tighten bolt after vehicle is resting on ground.

REAR AXLE ASSEMBLY

Removal & Installation – 1) Raise and support vehicle. Remove wheels. Remove brake fittings and retaining clips that hold the flexible brake lines. Remove parking brake cable adjusting nut. Release both parking brake cables from the bracket. Pull parking brake cables through the bracket.
2) Remove wheel bearing dust cap. Remove cotter pin, lock nut, adjusting nut, washer and outer wheel bearing. Remove brake drum assembly. Remove 4 brake assembly and spindle retaining bolts. Set spindle aside. Hang brake assembly out of the way using a piece of wire.
3) Support rear axle assembly with jacks. Remove shock absorber lower mounting bolts. Remove trailing arm-to-hanger bracket mounting bolt. Lower jacks and remove rear axle assembly.
4) To install, reverse removal procedure. Tighten mounting bolts to specification with weight of vehicle on the suspension. Bleed and readjust brakes.

WHEEL BEARINGS

NOTE: Under normal service, rear wheel bearings should be inspected, lubricated and adjusted whenever rear brakes are serviced or at least every 30,000 miles. Lubricate wheel bearings using high temperature wheel bearing grease.

Removal – Raise and support vehicle. Remove dust cap, cotter pin, lock nut, adjusting nut and washer. Remove outer bearing. Slide drum off spindle. Carefully drive out inner seal and remove inner bearing inner race. Remove inner and outer bearing races with a non-metallic rod.

Installation – 1) Seat new inner and outer bearing outer races against shoulder in hub. Force lubricant between all bearing rollers. Install inner bearing inner race and new seal. Position seal lip inward. Install seal flush with end of hub.
2) Install drum on spindle and install outer bearing, washer and adjusting nut. Adjust wheel bearings as previously described. Install lock nut and new cotter pin. Install wheel and tire assembly and lower vehicle.

TIGHTENING SPECIFICATIONS

Application	Ft. Lbs. (N.m)
Shock Absorber Lower Bolt	40 (55)
Upper Nut	20 (27)
Spindle Retaining Bolts	55 (75)
Trailing Arm-to-Hanger Nuts	40 (55)
Wheel Lug Nuts	85 (115)

Premier

DESCRIPTION

The rear axle and suspension consists of 2 trailing arms connected to a "V" shaped crossmember. Axle assembly is mounted to the body by the use of 2 torsion support brackets which contain rubber bushings. An axle shaft is attached to the trailing arms.

Hub and bearings are mounted on axle shaft. Hub and bearings are non-serviceable and must be replaced as a complete unit.

Gas charged (high pressure) shock absorbers are mounted on each trailing arm and to the body. Use of the 2 suspension torsion bars (front bars) and 2 anti-sway torsion bars (rear bars) are used for providing suspension action for the rear axle.

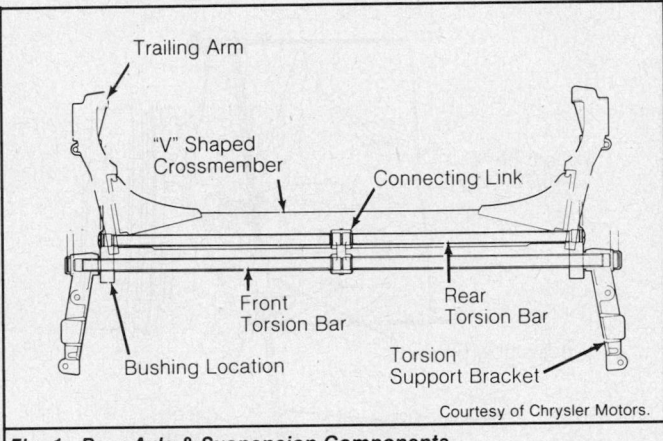

Courtesy of Chrysler Motors.

Fig. 1: Rear Axle & Suspension Components

ADJUSTMENTS

REAR WHEEL BEARINGS

The hub and bearings are non-serviceable and must be replaced as a complete unit. If axial play exceeds .001 (.03 mm), replace hub and bearing assembly.

RIDING HEIGHT

To check riding height, see RIDING HEIGHT in this article.

REMOVAL & INSTALLATION

REAR AXLE ASSEMBLY

CAUTION: Vehicle must not be raised under the "V" shaped channel on rear axle or damage to axle could result.

Removal – 1) Torsion bars DO NOT require removal prior to rear axle removal. Raise and support vehicle. Remove wheels. Support weight of rear axle at each trailing suspension arm. Disconnect shock absorbers at trailing arms.
2) Loosen emergency brake cable adjusting nuts to allow enough clearance for cable removal. Remove parking brake cables from adjusting bracket.

CAUTION: Damage to axle may result if a lifting force is applied to jack placed under rear axle.

3) Disconnect brake hoses at rear axle. Place jack under rear axle. Remove torsion support bracket retaining bolts from each side. Lower and remove rear axle.

Installation – To install reverse removal procedure. Tighten bolts to specification. See TIGHTENING SPECIFICATIONS table at end of this article. Adjust rear brakes and parking brake cable. Bleed brake system.

HUB & BEARING ASSEMBLY

Inspection – 1) Raise and support vehicle. Remove wheel. Remove plastic cap from center of hub. Install dial indicator on brake drum with stem resting against end of axle shaft
2) Rotate wheel hub and measure the wheel bearing axial play. Replace hub and bearing assembly if movement exceeds .001" (.03 mm).

Removal – 1) Raise and support vehicle. Remove wheel. Remove brake drum-to-axle shaft retaining clips (if equipped). Remove plastic cap from center of hub. Remove brake drum.
2) Remove axle shaft-to-hub lock nut. Remove hub assembly from axle shaft. If necessary, use a hub puller to remove hub from axle shaft.

Installation – To install, reverse removal procedure. Lightly oil axle shaft prior to hub installation. Install new axle shaft retaining nut. Tighten bolts to specification. See TIGHTENING SPECIFICATIONS table at end of this article. Adjust brakes if necessary.

NOTE: Always replace axle shaft retaining nut once removed.

AXLE SHAFT

Removal – Raise and support vehicle. Remove hub and bearing assembly. See HUB & BEARING ASSEMBLY under REMOVAL in this article. Remove axle shaft-to-trailing arm retaining bolts. Remove brake backing plate-to-axle shaft retaining bolt. Remove axle shaft. Remove the brake backing plate.

Installation – 1) Install brake backing plate bolt finger tight. Coat axle shaft retaining bolts with Loctite prior to installation.
2) Using a criss-cross pattern, tighten axle shaft retaining bolts to specification. Tighten brake backing plate bolt. Install hub & bearing assembly, See HUB & BEARING ASSEMBLY under INSTALLATION in this article. Use a new axle shaft lock nut. Tighten all bolts to specification. See TIGHTENING SPECIFICATIONS table at end of this article.

SHOCK ABSORBERS

Removal – 1) Raise and support vehicle. Place jack under trailing arm below shock absorber lower mounting area. Raise jack to release tension on shock absorber.
2) Remove upper and lower shock absorber retaining bolts. Remove shock absorber.

Installation – To install, reverse removal procedure. Tighten bolts to specification. See TIGHTENING SPECIFICATIONS table at end of this article.

TORSION BARS

Removal – 1) Raise and support vehicle. Remove wheels. Remove shock absorbers. See SHOCK ABSORBER under REMOVAL &

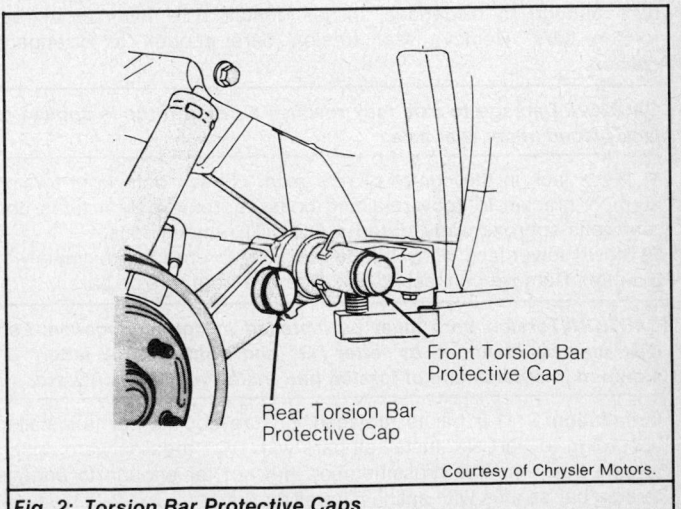

Courtesy of Chrysler Motors.

Fig. 2: Torsion Bar Protective Caps

INSTALLATION in this article. Pry protective caps from both ends of front torsion bars. Unscrew protective caps from ends of rear torsion bars. *See Fig. 2.*

bar mountings are marked "D" for initial positioning of suspension. *See Fig. 3.* Rear torsion bars must be marked prior to removal. This mark will be referred to as "E".

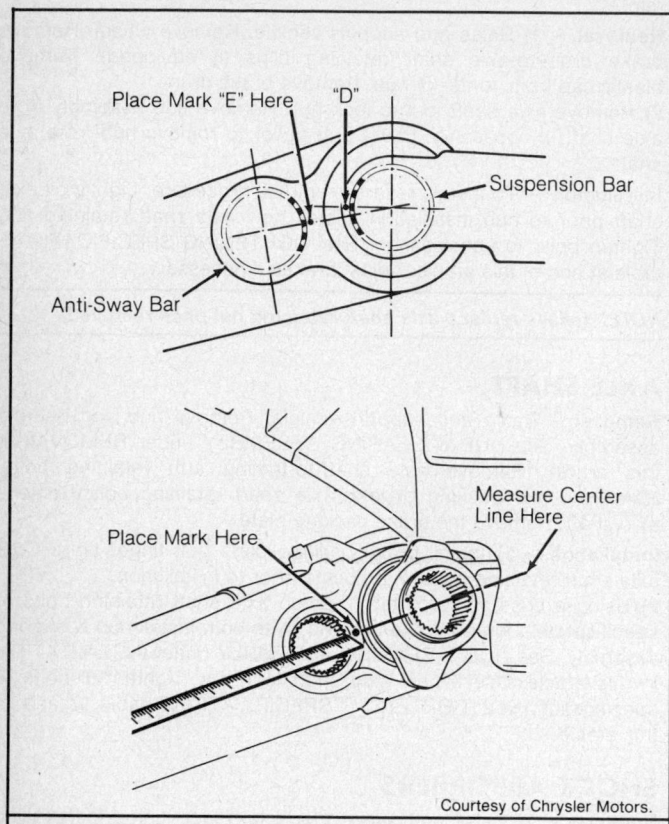

Fig. 3: Determining Torsion Bar Locations

3) Place straightedge on center line of the 2 mounting holes. Punch a mark into trailing arm adjacent to rear torsion bar spline groove. *See Fig. 3.* Note and record location of the DOTS located on the end of all torsion bars in relation to the "D" and "E" marks. *See Fig. 3.*

NOTE: Different DOT locations are determined by vehicle application. Location in relation to "D" and "E" marks may vary by application.

4) Install slide hammer in front torsion bars. Remove front torsion bars enough to disengage splines. Install slide hammer in rear torsion bars. Remove rear torsion bars enough to disengage splines.

CAUTION: Damage to axle may result if a lifting force is applied to jack placed under rear axle.

5) Place jack in the center of rear axle. Loosen both front torsion support bracket-to-body retaining bolts approximately 4 turns and rear bolts approximately 10 turns. DO NOT remove bolts.

6) Slowly lower jack, allowing the rear axle to drop approximately 1" (25 mm). Remove connecting link. Remove front torsion bars.

CAUTION: Torsion bars must be installed in correct location. Left side may be identified by letter "G" and right side by letter "D" stamped in outside end of torsion bar. Install with DOT outward.

Installation – 1) If bar is replaced, ensure correct bar is installed according to Part No. Install all bars with DOT area outward. Insert torsion bars into the crossmember, but not far enough to engage torsion bar splines with splines in trailing arm.

2) Ensure proper torsion bar is installed in correct location. Left side may be identified by letter "G" and right side by letter "D", stamped in outside end of torsion bar.

3) Raise jack and tighten front and rear torsion support bracket bolts to 68 ft. lbs. (92 N.m). Trailing arm distance must now be set. Adjust 2 Rods (Sus. Lm.02) to the dimension of 17 15/16" (456 mm). *See Fig. 4.*

4) Using trailing arm Positioning Tool (Sus. Lm.02), Insert upper attaching bolt through eyelet and loosely tighten it. Insert Spacer (T.Ar. 1056) into the lower shock absorber attaching bolt hole, and insert adjustable bracket hub into spacer. *See Fig. 4.* Apply all purpose lubricant to torsion bar splines.

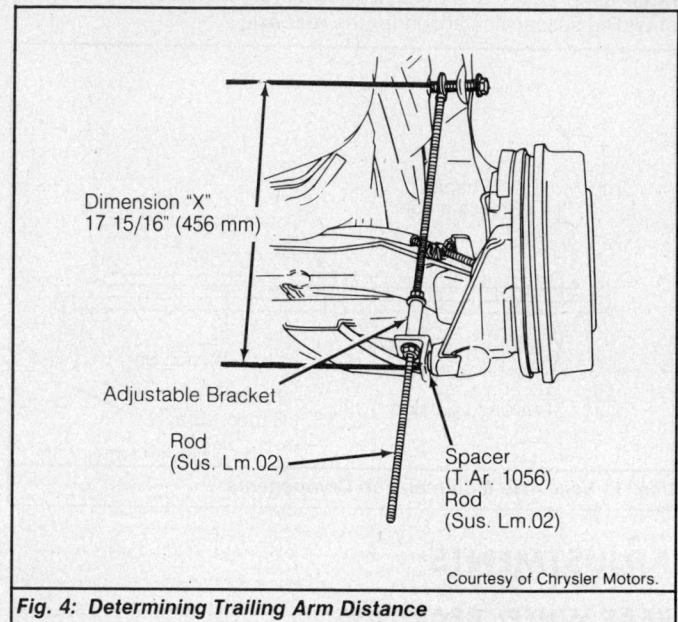

Fig. 4: Determining Trailing Arm Distance

5) Ensure DOT reference is located in original location and same on both sides of vehicle. Refer to previously noted torsion bar DOT reference positions. See TORSION BAR under REMOVAL in this article.

6) Correctly mesh spline of one of the rear torsion bars with trailing arm spline. Mesh the connecting link spline with spline of rear torsion bar. Make sure connecting link is correctly centered within V shaped channel in crossmember. *See Fig. 5.*

7) Mesh spline of opposite rear torsion bar with trailing arm spline and connecting link spline. Mesh spline of one of the front torsion bars with torsion support bracket spline and connecting link spline.

8) Mesh spline of opposite front torsion bar with torsion support bracket spline and connecting link spline.

NOTE: If torsion bars were not replaced, ensure that all four torsion bars are installed in their original position.

9) Once torsion bars are installed, all bars must be checked for correct centering. Using brass drift, tap outer end of front torsion bars so it is recessed 3/4"-7/8" (.750-.875 mm) from outer edge of torsion support bracket.

10) Tap on the ends of the rear torsion bar until outer end is recessed 3/16"-5/16" (.188-.313 mm) from outer edge of trailing arm. Insert retaining clips against the ends of torsion bars. Install protective caps at ends of torsion bars.

11) Remove trailing arm positioning tool. Install shock absorbers. See SHOCK ABSORBER under REMOVAL & INSTALLATION in this article. Tighten bolts to specification. See TIGHTENING SPECIFICATIONS at end of this article. Check riding height. See RIDING HEIGHT in this article.

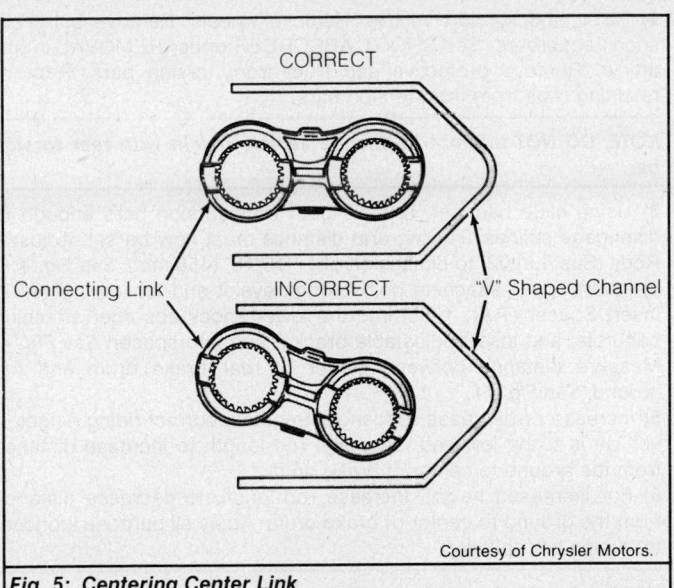

Fig. 5: Centering Center Link

Courtesy of Chrysler Motors.

TORSION SUPPORT BRACKET BUSHINGS

Removal – 1) Remove torsion bars from crossmember. See TORSION BAR in this article. Remove rear axle. See REAR AXLE ASSEMBLY in this article. Place Bushing Driver (T.Ar. 1056) against bushing and install a 2 jaw extractor puller on the trailing arm side of bushing. *See Fig. 6.*

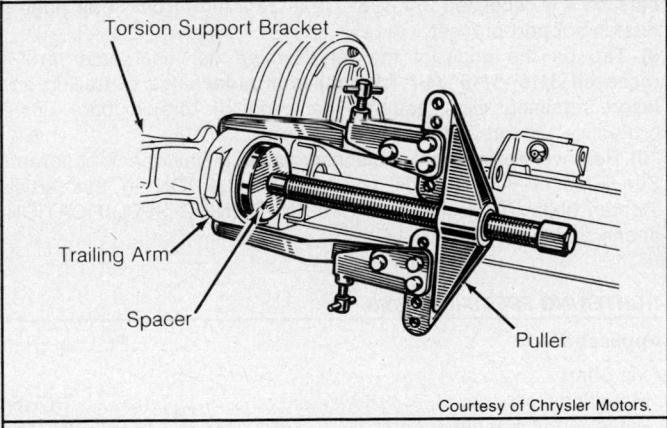

Fig. 6: Removing Torsion Support Bracket From Axle

Courtesy of Chrysler Motors.

2) To remove bushing, weld a 1" (26 mm) nut on inside of bushing. Using a press and Bearing Splitter (J-22912-01), press bushing from torsion support backet.

Installation – 1) Place bushing on trailing arm bushing bar. Using Bushing Installer (T.Ar. 1056), install bushing until it is even with outside of bore *See Fig. 7.*

2) Position torsion support bracket at trailing arm so that bracket bushing bore is mated with bushing. Torsion support bracket must be properly positioned. Measure dimension "X" by placing a straightedge across top of torsion support bracket-to-body contact area. Place torsion support bracket so that dimension "X" is 27/32"-29/32" (22-24 mm). *See Fig. 8.*

3) Once correct dimension is obtained, using Bushing Installer (T.Ar. 1056), press bushing into bushing bore, and press torsion support bracket against trailing arm. *See Fig. 9.*

4) Press bushings into left and right torsion support bracket bushing bores until distance between 2 rear bolt hole centerlines is 52" (1320.8 mm). *See Fig. 10.*

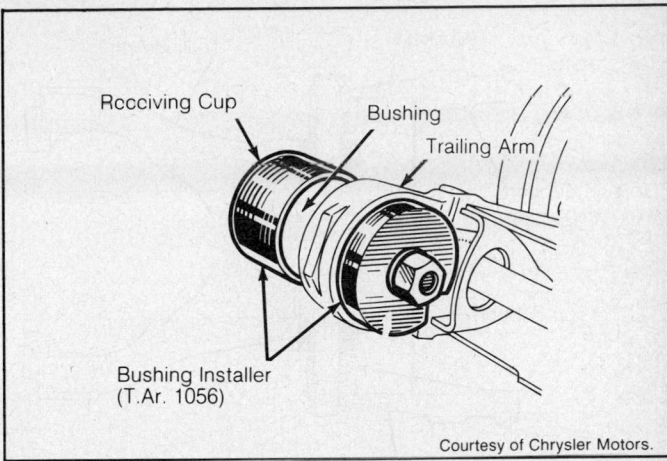

Fig. 7: Installing Torsion Support Bracket Bushing

Courtesy of Chrysler Motors.

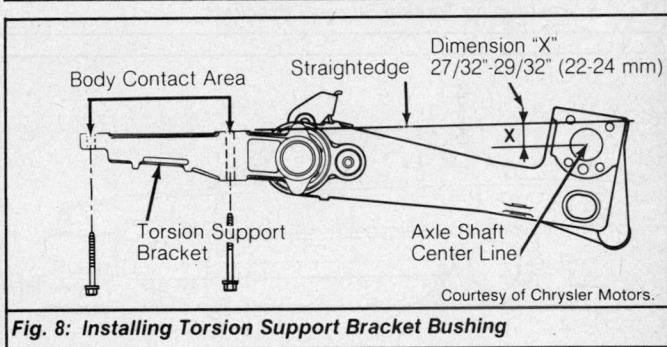

Fig. 8: Installing Torsion Support Bracket Bushing

Courtesy of Chrysler Motors.

NOTE: Distance between left and right bolt hole centerlines is critical. It establishes correct installation alignment between bolt holes and nut plates on vehicle chassis.

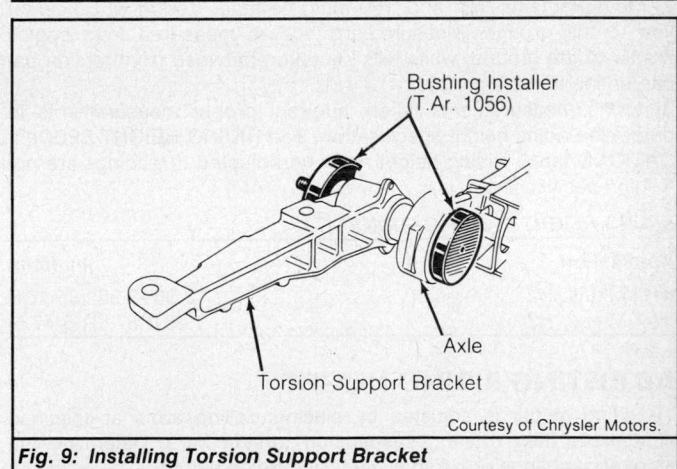

Fig. 9: Installing Torsion Support Bracket

Courtesy of Chrysler Motors.

5) To complete installation, reverse removal procedure for remaining components. Tighten bolts to specification. See TIGHTENING SPECIFICATIONS table at end of this article. Check riding height. See RIDING HEIGHT in this article.

RIDING HEIGHT

NOTE: Riding height should be measured with vehicle unloaded, on flat surface, full tank of gasoline, and tires having the same recommended pressure.

CHECKING RIDING HEIGHT

1) Measure riding height at locations indicated. *See Fig. 11.*

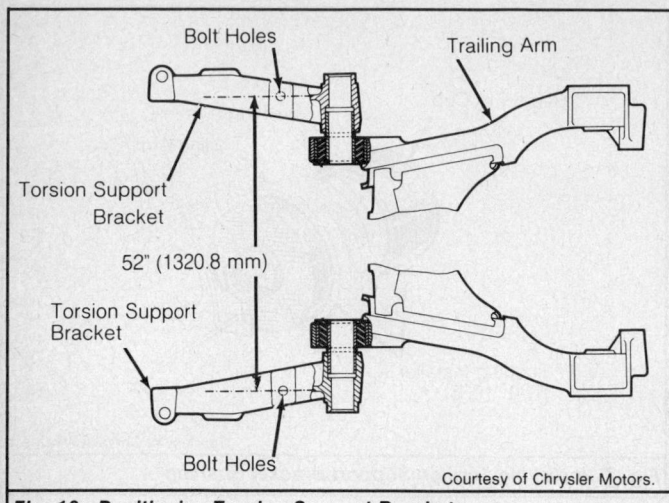

Fig. 10: Positioning Torsion Support Brackets

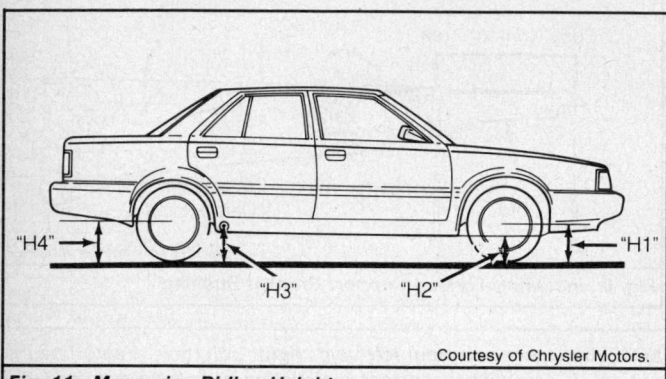

Fig. 11: Measuring Riding Height

2) Measurements "H1" and "H4" must be measured at wheel center line to the ground. Measurement "H2" is measured from engine cradle to the ground, while "H3 " is taken between front torsion bar center line and the ground.

3) Using measurements taken, subtract proper measurements to determine riding height specification. See RIDING HEIGHT SPECIFICATIONS table. Riding height must be adjusted if readings are not within specification.

RIDING HEIGHT SPECIFICATIONS

Application	In. (mm)
"H1" Minus "H2"	3.36"-3.98" (85-101)
"H4" Minus "H3"	1.25-1.87 (31.5-47.5)

ADJUSTING RIDING HEIGHT

1) Riding height is adjusted by placing trailing arms at specified dimension, then rotating suspension torsion bars. Determine the amount of change required by checking riding height.

2) Raise and support vehicle. Remove wheels. Remove both rear shock absorbers. See SHOCK ABSORBER under REMOVAL in this article. Remove protective cap from front torsion bars. Remove retaining clips from front torsion bars.

NOTE: DO NOT attempt to change vehicle height with rear torsion bar.

3) Using slide hammer, remove both front torsion bars enough to disengage splines. Trailing arm distance must now be set. Adjust 2 Rods (Sus. Lm.02) to dimension of 17 15/16" (456 mm). *See Fig. 4.*

4) Insert upper attaching bolt through eyelet and loosely tighten it. Insert Spacer (T.Ar. 1056) into the lower shock absorber attaching bolt hole, and insert adjustable bracket hub into spacer. *See Fig. 4.* Measure distance between center of rear brake drum and the ground. *See Fig. 11.*

5) Increase or decrease rod length to obtain correct riding height. If vehicle is to be lowered, decrease rod length to increase distance from the ground to center of brake drum.

6) For increased height, increase rod length to decrease distance from the ground to center of brake drum. Apply all purpose lubricant to torsion bar splines.

NOTE: DO NOT force torsion bar into position. This could cause spline damage.

7) Slowly rotate suspension bar until spline alignment is obtained and bar will slide in easily. Note the number of teeth from drilled hole in the end of torsion bar to the "D" mark. *See Fig. 3.* Install remaining suspension bar in the same spline location.

8) Once torsion bars are installed, all bars must be checked for correct centering. Using brass drift, tap outer end of front torsion bars so it is recessed 3/4"-7/8" (19.0- 22.2 mm) from outer edge of torsion support bracket.

9) Tap on the ends of the rear torsion bar until outer end is recessed 3/16"-5/16" (4.7-7.9 mm) from outer edge of trailing arm. Insert retaining clips against the ends of torsion bars. Install protective caps at ends of torsion bars.

10) Remove trailing arm positioning tools. Install shock absorbers. See SHOCK ABSORBER under INSTALLATION in this article. Tighten bolts to specification. See TIGHTENING SPECIFICATIONS at end of this article.

TIGHTENING SPECIFICATIONS

Application	Ft. Lbs. (N.m)
Axle Shaft	
Mounting Bolt	[1] 47 (64)
Wheel Hub Lock nut	123 (167)
Backing Plate	12 (16)
Shock Absorber Bolt	
Lower	85 (115)
Upper	60 (81)
Torsion Support Bracket Bolt	68 (92)
Wheel Lug Nut	63 (85)

[1] – Use crisscross pattern when tightening.

DESCRIPTION

These vehicles use a modified MacPherson strut independent rear suspension. Each side consists of a shock strut, lower control arm, tie rod, forged spindle and a coil spring mounted between the lower control arm and the body crossmember.

The shock strut assembly is attached to the body side panel by a rubber insulated top mount assembly and nut. The lower end is bolted to the spindle. The lower control arm attaches to the underbody and the spindle. The tie rod attaches to the underbody and the spindle.

ADJUSTMENTS

WHEEL ALIGNMENT

See appropriate article in WHEEL ALIGNMENT section.

RIDING HEIGHT

See RIDING HEIGHT SPECIFICATIONS article in WHEEL ALIGNMENT section.

REAR WHEEL BEARINGS

1) Raise and support vehicle. Remove wheel and tire. Remove grease cap and cotter pin. Remove nut retainer. Back off adjusting nut one full turn. Tighten nut to 17-25 ft. lbs. (23-34 N.m), while rotating hub and drum assembly to seat bearings.

2) Loosen adjusting nut 1/2 turn and retighten nut to 24-28 INCH lbs. (2.7-3.2 N.m), using an INCH lb. torque wrench. Position adjusting nut retainer over adjusting nut. Align slots in nut retainer flange with cotter pin hole in spindle.

3) Install new cotter pin. Check hub rotation. If hub rotates freely, install grease cap. If not, check bearings for damage and replace as necessary. Install wheel and tire assembly and wheel cover (if equipped). Lower vehicle and test drive.

REMOVAL & INSTALLATION

COIL SPRING

NOTE: If a twin-post hoist is used, support rear with jack stands placed under jack pads, forward of the tie rod bracket. Lower rear post out of way.

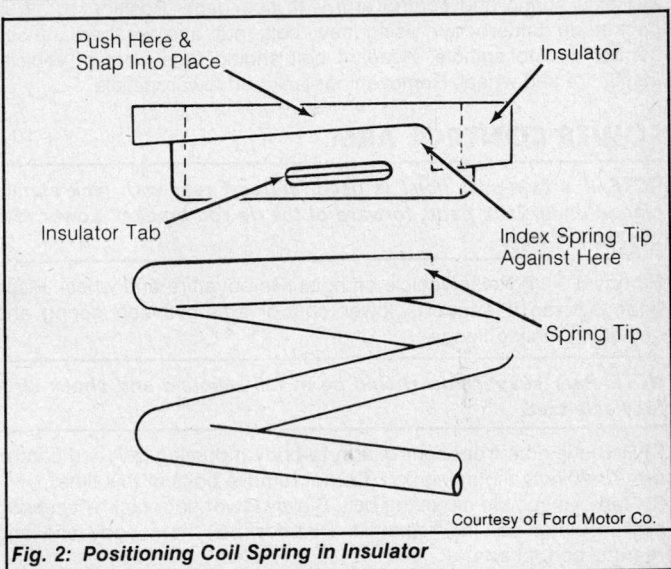

Courtesy of Ford Motor Co.

Fig. 2: Positioning Coil Spring in Insulator

Removal – Raise vehicle on hoist. Remove tire and wheel. Place floor jack under lower control arm. Raise lower control arm slightly. Remove nut, bolt, and washers retaining lower control arm to spindle. Slowly lower control arm with floor jack until spring can be removed.

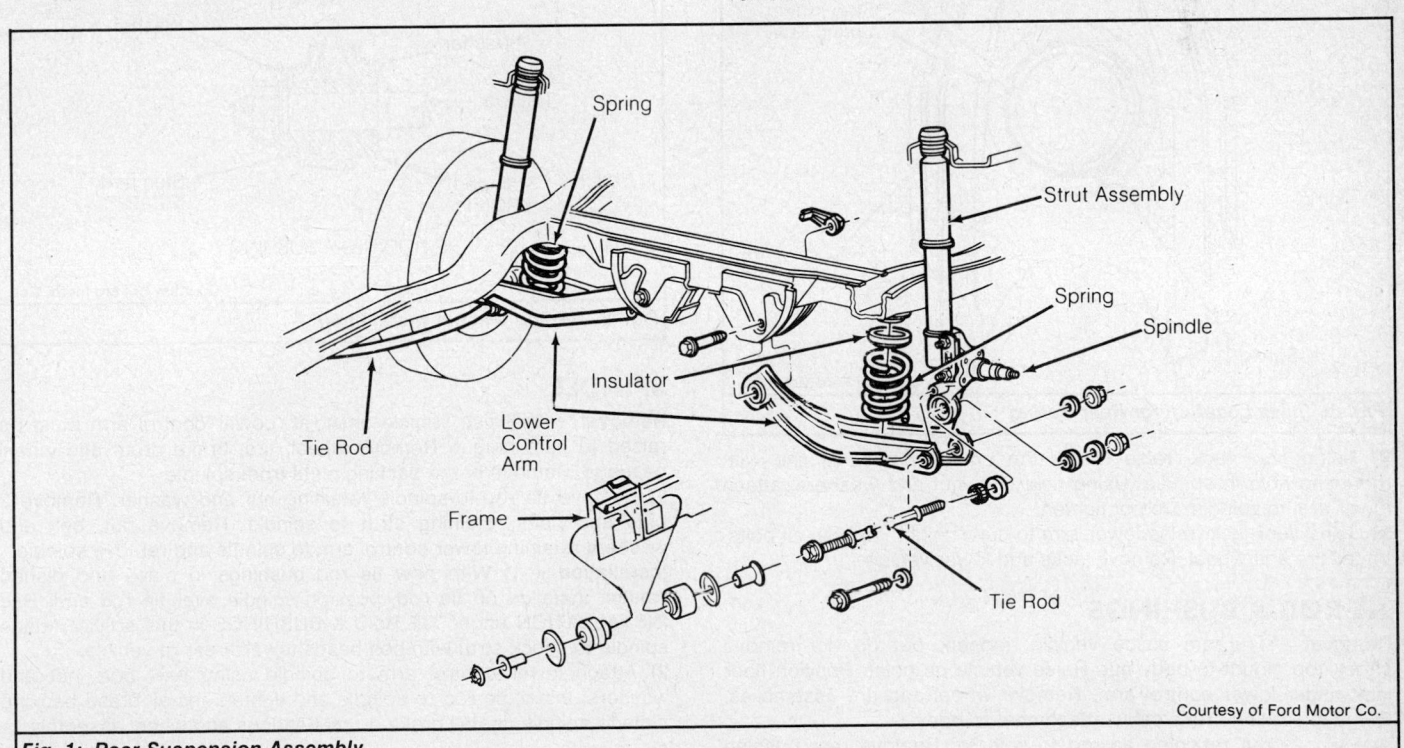

Courtesy of Ford Motor Co.

Fig. 1: Rear Suspension Assembly

Installation – 1) Using new spring insulator, index insulator against tip of spring and press down until it snaps into place. *See Fig. 2.* Install spring in control arm, making sure it is properly seated in spring pocket. *See Fig. 3.*

NOTE: Ensure spring is properly indexed in control arm and insulator is seated and indexed at top of spring. See Fig. 2.

2) Raise spring and control arm with floor jack. Position spring in pocket on underbody. Using new bolt, nut and washers, attach control arm to spindle. Head of bolt should face front of vehicle. Install tire and wheel. Remove floor jack and lower vehicle.

LOWER CONTROL ARM

NOTE: If a twin-post hoist is used, support rear with jack stands placed under jack pads, forward of the tie rod bracket. Lower rear post out of way.

Removal – 1) Raise vehicle on hoist. Remove tire and wheel. Place floor jack so it supports lower control arm between spring and spindle mounting flange.

NOTE: Rear suspension should be at full rebound and shock strut fully extended.

2) Remove nuts from control arm-to-body mounting bolt and control arm-to-spindle mounting bolt. Do not remove bolts at this time.
3) Remove spindle mounting bolt. Slowly lower floor jack until spring and insulator can be removed. Remove bolt from body end and remove control arm.
Installation – 1) Using new bolt and nut, attach lower control arm to body bracket. Do not tighten. Place spring in spring pocket in lower control arm.

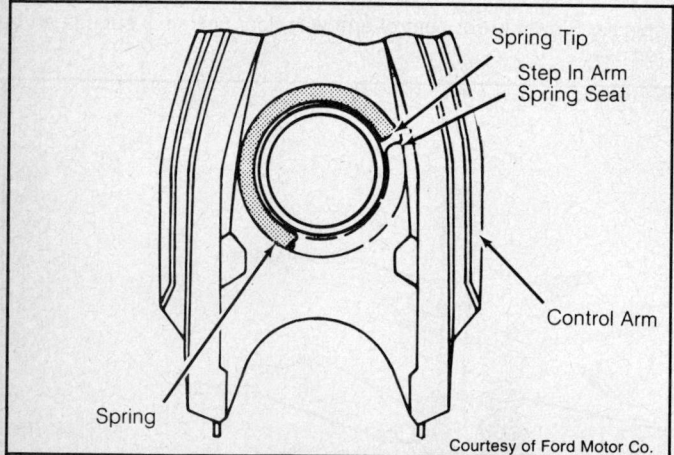

Fig. 3: Index Location for Rear Spring

Labels: Spring Tip, Step In Arm, Spring Seat, Control Arm, Spring
Courtesy of Ford Motor Co.

2) Using floor jack, raise lower arm until it comes in line with mounting hole in spindle. Using new bolt, nut and washers, attach lower arm to spindle. Do not tighten.
3) Using floor jack, raise lower arm to curb height. Tighten all bolts. Install tire and wheel. Remove jacks and lower vehicle.

TIE ROD & BUSHINGS

Removal – 1) From inside vehicle, loosen, but do not remove shock top mount-to-body nut. Raise vehicle on hoist. Position floor jack under lower control arm. Remove wheel and tire assemblies. Remove parking brake cable attachment to body.
2) Remove nut retaining tie rod to spindle. Remove rear bushing and washer from tie rod. Remove forward nut retaining tie rod to the body. Remove nut washers and bolt attaching lower control arm to spindle. Move spindle outward and rearward far enough to remove tie rod.

3) Using 2 pry bars, pry tie rod rearward to separate inner sleeve from outer sleeve. Remove bushings, washers, and inner and outer sleeve from the body bracket.
Installation – 1) Install new washer and bushing on rear of tie rod. Install outer sleeve (large inside diameter) on front end of tie rod. Insert front end of tie rod into body bracket. Install new bushing, washer, inner sleeve (small inside diameter) and nut. *See Fig. 4.* Do not tighten at this time.

NOTE: Remove .3-.5" (8-13 mm) from length of small diameter sleeve before installation.

2) Pull spindle outward and rearward far enough so that tie rod can be installed in spindle. Install new bushing, washer and nut. Do not tighten at this time. Attach lower control arm to the spindle using new bolt (with bolt head toward front of vehicle), washers and nut.
3) Install parking brake cable rear attachment to the body. Using floor jack, raise lower control arm to curb height. Tighten both tie rod nuts to specifications. Retighten top shock mount nuts. Remove floor jack. Install wheel and tire assemblies. Lower vehicle. Check rear wheel alignment.

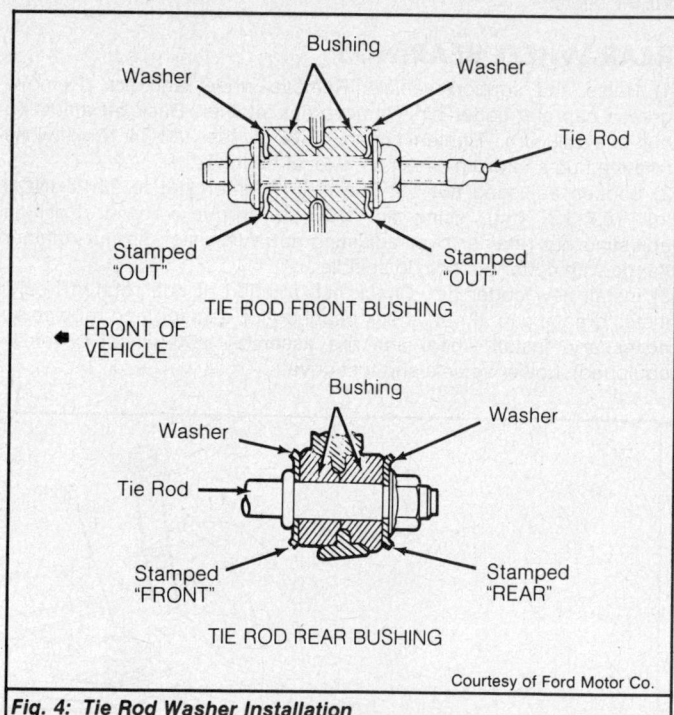

Labels: Bushing, Washer, Washer, Tie Rod, Stamped "OUT", Stamped "OUT"
TIE ROD FRONT BUSHING
FRONT OF VEHICLE

Labels: Bushing, Washer, Washer, Tie Rod, Stamped "FRONT", Stamped "REAR"
TIE ROD REAR BUSHING
Courtesy of Ford Motor Co.

Fig. 4: Tie Rod Washer Installation

SPINDLE

Removal – 1) Raise vehicle on hoist. Lower control arm must be raised to curb height. Remove wheel, tire, brake drum and wheel bearings. Remove brake backing plate from spindle.
2) Remove tie rod-to-spindle retaining nut and washer. Remove 2 nuts and bolts retaining strut to spindle. Remove nut, bolt and washers retaining lower control arm to spindle and remove spindle.
Installation – 1) With new tie rod bushings in place and dished washer installed on tie rod, position spindle over tie rod end. See INSTALLATION under TIE ROD & BUSHINGS in this article. Attach spindle to shock strut with bolt heads toward rear of vehicle.
2) Attach lower control arm to spindle using new bolt, nut and washers. Install tie rod to spindle and tighten. Install brake backing plate to spindle. Install brake drum, bearings and wheel assembly.

SHOCK ABSORBER STRUTS

Removal – 1) Remove rear compartment access panels on 2-door models, or quarter trim panels on 4-door models. Loosen, but do not remove, top shock absorber attaching nut with a 43 mm deep

External Drive Socket (T81P-18045-BH). Hold strut rod with an 8 mm deep socket while loosening.

2) Raise vehicle on hoist and remove tire and wheel. Remove clip retaining flexible brake hose to rear shock and move hose aside.

NOTE: If a frame contact hoist is used, support lower control arm with floor jack. If twin-post hoist is used, support body with floor jacks placed on lifting pads forward of tie rod body bracket.

3) Loosen 2 bolts retaining shock to spindle. Do not remove bolts at this time. Remove top mounting nut, washer and rubber insulator. Remove 2 bottom mounting bolts and remove shock.

Installation – 1) Extend shock absorber to maximum length. Install new lower washer and insulator assembly. Use tire lubricant to ease insertion into quarter panel shock tower.

2) Position upper part of shock shaft into shock tower opening in body and push slowly on lower part of shock until mounting holes are lined up with mounting holes in spindle.

3) Install, but do not tighten, new lower mounting bolts and nuts. Bolt heads should face to rear. Place new washer and upper insulator on upper shock shaft.

4) Using a 43 mm deep External Drive Socket (T81P-18045-BH), while holding strut shaft with an 8 mm deep socket, tighten upper shock nut. Tighten lower mounting bolts.

5) Install brake flex hose and retaining clip. Install wheel and tire assembly. Remove floor jacks and lower vehicle. Install quarter trim panels or rear access panels.

WHEEL BEARINGS

Removal – 1) Raise vehicle. Remove wheel from hub and drum. Remove grease cap, cotter pin, nut retainer, adjusting nut and flat washer from spindle.

2) Pull hub and drum off spindle without dropping outer bearing assembly. Remove outer bearing assembly. Using Seal Remover (1175-AC), remove and discard grease seal. Remove inner bearing from hub.

Installation – 1) If inner or outer bearing cups were removed, install new cups using Driver (T77F-1102-A and T77F-1217-A). Support drum on wood block to prevent damage.

2) Ensure spindle and bearing surfaces are clean. Thoroughly grease bearing. Install inner bearing and cone into inner cup. Apply light film of grease to lips of new seal. Install seal with Driver (T81P-1249-A).

3) Seat seal retainer flange. Apply light coat of grease to spindle shaft bearing surfaces. Install hub and drum assembly. Keep hub centered on spindle.

4) Install outer bearing assembly and flat washer on spindle. Install adjusting nut finger tight. Adjust bearings as described under ADJUSTMENTS in this article. Install grease cap. Install wheel and tire and lower vehicle.

TIGHTENING SPECIFICATIONS

Application	Ft. Lbs. (N.m)
Control Arm-to-Body Bolt	52-74 (70-100)
Control Arm-to-Spindle Bolt	70-96 (95-130)
Strut-to-Body Nut	35-55 (47-75)
Strut-to-Spindle Bolt	70-96 (95-130)
Tie Rod-to-Body Nuts	
Front	52-74 (70-100)
Rear	6-12 (8-16)
Tie Rod-to-Spindle Nut	35-50 (47-68)

1989 REAR SUSPENSION
Ford Motor Co. Probe

DESCRIPTION

The rear suspension is fully independent with a MacPherson strut at each wheel. Front and rear lateral links, a stabilizer bar and a single trailing arm eliminate undesired rear wheel movement.

The rear stabilizer bar attaches to the crossmember and front lateral link. The rear lateral link is adjustable for alignment purposes. Both lateral links and trailing arm have bushings at each end which are not replaceable.

Lateral links attach to rear crossmember and spindle with a common bolt and nut on each end. See Fig. 1. The trailing arm bolts to spindle and floor pan bracket.

If vehicle is Programmed Ride Control equipped, actuators (attached to upper strut mounting brackets) electronically adjust ride from soft to hard. PRC and conventional struts are NOT interchangeable. For more information on PRC, see ELECTRONIC SUSPENSIONS in this section.

ADJUSTMENTS

REAR WHEEL ALIGNMENT

See appropriate article in WHEEL ALIGNMENT section.

RIDING HEIGHT

See RIDING HEIGHT SPECIFICATIONS in WHEEL ALIGNMENT section.

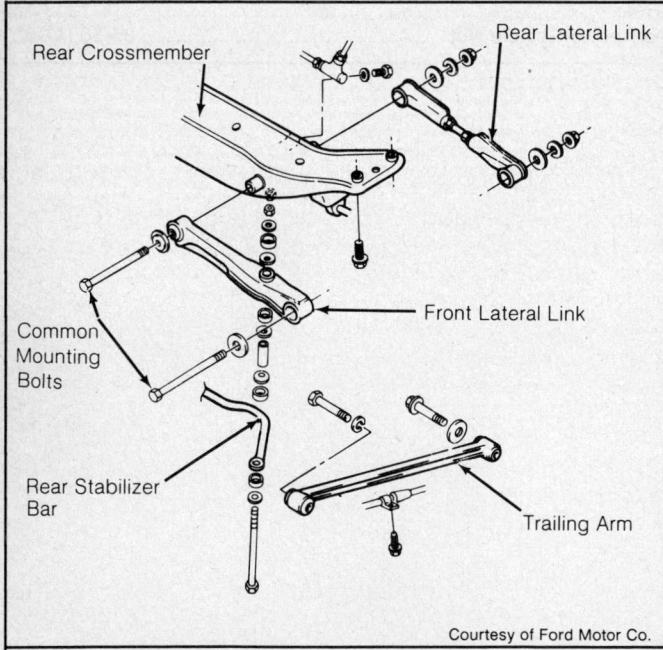

Courtesy of Ford Motor Co.

Fig. 1: Exploded View of Probe Rear Suspension

REMOVAL & INSTALLATION

STRUT & COIL SPRING ASSEMBLY

Removal – 1) Raise vehicle and remove wheel. Remove upper trunk side garnish and lower trunk side trim for access to strut. Disconnect and remove PRC actuator (if equipped).

2) Remove dust cap and staked axle nut. Remove rear brake drum. Remove parking brake return spring and attaching bolts. Disconnect parking brake cable. Loosen metal brake line to wheel cylinder. Remove 4 bolts and brake backing plate.

3) On rear disc brake system, remove caliper, parking brake cable, brake hose, rotor and backing plate. Remove anti-lock brake harness and bracket (if equipped). Remove brake line "U" clip from strut housing.

4) Loosen trailing arm bolt. Remove spindle to strut attaching bolts.

5) Remove strut attaching nuts from inside vehicle. Remove strut assembly.

Disassembly – 1) Place strut assembly in a vise. Loosen, but DO NOT remove, strut nut. Remove strut assembly from vise and compress spring using SPRING COMPRESSOR (D85P-76178-A or 086-00029).

2) Remove nut from strut assembly. Slowly release spring compressor being careful not to strip strut threads.

3) Remove strut mounting block, upper rubber spring seat, dust boot, bump stopper and coil spring. Inspect and replace parts as necessary.

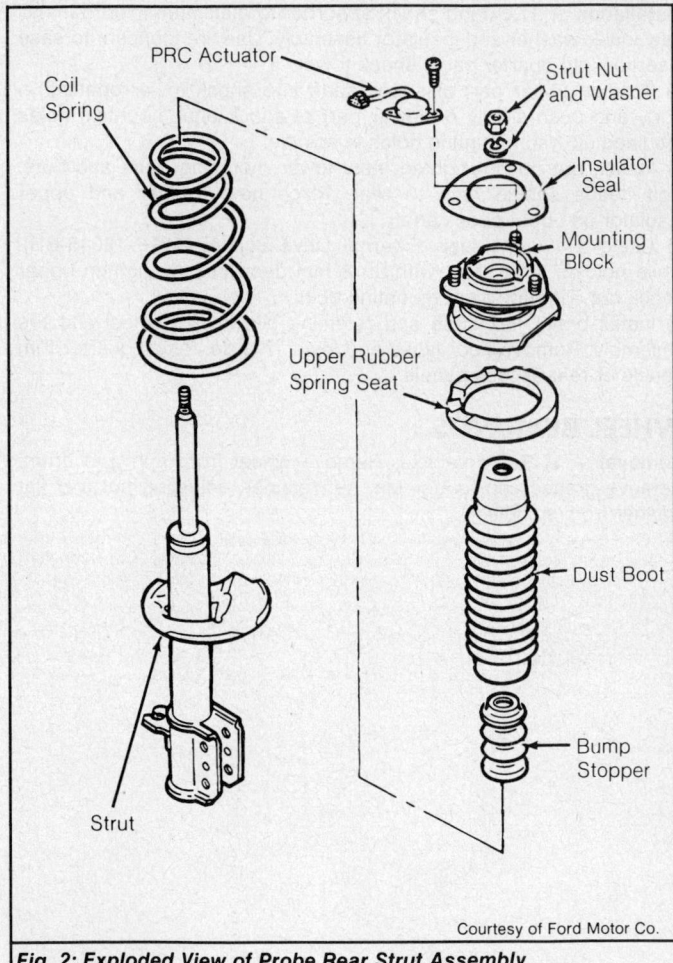

Courtesy of Ford Motor Co.

Fig. 2: Exploded View of Probe Rear Strut Assembly

Reassembly – 1) Install strut mounting block, upper rubber spring seat, dust boot, bump stopper and coil spring. Inspect and replace parts as necessary.

2) Install strut mounting block. The mounting block will not seat on strut unless notches on the block align with those on strut. Compress coil spring. Install strut nut. See Fig. 2. Tighten to specification.

3) Slowly release spring compressor. Remove strut assembly. Install strut assembly.

Installation – 1) Position strut assembly in strut tower and install attaching nuts from inside vehicle. Install PRC actuator (if equipped). Install lower trunk side trim and upper trunk side garnish.

2) Install spindle to strut mounting bolts. Install trailing arm. Tighten to specifications. Install backing plate and drum or rotor and caliper. Install brake hose "U" clip to strut.

3) Install anti-lock brake harness and bracket, if equipped. Tighten to specifications. Install wheel and lower vehicle.

REAR SPINDLE

Removal – 1) Raise vehicle and remove wheel. Remove dust cap and staked nut from spindle. Remove brake drum and backing plate on drum systems. Remove caliper and rotor if disc brake equipped.
2) Loosen, but DO NOT remove, spindle-to-strut mounting bolts. Remove common lateral link arm bolt and nut. Remove trailing arm mounting bolt at spindle. Remove spindle-to-strut mounting bolts. Remove spindle.

Installation – 1) Position spindle on strut mounting bracket. Install spindle-to-strut mounting bolts. Install trailing arm mounting bolt. Tighten to specifications.
2) Install backing plate and brake drum, if drum brake equipped. Install rotor and caliper, if rear disc equipped. Install staked axle nut and dust cap. Tighten to specifications. Install wheel and lower vehicle.

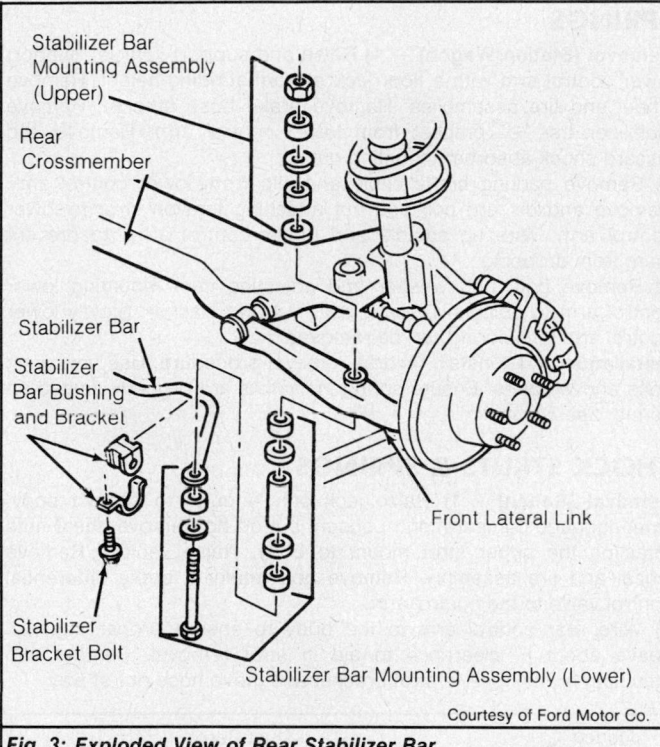

Courtesy of Ford Motor Co.

Fig. 3: Exploded View of Rear Stabilizer Bar

REAR STABILIZER BAR

Removal & Installation – Raise vehicle and remove wheel. Remove stabilizer bar mounting bolt assembly from front lateral link. Remove stabilizer bushing and bracket from rear crossmember. Remove stabilizer bar. See Fig. 3. To install, reverse removal procedure. Tighten to specifications.

LATERAL LINK, TRAILING ARM & REAR CROSSMEMBER

Removal – 1) Remove spindle. See REMOVAL under REAR SPINDLE. Remove rear stabilizer bar. See REMOVAL under REAR STABILIZER BAR.
2) Remove nut from common lateral link mounting bolt at rear crossmember. Remove rear lateral link.

NOTE: Because of close clearance between fuel tank and lateral link mounting bolt, the front lateral link and bolt must be removed with the crossmember.

3) Remove parking brake attaching bolt from trailing arm assembly. Remove trailing arm mounting bolt from body mounting bracket. Remove trailing arm.

4) Remove exhaust system mounting bolts and brake line retaining bracket from crossmember. Remove mounting bolts from end of crossmember. Remove crossmember and front lateral link together.
5) Remove common lateral link mounting bolt from crossmember and separate. Remove front lateral link from crossmember. See Fig. 4.

Installation – 1) Position front lateral link on rear crossmember. Install common lateral link mounting bolt.

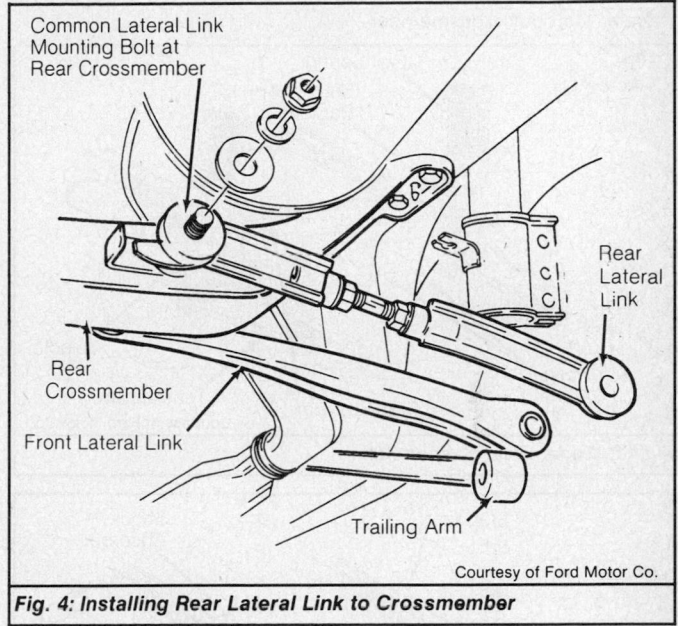

Courtesy of Ford Motor Co.

Fig. 4: Installing Rear Lateral Link to Crossmember

2) Install rear crossmember. Attach exhaust system mounting bolts and brake line retaining bracket to crossmember. Tighten crossmember bolts to specifications.
3) Install trailing arm. Install parking brake cable to trailing arm.
4) Install rear lateral link to crossmember with common mounting bolt. Install rear stabilizer bar. To complete installation, reverse removal procedure. Tighten to specification.

TIGHTENING SPECIFICATIONS

Application	Ft. Lbs. (N.m)
Axle Nut [1]	73-131 (98-117)
Brake	
Backing Plate Bolts	31-47 (45-67)
Caliper Anchor Bracket	33-49 (45-67)
Caliper Retaining Bolt	12-17 (16-24)
Flex Hose-to-Caliper	16-20 (22-26)
Parking Brake Lock nut	14-21 (20-28)
Line Retaining Bracket	13-20 (18-26)
Common Lateral Link Bolt	64-86 (86-117)
Crossmember Mounting Bolts	27-40 (36-54)
Front Lateral Link to Spindle	64-86 (86-117)
Rear Lateral Link-to-Crossmember	64-86 (86-117)
Stabilizer Bar	
Bracket-to-Crossmember	27-40 (36-54)
Mounting Bolt-to-Lateral Link	12-17 (16-23)
Strut	
Top Nut	47-67 (64-84)
Top Mount-to-Tower	34-46 (46-63)
Mount-to-Spindle	69-86 (93-117)
Trailing Arm-to-Spindle	64-86 (86-117)
Trailing Arm Mounting Bolts	46-69 (63-93)
Wheel Nuts	65-87 (88-118)

[1] – Install NEW axle shaft nut and tighten to specification. Stake axle nut using a rounded-edge cold chisel.

1989 REAR SUSPENSION
Ford Motor Co. Sable & Taurus

DESCRIPTION

Sable and Taurus sedan models utilize a MacPherson strut independent rear suspension. Each side consists of a strut assembly, 2 parallel control arms, tension strut, cast spindle and strut-mounted stabilizer bar.

Station wagon models use upper and lower control arms, shock absorber, 2-piece cast spindle, tension strut, control arm mounted stabilizer bar, and a coil spring mounted between the lower control arm and the body crossmember.

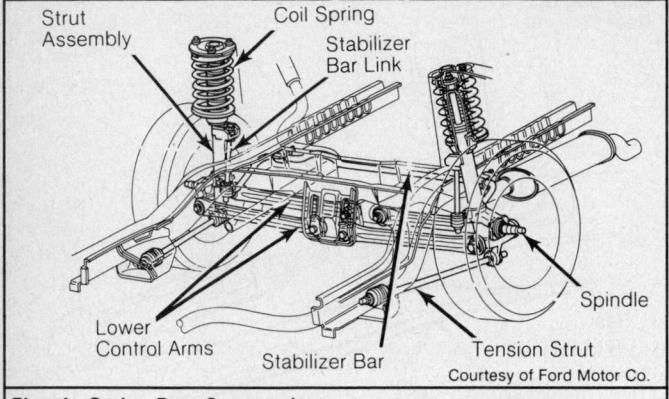

Fig. 1: Sedan Rear Suspension

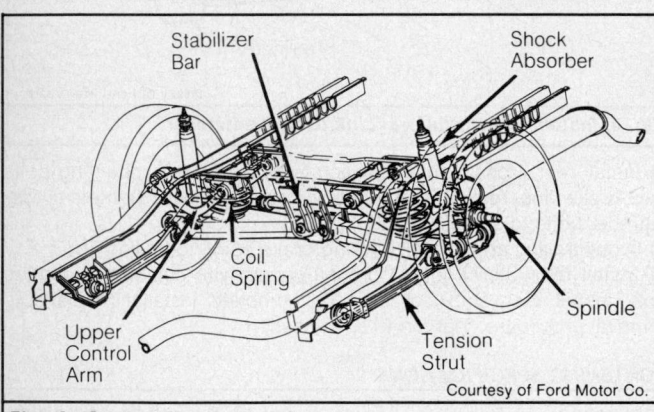

Fig. 2: Station Wagon Rear Suspension

ADJUSTMENTS

RIDING HEIGHT

See RIDING HEIGHT SPECIFICATIONS article in WHEEL ALIGNMENT section.

TOE ADJUSTMENT

See appropriate article in WHEEL ALIGNMENT section.

REAR WHEEL BEARING

1) Raise vehicle until tire clears floor. Remove wheel cover or ornament and nut covers. If vehicle has styled steel or aluminum wheels, remove wheel and tire assembly. Remove grease cap from hub.

2) Remove cotter pin and nut retainer. Back off adjusting nut one full turn. Tighten nut to 17-25 ft. lbs. (23-34 N.m), while rotating hub and drum assembly to seat bearings.

3) Loosen adjusting nut 1/2 turn and retighten nut to 24-28 INCH lbs. (2.7-3.2 N.m), using an INCH lb. torque wrench. Position adjusting nut retainer over adjusting nut. Ensure slots in nut retainer flange are in line with cotter pin hole in spindle.

4) Install new cotter pin. Check hub rotation. If hub rotates freely, install grease cap. If not, check bearings for damage and replace as

necessary. Install wheel and tire assembly and wheel cover (if equipped). Lower vehicle and test drive.

REMOVAL & INSTALLATION

SHOCK ABSORBER

Removal (Station Wagon) – 1) Remove rear compartment access cover. Loosen, but do not remove, upper shock mounting nut. Raise and support vehicle. Remove wheel and tire assembly. Support lower suspension arm with a floor jack.

2) Remove upper mounting nuts, washers and insulators. Lower floor jack. Remove 2 lower shock absorber mounting bolts. Compress shock and remove from vehicle.

Installation – To install, reverse removal procedure.

SPRINGS

Removal (Station Wagon) – 1) Raise and support vehicle. Support lower control arm with a floor jack at normal riding height. Remove wheel and tire assemblies. Remove brake hose bracket. Remove stabilizer bar "U" bracket from lower control arm. Remove and discard shock absorber mounting nuts.

2) Remove parking brake cable and clip from lower control arm. Remove and discard bolt and nut attaching tension strut to lower control arm. Wire up spindle and upper control arms to prevent them from dropping.

3) Remove bolt, nut, washer and adjusting cam mounting lower control arm to spindle. Discard bolt, nut and washer. Slowly lower control arm until spring can be removed.

Installation – To install, reverse removal procedure. Use new nuts, bolts and washers. Ensure spring insulators are properly seated on spring. *See Fig. 4.*

SHOCK STRUTS & SPRINGS

Removal (Sedan) – 1) Raise jack only enough to contact body. Open luggage compartment. Loosen, but do not remove, the 3 nuts retaining the upper strut mount to body. Raise vehicle. Remove wheel and tire assembly. Remove bolt retaining brake differential control valve to the control arm.

2) Wire rear control arm to the body to ensure proper support. Leave about 6" clearance to aid in strut removal. Remove clip attaching brake hose to strut bracket and move hose out of way.

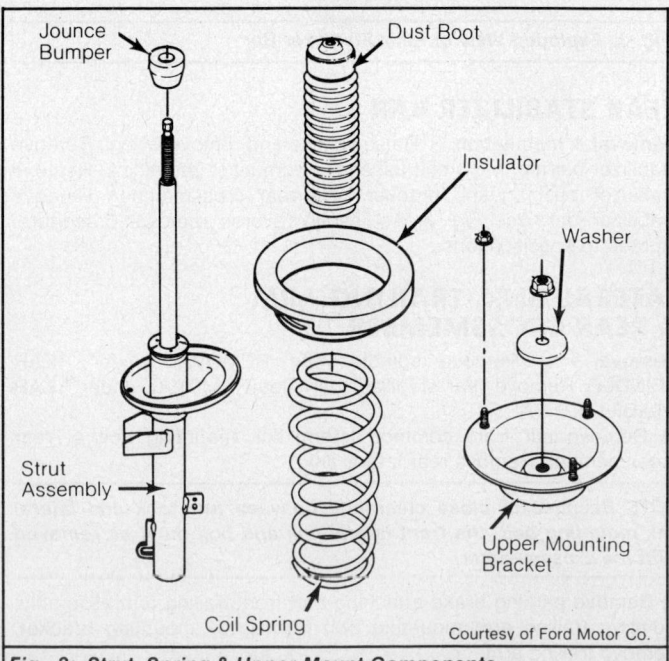

Fig. 3: Strut, Spring & Upper Mount Components

3) Remove stabilizer bar "U" bracket from body. Remove stabilizer bar link assembly from strut mounting bracket (if equipped). Disconnect tension strut from spindle. Move spindle rearward enough to separate it from tension strut.

4) Remove pinch bolt retaining strut to spindle. Spread strut-to-spindle pinch joint (if necessary). Separate strut from spindle. From inside luggage compartment, remove 3 nuts attaching upper mount to body and remove strut.

5) Mark insulator to top mount position for reassembly purposes. Compress spring with Spring Compressor (D85P-7178-A). With spring compressed, hold shaft stationary and remove strut shaft-to-mount nut. To avoid fracture of shaft at base of hex, DO NOT turn shaft. Remove spring, strut and mount from compressor.

Installation – To install, reverse removal procedure. Ensure spring is properly located in the upper and lower spring seats. *See Fig. 4.* Tighten all nuts and bolts to specification.

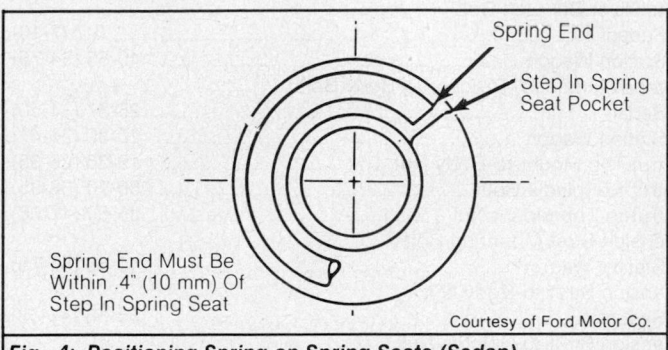

Fig. 4: Positioning Spring on Spring Seats (Sedan)

LOWER CONTROL ARM

Removal (Sedan) – Raise vehicle. Disconnect brake proportioning valve from left front arm. Disconnect parking brake cable from front control arm. Remove and discard control arm-to-spindle bolt, washer and nut. Remove and discard control arm-to-body bolt and nut. Remove control arm from vehicle.

Installation – To install, reverse removal procedure. Use new nuts, bolts and washers.

NOTE: When installing new control arms, offset on arms must face up. Control arms are stamped "BOTTOM" on lower edge. Flange edge of arm stamping must face front of vehicle on right rear arm. On all other arms, flange edge must face rear.

Removal (Station Wagon) – Raise and support vehicle at lifting pads. Remove wheel and tire assembly. Remove spring as previously described. Remove bolts and nuts mounting lower control arm to body and spindle. Remove lower control arm.

Installation – To install, reverse removal procedure. Install control arm-to-body bolt with head of bolt toward front of vehicle. Tighten mounting bolts and nuts to specification with vehicle at riding height.

UPPER CONTROL ARMS

Removal (Station Wagon) – 1) Raise and support vehicle. Support lower control arm at curb height. *See Fig. 5.* Remove wheel and tire assemblies. Remove brake line bracket from body. Loosen, but do not remove, spindle-to-upper arm and lower arm mounting nuts.

2) Remove bolts and nuts mounting front and rear upper control arms to body brackets. Ensure spindle does not fall outward. Carefully tilt top of spindle outward, until ends of upper control arms are clear of the body bracket.

3) Wire spindle to the body in this position. Remove nut mounting upper control arms to spindle. Remove upper control arms from vehicle.

Installation – To install, reverse removal procedure.

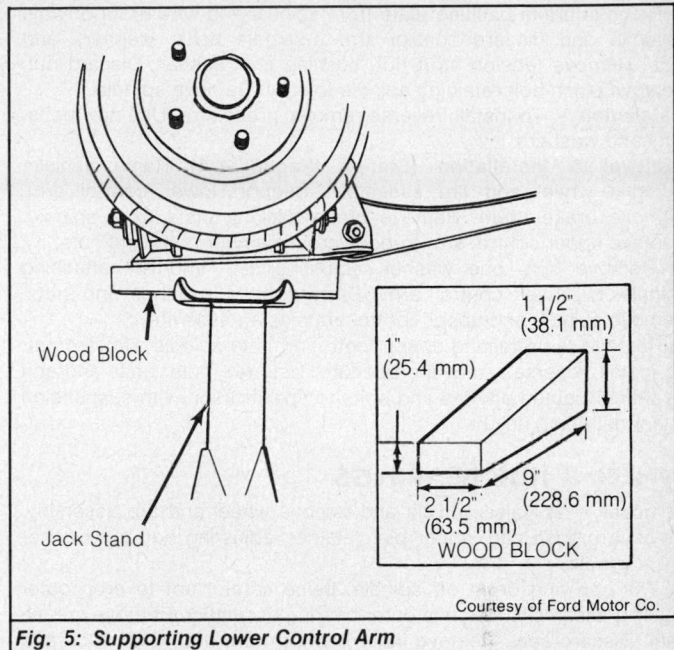

Wood Block

Jack Stand

1 1/2" (38.1 mm)

1" (25.4 mm)

9" (228.6 mm)

2 1/2" (63.5 mm)

WOOD BLOCK

Courtesy of Ford Motor Co.

Fig. 5: Supporting Lower Control Arm

TENSION STRUT

Removal & Installation (Sedan) – 1) Raise vehicle using lift pads located in front of rear wheels and rearward of front wheels. Loosen 3 upper strut nuts from inside luggage compartment. Remove tire and wheel assembly. Remove and discard tension strut-to-spindle and body nuts.

2) Move spindle rearward. Remove tension strut. To install, reverse removal procedure. Ensure rear bushings have indentations in them. Tighten bolts and nuts with vehicle at normal riding height.

Removal & Installation (Station Wagon) – 1) Raise and support vehicle. Support lower control arm at normal riding height. Remove wheel and tire assembly. Remove bolt and nut retaining tension strut to lower control arm. Remove bolt and nut retaining tension strut to body bracket. Remove tension strut assembly.

2) To install, reverse removal procedure. Install new mounting bolts and nuts. Tighten bolts and nuts to specification with vehicle at normal riding height. Perform rear wheel alignment.

STABILIZER BAR

Removal (Sedan) – Raise and support vehicle. Remove wheel and tire assemblies. Remove nut and insulator attaching stabilizer bar to end link assemblies. Remove 2 "U" brackets attaching stabilizer bar to the body. Remove stabilizer bar. Remove nut attaching link assembly to bracket and remove link.

Installation – To install, reverse removal procedure.

Removal (Station Wagon) – 1) Raise and support vehicle. Place jack stands under lower control arms to neutralize stabilizer bar lower arm insulators. Remove 2 "U" brackets and insulator retaining bolts and nuts. Discard bolts and nuts.

2) Slide "U" brackets and insulators off stabilizer bar. Separate "U" bracket from insulator. Replace insulator if damaged. Remove 2 bolts and nuts attaching link assemblies to the body brackets. Remove stabilizer bar and link assemblies from vehicle.

Installation – To install, reverse removal procedure. Thoroughly clean stabilizer bar before installing. Use new nuts, bolts and washers.

SPINDLE

Removal (Sedan) – 1) Raise vehicle. Remove wheel and tire assembly. Remove brake drum. Remove bolt retaining brake flex hose bracket to strut. Remove 4 bolts retaining brake backing plate to spindle.

2) Remove brake backing plate from spindle and wire it out of way. Remove and discard control arm-to-spindle bolts, washers and nuts. Remove tension strut nut, bushing and washer. Discard nut. Remove pinch bolt retaining spindle to strut. Remove spindle.

Installation – To install, reverse removal procedure. Use new bolts, nuts and washers.

Removal & Installation (Station Wagon) – **1)** Raise vehicle. Remove wheel and tire assembly. Support lower control arm. Remove brake drum. Remove brake backing plate from spindle. Remove upper control arm-to-body crossmember bolts and nuts.

2) Remove bolt, one washer, adjusting cam and nut attaching spindle to lower control arm. Discard bolts, washer and nuts. Remove spindle and upper control arms as an assembly.

3) Remove nut retaining upper control arms to spindle. Discard nut. To install, reverse removal procedure. Use new nuts, bolts and and washers. Tighten all nuts and bolts to specification with suspension at normal riding height.

WHEEL & HUB BEARINGS

Removal – **1)** Raise vehicle and remove wheel and tire assembly. Remove grease cap, cotter pin, retainer, adjusting nut and washer from spindle.

2) Pull hub and drum off spindle, being careful not to drop outer bearing assembly. Remove outer bearing assembly. Remove grease seal. Discard seal. Remove inner bearing from hub. Clean hub and spindle with clean cloth. Remove inner and outer races if necessary.

Installation – **1)** If bearing races were removed, install new inner and outer bearing races using Installer Set (T80T-4000-W, T77F-1217-B and T73F-1217-A). Support drum on wood block and ensure races are properly seated. DO NOT use cone and roller assembly to install races, as this will damage races.

2) Pack bearings with grease. Apply grease to race surfaces. Place inner bearing cone and roller assembly in inner race. Apply light film of grease to lips of new grease seal.

3) Install seal with Installer (T56T-4676-B). Ensure retainer flange is seated all around. Apply light film of grease on spindle bearing surfaces. Install hub and drum on spindle.

4) Install outer bearing and keyed flat washer on spindle. Install adjusting nut finger tight. Adjust wheel bearings. Install new cotter pin and grease cap. Install tire assembly. Lower vehicle and tighten lug nuts.

TIGHTENING SPECIFICATIONS

Application	Ft. Lbs. (N.m)
Lower Control Arm-to-Body Bolt	
Sedan	45-65 (61-88)
Station Wagon	40-55 (54-75)
Lower Control Arm-to-Spindle Bolt	
Sedan	42-57 (57-78)
Station Wagon	40-55 (54-75)
Lower Shock Absorber Nuts	13-20 (18-27)
Stabilizer Bar Link Bolt	
Sedan	5-7 (7-10)
Station Wagon	40-55 (54-75)
Stabilizer Bar "U" Bracket-to-Body Bolt	
Sedan	25-37 (34-50)
Station Wagon	20-30 (27-41)
Strut Top Mount-to-Body Nut	19-26 (26-35)
Strut-to-Spindle Bolt	50-70 (68-95)
Strut-to-Top Mount Nut	35-50 (47-68)
Tension Strut Mounting Bolts	
Station Wagon	40-55 (54-75)
Tension Strut-to-Body Nut	
Sedan	35-50 (47-68)
Tension Strut-to-Spindle Nut	
Sedan	35-50 (47-68)
Upper Control Arm-to-Body Bolt	70-95 (95-129)
Upper Control Arm-to-Spindle Bolt	150-190 (203-257)
Upper Shock Absorber Nut	19-27 (26-37)
Wheel Lug Nuts	80-105 (108-142)

DESCRIPTION

Tempo and Topaz utilize a MacPherson strut independent rear suspension. Each side consists of a gas pressurized shock absorber strut assembly, 2 parallel control arms, tie rod, forged spindle, shock bumper and dust shield.

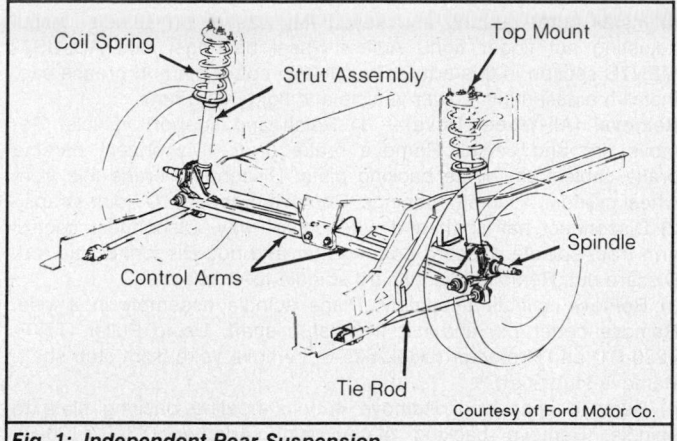

Fig. 1: Independent Rear Suspension

Courtesy of Ford Motor Co.

ADJUSTMENTS

WHEEL ALIGNMENT

See appropriate article in WHEEL ALIGNMENT section.

RIDING HEIGHT

See RIDING HEIGHT SECIFICATIONS article in WHEEL ALIGNMENT section.

REAR WHEEL BEARINGS

NOTE: Wheel bearings on all-wheel drive models are not adjustable.

1) Raise vehicle until tire clears floor. Remove wheel cover or ornament and nut covers. If vehicle has styled steel or aluminum wheels, remove wheel and tire assembly. Remove grease cap from hub.
2) Remove cotter pin and nut retainer. Back off adjusting nut one turn. Tighten nut to 17-25 ft. lbs. (23-34 N.m) while rotating hub and drum assembly.
3) Loosen adjusting nut 1/2 turn and retighten nut to 10-15 INCH lb. (1.0-1.7 N.m) using an INCH lb. torque wrench. Position adjusting nut retainer over adjusting nut. Ensure slots in nut retainer flange are in line with cotter pin hole in spindle.
4) Install new cotter pin and bend ends around retainer flange. Check hub rotation. If hub rotates freely, install grease cap. If not, check bearings for damage and replace as necessary.
5) Install wheel and tire assembly, wheel cover, ornament and nut covers as required. Lower vehicle and test drive.

REMOVAL & INSTALLATION

SHOCK STRUT & SPRING

CAUTION: Struts are gas charged. DO NOT apply heat or flame to strut during removal.

Removal – 1) Raise jack only enough to contact body. Open trunk lid. Loosen 2 nuts retaining the upper strut mount to body, but do not remove nuts. Raise vehicle. Remove wheel and tire assembly.
2) Place safety stand under control arm to support suspension. Remove bolt attaching brake hose bracket to strut and place it out of way. Use care not to stretch brake hose or damage metal brake line.

3) Remove 2 bolts retaining strut to spindle. Remove 2 upper mount-to-body nuts and remove strut.
4) Compress spring with Spring Compressor (D83P-5310-A). To avoid fracture of shaft at base of hex, hold shaft and remove strut shaft-to-mount nut. Remove spring, strut and mount from compressor.

Installation – To install, reverse removal procedure. Ensure spring is properly located in the upper and lower spring seats. *See Fig. 2.* Position lower washer correctly. *See Fig. 3.* Tighten all nuts and bolts to specifications.

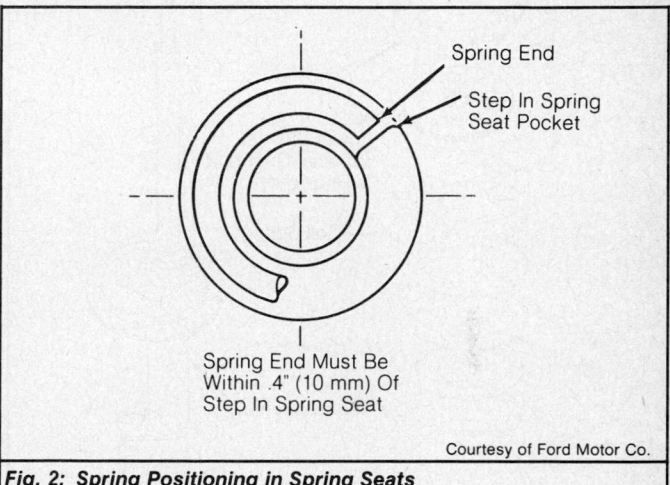

Courtesy of Ford Motor Co.

Fig. 2: Spring Positioning in Spring Seats

CONTROL ARMS

Removal – Raise vehicle. Remove and discard arm-to-spindle bolts and nuts. Remove and discard center mounting bolts and nuts. Remove arms from vehicle.
Installation – To install, reverse removal procedure. Use new nuts, bolts and washers. When installing new control arms, bushing with .39" (10 mm) hole is installed to center of vehicle and bushing with .48" (12 mm) hole is installed to spindle. Offset on arm must face up on right side of vehicle and down on left side. Flange edge of arm stamping must face rear of vehicle. Check wheel alignment.

TIE ROD

Removal – 1) Raise vehicle on a frame contact hoist using the lift pads located to the rear of the front wheels and the lift pads forward of the rear wheels. Raise hoist only enough to contact the body. From inside trunk, loosen, but do not remove, 2 strut top mount-to-body nuts.
2) Raise vehicle and place safety stand under suspension for support. Remove wheel and tire assembly. Remove 2 top mount nuts. Remove nut retaining tie rod to spindle. Remove nut retaining tie rod to body. Lower safety stand enough so that upper strut mount studs are out of holes in body. Move spindle rearward so that tie rod can be removed.
Installation – To install, reverse removal procedure. Note that front and rear tie rod bushings are different. Rear bushings have indentations in them. Replace washers and bushings if worn. Tighten 2 tie rod nuts with wheels at curb height. Washers must be installed with dish facing away from bushings.

SPINDLE

Removal – 1) Raise vehicle. Remove wheel and tire assembly. Remove brake drum. Remove bolt retaining brake flex hose bracket to strut. Remove 4 bolts retaining brake backing plate to spindle. Use care not to stretch brake hose or damage metal brake line.
2) Remove brake backing plate from spindle and wire it out of way. Remove control arm to spindle bolt, washers and nut. Remove tie rod nut, bushing and washer. Remove 2 bolts retaining spindle to strut and remove spindle.

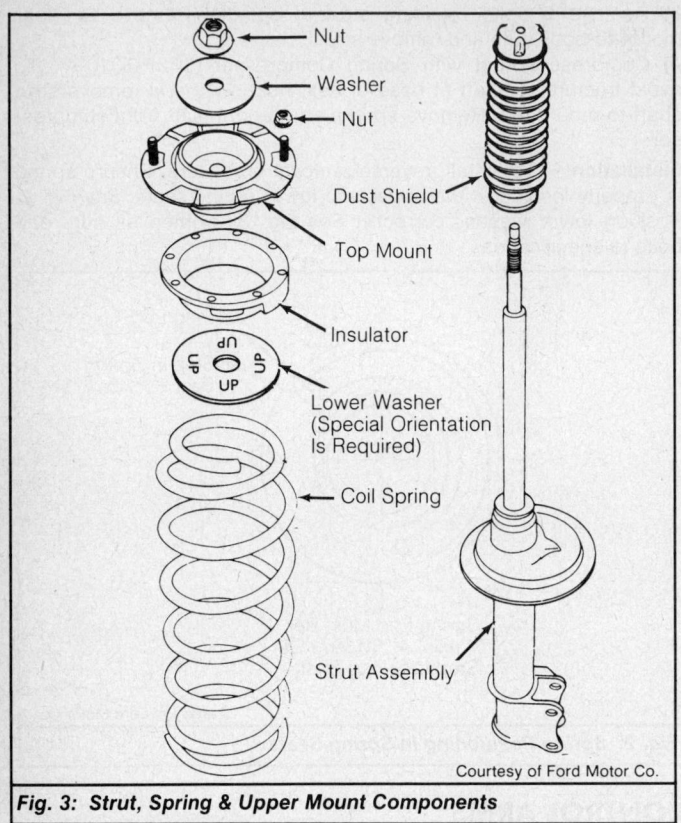

Fig. 3: Strut, Spring & Upper Mount Components

Installation – To install, reverse removal procedure. Use new nuts, bolts and washers. Tighten all nuts and bolts to specification.

WHEEL & HUB BEARINGS

Removal (2WD) – 1) Raise vehicle and remove wheel and tire assembly. Remove grease cap, cotter pin, retainer, adjusting nut and washer from spindle.
2) Pull hub and drum off spindle, being careful not to drop outer bearing assembly. Remove outer bearing assembly.
3) Using Remover (1175-AC), remove grease seal. Discard seal. Remove inner bearing from hub. Clean hub and spindle with clean cloth.
Installation – 1) If bearing cups were removed, install new inner and outer bearing cups using Installer Set (T80T-4000-W, T77F-1202-A and T73T-1217-A). Support drum hub on wood block and ensure cups are properly seated. DO NOT use cone and roller assembly to install cups, as this will damage cups.

2) Pack bearings with grease. Apply grease to cup surfaces. Place inner bearing cone and roller assembly in inner cup. Apply light film of grease to lips of new grease seal.
3) Install seal with Installer (T81P-1249-A). Ensure retainer flange is seated all around. Apply light film of grease on spindle bearing surfaces. Install hub and drum on spindle.
4) Install outer bearing and keyed flat washer on spindle. Install adjusting nut finger tight. Adjust wheel bearings. See ADJUST-MENTS section in this article. Install new cotter pin and grease cap. Install tire assembly. Lower vehicle and tighten lug nuts.
Removal (All-Wheel Drive) – 1) Raise and support vehicle. Remove tire and wheel. Remove brake drum. Disconnect parking brake cable from brake backing plate. Disconnect brake line from wheel cylinder. Plug all openings. Remove outboard "U" joint straps.
2) Disconnect half-shaft and wire out of way. Disconnect control arm from spindle. Discard bolt, washer and nut. Disconnect tie rod. Discard nut. Remove and discard spindle-to-strut bolts.
3) Remove spindle assembly. Place spindle assembly in a vise. Remove cotter pin and nut from stub shaft. Using Puller (T77F-4220-B1) and Protector (D80L-625-6), remove yoke from stub shaft. Remove stub shaft.
4) Remove snap ring. Remove 4 bolts holding backing plate to spindle. Remove backing plate. Using Adapter (T87P-7120-B), Handle (T80T-4000-W) and hydraulic press, remove bearing from spindle.
Installation – To install, reverse removal procedure. Use Step Plate Adapter (D80L-630-8) and handle to install bearing. Use new nuts, bolts and washers.

TIGHTENING SPECIFICATIONS

Application	Ft. Lbs. (N.m)
Control Arm-to-Body Bolt	30-40 (41-54)
Control Arm-to-Spindle Nut	60-80 (81-108)
Stabilizer "U" Bracket-to-Body Bolt	15-26 (20-35)
Strut Top Mount-to-Body Nut	20-30 (27-41)
Strut-to-Spindle Bolts	70-96 (95-130)
Strut-to-Top Mount Nut	35-50 (47-68)
Stub Shaft Nut	120-150 (163-204)
Tie Rod-to-Body Bolts	52-74 (71-100)
Tie Rod-to-Spindle Nut	52-74 (71-100)
"U" Joint Strap Bolt	15-17 (20-23)

LTD Crown Victoria, Grand Marquis, Mustang, Town Car, Wagon

NOTE: For Mark VII models, see Ford Motor Co. Air Suspension article in this section.

CAUTION: Unless otherwise noted, procedures and specifications for LTD Crown Victoria and Grand Marquis may generally be used on Station Wagon models.

DESCRIPTION

The rear axle housing is suspended from frame by 2 upper control arms which control side-to-side movement, and 2 lower control arms which control front-to-rear movement. Each coil spring is mounted between an upper and lower seat. Shock absorbers are attached to upper spring seat, or upper shock tower on floorpan, and at lower shock brackets welded to axle tube.

Mustang models with handling suspension package, use 2 hydraulic axle dampers. These axle dampers are mounted rearward of axle, between axle bracket and frame, to control rotational forces during power applications.

ADJUSTMENTS

RIDING HEIGHT

See RIDING HEIGHT SPECIFICATIONS article in WHEEL ALIGNMENT section.

PINION ANGLE

Checking – 1) Vehicle must be at normal curb height. Curb height is measured vertically from top of axle housing tube to outboard edge of frame side rail. *See Fig. 1.*

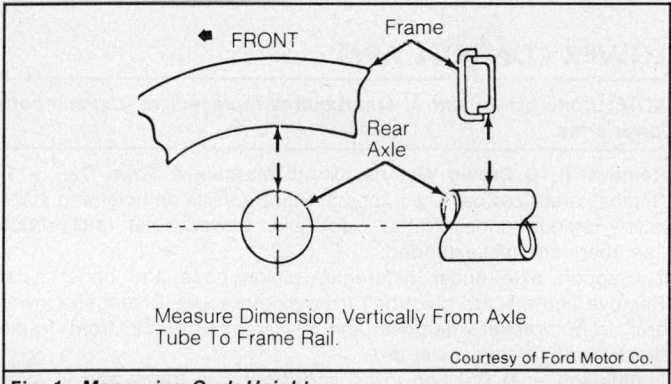

Fig. 1: Measuring Curb Height

2) Position "V" magnet of Pinion Angle Level Gauge (T86P-4602-A) on drive shaft. Make sure magnet is away from welds or balance weights. *See Fig. 2.*

3) From left side of vehicle, angle level gauge on magnet with adjusting screw to left. Adjust dial on tool until left hand edge of bubble is exactly on zero line.

4) Place angle level gauge on circular bearing cap of "U" joint with tool in same relative position as it was on drive shaft. *See Fig. 2.* Snap ring must be removed during reading.

5) Read position of bubble's left hand edge on scale to determine drive shaft angle. See PINION ANGLE SPECIFICATIONS table. If angle is not as specified, go to ADJUSTMENT.

Adjustment – 1) If pinion angle is not within specifications, install new upper control arm bushings equipped with adjustment cams. See REMOVAL & INSTALLATION in this article.

2) Eccentric cam in upper control arm can be rotated to change pinion angle. If cam is rusty, tap it with a drift to remove rust so cam will rotate. *See Fig. 3.*

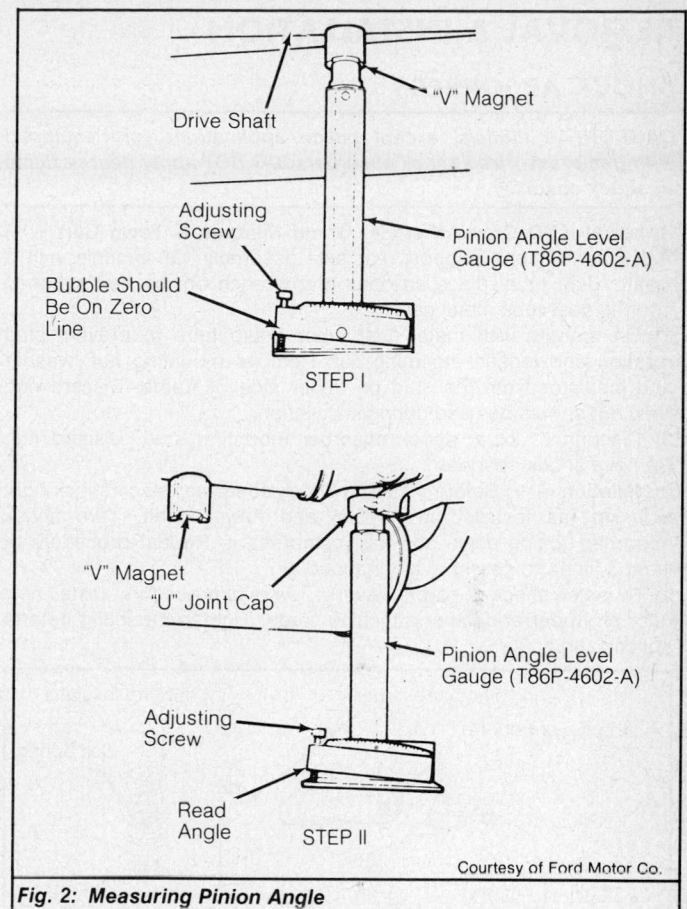

Fig. 2: Measuring Pinion Angle

PINION ANGLE SPECIFICATIONS

Model	Pinion Angle	Curb Height In. (mm)
Sedan		
LTD Crown Victoria	2°18′	6.02 (152.9)
Grand Marquis	2°18′	6.02 (152.9)
Wagon		
All	2°59′	6.47 (164.3)
Mustang		
Axle 6.75″	2°10′	5.29 (134.4)
Axle 7.50″	2°27′	5.07 (128.8)
Town Car	2°18′	5.58 (141.8)

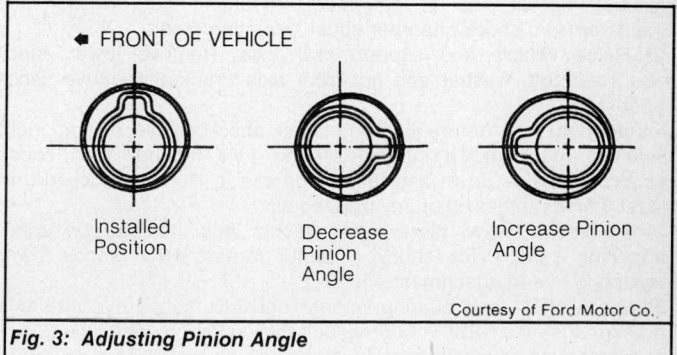

Fig. 3: Adjusting Pinion Angle

12-52

1989 REAR SUSPENSION
Ford Motor Co. Exc. Cougar & Thunderbird (Cont.)

REMOVAL & INSTALLATION

SHOCK ABSORBERS

CAUTION: All models, except police applications, are equipped with gas-pressurized shock absorbers. DO NOT apply heat or flame to shock absorber.

Removal (LTD Crown Victoria, Grand Marquis & Town Car) – 1) Raise vehicle and support rear axle assembly. On models with a plastic dust tube, place an open end wrench on the hex stamped into the dust tube metal cap.
2) On models with metal dust tube, grasp tube to prevent stud rotation and loosen mounting nut. Remove mounting nut, washer and insulator from the stud on upper side of frame. Discard nut. New nut should be used during installation.
3) Disconnect lower shock absorber mounting stud. Discard nut. Remove shock absorber.
Installation – 1) Before installing shock absorber, place shock right side up (as installed in vehicle) and fully extend. Turn shock absorber upside down and fully compress it. Repeat procedure at least 3 times to get rid of any trapped air.
2) To install shock absorber, reverse removal procedure. Install new nuts on upper and lower attaching studs. Tighten mounting nuts to specification.

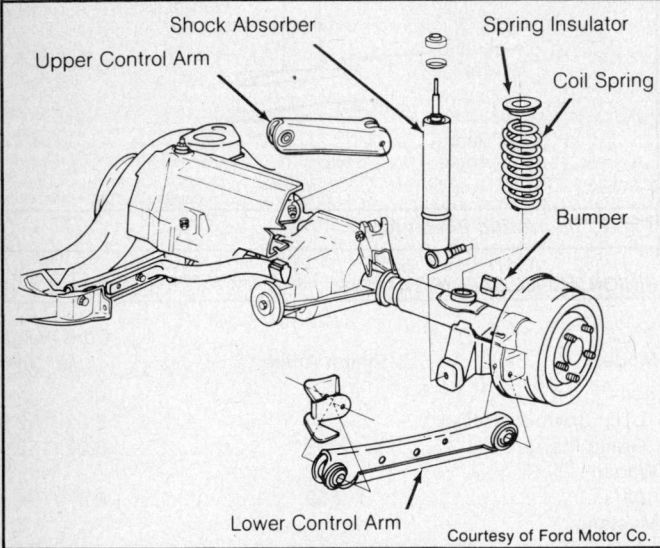

Shock Absorber — Spring Insulator — Upper Control Arm — Coil Spring — Bumper — Lower Control Arm

Courtesy of Ford Motor Co.

Fig. 4: Exploded View Typical Rear Suspension

Removal (Mustang) – 1) On all models except 3-door, open trunk to access upper shock absorber mounting stud. On 3-door models, open rear hatch and remove trim panel access door. On all models, remove rubber cap (if equipped), mounting nut, washer and insulator from shock absorber upper mounting stud.
2) Raise vehicle and support rear axle. Remove lower shock absorber bolt, washer and nut from axle bracket. Remove shock absorber.
Installation – 1) Before installing shock absorber, place shock right side up (as installed in vehicle) and fully extend. Turn shock absorber upside down and fully compress it. Repeat procedure at least 3 times to get rid of any trapped air.
2) To install shock, place inner washer and insulator on upper attaching stud. Place shock in upper mount. Align shock lower mounting eye to attachment.
3) Use a NEW load bearing washer between shock eye and axle bracket. Install a NEW Torx drive bolt through shock and axle.
4) Tighten lower mounting bolt while allowing self-wrenching nut to rotate freely so wrenching tab seats on outboard of axle bracket. DO NOT hold nut tab using any other method.

5) On models with handling suspension, lower mounting bolt head must seat on inboard side of shock bracket. Install a new nut. Tighten lower shock cross bolt to specification.
6) Lower vehicle. Install insulator, outer washer and NEW nut to upper shock stud. Tighten to specification.

COIL SPRINGS & INSULATORS

NOTE: If one spring must be replaced, replace both springs. Remove stabilizer bar (if equipped).

Removal (LTD Crown Victoria, Grand Marquis & Town Car) – 1) Place hoist under axle housing and raise vehicle. Place safety stands under frame side rails. Disconnect lower shock absorber mounts. Remove right side parking brake cable from upper arm retainer.
2) Lower hoist and axle housing until coil springs are released. Remove springs and insulators from vehicle.
Installation – To install coil spring, reverse removal procedure. Ensure coil spring insulator is installed between upper end of spring and upper seat. Use NEW nuts on shock absorber mounting stud.
Removal (Mustang) – 1) Raise vehicle and support body at rear crossmember. Lower hoist until shock absorbers are fully extended. Rear axle must be supported by stands. Place transmission jack under lower arm-to-axle pivot bolt.
2) Remove pivot bolt and nut. Lower transmission jack slowly to release spring load. Remove coil spring and insulator.
Installation – 1) Place upper spring insulator on top of spring. Tape in place if necessary. Place lower spring insulator on lower arm.
2) Position coil spring on lower seat so that pigtail is at rear and pointing toward left side of vehicle. *See Fig. 5.* Slowly raise transmission jack until arm is in position.
3) Install NEW rear pivot bolt with nut facing out. Lower jack and raise axle to curb height. Tighten pivot bolt. Reinstall stabilizer bar (if equipped). Remove supports and lower vehicle.

LOWER CONTROL ARM

NOTE: If one lower control arm requires replacement, replace both lower arms.

Removal (LTD Crown Victoria, Grand Marquis & Town Car) – 1) Remove stabilizer bar (if equipped). Raise vehicle on hoist and place safety stands under frame side rails. Lower hoist until shock absorbers are fully extended.
2) Support axle under differential pinion nose and under axle. Remove and discard pivot bolt from axle bracket. Disengage lower arm from bracket. Remove and discard pivot bolt from frame bracket and remove lower arm.
Installation – 1) Position lower control arm in frame and in axle. Install NEW pivot bolts and nuts. Install bolts so heads face outboard.
2) Raise axle. Tighten pivot bolts to specification. Install stabilizer bar. Lower vehicle.
Removal (Mustang) – 1) Remove stabilizer bar (if equipped). Raise vehicle and support at rear body crossmember. Support axle and lower hoist until shock absorbers are fully extended.
2) Place transmission jack under lower arm-to-axle pivot bolt and remove. Lower transmission jack slowly until coil spring can be removed. Remove lower control arm-to-frame pivot bolt and remove lower arm.
Installation – 1) Position lower arm assembly into front arm bracket. Install NEW arm-to-frame pivot bolt and nut with nut facing outward. DO NOT tighten yet.
2) Install coil spring and raise axle. Install NEW lower pivot bolt and nut with nut facing outward. Raise axle to curb height. Tighten upper and lower bolts to specification.

1989 REAR SUSPENSION
Ford Motor Co. Exc. Cougar & Thunderbird (Cont.)

12-53

UPPER CONTROL ARM

NOTE: If one upper control arm requires replacement, replace both upper arms. To ensure safety, replace one arm at a time.

Removal (LTD Crown Victoria, Grand Marquis & Town Car) – 1) Raise vehicle and place safety stands under frame side rails. Support axle. Lower axle and support under differential pinion nose as well as under axle.

2) Disconnect parking brake cable from upper arm retainer. Remove and discard upper arm-to-axle housing bolt. Disconnect arm from housing. Remove and discard upper arm-to-frame bracket bolt, and remove upper arm.

Bushing Replacement – Upper control arm bushings may be replaced using special tool set. *See Fig. 6.*

Installation – Install NEW upper pivot bolt and self-locking nut with bolt facing front of vehicle. Install NEW lower pivot bolt and nut so nut faces inboard. Tighten all pivot bolts with axle in normal riding height position.

Removal (Mustang) – Raise vehicle on hoist and support at rear body crossmember. Remove upper arm-to-axle and upper arm-to-frame pivot bolts. Discard bolts and nuts. Remove upper arm.

Bushing Replacement – Bushing replacement is similar to LTD Crown Victoria, Grand Marquis and Town Car. *See Fig. 6.*

Installation – Install NEW upper axle pivot bolt with nut facing outboard. Install NEW upper frame pivot bolt with nut facing inboard. Tighten pivot bolts with rear axle in curb height position. *See Fig. 5.*

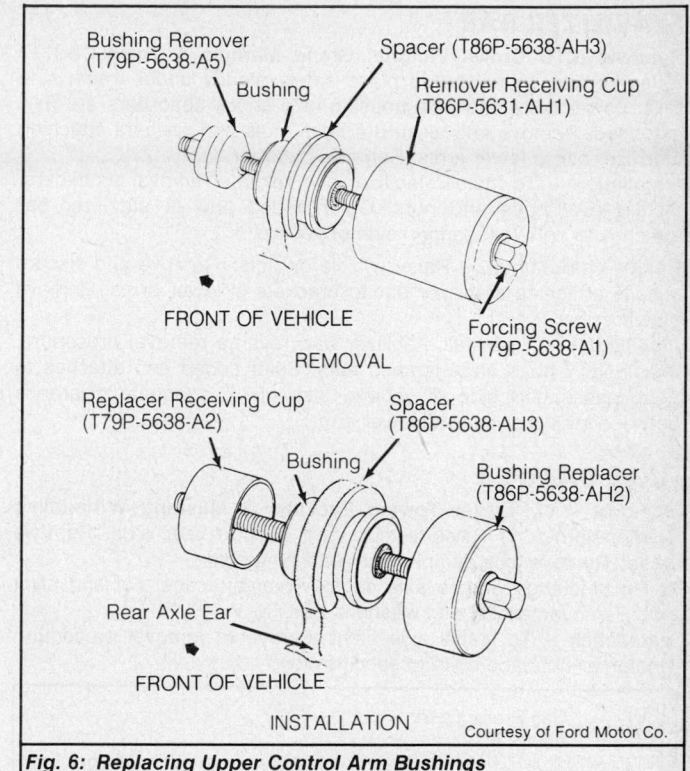

Courtesy of Ford Motor Co.

Fig. 6: Replacing Upper Control Arm Bushings

Courtesy of Ford Motor Co.

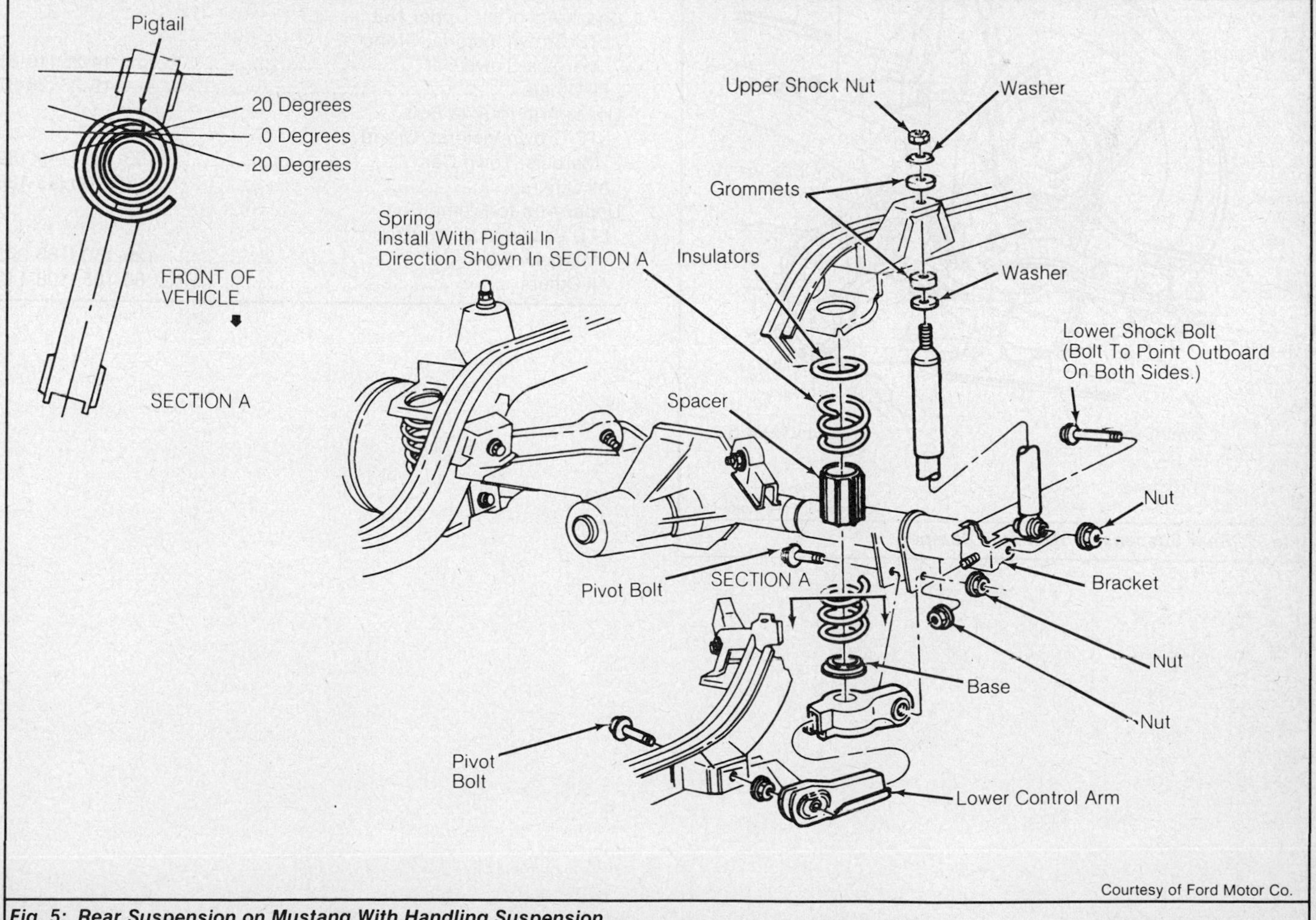

Fig. 5: Rear Suspension on Mustang With Handling Suspension

12-54

1989 REAR SUSPENSION
Ford Motor Co. Exc. Cougar & Thunderbird (Cont.)

STABILIZER BAR

Removal (LTD Crown Victoria, Grand Marquis & Town Car) – Raise vehicle on hoist and place safety stands under frame side rails. Lower hoist and axle housing until shock absorbers are fully extended. Remove and discard 4 bolts, nuts and spacers attaching stabilizer bar to lower arms. Remove stabilizer bar.

Installation – To install stabilizer bar, reverse removal procedure. Install NEW bolts and nuts. Color coded end of stabilizer bar attaches to right (passenger) side of vehicle.

Removal (Mustang) – Raise vehicle on hoist. Remove and discard 4 bolts attaching stabilizer bar to brackets in lower arms. Remove stabilizer bar.

Installation – To install stabilizer bar, reverse removal procedure. Install NEW bolts and stamped nuts. Color coded end attaches to right (passenger) side of vehicle. Inspect for adequate clearance between stabilizer bar and lower arm.

AXLE DAMPER

Removal (5.0L Trailer Towing Package & Mustang W/Handling Suspension) – **1)** Raise vehicle and support rear axle. Remove wheel. Remove axle damper front attaching bolt.

2) On Mustang, remove axle damper rear attaching nut and pivot bolt. Remove damper and washers. *See Fig. 7.*

Installation – To install axle damper, reverse removal procedure. Tighten all nuts and bolts to specification.

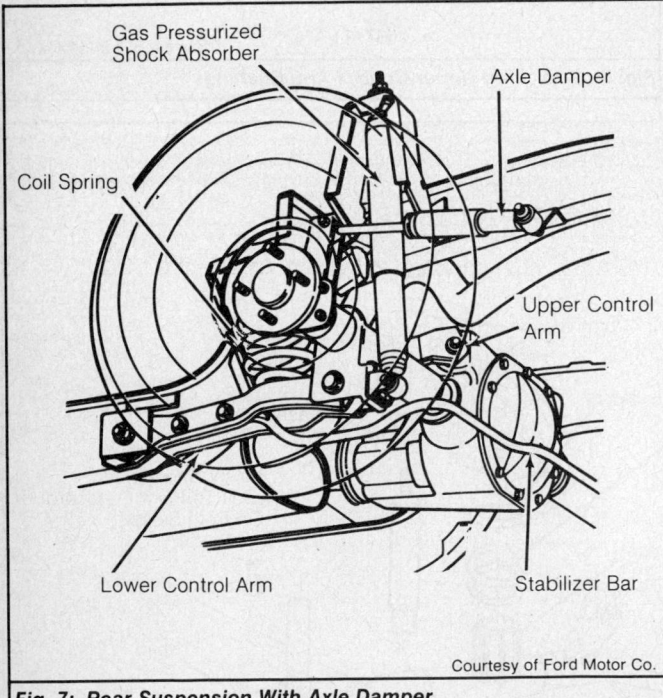

Courtesy of Ford Motor Co.

Fig. 7: Rear Suspension With Axle Damper

NOTE: Unless otherwise noted, procedures and specifications for LTD Crown Victoria and Grand Marquis may generally be used on Station Wagon models.

TIGHTENING SPECIFICATIONS

Application	Ft. Lbs. (N.m)
Axle Damper Bolt	
Mustang	55-70 (75-95)
Clevis Bracket-to-Axle Nut	
Mustang	55-70 (75-95)
Drive Shaft Flange-to-Pinion	
Flange Bolts	70-95 (95-129)
Lower Arm-to-Axle Bolt	
LTD Crown Victoria, Grand Marquis, Town Car	103-133 (140-180)
All Others	70-100 (95-136)
Lower Arm-to-Frame Bolt	
LTD Crown Victoria, Grand Marquis, Town Car	120-150 (163-203)
All Others	80-105 (108-142)
Rear Stabilizer Bar Bolt	
LTD Crown Victoria, Grand Marquis, Town Car	70-92 (95-125)
All Others	33-51 (45-70)
Shock Absorber Lower Nut	
LTD Crown Victoria, Grand Marquis, Town Car	52-85 (70-115)
All Others	55-70 (75-95)
Shock Absorber-to-Clevis Bracket Bolt	
Mustang	45-60 (61-81)
Shock Absorber Upper Nut	
LTD Crown Victoria, Grand Marquis, Town Car	14-26 (19-35)
All Others	19-27 (26-37)
Upper Arm-to-Axle Bolt	
LTD Crown Victoria, Grand Marquis, Town Car	103-133 (140-180)
All Others	70-100 (95-136)
Upper Arm-to-Frame Bolt	
LTD Crown Victoria, Grand Marquis, Town Car	120-150 (163-203)
All Others	80-105 (108-142)

DESCRIPTION

Suspension is mounted on isolated subframe and is fully independent. Two lower control arms limit front-to-rear movement while 2 upper control arms limit side-to-side movement. Upper and lower control arms are connected by a cast aluminum knuckle that houses the half-shaft bearing while also serving as a mount for rear brake calipers. Variable rate coil springs are mounted in the conventional manner between lower control arm and body.

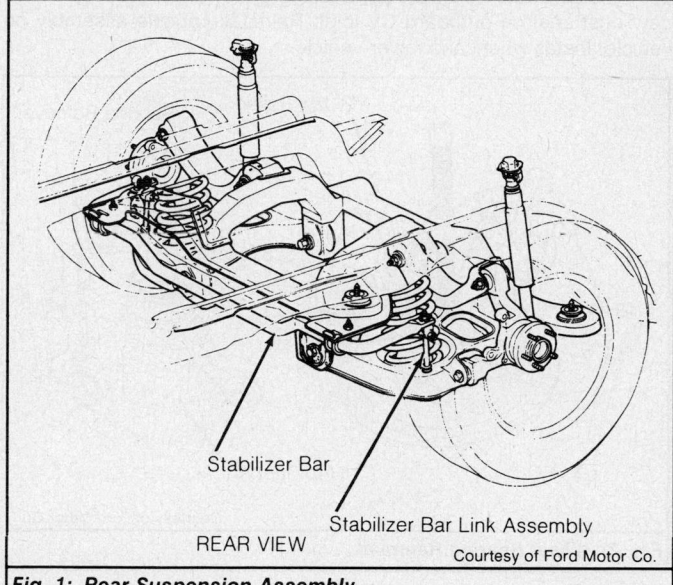

Stabilizer Bar
Stabilizer Bar Link Assembly
REAR VIEW
Courtesy of Ford Motor Co.

Fig. 1: Rear Suspension Assembly

ADJUSTMENTS

WHEEL ALIGNMENT

See appropriate article in WHEEL ALIGNMENT section.

RIDING HEIGHT

See RIDING HEIGHT SPECIFICATIONS article in WHEEL ALIGNMENT section.

REAR WHEEL BEARINGS

Rear wheel bearings are sealed nonadjustable units. Install NEW hub nut and washer whenever they are loosened or removed. See WHEEL BEARINGS under REMOVAL & INSTALLATION in this article.

REMOVAL & INSTALLATION

SHOCK ABSORBERS

NOTE: *Rear shock absorbers act to limit rear suspension travel. If shocks are removed or disconnected, it is necessary to use a drive-on rack or other means to raise vehicle while maintaining load on suspension.*

Removal – On Thunderbird Super Coupe and Cougar XR-7, see ACTUATOR under FORD MOTOR CO. AUTOMATIC RIDE CONTROL in this section. Position vehicle on hoist. Remove shock upper attachments from inside luggage compartment. Remove bolt and nut at lower control arm. Remove shock.

Installation – Before installing shock absorber, place shock right side up (as installed in vehicle) and fully extend. Turn shock absorber upside down and fully compress it. Repeat at least 3 times to get rid of any trapped air. To install, reverse removal procedure. Tighten nuts and bolts to specifications.

KNUCKLE

CAUTION: *Do not begin procedure unless NEW hub nut is available. Once removed, its torque holding ability is GREATLY reduced.*

Removal – 1) Raise vehicle. Remove wheel and tire assembly. Remove and discard hub nut and washer. Pull parking brake release lever while also pulling on cable. This will give cable enough slack to be removed from caliper or backing plate. Remove cable from caliper (disc brakes).

2) Remove both caliper bolts. Remove caliper and carefully wire out of way, so that brake cable is not stretched or damaged. Remove push-on nuts and remove brake rotor or drum. Disconnect parking brake cable and brake line from wheel cylinder (drum brakes).

3) Remove upper control arm nut and bolt. Wire upper control arm to body. Using Hub Remover (T81P-1104-C), remove hub from half-shaft. With upper control arm bolt removed, the lower control arm bushings are in relaxed or unloaded position. It is important to mark control arm-to-knuckle relation for reassembly. See Fig. 2.

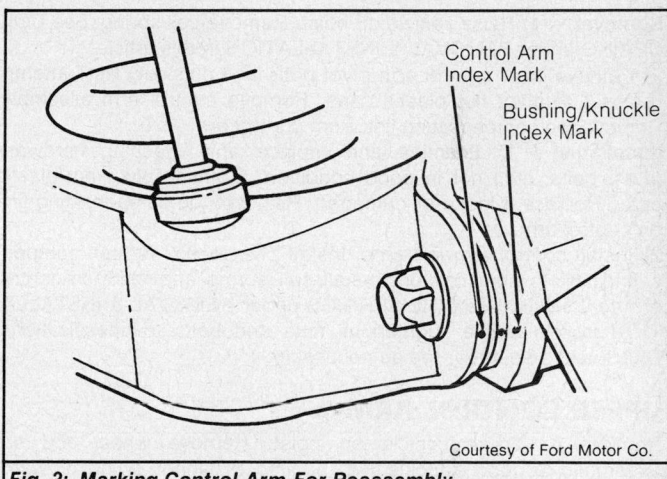

Control Arm
Index Mark

Bushing/Knuckle
Index Mark

Courtesy of Ford Motor Co.

Fig. 2: Marking Control Arm For Reassembly

4) If knuckle is being replaced, measure and record distance between upper bushing and any convenient point on vehicle body. Remove lower control arm-to-knuckle bolts and nuts. Remove knuckle assembly from half-shaft.

Installation – 1) Place hub and knuckle assembly on half-shaft and install lower control arm-to-knuckle bolts and nuts. Align index marks on control arm with marks on bushing. If new knuckle is being installed, set to measurement obtained during removal procedure.

2) Install upper control arm attaching bolt and nut. Tighten to specifications. Install NEW hub nut and washer. Install splash shield (disc brakes). Tighten 3 retaining bolts to specifications. On drum brakes, attach brake line to wheel cylinder and install parking brake cable.

3) Install rotor or drum and new push-on nuts. Install caliper. Tighten bolts to specifications. Install parking brake cable. Adjust as necessary. Bleed drum brakes. Install wheel and tire assembly. Lower vehicle and tighten hub retainer nut to specification.

COIL SPRING

Removal – 1) Raise vehicle on hoist. Support control arm with jack. Remove stabilizer bar link nuts and rotate bar upward out of way. Disconnect parking brake cable at caliper. Wire upper control arm assembly upward out of way.

2) Install 3 Rotunda Spring Cages (086-00031) or equivalent at 120 degree intervals around spring circumference. Remove lower shock absorber bolt and nut. Mark toe adjustment cam-to-subframe position for reassembly. Loosen but do not remove, both inboard pivot bolts on lower control arm.

NOTE: Control arm must not be lowered until pivot bolts are loosened. Do not attempt to remove plastic cap on pivot nuts.

3) Slowly lower jack supporting control arm. Be sure spring cages hold spring securely. Remove jack. Pull control arm down and remove spring assembly. Remove insulators if necessary.

Installation – 1) If a new spring is being installed, use Coil Spring Compressor (D78P-5310-A) to compress spring for removal or installation of cages. Install spring insulators before using spring compressor. Compress spring to approximately 10.5" (NOT including insulators).

2) Install 3 Rotunda Spring Cages (086-00031) at 120 degree intervals around spring circumference. Install cage and spring assembly. To install, reverse removal procedure. Tighten all nuts and bolts to specifications. Check toe adjustment and adjust as necessary.

LOWER CONTROL ARM

Removal – 1) Raise vehicle on hoist. Remove coil spring. See COIL SPRING under REMOVAL & INSTALLATION in this article.

2) Remove inner control arm pivot bolts and nuts. DO NOT attempt removal of pivot nut plastic caps. Remove control arm assembly. Remove toe compensating link from control arm.

Installation – 1) Examine and replace any attaching hardware (nuts, bolts, etc.) not in good condition. Examine pivot nut plastic caps. Replace if loose or damaged. Reinstall toe compensating link on control arm.

2) Install control arm in frame. Install pivot bolts. Tighten compensating link to specification. Install coil spring and reattach control arm to knuckle. See COIL SPRINGS under REMOVAL & INSTALLATION in this article. Tighten all nuts and bolts to specifications. Check and adjust rear toe as necessary.

UPPER CONTROL ARM

Removal – Raise vehicle on hoist. Remove wheel and tire assembly. Support knuckle and hub so it cannot swing outward. Remove inner and outer pivot bolts. Remove upper control arm.

NOTE: Inner pivot bolt is used for camber adjustment with special washer under bolt head. Install fasteners in original locations.

Installation – To install, reverse removal procedure. Tighten all fasteners to specifications. See TIGHTENING SPECIFICATIONS table. Install wheel and tire assembly. Lower vehicle. Check and adjust rear wheel alignment as necessary. See appropriate article in WHEEL ALIGNMENT section.

STABILIZER BAR

Removal – Raise vehicle on hoist. Remove wheel and tire assemblies. Remove both stabilizer bar link upper retaining bolts and nuts. Remove both stabilizer bracket bolts. Remove muffler hanger nuts. Remove stabilizer bar. Remove bushings if necessary.

Installation – To install, reverse removal procedure. Tighten all fasteners to specifications. See TIGHTENING SPECIFICATIONS table. Install wheel and tire assemblies. Lower vehicle.

WHEEL BEARINGS

Removal – 1) Remove knuckle and hub assembly. See KNUCKLE REMOVAL under REMOVAL & INSTALLATION in this article. Place knuckle and hub assembly in vise. On drum brakes, remove linings, springs and adjuster. Remove 4 bolts holding backing plate to knuckle.

2) Using a 3 jaw puller and Step Plate (D88L-1037-A), press hub out of knuckle assembly. *See Fig. 3.* Remove backing plate. Remove bearing retainer snap ring. Place bearing and knuckle assembly on press with Hub Support (T-89P-1104-A) and press bearing out.

Installation – 1) Place knuckle assembly on press bed. Using Bearing Installer (T-86P-1104-A3), press in new bearing. *See Fig. 4.*

Install snap ring. Place backing plate on knuckle and install 4 retaining bolts. Tighten backing plate bolts to 45-60 ft. lbs. (61-81 N.m).

2) Position hub on Spacer (T-83P-1104-AH3), with lugs facing downward. Place hub and spacer on press bed. Place knuckle assembly on hub with outboard side down. Press down on Bearing Remover (T-83P-1104-AH2) until bearing is fully seated. Hub should rotate freely in knuckle.

3) Reinstall brake hardware on backing plate (drum brakes). Install new dust seal on outboard CV joint. Reinstall knuckle assembly on vehicle. Install wheel and lower vehicle.

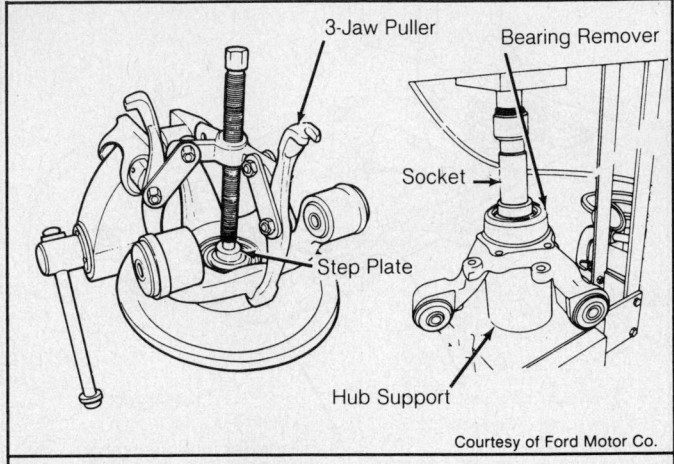

Fig. 3: Wheel Bearing Removal

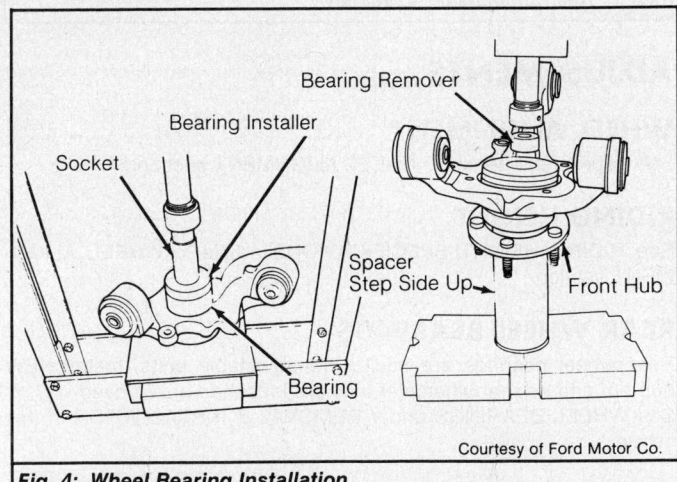

Fig. 4: Wheel Bearing Installation

TIGHTENING SPECIFICATIONS

Application	Ft. Lbs. (N.m)
Hub Retainer Nut	250 (340)
Jounce Bumper-to-Body	28-47 (38-64)
Lower Control Arm-to-Compensator Link Nut	118-148 (160-200)
Lower Control Arm-to-Knuckle Bolts	118-148 (160-200)
Lower Control Arm-to-Subframe Nut (Front)	184-229 (250-310)
Lower Control Arm-to-Subframe Nut (Rear)	125-170 (170-230)
Shock Absorber-to-Body (Upper Mount) Nut	27-35 (37-47)
Shock Absorber-to-Lower Control Arm Nut	110-120 (150-162)
Stabilizer Bar Link-to-Lower Control Arm Nut	6-12 (8-16)
Stabilizer Bar "U" Bracket-to-Subframe Bolt	26-34 (35-46)
Stabilizer Clevis-to-Stabilizer Bar Nut	28-40 (38-54)
Stabilizer Link-to-Stabilizer Bar Nut	34-46 (46-62)
Upper Control Arm-to-Knuckle Nut	118-148 (160-200)
Upper Control Arm-to-Subframe Nut	81-98 (110-133)

Dynasty, New Yorker

DESCRIPTION & OPERATION

Electronic height control system automatically raises or lowers rear of vehicle, according to vehicle's load. System consists of a compressor, control module, height sensor, air lines, relay, rear air shock absorbers, air drier and connecting wiring.

As load is added or removed to rear of vehicle, height sensor, located on right rear shock absorber, sends a signal to control module. Control module then opens ground circuit to compressor (to raise) or exhaust valve (to lower), located on compressor.

Height sensor signals control module when vehicle is at normal riding height. To prevent excess cycling between exhaust valve and compressor, control module has a 12-18 second delay between signal outputs. A residual of 10-22 psi (69-152 kPa) remains in system to improve ride under light load conditions.

TESTING

RESIDUAL AIR CHECK

1) Remove air line from air drier and right rear shock absorber. Using 2 test pieces of nylon tubing, attach pressure gauge (0-300 psi) between shock absorber and air drier. *See Fig. 1.*

2) A compression ball sleeve nut and sleeve for 3/16" tubing with ball sleeve connector and internal "T" fitting can be used as alternate way of attaching pressure gauge to system.

3) Cycle ignition off and on. Apply load of 300-325 lbs. (136-147 kg) to rear of vehicle. Compressor should operate and raise vehicle.

4) When compressor stops operating, remove load. System should exhaust air. When no more air is exhausted, pressure gauge should read 10-22 psi (69-152 kPa). If pressure is not as specified, check for air leaks. If no air leak can be found, replace air drier and retest.

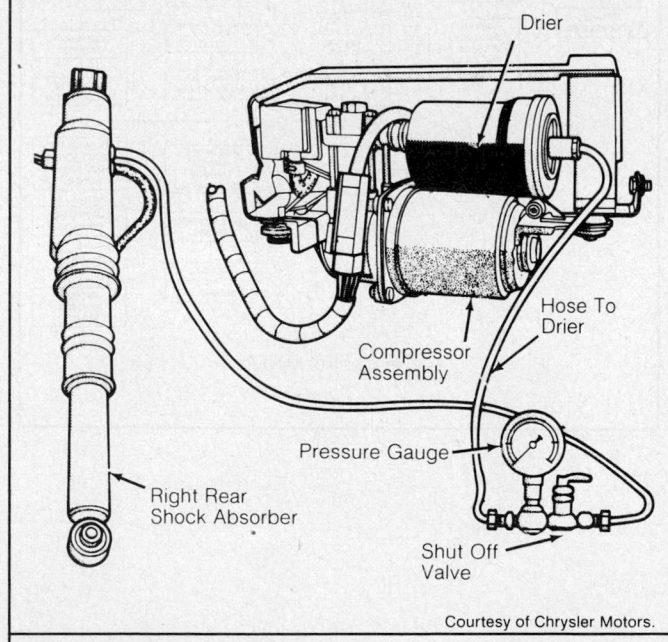

Fig. 1: Installing Pressure Gauge

LEAK CHECKS

1) Perform RESIDUAL AIR CHECK steps 1), 2) and 3) until pressure gauges reads 70-90 psi (483-621 kPa). DO NOT allow compressor to operate until it shuts down or exhaust valve will open resulting in leak-down. This will indicate false air leak.

2) Unplug control module connector, located on right rear panel, inside luggage compartment. Remove load from vehicle. Vehicle should rise as load is removed. Turn ignition off. Observe pressure gauge reading for 15 minutes.

3) If system pressure drops or will not inflate more than 50 psi (345 kPa), check for leaks or pinched lines. Use a soapy solution to check for leaks. If system maintains pressure, see TROUBLE SHOOTING charts in this article.

COMPRESSOR PERFORMANCE TEST

1) Unplug compressor connector. Disconnect air line between air drier and right shock absorber. Connect pressure gauge. See RESIDUAL AIR CHECK steps 1) and 2). Connect an ammeter in series between Red wire terminal, at compressor, and 12-volt source. *See Fig. 2.*

2) Connect a jumper wire between Black wire terminal, at compressor, and known good ground. If current draw is more than 21 amps, replace compressor. If current draw is okay, disconnect wiring when system stabilizes at 120 psi (827 kPa).

3) If system leaks down below 90 psi (612 kPa) before it stabilizes or pressure is less than 110 psi (758 kPa) when it stabilizes, replace compressor. Do not allow system pressure to reach 220 psi (1517 kPa). If system reaches specified pressure, exhaust valve will open, allow air to escape. This can lead to false leak.

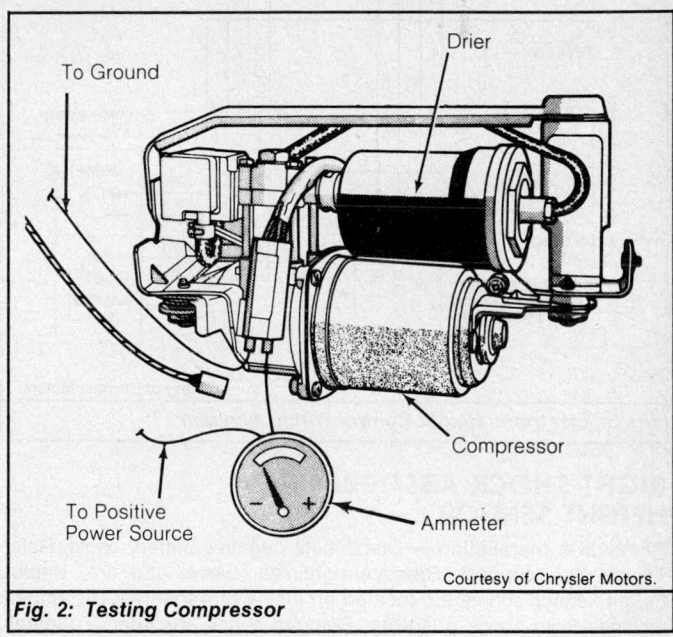

Fig. 2: Testing Compressor

NOTE: In addition to above testing procedure, see TROUBLE SHOOTING CHARTS in rear portion of this article.

REMOVAL & INSTALLATION

COMPRESSOR

Removal & Installation – 1) Disconnect negative battery cable. Raise vehicle and support. Remove cover from compressor. Unplug electrical connectors from compressor.

2) Disconnect air line. Remove compressor from vehicle. Remove mounting bracket from compressor. To install, reverse removal procedure. Check system operation.

CONTROL MODULE & RELAY

Removal & Installation – Disconnect negative battery cable. Remove trim panel on right rear panel, inside luggage compartment. Unplug control module and relay connectors. Remove control module and relay. To install, reverse removal procedure. Check system operation.

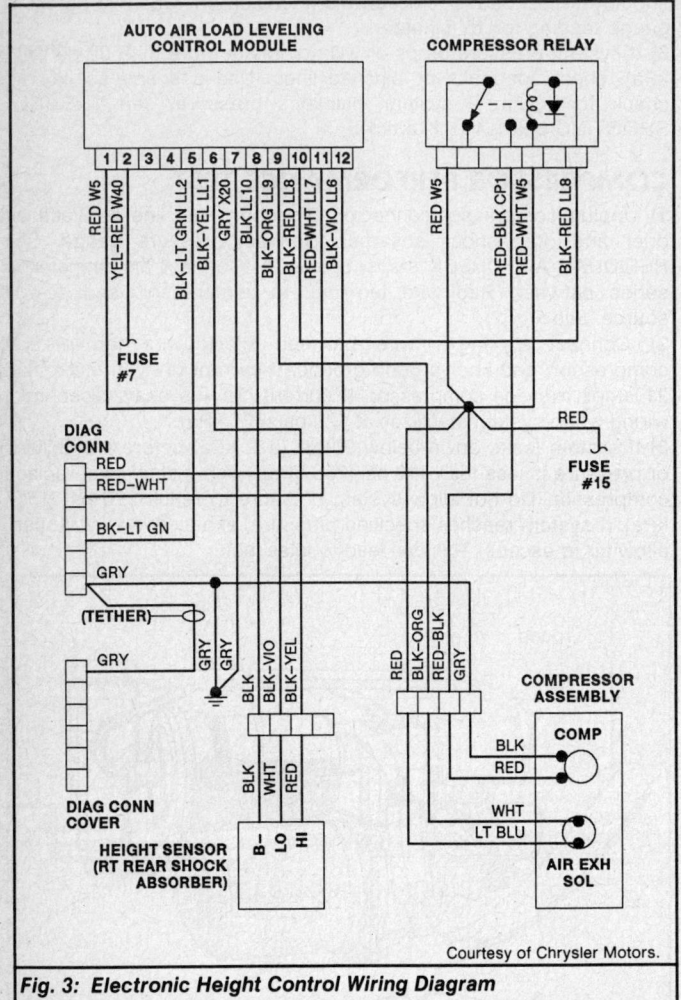

Fig. 3: Electronic Height Control Wiring Diagram

Courtesy of Chrysler Motors.

RIGHT SHOCK ABSORBER & HEIGHT SENSOR

Removal & Installation – Disconnect negative battery cable. Raise vehicle and support. Remove right rear wheel and tire. Unplug height sensor connector, located on inside of frame rail. Disconnect air lines from shock absorber. Remove shock absorber. To install, reverse removal procedure.

TIGHTENING SPECIFICATIONS

Applications	Ft. Lbs. (N.m)
Lower Shock Absorber Nut	40 (54)
Upper Shock Absorber Nut	45 (61)

	INCH Lbs. (N.m)
Control Module Mounting Screws	19-29 (2-3)
Mounting Bracket-to-Compressor Screw	70 (8)
Mounting Bracket-to-Frame Rail Screw	70 (8)

TROUBLE SHOOTING CHARTS

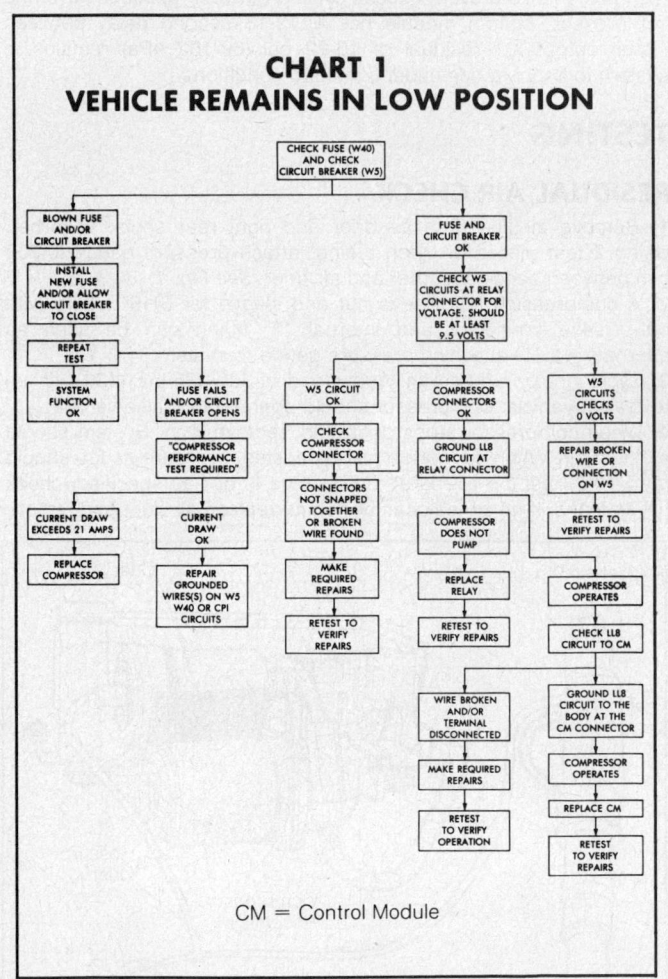

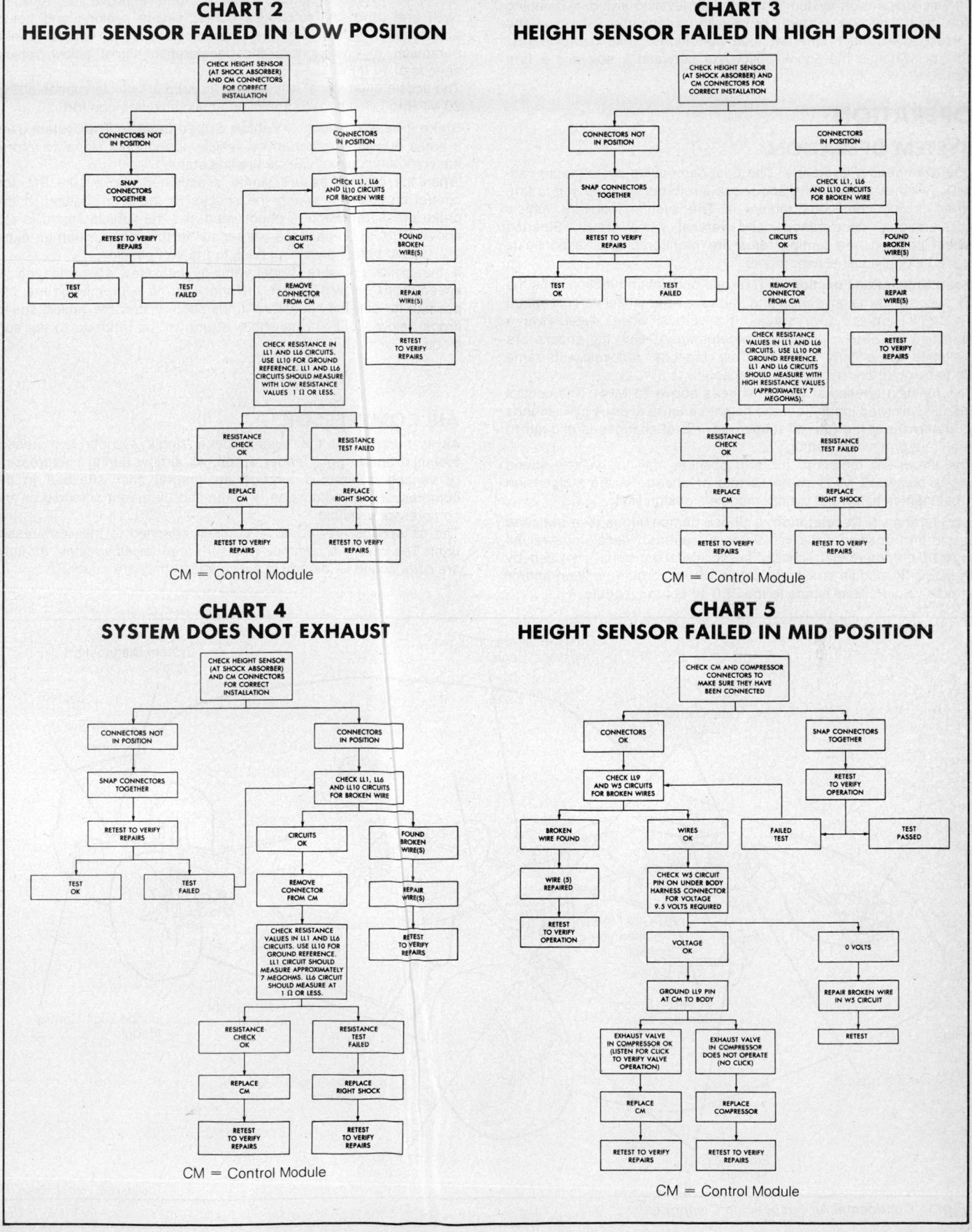

DESCRIPTION

The air suspension system combines air leveling and dual damping ride control in one system. Air leveling keeps the vehicle at the correct level under different load-conditions. Dual damping ride control switches the shock absorbers between a soft and a firm ride.

OPERATION

SYSTEM OPERATION

Dual Dampening System – The dual dampening system automatically switches the MacPherson shock strut settings from soft to firm when driving conditions require it. The system monitors vehicle accelerations, decelerations and vertical wheel travel. Steering wheel position and turning rates are monitored and response is issued to individual sensor inputs.

Road Undulation Function – The road undulation function uses the air suspension height sensors to measure road wheel vertical speed and travel (up-and-down travel). If a vertical wheel speed over a specified distance is above a predetermined level, the shocks are switched to a firm position. This function reduces sub-frame bottoming out on rough road surfaces.

The function is used at vehicle speeds above 16 MPH. The control module will read inputs fom the height sensors every 4 milliseconds to determine if the rate of suspension travel changes is enough to require a firm shock setting.

The struts will remain in the firm position until the vehicle speed drops below 10 MPH and/or a rate of change in the suspension movement is below the control module's design limit.

Acceleration & Deceleration – Shock dampening is also switched to the firm position if the vehicle acceleration or decelertion values exceed predetermined limits. The acceleration signal provided by the EEC-IV module is a combination of the throttle position and/or engine vacuum level inputs to the EEC-IV control module.

The deceleration signal is provided by a pressure switch located in the brake hydraulic circuit. These 2 inputs improve the vehicle's pitch and drive characteristics during severe braking and heavy acceleration. Inputs are then combined with a vehicle speed parameter that will ignore the deceleration signal below vehicle speeds of 10 MPH.

The acceleration signal will also be ignored at vehicle speeds above 20 MPH to minimize harshness and maximize ride comfort.

Brake Pressure Switch & Vehicle Speed Input – The system uses a brake pressure switch and a vehicle speed input signal to inform the control module of vehicle braking status.

When the brake pressure signal is activated above 10 MPH, the control module will switch the shocks to the firm position. If the brake pressure switch is deactivated and the vehicle speed is still above 10 MPH, the shocks will remain in the firm position an extra 1/2 second before switching back to the soft position.

If the brake pressure signal remains activated after the vehicle speed drops below 10 MPH, the shock struts will remain in the firm position for only 2.4 seconds. At one second after the vehicle speed drops below 10 MPH, the shock struts will be returned to the soft mode.

AIR COMPRESSOR

Air is supplied to the system by a single cylinder compressor mounted on the right fender apron. All airflow during compression or venting is directed through an integral drier attached to the compressor. Air exhaustion is controlled by a vent solenoid on the compressor manifold.

The air springs are fed by 4 air lines attached to the compressor drier. The drier is a common pressure feed for all air lines. Air lines are color coded to identify to which spring they are attached.

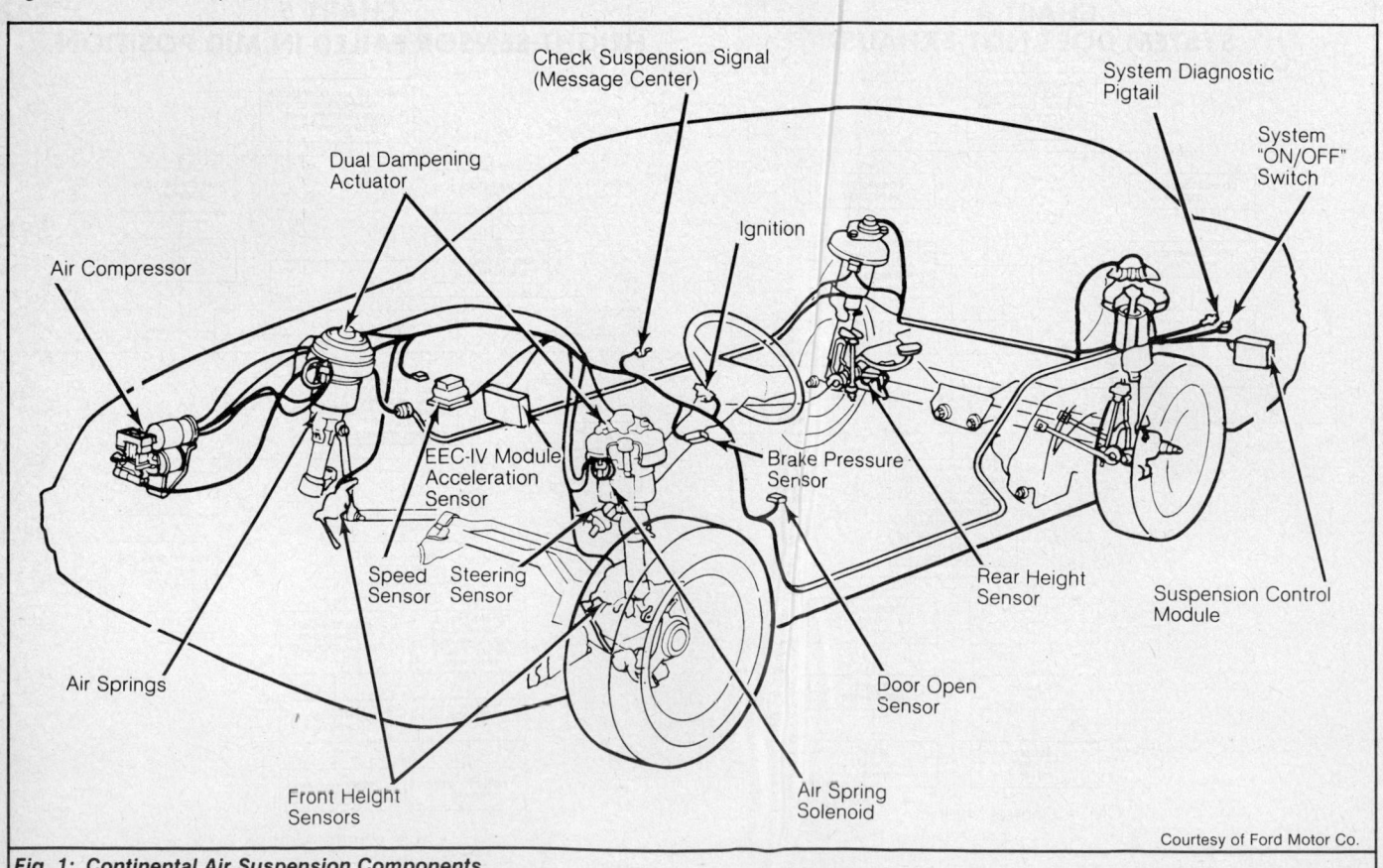

Fig. 1: Continental Air Suspension Components

Courtesy of Ford Motor Co.

1989 ELECTRONIC SUSPENSION
Ford Motor Co. Air Suspension – Continental (Cont.)

12-61

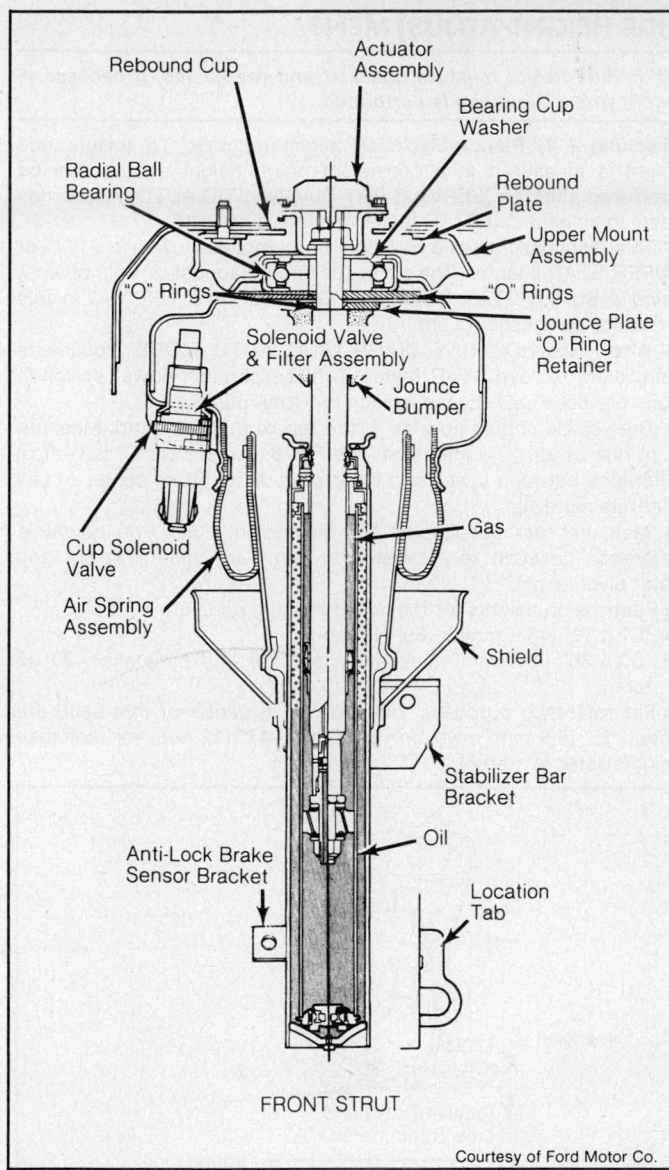

Fig. 2: Continental Front Strut Assembly
(Rear Strut Assembly Is Similar)

Courtesy of Ford Motor Co.

FRONT STRUT

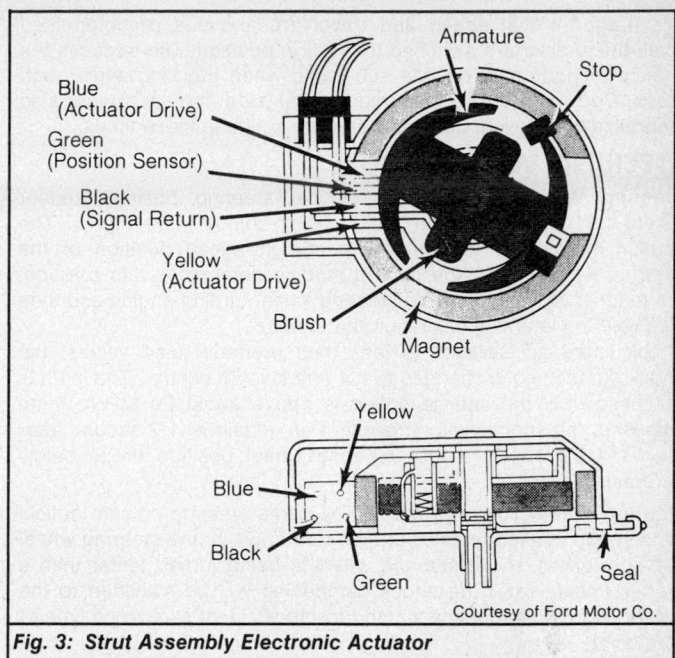

Fig. 3: Strut Assembly Electronic Actuator

Courtesy of Ford Motor Co.

AIR SPRING & STRUT ASSEMBLIES

Front and rear suspensions are equipped with MacPherson strut assemblies with integral air springs that incorporate 2-stage dampening mechanisms. A soft or firm ride (dual dampening) can be selected by changing piston orifice area with an externally mounted electronic rotary actuator. See Fig. 3. The front struts are attached to the body through a precision ball bearing and rubber mount system. Ball bearings provide a smooth pivot point for the strut and wheel assembly. See Fig. 2.

Oversize rubber mountings provides impact and noise isolation on the top of the strut. Rear struts have a dual path mount which separates the strut and air spring mounting surfaces for maximum isolation.

CONTROL MODULE

The control module is the electronic control center of the system. It receives signals from various sensors in the vehicle. The module uses sensor inputs to maintain desired ride height when vehicle is moving or stopped.

This is accomplished by opening or closing the air spring valves. The control module also operates the compressor through the compressor relay or opens the vent solenoids in response to signal inputs from height sensors.

The control module receives the following inputs:

- Vehicle speed.
- Steering wheel turning rotation.
- Engine vacuum level.
- Throttle position angle (supplied by EEC-IV system).
- Brake pressure sensor.
- Ignition switch position.
- Shock absorber damping position.
- Door switch position.
- Height sensor position.

ELECTRONIC HEIGHT SENSORS

The height sensors are a rotary style, Hall effect design that determines ride height. See Fig. 4. Sensors are located at the left front, right front and rear of the vehicle. Each sensor measures the difference between a set reference point and actual vehicle height so the control module can respond to variations in ride height.

In parking mode, additional height positions allow the control module to determine if an obstruction was found while parking the vehicle. In driving mode, road surface variations are sensed by checking road wheel vertical speed and vertical travel.

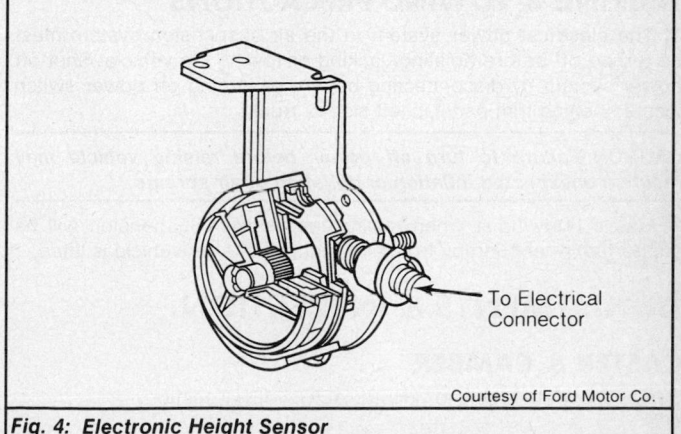

Courtesy of Ford Motor Co.

Fig. 4: Electronic Height Sensor

12-62

1989 ELECTRONIC SUSPENSION
Ford Motor Co. Air Suspension — Continental (Cont.)

If average vertical speed and travel are above a predetermined level, the shocks are switched to the firm position. This reduces the chance of bottoming out the sub-frame when traveling over rough roads. Body rolls during long, high lateral (side) force turns are also neutralized to prevent unwanted leveling action at these times.

STEERING WHEEL INPUTS

Steering Wheel Sensor – An optical steering position sensor (photo-cell) is mounted on the steering column. See Fig. 5. The sensor is used to determine the straight-ahead position of the steering wheel. Once the control module determines this position, the module can measure the steering wheel turning angles and then calculate the lateral acceleration that results.

If calculated acceleration is less than predetermined values, the shock dampening is changed to the firm level of control. The input is not used until the vehicle speed is above about 20 MPH. When activated, the shocks will remain firm an additional 1/2 second after the vehicle's speed and/or steering wheel position drops below parameter levers.

Steering Wheel Turning Rate – The same steering column optical sensor also is used to calculate the rate at which the steering wheel is being turned. If the steering wheel is being turned faster than a predetermined rate, the shock dampening will be switched to the firm postion. This function is used for an accident avoidance type of maneuver.

Under these conditions, the action is fast but the actual movement and/or displacement of the steering wheel may not be enough to activate the steering position function. The steering rate function is not used until the vehicle's speed is more than 20 MPH. After the shocks are activated, they will remain in the firm mode for 1/2-3/4 of a second after the vehicle's speed and/or steering wheel rate drops below parameter levels.

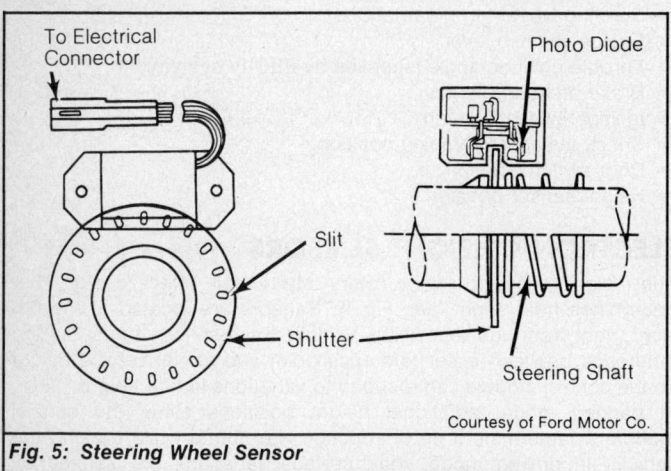

Fig. 5: Steering Wheel Sensor

JACKING & TOWING PRECAUTIONS

1) The electrical power system to the air suspension system must be turned off before hoisting, jacking or towing the vehicle. Shut off power system by disconnecting battery or turning off power switch located behind trim panel in left side of trunk.

CAUTION: Failure to turn off power before raising vehicle may result in unexpected inflation or deflation of air springs.

2) Use a body hoist when raising the vehicle. Suspension will be supported in rebound by front and rear struts after vehicle is lifted.

ADJUSTMENTS & INSPECTION

CASTER & CAMBER

See appropriate article in WHEEL ALIGNMENT section

RIDE HEIGHT ADJUSTMENT

NOTE: Ride height must be checked and readjusted, if necessary, before wheel alignment is performed.

Checking – 1) Place vehicle on alignment rack. To ensure ride height is measured at a consistent point, height should only be measured after the "SERVICE BAY DIAGNOSTIC AUTO MODE" has been completed and STAR tester displays a code 12.

2) This diagnostic routine can only be completed using a STAR or SUPER STAR II tester. The air suspension diagnostics will not work using a SUPER STAR tester. See DIAGNOSIS & TESTING in this article for diagnostic routine.

3) After "SERVICE BAY DIAGNOSTIC AUTO MODE" routine is completed, remove STAR tester. Turn suspension power switch in trunk off. See Fig. 1. Leave ignition in "RUN" position.

4) The vehicle should now be at the top of the trim band. Measure front ride height "C" dimension. See Fig. 6. Dimension "C" is vertical difference between lower arm inner pivot and bottom center of ball joint retainer disk.

5) Measure rear suspension "D" dimension. Rear ride height is difference between rear lower arm pivot attachment height and outer pivot height.

6) Suspension heights for the top of the trim band are:
- "C": 1.72" (43.6 mm) ± .39" (10 mm).
- "D": -.36" (-9.3 mm). Tolerance is +.39" (10 mm) and -.20" (5 mm).

7) For reference purposes, ride heights at center of trim band are about .35" (8.8 mm) lower for front, and .47" (12 mm) for rear than heights listed in step **6)**.

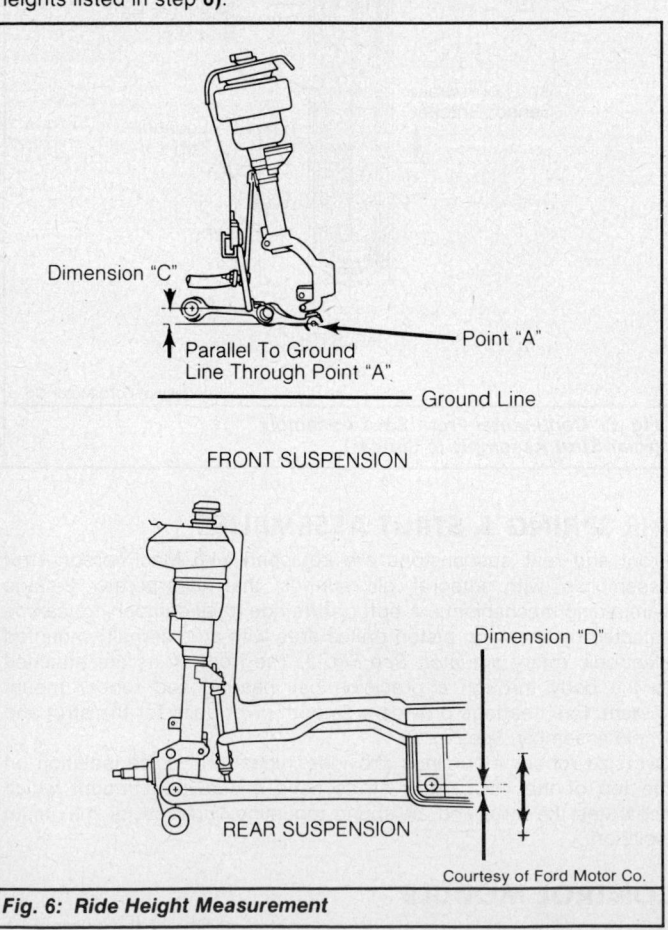

Fig. 6: Ride Height Measurement

Front Ride Height Adjustment – 1) Front ride height is adjusted by changing height sensor link. See FRONT RIDE HEIGHT SENSOR LINK DIMENSIONS table. See Fig. 7.

1989 ELECTRONIC SUSPENSION
Ford Motor Co. Air Suspension — Continental (Cont.)

12-63

2) When removing front link, carefully pry it off with a wide-bladed screwdriver. When installing link, support height sensor from behind to prevent sensor damage. Any front link change must be made with reference to the link that is to be removed.

FRONT RIDE HIDE HEIGHT SENSOR LINK DIMENSIONS

Part No. [1] Left Front	[1] Part No. Right Front	Sensor Link	Front Ride Height [2] Change In. (mm)
CA	GA	+1 (Green)	+.24 (6)
BA	FA	-1 (Red)	-.24 (6)
JA	KA	Nominal (Blue)	0
DA	HA	+2 (Yellow)	+47 (12)
AA	EA	-2 (White)	-.47 (12)

[1] – All part numbers are preceded by E80F-3C111-.
[2] – Ride height change is with respect to nominal link.

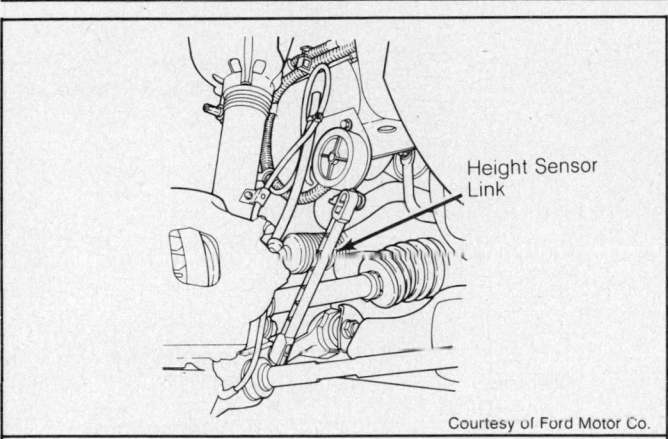

Fig. 7: Front Height Sensor Link

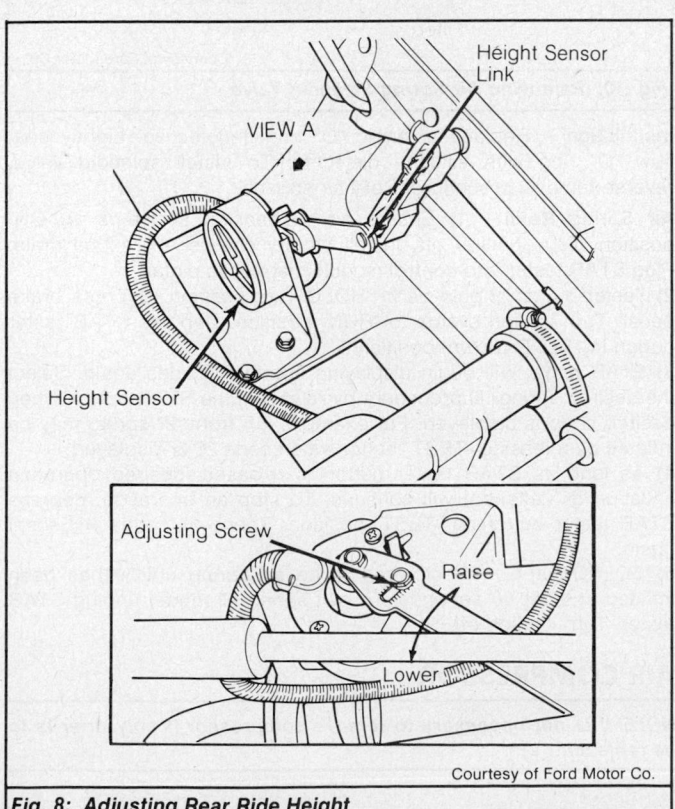

Fig. 8: Adjusting Rear Ride Height

Rear Ride Height Adjustment – To adjust rear height sensor, loosen and reposition height sensor lever adjustment screw. Each notch on rear height sensor lever gives about .60" (15 mm) of ride height adjustment. See Fig. 8.

FRONT WHEEL BEARINGS

Front wheel bearings do not require periodic adjustments.

BALL JOINT CHECKING

1) Turn off air suspension switch located in left side of trunk. Raise and support vehicle until front wheels are in fully extended position.
2) Move lower edge of tire in and out. Any movement at lower end of knuckle and lower control arm indicates ball joint wear. If any movement is seen, install new lower control arm and ball joint assembly.

STRUT & SPRING ASSEMBLY

Inspection – 1) The gas-filled hydraulic struts are nonadjustable and non-refillable and are serviced as assemblies. Before a strut is replaced because it is suspected to be defective, perform the following checks.
2) Check all tire pressures. Check the torque of all strut and suspension mounting bolts and nuts. Check strut for obvious external damage.
3) Check for fluid leakage by removing solenoid on top of strut. See AIR SPRING SOLENOID in REMOVAL & INSTALLATION (FRONT SUSPENSION) in this article. Check for oil film on solenoid or oil otaurated oil filter. Replace strut if leaking.
Strut Noise Check – 1) Bounce vehicle and try to isolate noise. Check spindle-to-fastener torque. Torque must exceed 55 ft. lbs. (75 N.m) on both rear strut lower mounting bolts. Front strut-to-knuckle torque must be greater than 70 ft. lbs. (95 N.m).

CAUTION: Strut lower mounting bolts use a locking material on threads. Loose bolts may appear to have correct torque. Replace fastener if equipped with locking material.

2) Check torque of strut upper mount-to-body nuts. Front torque must exceed 22 ft. lbs. (30 N.m). Rear torque must exceed 19 ft. lbs. (26 N.m).
3) Check torque of strut rod-to-mount nut. Torque must exceed 35 ft. lbs. (48 N.m). Rubber isolators must be in place.

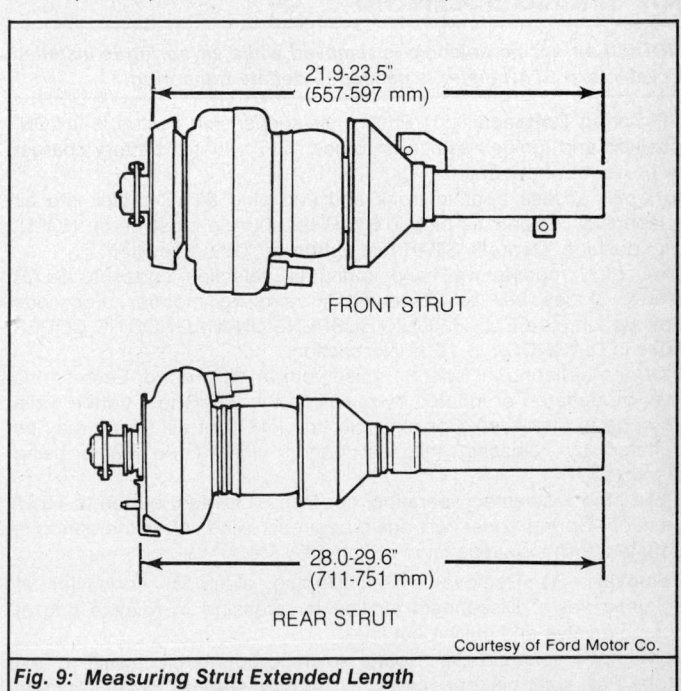

Fig. 9: Measuring Strut Extended Length

12-64

1989 ELECTRONIC SUSPENSION
Ford Motor Co. Air Suspension — Continental (Cont.)

4) Inspect connecting joints for damaged threads. Replace components as necessary. If noise is still present, remove strut and go to STRUT BENCH TEST.

Strut Bench Test – 1) Struts should be fully extended when out of vehicle and not restrained. If a strut does not fully extend, it should be replaced. *See Fig. 9.*

2) With the strut in normal upright position, compress it. Allow strut to extend 3 times to purge pressure chamber or any trapped gas.

3) Place shock absorber in vise. Hand stroke shock as fast as possible with as much travel as possible. Action should be smooth and uniform as possible on each stroke. Higher resistance on extension than on compression is normal.

4) Replace strut if any of the following conditions exist:
- A lag or skip at reversal of travel near mid-stroke when shock is properly primed and in installed position.
- Seizing.
- Noise other than faint "swish", such as clicking.
- Excessive fluid leakage.
- Any side-to-side motion with rod fully extended.

REMOVAL & INSTALLATION (AIR SUSPENSION)

CAUTION: Manufacturer recommends using new suspension fasteners whenever old fasteners are loosened or removed.

AIR LINES

Removal & Installation – 1) Air lines on air spring solenoids and compressor dryer are disconnected by pushing in plastic release ring where line meets quick connect fitting. Pull out air line while holding release ring. Install air line by pushing in tubing until flare on line is against release ring.

2) Quick connect fittings can be removed by disconnecting air line. Insert length of scrap air line into collet. Pull collet out by HAND. Remove "O" rings.

3) Clean "O" ring seat. Lightly coat "O" rings with silicone dielectric. Install new collet (prongs first) with finger pressure. Install release ring and line.

Repair – Service kits are available to repair damaged air lines. Sections of air line may be cut out and union installed.

AIR SPRING SOLENOID

NOTE: If air spring solenoid is removed while air spring is installed in vehicle, a STAR tester is needed to deflate the spring.

Air Spring Deflation – 1) Ensure air suspension switch is in "ON" position and ignition switch is turned "OFF". Install battery charger to prevent battery drain.

2) Open access door in trunk and and plug STAR tester into air suspension diagnostic pigtail. STAR test button must be in "HOLD" (up) position. Depress STAR test button to "TEST" position.

3) Control module will send spring fill selection codes to STAR tester. Codes will be displayed in scrolling manner. For code description, see ELECTRONIC SUSPENSION DIAGNOSTIC CODES table in DIAGNOSIS & TESTING section.

4) When deflating air springs, raise vehicle off ground. Each spring may be deflated or inflated by releasing the STAR test button while its code is displayed. For example, the left front air spring may be deflated by releasing the test button while code 22 is being displayed.

5) To stop a selected operation, depress STAR test button to TEST position. Spring codes will again begin scrolling. After the spring is deflated, turn air suspension switch off.

Removal – 1) Remove wheel. Unplug electrical connector at solenoid valve. Disconnect air line by pressing in release ring at solenoid valve and pulling out line.

2) Remove solenoid clip. Rotate solenoid counterclockwise to first stop. Pull solenoid out slowly to second stop to bleed air from system. *See Fig. 10.*

CAUTION: Do not remove solenoid until air spring is bled.

3) Bleed air from system. Rotate solenoid counterclockwise to third stop and remove from air spring. Inspect filter. Replace filter if oily. Very oily filter indicates a leaking air strut.

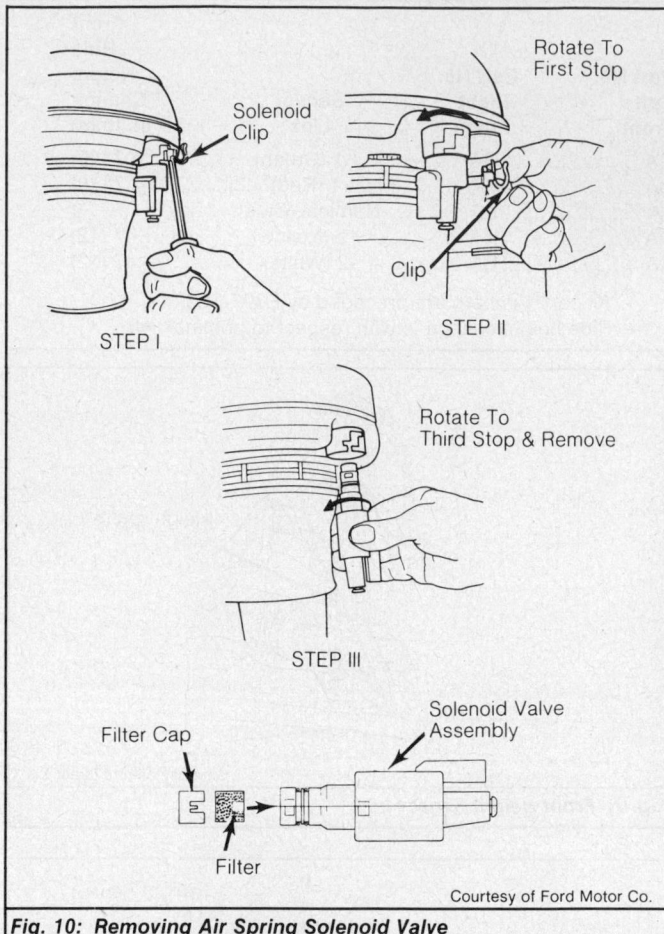

Courtesy of Ford Motor Co.

Fig. 10: Removing Air Spring Solenoid Valve

Installation – Replace solenoid "O" ring if defective. Lightly coat new "O" ring with silicone dielectric. To install solenoid valve, reverse removal procedure. Refill air springs.

Air Spring Refill – 1) Ensure air suspension switch is in "ON" position. Turn ignition off. Install battery charger to reduce drain. Plug STAR tester into control module diagnostic pigtail.

2) Tester button should be in "HOLD" (up) position. Depress brake pedal. Turn ignition switch to "RUN" position. Depress STAR tester button to "TEST" (down) position.

3) STAR tester will begin displaying spring fill codes again. Select the desired spring fill procedure by releasing the STAR button when desired code is displayed. For example, left front air spring may be inflated by releasing "TEST" button when code 25 is displayed.

4) As long as STAR tester button is released, desired operation (inflation or deflation) will continue. To stop an operation, depress STAR tester button to "TEST" position. Spring fill codes will scroll again.

5) DO NOT apply vehicle load to an air spring until it has been inflated at least 60 seconds. To exit spring fill mode, unplug STAR tester. Turn ignition off.

AIR COMPRESSOR

NOTE: It is not necessary to remove compressor if only drier is to be replaced.

1989 ELECTRONIC SUSPENSION
Ford Motor Co. Air Suspension — Continental (Cont.)

12-65

Removal – 1) Turn air suspension switch off. Unplug electrical connector on compressor. Remove air line protector cap from drier by releasing 2 latching pins located 180 degrees apart on bottom of cap.

2) Disconnect 4 air lines from drier. Remove 3 screws retaining air compressor to mounting bracket.

Installation – To install air compressor, reverse removal procedure. Turn on air suspension switch.

DAMPING ACTUATORS

NOTE: Strut assembly must be removed to replace rear actuator.

Removal – 1) Place vehicle on level surface. Set parking brake. Turn ignition off. On front actuators, remove plastic cover from top of shock tower.

2) On front and rear actuators, unplug actuator harness connector. Remove actuator clips from upper mount attaching studs. Remove 2 actuator-to-mounting bracket screws and lift off actuator.

Installation – Ensure flats of actuator and shock absorber are aligned. *See Fig. 11.* Align actuator screw attaching holes with mounting bracket. With wheels straight ahead, wire leads should point inboard. Install and tighten attaching screws to 10-14 INCH lbs. (1.1-1.6 N.m).

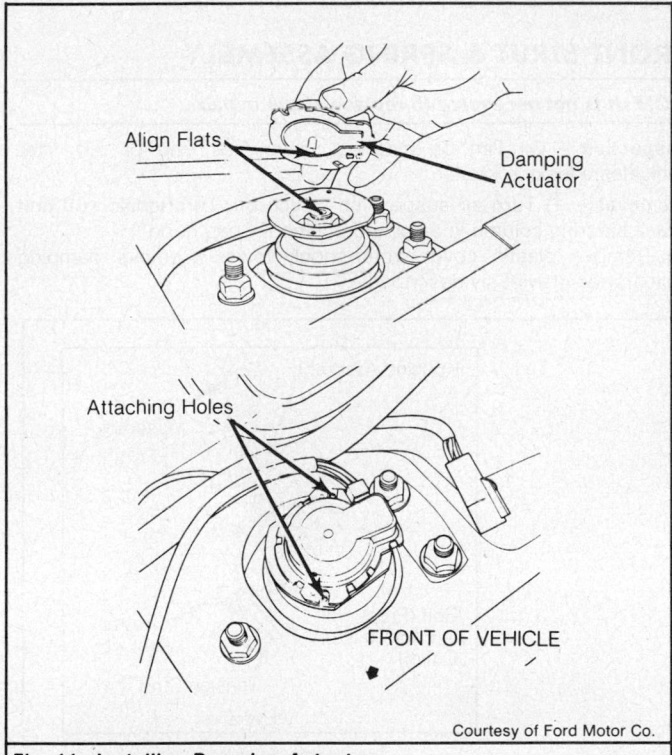

Courtesy of Ford Motor Co.

Fig. 11: Installing Damping Actuator

FRONT HEIGHT SENSOR

Removal – 1) Turn air suspension switch off. Unplug sensor electrical connectors. Left front sensor is in engine compartment behind shock tower. Right front connector is in engine compartment next to air compressor.

2) Push front sensor connector through access hole in rear of shock tower. Turn off air suspension switch in trunk. Raise and support vehicle.

3) Disconnect top and bottom of height sensor link from stud. *See Fig. 12.* Unplug anti-lock wire from bracket. Disconnect brake line from bracket. Remove attaching screws and remove sensor.

Installation – To install front height sensor, reverse removal procedure. Turn on air suspension switch.

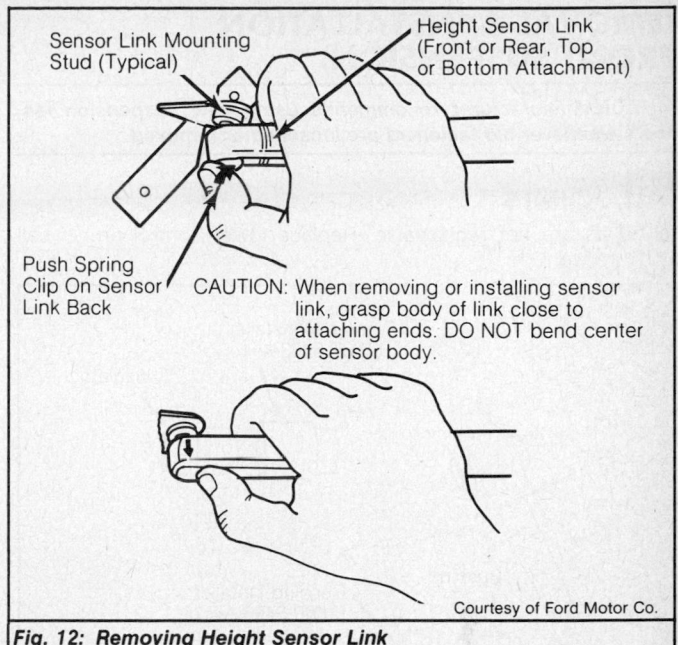

Courtesy of Ford Motor Co.

Fig. 12: Removing Height Sensor Link

REAR HEIGHT SENSOR

Removal – 1) Turn air suspension switch off. Unplug electrical connector in trunk in front of forward trim panel. Pull carpet back for access to sensor sealing grommet on floor pan.

2) Raise and support vehicle. Suspension must be at full rebound. Disconnect top and bottom end of height sensor link from attaching stud. *See Fig. 12.* Remove sensor attaching screws and lift off sensor.

Installation – To install height sensor, reverse removal procedure. Turn on air suspension switch.

STEERING SENSOR

Steering sensor is located at lower end of steering column. It may be replaced with steering column in or out of vehicle. Sensor and sensor rings are separate units. Sensor ring can only be removed by disassembling steering column.

Removal & Installation – 1) Unplug sensor electrical connector from wiring harness. Remove sensor electrical connector from shift control cable bracket under instrument panel. *See Fig. 13.*

2) Remove 2 retaining screws and lift off sensor. To install sensor, reverse removal procedure.

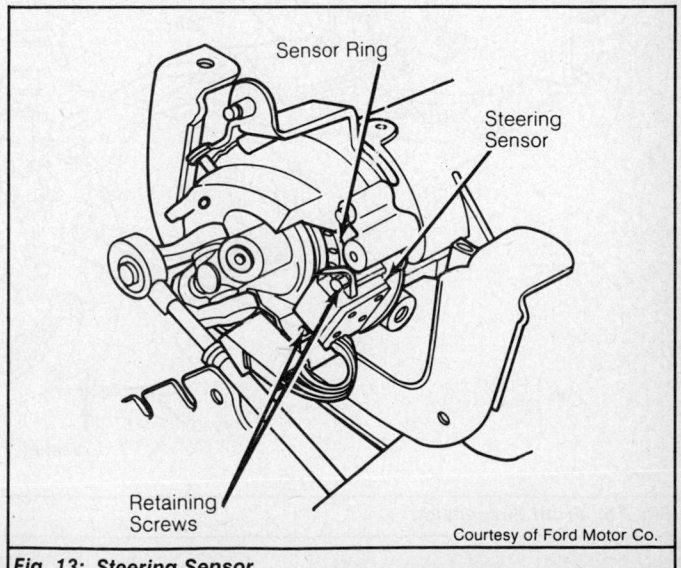

Courtesy of Ford Motor Co.

Fig. 13: Steering Sensor

12-66

1989 ELECTRONIC SUSPENSION
Ford Motor Co. Air Suspension – Continental (Cont.)

REMOVAL & INSTALLATION (FRONT SUSPENSION)

CAUTION: Manufacturer recommends using new suspension fasteners whenever old fasteners are loosened or removed.

BALL JOINTS

Ball joints are not replaceable. Replace lower control arm if ball joints are worn.

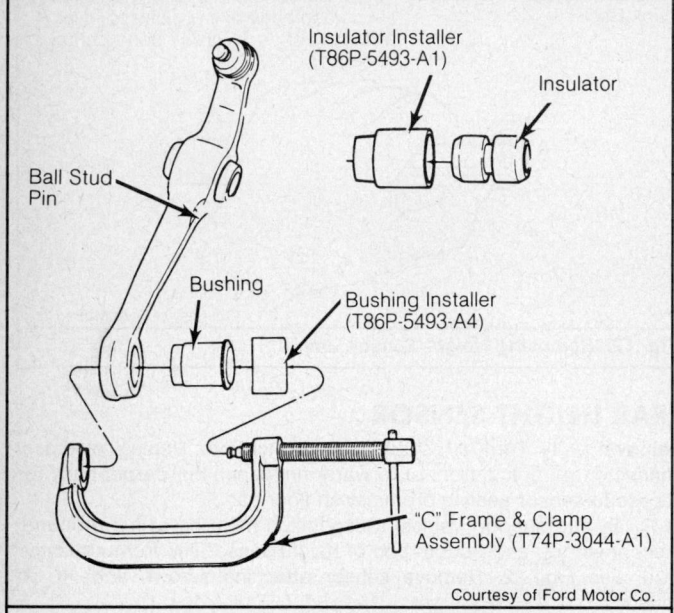

Fig. 14: Replacing Inner Pivot Bushing Or Tension Strut Insulator

Courtesy of Ford Motor Co.

LOWER CONTROL ARM (FRONT)

Removal – 1) Turn air suspension switch off. Raise vehicle and remove wheels. Disconnect height sensor link from ball stud pin. Remove and discard nut from tension strut. Remove dished washer. *See Fig. 15.*

2) Remove and discard lower control arm ball joint pinch bolt. Slightly spread knuckle pinch joint and separate control arm from steering knuckle. DO NOT damage bolt seal.

3) DO NOT use a hammer to separate ball joint from knuckle. Remove and discard lower control arm inner pivot bolt and nut. Remove lower control arm assembly from tension strut.

CAUTION: DO NOT allow outer drive axle shaft to extend. CV joint may separate causing failure.

Inner Pivot Bushing & Tension Strut Insulator – 1) Use "C" Frame and Clamp Assembly with correct adapters for removal and installation. *See Fig. 14.* Place "C" frame in bench vise when replacing bushings.

2) On inner pivot bushing, ensure bushing flange is at front of arm. Coat new insulator bushing with vegatable oil to ease installation. DO NOT use petroleum or mineral based oils.

Installation – Reverse removal procedure for installation. Always use NEW fasteners on lower control arm pivot and ball joint pinch bolts. Turn on air suspension switch.

FRONT STRUT & SPRING ASSEMBLY

NOTE: It is not necessary to replace struts in pairs.

Inspection – Oil film on solenoid valve filter cap or oily filter indicates a leaking strut.

Removal – 1) Turn air suspension switch off. Turn ignition off and place steering column in unlocked position. Open hood.

2) Remove plastic cover from shock tower. Remove damping actuator as previously described.

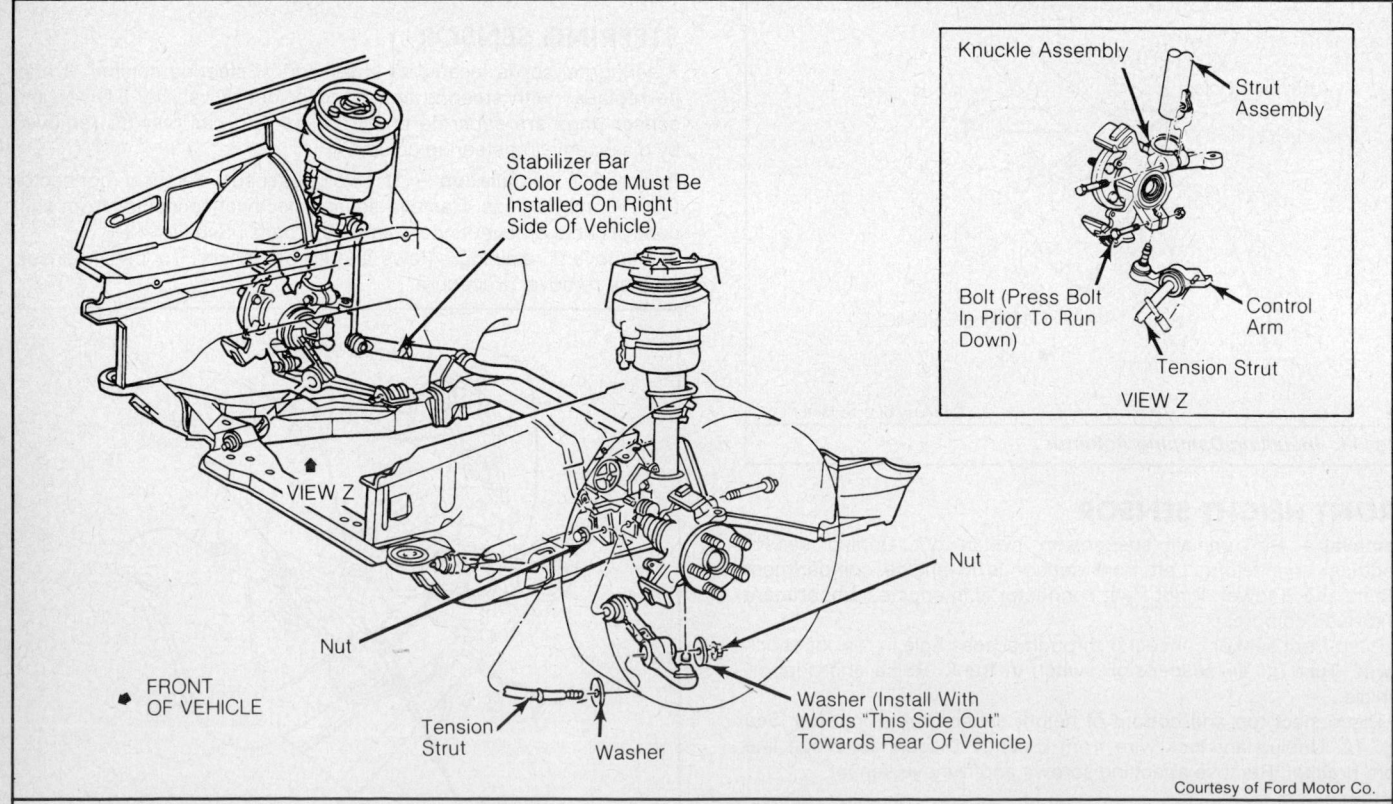

Courtesy of Ford Motor Co.

Fig. 15: Front Suspension

1989 ELECTRONIC SUSPENSION
Ford Motor Co. Air Suspension — Continental (Cont.)

12-67

CAUTION: Hub nut cannot be reused after removal. DO NOT loosen hub nut after it is tightened to final torque.

3) Remove hub cap. Loosen, but do not remove, wheel lug nuts. Remove hub nut by applying sufficient force to overcome prevailing torque feature of nut. DO NOT use an impact to remove nut.

4) DISCARD hub nut after removal. Remove hub nut washer. Loosen, but do not remove, 3 top mount-to-shock tower nuts. Raise and support vehicle. DO NOT support vehicle by lower control arm.

5) Remove wheel. Remove brake line bracket from strut assembly. Disconnect height sensor link from ball stud pin at lower control arm. Disconnect air line at solenoid valve.

6) Unplug electrical connector at solenoid valve. Move brake caliper out of way. Separate tie rod end from steering knuckle. DISCARD tie rod end nut. Remove stabilizer bar link nut.

7) Separate link from strut. Remove and DISCARD lower arm-to-steering knuckle pinch bolt and nut. Slightly spread knuckle-to-lower arm pinch joint. Separate lower arm from steering knuckle.

8) Press half-shaft from hub. *See Fig. 16.* Wire half-shaft so it supported in a level position. To prevent over extension of CV joint, do not allow half-shaft to move outward.

9) Remove shock strut-to-steering knuckle pinch bolt. Slightly spread knuckle-to-pinch strut joint and slip strut from knuckle. Remove 3 top mount-to-shock tower nuts. Remove strut assembly.

10) If air spring solenoid is to be replaced, remove solenoid clip. Rotate solenoid counterclockwise to first stop. Pull solenoid straight out slowly to second stop to bleed air from system.

11) DO NOT fully release solenoid until air is completely bled from air spring. After air is bled, rotate counterclockwise to third stop and remove solenoid from housing. Replace "O" ring if worn.

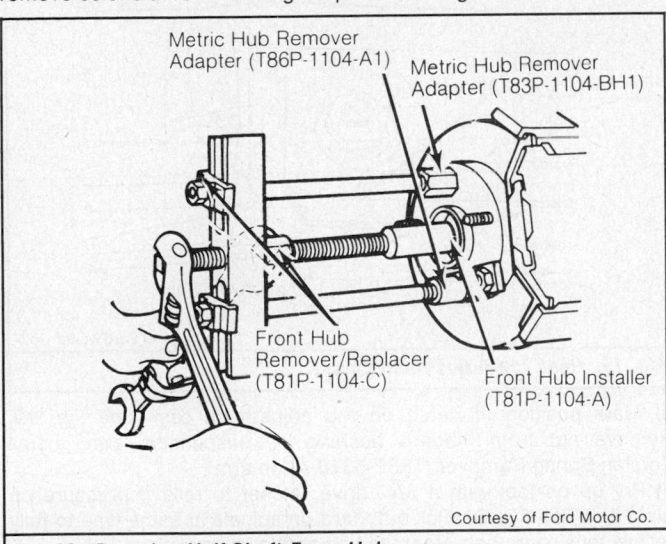

Fig. 16: Pressing Half-Shaft From Hub

Installation – 1) To install strut and spring assembly, reverse removal procedure. Use NEW attaching hardware on following components:
- Shock strut-to-steering knuckle pinch bolt.
- Lower arm-to-steering knuckle bolt and nut.
- Stabilizer bar link nut.
- Tie rod end slotted nut.

2) Use a puller to install half-shaft into hub. DO NOT use new hub nut to pull half-shaft into hub.

CAUTION: DO NOT impact wrench to tighten hub nut.

3) Fill air spring BEFORE lowering vehicle. See AIR SPRING REFILL under AIR SPRING SOLENOID in this article.

FRONT STABILIZER BAR

Removal – 1) Turn air suspension switch off. Raise and support vehicle. DO NOT support vehicle under front sub-frame. Remove and DISCARD stabilizer bar link-to-shock strut nut. Remove sub-frame-to-steering gear nuts.

2) Move gear off of sub-frame. Place a set of jack stands under sub-frame. Lower vehicle on to jack stands. Remove and DISCARD 2 rear sub-frame bolts. New bolts must be used on reassembly.

3) Lower sub-frame to gain access to stabilizer bar mounting brackets. Remove stabilizer bar "U" bracket bolts. Remove stabilizer bar or insulators as required.

Installation – 1) To install stabilizer bar, reverse removal procedure. If installing new stabilizer bar insulators, lubricate before installation. DO NOT use petroleum or mineral based grease.

2) USE NEW "U" bracket bolts, sub-frame bolts and stabilizer bar link nut on reassembly. Turn on air suspension switch after vehicle is lowered.

UPPER MOUNT & BEARING ASSEMBLY (FRONT)

Removal – 1) Remove front strut assembly. Remove solenoid clip. Rotate solenoid counterclockwise to first stop. Pull solenoid out slowly to second stop to bleed air from system.

2) DO NOT fully release solenoid until air is completely bled from air spring. After air is bled, rotate counterclockwise to third stop and remove solenoid from housing. Replace "O" ring if worn.

3) Place actuator mounting bracket (rebound cup) loosely in vise by flats. Other end of strut should be resting on bench. Remove nut and rebound cup. Remove upper nut mount and rebound assembly. Remove "O" ring retainer plate.

Installation – To install mount assembly, reverse removal procedure. Fill air spring BEFORE lowering vehicle to ground. See AIR SPRING REFILL under AIR SPRING SOLENOID in this article.

STEERING KNUCKLE

Removal – 1) Turn ignition to "OFF" position to unlock steering column. Remove hub cap. Loosen, but do not remove, wheel lug nuts. Remove hub nut. DO NOT use an impact to remove nut.

CAUTION: Hub nut cannot be reused after removal. DO NOT loosen hub nut after it is tightened to final torque.

2) DISCARD hub nut after removal. Remove hub nut washer. Raise vehicle and remove wheel. DO NOT support vehicle by lower control arm. Remove and DISCARD tie rod end nut and cotter pin.

3) New fastener must be installed on reassembly. Separate tie rod end from knuckle. Remove stabilizer bar link from strut assembly. Remove brake caliper. Wire caliper out of way. Remove brake rotor.

4) Remove plastic cover from shock tower. LOOSEN, but do not remove, 3 top mounting nuts. Remove and DISCARD lower arm-to-steering knuckle pinch bolt. Slightly spread knuckle to separate lower arm from knuckle. DO NOT use hammer to separate ball joint from knuckle.

5) Remove shock strut-to-knuckle pinch bolt. Slightly spread knuckle pinch joint. Press half-shaft from hub. *See Fig. 16.* Wire half-shaft so it supported in a level position. DO NOT allow half-shaft to extend outward.

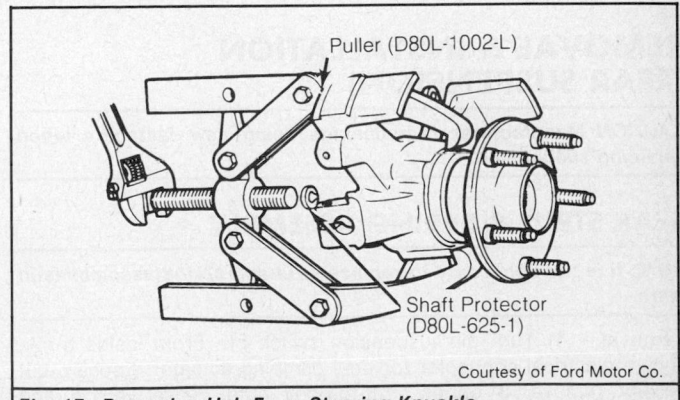

Fig. 17: Removing Hub From Steering Knuckle

12-68

1989 ELECTRONIC SUSPENSION
Ford Motor Co. Air Suspension – Continental (Cont.)

6) Remove rotor splash shield (if equipped). Remove knuckle from shock strut. If necessary, press hub from knuckle using puller in Fig. 17. Remove snap ring and press bearing from knuckle.

NOTE: A new bearing must be installed if original bearing is pressed out of knuckle.

Installation – 1) Install splash shield using new rivets. If removed, press NEW bearing into knuckle and install snap ring. Press hub into knuckle. If necessary, replace seal on outboard CV joint.

2) Install steering knuckle onto shock strut. Loosely install a NEW pinch bolt in knuckle to retain strut. Install knuckle and strut on half-shaft. Install lower control arm to knuckle. Ensure ball stud groove is aligned.

3) Tighten NEW strut-to-knuckle pinch bolt. Install rotor and brake caliper. Coat caliper pins with silicone grease. Tighten caliper locating pins. With steering wheel in straight ahead position, place tie rod into knuckle.

4) Install NEW slotted nut and tighten to specification. If needed, tighten tie rod nut slightly to align cotter pin holes. Install new cotter pin. Install stabilizer bar link to strut.

5) Install and tighten NEW nut to specification. Install wheels. Lower vehicle. Install and tighten 3 top mount-to-apron nuts. Use a puller to install half-shaft into hub. DO NOT use new hub nut to pull half-shaft into hub.

6) Use torque wrench and tighten by hand. DO NOT use impact wrench to tighten hub nut. Turn on air suspension. Pump brake prior to driving vehicle.

FRONT SUBFRAME

Removal – 1) Install Engine Support (D97L-6000-A) on engine lifting eyes to support engine. Turn air suspension off. Raise vehicle and remove front wheels. Support steering gear with wire from the tie rod end.

2) Disconnect exhaust system at flex coupling and lower. Remove and DISCARD lower control arm pinch bolts at ball joint. Remove 2 steering gear-to-crossmember bolts.

3) Remove attaching nuts from right front and right rear engine mounts. Remove stabilizer bar link from stabilizer bar. Remove left engine mount insulator at subframe through bolt.

4) Place jack stands at points where subframe meets body. Lower vehicle to jack stands. Remove 4 body mount attaching bolts. Raise vehicle enough to remove subframe.

Installation – 1) Align subframe to body. Ensure all rubber mounts are in position. Install, but do not tighten, 4 subframe bolts.

2) Install a 3/4" O.D. pipe or similar tool into driver's side subframe and body alignment holes. Slightly tighten driver's side front body mount bolt.

3) Repeat step **2)** on right side (passenger) alignment holes. After verifying subframe is aligned, tighten mounting bolts to 65-85 ft. lbs. (90-115 N.m).

4) To complete installation, reverse removal procedure. Use NEW pinch bolt and nut at ball joint. Turn on air suspension switch after vehicle is lowered to ground.

REMOVAL & INSTALLATION (REAR SUSPENSION)

CAUTION: Manufacturer recommends using new fasteners when servicing suspension.

REAR STRUT & SPRING ASSEMBLY

NOTE: It is not necessary to replace strut and spring assemblies in pairs.

Removal – 1) Turn air suspension switch off. From inside trunk, unplug electrical connector for dual damping actuator. Loosen, but do not remove, 3 upper strut-to-body nuts. Raise vehicle and remove wheel.

2) Disconnect air line from solenoid by pressing in release ring. Unplug electrical connector from solenoid valve. Remove brake hose retainer at strut bracket. Disconnect parking brake cable from brake caliper.

3) Remove all wire and parking brake cable retainers from lower control arm. Disconnect height sensor link from ball stud pin on lower control arm. See Fig. 18. Remove caliper assembly from spindle and support. Bleed air spring by removing solenoid clip.

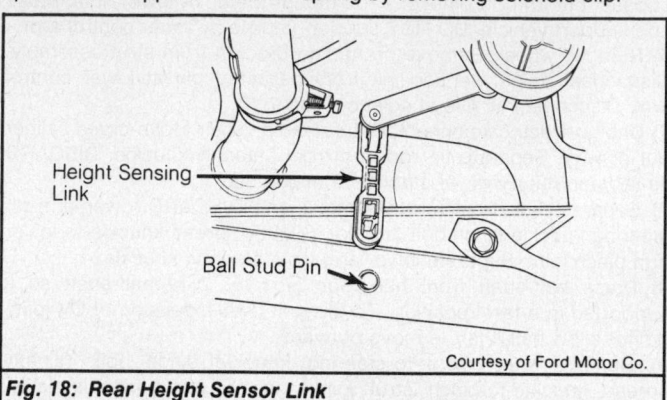

Courtesy of Ford Motor Co.

Fig. 18: Rear Height Sensor Link

4) Rotate solenoid to first stop. See Fig. 10. Pull solenoid outward to second stop to bleed air. After air is completely bled, rotate to third stop and remove solenoid from housing.

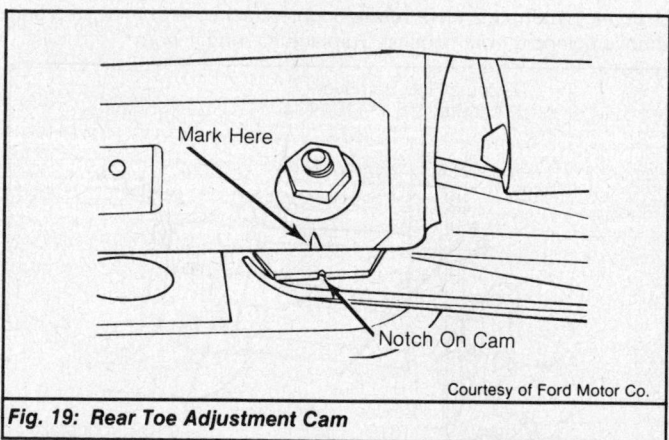

Courtesy of Ford Motor Co.

Fig. 19: Rear Toe Adjustment Cam

5) Mark position of notch on toe adjustment cam. See Fig. 19. Remove nut from inboard bushing on suspension arm. Install Torsion Spring Remover (T88P-5310-A) on arm.

6) Pry up on tool with a 3/4" drive ratchet to relieve pressure on pivot bolt. See Fig. 20. Pull outboard on spindle at same time to fully relieve tension on bolt. Remove bolt and lower arm.

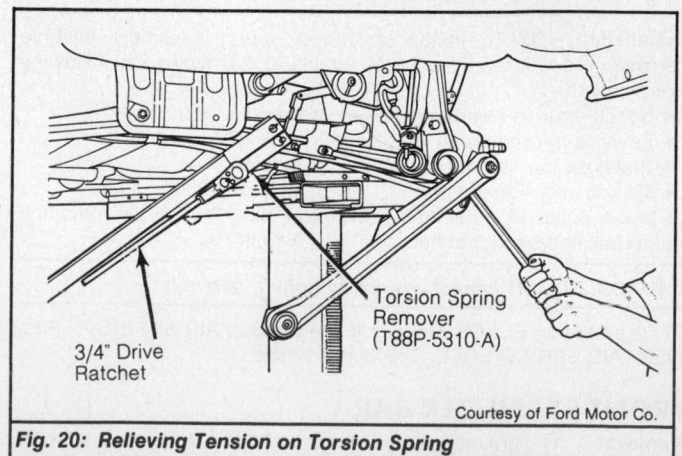

Courtesy of Ford Motor Co.

Fig. 20: Relieving Tension on Torsion Spring

1989 ELECTRONIC SUSPENSION
Ford Motor Co. Air Suspension — Continental (Cont.)

12-69

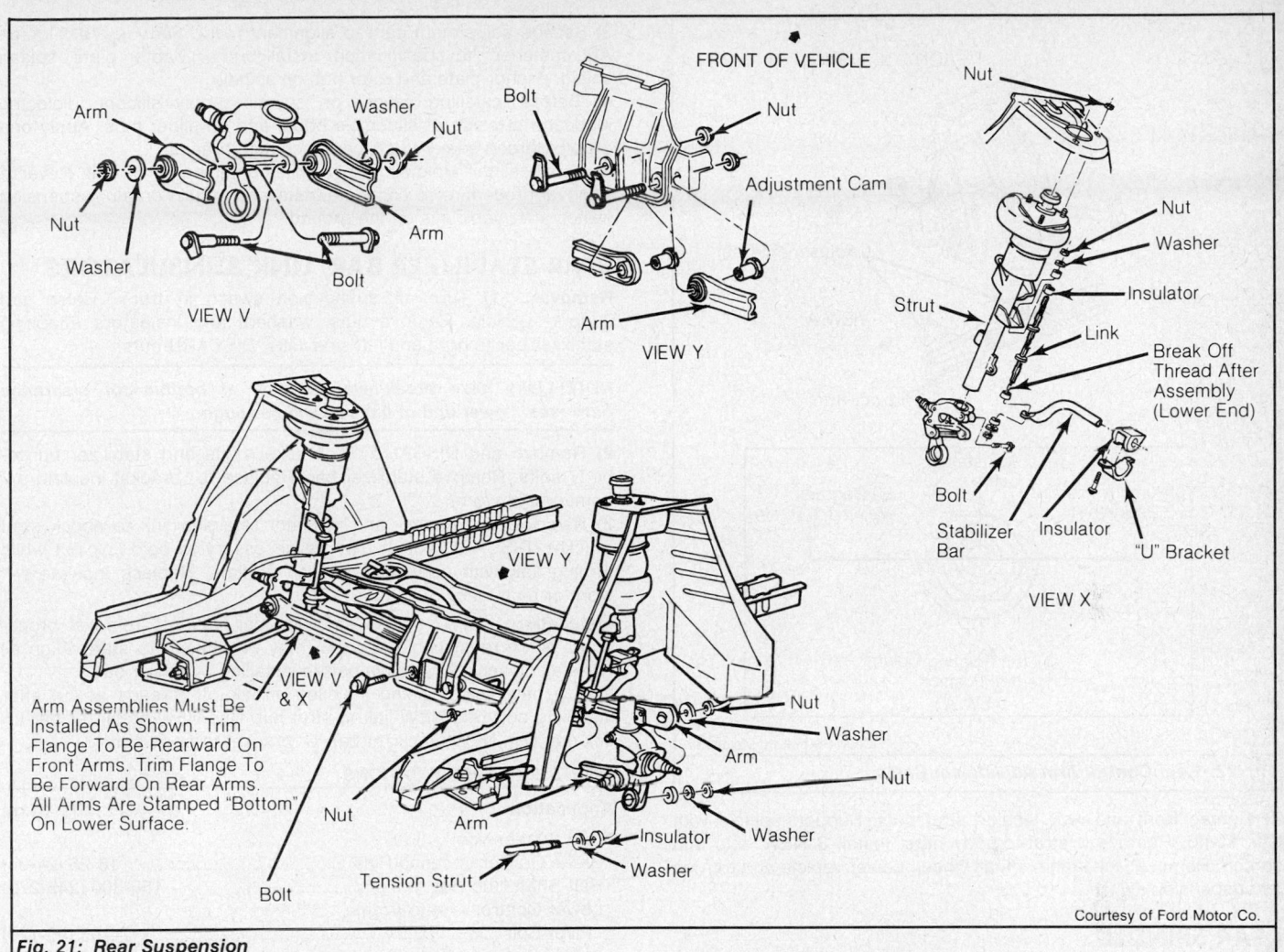

FRONT OF VEHICLE

VIEW V

VIEW Y

VIEW X

Arm Assemblies Must Be Installed As Shown. Trim Flange To Be Rearward On Front Arms. Trim Flange To Be Forward On Rear Arms. All Arms Are Stamped "Bottom" On Lower Surface.

VIEW V & X

Break Off Thread After Assembly (Lower End)

Courtesy of Ford Motor Co.

Fig. 21: Rear Suspension

7) Repeat steps **5)** and **6)** for opposite arm. Remove torsion spring from arms. Remove stabilizer "U" bracket from body. Remove nut, washer and insulator attaching stabilizer bar to link. Separate stabilizer bar from link.

8) Remove nut, washer and insulator holding tension strut to rear spindle. Move spindle enough to separate it from tension strut. Remove and DISCARD shock strut-to-spindle pinch bolt (if necessary).

10) Separate spindle from strut and remove as an assembly with arms attached. From inside trunk, remove and DISCARD 3 upper mount-to-body nuts. Guide electric actuator wire through body opening.

NOTE: New pinch bolt and nut must be installed during reassembly if they are loosened or removed.

Installation – Reverse removal procedure for installation. Before tightening nut on inboard bushing of lower control arm, ensure toe alignment mark aligns with notch on cam. *See Fig. 19.* Adjust toe as necessary.

CAUTION: Before lowering vehicle, fill air spring. See AIR SPRING REFILL under AIR SPRING SOLENOID.

LOWER CONTROL ARM (REAR)

Removal – **1)** Turn air suspension switch off. Raise vehicle. Remove wire retainers and parking brake cable retainers from lower control arm. Disconnect rear height sensor from link from ball stud pin on lower arm. *See Fig. 18.*

2) Mark position of notch on toe adjustment cam. *See Fig. 19.* Remove nut from inboard bushing on suspension arm. Install Torsion Spring Remover (T88P-5310-A) on arm. *See Fig. 20.* Pry up on tool with a 3/4" drive ratchet to relieve pressure on pivot bolt.

3) Pull out on spindle to at same time to relieve pressure on bolt. Remove bolt and lower arm. Remove nut retaining torsion spring to arm. Separate spring from arm. Remove outboard attaching bolt at spindle. Repeat for other arm(s).

Installation – **1)** When installing new control arms, offset must face up. Arms are stamped "BOTTOM" on lower edge. Rear control arm adjustment cams are installed from front of both arms. *See Fig. 22.*

2) To complete installation, reverse removal procedure. Turn on air suspension switch after lowering vehicle to ground.

TENSION STRUT (REAR)

Removal – **1)** Turn air suspension switch off. Place vehicle on frame hoist. Raise hoist only enough to contact body. From inside trunk, loosen but do not remove 3 upper shock strut-to-body nuts.

2) Raise vehicle and remove wheels. Remove and DISCARD tension strut-to-spindle nut. Remove and DISCARD tension strut-to-body. Move spindle rearward so tension strut can be removed.

Installation – **1)** Place new washers and bushings on both ends of tension strut. Front and rear bushings are different. Rear bushings have indentations. *See Fig. 21.* Insert one end into body bracket.

2) Install but do not tighten new bushing, washer and nut. Pull back spindle enough so tension strut end can be installed in spindle. Install new bushing, washer and nut. Ensure bushings are correctly installed.

12-70

1989 ELECTRONIC SUSPENSION
Ford Motor Co. Air Suspension – Continental (Cont.)

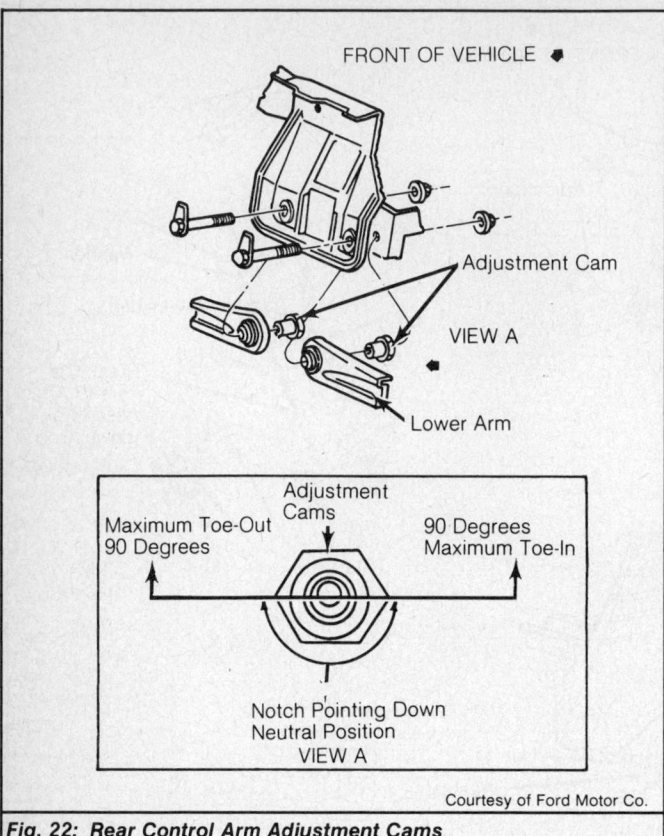

FRONT OF VEHICLE ◀

Adjustment Cam

VIEW A

Lower Arm

Adjustment Cams

Maximum Toe-Out
90 Degrees

90 Degrees
Maximum Toe-In

Notch Pointing Down
Neutral Position
VIEW A

Courtesy of Ford Motor Co.

Fig. 22: Rear Control Arm Adjustment Cams

3) Tighten front and rear tension strut nuts. Support spindle with jack stand. Remove 3 strut-to-body nuts. Install 3 NEW nuts and tighten. Remove jack stand. Install wheel. Lower vehicle and turn on air suspension switch.

REAR SPINDLE

Removal – 1) Turn air suspension switch off. From inside trunk, loosen, but do not remove, 3 upper strut-to-body nuts. Raise and support vehicle. Remove wheel. Remove brake hose retainer at strut bracket.

2) Disconnect parking brake cable from brake caliper. Remove all wire and parking brake cable retainers from lower arm. Disconnect height sensor link from ball stud pin on lower arm. *See Fig. 18.*

3) Remove caliper assembly from spindle and support with wire. Remove rotor, hub, anchor plate, splash shield and brake adapter plate from spindle. Mark position of notch on toe adjustment cam. *See Fig. 19.*

4) Remove nut from inboard bushing on suspension arm. Install Torsion Spring Remover (T88P-5310-A) on arm. *See Fig. 20.* Pry up on tool with a 3/4" drive ratchet to relieve pressure on pivot bolt.

5) Pull outboard on spindle at same time to fully relieve tension on bolt. Remove bolt and lower arm.

6) Repeat steps **4)** and **5)** on opposite lower arm. Remove torsion springs from arms. Remove arms from spindle. Remove and DISCARD shock strut-to-spindle pinch bolt. A new bolt must be installed on reassembly.

7) Slightly spread spindle pinch joint so strut can be removed. Remove nut, washer and insulator that retains tension strut to spindle. Slide tension strut from spindle. Remove spindle.

Installation – 1) Install spindle on shock strut. Install but do not tighten NEW shock strut-to-spindle pinch bolt. Position tension strut in spindle. Install insulator, washer and nut on tension strut. *See Fig. 21.*

2) Position spindle on lower arm. Install torsion spring on arms. Position inboard lower arm bushing in bracket using Torsion Spring Remover (T88P-5310-A). *See Fig. 20.* DO NOT tighten nut yet.

3) Set toe adjustment cam to alignment mark. *See Fig. 19.* Tighten ALL fasteners to specification. Install brake adapter plate, splash shield, anchor plate and rotor hub on spindle.

4) Before installing caliper on spindle, apply silicone dielectric lubricant to inside of slider pin boots and on slider pins. Apply one drop of thread sealer to caliper pinch bolt threads.

5) Install caliper. Hold slider pin while tightening pinch bolt. Reverse removal procedure to complete installation. Turn on air suspension switch after vehicle is on the ground.

REAR STABILIZER BAR, LINK & INSULATORS

Removal – 1) Turn air suspension switch in trunk. Raise and support vehicle. Remove nuts, washers and insulators attaching stabilizer bar to right and left side links. DISCARD nuts.

NOTE: Links have break-away threads at bottom for clearance purposes. Lower end of link rod will be rough.

2) Remove and DISCARD "U" bracket bolts and stabilizer bar-to-body bolts. Remove stabilizer bar. Replace "U" bracket insulators if damaged or worn.

3) Remove nut, washer and insulator retaining link to shock strut bracket. DISCARD nut. It may be necessary to hold link nut while turning link with open end wrench at flats. Replace insulators if worn or damaged.

Installation – 1) To install stabilizer bar, reverse removal procedure. When reusing old link, nut may be difficult to start. Align all parts as closely as possible before installing stabilizer bar.

2) If a new link is being installed, break off threads at cut after installing nut. Use NEW link-to-strut nut. Use NEW stabilizer bar-to-link nut. Use NEW stabilizer bar "U" bracket-to-body bolt.

TIGHTENING SPECIFICATIONS

Application	Ft. Lbs. (N.m)
Front Suspension	
Brake Caliper Locating Pins	18-25 (24-34)
Half-Shaft Hub Nut	180-200 (245-270)
Lower Control Arm-to-Frame	
Pivot Bolt	70-95 (95-129)
Lower Control Arm-to-Knuckle Nut	40-55 (54-75)
Stabilizer Bar-to-Stabilizer	
Bar Link Nut	35-48 (47-65)
Stabilizer Bar Link-to-Strut Nut	55-75 (75-101)
Strut-to-Knuckle Pinch Bolt	70-95 (95-129)
Strut-to-Top Mount Nut	35-50 (48-68)
Strut Top Mount-to-Shock	
Tower Nuts	22-32 (30-43)
Tension Strut Nut	70-95 (95-129)
Tie Rod End Nut	23-35 (31-47)
Rear Suspension	
Brake Caliper Pinch Bolt	[1] 30-35 (40-47)
Lower Control Arm-to-Body Nut	45-65 (62-88)
Lower Control Arm-to-Spindle Nut	42-57 (57-77)
Stabilizer Bar "U" Bracket-to-	
Body Bolt	25-37 (34-50)
Strut-to-Spindle Bolt	50-70 (68-95)
Strut Top Mount-to-Body	
Mount Nuts	19-26 (26-35)
Strut-to-Top Mount Nuts	35-50 (47-68)
Tension Strut-to-Body Nuts	52-74 (70-100)
Tension Strut-to-Spindle Nut	35-50 (48-68)

	INCH Lbs. (N.m)
Rear Suspension	
Stabilizer Bar Link-to-Strut Nut	72-144 (8-16)
Stabilizer Bar-to-Link Nut	72-144 (8-16)

[1] – Use one drop of thread sealer on caliper pinch bolts.

TESTING & DIAGNOSIS

ELECTRONIC SUSPENSION DIAGNOSTIC CODES

Code	Test	Description	Priority
10		Diagnostics Entered	
11		System Checked Okay	
12		No Faults Detected	
		Perform Manual Input	
13		Faults Detected	
		Perform Manual Input	
15		No Faults Detected	
21		Vent RF Air Spring	
22		Vent LF Air Spring	
23		Vent RR Air Spring	
24		Inflate RF Air Spring	
25		Inflate LF Air Spring	
26		Inflate RR Air Spring	
27		Vent LR Air Spring	
28		Inflate LR Air Spring	
31		Air Compressor Toggle	
32		Vent Solenoid Valve Toggle	
33		Air Spring Solenoid Valve Toggle	
34		Shock Actuator Toggle	
35		Door Position Detector	
40	EA	LF Solenoid Valve Short Circuit	2nd
41	EB	RF Solenoid Valve Short Circuit	2nd
42	EC	LR Solenoid Valve Short Circuit	2nd
43	ED	RR Solenoid Valve Short Circuit	2nd
44	EE	LF Solenoid Valve Short Circuit	2nd
45	EF	Air Comp. Relay Short Circuit	2nd
46	EG	Height Sensor Circuit Shorted	2nd
47	EH	Soft Shock Relay Circuit Shorted	2nd
48	EI	Firm Shock Relay Circuit Shorted	2nd
49	HA	No RF Corner Lowering Detection	2nd
50	HB	No LF Corner Lowering Detection	5th
51	HC	No RR Corner Lowering Detection	5th
51a		No Rear Lowering Detection	5th
52	IA	No RF Corner Rise Detection	6th
53	IB	No LF Corner Rise Detection	6th
54	IC	No RR Corner Rise Detection	6th
54a		No Rear Rise Detection	6th
55	JA	Speed Over 15 MPH Not Detected	7th
56	GA	LR Actuator "Soft" Not Detected	4th
57	GB	RF Actuator "Soft" Not Detected	4th
58	GC	LF Actuator "Soft" Not Detected	4th
59	GD	RR Actuator "Soft" Not Detected	4th
60	GA	LR Actuator "Firm" Not Detected	4th
61	GB	RF Actuator "Firm" Not Detected	4th
62	GC	LF Actuator "Firm" Not Detected	4th
63	GD	RR Actuator "Firm" Not Detected	4th
64	GE	All Actuator "Soft" Not Detected	4th
65	GE	All Actuator "Firm" Not Detected	4th
66	EJ	RF Height Sensor Short Circuit	2nd
67	EK	LF Height Sensor Short Circuit	2nd
68	EL	Rear Height Sensor Short Circuit	2nd
69	FA	RF Height Sensor Open Circuit	3rd
70	FB	LF Height Sensor Open Circuit	3rd
71	FC	Rear Height Sensor Open Circuit	3rd
72	JB	Door Position Signal Not Detected	7th
73	JB	Brake Switch Not Detected	7th
74	JC	Steering Wheel Rotation	7th
		Not Detected	
75	JE	Acceleration Signal Not Detected	7th
78	HD	No LR Corner Lowering Detection	5th
79	ID	No LR Corner Rise Detection	5th
80	DA	Battery Voltage to Low	1st
		to Run Diagnostics	

TESTING PRECAUTIONS

1) Compressor relay, compressor vent solenoid and all air spring solenoids have internal diodes for noise suppression. Do not switch battery and ground feeds when testing components.

2) When charging the battery, the ignition switch MUST be in the "OFF" position if air suspension switch in trunk is "ON". If ignition switch is "ON", air compressor relay or motor may be damaged.

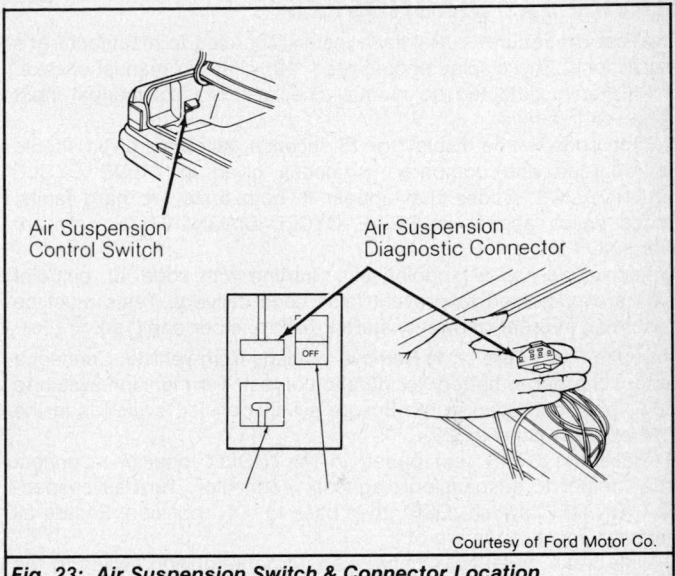

Air Suspension Control Switch

Air Suspension Diagnostic Connector

Courtesy of Ford Motor Co.

Fig. 23: Air Suspension Switch & Connector Location

TESTING PROCEDURES

Servicing an Air Suspension System malfunction involves 3 diagnostic levels to isolate the fault accurately and determine repair with the least amount of time. The correct procedure consists of Drive Cycle Diagnostics, Service Bay Diagnostics, and Spring Fill Diagnostics. A Rotunda STAR (007-00004) or Rotunda SUPER STAR II (007-00041) tester must be used to diagnose system. A Rotunda SUPER STAR tester will not work.

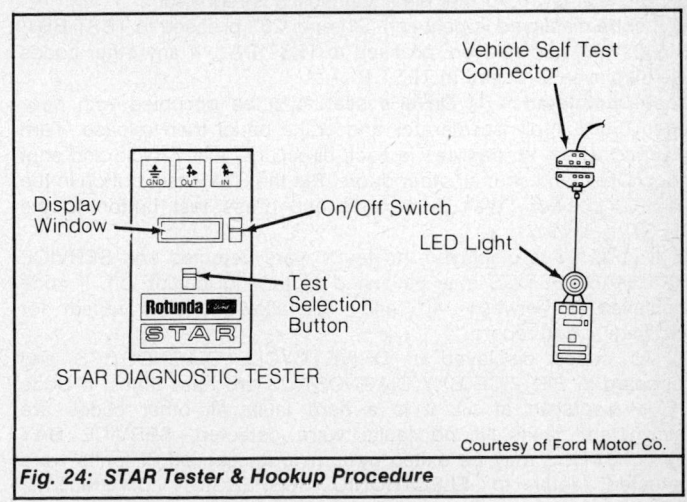

Vehicle Self Test Connector

Display Window

On/Off Switch

LED Light

Rotunda STAR

Test Selection Button

STAR DIAGNOSTIC TESTER

Courtesy of Ford Motor Co.

Fig. 24: STAR Tester & Hookup Procedure

DRIVE CYCLE DIAGNOSTICS

1) If a fault is detected in the system while the vehicle is in motion, the "RIDE CONTROL" light will be activated. A maximum of 32 codes can be stored for one hour after ignition is turned off. See ELECTRONIC SUSPENSION DIAGNOSTIC CODES table.

2) Codes can be obtained if the ignition remains off with the suspension switch on. Drive vehicle for a minimum of 4 minutes above 15 MPH. Verify suspension switch is in the "ON" position.

12-72

1989 ELECTRONIC SUSPENSION
Ford Motor Co. Air Suspension — Continental (Cont.)

3) Within 20 minutes the STAR tester should display code "15". Ensure test button is in the "HOLD" position and turn tester on. If code "40" or "71" are obtained, DRIVE CYCLE DIAGNOSTICS is completed and faults were found in the system.

4) Record codes and proceed to DRIVE CYCLE DIAGNOSTICS. If any other codes are found, proceed to TEST AA1. If no faults are found, remove tester and exit diagnostics

SERVICE BAY DIAGNOSTICS

Pre-Test Procedure – 1) Attach tester according to manufacturer's instructions. The display should read "12/ okay do manual checks" or "13/Faults detected do manual checks". Perform manual input checks at this time.

2) Each code will be display for 15 seconds. All codes given should be recorded and compared to codes given in DRIVE CYCLE DIAGNOSTICS. Codes that appear in both tests are hard faults. Codes which appear in DRIVE CYCLE DIAGNOSTICS only are intermittent faults.

3) Each code has a pinpoint test. Starting with code 40, pinpoint tests are prioritized to prevent false code delivery. Tests must be performed in order of priority starting with number one (1st).

Entrance Procedure – 1) Remove all loads from vehicle. Connect a battery charger to battery for duration of test. Turn ignition switch to "OFF" position. Open trunk. Ensure air suspension switch is in the "ON" position. *See Fig. 23.*

2) Place the STAR test button in the "HOLD" position. Connect STAR tester to suspension diagnostic connector. Turn air suspension "ON/OFF" switch "OFF", then back to "ON" position. Ensure all electrical accessories are off.

3) With brake pedal NOT depressed, turn the ignition switch to the "RUN" position. Wait 5 seconds and then depress STAR test button so it remains down in "TEST" position.

4) Within 20 seconds, STAR tester will display a code. If code 10 is displayed, air suspension module has completed a self-check and is conducting the automatic portion of diagnostics. DO NOT touch or lean on vehicle while automatic testing is being run.

5) Test will take about 3-4 minutes to complete if there are no problems. If problems are encountered, test will take up to 14 minutes. At end of test, STAR tester will display a code 12 or 13. Vehicle riding height can now be checked. If any code other than 12 or 13 is displayed, further electrical testing is required.

6) If code displayed is between "21" and "28", proceed to TEST BB1. If code "80" is displayed, proceed to TEST DA1. If any other codes are displayed, proceed to TEST BA1.

Test Completed – 1) Driver's seat must be occupied with door open. Fully apply accelerator and brake pedal then release. Turn steering wheel 90 degrees in each directions, exit vehicle and shut door. Open and shut all other doors. Put the STAR test button in the "HOLD" position. Wait 5 seconds and press test button to the "TEST" position.

2) If code 11 is displayed, no faults were detected and SERVICE BAY DIAGNOSTICS may be exited by turning ignition off. If code displayed is between "40" and "79", allow code to repeat for verification and record.

3) All codes displayed in DRIVE CYCLE DIAGNOSTICS and repeated in SERVICE BAY DIAGNOSTICS are hard faults. If Code 55 is displayed at all, it is a hard fault. All other codes are intermittent faults. If no faults were detected, SERVICE BAY DIAGNOSTICS may be exited by turning ignition off. If faults were detected, refer to ELECTRONIC SUSPENSION DIAGNOSTIC CODES table for correct order of procedure.

SPRING FILL DIAGNOSTICS

Description – Pinpoint tests will lead to SPRING FILL DIAGNOSTICS. This mode will allow the technician to operate each spring independantly to isolate problems by quadrant for individual testing.

Entrance Procedure – 1) Connect a battery charger to battery for duration of test. Turn ignition switch to "OFF" position. Open trunk. Ensure air suspension switch is in the "ON" position. *See Fig. 23.*

2) Place the STAR test button in the "HOLD" position. Connect STAR tester to suspension diagnostic connector in trunk. Turn air suspension "ON/OFF" switch "OFF", then back to "ON" position. Ensure all electrical accessories are on.

3) With brake pedal DEPRESSED HARD, turn the ignition switch to the "RUN" position. Wait 5 seconds and then release brake pedal. After 5 seconds, depress STAR test button so it remains down in "TEST" position. Within 20 seconds, STAR tester will display a code. If any code except "21" to "28" is displayed, proceed to TEST CA1.

4) If code "21" to "28" is displayed, SPRING FILL DIAGNOSTICS has been entered. To select and activate SPRING FILL test put Star test button in the "HOLD" position after desired code has been given for 5 seconds. This will retain the desired function.

5) To cancel SPRING FILL testing, put Star test button in the "TEST" position. Codes are displayed in numerical order from smallest to largest number. When the largest number has been displayed, the list will start over. This will continue as long as the Star test button is in the "TEST" position. See ELECTRONIC SUSPENSION DIAGNOSTIC CODES table.

TEST AA1

Unable To Enter Drive Cycle Diagnostics – Inability to enter drive cycle diagnostics is generally caused by a defective STAR tester, ignition switch or disruption in the positive side of the "B" (battery) power supply circuit. Additional possibilities are defective Self Test Input (STI) or Self Test Output (STO) circuit. Proceed to TEST AA2 for further inspection.

TEST AA2

STAR Tester Check – Replace STAR tester with a known working unit. With ignition in the "OFF" position, attach tester to air suspension diagnostic pigtail. Turn tester on and put test button in the "HOLD" position. Wait 5 seconds and put test button in the "TEST" position.

2) If Code 15 is displayed, diagnostic cycle has been completed and no faults were detected. If any Codes between "40" and "71" are displayed twice, record number and refer to SERVICE BAY DIAGNOSTICS. If neither of these conditions occur, proceed to TEST AA3.

TEST AA3

Power Supply Check – 1) Check power supply as possible source of inability to enter drive cycle diagnostics. Put test button in the "HOLD" position and separate tester from conector. Turn air suspension switch to the "OFF" Position. Separate control module from wire harness at connector.

2) Apply voltmeter positive lead to pin location 37 (circuit 418A) and negative lead to pin location 40 (circuit 430G). *See Air Suspension Control Module & STAR Tester Connector Identification.* If 11 volts or more are available, proceed to TEST AA4. If not, refer to wiring diagram to determine why voltage is not available.

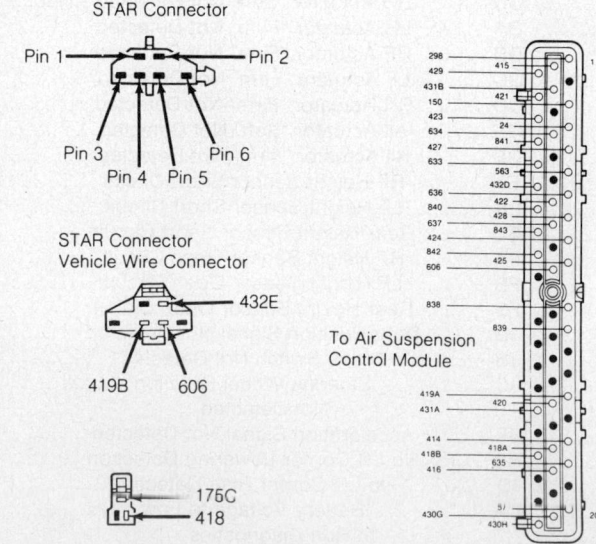

Air Suspension Control Module & Star Tester Connector Identification

1989 ELECTRONIC SUSPENSION
Ford Motor Co. Air Suspension — Continental (Cont.)

12-73

TEST AA4

Power Supply Circuit Check – Apply voltmeter positive lead to pin location 57 (circuit 418B) and negative lead to pin location 60 (circuit 430H). *See Air Suspension Control Module & Star Tester Connector Identification.* If 11 volts or more are available, proceed to TEST AA5. If not, refer to wiring diagram to determine why voltage is not available.

TEST AA5

Ignition Circuit Check – Turn ignition switch to the "OFF" position. Apply voltmeter positive lead to control module pin location 1 (circuit 298) and negative lead to pin location 40 (circuit 430G). *See Air Suspension Control Module & Star Tester Connector Identification.* If zero volts are available, proceed to TEST AA6. If not, refer to wiring diagram to determine why voltage is available.

TEST AA6

Ignition Circuit Check – Turn ignition switch to the "ON" position. Apply voltmeter positive lead to control module pin location 1 (circuit 298) and negative lead to pin location 40 (circuit 430G). *See Air Suspension Control Module & Star Tester Connector Identification.* If 11 volts or more are available, proceed to TEST AA7. If not, refer to wiring diagram to determine why voltage is not available.

TEST AA7

Self Test Input (STI) Circuit Check – Apply analog ohmmeter lead to control module pin location 30 (circuit 606). Apply other lead to pin location 40 (circuit 430G). *See Air Suspension Control Module & Star Tester Connector Identification.* If 10,000 ohms or more are available, proceed to TEST AA8. If not, the STI circuit is shorted to ground. Refer to wiring diagram to repair circuit.

TEST AA8

Self Test Input (STI) Circuit Check – Apply analog ohmmeter lead to air control module pin location 30 (circuit 606). Apply other lead to the wire harness connector (for Star tester) pin location 2 (circuit 432E). *See Air Suspension Control Module & Star Tester Connector Identification.* If 5 ohms or less are available, proceed to TEST AA9. If not, the STI circuit 606 or 432E has an open. Refer to wiring diagram to repair circuit.

TEST AA9

Self Test Output (STO) Circuit Check – Apply analog ohmmeter lead to air control module pin location 15 (circuit 419A). Apply other lead to pin location 40 (circuit 430G). *See Air Suspension Control Module & Star Tester Connector Identification.* If 10,000 ohms or more are available, proceed to TEST AA10. If not, the STO circuit 419A is shorted to ground. Refer to wiring diagram to repair circuit.

TEST AA10

Self Test Output (STO) Circuit Check – Apply analog ohmmeter lead to air control module pin location 15 (circuit 419A). Apply other lead to the wire harness connector (for Star tester) pin location 4 (circuit 419B). *See Air Suspension Control Module & Star Tester Connector Identification.* If 5 ohms or less are available, turn the air suspension switch off and replace the air suspension control module. If 5 ohms or less are not available, the STO circuit 419A/419B has an open. Refer to wiring diagram to repair circuit.

TEST BA1

Unable To Enter Service Bay Diagnostics – Inability to enter drive cycle diagnostics is generally caused by a defective STAR tester, ignition switch or disruption in the positive side of the "B" power supply circuit. Additional possibilities are defective Self Test Input (STI) or Self Test Output (STO) circuit. Proceed to TEST BA2 for further inspection.

TEST BA2

STAR Tester Check – 1) Replace STAR tester with a known working unit. Put test button in the "HOLD" position. Attach tester to air suspension diagnostic connector and turn tester on. With ignition in the "OFF" position, wait 10 seconds and turn ignition to the "ON" position.

TEST BA2 (Cont.)

2) Wait 5 seconds and put test button in the "TEST" position. Wait 20 seconds. If Code 10 is displayed, See SERVICE BAY DIAGNOSTIC ENTRANCE PROCEDURE step 4). If any Codes between "21" and "28" are displayed, record number and proceed to TEST BB1. If neither of these conditions occur, proceed to TEST BA3.

TEST BA3

Power Supply Check – 1) Check power supply as possible source of inability to enter drive cycle diagnostics. Put test button in the "HOLD" position. Turn air suspension switch to the "OFF" position. Separate air suspension control module from from wire harness at connector. Turn air suspension switch to the "ON" position.

2) Apply voltmeter positive lead to pin location 37 (circuit 418A) and negative lead to pin location 40 (circuit 430G). *See Air Suspension Control Module & STAR Tester Connector Identification.* If 11 volts or more are available, proceed to TEST BA4. If not, refer to wiring diagram to determine why voltage is not available.

TEST BA4

Power Supply Circuit Check – Apply voltmeter positive lead to pin location 57 (circuit 418B) and negative lead to pin location 60 (circuit 430H). *See Air Suspension Control Module & Star Tester Connector Identification.* If 11 volts or more are available, proceed to TEST BA5. If not, refer to wiring diagram to determine why voltage is not available.

TEST BA5

Ignition Circuit Check – Turn ignition switch to the "OFF" position. Apply analog voltmeter positive lead to control module pin location 1 (circuit 298) and negative lead to pin location 40 (circuit 430G). *See Air Suspension Control Module & Star Tester Connector Identification.* If zero volts are available, proceed to TEST BA6. If not, refer to wiring diagram to determine why voltage is available.

TEST BA6

Ignition Circuit Check – Turn ignition switch to the "ON" position. Apply analog voltmeter positive lead to control module pin location 1 (circuit 298) and negative lead to pin location 40 (circuit 430G). *See Air Suspension Control Module & Star Tester Connector Identification.* If 11 volts or more are available, proceed to TEST BA7. If not, refer to wiring diagram to determine why voltage is not available.

TEST BA7

Self Test Input (STI) Circuit Check – Apply analog ohmmeter lead to control module pin location 30 (circuit 606). Apply other lead to pin location 40 (circuit 430G). *See Air Suspension Control Module & Star Tester Connector Identification.* If 10,000 ohms or more are available, proceed to TEST BA8. If not, STI circuit 606 is shorted to ground. Refer to wiring diagram to repair circuit.

TEST BA8

Self Test Input (STI) Circuit Check – Apply analog ohmmeter lead to air control module pin location 30 (circuit 606). Apply other lead to the wire harness connector (for Star tester) pin location 2 (circuit 432E). *See Air Suspension Control Module & Star Tester Connector Identification.* If 5 ohms or less are available, proceed to TEST BA9. If not, the STI circuit 606 or 432E has an open. Refer to wiring diagram to repair circuit.

TEST BA9

Self Test Output (STO) Circuit Check – Apply analog ohmmeter lead to air control module pin location 15 (circuit 419A). Apply other lead to pin location 40 (circuit 430G). *See Air Suspension Control Module & Star Tester Connector Identification.* If 10,000 ohms or more are available, proceed to TEST BA10. If not, STO circuit 419A is shorted to ground. Refer to wiring diagram to repair circuit.

TEST BA10

Self Test Output (STO) Circuit Check – Apply analog ohmmeter lead to air control module pin location 15 (circuit 419A). Apply other lead to the wire harness connector (for Star tester) circuit 419B. *See Air Suspension Control Module & Star Tester Connector Identification.* If 5 ohms or less are available, turn the air suspension switch off and replace the air suspension control module. If 5 ohms or less is not available, the STO circuit 419A/419B has an open. Refer to wiring diagram to repair circuit.

12-74

1989 ELECTRONIC SUSPENSION
Ford Motor Co. Air Suspension – Continental (Cont.)

TEST BB1

Brake Pressure Switch Voltage Check – 1) To transfer from SERVICE BAY DIAGNOSTICS to SPRING FILL, put STAR tester test button in the "HOLD" position. Turn air suspension switch to the "OFF" position. Separate control module from from wire harness at connector.

2) Apply analog voltmeter positive lead to pin location 7 (circuit 636) and negative lead to pin location 40 (circuit 430G). *See Air Suspension Control Module & STAR Tester Connector Identification.* There should be no voltage. If no voltage is available, proceed to TEST BB2. If any voltage is available, refer to wiring diagram to determine why voltage is available.

TEST BB2

Brake Pressure Switch Resistance Check – Apply analog ohmmeter lead to pin location 7 (circuit 636). Apply other lead to pin location 40 (circuit 430G). *See Air Suspension Control Module & Star Tester Connector Identification.* If 10,000 ohms or more are available, replace the air suspension control module and run SERVICE BAY DIAGNOSTICS. If less than 10,000 ohms are available, proceed to TEST BB3.

TEST BB3

Brake Pressure Switch Check – 1) Separate brake pressure switch from wiring harness. Apply analog ohmmeter lead to air suspension control module wire harness connector pin location 7 (circuit 636) and negative lead to pin location 46 (circuit 432D). *See Air Suspension Control Module & Star Tester Connector Identification.*

2) If 10,000 ohms are available, replace brake pressure switch and run SERVICE BAY DIAGNOSTICS. If less than 10,000 ohms are available, circuit 636 has a short. Refer to wiring diagram to repair circuit.

TEST CA1

Unable To Enter Spring Fill Diagnostics – Inability to enter spring fill diagnostics is generally caused by a defective STAR tester, brake switch circuit, ignition switch or disruption in the positive side of the "B" power supply circuit. Additional possibilities are defective Self Test Input (STI) or Self Test Output (STO) circuit. Proceed to TEST CA2 for further inspection.

TEST CA2

STAR Tester Check – 1) Replace STAR tester with a known working unit. Put test button in the "HOLD" position. Attach tester to air suspension diagnostic connector and turn tester on. With ignition in the "OFF" position, wait 10 seconds and turn ignition to the "ON" position.

2) Wait 5 seconds and put test button in the "TEST" position. Wait 20 seconds. If any Codes between "21" and "28" are displayed, see SPRING FILL DIAGNOSTICS. If any other code is displayed, record number and proceed to TEST CA3.

TEST CA3

Brake Pressure Switch Circuit Check – 1) Put STAR tester test button in the "HOLD" position. Turn air suspension switch to the "OFF" position. Separate control module from from wire harness at connector. Turn air suspension switch to the "ON" position.

2) Apply analog voltmeter positive lead to pin location 7 (circuit 636) and negative lead to pin location 40 (circuit 430G). *See Air Suspension Control Module & STAR Tester Connector Identification.* There should be no voltage. If no voltage is available, proceed to TEST CA4. If any voltage is available, refer to wiring diagram to determine why voltage is available.

TEST CA4

Brake Pressure Switch Resistance Check – Apply analog ohmmeter lead to pin location 7 (circuit 636). Apply other lead to pin location 40 (circuit 430G). *See Air Suspension Control Module & Star Tester Connector Identification.* If 10,000 ohms or more are available, proceed to CA6. If less than 10,000 ohms are available, proceed to TEST CA5.

TEST CA5

Brake Pressure Switch Check – 1) Separate brake pressure switch from wiring harness. Apply analog ohmmeter lead to air suspension control module wire harness connector pin location 7 (circuit 636) and negative lead to pin location 46 (circuit 432D). *See Air Suspension Control Module & Star Tester Connector Identification.*

TEST CA5 (Cont.)

2) If 10,000 ohms are available, replace brake pressure switch and run SPRING FILL DIAGNOSTICS. If less than 10,000 ohms are available, circuit 636 has a short. Refer to wiring diagram to repair circuit.

TEST CA6

Power Supply Check – Check power supply as possible sourse of inability to enter SPRING FILL DIAGNOSTICS. Put Star test button in the "HOLD" position. Apply voltmeter positive lead to pin location 37 (circuit 418A) and negative lead to pin location 40 (circuit 430G). *See Air Suspension Control Module & Star Tester Connector Identification.* If 11 volts or more are available, proceed to TEST CA7. If not, refer to wiring diagram to determine why voltage is not available.

TEST CA7

Power Supply Circuit Check – Apply voltmeter positive lead to pin location 57 (circuit 418B) and negative lead to pin location 60 (circuit 430H). *See Air Suspension Control Module & Star Tester Connector Identification.* If 11 volts or more are available, proceed to TEST CA8. If not, refer to wiring diagram to determine why voltage is not available.

TEST CA8

Ignition Circuit Check – Turn ignition switch to the "OFF" position. Apply analog voltmeter positive lead to control module pin location 1 (circuit 298) and negative lead to pin location 40 (circuit 430G). *See Air Suspension Control Module & Star Tester Connector Identification.* If zero volts are available, proceed to TEST CA9. If not, refer to wiring diagram to determine why voltage is available.

TEST CA9

Ignition Circuit Check – Turn ignition switch to the "ON" position. Apply analog voltmeter positive lead to control module pin location 1 (circuit 298) and negative lead to pin location 40 (circuit 430G). *See Air Suspension Control Module & Star Tester Connector Identification.* If 11 volts or more are available, proceed to TEST CA10. If not, refer to wiring diagram to determine why voltage is not available.

TEST CA10

Self Test Input (STI) Ground Check – Apply analog ohmmeter lead to control module pin location 30 (circuit 606). Apply other lead to pin location 40 (circuit 430G). *See Air Suspension Control Module & Star Tester Connector Identification.* If 10,000 ohms or more are available, proceed to TEST CA11. If not, STI circuit 606 is shorted to ground. Refer to wiring diagram to repair circuit.

TEST CA11

Self Test Input (STI) Circuit Check – Apply analog ohmmeter lead to air control module pin location 30 (circuit 606). Apply other lead to the wire harness connector (for Star tester) pin location 2 (circuit 432E). *See Air Suspension Control Module & Star Tester Connector Identification.* If 5 ohms or less are available, proceed to TEST CA12. If not, the STI circuit 606 or 432E has an open. Refer to wiring diagram to repair circuit.

TEST CA12

Self Test Output (STO) Circuit Check – Apply analog ohmmeter lead to air control module pin location 15 (circuit 419A). Apply other lead to pin location 40 (circuit 430G). *See Air Suspension Control Module & Star Tester Connector Identification.* If 10,000 ohms or more are available, proceed to TEST CA13. If not, STO circuit 419A is shorted to ground. Refer to wiring diagram to repair circuit.

TEST CA13

Self Test Output (STO) Circuit Check – Apply analog ohmmeter lead to air control module pin location 15 (circuit 419A). Apply other lead to the wire harness connector (for Star tester) circuit 419B. *See Air Suspension Control Module & Star Tester Connector Identification.* If 5 ohms or less are available, turn the air suspension switch off and replace the air suspension control module. If 5 ohms or less is not available, the STO circuit 419A/419B has an open. Refer to wiring diagram to repair circuit.

1989 ELECTRONIC SUSPENSION
Ford Motor Co. Air Suspension — Continental (Cont.)

12-75

TEST DA1

Low Power Supply – 1) If the air suspension control module detects a low power supply, check by putting Star test button in the "HOLD" position. Turn air suspension switch to the "OFF" position. Separate air suspension control module from from wire harness at connector. Turn air suspension switch to the "ON" position.

2) Apply analog voltmeter positive lead to pin location 37 (circuit 418A) and negative lead to pin location 40 (circuit 430G). *See Air Suspension Control Module & Star Tester Connector Identification.* If 11 volts or more are available, proceed to TEST DA2. If not, refer to wiring diagram to determine why voltage is not available. Run SERVICE BAY DIAGNOSTICS after repair is made.

TEST DA2

Power Supply Circuit Check – Apply voltmeter positive lead to pin location 57 (circuit 418B) and negative lead to pin location 60 (circuit 430H) *See Air Suspension Control Module & Star Tester Connector Identification.* If 11 volts or more are available, proceed to TEST DA3. If not, refer to wiring diagram to determine why voltage is not available. Run SERVICE BAY DIAGNOSTICS after repair is made.

TEST DA3

Ignition Circuit Check – 1) Turn ignition switch to the "OFF" position. Apply analog voltmeter positive lead to control module pin location 1 (circuit 298) and negative lead to pin location 40 (circuit 430G). *See Air Suspension Control Module & Star Tester Connector Identification.* If one volt or less is available, turn the air suspension switch off.

2) Replace the air suspension control module. Run SERVICE BAY DIAGNOSTICS after repair is made. If one volt or less is not available, refer to wiring diagram to repair circuit. Run SERVICE BAY DIAGNOSTICS after repair is made.

TEST EA1 (CODE 40)

1) When the air suspension control module detects a short in the left front air spring solenoid valve Code 40 will be logged into memory. The possible causes of Code 40 are a defective air spring solenoid valve, air suspension control module or disruption in the positive side of the "B" power supply circuit.

2) To diagnose system, turn air suspension switch off. Disengage air suspension control module. Apply analog ohmmeter positive lead to the wire harness connector pin location 21 (circuit 415). *See Air Suspension Control Module & Star Tester Connector Identification.* Apply other lead to pin location 40 (circuit 430G).

3) Record readings. Apply analog ohmmeter positive lead to the wire harness connector pin location 40 (circuit 430G). Apply other lead to pin location 21 (circuit 415). If 8 ohms or more are available on one or both readings, proceed to TEST EA3. If not, proceed to TEST EA2.

TEST EA2

Wiring Harness Inspection – 1) Disengage left front air spring solenoid valve from wiring harness. Apply analog ohmmeter lead to the wire harness connector pin location 21 (circuit 415). *See Air Suspension Control Module & Star Tester Connector Identification.* Apply other lead to pin location 40 (circuit 430G).

2) If ohmmeter readings are greater than 10,000 ohms, replace left front air spring solenoid valve and run SERVICE BAY DIAGNOSTICS. If ohmmeter readings are less than 10,000 ohms, repair circuit 415/430 short to ground and run SERVICE BAY DIAGNOSTICS.

TEST EA3

Wiring Harness Inspection – Disengage left front air spring solenoid valve from wiring harness. Apply analog ohmmeter lead to solenoid valve wire harness connector circuit 430K. *See Air Spring Solenoid Connector Identification.* Apply other lead to ground. If ohmmeter readings are greater than 2 ohms, proceed to TEST EA4. If not, proceed to TEST EA5.

Left Front Solenoid Valve Wire Harness Connector

Right Front Solenoid Valve Wire Harness Connector

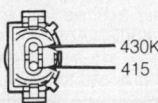
430K
415

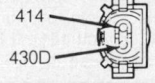
414
430D

TEST EA3 (Cont.)

Left Rear Solenoid Valve Wire Harness Connector

Right Rear Solenoid Valve Wire Harness Connector

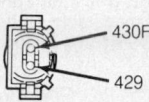
430F
429

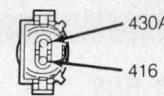
430A
416

Air Spring Solenoid Connector Identification

TEST EA4

Wiring Harness Inspection – 1) Inspect left front air spring solenoid valve circuit for correct routing by applying analog ohmmeter lead to solenoid valve wire harness connector circuit 415. *See Air Spring Solenoid Connector Identification.*

2) Apply other lead to ground. If ohmmeter readings are less than 2 ohms, air spring solenoid power circuit 415 and 430K are reversed. Repair as necessary and run SERVICE BAY DIAGNOSTICS.

3) If ohmmeter readings are greater than 2 ohms, air spring solenoid ground circuit 430K resistance is beyond acceptable range. Repair as necessary and run SERVICE BAY DIAGNOSTICS.

TEST EA5

Control Module & Solenoid Valve Inspection – 1) To diagnose system, turn air suspension switch off. Connect air suspension control module to wiring harness. Turn air suspension switch on. Run SERVICE BAY DIAGNOSTICS without connecting air suspension control module to wiring harness.

2) Disregard all codes except Code 40. If Code 40 is displayed, turn air suspension switch off. Replace control module and run SERVICE BAY DIAGNOSTICS. If Code 40 is not displayed, turn air suspension switch off. Replace air spring solenoid valve and run SERVICE BAY DIAGNOSTICS.

TEST EB1 (CODE 41)

1) When the air suspension control module detects a short in the right front air spring solenoid valve Code 41 will be logged into memory. The possible causes of Code 41 are a defective air spring solenoid valve, air suspension control module or disruption in the positive side of the "B" power supply circuit.

2) To diagnose system, turn air suspension switch off. Disengage air suspension control module. Apply analog ohmmeter positive lead to the wire harness connector pin location 17 (circuit 414). *See Air Suspension Control Module & Star Tester Connector Identification.* Apply other lead to pin location 40 (circuit 430G).

3) Record readings. Apply analog ohmmeter positive lead to the wire harness connector pin location 40 (circuit 430G). Apply other lead to pin location 17 (circuit 414). If 8 ohms or more are available on one or both readings, proceed to TEST EB3. If not proceed to TEST EB2.

TEST EB2

Wiring Harness Inspection – 1) Disengage right front air spring solenoid valve from wiring harness. Apply analog ohmmeter lead to the wire harness connector pin location 17 (circuit 414). *See Air Spring Solenoid Connector Identification.* Apply other lead to pin location 40 (circuit 430G).

2) If ohmmeter readings are greater than 10,000 ohms, replace right front air spring solenoid valve and run SERVICE BAY DIAGNOSTICS. If ohmmeter readings are less than 10,000 ohms, repair circuit 414/430G short to ground and run SERVICE BAY DIAGNOSTICS.

TEST EB3

Wiring Harness Inspection – Disengage right front air spring solenoid valve from wiring harness. Apply analog ohmmeter lead to solenoid valve wire harness connector circuit 430D. *See Air Spring Solenoid Connector Identification.* Apply other lead to ground. If ohmmeter readings are greater than 2 ohms, proceed to TEST EB4. If not, proceed to TEST EB5.

TEST EB4

Wiring Harness Inspection – 1) Inspect right front air spring solenoid valve circuit for correct routing by applying analog ohmmeter lead to solenoid valve wire harness connector circuit 414. *See Air Spring Solenoid Connector Identification.*

12-76

1989 ELECTRONIC SUSPENSION
Ford Motor Co. Air Suspension – Continental (Cont.)

TEST EB4 (Cont.)

2) Apply other lead to ground. If ohmmeter readings are less than 2 ohms, air spring solenoid power circuit 414 and 430D are reversed. Repair as necessary and run SERVICE BAY DIAGNOSTICS.

3) If ohmmeter readings are greater than 2 ohms, air spring solenoid ground circuit 430D resistance is beyond acceptable range. Repair as necessary and run SERVICE BAY DIAGNOSTICS.

TEST EB5

Control Module & Solenoid Valve Inspection – 1) To diagnose system, turn air suspension switch off. Connect air suspension control module to wiring harness. Turn air suspension switch on. Run SERVICE BAY DIAGNOSTICS without connecting air suspension control module to wiring harness.

2) Disregard all codes except Code 41. If Code 41 is displayed, turn air suspension switch off. Replace control module and run SERVICE BAY DIAGNOSTICS. If Code 41 is not displayed, turn air suspension switch off. Replace air spring solenoid valve and run SERVICE BAY DIAGNOSTICS.

TEST EC1 (CODE 42)

1) When the air suspension control module detects a short in the left rear air spring solenoid valve Code 42 will be logged into memory. The possible causes of Code 42 are a defective air spring solenoid valve, air suspension control module or disruption in the positive side of the "B" power supply circuit.

2) To diagnose system, turn air suspension switch off. Disengage air suspension control module. Apply analog ohmmeter positive lead to the wire harness connector pin location 41 (circuit 429). *See Air Suspension Control Module & Star Tester Connector Identification.* Record readings. Apply analog ohmmeter positive lead to the wire harness connector pin location 40 (circuit 430G). Apply other lead to pin location 41 (circuit 429). If 8 ohms or more are available on one or both readings, proceed to TEST EC3. If not proceed to TEST EC2.

TEST EC2

Wiring Harness Inspection – 1) Disengage left rear air spring solenoid valve from wiring harness. Apply analog ohmmeter lead to the control module wire harness connector pin location 41 (circuit 429). *See Air Suspension Control Module & Star Tester Connector Identification.* Apply other lead to pin location 40 (circuit 430G).

2) If ohmmeter readings are greater than 10,000 ohms, replace left rear air spring solenoid valve and run SERVICE BAY DIAGNOSTICS. If ohmmeter readings are less than 10,000 ohms, repair circuit 429/430G short to ground and run SERVICE BAY DIAGNOSTICS.

TEST EC3

Wiring Harness Inspection – Disengage left rear air spring solenoid valve from wiring harness. Apply analog ohmmeter lead to solenoid valve wire harness connector circuit 430F. *See Air Spring Solenoid Connector Identification.* Apply other lead to ground. If ohmmeter readings are greater than 2 ohms, proceed to TEST EC4. If not, proceed to TEST EC5.

TEST EC4

Wiring Harness Inspection – 1) Inspect left rear air spring solenoid valve circuit for correct routing by applying analog ohmmeter lead to solenoid valve wire harness connector circuit 429. *See Air Spring Solenoid Connector Identification.*

2) Apply other lead to ground. If ohmmeter readings are less than 2 ohms, air spring solenoid power circuit 429 and 430F are reversed. Repair as necessary and run SERVICE BAY DIAGNOSTICS.

3) If ohmmeter readings are greater than 2 ohms, air spring solenoid ground circuit 430F resistance is beyond acceptable range. Repair as necessary and run SERVICE BAY DIAGNOSTICS.

TEST EC5

Control Module & Solenoid Valve Inspection – 1) To diagnose system, turn air suspension switch off. Connect air suspension control module to wiring harness. Turn air suspension switch on. Run SERVICE BAY DIAGNOSTICS without connecting air suspension control module to wiring harness.

2) Disregard all codes except Code 42. If Code 42 is displayed, turn air suspension switch off. Replace control module and run SERVICE BAY DIAGNOSTICS. If Code 42 is not displayed, turn air suspension switch off. Replace air spring solenoid valve and run SERVICE BAY DIAGNOSTICS.

TEST ED1 (CODE 43)

1) When the air suspension control module detects a short in the right rear air spring solenoid valve Code 43 will be logged into memory. The possible causes of Code 43 are a defective right rear air spring solenoid valve, air suspension control module or disruption in the positive side of the "B" power supply circuit.

2) To diagnose system, turn air suspension switch off. Disengage air suspension control module. Apply analog ohmmeter positive lead to the wire harness connector pin location 38 (circuit 416). *See Air Suspension Control Module & Star Tester Connector Identification.* Apply other lead to pin location 40 (circuit 430G).

3) Record readings. Apply analog ohmmeter positive lead to the wire harness connector pin location 40 (circuit 430G). Apply other lead to pin location 38 (circuit 416). If 8 ohms or more are available on one or both readings, proceed to TEST ED3. If not proceed to TEST ED2.

TEST ED2

Wiring Harness Inspection – 1) Disengage right rear air spring solenoid valve from wiring harness. Apply analog ohmmeter lead to the control module wire harness connector pin location 38 (circuit 416). *See Air Suspension Control Module & Star Tester Connector Identification.* Apply other lead to pin location 40 (circuit 430G).

2) If ohmmeter readings are greater than 10,000 ohms, replace right rear air spring solenoid valve and run SERVICE BAY DIAGNOSTICS. If ohmmeter readings are less than 10,000 ohms, repair circuit 416/430G short to ground and run SERVICE BAY DIAGNOSTICS.

TEST ED3

Wiring Harness Inspection – Disengage right rear air spring solenoid valve from wiring harness. Apply analog ohmmeter lead to solenoid valve wire harness connector circuit 430A. *See Air Suspension Control Module & Star Tester Connector Identification.* Apply other lead to ground. If ohmmeter readings are greater than 2 ohms, proceed to TEST ED4. If not, proceed to TEST ED5.

TEST ED4

Wiring Harness Inspection – 1) Inspect right rear air spring solenoid valve circuit for correct routing by applying analog ohmmeter lead to solenoid valve wire harness connector circuit 416. *See Air Spring Solenoid Connector Identification.*

2) Apply other lead to ground. If ohmmeter readings are less than 2 ohms, air spring solenoid power circuit 416 and 430A are reversed. Repair as necessary and run SERVICE BAY DIAGNOSTICS.

3) If ohmmeter readings are greater than 2 ohms, air spring solenoid ground circuit 430A resistance is beyond acceptable range. Repair as necessary and run SERVICE BAY DIAGNOSTICS.

TEST ED5

Control Module & Solenoid Valve Inspection – 1) To diagnose system, turn air suspension switch off. Connect air suspension control module to wiring harness. Turn air suspension switch on. Run SERVICE BAY DIAGNOSTICS without connecting air suspension control module to wiring harness.

2) Disregard all codes except Code 43. If Code 43 is displayed, turn air suspension switch off. Replace control module and run SERVICE BAY DIAGNOSTICS. If Code 43 is not displayed, turn air suspension switch off. Replace air spring solenoid valve and run SERVICE BAY DIAGNOSTICS.

TEST EE1 (CODE 44)

1) When the air suspension control module detects a short in the vent solenoid valve circuit, Code 44 will be logged into memory. The possible causes of Code 44 are a defective vent solenoid valve, air suspension control module or disruption in the positive side of the "B" power supply circuit.

2) To diagnose system, turn air suspension switch off. Disengage air suspension control module. Apply analog ohmmeter positive lead to the wire harness connector pin location 42 (circuit 421). *See Air Suspension Control Module & Star Tester Connector Identification.* Apply other lead to pin location 40 (circuit 430G).

3) Record readings. Apply analog ohmmeter positive lead to the wire harness connector pin location 40 (circuit 430G). Apply other lead to pin location 42 (circuit 421). If 8 ohms or more are available on one or both readings, proceed to TEST EE3. If not proceed to TEST EE2.

1989 ELECTRONIC SUSPENSION
Ford Motor Co. Air Suspension – Continental (Cont.)

12-77

TEST EE2

Wiring Harness Inspection – **1)** Disengage air compressor assembly from wiring harness. Apply analog ohmmeter lead to the wire harness connector pin location 42 (circuit 421). *See Air Suspension Control Module & Star Tester Connector Identification.* Apply other lead to pin location 40 (circuit 430G).

2) If ohmmeter readings are greater than 10,000 ohms, replace air compressor assembly and run SERVICE BAY DIAGNOSTICS. If ohmmeter readings are less than 10,000 ohms, repair circuit 421/430G short to ground and run SERVICE BAY DIAGNOSTICS.

TEST EE3

Wiring Harness Inspection – Disengage left front air spring solenoid valve from wiring harness. Apply analog ohmmeter lead to solenoid valve wire harness connector circuit 430E. Apply other lead to ground. If ohmmeter readings are greater than 2 ohms, proceed to TEST EE4. If not, proceed to TEST EE5.

TEST EE4

Wiring Harness Inspection – **1)** Inspect vent solenoid valve circuit for correct routing by applying analog ohmmeter lead to vent solenoid valve wire harness connector circuit 421. *See Air Suspension Control Module & Star Tester Connector Identification.*

2) Apply other lead to ground. If ohmmeter readings are less than 2 ohms, vent solenoid power circuit 421 and 430E are reversed. Repair as necessary and run SERVICE BAY DIAGNOSTICS.

3) If ohmmeter readings are greater than 2 ohms, vent solenoid ground circuit 430E resistance is beyond acceptable range. Repair as necessary and run SERVICE BAY DIAGNOSTICS.

TEST EE5

Control Module & Vent Solenoid Valve Inspection – **1)** To diagnose system, turn air suspension switch off. Connect air suspension control module to wiring harness. Turn air suspension switch on. Run SERVICE BAY DIAGNOSTICS without connecting air suspension control module to wiring harness.

2) Disregard all codes except Code 44. If Code 44 is displayed, turn air suspension switch off. Replace control module and run SERVICE BAY DIAGNOSTICS. If Code 44 is not displayed, turn air suspension switch off. Replace air spring solenoid valve and run SERVICE BAY DIAGNOSTICS.

TEST EF1 (CODE 45)

1) When the air suspension control module detects a short in the air compressor activation relay circuit, Code 45 will be logged into memory. The possible causes of Code 45 are a defective air compressor relay, air suspension control module or disruption in the positive side of the "B" power supply circuit.

2) To diagnose system, turn air suspension switch off. Disengage air suspension control module. Apply analog ohmmeter positive lead to the wire harness connector pin location 35 (circuit 420). *See Air Suspension Control Module & Star Tester Connector Identification.* Apply other lead to pin location 40 (circuit 430G).

3) Record readings. Apply analog ohmmeter positive lead to the wire harness connector pin location 40 (circuit 430G). Apply other lead to pin location 35 (circuit 420). If 40 ohms or more are available on one or both readings, proceed to TEST EF3. If not proceed to TEST EF2.

TEST EF2

Wiring Harness Inspection – **1)** Disengage air compressor relay from wiring harness. Apply analog ohmmeter lead to control module wire harness connector pin location 35 (circuit 420). *See Air Suspension Control Module & Star Tester Connector Identification.* Apply other lead to pin location 40 (circuit 430G).

2) If ohmmeter readings are greater than 10,000 ohms, replace air compressor relay and run SERVICE BAY DIAGNOSTICS. If ohmmeter readings are less than 10,000 ohms, repair circuit 420/430G short to ground and run SERVICE BAY DIAGNOSTICS.

TEST EF3

Wiring Harness Inspection – Disengage air compressor relay from wiring harness. Apply analog ohmmeter lead to air compressor relay wire harness connector circuit 430B. *See Air Compressor & Relay Connector Identification.* Apply other lead to ground. If ohmmeter readings are greater than 2 ohms, proceed to TEST EF4. If not, proceed to TEST EF5.

TEST EF3 (Cont.)

Air Compressor & Relay Connector Identification

TEST EF4

Wiring Harness Inspection – **1)** Inspect air compressor relay circuit for correct routing by applying analog ohmmeter lead to air compressor relay wire harness connector circuit 420. *See Air Compressor & Relay Connector Identification.*

2) Apply other lead to ground. If ohmmeter readings are less than 2 ohms, air compressor relay power circuit 420 and 430B are reversed. Repair as necessary and run SERVICE BAY DIAGNOSTICS.

3) If ohmmeter readings are greater than 2 ohms, visually inspect air compressor relay wire arrangement. If okay, air compressor relay circuit 430B resistance is beyond acceptable range. Repair as necessary and run SERVICE BAY DIAGNOSTICS.

TEST EF5

Air Compressor Relay & Control Module Inspection – **1)** To diagnose system, turn air suspension switch off. Connect air suspension control module to wiring harness. Turn air suspension switch on. Run SERVICE BAY DIAGNOSTICS without connecting air suspension control module to wiring harness.

2) Disregard all codes except Code 45. If Code 45 is displayed, turn air suspension switch off. Replace control module and run SERVICE BAY DIAGNOSTICS. If Code 45 is not displayed, turn air suspension switch off. Replace air spring solenoid valve and run SERVICE BAY DIAGNOSTICS.

TEST EG1 (CODE 46)

1) When the air suspension control module detects a short in the height sensor circuit, Code 46 will be logged into memory. The possible causes of Code 46 are a defective height sensor, air suspension control module or disruption in the positive side of the "B" power supply circuit.

2) Ensure Star test button is in the "HOLD" position and turn tester on. Disconnect left front height sensor connector. Turn ignition switch and air suspension to the "ON" position and wait 5 seconds.

3) Turn ignition switch to the "OFF" position. Put Star test button is in the "TEST" position. If code 46 is displayed, go to TEST EG2. If not, replace left front height sensor and run SERVICE BAY DIAGNOSTICS.

TEST EG2

1) Ensure Star test button is in the "HOLD" position and turn tester on. Turn air suspension switch to the "OFF" position. Disconnect right front height sensor connector. Turn ignition switch and air suspension to the "ON" position and wait 15 seconds.

2) Turn ignition switch to the "OFF" position. Put Star test button is in the "TEST" position. If code 46 is displayed, go to TEST EG3. If not, replace right front height sensor and run SERVICE BAY DIAGNOSTICS.

12-78

1989 ELECTRONIC SUSPENSION
Ford Motor Co. Air Suspension — Continental (Cont.)

TEST EG3

1) Ensure Star test button is in the "HOLD" position and turn tester on. Turn air suspension switch to the "OFF" position. Disconnect rear height sensor connector. Turn ignition switch and air suspension to the "ON" position and wait 15 seconds.

2) Turn ignition switch to the "OFF" position. Put Star test button is in the "TEST" position. If code 46 is displayed, go to TEST EG4. If not, replace rear height sensor and run SERVICE BAY DIAGNOSTICS.

TEST EG4

Wiring Harness Inspection – 1) When the air suspension control module detects a short in the height sensor circuit and all height sensors have been eliminated as possibilities, 2 possible causes remain. Either the wiring harness has a short or the air suspension control module is defective.

2) Disengage air suspension control module connector and turn suspension switch off. Apply analog ohmmeter lead to the wire harness connector pin location 22 (circuit 431B). *See Air Suspension Control Module & Star Tester Connector Identification.* Apply other lead to pin location 40 (circuit 430G).

3) If ohmmeter readings are greater than 10,000 ohms, proceed to TEST EG5. If ohmmeter readings are less than 10,000 ohms, repair circuit 431B short to ground and run SERVICE BAY DIAGNOSTICS.

4) If ohmmeter readings are greater than 10,000 ohms, replace air suspension control module and run SERVICE BAY DIAGNOSTICS. If ohmmeter readings are less than 10,000 ohms, repair circuit 431B short to ground and run SERVICE BAY DIAGNOSTICS.

TEST EG5

Wiring Harness Inspection – 1) Apply analog ohmmeter lead to the wire harness connector pin location 55 (circuit 431A). *See Air Suspension Control Module & Star Tester Connector Identification.* Apply other lead to pin location 60 (circuit 430H).

2) If ohmmeter readings are greater than 10,000 ohms, replace air suspension control module and run SERVICE BAY DIAGNOSTICS. If ohmmeter readings are less than 10,000 ohms, repair circuit 431B short to ground and run SERVICE BAY DIAGNOSTICS.

TEST EH1 (CODE 47)

1) When the air suspension control module detects a short in the soft shock position relay circuit, Code 47 will be logged into memory. The possible causes of Code 47 are a defective soft shock relay, air suspension control module or disruption in the positive side of the "B" power supply circuit.

2) To diagnose system, turn air suspension switch off. Disengage air suspension control module. Apply analog ohmmeter positive lead to the wire harness connector pin location 12 (circuit 839). *See Air Suspension Control Module & Star Tester Connector Identification.* Apply other lead to pin location 40 (circuit 430G).

3) Record readings. Apply analog ohmmeter positive lead to the wire harness connector pin location 40 (circuit 430G). Apply other lead to pin location 12 (circuit 839). If 40 ohms or more are available on one or both readings, proceed to TEST EE3. If not proceed to TEST EE2.

TEST EH2

Wiring Harness Inspection – 1) Disengage soft shock relay from wiring harness. Apply analog ohmmeter lead to the control module wire harness connector pin location 12 (circuit 839). *See Air Suspension Control Module & Star Tester Connector Identification.* Apply other lead to pin location 40 (circuit 430G).

2) If ohmmeter readings are greater than 10,000 ohms, replace soft shock relay and run SERVICE BAY DIAGNOSTICS. If ohmmeter readings are less than 10,000 ohms, repair circuit 839/430G short to ground and run SERVICE BAY DIAGNOSTICS.

TEST EH3

Wiring Harness Inspection – Disengage soft shock relay from wiring harness. Apply analog ohmmeter lead to soft shock relay harness connector circuit 430B. *See Firm/Soft Shock Relay Connector Identification.* Apply other lead to ground. If ohmmeter readings are greater than 2 ohms, proceed to TEST EH4. If not, proceed to TEST EH5.

TEST EH3 (Cont.)

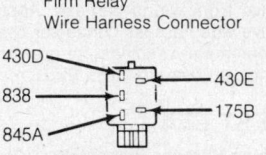

Firm/Soft Shock Relay Connector Identification

TEST EH4

Wiring Harness Inspection – 1) Inspect soft shock relay circuit for correct routing by applying analog ohmmeter lead to soft shock relay wire harness connector circuit 839. *See Firm/Soft Shock Relay Connector Identification.*

2) Apply other lead to ground. If ohmmeter readings are less than 2 ohms, soft shock relay circuit 839 and 430B are reversed. Repair as necessary and run SERVICE BAY DIAGNOSTICS.

3) If ohmmeter readings are greater than 2 ohms, soft shock relay circuit 430B resistance is beyond acceptable range. Repair as necessary and run SERVICE BAY DIAGNOSTICS.

TEST EH5

Control Module & Soft Shock Relay – 1) To diagnose system, turn air suspension switch off. Connect air suspension control module to wiring harness. Turn air suspension switch on. Run SERVICE BAY DIAGNOSTICS without connecting air suspension control module to wiring harness.

2) Disregard all codes except Code 47. If Code 47 is displayed, turn air suspension switch off. Replace control module and run SERVICE BAY DIAGNOSTICS. If Code 47 is not displayed, turn air suspension switch off. Replace air spring solenoid valve and run SERVICE BAY DIAGNOSTICS.

TEST EI1 (CODE 48)

1) When the air suspension control module detects a short in the firm shock position relay circuit, Code 48 will be logged into memory. The possible causes of Code 48 are a defective firm shock relay, air suspension control module or disruption in the positive side of the "B" power supply circuit.

2) To diagnose system, turn air suspension switch off. Disengage air suspension control module. Apply analog ohmmeter positive lead to the wire harness connector pin location 11 (circuit 838). *See Air Suspension Control Module & Star Tester Connector Identification.* Apply other lead to pin location 40 (circuit 430G).

3) Record readings. Apply analog ohmmeter positive lead to the wire harness connector pin location 40 (circuit 430G). Apply other lead to pin location 11 (circuit 838). If 40 ohms or more are available on one or both readings, proceed to TEST EI3. If not proceed to TEST EI2.

TEST EI2

Wiring Harness Inspection – 1) Disengage firm shock relay from wiring harness. Apply analog ohmmeter lead to the wire harness connector pin location 11 (circuit 838). *See Firm/Soft Shock Relay Connector Identification.* Apply other lead to pin location 40 (circuit 430G).

2) If ohmmeter readings are greater than 10,000 ohms, replace firm shock relay and run SERVICE BAY DIAGNOSTICS. If ohmmeter readings are less than 10,000 ohms, repair circuit 838/430G short to ground and run SERVICE BAY DIAGNOSTICS.

TEST EI3

Wiring Harness Inspection – Disengage firm shock relay from wiring harness. Apply analog ohmmeter lead to firm shock relay harness connector circuit 430D. *See Firm/Soft Shock Relay Connector Identification.* Apply other lead to ground. If ohmmeter readings are greater than 2 ohms, proceed to TEST EI4. If not, proceed to TEST EI5.

TEST EI4

Wiring Harness Inspection – **1)** Inspect firm shock relay circuit for correct routing by applying analog ohmmeter lead to soft shock relay wire harness connector circuit 838. *See Firm/Soft Shock Relay Connector Identification.*

2) Apply other lead to ground. If ohmmeter readings are less than 2 ohms, firm shock relay circuit 838 and 430D are reversed. Repair as necessary and run SERVICE BAY DIAGNOSTICS.

3) If ohmmeter readings are greater than 2 ohms, firm shock relay circuit 430D resistance is beyond acceptable range. Repair as necessary and run SERVICE BAY DIAGNOSTICS.

TEST EI5

Control Module & Firm Shock Relay – **1)** To diagnose components, turn air suspension switch off. Connect air suspension control module to wiring harness. Turn air suspension switch on. Run SERVICE BAY DIAGNOSTICS without connecting air suspension control module to wiring harness.

2) Disregard all codes except Code 48. If Code 48 is displayed, turn air suspension switch off. Replace control module and run SERVICE BAY DIAGNOSTICS. If Code 48 is not displayed, turn air suspension switch off. Replace air spring solenoid valve and run SERVICE BAY DIAGNOSTICS.

TEST EJ1 (CODE 66)

1) When the air suspension control module detects a short in the right height sensor circuit, Code 66 will be logged into memory. The possible causes of Code 66 are a defective height sensor, air suspension control module or short in the channel "A" or "B" return signal circuit.

2). Turn air suspension switch to the "OFF" position. Disconnect right front sensor connector. Turn ignition switch and air suspension to the "ON" position and wait 15 seconds.

3) Turn ignition switch to the "OFF" position. Put Star test button is in the "TEST" position. Disregard Code 55. If code 66 is displayed, go to TEST EG4. If not, replace right front height sensor and run SERVICE BAY DIAGNOSTICS.

TEST EJ2

Wiring Harness Inspection – **1)** Turn air suspension switch to the "OFF" position. Disengage air suspension control module connector. Apply analog ohmmeter lead to the air suspension control module wire harness connector pin location 9 (circuit 424). *See Air Suspension Control Module & Star Tester Connector Identification.* Apply other lead to ground.

2) If ohmmeter readings are greater than 10,000 ohms, proceed to TEST EJ3. If ohmmeter readings are less than 10,000 ohms, repair circuit 424 short to ground. Attach connectors and run SERVICE BAY DIAGNOSTICS.

TEST EJ3

Wiring Harness Inspection – **1)** Apply analog ohmmeter lead to the wire harness connector pin location 10 (circuit 425). *See Air Suspension Control Module & Star Tester Connector Identification.* Apply other lead to ground.

2) If ohmmeter readings are greater than 10,000 ohms, replace air suspension control module and run SERVICE BAY DIAGNOSTICS. If ohmmeter readings are less than 10,000 ohms, repair circuit 425 short to ground and run SERVICE BAY DIAGNOSTICS.

TEST EK1 (CODE 67)

1) When the air suspension control module detects a short in the left front height sensor circuit, Code 67 will be logged into memory. The possible causes of Code 67 are a defective left front height sensor, air suspension control module or short in the channel "A" or "B" return signal circuit.

TEST EK1 (Cont.)

2). Turn air suspension switch to the "OFF" position. Disconnect left front height sensor connector. Turn ignition switch and air suspension to the "ON" position and wait 15 seconds.

3) Turn ignition switch to the "OFF" position. Put Star test button is in the "TEST" position. Disregard Code 55. If code 67 is displayed, go to TEST EK4. If not, replace left front height sensor and run SERVICE BAY DIAGNOSTICS.

TEST EK2

Wiring Harness Inspection – **1)** Turn air suspension switch to the "OFF" position. Disengage air suspension control module connector. Apply analog ohmmeter lead to the air suspension control module wire harness connector pin location 27 (circuit 422). *See Air Suspension Control Module & Star Tester Connector Identification.* Apply other lead to ground.

2) If ohmmeter readings are greater than 10,000 ohms, proceed to TEST EK3. If ohmmeter readings are less than 10,000 ohms, repair circuit 422 short to ground. Attach connectors and run SERVICE BAY DIAGNOSTICS.

TEST EK3

Wiring Harness Inspection – **1)** Apply analog ohmmeter lead to the wire harness connector pin location 43 (circuit 423). *See Air Suspension Control Module & Star Tester Connector Identification.* Apply other lead to ground.

2) If ohmmeter readings are greater than 10,000 ohms, replace air suspension control module and run SERVICE BAY DIAGNOSTICS. If ohmmeter readings are less than 10,000 ohms, repair circuit 423 short to ground and run SERVICE BAY DIAGNOSTICS.

TEST EL1 (CODE 68)

1) When the air suspension control module detects a short in the rear height sensor circuit, Code 68 will be logged into memory. The possible causes of Code 68 are a defective rear height sensor, air suspension control module or short in the channel "A" or "B" return signal circuit.

2) Turn air suspension switch to the "OFF" position. Disconnect rear height sensor connector. Turn ignition switch and air suspension to the "ON" position and wait 15 seconds.

3) Turn ignition switch to the "OFF" position. Put Star test button is in the "TEST" position. Disregard Code 55. If code 68 is displayed, go to TEST EL4. If not, replace rear height sensor and run SERVICE BAY DIAGNOSTICS.

TEST EL2

Wiring Harness Inspection – **1)** Turn air suspension switch to the "OFF" position. Disengage air suspension control module connector. Apply analog ohmmeter lead to the air suspension control module wire harness connector pin location 5 (circuit 427). *See Air Suspension Control Module & Star Tester Connector Identification.* Apply other lead to ground.

2) If ohmmeter readings are greater than 10,000 ohms, proceed to TEST EL3. If ohmmeter readings are less than 10,000 ohms, repair circuit 427 short to ground. Attach connectors and run SERVICE BAY DIAGNOSTICS.

TEST EL3

Wiring Harness Inspection – **1)** Apply analog ohmmeter lead to the wire harness connector pin location 8 (circuit 428). *See Air Suspension Control Module & Star Tester Connector Identification.* Apply other lead to ground.

2) If ohmmeter readings are greater than 10,000 ohms, replace air suspension control module and run SERVICE BAY DIAGNOSTICS. If ohmmeter readings are less than 10,000 ohms, repair circuit 428 short to ground and run SERVICE BAY DIAGNOSTICS.

TEST FA1 (CODE 69)

1) When the air suspension control module detects a short in the right front height sensor circuit, Code 69 will be logged into memory. The possible causes of Code 69 are a defective right front height sensor, malfunctioning linkage arm, air suspension control module, a disruption in the "B" power supply circuit or open circuit in the channel "A" or "B" return signal.

TEST FA1 (Cont.)

2) A visual inspection should be made to verify that sensor connector and linkage arm are attached and not damaged. Disconnect right front height sensor connector. Apply analog voltmeter positive lead to circuit 431C. *See Height Sensor Connector Identification.* Apply other lead to ground. If voltage is greater than 4 volts, proceed to TEST FA2.

3) If voltage is less than 4 volts, turn air suspension switch to the "OFF" position. Disengage air suspension control module connector. Apply ohmmeter lead to the air suspension control module wire harness connector pin location 22 (circuit 431B). Apply other lead to right front height sensor circuit 431C.

4) If ohmmeter readings are less than 5 ohms, replace air suspension control module and run SERVICE BAY DIAGNOSTICS. If ohmmeter readings are greater than 5 ohms, resistance in circuit 431B and 431C is beyond acceptable range. Repair as necessary and run SERVICE BAY DIAGNOSTICS.

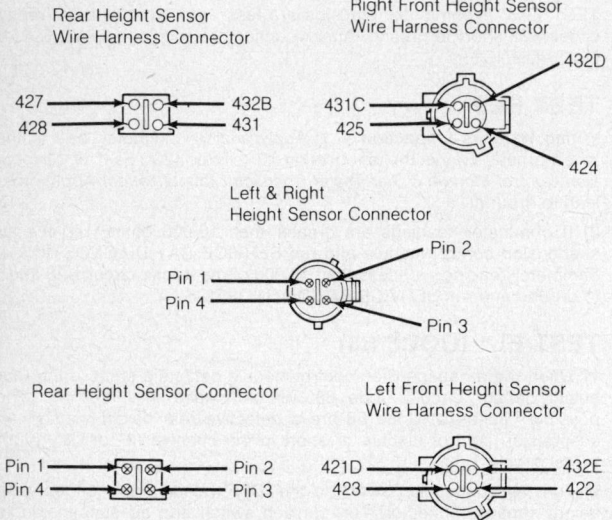

Height Sensor Connector Identification

TEST FA2

B+ Power Return Circuit Check – 1) Apply ohmmeter lead to the right front height sensor wire harness connector circuit 432D. *See Height Sensor Connector Identification.* Apply other lead to ground. If ohmmeter reading is less than 5 ohms, proceed to TEST FA3. If ohmmeter readings is greater than ohms, turn air suspension switch to the "OFF" position.

2) Disengage air suspension control module connector. Apply ohmmeter lead to the air suspension control module wire harness connector pin location 46 (circuit 432D). Apply other lead to right front height sensor connector circuit 432D.

3) If ohmmeter readings are less than 5 ohms, replace air suspension control module and run SERVICE BAY DIAGNOSTICS. If ohmmeter readings are greater than 5 ohms, resistance in circuit 432D is beyond acceptable range. Repair as necessary and run SERVICE BAY DIAGNOSTICS.

TEST FA3

Channel "A" Inspection – 1) Apply analog voltmeter positive lead to circuit 424 of right front height sensor connector. *See Height Sensor Connector Identification.* Apply other lead to ground. If voltage is greater than 4 volts, replace right front height sensor.

2) If voltage is less than 4 volts, turn air suspension switch to the "OFF" position. Disengage air suspension control module connector. Apply analog ohmmeter lead to the air suspension control module wire harness connector pin location 9 (circuit 424). *See Height Sensor Connector Identification.* Apply other lead to right front height sensor connector circuit 424.

3) If ohmmeter readings are less than 5 ohms, replace air suspension control module and run SERVICE BAY DIAGNOSTICS. If ohmmeter readings are greater than 5 ohms, resistance in right front sensor channel "A" circuit is beyond acceptable range. Repair as necessary and run SERVICE BAY DIAGNOSTICS.

TEST FA4

Channel "B" Inspection – 1) Apply analog voltmeter positive lead to circuit 425 of right front height sensor connector. *See Height Sensor Connector Identification.* Apply other lead to ground. If voltage is greater than 4 volts, replace the right front height sensor. If voltage is less than 4 volts, proceed to Step **2)**.

2) Turn air suspension switch to the "OFF" position. Disengage air suspension control module connector. Apply analog ohmmeter lead to the air suspension control module wire harness connector pin location 10 (circuit 425). Apply other lead to right front height sensor connector circuit 425.

3) If ohmmeter readings are less than 5 ohms, replace air suspension control module and run SERVICE BAY DIAGNOSTICS. If ohmmeter readings are greater than 5 ohms, resistance in right front sensor channel "B" circuit is beyond acceptable range. Repair as necessary and run SERVICE BAY DIAGNOSTICS.

TEST FB1 (CODE 70)

1) When the air suspension control module detects an open in the left front height sensor circuit, Code 70 will be logged into memory. The possible causes of Code 70 are a defective left front height sensor, malfunctioning linkage arm, air suspension control module, a disruption in the "B" power supply circuit or open circuit in the channel "A" or "B" return signal.

2) A visual inspection should be made to verify that sensor connector and linkage arm are attached and not damaged. Disconnect left front height sensor connector. Apply analog voltmeter positive lead to left front height sensor circuit 431D. *See Height Sensor Connector Identification.* Apply other lead to ground. If voltage is greater than 4 volts, proceed to TEST FB2.

3) If voltage is less than 4 volts, turn air suspension switch to the "OFF" position. Disengage air suspension control module connector. Apply ohmmeter lead to the air suspension control module wire harness connector pin location 22 (circuit 431B). *See Air Suspension Control Module & Star Tester Connector Identification.* Apply other lead to circuit 431D.

4) If ohmmeter readings are less than 5 ohms, replace air suspension control module and run SERVICE BAY DIAGNOSTICS. If ohmmeter readings are greater than 5 ohms, resistance in circuit 431B and 431D is beyond acceptable range. Repair as necessary and run SERVICE BAY DIAGNOSTICS.

TEST FB2

B+ Power Return Circuit Check – 1) Apply ohmmeter lead to the left front sensor wire harness connector circuit 432E. *See Height Sensor Connector Identification.* Apply other lead to ground. If ohmmeter reading is less than 5 ohms, proceed to TEST FB3. If ohmmeter readings is greater than ohms, turn air suspension switch to the "OFF" position.

2) Disengage air suspension control module connector. Apply ohmmeter lead to the air suspension control module wire harness connector pin location 46 (circuit 432D). *See Height Sensor Connector Identification.* Apply other lead to left front height sensor connector circuit 432E.

3) If ohmmeter readings are less than 5 ohms, replace air suspension control module and run SERVICE BAY DIAGNOSTICS. If ohmmeter readings are greater than 5 ohms, resistance in circuit 432D and 432E is beyond acceptable range. Repair as necessary and run SERVICE BAY DIAGNOSTICS.

TEST FB3

Channel "A" Inspection – 1) Apply voltmeter positive lead to circuit 422 of left front height sensor connector. *See Height Sensor Connector Identification.* Apply other lead to ground. If voltage is greater than 4 volts, proceed to TEST FB4.

2) If voltage is less than 4 volts, turn air suspension switch to the "OFF" position. Disengage air suspension control module connector. Apply analog ohmmeter lead to the air suspension control module wire harness connector pin location 27 (circuit 422). *See Height Sensor Connector Identification.* Apply other lead to left front height sensor connector circuit 422.

3) If ohmmeter readings are less than 5 ohms, replace air suspension control module and run SERVICE BAY DIAGNOSTICS. If ohmmeter readings are greater than 5 ohms, resistance in left front sensor channel "A" (circuit 422) circuit is beyond acceptable range. Repair as necessary and run SERVICE BAY DIAGNOSTICS.

1989 ELECTRONIC SUSPENSION
Ford Motor Co. Air Suspension – Continental (Cont.)

12-81

TEST FB4

Channel "B" Inspection – 1) Apply analog voltmeter positive lead to circuit 423 of left front height sensor connector. *See Height Sensor Connector Identification.* Apply other lead to ground. If voltage is greater than 4 volts, replace the left front height sensor. If voltage is less than 4 volts, proceed to Step **2).**

2) Turn air suspension switch to the "OFF" position. Disengage air suspension control module connector. Apply analog ohmmeter lead to the air suspension control module wire harness connector pin location 43 (circuit 423). *See Air Suspension Control Module & Star Tester Connector Identification.* Apply other lead to left front height sensor connector circuit 423.

3) If ohmmeter readings are less than 5 ohms, replace air suspension control module and run SERVICE BAY DIAGNOSTICS. If ohmmeter readings are greater than 5 ohms, resistance in left front sensor channel "B" circuit (circuit 423) is beyond acceptable range. Repair as necessary and run SERVICE BAY DIAGNOSTICS.

TEST GA1 (CODES 56 & 60)

1) When signal transmission to the air suspension control module from the left rear shock actuator is interrupted, Code 56 or 60 will be logged into memory. The possible component causes are a defective air suspension control module, left rear shock actuator, "SOFT" and/or "FIRM" relay or a binding in the left rear actuator. The possible circuit causes are a disruption in the left rear actuator power supply circuit or a defective "SOFT" or "FIRM" relay circuit.

2) A visual inspection should be made to verify that actuator connector is attached and wire harness is not damaged. If any defects are found, repair as necessary and run SERVICE BAY DIAGNOSTICS. If no defects are found, proceed to step **3).**

3) Disengage left rear actuator connector. Apply analog ohmmeter lead to actuator pin position "1" and "2". If ohmmeter readings are 5 ohms or less, proceed to TEST GA2. If ohmmeter readings are greater than 10,000 ohms, apply 12 volts to actuator pin position "3" with actuator pin position "4" grounded to drive actuator to "SOFT" position.

4) Remove power supply. Apply analog ohmmmeter leads to pin positions "1" and "2". If ohmmeter readings are 5 ohms or less, proceed to TEST GA3. If ohmmeter readings are greater than 10,000 ohms, apply 12 volts to actuator pin position "4" with actuator pin position "3" grounded for 2 seconds to drive actuator to "FIRM" position.

5) Remove power supply. Apply analog ohmmeter lead to pin positions "1" and "2". If ohmmeter readings are 10,000 ohms or greater, proceed to TEST GA2, step **2).** If ohmmeter readings are 5 ohms or less, replace left rear actuator and run SERVICE BAY DIAGNOSTICS.

TEST GA2

1) Apply 12 volts to actuator pin position "4" with actuator pin position "3" grounded for 2 seconds to drive actuator to "FIRM" position. Remove power supply. Apply analog ohmmeter lead to pin positions "1" and "2". If ohmmeter readings are 10,000 ohms or greater, proceed to TEST GA3.

2) If ohmmeter readings are 5 ohms or less, apply 12 volts to actuator pin position "3" with actuator pin position "4" grounded for 2 seconds to drive actuator to "SOFT" position. Remove power supply. Apply analog ohmmeter readings to pin positions "1" and "2". If ohmmeter readings are 10,000 ohms or greater, replace left rear actuator and run SERVICE BAY DIAGNOSTICS.

3) If ohmmeter readings are 5 ohms or less, remove strut actuator and rotate control tube to the "S" (soft) position. Apply analog ohmmeter lead to pin positions "1" and "2". If ohmmeter readings are 10,000 ohms or greater, replace left rear actuator and run SERVICE BAY DIAGNOSTICS.

4) If ohmmeter readings are 5 ohms or less, rotate control tube to the "H" (firm) position. Apply analog ohmmeter lead to pin positions "1" and "2". If ohmmeter readings are 5 ohms or less, replace left rear actuator and run SERVICE BAY DIAGNOSTICS.

5) If ohmmeter readings are 10,000 ohms or greater, verify control tube is in the "H" (firm) position. Apply 12 volts to actuator pin position "3" with actuator pin position "4" grounded for 2 seconds to drive actuator to the "S" (soft) position. If control tube does not rotate to "S" position, replace left rear actuator and run SERVICE BAY DIAGNOSTICS.

TEST GA2 (Cont.)

6) If control tube does rotate to "S" position, apply 12 volts to actuator pin position "4" with actuator pin position "3" grounded for 2 seconds to drive actuator to the "H" (firm) position. If control tube does not rotate to "H" position, replace left rear actuator and run SERVICE BAY DIAGNOSTICS.

7) If control tube does rotate to "H" position, install a functional rear actuator on strut assembly and run SERVICE BAY DIAGNOSTICS. If Code 56 and/or 60 are displayed, a binding situation exists in the strut assembly. If no codes are displayed, the problem has been corrected.

TEST GA3

Wire Harness Inspection – 1) Turn air suspension to the "OFF" position and wait 5 seconds. Ensure Star test button is in the "HOLD" position and turn tester off. Disconnect air suspension control module from wiring harness connector.

2) Apply analog ohmmeter lead to control module wire harness connector pin location 49 (circuit 842). *See Air Suspension Control Module & Star Tester Connector Identification.* Apply other lead to left rear actuator connector circuit 842. If ohmmeter readings are greater than 5 ohms, resistance in circuit is beyond acceptable range. Repair as necessary and run SERVICE BAY DIAGNOSTICS.

3) If ohmmeter readings are less than 5 ohms, apply analog ohmmeter lead to control module wire harness connector pin location 46 (circuit 432D). *See Air Suspension Control Module & Star Tester Connector Identification.* Apply other lead to left rear actuator connector circuit 432C. If ohmmeter readings are greater than 5 ohms, resistance in circuit is beyond acceptable range. Repair as necessary and run SERVICE BAY DIAGNOSTICS.

4) If ohmmeter readings are less than 5 ohms, disengage Soft Shock Relay wire harness connector. Apply analog ohmmeter lead to Soft Shock Relay wire harness connector circuit 846A. Apply other lead to left rear actuator connector circuit 846C. If ohmmeter readings are greater than 5 ohms, resistance in circuit is beyond acceptable range. Repair as necessary and run SERVICE BAY DIAGNOSTICS.

5) If ohmmeter readings are less than 5 ohms, disengage Firm Shock Relay wire harness connector. Apply analog ohmmeter lead to Soft Shock Relay wire harness connector circuit 845A. Apply other lead to left rear actuator connector circuit 845C. If ohmmeter readings are less than 5 ohms, replace air suspension control module. If ohmmeter readings are greater than 5 ohms, resistance in circuit is beyond acceptable range. Repair as necessary and run SERVICE BAY DIAGNOSTICS.

TEST GB1 (CODES 57 & 61)

1) When signal transmission to the air suspension control module from the right front shock actuator is interrupted, Code 57 or 61 will be logged into memory. The possible component causes are a defective air suspension control module, right front shock actuator, "SOFT" and/or "FIRM" relay or a binding in the right front actuator. The possible circuit causes are a disruption in the right front actuator power supply circuit or a defective "SOFT" or "FIRM" relay circuit.

2) A visual inspection should be made to verify that actuator connector is attached and wire harness is not damaged. If any defects are found, repair as necessary and run SERVICE BAY DIAGNOSTICS. If no defects are found, proceed to step **3).**

3) Disengage right front actuator connector. Apply analog ohmmeter lead to actuator pin position "1" and "2". If ohmmeter readings are 5 ohms or less, proceed to TEST GB2. If ohmmeter readings are greater than 10,000 ohms, apply 12 volts to actuator pin position "3" with actuator pin position "4" grounded to drive actuator to "SOFT" position.

4) Remove power supply. Apply analog ohmmeter leads to pin positions "1" and "2". If ohmmeter readings are 5 ohms or less, proceed to TEST GB3. If ohmmeter readings are greater than 10,000 ohms, apply 12 volts to actuator pin position "4" with actuator pin position "3" grounded for 2 seconds to drive actuator to "FIRM" position.

5) Remove power supply. Apply analog ohmmeter lead to pin positions "1" and "2". If ohmmeter readings are 10,000 ohms or greater, proceed to TEST GB2. If ohmmeter readings are 5 ohms or less, proceed to TEST G3.

12-82

1989 ELECTRONIC SUSPENSION
Ford Motor Co. Air Suspension – Continental (Cont.)

TEST GB2

1) Apply 12 volts to actuator pin position "4" with actuator pin position "3" grounded for 2 seconds to drive actuator to "FIRM" position. Remove power supply. Apply analog ohmmeter leads to pin positions "1" and "2". If ohmmeter readings are 5 ohms or less, replace right front actuator and run SERVICE BAY DIAGNOSTICS. If ohmmeter readings are 10,000 ohms or greater, proceed to step **4)**.

2) Apply 12 volts to actuator pin position "4" with actuator pin position "3" grounded for 2 seconds to drive actuator to "FIRM" position. Remove power supply. Apply analog ohmmeter lead to pin positions "1" and "2". If ohmmeter readings are 10,000 ohms or greater, proceed to TEST G3.

3) If ohmmeter readings are 5 ohms or less, apply 12 volts to actuator pin position "3" with actuator pin position "4" grounded for 2 seconds to drive actuator to "SOFT" position. Remove power supply. Apply analog ohmmeter lead to pin positions "1" and "2". If ohmmeter readings are 10,000 ohms or greater, replace right front actuator and run SERVICE BAY DIAGNOSTICS.

4) If ohmmeter readings are 5 ohms or less, remove actuator from strut assembly and rotate control tube to the "S" (soft) position. Apply analog ohmmeter lead to pin positions "1" and "2". If ohmmeter readings are 10,000 ohms or greater, replace right front actuator and run SERVICE BAY DIAGNOSTICS.

5) If ohmmeter readings are 5 ohms or less rotate control tube to the "H" (firm) position. Apply analog ohmmeter lead to pin positions "1" and "2". If ohmmeter readings are 5 ohms or less, replace right front actuator and run SERVICE BAY DIAGNOSTICS.

6) If ohmmeter readings are 10,000 ohms or greater, rotate control tube to the "H" (firm) position. Apply 12 volts to actuator pin position "3" with actuator pin position "4" grounded for 2 seconds to drive actuator to the "S" (soft) position. If control tube does not rotate to "S" position, replace right front actuator and run SERVICE BAY DIAGNOSTICS.

7) If control tube does rotate to "S" position, apply 12 volts to actuator pin position "4" with actuator pin position "3" grounded for 2 seconds to drive actuator to the "H" (firm) position. If control tube does not rotate to "H" position, replace right front actuator and run SERVICE BAY DIAGNOSTICS.

8) If control tube does rotate to "H" position, install a functional rear actuator on strut assembly and run SERVICE BAY DIAGNOSTICS. If Code 57 and/or 61 are displayed, a binding situation exists in the strut assembly. If no codes are displayed, the problem has been corrected.

TEST GB3

Wire Harness Inspection – 1) Turn air suspension to the "OFF" position and wait 5 seconds. Ensure Star test button is in the "HOLD" position and turn tester off. Disconnect air suspension control module from wiring harness connector.

2) Apply analog ohmmeter lead to control module wire harness connector pin location 44 (circuit 841). *See Air Suspension Control Module & Star Tester Connector Identification.* Apply other lead to right front actuator connector circuit 841. If ohmmeter readings are greater than 5 ohms, resistance in circuit is beyond acceptable range. Repair as necessary and run SERVICE BAY DIAGNOSTICS.

3) If ohmmeter readings are less than 5 ohms, apply analog ohmmeter lead to control module wire harness connector pin location 46 (circuit 432D). *See Air Suspension Control Module & Star Tester Connector Identification.* Apply other lead to right front actuator connector circuit 432C. If ohmmeter readings are greater than 5 ohms, resistance in circuit is beyond acceptable range. Repair as necessary and run SERVICE BAY DIAGNOSTICS.

4) If ohmmeter readings are less than 5 ohms, disengage Soft Shock Relay wire harness connector. Apply analog ohmmeter lead to Soft Shock Relay wire harness connector circuit 845A. Apply other lead to right front actuator connector circuit 845A. If ohmmeter readings are greater than 5 ohms, resistance in circuit is beyond acceptable range. Repair as necessary and run SERVICE BAY DIAGNOSTICS.

5) If ohmmeter readings are less than 5 ohms, disengage Firm Shock Relay wire harness connector. Apply analog ohmmeter lead to Soft Shock Relay wire harness connector circuit 845A. Apply other lead to right front actuator connector circuit 845A. If ohmmeter readings are less than 5 ohms, replace air suspension control module. If ohmmeter readings are greater than 5 ohms, resistance in circuit is beyond acceptable range. Repair as necessary and run SERVICE BAY DIAGNOSTICS.

TEST GC1 (CODES 58 & 62)

1) When signal transmission to the air suspension control module from the left front shock actuator is interrupted, Code 58 or 62 will be logged into memory. The possible component causes are a defective air suspension control module, left front shock actuator, "SOFT" and/or "FIRM" relay or a binding in the left front actuator. The possible circuit causes are a disruption in the left front actuator power supply circuit or a defective "SOFT" or "FIRM" relay circuit.

2) A visual inspection should be made to verify that actuator connector is attached and wire harness is not damaged. If any defects are found, repair as necessary and run SERVICE BAY DIAGNOSTICS. If no defects are found, proceed to step **3)**.

3) Disengage left front actuator connector. Apply analog ohmmeter lead to actuator pin position "1" and "2". If ohmmeter readings are 5 ohms or less, proceed to TEST GC2. If ohmmeter readings are greater than 10,000 ohms, apply 12 volts to actuator pin position "3" with actuator pin position "4" grounded to drive actuator to "SOFT" position.

4) Remove power supply. Apply analog ohmmmeter leads to pin positions "1" and "2". If ohmmeter readings are 5 ohms or less, proceed to TEST GC3. If ohmmeter readings are greater than 10,000 ohms, apply 12 volts to actuator pin position "4" with actuator pin position "3" grounded for 2 seconds to drive actuator to "FIRM" position.

5) Remove power supply. Apply analog ohmmeter lead to pin positions "1" and "2". If ohmmeter readings are 10,000 ohms or greater, proceed to TEST GC2, step **3)**. If ohmmeter readings are 5 ohms or less, replace left front actuator and run SERVICE BAY DIAGNOSTICS.

TEST GC2

Component Inspection – 1) Apply 12 volts to actuator pin position "4" with actuator pin position "3" grounded for 2 seconds to drive actuator to "FIRM" position. Remove power supply. Apply analog ohmmeter lead to pin positions "1" and "2". If ohmmeter readings are 10,000 ohms or greater, proceed to TEST GC3.

2) If ohmmeter readings are 5 ohms or less, apply 12 volts to actuator pin position "3" with actuator pin position "4" grounded for 2 seconds to drive actuator to "SOFT" position. Remove power supply. Apply analog ohmmeter lead to pin positions "1" and "2". If ohmmeter readings are 10,000 ohms or greater, replace left front actuator and run SERVICE BAY DIAGNOSTICS.

3) If ohmmeter readings are 5 ohms or less, remove strut actuator and rotate control tube to the "S" (soft) position. Apply analog ohmmeter lead to pin positions "1" and "2". If ohmmeter readings are 10,000 ohms or greater, replace left front actuator and run SERVICE BAY DIAGNOSTICS.

4) If ohmmeter readings are 5 ohms or less, rotate control tube to the "H" (firm) position. Apply analog ohmmeter lead to pin positions "1" and "2". If ohmmeter readings are 5 ohms or less, replace left front actuator and run SERVICE BAY DIAGNOSTICS.

5) If ohmmeter readings are 10,000 ohms or greater, verify control tube is in to the "H" (firm) position. Apply 12 volts to actuator pin position "3" with actuator pin position "4" grounded for 2 seconds to drive actuator to the "S" (soft) position. If control tube does not rotate to "S" position, replace left front actuator and run SERVICE BAY DIAGNOSTICS.

6) If control tube does rotate to "S" position, apply 12 volts to actuator pin position "4" with actuator pin position "3" grounded for 2 seconds to drive actuator to the "H" (firm) position. If control tube does not rotate to "H" position, replace left front actuator and run SERVICE BAY DIAGNOSTICS.

7) If control tube does rotate to "H" (firm) position, install a functional front actuator on strut assembly and run SERVICE BAY DIAGNOSTICS. If no codes are displayed, the problem has been corrected. If Code 58 and/or 62 are displayed, a binding situation exists in the strut assembly.

TEST GC3

Wire Harness Inspection – 1) Turn air suspension to the "OFF" position. Ensure Star test button is in the "HOLD" position and turn tester off. Disconnect air suspension control module from wiring harness connector.

2) Apply analog ohmmeter lead to control module wire harness connector pin location 47 (circuit 840). *See Air Suspension Control Module & Star Tester Connector Identification.* Apply other lead to left front actuator connector circuit 840. If ohmmeter readings are greater than 5 ohms, resistance in circuit is beyond acceptable range. Repair as necessary and run SERVICE BAY DIAGNOSTICS.

1989 ELECTRONIC SUSPENSION
Ford Motor Co. Air Suspension — Continental (Cont.)

12-83

TEST GC3 (Cont.)

3) If ohmmeter readings are less than 5 ohms, disengage Soft Shock Relay connector. Apply analog ohmmeter lead to connector circuit 846A. *See Fig. 28.* Apply other lead to left front actuator connector circuit 846B. If ohmmeter readings are greater than 5 ohms, resistance in circuit is beyond acceptable range. Repair as necessary and run SERVICE BAY DIAGNOSTICS.

4) If ohmmeter readings are less than 5 ohms, disengage Firm Shock Relay wire harness connector. Apply analog ohmmeter lead to Soft Shock Relay wire harness connector circuit 845A. Apply other lead to left front actuator connector circuit 845B. If ohmmeter readings are less than 5 ohms, replace air suspension control module. If ohmmeter readings are greater than 5 ohms, resistance in circuit is beyond acceptable range. Repair as necessary and run SERVICE BAY DIAGNOSTICS.

TEST GD1 (CODES 59 & 63)

1) When signal transmission to the air suspension control module from the right rear shock actuator is interrupted, Code 59 or 63 will be logged into memory. The possible component causes are a defective air suspension control module, right rear shock actuator, "SOFT" and/or "FIRM" relay or a binding in the right rear actuator. The possible circuit causes are a disruption in the right rear actuator power supply circuit or a defective "SOFT" or "FIRM" relay circuit.

2) A visual inspection should be made to verify that actuator connector is attached and wire harness is not damaged. If any defects are found, repair as necessary and run SERVICE BAY DIAGNOSTICS. If no defects are found, proceed to step 3).

3) Disengage right rear actuator connector. Apply analog ohmmeter lead to actuator pin position "1" and "2". If ohmmeter readings are 5 ohms or less, proceed to TEST GD2. If ohmmeter readings are greater than 10,000 ohms, apply 12 volts to actuator pin position "3" with actuator pin position "4" grounded to drive actuator to "SOFT" position.

4) Remove power supply. Apply analog ohmmeter leads to pin positions "1" and "2". If ohmmeter readings are 5 ohms or less, proceed to TEST GD3. If ohmmeter readings are greater than 10,000 ohms, apply 12 volts to actuator pin position "4" with actuator pin position "3" grounded for 2 seconds to drive actuator to "FIRM" position.

5) Remove power supply. Apply analog ohmmeter lead to pin positions "1" and "2". If ohmmeter readings are 10,000 ohms or greater, proceed to TEST GD2, step 4) . If ohmmeter readings are 5 ohms or less, replace right rear actuator.

TEST GD2

1) Apply 12 volts to actuator pin position "4" with actuator pin position "3" grounded for 2 seconds to drive actuator to "FIRM" position. Remove power supply. Apply analog ohmmeter leads to pin positions "1" and "2". If ohmmeter readings are 10,000 ohms or greater, proceed to TEST GD3.

2) If ohmmeter readings are 5 ohms or less, apply 12 volts to actuator pin position "3" with actuator pin position "4" grounded for 2 seconds to drive actuator to "SOFT" position. Remove power supply. Apply analog ohmmeter lead to pin positions "1" and "2". If ohmmeter readings are 10,000 ohms or greater, replace right rear actuator.

3) If ohmmeter readings are 5 ohms or less, remove actuator from strut assembly and rotate control tube to the "S" (soft) position. Apply analog ohmmeter lead to pin positions "1" and "2". If ohmmeter readings are 10,000 ohms or greater, replace right rear actuator and run SERVICE BAY DIAGNOSTICS.

4) If ohmmeter readings are 5 ohms or less rotate control tube to the "H" (firm) position. Apply analog ohmmeter lead to pin positions "1" and "2". If ohmmeter readings are 5 ohms or less, replace right rear actuator and run SERVICE BAY DIAGNOSTICS.

5) If ohmmeter readings are 10,000 ohms or greater, rotate control tube to the "H" (firm) position. Apply 12 volts to actuator pin position "3" with actuator pin position "4" grounded for 2 seconds to drive actuator to the "S" (soft) position. If control tube does not rotate to "S" position, replace right rear actuator and run SERVICE BAY DIAGNOSTICS.

6) If control tube does rotate to "S" position, apply 12 volts to actuator pin position "4" with actuator pin position "3" grounded for 2 seconds to drive actuator to the "H" (firm) position. If control tube does not rotate to "H" position, replace right rear actuator and run SERVICE BAY DIAGNOSTICS.

TEST GD2 (Cont.)

7) If control tube does rotate to "H" position, install a functional rear actuator on strut assembly and run SERVICE BAY DIAGNOSTICS. If Code 59 and/or 63 are displayed, a binding situation exists in the strut assembly. If no codes are displayed, the problem has been corrected.

TEST GD3

Wire Harness Inspection – 1) Turn air suspension to the "OFF" position and wait 5 seconds. Ensure Star test button is in the "HOLD" position and turn tester off. Disconnect air suspension control module from wiring harness connector.

2) Apply analog ohmmeter lead to control module wire harness connector pin location 48 (circuit 843). *See Air Suspension Control Module & Star Tester Connector Identification.* Apply other lead to left rear actuator connector circuit 843. If ohmmeter readings are greater than 5 ohms, resistance in circuit is beyond acceptable range. Repair as necessary and run SERVICE BAY DIAGNOSTICS.

3) If ohmmeter readings are less than 5 ohms, disengage Soft Shock Relay wire harness connector. Apply analog ohmmeter lead to Soft Shock Relay wire harness connector circuit 846A. Apply other lead to right rear actuator connector circuit 846B. If ohmmeter readings are greater than 5 ohms, resistance in circuit is beyond acceptable range. Repair as necessary and run SERVICE BAY DIAGNOSTICS.

4) If ohmmeter readings are less than 5 ohms, disengage Firm Shock Relay wire harness connector. Apply analog ohmmeter lead to Soft Shock Relay wire harness connector circuit 845A. Apply other lead to right rear actuator connector circuit 845C. If ohmmeter readings are less than 5 ohms, replace air suspension control module. If ohmmeter readings are greater than 5 ohms, resistance in circuit is beyond acceptable range. Repair as necessary and run SERVICE BAY DIAGNOSTICS.

TEST GE1 (CODES 64 & 65)

All Actuators Non-Responsive – 1) When signal transmission to the air suspension control module from all shock actuators is interrupted, Code 64 or 65 will be logged into memory. The possible component causes are a defective air suspension control module, or "SOFT" and/or "FIRM" relay. The possible electrical network causes are a disruption in the shock actuator relay wiring harness, or a defective "SOFT" or "FIRM" relay circuit.

2) Connect Star tester to air suspension diagnostic pigtail and put test button in the "HOLD" position. Wait 5 seconds and put button in the "TEST" position. If tester displays codes between 31 and 35 proceed to step 4)

3) If not, put test button in the "HOLD" position and wait 5 seconds. Put button in the "TEST" position. If tester does not display codes run SERVICE BAY DIAGNOSTICS. If unable to obtain functional test mode, replace air suspension control module.

4) If tester displays codes between 31 and 35, remove left front shock actuator. Put test button in the "HOLD" position after Code 34 is displayed and wait 5 seconds. If the control tube has little or no movement, proceed to TEST GE2. If the control tube continuously occillates between "H" and "S", turn Star tester off.

5) Turn the air suspension switch off and and disconnect module. Manually adjust left front actuator control tube to the "S" position. Apply analog ohmmeter lead to control module wiring harness connector pin position 47. Apply other lead to pin position 46.

6) If ohmmeter readings are greater than 5 ohms, reconnect module and all connectors. Run SERVICE BAY DIAGNOSTICS. If tester displays Codes 64 and/or 65, replace control module. If not, an open circuit exists in the actuator position circuit. Repair as necessary and run SERVICE BAY DIAGNOSTICS.

TEST GE2

1) Put Star test button in the "TEST" position. Remove "Soft" and "FIRM" relays from vehicle. Apply analog voltmmeter positive lead to soft actuator relay connector circuit 175A. Apply other lead to circuit 430C. If no battery voltage is available, a disruption in the wiring harness exists. Repair as necessary and run SERVICE BAY DIAGNOSTICS.

2) If battery voltage is available, apply analog voltmmeter positive lead to firm actuator relay connector circuit 175B. Apply other lead to circuit 430E. If no battery voltage is available, a disruption in the wiring harness exists. Repair as necessary and run SERVICE BAY DIAGNOSTICS.

12-84

1989 ELECTRONIC SUSPENSION
Ford Motor Co. Air Suspension — Continental (Cont.)

TEST GE2 (Cont.)

3) If battery voltage is available, apply analog ohmmeter lead to soft actuator relay connector circuit 846A. Apply other lead to ground. If resistance is less than 10,000 ohms, a short in the actuator activation exists. Replace "Soft" and "Firm" relays and run SERVICE BAY DIAGNOSTICS.

4) If resistance is more than 10,000 ohms, apply analog ohmmeter lead to firm actuator relay connector circuit 845A. Apply other lead to ground. If resistance is less than 10,000 ohms, a short in the actuator activation exists. Replace "Soft" and "Firm" relays and run SERVICE BAY DIAGNOSTICS.

5) If resistance is more than 10,000 ohms, apply analog ohmmeter lead to firm actuator relay connector circuit 845A. Apply other lead to soft actuator relay connector circuit 846A. If resistance is more than 10 ohms, an open in the actuator activation exists. Repair as necessary and run SERVICE BAY DIAGNOSTICS.

6) If resistance is less than 10 ohms, put Star test button in the "HOLD" position and wait 5 seconds after Code 34 is displayed. Apply voltmeter positive lead to circuit 839. Apply other lead to soft actuator relay connector circuit 430C. If voltage pulses between zero and 12 volts, proceed to step 8).

7) If voltage does not pulse between zero and 12 volts, turn Star tester and suspension switch to the "OFF" position. Disconnect control module. Apply analog ohmmeter lead to control module wiring harness connector pin position "12". Apply other lead to "SOFT" relay connector circuit 839.

8) If resistance is less than 5 ohms, replace control module and run SERVICE BAY DIAGNOSTICS. If resistance is more than 5 ohms, an open in circuit 839 exists. Repair as necessary and run SERVICE BAY DIAGNOSTICS.

9) If voltage pulses in step 6), apply voltmeter positive lead to circuit 838. Apply other lead to soft actuator relay connector circuit 430E. If voltage pulses between zero and 12 volts, replace "SOFT" and "FIRM" relays and run SERVICE BAY DIAGNOSTICS.

10) If voltage does not pulse between zero and 12 volts, turn Star tester and suspension switch to the "OFF" position. Disconnect control module. Apply analog ohmmeter lead to control module wiring harness connector pin position "11". Apply other lead to "FIRM" relay connector circuit 838.

11) If resistance is less than 5 ohms, replace control module and run SERVICE BAY DIAGNOSTICS. If resistance is more than 5 ohms, an open in circuit 838 exists. Repair as necessary and run SERVICE BAY DIAGNOSTICS.

TEST HA1 (CODE 49)

RF Lowering Non-Detectable – 1) When the air suspension control module does not receive a signal from the right front shock actuator has vented during SERVICE BAY DIAGNOSTIC check, Code 49 will be logged into memory. The possible component causes are a defective air suspension control module, right front air spring solenoid valve, vent solenoid, plugged air line or improperly attached height sensor linkage arm. The possible circuit causes are a disruption in the positive "B" power supply circuit or an open in the right front air spring and/or vent solenoid ground return circuit.

2) A visual inspection should be made to determine that height sensor and linkage are attached. Verify components and wire harness are not damaged. If any defects are found, repair as necessary and run SERVICE BAY DIAGNOSTICS. If no defects are found, connect Star tester to air suspension diagnostic pigtail.

3) Put Star test button in the "HOLD" position. Wait 5 seconds and put test button in the "TEST" position to enter system into FUNCTIONAL TEST mode. If tester displays codes from "31" to "35", proceed to step 4). If not, FUNCTIONAL TEST mode has not been entered. Check connections and repeat step 3). Run SERVICE BAY DIAGNOSTICS and replace control module (if necessary).

4) Put Star test button in the "HOLD" position and wait 5 seconds after Code 32 is displayed. If the air compressor vent solenoid continuously cycles on and off, proceed to step 9). If not, disconnect air compressor wiring harness connector to inspect for good contact and correct installation.

5) Put air suspension switch in the "OFF" position. Disconnect control module. Disconnect air compressor wiring harness connector. Apply analog ohmmeter lead to control module wiring harness connector pin position "42" (circuit 421). Apply other lead to air compressor wiring harness connector pin position "40" (circuit 430G). If resistance is less than 10,000 ohms, an short in circuit 421 exists. Repair as necessary and run SERVICE BAY DIAGNOSTICS.

TEST HA1 (Cont.)

6) If resistance is less than 10,000 ohms, apply analog ohmmeter lead to control module wiring harness connector pin position "42" (circuit 421). Apply other lead to air compressor wiring harness circuit 421. If resistance is more than 10 ohms, an open in circuit 421 exists. Repair as necessary and run SERVICE BAY DIAGNOSTICS.

7) If resistance is less than 10,000 ohms, apply analog ohmmeter lead to control module wiring harness connector pin position "40" (circuit 430G). Apply other lead to air compressor wiring harness circuit 430E. If resistance is more than 10 ohms, an open in circuit 430E exists. Repair as necessary and run SERVICE BAY DIAGNOSTICS.

8) If resistance is less than 10 ohms, apply 12 volts to air compressor wiring harness connector pin position "1". Apply air compressor wiring harness connector pin position "2" to ground for 3 seconds. If air compressor makes a "click" sound as voltage is applied, replace air suspension control module and run SERVICE BAY DIAGNOSTICS. If not, replace air compressor and run SERVICE BAY DIAGNOSTICS.

9) If the air compressor vent solenoid continuously cycled on and off, in step 4), put Star test button in the "HOLD" position and wait 5 seconds after Code 33 is displayed. If the right front air spring solenoid valve continuously cycles on and off, proceed to step 13). If not, disconnect air spring solenoid from wiring harness connector.

10) Apply voltmeter positive lead to air spring solenoid valve wiring harness connector circuit 414. Apply other lead to circuit 430D of the same connector. Observe voltmeter for one minute. If voltage pulses between zero and 12 volts, replace right front air spring solenoid and run SERVICE BAY DIAGNOSTICS.

11) If voltage does not pulse between zero and 12 volts, turn suspension switch to the "OFF" position. Disconnect control module connector. Apply analog ohmmeter lead to control module wiring harness connector pin position "17" (circuit 414). Apply other lead to right front air spring solenoid connector circuit 414.

12) If resistance is less than 10 ohms, an open in circuit 414 exists. Repair as necessary and run SERVICE BAY DIAGNOSTICS. If resistance is more than 10 ohms, apply analog ohmmeter lead to control module wiring harness connector pin position "60" (circuit 430H).

13) Apply other lead to right front air spring solenoid connector air compressor wiring harness circuit 430D. If resistance is less than 10 ohms, replace control module and run SERVICE BAY DIAGNOSTICS. If resistance is more than 10 ohms, an open in circuit 430H/430D exists. Repair as necessary and run SERVICE BAY DIAGNOSTICS.

14) Enter system into SPRING FILL DIAGNOSTICS. See SPRING FILL DIAGNOSTICS procedure. If tester displays any code from 21 to 28, proceed to step 15). If not, repeat step 14) until Code 21 to 28 is displayed.

15) Cause right front air spring to overinflate by putting Star tester in the "HOLD" position after Code 24 has been displayed for 5 seconds. The right front air spring should inflate until a 2" gap develops between the top of the tire and the bottom of fender lip. If not, repeat step 15) or inspect air line/spring for leak.

16) Put Star tester in the "TEST" position. To vent front spring, put Star tester in the "HOLD" position until Code 21 has been displayed for 5 seconds. When spring has vented enough, put Star tester in the "TEST" position. If spring does not vent, or vents slowly, replace air compressor and run SERVICE BAY DIAGNOSTICS.

17) If spring vents slowly or at a normal rate, malfunction in the left front system are indicated and should be serviced before continuing. If malfunction in the left front cannot be located, run SERVICE BAY DIAGNOSTICS. If problem is not eliminated, replace air suspension control module and run SERVICE BAY DIAGNOSTICS.

TEST HB1 (CODE 50)

LF Lowering Non-Detectable – 1) When the air suspension control module does not receive a signal from the left front shock actuator has vented during SERVICE BAY DIAGNOSTIC check, Code 50 will be logged into memory. The possible component causes are a defective air suspension control module, left front air spring solenoid valve, vent solenoid, plugged air line or improperly attached height sensor linkage arm. The possible circuit causes are a disruption in the positive "B" power supply circuit or an open in the left front air spring and/or vent solenoid ground return circuit.

2) A visual inspection should be made to determine that height sensor and linkage are attached. Verify components and wire harness are not damaged. If any defects are found, repair as necessary and run SERVICE BAY DIAGNOSTICS. If no defects are found, connect Star tester to air suspension diagnostic pigtail.

1989 ELECTRONIC SUSPENSION
Ford Motor Co. Air Suspension — Continental (Cont.)

12-85

TEST HB1 (Cont.)

3) Put Star test button in the "HOLD" position. Wait 5 seconds and put test button in the "TEST" position to enter system into FUNCTIONAL TEST mode. If tester displays codes from "31" to "35", proceed to step **4)**. If not, FUNCTIONAL TEST mode has not been entered. Check connections and repeat step **3)**. Run SERVICE BAY DIAGNOSTICS and replace control module (if necessary).

4) Put Star test button in the "HOLD" position and wait 5 seconds after Code 32 is displayed. If the air compressor vent solenoid continuously cycles on and off, proceed to step **9)**. If not, disconnect air compressor wiring harness connector to inspect for good contact and correct installation.

5) Put air suspension switch in the "OFF" position. Disconnect control module. Disconnect air compressor wiring harness connector. Apply analog ohmmeter lead to control module wiring harness connector pin position "42" (circuit 421). Apply other lead to air compressor wiring harness connector pin position "40" (circuit 430G). If resistance is less than 10,000 ohms, a short in circuit 421 exists. Repair as necessary and run SERVICE BAY DIAGNOSTICS.

6) If resistance is more than 10,000 ohms, apply analog ohmmeter lead to control module wiring harness connector pin position "42" (circuit 421). Apply other lead to air compressor wiring harness circuit 421. If resistance is more than 10 ohms, an open in circuit 421 exists. Repair as necessary and run SERVICE BAY DIAGNOSTICS.

7) If resistance is less than 10 ohms, apply analog ohmmeter lead to control module wiring harness connector pin position "40" (circuit 430G). Apply other lead to air compressor wiring harness circuit 430E. If resistance is more than 10 ohms, an open in circuit 430E exists. Repair as necessary and run SERVICE BAY DIAGNOSTICS.

8) If resistance is less than 10 ohms, apply 12 volts to air compressor wiring harness connector pin position "1". Apply air compressor wiring harness connector pin position "2" to ground for 3 seconds. If air compressor makes a "click" sound as voltage is applied, replace air suspension control module and run SERVICE BAY DIAGNOSTICS. If not, replace air compressor and run SERVICE BAY DIAGNOSTICS.

9) If the air compressor vent solenoid continuously cycled on and off, in step **4)**, put Star test button in the "HOLD" position and wait 5 seconds after Code 33 is displayed. If the left front air spring solenoid valve continuously cycles on and off, proceed to step **14)**. If not, disconnect air spring solenoid from wiring harness connector.

10) Apply voltmeter positive lead to air spring solenoid valve wiring harness connector circuit 415. Apply other lead to circuit 430K of the same connector. Observe voltmeter for one minute. If voltage pulses between zero and 12 volts, replace left front air spring solenoid and run SERVICE BAY DIAGNOSTICS.

11) If voltage does not pulse between zero and 12 volts, turn suspension switch to the "OFF" position. Disconnect control module connector. Apply analog ohmmeter lead to control module wiring harness connector pin position "21" (circuit 415). Apply other lead to left front air spring solenoid connector circuit 415.

12) If resistance is less than 10 ohms, an open in circuit 415 exists. Repair as necessary and run SERVICE BAY DIAGNOSTICS. If resistance is more than 10 ohms, apply analog ohmmeter lead to control module wiring harness connector pin position "60" (circuit 430H).

13) Apply other lead to left front air spring solenoid connector air compressor wiring harness circuit 430K. If resistance is less than 10 ohms, replace control module and run SERVICE BAY DIAGNOSTICS. If resistance is more than 10 ohms, an open in circuit 430H/430K exists. Repair as necessary and run SERVICE BAY DIAGNOSTICS.

14) Enter system into SPRING FILL DIAGNOSTICS. See SPRING FILL DIAGNOSTICS procedure. If tester displays any code from 21 to 28, proceed to step **15)**. If not, repeat step **14)** until Code 21 to 28 is displayed.

15) Cause left front air spring to overinflate by putting Star tester in the "HOLD" position after Code 25 has been displayed for 5 seconds. The left front air spring should inflate until a 2" gap develops between the top of the tire and the bottom of fender lip. If not, repeat step **15)** or inspect air line/spring for leak.

16) Put Star tester in the "TEST" position. To vent front spring, put Star tester in the "HOLD" position until Code 22 has been displayed for 5 seconds. When spring has vented enough, put Star tester in the "TEST" position. If spring does not vent, or vents slowly, replace air compressor and run SERVICE BAY DIAGNOSTICS.

TEST HB1 (Cont.)

17) If spring vents slowly or at a normal rate, malfunction in the left front system is indicated and should be serviced before continuing. If malfunction in the left front cannot be located, run SERVICE BAY DIAGNOSTICS. If problem is not eliminated, replace air suspension control module and run SERVICE BAY DIAGNOSTICS.

TEST HC1 (CODE 51)

RR Lowering Non-Detectable – 1) When the air suspension control module does not receive a signal from the left rear shock actuator has vented during SERVICE BAY DIAGNOSTIC check, Code 51 will be logged into memory. The possible component causes are a defective air suspension control module, left rear air spring solenoid valve, vent solenoid, plugged air line or improperly attached height sensor linkage arm. The possible circuit causes are a disruption in the positive "B" power supply circuit or an open in the left rear air spring and/or vent solenoid ground return circuit.

2) A visual inspection should be made to determine that height sensor and linkage are attached. Verify components and wire harness are not damaged. If any defects are found, repair as necessary and run SERVICE BAY DIAGNOSTICS. If no defects are found, connect Star tester to air suspension diagnostic pigtail.

3) Put Star test button in the "HOLD" position. Wait 5 seconds and put test button in the "TEST" position to enter system into FUNCTIONAL TEST mode. If tester displays codes from "31" to "35", proceed to step **4)**. If not, FUNCTIONAL TEST mode has not been entered. Check connections and repeat step **3)**. Run SERVICE BAY DIAGNOSTICS and replace control module (if necessary).

4) Put Star test button in the "HOLD" position and wait 5 seconds after Code 32 is displayed. If the air compressor vent solenoid continuously cycles on and off, proceed to step **9)**. If not, disconnect air compressor wiring harness connector to inspect for good contact and correct installation.

5) Put air suspension switch in the "OFF" position. Disconnect control module. Disconnect air compressor wiring harness connector. Apply analog ohmmeter lead to control module wiring harness connector pin position "42" (circuit 421). Apply other lead to air compressor wiring harness connector pin position "40" (circuit 430G). *See Air Suspension Control Module & Star Tester Connector Identification and Air Compressor & Relay Connector Identification.* If resistance is less than 10,000 ohms, a short in circuit 421 exists. Repair as necessary and run SERVICE BAY DIAGNOSTICS.

6) If resistance exceeds 10,000 ohms, apply analog ohmmeter lead to control module wiring harness connector pin position "42" (circuit 421). Apply other lead to air compressor wiring harness circuit 421. If resistance exceeds 10 ohms, an open in circuit 421 exists. Repair as necessary and run SERVICE BAY DIAGNOSTICS.

7) If resistance is less than 10 ohms, apply analog ohmmeter lead to control module wiring harness connector pin position "40" (circuit 430G). Apply other lead to air compressor wiring harness circuit 430E. If resistance exceeds 10 ohms, an open in circuit 430E exists. Repair as necessary and run SERVICE BAY DIAGNOSTICS.

8) If resistance is less than 10 ohms, apply 12 volts to air compressor wiring harness connector pin position "1". Apply air compressor wiring harness connector pin position "2" to ground for 3 seconds. *See Air Compressor & Relay Connector Identification.* If air compressor makes a is activated when voltage is applied, replace air suspension control module and run SERVICE BAY DIAGNOSTICS. If not, replace air compressor and run SERVICE BAY DIAGNOSTICS.

9) If the air compressor vent solenoid continuously cycled on and off, in step **4)**, put Star test button in the "HOLD" position and wait 5 seconds after Code 33 is displayed. If the left rear air spring solenoid valve continuously cycles on and off, proceed to step **14)**. If not, disconnect air spring solenoid from wiring harness connector.

10) Apply voltmeter positive lead to air spring solenoid valve wiring harness connector circuit 416. Apply other lead to circuit 430A of the same connector. *See Air Spring Solenoid Connector Identification.* Observe voltmeter for one minute. If voltage pulses between zero and 12 volts, replace left rear air spring solenoid and run SERVICE BAY DIAGNOSTICS.

11) If voltage does not pulse between zero and 12 volts, turn suspension switch to the "OFF" position. Disconnect control module connector. Apply analog ohmmeter lead to control module wiring harness connector pin position "38" (circuit 416). Apply other lead to left rear air spring solenoid connector circuit 416. *See Air Spring Solenoid Connector Identification.*

12-86

1989 ELECTRONIC SUSPENSION
Ford Motor Co. Air Suspension – Continental (Cont.)

TEST HC1 (Cont.)

12) If resistance is less than 10 ohms, an open in circuit 416 exists. Repair as necessary and run SERVICE BAY DIAGNOSTICS. If resistance exceeds 10 ohms, apply analog ohmmmeter lead to control module wiring harness connector pin position "60" (circuit 430H).

13) Apply other lead to left rear air spring solenoid connector air compressor wiring harness circuit 430A. If resistance is less than 10 ohms, replace control module and run SERVICE BAY DIAGNOSTICS. If resistance exceeds 10 ohms, an open in circuit 430H/430A exists. Repair as necessary and run SERVICE BAY DIAGNOSTICS.

14) Enter system into SPRING FILL DIAGNOSTICS. See SPRING FILL DIAGNOSTICS procedure. If tester displays any code from 21 to 28, proceed to step **15)**. If not, repeat step **14)** until Code 21 to 28 is displayed.

15) Cause left rear air spring to overinflate by putting Star tester in the "HOLD" position after Code 26 has been displayed for 5 seconds. The left rear air spring should inflate until a 2" gap develops between the top of th e tire and the bottom of fender lip. If not, repeat step **15)** or inspect air line/spring for leak.

16) Put Star tester in the "TEST" position. To vent front spring, put Star tester in the "HOLD" position until Code 23 has been displayed for 5 seconds. When spring has vented enough, put Star tester in the "TEST" position. If spring does not vent, or vents slowly, replace air compressor and run SERVICE BAY DIAGNOSTICS.

17) If spring vents slowly or at a normal rate, malfunction in the left rear system are indicated and should be serviced before continuing. If malfunction in the left rear cannot be located, run SERVICE BAY DIAGNOSTICS. If problem is not eliminated, replace air suspension control module and run SERVICE BAY DIAGNOSTICS.

TEST HD1 (CODE 78)

LR Lowering Non-Detectable – 1) When the air suspension control module does not receive a signal from the left rear shock actuator has vented during SERVICE BAY DIAGNOSTIC check, Code 78 will be logged into memory. The possible component causes are a defective air suspension control module, left rear air spring solenoid valve, vent solenoid, plugged air line or improperly attached height sensor linkage arm. The possible circuit causes are a disruption in the positive "B" power supply circuit or an open in the left rear air spring and/or vent solenoid ground return circuit.

2) A visual inspection should be made to determine that height sensor and linkage are attached. Verify components and wire harness are not damaged. If any defects are found, repair as necessary and run SERVICE BAY DIAGNOSTICS. If no defects are found, connect Star tester to air suspension diagnostic pigtail.

3) Put Star test button in the "HOLD" position. Wait 5 seconds and put test button in the "TEST" position to enter system into FUNCTIONAL TEST mode. If tester displays codes from "31" to "35", proceed to step **4)**. If not, FUNCTIONAL TEST mode has not been entered. Check connections and repeat step **3)**. Run SERVICE BAY DIAGNOSTICS and replace control module (if necessary).

4) Put Star test button in the "HOLD" position and wait 5 seconds after Code 32 is displayed. If the air compressor vent solenoid continuously cycles on and off, proceed to step **9)**. If not, disconnect air compressor wiring harness connector to inspect for good contact and correct installation.

5) Put air suspension switch in the "OFF" position. Disconnect control module. Disconnect air compressor wiring harness connector. Apply analog ohmmmeter lead to control module wiring harness connector pin position "42" (circuit 421). Apply other lead to air compressor wiring harness connector pin position "40" (circuit 430G). *See Air Compressor & Relay Connector Identification.* If resistance is less than 10,000 ohms, a short in circuit 421 exists. Repair as necessary and run SERVICE BAY DIAGNOSTICS.

6) If resistance exceeds 10,000 ohms, apply analog ohmmmeter lead to control module wiring harness connector pin position "42" (circuit 421). Apply other lead to air compressor wiring harness circuit 421. If resistance exceeds 10 ohms, an open in circuit 421 exists. Repair as necessary and run SERVICE BAY DIAGNOSTICS.

7) If resistance is less than 10 ohms, apply analog ohmmmeter lead to control module wiring harness connector pin position "40" (circuit 430G). Apply other lead to air compressor wiring harness circuit 430E. If resistance exceeds 10 ohms, an open in circuit 430E exists. Repair as necessary and run SERVICE BAY DIAGNOSTICS.

8) If resistance is less than 10 ohms, apply 12 volts to air compressor wiring harness connector pin position "1". Apply air compressor wiring harness connector pin position "2" to ground for 3 seconds. If air compressor makes a is activated when voltage is applied, replace air

TEST HD1 (Cont.)

suspension control module and run SERVICE BAY DIAGNOSTICS. If not, replace air compressor and run SERVICE BAY DIAGNOSTICS.

9) If the air compressor vent solenoid continuously cycled on and off, in step **4)**, put Star test button in the "HOLD" position and wait 5 seconds after Code 33 is displayed. If the left rear air spring solenoid valve continuously cycles on and off, proceed to step **14)**. If not, disconnect air spring solenoid from wiring harness connector.

10) Apply voltmeter positive lead to air spring solenoid valve wiring harness connector circuit 429. Apply other lead to circuit 430F of the same connector. *See Air Spring Solenoid Connector Identification.* Observe voltmeter for one minute. If voltage pulses between zero and 12 volts, replace left rear air spring solenoid and run SERVICE BAY DIAGNOSTICS.

11) If voltage does not pulse between zero and 12 volts, turn suspension switch to the "OFF" position. Disconnect control module connector. Apply analog ohmmmeter lead to control module wiring harness connector pin position "41" (circuit 429). Apply other lead to left rear air spring solenoid connector circuit 429.

12) If resistance is less than 10 ohms, an open in circuit 429 exists. Repair as necessary and run SERVICE BAY DIAGNOSTICS. If resistance exceeds 10 ohms, apply analog ohmmmeter lead to control module wiring harness connector pin position "60" (circuit 430H).

13) Apply other lead to left rear air spring solenoid connector air compressor wiring harness circuit 430F. *See Air Spring Solenoid Connector Identification.* If resistance is less than 10 ohms, replace control module and run SERVICE BAY DIAGNOSTICS. If resistance exceeds 10 ohms, an open in circuit 430H/430F exists. Repair as necessary and run SERVICE BAY DIAGNOSTICS.

14) Enter system into SPRING FILL DIAGNOSTICS. See SPRING FILL DIAGNOSTICS procedure. If tester displays any code from 21 to 28, proceed to step **15)**. If not, repeat step **14)** until Code 21 to 28 is displayed.

15) Cause left rear air spring to overinflate by putting Star tester in the "HOLD" position after Code 28 has been displayed for 5 seconds. The left rear air spring should inflate until a 2" gap develops between the top of th e tire and the bottom of fender lip. If not, repeat step **15)** or inspect air line/spring for leak.

16) Put Star tester in the "TEST" position. To vent front spring, put Star tester in the "HOLD" position until Code 27 has been displayed for 5 seconds. When spring has vented enough, put Star tester in the "TEST" position. If spring does not vent, or vents slowly, replace air compressor and run SERVICE BAY DIAGNOSTICS.

17) If spring vents slowly or at a normal rate, malfunction in the left rear system are indicated and should be serviced before continuing. If malfunction in the left rear cannot be located, run SERVICE BAY DIAGNOSTICS. If problem is not eliminated, replace air suspension control module and run SERVICE BAY DIAGNOSTICS.

TEST IA1 (CODE 52)

RF Rise Non-Detectable – 1) When the air suspension control module does not receive a signal that the right front shock actuator raised during SERVICE BAY DIAGNOSTIC check, Code 52 will be logged into memory. The possible component causes are a defective air suspension control module, air compressor, right front air spring solenoid valve, vent solenoid, air line or improperly attached height sensor linkage arm. The possible circuit causes are a disruption in the positive "B" power supply circuit or an open in the right front air spring and/or air compressor ground return circuit.

2) A visual inspection should be made to determine that height sensor and linkage are attached. Check under vehicle for obstructions preventing lowering of right front corner. Verify components and wire harness are not damaged. If any defects are found, repair as necessary and run SERVICE BAY DIAGNOSTICS. If no defects are found, connect Star tester to air suspension diagnostic pigtail.

3) Put Star test button in the "HOLD" position. Wait 5 seconds and put test button in the "TEST" position to enter system into FUNCTIONAL TEST mode. If tester displays codes from "31" to "35", proceed to step **4)**. If not, FUNCTIONAL TEST mode has not been entered. Check connections and repeat step **3)**. Run SERVICE BAY DIAGNOSTICS and replace control module (if necessary).

4) Put Star test button in the "HOLD" position and wait 5 seconds after Code 31 is displayed. If the air compressor continuously cycles on and off, put Star test button in the "TEST" position and proceed to step **16)**.

1989 ELECTRONIC SUSPENSION
Ford Motor Co. Air Suspension – Continental (Cont.)

12-87

TEST IA1 (Cont.)

5) If air compressor remains off, put Star test button in the "HOLD" position. Disconnect air compressor wiring harness connector. Examine connectors and service if necessary. Allow compressor to cool for a minimum of 15 minutes to reset internal thermal circuit breaker. Reconnect air compressor wiring harness connector.

6) If compressor remains off, proceed to step **7)**. If not, remove air compressor wiring harness connector. If compressor remains off, replace air compressor relay. If compressor remains on, a short exists between circuits 417 and "B" positive. Repair as necessary and run SERVICE BAY DIAGNOSTICS.

7) Put Star test button in the "HOLD" position and wait 5 seconds after Code 31 is displayed. If the air compressor continuously cycles on and off, put Star test button in the "TEST" position. Wait 30 minutes and run SERVICE BAY DIAGNOSTICS. If compressor remains off, proceed to step **8)**.

8) Disconnect air compressor wiring harness connector. Apply voltmeter positive lead to circuit 417 of air compressor wiring harness connector. Apply other lead to circuit 430F. *See Air Compressor & Relay Connector Identification.* Observe voltmeter for one minute. If voltage pulses between zero and 12 volts, replace air compressor and run SERVICE BAY DIAGNOSTICS.

9) If voltage does not pulse between zero and 12 volts, put Star tester in the "TEST" position. Disconnect air compressor wiring harness connector. Apply analog ohmmeter lead to compressor relay wiring harness connector circuit 417. Apply other lead to air compressor wiring harness circuit 417. If resistance exceeds 5 ohms, an open in circuit 417 exists. Repair as necessary and run SERVICE BAY DIAGNOSTICS.

10) If resistance is less than 5 ohms, apply analog ohmmeter lead to compressor relay circuit 430B. *See Air Compressor & Relay Connector Identification.* Apply other lead to ground. If resistance exceeds 5 ohms, an open in circuit 430B exists. Repair as necessary and run SERVICE BAY DIAGNOSTICS.

11) If resistance is less than 5 ohms, apply voltmeter positive lead to circuit 175 of air compressor relay wiring harness connector. Apply other lead to circuit 430B. The circuit has been disrupted if voltage is less than 10 volts. Repair as necessary and run SERVICE BAY DIAGNOSTICS.

12) If voltage exceeds 10 volts, put Star test button in the "HOLD" position and wait 5 seconds after Code 31 is displayed. Apply voltmeter positive lead to circuit 420 of air compressor relay wiring harness connector. Apply other lead to circuit 430B. Observe voltmeter for one minute. If voltage pulses between zero and 12 volts, replace air compressor relay and run SERVICE BAY DIAGNOSTICS.

13) If voltage does not pulse between zero and 12 volts, turn suspension switch off and disconnect control module from wiring harness. Apply analog ohmmeter lead to compressor relay wiring harness connector circuit 420. Apply other lead to pin position "35" (circuit 420) of the control module wiring harness connector.

14) If resistance is less than 5 ohms, replace control module and run SERVICE BAY DIAGNOSTICS. If resistance exceeds 5 ohms, an open in circuit 420 exists. Repair as necessary and run SERVICE BAY DIAGNOSTICS.

15) If resistance is less than 5 ohms, apply voltmeter positive lead to circuit 175 of air compressor relay wiring harness connector. Apply other lead to circuit 430B. The circuit has been disrupted if voltage is less than 10 volts. Repair as necessary and run SERVICE BAY DIAGNOSTICS.

16) Put Star test button in the "HOLD" position and wait 5 seconds after Code 33 is displayed. If the right front air spring solenoid valve continuously cycles on and off, proceed to step **15)**. If not, disconnect air spring solenoid from wiring harness connector.

17) Apply voltmeter positive lead to air spring solenoid valve wiring harness connector circuit 414. Apply other lead to circuit 430D of the same connector. Observe voltmeter for one minute. If voltage pulses between zero and 12 volts, replace right front air spring solenoid and run SERVICE BAY DIAGNOSTICS.

18) If voltage does not pulse between zero and 12 volts, turn suspension switch to the "OFF" position. Disconnect control module connector. Apply analog ohmmeter lead to control module wiring harness connector pin position "17" (circuit 414). Apply other lead to right front air spring solenoid connector circuit 414. *See Air Spring Solenoid Connector Identification.*

19) If resistance is exceeds 10 ohms, an open in circuit 414 exists. Repair as necessary and run SERVICE BAY DIAGNOSTICS. If resistance is less than 10 ohms, apply analog ohmmeter lead to

TEST IA1 (Cont.)

control module wiring harness connector pin position "60" (circuit 430H).

20) Apply other lead to right front air spring solenoid connector air compressor wiring harness circuit 430D. If resistance is less than 10 ohms, replace control module and run SERVICE BAY DIAGNOSTICS. If resistance exceeds 10 ohms, an open in circuit 430H/430D exists. Repair as necessary and run SERVICE BAY DIAGNOSTICS.

21) Enter system into SPRING FILL DIAGNOSTICS. See SPRING FILL DIAGNOSTICS procedure. If tester displays any code from 21 to 28, proceed to step **22)**. If not, repeat step **15)** until Code 21 to 28 is displayed.

22) Enter system into SPRING FILL DIAGNOSTICS. See SPRING FILL DIAGNOSTICS procedure. If tester displays any code from 21 to 28, proceed to step **22)**. If not, repeat step **15)** until Code 21 to 28 is displayed.

23) Cause right front air spring to over vent by putting Star tester in the "HOLD" position after Code 21 has been displayed for 5 seconds. The right front air spring should vent until a 1" or less gap develops between the top of the tire and the bottom of fender lip. If not, repeat step **16)** or inspect air line/spring for leak.

24) Put Star tester in the "TEST" position. To inflate front spring, put Star tester in the "HOLD" position until Code 25 has been displayed for 5 seconds. When spring has raised right front fender lip 3" above top of tire, put Star tester in the "TEST" position. If spring inflates slowly or at a normal rate, run SERVICE BAY DIAGNOSTICS. If problem is not eliminated, replace air suspension control module and run SERVICE BAY DIAGNOSTICS again.

25) If spring does not inflate or inflates slowly, put Star tester in the "TEST" position. Remove right front air spring solenoid valve air line and wiring harness connector. Put Star tester in the "HOLD" position until Code 24 has been displayed for 5 seconds. Compressor will continue running with tester in the "HOLD" position. If spring does not inflate or inflates slowly,

26) If pressure from air line is low or air line hads no pressure at all, disconnect another air line. If the pressure is the same or slightly higher, replace air compressor and run SERVICE BAY DIAGNOSTICS. If air pressure is higher, repair restriction in air line and run SERVICE BAY DIAGNOSTICS.

TEST HC2

Leak Test – 1) When air suspension pressure loss is suspected, the following components should be inspected for air leakage: air compressor, air lines, air spring bags, air spring solenoid valve, canister, dryer assembly and all connections.

2) If any leaks are detected, make necessary repairs and run SERVICE BAY DIAGNOSTICS. If no leaks are detected, replace air suspension control module and run SERVICE BAY DIAGNOSTICS.

TEST IB1 (CODE 53)

LF Rise Non–Detectable – 1) When the air suspension control module does not receive a signal that the left front shock actuator raised during SERVICE BAY DIAGNOSTIC check, Code 53 will be logged into memory. The possible component causes are a defective air suspension control module, air compressor, left front air spring solenoid valve, vent solenoid, air line or improperly attached height sensor linkage arm. The possible circuit causes are a disruption in the positive "B" power supply circuit or an open in the left front air spring and/or air compressor ground return circuit.

2) A visual inspection should be made to determine that height sensor and linkage are attached. Check under vehicle for obstructions preventing lowering of left front corner. Verify components and wire harness are not damaged. If any defects are found, repair as necessary and run SERVICE BAY DIAGNOSTICS. If no defects are found, connect Star tester to air suspension diagnostic pigtail.

3) Put Star test button in the "HOLD" position. Wait 5 seconds and put test button in the "TEST" position to enter system into FUNCTIONAL TEST mode. If tester displays codes from "31" to "35", proceed to step **4)**. If not, FUNCTIONAL TEST mode has not been entered. Check connections and repeat step **3)**. Run SERVICE BAY DIAGNOSTICS and replace control module (if necessary).

4) Put Star test button in the "HOLD" position and wait 5 seconds after Code 31 is displayed. If the air compressor continuously cycles on and off, put Star test button in the "TEST" position and proceed to step **15)**.

TEST IB1 (Cont.)

5) If air compressor remains off, put Star test button in the "HOLD" position. Disconnect air compressor wiring harness connector. Examine connectors and service if necessary. Allow compressor to cool for a minimum of 15 minutes to reset internal thermal circuit breaker. Reconnect air compressor wiring harness connector.

6) If compressor remains off, proceed to step **7)**. If not, remove air compressor wiring harness connector. If compressor remains off, replace air compressor relay. If compressor remains on, a short exists between circuits 417 and "B" positive. Repair as necessary and run SERVICE BAY DIAGNOSTICS.

7) Put Star test button in the "HOLD" position and wait 5 seconds after Code 31 is displayed. If the air compressor continuously cycles on and off, put Star test button in the "TEST" position. Wait 30 minutes and run SERVICE BAY DIAGNOSTICS. If compressor remains off, proceed to step **8)**.

8) Disconnect air compressor wiring harness connector. Apply voltmeter positive lead to circuit 417 of air compressor wiring harness connector. Apply other lead to circuit 430F. *See Air Compressor & Relay Connector Identification.* Observe voltmeter for one minute. If voltage pulses between zero and 12 volts, replace air compressor and run SERVICE BAY DIAGNOSTICS.

9) If voltage does not pulse between zero and 12 volts, put Star tester in the "TEST" position. Disconnect air compressor wiring harness connector. Apply analog ohmmeter lead to compressor relay wiring harness connector circuit 417. Apply other lead to air compressor wiring harness circuit 417. If resistance exceeds 5 ohms, an open in circuit 417 exists. Repair as necessary and run SERVICE BAY DIAGNOSTICS.

10) If resistance is less than 5 ohms, apply analog ohmmeter lead to compressor relay circuit 430B. Apply other lead to ground. If resistance exceeds 5 ohms, an open in circuit 430B exists. Repair as necessary and run SERVICE BAY DIAGNOSTICS.

11) If resistance is less than 5 ohms, apply voltmeter positive lead to circuit 175 of air compressor relay wiring harness connector. Apply other lead to circuit 430B. *See Air Compressor & Relay Connector Identification.* The circuit has been disrupted if voltage is less than 10 volts. Repair as necessary and run SERVICE BAY DIAGNOSTICS.

12) If voltage exceeds 10 volts, put Star test button in the "HOLD" position and wait 5 seconds after Code 31 is displayed. Apply voltmeter positive lead to circuit 420 of air compressor relay wiring harness connector. Apply other lead to circuit 430B. *See Air Compressor & Relay Connector Identification.* Observe voltmeter for one minute. If voltage pulses between zero and 12 volts, replace air compressor relay and run SERVICE BAY DIAGNOSTICS.

13) If voltage does not pulse between zero and 12 volts, turn suspension switch off and disconnect control module from wiring harness. Apply analog ohmmeter lead to compressor relay wiring harness connector circuit 420. Apply other lead to pin position "35" (circuit 420) of the control module wiring harness connector.

14) If resistance is less than 5 ohms, replace control module and run SERVICE BAY DIAGNOSTICS. If resistance exceeds 5 ohms, an open in circuit 420 exists. Repair as necessary and run SERVICE BAY DIAGNOSTICS.

15) If resistance is less than 5 ohms, apply voltmeter positive lead to circuit 175 of air compressor relay wiring harness connector. Apply other lead to circuit 430B. The circuit has been disrupted if voltage is less than 10 volts. Repair as necessary and run SERVICE BAY DIAGNOSTICS.

16) Put Star test button in the "HOLD" position and wait 5 seconds after Code 33 is displayed. If the left front air spring solenoid valve continuously cycles on and off, proceed to step **17)**. If not, disconnect air spring solenoid from wiring harness connector.

17) Apply voltmeter positive lead to air spring solenoid valve wiring harness connector circuit 415. Apply other lead to circuit 430K of the same connector. *See Air Spring Solenoid Connector Identification.* Observe voltmeter for one minute. If voltage pulses between zero and 12 volts, replace left front air spring solenoid and run SERVICE BAY DIAGNOSTICS.

18) If voltage does not pulse between zero and 12 volts, turn suspension switch to the "OFF" position. Disconnect control module connector. Apply analog ohmmeter lead to control module wiring harness connector pin position "21" (circuit 415). Apply other lead to left front air spring solenoid connector circuit 415.

19) If resistance is exceeds 10 ohms, an open in circuit 415 exists. Repair as necessary and run SERVICE BAY DIAGNOSTICS. If resistance is less than 10 ohms, apply analog ohmmeter lead to

TEST IB1 (Cont.)

control module wiring harness connector pin position "60" (circuit 430H).

20) Apply other lead to left front air spring solenoid connector air compressor wiring harness circuit 430K. If resistance is less than 10 ohms, replace control module and run SERVICE BAY DIAGNOSTICS. If resistance exceeds 10 ohms, an open in circuit 430H/430K exists. Repair as necessary and run SERVICE BAY DIAGNOSTICS.

21) Enter system into SPRING FILL DIAGNOSTICS. See SPRING FILL DIAGNOSTICS procedure. If tester displays any code from 21 to 28, proceed to step **23)**. If not, repeat step **15)** until Code 21 to 28 is displayed.

22) Enter system into SPRING FILL DIAGNOSTICS. See SPRING FILL DIAGNOSTICS procedure. If tester displays any code from 21 to 28, proceed to step **23)**. If not, repeat step **15)** until Code 21 to 28 is displayed.

23) Cause left front air spring to over vent by putting Star tester in the "HOLD" position after Code 22 has been displayed for 5 seconds. The left front air spring should vent until a 1" or less gap develops between the top of the tire and the bottom of fender lip. If not, repeat step **16)** or inspect air line/spring for leak.

24) Put Star tester in the "TEST" position. To inflate front spring, put Star tester in the "HOLD" position until Code 25 has been displayed for 5 seconds. When spring has raised left front fender lip 3" above top of tire, put Star tester in the "TEST" position. If spring inflates slowly or at a normal rate, run SERVICE BAY DIAGNOSTICS. If problem is not eliminated, replace air suspension control module and run SERVICE BAY DIAGNOSTICS again.

25) If spring does not inflate or inflates slowly, put Star tester in the "TEST" position. Remove left front air spring solenoid valve air line and wiring harness connector. Put Star tester in the "HOLD" position until Code 25 has been displayed for 5 seconds. Compressor will continue running with tester in the "HOLD" position. If spring does not inflate or inflates slowly,

26) If pressure from air line is low or air line hads no pressure at all, disconnect another air line. If the pressure is the same or slightly higher, replace air compressor and run SERVICE BAY DIAGNOSTICS. If air pressure is higher, repair restriction in air line and run SERVICE BAY DIAGNOSTICS.

TEST IB2

Leak Test – 1) When air suspension pressure loss is suspected, the following components should be inspected for air leakage: air compressor, air lines, air spring bags, air spring solenoid valve, canister, dryer assembly and all connections.

2) If any leaks are detected, make necessary repairs and run SERVICE BAY DIAGNOSTICS. If no leaks are detected, replace air suspension control module and run SERVICE BAY DIAGNOSTICS.

TEST IC1 (CODE 54)

RR Rise Non-Detectable – 1) When the air suspension control module does not receive a signal that the left front shock actuator raised during SERVICE BAY DIAGNOSTIC check, Code 54 will be logged into memory. The possible component causes are a defective air suspension control module, air compressor, left front air spring solenoid valve, vent solenoid, air line or improperly attached height sensor linkage arm. The possible circuit causes are a disruption in the positive "B" power supply circuit or an open in the left front air spring and/or air compressor ground return circuit.

2) A visual inspection should be made to determine that height sensor and linkage are attached. Check under vehicle for obstructions preventing lowering of left front corner. Verify components and wire harness are not damaged. If any defects are found, repair as necessary and run SERVICE BAY DIAGNOSTICS. If no defects are found, connect Star tester to air suspension diagnostic pigtail.

3) Put Star test button in the "HOLD" position. Wait 5 seconds and put test button in the "TEST" position to enter system into FUNCTIONAL TEST mode. If tester displays codes from "31" to "35", proceed to step **4)**. If not, FUNCTIONAL TEST mode has not been entered. Check connections and repeat step **3)**. Run SERVICE BAY DIAGNOSTICS and replace control module (if necessary).

4) Put Star test button in the "HOLD" position and wait 5 seconds after Code 31 is displayed. If the air compressor continuously cycles on and off, put Star test button in the "TEST" position and proceed to step **16)**.

1989 ELECTRONIC SUSPENSION
Ford Motor Co. Air Suspension — Continental (Cont.)

12-89

TEST IC1 (Cont.)

5) If air compressor remains off, put Star test button in the "HOLD" position. Disconnect air compressor wiring harness connector. Examine connectors and service if necessary. Allow compressor to cool for a minimum of 15 minutes to reset internal thermal circuit breaker. Reconnect air compressor wiring harness connector.

6) If compressor remains off, proceed to step **7)**. If not, remove air compressor wiring harness connector. If compressor remains off, replace air compressor relay. If compressor remains on, a short exists between circuits 417 and "B" positive. Repair as necessary and run SERVICE BAY DIAGNOSTICS.

7) Put Star test button in the "HOLD" position and wait 5 seconds after Code 31 is displayed. If the air compressor continuously cycles on and off, put Star test button in the "TEST" position. Wait 30 minutes and run SERVICE BAY DIAGNOSTICS. If compressor remains off, proceed to step **8)**.

8) Disconnect air compressor wiring harness connector. Apply voltmeter positive lead to circuit 417 of air compressor wiring harness connector. Apply other lead to circuit 430F. *See Air Compressor & Relay Connector Identification.* Observe voltmeter for one minute. If voltage pulses between zero and 12 volts, replace air compressor and run SERVICE BAY DIAGNOSTICS.

9) If voltage does not pulse between zero and 12 volts, put Star tester in the "TEST" position. Disconnect air compressor wiring harness connector. Apply analog ohmmeter lead to compressor relay wiring harness connector circuit 417. Apply other lead to air compressor wiring harness circuit 417. If resistance exceeds 5 ohms, an open in circuit 417 exists. Repair as necessary and run SERVICE BAY DIAGNOSTICS.

10) If resistance is less than 5 ohms, apply analog ohmmeter lead to compressor relay circuit 430B. Apply other lead to ground. If resistance exceeds 5 ohms, an open in circuit 430B exists. Repair as necessary and run SERVICE BAY DIAGNOSTICS.

11) If resistance is less than 5 ohms, apply voltmeter positive lead to circuit 175 of air compressor relay wiring harness connector. Apply other lead to circuit 430B. The circuit has been disrupted if voltage is less than 10 volts. Repair as necessary and run SERVICE BAY DIAGNOSTICS.

12) If voltage exceeds 10 volts, put Star test button in the "HOLD" position and wait 5 seconds after Code 31 is displayed. Apply voltmeter positive lead to circuit 420 of air compressor relay wiring harness connector. Apply other lead to circuit 430B. *See Air Compressor & Relay Connector Identification.* Observe voltmeter for one minute. If voltage pulses between zero and 12 volts, replace air compressor relay and run SERVICE BAY DIAGNOSTICS.

13) If voltage does not pulse between zero and 12 volts, turn suspension switch off and disconnect control module from wiring harness. Apply analog ohmmeter lead to compressor relay wiring harness connector circuit 420. Apply other lead to pin position "35" (circuit 420) of the control module wiring harness connector.

14) If resistance is less than 5 ohms, replace control module and run SERVICE BAY DIAGNOSTICS. If resistance exceeds 5 ohms, an open in circuit 420 exists. Repair as necessary and run SERVICE BAY DIAGNOSTICS.

15) If resistance is less than 5 ohms, apply voltmeter positive lead to circuit 175 of air compressor relay wiring harness connector. Apply other lead to circuit 430B. *See Air Compressor & Relay Connector Identification.* The circuit has been disrupted if voltage is less than 10 volts. Repair as necessary and run SERVICE BAY DIAGNOSTICS.

16) Put Star test button in the "HOLD" position and wait 5 seconds after Code 33 is displayed. If the left front air spring solenoid valve continuously cycles on and off, proceed to step **17)**. If not, disconnect air spring solenoid from wiring harness connector.

17) Apply voltmeter positive lead to air spring solenoid valve wiring harness connector circuit 415. Apply other lead to circuit 430K of the same connector. Observe voltmeter for one minute. If voltage pulses between zero and 12 volts, replace left front air spring solenoid and run SERVICE BAY DIAGNOSTICS.

18) If voltage does not pulse between zero and 12 volts, turn suspension switch to the "OFF" position. Disconnect control module connector. Apply analog ohmmeter lead to control module wiring harness connector pin position "21" (circuit 415). Apply other lead to left front air spring solenoid connector circuit 415.

19) If resistance is exceeds 10 ohms, an open in circuit 415 exists. Repair as necessary and run SERVICE BAY ELAGNOSTICS. If resistance is less than 10 ohms, apply analog ohmmeter lead to control module wiring harness connector pin position "60" (circuit 430H).

TEST IC1 (Cont.)

20) Apply other lead to left front air spring solenoid connector air compressor wiring harness circuit 430K. If resistance is less than 10 ohms, replace control module and run SERVICE BAY DIAGNOSTICS. If resistance exceeds 10 ohms, an open in circuit 430H/430K exists. Repair as necessary and run SERVICE BAY DIAGNOSTICS.

21) Enter system into SPRING FILL DIAGNOSTICS. See SPRING FILL DIAGNOSTICS procedure. If tester displays any code from 21 to 28, proceed to step **23)**. If not, repeat step **15)** until Code 21 to 28 is displayed.

22) Enter system into SPRING FILL DIAGNOSTICS. See SPRING FILL DIAGNOSTICS procedure. If tester displays any code from 21 to 28, proceed to step **23)**. If not, repeat step **15)** until Code 21 to 28 is displayed.

23) Cause left front air spring to over vent by putting Star tester in the "HOLD" position after Code 22 has been displayed for 5 seconds. The left front air spring should vent until a 1" or less gap develops between the top of the tire and the bottom of fender lip. If not, repeat step **16)** or inspect air line/spring for leak.

24) Put Star tester in the "TEST" position. To inflate front spring, put Star tester in the "HOLD" position until Code 25 has been displayed for 5 seconds. When spring has raised left front fender lip 3" above top of tire, put Star tester in the "TEST" position. If spring inflates slowly or at a normal rate, run SERVICE BAY DIAGNOSTICS. If problem is not eliminated, replace air suspension control module and run SERVICE BAY DIAGNOSTICS again.

25) If spring does not inflate or inflates slowly, put Star tester in the "TEST" position. Remove left front air spring solenoid valve air line and wiring harness connector. Put Star tester in the "HOLD" position until Code 25 has been displayed for 5 seconds. Compressor will continue running with tester in the "HOLD" position. If spring does not inflate or inflates slowly,

26) If pressure from air line is low or air line hads no pressure at all, disconnect another air line. If the pressure is the same or slightly higher, replace air compressor and run SERVICE BAY DIAGNOSTICS. If air pressure is higher, repair restriction in air line and run SERVICE BAY DIAGNOSTICS.

TEST IC2

Leak Test – 1) When air suspension pressure loss is suspected, the following components should be inspected for air leakage: air compressor, air lines, air spring bags, air spring solenoid valve, canister, dryer assembly and all connections.

2) If any leaks are detected, make necessary repairs and run SERVICE BAY DIAGNOSTICS. If no leaks are detected, replace air suspension control module and run SERVICE BAY DIAGNOSTICS.

TEST JA1 (CODE 55)

1) When signal transmission to the air suspension control module has not been recieved, indicating vehicle has reached 15 MPH during DRIVE CYCLE DIAGNOSTICS, Code 55 will be logged into memory. The possible component causes are a defective air suspension control module or vehicle speed sensor. The possible circuit causes are a disruption in the positive "B" circuit or speed sensor ground circuit.

2) A visual inspection should be made to verify that speed sensor connector is attached and wire harness is not damaged. If any defects are found, repair as necessary and run DRIVE CYCLE DIAGNOSTICS. If no defects are found, proceed to step **3)**.

3) Turn ignition and air suspension switch to the "OFF" position. Disengage air suspension control module connector. Apply analog ohmmeter lead to the air suspension control module wire harness connector pin location 6 (circuit 563). Apply other lead to circuit 430G. *See Air Suspension Control Module & Star Tester Connector Identification.*

4) If ohmmeter readings are greater than 5 ohms, ground circuit 563 of vehicle speed sensor is open. Repair as necessary and run DRIVE CYCLE DIAGNOSTICS. If ohmmeter readings are less than 5 ohms, proceed to step **5)**.

5) Apply analog ohmmeter lead to the air suspension control module wire harness connector pin location 3 (circuit 150). Apply other lead to speed sensor wire harness connector circuit 150A. *See Speed Sensor Connector Identification.*

6) If ohmmeter readings are more than 5 ohms, repair open in circuit 150 and run DRIVE CYCLE DIAGNOSTICS. If ohmmeter readings are less than 5 ohms, replace control module and run DRIVE CYCLE DIAGNOSTICS.

12-90

1989 ELECTRONIC SUSPENSION
Ford Motor Co. Air Suspension – Continental (Cont.)

TEST JA1 (Cont.)

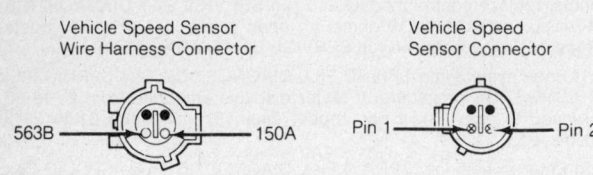

Vehicle Speed Sensor
Wire Harness Connector

Vehicle Speed
Sensor Connector

563B — 150A

Pin 1 — Pin 2

Vehicle Speed Sensor Connector Identification

TEST JB1 (CODE 73)

1) When a signal to the air suspension control module has not been received, indicating hard vehicle braking, Code 55 will be logged into memory. The possible component causes are a defective air suspension control module or brake pressure switch. The possible circuit causes are a disruption in the brake pressure switch circuit.

2) A visual inspection should be made to verify that brake pressure switch connector is attached and wire harness is not damaged. If any defects are found, repair as necessary and run SERVICE BAY DIAGNOSTICS. If no defects are found, proceed to step **3)**.

3) Attach Star tester and put selector in the "HOLD" position. Turn air suspension switch to the "OFF" position. Disengage air suspension control module connector. Apply analog ohmmeter lead to wire harness connector pin location 7 (circuit 636). Apply other lead to pin location 40 (circuit 430G).

4) If ohmmeter readings are more than 10,000 ohms, proceed to step **5)**. If ohmmeter readings are less than 10,000 ohms, repair ground in in brake pressure switch circuit.

5) Apply analog ohmmeter lead to wire harness connector pin location 7 (circuit 636). Apply other lead to wire harness pin location 46 (circuit 432D). If ohmmeter reading is less than 10,000 ohms, disengage brake pressure switch connector and apply analog ohmmeter lead to wire harness connector pin location 7 (circuit 636). Apply other lead to pin location 46 (circuit 432D).

6) If ohmmeter readings are less than 10,000 ohms, proceed to step **7)**. If ohmmeter readings are more than 10,000 ohms, replace brake pressure switch and run SERVICE BAY DIAGNOSTICS. If ohmmeter readings are less than 10,000 ohms, repair short to ground in in brake pressure switch circuit 636/432D.

7) Apply analog ohmmeter lead to wire harness connector pin location 7 (circuit 636). Apply other lead to wire harness pin location 46 (circuit 432D). If ohmmeter reading is less than 10,000 ohms, disengage brake pressure switch connector and apply analog ohmmeter lead to wire harness connector pin location 7 (circuit 636). Apply other lead to pin location 46 (circuit 432D).

8) Depress and hold brake pedal. If ohmmeter readings are more than 10,000 ohms, replace brake pressure switch and run SERVICE BAY DIAGNOSTICS. If ohmmeter readings are less than 10,000 ohms, replace control module and run SERVICE BAY DIAGNOSTICS.

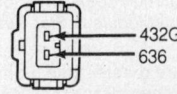

Brake Pressure Switch
Wire Harness Connector

432G
636

Brake Pressure Switch Connector Identification

TEST JC1 (CODE 74)

1) When the air suspension control module has not recieved a signal indicating dual directional rotation of vehicle steering wheel, Code 74 will be logged into memory. The possible component causes are a defective air suspension control module or steering wheel sensor. The possible circuit causes are a disruption in the positive "B" or steering channel circuit.

2) A visual inspection should be made to verify that steering sensor connector is attached and wire harness is not damaged. Check shutter for contamination or damage. If any defects are found, repair as necessary and run SERVICE BAY DIAGNOSTICS. If no defects are found, proceed to step **3)**.

3) Attach Star tester and put selector in the "OFF" position. Turn air suspension switch to the "OFF" position. Disengage air suspension control module connector. Use jumper wire to ground control module pin location 46.

4) Apply analog ohmmeter lead to wire harness connector pin location 1 (circuit 633). Apply other lead to ground. Slowly rotate steering wheel while observing ohmmeter. If ohmmeter readings oscillate from high to low every 9 degrees of steering wheel travel, proceed to step **5)**. If not, proceed to step **6)**.

5) Apply analog ohmmeter lead to wire harness connector pin location 1 (circuit 633). Apply other lead to ground. Slowly rotate steering wheel while observing ohmmeter. If ohmmeter readings oscillate from high to low every 9 degrees of steering wheel travel, connect control module and run SERVICE BAY DIAGNOSTICS. If tester still displays Code 74, replace control module.

6) Locate steering wheel sensor on lower steering wheel column. Disconnect sensor from wire harness. Apply voltmeter positive lead to steering sensor wire harness connector circuit 298H. Apply other lead to ground. If voltmeter reading is battery voltage, repair open in circuit 298H.

7) If not, apply analog ohmmeter lead to control module wire harness connector pin location 46 (circuit 432D). Apply other lead to steering sensor wire harness connector circuit 432A. If ohmmeter readings are more than 5 ohms, repair open in circuit 432A/432D and run SERVICE BAY DIAGNOSTICS.

8) If ohmmeter readings are more than 5 ohms, apply analog ohmmeter lead to control module wire harness connector pin location 45 (circuit 633). Apply other lead to steering sensor wire harness pin location circuit 633A. If ohmmeter reading is less than 5 ohms, repair open in circuit 633/633A and run SERVICE BAY DIAGNOSTICS.

9) If not, apply analog ohmmeter lead to control module wire harness connector pin location 24 (circuit 634). Apply other lead to steering sensor wire harness connector circuit 634A. If ohmmeter readings are more than 5 ohms, repair open in circuit 634/634A and run SERVICE BAY DIAGNOSTICS. If not, replace steering sensor and run SERVICE BAY DIAGNOSTICS.

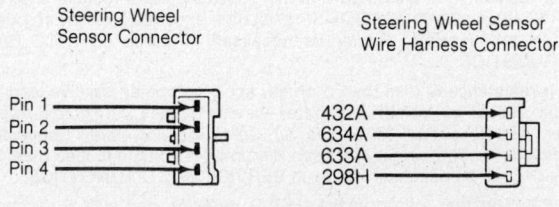

Steering Wheel
Sensor Connector

Steering Wheel Sensor
Wire Harness Connector

Pin 1
Pin 2
Pin 3
Pin 4

432A
634A
633A
298H

Steering Wheel Sensor Connector Identification

1989 ELECTRONIC SUSPENSION
Ford Motor Co. Air Suspension – Continental (Cont.)

12-91

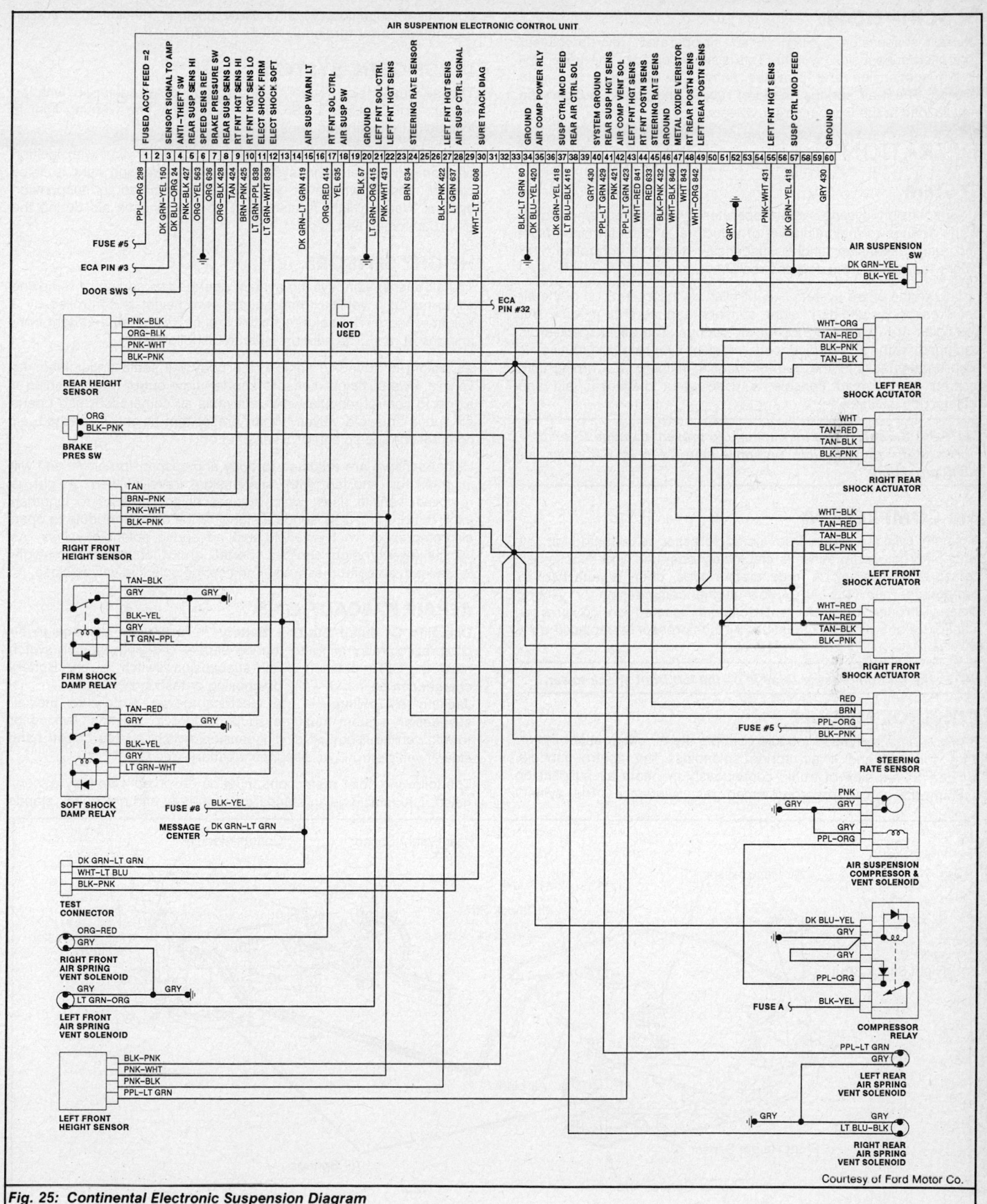

Fig. 25: Continental Electronic Suspension Diagram

Courtesy of Ford Motor Co.

1989 ELECTRONIC SUSPENSION
Ford Motor Co. Air Suspension – Mark VII

DESCRIPTION

The air suspension system is an air-operated, microprocessor controlled suspension system. This system replaces the usual coil spring suspension and provides automatic front and rear load leveling. The 4 air springs, made of rubber and plastic, support the vehicle load at the front and rear wheels.

OPERATION

SYSTEM

Air suspension leveling system operates by adding or removing air in the springs to maintain level of vehicle at a predetermined front and rear suspension height. Suspension height is controlled by 3 height sensors (2 front and one rear).

Airflow to the entire system is controlled by the interaction of the air compressor, solenoids, height sensors and control module. Air solenoids are located on top of air springs. The air suspension is equipped with a self-diagnostic system. An air fill routine is preprogrammed into the control module memory. A warning light located in overhead console is used as a diagnostic aid and malfunction indicator.

CAUTION: *Carefully read instructions to prevent damage to suspension system and possible personal injury due to automatic air filling procedure.*

AIR COMPRESSOR

A single cylinder piston-type air compressor is mounted on left fender apron. Compressor is electrically operated and supplies air pressure to system. A regenerative type drier is attached to compressor manifold. All airflow during compression or venting passes through drier. A vent solenoid, located on compressor manifold, controls air exhaustion. Air compressor is replaced as a unit.

NOTE: *The air compressor relay is on the left front shock tower.*

CONTROL MODULE

A microcomputer-based module controls the air compressor motor, vent solenoid and 4 air spring solenoids. The control module, located on left side of trunk, continuously monitors air suspension system through a preprogrammed test sequence. The system

operates with ignition switch in "RUN" position with limited operation for one hour after turning to "OFF" position.

DIAGNOSTIC SYSTEM

The air suspension system control module is equipped with an amber "CHECK SUSPENSION" warning light. The warning light is located in the overhead console.

Observation of warning light during normal operation with ignition on, can aid in detecting system problems. Warning light is lit by control module whenever a malfunction is noted in suspension system. Warning light is also used as a diagnostic aid during the preprogrammed test cycle.

HEIGHT SENSORS

The air suspension leveling system operates by adding or removing air to maintain vehicle (trim) height. Trim height is controlled by 3 height sensors. The height sensors are located at left and right front and one at rear. The sensors operate as follows:

As weight is added to vehicle, the body will settle under load. As vehicle lowers, height sensors shorten (low out-of-trim), sending a signal to control module which activates air compressor and opens air spring solenoid valves. When preset trim height is reached, air compressor and solenoid valves shut off.

Height sensors are attached to body and suspension arms, and will lengthen or shorten with suspension travel. When weight is removed, vehicle rises, which causes height sensors to lengthen (high out-of-trim). This sends a signal to the control module to open air compressor vent solenoid and air spring solenoid valves. As vehicle lowers, height sensors shorten, and when preset trim height is reached, air compressor vent and spring solenoid valves close.

REPAIR PRECAUTIONS

Charging Or Jump Starting Battery – To prevent damage to air compressor relay or motor during battery charging, ignition switch must in "OFF" position if air suspension switch is on. Battery charger can be in use while diagnosing or testing system.

Jacking & Towing – The electrical power supply to the air suspension system must be shut off prior to hoisting, jacking or towing vehicle. Turn off air suspension switch located on left hand side of vehicle trunk or disconnect battery. *See Fig. 7.*

The following hoist restrictions must be observed: Use only a "body hoist". Lift vehicle using standard procedures and place jack stands

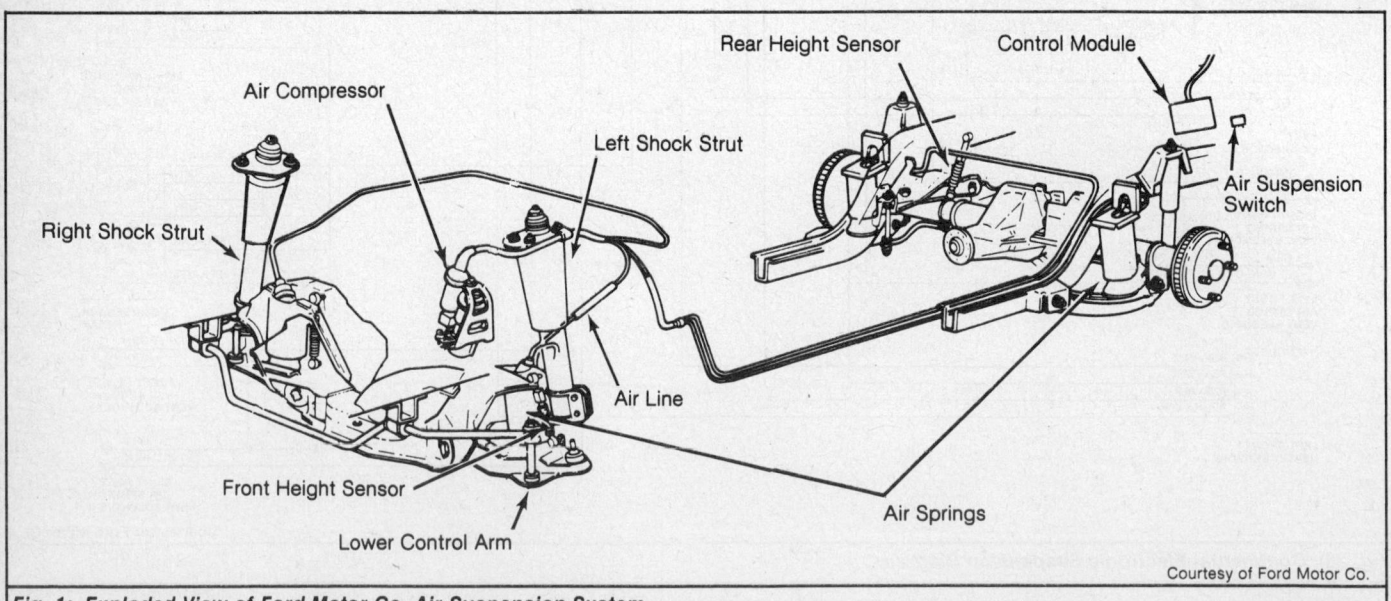

Fig. 1: Exploded View of Ford Motor Co. Air Suspension System

Rear Height Sensor

Control Module

Air Compressor

Left Shock Strut

Air Suspension Switch

Right Shock Strut

Air Line

Front Height Sensor

Lower Control Arm

Air Springs

Courtesy of Ford Motor Co.

1989 ELECTRONIC SUSPENSION
Ford Motor Co. Air Suspension — Mark VII (Cont.)

12-93

at each corner as a safety precaution. If "body hoist" is not available, use standard hydraulic floor jack. Raise front of vehicle at No. 2 crossmember and place jack stands at front corners of body. For rear, use same procedure, but use rear jacking location.

ADJUSTMENTS

CASTER & CAMBER

See appropriate article in WHEEL ALIGNMENT section.

RIDE HEIGHT ADJUSTMENT

NOTE: Pre-alignment procedure must be performed before alignment or ride height is checked so air suspension system will vent to trim. Vehicle temperature must be within 20°F (6°C) of alignment area temperature.

Pre-Alignment Procedure – 1) Drive onto alignment rack. Turn ignition off. Level rack as necessary. Turn ignition switch to the "RUN" position (DO NOT start).
2) Allow one minute for vehicle to level. Push trunk release, turn ignition off and exit vehicle. Allow 20 seconds for vehicle to vent to trim height (all doors closed).
3) Turn off air suspension system switch in trunk on left front side panel. *See Fig. 7.* Check for proper ride height. If necessary, adjust front ride height.

Adjusting Ride Height – 1) Measure ride height at front and rear suspensions. *See Fig. 2.*

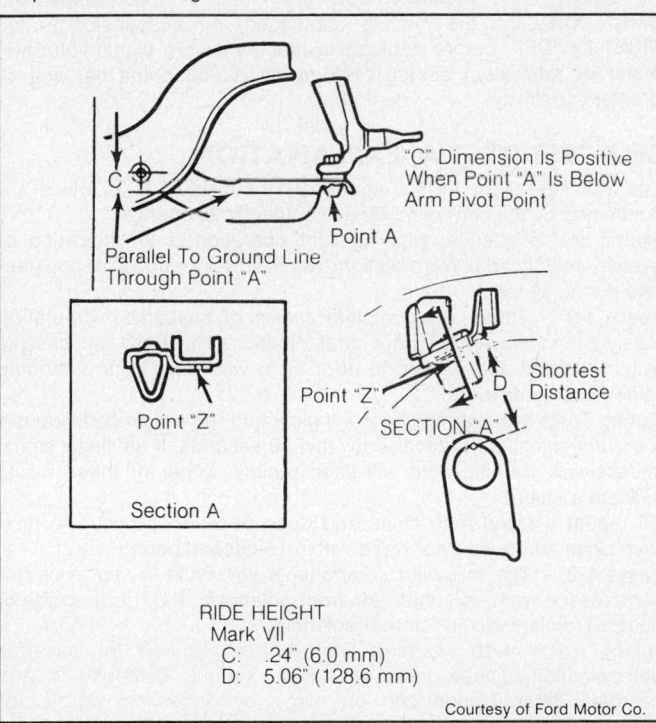

RIDE HEIGHT
Mark VII
  C: .24" (6.0 mm)
  D: 5.06" (128.6 mm)

Courtesy of Ford Motor Co.

Fig. 2: Riding Height Check Points

2) Adjust front ride height by moving front left and/or right lower sensor attaching stud.
3) There are 3 adjustment positions provided on bracket. Loosen attaching bolt and adjust as necessary. A one position change to sensor attachment point will result in 1/2" (12.7 mm) change, up or down. *See Fig. 3.*
4) Rear suspension ride height is adjusted by moving rear sensor attaching bracket up or down relative to right rear arm (slot adjustment is provided on bracket).
5) Loosen attaching nut and adjust up or down as required. One index mark change to sensor attachment point will result in 1/4" (6.4 mm) change up or down. *See Fig. 4.*

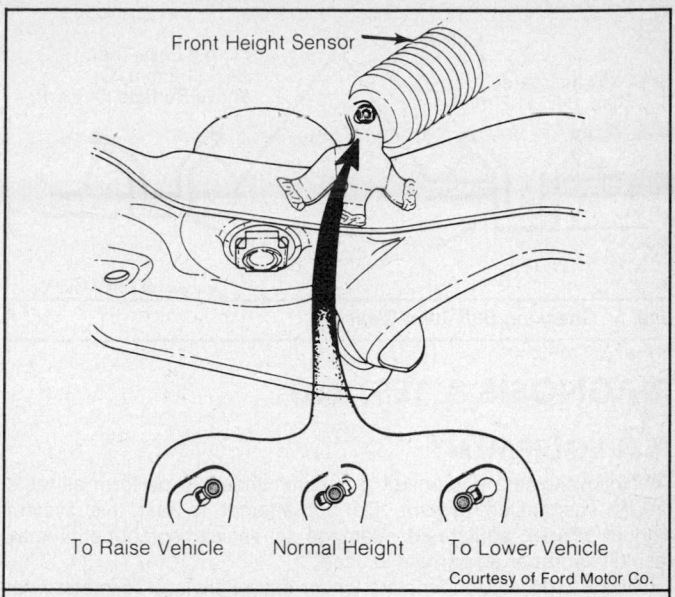

Courtesy of Ford Motor Co.

Fig. 3: Adjusting Front Ride Height

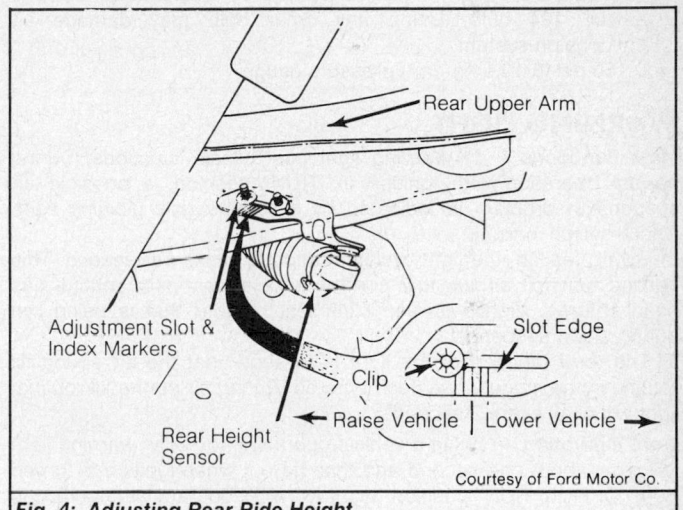

Courtesy of Ford Motor Co.

Fig. 4: Adjusting Rear Ride Height

FRONT WHEEL BEARINGS

1) Turn air suspension switch off. *See Fig. 7.* Raise vehicle as previously outlined and remove wheel cover and grease cap. Remove cotter pin and locking nut. Loosen adjusting nut 3 turns and rock wheel to relieve brake pad pressure from hub and rotor assembly.
2) Tighten adjusting nut to 17-25 ft. lbs. (23-34 N.m) while rotating wheel assembly. Loosen adjusting nut 1/2 turn, then retighten to 10-12 INCH lbs. (1.1-1.7 N.m).
3) Reinstall nut lock on adjusting nut and insert new cotter pin. Install grease cap and wheel cover. Lower vehicle. Before driving vehicle, pump brake pedal to restore normal brake pedal travel.

BALL JOINT CHECKING

1) Turn off air suspension switch. *See Fig. 7.* Support vehicle in normal driving position with vehicle weight on ball joints. Wipe off wear indicator and ball joint cover checking surface, so they are free of dirt and grease.
2) Checking surface should project outside cover. If checking surface is in cover, replace lower arm assembly. *See Fig. 5.*

NOTE: Lower control arm, including both end bushings, are replaceable as assemblies. Replace in pairs only.

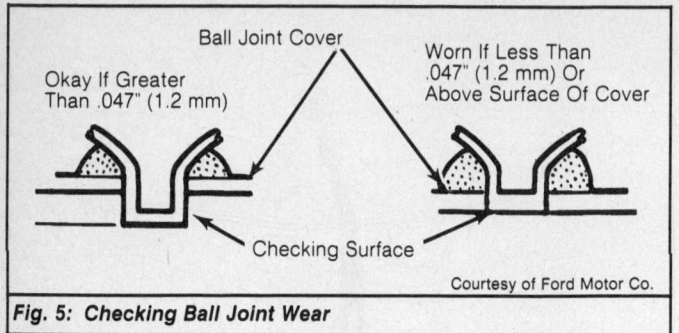

Ball Joint Cover

Okay If Greater Than .047" (1.2 mm)

Worn If Less Than .047" (1.2 mm) Or Above Surface Of Cover

Checking Surface

Courtesy of Ford Motor Co.

Fig. 5: Checking Ball Joint Wear

DIAGNOSIS & TESTING

TEST EQUIPMENT

The following test equipment is recommended to perform all tests on air suspension system. Do not attempt to test this system without proper equipment. Damage to vehicle components may result if improper equipment is used.

- Digital type volt/ohmmeters or an equivalent analog meter with 20,000 ohms per volt sensitivity.
- Fabricate a test light. Attach 2 test leads with pointed probes to a No. 194 bulb. Using any other bulb may damage air suspension system.
- 0-150 psi (0-10.5 kg/cm²) pressure gauge.

WARNING LIGHT

Main Functions – 1) Warning light has 3 main functions. During normal operation with ignition in "RUN" position, a possible air suspension problem is indicated by a continuously glowing light. Check switch in trunk.

2) During testing, the light cycles at about 2 blinks per second. This second function shows that control module diagnostic routine has been entered. Light will also blink test number that is being run during a test sequence.

3) The third function of the light is to show that the air spring fill routine in the module has been entered. During air spring fill routine, light will blink every 2 seconds.

Light Operation – 1) On a vehicle operating normally, warning light will glow about one second and then go out when ignition is turned from "OFF" to "RUN" position. Light will NOT operate with ignition in "OFF" or "START" positions.

2) If light will not go out after turning ignition to "OFF" or "RUN" position, this is an indication of no battery power to control module.

3) Light can show height sensor or harness problem in following manner: light glows for about 1/2 second, goes out, and then glows continuously after 5-8 seconds when ignition is turned from "OFF" to "RUN" position.

4) System problem is indicated if light comes on and glows continuously at any time after 8 seconds when ignition is turned from "OFF" to "RUN".

5) If light comes on during an ignition "ON" cycle, it will glow continuously for that particular cycle. Any erratic light operation indicates a system malfunction.

SYSTEM LOGIC

The following describes how the air suspension system should work when all systems are operating properly.

Ignition In "OFF" Position – System operates for one hour after ignition is turned off. System is inoperable after one hour.

Ignition In "RUN" Position (Less Than 45 Seconds) – System will raise front or rear of vehicle, if required. System will not lower vehicle.

Ignition In "RUN" Position (More Than 45 Seconds) – 1) If door is open with brake off, system will raise vehicle, but will not lower vehicle until door is closed. If doors are closed and brake is off, system will raise or lower vehicle over a 45 second period.

2) If brake is applied and a door is open, system will raise vehicle but not lower it. If brake is applied and doors are closed, system will NOT raise or lower vehicle. If rear of vehicle is in process of being raised, system will complete cycle.

General Operation – 1) Vehicle will not be lowered if ANY door is open. System responds to signals from height sensors in following order: rear up, front up, rear down and front down.

2) With ignition in "RUN" position, warning light will come on for that ignition cycle if any up or down request from sensors is not carried out within 3 minutes. ONLY request that triggered light will be affected; all other up and down functions will operate normally.

3) Rear spring solenoids are operated together; front spring solenoids can operate independently. Control module NEVER responds to front and rear signals at same time; front or rear height will be corrected separately.

4) Turning ignition from "RUN" to "OFF" clears all memory in module. Warning light may not immediately indicate a failure when ignition is turned to "RUN" position.

DIAGNOSTIC ROUTINE

How To Diagnose Air Suspension System – 1) A quick system check can be made by following the QUICK TEST procedure. If more detailed testing is required, go the SELF-TEST.

2) SELF-TEST will guide you to other tests (B through H) to repair the system. Follow all instructions in each step of the SELF-TEST.

QUICK TEST

All QUICK TEST measurements are made with air suspension switch "ON" and the module unplugged. Air suspension switch MUST be "OFF" before unplugging module. Use a digital volt/ohmmeter or equivalent analog meter with 20,000 ohms per volt or greater sensitivity.

SELF-TEST (TEST A) EXPLANATION

The Self-Test (Test A) is a series of 10 individual tests which are conducted by the control module in a specific sequence.

During test sequence, warning light operation is an indication of system malfunction. Warning light will flash test number at constant rate during all tests.

Tests 1-3 – These are complete cycles of suspension operation (raising and lowering; front first, then rear). Each successive transition from door closed to door open will cause control module to advance to next test.

During Tests 1-3, warning light will glow and remain on continuously if correct signal is not received within 30 seconds. If an illegal signal is received, warning light will flash rapidly. Either of these would indicate a failure.

To repeat a failed test, close and open door. To proceed to next test, close and open door twice within 15-second period.

Tests 4-9 – The following components will cycle in sequence: air compressor, vent solenoid, left front solenoid, right front solenoid, right rear solenoid and left rear solenoid.

During Tests 4-10, warning light is not required for pass/fail determination. These tests will cycle various components and pass/fail determination can be made by observing vehicle for automatic lowering, or listening to compressor and vent solenoid for operation. To advance to next test, close and open door.

Test 10 – This test checks brake circuit system and completes test sequence. Test is terminated either by actuating service brake, turning ignition switch to "OFF" position, or disconnecting diagnostic pigtail from control module. System returns to normal operating mode.

NOTE: Do not perform any other tests until SELF-TEST is completed.

CAUTION: Air fill and diagnostic routines are both activated in similar manner. DO NOT open and close driver's door unless specifically instructed to by routine.

1989 ELECTRONIC SUSPENSION
Ford Motor Co. Air Suspension — Mark VII (Cont.)

12-95

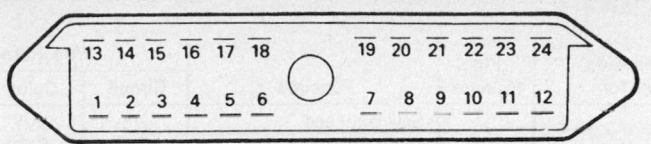

MODULE CONNECTOR

Circuit	Pin Number	Meter Reading
Module Circuit	20 and 1	Battery Voltage
	20 and 24	Battery Voltage
	7 and 1	Ignition Switch in RUN — Battery Voltage Ignition Switch OFF — Zero Volts
	15 and 1	Brake Switch On — Battery Voltage Brake Switch Off — Zero Volts
	19 and 1	Door Open — Battery Voltage All Doors Closed — Zero Volts
Air Spring Solenoid Valve Circuit	20 and 9	(Left Rear) — Approx. 15-16 ohms (No. 20 is Positive Lead)*
	20 and 10	(Right Rear) — Approx. 15-16 ohms (No. 20 is Positive Lead)*
	20 and 11	(Left Front) — Approx. 15-16 ohms (No. 20 is Positive Lead)*
	20 and 12	(Right Front) — Approx. 15-16 ohms (No. 20 is Positive Lead)*
Compressor Relay Coil Circuit	20 and 22	Approx. 60-70 ohms*
Vent Solenoid Circuit	20 and 23	Approx. 30 ohms

*To verify suppression diode across the coil of solenoid is good, ohmmeter will read as stated above with one meter polarity and less with the reverse polarity.

The following voltage measurements are made at the harness connector (for each sensor) with the sensor disconnected and the ignition switch in RUN and the air suspension switch on.

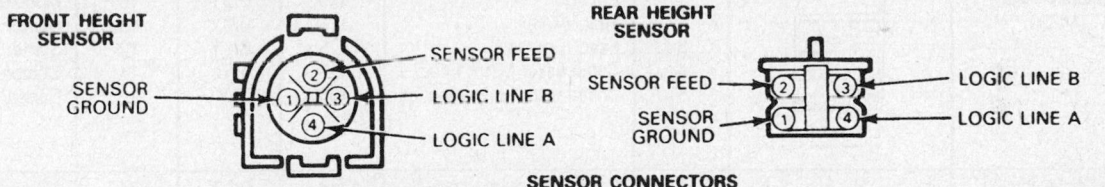

SENSOR CONNECTORS

Circuit	Pin Number	Meter Reading
Height Sensor Circuits	1 and 2	2-3 Volts
	1 and 3	Approx. 5 Volts
	1 and 4	Approx. 5 Volts

Courtesy of Ford Motor Co.

Fig. 6: Quick Test

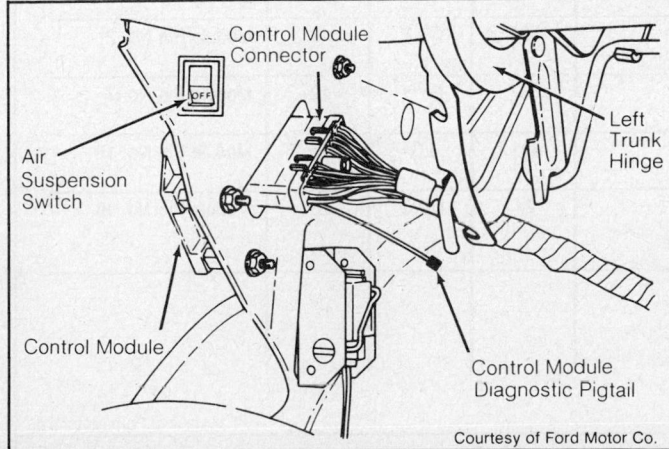

Courtesy of Ford Motor Co.

Fig. 7: Location of Air Suspension Control Module & Switch

Entering Diagnostics – 1) Turn on air suspension switch. Diagnostic pigtail located at rear of on/off switch in trunk must be ungrounded. *See Fig. 7.* Connect battery charger to battery to reduce drain.

2) Open driver's door with all other doors closed. Cycle ignition switch from "OFF" to "RUN" position, hold switch in "RUN" position for a minimum of 5 seconds. Turn ignition off.

3) Ground diagnostic pigtail on vehicle. Pigtail must remain grounded during diagnostic sequence.

4) Turn ignition switch to "RUN" position. Do not start vehicle. Warning light will blink continuously at a rate of about 1.8 blinks per second to indicate diagnostics routine has been entered.

5) Close driver's door once to start TEST No. 1. Warning light will alternately blink and pause until next test is started.

6) Each time driver's door is closed and then opened, module will advance to next test sequence. Warning light will blink current test number.

Exiting Diagnostics – Diagnostic mode may be stopped, and module returned to normal operation mode, by cycling the ignition, actuating service brake or removing diagnostic pigtail ground.

1989 ELECTRONIC SUSPENSION
Ford Motor Co. Air Suspension – Mark VII (Cont.)

Component (Harness Number)	Harness Side Connector	Pin Number	Function	Wire Harness			Circuit End Point
				Circuit	Color	Gauge	
Compressor (1) (14290)		1	Solenoid Feed	175	BK/Y	14	Starter Relay
		2	Motor Feed	417	P/O	14	Compressor Relay
		3	Motor Ground	430	GY	14	Battery Ground Cable
		4	Solenoid Control	578	LB/PK	18	Module Pin No. 23
Spring Solenoid (4) (14290 LF/RF) (12614 LR/RR)		1	Control — LR	429	P/LG	18	Module Pin No. 9
			Control — RR	416	LB/BK	18	Module Pin No. 10
			Control — LF	415	LG/O	18	Module Pin No. 11
			Control — RF	414	O/R	18	Module Pin No. 12
		2	Feed	175	BK/Y	16	Starter Relay
Front Height Sensor (2) (14290)	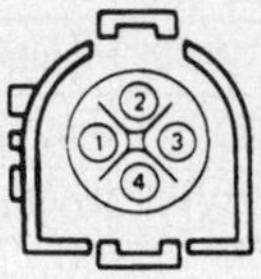	1	Ground	432	BK/PK	18	Module Pin No. 14
		2	Feed — LF (RF)	431	PK/W	18	Module Pin No. 4
		3	Logic Line B — RF	425	BR/PK	18	Module Pin No. 16
			Logic Line B — LF	423	P/LG	18	Module Pin No. 17
		4	Logic Line A — RF	424	T	18	Module Pin No. 5
			Logic Line A — LF	422	PK/BK	18	Module Pin No. 6
Rear Height Sensor (1) (12614)	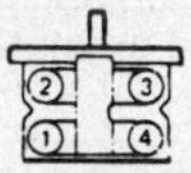	1	Ground	432	BK/PK	18	Module Pin No. 14
		2	Feed	426	R/BK	18	Module Pin No. 3
		3	Logic Line B	428	O/BK	18	Module Pin No. 18
		4	Logic Line A	427	PK/BK	18	Module Pin No. 13
Compressor Relay (1) (14290)	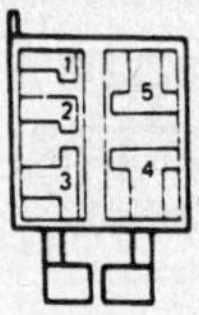	1	Control	420	DB/Y	18	Module Pin No. 22
		2	Feed (Coil)	175	BK/Y	18	Starter Relay
		3	Feed (Contacts)	175	BK/Y	12	Starter Relay
		4	Compressor Motor Feed	417	P/O	14	Compressor
		5	Compressor Motor Ground	430	GY	12	Battery Ground Cable
On/Off Switch (1) (12614)	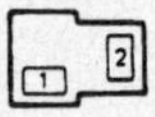	1	Feed to Module	418	DG/Y	14	Module Pin No. 20
		2	Feed to Switch	175	BK/Y	14	Starter Relay
Warning Lamp (1) (14A005)	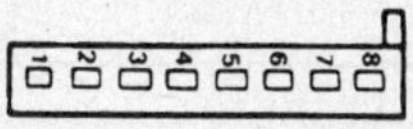	8	Control	419	DG/LG	20	Module Pin No. 21
		6	Feed	640	R/Y	20	Fuse Panel
Battery Ground Cable (14290)	—	—	System Ground	577	LG/RD	12	Module Pin No. 1 and 24
Diagnostic Pigtail	—	—	Access to System Diagnostics and Air Fill	606	W/LB	18	Module Pin No. 2
Ignition Switch (14401)	Branch of Existing Circuit	—	Ignition Sense	687	GY/Y	12	Module Pin No. 7
Stoplamp Switch (14A005)	Branch of Existing Circuit	—	Brake Sense	511	LG	18	Module Pin No. 15
Courtesy Lamp Door Switch (14488)	Branch of Existing Circuit	—	Door Sense	24	DB/O	20	Module Pin No. 19
Module (1) (12614)	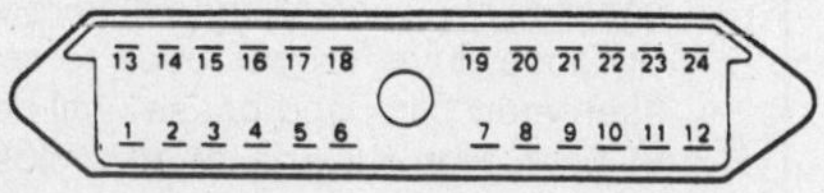						

Courtesy of Ford Motor Co.

Fig. 8: Air Suspension Connector Identification

1989 ELECTRONIC SUSPENSION
Ford Motor Co. Air Suspension — Mark VII (Cont.)

12-97

TEST A (SELF-TEST)

A1 (Check Vehicle Load) – Unload passenger and luggage compartments, as necessary. Allow vehicle to sit with ignition switch in "RUN" position for minimum of 5 minutes (doors closed, brake off). Level vehicle. Go to A2

A2 (Initialize System) – Turn ignition switch to "OFF" position, then turn ignition switch to "RUN" position. Observe air suspension warning light. If warning light blinks or turns on, go to A3. If warning light does not blink or glow, go to B1.

A3 (Enter Diagnostics) – 1) Before entering diagnostics, attach battery charger to vehicle and leave on until completion of diagnostics. After diagnostics are entered, DO NOT open the driver's door, step on brake pedal or start engine unless you are specifically told to do so.

2) Turn ignition off. Ground diagnostic pigtail in trunk. Turn ignition switch to "RUN" position; DO NOT start engine, open door or step on brake pedal.

3) If warning light blinks continuously, go to A4. If warning light blinks once, diagnostics are not entered; go to B10. If warning light stays on, light is not functioning properly. Go to B13.

A4 (TEST No. 1) – 1) To start TEST No. 1, open and close door. System raises rear evenly for 15-30 seconds, then lowers rear for 30 seconds (maximum). When a rear low signal is received by the control module, the rear of the vehicle will raise for a maximum of 30 seconds or until a rear trim signal is received at the control module. TEST No. 1 is completed.

2) Warning light will blink TEST No. 1 at a constant rate for a maximum test time of 90 seconds. After 90 seconds, observe warning light. If warning light flashes about 4 times per second or stays on, record TEST No.1 as a failure and go to A5. If warning light flashes TEST No. 1, go to A5. If warning light does not flash TEST No. 1, flashes rapidly or remains on, go to B22.

A5 (TEST No. 2) – 1) To start test, open and close door once. If TEST No. 1 failed, open and close door TWICE. System raises right front for 15-30 seconds, then lowers for 30 seconds (maximum). When right front low signal is received by control module, right front of vehicle will raise for maximum of 30 seconds or until right front trim signal is received by control module. Warning light will blink TEST No. 2 at a constant rate for a maximum test time of 90 seconds.

2) After 90 seconds, observe warning light. If warning light flashes about 4 times per second or stays on, record TEST No. 2 as a failure. Go to A6. If warning light flashes TEST No. 2, go to A6.

A6 (TEST No. 3, Left Front Suspension) – 1) To start test, open and close door once. If TEST No. 2 failed, open and close door TWICE. System raises left front for 15-30 seconds, then lowers for 30 seconds (maximum). When a vehicle high signal is received from left front sensor, left front of vehicle will raise for maximum of 30 seconds or until left front trim signal is received at control module. Warning light will blink TEST No. 3 at a constant rate for a maximum test time of 90 seconds.

2) After 90 seconds, observe warning light. If warning light flashes about 4 times per second or stays on, record TEST No. 3 as a failure. Go to A7. If warning light flashes TEST No. 3, system passed test. Go to A7.

A7 (TEST No. 4) – 1) To start test, open and close door once. If TEST No. 3 failed, open and close door TWICE. System cycles compressor on and off. Warning light will blink TEST No. 4 continuously. Compressor will only cycle 50 times during test. Rear of vehicle may raise during test.

2) If compressor does not cycle, runs continuously or doesn't run, system failed test. Record TEST No. 4 as a failure. Go to A8. If compressor cycles, system passed test. Go to A8.

A8 (TEST No. 5) – To start test, open and close door. System cycles vent solenoid on and off. Solenoid is part of compressor assembly. Warning light will blink TEST No. 5 continuously during test. If solenoid doesn't cycle, system failed test. Record TEST No. 5 as a failure. Go to A9 If solenoid cycles, system passed test. Go to A9.

A9 (TEST No. 6) – 1) To start test, open and close door. Listen for air escaping from vent solenoid and for left front spring solenoid to cycle. Left front of vehicle will drop during test.

2) If spring solenoid doesn't cycle or air is not venting, system has failed test. Record TEST No. 6 as a failure. Go to A10. If spring solenoid cycles and air is escaping from vent solenoid, system passed test. Go to A10.

TEST A (Cont.)

A10 (TEST No. 7 – 1) To start test, open and close door. Listen for air escaping from vent solenoid and for right front spring solenoid to cycle. Right front of vehicle will drop during test.

2) If spring solenoid doesn't cycle or air is not venting, system has failed test. Record TEST No. 7 as a failure. Go to A11. If spring solenoid cyles and air is escaping from vent solenoid, system has passed test. Go to A11.

A11 (TEST No. 8) – 1) To start test, open and close door. Listen for air escaping from vent solenoid and for right rear spring solenoid to cycle. Right rear of vehicle will drop during test.

2) If spring solenoid doesn't cycle or air is not venting, system has failed test. Record TEST No. 8 as a failure. Go to A12. If spring solenoid cycles and air is venting, system has passed test. Go to A12.

A12 (TEST No. 9) – 1) To start test, open and close door. Listen for air escaping from vent solenoid and for left rear spring solenoid to cycle. Left rear of vehicle will drop during test.

2) If spring solenoid doesn't cycle or air is not venting, system has failed test. Record TEST No. 9 as a failure. Go to A13. If spring solenoid cycles and air is escaping, system has passed test. Go to A13.

A13 (TEST No. 10) – To start test, open door. DO NOT close door. Sit in driver's seat and depress brake pedal. If warning light continues to blink, system has failed test. Go to B30. If warning light stops blinking, system has passed test. This completes diagnostic sequence. If system passed all SELF-TESTS, disconnect ground from pigtail.

A14 (Any Failures Recorded?) – If any failures were recorded during SELF-TEST, go to A15. If no failures were noted, system is working correctly. No further tests required.

A15 – If warning light flashed rapidly for any of the first 3 tests, go to C1. If sensors okay, go to A16.

A16 – If warning light stayed on after completion of TEST No. 1, check rear of vehicle. Go to D1. If light did not stay on, go to A17.

A17 – If warning light stayed on after completion of TEST No. 2, go to E1. If warning light did not stay on, go to A18.

A18 – If warning light stayed on after completion of TEST No. 3, go to F1. If light did not stay on, go to A19.

A19 – If left front solenoid cycled during TEST No. 6, solenoid is okay. Go to A20. If left front solenoid did NOT cycle during TEST No. 6, go to F1.

A20 – If right front solenoid cycled during TEST No. 7, solenoid is okay. go to A21. If right front solenoid did not cycle during TEST No. 7, go to E1.

A21 – If right rear solenoid did NOT cycle or air did not escape from vent solenoid during TEST No. 8, go to D1. If solenoid did cycle, solenoid is okay. Go to A22.

A22 – If left rear solenoids did NOT cycle or air did NOT escape from vent solenoid during TEST No. 9, go to D1. If solenoid did cycle, solenoid is okay.

TEST B (CANNOT ENTER, SEQUENCE OR EXIT DIAGNOSTIC TEST)

B1 – Check air suspension warning light bulb, and replace if defective. Repeat SELF-TEST. If bulb is not defective, go to B2.

B2 (Make Test Light) – Make a test light out of a No. 194 bulb and 2 leads. Any other bulb WILL DAMAGE SYSTEM. Go to B3.

B3 (Check Ignition Circuit) – Check ignition circuit. Turn ignition and air suspension switch (in trunk) off. If warning light is off, go to B4. If warning light stays on, repair short between battery to ignition in circuit No. 687. Circuit No. 687 is Gray/Yellow wire that ends at module pin No. 7. Turn air suspension switch on. Repeat SELF-TEST.

B4 (Check Ignition Circuit) – Check ignition circuit using test light, connect one lead to ignition circuit No. 640 (Red/Yellow wire) at warning light and other lead to ground. Turn ignition switch to "RUN" position. If test light is on, go to B6. If test light remains off, go to B5.

B5 (Check Fuse) – Check fuse in ignition circuit No. 640 (Red/Yellow wire on fuse panel). If fuse is okay, repair open in circuit No. 640. Repeat SELF-TEST. If fuse is blown, repair short in ignition circuit No. 640, and replace fuse. If second fuse fails, repeat SELF-TEST.

TEST B (Cont.)

B6 (Check Ignition Circuit) – 1) Check ignition circuit. Using test light, connect one lead to pin No. 7 (circuit No. 687) of control module connector and other lead to ground. Turn ignition switch to "RUN" position.

2) If test light is on, go to B7. If test light is off, repair short in ignition circuit No. 687. Turn air suspension switch on, and repeat SELF-TEST.

B7 (Check Module Ground Circuit) – 1) Connect one test light lead to pin No. 7 (circuit No. 687) of control module connector. Turn ignition switch to "RUN" position. Connect other test light lead to pin No. 1 (circuit No. 430) of control module connector. Move lead on pin No. 1 of control module connector to pin No. 24 on control module connector.

2) If test light is on, go to B8. If test light does NOT light, repair open in circuit No. 430 and repeat SELF-TEST.

B8 (Check Warning Light Circuit) – 1) Using volt/ohmmeter, connect negative test lead to ground. Connect positive lead to pin No. 21 (circuit No. 419) of control module connector. Turn ignition switch to "RUN" position.

2) If voltage is more than 5 volts, go to B9. If voltage is 5 volts or less, repair short in warning light circuit No. 419 from control module connector to warning light connector. Turn air suspension switch on and repeat SELF-TEST.

B9 (Check Battery Voltage) – 1) Connect negative lead to pin No. 24 (circuit No. 430) of control module connector and positive lead to pin No. 20 (circuit No. 418) of control module connector. Turn ignition switch to "RUN" position.

2) If voltage is less than 11 volts, check battery or faulty connection. Turn air suspension switch on and repeat SELF-TEST. If voltage is more than 11 volts, replace air suspension control module. Perform SELF-TEST.

B10 – Check for proper ground at pigtail. If warning light blinks only once, go to B11. If warning light blinks more than once, repeat SELF-TEST.

B11 (Test Light) – If not already done, fabricate test light from a No. 194 light. Go to B12.

B12 (Check Pigtail) – 1) Using test light, connect one lead to pin No. 2 (circuit No. 606) of control module connector and other lead to pin No. 7 (circuit No. 687) of control module connector. Turn ignition to "RUN" position. Ground and then unground the diagnostic pigtail.

2) If test light is on, then off, pigtail circuit is good. Go to B13. If test light is off, repair short in circuit No. 606 White/Lt. Blue on module pin No. 2 and repeat SELF-TEST.

B13 (Checking System In Diagnostic Mode) – Open and close door. If compressor starts running, go to B20. If compressor is already running or does not start, go to B14.

B14 (Test Light) – If not already done, fabricate test light from a No. 194 light. Go to B15.

B15 (Checking Battery Circuit) – Using test light, connect one lead to pin No. 20 (circuit No. 418) at control module connector and other lead to ground. If test light illuminates, go to B21. If test light is off, go to B16.

B16 (Check Fuse Link) – Check battery circuit No. 175 (Black/Yellow wire) at on/off switch in trunk. If fuse link is good, go to B17. If fuse link is blown, replace fuse link and repeat SELF-TEST.

B17 – Check that air suspension switch is on. If on, go to B18. If switch is off, turn air suspension switch on and repeat SELF-TEST.

B18 (Check Battery Circuit) – Using test light, connect one lead to Black/Yellow wire (circuit No. 175) at air suspension switch pin No. 2 and the other lead to ground. If test light is on, go to B19. If test light is off, repair short in battery circuit No. 175 from air suspension switch to battery and repeat SELF-TEST.

B19 (Checking On/Off Switch) – Using test light, connect one lead to on/off switch pin No. 1 (circuit No. 418) of switch (control module side) and other lead to ground. If test light is on, repair short in battery from pin No. 1 to battery and repeat SELF-TEST. If test light is off, replace switch. Repeat SELF-TEST.

B20 (Check Warning Light Circuit) – Unplug control module connector. If warning light is on, repair short in ground circuit No. 419 from control module connector to warning light. Plug in connector and repeat SELF-TEST. If warning light is off, go to B21.

TEST B (Cont.)

B21 (Checking Battery Voltage) – 1) Using volt/ohmmeter, connect negative lead to pin No. 24 (circuit No. 430) of control module connector and positive lead to pin No. 20 (circuit No. 418) of control module connector.

2) If voltage is less than 11 volts, check for low battery or faulty connections at battery and repeat SELF-TEST. If voltage is more than 11 volts, replace control module. Plug in connectors and repeat SELF-TEST.

B22 (Test Light) – If not already done, fabricate test light from a No. 194 light. Go to B23.

B23 (Checking Door Circuit) – Using test light, connect one lead to pin No. 19 (circuit No. 24) at control module connector and other lead to ground. Close door.

If test light is on, repair short in circuit No. 24 or replace faulty door switch. Repeat SELF-TEST. If test light is off, go to B24.

B24 (Checking Door Circuit) – Open door. If test light comes on, circuit is good. Go to B25. If test light is off, replace defective door switch or repair open or short circuit No. 24. Repeat SELF-TEST.

B25 (Checking Brake Circuit) – Depress and release brake pedal. If rear brake lights operate properly, go to B26. If brake lights do not operate properly, repair as necessary and repeat SELF-TEST.

B26 (Checking Compressor Circuit) – Disconnect compressor relay connector. Perform A2-A4 of SELF-TEST. Observe warning light. If light flashes rapidly, flashes test number or stays on, go to B27. If light does anything else, go to B21.

B27 (Checking Compressor Circuit) – 1) DO NOT reconnect compressor relay connector. Using volt/ohmmeter, connect negative lead to ground and positive lead to pin No. 2 (circuit No. 417) on harness side of connector.

2) Measure resistance. If reading is greater than 1000 ohms, go to B28. If reading less than 1000 ohms, repair short to ground on circuit No. 417 and repeat SELF-TEST.

B28 (Checking Compressor Current) – 1) Unplug compressor connector. Connect jumper wire (14 ga. minimum) between compressor connector (compressor side) pin No. 3 and a good ground. Using ammeter, (40 amps minimum) connect negative lead to pin No. 3 and positive lead to positive side of battery.

2) Measure amperage after compressor has run for 10 seconds. DO NOT allow compressor to run more than 60 seconds. If amperage is greater than 35 amps, replace compressor assembly and repeat SELF-TEST. If less than 35 amps, go to B29.

B29 (Checking Compressor Voltage) – Perform B28, except measure battery voltage with compressor running. If more than 11 volts, replace control module. Plug in connectors and repeat SELF-TEST. If less than 11 volts, check battery and charge if necessary. Repeat SELF-TEST.

B30 (Test Light) – If not already done, fabricate test light from a No. 194 light. Go to B31.

B31 (Checking Brake Circuit) – Depress and release brake pedal. If brake lights operate properly, go to B32. If brake lights do not operate properly, repair as necessary and repeat SELF-TEST.

B32 (Checking Brake Circuit) – Using test light, connect one lead to pin No. 15 (circuit No. 511) at control module connector and other lead to ground. Depress brake pedal. If test light is on, replace control module and repeat SELF-TEST. If light is off, repair short in brake circuit No. 511. and repeat SELF-TEST.

TEST C (SENSOR TESTS)

C1 – If warning light flashed for all 3 tests, go to C2. If not, go to C11.

C2 (Checking Sensor Ground Circuit) – Using test light, connect one lead to pin No. 1 (circuit No. 432) at left front sensor connector and connect other lead to the positive battery terminal. If test light is on, ground circuit is good. Go to C5. If light is off, go to C3.

C3 (Checking Sensor Ground Circuit) – Using test light, connect one lead to pin No. 14 (circuit No. 432) at control module connector. DO NOT disconnect control module. Attach other lead to pin No. 20. If test light is on, repair open in ground circuit No. 432 and perform SELF-TEST. If light is off, go to C4.

1989 ELECTRONIC SUSPENSION
Ford Motor Co. Air Suspension – Mark VII (Cont.)

12-99

TEST C (Cont.)

C4 – Unplug control module connector. Check sensor ground pin No. 14, and control module ground pins No. 1 and No. 24 for corrosion or damage. If damage or corrosion is found, repair or clean pins and perform SELF-TEST. If pins are good, replace control module and perform SELF-TEST.

C5 – **1)** Set volt/ohmmeter to read 3 volts DC. Connect negative lead to pin No. 14 (circuit No. 432) at control module connector. Connect positive lead to pin No. 4 (circuit No. 431) of control module connector. Turn ignition switch to "RUN" position.

2) If reading is less than one volt and steady, go to C6. If readings are erratic or greater than one volt, but less than 5 volts, repair open in sensor power circuits No. 426 or No. 431, between control module and sensors. Perform SELF-TEST. If reading is more than 5 volts, replace control module and perform SELF-TEST.

C6 (Checking Left Front Sensor) – Unplug harness at left front sensor and read volt/ohmmeter. If reading is less than one volt and steady, sensor is good. Go to C7. If reading is erratic or more than one volt, replace left front sensor and perform SELF-TEST.

C7 (Checking Right Front Sensor) – Do not reconnect left front sensor. Disconnect harness at right front sensor and read volt/ohmmeter. If reading is less than one volt and steady, sensor is good. Go to C8. If reading is erratic or more than one volt, replace sensor and perform SELF-TEST.

C8 (Checking Rear Sensor) – Do not reconnect left or right front sensor. Disconnect harness at rear sensor and read volt/ohmmeter. If reading is less than one volt and steady, sensor is good. Go to C9. If reading is erratic or more than one volt, replace sensor. Reconnect all sensors (except rear) and perform SELF-TEST.

C9 (Checking Sensor Power Circuit) – **1)** Do not reconnnect rear sensor. Disconnect control module. Using volt/ohmmeter, connect negative lead to pin No. 1 (circuit No. 430) of control module connector and positive lead to pin No. 3 (circuit No.426) at control module connector. Measure resistance.

2) If more than 1000 ohms, go to C10. If less than 1000 ohms, repair short in circuit No. 426. Reconnect all sensors and control module. Perform SELF-TEST.

C10 (Checking Sensor Power Circuit) – Move positive lead to pin No. 4 (circuit No. 431) at control module connector. Measure resistance. If more than 1000 ohms, replace control module and PERFORM SELF-TEST. If less than 1000 ohms, repair short to ground in circuit No. 431. Reconnect all sensors and control module and perform SELF-TEST.

C11 – If warning light flashed rapidly on C1, go to C12. If not, go to C23.

C12 (Checking Sensor Ground Circuit) – **1)** Turn air suspension switch off. Using volt/ohmmeter, connect positive lead to pin No. 1 (circuit No. 432) at rear sensor. Connect negative lead to ground. Measure resistance.

2) If more than 5 ohms, repair open in circuit No. 432 between control module connector and rear sensor. Perform SELF-TEST. If less than 5 ohms, go to C13.

C13 (Checking Sensor Power Circuit) – **1)** Turn air suspension switch on. Using volt/ohmmeter, connect negative test lead to pin No. 1 (circuit No. 432) at rear sensor connector and positive lead to pin No. 2 (circuit No. 426). Turn ignition switch to "RUN" position and read voltage.

2) If less than one volt and steady, repair open in circuit No. 426 from sensor to control module and perform SELF-TEST. If voltage is more than one volt or erratic, power circuit is good. Go to C14.

C14 (Checking Rear Sensor "A" Circuit) – Move positive lead to pin No. 4 (circuit No. 427) at rear sensor connector. Read voltage. If more than 1.5 volts or erratic, rear sensor circuit is good. Go to C15. If less than 1.5 volts, go to C15.

C15 (Checking Rear Sensor) – Unplug rear sensor connector and read voltage. If more than 1.5 volts, replace rear sensor. Perform SELF-TEST. If less than 1.5 volts, go to C16.

C16 (Checking Rear Sensor "A" Circuit) – **1)** Do not connect rear sensor. Using a volt/ohmmeter, connect negative lead to pin No. 14 (circuit No. 432) and positive lead to pin No. 13 (circuit No. 427). Read voltage.

2) If more than 1.5 volts, repair open in circuit No. 427 between control module and sensor. Connect sensor lead and perform SELF-TEST. If less than 1.5 volts, go to C17.

TEST C (Cont.)

C17 (Checking Rear Sensor "A" Circuit) – **1)** Unplug control module. Using volt/ohmmeter, connect negative lead to pin No. 1 (circuit No. 430) at control module connector and positive lead to pin No. 13 (circuit No. 427). Read resistance.

2) If more than 1000 ohms, replace control module unit. Connect rear sensor and perform SELF-TEST. If less than 1000 ohms, repair short to ground on circuit No. 427, between control module and rear sensor. Connect rear sensor and perform SELF-TEST.

C18 (Checking Rear Sensor "B" Circuit) – Move positive lead to pin No. 3 (circuit No. 428) at rear sensor connector and read voltage. If more than 1.5 volts, rear sensor circuit is good. Go to C19. If less than 1.5 volts, go to C20.

C19 (Checking Control Module Damage) – Repeat SELF-TEST A2-A4. If warning light flashes rapidly, replace control module and perform SELF-TEST. If warning light is NOT flashing rapidly, perform SELF-TEST.

C20 (Checking Rear Sensor) – Unplug rear sensor and read voltage. If more than 1.5 volts, replace rear sensor and perform SELF-TEST. If less than 1.5 volts, rear sensor is good. Go to C21.

C21 (Checking Rear Sensor "B" Circuit) – **1)** Do not connect rear sensor. Connect negative lead to pin No. 14 (circuit No. 432) at control module connector and positive lead to pin No. 18 (circuit No. 428) at module connector. Read voltage.

2) If more than 1.5 volts, repair open in circuit No. 428 between control module and sensor. Connect rear sensor and perform SELF-TEST. If less than 1.5 volts, go to C22.

C22 (Checking Rear Sensor "B" Circuit) – **1)** Unplug control module connector. Using volt/ohmmeter, connect negative lead to pin No. 1 (circuit No. 430) and positive lead to pin No. 18 (circuit No. 428). Read resistance.

2) If more than 1000 ohms, replace control module. Connect rear sensor and perform SELF-TEST. If less 1000 ohms, repair short in circuit No. 428 between control module and rear sensor. Connect control module and perform SELF-TEST.

C23 – If warning light flashed rapidly during SELF-TEST A2, go to C24. If not, go to C35.

C24 (Checking Sensor Ground Circuit) – **1)** Using test light, connect one lead to pin No. 1 (circuit No. 432) at right front sensor and other lead to positive side of battery.

2) If test light is on, sensor ground circuit is good. Go to C25. If test light is off, repair open in circuit No. 432 between control module and right front sensor. Connect sensor and perform SELF-TEST.

C25 (Checking Sensor Power Circuit) – **1)** Using volt/ohmmeter, connect negative lead to pin No. 1 (circuit No. 432) at right front sensor connector and positive lead to pin No. 2 (circuit No. 431) at right front sensor. Turn ignition switch to "RUN" position and read voltage.

2) If less than one volt and steady, repair open in circuit No. 431 from right front sensor to control module. Connect sensor and perform SELF-TEST. If voltage is more than one volt and erratic, sensor power is good. Go to C26.

C26 (Checking Right Front Sensor "A" Circuit) – Move positive lead to pin No. 4 (circuit No. 424) at right front sensor and read voltage. If more than 1.5 volts, right front sensor is good. Go to C30. If less than 1.5 volts, go to C27.

C27 (Checking Right Front Sensor) – Unplug right front sensor and read voltage. If more than 1.5 volts, replace right front sensor and perform SELF-TEST. If less than 1.5 volts, right front sensor is good. Go to C28.

C28 (Checking Right Front Sensor "A" Circuit) – **1)** Do not connect right front sensor. Using volt/ohmmeter, connect negative lead to pin No. 14 (circuit No. 432) at control module connector and positive lead to pin No. 5 (circuit 424) at module connector. Read voltage.

2) If more than 1.5 volts, repair open in sensor circuit No. 424 between control module and sensor. Connect sensor and perform SELF-TEST. If less than 1.5 volts, go to C29.

C29 (Checking Right Front Sensor "A" Circuit) – **1)** Do not connect control module. Using volt/ohmmeter, connect negative lead to pin No. 1 (circuit No. 430) at control module connector and positive lead to pin No. 5 (circuit No. 424) at control module connector. Read resistance.

TEST C (Cont.)

2) If more than 1000 ohms, replace control module. Connect right front sensor and perform SELF-TEST. If less than 1000 ohms, repair short in circuit No. 424 between control module and right front sensor. Connect sensor and perform SELF-TEST.

C30 (Checking Right Front Sensor "B" Circuit) – Move positive lead to right front sensor connector pin No. 3 (circuit No. 425) at right front sensor connector and read voltage. If more than 1.5 volts or erratic, replace right front sensor and go to C31. If less than 1.5 volts, go to C32.

C31 (Checking Control Module) – Repeat SELF-TEST A2-A5. If warning light flashes rapidly during test, replace control module. Perform SELF-TEST. If warning light is NOT flashing rapidly, perform SELF-TEST.

C32 (Checking Right Front Sensor) – Unplug right front sensor and read voltage. If more than 1.5 volts or erratic, replace sensor and perform SELF-TEST. If less than 1.5 volts, go to C33.

C33 (Checking Right Front Sensor "B" Circuit) – **1)** Do not connect right front sensor. Using volt/ohmmeter, connect negative lead to pin No. 14 (circuit No. 432) at control module connector and positive lead to pin No. 16 (circuit No. 425) at control module connector. Read voltage.

2) If more than 1.5 volts, repair short in sensor B circuit No. 425 between control module and sensor. Connect sensor and perform SELF-TEST. If less than 1.5 volts, go to C34.

C34 (Checking Right Front Sensor "B" Circuit) – **1)** Unplug control module. Using volt/ohmmeter, connect negative lead to pin No. 1 (circuit No. 430) at control module connector and positive lead to pin No. 16 (circuit No. 425). Read resistance.

2) If more than 1000 ohms, replace control module. Reconnect sensor and perform SELF-TEST. If less than 1000 ohms, repair short in circuit No. 425 between control module and right front sensor. Perform SELF-TEST.

C35 (Checking Sensor Ground Circuit) – **1)** Using test light, connect one lead to pin No. 1 (circuit No. 432) at left front sensor and other lead to positive battery terminal.

2) If test light is on, sensor ground is good. Go to C36. If test light is off, repair open in circuit No. 432 between control module and left front sensor. Connect sensor and perform SELF-TEST.

C36 (Checking Sensor Power Circuit) – **1)** Using volt/ohmmeter, connect negative lead to pin No. 1 (circuit No. 432) at left front sensor connector and positive lead to pin No. 2 (circuit No. 431) at left front sensor. Turn ignition switch to "RUN" position and read voltage.

2) If voltage is less than one volt, repair open in circuit No. 431 from left front sensor and control module. Connect sensor and perform SELF-TEST. If voltage is erratic or more than one volt, sensor circuit is good. Go to C37.

C37 (Checking Left Front Sensor "A" Circuit) – Move positive lead to pin No. 4 (circuit No. 422) at left front sensor connector and read voltage. If more than 1.5 volts or erratic, left front sensor is good. Go to C41. If less than 1.5 volts, go to C38.

C38 (Checking Left Front Sensor) – Unplug left front sensor connector and read voltage. If more 1.5 volts, replace sensor. Perform SELF-TEST. If less than 1.5 volts, go to C39.

C39 (Checking Left Front Sensor "A" Circuit) – **1)** Do not connect left front sensor. Using volt/ohmmeter, connect negative lead to pin No. 14 (circuit No. 432) at control module connector and positive lead to pin No. 6 (circuit No. 422) at control module connector. Read voltage.

2) If more than 1.5 volts, repair open in circuit No. 422 between control module and sensor. Connect sensor and perform SELF-TEST. If voltage is less than 1.5 volts, go to C40.

C40 (Checking Left Front Sensor "A" Circuit) – **1)** Unplug control module. Using volt/ohmmeter, connect negative lead to pin No. 1 (circuit No. 430) at control module connector and positive lead to Pin No. 6 (circuit No. 422) at control module connector. Read resistance.

2) If more than 1000 ohms, replace control module. Connect left sensor and perform SELF-TEST. If less than 1000 ohms, repair short in circuit No. 422 between control module and left sensor. Connect left front sensor and perform SELF-TEST.

C41 (Checking Left Front Sensor "B" Circuit) – Move positive lead to pin No. 3 (circuit No. 423) at left front sensor connector and read voltage. If more than 1.5 volts or erratic, replace sensor and go to C42. If less than 1.5 volts, go to C43.

TEST C (Cont.)

C42 (Checking Control Module) – Rerun SELF-TEST A2-A4. If warning light flashes rapidly during TEST No. 3, replace control module and perform SELF-TEST. If warning light is not flashing rapidly during TEST No. 3, perform SELF-TEST.

C43 (Checking Left Front Sensor) – Unplug left front sensor connector. Using volt/ohmmeter, check voltage. If more than 1.5 volts or erratic, install new left front sensor and perform SELF-TEST. If less than 1.5 volts, left front sensor is good. Go to C44.

C44 (Checking Left Front Sensor "B" Circuit) – **1)** Do not connect left front sensor. Using volt/ohmmeter, connect negative lead to pin No. 14 (circuit No. 432) at control module connector and positive lead to pin No. 17 (circuit No. 423). Read voltage.

2) If more than 1.5 volts, repair open in circuit No. 423 between control module and sensor. Connect sensor and perform SELF-TEST. If less than 1.5 volts, sensor is good. Go to C45.

C45 (Checking Left Front Sensor "B" Circuit) – **1)** Unplug control module. Using volt/ohmmeter, connect negative lead to pin No. 1 (circuit No. 430) at control module connector and positive lead to pin No. 17 (circuit No. 423) at control module connector. Read resistance.

2) If more than 1000 ohms, replace control module. Connect sensor and perform SELF-TEST. If less than 1000 ohms, repair short in circuit No. 423 between control module and sensor. Connect sensor and perform SELF-TEST.

TEST D (REAR SUSPENSION)

NOTE: Use soapy water solution to check for air leaks.

D1 – If compressor did NOT cycle during SELF-TEST No. 4, go to G1. If compressor did cycle, go to D2.

D2 – If right rear solenoid did NOT cycle during SELF-TEST No. 8, go to D12. If right rear solenoid did cycle, go to D3.

D3 – If left rear solenoid did NOT cycle during SELF-TEST No. 9, go to D23. If left rear solenoid did cycle, go to D4.

D4 – If vent solenoid did NOT cycle during SELF-TEST No. 5, go to H1. If vent solenoid did cycle, go to D5.

D5 (Checking Compressor) – **1)** Perform SELF-TEST A2 and A3. Disconnect all air lines at compressor. Plug 3 of the 4 air line fittings at compressor. Using a 0-150 psi (0-1034 kPa) pressure gauge, connect gauge to remaining open fitting on air compressor. Open and close door and observe pressure gauge.

2) If pressure is more than 120 psi (827 kPa), compressor is good. Go to D6. If pressure is less than 120 psi (827 kPa), replace compressor. Connect all air lines and repeat SELF-TEST.

D6 (Checking Rear Sensor Connection) – Check rear sensor, ball studs and bracket for secure mechanical connection. If all fittings are tight, go to D7. If all fittings are not tight, tighten as necessary and repeat SELF-TEST.

D7 (Checking Rear Air System) – **1)** Disconnect air lines going to rear suspension at compressor. Repeat SELF-TEST A2 and A3. Open and close door and verify that air is escaping from air lines.

2) If air is escaping from both air lines, go to D8. If air is not escaping from one rear air line, go to D10. If air is not escaping from either air line because of no air in air springs, go to D8.

D8 – If vehicle failed SELF-TEST A2 and A3, go to D9. If vehicle passed both tests, locate and repair air leaks in either spring or solenoid assembly.

D9 – If rear of vehicle is at rebound (high), replace compressor assembly and repeat SELF-TEST. If vehicle is not at rebound, check all air lines and fittings. Repair air leaks and repeat SELF-TEST.

D10 (Checking Air Restrictions At Rear Solenoids) – **1)** Connect air lines at compressor and remove air line from suspected rear solenoid. Open and close door and verify that air is escaping from suspected rear air spring.

2) If air is not escaping from rear solenoid air line, go to D11. If air is escaping from solenoid, repair leak and repeat SELF-TEST.

D11 – Check suspected air spring solenoid. If there are no air leaks, replace solenoid. Repeat SELF-TEST. If leaks are found, repair or replace as necessary and repeat SELF-TEST.

1989 ELECTRONIC SUSPENSION
Ford Motor Co. Air Suspension – Mark VII (Cont.)

12-101

TEST D (Cont.)

D12 (Cycle Right Rear Solenoid) – Perform SELF-TEST A2 and A3. Open and close door until warning light blinks TEST No. 8, then go to D13.

D13 (Checking Right Rear Solenoid Circuit) – 1) Using test light, connect one lead to solenoid circuit No. 416 (Light Blue/Black wire) at right rear solenoid connector and other lead to battery circuit No. 175 (Black/Yellow wire) at right rear solenoid connector.

2) If test light is blinking, replace right rear solenoid solenoid and repeat SELF-TEST. If test light is on, go to D21. If test light is off, go to D14.

D14 (Checking Connector Polarity) – Move test lead to pin No. 2 at right rear solenoid connector. Connect other test lead to ground. If test light is on, go to D17. If test light is off, go to D15.

D15 (Checking Connector Polarity) – Connect test lead to pin No. 1 on right rear solenoid connector. Connect other lead to ground. If light is off, go to D17. If light is on, repair crossed wires in solenoid connector and go to D16.

D16 (Checking Battery Circuit) – Move test lead connected to circuit No. 416 (Light Blue/Black wire) at right rear solenoid to ground. If test light is on, battery circuit is good. Go to D17. If light is off, repair open in circuit No. 175 (Black/Yellow wire) between right rear solenoid and fuse link. Repeat SELF-TEST.

D17 (Checking Control Module) – 1) Using test light, connect one lead to pin No. 10 (circuit No. 416) at control module connector and other lead to pin No. 20 (circuit No. 418) at control module connector. Do not disconnect control module connector.

2) If test light is blinking, repair open in circuit No. 416 between control module and right rear solenoid. Repeat SELF-TEST. If test light is off, go to D18.

D18 – If warning light is blinking TEST No. 8, go to D19. If light is off, go to D12.

D19 (Checking Control Module Connector Pins) – Disconnect control module connector and inspect pins. If pins are good. Go to D20. If pins are bad, repair and repeat SELF-TEST.

D20 (Checking Right Rear Solenoid) – 1) Using volt/ohmmeter, connect negative lead to pin No. 1 at right rear solenoid connector and positive lead to pin No. 2 of right rear solenoid connector. Read resistance.

2) If more than 13 ohms, replace control module unit and repeat SELF-TEST. If less than 13 ohms, replace solenoid and control module unit. Repeat SELF-TEST.

D21 – If warning light is blinking TEST No. 8, go to D22. If not, go to D12.

D22 (Checking Right Rear Solenoid Circuit) – Unplug control module connector. If test light is on, repair short in circuit No. 416 (Light Blue/Black wire) between control module and solenoid. Repeat SELF-TEST. If test light is off, replace control module and repeat SELF-TEST.

D23 (Cycle Left Rear Solenoid) – Perform SELF-TEST A2 and A3. Open and close door until warning light blinks TEST No. 9, go to D24.

D24 (Checking Left Rear Solenoid Circuit) – 1) Using test light, connect one lead to circuit No. 429 (Pink/Light Green wire) at left rear solenoid connector and other lead to battery circuit No. 175 (Black/Yellow wire) at left rear solenoid connector.

2) If test light is blinking, replace solenoid and repeat SELF-TEST. If test light is off, go to D25. If test light is on, go to D32.

D25 (Checking Connector Polarity) – Connect test lead to connector pin No. 2 at left rear solenoid. Connect other lead to ground. If test light is on, go to D28. If test light is off, go to D26.

D26 – Connect test lead to pin No. 1 at left rear solenoid. Connect other lead to ground. If test light is off, go to D28. If test light is on, repair crossed wires in solenoid connector and go to D27.

D27 (Checking Battery Circuit) – Move test lead connected to circuit No. 429 (Pink/Light Green wire) to ground. If test light is on, battery circuit is good. Go to D28. If test light is off, repair short or open in circuit No. 418 (Dark Green/Yellow wire) between air suspension switch and right rear solenoid. Repeat SELF-TEST.

D28 (Checking Control Module) – Using test light, connect one lead to pin No. 9 (circuit No. 429) at control module connector and other lead to pin No. 20 (circuit No. 418). Do not unplug control module connector. If test light is blinking, repair short in circuit No. 429 (Pink/Light Green wire) between control module and left rear solenoid. Repeat SELF-TEST. If test light is off, go to D29.

TEST D (Cont.)

D29 – If warning light is blinking TEST No. 9, go to D30. If warning light is off, go to D23.

D30 (Checking Control Module Connector Pins) – If pins are good, go to D31. If pins are bad, repair as necessary and repeat SELF-TEST.

D31 (Checking Left Rear Solenoid) – 1) Using volt/ohmmeter, connect negative lead to pin No. 1 at left rear solenoid connector. Connect positive lead to pin No. 2 at left rear solenoid connector. Read resistance.

2) If more than 13 ohms, replace control module unit and repeat SELF-TEST. If less than 13 ohms, replace solenoid and control module unit. Repeat SELF-TEST.

D32 – If warning light is blinking TEST No. 9, go to D33. If warning light is off, go to D23.

D33 (Checking Left Rear Solenoid Circuit) – Unplug control module connector. If test light is on, repair short to circuit No. 429 between control module connector and left rear solenoid. Repeat SELF-TEST. If light is off, replace control module and repeat SELF-TEST.

TEST E (RIGHT FRONT)

E1 – Did vehicle pass SELF-TEST No. 1. If so, go E2. If not, go to D1.

E2 – If right front solenoid passed SELF-TEST No. 7, go to E3. If system did not pass, go to E4. If system passes air but did not click, go to E16.

E3 (Checking Right Front Sensor) – Check sensor and ball studs for a tight mechanical connection. If connections are tight, go to E6. If loose, tighten and repeat SELF-TEST.

E4 (Checking Right Front Solenoid Circuit) – 1) Perform SELF-TEST A2 and A3. Open and close door until warning light blinks TEST No. 7. Using test light, connect one lead to circuit No. 414 (Orange/Red wire) at solenoid connector and other lead to battery circuit No. 175 (Black/Yellow wire) at solenoid connector.

2) If test light blinks, system is good. Go to E5. If test light is off, go to E7. If test light is on, go to E14.

E5 (Checking Restricted Right Front Air Line) – Perform SELF-TEST A2 and A3. Right front of vehicle will drop during this test. Disconnect air lines at air spring solenoid. Open and close door twice and verify that air is escaping from spring solenoid line. If air is escaping, repair air line as necessary and repeat SELF-TEST. If air is not escaping, go to E6.

E6 (Checking For Solenoid Or Air Spring Leaks) – Connect air lines and perform SELF-TEST A2 and A3. Open and close door twice and verify that air is not leaking from air spring or solenoid. If air is not leaking, repair or replace air spring solenoid due to obstruction. If air is leaking, repair or replace leaky spring or solenoid. Repeat SELF-TEST.

E7 (Checking Connector Polarity) – Connect test light to right front solenoid connector pin No. 2 and ground. If test light is on, go to E10. If test light is off, go to E8.

E8 – Connect test light to the solenoid connector pin No. 1 and ground. If test light is off, go to E10. If test light is on, repair crossed wires in solenoid connector and go to E9.

E9 (Checking Battery Circuit) – Move test lead from solenoid circuit No. 414 (Orange/Red wire) to ground. If test light is on, battery circuit is good. Go to E10. If test light is off, repair open or short in battery circuit No. 175 (Light Green/Orange wire) between battery and solenoid. Repeat SELF-TEST.

E10 (Checking Control Module) – Using test light, connect one lead to pin No. 12 at control module connector and other lead to pin No. 20. Do not unplug control module connector. If test light is blinking, repair open in circuit No. 414 (Orange/Red wire) between control module and right front solenoid. Repeat SELF-TEST. If test light is off, go to E11.

E11 – If warning light is blinking TEST No. 7, go to E12. If test light is not blinking, go to E4.

E12 (Checking Control Module Unit) – Unplug control module connector and inspect pins. If pins are good, go to E13. If pins are bad, repair as necessary and repeat SELF-TEST.

12-102

1989 ELECTRONIC SUSPENSION
Ford Motor Co. Air Suspension – Mark VII (Cont.)

TEST E (Cont.)

E13 (Checking Right Front Solenoid) – 1) Unplug solenoid connector. Using volt/ohmmeter, connect negative test lead to pin No. 1 at solenoid connector and positive test lead to pin No. 2. Read resistance.

2) If more than 13 ohms, replace control module unit and repeat SELF-TEST. If less than 13 ohms, replace solenoid and control module unit and repeat SELF-TEST.

E14 – If warning light blinks TEST No. 7, go to E15. If not, go to E4.

E15 – Unplug control module connector, leaving test light connected between circuits No. 414 and No. 175. If test light is on, repair short to ground in circuit No. 414 between control module connector and right front solenoid and repeat SELF-TEST. If test light is off, replace control module unit and repeat SELF-TEST.

E16 – Unplug right front solenoid connector. Connect one test light lead to circuit No. 414 on harness side of connector. Connect other lead to battery circuit No. 175 on harness side of connector. If test light is on, repair short to ground in circuit No. 414 between control module connector and solenoid. Repeat SELF-TEST. If test light is off, replace solenoid. Repeat SELF-TEST.

TEST F (LEFT FRONT)

F1 – If vehicle passed SELF-TEST No. 1, go to F2. If vehicle did not pass test, go to D1.

F2 – If left front solenoid passed SELF-TEST No. 6, go to F3. If solenoid did not pass air, go to F4. If solenoid passes air but does not click, go to F16.

F3 (Checking Left Front Sensor) – Check sensor and ball stud for tight mechanical connection. If loose, tighten sensor and repeat SELF-TEST. If sensor is good, go to F6.

F4 (Checking Left Front Solenoid Circuit) – 1) Perform SELF-TEST A2 and A3. Open and close door until warning light blinks TEST No. 6. Using test light, connect one lead to solenoid circuit No. 415 (Light Green/Orange wire) at left front solenoid connector and other lead to battery circuit No. 175 (Black/Yellow wire) at left front solenoid connector.

2) If test light is blinking, system is good. Go to F5. If test light is off, go to F7. If test light is on, go to F14.

F5 (Checking for Restrictions In Left Front Air Line) – 1) Perform SELF-TEST A2 and A3. Left front of vehicle will drop during this test. Disconnect air lines at left front air spring solenoid. Open and close door 3 times and verify that air is escaping spring solenoid.

2) If air is escaping from solenoid, repair air lines as necessary. Reconnect air lines and repeat SELF-TEST. If air is not escaping, go to F6.

F6 (Checking For Solenoid Or Air Spring Leaks) – 1) Connect air lines. Perform SELF-TEST A2 and A3. Open and close door 3 times and verify that air is not leaking from left front spring or solenoid.

2) If air is not leaking, repair or replace air spring solenoid due to obstruction. Repeat SELF-TEST. If air is leaking, repair or replace air spring or solenoid and repeat SELF-TEST.

F7 (Checking For Connector Polarity) – Connect test light lead to pin No. 2 at left front solenoid connector. Connect other test lead to ground. If test light is on, go to F10. If test light is off, go to F8.

F8 (Checking For Connector Polarity) – Connect test light lead to right front solenoid connector pin No. 1. Connect other test lead to ground. If test light is off, go to F10. If test light is on, repair or service crossed wires at solenoid connector and go to F9.

F9 (Checking Battery Circuit) – Move test lead from left front solenoid circuit No. 415 (Light Green/Orange) to ground. If test light is on, battery circuit is good. Go to F10. If light is off, repair short or open in circuit No. 175 (Black/Yellow) between the battery and solenoid. Repeat SELF-TEST.

F10 (Checking Control Module) – 1) Do not unplug control module connector. Using test light, connect one lead to pin No. 11 (circuit No. 415) at control module connector and the other lead to control pin No. 20 (circuit No. 418).

2) If test light is blinking, repair open in circuit No. 415 between control module and left front solenoid. Repeat SELF-TEST. If test light is off, go to F11.

F11 – If warning light is blinking TEST No. 6, go to F12. If not, go to F4.

TEST F (Cont.)

F12 – Unplug control module connector and inspect pins. If pins are good, go to F13. If pins are bad, repair as necessary and repeat SELF-TEST.

F13 – 1) Check left front solenoid. Unplug left front solenoid connector. Using a volt/ohmmeter, connect negative lead to pin No. 1 at left front solenoid connector and positive lead to pin No. 2 at left front solenoid connector.

2) Read resistance. If more than 13 ohms, replace control module and repeat SELF-TEST. If less than 13 ohms, replace left front solenoid and control module. Repeat SELF-TEST.

F14 – If warning light is blinking TEST No. 6, go to F15. If not, go to F4.

F15 – Unplug control module connector and leave test light connected to circuits No. 415 and No. 175. If test light is on, repair short in circuit No. 415 between control module connector and left front solenoid. Repeat SELF-TEST. If test light is off, replace control module and repeat SELF-TEST.

F16 – Unplug left front solenoid connector. Using test light, connect one lead to circuit No. 415 on harness side of connector and connect other lead to circuit No. 175 on harness side. If test light is on, repair short to ground in circuit No. 415 and repeat SELF-TEST. If test light is off, replace solenoid and repeat SELF-TEST.

TEST G (AIR SPRING FILL)

G1 (Checking Compressor Relay) – Perform SELF-TEST A2 and A3. Open and close door until warning light blinks TEST No. 4. Rear of vehicle may raise during this test. Compressor will cycle 50 times during TEST No. 4 (about 3 minutes) then shut off and will not restart until TEST No. 4 is reentered. If relay is cycling, go to G2. If relay is not cycling, go to G5.

G2 (Checking Compressor Circuit) – 1) Unplug compressor connector. Using test light, connect one lead to circuit No. 417 (Pink/Orange wire) at harness side of compressor connector. Connect other lead to ground.

2) If test light is blinking, compressor circuit is good. Go to G3. If test light is on, replace compressor relay and perform SELF-TEST. If test light is off, go to G4.

G3 (Checking Compressor Ground Circuit) – Move ground lead of test light to circuit No. 430 (Gray wire) at harness side of compressor connector. If light is blinking, install new compressor and perform SELF-TEST. If test light is off, repair open in circuit No. 430 between compressor and battery. Perform SELF-TEST.

G4 (Checking Compressor Circuit) – 1) Plug in compressor connector and repeat G1. Using test light, connect one lead to circuit No. 417 (Pink/Orange wire) at compressor relay. Connect other lead to ground.

2) If test light is blinking, repair open or short to ground in circuit No. 417 between compressor and compressor relay. Perform SELF-TEST. If test light is off, replace compressor relay and perform SELF-TEST.

G5 (Checking Compressor Relay Circuit) – Using test light, connect one lead to compressor relay circuit No. 420 (Dark Blue/Yellow wire) at relay and connect other lead to positive side of battery. If test light blinks, module relay circuit is good. Go to G6. If test light is on, go to G8. If test light is off, go to G9.

G6 (Checking Jumper Circuit) – Using test light, connect one lead of jumper to pin No. 2 (circuit No. 175A) at compressor relay. Connect other lead to ground. If test light is on, replace compressor relay and perform SELF-TEST. If test light is off, go to G7.

G7 (Checking Battery Circuit) – Using test light, connect one lead to pin No. 3 (circuit No. 175) at compressor relay and other lead to ground. If test light is on, repair short or open in circuit No. 175A and perform SELF-TEST. If test light is off, repair short or open in circuit No. 175 between relay and battery. Perform SELF-TEST.

G8 (Checking Control Module Unit) – Unplug control module connector. If test light is on, repair short to ground in circuit No. 420 (Dark Blue/Yellow wire) at compressor relay. Perform SELF-TEST. If test light is off, replace control module unit and perform SELF-TEST.

G9 (Checking Compressor Relay) – 1) Unplug compressor relay. Using volt/ohmmeter, connect negative lead to pin No. 2 at compressor relay connector. Connect other lead to pin No. 1 at compressor relay connector. Read resistance.

1989 ELECTRONIC SUSPENSION
Ford Motor Co. Air Suspension — Mark VII (Cont.)

12-103

TEST G (Cont.)

2) If more than 54 ohms, compressor relay is good. Go to G10. If less than 54 ohms, replace compressor relay and perform SELF-TEST.

NOTE: This failure may have damaged control module.

G10 (Checking Control Module) – 1) Perform G1. Do not unplug control module connector. Using test light, connect one lead to pin No. 22 (circuit No. 420) at control module connector and the other lead to pin No. 20 (circuit No. 418).

2) If test light is blinking, repair short in circuit No. 420 between compressor relay and control module. Perform SELF-TEST. If test light is off, replace control module unit. Perform SELF-TEST.

TEST H (VENT SYSTEM)

H1 (Checking Vent Solenoid Circuit) – 1) Perform SELF-TEST A2 and A3. Open and close door until warning light blinks TEST No. 5. Unplug air compressor connector. Using test light, connect one lead to pin No. 4 (circuit No. 421) at harness side of connector. Connect other lead to pin No. 1 (circuit No. 175) at harness side of connector.

2) If test light blinks, replace compressor assembly and perform SELF-TEST. If test light is off, go to H3. If test light is on, go to H2.

H2 (Checking Control Module) – Unplug control module connector. If test light is on, repair short in vent solenoid circuit No. 421 (Pink wire) between compressor and control module. Perform SELF-TEST. If test light is off, replace control module and perform SELF-TEST.

H3 (Checking Battery Circuit) – Move test light lead at vent solenoid circuit No. 421 (Pink wire) to ground. If test light is on, battery circuit is good. Go to H4. If test light is off, repair short or open in circuit No. 175 between vent solenoid and battery. Perform SELF-TEST.

H4 (Checking Control Module) – 1) Do not unplug control module connector. Using test light, connect one lead to pin No. 23 (circuit No. 421) at control module connector and other lead to pin No. 20 (circuit No. 418).

2) If test light is blinking, repair open in circuit No. 421 between control module and compressor relay. If test light is off, go to H5.

H5 (Checking Warning Light) – If warning light blinks TEST No. 5, go to H6. If not, go to H1.

H6 (Checking Vent Solenoid) – 1) Unplug connector at compressor. Using volt/ohmmeter, connect negative lead to pin No. 4 at compressor assembly and positive lead to pin No. 1 at compressor assembly. Read resistance.

2) If more than 27 ohms, replace control module and perform SELF-TEST. If less than 27 ohms, replace compressor unit and control module. Perform SELF-TEST.

TIGHTENING SPECIFICATIONS

Application	Ft. Lbs. (N.m)
Front Suspension	
Ball Joint-to-Spindle Nut	100-120 (136-163)
Lower Arm-to-Crossmember Nut	110-150 (149-203)
Sensor Upper Attachment-to-Frame Nut	26-34 (35-46)
Shock Strut-to-Upper Mount Nut	55-92 (75-125)
Shock Strut Upper Mount-to-Body Nut	62-75 (84-102)
Spindle-to-Shock Strut Nut	140-200 (190-271)
Stabilizer Bar Mounting Clamp-to-Bracket Bolt	40-55 (54-74)
Steering Gear-to-Crossmember Nut	90-100 (122-136)
Tie Rod End-to-Spindle Nut	35-47 (47-64)
Rear Suspension	
Air Spring-to-Lower Arm Bolt	25-35 (34-47)
Lower Arm-to-Axle Bolt	90-100 (122-136)
Lower Arm-to-Frame Bolt	80-105 (108-142)
Shock Absorber-to-Frame Nut	17-27 (23-37)
Stabilizer Bar-to-Axle Bolt	13-20 (18-27)
Stabilizer Bar-to-Body Nut	13-18 (18-24)
Upper Arm-to-Frame Bolt	80-105 (108-142)
Upper Arm-to-Axle Bolt	70-100 (95-136)

Application	INCH Lbs. (N.m)
Front Suspension	
Air Compressor-to-Bracket Bolt	27-44 (3-5)
Sensor Attachment-to-Lower Arm	96-144 (10-16)
Stabilizer Bar-to-Lower Arm Nut	106-144 (12-16)
Rear Suspension	
Sensor Lower Bracket-to-Arm Nut	84-120 (9-14)
Sensor Upper Bracket-to-Frame Bolt	106-150 (12-17)

12-104

1989 ELECTRONIC SUSPENSION
Ford Motor Co. Air Suspension – Mark VII (Cont.)

REMOVAL & INSTALLATION

AIR SPRING FILL PROCEDURE

NOTE: This routine is used only to add air to front or rear air springs. Do not perform this routine unless a mechanical problem is verified as a cause of air loss (hole in spring, defective solenoid, etc.) and leak has been corrected.

1) Raise vehicle as previously outlined. Do not apply a load to suspension. Disconnect ground from diagnostic pigtail and turn air suspension switch to "ON" position. *See Fig. 7.*

2) Install battery charger to reduce drain. Open driver's door. Turn ignition switch to "RUN" position. Hold in "RUN" position for 5 seconds, then turn ignition off.

3) Connect jumper lead between diagnostic pigtail and ground. Leave in grounded position during the entire filling procedure. Apply brake pedal and turn ignition switch to "RUN" position. Leave driver's door open. Warning light will blink continuously every 2 seconds indicating spring fill sequence has been entered.

4) To fill rear springs, close and open door once. After 6 seconds, rear springs will fill for 60 seconds. To fill front springs, close and open door twice. To fill front and rear springs, wait until rear springs are finished, then close and open door once.

5) After completion of air spring fill sequence, turn air suspension switch to "OFF" position. Inspect all air springs for proper inflation. Remove ground from pigtail. Any further leveling will done automatically when vehicle is on the ground, if the air suspension is on.

AIR SPRING SOLENOID

NOTE: Follow all precautions as previously outlined.

Removal – 1) Turn air suspension switch to "OFF" position. *See Fig. 7.* Raise vehicle as previously outlined. With suspension at full rebound, remove wheel and tire assembly. Unplug electrical connector. Remove air line.

2) The air spring solenoid has a 2-stage pressure relief fitting. First remove clip and rotate solenoid counterclockwise to first stop. Slowly pull solenoid straight out and release air out of air spring.

3) After air is fully bled from air spring, rotate solenoid to third stop. Remove solenoid from spring. Remove "O" ring from solenoid housing.

Installation – 1) Check "O" rings for cuts or abrasions. Replace as necessary. Lubricate "O" rings with silicone dielectric. Install "O" ring into housing. Insert solenoid into end cap and rotate clockwise to third stop. Push solenoid in until it reaches second stop, then rotate clockwise to first stop.

2) Install solenoid clip. Inspect wiring harness connector and ensure rubber gasket is in place at bottom of connector cavity. Connect air line and electrical connector. Refill air springs. Install wheel and tire assembly.

AIR SPRING

NOTE: If any air springs are found to be improperly folded while in service on vehicle, replace unit. Properly folded springs will have NO creases or folds on surface.

Removal (Front & Rear) – 1) Turn air suspension switch to "OFF" position. *See Fig. 7.* Raise vehicle as previously outlined. With suspension at full rebound, remove wheel and tire assembly. Remove air solenoid, as previously described.

2) Remove spring clips for front or bolts for rear. Push down spring clip on collar of air spring and rotate counterclockwise to release spring from body spring seat. Remove spring.

CAUTION: To prevent air spring failure during use, the following precautions must be followed.

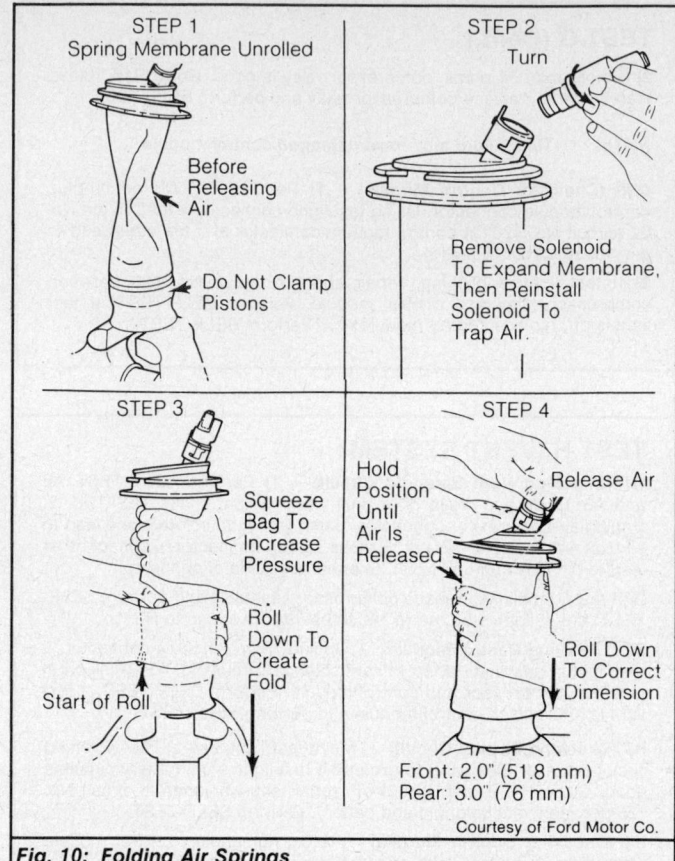

Fig. 10: Folding Air Springs

Installation Precautions – 1) DO NOT install or inflate any air spring that is unfolded. *See Fig. 10.*

2) Any unfolded spring must be refolded before being installed in vehicle. DO NOT try to refold air springs which were previously installed on vehicle and not folded correctly.

3) When installing a NEW air spring, do not apply load to suspension until springs have been inflated using AIR SPRING FILL PROCEDURE. When replacing front air springs, front height sensors must be inspected. Replace sensors if defective.

4) After air spring has been inflated in proper position, inspect it for correct shape. *See Fig. 11.*

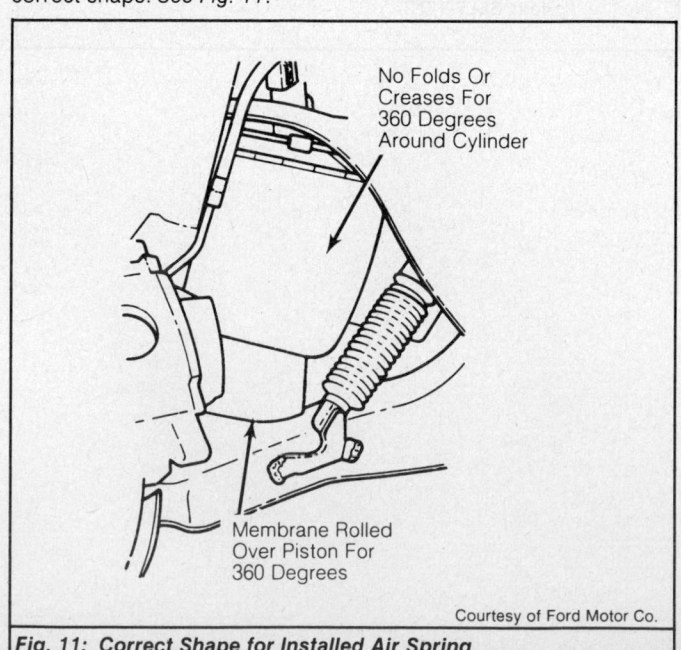

Fig. 11: Correct Shape for Installed Air Spring

1989 ELECTRONIC SUSPENSION
Ford Motor Co. Air Suspension — Mark VII (Cont.)

12-105

Installation – 1) Install air spring solenoid as previously described. Ensure air spring seats are installed properly. *See Fig. 12.* Install air spring into body spring seat, being careful not to damage solenoid or electrical connections

2) Rotate air spring collar until spring snaps into place. Ensure collar is retained by 3 roll tabs on body spring seat. Attach air line and electrical connector to solenoid.

3) With suspension at full rebound and supported by shock absorbers, align and secure lower arm to spring attachment.

CAUTION: To prevent spring damage, do not allow vehicle suspension to compress before air springs are filled.

4) Replace wheel. Lower vehicle to 3" above floor. Refill springs as previously outlined.

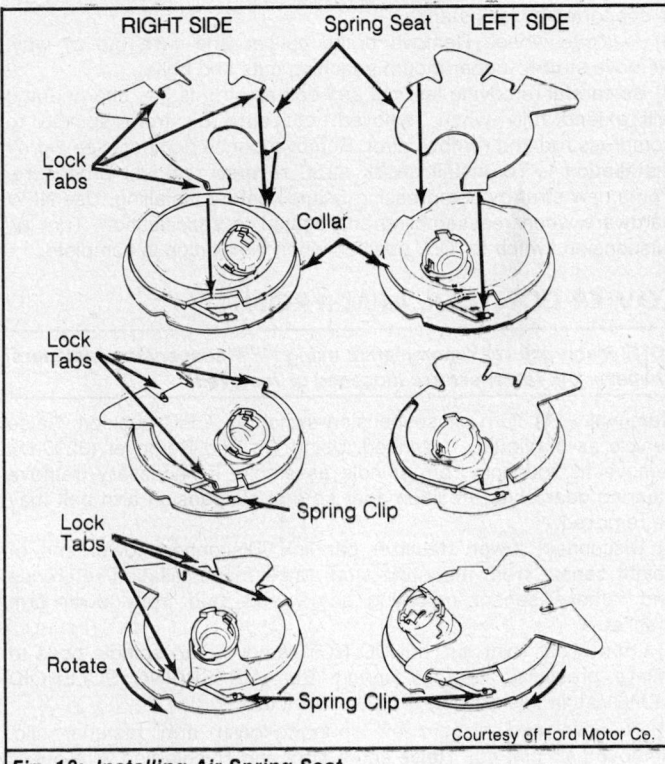

Fig. 12: Installing Air Spring Seat

Courtesy of Ford Motor Co.

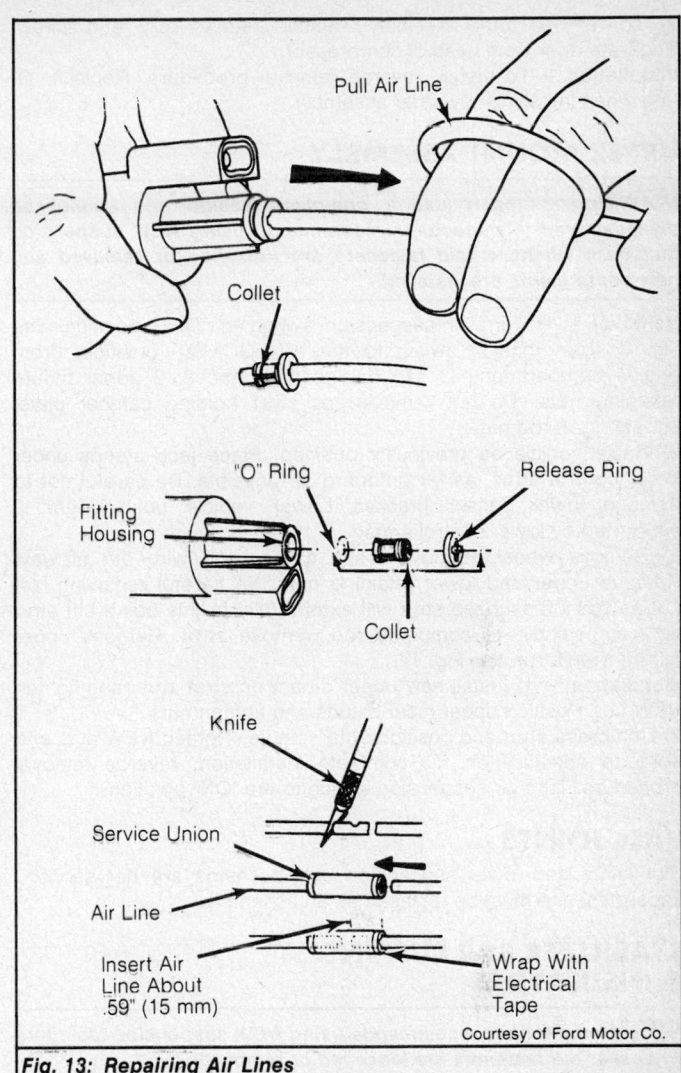

Fig. 13: Repairing Air Lines

Courtesy of Ford Motor Co.

AIR LINES

Removal & Installation – 1) Air lines on air spring solenoids and compressor dryer are disconnected by pushing in plastic release ring where line meets quick connect fitting. Pull out air line while holding release ring. Install air line by pushing in tubing until flare on line is against release ring.

2) Quick connect fittings can be removed by disconnecting air line. Insert length of scrap air line into collet. *See Fig. 13.* Pull collet out by HAND. Remove "O" rings.

3) Clean "O" ring seat. Lightly coat "O" rings with silicone dielectric grease. Install new collet (prongs first) with finger pressure. Install release ring and line.

Repair – Service kits are available to repair damaged air lines. Sections of air line may be cut out and union installed. *See Fig. 13.*

HEIGHT SENSOR

Removal (Front & Rear) – 1) Turn suspension switch to "OFF" position. *See Fig. 7.* Unplug electrical connector located in engine compartment behind shock tower. Push connector through access hole in shock tower.

2) For rear sensor, electrical connector is located in the luggage compartment in front of forward trim panel. Pull luggage compartment carpet back for access to sensor sealing grommet located on floor pan.

3) Raise vehicle as previously outlined until suspension is at full rebound. Detach top and bottom of sensor from attaching studs by gently pulling back on spring clip.

4) Disconnect sensor wiring harness from plastic clips on shock tower and remove sensor. For rear sensor, push upward on sealing grommet to unseat sensor. Push sensor through floor pan hole into luggage compartment.

Installation – To install, reverse removal procedure. Turn air suspension switch to "ON" position after installation.

ELECTRONIC CONTROL MODULE

Removal & Installation – Turn air suspension and ignition switches to the "OFF" position. *See Fig. 7.* Remove left luggage compartment trim panel and disconnect harness connector. Remove 3 attaching nuts and remove unit. To install, reverse removal procedure.

COMPRESSOR RELAY

Removal & Installation – Unplug electrical connector. Remove relay retaining screw at left front shock tower. Remove relay. To install, reverse removal procedure.

AIR COMPRESSOR & DRIER ASSEMBLY

Removal – 1) Turn air suspension switch to "OFF" position. *See Fig. 7.* Unplug electrical connection at compressor. Remove air line protector cap from drier by releasing 2 latching pins located at the bottom of cap, 180 degrees apart. Disconnect 4 air lines from drier. Remove 3 compressor bracket retaining screws and compressor.

12-106

1989 ELECTRONIC SUSPENSION
Ford Motor Co. Air Suspension — Mark VII (Cont.)

2) To remove drier assembly, remove retainer clip and screw. Separate drier from head of compressor.

Installation – To install, reverse removal procedure. Replace "O" ring when installing new drier assembly.

UPPER MOUNT ASSEMBLY

NOTE: Upper mounts use a one-piece design and cannot be disassembled. Manufacturer recommends using NEW suspension fasteners whenever old fasteners are loosened or removed and new components are installed.

Removal – **1)** Turn air suspension switch to "OFF" position. *See Fig. 7.* Turn ignition switch to the "UNLOCKED" position. From engine compartment, loosen but do not remove, 3 upper mount retaining nuts. Do not remove pop rivet holding camber plate. Loosen strut rod nut.

2) Raise vehicle as previously outlined. Place jack stands under lower control arms, as far outboard as possible. Be careful not to damage lower sensor bracket. Lower vehicle until weight is supported by lower control arms.

3) Remove wheel. Remove brake caliper and wire out of way. Remove upper and lower retaining nuts. Be careful removing last nut as gas pressurized strut will extend fully at this point. Lift strut up from spindle to compress rod, remove strut. Remove upper mount from strut. *See Fig. 14.*

Installation – **1)** Install new upper mount on strut and hand tighten NEW nut. Position upper mount studs and tighten nuts.

2) Compress strut and position onto spindle. Tighten NEW nuts and bolts to specification. To complete installation, reverse removal procedure. Turn air suspension switch to the "ON" position.

BALL JOINTS

Ball joints and lower suspension arm bushings are not serviced separately and must be replaced as an assembly.

STABILIZER BAR BUSHING & INSULATORS

NOTE: Manufacturer recommends using NEW suspension fasteners whenever old fasteners are loosened or removed.

Removal (Front & Rear) – **1)** Turn air suspension switch to "OFF" position. *See Fig. 7.* Raise vehicle as previously outlined. Remove nut, washer and insulator from end of stabilizer bar link attaching bolts.

2) Remove remaining hardware. Remove adapter brackets and "U" clamps. Cut worn bushings from stabilizer bar. *See Fig. 14.*

Installation – To install bushing, reverse removal procedure. Lubricate bushings and insulators with silicone rubber lubricant. Use NEW nuts and bolt and tighten to specification.

SPINDLE ASSEMBLY

NOTE: Manufacturer recommends using NEW suspension fasteners whenever old fasteners are loosened or removed.

Removal – **1)** Turn air suspension switch to "OFF" position. *See Fig. 7.* Raise vehicle as previously outlined. Remove wheel, brake caliper, rotor and dust shield. Remove stabilizer link from lower arm assembly. Using Tie Rod Remover (3290-D), remove tie rod end from spindle. Remove cotter pin from ball joint stud nut.

2) Loosen but DO NOT remove nut. Tap spindle boss to relieve stud pressure. Place floor jack under lower control arm. Compress air spring and remove stud nut. Remove 2 bolts and nuts attaching spindle to shock strut. Compress shock strut until clearance is obtained. Remove spindle assembly. *See Fig. 14.*

Installation – **1)** Place spindle on ball joint stud. Install NEW stud nut, but DO NOT tighten at this time. Lower shock strut until attaching holes are aligned with holes in spindle. Install 2 bolts and nuts.

2) Tighten ball joint stud nut and install cotter pin. To complete installation, reverse removal procedure. Use NEW nuts and bolts and tighten to specification.

SHOCK STRUT REPLACEMENT

NOTE: Manufacturer recommends using NEW suspension fasteners whenever old fasteners are loosened or removed.

Removal – **1)** Turn air suspension switch to "OFF" position. *See Fig. 7.* Turn ignition to the "UNLOCKED" position. From engine compartment, loosen but do not remove strut-to-upper mount attaching nut. Raise vehicle as previously outlined.

2) Place jack stands as far outboard as possible under control arms, clearing lower sensor mounting brackets. Lower vehicle until weight is supported by jack stands.

3) Remove wheel. Remove brake caliper and wire out of way. Remove strut-to-upper mount attaching nuts and bolts.

4) Be careful removing last nut and bolt as strut is gas charged and will extend fully when removed. Lift strut up from spindle to compress rod and remove strut. Remove jounce bumper. *See Fig. 7.*

Installation – To Install shock strut, reverse removal procedure. Prime new strut by compressing 5 times before installing. Use NEW hardware when reassembling and tighten to specification. Turn air suspension switch to "ON" position when installation is complete.

LOWER CONTROL ARM (FRONT)

NOTE: Manufacturer recommends using NEW suspension fasteners whenever old fasteners are loosened or removed.

Removal – **1)** Turn air suspension switch to "OFF" position. Raise vehicle as previously described. Using Tie Rod Remover (3290-D), remove tie rod end from spindle assembly. If necessary, remove steering gear bolts. Position gear so that suspension arm bolt may be removed.

2) Disconnect lower stabilizer bar link. Disconnect lower end of height sensor from mounting stud. Mark for installation reference and remove sensor mounting screw and stud from lower arm bracket.

3) Loosen ball joint nut, but DO NOT remove. Tap spindle boss to relieve pressure. Vent air spring. See AIR SPRING SOLENOID REMOVAL in this article. Reinstall solenoid.

4) Remove and discard air spring-to-lower arm fastener clip. Remove ball joint nut. Raise entire strut and spindle and wire out of way. Remove suspension arm-to-crossmember nuts and bolts. Remove arm from spindle. *See Fig. 14.*

Installation – **1)** Using new hardware, position arm into crossmember, but do not tighten. Attach ball joint to spindle, but do not tighten. Position air spring and install fastener.

2) Install sensor in original position. Connect lower end of sensor to lower mounting stud. Using floor jack, raise suspension arm to curb height. Tighten lower arm-to-crossmember nut. Tighten ball joint stud nut and install cotter pin. Remove floor jack.

3) If removed, install steering gear bolts. Position tie rod assembly into steering spindle. Tighten nut and install cotter pin. Connect stabilizer bar link to lower suspension and tighten nut

4) Install wheel. Lower vehicle, but do not allow wheels to touch floor. Refill air springs as previously outlined. If necessary, check front wheel alignment.

REAR SHOCK ABSORBERS

CAUTION: Shocks are gas-pressurized and will extend when removed.

Removal – **1)** Turn air suspension switch to "OFF" position. Remove inside trim panels from luggage compartment. Loosen, but do not remove shock rod attaching nut. Raise vehicle as previously outlined. Place jack stands in position and lower vehicle until weight is supported by rear axle.

1989 ELECTRONIC SUSPENSION
Ford Motor Co. Air Suspension — Mark VII (Cont.)

12-107

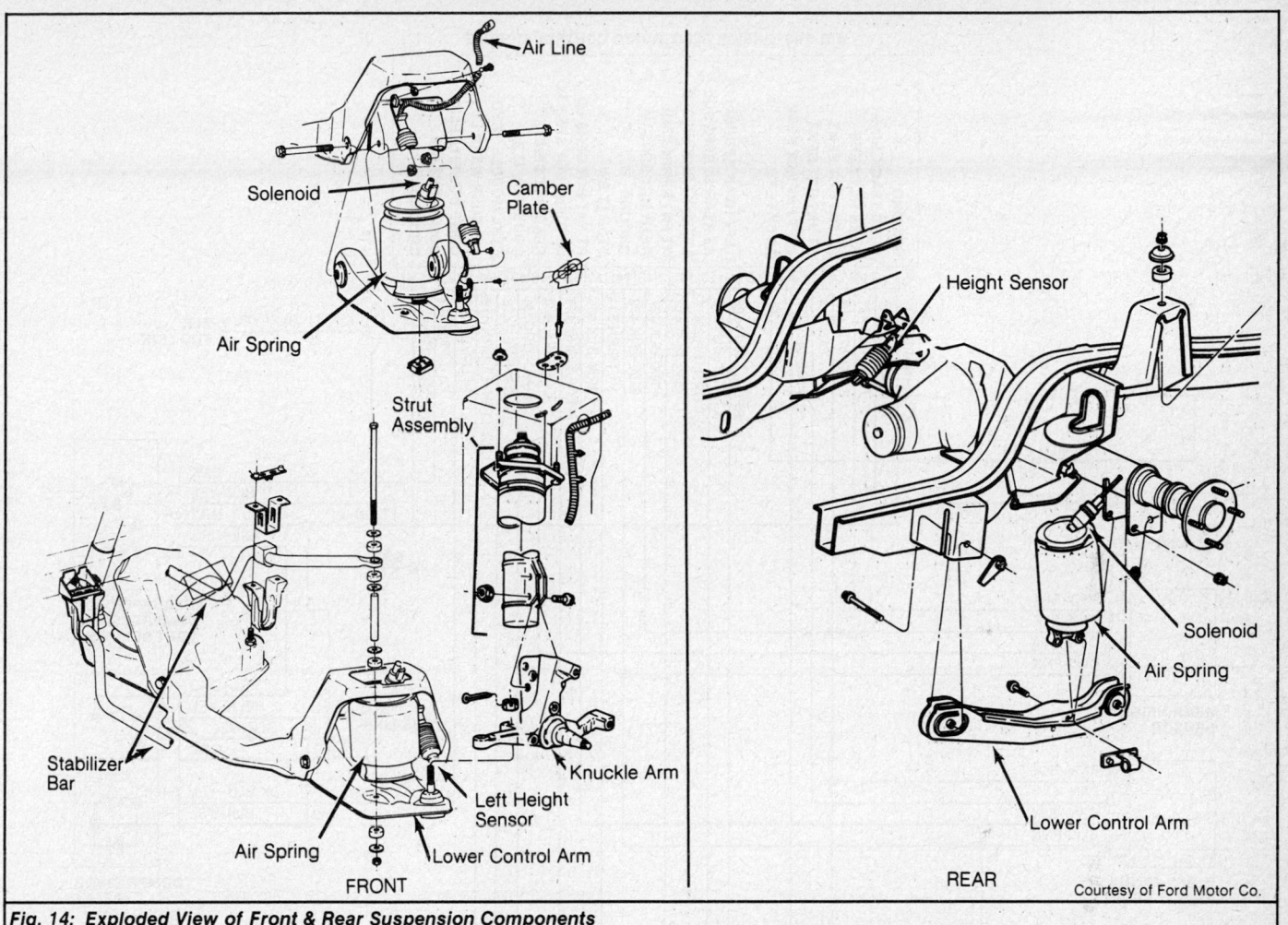

Fig. 14: Exploded View of Front & Rear Suspension Components

2) Remove upper attaching nut, washer and insulator. Remove right lower shock protective cover. Remove lower shock absorber cross bolt and nut. From beneath vehicle, compress shock absorber until clear from hole in upper shock tower.

Installation – To install rear shocks, reverse removal procedure. Prime new shocks by compressing 5 times before installation. Turn air suspension switch to "ON" position after installation is completed.

LOWER CONTROL ARM (REAR)

CAUTION: Replace lower control arm in sets only. Manufacturer recommends using NEW suspension fasteners whenever old fasterners are loosened or removed.

Removal – 1) Turn air suspension switch to "OFF" position. *See Fig. 7.* Raise vehicle until suspension is at full rebound. Remove wheel. Vent air spring. See AIR SPRING SOLENOID in this article.

2) Reinstall solenoid. Remove 2 air spring-to-lower arm bolts. Remove air spring. Remove frame-to-arm bolts. Remove axle-to-arm bolts. Discard all bolts. Remove arm from vehicle. *See Fig. 14.*

Installation – 1) Using new hardware, position lower control arm assembly into front arm brackets. Install NEW arm-to-frame pivot bolt and nut so nut faces outward. Do not tighten at this time.

2) Position rear bushing in axle bracket. Install NEW arm-to-axle pivot bolt and nut with nut facing outward. *See Fig. 14.* Carefully

reinstall air spring. Ensure air spring is folded correctly. See AIR SPRING in this article. Do not tighten bolts at this time.

3) Using floor jack, raise axle to curb height. Tighten all attaching bolts. Replace wheel and lower jack. Using previously outlined air spring fill sequence, fill air springs.

UPPER CONTROL ARM & AXLE BUSHING

NOTE: Upper control arms are replaced in sets only. Manufacturer recommends using NEW suspension fasteners whenever old fasterners are loosened or removed.

Removal – 1) Turn air suspension switch to "OFF" position. *See Fig. 7.* Raise vehicle to full rebound. Detach height sensor from right side arm. Note position of sensor adjustment bracket on upper arm for reinstallation reference.

2) Remove upper arm-to-axle and upper arm-to-frame bolts and nuts. Remove upper arm from vehicle. If necessary, use Remover (T78P-5638-A) to replace axle bushings.

Installation – 1) Place upper arm into frame and into axle. Install NEW bolts and nuts. Do not tighten yet.

2) When attaching right rear height sensor, place adjusting bracket in its original position and tighten bracket. Raise axle to curb height and tighten bolts and nuts.

3) Remove jack stands. Lower vehicle. Turn air suspension switch to "ON" position.

1989 ELECTRONIC SUSPENSION
Ford Motor Co. Air Suspension — Mark VII (Cont.)

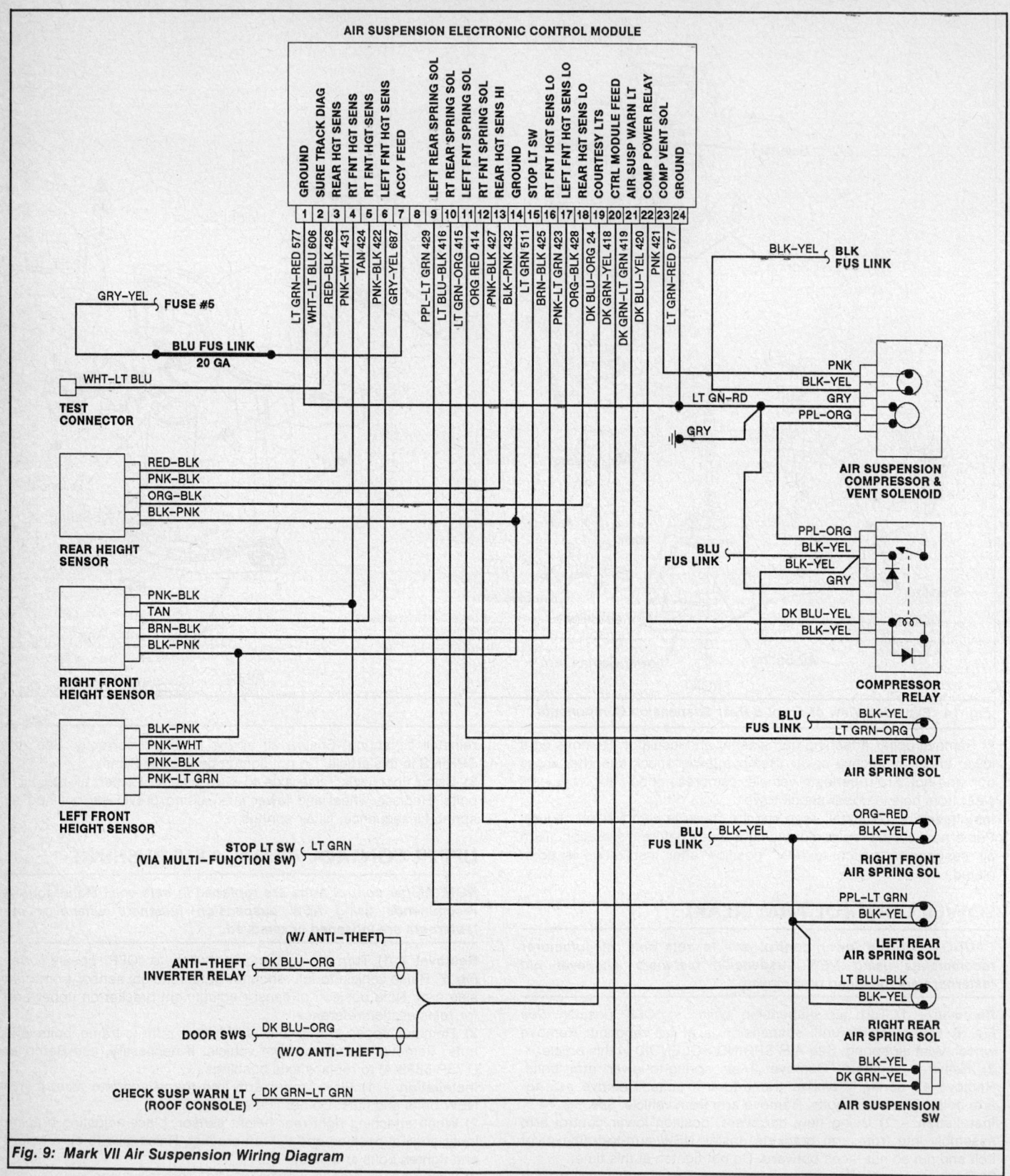

Fig. 9: Mark VII Air Suspension Wiring Diagram

Cougar XR-7, Thunderbird Super Coupe

DESCRIPTION

Automatic Ride Control (ARC) allows driver to select firm (sport) suspension or automatic ride control. The system consists of sensors for brakes, vehicle speed, steering and acceleration which relay information about driving conditions to a control module. See Fig. 1.

Also included is Electronic Variable Orifice (EVO) steering control which is controlled by the same module.

The ARC/EVO computer adjusts vehicle ride from soft to firm during periods of heavy braking, high speed driving, hard cornering, rapid acceleration or super charger boost. The green "FIRM RIDE" light on instrument panel will illuminate when system is in firm condition.

OPERATION

The ARC selector switch is located on center console. When driver selects "FIRM" ride, the control module signals actuators on each shock absorber to adjust to a firm ride. The actuators adjust to a softer ride in "AUTO" mode.

System automatically switches to "FIRM" during severe conditions:

- Brake system pressure of more than 400 psi (2758 kPa).
- Speeds of more than 83 MPH.
- Cornering (lateral acceleration) of more than 0.35g.
- More than 90 percent of full throttle.
- Rapid acceleration or super charger "boost".

The ARC system returns to automatic dampening a few seconds after vehicle speed, braking and cornering return to normal. "FIRM RIDE" light will flash to indicate system malfunction.

The EVO system uses varying current from ARC/EVO module to control fluid pressure to actuator/spool valve. This variable assist is dependent on steering wheel speed of rotation. The system provides full assist at low speed (parking lot maneuvers) and minimal assist at high speeds. This improves "road" feel and directional stability. Full power steering assist returns during evasive maneuvers.

The steering wheel rotation sensor (photo cell) measures wheel rotation and relays information to module for EVO actuator changes. The ARC/EVO control module is located on module packaging tray in trunk behind driver's side of back seat. During system malfunction, the EVO system will provide full power steering assist at all times.

TESTING

TEST EQUIPMENT

To test ARC system, SUPER STAR II (007-00019), STAR (007-00017) or equivalent should be used. A volt-ohmmeter is also required.

See QUICK TESTS & DIAGNOSIS and wiring diagram for diagnostic purposes. See Fig. 6.

REMOVAL & INSTALLATION

ACTUATORS

Removal (Front) – 1) Park vehicle on level surface. Apply parking brake. Turn ignition off. Unplug actuator connector from harness. Pry off plastic cover at screwdriver slot in front.

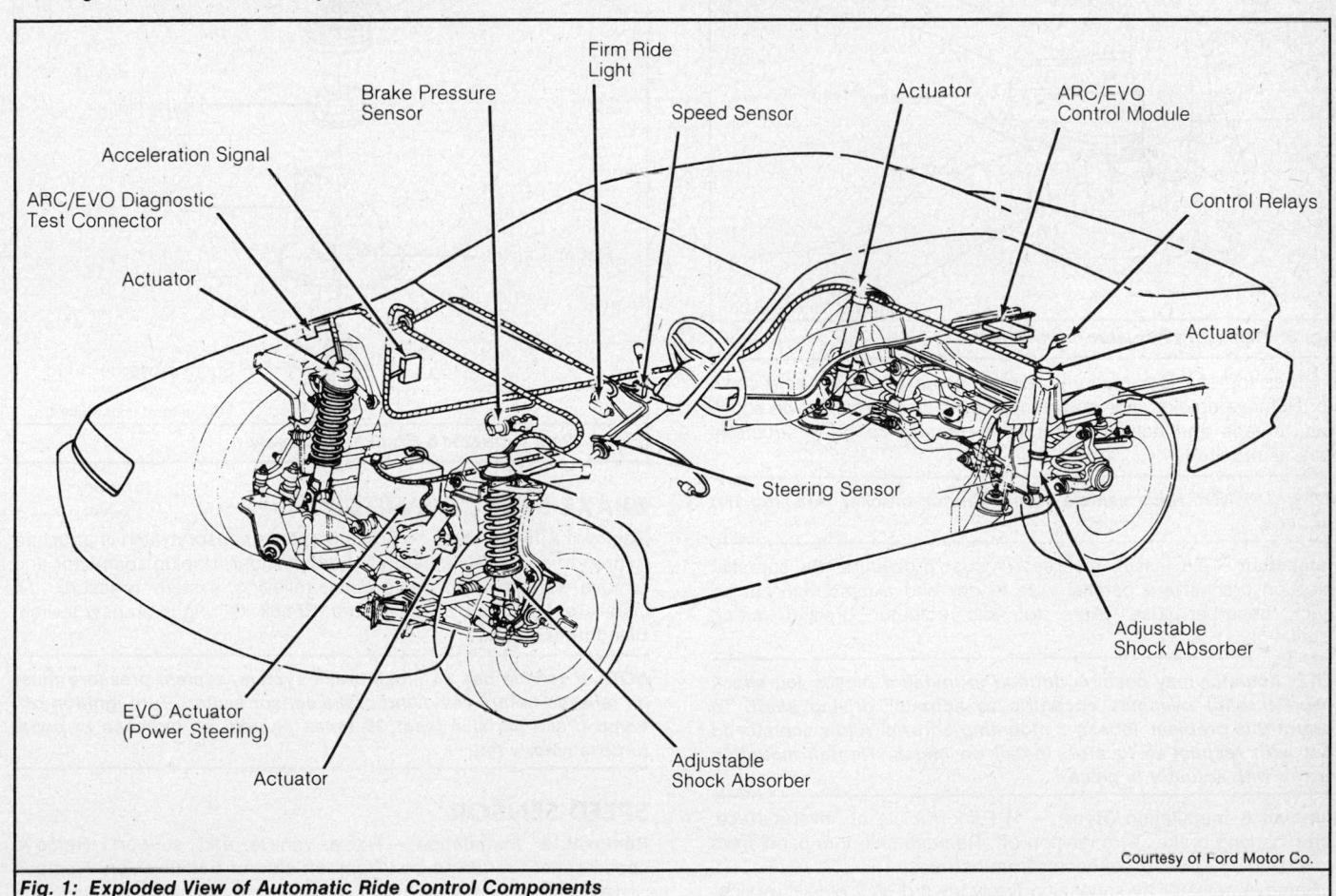

Courtesy of Ford Motor Co.

Fig. 1: Exploded View of Automatic Ride Control Components

1989 ELECTRONIC SUSPENSION
Ford Motor Co. Automatic Ride Control (Cont.)

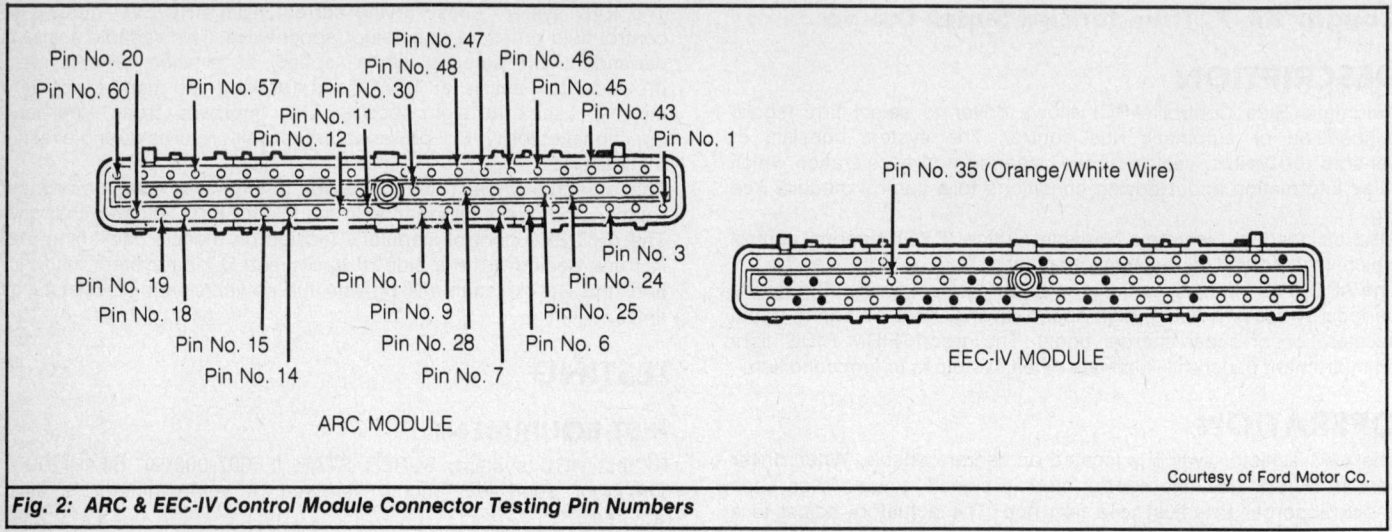

Pin No. 20
Pin No. 60
Pin No. 57
Pin No. 11
Pin No. 12
Pin No. 30
Pin No. 48
Pin No. 47
Pin No. 46
Pin No. 45
Pin No. 43
Pin No. 1

Pin No. 19
Pin No. 18
Pin No. 15
Pin No. 14
Pin No. 10
Pin No. 9
Pin No. 28
Pin No. 7
Pin No. 3
Pin No. 24
Pin No. 25
Pin No. 6

ARC MODULE

Pin No. 35 (Orange/White Wire)

EEC-IV MODULE

Courtesy of Ford Motor Co.

Fig. 2: ARC & EEC-IV Control Module Connector Testing Pin Numbers

2) Remove 2 actuator retaining screws. Remove actuator by squeezing firmly inward on 2 plastic retainer tabs with one hand and lifting with other hand. *See Fig. 3.*

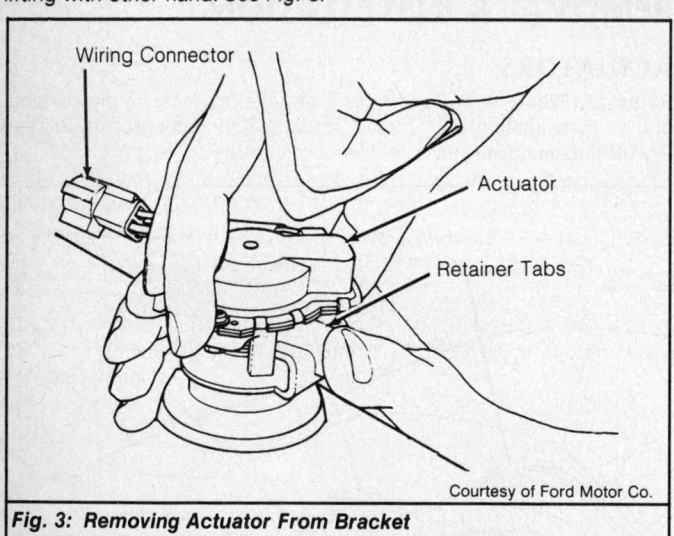

Wiring Connector

Actuator

Retainer Tabs

Courtesy of Ford Motor Co.

Fig. 3: Removing Actuator From Bracket

3) Grasp top of shock stud and remove actuator bracket hold-down nut. Remove bracket. For reassembly, note location of flat on shock stud threads and actuator bracket in relation to body structure. Mark as required.

NOTE: DO NOT raise vehicle with actuator bracket retaining nut removed.

Installation – To install, reverse removal procedure. Be sure flat sides on bracket are parallel with fender and aligned with flat on shock absorber. Use pliers to hold actuator bracket during installation.

NOTE: Actuator may become difficult to install if plastic (on shock absorber end) becomes eccentric to actuator driving shaft. To correct this problem, loosen 2 mounting screws. Allow actuator to float with respect to locator. Install on shock. Tighten mounting screws with actuator in place.

Removal & Installation (Rear) – **1)** Park vehicle on level surface. Apply parking brake. Turn ignition off. Remove side trim panel from trunk. Unplug actuator connector from harness.
2) Remove actuator by squeezing firmly inward on 2 plastic retainer tabs with one hand and lifting with other hand. Holding actuator

bracket with pliers, remove shock absorber upper nut. Remove bracket. *See Fig. 4.* To install, reverse removal procedure.

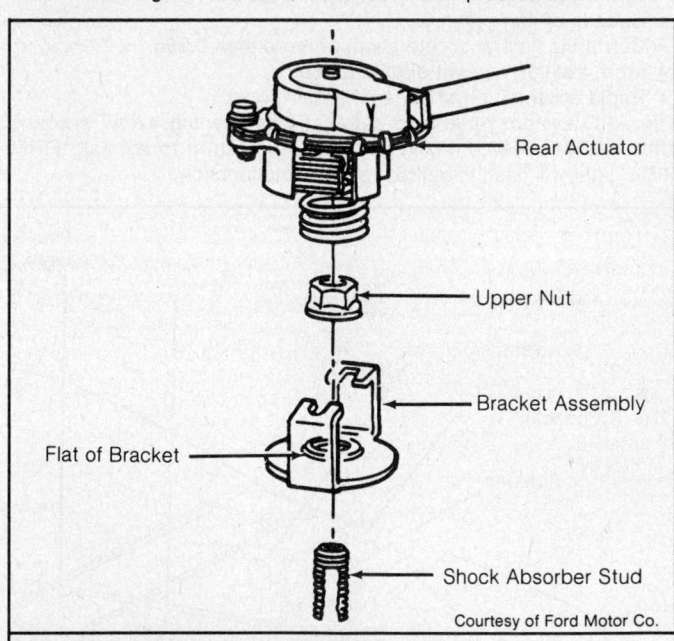

Rear Actuator

Upper Nut

Bracket Assembly

Flat of Bracket

Shock Absorber Stud

Courtesy of Ford Motor Co.

Fig. 4: Rear Actuator & Bracket Assembly

BRAKE SENSOR SWITCH

Removal & Installation – Brake pressure sensor switch is attached to proportioning valve, below master cylinder. Unplug connector and remove sensor from valve after relieving system pressure. To install, reverse removal procedure. Check "O" ring is on new switch. Bleed front brakes.

NOTE: If vehicle has anti-lock brake system, system pressure must be relieved before removing brake sensor switch. Turn ignition off. Pump brake pedal a least 20 times or until an increase in pedal force is clearly felt.

SPEED SENSOR

Removal & Installation – Raise vehicle and support. Remove speed sensor retaining bolt from left side of transmission. Remove sensor and driven gear. Unplug connector. Remove retainer and driven gear from sensor. To install, reverse removal procedure. Check "O" ring is properly seated.

1989 ELECTRONIC SUSPENSION
Ford Motor Co. Automatic Ride Control (Cont.)

12-111

CONTROL MODULE/RIDE CONTROL RELAYS

Removal & Installation – **1)** ARC control module and related relays are located in trunk on module packaging tray behind driver's side of back seat. Turn ignition off before disconnecting module.

2) Locate push pin left of tray and release. Pull down lightly on tray. Disconnect harness wiring connector. Remove control module or relays. To install, reverse removal procedure.

STEERING WHEEL ROTATION SENSOR

Removal & Installation – **1)** Steering sensor is located at lower end of steering column. It can be removed with or without steering column installed. See appropriate STEERING COLUMNS article.

2) Once column is out, disconnect sensor connectors from wiring harness and bracket under instrument panel. Remove sensor ring shield and 2 retaining screws. Remove sensor. Steering column must be removed to replace steering sensor ring. *See Fig. 5.* To install, reverse removal procedure.

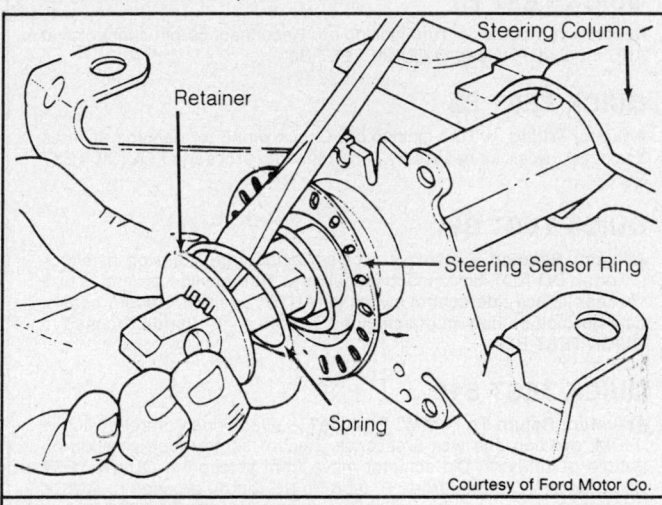

Courtesy of Ford Motor Co.

Fig. 5: Removing Steering Sensor Ring

EVO ACTUATOR ASSEMBLY

Removal – **1)** Disconnect wiring harness from EVO actuator on power steering pump. Disconnect power steering pressure and return hoses. Plug openings.

2) Carefully remove actuator from pump. The flow control valve and spring may come out.

Installation – **1)** Install flow control spring and valve. Install EVO actuator into pump. Tighten EVO actuator to 25-34 ft. lbs. (34-46 N.m).

NOTE: The EVO valve may stick in pump cover during installation. Do not force valve forward. Forcing valve may shear metal casing and release metal particles into valve bore.

2) Reconnect hoses. Reconnect EVO wiring harness. Fill with power steering fluid and purge system.

TIGHTENING SPECIFICATIONS

Application	Ft. Lbs. (N.m)
Upper Shock Nut	
Front	60-75 (82-102)
Rear	15-21 (20-29)

	INCH Lbs. (N.m)
Brake Sensor Switch	96-120 (10-14)

QUICK TESTS & DIAGNOSIS

ARC QUICK TEST [1] [2]

STAR TESTER/ LIGHT CODES	PROBLEM AREA	QUICK TEST/ACT
11/1 Then 1	No Problem Yet	TEST A2
10/1	[3] Faulty Left Rear Actuator	TEST B8
20/2	[3] Faulty Right Rear Actuator	TEST B8
30/3	[3] Faulty Right Front Actuator	TEST B8
40/4	[3] Faulty Left Front Actuator	TEST B8
50/5	Soft Relay Short	TEST B21
60/6	EVO Steering Circuit Open	TEST E1
70/7	Auto Ride Control Module	REPLACE
12/1, Then 2	Soft Relay Short/Open	TEST B21
13/1, Then 3	Hard Relay Short/Open	TEST B21
14/1, Then 4	Relay Control	TEST B25
15/Light Always On	Firm Ride Lamp Short	TEST C9
16/1, Then 6	EVO Steering Circuit Short	TEST E4
22/2, Then 2	Soft Relay Short	TEST B21
23/2, Then 3	Hard Relay Short	TEST B21
25/2, Then 5	Firm Ride Short	TEST C2
26/2, Then 6	EVO Steering Valve Bad	TEST E4
00/Dim or No Flash	Observe Key Sequence	TEST C1

[1] – The lamp will blink same code twice.
[2] – DO NOT move ride selector switch during test.
[3] – If 4 actuator circuit codes flash (1–4), proceed to TEST B1.

QUICK TESTS

QUICK TEST A1

Enter Diagnostics – Turn ignition off. Turn off headlights and parking lights during test. Place ride control switch to "AUTO." DO NOT move ride control switch during test. Connect Super Star II (007-00019, 007-00028), Star Tester (007-00017) or equivalent to test connector marked "ARC/EVO", near right front shock tower. Put tester in "HOLD" position. Turn on tester and put in "TEST" position.

NOTE: If using Super Star II tester, be sure mode switch is in EEC-IV MCU mode and NOT MECS or invalid codes will be obtained.

Start engine. Following procedure must be done within 20 seconds of starting engine. Go from "TEST" mode, to "HOLD", and back to "TEST" within 5 seconds. ARC/EVO module will run through self-test procedure and send error codes to Star tester. The "FIRM" ride green light will also flash error codes. The light will blink same codes twice, once every 9 seconds.

NOTE: Tests A2 and A3 may need to be repeated several times to ensure proper diagnosis. If ignition or ride control switch are inadvertently moved during test, proceed to QUICK TEST A4 or QUICK TEST A1.

QUICK TEST A2

Steering Sensor – Ensure green light stopped blinking. With engine running and vehicle stopped, turn steering wheel back and forth to each stop, 3 times or until light comes on. Light normally comes on before steering wheel reaches stop. If light comes on for 5 seconds, then goes out, proceed to QUICK TEST A3. If light does not come on, proceed to QUICK TEST D13.

QUICK TEST A3

Speed Sensor – Wait until green light is off. Drive vehicle at more than 15 MPH. If light comes on and stays on until vehicle speed is less than 15 MPH, proceed to QUICK TEST A4. If light does not come on, proceed to QUICK TEST D19.

12-112

1989 ELECTRONIC SUSPENSION
Ford Motor Co. Automatic Ride Control (Cont.)

QUICK TEST (Cont.)

QUICK TEST A4

Prepare For Remaining Test – Turn ignition off. Put ride control switch in "AUTO" position. Turn ignition on. Wait until Green light goes out (approximately 4 seconds). If light comes on, then goes out after 4 seconds, proceed to QUICK TEST A5. If light comes on and stays on while in "AUTO" position, proceed to QUICK TEST D6. If light comes on, then flashes code, record trouble code and proceed to QUICK TEST A1.

NOTE: QUICK TEST A5 and QUICK TEST A6 may have to be performed many times to ensure satisfactory results.

QUICK TEST A5

Ride Control Switch – Put ride control switch in "AUTO" position. After Green light turns off, place control switch in "FIRM" position. After light comes on, put control switch in "AUTO" position. If light is on in "FIRM" position and not in "AUTO" position, proceed to QUICK TEST A6. If light does not come on, proceed to QUICK TEST D23. If light flashes code, record trouble code and proceed to QUICK TEST A1.

QUICK TEST A6

Brake Sensor – Ensure ride control switch is in "AUTO" position. After Green light turns off, depress brake pedal firmly until light comes on. After light goes on, release brake pedal. If light comes on as indicated, proceed to QUICK TEST A7. If light comes does NOT come on, proceed to QUICK TEST D27. If light flashes code, record trouble code and proceed to QUICK TEST A1.

QUICK TEST A7

Acceleration Signal – Ensure ride control switch is in "AUTO" position. After green light turns off, depress accelerator pedal to floor (without engine running). Light should come on. Release accelerator pedal. Light should turn off. If light goes on and off as indicated, proceed to QUICK TEST A8. If light did not come on, proceed to QUICK TEST D31. If light flashes code, record trouble code and proceed to QUICK TEST A1.

QUICK TEST A8

Dimming Function – Move ride control switch to "FIRM" position. Turn on and off headlights while watching "FIRM" indicator. If light is bright with headlights off and dimmer with headlights on, vehicle passes diagnostics (only if QUICK TESTS A1–A7 were okay). If light does not dim, proceed to QUICK TEST C6.

ACTUATOR CONTROL CIRCUIT DIAGNOSIS

QUICK TEST B1

Actuator Wiring – Turn ignition off. Check wiring and connectors to left rear actuator for wear or damage. If wires damaged, repair as necessary. If no damage, proceed to QUICK TEST B2.

QUICK TEST B2

Disconnect Module – Turn ignition off. Proceed to trunk and lower module packaging tray behind driver's side of back seat. Disconnect 60-pin connector at ARC module. Proceed to QUICK TEST B3.

QUICK TEST B3

Energize Hard Relay – Turn ignition on. Connect a jumper wire between pins No. 11 to No. 60 at 60-pin connector at ARC module for 1-2 seconds. Proceed to QUICK TEST B4.

QUICK TEST B4

Position Switches Operation – Using an ohmmeter, check resistance between pins: No. 46 and No. 19, No. 46 and No. 25, No. 46 and No. 7, and No. 46 and No. 10. If resistance is more than 1000 ohms, switch is open. If resistance is less than 10 ohms, switch is closed. If 4 switches are open, proceed to QUICK TEST B5. If 4 switches are closed, proceed to QUICK TEST B17. If any individual switches are open, proceed to QUICK TEST B7.

ACTUATOR CONTROL CIRCUIT DIAGNOSIS (Cont.)

QUICK TEST B5

Energize Soft Relay – Connect a jumper wire between pins No. 12 and No. 60 at 60-pin connector at ARC module for 1-2 seconds. Proceed to QUICK TEST B6.

QUICK TEST B6

Do Position Switches Close? – Check resistance between following pins: No. 46 and No. 19, No. 46 and No. 25, No. 46 and No. 7, and No. 46 and No. 10. If resistance is more than 1000 ohms, switch is open. If resistance is less than 10 ohms, switch is closed. If 4 switches are closed, proceed to QUICK TEST B7. If any 4 switches are open, proceed to QUICK TEST B17. If any individual switch is closed, proceed to QUICK TEST B7.

QUICK TEST B7

Reconnect Module – Turn ignition off. Reconnect 60-pin connector at ARC module. Proceed to QUICK TEST B8.

QUICK TEST B8

Actuator Wiring – Turn ignition off. Check wiring for damage. If wires damaged, repair as necessary. If no damage, proceed to QUICK TEST B9.

QUICK TEST B9

Actuator Rotation – Remove problem actuator(s) from top of shock tower(s). DO NOT disconnect connectors. Turn ignition on and wait 5 seconds. Place ride control switch in "AUTO" position. Record control tube position on bottom of actuator, "S" (soft) or "H" (hard). Proceed to QUICK TEST B10.

QUICK TEST B10

Actuators Return To "FIRM" Position? – Place ride control switch in "FIRM" position and wait 5 seconds. Record control tube position on bottom of actuator. Did actuator move from position in QUICK TEST B9? If actuator rotated from "S" (soft) to "H" (hard), proceed to QUICK TEST B12. If actuator did not rotated, proceed to QUICK TEST B11. If actuator rotated from "H" to "S", circuits at actuator is reversed.

QUICK TEST B11

Does Actuator Rotate? – Turn ignition off. Disconnect problem actuator and replace with known good actuator. Turn ignition on. Place ride control switch to "AUTO" position and check control tube position.

Place control switch in "FIRM" position and check control tube position. If actuator does not move, replace actuator. If actuator does rotate, check wiring to actuator for short or open circuit.

QUICK TEST B12

Actuator Resistance – Disconnect problem actuator connector. Using a small blade screwdriver, rotate control tube on problem actuator to "S" position. Using an ohmmeter, check resistance between Tan/Black wire and each of following: Tan/Black on left front, White/Red on right front, White on right rear and White/Orange on left rear at connector terminals. Rotate control tube to "H" position. If resistance is greater than 1000 ohms, switch is open. If resistance is less than 10 ohms, switch is closed. If switch closed in "S" position and open in "H" position, proceed to QUICK TEST B13. If switch is always open or always closed, replace actuator.

QUICK TEST B13

Actuator Short – Using small blade screwdriver, rotate control tube to "H" position. Check resistance between Tan/Black and Tan/Red wires. If resistance is less than 10 ohms, replace actuator. If resistance is more than 1000 ohms, proceed to QUICK TEST B14.

QUICK TEST B14

Signal Return Circuit – Check resistance between following wires and ground: left front actuator White/Black, right front actuator White/Black, right rear actuator White, and left rear actuator White/Orange. If resistance at any wire is more than 1000 ohms, check open. If resistance at all 4 wires is less than 10 ohms, proceed to QUICK TEST B15.

1989 ELECTRONIC SUSPENSION
Ford Motor Co. Automatic Ride Control (Cont.)

12-113

ACTUATOR CONTROL CIRCUIT DIAGNOSIS (Cont.)

QUICK TEST B15

Disconnect Module – Turn ignition off. Proceed to trunk and lower module packaging tray behind driver's side of back seat. Disconnect 60-pin connector at ARC module. Proceed to QUICK TEST B16.

QUICK TEST B16

Sensor Position Circuit – Check pin No. 46 at ARC module for damage. Check continuity between pin No. 46 and Yellow/Black wire terminal at defective actuator. If there is no continuity, or pin is damage, repair as necessary. If there is continuity, proceed to QUICK TEST B37.

QUICK TEST B17

Relays Power Circuit – Turn ignition off. Disconnect soft and firm relay connectors. Turn ignition on. Check voltage from Black/Orange (power) and Black (ground) wires at both relay connectors. If zero volt, proceed to QUICK TEST B18. If 12 volts, proceed to QUICK TEST B19.

QUICK TEST B18

Relays Power Feed – Check voltage between Black/Orange wire and ground at each relay connector. If voltage, check open in Black wire circuit. If zero volt, check fuses or open in Black/Orange wire circuit.

QUICK TEST B19

Relays-To-Actuator Circuits – Disconnect right rear actuator connector. Check continuity between actuator and relays (Tan/Red and Tan/Black). If continuity, proceed to QUICK TEST B20. If no continuity, repair defective wire.

QUICK TEST B20

Crossed Relay Circuits – Check Light Green/Pink (circuit No. 838) and Tan/Black (circuit No. 845) wires are in connector to "FIRM" relay. Light Green/White (circuit No. 839) and Tan/Red (circuit No. 846) wires are in connector to "SOFT" relay. If wire locations okay, replace relay in question. If wire positions are not okay, repair as necessary.

QUICK TEST B21

Disconnect Module – Turn ignition off. Proceed to trunk and lower module packaging tray behind driver's side of back seat. Disconnect 60-pin connector at ARC module. Proceed to QUICK TEST B22.

QUICK TEST B22

Relay Control Circuit – Check Light Green/Purple wire (circuit No. 838) is connected to pin No. 11 at ARC module. Check Light Green/White wire (circuit No. 839) is connected to pin No. 12 at module. Turn ignition on. Check resistance between pins No. 11 and No. 60, and No. 12 and No. 60. If resistance is more than 1000 ohms at both circuits, replace ARC module. If resistance okay, proceed to QUICK TEST B23.

QUICK TEST B23

Disconnect Problem Relay – Disconnect problem relay. Check wiring to relay is not crossed or damaged. If wires crossed or damaged, repair as necessary. If wiring okay, proceed to QUICK TEST B24.

QUICK TEST B24

Retest Relay Circuit – Check resistance between pins No. 11 and No. 60, and No. 12 and No. 60. If resistance at both points is more than 1000 ohms, replace problem relay. If resistance is less than 10 ohms, check short in wiring.

QUICK TEST B25

Disconnect Module – Turn ignition off. Proceed to trunk and lower module packaging tray behind driver's side of back seat. Disconnect 60-pin connector at ARC module. Proceed to QUICK TEST B26.

ACTUATOR CONTROL CIRCUIT DIAGNOSIS (Cont.)

QUICK TEST B26

Light Control Circuit – Turn ignition on. Connect a jumper wire between pins No. 15 to No. 60 at 60-pin connector at ARC module. Observe Green light on instrument panel. If light comes on, proceed to QUICK TEST B27. If light does not come on, check fault in light control circuit. If wiring and light okay, replace ARC module.

QUICK TEST B27

Energize Hard Relay – Turn ignition on. Connect jumper wire between pins No. 11 and No. 60 for 1-2 seconds at 60-pin connector at ARC module. Proceed to QUICK TEST B28.

QUICK TEST B28

Position Switches Open? – Check resistance between following pins: No. 46 and No. 19, No. 46 and No. 25, No. 46 and No. 7, and No. 46 and No. 10. If resistance is more than 1000 ohms, switch is open. If resistance is less than 10 ohms, switch is closed. If 4 switches are open, proceed to QUICK TEST B29. If 4 switches are closed, problem is firm relay. Proceed to QUICK TEST B31.

QUICK TEST B29

Energize Soft Relay – Connect a jumper wire between pins No. 12 to No. 60 at 60-pin connector at ARC module for 1-2 seconds. Proceed to QUICK TEST B30.

QUICK TEST B30

Position Switches Close? – Check resistance between following pins: No. 46 and No. 19, No. 46 and No. 25, No. 46 and No. 7, and No. 46 and No. 10. If resistance is more than 1000, switch is open. If resistance is less than 10 ohms, switch is closed. If 4 switches are closed, replace ARC module. If 4 switches are open, fault in soft relay is indicated. Proceed to QUICK TEST B31.

QUICK TEST B31

Disconnect Problem Relay – Disconnect problem relay. Examine harness wires at relay connector for damage. If wires are damaged or crossed, repair as necessary. If no problem observed, proceed to QUICK TEST B32.

QUICK TEST B32

Coil Power Feed – Check voltage between Purple/Orange wire (circuit No. 298 between soft and firm relays) and ground. If zero volt, repair or replace Purple/Orange wire between ARC module and relays. If 12 volts, proceed to QUICK TEST B33.

QUICK TEST B33

Relay Control Circuit – Check problem relay circuit at 60-pin connector at ARC module. Check continuity between pins No. 11 (circuit No. 838) and No. 12 (circuit No. 839). If continuity, replace relay. If open circuit, repair wire as necessary and proceed to QUICK TEST B34.

QUICK TEST B34

Attach Problem Actuator – Attach problem actuator to shock absorber. Connect actuator to wiring harness. Proceed to QUICK TEST B36.

QUICK TEST B35

Energize Hard Relay – Turn ignition on. Connect a jumper wire between pins No. 11 and No. 60 for 1-2 seconds. Proceed to QUICK TEST B36.

QUICK TEST B36

Position Switch Open? – Check resistance between wiring harness pins for left rear actuator (No. 46 and No. 19), right rear actuator (No. 46 and No. 25), right front actuator (No. 46 and No. 7) and left front actuator (No. 46 and No. 10). If resistance is more than 1000 ohms, switch is open. If less than 10 ohms, switch is closed. If problem actuator switch is open, proceed to QUICK TEST B37. If problem actuator switch is closed, replace actuator and shock absorber (mechanical parts binding).

12-114

1989 ELECTRONIC SUSPENSION
Ford Motor Co. Automatic Ride Control (Cont.)

ACTUATOR CONTROL CIRCUIT DIAGNOSIS (Cont.)

QUICK TEST B37

Energize Soft Relay – Connect a jumper wire between pin No. 12 to pin No. 60 at 60-pin connector at ARC module for 1–2 seconds. Proceed to QUICK TEST B38.

QUICK TEST B38

Position Switch Closed? – Check resistance between wiring harness pins for left rear actuator (No. 46 and No. 19), right rear actuator (No. 46 and No. 25), right front actuator (No. 46 and No. 7) and left front actuator (No. 46 and No. 10). If problem actuator switch is closed, replace ARC module. If problem actuator switch is open, replace actuator and shock absorber (mechanical parts binding).

FIRM RIDE INDICATOR LIGHT CIRCUIT DIAGNOSIS

QUICK TEST C1

Key On Sequence – Turn ignition off. Place ride control switch in "FIRM" position. Shield Green light so it can be seen when dim. Turn ignition on. If light does not come on, replace bulb and proceed to QUICK TEST C2. If light is dim, proceed to QUICK TEST C6. If light comes on bright, proceed to QUICK TEST D1.

QUICK TEST C2

Disconnect Module – Turn ignition off. Proceed to trunk and lower module packaging tray behind driver's side of back seat. Disconnect 60-pin connector at ARC module. Proceed to QUICK TEST C3.

QUICK TEST C3

"FIRM RIDE" Light Operation – Turn ignition on. Connect a jumper wire between pins No. 15 and No. 60 at 60-pin connector at ARC module. Observe light. If light comes on, fault in module circuit, proceed to QUICK TEST C4. If light does not come on, proceed to QUICK TEST C5.

QUICK TEST C4

Module Power Circuit – Check voltage between pins No. 57 and No. 60 at 60-pin connector at ARC module. If zero volt, repair/replace Purple/Orange wire or 18-gauge fuse link between starter solenoid and pin No. 57 at ARC module. Circuit goes through 8-pin connector in right side kick panel. If 12 volts, replace ARC module.

QUICK TEST C5

Light Circuit – Locate "FIRM RIDE" light (Red/Black) wire on instrument panel connection and check continuity. If no continuity, service ground or open in Red/Black wire between pin No. 15 of ARC module and light. If continuity, check instrument panel power, ground and bulb.

QUICK TEST C6

Light Dimming – Move ride control switch to "FIRM" to turn on light. Turn headlights on and off while observing "FIRM RIDE" light. If light does not dim with headlights on, proceed to QUICK TEST C7.

QUICK TEST C7

Disconnect Module – Turn ignition off. Proceed to trunk and lower module packaging tray behind driver's side of back seat. Disconnect 60-pin connector at ARC module. Proceed to QUICK TEST C8.

QUICK TEST C8

Headlight Wiring – Check voltage between pins No. 1 (circuit No. 14 for headlights) and No. 60 at 60-pin connector at ARC module. Turn headlights on and off. If 12 volts with headlights on and zero volt with headlights off, replace ARC module. If 12 volts or zero volt always, repair problem in headlight switch circuit (brown wire between pin No. 1 of ARC module and headlight switch).

FIRM RIDE INDICATOR LIGHT CIRCUIT DIAGNOSIS (Cont.)

QUICK TEST C9

Disconnect Module – Turn ignition off. Proceed to trunk and lower module packaging tray behind driver's side of back seat. Disconnect 60-pin connector at ARC module. Proceed to QUICK TEST C10.

QUICK TEST C10

"Firm Ride" Circuit Short – Check circuit No. 133 (Tan/Red wire) is attached to pin No. 15 at 60-pin connector at ARC module. Check damage. Check resistance between pin No. 15 and pin No. 60 at 60-pin connector. If resistance is more than 1000 ohms, replace ARC module. If less than 10 ohms, repair short to ground between ARC module and "FIRM RIDE" light.

MODULE INPUT CIRCUIT DIAGNOSIS

QUICK TEST D1

Enter Diagnostics Again – Verify ARC/EVO test connector (right front shock tower) is clean and corrosion free. Repeat attempt to enter diagnostics (see QUICK TEST A1). Be sure tester switch positions and procedures are followed. If second attempt to enter diagnostics is successful, proceed from QUICK TEST A1. If second attempt fails, proceed to QUICK TEST D2.

QUICK TEST D2

Signal Wire Continuity – Check signal return wire (Gray/Red), diagnostic wire (Yellow/Black) and Star Tester wire (Dark Blue) at ARC/EVO diagnostic connector for damage. If wires are damaged, repair as necessary. Test continuity of Yellow/Black wire to chassis ground. If no continuity, repair open in Yellow/Black wire to pin No. 46 of ARC module. If no problems, proceed to QUICK TEST D3.

QUICK TEST D3

Disconnect Module – Turn ignition off. Proceed to trunk and lower module packaging tray behind driver's side of back seat. Disconnect 60-pin connector at ARC module. Proceed to QUICK TEST D4.

QUICK TEST D4

Diagnostic Circuit Short – Check circuit No. 844 (Gray/Red wire) is attached to pin No. 30 at 60-pin connector at ARC module. Check resistance from pin No. 30 to pin No. 60. If resistance is more than 1000 ohms, proceed to QUICK TEST D5. If less than 10 ohms, repair circuit short. Also, check for short in Dark Blue wire (circuit No. 930).

QUICK TEST D5

Diagnostic Circuit – Connect tester to ARC/EVO connector at right front shock tower. Check resistance between pins No. 30 and No. 46 at 60-pin connector at ARC module. Check resistance with tester button depressed and released. If resistance always more than 1000 ohms, repair open in Gray/Red wire (Circuit No. 844), or poor contact at connector. If more than 1000 ohms released and less than 10 ohms depressed, replace ARC module. Less than 10 ohms always, check STAR Tester.

QUICK TEST D6

Switch Positions – Move ride control switch to "FIRM" position. If ride light stays on, proceed to QUICK TEST D7. If firm light turns off, switch positions reversed. Replace control switch.

QUICK TEST D7

Disconnect Module – Turn ignition off. Set ride control switch to "AUTO" position. Proceed to trunk and lower module packaging tray behind driver's side of back seat. Disconnect 60-pin connector at ARC module. Proceed to QUICK TEST D8.

1989 ELECTRONIC SUSPENSION
Ford Motor Co. Automatic Ride Control (Cont.)

12-115

MODULE INPUT
CIRCUIT DIAGNOSIS (Cont.)

QUICK TEST D8

Brake Circuit Short – Check circuit No. 847 (Orange/Light Green wire) attached to pin No. 9 at 60-pin connector of ARC module. Check resistance between pins No. 9 and No. 60. If more than 1000 ohms, proceed to QUICK TEST D9. If less than 10 ohms, repair short to ground (Orange/Light Green wire between brake pressure switch and ARC module).

QUICK TEST D9

Brake Circuit Always Closed? – Check resistance between pins No. 9 and No. 46 at 60-pin connector at ARC module. If more than 1000 ohms, proceed to QUICK TEST D10. If less than 10 ohms, replace brake pressure switch.

QUICK TEST D10

Ride Control Switch Circuit – Put ride control switch to "AUTO". Check circuit No. 832 (Brown/Light Green wire) is attached to pin No. 18 at 60-pin connector at ARC module. Check voltage between pins No. 18 to No. 60. If zero volt, proceed to QUICK TEST D11. If 12 volts, replace shock select switch.

QUICK TEST D11

Acceleration Switch Always On? – Check circuit No. 836 (Orange/White wire) attached to pin No. 28 at 60-pin connector at ARC module. Check resistance between pins No. 28 and No. 60. If more than 1000 ohms, replace ARC module. If less than 10 ohms, proceed to QUICK TEST D12.

QUICK TEST D12

Acceleration Circuit Short – Turn ignition off. Disconnect EEC-IV control module (right side cowling) from wiring harness. Proceed to trunk and lower ARC module packaging tray behind driver's side of back seat. Check resistance between pins No. 28 and No. 60 at ARC module. If more than 1000 ohms, possible defective throttle position signal or EEC-VI module. If less than 10 ohms, repair short in circuit No. 836 Orange/White wire between ARC module and EEC IV module.

QUICK TEST D13

Disconnect Module – Turn ignition off. Proceed to trunk and lower module packaging tray behind driver's side of back seat. Disconnect 60-pin connector at ARC module. Proceed to QUICK TEST D14.

QUICK TEST D14

Steering Sensor Wires – Check circuit No. 834 (Red/Yellow wire) is attached to pin No. 45 and circuit No. 835 (Red/White wire) is attached to pin No. 24 at 60-pin connector at ARC module. If wires are damaged, repair as necessary. If no damage, proceed to QUICK TEST D15. These circuits can be reversed without problem.

QUICK TEST D15

Steering Sensor Signals – Connect a jumper wire between pins No. 46 and No. 60 at ARC module. Start engine. Check resistance with analog ohmmeter on 1000-ohm scale between pins No. 45 and No. 60. Also, check resistance between pins No. 24 and No. 60. Perform both checks while slowly rotating steering wheel. If meter needle does not swing for one or both circuits, proceed to QUICK TEST D16. If meter swings for both circuits, replace ARC module.

QUICK TEST D16

Disconnect Steering Sensor – Turn ignition off. Disconnect steering sensor near brake pedal at steering column. Check wiring to steering sensor for damage. Test continuity of Red/Yellow wire to pin No. 45 (circuit No. 834) and Red/White wire to pin No. 24 (circuit No. 835) from steering sensor at 60-pin connector at ARC module. If wires damaged, repair as necessary. If no continuity, repair open in Red/Yellow wire or Red/White wire as necessary. No problem found, proceed to QUICK TEST D17.

MODULE INPUT
CIRCUIT DIAGNOSIS (Cont.)

QUICK TEST D17

Steering Sensor Power – Turn ignition on. Check voltage between Pink/Orange wire (circuit No. 298) and Yellow/Black (circuit No. 837) at wiring harness side of steering sensor connector. If zero volt, proceed to QUICK TEST D18. If 12 volts, replace steering sensor.

QUICK TEST D18

Steering Sensor Circuit – Check voltage between Pink/Orange wire (circuit No. 298) at wiring harness side of steering sensor connector to chassis ground. If zero volt, repair short in Pink/Orange wire. If 12 volts, repair short in Yellow/Black wire.

QUICK TEST D19

Disconnect Module – Turn ignition off. Proceed to trunk and lower module packaging tray behind driver's side of back seat. Disconnect 60-pin connector at ARC module. Proceed to QUICK TEST D20.

QUICK TEST D20

Speed Sensor Signal – Check circuit No. 150 (Dark Green/White wire) is attached to pin No. 3 and circuit No. 563 (Orange/Yellow wire) is attached to pin No. 6 at 60-pin connector at ARC module. If wires are damaged, repair as necessary. If no damage, proceed to QUICK TEST D21.

QUICK TEST D21

Speed Sensor Ground – Test continuity of speed sensor ground (Orange/Yellow wire) circuit No. 563 from pin No. 6 and pin No. 60 at ARC module. If continuity, proceed to QUICK TEST D22. If open circuit, repair wire or ground as necessary.

QUICK TEST D22

Speed Sensor – Turn ignition on. Check speedometer operation. If problem with speedometer, check AC voltage between two output wires on transmission-mounted speed sensor. Check wiring to sensor and speedometer fuse. Check instrument cluster circuit for loose screws, bad terminals or damaged circuit board. If no problem is found, replace ARC module.

QUICK TEST D23

Disconnect Module – Turn ignition off. Proceed to trunk and lower module packaging tray behind driver's side of back seat. Disconnect 60-pin connector at ARC module. Proceed to QUICK TEST D24.

QUICK TEST D24

"FIRM" Signal – Check circuit No. 832 (Brown/Light Green wire) is attached to pin No. 18 at 60-pin connector at ARC module. Turn ignition on. Set ride control switch to "FIRM" position. Check voltage between pins No. 18 and No. 60 at 60-pin connector. If zero volt, got to QUICK TEST D25. If 12 volts, replace ARC module.

QUICK TEST D25

Ride Control Switch – Turn ignition off. Disconnect ride control switch at instrument panel. Check wires at switch for damage. If wires damaged, repair as necessary. If no damage, proceed to QUICK TEST D26.

QUICK TEST D26

Ride Control Switch Power Feed – Turn ignition on. Check voltage between Pink/Orange wire (circuit No. 298) at wiring harness side of shock select switch connector to chassis ground. If zero volt, repair open in Pink/Orange wire. If 12 volts, replace shock select switch.

QUICK TEST D27

Disconnect Module – Turn ignition off. Proceed to trunk and lower module packaging tray behind driver's side of back seat. Disconnect 60-pin connector at ARC module. Proceed to QUICK TEST D28.

12-116

1989 ELECTRONIC SUSPENSION
Ford Motor Co. Automatic Ride Control (Cont.)

MODULE INPUT
CIRCUIT DIAGNOSIS (Cont.)

QUICK TEST D28

Brake Switch Closed? – Check circuit No. 847 (Orange/Light Green wire) is attached to pin No. 9 at 60-pin connector at ARC module. Start engine and press brake firmly to floor. Check resistance between pins No. 9 and No. 60 on ARC harness while brake is down. If more than 1000 ohms, proceed to QUICK TEST D29. If less than 10 ohms, replace ARC module.

QUICK TEST D29

Disconnect Brake Switch – Turn ignition off. Disconnect brake pressure switch at the proportioning valve. Check wires at brake pressure switch connector for damage. If wires damaged, repair as necessary. If no problems, proceed to QUICK TEST D30.

QUICK TEST D30

Brake Switch Ground – Check resistance between Yellow/Black wire (circuit No. 837) at wiring harness side of brake switch connector to ground. If more than 1000 ohms, repair open or short in Yellow/Black wire. If less than 10 ohms, replace brake pressure switch.

QUICK TEST D31

Disconnect Module – Turn ignition off. Proceed to trunk and lower module packaging tray behind driver's side of back seat. Disconnect 60-pin connector at ARC module. Proceed to QUICK TEST D32.

QUICK TEST D32

Module Connector – Check circuit No. 836 (Orange/White wire) is attached to pin No. 28 at 60-pin connector at ARC module. Check wires for damage or crossed. If wires damaged, repair as necessary. If no problems, proceed to QUICK TEST D33.

QUICK TEST D33

EEC-IV Connector – Disconnect 60-pin connector at EEC-IV module. Check circuit No. 836 (Orange/White wire) is attached to pin No. 35 at 60-pin connector. Check wires for damage or crossed. If wires damaged, repair as necessary. If no problems, proceed to QUICK TEST D34.

QUICK TEST D34

Acceleration Circuit Continuity – Test for continuity of circuit No. 836 (Orange/White wire) from ARC module to EEC-IV module. If no continuity, service open circuit between ARC and EEC-IV modules. If no wiring problems, replace ARC module.

MODULE INPUT
CIRCUIT DIAGNOSIS (Cont.)

QUICK TEST E1

Connector Wires – Turn ignition off. Check EVO valve connector on power steering pump is properly seated. If connector is seated properly, proceed to QUICK TEST E2.

QUICK TEST E2

EVO Steering – Turn ignition off. Proceed to trunk and lower module packaging tray behind driver's side of back seat. Disconnect 60-pin connector at ARC module. Check continuity between pins No. 43 and No. 48. If resistance is more than 1000 ohms, proceed to QUICK TEST E3. If resistance is more than 18 ohms, proceed to QUICK TEST E4. If resistance is less than 18 ohms, proceed to QUICK TEST E3.

QUICK TEST E3

EVO Wiring Continuity – Disconnect EVO connector from EVO valve on power steering pump. Check continuity of module harness at pin No. 48 (circuit No. 330) and pin No. 43 (circuit No. 353). If no continuity, repair wiring as necessary. If continuity, proceed to QUICK TEST E4.

QUICK TEST E4

EVO Valve On Pump – Disconnect EVO connector from EVO valve on power steering pump. Check resistance of EVO valve across 2 valve connector pins. If resistance is more than 20 ohms, replace EVO valve. If resistance is less than 5 ohms, replace EVO valve. If resistance is greater than 5 ohms and less than 20 ohms, proceed to QUICK TEST E5.

QUICK TEST E5

Wire Harness Ground Short – Turn ignition off. Proceed to trunk and lower module packaging tray behind driver's side of back seat. Disconnect 60-pin connector at ARC module. Check resistance between pins No. 60 and No. 43. If resistance is more than 1000 ohms, proceed to QUICK TEST E6. If less than 10 ohms, inspect harness for short to ground.

QUICK TEST E6

EVO Wire Harness Short – Check resistance between pins No. 60 and No. 48 at 60-pin connector at ARC module. If resistance is greater than 1000 ohms, replace ARC/EVO module. If resistance is less than 10 ohms, inspect harness for short to ground.

1989 ELECTRONIC SUSPENSION
Ford Motor Co. Automatic Ride Control (Cont.)

12-117

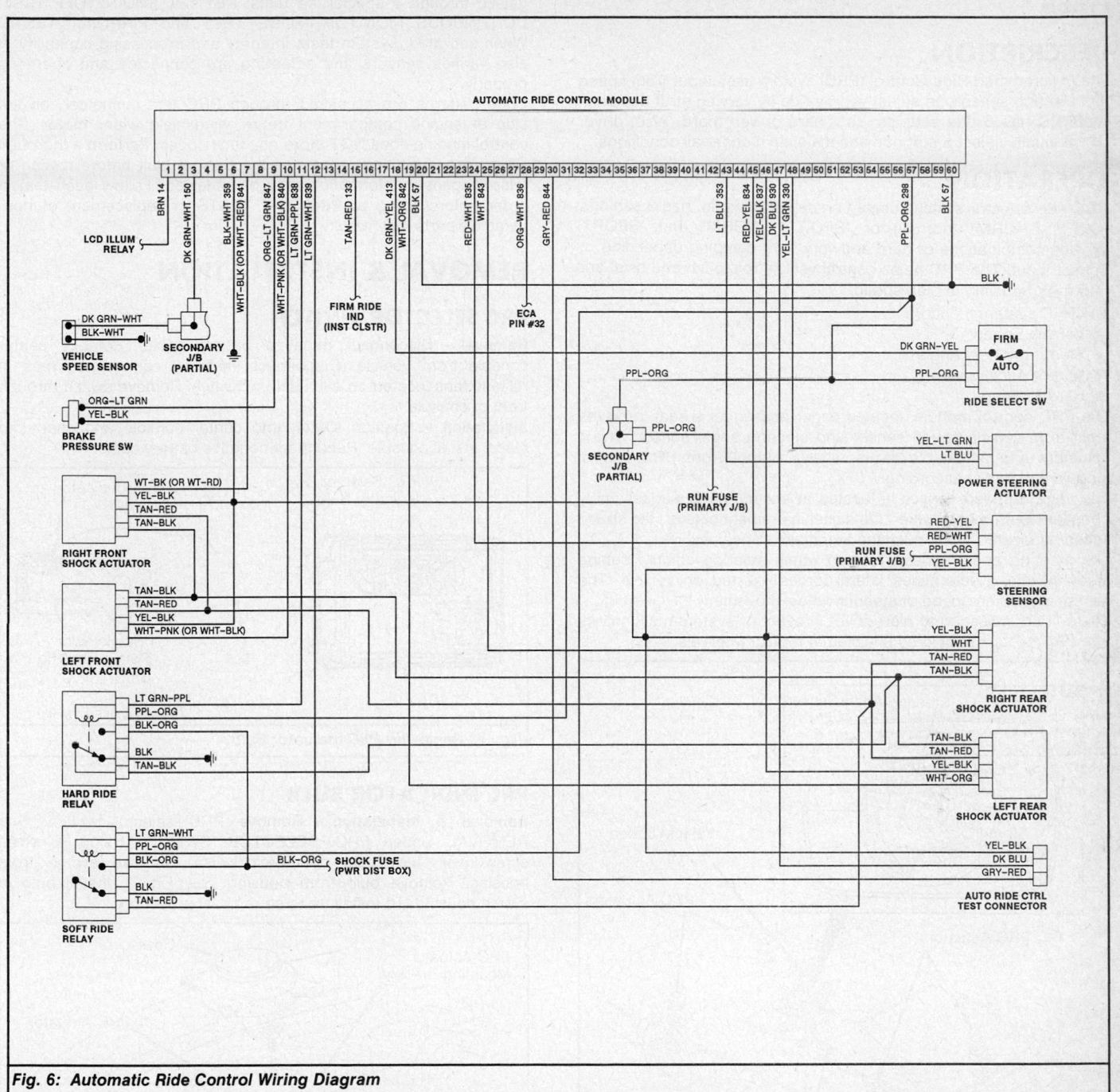

Fig. 6: Automatic Ride Control Wiring Diagram

Probe

DESCRIPTION

The Programmed Ride Control (PRC) system uses input from speed and steering sensors to adjust vehicle ride by varying strut damping. The PRC has 3 ride settings: soft, hard or very hard. Also, driver can manually select a soft ride and maintain it under all conditions.

OPERATION

PRC ride selector switch, located on center console, has 3 settings: "SOFT," "NORM" (normal) or "SPORT." "NORM" and "SPORT" provide combinations of hard and very hard damping depending on sensor input. The PRC helps control vehicle roll, pitch and dive, and improves handling at high speed.

The PRC system monitors:
- Vehicle Speed
- Steering Wheel Angle
- Abrupt Acceleration
- Hard Braking

The PRC control module, located under passenger's seat, receives input from vehicle speed sensor and steering angle sensor. The 4 actuators and adjustable struts receive output from PRC control module and adjust accordingly.

The vehicle speed sensor is located in speedometer subassembly of analog instrument cluster. On digital instrument cluster, the speed sensor is located on manual and automatic transaxles.

The steering angle sensor, located within steering column behind steering wheel, determines lateral forces exerted on vehicle. The sensor measures speed of steering wheel movement.

There is no indication to alert driver in event of system malfunction. The PRC system should be checked at regular intervals.

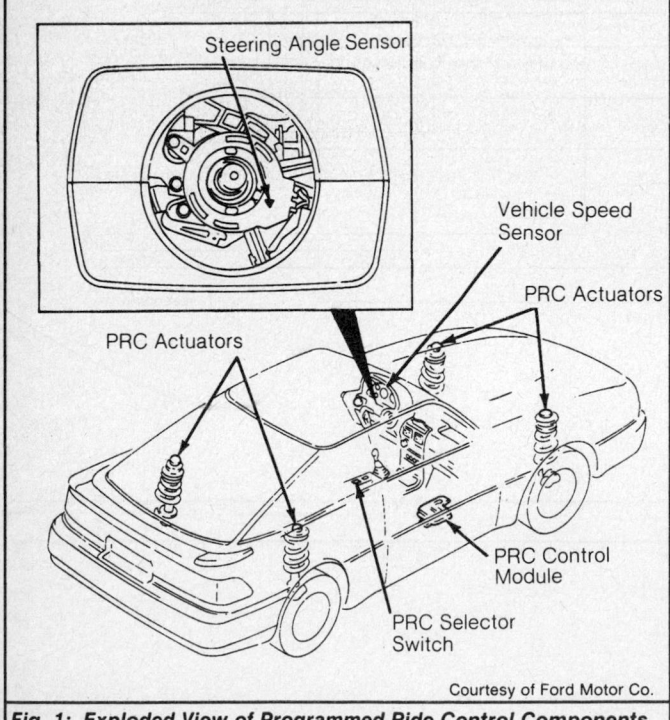

Fig. 1: Exploded View of Programmed Ride Control Components

TESTING

A thorough visual inspect should precede all testing. See SYMPTOM DIRECTORY and PRC SYSTEM SELF-DIAGNOSTICS. See Fig. 8. An Analog Volt-Ohm Meter (VOM), jumper wire and circuit tester are needed for testing.

The PRC system has no warning light to signal driver about ride control problems. Information concerning possible problems can be gained through 3 specialized tests: KEY ON, ENGINE OFF TEST, CONTINUOUS MONITOR MODE TEST and PINPOINT TESTS. When activated, system tests integrity and processing capability. It also varifies sensors and actuators are connected and operating properly.

Code patterns are accessed through PRC test connector, on left side of engine compartment below windshield wiper motor. The control module does NOT store any fault codes. Perform a thorough visual inspection and repair any mechanical fault before testing or false diagnostic information may be obtained. Follow each test in order before going to PINPOINT TESTS or replacement of non-defective parts may result.

REMOVAL & INSTALLATION

PRC SELECTOR SWITCH

Removal – Disconnect negative battery cable. Remove center console from vehicle. Disconnect electrical connector. Press in release tabs located on each side of switch. Remove switch through front of console.

Installation – Position switch into center console and snap into place. Install console. Reconnect negative battery cable.

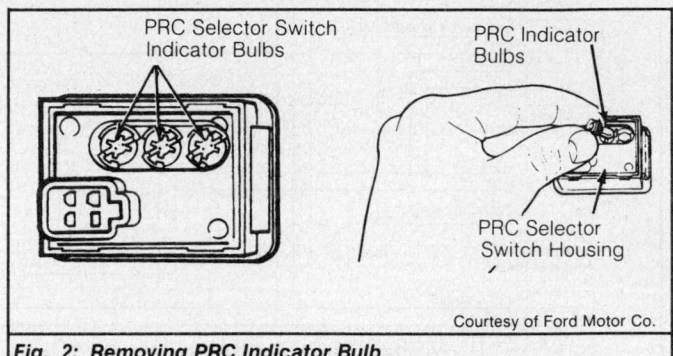

Fig. 2: Removing PRC Indicator Bulb

PRC INDICATOR BULB

Removal & Installation – Remove PRC selector switch. See REMOVAL under PRC SELECTOR SWITCH. Using a small screwdriver, turn bulb counterclockwise. Remove switch from housing. Remove bulb from housing. See Fig. 2. Install bulb in switch housing. To install, reverse removal procedure.

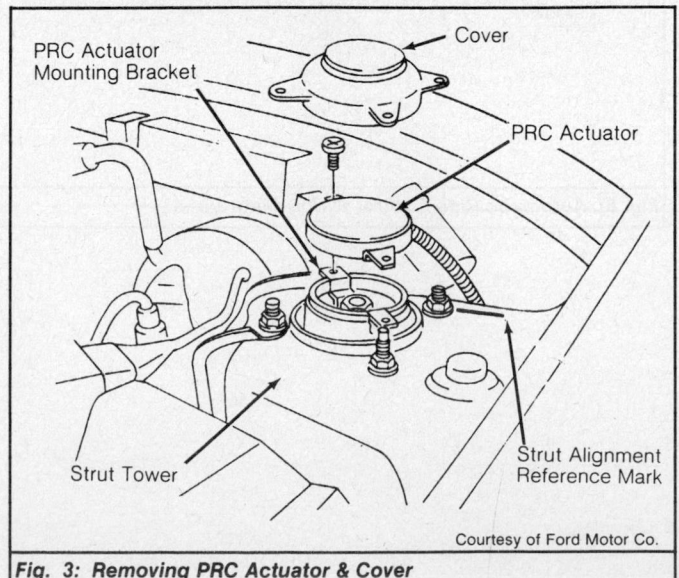

Fig. 3: Removing PRC Actuator & Cover

1989 ELECTRONIC SUSPENSION
Ford Motor Co. Programmed Ride Control (Cont.)

12-119

PRC ACTUATORS

Removal & Installation (Front) – Raise vehicle and remove tire. Remove rubber cap from strut mounting block. Disconnect actuator connector. Put an alignment mark on inside of strut mounting block and chassis strut tower. *See Fig. 3.* Remove actuator. To install, reverse removal procedure.

Removal & Installation (Rear) – Raise vehicle and remove tire. Remove upper trunk side trim and lower trunk side trim for access to strut assembly. Remove rubber cap from strut mounting block. Disconnect actuator connector. Put an alignment mark on inside of strut mounting block and chassis strut tower. Remove actuator. To install, reverse removal procedure.

STEERING ANGLE SENSOR

Removal & Installation – Sensor is located in steering column, behind steering wheel. It uses a 3-wire connector (Green, Green/White and Green/Yellow). *See Fig. 1.*

VEHICLE SPEED SENSOR

Removal & Installation (Digital Instrument Cluster) – Disconnect negative battery cable. Disconnect 2-wire electrical connector from speed sensor in transaxle. *See Fig. 4.* Remove sensor mounting bolt. Pull sensor out of housing. To install, reverse removal procedure.

Removal & Installation (Analog Instrument Cluster) – 1) Disconnect negative battery cable. Remove steering wheel. Remove 2 screws from steering column cover. Remove cover.

2) Remove 9 attaching screws from cluster module. Carefully pull cluster module for access to electrical connections. Disconnect 7 electrical connectors from cover. Remove ignition switch illumination bulb housing. Remove cluster module.

3) Loosen 2 cover hinge screws. Remove 6 screws from instrument cluster cover. Remove lower cluster cover panel.

NOTE: While removing lower cluster cover, be careful not to rip rubber seal between upper and lower cluster cover panels.

4) Remove 4 attaching screws from cluster. Disconnect 3 electrical connectors from back of cluster. Remove cluster.

5) Remove lens assembly. Remove 7 attaching screws and speedometer subassembly. To install, reverse removal procedure. *See Fig. 5.*

PRC CONTROL MODULE

Removal & Installation – Disconnect negative battery cable. Remove passenger's seat. PRC control module is to right of premium sound audio amplifier. Remove 3 control module mounting bolts. Disconnect PRC electrical connection. Remove control module. To install, reverse removal procedure.

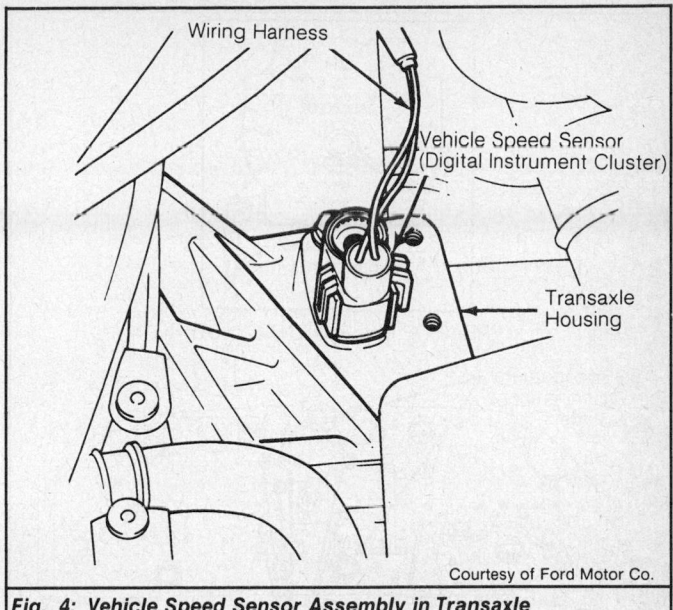

Courtesy of Ford Motor Co.

Fig. 4: Vehicle Speed Sensor Assembly in Transaxle

PRC SYSTEM SELF-DIAGNOSTICS

DESCRIPTION

Thoroughly inspect all PRC components and wiring visually before proceeding with tests. There will be 3 specific tests: KEY ON, ENGINE OFF TEST, CONTINUOUS MONITOR TEST and PINPOINT TEST. Follow specific order and instructions in each test before performing any repairs.

When directed to PINPOINT TESTS, look carefully at wiring diagram. Any time a repair is made, KEY ON, ENGINE OFF TEST should be repeated as a double check.

VISUAL INSPECTION

- Check front and rear struts for damage, leaks, cracks and proper mounting. Check tire pressure.
- Check PRC wiring harness for proper connections, bent or broken pins, corrosion, loose wires and proper routing. Check control module, sensors and actuators for physical damage.
- Make all necessary repairs before continuing with PRC SYSTEM SELF-DIAGNOSTICS.
- Set parking brake, place shifter in park position (neutral on manual transaxle) and block wheels. Turn off all electrical assessories. Proceed to EQUIPMENT CONNECTION.

SYMPTOM DIRECTORY

SYMPTOM	POSSIBLE CAUSE	ACTION TO TAKE
EXCESSIVE BODY ROLL	Steering angle sensor, control unit, wiring harness, actuators	Go to SELF-DIAGNOSTICS
EXCESSIVE DIVE OR SQUAT UNDER HARD BRAKING OR ACCELERATION	Vehicle speed sensor, control unit, actuators, wiring harness	Go to SELF-DIAGNOSTICS
SUSPENSION SETTING DOES NOT CORRESPOND TO SELECTOR SWITCH	Actuators, control unit, wiring harness, PRC switch	Go to SELF-DIAGNOSTICS
SUSPENSION SETTING DOES NOT CHANGE WHEN SWITCH IS CHANGED	Actuators, wiring harness, PRC switch, control unit	Go to SELF-DIAGNOSTICS

12-120

1989 ELECTRONIC SUSPENSION
Ford Motor Co. Programmed Ride Control (Cont.)

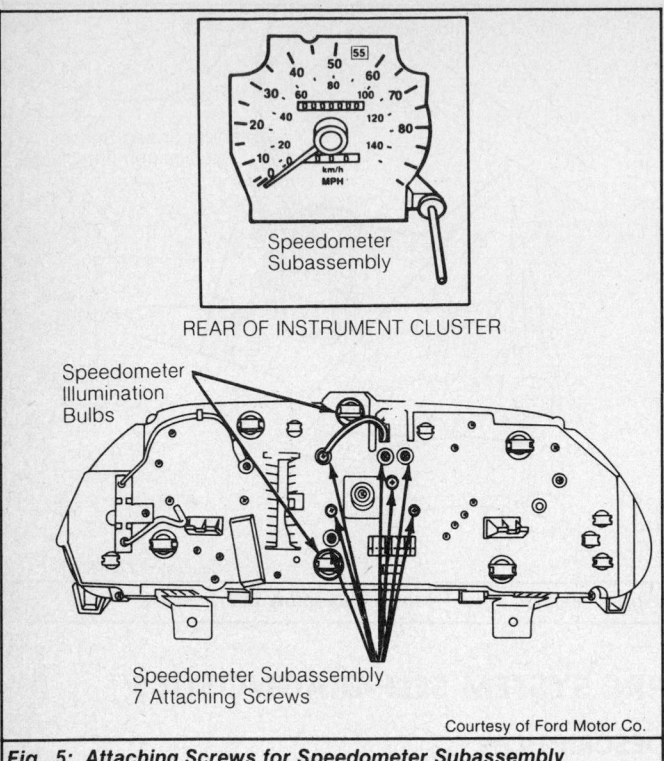

REAR OF INSTRUMENT CLUSTER

Speedometer Subassembly

Speedometer Illumination Bulbs

Speedometer Subassembly 7 Attaching Screws

Courtesy of Ford Motor Co.

Fig. 5: Attaching Screws for Speedometer Subassembly

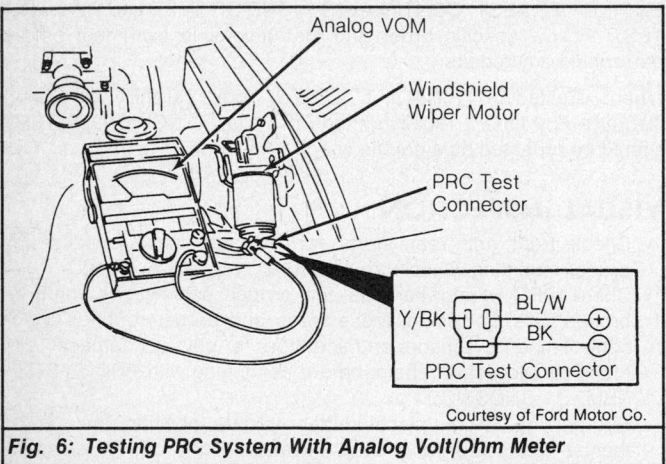

Analog VOM

Windshield Wiper Motor

PRC Test Connector

Y/BK   BL/W
         BK   (+)
                (−)

PRC Test Connector

Courtesy of Ford Motor Co.

Fig. 6: Testing PRC System With Analog Volt/Ohm Meter

EQUIPMENT CONNECTION

Set Analog Volt/Ohm Meter (VOM) to 20-volt (DC) scale. Locate PRC test connector under hood, below windshield wiper motor. Connect VOM positive lead to Blue/White wire terminal and negative lead to Black wire terminal. *See Fig. 6.*

KEY ON, ENGINE OFF TEST

Test Procedure – Turn ignition off to reset PRC control module before each test. Verify vehicle has completed VISUAL INSPECTION. Ensure steering wheel is straight. Turn on analog VOM. Turn on ignition to activate KEY ON, ENGINE OFF TEST. *See Fig. 7.* Refer to TEST STEPS in left column for procedure to follow. Then count needle sweeps and record all service codes. The chart shows voltmeter needle sweeps and durations. Notice same code pattern can sometimes indicate different faults in different test steps.

Test Results – After performing TEST STEP in left column, compare results with CODE PATTERN to determine appropriate

ACTION TO TAKE. *See Figs. 3 and 4.* While performing Test A, ignore code needle sweeps retrieved while steering wheel is centered.

A pass code in right column, under ACTION TO TAKE indicates no faults detected. Proceed to Test Step B. See Fig. 4. If directed to pinpoint tests, see PINPOINT TESTS listed in this article. (Example: Begin with PINPOINT TEST A1, then proceed to PINPOINT TEST A2, A3, etc.)

CONTINUOUS MONITOR TEST

Test Procedure – Verify pass code in all KEY ON, ENGINE OFF TEST steps before beginning CONTINUOUS MONITOR TEST. This test allows technician and an assistant to simulate intermittent faults not retrieved during KEY ON, ENGINE OFF TEST. Connect analog VOM to PRC test connector, on left side of engine compartment below windshield wiper motor. Turn ignition on to enter continuous monitor mode. Tap, move and wiggle suspect sensor and/or harness, while running all steps of KEY ON, ENGINE OFF TEST. Observe code patterns retrieved and follow appropriate ACTION TO TAKE in right column.

Using Continuous Monitor Mode – If a code pattern is displayed:

- Lightly tap on sensor.
- Push/pull on sensor harness connector. DO NOT disconnect connector at this time.
- Shake harness vigorously, working from sensor harness connector toward dash panel and from dash panel to PRC control module in short sections.
- If there is no positive sign of an intermittent, disconnect sensor from harness. Inspect harness at both ends for corrosion, bad crimps and improperly seated terminals. Reconnect after inspection.
- Disconnect PRC control module and inspect terminals. Remove only terminals associated with sensor being inspected. *See Fig. 8.*
- If VOM DOES NOT give a positive intermittent indication, reconnect all terminals and connectors.

Test Results – The CONTINUOUS MONITOR TEST can aid in diagnosing intermittent PRC circuit failures. If VOM indicates a fault (short or open), a corresponding code pattern will be indicated. After determining affected circuits, a close check of harness and connectors should be made.

PINPOINT TEST PREPARATION

Pre-Test Instructions – Run pinpoint tests only after completing VISUAL INSPECTION or being directed there through KEY ON ENGINE OFF TEST and CONTINUOUS MONITOR MODE TEST.

- Each pinpoint test assumes a fault has been detected. Failure to comply with correct testing order can result error.
- Test results depend on proper operation of related parts. Correct any defects in this area before entering pinpoint tests.
- DO NOT replace parts unless test results indicate it.
- When one or more service codes are shown, start with first code received.
- DO NOT measure voltage or resistance at PRC control module or connect any test lights unless specified.
- Isolate both ends of a circuit and turn ignition off whenever checking for shorts or continuity, unless specified.
- Disconnect solenoids and switches from harness before measuring for continuity, resistance or energizing with 12-volt source.
- In using Pinpoint Test, follow each step in order, starting from first step in appropriate test. Follow each step until fault is found.
- An open is defined as any resistance reading more than 5 ohms unless otherwise specified.
- A short is defined as any resistance reading less than 10,000 ohms to ground, unless otherwise specified.

1989 ELECTRONIC SUSPENSION
Ford Motor Co. Programmed Ride Control (Cont.)

12-121

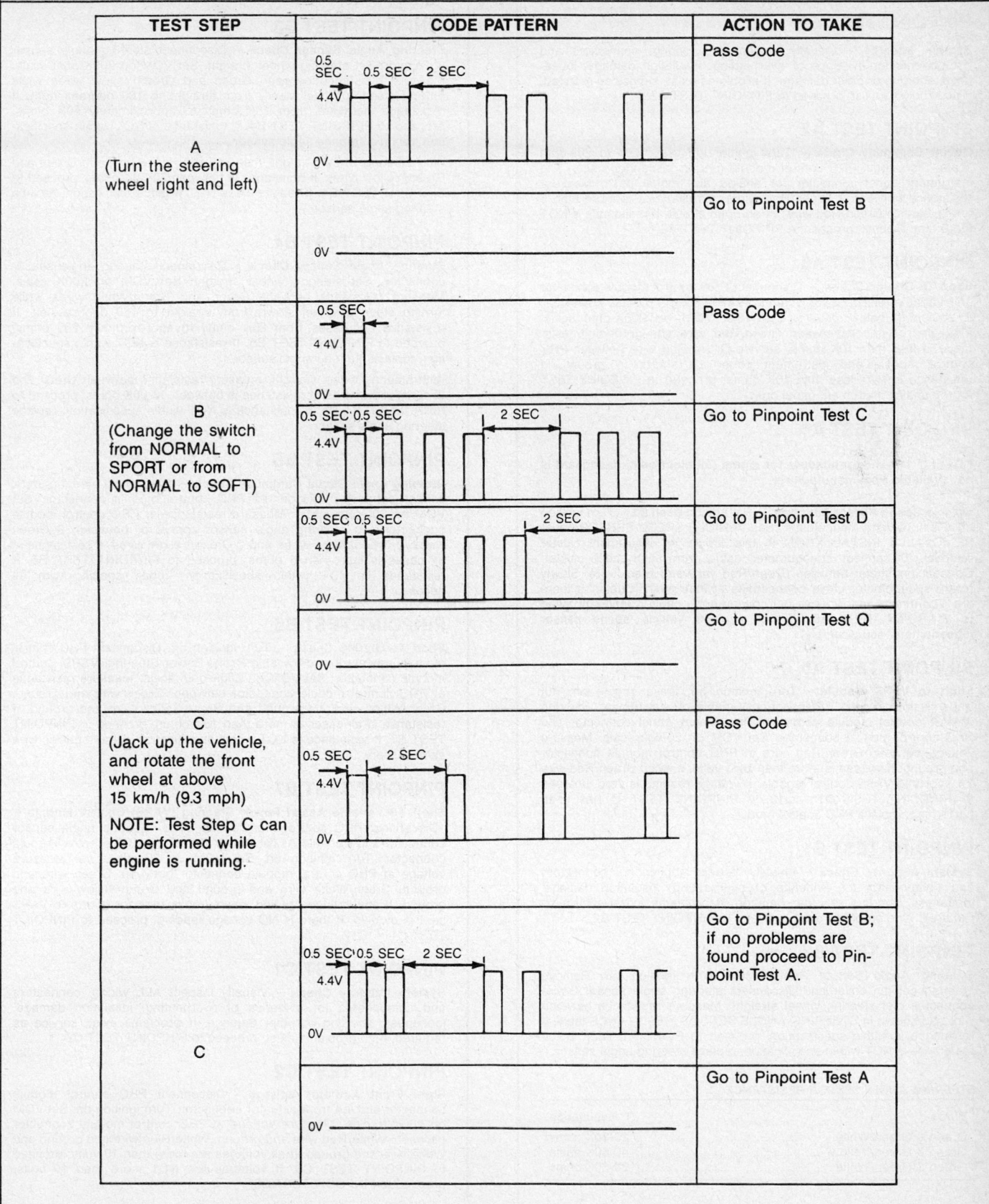

TEST STEP	CODE PATTERN	ACTION TO TAKE
A (Turn the steering wheel right and left)		Pass Code
		Go to Pinpoint Test B
B (Change the switch from NORMAL to SPORT or from NORMAL to SOFT)		Pass Code
		Go to Pinpoint Test C
		Go to Pinpoint Test D
		Go to Pinpoint Test Q
C (Jack up the vehicle, and rotate the front wheel at above 15 km/h (9.3 mph) NOTE: Test Step C can be performed while engine is running.		Pass Code
C		Go to Pinpoint Test B; if no problems are found proceed to Pinpoint Test A.
		Go to Pinpoint Test A

Courtesy of Ford Motor Co.

Fig. 7: Performing Key On, Engine Off Test

12-122

1989 ELECTRONIC SUSPENSION
Ford Motor Co. Programmed Ride Control (Cont.)

PINPOINT TEST A1

System Integrity – Visually inspect ALL wiring, connectors and components for evidence of overheating, insulation damage, looseness, shorting or other damage. If problems exist, service as required. If no problems exist, proceed to PINPOINT TEST A2.

PINPOINT TEST A2

Circuit Continuity Check – Turn ignition off. Set VOM to 200-ohm scale. Disconnect PRC control module (under passenger's seat) and instrument panel connector for analog and digital dash. Measure resistance between 2 Green/Red wires. If resistance is more than 5 ohms, service Green/Red wire for an open circuit. If resistance is NOT more than 5 ohms, proceed to PINPOINT TEST A3.

PINPOINT TEST A3

Short To Ground Check – Disconnect PRC control module connector and Variable Assist Power Steering (VAPS) control module connector, if equipped, below driver's seat. Set VOM on 200K-ohm scale. Measure resistance between Green/Red wire and ground. If resistance is less than 10K ohms, service Green/Red wire between PRC control module and instrument panel for shorts to ground. If resistance is NOT less than 10K ohms, proceed to PINPOINT TEST A4 (on analog instrument panel only.)

PINPOINT TEST A4

NOTE: Testing procedure for digital (all electronic) dashboard is not available from manufacturer.

Vehicle Speed Sensor Function – For analog dash only. Turn ignition off. Remove instrument cluster. See VEHICLE SPEED SENSOR under REMOVAL & INSTALLATION in this article for instrument cluster removal. Disconnect speedometer cable from instrument cluster. Connect ohmmeter between Green/Red wire and Black wire. Slowly rotate speedometer cable connections at instrument cluster. If there are 4 continuity interruptions per speedometer cable rotation, proceed to PINPOINT TEST A5. If not, replace vehicle speed sensor (speedometer subassembly).

PINPOINT TEST A5

Short to VAPS Module – Turn ignition on, leave engine off. Put transmission in park. Disconnect Variable Assist Power Steering (VAPS) control module connector, instrument panel connector and PRC control module connector. Set VOM on 20-volt scale. Measure voltage between Green/Red wire in PRC control module connector and ground. If voltage is more than zero volts, service Green/Red wire for shorts to VAPS control module. If voltage reading is zero, proceed to PINPOINT TEST Q1 – Q12. If PINPOINT TEST Q has been performed, replace PRC control module.

PINPOINT TEST B1

System Integrity Check – Visually inspect ALL wiring, connectors and components for evidence of overheating, insulation damage, looseness, shorting or other damage. If problems exist, service as required. If no problems exist, proceed to PINPOINT TEST B2.

PINPOINT TEST B2

Steering Angle Sensor Resistance – Turn ignition off. Remove steering column cover and disconnect steering angle sensor 3-wire connector. Set steering wheel straight. Measure resistance between wires as shown in STEERING ANGLE SENSOR RESISTANCE table. If resistance is within specification, proceed to PINPOINT TEST B3. If resistance is NOT within specification, replace steering angle sensor.

STEERING ANGLE SENSOR RESISTANCE

Wires	Resistance
Green & Green/White	20-30K ohms
Green & Green/Yellow	40-60K ohms
Green & Green/White	20-30K ohms

PINPOINT TEST B3

Steering Angle Sensor Check – Disconnect steering angle sensor connector. Set steering wheel straight. Set VOM on 200K-ohm scale. Measure resistance between Green and Green/Yellow wires while turning steering wheel slowly from straight to 180 degrees right. If resistance increases from 25K ohms to approximately 50K ohms, proceed to PINPOINT TEST B4. If resistance is NOT within specification, replace steering angle sensor.

With steering wheel straight, measure resistance between Green and Green/Yellow wires. If resistance is between 20-30K ohms, proceed to PINPOINT TEST B4. If resistance is NOT within specification, replace steering angle sensor.

PINPOINT TEST B4

Steering Angle Sensor Check – Disconnect steering angle sensor connector. Set steering wheel straight. Set VOM on 200K scale. Measure resistance between Green and Green/White wires while turning steering wheel slowly from straight to 180 degrees left. If resistance decreases from 25K ohms to approximately 200 ohms, proceed to PINPOINT TEST B5. If resistance is NOT within specification, replace steering angle sensor.

With steering wheel straight, measure resistance between Green and Green/Yellow wires. If resistance is between 40-60K ohms, proceed to PINPOINT TEST B5. If resistance is NOT within specification, replace steering angle sensor.

PINPOINT TEST B5

Steering Angle Circuit Continuity Check – Disconnect steering angle sensor connector. Disconnect PRC control module connector. Set VOM on 200-ohm scale. Measure resistance at PRC control module connector and steering angle sensor connector between: 2 Green wires, 2 Green/White wires and 2 Green/Yellow wires. If resistance in all cases is less than 5 ohms, proceed to PINPOINT TEST B6. If resistance is NOT within specification, repair specific wire as necessary.

PINPOINT TEST B6

Short To Ground Check – Turn ignition off. Disconnect PRC control module connector and Variable Assist Power Steering (VAPS) control module connector. Set VOM on 200K-ohm scale. Measure resistance at PRC control module connector between: Green wire and ground, Green/White wire and ground and Green/Yellow wire and ground. If resistance in all cases is more than 10K ohms, proceed to PINPOINT TEST B7. If resistance is NOT within specification, repair specific wire as necessary.

PINPOINT TEST B7

Short To Variable Assist Power Steering (VAPS) Control Module – Disconnect PRC control module connector, steering angle sensor connector and Variable Assist Power Steering (VAPS) control module connector. Turn ignition on. Set VOM on 20-volt scale. Measure voltage at PRC control module connector between: Green wire and ground, Green/White wire and ground and Green/Yellow wire and ground. If any voltage reading, check/repair wire for shorts to VAPS control module. If there is NO voltage reading, proceed to PINPOINT TEST Q1 – Q12.

PINPOINT TEST C1

System Integrity Check – Visually inspect ALL wiring, connectors and components for evidence of overheating, insulation damage, looseness, shorting or other damage. If problems exist, service as required. If no problems exist, proceed to PINPOINT TEST C2.

PINPOINT TEST C2

Right Front Actuator Voltage – Disconnect PRC control module connector and left front actuator connector. Turn ignition on. Set VOM on 20-volt scale. Measure voltage at PRC control module connector between: White/Red wire and ground, White/Blue wire and ground and White wire and ground. If all voltages are more than 10 volts, proceed to PINPOINT TEST C3. If voltages are NOT more than 10 volts, proceed to PINPOINT TEST C6.

1989 ELECTRONIC SUSPENSION
Ford Motor Co. Programmed Ride Control (Cont.)

12-123

PINPOINT TEST C3

Left Front Actuator Voltage – Disconnect PRC control module connector and right front actuator connector. Reconnect left front actuator connector. Turn ignition on. Set VOM on 20-volt scale. Measure voltage at PRC control module connector between: White-/Red wire and ground, White/Blue wire and ground and White wire and ground. If all voltages are more than 10 volts, proceed to PINPOINT TEST C4. If voltages are NOT more than 10 volts, proceed to PINPOINT TEST C8.

PINPOINT TEST C4

Right Front Actuator Integrity – Turn ignition off. Disconnect right front actuator connector. With a jumper wire, jump battery voltage to Yellow wire. With another jumper wire, ground White/Red wire, White/Blue and White/Yellow, one at a time. Verify motor operates as each terminal is grounded. If actuator motor operates when each terminal is grounded, proceed to PINPOINT TEST C5. If motor does NOT operate, replace right front actuator.

PINPOINT TEST C5

Left Front Actuator Integrity – Turn ignition off. Disconnect left front actuator connector. With a jumper wire, jump battery voltage to Yellow wire. With another jumper wire, ground White/Red wire, then White/Blue and then White/Yellow, one at a time. Verify motor operates as each terminal is grounded. If actuator motor operates when each terminal is grounded, proceed to PINPOINT TEST Q1 – Q12. If motor does not operate, replace left front actuator.

PINPOINT TEST C6

Right Front Actuator Voltage – Leave left front actuator disconnected. Turn ignition on. Set VOM on 20-volt scale. Check voltage from back of right front actuator connector between: White/Red wire and ground, White/Blue wire and ground and White/Yellow wire and ground. If all voltages are more than 10 volts, repair wire(s) as necessary. If voltages are NOT more than 10 volts, proceed to PINPOINT TEST C7.

PINPOINT TEST C7

Right Front Actuator Power – Disconnect right front actuator connector. Turn ignition on. Set VOM on 20-volt scale. Measure voltage between Yellow wire and ground. If voltage is more than 10 volts, replace right front actuator. If voltage is NOT more than 10 volts, repair Yellow wire between right front actuator and ignition relay as necessary.

PINPOINT TEST C8

Left Front Actuator Voltage – Leave right front actuator connector disconnected. Turn ignition on. Set VOM on 20-volt scale. Check voltage from back of left front actuator connector between: White/Red wire and ground, White/Blue wire and ground and White/Yellow wire and ground. If all voltages are more than 10 volts, repair wire(s) between left front actuator and PRC control module as necessary. If voltages are NOT more than 10 volts, proceed to PINPOINT TEST C9.

PINPOINT TEST C9

Left Front Actuator Power – Disconnect left front actuator connector. Turn ignition on. Set VOM on 20-volt scale. Measure voltage between Yellow wire and ground. If voltage is more than 10 volts, replace left front actuator. If voltage is NOT more than 10 volts, repair Yellow wire between actuator and ignition relay as necessary.

PINPOINT TEST D1

System Integrity Check – Visually inspect ALL wiring, connectors and components for evidence of overheating, insulation damage, looseness, shorting or other damage. If problems exist, service as required. If no problems exist, proceed to PINPOINT TEST D2.

PINPOINT TEST D2

Right Rear Actuator Voltage – Disconnect PRC module connector and left rear actuator connector. Turn ignition on. Set VOM on 20-volt scale. Measure voltage between: Yellow/Red wire and ground, Yellow/Green wire and ground and Yellow/Blue wire and ground. If all voltages are more than 10 volts, proceed to PINPOINT TEST D3. If voltages are NOT more than 10 volts, proceed to PINPOINT TEST D6.

PINPOINT TEST D3

Left Rear Actuator Voltage – Disconnect PRC module connector and right rear actuator connector. Reconnect left rear actuator connector. Turn ignition on. Set VOM on 20-volt scale. Measure voltage at PRC control module between: Yellow/Red wire and ground, Yellow/Green wire and ground and Yellow/Blue wire and ground. If all voltages are more than 10 volts, proceed to PINPOINT TEST D4. If voltages are NOT more than 10 volts, proceed to PINPOINT TEST D8.

PINPOINT TEST D4

Right Rear Actuator Integrity – Turn ignition off. Disconnect right rear actuator connector. With a jumper wire, jump battery voltage to Yellow wire. With another jumper wire, ground Yellow/Red wire, Yellow/Blue wire and Yellow/Green wire, one at a time. Verify motor operates as each terminal is grounded. If actuator motor operates when each terminal is grounded, proceed to PINPOINT TEST D5. If motor does NOT operate, replace right rear actuator.

PINPOINT TEST D5

Left Rear Actuator Integrity – Turn ignition off. Disconnect left rear actuator connector. With a jumper wire, jump battery voltage to Yellow wire. With another jumper wire, ground Yellow/Red wire, then Yellow/Blue and then Yellow/Green, one at a time. Verify motor operates as each terminal is grounded. If actuator motor operates when each terminal is grounded, proceed to PINPOINT TEST Q. If motor does NOT operate, replace left rear actuator.

PINPOINT TEST D6

Right Rear Actuator Voltage – Leave left rear actuator connector disconnected. Turn ignition on. Set VOM on 20-volt scale. Check voltage from back of right rear actuator connector between: Yellow/Red wire and ground, Yellow/Green wire and ground and Yellow/Black wire and ground. If all voltages are more than 10 volts, repair wire(s) between right rear actuator and PRC control module as necessary. If voltages are NOT more than 10 volts, proceed to PINPOINT TEST D7.

PINPOINT TEST D7

Right Rear Actuator Power – Disconnect right rear actuator connector. Turn ignition on. Set VOM on 20-volt scale. Measure voltage between Yellow wire and ground. If voltage is more than 10 volts, replace right rear actuator. If voltage is NOT more than 10 volts, repair Yellow wire between right rear actuator and ignition relay (in front of battery with black, 6-terminal connector) as necessary.

PINPOINT TEST D8

Left Rear Actuator Voltage – Leave right rear actuator connector disconnected. Turn ignition on. Set VOM on 20-volt scale. Check voltage from back of left front actuator connector between: Yellow/Red wire and ground, Yellow/Green wire and ground and Yellow/Blue wire and ground. If all voltages are more than 10 volts, repair wire(s) between left rear actuator and PRC control module as necessary. If voltages are NOT more than 10 volts, proceed to PINPOINT TEST D9.

PINPOINT TEST D9

Left Rear Actuator Power – Disconnect left rear actuator connector. Turn ignition on. Set VOM on 20-volt scale. Measure voltage between Yellow wire and ground. If voltage is more than 10 volts, replace left rear actuator. If voltage is NOT 10 volts, repair Yellow wire between left rear actuator and ignition relay (in front of battery with black, 6-terminal connector) as necessary.

PINPOINT TEST Q1

System Integrity Check – Visually inspect ALL wiring, connectors and components for evidence of overheating, insulation damage, looseness, shorting or other damage. If problems exist, service as required. If no problems exist, proceed to PINPOINT TEST Q2.

PINPOINT TEST Q2

PRC Control Module Power – Disconnect PRC control module connector. Turn ignition on. Set VOM on 20-volt scale. Measure voltage between Black/Yellow wire and ground. If voltage is more than 10 volts, proceed to PINPOINT TEST Q3. If voltage is NOT more than 10, check 15-amp fuse or repair Black/Yellow wire between PRC control module and fuse box at left-hand side of engine compartment as necessary.

PINPOINT TEST Q3

PRC Control Module Grounds – Leave PRC control module connector disconnected. Set VOM on 200-ohm scale. Measure resistance between 2 Black wires (near center of connector) and ground. If resistance is less than 5 ohms, proceed to PINPOINT TEST Q4. If resistance is NOT within specifications, repair Black wire between PRC control module and chassis ground, under front passenger seat near sill plate for opens, as necessary.

PINPOINT TEST Q4

Test Connector Ground – Disconnect PRC test connector, under hood below windshield wiper motor, from mounting. Set VOM on 200-ohm scale. Measure resistance between Black wire and ground. If resistance is less than 5 ohms, proceed to PINPOINT TEST Q5. If resistance is NOT less than 5 ohms, repair Black wire between test connector and chassis ground at right-hand fender apron as necessary.

PINPOINT TEST Q5

Test Connector Continuity – Disconnect PRC control module connector. Set VOM on 200-ohm scale. Measure resistance between Blue/White wires in PRC control module connector and PRC test connector. If resistance is less than 5 ohms, proceed to PINPOINT TEST Q6. If resistance is NOT less than 5 ohms, repair Blue/White wire between module and test connector for opens.

PINPOINT TEST Q6

Test Connector Short – Leave PRC control module connector disconnected. Turn ignition off. Set VOM on 200K-ohm scale. Measure resistance between Blue/White wire and ground. If resistance is more than 10K ohms, proceed to PINPOINT TEST Q7. If resistance is NOT more than 10K ohms, repair Blue/White wire between control module and test connector as necessary.

PINPOINT TEST Q7

Test Connector To VAPS Module – Leave PRC control module connector disconnected. Turn ignition on. Set VOM on 20-volt scale. Measure voltage between Blue/White wire and ground. If voltage reading is more than zero volt, repair Blue/White wire between module and PRC test connector as necessary. If voltage is NOT more than zero, proceed to PINPOINT TEST Q8.

PINPOINT TEST Q8

Ride Selector Switch Power – Disconnect PRC ride selector switch connector on center console. Turn ignition on. Set VOM on 20-volt scale. Measure voltage between Black/Yellow wire and ground. If voltage reading is less than 10 volts, check 15-amp fuse or Black/Yellow wire between fuse box and ride selector switch. If voltage is NOT less than 10 volts, proceed to PINPOINT TEST Q9.

PINPOINT TEST Q9

Ride Selector Switch Ground – Leave PRC ride selector switch connector disconnected. Set VOM on 200-ohm scale. Measure resistance between Black wire and ground. If resistance is less than 5 ohms, proceed to PINPOINT TEST Q10. If resistance is NOT less than 5 ohms, repair Black wire between ride selector switch and chassis ground at right-hand fender apron for opens.

PINPOINT TEST Q10

Module/Ride Selector Switch Continuity – Disconnect PRC control module connector and PRC ride selector switch connector. Set VOM on 200-ohm scale. Measure resistance between Blue/Yellow wires at 2 connectors. If resistance is less than 5 ohms, proceed to PINPOINT TEST Q11. If resistance is not less than 5 ohms, repair Blue/Yellow wire between control module and ride selector switch for opens as necessary.

PINPOINT TEST Q11

PRC Circuit Short To Ground – Disconnect PRC control module connector and PRC ride selector switch connector. Set VOM on 200K-ohm scale. Measure resistance between Blue/Yellow wire and ground. If resistance is more than 10K ohms, proceed to PINPOINT TEST Q12. If resistance is not more than 10K ohms, repair Blue/Yellow wire between control module and switch for shorts to ground as necessary.

PINPOINT TEST Q12

Ride Selector Switch Operation – Remove PRC ride selector switch from center console. Set VOM on 200-ohm scale. Measure continuity between ride selector switch terminals in all positions. Reverse polarity and check continuity twice between each terminal indicated in table. *See Fig. 9.* If selector switch functions properly, replace PRC control module. If switch does NOT function properly, replace PRC ride selector switch.

1989 ELECTRONIC SUSPENSION
Ford Motor Co. Programmed Ride Control (Cont.)

12-125

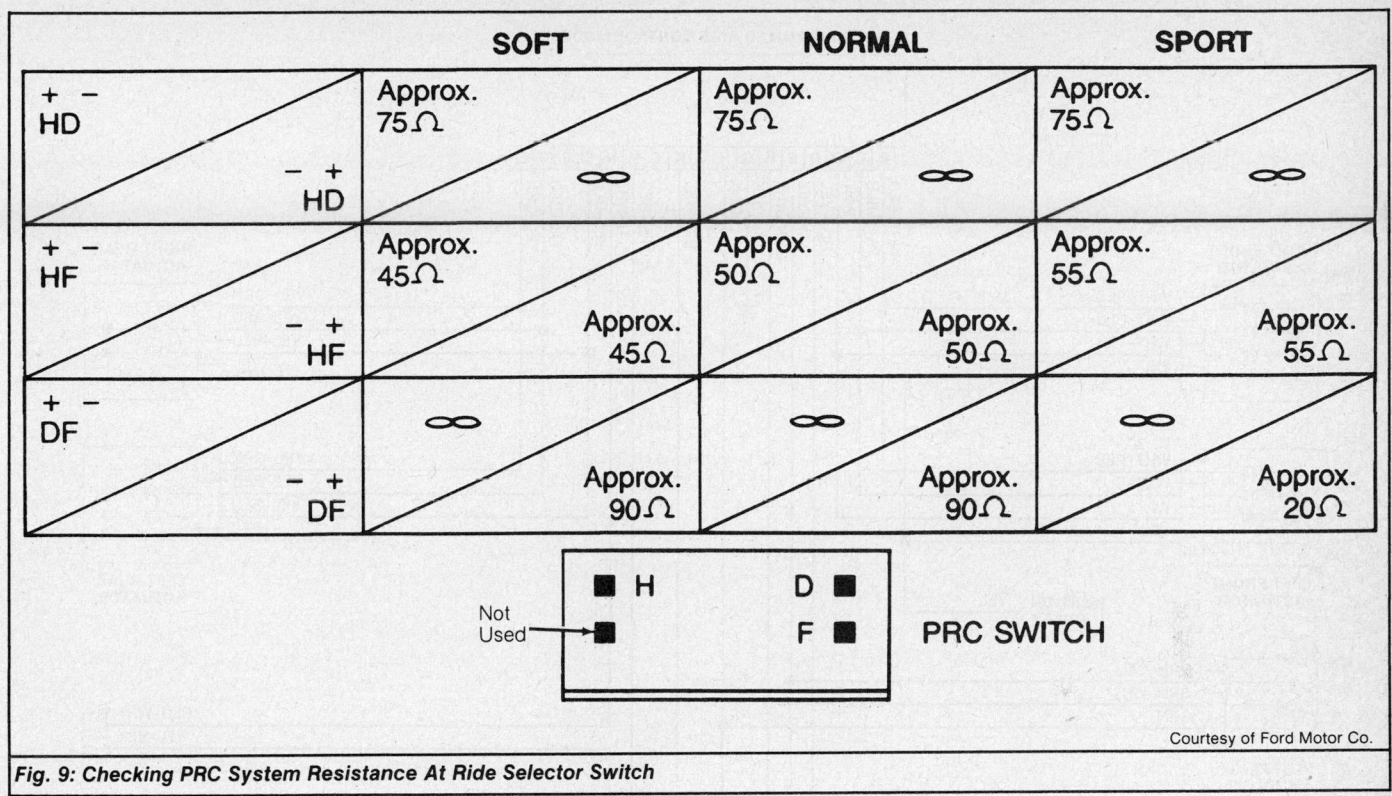

Fig. 9: Checking PRC System Resistance At Ride Selector Switch

Courtesy of Ford Motor Co.

1989 ELECTRONIC SUSPENSION
Ford Motor Co. Programmed Ride Control (Cont.)

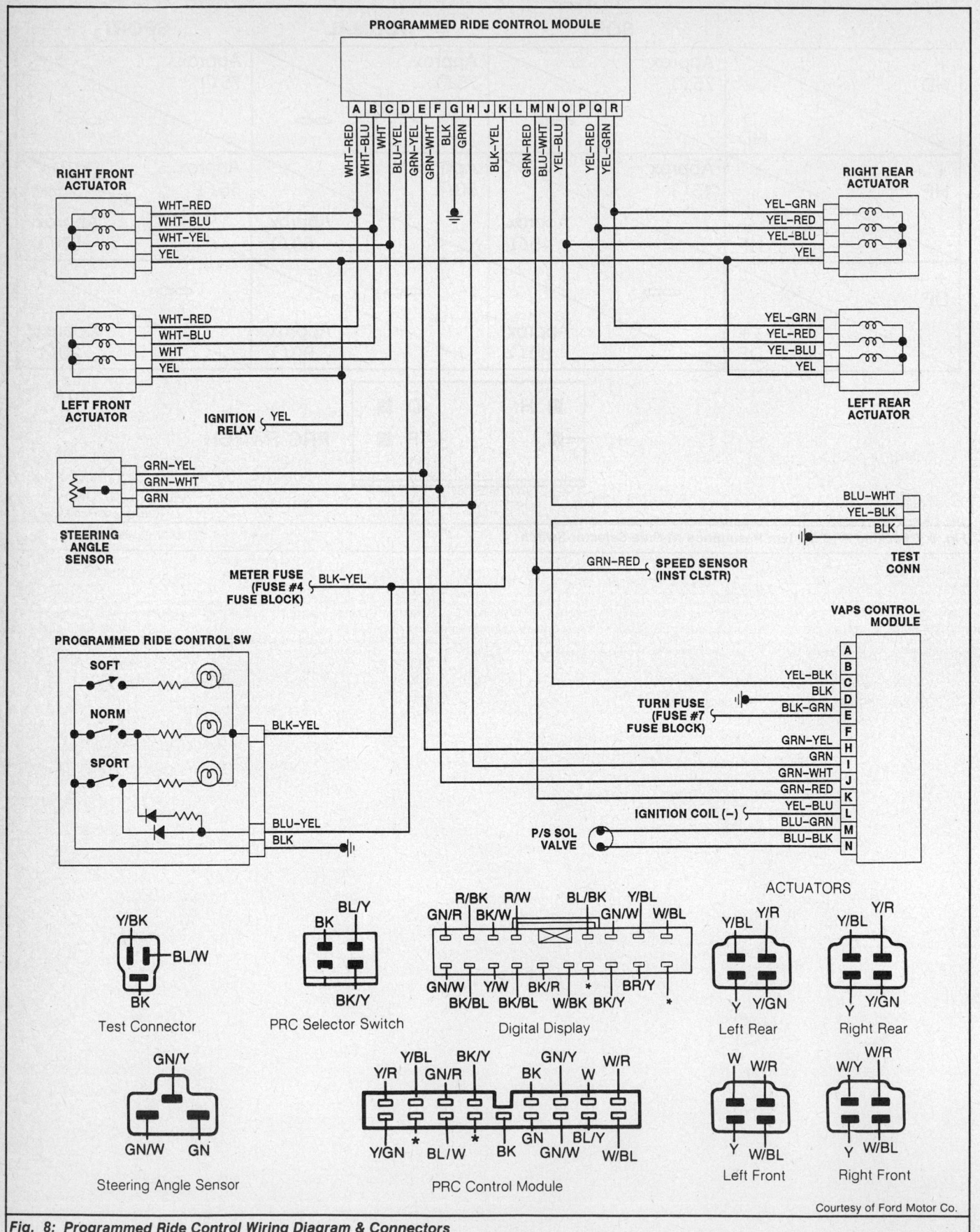

LTD Crown Victoria, Grand Marquis, Town Car, Wagon

CAUTION: DO NOT charge battery with ignition on. Damage to air compressor will occur.

DESCRIPTION

The automatic leveling system is an air-operated, computer-controlled leveling system. Components are in addition to the standard rear suspension. Vehicle ride height automatically adjusts to varying loads, with the aid of air shocks. The system consists of air-adjustable shocks, a compressor assembly, air drier with minimum retention valve, exhaust solenoid, compressor relay, rotary height sensor, microcomputer module, wiring and nylon tubing.

OPERATION

Air suspension leveling system operates by adding or removing air in the air shocks to maintain level of vehicle at a predetermined rear suspension height. The suspension height is controlled by a rotary height sensor. Airflow to the entire system is controlled by the interaction of the air compressor, vent solenoid, height sensor and microcomputer module.

AIR COMPRESSOR

A single cylinder piston-type air compressor is mounted on the left front wheelwell of all models. The compressor is electrically operated. A regenerative-type drier is attached to compressor manifold. The vent solenoid, located on compressor manifold, controls air expulsion. A minimum retention valve, located inside the air drier, maintains a minimum pressure in air shocks of 10-22 psi.

MICROCOMPUTER MODULE

The microcomputer module is mounted behind the right rear trim panel in the luggage compartment. It controls the compressor relay and vent solenoid. The microcomputer module also controls power and ground to the rotary sensor. The module provides a 7-13 second time delay before any circuit can be completed.

The microcomputer module monitors air suspension system through inputs from the height sensor and ignition circuits. It limits compressor run time to 2 minutes and exhaust solenoid time to one minute. This function is to limit continuous compressor operation in case of a severe system leak or a malfunctioning exhaust valve. The timer function is reset when ignition key is cycled through "OFF" and "RUN" positions.

ROTARY HEIGHT SENSOR

Ride height is controlled by the rotary height sensor. The sensor is located at the center of rear crossmember above the center section of the axle.

The sensor operates as follows: as vehicle lowers, height sensor arm is rotated upward (low out-of-trim), sending 2 signals to microcomputer. After 7-13 seconds of continuous height sensor signal, the air compressor activates to send air to the shocks.

When pre-set ride height is reached, the air compressor shuts off. As weight is removed from the vehicle, the body will raise. The height sensor arm is rotated downward (high out-of-trim). After sending a continuous 7-13 second signal to microcomputer, the vent solenoid is activated and allows air to escape. As vehicle lowers, height sensor rotates upward. When pre-set ride height is reached, vent solenoid valves close.

ADJUSTMENTS
RIDING HEIGHT

Ride height specification is adjusted by moving rear sensor arm ball stud to one of 3 positions. Raise and support vehicle. Loosen stud attaching nut at upper control arm. Move sensor attachment to

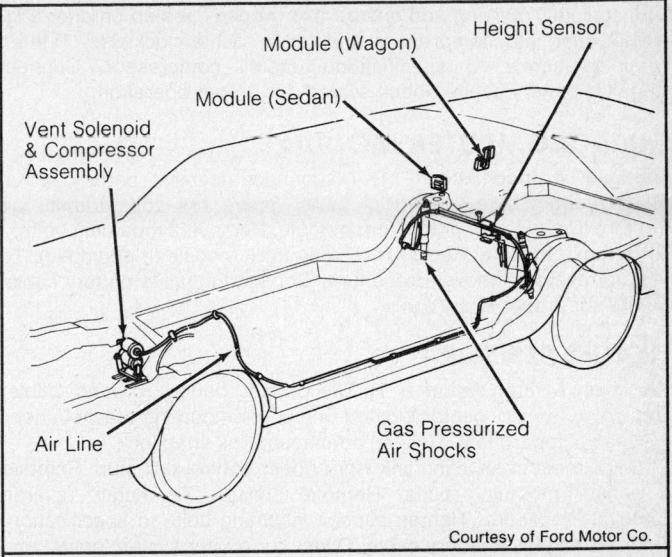

Courtesy of Ford Motor Co.

Fig. 1: Automatic Leveling Rear Suspension Components

desired position. There are 3 adjustment positions provided on the arm. Normally set in center position, one position change will provide .75" (19 mm) adjustment. *See Fig. 2.* Lower vehicle and turn ignition on. Check ride height. Ride height is measured vertically from rear axle tube to frame rail. See RIDE HEIGHT SPECIFICATIONS in this article.

NOTE: Ride height is measured vertically from axle tube to frame rail at this location on vehicle.

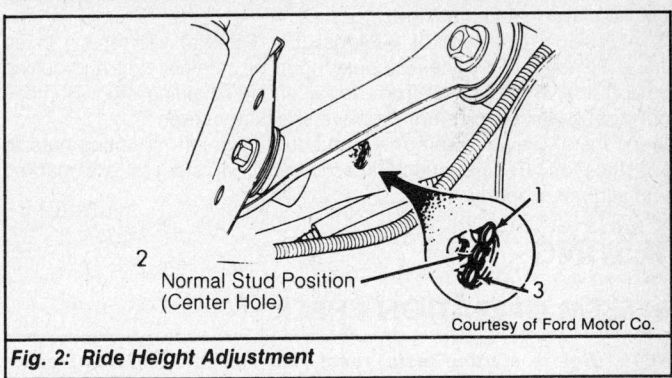

Courtesy of Ford Motor Co.

Fig. 2: Ride Height Adjustment

REMOVAL & INSTALLATION

AIR COMPRESSOR

NOTE: During installation always reconnect negative battery cable last.

Removal & Installation – 1) Disconnect negative battery cable. Remove air line from drier by pushing in on retainer and pulling air line out. Unplug wire connector from air compressor.

2) Remove air compressor. Remove mounting bracket. To install, reverse removal procedure. Reconnect negative battery cable. Check air lines for leakage. Check for proper system operation.

AIR DRIER

Removal & Installation – 1) Disconnect negative battery cable. Unplug wire connector from air compressor. Remove air compressor from mounting bracket.

2) Remove drier-to-compressor retaining screw. Twist drier clockwise to disengage from air compressor. Remove drier and "O" ring. Discard "O" ring.

12-128

1989 ELECTRONIC SUSPENSION
Ford Motor Co. Rear Level Control (Cont.)

3) Install new "O" ring and ensure it is properly seated on drier end. Install drier into compressor and twist counterclockwise. Tighten retaining screw to specification. Install compressor. Connect negative battery cable. Check system for proper operation.

MICROCOMPUTER MODULE

Removal & Installation – 1) Disconnect negative battery cable. Remove right side trunk trim panel (spare tire compartment on wagon). Unplug connector from module. Remove 2 mounting bolts. **2)** Remove module. Remove "U" nuts from module (if equipped). To install, reverse removal procedure. Connect negative battery cable. Check for proper operation.

HEIGHT SENSOR

Removal & Installation – 1) Disconnect battery ground cable. Unplug sensor connector located on sensor mounting bracket under luggage compartment. Unlatch connecting link snap lock.
2) Disconnect connecting link from upper control ball stud. Remove 2 sensor mounting bolts. Remove sensor. To install, reverse removal procedure. Tighten sensor mounting bolts to specification. Connect negative battery cable. Check for proper system operation.

REAR SHOCK ABSORBERS

CAUTION: Removal procedure must be followed carefully to avoid damage to components.

NOTE: Air shocks may be replaced individually. Replace faulty shock only.

Removal & Installation – 1) Turn ignition off. Disconnect height sensor connector link. Raise vehicle. The vent solenoid will vent air while vehicle is on jack or hoist. Wait until air has stopped "hissing" before disconnecting air lines.
2) A residual pressure of 8-24 psi (55-165 kPa) will remain in air lines. Disconnect air lines by pushing in on retainer ring and pulling out on line. Remove nut from upper shock retaining stud. Remove nut from lower shock stud. Remove shock absorber.
3) To install, reverse removal procedure. Tighten mounting nuts to specification. Ensure shock absorber rubber sleeves are marked and aligned properly.

TESTING

SYSTEM OPERATION CHECK

NOTE: Before starting tests, reset vent solenoid and compressor "on times" by turning ignition on then off.

1) Measure and record ride height. Adjust to specification (if necessary). Briefly start and run engine. Apply a load of 300-350 lbs. (136-159 kg) to the rear of the vehicle. There should be a 7-13 second delay before the compressor turns on and rear of vehicle starts to rise.
2) Vehicle should rise to within 1/2" (13 mm) of ride height set in step **1)** by the time the compressor shuts off. If vehicle does not rise to within 1/2" (13 mm) of the unloaded specification, check trunk for excess weight. If overloaded, remove load and retest.
3) Remove load applied in step **1)**. There should be a 7-13 second delay before vehicle starts to lower. Vehicle should lower to within 1/2" (13 mm) of ride height specification. If not, refer to DIAGNOSTIC TESTING in this article.

RESIDUAL PRESSURE CHECK

1) Remove the air line from the drier and attach it to one side of a pressure gauge. Connect the drier to the other side of the gauge using a short piece of nylon tubing. Turn ignition from off to on.
2) Apply a load of 300-350 lbs. (136-159 kg) to the rear of vehicle to run the compressor and raise vehicle. Remove load and allow system to exhaust air pressure and lower vehicle.

3) When no more air is being exhausted, the gauge should read 8-24 psi (55-165 kPa). Remove pressure gauge and reconnect the system. Turn ignition from off to on and repeat step **2)** to ensure there is system air pressure in the shocks.

LEAK CHECK

NOTE: If compressor is run to maximum pressure the vent solenoid valve will function as a relief valve. The leak-down, after compressor shut-down will indicate a false air leak.

1) Repeat steps **1)** and **2)** of RESIDUAL PRESSURE CHECK. Allow the system to fill until the gauge reads 70-100 psi (483-690 kPa). With load still applied, disconnect wiring harness connector from the microcomputer module and then remove the load.
2) Rear of vehicle should rise. Turn ignition on then off. Observe system for leaks for about 15 minutes. If system will not inflate to more than 50 psi (339 kPa), a severe air leak is indicated. Check air line between compressor and shocks for damage.
3) Check all connections with soap/water solution. If pressure is stable, perform diagnostic test.
4) Attach wire connector to module. Turn ignition switch from "OFF" to "RUN" position. Allow air to exhaust and vehicle to lower. Remove pressure gauge from system and reconnect drier. Turn ignition from "OFF" to "ON" and repeat step **2)** of RESIDUAL PRESSURE CHECK. Perform SYSTEM OPERATION CHECK.

MONITOR LIGHT OPERATION

1) Turning the ignition switch from "OFF" to "RUN" will cause monitor light to flash. The monitor light flashes once per second while compressor relay is on.
2) The light stays on while ignition is on and one or more of the following occur: height sensor wire connector is detached, an air line is removed, vent solenoid is on over one minute or compressor relay is on over 2 minutes.
3) Whenever an abnormal program run is detected, the microcomputer module suspends all controls and the monitor light stays on. All system functions of the module, except compressor relay on, are energized for 29-31 minutes after the ignition is turned off.
4) To reset the system, turn ignition switch from "OFF" to "RUN" position.

DIAGNOSTIC TESTING

NOTE: To perform diagnostic testing, an analog volt/ohmmeter, a jumper lead and a test light with No. 194 bulb must be used. Use of any other type of testing equipment may damage system or give false readings.

Construct test light using a No. 194 bulb, one lead with a pointed probe end and the other lead with a clip end. Leads should be 25-30" in length. Connect test light before turning ignition switch from "RUN" to "OFF" position.

When performing tests, observe that the module vent solenoid timer (1 minute) and compressor timer (2 minutes) are operating properly. Perform tests without disconnecting the harness at the module connector, unless stated in individual tests. The compressor relay, vent solenoid and height sensor have internal diodes for noise suppression. DO NOT reverse polarity.

QUICK REFERENCE TEST CHART

Description	Test
Vehicle Load	Test A
Power Monitor Light	Test B
Initialize System	Test C
Ignition Circuit	Test D
Battery Circuit	Test E
Vent Solenoid Circuit	Test F
Sensor Ground Circuit	Test G
Sensor Power Circuit	Test H
Sensor Logic Circuits	Test J
Compressor Relay/Motor	Test K

1989 ELECTRONIC SUSPENSION
Ford Motor Co. Rear Level Control (Cont.)

12-129

RIDE HEIGHT SPECIFICATIONS

Application	Inches (mm)
Crown Victoria, Grand Marquis (Sedan)	6.02 (152.9)
Crown Victoria, Grand Marquis (Wagon)	6.47 (164.3)
Town Car	5.58 (141.8)

TIGHTENING SPECIFICATIONS

Application	Ft. Lbs. (N.m)
Shock Absorber Lower Nut	52-85 (70-115)
Shock Absorber Upper Nut	14-26 (19-35)

Application	INCH Lbs. (N.m)
Air Drier Mounting Screw	15-25 (1.6-2.8)
Compressor Bracket-to-Body Nut	72-156 (8-17)
Compressor-to-Air Drier Screw	13-19 (1.5-2.1)
Compressor-to-Bracket Mounting Bolt	30-40 (3.4-4.5)
Control Module Bolt	72-156 (8-17)
Height Sensor Bolt	72-156 (8-17)

SYMPTOM	ACTION TO TAKE
• System inoperative: compressor does not run. • Vehicle low or high: vehicle rises and lowers OK when load is added or removed, but normal trim height seems high or low.	• CHECK vehicle load. • CHECK trim height as outlined. • PERFORM System Operation Check. • PERFORM diagnosis procedure.
• Vehicle rises OK, but gradually leaks down. • Compressor cycles On and Off intermittently while driving.	• REFER to Leak Checks. • PERFORM diagnosis procedure. • PERFORM System Operation Check.
• Compressor runs continuously for two minutes with ignition switch in RUN. • Compressor turns Off after two minutes of accumulated operating time. **NOTE: Vehicle rear may or may not rise during either situation.**	• REFER to Leak Checks. • CHECK sensor link attachment. • CHECK compressor relay and motor circuit for short to ground. • CHECK sensor circuits — Pinpoint Tests G, H and J. • PERFORM diagnosis procedure.
• Vehicle high or will not lower with ignition switch ON or OFF.	• CHECK vent solenoid circuit, Pinpoint Test F. • CHECK sensor circuits — Pinpoint Tests G, H and J. • CHECK ignition circuit — Pinpoint Test D. • CHECK sensor link attachment and ball stud position. • PERFORM diagnosis procedure.
• Vehicle low or compressor does not run with ignition switch ON and a load applied.	• CHECK sensor link attachment. • CHECK ignition circuit — Pinpoint Test D. • CHECK sensor circuits — Pinpoint Tests G, H and J. • CHECK compressor relay and motor circuits — Pinpoint Test K. • PERFORM diagnosis procedure.
• Excessive bottoming in rear with load.	• CHECK trim height as outlined. • REFER to Leak Checks. • PERFORM System Operational Check.

Courtesy of Ford Motor Co.

Fig. 3: Diagnosis Selection Chart

12-130

1989 ELECTRONIC SUSPENSION
Ford Motor Co. Rear Level Control (Cont.)

Wiring	Harness Side Connector	Pin Number	Function	Wire Harness			Circuit End Point
				Circuit	Color	Gauge	
Front Compressor and Vent Solenoid	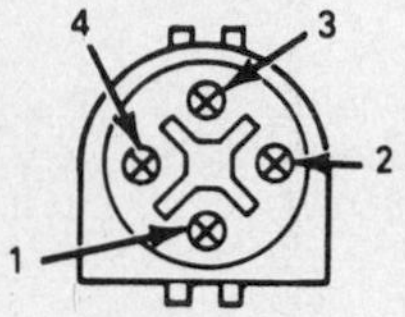	1	Solenoid Control	415	LG/O	14	Module Pin No. 9
		2	Motor Ground	57B	BK	12	Battery Ground Terminal
		3	Motor Feed	417	P/O	12	Compressor Relay
		4	Solenoid Feed	37F	Y	14	Starter Relay
Compressor Relay (1)	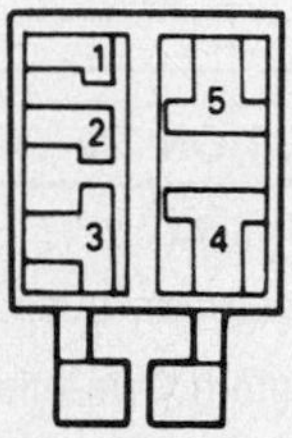	1	Control	420	DB/Y	18	Module Pin No. 8
		2	Feed (Coil)	298A	P/O	18	Compressor Relay
		3	Feed (Contacts)	37C	Y	12	Starter Relay
		4	Compressor Motor Feed	417	P/O	12	Compressor
		5	Compressor Motor Ground	57A	BK	12	Battery Ground Terminal
Front/Rear Harness Connector	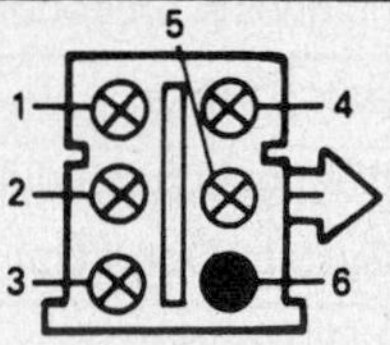	1	Control	420	DB/Y	18	Module Pin No. 8
		2	Ignition Sense	298A	P/O	18	Ignition Switch
		3	System Ground	57	BK	14	Battery Ground Terminal
		4	—	—	—	—	
		5	Module Power	37	Y	14	Module Pin No. 5
		6	Vent Solenoid Control	415	LG/O	14	Module Pin No. 9
Ignition Sense			Ignition Sense	298	P/O	18	Module Pin No. 4
				and 298A	P/O	18	Compressor Relay
Rear Height Sensor (1)		1	Logic Line B	428	O/BK	18	Module Pin No. 6
		2	Feed	431	PK/W	18	Module Pin No. 3
		3	Logic Line A	427	PK/BK	18	Module Pin No. 1
		4	Ground	430	GY	18	Module Pin No. 10
Module (1)			Diagnostic Monitor Lamp	693	O	18	Module Pin No. 7
	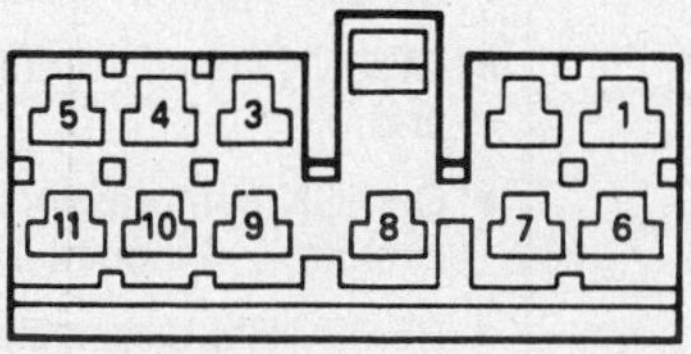			Wire Bundle			Control Module

Fig. 4: Harness Connector Chart

Courtesy of Ford Motor Co.

1989 ELECTRONIC SUSPENSION
Ford Motor Co. Rear Level Control (Cont.)

12-131

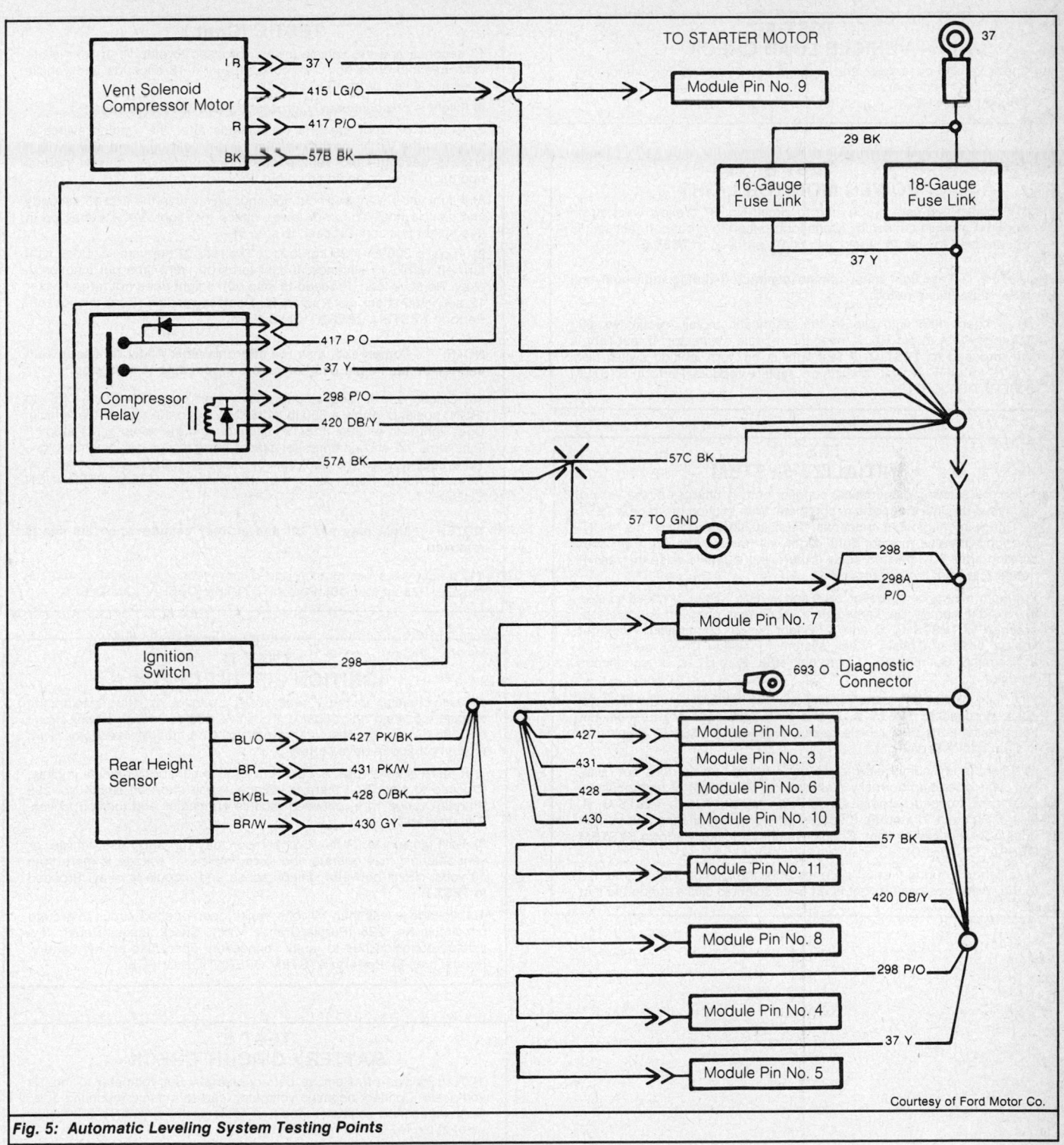

Fig. 5: Automatic Leveling System Testing Points

Courtesy of Ford Motor Co.

12-132

1989 ELECTRONIC SUSPENSION
Ford Motor Co. Rear Level Control (Cont.)

TEST A
VEHICLE LOAD CHECK

Check vehicle passenger and luggage compartments for overloading. Unload as necessary. If ride height is okay, perform SYSTEM OPERATION CHECK. Adjust ride height if necessary.

TEST B
POWER MONITOR LIGHT

1) Connect test light probe lead to circuit No. 37 (Yellow wire) at pin No. 5 on module connector. Connect clip lead to ground. If test light is on, proceed to step 2). If test light is off, proceed to **TEST E**.

NOTE: Test light must remain connected during individual test unless otherwise noted.

2) Connect lead with clip to the diagnostic pigtail, circuit No. 693 (Orange wire) at pin No. 7, near the module connector. If test light is off, proceed to **TEST C**. If test light is on, turn ignition switch from "RUN" to "OFF". If light remains on, replace module. Perform SYSTEM OPERATION CHECK.

TEST C
INITIALIZE SYSTEM

1) Before entering diagnostics, connect battery charger to the vehicle and leave on until diagnosis is complete. With ignition off, repeat **TEST B**. Check monitor light functions. Turn ignition switch to the "RUN" position. Observe monitor light. Light will normally be off, then start blinking after 7-13 second delay if there is a signal to raise the rear of the vehicle from the height sensor.

2) If light blinks, compressor runs and vehicle raises, proceed to step 5). If light comes on immediately, abnormal program is detected, proceed to **TESTS G, H and J**. If light blinks, compressor runs, but vehicle does not raise, check system for leaks. Check sensor link attachment. Compressor times out after 2 minutes of continuous running.

3) If light blinks, but compressor does not run and vehicle does not raise, proceed to **TESTS D, E and K**. If light does not turn on, but compressor runs and vehicle raises, proceed to **TEST B**. Reinitialize system and observe light.

4) If light is off, compressor does not run and vehicle does not raise, vehicle is operating normally. Vehicle is at ride height or high position. Check for crossed harness sensor logic circuits. Go to **TESTS G, H, and J**. Proceed to step 5). If light is off, compressor runs, but vehicle does not raise, check light. Check system for leaks. Perform SYSTEM OPERATION CHECK.

5) Is light off during first 60 seconds after the ignition switch is turned to the "RUN" position? If light is off, vent solenoid clicks during the first

TEST C (Cont.)

15 seconds and the vehicle lowers, proceed to step 7). If light is off, vent solenoid does not click during the first 15 seconds and vehicle does not lower, proceed to step 8).

6) If light is on continuously, proceed to **TESTS F, G, H and J**.

7) Is light on after the first 60 seconds after the ignition switch is turned to the "RUN" position? If light is on, vent solenoid clicks within first 15 seconds and vehicle does/does not lower, this is normal operation. Vent solenoid timed out. Proceed to step 9).

8) If light is off, vent solenoid does not click within the first 15 seconds and vehicle does/does not lower, check test light. Vehicle may be in ride height position. Proceed to step 9).

9) Apply a 300 lb. (136 kg) load to the rear of the vehicle. Does light turn off within 15 seconds. If light turns off, vent time out function is okay. Remove load. Proceed to step 10). If light does not turn off after 15 seconds, check vent solenoid. Replace module. Turn ignition off. Perform SYSTEM OPERATION CHECK.

NOTE: Compressor may run after this time. Allow vehicle to vent and reach ride height position before proceeding to next step.

10) Disconnect air line at drier. Turn ignition switch from "OFF" to "RUN" position. Apply a 300 lb. (136 kg) load to the rear of the vehicle. Does light turn on after 115-125 seconds and the compressor stop? If light turns on and compressor stops, compressor run timer is okay. Time begins when the compressor starts to run. Reconnect air line. Remove weight from rear of vehicle. Perform SYSTEM OPERATION CHECK.

NOTE: Light may turn off and air may escape when the line is removed.

11) If light does not turn on and compressor does not stop, replace module. Repeat step 10). Perform SYSTEM OPERATION CHECK.

TEST D
IGNITION CIRCUIT CHECK

1) Set voltmeter to the 12-volt scale. Connect negative lead to the module mounting bolt . Connect positive lead to ignition power circuit No. 298 (Purple/Orange wire) at pin No. 4 on module connector. Turn ignition off and remove battery charger.

2) If there is zero volts, circuit from ignition sensor to module is okay. Proceed to step 3). If there is voltage, repair short on circuit No. 298 (Purple/Orange wire) between module connector and ignition switch. Repeat step 1).

3) Turn ignition to "RUN". Compressor may run and raise vehicle, or vent solenoid may operate and lower vehicle. If voltage is more than 10 volts, circuit between ignition sense and module is okay. Proceed to **TEST E**.

4) If voltage is less than 10 volts, repair open or short circuit to ground on circuit No. 298 (Purple/Orange wire). Check fuses. Repair low voltage condition due to faulty connection, open fuse or low battery. Repeat step 3). Perform SYSTEM OPERATION CHECK.

TEST E
BATTERY CIRCUIT CHECK

1) Turn ignition off. Remove battery charger. Set voltmeter to the 12-volt scale. Connect negative voltmeter lead to module mounting bolt . Connect positive voltmeter lead to module power circuit No. 37 (Yellow wire) at pin No. 5 on module connector.

NOTE: With ignition off and 30-minute timer activated, solenoid may click and vehicle may or may not lower.

2) If voltage is more than 10 volts and steady, battery circuit to the module is okay. Perform **TEST B**. If voltage is less than 10 volts, repair low voltage condition due to faulty connection, low battery or fusible link at starter relay on circuit No. 37 (Yellow wire). Reconnect connectors as necessary. Repeat step 1).

1989 ELECTRONIC SUSPENSION
Ford Motor Co. Rear Level Control (Cont.)

12-133

TEST F
VENT SOLENOID SYSTEM CHECK

1) Check monitor light. Remove battery charger. Turn ignition switch to "OFF" position. If monitor light is off, test is okay. Go to step 2). If monitor light is on 55 seconds after ignition was turned off, vent time out is okay. Proceed to step 2).

2) Set voltmeter to the 12-volt scale. Connect negative voltmeter lead to module mounting bolt . Connect positive lead to circuit No. 415 (Light Green/Orange wire) at pin No. 9 on module connector. If voltage reading is more than 8.5 volts and steady, circuit between vent solenoid and module is okay. Proceed to step 3). If voltage is less than 8.5 volts, check battery voltage. Proceed to step 3).

3) Remove positive lead from voltmeter and touch to a good ground. If vent solenoid clicks, vent solenoid and circuit No. 415 to module are okay. Reconnect test lead and proceed to step 4). If vent solenoid does not click, reconnect test lead and proceed to test 5).

4) Raise rear bumper with floor jack. Turn ignition switch from "RUN" to "OFF" position. If light is on after 55 seconds, vent times out is okay. Proceed to step 6). If light is off after 55 seconds, check sensor circuits. Replace module. Perform SYSTEM OPERATION CHECK.

5) Move positive voltmeter lead to solenoid feed circuit No. 37 (Yellow wire) at the compressor connector. Disregard monitor light. If voltage is more than 8.5 volts and steady, solenoid feed circuit from battery relay is okay. Proceed to step 6). If voltage is less than 8.5 volts and steady, repair low voltage condition, or open in feed circuit No. 37 (Yellow wire) from starter relay to the connector. Repeat step 5).

6) Move positive voltmeter lead to solenoid control unit circuit No. 415 at the compressor connector. Disregard the monitor light. If voltage reading is more than 8.5 volts, and steady, vent solenoid is okay. Proceed to step 7). If voltage is less than 8.5 volts, vent solenoid is inoperative. Replace compressor assembly. Repeat step 6).

7) Move voltmeter lead to control circuit No. 415 (Light Green/Orange wire) at pin No. 9 on module connector. Disregard monitor light. If voltage is less than 8.5 volts, repair open in control circuit No. 415 (Light Green/Orange wire) between module connector and compressor connector. Repeat step 7). If voltage is more than 8.5 volts, solenoid circuit is okay. Proceed to TEST H.

TEST G
SENSOR GROUND CIRCUIT CHECK

1) Turn ignition switch from "ON" to "OFF" position. Remove battery charger. Unplug connector from module. Connect negative ohmmeter lead to module mounting bolt. Touch positive lead to module pin No. 10. Disregard monitor light. If resistance is more than 2 ohms, record reading. Proceed to step 2). If reading is less than 2 ohms, sensor ground circuit through module is okay. Proceed to step 2).

2) Connect ohmmeter lead to circuit No. 431 (Pink/White wire) at pin No. 3 on module connector. Move negative ohmmeter lead to ground circuit No. 430 (Gray wire) at pin No. 10 on module connector. If resistance is more than 8 ohms, proceed to step 3). If resistance is less than 8 ohms, sensor circuit to ground is okay. Proceed to TEST H.

3) Disconnect rear harness sensor connector at underbody. On sedan, push harness grommet up inside luggage compartment. On wagon, use longer test leads. Move positive test lead of ohmmeter to ground circuit No. 430 (Gray wire) at the height sensor connector. If resistance is more than 2 ohms, repair open in sensor ground circuit No. 430 (Gray wire) between module connector and height sensor connector. Repeat step 3). If resistance is less than 2 ohms, proceed to step 4).

4) Move positive voltmeter lead to circuit No. 431 (Pink/White wire) at height sensor connector. Move negative lead to circuit No. 431 (Pink/White wire) at pin No. 3 on module connector. If resistance is more than 2 ohms, repair open in sensor circuit No. 431 between module connector and height sensor connector. Repeat step 4). If resistance is less than 2 ohms, circuit No. 431 is okay, proceed to step 5).

5) Move positive test lead to sensor circuit No. 431 (sensor side). Move negative test lead to sensor circuit No. 430. (sensor side). If resistance is more than 18 ohms, replace sensor. Perform SYSTEM OPERATION CHECK. If resistance is less than 18 ohms, proceed to step 6).

6) Reconnect all separated connectors. Perform procedure outlined in step 1). If resistance is less than 20 ohms, system is okay. If resistance is more than 20 ohms, replace module. Perform SYSTEM OPERATION CHECK.

TEST H
SENSOR POWER CIRCUIT CHECK

1) Reconnect module, if disconnected. Set voltmeter to 5-volt scale. Connect voltmeter negative lead to module mounting bolt. Connect positive lead to sensor power circuit No. 431 (Pink/White wire) at pin No. 3 on module connector. Turn igniton switch from "RUN" to "OFF" position. Disregard monitor light. Vent solenoid may click. Observe voltmeter.

NOTE: Voltage check must be completed within 30 minutes of cycling ignition switch, or voltage will return to zero.

2) If voltage is 5 volts and steady, module output power is okay. Proceed to step 3). If voltage is more than 5.3 volts, replace module. Repeat step 1). Perform SYSTEM OPERATION CHECK. If voltage is less than 4.7 volts, repeat step 1). If voltage is still less than 4.7 volts, replace module. Perform SYSTEM OPERATION CHECK.

3) Move positive test lead to sensor circuit No. 427 at pin No. 1 on module connector. Disregard monitor light. If voltage is more than 4.1 volts, module output power is okay. Proceed to step 5). If voltage is 1.3-4.1 volts, sensor is switching electrically from low-to-high or high-to-low. Add 300 lbs. (136 kg) to rear of vehicle and repeat step 3).

4) If voltage is less than 1.3 volts, but more than zero volts, module output power is okay. Proceed to step 5). If there is zero volts, turn ignition switch to "RUN" and then to "OFF" position. Repeat step 3). If voltage is still zero volts, proceed to TEST G.

5) Move positive test lead to sensor circuit No. 428 at pin No. 6 on module connector. Disregard monitor light. If voltage is greater than 4.1 volts, or between zero and 1.3 volts, module power circuit is okay. Proceed to TEST J.

6) If voltage is 1.3-4.1 volts, add 300 lbs. (136 kg) to rear of vehicle. Repeat step 5). If there is zero volts, turn ignition switch to "RUN" and then to "OFF" position. Repeat step 5). If voltage is still zero volts, proceed to TEST G.

TEST J
SENSOR LOGIC CIRCUIT CHECK

1) Reconnect module. Disconnect rear harness sensor connector at underbody. Turn ignition off. Set voltmeter to 5-volt scale. Connect negative test lead to the module mounting bolt . Connect positive test lead to sensor circuit No. 427 at pin No. 1 on module connector. Disregard monitor light if connected. Test must be completed within 30 minutes. If not, turn ignition switch to "RUN" and then "OFF" position to reset timer, as required.

2) If voltage is more than 4.3 volts, proceed to step 3). If voltage is less than 4.3 volts, turn ignition switch to "RUN" and then to "OFF" position. Repeat step 1). Replace module. Perform SYSTEM OPERATION CHECK.

3) Move positive lead to sensor circuit No. 428 at pin No. 6 on module connector. If voltage is more than 4.3 volts, proceed to step 4). If voltage is less than 4.3 volts, turn ignition switch from "RUN" to "OFF" position. Repeat step 3). Replace module. Perform SYSTEM OPERATION CHECK.

4) Move positive test lead to sensor circuit No. 428 (Orange/Black wire) at height sensor connector. If voltage is more than 4.3 volts, harness circuit is okay. If voltage is less than 4.3 volts, repair open in circuit No. 428, between module connector and height sensor connector. Repeat step 4).

5) Move positive test lead to sensor circuit No. 427 (Pink/Black wire) at height sensor connector. If voltage is more than 4.3 volts, harness circuit is okay. If voltage is less than 4.3 volts, repair open in circuit No. 427, between module connector and height sensor connector. Repeat step 5).

6) Disconnect module connector, move negative lead of ohmmeter to circuit No. 427 at pin No. 1 on module connector. Ohmmeter should read less than 2 ohms to indicate circuit No. 427 is okay. Perform SYSTEM OPERATION CHECK. If ohmmeter reads more than 2 ohms, circuit No. 427 and circuit No. 428 are crossed. Switch circuit leads at module or height sensor connector. Repeat step 6).

12-134

1989 ELECTRONIC SUSPENSION
Ford Motor Co. Rear Level Control (Cont.)

TEST K
COMPRESSOR RELAY MOTOR CHECK

1) Turn ignition switch from "RUN" to "OFF" position. Set voltmeter to 12-volt scale. Disregard monitor light. Relay and/or vent relay may click. Connect negative test lead to module mounting bolt. Connect positive test lead to circuit No. 420 (Dark Blue/Yellow wire) at pin 8 on module connector. If voltage is less than one volt, proceed to step **2)**. If voltage is more than one volt, repair short on circuits No. 298 (pin No. 4) and No. 420 (pin No. 8), between ignition switch relay and module connector. Repeat step **1)**.

2) Disconnect module harness from control module connector. Turn ignition switch from "OFF" to "RUN" position. Connect positive test lead to circuit No. 420 (Dark Blue/Yellow wire) at pin No. 8 on module connector. If voltage is more than 8 volts, compressor relay control circuits No. 298 and No. 420 to the module are okay. Proceed to step **3)**. If voltage is less than 8 volts, repair low voltage condition due to faulty connection, relay, low battery or blown fuse on circuits No. 298 (Purple/Orange wire; pin No. 4) and 420 (Dark Blue/Yellow wire; pin No. 8). Repeat step **2)**.

3) Remove positive test lead from voltmeter and touch module mounting bolt . Compressor relay should click. If compressor relay clicks, compressor relay coil is okay. Reconnect test lead to voltmeter. Proceed to step **4)**. If compressor relay does not click, replace relay. Repeat step **3)**. Perform SYSTEM OPERATION CHECK.

4) Check compressor motor. Repeat step **3)**. If compressor motor cycles, compressor and ground are okay. Reconnect test lead to voltmeter. Proceed to **TEST G**. If compressor does not cycle, reconnect test lead to voltmeter. Proceed to step **5)**.

5) Move test lead to circuit No. 37 (Yellow wire) at the harness side of the compressor relay connector. If voltage is more than 8 volts, battery feed circuit to the compressor relay is okay. Proceed to step **6)**. If voltage is less than 8 volts, repair open or short to ground on circuit No. 37, between battery and relay connector. Check fusible link and battery condition. Repeat step **5)**.

6) Connect jumper lead between circuit No. 420 (Dark Blue/Yellow wire) at pin No. 8 on module connector located in luggage compartment and a mounting bolt . Relay should click. Compressor may cycle. If relay clicks, remove jumper wire from mounting bolt . Proceed to step **7)**. If relay does not click, proceed to step **7)**.

7) Move positive test lead to compressor motor feed circuit No. 417 (Purple/Orange wire) at the harness side of the compressor motor connector. Touch the meter lead to the module mounting bolt . Voltage reading should be more than 8 volts. Relay should click. Compressor may cycle. If voltage is more than 8 volts and relay clicks, remove jumper lead. Proceed to step **8)**. If voltage is less than 8 volts, and relay does not click, repair open or short to ground on circuit No. 417 (Purple/Orange wire) between relay and motor connector, or replace as necessary. Repeat step **7)**.

8) Touch test lead to module mounting bolt . Compressor motor should cycle. If motor cycles, motor circuit is okay. Replace module. Perform SYSTEM OPERATION CHECK. If motor does not cycle, remove jumper lead from mounting bolt . Proceed to step **9)**.

9) Disconnect compressor connector. Connect ohmmeter positive to feed circuit No. 417 (Purple/Orange wire) at motor connector. Connect negative lead to circuit No. 57 (Black wire) at motor connector. Ohmmeter reading should be less than 2 ohms. If ohmmeter reading is less than 2 ohms, compressor and circuit breaker are okay. Proceed to step **10)**. If reading is more than 2 ohms, replace compressor motor. Reconnect compressor and module connectors. Perform SYSTEM OPERATION CHECK.

10) Move negative test lead to motor ground circuit No. 57 (Black wire) at harness side of compressor connector. Move positive test lead to ground circuit No. 57 (Black wire) at pin No. 11 on module connector. Move positive test lead to body eyelet (in engine compartment), ground circuit No. 57. Ohmmeter should indicate less than 2 ohms at both points.

11) If ohmmeter reading is less than 2 ohms, ground circuit is okay. Reconnect motor and module connectors. Perform SYSTEM OPERATION CHECK. If readings are not less than 2 ohms, repair open in circuit No. 57 (Black wire) between motor harness and ground and/or between module pin No. 11 and ground. Repeat step **10)**.

Section 13

STEERING

CONTENTS

TROUBLE SHOOTING   Page

Standard Steering Column 13-2
Tilt Steering Column 13-2
Manual Steering Gear 13-3
Power Steering Gear 13-4

STEERING WHEEL & COLUMN SWITCHES

Chrysler Motors
  Except Horizon & Omni 13-6
  Horizon & Omni 13-8
Eagle 13-9
Ford Motor Co. 13-10

STEERING COLUMNS

Chrysler Motors
  Except Horizon & Omni 13-14
  Horizon & Omni 13-20
Eagle 13-21
Ford Motor Co. 13-25

MANUAL STEERING GEARS   Page

Chrysler Motors
  Rack & Pinion 13-33
Ford Motor Co.
  Rack & Pinion 13-34

POWER STEERING GENERAL SERVICING

All Manufacturers 13-37

POWER STEERING GEARS

Chrysler Motors
  Rack & Pinion 13-39
  Recirculating Ball 13-40
Eagle
  Center-Linked Rack & Pinion 13-44
Ford Motor Co.
  Integral Power Steering 13-49
  Integral Rack & Pinion 13-52

ELECTRONIC POWER STEERING GEAR

Ford Motor Co.
Electronic Variable Orifice (EVO)
  Cougar & Thunderbird 13-59
Variable Assist
  Continental 13-64
  Probe 13-68

POWER STEERING PUMPS

Chrysler Motors
  FWD Saginaw & "ZF" 13-75
  RWD Saginaw 13-78
Eagle
  Saginaw With Remote Reservoir 13-81
Ford Motor Co.
  C-II 13-84

STEERING LINKAGE

All Models 13-86

NOTE: ALSO SEE GENERAL INDEX

1989 STEERING
Standard Steering Column Trouble Shooting

CONDITION	POSSIBLE CAUSE	CORRECTION
Noise in Steering	Coupling pulled apart	See STEERING COLUMNS
	Column not correctly aligned	See STEERING COLUMNS
	Broken lower joint	Replace joint
	Horn contact ring not lubricated	See STEERING COLUMNS
	Bearings not lubricated	See STEERING COLUMNS
	Bearing worn or broken	Replace bearing and lubricate
	Shaft snap ring not properly seated	Reseat or replace snap ring
	Plastic spherical joint not lubricated	See STEERING COLUMNS
	Shroud or housing loose	Tighten holding screws
	Lock plate retaining ring not seated	See STEERING COLUMNS
	Loose sight shield	Tighten holding screws
High Steering Shaft Effort	Column assembly misaligned	See STEERING COLUMNS
	Improperly installed dust shield	Adjust or replace
	Damaged upper or lower bearing	Replace bearings
	Tight steering universal joint	See STEERING COLUMNS
High Shift Effort	Column is out of alignment	See STEERING COLUMNS
	Improperly installed dust shield	Adjust or replace
	Seals or bearings not lubricated	See STEERING COLUMNS
	Mounting bracket screws too long	Replace with new shorter screws
	Burrs on shift tube	Remove burrs or replace tube
	Lower bowl bearing assembled wrong	See STEERING COLUMNS
	Shift tube bent or broken	Replace as necessary
	Improper adjustment of shift levers	See STEERING COLUMNS
Improper Trans. Shifting	Sheared shift tube joint	Replace as necessary
	Sheared lower shaft lever weld joint	Replace as necessary
	Improper shift lever adjustment	See STEERING COLUMNS
	Improper gate plate adjustment	See STEERING COLUMNS
Excess Play in Column	Instrument panel bracket bolts loose	Tighten bolts and check bracket
	Broken weld nut on jacket	See STEERING COLUMNS
	Instrument bracket capsule sheared	See STEERING COLUMNS
	Column bracket/jacket bolts loose	Tighten bolts and check bracket
Steering Locks in Gear	Release lever mechanism damaged	See STEERING COLUMNS

Tilt Steering Column Trouble Shooting

CONDITION	POSSIBLE CAUSE	CORRECTION
Steering Wheel Loose	Excess clearance in support	Check and replace if necessary
	Excess clearance in housing/pivot pin	Check and replace if necessary
	Damaged anti-lash spring in spheres	See TILT STEERING COLUMNS
	Upper bearing not seated properly	See TILT STEERING COLUMNS
	Upper bearing inner race seal missing	Replace if necessary
	Improperly adjusted tilt/telescopic lock	See STEERING COLUMNS
	Loose support screws	Tighten and check bracket
	Bearing preload spring missing/broken	Replace spring
	Housing loose on jacket	Tighten and/or replace screws
Play in Column Mount	Loose support screws	Tighten and check bracket
	Loose shoes in housing	See TILT STEERING COLUMNS
	Loose tilt head pivot pins	See TILT STEERING COLUMNS
	Loose shoe lock pin in support	See TILT STEERING COLUMNS
Housing Scraping on Bowl	Bowl bent or out of round	See TILT STEERING COLUMNS
Wheel Will Not Lock	Shoe seized on its pivot pin	See TILT STEERING COLUMNS
	Shoe may have burrs/dirt in them	Clean or replace
	Shoe lock spring weak/broken	Replace if necessary

Tilt Steering Column Trouble Shooting (Cont.)

CONDITION	POSSIBLE CAUSE	CORRECTION
Wheel Fails to Return	Pivot pins are bound up	Clean or replace
	Wheel tilt spring is damaged	See TILT STEERING COLUMNS
	Turn signal switch wires too tight	Loosen and check operation
Noise When Tilting	Upper tilt bumpers worn	Replace if necessary
	Tilt spring rubbing in housing	Adjust and check operation
Hard Steering	Incorrect tire pressure	Inflate to proper pressure
	Lack of lubricant in steering linkage	Service Steering, Suspension and Linkage
	Improper front end alignment	See FRONT ALIGNMENT
	Improper steering gear adjustment	See STEERING GEARS

Manual Steering Gear Trouble Shooting

CONDITION	POSSIBLE CAUSE	CORRECTION
Rattle or Chucking Noise in Rack and Pinion	Rack and pinion mounting bracket loose	Tighten all mounting bolts
	Lack of/or incorrect lubricant	See RACK & PINION STEERING
	Steering gear mounting bolts loose	Tighten all mounting bolts
Excessive Play	Front wheel bearing improperly adjusted	See FRONT SUSPENSION
	Loose or worn steering linkage	See STEERING LINKAGE
	Loose or worn steering gear shaft	See MANUAL STEERING GEARS
	Steering arm loose on gear shaft	See MANUAL STEERING GEARS
	Steering gear housing bolts loose	Tighten all mounting bolts
	Steering gear adjustment too loose	See MANUAL STEERING GEAR
	Steering arms loose on knuckles	Tighten and check steering linkage
	Rack and pinion mounting loose	Tighten all mounting bolts
	Rack and pinion out of adjustment	See adjustment in STEERING
	Tie rod end loose	Tighten and check steering linkage
	Excessive Pitman shaft-to-ball nut lash	See STEERING
Poor Returnability	Lack of lubricant in ball joint or linkage	Lubricate and service systems
	Binding in linkage or ball joints	See STEERING LINKAGE and SUSPENSION
	Improper front end alignment	See WHEEL ALIGNMENT
	Improper steering gear adjustment	See STEERING
	Improper tire pressure	Inflate to proper pressure
	Tie rod binding	See FRONT SUSPENSION
	Shaft seal rubbing shaft	See STEERING COLUMNS
Excessive Vertical Motion	Improper tire pressure	Inflate to proper pressure
	Tires, wheels or rotors out of balance	Balance tires then check wheels and rotors
	Worn or faulty shock absorbers	Check and replace if necessary
	Loose tie rod ends or steering	Tighten or replace if necessary
	Loose or worn wheel bearings	See SUSPENSION
Steering Pulls to One Side	Improper tire pressure	Inflate to proper pressure
	Front tires are different sizes	Rotate or replace if necessary
	Wheel bearings not adjusted properly	See FRONT SUSPENSION
	Bent or broken suspension components	See FRONT SUSPENSION
	Improper wheel alignment	See WHEEL ALIGNMENT
	Brakes dragging	See BRAKES
Instability	Low or uneven tire pressure	Inflate to proper pressure
	Loose or worn wheel bearings	See FRONT SUSPENSION
	Loose or worn idler arm bushing	See FRONT SUSPENSION
	Loose or worn strut bushings	See FRONT SUSPENSION
	Incorrect front wheel alignment	See WHEEL ALIGNMENT
	Steering gear not centered	See MANUAL STEERING GEARS
	Springs or shock absorbers defective	Check and replace if necessary
	Improper cross shaft	See MANUAL STEERING GEARS

1989 STEERING
Power Steering Gear Trouble Shooting

CONDITION	POSSIBLE CAUSE	CORRECTION
Rattle or Chucking Noise in Steering	Pressure hoses touching engine parts	Adjust to proper clearance
	Loose Pitman shaft	Adjust or replace if necessary
	Tie rods ends or Pitman arm loose	Tighten and check system
	Rack and pinion mounts loose	Tighten all mounting bolts
	Free play in worm and piston assembly	See POWER STEERING GEARS
	Loose sector shaft or thrust bearing adjustment	See POWER STEERING GEARS
	Free play in pot coupling	See STEERING COLUMNS
	Worn shaft serrations	See STEERING COLUMNS
Growl in Steering Pump	Excessive pressure in hoses	Restricted hoses see POWER STEERING GEARS
	Scored pressure plates	See POWER STEERING GEARS
	Scored thrust plates or rotor	See POWER STEERING GEARS
	Extreme wear of cam ring	See POWER STEERING GEARS
Rattle in Steering Pump	Vanes not installed properly	See POWER STEERING PUMPS
	Vanes sticking in rotor slots	See POWER STEERING PUMPS
Swish Noise in Pump	Defective flow control valve	See POWER STEERING PUMPS
Groan in Steering Pump	Air in fluid	See POWER STEERING PUMPS
	Poor pressure hose connection	Tighten and check, replace if necessary
Squawk When Turning	Damper "O" ring on valve spool cut	See POWER STEERING PUMPS
Moan or Whine in Pump	Pump shaft bearing scored	Replace bearing and fluid
	Air in fluid or fluid level low	See POWER STEERING PUMPS
	Hose or column grounded	Check and replace if necessary
	Cover "O" ring missing or damaged	See POWER STEERING PUMPS
	Valve cover baffle missing or damaged	See POWER STEERING PUMPS
	Interference of components in pump	See POWER STEERING PUMPS
	Loose or poor bracket alignment	Correct or replace if necessary
Hissing When Parking	Internal leakage in steering gear	Check valve assembly first
Chirp in Steering Pump	Loose or worn power steering belt	Adjust or replace if neceesary
Buzzing When Not Steering	Noisy pump	See POWER STEERING PUMPS
	Free play in steering shaft bearing	See STEERING COLUMNS
	Bearing loose on shaft serrations	See STEERING COLUMNS
Clicking Noise in Pump	Pump slippers too long	See POWER STEERING PUMPS
	Broken slipper springs	See POWER STEERING PUMPS
	Excessive wear or nicked rotors	See POWER STEERING PUMPS
	Damaged cam contour	See POWER STEERING PUMPS
Poor Return of Wheel	Wheel rubbing against turn signal	See STEERING WHEEL SWITCHES
	Flange rubbing steering gear adjuster	See STEERING COLUMNS
	Tight or frozen steering shaft bearing	See STEERING COLUMNS
	Steering gear out of adjustment	See Adjustment in STEERING
	Sticking or plugged spool valve	See POWER STEERING PUMPS
	Improper front end alignment	See WHEEL ALIGNMENT
	Wheel bearings worn or loose	See FRONT SUSPENSION
	Ties rods or ball joints binding	Check and replace if necessary
	Intermediate shaft joints binding	See STEERING COLUMNS
	Kinked pressure hoses	Correct or replace if necessary
	Loose housing head spanner nut	See POWER STEERING GEARS
	Damaged valve lever	See POWER STEERING GEARS
	Sector shaft adjusted too tight	See ADJUSTMENTS in POWER STEERING GEARS
	Worm thrust bearing adjusted too tight	See ADJUSTMENTS in POWER STEERING GEARS
	Reaction ring sticking in cylinder	See POWER STEERING GEARS
	Reaction ring sticking in housing head	See POWER STEERING GEARS
	Steering pump internal leakage	See POWER STEERING PUMPS
	Steering gear-to-column misalignment	See STEERING COLUMNS
	Lack of lubrication in linkage	Service front suspension
	Lack of lubrication in ball joints	Service front suspension

CONDITION	POSSIBLE CAUSE	CORRECTION
Increased Effort When Turning Wheel Fast, Foaming, Milky Power Steering Fluid, Low Fluid Level or Low Pressure	High internal pump leakage	See POWER STEERING PUMPS
	Power steering pump belt slipping	Adjust or replace if necessary
	Low fluid level	Check and fill to proper level
	Engine idle speed to low	Adjust to correct setting
	Air in pump fluid system	See POWER STEERING PUMPS
	Pump output low	See POWER STEERING PUMPS
	Steering gear malfunctioning	See POWER STEERING GEARS
Wheel Surges or Jerks	Low fluid level	Check and fill to proper level
	Loose fan belt	Adjust or replace if necessary
	Insufficient pump pressure	See POWER STEERING PUMPS
	Sticky flow control valve	See POWER STEERING PUMPS
	Linkage hitting oil pan at full turn	Replace bent components
Kick Back or Free Play	Air in pump fluid system	See POWER STEERING PUMPS
	Worn poppet valve in steering gear	See POWER STEERING GEARS
	Excessive over center lash	See POWER STEERING GEARS
	Thrust bearing out of adjustment	See POWER STEERING GEARS
	Free play in pot coupling	See POWER STEERING PUMPS
	Steering gear coupling loose on shaft	See POWER STEERING PUMPS
	Steering disc mounting bolts loose	Tighten or replace if necessary
	Coupling loose on worm shaft	Tighten or replace if necessary
	Improper sector shaft adjustment	See POWER STEERING GEARS
	Excessive worm piston side play	See POWER STEERING GEARS
	Damaged valve lever	See POWER STEERING GEARS
	Universal joint loose	Tighten or replace if necessary
	Defective rotary valve	See POWER STEERING GEARS
No Power When Parking	Sticking flow control valve	See POWER STEERING PUMPS
	Insufficient pump pressure output	See POWER STEERING PUMPS
	Excessive internal pump leakage	See POWER STEERING PUMPS
	Excessive internal gear leakage	See POWER STEERING PUMPS
	Flange rubs against gear adjust plug	See STEERING COLUMNS
	Loose pump belt	Adjust or replace if necessary
	Low fluid level	Check and add proper amount of fluid
	Engine idle too low	Adjust to correct setting
	Steering gear-to-column misaligned	See STEERING COLUMNS
No Power, Left Turns	Left turn reaction seal "O" ring worn	See POWER STEERING GEARS
	Left turn reaction seal damaged/missing	See POWER STEERING GEARS
	Cylinder head "O" ring damaged	See POWER STEERING PUMPS
No Power, Right Turns	Column pot coupling bottomed	See STEERING COLUMNS
	Right turn reaction seal "O" ring worn	See POWER STEERING GEARS
	Right turn reaction seal damaged	See POWER STEERING GEARS
	Internal leakage through piston end plug	See POWER STEERING GEARS
	Internal leakage through side plugs	See POWER STEERING GEARS
Lack of Effort in Turning	Left and/or right reaction seal worn	Replace, see POWER STEERING GEARS
	Left and/or right reaction oil passageway not drilled	Check housing and cylinder head
	Left and/or right reaction seal sticking in cylinder head	See POWER STEERING GEARS
Wanders to One Side	Front end alignment incorrect	See WHEEL ALIGNMENT
	Unbalanced steering gear valve	See POWER STEERING GEARS
Low Pressure Due to Steering Pump	Flow control valve stuck or inoperative	See POWER STEERING
	Pressure plate not flat against cam ring	See POWER STEERING PUMPS
	Extreme wear of cam ring	Replace and check adjustments
	Scored plate, thrust plate or rotor	See POWER STEERING PUMPS
	Vanes not installed properly	See POWER STEERING PUMPS
	Vanes sticking in rotor slots	See POWER STEERING PUMPS
	Cracked/broken thrust or pressure plate	See POWER STEERING PUMPS

1989 STEERING WHEEL & COLUMN SWITCHES
Chrysler Motors Except Horizon & Omni

REMOVAL & INSTALLATION

PRECAUTION

Steering column must be lowered or removed for access to ignition switch on some vehicles. Steering wheel, turn signal switch and other components must be removed to gain access to lock cylinder retaining tab for lock cylinder removal.

HORN BUTTON

Removal & Installation – Disconnect negative battery cable. Remove horn pad. Disconnect horn electrical connectors. Remove horn switch. To install, reverse removal procedure.

STEERING WHEEL

Removal & Installation – Remove horn pad. Disconnect horn connectors. Remove steering wheel nut and washer. Remove wheel with Puller (C-3428B). To install, reverse removal procedure.

TURN SIGNAL SWITCH

Removal – 1) Disconnect negative battery cable. Remove horn pad. Remove steering wheel with Puller (C-3428B). Remove insulation from below steering column, if equipped. Remove lower instrument panel bezel. Loosen Allen screw on gearshift housing. Remove gearshift indicator.

2) If equipped with tilt column, position column at mid-point. Remove 2 column-to-lower panel reinforcement nuts. Remove mounting bracket from steering column by removing 4 attaching bolts.

3) Pry out plastic buttons retaining wiring trough to column. Remove trough. Disconnect turn signal wiring harness. Wrap a piece of tape around connector to prevent snagging when removing switch. *See Fig. 1.*

4) On standard columns, place gearshift lever in full clockwise position. Remove screw holding turn signal switch pivot. Leave this assembly in its installed location. Remove 3 screws and bearing retainer fastening turn signal switch to upper bearing housing.

5) On tilt columns, remove plastic cover from lock plate. While depressing lock plate with Lock Plate Depressor (C-4156), pry retaining ring from groove with screwdriver. DO NOT release full load of upper bearing spring.

6) On all models, remove lock plate, canceling cam and cam spring. Place turn signal switch in right turn position. Remove hazard warning switch knob attaching screw. Remove 3 turn signal switch-to-steering column screws.

7) Remove turn signal/hazard warning switch, Gently pull switch from column while straightening and guiding wires through column opening.

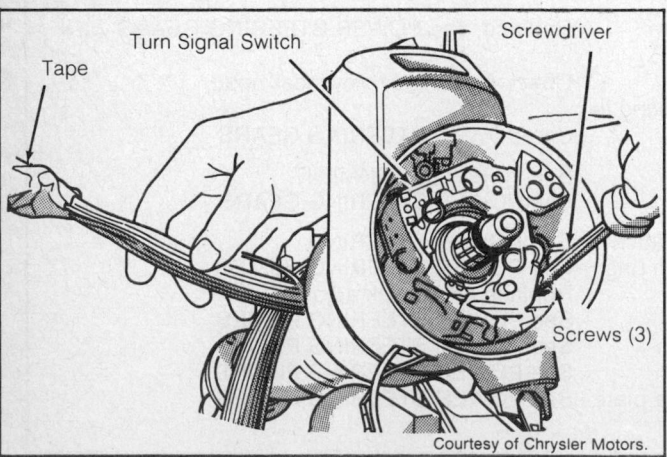
Fig. 1: *Removing Turn Signal Switch & Wiring*

Installation – 1) On fixed columns, lightly lubricate turn signal switch pivot with grease. Wrap a piece of tape around connector to ensure smooth installation. Guide connector and wires through opening in steering column.

2) Remove tape. Position turn signal switch and bearing retainer into upper bearing housing. Secure with 3 mounting screws. Place turn signal lever into switch pivot. Secure lever with screw through pivot.

3) On tilt columns, position turn signal switch in upper column housing. Place switch in right turn position. Secure with 3 mounting screws. Put link in position between turn signal switch and pivot. Secure link with screw.

4) On all models, install canceling cam, cam spring and lock plate. Using Lock Plate Depressor (C-4156), depress lock plate. Install new retaining ring, hazard warning knob and plastic cover on lock plate.

5) Connect wiring harness connectors. Position wiring trough around wires. Mount wiring trough to column jacket with 4 plastic buttons.

6) On tilt column, secure mounting bracket to column with 4 bolts. Tighten bolts to 110 INCH lbs. (12 N.m). Position steering column into place in lower reinforcement, install nuts. Tighten nuts to 110 INCH lbs. (12 N.m).

7) On all models, place gearshift lever into Reverse position. Position gearshift indicator at center of Reverse position. Tighten Allen screw. Place column shift into Park position.

8) Install instrument panel bezels and insulation. Install steering wheel. Install horn pad. Connect negative battery cable. Ensure proper operation of turn signal, hazard warning, horn, and beam selector.

WINDSHIELD WIPER/WASHER SWITCH

Removal – 1) Disconnect negative battery cable. Remove steering wheel as previously described. Remove lower instrument panel bezel.

2) On tilt columns, remove lock plate cover and lock plate. Remove gearshift indicator. Remove 2 nuts mounting column to lower panel reinforcement. Remove mounting bracket from steering column by removing 4 attaching bolts.

3) On all models, remove wiring trough from steering column by unsnapping 4 plastic retainer clips. Remove turn signal switch.

4) Remove 2 lock housing cover attaching screws. Remove cover. Gently pull wiper switch up from column while guiding wires up through column opening.

Installation – To install, reverse removal procedure.

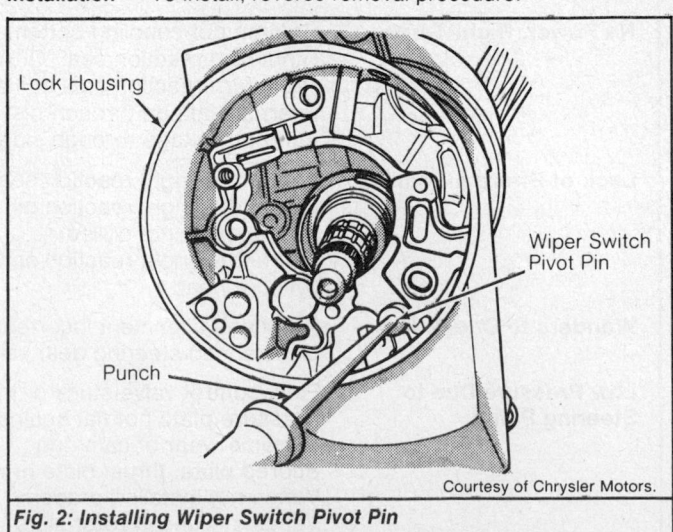
Fig. 2: *Installing Wiper Switch Pivot Pin*

CRUISE CONTROL SWITCH

Removal – 1) Disconnect negative battery cable. Remove lower steering column cover. On tilt column, lower column. DO NOT damage gear shift indicator cable. Remove 4 support bracket-to-column jacket screws. Remove wiring trough.

2) On fixed column, unsnap 4 wiring trough retainer clips. Remove wiring trough. Disconnect cruise control harness connector.

3) On all models, remove wiper control knob from end of lever. Remove 2 cruise control switch screws.

4) On tilt column, remove steering wheel. Attach flexible guide wire to lower end of cruise control switch harness. Pull wires up through lock housing between lock plate and side of housing. Disconnect guide wire. Remove switch.

5) On fixed column, remove 2 upper steering column lock housing cover retaining screws. Gently remove switch and harness from column, taking care to avoid damaging wires while pulling them through column.

Installation – 1) On fixed column, insert harness connector through turn signal lever opening in column. Pull harness connector down and out lower end.

2) On tilt columns, insert harness wires through turn signal lever opening in column. Pull harness upward through upper housing. Attach guide wire to switch wiring harness. Pull wires gently downward through steering column opening between lock plate and side of housing.

3) On all models, reconnect wiring harness connector. Install 2 screws to attach cruise control switch to column. Push wiper control knob into place. To complete installation, reverse removal procedure.

LOCK CYLINDER

Removal – 1) Remove turn signal switch, horn pad and key light ground wire. Remove ignition key light retaining screw. Lift key light assembly out of way.

2) Remove 4 bearing housing-to-lock housing screws. Remove snap ring, bearing housing, lock plate spring and lock plate from steering shaft.

3) Place cylinder in "LOCK" position. Remove key. Remove buzzer switch retaining screw. Lift out buzzer switch. Remove 2 ignition switch attaching screws, rotate switch 90 degrees. Slide switch off actuating rod.

4) Remove 2 screws from dimmer switch. Disengage switch from actuator rod. Remove 2 screws from bellcrank. Slide bellcrank up into lock housing until it can be disconnected from ignition switch actuator rod.

5) Insert small screwdrivers into lock cylinder release slots. Push in to release spring loaded lock retainers. Pull lock cylinder out of housing bore.

Installation – 1) Position bellcrank assembly into lock housing. Install ignition switch actuator rod into bellcrank. Pull ignition switch actuator rod down column. Install bellcrank onto its mounting surface.

2) Gearshift lever should be in Park (automatic) or Reverse (manual). Place ignition switch onto actuator rod. Rotate switch 90 degrees to lock rod into position.

3) To install ignition lock, turn key to "LOCK" position. Remove key. Insert cylinder into housing far enough to contact switch actuator. Press inward while moving switch actuator rod up and down to align parts.

4) When parts align, cylinder will move inward and a spring loaded retainer will snap into place, locking cylinder into housing. With key cylinder and ignition switch in the "LOCK" position (second detent from top), tighten ignition switch mounting screws.

5) Feed buzzer switch wires behind wiring post and down through space between housing and jacket. Remove ignition key. Install buzzer switch. Tighten buzzer switch screws.

IGNITION SWITCH

NOTE: The ignition switch is mounted on steering column and is connected to the key lock assembly by a remote lock rod.

Removal – 1) Disconnect negative battery cable. Disconnect ignition switch electrical connectors. Place lock cylinder in "LOCK" position. Remove key.

2) Remove screw and lift out buzzer/chime switch (if equipped). Remove 2 screws attaching ignition switch. Rotate switch 90 degrees and slide off actuating rod.

Installation – 1) Fit actuator rod into slider by turning switch 90 degrees, inserting rod, and rotating back 90 degrees. Mount switch on column. Install, but do not tighten screws.

2) Position ignition switch with actuator rod at second detent from top. Push down lightly to remove lash in actuator rod. Finger tighten screws.

3) Install buzzer/chime switch (if equipped). Tighten screws. Install wiring connectors. Connect battery cable. Check switch for proper operation.

DIMMER SWITCH

Removal – Disconnect negative battery cable. Remove lower steering column cover. Disconnect dimmer switch electrical connector. Remove mounting nut and screw from switch. Disengage switch from push rod. Remove switch.

Installation – 1) Firmly push rod into switch. Compressing switch, insert 2 3/32" drill bit shanks through alignment holes.

2) Reposition upper end of push rod into pocket of washer/wiper switch. With a light rearward pressure on switch, install nut and screw. Remove drill bits.

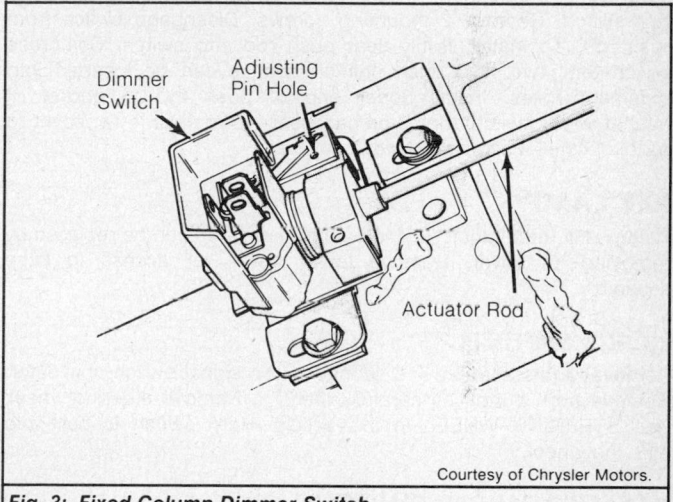

Courtesy of Chrysler Motors.

Fig. 3: Fixed Column Dimmer Switch

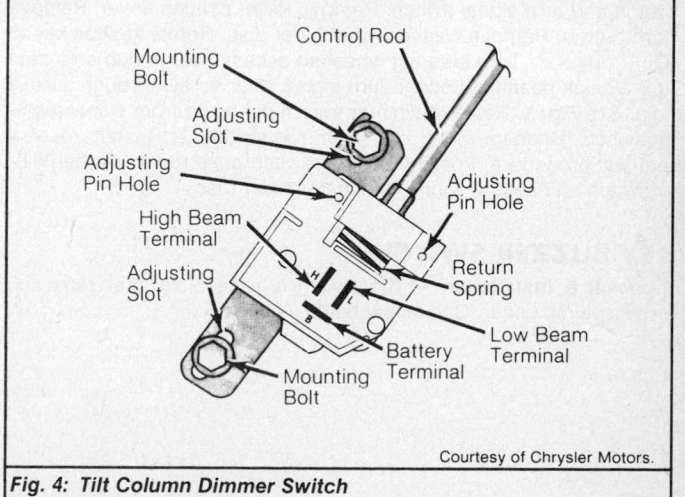

Courtesy of Chrysler Motors.

Fig. 4: Tilt Column Dimmer Switch

TIGHTENING SPECIFICATIONS

Application	Ft. Lbs. (N.m)
Steering Wheel Retaining Nut	45 (61)

REMOVAL & INSTALLATION

STEERING WHEEL

Removal & Installation – Remove horn button and horn switch. Remove steering wheel nut. Use Steering Wheel Puller (C-3428B) to remove wheel. To install, align master serration in wheel hub with missing tooth on shaft. Tighten nut to specification. Install horn button.

IGNITION SWITCH

Removal – Disconnect negative battery cable. Remove ignition switch connectors. Place lock cylinder in "LOCK" position. Remove key. Remove 2 ignition switch mounting screws. Allow switch and push rod to drop below lower cover. Rotate switch 90 degrees and disconnect switch from push rod.

Installation – Position switch in "LOCK" position, second detent from top. Place switch at right angle to column and insert push rod. Align switch on bracket. Install screws. Lightly, push switch rearward and tighten screws. Connect electrical connectors. Check switch operation.

DIMMER SWITCH

Removal & Installation – Remove electrical connector from dimmer switch. Remove 2 mounting screws. Disengage switch from push rod. To install, firmly seat push rod into switch. Compress switch until two .093" inch drill bit shanks can be inserted into alignment holes. Install upper end of push rod in pocket of washer/wiper switch. It may be necessary to remove lower cover to do this. Install 2 screws. Remove drill bits.

KEY LAMP

Removal & Installation – The bulb for key lamp can be replaced by removing its cover. Remove lower cover for access to lamp assembly.

HORN SWITCH

Removal & Installation – Disconnect turn signal switch connector. Remove horn button by carefully lifting it. Remove steering wheel. See STEERING WHEEL in this article. Horn switch is built into steering wheel.

WASHER/WIPER SWITCH

Removal & Installation – Disconnect connectors for washer/wiper switch and turn signal switch. Remove lower column cover. Remove horn button. Remove washer/wiper hider disc. Rotate ignition key to "OFF" position. Turn steering wheel so access hole in hub area sets at 9 o'clock position. Loosen turn signal lever screw through access hole. *See Fig. 1.* Remove dimmer switch push rod from washer/wiper switch. Unsnap wiring clip. Remove switch. To install, reverse removal procedure. Position dimmer switch push rod in washer/wiper switch and secure wiring clip. Install hider disc.

KEY BUZZER SWITCH

Removal & Installation – The switch is accessible after removing lower column cover. One screw holds it in place.

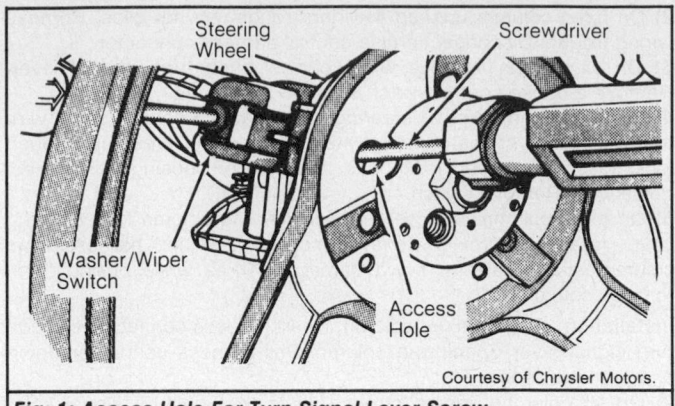

Fig. 1: Access Hole For Turn Signal Lever Screw

TURN SIGNAL SWITCH

Removal & Installation – Disconnect turn signal switch connector. Remove steering wheel and lower column. See STEERING WHEEL in this article. Remove 3 screws, wiring clip and switch. To install, reverse removal procedure.

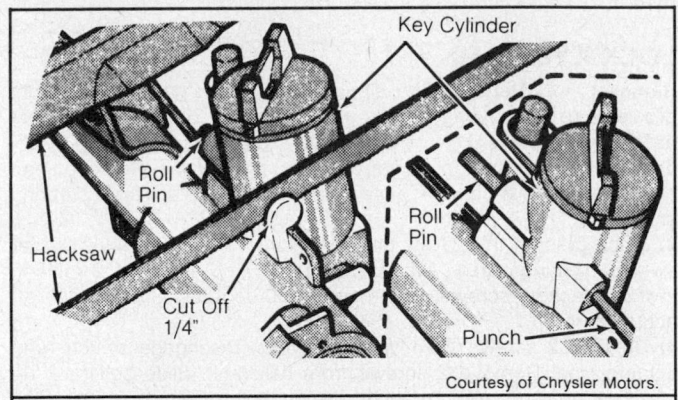

Fig. 2: Cutting Key Cylinder Retainer Boss

KEY CYLINDER

Removal & Installation – Remove steering wheel. Remove both column covers. Remove turn signal switch. Using a hacksaw blade, cut the upper 1/4 inch from the key cylinder retainer pin boss. *See Fig. 2.* Drive roll pin from housing with a punch. Remove key cylinder. To install, reverse removal procedure.

TIGHTENING SPECIFICATIONS

Application	Ft. Lbs. (N.m)
Steering Wheel Nut	45 (61)

Premier
REMOVAL & INSTALLATION
STEERING WHEEL

Removal – 1) Disconnect negative battery cable. Unsnap horn contact cover from steering wheel. Disconnect 2 horn wire connections. Remove cover.

2) Note alignment reference mark on steering shaft hub. Remove steering shaft hub nut. Disconnect speed control wire connector, if equipped. Remove steering wheel. It is NOT necessary to use puller to remove steering wheel from shaft.

Installation – To install, reverse removal procedure. Align reference marks. Tighten steering shaft hub nut to specification. See TIGHTENING SPECIFICATIONS table in this article. If steering wheel is off-center, loosen alignment screws to allow screw shanks to slide within alignment slots. Rotate wheel to center wheel. Tighten alignment screws.

IGNITION SWITCH

Removal – 1) Disconnect negative battery cable. Remove instrument panel lower cover. Remove steering wheel. See STEERING WHEEL in this artricle. Remove turn signal cancel cam by unhooking tabs. Hold tabs away from shaft with paper clips. Slide cancel cam off steering column.

2) If equipped with tilt wheel, remove tilt wheel control lever. Remove left switch pod rear cover. See Fig. 1. Small clips may fall off when switch pod cover is removed. Remove right switch pod assembly. Pry off ignition switch trim ring.

3) Pull switch pod assemblies from housing and remove mounting screws. Pull switch pods from housings. Separate and remove lower column shroud. Remove upper column shroud.

4) Remove ignition switch retaining screws. Separate ignition switch from key/lock cylinder housing. Remove harness anchor. Loosen hold-down nut in middle of dash panel harness connector. Separate connectors. Remove ignition switch and harness.

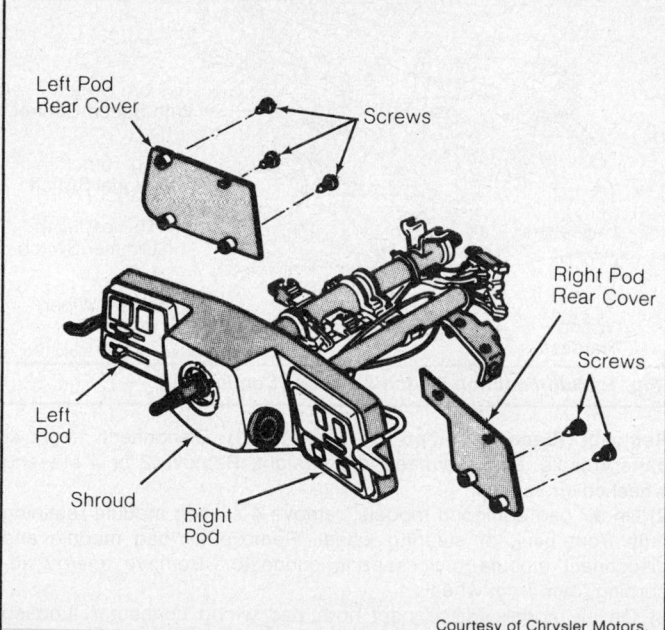

Fig. 1: Exploded View of Switch Pod Rear Covers

Installation – 1) Connect pod connectors to ignition switch connector from wire side of connector. Install dash panel harness connector. Tighten retaining nut.

2) Position ignition switch. Install and tighten screws. Secure harness with tie wraps. Install harness anchor. Install harness anchor screw. Install upper and lower column covers. Pass pods through pod housings. Install and tighten pod housing attaching screws. Snap ignition switch trim ring in place.

3) Install pods into pod housings. Install pod retaining screws. Install instrument panel lower cover, steering wheel and turn signal switch.

4) To complete installation, reverse removal procedure. Check operation of ignition switch, headlight pod, heating-AC pod and lock cylinder. Reconnect battery cable.

KEY/LOCK CYLINDER

Removal & Installation – Follow steps **1)** through **3)** from IGNITION SWITCH in this article. Insert ignition key in lock cylinder. Turn key to align key with groove in bottom of key/lock cylinder housing. Press in locking tab located in bottom of key/lock cylinder housing, pull out cylinder. See Fig. 2. To install, reverse removal procedure.

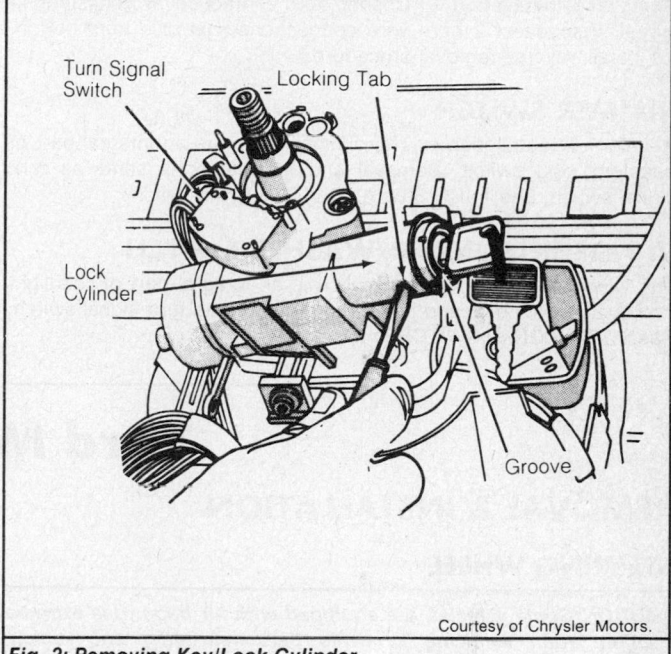

Fig. 2: Removing Key/Lock Cylinder

TURN SIGNAL SWITCH

Removal & Installation – 1) Disconnect negative battery cable. Remove instrument panel lower cover. Remove support bar. Pull aside air duct. Remove tie straps. Loosen hold-down nut for steering column connector and separate connector.

2) Separate turn signal/windshield wiper/light connector from steering column connector with a thin blade screwdriver. Remove 2 screws from bottom of left switch pod assembly. Remove switch pod housing rear cover. Small clips may fall off when switch pod cover is removed.

3) Pull switch pod far enough from housing to expose and remove 2 screws. Pull switch forward and pull harness out through housing. Remove switch.

4) To install, reverse removal procedure. Use wire ties to hold harness to column.

TURN SIGNAL CANCEL SWITCH

Removal & Installation – 1) Disconnect battery ground cable. Remove instrument panel lower cover. Unsnap horn pad and remove connectors. Remove steering wheel. See STEERING WHEEL in this article. Remove turn signal switch cancel cam by unhooking tabs. Hold tabs away from shaft with paper clips. Slide cam off steering column.

2) If equipped with tilt wheel, remove tilt wheel control lever. Remove left switch pod rear cover. Small clips may fall off when switch pod cover is removed. Remove right switch pod assembly. Pry off ignition switch trim ring.

3) Pull switch pod assemblies from housing and remove mounting screws. Remove screws and pass switch pod assemblies through housing. Remove lower column shroud. Remove upper column shroud. Remove 3 screws and turn signal cancel switch. To install, reverse removal procedure.

CRUISE CONTROL SWITCH

Removal & Installation – Unsnap horn contact cover from steering wheel. Disconnect 2 horn wire connections. Pry up on cruise control switch panel. Remove panel from steering wheel. To install, reverse removal procedure.

HORN BUTTON & SWITCH

Removal & Installation – Unsnap horn contact cover from steering wheel. Disconnect 2 horn wire connections. Remove horn button. To install, reverse removal procedure.

DIMMER SWITCH

Removal & Installation – The dimmer switch is an integral part of headlight pod switch. Removal and installation is same as turn signal switch. See TURN SIGNAL SWITCH in this article.

WINDSHIELD WIPER/WASHER SWITCH

The windshield wiper/washer switch is an integral part of headlight pod switch. Removal and installation is same as turn signal switch. See TURN SIGNAL SWITCH in this article.

HEATING-A/C SWITCH

Removal & Installation – **1)** Disconnect negative battery cable. Remove instrument panel lower cover. Remove knee bolster, if equipped with passive restaint.

2) Remove instrument panel support rod. Pull aside air duct. Remove tie strap. Loosen hold-down nut in middle of steering connectors. Separate heating-A/C pod connector and steering column connector. Push wire side of heating-A/C connector and slide out connector. Remove heating-A/C pod retaining screws.

3) Remove lower column shroud. Remove pod by pulling wires through housing. It may be necessary to remove 2 screws near ignition switch trim ring for clearance to remove connector.

4) To install, reverse removal procedure.

TIGHTENING SPECIFICATIONS

Application	Ft. Lbs. (N.m)
Steering Wheel Retaining Nut	52 (70)

Ford Motor Co.

REMOVAL & INSTALLATION

STEERING WHEEL

CAUTION: Some vehicles are equipped with air bags. Use extreme caution when servicing to avoid personal injury and vehicle damage.

Removal (Cougar & Thunderbird) – Disconnect negative battery cable. Remove horn pad and cover assembly. Disconnect horn wire and speed control switch wire from contact plate terminal. Remove and discard steering wheel attaching bolt. Remove steering wheel with Puller (T67L-3600-A). DO NOT use knock-off type steering wheel puller. Damage to upper bearing can occur.

Installation (Cougar & Thunderbird) – Install steering wheel. Tighten new attaching bolt to 23-33 ft. lbs. (31-45 N.m). To complete installation, reverse removal procedure.

Removal (Continental) – **1)** Ensure front wheels are straight. Disconnect negative battery cable. Remove lower instrument panel cover. Remove ignition lock cylinder. See IGNITION LOCK CYLINDER in this article. Remove tilt release lever. Remove lower steering column shroud.

2) Disconnect contact assembly connector at body wiring harness. *See Fig. 1.* Remove contact assembly ground screw at lock cylinder housing. Remove 4 air bag module retaining nuts. Remove air bag module from steering wheel. Disconnect contact assembly at module.

3) Remove and discard steering wheel attaching bolt. Remove steering wheel and contact assembly. Set contact assembly in straight ahead position. DO NOT allow contact assembly to rotate.

Installation (Continental) – **1)** Install steering wheel and contact assembly. Ensure drive pin on speed control/horn brush assembly engages in drive socket on contact assembly. Install and tighten new steering wheel attaching bolt to 23-33 ft. lbs. (31-45 N.m).

2) Install ground wire and retaining screw. Connect contact assembly wire harness and at air bag module. *See Fig. 2.* Install 4 air bag module retaining nuts. To complete installation, reverse removal procedure.

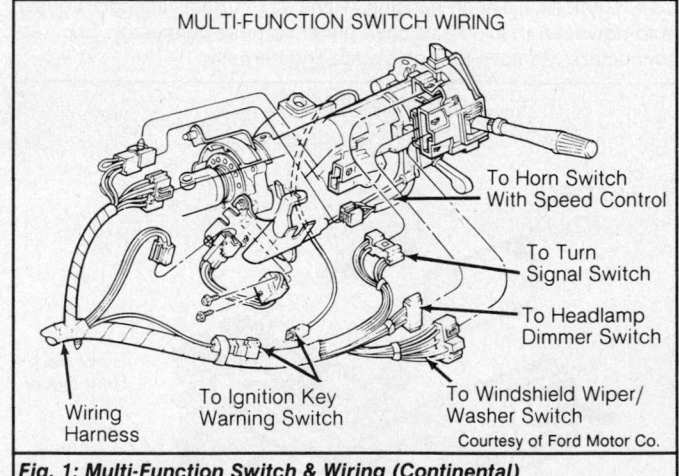

MULTI-FUNCTION SWITCH WIRING

To Horn Switch With Speed Control

To Turn Signal Switch

To Headlamp Dimmer Switch

To Windshield Wiper/ Washer Switch

To Ignition Key Warning Switch

Wiring Harness

Courtesy of Ford Motor Co.

Fig. 1: Multi-Function Switch & Wiring (Continental)

Removal (Escort, Tempo & Topaz) – **1)** Disconnect negative battery cable. Ensure wheels are straight. Remove 2 or 4 steering wheel cover screws.

2) On air bag equipped models, remove 4 air bag module retaining nuts from back of steering wheel. Remove air bag module and disconnect module-to-clockspring connector. Remove energy absorbing foam from wheel.

3) On all models, disconnect horn pad wiring connector. Loosen steering wheel attaching bolt 4-6 turns. DO NOT remove bolt.

4) On air bag equipped models, remove attaching bolt completely. Remove vibration damper. Reinstall attaching bolt loosely on shaft. On all models, use Puller (T67L-3600-A) to loosen steering wheel on shaft. Remove and discard steering wheel attaching bolt. Remove wheel.

Installation (Escort, Tempo & Topaz) – **1)** Align reference marks and install steering wheel on column. On air bag equipped vehicles, install vibration damper. On all models, tighten new attaching bolt to 23-33 ft. lbs. (31-45 N.m).

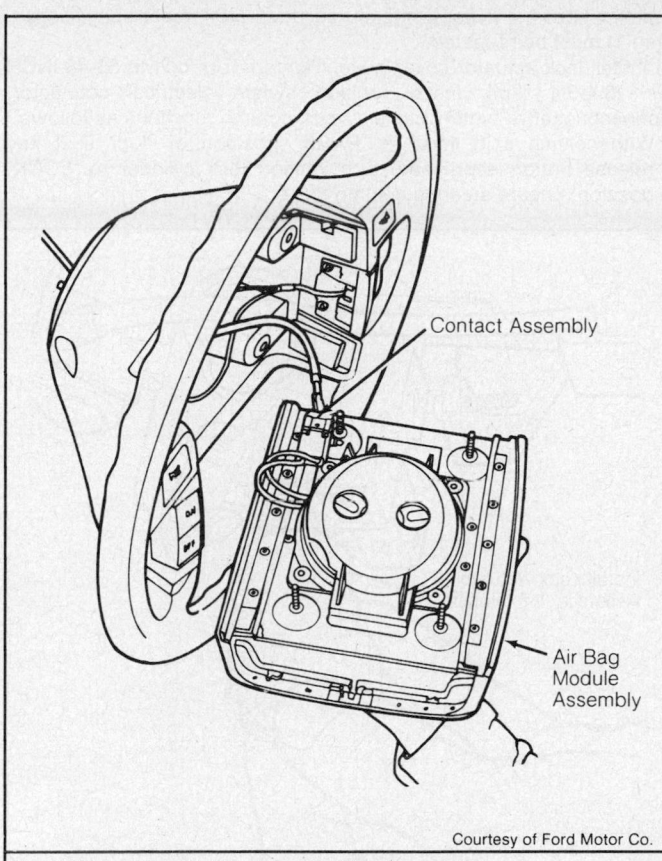

Courtesy of Ford Motor Co.

Fig. 2: Removing Air Bag Module (Continental)

2) On air bag equipped models, connect air bag module wire to clockspring connector. Install module on steering wheel. Install 4 module retaining nuts and tighten to 35-53 INCH lbs. (4-6 N.m). Connect horn pad wiring. Install energy absorbing foam, if equipped. Install horn pad and retaining screws. Connect negative battery cable.

Removal (Mark VII & Mustang) – Disconnect negative battery cable. Remove steering wheel cover. Loosen steering wheel attaching bolt 4-6 turns. DO NOT remove bolt. Remove steering wheel with Puller (T67L-3600-A). DO NOT use knock-off type steering wheel puller. Damage to upper bearing can occur.

Installation (Mark VII & Mustang) – Before installing steering wheel, lubricate slip ring and inspect slip ring brushes. Align master serrations and install steering wheel. Tighten new steering wheel attaching bolt to 21-33 ft. lbs. (29-45 N.m). Install steering wheel cover.

Removal (Grand Marquis, LTD Crown Victoria & Town Car) – Disconnect negative battery cable. Remove 2 horn pad screws from behind steering wheel. Disconnect 2 horn wires from horn switch. Loosen steering wheel attaching bolt 4-6 turns. Remove steering wheel with Puller (T67L-3600-A). DO NOT use knock-off type steering wheel puller. Damage to upper bearing can occur.

Installation (Grand Marquis, LTD Crown Victoria & Town Car) – Before installing steering wheel, lubricate slip ring and inspect slip ring brushes. Align master serrations and install steering wheel. Tighten new steering wheel attaching bolt to 30-35 ft. lbs. (41-47 N.m). Install steering wheel cover.

Removal (Probe) –Disconnect negative battery cable. Remove 2 steering wheel horn pad screws from back of steering wheel. Remove cover pad. Disconnect horn wire from cover pad. Remove steering wheel attaching nut. Scribe an reference mark on wheel and steering shaft for reassembly. Remove steering wheel with Puller (T67L-3600-A).

Installation (Probe) – Align reference marks on steering wheel and steering shaft. Install nut and tighten to 29-36 ft. lbs. (39-49 N.m). To complete installation, reverse removal procedure.

Removal (Sable & Taurus) – Disconnect negative battery cable. Remove steering wheel cover. Remove steering wheel attaching bolt. Pull steering wheel off steering shaft. A puller is NOT required.

Installation (Sable & Taurus) – Align reference marks on steering wheel and steering shaft. Install attaching bolt and tighten to 23-33 ft. lbs. (31-45 N.m). To complete installation, reverse removal procedure.

IGNITION LOCK CYLINDER

Removal & Installation (Continental, Sable & Taurus) – Disconnect negative battery cable. Turn key to "RUN" position. Put a 1/8" drift punch in trim shroud hole below lock cylinder. Depress pin while pulling on lock cylinder. To install, reverse removal procedure.

Removal & Installation (Escort, Tempo & Topaz) – **1)** Disconnect negative battery cable. On tilt column, remove upper shroud by unsnapping shroud from retaining clip at 9 o'clock position. On Tempo and Topaz, remove 5 shroud attaching screws. Remove 2 trim shroud halves. On Escort, remove lower shroud. On all models, disconnect key warning buzzer connector. Turn ignition key to "Run" position.

2) Place a 1/8" drift punch in hole surrounding lock cylinder. Depress retaining pin while pulling out on cylinder. Remove cylinder. To install, reverse removal procedure.

IGNITION SWITCH

Removal (Cougar & Thunderbird) – **1)** Disconnect negative battery cable. Remove lower column shroud. Remove 4 steering column-to-column mounting bracket nuts. Lower column until ignition switch screws are accessible.

2) Remove upper shroud. Disconnect ignition switch electrical connector. Turn key to "RUN" position. Remove 2 switch-to-lock housing screws. Remove ignition switch from actuator pin.

Installation (Cougar & Thunderbird) – Insure actuator pin slot on ignition switch is in "Run" position. *See Fig. 3.* "RUN" position location can be found by rotating keylock cylinder approximately 90 degrees from "LOCK" position. Move switch back and forth to align switch mounting holes with column lock housing threaded holes. Install screws. To complete installation, reverse removal procedure.

Removal & Installation (LTD Crown Victoria, Grand Marquis, Mark VII, Mustang, Town Car) – Disconnect negative battery cable. On tilt column models, remove upper extension shroud by unsnapping shroud from retaining clip at 9 o'clock position. Remove trim shroud halves. Disconnect ignition switch connectors. Turn key to "RUN" position. Remove 2 ignition switch-to-lock cylinder housing screws. Remove ignition switch. To install, reverse removal procedure.

Removal (Escort, Tempo & Topaz) – Disconnect negative battery cable. Remove 5 shroud screws. Remove steering column-to-bracket assembly bolts and nuts. Remove steering column shrouds. Disconnect ignition switch connector. Turn ignition keylock cylinder to "RUN" position. Remove 2 switch-to-keylock cylinder housing screws. Remove ignition switch from actuator pin.

Installation (Escort, Tempo & Topaz) – Insure actuator pin slot on ignition switch is in "RUN" position. *See Fig. 3.* "RUN" position can be located by rotating keylock cylinder approximately 90 degrees from "LOCK" position. Move switch back and forth to align switch mounting holes with column lock housing threaded holes. Install screws. To complete installation, reverse removal procedure.

Removal & Installation (Probe) – Disconnect negative battery cable. Remove steering column upper mounting bolts. Allow steering column to hang. Remove steering column pivot lock assembly. Remove ignition switch-to-ignition switch housing screw. Disconnect 4 ignition switch snap connectors on left of column. Remove ignition switch protective wire loom. Note location of each connector for installation. Disconnect 2 key warning buzzer wires (Green and Red/Orange wires) at 4-terminal connector. To install, reverse removal procedure.

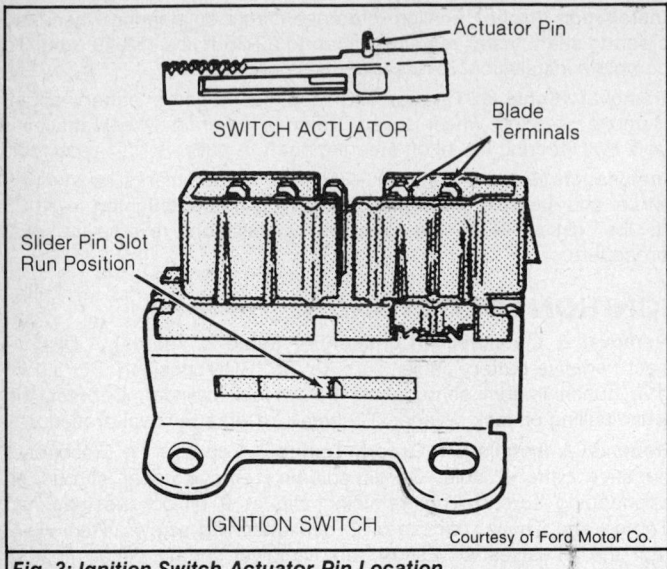

SWITCH ACTUATOR

Actuator Pin

Blade Terminals

Slider Pin Slot Run Position

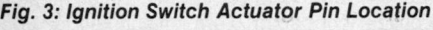

IGNITION SWITCH

Courtesy of Ford Motor Co.

Fig. 3: Ignition Switch Actuator Pin Location

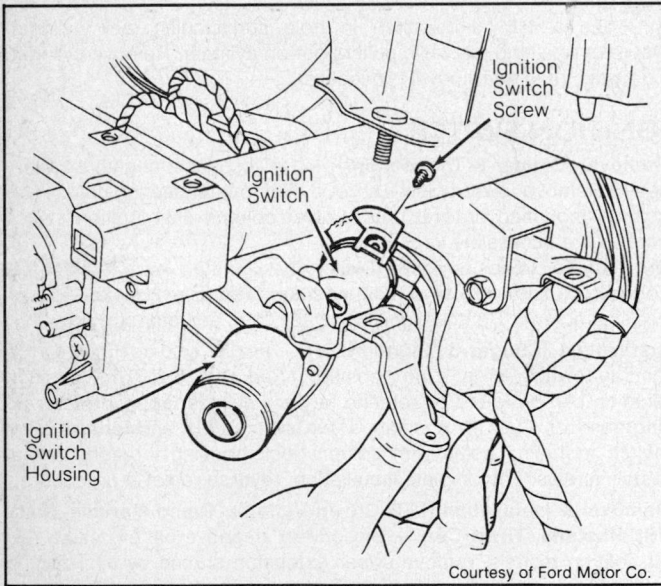

Ignition Switch Screw

Ignition Switch

Ignition Switch Housing

Courtesy of Ford Motor Co.

Fig. 4: Removing Probe Ignition Switch

Removal (Sable & Taurus) – **1)** Disconnect negative battery cable. Remove ignition lock cylinder. See IGNITION LOCK CYLINDER in this article. On tilt column models, remove tilt release lever capscrew. Remove tilt release lever. Remove instrument panel cover.

2) Remove column shroud. Remove 4 steering column-to-support bracket nuts. Lower steering column. Disconnect ignition switch electrical connector. Remove Torx bolt holding lock actuator cover plate. Lock actuator assembly will move freely out of cylinder after ignition switch is removed. See Fig. 5. Remove 2 Torx bolts holding ignition switch and cover. Remove switch.

Installation (Sable & Taurus) – **1)** Set ignition switch to "RUN" position by rotating shaft clockwise until it stops and release it. Install lock actuator assembly to .46-.52" (11.8-13.3 mm) from bottom of actuator assembly to bottom of lock cylinder housing. See Fig. 6. Install ignition switch while holding actuator assembly at proper depth. Install ignition switch and cover. Tighten Torx bolts to 30-48 INCH lbs. (3.4-5.4 N.m).

2) Install lock cylinder. Rotate ignition lock cylinder to "LOCK" position. Measure depth of actuator assembly as in step 1). The actuator assembly must be .92-1.00" (23.5-25.5 mm) inside lock

cylinder housing. If depth measured does NOT meet specification, step 1) must be repeated.

3) Install lock actuator cover plate. Tighten Torx bolt to 30-48 INCH lbs. (3.4-5.4 N.m). Install ignition switch electrical connector. Connect negative battery cable. Check column functions as follows:

• With column shift lever in "PARK" position or floor shift key release button depressed, turn ignition lock cylinder to "LOCK" position. Ensure steering column locks.

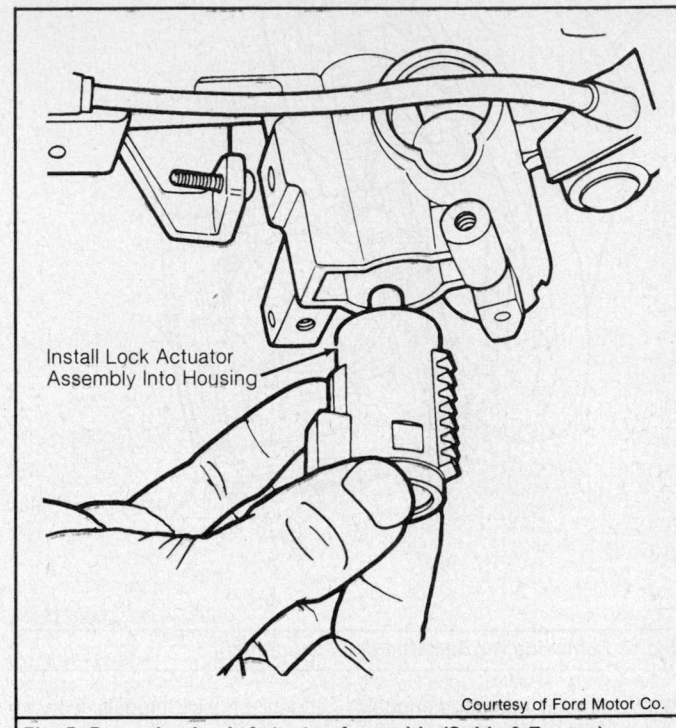

Install Lock Actuator Assembly Into Housing

Courtesy of Ford Motor Co.

Fig. 5: Removing Lock Actuator Assembly (Sable & Taurus)

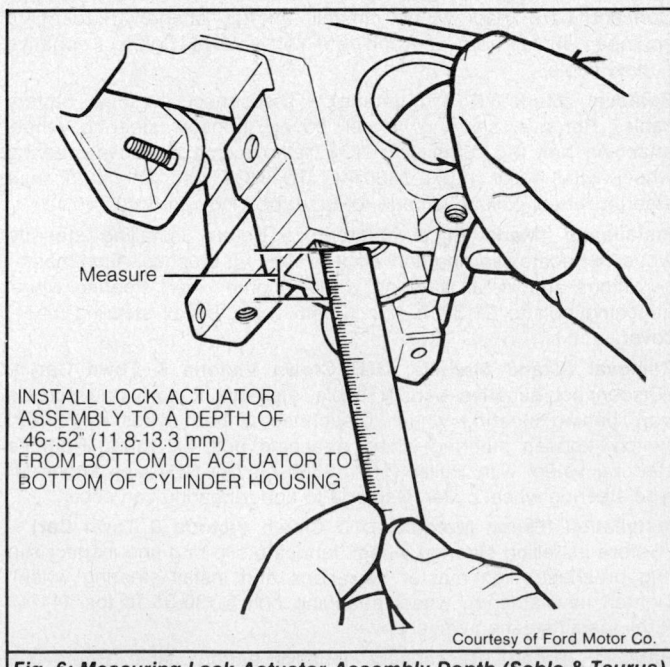

Measure

INSTALL LOCK ACTUATOR ASSEMBLY TO A DEPTH OF .46-.52" (11.8-13.3 mm) FROM BOTTOM OF ACTUATOR TO BOTTOM OF CYLINDER HOUSING

Courtesy of Ford Motor Co.

Fig. 6: Measuring Lock Actuator Assembly Depth (Sable & Taurus)

• Put column shift lever in "DRIVE" position or extend floor shift key release button. Put ignition switch to "RUN" position. Rotate ignition lock cylinder to "LOCK" position until it stops. Ensure engine electrical functions are off and steering shaft DOES NOT lock.

- Turn ignition switch to "ACCESSORY" position. Check radio operation.
- Place shift lever in "PARK" position. Turn ignition switch to "START" position. Ensure starter engages.

4) Remove ignition lock cylinder. Align steering column mounting holes with support bracket. Center steering column in instrument panel opening. Install 4 nuts and tighten to 15-25 ft. lbs. (20-34 N.m).

5) Install column trim shrouds. Install instrument panel lower cover. On tilt column models, install tilt release lever. Install ignition switch. On tilt column models, ensure there is no interference between column and instrument panel.

MULTI-FUNCTION SWITCH

NOTE: The multi-function switch incorporates turn signal, hazard warning, flash-to-pass and dimmer switch functions.

Removal & Installation (Escort, Tempo & Topaz) – Disconnect negative battery cable. Remove 5 shroud screws. Remove lower shroud. Remove upper shroud. Remove switch lever by pulling it straight out from switch. Peel back foam switch cover from turn signal switch. Disconnect 2 electrical connectors and air bag clockspring connector, if equipped. Remove 2 switch-to-lock housing self-tapping screws. Remove switch. To install, reverse removal procedure.

Removal & Installation (Cougar & Thunderbird) – 1) Disconnect negative battery cable. Remove lower right-hand finish panel retaining bolts. Carefully, pull lower right-hand finish panel to disengage retaining clips. Remove lower right-hand reinforcement panel retaining bolts. Remove reinforcement panel.

2) Remove steering column shroud retaining screws. Remove upper shroud. Disconnect multi-function switch electrical connector. Remove switch retaining bolts and switch. To install, reverse removal procedure.

Removal & Installation (Continental) – Disconnect negative battery cable. In tilt column models, tilt column to lowest position. Remove tilt lever. On all models, remove ignition switch. See IGNITION SWITCH in this article. Remove upper and lower steering column shrouds. Remove wiring harness retainer. Disconnect 3 electrical connectors. Remove 2 multi-function switch-to-steering column screws. Remove switch. To install, reverse removal procedure.

SPEED CONTROL SWITCH

Removal & Installation (Continental) – Disconnect negative battery cable. Remove 4 air bag module retaining nuts. Remove air bag module. Disconnect contact assembly at module. Disconnect connectors to speed control switch. Remove switch and wiring assembly. To install, reverse removal procedure.

Removal & Installation (Grand Marquis, LTD Crown Victoria & Town Car) – Remove horn pad cover by inserting a punch through holes behind steering wheel. Remove steering wheel. See STEERING WHEEL in this article. Remove 6 steering wheel-to-back cover screws. Disconnect speed control switch from horn pad cover. Remove speed control switch assembly. To install, reverse removal procedure.

Removal & Installation (Escort, Tempo & Topaz) – Remove 2 steering wheel pad cover screws from back of steering. Remove steering wheel pad cover. Remove energy absorbing foam, if equipped. Disconnect wiring connector from steering wheel. Disconnect 2 horn wire connectors. Remove 2 screws and speed control switches from steering wheel pad cover. To install, reverse removal procedure. Ensure wiring is on top of foam and not pinched.

Removal & Installation (Mark VII) – Remove steering wheel. See STEERING WHEEL in this article. Remove steering wheel back cover. Separate speed control switch connector from terminal on cover. Remove speed control switch by pressing on each post from rear of steering wheel until switch releases. Rotate switch and repeat procedure. To install, reverse removal procedure.

Removal & Installation (Mustang) – Remove horn cover assembly. Remove steering wheel. See STEERING WHEEL in this article. Remove 3 screws and slip ring. Carefully, separate speed control switch connector from slip ring terminals. Remove back cover. Remove speed control switch. To install, reverse removal procedure. Ensure slip ring grease is not contaminated. Inspect brush assembly.

Removal & Installation (Sable & Taurus) – Remove 2 screws for horn pad cover from behind steering wheel. Remove horn pad cover. Disconnect wiring from slip ring terminal. Remove screws from horn pad. Push on back of switch and rotate. To install, reverse removal procedure. When installing horn cover pad, snap latching hook at 12 o'clock position.

TURN SIGNAL SWITCHES

Removal & Installation (Probe) – Disconnect negative battery cable. Remove steering wheel and horn cover. See STEERING WHEEL in this article. Remove 2 center cover screws and cover. Remove attaching screws and electrical connections from cluster module. Remove cluster module. Remove turn signal arm screw and arm. Remove turn signal switch screws and switch. To install, reverse removal procedure.

Removal & Installation (Grand Marquis, LTD Crown Victoria, Mark VII, Mustang & Town Car) – On tilt column models, remove upper extension shroud by unsnapping shroud from retaining clip at 9 o'clock position. On all models, Remove 2 trim shroud halves. Remove turn signal lever by grasping and pulling straight out. Peel back shield from switch. Disconnect 2 electrical connectors. Remove turn signal-to-lock cylinder housing screws. Remove switch. To install, reverse removal procedure.

WINDSHIELD WIPER SWITCH

Removal & Installation (Gran Marquis, LTD Crown Victoria & Town Car) – Disconnect negative battery cable. Remove steering column cover. Remove 2 wiper switch retaining screws. Disconnect multiple connector at rear of switch. Remove switch. To install, reverse removal procedure.

Removal & Installation (Escort) – Disconnect negative battery cable. Remove upper and lower steering column shrouds. Disconnect electrical connector. Peel back shield from switch. Remove 2 switch-to-steering column screws. Remove switch. To install, reverse removal procedure.

Removal & Installation (Escort With Tilt Column) – Disconnect negative battery cable. Remove steering column shroud. Peel back shield from switch. Disconnect switch wiring. Remove wiring retainer-to-steering column screw. Grasp switch handle and pull straight out. To install, reverse removal procedure.

TIGHTENING SPECIFICATIONS

Steering Wheel Nut/Bolt	Ft. Lbs. (N.m)
Continental	23-33 (31-45)
Cougar & Thunderbird	23-33 (31-45)
Escort, Tempo & Topaz	23-33 (31-45)
Grand Marquis, LTD Crown Victoria & Town Car	30-35 (41-47)
Mark VII & Mustang	23-33 (31-45)
Probe	29-36 (39-49)
Sable & Taurus	23-33 (31-45)

Except Acclaim, Horizon, Omni, Spirit

DESCRIPTION

Three types of steering columns are covered in this article: tilt wheel, fixed with floor shift and fixed with column shift. This article will cover REMOVAL & INSTALLATION of standard column. Information about REMOVAL & INSTALLATION of other columns is similar.

OVERHAUL in this article will cover tilt wheel column and fixed column with column shift. Overhaul of fixed column with floor shift is not available from manufacturer. Design is similar for all columns. The difference is the addition of column shifters and tilt mechanisms. Steering columns use an integral ignition lock switch, which secures steering wheel and shift linkage on column shift. Upper and lower sections of steering shaft are connected by plastic collars and pins.

REMOVAL & INSTALLATION

CAUTION: Some vehicles are equipped with air bags. Use extreme caution when servicing to avoid personal injury and vehicle damage.

FIXED STEERING COLUMN

NOTE: Information on removal and installation of tilt columns is not available from manufacturer.

Removal – 1) Disconnect negative battery cable. On vehicles with column shift, disconnect link rod from grommet in shift lever. Remove steering shaft lower coupling-to-steering gear roll pin. Disconnect wiring connectors at steering column jacket.

2) Remove steering wheel center pad assembly. Disconnect horn wire(s). Remove horn switch, if applicable. Remove steering wheel retaining nut. Remove steering wheel with Puller (C-3428B). Remove floor plate-to-floor pan attaching screws to expose steering column bracket.

3) Remove instrument panel steering column cover and lower reinforcement. Remove steering column bracket-to-instrument panel support nuts. Remove lower coupling from steering gear shaft. Remove column assembly.

Installation – 1) Install ground clip on left column bracket slot. Insert column through floor pan opening and couple with steering gear shaft. Install roll pin. Connect column-to-mounting studs with nuts, but DO NOT tighten. Assure breakaway capsules are seated in column support bracket. Tighten upper bracket nuts to specification. See TIGHTENING SPECIFICATIONS in this article.

2) Install floor plate. Install steering wheel. Install horn switch and wire(s). Install wiring connectors at steering column jacket. Install link rod-to-shift lever by snapping rod into grommet with pliers. Adjust shift rod linkage.

3) Install gearshift indicator pointer to approximate original location and adjust as required. Install lower reinforcement. Install lower instrument panel steering column cover. Install negative battery cable. Test light and horn operation.

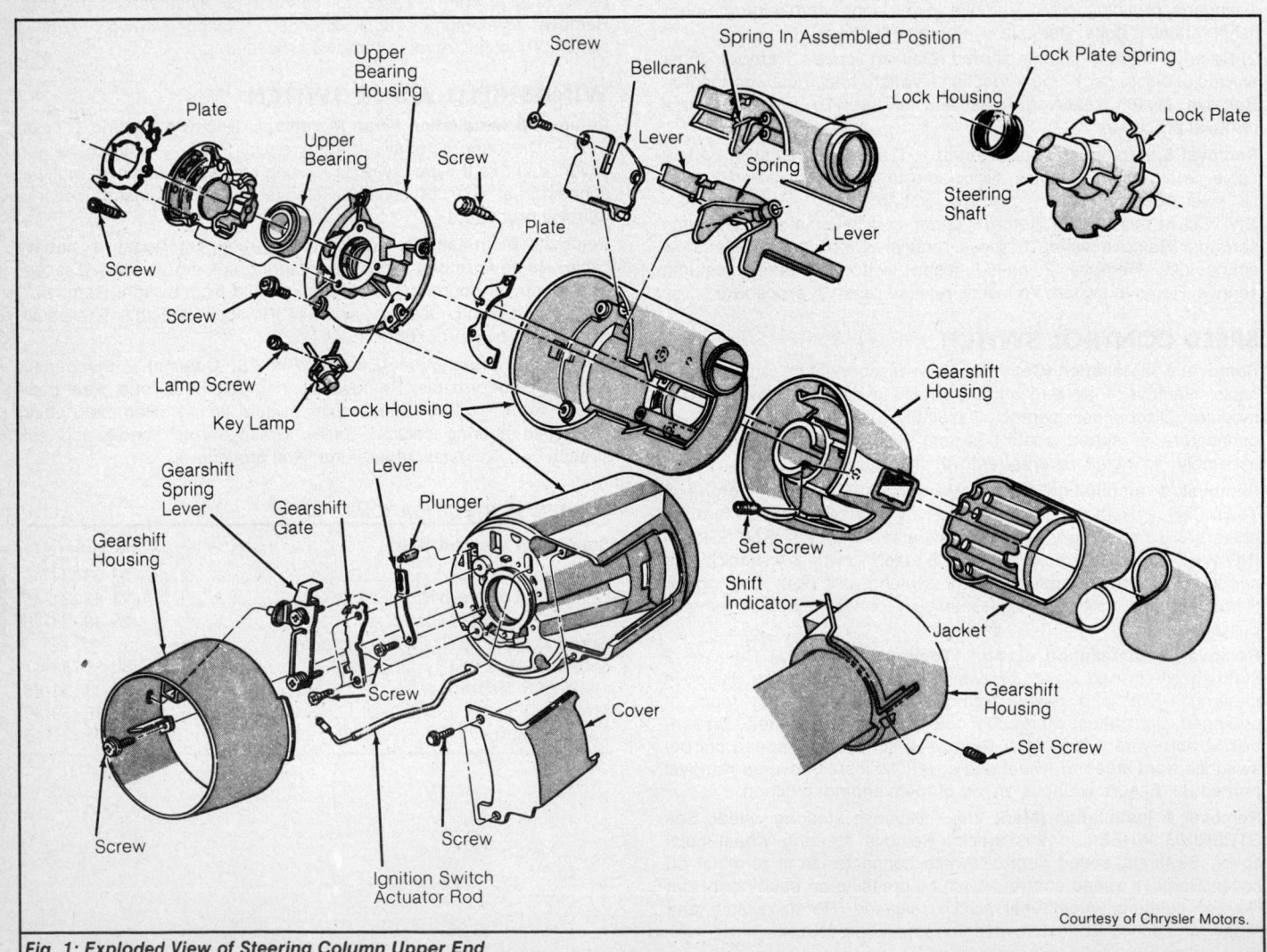

Courtesy of Chrysler Motors.

Fig. 1: Exploded View of Steering Column Upper End

OVERHAUL

FIXED COLUMN

CAUTION: Some vehicles are equipped with air bags. Use extreme caution when servicing to avoid personal injury and vehicle damage.

Disassembly – 1) Remove steering wheel. See appropriate STEERING WHEEL & COLUMN SWITCHES article in this section. Disconnect negative battery cable. Pry off retainers and remove wiring trough. Remove shift lever roll pin. Remove breakaway capsules. Secure steering column in a vise.

2) Remove 2 lock housing cover screws. Remove lock housing cover. Remove washer/wiper switch assembly. Pull plastic cover up control stalk. Remove 2 screws attaching control stalk sleeve to washer/wiper switch. Rotate control stalk shaft to full clockwise position. Remove shaft by pulling straight out. Remove turn signal switch and upper bearing retainer screws. Remove retainer and lift turn signal switch upward.

3) Unclip horn and key light ground wires. Remove retaining screw and lift ignition key lamp assembly out of way.

4) Remove 4 bearing housing-to-lock housing screws. Remove snap ring from upper end of steering shaft. DO NOT allow steering shaft to slide out of jacket. Remove bearing housing from shaft. Remove lock plate spring and lock plate from steering shaft. Remove steering shaft through bottom of column.

5) Remove ignition key. Remove screw and lift out buzzer/chime switch. Remove 2 ignition switch screws. Disconnect ignition switch wiring harness. Remove ignition switch by rotating it 1/4 turn and sliding it off actuator rod. Remove dimmer switch screws. Remove dimmer switch from actuator rod.

6) Remove 2 bellcrank mounting screws. Slide bellcrank in lock housing until it can be disconnected from ignition switch actuator rod. Place lock cylinder in "LOCK" position and remove key. Insert 2 small screwdrivers into both lock cylinder release holes. See Fig. 3. Push to release spring loaded lock retainers. The lock cylinder lower release hole is just above buzzer/chime switch mounting screw hole. Pull cylinder out of housing bore.

7) Grasp lock lever and spring assembly and pull from housing. Remove 4 lock housing-to-column jacket hex head retaining screws. Remove lock housing plate and housing from jacket. Turn lock housing 1/4 turn to disengage from ignition switch actuator rod.

8) Loosen shift tube set screw in housing. Remove shift tube through lower end of jacket. Remove floor plate and grommet from jacket. Remove 4 bolts and 2 cross straps from steering shaft flexible coupling. Note position of long and short coupling bolts for installation. Remove flexible coupling.

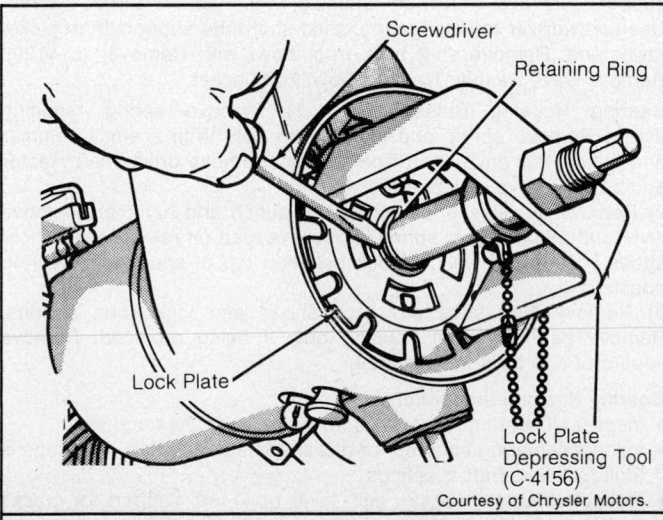

Fig. 2: Removing Lock Plate Retaining Ring

9) Pry cover tangs from steering shaft pot coupling. Lift seal and cover from body. Drive small short dowel pin at edge of coupling body down into coupling and discard. Pull body off shaft and shoe assembly.

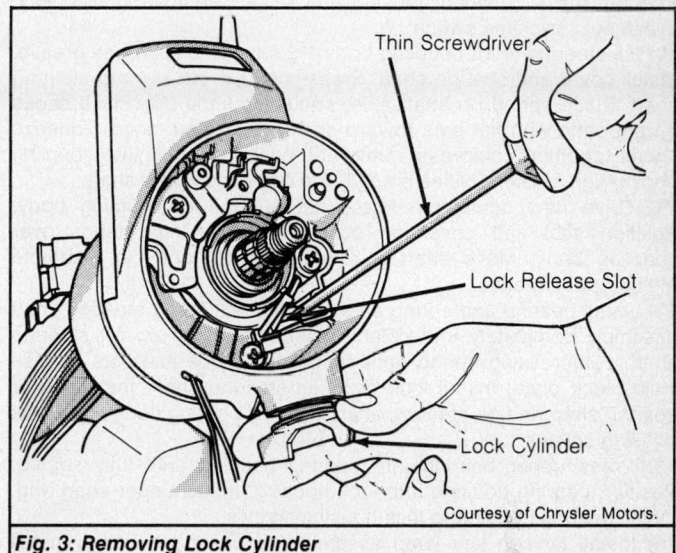

Fig. 3: Removing Lock Cylinder

Inspection – Check flexible coupling for cracks or deterioration. Check cross straps for warpage or distoration.

Inspect turn signal switch for distortion, broken or damaged parts. Inspect wiring insulation for worn or bare spots. Inspect steering shaft bearings for smooth operation. Lubricate bearings with multipurpose grease. Inspect floor plate grommet and replace if damaged.

Reassembly – 1) Install shift tube into shift tube housing. Tighten shift tube set screw. Connect flexible coupling to 2 cross straps with 4 bolts. Align master splines and place coupling assembly on flanges. Tighten to specification.

2) Coat all friction surfaces with multipurpose grease. Clamp column in vise so both ends are accessible. Check column tube-to-mandrel rivet tightness. Replace, if necessary, using 1/8" diameter by 1/4" long aluminum "blind" rivets. DO NOT use steel rivets. This joint must shear under impact.

3) Install floor plate and grommet on column lower jacket end. Position gearshift housing on column jacket. Ensure support is pressed in place against jacket tabs. Install dust seal and shift tube support on shift tube. Slide shift tube assembly into jacket. Guide key on upper end of tube into slot on gearshift housing. Hold together and tighten shift housing set screw.

4) Position crossover load spring and shift lever in gearshift housing. Tap pivot into place. Assemble key cylinder plunger spring. Install key cylinder on lock housing. Install shift lever gate on lock housing. Place ignition switch rod through shift housing.

5) Place shift lever in middle position. Place ignition switch rod through the oval hole in lock housing. Seat lock housing on top of jacket, aligning keyway in housing with slot in jacket. Insert 4 holding lock housing-to-jacket screws. Tighten to specification.

6) Lubricate and assemble 2 lock levers, lock lever spring and pin. Install lock lever assembly in lock housing. Seat pin firmly in bottom of slots. Ensure lock lever spring leg is firmly seated in lock casting notch. Install bellcrank assembly into lockhousing.

7) Install ignition switch actuator rod into bellcrank. While pulling ignition switch actuator rod down column, install bellcrank onto its mounting surface. Gearshift lever should be in "PARK." Connect ignition switch to actuator rod and rotate switch 1/4 turn to lock in position.

8) Install ignition lock by turning key to "LOCK" position and remove key. Insert lock cylinder far enough into housing to contact switch actuator. Insert key and press inward. When parts align, cylinder will move inward and spring loaded retainers will snap into place, locking cylinder into housing. Put key cylinder and ignition switch in "LOCK" position, second detent from top. Tighten ignition switch mounting screws.

9) Feed buzzer/chime switch wires behind wiring post, down through space between housing and jacket. Remove ignition key. Install buzzer/chime switch.

10) Fill steering shaft coupling body 1/2 full of multipurpose grease. Install cover and seal on shaft. Press shoe pin equally into steering shaft. Place spring on shaft side, straddling shoe pin. Place shoes on pin ends with flat side toward spring, engaging tangs. Squeeze shoes together, compress spring and push assembly into coupling body. Align master splines on coupling body and upper shaft.

11) Drive new dowel pin into outer surface of coupling body. Position seal and cover on coupling body. Crimp tangs over coupling body. Move shaft in and out of pot body to distribute multipurpose grease.

12) Install bearing and spring on steering shaft. Insert steering shaft assembly completely into column assembly. Push up on steering shaft, compressing spring until snap ring can be installed. Grease inside lock plate. Install lock plate on steering shaft. Install upper bearing snap ring on steering shaft. Install 4 bearing housing-to-lock housing screws.

13) Press upper bearing into bearing housing until fully seated. Position bearing housing into lock housing. Install upper snap ring. Install bearing housing to lock housing screws.

14) Install ignition key lamp assembly on bearing housing. Install turn signal switch. Feed turn signal and key lamp wires between bearing housing and lock housing. Install bearing retaining plate. Tighten to specification. Ensure turn signal switch assembly ground wires are positioned toward ground clips.

15) Assemble washer/wiper switch, washer/wiper shaft and switch cover. Assemble speed control switch, hider disc and knob. Place washer/wiper switch into lock housing. Feed wires through lock housing and shift housing.

16) Install dimmer switch actuator rod through housings and into washer/wiper switch pocket. Compress dimmer switch until 2 .093" drill shanks can be inserted into alignment holes. With actuator rod seated into dimmer switch and washer/wiper switch pockets, apply a slight upward pressure and connect dimmer switch to its bracket. Remove drill shanks.

17) Install turn signal lever cover. Install breakaway capsules. Install wiring trough in place over wires. Install new retainers, if required.

TILT COLUMN

Column Disassembly – 1) Remove 4 bracket assembly-to-column jacket bolts. Remove wiring protector from column jacket. Attach column to Holding Fixture (C-4132) and install in vise.

2) Remove tilt lever. Remove hazard warning knob. Remove hider and sleeve from washer/wiper switch. Rotate wiper/washer switch shaft to full clockwise position and pull straight out to remove. Remove lock plate plastic cover. Remove lock plate retaining ring with Lock Plate Depressing Tool (C-4156) and small screwdriver.

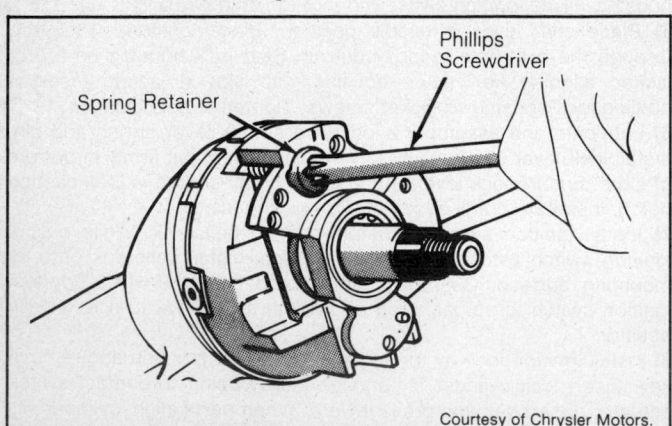

Fig. 4: Removing Tilt Spring Retainer

Courtesy of Chrysler Motors.

See Fig. 2. Remove lock plate, cancelling cam and upper bearing spring.

3) Remove switch actuator screw and arm. Remove 3 turn signal switch screws. Place gear shift in low position. Wrap tape around connector and wires. Remove turn signal switch and wiring. Remove key lamp. Put key in "LOCK" position. Insert a thin screwdriver into slot next to switch mounting screw and depress spring latch at bottom of slot. Remove lock cylinder. *See Fig. 3.*

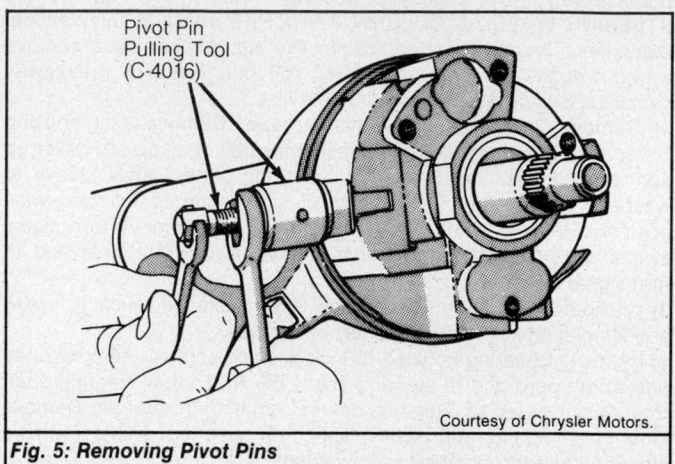

Fig. 5: Removing Pivot Pins

Courtesy of Chrysler Motors.

4) Remove buzzer/chime switch from housing. Remove 3 screws and housing cover. Remove washer/wiper switch. Place column in upright position. With a large Phillips head screwdriver, remove spring retainer, spring and guide. *See Fig. 4.* Remove 2 dimmer switch screws. Remove dimmer switch from rod.

5) Push in upper steering shaft enough to remove steering shaft inner race seat and inner race. Remove ignition switch. Place Pivot Pin Remover (C-4016) over pivot pin. *See Fig. 5.* Thread small portion of screw firmly into pivot pin. Hold screw from turning with one wrench, turn nut clockwise with a second wrench to withdraw pivot pin from support. Remove opposite pivot pin in similar manner.

6) Use tilt release lever to disengage lock shoes. Remove bearing housing assembly by pulling upward. Move housing assembly left to disengage rack from actuator. Rotate housing clockwise to free dimmer switch actuator rod. Remove actuator assembly.

7) Remove steering shaft coupling. Double coupling is held to shaft by roll pin. Remove steering shaft assembly from upper end. Remove center spheres and anti-lash springs from steering shaft. Remove 4 bolts holding support to lock plate.

8) Remove support from column jacket end. Remove shift gate from support. Remove shift tube retaining ring. Remove thrust washer. Use screwdriver to disengage plastic shift tube support from jacket lower end. Remove shift tube from bowl with Remover (C-4120). Remove wave washer. Remove bowl from jacket.

Bearing Housing Disassembly – 1) Remove spring retaining screw. Remove spring and lock spring bolt. With a small hammer and punch, tap drive shaft from sector. Remove drive shaft, sector and bolt. Remove rack and rack spring.

2) Remove tilt release lever pin with punch and hammer. Remove lever and release lever spring. To relieve load on release lever, hold shoes inward and wedge block between top of shoes and bearing housing.

3) Remove lock shoe pin, lock shoes and lock shoe springs. Remove bearings from housing only if being replaced. Remove separator and balls from bearing.

Bearing Housing Inspection:
- Inspect all bearings and races for nicks, scratches and wear.
- Inspect centering spheres for nicks, damage or wear. If damage is found, check shaft couplings.
- Inspect actuator housing, shift lever bowl and support for cracks and other damage.
- Inspect turn signal switch for distortion, broke or damaged parts.

Prem

DESC

Steerin
shift m
column
betwee
steering

REMO

FIXED

Remova
panel s
panel su
2) Disco
attachin

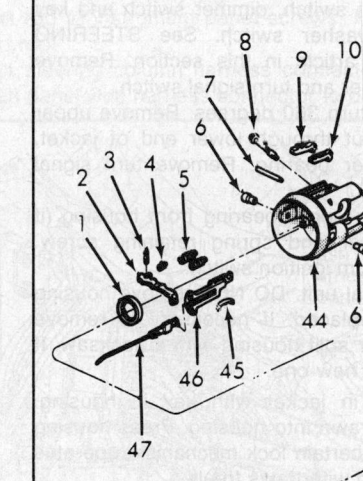

1. Bearing Assembly
2. Shoe Release Lever
3. Release Lever Pin
4. Release Lever Spring
5. Shoe Spring
6. Pivot Pin
7. Dowel Pin
8. Drive Shaft
9. Steering Wheel Lock Shoe
10. Steering Wheel Lock Shoe
11. Lock Bolt
12. Bearing Assembly
13. Tilt Lever Opening Shield
14. Dimmer Switch Actuating Rod
15. Lock Cylinder Set
16. Lock Housing Cover
17. Lock Retaining Screw
18. Buzzer Switch Retaining Clip
19. Buzzer Switch
20. Pan Head Cross Recess Screw
21. Inner Race
22. Upper Bearing Inner Race Seat
23. Turn Signal/Flasher Switch Asse
24. Turn Signal Arm

Fig. 10: Exploded View of Tilt Steer

Fig. 1: P

3) For ve
transaxle
pliers to
retainer c
bracket sc
2.

Fig. 2: Rem

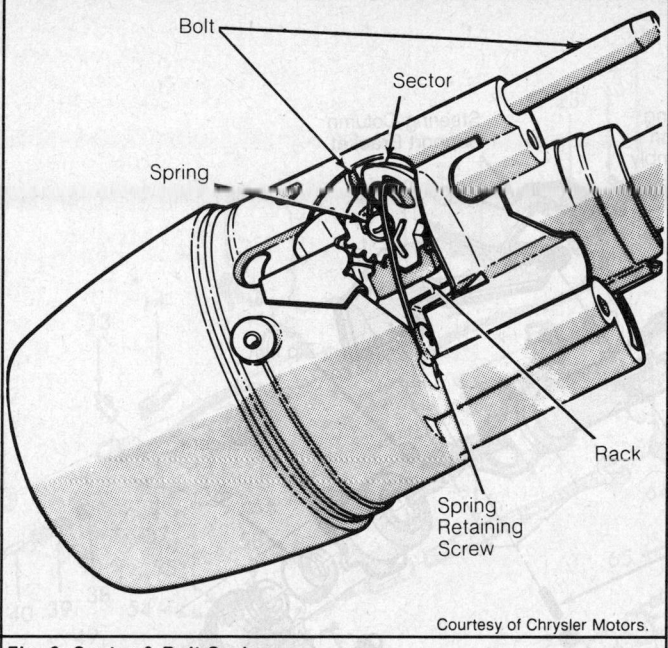

Fig. 6: Sector & Bolt Spring

Courtesy of Chrysler Motors.

- Inspect horn and turn signal wires for worn or bare spots.
- Inspect steering shaft and gearshift tube for loose or broken plastic shear joints.

Bearing Housing Reassembly – 1) Install bearings in bearing housing, if removed. Install lock shoes springs, lock shoes and shoe pin in bearing housing.
2) With tilt lever opening on left side, shoes facing up, the 4 slot shoe is on left. Install spring, release lever and pin in bearing housing. Install drive shaft in housing. Tap sector onto shaft.
3) Install lock bolt and engage with sector cam surface. Install rack and spring. Block tooth on rack to engage block tooth on sector. Install external tilt release lever.

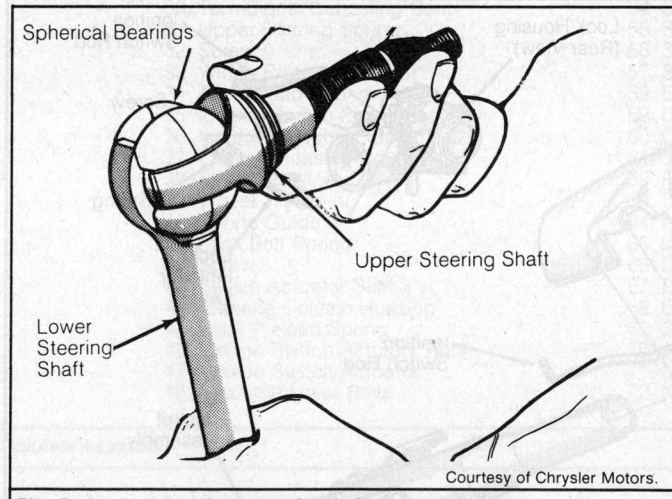

Fig. 7: Assembling Steering Shaft Centering Spheres

Courtesy of Chrysler Motors.

Column Reassembly – 1) Install bolt spring and spring retainer screw. Tighten to specification. Install shift lever spring in bowl. Slide bowl into jacket. Install wave washer and jacket mounting plate. Work jacket mounting plate into notches in jacket.

2) Install shift tube in lower end of jacket. Install thrust washer and retaining ring. Slide dimmer switch actuator rod through hole in support. Feed rod between bowl and jacket. Install support. Connect support to lock plate. Tighten to specification.
3) Install lower bearing 3/16" into lower end of jacket. Install centering spheres and anti-lash spring in upper steering shaft. See Fig. 7. Install lower steering shaft from same side of spheres as spring end protrudes. Ensure master serrations align.
4) Position shift bowl in Park. Install ignition switch actuator rod from bottom, between bowl and jacket. Guide back of coupling into support slot. Assemble bearing housing over steering shaft. Engage rack over end of ignition switch actuator. Position access hole of bearing housing over end of dimmer switch acuator rod. Rotate housing counterclockwise to assemble.
5) Hold locking shoes in disengaged position. Install bearing housing over steering shaft until pivot holes align with holes in support. Install pivot pins. Replace washer/wiper pivot assembly and press pivot pin in cover. Install washer/wiper switch.
6) Install tilt lever opening shield in cover. Position cap over dimmer switch actuator rod. Guide actuator rod into pivot slot during cover assembly. Hold cap so cover will slide over it.
7) Place housing in full up position. Lubricate guide, peg on support, tilt spring and tilt retainer spring. Install guide and retainer. Install bearing inner race and seat. Install lock housing cover and tighten 3 screws to specifications.
8) Install buzzer/chime switch. Install key lamp. Install turn signal switch wires and connectors through cover, bearing housing and shift bowl. Install hazard warning knob. Install canceling cam assembly and lock plate. Install new retaining with Remover/Installer (C-4156).
9) Install tilt release lever and turn signal lever. Install ignition lock by turning key to "LOCK" position and removing key. Insert cylinder into housing far enough to contact drive shaft. Press inward and move ignition switch actuator rod to align parts. The cylinder will move inward and spring loaded retainer will snap into place.
10) Install ignition switch and dimmer switch. Ensure actuator rods are firmly seated. Install wire protector on column jacket. Remove column from vise and fixture. Install column in vehicle.

TIGHTENING SPECIFICATIONS

Application	Ft. Lbs. (N.m)
Steering Wheel Retaining Nut	45 (61)

Application	INCH Lbs. (N.m)
Bearing Retaining Plate Screws	24 (3)
Bellcrank Screws	35 (4)
Column Bracket-to-Column Bolt	20 (2)
Column Clamp Bolt	105 (12)
Column Clamp Stud	110 (12)
Column Clamp Stud Nut	200 (23)
Column Upper Bracket Nut	110 (13)
Flexible Coupling Bolt	200 (23)
Gearshift Gate Spring Screw	24 (3)
Gearshift Housing Set Screw	18 (2)
Lock Housing Cover	100 (11)
Lock Housing-to-Jacket Screw	90 (10)
Sector Bolt	35 (4)
Support-to-Lock Plate Screw	60 (7)

1989 STEERING COLUMNS
Eagle (Cont.)

Steering
Wheel
Nut

Groun
Clip

Wiring Cove

Reta

Fig. 8: Exploded View of Chrysl

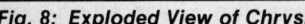

Fig. 1:

Acclaim

DESC

The ste
driver st
to steeri
the stee
actuates
is moun

REM

STEER

Remova
harness
2) Pull
coupling
pin.

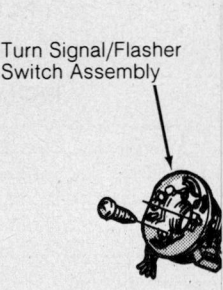

Turn Signal/Flasher
Switch Assembly

Upper Bearin

Ignition

Fig. 2: S

Fig. 9: Exploded View of Chrysl

OVERHAUL

STEERING COLUMN

NOTE: Overhaul procedures are for fixed and tilt steering column assemblies. Overhaul procedures for fixed columns are similar except for references to tilt mechanism components.

Disassembly – 1) Disconnect negative battery cable. Remove steering wheel. See STEERING WHEEL & COLUMN SWITCHES article in this section. Remove steering column. See FIXED & TILT STEERING COLUMNS under REMOVAL & INSTALLATION.

2) Remove rear covers from shroud pods. Remove lower cover-to-shroud bracket screw. Carefully separate lower and upper covers by removing upper cover tab fasteners from lower cover notches. Remove 2 shroud bracket-to-upper cover screws. Remove upper shroud cover.

3) Slide upper shroud cover over gearshift lever. Remove control modules from shroud. Detach key/lock cylinder bezel from shroud. Cover tilt lever stalk with shop towel and remove lever with pliers. Remove shroud from bracket.

4) Remove canceling cam and wave washer from turn signal switch. Remove turn signal switch from switch adapter.

5) Remove shroud bracket. Remove ignition switch from key/lock cylinder housing. Turn ignition key to unmarked position. Press lock tab and remove key/lock cylinder. Remove turn signal switch adapter from steering column housing.

CAUTION: Steering shaft retaining ring and upper bearing spring retainer compress strong spring tension from upper bearing spring. DO NOT remove retaining without relieving spring tension.

6) Remove upper steering shaft retaining ring, upper bearing spring retainer and upper bearing spring. Position Adapter (J-35899) on spring retainer. *See Fig. 4.* Thread Compressor (J-23653A) onto steering column shaft. Tighten spring compressor nut to compress bearing retainer spring. Remove and discard snap ring. Loosen spring compressor nut. Remove spring compressor and adapter. Remove bearing retainer and spring.

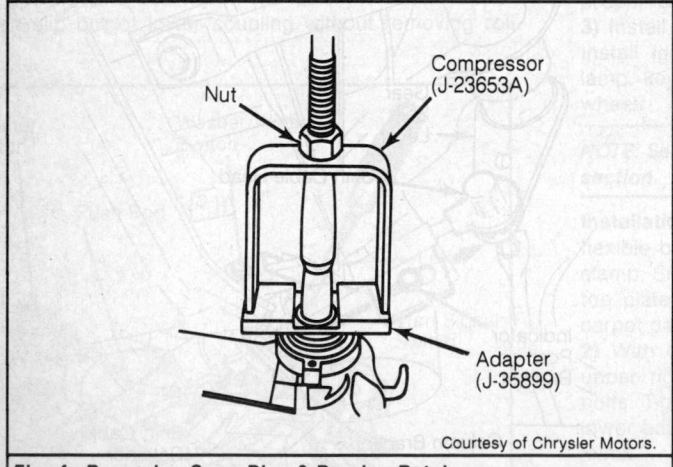

Nut

Compressor
(J-23653A)

Adapter
(J-35899)

Courtesy of Chrysler Motors.

Fig. 4: Removing Snap Ring & Bearing Retainer

7) On column shift models, remove gearshift cable by pressing in retaining tab. *See Fig. 8.* Temporarily remove tilt lever. Center punch and drill out lock cylinder shear bolts until drill bit reaches washers.

8) Remove lock cylinder housing. Using pliers, remove drilled-out bolts. Install tilt lever. Place column in full up position. Insert large Phillips screwdriver into tilt spring retainer recess.

CAUTION: Exercise extreme care when removing tilt spring retainer. Spring is under extreme pressure. The Phillips screwdriver tip should be large enough to snugly fit into cross-shaped retainer recess.

9) Press retainer inward and turn it clockwise to remove retainer and spring. Place column in center position. Using Puller (J-21854-1), remove housing pivot pins. Move tilt lever to disengage lock shoes.

10) Slide housing off support. DO NOT strike shaft to remove. Pull steering shafts out of column support and jacket. Remove 4 steering column support Torx-head screws. Remove support from column.

11) Separate steering shafts. Pivot upper and lower shafts to a 90 degree angle and separate at flexible joint.

Inspection – 1) Column and housing bearings are not serviceable separately. If column or housing bearings are damaged or worn, replace column or housing as a unit.

2) Measure distance between upper and lower steering column jackets if collapse of column is suspected. *See Fig. 5.* Measurement should be at least 3.54" (90 mm). If less than specification, replace steering column.

3) With steering shaft removed from steering column, check shaft straightness. If shaft is bent or warped more than .065" (1.65 mm), replace shaft. Check condition of steering shaft shear pins. If any are broken or damage, replace steering shaft.

4) Check steering column attaching bracket breakaway capsules. Measure clearance between capsules and bottom edge of slots in attaching bracket. If clearance is greater than 0.065" (1.65 mm), replace steering column jacket.

5) Check pivot pins, flex joint and support housing for looseness at pivot points. Check tilt lock shoes for worn teeth. Replace parts as necessary.

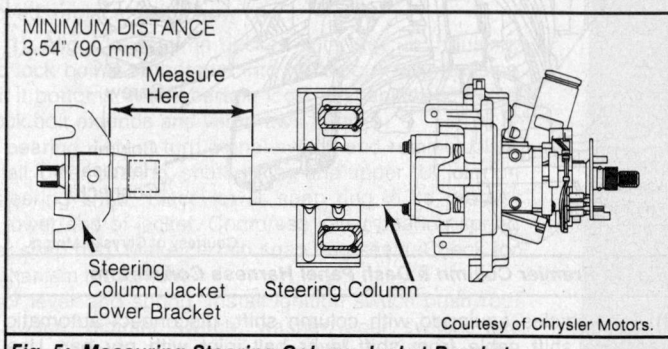

MINIMUM DISTANCE
3.54" (90 mm)

Measure
Here

Steering
Column Jacket
Lower Bracket

Steering Column

Courtesy of Chrysler Motors.

Fig. 5: Measuring Steering Column Jacket Bracket

Reassembly – 1) Lubricate column bearings. Install support on column. Install and tighten support-to-column Torx head screws. Install centering spheres in upper and lower steering shafts. Connect upper and lower shafts. Install snap ring to centering spheres. Slide steering shaft assembly into column from support side.

2) Position housing over shaft and onto support. Position steering column housing over steering shaft and mate with steering column support. Align tilt pivot pin holes in housing and support.

3) Retract tilt lock shoes by pulling on tilt lever to align pivot pin holes. Insert pivot pins. Using hammer and drift, seat pivot pins. Using hammer and punch, stake each pivot pin in 2 places.

4) Install tilt spring in column. Place retainer on spring. Insert large Phillips screwdriver into retainer. Push retainer and turn counterclockwise to lock in position.

5) Place ignition lock cylinder housing on tilt housing. Install and tighten new shear bolts until heads break off. On column shift models, press tab to install shift cable in housing. *See Fig. 7.*

6) Install upper bearing spring and spring retainer and against upper bearing. Position Adapter (J-35899) on shaft. Thread Compressor (J-23653A) on shaft. *See Fig. 4.*

7) Tighten compressor nut to compress spring. Install snap ring into second groove of steering shaft. Loosen compressor nut. Remove compressor and adapter.

8) Position ignition switch on key/lock cylinder housing and install 2 retaining screws. Install shroud mounting bracket on column. Install turn signal switch adapter and turn signal switch. Install wave washer and canceling cam.

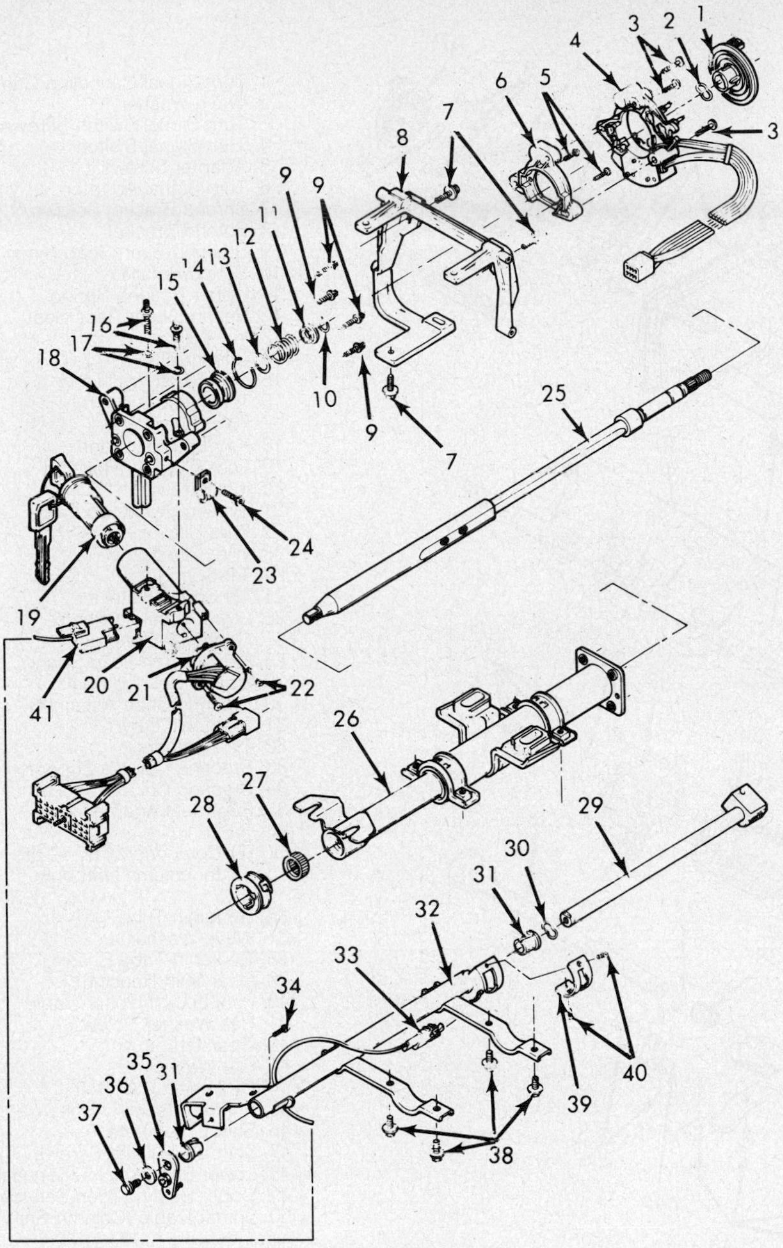

1. Turn Signal Canceling Cam
2. Wave Washer
3. Turn Signal Switch Screws
4. Turn Signal Switch
5. Adapter Screws
6. Turn Signal Adapter
7. Shroud Bracket Screws
8. Shroud Bracket
9. Housing Screws
10. Steering Shaft Snap Ring
11. Retainer Spring
12. Bearing Spring
13. Thrust Washer
14. Bearing Snap Ring
15. Upper Bearing
16. Shear Bolt
17. Shear Bolt Washer
18. Column Housing
19. Key/Lock Cylinder
20. Lock Cylinder Housing
21. Ignition Switch
22. Ignition Switch Screws
23. Wire Clip
24. Clip Screw
25. Steering Shaft
26. Column Jacket
27. Lower Bearing
28. Boot Seal Adapter

NOTE: Components 29-41 are for column shift only.

29. Gearshift Tube
30. Wave Washer
31. Tube Bearings
32. Shift Tube Assembly
33. Park Lock Inhibitor Cable
34. Hex Washer Screw
35. Gearshift Lever
36. Flat Washer
37. Shift Lever Bolt
38. Shifter Assembly Bolts
39. Shift Lever Gate
40. Gate Screws
41. Shifter Cable

Courtesy of Chrysler Motors.

Fig. 6: Exploded View of Premier Fixed Steering Column Assembly

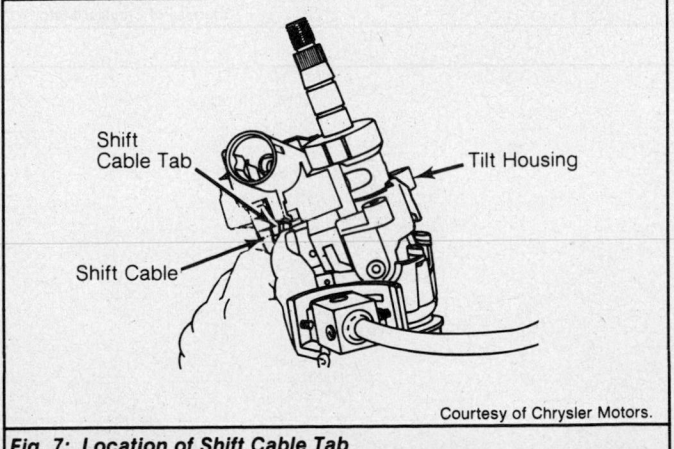

Shift Cable Tab

Tilt Housing

Shift Cable

Courtesy of Chrysler Motors.

Fig. 7: Location of Shift Cable Tab

9) With key in lock cylinder, turn key to unmarked position. Install lock cylinder into housing. Install ignition switch. Install shroud on shroud bracket and internal screws. Install key/lock bezel to shroud. Install tilt level stalk.

10) Install control modules in shroud. Install shroud upper cover over gearshift lever and adjacent to shroud bracket. Carefully mate upper and lower covers. Install rear covers on shroud pods.

11) Install steering column. See REMOVAL & INSTALLATION in this article. Install steering wheel. See STEERING WHEEL & COLUMN SWITCHES in this section. Ensure proper operation of steering column, column shifter (if equipped), ignition switch and headlight pod switches.

1989 STEERING COLUMNS
Eagle (Cont.)

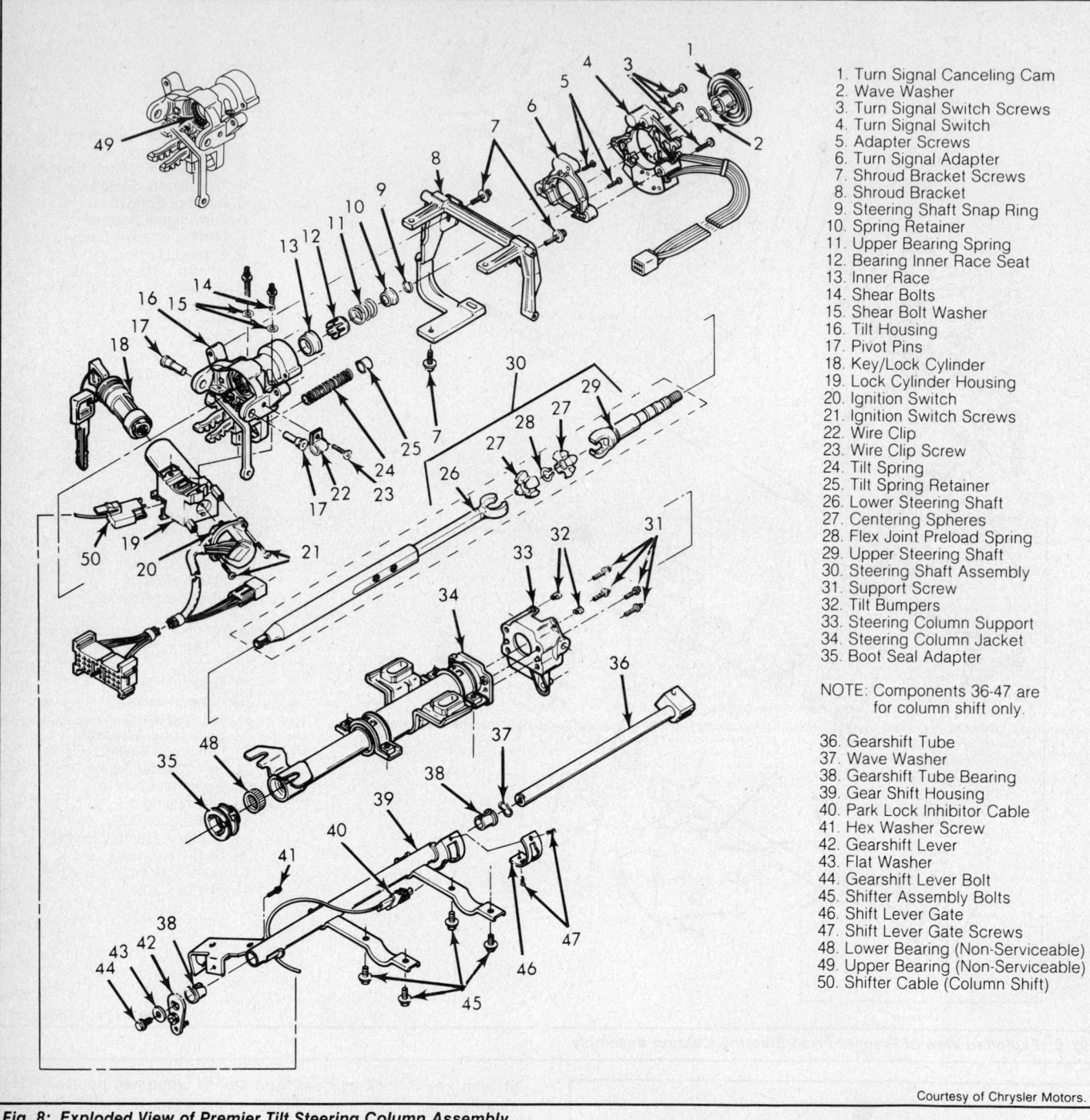

1. Turn Signal Canceling Cam
2. Wave Washer
3. Turn Signal Switch Screws
4. Turn Signal Switch
5. Adapter Screws
6. Turn Signal Adapter
7. Shroud Bracket Screws
8. Shroud Bracket
9. Steering Shaft Snap Ring
10. Spring Retainer
11. Upper Bearing Spring
12. Bearing Inner Race Seat
13. Inner Race
14. Shear Bolts
15. Shear Bolt Washer
16. Tilt Housing
17. Pivot Pins
18. Key/Lock Cylinder
19. Lock Cylinder Housing
20. Ignition Switch
21. Ignition Switch Screws
22. Wire Clip
23. Wire Clip Screw
24. Tilt Spring
25. Tilt Spring Retainer
26. Lower Steering Shaft
27. Centering Spheres
28. Flex Joint Preload Spring
29. Upper Steering Shaft
30. Steering Shaft Assembly
31. Support Screw
32. Tilt Bumpers
33. Steering Column Support
34. Steering Column Jacket
35. Boot Seal Adapter

NOTE: Components 36-47 are
for column shift only.

36. Gearshift Tube
37. Wave Washer
38. Gearshift Tube Bearing
39. Gear Shift Housing
40. Park Lock Inhibitor Cable
41. Hex Washer Screw
42. Gearshift Lever
43. Flat Washer
44. Gearshift Lever Bolt
45. Shifter Assembly Bolts
46. Shift Lever Gate
47. Shift Lever Gate Screws
48. Lower Bearing (Non-Serviceable)
49. Upper Bearing (Non-Serviceable)
50. Shifter Cable (Column Shift)

Courtesy of Chrysler Motors.

Fig. 8: Exploded View of Premier Tilt Steering Column Assembly

TIGHTENING SPECIFICATIONS

Application	Ft. Lbs. (N.m)
Dash Panel Protective Boot	10-12 (13-17)
Intermediate Shaft Clamp Bolt	26-33 (35-45)
Steering Column Bracket Bolts	30-37 (40-50)
Steering Wheel Hub Nut	50-53 (68-72)

	INCH Lbs.
Tilt Support-to-Column Screws	36 (4)
Tilt Wheel Lever	24-48 (3-5)

1989 STEERING COLUMNS
Ford Motor Co.

DESCRIPTION

Fixed columns as standard equipment on most vehicles with tilt columns optional. The exceptions are the Continental, Mark VII and Town Car, which come with a tilt column as standard equipment. Floor shift columns, both fixed and tilt, are identical to column shift columns. The only difference is the external shift mechanism and the addition of a key release button.

A multi-function switch, which incorporates turn signal, windshield wiper/washer, dimmer and flash-to-pass switch functions into one is on most columns.

This article will cover REMOVAL & INSTALLATION of steering columns, upper shaft bearings and lock cylinder housing. Complete tilt column overhaul procedures are not available from the manufacturer. Overhaul procedure for Probe steering column is not available from the manufacturer.

ADJUSTMENTS

Adjust shift indicator cable on Sable and Taurus models as follows:
- On CLC transmission, place shift lever in "DRIVE" position. On AXOD transmission, place shift lever in "OVERDRIVE." Hang an 8 lbs. weight on shift lever to hold lever completely against the shift detent.
- Adjust cable until pointer completely covers the proper letter or number. Tighten hex-head screw to 18-30 INCH lbs. (2-3.4 N.m).

REMOVAL & INSTALLATION

STEERING COLUMN

CAUTION: *Some vehicles are equipped with air bags. Use extreme caution when servicing to avoid personal injury and vehicle damage.*

Removal (Cougar & Thunderbird) – 1) Disconnect negative battery cable. Remove lower right-hand finish panel retaining bolts. Carefully pull lower right-hand finish panel to disengage retaining clips. Remove lower right-hand reinforcement panel retaining bolts. Remove reinforcement panel.

2) Remove steering column shroud retaining screws. Remove shroud. Disconnect ignition key courtesy light wire connector. Disconnect cruise control, ignition switch, multi-function switch and steering sensor wiring.

3) Remove steering shaft universal pinch joint. Remove steering column retaining nuts. Disconnect hazard warning connector. Remove starter interlock switch. Remove steering column.

Installation – 1) Position steering column and loosely install one retaining nut. Install starter interlock switch. Connect hazard warning wire connector. Install steering column upper shroud. Align steering shaft universal.

2) Install steering column retaining nuts. Install universal pinch bolt and tighten to 30-42 ft. lbs. (41-57 N.m). Connect all wire connectors. Secure wiring harness. Install lower steering column shroud and retaining screws. Install right-hand reinforcement panel and finish panel. Connect battery cable. Check column operation.

Removal (Continental, Sable & Taurus) – 1) Disconnect negative battery cable. Remove steering column lower cover. On tilt column models, remove release lever retaining. Remove release lever.

2) On all models, turn ignition lock cylinder to "RUN" position. Depress lock cylinder retaining pin from below through access hole with a 1/8" punch. Remove lock cylinder. Remove 3 self-tapping screws from lower shroud. Remove lower shroud. Remove steering wheel cover and steering wheel assembly. See appropriate STEERING WHEEL & COLUMN SWITCHES article in this section.

3) On column shift models, disconnect shift indicator cable from lock cylinder housing by removing retaining screw. Use a punch to remove shift lever roll pin. On all models, disconnect speed control/horn brush wiring connector from main harness. Remove multi-function switch wiring harness retainer from lock cylinder housing by squeezing end of retainer and pushing out.

4) Disconnect multi-function switch connector. Remove 2 self-tapping screws and multi-function switch from lock cylinder housing. Disconnect key warning buzzer switch connector from main harness. Disconnect ignition switch connector. Remove intermediate shaft "U" clamp. Remove intermediate shaft.

5) On column shift models, remove shift cable plastic terminal from column selector lever. Remove shift cable bracket from lock cylinder housing by removing 2 retaining screws.

6) Remove vacuum hoses for automatic parking brake release switch (if equipped). Remove 2 rear column retaining nuts. Loosen 2 front retaining nuts to end of studs. Pull column downward to release rear retainer clips. Remove front retaining nuts. Remove column.

Installation – 1) Align steering column brackets with 4 mounting holes and hand start 4 nuts. Center column in instrument panel. Tighten column bracket nuts to 15-25 ft. lbs. (21-33 N.m). Install vacuum hoses on automatic parking brake release switch, if removed.

2) On column shift models, install shift cable bracket to lock cylinder housing with 2 retaining screws. Tighten to 60-84 INCH lbs. (7-9 N.m). Snap shift cable terminal to pivot ball on steering column.

3) On all models, lubricate and install steering column to intermediate shaft with retainer assembly and 2 nuts. Ensure "V" angles of intermediate shaft and steering column yoke fit correctly. Tighten steering column-to-intermediate shaft nuts to 15-25 ft. lbs. (21-33 N.m).

4) Connect ignition switch and key warning buzzer connectors to main wiring harness. Install multi-function switch to lock cylinder housing. Tighten self-tapping screws to 18-26 INCH lbs. (2-3 N.m). Install multi-function switch wiring harness retainer over shroud mounting boss. Snap retainer into lock cylinder housing slot. Connect speed control/horn brush wiring connector to main wiring harness.

5) On column shift models, install shift indicator cable into retaining hook on lock cylinder housing. Connect shift indicator cable to shift socket. Loosely install shift indicator cable onto lock cylinder housing with one retaining screw.

6) Position shift lever into shift lever socket. Install new shift lever retaining pin. Install steering wheel and cover pad. Install shrouds.

7) On tilt column models, install tilt release lever. Install steering column cover. Connect negative battery cable. Check column functions.

Removal (Grand Marquis, LTD Crown Victoria & Town Car) – 1) Disconnect negative battery cable. Remove steering shaft-to-lower steering shaft bolt. Disengage "U" joint stub shaft from column shaft by collapsing intermediate shaft. Disconnect transmission shift rod from transmission control selector lever at bottom of shift tube.

2) Remove shift linkage grommet. Remove steering column trim shrouds. Remove steering column cover and hood release mechanism.

3) Disconnect all electrical connections to steering column switches. Loosen 4 nuts holding column to brake pedal support. Carefully, lower column enough to access shift indicator lever and cable assembly. DO NOT lower column too far or plastic lever or cable may break.

4) Lift shift indicator cable off cleat by reaching between steering column and instrument panel. Remove shift indicator cable clamp from steering column tube. Remove 4 dust boot-to-dash panel screws. Remove 4 steering column-to-brake pedal support nuts. Lower column to clear 4 mounting bolts and remove column.

Installation – 1) Position steering column through opening in dash panel. Align brake pedal support mounting holes with column collar and bracket. Loosely install nuts so shift indicator cable can be installed.

2) Loosely install shift indicator cable clamp to steering column tube. Reach between column and instrument panel and shift indicator cable over cleat on lever. Tighten 4 column support nuts to 20-37 ft. lbs. (28-50 N.m).

3) Move gearshift lever to "DRIVE." Rotate shift indicator bracket, located middle of column outer tube, until shift indicator aligns with "D." Tighten nut on bracket. Connect all electrical connections for column switches.

4) Slide lower steering shaft into steering column shaft. Tighten bolt and nut to 35-45 ft. lbs. (47-61 N.m). Install new grommet and connect shift rod to shift lever on lower end of steering column.

5) Raise vehicle. Loosen nut on automatic transmission shift rod. Move lever on transmission to "DRIVE" position by moving lever counterclockwise until it stops. Rotate lever clockwise 2 detents. Lower vehicle and varify indicator is in "DRIVE" position. Hang 8 lbs. weight on gearshift lever. Tighten shift rod adjusting nut. Lower vehicle.

6) Install dust boot-to-dash panel screws. Install trim shrouds. Install hood release mechanism and steering column cover. Install steering wheel. Connect negative battery cable. Check steering column operation.

Removal (Escort, Tempo & Topaz) – 1) Disconnect negative battery cable. Remove 2 steering column-to-instrument panel mounting screws. Remove 2 speed control module mounting screws (if equipped). Remove 5 lower steering column shroud mounting screws. Loosen steering column retaining bolts and nuts. Remove upper shroud.

2) Disconnect all electrical connections: ignition, wash/wipe, turn signal, key warning buzzer and speed control. On console shift automatic transmission, remove interlock cable retaining screw and disconnect cable from steering column.

3) Loosen steering column-to-intermediate shaft clamp. Remove bolt or nut. Remove steering column-to-support bracket retaining bolts and nuts. Pry open steering column shaft in area of clamp on each side of bolt groove with steering column locked. Inspect column bracket clips for distortion. If bracket clips are distorted, replace with new ones.

Installation – 1) Install lower steering shaft-to-intermediate shaft clamp bolt and nut. Align 2 steering column support bracket bolts with outer tube mounting holes and hand start 2 nuts. Ensure 2 clips are on outer bracket. Install outer tube upper bracket.

2) On console shift automatic transmission models, install interlock cable and retaining screw. Tighten to specification. On all models, connect all electrical connections. Install upper shroud. Tighten steering column mounting nuts and bolts.

3) On air bag equipped models, unlock steering column. Turn steering wheel, one turn right and one turn left, to align intermediate shaft into column shaft. Engine must be running to perform this step on vehicles with power steering.

4) On all models, tighten steering shaft clamp to specification. Install 5 lower trim shroud screws. Install 2 speed control module screws (if equipped). Install steering column cover. Connect negative battery cable.

Removal (Probe) – 1) Disconnect negative battery cable. Remove steering wheel, if necessary. See appropriate STEERING WHEEL & COLUMN SWITCHES article in this section. Remove 2 column cover retaining screws. Remove column cover. Remove 9 instrument cover attaching screws.

2) Carefully, pull instrument cover outward for access to electrical connections. Disconnect 7 electrical connections. Remove ignition switch illumination bulb. Remove instrument cover.

3) Loosen 2 instrument cluster cover hinge screws. Remove 6 instrument cover screws. Remove cover. Remove lower panel. Remove lap duct. Remove defrost duct. Disconnect 4 connectors at turn signal switch assembly.

4) Remove "U" joint pinch bolt from lower end of steering shaft. Remove hinge bracket mounting nuts. Remove 4 cluster support nuts. Remove 2 nuts and 4 bolts from upper steering column brackets. Remove steering shaft assembly.

5) Lift boot from intermediate shaft "U" joint at steering rack. Remove "U" joint pinch bolt. Remove 4 intermediate shaft dust cover assembly nuts. Remove intermediate shaft and dust cover. Remove steering column.

Installation – 1) Guide lower "U" joint onto steering rack pinion while an assistant holds steering column. Install pinch bolt. Tighten to 13-20 ft. lbs. (18-26 N.m). Install dust cover assembly nuts.

2) Guide steering column into upper intermediate "U" joint while an assistant holds column. Install hinge bracket nuts. DO NOT tighten nuts yet. Install 4 upper column bracket bolts. Tighten hinge nuts and upper column bracket bolts to 12-17 ft. lbs. (16-23 N.m).

3) Connect ignition switch electrical connectors. Install instrument cluster. Connect 7 connectors and ignition switch illumination bulb to instrument cover. Install instrument cover. Install column cover. Install steering wheel.

Removal (Mark VII & Mustang) – 1) Disconnect negative battery cable. Remove 2 flexible coupling-to-steering shaft flange nuts. Remove safety strap and bolt assembly from flexible coupling. Remove steering column trim shrouds. Remove steering column cover and hood release mechanism.

2) Disconnect electrical connections from column switches. Remove dust boot-to-dash panel screws. Remove 4 column-to-brake pedal support nuts. Lower column to clear mounting bolts. Remove column.

Installation – 1) Insert "U" joint assembly. Align brake pedal support with column collar and bracket. Install nuts and tighten to 20-37 ft. lbs. (27-50 N.m). Connect electrical connections to column switches.

2) Install safety strap and bolt assembly to steering gear input shaft. Tighten nuts to 20-37 ft. lbs. (27-50 N.m). DO NOT distort flexible coupling when tightening nuts. Pry steering shaft up-and-down to achieve approximately 1/8" (3 mm) coupling insulator flatness. To complete installation, reverse removal procedure.

UPPER SHAFT BEARING (FIXED COLUMN)

CAUTION: Some vehicles are equipped with air bags. Use extreme caution when servicing to avoid personal injury and vehicle damage.

Removal (Cougar, Mustang & Thunderbird) – 1) Remove steering wheel. See appropriate STEERING WHEEL & COLUMN SWITCHES article in this section. Remove steering column. See STEERING COLUMN under REMOVAL & INSTALLATION in this article.

2) Remove "U" joint assembly from steering shaft. Remove 2 multi-function switch retaining screws. Remove multi-function switch. Remove 2 upper bearing retainer plate retaining screws. Remove plate.

3) Remove upper bearing snap ring. Remove 2 lock cylinder housing assembly-to-column tube bolts. Remove housing assembly. Remove steering sensor ring shield from lower end of column (if equipped).

4) Remove 2 steering sensor switch retaining screws. Remove steering sensor switch. Remove spring retainer, spring and sensor ring. Discard retainer. Remove shaft bearing sleeve. Remove shaft. Remove lock cylinder housing assembly from column tube.

5) Support edge of lock cylinder housing assembly on edge of workbench or vise. Strike steering shaft with soft-faced hammer to drive shaft out of bearing. Remove bearing from lock cylinder housing.

Installation – 1) Slide lock cylinder housing assembly onto steering shaft assembly. Install shaft and lock cylinder assembly into column tube. Install 2 lock cylinder housing retaining bolts. Tighten to 12-21 ft. lbs. (16-28 N.m).

2) Place upper steering shaft bearing and sleeve over shaft end and into bearing bore of lock cylinder housing. Put a pipe 3/4" (19.05 mm) inside diameter by 3 1/2" (88.9 mm) long over upper steering shaft end. Install steering wheel attaching bolt. Tighten steering wheel attaching bolt until bearing is seated on steering shaft.

3) Remove steering wheel attaching bolt and pipe. Install new upper bearing snap ring. Install multi-function switch and 2 retaining screws. Install lower bearing sleeve, steering sensor ring, spring and new spring retainer on lower end of steering shaft.

4) Install steering sensor switch and 2 retaining screws. Install sensor ring shield. Install "U" joint assembly and tighten bolts to 30-42 ft. lbs. (41-57 N.m). Install steering column and steering wheel.

Removal (Escort, Tempo & Topaz Without Air Bag) – 1) Remove steering wheel. See appropriate STEERING WHEEL & COLUMN SWITCHES article in this section. Remove upper and lower shroud. Remove upper bearing retainer plate. Remove upper bearing retainer snap ring and discard.

2) Insert 2 screwdrivers under bearing. Using 2 slots provided, gently pry upper bearing and sleeve from steering shaft. Discard sleeve.

Installation – 1) Use a prick punch to rough surface of upper steering shaft where bearing rides. This ensures interference fit between bearing inner race and steering column upper shaft.

2) Position bearing and new sleeve on shaft. Work bearing and sleeve as far down shaft as possible. Put a pipe 3/4" (19.05 mm) inside diameter by 1.8" (45.7 mm) long over upper steering shaft end. Install steering wheel attaching bolt.

3) Tighten steering wheel attaching bolt until bearing is seated on steering shaft. Remove steering wheel attaching bolt and pipe. Install new upper bearing snap ring. Install upper bearing retainer. Install upper and lower shrouds. Install steering wheel.

Removal (Escort, Tempo & Topaz With Air Bag) – 1) Disconnect negative battery cable. Ensure wheels are straight. Turn ignition switch to "LOCK" position and rotate steering wheel counterclockwise until set in locked position.

CAUTION: On vehicles with air bags, whenever steering column is separated from steering gear, the column must be locked. This prevents steering wheel rotation which could damage air bag clockspring.

---

2) Remove horn pad cover screws. Remove emblem assembly by pushing out from behind emblem. Remove 4 air bag module retaining nuts from back of wheel. Remove air bag module and disconnect air bag module-to-clockspring connector. Remove energy absorbing foam from wheel. Remove vibration damper and reinstall bolt loosely on shaft. Use Remover (T67L-3600-A) or equivalent to remove steering wheel.

3) Remove upper and lower shroud. Disconnect air bag clockspring connector from column wiring harness.

4) Remove 2 clockspring-to-retaining plate screws. Remove clockspring. Remove upper bearing retainer plate. Remove upper bearing retainer snap ring and discard. Insert 2 screwdrivers under upper bearing, using 2 slots provided in casting. Pry upper bearing and sleeve from steering shaft. Discard sleeve.

Installation – 1) Use a prick punch to rough surface of upper steering shaft where bearing rides. This ensures interference fit between bearing inner race and steering column upper shaft.

2) Position bearing and insulator on shaft. Work bearing and insulator as far down shaft as possible. Put a pipe 3/4" (19.05 mm) inside diameter by 1 1/2" (38.1 mm) long over upper steering shaft end. Install steering wheel attaching bolt.

3) Tighten steering wheel attaching bolt until bearing is seated on steering shaft. Remove steering wheel attaching bolt and pipe. Install new upper bearing snap ring. Place air bag clockspring on steering shaft. Install 2 clockspring-to-retainer plate screws. Connect ground wire with lower retaining screw. Remove tape from clockspring.

4) Connect clockspring wire to column harness. To complete installation, reverse removal procedure. Tighten nuts, bolts and screws to specification. Verify air bag light operates.

Removal (Grand Marquis & LTD Crown Victoria) – 1) Remove steering wheel. See appropriate STEERING WHEEL & COLUMN SWITCHES article in this section. Remove trim shroud halves. Remove upper bearing retainer plate. Remove steering shaft-to-lower steering shaft assembly bolt(s). Remove upper bearing-to-steering shaft snap ring.

2) Pull on steering shaft to loosen upper bearing and sleeve. Gently pry bearing off shaft with 2 small screwdrivers.

Installation – 1) Use a prick punch to rough surface of upper steering shaft where bearing rides. This ensures interference fit between bearing inner race and steering column upper shaft.

2) Position bearing and insulator on shaft. Work bearing and insulator as far down shaft as possible. Put a pipe 3/4" (19.05 mm) inside diameter by 1 1/2" (38.1 mm) long over upper steering shaft end. Install steering wheel attaching bolt.

3) Tighten steering wheel attaching bolt until bearing is seated on steering shaft. Remove steering wheel attaching bolt and pipe. Install new upper bearing snap ring. Install upper bearing retainer.

4) Connect lower steering shaft with steering shaft. Install bolt and nut and tighten to 35-45 ft. lbs. (48-61 N.m). Ensure coupler insulation is uniform. To complete installation, reverse removal procedure.

Removal & Installation (Probe) – Information from manufacturer is not available.

UPPER SHAFT BEARING (TILT COLUMN)

Removal (Cougar, Escort, Grand Marquis, LTD Crown Victoria, Mark VII, Mustang, Tempo, Thunderbird, Topaz & Town Car) – 1) Remove steering wheel. See appropriate STEERING WHEEL & COLUMN SWITCHES article in this section. Remove upper extension shroud by unsnapping shroud from retainer clip at 9 o'clock position. Remove 3 screws attaching upper and lower shrouds. Remove shrouds.

2) Remove conical coil spring and upper bearing retainer plate. Remove "C" clip from shaft located on top of bearing. Move tilt casting to upper position. Use Pivot Pin Remover Handle (T67P-3D739-C) and Pivot Pin Removers (T67P-3D739-B or T70P-3D739-A) to remove pivot pins. Use care when removing pivot pins. The tilt spring is still under pressure and will expand rapidly.

3) Lift tilt casting from column. Tilt casting contains 2 bearings, tilt release lever and lock lever. Remove tilt spring. Working from bottom side using drift punch, remove upper bearing. Working from side-to-side in 2 casting relief areas, use drift punch to remove lower bearing.

Installation – 1) Install bearings into tilt casting, using care not to press on inner race. Install tilt spring between upper and lower tilt casting. Latch tilt release lever in upper position. Align 2 castings and insert pivot pins using "C" clamp. Pivot pins must be flush with casting surface.

2) Install upper bearing snap ring, retainer plate and conical spring. Ensure conical spring snaps into groove on shaft. Install upper and lower shrouds and secure with 3 screws. Install upper extension shroud. Install steering wheel. Check tilt operation.

UPPER SHAFT BEARING
(FIXED OR TILT COLUMN IN-VEHICLE SERVICE)

Removal & Installation (Continental, Sable & Taurus) – 1) Disconnect negative battery cable. Remove steering column cover from instrument panel. Remove ignition lock cylinder. See appropriate STEERING WHEEL & COLUMN SWITCHES article in this section. On tilt column, remove capscrew and tilt release lever.

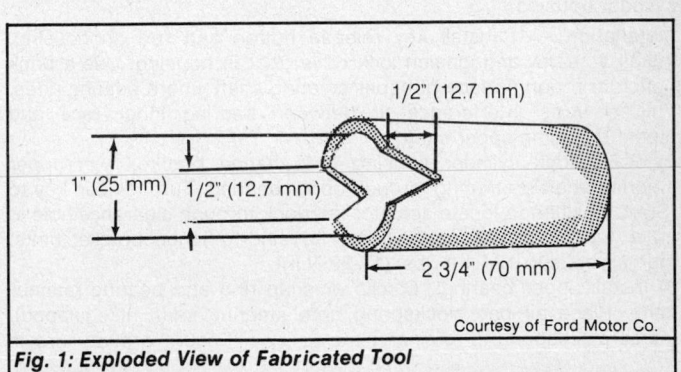

1" (25 mm)   1/2" (12.7 mm)   1/2" (12.7 mm)   2 3/4" (70 mm)

Courtesy of Ford Motor Co.

Fig. 1: Exploded View of Fabricated Tool

2) Remove shrouds. Remove multi-function switch. Remove horn pad and steering wheel. See appropriate STEERING WHEEL & COLUMN SWITCHES article in this section. Make a fabricated tool from tubing 1" X 2 1/2" (25 mm X 63.5 mm) *See Fig. 1.* Install fabricated tool on steering shaft, aligning clearance slot over shaft retaining pin. Install steering wheel bolt and appropriate washer (1/2" I.D. X 1 1/4" O.D.). Tighten bolt enough to relieve pressure and remove retaining pin with drift punch.

3) Remove steering wheel bolt, washer and tool. Remove steering shaft retaining washer and upper alignment wedge. Use a small screwdriver to pry bearing and sleeve from lock cylinder housing. To install, reverse removal procedure.

LOCK CYLINDER HOUSING (FIXED COLUMN)

Removal (Cougar, Mustang & Thunderbird) – 1) Remove steering column. See STEERING COLUMN under REMOVAL & INSTALLATION in this article. Remove 2 multi-function switch-to-lock cylinder housing screws. Remove multi-function switch. Remove 2 lock cylinder housing-to-outer tube flange bracket bolts.

2) Remove 2 upper bearing retainer plate screws. Remove upper bearing snap ring. Remove steering sensor ring shield from bottom of column. Remove steering sensor switch screws. Remove spring retainer and discard. Remove spring, sensor ring and shaft sleeve. Remove shaft and lock cylinder housing assembly from column tube.

Installation – 1) Slide lock cylinder housing onto upper steering shaft. Install lock cylinder housing-to-column tube bolts. Tighten to 12-21 ft. lbs. (16-28 N.m).

2) Put a piece of pipe 3/4" (19.05 mm) inside diameter by 3 1/2" (88.9 mm) long, over upper steering shaft end. Install steering wheel attaching bolt. Tighten steering wheel attaching bolt until bearing is seated on steering shaft. Install snap ring.

3) Remove steering wheel attaching bolt and piece of pipe from upper shaft. Install multi-function switch. Install lower bearing sleeve, sensor ring, spring and a new spring retainer on steering shaft lower end. Install "U" joint assembly and tighten bolts to 30-42 ft. lbs. (41-57 N.m). Install column.

Removal (Escort, Tempo & Topaz) – 1) Disconnect negative battery cable. Remove steering wheel and trim shrouds. See STEERING WHEEL & COLUMN SWITCHES article in this section. Disconnect wiper switch, turn signal switch and key warning buzzer connectors. Remove switches.

CAUTION: Before removing air bag clockspring from steering shaft, tape clockspring. This will prevent clockspring rotor from turning, causing damage to clockspring.

---

2) Disconnect air bag clockspring connector from column wiring harness (if equipped). Remove clockspring-to-retaining plate screws. Remove clockspring. Remove upper bearing retainer plate, "C" clip or snap ring and upper bearing. Remove lock cylinder housing-to-outer tube flange bracket.

3) Rotate ignition key to "Start" position. Pull actuator interlock from tube. Lift casting off upper steering shaft. Remove ignition lock drive gear. Remove key release and rod from housing. Remove lock cylinder housing.

Installation – 1) Install key release button and rod on housing. Install actuator and ignition lock drive gear in housing. Use a prick punch to rough surface of upper steering shaft where bearing rides. This ensures interference fit between bearing inner race and steering column upper shaft.

2) Place lock cylinder housing onto flange bracket with upper steering shaft protruding through upper bearing. Turn ignition key to "Start" position to locate actuator interlock through clearance hole in outer tube. Install 2 lock cylinder housing-to-flange bracket bolts. Tighten bolts to 12-21 ft. lbs. (17-28 N.m).

3) Install upper bearing, "C" clip or snap ring and bearing retainer plate. Place air bag clockspring onto steering shaft (if equipped). Install clockspring-to-retainer plate screws. Ensure ground wire is

secured with lower screw. Connect clockspring wire connector to column harness (if equipped). To complete installation, reverse removal procedure.

Removal (Grand Marquis & LTD Crown Victoria) – 1) With steering column removed, remove shift cane assembly. Remove 2 turn signal switch-to-lock cylinder housing attaching screws. Remove turn signal switch.

2) Remove 2 screws and washer/wiper switch. Remove upper steering shaft bearing. Remove 2 lock cylinder housing-to-outer tube flange bracket bolts. Remove lock cylinder.

Installation – 1) Install upper steering shaft bearing and sleeve in lock cylinder housing. Install upper bearing plate. Use a prick punch to rough surface of upper steering shaft where bearing rides. This ensures interference fit between bearing inner race and steering column upper shaft.

2) Place lock cylinder housing onto flange bracket with upper steering shaft protruding through upper bearing. Install 2 lock cylinder housing-to-flange bracket bolts. Tighten bolts to 12-21 ft. lbs. (17-28 N.m).

3) Put a piece of pipe 3/4" (19.05 mm) I.D. X 3 1/2" (88.9 mm) long, over upper steering shaft end. Install steering wheel attaching bolt. Tighten steering wheel attaching bolt until bearing is seated on steering shaft. Install snap ring. To complete installation, reverse removal procedure.

Removal & Installation (Probe) – Information from manufacturer is not available.

LOCK CYLINDER HOUSING (TILT COLUMN)

Removal (Cougar, Escort, Mark VII, Tempo, Thunderbird & Topaz) – 1) Remove steering column. See appropriate STEERING COLUMN under REMOVAL & INSTALLATION in this article. Remove turn signal or multi-function switch.

2) Remove washer/wiper switch (if equipped). Remove steering wheel. See appropriate STEERING WHEEL & COLUMN SWITCHES article in this section. Remove conical coil spring and upper bearing retainer plate.

3) Remove "C" clip from shaft. Move tilt lever to upper position. Use Pivot Pin Remover (T70P-3D739-A) to remove pivot pins. Use care when removing pivot pins. The tilt spring is still under pressure and will expand rapidly. Remove upper tilt casting from lock cylinder housing.

4) Remove "U" joint assembly from lower shaft. Remove steering sensor switch. Remove sensor ring shield. Remove spring retainer and discard. Remove spring, sensor ring and shaft sleeve. Remove steering shaft out top of column. Remove 2 lock cylinder housing-to-outer column tube bolts. Remove lock cylinder housing.

Installation – 1) Install lock cylinder housing onto upper steering flange bracket. Install lock cylinder housing bolts and tighten to 12-20 ft. lbs. (16-28 N.m). Install steering shaft.

2) With tilt spring in position, install upper casting assembly. Install pivot pins with "C" clamp. Pivot pins must be flush with surface. Install "C" clip on steering shaft groove. Install multi-function switch. To complete installation, reverse removal procedure. Tighten "U" joint assembly bolt to 30-42 ft. lbs. (41-57 N.m).

LOCK CYLINDER HOUSING (FIXED OR TILT COLUMN)

Removal (Grand Marquis, LTD Crown Victoria, Mustang & Town Car - For Zinc/Silver Lock Cylinder Housing) – 1) Remove trim shrouds and electrical connector for key warning switch. Turn lock cylinder to "Run" position. Put a 1/8" drift punch into slot in cylinder housing and remove lock cylinder.

2) Remove snap ring, washer and lock drive gear from lock cylinder housing. Carefully note lock drive gear relation to position of rack teeth. Remove lock cylinder housing.

Installation – 1) Install lock drive gear in base of lock cylinder housing in position noted during removal. The lock drive gear position is correct if the last teeth mesh with last teeth of rack.

2) Install washer and snap ring. Align drive gear flats with washer flats by pulling down on column actuator. Install lock cylinder assembly.

Removal (Grand Marquis, LTD Crown Victoria, Mustang & Town Car - For Magnesium/Gold Lock Cylinder Housing) – 1) Remove trim shrouds and electrical connector for key warning switch. Turn lock cylinder to "Run" position. Put a 1/8" drift punch into slot in cylinder housing and remove lock cylinder.

2) Carefully note white plastic bearing retainer position. Pry White plastic bearing retainer from bearing with small screwdriver. Insert tip if screwdriver into double "D" slot of bearing and rotate 90

degrees. Remove bearing. Carefully note relationship of lock drive gear to rack teeth. Remove lock drive gear.

Installation – 1) Install lock drive gear in base of lock cylinder housing in position noted during removal. The lock drive gear position is correct if the last teeth mesh with last teeth of rack.

2) Install bearing in lock cylinder housing. Insert tip of screwdriver into double "D" slot of bearing and rotate 90 degrees. Install White plastic bearing retainer into lock cylinder housing. Ensure retainer is in its original position. Align drive gear flats with washer flats by pulling down on column actuator. Install lock cylinder assembly.

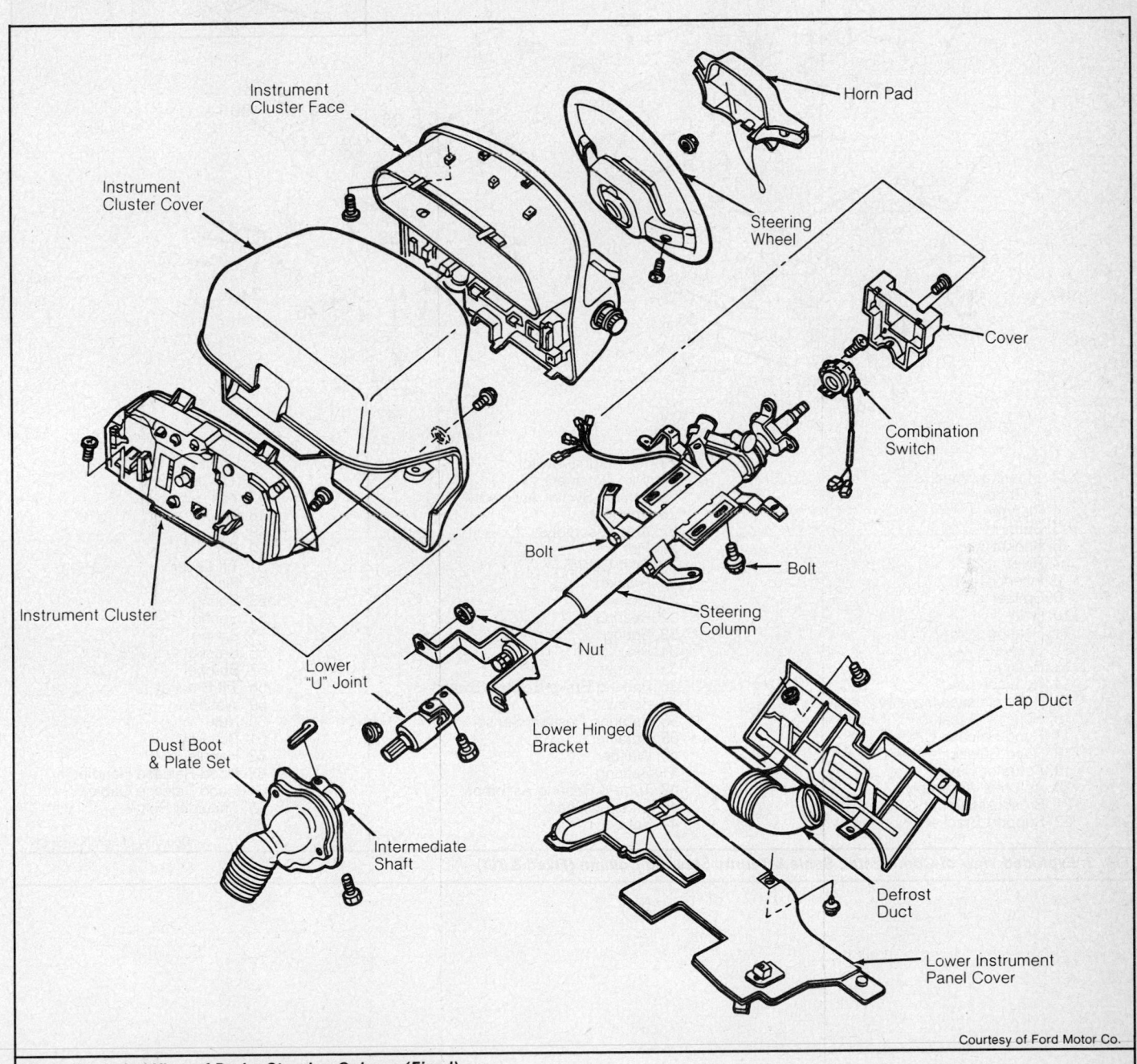

Courtesy of Ford Motor Co.

Fig. 2: Exploded View of Probe Steering Column (Fixed)

1989 Steering Columns
Ford Motor Co. (Cont.)

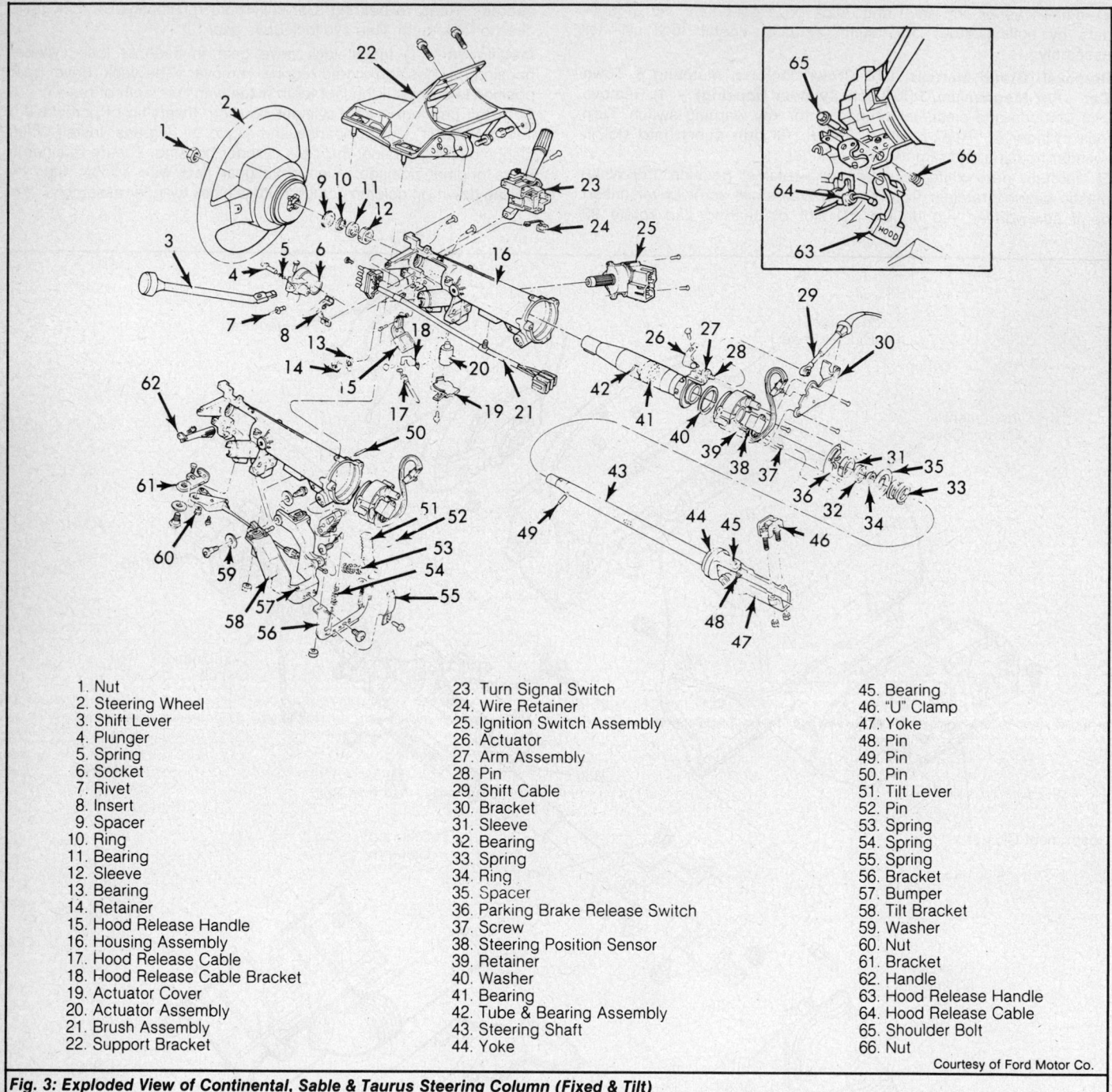

1. Nut	23. Turn Signal Switch	45. Bearing
2. Steering Wheel	24. Wire Retainer	46. "U" Clamp
3. Shift Lever	25. Ignition Switch Assembly	47. Yoke
4. Plunger	26. Actuator	48. Pin
5. Spring	27. Arm Assembly	49. Pin
6. Socket	28. Pin	50. Pin
7. Rivet	29. Shift Cable	51. Tilt Lever
8. Insert	30. Bracket	52. Pin
9. Spacer	31. Sleeve	53. Spring
10. Ring	32. Bearing	54. Spring
11. Bearing	33. Spring	55. Spring
12. Sleeve	34. Ring	56. Bracket
13. Bearing	35. Spacer	57. Bumper
14. Retainer	36. Parking Brake Release Switch	58. Tilt Bracket
15. Hood Release Handle	37. Screw	59. Washer
16. Housing Assembly	38. Steering Position Sensor	60. Nut
17. Hood Release Cable	39. Retainer	61. Bracket
18. Hood Release Cable Bracket	40. Washer	62. Handle
19. Actuator Cover	41. Bearing	63. Hood Release Handle
20. Actuator Assembly	42. Tube & Bearing Assembly	64. Hood Release Cable
21. Brush Assembly	43. Steering Shaft	65. Shoulder Bolt
22. Support Bracket	44. Yoke	66. Nut

Courtesy of Ford Motor Co.

Fig. 3: Exploded View of Continental, Sable & Taurus Steering Column (Fixed & Tilt)

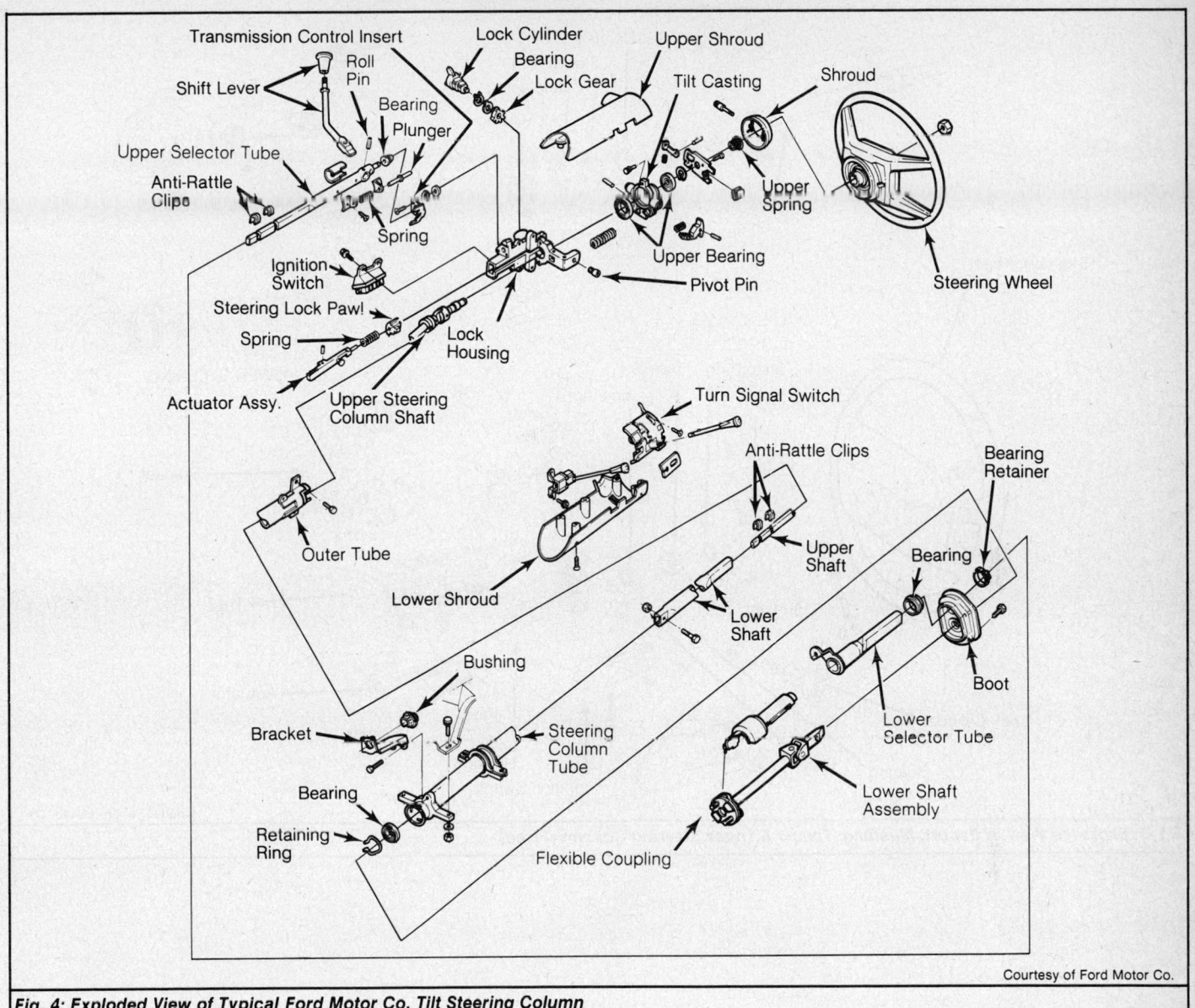

Fig. 4: Exploded View of Typical Ford Motor Co. Tilt Steering Column

1989 STEERING COLUMNS
Ford Motor Co. (Cont.)

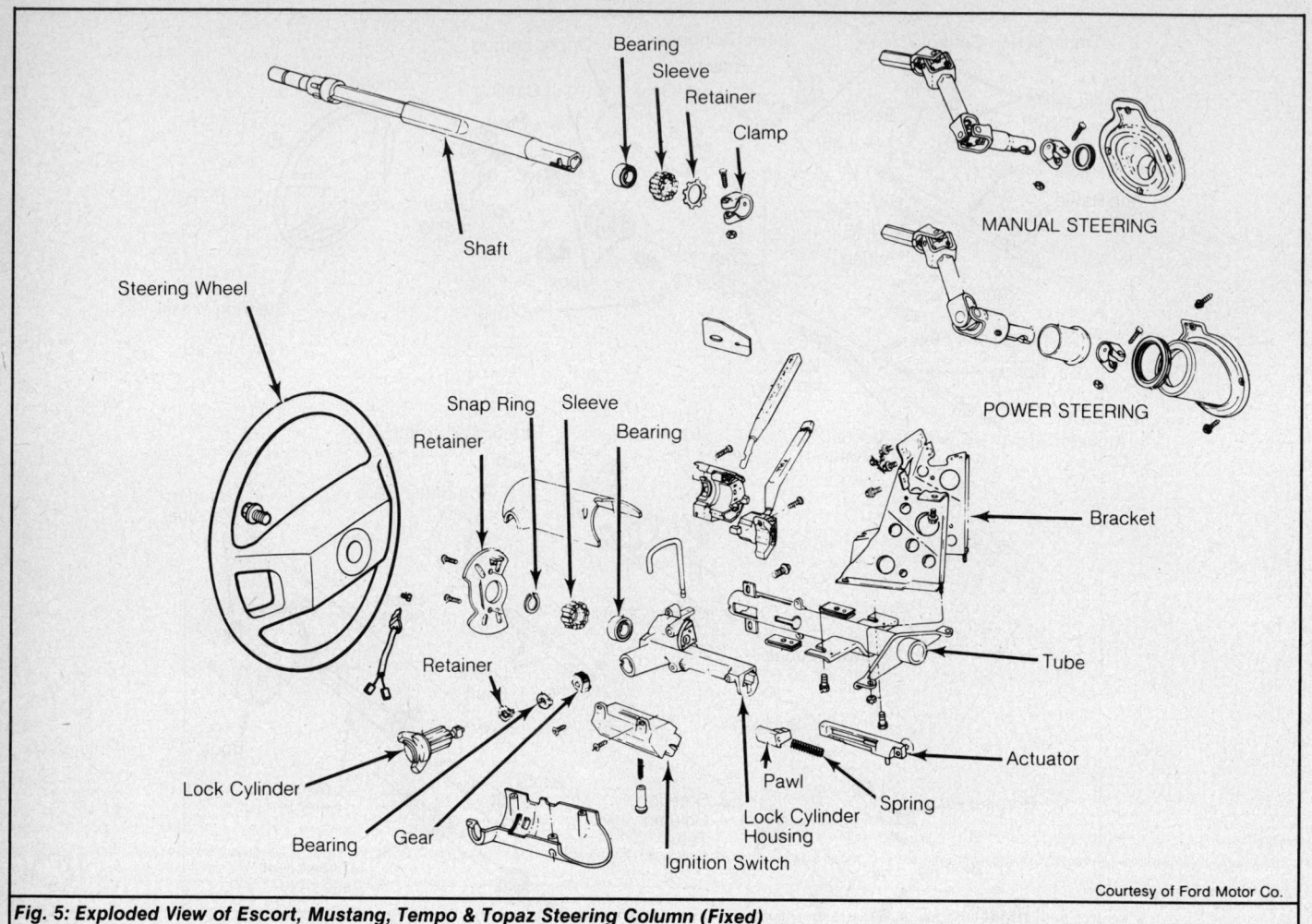

Courtesy of Ford Motor Co.

Fig. 5: Exploded View of Escort, Mustang, Tempo & Topaz Steering Column (Fixed)

Aries, Horizon, Omni, Reliant

DESCRIPTION

The rack and pinion assembly converts rotational movement of the pinion to transverse movement of the rack. Rack and pinion, connected to steering knuckles at the tie rods, is factory lubricated and sealed. It is not adjustable. Service is limited to replacement of tie rod ends and boots. Complete replacement is required in event of malfunction.

REMOVAL & INSTALLATION

RACK & PINION

Removal – 1) Raise and support vehicle. Remove front wheels. Remove cotter pins and castle nuts from tie rod ends. Using a puller, separate tie rod ends from knuckles. If equipped, disconnect engine damper strut from crossmember.

2) Remove 4 front suspension crossmember attaching bolts. Using transmission jack, lower crossmember. Drive out steering coupling roll pin.

3) Separate rack and pinion from steering shaft. Remove splash and boot seal shields. Remove bolts securing rack and pinion to front crossmember. Remove rack and pinion from crossmember.

Installation – To install, reverse removal procedure. An assistant will be needed in the vehicle to guide steering column coupling onto rack and pinion. Ensure master serrations align. Install right rear crossmember bolt first. Tighten crossmember mounting bolts to specification. Check and adjust toe-in. See appropriate article in WHEEL ALIGNMENT section.

TIE ROD END

Removal – Remove castle nut and cotter pin. Using a puller, separate tie rod end from steering knuckle. Loosen lock nut. Counting the number of turns necessary, remove tie rod ends from tie rods.

Installation – To install tie rod end, reverse removal procedure. Check and adjust toe-in.

BOOT SEAL

Removal & Installation – Remove tie rod end. Use pliers to expand outer boot clamp and remove. Remove inner boot clamp. Mark breather tube location before removing boot. Use a small screwdriver to carefully lift boot from groove. Remove boot. To install, reverse removal procedure. Lubricate boot groove with silicone before installing outer clamp.

TIGHTENING SPECIFICATIONS

Application	Ft. Lbs. (N.m)
Crossmember-to-Frame Bolts	90 (122)
Rack & Pinion-to-Crossmember Bolts	50 (68)
Tie Rod End-to-Knuckle Castle Nuts	38 (52)
Tie Rod End Lock Nuts	55 (75)

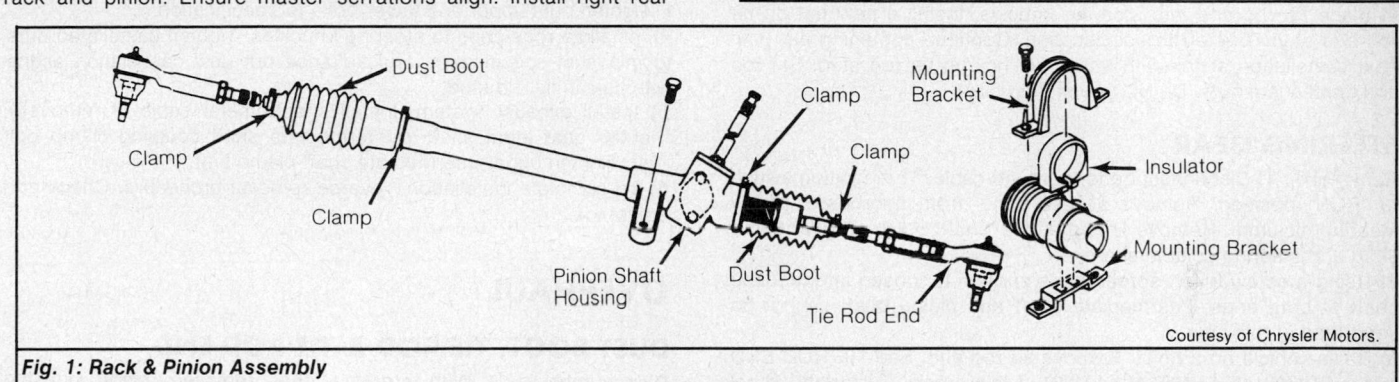

Courtesy of Chrysler Motors.

Fig. 1: Rack & Pinion Assembly

1989 MANUAL STEERING GEARS
Ford Motor Co. Rack & Pinion

Escort

DESCRIPTION

The steering system is rack and pinion type. Steering gear is connected to steering knuckles with tie rods. The input shaft connects to the steering shaft with double "U" joint intermediate shaft. The inner ball joints are preset and NOT adjustable.

ADJUSTMENT

RACK PRELOAD

Rack preload is adjusted during reassembly procedure. See OVERHAUL in this article.

REMOVAL & INSTALLATION

TIE ROD END

Removal – 1) Remove cotter pin and nut from tie rod end. Disconnect tie rod end from spindle using Tie Rod End Remover (TOOL-3290-D) and Adapter (T81P-3504-W).
2) Hold tie rod end with wrench and loosen tie rod lock nut. Grip tie rod flats with pliers. Remove tie rod end.
Installation – 1) Clean tie rod threads and apply light coat of grease. Thread new tie rod end on tie rod to approximately same depth as old tie rod.
2) Place tie rod end into steering knuckle. Install a new nut on tie rod end stud. Tighten to specification. Continue tightening nut until next castellation aligns with cotter pin hole in tie rod stud. Set toe and tighten jam nuts. Do NOT twist dust boot.

STEERING GEAR

Removal – 1) Disconnect battery ground cable. Turn ignition switch to "RUN" position. Remove access panel from floorboard, below steering column. Remove intermediate shaft bolts at gear input shaft and steering column shaft.
2) Using a screwdriver, spread slots enough to loosen intermediate shaft at both ends. Intermediate shaft and pinion shaft cannot be separated at this time.
3) Raise vehicle on a hoist. Remove tie rod end. See TIE ROD END under REMOVAL & INSTALLATION in this article. Turn right wheel to full left turn position.

4) Disconnect speedometer cable at transmission (automatic only). Disconnect secondary air tube at check valve. Disconnect exhaust system from exhaust manifold.
5) Remove steering gear mounting brackets and insulators. Left and right bushings and brackets are NOT interchangeable. Turn steering wheel full left. Separate gear intermediate shaft by having an assistant pull up on shaft from inside vehicle.
6) Carefully rotate gear forward and down to clear pinion shaft through floorboard opening. Ensure pinion shaft is in full left turn position.
7) Move gear through passenger side apron opening until left tie rod clears shift linkage. Lower gear left side. Remove steering gear.
Installation – 1) Rotate input shaft to full left turn stop. Position right wheel to full left turn. Start left side of gear through opening in right apron. Move gear until left tie rod clears all parts so it may be raised to left apron opening.
2) Raise gear and insert left side through apron opening. Rotate gear so joint shaft enters floorboard opening. With an assistant guiding intermediate shaft from inside vehicle, insert input shaft into intermediate shaft coupling. Insert intermediate shaft clamp bolts finger tight. DO NOT tighten at this time.
3) Install gear mounting bushings and brackets. Ensure flat in left mounting area is parallel to floor board. Tighten bracket bolts in the following sequence:
- Tighten left upper bolt halfway.
- Tighten left lower bolt to specification.
- Tighten left upper bolt to specification.
- Tighten right upper and lower bolts to specification.

4) Install tie rods ends to steering knuckles. Tighten castellated nuts to minimum specification and advance nut until castellation aligns with hole in tie rod stud.
5) Install exhaust system. Install speedometer cable (if removed). Tighten gear input shaft-to-intermediate shaft coupling clamp bolt first. Tighten upper intermediate shaft clamp bolt.
6) To complete installation, reverse removal procedure. Check and adjust toe.

OVERHAUL

DUST BOOT, TIE ROD & TIE ROD END

Disassembly – 1) With steering gear removed, clean housing exterior. Loosen tie rod end lock nuts. Remove tie rod ends. Remove outer boot clamps.

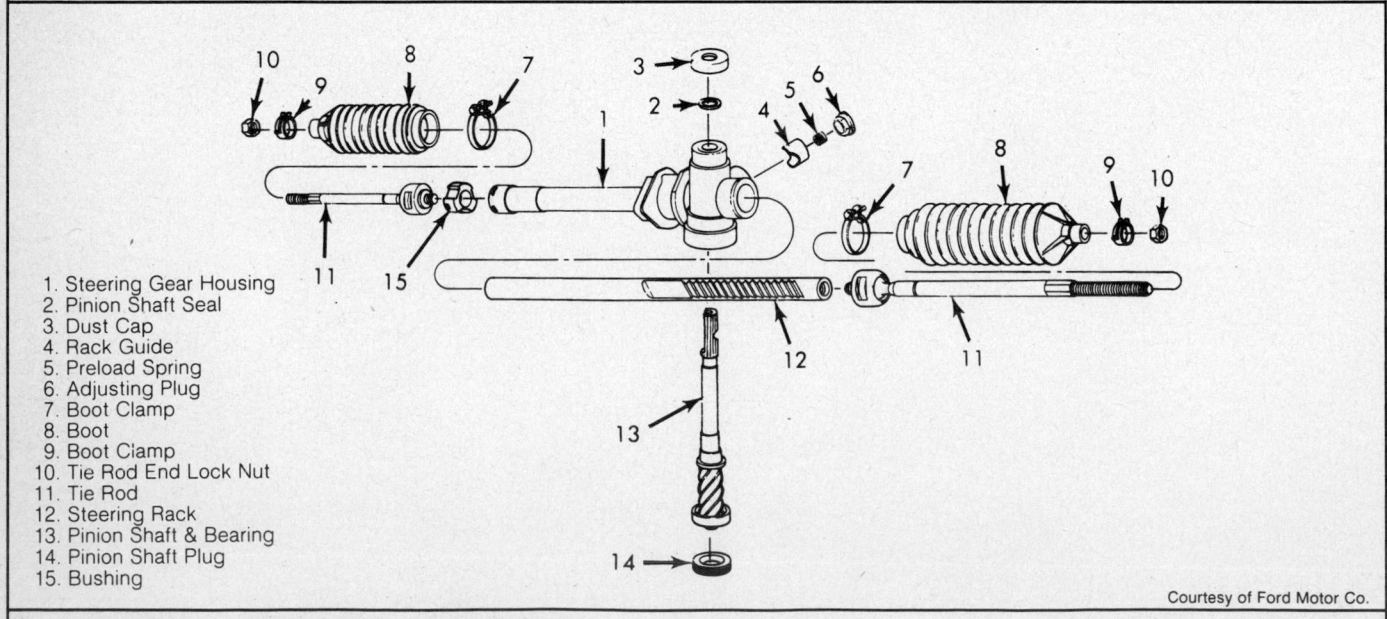

1. Steering Gear Housing
2. Pinion Shaft Seal
3. Dust Cap
4. Rack Guide
5. Preload Spring
6. Adjusting Plug
7. Boot Clamp
8. Boot
9. Boot Clamp
10. Tie Rod End Lock Nut
11. Tie Rod
12. Steering Rack
13. Pinion Shaft & Bearing
14. Pinion Shaft Plug
15. Bushing

Courtesy of Ford Motor Co.

Fig. 1: Exploded View of Rack & Pinion Steering Gear

1989 MANUAL STEERING GEARS
Ford Motor Co. Rack & Pinion (Cont.)

13-35

2) Remove and discard inner boot clamps. Remove boots. Turn gear full right to expose rack teeth. Mount rack teeth in soft-jawed vise. Using pipe wrench on inner tie rod ball socket, remove and discard tie rod.

NOTE: Replacement tie rod assemblies incorporate machined flats on inner ball joints for easier assembly. However, original equipment assemblies do not have this feature. The rack teeth must be placed in a soft-jawed vise. Use a pipe wrench to disconnect tie rod from rack at ball joint.

Inspection – Visually inspect rack for corrosion or contamination. If either is present, overhaul or replace steering gear. See STEERING GEAR under OVERHAUL in this article.

Reassembly – 1) Turn gear full right turn to expose rack teeth. Mount rack teeth in a soft-jawed vise. Before installing tie rods, inspect ends of rack. If burrs are present, remove with a file. Install new tie rods. Tighten to specification. Remove assembly from vise. Supporting ball socket, stake socket to rack with a punch.

2) Center of punch should be approximately .06" (1.5 mm) from rack end. *See Fig. 2.* Verify displacement of metal into rack slot.

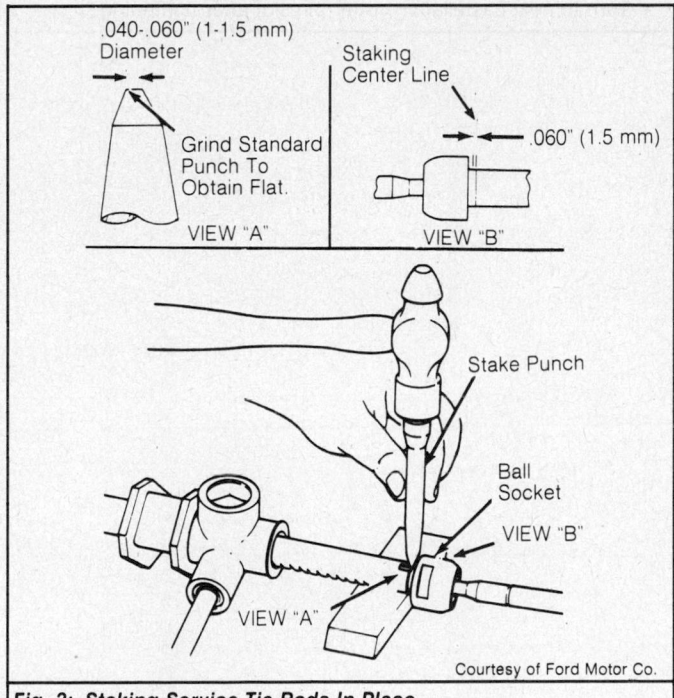

Fig. 2: Staking Service Tie Rods In Place

3) Grease rack and rack teeth. Coat remainder of rack with light film of grease. Install boots and boot clamps. Ensure small diameter of boot is in tie rod groove. Install lock nuts and tie rod ends.

STEERING GEAR

NOTE: If pinion is removed, the entire gear must be disassembled for cleaning. The pinion plug threads must be retapped and cleaned.

Disassembly – 1) With steering gear removed, remove tie rod ends, lock nuts, dust boots and tie rods. Mount rack assembly in soft-jawed vise. Remove and discard pinion shaft plastic cap.

2) Turn pinion fully right. Using Plug Remover (T86P-3504-A), remove and discard pinion plug. With plug remover reversed, remove and discard adjusting plug.

3) Remove spring and rack guide bearing. Remove pinion and bearing assembly by pushing out through the pinion plug opening. Use plastic mallet if necessary.

4) Remove rack from left side of housing. Using screwdriver, carefully pry out pinion shaft seal. DO NOT damage housing. Discard seal.

Cleaning & Inspection – 1) Using Plug Remover (T86P-3504-A), clean threads of adjusting plug and pinion plug bore. Wash all parts in mineral spirits. Air dry all parts.

2) DO NOT submerge right end of housing tube containing delrin rack bushing in solvent. Inspect rack bushing for wear. Check pinion teeth and rack for corrosion, wear, straightness, cracks, scoring, pitting or breaks.

3) Inspect lower pinion bearing for wear or roughness. If any of these conditions exist, replace the rack housing. Replace all other parts as necessary.

Reassembly – 1) If rack bearing was not removed, go to step **4)**. If rack bearing was removed, align 3 slots of Rack Bushing Guide (T86P-3504-C2) over dimples in rack tube. Align extra slot over one of tube slots. *See Fig. 3.*

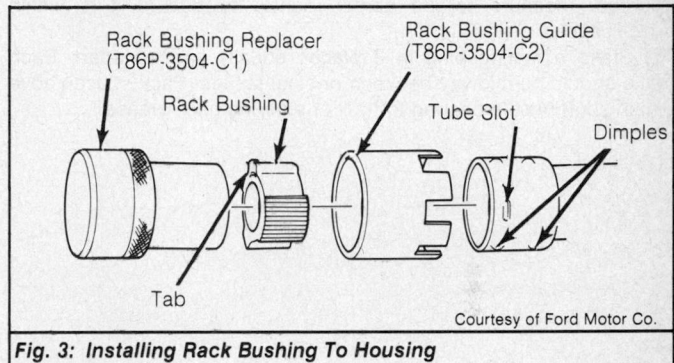

Fig. 3: Installing Rack Bushing To Housing

2) Lubricate new rack bushing outer diameter with steering gear grease. Insert new rack bushing into tool so tabs align with grooves in tool.

3) Using Rack Bushing Replacer (T86P-3504-C1) and hand pressure, push rack bushing into rack tube until tool bottoms. Remove rack bushing guide. Reapply hand pressure to rack bushing replacer to fully seat tabs in slots.

4) Fill rack teeth and cover rest of shaft with a light film of grease. Pack pinion shaft lower bearing and inboard of rack bushing with grease. Install rack into housing from left end.

5) Center the load slot in pinion bore. Coat all remaining sliding surfaces with grease. Coat pinion shaft teeth and bearing with grease. Install pinion shaft and bearing assembly from bottom through load slot in rack.

6) Install pinion shaft plug and tighten to specification. Install, but DO NOT tighten, left tie rod assembly to rack. Mount gear to Holding Fixture (T57L-500-B).

7) Hold pinion shaft flat in 9 o'clock position while pushing rack into housing. Jiggle rack to engage rack to pinion and to start rack in rack bushing. Push rack in all the way.

8) The pinion shaft flat should stop in the 6 o'clock position when left ball joint contacts the housing. *See Fig. 4.* If flat is not in the 6 o'clock position, repeat step **7)** until it is.

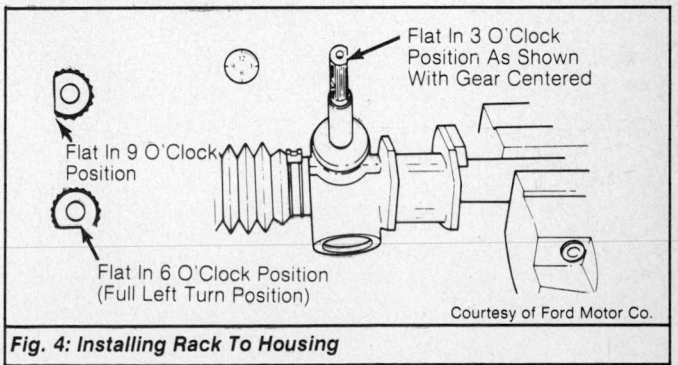

Fig. 4: Installing Rack To Housing

9) Install, but do not tighten, right tie rod to rack. Install rack guide, preload spring and adjusting plug. Tighten plug until most of play in rack is taken up.

10) Turn pinion lock-to-lock, counting number of turns necessary. Return pinion half the number of turns to center position. Pinion shaft flat should be at 3 o'clock position.

11) The pinion gear has only 4 teeth, so flat can only be in one of 4 positions, 90 degrees apart. If out of adjustment, repeat step **7)**.

12) Remove adjusting plug. Apply Loctite hydraulic sealant to plug threads. Tighten adjusting plug to specifications. With Pinion Torque Adapter (T86P-3504-B) mounted to a torque wrench, slowly turn pinion input shaft 1/2 turn in each direction from center.

13) Return to center position. Repeat twice, checking peak torque within 1/4 turn from center. Peak torque must be a minimum of 15 INCH lbs. (1.7 N.m) in either direction.

14) If not to specification, check adjusting plug bore threads for burrs. Repeat steps **12)** and **13)**. Back off adjusting plug 30 degrees. Measure torque across center to ensure it is within specification.

15) Stake adjusting plug in 3 places equally spaced apart. Each stake should be midway between original stakes. Pack space above pinion shaft needle bearing 2/3 full of steering gear grease.

16) Coat new pinion shaft seal lip with grease. Using Pinion Cover Installer (T81P-3504-Y) and hand pressure, press seal in until flush with top of housing.

17) Stake pinion plug in 2 places midway between original stakes. Fill plastic cap with grease. Using hand pressure, install cap until bottomed on gear housing.

18) Wipe off excess grease. Install new inner tie rods, boots and boot clamps. Install tie rod end lock nuts and tie rod ends.

TIGHTENING SPECIFICATIONS

Application	Ft. Lbs. (N.m)
Pinion Plug	52-73 (70-100)
Steering Gear Mounting Bolts	40-55 (54-75)
Tie Rod End Castle Nut	[1] 27-32 (36-43)
Tie Rod End Lock Nuts	35-50 (47-68)
Tie Rod End-to-Rack	50-60 (68-81)
"U" Joint-to-Pinion Shaft Clamp Bolt	20-37 (28-50)

	INCH Lbs. (N.m.)
Adjusting Plug	40 (4.5)

[1] – Turn to next castellation cotter pin slot after tightening.

LUBRICATION

SERVICE INTERVALS

Check fluid level every 7500 miles. If vehicle is driven less than 12,000 miles a year, check fluid every 3000 miles. Clean dirt and grease from filler cap area to avoid contaminating fluid. Check fluid level with engine off stopped. Depending upon dipstick mark, maintain fluid at either "FULL" level or above full "COLD" mark.

RECOMMENDED FLUID TYPE

Application	Fluid Type
Chrysler Motors	Mopar Power Steering Fluid P/N (431-8055)
Eagle	Jeep/Eagle Power Steering Fluid P/N (8982-200-946)
Ford Motor Co.	ATF Type F

BLEEDING & REFILLING SYSTEM

Chrysler Motors & Eagle – 1) Fill pump reservoir. Operate engine until power steering fluid reaches operating temperature. Stop engine. Recheck fluid level and add as necessary. Repeat procedure until fluid level stabilizes.

2) Raise and support vehicle so front wheels are off ground. Start engine. Turn steering wheel from side-to-side several times. Avoid hitting stops or holding wheel in full left or right position. Fluid level should remain visible.

3) Return wheels to center position. Operate engine for 2-3 minutes. Road test vehicle. Recheck fluid level. Fluid containing air will have a milky appearance. All air should be eliminated to obtain normal steering.

Ford Motor Co. – 1) Fill pump reservoir. Operate engine until power steering fluid reaches operating temperature. Stop engine. Recheck fluid level. Add fluid as necessary. Repeat procedure until fluid level stabilizes.

2) Raise and support vehicle so front wheels are off ground. Start engine. Turn steering wheel from side-to-side several times. Avoid hitting stops or holding wheel in full left or right position. Fluid level should remain visible.

3) Return wheels to center position. Operate engine for 2-3 minutes. Road test vehicle. Recheck fluid level. Fluid containing air will have a milky appearance. All air should be eliminated to obtain normal steering.

NOTE: Abnormal noise originating from the power steering system may be caused by air trapped in the system. Rotunda Vacuum Tester (021-00014) and following procedure will eliminate this condition.

4) Carefully remove pump filler adapter and dipstick. Check and fill reservoir to "COLD" mark. Disconnect ignition coil lead. Raise front wheels off ground.

5) Crank engine while cycling steering wheel. DO NOT hold wheel on stops. Add fluid if necessary. Attach coil lead. Install evacuation tool onto reservoir.

6) Start engine. Apply 15 in. Hg on reservoir for approximately 3 minutes with engine idling. As air is purged from system, vacuum will decrease.

7) Maintain sufficient vacuum with vacuum source. Release vacuum. Check fluid level. Install filler adapter assembly and dipstick. Start engine.

8) Turn steering wheel from stop to stop while checking for leaks. If condition is severe, repeat procedure until all air is removed. Lower vehicle. Road test vehicle.

SERVICING

BELT TENSION

Serpentine Belt – On vehicles with serpentine belts, belt tension is adjusted automatically.

Conventional Belt – Using a belt strand tension gauge, check tension of power steering belt. See POWER STEERING BELT TENSION SPECIFICATIONS table.

POWER STEERING BELT TENSION SPECIFICATIONS

Application	New Belt Lbs. (Kg)	Used Belt Lbs. (Kg)
Chrysler Motors		
FWD	95 (43)	70 (32)
RWD		
W/Air Pump	120 (54)	60 (27)
W/O Air Pump	50 (23)	40 (18)
Eagle	190 (86)	150 (68)
Ford Motor Co.		
1.9L	73 (33)	50 (23)
2.3L OHC	170 (77)	150 (68)
2.3L HSC	140 (63)	120 (54)
3.8L	170 (77)	150 (68)
5.0L	110 (50)	.....
H.D.	140 (63)	.....
2-Speed Belt	170 (77)	150 (68)
5.8L	170 (77)	150 (68)

TESTING

NOTE: Before testing, check fluid level, belt tension, pump pulley, tire pressure and engine idle speed.

PRESSURE TESTING

Chrysler Motors – 1) Remove high pressure hose at steering pump and connect a spare hose to pump fitting. Connect opposite end of spare hose to Test Gauge (C-3309E). Connect pressure hose from valve side of steering gear to valve side of gauge. Valve must be installed on outlet side of gauge.

NOTE: Replacement fittings are required on Test Gauge (C-3309E) for adapting to "O" ring type hose tube ends.

2) With a thermometer in fluid reservoir, start engine and warm fluid to 160°F (72°C). Turning wheels from stop to stop will aid in warming fluid. DO NOT hold wheels against stop.

3) With engine at idle speed, gauge open, record maximum pressure while turning steering wheel from stop to stop. The minimum pressure at idle should read 80-125 psi (5.6-8.8 kg/cm²) on RWD models, and 30-50 psi (2.1-3.5 kg/cm²) on FWD models.

4) If pressure is less than specifications, steering system is not functioning properly. To determine which unit is faulty, momentarily close pressure gauge valve and note maximum pressure registered on gauge.

5) If pressure reads less than maximum pressure, 1200-1300 psi (87.7-91.4 kg/cm²) on RWD models, or 1000-1100 psi (70.3-77.3 kg/cm²) on FWD models, the pump is faulty and should be reconditioned.

6) If pressure reads low at step 3), but not at step 4), steering gear is at fault. When removing test equipment, ensure hose is installed in original position to avoid interference with engine or sheet metal.

Eagle – 1) Remove high pressure line from pump. Attach Adapter Fitting (J-21567-5) to pump. Using Pressure Gauge (J-21567) and Adapter (J-5176-12), connect gauge to hose.

2) Open valve fully. Run engine until fluid reaches normal operating temperature. Check fluid level. Add if necessary. With engine at operating temperature, pressure reading should be 80-125 psi (5.6-8.8 kg/cm²).

3) If pressure is more than 200 psi (14 kg/cm²), inspect system for restrictions or faulty poppet valve. Alternately close and then open gauge valve fully 3 times while recording highest pressure obtained.

CAUTION: Do not hold valve closed for more than 5 seconds as pump damage may result.

4) If recorded pressures are all within 50 psi (3.5 kg/cm²), pump performance is acceptable. If pressures are high and not within 50 psi (3.5 kg/cm²) of each other, flow control valve is sticking.

5) If pressures are constant and more than 100 psi (7.0 kg/cm²), but less than 1350 psi (94.9 kg/cm²), replace flow control valve. Retest pump pressure.

6) If pump meets specification, leave valve open. Turn steering wheel from stop to stop. Record and compare highest pressure with maximum pump pressure.

7) If pressure at both stops is not similar to maximum pressure, steering gear is leaking internally. Shut off engine, remove testing equipment, check fluid level, or make necessary repairs.

NOTE: When testing pump flow and pressure on Ford Motor Co. vehicles, use Rotunda Analyzer (014-00207). Check entire system for damage. Check pulley size and pump model for proper application.

Ford Motor Co. – 1) Reservoir must be kept full and at normal operating temperature during testing. Attach tester between pressure line and pump with gauge between pump and tester valve. Start engine and let idle for 2 minutes.

2) With engine idling and fluid hot, record pressure (with tester valve open) and flow. If flow is less than 1.5 gals. (5.68L) per minute, pump may require service. However, proceed with testing at this point.

3) If pressure is more than 150 psi (10.5 kg/cm²), check hoses for restrictions. Partially close tester valve. Allow pressure to increase to 740 psi (52 kg/cm²). Record flow. If flow is less than minimum, pump cam pack requires replacement. Proceed with testing.

4) Close and partially open tester valve 3 times. Tester valve must not remain closed over 5 seconds. Observe and record pressure each time valve is closed. If readings vary more than 50 psi (3.5 kg/cm²), flow control valve may be sticking.

5) If pressure is less than minimum specification, replace flow control valve. If pressure is more than maximum specification, remove flow control valve. Clean or replace flow control valve as necessary.

6) Increase engine speed to about 1500 RPM. Observe and record flow. If flow exceeds maximum free flow listed in chart, remove flow control valve. Clean or replace flow control valve as necessary.

7) Return engine to idle speed. Turn wheel from stop to stop. Observe and record flow at both stops. Pressure readings should be near maximum pressure specification listed in chart.

8) Flow should drop to less than .5 gals./min. (1.9L/min.). If pressure fails to reach maximum or if flow does not drop to less than .5 gals./min. (1.9L/min.), excessive internal leakage of steering gear is occurring.

9) With engine running, attach pull scale to rim of steering wheel. Measure pull required to turn wheel one complete revolution in each direction. Pull should be approximately 9 lbs. (2.25 kg) during turning.

POWER STEERING PUMP TEST SPECIFICATIONS

Application	Pressure (psi)		¹ Flow (gpm)	
	Idle	Relief	Minimum	Maximum
Chrysler Motors				
FWD Models	30-50	1000-1100	.....	.....
RWD Models	80-125	1200-1300	....	....
Eagle				
Premier	80-125	1100-1200	.....	.....
Ford Motor Co.				
1.9L All Models	150	750-1030	1.10	2.20
2.2L Probe	²	²	²	²
2.3L Tempo & Topaz	150	1100-1380	.95	2.20
2.3L Mustang & Thunderbird	150	850-1130	1.30	2.60
2.5L & 3.0L Sable & Taurus (All)	150	1200-1480	.90	2.60
3.8L Continental	150	1300-1530	1.50	3.00
3.8L Cougar & Thunderbird				
With Handling Package	150	950-1230	1.40	2.60
Without Handling Package	150	950-1230	1.25	2.60
3.8L Sable & Taurus	150	1300-1530	.90	2.20
5.0L Cougar & Thunderbird	150	950-1230	1.40	2.60
5.0L LTD Crown Victoria & Grand Marquis	150	1100-1380	1.50	3.00
5.0L Mustang				
Auto. Trans.	150	950-1230	1.40	2.60
Man. Trans.	150	950-1230	1.35	2.60
5.0L Mark VII	150	1200-1480	1.60	2.60
5.0L Town Car	150	1100-1380	1.50	3.40
5.8L Police	150	1100-1380	1.50	3.40

¹ – Flow is measured in gallons per minute.
² – Information not available from manufacturer.

FWD Models

DESCRIPTION

A rotary valve in the pinion assembly directs fluid to either side of the integral rack piston. Tie rods connect the steering gear (rack and pinion) to the steering knuckles. Loosely fitted pinion drivetangs, will provide manual steering control in the event of a system malfunction. Steering wheel movement is transmitted by the shaft, mounted in the steering column, to the pinion through 2 universal joint couplings. The steering gear rack and pinion assembly converts rotational movement of the pinion to transverse movement of the rack.

LUBRICATION, TROUBLE SHOOTING & TESTING

See POWER STEERING GENERAL SERVICING and TROUBLE SHOOTING articles in this section.

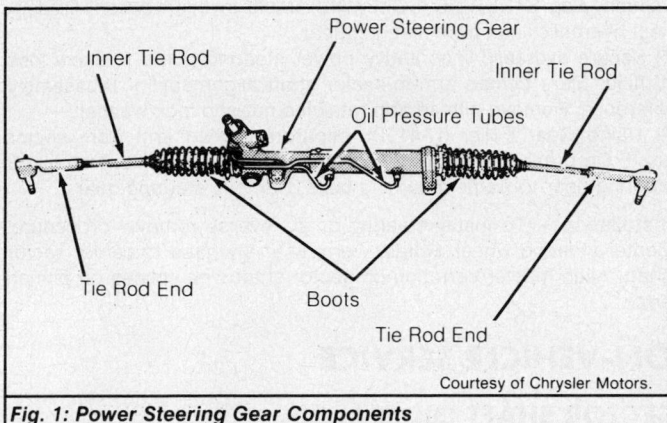

Fig. 1: Power Steering Gear Components

REMOVAL & INSTALLATION

STEERING GEAR

Removal – 1) Raise and support vehicle. Remove front wheels. Remove cotter pins and castle nuts from tie rod ends. Using a puller, separate tie rod ends from knuckles. If equipped, disconnect engine damper strut from crossmember.
2) Remove 4 front suspension crossmember attaching bolts. Using transmission jack, lower crossmember. Remove power steering hoses. Drive out steering coupling roll pin.
3) Separate steering gear from steering shaft. Remove splash and boot seal shields. Remove bolts securing steering gear to front crossmember. Remove steering gear from crossmember.

Installation – 1) To install, reverse removal procedure. An assistant will be needed in the vehicle to guide steering column coupling onto steering gear.
2) Install right rear crossmember bolt first. This correctly locates crossmember. Tighten crossmember mounting bolts to specification. Check for fluid leaks. Check and adjust toe-in.

TIE ROD END

Removal & Installation – Remove castle nut and cotter pin. Using a puller, separate tie rod end from steering knuckle. Loosen lock nut. Counting the number of turns necessary, remove tie rod ends from tie rods. To install, reverse removal procedure. Check and adjust toe-in.

BOOT SEAL

Removal & Installation – Remove tie rod end. Use pliers to expand outer boot clamp and remove. Remove inner boot clamp. Mark breather tube location before removing boot. Use a small screwdriver to carefully lift boot from groove. Remove boot. To install, reverse removal procedure. Lubricate boot groove with silicone before installing outer clamp.

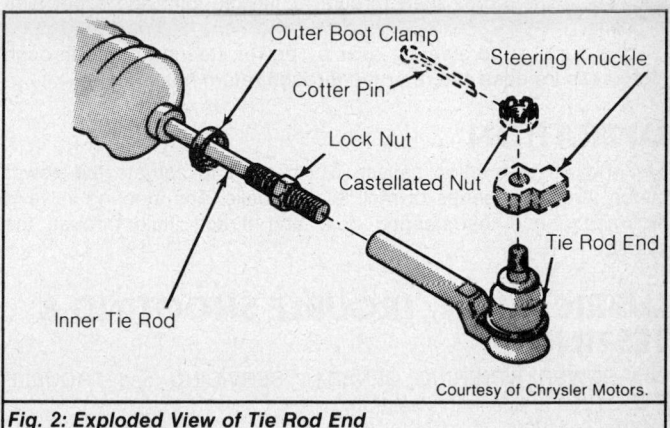

Fig. 2: Exploded View of Tie Rod End

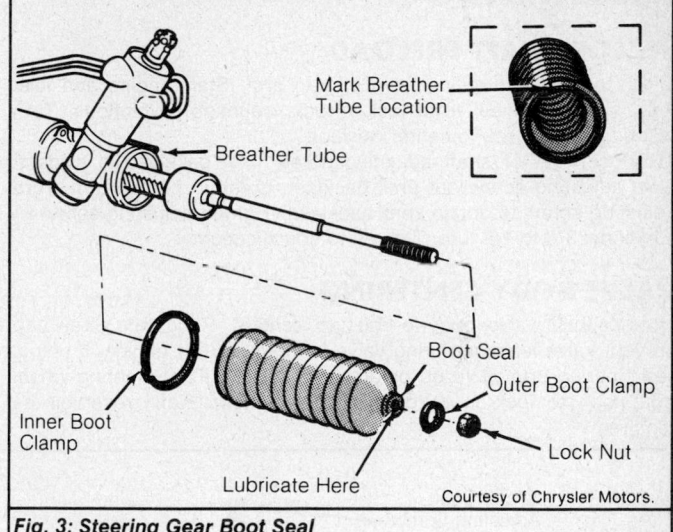

Fig. 3: Steering Gear Boot Seal

OVERHAUL

STEERING GEAR

The power steering gear should NOT be serviced or adjusted. If a malfunction or oil leak occurs, complete steering gear should be replaced.

TIGHTENING SPECIFICATIONS

Application	Ft. Lbs. (N.m)
Crossmember Bolts	90 (122)
Gear-to-Crossmember Bolts	50 (68)
Tie Rod End Lock Nut	55 (75)
Tie Rod End-to-Knuckle Castle Nut	38 (52)

1989 POWER STEERING GEARS
Chrysler Motors Recirculating Ball

Diplomat, Fifth Avenue, Gran Fury

DESCRIPTION

The power steering gear consists of a gear housing, a geared sector shaft, and a geared power piston which is in constant mesh with the sector shaft and the worm shaft. The steering wheel is coupled to the worm shaft through a flexible joint and a pot type coupling.

Fluid is supplied to steering gear by power steering pump through high pressure hose and returned through return hose.

OPERATION

Steering wheel rotation causes worm shaft to actuate the power piston through a series of recirculating balls. The steering valve is mounted above the steering gear and directs fluid through the system.

LUBRICATION, TROUBLE SHOOTING & TESTING

See POWER STEERING GENERAL SERVICING and TROUBLE SHOOTING article in this section.

ADJUSTMENTS

SECTOR SHAFT PRELOAD

1) Disconnect center-link from pitman arm. Start engine and idle. Turn steering wheel from lock-to-lock, counting revolutions. Turn steering wheel back to center position.

2) Loosen sector shaft adjusting screw until backlash is evident. Turn adjusting screw out until backlash is felt in pitman arm. Turn adjusting screw to obtain zero backlash. Tighten adjusting screw an additional 3/8 to 1/2 turn. Tighten to specification.

VALVE BODY CENTERING

1) Loosen 2 valve body-to-housing screws. Retighten screws to prevent valve leakage during valve centering. Start engine. If unit is self-steering, tap valve up or down to correct. Turn steering wheel from lock to lock to purge air from system. Refill reservoir as required.

CAUTION: Do not turn steering wheel hard against locks. High pressure may blow out "O" rings.

2) With steering wheel centered, start and stop engine several times. Tap valve body up and down as required until there is no movement of steering wheel when engine is started or stopped. The valve is now centered. Tighten 2 valve body-to-housing attaching screws to specification.

REMOVAL & INSTALLATION

STEERING GEAR

NOTE: It is recommended that steering column be completely detached from floor and instrument panel to prevent possible damage.

Removal – 1) Disconnect negative battery cable. Remove steering column. See STEERING COLUMNS article in this section. Disconnect hydraulic lines from steering gear.

2) Secure hydraulic lines above power steering pump to avoid loss of fluid. Mark pitman arm-to-sector shaft alignment for reassembly reference. Remove pitman arm retaining nut and lock washer.

3) Using Gear Puller (C-4150), separate pitman arm from sector shaft. Drop exhaust system. Remove starter heat shield. Remove 3 steering gear-to-frame mounting bolts. Remove steering gear.

Installation – To install steering gear, reverse removal procedure. Center steering wheel. Rotate worm shaft by hand to center sector shaft. Align master serration on sector shaft with splines on pitman arm.

ON-VEHICLE SERVICE

SECTOR SHAFT OIL SEAL

Removal – 1) Remove pitman arm nut. Using Gear Puller (C-4150), separate pitman arm from sector shaft. Position Adapter (SP-3056) of Seal Tool (C-3350-A) over sector shaft. Thread nut onto sector shaft.

2) Maintain pressure on threaded adapter with nut. Screw in adapter until it engages metal portion of grease retainer. Place the 2 half-

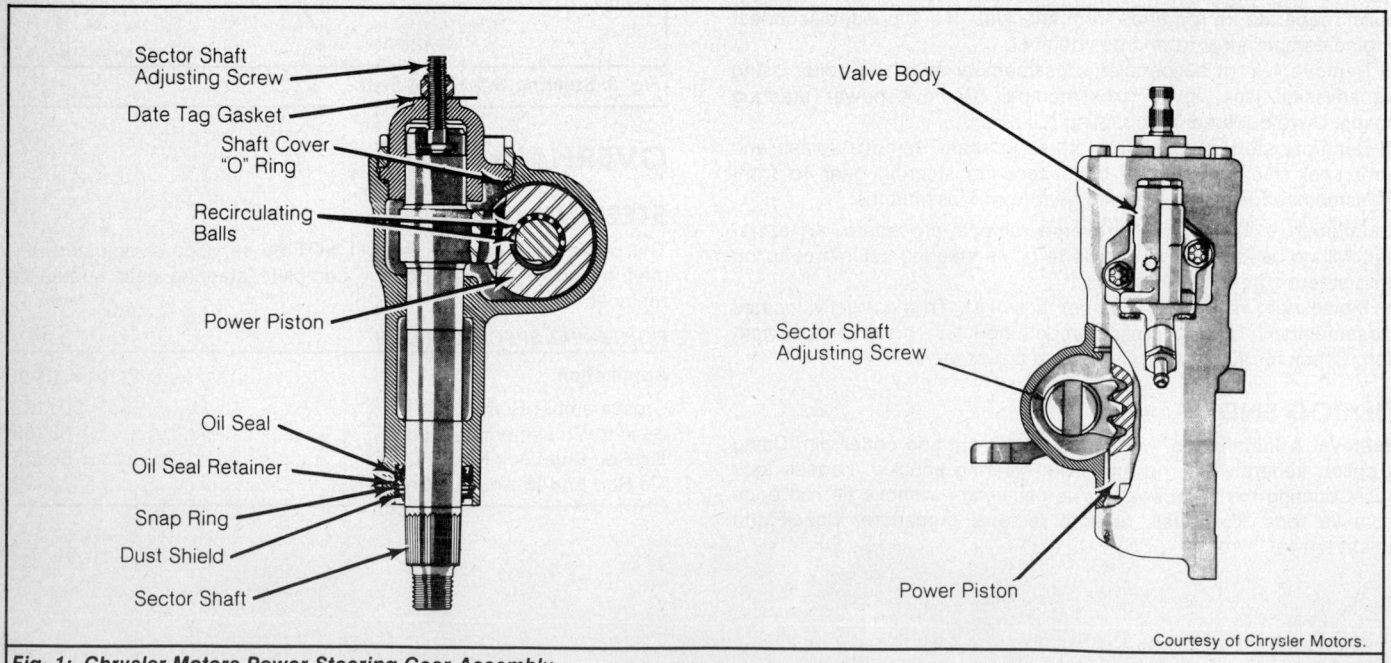

Courtesy of Chrysler Motors.

Fig. 1: Chrysler Motors Power Steering Gear Assembly

rings (SP-1932) of Seal Tool (C-3350-A) and retainer ring over both portions of seal tool.

3) Turn nut counterclockwise to remove retainer. Remove oil seal snap ring and seal back-up washer. Using Seal Tool (C-3350-A), remove grease retainer.

4) An alternate method of removing oil seal is as follows. Disconnect the pitman arm. Carefully pry grease seal out of housing. Remove oil seal retaining snap ring and seal retainer.

5) Place receptacle under gear. Start engine. Turn steering wheel to full left lock. Oil pressure will force seal out of steering gear housing.

Installation – 1) Place new seal on flat surface (lip down). Lubricate inner lip with power steering fluid. Insert Seal Protector Sleeve (SP-1601) into the seal.

2) Position new seal on sector shaft (seal lip in). Place Adapter (SP-5148) against new seal. Slide adapter over shaft with seal lip toward housing.

3) Install nut on sector shaft. Tighten nut until shoulder of adapter contacts housing. Remove nut, adapter and protector. Install seal back-up washer and oil seal snap ring (identification mark out).

4) Fill housing with multipurpose grease. Position grease retainer in housing bore. Place short-step surface of Tool Adapter (SP-5148) against retainer.

5) Install nut on sector shaft. Tighten nut until shoulder of adapter contacts housing. Remove adapter. With steering gear and wheels in straight-ahead position, install pitman arm and retaining nut.

WORM SHAFT OIL SEAL

Replacement – Remove steering column. Remove oil seal using Seal Remover (C-3638). Using Seal Installer (C-3650) and a soft-faced hammer, drive new oil seal in place (lip toward housing). Install and align steering column.

OVERHAUL

VALVE BODY

Disassembly – 1) Disconnect hydraulic lines from valve body. Secure hydraulic lines above power steering pump to avoid loss of fluid. Remove 2 valve body-to-housing screws. Raise valve body. Disengage valve body from valve lever.

2) Remove 2 steering valve-to-control valve mounting screws. Separate the 2 sub-assemblies. Remove outlet, spring and piston from control valve body. Remove spool valve from steering valve body. See Fig. 2.

Inspection & Cleaning – 1) Inspect spool valve for nicks and burrs. Use crocus cloth to clean up minor irregularities. DO NOT round-off any sharp edges on piston or spool valve.

2) Clean spool valve and piston in cleaning solvent. Blow-dry passages with compressed air. Lubricate pistons, valves and bores with power steering fluid. DO NOT use ATF.

Reassembly – 1) Install spool valve in valve body. Ensure valve lever hole lines up with lever opening in valve body. Valve must move freely in bore. Install end plug (if removed) with a new gasket. Tighten to specification.

2) Install short spring, piston, long spring and outlet fitting to control valve. Tighten to specification. Mount control valve body to steering valve body using new "O" rings. Tighten screws to specification.

3) Align spool valve lever hole with opening in valve body. Install valve body on housing. Ensure valve lever enters hole in spool and that keyed portion of valve body mates with keyway in housing. See VALVE BODY CENTERING.

STEERING GEAR

Disassembly – 1) Clean exterior of gear housing. Drain housing. Mount housing in a vise. Remove valve body retaining screws, valve body and 3 "O" rings. Remove valve lever and spring. Carefully pry spherical head with screwdriver.

CAUTION: Do not collapse valve lever slotted end. This will damage bearing tolerances of spherical head.

2) Loosen sector shaft adjusting screw lock nut. Using Spanner Wrench (C-3988), remove sector shaft cover spanner nut. Rotate worm shaft to position sector shaft teeth at center of piston travel. Using Power Train Wrench (C-3989), loosen steering power train retaining nut.

3) Compress power train parts by turning worm shaft to full left turn position. Remove power train retaining nut. While firmly compressing power train, pry on piston teeth with a flat-blade screwdriver, using sector shaft gear teeth as a fulcrum. Remove power train assembly.

NOTE: Cylinder head, center race and spacer assembly and housing head must be maintained in close contact with each other.

4) Place power train vertically in soft-jawed vise. Raise housing head until oil seal clears top of wormshaft. Position Arbor (C-3929) on top of wormshaft and into oil seal. Pull up on housing head until arbor is positioned in bearing. Remove housing head and arbor.

NOTE: If worm shaft seal is to be replaced, replace seal with housing head disassembled.

5) Remove large "O" ring from groove in housing head. Remove reaction seal from groove in face of housing head with compressed air directed into ferrule chamber. Remove reaction spring, reaction ring, worm balancing ring and spacer.

6) While holding worm shaft, turn nut until it releases from knurled section. Remove nut. Wire brush knurled sections to remove metal chips. Blow out nut and worm shaft to remove any metal particles.

7) Remove upper thrust bearing race and upper thrust bearing. Remove center bearing race. Remove lower thrust bearing and bearing race. Remove lower reaction ring and spring. Remove cylinder head.

8) Remove "O" rings from 2 outer grooves in cylinder head. Remove reaction "O" ring from groove in face of cylinder head by directing air pressure into oil hole between 2 "O" ring grooves.

9) Remove snap ring and seal. Test operation of worm shaft. Required torque to rotate wormshaft throughout its travel in or out of piston should not exceed 1.5 INCH lbs. (.17 N.m). Worm and piston are serviced as an assembly and should not be disassembled.

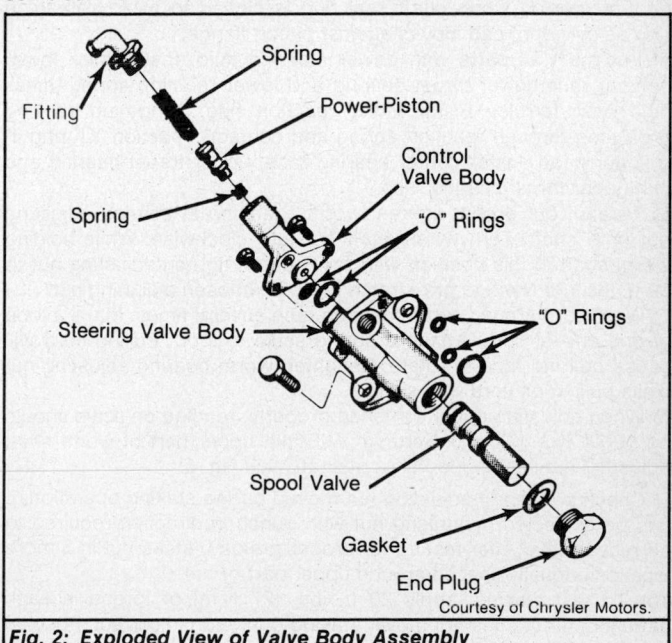

Courtesy of Chrysler Motors.

Fig. 2: Exploded View of Valve Body Assembly

10) Test for excessive side play with piston held in vise (rack teeth up) and worm in its approximate center of travel. Vertical side play measured at a point 2.31" (58.7 mm) from piston flange should not exceed .008" (.20 mm) when end of worm is lifted with a force of 1 lb. (.45 kg).

Inspection & Reassembly – 1) Inspect condition of Teflon seal ring. If replacement is necessary, install a new rectangular seal. Ensure seal is not twisted. Stretch Teflon ring as little as possible and slide ring into piston groove. Re-size Teflon ring by using a piston ring compressor.

2) Place piston assembly in vertical position (worm shaft up) in a soft-jawed vise. Inspect worm shaft Teflon seal for nicks and voids. To replace seal, cut with knife and remove. Replacement seal is split and should be installed using multipurpose grease to hold seal centered on shaft. Ensure end gap is closed.

3) Inspect cylinder head ferrule oil passages for obstructions and lands for burrs. Lubricate 2 large "O" rings. Install "O" rings in cylinder head grooves. Install lower reaction seal "O" ring in cylinder head groove. *See Fig. 3.*

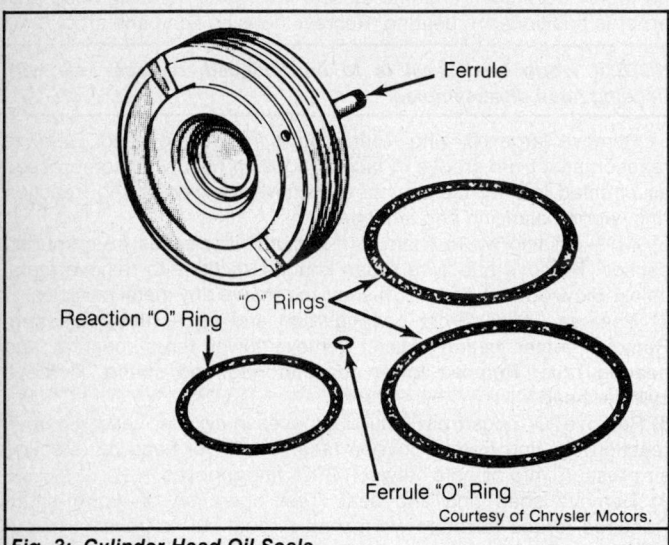

Fig. 3: Cylinder Head Oil Seals

4) Slide cylinder head assembly (ferrule up) onto worm shaft. Ensure gap on worm shaft seal ring is closed to avoid damaging ring as cylinder head moves against piston flange.

5) Lubricate all parts with power steering fluid. Install thick lower bearing race, lower thrust bearing and lower reaction spring (small hole over ferrule). Install lower reaction ring, flange up so ring protrudes through reaction spring and contacts reaction "O" ring in cylinder head. Install center bearing race, upper thrust bearing and thin upper thrust bearing race.

6) Thread, but do not tighten, worm shaft thrust bearing adjusting nut onto shaft. Turn worm shaft 1/2 turn clockwise. While holding worm shaft in this position with splined nut, tighten adjusting nut to 50 ft. lbs. (68 N.m.) to pre-stretch threads. Loosen adjusting nut.

7) Wrap cord around center bearing race several times. Make a loop in one end of cord. Attach a spring scale to loop. Pulling cord will cause bearing race to rotate. Retighten worm bearing adjusting nut while pulling on cord with scale.

8) When adjusting nut is tightened properly, reading on scale should be 16-24 ozs. (.28 kg). *See Fig. 4.* Stake upper part of worm shaft adjusting nut into knurled area of shaft. *See Fig. 5.*

9) Check preload. If adjusting nut moved during staking operation, it can be corrected by striking nut with punch in direction required to correct setting. After testing for proper preload, stake nut in 3 more locations equally spaced around upper part of nut.

10) To test staking, apply 20 ft. lbs. (27 N.m) of torque in each direction. If nut does not move, staking operation is correct. Position spacer assembly over center race. Dowel pin should engage slot in race and cylinder head ferrule should pass through slot in spacer.

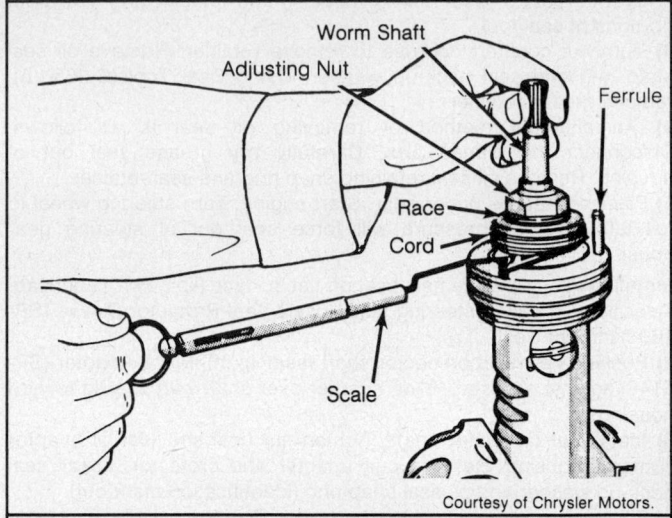

Fig. 4: Measuring Center Bearing Preload

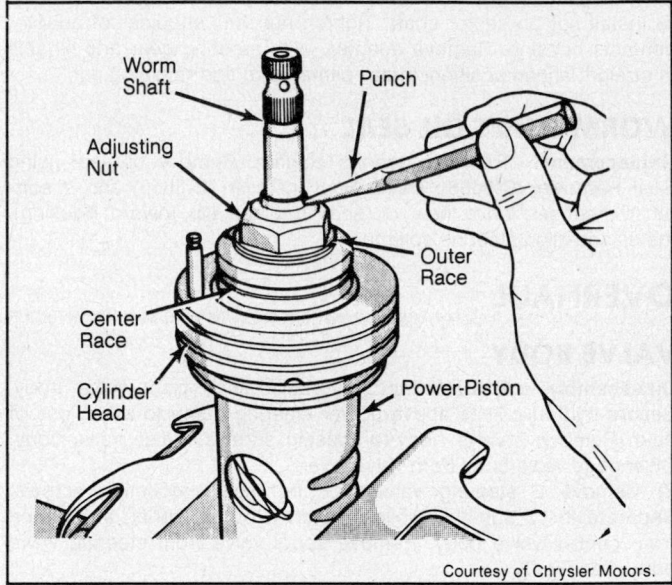

Fig. 5: Staking Adjusting Nut Onto Worm Shaft

11) Install upper reaction ring on center race and spacer with flange against spacer. Install upper reaction spring over reaction ring with cylinder head ferrule passing through hole in reaction spring. Install worm balancing ring (without flange) inside upper reaction ring.

12) Lubricate ferrule "O" ring with petroleum jelly. Install "O" ring in groove on cylinder head ferrule. If oil seal was removed from housing head, install new seal with lip facing bearing. Using Seal Driver (C-3650), drive seal into head until it bottoms on support.

13) Lubricate and install reaction seal in groove of housing head face with flat side of seal out. Install "O" ring in groove on housing head. Install the small "O" ring for the ferrule groove after upper reaction spring and spacer have been installed.

14) Slide housing head over worm shaft, carefully engaging cylinder head ferrule and "O" ring. Ensure reaction rings enter circular groove in housing head. Install power train in gear housing. If gear shaft needle bearings require replacement, turn adjusting screw clockwise until sector shaft becomes disengaged from cover.

15) Slide adjusting screw out of "T" slot in end of shaft. Do not remove sector shaft oil seal unless replacement is necessary. To remove seal, pry out grease retainer, remove oil seal snap ring and back-up washer. Pry out oil seal. Do not scratch seal bore.

16) Lubricate new seal with power steering fluid. Position seal with lip toward housing. Drive seal into housing. Install seal, back-up washer and snap ring (mark facing outward). Fill housing cavity with multipurpose grease. Position grease retainer on housing bore with metal side facing out.

17) Drive retainer into housing until shoulder of Driver (SP-5148) contacts gear housing. Insert sector shaft and adjusting screw into cover. Using an Allen wrench, turn screw counterclockwise to pull shaft completely into cover. Install gasket, date tag and lock nut, but do not tighten. Install "O" ring in undercut shelf of cover.

18) Lubricate power train bore of housing. Install power train. To keep reaction rings aligned in their grooves, keep worm turned fully counterclockwise. When installed in vehicle, piston teeth must face right side and valve lever hole in center race and spacer must face in upward direction.

19) Ensure cylinder head is bottomed on housing shoulder. Align valve lever hole in center bearing race with valve lever hole in gear housing. Install valve lever (double bearing end first) into center race and spacer through hole in gear housing. Engage center race and spacer.

20) Slots in valve lever must be parallel to worm shaft. Tap lightly on end of lever to seat lower pivot point in center race. Center lever by turning housing head. Install housing head tang washer so that it indexes with groove in housing. Install and tighten spanner nut.

21) Valve lever must remain centered in housing hole. Turn worm shaft until piston bottoms in both directions. Note action of lever. Valve lever must be centered in hole and snapped back to center position when worm shaft torque is relieved. Install valve lever spring (small end first).

22) Set power piston at center of travel. Install gear shaft and cover assembly with sector teeth indexed to rack piston teeth. Ensure cover "O" ring is installed correctly. Tighten cover spanner nut. Install valve body on housing. Ensure valve pivot lever enters hole in valve spool.

23) Ensure "O" ring seals are in place. Tighten valve mounting screws. If new worm shaft and piston assembly have been installed, master serration on power steering gear worm shaft spline must be machined to properly center steering shaft coupling.

24) To remove master serration, steering gear must be assembled and worm shaft centered in its travel. With steering gear in its normal upright position, use a file to remove one tooth of spline at the 12 o'clock position.

TIGHTENING SPECIFICATIONS

Application	Ft. Lbs. (N.m)
Control Valve Body-to-Steering Valve Bolt	17 (23)
Flexible Coupling Bolts	17 (23)
Housing Head Spanner Nut	200 (271)
Outlet Fitting-to-Valve	20 (27)
Pitman Arm Nut	175 (237)
Sector Shaft Adjusting Screw Lock Nut	28 (38)
Sector Shaft Cover Spanner Nut	150 (203)
Steering Column Clamp Stud Nut	17 (23)
Steering Gear Mounting Bolts	100 (136)
Steering Wheel Nut	45 (61)
Valve Body End Plug	50 (68)

	INCH Lbs. (N.m)
Steering Column Bracket-to-Column	20 (2)
Steering Column Clamp Stud	110 (12)
Steering Column Support Plate Bolts	60 (7)
Valve Body-to-Housing Attaching Bolts	108 (11)

1989 POWER STEERING GEARS
Eagle Center-Linked Rack & Pinion

Premier

DESCRIPTION

Power rack and pinion steering system uses a rotary control valve to direct hydraulic fluid to either side of rack piston. Rack piston is integral with rack gear and converts hydraulic pressure to linear force. This force assists rack gear to move either left or right. Power rack and pinion steering gear consists of an input pinion gear, steering rack gear, tube housing and a rotary valve assembly.

LUBRICATION, TROUBLE SHOOTING & TESTING

See POWER STEERING GENERAL SERVICING & TROUBLE SHOOTING articles in this section.

ADJUSTMENTS

RACK BEARING PRELOAD

1) Raise and support front of vehicle. Center steering wheel. Loosen adjusting plug lock nut. Turn adjusting plug clockwise until it bottoms in housing. Back off adjusting plug 45-50 degrees.
2) Tighten lock nut to specification while holding adjuster plug stationary. Check steering wheel movement for binding after adjustment.

REMOVAL & INSTALLATION

RACK & PINION ASSEMBLY

Removal – 1) Remove instrument panel lower cover to gain access to steering shaft boot. Unsnap steering shaft boot flange from dash panel opening. Slide boot up intermediate shaft out of the way.
2) Remove intermediate shaft-to-pinion "U" joint clamp bolt. Mark intermediate shaft and pinion shaft for reassembly reference. In engine compartment, pry out splash shield retaining clips with a screwdriver.
3) Remove splash shield. Fold back tabs on tie rod center link lock plate. Loosen tie rod retaining bolts one or 2 turns. DO NOT remove bolts. Unsnap hydraulic lines from rubber mounting block.
4) Place a drain pan under vehicle. Disconnect hydraulic lines from steering gear. Remove right front mounting nut. Raise and support vehicle. Remove left front wheel. Remove cotter pins and castle nuts from knuckles.
5) Using a tie rod end puller, separate tie rod ends from struts. Remove 3 remaining steering gear mounting bolts. Remove steering gear with tie rods through access opening in left fenderwell.
6) Keep tie rods parallel to steering gear during removal. If necessary, tape or tie wrap tie rods to steering gear to ease removal.
Installation – To install, reverse removal procedure. Replace hydraulic line "O" rings with new ones. Tighten nuts and bolts to specification.

TIE ROD END

Removal & Installation – Remove cotter pin and nut from tie rod end. Loosen tie rod end pinch bolt. Using tie rod end puller, separate tie rod end from strut. Unscrew tie rod end, counting number of turns for reassembly reference. To install, reverse removal procedure.

OVERHAUL

RACK & PINION ASSEMBLY

NOTE: *Manufacturer does not recommend service of rack and pinion without use of Overhaul Tool Kit (6118), which contains all tools mentioned in disassembly and reassembly procedures.*

Disassembly – 1) Remove end plug from steering gear shaft bore. Using Preload Adjustment Cap Remover (6103), remove preload adjustment cap lock nut and cap from steering gear housing bore. *See Fig. 1.* Using pliers, remove thrust bearing from steering gear housing bore. Remove steering gear shaft retaining ring from steering gear shaft bore in steering gear housing.

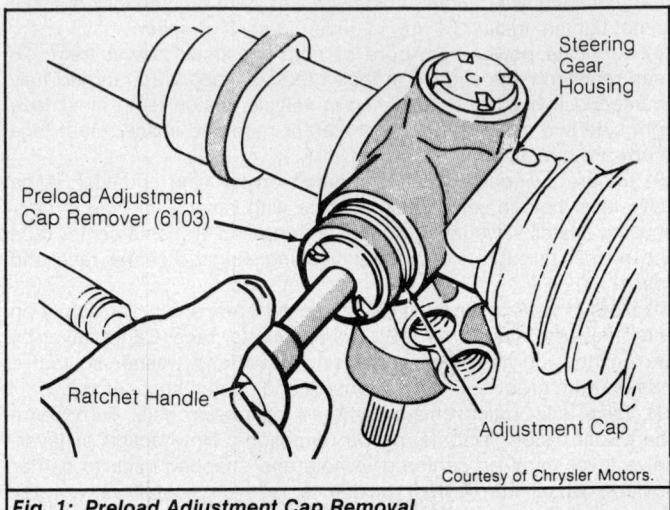

Fig. 1: Preload Adjustment Cap Removal

2) Hold steering gear shaft in place with a combination wrench and Steering Gear Shaft Holder (SP-3616) and remove steering gear shaft retaining nut. *See Fig. 2.* Using Steering Gear Shaft Remover (6095), remove steering gear shaft from steering gear shaft bore. Thread remover into steering gear shaft bore and tighten screw to force shaft from bore. Remove outer seal and outer bearing from shaft.

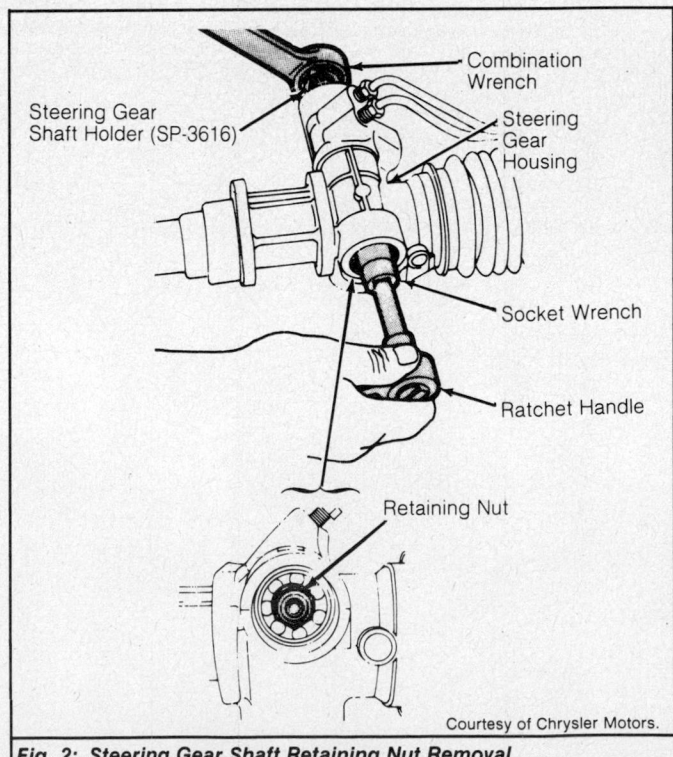

Fig. 2: Steering Gear Shaft Retaining Nut Removal

3) Remove ring seals from steering gear shaft by pushing seals to one side of groove and cutting with a knife. Use care not to nick or scratch steering gear shaft. Using a hammer and brass drift, remove steering gear shaft inner bearing from steering gear shaft bore. Using Seal Remover (C-4694), remove steering gear shaft inner seal

1989 POWER STEERING GEARS
Eagle Center-Linked Rack & Pinion (Cont.)

13-45

from steering gear shaft bore by inserting remover with threaded rod through steering gear shaft bore and inner seal.

4) Install and tighten remover lower nut to expand tool inside inner seal. Position cup (included with remover) over remover threaded rod against steering gear housing. Install and tighten remover upper nut to force inner seal from shaft bore. *See Fig. 3.*

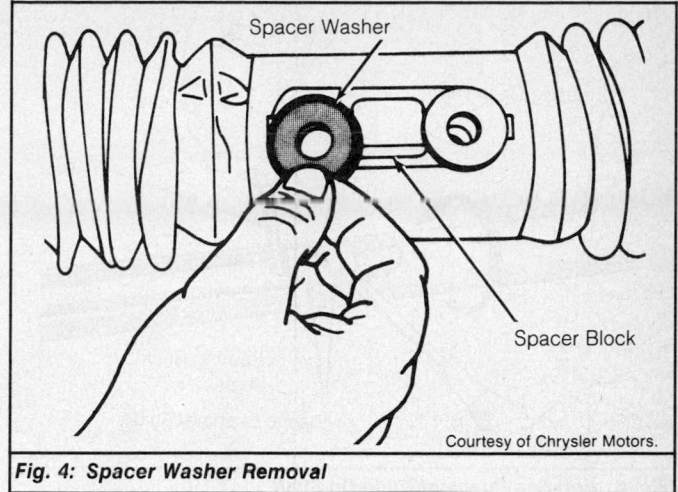

Fig. 4: *Spacer Washer Removal*

Courtesy of Chrysler Motors.

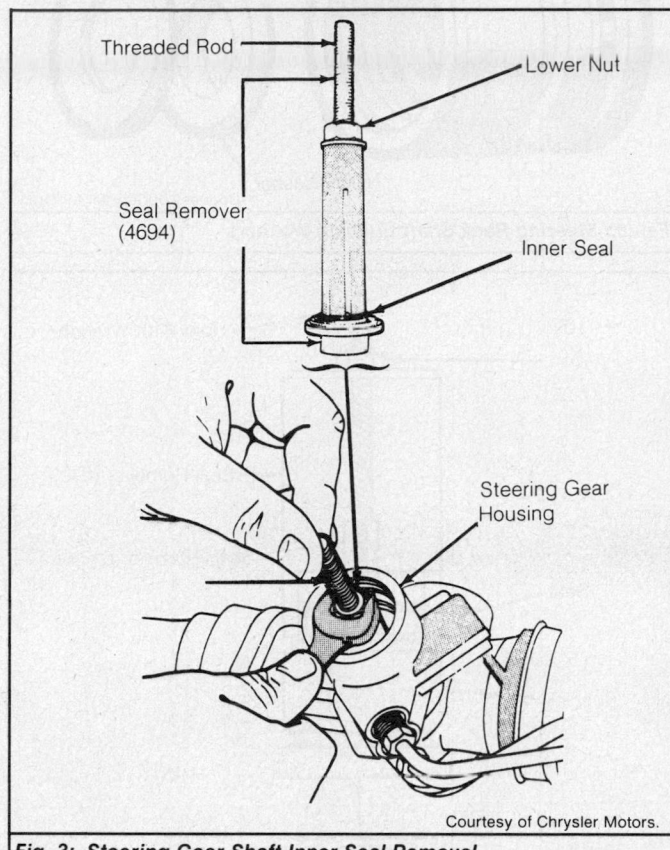

Fig. 3: *Steering Gear Shaft Inner Seal Removal*

Courtesy of Chrysler Motors.

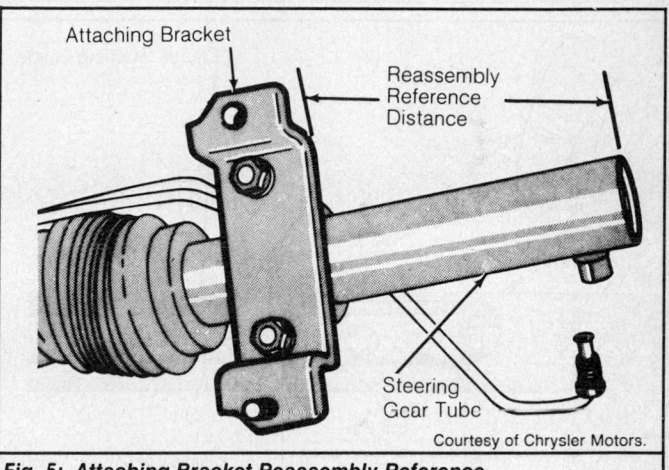

Fig. 5: *Attaching Bracket Reassembly Reference*

Courtesy of Chrysler Motors.

5) Remove steering gear tube end cap retaining wire with Wire Remover (6101). Insert wire remover into 2 holes in tube end cap. Rotate wire remover and end cap clockwise or counterclockwise to force retaining wire from tube. Disconnect fluid tubing outer fitting from steering gear tube. Do not disconnect any other tubing fitting at this time.

6) Remove steering gear tube end cap with compressed air. Use a cloth to catch end cap as it discharges from tube. Remove ring seal from end cap. Remove attaching bolts and tie rods from steering rack shaft spacer block. Remove spacer washers from spacer block. *See Fig. 4.* Cut and remove clamps that attach protective boot to steering gear tube and cast metal housing.

NOTE: Steering gear fluid tube fittings have ring seals and are not flared. When tube fittings are removed, ring seals must be replaced to avoid possible leakage. Ring seals must be enlarged for installation, then compressed back to original size after they have been fitted over tubing lips.

7) Remove remaining fluid tubing fittings from steering gear housing and tube. Before removing steering gear attaching bracket, measure distance from bracket to end of steering gear tube for reassembly reference. *See Fig. 5.* Remove steering gear attaching brackets and rubber isolators. To prevent damage during removal of steering gear boot, install protective Caps (6116) on fluid tubing fitting bosses located on steering gear tube.

8) Slide boot over caps and off tube. To prevent shaft from rotating, temporarily attach spacer block to steering rack shaft with a tie rod attaching bolt. Remove rivet from steering gear tube. Remove piston retaining nut located at end of steering rack shaft. Remove tie rod end attaching bolt and spacer block.

9) Relocate steering rack shaft plastic bushing/guide by first inserting a small pry bar into one tie rod bolt hole in steering rack shaft to prevent it from rotating. Using another small pry bar, rotate bushing/guide on shaft in a clockwise direction around roll pin until separation is aligned with roll pin. *See Fig. 6.* Slide bushing/guide approximately 2" along steering rack shaft. *See Fig. 7.*

10) Thread Steering Rack Shaft Remover (6099) onto end of slide hammer and onto steering rack shaft. Use slide hammer and remove steering rack shaft, bushing and piston as an assembly from steering gear tube. Remove slide hammer and rack shaft remover from steering rack shaft. Remove and discard 2 seals on steering rack shaft. Cut and remove "O" ring seals from steering rack shaft piston and bushing.

11) Using snap ring pliers, remove retaining ring from steering rack shaft bushing. Remove metal and nylon washers from inside steering rack shaft bushing. *See Fig. 8.* Using Seal Removers (6109 and 6124), remove seal from steering rack shaft bushing bore by first removing nut from threaded end of seal remover. Insert one seal remover through seal and bushing bore. Install other seal remover on top of bushing. *See Fig. 9.*

12) Install nut on threaded end of seal remover. Hold threaded end of seal remover with a wrench and tighten nut to force seal from bore.

Cleaning & Inspection – 1) Remove and discard all "O" ring seals. Clean all components and allow to air dry. Check steering gear housing and tube for cracks or leaks.

2) Check seal mating surfaces on steering rack shaft, steering gear shaft, rack shaft piston and bushing, and gear housing and tube. Replace any component that has excessive wear or damage at seal mating surfaces.

13-46

1989 POWER STEERING GEARS
Eagle Center-Linked Rack & Pinion (Cont.)

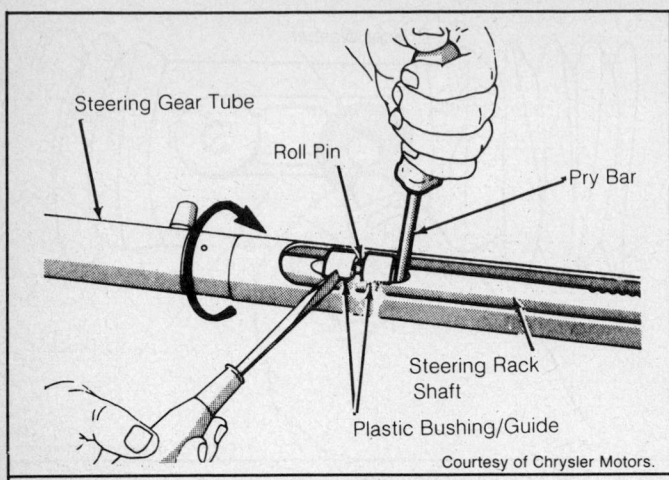

Fig. 6: Rotating Bushing/Guide On Shaft

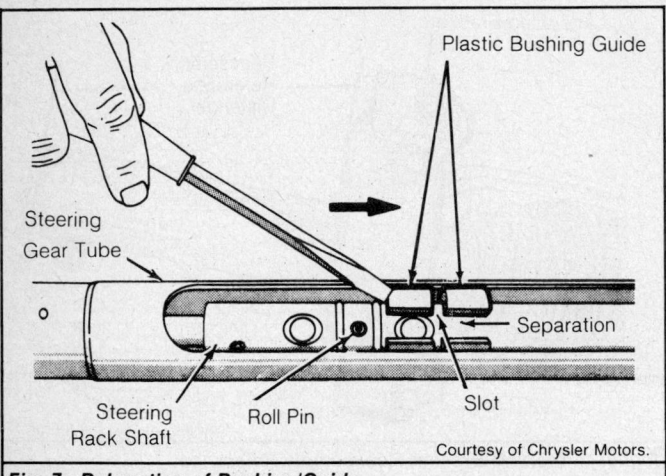

Fig. 7: Relocation of Bushing/Guide

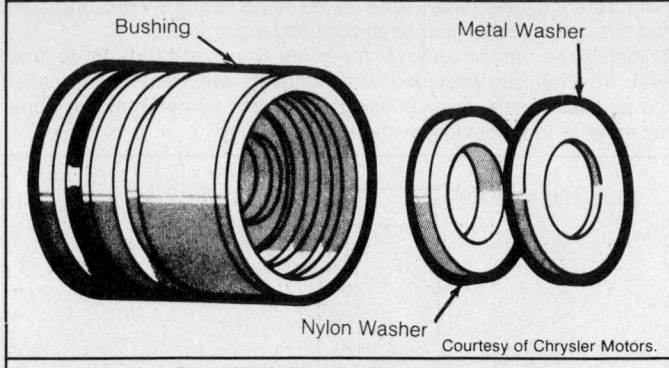

Fig. 8: Steering Rack Shaft Bushing Washers

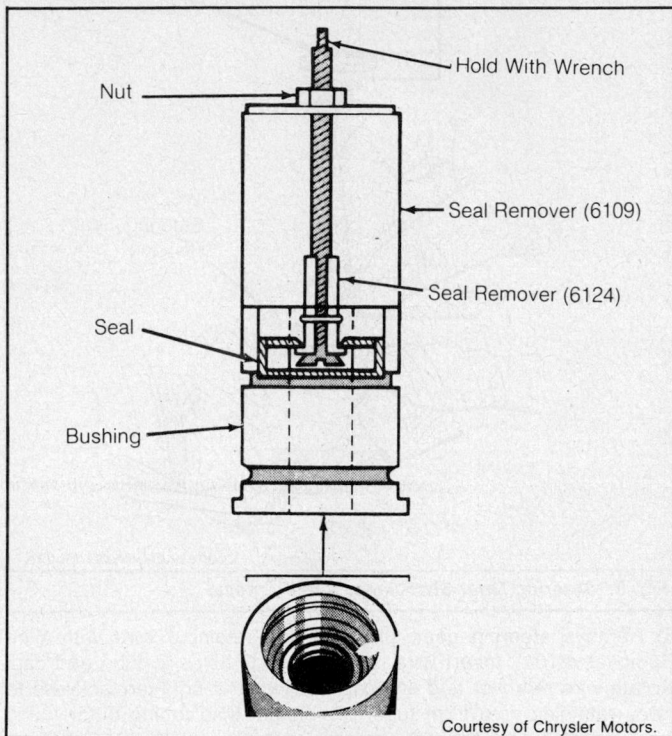

Fig. 9: Steering Shaft Bushing Seal Removal

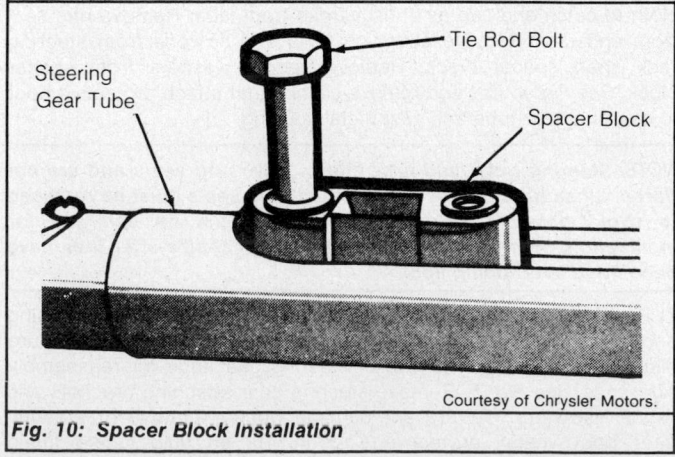

Fig. 10: Spacer Block Installation

Reassembly – 1) Install new "O" ring seals on steering rack shaft bushing. Using Driver Handle (6104) and Seal Installer (6110), install new seals in steering rack shaft bushing bore. Install new nylon washer, metal washer and retaining ring in steering rack shaft bushing. Install new "O" rings on steering rack shaft.

2) Use a long pry bar and force steering rack shaft bushing into tube until rivet groove in bushing aligns with rivet hole in steering gear tube. Install a replacement rivet in tube rivet hole. Install a new "O" ring on steering rack shaft piston. Insert piston and "O" ring into Piston Installer (6111).

CAUTION: Manufacturer does not recommend installation of steering rack shaft piston without use of Piston Installer (6111).

3) Position piston installer with piston and "O" ring into end of steering gear tube, ensuring piston installer is correctly aligned with steering gear tube bore. Using a brass drift, carefully force piston and "O" ring through piston installer and into end of steering gear tube until it contacts threaded end of steering rack shaft. Remove brass drift and piston installer.

4) Install piston retaining nut on threaded end of steering rack shaft. Do not tighten nut at this time. To prevent rotation, use a tie rod attaching bolt and temporarily install spacer block on steering rack shaft. *See Fig. 10.* Tighten steering rack shaft piston retaining nut and remove spacer block.

5) Position separation in plastic bushing/guide so it aligns with roll pin in steering rack shaft. Slide plastic bushing/guide toward roll pin until slot is aligned with roll pin. Rotate plastic bushing/guide slot toward roll pin until end of slot contacts roll pin.

6) Rotate steering rack shaft 180 degrees to position roll pin on opposite side of steering tube. Ensure steering rack shaft and bushing/guide are positioned properly. *See Fig. 11.*

1989 POWER STEERING GEARS
Eagle Center-Linked Rack & Pinion (Cont.)

13-47

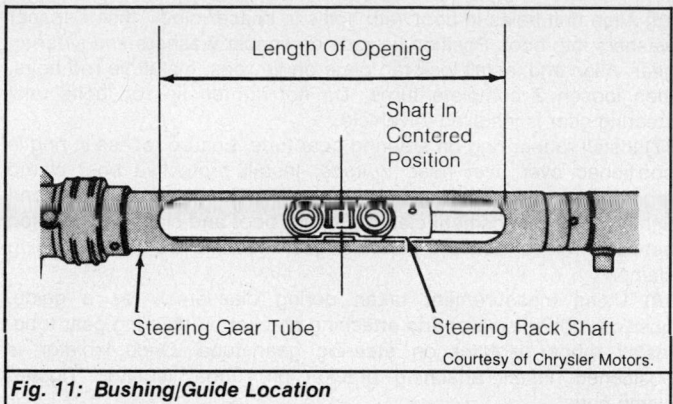

Fig. 11: **Bushing/Guide Location**

Courtesy of Chrysler Motors.

CAUTION: Manufacturer does not recommend installation of following seals without use of Ring Seal Installer (6102), Tube (6109), Ring Compressor (6108) and Spacers (6105 and 6106).

7) Install Ring Seal Installer (6102) on steering gear shaft. Installer will align with first ring seal groove. Slide first ring seal onto installer. Install Seal Remover/Installer (6109) over installer and force first ring seal into first ring seal groove. Remove tools from steering gear shaft and compress first ring seal to original size by sliding largest end of Ring Compressor (6108) onto shaft and over ring seal. Using appropriate Spacers (6105 and 6106), install other seals in same manner.

8) Center steering rack shaft in steering gear housing and tube. Measure length of oval opening in steering gear tube. Divide length by 2 and center steering rack shaft. Use center location between 2 steering rack shaft ring seals as center of steering rack shaft. See Fig. 12.

9) Temporarily install spacer block on steering rack shaft using a tie rod attaching bolt. Place steering gear shaft inner seal on Driver Handle (6104) and position flush against Seal Installer (6098). Install steering gear shaft inner seal on driver handle and position it flush against installer.

10) Install steering gear shaft inner seal in shaft bore until it is flush against machined shoulder in bore. Using same tools, install shaft inner bearing.

11) Ensure steering rack shaft is centered in steering gear housing and tube. Insert small diameter end of Steering Gear Shaft Installer (6108) in steering gear shaft bore. Insert steering gear shaft in installer. Ensure steering gear shaft is correctly indexed, then force steering gear shaft inward through installer and into shaft bore. See Fig. 13.

12) Install a new retaining nut on end of steering gear shaft. Hold shaft in place and tighten nut. Position steering gear shaft outer bearing over shaft and insert it into shaft bore. Install Seal Protector (6112) on end of steering gear shaft.

13) Position steering gear shaft outer seal over end of seal protector. Slide outer seal toward steering gear housing until flush with outer edge of shaft bore. Seat outer seal in shaft bore. Install steering gear shaft retaining ring. Install and tighten steering gear shaft end plug.

14) Install thrust bearing and thrust spring in steering gear housing bore. Using Adjustment Cap Installer (6103), install and tighten preload adjustment cap. After tightening, loosen plug 45-50 degrees. Install and tighten preload adjustment cap lock nut. Do not allow adjustment cap to rotate when tightening lock nut.

15) Install new "O" ring on steering gear tube end cap. Align retaining wire hole in end cap with oval slot in steering gear tube. Force end cap into tube. See Fig. 14. Install new end cap retaining wire. Insert wire into hole in end cap. Rotate end cap clockwise to force wire completely into tube. Install spacer block on steering rack shaft and install boot. See Fig. 15.

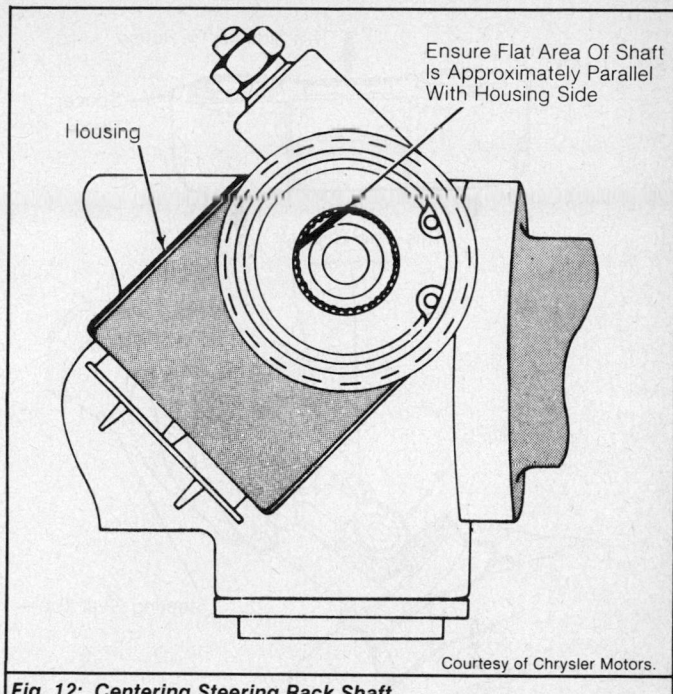

Courtesy of Chrysler Motors.

Fig. 12: **Centering Steering Rack Shaft**

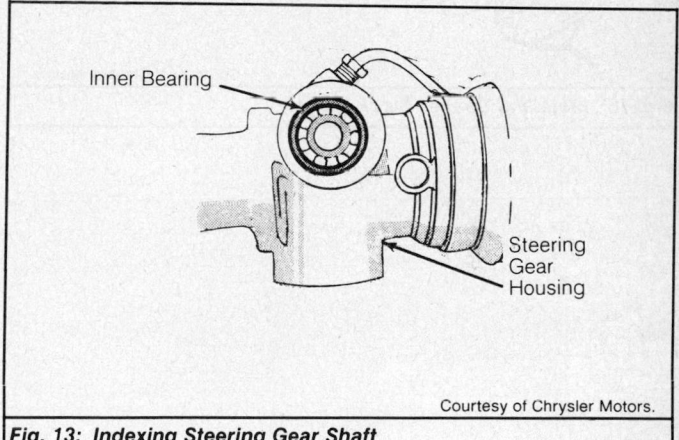

Courtesy of Chrysler Motors.

Fig. 13: **Indexing Steering Gear Shaft**

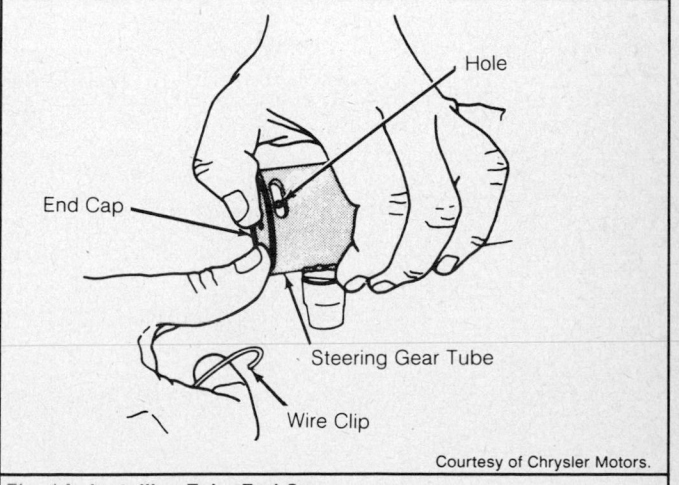

Courtesy of Chrysler Motors.

Fig. 14: **Installing Tube End Cap**

1989 POWER STEERING GEARS
Eagle Center-Linked Rack & Pinion (Cont.)

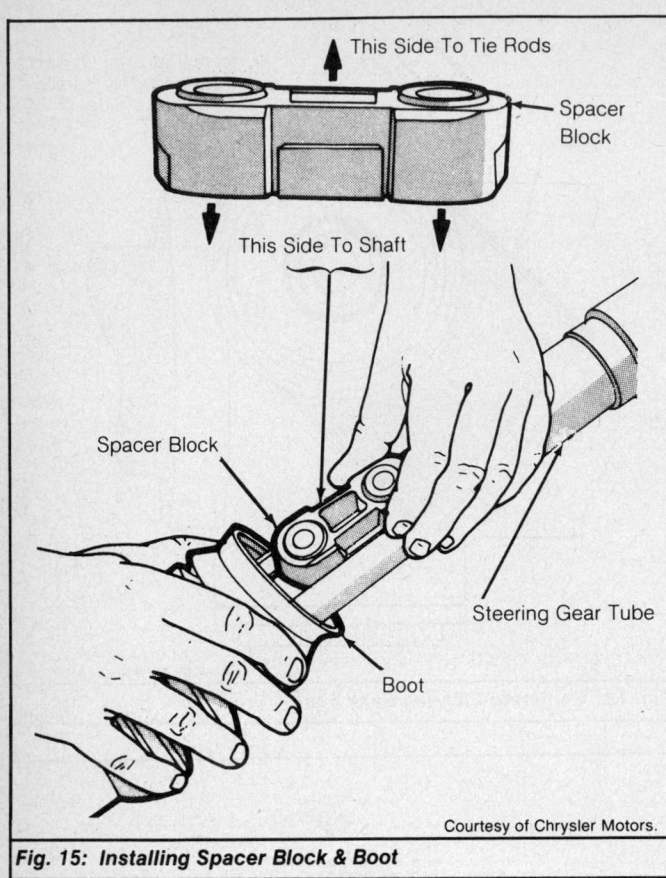

This Side To Tie Rods

Spacer Block

This Side To Shaft

Spacer Block

Steering Gear Tube

Boot

Courtesy of Chrysler Motors.

Fig. 15: Installing Spacer Block & Boot

16) Align bolt holes in boot with holes in spacer block. Insert spacer washers into boot. Position tie rods on spacer washers and steering gear. Align and install lock tab plate on tie rods. Install tie rod bolts, then loosen 2 complete turns. Do not tighten tie rod bolts until steering gear is installed in vehicle.

17) Install rubber ring on steering gear tube. Ensure recess in ring is positioned over rivet head in tube. Install protective boot clamp groove between raised ribs on steering gear housing. Install and tighten boot replacement clamp. Ensure boot and clamp are located between raised ribs on steering gear housing before tightening clamp.

18) Using measurement taken during diassembly as a guide, position rubber isolator and attaching bracket on steering gear tube. Install rubber isolator on steering gear tube. Once isolator is positioned, install attaching bracket on rubber isolator. Tighten clamp nuts.

19) Install new ring seals on steering gear fluid tubing fittings. Install fluid tubing fittings to steering gear. Install steering gear in vehicle.

TIGHTENING SPECIFICATIONS

Application	Ft. Lbs. (N.m)
Intermediate Shaft Clamp-to-Steering Gear Bolt	30 (40)
Steering Gear Bracket Bolt	40 (55)
Steering Gear Shaft End Plug	45 (61)
Tie Rod End Adjustment Sleeve Lock Nut	36 (49)
Tie Rod End-to-Strut Nut	35 (48)
Tie Rod Shaft-to-Steering Gear Spacer Block Bolt	55 (75)
Return Hose Fitting	25 (30)

	INCH Lbs. (N.m)
Preload Adjustment Cap	45-50 (5-6)

Grand Marquis, LTD Crown Victoria, Town Car

DESCRIPTION

System is a hydraulically assisted torsion bar type. It incorporates a rotary valve, pinion shaft, torsion bar, worm shaft, 1-piece rack piston, sector shaft and housing. Rotary valve is mounted on input shaft and controls fluid pressure to each side of rack piston.

OPERATION

Control valve uses rotational position of input shaft and valve sleeve to direct fluid flow. Valve is pinned to worm shaft, and input shaft is connected to worm shaft through torsion bar. During operation, the valve and housing cylinder are always full of fluid, which dampens road shock.

LUBRICATION, TROUBLE SHOOTING & TESTING

See POWER STEERING GENERAL SERVICING and TROUBLE SHOOTING articles in this section.

ADJUSTMENTS

SECTOR SHAFT MESH LOAD

1) Disconnect pitman arm from sector shaft. Disconnect fluid return line at reservoir and cap line fitting. Place return line in container and cycle steering wheel to drain fluid from gear.

2) Turn steering wheel to within 45 degrees of left stop. Using an INCH lb. torque wrench on steering wheel nut, measure rotational drag required to turn gear about 1/4 of a turn from left stop.

3) Record reading. If vehicle is equipped with a tilt wheel, place wheel in center tilt position. Turn steering wheel to center position and measure torque required to rotate shaft back and forth across center position. Reading should be 14-29 INCH lbs. (1.6-3.3 N.m).

4) If adjustment is necessary, loosen adjuster screw lock nut. Turn screw to adjust sector mesh load. To set torque, measure rocking across center to a value of 14-20 INCH lbs. (1.6-2.3 N.m) greater than that measured 45 degrees from left stop.

5) Tighten adjuster screw lock nut. Recheck rotational turning torque. Reconnect return line. Add fluid and reinstall pitman arm. Tighten nut to specification. Check and adjust power steering belt as necessary.

REMOVAL & INSTALLATION

STEERING GEAR

Removal – 1) Remove stone shield. Disconnect hydraulic lines from gear and mark for reassembly reference. Plug lines and ports to prevent contamination.

2) Remove flexible coupling bolts. Raise and support vehicle. Remove sector shaft nut. Mark pitman arm and sector shaft for reassembly reference (if necessary). Using Puller (T-64P-3590-F), remove pitman arm.

3) Support steering gear and remove gear attaching bolts. Remove flexible coupling clamp bolts. Separate gear from coupling and remove gear from vehicle.

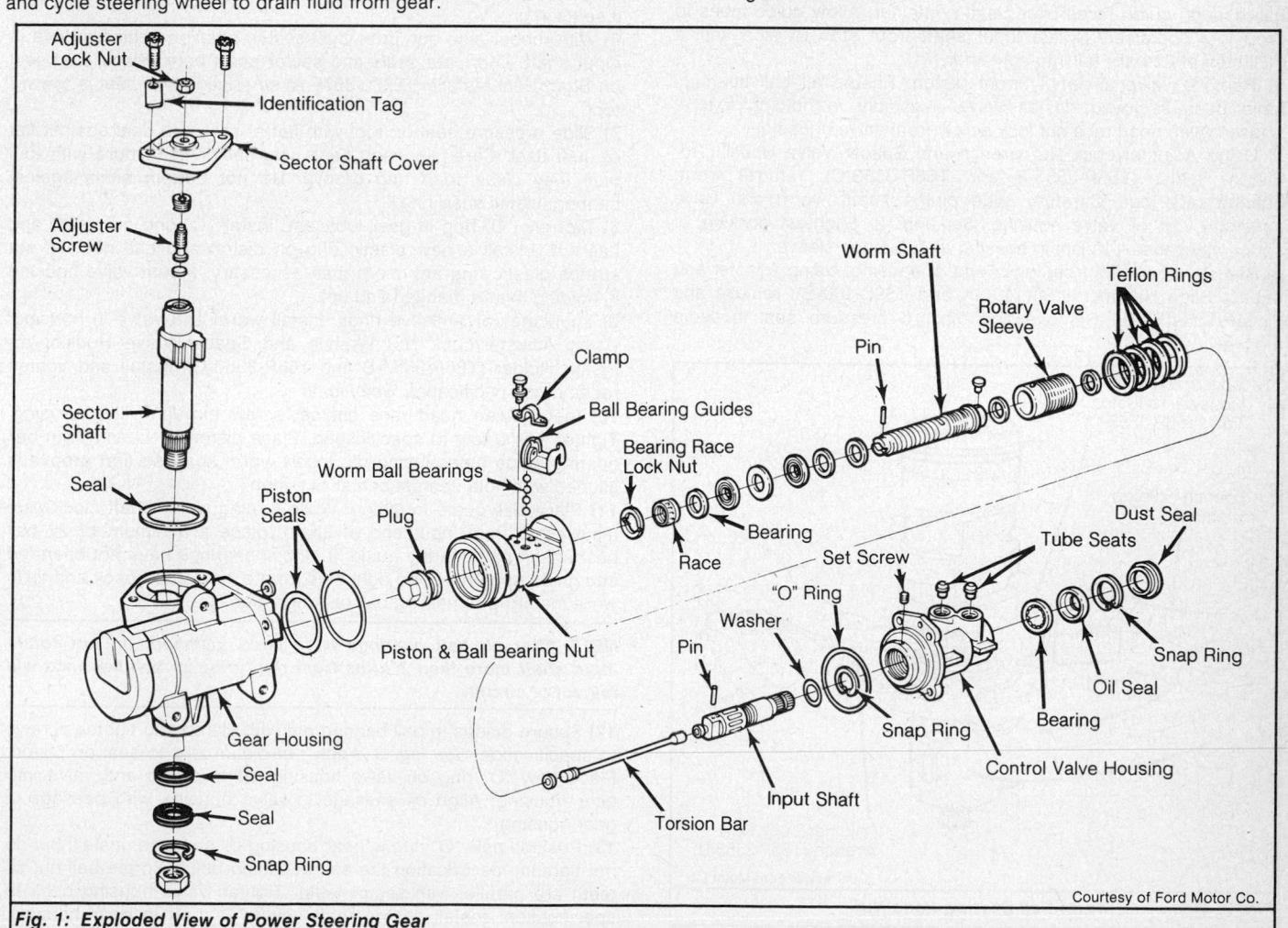

Courtesy of Ford Motor Co.

Fig. 1: Exploded View of Power Steering Gear

1989 POWER STEERING GEARS
Ford Motor Co. Integral Power Steering (Cont.)

13-50

Installation – 1) Turn steering wheel to straight ahead position. Center steering gear input shaft with indexing flat facing downward. Slide steering gear input shaft into flex coupling and into place on frame side rail. Install and tighten attaching bolts.

2) Ensure wheels are in straight ahead position and install pitman arm, lockwasher and nut on sector shaft. Tighten nut to specification. Move flex coupling into place on steering gear input shaft. Install attaching bolt and tighten to specification.

3) Install and tighten pressure and return lines to steering gear. Fill reservoir and bleed system. Reinstall stone shield.

OVERHAUL

STEERING GEAR

Disassembly – 1) Drain steering gear and mount in holding fixture. Remove lock nut and washer from adjusting screw. Turn input shaft to either stop. Turn back 1 5/8 turns to center gear. Indexing flat on pinion spline should face downward.

2) Remove sector shaft cover bolts. Tap lower end of sector shaft with a soft hammer. Lift cover and shaft from housing as an assembly. Discard "O" ring.

3) Turn sector shaft cover counterclockwise to remove cover from adjusting screw. Remove valve housing attaching bolts and identification tag. Lift valve housing from steering gear housing while holding piston to prevent it from rotating off worm shaft.

4) Remove and discard valve housing-to-gear "O" rings. Hold piston so ball bearing guide faces upward. Remove ball guide clamp screws and clamp.

5) Place finger over opening in ball bearing guide and turn piston so ball bearing guide faces over clean container. Allow guide tubes to drop into container. Rotate input shaft from stop to stop until a minimum of 27 balls fall into container.

6) Remove valve assembly from piston. Ensure all ball bearings have been removed. Install valve assembly in holding fixture. Loosen Allen head race nut lock screw from valve housing.

7) Using Adjuster/Lock Nut wrench and Spacer Valve Housing-to-Piston Holder (T66P-3553-B and T66P-3553-C), remove worm bearing race nut. Carefully slide pinion shaft, worm and valve assembly out of valve housing. *See Fig. 2.* Slightest cocking of spool may cause it to jam in housing and damage sleeve.

8) Remove snap ring from lower end of housing. Using Adapter and Impact Slide Hammer (T58L-101-A and T59L-100-B), remove and discard dust seal. Remove and discard pressure seal in same manner.

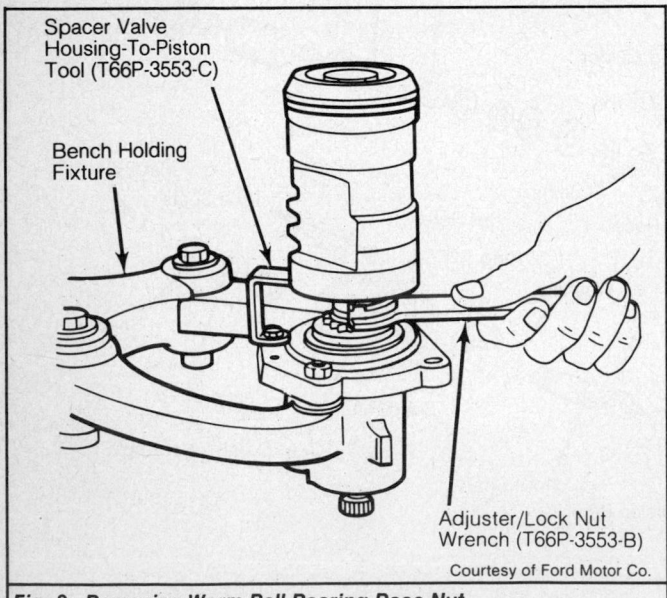

Spacer Valve Housing-To-Piston Tool (T66P-3553-C)

Bench Holding Fixture

Adjuster/Lock Nut Wrench (T66P-3553-B)

Courtesy of Ford Motor Co.

Fig. 2: Removing Worm Ball Bearing Race Nut

9) Using same adapter and impact slide hammer, remove and discard dust seal from rear of valve housing. Carefully insert Bearing Remover/Installer (T65P-3524-A2) in valve body assembly opposite oil seal. Gently tap bearing and seal out of housing and discard seal.

10) If valve bore is damaged, remove inlet and outlet tube seats with Brass Tube Remover (T-74P-3504-2). Remove valve sleeve Teflon rings only if scratched or worn. Insert a knife blade under rings and cut them off. Avoid scratching valve sleeve. Remove plastic ring and "O" ring from piston and ball nut.

Reassembly – 1) Install Mandrel (T75L-3517-A1) over valve sleeve. Slide one valve ring over mandrel. Slide Pusher (T75L-3517-A2) over mandrel. Rapidly push down on tool, forcing ring down ramp and into 4th groove of valve sleeve.

2) Repeat procedure 3 more times, adding a Spacer (T75L-3517-A3), under mandrel each time. After installing 4 valve sleeve rings, apply gear lubricant to sleeve and rings. Install one spacer over input shaft as a pilot for installing sizing tube.

3) Slowly install Sizing Tube (T75L-3517-A4) over sleeve valve end of worm shaft onto valve sleeve rings. Ensure rings are not being bent over as tube is slid over them. Remove sizing tube and check condition of rings. Rings must turn freely in grooves.

4) Coat new tube seats with petroleum jelly. Install new tube seals using Brass Tube Installer (T74P-3504-M). Coat bearing and seal surface of housing with petroleum jelly. Position bearing in housing. Press bearing with metal covered side facing outward. Ensure bearing rotates freely.

5) Dip new oil seal in gear lube. Place seal in housing, metal side out. Drive seal into housing until outer edge does not quite clear snap ring groove. Place snap ring in housing. Drive snap ring in until it seats in groove.

6) With rubber side out, drive dust seal in position behind groove in input shaft. Lubricate seals and sector shaft bore. Place dust seal on Shaft Seal Installer (T77L-3576-A) so raised lip of seal is toward tool.

7) Slide pressure seal on tool with flat of pressure seal against flat of dust seal. Carefully insert seals into sector shaft bore with tool until they clear snap ring groove. Do not bottom seals against bearing. Install snap ring.

8) Dip new "O" ring in gear lubricant. Install "O" ring on piston and ball nut. Install a new plastic ring on piston and ball nut. Do not stretch plastic ring any more than necessary. Mount valve housing in holding fixture (flanged end up).

9) Lubricate valve sleeve rings. Install worm and valve in housing. Using Adjuster/Lock Nut Wrench and Spacer Valve Housing-to-Piston Holder (T66P-3553-B and T66P-3553-C), install and tighten race nut to specification. *See Fig. 2.*

10) Install Allen head race nut set screw through valve housing. Tighten set screw to specification. Place piston on bench, with ball bearing guide holes facing up. Insert worm shaft so first groove is aligned with hole nearest center of piston.

11) Place ball guide in piston. While turning worm shaft clockwise, (as viewed from input end of shaft), place a minimum of 27 ball bearings in ball bearing guide. If all ball bearings have not been fed into guide upon reaching right stop, rotate input shaft back and forth while installing remaining ball bearings. *See Fig. 3.*

NOTE: After all ball bearings have been installed, do not rotate input shaft more than 3 turns from right stop or ball bearings will fall out of circuit.

---

12) Secure guides in ball bearing nut with clamp and tighten screws to specification. *See Fig. 3.* Apply petroleum jelly to seal on piston. Place new "O" ring on valve housing. Slide piston and valve into gear housing. Align oil passage in valve housing with passage in gear housing.

13) Position new "O" ring in gear housing oil passage. Install, but do not tighten, identification tag and attaching bolts. Rotate ball nut so teeth are parallel with sector teeth. Tighten valve housing bolts to specification. Install sector shaft cover "O" ring in gear housing. Turn input shaft to center piston.

1989 POWER STEERING GEARS
Ford Motor Co. Integral Power Steering (Cont.)

13-51

14) Apply petroleum jelly to sector shaft journal. Position sector shaft and cover assembly in gear housing. Rotate input shaft one turn on either side of center. Install and tighten cover bolts to specification. Perform sector shaft adjustment. See ADJUSTMENTS section in this article

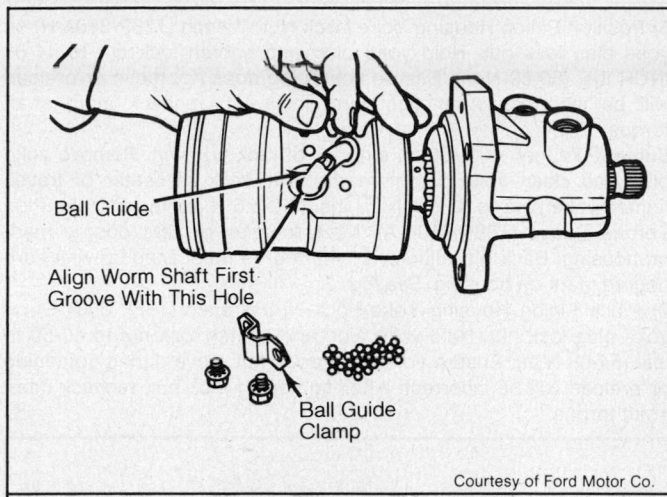

Ball Guide

Align Worm Shaft First Groove With This Hole

Ball Guide Clamp

Courtesy of Ford Motor Co.

Fig. 3: Installing Piston & Worm Shaft Ball Bearings

TIGHTENING SPECIFICATIONS

Application	Ft. Lbs. (N.m)
Flexible Coupling Bolt	20-30 (27-41)
Piston End Cap	70-110 (95-149)
Pitman Arm Retaining Nut	200-250 (271-339)
Presure Line-to-Steering Gear	16-25 (22-34)
Race Nut	55-90 (75-122)
Return Line-to-Steering Gear	25-34 (34-46)
Sector Shaft Adj. Screw Lock Nut	35-45 (47-61)
Sector Shaft Cover Bolts	55-70 (75-95)
Steering Gear Mounting Bolts	50-65 (68-88)
Valve Housing Bolts	30-45 (41-61)
Worm Bearing Race Nut	[1] 55-90 (75-122)

	INCH Lbs. (N.m)
Ball Bearing Return Guide Clamp Screws	42-70 (4.8-7.9)
Hose Clamps	12-24 (1.4-2.7)
Race Nut Allen Set Screw	15-25 (1.7-2.8)

[1] – To obtain proper torque reading when using Adapter (T66P-3553-B), multiply desired torque reading by torque wrench length. Divide result by total wrench and adapter length (5.5"). Example: With a 13" torque wrench, 5.5" adapter and a desired torque value of 55 ft. lbs. (75 N.m), the actual torque reading would be 39 ft. lbs. (52 N.m).

1989 POWER STEERING GEARS
Ford Motor Co. Integral Rack & Pinion

**Except Cougar, Continental, Grand Marquis,
LTD Crown Victoria, Probe, Thunderbird,
Town Car**

DESCRIPTION & OPERATION

All vehicles use a one-piece power steering gear unit. Gear and valve housing are combined into an aluminum die casting. Quick connect fittings are used for pressure and return lines. Fittings are designed to swivel and should not be overtightened.

A hydraulic-mechanical unit with an integral piston and rack provides power-assisted steering control. Internal valving directs pump flow and controls pressure. Unit contains a rotary fluid control valve and a boost cylinder integral with gear rack.

LUBRICATION, TROUBLE SHOOTING & TESTING

See POWER STEERING GENERAL SERVICING and TROUBLE SHOOTING articles in this section.

ADJUSTMENTS

RACK YOKE PLUG CLEARANCE

NOTE: This is not a normal service adjustment. It is only required when input shaft and valve assembly is removed. Steering gear unit must be removed from vehicle.

RWD Models – 1) Clean exterior of steering gear. Install 2 long bolts and washers through bushings and attach unit to Bench Mounted Holding Fixture (T57L-500-B).

2) Do not remove external pressure lines unless necessary. If lines are removed, they must be replaced with new ones. Drain fluid by rotating input shaft lock-to-lock twice using Pinion Shaft Torque Adjuster (T74P-3504-R). Cover ports on valve housing with a cloth while draining gear.

3) Insert an INCH lb. torque wrench in pinion shaft torque adjuster. Position adapter and wrench on input shaft splines. Loosen yoke plug lock nut using Pinion Housing Yoke Lock Nut Wrench (T78P-3504-H). *See Fig. 1.* Loosen yoke plug with a 3/4" socket wrench.

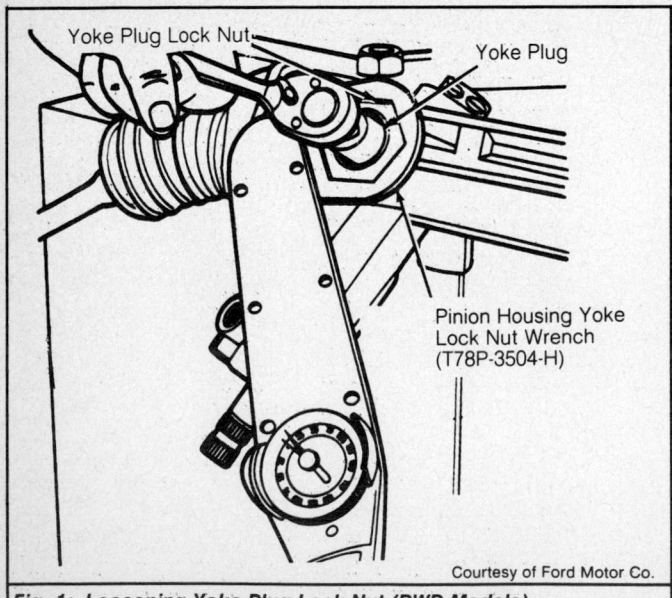

Yoke Plug Lock Nut

Yoke Plug

Pinion Housing Yoke Lock Nut Wrench (T78P-3504-H)

Courtesy of Ford Motor Co.

Fig. 1: Loosening Yoke Plug Lock Nut (RWD Models)

4) Clean yoke plug threads. With rack centered, tighten yoke plug to 45-50 INCH lbs. Loosen yoke plug approximately 1/8 turn, until torque is to specification. See INPUT SHAFT ROTATION TORQUE table.

INPUT SHAFT ROTATION TORQUE

Application	INCH Lbs. (N.m)
Standard Rack & Pinion	7-18 (.80-2.0)
Handling Rack & Pinion	7-24 (.80-2.7)

5) Position Pinion Housing Yoke Lock Nut Wrench (T78P-3504-H) on yoke plug lock nut. Hold yoke plug and tighten lock nut to 44-66 INCH lbs. (60-89 N.m). Ensure yoke plug does not move or preload will be incorrect. After tightening lock nut, recheck input shaft torque.

Sable & Taurus – 1) Clean exterior of rack housing. Remove yoke plug and clean yoke plug threads. With rack at center of travel, tighten yoke plug to 45-50 INCH lbs. (5.0-5.6 N.m). Install Yoke Plug Torque Gauge (T88P-3504-A). Mark location of zero degree mark on housing. Back off adjuster so 48 degree mark lines up with zero degree mark on housing. *See Fig. 2.*

2) Place Pinion Housing Yoke Lock Nut Wrench (T86P-3504-E) on yoke plug lock nut. Hold yoke plug and tighten lock nut to 40-50 ft. lbs. (54-68 N.m). Ensure yoke plug does not move during tightening or preload will be incorrect. After tightening lock nut, recheck input shaft torque.

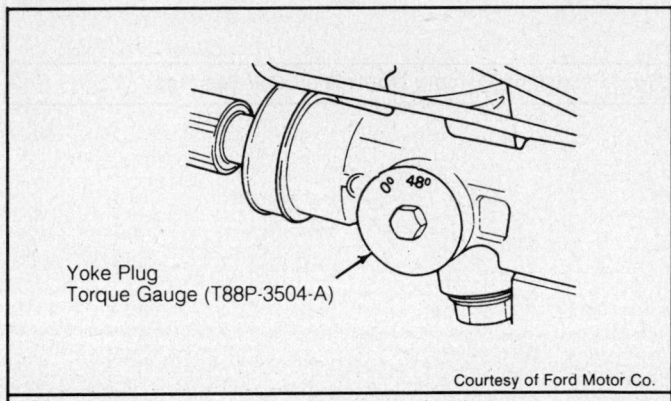

Yoke Plug Torque Gauge (T88P-3504-A)

Courtesy of Ford Motor Co.

Fig. 2: Sable & Taurus Rack Yoke Plug Clearance

Escort, Tempo & Topaz – 1) Clean exterior of rack housing. Mount steering gear in Rack Housing Holding Fixture (D87P-3504-B). Do not remove hydraulic lines unless necessary. If lines are removed, they must be replaced. Drain power steering fluid by rotating input shaft lock-to-lock twice using Input Shaft Torque Adapter (T81P-3504-R).

2) Position adapter and wrench on input shaft. Loosen yoke plug lock nut using Pinion Housing Yoke Lock Nut Wrench (T81P-3504-G). Loosen yoke plug with Yoke Plug Adapter (T87P-3504-G). *See Fig. 3.* With rack at center of travel, clean yoke threads and tighten yoke plug to 44-50 INCH lbs. (5.0-5.7 N.m).

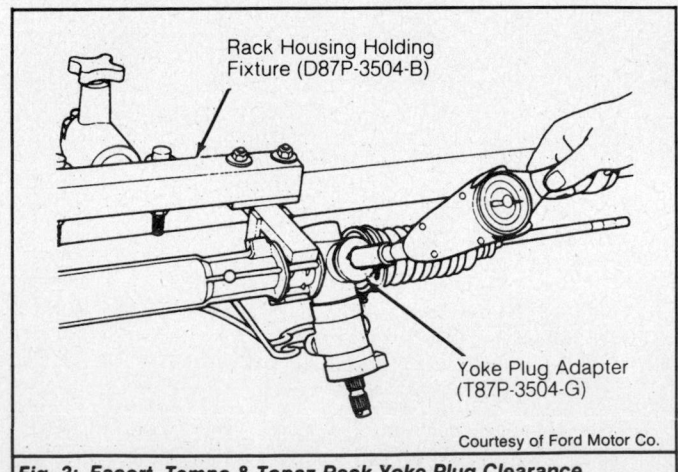

Rack Housing Holding Fixture (D87P-3504-B)

Yoke Plug Adapter (T87P-3504-G)

Courtesy of Ford Motor Co.

Fig. 3: Escort, Tempo & Topaz Rack Yoke Plug Clearance

1989 POWER STEERING GEARS
Ford Motor Co. Integral Rack & Pinion (Cont.)

13-53

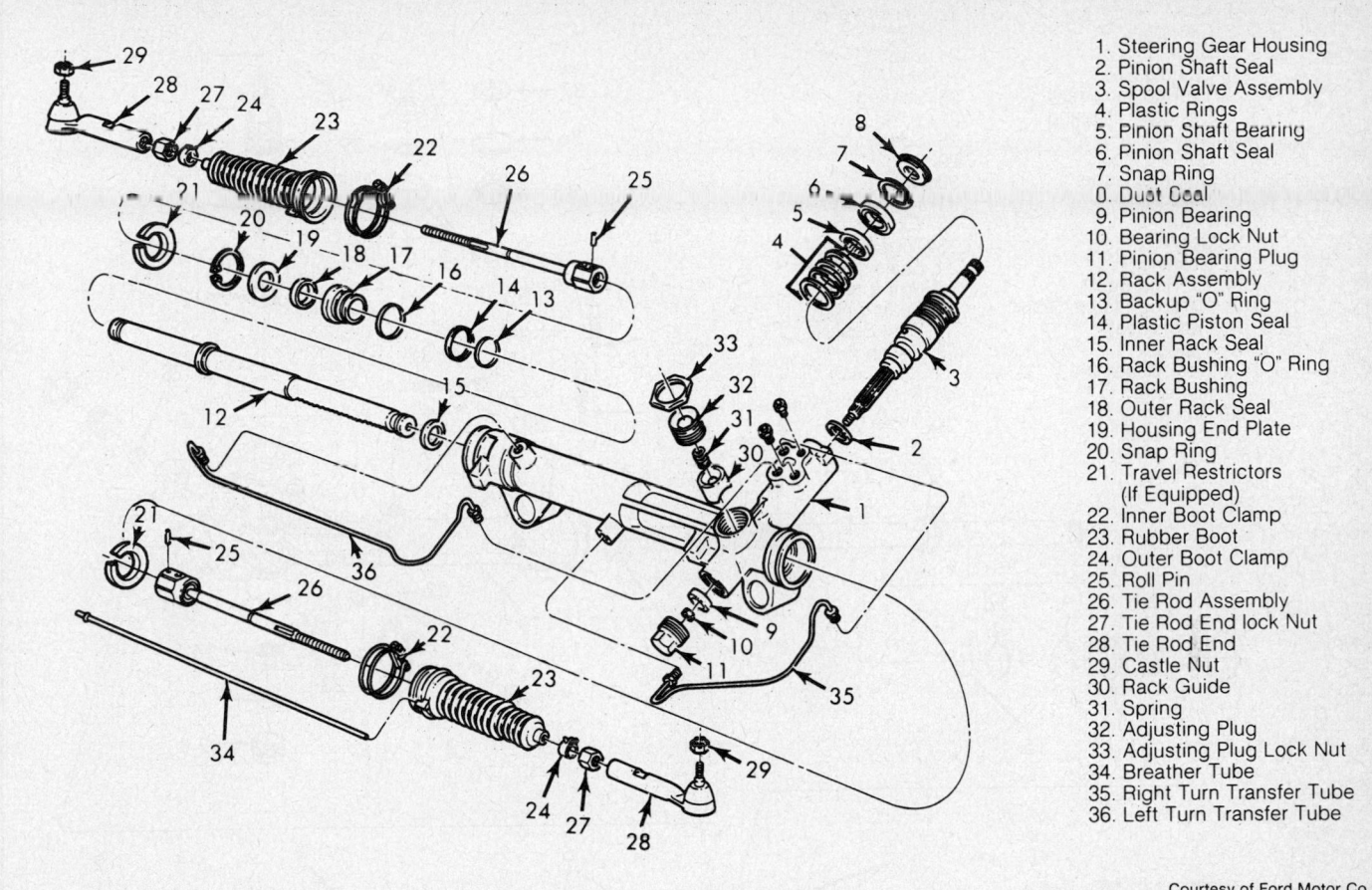

1. Steering Gear Housing
2. Pinion Shaft Seal
3. Spool Valve Assembly
4. Plastic Rings
5. Pinion Shaft Bearing
6. Pinion Shaft Seal
7. Snap Ring
8. Dust Seal
9. Pinion Bearing
10. Bearing Lock Nut
11. Pinion Bearing Plug
12. Rack Assembly
13. Backup "O" Ring
14. Plastic Piston Seal
15. Inner Rack Seal
16. Rack Bushing "O" Ring
17. Rack Bushing
18. Outer Rack Seal
19. Housing End Plate
20. Snap Ring
21. Travel Restrictors (If Equipped)
22. Inner Boot Clamp
23. Rubber Boot
24. Outer Boot Clamp
25. Roll Pin
26. Tie Rod Assembly
27. Tie Rod End lock Nut
28. Tie Rod End
29. Castle Nut
30. Rack Guide
31. Spring
32. Adjusting Plug
33. Adjusting Plug Lock Nut
34. Breather Tube
35. Right Turn Transfer Tube
36. Left Turn Transfer Tube

Courtesy of Ford Motor Co.

Fig. 4: Exploded View of RWD Steering Gear Assembly

3) Install Yoke Plug Adapter (T87P-3504-G), which has degree increments. Mark location of zero degree mark on housing. Back off adjuster so 48 degree mark lines up with zero degree mark on housing. Position Pinion Housing Yoke Lock Nut Wrench (T81P-3504-G) on yoke plug lock nut. While holding yoke plug, tighten lock nut to specification. Ensure yoke plug does not move or preload will be incorrect. After tightening lock nut, recheck input shaft torque.

REMOVAL & INSTALLATION

STEERING GEAR

Removal (Cougar & Thunderbird) – 1) Raise vehicle on hoist. Remove both front wheels. Remove cotter pins and castle nuts at outer tie rod ends. Separate tie rod end studs from spindles. Position a drain pan under vehicle. Disconnect and plug power steering return line hose. Disconnect power steering pressure line at intermediate fitting.

2) Remove steering shaft retaining bolt. Remove rack-to-subframe bolts and nuts. Lower rack as necessary to remove pressure line inlet tube. Remove and discard plastic seal on inlet tube. Cut tie strap securing pressure line to each tube. Remove steering rack from vehicle.

Installation – Install new seal on pressure line inlet tube. Install insulators from rear side of gear. Ensure insulators are fully seated. Install and position rack to front crossmember. Install pressure line inlet tube to rack. Align steering shaft so rack will seat on crossmember. To complete installation, reverse removal procedure.

Removal (Escort, Tempo 2WD & Topaz) – 1) Disconnect negative battery cable. Turn ignition switch to "RUN" position. Remove access panel from below steering column. Remove 4 screws from steering column boot at dash panel and slide boot up intermediate shaft.

2) Remove intermediate shaft bolt at gear input shaft. Loosen bolt at steering column shaft joint. Using a screwdriver, spread slots enough to loosen intermediate shaft at both ends. Intermediate shaft and gear input shaft cannot be separated at this time.

3) On Escort, remove air cleaner. On Escort with A/C, wire air conditioner liquid line above dash panel opening to provide clearance for gear input shaft removal and installation. Separate pressure and return lines at intermediate connections.

4) On Tempo and Topaz, separate pressure and return lines at steering gear and drain fluid. Remove pressure switch. Disconnect exhaust secondary tube at check valve. Disconnect exhaust system at intermediate connection. On Escort, disconnect exhaust system at exhaust manifold.

5) On all models, separate tie rod ends from steering knuckles. On manual transmission vehicles, mark and remove left tie rod end. On automatic transmission vehicles, disconnect speedometer cable, remove speed sensor and shift cable assembly. Turn steering wheel to full left stop.

6) On Escort, remove 2 screws holding heater water tube to shake brace below oil pan. Remove nut from lower of 2 bolts holding engine mount support bracket to transmission housing. Tap bolt out as far as possible.

7) On all models, remove gear mounting brackets and insulators. Put a cloth over both apron opening edges to protect bellows during gear removal. Separate gear from intermediate shaft.

8) Rotate gear forward and down to clear input shaft through dash panel opening. Ensure input shaft is in full left turn position. Move gear through right side apron opening until left tie rod clears left apron opening. Remove gear from vehicle, using care not to tear bellows.

Installation – 1) Rotate input shaft to full left turn stop. Position right load wheel to full left turn. Start right side of gear through

13-54

1989 POWER STEERING GEARS
Ford Motor Co. Integral Rack & Pinion (Cont.)

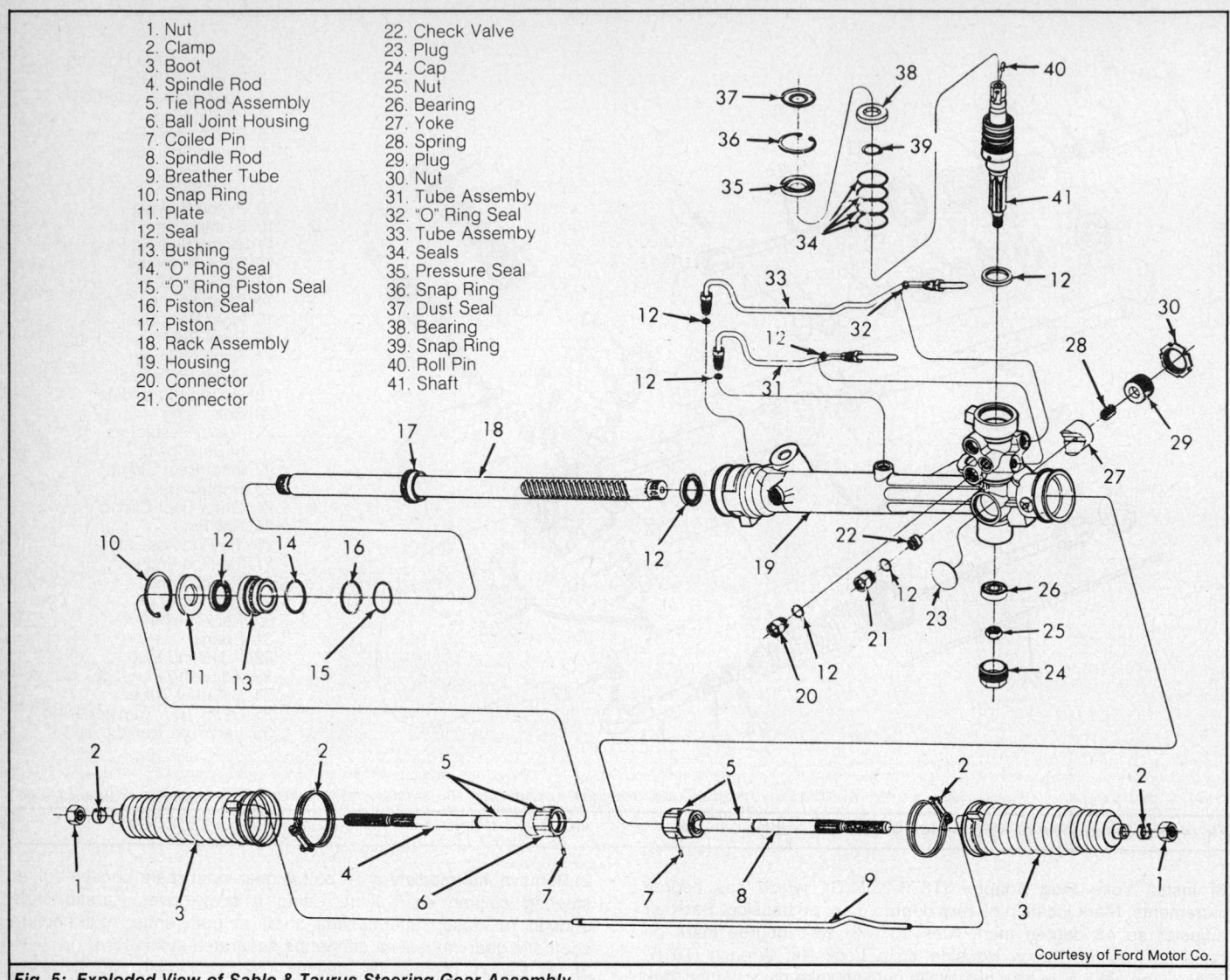

1. Nut
2. Clamp
3. Boot
4. Spindle Rod
5. Tie Rod Assembly
6. Ball Joint Housing
7. Coiled Pin
8. Spindle Rod
9. Breather Tube
10. Snap Ring
11. Plate
12. Seal
13. Bushing
14. "O" Ring Seal
15. "O" Ring Piston Seal
16. Piston Seal
17. Piston
18. Rack Assembly
19. Housing
20. Connector
21. Connector
22. Check Valve
23. Plug
24. Cap
25. Nut
26. Bearing
27. Yoke
28. Spring
29. Plug
30. Nut
31. Tube Assemby
32. "O" Ring Seal
33. Tube Assemby
34. Seals
35. Pressure Seal
36. Snap Ring
37. Dust Seal
38. Bearing
39. Snap Ring
40. Roll Pin
41. Shaft

Courtesy of Ford Motor Co.

Fig. 5: Exploded View of Sable & Taurus Steering Gear Assembly

opening in right apron. Install gear until left tie rod clears all components and can be raised upward to clear left apron opening. Raise gear and insert left side through apron opening. Guide power steering hoses into position at the same time.

2) Rotate gear so input shaft enters dash panel opening. With a helper guiding intermediate shaft from inside vehicle, insert input shaft into intermediate shaft coupling. Install intermediate shaft clamp bolts finger tight.

3) Install gear mounting insulators and brackets. Ensure flat in left mounting area is parallel to dash panel. Tighten left upper bracket bolt halfway. Tighten left lower bolt, left upper bolt and right bolts to specification. Attach tie rod ends to steering knuckles.

4) On Escort, install and tighten engine mount nut. Install heater water tube to shake brace. On automatic transmission vehicles, install transmission shift cable assembly, speedometer cable and vehicle speed sensor. Install exhaust system. Connect secondary air tube at check valve. Connect pressure and return lines at intermediate connections.

5) On Tempo and Topaz, connect pressure and return lines at steering gear. Using a crow's foot wrench, install pressure switch.

6) On Escort, install air cleaner. On all models, tighten coupling clamp bolt at gear input shaft. Tighten upper intermediate shaft clamp bolt. To complete installation, reverse removal procedure.

Removal (Tempo AWD) – 1) Disconnect negative battery cable. Position drain pan under vehicle. Remove right instrument panel sound insulator. Move front carpeting out of way. Loosen steering

gear input shaft-to-steering column shaft upper coupling. Disconnect steering gear input shaft-to-steering column shaft lower coupling.

2) Raise vehicle on a hoist. Remove right wheel. Disconnect catalytic converter air tube. Remove exhaust converter mounting bracket. Remove muffler, resonator and tailpipe assembly. Disconnect driveshaft, transaxle shift cable, speedometer cable and accessory feed wiring assemby. Remove pressure switch assembly.

3) Disconnect power steering pressure hose assembly, return line and front spindle connecting outer tie rod end. Remove steering gear mounting bracket. Remove steering gear through opening in right fender apron.

Installation – 1) Position steering gear assembly in vehicle. Connect power steering return line. Connect power steering pressure hose assembly. Install steering gear mounting bracket retaining bolts. Install pressure switch assembly. Connect accessory feed wiring assembly. Install speedometer cable assembly and transaxle shift cable.

2) Connect driveshaft assembly. Install muffler, resonator and tailpipe assembly. Install catalytic converter air tube. Install exhaust converter mounting bracket. To complete installation, reverse removal procedure.

Removal (Mark VII) – 1) Turn off air suspension switch located in luggage compartment. Disconnect battery ground cable. Turn ignition switch to "RUN" position. Raise and support vehicle. Position drain pan to catch fluid from steering gear.

1989 POWER STEERING GEARS
Ford Motor Co. Integral Rack & Pinion (Cont.)

13-55

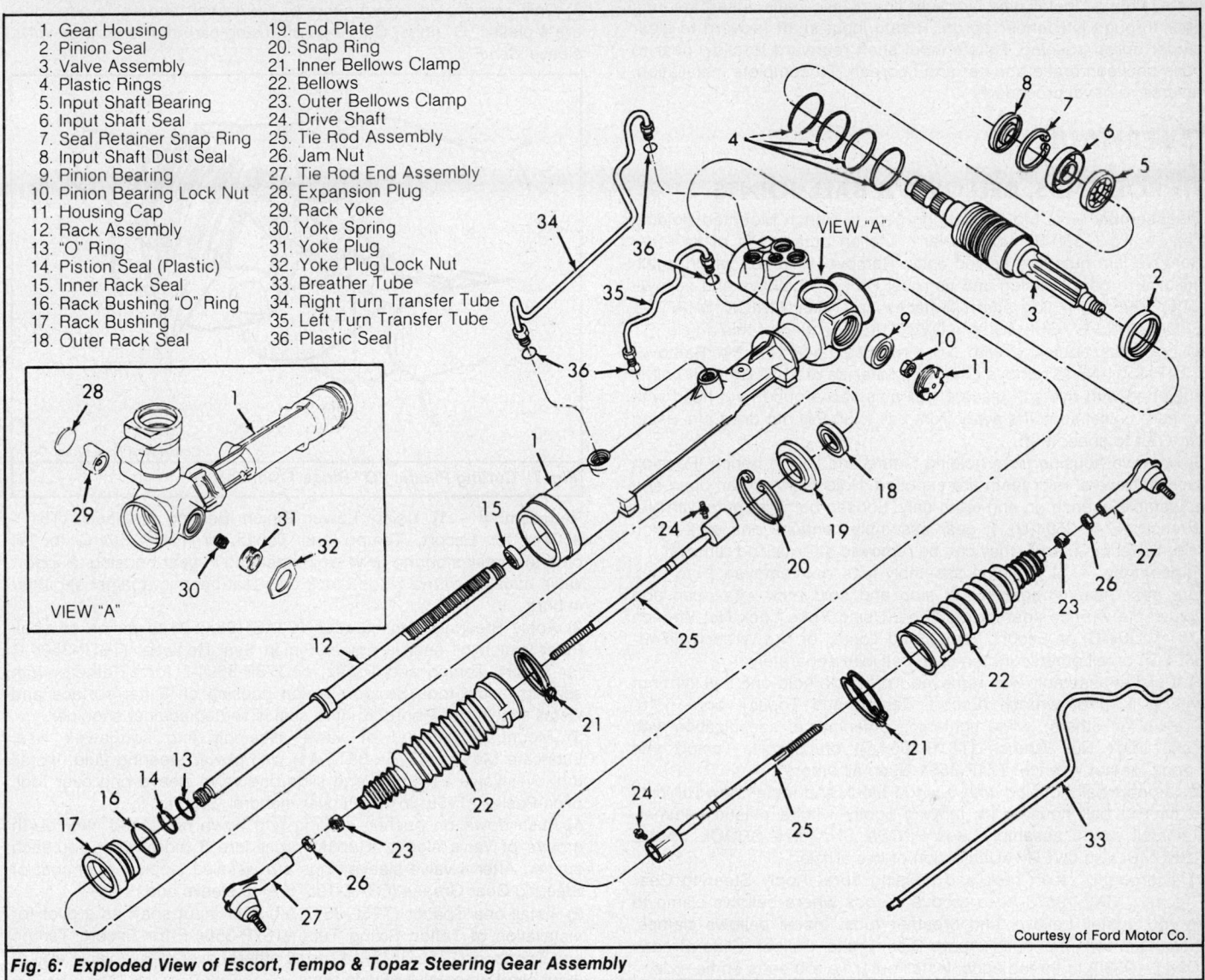

1. Gear Housing
2. Pinion Seal
3. Valve Assembly
4. Plastic Rings
5. Input Shaft Bearing
6. Input Shaft Seal
7. Seal Retainer Snap Ring
8. Input Shaft Dust Seal
9. Pinion Bearing
10. Pinion Bearing Lock Nut
11. Housing Cap
12. Rack Assembly
13. "O" Ring
14. Pistion Seal (Plastic)
15. Inner Rack Seal
16. Rack Bushing "O" Ring
17. Rack Bushing
18. Outer Rack Seal
19. End Plate
20. Snap Ring
21. Inner Bellows Clamp
22. Bellows
23. Outer Bellows Clamp
24. Drive Shaft
25. Tie Rod Assembly
26. Jam Nut
27. Tie Rod End Assembly
28. Expansion Plug
29. Rack Yoke
30. Yoke Spring
31. Yoke Plug
32. Yoke Plug Lock Nut
33. Breather Tube
34. Right Turn Transfer Tube
35. Left Turn Transfer Tube
36. Plastic Seal

VIEW "A"

Courtesy of Ford Motor Co.

Fig. 6: Exploded View of Escort, Tempo & Topaz Steering Gear Assembly

2) Remove flexible coupling-to-pinion shaft bolt. Remove cotter pins and castle nuts from tie rod ends. Using a tie rod end puller, separate tie rod ends from steering knuckles.

3) Remove steering gear-to-crossmember bolts and nuts. Position gear forward to remove grommets. Disconnect and plug hydraulic lines to prevent contamination. Remove steering gear from vehicle.

Installation – 1) Ensure rubber grommets are in position in gear housing. Position steering gear on crossmember. Loosely install mounting bolts. Install new plastic seals on hydraulic line fittings.

2) Install hydraulic lines. Insert pinion shaft into flexible coupling. Tighten mounting bolts and nuts to specification. Install tie rods to steering knuckles. Install nuts and cotter pins. Lower vehicle. Install flexible coupling-to-pinion shaft bolt. Turn ignition switch to "OFF" position.

3) Connect negative battery cable. Turn air suspension switch to "ON" position. Fill power steering pump reservoir. Check fluid level. Add fluid as required.

4) Start engine. Cycle steering wheel from lock to lock. Inspect seals and hoses for leaks at maximum pressure. Check and adjust wheel alignment as required. See WHEEL ALIGNMENT section.

Removal (Mustang) – 1) Disconnect negative battery cable. Turn ignition switch to "RUN" position. Raise vehicle and position drain pan. Remove one bolt retaining flexible coupling to input shaft. Remove 2 tie rod end retaining cotter pins and nuts. Separate studs from spindle arms.

2) Remove 2 nuts, insulator washers and bolts which retain steering gear to No. 2 crossmember. Remove front rubber insulators. Disconnect hydraulic lines and remove steering gear.

Installation – 1) Install new plastic seals on hydraulic line fittings. Install gear on mounting spikes. Install hydraulic lines. Install front rubber insulators. Ensure rubber insulators are pushed completely inside gear housing before installing mounting bolts.

2) Insert input shaft into flexible coupling. Install 2 mounting bolts, insulator washers and nuts. To complete installation, reverse removal procedure.

Removal (Sable & Taurus) – 1) Working from inside vehicle, remove nuts which retain steering shaft weather boot to dash panel. Remove 2 bolts retaining intermediate shaft to steering column shaft. Set weather boot aside. Remove pinch bolt at steering gear input shaft and remove intermediate shaft. Raise and support vehicle.

2) Remove left front wheel and heat shield. Cut strap which retains lines to gear. Remove rod ends from spindles. Position a drain pan under vehicle and remove hydraulic pressure and return lines from front of valve housing. Remove gear mounting bolt nut.

3) Push weather boot end into vehicle and lift gear out of mounting holes. Rotate gear so input shaft will pass between brake booster and floorpan. Using care, work steering gear out through left fender opening. Rotate input shaft so it clears left fender apron opening.

1989 POWER STEERING GEARS
Ford Motor Co. Integral Rack & Pinion (Cont.)

Installation – Install new hydraulic line plastic seals. Insert steering gear through left fender apron. Rotate input shaft forward to clear fender apron opening. Rotate input shaft rearward to allow gear to pass between brake booster and floorpan. To complete installation, reverse removal procedure.

OVERHAUL

TIE ROD ENDS, BELLOWS & BALL JOINTS

Disassembly – **1)** Mount steering gear in Bench Mounted Holding Fixture (T57L-500-B). Loosen jam nuts on outer ends of tie rods. Remove jam nuts and tie rod ends. Remove 4 clamps which retain bellows to gear housing and tie rods. Remove bellows and bellows tube. Remove pinion shaft (if necessary). See PINION SHAFT & SPOOL VALVE ASSEMBLY in OVERHAUL section of this article.

2) For units equipped with roll pins, use Lock Nut Pin Remover (D81P-3504-N), to remove pins from inner tie rod ball joints. If unit is equipped with rivets in place of roll pins, tap around rivet head with a sharp chisel so it lifts away from ball joint. Pry out drive pin, using care not to sheer it off.

3) Remove housing from holding fixture and lay on bench. Position rack so several rack teeth are exposed. Hold rack with an open end adjustable wrench on end teeth only. Loosen ball joint nuts with Nut Wrench (T74P-3504-U). If gear assembly contains one or 2 nylon rack travel restrictors, they can be removed after tie rod removal.

Reassembly – **1)** If pinion assembly was not removed from unit, turn gear near or against left stop and hold rack with open end adjustable wrench nearest rack end. Using Yoke Lock Nut Wrench (T81P-3504-G) on Escort, Tempo and Topaz, or Nut Wrench (T74P-3504-U) on all others, tighten each ball joint separately.

2) If pinion assembly was removed from rack, hold one ball joint nut with a 1 3/16" wrench (Escort, Tempo and Topaz), or 1 5/16" wrench (all others), while tightening other nut to specification with Yoke Lock Nut Wrench (T81P-3504-G) on Escort, Tempo and Topaz, or Nut Wrench (T74P-3504-U) on all others.

3) Support ball housing with a wood block and install new roll pins in tie rod ball housing by tapping lightly with a plastic hammer. Reinstall pinion assembly. See PINION SHAFT & SPOOL VALVE ASSEMBLY in OVERHAUL section of this article.

4) Thoroughly clean rack and housing bore. Apply Steering Gear Grease (C3AZ-19578-A) to groove in rods where bellows clamp to tie rod. Install bellows and breather tube. Install bellows clamps. Install tie rod jam nuts. Apply Disc Brake Caliper Slide Grease (D7AZ-19590) to tie rod ends. Install outer tie rod ends on tie rods.

PINION SHAFT & SPOOL VALVE ASSEMBLY

Disassembly – **1)** Clean input shaft valve housing, yoke lock nut and plug, and pinion bearing plug. Mount gear in holding fixture. Do not remove external pressure lines unless damaged. If lines are removed, new Teflon seals must be installed.

2) Relieve preload by loosening yoke plug lock nut and yoke plug. Remove pinion bearing plug. Install Pinion Shaft Torque Adjuster (T81P-3504-R on Escort, Tempo and Topaz or T74P-3504-R on all others) on input shaft. Hold input shaft. Using a socket, remove and discard pinion bearing lock nut. Ensure rack does not reach full travel when loosening or tighting lock nut.

3) Using a small, sharp chisel, pry input shaft dust seal out of valve housing. Ensure valve housing surface is not damaged. Remove retaining snap ring under dust seal. Attach Input Shaft and Valve Body Puller (T86P-3504-D and T81P-3504-T for Escort, Tempo and Topaz, or T78P-3504-B for all others) to input shaft. Turn nut to remove valve. Input shaft seal and bearing should come out with valve body.

4) Remove lower pinion shaft seal by inserting part of Lower Pinion Seal Remover (T78P-3504-E2 on RWD, T86P-3504-F on FWD) until it bottoms along with spacer collet.

5) Using 2 wrenches, hold large nut and turn small nut until expander fully tightens. Using Impact Slide Hammer (T50T-100-A), pull tool and seal from housing. Using Puller Attachment (T58L-101-B), remove pinion bearing from gear housing.

6) Only serviceable components of input shaft and valve assembly are 4 plastic "O" rings. Cut rings off, using care not to scratch valve sleeve. See Fig. 7.

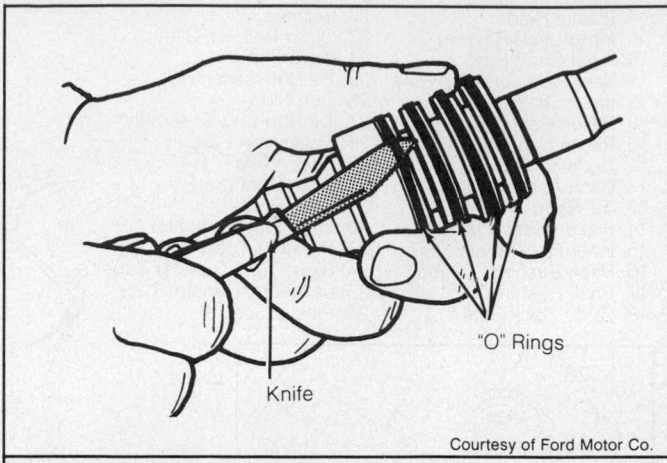

"O" Rings

Knife

Courtesy of Ford Motor Co.

Fig. 7: Cutting Plastic "O" Rings From Valve

Reassembly – **1)** Using Lower Pinion Bearing Replacer (T81P-3504-H for Escort, Tempo and Topaz, or T78P-3504-G for all others), install steering gear pinion bearing in gear housing. Support valve housing with a wood block and seat bearing against shoulder in bore.

2) Apply Steering Gear Grease (C3AZ-19578-A) to pinion oil seal. Place pinion oil seal in Lower Pinion Seal Replacer (T87P-3504-C for Escort, Tempo and Topaz, or T78P-3504-F for all others) with seal lip facing tool. Support pinion housing on a flat surface and install seal in valve bore. Ensure seal is seated against shoulder.

3) Mount pinion end of valve assembly into soft-jawed vise. Lubricate Mandrel (T75L-3517-A1) with power steering fluid. Install tool over valve assembly and slide one valve sleeve ring over tool. Slide Pusher (T75L-3517-A2) over mandrel. See Fig. 8.

4) Push down on pusher, forcing ring down ramp and into fourth groove of valve sleeve. Repeat procedure 3 more times for each spacer. After 4 valve sleeve rings are installed, apply a light coat of Steering Gear Grease (C3AZ-19578-A) to sleeve and rings.

5) Install one Spacer (T75L-3517-A3) over input shaft as a pilot for installation of Teflon Sizing Tube (T87P-3504-F for Escort, Tempo and Topaz, or T75L-3517-A4 for all others) over sleeve valve end of input shaft onto valve sleeve rings.

6) Ensure rings are not bent over as tube is slid over them. Remove sizing tool and check condition of rings. Ensure rings turn freely in grooves.

7) Insert Valve Body Inserter (T78P-3504-C) into valve housing. On Escort, Tempo and Topaz, and Sable and Taurus, ensure flats on input shaft are positioned as shown in illustration. See Fig. 9.

8) On all other models, line up flat spot on input shaft 180 degrees from yoke plug yoke center and install valve assembly into bore. Ensure flat spot points straight down when gear is installed in vehicle with gear in straight-ahead position. If necessary, rotate input shaft side-to-side to mesh pinion to rack teeth. Push valve assembly in by hand until it is seated.

9) On all models, turn input shaft with Pinion Shaft Torque Adjuster (T81P-3504-R on Escort, Tempo and Topaz, T74P-3504-K on Sable and Taurus, or T74P-3504-R on all others). Ensure pinion is centered by counting number of turns from center to each stop.

10) Number of turns should be approximately 1 1/2 turns for variable ratio gear or 1 1/4 turns for constant ratio. If turns are unequal, pull valve assembly out far enough to free pinion teeth. Rotate input shaft 45 degrees (Sable and Taurus), or 60 degrees (one tooth, all others) in direction that required fewer turns. Insert valve assembly and ensure it is centered. Repeat procedure as necessary.

11) Install nut on pinion end of valve assembly (if required). Hold input shaft with torque adjuster. Ensure rack is away from its stops.

1989 POWER STEERING GEARS
Ford Motor Co. Integral Rack & Pinion (Cont.)

13-57

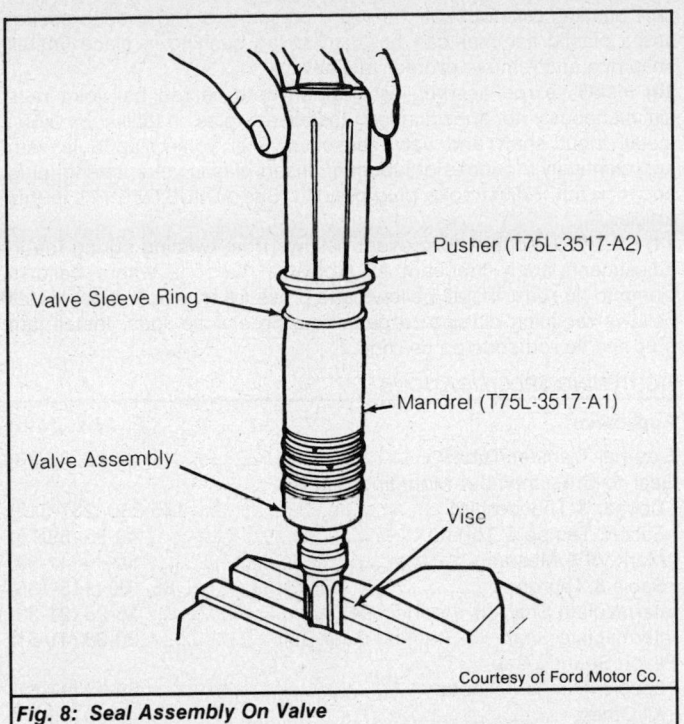

Fig. 8: *Seal Assembly On Valve*

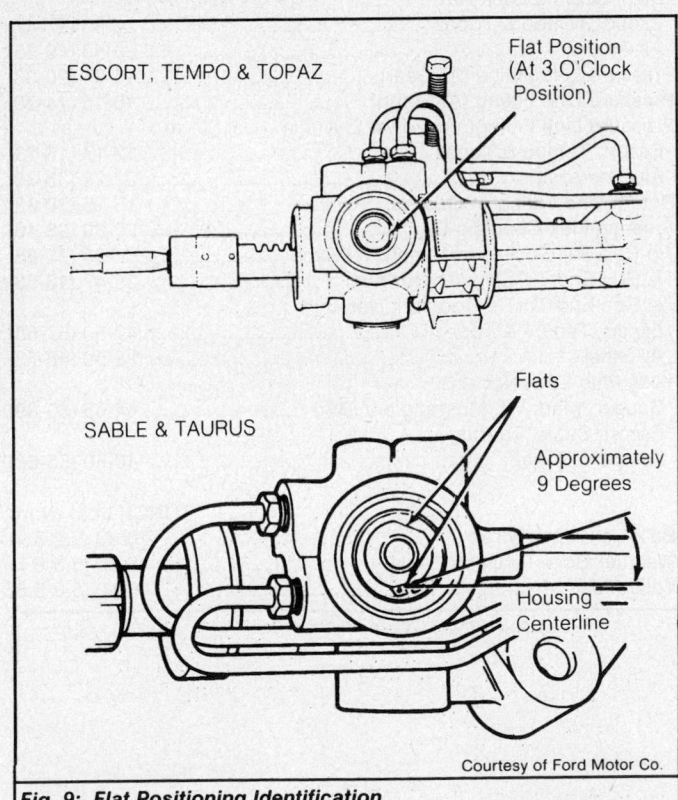

Fig. 9: *Flat Positioning Identification*

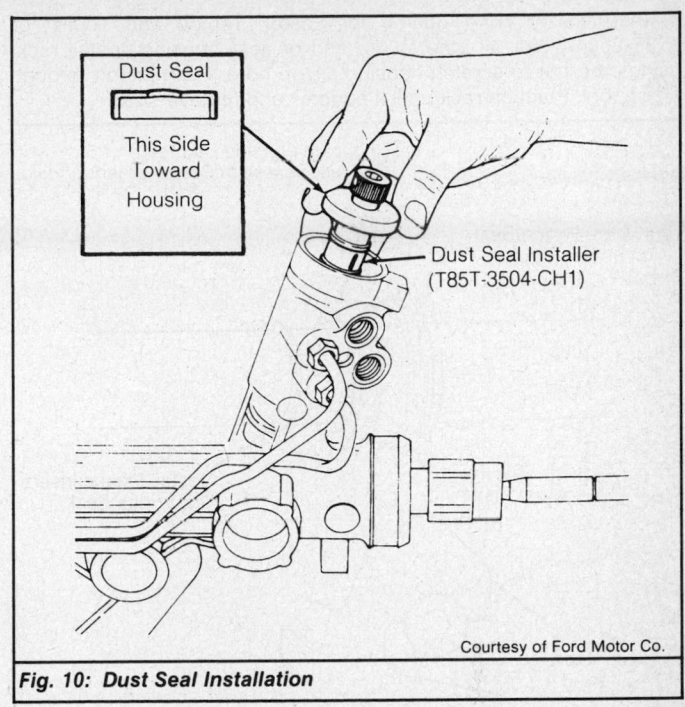

Fig. 10: *Dust Seal Installation*

Tighten nut to specification. Install bearing in valve bore. Seat bearing with Upper Pinion Bearing Seal Replacer (T78P-3504-D).

12) Apply a thin coat of Steering Gear Grease (C3AZ-19578-A) to input shaft seal. Install seal with lip toward valve. Seat seal with bearing/seal replacer. Install snap ring in valve bore. Coat input shaft in dust seal contact area with Multi-Purpose Grease (D0AZ-19584-AA). Drive input shaft dust seal into position, using Dust Seal Installer (T85T-3504-CH1). See Fig. 10. Install steering gear housing pinion bearing cap and tighten to specification.

13) Fill yoke housing with approximately 2 ounces of gear lubricant. Install plastic yoke, ensuring it seats against rack with finger pressure. If not, check for burrs in yoke housing.

14) Install yoke thrust spring, yoke plug and yoke plug lock nut. Before tightening lock nut, set rack yoke plug preload. See ADJUSTMENTS in this article.

GEAR HOUSING, RACK YOKE PLUG & RACK ASSEMBLY

Disassembly – 1) Remove yoke plug lock nut. Remove yoke spring, yoke, input shaft and valve assembly from gear housing. Remove tie rod and socket assemblies from both ends of rack. Working from right side of gear, push rack in far enough to remove snap ring.

2) Slowly pull rack out of right side of housing until rack piston contacts aluminum rack bushing. Do not hammer on rack until bushing is out of housing. Remove rack from housing.

3) Remove internal high-pressure rack oil seal by inserting Rack Oil Seal Remover (T87P-3504-A on Escort, Tempo and Topaz, or T78P-3504-J on all others) into housing until it bottoms. Turn expander on tool with a wrench until expander fully tightens. Using a slide hammer threaded into expander end, remove tool with oil seal from housing. Discard seal.

4) Remove plastic "O" ring and rubber "O" ring from rack piston. Insert rack bushing (seal end first) into Rack Bushing Holder (T78P-3504-L). Place holder and bushing in vise. Using oil seal remover and slide hammer, remove seal. Remove rubber "O" ring from bushing.

Reassembly – 1) To ease reassembly, use paint and mark center tooth space on rack where it will be visible through valve bore. Install rubber "O" ring in rack piston groove. Slide Teflon ring replacer on rack until it seats on piston. Slide "O" ring over tool into piston groove past rubber "O" ring.

2) Remove plastic insert from rack seal. Save plastic insert for installation. Install Rack Seal Protector (T87P-3504-H for Escort, Tempo and Topaz, or T85L-3504-B for all others) over rack teeth. Lubricate rack seal protector and rack with power steering fluid. Install seal with lip toward piston. Remove rack seal protector.

3) Install plastic insert in rack seal. See Fig. 11. Pack rack teeth with steering gear lubricant. Apply a light coat of lubricant to back of rack teeth. Lubricate outside diameter of piston cient and rack seal with power steering fluid.

13-58

1989 POWER STEERING GEARS
Ford Motor Co. Integral Rack & Pinion (Cont.)

4) Install Sizer (T87P-3504-F for Escort, Tempo and Topaz, or T78P-3504-M for all others) into end of gear housing. Install rack, using care not to scratch housing piston bore. Push piston through sizing tool. Push on rack until it bottoms and remove sizer.

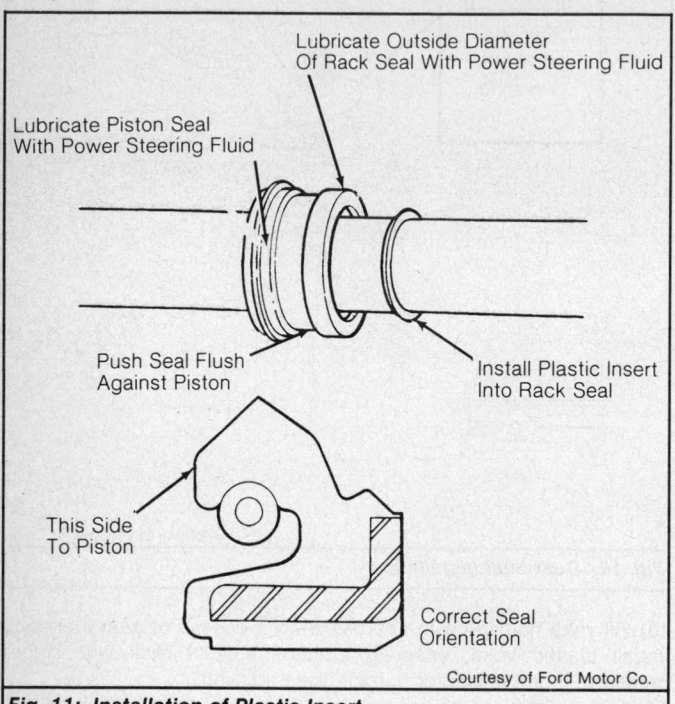

Lubricate Outside Diameter Of Rack Seal With Power Steering Fluid

Lubricate Piston Seal With Power Steering Fluid

Push Seal Flush Against Piston

Install Plastic Insert Into Rack Seal

This Side To Piston

Correct Seal Orientation

Courtesy of Ford Motor Co.

Fig. 11: Installation of Plastic Insert

5) Seat rack seal by driving end of rack with a drift and plastic hammer. Position rack so it is approximately centered in housing. On Escort, Tempo and Topaz, install rubber "O" ring on aluminum rack bushing. Apply power steering fluid to outer rack oil seal. Install oil seal in rack bushing using Rack Oil Seal Installer (T81P-3504-C). Lip spring must face inside of bushing.

6) On all models, thread Rack Seal Protection Sleeve (T81P-3504-N on Escort, Tempo and Topaz, T74P-3504-J on all others) over threads on right side of rack. Apply power steering fluid to protective sleeve. On all models except Escort, Tempo and Topaz, install rubber "O" ring to aluminum rack bushing. Apply gear lubricant to outer rack oil seal.

7) Using Outer Rack Seal Replacer (T74P-3504-F), install high-pressure oil seal in rack bushing. Ensure lip spring faces inside of bushing. Lubricate short protective sleeve on rack end and rubber "O" rings on rack bushing with gear lubricant.

8) On all models, install bushing, seal facing out, on rack. Install bushing and seal over protective sleeve and into housing bore. Position end plate against rack bushing.

9) Using Teflon Ring Sizer (T78P-3504-M), apply hand pressure to end plate and rack bushing until bushing seats in gear housing. If rack bushing will not seat with hand pressure, a 1 1/8" deep socket and a plastic hammer can be used to tap bushing in place. Install snap ring and remove protective sleeve.

10) Install tie rod assemblies. Tighten both tie rod ball joint nuts simultaneously to specification. Install roll pins in ball joint nuts. Install input shaft and valve assembly. Fill yoke plug hole with approximately 2 ounces of lubricant. Insert plastic yoke, spring, plug and lock nut. Adjust yoke plug preload. See ADJUSTMENTS in this article.

11) On RWD models, to prevent bellows from twisting during toe-in adjustment, apply lubricant to groove in tie rods where bellows clamp to tie rods. Install bellows and pressure equalizer tube. Install bellows retaining clamps to gear housing and tie rods. Install jam nuts and tie rod ends on tie rods.

TIGHTENING SPECIFICATIONS

Application	Ft. Lbs. (N.m)
External Transfer Tubes	22-28 (30-38)
Gear-to-Crossmember Mounting Bolt Nut	
Cougar & Thunderbird	175-230 (237-312)
Escort, Tempo & Topaz	40-55 (55-75)
Mark VII & Mustang	30-40 (41-54)
Sable & Taurus	85-100 (115-135)
Intermediate Shaft-to-Steering Column	15-25 (21-33)
Intermediate Shaft-To-Steering Gear Bolt	30-38 (41-51)
Pinion Bearing Cap	
Escort, Tempo & Topaz	35-45 (47-61)
All Others	40-60 (55-81)
Pinion Bearing Lock Nut	
Escort, Tempo & Topaz	20-35 (27-47)
All Others	30-40 (40-55)
Pressure Line Fitting (At Gear)	15-25 (20-33)
Pressure Line Fitting (At Pump)	10-15 (14-20)
Pressure Line Fittings At Power Cylinder	
Escort, Tempo & Topaz	12-17 (16-23)
All Others	22-28 (30-38)
Return Line Fitting At Gear	15-25 (20-33)
Steering Flex Coupling Bolt	20-30 (28-40)
Tie Rod Ball Socket Assembly-To-Rack	55-65 (75-88)
Tie Rod End-To-Spindle Arm Nut	35-47 (48-63)
Tie Rod End-To-Tie Rod Jam Nut	
Escort, Tempo & Topaz	42-50 (57-68)
All Others	35-50 (48-68)
Yoke Plug Lock Nut	
Cougar, Mark VII, Mustang & T-Bird	44-66 (60-89)
Escort, Sable, Taurus	
Tempo & Topaz	40-50 (55-68)

	INCH Lbs. (N.m)
Bellows Clamp Screw	20-30 (2.2-3.4)
Weather Boot-To-Dash Panel	48-60 (5.5-6.7)
Yoke Plug	45-50 (5.0-5.6)

DESCRIPTION

The Electronic Variable Orifice (EVO) system is designed to regulate power steering effort according to vehicle speed and steering wheel rotation rate. The system provides full assist at low vehicle speed for light parking effort and minimum assist at high vehicle speed for improved handling and road feel. Full power steering assist returns during evasive manuevers.

During periods of system malfunction, the system will provide full power steering assist at all times. Diagnostic codes are accessible through the service diagnostic connector, inside upper glove compartment. The EVO system consists of speed and steering sensors, a control module, an actuator and interconnecting wiring.

OPERATION

The steering wheel rotation sensor and vehicle speed sensor feed information to the EVO control module, which electronically regulates the EVO actuator valve assembly on the power steering pump.

The steering wheel rotation sensor is an optical or photo-cell sensor. The sensor mounts on the steering column and establishes the rate of steering wheel rotation. The steering wheel rotation sensor, located at lower end of the steering column, may be removed with the column in or out of the vehicle. The sensor and sensor ring are removed separately.

The vehicle speed sensor is mounted on the transmission and sends electrical signal to the control module. The current produced by the sensor increases and decreases linearly, according to vehicle speed. The current is constant at 80 MPH or faster.

The EVO actuator assembly generates a differential pressure, according to flow and current input, to control spool valve in C11 power steering pump. The electronic variable orifice is inside the actuator valve.

The EVO control module contains a microprocessor which analyzes input from vehicle speed and steering wheel rotation sensors.

On Thunderbird LX and Cougar LS with anti-lock brakes, the control module is located in the module tray in the trunk, behind driver's side of the back seat. On Cougar LS without anti-lock brakes, the module is mounted on a bracket below left rear speaker opening, immediately below package tray. On Thunderbird Super Coupe and Cougar XR7, the module is integrated within the Automatic Ride Control System.

NOTE: For Thunderbird Super Coupe and Cougar XR-7 system testing, see FORD MOTOR CO. AUTOMATIC RIDE CONTROL article in ELECTRONIC SUSPENSION section.

PUMP FLOW & PRESSURE TESTS

See appropriate table in POWER STEERING GENERAL SERVICING article in STEERING section.

REMOVAL & INSTALLATION

EVO CONTROL MODULE

Removal & Installation (Thunderbird LX & Cougar LS With Anti-Lock Brakes) – Turn ignition off. Locate module packaging tray in trunk, behind driver's side of the back seat. *See Fig. 1.* Disengage push-pin on left side of module tray. Swing tray down. Release lock tabs and remove control module. Disconnect wiring harness connector from module. To install, reverse removal procedure.

Removal & Installation (Cougar LS W/O Anti-Lock Brakes) – Turn ignition off. Locate module mounted with a bracket under left rear speaker opening, immediately below package tray. Disconnect wiring harness connector from module. Remove 2 plastic rivets on sides of module. Pull down rivets and head assembly from module retaining bracket. Remove control module. To install, reverse removal procedure.

EVO ACTUATOR ASSEMBLY

Removal – Remove windshield washer reservoir for access. Disconnect EVO wiring harness connector from actuator. Disconnect return hose from power steering pump. Disconnect pressure hose from actuator. Remove EVO actuator from pump. *See Fig. 2.* The flow control valve and spring may come out when the actuator is removed.

NOTE: If actuator is cocked, it may stick in valve cover. DO NOT force valve forward. If forced, valve may shear metal and carry metal chips into valve bore.

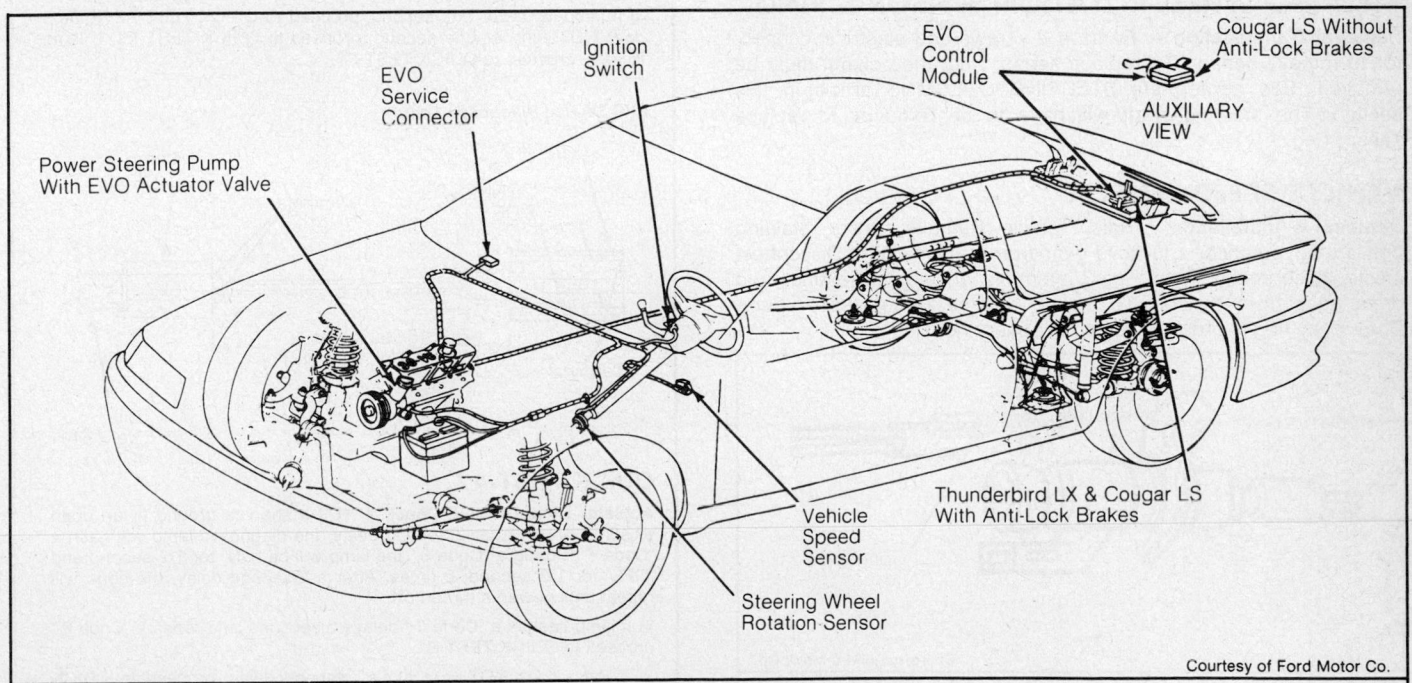

Fig. 1: Exploded View of Electronic Variable Orifice (EVO) Power Steering System

Courtesy of Ford Motor Co.

13-60

1989 ELECTRONIC POWER STEERING GEAR
Ford Motor Co. EVO – Cougar & Thunderbird (Cont.)

Installation – Install flow control valve, spring and EVO actuator into pump reservoir and valve cover. Tighten to specification. See TIGHTENING SPECIFICATION in this article. Connect power steering hoses. Connect EVO wiring. Install windshield washer reservoir.

Start-Up Procedure – 1) Disconnect coil wire. Fill reservoir with power steering fluid. Crank engine and fill reservoir until level remains constant. Raise vehicle. Turn steering wheel from lock-to-lock while cranking engine.

2) Check and add fluid, if necessary. Start engine and allow it to idle for several minutes. Rotate wheel from lock-to-lock. Turn engine off. Check fluid. If air is still present, use Vacuum Tester (021-00014) to purge system.

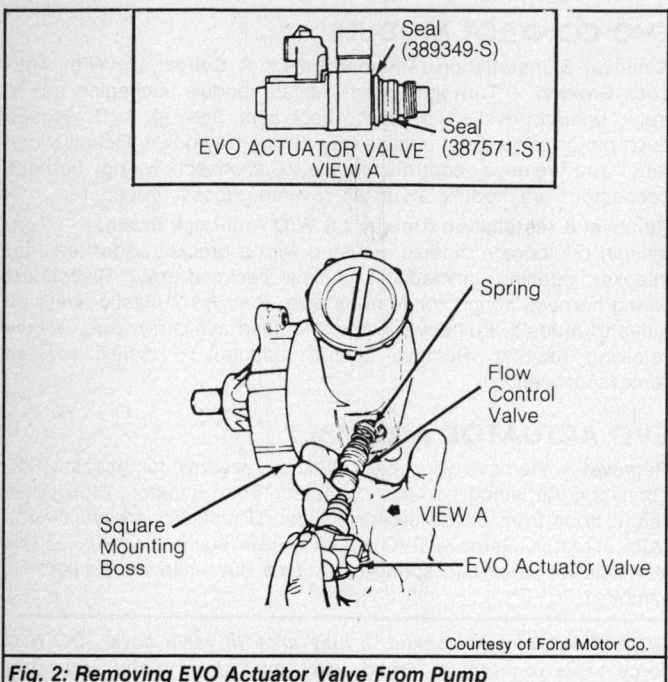

Fig. 2: Removing EVO Actuator Valve From Pump

STEERING WHEEL ROTATION SENSOR & RING

Removal & Installation – Remove 2 screws and electrical connector to remove sensor. To replace sensor ring, the column must be removed. See appropriate STEERING COLUMNS article in this section. The steering shaft will have to be removed to replace sensor ring.

VEHICLE SPEED SENSOR

Removal & Installation – Raise vehicle. Remove sensor retaining bolt. Remove sensor and drive gear from transmission. Disconnect electrical connector. *See Fig. 3.* Remove drive gear retainer and drive gear from sensor. To install, reverse removal procedure. Ensure "O" ring is properly seated in sensor housing.

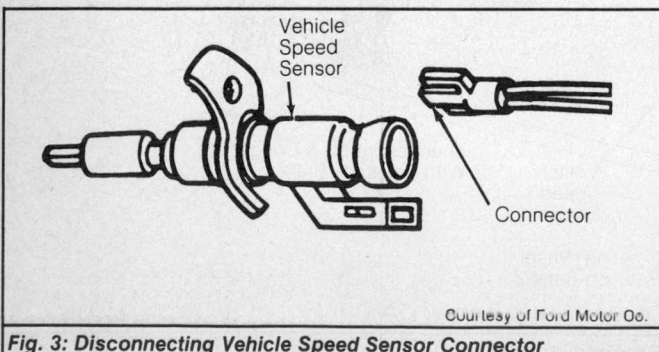

Fig. 3: Disconnecting Vehicle Speed Sensor Connector

TESTING

TESTING PROCEDURE

A series of QUICK TESTS and a wiring diagram are provided for diagnostic purposes. A fabricated tool will be needed to access EVO trouble codes. *See EVO Service Diagnostic Lamp Illustration.* After acquiring parts listed below, assemble according to figure.
The following parts will be needed to make the fabricated tool:
For Connector Side
- A 16-gauge wire, 18" long
- Connector (E9SB-14489-EA)
- 2 terminals (E8VB-14474-BA)

For Lamp Side
- A lamp socket (E2DB-13728-A)
- 2 terminals (D4AB-14490-D, E or F)
- No. 194 or No. 161 bulb.

An analog volt-ohmmeter and a digital volt-ohmmeter are also required for testing.

TIGHTENING SPECIFICATIONS

Application	Ft. Lbs. (N.m)
EVO Actuator Fitting	25-34 (34-46)

QUICK TESTS

QUICK TEST A0

Check Connections – Verify EVO actuator valve (on power steering pump) and EVO control module harness connectors (in trunk) are firmly seated. If connectors are NOT firmly seated, make proper connection and proceed to QUICK TEST A1. If connectors were seated properly, proceed to QUICK TEST A1.

QUICK TEST A1

Control Module Check – 1) Turn ignition off. Locate service diagnostic connector in upper glove compartment. Connect fabricated EVO service diagnostic lamp to service connector. See TESTING in this article for tool fabrication. See EVO SERVICE DIAGNOSTIC LAMP figure. Start engine.

2) When the engine starts, the control module should light the diagnostic lamp for one second. This indicates control module and bulb are functional.

3) If lamp lights for one second, proceed to QUICK TEST A2. If lamp does NOT light for one second, proceed to QUICK TEST E1. If lamp flickers, proceed to QUICK TEST E1.

EVO Service Diagnostic Lamp

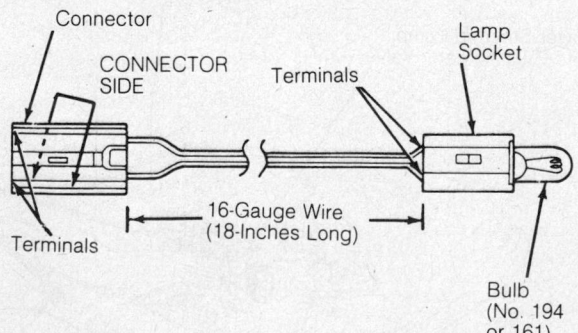

QUICK TEST A2

Actuator Output Circuit Check – 1) If a short to ground or an open exists in circuit, after 2 second delay, the diagnostic lamp will flash a "Code 6." During a "Code 6," the lamp will be "ON" for 1/2 second and "OFF" for 1/2 second, 6 times. After a 2-second delay, the code will repeat until power is turned off.

2) If lamp flashes a "Code 6," delays 2 seconds, and repeats "Code 6," proceed to QUICK TEST B1.

3) If lamp does NOT light after 2 second delay, proceed to QUICK TEST A3. Actuator output circuit is okay.

1989 ELECTRONIC POWER STEERING GEAR
Ford Motor Co. EVO — Cougar & Thunderbird (Cont.)

13-61

QUICK TEST A3

Steering Wheel Sensor Check – Start engine and idle. Rotate steering wheel from lock-to-lock. If diagnostic lamp lights for 3 seconds, proceed to QUICK TEST A4. If diagnostic lamp does NOT light, proceed to QUICK TEST C1.

QUICK TEST A4

Vehicle Speed Sensor Check – Raise back wheels off ground on jack stands. Start vehicle. Hold steering wheel straight. Increase speed to greater than 15 MPH. If lamp lights at greater than 15 MPH, proceed to QUICK TEST A4.1. If lamp does not light at greater than 15 MPH, proceed to QUICK TEST D1.

QUICK TEST A4.1

Vehicle Speed Sensor Check (Cont.) – Lower speed to less than 10 MPH. If diagnostic lamp turns off at less than 10 MPH, speed sensor electrical circuit is working properly. Proceed to QUICK TEST A5. If lamp does NOT turn off at less than 10 MPH, proceed to QUICK TEST D1.

QUICK TEST A5

Service Power Steering – Check power steering pump pressure and flow. Replace as required. Testing requires Power Steering System Analyzer (014-00207). For specifications, see POWER STEERING GENERAL SERVICING article in this section.

QUICK TEST B1

"Code 6" Activated During Actuator Check – Turn ignition off. Verify EVO actuator valve harness connector is firmly seated. If connector is NOT firmly seated, make proper connection and proceed to QUICK TEST A1. If connector is firmly seated, proceed to QUICK TEST B2.

QUICK TEST B2

Actuator Valve Resistance – Turn ignition off. Locate control module in the module packaging tray in the trunk. Measure resistance between pin No. 13 and pin No. 14 of the EVO control module 14-pin harness connector. See EVO CONTROL MODULE CONNECTOR PIN LOCATIONS figure. If resistance is greater than 1000 ohms, the circuit is open. Proceed to QUICK TEST B3. If resistance is more than 18 ohms, proceed to QUICK TEST B4. If resistance is less than 18 ohms, proceed to QUICK TEST B3.

EVO Control Module Connector Pin Locations

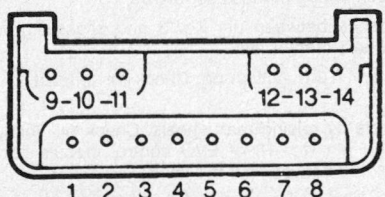

QUICK TEST B3

Wiring Continuity Check – Turn ignition off. Disconnect EVO actuator valve harness connector. Check the continuity of circuit No. 330 (Yellow/Light Green wire) and circuit No. 353 (Light Blue wire) from EVO actuator valve harness connector to EVO control module pin No. 14. If continuity exists, proceed to QUICK TEST B4. If continuity does NOT exist, service wires and proceed to QUICK TEST A0.

QUICK TEST B4

EVO Actuator Valve Resistance – Disconnect EVO actuator valve harness connector at pump. Measure resistance between 2 actuator valve connector pins. If resistance is between 5-20 ohms, proceed to QUICK TEST B5. If resistance is NOT within specification, replace EVO actuator valve.

QUICK TEST B5

Check Wiring Harness Shorts – Turn ignition off. Leave EVO actuator valve harness disconnected. Disconnect 14-pin connector from EVO control module. For component location, see EVO CONTROL MODULE under REMOVAL & INSTALLATION in this article. Proceed to QUICK TEST B5.1.

QUICK TEST B5.1

Check Wiring Harness Shorts (Cont.) – Check resistance between pin No. 5 (Black wire) and pin No. 13 (Yellow/Light Green wire) of the EVO harness connector. If resistance is greater than 1000 ohms, proceed to QUICK TEST B5.2. If resistance is less than 10 ohms, service wiring harness and proceed to QUICK TEST B5.2. If resistance is between 10-1000 ohms, proceed to QUICK TEST B6.

QUICK TEST B5.2

Check Wiring Harness Shorts (Cont.) – Measure resistance between pin No. 5 (ground) and pin No. 14 (Light Blue wire) of EVO harness connector. If resistance is less than 10 ohms, service EVO harness and proceed to QUICK TEST B6. If resistance is greater than 10 ohms, proceed to QUICK TEST B6.

QUICK TEST B6

Check Harness Short To B+ – Turn ignition to "Run" position. Disconnect EVO actuator valve harness connector at power steering pump. Measure voltage across pin No. 13 (Yellow/Light Green wire) and pin No. 5 (Black wire). Measure voltage across pin No. 14 (Light Blue wire) and pin No. 5. If voltage is more than 5 volts, a short is indicated. Service wires as necessary and proceed to QUICK TEST A0. If voltage is less than 5 volts, proceed to QUICK TEST B7.

QUICK TEST B7

Short Across Circuits No. 330 & No. 353 – Turn ignition off. Disconnect EVO actuator valve harness at power steering pump. Disconnect EVO control module 14-pin harness connector. Measure resistance across pin No. 13 (Yellow/Light Green wire) and pin No. 14 (Light Blue wire) of EVO control module connector. If resistance is less than 10 ohms, a short is indicated. Service wires and proceed to QUICK TEST A0. If resistance is more than 1000 ohms, replace EVO control module.

QUICK TEST C1

Steering Wheel Rotation Sensor Connector Check – Verify steering wheel rotation sensor connector, at base of steering column, is properly seated. If connector is properly seated, proceed to QUICK TEST C2. If connector is NOT properly seated, make proper connection and proceed to QUICK TEST A0.

QUICK TEST C2

Steering Wheel Rotation Sensor Check – 1) Turn ignition off. Disconnect EVO control module 14-pin harness connector. Examine wiring harness for damage. Verify the following wires correspond to these pin numbers:

- Red/Yellow wire (circuit No. 834) in pin No. 1
- Red/White wire (circuit No. 835) in pin No. 6
- Yellow/Black wire (circuit No. 837) in pin No. 12

2) If damaged or crossed wires are found, service wires and proceed to QUICK TEST A0. If wires are okay, proceed to QUICK TEST C3.

QUICK TEST C3

Steering Wheel Rotation Sensor Signal Check – 1) Use a jumper wire to connect pin No. 12 (Yellow/Black wire) and pin No. 5 (Black wire) of the 14-pin EVO connector. Start engine. Set analog ohmmeter to 1K/ohm scale. While rotating the steering wheel slowly, measure resistance between pin No. 1 (Red/Yellow wire) and pin No. 5 (Black wire). Measure resistance between pin No. 6 (Red/White wire) and pin No. 5.

NOTE: The resistance values will vary between meters. The needle on all meters should swing from a lower to higher resistance and back, approximately every 9 degrees of steering wheel rotation.

2) If meter needle swings for both circuits, the steering wheel rotation sensor is functional. Replace EVO control module and re-test system. If meter does NOT swing for both circuits, proceed to QUICK TEST C4. Disconnect jumper wire before proceeding.

13-62

1989 ELECTRONIC POWER STEERING GEAR
Ford Motor Co. EVO – Cougar & Thunderbird (Cont.)

QUICK TEST C4

Steering Wheel Rotation Sensor Wire Check – Turn ignition off. Disconnect steering wheel rotation sensor connector at lower steering column. Inspect sensor wires for damage. Test continuity of Red/Yellow wire (circuit No. 834), Red/White wire (circuit No. 835) and Yellow/Black wire (circuit No. 837) between steering sensor and EVO control module harness. If wires are damaged or crossed, service wires as necessary. If no continuity exists, service wires as necessary and proceed to QUICK TEST A0. If no problems found, proceed to QUICK TEST C5.

QUICK TEST C5

Check Shorts Across Circuits No. 834 and No. 835 – 1) Turn ignition off. Disconnect steering wheel rotation sensor. Disconnect EVO control module 14-pin connecter. Measure resistance between following pins in EVO harness:

- Pin No. 1 and pin No. 6
- Pin No. 1 and pin No. 12
- Pin No. 6 and pin No. 12

2) If resistance is more than 1000 ohms, proceed to QUICK TEST C6. If resistance is less than 10 ohms, service wires as necessary and proceed to QUICK TEST A0.

QUICK TEST C6

Testing Steering Wheel Rotation Sensor Power – Use a jumper wire to connect pin No. 12 and pin No. 5 of the 14-pin EVO harness connector. Turn ignition switch to "Run" position. Measure voltage between Purple/Orange wire and Yellow/Black wire of steering wheel rotation sensor connector. If 12 volts is present, proceed to QUICK TEST C7. If NO voltage is present, service Purple/Orange wire (circuit No. 298) between steering wheel rotation sensor and pin No. 7 of EVO control module. After servicing circuit, proceed to QUICK TEST A0.

QUICK TEST C7

Testing Steering Wheel Rotation Sensor Power Circuit – Remove jumper wire used in QUICK TEST C6. Measure voltage between Yellow/Black wire (circuit No. 837) and Purple/Orange wire (circuit No. 298) at steering wheel rotation sensor connector. If 12 volts is present, replace steering wheel rotation sensor. If NO voltage is present, replace EVO control module.

QUICK TEST D1

Vehicle Speed Sensor Connector Check – Verify vehicle speed sensor connector is properly seated. If connector is properly seated, proceed to QUICK TEST D2. If connector is NOT properly seated, make proper connection and proceed to QUICK TEST A0.

QUICK TEST D2

Speed Sensor Check – 1) Turn ignition off. Disconnect EVO control module 14-pin harness connector. Examine wiring harness for damage. Verify the following wires correspond to these pin numbers:

- Dark Green/White wire (circuit No. 150) in pin No. 9
- Black/White wire (circuit No. 359) in pin No. 8

2) If damaged or crossed wires are found, service wires and proceed to QUICK TEST A0. If wires are okay, proceed to QUICK TEST D3.

QUICK TEST D3

Testing Speed Sensor Ground Circuit – Test continuity of speed sensor ground circuit (No. 359). Check continuity from pin No. 8 to pin No. 5 of 14-pin EVO harness connector. If continuity is present, proceed to QUICK TEST D4. If circuit is open, service wire or ground eyelet, as necessary, and proceed to QUICK TEST A0.

QUICK TEST D4

Testing Speed Sensor – Raise vehicle on a lift. Start engine. Verify speedometer operation. If speedometer works properly, replace EVO control module. If speedometer reads zero at all times, proceed to QUICK TEST D4.1

QUICK TEST D4.1

Check Speed Control – Either road test or raise rear wheels to check operation of vehicle speed control. If vehicle does NOT have speed control, proceed to QUICK TEST D4.4. If speed control is inoperative, proceed to QUICK TEST D4.3 If speed control is okay, proceed to QUICK TEST D4.2.

QUICK TEST D4.2

Check Wiring – Check for loose wiring connections in engine compartment and at instrument cluster. If wiring connections are loose, repair as necessary. If wiring is okay, proceed to QUICK TEST D4.4.

QUICK TEST D4.3

Verify Speed Signal – Connect an AC voltmeter between 2 ouput wires of speed sensor, mounted on transmission. Raise rear wheels to check operation of vehicle speed control. If voltage is between 1.3-6.1 volts, proceed to QUICK TEST D4.4. If there is NO voltage output, replace speed sensor.

QUICK TEST D4.4

Check Speedometer Fuse – If fuse is blown, replace fuse and check speedometer operation. If fuse is okay, proceed to QUICK TEST D4.5.

Instrument Cluster Harness Connector

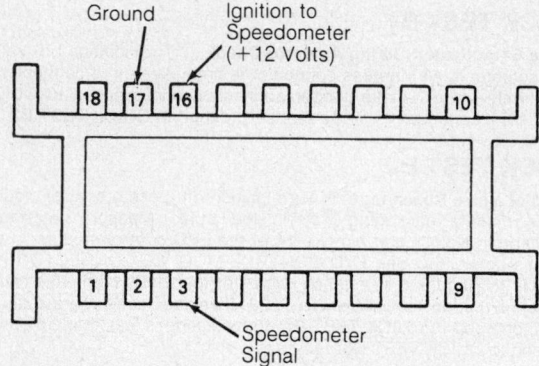

QUICK TEST D4.5

Instrument Cluster Resistance & Voltage – 1) Disconnect battery. Remove instrument cluster. See INSTRUMENT CLUSTER HARNESS CONNECTOR figure. Perform resistance and voltage checks on instrument cluster wiring harness as follows:

- Check resistance between pin No. 3 and chassis ground. Resistance should be 1 ohm or less.
- Connect battery. Turn ignition on. Check for at least 12 volts at pin No. 17.
- Operate vehicle by raising rear wheels. Check AC voltage between pin No. 3 and pin No. 16 of EVO control module connector. AC voltage should be between 1.3-6.1 volts.

2) If resistance and voltage are NOT within specifications, identify wiring harness problem and repair as necessary. If resistance and voltage are within specification, proceed to QUICK TEST D4.6.

QUICK TEST D4.6

Cluster Circuit Check – Check for loose/missing screws or clips to speedometer terminals on back of cluster. Check for damaged printed circuit boards. If there are loose retainers or damaged terminals, service as required. If retainers and terminals are okay, replace speedometer.

QUICK TEST E1

Diagnostic Lamp Check – Check lamp in EVO diagnostic tester. Check lamp connection within tool. If lamp is bad, replace lamp and proceed to QUICK TEST A1. If lamp is okay, but did NOT light during QUICK TEST A1, proceed to QUICK TEST F1. If lamp is okay and light flickered during QUICK TEST A1, proceed to QUICK TEST E2.

1989 ELECTRONIC POWER STEERING GEAR
Ford Motor Co. EVO – Cougar & Thunderbird (Cont.)

13-63

QUICK TEST E2

Control Module Retest – Turn ignition off. Connect EVO service diagnostic lamp to connector in upper glove compartment. Start engine. If lamp lights for 1 second, proceed to QUICK TEST A2. If lamp does NOT light, proceed to QUICK TEST F1. If lamp flickers, replace EVO control module.

QUICK TEST F1

EVO Control Module Check – Turn ignition off. Ensure 14-pin connector is properly connected to EVO module. If connector is proper, proceed to QUICK TEST F2. If connection is NOT proper, secure connection and proceed to QUICK TEST A1.

QUICK TEST F2

Control Module Power Feed Check – **1)** Turn ignition off. Disconnect EVO control module 14-pin connector. Turn ignition to "Run" position. Using a digital volt-ohmmeter measure voltage from pin No. 7 (ignition-run only, (Purple/Orange wire) and pin No. 5 (ground, Black wire) at 14-pin connector.

2) If 12 volts are present, replace EVO control module. If no voltage is present, repair short to ground or open in Purple/Orange wire (circuit No. 298). Return to QUICK TEST A0.

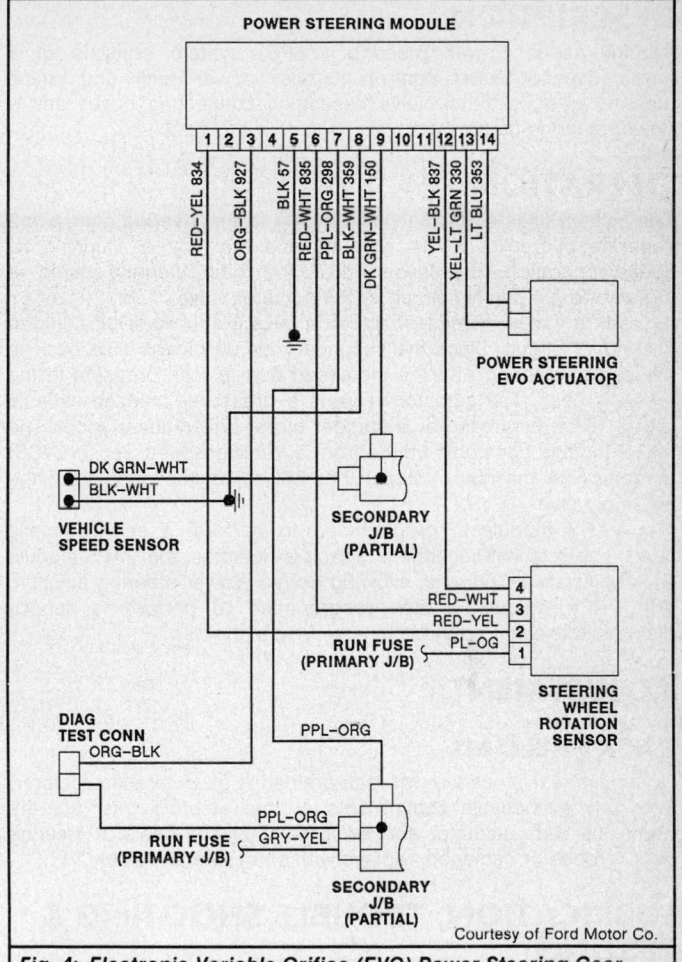

Fig. 4: Electronic Variable Orifice (EVO) Power Steering Gear Wiring Diagram

DESCRIPTION

Variable-Assist Power Steering (VAPS) system consists of a microprocessor-based control module, power rack and pinion steering gear, actuator valve assembly, connecting hoses and a power steering pump

OPERATION

The system uses a modified rotary valve in the steering gear with 2 separate hydraulic circuits (primary and secondary). During low-speed operation, pressurized fluid from the steering pump is directed to the primary circuit by the actuator valve.

As vehicle speed increases, actuator valve gradually diverts fluid to secondary circuit. Since the secondary circuit diverts fluid back to the pump, steering effort is increased due to less pressure in the steering gear. The actuator valve is a pressure-balanced variable orifice valve, controlled by a stepper motor-driven linear spool. The VAPS module computes inputs from a Vehicle Speed Sensor (VSS) to determine the output signal that will adjust the opening of the actuator valve.

The VAPS module is programmed to perform a self-diagnostic check every 16 milliseconds. If a fault is detected, the VAPS module will deactivate its outputs, allowing normal power steering function. The VAPS module is also programmed to perform a service diagnostic check if activated by a service technician.

ADJUSTMENTS

RACK PRELOAD

No adjustment procedure for rack preload is given by manufacturer. The only serviceable components on the steering gear are the boots, tie rods, actuator and actuator bolts and seals. If steering gear is loose or damaged, replace with short rack assembly.

LUBRICATION, TROUBLE SHOOTING & TESTING

If steering effort is excessive at low speeds or if steering effort is low at all speeds, VAPS system is malfunctioning. For electronic variable-assist related testing procedures refer to VAPS TESTING in this article.

For all non-electronic variable-assist related lubrication, trouble shooting or testing procedures, see POWER STEERING GENERAL SERVICING and TROUBLE SHOOTING articles in this section.

VAPS TESTING

Testing can be done with a Digital Volt/Ohmmeter (DVOM) and inductive dwell meter. The diagnostic connector is located in the engine compartment near the brake fluid reservoir and brake booster.

VAPS Module Test – 1) Turn ignition switch to "OFF" position. Connect DVOM positive lead to circuit No. 606. Connect DVOM negative lead to vehicle ground. *See Fig. 1.* Position DVOM so it can be observed from inside vehicle. Start vehicle and let idle. Observe reading on DVOM.

2) DVOM reading should be between 11-14 volts. If voltage reading is correct, proceed to step **4)**. If voltage reading is incorrect, check VAPS fuse located in fuse panel below left side of instrument panel.

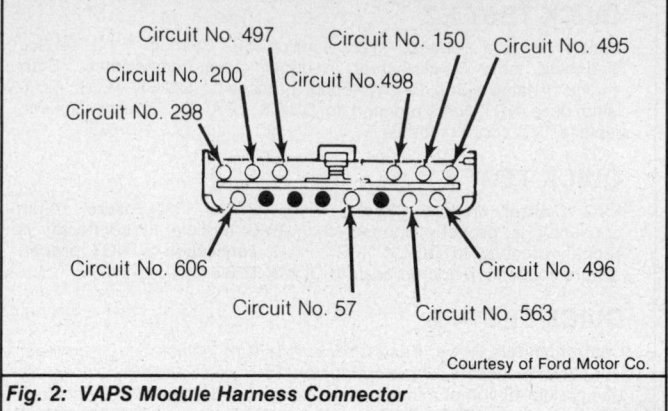

Courtesy of Ford Motor Co.

Fig. 2: VAPS Module Harness Connector

3) If fuse is good, proceed to VAPS HARNESS & CONNECTOR TEST NO. 3. If fuse is bad, replace fuse. Repeat steps **1)** and **2)**.

4) Turn engine off. Connect an analog voltmeter as in step **1)**. Using a jumper wire, jump circuit No. 200 to ground. Start engine and let idle. Rotate steering wheel for approximately 90 seconds while noting any changes in steering effort.

5) Continue rotating steering wheel. After 90 seconds, steering effort should change and voltmeter will show a sweep pattern 4 times between battery voltage and zero volts.

6) If steering effort changes and there are 4 sweeps from battery voltage to zero volts, VAPS module is functioning properly. Proceed to VEHICLE TEST DRIVE.

7) If steering effort changes, but there are no sweeps from battery voltage to zero volts, or if there is no change in steering effort, but there are 6 sweeps from battery voltage to zero volts, proceed to ACTUATOR ELECTRICAL TEST NO. 2.

8) If there is no change in steering effort, but there are 4 sweeps from battery voltage to zero volts, proceed to ACTUATOR ELECTRICAL TEST NO. 1.

Vehicle Test Drive – 1) Ensure VAPS system is connected. Drive vehicle up to 55 MPH. Note whether or not steering effort changes and if speedometer functions properly.

2) If steering effort increases as speed increases, decreases as speed decreases, and if speedometer functions properly, system is functioning properly.

3) If there is no change in steering effort, or if speedometer is not functioning properly, check speedometer and replace as necessary. See appropriate SWITCHES & INSTRUEMNT PANELS article in ACCESSORIES & EQUIPMENT section.

4) If there was no change in steering effort, but speedometer was functioning properly, proceed to SPEED SENSOR CIRCUIT TEST.

5) If steering effort is unequal for both right turns and left turns, replace steering gear. See STEERING GEAR REMOVAL & INSTALLATION in this article.

Speed Sensor Circuit Test – 1) Disconnect VAPS connector from module. Connect DVOM across circuits No. 150 and 563. *See Fig. 2.* Measure resistance.

2) If resistance is between 150-225 ohms, speed sensor is functioning properly. Replace VAPS module. If resistance is less than 150 ohms, or greater than 225 ohms, repair wiring harness.

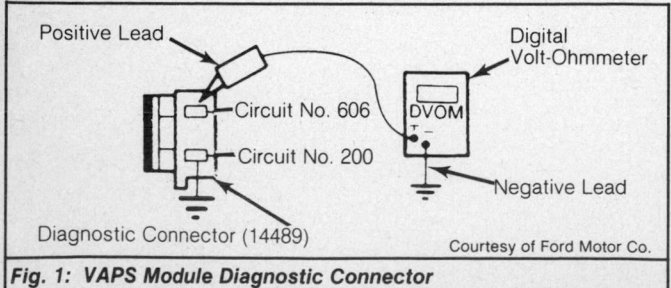

Courtesy of Ford Motor Co.

Fig. 1: VAPS Module Diagnostic Connector

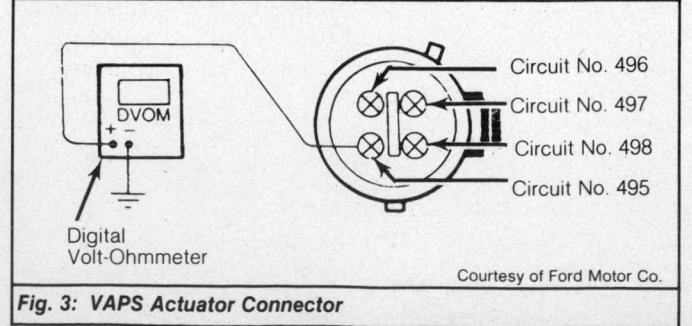

Courtesy of Ford Motor Co.

Fig. 3: VAPS Actuator Connector

Actuator Electrical Test No. 1 – 1) Turn ignition off. Disconnect VAPS connector from module. Connect DVOM leads to circuits No. 495 and 496 and then to circuits No. 497 and 498 on actuator side of connector. Note resistance values.

2) If resistance is between 43 and 70 ohms, proceed to HARNESS VOLTAGE AT ACTUATOR CONNECTOR TEST. If resistance is less than 43 ohms or greater than 70 ohms, Disconnect actuator connector from harness connector. Measure resistance between circuits No. 495 and 496, and circuits No. 497 and 498. If resistance is less than 43 or greater than 70 ohms, replace acutator.

3) If resistance is between 43 and 70 ohms, disconnect module connector from module. Disconnect actuator connector from actuator. Using a DVOM, check continuity of circuits No. 495, 496, 497 and 498 from module connector to actuator connector.

4) If all circuits are okay, go to ACTUATOR MECHANICAL TEST. If any or all circuits fail continuity check, repair harness and repeat VAPS MODULE TEST.

Harness Voltage At Actuator Connector Test – 1) Turn ignition switch to "OFF" position. Ensure VAPS connector is connected to VAPS module. Disconnect actuator connector from VAPS harness connector. Turn ignition switch to "RUN" position.

2) Wait 5 seconds. On the harness side of connector, measure voltage between circuit No. 495 and vehicle ground. Repeat procedure for circuit No. 496. One of these 2 circuits should be greater than 10 volts and the other less than 2 volts. Repeat steps for circuits No. 497 and 498.

3) If all voltage readings are correct, proceed to ACTUATOR MECHANICAL TEST. If not, replace VAPS module and repeat VAPS MODULE TEST.

Actuator Mechanical Test – 1) Turn ignition off. Remove actuator. See ACTUATOR REMOVAL & INSTALLATION in this article. Reconnect actuator connector to VAPS harness connector.

2) Attach positive lead of DVOM to diagnostic connector circuit No. 606. Using a jumper wire, ground circuit No. 200. Connect negative lead to vehicle ground. Turn ignition switch to "ON" position.

3) The actuator will perform a 90 second effort change sequence diagnostic check. If actuator is functioning properly, valve will move through its 2 travel limits. This can be observed by watching the spring move.

4) If spring moves, actuator is functioning properly. Replace steering gear. See STEERING GEAR REMOVAL & INSTALLATION in this article. Repeat VAPS MODULE TEST.

5) If spring does not move, actuator is malfunctioning, replace actuator. See ACTUATOR REMOVAL & INSTALLATION in this article. Repeat VAPS MODULE TEST.

VAPS Harness & Connector Test No. 1 – 1) Turn ignition switch to "OFF" position. Connect positive lead of DVOM to VAPS module harness connector ground circuit No. 57. Connect DVOM negative lead to vehicle ground. *See Fig. 2.* Measure resistance.

2) If resistance is between 0-15 ohms, connect negative lead of DVOM to circuit No. 57 and positive lead to circuit No. 298. Note resistance. Leave negative lead on circuit No. 57. Move positive lead to all remaining circuits while noting resistance. Refer to VAPS MODULE HARNESS CONNECTOR RESISTANCE VALUES (IGNITION OFF) table for correct resistance values.

3) If values are within specification, proceed to VAPS HARNESS & CONNECTOR TEST NO. 2. If values are not within specification, repair harness. Repeat test.

VAPS MODULE HARNESS CONNECTOR RESISTANCE VALUES (IGNITION OFF)

Circuit No.	Function	Ohms
298	Power	3.6
200	Diagnostic	Open
497	Actuator	Open
498	Actuator	Open
150	Speed Sensor	195
495	Actuator	Open
606	Diagnostic	Open
563	Speed Sensor	.6
496	Actuator	Open

VAPS Harness & Connector Test No. 2 – 1) Turn ignition switch to "ON" position. Connect DVOM negative lead to circuit No. 57. *See Fig. 2.* Using the negative lead, measure voltage between circuit No. 57 and other circuits. Note voltage readings.

2) Refer to VAPS MODULE HARNESS CONNECTOR VOLTAGE VALUES (IGNITION ON) table for correct voltage values. If voltage readings are within specification, replace module. Repeat VAPS MODULE TEST. If values are not within specification, repair harness. Repeat test.

VAPS MODULE HARNESS CONNECTOR VOLTAGE VALUES (IGNITION ON)

Circuit No.	Function	Volts
298	Power	12
200	Diagnostic	Less Than .1
497	Actuator	Less Than .1
498	Actuator	Less Than .1
150	Speed Sensor	
495	Actuator	Less Than .1
606	Diagnostic	Less Than .1
57	Ground	Less Than .1
563	Speed Sensor	
496	Actuator	Less Than .1

Actuator Electrical Test No. 2 – 1) Turn ignition switch to "OFF" position. Disconnect actuator connector from harness connector. *See Fig. 3.* Measure resistance between circuits No. 495 and 496, and between circuits No. 497 and 498 on harness side of connector.

2) If resistance is 43-70 ohms, replace VAPS module and repeat VAPS MODULE TEST. If resistance is less than 43 or greater than 70 ohms, repair harness and repeat VAPS MODULE TEST.

VAPS Harness & Connector Test No. 3 – Turn ignition off. Disconnect VAPS connector from module. Connect positive lead of DVOM to circuit No. 57 and negative lead to ground. Measure resistance. If resistance is between 0-15 ohms, go to VAPS HARNESS & CONNECTOR TEST NO. 4. If resistance is greater than 15 ohms, service harness and repeat test.

VAPS Harness & Connector Test No. 4 – 1) Connect positive lead of DVOM to circuit No. 298 and negative lead to circuit No. 57. Turn ignition switch to "ON" position. Measure voltage, then turn ignition off.

2) If 12 volts is present, check continuity of circuit No. 606 from diagnositc connector to module connector. If circuit No. 606 is okay, replace module and go to VAPS MODULE TEST. If circuit No. 606 is not okay, repair circuit and go to VAPS MODULE TEST.

REMOVAL & INSTALLATION
ACTUATOR

Removal – Remove air inlet duct. Disconnect VAPS electrical connector from actuator. Disconnect pressure switch connector. Remove 2 actuator-to-steering gear attaching bolts. Lift actuator from steering gear.

Installation – Ensure 2 seals between steering gear and actuator are in position. Align actuator on steering gear. Install and tighten 2 actuator-to-steering gear bolts to specification. Connect pressure switch and VAPS electrical connectors. Install air inlet duct.

STEERING GEAR

Removal – 1) Remove primary steering column boot retainers. Remove intermediate shaft retaining bolts. Remove intermediate shaft. See appropriate STEERING COLUMNS article in STEERING section.

2) Remove secondary steering column boot from inside passenger compartment. Raise vehicle on a twin post hoist and remove front wheels. Support vehicle with 2 jack stands, under rear edge of engine sub-frame, so sub-frame can be lowered.

3) Remove tie rod end cotter pins and castle nuts. Using Tie Rod Remover (TOOL-3290-D), separate tie rod ends from steering knuckles. Loosen tie rod end lock nuts. Mark tie rod end lock nut position for reassembly reference.

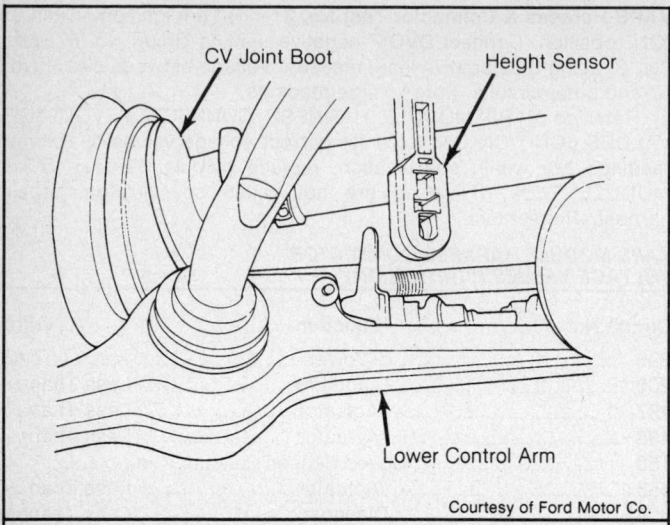

Fig. 4: *Location of Height Sensor*

4) Remove tie rod ends and lock nuts from tie rods. Remove steering gear-to-sub-frame retaining nuts. Remove both height sensors. *See Fig. 4.*

5) Remove rear sub-frame-to-body attaching bolts. Remove exhaust pipe-to-catalytic converter retaining bolts. *See Fig. 5.*

6) Lower stands to allow approximately 4" clearance between sub-frame and body. Remove heat shield retaining band. Fold heat shield down out of way. Disconnect VAPS electrical connector. *See Fig. 6.*

7) Rotate steering gear to clear bolts in sub-frame. Pull steering gear left to allow hydraulic line removal. Position drain pan under vehicle.

8) Remove hydraulic lines from steering gear. Remove left side sway bar link. *See Fig. 7.* Carefully remove steering gear through left wheel opening.

Installation – 1) Install manufacturer specified "O" rings on hydraulic line fittings. Install steering gear retaining bolts in steering gear. Insert steering gear through left wheel opening.

2) Install hydraulic lines to steering gear. *See Fig. 8.* Connect VAPS electrical connector. Position steering gear in sub-frame. Install tie rod end lock nuts and tie rod ends.

3) Install retaining band on heat shield. Attach tie rod ends on steering knuckles. Install and tighten NEW castle nut to specification. Tighten castle nut further to align cotter pin slot. Install NEW cotter pins. Attach left side sway bar link.

4) Raise stands until sub-frame contacts body. Install sub-frame attaching bolts. Install and tighten steering gear-to-sub-frame retaining nuts to specification.

5) Install catalytic converter. Attach height sensors. Install wheels. Remove jack stands and lower vehicle. Fill and bleed power steering system.

6) Install secondary steering column boot on steering gear from inside passenger compartment. Install primary steering column boot.

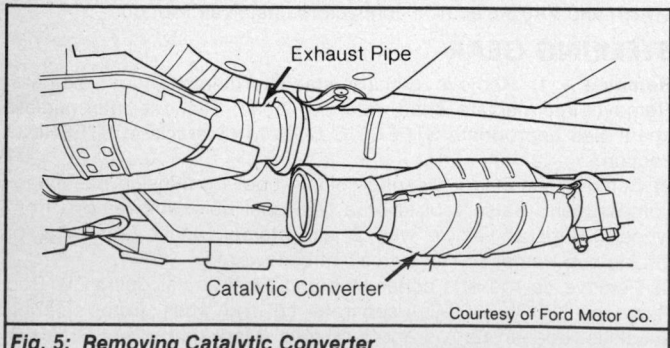

Fig. 5: *Removing Catalytic Converter*

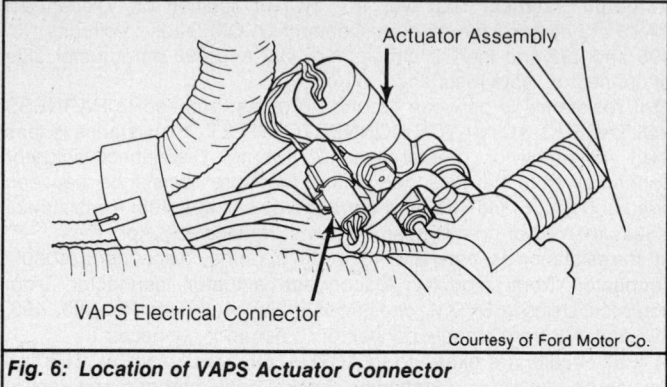

Fig. 6: *Location of VAPS Actuator Connector*

7) Attach intermediate steering column shaft. Refer to appropriate STEERING COLUMNS article in STEERING section. Align front end as necessary.

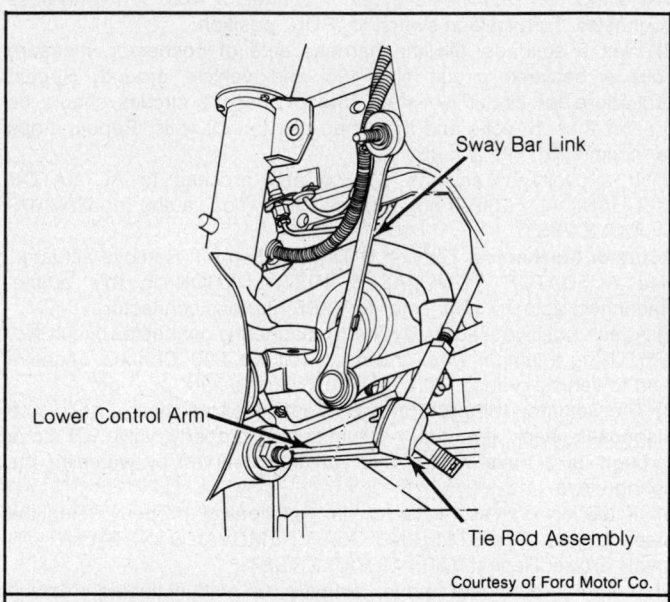

Fig. 7: *Location of Left Side Sway Bar Link*

TIE ROD ENDS

Removal – 1) Raise and support vehicle. Remove tie rod end cotter pins and castle nuts. Using Tie Rod Remover (TOOL-3290-D), separate tie rod ends from steering knuckles. Loosen tie rod end lock nuts.

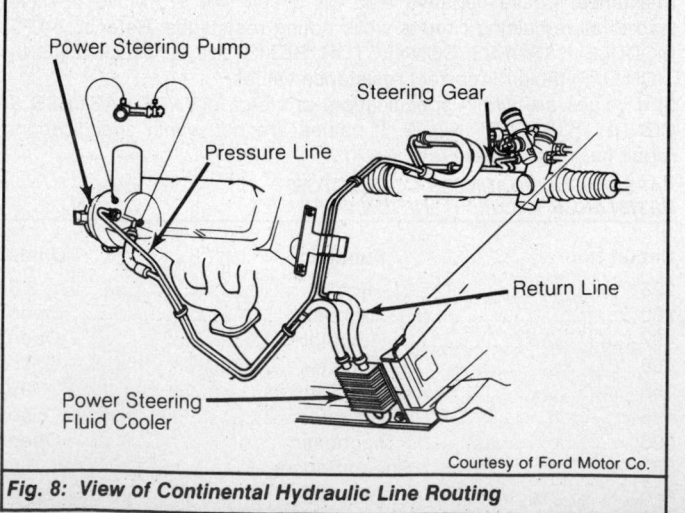

Fig. 8: *View of Continental Hydraulic Line Routing*

2) Mark tie rod end lock nut position for reassembly reference. Remove tie rod ends and lock nuts from tie rods.

Installation – To install, reverse removal procedure. Install and tighten NEW castle nut to specification. Tighten castle nut further to align cotter pin slot. Install NEW cotter pins. Adjust toe-in as necessary. Tighten tie rod end lock nut to specification.

VAPS MODULE

Removal – Module is located below instrument panel to right of steering column. To remove, disconnect wiring harness connector from VAPS module. Remove 3 module fixture attaching screws from column mounting fixture and remove module. *See Fig. 9.*

Installation – Align mounting holes of VAPS module to holes on column fixture. Install and tighten mounting screws to specification. Reconnect wiring harness.

OVERHAUL

STEERING GEAR

Serviceable components on steering gear are boots, tie rods, actuator and actuator bolts and seals. Manufacturer does not recommend steering gear overhaul. If necessary, replace steering gear with short rack assembly.

TIE RODS & BOOTS

Disassembly – **1)** With steering gear removed from vehicle, mount steering gear in Holding Fixture (T57L-500-B). It may be necessary to drill out holes in holding fixture with a 9/16" drill bit. Mount holding fixture in vise.

2) Remove inner and outer boot retaining clamps. Remove boots with breather tube. Using Lock Nut Pin Remover (D81P-3504-N), remove spring pin from tie rod inner ball joint.

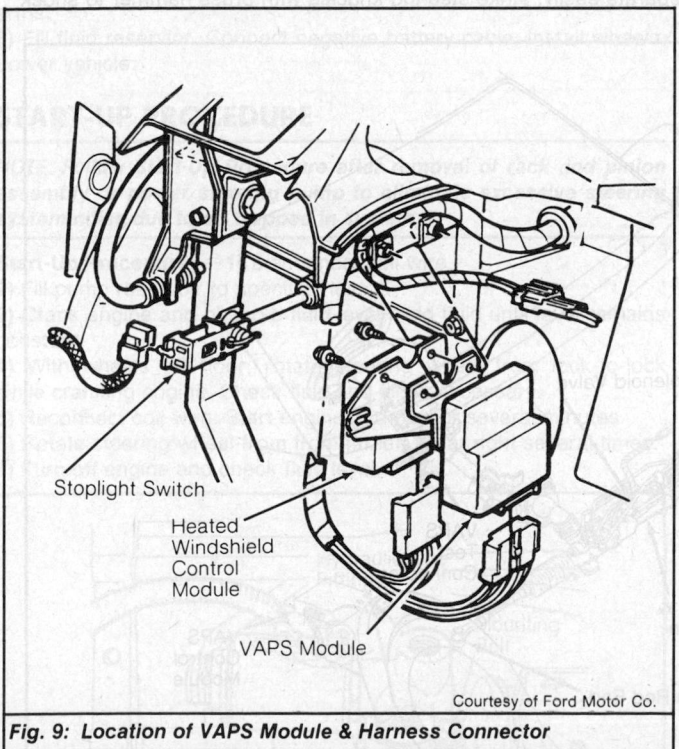

Stoplight Switch

Heated Windshield Control Module

VAPS Module

Courtesy of Ford Motor Co.

Fig. 9: Location of VAPS Module & Harness Connector

VARIABLE ASSIST POWER STEERING MODULE

| 1 | 2 | 3 | 4 | 5 | 6 | 7 | 8 | 9 | 10 | 11 | 12 | 13 | 14 |

ORG 496 | ORG-YEL 563 | WHT-BLK 200 | BLK 57 | DK GRN-WHT 150 | WHT LT BLU 606 | TAN 495 | PNK 498 | WHT 497 | PPL-ORG 298

FUSE #5

TEST CONN

1
2
3
4

VARIABLE ASSIST STEPPER MOTOR

ORG-YEL → ECA PIN #6
ORG-YEL
DK GRN-WHT
DK GRN-WHT → ECA PIN #7

VEHICLE SPEED SENSOR

Courtesy of Ford Motor Co.

Fig. 10: Variable Assist Power Steering Module Wiring Diagram

3) Position rack so several teeth are exposed. Using a wrench to hold end teeth only, turn ball joint with Nut Wrench (T74P-3504-U), and separate tie rod from rack.

Cleaning & Inspection – Clean rack and housing bore. Check steering gear housing for cracks or leakage. If steering gear is damaged, replace with a new unit. Inspect boots for cracking or signs of dryness. Check clamps for damage or corrosion.

Reassembly – **1)** Position rack so several teeth are exposed. Using a wrench to hold end teeth only, turn ball joint with Nut Wrench (T74P-3504-U) to install tie rod onto rack.

2) Tighten ball joints to specification. Using a small hammer, install new spring pins into ball joints. Replace any grease that may have been removed with Steering Gear Grease (C3AZ-19578-A).

3) Apply steering gear grease to groove in rods where boots clamp to tie rod to allow toe-in adjustment without twisting boots. Install boots and breather tube.

4) Install and tighten inner boot retaining clamps. Install, but do not tighten, outer boot retaining clamps. Install steering gear in vehicle. Adjust toe-in as necessary. Tighten outer boot retaining clamps.

TIGHTENING SPECIFICATIONS

Application	Ft. Lbs. (N.m)
Actuator-to-Steering Gear Bolt	20-25 (28-33)
Flexible Coupling-to-Pinion Bolt	30-38 (41-51)
Hydraulic Fittings-to-Steering Gear	10-15 (14-21)
Hydraulic Transfer Tubes	22-28 (30-38)
Intermediate Shaft-to-Steering Shaft Nuts	15-25 (21-33)
Steering Gear-to-Sub-Frame Mounting Bolts & Nuts	85-100 (115-135)
Sub-Frame-to-Body Attaching Bolts	65-85 (90-115)
Tie Rod Ball Joint-to-Rack Nut	55-65 (75-90)
Tie Rod End Lock Nut	35-50 (48-68)
Tie Rod End-to-Steering Knuckle Nut	35-47 (48-64)

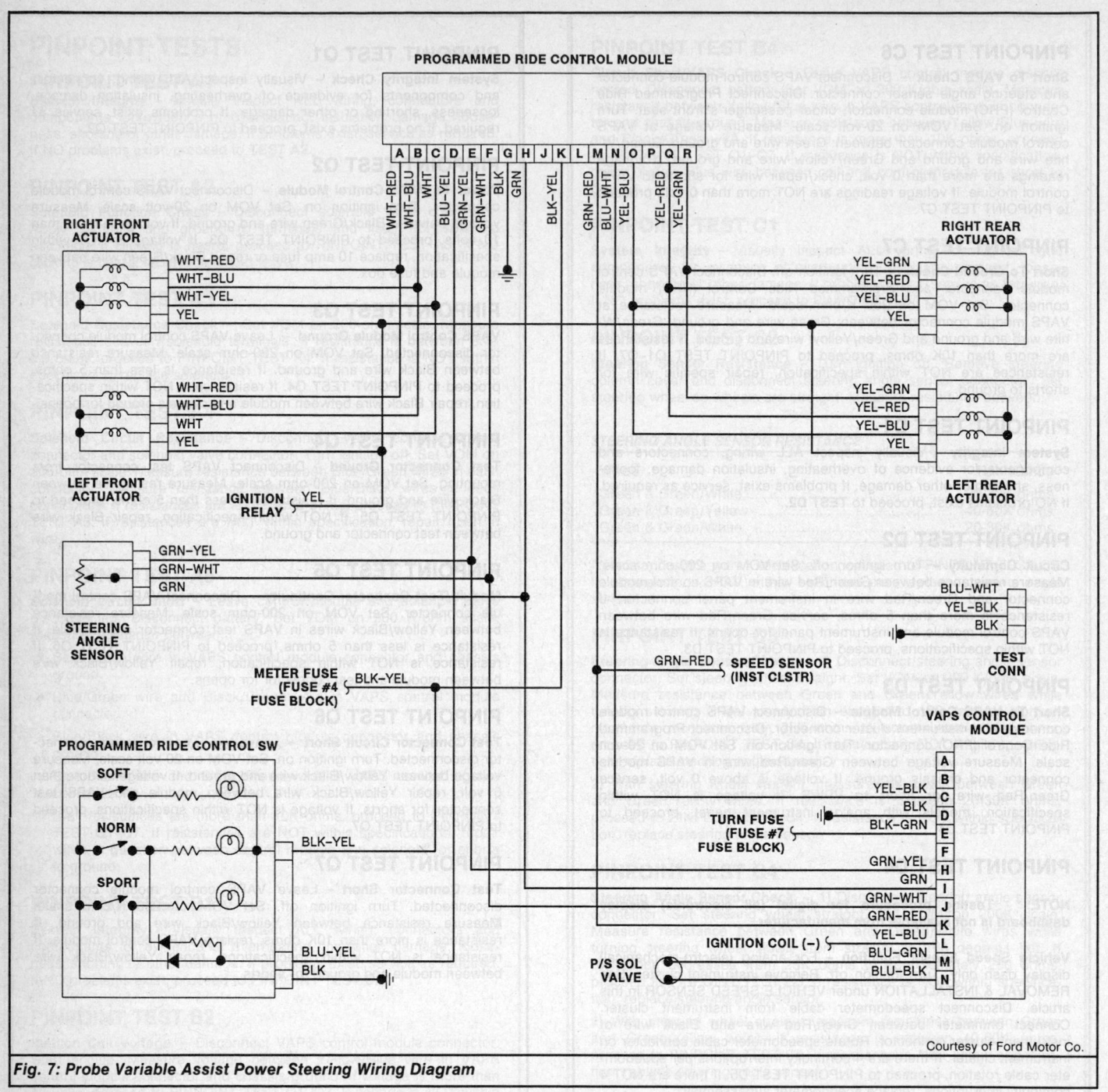

Fig. 7: Probe Variable Assist Power Steering Wiring Diagram

Courtesy of Ford Motor Co.

DESCRIPTION

Chrysler uses 2 different power steering pumps on its FWD cars: Saginaw and "ZF" type. The Saginaw power steering pump is serviceable. The "ZF" pump is NOT serviceable.

The Saginaw vane power steering pump is a constant displacement, vane type pump with an integral fluid reservoir. Shaft-driven pumping vanes move the fluid. When pressure exceeds set limits, the flow control pressure relief valve opens and allows fluid to return to the inlet side of the pump. Under normal conditions, both pressure relief and flow control valves are closed.

POWER STEERING PUMP APPLICATION

Body Code	Models	Pump Type
"A"	Acclaim, Spirit	Saginaw/"ZF"
"C"	Dynasty, New Yorker	Saginaw
"G"	Daytona	"ZF"
"H"	Lancer, LeBaron GTS	"ZF"
"J"	LeBaron	"ZF"
"K"	Aries, Reliant	Saginaw
"L"	Horizon, Omni	Saginaw
"M"	Diplomat, 5th Ave, Gran Fury	Saginaw
"P"	Shadow, Sundance	"ZF"

LUBRICATION, TROUBLE SHOOTING & TESTING

See POWER STEERING GENERAL SERVICING and TROUBLE SHOOTING articles in this section.

TESTING

PUMP TEST

This procedure tests power steering system on vehicle:
- With engine off, inspect fluid level. Fill if needed.
- Check belt tension. Adjust if needed.
- Disconnect pressure hose and connect spare pressure hose to pump fitting.
- Connect spare hose to gauge side of Hydraulic Pump Pressure Tester and Tube Assembly Adapters (C-3309E and L-4601). Ensure valve on tool is on outlet side of gauge. New fittings are required on hydraulic pump pressure tester to adapt to new "O" ring-type hose tube ends.
- Open hand valve on hydraulic pump pressure.
- Insert thermometer in fluid reservoir. Start engine. Turn steering wheel from lock-to-lock to warm fluid to between 150-170°F (66-77°C).
- With engine idling and gauge valve open, initial pressure should be between 30-50 psi (207-345 kPa). If pressure exceeds 100 psi (690 kPa), check hoses for crimps and/or restricted hoses.
- Close and open gauge valve completely 3 times for 5 seconds and record highest pressure reached.
- If recorded pressures are within specifications and range of readings is within 50 psi (345 kPa), pump is operating properly.
- If pressure is high but does NOT repeat within 50 psi (345 kPa), flow control valve in pump is sticking. On Saginaw pump, control valve can be removed and cleaned. Replace "ZF" pump.
- If pressures recorded are constant but low, clean or replace pressure relief valve and flow control assembly on Saginaw pump. If pressures are still low, replace pump. Replace "ZF" pump.
- If pump checks okay, leave gauge open and turn wheel from lock-to-lock with engine idling. Record highest pressure attained at each lock. If pressure cannot be built up at either lock, the steering gear is leaking internally. Replace steering gear.

REMOVAL & INSTALLATION

POWER STEERING PUMP

Removal (FWD Models) – 1) Remove drive belt. Raise vehicle on hoist. Disconnect return hose from gear tube and drain oil from pump. Remove right side splash shield. Disconnect both hoses from pump. Cap open end of hoses. Remove lower stud nut and pivot screw from pump.

2) Lower vehicle and remove belt from pulley. Move pump rearward to clear mounting bracket. Remove adjustment bracket. Rotate pump clockwise so pulley faces rear of vehicle. Pull upward to remove pump.

Installation – 1) Turn pump so it faces rear of vehicle and lower into position. Install adjustment bracket onto pump with tab in lower left front housing mounting hole.

2) Raise vehicle and install lower pump stud nut and pivot bolt. DO NOT tighten. Install new "O" rings on pressure hose. Connect both hoses. Install drive belt into pulley groove. Lower vehicle. Install belt adjustment screw. Adjust belt tension. Tighten adjustment bolt.

3) Raise vehicle. Tighten lower stud nut and pivot screw. Install splash shield. Fill reservoir with power steering fluid. Start engine. Turn steering wheel from lock-to-lock to bleed system. Stop engine. Check fluid. Check for leaks.

Removal (RWD Models) – Loosen pump mounting and locking bolts. Remove power steering belt. Disconnect pressure and return hoses at pump. Remove mounting and locking bolts. Remove pump and bracket.

Installation – Position pump and mounting bracket on engine. Install and adjust belt. DO NOT pry on pump reservoir. Tighten pump mounting bolts to specification. Replace and lubricate "O" ring on pressure hose pump end. Install hoses. Tighten hoses to specification. Fill pump reservoir with power steering fluid. Start engine and turn wheel from lock-to-lock to bleed system. Stop engine. Check fluid. Repeat procedure.

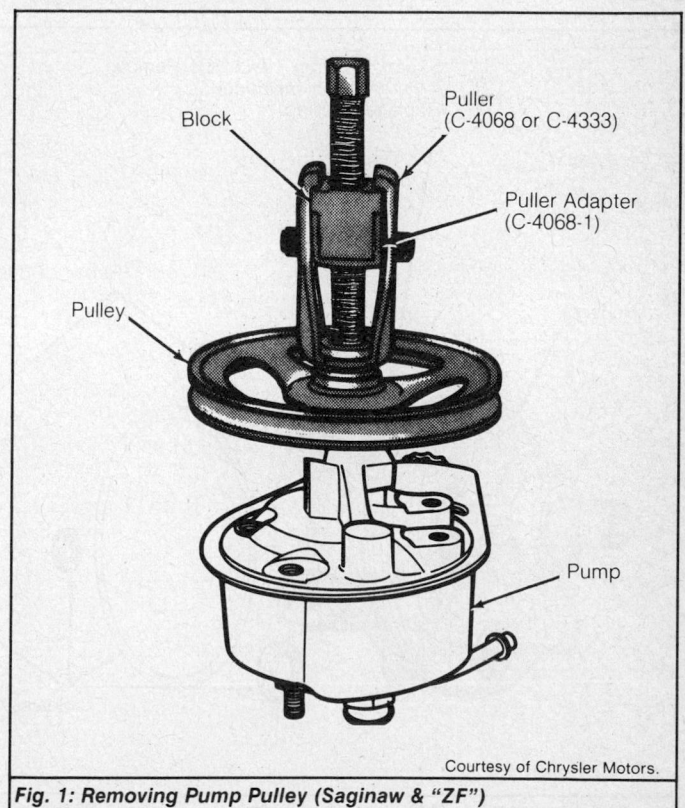

Courtesy of Chrysler Motors.

Fig. 1: Removing Pump Pulley (Saginaw & "ZF")

13-76

1989 POWER STEERING PUMPS
Chrysler Motors FWD — Saginaw & "ZF" (Cont.)

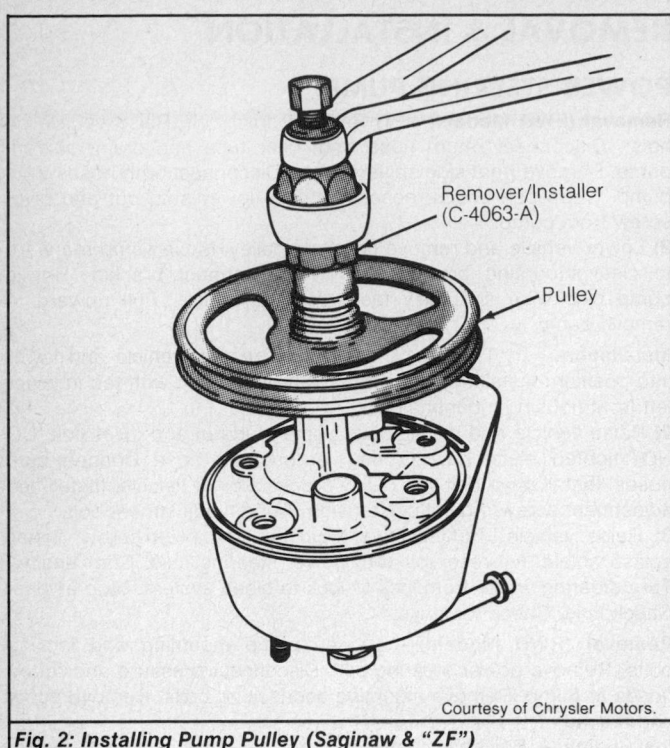

Fig. 2: Installing Pump Pulley (Saginaw & "ZF")

Courtesy of Chrysler Motors.

PUMP PULLEY

Removal & Installation – Remove pulley on Saginaw pump with Puller (C-4068 or C-4333) and Puller Adapter (C-4068-1). Remove pulley from "ZF" pump with Remover/Installer (C-4063-A). *See Figs.*

1 and 2. Replace pulley if bent, cracked or loose. Install Saginaw and "ZF" pump pulleys with Remover/Installer (C-4063-A). Press pulley until flush with shaft end.

PUMP SEAL

Removal & Installation – To replace drive shaft oil seal, it is necessary to remove and disassemble pump assembly. See OVERHAUL in this article.

OVERHAUL

POWER STEERING PUMP (SAGINAW)

Disassembly – **1)** Remove filler cap. Drain oil from reservoir before removing parts. Remove pulley. See PUMP PULLEY under REMOVAL & INSTALLATION in this article. Remove hose fitting and 2 studs from back of housing. *See Fig. 3.*

2) Rock reservoir by hand or tap with soft-faced hammer to separate from housing. Remove "O" ring. Remove end plate retaining ring. Remove end plate, control valve and control valve spring.

3) Clamp land end of pressure relief valve in soft-jawed vise. Remove hex-head ball seat. Remove 2 shims, pressure relief ball, guide, spring and flow control valve.

4) With plastic hammer, tap shaft end lightly until pressure plate is free. Remove pressure plate, cam ring, 10 vanes, rotor, thrust plate and shaft. Remove rotor lock ring and discard.

Reassembly – Inspect all wearing surfaces. Replace parts with excessive wear, scuffing and scoring. Lubricate all seals with power steering fluid before installation. DO NOT use automatic transmission fluid. To reassemble, reverse reassembly procedure. See TIGHTENING SPECIFICATIONS table in this article.

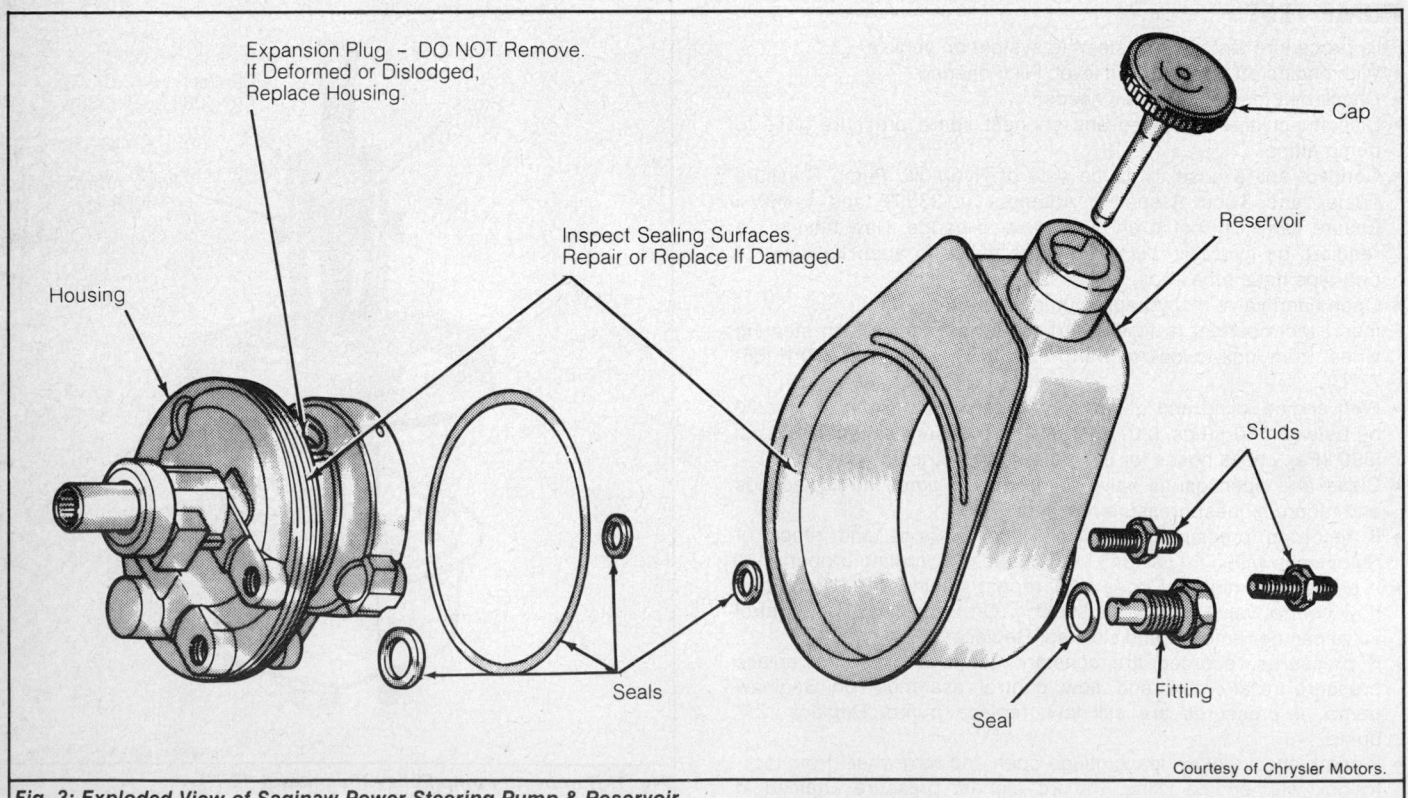

Fig. 3: Exploded View of Saginaw Power Steering Pump & Reservoir

Courtesy of Chrysler Motors.

1989 POWER STEERING PUMPS
Chrysler Motors FWD — Saginaw & "ZF" (Cont.)

13-77

POWER STEERING PUMP ("ZF")

NOTE: The "ZF" pump is NOT serviceable. Only reservoir can be replaced.

Disassembly – Remove 2 rear bolts and 2 retaining plates. Drive 2 pins out from front. DO NOT enlarge front access hole. Lift off reservoir. Inspect pump inlet. Replace pump if inlet is damaged or worn.

Reassembly – Inspect "O" ring. Coat "O" ring with power steering fluid. Carefully snap reservoir into place. Install new pins from rear of pump. Push in until flush with back plate. Install pin retaining plates. Tighten bolts to specification.

TIGHTENING SPECIFICATIONS

Application	Ft. Lbs. (N.m)
Hoses	
Pump End Fitting	32 (43)
Gear End Fitting	19 (26)
Power Steering Pump	
Adjustment Bolt	30 (41)
Discharge Fitting ("ZF")	37 (50)
Fitting Nut	40 (54)
Lower Stud Nut/Pivot Screw	40 (54)
Mounting Bracket Nut	30 (41)
Mounting Bracket Bolts	30 (41)
Pressure Hose ("O" Ring Type)	25 (34)
Rear Studs	35 (48)

	INCH Lbs. (N.m)
Ball Seat (Saginaw Pump)	50 (6)
Pin Retaining Plate Bolts ("ZF" Pump)	90 (10)

1989 POWER STEERING PUMPS
Chrysler Motors RWD – Saginaw

DESCRIPTION

The Saginaw vane power steering pump is a constant displacement, vane type pump with an integral fluid reservoir. Shaft-driven pumping vanes move the fluid from the intake to cam ring pressure cavities. As the rotor turns, the vanes pick up residual fluid. The rotor forces the fluid into a high pressure area.

Fluid is then forced into the cavities of the thrust plate through 2 crossover holes in the cam ring and pressure plate. The crossover holes empty into a high pressure area between the pressure plate and housing end cover.

When pressure exceeds set limits, the flow control pressure relief valve opens and allows fluid to return to the inlet side of the pump. Under normal conditions, both pressure relief and flow control valves are closed.

LUBRICATION, TROUBLE SHOOTING & TESTING

See POWER STEERING GENERAL SERVICING and TROUBLE SHOOTING articles in this section.

REMOVAL & INSTALLATION

POWER STEERING PUMP

Removal & Installation – Place container under vehicle. Disconnect power steering hoses and plug fittings. Remove drive belt. Remove pump mounting hardware and pump. Because of different engines and air conditioning configurations, it may be necessary to remove additional components. On some models, power steering pump pulley may be removed to ease removal of pump. To install, reverse removal procedure.

NOTE: On some models, it may be necessary to remove pump bracket with pump. Bracket mounting bolts may extend into water jacket.

POWER STEERING PUMP PULLEY

Removal & Installation – Pump pulley is a press fit and must be removed and installed with a puller. See PUMP PULLEY SERVICE TOOLS table. Clamp pump in vise at mounting bracket or front hub. Avoid clamping front hub too tightly. *See Figs. 2 and 3.*

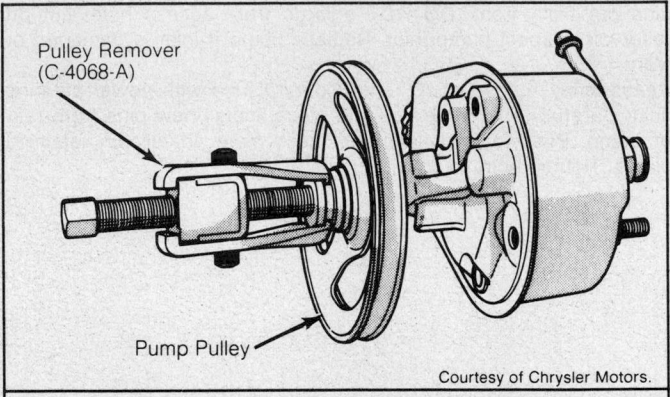

Pulley Remover (C-4068-A)

Pump Pulley

Courtesy of Chrysler Motors.

Fig. 2: Removing Power Steering Pump Pulley

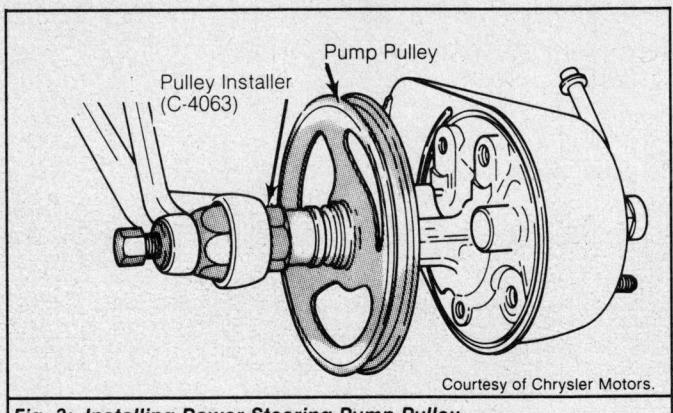

Pump Pulley

Pulley Installer (C-4063)

Courtesy of Chrysler Motors.

Fig. 3: Installing Power Steering Pump Pulley

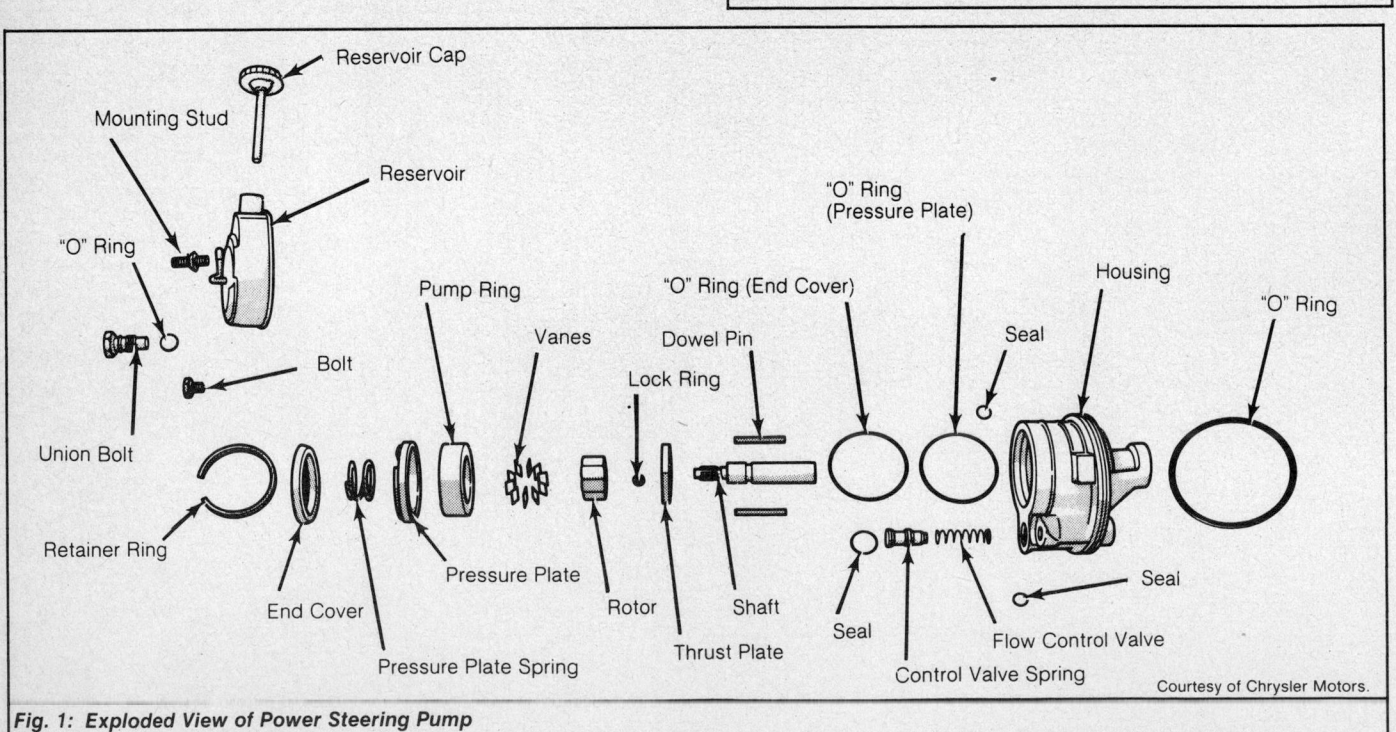

Reservoir Cap

Mounting Stud

Reservoir

"O" Ring

"O" Ring (Pressure Plate)

Pump Ring

Housing

"O" Ring

Bolt

Vanes

"O" Ring (End Cover)

Seal

Union Bolt

Dowel Pin

Lock Ring

Retainer Ring

End Cover

Pressure Plate

Rotor

Shaft

Seal

Seal

Pressure Plate Spring

Thrust Plate

Control Valve Spring

Flow Control Valve

Courtesy of Chrysler Motors.

Fig. 1: Exploded View of Power Steering Pump

PUMP PULLEY SERVICE TOOLS

Application	Remover Tool No.	Installer Tool No.
Chrysler Motors	C-4068-A	C-4063

DRIVE SHAFT SEAL

Removal & Installation – Remove pump from vehicle and remove pump pulley. Protect pump shaft with shim stock. Using a chisel, cut and remove seal. To install, coat shaft seal with power steering fluid. Using a socket, drive new seal in place until it bottoms on shoulder.

RESERVOIR

Removal – **1)** Remove pump from vehicle and drain fluid. Mount pump in vise with shaft facing down. Do not allow vise jaws to contact reservoir.

2) Remove 2 reservoir-to-pump mounting studs at rear of pump. Remove pressure line outlet fitting. Using a soft mallet, tap on filler neck of reservoir. Move reservoir back and forth until free of pump.

Installation – **1)** Use new "O" rings. Lubricate and install pump housing "O" ring, 2 pump-to-reservoir stud "O" rings and outlet fitting "O" ring. Slide reservoir over pump. Ensure reservoir is seated properly.

2) Install pump-to-reservoir mounting studs and tighten to 26 ft. lbs. (35 N.m). Install outlet fitting and tighten to 55 ft. lbs (75 N.m). Install pump in vehicle, adjust belt tension, refill and bleed pump, and check for leaks.

OVERHAUL

CAUTION: When clamping pump in vise or mounting fixture, do not exert excessive force on front hub as housing may be distorted.

POWER STEERING PUMP

Disassembly – **1)** Remove pulley from shaft. Remove brackets from pump. Drain reservoir. Clean exterior of pump. Clamp pump in a soft-jawed vise, shaft down, between square boss and shaft housing.

2) Remove pressure fitting and "O" ring seal. Remove retaining studs. Rock filler tube back and forth gently to loosen. Work reservoir off pump body. Remove and discard all "O" rings.

3) Using a punch, tap end cover retaining ring until one end of ring is near hole in pump body. Insert punch in hole far enough to disengage ring from groove in pump bore. Pry ring out of pump body.

4) Tap end cover with plastic hammer to jar it loose. Spring located under cover should push it up. Remove pump body from vise. Place pump in an inverted position on a clean, flat surface.

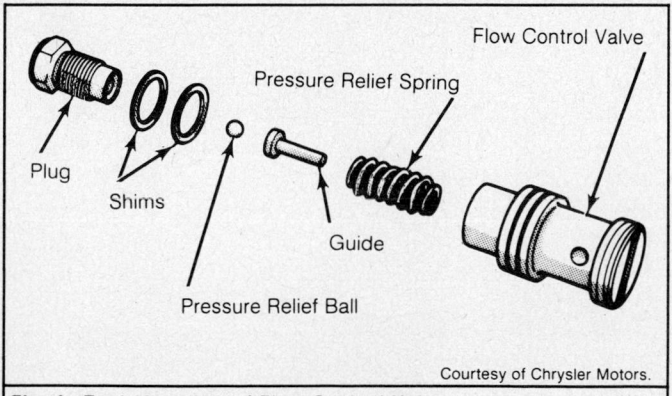

Fig. 4: Exploded View of Flow Control Valve

Plug
Shims
Pressure Relief Ball
Guide
Pressure Relief Spring
Flow Control Valve

Courtesy of Chrysler Motors.

5) Tap end of drive shaft with plastic hammer to loosen pressure plate, rotor, and thrust plate assembly from body. Lift pump body off rotor assembly.

6) Flow control valve and spring should slide out of bore. Remove and discard end plate and pressure plate "O" rings. Remove drive shaft oil seal.

7) Lift pressure plate and cam ring from rotor. Remove 10 vanes from slots. Clamp drive shaft in soft-jawed vise with rotor and thrust plate up.

8) Remove and discard rotor lock ring. Use care to avoid nicking rotor end face. Slide rotor and thrust plate off shaft. Remove shaft from vise.

NOTE: Individual control valve parts are not available. Replace flow control valve as an assembly if worn or damaged. If pump is being overhauled because of contamination in system, valve can be disassembled for cleaning.

Cleaning & Inspection – **1)** Clean all parts in solvent. Inspect flow control valve for wear or damage. Inspect seal bore in housing for burrs, nicks or scoring. Inspect fit of vanes in rotor. Vanes must slide freely into slots of rotor without binding.

2) Excessively loose vanes require replacement of rotor and/or vanes. Examine inner surface of cam ring for heavy scuff or chatter marks. Inspect flat surfaces of pressure and thrust plates for wear or scoring.

3) Light scoring can be removed by lapping on a flat surface. Inspect pump body drive shaft bushing for excessive wear. Replace pump body and bushing as an assembly if badly worn or scored. Replace any damaged or worn parts.

NOTE: If pump is equipped with magnet, ensure all residue is cleaned from magnet.

Reassembly – **1)** Lubricate all "O" ring seals and seal areas with power steering fluid. Place pump body on flat surface. Drive new pump shaft seal into bore with a 7/8" or 15/16" socket until seal bottoms on shoulder. Do not use excessive force as seal can be distorted.

2) Clamp pump body in vise with shaft down. Install end cover and pressure plate "O" rings in grooves in pump cavity. With drive shaft clamped, splined shaft up, install thrust plate on drive shaft with ported side up. See Fig. 5.

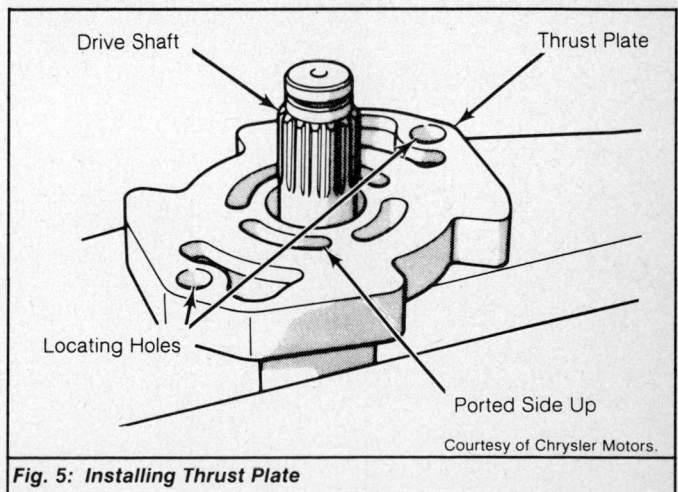

Drive Shaft
Thrust Plate
Locating Holes
Ported Side Up

Courtesy of Chrysler Motors.

Fig. 5: Installing Thrust Plate

3) Slide rotor over splines with counterbore of rotor facing down. Install rotor lock ring. Insert both dowel pins in holes of pump cavity. Rotor must move freely on splines. Install pump shaft assembly in pump body, ensuring dowel pins are properly engaged in thrust plate.

4) Slide cam ring over rotor on dowel pins with arrow facing up. See Fig. 6. Install 10 vanes in rotor slots. Position pressure plate on dowel pins with plate spring groove facing upward. Place a 1 1/4" socket in groove of pressure plate. Seat entire assembly on "O" ring in pump cavity by pressing down with both thumbs.

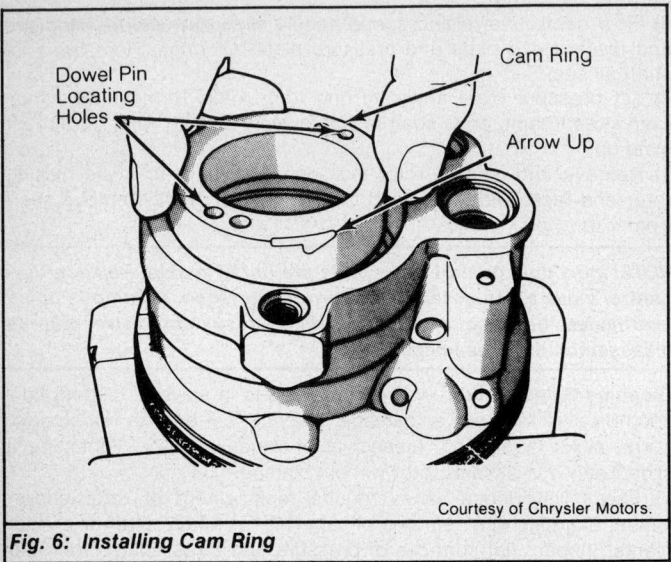

Dowel Pin
Locating
Holes

Cam Ring

Arrow Up

Courtesy of Chrysler Motors.

Fig. 6: Installing Cam Ring

5) Place spring in groove in pressure plate. Position end cover lip edge up over spring. Press end cover down below retaining ring

groove with thumb. Install ring. Ensure ring is seated in groove. Use care to avoid cocking end cover in bore or distorting assembly.

6) Install flow control valve, if removed, in pump bore with spring and hex end of valve facing interior of bore. Using a punch, tap retainer ring end around groove until opening is opposite flow control valve bore. This is important for maximum retention of retainer ring.

7) Replace reservoir "O" ring seal, 2 mounting stud "O" ring seals and flow control valve "O" ring seal on pump body. Carefully position reservoir on pump body. Visually align mounting stud holes until studs can be started in threads.

8) Press reservoir down on pump to seat on pump body. Place new seal on pump union. Install union in flow control valve bore. Tighten mounting studs. Install pump pulley.

TIGHTENING SPECIFICATIONS

Application	Ft. Lbs. (N.m)
Flow Control Valve Fitting	55 (75)
High Pressure Line-to-Union Fitting	30 (41)
High Pressure Union Fitting	35 (47)
Mounting Bracket Bolts	30 (41)
Reservoir Mounting Bolt	26 (35)
	INCH Lbs. (N.m)
Flow Control Valve Plug	4 (.45)

Premier

DESCRIPTION

This pump uses a fluid reservoir separate from the pump. Two types of pumps are used. The "N" series pump is used on 3.0L engines and the "TC" series pump is used on 2.5L engines. Both series pumps are similar and are overhauled in the same manner.

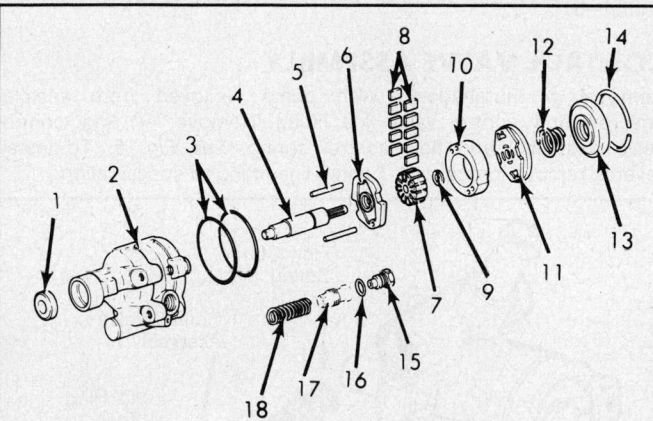

1. Pump Shaft Seal
2. Pump Housing
3. "O" Rings
4. Pump Shaft
5. Dowel Pins
6. Thrust Plate
7. Pump Rotor
8. Pump Vanes (10)
9. Shaft Retaining Ring
10. Cam Ring
11. Pressure Plate
12. Pressure Plate Spring
13. End Plate
14. End Plate Retaining Ring
15. Fitting
16. "O" Ring
17. Flow Control Valve
18. Flow Control Spring

Courtesy of Chrysler Motors.

Fig. 1: Exploded View Of "N" Series Power Steering Pump Components

OPERATION

Rectangular pumping vanes, carried by a shaft driven rotor, move fluid from intake to pressure cavities of the cam ring. As the rotor begins to rotate, centrifugal force throws the vanes against the inside surface of the cam ring to pick up residual oil, which is then forced into the high pressure area.

Oil is forced into cavities of the thrust plate and through 2 cross-over holes in the cam ring and pressure plate. This oil empties into the high pressure area between the pressure plate and housing end plate. Filling the high pressure area causes oil to flow under vanes in slots of rotor, forcing the vanes to follow the inside oval surface of cam ring. As the vanes rotate to the small area of cam ring, oil is forced out from between the vanes, creating high pressure.

LUBRICATION, TROUBLE SHOOTING & TESTING

For further information, see POWER STEERING GENERAL SERVICING article in this section.

REMOVAL & INSTALLATION

POWER STEERING PUMP

Removal (2.5L Engine) – **1)** To release drive belt tension, loosen power steering pump adjustment slot nut and pivot bolt. Loosen rear bracket-to-pump bolts. Turn power steering pump adjustment screw counterclockwise until belt is slack enough to allow pump removal. Position a drain pan under power steering pump. Install a clamp on pump fluid return hose to prevent excess fluid leakage. Disconnect return hose and high pressure tubing fitting from pump.

2) Remove rear bracket-to-pump bolts. Remove adjustment bracket-to-rear bracket bolts and pivot bolt. Remove power steering pump, front bracket and adjustment bracket as a unit.

Installation – To install, reverse removal procedure. Ensure "O" ring at end of high pressure fitting is replaced before connecting fitting to power steering pump.

Removal (3.0L Engine) – **1)** To release drive belt tension, loosen alternator pivot bolt and alternator adjustment bolt. Turn belt adjustment screw counterclockwise until belt is slack enough to allow pump removal.

2) Position a drain pan under power steering pump. Install a clamp on pump fluid return line to prevent excessive fluid leakage. Disconnect fluid line hose from pump.

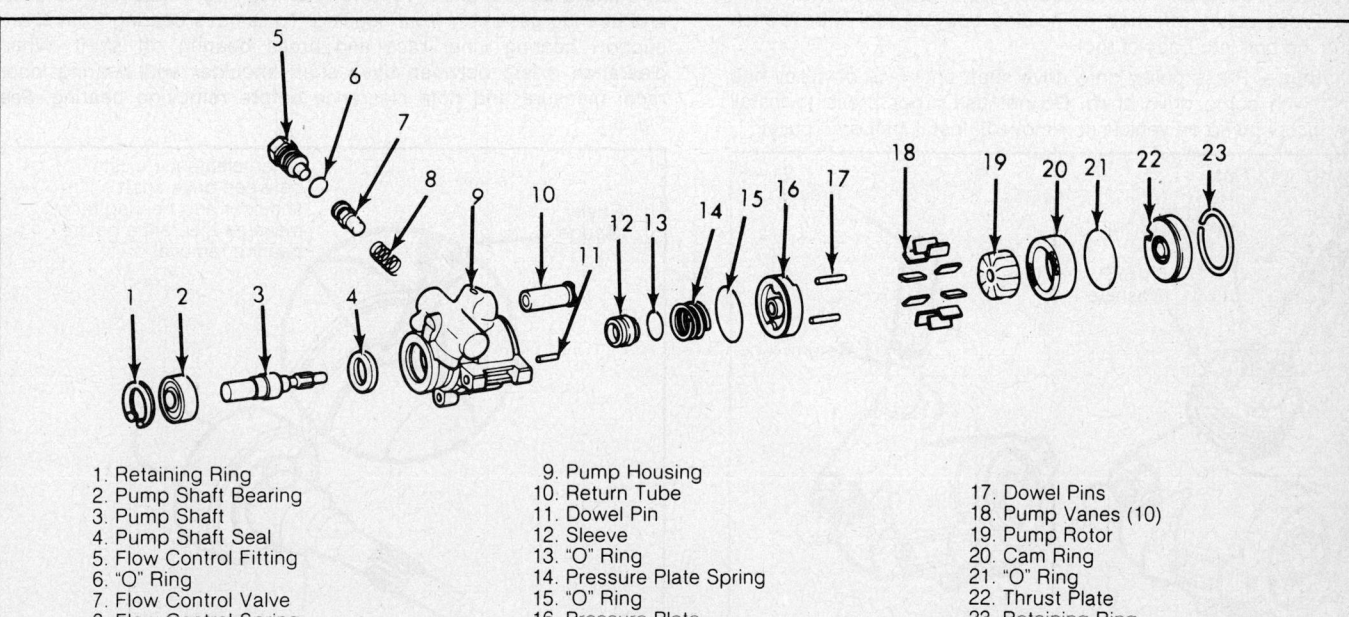

1. Retaining Ring
2. Pump Shaft Bearing
3. Pump Shaft
4. Pump Shaft Seal
5. Flow Control Fitting
6. "O" Ring
7. Flow Control Valve
8. Flow Control Spring
9. Pump Housing
10. Return Tube
11. Dowel Pin
12. Sleeve
13. "O" Ring
14. Pressure Plate Spring
15. "O" Ring
16. Pressure Plate
17. Dowel Pins
18. Pump Vanes (10)
19. Pump Rotor
20. Cam Ring
21. "O" Ring
22. Thrust Plate
23. Retaining Ring

Courtesy of Chrysler Motors

Fig. 2: Exploded View Of "TC" Series Power Steering Pump Components

13-82

1989 POWER STEERING PUMPS
Eagle – Saginaw With Remote Reservoir (Cont.)

3) Remove pump rear bracket-to-sump bolts. Remove pump front bracket-to-timing cover bolt. Remove power steering pump and brackets as a unit.

Installation – 1) Install front and rear pump brackets to pump. Install, but do not tighten front bracket-to-rear bracket bolts/nuts at this time. Position pump, with brackets attached, at installation position on engine. Install 3 rear bracket-to-timing cover bolts finger tight.

2) Install pump front bracket-to-timing cover bolt and tighten to specification. Tighten remaining bracket-to-timing cover bolts in correct order and to specification. *See Fig. 3.*

3) To complete installation, reverse removal procedure. Ensure "O" ring at end of high pressure fitting is replaced before connecting fitting to power steering pump.

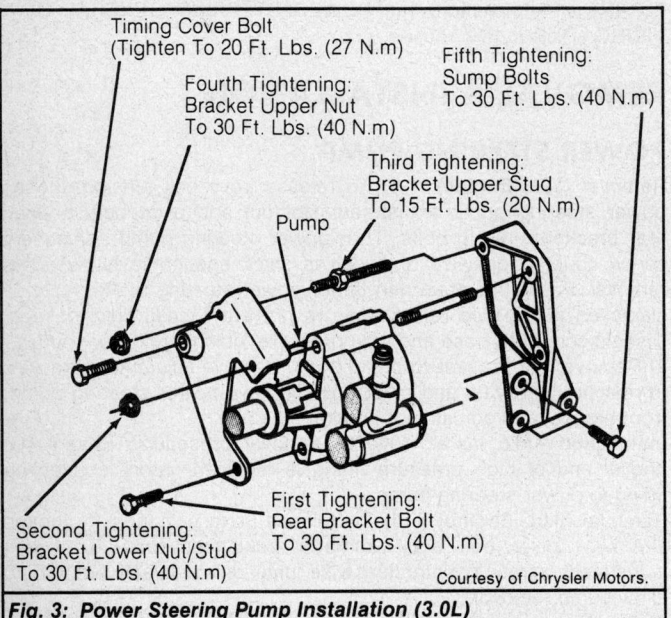

Fig. 3: Power Steering Pump Installation (3.0L)

POWER STEERING PUMP PULLEY

Removal & Installation – Remove belt from pump. Remove pump as previously described (if necessary). Install a pulley remover on pulley. Press pulley off shaft by holding body of tool with wrench and turning bolt into body of tool.

Installation – Press pulley onto drive shaft until face of pulley hub is flush with pump drive shaft. Do not use arbor press to install pulley. Install pump on vehicle (if removed). Install belt onto pulley.

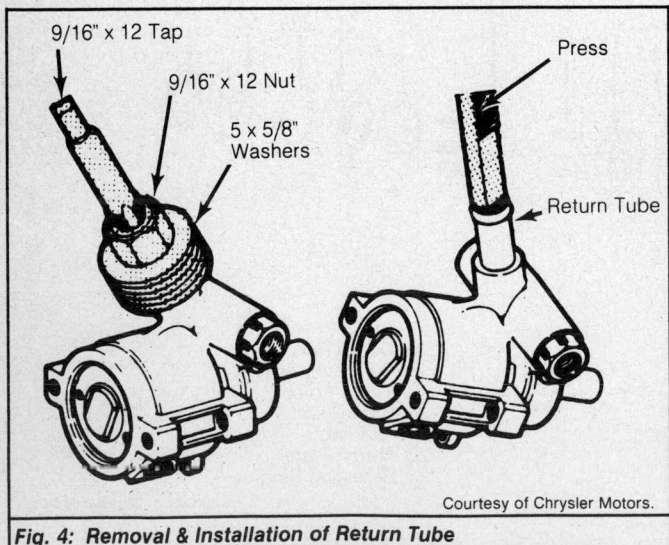

Fig. 4: Removal & Installation of Return Tube

RETURN TUBE

Removal & Installation – 1) Plug return tube to prevent chips from entering pump. Using a 9/16" x 12 thread per inch tap, a 9/16" x 12 thread per inch nut and five 5/8" washers, screw tap into tube, slide washers over end of tap and use the nut to draw tube out of pump body. *See Fig. 4.*

2) Using Loctite Solvent (75559) and Loctite Adhesive (290), coat end of the return tube. Using a press, press tube into housing until bottomed.

CONTROL VALVE ASSEMBLY

Removal & Installation – With pump removed from vehicle, unscrew flow control valve line fitting. Remove "O" ring, control valve assembly and flow control spring. *See Fig. 5.* To install reverse removal procedure. Tighten line fitting to specification.

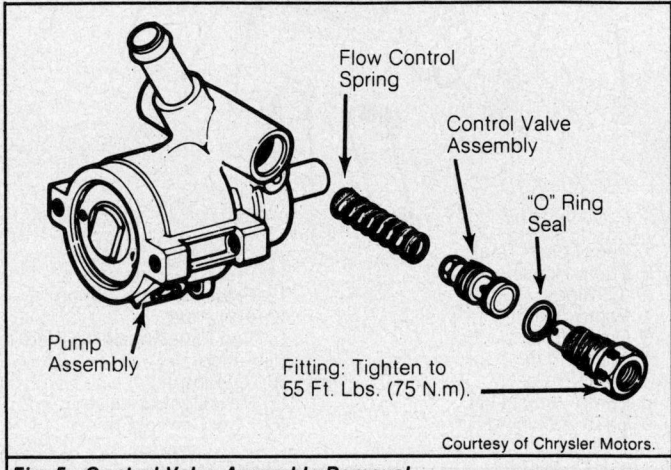

Fig. 5: Control Valve Assembly Removal

DRIVE SHAFT & BALL BEARING ASSEMBLY

Removal – 1) Remove pump from vehicle. See POWER STEERING PUMP under REMOVAL & INSTALLATION in this article. Remove pump pulley. See POWER STEERING PUMP PULLEY under REMOVAL & INSTALLATION in this article.

2) Using snap ring pliers, remove retaining ring. Remove drive shaft and bearing assembly from housing. To remove bearing from shaft, support bearing inner race and press bearing off shaft. When clearance exists between drive shaft shoulder and bearing inner race, measure and note clearance before removing bearing. *See Fig. 6.*

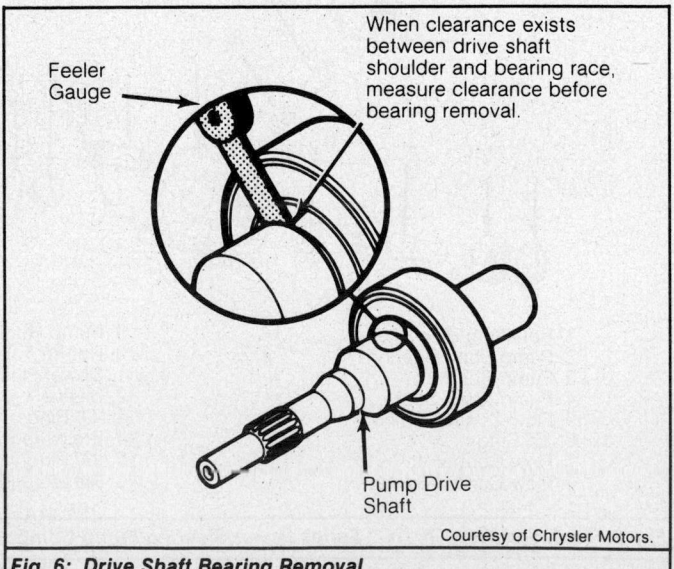

Fig. 6: Drive Shaft Bearing Removal

1989 POWER STEERING PUMPS
Eagle – Saginaw With Remote Reservoir (Cont.)

13-83

Installation – To install, press bearing to shoulder of drive shaft or to clearance measured prior to disassembly. *See Fig. 7.* Slide assembly into housing while rotating drive shaft so shaft serations engage with rotor. Bottom bearing in housing. Install retaining ring with beveled side down. *See Fig. 7.*

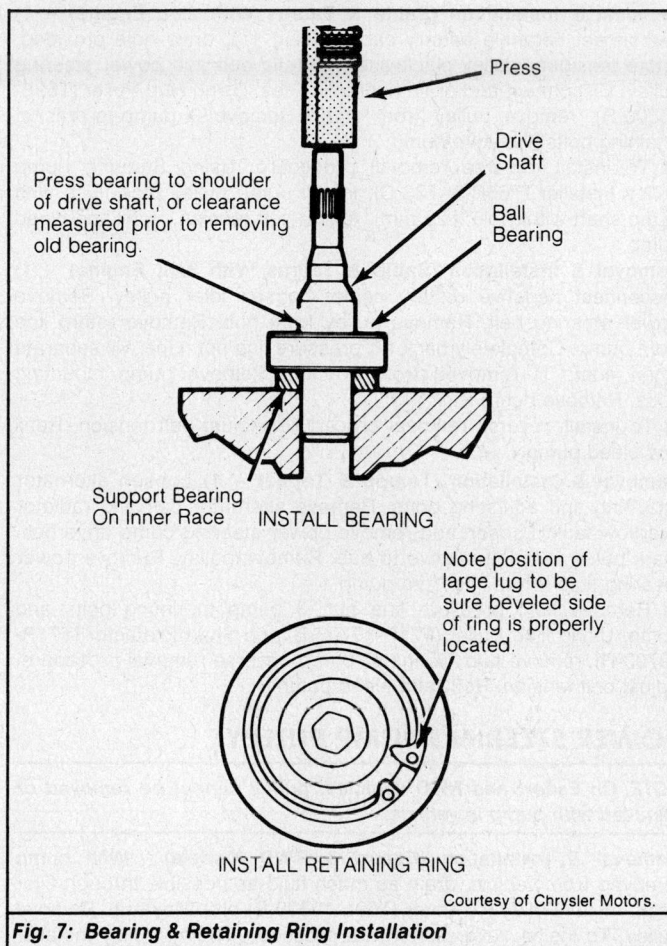

Fig. 7: Bearing & Retaining Ring Installation

Courtesy of Chrysler Motors.

DRIVE SHAFT SEAL

Removal & Installation – **1)** Remove pump from vehicle. Remove pump pulley and drive shaft assembly as previously described.

2) Using a screwdriver, pry old seal from housing. To install, use a suitable socket to drive oil seal into housing until bottomed. Install drive shaft, pump pulley and pump as previously described.

ROTATING GROUP

Removal – **1)** Remove pump from vehicle. Remove pump pulley and drive shaft assembly. Using a small punch in access hole, remove retaining ring.

2) Using a 5/8" piece of bar stock, press on pressure plate hub from drive shaft side of housing until thrust plate can be removed. Remove "O" ring seal from housing.

3) Remove pump rotor, rotor vanes, pump ring dowel pins, pump ring, pressure plate and pressure plate spring from housing. Use a press to remove pressure plate from pump cavity (if necessary).

Installation – **1)** Lubricate and install new "O" ring seal into sleeve assembly. Insert small dowel pin into housing. Install pressure plate spring over sleeve assembly into housing. Lubricate and install new "O" ring seal onto pressure plate.

2) Mark top of pressure plate directly over dowel pin hole in plate. This will aid in aligning dowel pin. Install pressure plate in housing. Be sure dowel pin and hole in pressure plate properly engage.

3) Install 2 pump ring dowel pins in holes in pressure plate. Slide pump ring over these 2 pins. Be sure identification marks on pump ring are facing upward. Install rotor with counter bore side toward drive shaft end of housing. Add the 10 pump vanes.

4) Lubricate thrust plate "O" ring seal and install in housing. Install thrust plate in housing. Be sure that dimples in thrust plate line up with bolt holes in housing and that thrust plate engages pump ring dowel pins.

5) Using a press, press thrust plate in only as far as necessary to install retaining ring. Install retaining ring with opening of ring centered with bolt hole in housing nearest to access hole.

6) Install pump pulley. Install pump in vehicle. Adjust belt tension, refill fluid reservoir. Bleed system.

TIGHTENING SPECIFICATIONS

Application	Ft. Lbs. (N.m)
Pressure Line Fitting	55 (75)
Pump Bracket-to-Bracket Lower Nut/Stud [1]	30 (40)
Pump Bracket-to-Bracket Upper Nut [1]	30 (40)
Pump Bracket-to-Bracket Upper Stud [1]	15 (20)
Pump Front Bracket-to-Rear Bracket Bolt [1]	30 (40)
Pump Rear Bracket-to-Sump Bolts [1]	30 (40)
Pump Front Bracket-to-Timing Cover Bolt [1]	20 (27)

[1] – For tightening sequence, See Fig. 3.

1989 POWER STEERING PUMPS
Ford Motor Co. C-II

DESCRIPTION

The C-II pump is a 10-slipper pump with an integral reservoir. Spring loaded slippers within cam and rotor create the pumping action. A flow control relief valve maintains pump volume and pressure.

The pump design incorporates a swiveled pressure fitting. An identification tag attached to reservoir body indicates pump model. Use model code when ordering service parts, as some differences in internal components do exist.

LUBRICATION, TROUBLE SHOOTING & TESTING

See POWER STEERING GENERAL SERVICING and TROUBLE SHOOTING articles in this section.

ADJUSTMENTS

PUMP BELT TENSION (IF NECESSARY)

See POWER STEERING GENERAL SERVICING article in this section.

REMOVAL & INSTALLATION

POWER STEERING PUMP

NOTE: Do not pry against reservoir to tighten conventional belt. Pressure may crack reservoir.

Removal & Installation (RWD Models) – Drain reservoir by disconnecting fluid return line at reservoir. Disconnect pressure hose at pump. Remove mounting bracket retaining bolts. To install, reverse removal procedure. Adjust belt tension if necessary. Refill and bleed pump.

Removal & Installation (Escort) – 1) Remove air cleaner, thermactor air pump and belt. Remove reservoir filler extension. Cover dipstick opening. On vehicles with EFI and remote reservoir, remove reservoir supply hose at pump.

2) Drain fluid. Cap opening. From under vehicle, loosen pump adjusting bolt. Remove pump-to-bracket mounting bolt. Disconnect return line.

3) Loosen adjusting and pivot bolts. Remove belt. Remove pump-to-bracket bolts. Remove pump by passing pulley through adjusting bracket opening. Remove pressure hose from pump.

4) To install pump, reverse removal procedure. Adjust belt tension. Refill and bleed pump.

Removal & Installation (Sable & Taurus With 2.5L Engine) – 1) Disconnect negative battery cable. Using 1/2" drive hole provided, rotate tensioner pulley clockwise. Remove belt and power steering pulley. Disconnect and drain hydraulic lines. Using Hub Puller (T69L-10300-B), remove pulley from shaft. Remove 3 pump-to-bracket retaining bolts. Remove pump.

2) To install, reverse removal procedure. Using Steering Pump Pulley Installer (T65P-3A733-C), install pump pulley face flush with pump shaft within .10" (.25 mm). Adjust belt tension. Refill and bleed pump.

Removal & Installation (Sable & Taurus With 3.0L Engine) – 1) Disconnect negative battery cable. Loosen idler pulley. Remove power steering belt. Remove pulley from hub. Remove return line from pump. Completely back off pressure line nut. Line will separate when pump is removed from bracket. Remove pump mounting bolts. Remove pump.

2) To install, reverse removal procedure. Adjust belt tension. Refill and bleed pump.

Removal & Installation (Tempo & Topaz) – 1) Loosen alternator attaching and adjusting bolts. Remove alternator belt and radiator overflow tank. Loosen and remove power steering pump drive belt. Mark pulley location relative to hub. Remove pulley. Remove power steering fluid return line from pump.

2) Remove fluid pressure line nut, 3 pump mounting bolts and pump. Using Hub Puller (T71P-19703-B) and Shaft Protector (T71P-19703-H), remove hub. To install pump, reverse removal procedure. Adjust belt tension. Refill and bleed pump.

POWER STEERING PUMP PULLEY

NOTE: On Escort and RWD vehicles, pulley cannot be removed or installed with pump in vehicle.

Removal & Installation (Escort & RWD Models) – With pump removed from vehicle, drain as much fluid as possible through filler neck. Install Pulley Remover (T69L-10300-B) on pulley hub. Remove pulley. To install, reverse removal procedure. Using Pulley Installer (T65P-3A733-C), install pulley flush with shaft.

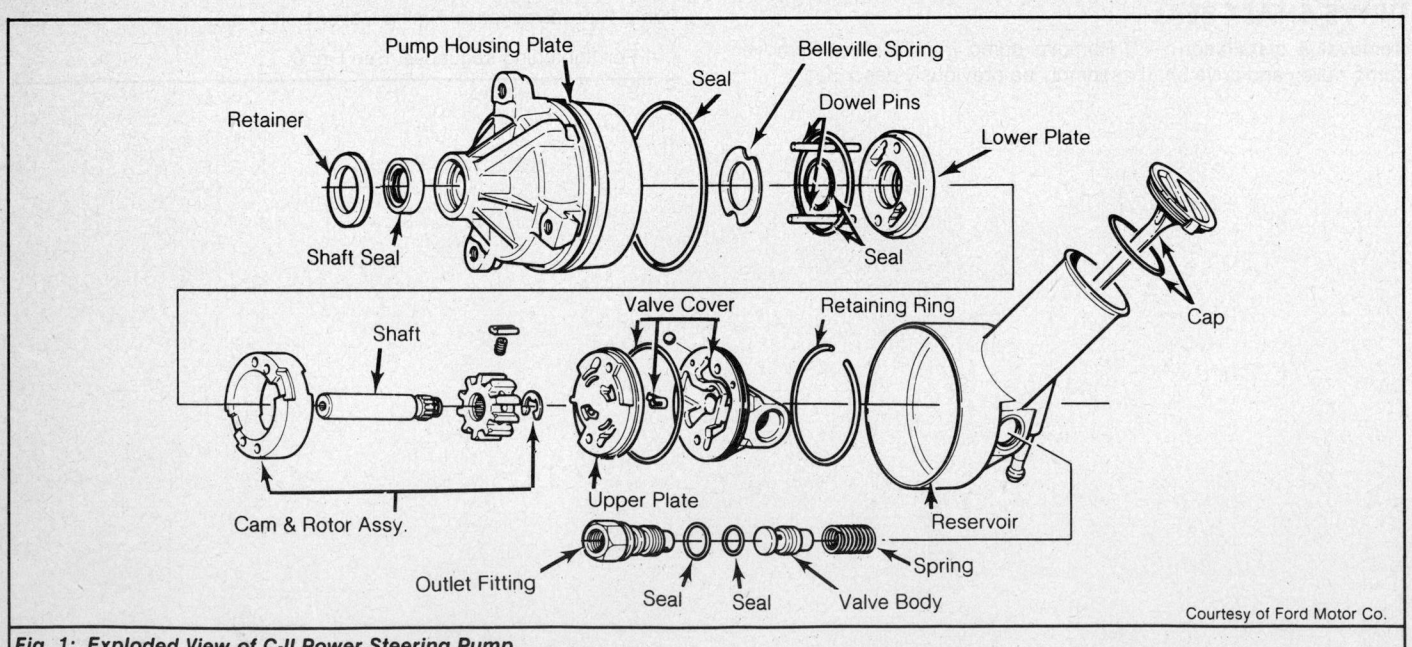

Courtesy of Ford Motor Co.

Fig. 1: Exploded View of C-II Power Steering Pump

NOTE: *When removing pulley, do not apply in and out pressure on pump shaft. Damage to internal thrust areas could result.*

Removal & Installation (All Other Models) – Remove radiator overflow tank. Mark pulley and hub position for reassembly reference. Remove pulley retaining bolts and pulley(s) from pump. To install pulley, align pulley and hub. Install pulley retaining bolts. To complete installation, reverse removal procedure.

PUMP RESERVOIR

Removal & Installation – Place pump in vise. Remove outlet fitting, flow control valve and spring. Remove reservoir by twisting side to side and lifting. Discard "O" ring. To install reservoir, apply petroleum jelly to new "O" ring. To complete installation, reverse removal procedure.

OVERHAUL

POWER STEERING PUMP

Disassembly – 1) Remove pulley, outlet fitting, flow control valve and spring. Remove reservoir from pump. Mount "C" Clamp (T74P-3044-A1) vertically in vise with screw at top.

2) Place Lower Support Plate (T78P-3733-A2) over pump rotor shaft. Install Upper Support Plate (T78P-3733-A1) into upper portion of "C" clamp. Place pump, shaft down, into "C" clamp. Tighten until a slight bottoming of valve cover is felt.

3) Using small drift punch, push inward on retaining ring through hole in side of pump housing. Using a screwdriver, pry retaining ring from housing. Loosen "C" clamp. Remove upper compressor plate and remove pump. Remove pump valve cover and discard "O" ring seal.

4) Push on rotor shaft to remove shaft, upper plate, rotating group assembly and 2 dowel pins. To remove cover plate and Belleville spring, slam pump housing on flat surface. Discard "O" rings and pry rotor shaft seal and seal retainer from housing.

Reassembly – 1) If rotating group was disassembled, place rotor on spline shaft. Rotor is symetrical, and can be installed either way. *See Fig. 2.* Install retaining ring on end of shaft. Place insert cam over rotor with recessed notch on cam facing up.

2) With rotor extended approximately halfway out of cam, insert one spring and slipper (groove facing cam) into one rotor cavity beneath recessed cam flats. Repeat procedure on opposite cavity.

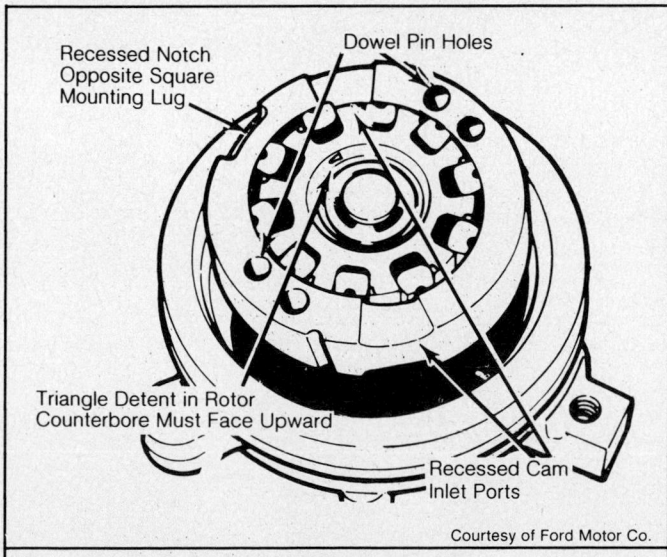

Courtesy of Ford Motor Co.

Fig. 2: Assembling Cam & Rotating Assembly

3) Index cam one space at a time, either right or left, around rotor. Insert remaining springs and slippers until all 10 cavities are filled. Turn rotor carefully so previously installed springs and slippers do not fall out.

4) Using Seal Driver (T78P-3733-A3), install rotor shaft seal into bore until it bottoms. Install seal retainer in same manner. With pulley side of housing facing down, insert 2 dowel pins and Belleville spring (dished surface upward) into housing.

5) Lubricate inner and outer "O" rings with power steering fluid and install on lower pressure plate. Insert lower pressure plate over dowels and into housing with seals facing front of pump.

6) Install pump into "C" clamp. Using Seal Driver (T78P-3733-A3), press lower plate lightly into housing until it bottoms. Install cam, rotor and slippers, and rotor shaft assembly over dowel pins and into housing. *See Fig. 2.*

7) Place upper pressure plate over dowel pins with recess directly over recessed notch on cam insert and approximately 180 degrees opposite square mounting lug. *See Fig. 3.*

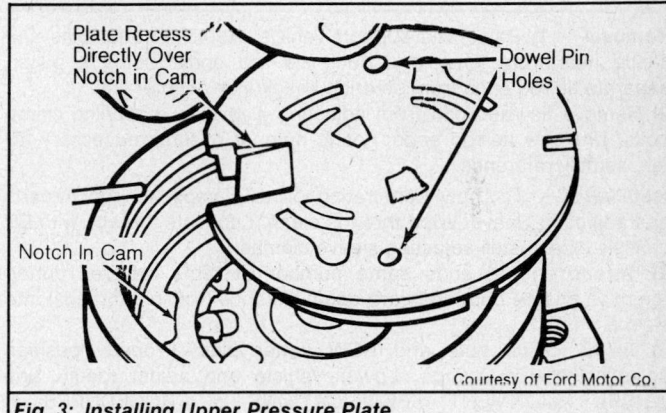

Courtesy of Ford Motor Co.

Fig. 3: Installing Upper Pressure Plate

8) Lubricate and place new "O" ring on valve cover. If plastic baffle is loose in valve cover, apply petroleum jelly to baffle. Install baffle into position on valve cover.

9) Insert valve cover over dowel pins with outlet fitting hole directly in line with square mounting lug on housing. Place assembly in "C" clamp. Compress valve cover into pump housing. Install retaining ring with ends near access hole in housing.

10) Lubricate and install "O" ring on pump housing. Install reservoir. Install flow control valve and spring into valve cover. Use new "O" ring seals on outlet fitting and install into valve cover to specified torque.

CAUTION: If flow control valve is cocked, it may become stuck in valve cover. Do not force valve forward since chips may shear off and carry into valve bore.

11) Lubricate and place new "O" ring seals in the outlet fitting. Install outlet fitting into valve cover. Tighten outlet fitting to specification.

TIGHTENING SPECIFICATIONS

Application	Ft. Lbs. (N.m)
Bracket-to-Engine Bolts	30-45 (41-61)
Outlet Fitting	25-34 (34-46)
Pivot Bolt	30-45 (41-61)
Pressure Hose Nut-to-Pump	10-15 (14-20)
Pump-to-Bracket	30-45 (41-61)
Quick Connect Fitting	10-15 (14-20)

Chrysler Motors, Eagle, Ford Motor Co.

GENERAL INFORMATION

Do not weld, heat or bend steering linkage to repair or straighten. When installing cotter pins, tighten nut to lower specified torque, then tighten nut to next slot that lines up with stud hole. Use new cotter pins during reassembly. Do not hammer on ball studs. Ensure threads are clean and lubricated before tightening.

REMOVAL & INSTALLATION

TIE RODS

NOTE: For removal and installation procedures for rack and pinion type steering gear, see appropriate STEERING GEARS article in this section.

Removal – 1) Raise and support vehicle. Remove cotter pins and castle nuts from inner and outer tie rod ends. Using a puller, separate tie rod ends from steering knuckle and center link.

2) Remove tie rod ends from adjusting sleeve by loosening clamp bolts. Unscrew tie rod ends, noting number of turns necessary for reassembly reference.

Installation – 1) Apply penetrating oil to clamps, tie rod threads and adjusting sleeve. Wipe threads clean. Lubricate threads with EP chassis lube. Install adjusting sleeve clamps.

2) Thread tie rod ends same number of turns required during removal. Ensure both ends are equal distance (within 3 threads) into sleeve.

3) Install castle nuts and NEW cotter pins. Properly position adjusting sleeve clamps. Lower vehicle and adjust toe-in. See WHEEL ALIGNMENT SPECIFICATIONS & PROCEDURES in WHEEL ALIGNMENT section. Tighten clamp bolts.

CENTER LINK

Removal & Installation – Raise and support vehicle. Remove cotter pins and castle nuts. Using a puller, separate inner tie rod ends, idler arm and pitman arm from center link. Remove center link from vehicle. Reverse removal procedure to install. Ensure idler arm stud seal is in place. Lower vehicle. Adjust toe-in.

IDLER ARM

Removal & Installation – 1) Raise vehicle. Separate center link from idler arm. Remove 2 idler arm mounting bolts. If idler arm support is disconnected from frame for other work, wire support to idler arm to prevent rotation if equipped with a threaded type bushing.

2) Idler arm should be replaced when a vertical force of 25 lbs. (11 kg) is applied at center link end of idler arm, and vertical lash exceeds .13" (3.3 mm).

PITMAN ARM

Removal & Installation – 1) Raise and support vehicle. Mark pitman arm-to-steering shaft for reassembly reference.

2) Remove center link ball joint stud cotter pin and nut. Using a puller, separate center link from pitman arm. DO NOT hammer on end of puller.

3) Remove pitman arm retaining nut. Using a puller, separate pitman arm from steering gear. To install, reverse removal procedure.

TIGHTENING SPECIFICATIONS

Application	Ft. Lbs. (N.m)
Idler Arm-to-Center Link Nut	
Chrysler Motors	40 (54)
Ford Motor Co.	60-70 (81-95)
Idler Arm-to-Frame	
Chrysler Motors	70 (95)
Ford Motor Co.	85-95 (115-129)
Pitman Arm-to-Center Link Nut	
Chrysler Motors	40 (54)
Ford Motor Co.	43-47 (58-64)
Tie Rod End Castle Nut	
Chrysler Motors	38 (52)
Eagle	35 (47)
Ford Motor Co.	35-47 (47-64)
Tie Rod End Lock Nut	
Chrysler Motors	38 (52)
Eagle	36 (49)
Ford Motor Co.	35-50 (47-68)

Section 14

TRANSMISSION SERVICING

CONTENTS

TRANSMISSION APPLICATIONS	Page
Automatic Transmissions	14-2
Manual Transmissions	14-2

OIL PAN GASKET IDENTIFICATION

All Models	14-3

AUTOMATIC TRANSMISSION SERVICING

Chrysler Motors	14-5
Eagle	14-7
Ford Motor Co.	14-9

AUTOMATIC TRANSMISSION REMOVAL

Chrysler Motors	14-15
Eagle	14-16
Ford Motor Co.	14-17

MANUAL TRANSMISSION SERVICING

Chrysler Motors	14-21
Ford Motor Co.	14-23

IMPORTANT: For information on manual transmission removal and installation, see CLUTCHES section.

NOTE: ALSO SEE GENERAL INDEX.

1989 TRANSMISSION APPLICATIONS
Domestic Cars – Automatic

DOMESTIC AUTOMATIC TRANSMISSION APPLICATIONS

Manufacturer & Model	Transmission
CHRYSLER MOTORS	
FWD	
Acclaim	A-413 & A-604 Transaxle
Aries	A-413 Transaxle
Daytona	A-413 Transaxle
Dynasty	A-413 & A-604 Transaxle
Horizon	A-413 Transaxle
Lancer	A-413 Transaxle
LeBaron	A-413 Transaxle
New Yorker	A-604 Transaxle
Omni	A-413 Transaxle
Reliant	A-413 Transaxle
Shadow	A-413 Transaxle
Spirit	A-413 & A-604 Transaxle
Sundance	A-413 Transaxle
RWD	
Diplomat	A-904-LA & [1] A-727
Fifth Avenue	A-904-LA
Gran Fury	A-904-LA

DOMESTIC AUTOMATIC TRANSMISSION APPLICATIONS (Cont.)

Manufacturer & Model	Transmission
EAGLE	
Premier	AR-4 & ZF 4HP-18 Transaxle
FORD MOTOR CO.	
FWD	
Continental	AXOD Transaxle
Escort	ATX Transaxle
Probe	G4A-EL (EC-AT) Transaxle
Sable	ATX & AXOD Transaxle
Taurus	ATX & AXOD Transaxle
Tempo	ATX Transaxle
Topaz	ATX Transaxle
RWD	
Cougar	AOD
Grand Marquis	AOD
LTD Crown Victoria	AOD
Mark VII	AOD
Mustang	AOD & [2] A4LD
Thunderbird	AOD
Town Car	AOD
Wagon	AOD

[1] – Police vehicles only.
[2] – 2.3L only.

Domestic Cars – Manual

DOMESTIC MANUAL TRANSMISSION APPLICATIONS

Manufacturer & Model	Transmission
CHRYSLER MOTORS	
FWD	
Acclaim	5-Speed A-520 & A-555 Transaxle
Aries	5-Speed A-520 Transaxle
Daytona	5-Speed A-555 Transaxle
Horizon	5-Speed A-525 Transaxle
Lancer	5-Speed A-555 Transaxle
LeBaron	5-Speed A-555 Transaxle
Omni	5-Speed A-525 Transaxle
Reliant	5-Speed A-520 Transaxle
Shadow	5-Speed A-520 Transaxle
Spirit	5-Speed A-520 & A-555 Transaxle
Sundance	5-Speed A-520 Transaxle

DOMESTIC MANUAL TRANSMISSION APPLICATIONS (Cont.)

Manufacturer & Model	Transmission
FORD MOTOR CO.	
FWD	
Escort	4-Speed MTX II Transaxle
Probe	5-Speed Transaxle
Tempo	4-Speed MTX II Transaxle
	5-Speed MTX III Transaxle
Topaz	5-Speed MTX III Transaxle
RWD	
Cougar	5-Speed M5R2
Mustang	5-Speed T50D
Thunderbird	5-Speed M5R2

1989 AUTOMATIC TRANSMISSIONS
Oil Pan Gasket Identification

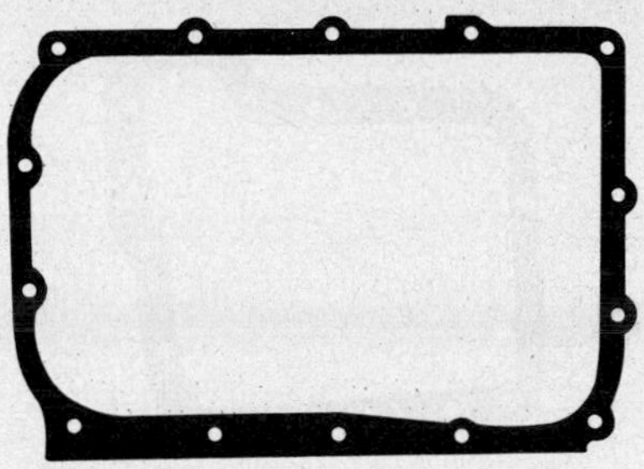

Fig. 1: Chrysler Motors A-413

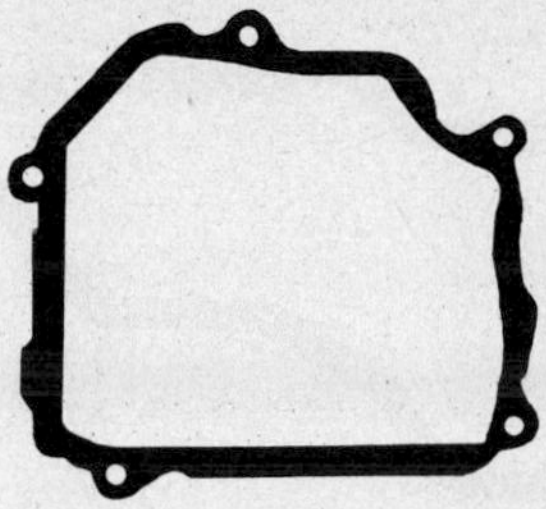

Fig. 5: Eagle Premier AR-4

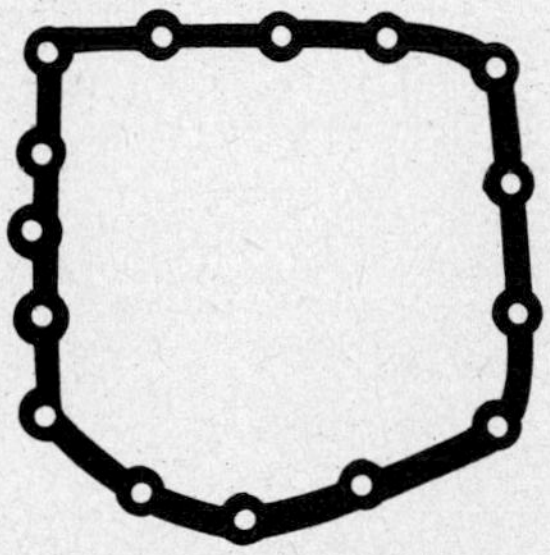

Fig. 2: Chrysler Motors A-604

Fig. 6: Eagle Premier ZF 4HP-18

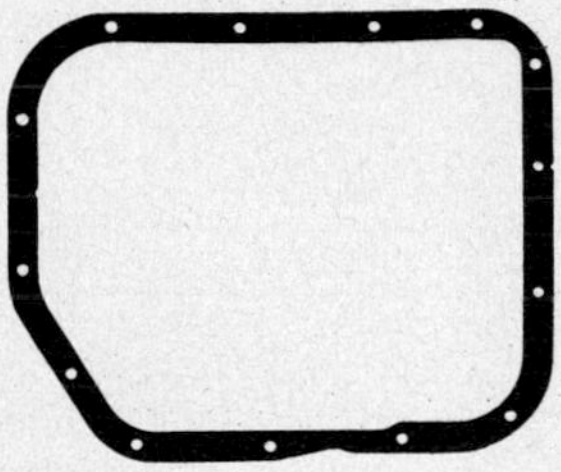

Fig. 3: Chrysler Motors A-904-LA

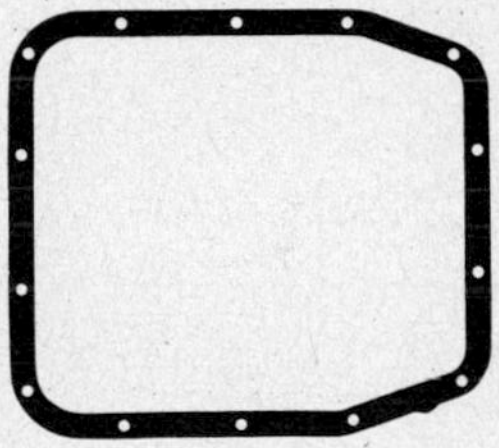

Fig. 7: Ford Motor Co. AOD

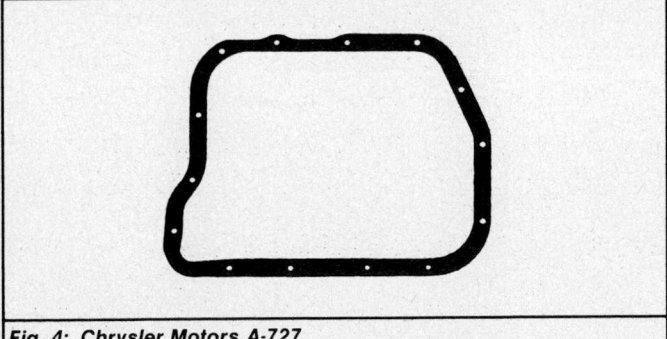

Fig. 4: Chrysler Motors A-727

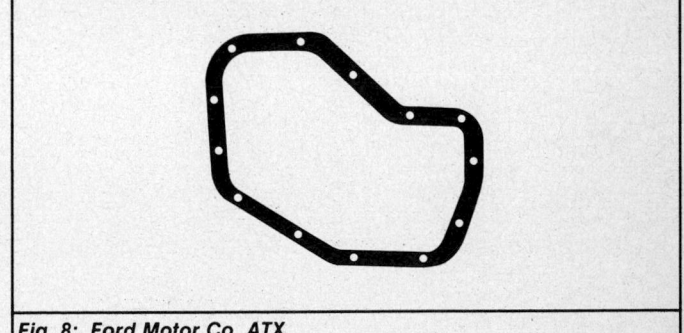

Fig. 8: Ford Motor Co. ATX

1989 AUTOMATIC TRANSMISSIONS
Oil Pan Gasket Identification (Cont.)

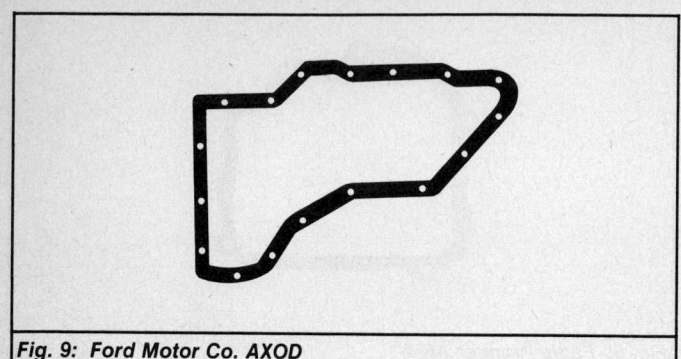

Fig. 9: Ford Motor Co. AXOD

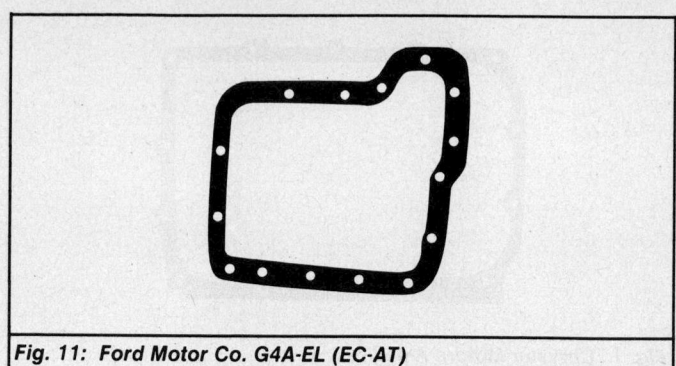

Fig. 11: Ford Motor Co. G4A-EL (EC-AT)

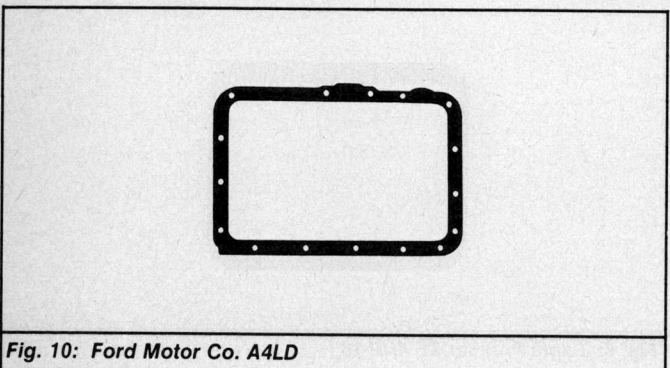

Fig. 10: Ford Motor Co. A4LD

IDENTIFICATION

CHRYSLER MOTORS AUTOMATIC TRANSMISSION APPLICATIONS

Model	Transmission
FWD	
Acclaim	A-413 & A-604 Transaxle
Aries	A-413 Transaxle
Daytona	A-413 Transaxle
Dynasty	A-413 & A-604 Transaxle
Horizon	A-413 Transaxle
Lancer	A-413 Transaxle
LeBaron	A-413 Transaxle
New Yorker	A-604 Transaxle
Omni	A-413 Transaxle
Reliant	A-413 Transaxle
Shadow	A-413 Transaxle
Spirit	A-413 & A-604 Transaxle
Sundance	A-413 Transaxle
RWD	
Diplomat	A-904-LA & [1] A-727
Fifth Avenue	A-904-LA
Gran Fury	A-904-LA

[1] – Police vehicles only.

LUBRICATION

SERVICE INTERVALS

Check fluid level whenever performing other underhood services. Draining, refilling and band adjustments are not required under normal driving conditions. Under heavy duty (severe service) conditions, change fluid, replace filter, and adjust bands (if applicable) every 15,000 miles.

CHECKING FLUID LEVELS

RWD Models – 1) With vehicle on level ground, apply parking brake. Start engine and run at curb idle. Shift gear selector through all positions, ending in Neutral.

2) Fluid level should be in crosshatch area on dipstick. Check condition of fluid for contamination or burned smell. Do not overfill. Fully seat dipstick.

FWD Models – 1) With vehicle on level ground, apply parking brake and run engine at curb idle for at least 60 seconds. Gear selector through all positons, ending in Park.

2) Fluid level should be in crosshatch area of dipstick marked "WARM" or "HOT", depending on fluid temperature. Check condition of fluid for contamination or burned smell. Do not overfill. Fully seat dipstick.

RECOMMENDED FLUID

Use only Dexron II ATF. Chrysler Motors does not recommend the use of any additives to transmissions.

FLUID CAPACITY

NOTE: *Transmission and converter assembly capacities given below are approximate. Correct fluid level should be determined by mark on dipstick.*

TRANSMISSION REFILL CAPACITIES

Application	Qts. (L)
A-413	
(Except Fleet)	8.9 (8.4)
(Fleet)	9.2 (8.7)
(Lock-Up)	8.5 (8.0)
A-604	9.1 (8.6)
A-727 (Lock-Up)	[1] 8.4 (8.0)
A-904-LA (Lock-Up)	[1] 8.1 (7.7)

[1] – Add .5 pts. (.2L) for auxiliary oil coolers.

DRAINING & REFILLING

1) Raise and support vehicle. Remove oil pan bolts to gradually lower and drain pan at one corner. Remove oil filter screws and remove filter. Adjustment of rear band can be made at this time (if required).

2) Install new filter and filter gasket or "O" ring (if equipped) on bottom of valve body and tighten screws (if equipped) to 40 INCH lbs. (5 N.m) on FWD models, and 35 INCH lbs. (4 N.m) on RWD models. Clean pan with solvent and blow dry with compressed air.

3) On RWD models, install pan with new gasket. Make sure round magnet is over boss in right front corner of oil pan. On FWD models, install pan using new RTV sealant to form gasket. Tighten pan bolts to specifications.

4) Lower vehicle. On FWD models, add 4 qts. (3.8L) of ATF. On RWD models, add 2 qts. (1.9L) of ATF. Start engine and allow to idle for at least 2 minutes.

5) With engine at curb idle and parking brake applied, move gear selector lever through all positions, ending in the "N" position ("P" position on FWD models). Add enough fluid to bring level to "ADD" mark on dipstick (1/8" below ADD on FWD models).

6) Recheck fluid level after transmission/transaxle has reached normal operating temperature. Add required amount of fluid. Do not overfill. Ensure dipstick is fully seated.

OIL PAN TIGHTENING SPECIFICATIONS

Transmission	INCH Lbs. (N.m)
FWD Models	165 (19)
RWD Models	150 (17)

ADJUSTMENTS

KICKDOWN BAND (FRONT)

NOTE: *The A-604 transaxle does not have any bands. Kickdown band adjustment screw for A-413 is located on left side (top front) of transaxle case, and on left side of transmission case above throttle linkage lever on A-727 & A-904 models.*

All Models – 1) Loosen adjustment screw lock nut (while preventing adjustment screw from turning) and back off 5 turns. After making sure adjustment screw turns freely in case.

2) Tighten adjustment screw to 72 INCH lbs. (8 N.m), then back off adjustment screw 2 1/2 turns. Hold adjustment screw in this position and tighten lock nut to 35 ft. lbs. (47 N.m).

LOW-REVERSE BAND (REAR)

NOTE: *Low-Reverse band adjustment screws for both FWD and RWD models are located on rear servo lever. Band adjustment screw is not accessible unless oil pan is removed. See Fig. 1.*

1) Drain transmission/transaxle and remove oil pan. Loosen band adjustment screw lock nut (while preventing adjustment screw from turning) and back off nut 5 turns. Ensure adjustment screw turns freely in case.

2) When tightening adjustment screw on RWD models, tighten screw to 72 INCH lbs. (8 N.m). On FWD models, tighten adjustment screw to 41 INCH lbs. (5 N.m).

3) On all models, back off adjustment screw the specified number of turns given in LOW-REVERSE BAND ADJUSTMENT table. Hold in this position and tighten lock nut to 10 ft. lbs. (14 N.m) on FWD models, and 30 ft. lbs. (41 N.m) on RWD models.

4) Clean oil pan and remove all gasket material from pan and case. Install oil pan using new pan gasket (or new RTV sealant) and add the required amount of fluid to fill transmission/transaxle. Road test vehicle.

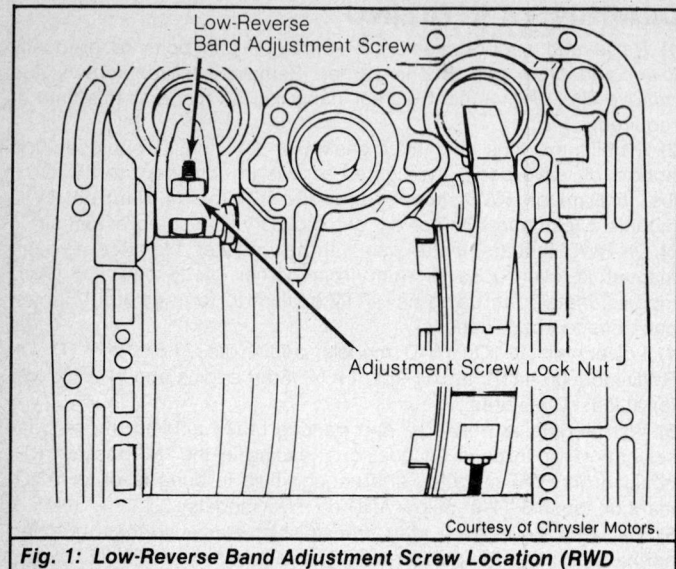

Fig. 1: Low-Reverse Band Adjustment Screw Location (RWD Models)

LOW-REVERSE BAND ADJUSTMENT

Application	Back Off Screw
A-904-LA	4 Turns
A-727	2 Turns
A-413	3 1/2 Turns

TRANSMISSION THROTTLE ROD

RWD Models – 1) Make sure carburetor is not on fast idle cam and idle speed is correctly set. Raise vehicle on hoist to make adjustment at transmission throttle lever.

2) Loosen adjustable swivel lock screw. Swivel must be free to slide along flat end of throttle rod so that preload spring action is not restricted. Hold transmission lever firmly forward against its internal stop, and tighten swivel lock screw. This completes throttle rod adjustment, as linkage backlash was automatically removed by the preload spring.

3) To check linkage freedom of operation, move throttle rod rearward and release slowly. Ensure that rod retracts to its full forward position. *See Fig. 2.*

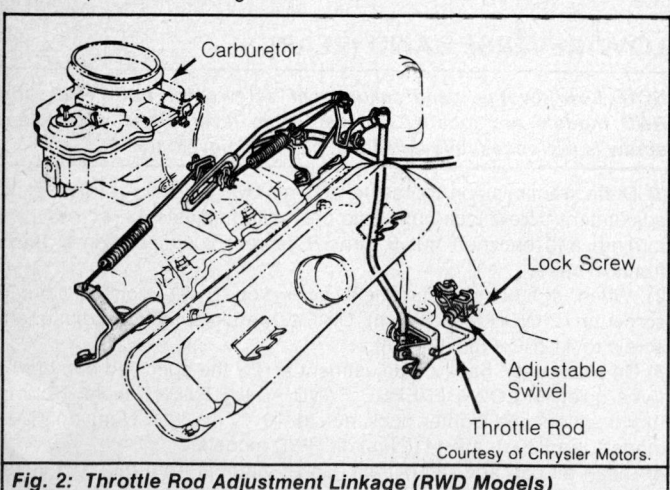

Fig. 2: Throttle Rod Adjustment Linkage (RWD Models)

TRANSMISSION THROTTLE CABLE

FWD Models – 1) Ensure engine idle speed is correct and engine is at normal operating temperature. Loosen adjustment bracket lock screw. Bracket must have both bracket alignment tabs touching

transaxle cast surface. Tighten lock screw to 105 INCH lbs. (12 N.m). *See Fig. 3.*

2) Release cross-lock on cable assembly by pulling upward. To ensure correct adjustment, cable must be free to slide toward engine, against its stop, after cross-lock is released.

3) Move transaxle throttle control lever fully clockwise against its internal stop. Press cross-lock downward into locked position.

4) Move transaxle throttle lever counterclockwise. Slowly release it to ensure it will return to full clockwise position.

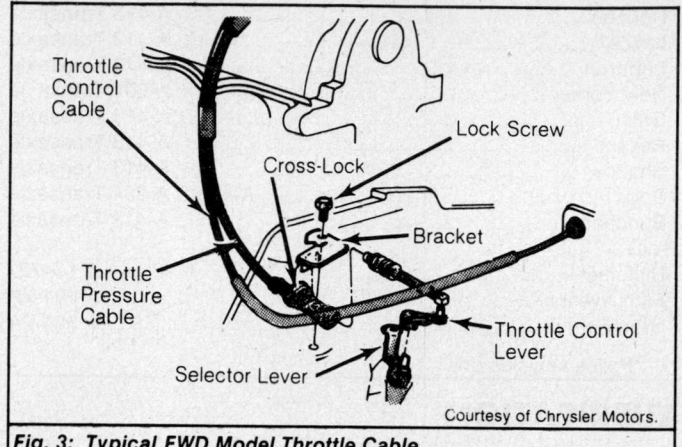

Fig. 3: Typical FWD Model Throttle Cable

SHIFT LINKAGE

Column Shift (RWD Models) – 1) Place gear selector in "P" position. Loosen adjustment swivel lock screw, making sure swivel block is free to turn on shift rod. Move shift lever on transmission all the way to rear detent position (Park). Tighten swivel lock screw to 100 INCH lbs. (11 N.m).

2) Check adjustment by moving gear selector. Detents for Drive and Neutral should be within limits of selector gate stops. Starter should operate only with gear selector in Park or Neutral. *See Fig. 4.*

CAUTION: On FWD and RWD models, whenever it is necessary to remove linkage cable from lever, replace old plastic grommets with new ones. Use pliers to snap new grommet onto lever and rod into grommet.

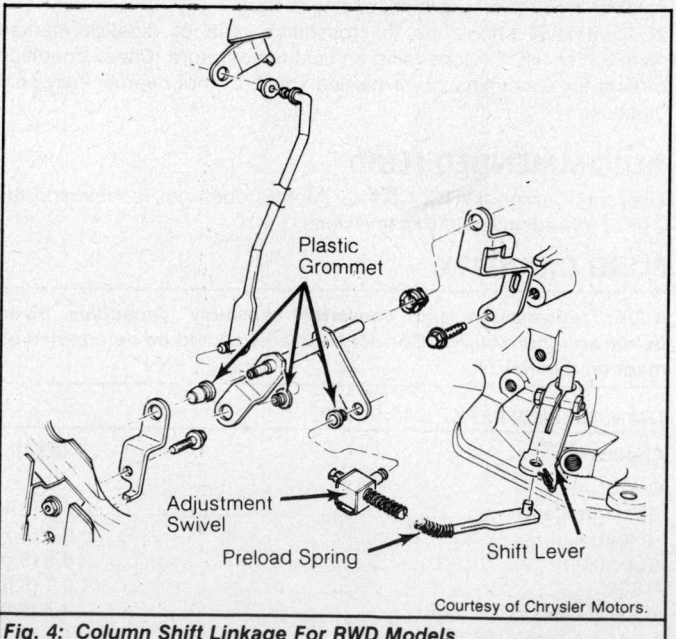

Fig. 4: Column Shift Linkage For RWD Models

Console or Column Shift (FWD Models) – 1) Place gear selector in the "P" position. Loosen lock bolt on cable adjusting bracket on transaxle. *See Fig. 5.* On column shift models, ensure preload adjustment spring engages fork on transaxle bracket.

2) On all models, pull shift lever by hand all the way to front detent position (Park). Tighen lock screw to 100 INCH lbs. (11 N.m).

3) To check adjustment, gearshift lever should be within limits of hand lever gate stops when shifted through gear positions. Vehicle must only start in Park or Neutral.

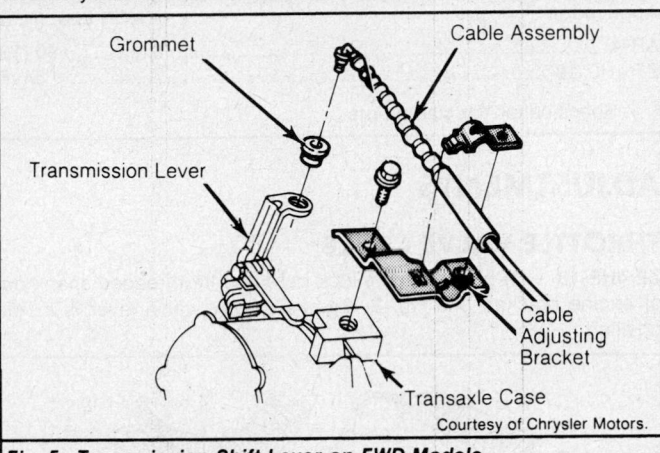

Fig. 5: Transmission Shift Lever on FWD Models

NEUTRAL SAFETY SWITCH

Combination neutral safety and back-up light switch is screwed into side of transmission case. Switch is nonadjustable. Switch may be tested for continuity using following method.

Testing – 1) Center terminal of 3 terminal neutral safety and back-up light switch provides ground for starter solenoid circuit through shift lever in Park or Neutral positions only.

2) To test, remove wiring connector from switch and check for continuity between center pin of switch and case. Continuity should exist only when transmission is in Park or Neutral.

NOTE: Check shift linkage adjustment before replacing a switch that tests bad.

3) The back-up light switch circuit is through the 2 outside terminals of the switch. Continuity should exist between the 2 terminals only when transmission is in reverse. No continuity should exist from either terminal to case.

4) To replace, unscrew switch from case (some fluid will escape). Move gear selector lever to Park, and then to Neutral position. Check to see that switch operating fingers are centered in switch opening in case.

5) Install switch with new seal into case and tighten. Check transmission fluid level.

Eagle

Premier

IDENTIFICATION

EAGLE AUTOMATIC TRANSMISSION APPLICATIONS

Application	Transaxle
Premier	AR-4 & ZF 4HP-18

The AR-4 transaxle is used with the 2.5L engine. Transaxle I.D. tag is located next to transaxle oil cooler on passenger side of case. The ZF 4HP-18 transaxle is used with 3.0L V6 engine. Transaxle I.D. tag is on driver's side of case above oil pan.

LUBRICATION

SERVICE INTERVALS

Transaxle – Transaxle fluid and filter screen should be changed every 30,000 miles.

Differential – Synthetic fluid does not require replacement. Check level when servicing transaxle.

CHECKING FLUID LEVELS

Transaxle – 1) Place vehicle on level surface. Start and run engine at idle speed. Move gear selector lever through all gear positions ending in Park.

2) If transaxle is cold, fluid level should be at "FULL COLD" mark on dipstick. If transaxle is at normal operating temperature, fluid level should be at "FULL HOT" mark on other side of dipstick. About 1/4 quart is needed to increase level from "ADD" to "FULL" mark.

Differential – With vehicle on level surface, fluid level should be at bottom of fill plug hole. *See Fig. 1.*

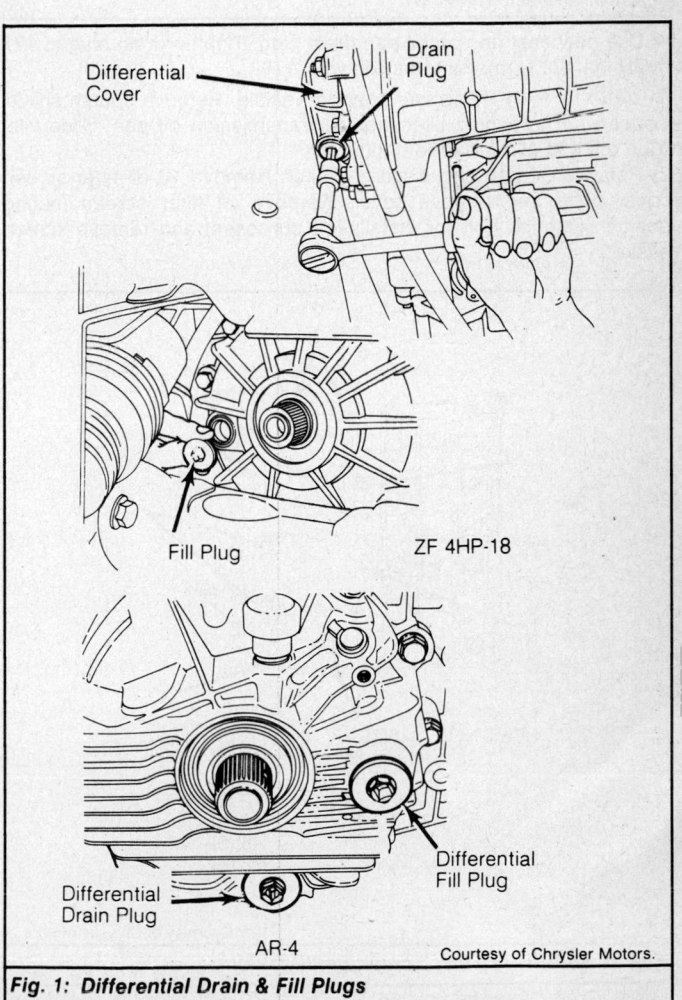

Fig. 1: Differential Drain & Fill Plugs

RECOMMENDED FLUID

Transaxle – Use only Mopar Mercon type fluid.

Differential – Use SAE 75W-140 synthetic gear oil (Part No. 89982 200 945).

NOTE: *Transaxle and differential are separate and require different lubricants.*

TRANSMISSION REFILL CAPACITIES

Application	Dry Fill Qts. (L)	Overhaul Qts. (L)
Transaxle		
AR-4	2.8 (2.6)	7.4 (7.0)
ZF 4HP-18	5.6 (5.3)	2.8 (2.6)
Differential		
AR-4	.89 (.85)	.89 (.85)
ZF 4HP-18	.73 (.70)	.73 (70)

DRAINING & REFILLING

AR-4 – 1) Raise and support vehicle. Remove splash pan. Remove drain plug on transaxle oil pan and drain fluid. Remove oil pan and discard gasket.
2) Remove 2 oil filter screen bolts. Discard screen and gasket.
3) Use petroleum jelly to hold oil filter screen gasket in place. Install filter screen and tighten bolts to 46 INCH lbs. (5 N.m). Install oil pan with new gasket. Do not use any sealant.

NOTE: *To prevent leaks, ensure all oil pan gasket hole spacers are in place before installation.*

4) Use new seal ring on oil pan drain plug. Tighten drain plug to 177 INCH lbs. (20 N.m). Fill transaxle with ATF.
ZF 4HP-18 – 1) Raise and support vehicle. Remove splash shield. Loosen nut attaching filler tube to transmission oil pan. Slide filler tube out and allow fluid to drain.
2) Remove oil pan and discard gasket. Remove 10 oil filter screen cover bolts and remove cover. Remove oil filter screen (noting position of each bolt for installation purposes) and remove screen gasket.

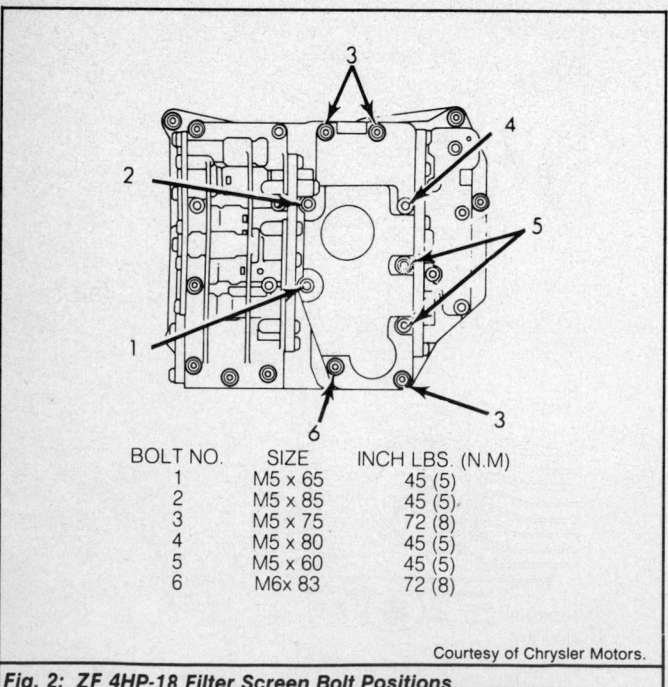

BOLT NO.	SIZE	INCH LBS. (N.M)
1	M5 x 65	45 (5)
2	M5 x 85	45 (5)
3	M5 x 75	72 (8)
4	M5 x 80	45 (5)
5	M5 x 60	45 (5)
6	M6x 83	72 (8)

Courtesy of Chrysler Motors.

Fig. 2: ZF 4HP-18 Filter Screen Bolt Positions

3) Clean oil pan and magnet. Replace all parts using new gaskets and oil filter screen "O" ring. Ensure oil filter screen bolts are installed in correct position and tightened to correct torque. *See Fig. 2.* Fill transaxle with ATF.

NOTE: *ZF 4HP-18 oil filter screen bolts are different lengths and must be replaced in their original positions.*

OIL PAN TIGHTENING SPECIFICATIONS

Application	INCH Lbs. (N.m)
AR-4	90 (10)
ZF 4HP-18	[1] 54 (6)

[1] – Specification for clamp nuts.

ADJUSTMENTS

THROTTLE VALVE CABLE

ZF 4HP-18 – 1) Loosen cable lock nuts and lift threaded shank out of engine bracket. *See Fig. 3.* Ensure throttle valve lever is in idle position.

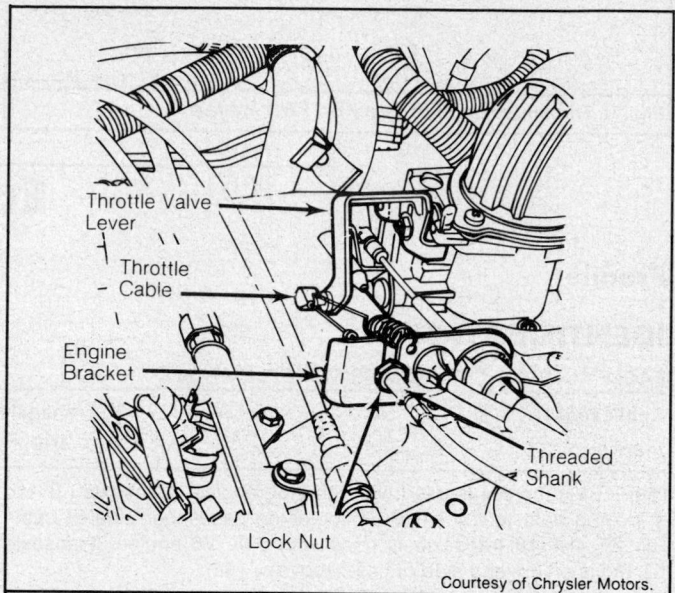

Courtesy of Chrysler Motors.

Fig. 3: ZF 4HP-18 Throttle Cable

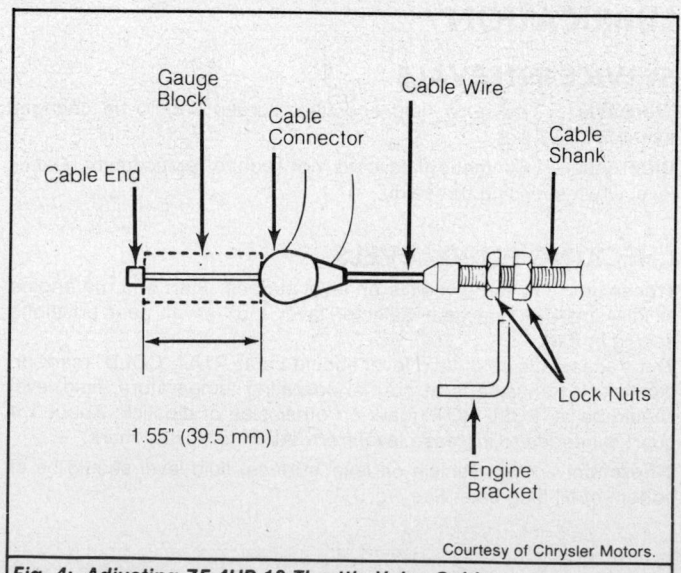

Courtesy of Chrysler Motors.

Fig. 4: Adjusting ZF 4HP 18 Throttle Valve Cable

2) Pull cable wire forward. Place a fabricated 1.55" (39.5 mm) gauge block between cable connector and cable end. Vernier calipers can be used to measure cable distance. *See Fig. 4.*

3) Pull cable shank rearward to detent position, but NOT to wide open throttle position. Detent position will have a definite feel, similiar to stop, when it is reached.

4) Hold shank at detent position and place it in engine bracket. Tighten lock nuts to lock shank in position. Remove gauge block. Detent position should be reached when cable travel is 1.52-1.59" (38.5-40.5 mm).

SHIFT CABLE

1) Ensure that shift cable is securely connected to column shift arm before proceeding with adjustment. Shift gear selector lever into the "P" position. Raise and support vehicle.

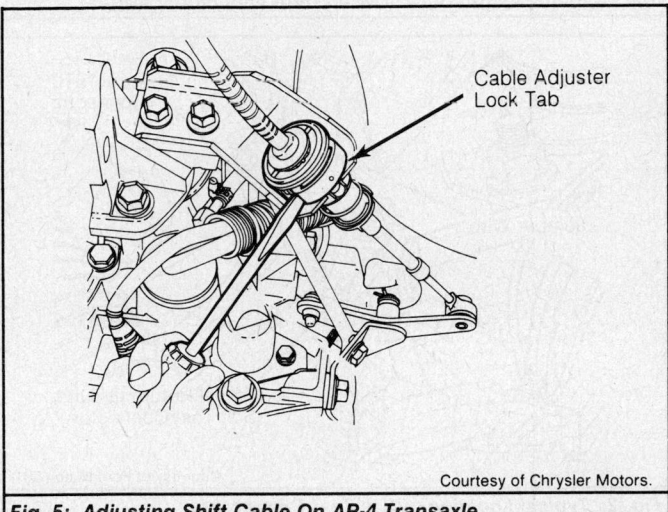

Cable Adjuster
Lock Tab

Courtesy of Chrysler Motors.

Fig. 5: Adjusting Shift Cable On AR-4 Transaxle

2) Release shift cable adjuster lock tab by prying it outward with a screwdriver. *See Fig. 5.* Move transaxle lever all the way rearward into the "P" position and ensure that it is centered in the detent.

3) Verify that cable is properly routed and secured. Check that wheels do not turn when in the Park position. Pull shift cable rearward until a distance of .300" (7.62 mm) is reached; then press cable adjuster tab inward until it snaps into place. *See Fig. 6.*

4) Lower vehicle and check that shift cable is properly adjusted. Engine should only start in the "P" and "N" positions. Repeat procedure if readjustment is necessary. Move shift cable (in either direction) in .040" (1 mm) increments until properly adjusted.

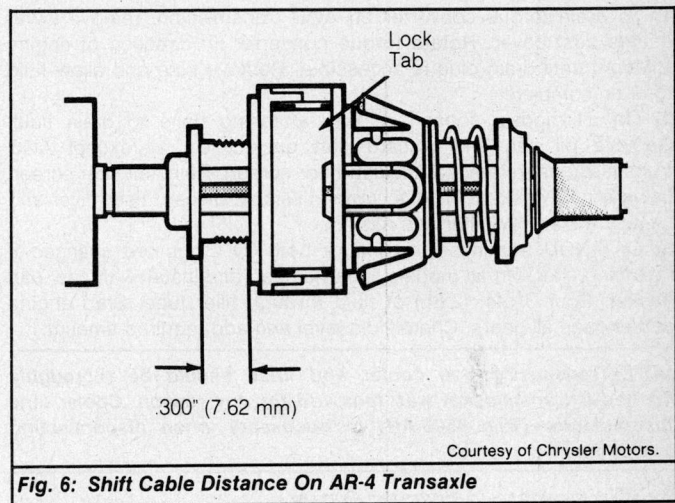

Lock
Tab

.300" (7.62 mm)

Courtesy of Chrysler Motors.

Fig. 6: Shift Cable Distance On AR-4 Transaxle

NEUTRAL SAFETY SWITCH

Neutral safety switches for both transaxles are mounted on outside of case and are nonadjustable.

Ford Motor Co.

IDENTIFICATION

FORD MOTOR CO. AUTOMATIC TRANSMISSION APPLICATIONS

Model	Transmission
FWD	
Continental	AXOD Transaxle
Escort	ATX Transaxle
Probe	G4A-EL (EC-AT) Transaxle
Sable	ATX & AXOD Transaxle
Taurus	ATX & AXOD Transaxle
Tempo	ATX Transaxle
Topaz	ATX Transaxle
RWD	
Cougar	AOD
Grand Marquis	AOD
LTD Crown Victoria	AOD
Mark VII	AOD
Mustang	AOD & [1] A4LD
Thunderbird	AOD
Town Car	AOD
Wagon	AOD

[1] – 2.3L only.

LUBRICATION

SERVICE INTERVALS

Check fluid level at every engine oil change. Fluid, filter changes and band adjustments are not required under normal operation. Under heavy duty (severe service), change fluid and filter every 30 months or 30,000 miles. On A4LD transmissions, adjust bands when fluid is changed.

CHECKING FLUID LEVEL

1) Transmission must be at normal operating temperature with vehicle on level ground. Apply parking brake, and run engine at curb idle. Shift gear selector lever through all positions, ending in Park.

2) Fluid level should be in crosshatch area if checked at operating temperature. If transmission is at room temperature, fluid level should be between two dimples on bottom of dipstick.

3) Do not overfill. Check condition of fluid for contamination or burned smell. Fully reseat dipstick.

NOTE: On AXOD transaxle, fluid level should only be checked at normal operating temperature.

RECOMMENDED FLUID

On all 1989 transmissions and transaxles, Ford Motor Co. recommends using the new Mercon (E4AZ-19582-B) automatic transmission fluid. Mercon is NOT recommended for power steering systems.

FLUID CAPACITY

NOTE: Transmission and converter assembly capacities given below are approximate. Correct fluid level should be determined by mark on dipstick, rather than by amount given.

TRANSMISSION REFILL CAPACITIES

Application	¹ Qts. (L)
AOD	12.3 (11.6)
ATX	8.3 (7.9)
AXOD	12.8 (12.1)
A4LD	9.5 (9.0)
G4A-EL	8.3 (7.9)

¹ – Includes oil cooler (if equipped).

DRAINING & REFILLING

1) To drain torque converter on AOD transmission, remove lower engine dust cover. Rotate torque converter (in direction of engine rotation) until drain plug is accessible. Remove plug and allow fluid to drain completely.

2) On all models, loosen oil pan attaching bolts to drain fluid. Remove oil pan and discard pan gasket. On all except AOD transmissions, remove and clean filter screen. Reinstall filter screen using a new gasket. On AOD transmissions, discard used filter and gasket. Install new filter and gasket.

3) On AXOD transmission, ensure both "O" rings are changed if replacing filter. On all models, clean oil pan and install with new pan gasket. Pour 3 qts. (2.8L) of fluid through filler tube. Start engine and engage all gears. Check fluid level and add required amount.

NOTE: Transmission oil cooler and lines should be thoroughly flushed if transmission was removed for any reason. Cooler Line Disconnector (T82L-9500-AH) is necessary when disconnecting cooler lines.

OIL PAN TIGHTENING SPECIFICATIONS

Transmission	INCH Lbs. (N.m)
AOD	72-124 (8-14)
ATX	144-204 (16-23)
AXOD	124-144 (14-16)
A4LD	96-124 (11-14)
G4A-EL	71-97 (8-11)

FILTER SCREEN TIGHTENING SPECIFICATIONS

Transmission	INCH Lbs. (N.m)
AOD	80-97 (9-11)
ATX	80-108 (9-12)
A4LD	71-97 (8-11)
G4A-EL	71-97 (8-11)

ADJUSTMENTS

INTERMEDIATE & OVERDRIVE BAND

A4LD – 1) Clean all dirt from band adjusting screw area. Remove and discard adjusting screw lock nut. Install a new lock nut on adjusting screw, leaving lock nut loose.

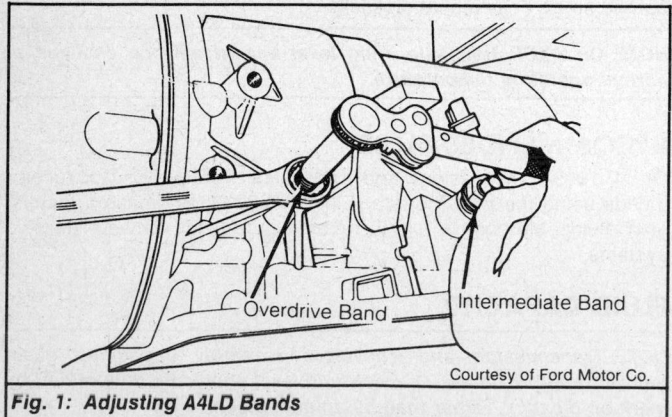

Fig. 1: Adjusting A4LD Bands

2) Tighten band adjusting screw to 10 ft. lbs. (14 N.m). Back off adjusting screw EXACTLY 2 turns. Hold adjusting screw in this position and tighten lock nut to 40 ft. lbs. (54 N.m). *See Fig. 1.*

THROTTLE CONTROL LINKAGE (ATX)

ATX (1.9L & 2.5L) – 1) Vehicle must be at idle with parking brake set. Transaxle must be in Park. Remove any corrosion from control rod and free-up trunnion block so it slides freely on control rod.

2) Connect a jumper wire between Self-Test Input (STI) connector and signal return ground on self-test connector. *See Fig. 2.* Turn ignition switch to the "RUN" position. DO NOT start engine. The ISC plunger will retract. Wait until plunger is fully retracted (about 10 seconds).

NOTE: STI connector is usually located near firewall on passenger side of engine compartment, or on right side fender apron.

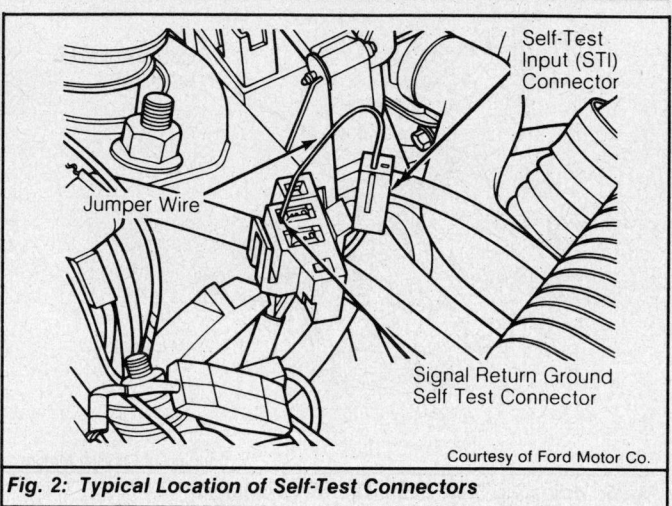

Self-Test Input (STI) Connector

Jumper Wire

Signal Return Ground Self Test Connector

Courtesy of Ford Motor Co.

Fig. 2: Typical Location of Self-Test Connectors

3) Turn ignition switch to the "OFF" position and remove jumper wire. Pull up on transaxle T.V. control rod using light force to ensure that T.V. control lever is against its internal idle stop.

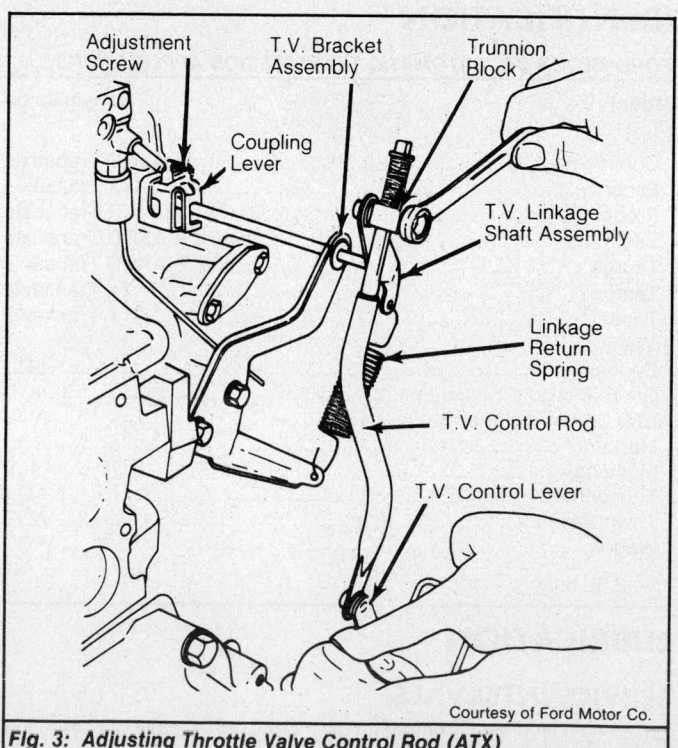

Adjustment Screw

T.V. Bracket Assembly

Trunnion Block

Coupling Lever

T.V. Linkage Shaft Assembly

Linkage Return Spring

T.V. Control Rod

T.V. Control Lever

Courtesy of Ford Motor Co.

Fig. 3: Adjusting Throttle Valve Control Rod (ATX)

4) Allow trunnion to slide on rod to its natural position. Without relaxing force on T.V. control lever, tighten bolt on trunnion block to 48-84 INCH lbs. (5-9 N.m). *See Fig. 3.*

ATX (2.3L) – 1) Vehicle must be at idle with parking brake set. Transaxle must be in Park. Remove any corrosion from control rod and free-up trunnion block so it slides freely on control rod.

2) Hold control rod stationary to prevent it from telescoping during adjustment. Hold T.V. lever against its internal idle stop. To hold control rod, either install T.V. linkage return spring, or apply a light force on linkage.

3) While holding control rod and T.V. lever, hold throttle lever against idle stop and tighten T.V. rod bolt to 48-84 INCH lbs. (5-9 N.m). Verify that T.V. linkage return spring is in place and control rod is free to travel (telescope). *See Fig. 3.*

THROTTLE CONTROL LINKAGE (AOD)

Checking Throttle Control Pressure (Cable Type) – 1) The T.V. control pressure should be checked using an accurate (0-60 psi) oil pressure gauge. Attach pressure gauge to T.V. throttle pressure tap port on right side of transmission. *See Fig. 4.* It may be necessary to use a 90 degree elbow adapter to avoid contact with exhaust system.

NOTE: Pressure gauge should have about 8 ft. of flexible hose attached so it can be read from passenger compartment.

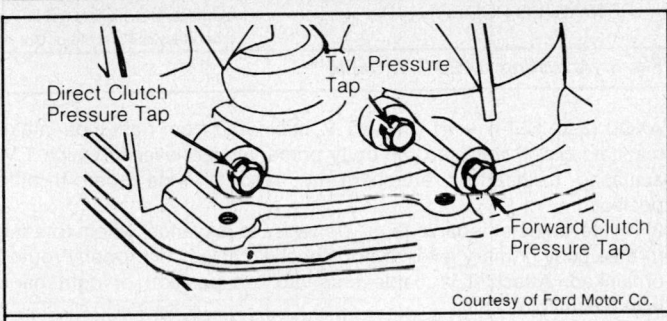

Courtesy of Ford Motor Co.

Fig. 4: T.V. Throttle Pressure Tap Port On AOD

2) Insert Cable T.V Gauge (T86L-70332-A) between crimped slug on end of cable and plastic notched rod attached to throttle lever. *See Fig. 5.* Force crimped slug away from plastic fitting. Ensure T.V. gauge is pushed in as far as possible.

3) Engine and transmission must be at normal operating temperature. Set parking brake and place gear selector lever in Neutral. With gauge tool in place and engine idling in Neutral, T.V. pressure should be 30-40 psi (207-276 kPa). If adjustment is necessary, see ADJUSTING THROTTLE CONTROL PRESSURE (CABLE TYPE) in this article.

NOTE: Do not check or set T.V. pressure in Park.

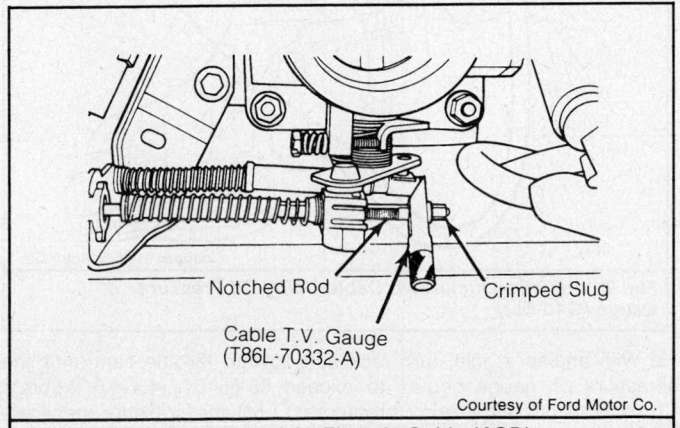

Courtesy of Ford Motor Co.

Fig. 5: T.V. Gauge Installed On Throttle Cable (AOD)

Adjusting Throttle Control Pressure (Cable Type) – 1) Remove air cleaner cover and inlet tube from throttle body inlet for easier access to throttle lever.

2) Using a wide blade screwdriver, pry grooved pin on cable assembly out of grommet on throttle body lever. *See Fig. 6.* Using a small screwdriver, push out White locking tab.

3) Check to ensure plastic block with pin and tab slides freely on notched rod. If it does not slide freely, White tab may not be pushed out far enough. Repeat procedure until tab slides freely.

4) While holding throttle lever firmly against its idle stop, push grooved pin back into grommet on throttle lever as far as it will go. Ensure that throttle lever does not move away from idle stop when installing pin.

5) If adjusting control pressure using oil gauge, check pressure at this time. If readjustment is required, go to step 6). If adjustment is within specifications, install air cleaner cover and air inlet tube.

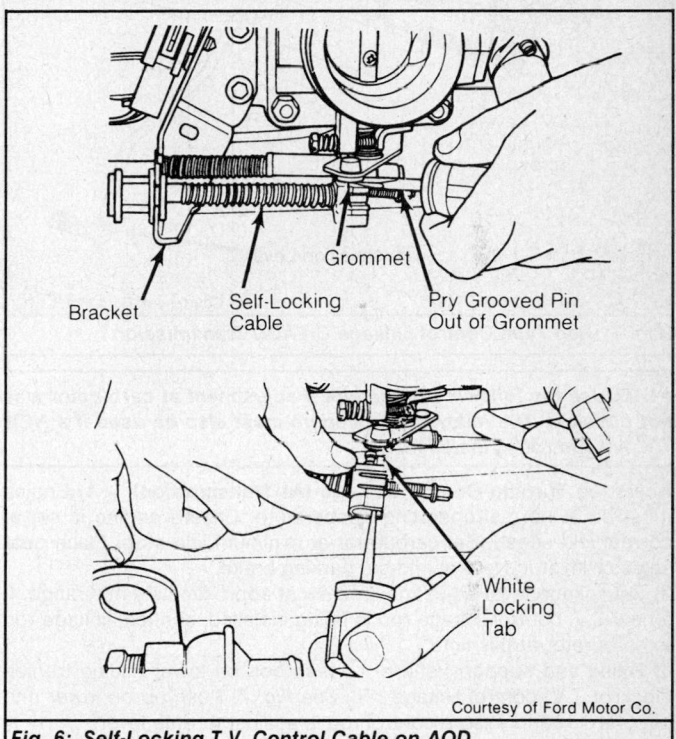

Fig. 6: Self-Locking T.V. Control Cable on AOD

Courtesy of Ford Motor Co.

6) Pry grooved pin out of grommet on throttle lever. Measure or mark location of plastic block on notched rod. Push out White locking tab.

7) Using mark or measurement on plastic block as reference, move plastic block towards throttle body to raise T.V. pressure. Move plastic block away from bracket to lower T.V. pressure. Push in White locking tab to secure block in position. Moving block one notch (in either direction) will change pressure approximately 2 psi.

NOTE: For best results, pressure should be as close to 33 psi (227 kPa) as possible when gauge tool is installed with transmission in Neutral. When shifted into forward gear, T.V. pressure will rise about 2 psi to desired 35 psi (241 kPa).

8) Insert grooved pin into throttle body grommet. Ensure throttle lever is held firmly against its idle stop position while installing grooved pin. Check T.V. pressure and readjust if necessary. Install air cleaner cover and inlet tube.

9) If correct pressure is present, remove gauge tool. Allow engine to return to idle. With engine idling and transmission in Neutral, T.V. pressure must drop to less than 0-5 psi (0-35 kPa). If not, readjust to compensate for high pressure reading.

Adjusting Throttle Control Pressure (Rod Type) – 1) Engine must be at normal operating temperature. Remove air cleaner. Throttle lever must be resting on idle stop or throttle solenoid positioner stop. Place gear selector lever in Neutral and set parking brake.

2) Back out T.V. lever adjustment screw so that screw end is flush with lever face. *See Fig. 7.* Turn in adjusting screw until a .005" (.127 mm) shim, or piece of writing paper fits snug between end of screw and throttle lever. Do not apply any load on lever when checking gap.

3) Turn adjustment screw in 3 turns. One turn minimum is permissible if screw travel is limited. If adjustment screw will not turn at least one turn or if it was not possible to obtain an initial gap as described in step **2)**, go to ADJUSTING THROTTLE CONTROL LINKAGE (AT TRANSMISSION).

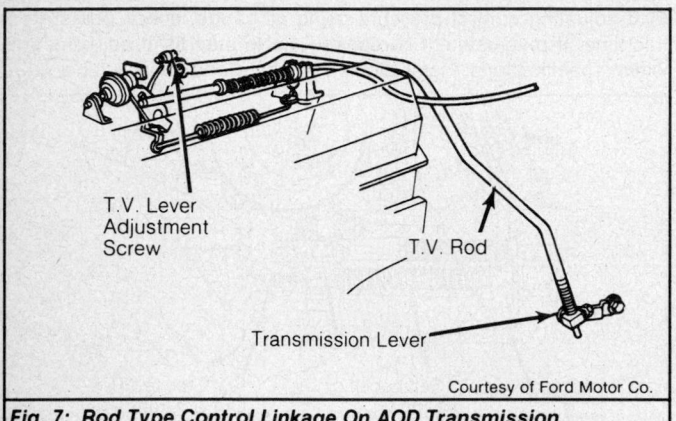

T.V. Lever Adjustment Screw

T.V. Rod

Transmission Lever

Courtesy of Ford Motor Co.

Fig. 7: Rod Type Control Linkage On AOD Transmission

NOTE: Use the following procedure if adjustment at carburetor was not possible. The following procedure must also be used if a NEW T.V. linkage rod is installed.

Adjusting Throttle Control Linkage (At Transmission) – 1) Engine must be at normal operating temperature. Ensure engine is set at correct idle speed. Set carburetor at minimum idle stop. Place gear selector lever in Neutral and set parking brake.

2) Set linkage lever adjustment screw at approximately mid-range. If a new T.V. control linkage rod is being installed, connect linkage rod to carburetor at this time.

3) Raise and support vehicle. Loosen bolt on lower sliding trunion block of T.V. control linkage rod. *See Fig. 7.* Push up on lower end of control rod to ensure control rod is against throttle lever.

4) Release force on rod. Rod must stay up. Push transmission T.V. control lever firmly against its internal idle stop. Tighten bolt on trunnion block.

5) Lower vehicle. Ensure throttle lever is still against minimum idle stop or throttle position solenoid stop. If not, repeat steps **2)** through **5)**.

THROTTLE CONTROL LINKAGE (ALL OTHERS)

A4LD Downshift Linkage (2.3L EFI) – Ensure bracket and cable are installed at transmission kickdown lever. Open throttle valve to WOT. While holding throttle at wide open throttle, install White locking cam to lock cable adjustment.

AXOD (3.0L) – 1) Ensure T.V. cable eye is connected to throttle control lever link. Ensure cable boot is attached to chain cover.

2) With T.V. cable mounted in engine bracket, ensure threaded shank is fully retracted. *See Fig. 8.* To retract shank, hold spring rest and wiggle top of threaded shank while pressing shank toward spring.

3) Attach end of T.V. cable to throttle body. Rotate throttle lever to wide open throttle position and release. Threaded shank must show movement or "ratchet" out of grip jaws. If no movement is observed, inspect T.V. cable system for broken or disconnected components and repeat procedure.

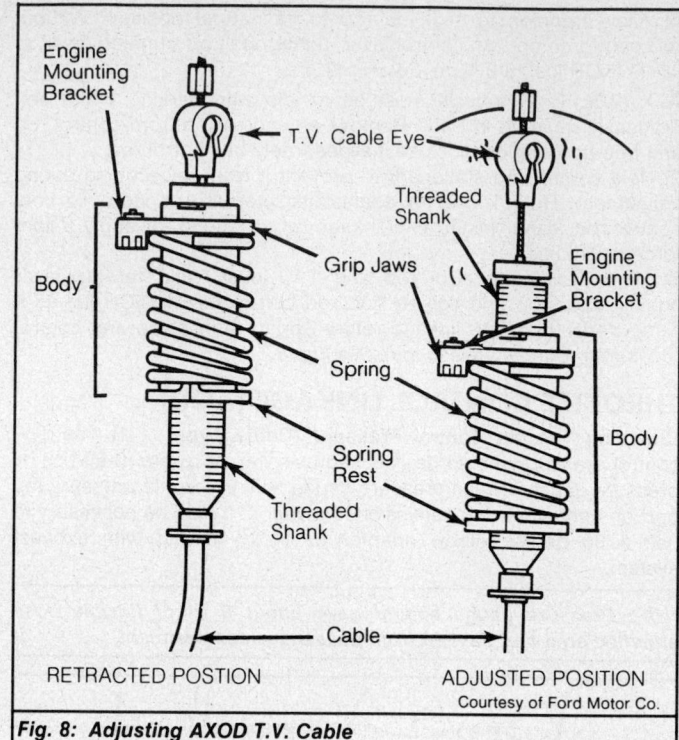

Engine Mounting Bracket

T.V. Cable Eye

Threaded Shank

Grip Jaws

Body

Engine Mounting Bracket

Spring

Body

Spring Rest

Threaded Shank

Cable

RETRACTED POSTION

ADJUSTED POSITION

Courtesy of Ford Motor Co.

Fig. 8: Adjusting AXOD T.V. Cable

AXOD (3.8L SEFI) – 1) Unclip T.V. cable end from right side intake manifold clip. Rotate throttle body primary lever (lever to which T.V. actuating nailhead is attached) by hand to wide open throttle position.

2) White adjuster shank must be seen to advance when rotating throttle body primary lever. If not, check if cable is improperly routed or kinked. Attach T.V. cable end into top position of right hand intake manifold clip.

G4A-EL – 1) Remove splash shield next to left front tire. Remove square head plug from pressure port marked "L" and attach transmission oil pressure gauge to pressure port. *See Fig. 9.*

2) Turn kickdown cable lock nuts to furthest point away from throttle cam (loosen cable all the way). Start engine and warm to operating temperature. Engine should idle between 700-800 RPM in Park.

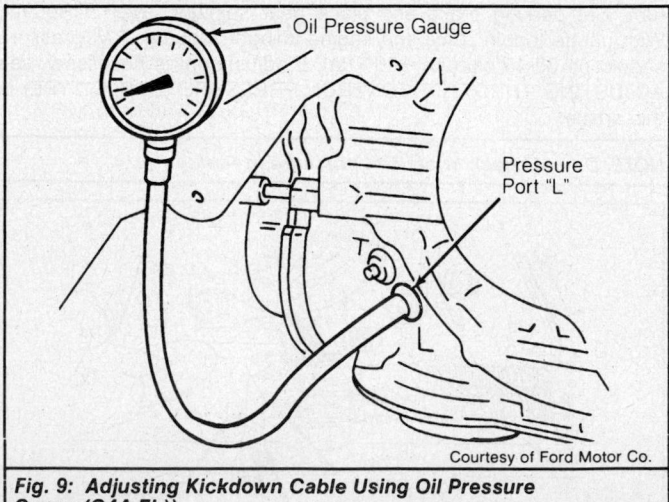

Oil Pressure Gauge

Pressure Port "L"

Courtesy of Ford Motor Co.

Fig. 9: Adjusting Kickdown Cable Using Oil Pressure Gauge (G4A-EL))

3) With engine at idle, turn lock nuts toward throttle cam until line pressure on gauge begins to exceed 63-66 psi (4.4-4.6 kg/cm²). Turn lock nuts away from throttle cam until line pressure stabilizes at 63-66 psi (4.4-4.6 kg/cm²). Tighten lock nuts and turn engine off.

4) Remove oil pressure gauge, install square head plug and tighten to 44-88 INCH lbs. (5-10 N.m). Road test vehicle.

SHIFT LINKAGE (FWD)

ATX (Escort, Taurus, Tempo & Topaz) – 1) Place gear selector lever in Drive. Gear selector lever must be held in rearward position during linkage adjustment.

2) Working at transaxle, loosen transaxle lever-to-control cable retaining nut. Move transaxle lever to Drive position (second detent from rear).

3) Tighten attaching nut to 16-27 ft. lbs. (12-20 N.m) on Taurus and 10-15 ft. lbs. (14-20 N.m) on all others. Ensure all gears engage correctly and vehicle will only start in Park or Neutral.

AXOD (Continental, Sable & Taurus) – 1) Place gear selector lever in "OVERDRIVE" position. Selector lever must be held in this position while adjusting linkage. Loosen manual lever-to-control cable retaining nut. *See Fig. 10.*

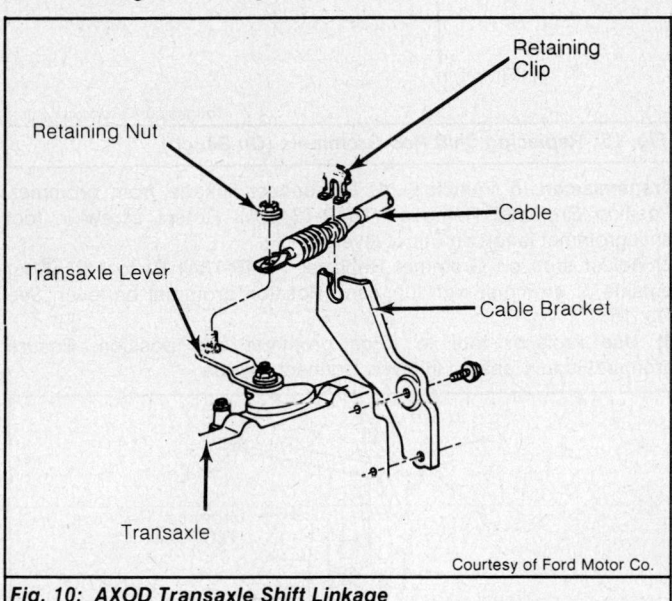

Fig. 10: *AXOD Transaxle Shift Linkage*

2) Move transaxle manual lever to "OVERDRIVE" position, second detent from most rearward position. Tighten attaching nut to 10-15 ft. lbs. (14-20 N.m). Check operation of transaxle in each gear position.

SHIFT LINKAGE (RWD)

Console (Floor) Shift – 1) Move gear selector lever rearward against stop in the Overdrive position (AOD and A4LD). Ensure lever is tight against rearward drive/overdrive stop. Raise vehicle. Loosen transmission lever-to-control cable (or rod) retaining nut.

2) Move transmission lever to Overdrive position (third detent from full counterclockwise). Hold selector in this position and tighten retaining nut. Check for normal operation in all selected positions. *See Fig. 11.*

Column Shift – 1) Place gear selector lever in the Overdrive position. Make sure selector lever remains against stop by hanging an 8 lb. (3.6 kg) weight on selector lever.

2) Loosen selector rod adjusting bolt (or nut). Push transmission lever downward to lowest position (third detent from full counterclockwise position).

3) Ensure the slotted rod end has flats aligned with flats on mounting stud, (if equipped). Ensure gear selector lever has not moved from the Overdrive position. Tighten bolt (or nut) and check operation in all selector (detent) positions. *See Figs. 12 and 13.*

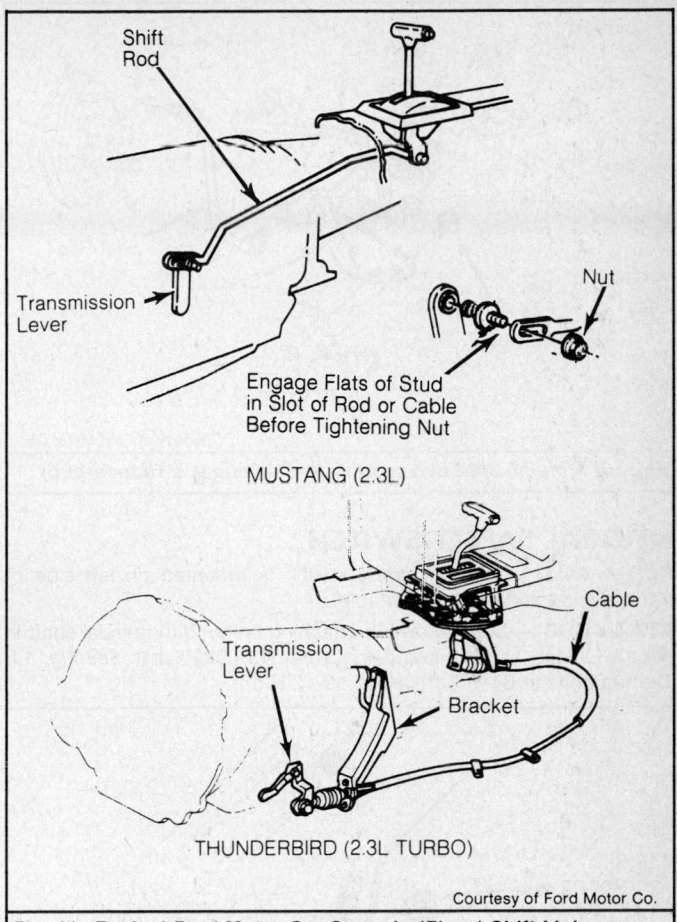

Fig. 11: *Typical Ford Motor Co. Console (Floor) Shift Linkage*

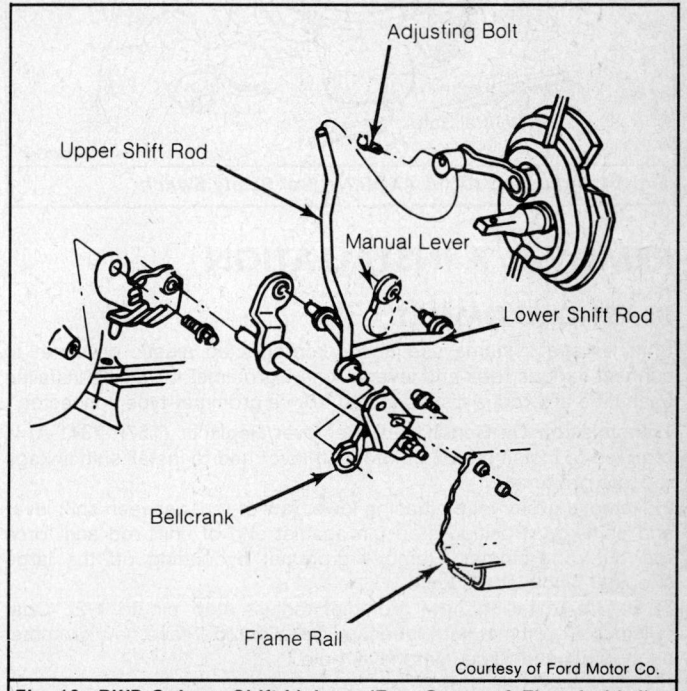

Fig. 12: *RWD Column Shift Linkage (Exc. Cougar & Thunderbird)*

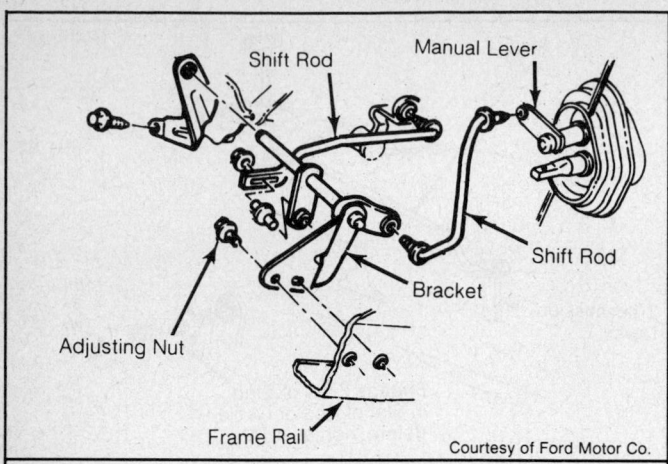

Fig. 13: Column Shift Linkage For RWD (Cougar & Thunderbird)

NEUTRAL SAFETY SWITCH

AOD & A4LD – Neutral safety switch is mounted on left side of transmission and is not adjustable.

ATX & AXOD – Loosen switch attaching bolts. With manual shaft in neutral detent, align switch using a No. 43 (.089") drill. *See Fig. 14.* Tighten bolts to 84-108 INCH lbs. (9-12 N.m).

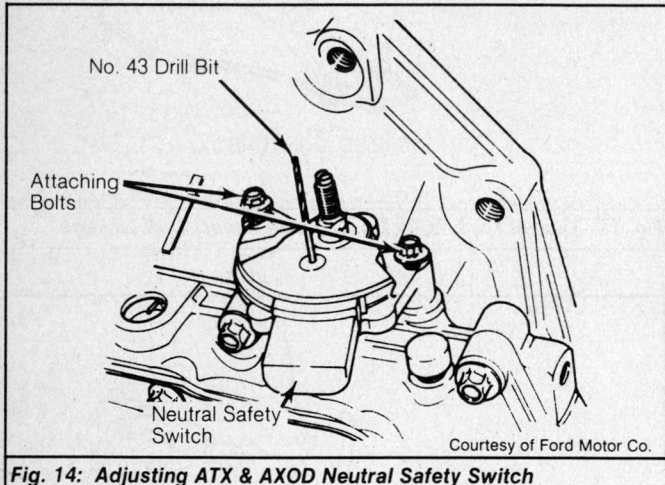

Fig. 14: Adjusting ATX & AXOD Neutral Safety Switch

REMOVAL & INSTALLATION

PLASTIC GROMMET

Shift linkage systems use an oil impregnated plastic grommet to connect various rods and levers. A new grommet MUST be installed each time any rod is disconnected from a grommet-type connector.

Transmission On Bench – 1) Remover/Replacer (T67P-7341-A) is required to install grommet into shift lever and to install shift linkage rod into grommet.

2) Remove grommet by placing lower jaw of tool between shift lever and shift rod. Position stop pin against end of shift rod and force rod out of grommet. Remove grommet by cutting off the large shoulder with a sharp knife.

3) Before installing new grommet, adjust stop pin to 1/2". Coat outside of grommet with lubricant. *See Fig. 15.* Place new grommet on stop pin and force it into lever hole.

4) Turn grommet several times to ensure proper seating. Squeeze rod into bushing until stopwasher seats against bushing.

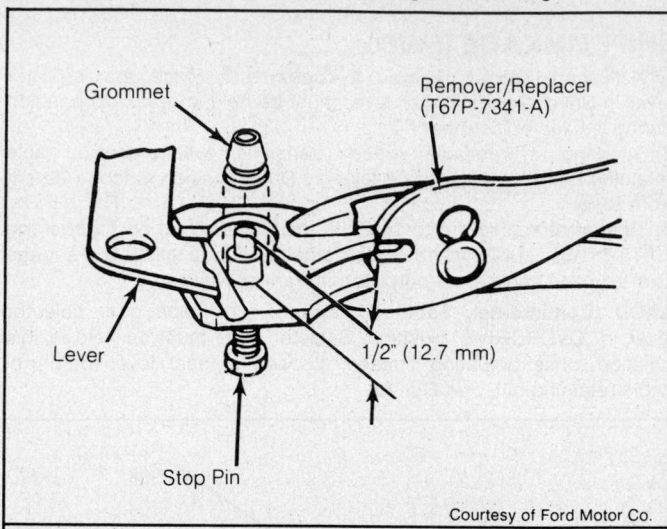

Fig. 15: Replacing Shift Rod Grommets (On Bench)

Transmission In Vehicle – 1) Disconnect linkage from grommet. Position Grommet Remover (T84P-7341-A). Rotate screw in tool until grommet is forced out of lever.

2) Adjust stop on Grommet Replacer (T84P-7341-B) to 1/2". Coat outside of grommet with lubricant. Position grommet on lever. *See Fig. 16.*

3) Use replacer tool to force grommet into position. Ensure grommet is fully seated in lever. Connect linkage.

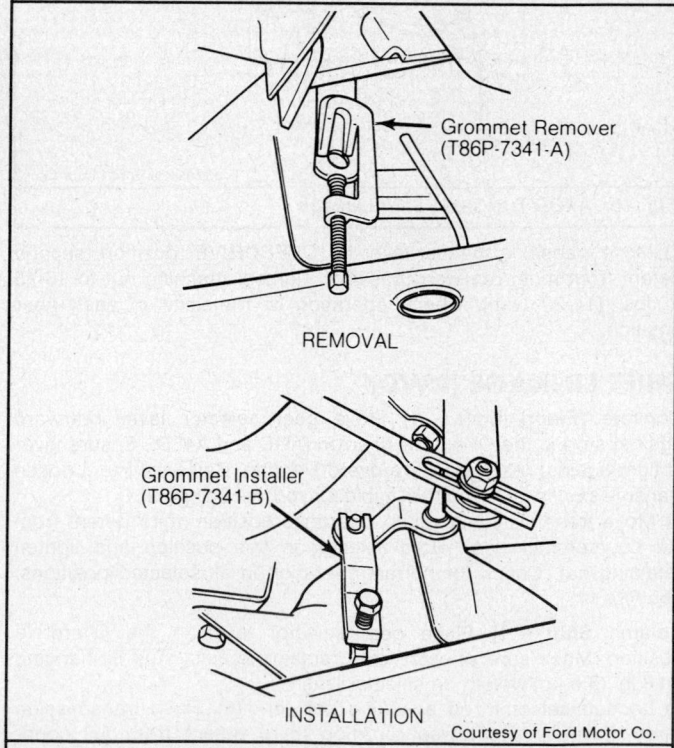

Fig. 16: Replacing Shift Rod Grommets (On Vehicle)

REMOVAL & INSTALLATION

FWD MODELS A-413 & A-604

Removal – 1) Disconnect negative battery cable. On vehicles using A-604 transaxles, drain engine cooling system and remove coolant return extension pipe. On all models, disconnect throttle linkage and shift linkage from transaxle. Disconnect cooler line hoses.

2) Attach engine support fixture to upper engine compartment and support engine. Remove upper bellhousing bolts. Raise and support vehicle and remove front wheels. Remove oil pan bolts and drain transaxle. Replace oil pan.

3) Remove axle nut cotter pin, nut lock and spring washer. Remove axle nut. Remove speedometer pinion gear and cable assembly from transaxle. Remove ball joint-to-steering knuckle clamp bolt.

4) Remove clamp bolt securing ball joint stud into steering knuckle. Separate ball joint stud from steering knuckle by prying against knuckle leg and control arm. Do not damage ball joint or CV joint boots.

5) Separate outer CV joint splined shaft from hub by holding CV housing while pushing knuckle assembly away from shaft. Support CV joint housing assemblies out of the way.

6) Remove left splash shield. Remove torque converter dust cover and index mark torque converter to drive plate. Remove access plug in right splash shield to rotate engine crankshaft and remove torque converter mounting bolts.

7) Disconnect neutral safety switch connector from neutral safety switch and disconnect all other sensor connectors. Remove engine mount bracket from front crossmember and remove front mount insulator through-bolt.

8) Support transaxle with transmission jack. Remove left engine mount near transaxle differential cover. Remove starter mounting bolts and lower bellhousing bolts.

9) Pry transaxle away from engine and slightly lower from engine. Pry transaxle from engine at extension housing (if needed). Ensure all external connections are clear from transaxle and lower unit from vehicle.

Installation – To install transaxle, reverse removal procedures. Adjust throttle cable and shift linkage as necessary. Replace pan gasket and fill transaxle with required amount of fluid to correct level. See appropriate AUTOMATIC TRANSMISSION SERVICING article in this section.

TIGHTENING SPECIFICATIONS (FWD MODELS)

Application	Ft. Lbs. (N.m)
Axle Nut	180 (245)
Bellhousing Bolts	70 (95)
Control Arm Pinch Bolts	70 (95)
Pan Bolts	14 (19)
Shift Linkage Bolts	20 (27)
Starter Mounting Bolts	40 (54)
Sway Bar Bolts	40 (54)
Wheel Lug Nuts	95 (129)

RWD MODELS A-904-LA & A-727

Removal – 1) Disconnect negative battery cable. Some models require the exhaust system be dropped for clearance. Remove engine to transmission struts (if equipped).

2) Remove cooler lines at transmission. Remove cooler line bracket, starter motor and torque converter cover. Loosen oil pan bolts, tap pan to break it loose allowing fluid to drain. Reinstall pan.

3) Index mark torque converter and drive plate for installation reference. Using socket on crankshaft vibration damper bolt, manually rotate engine clockwise for torque converter mounting bolts for removal. Index mark propeller shaft and rear yoke for installation reference. Remove propeller shaft.

4) Unplug neutral safety switch harness from transmission switch. Disconnect gearshift rod, torque shaft assembly and throttle rod lever from left side of transmission. Remove linkage at bellcrank from transmission (if equipped).

NOTE: Replace plastic grommets if linkage rods are disassembled.

5) Remove oil filler tube and speedometer cable. Support rear of engine with jack stand. Raise transmission slightly with jack to relieve load on mounts. Remove bolts securing transmission mount to crossmember and crossmember to frame. Remove crossmember.

6) Remove bellhousing bolts. Pull transmission assembly back. Attach a small "C" clamp to edge of converter housing to hold torque converter in place during transmission removal. Slowly lower transmission from vehicle.

CAUTION: Flush oil cooler and lines before replacing transmission.

Installation – 1) To install, reverse removal procedures. Ensure converter fully engages pump inner rotor lugs. Surface of converter front cover lug should be at least 1/2" below front edge of bellhousing when converter is installed.

2) Attach small "C" clamp to converter housing. Inspect converter flex plate for distortion or cracks and replace if necessary. Coat converter hub hole in crankshaft with multipurpose grease.

NOTE: When flex plate replacement is necessary, ensure both transmission dowel pins are in engine block.

3) Place transmission with converter on a transmission jack. Rotate converter so mark on converter (made during removal) will align with mark on drive plate. Offset holes in drive plate are located next to 1/8" hole in inner circle of plate. A stamped "O" identifies offset hole in converter.

4) Position transmission at rear of engine. Install and tighten all bolts to specifications. Clean oil pan and replace pan gasket. See appropriate AUTOMATIC TRANSMISSION SERVICING article in this section. Adjust shift and throttle linkage. Refill transmission with required amount of fluid.

5) To complete installation, reverse removal procedure. Tighten bolts holding struts to transmission before tightening strut to engine bolts (if equipped).

TIGHTENING SPECIFICATIONS (RWD MODELS)

Application	Ft. Lbs. (N.m)
Bellhousing Bolts	30 (40)
Cooler Line Flange Nuts	13 (18)
Crossmember-to-Frame Bolts	30 (40)
Exhaust Manifold-to-Pipe Flange Nuts	19 (26)
Mount-to-Crossmember Bolts	50 (68)
Mount-to-Transmission Bolts	50 (68)
Oil Pan Bolts	12 (16)
Propeller Shaft Strap Screws	14 (19)
Starter Motor Bolts	50 (68)
Tailhousing Exhaust Bracket Nuts	14 (19)
Torque Converter Mounting Bolts	22 (30)

1989 AUTOMATIC TRANSMISSION REMOVAL
Eagle

REMOVAL & INSTALLATION

AR-4

Removal – 1) Disconnect negative battery cable and remove windshield washer reservoir. Mark and disconnect harness connectors at TCU and disconnect cooler line hoses. Remove engine timing sensor.

2) Raise and support vehicle. Remove front wheels and drain fluid from transaxle. Remove pins attaching drive axle shafts to transaxle using a pin punch. Remove steering knuckle-to-strut upper nuts and bolts. Do not turn bolts (bolts are splined and must be tapped out with a brass or rubber mallet when removing).

3) Loosen (do not remove) steering knuckle-to-strut bottom nuts. Tap each bolt 3/4 of the way out of knuckle and strut until bolt splines are clear. Tilt steering knuckle outward and remove transaxle splash shield. Pull drive axle shafts off of transaxle shafts.

4) Disconnect and remove all brackets, retainers, tie straps or clips securing transaxle electrical wiring harnesses to vehicle body. Do not remove transaxle sensors or wire harnesses connected to transaxle.

5) Remove starter motor bolts and pull starter out of housing. Disconnect wires from starter motor. Remove starter heat shield nuts and remove shield. Remove torque converter housing access plug. Rotate engine manually and remove 3 torque converter bolts.

6) Remove exhaust pipe clamp and bracket. Support transaxle with transmission jack. Remove bolts and nuts attaching transaxle crossmember to engine cradle. Remove bolt attaching rear mount to transaxle bracket and remove crossmember and rear mount together as an assembly.

7) Disconnect shift cable from bellcrank. Remove brace rod and remaining bolts attaching shift cable bracket to transaxle case. Disconnect link rod from transaxle shift lever. Remove bellcrank bracket bolts and remove bellcrank, link rod, bracket and shift cable. Support bracket aside for working clearance.

8) Remove transaxle mount bracket bolts and remove bracket. Remove transaxle-to-engine attaching bolts. Pull transaxle assembly rearward and lower transmission jack to remove transaxle from vehicle.

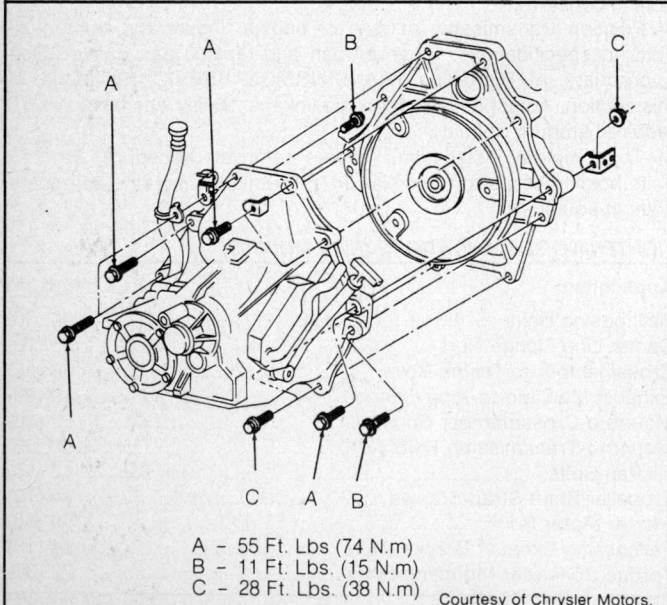

A – 55 Ft. Lbs (74 N.m)
B – 11 Ft. Lbs. (15 N.m)
C – 28 Ft. Lbs. (38 N.m)

Courtesy of Chrysler Motors.

Fig. 1: Tightening Specifications For Transaxle-to-Engine Bolts (AR-4 Transaxle)

Installation – 1) Inspect torque converter drive plate and replace if worn or damaged. Lubricate inside of torque converter pilot bore with grease before installing transaxle. Apply Locktite 271 to torque converter bolts before installing bolts.

2) To install transaxle, reverse removal procedure. For proper tightening specifications for transaxle-to-engine bolts, *See Fig. 1.* For other tightening specifications, use appropriate TIGHTENING SPECIFICATIONS table for each transaxle.

3) Ensure transaxle output shaft "O" rings are in recess on shaft. Replace "O" rings if damaged. Gradually fill transaxle with required amount of fluid. Make any necessary shift cable or throttle linkage adjustments and road test vehicle.

TIGHTENING SPECIFICATIONS (AR-4)

Application	Ft. Lbs. (N.m)
Bellcrank Bracket Bolts	31 (42)
Crossmember-to-Engine Cradle	31 (42)
Drive Plate-to-Crankshaft Bolts	[1] 40 (54)
Exhaust Pipe Bracket	31 (42)
Rear Mount Bolt	49 (66)
Shift Cable Bracket Bolts	31 (42)
Starter Motor Bolts	31 (42)
Steering Knuckle-to-Strut Nuts	148 (200)
Torque Converter Bolts	24 (33)

	INCH Lbs. (N.m)
Engine Timing Sensor	72 (8)
Starter Heat Shield Nuts	96 (11)

[1] – Turn an additional 60 degrees after torque is reached.

ZF 4HP-18

Removal – 1) Disconnect negative battery cable. Loosen throttle valve cable lock nuts, disconnect cable and remove from engine bracket. Raise and support vehicle.

2) Remove front wheels. Remove steering knuckle upper nut and bolt. Only loosen nut from lower knuckle connection. Do not rotate steering knuckle bolts; bolts are splined and can be removed by tapping with a soft mallet.

3) Tilt steering knuckle outward and remove splash shield. Position drain pan under transmission oil pan. Loosen nut attaching transmission filler tube to oil pan and allow fluid to drain completely. Remove filler tube and install plug into hole.

4) Remove torque converter housing bottom and side covers. Remove 3 torque converter bolts. Remove roll pins attaching drive axle shafts to differential output shafts. Pull axle shafts off differential output shafts and support out of the way.

5) Support transaxle with transmission jack. Remove nuts attaching crossmember to side supports. Remove long bolt attaching rear mount to transaxle bracket. Remove exhaust pipe bracket from rear mount. Remove crossmember and mount as an assembly.

6) Remove nuts attaching exhaust pipe bracket to front "Y" pipe. Remove nuts attaching catalytic converter to "Y" pipe. Disconnect oxygen sensor wires. Loosen (do not remove) engine cradle bolts until there is 1/2-7/8" working clearance space between cradle and side supports.

7) Remove front exhaust pipe assembly from manifolds. Disconnect starter cables and relay wires. Remove bolts and remove starter, starter plate and alignment dowel. Disconnect shift cable at transaxle lever. Remove shift cable bracket bolts and remove cable bracket.

8) Remove brace rod. After removing brace rod, reinstall rear bolt to hold neutral switch in place. Squeeze lock tabs on shift selector cable and remove cable from bracket. Remove engine speed sensor.

9) Disconnect transmission fluid cooler hoses. Plug off hoses to prevent fluid loss. Disconnect speedometer sensor wire and remove sensor. Remove engine-to-converter housing bolts and remaining engine-to-converter bolts. Pull transaxle away from engine and lower transaxle.

Installation – 1) Inspect drive plate for warpage, wear or damage and replace if necessary. To install transaxle, reverse removal procedure. Before installing transaxle, coat torque converter pilot hub with bearing grease and ensure that torque converter is fully into transaxle pump.

2) Use Loctite No. 271 on torque converter mounting bolts. When installing inner ends of drive axle shafts into transaxle, ensure roll pin holes of axle shafts and output shafts are aligned. Refill transaxle and differential. Ensure proper adjustment of shift cable and throttle valve cable.

TIGHTENING SPECIFICATIONS (ZF 4HP 18)

Application	Ft. Lbs. (N.m)
Catalytic Converter-to-Exhaust "Y" Pipe	25 (34)
Crossmember-to-Side Support Nuts	44 (60)
Engine Cradle Bolts	44 (60)
Exhaust Pipe Bracket	23 (31)
Exhaust-to-Manifold Nuts	23 (31)
Filler Tube Nut	74 (100)
Splash Shield Bolts	21 (28)
Starter Bolts	31 (42)
Steering Knuckle Nuts	148 (200)
Throttle Cable Nuts	11 (15)
Torque Converter Bolts	24 (32)
Transaxle-to-Engine Bolts	32 (43)

Ford Motor Co.

REMOVAL & INSTALLATION

ATX

Removal (Escort, Tempo & Topaz) – 1) Disconnect negative battery cable. Remove air cleaner assembly. Disconnect wiring from neutral safety switch. Harness connector is near distributor. Disconnect throttle valve linkage and manual lever cable at transaxle.

2) Cover up timing window in converter housing to prevent contamination. Remove bolts retaining air injection system hoses (if equipped). Position valve and hoses away from tubing and master cylinder. Remove ground strap above engine mount (if equipped).

3) Remove coil and bracket assembly. Remove the 2 upper transaxle-to-engine attaching bolts. Raise and support vehicle. Remove wheels.

4) Remove control arm-to-steering knuckle attaching bolt and nut (at both ball joints) and discard. A NEW bolt and nut must be used during transalxe installation. Using pry bar, carefully separate control arms from steering knuckles.

CAUTION: Use care not to damage ball joint boot. Pry bar must not contact control arm. DO NOT use hammer on ball joints.

5) Remove bolts attaching stabilizer bar brackets to frame. Remove stabilizer bar-to-control arm nut and washer. Discard bolts and washer. Manufacturer recommends using NEW hardware on installation.

6) Pull stabilizer bar out of control arms. Remove bolts attaching brake hose routing clips to suspension strut brackets. Disconnect tie rod ends from steering knuckles.

7) Pry right side drive axle shaft out of transaxle using Halfshaft Remover (D83P-4026-A). See FWD AXLE SHAFTS in DRIVE AXLES section for removal procedure. Position shaft on transaxle housing.

8) Insert Differential Rotator (T81P-4026-A) into right side differential side gear. Drive left drive axle shaft from differential side gear. Pull drive axle shaft from transaxle and support out of way.

CAUTION: Do not let axle shaft hang unsupported. Damage to outboard CV joint may result.

9) Install Seal Plugs (T81P-1177-B) into differential seals to prevent spline misalignment. Remove starter. On throttle body equipped vehicles, remove 2 hose/bracket bolts on starter and one (1) bolt attached to converter. Disconnect hoses.

10) Remove transaxle support bracket. Remove torque converter housing dust cover. Remove flex plate-to-converter nuts. Position transmission jack under transaxle. Remove rear support bracket nuts. Remove nuts attaching left front insulator to body bracket. Remove bracket-to-body bolts and remove bracket.

11) Disconnect oil cooling lines at transaxle using Cooler Line Disconnector (T82L-9500-AH). Remove bolts attaching manual lever bracket to transaxle case. Support engine. Position transmission jack under transaxle and remove 4 remaining transaxle-to-engine bolts.

12) Insert screwdriver between flex plate and converter. Carefully move transaxle and converter away from engine. When converter studs are clear of flex plate, lower transaxle about 3". Disconnect speedometer cable and lower transaxle from vehicle.

NOTE: If left-front insulator contacts body before converter studs clear flex plate, remove left-front insulator.

Installation – 1) To install transaxle, reverse removal procedure. ALWAYS replace snap ring on CV joint stub shaft.

2) To install drive axle shafts, carefully align splines on shaft with differential splines. Push CV joint until snap ring is felt to seat in groove in side gear.

3) Attach lower ball joint to steering knuckle, taking care not to damage or cut ball joint boot. Install NEW pinch bolt and NEW nut. DO NOT tighten bolt, tighten NUT to specification.

4) Fill transaxle with ATF. See AUTOMATIC TRANSMISSION SERVICING in this section.

Removal (Sable & Taurus) – 1) Disconnect negative battery cable. Remove air cleaner assembly. Position engine control wiring assembly away from transaxle converter housing area. Disconnect throttle valve linkage and manual lever cable. Remove power steering hose brackets. Remove 2 upper transaxle-to-engine bolts.

2) Install Engine Lifting Bracket (D81L-6001-D) to right side rear area of cylinder with a M10 x 1.5 x 20 bolt. Install a second engine lifting bracket to left side front area of cylinder with same size bolt. Install 2 Engine Support Bars (D79P-6000-A).

NOTE: An engine support bar can be fabricated from a length of 4" x 4" wood cut to approximately 57".

3) Place one (1) engine support bar across vehicle in front of each shock tower. Place the other support bar between alternator and valve cover. Attach chains from each support bar to engine lifting brackets. Raise and support vehicle. Remove both wheels.

4) Remove catalytic converter inlet pipe. Disconnect engine exhaust air hose assembly. Remove each tie rod end from its spindle. Remove bolts and nuts attaching lower ball joints to struts. Separate and remove ball joints. Remove lower control arm from each spindle.

5) Remove stabilizer bar nuts and disconnect stabilizer bar. Remove nuts securing steering rack to subframe. Disconnect and remove auxiliary cooler from subframe. Position steering rack away from subframe and secure with wire. Remove right side front axle support and bearing assembly bolts.

6) Remove right side front drive axle shaft support and bearing assembly. Remove axle shaft assembly out of right side of transaxle. See DRIVE AXLES section for removal procedure.

7) Disengage left side halfshaft from differential side gear using Differential Rotator (T81P-4026-A). Pull halfshaft out of transaxle. Support and secure halfshaft. DO NOT allow halfshafts to hang unsupported.

8) Install Seal Plugs (T81P-1177-B) in transaxle to prevent spline misalignment. Remove front support insulator. Move left side front splash shield aside. Position bench or jack stands to support subframe after it is disconnected.

9) Lower vehicle to bench or jack stand. Block or support as needed. Remove subframe bolts and subframe.

10) Disconnect neutral safety switch wire assembly. Disconnect speedometer cable. Remove shift cable bracket bolts and bracket from transaxle. Disconnect oil cooler lines using Cooler Line Disconnector (T86P-77265-AA). Remove starter.

11) Remove dust cover from torque converter housing. Remove flex plate-to-converter nuts. Position transmission jack under transaxle and secure transaxle to jack. Remove remaining transaxle-to-engine bolts.

12) Insert a screwdriver between flex plate and torque converter. Carefully move transaxle and converter away from engine. When torque converter studs are clear of flex plate, lower transaxle and remove from vehicle.

Installation – 1) To install transaxle, reverse removal procedure. Prior to installing drive axle shafts, replace snap ring on CV joint stub shaft.

2) To install halfshafts, carefully align splines on shaft with differential splines. See DRIVE AXLES in this section for installation procedure.

3) Attach lower ball joint to steering knuckle, taking care not to damage or cut ball joint boot. Install NEW BOLT and NEW NUT. DO NOT tighten bolt, tighten nut to specification.

4) Converter is correctly seated when pilot is 7/16-9/16" (11-14 mm) from engine mounting surface. Prevent converter from moving forward during installation.

5) Readjust T.V. linkage and manual linkage. Fill transaxle with ATF to proper level. See AUTOMATIC TRANSMISSION SERVICING in this section.

TIGHTENING SPECIFICATIONS (ATX)

Application	Ft. Lbs. (N.m)
Ball Joint Nut-to-Steering	
Knuckle Bolt	40-54 (54-74)
Converter-to-Flex Plate	23-39 (31-53)
Cooler Line Nut	
At Radiator & Transaxle	12-18 (16-24)
Cooler Line Push Connector	
At Transaxle	18-23 (24-31)
Flex Plate-to-Crankshaft Bolts	
1.9L, 2.3L, 2.5L	54-64 (73-87)
3.0L, 3.8L	54-64 (73-87)
Insulator Mount-to-Transaxle Bolts	25-33 (34-45)
Insulator-to-Bracket Bolts	55-70 (75-95)
Insulator Bracket-to-Frame Bolts	40-50 (54-68)
Tie Rod-to-Knuckle Nut	[1] 23-35 (31-47)
Transaxle-to-Engine Bolts	25-33 (34-45)

[1] – Tighten to minimum torque; continue tightening to nearest cotter pin slot.

AXOD

Removal (Continental, Sable & Taurus) – 1) Remove negative battery cable and air cleaner assembly. Remove shifter cable and bracket from transaxle. Disconnect neutral safety switch and bulkhead connector from rear of transaxle.

2) Remove T.V. cable from throttle body and transaxle. Remove through bolt from left motor mount strut. Remove upper transaxle-to-engine bolts. On Sable and Taurus, attach Engine Lifting Bracket (D81L-6001-D) to rear of left side cylinder head. Lifting bracket should already be installed on front of right side cylinder head.

3) On all models, attach Engine Support Bar (D87L-6000-A) across shock towers. Attach engine to support bar. Raise engine to take pressure off engine mounts.

4) Raise vehicle on hoist. Remove front wheels. Separate tie rod ends from spindles. Remove bolts and nuts securing ball joints. Remove lower ball joints.

5) Remove lower control arms from each spindle. Remove sway bar link-to-body bolts. Remove steering rack-to-subframe bolts.

6) Remove all subframe-to-engine mount bolts. Disconnect oxygen sensor lead. Remove exhaust system section under subframe and transaxle. Support subframe. Remove remaining subframe-to-body bolts and lower subframe.

7) Position transaxle jack under transaxle. Remove speedometer or vehicle speed sensor from transaxle. Remove transaxle-to-engine supports and transaxle mount. Remove starter and dust cover.

8) Remove 4 flex plate-to-torque converter nuts. Disconnect transaxle cooler lines. Pull CV joints from transaxle using a slide hammer with a CV Joint Puller (T86P-3514-A1) and Extension (T86P-3514-A2). See DRIVE AXLES section for removal procedure.

9) Remove remaining transaxle-to-engine bolts. Separate transaxle from engine and lower out of vehicle. Remove torque converter from transmission.

Installation – To install transaxle, reverse removal procedure. Adjust T.V. cable and shift linkage. A NEW circlip MUST be used on drive axle inboard stub shaft before installation. Fill transaxle with ATF. See AUTOMATIC TRANSMISSION SERVICING in this section.

TIGHTENING SPECIFICATIONS (AXOD)

Application	Ft. Lbs. (N.m)
Ball Joint Nut-to-Steering	
Knuckle Bolt	37-44 (50-60)
Converter-to-Flex Plate Nuts	23-39 (31-53)
Cooler Line Nut	
At Radiator	12-18 (16-24)
Cooler Line Push Connector	
At Transaxle	18-23 (24-31)
Flex Plate-to-Crankshaft Bolts	
2.5L	54-64 (73-87)
3.0L & 3.8L	54-64 (73-87)
Insulator Mount-to-Transaxle Bolts	25-33 (34-45)
Insulator-to-Bracket Bolts	55-70 (75-95)
Insulator Bracket-to-Frame Bolts	40-50 (54-68)
Stabilizer-to-Control Arm Bolts	98-125 (133-169)
Tie Rod-to-Knuckle Nuts	[1] 23-35 (31-47)
Transaxle-to-Engine Bolts	41-50 (55-68)

[1] – Tighten to minimum torque; continue tightening to nearest cotter pin slot.

G4A-EL

Removal (Probe) – 1) Disconnect battery terminals and remove battery and battery carrier. Disconnect main fuse block. Disconnect lead from center distributor terminal.

2) Disconnect airflow meter connector and remove air cleaner assembly. Remove resonance chamber and bracket. Disconnect speedometer cable (electro-mechanical cluster), or harness (electronic cluster).

3) Disconnect 4 electrical connectors and separate harnesses from transaxle clips. Disconnect 2 ground wires from transaxle case and range selector cable from transaxle lever.

4) Disconnect kickdown cable. Raise and support vehicle. Remove front wheels and splash shields. Drain transaxle fluid. Disconnect oil cooler outlet and inlet hoses and insert plugs to prevent fluid leakage.

5) Remove stabilizer link assemblies and remove cotter pins and tie rod nuts. Disconnect tie rod ends. Remove bolts and nuts from lower control arm ball joints. Pull lower control arms to separate them from knuckles.

6) Remove right joint shaft bracket. Remove drive axle shafts from transaxle by prying with bar inserted between shaft and transaxle case. Install 2 Transaxle Plugs (T88C-7025-AH) into differential side gears.

CAUTION: Failure to install transaxle plugs may allow the differential side gears to become mispositioned.

7) Remove gusset plate-to-transaxle bolts. Remove torque converter cover. Index mark torque converter to drive plate and remove torque converter nuts. Remove starter motor and access brackets.

8) Lower vehicle and mount an engine support bar over engine compartment. Attach engine (by engine hanger) with a chain to support bar. Remove center transaxle nount and bracket. Remove left transaxle mount.

9) Remove nut and bolt attaching right transaxle mount to frame. Remove crossmember and left lower arm as an assembly. Position a transmission jack under transaxle and secure transaxle to jack.

10) Remove engine-to-transaxle mounting bolts. Before transaxle can be lowered out of vehicle, torque converter studs must be clear of drive plate. Insert a screwdriver between drive plate and converter and carefully disengage studs. Lower transaxle out of vehicle.

Installation – **1)** Inspect torque converter drive plate for damage or abnormal wear and replace if necessary. To install transaxle, reverse removal procedure. Align index mark (previously made) on torque converter to drive plate.

2) A NEW circlip MUST be used on drive axle shaft inboard stub shaft before installation. Fill transaxle with required amount of fluid and adjust T.V. cable and shift linkage. See AUTOMATIC TRANSMISSION SERVICING in this section.

TIGHTENING SPECIFICATIONS (G4A-EL)

Application	Ft. Lbs. (N.m)
Center Mount	
Bolts	27-40 (37-54)
Nuts	47-66 (64-89)
Crossmember	
Bolts	27-40 (37-54)
Nuts	55-69 (75-93)
Drive Plate-to-Crankshaft Bolts	71-76 (96-103)
Engine-to-Transaxle Bolts	66-86 (89-117)
Left Mount Nut	63-86 (85-117)
Left Mount-to-Bracket	
Bolt & Nut	49-69 (66-93)
Lower Control Arm Ball Joint	
Bolts & Nuts	32-40 (43-54)
Lower Control Arm	
Bolts	27-40 (37-54)
Nuts	55-69 (75-93)
Right Mount Bolt & Nut	63-86 (85-117)
Selector Cable Bolts	22-29 (30-39)
Stabilizer Link Nuts	12-17 (16-23)
Starter Mounting Bolts	23-34 (31-46)
Tie Rod End Nuts	22-33 (30-45)
Torque Converter Nuts	32-45 (43-61)
Transaxle-to-Engine Bracket Bolts	27-38 (37-51)
Wheel Lug Nuts	65-87 (88-118)

AOD

Removal (Cougar, Grand Marquis, LTD Crown Victoria, Mark VII, Mustang, Thunderbird, Town Car & Wagon) – **1)** Raise and support vehicle. Drain transmission fluid (including converter). Remove converter access cover and adapter plate bolts from lower left side of converter housing. Remove 4 converter-to-flex plate nuts. Turn crankshaft clockwise (as viewed from front) to gain access to nuts.

CAUTION: On belt driven overhead cam engines, NEVER turn engine counterclockwise (as viewed from front).

2) Mark position of yokes and remove propeller shaft. Install Seal Replacer (T74P-77052-A) in extension housing to prevent leakage. Disconnect and remove speedometer sensor from extension housing. Remove starter.

3) Remove rear mount-to-crossmember bolts and 2 crossmember-to-frame bolts. Remove 2 engine rear support-to-extension housing attaching bolts.

4) Disconnect T.V. linkage rod or cable from transmission. On Thunderbird and Cougar models, disconnect cable from bellcrank lever stud and remove self-tapping bolt from bellhousing bracket.

5) On all models, disconnect manual rod from transmission manual lever. Remove 2 bolts securing bellcrank bracket-to-converter housing. Disconnect neutral safety switch wires.

6) Position jack under transmission and raise it slightly. Remove engine support-to-crossmember bolts. Remove crossmember-to-frame bolts. Remove crossmember, insulator support and damper.

7) Disconnect and remove any interfering exhaust system hardware. Lower jack slightly to gain access to oil cooler lines. Disconnect oil cooler lines from transmission using Cooler Line Disconnector (T86P-77265-AH). Plug openings.

8) Remove lower converter-to-housing bolts. Remove transmission filler tube. Secure transmission to jack with a safety chain. Slide transmission to the rear and lower from vehicle.

Installation – **1)** To install transmission, reverse removal procedure. Ensure converter is fully seated in pump. Lubricate converter pilot with chassis grease. Align Orange balancing marks (if present) on converter and flex plate.

2) Align converter drive studs and drain plug with holes in flex plate. Readjust manual and downshift linkage.

3) Fill transmission with ATF to proper level. If any shift rods were disassembled, new plastic grommets must be installed. See appropriate AUTOMATIC TRANSMISSION SERVICING article in this section.

TIGHTENING SPECIFICATIONS (AOD)

Application	Ft. Lbs. (N.m)
Converter-to-Flex Plate Nuts	20-34 (27-46)
Converter Drain Plug	8-28 (11-38)
Cooler Lines-to-Transmission	18-23 (24-31)
Crossmember-to-Side Support Bolts	70-100 (95-136)
Flex Plate-to-Crankshaft Bolts	
2.3L (OHC), 3.8L	56-64 (76-87)
5.0L, 5.8L	75-85 (102-115)
Transmission-to-Engine Bolts	40-50 (54-68)

A4LD

Removal (Grand Marquis, LTD Crown Victoria, Mustang & Town Car) – **1)** Raise and support vehicle. Remove oil pan and drain transmission fluid. Remove converter access cover and adapter plate bolts from lower left side of converter housing.

CAUTION: On belt driven overhead cam engines, never rotate pulley in a counterclockwise direction (as viewed from the front).

2) Remove torque converter drain plug and drain remaining fluid from torque converter. Turn engine crankshaft clockwise (as viewed from front) to gain access to torque converter drain plug and nuts. Remove 4 converter-to-flex plate nuts.

3) Mark position of yokes and remove propeller shaft. Install correct size plug into extension housing to prevent leakage. Disconnect and remove speedometer sensor from extension housing (if equipped). Disconnect and remove starter motor.

4) Disconnect neutral safety switch plug connector. Remove rear mount-to-crossmember attaching bolts and 2 crossmember-to-frame attaching bolts. Remove 2 engine rear support-to-extension housing attaching bolts.

5) Disconnect T.V. linkage rod or cable from transmission T.V. lever ball stud. Disconnect selector rod from transmisson lever at transmission using Shift Linkage Grommet Removal Tool (T84P-7341-A).

6) Remove 2 bolts securing bellcrank bracket to converter housing. Raise transmission with a transmission jack to provide clearance to remove crossmember. Remove rear mount from crossmember and remove crossmember from side supports.

7) Disconnect any interfering exhaust system hardware at this time. Lower transmission to gain access to oil cooler lines. Disconnect oil cooler line from fittings on transmission using Cooler Line Disconnect Tool (T86P-77265-AH).

8) Disconnect speedometer cable from extension housing. Remove bolt that secures transmission filler tube to engine block. Lift filler tube and dipstick from transmission. Secure transmission to transmission jack with a chain. Remove transmission-to-engine bolts.

9) Move transmission and converter assembly away from engine while lowering jack to clear underside of vehicle. Tighten torque converter drain plug to 8-28 ft. lbs. (11-38 N.m). Remove converter and place transmission on bench.

Installation – 1) Inspect torque converter flex plate for signs of wear or damage and replace if necessary. To install transmission, reverse removal procedure. Torque converter is properly installed when pilot hub is 7/16-9/16" (11-14 mm) from engine mating surface of converter housing.

2) Fill transmission with required amount of fluid. Adjust shift cable and throttle valve cable as needed. See appropriate AUTOMATIC TRANSMISSION SERVICING article in this section.

TIGHTENING SPECIFICATIONS (A4LD)

Application	Ft. Lbs. (N.m)
Access Cover/Adapter Plate Bolts	12-16 (16-22)
Converter-to-Flex Plate Nuts	20-34 (27-46)
Crossmember-to-Frame Bolts	20-30 (27-41)
Engine Support-to-Crossmember Nuts	60-80 (81-108)
Filler Tube Bolt	28-38 (38-51)
Propeller Shaft Nuts	70-95 (95-129)
Starter Mounting Bolts	15-20 (20-27)
Transmission-to-Engine Bolts	26-38 (38-51)

IDENTIFICATION

CHRYSLER MOTORS TRANSMISSION APPLICATIONS

Model	Transmission
Acclaim	5-Speed A-520 & A-555 Transaxle
Aries	5-Speed A-520 Transaxle
Daytona	5-Speed A-555 Transaxle
Horizon	5-Speed A-525 Transaxle
Lancer	5-Speed A-555 Transaxle
LeBaron	5-Speed A-555 Transaxle
Omni	5-Speed A-525 Transaxle
Reliant	5-Speed A-520 Transaxle
Shadow	5-Speed A-520 Transaxle
Spirit	5-Speed A-520 & A-555 Transaxle
Sundance	5-Speed A-520 Transaxle

LUBRICATION

SERVICE INTERVALS

Check fluid level whenever other underhood services are performed. Under normal driving conditions, factory installed fluid will give satisfactory lubrication for the life of the vehicle. Under severe driving conditions, drain and refill at 15,000 mile intervals.

CHECKING FLUID LEVEL

1) Check lubricant level at filler plug hole on left side of transaxle (on rear end cover). Lubricant should be level with bottom of filler plug hole.
2) Fluid is drained by removing differential cover. Clean magnet. Use RTV sealant on differential cover.

RECOMMENDED FLUID

A-520 & A-555 Transaxles – Use SAE 5W-30 engine oil.
A-525 Transaxle – Use Dexron II ATF.

FLUID CAPACITY

TRANSAXLE REFILL CAPACITIES

Application	Pts. (L)
5-Speed	
A-525	4.4 (2.1)
A-520 & A-555	4.8 (2.3)

ADJUSTMENTS

SHIFT LINKAGE

Rod Operated Transaxles (Horizon & Omni) – **1)** Place transaxle in Neutral position. Working over left front fender, remove lock pin from transaxle selector shaft housing. *See Fig. 1.*
2) Invert lock pin (long end down) and insert into same threaded hole while pushing selector shaft into selector housing. Hole in selector shaft will align with lock pin, allowing lock pin to be inserted in housing. Selector shaft will be locked in Neutral position.
3) Raise and support vehicle. Loosen clamp bolt that secures gearshift tube to gearshift connector. Ensure gearshift connector slides and turns freely in gearshift tube. *See Fig. 2.*
4) Position shifter mechanism connector assembly so isolator is contacting upstanding flange, and rib on isolator is aligned fore and aft with the hole in lock-out bracket. Hold in this position while tightening clamp bolt on gearshift tube to 14 ft. lbs. (19 N.m). No force should be exerted on linkage during this operation.
5) Lower vehicle. Remove lock pin from selector shaft housing, and reinstall lock pin upside down (long end up) in selector shaft housing. Tighten lock pin to 105 INCH lbs. (12 N.m). Check for shift into 1st and Reverse. Check for Reverse lock-out function.

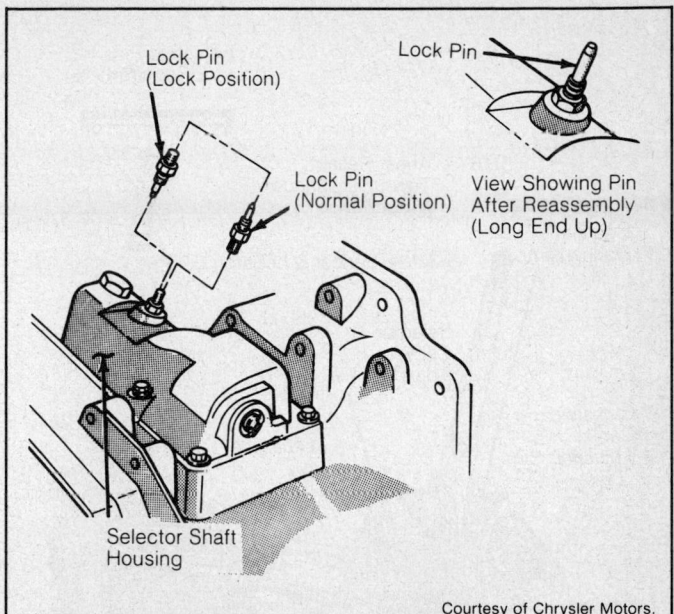

Courtesy of Chrysler Motors.

Fig. 1: Removing Lock Pin From Transaxle Selector Shaft Housing

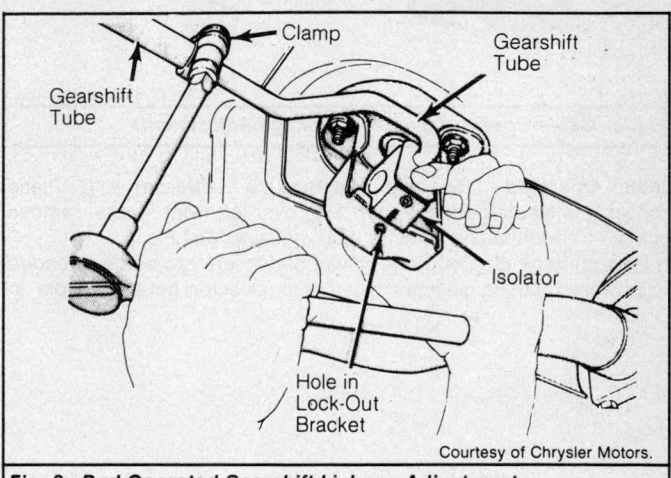

Courtesy of Chrysler Motors.

Fig. 2: Rod Operated Gearshift Linkage Adjustment

Cable Operated Transaxle (Except Daytona & LeBaron) – **1)** Place transaxle in Neutral position. Working over left front fender, remove lock pin from transaxle selector shaft housing. *See Fig. 1.*
2) Reverse lock pin (long end down) and insert into same threaded hole while pushing selector shaft into selector housing. Hole in selector shaft will align with lock pin, allowing lock pin to be inserted in housing. Selector shaft will be locked in Neutral position.
3) Remove gearshift knob, retaining nut and pull-up ring. Remove screws attaching center console and remove console. Fabricate 2 adjustment pins from 3/16" or 5/32" diameter rod, depending on model application. *See Fig. 3.*
4) Loosen crossover and selector cable adjustment screws. Allow both cables to center themselves in the adjustment slot. Install adjustment pins in gear shifter mechanism. Retighten cable adjustment set screws to 70 INCH lbs. (8 N.m).

CAUTION: Proper torque on crossover and selector cable set screws is very important.

5) Remove lock pin from selector shaft housing, and reinstall lock pin upside down (long end up) in selector shaft housing. Tighten lock pin to 105 INCH lbs. (12 N.m). Check for shift into 1st and Reverse. Check for lock-out into Reverse.

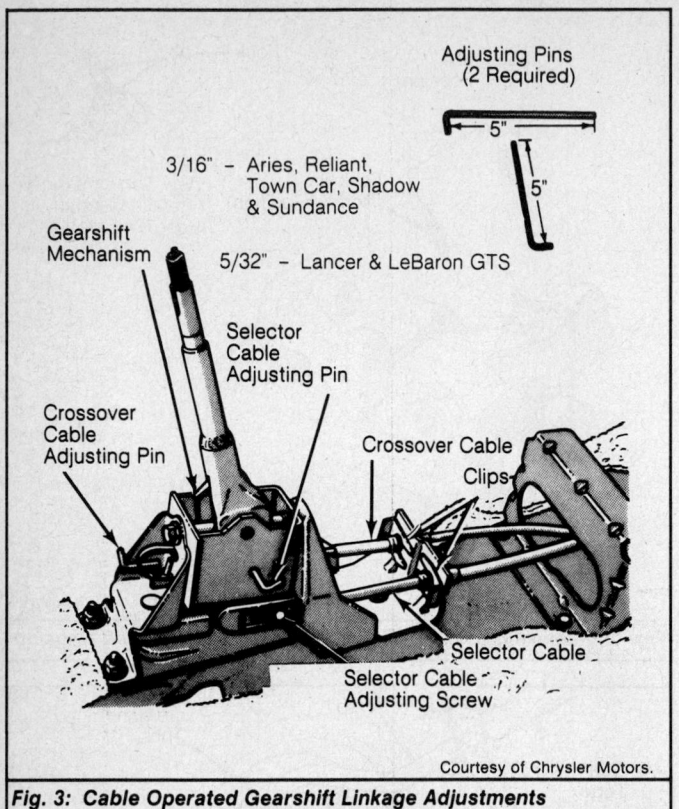

Fig. 3: Cable Operated Gearshift Linkage Adjustments

Cable Operated Transaxle (Daytona & LeBaron) – 1) Place transaxle in Neutral position. Working over left front fender, remove lock pin from transaxle selector shaft housing. *See Fig. 1.*

2) Reverse lock pin (long end down) and insert into same threaded hole while pushing selector shaft into selector housing. Hole in selector shaft will align with lock pin, allowing lock pin to be inserted in housing. Selector shaft will be locked in Neutral position.

3) Remove gearshift knob, retaining nut and pull-up ring. Remove center console. An adjusting screw tool (with left-hand threads) is taped to shifter suport bracket. Remove tool from bracket. Loosen crossover and selector cable adjustment screws.

4) Insert and tighten adjusting screw tool to 20 INCH lbs. (2 N.m). *See Fig. 4.* Retighten cable adjustment set screws to 70 INCH. lbs. (8 N.m).

5) Remove adjusting screw tool and fasten to support bracket. Remove lock pin from selector shaft housing, and reinstall lock pin upside down (long end up) into selector shaft housing. Tighten lock pin to 105 INCH lbs. (12 N.m). Check for shift into 1st and Reverse. Check for lock-out function in Reverse.

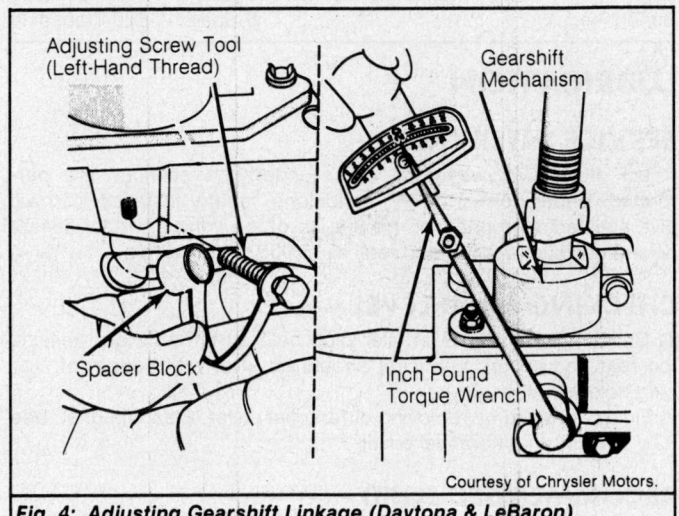

Fig. 4: Adjusting Gearshift Linkage (Daytona & LeBaron)

IDENTIFICATION

FORD MOTOR CO. MANUAL TRANSMISSION APPLICATION

Model	Transmission
Cougar	5-Speed M5R2
Escort	4-Speed MTX II Transaxle
Mustang	5-Speed T50D
Probe	5-Speed Transaxle
Tempo	4-Speed MTX II Transaxle
	5-Speed MTX III Transaxle
Thunderbird	5-Speed M5R2
Topaz	5-Speed MTX III Transaxle

LUBRICATION

SERVICE INTERVALS

Check fluid level at 15 month/15,000 mile intervals. Draining and refilling are not required, except at time of overhaul or service.

CHECKING FLUID LEVEL

CAUTION: Drain and fill plugs for T50D are on right side of case. Do not remove reverse shift lever pin (top hex bolt) on left side of case. Damage may result.

All Models (Exc. Probe) – Check lubricant level at filler plug hole on side of transmission. Lubricant should be level with bottom of filler plug hole. Add lubricant as necessary to bring to correct level.

Probe – To check fluid, remove retaining bolt and pry out speedometer driven gear assembly (analog cluster) or vehicle speed sensor (digital cluster) from transaxle. Wipe fluid from driven gear and housing. Reinsert assembly into transaxle and withdraw again checking fluid level as shown in *Fig. 1*.

RECOMMENDED FLUID

MTX Transaxle & T5OD – Use Type F, Dexron II, or Mercon ATF.
M5R2 – Use Dexron II ATF.
Probe Transaxle – Use Mercon, Type F, or Dexron II ATF.

FLUID CAPACITY

TRANSMISSION REFILL CAPACITIES

Application	Pts. (L)
MTX	
4 & 5-Speed	6.1 (2.9)
M5R2	6.3 (3.0)
Probe Transaxle	
Non-Turbo	7.1 (3.4)
Turbo	7.7 (3.7)
T5OD 5-Speed Overdrive	5.6 (2.6)

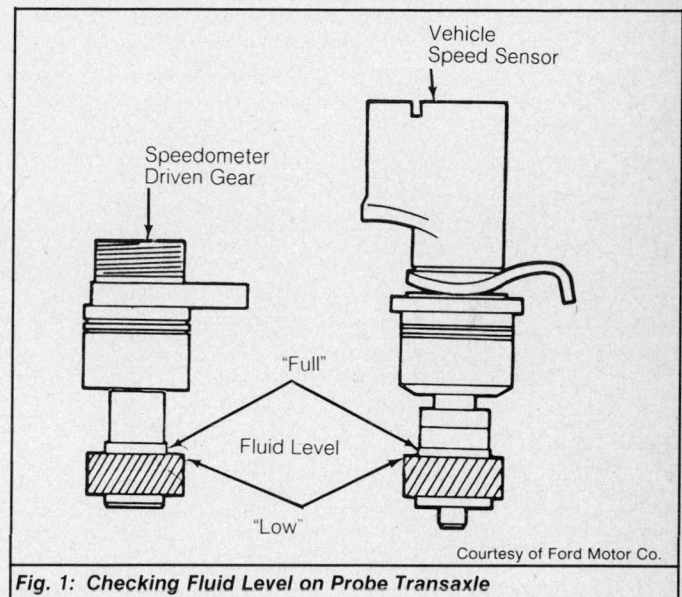

Courtesy of Ford Motor Co.

Fig. 1: Checking Fluid Level on Probe Transaxle

ADJUSTMENTS

SHIFT LINKAGE

No in-service adjustment of shift linkage is necessary.

LATEST CHANGES & CORRECTIONS

CAUTION

CONTENTS

	Page
Alignment	5
Brakes	3
Computerized Engine Control	2
Engines	3
Fuel Systems	3
Suspension	5
Tune-Up	2

NOTE: *The Latest Changes & Corrections represent a collection of last minute manual revisons and relevant technical bulletins. It may be useful to read through this section and find any changes or helpful information. Then, go to the manual and note the changes on the appropriate page.*

TUNE-UP

CHRYSLER MOTORS

▷1 *1986-88 CHRYSLER MOTORS WITH 5.2L V8 ENGINE: IGNITION TIMING PROCEDURE REVISION* – When setting the ignition timing on 5.2L 2-Bbl models, the vacuum hose to the Spark Control Computer must be disconnected and plugged. Also, ensure a jumper wire is connected from the idle switch to ground. Please add this information to the following publications:
DOMESTIC CARS SERVICE & REPAIR manual and TUNE-UP SERVICE & REPAIR supplement
- 1987 – Page 1-14, step **1)**.
- 1988 – Page 1-21, step **1)**.
EMISSION CONTROL SERVICE & REPAIR DOMESTIC CARS supplement
- 1987 – Page 59, 5.2L V8, step **1)**.
- 1988 – Page 1-3, 5.2L V8, step **1)**.

▷2 *1986-87 CHRYSLER MOTORS THROTTLE BODY FUEL INJECTION: FUEL PRESSURE SPECIFICATION REVISION* – In 1986 and 1987, the correct fuel pressure for the throttle body fuel injection should be 14.5 psi (1.02 kg/cm²), NOT 43-47 psi (3.02-3.30 kg/cm²) as listed on page 1-17 in the 1986 and 1987 DOMESTIC CARS SERVICE & REPAIR manual and TUNE-UP SERVICE & REPAIR supplement.

EAGLE

▷3 *1988 EAGLE PREMIER V6 TUNE-UP: FIRING ORDER REVISION* – The Eagle Premier V6 firing order as shown on page 1-22 in the DOMESTIC CARS SERVICE & REPAIR manual and TUNE-UP SERVICE & REPAIR supplement is incorrect. For correct firing order, *See Fig. 1.*

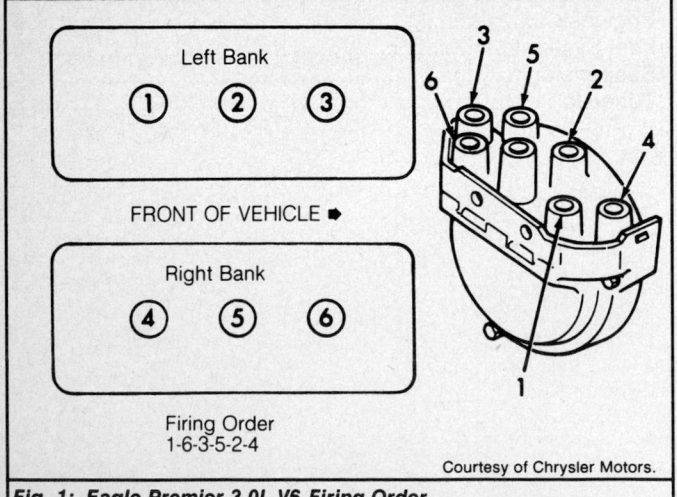

Left Bank

① ② ③

FRONT OF VEHICLE ➡

Right Bank

④ ⑤ ⑥

Firing Order
1-6-3-5-2-4

Courtesy of Chrysler Motors.

Fig. 1: Eagle Premier 3.0L V6 Firing Order

COMPUTERIZED ENGINE CONTROL

CHRYSLER MOTORS

▷4 *1984-88 CHRYSLER MOTORS FWD ENGINE CONTROL SYSTEM: SETTING CODE 88* – On 1984-88 Chrysler Motors vehicles, YOU WILL NOT get a Code 88 if you are using the check engine light to diagnose the engine control system. There will be a 2-second bulb check, followed by the codes, ending with a Code 55. A Code 88 will only be set when using Chrysler's DRB: II tester. Some other "Scan" testers may also set a Code 88 under certain conditions. Check equipment manufacturer for specific instructions.

▷5 *1987 CHRYSLER MOTORS FWD ELECTRONIC FUEL CONTROL: IGNITION SYSTEM TEST REVISION* – Under the "FAILURE TO START TEST," please revise step 6) to read as follows:

6) If in step **3)** the correct spark was obtained but engine would not start, hold carburetor switch open with a thin cardboard insulator. Measure voltage between carburetor switch and ground. Reading should be within one volt of battery voltage. If so, proceed to step **10)**.

Please note this revision in the following publications:
DOMESTIC CARS SERVICE & REPAIR manual and TUNE-UP SERVICE & REPAIR supplement
- 1987 – Page 1a-34.
EMISSION CONTROL SERVICE & REPAIR DOMESTIC CARS supplement
- 1987 – Page 77.
COMPUTERIZED ENGINE CONTROLS manual
- 1987 – Page 36.

▷6 *1981-88 CHRYSLER MOTORS DUAL PICK-UP COIL DISTRIBUTOR: SERVICE MANUAL REVISION* – The component callouts for the dual pick-up coil distributor illustration in the Domestic Cars Service & Repair manual are incorrect. See following list for year and page number.
- 1981 – page 1a-39.
- 1982 – page 1a-40.
- 1983 – page 1a-41.
- 1984 – page 1a-48.
- 1985 – page 1a-99.
- 1986 – page 1a-92.
- 1987 – page 1a-91.
- 1988 – page 1a-93.
See the 1989 Domestic Cars Service & Repair manual, page 1a-170 for the correct illustration.

FORD MOTOR CO.

▷7 *1985 FORD MOTOR CO. EEC-IV: MANUAL REVISION* – Revise CIRCUIT TEST A, step 13) to read as follows:

13) Turn key off and wait 10 seconds. Disconnect ECA 60-pin connector and inspect for damage, loose or corroded pins or wires. Repair wiring and connect ECA. Set DVOM to 20-volt scale and make sure breakout box timing switch is set in "Computed" position. Measure voltage between test pin No. 36 and chassis ground while cranking engine. If between 3.0-6.0 volts, on 2.3L OHC/FBC models, check carburetor for cause of no start condition. Go to next step on all other models. If less than 3.0 volts or over 6.0 volts, go to step **10)** of this test.
Note this revision in the following publications:

DOMESTIC CARS SERVICE & REPAIR manual and TUNE-UP SERVICE & REPAIR supplement
- 1985 – Page 1a-136.
COMPUTERIZED ENGINE CONTROLS manual
- 1985 – Page 223.

⑧ *FORD MOTOR CO. EEC-IV: MANUAL REVISION* – The EEC-IV CONTINUOUS SELF-TEST code charts refer Code 14 to CIRCUIT TEST C2 for all engine sizes. This information has been revised. Code 14 faults should be referred to CIRCUIT TEST D 23, for all engine sizes.
Note this revision in the following publications:
DOMESTIC CARS SERVICE & REPAIR manual
- 1988 – Page 1a-133 and 1a-134.
TUNE-UP SERVICE & REPAIR supplement
- 1988 – Page 1a-133 and 1a-134.
COMPUTERIZED ENGINE CONTROLS manual
- 1988 – Page 135 and 136.

⑨ *1987 FORD MOTOR CO. EEC-IV: WIRING DIAGRAM REVISION* – The 2.5L HSC/CFI EEC-IV Wiring Diagram lists 2 pins No. 15 on the integrated controller module. The bottom pin No. 15 (Pink/Black wire) is incorrectly labeled and should be changed to pin No. 5.
Note this revision in the following publications:
DOMESTIC CARS SERVICE & REPAIR manual
- 1987 – Page 1a-141.
TUNE-UP SERVICE & REPAIR supplement
- 1987 – Page 1a-141.
COMPUTERIZED ENGINE CONTROLS manual
- 1987 – Page 143.

⑩ *1988 FORD MOTOR CO. TEMPO & TOPAZ 2.3L MPFI: WIRING DIAGRAM REVISION* – The wiring diagram for the Tempo and Topaz 2.3L MPFI is incorrect. For the correct diagram, *See Fig. 2.*
Note this revision in the following publications:
DOMESTIC CARS SERVICE & REPAIR manual
- 1988 – Page 1a-187.
- 1988 – Page 2-63.
ELECTRONIC FUEL INJECTION manual
- 1988 – Page 233.

FUEL SYSTEMS

CHRYSLER MOTORS

⑪ *1986 CHRYSLER MOTORS THROTTLE BODY FUEL INJECTION: FUEL PUMP PRESSURE REVISION* – The fuel pressure specification for throttle body injection systems should be 14.5 psi (1.02 kg/cm²), NOT 34-38 psi (2.4-2.7 kg/cm²) as listed in the FUEL PUMP SPECIFICATIONS (TYPICAL) table.
Note this revision in the following publications:
DOMESTIC CARS SERVICE & REPAIR manual
- 1986 – Page 2-195.
TUNE-UP SERVICE & REPAIR manual
- 1986 – Page 2-195.

FORD MOTOR CO.

⑫ *1988 FORD MOTOR CO. TEMPO & TOPAZ 2.3L MPFI: WIRING DIAGRAM REVISION* – The wiring diagram for the Tempo and Topaz 2.3L MPFI is incorrect. For the correct diagram, *See Fig. 2.*
Note this revision in the following publications:
DOMESTIC CARS SERVICE & REPAIR manual
- 1988 – Page 1a-187.
- 1988 – Page 2-63.
ELECTRONIC FUEL INJECTION manual
- 1988 – Page 233.

ENGINES

FORD MOTOR CO.

⑬ *1982-83 FORD MOTOR CO. 2.3L OHC ENGINE: REAR MAIN SEAL* – The rear main seal in this engine was changed from a 2-piece to a one-piece design for the 1983 model year. However, some late production 1982 1.9L engines may be equipped with the

2-piece seal. Always check the type of seal used in the engine before removing the oil pan and rear main bearing cap.

⑭ *1988 FORD MOTOR CO. 1.9L ENGINE: SERVICE MANUAL REVISION* – On page 6-57 of the 1988 DOMESTIC CARS SERVICE & REPAIR manual, the GENERAL SPECIFICATIONS table for the 1.9L engine is incorrect. For correct specifications, refer to the 1.9L engine article in the 1989 edition of this manual. The correction should also be noted on page 6-57 in the *1988* ENGINE, CLUTCH & DRIVE AXLE SERVICE & REPAIR supplement.

⑮ *1986 FORD MOTOR CO. 1.9L ENGINE: CONNECTING ROD JOURNAL REVISION* – On page 6-68 of the 1986 DOMESTIC CARS SERVICE & REPAIR manual, please revise the connecting rod journal diameter to read 1.8854-1.8862" (47.889-47.909 mm). This correction should also be noted on page 6-68 in the 1986 ENGINE, CLUTCH & DRIVE AXLE SERVICE & REPAIR supplement.

⑯ *1984-85 FORD MOTOR CO. 1.6L ENGINE: CONNECTING ROD INSTALLATION REVISION* – In the 1984 and 1985 editions of the DOMESTIC CARS SERVICE & REPAIR manual, the procedure under PISTON PINS states the connecting rod oil squirt hole should face the exhaust side of engine. The oil squirt hole should face toward the INTAKE side of engine. Please change this procedure on the following pages:
- 1984 – Page 6-76.
- 1985 – Page 6-76.
The procedure should also be revised on page 6-76 in the 1984 and 1985 ENGINE, CLUTCH & DRIVE AXLE SERVICE & REPAIR supplements.

⑰ *1983-84 FORD MOTOR 3.8L V8: REAR CRANKSHAFT SEAL REVISION* – In 1983, the rear crankshaft seal was changed from a 2-piece to a 1-piece design. Please note this change in the DOMESTIC CARS SERVICE & REPAIR manual and the ENGINE, CLUTCH & DRIVE AXLE supplement on the following pages:
- 1983 – Page 6-101.
- 1983 – Page 6-114.

BRAKES

CHRYSLER MOTORS

⑱ *CHRYSLER MOTORS ABS CODES & OHM SPECIFICATION: MANUAL REVISION* – There is a revision in the CHRYSLER ABS CODES 1-4 in the WHEEL CIRCUIT VALVE CHART on page 9-17 of the 1988 DOMESTIC CARS SERVICE & REPAIR manual and 1988 CHASSIS SERVICE & REPAIR supplement. The code identification is as follows in the manual:
CODE 1 – LF VALVE
CODE 2 – RR VALVE
CODE 3 – RF VALVE
CODE 4 – LR VALVE

The codes should read as follows:
CODE 1 – LF VALVE
CODE 2 – RF VALVE
CODE 3 – RR VALVE
CODE 4 – LR VALVE
In addition, the flow charts throughout the article specify 1.8 ohms This specification should be revised to 2.5 ohms.

FORD MOTOR CO.

⑲ *FORD MOTOR CO. TEVES ANTI-LOCK BRAKE SYSTEM (ABS): PIN IDENTIFICATION REVISION* – In the 1988 DOMESTIC CARS SERVICE & REPAIR manual and 1988 CHASSIS SERVICE & REPAIR supplement, page 9-38, on the Anti-Lock Quick

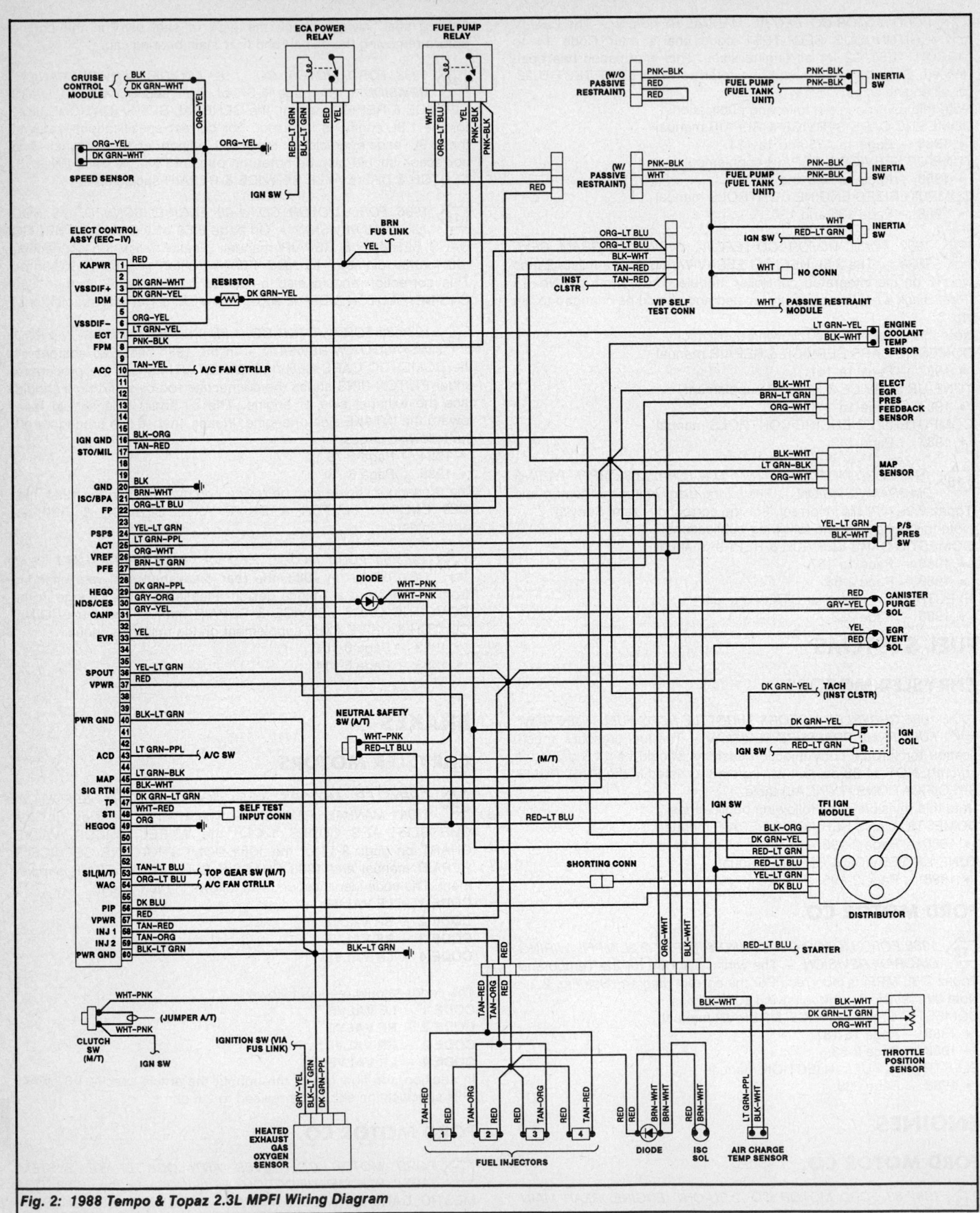

Fig. 2: 1988 Tempo & Topaz 2.3L MPFI Wiring Diagram

Check Sheet under "Item To Be Tested", it states "Remove jumper from Pins 2 and 8". This should read "Remove jumper from Pins 9 and 18." Also, on page 9-52 a ground wire was omitted from the wiring diagram. The ground wire should be present from ABS Control Module Pin "1" to chassis ground.

ALIGNMENT

FORD MOTOR CO.

[20] *TEMPO & TOPAZ: RIDING HEIGHT SPECIFICATION REVISION* – The manufacturer has revised the riding height specification for all Ford Tempo and Topaz models. The correct specification is 20.3" for the front height and 20.8" for the rear height. Both front and rear should be measured from the floor to the bottom of the bumper.

SUSPENSION

FORD MOTOR CO.

[21] *1988 FORD MOTOR CO. FWD FRONT SUSPENSION: ILLUSTRATION REVISION* – In the 1988 edition of the DOMESTIC CARS SERVICE & REPAIR manual, page 11-16 shows the front suspension for FWD Fords in Figs. 1 and 2. Sable and Taurus are shown in Fig. 2, not Fig. 1.

GENERAL INDEX

CONTENTS

AUTOMOBILE MANUFACTURERS   Page
Chrysler Motors I-2
Eagle I-7
Ford Motor Co. I-10

1989 CHRYSLER MOTORS INDEX

A

ABBREVIATIONS
Mitchell's Abbreviations G-7

AIR BAGS
Description & Operation 6-2
Removal & Installation 6-3
Testing & Diagnosis 6-4

ALIGNMENT – *See Wheel Alignment*

ALTERNATOR
Chrysler Motors 90 & 120 Amp
  With External Regulator
    Bench Tests 4-32
    Description 4-31
    On-Vehicle Test 4-31
    Specifications 4-33
Bosch 90 Amp
  Description 4-27
  Operation 4-27
  Specifications 4-30
  Testing & Diagnosis 4-27
Nippondenso 75, 90 & 120 Amp
  With Internal Regulator
    Description 4-34
    Operation 4-34
    Specifications 4-37
    Testing & Diagnosis 4-34
Nippondenso 90 & 120 Amp
  With External Regulator
    Bench Tests 4-40
    Description 4-38
    On-Vehicle Test 4-38
    Specifications 4-41
Regulator
  Diplomat, Fifth Avenue
  & Grand Fury
    Description 4-42
Trouble Shooting
  All Models 4-26

ANTENNA
Description 6-63
Removal & Installation 6-63
Teating & Trouble Shooting 6-63

ANTI-THEFT SYSTEM
Description & Operation 6-15
Removal & Installation 6-16
Teating & Trouble Shooting 6-15

APPLICATIONS
Tool Applications G-12

AUTOMATIC CHOKE – *See Carburetor*

AXLE
FWD – *See Drive Axle Shaft*
RWD
  7 1/4" & 8 1/4" Ring Gear
    Axle Ratio & Identification 9-5
    Description 9-5
    Gear Tooth Patterns 9-4
    Overhaul 9-6
    Removal & Installation 9-5
  Positive Traction
    Description 9-17
    Gear Tooth Patterns 9-4
    Identification 9-17
    Lubrication 9-17
    Overhaul 9-17
    Removal & Installation 9-17

B

BALL JOINT
FWD
  Checking 12-3
  Removal & Installation 12-4
RWD
  Checking 12-8
  Removal & Installation 12-8

BATTERY
Specifications
  4-Cylinder 1-7
  3.0L V6 1-9
  5.2L V8 1-13

BELT
Serpentine Drive Belts
  All Models 7-153

BRAKES
Anti-Lock Brake Systems (ABS)
  Bleeding Brake System 10-3, 10-10
  Description 10-9
  Operation 10-9
  Removal & Installation 10-9
  Safety Precautions 10-8
  Testing 10-9
  Trouble Shooting Charts 10-11
Hydraulic Brake System Bleeding
  Description 10-3
  Servicing 10-3
Disc
  Single Pision – Front
    Adjustments 10-43
    Description 10-43
    Overhaul 10-44
    Removal & Installation 10-43
    Servicing 10-43
  Single Piston – Rear
    Adjustments 10-46
    Description 10-46
    Overhaul 10-47
    Removal & Installation 10-46
    Servicing 10-46
Drum
  Bendix Single Anchor
    Automatic Adjuster
      Adjustments 10-54
      Cleaning & Inspection 10-55
      Description 10-54
      Overhaul 10-55
Master Cylinder
  Bendix/Delco-Moraine
    Description 10-6
    Overhaul 10-6
    Removal & Installation 10-6
Power Brake Units
  Single Diaphragm
    Adjustments 10-4
    Description 10-4
    Removal & Installation 10-4
  Trouble Shooting 10-2

C

CAMSHAFT TIMING – *See Engine*

CAMSHAFT – *See Engine*

CAPACITIES – *See Axle, Cooling, Oil, Transaxle
Servicing or Transmission Servicing*

CARBURETOR
5.2L V8 Holly 6280
  Adjustments 2-6

Application 2-6
Description 2-6
Identification 2-6
Overhaul 2-7
Specifications 2-8
Trouble Shooting 2-2
5.2L V8 Rochester E4ME
  Adjustments 2-15
  Application 2-15
  Description 2-15
  Identification 2-15
  Overhaul 2-18
  Specifications 2-21
  Testing 2-15
  Trouble Shooting 2-2

CATALYTIC CONVERTERS – *See Emission*

CLUTCH
All Models 8-4

COMPRESSION PRESSURE
4-Cylinder 1-5
3.0L V6 1-8
5.2L V8 1-10

COMPUTERIZED ENGINE CONTROL
Introduction 1a-2
Body Control Computer
  Dynasty & New Yorker
    Description 1a-189
    Testing & Diagnosis 1a-190
    Diagnostic Test Outline 1a-190
    Removal & Installation 1a-191
    Wiring Diagrams 1a-192
2.2L Turbo II MPFI
  Description 1a-4
  Operation 1a-4
  Removal & Installation 1a-5
  Testing & Diagnosis 1a-6
2.2L & 2.5L SPFI
  Description 1a-37
  Fault Codes 1a-41
  Model Identification 1a-37
  Operation 1a-37
  Removal & Installation 1a-38
  Testing & Diagnosis 1a-39
2.5L Turbo I MPFI
  Description 1a-83
  Fault Codes 1a-87
  Operation 1a-83
  Removal & Installation 1a-84
  Testing & Diagnosis 1a-85
3.0L MPFI
  Description 1a-126
  Fault Codes 1a-130
  Operation 1a-126
  Removal & Installation 1a-127
  Testing & Diagnosis 1a-127
RWD Models
  Adjustments 1a-171
  Description 1a-169
  Removal & Installation 1a-171
  Testing 1a-171

CONNECTING ROD – *See Engine*

CONSTANT VELOCITY JOINT – *See Drive Axle Shaft*

CONVERSION
Engine & Model Conversion G-6

CONVERTIBLE TOPS
Power
  Adjustments 6-6
  Description & Operation 6-6

CONVERTIBLE TOPS (Cont.)
Removal & Installation 6-67
Trouble Shooting 6-66

COOLING
Capacities 7-130
Electric Cooling Fans 7-132
Recovery Systems 7-129
Servicing 7-129

CRANKCASE – See Oil

CRANKSHAFT – See Engine

CRUISE CONTROL
Adjustments 6-20
Description & Operation 6-20
Removal & Installation 6-23
Testing 6-21
Trouble Shooting 6-20

CYLINDER HEAD – See Engine

D

DEFOGGER
Description, Operation & Testing 6-36

DIFFERENTIAL – See Axle

DISTRIBUTOR
Electronic Spark Control (ESC)
RWD Models
Adjustments 4-4
Description 4-3
Operation 4-3
Overhaul 4-5
Testing 4-4
Hall Effect Electronic Ignition
2.2L & 2.5L
Adjustments 4-7
Description & Operation 4-7
Testing 4-7
Optical Ignition
3.0L
Adjustments 4-8
Description 4-8
Operation 4-8
Testing 4-8
Trouble Shooting
All Models 4-2

DOOR
Electric Locks 6-39

DRIVE AXLE SHAFT
FWD
Description & Identification 9-25
Lubrication 9-25
Overhaul 9-27
Service (In Vehicle) 9-25
RWD – See Axle

E

Electronic Height Control (FWD) – See Suspension

EMISSIONS
Air Injection Systems
Description 3-12
Operation 3-12
Service Procedures 3-12
Testing 3-13
Catalytic Converters
Description & Operation 3-4
Service Procedures 3-4
Testing 3-4
Electric Assist Choke
Description 3-14
Operation 3-14
Testing 3-14
Emission Application Table 3-7
Emission Components 3-8
Emission Standards 3-2
Exhaust Gas Recirculation (EGR)
Description 3-10
Operation 3-10
Servicing 3-11
Testing 3-10
Fuel Evaporation Control System
Description 3-15
Operation 3-15
Maintenance 3-15
Maintenance Reminder Light
1980-89 Reset Procedures G-2
Positive Crankcase Ventilation
Description 3-3
Operation 3-3
Service Procedures 3-3
Thermostatic Air Cleaners
Description 3-5
Operation 3-5
Testing 3-5
Vacuum Diagrams 3-16

ENGINES
Engine Overhaul Procedures 7-5
2.2L & 2.5L 4-Cylinder
Adjustments 7-17
Balance Shafts 7-20
Camshaft 7-21, 7-22
Cooling System 7-130
Crankshaft Front Seal 7-20
Cylinder Block Assembly 7-23
Cylinder Head 7-18, 7-22
Electric Cooling Fans 7-132
Engine Removal 7-32
Engine Identification 7-17
Front Crankshaft Sprocket Oil Seal 7-20
Intake & Exhaust Manifolds 7-17
Intermediate Shaft 7-21, 7-22
Oil Pan Removal 7-126
Oil Pump 7-24
Rear Crankshaft Oil Seal 7-19
Specifications 7-25
Thermostat 7-130
Tightening Specifications 7-25
Timing Belt 7-19
Valve Train 7-22
Water Pump 7-22
3.0L V6
Adjustments 7-27
Camshaft 7-30
Cooling System 7-130
Cylinder Block Assembly 7-31
Cylinder Head 7-28, 7-30
Electric Cooling Fans 7-132
Engine Removal 7-118
Engine Identification 7-27
Exhaust Manifolds 7-28
Front Cover & Timing Belt 7-29
Intake Manifolds 7-27
Oil Pan Removal 7-126

Oil Pump 7-32
Rear Crankshaft Oil Seal 7-29
Specifications 7-32
Thermostat 7-130
Tightening Specifications 7-32
Valve Train 7-30
Water Pump 7-30
5.2L V8
Adjustments 7-34
Camshaft 7-36
Cooling System 7-130
Crankshaft Front Seal 7-35
Cylinder Block Assembly 7-37
Cylinder Head 7-34, 7-37
Electric Cooling Fans 7-132
Engine Removal 7-118
Engine Identification 7-34
Exhaust Manifolds 7-34
Front Cover Oil Seal 7-35
Front Timing Cover 7-35
Intake Manifold 7-34
Oil Pan Removal 7-126
Oil Pump 7-38
Rear Crankshaft Oil Seal 7-36
Specifications 7-39
Thermostat 7-130
Tightening Specifications 7-39
Timing Chain 7-35
Valve Train 7-37
Water Pump 7-36

F

FILTER
Service Intervals
4-Cylinder 1-7
3.0L V6 1-9
5.2L V8 1-13

FIRING ORDER
4-Cylinder 1-6
3.0L V6 1-9
5.2L V8 1-11

FUEL GAUGE – See Gauge

FUEL INJECTION
2.2L Turbo, 2.5L Turbo & 3.0L
Multi-Point Fuel Injection
Description 2-22
Operation 2-22
Removal & Installation 2-24
Testing & Diagnosis 2-24
Trouble Shooting 2-3, 2-24
Turbocharger 2-49
2.2L & 2.5L
Throttle Body Injection
Description 2-26
Operation 2-26
Removal & Installation 2-28
Testing & Diagnosis 2-27
Trouble Shooting 2-3, 2-27

FUEL PUMP
Specifications
4-Cylinder 1-6
3.0L V6 1-9
5.2L V8 1-13
Testing
Multi-Point Fuel Injection 2-24
Throttle Body Fuel Injection 2-27

1989 CHRYSLER MOTORS INDEX

G

GAUGE
Electronic Instrument Panel
Adjustments 6-126
Description & Operation 6-122
Removal & Installation 6-126
Testing & Diagnosis 6-124
Standard Instrument Panel
Description & Operation 6-112
Removal & Installation 6-120
Testing & Diagnosis 6-112

H

HEADLIGHT
Switch Removal 6-120

HORN BUTTON
Except Horizon & Omni
Removal & Installation 13-6
Horizon & Omni
Removal & Installation 13-8

I

IDENTIFICATION – *See Engine, Tune-Up or Vehicle Identification Number*

IGNITION
Electronic Spark Control (ESC)
RWD Models
Adjustments 4-4
Description 4-3
Operation 4-3
Overhaul 4-5
Testing 4-4
Hall Effect Electronic Ignition
2.2L & 2.5L
Adjustments 4-7
Description & Operation 4-7
Testing 4-7
Optical Ignition
3.0L
Adjustments 4-8
Description 4-8
Operation 4-8
Testing 4-8
Trouble Shooting
All Models 4-2

IGNITION SWITCH – *See Steering Column Switches*

INJECTION – *See Fuel Injection*

INSTRUMENT PANEL
Electronic Instrument Panel
Adjustments 6-126
Description & Operation 6-122
Removal & Installation 6-126
Testing & Diagnosis 6-124
Standard Instrument Panel
Description & Operation 6-112
Removal & Installation 6-120
Testing & Diagnosis 6-112

J

JACKING & HOISTING
All Models 11-10

L

LINKAGE
Automatic Transmission 14-5
Manual Transmission 14-21
Steering 13-86

LUBRICATION – *See Axle, Engine, Oil Transaxle Servicing or Transmission Servicing*

LUG NUTS
Tightening Specifications 11-4

M

MANIFOLDS – *See Engine*

MANUAL STEERING – *See Steering*

MASTER CYLINDER – *See Brakes*

N

NEUTRAL SAFETY SWITCH – *See Switch*

O

OIL
Capacity
4-Cylinder 1-7
3.0L V6 1-9
5.2L V8 1-13

OIL PAN REMOVAL
All Models 7-126

OIL PUMP – *See Engine*

OIL PRESSURE GAUGE – *See Gauge*

P

PARKING BRAKE – *See Brakes*

PISTON – *See Engine*

PISTON RING – *See Engine*

POSITIVE TRACTION DIFFERENTIAL – *See Axle*

POWER
Brake Unit – *See Brakes*
Convertible Tops – *See Convertible Tops*
Steering - *See Steering*
Seat – *See Seat*
Window – *See Window*

PROPELLER SHAFT
RWD Models 9-20

R

RADIATOR – *See Cooling*

REAR
Axle – *See Axle*
Suspension – *See Suspension*
Window Defogger – *See Defogger*

REGULATOR
Diplomat, Fifth Avenue & Grand Fury 4-42

RIDING HEIGHT
All Models 11-5

RING – *See Engine*

S

SEAT
Acclaim & Spirit Power Seat
Description & Operation 6-78
Removal & Installation 6-79
Testing 6-78
Dynasty & New Yorker Power Memory Seat
Description & Operation 6-80
Removal & Installation 6-82
Testing 6-80

SPARK PLUG
Application & Torque
4-Cylinder 1-5
3.0L V6 1-8
5.2L V8 1-10

SPEED CONTROL – *See Cruise Control*

SPEEDOMETER – *See Gauge*

STARTER
Bosch & Nippondenso
FWD
Bench Testing 4-6
Description 4-6
On-Vehicle Tests 4-6
Specifications 4-6
Nippondenso
RWD
Bench Testing 4-6
Description 4-6
On-Vehicle Testing 4-6
Specifications 4-6
Trouble Shooting 4-6
Removal
All Models 4-6
Trouble Shooting
All Models 4-5

STEERING
Columns
Standard Column
Except Acclaim, Horizon,
Omni & Spriit
Description 13-14
Overhaul 13-15
Removal & Installation 13-14
Tightening Specifications 13-17
Trouble Shooting 13-2
Acclaim, Horizon, Omni & Spirit
Description 13-20
Overhaul 13-20
Removal & Installation 13-20
Tightening Specifications 13-20
Trouble Shooting 13-2
Tilt Column
Except Horizon & Omni
Description 13-14
Overhaul 13-16
Tightening Specifications 13-17
Trouble Shooting 13-2
Gears
Manual Steering Gears
Description 13-33
Removal & Installation 13-33
Tightening Specifications 13-33
Trouble Shooting 13-3
Power Steering Gears – FWD
Rack & Pinion
Description 13-39
General Servicing 13-37
Overhaul 13-39
Removal & Installation 13-39
Tightening Specifications 13-39
Trouble Shooting 13-4
Recirculating Ball – RWD
Adjustments 13-40
Description 13-40
General Servicing 13-37
On-Vehicle Service 13-40
Operation 13-40
Overhaul 13-41
Removal & Installation 13-40
Tightening Specifications 13-43
Trouble Shooting 13-4
Linkage – See Linkage
Pump
FWD
Description 13-75
General Servicing 13-37
Overhaul 13-76
Removal & Installation 13-75
Testing 13-75
Tightening Specifications 13-77
RWD
Description 13-78
General Servicing 13-37
Overhaul 13-79
Removal & Installation 13-78
Tightening Specifications 13-80
Wheel
Except Horizon & Omni 13-6
Horizon & Omni 13-8

SUNROOF
Adjustment 6-107
Description & Operation 6-107
Maintenance 6-107
Removal & Installation 6-107

SUSPENSION
Front
FWD
Adjustments 12-3
Description 12-3
Removal & Installation 12-3
Tightening Specifications 12-7
RWD
Adjustments 12-8
Description 12-8
Removal & Installation 12-8
Tightening Specifications 12-11
Rear
FWD Exc. Horizon & Omni
Adjustments 12-33
Description 12-33
Removal & Installation 12-33
Tightening Specifications 12-35
FWD Horizon & Omni
Adjustments 12-36
Description 12-36
Removal & Installation 12-36
Tightening Specifications 12-36
Electronic Suspension
Rear
Description & Operation 12-57
Removal & Installation 12-57
Testing 12-57
Trouble Shooting Charts 12-58

SWITCH
Dimmer
Except Horizon & Omni 13-7
Horizon & Omni 13-8
Headlight 6-120
Ignition
Except Horizon & Omni 13-7
Horizon & Omni 13-8
Ignition Lock
Except Horizon & Omni 13-7
Horizon & Omni 13-8
Neutral Safety 14-7
Speed Control
Except Horizon & Omni 13-6
Turn Signal
Except Horizon & Omni 13-6
Wiper/Washer
Except Horizon & Omni 13-6
Horizon & Omni 13-8

T

THERMOSTAT – See Engine

TIMING
Belt – See Belt
Chain – See Engine
Ignition
4-Cylinder 1-6
3.0L V6 1-8
5.2L V8 1-11

TRANSAXLE SERVICING
Application 14-2
Automatic
Adjustments 14-5
Identification 14-5
Lubrication & Capacities 14-5
Removal & Installation 14-15

Manual
Adjustments 14-21
Identification 14-21
Lubrication 14-21
Removal & Installation 8-4

TRANSMISSION SERVICING
Application 14-2
Automatic
Adjustments 14-5
Identification 14-5
Lubrication & Capacities 14-5
Removal & Installation 14-15

TROUBLE SHOOTING
Air Bag 6-4
Anti-Theft 6-15
Axles 9-2
Brakes 10-2
Carburetor 2-2
Charging System 4-26
Clutch 8-2
Cooling System 7-128
Cruise Control 6-20
Engine 7-2
Fuel Injection 2-3
Ignition System 4-2
Manual Steering Gear 13-3
Power Steering 13-4
Starting System 4-58
Steering Column 13-2
Suspension 12-2
Turbocharger 2-4
Tune-Up 1-2
Wheel Alignment 11-2

TURBOCHARGER
Application 2-49
Description 2-49
Internal Inspection 2-50
Operation 2-49
Removal & Installation 2-50
Testing 2-49
Trouble Shooting 2-4

TURN SIGNAL
Flasher – See Fuse
Switch – See Switch

TUNE-UP
4-Cylinder 1-5
3.0L V6 1-8
5.2L V8 1-10

U

UNIVERSAL JOINT
All Models 9-24

V

VALVE
Adjustment
4-Cylinder 7-17
3.0L V6 7-27
5.2L V8 7-34
Train – See Engine

VEHICLE IDENTIFICATION NUMBER
Engine Identification
4-Cylinder 1-5
3.0L V6 1-8
5.2L V8 1-10
VIN Code Explanation G-5

VOLTAGE REGULATOR – *See Alternator*

W

WATER PUMP
2.2L & 2.5L 4-Cylinder
Removal & Installation 7-22
3.0L V6
Removal & Installation 7-30
5.2L V8
Removal & Installation 7-36

WHEEL
Alignment
Procedures 11-3
Specifications 11-6
Trouble Shooting 11-2
Bearings
Front
FWD
Adjustment 12-3
Removal & Installation 12-5
RWD
Adjustment 12-8
Rear
Except Horizon & Omni
Adjustment 12-33
Removal & Installation 12-34
Horizon & Omni
Adjustment 12-36
Removal & Installation 12-36
Steering – *See Steering*

WINDOW
Acclaim & Spirit Power Window
Description & Testing 6-95
Removal & Installation 6-95
All Other FWD Power Window
Description & Testing 6-97
Removal & Installation 6-98
RWD Power Window
Description & Testing 6-100
Removal & Installation 6-100

WIPER/WASHER SYSTEM
Liftgate
Description & Operation 6-194
Removal & Installation 6-194
Testing 6-194
Dynasty & New Yorker (Windshield)
Adjustments & Testing 6-189
Description & Operation 6-189
Removal & Installation 6-190
All Others (Windshield)
Adjustments & Testing 6-194
Description & Operation 6-194
Removal & Installation 6-192

WIRING DIAGRAM
Explanation & Symbology 5-2
Chassis
Acclaim & Spirit 5-4
Aries & Reliant 5-14
Daytona 5-19
Diplomat, Fifth Avenue
& Gran Fury 5-26
Dynasty & New Yorker 5-31
Horizon & Omni 5-43
Lancer & LeBaron Sedan 5-47
LeBaron Coupe & Convertible 5-55
Shadow & Sundance 5-63

A

ABBREVIATIONS
Mitchell's Abbreviations G-7

ALIGNMENT – *See Wheel Alignment*

ALTERNATOR
Delco-Remy
Adjustments 4-44
Description 4-44
On-Vehicle Tests 4-44
Trouble Shooting 4-26, 4-44

AMMETER – *See Gauge*

APPLICATIONS
Tool Applications G-12

AXLE
Description 9-31
Lubrication 9-31
Overhaul 9-31
Service (In-Vehicle) 9-31
Trouble Shooting 9-2

B

BALL JOINT
Removal & Installation 12-12

BATTERY
Specifications
2.5L 4-Cylinder 1-15
3.0L V6 1-17

BELT
Accessory Drive
2.5L 4-Cylinder 1-15
3.0L V6 1-17
Serpentine Drive
All Models 7-153

BRAKES
Hydraulic Brake System Bleeding
Description 10-3
Servicing 10-3
Disc
Single Pision – Front
Adjustments 10-48
Description 10-48
Overhaul 10-49
Removal & Installation 10-48
Servicing 10-48
Drum
Bendix Single Anchor
Automatic Adjuster
Adjustments 10-54
Cleaning & Inspection 10-55
Description 10-54
Overhaul 10-55
Master Cylinder
Bendix/Delco-Moraine
Description 10-6
Overhaul 10-6
Removal & Installation 10-6

Power Brake Units
Single Diaphragm
Adjustments 10-4
Description 10-4
Removal & Installation 10-5
Trouble Shooting 10-2

C

CAMSHAFT – *See Engine*

CAMSHAFT TIMING – *See Engine*

CAPACITIES – *See Axle, Cooling, Oil, Transaxle
Servicing or Transmission Servicing*

CATALYTIC CONVERTERS – *See Emission*

COMPRESSION RATIO
2.5L 4-Cylinder 1-14
3.0L V6 1-16

COMPUTERIZED ENGINE CONTROL
Introduction 1a-2
2.5L 4-Cylinder
Description 1a-275
Fault Codes 1a-324
Operation 1a-275
Removal & Installation 1a-276
Testing & Diagnosis 1a-277
3.0L 6-Cylinder
Description 1a-320
Fault Codes 1a-324
Operation 1a-320
Removal & Installation 1a-321
Testing & Diagnosis 1a-322

CONNECTING ROD – *See Engine*

CONSTANT VELOCITY JOINT – *See Drive Axle Shaft*

CONVERSION
Engine & Model Conversion G-6

COOLING
Capacities 7-130
Electric Cooling Fans 7-134
Recovery Systems 7-129
Servicing 7-129

CRANKCASE – *See Oil*

CRANKSHAFT – *See Engine*

CRUISE CONTROL
Description & Operation 6-24
Removal & Installation 6-25
Testing 6-24
Trouble Shooting 6-24

CYLINDER HEAD – *See Engine*

D

DIFFERENTIAL – *See Axle*

DISTRIBUTOR
Electronic Ignition
Description 4-11

Adjustment & Description 3-4
Operation 3-4
Overhaul 4-11
Testing 4-11
Trouble Shooting 4-2

DOOR
Power Locks
Side Door 6-40
Trunk Release 6-41

DRIVE AXLE SHAFT
Description 9-31
Lubrication 9-31
Overhaul 9-31
Service (In-Vehicle) 9-31
Trouble Shooting 9-2

E

Electronic Level Control – *See Suspension*

EMISSIONS
Catalytic Converters
Description & Operation 3-4
Service Procedures 3-4
Testing 3-4
Emission Application Table 3-18
Emission Components 3-19
Emission Standards 3-2
Exhaust Gas Recirculation (EGR)
Description & Operation 3-21
Testing 3-21
Evaporative Emission Control
Description & Operation 3-22
Maintenance Reminder Light
1980-89 Reset Procedures G-3
Positive Crankcase Ventilation
Description 3-3
Operation 3-3
Service Procedures 3-3
Thermostatic Air Cleaners
Description 3-5
Operation 3-5
Testing 3-5
Vacuum Diagrams 3-23

ENGINES
Overhaul Procedures 7-5
2.5L 4-Cylinder
Adjustments 7-42
Camshaft 7-44
Cooling System 7-130
Crankshaft Front Seal 7-43
Cylinder Block Assembly 7-44
Cylinder Head 7-43, 7-44
Electric Cooling Fans 7-134
Engine Removal 7-120
Engine Identification 7-42
Front Timing Cover 7-43
Intake & Exhaust Manifold 7-42
Oil Pan Removal 7-126
Oil Pump 7-45
Rear Main Bearing Oil Seal 7-44
Specifications 7-47
Tightening Specifications 7-46
Timing Chain & Gears 7-43
Valve Cover & Rocker Arms 7-43
Water Pump 7-44
3.0L V6
Adjustments 7-49
Camshaft 7-49

ENGINES (Cont.)
Cooling System 7-130
Cylinder Block Assembly 7-55
Cylinder Head 7-50, 7-55
Electric Cooling Fans 7-134
Engine Removal 7-120
Engine Identification 7-49
Exhaust Manifold 7-49
Front Timing Case Cover 7-52
Intake Manifold 7-49
Oil Pan Removal 7-126
Oil Pump 7-57
Rocker Arm & Lash Adjuster 7-54
Specifications 7-57
Tightening Specifications 7-57
Timing Chain & Sprockets 7-52
Valve Covers 7-50
Water Pump 7-54

F

FILTER
Service Intervals
2.5L 4-Cylinder 1-15
3.0L V6 1-17

FIRING ORDER
2.5L 4-Cylinder 1-14
3.0L V6 1-16

FUEL GAUGE – *See Gauge*

FUEL INJECTION
2.5L 4-Cylinder – TBI
Adjustments 2-33
Description 2-32
Operation 2-32
Removal & Installation 2-34
Testing & Diagnosis 2-33
Trouble Shooting 2-3, 2-33
3.0L V6 – MPFI
Adjustments 2-29
Description 2-29
Operation 2-29
Removal & Installation 2-30
Testing & Diagnosis 2-30
Trouble Shooting 2-3, 2-29

FUEL PUMP
Specifications
2.5L 4-Cylinder 1-15
3.0L V6 1-16
Testing
2.5L 4-Cylinder 2-33
3.0L V6 2-30

G

GAUGES
Eagle
Description & Operation 6-127
Removal & Installation 6-129
Testing 6-127

H

HORN BUTTON
Removal & Installation 13-10

I

IDENTIFICATION – *See Engine, Tune-Up or Vehicle Identification Number*

IGNITION
Electronic Ignition
Description 4-11
Adjustment & Description 3-4
Operation 3-4
Overhaul 4-11
Testing 4-11
Trouble Shooting 4-2

IGNITION LOCK CYLINDER – *See Steering Column Switches*

IGNITION SWITCH – *See Steering Column Switches*

INJECTION – *See Fuel Injection*

INSTRUMENT PANEL
Eagle
Description & Operation 6-127
Removal & Installation 6-127
Testing 6-127

J

JACKING & HOISTING
All Models 11-11

L

LINKAGE
Automatic Transmission 14-8
Steering 13-86

LUBRICATION – *See Axle, Engine, Oil, Transaxle Servicing or Transmission Servicing*

LUG NUT
Tightening Specifications 11-4

M

MANIFOLD – *See Engine*

MANUAL STEERING – *See Steering*

MASTER CYLINDER – *See Brakes*

MIRROR
Power Side Mirror 6-74

N

NEUTRAL SAFETY SWITCH – *See Switch*

O

OIL
Capacity
2.5L 4-Cylinder 1-15
3.0L V6 1-17

OIL PAN REMOVAL
All Models 7-40

OIL PRESSURE GAUGE – *See Gauge*

OIL PUMP – *See Engine*

P

PARKING BRAKE – *See Brakes*

PISTON – *See Engine*

PISTON RING – *See Engine*

POSITIVE TRACTION DIFFERENTIAL – *See Axle*

POWER
Brake Unit – *See Brakes*
Mirror – *See Mirror*
Seat – *See Seat*
Steering – *See Steering*
Window – *See Window*

R

RADIATOR – *See Cooling*

REAR
Axle – *See Axle*
Suspension – *See Suspension*

RIDING HEIGHT
All Models 11-5

RING – *See Engine*

S

SEAT
Power
Description & Operation 6-87
Testing 6-87

SPARK PLUGS
Application & Torque
 2.5L 4-Cylinder 1-14
 3.0L V6 1-16
Wire Resistance
 2.5L 4-Cylinder 1-14
 3.0L V6 1-16

SPEED CONTROL – *See Cruise Control*

SPEEDOMETER – *See Gauge*

STARTER
Bosch & Mitsubishi
 Bench Tests 4-67
 Description 4-67
 On-Vehicle Tests 4-67
 Removal 4-60
 Specifications 4-69
 Trouble Shooting 4-59

STEERING
Column
 Description 13-21
 Overhaul 13-22
 Removal & Installation 13-21
 Tightening Specifications 13-24
 Trouble Shooting 12-2
Gear
 Power Steering Gears
  Adjustments 13-44
  Description 13-44
  General Servicing 13-37
  Overhaul 13-44
  Removal & Installation 13-44
  Tightening Specifications 13-48
  Trouble Shooting 12-3
Linkage – *See Linkage*
Pump
 Description 13-81
 General Servicing 13-37
 Operation 13-81
 Removal & Installation 13-81
 Tightening Specifications 13-83
Wheel 13-9

STEERING COLUMN SWITCHES
All Models 13-9

STOP LIGHT SWITCH – *See Switch*

SUSPENSION
Front
 Adjustments 12-12
 Description 12-12
 Removal & Installation 12-12
 Tightening Specifications 12-14
Rear
 Adjustments 12-37
 Description 12-37
 Removal & Installation 12-37
 Riding Height 12-39
 Tightening Specifications 12-40

SWITCH
Dimmer 13-10
Ignition 13-9
Ignition Lock 13-9
Neutral Safety 14-9
Speed Control 13-10
Turn Signal 13-9
Wiper/Washer 13-10

T

TAILGATE – *See Power Window*

THERMOSTAT – *See Engine*

TIMING
Chain – *See Engine*
Ignition
 2.5L 4-Cylinder 1-14
 3.0L V6 1-16

TRANSAXLE SERVICING
Application 14-2
Automatic
 Adjustments 14-8
 Identification 14-7
 Lubrication & Capacities 14-7
 Removal & Installation 14-16

TROUBLE SHOOTING
Axle 9-3
Brakes 10-2
Charging System 4-26
Cooling System 7-128
Cruise Control 6-24
Engine 7-2
Ignition System 4-2
Manual Steering Gear 13-3
Power Steering 13-4
Power Windows 6-101
Starting System 4-59
Steering Column 13-2
Suspension 12-2
Tune-Up 1-2
Wheel Alignment 11-2

TUNE–UP
2.5L 4-Cylinder 1-14
3.0L V6 1-16

TURN SIGNAL
Flasher – *See Fuse*
Switch – *See Switch or Steering*

V

VALVE
Adjustment
 2.5L 4-Cylinder 1-14, 7-42
 3.0L V6 .... 1-16, 7-49

VEHICLE IDENTIFICATION NUMBER
Engine Identification
 2.5L 4-Cylinder 1-14
 3.0L V6 1-16
VIN Code Explanation G-5

W

WATER PUMP
2.5L 4-Cylinder
 Removal & Installation 7-44
3.0L V6
 Removal & Installation 7-54

WHEEL
Alignment
 Procedures 11-3
 Specifications 11-6
 Trouble Shooting 11-2
Bearings
 Front
  Removal & Installation 12-12
 Rear
  Removal & Installation 12-37

WINDOW
Power Side Window
 Description & Trouble Shooting 6-101
 Testing 6-101

WIRE RESISTANCE – *See Spark Plug*

WIRING DIAGRAM
Explanation & Symbology 5-2
Chassis
 Premier 5-69

1989 FORD MOTOR CO. INDEX

STEERING (Cont.)
Removal & Installation 13-52
Tightening Specifications 13-58
Trouble Shooting 13-4
Electronic Power Steering Gears
Electronic Variable Orifice
Description 13-59
Operation 13-59
Removal & Installation 13-59
Testing 13-60
Quick Tests 13-60
Variable Assist – Continental
Adjustments 13-64
Description 13-64
Lubrication, Trouble Shooting
& Testing 13-64
Operation 13-64
Overhaul 13-67
Removal & Installation 13-65
Tightening Specifications 13-67
Variable Assist – Probe
Adjustments 13-68
Description 13-68
Operation 13-68
Overhaul 13-70
Removal & Installation 13-68
Testing 13-70
Tightening Specifications 13-70
Trouble Shooting 13-70
Linkage – *See Linkage*
Pumps
Adjustments 13-84
Description 13-84
General Servicing 13-37
Overhaul 13-85
Removal & Installation 13-84
Tightening Specifications 13-85
Wheel 13-10

STOP LIGHT SWITCH – *See Switch*

SUN & MOON ROOFS
Adjustments 6-109
Description & Operation 6-109
Removal & Installation 6-111
Testing 6-110

SUPERCHARGER
3.8L Cougar XR7 & Thunderbird Super Coupe
Description 2-53
Operation 2-53
Removal & Installation 2-53
Trouble Shooting 2-5, 2-53

SUSPENSION
Electronic Suspension
Air Suspension
Continental
Adjustments & Inspection 12-62
Description 12-60
Operation 12-60
Removal & Installation
Air Suspension 12-64
Front Suspension 12-66
Rear Suspension 12-68
Testing & Diagnosis 12-71
Tightening Specifications 12-70
Mark VII
Adjustments & Inspection 12-93
Description 12-92
Diagnosis & Testing 12-94
Operation 12-92
Removal & Installation 12-104
Tightening Specifications 12-103

Automatic Ride Control
Cougar XR-7 & Thunderbird Super Coupe
Description 12-109
Operation 12-109
Removal & Installation 12-109
Tightening Specifications 12-111
Testing 12-109
Quick Tests & Diagnosis 12-111
Programmed Ride Control
Probe
Description 12-118
Operation 12-118
Removal & Installation 12-118
Testing 12-118
Rear Level Control
LTD Crown Victoria, Grand Marquis,
Town Car & Wagon
Adjustments 12-127
Description 12-127
Operation 12-127
Removal & Installation 12-127
Ride Height Specifications 12-129
Testing 12-128
Tightening Specifications 12-129
Front
FWD
Escort, Tempo & Topaz
Adjustments 12-15
Description 12-15
Removal & Installation 12-15
Tightening Specifications 12-17
Probe
Adjustments 12-18
Description 12-18
Removal & Installation 12-18
Tightening Specifications 12-20
Sable & Taurus
Adjustments 12-21
Description 12-21
Removal & Installation 12-21
Tightening Specifications 12-24
RWD
Cougar & Thunderbird
Adjustments 12-25
Description 12-25
Removal & Installation 12-25
Tightening Specifications 12-26
LTD Crown Victoria, Grand Marquis,
Town Car & Wagon
Adjustments 12-27
Description 12-27
Removal & Installation 12-27
Tightening Specifications 12-20
Mustang
Adjustments 12-30
Description 12-30
Removal & Installation 12-30
Tightening Specifications 12-32
Rear
FWD
Escort
Adjustments 12-41
Description 12-41
Removal & Installation 12-41
Tightening Specifications 12-43
Probe
Adjustments 12-44
Description 12-44
Removal & Installation 12-44
Tightening Specifications 12-45
Trouble Shooting 12-2
Sable & Taurus
Adjustments 12-46
Description 12-46
Removal & Installation 12-46
Tightening Specifications 12-48

Tempo & Topaz
Adjustments 12-49
Description 12-49
Removal & Installation 12-49
Tightening Specifications 12-50
RWD
Cougar & Thunderbird
Adjustments 12-55
Description 12-55
Removal & Installation 12-55
Tightening Specifications 12-56
LTD Crown Victoria, Grand Marquis,
Mustang, Town Car & Wagon
Adjustments 12-51
Description 12-51
Removal & Installation 12-52
Tightening Specifications 12-54

SWITCH
Dimmer 13-13
Headlight 6-133, 6-138
Ignition 13-11
Ignition Lock 13-11
Neutral Safety 13-16
Speed Control 13-13
Turn Signal 13-13
Wiper/Washer 13-13

T

THERMOSTAT – *See Engine*

TIMING
Belt – *See Belt*
Chain – *See Engine*
Ignition
4-Cylinder 1-20
V6 1-25
V8 1-29

TRANSAXLE SERVICING
Automatic
Adjustment 13-13
Application 13-2
Capacity 13-13
Lubrication 13-13
Removal & Installation 13-28
Manual
Adjustment 13-35
Application 13-2
Capacity 13-35
Lubrication 13-35
Removal & Installation 13-40

TRANSMISSION SERVICING
Automatic
Adjustment 13-13
Application 13-2
Capacity 13-13
Lubrication 13-13
Removal & Installation 13-28
Manual
Adjustment 13-35
Application 13-2
Capacity 13-35
Lubrication 13-35
Removal & Installation 13-40

TROUBLE SHOOTING
Anti-Theft System 6-17
Automatic Headlight Dimmer 6-53
Axle 9-2

1989 FORD MOTOR CO. INDEX

TROUBLE SHOOTING (Cont.)
Brakes 10-2
Carburetor 2-2
Charging System 4-26
Clutch 8-2
Cooling System 7-128
Cruise Control 6-27, 6-34
Engine 7-2
Fuel Injection 2-3
Ignition System 4-2
Manual Steering Gear 13-3
Power Steering 13-4
Starting System 4-58
Steering Column 13-2
Supercharger 2-5
Suspension 12-2
Tune-Up 1-2
Turbocharger 2-4
Wiper/Washer System 6-195, 6-198
Wheel Alignment 11-2

TUNE-UP
4-Cylinder 1-18
V6 1-24
V8 1-28

TURBOCHARGER
2.2L Probe
Description 2-51
Operation 2-51
Removal & Installation 2-51
Testing 2-52
Trouble Shooting 2-4, 2-52

TURN SIGNAL
Switch – *See Switch or Steering*

U

UNIVERSAL JOINT
All Models 9-24

V

VALVE
Clearance
1.9L 4-Cylinder Gas 7-60
2.2L 7-68
2.3L & 2.5L HSC 4-Cylinder 7-75
2.3L OHC 4-Cylinder 7-82
3.0L V6 7-89
3.0L SHO V6 7-97
3.8L & 3.8L Supercharged V6 7-103
5.0L & 5.8L V8 7-111

VEHICLE IDENTIFICATION NUMBER
Engine Identification
4-Cylinder 1-18
V6 1-24
V8 1-28
VIN Code Explanation G-5

VOLTAGE REGULATOR – *See Regulator*

W

WATER PUMP
1.9L 4-Cylinder
Removal & Installation 7-64
2.2L 4-Cylinder
Removal & Installation 7-71
2.3L & 2.5L HSC 4-Cylinder
Removal & Installation 7-77
2.3L OHC 4-Cylinder
Removal & Installation 7-85
3.0L V6
Removal & Installation 7-90
3.0L SHO V6
Removal & Installation 7-98
3.8L & 3.8L Supercharged V6
Removal & Installation 7-105
5.0L & 5.8L V8
Removal & Installation 7-112

WHEEL
Alignment
Procedures 11-3
Specifications 11-6
Trouble Shooting 11-2

Bearings
Front
FWD
Escort, Tempo & Topaz
Adjustment 12-15
Removal & Installation 12-16
Probe
Adjustment 12-18
Removal & Installation 12-18
Sable & Taurus
Adjustment 12-21
Removal & Installation 12-23
RWD
Cougar & Thunderbird
Adjustment 12-25
Removal & Installation 12-26
LTD Crown Victoria, Grand Marquis,
Town Car & Wagon
Adjustment 12-27
Removal & Installation 12-29
Mustang
Adjustment 12-30
Removal & Installation 12-32
Rear
FWD
Escort
Adjustment 12-41
Removal & Installation 12-43
Sable & Taurus
Adjustment 12-46
Removal & Installation 12-48
Tempo & Topaz
Adjustment 12-49
Removal & Installation 12-50

WIRE RESISTANCE – *See Spark Plug*

WIRING DIAGRAM
Explanation & Symbology 5-2
Chassis
Continental 5-80
Cougar & Thunderbird 5-92
Escort 5-106
LTD Crown Victoria, Grand Marquis
& Wagons 5-114
Mark VII 5-124
Mustang 5-134
Probe 5-141
Sable & Taurus 5-153
Tempo & Topaz 5-166
Town Car 5-174

METRIC CONVERSIONS

Metric conversions are making life more difficult for the mechanic. In addition to doubling the number of tools required, metric-dimensioned nuts and bolts are used alongside English components in many new vehicles. The mechanic has to decide which tool to use, slowing down the job. The tool problem can be solved by trial and error, but some metric conversions aren't so simple.

Converting temperature, lengths or volumes requires a calculator and conversion charts, or else a very nimble mind. Conversion charts are only part of the answer though, because they don't help you "think" metric, or "visualize" what you are converting. The following examples are intended to help you "see" metric sizes:

LENGTH

Meters are the standard unit of length in the metric system. The smaller units are 10ths (decimeter), 100ths (centimeter), and 1000ths (millimeter) of a meter. These common examples might help you to visualize the metric units:

* A meter is slightly longer than a yard (about 40 inches).
* An aspirin tablet is about one centimeter across (.4 inches).
* A millimeter is about the thickness of a dime.

VOLUME

Cubic meters and centimeters are used to measure volume, just as we normally think of cubic feet and inches. Liquid volume measurements include the liter and milliliter, like the English quarts or ounces.

* One teaspoon is about 5 cubic centimeters.
* A liter is about one quart.
* A liter is about 61 cubic inches.

WEIGHT

The metric weight system is based on the gram, with the most common unit being the kilogram (1000 grams). Our comparable units are ounces and pounds:

* A kilogram is about 2.2 pounds.
* An ounce is about 28 grams.

TORQUE

Torque is somewhat complicated. The term describes the amount of effort exerted to turn something. A chosen unit of weight or force is applied to a lever of standard length. The resulting leverage is called torque. In our standard system, we use the weight of one pound applied to a lever a foot long– resulting in the unit called a foot-pound. A smaller unit is the inch-pound (the lever is one inch long). Metric units include the meter kilogram (lever one meter long with a kilogram of weight applied) and the Newton-meter (lever one meter long with force of one Newton applied). Some conversions are:

* A meter kilogram is about 7.2 foot pounds.
* A Newton-meter is about 1.4 foot pounds.
* A centimeter kilogram (cmkg) is equal to .9 inch pounds.

English-Metric Conversion Chart

CONVERSION FACTORS

Unit	To	Unit	Multiply By
LENGTH			
Millimeters		Inches	.03937
Inches		Millimeters	25.4
Meters		Feet	3.28084
Feet		Meters	.3048
Kilometers		Miles	.62137
Miles		Kilometers	1.60935
AREA			
Square Centimeters		Square Inches	.155
Square Inches		Square Centimeters	6.45159
VOLUME			
Cubic Centimeters		Cubic Inches	.06103
Cubic Inches		Cubic Centimeters	16.38703
Liters		Cubic Inches	61.025
Cubic Inches		Liters	.01639
Liters		Quarts	1.05672
Quarts		Liters	.94633
Liters		Pints	2.11344
Pints		Liters	.47317
Liters		Ounces	33.81497
Ounces		Liters	.02957

Unit	To	Unit	Multiply By
WEIGHT			
Grams		Ounces	.03527
Ounces		Grams	28.34953
Kilograms		Pounds	2.20462
Pounds		Kilograms	.45359
WORK			
Centimeter Kilograms		Inch Pounds	.8676
Inch Pounds		Centimeter Kilograms	1.15262
Meter Kilograms		Foot Pounds	7.23301
Foot Pounds		Newton Meters	1.3558
PRESSURE			
Kilograms/Sq. Centimeter		Pounds/Sq. Inch	14.22334
Pounds/Sq. Inch		Kilograms/Sq. Centimeter	.07031
Bar		Pounds/Sq. Inch	14.504
Pounds/Sq. Inch		Bar	.06895
Atmosphere		Pounds/Sq. Inch	14.696
Pounds/Sq. Inch		Atmosphere	.06805
TEMPERATURE			
Centigrade Degrees		Fahrenheit Degrees	$(C° \times \frac{9}{5}) + 32$
Fahrenheit Degrees		Centigrade Degrees	$(F° - 32) \times \frac{5}{9}$

Inches	Decimals	MM
1/64	.016	.397
1/32	.031	.794
3/64	.047	1.191
1/16	.063	1.588
5/64	.078	1.984
3/32	.094	2.381
7/64	.109	2.778
1/8	.125	3.175
9/64	.141	3.572
5/32	.156	3.969
11/64	.172	4.366
3/16	.188	4.763
13/64	.203	5.159
7/32	.219	5.556
15/64	.234	5.953
1/4	.250	6.350
17/64	.266	6.747
9/32	.281	7.144
19/64	.297	7.541
5/16	.313	7.938
21/64	.328	8.334
11/32	.344	8.731
23/64	.359	9.128
3/8	.375	9.525
25/64	.391	9.922
13/32	.406	10.319
27/64	.422	10.716
7/16	.438	11.113
29/64	.453	11.509
15/32	.469	11.906
31/64	.484	12.303
1/2	.500	12.700

Inches	Decimals	MM
33/64	.516	13.097
17/32	.531	13.494
35/64	.547	13.891
9/16	.563	14.288
37/64	.578	14.684
19/32	.594	15.081
39/64	.609	15.478
5/8	.625	15.875
41/64	.641	16.272
21/32	.656	16.669
43/64	.672	17.066
11/16	.687	17.463
45/64	.703	17.859
23/32	.719	18.256
47/64	.734	18.653
3/4	.750	19.050
49/64	.766	19.447
25/32	.781	19.844
51/64	.797	20.241
13/16	.813	20.638
53/64	.828	21.034
27/32	.844	21.431
55/64	.859	21.828
7/8	.875	22.225
57/64	.891	22.622
29/32	.906	23.019
59/64	.922	23.416
15/16	.938	23.813
61/64	.953	24.209
31/32	.969	24.606
63/64	.984	25.003

PRESSURE

Pressure is another complicated measurement. Pressure is described as a force or weight applied to a given area. Our common unit is pounds per square inch. Metric units can be expressed in several ways. One is the kilogram per square centimeter (kg/cm²). Another unit of pressure is the Pascal (force of one Newton on an area of one square meter), which equals about 4 ounces on a square yard. Since this is a very small amount of pressure, we usually see the kiloPascal, or kPa (1000 Pascals). Another common automotive term for pressure is the bar (used by German manufacturers), which equals 10 Pascals. Thoroughly confused? Try the examples below:

*   Atmospheric pressure at sea level is about 14.7 psi.
*   Atmospheric pressure at sea level is about 1 bar.
*   Atmospheric pressure at sea level is about 1 kg/cm².
*   One pound per square inch is about 7 kPa.

NOTES

NOTES

NOTES

NOTES

NOTES

NOTES

NOTES

NOTES